D1336532

THE GREAT ROCK DISCOGRAPHY

SEVENTH EDITION

MARTIN C. STRONG

With a foreword by
John Peel

CANONGATE

Seventh edition first published in the UK in 2004 by Canongate Books Ltd,
14 High Street, Edinburgh EH1 1TE

10 9 8 7 6 5 4 3 2 1

British Library Cataloguing-in-Publication Data
A catalogue record for this book is available upon request from the British Library

ISBN 1 84195 551 5

Typeset by TexturAL, Dundee

Printed and bound in Finland by WS Bookwell

This book is dedicated to ...

my mother JEAN FOTHERINGHAM
(born: 6th of January 1929,
died of cancer: 31st of August 1985)

Still missing you
and thanks for still
guiding me through all
the hard times.

my dad GERRY/GEOFF STRONG
(born: 28th of July 1930,
died of a heart attack: 20th October 1998)

Will miss you always.
You were also a great friend, inspiration
and someone who could make me laugh.

Hope you're both getting on up there.
If only ...

* * * * *

Acknowledgements

Due to certain pressures I'm going to keep this book's credits down to a minimum. Firstly much appreciation to hard-grafting co-biographers Brendon Griffin and Adam Stafford, plus busy typesetter Alan Lawson. Secondly I'd like to thank my understanding partner of the last few years, Dawn Ford, and our wee newly-born bairn, Samantha. And finally, I'd like to thank all my closest friends – they know who they are (if they/you don't, see back editions).

* * * * *

Foreword

When I first received my hardback copy of *The Great Rock Discography* and being familiar with what I'm afraid you might feel compelled to style the obsessive attention to detail of Martin C. Strong, I turned to the Bob Seger section in the faint hope that I might read something like, "In the seventies and eighties an unknown middle-aged woman was often spotted in London's bustling Notting Hill Gate area wearing an ill-fitting Bob Seger Band tour jacket". That would have been my mother but, alas, Martin has chosen – recklessly in my view – not to include her in his book. So far, that is about the only notable omission I have spotted.

There is, inevitably, a lot of stuff here you're not going to need. Not for a while anyway. I mean Rhyl's The Alarm apparently started out as The Toilets. And Robert Palmer was in Mandrake Paddle Steamer. I've got two copies of their single, if you're interested.

But there are things here about people I thought I knew. I have always believed that The Fall – and I hope you'll excuse what may seem unpleasantly like bragging – had released their debut single by the time they came to record their first session for Radio 1. Not so, it seems. And I never knew that Captain Beefheart, as a child – and what can he have been like as a child? – made clay figurines for a local television programme. What a guy! And what's this? Did you know that Bill Oddie, the bird-watching former Goodie, sang on two Rick Wakeman albums? Armed with that fact alone, you could bring conversation to an awe-struck silence in most pubs in Britain.

I don't know, of course, what you're going to use this extraordinary work of scholarship for, but I suggest you use it for something. If nothing else, you'll know the answer the next time someone stops you on the street and asks, "Whatever happened to Fred Neil?"

I'm going to keep my copy by the bed, and plan to learn a fact a day. You have been warned.

John Peel

Introduction

Hello readers,

Being a tad superstitious, it is something of a relief to overtake Book No.13, which THE GREAT INDIE DISCOGRAPHY (2nd Edition) had the honour of being. And here we are now looking at THE GREAT ROCK DISCOGRAPHY 7th Edition and Book No.14 in the GRD series.

You can thank Canongate again for their insistence on publishing the GRD biennially when I wanted to ease down for about a year so that I could concentrate on my newly-born- to-be and putting the finishing touches to my recently renovated two-bedroomed flat. But money needed to pay off the dreaded taxman helped me to change my mind. So with the renovation of my flat put aside for several months while I worked the old 60–70 hours a week again, here it is...

The first major change that'll hit you about the revised and updated 7th Edition is the all-new compact format complete with over 1700 pages – the last edition had just 1185 A4-size pages. I'll let you the reader decide about this modification; the jury's still out with my views.

With this new edition I have had to balance new additions against entries already in previous editions, so that the book didn't expand to an unwieldy 2,000-plus pages. Unfortunately, this means just over 150 artists have been excluded, and I have also selectively edited down approximately 100 "golden oldie" compilations; the reader will now have to revert to past editions to view them in full. What I'm going to do for the 8th Edition, God (and/or Canongate) only knows!

On the plus front though (lucky for me there is one), additions to the new book included over 60 newcomers (i.e. The DARKNESS, The CORAL, EVANESCENCE, KINGS OF LEON, The STREETS, etc.), 400 new biography updates, two years' worth of new releases to the discographies, several years' worth of CD re-issues, compilations, and not forgetting the UK + US charts – the cut-off date being 31/12/03. Sadly, this meant that hits of 2004, FRANZ FERDINAND, KEANE, SCISSOR SISTERS and The RASMUS, missed the cut by a whisker.

For disgruntled CLIFF RICHARD fans who religiously wrote to me in droves, sorry I couldn't take time off my GRD work to return some correspondence. However, here's an edited version of what I might've written:-

> This is The Great ROCK Discography and fans of CLIFF will just have to wait for the publication of The Great POP Discography – notice the words ROCK and POP emphasised! – hopefully in a few years from now. Any fans of Sir CLIFF and other Pop Idols should forward their grievances and possibly even a signed petition to Canongate Books (c/o MC & Cliff) and maybe the demand will change their objections to publishing such a tome. For Christ's sake man, this has got me humming 'Mistletoe & Wine' – aarrgghh!!

Getting away from this bit of caustic wit for a moment, one thing that has annoyed me during the past few years is those undoubtedly bullshitting Internet businessmen who've wasted my valuable time telling me (and Canongate) of great money-spinning ventures for my GREAT ROCK data. These people should pay up and allow the book and myself to move on to better things. Hopefully, I'll get over this when someone decent hits me with a proposition that will give Internet readers the chance to read ALL my work.

What's next then? I wish I could tell you but

I'm keeping my new project underneath my baseball cap for now, although it should be on Canongate's desk by the time you read this. There'll be a post vacant soon...

Is there anyone out there foolish enough to apply in writing wishing to be my apprentice discographer? The pay is average, the work initially brain-numbing, but it could in the long run benefit the prospective victor. But remember... many have tried and failed before, so time and patience will be a virtue.

Yours once again,

Martin C. Strong

Falkirk, Sept 2004

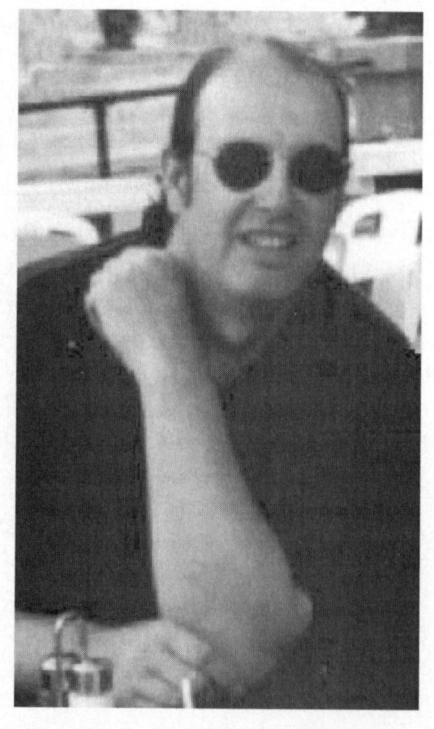

P.S. By the way, *THE GREAT SCOTS MUSICOGRAPHY* is still available from Mercat Press and some wee book shops in Scotland. If you can't get a hold of it for any reason, report to me and I'll try and get you a copy.

How To Read The Book

If you're struggling in any way to comprehend some of the more complex parts of each discography, here are some examples to make it easier. Read below for around 10 minutes, taking a step at a time. The final lines/examples you see will give you a good guide before you proceed with the actual chronological discographies. However, I think that once you've read your own favourites you'll have a good idea.

GROUP / ARTIST

Formed/Born: Where/When . . . biography including style/analysis, songwriters, cover versions, trivia, etc.

Album rating: a rating between 1 and10 – an amalgamation between music press reviews, your letters and my own personal opinion.

SINGER (born; b. day/month/year, town/city, country) – vocals, whatever (ex-GROUP; if any) / **MUSICIAN** (b. BIRTH NAME, 8 Sep'60, Musselburgh, Scotland) – instruments / **OTHER MUSICIANS** – other instruments, vocals, etc.

UK Label US Label

UKdate. (single, ep or album) *(UK cat.no.)* <*US cat.no.*> **THE RELEASE TITLE** [ ] US date [ ]

Note:– UK label – might be another country's label if not released in UK.
also:- Labels only appear when the group signs to a new one.

Note:– UK date – might be foreign, <even American at times>, if not initially issued in Britain.

Note:– (UK catalogue number in curved brackets) <US cat.no. in angle brackets>

Note:– chart positions, UK and US, are in the boxes below record-labels.
also:- the boxes in the above example have been left blank, meaning they did not hit either UK or US charts.

Note:– US date between the boxes indicates a variation from its UK counterpart.
also:- Any other info between the boxes (e.g. German) indicates it was not issued in the US.

UKdate. (7") *(UK cat.no.)* **A-SIDE. / B-SIDE** [ ] [–]
US date. (7") <*US cat.no.*> **A-SIDE. / DIFFERENT B-SIDE** [–] [ ]

Note:– The two examples above show that the UK + US release did not have an identical A-side & B-side, thus the chart boxes are marked with a – to indicate it was not released in the UK or not released in the US.

UKdate. (7"/c-s) *(CATNO 1/+C)* **A-SIDE. / B-SIDE** [ ] [–]

Note:– above had two formats with the same tracks (i.e. 7"/c-s). However, catalogue numbers will always vary among different formats – often only slightly (e.g. CATNO 1/+C). Each cat.no. would read thus:- (7")=*(CATNO 1)* and (c-s)=*(CATNO 1C)*. To save space the (/) slash comes into effect. The (/) means "or" and in this case it is prefixed with a + sign for the equivalent cassette (c-s).

UKdate. (7"/c-s) *(example same as above)* **SEE ABOVE** [ ] [–]
(12"+=/cd-s+=) *(CATNO 1-12/1-CD)* – Extra tracks.

Note:– If there are more formats with extra or different tracks, a new line would be used. Obviously there would also be alternative catalogue numbers utilising the "(/)" as before. Extra tracks would therefore mean the addition of the sign "(+=)" to each format.

UKdate. (lp/c/cd) *(CATNO 200/+MC/CD)* <*US cat. no. 4509*>
ALBUM TITLE [ ] [ ]
– Track listing / Track 1 / Track 2 / And so on. *(re-issued = re-iss. A later date, and other 'Label' mentioned, if different from original; new cat.no.) (could be re-iss. many times and if "(+=)" sign occurs there will be extra tracks from the original) <could also apply to the US release if in angle brackets>*

Note:– Album above released in 3 formats, thus 3 catalogue numbers are neccessary. The "long-player" lp *(CATNO 200)* is obvious. The "cassette" c = +MC *(CATNO 200MC)* or "compact disc" CD *(CATNO 200CD)*. The US <*cat.no.*> will normally be just one set of numbers (or see further below for other details).

UKdate. (cd/c/lp) *(CD/TC+/CATNO+200)* <*US cat. no. 4509*>
ALBUM TITLE [ ] US date [ ]

Note:– This time a prefix is used instead of a suffix, hence the difference before the standard lp catalogue number. For instance, the cd would read as *(CDCATNO 200)*.

Jun 97. (cd/c/lp) <*(5557 49860-2/-4/-1)*> **ALBUM TITLE** [1] May97 [1]

Note:– Some catalogue numbers don't include any letters, but instead consist of a number sequence followed by one digit which universally corresponds with the format (i.e. 2 = cd / 4 = c / 1 = lp).
also:- If the US numbers are identical, there is no need to list them separately, i.e. <*(the numbers)*>

Note:– I've also marked down an actual date of release and its variant in the US (you'll find this fictitious album also hit No.1 in both charts "and ah've no even heard it yet, man!")

— **NEW MUSICIAN/SINGER** (b.whenever, etc.) – instruments (ex-GROUP(s)) replaced (repl.) DEPARTING MUSICIAN/SINGER, who joined whatever.

The above denotes a line-up change.

GROUP or ARTIST with major change of name

UK Label US Label

Jun 97. (cd/c/lp; GROUP or ARTIST with minor change of name) <*(5557 49860)*> **ALBUM TITLE** [1] May97 [1]

– compilations, etc. –

UKdate. (cd) *compilation Label only; (cat.no.)* **ALBUM TITLE** [100] [–]
– Track listing would be selective, only included if the release was deemed essential.

☐ PERSONAL NAME (see under ⇒ GROUP-NAME)

The above is a cross-reference.

Formats & Abbreviations

VINYL (black coloured unless stated)

(lp)	=	The (LONG PLAYER) record ... circular 12" plays at $33^{1/3}$ r.p.m., and has photo or artwork sleeve. Approximate playing time ... 30–50 minutes with average 10 tracks. Introduced in the mid-'50s on mono until stereo took over in the mid-'60s. Quadrophonic had a spell in the '70s, but only on mainly best-selling lp's, that had been previously released. Because of higher costs to the manufacturer and buyer, the quad-sunk around 1978. Also note that around the mid-'50s, some albums were released on 10 inch. Note:– average cost to the customer as of now = £9.00 (new). Collectors can pay anything from £1 to over £500, depending on the quality of the recording. Very scratched records can be worthless, but unplayed mint deletions are worth a small fortune to the right person. Auctions and record fairs can be the place to find that long lost recording that's eluded you. This applies to all other vinyl below.
(d-lp)	=	The (DOUBLE-LONG PLAYER) record ... as before. Playing time 50–90 minutes on 4 sides, with average 17 tracks. Introduced to rock/pop world in the late '60s, to complement compilations, concept & concert (aka live) albums.[1] Compilations:– are a selection of greatest hits or rare tracks, demos, etc. Concepts:– are near-uninterrupted pieces of music, based around a theme. Note that normal lp's could also be compilations, live or concept. Some record companies through the wishes of their artists, released double lp's at the price of one lp. If not, price new would be around £15.
(t-lp)	=	The (TRIPLE-LONG PLAYER) record ... as before. Playing time over 100 minutes with normally over 20 tracks. Because of the cost to the consumer, most artists steered clear of this format. Depending on the artwork on the sleeve, these cost over £17.50. (See its replacement, the CD.)
(4-lp-box)	=	The (BOXED-LONG PLAYER) record (could be between 4 and 10 in each boxed-set). As the triple album would deal with live, concept or compilation side, the boxed-set would be mostly re-issues of all the artist's album material, with probably a bonus lp thrown in, to make it collectable. Could be very pricey, due to lavish outlay in packaging. They cost over £25 new.
(m-lp)	=	The (MINI-LONG PLAYER) record ... playing time between 20 and 30 minutes and containing on average 7 tracks. Introduced for early '80s independent market, and cost around £5.
	=	Note:– This could be confused at times with the extended-play 12" single.
(pic-lp)	=	The (PICTURE DISC-LONG PLAYER) record... as before but with album artwork/design on the vinyl grooves. Mainly for the collector because of the slightly inferior sound quality. If unplayed, these can fetch between £10 and £250.
(coloured lp)	=	The (COLOURED-LONG PLAYER) record; can be in a variety of colours including ... white / blue / red / clear / purple / green / pink / gold / silver.
(red-lp)	=	The (RED VINYL-LONG PLAYER) record would be an example of this.
(7")	=	The (7-INCH SINGLE). Arrived in the late '50s, and plays at 45 r.p.m. Before this its equivalent was the 10" on 78 r.p.m. Playing time now averages 4 minutes per side, but during the late '50s up to mid-'60s, each side averaged $2^{1/2}$ minutes. Punk rock/new wave in 1977/78 resurrected this idea. In the '80s, some disco releases increased playing time. Another idea that was resurrected in 1977 was the picture sleeve. This had been introduced in the '60s, but mostly only in the States.

1: **Note**:– Interview long players, mainly released on 'Babatak' label, have not been included due to the fact this book only gives artists' music discography.

Note:– cost in mid-98 was just under £2.50; second-hand rarities can cost between 25p and £200, depending again on their condition. These might also contain limited freebies/gifts (i.e. posters, patches, stickers, badges, etc). Due to the confusion this would cause, I have omitted this information, and kept to the vinyl aspect in this book. Another omission has been DJ promos, demos, acetates, magazine freebies, various artists' compilations, etc. Only official shop releases get a mention.

(7" m) = The (7-INCH MAXI-SINGLE). Named so because of the extra track, mostly on the B-side. Introduced widely during the early '70s; one being ROCKET MAN by ELTON JOHN.

(7" ep) = The (7-INCH EXTENDED PLAY SINGLE). Plays mostly at $33^{1/3}$ r.p.m., with average playing time 10–15 minutes and 4 tracks. Introduced in the late '50s as compilations for people to sample their albums. These had a *title* and were also re-introduced from 1977 onwards, but this time for punk groups' new songs.

(d7") = The (DOUBLE 7-INCH SINGLE). Basically just two singles combined ... 4 tracks. Introduced in the late '70s for the "new wave/romantics", and would cost slightly more than normal equivalent.

(7" pic-d) = The (7-INCH PICTURE-DISC SINGLE). This was vinyl that had a picture on the grooves, which could be viewed through a see-through plastic cover.

(7" sha-pic-d) = The (7-INCH SHAPED-PICTURE-DISC SINGLE). Vinyl as above but with shape (i.e. gun, mask, group) around the edge of the groove. Awkward because it would not fit into the collector's singles box. Initially limited, and this can still be obtained at record fairs for over £3. Note:– However, in the book the type of shape has not been mentioned, to save space.

(7" coloured) = The (7-INCH COLOURED SINGLE). Vinyl that is not black (i.e. any other colour; red, yellow, etc). Note:– (7" multi) would be a combination of two or more colours (i.e. pink/purple).

(7" flexi) = The (7-INCH FLEXIBLE SINGLE). One-sided freebies, mostly given away by magazines, at concerts or as mentioned here; free with single or lp. Worth keeping in mint condition and well protected.

(12") = The (12-INCH SINGLE). Plays at 45 r.p.m., and can have extended or extra tracks to its 7" counterpart (+=) or (++=). B-side's playing speed could be at 33 r.p.m. Playing time could be between 8 and 15 minutes. Introduced in 1977 with the advent of new wave and punk. They were again a must for collectors, for the new wave of British heavy metal scene.

(12" ep) = The (12-INCH EXTENDED PLAY SINGLE). Virtually same as above but *titled* like the 7" ep. Playing time over 12 minutes, and could have between 3 and 5 tracks.

(d12") = The (DOUBLE 12-INCH SINGLE). See double 7". Can become very collectable and would cost new as normal 12", £4.50.

(12" pic-d) = The (12-INCH PICTURE-DISC SINGLE). As with 7" equivalent ... see above.

(12" sha-pic-d) = The (12-INCH SHAPED-PICTURE-DISC SINGLE). See above 7" equivalent.

(12" colrd) = The (12-INCH COLOURED SINGLE). Not black vinyl ... see above 7" equivalent.

(10") = The (10-INCH SINGLE). Plays at 45 r.p.m. and, like the 12", can have extra tracks (+=). Very collectable, it surfaced in its newer form around the early '80s, and can be obtained in shops at £4.50. Note:– also (10" ep) / (d10") / (10" coloured) / (10" pic-d) / (10" sha-pic-d).

CASSETTES

(c) = The (CASSETTE) album ... size in case $4^{1/2}$ inches high. Playing-time same as lp album, although after the mid-'80s cd revolution, some were released with extra tracks. Introduced in the late '60s, to compete with the much bulkier lp. Until the '80s, most cassettes were lacking in group info, lyric sheets, and freebies. Note:– cost to the consumer as of now = £8 new. But for a few exceptions, most do not increase in price, and can be bought second-hand or budget-priced for around £5.

(d-c) = The (DOUBLE-CASSETTE) album ... as above, and would hold same tracks as d-lp or even t-lp. Price between £12 and £16.

(c-s) = The (CASSETTE-SINGLE). Now released mostly with same two tracks as 7" equivalent. The other side played the same 2 or 3 tracks. Introduced unsuccessfully in the US around the late '60s. Re-introduced there and in Britain in the mid-'80s. In the States, it and its cd counterpart have replaced the charting 7" single for the '90s. Cost new is around £1.50–£2.50, and might well become quite collectable.

(c-ep) = The (CASSETTE-EXTENDED PLAY SINGLE). Same as above but *titled* as 12".

COMPACT DISCS

(cd) = The (COMPACT DISC) album. All 5" circular and mostly silver on its playing side. Perspex casing also includes lyrics & info, etc. Introduced late in 1982, and widely the following year (even earlier for classical music). Initially for top recording artists, but now in 2004 nearly every release is in cd format. Playing time normally over 50 minutes with some containing extra tracks or mixes. Possible playing time is just over 75 minutes. Marketed as unscratchable, although if they go uncleaned, they will stick just as vinyl. Average price now is £15, and will become collectable if, like most gloomy predictions, they do not deteriorate with time.

(d-cd) = The (DOUBLE-COMPACT DISC) album ... same as above although very pricey, between £20 and £25.

(cd-s) = The (COMPACT DISC-SINGLE). Mainly all 5" (but some 3" cd-s could only be played with a compatible gadget inside the normal cd player). Playing time over 15 minutes to average 25 minutes, containing 4 or 5 tracks. Introduced in 1986 to compete with the 12" ep or cassette. 99% contained extra tracks to normal formats. Cost new: over £4.50.

(pic-cd-s) = The (PICTURE-COMPACT DISC-SINGLE). Has picture on disc, which gives it its collectability. Also on (pic-cd-ep).

(vid-pic-s) = The (VIDEO-COMPACT DISC-SINGLE). A video cd, which can be played through stereo onto normal compatible TV screen. Very costly procedure, but still might be the format of the future. Promo videos can be seen on pub jukeboxes, which has made redundant the returning Wurlitzer style.

DIGITAL AUDIO TAPE

(dat) = The (DIGITAL AUDIO TAPE) album. Introduced in the mid-'80s and, except for Japan and the rich yuppie, are not widely issued. It is a smaller version of the cassette, with the quality of the cd.

Another format (which I have not included) is the CARTRIDGE, which was available at the same time as the cassette. When the cassette finally won the battle in the early '80s, the cartridge became redundant. All car-owners of the world were happy when thieves made them replace the stolen cartridge player with the resurrected cassette. You can still buy these second-hand, but remember you'll have to obtain a second-hand 20-year-old player, with parts possibly not available.

Other abbreviations: repl. = replaced / comp. = compilation / re-iss. = re-issued / re-dist. = re-distributed

AC/DC

'A'

Formed: Suffolk, England . . . 1994 by the Leeds-born PERRY brothers, JASON, GILES and ADAM, who duly recruited MARK CHAPMAN and STEVIE SWINDON. Initially VAN HALEN obsessives, they progressed into an alternative heavy/punk fun-rock outfit influenced by JANE'S ADDICTION, GREEN DAY and The MANIC STREET PREACHERS. 'A' – they probably picked this short moniker because they'd be first in every Rock book – proceeded to tour with everyone from the re-formed SEX PISTOLS, ASH and SYMPOSIUM before being shipped off to California on a new recording mission courtesy of 'London' (via their own 'Tycoon' label). A's debut single in the summer of '96, '5 IN THE MORNING', was received favourably by critics into prozac-punk pop. During the next year, they released three more (including 'No.1', which used lyrics from Billy Joel's 'My Life') and an album 'HOW ACE ARE BUILDINGS', which was given rave reviews in Kerrang! In 1999, 'A' were back with a sophomore effort, 'vs MONKEY KONG'. However, despite three further minor hits, 'SUMMER ON THE UNDERGROUND', 'OLD FOLKS' and 'I LOVE LAKE TAHOE', it fell just short of giving the band a Top 60 place. Taking a leaf out of the emo book of rock, A went on to issue their finest album to date, 'HI-FI SERIOUS' (2002), a fun, uptempo record with some hot-headed riffs to boot. Lead single 'STARBUCKS' aside, there was hardly one duff track on this killer rock album or anything to suggest that the band had lost their punk edge. The group even slid into anthemic stadium rock mode for the metal wig-out 'THE DISTANCE', out-riffing The DARKNESS a year earlier. Mixing thick-ass synths with bellowing punk-metal reminiscent of POISON, A showed us their mellower side with 'TOOK IT AWAY' displaying soft, sun-drenched melodies West Coast surf style. For anybody who enjoyed the subtleties of emo and appreciated the kick-ass tantrums of juggernaut pop-punk 'HI-FI SERIOUS' had it all. • **Covered:** OWNER OF A LONELY HEART (Yes).

Album rating: HOW ACE ARE BUILDINGS (*6) / vs MONKEY KONG (*5) / HI-FI SERIOUS (*7)

JASON PERRY – vocals / **MARK CHAPMAN** – guitar / **GILES PERRY** – keyboards, vocals / **STEVIE SWINDON** – bass, vocals / **ADAM PERRY** – drums

Tycoon | not iss.

Jul 96. (7") *(TY 1)* **FIVE IN THE MORNING. / ALMOST EVERYTHING IS GREAT** [ ] [–]
(cd-s+=) *(TYCD 1)* – 8 fingers.

Nov 96. (7") *(TY 2)* **HOUSE UNDER THE GROUND. / "40"** [ ] [–]
(cd-s+=) *(TYCD 2)* – Demolished house.

May 97. (7") *(TY 3)* **BAD IDEA. / "40"** [ ] [–]
(cd-s+=) *(TYCD 3)* – Look what you made me do.

Aug 97. (7") *(TY 4)* **No.1. / ALRIGHT** [ ] [–]
(cd-s+=) *(TYCD 4)* – Ouch! / ('A'version).

Sep 97. (cd/c) *(828 916-2/-4)* **HOW ACE ARE BUILDINGS** [ ] [–]
– Turn it up / Foghorn / Cheeky monkey / No.1 / Bad idea / Sing-a-long / Winter of '96 / Out of tune / Fistral / House under the ground / 5 in the morning / Ender. *(re-iss. Jun98; same)*

—— (summer '97) **DANIEL P. CARTER** – bass; repl. SWINDON

Oct 97. (cd-s) *(COUP 06)* **HOUSE UNDER THE GROUND / (track by Glitterbox)** [ ] [–]
(above issued on 'Revolution')

Jan 98. (7") *(TY 5)* **FOGHORN. / LAST GIRL** [63] [–]
(cd-s+=) *(TYCD 5)* – A demolished house.

Mar 98. (7") *(TY 6)* **NUMBER ONE. / GOOD IDEA** [47] [–]
(cd-s+=) *(TYCD 6)* – Alright / Sasqatch.
(cd-s) *(TYCDP 6)* – ('A'side) / ('A'-Happy Valley ranch mix) / Foghorn / Foghorn (video).

Jun 98. (7"pic-d) *(TY 7)* **SING-A-LONG. / I'M OVER IT** [57] [–]
(cd-s+=) *(TYCD 7)* – Callhimyin / Photo finger.
(cd-s) *(TYCDP 7)* – ('A'side) / ('A'-post-term audio mix) / Singing out of tune (literally, in a castle) / Number One (video).

London | Mammoth

Oct 98. (7"/c-s) *(TY/+CS 8)* **SUMMER ON THE UNDERGROUND. / OWNER OF A LONELY HEART** [72] [–]
(cd-s+=) *(TYCD 8)* – I can't wait until morning.
(cd-s) *(TYCDP 8)* – ('A'side) / For starters / Charlie Jordan.

May 99. (7"pic-d) *(TY 9)* **OLD FOLKS. / ONE DAY** [54] [–]
(cd-s+=) *(TYCD 9)* – Don't be punks (acapella version).
(cd-s) *(TYCDP 9)* – ('A'side) / She said / We're equal.

Aug 99. (7"pic-d) *(TY 10)* **I LOVE LAKE TAHOE. / MONKEY KING JR.** [59] [–]
(cd-s) *(TYCD 10)* – ('A'-version).
(cd-s) *(TYCDP 10)* – ('A'side) / Turn it down / Old folks / Old folks (video).

Aug 99. (cd) *(3984 27695-2)* *<65501>* **vs MONKEY KONG** [62] Sep00 [ ]
– For starters / Monkey Kong / A / Old folks / Hopper Jonnus fang / Summer on the underground / Warning / If it ain't broke, fix it anyway / I love Lake Tahoe / Don't be punks / Down on the floor / Jason's addiction / Miles away / Getting around. *<US+=>* – She said / One day / If it ain't broke (live). *(re-iss. Nov02 on 'B-Unique'; BUN 041)*

May 00. (m-cd) *(8573 83098-2)* **EXIT STAGE RIGHT (live)** [ ] [–]
– Intro / If it ain't broke, fix it anyway / Monkey Kong / A / Old folks / I love Lake Tahoe / Over it / Foghorn.

Feb 02. (12") *(LONX 463)* **NOTHING. / T-SHIRT MONEY / EVERYBODY IN** [9] [–]
(cd-s+=) *(LOCDP 463)* – ('A'-video).
(cd-s) *(LONCD 463)* – ('A'side) / Getting me off / The distance / The distance (video).

Mar 02. (cd) *(0927 44776-2)* *<165530>* **HI-FI SERIOUS** [18] Jul02 [ ]
– Nothing / Something's going on / 6 o'clock on a tube stop / Going down / Took it away / Starbucks / The springs / Shut yer face / Pacific ocean blue / The distance / W.D.Y.C.A.I. / Hi-fi serious. *<US+=>* – Champions of endings / Nothing.

May 02. (cd-s) *(LONCD 467)* **STARBUCKS / SOME PEOPLE / CHAMPIONS OF ENDINGS / STARBUCKS (video)** [20] [–]
(cd-s) *(LOCDP 467)* – ('A'side) / Monterey / Coming around / Coming around (video).

Nov 02. (7") *(LON 471)* **SOMETHING'S GOING ON. / ROCK** [51] [–]
(cd-s+=) *(LONCD 471)* – Human condition.
(cd-s) *(LOCDP 471)* – ('A'side) / Just like paradise / Sorry but . . .

Sep 03. (cd-s) *(LONCD 480)* **GOOD TIMES / SIX O'CLOCK (live) / FULL PEKT / GOOD TIME (live video)** [23] [–]
(cd-s) *(LONCP 480)* – ('A'side) / Starbucks (live) / Why don't you (live) / ('A'-video).

AALIYAH

Born: AALIYAH DANI HOUGHTON, 16 Jan'79, Brooklyn, New York, USA; pronounced Ah-lee-yah. Tragedy was to befall one of R&B's most talented and gifted young artists in August 2001, when AALIYAH, a revered and respected figure in the music industry was killed in a plane crash after a video shoot in the Bahamas. She was only twenty-two, but left an amazing legacy behind her with everyone from SEAN COMBS, R. KELLY and USHER expressing their deep regrets that such a blossoming talent had to die so young. AALIYAH was raised in Detroit by her musical mother, who was also a soul singer. She had other musical connections in her family; her uncle, an entertainment lawyer, was married to GLADYS KNIGHT, whom AALIYAH appeared on stage with aged only eleven. She resurfaced after this introduction on the scene four years later with her debut album 'AGE AIN'T NOTHING BUT A NUMBER' (1994), an R. KELLY produced R&B record that spawned the hit singles 'AT YOUR BEST (YOU ARE LOVE)' and 'BACK AND FORTH' which both made it to the Top 10 in the American Billboard charts. She also courted controversy, quite literally, when she married R. KELLY at the tender age of fifteen. However, the relationship was not to last, with AALIYAH departing from the R&B millionaire in 1996. She collaborated with rising stars TIMBALAND and MISSY ELLIOTT on her sophomore set 'ONE IN A MILLION' (1996), a collection of sassy R&B tracks, mixed with Hip-Hop and a fruity dance, funk/soul style. The album was another hit, with 'IF YOUR GIRL ONLY KNEW' becoming one of the most important R&B tracks of the year. Eventually, AALIYAH made her way into films, starring in the Jet Li vehicle 'Romeo Must Die' and signing up to star in the two sequels in 'The Matrix' series. She issued her self titled album in 2001, after a long recording hiatus and began work on her second feature film 'Queen Of The Damned', in which she played a sexy, femme fatale, who just so happened to be a vampire. The young actress/artist's career was finally reaching boiling point when the tragedy struck. But with such a detailed and enigmatic legacy, she was becoming the most respected and dearly missed artist of her generation. 2002's 'I CARE 4 U' paid tribute to that legacy with a measured selection of past glories – from early hits like 'BACK AND FORTH', right through to cuts from 2001's eponymous 'AALIYAH' album – and unreleased tracks, the bulk of which comprised ballad material penned by Johnta Austin, of 'I DON'T WANNA' fame.

Album rating: AGE AIN'T NOTHING BUT A NUMBER (*6) / ONE IN A MILLION (*7) / AALIYAH (*7) / I CARE 4 U (*6)

AALIYAH – vocals / with session people/producers

Jive — Be!-Jive

Jun 94. (7"/c-s) *(JIVE/+C 357)* <42174> **BACK AND FORTH. / (Mr Lee & R Kelly's remix)** [16] Apr94 [5]
(12"+=/cd-s+=) *(JIVE T/CD 357)* – ('A'-Ms Mello & Mr. Lee's club + instrumental + bonus beats mixes).

Jul 94. (cd/c/lp) *(CHIP/HIPC/HIP 149)* <41533> **AGE AIN'T NOTHING BUT A NUMBER** [23] May94 [18]
– Throw your hands up / Back and forth / Age ain't nothing but a number / Down with the clique / At your best (you are love) / Me quite like you do / I'm so into you / Street thing / Young nation / Old school / I'm down.

Oct 94. (7"/c-s) *(JIVE/+C 359)* <42239> **AT YOUR BEST (YOU ARE LOVE). / (mix)** [27] Aug94 [6]
(12"+=/cd-s+=) *(JIVE T/CD 359)* – ('A'mix) / Back + forth (Ms. Mello mix).

Feb 95. (7"/c-s) *(JIVE/+C 369)* <42273> **AGE AIN'T NOTHING BUT A NUMBER. / I'M DOWN** [32] Jan95 [75]
(12"+=/cd-s+=) *(JIVE T/CD 369)* – ('A'mixes).

May 95. (7"/c-s) *(JIVE/+C 377)* **DOWN WITH THE CLIQUE. / (instrumental mix)** [33] [ ]
(12"+=/cd-s+=) *(JIVE T/CD 377)* – ('A'-Maghouse mixes).

Aug 95. (7"/c-s) *(JIVE/+C 382)* **THE THING I LIKE. / (Paul Gotel mix)** [33] [ ]
(12"+=/cd-s+=) *(JIVE T/CD 382)* – ('A'-Paul Gotel's mixes).

—— in Feb'96, she featured on JUNIOR M.A.F.I.A.'s minor hit, 'I Need You Tonight'

Atlantic — Atlantic

Aug 96. (c-s) *(A 5669C)* <98067> **IF YOUR GIRL ONLY KNEW / (mix)** [21] [11]
(cd-s+=) *(A 5669CD)* – ('A'-mixes; instrumental, etc.)

Aug 96. (cd/c) <*(7567 92715-2/-4)*> **ONE IN A MILLION** [ ] [18]
– Beats 4 da street (intro) / Hot like fire / One in a million / A girl like you / If your girl only knew / Choosey lover (old school – new school) / Got to give it up / 4 page letter / Everything's gonna be alright / Giving you more / I gotcha' back / Never givin' up / Heartbroken / Never comin' back / Ladies in da house / The one I gave my heart to / Came to give love (outro). *(cd re-iss. Aug01 on 'Virgin America'; CDVUS 211)*

Nov 96. (c-s) *(A 5632C)* **GOT TO GIVE IT UP / (TNT's house mix)** [37] [ ]
(cd-s+=) *(A 5632CD)* – No days go by / ('A'-Tee's freeze mix).

May 97. (c-s) *(A 5610C)* **IF YOUR GIRL ONLY KNEW / ONE IN A MILLION** [15] [–]
(12"+=/cd-s+=) *(A 5610 T/CD)* – ('A'-dark child remix) / ('B'-Armand's drum'n'bass mix).

Aug 97. (c-s) *(AT 0010C)* **4 PAGE LETTER / (Quiet Storm mix)** [24] [ ]
(cd-s+=) *(AT 0010CD1)* – ('A'-Timbaland mix).
(cd-s) *(AT 0010CD2)* – ('A'mixes).

Nov 97. (c-s/cd-s) *(AT 0017 C/CD1)* <95567> **THE ONE I GAVE MY HEART TO / HOT LIKE FIRE** [30] Sep97 [9]
(cd-s+=) *(AT 0017CD2)* – ('A'mixes).

Apr 98. (c-s) *(AT 0026C)* **JOURNEY TO THE PAST / (mix)** [22] [ ]
(12"+=/cd-s+=) *(AT 0026 T/CD)* – ('A'mixes).

Aug 98. (c-s) *(AT 0047C)* **ARE YOU THAT SOMEBODY? / (instrumental)** [11] [21]
(12"+=/cd-s+=) *(AT 0047 T/CD)* – ('A'-acappella).

Virgin — Priority

Jan 00. (-) <*radio cut*> **I DON'T WANNA** [–] [35]

Jul 00. (c-s) *(VUSC 167)* <*radio cut*> **TRY AGAIN / (Timbaland mix)** [5] Mar00 [1]
(12"+=/cd-s+=) *(VUSCD 167)* – (D'jam Hassam mix) / (instrumental).

Nov 00. (c-s) *(VUSC 179)* **I DON'T WANNA / COME BACK IN ONE PIECE** [ ] [–]
(12"+=/cd-s+=) *(VUS T/CD 179)* – ('B'extended).

Jul 01. (c-s; by AALIYAH featuring TIMBALAND) *(VUSC 206)* <38781> **WE NEED A RESOLUTION / ARE YOU FEELIN' ME** [20] May01 [59]
(cd-s+=) *(VUST 206)* – Messed up.
(12"+=) *(VUST 206)* – ('A'-instrumental).

Jul 01. (cd/d-lp) *(CDVUS/VUSLP 199)* <10082> **AALIYAH** [5] [1]
– We need a resolution / Loose rap / Rock the boat / More than a woman / Never no more / I care 4 U / Extra smooth / Read between the lines / U got nerve / I refuse / It's whatever / I can be / Those were the days / What if. *(bonus+=)* – Messed up. *(ltd-cd w/ dvd+=; CDVUSY 199)*

—— On the 25th August 2001, AALIYAH was killed in a plane crash

Jan 02. (c-s) *(VUSC 230)* <546042> **MORE THAN A WOMAN / ('A'-Bump & Flex mix)** [1] Nov01 [25]
(12"+=/cd-s+=) *(VUS T/CD 230)* – ('A'-MAW main mix).

May 02. (c-s) *(VUSC 243)* <546109> **ROCK THE BOAT / (edit)** [12] Jan02 [14]
(12"+=/cd-s+=) *(VUS T/CD 243)* – ('A'-Mixso club mix) / ('A'-instrumental).

Independiente — Blackground

Feb 03. (cd) *(ISOM 37CD)* <06008-2> **I CARE 4 U** [4] Dec02 [3]
– Back and forth / Are you that somebody / One in a million / I care 4 U / More than a woman / Don't know what to yell ya / Try again / All I need / Miss you / Don't worry / Come over / Erica Kane / At your best / Got to give up (remix) / We need a revolution (with TIMBALAND) / Rock the boat / Miss you (video). *(ltd-cd w/ dvd+=; ISOM 37CDL)*

Apr 03. (12") <*2411-1*> **I CARE 4 U. / DON'T WORRY** [–] [16]

Apr 03. (cd-s) <*584610*> **MISS YOU / MISS YOU (remix with JAY-Z)** [–] [3]

Apr 03. (12") *(ISOM 73T)* **DON'T KNOW WHAT TO TELL YA. / (handcuff remix) / TRY AGAIN** [22] [–]
(cd-s) *(ISOM 73MS)* – (first 2 tracks) / Miss you (video).

– compilations, etc. –

Nov 01. (12"; AALIYAH & PIKACHU) *Eva; (VO 010)* **TRY AGAIN** [ ] [–]

ABBA

Formed: Stockholm, Sweden … 1971 by songwriting buddies BJORN and BENNY with partners AGNETHA and ANNI-FRID, each individual member already established in their own right previous to this inevitable formation (see further solo). In 1973, they entered for The Eurovision Song Contest with 'RING RING'. It didn't win, but the following year's 'WATERLOO' did, soon topping the UK charts. The accompanying album of the same name didn't perform so well, struggling to make the Top 30, and it took more than a year for them to get back on track commercially. The plangent 'S.O.S.' achieved this in fine style, while 'MAMMA MIA' made No.1 at Christmas '75 and the ABBA phenomenon really kicked into gear. Simultaneously one of the most cherished groups ever to come out of the continent and one of the most readily identifiable icons of 70's cheesiness, ABBA were a one-off, plain and simple. With their gorgeous lovelorn melodies, glossy harmonies, kissing couples charm and occasionally pigeon English, ABBA captured the hearts of everyone from teenyboppers to grannies, hell, even John Peel! In their mid-late 70's heyday, the group scored an incredible amount of No.1's including 'FERNANDO', 'DANCING QUEEN', 'KNOWING ME, KNOWING YOU', 'THE NAME OF THE GAME' and 'TAKE A CHANCE ON ME'. There was something about the ABBA sound, something undefinable that made their records magical, timeless; there are songs which, for anyone who grew up in the 70's, can conjure up long forgotten memories more vividly than any photograph. The albums, 'ARRIVAL' (1977), 'THE ALBUM' (1978), 'VOULEZ VOUS' (1979) and 'SUPER TROOPER' (1980) all made the UK No.1, achieving massive sales all over the world. In fact, at their peak, ABBA were one of the country's top exports, listed on the national stock exchange. Like FLEETWOOD MAC, the stormy inter-band relationships in ABBA fuelled their most affecting, poignant work, and, as the decade wore on, the sad songs became even sadder; the dreamy Euro-pop of 'ANGELEYES' and the cod-disco of 'DOES YOUR MOTHER KNOW' belied a band in emotional turmoil. The heartbroken opening piano chords of 'WINNER TAKES IT ALL' spoke volumes, a song of lost love as powerful as any ever written; the track gave ABBA yet another No.1. After a final long-player, 'THE VISITORS' (1981), the band drifted apart to solo ventures. Unmentionable in the style-conscious 80's, the ABBA legend had become almost an industry in itself by the mid-90's. Part of an overall 70's revival, ABBA's elevation to gurus of "the decade that taste forgot" was fuelled by Australian parody outfit BJORN AGAIN as well as multi-million selling retrospective compilation 'ABBA GOLD' (1992).

Best CD compilation: THE DEFINITIVE COLLECTION (*9)

AGNETHA FALTSKOG (-ULVAEUS) (b. 5 Apr'50, Jonkopping, Sweden) – vocals / **BJORN ULVAEUS** (b.25 Apr'45, Gothenburg, Sweden) – guitar, vocals / **BENNY ANDERSSON** (b.16 Dec'46, Stockholm, Sweden) – keyboards, synth, vocals (both ex-HEP STARS, ex-HOOTENANNY SINGERS) / **ANNI-FRID LYNGSTAD-FREDRIKSSON** (b.15 Nov'45, Norway) – vocals

—— In May'72, a single by **BJORN, BENNY, AGNETHA + FRIDA** hit Swedish No.2

(below debut single was released in Sweden Feb '73 + hit No.1)

Epic / Atlantic

Oct 73. (7") *(EPC 1793)* **RING RING. / ROCK'N'ROLL BAND** [ ] [–]

Apr 74. (7") *(EPC 2040) <3035>* **WATERLOO. / WATCH OUT** [1] May74 [6]

(re-iss. Feb78; EPC 5961) (re-iss. 1986; 650252-7)

May 74. (lp/c) *(EPC/40 80179) <18101>* **WATERLOO** [28] Aug74 [ ]

– Waterloo / Watch out / King Kong song / Hasta manana / My mama said / Dance (while the music still goes on) / Honey, honey / What about Livingstone / Gonna sing you my love song / Suzy hang around / Ring ring. *(re-iss. Mar81 lp/c; EPC/40 32009) (re-iss. Sep92 on 'Polydor' cd/c; 843643-2/-4) (re-iss. Jun93 on 'Spectrum' cd/c; 550034-2/-4)*

Jul 74. (7") *(EPC 2452)* **RING RING. / ROCK'N'ROLL BAND** [32] [–]

Sep 74. (7") *<3209>* **HONEY, HONEY. / DANCE (WHILE THE MUSIC STILL GOES ON)** [–] [27]

Nov 74. (7") *(EPC 2848)* **SO LONG. / I'VE BEEN WAITING FOR YOU** [ ] [–]

Apr 75. (7") *(EPC 3229)* **I DO I DO I DO I DO I DO. / ROCK ME** [38] [–]

Jun 75. (7") *<3240>* **RING RING. / HASTA MANANA** [–] [ ]

Aug 75. (7") *(EPC 3576) <3265>* **S.O.S. / MAN IN THE MIDDLE** [6] [15]

Dec 75. (7") *(EPC 3790)* **MAMMA MIA. / INTERMEZZO No.1** [1] [–]

Jun 75. (lp/c) *(EPC/40 80835) <18146>* **ABBA** [13] Nov75 [ ]

– Mamma mia / Hey, hey Helen / Tropical loveland / S.O.S. / Man in the middle / Bang-a-boomerang / I do, I do, I do, I do, I do / Rock me / Intermezzo No.1 / I've been waiting for you / So long. *(re-iss. Nov81 lp/c; EPC/40 32052) (re-iss. Sep92 on 'Polydor' cd/c+=; 831596-2/-4)* – Waterloo / Hasta manana / Honey honey / Ring ring / Nina, pretty ballerina. *(lp re-iss. Aug99 on 'Simply Vinyl'; SVLP 103)*

Jan 76. (7") *<3310>* **I DO I DO I DO I DO I DO. / BANG-A-BOOMERANG** [–] [15]

Mar 76. (7") *<3315>* **MAMMA MIA. / TROPICAL LOVELAND** [–] [ ]

Mar 76. (7") *(EPC 4036) <3346>* **FERNANDO. / HEY HEY HELEN** [1] Aug76 [13]

(re-iss. Feb78; EPC 5962)

Apr 76. (lp/c) *(EPC/40 69218) <18189>* **GREATEST HITS** (compilation) [1] Sep76 [48]

– Fernando / S.O.S. / He is your brother / Hasta manana / Dance (while the music still goes on) / Another town, another train / Mamma mia / Waterloo / I do I do I do I do I do / Honey honey / People need love / Ring ring / Bang-a-boomerang / Nina, pretty ballerina / So long. *(re-iss. Apr85 lp/c; EPC/40 32571)*

May 76. (7") *<3315>* **MAMMA MIA. / TROPICAL LOVELAND** [–] [32]

Aug 76. (7") *(EPC 4499) <3372>* **DANCING QUEEN. / THAT'S ME** [1] Nov76 [1]

Nov 76. (7") *(EPC 4713) <3434>* **MONEY MONEY MONEY. / CRAZY WORLD** [3] Oct77 [56]

Nov 76. (lp/c) *(EPC/40 86018) <18207>* **ARRIVAL** [1] Jan77 [20]

– My love my life / When I kissed the teacher / Dancing queen / Dum dum diddle / Knowing me knowing you / Money, money, money / That's me / Why did it have to be me / Tiger / Arrival. *(re-iss. Jul83 lp/c; EPC/40 32320) (cd-iss. 1986; CD 86018) (re-iss. Sep92 on 'Polydor' cd/c; 821319-2/-4)*

Feb 77. (7") *(EPC 4955) <3387>* **KNOWING ME KNOWING YOU. / HAPPY HAWAII** [1] May77 [14]

Oct 77. (7") *(EPC 5750) <3449>* **THE NAME OF THE GAME. / I WONDER (DEPARTURE)** [1] Dec77 [12]

Jan 78. (7") *(EPC 5950) <3457>* **TAKE A CHANCE ON ME. / I'M A MARIONETTE** [1] Apr78 [3]

(re-iss. May82; EPC 8088)

Jan 78. (lp/c) *(EPC/40 86052) <19164>* **THE ALBUM** [1] Feb78 [14]

– Eagle / Take a chance on me / One man, one woman / The name of the game / Move on / Hole in your soul / The girl with the golden hair (three scenes from a mini musical): Thank you for the music – I wonder (departure) – I'm a marionette. *(re-iss. Mar84 lp/c; EPC/40 32321) (cd-iss. 1986; CD86052) (cd re-iss. Jun89; CD 32321) (re-iss. Sep92 on 'Polydor' cd/c; 821217-2/-4)*

Sep 78. (7") *(EPC 6595) <3515>* **SUMMER NIGHT CITY. / MEDLEY (PICK A PALE OF COTTON – OLD SMOKEY – MAKING IT SPECIAL)** [5] [ ]

Jan 79. (7") *(EPC 7030) <3629>* **CHIQUITITA. / LOVELIGHT** [2] Nov79 [29]

(re-iss. May82; EPC 7030)

Apr 79. (7") *(EPC 7316) <3574>* **DOES YOUR MOTHER KNOW. / KISSES OF FIRE** [4] May79 [19]

May 79. (lp/c/pic-lp) *(EPC/40/EPC11 86086) <16000>* **VOULEZ VOUS** [1] Jun79 [19]

– As good as new / Voulez-vous / I have a dream / Angeleyes / The king has lost his crown / Does your mother know / If it wasn't for the night / Chiquitita / Lovers (like a little longer) / Kisses of fire. *(re-iss. Jul86 lp/c; EPC/40 32322) (cd-iss. Nov86; CD 86086) (cd re-iss. Jun89; CD 32322) (re-iss. Sep92 on 'Polydor' cd/c; 821320-2/-4)*

Jul 79. (7") *(EPC 7499) <3609>* **ANGELEYES. / VOULEZ-VOUS** 3 64
80
(re-iss. Feb89 on 'Old Gold'; OG 9856)

Oct 79. (7") *(EPC 7914) <3652>* **GIMME GIMME GIMME (A MAN AFTER MIDNIGHT). / THE KING HAS LOST HIS CROWN** 3

Nov 79. (lp/c) *(EPC/40 10017) <16009>* **GREATEST HITS VOL.2** (compilation 1976-1979) 1 Dec79 46
– Take a chance on me / Gimme gimme gimme (a man after midnight) / Money money money / Rock me / Eagle / Angeleyes / Dancing queen / Does your mother know / Chiquitita / Summer night city / I wonder / Name of the game / Thank you for the music / Knowing me knowing you. *(cd-iss. 1984; CD 10017) (re-iss. May87 lp/c; 450915-1/-4)*

Dec 79. (7") *(EPC 8088)* **I HAVE A DREAM. / TAKE A CHANCE ON ME (live)** 2 –

Jul 80. (7"/12") *(EPC/+12 8835) <3776>* **THE WINNER TAKES IT ALL. / ELAINE** 1 Nov80 8

Nov 80. (7") *(EPC 9089) <3806>* **SUPER TROUPER. / THE PIPER** 1 Mar81 45

Nov 80. (lp/c) *(EPC/40 10022) <16023>* **SUPER TROUPER** 1 Dec80 17
– Super trouper / The winner takes it all / On and on and on / Andante andante / He and I / Happy New Year / Our last summer / The piper / Lay all your love on me / The way old friends do. *(also box-lp; ABBOX 1) (cd-iss. May83; CD 10022) (re-iss. Sep92 on 'Polydor' cd/c; 800023-2/-4)*

Jun 81. (7") *(EPCA 1314) <3826>* **LAY ALL YOUR LOVE ON ME. / ON AND ON AND ON** 7 B-side 90

Dec 81. (7"/7"pic-d) *(EPCA/+11 1740) <89881>* **ONE OF US. / SHOULD I LAUGH OR CRY** 3

Dec 81. (lp/c) *(EPC/40 10032) <19332>* **THE VISITORS** 1 Jan82 29
– The visitors / Head over heels / When all is said and done / Soldiers / I let the music speak / One of us / Two for the price of one / Slipping through my fingers / Like an angel / Passing through my room / Eagle. *(cd-iss. May83; CD 10032) (re-iss. Sep92 on 'Polydor' cd/c; 800011-2/-4)*

Jan 82. (7") *<3889>* **WHEN ALL IS SAID AND DONE. / SHOULD I LAUGH OR CRY** – 27

Feb 82. (7") *(EPCA 2037) <4031>* **HEAD OVER HEELS. / THE VISITORS** 25 B-side 63

Oct 82. (7") *(EPCA 2847) <89948>* **THE DAY BEFORE YOU CAME. / CASSANDRA** 32

Nov 82. (d-lp/d-c) *(ABBA/+40 10) <80036>* **THE SINGLES – THE FIRST TEN YEARS** (compilation) 1 62
– Ring ring / Waterloo / So long / I do I do I do I do I do / S.O.S. / Mamma mia / Fernando / Ancing queen / Money money money / Knowing me knowing you / The name of the game / Take a chance on me / Summer night city / Chiquitita / Does your mother know / Voulez-vous / Gimme gimme gimme (a man after midnight) / I have a dream / The winner takes it all / Super trouper / One of us / The day before you came / Under attack. *(also iss.d-pic-lp; ABBOX 11-1/2) (cd-iss. Sep83; ABBACD 10)*

Dec 82. (7"/7"pic-d) *(EPCA/+11 2971)* **UNDER ATTACK. / YOU OWE ME ONE** 26 –

—— broke up late '82, FALTSKOG + FRIDA both had successful solo careers

– compilations, others, etc. –

on 'Epic' UK / 'Atlantic' unless mentioned otherwise

Aug 82. (7"ep/c-ep) *(EPCA/40 2618)* **GREATEST ORIGINAL HITS (EP)** –
– Super trouper / The winner takes it all / Lay all your love on me.

Nov 83. (7"/7"sha-pic-d) *(A/WA 3894)* **THANK YOU FOR THE MUSIC (live). / OUR LAST SUMMER (live)** 33

Nov 83. (lp/c) *(EPC/40 10043)* **THANK YOU FOR THE MUSIC – A COLLECTION OF LOVE SONGS (live)** 17 –
– My love, my life / I wonder / Happy New Year / Slipping through my fingers / Fernando / One man, one woman / Eagle / I have a dream / Our last summer / The day before you came / Chiquitita / Should I laugh or cry / The old way friends do / Thank you for the music. *(originally rel.Mar81 as 'GRACIAS POR LA MUSICA'; EPC 86123) (re-iss. Aug92 on 'Ariola Express' cd/c; 2/4 90928)*

Apr 84. (26x7"box) *(ABBA 26)* **ANNIVERSARY BOX SET** –
– (all 26 singles)

Aug 86. (lp/c)(cd) *Polydor; (POLH/+C 29)(829 951-2)* **ABBA LIVE (live)** –
(re-iss. Sep92 cd/c; 829951-2/-4)

Sep 87. (lp/c) *Hallmark; (SHM/HSC 3215)* **THE HITS** –
(cd-iss. Jan89 on 'Pickwick' PCD 866)

Nov 87. (7") *Old Gold; (OG 9726)* **DANCING QUEEN. / FERNANDO** –

Nov 87. (7") *Old Gold; (OG 9727)* **TAKE A CHANCE ON ME. / CHIQUITITA** –

Dec 87. (d-lp/c/cd) *Castle; (CCS LP/MC/CD 176)* **ABBA – THE COLLECTION** –

Jan 88. (7") *Old Gold; (OG 9741)* **WATERLOO. / MAMMA MIA** –

Feb 88. (lp/c) *Hallmark; (SHM/HSC 3229)* **THE HITS 2** –
(cd-iss. Jan89 on 'Pickwick'; PWKS 500)

Sep 88. (lp/c) *Hallmark; (SHM/HSC 3241)* **THE HITS 3** –
(cd-iss. Jan89 on 'Pickwick'; PWKS 15)

Nov 88. (d-lp/c/cd) *Castle; (CCS LP/MC/CD 198)* **ABBA – THE COLLECTION 2** –

Nov 88. (lp/c/cd) *Telstar; (STAR/STAC/TCD 2329)* **ABSOLUTE ABBA** 70 –

Feb 89. (7") *Old Gold; (OG 9858)* **KNOWING ME KNOWING YOU. / THE WINNER TAKES IT ALL** –

Feb 89. (7") *Old Gold; (OG 9860)* **GIMME GIMME GIMME (A MAN AFTER MIDNIGHT). / DOES YOUR MOTHER KNOW** –

Dec 89. (lp/c) *Hallmark; (SHM/HSC 3297)* **THE LOVE SONGS** –
(cd-iss. on 'Pickwick'; PWKS 564)

Jan 90. (12") *Old Gold; (OG 4151)* **LAY ALL YOUR LOVE ON ME. / SUMMER NIGHT CITY** –

Nov 91. (t-cd/t-c;box) *Carlton; (BOX D/C 1)* **THE HITS BOX** –

Aug 92. (7"/c-s) *Polydor; (PO/+CS 231)* **DANCING QUEEN. / LAY YOUR LOVE ON ME** 16
(12"+=/cd-s+=) *(PZ/+CD 231)* – The day before you came / Eagle.

Sep 92. (cd/c/d-lp) *Polydor; (<517007-2/-4/-1>)* **ABBA – GOLD GREATEST HITS** 1 63
– Dancing queen / Knowing me, knowing you / Take a chance on me / Mamma mia / Lay all your love on me / Super trouper / I have a dream / The winner takes it all / Money, money, money / S.O.S. / Chiquitita / Fernando / Voulez vous / Gimme, gimme, gimme (a man after midnight) / Does your mother know / One of us / The name of the game / Thank you for the music / Waterloo. *(re-iss. Feb99; same)*

Nov 92. (7"/c-s) *Polydor; (PO/+CS)* **THANK YOU FOR THE MUSIC. / HAPPY NEW YEAR**
(cd-s+=) *(PZCD)* – The way old friends do.

Dec 92. (cd-s) *Polydor;* **VOULEZ VOUS /**

May 93. (cd/c/lp) *Polydor; (<519353-2/-4/-1>)* **ABBA GOLD VOL.2 – MORE ABBA HITS** 14
(re-iss. Jul99; same) – hit No.13

Nov 94. (4xcd-box) *Polydor; (<523472-2>)* **THANK YOU FOR THE MUSIC**
(re-iss. May99; same)

Nov 95. (3xcd-box) *Polydor;* **VOULEZ VOUS / SUPER TROUPER / ARRIVAL** –

Mar 96. (cd/c) *Spectrum; (551109-2/-4)* **AND THE MUSIC STILL GOES ON** –

Oct 96. (d-cd) *Polydor; (<533083-2>)* **FOREVER GOLD**

Oct 98. (cd/c) *Polydor; (<559221-2/-4>)* **LOVE SONGS** 51

Nov 98. (cd/c) *Spectrum; (551109-2/-4)* **THE MUSIC STILL GOES ON** –

Apr 99. (28xcd-s-box) *Polydor; (563286-2)* **THE SINGLES COLLECTION 1972-1982** –

Nov 99. (27xcd-s-box) *Polydor; (561252-2)* **THE SINGLES COLLECTION 1972-1982** –

Oct 01. (d-cd) *Polydor; (<549974-2>)* **THE DEFINITIVE COLLECTION** 17 Nov01
– People need love / He is your brother / Ring ring / Love isn't easy (but it sure is hard enough) / Waterloo / Honey, honey / So long / I do, I do, I do, I do, I do / S.O.S. / Mamma mia / Fernando / Dancing queen / Money, money, money / Knowing me, knowing you / The name of the game / Take a chance on me / Eagle / Summer night city / Chiquitita / Does your mother know / Voulez-vous / Angeleyes / Gimme! gimme! gimme! (a man after midnight) / I have a dream / The winner takes it all / Super trouper / On and on and on / Lay all your love on me / One of us / When all is said and done / Head over heels / The visitors (crackin' up) / The day before you came / Under attack / Thank you for the music. *(bonus+=)* – Ring ring (single remix) / Voulez-vous (extended).

—— BENNY & BJORN in 1984 collaborated with TIM RICE on 'CHESS' stage show. Released as d-lp,d-c,d-cd on 'RCA' Oct84; it hit UK No.10. It featured many singers, including MURRAY HEAD who scored UK No.12 / US No.3 hit with ONE NIGHT IN BANGKOK. To end the year '84, ELAINE PAIGE & BARBARA DICKSON hit UK No.1 duetting on I KNOW HIM SO WELL. ELAINE was to release more solo flops from the musical between late 1984-Spring 1986. In Oct85 'Telstar' issued lp,c,cd. 'CHESS PIECES –

THE BEST OF CHESS' to attemt to cash in musicals' success. In 1986, both wrote and backed brother/sister duo GEMINI. An eponymous album was issued on 'Polydor', as were 2 singles 'JUST LIKE THAT' & 'ANOTHER YOU, ANOTHER ME'. The following year, another album GEMINISM was released on 'Polar' in Sweden only. Later in '87, BENNY released debut solo album 'KLINGA MINA KLOCKOR' on own label 'Mono Music' in Sweden. BENNY and BJORN went on to work with and produce most artists on that label.

☐ ABBC (see under ⇒ CALEXICO)

ABC

Formed: Sheffield, England . . . 1979 as VICE VERSA by STEPHEN SINGLETON and MARK WHITE. In late 1980, they found 'Modern Drugs' fanzine editor, MARTIN FRY, and became ABC, starting their own 'Neutron' label which was soon (early 1982) distributed by Phonogram. Their first 45, 'TEARS ARE NOT ENOUGH', broke through into the UK Top 20 and they soon became leading contenders in the New Romantic attempt to dethrone DURAN DURAN and SPANDAU BALLET. ABC touted unashamed glamour-pop to former punks who'd become tired of tuneless grimacing. A follow-up single, 'POISON ARROW', narrowly missed the Top 5 in addition to cracking the US Top 30, the Americans rapidly developing a taste for all things New Romantic. A third single, 'THE LOOK OF LOVE' remains the defining ABC moment, a lavish lame' suit of a record. This Top 5 success saw the debut album, 'THE LEXICON OF LOVE' unsurprisingly clinch a No.1 spot. Produced by ubiquitous 80's guru, TREVOR HORN, the record remains one of the most popular albums of the early 80's, not only a lexicon of love, but a kaleidoscope of kitsch and a dictionary of debonair cool. It spawned one further single, 'ALL OF MY HEART', later that year, FRY and Co. touring extensively before entering the studio for a follow-up set, 'BEAUTY STAB'. A more rock-centric affair, the album met with frowning reviews, although it did make the Top 20. With DAVID YARRITH and EDEN replacing SINGLETON and bassist MARK LICKLEY respectively, a further effort, the kitschy 'HOW TO BE A ZILLIONAIRE' (1985) reclaimed at least some of the lost ground with a Top 10 US hit in 'BE NEAR ME'. Although FRY was subsequently diagnosed with Hodgkin's Disease (a form of cancer), the group bounced back with a Top 10 album, 'ALPHABET CITY' (1987) and a transatlantic smash with the SMOKEY ROBINSON tribute song, 'WHEN SMOKEY SINGS'. Though a further couple of low-key sets followed, the group were fairly inactive for most of the 90's, a comeback album 'SKYSCRAPING' – produced by GLENN GREGORY of HEAVEN 17 – in 1997 failing to register any commercial success.

Album rating: THE LEXICON OF LOVE (*9) / BEAUTY STAB (*5) / HOW TO BE A . . . ZILLIONAIRE! (*6) / ALPHABET CITY (*5) / UP (*4) / ABSOLUTELY ABC (compilation) (*7) / ABRACADABRA (*4) / SKYSCRAPING (*5) / LOOK OF LOVE – THE VERY BEST OF ABC compilation (*7)

VICE VERSA

MARK WHITE (b. 1 Apr'61) – guitar, synthesizers / **STEPHEN SINGLETON** (b.17 Apr'59) – saxophone, synthesizers / **DAVE WYNDHAM** – vocals

Neutron | not iss.

Jan 80. (7"ep) *(NT 001)* **MUSIC 4** [ ] [–]
– New girls / Neutrons / Science-fact / Riot squad / Camille.

—— added **MARTIN FRY** (b. 9 Mar'58, Manchester) – vocals

Jun 81. (7") *(NT 003)* **STILYAGI. / EYES OF CHRIST** [–] Dutch [–]

ABC

—— added **MARK LICKLEY** – bass / **DAVID ROBINSON** – drums

Neutron | Mercury

Oct 81. (7") *(NT 101)* **TEARS ARE NOT ENOUGH. / ALPHABET SOUP** [19] [ ]
(12"+=) *(NTX 101)* – ('A'+'B'extended).

Feb 82. (7") *(NT 102) <810340>* **POISON ARROW. / THEME FROM MANTRAP** [6] Jan83 [25]
(12"+=) *(NTX 102)* – Mantrap (The Lounge Sequence).

—— **DAVID PALMER** (b.29 May'61, Chesterfield) – drums; repl. ROBINSON

May 82. (7") *(NT 103) <76168>* **THE LOOK OF LOVE. / (part 2)** [4] Aug82 [18]
(12"+=) *(NTX 103)* – (parts 3 & 4). *(re-iss. Oct83; same)*

Jun 82. (lp/c) *(NTRS/+C 1) <4059>* **THE LEXICON OF LOVE** [1] Sep82 [24]
– Show me / Poison arrow / Many happy returns / Tears are not enough / Valentine's day / The look of love / Date stamp / All of my heart / 4 ever 2 gether / The look of love. *(cd-iss. Feb83; 810003-2) (remastered Mar96; 514942-2)*

Aug 82. (7") *(NT 104)* **ALL OF MY HEART. / OVERTURE** [5] [ ]

—— guest session man **ANDY NEWMARK** – drums repl. PALMER

Oct 83. (7"/12") *(NT/+X 105) <814631>* **THAT WAS THEN BUT THIS IS NOW. / VERTIGO** [18] Jan84 [89]

Nov 83. (lp/c)(cd) *(NTRL/+C 2)(<814661>)* **BEAUTY STAB** [12] [69]
– That was then but this is now / Love's a dangerous language / If I ever thought you'd be lonely / The power of persuasion / Beauty stab / By default by design / Hey citizen / King money / Bite the hand / Unzip / S.O.S. / United kingdom. *(cd re-iss. Jul02 on 'Mercury'; 536397-2)*

Jan 84. (7"/7"pic-d/12") *(NT/+P/X 106)* **S.O.S. / UNITED KINGDOM** [39] [ ]

—— **FRY + WHITE** recruited new members (alongside other sessioners) **DAVID YARRITH** – keyboards; repl. SINGLETON / **EDEN** (b. FIONA RUSSELL-POWELL) – keyboards; repl. LICKLEY

Oct 84. (7") *(NT 107) <884382>* **HOW TO BE A MILLIONAIRE. / HOW TO BE A BILLIONAIRE** [49] Jan86 [20]
(ext.12"+=) *(NTX 107)* – ('A'-acappella version) / How to be a . . . zillionaire (mix).
(12") *(NTXR 107)* – ('A'acappella & Zillionaire mixes only).

Mar 85. (7") *(NT 108) <880626>* **BE NEAR ME. / A TO Z** [26] Aug85 [9]
(d7"+=) *(NTD 108)* – Poison arrow / The look of love (US mix).
(12") *(NTX 108)* – ('A'disco mix) / What's your destination.

Jun 85. (7"/7"sha-pic-d) *(NT/+P 109) <884714>* **VANITY KILLS. / JUDY'S JEWELS** [70] May86 [91]
(d7"+=) *(NTD 109)* – S.O.S. / United Kingdom.
(12"+=) *(NTX 109)* – You love you (instrumental).
(12"+=) *(NTXR 109)* – Be near me (ecstacy mix).

Oct 85. (lp/c)(cd) *(NTRH/+C 3)(<824904>)* **HOW TO BE A . . . ZILLIONAIRE!** [28] [30]
– Tower of London / How to be a millionaire / Ocean blue / Fear of the world* / Vanity kills* / Be near me* / A to Z / So hip it hurts / Between you and me / 15 storey halo. *(c+=/cd+=)* – (diff.track mixes*)

Jan 86. (7") *(NT 110)* **OCEAN BLUE. / TOWER OF LONDON (instrumental)** [51] [ ]
(d7"+=) *(NTD 110)* – All of my heart / The look of love.
(12"+=) *(NTX 110)* – ('A'mix) / Be near me (mix).
(12"+=) *(NTXR 110)* – ABC Megamix.

—— trimmed to **FRY + WHITE** duo plus sessioners (unknown)

May 87. (7") *(NT 111) <888604>* **WHEN SMOKEY SINGS. / CHICAGO (pt.1)** [11] [5]
(12"+=) *(NTX 111)* – Chicago (pt.2).
(cd-s+=) *(NTCD 111)* – All of my heart (live).

Aug 87. (7") *(NT 112)* **THE NIGHT YOU MURDERED LOVE. / MINNEAPOLIS** [31] [ ]
(12"+=/c-s+=) *(NT X/C 112)* – ('A'version).

Oct 87. (lp/c)(cd) *(NTRH/+C 4)(<832391>)* **ALPHABET CITY** [7] Aug87 [48]
– Avenue A / When Smokey sings / The night you murdered love / Think again / rage and then regret / Arkangel / King without a crown / Bad blood / Jealous lover / One day / Avenue Z. *(cd+=)* – (4 versions of last 2 singles 7")

Nov 87. (7") *(NT 113)* **KING WITHOUT A CROWN. / THE LOOK OF LOVE (live)** [44] [ ]
(c-s+=/12"pic-d+=) *(NT MC/XR 113)* – Poison arrow (live).
(12"++=/cd-s++=) *(NT X/CD 113)* – All of my heart (live).

May 89. (7") *(NT 114)* **ONE BETTER WORLD. / ('A'-percapella mix)** [32] [ ]
(12"+=/cd-s+=) *(NT X/CD 114)* – ('A'club mix) / ('A'garage mix).
(12"+=) *(NTXR 114)* – (above 3 extra mixes only; not 7" version)

Aug 89. (lp/c/cd) *(<838646-1/-4/-2>)* **UP** [58] [ ]

– Never more than now / The real thing / One better world / Where is the Heaven? / The greatest love of all / I'm in love with you / Paper thin. *(re-iss. cd Aug94; same)*

Sep 89. (7") *(NT 115)* **THE REAL THING. / THE GREATEST LOVE OF ALL** [68] [ ]
(c-s+=) *(NTMC 115)* – North.
(cd-s++=) *(NTCD 115)* – The look of love (pt.5).
(12"+=/12"pic-d+=) *(NTX/+R 115)* – When Smokey sings / Be near me.

Mar 90. (7") *(NT 116)* **THE LOOK OF LOVE (1990 remix). / OCEAN BLUE** [68] [ ]
(12"+=/cd-s+=) *(NT X/CD 116)* – Vanity kills.

Apr 90. (cd/c/lp) *(<842967-2/-4/-1>)* **ABSOLUTELY ABC** (compilation) [7] [ ]
– Poison arrow / The look of love / All of my heart / Tears are not enough / That was then but this is now / S.O.S. / How to be a millionaire / Be near me / When Smokey sings / The night you murdered love / King without a crown / One better world. *(c+=/cd+=)* – Look of love (1990 remix) / When Smokey sings (12"remix) / Be near me (12"remix) / One better world (12"remix) / Ocean blue.

Parlophone M.C.A.

Jun 91. (c-s/7") *(TC+/R 6292)* **LOVE CONQUERS ALL. / WHAT'S GOOD ABOUT GOODBYE** [47] [ ]
(cd-s+=) *(CDR 6292)* – ('A'extended) / ('A'percapella).

Aug 91. (cd/c/lp) *(CD/TC+/PCS 7355)* **ABRACADABRA** [50] Oct91 [ ]
– Love conquers all / Unhook the secrets of your heart / Answered prayer / Spellbound / Say it / Welcome to the real world / Satori / All that matters / This must be magic.

Aug 91. (c-s/7") *(TC+/R 6298) <54040>* **SAY IT (Black Box mix). / ('A'-Abracadabra mix)** [ ] [ ]
(12"+=) *(12R 6298) <54055>* – Satori.
(cd-s+=) *(CDR 6298)* – ('A'-piano mix / ('A'instrumental).
(re-iss. Jan92, hit UK No.42; same)

—— re-formed for one-off in 1996

Blatant-Arista Deconstr.

Mar 97. (c-s) *(74321 45363-4)* **STRANGER THINGS / THE WORLD SPINS ON** [57] [–]
(cd-s+=) *(74321 45363-2)* – All we need.

Apr 97. (cd/c) *(<74321 45653-2/-4>)* **SKYSCRAPING** [ ] [ ]
– Stranger things / Ask a thousand times / Skyscraping / Who can I turn to / Rolling sevens / Only the best will do / Love is its own reward / Light years / Seven day weekend / Heaven knows / Faraway.

May 97. (10"/cd-s) *(74321 48525-1/-2)* **SKYSCRAPING / LIGHT YEARS. / SKYDUBBING / STRANGER THINGS (live)** [ ] [–]

Jul 97. (c-s) *(74321 49807-4)* **ROLLING SEVENS / ALL OF MY HEART (live)** [ ] [–]
(cd-s+=) *(74321 49807-2)* – The look of love (live) / Heaven knows.

– compilations, etc. –

Mar 93. (cd/c) *Connoisseur; (VSOP CD/MC 182)* **THE REMIX COLLECTION** [ ] [–]

May 93. (cd/c) *Spectrum; (550000-2/-4)* **TEARS ARE NOT ENOUGH** [ ] [–]

Aug 95. (d-cd) *Neutron; (528600-2)* **LEXICON OF LOVE / BEAUTY STAB** [ ] [–]

Mar 96. (cd/c) *Spectrum; (551831-2/-4)* **THE COLLECTION** [ ] [–]

Sep 99. (cd) *Blatant; (BLATCD 1)* **THE LEXICON OF LIVE (live)** [ ] [–]

Nov 99. (cd) *Universal; (546804-2)* **UNIVERSAL MASTERS COLLECTION** [ ] [–]

Jun 00. (cd) *Mercury; <542459>* **THE BEST OF ABC: THE MILLENNIUM COLLECTION** [–] [ ]

Jul 00. (cd) *Delta No.1; (CD 23105)* **ONE BETTER WORLD** [ ] [–]

Mar 01. (cd) *Neutron; (548522-2)* **HELLO! – AN INTRODUCTION TO ABC** [ ] [–]

Jul 01. (cd) *Universal; (<586237-2>)* **LOOK OF LOVE – THE VERY BEST OF ABC** [69] Nov01 [ ]
– The look of love / All of my heart / Poison arrow / When Smokey sings / That was then but this is now / Tears are not enough / How to be a millionaire / The night you murdered love / Peace and tranquility / One better world / S.O.S. / King without a crown / Be near me / Ocean blue / Vanity kills / The real thing / Blame.

Apr 02. (cd) *Spectrum; (554858-2)* **POISON ARROW** [ ] [ ]

☐ A CAMP (see under ⇒ CARDIGANS)

AC/DC

Formed: Sydney, Australia ... 1973, by ex-pat Scots brothers MALCOLM and ANGUS YOUNG. After an initial single, 'CAN I SIT NEXT TO YOU', the siblings headed for Melbourne where they recruited another Caledonian exile, wildman BON SCOTT. Stabilizing the line-up with MARK EVANS and PHIL RUDD, the band signed up with 'Albert' records, a company run by the eldest YOUNG brother, GEORGE, and HARRY VANDA (both ex-EASYBEATS). AC/DC's first two releases, 'HIGH VOLTAGE' (1975) and 'TNT' (1976) were Australia-only affairs, competent boogie-rock that established their name on the domestic scene and generated enough interest for 'Atlantic' UK to come sniffing with chequebook in hand. With major label muscle behind them, the band relocated to London just as punk was rearing its snotty, vomit-encrusted head. With their particular brand of no-frills rock and ANGUS' school uniform stage gear, the band were initially loosely affiliated to the scene. But with ANGUS' bowel-quaking riffs and SCOTT's high-pitched bellow, their eventual status as one of the archetypal heavy metal acts was almost inevitable from the off. 'Atlantic' introduced the band to Britain with a compilation drawn from the group's first two Australian releases (confusingly also titled 'HIGH VOLTAGE') and AC/DC's first album proper was 1976's 'DIRTY DEEDS DONE DIRT CHEAP'. While its follow-up, 'LET THERE BE ROCK' gave the band their first taste of chart action, AC/DC were first and foremost a live band. The bare-legged cheek of ANGUS was eminently entertaining, his body contorting and jerking like a clockwork toy on speed (NEIL YOUNG's more frenetic noodlings bear a striking similarity, long lost brothers perhaps?!). After a corking live album, 'IF YOU WANT BLOOD, YOU'VE GOT IT' (featuring that classic paeon to the larger woman, 'WHOLE LOTTA ROSIE', no anorexic waifs for this lot!), the band hit the big time with 'HIGHWAY TO HELL' (1979). Despite a more commercial sheen courtesy of producer Mutt Lange, the likes of 'TOUCH TOO MUCH' and the title track were unforgettable AC/DC moments, utilising the band's trademark steamrolling rhythm section and their inimitable way with a testosterone-saturated chorus. As ever, the group's lyrics were, for the most part, positively neolithic although their reliably unreconstructed, femininst-baiting songs were never without humour, something of a novelty in the metal scene of that era. Being Scottish/Australian, and a rock star to boot, BON SCOTT wasn't exactly a lager shandy man, the 'Uisge Beath' ('Water of life', or whisky to sassenach readers) rather taking away his life after he drank himself into an early grave the following February (1980). Yet incredibly, by July, the band were back with a No. 1 album, 'BACK IN BLACK', a record that saw the band finally break big in America. Ex-GEORDIE singer, BRIAN JOHNSON, had been recruited on vocal duties and his gravelly yelp carried on where SCOTT left off. The likes of 'HELL'S BELLS' and the irrepressible 'YOU SHOOK ME ALL NIGHT LONG' were staples of rock discos (remember them?) up and down the land and the band became a top drawer draw in the age of stadium rock, headlining the legendary Castle Donington Festival in its heyday. Yet from here on in, AC/DC lost their spark somewhat. 'FLICK OF THE SWITCH' and 'FLY ON THE WALL' were metal by numbers although 'WHO MADE WHO' (1986) was an interesting hotch-potch of new and old. 'BLOW UP YOUR VIDEO' (1988) and 'THE RAZOR'S EDGE' (1990) saw a resurgence of sorts, the respective sets making Top 5. The band continued to tour for the metal faithful, 1992's 'LIVE' documenting the visceral thrill of the AC/DC concert experience. But while their formula was wearing a bit thin, nobody seemed to have informed the band, 1995's hilariously titled 'BALLBREAKER' crudely retreading over-familiar ground. Still, in the (supposedly) sophisticated PC world of the 90's, you had to hand it to a band who could still get away with titles like 'COVER YOU IN OIL', 'HARD AS A ROCK' and 'LOVE BOMB'. Signed to 'Liberty' at the turn of the millennium, AC/DC delivered a much improved and even tastier set of numbers via 'STIFF UPPER LIP' (2000). Vive le rock! • **Songwriters:** Most by YOUNG brothers, some with SCOTT or JOHNSON. Covered; BABY PLEASE DON'T GO / BONNY (trad).

Album rating: HIGH VOLTAGE (UK *8) / DIRTY DEEDS DONE DIRT CHEAP (*6) / LET THERE BE ROCK (*8) / POWERAGE (*6) / IF YOU WANT BLOOD – YOU'VE GOT IT (*8) / HIGHWAY TO HELL (*8) / BACK IN BLACK (*8) / FOR THOSE ABOUT TO ROCK (WE SALUTE YOU) (*4) / FLICK OF THE SWITCH (*5) / FLY ON THE WALL (*5) / WHO MADE WHO (*5) / BLOW UP YOUR VIDEO (*7) / THE RAZOR'S EDGE (*5) / LIVE (*7) / BALLBREAKER (*6) / STIFF UPPER LIP (*7)

ANGUS YOUNG (b.31 Mar'59, Glasgow, Scotland) – guitar / **MALCOLM YOUNG** (b. 6 Jan'53, Glasgow) – guitar / **DAVE EVANS** – vocals / **ROB BAILEY** – bass / **PETER CLACK** – drums

not iss. — Albert

Jul 74. (7") **CAN I SIT NEXT TO YOU. / ROCKIN' IN THE PARLOUR** [–] Aust. [–]

— When all but the brothers departed, they recruited (i.e.DAVE joined RABBIT) **BON SCOTT** (b.RONALD SCOTT, 9 Jul'46, Kirriemuir, Scotland) – vocals (ex-VALENTINES, ex-FRATERNITY, ex-SPECTORS, ex-MOUNT LOFTY RANGERS) / **MARK EVANS** – (b. 2 Mar'56, Melbourne) – bass (ex-BUSTER BROWN) / **PHIL RUDD** (b.19 May'54, Melbourne) – drums

Jan 75. (lp) *<APLP 009>* **HIGH VOLTAGE** [–] Austra [–]
– Baby please don't go / She's got balls / Little lover / Stick around / Soul stripper / You ain't got a hold of me / Love song / Show business.

1975. (7") **DOG EAT DOG. / CARRY ME HOME** [–] Austra [–]

Dec 75. (lp) *<APLP 016>* **T.N.T.** [–] Austra [–]
– It's a long way to the top (if you wanna rock'n'roll) / The Rock'n'roll singer / The jack / Live wire / T.N.T. / Rocker / Can I sit next to you girl / High voltage / School days.

Atlantic — Atco

Apr 76. (7") *(K 10745)* **IT'S A LONG WAY TO THE TOP (IF YOU WANNA ROCK'N'ROLL). / CAN I SIT NEXT TO YOU GIRL** [ ] [–]
(re-iss. Jun80 on 'Heavy Metal-Atlantic'; HM 3) (hit UK 55)

May 76. (lp/c) *(K/K4 50257)* **HIGH VOLTAGE** (compilation from two above) [ ] [–]
– It's a long way to the top (if you wanna rock'n'roll) / The rock'n'roll singer / The jack / Live wire / T.N.T. / Can I sit next to you girl / Little lover / She's got balls / High voltage. *<US-iss.Apr81; 142> (cd-iss. Oct87; K2 50257) (re-iss. Jul94 cd/c; 7567 92413-2/-4) (cd re-iss. May98 on 'E.M.I.'; 494671-2)*

Aug 76. (7") *(K 10805)* **JAILBREAK. / FLING THING** [ ] [–]
(re-iss. Mar80)

Oct 76. (7") *(K 10860)* **HIGH VOLTAGE. / LIVE WIRE** [ ] [–]
(re-iss. Jun80 on 'Heavy Metal-Atlantic'; HM 1) (hit UK 48)

Dec 76. (7") *<7068>* **HIGH VOLTAGE. / IT'S A LONG WAY TO THE TOP (IF YOU WANNA ROCK'N'ROLL)** [–] [ ]

Dec 76. (lp/c) *(K/K4 50323)* **DIRTY DEEDS DONE DIRT CHEAP** [ ] [–]
– Dirty deeds done dirt cheap / Love at first feel / Big balls / Rocker / Problem child / There's gonna be some rockin' / Ain't no fun (waiting round to be a millionaire) / Ride on / Squealer. *<US-iss.Apr81; 16033>* – <hit No.3> *(cd-iss. Aug87; K2 50323) (re-iss. Jul94 cd/c; 7567 92448-2/-4) (cd re-iss. May98 on 'E.M.I.'; 494670-2)*

Jan 77. (7"m) *(K 10899)* **DIRTY DEEDS DONE DIRT CHEAP. / BIG BALLS / THE JACK** [ ] [–]
(re-iss. Jun80 on 'Heavy Metal-Atlantic'; HM 2) (hit UK 47)

— **CLIFF WILLIAMS** (b.14 Dec'49, Romford, England) – bass (ex-HOME, ex-BANDIT) repl. MARK

Sep 77. (7") *(K 11018)* *<7086>* **LET THERE BE ROCK. / PROBLEM CHILD** [ ] [ ]
(re-iss. Mar80)

Oct 77. (lp/c) *(K/K4 50366)* *<151>* **LET THERE BE ROCK** [17] [ ]
– Go down / Dog eat dog / Let there be rock / Bad boy boogie / Overdose / Crapsody in blue / Hell ain't a bad place to be / Whole lotta Rosie. *(cd-iss. Jun89; K2 50366) (re-iss. Oct94 cd/c; 7567 92445-2/-4) (cd re-iss. Sep98 on 'E.M.I.'; 497316-2)*

Atlantic — Atlantic

May 78. (lp/c) *(K/K4 50483)* *<19180>* **POWERAGE** [26] [ ]
– Gimme a bullet / Down payment blues / Gone shootin' / Riff raff / Sin city / Up to my neck in you / What's next to the moon / Cold hearted man / Kicked in the teeth. *(cd-iss. Jun89; K 781 548-2) (re-iss. Oct94 cd/c; 7567 92446-2/-4) (cd re-iss. May98 on 'E.M.I.'; 494672-2)*

May 78. (7"/12") *(K 11142/+T)* **ROCK'N'ROLL DAMNATION. / SIN CITY** [24] [–]
(re-iss. Mar80; same)

Jun 78. (7") *<3499>* **ROCK'N'ROLL DAMNATION. / KICKED IN THE TEETH** [–] [ ]

Oct 78. (lp/c) *(K/K4 50532)* *<19212>* **IF YOU WANT BLOOD, YOU'VE GOT IT (live)** [13] [ ]
– Riff raff / Hell ain't a bad place to be / Bad boy boogie / The jack / Problem child / Whole lotta Rosie / Rock'n'roll damnation / High voltage / Let there be rock / Rocker. *(re-iss. Mar80; same) (cd-iss. Jun89; K 781 553-2) (re-iss. Oct94; 7567 92447-2/-4) (cd re-iss. May98 on 'E.M.I.'; 494669-2)*

Oct 78. (7"/12") *(K 11207/+T)* *<3553>* **WHOLE LOTTA ROSIE (live). / HELL AIN'T A BAD PLACE TO BE (live)** [ ] [ ]
(re-iss. Mar80; same) (re-iss. Jun80 on 'Heavy Metal-Atlantic'; HM 4) (hit UK 36)

Aug 79. (lp/c) *(K/K4 50628)* *<19244>* **HIGHWAY TO HELL** [8] [17]
– Highway to Hell / Girls got rhythm / Walk all over you / Touch too much / Beating around the bush / Shot down in flames / Get it hot / If you want blood (you've got it) / Love hungry man / Night prowler. *(cd-iss. Jul87; 250 628-2) (cd re-iss. 1989; K2 50628) (cd re-iss. Jan98 on 'E.M.I.'; 477088-2)*

Aug 79. (7") *(K 11321)* **HIGHWAY TO HELL. / IF YOU WANT BLOOD (YOU'VE GOT IT)** [56] [–]
(re-iss. Mar80; same)

Aug 79. (7") *<3617>* **HIGHWAY TO HELL. / NIGHT PROWLER** [–] [47]

Oct 79. (7") *(K 11406)* **GIRLS GOT RHYTHM. / GET IT HOT** [ ] [–]
(7"ep) *(K 11406E)* – ('A'side) / If you want blood (you've got it) / Hell ain't a bad place to be (live) / Rock'n'roll damnation.

Jan 80. (7"m) *(K 11435)* **TOUCH TOO MUCH (live). / LIVE WIRE (live) / SHOT DOWN IN FLAMES (live)** [29] [–]

Feb 80. (7") *<3644>* **TOUCH TOO MUCH (live). / WALK ALL OVER YOU (live)** [–] [ ]

— **BRIAN JOHNSON** (b.5 Oct'47, Newcastle, England) – vocals (ex-GEORDIE) repl. BON SCOTT who died 20 Feb'80 after drunken binge.

Jul 80. (lp/c) *(K/K4 50735)* *<16018>* **BACK IN BLACK** [1] [4]
– Hells bells / Shoot to thrill / What do you do for money honey / Give the dog a bone / Let me put my love into you / Back in black / You shook me all night long / Have a drink on me / Shake a leg / Rock and roll ain't noise pollution. *(cd-iss. Feb87; K2 50735) (re-iss. Aug94 cd/c; 7567 92418-2/-4) (cd re-iss. Jun98 on 'E.M.I.'; 495153-2)*

Sep 80. (7") *(K 11600)* *<3761>* **YOU SHOOK ME ALL NIGHT LONG. / HAVE A DRINK ON ME** [38] [35]

Nov 80. (7"/12") *(K 11630/+T)* **ROCK'N'ROLL AIN'T NOISE POLLUTION. / HELL'S BELLS** [15] [ ]

Feb 81. (7") *<3787>* **BACK IN BLACK. / WHAT DO YOU DO FOR MONEY HONEY** [–] [37]

Nov 81. (lp/c) *(K/K4 50851)* *<11111>* **FOR THOSE ABOUT TO ROCK (WE SALUTE YOU)** [3] [1]
– For those about to rock (we salute you) / Put the finger on you / Let's get it up / Inject the venom / Snowballed / Evil walk / C.O.D. / Breaking the laws / Night of the long knives / Spellbound. *(cd-iss. Jul87; K2 50851) (re-iss. Jul94 cd/c; 7567 92412-2/-4) (cd re-iss. Jan98 on 'E.M.I.'; 477090-2)*

Jan 82. (7") *(K 11706)* **LET'S GET IT UP. / BACK IN BLACK (live)** [13] [–]
(12"+=) *(K 11706T)* – T.N.T. (live).

Jan 82 (7")(12") *<3894><3898>* **LET'S GET IT UP. / SNOWBALLED** [–] [44]

Jun 82 (7") *<4029>* **FOR THOSE ABOUT TO ROCK (WE SALUTE YOU). / T.N.T.** [–] [ ]

Jun 82. (7"/ext.12") *(K 11721/+T)* **FOR THOSE ABOUT TO ROCK (WE SALUTE YOU). / LET THERE BE ROCK (live)** [15] [ ]

Aug 83. (lp/c) *(780 100-1/-4)* *<80100>* **FLICK OF THE SWITCH** [4] [15]

– Rising power / This house is on fire / Flick of the switch / Nervous shakedown / Landslide / Guns for fire / Deep in the hole / Bedlam in Belgium / Badlands / Brain shake. *(re-iss. Jul87 lp/c/cd; K781 455-1/-4/-2) (re-iss. Oct94 cd/c; 7567 92448-2/-4) (cd re-iss. Jan98 on 'E.M.I.'; 477091-2)*

Sep 83. (7"/7"sha-pic-d) *(A 9774/+P)* <89774> **GUNS FOR HIRE. / LANDSLIDE** [37] [84]

Mar 84. (7") <89722> **FLICK OF THE SWITCH. / BADLANDS** [-] [ ]

—— **SIMON WRIGHT** (b.19 Jun'63) – drums (ex-A II Z, ex-TYTAN) repl. RUDD

Jul 84. (7"/7"sha-pic-d) *(A 9651/+P)* **NERVOUS SHAKEDOWN. / ROCK'N'ROLL AIN'T NOISE POLLUTION (live)** [35] [ ]
(12"+=/c-s+=) *(A 9651 T/C)* – Sin city (live) / This house is on fire (live).

Jun 85. (7"/7"w-poster/7"sha-pic-d/12") *(A 9532/+W/P/T)* <89532> **DANGER. / BACK IN BUSINESS** [48] [ ]

Jul 85. (lp/c/cd) *(781 263-1/-4/-2)* <81263> **FLY ON THE WALL** [7] [32]
– Fly on the wall / Shake your foundations / First blood / Danger / Sink the pink / Playing with the girls / Stand up / Hell or high water / Back in business / Send for the man. *(cd re-iss. Jan98 on 'E.M.I.'; 477092-2)*

Nov 85. (7") **SHAKE YOUR FOUNDATIONS. / SEND FOR THE MAN** [-] [ ]

Jan 86. (7"/7"w-poster/7"sha-pic-d) *(A 9474/+C/P)* **SHAKE YOUR FOUNDATIONS. / STAND UP** [24] [ ]
(12"+=) *(A 9474T)* – Jailbreak.

May 86. (7"/7"sha-pic-d) *(A 9425/+P)* <89425> **WHO MADE WHO. / GUNS FOR HIRE (live)** [16] [ ]
(12"+=/12"w-poster) *(A 9425T/+W)* – ('A'-Collectors mix).

May 86. (lp/c) *(WX 57/+C)* <81650> **WHO MADE WHO (Soundtrack; Maximum Overdrive)** (part compilation) [11] [33]
– Who made who / You shook me all night long / DT / Sink the pink / Ride on / Hells bells / Shake your foundations / Chase the ace / For those about to rock (we salute you). *(cd-iss. 1988; 781 650-2) (cd re-iss. Sep98 on 'E.M.I.'; 746299-2)*

Aug 86. (7"/7"sha-pic-d) *(A 9377/+P)* <89377> **YOU SHOOK ME ALL NIGHT LONG (live). / SHE'S GOT BALLS (live)** [46] [ ]
(12"/12"sha-pic-d) *(A 9377 T/TP)* – ('B'extended) / ('A'live).

Jan 88. (7") *(A 9136)* <89136> **HEATSEEKER. / GO ZONE** [12] [ ]
(12"+=/12"g-f+=/12"pic-d+=/3"cd-s+=) *(A 9136 T/TW/TP/CD)* – Snake high.

Feb 88. (lp/c)(cd) *(WX 144/+C)(781 828-2)* <81828> **BLOW UP YOUR VIDEO** [2] [12]
– Heatseeker / That's the way I wanna rock'n'roll / Meanstreak / Go zone / Kissin' dynamite / Nick of time / Some sin for nuthin' / Ruff stuff / Two's up / Some sin for nuthin' / This means war. *(cd re-iss. Sep98 on 'E.M.I.'; 748977-2)*

Mar 88. (7") *(A 9098)* <89098> **THAT'S THE WAY I WANNA ROCK'N'ROLL. / KISSIN' DYNAMITE** [22] [ ]
(12"+=/12"g-f+=/12"pic-d+=) *(A 9098T/+W/P)* – Borrowed time.
(3"cd-s+=) *(A 9098CD)* – Shoot to thrill (live) / Whole lotta Rosie (live).

—— (Apr88) cousin **STEVE YOUNG** – guitar briefly replaced MALCOLM on tour

—— (1989) (ANGUS, MALCOLM, BRIAN & CLIFF) bring in **CHRIS SLADE** (b.30 Oct'46) – drums (ex-GARY MOORE, ex-MANFRED MANN EARTHBAND, ex-FIRM) repl. WRIGHT who had joined DIO.

Atco Atco

Sep 90. (7"/c-s/10"pic-d) *(B 8907/+C/P)* **THUNDERSTRUCK. / FIRE YOUR GUNS** [13] [ ]
(12"+=/cd-s+=) *(B 8907 T/CD)* – DT / Chase the ace.

Oct 90. (cd)(lp/pic-lp/c) *(<91413>)(WX 364/+P/+C)* **THE RAZOR'S EDGE** [4] [2]
– Thunderstruck / Fire your guns / Moneytalks / The razor's edge / Mistress for Christmas / Rock your heart out / Are you ready / Got you by the balls / Shot of love / Let's make it / Goodbye & good riddance to bad luck / If you dare. *(cd re-iss. Jun98 on 'E.M.I.'; 495144-2)*

Nov 90. (7"/c-s) *(B 8886/+C)* **MONEYTALKS. / MISTRESS FOR CHRISTMAS** [36] [-]
(12"+=/12"sha-pic-d+=/cd-s+=) *(B 8886 T/P/CD)* – Borrowed time.

Nov 90. (c-s) <98881> **MONEYTALKS. / BORROWED TIME** [-] [23]

Apr 91. (7"/7"w-patch/7"s/c-s) *(88830/+X/W/C)* **ARE YOU READY. / GOT YOU BY THE BALLS** [34] [ ]
(12"+=/12"g-f+=/cd-s+=) *(88830 T/TW/CD)* – The razor's edge.

Oct 92. (7") *(B 8479)* **HIGHWAY TO HELL (live) / HELL'S BELLS (live)** [14] [ ]
(12"pic-d) *(B 8479TP)* – ('A'side) / High voltage (live).
(cd-s) *(B 8479CD)* – ('A'side) / High voltage (live) / Hell ain't a bad place to be (live).
(cd-s) *(B 8479CDX)* – ('A'side) / High voltage (live) / The jack (live).

Oct 92. (cd/c/d-lp) *(<7567 92212-2/-4/-1>)* **LIVE (live)** [5] [15]
– Thunderstruck / Shoot to thrill / Back in black / Sin city / Who made who / Fire your guns / Jailbreak / The jack / The razor's edge / Dirty deeds done dirt cheap / Hells bells / Heatseeker / That's the way I wanna rock'n'roll / High voltage / You shook me all night long / Whole lotta Rosie / Let there be rock / Medley:- Bonny – Highway to Hell / T.N.T. / For those about to rock (we salute you). *<in the US, a SPECIAL COLLECTOR'S EDITION hit No.26; 92215-2> (cd/d-cd re-iss. Jun98 on 'E.M.I.'; 49514 5/6-2)*

Feb 93. (12"/cd-s) *(B 6073 T/CD)* **DIRTY DEEDS DONE DIRT CHEAP (live). / SHOOT TO THRILL (live) / DIRTY DEEDS DONE DIRT CHEAP** [68] [ ]

Jun 93. (7"/c-s) *(88396/+C)* <98406> **BIG GUN. / BACK IN BLACK (live)** [23] [65]
(12"+=) *(88396T)* – For those about to rock (live).
(cd-s) *(88396CD)* – ('A'side) / For those about to rock (live).

Sep 95. (7"yellow/cd-s/s-cd-s) *(A 4368 X/CD/CDX)* **HARD AS A ROCK. / CAUGHT WITH YOUR PANTS DOWN** [33] [ ]

Sep 95. (cd/c/lp) *(<7559 61780-2/-4/-2>)* **BALLBREAKER** [6] [4]
– Whisky on the rocks / The honey roll / The furor / Love bomb / Hard as a rock / Hail Caesar / Cover you in oil / Caught with your pants down / Burnin' alive / Boogie man / Ballbreaker. *(cd re-iss. Jun98 on 'E.M.I.'; 495149-2)*

Apr 96. (c-s) *(A 6051C)* **HAIL CAESAR / WHISKEY ON THE ROCKS** [56] [ ]
(cd-s+=) *(A 6051CD)* – Whole lotta Rosie (live).

Jul 96. (cd-s) *(7559-64286-2)* **COVER YOU IN OIL / LOVE BOMB / BALLBREAKER** [ ] [ ]

Liberty Liberty

Feb 00. (cd/c) *(525667-2/-4)* <62494> **STIFF UPPER LIP** [12] [7]
– Stiff upper lip / Meltdown / House of jazz / Hold me back / Safe in New York City / Can't stand still / Can't stop rock'n'roll / Satellite blues / Damned / Come and get it / All screwed up / Give it up.

Apr 00. (cd-s) *(CDSTIFF 100)* **STIFF UPPER LIP / HARD AS A ROCK (live) / BALLBREAKER (live)** [65] [-]

– compilations, others, etc. –

Aug 84. (m-lp) *Atco;* <80178> **JAILBREAK '74** (early demos..) [-] [76]
(UK re-iss. cd Oct94; 7567 92449-2)

Sep 84. (7") *Atlantic;* <89616> **JAILBREAK. / SHOW BUSINESS** [-] [ ]

1991. (3xcd-box) *Atco;* **BOX SET** [ ] [-]
– HIGHWAY TO HELL / BACK IN BLACK / FOR THOSE ABOUT TO ROCK

Nov 97. (d-cd; BON SCOTT & THE FRATERNITY) *Raven; (RVCD 56)* **COMPLETE SESSIONS 1971-1972** [ ] [ ]

Dec 97. (5xcd-box) *(493273-2)* **BONFIRE** [ ] [90]

Jan 98. (cd-s; BON SCOTT) *Head Office; (HOR 002)* **ROUND AND ROUND AND ROUND. /** [ ] [-]

Sep 98. (cd; by BON SCOTT & THE FRATERNITY) *Connoisseur; VSOPCD 261)* **LIVESTOCK – BON SCOTT WITH FRATERNITY** [ ] [-]

David ACKLES

Born: 27 Feb'37, Rock Island, Illinois, USA. Raised by his showbiz parents (he was also a child-star of B-movies) DAVID found his niche as a 30-something singer/songwriter in sunny California. Having signed a solo deal with 'Elektra', the man's first work surfaced in 1968 when his eponymous debut album (sometimes called 'THE ROAD TO CAIRO') made it to the shops. It disclosed a schooling in the tradition of BOB DYLAN or JACQUES BREL, although for this reason it didn't meet too well with the unassuming Stateside press; one of its best known songs 'DOWN RIVER' was subsequently covered by SPOOKY TOOTH. 1969's follow-up set,

'SUBWAY TO THE COUNTRY', was a shade better, his deep lyricism highlighted without question on 'THE CANDY MAN' track. Licking his proverbial wounds, ACKLES returned in July '72 after a short hiatus. Augmented this time by (ELTON JOHN co-pensmith) BERNIE TAUPIN on production, 'AMERICAN GOTHIC' showed the singer at his most dramatic and melancholic best. Although it made the US Top 200 listings – his only LP to do so! – the masterpiece suffered moderately poor sales resulting in a change of label ('Columbia'). A fourth album, 'FIVE & DIME' (1973), was virtually most of America in a nutshell (the people and their environment, that is!), his lyrical RANDY NEWMAN-esque insights maturer than his more youthful, richer peers. One of its more tongue-in-cheek numbers, 'SURF'S DOWN' (a BRIAN WILSON parody of sorts!), checklisted DEAN TORRANCE (of JAN & DEAN) on harmonies, although this set would mark the end of ACKLES' brief musical lifespan. ACKLES went on to be a lecturer, among other things, while also writing ballets! Sadly, the man died of lung cancer on the 2nd March, 1999.

Album rating: DAVID ACKLES (*8) / SUBWAY TO THE COUNTRY (*6) / AMERICAN GOTHIC (*7) / FIVE & DIME (*5)

DAVID ACKLES – vocals, acoustic guitar / with session people

Elektra Elektra

Sep 68. (lp) <*(EKS 74002)*> **DAVID ACKLES**
– The road to Cairo / When love is gone / Sonny come home / Blue ribbons / What a happy day / Down river / Laissez-faire / Lotus man / His name is Andrew / Be my friend. *(re-iss. 1971; K42020) (cd-iss. Oct93 & Sep00; 7559 61595-2) (cd re-iss. Sep02 on 'Collector's Choice'; CCM 0312-2)*

1968. (7") *(EKSN 45-039)* **DOWN RIVER. / LA ROUTE TO CHICAGO**

Mar 69. (7") *(EKSN 45-054)* **LAISSEZ-FAIRE. / BLUE RIBBONS**

Jan 70. (lp) <*(EKS 74060)*> **SUBWAY TO THE COUNTRY** Nov69
– Mainline saloon / That's no reason to cry / The candy man / Out on the road / Cabin in the mountain / Woman river / Inmates of the institution / Subway to the country. *(re-iss. 1971; K 42092) (cd-iss. Oct93 & Sep00; 7559 61596-2) (cd re-iss. Sep02 on 'Collector's Choice'; CCM 0313-2)*

Jan 70. (7") *(EKSN 45-079)* **SUBWAY TO THE COUNTRY. / THAT'S NO REASON TO CRY**

Jul 72. (lp) *(EKS 75032)* <*42112*> **AMERICAN GOTHIC**
– American gothic / Love's enough / Ballad of the ship of state / One night stand / Oh, California! / Another Friday night / Family band / Midnight carousel / Waiting for the moving van / Blues for Billy Whitecloud / Montana song. *(cd-iss. Oct93 & Sep00; 7559 61597-2) (cd re-iss. Sep02 on 'Collector's Choice'; CCM 0311-2)*

— now with many newly introduced session people

not iss. C.B.S.

1973. (lp) <*32466*> **FIVE & DIME** [-]
– Everybody has a story / I've been love / Jenna saves / Surf's down / Berry tree / One good woman's man / Run pony run / Aberfan / House above the strand / Photograph of you / Such a woman / Postcards.

— retired from the music scene; he died of lung cancer on 2nd March '99

ADAM & THE ANTS

Formed: London, England . . . April '77 by STUART GODDARD (aka ADAM ANT) along with LESTER SQUARE, ANDY WARREN and PAUL FLANAGAN. Initially a fairly rote punk act with attitude, what got the band noticed was their lurid stage show and penchant for S&M trappings. Derek Jarman was sufficiently enamoured to offer ADAM a part in his controversial punk flick, 'Jubilee' (released Feb '78), a revised ANTS line-up (featuring new members DAVE BARBE and MARK GAUMONT) recording two songs for the soundtrack, 'Plastic Surgery' and 'Deutcher Girls'. Later that year, the group released a one-off debut single for 'Decca', 'YOUNG PARISIANS', before releasing their rated debut album, 'DIRK WEARS WHITE SOX' in late '79. A morose slab of post-punk doom-mongering, the record stood in stark contrast to their later albums by a remodelled ADAM & THE ANTS. The shake-up came courtesy of none other than ex-SEX PISTOLS svengali, MALCOLM McLAREN, who, after dreaming up the flamboyant new image (a surprisingly effective if retrospectively ridiculous Native Indian cum swashbuckling pirates concept), whisked ADAM's band off to become BOW WOW WOW. Virtually written off by his critics, ADAM came swaggering back with a new line-up (MARCO PIRRONI, CHRIS HUGHES aka MERRICK, KEVIN MOONEY and TERRY LEE MIALL), a new sound and a new album (his first for 'C.B.S.'), 'KINGS OF THE WILD FRONTIER' (1980). Taking their cue from the Burundi drummers of Africa, the band had stumbled on a unique musical mutant which combined retro rock'n'roll with pseudo-tribal, dayglo pouting pop; teenyboppers loved it and a string of anthemic singles, 'DOG EAT DOG', 'ANT MUSIC' and the thundering title track all made the UK Top 5. The album itself rode to the top of the charts (even scaping into the US Top 50) and for a brief but warpainted period, Britain was gripped with "Antmania". The sight of the ever photogenic ADAM striding boldly through his video adventures like some dandy Indiana Jones was the stuff of girly fantasy and if you didn't have a white stripe across your nose, well, you could forget about getting lucky at the school disco. ANT was clever enough to slightly tweak his image on the follow-up set, 'PRINCE CHARMING' (1981), this time going for a dashing highwayman cum 18th century courtier get-up. It was even more effective, the group scoring two No.1 singles in quick succession with 'STAND AND DELIVER' and the title track, while 'ANT RAP' made the Top 3. To be fair to the man, he had the good sense to disband ADAM & THE ANTS at the height of their fame, although by carrying on as ADAM ANT in a vaguely similar vein, he was bound to suffer a backlash sooner or later. Retaining sidekick, PIRRONI, ANT's solo career nevertheless got off to an auspicious start with No.1 single, 'GOODY TWO SHOES', while the accompanying album, 'FRIEND OR FOE' (1982) made the Top 5 (and bizarrely the US Top 20). The following three years brought only one major hit in 'PUSS 'N' BOOTS' and after the 'VIVE LE ROCK' (1985) set, ANT took four years off to develop his acting career while PIRRONI joined SPEAR OF DESTINY. By the turn of the decade, the pair were back with an underwhelming new single, 'ROOM AT THE TOP', and album, 'MANNERS & PHYSIQUE', both enjoying a brief stint in the charts but largely ignored as the nation's pop kids raved to acid house. Of late, the ageing ADAM/STUART has run into a bit of trouble due to him brandishing a WWII gun in a pub when he was refused entry. Early in 2002, he was arrested by police and taken to a mental unit of the Royal Free Hospital in Hampstead, North London. • **Trivia:** He acted in stage production of 'Entertaining Mr. Sloane'. After retiring to the States in 1986 he took parts in 'Slam Dance' film, and 'Equalizer' TV serial.

Album rating: DIRK WEARS WHITE SOX (*7) / KINGS OF THE WILD FRONTIER (*7) / PRINCE CHARMING (*5) / FRIEND OR FOE (*5) / STRIP (*4) / VIVE LE ROCK (*4) / MANNERS AND PHYSIQUE (*4) / WONDERFUL (*5) / HITS (1980-1985) compilation (*7)

ADAM ANT (b. STUART GODDARD, 3 Nov'54) – vocals, guitar / **MATTHEW ASHMAN** (b.'62) – guitar, vocals (ex-KAMERAS) / **ANDY WARREN** (b.'61) – bass, vocals / **DAVE BARBE** (b.'61) – drums (ex-DESOLATION ANGELS)

Decca not iss.

Oct 78. (7") *(F 13803)* **YOUNG PARISIANS. / LADY** [-]
(re-act.Dec80; hit No.9)

Do-It not iss.

Jun 79. (7") *(DUN 8)* **ZEROX. / WHIP IN MY VALISE** [-]

— (some copies had B-side playing 'PHYSICAL (YOU'RE SO)')
(re-act.Jan81; hit No.45)

Nov 79. (lp/c) *(RIDE 3/+M)* **DIRK WEARS WHITE SOX** [ ] [–]
– Cartrouble (part 1 & 2) / Digital tenderness / Nine plan failed / Day I met God * / Tabletalk / Cleopatra / Catholic day / Never trust a man (with egg on his face) / Animals and men / Family of noise / The idea. *(re-act.Jan81; hit No.16) (remixed & re-iss. Apr83 on 'C.B.S.' lp/c; CBS/40 25361) (track * replaced by)* – Zerox / Kick! / Whip in my valise. *(cd-iss. Jul95 on 'Columbia'; 480521-2)*

—— **LEIGH GORMAN** – bass (on B-side) repl. WARREN who joined MONOCHROME SET

Feb 80. (7") *(DUN 10)* **CARTROUBLE. / KICK!** [ ] [–]
(re-act.Jan81; hit No.33)

—— (Jan80) until (Mar'80 when ADAM brought in entire new group) **MARCO PIRRONI** (b.27 Apr'59) – guitar, vocals (ex-MODELS) repl. ASHMAN / **MERRICK** (b.CHRIS HUGHES, 3 Mar'54) – drums repl. BARBE / **KEVIN MOONEY** – bass, vocals repl. GORMAN (who with above 2 formed BOW WOW WOW) / added **TERRY LEE MIALL** (b. 8 Nov'58) – 2nd drummer (ex-MODELS)

C.B.S. Columbia

Jul 80. (7") *(CBS 8877)* **KINGS OF THE WILD FRONTIER. / PRESS DARLINGS** [48] [–]
(re-act.Feb81; hit No.2)

Sep 80. (7") *(CBS 9039)* **DOG EAT DOG. / PHYSICAL (YOU'RE SO)** [4] [–]

Nov 80. (lp/c) *(CBS/40 84549)* *<37033>* **KINGS OF THE WILD FRONTIER** [1] Feb81 [44]
– Dog eat dog / Ant music / Feed me to the lions / Los Rancheros / Ants invasion / Killer in the home / Kings of the wild frontier / The magnificent five / Don't be square (be there) / Jolly Roger / Making history / The human beings. *(cd-iss. Oct93 & Dec98 on 'Sony Europe'; 477902-2)*

Nov 80. (7") *(CBS 9352)* **ANT MUSIC. / FALL IN** [2] [–]

Jan 81. (7")(12") *<02042><01061>* **ANT MUSIC. / DON'T BE SQUARE (BE THERE)** [–] [ ]

—— **GARY TIBBS** (b.25 Jan'58)- bass (ex-ROXY MUSIC, ex-VIBRATORS) repl. MOONEY

May 81. (7")<US-12"> *(A-1065)* *<02193>* **STAND AND DELIVER. / BEAT MY GUEST** [1] [ ]

Sep 81. (7") *(A-1408)* **PRINCE CHARMING. / CHRISTIAN D'OR** [1] [–]

Nov 81. (lp/c) *(CBS/40 85268)* *<37615>* **PRINCE CHARMING** [2] [94]
– Prince Charming / The Scorpios / Picasso visita el Planeta de los Simios / 5 guns west / That voodoo / Stand and deliver / Mile high club / Ant rap / Mowhok / S.E.X. *(re-iss. cd Mar96 on 'Columbia'; 474606-2)*

Dec 81. (7"/7"pic-d) *(A/+11 1738)* **ANT RAP. / FRIENDS** [3] [–]

—— they broke up early '82

ADAM ANT

continued solo augmented by **PIRRONI** and sessioners

C.B.S. Epic

May 82. (7"/7"pic-d) *(A/+11 2367)* **GOODY TWO SHOES. / RED SCAB** [1] [–]

Sep 82. (7"/7"pic-d) *(A/+11 2736)* **FRIEND OR FOE. / JUANITO THE BANDITO** [9] [–]

Oct 82. (lp/c) *(CBS/40 25040)* *<38370>* **FRIEND OR FOE** [5] [16]
– Friend or foe / Something girls / Place in the country / Desperate but not serious / Here comes the grump / Hello I love you / Goody two shoes / Crackpot history and the right to lie / Made of money / Cajun twisters / Try this for sighs / A man called Marco. *(cd-iss. Jul96 on 'Columbia'; 484436-2)*

Oct 82. (7") *<03367>* **GOODY TWO SHOES. / CRACKPOT HISTORY** [–] [12]

Nov 82. (7"/7"pic-d) *(A/+11 2892)* **DESPERATE BUT NOT SERIOUS. / WHY DO GIRLS LOVE HORSES?** [33] [–]

Feb 83. (7") *<03688>* **DESPERATE BUT NOT SERIOUS. / PLACE IN THE COUNTRY** [–] [66]

Oct 83. (7"/7"pic-d/ext.12") *(A/WA/TA 3614)* *<04461>* **PUSS 'N' BOOTS. / KISS THE DRUMMER** [5] May84 [ ]

Nov 83. (lp/c) *(CBS/40 25705)* *<39108>* **STRIP** [20] [65]
– Baby let me scream at you / Libertine / Spanish games / Vanity / Puss'n'boots / Playboy / Strip / Montreal / Navel to neck / Amazon. *(cd-iss. Jul84; CD 25705)*

Dec 83. (7"/7"pic-d/ext.12") *(A/WA/TA 3589)* *<04337>* **STRIP. / YOURS, YOURS, YOURS** [41] [42]

Sep 84. (7"/'A'-Orbit mix-12") *(A/TA 4719)* **APOLLO 9. / B SIDE BABY** [13] [ ]
(12") *(QTA 4719)* – ('A'-Splashdown remix & acappella instrumental).

Jul 85. (7") *(A 6367)* *<05574>* **VIVE LE ROCK. / GRETA X** [50] [ ]
(12"+=) *(TA 6367)* – ('A'instrumental dub mix).

Sep 85. (lp/c) *(CBS/40 26583)* *<40159>* **VIVE LE ROCK** [42] [ ]
– Vive le rock / Miss Thing / Razor keen / Rip down / Scorpio rising / Apollo 9 / Hell's eight acres / Mohair lockeroom pin-up boys / No zap / P.O.E. *(c+=)* – Human bondage den. *(cd-iss. 1988+=; CD 26583)* – Apollo 9 (acappella). *(re-iss. cd Mar95 on 'Rewind'; 478504-2)*

—— ADAM retired for 4 years. MARCO joined SPEAR OF DESTINY

ADAM ANT

brought back MARCO to resurrect career.

M.C.A. M.C.A.

Feb 90. (7"/7"s/c-s) *(MCA/+R/C 1387)* *<53679>* **ROOM AT THE TOP. / BRUCE LEE** [13] [17]
(cd-s+=/12"+=) *(D+/MCAT 1387)* – ('A'house vocals).
(cd-s+=) *(DMCAX 1387)* – ('A'mixes).

Mar 90. (cd/lp)(c) *(D+/MCG 6068)(MCGC 6068)* *<6315>* **MANNERS & PHYSICIQUE** [19] [57]
– Room at the top / If you keep on / Can't set rules about love / Bright lights black leather / Young dumb and full of it / Rough stuff / Manners & physicique / U.S.S.A. / Piccadilly / Anger Inc.

Apr 90. (7"/c-s) *(MCA/+C 1404)* **CAN'T SET RULES ABOUT LOVE. / HOW TO STEAL THE WORLD** [47] [ ]
(cd-s+=/12"+=) *(D+/MCAT 1404)* – Brand new torso.
(cd-s++=) *(DMCAP 1404)* – ('A'-lp version).

Jun 90. (7") *<79042>* **BRIGHT LIGHTS BLACK LEATHER. / ROUGH STUFF** [–] [ ]

—— w/ **PIRRONI** / **BOZ BOORER** – guitars / **BRUCE WITKIN** – bass / **DAVE RUFFY** – drums

E.M.I. Capitol

Jan 95. (c-s/7") *(TC+/EM 366)* *<58239>* **WONDERFUL. / GOES AROUND** [32] Mar95 [39]
(cd-s+=) *(CDEMS 366)* – Norman / Woman love run through me.
(cd-s) *(CDEM 366)* – ('A'side) / If / Phoenix.

Mar 95. (c-s/7"; withdrawn) **BEAUTIFUL DREAM. / LET'S HAVE A FIGHT** [ ] [ ]
(cd-s+=; w-drawn) – Billy boy / Wonderful (acoustic).
(cd-s; w-drawn) – ('A'side) / Shake your hips / Ant music (acoustic) / ('A'-Lucas master mix).

Apr 95. (cd/c) *(CD/TC EMC 3687)* *<30335>* **WONDERFUL** [24] [39]
– Won't take that talk / Beautiful dream / Wonderful / 1969 again / Yin & Yang / Image of yourself / Alien / Gotta be a sin / Vampires / Angel / Very long ride. *(cd re-iss. Sep97; same)*

May 95. (c-s) *(TCEM 379)* **GOTTA BE A SIN / DOG EAT DOG (live)** [48] [ ]
(cd-s) *(CDEM 379)* – ('A'side) / Cleopatra (live) / Beat my guest (live) / Red scab (live).
(cd-s) *(CDEMS 379)* – ('A'side) / Desperate but not serious (live) / Car trouble (live) / Physical (you're so) (live).

– compilations, others, etc. –

Feb 82. (7") *E.G.; (EGO 5)* **DEUTCHER GIRLS. / PLASTIC SURGERY** [13] [–]

Mar 82. (7"ep/7"pic-ep) *Do-It; (DUN/+X 20)* **THE B-SIDES** [46] [–]
– Friends / Kick! / Physical (you're so).
(12"ep+=) **ANTMUSIC** *(DUNIT 20)* – Cartrouble (pts. 1 & 2).

1982. (7"; as MANEATERS) *E.G.; (EGO 8)* **NINE TO FIVE. / (SUZI PINNS: Jerusalem)** [ ] [–]
(above another from the film 'Jubilee' & featuring TOYAH)

Sep 86. (lp/c) *C.B.S.; (CBS/40 450074-1/-4)* **HITS** [ ] [ ]
– Kings of the wild frontier / Dog eat dog / Ant music / Stand and deliver / Prince Charming / Ant rap / Goody two shoes / Friend or foe / Desperate but not serious / Puss 'n' boots / Strip / Apollo 9 / Vive le rock. *(re-iss. Jul90 & Jul98 on 'Columbia' cd/c; R 450074-2/-4)*

Jan 88. (7") *Old Gold; (OG 9739)* **ANT MUSIC. / STAND AND DELIVER** [ ] [–]

Oct 89. (12"white/12"pic-d) *Damaged Goods; (FNARR/+P 7)* **YOUNG PARISIANS / LADY. / (interview)** [ ] [–]

Nov 90. (7") *Old Gold; (OG 9953)* **PRINCE CHARMING. / GOODY TWO SHOES** [ ] [–]

Feb 91. (cd/c/lp) *Strange Fruit; (SFR CD/MC/LP 115)* **THE PEEL SESSIONS** (early 1979 material) [ ] [–]

Jun 91. (cd/c) *Columbia; (468762-2/-4)* **ANTICS IN THE FORBIDDEN ZONE** [ ] [–]
Aug 93. (cd/c) *Arcade; (ARC 31000 5-2/6-4)* **ANTMUSIC – THE VERY BEST OF ADAM ANT** [6] [–]
(re-iss. Mar94 d-cd+ 'LIVE'; ARC 310000-2); hit No.30)
Oct 94. (cd) *Columbia; (477513-2)* **THE BEST (ADAM ANT)** [ ] [ ]
May 95. (cd) *Columbia; (480362-2)* **B SIDES BABIES** [ ] [–]
Mar 99. (cd) *Columbia; (494229-2)* **THE VERY BEST OF . . .** [56] [ ]

Bryan ADAMS

Born: 5 Nov'59, Vancouver, Canada. In 1977 he set up a writing partnership with JIM VALLANCE, drummer with techno-rock band, PRISM. Numerous groups, including LOVERBOY, KISS, BACHMAN-TURNER OVERDRIVE, etc. used their songs before ADAMS signed a contract with 'A&M' early in 1979. While VALLANCE recorded with ADAMS on the low-key debut single and eponymous album, he soon bowed out (the writing partnership continued) and ADAMS assembled a new band for the follow-up, 'YOU WANT IT YOU GOT IT' (1982). However, it wasn't until Spring 1983, with the release of 'STRAIGHT FROM THE HEART', that ADAMS made a significant impact on the US charts. His gravel-voiced, sub-SPRINGSTEEN rock was soon to enter into an ongoing love affair with coffee tables the world over, the follow-up album, 'CUTS LIKE A KNIFE' making the Top 10 album chart in America. ADAMS really hit his stride with 'RECKLESS' (1984), a sturdy, professional set of soft-rockers and ballads. While 'SUMMER OF '69' was an entertaining piece of anthemic pop/rock and the album possessed just enough rough-edged charm to offset the cheese factor, the likes of 'THE KIDS WANNA ROCK' was downright cringeworthy. ADAMS also beat ELTON to a Princess Di tribute with the B-side of the 'HEAVEN' single, entitled, funnily enough, 'DIANA'. The album made the man a household name while the follow-up effort, 'INTO THE FIRE' (1987) marked the end of his songwriting partnerhip with VALLANCE and saw ADAMS lyrics take on a more political bent (the following year saw ADAMS playing the Nelson Mandela benefit concert at Wembley Stadium). Still, any hopes of a radical new direction were dashed several years later upon the release of the unashamed slush-pop ballad, '(EVERYTHING I DO) I DO IT FOR YOU'. The record (featured on the soundtrack to the Kevin Costner film, 'Robin Hood, Prince Of Thieves') went to No. 1 on both sides of the Atlantic for what seemed like an eternity. After 16 weeks of radio overkill, one might have suspected that the populace had satiated their Adams appetite, so to speak, but no, the follow-up, 'CAN'T STOP THIS THING WE STARTED' (more uptempo but equally bland) almost breached the UK Top 10. The album, 'WAKING UP THE NEIGHBOURS' (1992) went to the top of the album charts, although it's safe to say that by now, ADAMS was probably appealing to a slightly different market and had lost any credibility (if, that is, he actually had any in the first place!) with a younger, more discerning audience. More nauseatingly saccharine ballads followed ('ALL FOR LOVE', 'HAVE YOU EVER REALLY LOVED A WOMAN' etc., you get the picture) into the singles charts while his most recent attempts at rock (in the loosest sense of the term, naturally) make HANSON sound dangerous. The icing on ADAMS' sickly-sweet cake came with 'SPIRIT: STALLION OF THE CIMARRON' (2002), a soundtrack for a Disney-style cartoon about a runaway horse. With a single, 'HERE I AM', making the UK Top 5, and the album itself making both the UK Top 10 and the US Top 40, it seems fair to say that come the summer of 2009, ADAMS will still have them rocking in the (cinema) aisles. • **Covered:** WALKING AFTER MIDNIGHT (D. Hecht / A. Block) / I FOUGHT THE LAW (Sonny Curtis) / LITTLE RED ROOSTER (Willie Dixon).

Album rating: BRYAN ADAMS (*3) / YOU WANT IT YOU GOT IT (*5) / CUTS LIKE A KNIFE (*7) / RECKLESS (*7) / INTO THE FIRE (*5) / WAKING UP THE NEIGHBOURS (*5) / SO FAR SO GOOD compilation (*6) / LIVE! LIVE! LIVE! (*4) / 18 TIL I DIE (*4) / UNPLUGGED (*4) / ON A DAY LIKE TODAY (*4) / THE BEST OF ME compilation (*8) / SPIRIT: STALLION OF THE CIMARRON soundtrack w/ Hans Zimmer (*5)

BRYAN ADAMS – vocals, guitar / with **JIM VALLANCE** – drums, keyboards, guitar, bass

A&M A&M

Jul 79. (7"/ext.12") *(AMS/+P 7460)* <2163> **LET ME TAKE YOU DANCIN'. / DON'T TURN ME AWAY** [ ] [ ]
Apr 80. (7") *(AMS 7520)* <2220> **HIDIN' FROM LOVE. / WAIT AND SEE** [ ] [ ]
Mar 81. (lp) *(AMLH 64800)* <4800> **BRYAN ADAMS** [ ] Nov80 [ ]
– Hidin' from love / Win some, lose some / Wait and see / Give me your love / Wastin' time / Don't ya say it / Remember / State of mind / Try to see it my way. *(cd-iss. Jan87; CDA 3100) (re-iss. cd 1988; CDMID 100)*
Apr 81. (7") <2249> **GIVE ME YOUR LOVE. / WAIT AND SEE** [–] [ ]

— now with **TOMMY HANDEL** – keyboards / **BRIAN STANLEY** – bass + **MICKEY CURRY** – drums repl. VALLANCE (he continued to co-write + play piano + percussion for ADAMS until '88).

Mar 82. (7") *(AMS 8183)* <2359> **LONELY NIGHTS. / DON'T LOOK NOW** [ ] [84]
Apr 82. (lp) *(AMLH 64864)* <4864> **YOU WANT IT, YOU GOT IT** [78] Jan82 [ ]
– Lonely nights / One good reason / Don't look now / Jealousy / Coming home / Fits ya good / Tonight / You want it, you got it / Last chance / No one makes it right. *(cd-iss. Aug85; CDA 3154) (re-iss. cd 1988; CDMID 100)*
Jul 82. (7") <2409> **COMING HOME. / FITS YA GOOD** [–] [ ]

— **DAVE TAYLOR** – bass repl. STANLEY

— added **KEITH SCOTT** – guitar, vocals

Mar 83. (lp) *(SMLH 64919)* <4919> **CUTS LIKE A KNIFE** [ ] Feb83 [8]
– The only one / Take me back / This time / Straight from the heart / Cuts like a knife / I'm ready / What's it gonna be / Don't leave me lonely / The best has yet to come. *(re-iss. Mar86; same); hit UK 21) (cd-iss. Mar86; CDA 4919)* (cd re-iss. 1988; *CDMID 102)*
Mar 83. (7") <2536> **STRAIGHT FROM THE HEART. / ONE GOOD REASON** [–] [10]
Apr 83. (7"/12") *(AM/+X 103)* **STRAIGHT FROM THE HEART. / LONELY NIGHTS** [ ] [–]
Jun 83. (7") <2553> **CUTS LIKE A KNIFE. / LONELY NIGHTS** [–] [15]
Jul 83. (7") *(AM 129)* **CUTS LIKE A KNIFE. / FITS YA GOOD** [ ] [–]
(12"+=) *(AMP 129)* – Hidin' from love.
Aug 83. (7") <2574> **THIS TIME. / FITS YA GOOD** [–] [24]
Nov 83. (7") <26??> **THE BEST HAS YET TO COME. / I'M READY** [–] [ ]
Dec 84. (7") *(AM 224)* <2686> **RUN TO YOU. / I'M READY** [11] Oct84 [6]
(12"+=) *(AMD 224)* – Cuts like a knife.
(d7"++=) *(AMY 224)* – Lonely nights.
Feb 85. (lp/c/cd) <*(AMA/AMC/CDA 5013)*> **RECKLESS** [7] Nov84 [1]
– One night love affair / She's only happy when she's dancin' / Run to you / Heaven / Somebody / Summer of '69 / It's only love / Kids wanna rock / Long gone / Ain't gonna cry. *(re-iss. Jul92 & Sep97; 395013-2)*
Feb 85. (7"/7"pic-d/12") *(AM/+P/Y 236)* <2701> **SOMEBODY. / LONG GONE** [35] Jan85 [11]
Mar 85. (7") <2722> **DIANA. / ('A'live)** [–] [ ]
Apr 85. (7") <2729> **HEAVEN. / ('A'live)** [–] [1]
May 85. (7") *(AM 256)* **HEAVEN. / DIANA** [38] [–]
(12"+=) *(AMY 256)* – Fits ya good / ('A'version).
(d7"+=) *(AMD 256)* – Straight from the heart / You want it, you got it.
Jun 85. (7") <2739> **SUMMER OF '69. / THE BEST HAS YET TO COME** [–] [5]
Jul 85. (7") *(AM 267)* **SUMMER OF '69. / KIDS WANNA ROCK (live)** [42] [–]
(12"+=) *(AMY 267)* – The Bryan Adamix.
Sep 85. (7") <2770> **ONE NIGHT LOVE AFFAIR. / LONELY NIGHTS** [–] [13]
Oct 85. (7"/12"; by BRYAN ADAMS & TINA TURNER) *(AM/+Y 285)* **IT'S ONLY LOVE. / THE BEST WAS YET TO COME** [29] [–]
(d7"+=) *(AMD 285)* – Somebody. / Long gone.

Nov 85. (7"; by BRYAN ADAMS & TINA TURNER) *<2791>*
IT'S ONLY LOVE. / THE ONLY ONE [–] [15]
Dec 85. (7"/12") *(AM/+Y 297)* **CHRISTMAS TIME. / REGGAE CHRISTMAS** [55] [–]
Feb 86. (7") *(AM 295)* **THIS TIME. / I'M READY** [41] [–]
(12"+=) *(AMY 295)* – Lonely nights.
Jul 86. (7") *(AM 322)* **STRAIGHT FROM THE HEART. / FITS YA GOOD** [51] [–]
(12"+=) *(AMY 322)* – ('A'live).
Mar 87. (7") *(ADAM 2) <2921>* **HEAT OF THE NIGHT. / ANOTHER DAY** [50] [6]
(12"+=) *(ADAM 2-12)* – ('A'extended remix).
Apr 87. (lp/c/cd) *<(AMA/AMC/CDA 3907)>* **INTO THE FIRE** [10] [7]
– Heat of the night / Into the fire / Victim of love / Another day / Native son / Only the strong survive / Remembrance day / Rebel rebel / Hearts on fire / Home again. *(re-iss. Mar93 cd/c; CD/C MID 185)*
May 87. (7") *<2948>* **HEARTS ON FIRE. / THE BEST HAS YET TO COME** [–] [26]
May 87. (7"/c-s) *(ADAM/+C 3)* **HEARTS ON FIRE. / RUN TO YOU** [57] [–]
(12"+=) *(ADAM 3-12)* – Native sun.
Aug 87. (7") *<2964>* **VICTIM OF LOVE. / INTO THE FIRE** [–] [32]
Oct 87. (7"/7"box/c-s) *(AM/+F/C 407)* **VICTIM OF LOVE. / HEAT OF THE NIGHT (live)** [68] [–]
(12"+=) *(AMY 407)* – ('A'live).

—— BRYAN now used session people?

Jun 91. (7"/c-s) *(AM/+MC 789) <1567>* **(EVERYTHING I DO) I DO IT FOR YOU. / SHE'S ONLY HAPPY WHEN SHE'S DANCING (live)** [1] [1]
(12"+=/cd-s+=) *(AM Y/CD 789)* – ('A'extended) / Cuts like a knife.
Aug 91. (7"/c-s) *(AM/+MC 812) <1576>* **CAN'T STOP THIS THING WE STARTED. / IT'S ONLY LOVE (live)** [12] [2]
(etched-12"+=/cd-s+=) *(AM Y/CD 812)* – Hearts on fire.
Sep 91. (cd/c/lp) *(397164-2/-4/-1) <5367>* **WAKING UP THE NEIGHBOURS** [1] [6]
– Is your mama gonna miss ya? / Hey honey – I'm rockin' you in! / Can't stop this thing we started / Thought I'd died and gone to Heaven / Not guilty / House arrest / Vanishing / Do I have to say the words? / There will never be another tonight / All I want is you / Depend on me / (Everything I do) I do it for you / If you wanna leave me (can I come too?) / Touch the hand / Don't drop that bomb on me.
Nov 91. (7"/c-s) *(AM/+C 838) <1588>* **THERE WILL NEVER BE ANOTHER TONIGHT. / INTO THE FIRE (live)** [32] [31]
(etched-12"+=/pic-cd-s+=) *(AM Y/CD 838)* – One night love affair (live).
Feb 92. (7"/c-s) *(AM/+C 848) <1592>* **I THOUGHT I'D DIED AND GONE TO HEAVEN. / SOMEBODY (live)** [8] [13]
(12"+=) *(AMY 848)* – (Everything I do) I do it for you.
(cd-s+=) *(AMCD 848)* – Heart of the night (live).
Jul 92. (7"/c-s) *(AM/+C 879)* **ALL I WANT IS YOU. / RUN TO YOU** [22] [–]
(12"+=/cd-s+=) *(AM Y/CD 879)* – Long gone.
Sep 92. (7"/c-s) *(AM/+C 0068) <1611>* **DO I HAVE TO SAY THE WORDS?. / SUMMER OF '69** [30] Jul92 [11]
(12"+=/cd-s+=) *(AM T/CD 0068)* – Kids wanna rock / Can't stop this thing we started.
Oct 93. (7"/c-s) *(580423-7/-4) <0422>* **PLEASE FORGIVE ME. / C'MON EVERYBODY** [2] [7]
(cd-s+=) *(580423-2)* – Can't stop this thing we started / There will never be another tonight.
Nov 93. (cd/c/lp) *(540157-2/-4/-1) <0157>* **SO FAR SO GOOD** (compilation) [2] [7]
– Summer of '69 / Straight from the heart / It's only love / Can't stop this thing we started / Do I have to say the words? / This time / Run to you / Heaven / Cuts like a knife / (Everything I do) I do it for you / Somebody / Kids wanna rock / Heat of the night / Please forgive me.
Jan 94. (7"/c-s; BRYAN ADAMS, ROD STEWART & STING) *(580477-7/-4) <0476>* **ALL FOR LOVE. / ('A'instrumental)** [2] Nov93 [1]
(cd-s) *(580477-2)* – ('A'side) / Straight from the heart (live) (BRYAN ADAMS) / If only (ROD STEWART) / Love is stronger than justice (live) (STING).
(above hit from the film 'The Three Musketeers')
Jul 94. (cd/c) *(397094-2/-4)* **LIVE! LIVE! LIVE!** (rec.live Belgium 1988) [17] [–]
– She's only happy when she's dancin' / It's only love / Cuts like a knife / Kids wanna rock / Hearts on fire / Take me back / The best was yet to come / Heaven / Heat of the night / Run to you / One night love affair / Long gone / Summer of '69 / Somebody / Walking after midnight / I fought the law / Into the fire.
Apr 95. (7"/c-s/cd-s) *(581028-7/-4/-2) <1028>* **HAVE YOU EVER REALLY LOVED A WOMAN? / LOW LIFE** [4] [1]
May 96. (c-s/cd-s) *(581579-4/-2) <1578>* **THE ONLY THING THAT LOOKS GOOD ON ME IS YOU / HEY ELVIS / I WANT IT ALL** [6] [52]
(cd-s) *(581639-2)* – ('A'side) / Summer of '69 / Cuts like a knife / Thought I'd died and gone to Heaven.
Jun 96. (cd/c) *(540675-2/-4) <0551>* **18 TIL I DIE** [1] [31]
– The only thing that looks good on me is you / Do to you / Let's make a night to remember / 18 til I die / Star / (I wanna be) Your underwear / We're gonna win / I think about you / I'll always be right there / It ain't a party . . . if you can't come 'round / Black pearl / You're still beautiful to me / Have you ever really loved a woman?
Aug 96. (c-ep) *(581865-4)* **LET'S MAKE A NIGHT TO REMEMBER / ROCK STEADY / HEY LITTLE GIRL / IF YA WANNA BE BAD YA GOTTA BE GOOD** [10] [–]
(cd-ep) *(581865-2)* – (first 3 tracks) / ('A'version).
(cd-ep) *(581867-2)* – ('A'side) / ('A'version) / If ya wanna be bad ya gotta be good / Little red rooster.
Aug 96. (c-s,cd-s) *<1862>* **LET'S MAKE A NIGHT TO REMEMBER / STAR** [–] [24]
Nov 96. (cd-ep) *(582027-2)* **STAR / THE ONLY THING THAT LOOKS GOOD ON ME IS YOU / IT'S ONLY LOVE (with MELISSA ETHERIDGE) / RUN TO YOU** [13] [–]
(c-ep/cd-ep) *(582025-4/-2)* – ('A'side) / Let's make it a night to remember / All for love / (Everything I do) I do it for you.
Jan 97. (c-s; by BARBRA STREISAND & BRYAN ADAMS) *(582083-4) <78480>* **I FINALLY FOUND SOMEONE / 18 TIL I DIE** [10] Nov96 [8]
(cd-s) *(582083-2)* – ('A'side) / Star / I think about you / Do to you.
(above issued on 'Columbia' US)
Apr 97. (c-s/cd-s) *(582183-4/-2)* **18 TIL I DIE / DO TO YOU** [22] [ ]
(cd-s+=) *(582183-5)* – Can't stop this thing we started / Touch the hand.
Dec 97. (cd/c) *<(540831-2/-4)>* **UNPLUGGED (live)** [19] [88]
– Summer of '69 / Back to you / Cuts like a knife / I'm ready / Fits ya good / When you love someone / 18 til I die / I think about you / If ya wanna be bad ya gotta be good / Let's make a night to remember / The only thing that looks good on me is you / A little love / Heaven / I'll always be right there.
Dec 97. (c-s/cd-s) *(582475-4/-2)* **BACK TO YOU / HEY ELVIS / CAN'T STOP THIS THING WE STARTED – IT AIN'T A PARTY . . . IF YOU CAN'T COME 'ROUND (medley)** [18] [ ]
Mar 98. (c-s/cd-s) *(582535-4/-2)* **I'M READY / (IN WANNA BE YOUR) UNDERWEAR / BACK TO YOU (original) / I'LL ALWAYS BE RIGHT THERE** [20] [–]
Mercury Mercury
Sep 98. (c-s) *(MERMC 516)* **ON A DAY LIKE TODAY / SHE BELIEVES IN ME** [13] [–]
(cd-s+=) *(MERCD 516)* – ('A'-Pants down mix).
(cd-s) *(MERDD 516)* – ('A'side) / The only thing that looks good on me (is you) / Bin there, done that.
Oct 98. (cd/c) *<(541016-2/-4)>* **ON A DAY LIKE TODAY** [11] [ ]
– How do ya feel tonight / C'mon c'mon c'mon / Getaway / On a day like today / Fearless / I'm a liar / Cloud number nine / When you're gone (with MELANIE C) / Inside out / If I had you / Before the night is over / I don't wanna live forever / Where angels fear to tread / Lie to me.
Nov 98. (c-s; by BRYAN ADAMS & MEL C) *(582818-4)* **WHEN YOU'RE GONE / HEY BABY** [3] [–]
(cd-s+=) *(582819-2)* – When you're gone (without Melanie C).
(cd-s) *(582821-2)* – ('A'side) / I love ya too much / What does it do to your heart.
Apr 99. (c-s) *(582646-4)* **CLOUD NUMBER NINE / Bryan Adams & Mel C: WHEN YOU'RE GONE (acoustic)** [6] [–]
(cd-s+=) *(582849-2)* – Let's talk about love.
(cd-s) *(582847-2)* – ('A'mixes; Chicane / Bascombe / medley).
Nov 99. (cd/c) *(490522-2/-4)* **THE BEST OF ME** (compilation) [12] [–]
– The best of me / Can't stop this thing we started / I'm ready / Summer of '69 / Let's make a night to remember / All for love / Have you ever really loved a woman? / Run to you / Cloud number nine / (Everything I do) I do it for you / Back to you / When you're gone / Please forgive me / The only thing that looks good on me is you / Inside out. *(special cd+=; 490559-2)* – South Africa live:- Summer of '69 / Back to you / Can't stop this thing we started / Have you ever really loved a woman / Rock steady.
<US cd-iss. Sep01; 540157>

Nov 99. (c-s) *(497023-4)* **THE BEST OF ME / CLOUD NUMBER NINE** [47] [–]
(cd-s+=) *(497196-2)* – Fearless.
(cd-s) *(497195-2)* – ('A'side) / Inside out / How do ya feel tonight.

— In Mar'00, ADAMS was credited with CHICANE on their UK No.1 single, 'Don't Give Up'.

Jul 02. (c-s) *(497743-4)* **HERE I AM – END TITLE / I'M READY (live at Slane Castle)** [5] [–]
(cd-s+=) *(497743-2)* – ('A'-soundtrack version) / Cloud number 9 (live at Slane Castle).
(cd-s) *(497744-2)* – ('A'side) / ('A'-instrumental) / You can't take me (alt. version) / ('A'-video).

Jul 02. (cd) *(493362-2)* *<493304-2>* **SPIRIT: STALLION OF THE CIMARRON** (soundtrack with Hans Zimmer) [8] May02 [40]
– Here I am – end title / I will always return / You can't take me / Get off my back / Brothers under the sun / Don't let go (SARAH McLACHLAN) / This is where I belong / Here I am / Sound the bugle (instrumental) / Run free (instrumental) / Homeland – main title (instrumental) / Rain (instrumental) / The long road back (instrumental) / Nothing I've ever known / I will always return – finale.

– compilations, others, etc. –

Jun 89. (c) *A&M; (AMC 24101)* **CUTS LIKE A KNIFE / RECKLESS** [ ] [–]

— on the 2nd lp below he had replaced NICK GILDER

Jan 92. (cd/lp; SWEENEY TODD featuring BRYAN ADAMS) *Receiver; (RR CD/LP 154)* **IF WISHES WERE HORSES** [ ] [–]
– Tantalize / If wishes were horses / Until I find you / Pushin' and shovin'/ No.5243605 Smith / Song for a star / Shut up / All of a sudden / Wastin' time / Say hello wave goodbye.

Ryan ADAMS

Born: DAVID RYAN ADAMS, 5 Nov'74, Jacksonville, North Carolina, USA. Before turning into a music industry brat and hanging around the likes of Elton John and Jon Bon Jovi, RYAN ADAMS used to be a highy respected and low-key member of America's thriving mid-west alt Country scene and the co-founder of the excellent WHISKEYTOWN. After his split with the aforementioned, however, ADAMS cleaned up his act, stopped partying and became friendly with the rich and famous. Luckily for us, he still managed to write songs that could smash most of today's modern singer/songwriter types into tiny pieces. 'HEARTBREAKER' (2000) was a fine example of this: recorded in seventeen days and featuring the likes of EMMYLOU HARRIS, GILLIAN WELCH and her husband DAVID RAWLINGS, the album was full of sweetness, bitterness and of course, downright heartbreak. 'TO BE YOUNG (IS TO BE SAD, IS TO BE HIGH)' was a good ol' country rock'n'roll track, while 'AMY' wouldn't have sounded out of place on The BEATLES 'WHITE ALBUM'. But most impressive of all was the sheer poignancy shot through most of ADAMS' songs, whether it be the soloistic flare of 'IN MY TIME OF NEED' or HARRIS' timely western vocals on the haunting 'OH MY SWEET CAROLINA' (perhaps one of the greatest songs of ADAMS' career, if not one of the greatest ballads ever written). The set also displayed an impressive array of songs and not one would fail to move the listener. After the critical acclaim of 'HEARTBREAKER', ADAMS began work on a more commercial affair, 'GOLD' (2001), a follow-up which saw him moving slowly towards the mainstream and abandoning his lo-fi country roots. To call him a sell-out would be unfair, but ADAMS certainly must have been tempted by the overground to issue such a MOR-tinged, conformist album. Some tracks still hit through (especially in America where it hit the Top 20). For instance 'RESCUE BLUES' and the sweet ballad 'WHEN THE STARS GO BLUE' lived up to the standards of his previous set, but single 'NEW YORK, NEW YORK' (accompanied by a terrible 'nostalgic' music video) was strictly for the Starbucks generation and could've easily featured on BON JOVI's latest. Here's hoping RYAN ADAMS' next venture will be more of his own style, not for the sake of his fans but for the sake of himself. Otherwise he might be one letter short of a dull radio-friendly rock star. To try to win back some of his indie cred, somewhat lost after 'GOLD', ADAMS set to releasing the quietly admirable demos and rarities compendium 'DEMOLITION' in 2002. Comprised of hastily written and recorded tracks, the album boasted a number of stripped down songs, which, with better production, could've proved to be a hit with his newfound mainstream audience. Whereas 'GOLD' saw him isolate his mawkish fanbase, 'DEMOLITION' did the opposite – not sitting well with the people who made 'NEW YORK . . .' a hit. Nevertheless, a fine addition to his back catalogue and proof that the prolific troubadour was capable of some pretty good stuff, it was back to the usual come the release of the shaky 'ROCK N ROLL' (2003). The "official" follow-up to 'GOLD', ADAMS wanted to issue his "death-threat to himself" album, 'LOVE IS HELL', as the set which would follow hot on its heels. Not if label 'Lost Highway' had anything to do with it; they rejected the album and sent ADAMS back to the studio, with the result being the aforementioned 'ROCK N ROLL'. Slightly hurried and, in some parts, sounding rather drab, the much rawer, depressing 'LOVE IS HELL' was finally available when it was released in two parts at the end of 2003. Sounding somewhat like an ode to those rainy day SMITHS albums ADAMS was so much in love with (and with a production by SMITHS collaborator John Porter), the two mini-LP's delved deeper into his dark psyche and with some impressive submissions aside, you couldn't help wonder if 'Lost Highway' had a point when they noted that the album was "too bleak". • **Covers:** LOVESICK BLUES (Hank Williams) / WONDERWALL (Oasis).

Album rating: HEARTBREAKER (*9) / GOLD (*6) / DEMOLITION (*5) / ROCK N ROLL (*5) / LOVE IS HELL PT.1 mini (*6) / LOVE IS HELL PT.2 mini (*4)

RYAN ADAMS – vocals, acoustic guitar, banjo

Cooking Vinyl / Cooking Vinyl

Oct 00. (cd) *<(COOKCD 205)>* **HEARTBREAKER** [ ] [ ]
– (Argument with David Rawlings concerning Morrissey) / To be young (is to be sad, is to be high) / My winding wheel / AMY / Oh my sweet Carolina / Bartering lines / Call me on your way back home / Damn, Sam (I love a woman that rains) / Come pick me up / To be the one / Why do they leave / Shakedown on 9th Street / Don't ask for the water / In my time of need / Sweet lil gal (23rd/1st). *(lp-iss.Jun02; COOK 205)*

Lost Highway / Lost Highway

Sep 01. (cd) *<(170235-2)>* **GOLD** [20] [59]
– New York, New York / Firecracker / Answering bell / Le cienega just smiled / The rescue blues / Somehow, someday / When the stars go blue / Nobody girl / Sylvia Plath / Enemy fire / Gonna make you love me / Wild flowers / Harder now that it's over / Touch, feel & lose / The Toledo's street walkin' blues / Goodnight Hollywood Blvd. *(d-cd+=; 170252-2)* – Rosalie come and go / Fool we are as men / Sweet black magic / Cannonball days / The bar is a beautiful place. *(cd/d-lp-iss.Apr02; 170 262-2/235-1)*

Nov 01. (cd-s) *(172223-2)* **NEW YORK NEW YORK / MARA LISA / FROM ME TO YOU / ('A'-video)** [53] [ ]

Apr 02. (cd-s) *(172239-2)* **ANSWERING BELL / SWEET BLACK MAGIC / THE BAR IS A BEAUTIFUL PLACE / ('A'-video)** [39] [ ]
(cd-s) *(172240-2)* – ('A'live) / New York New York (live) / To be young (is to be sad is to be high) (live) / New York New York (video).

Sep 02. (7") *(172259-7)* **NUCLEAR. / SONG FOR KEITH** [37] [–]
(cd-s) *(172259-2)* – ('A'side) / Blue.

Sep 02. (cd/lp) *<(170333-2/-1)>* **DEMOLITION** [22] [28]
– Nuclear / Hallelujah / You will always be the same / Desire / Cry on demand / Starting to hurt / She wants to play hearts / Tennessee sucks / Dear Chicago / Gimme a sign / Tomorrow / Chin up, cheer up / Jesus (don't touch my baby).

Nov 03. (cd)(lp) *(9861324)(9861004) <13760-2/-1>* **ROCK N ROLL** [41] [33]
– This is it / Shallow / 1974 / Wish you were here / So alive / Luminol / Burning photographs / She's lost total control / Note to self: don't die / Rock n roll / Anybody wanna take me home / Do Miss America / Boys / The drugs not working. *(UK cd+=)* – Hypnotised.

Nov 03. (m-cd) *(9812782) <15480-2>* **LOVE IS HELL PT.1** [62] [78]
– Political scientist / Afraid not scared / This house is not for sale / Love is hell / Wonderwall / The shadowlands / World War 24 / Avalanche.

Dec 03. (m-cd) *(9813667) <15490-2>* **LOVE IS HELL PT.2** [ ] [ ]
– My blue Manhattan / Please do not let me go / City rain, city streets / I see monsters / English girls approximately / Thank you Louise / Hotel Chelsea nights.

Dec 03. (d-10"lp) *(9861361) <17020-2>* **LOVE IS HELL PT.1 & PT.2** [ ] [ ]
– (above tracks +) / Fuck the universe / Twice as bad as love.

ADD N TO (X)

Formed: South London, England . . . 1994 by former Radio Prague DJ, BARRY SMITH, alongside ANN SHENTON and STEVEN CLAYDON, taking their puzzling moniker from a mathematical formula. Moog and theremin dole-meisters of the Nth degree, ADD N TO X debuted early in 1996 with 'VERO ELECTRONICS', a strangely strange set of mind-blowing knob twiddling. The following year, after inking a deal with 'Satellite', the eardrum-bashing futurists had two NME Singles Of The Week, 'THE BLACK REGENT' and 'KING WASP'. Early in 1998, they established themselves with an innovative electro A-Bomb of sound in their second long-player, 'ON THE WIRES OF OUR NERVES'. Extreme and trailblazing, like STEREOLAB/SUICIDE with a rocket shoved up their rectum, the album's lengthy, disorientated tracks were a prime feature of DJ, Mary Ann Hobbs' Radio One "Breeze Block" show. After turning down the majors, ADD N TO X subsequently signed to semi-seminal indie, 'Mute', their first outing being the wonderful 'LITTLE BLACK ROCKS IN THE SUN'. In September that year, they were probably the first band ever to play underground at a nuclear shelter, the bunker in question being in the rural backwaters of north east Fife near Anstruther. ADD N TO (X) caused a little rumpus the following Spring with the single 'METAL FINGERS IN MY BODY', due to the accompanying animated porn clip. This track, alongside classic electro-gems such as 'ROBOT NEW YORK' and 'REVENGE OF THE BLACK REGENT', made their third set 'AVANT HARD' (1999), the most pioneering cyberpunk since DEVO donned their boiler-suits. SHENTON, CLAYDON, SMITH and HIGH LLAMAS drummer ROB ALLUM returned with more 'tronic frolics of sorts, 'ADD INSULT TO INJURY' (2000), created an eclectic barrage of synth-punk that ear-bashed its way (at times) through the black holes of your mind. 'LOUD LIKE NATURE' in 2002, saw the group expand their electronica-meets-punk brand of sexy post-rock and it even saw the inclusion of rock icon KIM FOWLEY singing on two numbers.

Album rating: VERO ELECTRONICS (*5) / ON THE WIRES OF OUR NERVES (*8) / AVANT HARD (*9) / ADD INSULT TO INJURY (*7) / LOUD LIKE NATURE (*7)

BARRY SMITH – synthesizer / **ANN SHENTON** – programming/ **STEVEN CLAYDON** – synthesizer

Blow Up — not iss.

Jan 96. (cd/lp) *(BLOW UP 004 CD/LP)* **VERO ELECTRONICS** [ ] [-]
– Inevitable fast access / A silhouette of a man and a wasp / Meetings in compact boxes / A very uncomfortable status (wet disco) / Inevitable fast access (sleeze) / A very uncomfortable status (mathematical) / Aphine repetition. *(cd re-iss. Aug97 & Nov99; same)*

Satellite — Mute

Jun 97. (12") *(STL 003)* **THE BLACK REGENT. / MURMUR ONE** [ ] [-]

Oct 97. (12") *(STL 007)* **KING WASP./ HIT ME** [ ] [-]

Nov 97. (ltd-12") *(PIAO 10)* **DEMON SEED. / (a track by FRIDGE)** [ ] [-]
(above single issued on 'Piao!')

—— added **ROB HALLUM** (of the HIGH LLAMAS)

Feb 98. (cd/d-lp) *(STL 010 CD/LP) <69053>* **ON THE WIRES OF OUR NERVES** [ ] [May98]
– We are Add N To X / Murmur one / Sound of accelerating concrete / Gentle Germans / The black regent / Planet Munich / Nevermind / King Wasp / Orgy of Bubastus / Grey body, green gun / On the wires of our nerves / Hit me / Sir Ape.

—— all above as **ADD N TO X**

Mute — Mute

Jul 98. (10"ep/cd-ep) *(10/CD MUTE 219)* **LITTLE BLACK ROCKS IN THE SUN. / VOICES 1-3** [ ] [-]

Mar 99. (12"/cd-s) *(12/CD MUTE 224)* **METAL FINGERS IN MY BODY. / THIS IS THE FLEX (Hi-Fi & Lo-Fi mixes)** [ ] [-]

Apr 99. (cd/d-lp) *(CD+/STUMM 170) <9091>* **AVANT HARD** [ ] [ ]
– Barry 7's contraption / Robot New York / Skills / Steve's going to teach himself who's boss / FYUZ / Buckminster fuller / Revenge of the black regent / Metal fingers in my body / Ann's eveready equestrian / Oh yeah, oh no / Machine is bored with love.

Aug 99. (7") *(7MUTE 231)* **REVENGE OF THE BLACK REGENT. / IRON MAN** [ ] [-]
(12"+=) *(12MUTE 213)* – ('A'side) / Old lady Ealing does man experiments / Is that alright FYUZ / March of the pure mathematical genius that ends (and results in war).
(cd-ep+=) *(CDMUTE 231)* – Metal fingers in my body (CD-Rom).

Oct 99. (7") *(SMALL 008)* **LIVE 1940 (Rommel & Raisin mix). / Canter: VOTEL, ANDY** [ ] [-]
(above issued on 'Slut Smalls')

—— now with **ROB ALLUM** – drums (of HIGH LLAMAS)

Oct 00. (7") *(MUTE 254)* **PLUG ME IN. / VIC HALLAM SYSTEM** [ ] [-]
(12"/cd-s) *(12/CD MUTE 254)* – ('A'side) / Murray's space shoes (Plug Me In disco remix) / Hey double double.

Oct 00. (cd/lp) *(CD+/STUMM 187) <9137>* **ADD INSULT TO INJURY** [ ] [ ]
– Adding N to X / Brothel charge / You must create / Kingdom of shades / Mister Bobby / The poke 'er 'ole / Plug me in / Hit for cheese / MDMH / BP Perine / Incenerator No.1 / Regent is dead.

Mar 01. (12"/cd-s) *(12/CD MUTE 258)* **THE POKE 'ER 'OLE. / WHITE SCRAPIE / PLUG ME IN** [ ] [-]
(cd-s) *(LCDMUTE 258)* – ('A'mixes).

May 01. (cd-s; as ADD N TO FU(X)A) *(RGIRL 22) <69822>* **AND ANOTHER THING!** [ ] [Jun02]
– (2 untitled tracks).
(above on 'Rocket Girl')

Oct 02. (12"/cd-s) *(12/CD MUTE 278)* **TAKE ME TO YOUR LEADER. / THE TREES ARE DREAMLESS LEAFLESS GENIUS / THE MONKEY SKIRT MARTYRS** [ ] [-]

Oct 02. (cd/lp) *(CD+/STUMM 204) <9194>* **LOUD LIKE NATURE** [ ] [ ]
– Total all out water / Electric village / Sheez mine / Invasion of the polaroid people / Party bag / Quantum leap / Pink light / Up the punks / Take me to your leader (make me really happy) / Lick a battery (tongues across the terminals) / U baby / Large number / All night lazy.

– compilations, etc. –

Oct 01. (cd/d-lp; Various Artists) *Lo; (LCD/LLP 25)* **BARRY 7'S CONNECTORS** (mixes) [ ] [-]

☐ AERIAL-M (see under ⇒ SLINT)

AEROSMITH

Formed: Sunapee, New Hampshire, USA . . . summer 1970, by JOE PERRY and STEVEN TYLER, who, with others (BRAD WHITFORD, TOM HAMILTON and JOEY KRAMER) moved to Boston, Massachusetts. By 1972, through a Max's Kansas City gig, they were signed to 'Columbia' by Clive Davis for a six figure sum. The band released their eponymous debut album the following year and the ROLLING STONES comparisons were inevitable from the off. While The 'Stones had taken American music, translated it and shipped it back across the water, AEROSMITH took the 'Stones interpretation of the Blues and customized it for a younger generation. Comparisons with LED ZEPPELIN were somewhat off the mark, the PERRY/TYLER partnership closely mimicking that of JAGGER and RICHARDS and while the latter two proclaimed themselves the 'Glimmer Twins', so it came to pass that Perry and Tyler were duly christened the 'Toxic Twins' in recognition of their legendary mid-70's decadence. 'MAMA KIN' and the Rufus Thomas cover, 'WALKIN' THE DOG' were fine examples of AEROSMITH's early revved-up R&B strut while the ballad, 'DREAM ON', scraped the lower regions of the US singles chart. The follow-up album, 'GET YOUR WINGS' (1974), consolidated the band's rock'n'raunch but it wasn't until the release of 'TOYS IN THE ATTIC' the following year that the band staked their claim as one of America's biggest and sexiest rock acts. Featuring the swaggering 'SWEET EMOTION' and the supple funk-rock of 'WALK THIS WAY', the record made AEROSMITH a household name, Stateside at least, going on to sell millions. Quintessentially American, the band cut little ice in Britain where punk was the order of the day. While Britain was pogoing to the strains of 'Anarchy in the UK', American heavy metal kids were skinning up to Aerosmith's 'ROCKS' (1976), a seminal record that saw the band at the peak of their powers. Dirty, sinewy riffs gyrated provocatively against diamond melodies, TYLER's pout almost audible as he casually reeled off his lurid tales of life on the road. While the band continued to pack out stadiums across America, their fabled penchant for nose candy was beginning to take its toll on their creative output. 'DRAW THE LINE' (1978) and 'NIGHT IN THE RUTS' (1980) fell woefully short of the band's capabilities, tension between TYLER and PERRY eventually leading to the latter leaving and forming The JOE PERRY PROJECT. Despite a near-fatal road accident, TYLER soldiered on with a revamped line-up for the equally uninspired 'ROCK IN A HARD PLACE' (1982). The all-important chemistry was gone while the chemicals seemingly continued to take their toll. Just as it looked like the end for the band, PERRY and TYLER settled their differences and the original AEROSMITH line-up signed to 'Geffen', getting it together for the 'DONE WITH MIRRORS' (1985) album, their best effort since the 70's heyday. AEROSMITH always had the funk and it seemed fitting that their miraculous commercial and creative rebirth was kickstarted by black hip hop crew RUN DMC. Their reworking of 'WALK THIS WAY' was released at the height of the rock/rap crossover in 1986 when 'Def Jam' was a force to be reckoned with and VW badges were in short supply, duly exposing AEROSMITH to a generation of kids who had never even heard of the band. Bang on cue, the band released 'PERMANENT VACATION' (1987), a masterful return to form which spawned a classic slice of AEROSMITH sleaze in 'DUDE (LOOKS LIKE A LADY)'. Moreover, the band had almost singlehandedly inspired a whole scene; almost every band in the late 80's glam-metal movement modelled themselves on prime 70's AEROSMITH (i.e. GUNS N' ROSES, FASTER PUSSYCAT, JUNKYARD, L.A. GUNS etc.). While the majority of these bands quickly faded into obscurity, AEROSMITH left the young pretenders for dust, releasing the adventurous and critically acclaimed 'PUMP' (1989). The single 'LOVE IN AN ELEVATOR', TYLER's tongue planted, as ever, firmly in cheek (probably not his own though), gave the band their first Top 20 hit in the UK. With the album reaching No.3, it finally seemed Britain had cottoned on, albeit fifteen years later. If 1993's 'GET A GRIP' sounded somewhat formulaic, it was another massive hit nevertheless. After just more than three years away, they returned to 'Columbia', releasing the wittily titled Top 50 hit, 'FALLING IN LOVE (IS HARD ON THE KNEES)', previewing yet another massive selling opus, 'NINE LIVES' (1997). Having scored a modest hit with 'PINK' (an ever bigger UK hit in '99), AEROSMITH unplugged their amps to power-ballad to the top of the Hot 100 with 'I DON'T WANT TO MISS A THING'. Almost as sentimental as the film it was lifted from ('Armageddon'), TYLER and his cohorts crooned through every filled up wrinkle whilst leaving a few mascara stains on their female fans. While The ROLLING STONES continue to roll (bankroll, that is), there's no reason to suggest that AEROSMITH won't continue in a creakily similar fashion. Come the new millennium, the veteran campaigners were back to the hard stuff (music, that is) with 'JUST PUSH PLAY' (2001), the BONEYARD BOYS (aka producers Mark Hudson and Marti Frederiksen) helping tease out a set which many believed AEROSMITH's best since 'PUMP' more than a decade earlier. • **Songwriters:** PERRY / TYLER (aka TOXIC TWINS) except; COME TOGETHER (Beatles) / REMEMBER WALKIN' IN THE SAND (Shangri-la's) / TRAIN KEPT A-ROLLIN' (Johnny Burnette Trio) / MILK COW BLUES (Kokomo Arnold) / CRY ME A RIVER (Julie London) / MY ADIDAS (Run-DMC) / LOVE ME TWO TIMES (Doors). THE JOE PERRY PROJECT:- GET IT ON (BANG A GONG) (T. Rex) / BIG TEN-INCH RECORD (F.Weismantel; blues artist?) / ALL YOUR LOVE (Otis Rush) / HELTER SKELTER (Beatles) / CHIP AWAY THE STONE (Richie Supa). • **Miscellaneous:** In 1978 the group appeared in the 'SGT. PEPPER' Beatles film.

Album rating: AEROSMITH (*8) / GET YOUR WINGS (*7) / TOYS IN THE ATTIC (*9) / ROCKS (*8) / DRAW THE LINE (*7) / LIVE BOOTLEG (*7) / AEROSMITH'S GREATEST HITS compilation (*9) / NIGHT IN THE RUTS (*6) / ROCK IN A HARD PLACE (*6) / DONE WITH MIRRORS (*6) / CLASSICS LIVE collection (*4) / CLASSICS LIVE 2 collection (*5) / PERMANENT VACATION (*8) / GEMS collection (*6) / PUMP (*8) / PANDORA'S BOX compilation boxed-set (*9) / GET A GRIP (*6) / BIG ONES compilation (*8) / NINE LIVES (*6) / JUST PUSH PLAY (*5) / YOUNG LUST – THE AEROSMITH ANTHOLOGY compilation (*8) / O, YEAH! ULTIMATE AEROSMITH ANTHOLOGY compilation (*8)

STEVEN TYLER (b. STEVEN TALLARICO, 26 Mar'48, New York City) – vocals / **JOE PERRY** (b.10 Sep'50, Lawrence, Mass.) – guitar (ex-JAM BAND) / **BRAD WHITFORD** (b.23 Feb'52, Winchester, Mass.) – guitar repl. RAY TABANO / **TOM HAMILTON** (b.31 Dec'51, Colorado Springs) – bass (ex-JAM BAND) / **JOEY KRAMER** (b.21 Jun'50, New York City) – drums

		C.B.S.	Columbia
Jun 73.	(lp) *<32005>* **AEROSMITH**	–	
	– Make it / Somebody / Dream on / One way street / Mama kin / Write me a letter / Movin' out / Walkin' the dog. *(UK-iss.Sep74; CBS 65486) <US re-dist.Mar76 hit No.21> <US re-iss. Sep87/ cd-May88; PC/CK 32005>(cd-iss. Mar92 & Dec93 on 'Columbia'; 469011-2) (cd re-iss. Nov94; CK 64401) (cd re-iss. May97 on 'Columbia'; 474962-2)*		
Nov 73.	(7") *(CBS 1898) <45894>* **DREAM ON. / SOMEBODY**		Oct73 59
	<US ext.re-iss. Jan76; 10278> ; hit No.6 *(re-iss. Apr76; CBS 4000)*		
Feb 74.	(7") *<46029>* **SAME OLD SONG AND DANCE. / PANDORA'S BOX**	–	
Apr 74.	(7") *<10034>* **SPACED. / TRAIN KEPT A-ROLLIN'**	–	
Jun 74.	(7") *<10105>* **S.O.S. (TOO BAD). / LORD OF THE THIGHS**	–	
Nov 74.	(lp/c) *(CBS/40 80015) <32847>* **GET YOUR WINGS**		Mar74 74

– Same old song and dance / Lord of the thighs / Spaced / Woman of the world / S.O.S. (too bad) / Train kept a-rollin' / Seasons of wither / Pandora's box. *<US re-iss. Sep87/ cd-May88; PC/CK 32847> (UK-cd Mar92 & Dec93 & May97 on 'Columbia'; 474963-2)*

May 75. (7") *<10155>* **SWEET EMOTION. / UNCLE SALTY** [–] [36]

Jul 75. (lp/c) *(CBS/40 80773) <33479>* **TOYS IN THE ATTIC** [ ] Apr75 [11]
– Toys in the attic / Uncle Salty / Adam's apple / Walk this way / Big ten inch record / Sweet emotion / No more no more / Round and round / You see me crying. *(re-iss. Feb88 on 'Castle' lp/c/cd; CLA LPX/MCX/CDX 135) <US re-iss. Sep87/ cd-iss. May88; PC/CK 33479) (UK re-iss. Apr91 & Nov93 & Jul95 & May97 on 'Columbia'; 480414-2) (re-iss. Oct97 on 'Simply Vinyl'; SVLP 0001)*

Sep 75. (7") *<10206>* **WALK THIS WAY. / ROUND AND ROUND** [–] [ ]

Nov 75. (7") *<10253>* **TOYS IN THE ATTIC. / YOU SEE ME CRYING** [–] [ ]

Jun 76. (lp/c) *(CBS/40 81379) <34165>* **ROCKS** [ ] May76 [3]
– Back in the saddle / Last child / Rats in the cellar / Combination / Sick as a dog / Nobody's fault / Get the lead out / Lick and a promise / Home tonight. *<US re-iss. Sep87/ May88; PC/CK 34165> (cd-iss. Jul89; CD 32517) (re-iss. cd Dec93 & May97 on 'Columbia'; 474965-2) (lp re-iss. Feb99 on 'Simply Vinyl'; SVLP 65)*

Aug 76. (7") *(CBS 4452) <10359>* **LAST CHILD. / COMBINATION** [ ] Jun76 [21]

Sep 76. (7") *<10407>* **HOME TONIGHT. / PANDORA'S BOX** [–] [71]

Feb 77. (7") *(CBS 4878) <10449>* **WALK THIS WAY. / UNCLE SALTY** [ ] Nov76 [10]

Apr 77. (7") *<10516>* **BACK IN THE SADDLE. / NOBODY'S FAULT** [–] [38]

Oct 77. (7") *<10637>* **DRAW THE LINE. / BRIGHT LIGHT FRIGHT** [–] [42]

Jan 78. (lp/c) *(CBS/40 82147) <34856>* **DRAW THE LINE** [ ] Dec77 [11]
– Draw the line / I wanna know why / Critical mass / Get it up / Bright light fright / Kings and queens / The hand that feeds / Sight for sore eyes / Milk cow blues. *<US re-iss. Sep87; PC 34856> (re-iss. cd Dec93 & May97 on 'Columbia'; 474966-2)*

Mar 78. (7") *<10699>* **KINGS AND QUEENS. / CRITICAL MASS** [–] [70]

Jun 78. (7") *<10727>* **GET IT UP. / MILK COW BLUES** [–] [ ]

Aug 78. (7") *<10802>* **COME TOGETHER. / KINGS AND QUEENS** [ ] [23]

Jan 79. (d-lp) *(CBS 88325) <35564>* **LIVE! BOOTLEG (live)** [ ] Nov78 [13]
– Back in the saddle / Sweet emotion / Lord of the thighs / Toys in the attic / Last child / Come together / Walk this way / Sick as a dog / Dream on / Chip away the stone / Sight for sore eyes / Mama kin / S.O.S. / I ain't got you / Mother popcorn / Train kept a rollin'. *<US re-iss. Dec87; PC 35564> (re-iss. cd Aug93/Dec93/May97 on 'Columbia'; 469004-2/474967-2)*

Jan 79. (7") *<10880>* **CHIP AWAY THE STONE (live). / CHIP AWAY THE STONE (studio)** [–] [77]

Jan 80. (lp/c) *(CBS/40 83680) <36050>* **NIGHT IN THE RUTS** [ ] Nov79 [14]
– No surprize / Chiquita / Remember (walkin' in the sand) / Cheesecake / Three mile smile / Reefer head woman / Bone to bone (Coney Island white fish boy) / Think about it / Mia. *<US re-iss. Sep87; PC 36050> (cd-iss. Mar92 & Dec93 & May97 & Feb01 on 'Columbia'; 474968-2)*

Feb 80. (7") *(CBS 8220) <11181>* **REMEMBER (WALKIN' IN THE SAND). / BONE TO BONE (CONEY ISLAND WHITE FISH BOY)** [ ] Jan80 [67]

—— (Dec79) **JIMMY CREPSO** – guitar (ex-FLAME) repl. JOE PERRY who went solo

—— (Feb80) **RICK DUFAY** – guitar repl. WHITFORD who teamed up with ST. HOLMES

Oct 82. (lp/c) *(CBS/40 85931) <38061>* **ROCK IN A HARD PLACE** [ ] Sep82 [32]
– Jailbait / Lightning strikes / Bitch's brew / Bolivian ragamuffin / Cry me a river / Prelude to Joanie / Joanie's butterfly / Rock in a hard place (Cheshire cat) / Jig it up / Push comes to shove. *<US re-iss. Sep87; PC 38061> (cd-iss. Aug93/Dec93/May97 on 'Columbia'; 469006-2/474970-2)*

—— (Mar84) original 1970's line-up reform (see above)

Geffen Geffen

Nov 85. (7") *<28814>* **SHEILA. / GYPSY BOOTS** [–] [ ]

Dec 85. (lp/c) *(GEF/40 26695) <24091>* **DONE WITH MIRRORS** [ ] Nov85 [36]
– Let the music do the talking / My fist your face / Shame on you / The reason a dog / Shela / Gypsy boots / She's on fire / The hop / Darkness. *<US cd-iss. Oct87; 20491-2> (UK re-iss. Jun89 on 'W.E.A.'; 924 091-1/-4/-2) (re-iss. Apr92 & Jun94 & Feb98 cd/c; GFLD/GFLC 19052)*

—— In Aug'86, AEROSMITH were credited on RUN DMC's hit version of 'WALK THIS WAY'.

Aug 87. (lp/c)(cd) *(WX 126/+C)(924 162-2) <24162>* **PERMANENT VACATION** [37] [11]
– Heart's done time / Magic touch / Rag doll / Simoriah / Dude (looks like a lady) / St. John / Hangman jury / Girl keep coming apart / Angel / Permanent vacation / I'm down / The movie. *(re-iss. Jun94 cd/c; ; GFLD/GFLC 19254) (lp re-iss. Jul98 on 'Simply Vinyl'; SVLP 35)*

Oct 87. (7") *(GEF 29) <28240>* **DUDE (LOOKS LIKE A LADY). / SIMORIAH** [45] Sep87 [14]
(12"+=/12"pic-d+=) *(GEF 29T/+P)* – Once is enough.

Apr 88. (7"/12"/12"pic-d) *(GEF 34/+T/TP) <28249>* **ANGEL. / GIRL KEEPS COMING APART** [69] Jan88 [3]
(3"cd-s+=) *(GEF 34CD)* – Angel (A.O.R. remix) / Dude (looks like a lady).

Jun 88. (12") *<27915>* **RAG DOLL. / ST.JOHN** [–] [17]

Aug 89. (7"/7"s/c-s) *(GEF 63/+X/C) <22845>* **LOVE IN AN ELEVATOR. / YOUNG LUST** [13] [5]
(10"pic-d+=/12"+=/3"cd-s+=) *(GEF 63 TP/T/CD)* – Ain't enough.

Sep 89. (lp/c)(cd) *(WX 304/+C)(924 254-2) <24254>* **PUMP** [3] [5]
– Young lust / F.I.N.E. / Love in an elevator / Monkey on my back / Janie's got a gun / The other side / My girl / Don't get mad, get even / Voodoo medicine man / What it takes. *(re-iss. Jun94 cd/c; GFLD/GFLC 19255) (lp re-iss. Nov98 on 'Simply Vinyl'; SVLP 45)*

Nov 89. (7"/7"sha-pic-d/c-s) *(GEF 68/+P/C) <22727>* **JANIE'S GOT A GUN. / VOODOO MEDICINE MAN** [ ] [4]
(12"+=/3"cd-s+=) *(GEF 68 T/CD)* – Rag doll (live).

Feb 90. (7"/7"sha-pic-d) *(GEF 72/+P)* **DUDE (LOOKS LIKE A LADY) (remix). / MONKEY ON MY BACK** [20] [–]
(12"/cd-s) *(GEF 72 T/CD)* – ('A'extended) / Love in an elevator (live) / Walk this way (live).

Mar 90. (7"/c-s) *<19944>* **WHAT IT TAKES. / MONKEY ON MY BACK** [–] [9]

Apr 90. (7") *(GEF 76)* **RAG DOLL. / SIMORIAH** [42] [–]
(12"/12"s) *(GEF 76 T/TW)* – ('A'side) / Mama kin (live) / Let it rain (live).
(cd-s) *(GEF 76CD)* – ('A'side) / Mama kin (live) / Dream on (live).

Aug 90. (7"/c-s) *(GEF 79/+C) <19927>* **THE OTHER SIDE. / MY GIRL** [46] Jun90 [22]
(12"+=) *(GEFT 79)* – Theme from 'Wayne's World' / ('A'-honky tonk).
(12") *(GEFTW 79)* – ('A'side) / Love in an elevator / Dude (looks like a lady) / Walk this way.

Apr 93. (12"pic-d/cd-s) *(GFST/+D 35) <19149>* **LIVIN' ON THE EDGE. / DON'T STOP / FLESH** [19] [18]
(cd-s) *(GFSTX 35)* – ('A'side) / ('A'acoustic) / Can't stop messin'.

Apr 93. (cd/c/lp) *(GED/GEC/GEF 24444) <24455>* **GET A GRIP** [2] [1]
– Intro / Eat the rich / Get a grip / Fever / Livin' on the edge / Flesh / Walk on down / Shut up and dance / Cryin' / Gotta love it / Crazy / Line up / Can't stop messin' / Amazing / Boogie man.

Jun 93. (10"colrd) *(GFST 46)* **EAT THE RICH. / FEVER / HEAD FIRST** [34] [–]
(cd-s+=) *(GFSTD 46)* – Livin' on the edge (demo).

Oct 93. (c-s) *(GFSC 56) <19256>* **CRYIN' / WALK ON DOWN** [17] Jul93 [12]
(12"white+=) *(GFST 56)* – I'm down.
(cd-s++=) *(GFSTD 56)* – My fist your face.
(cd-s+=) *(GFSXD 56)* – Love in an elevator / Janie's got a gun.

Nov 93. (c-s,cd-s) *<19264>* **AMAZING / FEVER** [–] [24]

Dec 93. (c-s) *(GFSC 63) <19264>* **AMAZING / GOTTA LOVE IT** [57] [–]
(12"colrd+=) *(GFST 63)* – ('A'acoustic).
(cd-s+=) *(GFSTD 63)* – ('A'orchestral).

May 94. (c-s,cd-s) *<19267>* **CRAZY / GOTTA LOVE IT** [–] [17]

Jun 94. (c-s) *(GFSC 75)* **SHUT UP AND DANCE. / DEUCES ARE WILD** [24] [–]
(7"+=) *(GFS 75)* – Crazy (orchestral).
(cd-s++=) *(GFSTD 75)* – Line up.

Oct 94. (c-s) *(GFSC 80)* **CRAZY / BLIND MAN** [23] [–]
(cd-s+=) *(GFSTD 80)* – Shut up and dance (live) / Blind man (mix).

Nov 94. (cd/c/d-lp) *(GED/GEC/GEF 24546) <24716>* **BIG ONES** (compilation) [7] [6]
– Walk on water / Love in an elevator / Rag doll / What it takes / Dude (looks like a lady) / Janie's got a gun / Cryin' / Amazing / Blind man / Deuces are wild / The other side / Crazy / Eat the rich / Angel / Livin' on the edge / Dude (looks like a lady) (live).

Dec 94. (c-s,cd-s) *<19377>* **BLIND MAN / HEAD FIRST** [–] [49]

Columbia Columbia

Mar 97. (7"/c-s) *(664075-7/-4)* **FALLING IN LOVE (IS HARD ON THE KNEES). / FALL TOGETHER** [22] Feb97 [35]
(cd-s+=) *(664075-2)* – Sweet emotion / Seasons of wither.

Mar 97. (cd/c) *(485020-2/-4) <67547>* **NINE LIVES** [4] [1]
– Nine lives / Falling in love (is hard on the knees) / Hole in my soul / Taste of India / Full circle / Something's gotta give / Ain't that a bitch / Farm / Crash / Kiss your past good-bye / Pink / Falling off / Attitude adjustment / Fallen angels.

Jun 97. (7"pic-d) *(664501-7)* **HOLE IN MY SOUL. / NINE LIVES (live)** [29] Aug97 [51]
(cd-s+=) *(664501-2)* – Falling in love (is hard on the knees) (Butcher mix) / Falling in love (is hard on the knees) (Moby flawed mix).
(cd-s) *(664501-5)* – ('A'side) / Falling in love (is hard on the knees) (Moby f**kee mix) / Falling in love (is hard on the knees) (live) / Walk this way (live).

Dec 97. (7"pink) *(664872-7) <78830>* **PINK. / PINK (Chulo mix)** [38] Feb98 [27]
(cd-s) *(664872-2)* – ('A'side) / ('A'-South Beach mix) / ('A'live).

Sep 98. (7"/cd-s) *(666408-7/-2) <78952>* **I DON'T WANT TO MISS A THING. / TASTE OF INDIA (rock remix)** [4] Aug98 [1]
(cd-s+=) *(6664087-5)* – Pink (live) / Crash.

Jun 99. (c-s) *(667534-4)* **PINK / I DON'T WANT TO MISS A THING (live)** [13] [–]
(cd-s+=) *(667534-2)* – Hole in my soul.
(cd-s) *(667534-5)* – ('A'side) / ('A'mix) / ('A'mix).

Mar 01. (7") *(670931-7) <79555>* **JADED. / ANGEL'S EYE** [13] [7]
(cd-s+=) *(670931-2)* – ('A'-stripped down acoustic mix) / ('A'-guitars mix) / Under my skin.
(cd-s+=) *(670931-5)* – ('A'-acoustic mix) / Under my skin (reprise).

Mar 01. (cd/c/lp) *(501535-2/-4/-1) <62088>* **JUST PUSH PLAY** [7] [2]
– Beyond beautiful / Just push play / Jaded / Fly away from here / Tip hoppin' / Sunshine / Under my skin / Luv lies / Outta your head / Drop dead gorgeous / The light inside / Avant garden / The face.

– compilations, others, etc. –

on 'CBS' UK / 'Columbia' US + UK (90's) unless otherwise mentioned

Jan 81. (lp/c) *(CBS/40 84704) <36865>* **AEROSMITH'S GREATEST HITS** [ ] Nov80 [53]
– Dream on / Same old song and dance / Sweet emotion / Walk this way / Remember (walking in the sand) / Back in the saddle / Draw the line / Kings and queens / Come together / Last child. *<US re-iss. Sep87/ cd-Feb88; CK/CS 36865> (re-iss. Nov89 pic-lp/cd; 460703-8/-2) (re-iss. cd Dec93 & Jan01 on 'Columbia'; 474969-2)*

Sep 86. (lp/c) *(CBS/40 26901) <40329>* **CLASSICS LIVE!** (live 1977-1983) [ ] Apr86 [84]
– Train kept a-rollin' / Kings and queens / Sweet emotion / Dream on / Mama kin / Three mile smile / Reefer head woman / Lord of the thighs / Major Barbra. *<US re-iss. Nov87 lp/c/cd; FC/FCT/CK 40329> (re-iss. cd Dec93 on 'Columbia'; 474971-2)*

Aug 87. (lp/c) *<FC/+T 40855>* **CLASSICS LIVE II (live)** [–] [ ]
– Back in the saddle / Walk this way / Movin' out / Draw the line / Same old song and dance / Last child / Let the music do the talking / Toys in the attic. *(UK cd-iss. Nov89; 460037-2) (cd re-iss. Dec92 on 'Columbia'; 474972-2)*

Jun 88. (d-lp/c/cd) *Raw Power; (RAW LP/TC/CD 037)* **ANTHOLOGY** [ ] [–]

1988. (7") *<08536>* **CHIP AWAY THE STONE. / S.O.S. (TOO BAD)** [–] [ ]

Aug 88. (3"cd-s) *<38K 0795-2>* **WALK THIS WAY / DREAM ON** [–] [ ]

Nov 89. (lp/c/cd) *(463224-1/-4/-2) <44487>* **GEMS** [ ] Dec88 [ ]
– Rats in the cellar / Lick and a promise / Chip away the stone / No surprize / Mama kin / Adam's apple / Nobody's fault / Round and round / Critical mass / Lord of the thighs / Jailbait / Train kept a rollin'. *(re-iss. Apr91 & Dec93 on 'Columbia'; 474973-2) (cd re-iss. May98; 491236-2)*

Dec 91. (t-cd/t-c) *(469293-2/-4) <46209>* **PANDORA'S BOX** [ ] [45]
– When I needed you / Make it / Movin' out / One way street / On the road again / Mama kin / Same old song and dance / Train kept a-rollin' / Seasons of wither / Write me a letter / Dream on / Pandora's Box / Rattlesnake shake / Walkin' the dog / Lord of the thighs // Toys in the attic / Round and round / Krawhitham / You see me crying / Sweet emotion / No More no more / Walk this way / I wanna know why / Big ten inch record / Rats in the cellar / Last child / All your love / Soul saver / Nobody's fault / Lick and a promise / Adam's apple / Draw the line / Critical mass // Kings and queens / Milk cow blues / I live in Connecticut / Three mile smile / Let it slide / Cheese cake / Bone to bone (Coney Island white fish boy) / No surprize / Come together / Downtown Charlie / Sharpshooter / Shit house shuffle / South station blues / Riff & roll / Jailbait / Major Barbara / Chip away the stone / Helter skelter / Back in the saddle / Circle jerk. *(3xcd-iss. Nov98; 487480-2)*

Jun 93. (cd) *(474038-2)* **TOYS IN THE ATTIC / CLASSICS LIVE** [ ] [–]

Jul 93. (cd) *(463224-2)* **ROCKS / GEMS** [ ] [ ]

Jun 94. (cd/c) *(476956-2/-4)* **PANDORA'S TOYS (BEST)** (compilation of 'PANDORA'S BOX') [ ] [ ]
– Sweet emotion / Draw the line / Walk this way / Dream on / Train kept a rollin' / Mama kin / Nobody's fault / Seasons of wither / Big ten-inch record / All your love / Helter skelter / Chip away the stone.

Aug 94. (c-s) *(660449-4) <74101>* **SWEET EMOTION / SUBWAY** [74] Dec91 [ ]
(cd-s+=) *(660449-2)* – Circle jerk.

Dec 94. (12xcd-box) *(477803-2)* **BOX OF FIRE** [ ] [ ]
– (AEROSMITH / GET YOUR WINGS / TOYS IN THE ATTICS / ROCKS / DRAW THE LINE / LIVE BOOTLEG / NIGHT IN THE RUTS / GREATEST HITS / ROCK IN A HARD PLACE / CLASSICS LIVE / CLASSICS LIVE II / GEMS / bonus cd)

May 97. (13xcd-box) *(477803-2)* **BOX OF FIRE** [ ] [ ]

Nov 97. (3xcd-box) *(485312-2)* **TOYS IN THE ATTIC / DRAW THE LINE / ROCKS** [ ] [ ]

Aug 98. (cd) *(487351-2)* **CLASSICS LIVE VOL.1 & 2** [ ] [ ]

Oct 98. (d-cd/d-c) *Geffen; <(GED/GEC 25221)>* **A LITTLE SOUTH OF SANITY (live)** [36] [12]
– Eat the rich / Love in an elevator / Falling in love (is hard on the knees) / Same old song and dance / Hole in my soul / Monkey on my back / Livin' on the edge / Cryin' / Rag doll / Angel / Janie's got a gun / Amazing // Back in the saddle / Last child / The other side / Walk on down / Dream on / Crazy / Mama kin / Walk this way / Dude (looks like a lady) / What it takes / Sweet emotion.

Sep 00. (cd) *(499855-2)* **AEROSMITH / TOYS IN THE ATTIC** [ ] [–]

Oct 00. (d-cd) *Universal; <(E 490433-2)>* **PERMANENT VACATION / DONE WITH MIRRORS** [ ] [ ]

Oct 00. (t-cd) *Universal; <(E 424935-2)>* **PERMANENT VACATION / DONE WITH MIRRORS / PUMP** [ ] [ ]

Nov 00. (t-cd) *Universal; <(E 485312-2)>* **TOYS IN THE ATTIC / DRAW THE LINE / ROCKS** [ ] [ ]

Jan 01. (cd) *Universal; <(E 497441-2)>* **THE UNIVERSAL MASTERS COLLECTION** [ ] [ ]

Nov 01. (d-cd) *Geffen; <(493119-2)>* **YOUNG LUST – THE AEROSMITH ANTHOLOGY** [32] [ ]
– Let the music do the talking / My fist your face / Shame on you / Heart's done time / Rag doll / Dude (looks like a lady) / Angel / Hangman jury / Permanent vacation / Young lust / The other side / What it takes / Monkey on my back / Love in an elevator / Janie's got a gun / Ain't enough / Walk this way (with RUN-D.M.C.) / Eat the rich / Love me two times / Head first / Livin' on the edge (acoustic) / Don't stop / Can't stop messin' / Amazing (orchestral) / Cryin' / Crazy / Shut up and dance / Deuces are wild / WAlk on water / Blind man / Falling in love (is hard on the knees) (live) / Dream on (live) / Hole in my soul (live) / Sweet emotion (live).

Jul 02. (d-cd) *Columbia; (508467-2) / Sony; <86700>* **O, YEAH! – ULTIMATE AEROSMITH HITS** [6] [4]
– Mama kin / Dream on / Same old song and dance / Seasons of wither / Walk this way / Big ten inch record / Sweet emotion / Last child / Back in the saddle / Draw the line / Dude (looks like a lady) / Angel / Rag doll / Janie's got a gun / Love in an elevator / What it takes / The other side / Livin' on the edge / Cryin' / Amazing / Deuces are wild / Crazy / Falling in love (is hard on the knees) / Pink (the South Beach mix) / I don't want to miss a thing / Jaded / Just push play (radio remix) / Walk this way (with RUN-D.M.C.) / Girls of summer / Lay it down.

AFGHAN WHIGS

Formed: Denver, Colorado, USA . . . Autumn '86, by GREG DULLI and RICK McCOLLUM who met in a prison. The pair moved to Cincinatti, Ohio, after signing for Seattle based indie label 'Sub Pop' in 1989, their independently released debut set, 'BIG TOP HALLOWEEN' (1988), having caused something of a stir with its proto-grunge exhortations. Produced by Seattle maestro, Jack

Endino, the album, 'UP IN IT', worked around the same formula, hinting at their wider country and soul influences. After a further set for 'Sub Pop', 'CONGREGATION' (1992), and an EP of soul covers, 'UPTOWN AVONDALE', the group were plucked from the mire of grunge cultdom by 'Elektra' in the major label stampede following NIRVANA's success. A former film student, DULLI cannily negotiated the right to creative control over the band's videos, his acting ambitions duly realised in 1994 when he scored the part of JOHN LENNON in Stuart Sutcliffe's story, 'Backbeat'. The 'WHIGS major label debut, 'GENTLEMEN', pushed all the right critical buttons, fleshing out their grungy noir-soul sound against a typically hard-bitten lyrical background. Although the record surprisingly failed to make the US charts, it scored a Top 60 placing in the UK. DULLI's rendition of Barry White's 'CAN'T GET ENOUGH OF YOUR LOVE', was an indication of where AFGHAN WHIGS were headed with 'BLACK LOVE'. An even more soul-centric offering, the album almost scraped into the British Top 40, the band now signed to 'Mute' (still on 'Elektra' US). 'Columbia' took up the reins for er . . . 1998's '1965', a celebration of rock music's debt to the power of sex. Recorded in New Orleans, the record was hailed as their long promised masterpiece, a writhing, sweaty slab of post-grunge voodoo soul. DULLI matched this aggression later in the year, after a brawl with a steward earned him a few days in intensive care and a fractured skull . . . er to boot. Subsequently the singer threatened action on the Texas nightclub even though it was alleged that he was the main instigator. Early in 2001, DULLI and Co disbanded. • **Covered:** MY WORLD IS EMPTY WITHOUT YOU + I HEAR A SYMPHONY + COME SEE ABOUT ME (Diana Ross & The Supremes) / CHALK OUTLINE (Paul K & The Weathermen) / BEWARE (Al Green) / TRUE LOVE TRAVELS ON A GRAVEL ROAD (Percy Sledge) / BAND OF GOLD (Freda Payne) / THE DARK END OF THE STREET (Dan Penn) / READY (Scrawl) / LITTLE GIRL BLUE (Rodgers-Hart) / I KEEP COMING BACK (Austell-Graham) / IF I ONLY HAD A HEART (from 'The Wizard Of Oz') / CREEP (Radiohead) / LITTLE GIRL BLUE (Hart-Rodgers) / CREEP (TLC) / MR. SUPERLOVE (Ass Ponys) / REVENGE (Patti Smith) / EASILY PERSUADED (Martha Reeves & The Vandellas) / YOU'VE CHANGED (Carey-Fisher) / I WANT TO GO TO SLEEP (Harold Chichester) / MOON RIVER (Henry Mancini) / IF THERE'S A HELL BELOW (WE'RE ALL GOING TO GO) (Curtis Mayfield) / SUPERSTITION (Stevie Wonder) / MISS WORLD (Hole) / PAPA WAS A RASCAL (James Booker) / LOST IN THE SUPERMARKET (Clash).

Album rating: BIG TOP HALLOWEEN (*4) / UP IN IT (*6) / CONGREGATION (*8) / GENTLEMEN (*8) / BLACK LOVE (*6) / 1965 (*8)

GREG DULLI – vocals, guitar / **RICK McCOLLUM** – guitar / **JOHN CURLEY** – bass / **STEVE EARLE** – drums

not iss. Ultrasuede

Oct 88. (lp) *<001>* **BIG TOP HALLOWEEN** [–] [ ]
– Here comes Jesus / In my town / Priscilla's wedding day / Push / Scream / But listen / Big top Halloween / Life in a day / Sammy / Doughball / Back o' the line / Greek is extra.

Sub Pop Sub Pop

Apr 89. (7") *<SP 32>* **I AM THE STICKS. / WHITE TRASH PARTY** [–] [ ]

Apr 90. (cd/c/lp/orange-lp) *<SP 60>* **UP IN IT** [–] [ ]
– Retarded / White trash party / Hated / Southpaw / Amphetamines and coffee / Now can we begin / You my flower / Son of the south / I know your secret. *(cd/c+=)* – I am the sticks. *(UK-iss.Aug90 on 'Glitterhouse'; GR 0092) (cd re-iss. Sep98; SPCD 60)*

Oct 90. (7",7"red) *<SP 84>* **SISTER BROTHER. / HEY CUZ** [–] [ ]

Dec 90. (12"ep) *(SP 4-115)* **THE RETARD EP** [ ] [–]
– Retarded / Sister brother / Hey cuz / Turning in two. *(cd-ep May93; SPCD 4-115)*

Jan 92. (cd-s) *<SP 133>* **TURN ON THE WATER / CHALK OUTLINE / MILES IZ DED** [–] [ ]

Jan 92. (lp/cd) *<(SP 183/+CD)>* **CONGREGATION** [ ] [ ]
– Her against me / I'm her slave / Turn on the water / Conjure me / Kiss the floor / Congregation / This is my confession / Dedicate it / The temple / Let me lie to you / Tonight. *(cd re-iss. Sep98; same)*

Jan 92. (7") *<(SP32,5/187)>* **TURN ON THE WATER. / MILES IZ DED** [ ] [–]
(12"+=/cd-s+=) *(SP32/+CD 187)* – Delta kong / Chalk outline.

May 92. (7"white,7"lavender) *<SP 142>* **CONJURE ME. / MY WORLD IS EMPTY WITHOUT YOU** [–] [ ]

Aug 92. (12"/cd-s) *(SP42/+CD 203)* **MY WORLD IS EMPTY WITHOUT YOU. / CONJURE ME / YOU MY FLOWER** [ ] [–]

Oct 92. (7"ep) *<(SP54 216)>* **UPTOWN AVONDALE EP: BAND OF GOLD. / COME SEE ABOUT ME** [ ] [ ]
(12"+=/cd-s+=) *<(SP53/+CD 215)>* – True love travels on a gravel road / Beware.
(cd-s++=) *<(SP 175b)>* – Rebirth of the cool.

Blast First Elektra

Sep 93. (7") *(BFFP 89)* **GENTLEMEN. / MR. SUPERLOVE** [ ] [–]
(12"+=/cd-s+=) *(BFFP 89 T/CD)* – The dark end of the street.

Oct 93. (lp/cd) *(BFFP 90/+CD) <7559 61501-2>* **GENTLEMEN** [58] [ ]
– If I were going / Gentlemen / Be sweet / Debonair / When we two parted / Fountain and fairfax / What jail is like / My curse / Now you know / I keep coming back / Brother Woodrow – Closing prayer. *(lp w /free 7"ep)* – ROT. / TONIGHT

— guests on the album: **HAROLD CHICHESTER** – keyboards / **BARB HUNTER** – cello / **JODY STEPHENS** – vocals / **MARCY MAYS** – vocals

Feb 94. (7"ep/12"ep/cd-ep) *(BFFP 95/+T/CD)* **BROKEN PROMISES EP** [ ] [–]
– Debonair / My curse / Little girl blue / Ready.
(cd-ep) *(BFFP 95CDL)* – ('A'side) / Rot / I keep coming back / Tonight.

— In Mar'94, 'MR. SUPERLOVE' was issued on B-side of ASS PONY's single on 'Monocat'.

Aug 94. (7"ep/cd-ep) *(BFFP 96/+CD)* **WHAT JAIL IS LIKE EP** [ ] [ ]
– What jail is like / Revenge / Easily persuaded / My curse.
(10"ep) *(BFFP 96T)* – ('A'side) / Now you know (live) / Gentlemen (live) / My world is empty without you – I hear a symphony (live).
(12"ep/cd-ep) *<61708-1/-2>* – What jail is like / Mr. Superlove / The dark end of the street / Little girl blue / What jail is like (live) / Now you know (live) / My world is empty without you – I hear a symphony (live).

— **PAUL BUCHIGNANI** – drums; repl. EARLE

Mute Elektra

Feb 96. (10"ep/cd-ep) *(10/CD MUTE 128)* **HONKY'S LADDER E.P.** [ ] [ ]
– Honky's ladder / Blame, etc. / If I only had a heart / Creep.

Mar 96. (cd/c/lp) *(CD/C+/STUMM 143) <61896>* **BLACK LOVE** [41] [79]
– Crime scene part one / My enemy / Double day / Blame, etc. / Step into the light / Going to town / Honky's ladder / Night by candlelight / Bulletproof / Summer's kiss / Faded.

Aug 96. (cd-ep) *(CDMUTE 199)* **GOING TO TOWN / GOING TO TOWN (live at Modern Rock) / YOU'VE CHANGED / I WANT TO GO TO SLEEP / MOON RIVER** [ ] [–]

— **MICHAEL HORRIGAN** – drums; repl. PAUL

Columbia Columbia

Oct 98. (cd-s) *(COL 666576-2)* **SOMETHIN' HOT (album version) / SOMETHIN' HOT (12" remix) / MISS WORLD / PAPA WAS A RASCAL** [ ] [–]

Oct 98. (cd/c) *(491486-2/-4) <69450>* **1965** [ ] [ ]
– Somethin' hot / Crazy / Uptown again / Sweet son of a bitch / 66 / City soleil / John the baptist / The slide song / Neglekted / Omerta / The vampire Lanois.

— added **JOSH PAXTON** – keyboards / **SUSAN MARSHALL + DOUG FALSETTI** – backing vocals

— disbanded in February 2001

AFI

Formed: Ukiah, Northern California, USA . . . 1991 by high school friends DAVEY HAVOK, MARKUS STOPHOLESE, VICK and ADAM CARSON. One split 7" single (wih LOOSE CHANGE) and a debut EP, 'BEHIND THE TIMES', later, college commitments led to an inevitable break up. A chance reunion show subsequently went down so well that the AFI crew (now featuring GEOFF KRESGE in place of VICK) got back together permanently, relocating to Berkeley where the likes of RANCID and GREEN DAY had cut their teeth at fabled punk venue, Gillman Street; a debut set, 'ANSWER THAT AND STAY FASHIONABLE' was delivered for 'Wingnut' in '95. After spotting the band at a show in Hollywood, DEXTER HOLLAND (of OFFSPRING fame) snapped them up for his 'Nitro' label and proceeded to release their follow-up album, 'VERY PROUD OF YA' (1996). Another set of bullseye-aim hardcore followed in 1997: 'SHUT YOUR MOUTH & OPEN YOUR EYES'. While the band's acronym has been subject to many and varied interpretations over the years, the official line is that it stands for A FIRE INSIDE, the title of a 1998 EP and also the name of AFI's website. Judging by the musical contents of 'BLACK SAILS IN THE SUNSET' (1999), that fire was at least partly fuelled by Old Nick himself. Well, not really, but influences form the darker side of punk – MISFITS, JOY DIVISION etc – were definitely infiltrating the band's previously straight up sound. Hardcore fans' suspicions were also raised by the fact that HAVOK (now backed by a slightly altered line-up of CARSON, HUNTER and JADE PUGET) had taken to wearing make-up and black PVC. The transformation was even more pronounced on 'THE ART OF DROWNING' (2000), HAVOK's angst-ridden lyrics mirroring the tortured music. A subsequent deal with 'Dreamworks' meant even more scope for studio experimentation which the band utilised to the full on 'SING THE SORROW' (2003). With Butch Vig and Jerry Finn tweaking the sound into even more of a contemporary mould and the band accommodating luxuries like cello and piano, the record was another sizeable step in AFI's evolution and a canny move into the US Top 5. HAVOK had also been exorcising his more gothic tendencies in SON OF SAM, a side project (featuring hardcore veterans like TODD YOUTH, STEVE ZING and even GLENN DANZIG himself) which released 'SONGS FROM EARTH' in 2001. • **Covered:** MAN IN A SUITCASE (Police) / OPEN YOUR EYES (Circust Tents) / VALUES HERE (Dag Nasty) / WHATEVER I DO (Negative Approach) / THE HANGING GARDEN (Cure) / HALLOWEEN + LAST CARESS + DEMONOMANIA (Misfits) / MY MACHINE (Guns 'N Roses) / TODAY'S LESSON (Filth)

Album rating: ANSWER THAT AND STAY FASHIONABLE (*6) / VERY PROUD OF YA (*5) / SHUT YOUR MOUTH AND OPEN YOUR EYES (*6) / BLACK SAILS IN THE SUNSET (*7) / THE ART OF DROWNING (*6) / SING THE SORROW (*7)

DAVEY HAVOC – vocals / **MARKUS STOPHOLESE** – guitar / **VICK** – bass / **ADAM CARSON** – drums

not iss. Key Lime Pie

1993. (7"split w/ LOOSE CHANGE) **DORK** –
– Self pity / Ny-quil / Red heat.

1993. (7"ep) **BEHIND THE TIMES EP** –
– Who said you could touch me? / Rolling balls / High school football hero / Rizzo in the box / Cereal wars / Born in the USA.

1994. (7"ep) **EDDIE PICNIC'S ALL WET EP (live)** –
– Ny-quil / Rizzo in the box / Who said you could touch me? / I wanna mohawk (but mom won't let me get one) / Love is a many splendored thing.

not iss. Wedge

1995. (7"ep) **FLY IN THE OINTMENT** –
– Theory of a revolution / Crop tub / Cruise control / Open your eyes.

not iss. Wingnut

1995. (7"split) **HECKLE split** –
– Aspirin free / Advances in modern technology.

1995. (7"split) **BOMBING THE BAY. / (other by SWINGIN' UTTERS)** –

—— **GEOFF KRESGE** – bass; repl. VICK

1995. (cd/lp) *<1370>* **ANSWER THAT AND STAY FASHIONABLE** –
– Two of a kind / Half-empty bottle / Yurf rendenmein / I wanna get a Mohawk (but mom won't let me) / Brownie bottom sundae / The chequered demon / Cereal wars / The mother in me / Rizzo in the box / Kung-fu devil / Your name here / Ny-quil / Don't make me ill / Open your eyes / Highschool football hero. *<(re-iss. Apr97 on 'Nitro' cd/c/lp; 15811-2/-4/-1)>*

Nitro Nitro

Oct 96. (cd/c/lp) *<(15805-2/-4/-1)>* **VERY PROUD OF YA** Jun96
– No Dave party / He who laughs last . . . / File 13 / Wake-up call / Cult status / Perfect fit / Advances in modern technolgy / Theory of revolution / This secret Ninja / Soap box derby / Fishbowl / Charles Atlas / Crop tub / Consult my lover / Take the test / Two of a kind / Shatty Fatmas / Yurf Rendenmein / Cruise control / Modern epic.

Nov 97. (cd/c/lp) *<(15815-2/-4/-1)>* **SHUT YOUR MOUTH AND OPEN YOUR EYES**
– Keeping out of direct sunlight / Three reasons / A single second / ph Low / Let it be broke / Third season / Lower your head and take it in the body / Coin return / The new patron saints and angels / Three seconds notice / Salt for your wounds / Today's lesson / The Devil loves you / Triple zero.

May 99. (7"ep/cd-ep) *<(ADELINE 002/+CD)>* **A FIRE INSIDE EP** Sep98
– 3 1/2 / Over exposure / The hanging garden / Demonomania.
(above issued on 'Adeline')

—— **JADE PUGET** – guitar; repl. MARKUS

—— **HUNTER** – bass; repl. GEOFF

Jun 99. (cd-ep) **BLACK SAILS** –
– Porphyria cutanea tarda / Who knew?

Jun 99. (cd/lp) *<(15824-2/-1)>* **BLACK SAILS IN THE SUNSET**
– Strength through wounding / Porphyria cutanea tarda / Esanguination / Malleus maleficarum / Narrative of soul against soul / Clove smoke catharsis / The prayer position / No poetic device / Weathered tome / The last kiss / At a glance / God called in sick today.

Dec 99. (cd-ep) *<(15829-2)>* **ALL HALLOWS EP**
– Porphryia / Malleus maleficarum / Prayer position / Who knew.

Sep 00. (cd/lp) *<(15835-2/-1)>* **THE ART OF DROWNING**
– Initiation / The lost souls / The nephilim / Ever and a day / Sacrifice theory / Of greetings and goodbyes / Smile / A story at three / The days of the phoenix / Catch a hot one / Wester / 6 to 8 / The despair factor / Morningstar / Battled *[cd-only]* / Dream of waking *[lp-only]*.

Apr 01. (cd-ep) *<(15843-2)>* **THE DAYS OF THE PHOENIX E.P.**
– The days of the phoenix / A winter's tale / Wester.

—— in 2001, HAVOK featured in punk supergroup SON OF SAM

Polydor Universal

Mar 03. (cd) *(450448-2)* *<450380>* **SING THE SORROW** 52 5
– Miseria cantare – The beginning / The leaving song pt.II / Bleed black / Silver and cold / Dancing through Sunday / Girl's not grey / Death of seasons / The great disappointment / Paper airplanes (makeshift wings) / This celluloid dream / The leaving song / . . .But home is nowhere. *(lp-iss.Mar03 on 'Adeline'; 026)*

Jun 03. (7"grey) *(4504602)* **GIRL'S NOT GREY. / THE HANGING GARDEN** 22 –
(cd-s+=) *(4504600)* – Synesthesia (demo) / ('A'-video).
(cd-s) *(4504601)* – ('A'side) / Reivers music / Now the world (alt. take) / ('A'-prelude / video).

Sep 03. (7") *(4504626)* **THE LEAVING SONG PT.II. / THE GREAT DISAPPOINTMENT (demo)** 43 –
(cd-s+=) *(4504627)* – Paper Airplanes (makeshift wings) (demo) / ('A'-video).
(cd-s) *(4504625)* – ('A'side) / . . .But home is nowhere (demo) / ('A'-demo).

Christina AGUILERA

Born: 18 Dec'80, Staten Island, New York, USA. AGUILERA was a precocious singing talent; by the age of eight she had appeared on talent-spotting television shows in the States, and by the age of 12 she was a regular star on Disney's The New Mickey Mouse Club. This would seal a hot-bed of US pop talent as three of her co-stars went on to find major fame in the charts; JC CHASEZ and JUSTIN TIMBERLAKE (of 'N SYNC), and perhaps most famously BRITNEY SPEARS. AGUILERA's first foray into the real world of pop came with 'ALL I WANNA DO' in 1998, which was a duet with KEIZO NAKANISHI, and sold well in Japan. Her eponymous debut album the following year sold massively within its first year, and the single, 'GENIE IN A BOTTLE' rocketed to pole-position in the US charts. AGUILERA shares SPEARS style of dance inflected pop, but some critics actually place her in higher esteem than SPEARS due to the natural quality of her vocals. Unfortunately for her she was not quite the sensation of her aforementioned rival; in many ways this was down to her being marketed initially as more sultry and raunchy which made her slightly less accessible for the teenage market. This was certainly not saying she did not have a huge share of the pop market, and also won a grammy as best newcomer within her genre. 2000 saw the release of the album 'MI REFLEJO', sung in Spanish, which was a huge market Stateside, due to the large amount of immigrants from Central and South America. 2001's album release, 'JUST TO BE FREE' was probably something the young singer would have rather forgotten. The album consisted of near-demo recordings of the singer from her mid-teens, and was mainly panned by critics, and was something that AGUILERA fought the record company not to release. The temptress found a new adult market via the collaborative chart-topping version of 'LADY MARMALADE', taken from the hit movie, 'Moulin Rouge'. AGUILERA returned in 2002 with her long-awaited sophomore album 'STRIPPED', the title refering to her newfound emotional identity, rather than her lack of clothes (apparently). Not much could be said for the album, apart from the fact that XTINA's new material was slightly more mature than her previous efforts. The album produced a string of Top 10 singles 'DIRRTY', 'FIGHTER' (an anthem for the wronged women all over the world) and the No.1 'BEAUTIFUL' (more of an anthem for freaks and misfits). Guest producers were scattered across the album's credits, with the most prominent being ROCKWILDER and Pink collaborator LINDA PERRY (ex-4 NON BLONDES), but ultimately it was AGUILERA's gig, with the diva herself sharing many of the writing credits. 'STRIPPED' subsequently went on to become a smash hit album, and proved that the one-time saucy teenage temptress had matured and almost out-diva'd her contemporaries BRITNEY and BEYONCe.

Album rating: CHRISTINA AGUILERA (*5) / STRIPPED (*6)

CHRISTINA AGUILERA – vocals / with various backers

R.C.A. R.C.A.

Sep 99. (cd-s; import) *<70106-2>* *<65692>* **GENIE IN A BOTTLE** [50] Jun99 [1]

Oct 99. (c-s/cd-s) *(74321 70548-4/-2)* **GENIE IN A BOTTLE / BLESSED** [1] [–]
(cd-s) *(74321 70549-2)* – ('A'side) / ('A'-video).

Oct 99. (cd/c) *<(07836 67690-2/-4)>* **CHRISTINA AGUILERA** [14] Aug99 [1]
– Genie in a bottle / What a girl wants / I turn to you / So emotional / Come on over baby / Reflections / Love for all seasons / Somebody's somebody / When you put your hands on me / Blessed / Love will find a way / Obvious. *(d-cd-iss. Nov00 +=; 74321 78054-2)* – (bonus mixes).

Feb 00. (c-s/cd-s) *(74321 73752-4/-2)* *<65960>* **WHAT A GIRL WANTS / (mixes)** [3] Nov99 [1]
(cd-s+=) *(74321 73735-2)* – Medley:- I turn to you – So emotional – Somebody's somebody – Genie in a bottle – Come on over baby – We're a miracle.

Jul 00. (c-s) *(74321 76547-4)* *<60251>* **I TURN TO YOU / WHAT A GIRL WANTS** [19] Apr00 [3]
(cd-s+=) *(74321 76547-2)* – ('A'-video).

Oct 00. (c-s) *(74321 79991-4)* *<60341>* **COME ON OVER BABY (ALL I WANT IS YOU) / (album version)** [8] Jul00 [1]
(cd-s+=) *(74321 79991-2)* – ('A'-Blacksmith club mix) / ('A'-Sunship vocal mix).
(12"++=) *(74321 79991-1)* – ('A'-Blacksmith & Sunship dubs).

— in Jan'01, CHRISTINA hit the charts with 'Nobody Wants To Be Lonely' alongside RICKY MARTIN

— In Apr'01, she was part of the female collaboration No.1 single, 'LADY MARMALADE' – taken from the 'Moulin Rouge' movie; it also hit UK No.1 that June

Oct 02. (cd/c) *(74321 96125-2/-4)* *<68037>* **STRIPPED** [2] [2]
– Stripped (part 1) / Can't hold us down / Walk away / Fighter / Primer amor (interlude) / Infatuation / Loves embrace (interlude) / Loving me 4 me / Impossible / Underappreciated / Beautiful / Make over / Cruz / Soar / Get mine, get yours / Dirrty (with REDMAN) / Stripped (part 2) / The voice within / I'm OK / Keep on singin' my song.

Nov 02. (c-s; as CHRISTINA AGUILERA & REDMAN) *(74321 97521-4)* *<97635>* **DIRRTY / I WILL BE** [1] Oct02 [48]
(12"+=/cd-s+=) *(74321 97521-1/-2)* – ('A'-extended).

Feb 03. (c-s) *(82876 50246-4)* *<98364>* **BEAUTIFUL / DIRRTY (MaUVe remix with REDMAN)** [1] Dec02 [2]
(cd-s+=) *(82876 50246-2)* – ('A'-video).
(12"+=) *(82876 50246-1)* – ('A'-Peter Rauhofer remix).

Jun 03. (c-s) *(82876 52429-4)* *<radio>* **FIGHTER / FIGHTER (valentine mix)** [3] [20]
(cd-s+=) *(82876 52429-2)* – ('A'-Freelance Hellraiser mix).

Sep 03. (12"; as CHRISTINA AGUILERA featuring LIL' KIM) *(82876 55633-1)* *<54526>* **CAN'T HOLD US DOWN. / BEAUTIFUL (Brother Brown remix)** [6] Aug03 [12]
(cd-s) *(82876 55633-2)* – ('A'side) / ('A'-remix).

Dec 03. (12"/cd-s) *(82876 58429-1/-2)* **THE VOICE WITHIN / BEAUTIFUL (Fug mix) / CAN'T HOLD US DOWN (Da yard riddim mix) / CAN'T HOLD US DOWN (medasyn mix)** [9] [33]

– US imports, etc. –

Dec 99. (cd-s) *<65943>* **THE CHRISTMAS SONG (CHESTNUTS ROASTING ON AN OPEN FIRE) /** [–] [18]

Nov 00. (cd) *B.M.G.; <(07863 69343-2)>* **MY KIND OF CHRISTMAS** [ ] [28]

Dec 00. (cd) *B.M.G.; <(07863 69323-2)>* **MI REFLEJO** [ ] Sep00 [27]

Jun 01. (cd) *Warlock; <2844>* **JUST BE FREE** (early recordings) [–] [71]

A-HA

Formed: Manglerud, Oslo, Norway . . . 1982 by songwriters MAGNE FURUHOLMEN and PAL WAAKTAAR (both ex-BRIDGES and DOORS-inspired SPIDER EMPIRE), who invited singer MORTEN HARKET to make up the trio. Relocating to London early the following year, A-HA secured the services of manager, Terry Slater and it was through him and a demo of 'LESSON ONE' that the band would sign to 'Warners'. Subsequently remixed by Tony Mansfield and renamed as 'TAKE ON ME', the song initially failed to impress the British buying public when issued in October 1984. The following summer, with Alan Tarney overseeing production, it bombed yet again and led to the lads returning for a summer solstice in Norway. However, things looked brighter in the States when the song received a Steve Barron-directed $100,000 animated video facelift. This resulted in some precious MTV airtime and a trip to L.A. which paved the way for a surprise US chart entry. Topping Billboard in October, it was immediately given a third release in Britain where it peaked at No.2, MORTEN, PAL and MAGNE becoming pin-up boys in the process.

The album 'HUNTING HIGH AND LOW' was finally unleashed in the UK towards the end of 1985, its blend of electro-pop and HARKET's falsetto vox setting it up nicely for a Top 3 chart placing. In 1986, the Norwegians had no less than five British Top 10 hits, 'THE SUN ALWAYS SHINES ON TV' (their only UK No.1), 'TRAIN OF THOUGHT', 'HUNTING HIGH AND LOW', 'I'VE BEEN LOSING YOU' and 'CRY WOLF', the latter two lifted from that year's sophomore Top 3 set, 'SCOUNDREL DAYS'. Although fading fast in America, the trio were still one of the most popular acts in Britain and continued to have hits right up until their split-up in 1994. One of these, 'THE LIVING DAYLIGHTS' was co-written by JOHN BARRY and used for the similarly-titled James Bond movie in 1987, while three years later they covered the Everly Brothers' classic 'CRYING IN THE RAIN'. In 1995 – while the other two moonlighted with TIMBERSOUND and SAVOY – HARKET delivered his only solo album to date, 'WILD SEED', which was unsurprisingly given the thumbs down by critics and public alike. A-HA re-formed for a one-off Nobel Peace Prize concert on the 11th of December 1998 and were threatening to go full-time again in 2000 (not a laughing matter me thinks!?). The long lost vikings of 80's pop did indeed strike out across the treacherous waters of the music biz once more come the new millennium. Granted, there was little hope of pillaging a decent chart placing (Top 30, to be exact) but in 'MINOR EARTH MAJOR SKY' (2000) longtime fans – who'd now presumably grown up – could content themselves with a suitably grown up set of MOR pop from a still angelic sounding HARKET and Co. Just to prove that the music business had indeed wanted them back for good, the lads followed up within two years courtesy of 'LIFELINES' (2002), an even more mature effort with allusions to an unheralded darker side. A brace of top name producers made for an interesting if uneven listen, with layers of studio gloss failing to dampen HARKET's vocal ardour.

Album rating: HUNTING HIGH AND LOW (*6) / SCOUNDREL DAYS (*5) / STAY ON THESE ROADS (*4) / EAST OF THE SUN, WEST OF THE MOON (*5) / HEADLINES & DEADLINES – THE HITS OF A-HA compilation (*6) / MEMORIAL BEACH (*3) / Morten Harket: WILD SEED (*3) / A-ha: MINOR EARTH MAJOR SKY (*5) / LIFELINES (*5)

PAL WAAKTAAR (b. 6 Sep'61) – guitar, vocals / **MAGNE "MAGS" FURUHOLMEN** (b. 1 Nov'62) – keyboards / plus **VIGGO BONDI** – bass / **OYSTEIN JEVANORD** – drums

Vakenatt not iss.

Oct 80. (lp; as BRIDGES) **FAKKELTOG** (means TORCHLIGHT PROCESSION) [–] Norway [–]
– The oncoming of day:- The oncoming of day (instrumental) / Somebody's going away / May the last be mine / Divided we fall / Vagrants / The oncoming:- The stranger's town / Pavillion of the luxuriant trees / The oncoming of night:- The oncoming of night (instrumental) / The vacant / Guest on Earth / Death of the century / The melancholic chevaliers / Scared, bewildered, wild / Every mortal night / September.

—— (1982) **PAL + MAGS** (let go OYSTEIN and VIGGO; former still on session) + introduced **MORTEN HARKET** (b.14 Sep'59, Konigsberg, Norway) – vocals

Warners Warners

Oct 84. (7") *(W 9146)* **TAKE ON ME. / AND YOU TELL ME** [ ] [ ]
(12"+=) *(W 9146T)* – Stop and make your mind up.

May 85. (7") *(W 9006) <29011>* **TAKE ON ME. / LOVE IS REASON** [ ] Jun85 [1]
(12"+=) *(W 9006T)* – ('A'extended).
(re-iss. Sep85 – hit UK No.2)

Nov 85. (lp/c)(cd) *(WX 30/+C)(925300-2) <25300>* **HUNTING HIGH AND LOW** [2] Jun85 [15]
– Take on me / Train of thought / Hunting high and low / The blue sky / Living a boy's adventure tale / The sun always shines on TV / And you tell me / Love is reason / Dream myself alive / Here I stand and face the rain.

Dec 85. (7"/7"sha-pic-d) *(W 8846/+P) <28846>* **THE SUN ALWAYS SHINES ON TV. / DRIFTWOOD** [1] Nov85 [20]
(12"+=) *(W 8846T)* – ('A'instrumental).

Mar 86. (7"/7"sha-pic-d/12") *(W 8736/+P/T)* **TRAIN OF THOUGHT. / AND YOU TELL ME** [8] [ ]

May 86. (7") *(W 6663)* **HUNTING HIGH AND LOW. / THE BLUE SKY (demo)** [5] [ ]
(12"+=/12"pic-d+=) *(W 6663 T/+P)* – ('A'version).

Sep 86. (7") *(W 8594)* **I'VE BEEN LOSING YOU. / THIS ALONE IS LOVE** [8] [ ]
(12"+=/12"pic-d+=) *(W 8594 T/+P)* – ('A'dub version).

Oct 86. (lp/c)(cd) *(WX 62/+C)(925501-2) <25501>* **SCOUNDREL DAYS** [2] [74]
– Scoundrel days / The swing of things / I've been losing you / October / Manhattan skyline / Cry wolf / Looking for the whales / The weight of the wind / Maybe maybe / Soft rains of April. *(cd re-iss. Feb95; same)*

Nov 86. (7"/7"g-f) *(W 8500/+V) <28500>* **CRY WOLF. / MAYBE MAYBE** [7] Jan87 [50]
(12"+=/12"pic-d+=) *(W 8500 T/+P)* – ('A'extended).

Feb 87. (7") *(W 8405)* **MANHATTAN SKYLINE. / WE'RE LOOKING FOR THE WHALES (live)** [13] [ ]
(12"+=/12"pic-d+=) *(W 8405 T/+P)* – ('A'extended remix).

Jul 87. (7"/7"g-f) *(W 8305/+V)* **THE LIVING DAYLIGHTS. / ('A'instrumental)** [5] [ ]
(12"+=/12"pic-d+=) *(W 8305 T/+P)* – ('A'extended).

Apr 88. (7") *(W 7936)* **STAY ON THESE ROADS. / SOFT RAINS OF APRIL (mix)** [5] [ ]
(12"+=/12"pic-d) *(W 7936 T/+P)* – ('A'extended).
(3"cd-s++=) *(W 7936CD)* – Cry wolf / Take on me.

Apr 88. (lp/c)(cd) *(WX 166/+C)(925733-2) <25733>* **STAY ON THESE ROADS** [2] [ ]
– The blood that moves the body / Touchy! / This alone is love / Hurry home / The living daylights / There's never a forever thing / Out of blue comes green / You are the one / You'll end up crying / Stay on these roads.
(cd re-iss. Feb95; same)

May 88. (7"/7"s) *(W 7840/+W)* **THE BLOOD THAT MOVES THE BODY. / THERE'S NEVER A FOREVER THING** [25] [ ]
(12"+=/12"pic-d+=) *(W 7840 T/+P)* – ('A'extended).
(3"cd-s++=) *(W 7840CD)* – The living daylights.

Aug 88. (7"/7"s) *(W 7749/+W)* **TOUCHY!. / HURRY HOME** [11] [ ]
(12"+=) *(W 7749T)* – ('A'-Go-Go mix).
(3"cd-s++=) *(W 7749CD)* – Hunting high and low.

Nov 88. (7") *(W 7636)* **YOU ARE THE ONE (remix). / OUT OF BLUE COMES GREEN** [13] [ ]
(12"+=/12"pic-d+=/cd-s+=) *(W 7636 T/TP/CD)* – ('A'instrumental).

Oct 90. (7"/c-s) *(W 9547/+C)* **CRYING IN THE RAIN. / (SEEMINGLY) NON-STOP JULY** [13] [ ]
(12"+=/cd-s+=) *(W 9547 T/CD)* – Cry wolf.

Oct 90. (cd)(lp/c) *(<7599 26314-2>)(WX 378/+C)* **EAST OF THE SUN, WEST OF THE MOON** [12] [ ]
– Crying in the rain / Early morning / I call your name / Slender frame / East of the sun / Sycamore leaves / Waiting for her / Cold river / The way we talk / Rolling thunder / (Seemingly) Non-stop July.

Dec 90. (7") *(W 9462)* **I CALL YOUR NAME. / THE WAY WE TALK** [44] [ ]
(12"+=/cd-s+=) *(W 9462 T/CD)* – The blood that moves the body.
(d7"+=) *(W 9462D)* – Hunting high and low / The Sun always shines on TV.

Feb 91. (7"/c-s) *(W 0012/+C)* **EARLY MORNING. / EAST OF THE SUN** [ ] [ ]
(12"+=/cd-s+=) *(W 0012 T/CD)* – Train of thought.

Oct 91. (7"/c-s) *(W 0070/+C)* **MOVE TO MEMPHIS. / CRYING IN THE RAIN (live)** [47] [ ]
(cd-s+=) *(W 0070CD)* – Early morning (live) / Manhattan skyline (live).
(12") *(W 0070T)* – ('A'side) / I've been losing you (live) / East of the sun (live) / (Seemingly) Non-stop July (live).

Nov 91. (cd)(lp/c) *(<7599 26773-2>)(WX 450/+C)* **HEADLINES & DEADLINES, THE HITS OF A-HA** (compilation) [12] [ ]
– Take on me / Cry wolf / Touchy! / You are the one / Manhattan skyline / The blood that moves the body / Hunting high and low / Move to Memphis / I've been losing you / The living daylights / Crying in the rain / I call your name / Stay on these roads / The sun always shines on TV. *(cd+=/c+=)* – Early morning / Train of thought.

Mar 92. (7") *(W 0089)* **THE BLOOD THAT MOVES THE BODY (The Gun mix). / ('A'-Two-Time Gun Mix)** [ ] [ ]
(12"+=/cd-s+=) *(W 0089 T/CD)* – ('A' mixes).

—— added **J.B. BOGEBERG** – bass / **PER HILLESTAD** – drums

May 93. (7"/c-s) *(W 0175/+C)* **DARK IS THE NIGHT. / ANGEL IN THE SNOW** [19] [ ]
(cd-s+=) *(W 0175CD)* – I've been losing you – Cry wolf (live).

(cd-s) *(W 0175CD2)* – ('A'side) / The sun always shines on TV / Hunting high and low / Crying in the rain.

Jun 93. (cd/c) *(<9362 45229-2/-4>)* **MEMORIAL BEACH** [17] [ ]
– Dark Is The Night / Move To Memphis / Cold As Stone / Angel In The Snow / Locust / Lie Down In Darkness / How Sweet It Was / Lamb To The Slaughter / Between Your Mama And Yourself / Memorial Beach

Sep 93. (7") *(W 0195/+C)* **ANGEL. / I CALL YOUR NAME** [41] [ ]
(cd-s) *(W 0195CD1)* – ('A'side) / Stay on these roads / Manhattan skyline / Scoundrel days (live).
(cd-s+=) *(W 0195CD2)* – The sun always shines on TV (live) / I call your name (live) / Early morning (live).

Mar 94. (7"/c-s) *(W 0236/+C)* **SHAPES THAT GO TOGETHER. / COLD AS STONE (remix)** [27] [ ]
(cd-s) *(W 0236CD)* – ('A'side) / Touchy! (live) / Slender frame (live) / Rolling thunder (live).

— after A-HA split, HARKET released a solo album, 'WILD SEED', in '95, he is currently filling in the singing position for BOOLA-BOSS. FURUHOLMEN, meanwhile has been linked with the band TIMBERSOUND and WAAKTAAR with SAVOY (he also took the moniker PAUL SAVOY for a solo venture)

MORTEN HARKET

WEA WEA

Aug 95. (c-s/cd-s) *(W 0304 C/CD)* **A KIND OF CHRISTMAS CARD / A CHANGE IS GONNA COME / LAY ME DOWN TONIGHT** [53] [–]
(re-iss. Dec95; same)

Sep 95. (cd/c) *(<9362 45912-2/-4>)* **WILD SEED** [ ] [ ]
– A kind of Christmas card / Spanish steps / Half in love half in hate / Brodsky tune / Wild seed / Los Angeles / East Tinor / Lay me down tonight / Tell me what you see / Stay / Lord / Ready to go home.

Feb 96. (c-s) *(W 0321/+C)* **SPANISH STEPS / GIRL** [ ] [–]
(cd-s+=) *(W 0321CD)* – Lord.

Arista not iss.

Jun 96. (c-s/cd-s) *(74321 39011-4/-2)* **HEAVEN'S NOT FOR SAINTS / (instrumental)** [ ] [–]

— MORTEN had no other solo UK releases

a-ha

— re-formed with the usual trio

WEA WEA

May 00. (c-s) *(WEA 275C)* **SUMMER MOVED ON / BARELY HANGING ON** [33] [–]
(cd-s+=) *(WEA 275CD)* – ('A'mixes).

Jun 00. (cd/c) *(<8573 82183-2/-4>)* **MINOR EARTH MAJOR SKY** [27] [ ]
– Minor earth major sky / Little black heart / Velvet / Summer moved on / The sun never shone that day / To let you win / The company man / Thought that it was you / I wish I cared / Barely hangin' on / You'll never get over me / I won't forget her / Mary Ellen makes the moment count.

Jun 02. (cd) *(<0927 44849-2>)* **LIFELINES** [67] [ ]
– Lifelines / You wanted more / Forever not yours / There's a reason for it / Time and again / Did anyone approach you? / Afternoon high / Oranges on apple trees / A little bit / Less than pure / Turn the lights down / Cannot hide / White canvas / Dragonfly / Solace.

Jul 02. (cd-s) *(W 353CDX)* **LIFELINES / HUNTING HIGH AND LOW (live) / MANHATTAN SKYLINE (live) / ('A'-video)** [ ] [–]

AIR

Formed: Paris, France . . . 1995 by NICOLAS GODIN and JEAN-BENOIT DUNCKEL, who had cut their proverbial teeth waking the neighbours up in punk outfit, ORANGE. Preceded by a string of highly desirable 12" singles and a mini-set 'PREMIERS SYMPTOMES', the gallic duo's sublime 'MOON SAFARI' album ranks as one of 1998's most hypnotic, emotive and consistently listenable long players; the Moog was back. With the added kudos of being an essential purchase for any self respecting fashion victim, the record's unearthly ELO / BURT BACHARACH / CARPENTERS hybrid (be assured that this works considerably more effectively on disc than it does on paper!) had music journalists of all persuasions (with the possible exception of the metal press) reaching for the thesaurus. Those that portrayed AIR as mere faux-space age lounge revivalists were surely missing the point, however; they might've doffed their cap to classic French pop but Messrs GODIN and DUNCKEL were in the business of making music to last, serious business. Seriously sexy in fact, sexy in the way that SAINT ETIENNE used to be, all throbbing bass and breathless melodies. While the likes of 'SEXY BOY' might actually have you questioning your closely guarded conviction that the 80's were shite, the liberal sprinkling of moog synth throughout places the record in a kind of vacuum-packed 70's no-man's land. A damn good place to be, especially if you happen to have a king-sized spliff, a decent pair of "cans" and your favourite armchair to hand. No surprise then, that the album made the UK Top 20, as did the attendant 'KELLY WATCH THE STARS' single. If there was a World Cup for music, AIR would definitely be in there with a shout, the French redrawing of contemporary musical battle lines continuing unabated. At the height of AIR's popularity, 'Virgin' squeezed out their 1997 mini-set for eager fans who surprisingly sent it into the UK Top 20. Meanwhile, the duo were busy constructing the soundtrack to Sofia Coppola's debut movie, 'THE VIRGIN SUICIDES' (2000). This brought AIR into the new millennium although its edited electronica held few surprises (bar hit single, 'PLAYGROUND LOVE') functioning primarily as a cinematic companion. The Gallic duo emerged again the following year with '10,000 Hz LEGEND' (2001), a worthy if more deliberately inscrutable follow-up to 'MOON SAFARI'. The prog-rock cover art was a bit of a giveaway, AIR opting to hue their electronic tapestries from much darker, unsettling source material than the moog-pop references of their debut. It was nevertheless immaculately crafted, flawlessly executed and often eerily beautiful, the likes of BECK and JASON FALKNER enhancing its post-modern appeal. What the album didn't need – in fact what most albums don't need – was a collection of tired remixes, even if the reworkings came from such in demand studio names as The NEPTUNES. 'EVERYBODY HERTZ' (2002) also gets nil points for its title, as insipid as the grooves contained within it. • **Note:** To avoid confusion with another outfit named AIR, "French Band" was incidentally the prefix printed in small writing next to their moniker.

Album rating: PREMIERS SYMPTOMES (*7) / MOON SAFARI (*9) / THE VIRGIN SUICIDES soundtrack (*6) / 10,000hz LEGEND (*8) / EVERYBODY HERTZ remixes (*4)

NICOLAS GODIN (b.1970) – bass, guitar, organ, Minimoog, Vocoder, Korg, percussion, harmonica / **JEAN-BENOIT DUNCKEL** (b.1970) – organ, piano, Rhodes, Korg MS23, Moog, Solins string ensemble, clavinet / with guest vocals **BETH HIRSCH** (on '98 lp)

Source not iss.

1995. (m-lp) *(894426)* **LE SOLIEL EST PRES DE MOI** [–] French [–]
(UK-iss.Jul97 on 'Source/Virgin'; same)

Nov 95. (12"ep) **MODULAR (mixes)** [–] French [–]
(UK-iss.Aug96 on 'Mo Wax' 12"/cd-s; MW 047/+CD)

Jul 96. (12"ep) *(936576)* **CASANOVA '70 / LES PROFESSIONNELS** [ ] [–]
(re-iss. Jan98; same)

Jul 97. (m-lp/m-cd) **PREMIERS SYMPTOMES** [–] French [–]
– Modular mix / Casanova 70 / Les professionels / J'ai dormi sous l'eau / Le soleil est pres de moi / California / Gordni mix (Brakes on mix). *(UK-iss.Jan98 on 'Source'; 7243-89428766/+CD) (re-iss. Sep99 on 'Virgin' cd/c/lp; CD/TC+/V 2895)* – Hit UK No.12

Source – Virgin Caroline

Jan 98. (cd/c/lp) *(CD/TC+/V 2848)* <CAR 6644-2> **MOON SAFARI** [6] [ ]
– La femme d'argent / Sexy boy / All I need / Kelly watch the stars /

Talisman / Remember / You make it easy / Ce matin la / New star in the sky / Le voyage de Penelope.

Feb 98. (12"/c-s) *(VST/VSC 1672)* **SEXY BOY (mixes; Cassius / Etienne De Crecy & the Flower Pistols)** 13 [ ]
(cd-s) *(VSCDT 1672)* – ('A'side) / Jeanne / New star in the sky.

May 98. (c-s) *(VSC 1690)* **KELLY WATCH THE STARS / ('A'mix)** 18 [ ]
(12"+=/cd-s+=) *(VS T/CDT 1690)* – Sexy boy (sex kino mix) / Remember (D Whitaker version).
(UK re-iss. Jun98 on 'Source' 7"; 8950727)

Nov 98. (c-s/12"/cd-s) *(VSC/VST/VSCDT 1702)* **ALL I NEED / KELLY WATCH THE STARS (Moog Cookbook mix) / KELLY WATCH THE STARS (American Girls remix by Phoenix)** 29 [ ]

Mar 99. (cd-s) <*CAR 6645-2*> **SEXY BOY (Beck remix)** – [ ]

Virgin / Astralwerks

Feb 00. (c-s) *(VSC 1764)* **PLAYGROUND LOVE / BATHROOM GIRL** 25 [ ]
(cd-s+=) *(VSCDT 1764)* – ('A'mix).
(12") *(VST 1764)* – ('A'side) / Nosferatu / Highschool prom.
(above sung by GORDON TRACKS)

Feb 00. (cd/c/lp) *(CD/TC+/V 2910)* <48848> **THE VIRGIN SUICIDES** (soundtrack) 14 Mar00 [ ]
– Playground love / Clouds up / Bathroom girl / Cemetary party / Dark messages / The word 'hurricane' / Dirty trip / Highschool lover / Afternoon sister / Ghost song / Empty house / Dead bodies / Suicide underground.

Virgin / Source

May 01. (7") *(VS 1803)* **RADIO NO 1. / FLOWERHEAD** 31 –
(cd-s+=) *(VSCDT 1803)* – ('A'-JP Cristal remix).
(12") *(VST 1803)* – ('A'side) / ('A'-JP Cristal remix) / ('A'-Senor Coconut's rumbamambochachacha remix).

May 01. (cd/lp) *(CD+/V 2945)* <10332> **10,000Hz LEGEND** 7 Jun01 88
– Electronic performers / How does it make you feel / Radio No 1 / Vagabond / Radian / Lucky and unhappy / Sex born poison / People in the city / Wonder milky bitch / Don't be light / Caramel prisoner.

Feb 02. (cd/d-lp) *(CDV/VD 2956)* <11833> **EVERYBODY HERTZ** (remixes) 67 [ ]
– Don't be light (edit) / Don't be light (Mr Ozio remix) / How does it make you feel? (Sherwood remix) / Don't be light (Neptunes remix) / People in the city (Modjo remix) / Don't be light (Hacker remix) / How does it make you feel? (edit) / Don't be light (Malibu remix) / People in the city (Jack Lahana remix) / The way you look tonight / People in the city.

– compilations, etc. –

Oct 01. (d-cd) *Virgin; (810875-2)* **MOON SAFARI / PREMIER SYMPTOMES** [ ] –

Nov 01. (d-cd) *Virgin; (810850-2)* **10,000hz LEGEND / THE VIRGIN SUICIDES** [ ] –

☐ AIRFORCE (see under ⇒ BAKER, Ginger)

ALARM

Formed: Rhyl, Wales . . . 1977 as punk band The TOILETS by MIKE PETERS, DAVE SHARP, EDDIE McDONALD and NIGEL TWIST. They became "mod" outfit "17" before the same quartet changed name again to The ALARM in 1981. After one indie 45 on the 'White Cross' label, they signed to Miles Copeland's US based 'I.R.S.' in summer '82. Just over a year later and now living in London, they entered the UK Top 20, not for the last time, with single '68 GUNS'. Compared to The CLASH, but inspired by the earnest passion of U2, the group's music was at odds with the limp synth-pop of the day, attracting fans who were too young to have experienced punk's heyday but still wanted energetic anthems that eschewed clever lyrics for a populist sensibility. Premiered by another banner-waving hit, 'WHERE WERE YOU HIDING WHEN THE STORM BROKE', the debut album, 'DECLARATION', arrived in early '84. Part of a kind of Celtic triumvirate (completed by Ireland's U2 and Scotland's BIG COUNTRY), The ALARM were essentially a rock extension of the folk tradition, their acoustic rendition of mining ballad (previously recorded by PETE SEEGER and The BYRDS amongst others), 'THE BELLS OF RHYMNEY' hardly seeming out of place. As with U2, there was always the possibility of taking things too far down the road of grandiose stadium rock, The ALARM coming perilously close on follow-up set, 'STRENGTH' (1985). Another UK Top 20 hit (it also cracked the US Top 40, where their big sound was much appreciated), the record spawned a futher epic Top 20 single in 'SPIRIT OF '76'. That self-same spirit seemed to be lacking on subsequent releases, although the 'CHANGE' album saw them adopt a more rootsy approach, even looking to their native heritage with the help of a Welsh male choir and The Welsh Symphony Orchestra. Although the band continued to cut little ice with the more snobbish critics, they soldiered on for a final set, 'RAW' (1991), before PETERS embarked on a solo career. • **Songwriters:** McDONALD / PETERS or SHARP / TWIST, except; KNOCKIN' ON HEAVEN'S DOOR (Bob Dylan) / WORKING CLASS HERO + HAPPY XMAS (WAR IS OVER) (John Lennon) / ROCKIN' IN THE FREE WORLD (Neil Young).

Album rating: DECLARATION (*5) / STRENGTH (*6) / EYE OF THE HURRICANE (*5) / ELECTRIC FOLKLORE LIVE mini (*5) / CHANGE (*5) / STANDARDS compilation (*7) / RAW (*4) / THE BEST OF THE ALARM AND MIKE PETERS compilation (*7) / Mike Peters: BREATHE (*4) / FEEL FREE (*4) / RISE (*5)

MIKE PETERS (b.25 Jan'59, Prestatyn, Wales) – vocals, guitar / **DAVE SHARP** (b.28 Jan'59) – guitar / **EDDIE McDONALD** (b. 1 Nov'59) – bass / **NIGEL TWIST** (b. 18 Jul'58) – drums

Vendetta / not iss.

Mar 80. (7"; as SEVENTEEN) *(VD 001)* **DON'T LET GO. / BANK HOLIDAY WEEKEND** [ ] –

White Cross / not iss.

Sep 81. (7") *(W 3-4)* **UNSAFE BUILDINGS. / UP FOR MURDER** [ ] –

Illegal / not iss.

Oct 82. (7"m) *(ILS 032)* **MARCHING ON. / ACROSS THE BORDER / LIE OF THE LAND** [ ] –

I.R.S. / I.R.S.

Apr 83. (7") *(PFP 1014)* **THE STAND. / THIRD LIGHT** [ ] –
(12") *(PFPX 1014)* – ('A'side) / For freedom / Reason 41.

Jun 83. (7") **THE STAND. / REASON 41** – [ ]

Jul 83. (m-lp) <*70504*> **THE ALARM (live)** – [ ]
– The stand / Across the border / Marching on / Lie of the land / For freedom.

Sep 83. (7") *(PFP 1023)* **68 GUNS. / (part 2)** 17 –
(w/ free c-s) *(PFPC 1023)* – (see mini-lp for tracks).
(12") *(PFPX 1023)* – ('A'extended) / Thoughts of a young man.

Nov 83. (7") **68 GUNS. / PAVILLION STEPS** – [ ]

Jan 84. (7") *(IRS 101)* **WHERE WERE YOU HIDING WHEN THE STORM BROKE? / PAVILLION STEPS** 22 [ ]
(12"+=) *(IRSX 101)* – What kind of Hell.

Feb 84. (lp/c) *(IRS A/C 7044)* <70608> **DECLARATION** 6 50
– Declaration / Marching on / Where were you hiding when the storm broke? / Third light / 68 guns / We are the light / Shout to the Devil / Blaze of glory / Tell me / The deceiver / The stand (prophecy) / Howling wind. *(cd-iss. Oct88; CDILP 25887) (re-iss. Oct92 on 'A&M' cd/c; CD/C MID 103) (cd re-mast.Nov01 on '21st Century'+=; 21C 011)* – (extra tracks).

Mar 84. (7"clear) *(IRS 103)* **THE DECEIVER. / REASON 41** 51 [ ]
(12"+=) *(IRSX 103)* – Second generation.
(ltd.d7"+=) *(IRSD 103)* – Lie of the land / Legal matter.

May 84. (7") **THE DECEIVER. / SECOND GENERATION** – [ ]

Oct 84. (7") *(IRS 114)* **THE CHANT HAS JUST BEGUN. / THE BELLS OF RHYMNEY** 48 [ ]
(12"+=) *(IRSY 114)* – The stand (extended).

Feb 85. (7"/12") *(ALARM 1/+2)* **ABSOLUTE REALITY. / BLAZE OF GLORY** 35 [ ]
(ltd.d7"+=) *(ALARMD 1)* – Room at the top / Reason 36.

Sep 85. (7") *(IRM 104)* <52736> **STRENGTH. / MAJORITY** 40 Dec85 61
(12"+=) *(IRT 104)* – ('A'side) / Absolute reality (acoustic).

Oct 85. (lp/c) *(MIRF/+C 1004) <5666>* **STRENGTH** [18] [39]
– Knife edge / Strength / Dawn chorus / Spirit of '76 / The day the ravens left the tower / Deeside / Father to son / Only the thunder / Walk forever by my side. *(cd-iss. Apr87; DMIRF 1004) (cd re-iss. Jan90 on 'M.C.A.'; DMIRL 1504) (re-iss. Apr92 cd/c; IRLD/IRLC 19006) (cd re-mast.Dec01 on '21st Century'+=; 21C 012)* – (extra tracks).

Jan 86. (7") *(IRM 109)* **SPIRIT OF '76. / WHERE WERE YOU HIDING WHEN THE STORM BROKE? (live)** [22] [ ]
(12"+=) *(IRMT 109)* – Deeside (live).
(d12"++=) *(IRMTD 109)* – Knockin' on Heaven's door (live) / 68 guns (live).

Apr 86. (7"/7"sha-pic-d) *(IRM/+SP 112)* **KNIFE EDGE. / CAROLINE ISENBERG** [43] [ ]
(12"+=) *(IRMT 112)* – Howling wind / Unbreak the promise.

Sep 87. (7") *(IRM 144) <53219>* **RAIN IN THE SUMMERTIME. / ROSE BEYOND THE WALL** [18] Nov87 [71]
(12"+=) *(IRMT 144)* – The bells of Rhymney / Time to believe.
(12") *(IRMX 144)* – ('A'-Through the haze mix) / ('A'-Lightning mix).

Nov 87. (lp/c/cd) *(MIRG/MIRGC/DMIRG 1023) <42061>* **EYE OF THE HURRICANE** [23] [77]
– Rain in the summertime / Newtown Jericho / Hallowed ground / One step closer to home / Shelter / Rescue me / Permanence in change / Presence of love / Only love can set me free / Eye of the hurricane. *(cd re-iss. May90 on 'M.C.A.'; DMIRL 1506) (cd re-mast.Dec01 on '21st Century'+=; 21C 013)* – (extra tracks).

Nov 87. (7"/7"blue) *(IRM/+BV 150)* **RESCUE ME. / MY LAND YOUR LAND** [48] [ ]
(12"+=) *(IRMT 150)* – The Hurricane sessions.

Feb 88. (7"/7"pic-d) *(IRM/+P 155) <53259>* **PRESENCE OF LOVE (LAUGHARNE). / KNIFE EDGE (live)** [44] [77]
(12"+=) *(IRMT 155)* – This train is bound for glory (live) / Dawn chorus (live).
(cd-s+=) *(DIRM 155)* – Rain in the summertime (Through The Haze mix).

Oct 88. (m-lp/m-c/m-cd) *(MIRM/MIRMC/DMIRM 5001) <39108>* **ELECTRIC FOLKLORE LIVE (live)** [62] [ ]
– Rescue me / Rain in the summertime / Permanence in change / Strength / Spirit of '76 / Blaze of glory. *(cd re-mast.Dec01 on '21st Century'+=; 21C 014)* – (extra tracks).

Sep 89. (7"/7"s) *(EIRS/+P 123) <73002>* **SOLD ME DOWN THE RIVER. / GWETHOCH FI I YR AFON** [43] [50]
(10"+=) *(EIRS10 123)* – Firing line.
(12"+=/cd-s+=) *(EIRS T/CD 123)* – Corridors of power.

Sep 89. (lp/c/cd) *(EIRSA X/C/CD 1020) <82018>* **CHANGE** [13] [75]
– Rivers to cross / A new South Wales / Sold me down the river / The rock / Devolution / Workin' man blues / Love don't come easy / Hard land / Change II / No frontiers / Scarlet / Where a town once stood / Prison without prison bars. *(cd re-mast.Dec01 on '21st Century'+=; 21C 015)* – (extra tracks).

Oct 89. (7"/12") *(EIRS/+T 129)* **A NEW SOUTH WALES. / THE ROCK (long version)** [31] [ ]
(cd-s+=) *(EIRSCD 129)* – Working class hero.
(10"white++=) *(EIRSTEN 129)* – Rivers to cross (new version).
(7" also in Welsh) *(EIRSB 129)* – HWYLIO DROS Y MOR. / Y GRAIG

Jan 90. (7"/c-s) *(EIRS/+C 134)* **LOVE DON'T COME EASY. / CROESI'R AFON** [48] [ ]
(12"+=/cd-s+=) *(EIRS T/CD 134)* – No frontiers.
(10"pic-d+=) *(EIRSPD 134)* – Change II.

Oct 90. (7"/12") *(ALARME 2/+T)* **UNSAFE BUILDINGS (1990). / UP FOR MURDER (1990)** [54] [ ]
(c-s+=/cd-s+=) *(ALARME 2 C/CD)* – Unsafe Buildings (original).

Nov 90. (lp/c/cd) *(EIRSA/+C/CD 1043) <13056>* **STANDARDS** (compilation) [47] [ ]
– The road / Unsafe buildings / The stand / 68 guns / Where were you hiding when the storm broke? / Absolute reality / Strength / Spirit of '76 / Rain in the summertime / Rescue me / Sold me down the river / A new south Wales / Happy Xmas (war is over). (cd/c+=) – Marching on / Blaze of glory.

Apr 91. (7") *(ALARM 3)* **RAW. / CHANGE 1** [51] [ ]
(12"+=/cd-s+=) *(ALARM 3 T/CD)* – Devolution / Workin' man's blues.

Apr 91. (lp/c/cd) *(EIRSA/+C/CD 1055) <13087>* **RAW** [33] [ ]
– Raw / Rockin' in the free world / God save somebody / Moments in time / Hell or high water / Lead me through the darkness / The wind blows away my words / Let the river run its course / Save your crying / Wonderful world. *(cd re-mast.Dec01 on '21st Century'+=; 21C 016)* – (extra tracks).

— in mid '91, MIKE PETERS went solo and the band folded

– compilations, others, etc. –

Apr 88. (cd-ep) *I.R.S.; (AMCD 906)* **COMPACT HITS** [ ] [–]
– 68 guns / Blaze of glory / Shout to the Devil / Where were you hiding when the storm broke?

Apr 98. (cd) *E.M.I.; (7243-493751-2)* **THE BEST OF THE ALARM AND MIKE PETERS** [ ] [–]
– 68 guns / Spirit of '76 / Down the road / Rain in the summertime / Strength / Breathe / Sold me down the river / New South Wales / 21st century / Stand / Where were you hiding when the storm broke / Majority / Deceiver / Blaze of glory / Walk forever by my side / One step closer to home / No better than this / Presence of love / Absolute reality / Rescue me (tearing the bonds asunder).

Jun 99. (cd) *King Biscuit; (KBFHCD 028)* **KING BISCUIT PRESENTS . . .** [ ] [–]

Nov 01. (cd) *21st Century; (21C 010)* **EPONYMOUS (1981-1983 remastered)** [ ] [–]

MIKE PETERS

Crai — not iss.

Jan 94. (c-ep/12"ep/cd-ep) *(CRAI 040 MC/T/CD)* **BACK INTO THE SYSTEM. / 21st CENTURY (demo) / A NEW CHAPTER** [ ] [–]
(cd-ep) *(CRAI 040CDW)* – (Welsh language version).

Apr 94. (c-ep/12"ep/cd-ep) *(CRAI 041 MC/T/CD)* **IT JUST DON'T GET ANY BETTER THAN THIS. / DEVIL'S WORLD / WHITE NOISE** [ ] [–]

Oct 94. (cd/c/2x10"lp; as MIKE PETERS & THE POETS) *(CRAI 042CD/042MC/10-42)* **BREATHE** [ ] [–]
– Poetic justice / All I wanted / If I can't have you / Breathe / Love is a revolution / Who's gonna make the piece / Spiritual / What the world can't give me / Levis & bibles / Beautiful thing / Into the 21st century / This is war / The message / Back into the system * / It just don't get any better than this * / Train a comin' / A new chapter (reprise). *(d-lp += *) (re-iss. Jan95 as Welsh language; CRAICD 047)*

Transatla. — not iss.

Aug 96. (cd) *(TRACD 233)* **FEEL FREE** [ ] [–]
– Shine on (13th dream) / The message / Feel free / All is forgiven / My calling / Regeneration / R.I.P. / What is it for / Psychological combat zone / The love we made / Breathe / Broken silence.

Nov 96. (cd-s) *(TRAX 1033)* **SHINE ON / (instrumental)** [ ] [–]

Mar 97. (cd-s) *(TRAX 1038)* **MY CALLING** [ ] [–]

— with **CHRIS LEWIS** – guitars / **RICHARD LLEWELLYN** – bass / **OWEN THOMAS** – drums / **MARK O'GRADY** – electronica

Eagle — not iss.

Feb 98. (cd) *(EAGCD 019)* **RISE** [ ] [–]
– In circles / Transcendental / Rise / You are to me / My calling / First light / High on the hill / Ground zero / White noise (part II) / The wasting land / Burnout syndrome.

☐ ALICE COOPER (see under ⇒ COOPER, Alice)

ALICE IN CHAINS

Formed: Seattle, Washington, USA ... 1987 as glamsters DIAMOND LIE, then FUCK by main songwriters, LAYNE STALEY and JERRY CANTRELL, who soon opted for the more palatable moniker of ALICE N' CHAINS. They altered this name slightly after enlisting SEAN KINNEY and MIKE STARR, subsequently signing to 'Columbia' in 1989 and debuting the following year with promo EP, 'WE DIE YOUNG. Their debut album, 'FACELIFT' was released to widespread favourable reviews, although it took some time to scale the Billboard Top 100. Later in '91, they finally cracked the Top 50, their cause furthered by the success of new groundbreaking grunge acts like NIRVANA and SOUNDGARDEN giving metal/hard rock a breath of fresh air. A Grammy nomination under their belt (for the track 'MAN IN THE BOX'), the group enjoyed a flurry of activity in '92 with both the release of the easier going 'SAP' EP and a Top

10 follow-up album, 'DIRT', the latter also breaking the band in Britain. In 1993, they lifted no less than four major hits ('WOULD?', 'THEM BONES', 'ANGRY CHAIR' and 'DOWN IN A HOLE') from this critically acclaimed opus. With acoustic sets all the rage, ALICE IN CHAINS then delivered a stripped-down EP, 'JAR OF FLIES', the set being the first mini-cd to top the US charts. When STALEY subsequently formed grunge 'supergroup', The GACY BUNCH (later changing the name to MAD SEASON) alongside PEARL JAM's MIKE McCREADY and BARRETT MARTIN of The SCREAMING TREES, speculation was rife about an ALICE IN CHAINS split. After a one-off album, 'ABOVE' (1995), however, STALEY, CANTRELL & Co. stormed back with the eponymous 'ALICE IN CHAINS' (1995), the record giving the group their second US No.1. The obligatory 'MTV UNPLUGGED' set followed in 1996, ALICE IN CHAINS being only one of a handful of similar acts to be bestowed with such an 'honour'. With AIC out of action for a few years, JERRY CANTRELL decided it was time for a solo piece. 'BOGGY DEPOT' (1998) – which included a track from the earlier made Jim Carrey film, 'The Cable Guy' – hit the US Top 30 for a week and failed miserably to gain much interest in Britain bar Kerrang(!), of course. With ALICE IN CHAINS on hold while STALEY deteriorated into a life of reclusive drug taking, CANTRELL set about recording his sophomore set. Naming it 'DEGRADATION TRIP' (2002), it would be released by 'Roadrunner' a few months after the untimely – but nevertheless expected – drugs death of STALEY c. 5 April 2002 (the anniversary of KURT COBAIN). The aforementioned set fared a little better than his previous effort and, with the help from some top notch backing on session (ROBERT TRUJILLO, CHRIS DeGARMO and MIKE BORDIN), the album peaked into the US Top 40. • **Songwriters:** CANTRELL solo covered, 'I'VE SEEN ALL THIS WORLD I CARE TO SEE' (Willie Nelson; on a tribute album).

Album rating: FACELIFT (*6) / SAP (*5) / DIRT (*8) / JAR OF FLIES (*7) / ALICE IN CHAINS (*5) / MTV UNPLUGGED (*4) / NOTHING SAFE compilation (*6) / Mad Season: ABOVE (*5) / Jerry Cantrell: BOGGY DEPOT (*5) / DEGRADATION TRIP (*6)

LAYNE STALEY (b.22 Aug'67, Bellevue, WA.) – vocals / **JERRY CANTRELL** (b.18 Mar'66, Tacoma, WA.) – guitar, vocals / **MICHAEL STARR** (b. 4 Apr'66, Honolulu, Hawaii) – bass (ex-SADO) / **SEAN KINNEY** (b.27 May'66, Seattle) – drums, percussion, megaphone

Columbia Columbia

Jul 90. (c-ep/12"ep) *<CAS/CAT 2095>* **WE DIE YOUNG EP** [–] [ ]
– We die young / It ain't like that / Killing yourself.

Sep 91. (cd/c/lp) *(467201-2/-4/-1) <46075>* **FACELIFT** [ ] Mar91 [42]
– We die young / Man in the box / Sea of sorrow / Bleed the freak / I can't remember / Love, hate, love / It ain't like that / Sunshine / Put you down / Confusion / I know somethin' ('bout you) / Real thing.

Oct 91. (cd-ep) *<73851>* **MAN IN THE BOX / SEA OF SORROW / BLEED THE FREAK / SUNSHINE** [–] [ ]

Feb 92. (c-ep)(cd-ep) *<74182><74305>* **SAP** [–] [ ]
– Brother / Got me wrong / Right turn / Am I inside / Love song.

—— **MIKE INEZ** (b.14 May'66, San Fernando, California) – bass; repl. MIKE STARR. He formed MY SISTER'S MACHINE, who released album in May'92 'DIVA' on 'Caroline'.

Oct 92. (cd/c/lp) *(472330-2/-4/-1) <52475>* **DIRT** [42] [6]
– Them bones / Dam that river / Rain when I die / Down in a hole / Sickman / Rooster / Junkhead / Dirt / God smack / Hate to feel / Angry chair / Would?

Jan 93. (7") *(658888-7)* **WOULD?. / MAN IN THE BOX** [19] [ ]
(12"green+=/pic-cd-s+=) *(658888-6/-2)* – Brother / Right Turn.

Mar 93. (7") *(659090-7)* **THEM BONES. / WE DIE YOUNG** [26] [ ]
(cd-s+=) *(659090-2)* – Got me wrong / Am I inside.

May 93. (7") *(659365-7)* **ANGRY CHAIR. / I KNOW SOMETHIN' ('BOUT YOU)** [33] [ ]
(12"+=) *(659365-6)* – Bleed the freak / It ain't like that.
(cd-s+=) *(659365-2)* – It ain't like that / Hate to feel.

Oct 93. (7"pic-d) *(659751-7)* **DOWN IN A HOLE. / ROOSTER** [36] [ ]
(12"+=) *(659751-6)* – A little bitter / Love, hate, love.
(cd-s+=) *(659751-2)* – What the hell I have I / ('A'radio edit).

Dec 93. (cd-s; w-drawn) *(660047-2)* **ROTTEN APPLE /** [–] [–]

Jan 94. (cd/c/lp) *(475713-2/-4/-1) <57628>* **JAR OF FLIES / SAP** [4] [1]
– Rotten apple / Nutshell / I stay away / No excuses / Whale & wasp / Don't follow / Swing on this. (US-version w /out 'SAP')

Oct 95. (7"/c-s) *(662623-7/-4)* **GRIND. / NUTSHELL** [23] [ ]
(cd-s+=) *(662823-2)* – So close / Love, hate, love.

Nov 95. (cd/c/d-lp) *(481114-2/-4/-1) <67248>* **ALICE IN CHAINS** [37] [1]
– Grind / Brush away / Sludge factory / Heaven beside you / Head creeps / Again / Shame in you / God am / So close / Nothin' song / Frogs / Over now.

Jan 96. (7"white) *(662893-7)* **HEAVEN BESIDE YOU. / WOULD? (live)** [35] [ ]
(cd-s+=) *(662893-2)* – Rooster (live) / Junkhead (live).
(cd-s) *(662893-5)* – ('A'side) / Angry chair (live) / Man in a box (live) / Love, hate, love (live).

—— added for below only; **SCOTT OLSEN** – guitar

Jul 96. (cd/c/d-lp) *(484300-2/-4/-1) <67703>* **MTV UNPLUGGED (live)** [20] [3]
– Nutshell / Brother / No excuses / Sludge factory / Down in a hole / Angry chair / Rooster / Got me wrong / Heaven beside you / Would? / Frogs / Over now / Killer is me.

Jul 99. (cd/c) *(494005-2/-4) <63649>* **NOTHING SAFE** (compilation) [ ] [20]
– Get born again / We die young / Man in the box / Them bones / Iron gland / Angry chair / Down in a hole / Rooster / Got me wrong / No excuses / I stay away / What the hell have I / Grind / Again / Would?

– compilations, etc. –

Oct 99. (4xcd-box) *Columbia; (CKX 69580)* **MUSIC BANK** [ ] [ ]

Dec 00. (cd) *Columbia; <85274>* **LIVE (live)** [–] [ ]

MAD SEASON

—— were originally called GACY BUNCH with **LAYNE STALEY** – vocals / **MIKE McCREADY** – guitar (of PEARL JAM) / **BARRETT MARTIN** – drums (of SCREAMING TREES)

Mar 95. (cd/c/lp) *(478507-2/-4/-1) <67057>* **ABOVE** [41] [24]
– Wake up / X-ray mind / I'm above / River of deceit / Lifeless dead / Artificial red / Long gone day / I don't know anything / November hotel / All alone.

JERRY CANTRELL

with **SEAN KINNEY** + **MIKE INEZ** / plus bassists **REX BROWN** (PANTERA), **NORWOOD FISHER** (FISHBONE) + **LES CLAYPOOL** (PRIMUS) / guest **ANGELO MOORE** (FISHBONE) – sax

Columbia Columbia

Apr 98. (cd/c/lp) *(488705-2/-4/-1) <68147>* **BOGGY DEPOT** [ ] [28]
– Dickeye / Cut you in / My song / Settling down / Breaks my back / Jesus hands / Devil by his side / Keep the light on / Satisfy / Hurt a long time / Between / Cold piece.

May 98. (cd-ep) *<4704>* **CUT YOU IN** [–] [ ]
– My song / Leave me alone (remix) / Cut you in.

Roadrunner Roadrunner

Jun 02. (cd) *<(RR 8451-2)>* **DEGRADATION TRIP** [ ] [33]
– Psychotic break / Bragain basement Howard Hughes / Anger rising / Angel eyes / Solitude / Mother's spinning in her grave / Hellbound / Give it a name / Castaway / She was my girl / Chemical tribe / Spiderbite / Locked on / Gone.

ALIEN ANT FARM

Formed: Riverside, California . . . 1996 by DRYDEN MITCHELL, TERRY CORSA, TYE ZAMORA and MIKE COSGROVE. After their debut album, 'GREATEST HITS' (1999) scooped Best Independent Album at the 1999 L.A. Music Awards, the PRIMUS/ALICE IN CHAINS/METALLICA-influenced quartet became the first act signed to PAPA ROACH's 'New Noise' label. The two bands had been friends since their mid-90's beginnings on the Californian club circuit although AAF plough a slightly less intense furrow than their more famous brethren. The 'ANThology' (2001) album brought general critical acclaim with many fans warming to an inventive if unlikely cover of Michael Jackson's 'SMOOTH CRIMINAL'. The band were subsequently dealt a near fatal blow when their bus crashed in Europe in 2001, with singer DRYDEN MITCHELL suffering a broken neck. Eventually they went back into the studio to record 'truANT' (2003), an urgent, vital collection of songs which underlined their determination to carry on.

Album rating: GREATEST HITS (*5) / ANThology (*6) / truANT (*7)

DRYDEN MITCHELL (b.15 Jun'76) – vocals / **TERENCE CORSO** (b.28 Nov'71) – guitar / **TYE ZAMORA** (b.30 May'77) – bass, vocals / **MIKE COSGROVE** (b. 7 Nov'75) – drums

not iss. own label

Nov 99. (cd) **GREATEST HITS** [–] [ ]
– These days / Pink tea / Movies / Dole roll / Denigrate / Solution time / S.S. recognize / Nova hands / Universe / Sick thief.

Dreamworks Dreamworks

Mar 01. (cd) *<(450293-2)>* **ANThology** [ ] [11]
– Courage / Movies / Flesh and bone / Whisper / Summer / Sticks and stones / Attitude / Stranded / Wish / Calico / Happy death day / Smooth criminal / Universe. *(re-dist.Aug01)* – hit UK No.11

Jun 01. (c-s) *(450899-4)* **MOVIES / PINK TEE** [53] [–]
(cd-s+=) *(450899-2)* – ('A'-acoustic live on KROQ) / ('A'-video).

Sep 01. (c-s) *(450888-4) <radio cut>* **SMOOTH CRIMINAL / DENIGRATE** [3] Aug01 [23]
(cd-s+=) *(450887-2)* – Orange appeal / ('A'-video).

Feb 02. (c-s) *(450849-4)* **MOVIES / SMOOTH CRIMINAL (live)** [5] [–]
(cd-s+=) *(450849-2)* – ('A'-live) / ('A'-video).

May 02. (c-s) *(450829-4)* **ATTITUDE / ATTITUDE (acoustic live)** [66] [–]
(cd-s+=) *(450829-2)* – Universe (video).
(cd-s) *(450828-2)* – ('A'side) / Universe (live) / Stranded (acoustic) / ('A'-video).

Polydor El Tonal

Aug 03. (cd) *(450501-2) <00005681-2>* **truANT** [68] [42]
– 1000 days / Drifting apart / Quiet / Glow / These days / Sarah Wynn / Never meant / Goodbye / Tia Lupe / Rubber mallet / S.S. Recognize / Hope.

ALKALINE TRIO

Formed: Chicago, Illinois, USA . . . 1997 by MATT SKIBA, GLENN PORTER and ROB DORAN. Inspired by 70's punk/pop and drinking, the 'TRIO were all the rage in the late 90's. From 1998's 'GODDAMMIT' to the recent 'FROM HERE TO INFIRMARY' (2001), these square-chinned lads from the Windy City finally came of age by supporting BLINK-182 around the US. However, by the dawn of 2000, they had lost PORTER who was superseded by MIKE FELUMLEE; DAN ANDRIANO had taken DORAN's place a few years earlier (see discography). The group issued 2003's 'GOOD MOURNING', with an album cover that featured all three members dressed in black and looking suspiciously like shifty bouncers at a secret goth club. The music inside was a blaring blend of squeal-metal and downright catchiness; infusing punk-pop melodies with atmospheric emo-rock. The only time The ALKALINE TRIO let down their guard was with the set's closing number 'BLUE IN THE FACE', an acoustic-tinged dirge paying homage to broken relationships. In turn AT managed to mix and match sour glumness with gigantic pop-rock melodies for the masses and also hit Top 40 into the bargain.

Album rating: GODAMMIT (*8) / MAYBE I'LL CATCH FIRE (*6) / ALKALINE TRIO collection (*7) / FROM HERE TO INFIRMARY (*8) / GOOD MOURNING (*7)

MATT SKIBA – vocals, guitar (ex-JERKWATER drummer) / **GLENN PORTER** – drums, vocals (ex-88 FINGER LOUIE) / **ROB DORAN** – bass, vocals

Asian Man Asian Man

Jun 98. (m-cd) *<(AM 028CD)>* **FOR YOUR LUNGS ONLY** [ ] May98 [ ]
– Snake oil tanker / Southern rock / Cooking wire / For your lungs only.

—— **DAN ANDRIANO** – bass (of SLAPSTICK) repl. DORAN

Oct 98. (lp/cd) *<(AM 034/+CD)>* **GODDAMMIT** [ ] [ ]
– Cringe / Cop / San Francisco / Nose over tail / As you were / Enjoy your day / Clavicle / My little needle / Southern rock / Message from Kathleen / Trouble breathing / Sorry about that. *(cd re-iss. Apr03 on 'Kung Fu'+=; 78814-2)* – Bleeder / Cooking wine / My friend Peter / 97.

Feb 00. (lp/cd) *<(AM 055/+CD)>* **MAYBE I'LL CATCH FIRE** [ ] [ ]
– Keep 'em coming Madam me / You've got so far to go / Fuck you Aurora / Sleepyhead / Maybe I'll catch fire / Tuck me in / She took him to the lake / 5-3-10-4 / Radio. *(cd re-iss. Apr03 on 'Kung Fu'+=; 78813-2)*

Apr 00. (lp/cd) *<(AM 058/+CD)>* **ALKALINE TRIO** (collection) [ ] [ ]
– Goodbye forever / This is getting over you / Bleeder / I lied my face off / My friend Peter / Snake oil tanker / Southern rock / Cooking wine / For your lungs only / Exploding boy / Sun dials / Nose over tail / '97.

—— **MIKE FELUMLEE** – drums (ex-SMOKING POPES) repl. PORTER

Lookout! Lookout!

Apr 01. (7") *<(L 264)>* **HELL YES. / MY STANDARD BREAK FROM LIFE** [ ] Mar01 [ ]

Vagrant Vagrant

Apr 01. (lp/cd) *<(VR 353/+CD)>* **FROM HERE TO INFIRMARY** [ ] [ ]
– Private eye / Mr chainsaw / Take lots with alcohol / Stupid kid / Another innocent girl / Steamer trunk / You're dead / Armageddon / I'm dying tomorrow / Bloodied up / Trucks and trains / Crawl. *(cd re-iss. Aug01 on 'B-Unique'+=; BUN 008)* – Standard break / Hell yes. *(cd re-iss. May03 on 'Universal'; 910353-2)*

B-Unique not iss.

Aug 01. (cd-s) *(BUN 007)* **STUPID KID / TRUCKS AND TRAINS / ARMAGEDDON** [ ] [–]

Jan 02. (7") *(BUN 013-7)* **PRIVATE EYE. / PRIVATE EYE (original)** [51] [–]
(cd-s+=) *(BUN 013CDS)* – ('A'-video).
(cd-s) *(BUN 013CDX)* – ('A'-side) / Mr. Chainsaw (live) / Cringe (live).

Mar 02. (7"pic-d/cd-s) *(BUN 016-7/CDS)* **STUPID KID. / METRO** [53] [–]
(cd-s) *(BUN 016CDX)* – ('A'-side) / She took him to the lake (live) / We've got so far to go (live) / Private eye (video).

Universal Vagrant

May 03. (cd/lp) *(980123-8/-9) <VR 381>* **GOOD MOURNING** [32] [20]
– This could be love / We've had enough / One hundred stories / Continental / All on black / Emma / Fatally yours / Every thug needs a lady / Blue Carolina / Dooner party (all night) / If we never go inside / Blue in the face. *(cd+=)* – Dead end road / Old school reasons.

Jul 03. (7"pic-d) *(9809024)* **WE'VE HAD ENOUGH. / BLUE IN THE FACE (demo)** [50] [–]
(cd-s+=) *(9809023)* – One hundred stories (demo) / ('A'-video).

Oct 03. (7"pic-d) *(9811507)* **ALL ON BLACK. / THIS COULD BE LOVE (acoustic SBN session)** [60] [–]
(cd-s+=) *(9811506)* – ('A'-SBN session).

ALL-AMERICAN REJECTS

Formed: Stillwater, Oklahoma, USA . . . 2000 by TYSON RITTER and NICK WHEELER. With the addition of MIKE KENNERTY and CHRIS GAYLOR, the 'REJECTS became operative, hooking up with Tim O'Heir for the recording of an eponymous debut album. Released on indie label 'Doghouse' in October 2002 (later picked up and re-released into the US Top 30 by 'DreamWorks'), the album was bursting at the seams with adolescent attitude, well-schooled rock classicism and hormome-saturated harmonies.

Album rating: ALL-AMERICAN REJECTS (*7)

TYSON RITTER – vocals, bass / **NICK WHEELER** – guitar, programming / **MIKE KENNERTY** – guitar / **CHRIS GAYLOR** – drums

Doghouse Doghouse

Nov 02. (cd) <(*DOG 092CD*)> **THE ALL-AMERICAN REJECTS** [ ] Oct02 [ ]
– My paper heart / Your star / Swing, swing / Time stands still / One more sad song / Why worry / Don't leave me / Too far gone / Drive away / Happy endings / The last song. <(*re-iss. Jun03 on 'DreamWorks'+=; 450460-6*)> – The cigarette song (acoustic). (*hit US No.25 + UK No.50*)

DreamWorks DreamWorks

Jul 03. (7") (*450461-7*) **SWING, SWING. / TOO FAR GONE (bedroom demo session version)** [13] Aug03 [60]
(cd-s+=) <(*450461-6*)> – The cigarette song (acoustic) / ('A'-video).

Nov 03. (7") (*4504642*) **THE LAST SONG. / TIME STANDS STILL (bedroom demo)** [69] [–]
(cd-s+=) (*4504641*) – Why worry (bedroom demo) / ('A'-video).

☐ Daevid ALLEN (see under ⇒ GONG)

ALLMAN BROTHERS BAND

Formed: Jacksonville, Florida, USA . . . 1967 by brothers DUANE and GREGG. They became The HOURGLASS, after previously gigging under the ALLMAN JOYS banner with others:- BOB KELLER (bass), BILLY CANELL or MANARD PORTWOOD (drums). HOURGLASS released two albums and nearly a third for 'Liberty' before disbanding in 1968. They then returned to their homeland to augment BUTCH TRUCKS in his outfit, 31st OF FEBRUARY, with DUANE also relying on session work for 'Atlantic'. In 1969, all three formed The ALLMAN BROTHERS BAND and moved to Macon, Georgia. The brothers had already signed to the 'Atlantic' distributed label 'Capricorn', run by one-time OTIS REDDING manager, Phil Walden. With a final line-up of GREGG, DUANE, BUTCH TRUCKS, BERRY OAKLEY (bass) and a second percussionist, JAIMO JOHANSON, the band cut their self-titled debut in 1969, following it up a year later with 'IDLEWILD SOUTH'. All the elements that would make the ALLMAN's a legend were in place; the smooth fluidity of the guitar runs, bible belt country and gospel in abundance, jazz-influenced explorations and dyed in the wool Southern-soaked vocals. During this time, DUANE continued his session work for the likes of LAURA NYRO and DELANEY & BONNIE, as well as lending an unmistakable hand to ERIC CLAPTON on DEREK AND THE DOMINOES' 'LAYLA' project (yes, that most famous of English rock refrains was created by the blonde maned all-American boy). Like their spiritual brothers The GRATEFUL DEAD, it was in a live setting that The ALLMAN BROTHERS BAND could really cook up a soulful gumbo stew and 'THE ALLMAN BROTHERS BAND AT FILLMORE EAST' (1971) was possibly the band's defining moment as well as one of rock's great live albums. A sprawling double set, the free flowing jams often tripped out on their own momentum and despite being spaced out over a whole side of vinyl, 'WHIPPING POST' (from the debut) lost none of its hypnotic power. Less than three months later, the band were dealt a potentially fatal blow when DUANE was killed in a motorbike accident. Bloodied but unbowed, the band released the 'EAT A PEACH' (1972) album, a mixture of live tracks left over from the Fillmore recordings and new studio material. Another double set, three tracks had been recorded prior to the accident, including DUANE's fragile 'LITTLE MARTHA'. The indulgence of the side-long DONOVAN adaptation, 'MOUNTAIN JAM', was balanced by the pastoral beauty of tracks like BETTS' 'BLUE SKY'. After BERRY OAKLEY was killed later that year in a crash spookily reminiscent of DUANE's, BETTS' influence was even more pronounced as the band struggled bravely on with the triumphant 'BROTHERS AND SISTERS' (1973) album. Replacing OAKLEY with LAMAR WILLIAMS and drafting in pianist CHUCK LEAVELL, the rootsier sounding album gave The ALLMAN BROTHERS BAND their first and only No.1. BETTS' glorious country-flavoured 'RAMBLIN' MAN' provided their biggest hit single to date and 'JESSICA' fuelled countless boy racer fantasies after it was used as the theme for Britain's 'Top Gear' TV show. The band then returned to their natural habitat, the tourbus, playing a landmark gig to a crowd of over half a million people in Watkins Glen, New York, alongside The GRATEFUL DEAD and The BAND. Patchy solo projects followed in the shape of GREG's 'LAID BACK' (1973) and BETTS' 'HIGHWAY CALL' (1974), while the next band effort 'WIN, LOSE OR DRAW' (1975) signalled that The ALLMANS' infamous fast living was beginning to sap their creativity. GREG began a brief, torrid marriage with CHER in 1975, releasing the 'TWO THE HARD WAY' album in 1977 under the moniker of ALLMAN AND WOMAN (no, seriously!). The turning point, however, came when GREG testified against his road manager/pusher, SCOOTER HERRING, who was up on a serious drugs rap. After HERRING was sentenced to 75 years(!) in prison, the rest of the band turned their backs on GREG, the all-brothers together bravado gone, at least until the reunion. Splitting and reforming numerous times throughout the 80's, their studio output trawled a creative nadir on their 'Arista' albums. Nevertheless, they can still put bums on seats in the American heartlands and their Southern fried innovation was given official recognition in 1995 when they were inducted into the Rock 'n' Roll Hall Of Fame. In fact they were still cutting it live come the dawn of the new millennium, as 'PEAKIN' AT THE BEACON' (2000) testified. Recorded at one of their annual gigs at New York's Beacon Theater, the record was notable for the last stand of BETTS who was subsequently replaced. While there were rumours that the guitarist was allegedly dropped due to a poor performance on stage, that didn't stop the band trawling through all twenty seven and a half minutes of the man's 'HIGH FALLS'. In the event, BETTS' absence didn't prevent the ALLMANS from turning in one of their best studio outings in the last two decades with 'HITTIN' THE NOTE' (2003). A US Top 40 entry no less, the record was as gritty, soulful, and ambitous as many of their 70's classics, particularly on the more acoustic, country flavoured tracks like 'OLD BEFORE MY TIME'. Even the cover of The Rolling Stones' 'HEART OF STONE' was startling in its delivery. • **Songwriters:** The ALLMANS and BETTS. In the 90's most were written by BETTS, HAYNES and NEEL. Covered; STATESBORO BLUES (Blind Willie McTell) / ONE WAY OUT (Elmore James) / I'M YOUR HOOCHIE COOCHIE MAN (Muddy Waters) / SLIP AWAY (Clarence Carter). • **Trivia:** DUANE sessioned for WILSON PICKETT, BOZ SCAGGS, ARETHA FRANKLIN, KING CURTIS, etc, etc . . .

Album rating: THE ALLMAN BROTHERS BAND (*8) / IDLEWILD SOUTH (*7) / AT FILLMORE EAST (*9) / EAT A PEACH (*9) / BROTHERS AND SISTERS (*8) / WIN, LOSE OR DRAW (*4) / WIPE THE WINDOWS, CHECK THE OIL, DOLLAR GAS (*5) / ENLIGHTENED ROGUES (*5) / REACH FOR THE SKY (*4) / BROTHERS OF THE ROAD (*4) / DREAMS boxed-set (*7) / SEVEN TURNS (*6) / A DECADE OF HITS 1969-1979 (*8) / AN EVENING WITH THE ALLMAN BROTHERS (*6) / WHERE IT ALL BEGINS (*5) / PEAKIN' AT THE BEACON (*5) / HITTIN' THE NOTE (*7) / Gregg Allman: LAID BACK (*5) / GREGG ALLMAN TOUR (*3) / PLAYIN' UP A STORM (*4) / TWO THE HARD WAY as Allman & Woman (*3) / I'M NO ANGEL (*5) / JUST BEFORE THE BULLETS FLY (*4) / SEARCHING FOR SIMPLICITY (*5)

HOURGLASS

GREGG ALLMAN (b. 8 Dec'48, Nashville, Tenn.) – vocals, keyboards, guitar / **DUANE ALLMAN** (b.20 Nov'46, Nashville) – guitars / **PAUL HORNSBY** – keyboards, guitar, vocals / **MABRON McKINNEY** – bass / **JOHN SANDLIN** – drums

Liberty Liberty

Feb 68. (7") *<56002>* **HEARTBEAT. / NOTHING BUT TEARS** [–] [ ]
Aug 68. (lp; mono/stereo) *(LBL/LBS 83219E) <7536>* **THE HOUR GLASS** [ ] Feb68 [ ]
– Out of the night / Nothing but tears / Love makes the world 'round / Cast off all my fears / I've been trying / No easy way down / Heartbeat / So much love / Got to get away / Silently / Bells.

—— **JESSE WILLARD CARR** – bass, vocals repl. MABRON McKINNEY

Jul 68. (7") *<56029>* **POWER OF LOVE. / I STILL WANT YOUR LOVE** [–] [ ]
Aug 68. (lp) *<7555>* **POWER OF LOVE** [–] [ ]
– Power of love / Changing of the guard / To things before / I'm not afraid / I can stand alone / Down in Texas / I still want your love / Home for the summer / I'm hangin' up my heart for you / Going nowhere / Norwegian wood / Now is the time. *(re-iss. the 1968 lp's; Mar74 on 'United Artists'; USD 303/4)<013G2>*
Sep 68. (7") *<56053>* **CHANGING OF THE GUARD. / D-I-V-O-R-C-E** [–] [ ]
Nov 68. (7") *<56065>* **GOING NOWHERE. / SHE'S MY WOMAN** [–] [ ]
Dec 68. (7") *<56072>* **NOW IS THE TIME. / SHE'S MY WOMAN** [–] [ ]
Feb 69. (7") *<56091>* **I'VE BEEN TRYING. / SILENTLY** [–] [ ]

—— 3rd album was withdrawn

31st FEBRUARY

DUANE and **GREGG** with **BUTCH TRUCKS** – drums / **SCOTT BOYER** – guitar, vocals / **DAVID BROWN** – bass

not iss.

Mar 69. (7") **IN THE MORNING WHEN I'M REAL. / PORCELAIN MIRRORS** [–] [ ]

—— An album DUANE AND GREGG was released 1973 on 'Polydor UK'/'Bold' US cont. these demos.

The ALLMAN BROTHERS BAND

(**GREGG** and **DUANE**) plus **DICKEY BETTS** (b.RICHARD, 12 Dec'43, West Palm Beach, Florida) – guitar, vocals / **BERRY OAKLEY** (b. 4 Apr'48, Chicago, Illinois) – bass / **BUTCH TRUCKS** (b.Jacksonville, Florida) – drums, timpani / **JAIMOE JOHANSON** (b.JOHN LEE JOHNSON, 8 Jul'44, Ocean Springs, Miss.) – percussion

Atco Atco

Nov 69. (lp) *(228 033) <308>* **THE ALLMAN BROTHERS BAND** [ ] [ ]
– Don't want you no more / It's not my cross to bear / Black hearted woman / Trouble no more / Every hungry woman / Dreams / Whipping post. *(cd-iss. 1994 on 'Polydor'; 823 653-2) (cd re-iss. Jun98; 531257-2)*
Mar 70. (7") *(226 013) <8803>* **BLACK HEARTED WOMAN. / EVERY HUNGRY WOMAN** [ ] [ ]
Nov 70. (lp) *(2400 032) <342>* **IDLEWIND SOUTH** [ ] [38]
– Revival (love is everywhere) / Don't keep me wonderin' / Midnight rider / In memory of Elizabeth Reed / I'm your hoochie coochie man / Please call home / Leave my blues at home. *(cd-iss. Mar89 on 'Polydor'; 833 334-2) (cd re-iss. Jun98; 531258-2)*
Nov 70. (7") *(2091 040) <8011>* **REVIVAL (LOVE IS EVERYWHERE). / LEAVE MY BLUES AT HOME** [ ] [92]
Mar 71. (7") *(2091 070) <8014>* **MIDNIGHT RIDER. / WHIPPING POST** [ ] [ ]

Capricorn Capricorn

Jul 71. (d-lp) *(2659 005) <802>* **AT FILLMORE EAST (live)** [ ] [13]
– Statesboro blues / Done somebody wrong / Stormy Monday / You don't love me / Hot 'Lanta / In memory of Elizabeth Reed / Whipping post. *(re-iss. Nov74;) (d-cd-iss. 1986 on 'Polydor'; 823 273-2) (d-cd re-iss. Jun98; 531260-2)*

—— On 29 Oct'71, DUANE was killed in a motorcycle accident in Macon. He had already contributed to 3 tracks on below album.

Feb 72. (d-lp) *(67501) <0102>* **EAT A PEACH** [ ] [4]
– Ain't wastin' time no more / Les brers in A minor / Melissa / Mountain jam / One way out / Trouble no more / Stand back / Blue sky / Little Martha / Mountain jam (reprise). *(re-iss. Nov74;) (cd-iss. 1986 on 'Polydor'; 823 654-2) (cd re-iss. Jun98; 531261-2)*
Apr 72. (7") *<0003>* **AIN'T WASTIN' TIME NO MORE. / MELISSA** [–] [77]
Jul 72. (7") *<0007>* **MELISSA. / BLUE SKY** [–] [86]
Nov 72. (7") *<0014>* **ONE WAY OUT. / STAND BACK** [–] [86]

—— (Jan'73) **LAMAR WILLIAMS** (b.1947) – bass; repl. BERRY OAKLEY who also died in a motorcyle accident, again in Macon, 11 Nov'72.

Sep 73. (lp/c) *(2429/3129 102) <0111>* **BROTHERS AND SISTERS** [42] Aug73 [1]
– Wasted words / Ramblin' man / Come and go blues / Jelly jelly / Southbound / Jessica / Pony boy. *(re-iss. Jun81; 2482 504) (cd-iss. 1986 on 'Polydor'; 825 092-2) (cd re-iss. Jun87 on 'Polydor'; 823 721-2) (cd re-iss. Jun98; 531262-2)*
Oct 73. (7") *(2089 005) <0027>* **RAMBLIN' MAN. / PONY BOY** [ ] Aug73 [2]
Jan 74. (7") *<0036>* **JESSICA. / WASTED WORDS** [–] [65]
Oct 74. (7") *(2089 006)* **JESSICA. / COME AND GO BLUES** [ ] [–]
Sep 75. (lp) *(2476 116) <0156>* **WIN, LOSE OR DRAW** [ ] [5]
– Can't lose what you never had / Just another love song / Nevertheless / Win, lose or draw / Louisiana Lou And Three Card Monty John / High falls / Sweet mama. *(cd-iss. Aug87; 827586-2) (cd re-iss. Jun98; 531263-2)*
Sep 75. (7") *<0246>* **NEVERTHELESS. / LOUISIANA LOU AND THREE CARD MONTY JOHN** [–] [67] [78]

—— Jul 76 when GREGG was ostracized by others for giving evidence against convicted drug trafficker and road manager Scooter Herring. GREGG formed his own band. BETTS formed GREAT SOUTHERN and others formed SEA LEVEL who hit US No. 31 Mar 78 with lp 'CATS ON THE COAST'. When rifts were settled **The ALLMAN BROTHERS BAND** re-united early '79. GREGG, DICKEY, BUTCH, JAIMO plus newcomers **DAN TOLER** – guitar / **DAVID GOLDFLIES** – bass (both ex-GREAT SOUTHERN)

Polydor Capricorn

Mar 79. (lp) *(2429 185) <0218>* **ENLIGHTENED ROGUES** [ ] [9]
– Crazy love / Can't take it with you / Pegasus / Need your love so bad / Blind love / Try it one more time / Just ain't easy / Sail away. *(cd-iss. 1987 on 'Polydor'; 831 589-2) (cd re-iss. Jun98; 531265-2)*
Apr 79. (7") *(2089 068) <0320>* **CRAZY LOVE. / IT JUST AIN'T EASY** [ ] Mar79 [29]
Jun 79. (7") *<0326>* **CAN'T TAKE IT WITH YOU. / SAIL AWAY** [–] [ ]

Arista Arista

Sep 80. (lp) *(SPART 1146) <9535>* **REACH FOR THE SKY** [ ] Aug80 [27]
– Hell & high water / Mystery woman / From the madness of the west / I got a right to be wrong / Angeline / Famous last words / Keep on keepin' on / So long. *(cd-iss. Aug97 on 'Razor & Tie'; RE 2131)*
Sep 80. (7") *<0555>* **ANGELINE. / SO LONG** [–] [58]
Jan 81. (7") *<0584>* **MYSTERY WOMAN. / HELL OR HIGH WATER** [–] [ ]
Sep 81. (lp) *<9564>* **BROTHERS OF THE ROAD** [ ] Aug81 [44]
– Brothers of the road / Leavin' / Straight from the road / The heat is on / Maybe we can go back to yesterday / The judgement / Two rights / Never knew how much (I needed you) / Things you used to do / I beg of you. *(cd-iss. Aug97 on 'Razor & Tie'; RE 2132)*
Sep 81. (7") *(ARIST 432) <0618>* **STRAIGHT FROM THE HEART. / LEAVING** [ ] Aug81 [39]
Nov 81. (7") *<0643>* **TWO RIGHTS. / NEVER KNEW HOW MUCH** [–] [ ]

—— **CHUCK LEAVELL** rejoined but they soon disbanded once again. Past member **LAMAR** died of cancer on 25 Jan'83.

GREGG ALLMAN BAND

went solo again in 1987 with **DAN TOLER** – guitar / **DAVID 'FRANKIE' TOLER** – drums / **TIM HEDING** – keyboards / **BRUCE WAIBEL** – bass, vocals / **CHAZ TRIPPY** – percussion

Epic Epic

May 87. (lp/c/cd) *<(450392-1/-4/-2)>* **I'M NO ANGEL** [ ] Feb87 [30]
– I'm no angel / Anything goes / Evidence of love / Yours for the asking / Things that might have been / Can't keep running / Faces without names / Lead me on / Don't want you no more / It's not my cross to bear.
Jul 87. (7") *(6507 517) <06998>* **I'M NO ANGEL. / LEAD ME ON** [ ] Mar87 [49]

Jul 87. (7") *<07215>* **CAN'T KEEP RUNNING. / ANYTHING GOES** – –

Sep 87. (7") *<07430>* **EVIDENCE OF LOVE. / ANYTHING GOES** – –

Apr 89. (lp/c/cd) *(462 477-1/-4/-2) <44033>* **JUST BEFORE THE BULLETS FLY** Aug88
– Demons / Before the bullets fly / Slip away / Thorn and a wild rose / Ocean awash the gunwale / Can't get over you / Island / Fear of falling / Night games / Every hungry woman.

Apr 89. (7") *<08041>* **SLIP AWAY. / EVERY HUNGRY WOMAN** –

Jan 98. (cd/c) *(481691-2/-4) <67143>* **SEARCHING FOR SIMPLICITY** Nov97
– Whipping post / House of blues / Come back and help me / Silence ain't golden no more / Rendezvous with the blues / Wolf's a-howlin' / Love the poison / Don't deny me / Dark end of the street / Neighbor neighbor / I've got news for you / Memphis in the meantime / Startin' over.

– other GREGG ALLMAN releases, etc. –

—— with **SCOTT BOYER** – guitar, vocals / **TOMMY TALTON** – slide guitar / **CHUCK LEAVELL** – keyboards / **DAVID BROWN** – bass / **BILL STEWART** – drums / etc.

Capricorn Capricorn

Nov 73. (lp) *(47508) <0116>* **LAID BACK** 13
– Will the circle be unbroken / Don't mess up a good thing / Multi-colored lady / Please call home / Queen of hearts / Midnight rider / Don't mess up a good thing / All my friends / These days. *(cd-iss. Aug87 on 'Polydor'; 831 941-2)*

Jan 74. (7") *(2089 002) <0035>* **MIDNIGHT RIDER. / MULTI-COLORED LADY** Dec73 19

—— (above releases were issued approx.half a year later in UK).

Mar 74. (7") *<0042>* **PLEASE CALL HOME. / DON'T MESS UP A GOOD THING** –

Oct 74. (7") *<0053>* **DON'T MESS WITH A GOOD THING. / MIDNIGHT RIDER** –

Nov 74. (d-lp) *(2659 038) <0141>* **GREGG ALLMAN TOUR (live)** 50
– Don't mess up a good thing / Queen of hearts / Feel so bad / Stand back / Time will take us / Where can you go / Double cross / Dreams / Are you lonely for me / Turn on your love light / Oncoming traffic / Will the circle be unbroken?. *(cd-iss. Oct87 on 'Polydor'; 831 940-2)*

—— retained **BILL STEWART** and brought in **STEVE BECKMEIER + JOHN HUG** – guitar / **RICKY HIRSCH** – slide guitar / **NEIL LARSEN** – piano / **WILLIE WEEKS** – bass

Jun 77. (lp) *(2476 131) <0181>* **PLAYIN' UP A STORM** 42
– Come and go blues / Let this be a lesson to ya / The brightest smile in town / Bring it on back / Cryin' shame / Sweet feelin' / It ain't no use / Matthew's arrival / One more try.

Aug 77. (7") *<0279>* **CRYIN' SHAME. / ONE MORE TRY** –

ALLMAN AND WOMAN

the (Woman being GREGG's wife and singer CHER) (same line-up)

Warners Warners

Nov 77. (lp) *(K 56436) <3120>* **TWO THE HARD WAY**
– Move me / I found you love / Can you fool / You've really got a hold on me / We're gonna make it / Do what you gotta do / In for the night / Shadow dream song / Island / I love makin' love to you / Love me.

Dec 77. (7") *(K 17057) <8504>* **LOVE ME. / MOVE ME**

—— they subsequently split and were divorced on 16th of January '79

The ALLMAN BROTHERS BAND

—— re-formed 1989, **GREGG, DICKEY, JAIMO, BUTCH** and newcomers **ALLEN WOODY** – bass / **WARREN HAYES** – guitar / **JOHNNY NEEL** – keyboards

Epic Epic

Jul 90. (7") *<73504>* **GOOD CLEAN FUN. / SEVEN TURNS** –

Jul 90. (cd/c/lp) *(466850-2/-4/-1) <46144>* **SEVEN TURNS** 53
– Good clean fun / Let me ride / Low down dirty mean / Shine it on / Loaded dice / Seven turns / Gambler's roll / True gravity / It ain't over yet.

Sep 90. (7") *<73583>* **SEVEN TURNS. / LET ME RIDE** –

Jul 91. (cd/c/lp) *(468525-2/-4/-1) <47877>* **SHADES OF TWO WORLDS** 85
– End of the line / Bad rain / Nobody knows / Desert blues / Get on with your life / Midnight man / Kind of bird / Come on in my kitchen.

Jun 92. (cd/c) *<48998-2/-4>* **AN EVENING WITH THE ALLMAN BROTHERS BAND** –
– Southbound / Nobody knows / Revival (love is everywhere) / Midnight blues / Get on with your life / Dreams / End of the line / Blue sky.

—— **MARC QUINONES** – congas, percussion; repl. NEEL

Jul 94. (cd/c) *(476884-2/-4) <64232>* **WHERE IT ALL BEGINS** May94
– All night train / Sailin' 'cross the Devil's sea / Back where it all begins / Soulshine / No one to run with / Change my way of living / Mean woman blues / Everybody's got a mountain to climb / What's done is done / Temptation is a gun.

May 95. (cd,c) *<66795>* **2ND SET – AN EVENING WITH THE ALLMAN BROTHERS BAND** – 88
– Sailin' 'cross the Devil's sea / You don't love me / Soul shine / Back where it all begins / In memory of Elizabeth Reed / Same thing / No one to run with / Jessica. *(UK-iss.Apr99; 480606-2)*

—— added **DEREK TRUCKS** – guitar

Nov 00. (cd) *<85205>* **PEAKIN' AT THE BEACON (live)** –
– Don't want you no more / It's not my cross to bear / Ain't wastin' time no more / Every hungry woman / Please call home / Stand back / Black hearted woman / Leave my blues alone / Seven turns / High falls.

—— **GREGG** plus **WARREN HAYNES** – guitars, vocals / **DEREK TRUCKS** – guitars / **OTEIL BURBRIDGE** – bass / **JAIMOE** – drums / **MARC QUINONES** – percussion

Sanctuary Sanctuary

Apr 03. (cd) *(SANCD 170) <84599>* **HITTIN' THE NOTE** Mar03 37
– Firing line / High cost of low living / Desdemona / Woman across the river / Old before my time / Who to believe / Maydell / Rockin' horse / Heart of stone / Instrumental illness / Old friend.

– DUANE & GREGG ALLMAN compilations, etc. –

1972. (7") *Bold;* **MORNING DEW. / (pt. 2)** –

1973. (lp) *Polydor; (2310 235) / Bold; <33-301>* **DUANE & GREGG ALLMAN** (rec.'68)
– Morning dew / God rest his soul / Nobody knows when you're down and out / Come down and get me / Melissa / I'll change for you / Back down home with you / Well I know too well / In the morning when I'm real.

– ALLMAN BROTHERS compilations, etc. –

Oct 73. (lp; as ALLMAN JOYS) *Mercury; (6398 005) / Dial; <6005>* **EARLY ALLMANS**

Nov 74. (d-lp) *Capricorn; (60046) / Atco; <805>* **BEGINNINGS** Mar73 25
– (first 2 ALLMAN BROTHERS BAND lp's) *(cd-iss. Oct87 on 'Polydor'; 827 588-2) (cd re-iss. Jun98; 531259-2)*

1974. (7") *Capricorn; <0050>* **AIN'T WASTIN' TIME NO MORE. / BLUE SKY** –

1974. (7") *Capricorn; <0051>* **MELISSA. / RAMBLIN' MAN** –

Feb 76. (d-lp) *Capricorn; (2637 101) <0164>* **THE ROAD GOES ON FOREVER** 54 Dec75 43
– Black hearted woman / Dreams / Whipping post / Midnight rider / Statesboro blues / Stormy Monday / Hoochie coochie man / Stand back / One way out / Blue sky / Hot 'Lanta / Ain't wastin' time no more / Melissa / Wasted words / Jessica / Ramblin' man / Little Martha.

Dec 76. (d-lp) *Capricorn; (2637 103) <0177>* **WIPE THE WINDOWS, CHECK THE OIL, DOLLAR GAS** (demos, rarities recorded live) 75
– (introduction) / Wasted words / Southbound / Ramblin' man / In memory of Elizabeth Reed / Ain't wastin' time no more / Come and go blues / Can't lose what you never had / Don't want you no more / It's not my cross to bear / Jessica. *(cd-iss. Jun98; 531264-2)*

Aug 80. (lp) *Capricorn; <6339>* **THE BEST OF THE ALLMAN BROTHERS BAND** Nov81

Jun 81. (d-lp) *Capricorn; (2637 105)* **THE STORY OF THE ALLMAN BROTHERS BAND**

Sep 83. (12"ep) *Polydor; (POSP 607)* **JESSICA / SOUTHBOUND. / WHIPPIN' POST / RAMBLIN' MAN** –

Jul 84. (7") *Old Gold; (OG 9437)* **JESSICA. / RAMBLIN' MAN** –

Sep 85. (lp; as HOURGLASS) *C5; (C5-524)* **THE SOUL OF TIME** –

Feb 88. (7") *Old Gold; (OG 4046)* **JESSICA. / (b-side by; Derek & The Dominoes')** –

Jul 88. (lp/c) *Knight; (KNLP/KNMC 10004)* **NIGHTRIDING** –
(cd-iss. Sep89; KNCD 10004)

Apr 89. (6xlp/4xc/4xcd) *Polydor; <(839417-1/-4/-2)>* **DREAMS** Jul89

Jul 90. (d-cd) *Polydor; (843260-2)* **LIVE AT LUDLOW GARAGE 1970 (live)** –

May 92. (cd/c) *Polydor; (511156-2/-4)* **A DECADE OF HITS 1969-1979** ☐ Nov91 ☐
– Statesboro blues / Ramblin' man / Midnight rider / Southbound / Melissa / Jessica / Ain't wastin' time no more / Little Martha / Crazy love / Revival / Wasted words / Blue sky / One way out / In memory of Elizabeth Reed / Dreams / Whipping post.

May 92. (cd/c) *Castle; (CCS CD/MC 327)* **THE COLLECTION** ☐ -
Sep 94. (cd) *R.C.A.; (0782 218724-2)* **HELL & HIGH WATER (The Best Of The Arista Years)** ☐ -
Mar 93. (d-cd) *Polydor; (517 294-2)* **THE FILLMORE CONCERTS (live)** ☐ ☐
Mar 98. (cd) *Camden; (74321 5696124)* **MADNESS OF THE WEST** ☐ -
Jun 98. (cd/c) *Epic; (489087-2/-4)* **MYCOLOGY** ☐ ☐
Sep 98. (cd) *Spectrum; (551824-2)* **THE BEST OF THE ALLMAN BROTHERS BAND LIVE (live)** ☐ -
Jan 00. (cd) *Universal; (E 543405-2)* **UNIVERSAL MASTERS COLLECTION** ☐ -
Mar 03. (cd) *Universal; (AA314 547899-2)* **20th CENTURY MASTERS** ☐ ☐

DUANE ALLMAN

exploitation compilations featuring all his guitar/sessions

Oct 74. (d-lp) *Capricorn; <2CP 0108>* **AN ANTHOLOGY** ☐ Dec72 28
– B.B. King medley / Hey Jude / The road of love / Goin' down slow / The weight / Games people play / Shake for me / Loan me a dime / Rollin' stone / Livin' on the open road / Down along the cove / lease be with me / Mean old world / Layla / Statesboro blues / Don't keep me wondering / Stand back / Dreams / Little Martha. *(d-cd.iss.Oct87 on 'Polydor'; 831 444-2)*

Jan 75. (d-lp) *Capricorn; <CPN2-0139>* **AN ANTHOLOGY VOL.2** ☐ Jul74 49
– Happily married man / It ain't fair / The weight / You reap what you sow / Matchbox / Born to be wild / No money down / Been gone too long / Stuff you gotta watch / Push push / Walk on gilded splinters / Waiting for a train / Don't tell me your troubles / Goin' upstairs / Come on in my kitchen / Dimples / Goin' up the country / Done somebody wrong / Leave my blues at home / Midnight rider. *(d-cd.iss.Oct87 on 'Polydor'; 831 445-2)*

Sep 79. (lp) *Capricorn; (242 919-8)* **THE BEST OF DUANE ALLMAN** ☐ -

Marc ALMOND

Born: PETER MARC ALMOND, 9 Jul'59, Southport, England. Having met DAVE BALL at Leeds Polytechnic, the pair formed SOFT CELL and with the help of visual technician, STEVEN GRIFFITHS, they embarked on studio and live work in 1980 with the 'MUTANT MOMENTS' EP. After appearing on the infamous 'Some Bizzare Album', with cut, 'The Girl With The Patent Leather Face', they secured a bonafide deal with the 'Some Bizzare' label. The following year, after a debut single, 'MEMORABILIA' failed to make an impression, a darkly compelling, electro-fuelled cover of 'TAINTED LOVE' (once the dancefloor domain of disco diva, GLORIA JONES) slipped in to the UK chart, peaking at No.1 for two weeks. To end the year, SOFT CELL cracked the Top 5 with both 'BEDSITTER' and their debut album, 'NON-STOP EROTIC CABARET', an early 80's classic which trawled the depths of ALMOND's black-leather, neon-lit fantasies to a sleazy musical backdrop of low-rent alternative disco. Apart from the aforementioned singles, tracks such as 'YOUTH', 'SEX DWARF', 'SEEDY FILMS', 'CHIPS ON MY SHOULDER' and the forthcoming hit, 'SAY HELLO, WAVE GOODBYE', even found a rampant audience in the gay disco community of New York. The extroverted ALMOND was a figurehead for young homosexuals, although the media were scathing in their criticism of what they saw as the singer's effeminate posturing. Nevertheless, SOFT CELL continued to chalk up the hits, 'TORCH' (an exquisite duet featuring CINDY ECSTACY) narrowly missing No.1, while a revamped dance model of the debut, 'NON-STOP ECSTATIC DANCING', marked time as BALL and ALMOND worked on a follow-up. Early in '83, their second set proper, 'THE ART OF FALLING APART', hit the shops and subsequently the Top 5, the record coming with a free 12" single that saw ALMOND bravely attempting a HENDRIX medley. As the pair increasingly concentrated on separate projects, MARC & THE MAMBAS and DAVE BALL solo, a split seemed imminent; by the release of 'THIS LAST NIGHT . . . IN SODOM' in January '84, SOFT CELL was no more. After many threats of impending retirement, ALMOND was back in his beloved spotlight with the 'VERMIN IN ERMINE' (1984) album, cut with new backing band, The WILLING SINNERS. Developing further as an interpretive balladeer/torch singer with each successive release, ALMOND's mid-late 80's output found him marginalised to cult appeal despite an impressive array of cover material from such luminaries as JACQUES BREL, SCOTT WALKER and JOHNNIE RAY. This approach finally resulted in a massive comeback hit duet with GENE PITNEY, the melodramatic 'SOMETHING'S GOTTEN HOLD OF MY HEART', originally a Top 5 hit in 1967 for the singing/songwriting heart-throb. In the early 90's, SOFT CELL enjoyed a bit of a renaissance, remixed versions of 'SAY HELLO WAVE GOODBYE' and 'TAINTED LOVE' making the charts, while ALMOND scored a surprise Top 20 hit with a dancefloor reworking of Jacques Brel's 'JACKY'. Taken from the album, 'TENEMENT SYMPHONY' (1991), this return to form also numbered future hits, 'MY HAND OVER MY HEART' and 'THE DAYS OF PEARLY SPENCER', the latter another blast from the 60's past and originally a hit for DAVID McWILLIAMS. ALMOND continued to work on various idiosyncratic projects, including a set of old French songs and poems, 'ABSINTHE' (1993). Having delivered what was to be a one-off album ('FANTASTIC STAR') for 'Mercury' in early '96, the long-suffering tainted soul that was MARC ALMOND made his re-appearance with the single 'BLACK KISS' in late '98. Having set up his own record label, 'Blue Star', the wee man unleashed his most advanced work since the early days in the shape of 'OPEN ALL NIGHT' (1999). With rave reviews (for once!), ALMOND set about publishing two works, the first a lyrics/poems collection entitled 'A Beautiful Twisted Night', the second an autobiography 'Tainted Life'. 'STRANGER THINGS' (2001) happened to ALMOND in the new millennium as he joined forces with Icelandic leftfield beats merchant JOHAN JOHANNSON. Well, not that strange, merely a trip into more widescreen territory courtesy of JOHANNSON's luxuriant string arrangements, the record even featuring the obligatory guest spot from SHIRLEY BASSEY to add that crucial 007 touch. Spurred on by a UK Top 40 "BEST OF . . ." compilation and with nearly every other post-New Wave outfit re-forming to rake in the spoils of money (or credibility!), it was no surprise that messrs ALMOND and BALL would resurrect SOFT CELL; it had been a full 18 years since their . . . er 'LAST NIGHT IN SODOM' came out. 'CRUELTY WITHOUT BEAUTY' (2002), stepped back to these heady days of yore. Opening with 'DARKER TIMES' and the minor hit single, 'MONOCULTURE', the set showed what might've been had ALMOND not ventured to croon land. • **Covered:** WHERE DID OUR LOVE GO (Supremes). MARC & THE MAMBAS covered IF YOU GO AWAY + THE BULLS (Jacques Brel) / CAROLINE SAYS (Lou Reed) / TERRAPIN (Syd Barrett) / CATCH A FALLEN STAR (Perry Como). MARC ALMOND solo:- A WOMAN'S STORY (Cher) / A SALTY DOG (Procol Harum) / THE LITTLE WHITE CLOUD THAT CRIED (Johnnie Ray) / THE PLAGUE (Scott Walker). • **Trivia:** In 1983, DAVE BALL scored the music for

Tennessee Williams' play 'Suddenly Last Summer'. In mid 1987, ALMOND guested and wrote on SALLY TIMMS' single 'This House Is A House Of Tears'.

Album rating: Soft Cell: NON-STOP EROTIC CABARET (*8) / NON-STOP ECSTATIC DANCING remix collection (*4) / THE ART OF FALLING APART (*6) / THIS LAST NIGHT ... IN SODOM (*5) / MEMORABILIA – THE SINGLES compilation (*8) / Marc And The Mambas: UNTITLED (*8) / TORMENT AND TOREROS (*5) / Marc Almond: VERMIN IN ERMINE (*5) / STORIES OF JOHNNY (*5) / MOTHER FIST AND HER FIVE DAUGHTERS (*4) / THE STARS WE ARE (*5) / JACQUES (*5) / ENCHANTMENT (*5) / TENEMENT SYMPHONY (*4) / TWELVE YEARS OF TEARS (*5) / ABSINTHE (*5) / FANTASTIC STAR (*5) / THE SINGLES (1984-1987) compilation (*7) / THE BEST OF MARC ALMOND compilation (*6) / OPEN ALL NIGHT (*7) / STRANGER THINGS (*6)

SOFT CELL

MARC ALMOND – vocals / **DAVE BALL** – keyboards, synthesizer, drum programming

Big Frock / not iss.

1980. (7"ep) *(ABF 1)* **MUTANT MOMENTS** [ ] [–]
– Potential / L.O.V.E. feelings / Metro MRX / Frustration.

Some Bizzare / Sire

Mar 81. (7") *(HARD 1)* **MEMORABILIA. / A MAN CAN GET LOST** [ ] [–]
(12") *(HARD 12)* – ('A'extended) / Persuasion (extended).

Jul 81. (7") *(BZS 2)* <49855> **TAINTED LOVE. / WHERE DID OUR LOVE GO** [1] Dec81 [8]
(12"+=) *(BZS 2-12)* – Tainted dub / Memorabilia.
(re-iss. Jul82; hit 50, re-iss. Jan85; hit 43)

Nov 81. (7"/ext-12") *(BZS 6/+12)* **BEDSITTER. / FACILITY GIRLS** [4] [ ]

—— guests **CINDY ECSTACY** – dual vox / **DAVE TOFANI** – sax / **JOHN GATHELL** – trumpet

Dec 81. (lp/c) *(BZ LP/MC 2)* <3647> **NON-STOP EROTIC CABARET** [5] Jan82 [22]
– Frustration / Tainted love / Seedy films / Youth / Sex dwarf / Entertain me / Chips on my shoulder / Bedsitter / Secret life / Say hello, wave goodbye. *(re-iss. May90 on 'Vertigo' cd/c/lp; 800 061-2/-4/-1)*

Jan 82. (7"/ext-12") *(BZS 7/+12)* **SAY HELLO, WAVE GOODBYE. / FUN CITY** [3] [ ]

May 82. (7"/ext-12") *(BZS 9/+12)* **TORCH. / INSECURE ME** [2] [ ]

—— duo carried on without CINDY, who later formed SIX SEE RED

Jun 82. (m-lp/m-c) *(BZ X/M 1012)* <23694> **NON-STOP ECSTATIC DANCING** (remixes) [6] Jul82 [57]
– Memorabilia / Where did our love go / What! / A man could get lost / Chips on my shoulder * / Sex dwarf. *<US version repl.* with =)* – Insecure ... me? *(re-iss. Mar92 on 'Mercury' cd/c; 510 295-2/-4)* – (extra tracks).

Aug 82. (7"/ext-12") *(BZS 11/+12)* **WHAT! / ... SO (remix)** [3] [ ]

Nov 82. (7"/ext-12") *(BZS 16/+12)* **WHERE THE HEART IS. / IT'S A MUG GAME** [21] [ ]

Feb 83. (lp/c) *(BIZL/+C 3)* <23769> **THE ART OF FALLING APART** [5] [84]
– Forever the same / Where the heart is / Numbers / Heat / Kitchen sink drama / Baby doll / Loving you, hating me / The art of falling apart. *(12"ep with above +=)* – MARTIN. / HENDRIX MEDLEY: HEY JOE – PURPLE HAZE – VOODOO CHILE *(re-iss. Nov87; SOD 2) (re-iss. Mar92 on 'Mercury' cd/c; 510 296-2/-4)* – (extra tracks).

Feb 83. (7"/ext-12") *(BZS 16/+12)* **NUMBERS. / BARRIERS** [25] [–]

Apr 83. (7") **HEAT. / IT'S A MUGS GAME** [–] [ ]

Sep 83. (7") *(BZS 20)* **SOUL INSIDE. / YOU ONLY LIVE TWICE** [16] [–]
(12"+=) *(BZS 20-12)* – Loving you, hating me / 007 theme.
(d7"+=) *(BZS 20-20)* – Loving you, hating me / Her imagination.

Feb 84. (7") *(BZS 22)* **DOWN IN THE SUBWAY. / DISEASE AND DESIRE** [24] [–]
(ext-12"+=/12"remix+=) *(BZS/+R 22-12)* – Born to lose.

Mar 84. (lp/c) *(BIZL/+C 6)* **THIS LAST NIGHT ... IN SODOM** [12] [–]
– Mr. Self destruct / Slave to this / Little rough rhinestone / Meet murder my angel / The best way to kill / L'Esqualita / Down in the subway / Surrender (to a stranger) / Soul inside / Where was your heart (when you needed it most). *(cd-iss. Aug84; 818 436-2)*

—— split just prior to the above album

– compilations, others, etc. –

1982. (6x12"box) *Some Bizzare; (CELBX 1)* **THE 12" SINGLES** [ ] [–]

Dec 86. (lp/c)(cd) *Some Bizzare; (BZ LP/MC 3)(830 708-2)* **SOFT CELL – THE SINGLES** [58] [–]

Mar 91. (7"/c-s) *Mercury; (SOF T/MC 1)* **SAY HELLO, WAVE GOODBYE '91. / MEMORABILIA (Grid remix)** [38] [–]
(12"+=)(cd-s+=) *(SOFT 1-12)(SOFCD 1)* – ('A'-Mendelsohn extended remix).
(cd-s) *(SOFCP 1)* – ('A'side) / Numbers / Torch (12"version).

May 91. (7"/c-s)(12") *Mercury; (SOF T/MC 2)(SOFT 2-12)* **TAINTED LOVE ('91 remix). / ('A'-Original)** [5] [–]
(cd-s+=) *(SOFCP 2)* – Where did our love go?
(cd-s) *(SOFCD 2)* – Tainted love – Where the heart is / Loving you – hating me / Where the heart is.

May 91. (cd/c/lp) *Mercury; (848 512-2/-4/-1)* **MEMORABILIA – THE SINGLES** [8] [ ]
– Memorabilia '91 / Tainted love / Bedsitter / Torch / What was the matter with Rachmaninov? / Say hello wave goodbye '91 / Where the heart is / I feel love / Tears run rings / A lover spurned / Something's gotten hold of my heart. *(cd+=)* – (Soul inside / Say hello wave goodbye (12"mix) / Waifs and strays (Grid twilight mix).

Mar 94. (cd/c) *Spectrum; (550 189-2/-4)* **DOWN IN THE SUBWAY** [ ] [–]

Mar 96. (cd) *Some Bizarre; (552 086-2)* **SAY HELLO TO SOFT CELL** [ ] [–]

Feb 99. (12"; as SOFT CELL vs CLUB 69) *Twisted; (TWD 55530)* **TAINTED LOVE** [ ] [–]

Apr 02. (cd) *Mercury; (586834-2)* <586912> **THE VERY BEST OF SOFT CELL** [37] [ ]
– Memorabilia / Tainted love / Where did our love go? / Bedsitter / Say hello, wave goodbye / Sex dwarf / Torch / Insecure me / What? / Where the heart is / It's a mugs game / Numbers / Loving you hating me / Soul inside / Down in the subway / Somebody, somewhere, sometime / Divided soul / Tainted love (2XS remix) / Say hello, wave goodbye (almighty radio mix).

MARC AND THE MAMBAS

with **ANNIE HOGAN** – piano / **TIM TAYLOR** – bass / **DAVE BALL** – multi instruments

Mar 82. (12"; mail order) *(BZS 5-12)* **FUN CITY. / SLEAZE (TAKE IT, SHAKE IT) / TAKING IT SHAKING IT** [–] [–]

—— guests on next 2 albums were **GENESIS P. ORRIDGE + MATT JOHNSON**

Oct 82. (lp/c) *(BZA/BZC 13)* **UNTITLED** [42] [–]
– Untitled / Empty eyes / Angels / Big Louise / Caroline says / Margaret / If you go away. *(free-12"ep with above +=)* – Terrapin / Twilights and lowlifes (street walking soundtrack) / Twilights and lowlifes. *(re-iss. Mar92 on 'Mercury' cd/c; 510 298-2/-4)*

Nov 82. (7";w-drawn) *(BZS 15)* **BIG LOUISE. / EMPTY EYES** [–] [–]
(12";w-drawn+=) *(BZS 15-12)* – The dirt behind the neon.

Jun 83. (7") *(BZS 19)* **BLACK HEART. / YOUR AURA** [49] [–]
(12"+=) *(BZS 19-12)* – Mamba.

Aug 83. (d-lp/c) *(BIZL/+C 4)* **TORMENT AND TOREROS** [28] [–]
– The animal in you / Narcissus / Gloomy Sunday / Vision / Your love is a lesson / The untouchable one / My little book of sorrows / In my room / First time / The bulls / Boss cat / Intro / Catch a fallen star / Beat out dat rhythm on a drum / A million manias / Torment / Black heart. *(re-iss. Mar92 on 'Mercury' cd/c; 812 872-2/-4) (cd re-iss. Oct97; SBZCD 028CD)*

Nov 83. (12"ep) *(BZS 21-12)* **TORMENT / FIRST TIME. / YOU'LL NEVER SEE ME ON A SUNDAY / MAGAMILLIONMANIA-MULTIMANIAMIX** [ ] [–]

MARC ALMOND

—— went solo augmented by **The WILLING SINNERS: ANNIE HOGAN** – piano / **BILLY McGEE** – bass / **RICHARD RILEY** – guitar / **STEPHEN HUMPHRIES** – drums / **MARTIN McCARRICK** – cello

May 84. (7") *(BZS 23)* **THE BOY WHO CAME BACK. / JOEY DEMENTO** [52] [ ]
(10"/12") *(BZS 23 10/12)* – ('A'-Loud cut) / ('B'extended).

Sep 84. (7") *(BZS 24)* **YOU HAVE. / SPLIT UP** [57] [ ]
(ext-10"+=) *(BZS 24-10)* – Black mountain blues.
(ext-12"+=) *(BZS 24-12)* – Joey Demento.

Oct 84. (lp/c)(cd) *(BIZL/+C 8)(<822 832-2>)* **VERMINE IN ERMINE** [36] [ ]

– Shining sinners / Hell was a city / You have / Crime sublime / Gutter hearts / Ugly head / The boy who came back / Solo adultos / Tenderness is a weakness. *(c+=/cd+=)* – Pink shack blues / Split lip / Joey Demento.

Nov 84. (7") *(BZS 25)* **TENDERNESS IS A WEAKNESS. / LOVE FOR SALE** [ ] [–]
(10"+=) *(BZS 25-10)* – Pink shack blues (live) / The heel (live).

—— In April '85, he teamed up with BRONSKI BEAT on Top 3 version of 'I FEEL LOVE'. Two months later, he featured anonymously on 12" 'SKIN' as The BURMOE BROTHERS

Aug 85. (7") *(BONK 1)* **STORIES OF JOHNNY. / STORIES OF JOHNNY (with The Westminster City School Choir)** [23] [–]
(12"+=) *(BONK 1-12)* – Take my heart.
(d7"++=/10"++=) *(BONK 1/+10)* – Blond boy.

Sep 85. (lp/c/cd) *(FAITH/TFTH/CDFTH 1)* **STORIES OF JOHNNY** [22] [–]
– Traumas, traumas, traumas / Stories of Johnny / The house is haunted (by the echoes of your last goodbye) / Love letter / The flesh is willing / Always / Contempt / I who never / My candle burns / Love and little white lies. *(c+=/cd+=)* – Take my heart / Blond boy / Stories of Johnny (with The Westminster City School Choir). *<US cd-iss. 1997 on 'Thirsty Ear'; 57039>*

Oct 85. (7") *(BONKP 2)* **LOVE LETTER. / LOVE LETTER (with The Westmonster City School Choir)** [68] [–]
(10"/12") *(BONK 2 10/12)* – ('A'-Special mix) / ('B'side).

Jan 86. (d7") *(GLOW D1)* **THE HOUSE IS HAUNTED (BY THE ECHO OF YOUR LAST GOODBYE). / BROKEN BARRICADES // CARA A CARA (FACE TO FACE). / MEDLEY: (UNCHAIN MY HEART – BLACK HEART – TAKE MY HEART)** [55] [–]
('A'-Ectoplasm mix-12"+=) *(GLOW 1-12)* – Burning boats.

May 86. (7") *(GLOW 2)* **A WOMAN'S STORY. / FOR ONE MOMENT** [41] [ ]
(c-ep+=)(10"pic-d-ep+=)(12"ep+=) **SOME SONGS TO TAKE TO THE TOMB EP** *(TGLOW 2-12)(GLOWY 2-10)(GLOW 2-12)* – The heel / A salty dog / The plague / The little white cloud that cried / Just good friends.

Oct 86. (7") *(GLOW 3)* **RUBY RED. / I'M SICK OF YOU TASTING OF SOMEONE ELSE** [47] [–]
('A'-Arnacoma mix-12"+=) *(GLOW 3-12)* – Broken hearted and beautiful / Jackal jackal (Mustapha Tomb Stone Teeth).
('A'ext.dance mix-12") *(GLOW 3-13)* – ('A'instrumental).

Jan 87. (7") *(GLOW 4)* **MELANCHOLY ROSE. / GYP THE BLOOD** [71] [–]
(12"+=) *(GLOW 4-12)* – A world full of people / Black lullaby.
(d7+=) *(GLOWD 4)* – Surabaya Johnny / Pirate Jenny.

Mar 87. (lp/c/cd) *(FAITH/TFTH/CDFTH 2)* **MOTHER FIST AND HER FIVE DAUGHTERS** [40] [–]
– Mother Fist / There is a bed / Saint Judy / The room below / Angel in her kiss / The hustler / Melancholy rose / Mr. Sad / The sea says / Champ / Ruby red / The river. *<US cd-iss. 1997 on 'Thirsty Ear'; 57038>*

Mar 87. (7") *(GLOW 5)* **MOTHER FIST. / TWO SAILORS ON THE BEACH** [ ] [–]
(12"+=) *(GLOW 5-12)* – The hustler.

Nov 87. (lp/c/cd) *(FAITH/TFTH/CDFTH 3)* **THE SINGLES 1984-1987** (compilation) [ ] [–]
– The boy who came back / You have / Tenderness is a weakness / Stories of Johnny / Love letters / The house is haunted / A woman's story / Ruby red / Melancholy rose / Mother Fist.

—— He was now backed by LA MAGIA. (aka HOGAN, HUMPHRIES + McGEE)

Parlophone Capitol

Aug 88. (7"/7"box) *(R/RX 6186)* *<44240>* **TEARS RUN RINGS. / EVERYTHING I WANTED LOVE TO BE** [26] Jan89 [67]
(12"+=/cd-s+=) *(12R/CDR 6186)* – ('A'extended).
('A'-Justin Strauss mix-12"+=) *(12RX 6186)* – ('A'-La Magia dance mix).

Sep 88. (cd/c/lp) *(CD/TC+/PCS 7324)* *<91042>* **THE STARS WE ARE** [41] Jan89 [ ]
– The stars we are / These my dreams are true / Bitter sweet / Only the moment / Your kisses burn / Tears run rings / Something's gotten hold of my heart / The sensualist / She took my soul in Instanbul. *(c+=/cd+=)* – The frost comes tomorrow / Kept boy. *(cd re-iss. Apr02 on 'E.M.I.'+=; 539176-2)* – Something's gotten hold of my heart (w/ GENE PITNEY).

Oct 88. (7"/7"g-f/7"clear) *(R/RG/RC 6194)* **BITTER SWEET. / KING OF THE FOOLS** [40] [–]
(12"+=/12"g-f+=/12"etched+=/'A'-Big Beat mix-12"+=/cd-s+=) *(12R/12RG/12RS/12RX/CDR 6194)* – Tears run rings (Justin Strauss remix).

Jan 89. (7"/7"box; by MARC ALMOND & GENE PITNEY) *(R/RX 6201)* **SOMETHING'S GOTTEN HOLD OF MY HEART. / ('A'-solo version)** [1] [ ]
(12"+=/12"etched+=/cd-s+=) *(12R/12RS/CDR 6201)* – The frost comes tomorrow.

Mar 89. (7",7"clear) *(R 6210)* **ONLY THE MOMENT. / REAL EVIL** [47] [–]
(cd-s+=) *(CDR 6210)* – She took my soul in Instanbul (The Blue Mosque mix).
(12"/12"etched) *(12R/+S 6210)* – ('A'-All The Time In The World mix) / She took my soul in Istanbul (The Blue Mosque mix).

Feb 90. (7"/ext-7"square-pic-d/ext-c-s) *(R/RPD/TCR 6229)* **A LOVER SPURNED. / EXOTICA ROSE** [29] [–]
(12"+=/cd-s+=) *(12R/CDR 6229)* – ('A'version).

May 90. (c-s/7") *(TC+/R 6252)* **THE DESPERATE HOURS. / THE GAMBLER** [45] [–]
(12"+=/12"clear-pic-d+=/cd-s+=) *(12R/12RPD/CDR 6252)* – ('A'extended Flamenco mix).

Jun 90. (cd/c/lp) *(CD/TC+/PCS 7344)* *<94404>* **ENCHANTED** [52] [ ]
– Madame de la luna / Waifs and strays / The desperate hours / Toreador in the rain / Widow weeds / A lover spurned / Death's diary / Sea still sings / Carnival of life / Orpheus in red velvet. *(cd re-iss. Apr02 on 'E.M.I.'; 539177-2)*

Oct 90. (c-s/7") *(TC+/R 6263)* **WAIFS AND STRAYS. / OLD JACK'S CHARM** [ ] [–]
(12") *(12R 6263)* – (2 'A'-Grid mixes).
(cd-s+=) *(CDR 6263)* – City of nights.

—— Wrote w/**DAVE BALL + NORRIS** (The GRID)

W.E.A. Sire

Sep 91. (7"/c-s) *(YZ 610/+C)* **JACKY. / DEEP NIGHT** [17] [–]
(12"+=) *(YZ 610T)* – ('A'-Alpine dub).
(cd-s+=) *(YZ 610CD)* – A love outgrown.

Oct 91. (cd/c/lp) *(9031 75518-2/-4/-1)* *<26764>* **TENEMENT SYMPHONY** [39] [ ]
– Meet me in my dream / Beautiful brutal thing / I've never seen your face / Vaudeville and burlesque / Champagne / Tenement symphony (i) Prelude, (ii) Jacky, (iii) What is love?, (iv) Trois Chansons de Bilitis – extract, (v) The days of Pearly Spencer, (vi) My hand over my heart. *(re-iss. cd Feb95; same)*

Dec 91. (7"/c-s) *(YZ 633/+C)* **MY HAND OVER MY HEART. / DEADLY SERENADE** [33] [–]
(12"pic-d) *(YZ 633TP)* – ('A'-Grit & Glitter mix) / Money for love (2 versions).
(cd-s) *(YZ 633CD)* – (above 3 tracks) / Night and no morning.

Apr 92. (7"/c-s) *(YZ 638/+C)* **THE DAYS OF PEARLY SPENCER. / BRUISES** [4] [–]
(cd-s+=) *(YZ 638CD)* – Dancing in a golden cage / Extract from 'Trois Chanson De Bilitis'.

—— with **DAVE CLAYTON** – keyboards, musical director / **MARTIN WATKINS** – piano / **ANDY HAMILTON** – saxophone / **MICHELE DREES** – drums, perc. / **CRIS BONACCI** – guitars / **SHIRLEY LEWIS, ANNA ROSS & AILEEN McLAUGHLIN** – b.vox / **TENEMENT SYMPHONY ORCH.**

Mar 93. (7"/c-s) *(YZ 720/+C)* **WHAT MAKES A MAN A MAN (live). / TORCH (live)** [60] [–]
(cd-s+=) *(YZ 720CD)* – The stars we are (live).
(cd-s) *(YZ 720CDX)* – ('A'side) / Tainted love (live) / Vision (live) / Only the moment (live).

Apr 93. (cd/c/lp) *(4509 92033-2/-4/-1)* *<45247>* **12 YEARS OF TEARS – LIVE AT THE ROYAL ALBERT HALL (live)** [ ] May93 [ ]
– Tears run rings / Champagne / Bedsitter / Mr. Sad / There is a bed / Youth / If you go away / Jacky / Desperate hours / Waifs and strays / Something's gotten hold of my heart / What makes a man a man / Tainted love / Say hello wave goodbye.

Some Bizzare not iss.

Sep 93. (cd/c/lp) *(SBZ CD/MC/LP 10)* **ABSINTHE: THE FRENCH ALBUM** [ ] [–]
– Undress me / Abel and Cain / Lost Paradise / Secret child / Rue Des Blancs Manteaux / The slave / Remorse of the dead / Incestuous love / A man / My little lovers / In your bed / Yesterday when I was young. *<US cd-iss. 1996 on 'Thirsty Ear'; 57026>*

Mercury Mercury

Apr 95. (c-s) *(MERMC 431)* **ADORED AND EXPLORED / ('A'-original)** [25] [–]
(cd-s) *(MERCD 431)* – ('A'side) / The user / Loveless world / ('A'-Andy Meecham's Slow Fat dub).

(cd-s) *(MERDD 431)* – ('A'side) / ('A'-Beatmasters 12 take 1) / ('A'-Andy Meecham club mix) / ('A'-X-Press 2 extre,me excess mix).

Jul 95. (c-s) *(MERMC 437)* **THE IDOL / ('A'-Tin Tin Out mix)** [44] [–]
(cd-s+=) *(MERDD 437)* – ('A'-Idolized mix) / ('A'-Teenage dream mix).
(cd-s) *(MERCD 437)* – ('A'-part 1) / Law of the night / Adored and explored (live) / Bedsitter (live).

Nov 95. (c-s) *(MERMC 450)* **CHILD STAR / EDGE OF HEARTBREAK** [41] [–]
(cd-ep+=) **CHILD STAR EP** *(MERCD 450)* – Christmas in Vegas / My guardian angel.
(cd-ep) **CHILD STAR EP** *(MERDD 450)* – ('A'side) / We need jealousy (live) / The idol (live) / Out there (live).

Feb 96. (c-s) *(MERMC 444)* **OUT THERE / BRILLIANT CREATURES** [ ] [–]
(cd-s+=) *(MERCD 444)* – Lie (Beatmasters mix) / Lie.
(12") *(MERX 444)* – ('A'mixes:- Tony De Vite parts 1 & 2 / Non Eric / House Of Usher / Valerie Singleton).

Feb 96. (cd/c) *(528 659-2/-4)* **FANTASTIC STAR** [54] [–]
– Caged / Out there / We need jealousy / Idol (parts 1 & 2) / All gods fall / Baby night eyes / Adored and explored / Child star / Looking for love (in all the wrong places) / Addicted / Edge of heartbreak / Love to die for / Betrayed / On the prowl / Come in sweet assassin / Brilliant creatures / Shining brightly. *(cd re-iss. Sep97; same)*

—— In Dec'96, MARC was credited on PJ PROBY minor hit single 'YESTERDAY HAS GONE' on 'EMI Premier' (PRESTC/CDPRES/CDPRESX 13).

Echo Instinct

Nov 98. (7"pic-d) *(ECS 58)* **BLACK KISS. / ('A'-DJ mix)** [ ] [–]
(cd-s) *(ECSCD 58)* – ('A'side) / Satan's child / ('A'live).

Blue Star Incense

Mar 99. (cd-s) *(BSRS 001)* **TRAGEDY (TAKE A LOOK AND SEE) / BEAUTIFUL LOSERS / BLACK KISS (hard vocal mix)** [ ] [–]

Apr 99. (cd) *(BSRCD 01) <INS 435-2>* **OPEN ALL NIGHT** [ ] Aug99 [ ]
– Night & dark / Bedroom shine / Tragedy (take a look and see) / Black kiss / Almost diamonds / Scarlet bedroom / My love / Heart in velvet / Open all night / Threat of love / Bad people kiss / Sleepwalker / Midnight soul. *<US+=>* – Satan's child / Lonely go-go dancer / Beautiful losers.

Nov 99. (cd-s) *(BRSCD 002)* **MY LOVE / THREAT OF LOVE / ONE BIG SOUL** [ ] [–]

—— next with **JOHANN JOHANNSON** – keyboards, etc / **JOHNNY GREEN** – strings, keyboards, etc / **PETUR HALLGRIMSSON** – guitar

XIII Bis XIII Bis

Jun 00. (cd) *(<533800-2>)* **STRANGER THINGS** [ ] Jul00 [ ]
– Glorious / Born to cry / Come out / Under your wing / Lights / Tantalise me / Moonbathe skin / Dancer / When it's your time / End in tears / Love in a time of science / Glorious (reprise).

– compilations, etc. –

Dec 89. (lp/c/cd) *Some Bizzare; (BREL/+C/CD 001)* **JACQUES** (most rec.1986) [ ] [–]
– The Devil (okay) / If you need / The lockman / We must look / Alone / I'm coming / Litany for a return / If you go away / The town fell asleep / The bulls / (Never to be) Next / My death. *<US cd-iss. 1996 on 'Thirsty Ear'; 57025>*

Sep 92. (cd/c) *Virgin; (CD/TC VM 9010)* **A VIRGIN'S TALE VOL.1 (1985-1988)** [ ] [–]

Sep 92. (cd/c) *Virgin; (CD/TC VM 9011)* **A VIRGIN'S TALE VOL.2 (1988-1991)** [ ] [ ]
(re-iss. both above Nov92 as d-cd; DCDVM 901 0/1) (both re-iss. Nov97; SBZ 032/033 CD)

Aug 95. (d-cd) *E.M.I.; (CDMATBOX 1)* **TREASURE BOX** [ ] [–]
(re-iss. Apr02 on 'E.M.I.'; 538915-2)

Sep 97. (cd; MARC ALMOND & FOETUS) *Some Bizzare; (SBZ 022CD)* **VIOLENT SILENCE** [ ] [ ]

Nov 97. (cd; MARC ALMOND & FOETUS) *Some Bizzare; (SBZ 034CD)* **FLESH VOLCANO / SLUT** [ ] [–]

Nov 98. (cd-enhanced) *Some Bizzare; (SBZ 037)* **LIVE IN CONCERT AT THE ASTORIA (with LA MAGIA)** [ ] [–]

Jun 03. (cd) *Cherry Red; (CDMRED 233)* **THE WILLING SINNER: LIVE AT THE PASSIONCHURCH – BERLIN (live)** [ ] [ ]

Aug 03. (cd) *Strange Fruit; (SFRSCD 121)* **THE RADIO 1 SESSIONS VOL.1 1983-1984** [ ] [–]

SOFT CELL

—— re-formed with **ALMOND + BALL**

Cooking Vinyl SpinArt

Sep 02. (12")(cd-s) *(FRY 132T)(FRYCD 132)* **MONOCULTURE / MONOCULTURE (extended). / ALL OUT OF LOVE / DANCING ALONE** [52] [–]
(cd-s) *(FRYCD 132X)* – ('A'-mixes; radio / Playgroup / Antoine 909 & Oggie-B).

Sep 02. (cd) *(COOKCD 245) <SPIN 116>* **CRUELTY WITHOUT BEAUTY** [ ] Oct02 [ ]
– Darker times / Monoculture / Le grand guignol / The night / Last chance / Together alone / Desperate / Whatever it takes / All out of love / Sensation nation / Caligula syndrome / On an up.

Jan 03. (cd-s) *(FRYCD 135)* **THE NIGHT / PERVERSITY / THE NIGHT (almighty mix)** [39] [–]
(cd-s+=) *(FRYCD 135X)* – ('A'-Wayne G Heaven anthem dub) / Say hello wave goodbye (live).

☐ ALONE AGAIN OR (see under ⇒ SHAMEN)

☐ ALT (see under ⇒ CROWDED HOUSE)

☐ AMATEUR NIGHT IN THE BIG TOP (see under ⇒ HAPPY MONDAYS)

☐ AMBOY DUKES (see under ⇒ NUGENT, Ted)

☐ AMBROSE SLADE (see under ⇒ SLADE)

AMERICA

Formed: By sons of American servicemen DAN PEEK, GERRY BECKLEY and DEWEY BUNNELL based in London, England . . . 1969. Signing to 'Warner Brothers', their debut release, 'A HORSE WITH NO NAME' became a massive hit on both sides of the Atlantic. Very much in the mould of CROSBY, STILLS & NASH, they delivered vocal harmonies reminiscent of NEIL YOUNG's more folk-orientated meanderings. The singles success precipitated a chart topping album and a string of Top 10 singles and worldwide concert sell-outs. Subsequent albums, 'HOMECOMING' (1972), 'HOLIDAY' (1974), 'HEARTS' (1975) and a compilation all made the US Top 10; only the more experimental 'HAT TRICK' in '73 failed to make the commercial grade. They also scored another US No.1 in summer '75 with the GEORGE MARTIN-produced 'SISTER GOLDEN HAIR' single. Never the greatest market for country-rock, Britain was ironically one of the few European territories where AMERICA failed to make an impact, at least after the initial success of their first two albums. The latter half of the 70's saw their dominance diminishing, the 'HARBOR' (1977) set just missing the US Top 20, while PEEK's departure (for born-again Christian-type activities) saw the duo of BECKLEY and BUNNELL taking a more commercial direction after signing to 'Capitol'. They persevered through a largely barren early 80's period, managing only one significant US hit with the RUSS BALLARD-penned 'YOU CAN DO MAGIC' in '82. Although a split finally came in 1985, the original trio reunited in 1993 to support The BEACH BOYS, subsequently recording a comeback album, 'HOURGLASS', in '94.

Album rating: AMERICA (*6) / HOMECOMIMNG (*5) / HAT TRICK (*4) / HOLIDAY (*5) / HEARTS (*5) / HISTORY: GREATEST HITS compilation (*6) / HIDEAWAY (*5) / HARBOR (*4) / AMERICA – LIVE (*2) / THE SILENT LETTER (*3) / ALIBI (*3) / VIEW FROM THE GROUND (*3) / YOUR MOVE (*3) / PERSPECTIVE (*3) / IN CONCERT (*3) / HOURGLASS (*3) / THE BEST

OF AMERICA – The Centenary Collection (*5) / HIGHWAY – 30 YEARS OF AMERICA boxed compilation (*7) / THE DEFINITIVE AMERICA compilation (*6)

DAN PEEK (b. 1 Nov'50, Panama City, Florida) – vocals, guitar / **GERRY BECKLEY** (b.12 Sep'52, Fort Worth, Texas) – vocals, guitar / **DEWEY BUNNELL** (b.19 Jan'52, Yorkshire, England) – vocals, guitar with guest drummer and bassmen.

Warners Warners

Nov 71. (7") *(K 16128)* <7555> **A HORSE WITH NO NAME. / EVERYONE: MEET IS FROM CALIFORNIA** 3 Jan72 1
Jan 72. (lp/c) *(K/K4 46093)* <2576> **AMERICA – HORSE WITH NO NAME** 14 1
– A horse with no name / Here / Riverside / Sandman / Three roses / Children / I need you / Rainy day / Never found the time / Clarice / Donkey jaw / Pigeon song. *(cd-iss. Jan93 on 'WEA'; 7599 27257-2)*
Aug 72. (7") *(K 16178)* <7580> **I NEED YOU. / RIVERSIDE** May72 9
Nov 72. (7") *(K 16219)* <7641> **VENTURA HIGHWAY. / SATURN NIGHTS** 43 Oct72 8
Dec 72. (lp/c) *(K/K4 46180)* <2655> **HOMECOMING** 21 Nov72 9
– Ventura highway / To each his own / Don't cross the river / Moon song / Only in your heart / Till the sun comes up again / Cornwall blank / Head & heart / California revisited / Saturn nights. *(cd-iss. Mar95;)*
Jan 73. (7") <7670> **DON'T CROSS THE RIVER. / TO EACH HIS OWN** – 35
Apr 73. (7") *(K 16259)* **DON'T CROSS THE RIVER. / TILL THE SUN COMES UP AGAIN** –
Apr 73. (7") <7694> **ONLY IN YOUR HEART. / MOON SONG** – 62
Aug 73. (7") *(K 16302)* <7725> **MUSKRAT LOVE. / CORNWALL BLANK** 67
Nov 73. (lp/c) *(K/K4 56016)* <2728> **HAT TRICK** 41 28
– Muskrat love / Wind wave / She's gonna let you down / Rainbow song / Submarine ladies / It's life / Hat trick / Molten love / Green monkey / Willow tree lullaby / Goodbye.
Nov 73. (7") <7760> **RAINBOW SONG. / WILLOW TREE LULLABY** –
Jan 74. (7") <7785> **GREEN MONKEY. / SHE'S GONNA LET YOU DOWN** –
Feb 74. (7") *(K 16348)* **GREEN MONKEY. / RAINBOW SONG** –
Jul 74. (lp/c) *(K/K4 56045)* <2808> **HOLIDAY** 3
– Miniature / Tin man / Another try / Lonely people / Glad to see you / Mad dog / Hollywood / Baby it's up to you / You / Old man Took / What does it matter / In the country.
Apr 74. (7") *(K 16419)* **TIN MAN. / MAD DOG** –
Aug 74. (7") <7839> **TIN MAN. / IN THE COUNTRY** – 4
Dec 74. (7") <8048> **LONELY PEOPLE. / MAD DOG** – 5
Apr 75. (7") *(K 16539)* **LONELY PEOPLE. / IN THE COUNTRY** –
Apr 75. (lp/c) *(K/K4 56115)* <2852> **HEARTS** 4
– Daisy Jane / Half a man / Midnight / Bell tree / Old Virginia / People in the valley / Company / Woman tonight / Story of a teenager / Sister golden hair / Tomorrow / Seasons. *(cd-iss. Mar95 on 'WEA'; 9362 45986-2)*
Jun 75. (7") *(K 16547)* <8086> **SISTER GOLDEN HAIR. / MIDNIGHT** Mar75 1
Jul 75. (7") <8118> **DAISY JANE. / TOMORROW** – 20
Aug 75. (7") *(K 16597)* **DAISY JANE. / WOMAN TONIGHT** –
Nov 75. (7") <8157> **WOMAN TONIGHT. / BELL TREE** – 44
Jan 76. (lp/c) *(K/K4 56169)* <2894> **HISTORY – AMERICA'S GREATEST HITS** (compilation) 60 Nov75 3
– A horse with no name / I need you / Sandman / Ventura highway / Don't cross the river / Only in your heart / Muskrat love / Tin man / Lonely people / Sister golden hair / Daisy Jane / Woman tonight. *(cd-iss. Jan87; 256 169)*
Apr 76. (lp/c) *(K/K4 56236)* <2932> **HIDEAWAY** 11
– Lovely night / Amber cascades / Don't let it get you down / Watership Down / She's beside you / Hideaway (part 1) / She's a liar / Letter / Today's the day / Jet boy blue / Who loves you / Hideaway (part 2).
May 76. (7") <8212> **TODAY'S THE DAY. / HIDEAWAY (part 2)** – 23
Aug 76. (7") <8238> **AMBER CASCADES. / WHO LOVES YOU** – 75
Aug 76. (7") *(K 16774)* **TODAY'S THE DAY. / AMBER CASCADES** –
Nov 76. (7") <8285> **SHE'S A LIAR. / SHE'S BESIDE YOU** –
Feb 77. (7") <8373> **DOWN TO THE WATER. / GOD OF THE SUN** –
Mar 77. (lp/c) *(K/K4 56351)* <3017> **HARBOR** 21
– God of the Sun / Sergeant Darkness / Sarah / These brown eyes / Don't you cry / Are you there / Monster / Down to the water / Hurricane / She's gone / Slow down / Political poachers.
Apr 77. (7") *(K 16931)* **SLOW DOWN. / SARAH** –
Jun 77. (7") <8397> **DON'T CRY BABY. / MONSTER** –
Jan 78. (lp/c) *(K/K4 56434)* <3136> **AMERICA/LIVE (live at Greek Theater, LA)** Dec77
– Tin man / Muskrat love / I need you / Old man Took / Daisy Jane / Company / Hollywood / Sergeant Darkness / Amber cascades / To each his own / Another try / Ventura highway / Sister golden hair / A horse with no name. *(cd-iss. Jan96 on 'WEA'; 7599 26690-2)*

—— Now a duo when DAN PEEK went solo (released an album and a handful of 45's) and also a became Christian.

not iss. American Int.

1978. (7") <5001> **DON'T FORGET ABOUT ME. / DON'T MAKE ME OVER** –
Mar 79. (7") <700> **CALIFORNIA DREAMIN'. / SEE IT MY WAY (BY FAR)** – 56

Capitol Capitol

Jul 79. (lp/c) <(EST/TC-EST 11950)> **THE SILENT LETTER**
– Tall treasures / No fortune / 1960 / All night / Only game in town / Foolin' / And forever / One morning / All around / All my life / High in the city. *(re-iss. Nov83 on 'Fame' lp/c; FA/TC-FA 413078-1/-4) (cd-iss. Nov98 on 'One Way'; 72438 19358-28) (cd re-iss. Jun99 on 'Magic'; 520116-2)*
Aug 79. (7") *(CL 16094)* <4752> **ONLY GAME IN TOWN. / HIGH IN THE CITY**
Oct 79. (7") *(CL 16109)* <4777> **ALL MY LIFE. / ONE MORNING**
Dec 79. (7") <4915> **CATCH THAT TRAIN. / HE COULD HAVE BEEN THE ONE** –
Nov 80. (7") <4950> **ONE IN A MILLION. / HANGOVER** –
Nov 80. (lp/c) <(EST/TC-EST 12098)> **ALIBI** Sep80
– Survival / Might be your love / Catch that train / You could've been the one / I don't believe in miracles / I do believe in you / Hangover / Right back to me / Coast-line / Valentine / One in a million. *(cd-iss. Mar98 on 'Magic'; 17657-2) (cd re-iss. Jun99 on 'Magic'; 520119-2)*
Oct 82. (7") *(CL 264)* <5142> **YOU CAN DO MAGIC. / EVEN THE SCORE** 59 Jul82 8
Nov 82. (lp/c) <(EST/TC-EST 12209)> **VIEW FROM THE GROUND** Aug82 41
– You can do magic / Never be lonely / You girl / Inspector Mills / Love on the vine / Desperate love / Right before your eyes / Jody / Sometimes lovers / Even the score. *(cd-iss. Apr95 on 'Connoisseur'; NSPCD 509) (cd re-iss. Jun99 on 'Magic'; 520115-2)*
Nov 82. (7") <5177> **RIGHT BEFORE YOUR EYES. / INSPECTOR MILLS** – 45
Jan 83. (7") *(CL 274)* **JODY. / INSPECTOR MILLS** –

—— guest **RUSS BALLARD** – keyboards, etc. (ex-ARGENT, solo artist)

Jul 83. (7") *(CL 301)* <5236> **THE BORDER. / SOMETIMES LOVERS** Jun83 33
Jul 83. (lp/c) <(EST/TC-EST 12277)> **YOUR MOVE** 81
– My kinda woman / She's a runaway / Cast the spirit / Love's worn out again / The border / Your move / Honey / My dear / Tonight is for dreamers / Don't let me be lonely / Someday woman. *(cd-iss. Mar98 on 'Magic'; 17658-2) (cd re-iss. Jun99 on 'Magic'; 520114-2)*
Oct 83. (7") <5275> **CAST THE SPIRIT. / MY DEAR** –
Nov 84. (lp) *(240216-1)* <12370> **PERSPECTIVE**
– We got all night / See how the love goes / (Can't fall asleep to a) Lullaby / Special girl / 5th Avenue / (It's like you) Never left at all / Stereo / Lady with a bluebird / Cinderela / Unconditional love / Fallin' off the world. *(cd-iss. Oct97 on 'Magic'; 17659-2) (cd re-iss. Jun99 on 'Magic'; 520118-2) (cd re-iss. Feb01 on 'EMI Plus'; 576087-2)*
Nov 84. (7") <5398> **SPECIAL GIRL. / UNCONDITIONAL LOVE** –
Feb 85. (7") <5430> **(CAN'T FALL ASLEEP TO A) LULLABY. / FALLIN' OFF THE WORLD** –

—— with **LEACOX** / **MICHAEL WOODS** – guitar, vocals / **BRAD PALMER** – bass, vocals

1985. (lp) *(064-240385-1)* **AMERICA IN CONCERT (live)** – German –
– Tin man / I need you / The border / Sister golden hair / Company / You can do magic / Ventura highway / Daisy Jane / A horse with no name / Survival. *(UK cd-iss. Oct96 on 'EMI Gold'; CDGOLD 1072) (cd re-iss. May03 on 'King Biscuit'; KBCCD 137)*

—— split later in 1985 and then '88, although the original trio re-formed in 1993 to support The BEACH BOYS

— in 1988, the duo had also featured on the soundtrack of the animated movie, 'The Last Unicorn'

American Gramaphone / American Gramaphone

Jun 94. (c/cd) *<AGC/+D 494>* **HOURGLASS**
– Young moon / Hope / Sleeper train / Mirror to mirror / Garden of peace / Call of the world / Whole wide world / Close to the wind / Greenhouse / Ports-of-call / Everyone I meet is from California / You can do magic.

Oxygen / Oxygen

Nov 98. (cd) *<(90004-2)>* **HUMAN NATURE**
– From a moving train / Wednesday morning / Town and country / Moment to moment / Hidden talent / The wheels are turning / World alone / Overwhelming world suite: Overwhelming world – Come back – Barstow / Pages / Hot town / Whispering / Oloololo.

— **BECKLEY + BUNNELL** recruited producer/session man ANDREW GOLD

Rhino / Rhino

Nov 02. (cd) *<(8122 74498-2)>* **HOLIDAY HARMONY** (festive) — Oct02

– compilations, others, etc. –

1974. (7"ep) *Warners; (K 16408)* **A HORSE WITH NO NAME / SANDMAN. / VENTURA HIGHWAY / RIVERSIDE** — [-]

Jul 81. (7") *Warners; (K 17814)* **A HORSE WITH NO NAME. / VENTURA HIGHWAY** — [-]
(re-iss. Sep85 on 'Old Gold'; OG 9525)

Sep 91. (cd/c) *Rhino; <R2/R4 70529>* **ENCORE: MORE GREATEST HITS** [-]

Mar 96. (cd) *Disky; (DC 86435-2)* **YOU CAN DO MAGIC** — [-]

Feb 97. (cd) *E.M.I.; (CTMCD 307)* **THE BEST OF AMERICA (The Centenary Collection)** — [-]
– You can do magic / The border / The last unicorn / All my life / Survival / Tall treasures / One morning / Honey / My dear / One in a million / Right before your eyes / We got all night / Lady with a bluebird / Only game in town / Ventura highway / Daisy Jane / I need you / Tin man / Sister golden hair / A horse with no name.

Jul 98. (cd) *King Biscuit; <(KBFHCD 012)>* **KING BISCUIT PRESENTS . . .**

Aug 00. (3xcd-box) *Rhino; <(8122 79887-2)>* **HIGHWAY – 30 YEARS OF AMERICA** — Jul00

Apr 01. (cd) *E.M.I.; <837638>* **PREMIUM GOLD COLLECTION** [-]

Sep 01. (cd) *Rhino; <(8122 73552-2)>* **THE DEFINITIVE AMERICA** — Jul01

May 02. (cd) *Disky; (SI 79411-2)* **VENTURA HIGHWAY LIVE (live)** — [-]

Apr 03. (cd) *King Biscuit; (KBCCD 129)* **OHIO** — [-]

AMERICAN HI-FI

Formed: Boston, Massachusetts, USA . . . late 90's by STACY JONES (former drummer with LETTERS TO CLEO and who'd worked with NINA GORDON of VERUCA SALT). Settling with a line-up that consisted of JAIME ARENTZEN (on guitar), DREW PARSONS (on bass) and BRIAN NOLAN (on sticks), AMERICAN HI-FI were well-named to pull the music world into their CHEAP TRICK-meets-FOO FIGHTERS type alt-pop/rock. The quartet soon inked a deal with 'Island' records ('Mercury' in the UK), their debut single, 'FLAVOR OF THE WEAK', hitting the charts in the summer of 2001 around the same time as their eponymous set was climbing into the US Top 100.

Album rating: AMERICAN HI-FI (*6) / THE ART OF LOSING (*)

STACY JONES – vocals, guitar (ex-LETTERS TO CLEO) / **JAIME ARENTZEN** – guitar / **DREW PARSONS** – bass / **BRIAN NOLAN** – drums

Mercury / Island

Aug 01. (c-s) *(588672-4) <radio cut>* **FLAVOR OF THE WEAK /** — 31 — Jun01 — 41

Sep 01. (cd) *(586457-2) <542871>* **AMERICAN HI-FI** — Feb01 — 81
– Surround / Flavor of the weak / A bigger mood / Safer on the outside / I'm a fool / Hi-fi killer / Blue day / My only enemy / Don't wait for the sun / Another perfect day / Scar / What about today / Wall of sound. *(bonus+=)* – Black satellite (demo) / Flavor of the weak (demo).

Feb 03. (cd) *(63657-2)* **THE ART OF LOSING**
– The art of losing / Break up song / Beautiful disaster / Save me / Nothing left to lose / Teenage alien nation / Rise / This is the sound / Gold rush / Built for speed / Happy. *(bonus+=)* – The art of losing (video + the making of the . . .). *(re-iss. Mar03 +=; 77146-2)* – Bigger mood (live) / Hi-fi killer (live).

Apr 03. (cd-s) *(077915-2)* **THE ART OF LOSING / FLAVOR OF THE WEAK (live) / WHEN THE BREEDERS WERE BIG / ('A'-video)** — 75

AMERICAN MUSIC CLUB

Formed: Burbank, California, USA . . . 1983 by MARK EITZEL, who had set up home in San Francisco after his Columbus, Ohio band The NAKED SKINNIES broke up in '82; they released one US-only single, 'ALL MY LIFE' / 'THIS IS THE BEAUTIFUL NIGHT' for 'Naked House'; (103457). With a line-up of MARK 'VUDI' PANKLER, DAN PEARSON, BRAD JOHNSON and MATT NORELLI, the AMERICAN MUSIC CLUB cut a debut album, 'RESTLESS STRANGER', for the small 'Grifter' label in 1985, before signing to 'Zippo' for the 'THE ENGINE' (1987). Regularly cited as one of the most criminally undervalued songwriters in the US, EITZEL has captured many a critic's ear with his neon-lit meditations on the tragic futility of human existence and the fleeting consolation of romantic love. Apart from a cult fanbase, however, AMC's appeal never translated to a wider audience, even after the band were picked up by 'Virgin' in the early 90's. By this point, the group had a clutch of austere, country-tinged classics under their belt, namely 'CALIFORNIA', 'UNITED KINGDOM' (1989) and 'EVERCLEAR' (1991), the latter set especially haunting in spite of its more accessible approach. EITZEL's wracked outpourings were often shot through with a kind of outraged desperation, the 'RISE' single, a poignant tribute to a friend who died of AIDS. Also featuring such bleakly beautiful material as 'SICK OF FOOD', the album saw EITZEL named as Rolling Stone magazine's songwriter of the year in 1991. The acclaim didn't sit particularly well with the AMC frontman; EITZEL, perhaps in response, accentuated the self-mocking tone of his work on the major label debut, 'MERCURY' (1993). Critically acclaimed once again, the album failed to sell, although it did almost scrape into the UK Top 40. It was the same story with 'SAN FRANCISCO' (1994). Parting company with 'Virgin', the band also saw fit to part company with each other, at least they'd given it their best shot. EITZEL remained with the label for a further solo album, '60 WATT SILVER LINING' (1996), another critical success seemingly doomed to obscurity. Switching labels for 'WEST' (1997 for 'Warners') and 'I CAN'T HOLD BACK . . .' (1998 for 'Matador'), EITZEL took a three-year hiatus before setting out his stall once more. 2001's 'THE INVISIBLE MAN' was a fine comeback encompassing all modern trites such as electronic sampling, etc. Indeed, his best song for some time, 'PROCLAIM YOUR JOY', closed the album and might've just given him a deserved hit single. The arch miserabilist was back in 2002 with 'MUSIC FOR COURAGE AND CONFIDENCE', presumably not a wholly ironic title for a record that, by its eclectic sweep alone, was worthy of close attention. Unsurprisingly perhaps, it was the countrified material which worked best, especially John Hartford's classic 'GENTLE ON MY MIND', although EITZEL reconstructed the likes of Bill Withers' 'AIN'T NO SUNSHINE' and even Culture Club's 'DO YOU REALLY WANT TO HURT ME' in his trademark skeletal style. While 'THE UGLY AMERICAN' (2003) wasn't likely to spawn any hits, its journey into Greek music at least made for one of the more adventurous recordings of EITZEL's career. Comprising remodelled versions of both songs from his AMC days and a choice selection of his latter day solo work, the album found EITZEL playfully messing with both the arrangements and the lyrics, setting the material to backdrops of Greek stringed instruments and, in the process, complementing some of the most gut-wrenching vocal performances of his career. • **Covered:** CALIFORNIA DREAMIN' (Mamas & The Papas). EITZEL covered THERE IS NO EASY WAY DOWN (Carole King) / SNOWBIRD (Anne Murray) / HELP ME MAKE IT THROUGH THE NIGHT (Kris Kristofferson) / I ONLY HAVE EYES FOR YOU (Flamingos) / MORE, MORE, MORE (Neil Diamond) / MOVE ON UP (Curtis Mayfield) / REHEARSALS FOR RETIREMENT (Phil Ochs) / I'LL BE SEEING YOU (Billie Holiday). • **Trivia:** EITZEL also moonlighted with The TOILING MIDGETS (a 5-piece also featuring early 90's AMC newcomer TIM MOONEY; he had always been part of the early 80's combo). They released an album, 'SON' (1993), before signing to 'Reprise' the same year.

Album rating: THE RESTLESS STRANGER (*5) / ENGINE (*6) / CALIFORNIA (*7) / UNITED KINGDOM (*7) / EVERCLEAR (*8) / MERCURY (*7) / SAN FRANCISCO (*6) / Mark Eitzel: SONGS OF LOVE: LIVE AT THE BORDERLINE – 1/19/91 (*6) / 60 WATT SILVER LINING (*6) / WEST (*7) / CAUGHT IN A TRAP AND I CAN'T BACK OUT (*5) / THE INVISIBLE MAN (*7) / MUSIC FOR COURAGE AND CONFIDENCE (*4) / THE UGLY AMERICAN (*6)

MARK EITZEL (b.30 Jan'59, Walnut Creek, Calif.) – vocals, guitar, keyboards / **MARK "VUDI" PANKLER** (b.22 Sep'52, Chicago, Illinois) – guitar, accordion, bass / **DAN PEARSON** (b.31 May'59, Walnut Creek) – bass, guitar, dulcimer, vocals, etc. / **BRAD JOHNSON** – keyboards / **MATT NORELLI** – drums

not iss. Grifter

Jan 86. (lp) *<GR 001>* **THE RESTLESS STRANGER** [–] [ ]
– $1,000,000 song / Away down my street / Yvonne gets dumped / Ms. Lucky / Point of desire / Goodbye reprise #54 / Tell yourself / When your love is gone / Heavenly smile / Broken glass / Hold on to your love. *<US cd-iss. 1999 on 'Reprise'; 46675>*

—— **TOM MALLON** – guitar, drums, vocals / **DAVE SCHEFF** – drums repl. JOHNSON + NORELLI

Zippo Frontier

Oct 87. (lp/cd) *(ZONG/+CD 020) <4612-1/-2>* **ENGINE** [ ] [ ]
– Big night / Outside this bar / At my mercy / Gary's song / Nightwatchman / Lloyd / Electric light / Mom's TV / Art of love / Asleep / This year.

—— now without SCHEFF

Demon Frontier

Oct 88. (lp/cd) *(FIEND/+CD 134) <4619-1/-2>* **CALIFORNIA** [ ] [ ]
– Firefly / Somewhere / Laughing stock / Lonely / Pale skinny girl / Blue and grey shirt / Bad liquor / Now you're defeated / Jenny / Western sky / Highway 5 / Last harbor. *(cd re-iss. Apr93; FMCD 1)*

—— **MIKE SIMMS** – drums; repl. MALLON

Oct 89. (lp/cd) *(FIEND/+CD 151)* **UNITED KINGDOM** [ ] [–]
– Here they roll down / Dreamers of the dream / Never mind / United kingdom / Dream is gone / Heaven of your hands / Kathleen / The hula maiden / Animal pen. *(cd+=)* – California (album). *(cd re-iss. Apr93; FMCD 2)*

—— added **BRUCE KAPHAN** (b. 7 Jan'55, San Francisco) – pedal steel guitar, keyboards, bass, producer (now full-time)

Alias Alias

Oct 91. (lp/c/cd) *<(A 015/+C/D)>* **EVERCLEAR** [ ] [ ]
– Why won't you stay / Rise / Miracle on 8th Street / Ex-girlfriend / Crabwalk / The confidential agent / Sick of food / The dead part of you / Royal cafe / What the pillar of salt held up / Jesus' hands.

Nov 91. (cd-ep) *<(A 014D)>* **RISE / CHANNEL NUMBER / THE RIGHT THING / CRABWALK** [ ] [ ]

—— **TIM MOONEY** (b. 6 Oct'58, Las Vegas, Nevada) – drums (of TOILING MIDGETS) repl. SIMMS

Virgin Reprise

Mar 93. (cd/c/lp) *(CD/TC+/V 2708) <45226>* **MERCURY** [41] [ ]
– Gratitude walks / If I had a hammer / Challenger / I've been a mess / Hollywood 4-5-92 / What Godzilla said to God when his name wasn't found in the book of life / Keep me around / Dallas, airports, bodybags / Apology for an accident / Over and done / Johnny Mathis' feet / The hopes and dreams of Heaven's 10,000 whores / More hopes and dreams / Will you find me?

Apr 93. (c-s) *(VSC 1445)* **JOHNNY MATHIS' FEET / WILL YOU FIND ME / THE HOPES AND DREAMS OF HEAVEN'S 10,000** [58] [–]
(cd-s+=) *(VSCDX 1445)* – The amylnitrate dream of Pat Robertson.
(cd-s) *(VSCDT 1445)* – ('A'side) / What Godzilla said to God when his name wasn't found in the book of life / Dallas, airports, bodybags (demo).

Jun 93. (c-ep) *(VSC 1464)* **KEEP ME AROUND / CHALLENGER / IN MY ROLE AS THE MOST HATED SINGER IN THE LOCAL UNDERGROUND MUSIC SCENE / MEMO FROM AQUATIC PARK** [ ] [–]
(cd-ep+=) *(VSCDG 1464)* – (no 2nd track) / Walking tune.

Aug 94. (7"/c-s) *(VS/+C 1512)* **WISH THE WORLD AWAY. / I JUST TOOK TWO SLEEPING PILLS AND NOW I'M LIKE A BRIDEGROOM** [46] [–]
(cd-s+=) *(VSCDT 1512)* – The revolving door (demo).
(cd-s) *(VSCDX 1512)* – ('A'side) / The President's test for physical fitness / Cape Canaveral.

Sep 94. (cd/c/lp) *(CD/TC+/V 2752) <45721>* **SAN FRANCISCO** [72] [ ]
– Fearless / It's your birthday / Can you help me / Love doesn't belong to anyone * / Wish the world away / How many six packs to screw in a light? / Cape Canaverai * / Hello Amsterdam / The revolving door / In the shadow of the valley * / What holds the world together / I broke my promise / The thorn in my side is gone / I'll be gone / Fearless (reprise) * / I just took my two sleeping pills and now I'm like a bridegroom. *(cd+=/c+= *)*

Feb 95. (7"/c-s) *(VS/+C 1523)* **CAN YOU HELP ME. / THE THORN IN MY SIDE IS GONE** [ ] [–]
(cd-s+=) *(VSCDT 1523)* – California dreamin' (alt.version).

MARK EITZEL

not iss. own label

1982. (c) *<#1>* **MEAN MARK EITZEL GETS FAT** [–] [ ]
– Swing low / You can be beautiful / Hold on to your love / I speak French / A tall black lady / Keep this dance for me / Shadow of my name.

Demon Matador

Apr 91. (lp/cd) *(FIEND/+CD 213)* **SONGS OF LOVE: LIVE AT THE BORDERLINE 1/19/91 (live)** [ ] [–]
– Firefly / Chanel No.5 / Western sky / Blue and grey shirt / Gary's song / Outside this bar / Room above the club / Last harbour / Kathleen / Crabwalk / Jenny / Take courage / Nothing can bring me down. *(cd re-iss. Nov97 on 'Diablo'; DIAB 838) (lp re-iss. Aug98 on 'Fruit Tree'; FRUITTREE 801)*

Jul 92. (12") *<OLE 016>* **TAKE COURAGE** [–] [ ]
– On the emblematic use of jewelry as a metaphor for the disolution of our hopes and dreams / The ecstatic epiphany: A celebration of youth and beauty past, present, and future.

Virgin Warners

Mar 96. (cd/c/lp) *(CD/TC+/V 2798) <46152>* **60 WATT SILVER LINING** [ ] [ ]
– There is no way down / Sacred heart / Always turn away / Saved / Cleopatra Jones / When my plane finally goes down / Mission rock / Wild sea / Aspirin / Some bartenders have the gift of pardon / Southend on sea / Everything is beautiful.

Warners Warners

Jun 97. (cd) *<(9362 46602-2)>* **WEST** [ ] May96 [ ]
– If you have to ask / Free of harm / Helium / Stunned and frozen / Then it really happens / In your life / Lower Eastside tourist / Three inches of wall / Move myself ahead / Old photographs / Fresh screwdriver / Live or die.

Matador Matador

Feb 98. (cd/lp) *<(OLE 179-2/-1)>* **CAUGHT IN A TRAP AND I CAN'T BACK OUT** [ ] Jan98 [ ]
– Are you the trash / Xmas lights spin / Auctioneer's song / White rosary / If I had a gun / Goodbye / Queen of no one / Cold light of day / Go away / Atico 18 / Sun smog seahorse.

Apr 01. (7") *(OLE 515-7)* **IT IS IMPORTANT THROUGHOUT YOUR LIFE TO PROCLAIM YOUR JOY. / THE MAN WITH THE HOLE IN HIS FOOT** [ ] [–]
(cd-s) *(OLE 515-2)* – ('A'side) / Tell it to the lonely fairy in the forest (a rural gambol) / Proclaim your joy (swinging version).

May 01. (cd) *<(OLE 505-2)>* **THE INVISIBLE MAN** [ ] [ ]
– The boy with the hammer in the paper bag / Can you see? / Christian science reading room / Sleep / To the sea / Shine / Steve I always knew /

Bitterness / Anything / Without you / The global sweep of human history / Seeing eye to eye / Proclaim your joy.

New West New West

Apr 02. (cd) <*(NWCD 6038)*> **MUSIC FOR COURAGE AND CONFIDENCE**
– Snowbird / Ain't no sunshine / Do you really want to hurt me / Help me make it through the night / I only have eyes for you / Gentle on my mind / More, more, more / Move on up / Rehearsals for retirement / I'll be seeing you.

Tongue Master Thirsty Ear

Feb 03. (cd) *(TMAST 001)* <57135> **THE UGLY AMERICAN**
– Western sky / Here they roll down / Jenny / Nightwatchman / Take courage / Anything / What good is love / Will you find me / Last harbor / Love's humming.

AMON DUUL II

Formed: Munich, Germany . . . Autumn 1968 from the original AMON DUUL commune. While the aforesaid outfit remained as a separate musical entity, CHRIS KARRER set-up AMON DUUL II with JOHN WEINZIERL, FALK-ULRICH ROGNER, RENATE KNAUP, CHRISTIAN 'SHRAT' THIERFELD an DIETER SERFAS. Securing a deal with 'Liberty', they released their first album in 1969, 'PHALLUS DEI' (God's Penis), which introduced a further two members, PETER LEOPOLD (from AMON DUUL I) and Englishman DAVE ANDERSON. Avant-garde space-rock in the mould of PINK FLOYD and GRATEFUL DEAD, the album brought home-produced, psychedelic improvisation to the German market. 'YETI', the follow-up in 1970, was a much more structured double-set featuring some excellent acid-rock numbers including the weird but wonderful single 'ARCHANGELS THUNDERBIRD'. Their next effort, 'DANCE OF THE LEMMINGS' (1971), concentrated more on lengthy, segued collages, including the outrageously brilliant, 'SYNTELMAN'S MARCH OF THE ROARING SEVENTIES'. With members coming and going at their leisure, it was difficult for the band to maintain any degree of consistency and records like 'CARNIVAL IN BABYLON' (1972), 'WOLF CITY' (1972), etc, sounded uninspired in comparison to their earlier work. Even a deal with 'Atlantic' in 1974, failed to result in a return to form. The band continued into the 90's, WEINZEIRL having brought back past members KARRER, ROGNER, RENATE, LEOPOLD and MEID for Christmas concerts in 1992. • **Trivia:** AMON DUUL II members guested on releases by POPOL VUH and EMBRYO.

Album rating: PHALLUS DEI (*6) / YETI (*8) / DANCE OF THE LEMMINGS (*6) / WOLF CITY (*6) / CARNIVAL IN BABYLON (*5) / LIVE IN LONDON (*6) / VIVE LA TRANCE (*4) / HIJACK (*4) / MADE IN GERMANY (*4) / PYRAGONY X (*4) / ALMOST ALIVE (*4) / ONLY HUMAN (*4) / VORTEX (*4) / HAWK MEETS PENGUIN (*4) / NADA MOONSHINE (*4) / ANTHOLOGY compilation (*7)

JOHN WEINZIERL – lead guitar, vocals, violin / **RENATE KNAUP-KROTENSCHWANZ** – vocals / **CHRIS KARRER** – violin, guitar, vocals, sax / **FALK ROGNER** – keyboards, synthesizers / **DAVE ANDERSON** – bass / **SHRAT** (b. CHRISTIAN THIELE) – bongos, vocals, violin / **PETER LEOPOLD** – drums / **DIETER SERFAS** – drums and guests / **HOLGER TRULZSCH** – Turkish drums / **CHRISTIAN BUCHARD** – vibraphone

Liberty Liberty

1969. (lp) *(LSB 83279)* **PHALLUS DEI** –
– Kanaan / Dem guten, Schonen, wahren / Luzifers ghilom / Henriette Krotenschwantz / Phallus dei. *(re-iss. Feb72 on 'Sunset'; SLS 50257) (cd-iss. Nov92 on 'Repertoire' Germany; REP 4274-WY) (cd re-iss. Apr97 & Jun98 on 'Mantra'; MANTRA 012) (cd re-iss. Jan99 & Dec00 on 'Repertoire'; REP 4747) <US cd-iss. 2001 on 'Repertoire'+=; REP 4872>* – Freak out requiem I, II, III & IV / Cymbals in the end.

— now without SERFAS, but with new guests **ULRICH LEOPOLD** – bass / **RAINER BAUER** – guitar, vocals (both of other AMON DUUL) + **THOMAS** – flute

1970. (7") *(15355)* **ARCHANGELS THUNDERBIRD. / SOAP SHOP ROCK** – German –

1970. (7") *(15417)* **RATTLESNAKEPLUMCAKE. / BETWEEN THE EYES** – German –

1971. (7") *(15468)* **LIGHT. / LEMMINGMANIA** – German –

Sep 70. (7") *(LBF 15355)* **ARCHANGELS THUNDERBIRD. / BURNING SISTER** –

Nov 70. (d-lp) *(LSP 101)* **YETI**
– Soda shop rock:- a. Burning sister – b. Halluzination guillotine – c. Gulp a sonata – d. Flesh-coloured anti-aircraft alarm / She came through the chimney / Archangels thunderbird / Cerberus / The return of Ruebezahl / Eye-shaking king / Pale gallery / Yeti (improvisation) / Yeti talks to Yogi (improvisation) / Sandoz in the rain (improvisation). *(cd-iss. Nov92 on 'Repertoire' Germany; REP 4275) (cd re-iss. Aug97 & Jun98 on 'Mantra'; MANTRA 010) (cd re-iss. Jan99 on 'Repertoire'; RR 4748) <Us cd-iss. 2001 on 'Repertoire'+=; REP 4914>* – Rattlesnakeplumcake / Between the eyes.

— **LOTHAR MEID** – bass, vocals; repl. ANDERSON who joined HAWKWIND

— **KARL-HEINZ HAUSMANN** – keyboards; repl. SCHRAT who formed SAMETI / added guests / **JIMMY JACKSON** – mellotron / **AL GROMER** – sitar / **HENRIETTE KROTENSCHWANZ** – vocals / **ROLF ZACHER** – vocals

U.A. U.A.

Jun 71. (d-lp) *(UAD 60003-4)* **DANCE OF THE LEMMINGS**
(German title 'TANZ DER LEMMING') –
– Syntelman's march of the roaring seventies: (a) In the glass garden – (b) Pull down your mask – (c) Prayer to the silence – (d) Telephonecomplex / (a) Restless skylight – transistor child – Landing in a ditch – (b) Dehypnotized toothpaste – (c) A short stop to the Transylvanian brain surgery / Race from here to your ears: (a) Little tornados – (b) Overheated tiara – (c) The flyweighted five – (d) Riding on a cloud – (e) Paralized Paradise – (f) H.G. Well's take off / Chamsin soundtrack; The Marilyn Monroe memorial church / Chewing gum telegram / Stumbling over melted moonlight / Toxicological whispering. *(cd-iss. Nov92 on 'Repertoire' Germany; REP 4276-WY) (cd re-iss. Sep98 on 'Mantra'; MANTRA 014) (cd re-iss. Jan99 as 'TANZ DER LEMMINGE' on 'Repertoire' REP 4749)*

— added **D. SECUNDUS FICHELSCHER** – drums, congas

Apr 72. (lp) *(UAG 29327)* **CARNIVAL IN BABYLON**
– C.I.D. in Urik / All the years round / Shimmering sands / Kronwinkl 12 / Tables are turned / Hawknose harlequin. *(cd-iss. Jun98 on 'Mantra'; MANTRA 063) (cd re-iss. Mar99 on 'Repertoire'; REP 4581) (cd re-iss. Jul00 on 'Captain Trip'; CTCD 033)*

1972. (7") *(UA 35338)* **ALL THE YEARS ROUND. / TABLES ARE TURNED** – German –

— now w/ out HAUSMANN

Nov 72. (lp) *(UAG 29406)* **WOLF CITY**
– Surrounded by the stars / Jail-house frog / Green-bubble-raincoated man / Wolf city / Wie der wind am ende einer strasse / Deutsch Nepal / Sleepwalker's timeless bridge. *(cd-iss. Apr97 & Jun98 on 'Mantra'; MANTRA 013) (cd re-iss. Feb99 on 'Repertoire'; RR 4750)*

1973. (lp) *(USP 102)* **LIVE IN LONDON (live)**
– Archangels thunderbird / Eye shaking king / Soap shop rock / Improvisation / Syntelman's march of the roaring seventies: (a) Pull down your mask – (b) Prayer to the silence – (c) Telephonecomplex) / (a) Restless skylight – Transistor child – Landing in a ditch – (b) Dehypnotized toothpaste – (c) A short stop at the Transylvanian brain surgery / Race from here to your ears: (a) Little tornadoes – (b) Riding on a cloud (c) Paralized paradise. *(cd-iss. Nov98 on 'Mystic'; MYSCD 128)*

— **ROBBY HEIBL** – bass repl. MEID (although he later returned)

1974. (lp) *(UAS 29504)* **VIVE LA TRANCE**
– A morning excuse / Fly united / Jalousie / Im krater bluhn weider die baume / Mozambique (dedicated to Monika Ertt) / Apocalyptic bore / Dr. Trap / Pigman / Manana / Ladies mimikry. *(cd-iss. Jun98 on 'Mantra'; MANTRA 062) (cd re-iss. Jan99 on 'Repertoire'; RR 4752)*

1974. (7") *(UA 35466)* <419> **PIGMAN. / MOZAMBIQUE** – German

— **ROBBY HEIBL** returned to replace MEID, KRAMPER and SECUNDUS

— (signed to 'Nova' in Germany)

Atlantic Atco

1975. (lp) *(K 50136)* **HIJACK** –
– I can't wait (parts 1 & 2) / Mirror / Traveller / You're not alone / Explode like a star / Da Guadeloop / Lonely woman / Liquid whisper / Archy the robot.

1975. (7") *(6.11579)* **MIRROR. / LIQUID WHISPER** – German –

1975. (d-lp) *(K 50182)* **MADE IN GERMANY** ☐ ☐
– Dreams / Ludwig / The king's chocolate waltz / Blue grotto / 5.5.55 / Emigrant song / La krautoma / Metropolis / Loosey girls / Gala gnome / Top of the mud / Mr.Kraut's jinx.

— **KARRER, WEINZIERL** and **LEOPOLD** were joined by **KLAUS EBART** – bass who repl. ROGNER and **STEFAN ZAUNER** – keyboards repl. KNAUP and BALDERSON

1976. (lp) *(622 890)* **PYRAGONY X** ☐ German ☐
– Flower of the Orient / Merlin / Crystal hexagram / Lost in space / Sally the seducer / Telly vision / The only thing / Capuccino.

1977. (lp) *(623 305)* **ALMOST ALIVE** ☐ German ☐
– One blue morning / Goodbye my love / Ain't today tomorrow's yesterday / Hallelujah / Feeling uneasy / Live in Jericho.

— now w/out WEINZIERL

— (signed to 'Strand' in Germany)

Vinyl not iss.

Jan 79. (lp) *(LV 1004)* **ONLY HUMAN** ☐ ☐
– Another morning / Don't turn to stone / Kirk Morgan / Spaniards & spacemen / Kismet / Pharaoh / Ruby lane.

1979. (7") *(6.12459)* **DON'T TURN TO STONE. / SPANIARDS & SPACEMEN** ☐ German ☐

— line-up **CHRIS KARRER / RENATE ASCHAUER KNAUP / JOERG EVERS** – bass, guitar, synthesizers / **DANIEL FICHELSCHER** – drums, percussion / **FALK ROGNER** – synth / plus **JOHN WEINZIERI** – guitar / **LOTHAR MEID** – bass / **STEFAN ZAUNER** – piano, synth

Telefunken not iss.

1981. (lp) *(624 852)* **VORTEX** ☐ German ☐
– Vortex / Holy west / Die 7 fetten Jahr / Wings of the wind / Mona / We are machines / Das gestern ist das heute von Morgen / Vibes in the air.

— Broke-up but reformed in the 80's with line-up below **JOHN WEINZIERL, DAVE ANDERSON, JULIE WAREING** – vocals / **ROBERT CALVERT** – vocals / **GUY EVANS** – drums (ex-VAN DER GRAAF GENERATOR)

Illuminated not iss.

Jan 83. (lp) *(JAMS 024)* **HAWK MEETS PENGUIN** ☐ ☐
– One moment of anger is two pints of blood / Meditative music from the third o before the producers pt.1 & 2. *(re-iss. as 'HAWK MEETS PENGUIN VOL.1' Dec85 on 'Demi-Monde'; DM 04) (cd-iss. 1992 on 'Thunderbolt'; CDTB 102) (cd re-iss. Apr97 on 'Spalax'; 14848)*

Jan 85. (lp) *(JAMS 27)* **MEETING WITH MEN MACHINES** ☐ ☐
– Pioneer / Old one / Marcus lied / Song / Things aren't always what they seem / Burundi drummer's nightmare. *(re-iss. 1985 on 'Demi-Monde'; DM 006) (cd-iss. Mar93 on 'Thunderbolt'; CDTB 107) (cd re-iss. Jun97 on 'Spalax'; 14820)*

Demi-Monde not iss.

Jan 89. (lp) *(DMLP 1013)* **FOOL MOON** ☐ ☐
– Fool moon / Tribe / Tik tok song / Haupmotor / Hymn for the hardcore. *(cd-iss. Nov89 on 'The CD Label'; CDTL 011) (cd re-iss. Jun97 on 'Spalax'; 14516)*

— disbanded again, but re-formed for gigs late 1992 with **KARRER, WEINZIERL, ROGNER, RENATE, LEOPOLD & MEID**

Mantra not iss.

Jun 93. (cd) **SURROUNDED BY THE STARS / BARS** ☐ ☐

Mystic Resurgent

Aug 96. (cd) *(MYS 106CD)* **NADA MOONSHINE** ☐ ☐

Aug 97. (cd) *(MYS 113CD)* <4175> **FLAWLESS** ☐ Nov98 ☐
– Nada Cairo / Surrounded by the stars / Castaneda daDream (In another world) / Wie der wind am ende einer strasse / Kiss ma eee / Cerberus / Speed inside my shoes / La paloma / Nada moonshine union / Dancing on fire / Jam 71 / What you gonna do? / Jim hai jam UK 96.

– compilations, others –

May 75. (lp) *United Artists; (UAS 29723)* **LEMMINGMANIA** ☐ ☐

Mar 87. (d-lp) *Raw Power; (RAWLP 032)* **ANTHOLOGY** ☐ ☐
– Soup shock rock / Burning sister / Halluzination guillotine / Gulp a sonata / Flesh-coloured anti-aircraft alarm / Kanaan / Trap / Phallus dei / Yet (improvisation) / Wolf city / C.I.D. in Uruk / Morning excuse / Apocalyptic bone / Jailhouse frog.

Nov 92. (cd) *Windsong; (WINCD 026)* **LIVE IN CONCERT (live BBC '73)** ☐ ☐

Jan 97. (cd) *Cleopatra; (CLP 9902-2)* **THE BEST OF AMON DUUL II 1969-1974** ☐ ☐

Jan 99. (cd) *Repertoire; (REP 4753)* **LIVE IN TOKYO (live)** ☐ ☐

Nov 00. (cd) *Strange Fruit; (SFRSCD 097)* **THE COMPLETE BBC RECORDINGS** ☐ ☐

UTOPIA

WEINZIERI, MEID, KROTEN SCHWANTZ, FICHELSCHER, OLAF KUSLER (producer) / **ROGNER, KARRER**

U.A. U.A.

1973. (lp) *(UAG 29438)* **UTOPIA** ☐ ☐
– What you gonna do / The Wolf-man Jack show / Alice / Las Vegas / Deutsch Nepal / Utopiat No. 1 / Nasi Goreng / Jazz kiste.

Tori AMOS

Born: MYRA ELLEN AMOS, 22 Aug'63, Newton, North Carolina, USA. Daughter of a preacher father and part-Cherokee Indian mother, she incredibly scored a scholarship to 'Peabody Conservatory' in Baltimore at five years old (youngest ever admitee!), studying classical piano. Parting company with this illustrious establishment at the age of eleven, AMOS embarked upon her rebellious phase, playing bars and subsequently relocating to L.A. where she was discovered by early 80's sophisto-disco star, NARADA MICHAEL WALDEN. Despite recording some professional demos and releasing a one-off independently released 45, 'BALTIMORE' (1981), it would be a few years down the line before AMOS's career really began. Reinventing herself as TORI, AMOS formed a gaudy glitz-metal band, Y KANT TORI READ, eventually signing to 'Atlantic' and releasing a dodgy eponymous album in 1988. Almost universally lambasted by the critics, TORI underwent a considerably more horrific ordeal when she was raped at gunpoint by a would-be fan after offering him a lift home (this experience was later detailed in the song, 'ME AND A GUN'). Making the transition from leather-clad frontwoman to soul searching singer-songwriter, TORI AMOS "moved along the corridor" to the 'East West' stable and released her solo debut, 'LITTLE EARTHQUAKES' (1991). Breaking initially in Britain, the album's deep subject matter and orchestrated, piano-led atmospherics were the backdrop for AMOS's eye-of-the-hurricane emotional turmoil; from heavy-lidded lullaby to howling, KATE BUSH-esque melodrama, the singer exorcised her demons in compelling fashion. Tracks such as 'SILENT ALL THESE YEARS', 'CHINA', 'WINTER' and 'CRUCIFY' (all UK hit singles in their own right) saw the album eventually scale the American charts; it has since become regarded as one of the all-time classic rock/pop records. AMOS's career trajectory was given a turbo boost in the first days of '94 with the strangely-titled 'CORNFLAKE GIRL', a Top 5 UK hit which helped propel her accompanying album, 'UNDER THE PINK' to the top of the British charts (Top 20 in America). A more probing exploration of the female psyche, the album attempted to reconcile AMOS's religious upbringing and developing identity with songs such as 'PAST THE MISSION', 'GOD' and 'PRETTY GOOD YEAR' (her second Top 10 hit in Britain). In early '96, AMOS released her most commercially successful album to date, 'BOYS FOR PELE' narrowly missing the top slot in both Britain and America despite its overtly experimental nature. Once again it was littered with classy hit singles (albeit with oblique lyrics), 'CAUGHT A LITE SNEEZE', 'TALULA' and double A side 'HEY JUPITER' / 'PROFESSIONAL WIDOW'. The latter track (allegedly written about the death of KURT COBAIN and its controversial aftermath) was subsequently deconstructed in stunning style from its more subdued album counterpart, dance guru ARMAND VAN HELDEN possibly inspired by BT's (BRIAN TRANSEAU) impressive use/sample of TORI's voice on his Top 30 hit, 'Blue Skies'. The remix scaled the British charts in early '97, exposing

AMOS's uniquely challenging work to a whole new E-poppin' audience. On the 22nd of February, 1998, she married Mark Hawley, the engineer on her last two albums, her new husband also worked on a mooted fourth set, tentatively titled 'FROM THE CHOIRGIRL HOTEL'. When released that Spring, the record shifted enough units to hit the Top 10 on both sides of the Atlantic, subsequently bringing further well-deserved acclaim to this eclectic but troubled lady; Jools Holland and his TV programme 'Later With . . .' intensified her complex image with a ubiquitous piano-playing performance that would put even RICK WAKEMAN to shame. Just over a year later, she followed this with a double-set helping 'TO VENUS AND BACK', which fused live gems with new studio work. It might have been the new millennium but come 2001, AMOS was not exactly doing anything new. Well, not unless you regard covers set (as in entire covers set) 'STRANGE LITTLE GIRLS' (2001) as breaking new ground. Constructed around a paper thin theme of recapturing the female perspective of songs originally sung about women by men, the record straddled the musical map from NEIL YOUNG to SLAYER, reaching the UK Top 20 and, surprisingly, the US Top 5. While it's unlikely that any TORI AMOS album will ever be described as easily digestible, 'SCARLET'S WALK' (2002) was a tentative return to the cryptic, guardedly accessible alternative pop she excelled at in the early 90's. 'TALES OF A LIBRARIAN: A TORI AMOS COLLECTION' (2003), meanwhile, apart from having a great title, was a more imaginative hits package than most, creatively revising her work rather than just throwing it together. • **Covers:** SMELLS LIKE TEEN SPIRIT (Nirvana) / RING MY BELL (Anita Ward) / ANGIE (Rolling Stones) / THANK YOU (Led Zeppelin) / LITTLE DRUMMER BOY (UK-hit 1959) / HOME ON THE RANGE + HAVE YOURSELF A MERRY LITTLE CHRISTMAS (trad.) / IF SIX WAS NINE (Jimi Hendrix Experience) / STRANGE FRUIT (Billie Holliday) / FAMOUS BLUE RAINCOAT (Leonard Cohen) / NEW AGE (Velvet Underground) / '97 BONNIE & CLYDE (Eminem) / STRANGE LITTLE GIRL (Stranglers) / ENJOY THE SILENCE (Depeche Mode) / I'M NOT IN LOVE (10cc) / RATTLESNAKES (Lloyd Cole & The Commotions) / TIME (Tom Waits) / HEART OF GOLD (Neil Young) / I DON'T LIKE MONDAYS (Boomtown Rats) / HAPPINESS IS A WARM GUN (Beatles) / RAINING BLOOD (Slayer) / REAL MEN (Joe Jackson). • **Trivia:** TORI sang backing for AL STEWART on 'Last Days of the Century' album, plus STAN RIDGWAY's 'Mosquitos'.

Album rating: LITTLE EARTHQUAKES (*9) / UNDER THE PINK (*7) / BOYS FOR PELE (*7) / FROM THE CHOIRGIRL MOTEL (*7) / TO VENUS AND BACK (*5) / STRANGE LITTLE GIRLS (*4) / SCARLET'S WALK (*6) / TALES OF A LIBRARIAN compilation (*8)

ELLEN AMOS

not iss. — MEA

Dec 80. (7") *<MEA 5290>* **BALTIMORE. / WALKING WITH YOU** [–] [ ]

Y KANT TORI READ

TORI AMOS – vocals, piano with group: **STEVE FARRIS** – guitar (ex-MR. MISTER) / **MATT SORUM** – drums

not iss. — Atlantic

Jun 88. (7") *<7-89086>* **THE BIG PICTURE. / YOU GO TO MY HEAD** [–] [ ]

Jul 88. (cd,c,lp) *<81845>* **Y KANT TORI READ** [–] [ ]
– The big picture / God on your island / Fayth / Fire on the side / Pirates / Floating city / Heart attack at 23 / On the boundary / You go to my head / Etienne trilogy

Aug 88. (7") *<7-89021>* **COOL ON YOUR ISLAND. / HEART ATTACK AT 23** [–] [ ]

TORI AMOS

—— with **STEVE CATON** – guitar / **WILL McGREGOR** – bass / **ERIC ROSSE** – keyboards, co-producer / **JEFF SCOTT** – bass, guitar / **PAULINHO DaCOSTA** – percussion

East West — Atlantic

Nov 91. (7") *(YZ 618/+C)* **SILENT ALL THESE YEARS. / ME AND A GUN** [51] [–]
(12"ep+=)(cd-ep+=) *(YZ 618 T/CD)* – Upside down / Thoughts.

Jan 92. (cd/c/lp) *<(7567 82358-2/-4/-1)>* **LITTLE EARTHQUAKES** [14] Dec91 [54]
– Crucify / Girl / Silent all these years / Precious things / Winter / Happy phantom / China / Leather / Mother / Tear in your hand / Me and a gun / Little earthquakes. *(lp re-iss. Jun99; same)*

Jan 92. (7"/c-s) *(A 7531/+C)* **CHINA. / SUGAR** [51] [–]
(12"+=/cd-s+=) *(A 7531 T/CD)* – Flying Dutchman / Humpty Dumpty.

Mar 92. (7"/c-s) *(A 7504/+C)* **WINTER. / THE POOL** [25] [–]
(cd-s+=) *(A 7504CD)* – Take to the sky / Sweet dreams.
(cd-s) *(A 7504CDX)* – ('A'side) / Angie / Smells like teen spirit / Thank you.

May 92. (cd-ep) *<82399-2>* **CRUCIFY (remix) / WINTER / ANGIE / SMELL LIKE TEEN SPIRIT / THANK YOU** [–] [ ]

Jun 92. (7"/c-s) *(A 7479/+C)* **CRUCIFY (remix). / HERE, IN MY HEAD** [15] [–]
(cd-s+=) *(A 7479CD)* – Mary / Crucify (version).
(cd-s) *(A 7479CDX)* – CRUCIFY LIVE EP – Crucify / Little earthquakes / Precious things / Mother.

Aug 92. (7"/c-s) *(A 7433/+C)* **SILENT ALL THESE YEARS. / SMELLS LIKE TEEN SPIRIT** [26] [–]
(cd-s) *(A 7433CD)* – ('A'side) / Upside down / Me and a gun / Thoughts.
(cd-s) *(A 7433CDX)* – ('A'side) / Ode to the banana king (part 1) / Song for Eric / Happy phantom (live).

Nov 92. (cd-ep) *<85799-2>* **WINTER / THE POOL / TAKE TO THE SKY / SWEET DREAMS / UPSIDE DOWN** [–] [ ]

—— now w/ **GEORGE PORTER JR.** – bass / **CARLO NUCCIO** – drums / **ERIC ROSSE** – programming / **STEVE CATON** – drums / **PAULINHO DaCOSTA** – percussion

Jan 94. (7"/c-s) *(A 7281/+C)* **CORNFLAKE GIRL. / SISTER JANET** [4] [–]
(cd-s+=) *(A 7281CD)* – Piano suite: All the girls hate her – Over it.
(cd-s) *(A 7282CDX)* – ('A'side) / A case of you / If 6 was 9 / Strange fruit.

Feb 94. (c-s) *<87250>* **GOD / SISTER JANET** [–] [72]
(cd-s) *<PRCD 5408>* – ('A'side) / Home on the range (Cherokee edition) / Hand suite: All the girls hate her – Over it.

Feb 94. (cd/c/lp) *<(7567 82567-2/-4/-1)>* **UNDER THE PINK** [1] [12]
– Pretty good year / God / Bells for her / Past the mission / Baker baker / The wrong band / The waitress / Cornflake girl / Icicle / Cloud on my tongue / Space dog / Yes, Anastasia.

Mar 94. (7"/c-s) *(A 7263/+C)* **PRETTY GOOD YEAR. / HONEY** [7] [–]
(cd-s+=) *(A 7263CD)* – The black swan.
(cd-s) *(A 7263CDX)* – ('A'side) / Daisy dead petals / Home on the range (Cherokee version).

Apr 94. (cd-ep) *<85655-2>* **CORNFLAKE GIRL / SISTER JANET / DAISY DEAD PETALS / HONEY** [–] [ ]

—— TRENT REZNOR of NINE INCH NAILS guested vox on 'Past The Mission'.

May 94. (7"/c-s) *(A 7257/+C)* **PAST THE MISSION. / ('A'live)** [31] [–]
(cd-s) *(A 7257CD)* – Winter (live) / The waitress (live) / Here in my head (live).
(cd-s) *(A 7257CDX)* – ('A'live) / Upside down (live) / Icicle (live) / Flying Dutchman (live).

Oct 94. (7"pic-d/c-s) *(A 7251/+C)* **GOD. / ('A'-Acapella vocal & rain mix)** [44] [–]
(12"+=/cd-s+=) *(A 7251 T/CD)* – ('A'remixes from;- The Joy / Carl Craig / CJ Bolland).

Atlantic — Atlantic

Jan 96. (c-s) *(A 5524C)* **CAUGHT A LITE SNEEZE / GRAVEYARD / TOODLES MR JIM** [20] [–]
(cd-s) *(A 5524CD1)* – ('A'side) / London girls / That's what I like Mick (sandwich song) / Samurai.
(cd-s) *(A 5524CD2)* – ('A'side) / Toodles Mr. Jim / Hungarian wedding song / This old man.

Jan 96. (cd-ep) *<85519>* **CAUGHT A LITE SNEEZE. / SILLY SONGS (medley:- THIS OLD MAN – THAT'S WHAT I LIKE MICK – GRAVEYARD – TOODLES MR. JIM)** [–] [60]

Jan 96. (cd/c) *<(7567 82862-2/-4)>* **BOYS FOR PELE** [2] [2]
– Beauty queen – Horses / Blood roses / Father Lucifer / Professional widow / Mr Zebra / Marianne / Caught a lite sneeze / Muhammed my

friend / Hey Jupiter / Way down / Little Amsterdam / Talula / Not the Red Baron / Agent Orange / Doughnut song / In the spring of his voodoo / Putting the damage on / Twinkle.

Mar 96. (c-s) *(A 8512C)* **TALULA / SISTER NAMED DESIRE** [22] [-]
(cd-s+=) *(A 8512CD2)* – Frog on my toe / Alamo.
(cd-s) *(A 8512CD1)* – ('A'-Tornado mix) / ('A'-Synethasia mix) / Til the chicken / Amazing Grace.

May 96. (cd-ep) *<85504>* **TALULA (Tornado version) / SAMURAI / FROG ON MY TOE / LONDON GIRLS / TATULA (BT's synethasia mix)** [-] [ ]

Jul 96. (c-s/12") *(A 5494 C/T)* **HEY JUPITER. / TALULA** [20] Aug96 [94]
(cd-s) *(A 5494CD) <82955-2>* – ('A'-Dakota version) / Professional widow / Sugar (live) / Honey (live). *<US ep+=, hit album chart>* – Somewhere over the rainbow.

Sep 96. (cd-s) *<2-85475>* **IN THE SPRINGTIME OF HIS VOODOO (mixes)** [-] [ ]

—— Nov'96, she featured on BT single 'BLUE SKIES', which hit UK 26.

Dec 96. (c-s/12"/cd-s) *(A 5450 C/T/CD) <2-85499>* **PROFESSIONAL WIDOW (IT'S GOT TO BE BIG). / (remixes by Armand Van Helden & Mr. Roy)** [1] Jul96 [ ]

Mar 97. (cd-s) *<2-83001>* **SILENT ALL THESE YEARS (live) / ('A'-album version)** [-] [65]

—— now with **MATT CHAMBERLAIN** – drums / **JUSTIN MELDAL-JOHNSEN + GEORGE PORTER JR.** – bass / **STEVE CATON** – guitars / **ANDY GRAY** – programming / etc

Apr 98. (c-s) *(AT 0031C) <84104>* **SPARK / PURPLE PEOPLE** [16] Jun98 [49]
(cd-s+=) *(AT 0031CD1)* – Have yourself a merry little Christmas / Bachelorette.
(cd-s) *(AT 0031CD2)* – ('A'side) / Do it again / Cooling.

May 98. (cd/c/lp) *<(7567 83095-2/-4/-1)>* **FROM THE CHOIRGIRL HOTEL** [6] [5]
– Spark / Cruel / Black-dove (January) / Raspberry swirl / Jackie's strength / iieee / Liquid diamonds / She's your cocaine / Northern lad / Hotel / Playboy mommy / Pandora's aquarium.

Aug 98. (cd-s) *<2-84163>* **JACKIE'S STRENGTH / NEVER SEEN BLUE / BEULAH LAND** [-] [54]

Aug 98. (cd-ep) *(AT 0041CD)* **JACKIE'S STRENGTH (Wedding Cake mixes) / FATHER LUCIFER (Silkscreen mixes)** [ ] [-]

Aug 98. (c-s; w-drawn) *(AT 0045C)* **RASPBERRY SWIRL (Lip Gloss version) / ('A'extended)** [ ] [-]
(12"+=/cd-s+=; w-drawn) *(AT 0045 T/CD)* – ('A'-Scarlet Spectrum Feels mix).

Apr 99. (cd-ep) *<2-84412>* **CRUEL (Shady Feline mix) / RASPBERRY SWIRL (Lip Gloss version) / AMBIENT RASPBERRY SWIRL (Scarlet Spectrum Feels) / MAINLINE CHERRY – AMBIENT SPARK** [-] [ ]

Aug 99. (cd-s) *<2-84533>* **BLISS / HEY JUPITER (live) / UPSIDE DOWN (live)** [-] [91]

Sep 99. (d-cd/d-c) *(7567 83242-2) <83230>* **TO VENUS AND BACK** [22] [12]
– Bliss / Juarez / Concertina / Glory of the 80's / Lust / Suede / Riot proof / Datura / Spring haze / 1000 oceans / Precious things / Cornflake girl / Bells for her / Girl / Cooling / Mr. Zebra / Cloud on my tongue / Sugar / Little earthquakes / Space dog / Waitress / Purple people.

Nov 99. (c-s) *(AT 0077 C/CD2)* **GLORY OF THE 80's / BAKER BAKER (live) / WINTER (live)** [46] [-]
(cd-s) *(AT 0077CD)* – ('A'side) / Blue raincoat (live) / Twinkle (live).

Nov 99. (cd-s) *<2-84534>* **1000 OCEANS / BAKER BAKER (live)** [-] [ ]

Sep 01. (cd/c) *<(7567 83486-2/-4)>* **STRANGE LITTLE GIRLS** [16] [4]
– New age / '97 Bonnie and Clyde / Strange little girl / Enjoy the silence / Rattlesnakes / I'm not in love / Time / Heart of gold / I don't like Mondays / Happiness is a warm gun / Raining blood / Real men. *(cd re-iss. Aug02; same)*

Epic Sony

Oct 02. (cd-s) *(673043-2)* **A SORTA FAIRYTALE (route 101 mix) / OPERATION PETER PAN / A SORTA FAIRYTALE / A SCARLET STORY (video)** [41] [ ]

Oct 02. (cd) *(508782-2) <86939>* **SCARLET'S WALK** [26] [7]
– Amber waves / A sorta fairytale / Wednesday / Strange / Carbon / Crazy / Wampum prayer / Don't make me come to Vegas / Sweet sangria / Your cloud / Pancake / I can't see New York / Mrs. Jesus / Taxi ride / Another girl's paradise / Scarlet's walk / Virginia / Gold dust. *(cd w/ free dvd; 508782-9)* – (video footage).

– compilations, etc. –

Nov 03. (cd) *Atlantic; <(7567 83658-2)>* **TALES OF A LIBRARIAN: A TORI AMOS COLLECTION** (re-workings) [74] [40]
– Precious things / Angels / Silent all these years / Cornflake girl / Mary / God / Winter / Spark / Way down / Professional widow / Mr. Zebra / Crucify / Me and a gun / Bliss / Playboy mommy / Baker, baker / Tear in your hand / Sweet dreams / Jackie's strength / Snow cherries from France. *(dvd+=; 7567 83658-2)* – Pretty good year / Honey / Northern lad / Putting the damage on / Mr. Zebra.

☐ AMPS (see under ⇒ BREEDERS)

ANASTACIA

Born: ANASTACIA NEWKIRK, 17 Sep'75, New York City, New York, USA. Despite being diagnosed with Crohn's disease at a very early age, ANASTACIA – who was raised in Chicago by her actress mother and singer father – made a name for herself as a teenage dancer on such programmes as MTV's 'Dance Club' and in various music videos (one of which was SALT'N'PEPA's 'Everybody Get Up'). In 1999, she graduated musically when she got to the final of US TV talent show 'The Cut'. This would mark a turning point in her career as it resulted in her inking a deal with 'Sony' offshoot 'Daylight'. Her debut album, 'NOT THAT KIND' was issued late in 2000, and although not a massive success in America, it sold two million copies in Europe and Asia thanks to the smash-hit single 'I'M OUTTA LOVE' (subsequently sung to death by hopefuls on the UK talent contest 'Pop Idols'). Even though she was American herself, the US of A still hadn't taken to ANASTACIA's loud, brash and vocally powerful ARETHA FRANKLIN-meets-MACY GRAY-like R&B/pop songs, not to mention her sexy and extroverted personality. Her only success to date, has been a dance version of 'I'M OUTTA LOVE' which was a massive club hit. ANASTACIA went on to record and release the sophomore album 'FREAK OF NATURE' in 2001, backed by the single 'PAID MY DUES', which entered the UK Top 20.

Album rating: NOT THAT KIND (*7) / FREAK OF NATURE (*5)

ANASTACIA – vocals / with various back-up

Epic Daylight

Sep 00. (c-s) *(669578-4) <79343>* **I'M OUTTA LOVE / I'M OUTTA LOVE (Rhythm Masters radio mix)** [6] Apr00 [92]
(cd-s+=) *(669578-2)* – ('A'-Ron Trent mix) / ('A'-video).

Oct 00. (cd/c) *(497412-2/-4) <69948>* **NOT THAT KIND** [2] Mar00 [ ]
– Not that kind / I'm outta love / Cowboys and kisses / Who's gonna stop the rain / Love is alive / I ask of you / Wishing well / Made for lovin' you / Black roses / Yo trippin' / One more chance / Same old story. *<re-iss. Apr01 & Dec02; same>*

Jan 01. (c-s) *(669722-4)* **NOT THAT KIND / NOTHIN' AT ALL / I'M OUTTA LOVE** [11] [-]
(cd-s+=) *(669722-2)* – ('A'-mixes).

May 01. (c-s) *(671262-4)* **COWBOYS AND KISSES / I'M OUTTA LOVE (Hex Hector mix)** [28] [-]
(cd-s+=) *(671262-2)* – ('A'-Tin Tin Out remix) / ('A'-Hex Hector main club mix) / ('A'-video).

Aug 01. (c-s) *(671717-4)* **MADE FOR LOVIN' YOU / MADE FOR LOVIN' YOU (Tin Tin Out mix) / UNDERDOG** [27] [-]
(cd-s+=) *(671717-2)* – ('A'-video).

Nov 01. (c-s) *(672125-4)* **PAID MY DUES / ('A'-S-man's darkstar radio mix)** [14] [-]
(cd-s+=) *(672125-2)* – I dreamed you.

Nov 01. (cd) *<(504757-2)>* **FREAK OF NATURE** [14] [27]
– Freak of nature / Paid my dues / Overdue goodbye / You'll never be alone / One day in your life / How come the world won't stop / Why'd you lie to me / Don't cha wanna / Secrets / Don't stop (doin' it) / I dreamed of you / Overdue goodbye (reprise). *(ltd d-cd+=; 504757-0)* – I thought I told

you that (with FAITH EVANS) / Someday my prince will come / Paid my dues (S-man's darkstar remix) / One day in your life ((Hex Hector & Mac Quale club mix) / Why's you lie to me (Maurice Joshua remix) / Freak of nature (live in Japan 9/13/02) / Overdue goodbye (live in Japan 9/13/02).

Mar 02. (c-s) *(672456-4)* **ONE DAY IN YOUR LIFE / (MASH radio mix)** 11 –
(cd-s+=) *(671717-2)* – ('A'-Almighty mix) / ('A'-video).

Jun 02. (c-s) *(673111-4)* **WHY'D YOU LIE TO ME / (MASH remix) / (Maurice J mix)** 25 –
(cd-s+=) *(673111-2)* – Bad girls (with JAMIROQUAI) / ('A'-video).
(cd-s) *(673111-5)* – ('A'side) / ('A'-Omar's UK Kardinal) / Boom / Boom (video).

Nov 02. (cd-s) *(673380-2)* **YOU'LL NEVER WALK ALONE / YOU SHOOK ME ALL NIGHT (with CELINE DION) / LORD IS BLESSING ME (live on stage at 6 years old) / ('A'-video)** 31 –

☐ Trey ANASTASIO (see under ⇒ PHISH)

☐ Ian ANDERSON (see under ⇒ JETHRO TULL)

☐ Jon ANDERSON (see under ⇒ YES)

Laurie ANDERSON

Born: LAURA PHILLIPS ANDERSON, 5 Jun'47, Chicago, Illinois, USA. Graduating from Columbia University in the early 70's, she soon became the Mother Superior of the New York art-rock cognescenti, after moving there to sculpture in the mid 70's. In 1977, a debut 45 'IT'S NOT THE BULLET THAT KILLS YOU', saw her turn her talents to music although the single did nothing. Gave up history tuition to concentrate more on performance art and fashion, utilising her weird violin playing to great effect. It wasn't until 1981 that her recording career took off, when a surprise 8-minute nauseating UK hit, 'O SUPERMAN', paved the way for debut 'Warners' album 'BIG SCIENCE'. This highlighted her speech-based, hypnotic minimalism, rounding on such topics as technology, culture and alienation with a wry, unsightful ease. The follow-up, 'MR HEARTBREAK', was a slightly more mainstream effort, due in part to BILL LASWELL's production on a couple of tracks. Two live albums were released during the mid-80's, one of them the latter 'HOME OF THE BRAVE', with its accompanying concert film, was a flop despite garnering critical plaudits at Cannes. 'STRANGE ANGELS' (1989) saw ANDERSON move towards "real" singing and a more melodious approach while 1994's 'BRIGHT RED', co-produced by BRIAN ENO was characterised by a more claustrophobic feel. Another live album and tour cemented her reputation as a witty and succinct cultural commentator, although her recorded output, while often being innovative, sometimes veered too close to theatre to warrant repeated listening. Another hiatus for LAURIE ended in 2001 when she released 'LIFE ON A STRING', a musical theatre work based on the novel 'Moby Dick'. The violinist (complete with numerous other string-ed instrumentation) developed her experimental side to the fore on the majority on the set while a song, 'SLIP AWAY', saw her depicting the recent death of her father. A month later, and to mark the horrific terrorist act that befell her native city on the 11th of September 2001, she performed 'LIVE AT THE TOWN HALL, NEW YORK CITY, SEPTEMBER 19-20, 2001' (the title of her next set in 2002), her lyrics "here comes the planes . . ." from 'O SUPERMAN' poignant to these fearful days as when they were written by her over 20 years ago. • **Trivia:** Her audio-visual concerts, complete with orchestra lasted for around 7 hours. Guests on her 1984 set were PETER GABRIEL, NILE RODGERS and WILLIAM S. BURROUGHS. She was romantically involved with LOU REED in the early 90's. • **Bibliography:** THE PACKAGE: A MYSTERY (1971) / TRANSPORTATION (1974) / NOTEBOOK (1977) / WORDS IN REVERSE (1979) / HOME OF THE BRAVE (1979) / EMPTY PLACES (1991) / STORIES FROM THE NERVE BIBLE (1994).

Album rating: BIG SCIENCE (*6) / UNITED STATES LIVE (*5) / MISTER HEARTBREAK (*7) / HOME OF THE BRAVE (*6) / STRANGE ANGELS (*7) / BRIGHT RED (*6) / THE UGLY ONE WITH THE JEWELS AND OTHER STORIES (*7) / TALK NORMAL – THE LAURIE ANDERSON ANTHOLOGY compilation (*7) / LIFE ON A STRING (*4) / LIVE AT TOWN HALL . . . (*5)

LAURIE ANDERSON – vocals, multi-instrumentalist (violin / synthesizers)

— with many on session incl. **DAVID VAN TIEGHEM** – percussion, drums / **ROMA BARAN** – accordian / **BILL OBRECHE** – sax, flute / **CHICK FISHER** – sax, clarinet / **PETER GORDON** – clarinet, sax / etc

not iss. Holly Solomon Gallery

1977. (7"ltd) <*004*> **IT'S NOT THE BULLET THAT KILLS YOU – IT'S THE HOLE** –

not iss. One-Ten

Sep 81. (7") <*OT 005*> **O SUPERMAN. / WALK THE DOG** –

Warners Warners

Oct 81. (7") *(K 17870)* <*49876*> **O SUPERMAN. / WALK THE DOG** 2

Jan 82. (7") *(K 17941)* **BIG SCIENCE. / EXAMPLE 22** –

Apr 82. (lp/c) *(K/K4 57002)* <*3674*> **BIG SCIENCE** 29
– From the air / Big science / Sweaters / Walking and falling / Born, never asked / O Superman (for Massenet) / Example #22 / Let x = x / It tango. *(cd-iss. Apr84; K2 57002)*

Jul 82. (7") *(K 17956)* **LET X = X. / IT TANGO** –
(12"+=) *(K 17956)* – Sweaters.

Feb 84. (lp/c) *(925077-1/-4)* <*25077*> **MISTER HEARTBREAK** 93 60
– Sharkey's day / Language d'amour / Gravity's angel / Kokoku / Excellent birds / Blue lagoon / Sharkey's night. *(cd-iss. Jul84; 925077-2)*

Jan 85. (5-lp-box) *(925192-1)* <*25192*> **UNITED STATES LIVE (live)**
– Say hello / Walk the dog / Violin solo / Closed circuits / For a large and changing rooms / Pictures of it / The language of the future / Cartoon song / Small voice / Three walking songs / The healing horn / New Jersey turnpike / So happy birthday / English / Dance of electricity / Three songs for paper, film and video / Sax solo / Sax duet / Born, never asked / From the air / Beginning French / O Superman (for Massenet) / Talkshow / Frames for the pictures / Democratic why / Looking for you walking and falling / Private property / Neon duet / Let x = x / The Mailman's nightmare / Difficult listening hour / Language is a virus from Outer Space – (William S. Burroughs) / Reverb / If you can't talk about it, point to it / Violin walk / City song / Finnish farmers / Red map / Hey ah / Bagpipe solo / Steven Weed / Time and a half / Voices on paper / Example #22 / Strike / False documents / New York social life / A curious phenomenon / Yankee see / I dreamed I had to take a test . . . / Running dogs / Four, three, two, one / The big top / It was up in the mountains / Odd objects / Dr. Miller / Big science / Big science (reprise) / Cello solo / It tango / Blue lagoon / Hothead (la langue d'amour) / Stiff neck / Telephone song / Sweaters / We've got four big clocks (and they're all ticking) / Song for two Jims / Over the river / Mach 20 / Rising sun / The visitors / The stranger / Classified / Going somewhere / Fireworks / Dog show / Lighting out for the territories.

Apr 86. (lp/c/cd) *(925400-1/-4/-2)* <*25400*> **HOME OF THE BRAVE**
– Smoke rings / White lily / Late show / Talk normal / Radar / Language is a virus from outer space / Sharkey's night / Credit racket.

May 86. (7"/12") *(W 8701/+T)* **LANGUAGE IS A VIRUS FROM OUTER SPACE (edit). / WHITE LILY** –

Nov 89. (lp/c)(cd) *(WX 258/+C)(K 925900-2)* <*25900*> **STRANGE ANGELS**
– Strange angels / Monkey's paw / Coolsville / Ramon / Babydoll / Beautiful red dress / The day the Devil / The dream before / My eyes / Hiawatha.

Oct 94. (cd/c) <*(9362 45534-2/-4)*> **BRIGHT RED**
– Speechless / Bright red / The puppet motel / Speak my language / World without end / Freefall / Muddy river / Beautiful pea green boat / Love

among the sailors / Poison / In our sleep / Night in Baghdad / Tightrope / Same time tomorrow.

Mar 95. (cd/c) <(9362 45347-2/-4)> **THE UGLY ONE WITH THE JEWELS & OTHER STORIES FROM THE NERVE BIBLE** ☐ ☐
– The end of the world / The salesman / The night flight from Houston / Word of mouth / The soul is a bird / The ouija board / The ugly one with the jewels / The geographic North Pole / John Lilly / The rotowhirl / On the way to Jerusalem / The Hollywood strangler / Maria Teresa Teresa Maria / Someone else's dream / White lily / The mysterious "J" / The cultural ambassador / Same time tomorrow. *(re-iss. Jul00; same)*

Apr 95. (cd-ep) <43515> **IN OUR SLEEP** - ☐
– In our sleep / Poison / The ouija board / In our sleep (trance mix) / Poison (trance mix) / The ugly one with jewels / Poison (instrumental) / In our sleep (instrumental).

Nonesuch – Atlantic | Nonesuch – Atlantic

Aug 01. (cd) <(7559 75939-2)> **LIFE ON A STRING** ☐ ☐
– One white whale / The island where I come from / Pieces and parts / Here with you / Slip away / My compensation / Dark angel / Broken / Washington Street / Statue of liberty / One beautiful evening / Life on a string.

Jun 02. (d-cd) <(7559 79681-2)> **LIVE AT TOWN HALL, NEW YORK CITY, SEPTEMBER 19-20, 2001 (live)** ☐ May02 ☐
– Here with you / Statue of liberty / Let x=x / Sweaters / My compensation / Washington Street / Pieces and parts / Strange angels / Dark angel / Wildebeests / One beautiful evening / Poison / Broken / Progress / Animals / Life on a string / Beginning French / O Superman / Slip away / White lily / Puppet motel / Love among the sailors / Coolsville.

– compilations, etc. –

Nov 00. (d-cd) *Rhino*; <(8122 76648-2)> **TALK NORMAL – THE LAURIE ANDERSON ANTHOLOGY** ☐ ☐
– o Superman (for Massenet) / From the air / Big science / Born, never asked / It tango / Gravity's angel / Excellent birds / Langue d'amour / Sharkey's day / Walk the dog / Cartoon song / So happy birthday / City song / The big top / Dr. Miller / Lighting out for the territories / Smoke rings / Talk normal / Language is a virus / Credit racket / Strange angels / Babydoll / Coolsville / My eyes / The dream before / The day the Devil / Speak my language / Love among the sailors / Poison / In our sleep / Night in Baghdad / The night flight from Houston / The rotowhirl / The ouija board / The end of the world.

☐ ANDERSON BRUFORD WAKEMAN HOWE
(see under ⇒ YES)

ANIMALS

Formed: Newcastle, England ... 1960, as The ALAN PRICE COMBO. BURDON's arrival in 1962 led to tension in the ranks, no doubt a major contributing factor to the band's increasingly manic stage show. After supporting the likes of legendary bluesmen SONNY BOY WILLIAMSON and JOHN LEE HOOKER, they moved to London early in '64 and were promptly signed to EMI's 'Columbia' label by then virtually unknown producer MICKIE MOST. Re-christened The ANIMALS by the fans, the band adopted the name with glee and hit paydirt in summer '64 with the blues standard, 'HOUSE OF THE RISING SUN'. A massive hit on both sides of the Atlantic, with BURDON's ominous vocal phrasing and PRICE's wailing organ, the record remains the band's defining moment. Rarely, if ever, has the United Kingdom produced a white guy who could sing the blues like ERIC BURDON. The whisky-soaked menace of his voice sounded at times like Old Nick incarnate and was a key component in The ANIMALS feisty challenge to The ROLLING STONES' throne at the height of the 60's R&B Boom. Much like The BYRDS, The ANIMALS had an uncanny knack of covering material which, on paper, seemed less than obvious, but worked a treat on vinyl. 'DON'T LET ME BE MISUNDERSTOOD' and 'WE GOTTA GET OUT OF THIS PLACE' both went Top 5 in the UK, ensuring respectable sales of their second album, 'ANIMAL TRACKS'. PRICE left in 1965, beginning a dispute (incredibly still ongoing after more than 30 years) with BURDON over the publishing rights to 'HOUSE OF THE RISING SUN'. With DAVE ROWBERRY as PRICE's replacement, the band cut a few more albums including the semi-classic 'ANIMALIZATION', which contained such powerful tracks as 'INSIDE – LOOKING OUT' and 'GIN HOUSE BLUES'. The original ANIMALS fell apart towards the end of '66, CHAS CHANDLER going on to manage JIMI HENDRIX. BURDON moved to San Francisco, where he immersed himself in the nascent psychedelic scene, consuming liberal quantities of LSD. Under the new and improved moniker ERIC BURDON & THE ANIMALS, he released in 1967 his paeon to the emerging hippy culture, 'WINDS OF CHANGE'. Other highlights of this period include BURDON's tribute to the narcotic delights of the Swiss pharmaceutical industry, 'A GIRL NAMED SANDOZ' and 'MONTEREY', his reverential recollection of the legendary pop festival. BURDON kept his third eye in check enough to release a handful of introspective albums before this particular version of The ANIMALS split at the end of '68. He tasted major success for the last time with soul/funk band WAR, their debut single 'SPILL THE WINE', climbing into the Top 3 in the States mid 1970. The collaboration was short-lived, however, and BURDON went solo with weak support from the public. The original ANIMALS line-up (minus PRICE, of course) re-formed in 1977 and again in '83, although the new material was met with a lukewarm response in the UK. CHAS CHANDLER, who also went onto work with SLADE and others, died of a heart attack on the 17th July '96. • **Songwriters:** BURDON lyrics / PRICE arrangements songs, with covers BOOM BOOM + DIMPLES + I'M MAD AGAIN (John Lee Hooker) / I'M IN LOVE AGAIN (Fats Domino) / TALKIN' ABOUT YOU (Ray Charles) / GONNA SEND YOU BACK TO GEORGIA (Timmy Shaw) / DON'T LET ME BE MISUNDERSTOOD (Nina Simone) / PRETTY THING (Bo Diddley) / BABY LET ME TAKE YOU HOME (Russell-Farrell) / BRING IT ON HOME TO ME (Sam Cooke) / WE'VE GOTTA GET OUT OF THIS PLACE (Mann-Weil) / DON'T BRING ME DOWN (Goffin-King) / RIVER DEEP MOUNTAIN HIGH (Phil Spector) / PAINT IT BLACK (Rolling Stones) / etc.

Best CD compilation: THE COMPLETE ANIMALS (*9)

ERIC BURDON (b.11 May'41, Walker, nr.Newcastle, England) – vocals / **ALAN PRICE** (b.19 Apr'41, Fairfield, Durham, England) – keyboards, vocals / **HILTON VALENTINE** (b.21 May'43, North Shields, England) – guitar / **CHAS CHANDLER** (b.18 Dec'38, Heaton, nr.Newcastle, England) – bass / **JOHN STEEL** (b. 4 Feb'41, Gateshead, England) – drums

Columbia | M.G.M.

Apr 64. (7") *(DB 7247)* <K 13242> **BABY LET ME TAKE YOU HOME. / GONNA SEND YOU BACK TO WALKER** (US 'A'side) 21 Sep64 57

Jun 64. (7") *(DB 7301)* <K 13264> **THE HOUSE OF THE RISING SUN. / TALKIN' 'BOUT YOU** 1 Jul64 1

Sep 64. (7") *(DB 7354)* <K 13274> **I'M CRYING. / TAKE IT EASY** 8 Oct64 19

Oct 64. (lp; mono/stereo) *(33SX 1669)* <E/SE 4264> **THE ANIMALS** 6 Sep64 7
– Story of Bo Diddley / Bury my body / Dimples / I've been around / I'm in love again / The girl can't help it / I'm mad again / She said yeah / The right time / Memphis / Boom boom / Around and around. *(US diff. tracks +=> – The house of the rising sun. (re-iss. Oct69 on 'Regal Starline'; SRS 5006) (cd-iss. Oct97 on 'E.M.I.'; DORIG 125)*

Nov 64. (7") <K 13298> **BOOM BOOM. / BLUE FEELING** - 43

Jan 65. (7") *(DB 7445)* <K 13311> **DON'T LET ME BE MISUNDERSTOOD. / CLUB A-GO-GO** 3 Feb65 15

Mar 65. (lp; mono/stereo) <E/SE 4281> **THE ANIMALS ON TOUR (live)** - 99
– Boom boom / How you've changed / I believe to my soul / Mess around

bright lights / Big city / Worried life blues / Let the good times roll / Crying dimples / She said yeah.

Apr 65. (7") *(DB 7539)* *<K 13339>* **BRING IT ON HOME TO ME. / FOR MISS CAULKER** [7] May 65 [32]

May 65. (lp; mono/stereo) *(33SX 1708)* *<E/SE 4305>* **ANIMAL TRACKS** [6] Sep65 [57]
– Mess around / How you've changed / Hallelujah, I love her so / I believe to my soul / Worried life blues / Roberta / I ain't got you / Bright lights, big city / Let the good times roll / For Miss Caulker / Roadrunner. *(re-iss. Sep84 on 'Fame' lp/c; FA/TCFA 413110) (cd-iss. Jan99 on 'E.M.I.'; 498936-2)*

Jul 65. (7") *(DB 7639)* *<K 13382>* **WE'VE GOTTA GET OUT OF THIS PLACE. / I CAN'T BELIEVE IT** [2] Aug65 [13]

Oct 65. (7") *(DB 7741)* *<K 13414>* **IT'S MY LIFE. / I'M GONNA CHANGE THE WORLD** [7] Nov65 [23]

— **DAVE ROWBERRY** (b.27 Dec'43, Newcastle, England) – keyboards (ex-MIKE COTTON SOUND) repl. PRICE who went solo

Decca M.G.M.

Feb 66. (7") *(F 2332)* **INSIDE – LOOKING OUT. / OUTCAST** [12] [–]

Mar 66. (7") *<K 13468>* **INSIDE – LOOKING OUT. / YOU'RE ON MY MIND** [–] [34]

— **BARRY JENKINS** (b.22 Dec'44, Leicester, England) – drums (ex-NASHVILLE TEENS) repl. STEEL

May 66. (7") *(F 12407)* *<K 13514>* **DON'T BRING ME DOWN. / CHEATING** [6] [12]

May 66. (lp) *(LK 4797)* **ANIMALISMS** [4] [–]
– One monkey don't stop no show / Maudie / Outcast / Sweet little sixteen / You're on my mind / Clapping / Gin house blues / Squeeze her – Tease her / What am I living for / I put a spell on you / That's all I am to you / She'll return it. *(cd-iss. Sep99 on 'Repetoire'; RR 4772)*

Aug 66. (lp; mono/stereo) *<E/SE 4384>* **ANIMALIZATION** [–] [20]
– Don't bring me down / One monkey don't stop no show / You're on my mind / She'll return it / Cheating / Inside – looking out / See see rider / Gin house blues / Maudie / What am I living for / Sweet little sixteen / I put a spell on you.

Sep 66. (7") *<K 13582>* **SEE SEE RIDER. / SHE'LL RETURN IT** [–] [10]

Nov 66. (lp; mono/stereo) *<E/SE 4414>* **ANIMALISM** [–] [33]
– All night long / Shake / Other side of this life / Rock me baby / Lucille / Smokestack lightning / Hey Gyp / Hit the road Jack / Outcast / Louisiana blues / That's all I am to you / Going down slow. *(cd-iss. Apr03 on 'Repertoire'; REP 4772)*

ERIC BURDON & THE ANIMALS

— ERIC with session musicians incl. BENNY GOULSON

Oct 66. (7") *(F 12502)* **HELP ME GIRL. / SEE SEE RIDER** [14] [–]

Dec 66. (7") *<K 13636>* **HELP ME GIRL. / THAT AIN'T WHERE IT'S AT** [–] [29]

Mar 67. (lp; mono/stereo) *<E/SE 4433>* **ERIC IS HERE** [–] [ ]
– Help me girl / In the night / Mama told me not to come / I think it's gonna rain today / This side of goodbye / That ain't where it's at / Wait till next year / Losin' control / It's not easy / Biggest bundle of them all / It's been a long time coming / True love.

— ERIC who had earlier moved to California brought back **BARRY JENKINS** in Jan '67

— recruited **VIC BRIGGS** (b.14 Feb'45, London) – guitar (ex-STEAMPACKET) to finally repl ROWBERRY / **JOHN WIEDER** (b.21 Apr'47, London) – guitar, violin repl. VALENTINE who went solo / **DANNY McCULLOCH** (b.18 Jul'45, London) – bass repl. CHANDLER who became producer

M.G.M. M.G.M.

May 67. (7") *(MGM 1340)* *<K 13721>* **WHEN I WAS YOUNG. / A GIRL NAMED SANDOZ** [45] Apr67 [15]

Aug 67. (7") *(MGM 1344)* **GOOD TIMES. / AIN'T THAT SO** [20] [–]

Aug 67. (7") *<K 13769>* **SAN FRANCISCAN NIGHTS. / GOOD TIMES** [–] [9]

Oct 67. (lp; mono/stereo) *(C/CS 8052)* *<E/SE 4454>* **WINDS OF CHANGE** [ ] Sep67 [42]
– San Franciscan nights / Good times / Winds of change / Poem by the sea / Paint it black / Black plague / Yes I am experienced / Man-woman / Hotel hell / Anything / It's all meat. *(re-iss. Apr71; 2354 001) (cd-iss. Oct85 on 'Polydor'; 825 717-2)*

Oct 67. (7") *(MGM 1359)* **SAN FRANCISCAN NIGHTS. / GRATEFULLY DEAD** [7] [–]

Nov 67. (7") *<K 13868>* **MONTEREY. / AIN'T IT SO** [–] [15]

Feb 68. (7") *(MGM 1373)* *<K 13939>* **SKY PILOT (pt.1). / SKY PILOT (pt.2)** [40] Jun68 [14]

Mar 68. (7") *<K 13917>* **ANYTHING. / IT'S ALL MEAT** [–] [80]

May 68. (7") *(MGM 1412)* **MONTEREY. / ANYTHING** [ ] [–]

May 68. (lp; mono/stereo) *(C/CS 8075)* *<E/SE 4537>* **THE TWAIN SHALL MEET** [ ] Mar68 [79]
– Just the thought / Closer to the truth / No self pity / Orange and red beans / Sky pilot / We love you Lil / All is one.

— **ZOOT MONEY** – keyboards (ex-BIG ROLL BAND, ex-DANTALIAN'S CHARIOT) / **ANDY SOMERS** (aka SUMMERS) – guitar, bass (ex-BIG ROLL BAND, ex-DANTALIAN'S CHARIOT) repl. BRIGGS and McCULLOCH

Aug 68. (lp; mono/stereo) *<E/SE 4553>* **EVERY ONE OF US** [–] [ ]
– Uppers and downers / Serenade to a sweet lady / The immigrant lad / Year of the guru / St.James infirmary / New York 1963 – America 1968 / White houses.

Nov 68. (7") *<K 14013>* **WHITE HOUSES. / RIVER DEEP MOUNTAIN HIGH** [–] [67]

Jan 69. (7") *(MGM 1461)* **RING OF FIRE. / I'M AN ANIMAL** [25] [–]

Dec 68. (lp; mono/stereo) <d-lp> *(C/CS 8105)* *<SE 4591-2>* **LOVE IS** [ ] [ ]
– River deep, mountain high / I'm the animal / I'm dying, or am I / Gemini / The madman / Ring of fire / Coloured rain / To love somebody / As tears go passing by. *(UK re-iss. Apr71; 2354 006-007) (re-iss. 1973; 2619 002) (cd re-iss/Sep94 on 'One Way'; OW 30338)*

May 69. (7") *(MGM 1481)* **RIVER DEEP, MOUNTAIN HIGH. / HELP ME GIRL** [ ] [–]

— Split Feb69. WIEDER joined FAMILY, ZOOT went solo, JENKINS joined HEAVY JELLY, SOMERS became SUMMERS and joined KEVIN AYERS then KEVIN COYNE. He later helped form The POLICE

ERIC BURDON & WAR

ERIC BURDON – vocals, and WAR: – **LONNIE (LEROY) JORDAN** – keyboards, vocals / **HOWARD SCOTT** – guitar, vocals / **CHARLES MILLER** – saxophone, clarinet / **HAROLD BROWN** – drums, percussion / **B.B. DICKERSON** – bass / **THOMAS 'PAPA DEE' ALLEN** – keyboards / **LEE OSKAR** – harmonica

Polydor M.G.M.

Sep 70. (lp) *(2310 041)* *<SE 4663>* **ERIC BURDON DECLARES WAR** [50] May70 [18]
– Dedication / Roll on Kirk / Tobacco road / I have a dream / Spill the wine / Blues for Memphis Slim / Birth / Mother Earth / Mr.Charlie / Danish pastry / You're no stranger. *(re-iss. Oct79 on 'MCA'; MCF 3026) <cd-iss. Oct95 on 'Avenue'; 74321 30526-2)*

Jul 70. (7") *(2001 072)* *<K 14118>* **SPILL THE WINE. / MAGIC MOUNTAIN** [ ] [3]

Liberty M.G.M.

Dec 70. (7") *(LBF 15434)* *<K 14196>* **THEY CAN'T TAKE AWAY OUR MUSIC. / HOME COOKIN'** [ ] [50]

Feb 71. (d-lp) *(LDS 84003-4)* *<SE 4710-2>* **BLACK MAN'S BURDON** [ ] Dec70 [82]
– Black on black in black / Paint it black / Laurel and Hardy / P.C. 3 / Black bird / Paint it black / Spirit / Beautiful new born child / Nights in white satin / Bird and the squirrel / Nuts seed and life / Out of nowhere / Sun – Moon / Pretty colours / Gun / Jimbo / Bare back ride / Home cookin' / They can't take away our music. *(re-iss. Oct79 on 'MCA'; MCSP 306) <US-cd 1993 on 'Avenue'; R2 71193>*

U.A. M.G.M.

Jun 71. (7") *(UP 35217)* **PAINT IT BLACK. / SPIRIT** [ ] [–]

ERIC BURDON & JIMMY WITHERSPOON

JIMMY WITHERSPOON – blues guitarist + WAR backing.

U.A. M.G.M.

Aug 71. (7") *(UP 35287)* *<K 14296>* **SOLEDAD. / HEADIN' FOR HOME** [ ] [ ]

Dec 71. (lp) *(UAG 29251)* *<SE 4791>* **GUILTY!** [ ] [ ]
– I've been drinking / Once upon a time / Steam roller / The laws must change / Have mercy judge / Goin' down slow / Soledad / Home dream / Wicked wicked man / Headin' for home / The time has come. *<US re-iss. 1976 as 'BLACK AND WHITE BLUES' on 'LA'; GG 58001> (re-iss. Oct79 as 'BLACK AND WHITE BLUES' on 'M.C.A.'; MCF 3024)*

ERIC BURDON BAND

performed at Reading festival (Aug73), backed by **AARON BUTLER** – guitar / **RANDY RICE** – bass / **ALVIN TAYLOR** – drums. This line-up also featured on his next long awaited album

Capitol Capitol

Dec 74. (7") *<3997>* **THE REAL ME. / LETTER FROM THE COUNTY FARM** –

Feb 75. (lp) *(<E-ST 11359>)* **SUN SECRETS** Dec74 51
– It's my life / Ring of fire / Medley: When I was young – Warchild – The real me / Don't let me be misunderstood – Nina's school / Letter from the county farm / Sun secrets.

Feb 75. (7") *<4007>* **RING OF FIRE. / THE REAL ME** –

— added **JOHN STERLING** – guitar / **TERRY RYAN** – keyboards / **MOSES WHEELOCK** – percussion / **GEORGE SURANOVICH** – drums / and **KIM KESTERSON** – bass (repl. AARON BUTLER)

Aug 75. (lp/<lp>) *(E-ST/<SMAS 11426>)* **STOP**
– City boy / Gotta get it on / The man / I'm lookin' up / Rainbow / All I do / Funky fever / By mine / The way it should be / Stop.

ORIGINAL ANIMALS

reformed to record below **BURDON, PRICE, VALENTINE, CHANDLER + STEEL**

Barn U.A.

Aug 77. (7") *(2014 109)* **PLEASE SEND ME SOMEONE TO LOVE. / RIVERSIDE COUNTY** –

Aug 77. (lp/c) *(2314 104) <790>* **BEFORE WE WERE SO RUDELY INTERRUPTED** 70
– Brother Bill (the last clean shirt) / Many rivers to cross / Lonely avenue / Please send me someone to love / Riverside county / It's all over now, baby blue / Fire on the sun / As the crow flies / Just a little bit / The fool. *(cd-iss. Feb00 on 'Repertoire'; REP 4845)*

Oct 77. (7") *(2014 115)* **MANY RIVERS TO CROSS. / BROTHER BILL (THE LAST CLEAN SHIRT)** –

Nov 77. (7") *<1070>* **FIRE ON THE SUN. / RIVERSIDE COUNTY** –

— PRICE returned to solo work.

ERIC BURDON

— solo with many session people.

Polydor not iss.

Mar 78. (lp) *(2302 078)* **SURVIVOR** –
– Rocky / Woman of the rings / The kid / Tomb of the unknown singer / Famous flames / Hollywood woman / Hook of Holland / I was born to live the blues / Highway dealer / P.O. box 500.

1980. (lp) *(2344 147)* **DARKNESS – DARKNESS** –
– Darkness darkness / On the horizon / Rat race / Gospel singer / Ride on / Baby what's wrong / Cry to me / So much love / Ecstasy / Too late.

Ariola not iss.

1981. (lp; as ERIC BURDON'S FIRE DEPT.) *(S 202 800-320)* **THE LAST DRIVE** – German –
– The last drive / Power company / Bird on the beach / The rubbing out of long hair / Atom-most-fear / Dry / Female terrorist / The last poet.

ANIMALS

reformed again in 1983.

I.R.S. I.R.S.

Sep 83. (7") *(PFP 1019) <9920>* **THE NIGHT. / NO JOHN NO** 48
(12"+=) *(PFXS 1019)* – Melt down.

Sep 83. (lp) *(<SP 70037>)* **ARK** 66
– Loose change / Love is for all time / My favourite enemy / Prisoner of the light / Being there / Hard times / The night / Trying to get to you / Just can't get enough / Melt down / Gotta get back to you / Crystal nights. *(cd-iss. Nov96 on 'Castle'; CLACD 412) (cd re-iss. Jan00 on 'Essential'; ESMCD 801)*

Nov 83. (7"/12") *(PFP/+X 1030) <9923>* **LOVE IS FOR ALL TIME. / JUST CAN'T GET ENOUGH**

Sep 84. (lp) *(<IRSA 70043>)* **RIP IT TO SHREDS – THE GREATEST HITS LIVE (live 1983)**
– It's too late / House of the rising Sun / It's my life / Don't bring me down / Don't let me be misunderstood / I'm cryin' / Bring it on home to me / O lucky man / Boom boom / We've gotta get out of this place.

— (split though they did reunion gigs)

ERIC BURDON BAND

with **JOHN STERLING + SNUFFY WALDEN** – guitar / **STEVE GOLDSTEIN + LUIS CABAZA + RONNIE BARRON** – keyboards / **BILL McCUBBIN + TERRY WILSON** – bass / **TONY BRUANAGLE** – drums

Blackline not iss.

1983. (lp) *(BL 712)* **COMEBACK** –
– No more Elmore / The road / Crawling King Snake / Take it easy / Dey won't / Wall of silence / Streetwalker / It hurts me too / Lights out / Bird on the beach. *(UK-iss.Jun84 as 'THE ROAD' on 'Thunderbolt'; THBL 1017) (cd-iss. Sep94 on 'Line'; LICD 900058)*

Bullfrog Carrere

Mar 84. (lp) *(BDL 4006) <267.003>* **POWER COMPANY** Dec83
– Power company / Devil's daughter / You can't kill my spirit / Do you feel it (today) / Wicked man / Heart attack / Who gives a f*** / Sweet blood call / House of the rising Sun / Comeback. *<US-iss.1988 as 'WICKED MAN on 'GNP Crescendo' lp/c/cd; GNP S/C/D 2194)*

Striped Horse not iss.

Aug 88. (12") *(SH12 615)* **RUN FOR YOUR LIFE (extended). / RUN FOR YOUR LIFE / RUN FOR YOUR LIFE (instrumental)** –
(cd-s+=) *(SHCD 615)* – Run for your life (Animal remix).

Aug 88. (cd) *<SHD 5006>* **I USED TO BE AN ANIMAL** –
– I used to be an animal / The dream / American dreams / Going back to Memphis / Leo's place / Run for your life / Don't give a damn / Living in fear / I will be with you again. *(re-iss. Jul94 on 'Success' cd/c; 2326)*

Rhino Rhino

1990. (c-s) *(4JM 74425)* **SIXTEEN TONS / ('A'instrumental)** –

– (selective) compilations, etc. –

on 'Columbia' UK / 'MGM' US, unless stated otherwise

Feb 66. (lp; mono/stereo) *<E/SE 4324>* **THE BEST OF THE ANIMALS** – 6
– It's my life / Gonna send you back to Walker / Bring it on home to me / I'm mad again / The house of the rising sun / We've gotta get out of this place / Boom boom / I'm in love again / I'm crying / Don't let me be misunderstood. *(UK iss.Mar89 on 'Crusader')*

Apr 66. (lp) *(SX 6035)* **MOST OF THE ANIMALS** 4 –
– The house of the rising sun / We've gotta get out of this place / Roadrunner / Let the good times roll / Hallelujah I love her so / It's going to change the world / Bring it on home to me / Worried life blues / Baby let me take you home / For Miss Caulker / I believe to my soul / How you've changed. *(re-iss. Sep71 on 'Music For Pleasure'; MFP 5218, hit no.18) (cd-iss. Feb92; CDMFP 5218) (cd re-iss. Mar02 on 'EMI Gold'+=; 538296-2)* – Don't let me be misunderstood / It's my life / Club a-go-go / I'm crying.

Jun 67. (lp; mono/stereo) *<E/SE 4454>* **THE BEST OF ERIC BURDON & THE ANIMALS VOL.2** – 71

Sep 72. (7"m) *R.A.K.; (RR 1)* **THE HOUSE OF THE RISING SUN. / DON'T LET ME BE MISUNDERSTOOD / I'M CRYING** 25 –
(re-iss. Sep82 7",7"pic-d; RR/+P 1, hit UK No.11)

Apr 76. (lp) *D.J.M.; (DJSL 069)* **IN CONCERT FROM NEWCASTLE (live '63)** –
(re-iss. Dec 76 as 'LIVE IN NEWCASTLE'; DJB 26069) (re-iss. Jan 77 as 'NEWCASTLE '63 on 'Charly'; CR 30016) (re-iss. Feb81; CR 30197) (re-iss. Nov88 as 'LIVE AT THE CLUB A GO GO, NEWCASTLE' on 'Decal'; LIK 88) (cd-iss. Feb93 on 'Charly'; CDCD 1037) (cd re-iss. Jun97 on 'Spalax'; 14550) (re-iss. Oct97 on 'Hallmark' cd/c; 30814-2/-4)

Dec 88. (lp/c/cd) *See For Miles; (SEE/+K/CD 244)* **THE EP COLLECTION** –
(cd re-iss. Mar99; same)

Jul 90. (d-cd/d-c/d-lp) *E.M.I.; (CD/TC+/EM 1367)* **THE COMPLETE ANIMALS** –

Dec 90. (cd/c/lp) *Decal; (CD/C+/LIK 72)* **TRACKIN' THE HITS** –

Mar 91. (cd/d-lp) *Sequel; (NEXCD/NEDLP 153)* **INSIDE LOOKING OUT (THE 1965-1966 SESSIONS)**(cd+= extra tracks) –

1993. (cd; ERIC BURDON) *Avenue; <R2 71219>* **SUN SECRETS / STOP** –

Jun 95. (cd) *Disky; (BA 86007-2)* **BASIC ORIGINALS** –

Nov 96. (cd) *Castle; (CLACD 424)* **GREATEST HITS LIVE** –
(re-iss. Jan00 on 'Essential'; ESMCD 802)

Apr 99. (cd) *Magic; (499689-2)* **THE ANIMALS VOL.1** –

Sep 99. (d-cd) *B.R. Music; (BS 81122)* **THE STORY OF THE ANIMALS** –

Sep 99. (cd) *Akarma; (AK 074)* **GUNSIGHT** –

Feb 00. (10"lp) *Get Back; (GET 580)* **THE BEGINNING** □ ⊟
Mar 00. (cd; ERIC BURDON) *Target; (CD 6211)* **ERIC BURDON SINGS THE BEST OF THE ANIMALS** □ ⊟
Jun 00. (cd) *Liberty; (527084-2)* **THE BEST OF THE ANIMALS** □ □
Jul 00. (cd) *Disky; (SI 25072-2)* **THE BEST OF THE 60'S** □ □
Apr 02. (cd) *Disky; (GO 79355-2)* **BOOM BOOM** □ □
Jun 02. (cd) *A.Z.; (AZCD 04)* **INTERESTING LIFE: NEW RECORDINGS OF THEIR GREATEST HITS** □ □
Mar 03. (cd) *Magic; (3930295)* **THE COMPLETE FRENCH CD EP COLLECTION** □ ⊟
Apr 03. (cd) *Snapper; (SNAP 135CD)* **LET IT ROCK** □ □
May 03. (cd) *E.M.I.; 583114-2)* **A'S B'S & EP'S** □ □
Aug 03. (cd) *Castle; (CMRCD 766)* **DON'T BRING ME DOWN: THE DECCA YEARS** □ □

□ ANOTHER PRETTY FACE (see under ⇒ WATERBOYS)

□ Adam ANT (see under ⇒ ADAM & THE ANTS)

ANTHRAX

Formed: Queens, New York, USA . . . mid'81, by NEIL TURBIN and DAN LILKER. SCOTT 'NOT' IAN, CHARLIE BENANTE and the diminutive DAN SPITZ completed the line-up, the band consequently spotted and signed to the 'Megaforce' label (licensed to 'Music For Nations' in Europe) by the legendary JOHNNY Z. The 1984 debut, 'FISTFUL OF METAL' (if you think the title's cheesy, wait till you see the cover!) hardly set the rock world alight, although 'METAL THRASHING MAD' was good for a laugh and the ALICE COOPER cover, 'I'M EIGHTEEN' was passable. By the release of the mini album, 'ARMED AND DANGEROUS', the following year, the more traditional metal tonsils of JOEY BELLADONNA were employed, a canny move that lent the band a modicum of style and sophistication. This was evident on ANTHRAX's first outing for 'Island', 'SPREADING THE DISEASE', a classy thrash metal affair that frequently rose above the narrow confines of the genre. By turns humorous, impassioned, and bloody loud, the likes of 'MADHOUSE' (a must-see video), 'AFTERSHOCK', 'ARMED AND DANGEROUS' and 'MEDUSA' made this one of the key metal releases of the 80's. 'AMONG THE LIVING' (1987) was almost as good and for many aging metallers, 'I AM THE LAW' is the definitive ANTHRAX track, a tribute to the meanest cop in Mega City One, Judge Dredd. 'INDIANS', meanwhile, was a more serious affair, dealing with the plight of their Native American brethren. Yet accomplished as the music was, it was almost overshadowed by the band's image. A case of bullet belts (!) out, skateboards and surf shorts in; for a brief, heady time in the late 80's, ANTHRAX almost made metal (whisper it now) trendy. Proving there was always a hip-hop element to their hardcore, the band released 'I'M THE MAN', a rap/metal pastiche that quite probably pissed off SAXON fans everywhere. At this point, the band were up there with METALLICA as the great white hopes of thrash and fans waited with baited breath for their next album, 'STATE OF EUPHORIA' (1988). Inevitably, perhaps, the record was a letdown; on first listen it sounded dense, promising, on repeated listening it became obvious the songs just weren't there. Equally inevitably, the band's dayglo image prompted a backlash. They retaliated with a considerably darker, more introspective opus, 'PERSISTENCE OF TIME' (1990). While the JOE JACKSON cover, 'GOT THE TIME', was engaging, the songwriting still wasn't up to scratch. A 1991 collaboration with CHUCK D on a storming cover of PUBLIC ENEMY's 'BRING THE NOISE' was the band's most effective effort for years and showed what they were obviously still capable of. The single was included on 'ATTACK OF THE KILLER B's', a compilation of B-sides and rare tracks, while ANTHRAX went on to tour with PUBLIC ENEMY on a genre busting double bill. Signing a new contract with 'Elektra', the band promptly ditched BELLADONNA in favour of ex-ARMOURED SAINT man, JOHN BUSH. These were tough times for ANTHRAX, as every metal band on the planet purchased a distortion pedal, grew a goatee, and insisted they weren't actually metal after all, no, they were GRUNGE!! (of course). All credit to ANTHRAX then, for sticking to their metal guns and releasing 'THE SOUND OF WHITE NOISE' (1993), a barrage of furious riffing that almost topped the work of their mid-80's golden period. 'STOMP 442' (1995) was equally ferocious, and while ANTHRAX mightn't sell as many records as they used to, they remain one of metal's best loved bands. The ever productive IAN had also turned his hand to side project STORMTROOPERS OF DEATH aka S.O.D. back in the mid-80's. A collaboration with BENANTE, LILKER and ANTHRAX roadie BILLY MILANO, the project came to life with the release of 1985's legendary 'SPEAK ENGLISH OR DIE'. Regarded as one of the pivotal records in the cross-fertilisation of punk/hardcore and thrash metal, the album was a riot of 2-minute-wonder noise, fury and irreverent humour which brought charges (not altogether unjustified) of sexism and racism. Incredibly, sales of this cult record eventually topped one million and prompted 'Megaforce' to release a millennial remastered edition complete with new studio tracks and live material. While it was originally intended as a one-off affair – MILANO going off to form M.O.D. – the group reformed in 1992 for the ironically titled 'LIVE AT BUDOKAN' (actually recorded live in New York). From the hilarious IRON MAIDEN pastiche of the cover art to MILANO's crowd baiting, the record was a treat for fans of the original album from which much of the material was used (alongside a few choice covers). Finally, the cult of S.O.D. demanded a follow-up studio album and in 1999, possibly the most belated sophomore effort in recorded history hit the shelves. 'BIGGER THAN THE DEVIL' carried on where their debut had left off all those years ago, showing the young pretenders how to really mosh and how to get a proper sense of humour. No target was too soft for MILANO's caustic gaze with both mealy-mouthed liberals and bigots coming under attack; they mightn't be bigger than the Devil but SOD probably have all the best jokes. Given the musical climate into which ANTHRAX returned in 2003, 'WE'VE COME FOR YOU ALL' was almost revolutionary in its no-frills thrash metal. While new guitarist and co-producer ROB CAGGIANO lent a competitive edge to proceedings, there were precious few, if any, concessions to contemporary trends. But then ANTHRAX were always one step removed from their peers. With spandex-rock the unlikliest of candidates for a fashion resurrection, it wouldn't be so surprising to see an 80's back-to-the-roots thrash revival in the not too distant future. What certainly was surprising was the appearance of ROGER DALTREY (on 'TAKING THE MUSIC BACK'), not quite as revolutionary a collaboration as the CHUCK D one, but effective nonetheless. • **Songwriters:** SCOTT IAN except; I'M EIGHTEEN (Alice Cooper) / SABBATH BLOODY SABBATH (Black Sabbath) / GOD SAVE THE QUEEN and FRIGGIN' IN THE RIGGIN' (Sex Pistols) / GOT THE TIME (Joe Jackson) / BRING THE NOISE (Public Enemy) / PROTEST AND SURVIVE (Discharge), LOOKING DOWN THE BARREL OF A GUN (Beastie Boys) / SHE (Kiss) / THE BENDS (Radiohead). • **Trivia:** DAN SPITZ's older brother DAVID played bass in the mid'80's with BLACK SABBATH. ANTHRAX an acting/ singing appearance on a 1992 showing of US TV sit-com 'Married With

Children'. • **Note:** Not to be confused with UK "oi" band of the same name.

Album rating: FISTFUL OF METAL (*4) / SPREADING THE DISEASE (*8) / AMONG THE LIVING (*8) / STATE OF EUPHORIA (*5) / PERSISTENCE OF TIME (*7) / SOUND OF WHITE NOISE (*6) / STOMP 442 (*5) / WE'VE COME FOR YOU ALL (*6)

NEIL TURBIN – vocals / **DAN SPITZ** (b.28 Jan'63) – lead guitar / **SCOTT 'Not' IAN** (b.31 Dec'63) – rhythm guitar / **DAN LILKER** (b.18 Oct'64) – bass / **CHARLIE BENANTE** (b.27 Nov'62, The Bronx) – drums

Music For Nations — Megaforce

Nov 83. (7") **SOLDIERS OF DEATH. / HOWLING FURIES** –

Jan 84. (lp) *(MFN 14) <MRS 469>* **FISTFUL OF METAL**
– Deathrider / Metal thrashing mad / I'm eighteen / Panic / Subjagator / Death from above / Across the river / Anthrax. *(re-iss. Apr87 lp/pic-lp; MFN 14DM/P) (c+=/cd+=; CD/T MFN 14)* – Soldiers of metal / Howling furies. *<US-cd-iss. 1987 on 'Caroline'; CAROLCD 1383> (re-iss. cd Sep95 on 'Bulletproof'; CDMVEST 56)*

(Mid'84) **MATT FALLON** – vocals repl. TURBIN

—— **FRANK BELLO** (b. 7 Sep'65) – bass (ex-roadie) repl. LILKER

—— (Aug'84) **MATT** was replaced by **JOEY BELLADONNA** (b.30 Oct'60, Oswego, NY) – vocals (ex-BIBLE BLACK)

Feb 85. (m-lp/pic-m-lp) *<MRS 05/+P>* **ARMED AND DANGEROUS** –
– Armed and dangerous / Raise Hell / God save the Queen / Metal thrashing mad / Panic. *(UK-iss.Aug87 on 'Music For Nations' lp/c; MFN/CMFN 123) (cd-iss. Nov91; CDMFN 123) (cd re-iss. Sep95 on 'Bulletproof'; CDMVEST 55)*

Music For Nations — Megaforce-Island

Feb 86. (lp/c) *(MFN/TMFN 62) <90460>* **SPREADING THE DISEASE** — Dec85
– A.I.R. / Lone justice / Madhouse / S.S.C – Stand or fall / The enemy / Aftershock / Armed and dangerous / Medusa / Gung ho. *(cd-iss. May86 on 'Island'; CID 9806) (pic-lp Sep87; MFNP 62) (re-iss. Aug91 on 'Island' cd)(c; IMCD 136)(ICM 9806)*

Island — Island

May 86. (12"/12"s/12"pic-d) *(12IS/+B/P 285)* **MADHOUSE. / A.I.R. / GOD SAVE THE QUEEN**

Feb 87. (7"pic-d)(12") *(LAWP 1)(12IS 316)* **I AM THE LAW. / BUD E. LUVBOMB AND SATAN'S LOUNGE BAND** 32
('A'live-7"red+=) *(ISX 316)* – Madhouse (live).

Apr 87. (lp/pic-lp/c/cd) *(ILPS/PILPS/ICT/CID 9865) <90584>* **AMONG THE LIVING** 18 62
– Among the living / Caught in the mosh / I am the law / Efilnikufesin (N.F.L.) / A skeleton in the closet / One world / A.D.I.- horror of it all / Imitation of life. *(cd re-iss. Mar94; IMCD 186)*

Jun 87. (7"orange/7"pic-d) *(IS/+P 325)* **INDIANS. / SABBATH BLOODY SABBATH** 44
(12"+=/12"pic-d+=) *(12IS/+P 325)* – Taint.

Nov 87. (7"/7"sha-pic-d) *(IS/+P 338)* **I'M THE MAN. / CAUGHT IN THE MOSH** 20 –
(12"+=) *(12IS 338)* – I am the law (live).

Dec 87. (m-lp,c,cd) *<90685>* **I'M THE MAN** – 53
– I'm the man (censored version) / I'm the man (Def uncensored version) / Sabbath bloody sabbath / I'm the man (live & extremely Def II uncensored version) / Caught in a mosh (live) / I am the law (live).

Sep 88. (7"yellow) *(IS 379)* **MAKE ME LAUGH. / ANTI SOCIAL (live)** 26
(12"+=/cd-s+=) *(12IS/CIDP 379)* – Friggin' in the riggin'.

Sep 88. (lp/c/cd) *(ILPS/ICT/CID 9916) <91004>* **STATE OF EUPHORIA** 12 30
– Be all, end all / Out of sight, out of mind / Make me laugh / Anti-social / Who cares wins / Now it's dark / Schism / Misery loves company / 13 / (finale). *(re-iss. cd Apr94; IMCD 187)*

Mar 89. (7"/7"amber/7"blue/7"red) *(IS/+A/B/R 409)* **ANTI-SOCIAL. / PARASITE** 44
(12"+=/12"amber+=/12"blue+=/12"red+=)(3"cd-s+=) *(12IS/+A/B/R 409)(CIDX 409)* – Le sects.

Island — Megaforce

Aug 90. (7") *(IS 470)* **IN MY WORLD. / KEEP IT IN THE FAMILY** 29
(10"+=/12"+=/cd-s+=) *(10IS/12IS/CID 470)* – ('A'&'B'extended).

Aug 90. (cd/c/lp) *(CID/ICT/ILPS 9967) <846480>* **PERSISTENCE OF TIME** 13 24
– Time / Blood / Keep it in the family / In my world / Gridlock / Intro to reality / Belly of the beast / Got the time / H8 red / One man stands / Discharge. *(pic-lp.Jan91; ILPSP 9967) (re-iss. Apr94 cd)(c; IMCD 178)(ICM 9967)*

Nov 90. (c-s/10"/7") *(C/10+/CIS 476)* **GOT THE TIME. / WHO PUT THIS TOGETHER** 16
(12"+=/cd-s+=) *(12IS/CID 476)* – I'm the man (live).

Jun 91. (c-s/7"; ANTHRAX featuring CHUCK D) *(C+/IS 490)* **BRING THE NOISE. / I AM THE LAW '91** 14
(10"+=/12"+=/cd-s+=)(10"pic-d+=/12"pic-d+=) *(10IS/12IS/CID 490)(10/12 ISP 490)* – Keep it in the family (live).

—— CHUCK D. (of-PUBLIC ENEMY)

Jun 91. (cd/c/lp) *(CID/ICT/ILPS 9980) <848804>* **ATTACK OF THE KILLER B's** (rare studio) 13 27
– Milk (ode to Billy) / Bring the noise / Keep it in the family (live) / Startin' up a posse / Protest and survive / Chromatic death / I'm the man '91 / Parasite / Pipeline / Sects / Belly of the beast (live) / N.F.B. (dallabnikufesin). *(re-iss. Apr94 cd)(c; IMCD 179)(ICM 9980)*

—— (May92) **JOHN BUSH** (b.24 Aug'63, L.A.) – vocals (ex-ARMOURED SAINT) repl. MARK OSEGUEDA who had replaced BELLADONNA

Elektra — Elektra

Apr 93. (7"/c-s) *(EKR 166/+C)* **ONLY. / ONLY (mix)** 36
(cd-s+=) *(EKR 166CD1)* – Cowboy song / Sodium pentaghol.
(cd-s) *(EKR 166CD2)* – ('A'side) / Auf wiedersehen / Noisegate.

May 93. (cd/c/lp) *<(7559 61430-2/-4/-1)>* **SOUND OF WHITE NOISE** 14 7
– Potter's field / Only / Room for one more / Packaged rebellion / Hy pro glo / Invisible / 1000 points of hate / C11 H17 N2 O2 SNA / Burst / This is not an exit. *(cd+=)* – Black lodge. *(cd re-iss. Jap version Apr98 on 'Victor'; VICP 80320)*

Sep 93. (7"/c-s) *(EKR 171/+W)* **BLACK LODGE. / ('A'-Black strings mix)** 53
(10"+=/12"pic-d+=/cd-s+=) *(EKR 171 TE/TP/CD)* – Pottersfield / Love her all I can.

Nov 93. (7"/c-s) *(EKR 178/+C)* **HY PRO GLO. / LONDON**
(12"+=/cd-s+=) *(EKR 178 T/CD)* – Room for one more (live).

Oct 95. (cd/c) *<(7559 61856-2/-4)>* **STOMP 442** 47
– Random acts of senseless violence / Fueled / King size / Riding shotgun / Perpetual motion / In a zone / Nothing / American Pompeii / Drop the ball / Tester / Bare.

Jan 96. (c-s) *(EKR 216C)* **NOTHING / FUELLED (remix)**
(cd-s+=) *(EKR 216CD1)* – Remember tomorrow / Grunt and click.
(cd-s) *(EKR 216CD2)* – ('A'side) / Dethroned emperor / No time this time.

Ignition – Tommy Boy — Ignition – Tommy Boy

Jul 98. (cd/c) *<(IGN7 4034-3/-4)>* **VOLUME 8 – THE THREAT IS REAL!** 73
– Crush / Catharsis / Inside out / Piss n vinegar / 604 / Toast to the extras / Born again idiot / Killing box / Harms way / Hog tied / Big fat / Cupajoe / Alpha male / Stealing from a thief.

Oct 98. (7") *(IGN 740516)* **INSIDE OUT. / GIVING THE HORNS** –
(cd-s+=) *(IGN 740513)* – The bends.

—— line-up:- **JOHN BUSH + SCOTT IAN + CHARLIE BENANTE + FRANK BELLO** recruited **ROB CAGGIANO** – lead guitar

Nuclear Blast — Sanctuary

Feb 03. (cd) *(NB 699DP) <84609>* **WE'VE COME FOR YOU ALL** — May03
– Contact / What doesn't lie / Superhero / Refuse to be denied / Safe home / Any place but here / Nobody knows anything / Strap it on / Black dahlia / Cadillac rock box / Taking the music back / Crash / Think about an end / W.C.F.Y.A. *(lp-iss.Apr03; 121095) (d-cd-iss. Jun03 +=; NB 6995)*

Aug 03. (cd-s) *(NB 1175CD)* **TAKING THE MUSIC BACK** –

– compilations, others, etc. –

Nov 92. (d-cd) *Island; (ITSCD 6)* **AMONG THE LIVING / PERSISTENCE OF TIME** –

Apr 94. (cd/c/lp) *Island; (CID/ICT/ILPS 8027) <518920>* **ANTHRAX LIVE – THE ISLAND YEARS (live)**

Mar 98. (cd) *Connoisseur; (VSOPCD 252)* **MOSHERS 1986-1991** –

Feb 99. (d-cd) *S.P.V.; (SPV 0761818-2)* **FISTFUL OF METAL / ARMED AND DANGEROUS** –

Nov 99. (cd) *Beyond; <(63985 78067-2)>* **RETURN OF THE KILLER A's**
(re-iss. Jan00 on 'Spitfire'; SPITCD 057)

Oct 01. (cd) *Universal; <(E 586324-2)>* **CLASSIC ANTHRAX: THE UNIVERSAL MASTERS COLLECTION** — Feb02

Aug 02. (cd) *Universal; <(5 44991-2)>* **THE COLLECTION** ☐ Jun02 ☐
Mar 03. (cd) *Universal; <(AA314 586004-2)>* **MADHOUSE – THE VERY BEST OF ANTHRAX** ☐ Jun01 ☐

☐ A PERFECT CIRCLE (see under ⇒ TOOL)

APHEX TWIN

Born: RICHARD JAMES, 18 Aug'71, Limerick, Ireland. Isolated in the wilds of the South West of Cornwall, James began his precocious electronic tinkering at an early age. In true bedroom boffin style, he made his first recordings using customised analog synths at a cherubic 14 years old. Credited to AFX, his first release was 'ANALOGUE BUBBLEBATH VOL.1' (1991), released on the small dance indie label, 'Rabbit City'. The record created something of a buzz but it was 'DIDGERIDOO', included on 'ANALOGUE BUBBLEBATH VOL.2' (1991) which had legendary dance label 'R&S' chasing JAMES' signature. A sinister, didgeridoo-driven bpm marathon, it still sounds unique today. 'XYLEM TUBE' (1992) wasn't quite so scary while 'SELECTED AMBIENT WORKS '85-'92' (1992) was a largely beatless compilation containing some of his earliest creations. Signing to 'Warp', he recorded 'SURFING ON SINE WAVES' (1992) under the pseudonym POLYGON WINDOW. The album spawned the punishing rhythmical workout of the 'QUOTH' (1993) single, its dark intensity recalling 'DIGERIDOO'. By this point, APHEX TWIN was something of a cause celebre among the press, the indie papers surprisingly vocal in their support. With previous single releases, JAMES had missed the top 40 by a small margin but 'ON' (1993) gave him his first chart hit, reaching No.32. The second volume of 'SELECTED AMBIENT WORKS' was released the following year, the record concentrating on darker, more avant-garde material. This went down none too well with the critics and a backlash started to form. Silencing at least some of his detractors with 1995's 'I CARE BECAUSE YOU DO', the record featured equally dark but more consumer friendly fare reflecting the (then) current penchant for trip hop. With 1996's 'RICHARD D. JAMES' album, the boy wonder explored drum 'n' bass textures replete with lush strings and the requisite exotic electronica. Having already caused a little controversy with his weirdo 'COME TO DADDY' video/single in '97, the APHEX TWIN took a break until 1999's Chris Cunningham-directed 'WINDOWLICKER'. This time the video/promo shoots saw his face superimposed on the bodies of bikini-clad models, although this first new track for three years hit the Top 20. RICHARD D. JAMES kept a low profile inbetween the release of the aforementioned single and his long-awaited double album, aptly entitled 'DRUKQS' (2001). The set, which was borderline between the man's 'SELECTED AMBIENT WORKS 85-92' and the 'RICHARD D. JAMES' album, was apparently never going to see the light of day as these were private tracks stored on his laptop. But a hacker downloaded them from the internet, forcing a very miffed JAMES to issue what seemed like a random collection of 'lost' tracks. Not in any particular order, and all with incomprehensible titles, 'DRUKQS' was a staggering work with all the usual 'TWIN motifs and twists. Opener 'JYNWEYTHEK' was reminiscent of 'NANOU', from the 'WINDOWLICKER' single, with its eerie/childlike, wind-up toy home-made piano sound. 'OMGYJYA-SWITCH' sounded like JAMES had sampled 2000 different kung-fu fights and stuck them together to create one big techno brawl, whilst avant garde, ERIK SATIE-led piano pieces such as 'STROTHA TYNHE', 'AVRIL 14TH' and the beautifully simplistic 'KESSON DALEF' would not sound out of place at a classical piano concert. The album, despite this display of raw, sometimes skeletal, but never boring work, received mixed reactions from critics who were expecting JAMES to issue something slightly more consistant. However, the album peaked at No.22 in the UK charts and was praised by fans and fellow electroids alike. • **Songwriters:** Ideas JAMES; sampled various and covered; FILM ME (Luxuria) / ONE DAY (Bjork). • **Trivia:** Was credited on SEEFEEL's 12" 'Time To Find Me (remixes)'.

Album rating: SELECTED AMBIENT WORKS '85-'92 (*8) / ANALOGUE BUBBLEBATH III (*6) / SELECTED AMBIENT WORKS, VOL.2 (*6) / CLASSICS compilation (*6) / . . . I CARE BECAUSE YOU DO (*7) / RICHARD D. JAMES (*6) / DRUKQS (*8) / 26 MIXES FOR CASH compilation (*8)

RICHARD D. JAMES (aka The APHEX TWIN) – keyboards, synthesizer

Rabbit City | not iss.

Dec 91. (12"ep; as AFX) *(CUT 001)* **ANALOGUE BUBBLEBATH VOL.1** ☐ ☐-
– Analogue bubblebath / Isopropopphlex / Entrance to exit / AFX 2.

Dec 91. (12"promo) *(009)* **ANALOGUE BUBBLEBATH VOL.2 (DIDGERIDOO 'Aboriginal' mix)** ☐- ☐-
(re-iss. 1993 as 12"ep; CUT 002)

Outer Rhythm – R&S | Apollo

Apr 92. (12"ep) *(RSUK 12)* **ANALOGUE BUBBLEBATH VOL.2** 55 ☐-
– Didgeridoo / Flaphead / Isoproplex.
(cd-ep+=) *(RSUK 12CD)* – Analogue bubblebath 1.

Jul 92. (12"ep/cd-ep) *(9209)* **XYLEM TUBE EP** ☐ ☐-
– Polynomial-C / Tamphex (headphuq mix) / Phlange phace / Dodeccaheedron.

Nov 92. (cd/c/d-lp) *(<AMB 3922 CD/MC/LP>)* **SELECTED AMBIENT WORKS '85-'92** ☐ ☐
– Xtal / Tha / Pulsewidth / Ageispolis / I won't let the Sun go down on me / Greencalx / Heliosphan / We are the music makers / Schotkey / Hedphelym / Delphium / Actium / Ptolemy. *(re-iss. Feb98 cd/d-lp; same)*

Warp | Sire

Dec 92. (cd/c/clear-lp; as POLYGON WINDOW) *(WARP CD/MC/LP 7)* **SURFING ON SINE WAVES** ☐ ☐-
– Polygon window / Audax powder / Quoth / If it really is me / Supremacy II / UT 1 – Dot / (0.07) / Quixote / Quino – Phec. *(cd re-iss. Apr96; same)*

Mar 93. (12"ep/cd-ep; as POLYGON WINDOW) *(WAP 33/+CD)* **QUOTH / IKEATA. / QUOTH (wooden thump mix) / QUOTH (bike pump meets bucket)** 49 ☐-

—— In Jul'93, he teamed up with SEEFEEL on 'PURE / IMPURE' EP for 'Too Pure' 12"/cd-s; *PURE/+CD 025)*

Dec 93. (12"ep/cd-ep) *(WAP 39/+CD)* **ON. / 73 YIPS. / D-SCAPE / XEPHA** 32 ☐
(12"ep/cd-ep) *(WAP 39 R/CDR)* – ('A'-D-Scape mix) / ('A'-Reload mix) / ('A'-M-21Q) / ('A'-28 mix).

Mar 94. (d-cd/d-c/2xd-lp) *(WARP CD/MC/LP 21) <45482>* **SELECTED AMBIENT WORKS VOLUME II** 11 ☐
– (12 + 13 of mostly untitled tracks; 1 of them 'Blue Calx')

Warp | Elektra

Mar 95. (12"ep/cd-ep) *(WAP 60/+CD)* **VENTOLIN / ('A'-Salbutanol mix) / ('A'-Marazanovose mix) / ('A'-Plain-an-guarry mix) / ('A'-The Coppice mix) / ('A'-Crowsnegods mix)** 49 ☐-
(12"ep/cd-ep; remixes) *(WAP 60 R/CDR)* – ('A'-Wheeze mix) / ('A'-Carnarack mix) / ('A'-Cyclob mix) / ('A'-Deep gong mix) / ('A'-Asthma beats mix).

Apr 95. (cd/c/d-lp) *(WARP CD/MC/LP 30) <61790>* **. . .I CARE BECAUSE YOU DO** 24 ☐
– Acrid avid Jan Shred / The waxen path / Wax the nip / Icct Hedral / Ventolin / Come on you slags / Start as you mean to go one / Wet tip hen ax / Mookid / Alberto Balsan / Cow cud is a twin / Next heap with.

Aug 95. (12"ep/cd-ep) *(WAP 63/+CD)* **DONKEY RHUBARB EP** ☐ ☐-
– Icct Hedral (credited with PHILIP GLASS) / Pancake lizard / Mass observation (the crackdown) / Film me and finish off / One day (Sabres of Paradise mix) / Vaz deferenz.

—— In Jul'96, he collaborated with The MIKE FLOWERS POPS on a 'Lo Recordings' 12"/cd-s release, 'FREEBASE'

Warp — Elektra

Oct 96. (12"/cd-s) *(WAP 78/+CD)* **GIRL/BOY EP** 64 –
– Girl/boy (NLS mix) / Milk man / Inkey $ / Girl/boy (#18 snare rush mix) / Beatles under my carpet / Girl/boy (redruth mix).

Nov 96. (cd/c/lp) *(WARP CD/MC/LP 43) <62010>* **RICHARD D. JAMES ALBUM** 62
– 4 / Cornish acid / Peek 824545201 / Fingerbob / Corn mouth / To cure a weakling child / Goon gumpos / Yellow calx – Girl/boy song / Local fock witch.

Oct 97. (12"/cd-s) *(WAP 094/+CD)* **COME TO DADDY (Pappy & Little Lord Faulteroy mixes). / FILM / BUCEPHALUS BOUNCING BALL** 36 –
(cd-s) *(WAP 094CDR)* – ('A'side) / To cure a weakling child (contour regard) / Funny little man / IZ-US.

Mar 99. (12"/cd-s) *(WAP 105/+CD)* **WINDOWLICKER. / (FORMULA) / NANNOU** 16 –
(cd-s+=) *(WAP 105CDR)* – ('A'-CD-Rom video).

Jul 01. (12"/cd-s; as AFX) *(MEN 1/+CD)* **2 REMIXES BY AFX** 69 –
(above issued on 'Men 1')

Oct 01. (d-cd/q-lp) *(WARP CD/LP 92) <31174>* **DRUKQS** 22
– Jynweythek / Vordhosbn / Kladfvgbung micshk / Omgyiya switch 7 / Strotha tynhe / Gwely mernans / Bbydhyonchord / Coc – Ver 10 / Avril 14th / Mt. Saint Michel mix + St. Michaels mount / Gwarek 2 / Orban eq trx 4 / Aussois / Hy a scullyas lyf a dhagrow / Kesson daslef / 54 Cymru beats / Btoum-roumada / Lornaderek / Penty harmonium / Meltphace 6 / Bit 4 / Prep gwarlek 3B / Father / Taking control / Petiatil cx htdui / Ruglen holon / Afx237 V7 / Ziggomatic V17 / Nanou 2.

Warp — Warp

Mar 03. (d-cd) *<(WARPCD 102)>* **26 MIXES FOR CASH**
(compilation of Various Artists remixes) 63

Men 1/2 — Rephlex

Jun 03. (12"/cd-s; as AFX) *(MEN 2/+CD) <80736>* **SMOJPHACE EP**
– Run the place red / Ktpa 1 / Ktpa 2.

– compilations, others, etc. –

(all on 'Rephlex' unless mentioned otherwise)

1992. (d-12"ep; as Q-CHASTIC) *(002EP)* **Q-CHASTIC EP** –
– Q-chastic #1 / Q-chastic #2 / Q-chastic #3 / Q-chastic #4.

1994. (12"; as KOSMIC KOMMANDO) *(CAT 007)* **THE KOSMIC KOMMANDO** –
(also issued 1994 same label; MC 202)

1994. (12"ep/cd-ep; as AFX) *(CAT 008/+CD)* **ANALOGUE BUBBLEBATH VOL.3** –
– (track numbers) *(re-iss. Nov97; same)*

1994. (12"; as CAUSTIC WINDOW) *(CAT 009)* **JOYREX 1. / JOYREX 2** –

Aug 94. (12"ep/cd-ep; as AFX) *(CAT 019/+CD)* **ANALOGUE BUBBLEBATH VOL.4** –
– I / II / III / IV. *(re-iss. Apr98; same)*

Jan 95. (blue-d-lp/c/cd) *R&S; (RS 95035/+MC/CD) / Distance; <0421>* **CLASSICS** 24
– Digeridoo / Flaphead / Phloam / Isoproplex / Polynomial-C / Tamphex / Phlange phace / Dodeccaheedron / Analogue bubblebath / En trance to exit / AFX 2 / Metapharstic / Digeridoo (live). *(re-iss. Feb98; same)*

☐ APHRODITE'S CHILD (see under ⇒ VANGELIS)

☐ APOLLO XI (see under ⇒ ORB)

APOLLO 440

Formed: Liverpool, England . . . 1990 by GRAY brothers TREVOR & HOWARD, plus NOKO. Initially, they set up their own label, 'Stealth Sonic', to release early singles 'BLACKOUT', 'DESTINY' & 'LOLITA'. Their rock sampling sound was a hit with many established bands and they were soon to become remixers of some repute for the likes of U2, POP WILL EAT ITSELF, EMF, etc. Early in 1994, they had the first of many chart entries with 'ASTRAL AMERICA', sampling The NICE's controversial version of BERNSTEIN & SONDHEIM's 'America'. Frontier mix 'n' match, techno 'n' roll, heavily influenced by french philosopher, Jean Baudrillard, 'MILLENNIUM FEVER' was eventually released early in '95. After the following years' novelty jazz cut-up, 'KRUPA', the techno terrorists took a heavier turn with early 1997's Top 10 hit, 'AIN'T TALKIN BOUT DUB', the single deriving the greater part of its not inconsiderable genius from a looped EDDIE VAN HALEN guitar riff. The 'ELECTRO GLIDE IN BLUE' album followed soon after, taking its name a la PRIMAL SCREAM's 'Vanishing Point', from a cult 70's movie. One track, 'PAIN IN ANY LANGUAGE', featured a vocal by the late, great BILLY MACKENZIE who admired them so much he'd requested their production skills for his next album prior to his untimely death. In August 1999, APOLLO FOUR FORTY once again rocketed up the charts, this time utilizing a sample of Status Quo's 'CAROLINE' on their Top 10 smash, 'STOP THE ROCK'. This previewed their third and best set to date, 'GETTIN' HIGH ON YOUR OWN SUPPLY', which resulted in their first major album chart appearance. Save for a timely resurrection of the Lightnin' Rod classic, 'HUSTLER'S CONVENTION' – renamed 'HUSTLER GROOVE' and featuring the super-smooth ROD himself – 'DUDE DESCENDING A STAIRCASE' (2003) was pretty much business – if a little funkier and more psychedelically pie-eyed – than usual for the Scouse electroids.

Album rating: MILLENNIUM FEVER (*6) / ELECTRO GLIDE IN BLUE (*6) / GETTIN' HIGH ON YOUR OWN SUPPLY (*7) / DUDE DESCENDING A STAIRCASE (*5)

TREVOR GRAY – keyboards, vocals / **HOWARD GRAY** – backing vocals / **NOKO** – vocals, guitar, keyboards (ex-LUXURIA)

Reverb — not iss.

1991. (12") *(RVBT 001)* **LOLITA. / ('A'-ambient)** –

1991. (12") *(RVBT 002)* **DESTINY (definitive hardcore mix). / DESTINY (theta wave immorality mix)** –

1991. (12") *(RVBT 006)* **LOLITA (original hardcore mix). / DESTINY (definitive digital hardcore mix)** –
(cd-s+=) *(RVBCDS 006)* – Lolita (USA '92) / Destiny (USA '92).
(12"/cd-s) *(RVB T/CDS 006R)* – Lolita (USA '92) / Lolita (USA instrumental '92) / Destiny (USA '92).

Nov 91. (12") *(RVBT 009)* **BLACK OUT. / ('A'mix)** –

Stealth Sonic-Epic — Epic-550

1993. (12"/cd-s) *(SSX T/CD 1)* **RUMBLE / HYDRAGLIDE. / LIQUID COOL (tune for cryonic suspension) (remix)** –

Jan 94. (c-s) *(SSXM 2)* **ASTRAL AMERICA / ('A'-Spirit Of America mix)** 36
(12"+=/cd-s+=) *(SSX T/CD 2)* – ('A'-Orgone accumulator mix) / ('A'-Acid America mix).

Oct 94. (12"ep) *(SSXT 3)* **LIQUID COOL (Deep Forest Ice Cold @ The Equator mix) / ('A'-Future Sound Of London remix) / ('A'-theme from Cryonic suspension) / ('A'-Jah Wobble remix)**
(cd-s+=) *(SSXCDX 3)* – ('A'-Re-animation mix).
(cd-s) *(SSXCD 3)* – ('A'-Deep Forest trans Afrique life extension express) / ('A'-Space colonization) / ('A'-Ollie J's live dubs) / ('A'-Space – 320 degrees F biostatic ambient mix).

Feb 95. (d-lp/c/cd) *(SSX/+C/CD 440)* **MILLENNIUM FEVER**
– Rumble – Spirit of America / Liquid cool / Film me and finish me off / I need something stronger / Pain is a close up / Omega point / (Don't fear) The reaper / Astral America / Millennium fever / Stelth requiem. *(cd re-iss. Aug98; same)*

Mar 95. (c-s) *(SSXM 4)* **(DON'T FEAR) THE REAPER / HOLD ON (2 WOT U GOT)** 35
(cd-s+=) *(SSXCD 4)* – ('A'-@ 440 Reaper remix) / Reaper Hoodlum Priest remix.
(12") *(SSXT 4)* – (3 versions above; but not c-s 2nd track).

APOLLO FOUR FORTY

Jul 96. (c-s) *(SSXM 5)* **KRUPA (edit) / KRUPA (original)** [23] [ ]
(cd-s+=) *(SSXCD 5)* – ('A'-Serotina) / ('A'-Alcatraz within the joint mix) / ('A'-Narcotic trust remix).
(12") *(SSXT 5)* – (no edit version).
(re-entered chart at No.24 in Sep'96)

Feb 97. (c-s) *(SSXM 6)* **AIN'T TALKIN' 'BOUT DUB / GLAM (Rock'n'roll part III)** [7] [ ]
(cd-s+=) *(SSXCD 6)* – ('A'-Matrix remix) / ('A'-Nok-hop remix).
above vocals, supplied by MARY MARY (ex-GAYE BIKERS ON ACID)

Mar 97. (cd/c/lp) *(SSX 2440 CD/C/LP)* **ELECTRO GLIDE IN BLUE** [62] [ ]
– Stealth overture / Ain't talkin' 'bout dub / Altamont super-highway revisited / Electro glide in blue / Vanishing point / Tears of the gods / Krupa / White man's throat / Pain in any language / Stealth mass in F/m. *(cd re-iss. Jan00; SSX 2440CDR)*

Jun 97. (c-s) *(SSXM 7)* **RAW POWER / (instrumental)** [32] [ ]
(12"+=/cd-s+=) *(SSX T/CD 7)* – ('A'-Urban takeover mix) / ('A'-Matthew Roberts bass in your face mix) / ('A'-Aquanauts black ark mix).

Nov 97. (12"/d-cd-s) *(SSX 8 T/CDX)* **CARRERA RAPIDA (mixes). / (excerpts:- STEALTH OVERTURE – AIN'T TALKIN' 'BOUT DUB – VANISHING POINT – TEARS OF GODS) / (excerpts: WHITE MAN'S THROAT – PAIN IN ANY LANGUAGE – STEALTH MASS IN FM – RAW POWER)** [ ] [–]

—— In June '98, the group were credited alongside JEAN-MICHEL JARRE's on his new UK Top 20 version of 'RENDEZVOUS'.

Jul 98. (c-s) *(SSX 9C)* **LOST IN SPACE / ('A'-Jason Nevins Lunar Landing mix) / ('A'-Will & Penny's theme)** [4] [–]
(cd-s) *(SSX 9CD)* – (first & third tracks) / Alpha point.
(cd-s) *(SSX 9CDX)* – (First & second tracks) / Imaginary forces.

—— the trio added guests:- MARY MARY (vocals), HARRY K (vinyl) / CLIFF HEWITT (drums), KODISH (drums) + KENNY COUGAR (bass, melodica)

Aug 99. (c-s) *(SSX 10CA)* **STOP THE ROCK / RAW POWER** [10] [ ]
(cd-s+=) *(SSX 10CD)* – ('A'mixes).
(cd-s+=) *(SSX 10CDX)* – ('A'mixes).

Sep 99. (cd/c) *(SSX 3440 CD/C) <BK 62238>* **GETTIN' HIGH ON YOUR OWN SUPPLY** [20] [ ]
– "Are we a rock band or what..?" / Stop the rock / Crazee horse / Cold rock the mic / Lost in space (theme) / For forty days / Heart go boom / The machine in the ghost / Blackbeat / Stadium parking lot / Yo! future / High on your own supply / The perfect crime.

Nov 99. (c-s) *(SSX 11CA)* **HEART GO BOOM / THE MACHINE IN THE GHOST (live) / HEART GO BOOM (Olav Basoski mix)** [57] [–]
(cd-s) *(SSX 11CD)* – ('A'side) / Anatomy (live) / The machine in the ghost (live).
(cd-s) *(SSX 11CDX)* – ('A'side) / ('A'-Lionrock mix) / ('A'Bad Company recordings mix) / ('A'-Harry K mix).
(12") *(SSX 11T)* – ('A'mixes).

Nov 00. (c-s) *(SSX 13MC)* **CHARLIE'S ANGELS 2000 / WALL OF DEATH** [29] [–]
(cd-s) *(SSX 13CD)* – ('A'side) / Escape to beyond the planet of the super ape / ('A'-Jetstream mix) / ('A'-video).

Jun 03. (cd-s; as APOLLO FOUR FORTY featuring The BEATNUTS) *(SSX 14CD)* **DUDE DESCENDING A STAIRCASE (mixes; radio / Stanton Warriors / Beginerz / PlastiqHouse / video)** [58] [–]
(cd-s) *(SSX 14CDX)* – ('A'-mixes; original / West London deep screamin' club / Stanton Warriors dub / DND nutty).
(12") *(SSX 14T)* – ('A'-mixes; West London deep screamin' club / Stanton Warriors vocal + fabric dub).

Jun 03. (d-cd) *(SSR 4440CD)* **DUDE DESCENDING A STAIRCASE** [ ] [–]
– Dude descending a staircase / Hustler groove / Disco sucks / N'existe pas / Electronic civil disobedience / 1, 2, 3, 4 / Escape to beyond the planet of the super ape / Time is running out / Children of the future // Diamonds in the sidewalk / Something's got to give / Christiane / Existe / Bulletproof blues / Suitcase '88 / Check your ego / Ropem rapture & the rising sun / Bad chemistry.

Fiona APPLE

Born: FIONA APPLE MAGGART, 13 Sep'77, New York City, New York, USA; her unmarried parents were separated when she was four. Raised most of her childhood by her jazz-loving mother and her BEATLES-obsessed step-father, FIONA found her solace in the poetry of Maya Angelou. However, more trauma was just around the corner when at the age of only twelve, she was raped outside her mother's apartment. Taking up singing as a way of channeling her emotions, FIONA was discovered by music publicist, Kathy Schenker (her babysitter at the time!), who sent her bedroom-cut demo on to 'Clean Slate' records boss, Andy Slater ('Sony'/'Work' would subsequently give it backing). In July '96 and after over eighteen months in the making, FIONA's debut album 'TIDAL' made the shops. Described as ALANIS MORISSETTE or TANITA TIKARAM with further angst to boot, the impressive album subsequently caught the attention of the American buying public and finally crawled all the way up to No.15 in the charts. One of it's highlights, 'CRIMINAL', took the Best Female Rock Performance Award at the 1998 Grammies, while another 'SLEEP TO DREAM' was released as a UK single. At the turn of the century, FIONA was already setting new boundaries by releasing her follow-up set, 'WHEN THE PAWN HITS . . .', the longest album title ever! (the full title taken from a poem). Released late into 1999 (early 2000 in Britain), the album hit No.13 in the Billboard charts, producer Jon Brion getting results from the youngest and most promising lady in recent years to grace the jazz-pop music world.

Album rating: TIDAL (*7) / WHEN THE PAWN . . . (*8)

FIONA APPLE – vocals, piano / with session people

Columbia / Sony

Sep 96. (cd/c) *(483750-2/-4) <67439>* **TIDAL** [ ] Jul96 [15]
– Sleep to dream / Sullen girl / Shadowboxer / Criminal / Slow like honey / The first taste / Never is a promise / The child is gone / Pale September / Carrion. *(cd re-iss. Apr00; same)*

Apr 97. (c-s) *(664428-4)* **SLEEP TO DREAM / PALE SEPTEMBER** [ ] [–]
(10"+=/cd-s+=) *(664428-0/-2)* – Never is a promise / Sullen girl.

Jun 98. (c-s/cd-s) *(6834) <78595>* **CRIMINAL / SLEEP TO DREAM (live)** [ ] Sep97 [21]

Jul 98. (c-s/cd-s) *<110509>* **SHADOWBOXER / (version) / NEVER IS A PROMISE / CARRION (live)** [–] [ ]

Feb 00. (cd-s) *(668996-2) <4630>* **FAST AS YOU CAN / SLEEP TO DREAM / I KNOW** [ ] Nov99 [33]
(cd-s) *(668996-5)* – ('A'side) / Never is a promise (live) / Across the universe (live).

Feb 00. (cd/c) *(496428-2/-4) <69195>* **WHEN THE PAWN . . .** [46] Nov99 [13]
– On the bound / To your love / Limp / Love ridden / Paper bag / A mistake / Fast as you can / The way things are / Get gone / I know.

Jul 00. (cd-s) *(669633-2)* **PAPER BAG / FAST AS YOU CAN (video) / LIMP (video) / PAPER BAG (video)** [ ] [ ]

ARAB STRAP

Formed: Falkirk, Scotland ... 1995 by AIDAN MOFFAT and MALCOLM MIDDLETON. The former had already given up his day job at the local Sleeves record shop to team up with songwriter, JASON "JT" TAYLOR, in his outfit, BAY. This low-key band with drummer! AIDAN (augmented on their second release by RONNIE YOUNG, WILL HEGGIE – ex-COCTEAU TWINS – and ROSS BALLANY), released a couple of RED HOUSE PAINTERS-esque CD's, namely 'HAPPY BEING DIFFERENT' (1994) and 'ALISON RAE' (1995), the latter including a Lo-Fi cover of Roxy Music's 'IN

EVERY DREAM HOME A HEARTACHE' and also coming free with an acoustic CD featuring a version of Nick Drake's 'WHICH WILL'. AIDAN, meanwhile, was plotting his own breakaway group, ARAB STRAP (named after a device used for horse-breeding and better known for something bought from a sex shop), re-establishing a friendship with MALCOLM while writing songs together in the latter's bedroom. A debut ARAB STRAP single, 'THE FIRST BIG WEEKEND', was warmly received by the music press in September '96, critics describing it as "trainspotting for the music world". AIDAN's drug/drink-fuelled life was portrayed in painful detail in a couple of the narrative songs from debut album, 'THE WEEK NEVER STARTS ROUND HERE' (incidentally the rhythm section was completed by GARY MILLER and DAVID GOW). His bittersweet, off-the-cuff, Scots-accented sagas of broken romance were squeezed between Lo-Fi mumblings of occasional pure genius – several of these provided by their equally wasted pal, JOHN MAUCHLINE. MALCOLM's guitar-plucking, meanwhile, came from the laid back school of cool, often played while literally lying on his back. The album was heralded by many (including John Peel) as the next big thing in exotic sound. It included seminal classics, 'THE CLEARING', 'COMING DOWN', 'I WORK IN A SALOON', 'WASTING' and 'DEEPER'. Their live set (including an early afternoon spot at Scotland's 'T In The Park' that added a host of singalong friends), was a mixture of apathy-in-concrete attitude with most people shouting for their favourite, 'THE FIRST BIG WEEKEND'; the track was subsequently used as the backing (with a new coherent talker!) on the Guinness ad (yes, that one that says about 38 per cent of all strippers were educated in a convent!). A year on, with word of mouth cult status ensured, ARAB STRAP finally achieved minor chart glory when 'THE GIRLS OF SUMMER' EP dented the Top 75. Following on from a double header tour with drinking buddies, MOGWAI, the now bearded AIDAN and Co delivered a surprise Top 50 hit, 'HERE WE GO' (a double A-side with 'TRIPPY'), one of the many low-rent, X-rated classics on their Top 40 Spring 1998 follow-up, 'PHILOPHOBIA'. Having signed up with 'Go Beat' early in '99, ARAB STRAP proceeded to deliver a disappointing stop-gap limited-edition live set, 'MAD FOR SADNESS'. Four months later, the 'CHERUBS' EP made amends and was one of the highlights of their rush-released third studio album, the over commercialised 'ELEPHANT SHOE'. However, after a two year vacation from the music scene, The 'STRAP returned in 2001 with their deeply poetic fourth outing 'THE RED THREAD'. Theme'd, as ever, around sex and love and drinking in the central belt of Scotland, the duo refused to change their style of song structure. But with single 'LOVE DETECTIVE' harking back to ARAB STRAP's earlier moments (thumping house beats, accompanied by MIDDLETON's sparse guitar playing) and closing track 'TURBULENCE' delivering a fine closure – if not conclusion – it's a wonder why this pair of talented musicians even strayed from their nest in the first place. Of late, AIDAN and a plethora of other, mainly Scottish musicians/singers, have got together for one set, 'Y'ALL GET SCARED NOW, YA HEAR' (2001) under the REINDEER SECTION banner. September 2002 was certainly an eventful month for MOFFAT and MIDDLETON with the release of both solo projects: the former with the LUCKY PIERRE minimalist instrumental set, 'HYPNOGOGIA', the latter with his solo effort, '5.14 FLUOXYTINE SEAGULL ALCOHOL JOHN NICOTINE' – the jury was certainly out on MOFFAT's noodlings. The Falkirk duo returned in 2003 with possibly their most courageous and adventurous work to date, the brilliant 'MONDAY AT THE HUG AND PINT'. A gloomy affair in places, but uplifting in others, MOFFAT and MIDDLETON added local jazzman BILL WELLS to the mix along with pipers, wind instruments and celloists to create an altogether alt-Celtic album (check out the beautiful chanter solo of 'LOCH LEAVEN INTRO'). Highlights included the stinging revenge song 'FUCKING LITTLE BASTARDS' in which MOFFAT rebuked his "fake friends", the eerie slide-guitar driven 'PEEP-PEEP', which was just classic STRAP, and the fact that AIDAN attempted to sing in tune and pulled it off added to its appeal.
• **Covers:** IS YOUR LOVE IN VAIN? (Bob Dylan) / YOU ONLY TELL ME YOU LOVE ME WHEN YOU'RE DRUNK (Pet Shop Boys) / NEW YEAR (Sugababes) / WHY CAN'T THIS BE LOVE (Van Halen) / YOU SHOOK ME ALL NIGHT LONG (Ac/Dc).

Album rating: THE WEEK NEVER STARTS ROUND HERE (*8) / PHILOPHOBIA (*8) / MAD FOR SADNESS (*6) / ELEPHANT SHOE (*7) / THE RED THREAD (*8) / MONDAY AT THE HUG AND PINT (*7) / Lucky Pierre: HYPNOGOGIA (*4) / Malcolm Middleton: 5.14 FLUOXYTINE SEAGULL ALCOHOL JOHN NICOTINE (*6)

AIDAN MOFFAT – vocals, keyboards / **MALCOLM MIDDLETON** – guitar / **GARY MILLER** – bass / **DAVID GOW** – drums

		Chemikal U/ground	Chemikal U/ground
Sep 96.	(7") *(CHEM 007)* **THE FIRST BIG WEEKEND. / GILDED**		–

—— interruptions/tape narrative by **JOHN MAUCHLINE**

Nov 96.	(lp/cd) *(<CHEM 010/+CD>)* **THE WEEK NEVER STARTS ROUND HERE**		1997
	– Coming down / The clearing / Driving / Gourmet / I work in a saloon / Wasting / General plea to a girlfriend / The first big weekend / Kate Moss / Little girls / Phone me tonight / Blood / Deeper.		
Mar 97.	(12"/cd-s) *(CHEM 013/+CD)* **THE CLEARING (guest starring Isobel Campbell & Chris Geddes). / (remixed by Hungry Lions) (remixed by Iain Hanlon & Jonathan Hilditch)**		–
Sep 97.	(12"ep/cd-ep) *(CHEM 017/+CD)* **THE GIRLS OF SUMMER E.P.**	74	–
	– Hey! fever / Girls of summer / The beautiful barmaids of Dundee / One day, after school.		
Nov 97.	(7"m) *(LISS 22)* **THE SMELL OF OUTDOOR COOKING. / THEME TUNE / BLACKSTAR**		–
	(above issued on 'Lissy's', below on 'Too Many Cooks')		
1998.	(7") *(BROTH 001)* **LIVE: PACKS OF THREE. / BLOOD**		–

		Chemikal U/ground	Matador
Mar 98.	(10"/cd-s) *(CHEM 20 T/CD)* **HERE WE GO. / TRIPPY**	48	–
Apr 98.	(cd) *(CHEM 21CD)* <OLE 315> **PHILOPHOBIA**	37	May98
	– Packs of three / Soaps / Here we go / New birds / One day, after school / Islands / The night before the funeral / Not quite a yes / Piglet / Afterwards / My favourite muse / I would've liked me a lot last night / The first time you're unfaithful.		
Sep 98.	(7") *(CHEM 27)* **(AFTERNOON) SOAPS. / PHONE ME TOMORROW**	74	–
	(12"+=/cd-s+=) *(CHEM 27 T/CD)* – ('A'side) / Toy fights / Forest hills.		

		Go Beat	not iss.
May 99.	(cd/lp) *(547387-2/-1)* **MAD FOR SADNESS (live)**		–
	– Intro – My favourite muse / Packs of three / New birds / Toy fights / Here we go / Phone me tomorrow / Girls of summer / Piglet / Blood / Afterwards. *<US cd-iss. Jul00 on 'Jetset'; 029>*		
Aug 99.	(12"ep/cd-ep) *(GOB X/CD 21 – 561263-1/-2)* **CHERUBS E.P.**		–
	– Cherubs / Motown answers / An eventful day / Pulled.		

—— next with guests, CORA BISSETT, BARRY BURNS + ALAN WYLIE

Sep 99.	(cd/lp) *(547805-2/-1)* **ELEPHANT SHOE**		–
	– Cherubs / One four seven one / Pyjamas / Autumnal / Lay the day free / Direction of strong man / Tanned / Aries the ram / The drinking eye / Pro-(your) life / Hello daylight. *<US cd-iss. Jun00 on 'Jetset'; 028>*		

		Chemikal U/ground	Matador
Nov 00.	(12"/cd-s) *(CHEM 048/+CD)* **FUKD ID VOL.2 EP**		–
	– Rocket, take your turn / Blackness.		
Jan 01.	(12"/cd-s) *(CHEM 049/+CD)* **LOVE DETECTIVE. / BULLSEYE / WE KNOW WHERE YOU LIVE**	66	–
Feb 01.	(lp/cd) *(CHEM 050/+CD)* <OLE 503> **THE RED THREAD**		
	– Amor veneris / Last orders / Scenery / The Devil-tips / The long sea / Love		

detective / Infrared / Screaming in the trees / Haunt me / Turbulence.

May 01. (12"/cd-s) *(CHEM 051/+CD)* **TURBULENCE (mixes by BIS, ARAB STRAP & JASON FAMOUS)** [ ] [-]

—— now without GOW + MILLER

Apr 03. (lp/cd) *(CHEM 065/+CD) <OLE 577>* **MONDAY AT THE HUG AND PINT** [ ] [ ]
– The shy retirer / Meanwhile, at the bar, a drunkard muses / Fucking little bastards / Peep-peep / Flirt / Who named the days? / Loch Leven intro / Loch Leven / Glue / Act of war / Serenade / The week never starts round here / Pica Luna.

Sep 03. (12"ep/cd-ep) *(CHEM 067/+CD)* **THE SHY RETIRER** [ ] [-]
– The shy retirer (radio mix) / Why can't this be love / The good part / The new Saturday / You shook me all night long / The shy retirer (Dirty Hospital remix).

LUCKY PIERRE

—— aka (French DJ) AIDAN MOFFAT with the FORCE

Lucky | not iss.

Feb 99. (7") *(LUCKY 001)* **PIERRE'S FINAL THOUGHT. / SOMETIMES I FEEL LIKE A MOTHERLESS CHILD** [ ] [-]

Jul 99. (12") *(LUCKY 02)* **BLANK FOR YOUR OWN MESSAGE** [ ] [-]

Melodic | not iss.

May 02. (12") **ANGELS ON YOUR BODY. / BOGEY ON MY SIX** [ ] [-]

Sep 02. (lp/cd) *(MELO 013/+CD)* **HYPNOGOGIA** [ ] [-]
– Angels of your body / Nurse flamingo / Shatterproof / Ghost two / The heart of all that is / The bit in the woods / Sometimes I feel like a motherless child / White Heaven in Hell / Ghost one / Bedwomb.

MALCOLM MIDDLETON

Chemikal U/ground | not iss.

Sep 02. (cd) *(chem 062cd)* **5.14 FLUOXYTINE SEAGULL ALCOHOL JOHN NICOTINE** [ ] [-]
– Crappo the clown / Wake up / The loneliest night of my life come calling / Best in me / Cold winter / Bring down (preprise) / Rotten heart / Speed on the M9 / 1, 2, 3, 4 / Birdwatcher / The king of bring / Devil and the angel.

☐ ARCADIA (see under ⇒ DURAN DURAN)

Joan ARMATRADING

Born: 9 Dec'50, Basseterre, St. Kitts, West Indies, although she and her family moved to Birmingham, England in '58. In 1969, she befriended PAM NESTOR (b. 28 Apr'48, Berbice, Guyana) with whom she initiated songwriting and stage partnership. They severed this arrangement when ARMATRADING alone was credited on debut album in '73 for 'Cube'. Two years later she signed to 'A&M', releasing a belated follow-up set, 'BACK TO THE NIGHT', in 1975. However, it was with third set, 'JOAN ARMATRADING' (1976), that the black singer/songwriter/guitarist fully realised her distinctive blend of folk, rock, pop and soul. While JONI MITCHELL was an obvious reference point, ARMATRADING had patented her own, richly resonant style which latter day singers such as TRACY CHAPMAN would subsequently draw on for inspiration. Buoyed by the British Top 10 success of the classic 'LOVE AND AFFECTION' single, the album made the UK Top 20. Further success followed with 'SHOW SOME EMOTION' (1977) and 'TO THE LIMIT' (1978), veteran producer GLYNN JOHNS at the helm for the bulk of this developmental late 70's period. Despite a harder-edged direction, 1980's 'ME, MYSELF, I' became her most successful album to date, making the UK Top 5. Other early 80's sets such as 'WALK UNDER LADDERS' (1981) and 'THE KEY' (1983) were also well received, while the latter represented ARMATRADING's sole sojourn into the American Top 40. While never maintaining a particularly high profile, ARMATRADING has continued to record and release albums at regular intervals throughout the 80's and the 90's. Though she didn't enjoy the commercial success of her earlier period, a loyal core of fans ensured that she usually made the British Top 40. ARMATRADING's first album of the new millennium and indeed her first in half a decade was the acclaimed 'LOVERS SPEAK' (2003), a late blossoming tour de force of emotional examination and exorcism. Self-produced and unflinching in its scrutiny of the multifarious dimensions, consequences and possibilities of love, the record outshone almost anything the singer had done since the 70's. Musically, its folk diversions, skirting the delicate outer fringes of pop, jazz-inflected meditations and even country flirtations delved deep into the very fabric of her personal vision. • **Songwriters:** She writes all material, except when PAM NESTOR wrote lyrics until '75. Covered; MOONDANCE (Van Morrison). • **Trivia:** MARK KNOPFLER (Dire Straits) and MARK BRZEZICKI (Big Country) guested on her 1988 album 'THE SHOUTING STAGE'.

Album rating: WHATEVER'S FOR US (*4) / BACK TO THE NIGHT (*5) / JOAN ARMATRADING (*7) / SHOW SOME EMOTION (*5) / TO THE LIMIT (*5) / STEPPIN' OUT (*5) / ME MYSELF, I (*6) / WALK UNDER LADDERS (*5) / THE KEY (*6) / TRACK RECORD compilation (*7) / SECRET SECRETS (*5) / SLEIGHT OF HAND (*4) / THE SHOUTING STAGE (*4) / HEARTS AND FLOWERS (*4) / THE VERY BEST OF JOAN ARMATRADING compilation (*7) / SQUARE THE CIRCLE (*5) / WHAT'S INSIDE (*4) / LOVE AND AFFECTION compilation (*7) / LOVERS SPEAK (*7)

JOAN ARMATRADING – vocals, acoustic guitar with various session people

Cube | A&M

Nov 72. (lp/c) *(HIFLY/ZCFLY 12) <4382>* **WHATEVER'S FOR US** [ ] [ ]
– My family / City girl / Spend a little time / Whatever's for us / Child star / Mean old man / Visionary mountains / It could have been better / Head of the table / Mister remember me / Give it a try / Alice / Conversation / Mean old man / All the King's garden. *(re-iss. Oct81 lp/c; same) (re-iss. Apr89 on 'Castle' lp/c/cd; CLA LP/MC/CD 143) (cd re-iss. Feb01 on 'Metro'; METRCD 047)*

Jul 73. (7") *(BUG 31)* **LONELY LADY. / TOGETHER IN WORDS AND MUSIC** [ ] [-]

A&M | A&M

Apr 75. (lp/c) *(AMLH/CAM 68305) <4525>* **BACK TO THE NIGHT** [ ] [ ]
– No love for free / Travelled so far / Steppin' out / Dry land / Cool blue / Stole my heart / Get in touch with Jesus / Body to dust / Back to the night / So good / Let's go dancing / Come when you need me. *(re-iss. Mar82; AMID 112) (re-iss. Sep84 on 'Hallmark' lp/c; SHM/HSC 3153)*

Jun 75. (7") *(AMS 7181)* **BACK TO THE NIGHT. / SO GOOD** [ ] [-]

Nov 75. (7") *(AMS 7205)* **DRY LAND. / BODY INTO DUST** [ ] [-]

Aug 76. (lp/c) *(AMLH/CAM 64588) <4588>* **JOAN ARMATRADING** [12] [67]
– Down to zero / Help yourself / Water with the vine / Love and affection / Save me / Join the boys / People / Somebody who loves you / Like fire / Tall in the saddle. *(cd-iss. 1988; CDA 3228) (re-iss. Aug91 cd/c; CD/C MID 104)*

Aug 76. (7") *(AMS 7249) <1865>* **LOVE AND AFFECTION. / HELP YOURSELF** [10] [ ]
(re-iss. 1988)

Jan 77. (7") *(AMS 7270) <1898>* **DOWN TO ZERO. / LIKE FIRE** [ ] [ ]

Apr 77. (7") *<1914>* **WATER WITH THE WINE. / PEOPLE** [-] [ ]

Sep 77. (lp/c) *(AMLH/CAM 68433) <4663>* **SHOW SOME EMOTION** [6] [52]
– Woncha come on home / Show some emotion / Warm love / Never is too late / Peace in mind / Opportunity / Mama mercy / Get in the sun / Willow / Kissin' and a huggin'. *(cd-iss. 1988; CDA 4663) (cd re-iss. Aug89; 394 663-2) (re-iss. Oct92 cd/c; CD/C MID 105)*

Oct 77. (7") *(AMS 7316)* **WILLOW. / NO WAY OUT** [ ] [-]

Jan 78. (7") *(AMS 7331)* **SHOW SOME EMOTION. / PEACE IN MIND** [ ] [-]

Feb 78. (7") *<1994>* **SHOW SOME EMOTION. / NO WAY OUT** [-] [ ]

Mar 78. (7") *(AMS 7346)* **WARM LOVE. / GET IN THE SUN** [ ] [–]
May 78. (7") *<2018>* **WARM LOVE. / NO WAY OUT** [–] [ ]
Jun 78. (7") *(AMS 7365)* **FLIGHT OF THE WILD GEESE. / NO WAY OUT** [ ] [ ]
Sep 78. (lp/c) *(AMLH/CAM 64732) <4732>* **TO THE LIMIT** [13] [ ]
– Barefoot and pregnant / Your letter / Am I blue for you / You rope you tie me / Baby I / Bottom to the top / Taking my baby up town / What do you want / Wishing / Let it last. *(cd-iss. 1988; CDA 4732)*
Oct 78. (7") *(AMS 7393) <2102>* **BOTTOM TO THE TOP. / YOUR LETTER** [ ] [ ]
Jan 79. (7") *<2113>* **BAREFOOT AND PREGNANT. / YOUR LETTER** [–] [ ]
Aug 79. (lp/c) *(AMLH/CAM 64789)* **STEPPING OUT (live)** [ ] [–]
– Mama mercy / Cool blue / Stole my heart / How cruel / Kissin' and a huggin' / Love song / Love and affection / Stepin' out / You rope you tie me / Kissin' and a huggin' / Tall in the saddle. *(re-iss. Sep85 on 'Hallmark' lp/c; SHM/HSC 3176)*
Dec 79. (m-lp) *<3302>* **HOW CRUEL** [–] [ ]
– How cruel / He wants her / I really must be going / Rosie.
Jan 80. (7") *(AMS 7506) <2210>* **ROSIE. / HOW CRUEL** [49] [ ]
Apr 80. (7") *<2224>* **HE WANTS HER. / SHOW SOME EMOTION** [–] [ ]
May 80. (lp/c) *(AMLH/CAM 64809) <4809>* **ME MYSELF, I** [5] [28]
– Me myself, I / Ma-me-o-beach / Friends / Is it tomorrow yet / Turn out the light / When you kisses me / All the way from America / Feeling in my heart (for you) / Simon / I need you. *(cd-iss. Sep86; CDA 4809) (re-iss. May93 on 'Spectrum' cd/c; 550058-2/-4) (cd re-iss. Feb01; 394809-2)*
Jun 80. (7") *(AMS 7527)* **ME MYSELF, I. / WHEN YOU KISS ME** [21] [–]
Jun 80. (7") *<2240>* **ME MYSELF, I. / FRIENDS** [–] [ ]
Aug 80. (7") *(AMS 7552)* **ALL THE WAY FROM AMERICA. / IS IT TOMORROW YET** [54] [–]
Sep 80. (7") *<2262>* **IS IT TOMORROW YET. / MA-ME-O-BEACH** [–] [ ]
Oct 80. (7") *(AMS 7571)* **SIMON. / HE WANTS HER** [ ] [–]
Aug 81. (7") *(AMS 8163)* **I'M LUCKY. / SHINE** [46] [–]
Sep 81. (lp/c) *(AMLH/CAM 64876) <4876>* **WALK UNDER LADDERS** [6] [88]
– I'm lucky / When I get it right / Romancers / I wanna hold you / The weakness in me / No love / At the hop / I can't lie to myself / Eating the bear / Only one. *(cd-iss. Nov88; 394 876-2)*
Oct 81. (7") *(AMS 8180)* **WHEN I GET IT RIGHT. / CRYING** [ ] [–]
Jan 82. (7") *(AMS 8179)* **NO LOVE. / DOLLARS** [50] [–]
Jan 82. (7") *<2381>* **THE WEAKNESS IN ME. / CRYING** [–] [ ]
Apr 82. (7") *<2400>* **I WANNA HOLD YOU. / CRYING** [–] [ ]
Feb 83. (7") *(AMS 8306) <2538>* **DROP THE PILOT. / BUSINESS IS BUSINESS** [11] May83 [78]
Mar 83. (lp/c) *(AMLX/CXM 64912) <4912>* **THE KEY** [10] [32]
– (I love it when you) Call me names / Foolish pride / Drop the pilot / The key / Everybody gotta know / Tell tale / What do boys dream / The game of love / The dealer / Bad habit / I love my baby. *(cd-iss. Jun86; CDA 64912)*
May 83. (7") *(AM 116)* **(I LOVE IT WHEN YOU) CALL ME NAMES. / FOR THE BEST** [ ] [ ]
Nov 83. (7") *<2622>* **HEAVEN. / FRUSTRATION** [–] [ ]
Nov 83. (7") *(AM 162)* **HEAVEN. / BACK TO THE NIGHT** [14] [–]
Nov 83. (lp/c) *(JA/+C 2001)* **TRACK RECORD** (compilation) [18] [–]
– Drop the pilot / (I love it when you) Call me names / Frustration / When I get it right / I'm lucky / Me myself I / The weakness in me / Heaven / Down to zero / Love and affection / Show some emotion / Willow / Rosie. *(cd-iss. Oct84; CDA 63725)*
Feb 85. (lp/c/cd) *(<AMA/AMC/CDA 5040)>* **SECRET SECRETS** [14] [73]
– Persona grata / Temptation / Moves / Talking to the wall / Love by you / Thinking man / Friends not lovers / One night / Secret secrets / Strange.
Feb 85. (7") *(AM 238) <2712>* **TEMPTATION. / TALKING TO THE WALL** [65] [ ]
(12"+=) *(AMY 238)* – Spanking brand new.
May 85. (7") *(AM AM 250) <2751>* **THINKING MAN. / LOVE GROWS** [ ] [ ]
Aug 85. (7"/12") *(AM/+Y 269)* **LOVE BY YOU. / READ IT WRITE** [ ] [–]
Apr 86. (7"/12") *(AM/+Y 315) <2837>* **KIND WORDS (AND A REAL GOOD HEART). / FIGURE OF SPEECH** [ ] [ ]
May 86. (lp/c/cd) *(<AMA/AMC/CDA 5130>)* **SLEIGHT OF HAND** [34] [68]
– Kind words (and a real good heart) / Reach out / Killing time / Angel man / Laurel and the rose / One more chance / Russian roulette / Jesse / Figure of speech / Don Juan.
Jun 86. (7") *<2868>* **ANGEL MAN. / RIVERS OF FIRE** [–] [ ]
Jul 86. (7") *(AM 338)* **REACH OUT. / RIVERS ON FIRE** [ ] [–]
Sep 86. (7") *(AM 350)* **JESSE. / DON JUAN** [ ] [–]
(d7"+=/12"+=) *(AM S/Y 350)* – Love and affection / Willow.
Jul 88. (7") *(AM 460)* **LIVING FOR YOU. / INNOCENT REQUEST** [ ] [–]
(12"+=/cd-s+=) *(AM Y/CD 460)* – Cool Blue stole my heart.
Jul 88. (lp/c/cd) *(<AMA/AMC/CDA 5211>)* **THE SHOUTING STAGE** [28] [100]
– The Devil I know / Living for you / Did I make you up / Stronger love / The shouting stage / Words / Straight talk / Watch you step / All a woman needs / Dark truths. *(cd+=)* – Innocent request.
Jul 88. (7") *<1235>* **LIVING FOR YOU. / I REALLY MUST BE GOING** [–] [ ]
Sep 88. (7") *(AM 449) <1259>* **THE SHOUTING STAGE. / I REALLY MUST BE GOING** [ ] [ ]
(12"+=/cd-s+=) *(AM Y/CD 449)* – He wants her.
Nov 88. (7") *(AM 482)* **STRONGER LOVE. / THE DEVIL I KNOW** [ ] [–]
May 90. (7"/c-s) *(AM/+C 561)* **MORE THAN ONE KIND OF LOVE. / GOOD TIMES** [75] [–]
(12"+=/cd-s+=) *(AM Y/CD 561)* – Love and affection.
Jun 90. (cd/c/lp) *(395298-2/-4/-1) <5298>* **HEARTS AND FLOWERS** [29] [ ]
– More than one kind of love / Hearts and flowers / Promise land / Someone's in the background / Can't let go / Free / Something in the air tonight / Always / Good times / The power of dreams.
Jun 90. (7"/c-s) *(AM/+C 567)* **PROMISE LAND. / DOWN TO ZERO (live)** [ ] [–]
(12"+=/cd-s+=) *(AM Y/CD 567)* – Dark truths (live).
Aug 90. (7") *(AM 595)* **FREE. / THE SHOUTING STAGE (live)** [ ] [–]
(cd-s+=) *(AMCD 595)* – Always.
May 92. (7") *(AM 877)* **WRAPPED AROUND HER. / PROMISE LAND (live at the BBC)** [56] [–]
(cd-s) *(AMCD 877)* – ('A'side) / All the way from America / I'm lucky / Can't lie to myself (all live at the BBC).
Jun 92. (cd/c/lp) *(395888-2/-4/-1)* **SQUARE THE CIRCLE** [34] [ ]
– True love / Crazy / Wrapped around her / Sometimes I don't wanna go home / Square the circle / Weak woman / Can I get next to you / Can't get over (how I broke your heart) / If women ruled the world / Cradled in your love.
Jul 92. (7") *(AM 881)* **TRUE LOVE. / MORE THAN ONE KIND OF LOVE (live)** [ ] [–]
(12"+=/cd-s+=) *(AM Y/CD 881)* – Love and affection (live) / Something in the air (live).

R.C.A. R.C.A.

May 95. (cd/c) *(<74321 27269-2/-4>)* **WHAT'S INSIDE** [48] [ ]
– In your eyes / Everyday boy / Merchant of love / Shapes and sizes / Back on the road / Lost the love / Songs / Would you like to dance / Recommend my love / Beyond the blue / Can't stop loving you / Shape of a pony / Trouble.
Feb 96. (c-s) *(74321 34112-4)* **EVERYDAY BOY / ('A'live)** [ ] [–]
(cd-s+=) *(74321 34112-2)* – Merchant of love (live) / Shapes and sizes (live).

not iss. Denon

Mar 03. (cd) *<17185>* **LOVERS SPEAK** [–] [ ]
– Lovers speak / Physical pain / In these times / Waiting / Prove yourself / Fire and ice / Love bug / Let's talk about us / Ocean / Tender trap / Less happy more often / Crazy for you / You made your bed / Blessed.

– compilations, others –

Dec 76. (7") *Cube; (BUG 74)* **ALICE. / ALL THE KING'S GARDEN** [ ] [–]
Jun 82. (7") *Cube; (BUG 93)* **LONELY LADY. / VISIONARY MOUNTAINS** [ ] [–]
May 81. (d-c) *A&M; (CAMCR 2)* **JOAN ARMATRADING / TO THE LIMIT** [ ] [–]
Feb 85. (lp/c) *Sierra; (FEDB/CFEDB 5005)* **REPLAY OF JOAN ARMATRADING** [ ] [–]
Apr 88. (cd-ep) *A&M; (AMCD 903)* **COMPACT HITS** [ ] [–]
– Love and affection / All the way from America / Willow / Flight of the wild geese.
Jun 89. (c) *A&M; (AMC 24107)* **ME MYSELF I / TRACK RECORD** [ ] [–]

Jun 90. (cd/c) *Knight;* **THE GOLDEN HOUR OF JOAN ARMATRADING** [ ] [–]

Feb 91. (7") *A&M;* **LOVE AND AFFECTION (remix). / ALL THE WAY FROM AMERICA** [ ] [–]
(12"+=/cd-s+=) – Promise land.

Mar 91. (cd/c/lp) *A&M; (397122-2/-4/-1)* **THE VERY BEST OF JOAN ARMATRADING** [9] [ ]
– Love and affection / Down to zero / Drop the pilot / Show some emotion / The shouting stage / Willow / Rosie / I'm lucky / Me, myself, I / (I love it when you) Call me names / Bottom to the top / More than one kind of love / The weakness in me / All the way from America.

Oct 93. (cd) *A&M;* **ME MYSELF I / WALK UNDER LADDERS** [ ] [–]

Sep 95. (d-cd) *A&M; (540 405-2)* **LOVE AND AFFECTION (A JOAN ARMATRADING ANTHOLOGY)** [ ] [ ]
(re-iss. Jan97; same)

Nov 99. (cd) *Spectrum; (554423-2)* **THE COLLECTION** [ ] [–]

Sep 00. (cd) *Universal; (AA694 90696-2)* **THE MILLENNIUM COLLECTION** [ ] [–]

Jul 01. (cd) *Universal; (E 490789-2)* **UNIVERSAL MASTERS COLLECTION** [ ] [–]

Mar 03. (cd) *Disky; (EMI 76290-2)* **SINGER/SONGWRITER** [ ] [–]

☐ ARMS AND LEGS (see under ⇒ JACKSON, Joe)

ASH

Formed: N. Ireland . . . 1989 by TIM WHEELER (then 12 years of age) and MARK HAMILTON, relocating to Downpatrick, County Down a few years later where they officially formed the trio with RICK McMURRAY. ASH's precocious talents were quickly spotted by American record moguls eager for more punk-centric guitar music which would also cross over to the pop market. Though they eventually opted to sign with 'Reprise', the trio had already released their debut set, 'TRAILER' on 'Infectious'. Their starry-eyed, bushy-tailed but ultimately derivative blend of indie punk finally became a part of the pop vocabulary when the catchy 'GIRL FROM MARS' sky-rocketed into the UK Top 20 in summer '95. This was pursued by another Top 20 hit later that year in 'ANGEL INTERCEPTOR'. With the hype machine going into overload, the group hit the UK Top 5 in Spring of the following year with 'GOLDFINGER', the single trailing a No.1 album, '1977' (1996). Apparently a reference to the year 'Star Wars' was released rather than any reference to safety-pins and saliva, the record included all their hit singles to date and confirmed their increasingly melodic approach. Keeping their profile high with festival appearances, the band later added another guitarist, CHARLOTTE HATHERLEY in summer '97. She made her debut on ASH's theme for the much lauded Ewan McGregor/Cameron Diaz film, 'A LIFE LESS ORDINARY', another Top 10 in late '97. While the indie scene continues to cry out for something innovative, it remains difficult to envisage any figureheads less ordinary than ASH (songs!). Surprisingly 'Kerrang!-friendly, the quartet lost a little of their indie cred with the release of their third album proper, 'NU-CLEAR SOUNDS' (1998), a record that quickly vacated the Top 10 with the accompanying single, 'JESUS SAYS', only managing to make a Top 20 placing. With sex (group, that is), drugs (abuse) and rock'n'roll (Tim Wheeler in the buff!) all the ingredients were in the latest promo instalment for ASH's single 'NUMBSKULL'. Unfortunately the viewing public, and for that matter the buying public, didn't get much of a look-in, as the EP (like many others at the turn of the century) was ineligible for the charts via a new ruling by those pesky compilers. Older and wiser, the ASH posse returned in 2001 with their first material of the new millennium, 'FREE ALL ANGELS'. Previewed by the hit singles, 'SHINING LIGHT' and 'BURN BABY BURN', the record recaptured some of their mid-period spunk and used it to temper the aural hangover of its predecessor. • **Songwriters:** WHEELER or w/ HAMILTON except covers; PUNKBOY (Helen Love) / GET READY (Temptations) / DOES YOUR MOTHER KNOW (Abba) / LOSE CONTROL (Backwater) / BLEW (Nirvana) / WHO YOU DRIVIN' NOW? (Mudhoney). • **Trivia:** The cover sleeve of their single, 'KUNG FU', had a photo of French former Man U star footballer, ERIC CANTONA, giving his famous throat and neck tackle on an abusive Crystal Palace supporter in 1995.

Album rating: TRAILER mini (*7) / 1977 (*9) / LIVE AT THE WIRELESS live official bootleg (*5) / NU-CLEAR SOUNDS (*7) / FREE ALL ANGELS (*6) / INTERGALACTIC SONIC SEVENS compilation (*8)

TIM WHEELER – vocals, guitar / **MARK HAMILTON** – bass / **RICK McMURRAY** – drums

La La Land — not iss.

Feb 94. (7") *(LA LA 001)* **JACK NAMES THE PLANETS. / DON'T KNOW** [ ] [–]

Infectious — Reprise

Aug 94. (7"ep) *(INFECT 13S)* **PETROL. / THE LITTLE POND / A MESSAGE FROM OSCAR WILDE AND PATRICK THE BREWER** [ ] [–]
(cd-s+=) *(INFEVT 13CD)* – Things. *(re-iss. Nov96; same)*

Oct 94. (cd/c/lp) *(INFECT 14 CD/MC/LP)* <45985> **TRAILER** [ ] Oct95 [ ]
– Season / Message from Oscar Wilde and Patrick the brewer / Jack names the planets / Intense thing / Uncle Pat / Message from Mr. Waterman / Get out / Petrol / Obscure thing. *(lp w/ free 7"yellow) (INFECT 14S)* SILVER SURFER. / JAZZ '59 *<diff.tracks US> (re-iss. Jan01 cd/c/lp; INFECT 14 CD/MC/LPX)*

Oct 94. (7") *(INFECT 16S)* **UNCLE PAT. / DIFFERENT TODAY** [ ] [–]
(cd-s+=) *(INFECT 16CD)* – Hulk Hogan bubble bath. *(re-iss. Nov96; same)*

Mar 95. (7") *(INFECT 21J)* <17706> **KUNG FU. / DAY OF THE TRIFFIDS** [57] Nov95 [ ]
(cd-s+=) *(INFECT 21CD)* – Luther Ingo's star cruiser. *(re-iss. Nov96 & Jan01; same)*

Jul 95. (7"/c-s) *(INFECT 24S/24MC)* **GIRL FROM MARS. / CANTINA BAND** [11] [–]
(cd-s+=) *(INFECT 24CD)* – Astral conversations with Toulouse Lautrec. *(re-iss. Nov96 & Jan01; same)*

Sep 95. (7"colrd-various) <G26> **PETROL. / PUNKBOY** [–] [ ]

Oct 95. (7"/c-s/cd-s) *(INFECT 27S/27MC/27CD)* **ANGEL INTERCEPTOR. / 5 A.M. ETERNAL / GIVE ME SOME TRUTH** [14] [–]
(re-iss. cd-s Nov96 & Jan01; same)

Dec 95. (7"red) *(FP 004)* **GET READY. / ZERO ZERO ZERO** [ ] [–]
(above 45 issued on 'Fantastic Plastic')

Apr 96. (7"/c-s) *(INFECT 39 S/MC)* **GOLDFINGER. / I NEED SOMEBODY / SNEAKER** [5] [–]
(cd-s+=) *(INFECT 39CD)* – Get ready. *(re-iss. Nov96 & Jan01; same)*

May 96. (cd/c/lp) *(INFECT 40 CD/MC/LP)* <46191> **1977** [1] [ ]
– Lose control / Goldfinger / Girl from Mars / I'd give you anything / Gone the dream / Kung Fu / Oh yeah / Let it flow / Innocent smile / Angel interceptor / Lost in you / Darkside lightside. *(cd+=hidden track)* – Sick of vomiting. *(lp re-iss. Jan01; same)*

Jun 96. (7"yellow/c-s) *(INFECT 41 S/MC)* **OH YEAH / T. REX / EVERYWHERE IS ALL AROUND / OH YEAH (quartet version)** [6] [–]
(cd-s) *(INFECT 41CD)* – (first 3 tracks) / Does your mother know. *(re-iss. Nov96 & Jan01; same)*

—— added **CHARLOTTE HATHERLEY** – guitar (ex-NIGHTNURSE)

Infectious — Dreamworks

Oct 97. (7"blue/c-s) *(INFECT 50 S/MC)* **A LIFE LESS ORDINARY. / WHERE IS LOVE GOING / WHAT DEANER WAS TALKING ABOUT** [10] [–]
(cd-s+=) *(INFECT 50CD)* – Halloween. *(re-iss. Jan01; same)*

Sep 98. (7") *(INFECT 059S)* **JESUS SAYS. / TAKEN OUT** [15] [–]
(c-s+=/cd-s+=) *(INFECT 059 MCS/CDS)* – Heroin, vodka, white noise.
(cd-s) *(INFECT 059CDSX)* – ('A'side) / Radiation / Dancing on the Moon. *(re-iss. Jan01; same)*

Oct 98. (cd/c/lp) *(INFECT 060 CD/MC/LP)* <50121> **NU-CLEAR SOUNDS** [7] Sep99 [ ]
– Projects / Low ebb / Jesus says / Wild surf / Death trip 21 / Folk song / Numbskull / Burn out / Aphrodite / Fortune teller / I'm gonna fall. *(re-iss. Jan01; same)*

Nov 98. (7") *(INFECT 061S)* **WILD SURF. / STORMY WATERS** [31] [-]
(c-s+=/cd-s+=) *(INFECT 061 MCS/CDS)* – When I'm tired.
(cd-s) *(INFECT 061CDSX)* – ('A'side) / Lose control / Gonna do it soon.
(re-iss. Jan01; same)

—— added on tour **DJ DICK KURTAINE** – turntables

Apr 99. (d7"red-ep) *(INFECT 62)* **NUMBSKULL EP** [ ] [-]
– Numbskull / Blew / Who you drivin' now? / Jesus says (live).
(cd-ep+=) *(INFECT 62EP)* – Girl from Mars (live) / Fortune teller (live).
(re-iss. Jan01; same)

Jan 01. (7"/c-s) *(INFECT 98 S/MCS)* **SHINING LIGHT. / WARMER THAN FIRE** [8] [-]
(cd-s+=) *(INFECT 98CDS)* – Gabriel.
(cd-s) *(INFECT 98CDSX)* – ('A'side) / Feel no pain / Jesus says (headrock valley beats lightyear 12"mix) / ('A'-CD-ROM video).

Apr 01. (7") *(INFECT 99S)* **BURN BABY BURN. / THINKING ABOUT YOU** [13] [-]
(cd-s+=) *(INFECT 99CDSX)* – Submission (Arthur Baker remix).
(cd-s) *(INFECT 99CDS)* – ('A'side) / 13th floor (session) / Only in dreams (session).

Apr 01. (cd/c/lp) *(INFECT 100 CD/MC/LP)* **FREE ALL ANGELS** [1] [-]
– Walking barefoot / Shining light / Burn baby burn / Candy / Submission / Someday / Pacific palisades / Shark / Sometimes / Nicole / There's a star / World domination.

Jul 01. (d7") *(INFEC 101S)* **SOMETIMES. / SKULLFULL OF SULPHUR / SO THE STORY GOES. / TEENAGE KICKS** [21] [-]
(cd-s) *(INFEC 101CDS)* – (first 3 tracks) / ('A'-video).
(cd-s) *(INFEC 101CDSX)* – (first & fourth tracks) / Melon farmer (live) / (video mixer update).

Oct 01. (d7") *(INFEC 106S)* **CANDY. / WATERFALL // NOCTURNE. / STAY IN LOVE FOREVER** [20] [-]
(cd-s) *(INFEC 106CDS)* – (first 3 tracks) / ('A'-video).
(cd-s) *(INFEC 106CDSX)* – (first & fourth tracks) / Sweetness of death by the obsidian knife.

Jan 02. (cd-s) *(INFEC 112CDS)* **THERE'S A STAR / NO PLACE TO HIDE / COASTING / THERE'S A STAR (video)** [13] [-]
(cd-s) *(INFEC 112CDSX)* – ('A'side) / Here comes the music / Grey will fade / (video excerpts).

Aug 02. (cd-s) *(INFEC 119CDS)* **ENVY / TONIGHT YOU BELONG TO ME / I SHALL NOT DIE** [21] [-]
(cd-s) *(INFEC 119CDSX)* – ('A'side) / Bad karma blues / I don't mind.
(d7"+=) *(INFEC 119S)* – I shall not die.

Sep 02. (cd/d-lp) *(INFEC 120 CD/LP)* **INTERGALACTIC SONIC SEVENS** (compilation) [3] [-]
– Burn baby burn / Envy / Girl from Mars / Shining light / A life less ordinary / Goldfinger / Jesus says / Oh yeah / Jack names the planets / Sometimes / Kung Fu / Candy / Angel interceptor / Uncle Pat / Wildsurf / Walking barefoot / Petrol / There's a star / Numbskull. *(2xcd+=/4xlp+=; INFEC 120CDB)* – No place to hide / Warmer than fire / Where is our love going / Taken out / 13th floor / Stormy waters / Message from Oscar Wilde / Who you drivin' now / Stay in love forever / Sweetness of death by the obsidian knife / Melon farmer / Nocturne / Gabriel / Coasting / Lose control / I need somebody / Sneaker / Cantina band / Astral conversations with Toulouse Lautrec / Day of the triffids / Hallowe'en / Thinking about you.

– compilations, etc. –

Feb 97. (cd) *Death Star; (DEATH 3)* **LIVE AT THE WIRELESS (live)** [ ] [-]
– Darkside lightside / Girl from Mars / Oh yeah / T.Rex / I'd give you anything / Kung Fu / What Deaner was talking about / Goldfinger / Petrol / A clear invitation to party. *(lp-iss.Jan01; DEATH 3LP)*

Dec 02. (cd-s) *Double Dragon; (DD 2007)* **JACK NAMES THE PLANETS** [ ] [-]

☐ Daniel ASH (see under ⇒ BAUHAUS)

☐ Richard ASHCROFT (see under ⇒ VERVE)

ASIA

Formed: London, England . . . early 1981 by seasoned pomp-rockers, JOHN WETTON, STEVE HOWE, CARL PALMER and GEOFFREY DOWNES. These supergroup stadium fillers had no trouble finding a record contract with 'Geffen', their eponymous debut soon climbing to No.1 in the States, supplanting them as top dogs over similar challengers, YES. Their smooth FM friendly AOR blend fared particularly well in the US, 'HEAT OF THE MOMENT', 'ONLY TIME WILL TELL' and 'DON'T CRY', all becoming Top 20 hits in 1982. The follow-up, 'ALPHA', didn't live up to the high expectations afforded it, although it still reached the Top 10 on both sides of the Atlantic. For a brief two year period, GREG LAKE filled in for the absent WETTON, the singer returning to record a third album, 'ASTRA' in '85. HOWE was also missing, having returned to YES, his replacement being MANDY MEYER. All this disruption clearly had a knock-on effect on album sales, the record stiffing in the lower regions of the chart. With another experienced campaigner, PAT THRALL, drafted in, the group recorded 'THEN & NOW', a 1990 set of re-worked favourites and a handful of new tracks. In 1992, with only DOWNES and PALMER remaining from the original line-up, they left 'Geffen' and recorded a fifth album, 'AQUA', which was followed by some more unremarkable cd outings, DOWNES having taken on full control when PALMER returned to ELP. • **Trivia:** Their "Asia In Asia" concert at Budokan, Tokyo 6 Dec'83, went live to over 20 million people in US through MTV station.

Album rating: ASIA (*6) / ALPHA (*4) / ASTRA (*3) / THEN & NOW (*5) / AQUA (*3) / ARIA (*3)

JOHN WETTON (b.12 Jul'49, Derby, England) – vocals, bass (ex-URIAH HEEP, ex-ROXY MUSIC, ex-BRYAN FERRY, ex-KING CRIMSON, ex-FAMILY, ex-U.K.) / **STEVE HOWE** (b. 8 Apr'47) – guitar, vocals (ex-YES, ex-BODAST, ex-TOMORROW) / **GEOFFREY DOWNES** – keyboards, vocals (ex-YES, ex-BUGGLES, ex-ISOTOPE) / **CARL PALMER** (b.20 Mar'47, Birmingham, England) – drums, percussion (ex-EMERSON, LAKE & PALMER, ex-P.M.)

Geffen Geffen

Apr 82. (lp/pic-lp/c) *(GEF/+11/40 85577)* <2008> **ASIA** [11] [1]
– Heat of the moment / Only time will tell / Sole survivor / One step closer / Time again / Wildest dream / Without you / Cutting it fine / Here comes the feeling. *(cd-iss. Apr83; CDGEF 85577) (re-iss. Sep86 lp/c; 902008-1/-4) (cd-iss. Feb87; 902008-2)* (re-iss. Apr91 cd/c; *GEFD/GEFC 02008) (re-iss. cd Apr92; GFLD 19054)*

Jun 82. (7") *(A 2494)* <50040> **HEAT OF THE MOMENT. / TIME AGAIN** [46] Apr82 [4]

Aug 82. (7"/7"pic-d) *(A/+11 2228)* <29970> **ONLY TIME WILL TELL. / RIDE EASY** [54] Jul82 [17]

Oct 82. (7") *(A 2884)* **SOLE SURVIVOR. / HERE COMES THE FEELING** [ ] [ ]

Aug 83. (7"/7"sha-pic-d) *(A/WA 3580)* <29571> **DON'T CRY. / DAYLIGHT** [33] Jul83 [10]
(12"+=) *(TA 3580)* – True Colours.

Aug 83. (lp/c) *(GEF/GEC 25508)* <4008> **ALPHA** [5] [6]
– Don't cry / The smile has left your eyes / Never in a million years / My own time (I'll do what I want) / The heat goes on / Eye to eye / The last to know / True colours / Midnight Sun / Open your eyes. *(c+=)* – Daylight. *(re-iss. Sep86 lp/c; 940008-1/-4) (cd-iss. Jun89; 94008-2) (re-iss. Apr91 & Aug99 cd/c; GEFD/GEFC 04008)*

Oct 83. (7") *(A 3836)* <29475> **THE SMILE HAS LEFT YOUR EYES. / LYING TO YOURSELF** [ ] [34]
(12"+=,12"red+=) *(TA 3836)* – Midnight Sun.

—— (Oct83) **GREG LAKE** (b.10 Nov'48, Bournemouth, England) – vocals, bass (ex-EMERSON, LAKE & PALMER, ex-Solo Artist, ex-KING CRIMSON) repl. WETTON

—— (Mar84). **ARMAND 'Mandy' MEYER** – guitar (ex-KROKUS) repl. HOWE who returned to YES and formed G.T.R.

—— **JOHN WETTON** returned to replace LAKE (re-joined E.L.P.)

Nov 85. (7") *(A 6737)* <28872> **GO. / AFTER THE WAR** [ ] [46]
(A-remix-12"+=) *(TA 6737)* – ('A'instrumental).
Dec 85. (lp/c/cd) *(GEF/40GEF/CDGEF 26413)* <24072> **ASTRA** [68] [67]
– Go / Voice of America / Hard on me / Wishing / Rock and roll dream / Countdown to zero / Love now till eternity / Too late / Suspicion / After the war.
Jan 86. (7") **WISHING. / TOO LATE** [–] [ ]
—— (early 1986, disbanded) **WETTON** teamed up with **PHIL MANZANERA**
—— In Sep87, GEOFFREY DOWNES released solo lp/cd 'THE LIGHT PROGRAMME' on 'Geffen'; *K 924156-1/-2)*
—— re-formed late 1989 (WETTON, DOWNES, PALMER plus **PAT THRALL** – guitar (ex-AUTOMATIC MAN). He was replaced by session men **STEVE LUKATHER, RON KOMIE, MANDY MEYER** and **SCOTT GORHAM**
Aug 90. (cd/c/lp) *(CD/40+/GEF 24298)* **THEN & NOW** (hits compliation & new songs) [ ] [ ]
– (THEN) Only time will tell / Wildest dreams / The smile has left your eyes / Heat of the moment / Don't cry / (NOW) – Days like these / Prayin' 4 a miracle / Am I in love? / Voice of America / Summer (can't last too long). *(re-iss. Aug91 cd/c; GEF D/C 24298)*
Sep 90. (c-s,cd-s) *<19677>* **DAYS LIKE THESE. / VOICE OF AMERICA** [–] [64]
—— **JOHN PAYNE** – vocals, bass; repl. WETTON
—— **AL PITRELLI** – guitar (ex-DANGER DANGER) repl. THRALL
—— **STEVE HOWE** also made guest appearance

FM Coast To Coast — JRS

Jun 92. (cd/c/lp) *(WKFM XD/XC/LP 180)* **AQUA** [ ] Mar92 [ ]
– Aqua (part one) / Who will stop the rain / Back in town / Love under fire / Someday / Little rich boy / The voice of reason / Lay down your arms / Crime of the heart / A far cry / Don't call me / Heaven on Earth / Aqua (part two). *(cd re-iss. Feb98 on 'Snapper'; SMMCD 521)*

Musidisc — Sony

Aug 92. (7") *(10952-7)* **WHO WILL STOP THE RAIN. / AQUA (part 1)** [ ] [ ]
(10"pic-d+=/12"+=) *(10952-1/-6)* – Heart of gold.
(cd-s++=) *(10952-2)* – Obsessing.
—— **MICHAEL STURGIS** – drums; repl. PALMER

Bulletproof — M.F.N.

May 94. (cd-ep) *(CDVEST 1001)* **ANYTIME / REALITY / ANYTIME (extended) / FEELS LIKE LOVE** [ ] [ ]
May 94. (cd/c/lp) *(CD/C+/VEST 8)* **ARIA** [ ] [ ]
– Anytime / Are you big enough? / Desire / Summer / Sad situation / Don't cut the wire (brother) / Feels like love / Remembrance day / Enough's enough / Military man / Aria. *(cd re-iss. Feb98 on 'Snapper'; SMMCD 523)*
—— **VINNIE BURNS + TREVOR THORNTON** repl. PITRELLI plus injured HOWE

– compilations, etc. –

Jun 92. (cd) *Essential; (ESSCD 174) / Rhino; <R2 70377>* **ASIA LIVE MOCKBA 09-XI-90 (live)** [ ] Nov90 [ ]
May 97. (d-cd) *Blueprint; (BP 252CD)* **LIVE IN OSAKA 1992 (live)** [ ] [–]
(re-iss. Feb01 on 'Recognition'; CDREC 507)
Mar 97. (cd) *Blueprint; (BP 253CD)* **ASIA NOW – LIVE IN NOTTINGHAM 1990 (live)** [ ] [–]
Jul 97. (cd) *Blueprint; (BP 254CD)* **LIVE IN KOLN (live)** [ ] [–]
(re-iss. Feb01 on 'Recognition'; CDREC 506)
Nov 97. (d-cd) *Blueprint; (BP 255CD)* **LIVE IN PHILADELPHIA (live)** [ ] [–]
(re-iss. Feb01 on 'Recognition'; CDREC 505)
Feb 98. (cd) *Snapper; (SMMCD 522)* **ARENA** [ ] [–]
<(re-iss. May98 on 'Resurgence'; LV 103CD)>
Mar 98. (cd) *Eagle; (EAMCD 037)* **LIVE IN MOSCOW (live)** [ ] [ ]
Jun 98. (cd) *Resurgence; (LV 104CD)* **ARCHIVA VOL.1** [ ] [ ]
(re-iss. Sep99 on 'Snapper'; SMMCD 596)
Jun 98. (cd) *Resurgence; (LV 105CD)* **ARCHIVA VOL.2** [ ] [ ]
(re-iss. Sep99 on 'Snapper'; SMMCD 597)
Feb 99. (d-cd) *Recall; (SMDCD 217)* **AXIOMS** [ ] [–]
– Bella nova / Who will stop the rain / Heaven on Earth / Words / Turn it around / Summer / Heaven / Far cry / Love under fire / Tell me why / Anytime / Aqua part two / Into the arena / Military man / Hunter / Desire / Sad situation / The day before the war / Feels like love / Different worlds / Remembrance day / U bring me down / Aria.
Jul 99. (cd) *Snapper; (SMMCD 519)* **ANTHOLOGY** [ ] [–]
Oct 99. (cd) *Resurgence; (LV 107CD)* **LIVE AT THE TOWN & COUNTRY CLUB (live)** [ ] [ ]
Nov 99. (cd) *Resurgence; (LV 108CD)* **LIVE ACOUSTIC (live)** [ ] [ ]
Feb 00. (cd) *Brilliant; (BT 33039)* **LIVE IN RUSSIA (live)** [ ] [–]
Apr 00. (cd) *Connoisseur; (VSOPCD 285)* **THE COLLECTION** [ ] [–]
Apr 00. (cd) *Resurgence; (LV 106CD)* **RARE** [ ] [–]
May 00. (3xcd-box) *Snapper; <(SMXCD 101)>* **THE BOX** [ ] Jul00 [ ]
– (AQUA / ARIA / ARENA)
Jul 00. (cd) *Interscope; <(490554-2)>* **HEAT OF THE MOMENT 1982-1990 – THE VERY BEST OF ASIA** [ ] Jun00 [ ]
Sep 00. (cd) *Music Club; (MCCD 443)* **ARCHIVES (THE BEST OF ASIA)** [ ] [–]
Oct 00. (cd) *Eagle; (EDMCD 110)* **LIVE** [ ] [–]
Mar 01. (cd) *Zoom Club; (ZCRCD 50)* **ALIVE IN THE HALLOWED HALLS (live 1983)** [ ] [–]
Jun 01. (cd) *Burning Airlines; (<PILOT 87)>* **ASIA IN ASIA (live in Tokyo 1983)** [ ] [ ]

ASIAN DUB FOUNDATION

Formed: Farringdon, London, England ... 1993 by DR. DAS, PANDIT G and MASTER D, a tutor, an assistant and a student respectively at an inner city community music programme designed for young aspiring Asian musicians/DJ's/MC's/etc. Initially trading as a sound system, ADF began making their own records the following year. Signed to 'Nation' (home of TRANSGLOBAL UNDERGROUND), the trio issued the 'CONSCIOUS' EP prior to adding unorthodox sitar-influenced guitarist, CHANDRASONIC, synth man SUN-J and stage dancer, BUBBLE-E. Taking up the agit-prop, slash'n'burn politico-musical baton from the ailing SENSER, ADF fought off the neo-Nazis with an inflammatory combination of Bengali folk, drum'n'bass and punk that strangely and uniquely recalled the spirit of ALTERNATIVE TV's MARK PERRY. In 1995, this radical troupe unleashed their debut long player, 'FACTS AND FICTIONS', a surprising cohesive set given the amount of disparate musical strands running through each track. Amassing a cult following drawn from both the indie and dance communities (much in the same way that The PRODIGY rose to such giddy heights a few years earlier), ADF soon found themselves under the wing of 'London' offshoot, 'FFRR' in 1997. Gaining more column inches and higher chart placings with each successive release via the incendiary singles, 'NAXALITE', 'BUZZIN', 'FREE SATPAL RAM' and 'BLACK WHITE', the long awaited follow-up set, 'RAFI'S REVENGE' (1998; 1997 in France!) blazed a trail into the UK Top 20. Nominated for a 'Mercury Award', the album didn't win but received some free televised publicity/criticism courtesy of Fantasy Football thingy/ 3 Lions/"comedian", David Baddiel, who obviously prefers the fluffier sounds of the LIGHTNING SEEDS. While working on their follow-up set, ADF were trying to convince the Home Office to "Free SATPAL RAM", the Asian man still in prison after 13 years. While 'COMMUNITY MUSIC' (2000) put the band back in the UK album charts, the underwhelming 'ENEMY OF THE ENEMY' (2003) was something of a false start to the new decade. While throwing everything from drum'n'bass and agit-samples to reggae melodies and would-be anthemic lyrics into the mix and hoping it would stick has worked for the band in the past, there was a jadedness about this record. At times, the disparate ingredients come together – especially when galvanised by an external influence such as the SINEAD O'CONNOR vocal on '1000 MIRRORS'.

Album rating: FACTS AND FICTIONS (*7) / RAFI'S REVENGE (*9) / COMMUNITY MUSIC (*7) / ENEMY OF THE ENEMY (*5)

MASTER D (DEEDER SAIDULLAH ZAMAN) – rapping / **PANDIT G** (JOHN ASHOK PANDIT) – turntables, voice / **DR. DAS** (ANIRUDDHA DAS) – bass, programming, voice

Nation / not iss.

Aug 94. (12"ep/cd-ep) *(NR 42 T/CD)* **CONSCIOUS EP.** [ ] [–]
– Debris / Tu meri / Jericho / Witness.

—— added **CHANDRASONIC (STEVE CHANDRA SAVALE)** – guitar, programming, vocals (ex-HEADSPACE, ex-The HIGHER INTELLIGENCE AGENCY)

—— added **SUN-J** (SANJAY GULABHAI TAILOR) – synths / + dancer **BUBBLE-E**

Apr 95. (12"ep/cd-ep) *(NR 51 T/CD)* **REBEL WARRIOR** [ ] [–]
– Rebel warrior / Nazrul dub / Strong culture / Rivers of dub.

Oct 95. (cd/lp) *(NAT CD/LP 58)* **FACTS AND FICTIONS** [ ] [–]
– Witness / PKNB / Jericho / Rebel warrior / Journey / Strong culture / Th9 / Tu meri / Debris box / Thacid 9 (dub version) / Return to Jericho (dub version). *(cd re-iss. Aug98; NATCDM 058)*

May 96. (12"ep/cd-ep) *(NR 61 T/CD)* **CHANGE A GONNA COME** [ ] [–]
– Change a gonna come / Operation eagle eye / C.A.G.C. (via pirate satellite) / Jerico (CAPA D dub).

Damaged Goods / not iss.

Jul 97. (7"; split with ATARI TEENAGE RIOT) *(DAMGOOD 132)* **split** [ ] [–]

Sub Rosa / not iss.

Jul 97. (12"; split with EUPHONIC) *(QUANTUM 605)*
TRIBUTE: . . . SOUND SYSTEM / WAY OF THE EXPLODING FIST [ ] [–]

—— now as ASIANDUBFOUNDATION

FFRR / Polygram

Oct 97. (7") *(F 320)* **NAXALITE. / CHARGE** [ ] [–]
(12"+=/cd-s+=) *(FX/FCD 320)* – ('A'+'B'mixes).

Feb 98. (7") *(F 326)* **FREE SATPAL RAM. / TRIBUTE TO JOHN STEPHENS** [56] [–]
(12"+=/cd-s+=) *(FX/FCD 326)* – ('A'-Primal Scream & Brendan Lynch mix) / ('A'-ADF Sound System mix).

Apr 98. (12"ep/cd-ep) *(FX/FCD 335)* **BUZZIN' (mixes) / DIGITAL UNDERCLASS** [31] [ ]
(cd-ep) *(FCDP 335)* – ('A'extended) / Free Satpal Ram (live) / Charge (live) / Naxalite (live).

May 98. (cd/c/d-lp) *(556 006-2/-4/-1)* <556 053> **RAFI'S REVENGE** [20] [ ]
– Naxalite / Buzzin' / Black white / Assassin / Hypocrite / Charge / Free Satpal Ram / Dub mentality / Culture move / Operation eagle lie / Change / Tribute to John Stevens. *(cd re-iss. Sep99; 3984 28193-2)*

Jun 98. (12"/cd-s) *(FX/FCDP 337)* **BLACK WHITE / BLACK WHITE (maximum roach mix). / NAXALITE (Underdog mix) / NAXALITE (Underdog instrumental)** [52] [–]
(cd-s) *(FCD 337)* – ('A'side) / Rafi / Assassin (live) / Buzzin' (live).

Sep 98. (12"ep/cd-ep) *(FX/FCD 348)* <570289> **NAXALITE / CULTURE MOVE EP** [ ] Nov98 [ ]
– Naxalite (main mix) / Culture move (pusher sound mix) / Free Satpal Ram (Russell Simmons mix) / Culture move (urban decay mix) / Culture move (silver haze mix).

FFRR / E.M.I.

Mar 00. (12"/cd-s) *(FX/FCD 376)* **REAL GREAT BRITAIN. / ('A'-Freqnasty acid monsta mix & dub)** [41] [–]
(cd-s) *(FCDP 376)* – ('A'side) / Officer XX (ADF jump up version) / ('A'-Jazzwad real Jamaica mix).

Mar 00. (cd) *(8573 82042-2)* <38204-2> **COMMUNITY MUSIC** [20] May00 [ ]
– Real Great Britain / Memory war / Officer XX / New way, new life / Riddim I like / Collective mode / Crash / Colour line / Taa deem / The judgement / Truth hides / Rebel warrior / Committed to life / Scaling new heights.

May 00. (12"/cd-s) *(FX/FCD 378)* **NEW WAY, NEW LIFE. / ('A'-Dry & Heavy vocal & dub mixes)** [49] [–]
(cd-s) *(cd-s) (FCDP 378)* – ('A'side) / Real Great Britain (live) / Crash (live).

DinDisc / E.M.I.

Jan 03. (cd-s) *(DINSDY 253)* **FORTRESS EUROPE / (Jazzwad remix) / (Sun J remix) / (video)** [57] [–]
(cd-s) *(DINSDX 253)* – ('A'side) / (Adrian Sherwood dub) / (Chandrasonic remix).
(12") *(DINST 253)* – ('A'-mixes; Jazzwad / Sun-J / Adrian Sherwood dub / Chandrasonic).

Feb 03. (cd/d-lp) *(CD/LP VIR 201)* <81283> **ENEMY OF THE ENEMY** [ ] [ ]
– Intro – Fortress Europe / Rise to the challenge / La haine / 1000 mirrors / 19 rebellions / Blowback / 2 face / Power to the small massive / Dhol rinse / Basta / Cyberabad / Enemy of the enemy. *(ltd-d-cd+=; CDVIRX 201)* – (remixes).

Apr 03. (10"; by ASIAN DUB FOUNDATION & SINEAD O'CONNOR) *(DINSA 259)* **1000 MIRRORS. / 1000 MIRRORS (Ils mix)** [ ] [–]
(cd-s+=) *(DINSD 259)* – ('A'-Visionary underground mix).

☐ ASPHALT RIBBONS (see under ⇒ TINDERSTICKS)

☐ ASSEMBLY (see under ⇒ YAZOO)

ASSOCIATES

Formed: Dundee, Scotland . . . 1979 by BILLY MACKENZIE and ALAN RANKINE, who had worked as a duo in 1976 (the ABSORBIC ONES). After a debut single on their own 'Double-Hip' label, they signed to Chris Parry's 'Fiction', a subsidiary of 'Polydor' records. Their glorious debut set, 'THE AFFECTIONATE PUNCH', was followed by a series of highly rated 45's for the independent 'Situation 2' label. In 1982, they enjoyed their first taste of success when stylish 'PARTY FEARS TWO' and 'CLUB COUNTRY' both hit the UK Top 20. Energetic alternative dance rock, featuring high, passionate vocals of MACKENZIE, The ASSOCIATES inimitable, unclassifiable sound enjoyed only a very brief liaison with the pop charts. Now signed to 'Warners', the group's more accessible 'SULK' (1982) album made the UK Top 10, its lavish arrangements, white funk and stirring vocal histrionics going down well amid the craze for all things "New Romantic". Despite this belated recognition, the pair subsequently went their separate ways, losing their commercial momentum in the process. When they finally got back together in 1984 (with a line-up of STEVE GOULDING, IAN McINTOSH, ROBERT SUAVE and L. HOWARD JONES), MACKENZIE and RANKINE recorded only one further single together, 'THOSE FIRST IMPRESSIONS', before the latter finally bowed out. The remaining members recorded the 'PERHAPS' (1985) album, a relative flop which saw a further set, 'THE GLAMOUR CHASE' shelved and MACKENZIE returned in 1990 with an album on the 'Circa' label, 'WILD AND LONELY', to little reaction. The ASSOCIATES name had seemingly been laid to rest when, a couple of years later, the singer released a solo set, 'OUTERNATIONAL'. The next five years were quiet as MACKENZIE attended to his beloved greyhounds in his native Dundee. The music world was shocked, when, on the 22nd January '97, it was announced that he had taken his own life, reportedly depressed after the death of his mother a little earlier. Ironically, MACKENZIE had signed to the hip 'Nude' label (home of SUEDE), and had been working on new material at the time of his death. This material was posthumously released as 'BEYOND THE SUN', pundits and public alike mourning the death at 39 of one of music's forgotten geniuses. • **Songwriters:** Lyrics / music by duo (until RANKINE's departure), except BOYS KEEP SWINGING (David Bowie) / LOVE HANGOVER (Diana Ross) / GLOOMY SUNDAY (Lewis-Seress) / GOD BLESS THE CHILD (Billie Holiday) / HEART OF GLASS (Blondie) / KITES (Simon Dupree & The Big Sound) / GROOVIN' WITH MR. BLOE (Mr. Bloe) / GREEN TAMBOURINE

(Lemon Pipers) / I'M GONNA RUN AWAY FROM YOU (Tammi Lynn). • **Trivia:** MACKENZIE featured on B.E.F.'s (HEAVEN 17) single 'IT'S OVER' circa '82.

Album rating: THE AFFECTIONATE PUNCH (*6) / FOURTH DRAWER DOWN singles compilation (*9) / SULK (*7) / PERHAPS (*5) / WILD AND LONELY (*4) / POPERA: THE SINGLES COLLECTION compilation (*8) / DOUBLE HIPNESS collection (*4) / Billy MacKenzie: OUTERNATIONAL (*5) / BEYOND THE SUN (*8)

BILLY MACKENZIE (b.27 Mar'57) – vocals / **ALAN RANKINE** – keyboards, guitar, etc

Double Hip — not iss.

Oct 79. (7") *(DHR 1)* **BOYS KEEP SWINGING. / MONA PROPERTY GIRL** [ ] [–]
(re-iss. Dec79 on 'M.C.A.'; MCA 537)

— added **NIGEL GLOCKER** – drums / guest **ROBERT SMITH** – guitar (of-CURE) who replaced unknown guitarist

Fiction — not iss.

Aug 80. (7") *(FICS 11)* **THE AFFECTIONATE PUNCH. / YOU WERE YOUNG** [ ] [–]
Aug 80. (lp/c) *(FIX/+C 5)* **THE AFFECTIONATE PUNCH** [ ] [–]
– The affectionate punch / Amused as always / Logan time / Paper house / Trans-port to Central / A matter of gender / Even dogs in the wild / Would I . . . bounce back / Deeply concerned / A. *(remixed & re-iss. Nov82; FIXD 5) (re-iss. Aug83 on 'Polydor' lp/c; SPE LP/MC 33)*

— **JOHN MURPHY** (b. Australia) – drums repl. GLOCKER (to TOYAH)

Situation 2 — not iss.

Apr 81. (7"/12") *(SIT 1/+12)* **TELL ME EASTER'S ON FRIDAY. / STRAW TOWELS** [ ] [–]
(re-iss. but w-drawn Nov82 on 'Beggars Banquet'; BEG 86)
Jun 81. (7") *(SIT 4)* **Q: QUARTERS. / KISSED** [ ] [–]
(12"+=) *(SIT 4T)* – Q: Quarters (original).
Aug 81. (7"/12") *(SIT 7/+T)* **KITCHEN PERSON. / AN EVEN WHITER CAR** [ ] [–]
Oct 81. (7"/12") *(SIT 10/+T)* **MESSAGE OBLIQUE SPEECH. / BLUE SOAP** [ ] [–]
Nov 81. (7"/12") *(SIT 11/+T)* **WHITE CAR IN GERMANY. / THE ASSOCIATE** [ ] [–]
Jan 82. (lp/c) *(SITU 2/+C)* **FOURTH DRAWER DOWN** [ ] [–]
– White car in Germany / A girl named Property / Kitchen person / Q; quarters / Tell me Easter's on Friday / The associate / Message oblique speech / An even whiter car. *(re-iss. Nov82 on 'Beggars Banquet' lp/c; BEGA/BEGC 43) (cd-iss. Apr02 on 'V2'; VVR 101202-2)*

R.S.O. — not iss.

1981. (7"/12"; as 39, LYON STREET) *(RSO/+X 78)* **KITES. / A GIRL NAMED POVERTY** [ ] [–]

— added **MICHAEL DEMPSEY** – bass (of CURE) / **MARTHA LADLY** – backing vocals (ex-MARTHA & THE MUFFINS)

Associates — WEA

Mar 82. (7"/12") *(ASC 1/+T)* **PARTY FEARS TWO. / IT'S BETTER THIS WAY** [9] [ ]
May 82. (7") *(ASC 2)* **CLUB COUNTRY. / IT'S YOU AGAIN** [13] [ ]
(12"+=) *(ASC 2T)* – Ulcragyceptemol.
Jun 82. (lp/c) *(ASCL/ASCC 1)* **SULK** [10] [–]
– It's better this way / Party fears two / Club country / Love hangover / 18 carat love affair / Arrogance gave him up / No / Skipping / Nothing in something particular / Arrogance gave him up / White car in Germany / Gloomy Sunday / The associate. *(re-iss. Oct82 on 'WEA' lp/c; 240 005-1/-4) (cd-iss. Jul88 on 'WEA'; K 240005-2) (cd re-iss. Apr02 on 'V2'; VVR 101201-2)*
Jul 82. (7") *(ASC 3)* **18 CARAT LOVE AFFAIR. / LOVE HANGOVER** [21] [ ]
(12"+=) *(ASC 3T)* – Voluntary wishes, swapit production.

— split & re-formed 1984 by **MACKENZIE + RANKINE** recruiting **STEVE GOULDING** – drums / **IAN McINTOSH** – rhythm guitar / **ROBERT SUAVE** – bass / **L. HOWARD JONES** – keyboards

WEA — WEA

May 84. (7"/ext.12") *(YZ 6/+T)* **THOSE FIRST IMPRESSIONS. / THIRTEEN FEELINGS** [43] [ ]

— **STEPHEN REID** – guitar; repl. RANKINE who joined PAUL HAIG. He also had a solo career between 1986-87, releasing two albums, 'THE WORLD BEGINS TO LOOK HER AGE' for 'Crepescule' and 'SHE LOVES ME NOT' for 'Virgin'

Aug 84. (7"/ext.12") *(YZ 16/+T)* **WAITING FOR THE LOVE BOAT. / SCHAMP OUT** [53] [ ]
Jan 85. (7"/7"pic-d) *(YZ 28/+P)* **BREAKFAST. / BREAKFAST ALONE** [49] [ ]
(12"+=) *(YZ 28T)* – Kites.
Feb 85. (lp/c) *(WX 9/+C)* **PERHAPS** [23] [ ]
– Those first impressions / Waiting for the love boat / Perhaps / Schampout / Helicopter helicopter / Breakfast / Thirteen feelings / The stranger in your voice / The best of you / Don't give me that I told you so look.
Oct 85. (7") *(YZ 47)* **TAKE ME TO THE GIRL. / PERHAPS** [ ] [–]
(ext.12"+=) *(YZ 47T)* – The girl that took me / ('A'instrumental).
(10"+=) *(YZ 47TE)* – God bless the child (live) / Even dogs in the wild (live) / The boy that Santa Claus forgot (live).

— The above 'A'side was later (in Mar88) covered by group/artist JIH.

— (early 1986) HUGHES and SUAVE joined PETE MURPHY

— **MACKENZIE** now used session people under The ASSOCIATES

Sep 88. (7") *(YZ 310)* **HEART OF GLASS. / HER ONLY WISH** [56] [ ]
(3"cd-s+=) *(YZ 310CD)* – Breakfast / Those first impressions.
('A'-Auchterhouse mix-12"+=) *(YZ 310T)* – ('A'-Auchterhouse instrumental).
(12"+=) *(YZ 310TX)* – ('A'-Temperamental mix) / Heavens blue.
Nov 88. (w-drawn lp/c)(cd) *(WX 222/+C)(244619-2)* **THE GLAMOUR CHASE** [–] [–]
Jan 89. (w-drawn 7") *(YZ 329)* **COUNTRY BOY. / JUST CAN'T SAY GOODBYE** [–] [–]
(w-drawn 12"+=) *(YZ 329T)* – Heart of glass (dub mix).
(w-drawn 3"cd-s++=) *(YZ 329CD)* – Take me to the girl.

Circa — Charisma

Mar 90. (c/cd/lp) *(CIRC/+D/A 11)* **WILD AND LONELY** [71] [ ]
– Fire to ice / Fever / People we meet / Just can't say goodbye / Calling all around the world / The glamour chase / Where there's love / Something's got to give / Strasbourg Square / Ever since that day / Wild and lonely / Fever in the shadows.
Apr 90. (7"/c-s) *(YR/+C 46)* **FEVER. / FEVER IN THE SHADOWS** [ ] [–]
(12"+=/s12"+=/3"cd-s+=/cd-s+=) *(YR T/TB/CD/CDT 46)* – Groovin' with Mr.Bloe.
Aug 90. (7"/c-s) *(YR/+C 49)* **FIRE TO ICE. / GREEN TAMBOURINE** [ ] [–]
(ext.12"+=) *(YRT 49)* – The glamour chase.
(10"++=/ext.cd-s++=) *(YR TX/CD 49)* – Groovin' with Mr.Bloe.
Sep 90. (12"ep) *<096448>* **FIRE TO ICE (mixes) / GREEN TAMBOURINE** [–] [ ]
Jan 91. (7"/c-s) *(YR/+C 56)* **JUST CAN'T SAY GOODBYE. / ONE TWO THREE** [ ] [–]
(12") *(YRT 56)* – ('A'-Time Unlimited mix) / ('A'-Time Unlimited instrumental) / ('A'-US mix).
(12") *(YRTX 56)* – ('A'-Time Unlimited mix) / ('A'-Time Unlimited instrumental) / ('A'-Karma mix).
(cd-s) *(YRCD 56)* – ('A'side) / ('A'-Time Unlimited piano mix) / ('A'-US version) / I'm gonna run away from you.

BILLY MACKENZIE

Jun 92. (7") *(YR 86)* **BABY. / SACRIFICE AND BE SACRIFICED (CH 8032 mix)** [ ] [–]
(cd-s+=) *(YRCD 86)* – Grooveature (D 1000 mix) / Colours will come (US 60659 mix).
(12") *(YRT 86)* – ('A'side) / Colours will come (Larry Heard remix) / Opal krush / Colours will come (Raw Stylus remix).
Aug 92. (7") *(YR 91)* **COLOURS WILL COME. / OPAL KRUSH** [ ] [–]
(12"+=/cd-s+=) *(YRT/YRCD 91)* – Look what you've done / Feels like the richtergroove.
Sep 92. (c/cd) *(CIRC/+D 22)* **OUTERNATIONAL** [ ] [–]
– Outernational / Feels like the richtergroove / Opal krusch / Colours wil come / Pastime paradise / Groovecture / Sacrifice and be sacrificed / Baby / What made me turn on the lights / Windows cell.

— In Jul'96, BILLY was featured on a single by LOOM, 'ANACOSTIA BAY'.

— Tragically on the 22nd January 1997, BILLY committed suicide in his father's garden shed; he had recently signed to 'Nude' records.

Nude — not iss.

Oct 97. (cd) *(NUDE 8CD)* **BEYOND THE SUN** [64] [–]
– Give me time / Winter academy / Blue it is / 14 mirrors / At the edge of the world / Beyond the sun / And this she knows / Sour jewel / 3 gypsies in a restaurant / Nocturne VII.

— early in 2000, a posthumous CD-album, 'MEMORY PALACE' (credited with PAUL HAIG) was released on 'Rhythm Of Life' *(ROL 003)*

Rhythm Of Life / not iss.

Mar 01. (cd; as BILLY MACKENZIE & STEVE AUNGLET) *(ROL 005)* **EUROCENTRIC** [ ] [–]
– Falling out with the future / Homophobic / 14th Century nightlife / Liberty lounge / When the world was young / Sing that song again / Soul that sighs / Wild is the wind / Mother Earth / Return to love.

– (ASSOCIATES) compilations, others, etc. –

Sep 81. (7"/12") *Fiction; (FICS/+X 13)* **A. / WOULD I . . . BOUNCE BACK** [ ] [–]

Nov 82. (7"/12") *Fiction; (FIXS/+X 16)* **A MATTER OF GENDER. / EVEN DOGS IN THE WILD** [ ] [–]

Oct 89. (12"ep/cd-ep) *Strange Fruit; (SFPS/+CD 075))* **THE PEEL SESSIONS** ('82) [ ] [–]
– It's better this way / Nude spoons / Me myself and the tragic story / Natural gender / Ulcragyceptemol.

Jan 91. (cd)(lp/c) *East West; (9031 72414-2)(WX 363/+C)* **POPERA** [ ] [–]
– Party fears two / Club country / 18 Carat love affair / Love hangover / Those first impressions / Waiting for the loveboat / Breakfast / Take me to the girl / Heart of glass / Country boy / The rhythm divine / Waiting for the loveboat (slight return) / Tell me Easter's on Friday / Q; quarters / Kitchen person / Message oblique speech / White car in Germany.

Jan 91. (7"/c-s) *East West; (YZ 534/+C)* **POPERETTA EP: WAITING FOR THE LOVEBOAT (Slight Return). / CLUB COUNTRY CLUB** [ ] [–]
(12"+=/cd-s+=) *(YZ 534 T/CD)* – Waiting for the loveboat (extended voyage) / Club country club (Time Unlimited).

Sep 94. (cd) *Nighttracks; (CDNT 006)* **THE RADIO ONE SESSION** [ ] [–]

Apr 02. (d-cd) *V2; (VVR 101203-2)* **DOUBLE HIPNESS** (outtakes) [ ] [–]

May 02. (d-cd) *Warners; (8573 88496-2)* **THE GLAMOUR CHASE / PERHAPS** [ ] [–]

☐ Ian ASTBURY (see under ⇒ CULT)

ATARIS

Formed: Anderson, Indiana, USA ... mid 90's by KRIS ROE. Having been handed a deal (on the strength of a demo tape) by JOE ESCALANTE (of VANDALS fame) and his 'Kung-Fu' label, ROE subsequently relocated to California where he recruited MARCO PENA, MIKE DAVENPORT and ex-LAGWAGON man, DERRICK PLOURDE. The latter was soon replaced by CHRIS KNAPP while debut set, ' . . .ANYWHERE BUT HERE' (1997) brought ATARIS to the attention of Cal-punk institution, 'Fat Wreck Chords'. The cheerily titled 'LOOK FORWARD TO FAILURE' EP in '98 was in turn followed by a sophomore album, 'BLUE SKIES, BROKEN HEARTS ... NEXT 12 EXITS' (1999). With a decidedly more sentimental streak and a more easygoing sound than your average punk act, ATARIS' nice guy reputation preceded them. Further albums, 'LET IT BURN' (2000) and 'END IS FOREVER' (2001) continued in a similar vein, marking them out from the tired posturing of their spike-haired brethren.

Album rating: . . .ANYWHERE BUT HERE (*6) / LOOK FORWARD TO FAILURE mini (*5) / BLUES SKIES BROKEN HEARTS NEXT 12 EXITS (*6) / END IS FOREVER (*6) / SO LONG, ASTORIA (*6)

KRIS ROE – vocals / **MARCO PENA** – guitar / **MIKE DAVENPORT** – bass / **CHRIS KNAPP** – drums; repl. DERRICK PLOURDE (ex-LAGWAGON)

Kung Fu / Kung Fu

Jun 98. (cd/c/lp) <*(78763-2/-4/-1)*> **. . .ANYWHERE BUT HERE** [ ] Apr97 [ ]
– Four chord wonders / Are we there yet? / Bite my tongue / Perfectly happy / Hey kid / Ray / As we speak / Sleepy / Lately / Let it go / Neilhouse / Make it last / Alone in Santa Cruz / Angry nerd rock / Take me back / Blind and unkind / Clara.

Nov 98. (m-cd) <*(FAT 581CD)*> **LOOK FORWARD TO FAILURE** [ ] [ ]
– San Dimas high school football rules / Not a worry in the world / My hotel year / Between you and me / That special girl / My so called life.
(above issued on 'Fat Wreck Chords')

Jun 99. (cd/lp) <*(78769-2)*> **BLUE SKIES BROKEN HEARTS NEXT 12 EXITS** [ ] [ ]
– Losing streak / 1-15-96 / San Dimas high school football rules / Your boyfriend sucks / I won't spend another night alone / Broken promise ring / Angry nerd rock / The last song I will ever write about a girl / Choices / Better way / My hotel year / Life makes no sense / Answer / In spite of the world.

Jun 00. (cd; shared w/ USELESS I.D.) <*(78779-2)*> **LET IT BURN** [ ] Apr00 [ ]
– The radio still sucks / Song for a mix tape / P.S. the scene is dead / Blue skies, broken hearts . . . next 12 exits / Let it burn / How I spend my summer vacation / On with the show / San Dimas high school football rules / (other tracks by USELESS I.D.).

Sep 00. (7") *(ATOM 016)* **split** [ ] [–]
(above issued on 'Speedowax')

Mar 01. (cd/lp) <*(78782-2)*> **END IS FOREVER** [ ] [ ]
– Giving up on love / Summer wind was always our song / I.O.U. one galaxy / Bad case of broken heart / Up, up, down, down, left, right, left, right, B, A, start / Road signs and rock songs / If you really want to hear about it . . . / Fast times at Drop-out High / Song for a mix tape / You need a hug / How I spent my summer vacation / Teenage riot / Song #13 / Hello & goodbye.

Feb 03. (m-cd) *(CTX 189CD)* **ALL YOU CAN EVER LEARN IS WHAT YOU ALREADY KNOW** [ ] [ ]
– Takeoffs and landings / Eight of nine (demo) / Teenager of the year / 1*15*96 (acoustic) / Pretty pathetic / Fast times at Dropout High (acoustic).

Columbia / Columbia

Mar 03. (cd) *(510530-2)* <*86184*> **SO LONG, ASTORIA** [ ] [24]
– So long, Astoria / Takeoffs and landings / In this diary / My reply / Unopened letter to the world / The saddest song / Summer '79 / The hero dies in this one / All you can ever learn is what you already know / The boys of summer / Radio #2 / Looking back on today / Eight of nine.

May 03. (7") *(673899-7)* **IN THIS DIARY. / A BEAUTIFUL MISTAKE** [ ] [–]
(cd-s+=) *(673899-2)* – ('A'-live) / ('A'-video).

Sep 03. (7") *(674340-7)* <*radio*> **THE BOYS OF SUMMER. / EIGHT OF NINE** [49] [20]
(cd-s+=) *(674340-2)* – Unopened letter / ('A'-video).

ATHLETE

Formed: Deptford, South London, England ... early 2000 by longtime friends JOEL POTT, CAREY WILLETS, TIM WANSTALL and STEVE ROBERTS. Alternative-type mavericks with a sound which can readily be deemed undefinable in the same way that the likes of The BETA BAND and SUPER FURRY ANIMALS defy lazy categorization, ATHLETE limbered up in style with their debut EP, 'WESTSIDE'. Released on 'Regal', the track earned a Single Of The Week award from Radio 1's Jo Whiley, with follow-up 'YOU GOT STYLE' entering the UK Top 40 a few months later and engendering a major label deal with 'Parlophone' – 'BEAUTIFUL' and 'EL SALVADOR' continuing the minor hit formula. Debut UK Top 20 album 'VEHICLES & ANIMALS' (2003) was unsurprisingly the kind of loose-limbed, horizontally chilled noodling that could only have been made in Britain, with gloriously insinuating hooks and midsummer harmonies easily taking up the slack.

Album rating: VEHICLES & ANIMALS (*6)

JOEL POTT – vocals, guitar / **CAREY WILLETS** – bass, vocals / **TIM WANSTALL** – keyboards, vocals / **STEVE ROBERTS** – drums, vocals

Regal | not iss.

Mar 02. (10"/cd-s) *(REG 72/+CD)* **WESTSIDE. / DUNGENESS / ONE OF THOSE DAYS** [ ] [–]

Parlophone | Astralwerks

Jun 02. (etched-10"/cd-s) *(10/CD ATH 001)* **YOU GOT THE STYLE. / A FEW DIFFERENCES / YOU GOT THE STYLE (remix)** [37] [–]

Nov 02. (7") *(ATH 002)* **BEAUTIFUL. / ON AND ON** [41] [–]
(cd-s+=) *(CDATH 002)* – Another kind of beautiful / ('A'-video).

Mar 03. (7") *(ATH 003)* **EL SALVADOR. / MOVING OUT** [31] [–]
(cd-s+=) *(CDATH 003)* – Loose change.
(cd-s) *(CDATHS 003)* – ('A'side) / Dungeness (live) / You got the style (live) / ('A'-video).

Apr 03. (cd/lp) *(582291-2/-1)* *<82291>* **VEHICLES & ANIMALS** [19] Feb04 [ ]
– El Salvador / Westside / One million / Shake those windows / Beautiful / New project / You got the style / Vehicles and animals / Out of nowhere / Dungeness / You know / Le casio.

Jun 03. (12") *(12ATH 005)* **WESTSIDE. / COUNT ME IN / WESTSIDE (Elbow mix)** [42] [–]
(cd-s+=) *(CDATHS 005)* – ('A'-video).
(cd-s) *(CDATH 005)* – ('A'live) / Vehicles and animals (live) / One million (live).

Sep 03. (7") *(ATH 006)* **YOU GOT THE STYLE. / HOT SUN PAVEMENT** [42] [–]
(cd-s) *(CDATH 006)* – ('A'side) / Beautiful (live).

AT THE DRIVE-IN

Formed: El Paso, Texas, USA . . . 1994 by frontman CEDRIC BIXLER and twin guitarists OMAR RODRIGUEZ and JIM WARD. Recorded between bouts of hard-bitten touring, the band's first two 7" singles, 'HELL PASO' and 'ALFARO VIVE, CARAJO' served notice of a hardcore storm brewing in the Texas badlands. Night after night spent playing to dismal crowds was rewarded when 'Flipside' caught them at an empty L.A. bar and signed them up for a debut album, 'ACROBATIC TENEMENT'. Released in early '97, the record's blistering emotional outpourings and precocious mastery of punk dynamics won over critics across the board while another stint of touring – with new recruits TONY and PALL – cultivated a grassroots fanbase. A subsequent mini-set, 'EL GRAN ORGO' was issued on the 'Offtime' imprint later that year, after which followed a period of insecurity as the band searched in vain for a label willing to take on their sophomore album. 'IN CASINO OUT' (1998) was finally sponsored by the independent 'Fearless' operation, a label more often associated with pop/punk fare. Nevertheless, the album – recorded almost entirely live with only a few overdubs – represented the closest ATDI had yet come to capturing the passionate drive of their live work. Yet more touring ensued as the band played with the likes of FUGAZI and ARCHERS OF LOAF before undertaking their first European jaunt in Spring '99. Later that summer the 'VAYA' EP showed that their relentless road schedule was paying handsome dividends in terms of musical sharpness and songwriting depth, 'Virgin' records signing up the Texas troopers for their third and most highly acclaimed album to date, 'RELATIONSHIP OF COMMAND' (2000). Released on the BEASTIE BOYS' 'Grand Royal' (with whom 'DEN' had merged), produced by Ross 'SLIPKNOT' Robinson and mixed by Andy Wallace, the record had critics reaching for the superlatives in an attempt to describe their unflinchingly honest and unrelentingly intense sound. After disclaiming "indefinite hiatus", ATD had literally split into two camps, The MARS VOLTA, which featured members BIXLER and RODRIGUEZ, and SPARTA, set up by WARD, HINOJOS and HAJJAR. The former, who issued the brilliant 'TREMULANT' EP in 2002, had strayed away from their restrictive "emo" tag and began performing rambunctious live shows which often leaned towards the experimental. IKEY OWENS of The Long Beach Dub All-Stars lended a hand, as did MICHAEL WARD (both flirted with prog-dub outfit DE FACTO). While The MARS VOLTA recreated the same volatile intensity as SCRATCH ACID and MELT BANANA, SPARTA would ultimately stick with the hard-edged punk formula of early BLACK FLAG and FUGAZI (circa 'Repeater'). After issuing the heavily criticised 'AUSTERE' EP on Spielberg/Geffen's 'Dreamworks' imprint, the group issued the overtly angst and typically difficult 'WIRETAP SCARS' (2002), a mixed bag of guitar-fuelled disdain and post-punk noise that had a distinct aftertaste of regret, worry and self-doubt. After ATD-I went their separate ways, much was hanging on what its abandoned members would do next. RODRIGUEZ and CEDRIC BIXLER were obviously going to stick together, as they had been best friends since childhood and shared the same enthusiastic and diverse musical tastes. It came as no surprise then when they announced their new project, The MARS VOLTA and issued an EP 'TREMULANT' in 2002, a record which whet the appetites of music critics and fans alike. Also recruiting JEREMY MICHEAL WARD and IKEY OWENS, they headed into the studio to record the schizophrenic and fractured debut album 'DE-LOUSED IN THE COMATORIUM' (2003), which took ATD-I's hardcore punk edge, put it in a blender and mixed it all up until it was practically unrecognisable. Mixing free-jazz, funk, metal and prog, the album truly did amaze and The MARS VOLTA were critically hailed by many as the new KING CRIMSON. After touring with The RED HOT CHILI PEPPERS, WARD sadly died of a drug overdose at the age of 27.

Album rating: ACROBATIC TENEMENT (*7) / IN/CASINO/OUT (*7) / RELATIONSHIP OF COMMAND (*7) / Sparta: WIRETAP SCARS (*7) / the Mars Volta: DE-LOUSED IN THE COMATORIUM (*7)

CEDRIC BIXLER – vocals / **OMAR RODRIGUEZ** – guitar / **JIM WARD** – guitar, vocals

not iss. | Western Breed – Offtime

Dec 94. (7"m) **HELL PASO. / EMPTINESS IS A MULE / RED PLANET** [–] [ ]

Jun 95. (7"ep) **ALFARO VIVE, CARAJO!. / BRADLEY SMITH / INSTIGATE THE ROLE** [–] [ ]
<re-iss. 1990's on 'Headquarter'>

not iss. | Flipside

Feb 97. (cd) *<FLIP 94CD>* **ACROBATIC TENEMENT** [–] [ ]
– Star flight / Schaffino / Ebroglio / Initiation / Communication drive-in / Skips on the record / Paid vacation time / Ticklish / Blue tag / Coating of arms / Porfirio Diaz. *(UK-iss.Jan00; same as US)*

—— added **PALL HINOJOS** – bass / **TONY HAJJAR** – drums

not iss. | One Foot – Offtime

Sep 97. (cd-ep) *<62>* **EL GRAN ORGO** [–] [ ]
– Give it a name / Honest to a fault / Winter month novelty / Fahrenheit / Picket fence cartel / Speechless.

Fearless | Fearless

Jul 98. (cd) *<F 034CD>* **IN/CASINO/OUT** [–] [ ]
– Alpha Centauri / Chanbara / Hulahoop wounds / Napoleon Solo / Pickpocket / For now . . . we toast / A devil among tailors / Shaking hand incision / Lopsided / Hourglass / Transatlantic foe. *(UK-iss.Aug00; same as US)*

Nov 98. (7") **DOORMAN'S PLACEBO. / (other track by AASSEE LAKE)** [–] [ ]

—— <above iss. on 'Nerd' records>

Oct 99. (12"ep) *(F 040-1)* **VAYA** [–] [ ]
– Rascuache / Proxima centauri / Ursa minor / Heliotrope / Metrognome arthritis / 300 MHz / 198d. *(UK-iss.Oct99; same as US) (cd-ep iss.Aug00; FO 40CD)*

Thick | Thick

Mar 00. (7"pic-d) *<(THK 066)>* **CATACOMBS. / (other by Burning Airlines)** [ ] [ ]
(UK re-iss. Oct00; same)

Big Wheel Big Wheel

May 00. (12"ep/cd-ep) <*(BWR 0223/+CD)*> **BIG WHEEL RECREATION** [ ] [ ]
– Extracurricular / Autorelocator / (two others by Sunshine).

Grand Royal Grand Royal

Aug 00. (7") <*(GR 91)*> **ONE ARMED SCISSOR. / PATTERN AGAINST USER** [64] [ ]
(cd-s+=) <*(GR 91CD)*> – Incetardis.

Virgin Virgin

Sep 00. (cd/lp) *(CDVUS/VUSLP 184)* <49999> **RELATIONSHIP OF COMMAND** [33] [ ]
– Arcarsenal / Pattern against user / One armed scissor / Sleepwalk capsules / Invalid litter dept. / Mannequin republic / Enfilade / Rolodex propaganda / Quarantined / Cosmonaut / Non-zero possibility / Catacombs.

Oct 00. (7"colrd) **BUDDYHEAD. / (other by Murder City Devils)** [–] [ ]

Dec 00. (7") *(VUS 189)* **ROLODEX PROPAGANDA. / EXTRACURRICULAR** [54] [–]
(cd-s+=) *(VUSCD 189)* – One armed scissor (Lamacq version).

Mar 01. (7") *(VUS 193)* **INVALID LITTER DEPT. / INITIATION (Lamacq version)** [50] [–]
(cd-s+=) *(VUSCD 193)* – Quarantined (Lamacq version).
(cd-s) *(VUSDX 193)* – ('A'side) / Take up thy stethoscope and walk (Lamacq version) / Metrognome arthritis.

— split later in 2001

MARS VOLTA

CEDRIC BIXLER + OMAR RODRIGUEZ with **JEREMY MICHAEL WARD + IKEY OWENS**

Gold Standard Gold Standard

Mar 02. (12"ep/cd-ep) <*(GSL 54/+CD)*> **TREMULANT EP** [ ] [ ]
– Cut that city / Concertina / Eunuch provocateur.

Universal Universal

Jun 03. (cd) *(9860460)* <*59302*> **DE-LOUSED IN THE COMATORIUM** [43] [39]
– Son et lumiere / Inertiatic ESP / Roulette dares (the haunt of) / Tira me a las Aranas / Drunkship of lanterns / Eriatarka / Cicatriz ESP / This apparatus must be unearthed / Televators / Take the veil Cerpin taxt. *(d-lp iss.Jul03 on 'Gold Standard' +=; GSL 75LP)* – Ambuletz.

M.C.A. Universal

Sep 03. (10") *(MCST 40352)* **INERTIATIC ESP. / DRUNKSHIP OF LANTERNS (FM session)** [42] [–]
(cd-s) *(MCSTD 40352)* – ('A'side) / Roulette dares (the haunt of) (XFM session) / ('A'-video).

SPARTA

JIM WARD – vocals, guitar / **PAUL HINOJOS** – guitar / **TONY HAJJAR** – drums / **MATT MILLER** – bass (ex-BELKNAP)

Dreamworks Dreamworks

Apr 02. (cd-s) *(450844-2)* **AUSTERE EP** [ ] [–]
– Mye / Cataract / Vacant skies / Echodyne harmonic (de-mix).

Aug 02. (cd) *(450393-2)* <*450366*> **WIRETAP SCARS** [ ] [ ]
– Cut your ribbon / Air / Mye / Collapse / Sans cosm / Light burns clear / Cataract / Red alibi / Rx coup / Glasshouse tarot / Echodyne harmonic / Assemble the empire.

□ ATTILA / HASSLES (see under ⇒ JOEL, Billy)

□ AUDIOSLAVE
(see under ⇒ RAGE AGAINST THE MACHINE)

AUTEURS

Formed: Southgate, London, England . . . early 1992 by LUKE HAINES (ex-SERVANTS) and girlfriend ALICE READMAN. They quickly signed to 'Fire', soon moving to Virgin off-shoot label, 'Hut', and indie chart surfing with their debut single, 'SHOWGIRL' later in the year. Glossy garage indie/punk merchants, fronted by the flamboyant but cynical HAINES, The AUTEURS sound was characterised by the singer's brooding lyrical complexities. The addition of cellist, JAMES BANBURY produced an extra dimension to their standard guitar, bass, drums approach and the debut album's encouragingly critical reception was matched by a UK Top 40 placing for 'NEW WAVE' (1993) and a nomination for the Mercury Music Award. Their third single, 'LENNY VALENTINO', almost scraped into the UK Top 40, the track relating to the debut album sleeve, which depicted Lenny Bruce dressed as Rudolph Valentino. HAINES preoccupations both, another favoured subject of the controversial frontman was the British Class System, 'THE UPPER CLASS' appearing on the follow-up set, 'NOW I'M A COWBOY' (1994). The record secured a Top 30 placing, although the group's critical acclaim continued to outweigh their commercial appeal. A remix set, 'THE AUTEURS VS U-ZIQ' appeared, although it wasn't until 1996 that a long-awaited third album materialised. Produced by STEVE ALBINI, this atmospheric offering combined HAINES' downbeat tales of intrigue with grinding organs, discordant guitars and mournful strings to often hypnotic effect. Despite garnering further plaudits, the record sold poorly and after a clutch of final gigs, HAINES wound the band up, subsequently releasing an album under the moniker of BAADER-MEINHOF (first mentioned on the bleak 'TOMBSTONE' track). In 1998, HAINES teamed up with two former members of BALLOON, JOHN MOORE (ex-EXPRESSWAY) and singer, SARAH NIXEY, in the more melodic, BLACK BOX RECORDER. Signing a major deal with 'Chrysalis', it didn't look likely that either their singles, 'CHILD PSYCHOLOGY' and 'ENGLAND MADE ME' or the latterly-titled accompanying album, would return the moody HAINES to earlier heights. 1999 saw the man discarding previous projects to reincarnate The AUTEURS. Comeback set, 'HOW I LEARNED TO LOVE THE BOOTBOYS', included their nostalgic look back to 70's glam-rock in the shape of minor hit single, 'THE RUBETTES'. The turn of the millennium saw the turn of BLACK BOX RECORDER again, 'THE FACTS OF LIFE' (2000) hitting the Top 40 after its title track made it all the way into the Top 20. A well-received comeback shimmered with SAINT ETIENNE-esque riffs along with jazzy piano trills that would be more at home in a fifties noir film. The ever prolific LUKE HAINES set about creating his own solo sojourn, two albums, 'CHRISTIE MALRY'S OWN DOUBLE ENTRY' soundtrack and 'THE OLIVER TWIST MANIFESTO' (both 2001). The former was based on a novel by B.S. Johnson and featuring his rendition of Nick Lowe's 'I LOVE THE SOUND OF BREAKING GLASS', while the latter veered towards a slightly more electronic sound with HAINES' predictable angst directed at wrong- do'ers all over the world. Surely not! • **Covers:** Black Box Recorder: SEASONS IN THE SUN (Jacques Brel) / ROCK'N'ROLL SUICIDE (David Bowie) / UPTOWN TOP RANKING (hit; Althea & Donna) / LORD LUCAN IS MISSING (Potter-Zuban).

Album rating: NEW WAVE (*7) / NOW I'M A COWBOY (*8) / AFTER MURDER PARK (*7) / HOW I LEARNED TO LOVE THE BOOT BOYS (*6) / Baader-Meinhof: BAADER-MEINHOF (*5) / Black Box Recorder: ENGLAND MADE ME (*6) / THE FACTS OF LIFE (*7) / THE WORST OF . . . compilation (*6) / Luke Haines: CHRISTIE MALRY'S OWN DOUBLE ENTRY soundtrack (*6) / THE OLIVER TWIST MANIFESTO (*7) / DAS CAPITAL compilation (*6)

LUKE HAINES (b. 7 Oct'67, Walton-On-Thames, Surrey, England) – vocals, guitar (ex-SERVANTS) / **ALICE READMAN** (b. 1967, Harrow, England) – bass (ex-SERVANTS) / **GLENN COLLINS** (b. 7 Feb'68, Cheltenham, England) – drums (ex-DOG UNIT, ex-VORT PYLON)

Hut — Caroline

Dec 92. (12"ep/cd-ep) *(HUT T/CD 24)* **SHOWGIRL. / GLAD TO BE GONE / STAYING POWER** [ ] [–]

— added **JAMES BANBURY** – cello

Mar 93. (cd/c/lp) *(CDHUT/HUTMC/HUTLP 7) <1735>* **NEW WAVE** [35] [ ]
– Showgirl / Bailed out / American guitars / Junk shop clothes / Don't trust the stars / Starstruck / How could I be wrong / Housebreaker / Valet parking / Idiot brother / Early years / Home again. *(free 7"w/lp on cd+c+=)* – Untitled.

May 93. (10"ep/12"ep/cd-ep) *(HUT EN/T/CD 28)* **HOW COULD I BE WRONG. / HIGH DIVING HORSES / WEDDING DAY** [ ] [–]

— **BARNEY CROCKFORD** – drums; repl. COLLINS

Hut — Vernon Yard

Nov 93. (7") *(HUT 36)* **LENNY VALENTINO. / DISNEY WORLD** [41] [–]
(12"/cd-s) *(HUT T/CD 36)* – ('A'side) / Car crazy / Vacant lot / ('A'original mix).

Apr 94. (7") *(HUTG 41)* **CHINESE BAKERY. / ('A'acoustic)** [42] [–]
(7"/cd-s) *(HUT/+CD 41)* – ('A'side) / Government bookstore / Everything you say will destroy you.
(12") *(HUTDX 41)* – ('A'side) / ('A'acoustic) / Modern history.

May 94. (cd/c/lp) *(CDHUT/HUTMC/HUTLP 16) <39597>* **NOW I'M A COWBOY** [27] [ ]
– Lenny Valentino / Brainchild / I'm a rich man's toy / New French girlfriend / The upper classes / Chinese bakery / A sister like you / Underground movies / Life classes – Life model / Modern history / Daughter of a child. *(lp w /free 1-sided 7") (HUTLPX 16)* – MODERN HISTORY (acoustic).

Nov 94. (m-cd/m-lp) *(DGHUTM/HUTMLP 20)* **THE AUTEURS VS U-ZIQ** (remixes) [ ] [–]
– Lenny Valentino No.3 / Daughter of a child / Chinese bakery / Lenny Valentino No.1 / Lenny Valentino No.2 / Underground movies.

Hut — Hut

Dec 95. (7"ep/c-ep/cd-ep) *(HUT/+C/CD 65)* **BACK WITH THE KILLER E.P.** [45] [–]
– Unsolved child murder / Back with the killer again / Former fan / Kenneth Anger's bad dream.

Feb 96. (10"ep/cd-ep) *(<HUT EN/CD 66>)* **LIGHT AIRCRAFT ON FIRE / BUDDHA (demo). / CAR CRASH / X – BOOGIE MAN** [58] [–]

Mar 96. (cd/c/lp) *(<DGHUT/HUTMC/HUTLP 33>)* **AFTER MURDER PARK** [53] [ ]
– Light aircraft on fire / The child brides / Land lovers / New brat in town / Everything you say will destroy you / Unsolved child murder / Married to a lazy lover / Buddha / Tombstone / Fear of flying / Dead Sea navagators / After Murder Park.

May 96. (10"ep/cd-ep) *(<HUT EN/CD 68>)* **"KID'S ISSUE" EP** [ ] [–]
– Buddha / A new life a new family / After murder park.

BAADER-MEINHOF

— **HAINES** with others **JAMES BANBURY + ANDY NICE** – cello / **JUSTIN ARMITAGE** – violin / **GARY STRASBOURG** – drums / **KULJIT BHAMRA** – percussion, tabla

Hi-Rise — not iss.

Nov 95. (7") *(FLAT 24)* **BAADER MEINHOFF. / MEET ME AT THE AIRPORT** [ ] [–]

Hut — Hut

Oct 96. (cd/lp) *(<CDHUT/HUTLP 36>)* **BAADER-MEINHOF** [ ] Feb97 [ ]
– Baader Meinhof / Meet me at the airport / There's gonna be an accident / Mogadishu / Theme from Burn Warehouse Burn / GSG-29 / . . .It's a moral issue / Back on the farm / Kill Ramirez / Baader Meinhof.

BLACK BOX RECORDER

— **HAINES** with **JOHN MOORE** – guitar (ex-JESUS & MARY CHAIN, ex-EXPRESSWAY, ex-REVOLUTION 9, ex-BALLOON) / **SARAH NIXEY** – vocals (ex-BALLOON)

Chrysalis — Jetset

May 98. (7") *(CHS 5082)* **CHILD PSYCHOLOGY. / GIRL SINGING IN THE WRECKAGE** [ ] [–]
(cd-s+=) *(CDCHS 5082)* – Seasons in the sun.

Jul 98. (7") *(CHS 5091)* **ENGLAND MADE ME. / LORD LUCAN IS MISSING** [ ] [–]
(cd-s) *(CDCHS 5091)* – ('A'side) / Factory radio / Child psychology (audio) / Child psychology (video).

Jul 98. (cd/d-lp) *(493907-2/-1) <TWA 21CD>* **ENGLAND MADE ME** [ ] 1999 [ ]
– Girl singing in the wreckage / England made me / New baby boom / It's only the end of the world / Ideal home / Child psychology / I C one female / Uptown top ranking / Swinging / Kidnapping an heiress / Hated Sunday.

— JOHN MOORE would soon form ABSINTHE EXPORTER

AUTEURS

— **HAINES** with old line-up

Hut — not iss.

May 99. (cd/c) *(HUT CD/MC 53)* **HOW I LEARNED TO LOVE THE BOOTBOYS** [ ] [–]
– The Rubettes / 1967 / How I learned to love the bootboys / Your gang, our gang / Some changes / School / Johhny and the Hurricanes / The south will rise again / Asti Spumante / Sick of Hare Krishna / Lights out / Future generation.

Jun 99. (7"/c-s) *(HUT/+MC 113)* **THE RUBETTES. / GET WRECKED AT HOME** [66] [–]
(cd-s+=) *(HUTCD 113)* – Breaking up.

BLACK BOX RECORDER

— with the main/same line-up/trio

Nude — Jetset

Apr 00. (7") *NUD 48S)* **THE FACTS OF LIFE. / SOUL BOY** [20] [–]
(cd-s+=) *(NUD 48CD1)* – Start as you mean to go on.
(cd-s) *(NUD 48CD2)* – ('A'side) / Brutality / Watch the angel, not the wine.

May 00. (cd) *(NUDE 16CD) <TWA 36CD>* **THE FACTS OF LIFE** [37] [ ]
– The art of driving / Weekend / The English motorway system / May queen / Sex life / French rock'n'roll / The facts of life / Straight life / Gift horse / The Deverall twins / Goodnight kiss. *<US+=>* – Start as you mean to go / Brutality.

Jul 00. (7") *(NUD 51S)* **THE ART OF DRIVING. / THE FACTS OF LIFE (remixed by the Chocolate Layers)** [53] [–]
(cd-s+=) *(NUD 51CD1)* – Rock'n'roll suicide.
(cd-s) *(NUD 51CD2)* – ('A'side) / Uptown top ranking (remix) / The facts of life (radio) / The facts of life (video).

Jetset — Jetset

Aug 01. (cd) *(<TWA 40CD>)* **THE WORST OF BLACK BOX RECORDER** (compilation B-sides, etc) [ ] [ ]
– Seasons in the sun / Watch the angel not the wire / Jackie sixty / Start as you mean to go on / The facts of life (Pulp remix) / Lord Lucan is missing / Wonderful life / Uptown top ranking (BBR remix) / Brutality / Factory radio / Soul boy / Rock'n'roll suicide / The facts of life (video) / Child psychology (video) / The art of driving (video) / England made me (video).

LUKE HAINES

— with **JAMES BANBURY** – cello, drums, programming

Hut — not iss.

Jun 01. (cd) *(CDHUT 65)* **CHRISTIE MALRY'S OWN DOUBLE ENTRY** (soundtrack) [ ] [–]
– Discomania / In the bleak midwinter / How to hate the working classes / The ledger / Bernie's funeral – Auto asphixiation / Discomaniax / Alchemy / Art will save the world / I love the sound of breaking glass / England, Scotland and Wales / Celestial discomania / Essexmania.

Jul 01. (cd) *(CDHUT 66)* **THE OLIVER TWIST MANIFESTO** [ ] [–]
– Rock'n'roll communique No.1 / Oliver Twist / Death of Satah Lucas / Never work / Discomania / Mr. and Mrs. Solanas / What happens when we die / Christ / The spook manifesto / England vs. America / The Oliver Twist manifesto.

– compilations, etc. –

Jul 03. (cd) *Hut; (CDHUT 81)* **DAS CAPITAL: THE SONGWRITING GENIUS OF LUKE HAINES** [ ] [–]
– Intro / How could I be wrong / Showgirl / Baader-Meinhof / Lenny Valentino / Starstruck / Satan wants me / Unsolved child murder / Junk shop clothes / Michael Powell / Bigger Bognor / Future generation.

AVALANCHES

Formed: Melbourne, Australia . . . 1995 by DARREN SELTMANN and ROBBIE CHATER who were both part of a short-lived, but interestingly titled collective The SWINGING MONKEY COCKS. Getting bored of playing punk and apeing experimental noisekins SONIC YOUTH, both CHATER and SELTMANN met GORDON McQUILTEN, TONI DIBLASI and DJ champion DEXTER FABAY to create sample-driven music leaning towards funk, or even trance hip-hop. In the early days, the group would simply experiment with sounds, cutting and pasting bits of other people's records and backing it with a swinging dance beat. This formula was to become the outfit's trademark, and their Australian-only debut EP 'ROCK CITY' (in 1997) helped secure a place with local independent 'Modular'. In turn, the impressive mini-album 'EL PRODUCTO' (1997; 1998 UK) was issued to critical acclaim and soon saw The AVALANCHES supporting the likes of The BEASTIE BOYS (who the band have been likened to, especially the 'Paul's Boutique' period) and PUBLIC ENEMY. Keyboardist JAMES DE LA CRUZ was added to the mix in early '98, just after the re-issue of a 'Demos and rarities' collection 'UNDERSEA COMMUNITY' at the end of the year. In the Autumn of 2000, their first bonafide single, 'SINCE I LEFT YOU' was released just prior to a low-key eponymous set; it would be a further six months or so before a wiser record imprint, 'X.L.' (home to The PRODIGY) would re-distribute it as 'SINCE I LEFT YOU' (2001). In the vein of DJ SHADOW and DAVID HOLMES (but much, much more meticulous), the set was a sunny psychedelic record comprising of insane and intricately juxtaposed samples/sounds/noises. Beginning with the breezy aforementioned title track, 'SINCE I LEFT YOU', one could only imagine a swinging pool-side party held by Hugh Hefner way back in the mid-seventies. 'TWO HEARTS IN 3/4 TIME' brilliantly blended funk with hip-hop and calypso jazz to create something entirely out of sync even by today's standards. It was The AVALANCHES' painstaking attention to detail that impressed the most: at some points during the set you could feel yourself asking, how can one group of people own so many bizarre records? Everything managed to blend together, even when things sounded out of place, the group would meld songs so the finished product sounded like one swinging mix. A highlight was the absolute madness of hit single 'FRONTIER PSYCHIATRIST', a possible theme tune to the first LSD-inspired spaghetti western. The ensemble also had permission from MADONNA to use a sample from the song 'Holiday', as well as samples supplied by JIMMY WEBB and ENNIO MORRICONE (who else!). 'SINCE I LEFT YOU' was a fine example of some serious ear-candy and an essential buy for any bored, tripped-out stoners, tired of waiting for the arrival of summer.

Album rating: EL PRODUCTO mini (*7) / THE AVALANCHES – SINCE I LEFT YOU (*9)

DARREN SELTMAN – vocals / **ROBBIE CHATER** – producer / **GORDON McQUILTEN** – percussion, piano / **TONI DIBLASI + DJ DEXTER FABAY**

Trifeka | not iss.

Sep 97. (7") *(001)* **ROCK CITY. / THANK YOU CAROLINE** [-] Austra [-]

Epigram | not iss.

Apr 98. (m-cd) *(001 GRAM)* **EL PRODUCTO** [ ] [-]
– Oening / Rolling high / Rap fever / Rock city / Under inspection / Run DNA / Closing.

— added **JAMES DE LA CRUZ** – turntables

Rex | not iss.

Feb 99. (10"ep) *(REKD 001T)* **UNDERSEA COMMUNITY EP** [ ] [-]
– Undersea community / Yamaha superstar / Slow walking / Thankyou Caroline

Sep 00. (12"/cd-s) *(REKD 014 T/CD)* **SINCE I LEFT YOU. / THANKYOU CAROLINE** [ ] [-]
(cd-s) *(REKD 014CD2)* – Everyday.

Oct 00. (cd/d-lp) *(REKD CD/LP 018)* **THE AVALANCHES** (see below) [ ] [-]

Nov 00. (d10") *(REKD 11T/12T)* **A DIFFERENT FEELING. / TWO HEARTS IN 3/4 TIME // ELECTRICITY (version). / RADIO** [ ] [-]

X.L. | Sire

Mar 01. (7") *(XLS 128)* **SINCE I LEFT YOU. / THANKYOU CAROLINE (Andy Votel mix)** [16] [-]
(c-s+=/12"+=/cd-s+=) *(XLC/XLS/XLT 128)* – Everyday.

Apr 01. (cd/d-lp) *(XLCD/XLLP 138)* <31177> **SINCE I LEFT YOU** [8] Nov01 [ ]
– Since I left you / Stay another season / Radio / Two hearts in 3/4 time / Avalanche rock / Flight tonight / Close to you / Diners only / A different feeling / Electricity / Tonight / Pablo's cruise / Frontier psychiatrist / Etoh / Summer crane / Little journey / Live at Dominoes / Extra kings.

Jul 01. (cd-s) *(XL 134CD)* **FRONTIER PSYCHIATRIST / SLOW WALKING / YAMAHA SUPERSTAR** [18] [-]
(12")(cd-s) *(XLT 134)(XLS 134CD)* – ('A'extended) / ('A'-Mario Caldata 85% remix & instrumental).

Dec 01. (cd-s) *(XLS 137CD)* **ELECTRICITY / ELECTRICITY (Dr. Rockit's dirty kiss) / A DIFFERENT FEELING (Ernest Saint Laurent mix) / ELECTRICITY (original) / ELECTRICITY (video)** [ ] [-]
(12") *(XLT 137)* – ('A'-Harvey's nightclub edit) / ('A'-DJ Sneak's electric mix).

AVERAGE WHITE BAND

Formed: Dundee/Glasgow, Scotland . . . early 1972 by ALAN GORRIE and other noted session men, HAMISH STUART, ONNIE McINTYRE, ROBBIE McINTOSH, ROGER BALL and MALCOLM 'MOLLY' DUNCAN. After supporting ERIC CLAPTON at his comeback Rainbow concert in '73, they gained enough attention to attract 'M.C.A.'. After one album, 'SHOW YOUR HAND', they moved to Los Angeles and signed to 'Atlantic', where the US audiences related more easily to their sound. Early in 1975, they scored a US No.1 with chant-orientated 'PICK UP THE PIECES', which was lifted from their self-titled top selling album. One of the few bands from Scotland (never mind Dundee!) to make it big in the States, what was even more ironic was that they didn't fit the usual Celtic musical stereotypes (i.e. folky, anthemic etc.), instead opting for a white funk/soul sound with top flight harmonies inspired by black artists of the 60's e.g. The ISLEY BROTHERS, MARVIN GAYE etc. The lock-tight rhythmic shuffle and classy horn stabs of the aforementioned 'PICK UP THE PIECES' assured the track a place in funk history, the record still being played out on dancefloors today. Although celebrations were cut short with the shock heroin overdose of McINTOSH later that summer, AWB eventually found a replacement in STEVE FERRONE and began work on a follow-up set, 'CUT THE CAKE' (1975). Another sizeable Stateside success, the record's largely instrumental workouts weren't so enthusiastically embraced by a British audience. As the UK musical climate changed during the ensuing few years, AWB concentrated on America, their laidback, sun-kissed soul continuing to soundtrack Californian idyll. The creamy-rich 'QUEEN OF MY SOUL' was the group's last hit in Britain for almost five years, the band eventually storming back into the UK Top 20 in 1979 with the strong 'FEEL NO FRET' album, the evocative 'ATLANTIC AVENUE' another defining AWB moment. After 'PICK UP THE PIECES', however, their most enduring track remains the yearning disco classic, 'LET'S GO ROUND AGAIN', only their second UK Top 20 hit. The accompanying album, 'SHINE' (1980) also went Top 20, although it marked a last stand of sorts, a subsequent effort, 'CUPID'S IN FASHION' (1982) seeing them floundering in tepid waters. Inevitably, they split the following year, while equally inevitably, perhaps, reforming at the end of the decade. A line-up of GORRIE, McINTYRE and BALL recruited ALEX LIGERTWOOD and a couple of session players, cutting a sole flop album, 'AFTERSHOCK' (1989). Though they've since turned their backs on the studio, AWB continue to draw in the crowds every year with regular tours of the UK including a residency at London's Jazz Cafe. They continued to release the odd album, 'SOUL TATTOO' (1997) and the concert CD, 'FACE TO FACE LIVE' (1999). • **Songwriters:** GORRIE and STUART, except I HEARD IT THROUGH THE GRAPEVINE (Marvin Gaye) / IMAGINE (John Lennon) / WALK ON BY (Burt Bacharach) / etc. • **Trivia:** McINTYRE and McINTOSH sessioned on CHUCK BERRY's 'My Ding-A-Ling'.

Album rating: SHOW YOUR HAND (*5) / AVERAGE WHITE BAND (*7) / CUT THE CAKE (*5) / SOUL SEARCHING (*6) / PERSON TO PERSON (*5) / BENNY AND US with Ben E. King (*5) / WARMER COMMUNICATIONS (*4) / FEEL NO FRET (*7) / SHINE (*4) / THE BEST OF THE AVERAGE WHITE BAND compilation (*7) / CUPID'S IN FASHION (*4) / AFTER SHOCK (*5) / THE BEST OF THE AVERAGE WHITE BAND – LET'S GO ROUND AGAIN compilation (*8) / SOUL TATTOO (*4) / FACE TO FACE LIVE (*5)

HAMISH STUART (b. 8 Oct'49, Glasgow, Scotland) – vocals, guitar / **ALAN GORRIE** (b.19 Jul'46, Perth, Scotland) – vocals, bass / **ONNIE McINTYRE** (b.25 Sep'45, Lennoxtown, Scotland) – lead guitar / **ROBBIE McINTOSH** (b. 1950) – drums / **ROGER BALL** (b. 4 Jun'44, Dundee, Scotland) – saxophone / **MALCOLM 'MOLLY' DUNCAN** (b.24 Aug'44, Montrose, Scotland) – tenor/soprano sax

M.C.A. M.C.A.

Apr 73. (7") *(MUS 1187)* **PUT IT WHERE YOU WANT IT. / REACH OUT** [ ] [–]

Jun 73. (7") *(MUS 1208)* **SHOW YOUR HAND. / THE JUGGLERS** [ ] [–]

Jun 73. (lp) *(MCF 2514)* <345> **SHOW YOUR HAND** [ ] [ ]
– The jugglers / This world has music / Twilight zone / Put it where you want it / Show your hand / How can you go home / Back in '67 / Reach out / T.L.C. *<US re-iss. Apr75 as 'PUT IT WHERE YOU WANT IT'; 475>* – hit No.39 *(UK re-iss. Feb82 under US title; MCL 1650) (re-iss. May83 on 'Fame' lp/c; FA/TC-FA 3062)*

Jul 73. (7") <40168> **THE JUGGLERS. / THIS WORLD HAS MUSIC** [–] [ ]

Jan 74. (7") *(MCA 86)* **HOW CAN YOU GO HOME. / TWILIGHT ZONE** [ ] [–]
(re-iss. May75; MCA 102)

Atlantic Atlantic

Jul 74. (lp/c) *(K/K4 50058)* <7308> **AVERAGE WHITE BAND** [6] Sep74 [1]
– You got it / Got the love / Pick up the pieces / Person to person / Work to do / Nothing you can do / Just wanna love you tonight / Keepin' it to myself / I just can't give you up / There's always someone waiting. *(re-iss. Oct80 on 'RCA Int.'; INTS 5049) (re-iss. Jun86 on 'Fame' lp/c; FA/TC-FA 3157) (cd-iss. 1987; 781515-2) (cd re-iss. Oct96 as 'THE WHITE ALBUM' on 'Essential'; ESMCD 439) (cd re-iss. Jan02 on 'Hit'; AHLCD 020)*

Jul 74. (7") *(K 10489)* **PICK UP THE PIECES. / YOU GOT IT** [ ] [–]
(re-dist.Feb75, hit UK No.6)

Oct 74. (7") *(K 10498)* <3044> **NOTHING YOU CAN DO. / I JUST CAN'T GIVE YOU UP** [ ] [ ]

Nov 74. (7") <3229> **PICK UP THE PIECES. / WORK TO DO** [–] [1]

—— **STEVE FERRONE** (b.25 Apr'50, Brighton, England) – drums (ex-BRIAN AUGER) repl. ROBBIE who died of a heroin overdose 23rd Sep'74

Apr 75. (7") *(K 10605)* <3261> **CUT THE CAKE. / PERSON TO PERSON** [31] [10]

Jun 75. (lp/c) *(K/K4 50146)* <18140> **CUT THE CAKE** [28] [4]
– Cut the cake / School boy crush / It's a mystery / Groovin' the night away / If I ever lose this Heaven / Why? / High flyin' woman / Cloudy / How sweet can you get / When they bring down the curtain. *(cd-iss. Sep97 on 'Snapper'; SMMCD 508) (cd re-iss. Jan02 on 'Hit'; AHLCD 030)*

Aug 75. (7") *(K 10655)* <3285> **IF I EVER LOSE THIS HEAVEN. / HIGH FLYIN' WOMAN** [ ] [39]

Nov 75. (7") *(K 10701)* <3304> **SCHOOL BOY CRUSH. / GROOVIN' THE NIGHT AWAY** [ ] [33]

May 76. (7") *(K 10778)* **EVERYBODY'S DARLING. / WHY?** [ ] [ ]

Jul 76. (lp/c) *(K/K4 50272)* <18179> **SOUL SEARCHING** [60] [8]
– Overture / Love your life / I'm the one / A love of your own / Queen of my soul / Soul searching / Goin' home / Everybody's darling / Would you say / Sunny days (make me think of you) / Digging deeper. *(re-iss. Nov80 on 'RCA Int.' lp/c; INTS/INTK 5058)*

Aug 76. (7") *(K 10825)* <3354> **QUEEN OF MY SOUL. / WOULD YOU STAY** [23] [40]

Dec 76. (7") *(K 10880)* **A LOVE OF YOUR OWN. / SOUL SEARCHIN'** [ ] [–]

Jan 77. (d-lp/d-c) *(K/K4 60127)* <1002> **PERSON TO PERSON (live)** [ ] [28]
– Person to person / Cut the cake / If I ever lose this Heaven / Cloudy / T.L.C. / I'm the one / Pick up the pieces / Love your life / School boy crush / I heard it through the grapevine.

Mar 77. (7") *(K 10912)* **GOIN' HOME (live). / I'M THE ONE (live)** [ ] [–]

Mar 77. (7") <3388> **CLOUDY (live). / LOVE YOUR LIFE (live)** [–] [ ]

AVERAGE WHITE BAND / BEN E. KING

Jun 77. (7") <3402> **KEEPIN' IT TO MYSELF. / GET IT UP FOR LOVE** [–] [ ]

Jul 77. (lp/c) *(K/K4 50384)* <19162> **BENNY AND US** [ ] [33]
– Get it up for love / Fool for you anyway / A star in the ghetto / The message / What is soul / Someday we'll all be free / Imagine / Keepin' it to myself.

Jul 77. (7") *(K 10977)* **A STAR IN THE GHETTO. / KEEPIN' IT TO MYSELF** [ ] [–]

Aug 77. (7") <3427> **A STAR IN A GHETTO. / WHAT IS SOUL** [–] [ ]

Dec 77. (7") <3444> **FOOL FOR YOU ANYWAY. / THE MESSAGE** [–] [ ]

AVERAGE WHITE BAND

R.C.A. Atlantic

Jun 78. (lp/c) *(XL/XC 13053)* <19162> **WARMER COMMUNICATIONS** [ ] Mar78 [28]
– Your love is a miracle / Same feeling, different song / Daddy's all gone / Big city lights / She's a dream / Sweet and sour / One look over my shoulder (is this really goodbye?). *(cd-iss. Jan02 on 'Hit'; AHLCD 029)*

Jun 78. (7") <3481> **ONE LOOK OVER MY SHOULDER. / LOVE IS A MIRACLE** [–] [ ]

Jun 78. (7"/7"colrd) *(XB/XC 9270)* **ONE LOOK OVER MY SHOULDER (IS THIS REALLY GOODBYE?). / BIG CITY LIGHTS** [ ] [–]

Aug 78. (7") <3500> **SHE'S A DREAM. / BIG CITY LIGHTS** [–] [ ]

Feb 79. (7") *(XB 1061)* **ATLANTIC AVENUE. / SHE'S A DREAM** [ ] [–]

Feb 79. (lp/c) *(XL/ZX 13063)* <19207> **FEEL NO FRET** [15] [32]
– When will you be mine / Please don't fall in love / Walk on by / Feel no fret / Stop the rain / Atlantic avenue / Ace of hearts / Too late to cry / Fire burning. *(re-iss. Sep81 lp/c; INTS/INTK 5140)*

Apr 79. (7"/7"colrd) *(XB/XC 1087)* <3563> **WALK ON BY. / TOO LATE TO CRY** [46] [92]

May 79. (7") <3581> **FEEL NO FRET. / FIRE BURNING** [–] [ ]

Jul 79. (7"/7"colrd) *(XB/XC 1096)* **WHEN WILL YOU BE MINE. / ACE OF HEARTS** [49] [ ]

R.C.A. Arista

Apr 80. (7"/12") *(AWB/+12 1)* **LET'S GO 'ROUND AGAIN. / (art 2)** [12] [–]

May 80. (lp/c) *(XL/XC 13123)* <9523> **SHINE** [14] [ ]
– Catch me / Let's go 'round again / Whatcha gonna do for me / Help is on the way / Shine / For you, for love / Into the night / Our time has come / If love only lasts for one night.

Jun 80. (7") <0515> **LET'S GO 'ROUND AGAIN. / SHINE** [–] [53]

Jul 80. (7"/12") *(AWB/+12 2)* **FOR YOU, FOR LOVE. / HELP IS ON THE WAY** [46] [–]

Jul 80. (7") <0553> **FOR YOU, FOR LOVE. / WHATCHA GONNA DO FOR ME** [–] [ ]

Jul 80. (7") <0580> **INTO THE NIGHT. /** [–] [ ]

—— added guest **RITCHIE STOTTS** – guitar (ex-PLASMATICS)

Jul 82. (7"/12") *(RCA/+T 250)* **YOU'RE MY NUMBER ONE. / THEATRE OF EXCESS** [ ] [–]

Sep 82. (lp/c) *(RCA LP/K 6052)* **CUPID'S IN FASHION** [ ] [ ]
– You're my number one / Easier said than done / You wanna belong /

Cupid's in fashion / Theatre of excess / I believe / Is it love that you're running from? / Reach out I'll be there / Isn't it strange / Love's a heartache.

Sep 82. (7"/12") *(RCA/+T 274)* **I BELIEVE. / REACH OUT I'LL BE THERE** ☐ ⊟

—— split 1983 but reformed in 1989 with **GORRIE, McINTYRE, BALL** recruited **ALEX LIGERTWOOD** (b.18 Dec'46, Glasgow) – guitar, vocals (ex-SANTANA, ex-BRIAN AUGER'S OBLIVION EXPRESS) / + on session **ELLIOT LEWIS** – keyboards / **TIGER McNEIL** – drums

—— HAMISH joined ERIC CLAPTON's band in 1990 and went solo

Polydor TRK

Aug 89. (lp/c/cd) *(839 466-1/-4/-2)* **AFTERSHOCK** ☐ ☐
– The spirit of love / Aftershock / I'll get over you / Let's go all the way / Sticky situation / Love at first sight / Later we'll be greater / We're in too deep.

Oct 89. (7") *(PO 56)* **THE SPIRIT OF LOVE. / ('A'beat mix)** ☐ ⊟
(12"/cd-s) *(PZ/+CD 56)* – ('A'dance) / ('A'-long beat) / ('A'-New York mix).

—— In 1985, ALAN GORRIE released album **SLEEPLESS NIGHTS** for 'A&M-US', plus single; 'AGE OF STEAM / I CAN TAKE IT (after) / DIARY OF A FOOL / IN THE JUNGLE

—— re-formed spring 1994 after the success of their compilation album

Hit Label not iss.

Mar 94. (cd/c) *(AHL CD/MC 15)* **THE BEST OF THE AVERAGE WHITE BAND – LET'S GO ROUND AGAIN** 38 ⊟
(cd re-iss. Oct96 on 'Music Club'; MCCD 274) (cd re-iss. Jan02 on 'Red Bullet'; RB 6695)

Mar 94. (7"/c-s) *(HL/+C 5)* **LET'S GO ROUND AGAIN (the CCN mix). / ('A'mix)** 56 ⊟
(cd-s+=) *(HLCD 5)* – ('A'mixes).

—— **ALAN GORRIE, ONNIE McINTYRE, ROGER BALL** plus **ELIOT LEWIS** – vocals, keyboards, bass, guitar / **PETE ABBOTT** – drums, percussion

Artful Foundation

Feb 97. (cd) *(ARTFULCD 7) <1601>* **SOUL TATTOO** ☐ ☐
– Soul mine / Back to basics / Livin' on borrowed time / Every beat of my heart / Oh Maceo / Do ya really / I wanna be loved / No easy way to say goodbye / Love is the bottom line / Welcome to the real world / Window to your soul. *(re-iss. Feb02 on 'S.P.V.'; SPV 0763375-2)*

Millennium Millennium

Jul 99. (cd) *(<MMPCD 002>)* **FACE TO FACE LIVE (live)** ☐ ☐
– Pick up the pieces / Let's go round again (pt.1) / Got the love / Love of your own / Work to do / Soul mine / Oh Maceo (dedicated to Maceo Parker) / Back to basics / Every beat of my heart.

– compilations etc. –

Jul 81. (7") *RCA-Gold; (GOLD 514)* **PICK UP THE PIECES. / CUT THE CAKE** ☐ ⊟

Sep 80. (lp) *Atlantic; <19266>* **VOLUME VIII** ⊟ ☐

Sep 81. (lp) *R.C.A.; (RCA 5139)* **THE BEST OF THE AVERAGE WHITE BAND** ☐ ⊟
– Pick up the pieces / Cut the cake / Queen of my soul / A love of your own / Person to person / I heard it through the grapevine / Walk on by / You got it / Cloudy / Work to do / Atlantic avenue / When will you be mine. *(re-iss. Aug84 lp/c; NL/NK 89091) (re-iss. May94 on 'Repertoire';)*

Aug 94. (cd) *Windsong; (WHISCD 005)* **LIVE ON THE TEST (live)** ☐ ⊟

Oct 96. (cd) *Castle; (CCSCD 438)* **ABOVE AVERAGE** ☐ ⊟

Feb 97. (cd) *Laserlight; (12891)* **THE VERY BEST OF THE AVERAGE WHITE BAND** ☐ ⊟

May 97. (d-cd) *Snapper; (SMDCD 173)* **AVERAGE WHITE BAND** ☐ ⊟

Aug 97. (cd-ep) *Club Classics; (CLCL 001)* **PICK UP THE PIECES / LET'S GO 'ROUND AGAIN / QUEEN OF MY SOUL** ☐ ⊟

Kevin AYERS

Born: 16 Aug'45, Herne Bay, Kent, England; raised in Malaysia. Left school and moved to Canterbury, where he and ROBERT WYATT helped form SOFT MACHINE in 1966. Burned out after a gruelling American tour supporting JIMI HENDRIX, the singer/songwriter decamped in 1968 to Ibiza to write material for the fledgling 'Harvest' label, the fruits of his labour being the following years' 'JOY OF A TOY' (title taken from an ORNETTE COLEMAN track). The album's idiosyncratic flair was indicative of the direction AYERS would take in his later work and contained some of his most enduring songs. In 1970, he hooked up with a young MIKE OLDFIELD to form KEVIN AYERS AND THE WHOLE WIDE WORLD. The unit, including saxophonist LOL COXHILL and keyboardist DAVID BEDFORD, released the experimental classic 'SHOOTING FOR THE MOON', setting the standard for the emergent progressive rock of the 70's. Critics complained that his monotone vox lay too close to SYD BARRETT, NICK DRAKE or even NICO, although he did manage to retain a distinctive character on such songs as 'CLARENCE IN WONDERLAND' and 'COLORES PARA DOLORES'. While 'WHATEVERSHEBRINGSWESING' (1972) and 'BANANAMOUR' (1973) contained moments of inspired exprimentation, AYERS began to move towards more straightforward writing. He appeared on the 'Island' live recording 'JUNE 1, 1974' alongside JOHN CALE, ENO and NICO, but he increasingly shied away from from publicity. The quality of his recorded output became inconsistent and directionless throughout the rest of the 70's and 80's, although he retained a diehard cult following. On the 1976 album 'YES WE HAVE NO MANANAS', he unwisely chose to record an appalling version of 'FALLING IN LOVE AGAIN' (made famous in the 30's by MARLENE DIETRICH). • **Covered:** LAY LADY LAY (Bob Dylan) / etc. • **Trivia:** In 1987, he contributed vocals to a MIKE OLDFIELD song, 'FLYING START', from the album 'ISLANDS'. AYERS had also largely contributed to an album (LINGUISTIC LEPROSY) in 1974 by friend and Deia neighbour LADY JUNE.

Album rating: JOY OF A TOY (*7) / SHOOTING AT THE MOON (*7) / WHATEVERSHEBRINGSWESING (*6) / BANANAMOUR (*5) / THE CONFESSIONS OF DR. DREAM (*5) / SWEET DECEIVER (*5) / ODD DITTIES collection (*5) / YES WE HAVE NO MANANAS (*5) / RAINBOW TAKEAWAY (*4) / THAT'S WHAT YOU GET BABE (*3) / DIAMOND JACK AND THE QUEEN OF PAIN (*3) / DEIA . . . VU (*4) / AS CLOSE AS YOU THINK (*4) / FALLING UP (*5) / STILL LIFE WITH GUITAR (*5) / BANANA PRODUCTIONS – BEST OF KEVIN AYERS compilation (*8) / THE GARDEN OF LOVE mini (*40

KEVIN AYERS – vocals, guitar (ex-SOFT MACHINE, ex-WILDE FLOWERS) / with **DAVID BEDFORD** – keyboards / **MIKE RATLEDGE** – keys / **HUGH HOPPER** – bass / **ROB TAIT** and **ROBERT WYATT** – drums / etc.

Harvest not iss.

Nov 69. (lp) *(SHVL 763)* **JOY OF A TOY** ☐ ⊟
– Joy of a toy . . . / Town feeling / Clarietta rag / Girl on a swing / Song for insane times / Stop this train again doing it / Eleanor's cake which ate her / Lady Rachel / Oleh olah bandu bandong / All this crazy gift of time. *(re-iss. Jun89 on 'Beat Goes On' lp/cd; BGO LP/CD 78) (cd re-mast.Jun03 on 'E.M.I.'+=; 582776-2)* – Religious experience (Syd Barrett session) / Lady Rachel (USA remix) / Soon soon soon / Religious experience / Lady Rachel / Singing a song in the morning.

Feb 70. (7") *(HAR 5011)* **SINGING A SONG IN THE MORNING. / ELEANOR'S CAKE WHICH ATE HER** ☐ ⊟

—— After being augmented on last single by CARAVAN members, he formed backing group The WHOLE WIDE WORLD, which included **DAVID BEDFORD** – keyboards / **MIKE OLDFIELD** – bass / **LOL COXHILL** – saxophone / **MICK FINCHER** – drums

Oct 70. (lp; as KEVIN AYERS & THE WHOLE WORLD) *(SHSP 4005)* **SHOOTING AT THE MOON** ☐ ⊟

– May I? / Rheinhardt and Geraldine / Colores para Dolores / Lunatics lament / Pisser dans un violin / The oyster and the flying fish / Underwater / Clarence in wonderland / Red, green and you, blue / Shooting at the Moon. *(re-iss. Jun89 on 'Beat Goes On' lp/cd; BGO LP/CD 13) (cd re-mast.Jun03 on 'E.M.I.'+=; 582777-2)* – Gemini child / Puis je? / Butterfly dance (version) / Jolie madame / Hat (take 4).

Oct 70. (7") *(HAR 5027)* **BUTTERFLY DANCE. / PUIS-JE?** ☐ [–]

Aug 71. (7") *(HAR 5042)* **STRANGER IN BLUE SUEDE SHOES. / STARS** ☐ [–]

—— The WHOLE WIDE WORLD were augmented by GONG members **DIDIER MALHERBE** – sax / **STEVE HILLAGE** – guitar / also session drummers **WYATT, DUFORT & TONY CARR**

Jan 72. (lp) *(SHVL 800)* **WHATEVERSHEBRINGSWESING** ☐ [–]
– There is loving – Among us – There is loving / Margaret / Oh my / Song from the bottom of a well / Whatevershebringswesing / Stranger in blue suede shoes / Champagne cowboy blues / Lullaby. *(re-iss. Jun89 on 'Beat Goes On' lp/cd; BGO LP/CD 11) (cd re-mast.Jun03 on 'E.M.I.'+=; 582778-2)* – Stars / Don't sing no more sad songs / Fake Mexican tourist blues / Stranger in blue suede shoes (early mix).

—— **ARCHIE LEGGAT** – bass (ex-WONDERWHEEL) repl. OLDFIELD who went solo / **EDDIE SPARROW** – drums / etc.

Nov 72. (7") *(HAR 5064)* **OH! WOT A DREAM. / CONNIE ON A RUBBER BAND** ☐ [–]

Harvest Sire

Apr 73. (7") *(HAR 5071)* **CARIBBEAN MOON. / TAKE ME TO TAHITI** ☐ ☐
(re-iss. Jul75; HAR 5100) (re-iss. May76; HAR 5109)

May 73. (lp) *(SHVL 807)* *<SAS 7406>* **BANANAMOUR** ☐ ☐
– Don't let it get you down / Shouting in a bucket-blues / When your parents go to sleep / Interview / International anthem / Decadence / Oh! wot a dream / Hymn / Beware of the dog. *<US-iss.+=)* – CARIBBEAN MOON (lp). *(re-iss. May86 on 'E.M.I.'; EMS 1124) (cd-iss. Oct92 on 'Beat Goes On'; BGOCD 142) (cd re-mast.Jun03 on 'E.M.I.'+=; 582780-2)* – Connie on a rubber band / Decadence / Take me to Tahiti / Caribbean moon.

—— His touring '747' band incl. **HENRY CRALLAN** – keyboards / **FREDDIE SMITH** – drums / **CAL BATCHELOR** – guitar. In the studio he now used many session people.

Island not iss.

Apr 74. (7") *(WIP 6194)* **THE UP SONG. / EVERYBODY'S SOMETIMES AND SOME PEOPLE'S ALL THE TIME BLUES** ☐ [–]

May 74. (lp) *(ILPS 9263)* **THE CONFESSIONS OF DR.DREAM AND OTHER STORIES** ☐ [–]
– Day by day / See you later / Didn't feel lonely till I thought of you / Everybody's sometimes and some people's all the time blues / It begins with a blessing, but it ends with a curse / Once I awsheared / Ball bearing blues / The confessions of Dr.Dream (a) Irreversible neural damage, (b) Invitation, (c) The one chance dance, (d) Doctor Dream theme, (e) Two into 4 goes. *(re-iss. Nov90 on 'Beat Goes On' cd/lp; BGO CD/LP 86)*

Jul 74. (7") *(WIP 6201)* **AFTER THE SHOW. / THANK YOU VERY MUCH** ☐ [–]

—— He was credited alongside ENO, NICO and JOHN CALE on 'Island' Various Artists album 'JUNE 1st, 1974'; *ILPS 9291*, released that month. *(cd-iss. Feb90; IMCD 92)*

—— He formed backing group, which included **ZOOT MONEY** – keyboards / **RICK WILLS** – bass / **TONY NEWMAN** – drums / **OLLIE HALSALL** – guitar

Mar 75. (lp) *(ILPS 9322)* **SWEET DECEIVER** ☐ [–]
– Observations / Guru banana / City waltz / Toujours la voyage / Sweet deceiver / Diminished but not finished / Circular lather / Once upon an ocean / Farewell again / Another dawn. *(cd-iss. Oct92 on 'Beat Goes On'; BGOCD 98)*

Feb 76. (7") *(WIP 6271)* **FALLING IN LOVE AGAIN. / EVERYONE KNOWS THE SONG** ☐ [–]

—— Retained ZOOT, calling in **ANDY SOMERS** – guitar / **CHARLIE McCRACKEN** – bass / **ROB TOWNSEND** – drums

Harvest A.B.C.

Feb 76. (7") *(HAR 5107)* **STRANGER IN BLUE SUEDE SHOES. / FAKE MEXICAN TOURIST BLUES** ☐ [–]

Jun 76. (lp) *(SHSP 4057)* **YES WE HAVE NO MANANAS** ☐ ☐
– Star / Mr. Cool / The owl / Love's gonna turn you 'round / Falling in love again (ich bin von kopf bis fuss duf liebe eingesteldt) / Help me / Ballad of Mr. Snake / Everyone knows the song / Yes I do / Blue. *(cd-iss. Apr93 on 'Beat Goes On'; BGOCD 143)*

1976. (7") *<12303>* **MR. COOL. /** [–] ☐

Apr 77. (7") *(HAR 5124)* **STAR. / THE OWL** ☐ [–]

—— **BILL LIVESY** – keyboards repl. ZOOT, etc.

Apr 78. (lp/c) *(SHSP/TC-SHSP 4085)* **RAINBOW TAKEAWAY** ☐ [–]
– Blaming it all on love / Ballad of a salesman who sold himself / A view from a mountain / Rainbow takeaway / Waltz for you / Beware of the dog 2 / Strange song / Goodnight goodnight / Hat song. *(cd-iss. May93 on 'Beat Goes On'; BGOCD 189)*

Feb 80. (lp/c) *(SHSP/TC-SHSP 4106)* **THAT'S WHAT YOU GET, BABE** ☐ [–]
– That's what you get, babe / Where do I go from here / You never outrun your heart / Given and taken / Idiots / Super salesman / Money, money, money / Miss Hanagal / I'm so tired / Where do the stars end. *(cd-iss. Jun93 on 'Beat Goes On'; BGOCD 190)*

Feb 80. (7") *(HAR 5198)* **MONEY, MONEY, MONEY. / STRANGER IN BLUE SUEDE SHOES** ☐ [–]

—— Retired to Majorca in Spain. Still retained **FOLLIE** + employed new Spanish musicians.

not iss. Columbia

1982. (7") *(MO 2113)* **ANIMALS. / DON'T FALL IN LOVE WITH ME** [–] Spain [–]

Charly not iss.

Jun 83. (lp) *(CR 30224)* **DIAMOND JACK AND THE QUEEN OF PAIN** ☐ [–]
– Madame Butterfly / Lay lady lay / Who's still crazy / You keep me hangin' on / You are a big girl / Steppin' out / My speeding heart / Howling man / Give a little bit / Champagne and valium.

Jul 83. (7") *(CYZ 7107)* **MY SPEEDING HEART. / CHAMPAGNE AND VALIUM** ☐ [–]

Blau not iss.

1984. (lp) *(A-014)* **DEIA . . . VU** [–] Spain [–]
– Champagne and valium / Thank God for a sense of humour / Take it easy / Stop playing with my heart (you are a big girl) / My speeding heart / Lay lady lay / Stop playing with my heart II / Be aware of the dog. *(UK cd-iss. Aug00; BLAUCD 148)*

Illuminated not iss.

May 86. (7"promo) *(LEV 71)* **STEPPIN' OUT. / ONLY HEAVEN KNOWS** [–] [–]

Jun 86. (lp) *(AMA 25)* **AS CLOSE AS YOU THINK** ☐ [–]
– Steppin' out / Fool after midnight / Wish I could fall / Heaven only knows / Too old to die young / The howling man / Never my baby / Budget tours (part one) / Budget tours (part two).

Virgin not iss.

Feb 88. (lp/c/cd) *(V/TCV/CDV 2510)* **FALLING UP** ☐ [–]
– Saturday night (in Deya) / Flying start / The best we have / Another rolling stone / Do you believe? / That's what we did / Night fighters / Am I really Marcel?

Permanent not iss.

Feb 92. (cd/c/lp) *(PERM CD/MC/LP 5)* **STILL LIFE WITH GUITAR** ☐ [–]
– Feeling this way / Something inbetween / Thank you very much / There goes Johnny / Ghost town / I don't depend on you / When your parents go to sleep / M16 / Don't blame them / Irene goodnight. *(cd re-iss. Mar98 on 'Indelible'; INDELCD 2) (cd re-iss. Feb02 on 'Market Square'+=; MSMCD 112)* – I don't depend on you (alt.) / Don't blame them (alt.) / Work in progress.

Voiceprint not iss.

Jun 98. (m-cd) *(VP 180CD)* **THE GARDEN OF LOVE** ☐ [–]
– The garden of love.

– compilations, etc. –

on 'Harvest' unless mentioned otherwise

Jun 75. (d-lp) *(SHDW 407)* **JOY OF A TOY / SHOOTING AT THE MOON** ☐ [–]

Feb 76. (lp) *(SHSM 2005)* **ODD DITTIES** ☐ [–]

Jul 83. (lp) *See For Miles; (CM 117)* **THE KEVIN AYERS COLLECTION** ☐ [–]
(re-iss. Jun86; same) (re-iss. Jul90 & Jun97 lp/cd; same/SEECD 117)

Jun 89. (d-lp/c)(cd) *(EM/TC-EM 2032)(CZ 176)* **BANANA PRODUCTIONS – THE BEST OF KEVIN AYERS** ☐ [–]
– Butterfly dance / Girl on a swing / Soon soon soon / Sweet deceiver / Caribbean moon / Decadence *[not on cd]* / Irreversible neural damage / Gemini child / The lady Rachel / Toujours le voyage *[not on cd]* / Stranger in blue suede shoes / There is loving – Among us – There is loving / The Clarietta rag / Reinhardt & Geraldine – Colores para Dolores / Stars /

Don't let it get you down / Hat song / Singing a song in the morning / Ballad of a salesman who sold himself / Clarence in Wonderland / Diminished but not finished / Blue *[not on cd]* / Song from the bottom of a well. *(cd re-iss. Sep00; CDP 792618-2)*

Jul 92. (cd) *Windsong; (WINCD 018)* **THE BBC RADIO LIVE IN CONCERT (live)** [ ] [-]

Oct 92. (cd) *Connoisseur; (CSAPCD 110)* **DOCUMENT SERIES PRESENTS (CLASSIC ALBUM & SINGLE TRACKS 1969-1980)** [ ] [-]

Sep 96. (cd) *Band Of Joy; (<BOJCD 019>)* **SINGING THE BRUISE: BBC SESSIONS 1970-1972** [ ] [ ]

Nov 96. (cd) *Band Of Joy; (<BOJCD 020>)* **1ST SHOW IN THE APPEARANCE BUSINESS: BBC SESSIONS 1973-1976** [ ] [ ]

Jul 98. (d-cd) *Hux; (<HUX 006>)* **TOO OLD TO DIE YOUNG** [ ] [ ]

Jul 98. (cd) *Hux; (<HUX 007>)* **BANANA FOLLIES** [ ] [ ]

Nov 99. (d-lp) *Turning Point; (TPM 99203)* **RADIO SESSIONS** [ ] [-]

Feb 00. (cd; as KEVIN AYERS & THE WIZARDS OF TWIDDLY) *Market Square; (MSMCD 105)* **TURN THE LIGHTS DOWN: LIVE IN LONDON (live 10th March 1995)** [ ] [-]

AZTEC CAMERA

Formed: East Kilbride, Scotland ... early 1980 by 15 year-old, RODDY FRAME, who released two independent 45's on ALAN HORNE's now semi-famous 'Postcard' label, before moving on to 'Rough Trade' in 1982. The following year, RODDY and Co. hit the top of the indie charts (reached Top 30 nationally) with debut album, 'HIGH LAND, HARD RAIN', a largely acoustic-based affair combining folkish flights of fancy, Latin/jazz rhythms and an incisive lyrical flair with stunning results. The record's breezy lead track, 'OBLIVIOUS', was re-issued by new label 'Warners' later that year on the back of the album's success, one of the few AZTEC CAMERA singles to break the Top 20. FRAME brought in a new cast of musicians for 1984's MARK KNOPFLER-produced 'KNIFE' set, including seasoned Scots players CRAIG GANNON and MALCOLM ROSS. A more commercial offering, the record almost made the UK hit in 'ALL I NEED IS EVERYTHING'. After a world tour, FRAME laid low for more than two years, penning material for 'LOVE' (1987), the most successful album of his career. Initially something of a non-starter, this over-produced yet affecting album eventually made the Top 10 almost a year after its release following the massive Top 5 success of the plaintive 'SOMEWHERE IN MY HEART' single. Despite courting the pop mainstream, FRAME's subsequent effort, 'STRAY' (1990) veered off into more eclectic territory, the Top 20 hit, 'GOOD MORNING BRITAIN', featuring MICK JONES of BIG AUDIO DYNAMITE / CLASH fame. The 90's witnessed FRAME developing his earlier style, especially on the 1995 set, 'FRESTONIA'. Come 1998, the Scots veteran had signed to 'Independiente', releasing a minor hit, 'REASON FOR LIVING' which accompanied the relatively low-key pop-rock album, 'THE NORTH STAR'. FRAME was back in 2002 with 'SURF', his most unassuming and low-key recording to date. Stripped back to the bare bones of vocals and acoustic guitar, the record proved that the Scotsman's astute, shrewdly observed and lovingly crafted material needed little or no sonic froth to get its point across. • **Covered:** JUMP (Van Halen) / DO I LOVE YOU (Cole Porter) / I THREW IT ALL AWAY (Bob Dylan) / BAD EDUCATION (Blue Orchids) / IF PARADISE WAS HALF AS NICE (Amen Corner). • **Trivia:** In Autumn '83, while in the States supporting ELVIS COSTELLO, he lied about his age (19) to get into the country.

Album rating: HIGH LAND, HARD RAIN (*8) / KNIFE (*6) / LOVE (*5) / STRAY (*6) / DREAMLAND (*6) / FRESTONIA (*5) / THE BEST OF AZTEC CAMERA compilation (*8) / Roddy Frame: THE NORTH STAR (*5) / SURF (*7)

RODDY FRAME (b.29 Jan'64) – vocals, acoustic guitar / **DAVE MULHOLLAND** – drums / **CAMPBELL OWENS** – bass; who repl. ALAN WELSH late in 1980

Postcard not iss.

Mar 81. (7") *(81-3)* **JUST LIKE GOLD. / WE COULD SEND LETTERS** [ ] [-]

Jul 81. (7") *(81-8)* **MATTRESS OF WIRE. / LOOK OUTSIDE THE TUNNEL** [ ] [-]

Sep 81. (lp; w-drawn) *(81-13)* **GREEN JACKET GREY** [-] [-]

— (mid-'82) added temp. member **BERNIE CLARK** – keyboards / **DAVE RUFFY** – drums (ex-RUTS) repl. MULHOLLAND

Rough Trade Sire

Aug 82. (7"/7"pic-d) *(RT 112/+P)* **PILLAR TO POST. / QUEEN'S TATTOO** [ ] [-]

Jan 83. (7") *(RT 122)* **OBLIVIOUS. / ORCHARD GIRL** [47] [-]
(12"+=) *(RT 122T)* – Haywire.

Apr 83. (lp) *(ROUGH 47) <23899>* **HIGH LAND, HARD RAIN** [22] Aug83 [ ]
– Oblivious / The boy wonders / Walk out to winter / The bugle sounds again / We could send letters / Pillar to post / Release / Lost outside the tunnel / Back on board / Down the dip. *(cd-iss. Feb87 +=; ROUGHCD 47)* – Haywire / Queen's tattoo / Orchard girl. *(re-iss. Sep93 on 'WEA' cd/c; 4509 92849-2/-4)*

May 83. (7"/12") *(RT/+T 132)* **WALK OUT TO WINTER. / SET THE KILLING FREE** [64] [ ]

WEA Sire

Oct 83. (d7") *(AZTEC 1)* **OBLIVIOUS. / ORCHARD GIRL // WE COULD SEND LETTERS (live). / BACK ON BOARD (live)** [18] [ ]

— **RODDY FRAME** retained **RUFFY** and brought into line-up:- **CRAIG GANNON** – bass (ex-BLUEBELLS) repl. OWENS / added **MALCOLM ROSS** – guitar (ex-ORANGE JUICE, ex-JOSEF K) / guest / **GUY FLETCHER** – keyboards

Aug 84. (7") *(AC 1)* **ALL I NEED IS EVERYTHING. / JUMP** [34] [ ]
(12") *(AC 1T)* – ('A'-Latin mix) / Jump (Loaded version).

Sep 84. (lp/c)(cd) *(WX 8/+C)(240 483-2) <25183>* **KNIFE** [14] [ ]
– Still on fire / Just like the U.S.A. / Head is happy (heart's insane) / The back door to Heaven / All I need is everything / Backwards and forwards / Birth of the true / Knife. *(cd-iss. Sep93; same) (cd re-iss. Jun02 on 'Wounded Bird'+=; WOU 5183)* – AZTEC CAMERA mini-lp tracks.

Nov 84. (7"/7"sha-pic-d) *(AC 2/+P)* **STILL ON FIRE. / WALK OUT TO WINTER** [ ] [ ]
(12"+=) *(AC 2T)* – Mattress of wire (live) / The boy wonders (live) / The bugle sounds again (live).

Apr 85. (10"m-lp) *<25285>* **AZTEC CAMERA (live)** [-] [ ]
– Birth of the true / Mattress of wire / Jump / The bugle sounds again / Backwards and forwards.

— **FRAME + RUFFY** alongside other session musicians **MARCUS MILLER** – bass / **DAVID FRANK** – keyboards (ex-SYSTEM) / **STEVE JORDAN** – guitar

Sep 87. (7"/ext-12") *(YZ 154/+T)* **DEEP AND WIDE AND TALL. / BAD EDUCATION** [ ] [ ]

Oct 87. (lp/c)(cd) *(WX 128/+C)(242 202-2) <25646>* **LOVE** [10] [ ]
– Deep and wide and tall / How men are / Everybody is a number one / More than a law / Somewhere in my heart / Working in a goldmine / One and one / Paradise / Killermont Street. *(cd-iss. Sep93; same)*

Jan 88. (7") *(YZ 168)* **HOW MEN ARE. / THE RED FLAG** [25] [ ]
(12"+=) *(YZ 168T)* – Killermont Street (live) / Pillar to post (live).
(cd-s+=) *(248 028-2)* – Oblivious / All I need is everything.

Apr 88. (7") *(YZ 181)* **SOMEWHERE IN MY HEART. / EVERYBODY IS A NUMBER ONE '86** [3] [ ]
(12"+=) *(YZ 181T)* – Down the dip / Jump.
(cd-s+=) *(YZ 181CD)* – Walk out to winter / Still on fire.

Jul 88. (7") *(YZ 199)* **WORKING IN A GOLDMINE. / I THREW IT ALL AWAY** [31] [ ]
(12"+=/12"s+=) *(YZ 199 T/W)* – ('A'version).
(cd-s++=) *(YZ 199CD)* – How men are.

Sep 88. (7") *(YZ 154)* **DEEP AND WIDE AND TALL. / BAD EDUCATION** [55] [ ]
(12"+=/cd-s+=) *(YZ 154 T/CD)* – More than a law.

— (live band '88: augmenting **FRAME + RUFFY**) **EDDIE KULAK** – keyboards / **GARY SANFORD** – guitar / **PAUL POWELL** – bass

— (by 1990, **FRAME** had lost RUFFY but retained **POWELL** / and new **GARY SANCTUARY** – keyboards / **FRANK TONTOH** – drums / guests **PAUL**

CARRACK, EDWYN COLLINS, MICKEY GALLAGHER & STEVE SIDELYNK.

Jun 90. (cd)(lp/c) *(<9031 71694-2>)(WX 350/+C)* **STRAY** 22
– Stray / The crying scene / Get outta London / Over my head / How it is / Good morning Britain (featuring MICK JONES) / The gentle kind / Notting Hill blues / Song for a friend. *(re-iss. cd+c Sep93)*

Jun 90. (7") *(YZ 492)* **THE CRYING SCENE. / TRUE COLOURS** 70
(12"+=/cd-s+=) *(YZ 492 T/CD)* – Salvation.
(10"+=) *(YZ 492X)* – I threw it all away (live).

Sep 90. (7"/c-s; AZTEC CAMERA and MICK JONES) *(YZ 521/+C)* **GOOD MORNING BRITAIN. / ('A'live version)** 19
(12"+=) *(YZ 521T)* – ('A'remix)
(cd-s+=) *(YZ 521CD)* – Consolation prize. (with EDWYN COLLINS)

Jul 92. (7"/c-s) *(YZ 688/+C)* **SPANISH HORSES. / JUST LIKE THE U.S.A. (live)** 52
(cd-s) *(YZ 688CD1)* – ('A'side) / Killermont street (live) / The birth of the true (live) / Song for a friend (live).
(cd-s) *(YZ 688CD2)* – ('A'live version) / Stray (live) / The bugle sounds again (live) / Dolphins (live).

Apr 93. (7"/c-s) *(YZ 740/+C)* **DREAM SWEET DREAMS. / GOOD MORNING BRITAIN (live)** 67
(cd-s+=) *(YZ 740CD1)* – Sister Anne (live) / How men are (live).
(cd-s) *(YZ 740CD2)* – ('A'side) / Mattress of wire (live) / Let your love decide (live) / Orchid girl (live).

May 93. (cd/c/lp) *(<4509 92492/-2/-4/-1>)* **DREAMLAND** 21
– Birds / Safe in sorrow / Black Lucia / Let your love decide / Spanish horses / Dream sweet dreams / Piano's and clocks / Sister Ann / Vertigo / Valium Summer / Belle of the ball.

Jun 93. (7"/c-s) *(YZ 754/+C)* **BIRDS. / DEEP AND WIDE AND TALL**
(cd-s) *(YZ 754CD1)* – ('A'side) / Working in a goldmine / Knife.
(cd-s) *(YZ 754CD2)* – ('A'side) / Somewhere in my heart / Oblivious / Good morning Britain.

WEA Reprise

Oct 95. (c-s) *(WEA 007C)* **SUN / SUNSET**
(cd-s+=) *(WEA 007CD)* – The crying scene (live).
(cd-s) *(WEA 007CDX)* – ('A'side) / We could send letters (live) / Black Lucia (live) / The rainy season (live).

Nov 95. (cd/c) *(<0630 11929-2/-4>)* **FRESTONIA**
– The rainy season / Sun / Crazy / On the avenue / Imperfectly / Debutante / Beautiful girl / Phenomenal world / Method of love / Sunset.

– compilations, etc. –

Sep 90. (7") *Old Gold; (OG 9945)* **SOMEWHERE IN MY HEART. / OBLIVIOUS** -

—— In Nov'90, 'DO I LOVE YOU?' appeared as the extra track on the 12" & cd-s of a Cole Porter tribute by The POGUES and KIRSTY MacCOLL

Oct 94. (cd) *Windsong; (WHISCD 006)* **LIVE ON THE TEST (live)** -

Jul 99. (cd/c) *WEA; (3984 28984-2/-4)* **THE BEST OF AZTEC CAMERA** 36 -
– Oblivious / Good morning Britain / Somewhere in my heart / Working in a goldmine / How men are / Birth of the true / Walk out to winter / Jump / All I need is everything / Deep & wide & tall / The crying scene / Killermont street / Spanish horses / Reason for living.

RODDY FRAME

Independiente Sony

Sep 98. (c-s) *(ISOM 18CS)* **REASON FOR LIVING / WINTER HAVEN HIGH** 45 Nov98
(cd-s) *(ISOM 18MS)* <66231A> – Rainy greys and blues.
(cd-s) *(ISOM 18SMS)* <66231B> – ('A'side) / Biba nova / The sea is wide.

Sep 98. (cd) *(ISOM 7CD)* <120123> **THE NORTH STAR** 55 Nov98
– Back to the one / The north star / Here comes the ocean / River of brightness / Strings / Bigger brighter better / Autumn flower / Reason for living / Sister shadow / Hymn to grace.

Redemption Cooking Vinyl

Aug 02. (cd) *(RRUK 2)* <COOKCD 117> **SURF** Oct02
– Over you / Surf / Small world / I can't start now / Abloom / Tough / Big Ben / High class music / Turning the world around / Mixed up love / For what it was.

The BEATLES

Eric B. & RAKIM

Formed: Long Island, New York, USA . . . 1985 by DJ ERIC BARRIER and rapper WILLIAM 'RAKIM' GRIFFIN. The pair met while BARRIER was working at New York radio station, WBLS, the dextrous turntable manipulator finally finding the MC skills he was looking for in the subtle but deadly RAKIM. Their debut effort, 'ERIC B. FOR PRESIDENT', stripped hip hop to its bare bones with merciless intensity, RAKIM's understated but effective vocal delivery heightening the impact. Initially released on the obscure 'Zakia' label, the track caught the attention of '4th and Broadway', who released the landmark 'PAID IN FULL' in 1987. A low-slung, sample happy classic propelled by a hypnotically funky rhythm track and focused on RAKIM's mantra like lyrical flow, the cut remains one of the genre's defining moments. A transatlantic singles chart sucess, the track inspired a brace of remixes as the emerging house culture cross pollinated with rap and hip hop; the most famous of these, the COLDCUT "Seven Minutes Of Madness" epic, embellished the original with the ubiquitous sample of Arabic singer OFRA HAZA, ERIC B. & RAKIM's cool reception of the makeover well documented. The accompanying album of the same name was released to just as much controversy, JAMES BROWN and BOBBY BYRD's legal team none too happy at the splicing of their early 70's funk classic in 'I KNOW YOU GOT SOUL' (another brilliantly conceived sample fest that also borrowed from The JACKSON 5 and KOOL & THE GANG amongst others). Yet the result was a literal exhumation of 'The Godfather's work for "reappraisal" by rap artists, just one of the seismic effects felt by hip hop in the wake of this pivotal album. A second set, 'FOLLOW THE LEADER' (1988) changed tack without losing the effect, its denser collages and harder hitting rhymes seeing the duo stay ahead of the game, almost; a US Top 30 hit, the record was nevertheless overshadowed by the unstoppable momentum of PUBLIC ENEMY. Despite a brave attempt at getting back to basics on the sinewy funk of 'LET THE RHYTHM HIT 'EM' (1990), ERIC B. & RAKIM were inevitably being overtaken by the emerging gangsta rappers, the pair finally splitting after a final album, 'DON'T SWEAT THE TECHNIQUE' (1992). By this point, RAKIM had matured into a lyricist of biting depth, the rapper embarking on a low key solo career before criminally fading into obscurity; his comeback album 'THE 18th LETTER' in 1997 gave him his first trip into US Top 5 territory. ERIC B. & RAKIM are up there with GRANDMASTER FLASH, AFRIKA BAMBAATAA, CHUCK D, pioneers in an era of hip hop creativity unrivalled since.

Album rating: PAID IN FULL (*8) / FOLLOW THE LEADER (*7) / LET THE RHYTHM HIT 'EM (*5) / DON'T SWEAT THE TECHNIQUE (*6) / Rakim: THE 18th LETTER (*6) / THE MASTER (*6)

ERIC B. (b. ERIC BARRIER, 8 Nov.64) – turntables / **RAKIM** (b. WILLIAM GRIFFIN Jr., 28 Jan'68) – vocals

Date	Release	UK	US
		Cooltempo	Cooltempo
Aug 86.	(12") *(COOLX 129)* **ERIC B. FOR PRESIDENT. / ('A'instrumental)**		
Nov 86.	(7") **MY MELODY. / ('A'instrumental)**	-	
Jun 87.	(7"/12") *(COOL/+X 146)* **I KNOW YOU GOT SOUL. / ('A'instrumental)** *(remixed versions Feb88 hit UK No.13, 7"/12"; COOLR/+X 146)*		
		4th & Broad	4th & Broad
Aug 87.	(lp/c/cd) *(BR LP/CA/CD 514) <4005>* **PAID IN FULL** – I ain't no joke / Eric B. is on the cut / My melody / I know you got soul / Move the crowd / As the rhyme goes on / Chinese arithmetic / Eric B. for president / Extended beat / Paid in full. *(cd re-iss. Jun89; IMCD 9)*	85	58
Oct 87.	(7") *(BRW 78)* **PAID IN FULL. / ERIC B IS ON THE CUT** (12"+=) *(12BRW 78)* – ('A'extended).	15	
Feb 88.	(7") *(BRW 88)* **MOVE THE CROWD. / ('A'mix)** (ext-12"+=) *(12BRW 88)* – ('A'-Wild Bunch mix).	53	
May 88.	(7") *(BRW 106)* **AS THE RHYME GOES ON. / CHINESE ARITHMETIC** (12"+=) *(12BRW 106)* – ('A'mixes).		
		M.C.A.	Uni
Jun 88.	(7") *(MCA 1256)* **FOLLOW THE LEADER. / ('A'dub)** (12"+=) *(MCAT 1256)* – ('A'extended). (cd-s++=) *(DMCA 1256)* – ('A'-Accapella mix).	21	
Aug 88.	(lp/c/cd) *(MCG/MCGC/DMCG 6031) <UNI 3>* **FOLLOW THE LEADER** – Follow the leader / Microphone fiend / Lyrics of fury / Eric B. never scared / Just a beat / Put your hands together / To the listeners / No competition / The R / Musical massacre / Beats for the listeners.	25	22
Nov 88.	(7") *(MCA 1300)* **MICROPHONE FIEND. / ('A'mix)** (12"+=/cd-s+=) *(MCAT/DMCA 1300)* – ('A'mixes).	74	
Jan 89.	(7") *(MCA 1303)* **THE R. / ('A'mix)** (12"+=/cd-s+=) *(MCAT/DMCA 1303)* – ('A'mixes).		

—— In Aug'89, ERIC B. & RAKIM were credited on JODY WATLEY's hit single, 'FRIENDS' *(MCA 1352)<53669>*

Date	Release	UK	US
		M.C.A.	M.C.A.
May 90.	(12") *<MCA 24026>* **LET THE RHYTHM HIT 'EM (mixes)**	-	
Jun 90.	(cd/c/lp) *(DMCG/MCGC/MCG 6097) <6416>* **LET THE RHYTHM HIT 'EM** – Let the rhythm hit 'em / No omega / In the ghetto / Step back / Eric B. made my day / Run for cover / Untouchables / Mahogany / Keep 'em eager to listen / Set 'em straight. *(cd+=)* – Let the rhythm hit 'em (12" remix).	58	32
Feb 92.	(cd-s) *<54333>* **JUICE (KNOW THE LEDGE) / ('A'instrumental)** (above from the film, 'Juice')	-	96
Jun 92.	(lp/c/cd) *<(MCA/+C/D 10594)>* **DON'T SWEAT THE TECHNIQUE** – What's on your mind / Teach the children / Pass the hand grenade / Casualties of war / Rest assured / The punisher / Relax with Pep / Keep the beat / What's going on / Know the ledge / Don't sweat the technique / Kick along.	73	22

RAKIM

Date	Release	UK	US
		Universal	Universal
Nov 97.	(d-cd/d-c) *<(UD2/UC2 53111)>* **THE 18th LETTER / THE BOOK OF LIFE** – (intro) / 18th letter (always and forever) / (skit) / It's been a long time /	72	4

Remember that / The saga begins / (skit 2) / Guess who's back / Stay a while / New York (ya' out there) / Show me love / (skit) / Mystery (who is God?) / When I'm flowin' / It's been a long time (suave house mix) / Guess who's back / (outro). *(w/ free cd 'THE BOOK OF LIFE' by ERIC B. & RAKIM)* – I know you got soul / Follow the leader / Eric B. is president / Microphone fiend / I ain't no joke / Lyrics of fury / My melody / Know the ledge / Move the crowd / Let the rhythm hit 'em / Mahogany / In the ghetto / Casualties of war / The punisher / Paid in full.

Dec 97. (c-s) *(UNC 56151)* **GUESS WHO'S BACK / IT'S BEEN A LONG TIME** [32] [–]
(12"+=/cd-s+=) *(UNT/UND 56151)* – ('A'mixes).

Aug 98. (c-s/12"/cd-s) *(UNC/UNT/UND 56203)* **STAY A LITTLE WHILE. / THE SAGA BEGINS (Desert Island Discs mix) / NEW YORK (ya out there mix)** [53] [ ]

Nov 99. (cd/c) <542082-2/-4> **THE MASTER** [ ] [72]
– Intro / Flow forever / When I B on tha mic / Finest ones / All night long / State of hip ho interlude / Uplift / I know / It's the R / I'll be there / It's a must / Real shit / How I get down / L.I. interlude / Strong island / Waiting for the world to end / We'll never stop.

Dec 99. (12") <156619> **WHEN I BE ON THA MIC** [–] [ ]

☐ BAADER-MEINHOF (see under ⇒ AUTEURS)

BABES IN TOYLAND

Formed: Minneapolis, Minnesota, USA ... 1987 by KAT BJELLAND, MICHELLE LEON and LORI BARBELO. Signing to influential local label, 'Twintone', the all-girl group released an early proto-grunge classic in the Jack Endino-produced 'SPANKING MACHINE' (1990). Featuring such white hot blasts of feminine subversiveness as 'HE'S MY THING' and 'PAIN IN MY HEART', the album opened the floodgates for a slew of similar angry young women (i.e. L7 and HOLE, whose JENNIFER FINCH and COURTNEY LOVE respectively, LYDIA LUNCH soundalike BJELLAND had previously played with in SUGAR BABY DOLL). Over the course of the next year, they released a mini-album, 'TO MOTHER', replaced MICHELLE with MAUREEN HERMAN and signed to 'Warner Bros', releasing a second album proper, 'FONTANELLE' in the Spring of '92. Produced by LEE RANALDO of SONIC YOUTH, the record breached the UK Top 30 on the back of rave reviews from both the inkies and the metal press. Following a stop-gap part live set, 'PAINKILLERS', the BABES took a sabbatical, BJELLAND turning up in STUART GRAY's (her husband) outfit, LUBRICATED GOAT, while moonlighting with CRUNT. BABES IN TOYLAND returned in 1995 with 'NEMESISTERS', which disappointed many of their more hardcore following by including covers of 'WE ARE FAMILY' (Sister Sledge), 'DEEP SONG' (Billie Holiday) and 'ALL BY MYSELF' (Eric Carmen). In 2001, KAT resurfaced once again with KATASTROPHY WIFE – album 'AMUSIA' – featuring her new husband GLEN/RICH MATTSON. • **Other BIT covers:** WATCHING GIRL (Shonen Knife) / THE GIRL CAN'T HELP IT (Little Richard) / CALLING OCCUPANTS OF INTERPLANETARY CRAFT (Klaatu) / HUBBLE BUBBLE TOIL AND TROUBLE (Manfred Mann).

Album rating: SPANKING MACHINE (*7) / TO MOTHER (*7) / FONTANELLE (*8) / PAINKILLERS (*5) / NEMESISTERS (*6) / LIVED collection (*5) / VILED collection (*5) / Katastrophy Wife: AMUSIA (*5)

KAT BJELLAND (b. KATHERINE, 9 Dec'63, Woodburn, Oregon) – vocals, guitar / **MICHELLE LEON** – bass / **LORI BARBERO** (b.27 Nov'60) – drums, vocals

not iss. Treehouse

Jul 89. (7",7"green) <TR 017> **DUST CAKE BOY. / SPIT TO SEE THE SHINE** [–] [ ]

not iss. Sub Pop

Apr 90. (7",7"gold) <SP 66> **HOUSE. / ARRIBA** [–] [ ]

Twin Tone Twin Tone

Jul 90. (cd/lp/mauve-lp) <TTR 89183-2/-4/-1> **SPANKING MACHINE** [–] [ ]
– Swamp pussy / He's my thing / Vomit heart / Never / Boto (w)rap / Dogg / Pain in my heart / Lashes / You're right / Dust cake boy / Fork down throat. *(re-iss. +c Dec91 on purple-lp)*

Jun 91. (m-cd/m-c/m-lp) <(TTR 89208-2/-4/-1)> **TO MOTHER** [ ] [ ]
– Catatonic / Mad pilot / Primus / Laugh my head off / Spit to see the shine / Pipe / The quiet room.

— (Mar'92) **MAUREEN HERMAN** (b.25 Jul'66, Philadelphia, Pennsylvania) – bass (ex-M+M STIGMATA drummer) repl. MICHELLE whose roadie boyfriend John Cole was killed by a burglar

Strange Fruit Dutch East India

Mar 92. (cd/10"m-lp) *(SFPMCD/SFPMA 211)* <8413> **THE PEEL SESSIONS (live on John Peel show)** [ ] [ ]
– Catatonic / Ripe / Primus / Spit to see the shine / Pearl / Dogg / Laugh my head off / Mad pilot.

Southern Warners

Aug 92. (cd/c/red-lp) *(18501-2/-4/-1)* <2-/4-26998> **FONTANELLE** [24] [ ]
– Bruise violet / Right now / Blue bell / Handsome & Gretel / Blood / Magick flute / Won't tell / The quiet room / Spun / Short song / Jungle train / Pearl / Real eyes / Mother / Gone.

Nov 92. (7"purple) *(18503-7)* **BRUISE VIOLET. / GONE** [ ] [ ]
(12"+=/cd-s+=) *(18503-6/-2)* – Magick flute.

Jun 93. (cd/c/lp) *(18512-2/-4/-1)* <45339> **PAINKILLERS (part live)** [53] [ ]
– He's my thing / Laredo / Istigkeit / Ragweed / Angel hair / Fontanellette (live at CBGB's): Bruise violet – Bluebell – Angel hair – Pearl – Blood – Magick flute – Won't tell – Real eyes – Spun – Mother – Handsome & Gretel.

— KAT married STUART GRAY and sidelined with bands, CRUNT and KATSTU

CRUNT

— **KAT BJELLAND / STUART GRAY** (of LUBRICATED GOAT) + **RUSSELL SIMINIS** (of JON SPENCER BLUES EXPLOSION)

Insipid Insipid

1993. (7") *(IV-31)* **SWINE. / SEXY** [ ] [ ]

Trance Syndicate Trance Syndicate

Mar 94. (lp,blue-lp/cd) <(TR 19/+CD)> **CRUNT** [ ] Feb94 [ ]
– Theme from Crunt / Swine / Black heart / Unglued / Changing my mind / Snap out of it / Sexy / Punishment / Spam / Elephant.

BABES IN TOYLAND

— re-formed (see last line-up)

Reprise Reprise

Apr 95. (cd/c/lp) <(9362 45868-2/-4/-1)> **NEMESISTERS** [ ] [ ]
– Hello / Oh yeah! / Drivin' / Sweet '69 / Surd / 22 / Ariel / Kiler on the road / Middle man / Memory / S.F.W. / All by myself / Deep song / We are family.

May 95. (12"ep/c-ep/cd-ep) *(W 0291 TEX/C/CD)* **SWEET '69 / S.F.W. (live) / SWAMP PUSSY (live)** [ ] [–]

Sep 95. (c-s/cd-s) *(W 0313 C/CD)* **WE ARE FAMILY (Arthur Baker remix) / ('A'-Ben Grosse remix)** [ ] [–]
(12"+=) *(W 0313T)* – (2 other Baker & Grosse mixes).

— In 1998, KAT's alternative/metal supergroup rock opera, Songs Of The Witchblade: A Soundtrack To The Comic Books', was released on CD (Dreamworks; DRMD 50102) featuring her alongside PETER STEELE (Type O Negative), BUZZ OSBORNE (Melvins), JIM THIRLWELL (Foetus), among others.

– compilations, etc. –

Mar 00. (cd) *Almafame; (ALMACD 11)* **LIVED (live)** [ ] [–]
– Dr. Timothy Leary (intro) / He's my thing / Handsome and Gretel / Blue bell / Sweet 69 / Ripe / Mad pilot / Right now / Dogg / Fork down throat / Ya' know that guy / Hubble bubble toil and trouble / Fair is foul and foul is fair / Big top astroanquility (video) / Bruised violet (video) / Memory (video).

May 00. (d-cd) *Snapper; (SMDCD 299)* **NATURAL BABE KILLERS** [ ] [–]

– Bruised violet / Won't tell / Jungle train / We are family / Big top / Magic flute / Memory / Dogg / Fork down throat / Mad pilot / Ripe / Ya know that guy / Spun / Primus / Sweet 69 / Hubble bubble toil and trouble / Fair is foul and foul is fair / Flesh crawl.

Aug 00. (cd) *Almafame; (ALMACD 12)* **DEVIL** [ ] [–]
– Oh yeah! / Spun / Bruised violet / Primus / Fake fur condo / Won't tell / Magick flute / So fucking what / Jungle train / Knife song / Flesh crawl / Intermentstral / We are family / More, more, more (demo) / Calling occupants of interplanetary craft (demo) / Babes In Toyland photo album.

Apr 01. (cd) *Cherry Red; <(CDMRED 181)>* **MINNEAPOLISM: LIVE – THE LAST TOUR** [ ] Apr01 [ ]

Apr 01. (cd) *Almafame; (ALMACD 15)* **VILED** [ ] [–]

Jun 01. (cd) *Fuel 2000; <061125>* **THE FURTHER ADVENTURES OF . . .** [–] [ ]

Nov 01. (cd) *Cherry Red; (CDMRED 199)* **THE BBC JOHN PEEL SESSIONS 1990-92** [ ] [ ]

Nov 01. (3xcd-box) *Dressed To Kill; (MIDRO 783)* **INTERMENSTRAL** [ ] [–]

Jan 02. (cd) *Brilliant; (BT 33084)* **COLLECTOR'S ITEM** [ ] [–]

KATASTROPHY WIFE

BJELLAND + RICH MATTSON – guitar / **MARK MALLMAN** – organ / **KEITH ST. LOUIS** – bass

Almaflame | Yeaah

Aug 01. (cd-s) *(KATWIF 01)* **GONE AWAY / HAPPY PICK-UP TRUCK / GONE AWAY (Fierce Elvis' suicide wedding mix)** [ ] [–]

Mar 02. (cd) *<19>* **AMUSIA** [–] [ ]
– Gone away / Bommerang doll / Git go / Rosacea / Pretty car / Anathema / Knife fight / Haunted / Window / Widdershins.

Integrity | Integrity

Jun 03. (7") *(INT 016V)* **LIBERTY BELLE. / ICE CREAM AND CIGARETTES** [ ] [–]
(cd-s+=) *(INT 016)* – Liberty belle (Bis remix).

BABYBIRD

Formed: Sheffield, England . . . 1988 by Telford born singer STEPHEN JONES. He had been a prolific writer in his bedroom, composing over 400 songs, some of which appeared on five well-received albums between mid-'95 and mid-'96. Each album came with a voting section on which the buyer was asked to write in with their "best of" lists. The top 12 appeared on BABYBIRD's "GREATEST HITS" later in '96, JONES finally coming to prominence that summer as he signed to 'Echo', roped in a full band (JOHN PEDDER, ROBERT GREGORY, LUKE SCOTT and HUW CHADBOURN) and had his first bonafide Top 30 hit with the 'GOODNIGHT' single. BABYBIRD only really took flight with 'YOU'RE GORGEOUS', however, a massive Top 3 hit and a masterstroke of pop genius which managed to weld JONES' wonderfully subversive lyrics to a twinkling, soaring melody and chorus. A simultaneous album, 'UGLY BEAUTIFUL' (1996) made the Top 10, although critics who'd praised his more endearing amateurish early recordings were unsure about this leap into semi-accessible chartbound territory. Nevertheless, a growing army of fans who'd never even heard the other albums (mainly because they were so rare it was impossible to get hold of them!) put a third single, 'CANDY GIRL' into the Top 10. A series of much talked about live appearances emphasized JONES performance-arty background, the singer drawing comparisons with PULP's JARVIS COCKER. Of late, STEPHEN and Co have been back in the public eye, 1998 seeing them hovering around the fringes of the UK Top 30 with a couple of singles and an album, 'THERE'S SOMETHING GOING ON'. Forgetting about all commercial interferences, mainman STEPHEN JONES put his head down to create some of the best work of his career and issued it as 'BUGGED' (2000), a collection of ten dark pop songs ranging from the sinister (and brief charting single) 'THE F-WORD' to the calm and lyrical 'OUT OF SIGHT'. JONES, taking a nod from artists such as MERCURY REV and The FLAMING LIPS, created something that was life-like, abstract and poignant all at once; ballad 'ALL I WANT IS LOVE' fitted this criteria, while 'THE WAY YOU ARE' was a fine example of dedicated songwriting. Something of a diversion, and under his own name, JONES issued his ambient masterpiece, '1985-2001' the following year. Obviously taking a wink at The APHEX TWIN's 'Selected Ambient Works 85-92', the set was such a departure from JONES' normal indie fare, that many critics and fans could not believe it was his own work. The album consisted of three CD's, all featuring breakbeats, clicks, beeps, samples and a whole host of weird sounds – some even went to the lengths of comparing it to AUTECHRE and MATMOS. Further 'TWIN comparisons were made in conjuction with the minimalist piano segues on the album and vocal samples/hooks. All in all, a fantastic break from the norm for somebody who had unfairly been dubbed a 'one hit wonder' in the past. Perhaps it was true in the pop sense, but ultimately STEPHEN JONES had a lot more to offer.

Album rating: I WAS BORN A MAN (*8) / BAD SHAVE (*7) / FATHERHOOD (*6) / THE HAPPIEST MAN ALIVE (*8) / UGLY BEAUTIFUL (*6) / THERE'S SOMETHING GOING ON (*7) / BUGGED (*7) / Stephen Jones: 1985-2001 collection (*8) / ALMOST CURED OF SADNESS (*5)

STEPHEN JONES (b.16 Sep'62) – vocals, guitar – with band; **LUKE SCOTT** (b.25 Aug'69) – guitar / HUW CHADBOURN (b. 7 Dec'63) – keyboards / **JOHN PEDDER** (b.29 May'62) – bass / **ROBERT GREGORY** (b. 2 Jan'67) – drums

Baby Bird | not iss.

Jul 95. (cd) *(BABYBIRD 001)* **I WAS BORN A MAN** [ ] [–]
– Blow it to the Moon / Man's tight vest / Lemonade baby / C.F.C. / Cornershop / Kiss your country / Hong Kong blues / Dead bird sings / Baby bird / Farmer / Invisible tune / Alison / Love love love.

Oct 95. (cd/d-lp) *(BABYBIRD CD/LP 002)* **BAD SHAVE** [ ] [–]
– KW Jesus TV roof appeal / Bad jazz / Too handsome to be homeless / Steam train / Bad shave / Oh my God, you're a king / The restaurant is guilty / Valerie / Shop girl / W.B.T. / Hate song / 45 & fat / Sha na na / Bug in a breeze / It's okay / Happy bus / Swinging from tree to tree.

Dec 95. (cd/d-lp) *(BABYBIRD CD/LP 003)* **FATHERHOOD** [ ] [–]
– No children / Cooling towers / Cool and crazy things to do / Bad blood / Neil Armstrong / I was never here / Saturday / Goodnight / I don't want to wake up with you / Iceberg / Aluminium beach / Goddamn it, you're a kid / Daisies / Failed old singer / Fatherhood / Dustbin liner / Not about a girl / Good weather / But love / May me.

Apr 96. (cd/lp) *(BABYBIRD CD/LP 004)* **THE HAPPIEST MAN ALIVE** [ ] [–]
– Razorblade shower / Sundial in a tunnel / Little white man / Halfway up the hill / Horsesugar / Please don't be famous / Louse / Copper feel / Seagullably / Dead in love / Candy girl / Gunfingers / Married / In the country / Planecrash Xmas / This beautiful disease / You'll get a slap / In the morning.

Echo | Atlantic

Jul 96. (7") *(ECS 024)* **GOODNIGHT. / JULY** [28] [–]
(cd-s+=) *(ECSCD 024)* – Harry and Ida swop teeth.
(cd-s) *(ECSCX 024)* – ('A'side) / Shellfish / Girl with money.

Oct 96. (c-s) *(ECSMC 026)* **YOU'RE GORGEOUS / BEBE LIMONADE** [3] [–]
(cd-s+=) *(ECSCX 026)* – Ooh yeah / Car crash.
(cd-s) *(ECSCD 026)* – ('A'side) / You're gorgeous too / Honk Kong blues / KW Jesus TV roof appeal.

Oct 96. (cd/c/d-lp) *(ECH CD/MC/LP 011) <83049>* **UGLY BEAUTIFUL** [9] 1997 [ ]
– Goodnight / Candy girl / Jesus is my girlfriend / I didn't want to wake you up / Dead bird sings / Atomic soda / You're gorgeous / Bad shave 2 / Cornershop / King Bing / You & me / 45 & fat / Too handsome to be homeless / July / Baby bird. *(cd re-iss. Mar99; same)*

Jan 97. (c-s) *(ECSMC 031)* **CANDY GIRL / FARMER** [14] [–]
(cd-s+=) *(ECSCD 031)* – You're gorgeous (BBC session) / Oh what a beautiful day.
(cd-s) *(ECSCX 031)* – ('A'side) / Bad shave (BBC session) / Cooling towers (BBC session) / Amtrack.

Apr 97. (ltd-7"pic-d) *(ECSPD 033)* **CORNERSHOP. / ALUMINIUM** [ ] [–]

May 97. (c-s) *(ECSMC 033)* **CORNERSHOP / HAPPIEST MAN ALIVE** [37] [ ]
(cd-s) *(ECSCD 033)* – ('A'side) / Death of the neighbourhood II / Shop girl / You're gorgeous (original demo – 1991).
(cd-s) *(ECSCX 033)* – ('A'side) / Death of the neighbourhood I / Pretty little graves / Cornershop (original demo – 1987).

—— now without HUW who left left early in '98

Echo Imprint

Apr 98. (7"pic-d) *(ECS 060)* **BAD OLD MAN. / FUCKLOVE** [31] [–]
(cd-s+=) *(ECSCD 060)* – Hospital bed.
(cd-s) *(ECSCX 060)* – ('A'side) / All I know / Comeback scumbag.

Aug 98. (7"pic-d) *(ECS 065)* **IF YOU'LL BE MINE. / POOLSIDE** [28] [–]
(c-s+=/cd-s+=) *(ECS MC/CD 065)* – Worn.
(cd-s) *(ECSCX 065)* – ('A'side) / Memorise / I want nothing.

Aug 98. (cd/c/lp) *(ECH CD/MC/LP 024)* <111059> **THERE'S SOMETHING GOING ON** [28] [ ]
– Bad old man / If you'll be mine / Back together / I was never here / First man on the sun / You will always love me / The life / All men are evil / Take me back / It's not funny anymore / There's something going on.

Feb 99. (7"clear) *(ECS 073)* **BACK TOGETHER. / IF YOU'LL BE MINE (acoustic)** [22] [–]
(cd-s) *(ECSCD 073)* – ('A'side) / Like before / C.F.C.
(cd-s) *(ECSCX 073)* – ('A'side) / Sunshine / Hate song.

Jul 99. (7") *(MUSE 006)* **DRUNK CAR. / East River Pipe: CYBERCAR** [ ] [–]
(above issued on 'Easy Tiger')

Mar 00. (7") *(ECS 92)* **THE F-WORD. / JUST A LITTLE** [35] [–]
(cd-s+=) *(ECSCD 92)* – ('A'-Steve Osborne mix).
(cd-s) *(ECSCX 92)* – ('A'side) / Beat the boys up / Bad old man (video).

May 00. (7") *(ECS 97)* **OUT OF SIGHT. / IN THE COUNTRY** [58] [–]
(cd-s+=) *(ECSCD 97)* – Love love love.
(cd-s) *(ECSCX 97)* – ('A'side) / 1 4 U / The F-word (video).

Jun 00. (cd/c/lp) *(ECH CD/MC/LP 32)* **BUGGED** [ ] [–]
– The F-word / Getaway / Out of sight / Fireflies / Eyes in the back of my head / Till you die / Wave your hands / All I want / The way you are / One dead groove. *(cd hidden+=)* – The Xmas god of New York.

STEPHEN JONES

Santuary not iss.

Aug 02. (cd) *(SANCD 121)* **ALMOST CURED OF SADNESS** [ ] [–]
– Key to the brain / Under the rainbow / Radio's been thinking again / Good day in a bad world / Friend / Pretty fucking happy / Your time / Little thug / Sitting in my graveyard / Jesus freaks and candy asses / Someplace far away / Quaaludes / Almost cured of sadness. *(hidden track+=)* – I can sing a rainbow.

– (BABYBIRD) compilations, etc. –

Aug 97. (cd) *Baby Bird; <60804>* **GREATEST HITS** [–] [ ]
– Goddamn it, you're a kid / Man's tight vest / KW Jesus TV roof appeal / Bad blood / Kiss your country / Hong Kong blues / Razor blade shower / Sha na na / Aluminium beach / Alison / Grandma begs to be 18 again / I was never here / Petrol cigarette / Losing my hair / Saturday / Invisible tune / Failed old singer / Swinging from tree to tree / Anot about a girl / In the morning.

Dec 97. (cd) *Babybird; (BABYBIRD 005)* **DYING HAPPY** [–] mail-o [–]
– Metal waterpistol / Cheap astronaut / Lead cloud / It's alright dad, isn't it / Grandma begs to be 18 again / The unemployable rub oil on her coffin / TV / Homesick satellites / When everyone speaks English, the world will explode / Petrol cigarette / Tomorrow's gone / Losing my hair.

Sep 00. (cd-ep) *Animal House; (AN!CD 110)* **DOUBLE A EP** [ ] [–]

Oct 01. (d-cd; as STEPHEN JONES) *Easy Tiger; (ETA 002CD)* **1985-2001** [ ] [–]
– Nevercoming home / The rice trail / 0-1-800 Jesus / Sawcuts / Nervous ice in cheap cola / Do you think he was singing it? / The broken 88 / Squeeze the trigger gently / Arthritis kid / Jokeshop bullethole / Tolls on the freeway / Gang cult No.5: the black reindeers / Here we attack / 17 Blue Sun Road, Yellow Hill / 25 watt halo / Baby's coming / Hai / The restaurant is guilty II / Baby Jesus opens his presents / Tealeaves on the rooftiles / Waking up in the coffin / Always bright / Loveable thug / Commercial suicide.

Nov 02. (6xcd-box) *Castle; CMYBOX 560)* **THE LO-FI ALBUMS REMASTERED/BOXED** [ ] [–]
– (I WAS BORN A MAN / BAD SHAVE / FATHERHOOD / THE HAPPIEST MAN ALIVE / GREATEST HITS / UNTITLED)

BACHMAN-TURNER OVERDRIVE

Formed: Winnipeg, Canada . . . 1972 by the BACHMAN brothers, RANDY, ROBBIE and TIM. The former had been part of late 60's rock outfit, GUESS WHO, before releasing a 1970 solo album, 'AXE'. He also formed a short-lived country-rock band, BRAVE BELT, who issued two albums for 'RCA' in the early 70's. Together with FRED TURNER, BACHMAN-TURNER OVERDRIVE signed to 'Mercury' in 1973, making steady inroads onto the US airwaves. By late '74, they had a No.1 US hit with the stuttering hard-rock anthem, 'YOU AIN'T SEEN NOTHING YET'. (In the 90's, its intro featured on Harry Enfield's UK TV show DJ creations, Chas Smash and Nicey Nice). The single formed the centrepiece of the album, 'NOT FRAGILE', which also topped the chart. Being of the Mormon persuasion, the BACHMAN's unfortunately couldn't live the rock'n'roll lifestyle to the hilt, their faith forbidding alcohol, drugs, tea or coffee. Nevertheless, they were adopted by the "blue collar" brigade (actually a title of one of their songs), enjoying a brief run of successful albums in the mid 70's. In 1978, without the departed RANDY, the BACHMAN's abbreviated their moniker to BTO, releasing a few more albums while the former formed the similar sounding IRON HORSE. BACHMAN-TURNER OVERDRIVE were re-united in the mid 80's, with RANDY back at the helm.

Album rating: Brave Belt: BRAVE BELT (*3) / BRAVE BELT II (*3) / Bachman-Turner Overdrive: BACHMAN-TURNER OVERDRIVE (*4) / BACHMAN-TURNER OVERDRIVE II (*5) / NOT FRAGILE (*6) / FOUR WHEEL DRIVE (*6) / THE BEST OF BTO (SO FAR) (*6) / HEAD ON (*4) / THE BEST OF B.T.O. compilation (*6) / FREEWAYS (*3) / STREET ACTION (*2) / ROCK'N'ROLL NIGHTS (*2) / GREATEST HITS compilation (*5)

RANDY BACHMAN

with **DAN TROIANO** – guitar / **GARRY PETERSON** – drums / **WES DAKUS** – steel guitar

not iss. R.C.A.

1970. (lp) *<SP 4348>* **AXE** [–] [ ]
– Zarahemia / Not to return / Pookie's shuffle / Tally's tune / Take the long way home / La Jolla / Tin Lizzie / Suite theam / Noah.

BRAVE BELT

RANDY BACHMAN (b.27 Sep'43) – vocals, guitar (ex-GUESS WHO) / **CHAD ALLAN** – keyboards, vocals (ex-GUESS WHO) / **C.F. (FRED) TURNER** (b.16 Oct'43) – bass, vocals / **ROBBIE BACHMAN** (b.18 Feb'53) – drums, percussion

not iss. Reprise

1971. (7") **ROCK AND ROLL BAND. / ANY DAY MEANS TOMORROW** [–] [ ]

1971. (lp) *<6447>* **BRAVE BELT** [–] [ ]
– Crazy arms, crazy eyes / Lifetime / Waitin' there for me / I am the man / French kin / It's over / Rock and roll band / Wandering fantasy girl / I wouldn't give up my guitar for a woman / Holy train / Anyday means tomorrow / Scarecrow.

1971. (7") *<1039>* **CRAZY ARMS, CRAZY EYES. / HOLY TRAIN** [–] [ ]

1972. (7") *<1061>* **NEVER COMIN' HOME. / CAN YOU FEEL IT** [–] [ ]

1972. (lp) *<2057>* **BRAVE BELT II** [–] [ ]

– Too far away / Dunrobin's gone / Can you feel it / Put it in a song / Summer soldier / Never comin' home / Be a good man / Long way round / Another way out / Waterloo country.

1972. (7") *<1083>* **ANOTHER WAY OUT. / DUNROBIN'S GONE** [–] [ ]

BACHMAN-TURNER OVERDRIVE

TIM BACHMAN – guitar repl. CHAD

Mercury Mercury

Aug 73. (7") *<73383>* **GIMME YOUR MONEY PLEASE. / LITTLE GAWDY DANCER** [–] [ ]

Aug 73. (lp) *(6499 509) <SRMI 673>* **BACHMAN-TURNER OVERDRIVE** [ ] [70]
– Gimme your money please / Hold back the water / Blue collar / Little gandy dancer / Stayed awake all night / Down and out man / Don't get yourself in trouble / Thank you for the feelin'. *(cd-iss. Jan93;)*

Sep 73. (7") *(6052 357)* **STAYED AWAKE ALL NIGHT. / DOWN AND OUT MAN** [ ] [–]

Nov 73. (7") *<73417>* **BLUE COLLAR. / HOLD BACK THE WATER** [–] [68]

Feb 74. (7") *<73457>* **LET IT RIDE. / TRAMP** [–] [23]

Mar 74. (7") *(6052 605)* **LET IT RIDE. / BLUE COLLAR** [ ] [–]

Mar 74. (lp) *(6338 482) <SRMI 693>* **BACHMAN-TURNER OVERDRIVE II** [ ] Jan74 [4]
– Blown / Welcome home / Stonegates / Let it ride / Give it time / Tramp / I don't have to / Takin' care of business.

Aug 74. (7") *(6052 627) <73487>* **TAKIN' CARE OF BUSINESS. / STONEGATES** [ ] May74 [12]

—— **BLAIR THORNTON** (b.23 Jul'50, Vancouver) – guitar repl. TIM who became producer

Oct 74. (7") *(6167 025) <73622>* **YOU AIN'T SEEN NOTHING YET. / FREE WHEELIN'** [2] Sep74 [1]

Oct 74. (lp/c) *(9100 007) <SRMI 1004>* **NOT FRAGILE** [12] Aug74 [1]
– Not fragile / Rock is my life, and this is my song / Roll on down the highway / You ain't seen nothing yet / Free wheelin' / Sledgehammer / Blue moanin' / Second hand / Givin' it all away. *(cd-iss. Mar91; 830178-2)*

Jan 75. (7") *(6167 071) <73656>* **ROLL ON DOWN THE HIGHWAY. / SLEDGEHAMMER** [22] [14]

May 75. (7") *(6167 173) <73683>* **HEY YOU. / FLAT BROKE LOVE** [ ] [21]

Jun 75. (lp/c) *(9100 012) <SRMI 1027>* **FOUR WHEEL DRIVE** [ ] May75 [5]
– Four wheel drive / She's a devil / Hey you / Flat broke love / She's keepin' time / Quick change artist / Lowland fling / Don't let the blues get you down.

Nov 75. (7") *<73724>* **DOWN TO THE LINE. / SHE'S A DEVIL** [–] [43]

Jan 76. (7") *(6167 320)* **AWAY FROM HOME. / DOWN TO THE LINE** [ ] [–]

Feb 76. (lp/c) *(9100 020) <SRMI 1067>* **HEAD ON** [ ] Jan76 [23]
– Find out about love / It's over / Average man / Woncha take me for a while / Wild spirit / Take it like a man / Lookin' out for #1 / Away from home / Stay alive.

Feb 76. (7") *<73766>* **TAKE IT LIKE A MAN. / WONCHA TAKE ME FOR A WHILE** [–] [33]

Apr 76. (7") *<73784>* **LOOKING OUT FOR #1. / FIND OUT ABOUT LOVE** [–] [65]

May 77. (7") *<73903>* **MY WHEELS WON'T TURN. / FREE WAYS** [–] [ ]

May 77. (7") *(6167 520)* **MY WHEELS WON'T TURN. / LIFE STILL GOES ON** [ ] [–]

May 77. (lp/c) *(9100 035) <SRMI 3700>* **FREEWAYS** [ ] Mar77 [70]
– Can we all come together / Life still goes on (I'm lonely) / Shotgun rider / Just for you / My wheels won't turn / Down, down / Easy groove / Freeways.

Sep 77. (7") *<73926>* **SHOTGUN RIDER. / DOWN, DOWN** [–] [ ]

Sep 77. (7") *(6167 567)* **SHOTGUN RIDER. / JUST FOR YOU** [ ] [–]

Dec 77. (7") *<73951>* **LIFE STILL GOES ON. / JUST FOR YOU** [–] [ ]

B.T.O.

—— **JIM CLENCH** – bass, vocals (ex-APRIL WINE) repl. RANDY who went solo

Mar 78. (lp/c) *(9100 051) <SRMI 3713>* **STREET ACTION** [ ] [ ]
– I'm in love / Down the road / Takes a lot of people / A long time for a little while / Street action / For love / Madison Avenue / You're gonna miss me / The world is waiting for a love song.

Mar 78. (7") *<73987>* **DOWN THE ROAD. / A LONG TIME FOR A LITTLE WHILE** [–] [ ]

Mar 79. (7") *<74046>* **HEARTACHES. / HEAVEN TONIGHT** [–] [60]

Mar 79. (7") *(6167 759)* **HEARTACHES. / ROCK'N'ROLL NIGHTS** [ ] [–]

Apr 79. (lp/c) *<SRMI 3748>* **ROCK'N'ROLL NIGHTS (live)** [ ] [ ]
– Jamaica / Heartaches / Heaven tonight / Rock and roll nights / Wastin' time / Here she comes again / End of the line / Rock and roll hell / Amelia Earhart.

Jun 79. (7") *<74062>* **END OF THE LINE (live). / JAMAICA (live)** [–] [ ]

—— Broke-up in 1979

BACHMAN-TURNER OVERDRIVE

Re-united mid-84 with below line-up 1984. **RANDY, TIM, FRED TURNER** and newcomer **GARRY PETERSON** – drums

Compleat Compleat

Sep 84. (7") *(CLT 6) <127>* **FOR THE WEEKEND. / JUST LOOK AT ME NOW** [ ] [ ]

Nov 84. (lp/c) *(CLTLP/ZCCLT 353) <1010>* **BACHMAN-TURNER OVERDRIVE** [ ] Sep84 [ ]
– For the weekend / Just look at me now / My sugaree / City's still growin' / Another fool / Lost in a fantasy / Toledo / Service with a smile.

Jan 85. (7") *<133>* **SERVICE WITH A SMILE. / MY SUGAREE** [–] [ ]

Mar 85. (7") *<137>* **MY SUGAREE. / (part 2)** [–] [ ]

M.C.A. Curb

Aug 86. (lp/c) *(IMCA/+C 5760)* **LIVE!-LIVE!-LIVE! (live)** [ ] [ ]
– Hey you / Mississippi queen / Sledgehammer / Fragile man / Bad news travels fast / You ain't seen nothin' yet / Roll on down the highway / Takin' care of business.

—— RANDY later joined with (ex-TROOPER), FRANK LUDWIG, in UNION. He also became a songwriter for BEACH BOYS, etc.

– compilations, others, etc. –

Mar 75. (lp) *Warners; (K 54036) <MS 2210>* **BACHMAN-TURNER OVERDRIVE AS BRAVE BELT** [ ] [ ]

Sep 76. (7") *Mercury; <73843>* **GIMME YOUR MONEY PLEASE. / FOUR WHEEL DRIVE** [–] [70]

Sep 76. (7") *Mercury; (6167 425)* **TAKIN' CARE OF BUSINESS. / WON'T CHA TAKE ME FOR A WHILE** [ ] [–]

Nov 76. (lp) *Mercury; (9100 026) <SRMI 1101>* **THE BEST OF B.T.O. (SO FAR)** [ ] Aug76 [19]
(cd-iss. Aug98; 558234-2)

1977. (lp) *Mercury;* **JAPAN TOUR (live)** [–] [ ]

Aug 81. (lp)(c) *Mercury; (6430 151)(7420 043)* **GREATEST HITS** [ ] [–]
– Lookin' out for #1 / Hey you / Takin' care of business / You ain't seen nothin' yet / Flat broke love / Rock'n'roll nights / Roll on down the highway / Freeways / Down, down / Let it ride / Can we all come together / Jamaica. *(cd-iss. Jan86; 830039-2)*

Oct 83. (lp/c) *Mercury; (PRICE/PRIMC 46)* **YOU AIN'T SEEN NOTHIN' YET** [ ] [–]

Oct 84. (7") *Mercury; (CUT 109)* **YOU AIN'T SEEN NOTHIN' YET. / ROLL ON DOWN THE HIGHWAY** [ ] [–]

Mar 88. (7") *Old Gold; (OG 9764)* **YOU AIN'T SEEN NOTHIN' YET. / (other track by – Thin Lizzy)** [ ] [–]

Jul 88. (lp/c) *Knight; (KNLP/KNMC 10008)* **NIGHTRIDING** [ ] [–]

Aug 93. (d-cd) *Polygram; (514902-2)* **ANTHOLOGY** [ ] [–]

Aug 94. (cd/c) *Spectrum; (550421-2/-4)* **ROLL ON DOWN THE HIGHWAY** [ ] [–]

Jun 97. (cd) *Go On Deluxe; (1031-2)* **THE VERY BEST OF BACHMAN-TURNER OVERDRIVE** [ ] [–]

Aug 98. (cd) *King Biscuit; (KBFHCD 013)* **KING BISCUIT PRESENTS . . .** [ ] [–]

Apr 00. (m-cd) *Capitol; <24505>* **LIVE** [–] [ ]

Sep 00. (cd) *M.C.A.; <548096>* **THE BEST OF BACHMAN-TURNER OVERDRIVE: THE MILLENNIUM COLLECTION** [–] [ ]

Feb 01. (m-cd) *Madacy; <3530>* **HITS YOU REMEMBER: LIVE** [–] [ ]

Mar 01. (cd) *Spectrum; (544429-2)* **THE COLLECTION** [ ] [–]

RANDY BACHMAN

solo with **BURTON CUMMINGS** – keyboards / **IAN GARDINER** – bass / **JEFF PORCARO** – drums / **TOM SCOTT** – saxophone

Polydor Polydor

Jun 78. (7") *(2066 954)* **JUST A KID. / SURVIVOR**

Jul 78. (lp/c) *(2490 146) <PDI 6141>* **SURVIVOR**
– Just a kid / One hand clappin' / Lost in the shuffle / Is the night too cold for dancin' / You moved me / I am a star / Maybe again / Survivor.

IRONHORSE

was formed by **RANDY** with **TOM SPARKS** – guitar / **JOHN PIERCE** – bass / **MIKE BAIRD** – drums / **BARRY ALLEN** – vocals

Warners Scotti Bros

Mar 79. (7") *(K 11271) <406>* **SWEET LUI-LOUISE. / WATCH ME FLY** 60 36

May 79. (lp/c) *(K 50598) <7103>* **IRONHORSE**
– One and only / Sweet Lui-Louise / Jump back in the light / You gotta let go / Tumbleweed / Stateline blues / Watch me fly / Old fashioned / Dedicated to Slowhand / She's got it / There ain't no clue.

Jul 79. (7") *(K 11319) <408>* **ONE AND ONLY. / SHE'S GOT IT**

— **FRANK LUDWIG** – vocals, keyboards repl. BARRY / **RON FOOS** – bass / **CHRIS LEIGHTON** – drums repl. JOHN + MIKE

Nov 80. (7") *(K 11497) <512>* **WHAT'S YOUR HURRY DARLIN'. / TRY A LITTLE HARDER** Apr80 89

Nov 80. (lp/c) *(K 50730) <7108>* **EVERYTHING IS GREY**
– Everything is grey / What's your hurry darlin' / Symphony / Only way to fly / Try a little harder / I'm hurting inside / Playin' that same old song / Railroad love / Somewhere sometime / Keep your motor running.

BACHMAN

— **RANDY** with various guests incl. NEIL YOUNG + MARGO TIMMINS

Koch Int. Legend

Sep 93. (cd) *(34108-2) <1>* **ANY ROAD** 1997
– Prairie road / Any road / I wanna shelter you / Overworked & underpaid / 15 minutes of fame / Tailspin / Vanishing heroes / One step ahead of the law / It's only money / One night in Texas / Why am I lonely / Prairie town.

RANDY BACHMAN

True North True North

Sep 97. (cd) *<(TNSD 0117)>* **MERGE**
– Born to ride / There ain't nothin' like it / Bad news travels fast / I play the fool for you / Anthem for the young / Please come to Paris / No reason to cry / Can't go back to Memphis / Burnin' up the floor / Made in Canada.

BAD BRAINS

Formed: Washington DC, USA . . . 1978 by Afro-Americans, H.R., his brother EARL, DR. KNOW and DARRYL JENNIFER. Prior to the advent of the punk rock movement in 1976/77, they had all played together in a jazz fusion outfit, carrying over the jazz dynamic to their frenetic, dub-wise hardcore. Subsequently relocating to New York, the late 70's saw the release of two classic 45's, 'PAY TO CUM' and 'BIG TAKEOVER'. These virtually went unnoticed, the band's UK profile remaining low after being refused work permits to support The DAMNED on a British tour. In 1983, they finally delivered their debut album, 'ROCK FOR LIGHT' (produced by RIC OCASEK of The CARS), a set that featured one side of hardcore and the other reggae. For three years, H.R. went solo, returning to the fold for 1986's 'I AGAINST I', a more metallic affair which anticipated the funk-rock explosion of the late 80's. H.R. (with EARL) subsequently departed to realise his more reggae orientated ambitions, releasing several albums for 'S.S.T.'. The remainder of BAD BRAINS parted company with this label, eventually reactivating the band for touring purposes with the addition of CHUCK MOSELEY (ex-FAITH NO MORE). H.R. and EARL returned to the fold for the 'QUICKNESS' album in 1989, remaining for the live set, 'THE YOUTH ARE GETTING RESTLESS'. Once again, H.R. and EARL decided to take off, their replacements being ISRAEL JOSEPH-I and the returning MACKIE. This line-up was in place for their major label debut for 'Epic', 'RISE' (1993), although incredibly yet again H.R. and EARL were invited back as BAD BRAINS were offered a place on MADONNA's 'Maverick' label. The resulting 1995 album, 'GOD OF LOVE' (again produced by OCASEK) focused more on dub reggae stylings, proving that the band were as open to experimentation as ever. However, during the accompanying tour, the athletic H.R. left the band for good in controversial circumstances, fighting with his fellow musicians and eventually being pulled up on a drugs charge (BAD BRAINS right enough!). With 'I & I SURVIVED (DUB)' (2002), meanwhile, the group – perhaps inevitably – cut a full-on dub record with enjoyable if hardly revelatory results. Sounding pretty much as you'd expect in the context of their increasing dabblings in the genre, the record benefitted from a busy brass section while JENIFER turned his hand to melodica. • **Songwriters:** H.R. / DR. KNOW / group, except DAY TRIPPER (Beatles) / SHE'S A RAINBOW (Rolling Stones).

Album rating: BAD BRAINS (*7) / ROCK FOR LIGHT (*8) / I AGAINST I (*8) / LIVE (*5) / QUICKNESS (*4) / RISE (*4) / GOD OF LOVE (*6) / I AND I SURVIVED (DUB) (*5) / BANNED IN D.C. – BAD BRAINS GREATEST RIFFS compilation (*8)

H.R. (b. PAUL HUDSON, 11 Feb'56, London, England) – vocals / **DR. KNOW** (b. GARY WAYNE MILLER, 15 Sep'58, Washington) – guitar, keyboards / **DARRYL AARON JENIFER** (b.22 Oct'60, Washington) – bass, vocals / **EARL HUDSON** (b.17 Dec'57, Alabama) – drums, percussion

not iss. Bad Brains

Jun 80. (7") *<BB 001>* **PAY TO CUM. / STAY CLOSE TO ME** –

Alternative Tentacles Alternative Tentacles

Jun 82. (12"ep) *(VIRUS 13)* **THE BAD BRAINS EP**
– I luv jah / Sailin' on / Big takeover.

R.O.I.R. R.O.I.R.

Dec 82. (c) *(A 106)* **BAD BRAINS**
– Sailin' on / Don't need it / Attitude / The regulator / Banned in D.C. / Jah calling / Supertouch / FVK / Big take over / Pay to cum / Right brigade / I love I jah / Intro / Leaving Babylon. *(cd-iss. Dec89 as 'ATTITUDE – THE ROIR SESSIONS' on 'We Bite' lp/cd; WB 056/+CD) <US re-iss. Nov89 on 'In-Effect'> (re-iss. cd/c/lp 1991 on 'Dutch East Wax'/ re-iss. lp Mar93) (re-iss. cd Apr96; RUDCD 8223) (lp re-iss. Jul98 & Nov99; RUSLP 8223R)*

Food For Thought Important

Mar 83. (12"ep) *(YUMT 101)* **I AND I SURVIVE / DESTROY BABYLON EP**

Abstract P.V.C.

Mar 83. (lp) *(ABT 007) <PVC 8933>* **ROCK FOR LIGHT**
– Coptic times / Attitude / We will not / Sailin' on / Rally around jah throne / Right brigade / F.V.K. (Fearless Vampire Killers) / Riot squad / The meek shall inherit the Earth / Joshua's song / Banned in D.C. / How low can a punk get / Big takeover / I and I survive / Destroy Babylon / Rock for light / At the movies. *(re-mixed re-iss. Feb91 on 'Caroline' cd/c/lp; CAR CD/MC/LP 4) (re-iss. cd Sep91; same) (cd re-iss. Jun97; CAROLCD 1375)*

S.S.T. S.S.T.

Feb 87. (lp/c) *<(SST 065/+C)>* **I AGAINST I** Nov86
– Intro / I against I / House of suffering / Re-ignition / Secret '77 / Let me help / She's calling you / Sacred love / Hired gun / Return to Heaven. *(cd-iss. Feb88 & May93; SST 065CD)*

— **CHUCK MOSELEY** – vocals (ex-FAITH NO MORE) repl. H.R.

— **MACKIE JAYSON** (b.27 May'63, New York City) – drums repl. EARL

Nov 88. (lp/c/cd) *<(SST 160 LP/C/CD)>* **LIVE (live)**
– I cried / At the movies / The regulator / Right brigade / I against I / I and I survive / House of suffering / Re-ignition / Sacred love / She's calling you / Coptic times / F.V.K. (Fearless Vampire Killers) / Secret 77 / Day tripper. *(re-iss. May93; same)*

— both **H.R. + EARL** returned

Caroline Caroline

Jul 89. (lp/c/cd) *<CAR LP/C/CD 4>* **QUICKNESS** ☐ ☐
– Soul craft / Voyage into infinity / The messengers / With the quickness / Gene machine – Don't bother me / Don't blow bubbles / Sheba / Yout' juice / No conditions / Silent tears / The prophet's eye / Endtro. *(re-iss. cd Sep91; same) (cd re-iss. Jun97; CAROLCD 1375)*

S.S.T. S.S.T.

Oct 89. (10"m-lp/m-c/m-cd) *<SST 228>* **SPIRIT ELECTRICITY** – ☐
– Return to Heaven / Let me help / Day tripper / She's a rainbow / Banned in D.C. / Attitude / Youth are getting restless.

— **ISRAEL JOSEPH-I** (b. DEXTER PINTO, 6 Feb'71, Trinidad) – vocals repl. H.R. / **MACKIE** returned EARL

Epic Epic

Sep 93. (cd/c/lp) *<(474265-2/-4/-1)>* **RISE** ☐ ☐
– Rise / Miss Freedom / Unidentified / Love is the answer / Free / Hair / Coming in numbers / Yes jah / Take your time / Peace of mind / Without you / Outro.

— **H.R. + EARL** returned to repl. JOSEPH-I + JAYSON

Maverick Maverick

May 95. (cd/c) *<(9362 45882-2/-4)>* **GOD OF LOVE** ☐ ☐
– Cool mountaineer / Justic keepers / Long time / Rights of a child / God of love / Over the water / Tongue tee tie / Darling I need you / To the heavens / Thank jah / Big fun / How I love thee.

— BAD BRAINS have since split, until . . .

Reggae Lounge Reggae Lounge

Nov 02. (d-lp/cd) *<(RLG 007/+CD)>* **I AND I SURVIVED (DUB)** ☐ ☐
– Jah love / Overdub / How low can a punk get? / I and I survive / Cowboy / Gene machine / Ghetto / Rally / September / Ragga dub / Gene machine (remix) / I and I survive (remix).

– compilations, etc. –

May 90. (cd/lp) *Caroline; (CARCD/LP 8) <CAROL 1617>* **THE YOUTH ARE GETTING RESTLESS (live in Amsterdam 1987)** ☐ ☐
– I / Rock for light / Right brigade / House of suffering / Day tripper – She's a rainbow / Coptic times / Sacred love / Re-ignition / Let me help / The youth are getting restless / Banned in D.C. / Sailin' on / Fearless vampire killer / At the movies / Revolution / Pay to cum / Big takeover. *(cd re-iss. Jun97; CAROLCD 1617)*

May 92. (d-cd) *Line; (LICD 921176)* **ROCK FOR LIGHT / I AGAINST I** – German –

Oct 96. (cd/lp) *Caroline; (PCAROL 005CD/LP) <7534>* **BLACK DOTS** (rec.1979) ☐ ☐
– Don't need it / At the Atlantis / Pay to cum / Supertouch – Shitfit / Regulator / You're a migraine / Don't bother me / Banned in D.C. / Why'd you have to go / Man won't annoy ya / Redbone in the city / Black dots / How low can a punk get / Just another damn song / Attitude / Send you no flowers.

Nov 97. (10"ep/cd-ep) *Victory; <(VR 064/+CD)>* **THE OMEGA SESSIONS** ☐ ☐
– I against you / Stay close to me / I love jah / At the movies / Attitude.

Aug 03. (cd) *Caroline; <(5 83049)>* **BANNED IN D.C. – BAD BRAINS GREATEST RIFFS** ☐ Apr03 ☐
– Pay to cum / I against I / Don't bother me / I / Regulator / F.V.K. (Fearless Vampire Killers) / Re-ignition / Sailin' on / How low can a punk get? / At the movies / With the quickness / Sacred love / Soul craft / Voyage into infinity / Banned in D.C. / Big takeover / Joshua's song / I and I survive / The meek / I luv I jah / The prophet's eye / Riot squad / I against I (dub).

BAD COMPANY

Formed: In late Summer 1973, by the English seasoned-pro foursome of PAUL RODGERS and SIMON KIRKE (both ex-FREE), plus MICK RALPHS and BOZ BURRELL. They got together to form this power-rock supergroup, taking their name from a 1972 Western film starring Jeff Bridges. LED ZEPPELIN manager, PETER GRANT, signed the band to his new 'Swan Song' label in 1974 and they hit the big time almost immediately. No.1 in America, No.3 in the UK, their eponymous debut album set the blueprint; driving music par excellence with RODGERS' heavy, soulful vocals set against a rock solid musical backdrop. These were songs that were built to last, and indeed they have, it's just a pity the cock-rock lyrics haven't aged quite so well. Then again, with such timeless melodic fare as 'CAN'T GET ENOUGH OF YOUR LOVE' and 'BAD COMPANY', maybe the lyrics are beside the point (it was the 70's after all). 'STRAIGHT SHOOTER' (1975) was a bit tougher, yet ultimately more of the same. No bad thing, with the classic 'FEEL LIKE MAKIN' LOVE' on a par with FREE's best efforts. Within such a limited framework, however, there was never much room for experimentation and it was probably inevitable that BAD COMPANY would begin to tread water as they waded through the murky tail end of the 70's. Nevertheless, they continued to sell bucketloads of records and put bums on seats right up until their 1983 parting shot, 'ROUGH DIAMONDS'. While RODGERS went on to solo work, BAD CO. reformed three years later with ex-TED NUGENT frontman, BRIAN HOWE, taking RODGERS' place. Their subsequent releases were lukewarm AOR fodder without the saving grace of the latter's voice, although they sold moderately. Come the 90's, RALPHS was the only remaining member from the original line-up, 'COMPANY OF STRANGERS' in '95 being their last new UK-issued effort to date. • **Songwriters:** RALPHS penned most. In the 90's RALPHS and HOWE individually co-wrote with THOMAS. • **Note:** watch out! a dance act going by the name of BAD COMPANY exists.

Album rating: BAD CO. (*7) / STRAIGHT SHOOTER (*8) / RUN WITH THE PACK (*4) / BURNIN' SKY (*4) / DESOLATION ANGELS (*5) / ROUGH DIAMONDS (*4) / 10 FROM 6 compilation (*7) / FAME AND FORTUNE (*3) / DANGEROUS ACE (*3) / HOLY WATER (*4) / HERE COMES TROUBLE (*3) / THE BEST OF BAD COMPANY LIVE . . . WHAT YOU HEAR IS WHAT YOU GET collection (*5) / COMPANY OF STRANGERS (*4) / STORIES TOLD AND UNTOLD (*4) / THE ORIGINAL BAD CO. ANTHOLOGY compilation (*8) / IN CONCERT – MERCHANTS OF COOL (*5)

PAUL RODGERS (b.12 Dec'49) – vocals, piano (ex-FREE) / **MICK RALPHS** (b.31 Mar'48) – guitar, piano (ex-MOTT THE HOOPLE) / **BOZ BURRELL** (b. RAYMOND BURRELL, 1946) – bass, vocals (ex-KING CRIMSON, ex-SNAFU) / **SIMON KIRKE** (b.28 Jul'49) – drums (ex-FREE)

Island Swan Song

May 74. (7") *(WIP 6191) <70015>* **CAN'T GET ENOUGH. / LITTLE MISS FORTUNE** 15 5

Jun 74. (lp/c) *(ILPS/ICT 9279) <8410>* **BAD CO.** 3 1
– Can't get enough / Rock steady / Ready for love / Don't let me down / Bad company / The way I choose / Movin' on / Seagull. *(cd-iss. Oct94 on 'Atlantic'; 7567 92441-2)*

Jan 75. (7") *<70101>* **MOVIN' ON. / EASY ON MY SOUL** – 19

Mar 75. (7") *(WIP 6223) <70103>* **GOOD LOVIN' GONE BAD. / WHISKEY BOTTLE** 31 36

Apr 75. (lp/c) *(ILPS/ICT 9304) <8413>* **STRAIGHT SHOOTER** 3 3
– Good lovin' gone bad / Feel like makin' love / Weep no more / Shooting star / Deal with the preacher / Wild fire woman / Anna / Call on me. *(cd-iss. Oct88 on 'Swan Song'; SS 8502-2) (cd re-iss. Jul94 on 'Atlantic'; 7567 82637-2)*

Aug 75. (7") *(WIP 6242) <70106>* **FEEL LIKE MAKIN' LOVE. / WILD FIRE WOMEN** 20 Jul75 10

Feb 76. (lp/c) *(ILPS/ICT 9346) <8415>* **RUN WITH THE PACK** 4 5
– Live for the music / Simple man / Honey child / Love me somebody / Run with the pack / Silver, blue & gold / Young blood / Do right by your woman / Sweet lil' sister / Fade away. *(cd-iss. Oct88 on 'Swan Song'; SS 8503-2) (cd re-iss. Jul94 on 'Atlantic'; 7567 92435-2)*

Mar 76. (7") *(WIP 6263)* **RUN WITH THE PACK. / DO RIGHT BY YOUR WOMAN** ☐ –

Mar 76. (7") *<70108>* **YOUNG BLOOD. / DO RIGHT BY YOUR WOMAN** – 20

Jul 76. (7") *<70109>* **HONEY CHILD. / FADE AWAY** – 59

Feb 77. (7") *(WIP 6381)* **EVERYTHING I NEED. / TOO BAD** ☐ ☐

Mar 77. (lp/c) *(ILPS/ICT 9441) <8500>* **BURNIN' SKY** 17 15

– Burnin' sky / Morning Sun / Leaving you / Like water / Everything I need / Heartbeat / Peace of mind / Passing time / Too bad / Man needs a woman / Master of ceremony. *(cd-iss. Oct94 on 'Atlantic'; 7567 92450-2)*

May 77. (7") *<70112>* **BURNIN' SKY. / EVERYTHING I NEED** – 78

Swan Song Swan Song

Mar 79. (7") *(K 19416) <70119>* **ROCK'N'ROLL FANTASY. / CRAZY CIRCLES** 13

Mar 79. (lp/c) *(SS K/4 59408) <8506>* **DESOLATION ANGELS** 10 3
– Rock'n'roll fantasy / Crazy circles / Gone, gone, gone / Evil wind / Early in the morning / Lonely for your love / Oh, Atlanta / Take the time / Rhythm machine / She brings me love. *(cd-iss. Sep94 on 'Atlantic'; 7567 92451-2)*

Jul 79. (7") *<71000>* **GONE, GONE, GONE. / TAKE THE TIME** – 56

Aug 82. (lp/c) *(SS K/4 59419) <90001>* **ROUGH DIAMONDS** 15 26
– Electricland / Untie the knot / Nuthin' on T.V. / Painted face / Kickdown / Ballad of the band / Cross country boy / Old Mexico / Downhill ryder / Racetrack. *(cd-iss. Oct94 on 'Atlantic'; 7567 92452-2)*

Sep 82. (7") *<99966>* **ELECTRICLAND. / UNTIE THE KNOT** – 74

— (mid'83) Disbanded. RODGERS went solo before joining The FIRM. KIRKE played with WILDFIRE. BURRELL sessioned for ROGER CHAPMAN.

— **BAD COMPANY** reformed 1986. **RALPHS, KIRKE, BURRELL** and the incoming **BRIAN HOWE** – vocals (ex-TED NUGENT)

Atlantic Atlantic

Jan 86. (lp/c)(cd) *(WX 31/+C)(781625-2) <81625>* **10 FROM 6** (compilation)
– Can't get enough / Feel like makin' love / Run with the pack / Shooting star / Movin' on / Bad company / Rock'n'roll fantasy / Electricland / Ready for love / Live for the music.

Oct 86. (lp/c)(cd) *(WX 69/+C)(781684-2) <81684>* **FAME AND FORTUNE**
– Burning up / This love / Fame and fortune / That girl / Tell it like it is / Long walk / Hold on my heart / Valerie / When we made love / If I'm sleeping.

Nov 86. (7") *(A 9355) <89355>* **THIS LOVE. / TELL IT LIKE IT IS** Oct86 85
(12"+=) *(TA 9355)* – Burning up / Fame & fortune.

Feb 87. (7") *(A 9296)* **FAME AND FORTUNE. / WHEN WE MADE LOVE** –

Feb 87. (7") *<89299>* **THAT GIRL. / IF I'M SLEEPING** –

Aug 88. (7") *<89035>* **NO SMOKE WITHOUT FIRE. / LOVE ATTACK** –

Aug 88. (lp/c/cd) *(K 781884-1/-4/-2) <81884>* **DANGEROUS AGE** 58
– One night / Shake it up / No smoke without fire / Bad man / Dangerous age / Dirty boy / Rock of America / Something about you / The way it goes / Love attack. *(cd+=)* – Excited.

Apr 89. (7") *<88939>* **SHAKE IT UP. / DANGEROUS AGE** – 82

Mar 90. (7"/c-s) *(A 7954/+MC)* **CAN'T GET ENOUGH. / BAD COMPANY** –
(12"+=/cd-s+=) *(A 7954 T/CD)* – No smoke without fire / Shake it up.

— **GEOFF WHITEHORN** – guitar (ex-BACK STREET CRAWLER) repl. RALPHS / **PAUL CULLEN** – bass repl. BURRELL / added **DAVE COLWELL** – keyboards (ex-ASAP)

Atco Atco

Jul 90. (cd/c/lp) *(<7567 91371-2/-4/-1>)* **HOLY WATER** Jun90 35
– Holy water / Walk through fire / Stranger stranger / If you needed somebody / Fearless / Lay your love on me / Boys cry tough / With you in a heartbeat / I don't care / Never too late / Dead of the night / I can't live without you / 100 miles.

Jul 90. (7") *<98944>* **HOLY WATER. / I CAN'T LIVE WITHOUT YOU** – 89
(12"+=/cd-s+=) – Love attack.

Apr 91. (7") *<98914>* **IF YOU NEEDED SOMEBODY. / DEAD OF THE NIGHT** Nov90 16
(12"+=/cd-s+=) – Love attack.

Jul 91. (c-s,cd-s) *<98748>* **WALK THROUGH FIRE / LAY YOUR LOVE ON ME** – 28

— (May'91) **STEVE WALSH** – vocals (ex-KANSAS) repl. HOWE / **MICK RALPHS** also returned

Sep 92. (c-s,cd-s) *<98509>* **HOW ABOUT THAT / BROKENHEARTED** – 38

Sep 92. (7"/c-s) **HOW ABOUT THAT. / HERE COMES TROUBLE** –
(12") – No smoke without a fire (remix) / Stranger stranger.
(cd-s+=) – No smoke without a fire (remix) / If you needed somebody.

Sep 92. (cd/c/lp) *(<7567 91759-2/-4/-1>)* **HERE COMES TROUBLE** 40
– How about that / Stranger than fiction / Here comes trouble / This could be the one / Both feet in the water / Take this town / What about you / Little angel / Hold on to my heart / Brokenhearted / My only one.

Nov 92. (c-s,cd-s) *<98463>* **THIS COULD BE THE ONE / BOTH FEET IN THE WATER** – 87

— **RICK WILLS** – bass (ex-ROXY MUSIC, ex-FOREIGNER, ex-PETER FRAMPTON) repl. WALSH

Dec 93. (cd/c) *(<7567 92307-2/-4>)* **WHAT YOU HEAR IS WHAT YOU GET (The Best Of Bad Company – live)**
– How about that / Holy water / Rock'n'roll fantasy / If you needed somebody / Here comes trouble / Ready for love / Shooting star / No smoke without a fire / Feel like makin' love / Take this town / Movin' on / Good lovin' gone bad / Fist full of blisters / Can't get enough / Bad company.

— **RALPHS, KIRKE, COLWELL + WILLS** recruited **ROBERT HART** – vox

Jul 95. (cd/c) *(<7559-61808-2/-4>)* **COMPANY OF STRANGERS**
– Company of strangers / Clearwater highway / Judas my brother / Little Martha / Gimme gimme / Where I belong / Down down down / Abandoned and alone / Down and dirty / Pretty woman / You're the only reason / Dance with the Devil / Loving you out loud.

Nov 96. (cd) *(7559 61976-2)* **STORIES TOLD & UNTOLD** (new & old) – German –
– One on one / Oh Atlanta / You're never alone / I still believe in you / Ready for love / Waiting on love / Can't get enough / Is that all there is to love / Love so strong / Silver, blue and gold / Downpour in Cairo / Shooting star / Simple man / Weep no more. *(UK-iss.Jan98; same)*

Mar 99. (d-cd) *<(7559 62391-2)>* **THE ORIGINAL BAD CO. ANTHOLOGY** (compilation)
– Can't get enough / Rock steady / Bad company / Seagull / Superstar woman / Little Miss Fortune / Good lovin' gone bad / Shooting star / Deal with the preacher / Wildfire woman / Easy on my soul / Whiskey bottles / Honey child / Run with the pack / Silver, blue and gold / Do right by your woman / Burnin' sky / Heartbeat / Too bad / Smoking / Rock'n'roll fantasy / Evil wind / Oh Atlanta / Rhythm machine / Untie the knot / Downhill rider / Track down a runaway / Ain't it good / Hammer of love / Hey hey.

— **RODGERS + KIRKE** now with **DAVE COLWELL** – guitar / **JAZ LOCHRIE** – bass

Sanctuary SAnctuary

May 02. (cd) *(SANCD 115) <84549>* **IN CONCERT: MERCHANTS OF COOL (live)**
– Burnin' sky / Can't get enough / Feel like makin' love / Rock steady / Movin' on / Deal with the preacher / Ready for love / Rock'n'roll fantasy – Ticket to ride / All right now / Bad company / Silver, blue and gold / Shooting star / Joe Fabulous / Saving grace.

BADFINGER

Formed: Swansea, South Wales . . . 1964 as The IVEYS by PETER HAM, RON GRIFFITHS, DAVID JENKINS and drummer TERRY GLEASON; the following year MIKE GIBBINS replaced the latter. The IVEYS were a melodic pop group in the vein of The HOLLIES. By the time they'd signed to The BEATLES' fledgling 'Apple' London-based label in 1968, Liverpudlian TOMMY EVANS had joined the group, replacing DAVID JENKINS. After one minor hit 'MAYBE TOMORROW', they ditched the IVEYS moniker in favour of the more late 60's sounding BADFINGER. They scored their first major hit in the first month of the new decade with the PAUL McCARTNEY-penned 'COME AND GET IT'. JOEY MOLLAND then replaced other original RON GRIFFITHS during its chart run, while EVANS switched to bass. The BEATLES comparisons were unavoidable and their next 45, 'NO MATTER WHAT', was as close an approximation of The Fab Four's mid-60's amphetamine kick as you're likely to hear. The BEATLES' connection continued with contributions to the soundtrack for the movie, 'MAGIC

CHRISTIAN MUSIC' and guest appearances on GEORGE HARRISON's 'All Things Must Pass' and JOHN LENNON's 'Imagine'. HARRISON returned the favour by producing 'DAY AFTER DAY', an American Top 5 hit from the 'STRAIGHT UP' album late in '71. The songwriting skills of the HAM-EVANS team were finally recognised in 1972, when NILSSON transformed their 'WITHOUT YOU' into his own tortured No.1 classic. Ironically, the band failed to capitalise on this and their subsequent material was fairly lacklustre. A reputed deal with 'Warner Bros.' for a $3 million advance was struck prior to their last album for 'Apple', 1973's 'ASS'. However, their 'WISH YOU WERE HERE' album in '74 was shifting plenty of units in the States when money in their account went mysteriously missing, the record removed from retail sale soon after. Frustrated by his band's lack of success and MOLLAND's departure, and troubled by personal worries, PETE HAM hanged himself on the 23rd April '75 in his London home. Reeling from this tragedy, the band split, only to be re-formed by EVANS and part-time pipefitter, MOLLAND, in 1978. They even secured a deal with 'Elektra' but again failed to achieve any real success. Incredibly, history repeated itself when, on the 19th of November '83, TOMMY EVANS also hanged himself amid fits of depression and financial troubles. Business problems were sorted out around a year and a half later, too late, of course, to bring back these lost songwriters of the 70's. Fans had to wait a decade and a half for the belated release of long lost album, 'HEAD FIRST' (2000), the record which the band had dutifully recorded – and then had rejected – by Warners after 'WISH YOU WERE HERE' was taken out of circulation back in the mid-70's. While it's difficult to listen to without the weight of attendant events hanging over it, this double disc set (compete with outtakes and demos) proved that BADFINGER were far from a spent force when they recorded it. On the contrary, its musclebound pop was among the best of the day, begging the unavoidable what if.. question. Another greatest hits package was released around the same time, only underlining the band's underrated talent.

Album rating: MAGIC CHRISTIAN MUSIC (*5) / NO DICE (*7) / STRAIGHT UP (*7) / ASS (*5) / BADFINGER (*3) / WISH YOU WERE HERE (*5) / AIRWAVES (*4) / SAY NO MORE (*3) / COME AND GET IT – THE BEST OF . . . compilation (*7) / THE VERY BEST OF . . . compilation (*8) / HEAD FIRST (*7) / Pete Ham: 7 PARK AVENUE (*7)

The IVEYS

PETE HAM (b.27 Apr'47, Swansea, Wales) – guitar, vocals / **TOM EVANS** (b. 5 Jun'47, Liverpool, England) – guitar; repl. DAVID JENKINS / **RON GRIFFITHS** – bass, vocals / **MIKE GIBBINS** (b.12 Mar'49, Swansea) – drums; repl. TERRY GLEASON

Apple Apple

Nov 68. (7") *(APPLE 5)* *<1803>* **MAYBE TOMORROW. / AND HER DADDY'S A MILLIONAIRE** [ ] Jan69 [67]

Jul 69. (lp) *(SAPCOR 8)* **MAYBE TOMORROW** [–] Europe [–]
(UK-iss.Jun92; same) (with free 12"; SAPCOR 82)

Jul 69. (7") *(APPLE 14)* **DEAR ANGIE. / NO ESCAPING YOUR LOVE** [–] Europe [–]

— Also appeared on Various Artists 'Apple' records comp. EP for Walls ice cream, singing 'STORM IN A TEACUP'.

BADFINGER

supplied 3 tracks (*) for THE MAGIC CHRISTIAN film soundtrack released Apr'70.

Dec 69. (7") *(APPLE 20)* *<1815>* **COME AND GET IT. / ROCK OF ALL AGES** [4] Jan70 [7]

— **JOEY MOLLAND** (b.21 Jun'47, Liverpool) – lead guitar (ex-MERSEYS, etc) repl. GRIFFITHS. (EVANS switched to bass guitar)

Jan 70. (lp) *(SAPCOR 12)* *<3364>* **MAGIC CHRISTIAN MUSIC** [ ] Mar70 [55]
– Come and get it / Crimson ship / Dear Angie / Fisherman / Midnight sun / Beautiful and blue / Rock of all ages / Carry on till tomorrow / Fisherman / I'm in love / Walk out in the rain / Knocking down our home / Give it a try / Maybe tomorrow. *(re-iss. Oct91 cd+=/c/d-lp; same)* – Storm in a teacup / Arthur.

Oct 70. (7") *<1822>* **NO MATTER WHAT. / CARRY ON UNTIL TOMORROW** [–] [8]

Dec 70. (7") *(APPLE 31)* **NO MATTER WHAT. / BETTER DAYS** [5] [–]

Dec 70. (lp) *(SAPCOR 16)* *<3367>* **NO DICE** [ ] Nov70 [28]
– I can't take it / I don't mind / Love me do / Midnight caller / No matter what / Without you / Blodwyn / Better days / It had to be / Watford John / Believe me / We're for the dark. *(cd-iss. Jun92+=;)* – Get down / Friends are hard to find / Mean mean Jemima / Loving you / I'll be the one.

Nov 71. (7") *<1841>* **DAY AFTER DAY. / MONEY** [–] [4]

Dec 71. (lp) *(SAPCOR 19)* *<3387>* **STRAIGHT UP** [ ] [31]
– Money / Flying / Suitcase / Sweet Tuesday morning / Perfection / I'd die babe / Take it all / Baby blue / Name of the game / Day after day / Sometimes / It's over. *(cd-iss. Mar93 cd/c/lp; same)* – (original sessions of songs).

Jan 72. (7") *(APPLE 40)* **DAY AFTER DAY. / SWEET TUESDAY MORNING** [10] [–]

Apr 72. (7"; w-drawn UK) *(APPLE 42)* *<1844>* **BABY BLUE. / FLYING** [ ] Mar72 [14]

Mar 74. (7") *(APPLE 49)* **APPLE OF MY EYE. / BLIND OWL** [ ] [ ]

Mar 74. (lp) *(SAPCOR 27)* *<3411>* **ASS** [ ] Dec73 [ ]
– Apple of my eye / Get away icicles / The winner / Blind owl / Constitution / When I say / Cowboy / Timeless / I can love you. *(cd-iss. Feb97; CDSAPCOR 27)*

Warners Warners

Jun 74. (lp) *(K 56023)* *<2762>* **BADFINGER** [ ] Mar74 [ ]
– I miss you / Shine on / Love is easy / Song for a lost friend / Why don't we talk / Island / Matted spam / Where do we go from here? / My heart goes out / Lonely you / Give it up / Andy Norris. *(<cd-iss. Mar00; 7599 26539-2>)*

Jul 74. (7") **I MISS YOU. / SHINE ON** [–] [ ]

Oct 74. (7") *(K 16323)* **LOVE IS EASY. / MY HEART GOES OUT** [ ] [ ]

Oct 74. (lp) *(K 56076)* *<2827>* **WISH YOU WERE HERE** [ ] [ ]
– Just a chance / You're so fine / Got to get out of here / Know one knows / Dennis / In the meantime / Love time / Some other time / King of the load (T) / Meanwhile, back at the ranch – Should I smoke. *(<cd-iss. Mar00; 7599 26540-2>)*

— added **BOB JACKSON** – keyboards (MOLLAND also left to join NATURAL GAS) They split just after PETE HAM commited suicide on 23rd April. EVANS joined DODGERS. Re-formed '76 by **MOLLAND + EVANS** who recruited new members / **KENNY HARCK** – drums / **JOE TANZIN** – guitar / session man **ANDY NEWMARK** – drums repl. HARCK on half of album

Elektra Elektra

Apr 79. (7") *(K 12345)* **LOST INSIDE YOUR LOVE. / COME DOWN HARD** [ ] [ ]

Apr 79. (lp) *(K 52129)* *<6E 175>* **AIRWAVES** [ ] [ ]
– Airwaves / Look out California / Lost inside your love / Love is gonna come at last / Sympathy / The winner / The dreamer / Come down hard / Sail away. *(cd-iss. Mar99 on 'Permanent Press'; 70267 52712-2)*

Jun 79. (7") *(K 12369)* *<46025>* **LOVE IS GONNA COME AT LAST. / SAIL AWAY** [ ] Mar79 [69]

— **MOLLAND + EVANS** brought in **TONY KAYE** – keyboards (ex-YES, ex-BADGER) / **GLENN SHERBA** – guitar / **RICHARD BRYANS** – drums

not iss. Radio-Atlantic

Feb 81. (7") *<3793>* **HOLD ON./ PASSIN' TIME** [–] [56]

Mar 81. (lp) *<16030>* **SAY NO MORE** [–] [ ]
– Hold on / I got you / Come on / Because I love you / Rock'n'roll contract / Passin' time / Three time loser / Too hung up on you / Crocadillo / No more.

May 81. (7") *<3815>* **I GOT YOU. / ROCK'N'ROLL CONTRACT** [–] [ ]

Jul 81. (7") *<3833>* **BECAUSE I LOVE YOU. / TOO HUNG UP ON YOU** [–] [ ]

— They split again in '83. JOEY MOLLAND released solo album AFTER THE PEARL. He later (1992) released cd 'THE PILGRIM' for 'Rykodisc'. TOM EVANS also tragically killed himself 23 Nov'83. MOLLAND and MIKE GIBBINS still tour as BADFINGER in US 60's tour.

— they reformed with **MOLLAND, GIBBINS** plus **RANDY ANDERSON** – guitar / **A.J. NICHOLAS** – bass

not iss. Independent

1988. (lp) **TIMELESS** –

– compilations, others, etc. –

Apr 89. (lp/cd) *Edsel; (ED/+CD 302)* **SHINE ON** –

Nov 90. (cd/c/lp) *Essential; (ESS CD/MC/LP 135)* **DAY AFTER DAY (live)** –
– Sometimes / I don't mind / Blind owl / Give it up / Constitution / Baby blue / Name of the game / Day after day / Timeless / I can't take it.

Jul 92. (cd) *Raven;* **APPLE DAZE** (TOM EVANS interview) –

Sep 93. (cd/c) *Gipsy;* **THE FINAL TRACKS** –

Apr 95. (cd/lp) *Apple; (CD+/SAPCOR 28)* **COME AND GET IT – THE BEST OF BADFINGER** –
– Come and get it / Maybe tomorrow / Rock of all ages / Dear Angie / Carry on till tomorrow / No matter what / Believe me / Midnight caller / Better days / Without you / Take it all / Money / Flying / The name of the game / Suitcase / Day after day / Baby blue / When I say / Icicles / I can love you / Apple of my eye.

Jun 97. (cd) *Strange Fruit; (SFRSCD 031)* **BBC LIVE IN CONCERT (live)** –
(d-lp re-iss. Dec99 on 'Turning Point'; TPM 99201)

Oct 00. (cd) *Apple/Capitol; (<5 26974-2>)* **THE VERY BEST OF BADFINGER** Sep00
– No matter what / Day after day / Baby blue / Name of the game / Maybe tomorrow / Come and get it / Rock of all ages / Carry on till tomorrow / Midnight caller / We're for the dark / I'll be the one / Without you / I'd die babe / It's over / When I say / Dennis / Lonely you / Love time / Meanwhile, back at the ranch – Should I smoke.

Nov 00. (d-cd) *Artisan – Snapper; (<SMADD 829>)* **HEAD FIRST** (shelved LP)
– Lay me down / Hey, Mr. Manager / Keep believing / Passed first / Rock'n'roll contract / Saville Row / Moonshine / Back again / Turn around / Rockin' machine / Time is mine / Smokin' gun / Old fashioned notions / Nothing to show / You ask yourself why / Keep your country tidy / To say goodbye / Queen of darkness / I can't believe in / Thanks to you all / Lay me down. *(re-iss. Sep02; SMDCD 395)*

PETE HAM

— posthumous solo release

Rykodisc Rykodisc

Apr 97. (cd) *<(RCD 10349)>* **7 PARK AVENUE**
– Catherine cares / Coppertone blues / It really doesn't matter / Live love all of your days / Would you deny / Dear father / Matted spam / No matter what / Leaving on a midnight train / Weep baby / Hand in hand / Sille veb / I know that you should / Island / Just look inside the cover / Just how lucky we are / No more / Ringside.

BADLY DRAWN BOY

Formed: Early 1997, as a one-man vehicle for the highly charged but eccentric DAMON GOUGH. The Bolton-born – or at least in a village outside it – first initiated his weird brand of gnome-ish psychedelia when he self-financed (with graphic designer ANDY VOTEL) an EP on his own 'Twisted Nerve' label. 'EP1' (released in September '97) was quickly pursued by the following year's 'EP2', a contract with 'XL Recordings' (home of The PRODIGY) just around the corner. In the Autumn of '98, his third set, the imaginatively titled 'EP3' hit the shops, this BECK-esque trio of tracks finally making the more discerning music punter sit up and listen. Prior to this, GOUGH had contributed the track, 'Nursery Rhyme', to the acclaimed UNKLE album, 'Psyence Fiction'. Minor hits 'ONCE AROUND THE BLOCK' and 'ANOTHER PEARL' preceded a long-awaited debut set, 'THE HOUR OF THE BEWILDERBEAST' (2000), the UK Top 20 entry a mixture of NICK DRAKE's quiet, cello-driven folk and SPRINGSTEEN's poor-man's blues. Three Top 30 singles followed the Mercury Prize-winning album; 'DISILLUSION', 'ONCE AROUND THE BLOCK' and 'PISSING IN THE WIND', with the latter video starring Joan Collins.

Album rating: THE HOUR OF THE BEWILDERBEAST (*8) / ABOUT A BOY soundtrack (*7) / HAVE YOU FED THE FISH? (*5)

DAMON GOUGH – vocals, instruments & things / with various session people

Twisted Nerve not iss.

Sep 97. (7"ep) *(TN 001)* **EP1** –
– Riding with Gabriel Greenburg / Shake the rollercoaster / No point in living / Sugarstealer / No point in living (reprise).

Apr 98. (7"ep) *(TN 002)* **EP2** –
– I love you all / The treeclimber / I love you all (I loop you all Andy Votel mix) / Thinking of you.

Twisted Nerve – X.L. Toy

Oct 98. (7") *(TNXL 001R)* **ROAD MOVIE. / MY FRIEND CUBILAS** –
(10"ep) *(TNXL 001T)* – ('A'side) / Spooky driver / I need a sign / Meet me on the horizon.
(cd-ep) *(TNXL 001CD)* – ('B'side) / Interlude / Kerplunk by candlelight / Meet me on the horizon.

Mar 99. (10"ep) *(TNXL 002T)* **IT CAME FROM THE GROUND / WALKMAN (demo 1) / OUTSIDE A LIGHT (1 & 2) / WALKMAN (demo 2)** –
(cd-ep+=) *(TNXL 002CD)* – ('A'-Andy Votel remix).
(7") *(TNXL 002R)* – (above remix) / Whirlpool.

Aug 99. (7") *(TNXL 003)* **ONCE AROUND THE BLOCK. / SOUL ATTITUDE** 46 –
(cd-s+=) *(TNXL 003CD)* – ('A'-Radio Luxembourg mix).
(7") *(TNXL 003R)* – ('A'-Andy Votel mix) / Another pearl.

Dec 99. (cd) *<1>* **HOW DID I GET HERE?** –
– My friend Cubilas / I need a sign / Interlude / Meet on the horizon / Road movie / Kerplunk by candlelight / It came from the ground / Outside is a light (one) / Soul attitude / Whirlpool / It came from the ground (Andy Votel mix).

Twisted Nerve – X.L. Twisted Nerve – X.L.

Jun 00. (10"/cd-s) *(TNXL 004 T/CD)* **ANOTHER PEARL. / DISTANT TOWN / CHAOS THEORY** 41 –
(cd-s) *(TNXL 004CD2)* – ('A'mixes).

Jun 00. (cd/c/lp) *(TNXL CD/MC/LP 133) <87211>* **THE HOUR OF THE BEWILDERBEAST** 13
– The shining / Everybody's stalking / Bewilder / Fall in a river / Camping next to water / Stone on the water / Another pearl / Body rap / Once around the block / This song / Bewilderbeast / Magic in the air / Cause a rockslide / Pissing in the wind / Blistered heart / Disillusion / Say it again / Epitaph.

Sep 00. (10") *(TNXL 005T)* **DISILLUSION. / WERECKING THE STAGE / DISILLUSION (Mr Scruff mix)** 26 –
(cd-s) *(TNXL 005CD)* – (first 2) / Bottle of tears.
(cd-s) *(TNXL 005CD2)* – ('A'side) / ('A'-Blue States mix) / ('A'-Black lodge mix).

Nov 00. (ltd-10") *(TNXL 008T)* **THE SHINING** – wdrawn –

Nov 00. (7") *(TNXL 009)* **ONCE AROUND THE BLOCK. / TUMBLEWEED / THE SHINING (Avalanches good for the weekend mix)** 27 –
(cd-s+=) *(TNXL 009CD)* – (first & third tracks) / The shining (Capitol K mix).
(cd-s) *(TNXL 009CD2)* – ('A'side) / ('A'-Andy Votel mix) / ('A'-Nick Faber mix).

May 01. (10"/cd-s) *(TNXL 010 T/CD)* **PISSING IN THE WIND. / SPITTING IN THE WIND / THE SHINING (minotaur shock mix)** 22 –
(cd-s) *(TNXL 010CD2)* – ('A'side) / Magic in the air (WDET Detroit mix) / Everybody's stalking (WDET Detroit mix).

Twisted Nerve Artist Direct

Mar 02. (7") *(TNXL 012)* **SILENT SIGH. / DONNA AND BLITZEN (KCRW acoustic session) / PIANO MEDLEY (KCRW acoustic session)** 16 –
(cd-s) *(TNXL 012CD)* – ('A'side) / ('A'-acoustic) / Better way / ('A'-version).
(cd-s) *(TNXL 012CD2)* – ('A'side) / ('A'-Broadway project mix) / ('A'-Zongamin remix).

Apr 02. (cd/lp) *(TNXL CD/LP 152) <1019>* **ABOUT A BOY (soundtrack)** 6
– Exit stage right / A peak you reach / Something to talk about / Dead duck / Above you, below me / I love N.Y.E. / Silent sigh / Wet, wet, wet / River, sea, ocean / S.P.A.T. / Rachel's flat / Walking out of stride / File me away / A minor incident / Delta (little boy blues) / Donna and Blitzen.

Jun 02. (7") *(TNXL 014)* **SOMETHING TO TALK ABOUT. / WALK IN THE PARK WITH ANGIE / HAMSTER COUNTDOWN** [28] [–]
(cd-s) *(TNXL 014CD)* – ('A'-side) / ('A'-Four Tet convention mix) / ('A'-Misty Dixon mix).
(cd-s) *(TNXL 014CD2)* – ('A'side) / Above you below me (electric bedroom version) / My name's not down.

Oct 02. (7") *(TNXL 015)* **YOU WERE RIGHT. / LAST FRUIT** [9] [–]
(cd-s+=) *(TNXL 015CD)* – You were right (live at Glastonbury).

Nov 02. (cd/lp) *(TNXL CD/LP 156)* <1066> **HAVE YOU FED THE FISH?** [10] [ ]
– Coming in to land / Have you fed the fish? / Born again / 40 days, 40 nights / All possibilities / I was wrong / You were right / Centrepeace / How? / The further I slide / Imaginary lines / Using our feet / Tickets to what you need / What is it now? / Bedside story.

Jan 03. (7") *(TNXL 016)* **BORN AGAIN. / THERE'S A STORM** [16] [–]
(cd-s+=) *(TNXL 016CD)* – Golden days.

Apr 03. (7") *(TNXL 017)* **ALL POSSIBILITIES. / WALK AWAY RENEE** [24] [–]
(cd-s) *(TNXL 017CD)* – ('A'side) / Where were you (live) / Let the sunshine (live).

BAD RELIGION

Formed: Los Angeles, California, USA ... 1980 by teenagers, GREG GRAFFIN, BRETT GUREWITZ, JAY BENTLEY and JAY ZISKROUT. To combat disinterest from major labels, the group initiated their own label, 'Epitaph', which has since become a proverbial pillar of the US hardcore/punk fraternity (i.e. OFFSPRING, etc). After one self-titled EP in '81, they unleashed their cheerily-titled debut, 'HOW COULD HELL BE ANY WORSE'. After they withdrew their next album, 'INTO THE UNKNOWN' from sale, BAD RELIGION disappeared for a long spell in the mid 80's. GRAFFIN returned with a new line-up in '87, numbering GREG HETSON, PETE FINESTONE and TIM GALLEGOS. An album, 'SUFFER' was a triumphant comeback effort, defining the new BAD RELIGION sound, a hybrid of melodic punk and machine-gun metal. In 1989, the band consolidated their newfound cult popularity with the follow-up, 'NO CONTROL', although their early 90's output suffered a slight decline. After 'Epitaph' experienced problems with distribution in '93, they signed to 'Columbia', with the result that they cracked the US Top 100 with their album, 'STRANGER THAN FICTION'. Two years later, GUREWITZ having earlier bailed out, they released 'THE GRAY RACE' (produced by RIC OCASEK, ex-CARS), re-establishing them at the forefront of the burgeoning hardcore/metal scene. Following 1997's stop-gap live set, 'TESTED', the band were back with the ironically titled 'NO SUBSTANCE' (1998). If substance is weighed in terms of polemic then BAD RELIGION have it in spades, still railing at American hypocrisy with all guns blazing. However, if substance is weighed in terms of musical innovation then these politico-punks might indeed be found wanting. It took veteran producer TODD RUNDGREN to bring out the latent accessibility within the band's uncompromising grooves, lending his unwaveringly midas touch to 'THE NEW AMERICA' (2000). BAD RELIGION's umpteenth album, the record finally saw them placing their longtime vision in a more musically interesting, melodic framework without losing any of their trademark bite. 2002's 'THE PROCESS OF BELIEF' slipped a little although it did give them their first US Top 50 entry.

Album rating: HOW COULD HELL BE ANY WORSE mini (*5) / INTO THE UNKNOWN (*7) / SUFFER (*7) / NO CONTROL (*8) / AGAINST THE GRAIN (*7) / GENERATOR (*6) / RECIPE FOR HATE (*6) / STRANGER THAN FICTION (*7) / THE GRAY RACE (*6) / ALL AGES compilation (*8) / TESTED (*5) / NO SUBSTANCE (*5) / THE NEW AMERICA (*6) / THE PROCESS OF BELIEF (*5)

GREG GRAFFIN – vocals / **BRETT GUREWITZ** – guitar / **JAY BENTLEY** – bass / **JAY ZISKROUT** – drums

Epitaph Epitaph

Sep 81. (7"ep) <*EP1*> **BAD RELIGION** [–] [ ]
– Bad religion / Politics / Sensory overload / Slaves / Drastic actions / World War III.

— **PETE FINESTONE** – drums; repl. ZISKROUT

Apr 82. (m-lp) <*BRLP 1*> **HOW COULD HELL GET ANY WORSE** [–] [ ]
– We're only gonna die / Latch key kids / Part III / Faith in God / Fuck armageddon . . . this is hell / Pity / In the night / Damned to be free / White trash (2nd generation) / American dream / Eat your dog / Voice of God is government / Oligarchy / Doing time.

— **PAUL DEDONA** – bass + **DAVY GOLDMAN** – drums; repl. JAY + PETE

Dec 83. (lp) <*BR 1*> **INTO THE UNKNOWN** [–] [ ]
– It's only over when . . . / Chasing the wild goose / Billy Gnosis / Time and disregard / The dichotomy / Million days / Losing generation / . . .You give up.

— **GRAFFIN** the sole survivor recruited **GREG HETSON** – guitar / **TIM GALLEGOS** – bass / **PETE FINESTONE** – drums (returned) / GUREWITZ joined CIRCLE JERKS

1984. (7"ep) <*BREP 2*> **BACK TO THE KNOWN** [–] [ ]
– Yesterday / Frogger / Bad religion / Along the way / New leaf.

— **GUREWITZ** + **BENTLEY** rejoined to repl. GALLEGOS

1988. (lp) <*6404-1*> **SUFFER** [–] [ ]
– You are (the government) / 1000 more fools / How much is enough / When? / Give you nothing / Land of competition / Forbidden beat / Best for you / Suffer / Delirium of disorder / Part II (the numbers game) / What can you do? / Do what you want / Part IV (the index fossil) / Pessimistic lines. *(UK-iss.cd/lp Mar91 & Jun93; same)*

1989. (lp) <*6406-1*> **NO CONTROL** [–] [ ]
– Change of ideas / Big bang / No control / Sometimes it feels like *?%+! / Automatic man / I want to conquer the world / Sanity / Henchman / It must look pretty appealing / You / Progress / I want something more / Anxiety / Billy / The world won't stop without you. *(UK-iss.cd/lp Mar91 & Jun93; same)*

Jan 91. (cd/c/lp) <*(6409-2/-4/-1)*> **AGAINST THE GRAIN** [ ] [ ]
– Modern man / Turn on the light / Get off / Blenderhead / Positive aspect of negative thinking / Anesthesia / Flat Earth Society / Faith alone / Entropy / Against the grain / Operation rescue / God song / 21st century digital boy / Misery and famine / Unacceptable / Quality or quantity / Walk away.

Mar 92. (cd/c/lp) <*(6416-2/-4/-1)*> **GENERATOR** [ ] [ ]
– Generator / Too much to ask / No direction / Tomorrow / Two babies in the dark / Heaven is falling / Atomic garden / Answer / Fertile crescent / Chimaera / Only entertainment.

Jun 93. (cd/c/lp) <*(6420-2/-4/-1)*> **RECIPE FOR HATE** [ ] [ ]
– Recipe for hate / Kerosene / American Jesus / Portrait of authority / Man with a mission / All good soldiers / Watch it die / Struck a nerve / My poor friend me / Lookin' in / Don't pray on me / Modern day catastrophists / Skyscraper / Sheath.

— GUREWITZ retired to spend time with his record label 'Epitaph'.

— line-up:- **GRAFFIN / HETSON / BENTLEY / + BRIAN BAKER** – guitar (ex-MINOR THREAT, ex-DAG NASTY) / **BOBBY SCHAYER** – drums

Plastic Head Plastic Head

1993. (7") *(MRR 006)* **NOAM. /** [ ] [–]

not iss. Sympathy F

1990's. (one-sided-7") <*SFTRI 158*> **ATOMIC GARDEN** [–] [ ]
1990's. (7") <*SFTRI 232*> **AMERICAN JESUS. / STEALTH** [–] [ ]
Aug 94. (7") <*SFTRI 326*> **STRANGER THAN FICTION. / MARKOVIAN PROCESS** [–] [ ]

Columbia Atlantic

Sep 94. (cd/c/lp) *(477343-2/-4/-1)* <*82658*> **STRANGER THAN FICTION** [ ] [87]
– Incomplete / Leave mine to me / Stranger than fiction / Tiny voices / The handshake / Better off dead / Infected / Television / Individual / Hooray for me / Slumber / Marked / Inner logic. *(cd re-iss. Jan99; same)*

Jan 95. (10"pic-d-ep) *(661143-0)* **21st CENTURY (DIGITAL BOY) / AMERICAN JESUS (live). / NO CONTROL (live) / WE'RE ONLY GONNA DIE (live)** [41] [ ]
(c-ep/cd-ep) *(661143-8/-2)* – ('A'side) / Leaders and followers (live) / Mediocrity (live) / American Jesus (live).

Mar 96. (cd/c)(grey-lp) *(493524-2/-4)(483652-0)* **THE GRAY RACE**
– The gray race / Them and us / Walk / Parallel / Punk rock songs / Empty causes / Nobody listens / Pity the dead / Spirit shine / Streets of America / Ten in 2010 / Victory / Drunk sincerely come join us / Cease / Punk rock song (German version).

Jun 96. (7") *(6628677-7)* **PUNK ROCK SONG. / CEASE**
(cd-s+=) *(6628677-5)* – Leave mine to me (live) / Change of ideas (live).
(cd-s) *(6628677-2)* – ('A'-German version) / The universal cynic / The dodo.
(above was shelved when they decided to do some more German gigs)

Apr 97. (cd/lp) *(486986-2/-1)* *<82870-2/-1>* **TESTED (live)** 56
– Operation rescue / Punk rock song / Tomorrow / A walk / God song / Pity the dead / One thousand more fool / Drunk sincerity / Generator / Change of ideas / Portrait of authority / What it is / Dream of unity / Sanity / American Jesus / Do what you want / Part III / 10 in 2010 / No direction / Along the way / Recipe for hate / Fuck armageddon / It's reciprocal / Struck a nerve / Leave mine to me / Tested / No control.

May 98. (cd/c) *(489570-2/-4)* *<83094>* **NO SUBSTANCE** 78
– Hear it / Shades of truth / All fantastic images / The biggest killer in American history / No substance / Raise your voice / Sowing the seeds of Utopia / The hippy killers / The state of the end of the millennium / The vocacious march of godliness / Mediocre minds / Victims of the revolution / Strange denial / At the mercy of imbeciles / The same person / In so many ways.

May 00. (cd/c/lp) *<83303>* **THE NEW AMERICA** – 88
– You've got a chance / It's a long way to the promise land / A world without melody / The new America / 1000 memories / A streetcar named Desire / Whisper in time / Believe it / I love my computer / The hopeless housewife / There will be a way / Let it burn / Don't sell me short.

Feb 02. (cd/lp) *<(6635-2/-1)>* **THE PROCESS OF BELIEF** 49
– Supersonic / Prove it / Can't stop it / Broken / Destined for nothing / Materialist / Kyoto now! / Sorrow / Epiphany / Evangeline / The defense / The lie / You don't belong / Bored and extremely dangerous.

– compilations, etc. –

Nov 91. (cd/c) *Epitaph; <(86407-2X/4X)>* **(1980-1985)**
– We're all gonna die / Latch key kids / Part III / Faith in God / F*** armageddon . . . this is Hell / Pitty / Into the night / Damned to be free / White trash (2nd generation) / American dream / Eat your dog / Voice of God is government / Oligarchy / Doing time / Politics / Sensory overload / Slaves / Drastic actions / World War III / Yesterday / Frogger. *(w/ free cd)* – HOW COULD HELL BE ANY WORSE

Nov 95. (cd/c/lp) *Epitaph; <(86443-2/-4/-1)>* **ALL AGES** (1988-1992 + 2 from '94)
– I want to conquer the world / Do what you want / You are (the government) / Modern man / We're only gonna die / Answer / Flat Earth society / Against the grain / Generator / Anesthesia / Suffer / Faith alone / No control / 21st century digital boy / Atomic garden / No direction / Automatic man / Change of ideas / Sanity / Walk away / Best for you / Fuck armageddon . . . this is Hell.

Erykah BADU

Born: ERICA WRIGHT, 26 Feb'72, Memphis, Tennessee, USA. On a diet of Motown/"real-soul" greats STEVIE WONDER and MARVIN GAYE, ERYKAH studied at the Dallas School Of Arts, where she crafted her smooth blend of BILLIE HOLIDAY jazz-soul/hip-hop poetry while crafting her choreography and acting. She performed frequently as ERYKAH FREE prior to working in 1996 with ROOTS D'ANGELO collaborator BOB POWER on her self-penned debut set, 'BADUIZM' (1997). It gained critical then commercial acclaim almost immediately after. Having nearly made the top spot in the States it charted in the UK Top 20, aided by hit singles, 'ON AND ON', 'NEXT LIFETIME' and 'APPLETREE'. Back after a three year maternity absence, the sexiest mother in showbusiness reclaimed her crown as nu-soul's guiding light with the JAY DEE-produced 'MAMA'S GUN' (2000). Firing on all cylinders, the foxy lady called down the spirit of JIMI HENDRIX for 'PENITENTIARY PHILOSOPHY' while rounding up living legends like ROY AYERS to boost her already considerable soul power. 2003's 'WORLDWIDE UNDERGROUND', meanwhile, made little concession to contemporary R&B trends, favouring instead an elongated sequence of easy going, collaborative workouts featuring the likes of QUEEN LATIFAH, ANGIE STONE and BAHAMADIA. Despite its loose production and lengthy songs, the record actually climbed to No.3 in the US chart, BADU's best position since her debut.

Album rating: BADUIZM (*7) / LIVE (*6) / MAMA'S GUN (*6) / WORLDWIDE UNDERGROUND (*5)

ERYKAH BADU – vocals / with **RON CARTER** – bass / etc

Kedar-Universal | Universal

Mar 97. (cd/c) *<UND/UNC 53027>* **BADUIZM** 17 Feb97 2
– Rim shot (intro) / On and on / Appletree / Other side of the game / Sometimes (mix #9) / Afro (freestyle skit) / Certainly / Touch a four leaf clover / No love / Drama / Sometimes / Certainly (flipped it) / Rim shot (outro).

Apr 97. (c-s) *(UNC 56117)* **ON AND ON / ('A'mix)** 12 Jan97 12
(12"+=/cd-s+=) *(UNT/UND 56117)* – ('A'mixes; acappella & instrumental).

Jun 97. (c-s) *(UNC 56132)* **NEXT LIFETIME / ('A'mix)** 30
(12"+=/cd-s+=) *(UNT/UND 56132)* – ('A'mixes; Linslee / live / instrumental).

Nov 97. (c-s) *(UNC 56150)* **APPLETREE / ('A'-hip hop mix)** 47
(12"+=/cd-s+=) *(UNT/UND 56150)* – Other side of the game (live at the Jazz Cafe) / Next lifetime (Linslee remix).
(cd-s+=) *(UNDX 56150)* – ('A'live) / Sometimes (live).

Nov 97. (cd) *<(UND 53109)>* **LIVE (live)** 4
– Rimshot (intro) / Other side of the game / On and on / Reprise / Appletree / Ye yo / Searching / Boogie nights – All night / Certainly / Stay / Next lifetime (interlude) / Tyrone / Next lifetime / Tyrone (extended).

— ERYKAH resurfaced early in '99 augmenting The ROOTS on their hit single, 'You Got Me'.

Kedar – Motown | Kedar – Motown

Aug 99. (c-s/cd-s; as ERYKAH BADU featuring RAHZEL) *<56360>* **SOUTHERN GUL (mixes; radio / album / acappella)** – 76

Aug 00. (cd-s) *<158326>* **BAG LADY / BAG LADY (cheebah sac mix)** – 6

Nov 00. (cd) *<(153259-2)>* **MAMA'S GUN** 11
– Penitentiary philosophy / Didn't cha know / My life / . . .And on / Cleva / Hey sugah (interlude) / Booty / Kiss me on my neck / A.D. 2000 / Orange moon / In love with you / Bag lady / Time's a wastin' / Green eyes. *(re-iss. Mar01 +=; 013938-2)*

Sep 01. (cd-s) *<158754>* **DIDN'T CHA KNOW** –

— in Sep'01, ERYKAH featured on MACY GRAY's Top 30 hit, 'Sweet Baby'

not iss. | M.C.A.

Aug 02. (12") *<113987>* **LOVE OF MY LIFE (AN ODE TO HIP HOP)** – 9

Motown | Motown

Aug 03. (12"; as BADU & COMMON) *<10521-1>* **DANGER (mixes)** – 82

Sep 03. (cd)<lp> *(986087-5)* *<7390-2/-1>* **WORLDWIDE UNDERGROUND** 3
– World keeps turnin' (intro) / Bump it / Back in the day (puff) / I want you / Woo / The grind / Danger / Think twice / Love of my life worldwide / World keeps turnin' (outro).

Joan BAEZ

Born: 9 Jan'41, Staten Island, New York, USA. After a successful 1959 Newport festival appearance, she signed to the 'Vanguard' label in the States. An innovator of protest folk music that leant on early PETE SEEGER, BAEZ was an inspiration to the likes of DYLAN etc. Her defiant protest anthems made her the darling of the intellectual beatnik scene developing in America at the time. Although her early material concentrated on traditional folk fare delivered in a crystal pure vocal style, BAEZ became a figurehead for the protest movement in the mid-60's with her anthemic 'WE SHALL OVERCOME'. On 'JOAN BAEZ 5' (1965), she showcased her move towards interpreting more contemporary artists, covering Phil Och's 'THERE BUT FOR FORTUNE' and Bob Dylan's 'IT AIN'T ME BABE'. As well as becoming a celebrated interpreter of the latter's work, BAEZ and DYLAN became lovers, the King and Queen of folk, as the couple were dubbed (their relationship was well documented in the film, 'Don't Look Back'). The aforementioned album went Top 5 in the UK as did her sixth set 'FAREWELL ANGELINA' (1965), a record featuring a further two DYLAN covers in 'IT'S ALL OVER NOW, BABY BLUE' and 'A HARD RAIN'S A-GONNA FALL'. The same year, BAEZ founded the Institute For The Study Of Nonviolence in California, her increasingly political activism directed mainly against US involvement in the Vietnam war. In 1968, the singer married fellow protest leader DAVID HARRIS, although he was subsequently jailed for resisting the draft. '68 also saw BAEZ's most ambitious album to date, 'BAPTISM – A JOURNEY THROUGH OUR TIME' (1968), wherein she turned her head to spoken word poems etc. The early 70's found the folk veteran covering material by more mainstream artists such as The BEATLES and The BAND, her reading of the latter's 'THE NIGHT THEY DROVE OLD DIXIE DOWN', making the US Top 3. Her commitment to humanitarian protest remained steadfast and indeed, throughout the first half of the 70's, the singer's political activities (she was a high profile opponent of the military coup in Chile) overshadowed her recorded output. With 'DIAMONDS AND RUST' (1975), however, BAEZ emerged as an important figure in the American singer/songwriter movement, the album making the US Top 20 and becoming one of her best loved works. The mid-70's also saw a belated reunion with DYLAN, the pair hooking up in the Rolling Thunder Revue. Autobiographical efforts such as 'GULF WINDS' (1976) and 'BLOWIN' AWAY' (1977) marked the end of BAEZ's career for almost a decade as she found herself without a record label. She nevertheless continued to perform throughout the 80's, playing benefit concerts for Amnesty International and, of course, appearing at Live Aid in 1985. Perhaps inspired by the new wave of young female troubadours (SUZANNE VEGA, TRACY CHAPMAN etc.), BAEZ returned to the recording front in the late 80's/early 90's, the 'PLAY ME BACKWARDS' (1993) set seeing her court an adult MOR audience, while a live set, 'RING THEM BELLS' (1995) featured duets with JANIS IAN, MARY CHAPIN-CARPENTER and MARY BLACK amongst others. Of late, BAEZ has completed a further studio set, 'GONE FROM DANGER' (1997), which didn't see light of day in the UK until a few years later. 'DARK CHORDS ON A BIG GUITAR' (2003) meanwhile, built on the achievements of its predecessor, bravely taking on material by such free musical spirits as STEVE EARLE, JOSH RITTER, RYAN ADAMS, NATALIE MERCHANT and GILLIAN WELCH. Bringing the whole weight and depth of her considerable talent and experience to bear on the likes of Earle's 'CHRISTMAS IN WASHINGTON' and Merchant's 'MOTHERLAND', BAEZ succeeded in infusing them with the kind of crackling emotional charge their original authors had perhaps only partly realised.

• **Songwriters:** She writes her own work interspersed with covers:- (Her debut album contained some Scottish traditional ballads). She recorded a whole lp 'ANY DAY NOW' of DYLAN material) and 'PACK UP YOUR SORROWS' (Richard Farina, her brother-in-law, who was killed in a motorcycle accident, summer '66) / IN THE QUIET MORNING (Mimi Farina, her sister) / LET IT BE (Beatles) / AMSTERDAM (Janis Ian) / STONES IN THE ROAD (Mary-Chapin Carpenter) / STRANGE RIVERS (John Stewart) / STEAL ACROSS THE BORDER (Ron Davies) / THROUGH YOUR HANDS (John Hiatt) / lots more . . .

Album rating: JOAN BAEZ (*8) / JOAN BAEZ 2 (*5) / JOAN BAEZ IN CONCERT (*7) / JOAN BAEZ IN CONCERT PART 2 (*5) / JOAN BAEZ 5 (*6) / FAREWELL ANGELINA (*6) / PORTRAIT (*5) / NOEL (*4) / JOAN (*5) / BAPTISM (*5) / ANY DAY NOW (*5) / DAVID'S ALBUM (*4) / ONE DAY AT A TIME (*5) / BLESSED ARE (*5) / CARRY IT ON (*5) / COME FROM THE SHADOWS (*5) / WHERE ARE YOU NOW, MY SON? (*4) / GRACIAS A LA VIDA (*4) / DIAMONDS AND RUST (*7) / FROM EVERY STAGE (*4) / GULF WINDS (*4) / BLOWING AWAY (*5) / HONEST LULLABY (*4) / LIVE EUROPE 83 (*5) / RECENTLY (*6) / DIAMONDS AND RUST IN THE BULLRING (*3) / SPEAKING OF DREAMS (*5) / PLAY ME BACKWARDS (*5) / RING THEM BELLS (*4) / GONE FROM DANGER (*5) / GREATEST HITS compilation (*7) / DARK CHORDS ON A BIG GUITAR (*6)

JOAN BAEZ – vocals, acoustic guitar

Fontana Vanguard

Nov 60. (lp) *(STFL 6002)* <*VSD 2077*> **JOAN BAEZ** [ ] [ ]
– Silver dagger / East Virginia / Ten thousand miles / House of the rising sun / All my trials / Wildwood flower / Donna Donna / John Riley / Rake and rambling boy / Little Moses / Mary Hamilton / Henry Martin / El preso numero nuevo (the ninth prisoner). *<re-dist.US Apr62 hit No.15> (re-iss. UK Jun65 hit No.9) (re-iss. 1973 on 'Vanguard'; VSD 79073) (cd-iss. Oct88 on 'Start'; VFCD 7101) (cd-iss. Jan94 & Oct95 on 'Vanguard'; VMD 2077) <(cd re-mast.Nov01 +=; VMD 79594)>* – Girl of constant sorrow / I know you rider / John Riley.

Oct 61. (lp) *(STFL 6025)* <*VSD 2097*> **JOAN BAEZ 2** [ ] [13]
– Wagoner's lad / The trees they do grow high / The lily of the west / Silkie / Engine 143 / Once I knew a pretty girl / Lonesome road / Banks of the Ohio / Pal of mine / Barbara Allen / The cherry tree carol / Old blue / Railroad boy / Plaisir d'amour. *(re-iss. 1973 on 'Vanguard'; VSD 79094) (cd-iss. Oct88 on 'Start'; VFCD 7102) (cd-iss. Jan94 & Oct95 on 'Vanguard'; VMD 2097) <(cd re-mast.Nov01 +=; VCD 79595)>* – I once loved a boy / Poor boy / The longest train I ever saw.

Oct 61. (7") <*35012*> **BANKS OF THE OHIO. / OLD BLUE** [–] [ ]

Feb 62. (7") <*35013*> **LONESOME ROAD. / PAL OF MINE** [–] [ ]

Oct 62. (lp) *(STFL 6035)* <*VSD 2122*> **JOAN BAEZ IN CONCERT (live)** [ ] [10]
– Babe, I'm gonna leave you / Geordie / Copper kettle / Kumbaya / What have they done to the rain / Black is the colour of my true love's hair / Danger waters / Gospel ship / The house carpenter / Pretty Boy Floyd / Lady Mary / Ate Amanha / Matty Groves. *(re-iss. 1973 on 'Vanguard'; VSD 79112) (cd-iss. Jan96 on 'Vanguard'; VMD 2122) <(cd re-mast.May02 +=; VMD 79598)>* – Streets of Laredo / My good old man / My Lord what a morning.

Nov 62. (7") <*35018*> **WHAT HAVE THEY DONE TO THE RAIN. / DANGER WATERS** [–] [ ]

Oct 63. (7") <*35023*> **WE SHALL OVERCOME (live). / WHAT HAVE THEY DONE TO THE RAIN (live)** [–] [90]

May 64. (lp) *(STFL 6033)* <*VSD 2123*> **JOAN BAEZ IN CONCERT, PART 2 (live)** [8] Dec63 [7]
– Once I had a sweetheart / Jackaroe / Don't think twice, it's all right / We shall overcome / Portland town / Queen of hearts / Manha de carnaval – Te ador / Long black veil / Fennario / 'Nu bello cardillo / With God on our side / Three fishers / Hush little baby / Battle hymn of the republic. *(re-iss. 1973 on 'Vanguard'; VSD 79113) (cd-iss. Jan96 on 'Vanguard'; VMD 2123) <(cd re-mast.May02 +=; VMD 79240)>* – Rambler gambler / Railroad Bill / Death of Emmett Till / Tomorrow is a long time / When first unto this country a stranger I came.

Jun 64. (7") <*35026*> **WITH GOD ON OUR SIDE. / RAILROAD BILL – DADDY YOU BEEN ON MY MIND (MEDLEY)** [–] [ ]

Nov 64. (7") *(TF 561)* **IT AIN'T ME BABE. / GO 'WAY FROM MY WINDOW** [ ] [–]

Apr 65. (lp) *(STFL 6043)* <*VSD 79160*> **JOAN BAEZ 5** [3] Nov64 [12]
– There but for fortune / Stewball / It ain't me babe / The death of Queen Jane / Villa lobos: Bachianas Brasileias No.5 – aria / Go 'way from my window / I still miss someone / When you hear them cuckoos hollerin' / Birmingham Sunday / So we'll go no more a-rovin' / O'cangaceiro / The unquiet grave. *(re-iss. 1973 on 'Vanguard'; VSD 79160) (cd-iss. Apr97 on 'Vanguard'; VMD 79160) <(cd re-mast.Sep02 on 'Vanguard'+=; VMD 79700)>* – Tramp on the street / Long black veil.

Mar 65. (7") *(TF 564)* **WE SHALL OVERCOME. / DON'T THINK TWICE** [26] [–]

Jun 65. (7") *<35031>* **THERE BUT FOR FORTUNE. / DADDY YOU BEEN ON MY MIND** [–] [50]

Jul 65. (7") *(TF 587)* **THERE BUT FOR FORTUNE. / PLAISIR D'AMOUR** [8] [–]

Aug 65. (7") *(TF 604)* **IT'S ALL OVER NOW, BABY BLUE. / DADDY YOU'VE BEEN ON MY MIND** [22] [–]

Nov 65. (lp) *(STFL 6058)* *<VSD 79200>* **FAREWELL ANGELINA** [5] Oct65 [10]
– Farewell Angelina / Daddy, you been on my mind / It's all over now, baby blue / The ranger's command / Colours / A satisfied mind / The river in the pines / Pauvre Ruteboeuf / Sagt mir wo die blumen sind / A hard rain's a-gonna fall. *(re-iss. 1973 on 'Vanguard'; VSD 23006) (re-iss. Oct88 on 'Start' lp/c/cd; VFLP5/VFTC6/VFCD7 105) (cd-iss. Jan94 & Oct95 on 'Vanguard'; VMD 79200) <(cd re-mast.Sep02 +=; VMD 79701)>* – One too many mornings / Rock, salt and nails / Water is wide.

Dec 65. (7") *(TF 639)* **FAREWELL ANGELINA. / QUEEN OF HEARTS** [35] [–]

Jun 66. (7") *(TF 727)* *<35040>* **PACK UP YOUR SORROWS. / SWALLOW SONG** [50] [ ]

Aug 66. (lp) *(STFL 6082)* *<VSD 79240>* **JOAN** [ ] [38]
– Be not too hard / Eleanor Rigby / Turquoise / La colombe – the dove / Dangling conversation / The lady came from Baltimore / North / Children of darkness / The greenwood side / If you were a carpenter / Annabel Lee / Saigon bride. *(re-iss. 1973 on 'Vanguard'; VSD 23011) (cd-iss. Apr97 on 'Vanguard'; VMD 79240)*

Nov 66. (7") *<35046>* **CANTIQUE DE NOEL. / LITTLE DRUMMER BOY** [–] [ ]

Nov 66. (lp) *(STFL 6082)* *<VSD 79240>* **NOEL** (festive album) [ ] [ ]
– O come, o come Emmanuel / Coventry carol / Good King Wencelas / Little drummer boy / Wonder as I wander, bring a torch Jeanette Isabella / Down in yon forest / Carol of the birds / Angels we have heard on high / Ave Maria / Medley:- Deck the halls – Mary's wandering – Away in a manger – Adieste fidelis / Cantique de noel (O holy night) / What child is this / Silent night. *(re-iss. 1973 on 'Vanguard'; VSD 23018) (re-iss. Oct88 on 'Start' lp/c/cd; VFLP5/VFTC6/VFCD7 107) (cd re-iss. Oct96 on 'Vanguard'; VMD 79230) <(cd re-mast.Nov01 +=; VMD 79596)>* – The first noel / We three kings / Virgin Mary / Good christian men / Burgundian carol / Away in a manger (French version).

Jun 67. (7") *(TF 865)* *<35055>* **BE NOT TOO HARD. / NORTH** [ ] [ ]
Vanguard Vanguard

Aug 68. (lp) *(SVRL 19000)* *<VSD 79275>* **BAPTISM – A JOURNEY THROUGH OUR TIME** [ ] [84]
– Old Welsh song / I saw the vision of armies / Minister of war / Casida of the lament / Of the dark past / London / In Guernica / Who murdered the minutes / Oh, little child / No man is an island / From portrait of the artist as a young man / All the pretty little horses / Childhood III / The magic wood / Poems from the Japanese / Colours / All in green went my love riding / Gacela of the dark death / The parable of the old man and the young / Evil / Epitaph for a poet / Old Welsh song (reprise). *(re-iss. Aug89 on 'Start' lp/c/cd; VFLP5/VFTC6/VFCD7 103) <(cd re-iss. Jun98 on 'Vanguard';* **VMD 79275)>**

—— added many session people **NORMAN PUTTNAM** – bass / **KEN BUTTREY** – drums / **DAVID BRIGGS** – keyboards / **GRADY MARTIN** – dobro / **PETE WADE** – guitar / etc.

Jan 69. (d-lp) *(55-66)* *<VSD 79306-7>* **ANY DAY NOW** [ ] [30]
– Love minus zero – No limit / North country blues / You ain't goin' nowhere / Drifter's escape / I pity the poor immigrant / Tears of rage / Sad eyed lady of the Lowlands / Love is just a four-letter word / I dreamed I saw St. Augustine / The walls of Redwing / Dear landlord / One too many mornings / I shall be released / Boots of Spanish leather / Walkin' down the line / Restless farewell. *(re-iss. Sep89 on 'Start' d-lp/d-c/cd; VSD/CVSD/VCD 79306-7)*

Apr 69. (7") *(VA 2)* *<35088>* **LOVE IS JUST A FOUR-LETTER WORD. / LOVE MINUS ZERO – NO LIMIT** [ ] [86]

Jun 69. (7") *<35092>* **IF I KNEW. / ROCK, SALT AND NAILS** [–] [ ]

Jun 69. (lp) *(SVRL 19050)* *<VSD 79308>* **DAVID'S ALBUM** [ ] [36]
– If I knew / Rock / Salt and nails / Glad bluebird of happiness / Green, green grass of home / Will the circle be unbroken / Tramp on the street / I'm a poor wayfaring stranger / Just a closer walk with thee / Hickory wind / My home's across the blue ridge mountains. *<(cd-iss. Jan94 & Oct98; VMD 79308)>*

Aug 69. (7") *<35098>* **HICKORY WIND. / FOUR DAYS GONE** [–] [ ]

Mar 70. (7") *<35103>* **NO EXPECTATIONS. / ONE DAY AT A TIME** [–] [ ]

Apr 70. (lp) *(VSD 23010)* *<VSD 79310>* **ONE DAY AT A TIME** [ ] Mar70 [80]
– Seven bridges road / David's song / Sweet Sir Galahad / Long black veil / Ghetto / Carry it on / Jolie blonde / Joe Hill / No expectations / Take me back to the sweet sunny south / One day at a time. *(cd-iss. Oct96; VMD 79310)*

Jun 70. (7") *<35106>* **SWEET SIR GALAHAD. / GHETTO** [–] [ ]

Jan 71. (7") *<35114>* **CARRY IT ON. / ROCK SALT & NAILS** [–] [ ]

Sep 71. (7") *<(VRS 35138)>* **THE NIGHT THEY DROVE OLD DIXIE DOWN. / WHEN TIME IS STOLEN** [6] Aug71 [3]

Sep 71. (d-lp) *<(VSD 6570-1)>* **BLESSED ARE** [ ] [11]
– Blessed are . . . / The night they drove old Dixie down / The salt of the Earth / Three horses / Brand new Tennessee waltz / Lost lonely and wretched / Lincoln freed me today / Outside the Nashville limits / San Francisco Mabel Joy / When time is stolen / Heaven help us all / Angeline / Help me make it through the night / Let it be / Put your hand in the hand / Gabriel and me / Milanese waltz / Marie Flore / The hitch-hiker's song / The 23rd of August / Fifteen months. *(d-cd-iss. Jan97; VCD2 6570)*

Nov 71. (7") *<35145>* **LET IT BE. / POOR WAYFARING STRANGER** [–] [49]

Nov 71. (7") *(VAN 1002)* **LET IT BE. / GABRIEL AND ME** [ ] [–]

Dec 71. (lp) *(VSD 519042)* *<VSD 79313>* **CARRY IT ON** (Soundtrack compilation) [ ] [ ]
– Oh, happy day / Carry it on / In forty days / Hickory wind / Last thing on my mind / Life is sacred / Joe Hill / I shall be released / Do right woman, do right man / Love is just another four-letter word / Suzanne / Idols and heroes / We shall overcome. *<(cd-iss. Sep99; VCD 79313)>*

Jan 72. (7") *<35148>* **WILL THE CIRCLE BE UNBROKEN. / JUST A CLOSER WALK WITH THEE** [–] [ ]

Apr 72. (7") *<35158>* **BLESSED ARE. / THE BRAND NEW TENNESSEE WALTZ** [–] [ ]

—— she also issued 2 film s-tracks 'Sacco & Vanzetti' & 'Silent Running'
A&M A&M

Apr 72. (7") *<1334>* **PRISON TRILOGY (BILLY ROSE). / SONG OF BANGLADESH** [–] [ ]

May 72. (lp/c) *(AMLH/CAM 64339)* *<4339>* **COME FROM THE SHADOWS** [ ] [48]
– Prison trilogy (Billy Rose) / Rainbow road / Love song to a stranger / Myths / In the quiet morning / Weary mothers / To Bobby / Song of Bangladesh / A stranger in my place / Tumbleweed / The partisan / Imagine.

Jul 72. (7") *(AMS 7011)* **IN THE QUIET MORNING. / SONG OF BANGLADESH** [ ] [–]

Jul 72. (7") *<1362>* **IN THE QUIET MORNING. / TO BOBBY** [–] [69]

Sep 72. (7") *<1393>* **LOVE SONG TO A STRANGER. / TUMBLEWEED** [–] [ ]

Mar 73. (7") *<1454>* **BEST OF FRIENDS. / MARY CALL** [–] [ ]

Apr 73. (lp/c) *(AMLH/CAM 64390)* *<4390>* **WHERE ARE YOU NOW, MY SON?** [ ] [ ]
– Only Heaven knows / Less than the song / A young gypsy / Mary call / Rider pass by / Best of friends / Windrose / Where are you now, my son? / *(one side was devoted to Vietnam bombing noises).*

—— now with complete new set of session people.

Jun 73. (7") *<1472>* **LESS THAN A SONG. / WINDROSE** [–] [ ]

Jun 73. (7") *(AMS 7072)* **LESS THAN A SONG. / MARY CALL** [ ] [–]

May 74. (lp/c) *(AMLH 63614)* **GRACIAS A LA VIDA (HERE'S TO LIFE)** [ ] [–]
– Gracias a la vida / Ilego contres heridas (Come with three wounds) / La Ilorona (The weeping woman) / El preso numero (Prisoner number nine) / Guantanamera / Te recuerdo Amanda (I remember Amanda) / Dida / Cucurrucucu Paloma / Paso Rio (I pass a river) / El rossinyol (The nightingale) / De colores (In colours) / Las madras cansades (All the weary mothers of the Earth) / No nos moveran (We shall not be moved) / Esquinazo del guerrillo (The guerilla's serenade). *<(cd-iss. Mar03 on 'Universal'; E 393614-2)>*

Jun 74. (7") *<1516>* **GUANTANAMERA. / FOREVER YOUNG** [–] [ ]

May 75. (lp/c) *(AMLH 64527)* *<4527>* **DIAMONDS & RUST** [ ] [11]
– Diamonds and rust / Fountain of sorrow / Never dreamed you'd leave me in summer / Children and all that jazz / Simple twist of fate / Blue sky / Hello in there / Jesse / Winds of the old days / Dida / I dream of Jeannie / Danny boy. *(cd-iss. Feb03 on 'Spectrum'; 393233-2)*

Jun 75. (7") *<1703>* **BLUE SKY. / DIDA** [–] [57]

Jul 75. (7") **NEVER DREAMED YOU'D LEAVE ME IN SUMMER. / LAST SUMMER** [ ] [–]

Oct 75. (7") *(AMS 7200)* *<1737>* **DIAMONDS AND RUST. / WINDS OF THE OLD DAYS** [ ] Sep75 [35]

Jan 76. (7") **CHILDREN AND ALL THAT JAZZ. / NEVER DREAMED YOU'D LEAVE ME IN SUMMER** [–] [ ]

Mar 76. (d-lp) *(AMLH 64704)* <3704> **FROM EVERY STAGE (live)** [ ] Jan76 [34]
– (Ain't gonna let nobody) Turn me around / Blessed are . . . / Suzanne / Love song to a stranger / I shall be released / Blowin' in the wind / Stewball / Natalia / The ballad of Sacco & Vanzetti / Joe Hill / Love is just a four-letter word / Forever young / Diamonds and rust / Boulder to Birmingham / Swing low sweet chariot / Oh, happy day / Please come to Boston / Lily, Rosemary and the jack of hearts / The night they drove old Dixie down / Amazing Grace. *<(d-cd-iss. Jul94 on 'Universal'; E 396506-2)>*

Apr 76. (7") *(AMS 7226)* <1802> **PLEASE COME TO BOSTON. / LOVE SONG TO A STRANGER** [ ] [ ]

Nov 76. (lp/c) *(AMLH/CAM 64603)* <4603> **GULF WINDS** [ ] [62]
– Sweeter for me / Seabirds / Caruso / Still waters at night / Kingdom of childhood / O brother! / Time is passing us by / Stephanie's room / Gulf winds.

Nov 76. (7") <1884> **CARUSO. / TIME IS PASSING US BY** [–] [ ]

Feb 77. (7") <1906> **O BROTHER!. / STILL WATERS AT NIGHT** [–] [ ]

Portrait Portrait

Jul 77. (lp/c) *(PRT/40 82011)* <34697> **BLOWIN' AWAY** [ ] Jun77 [54]
– Sailing / Many a mile to freedom / Miracles / Yellow coat / Time rag / A heartfelt line or two / I'm blowin' away / Luba the baroness / Alter boy and the thief / Cry me a river.

Jul 77. (7") <70006> **I'M BLOWIN' AWAY. / ALTAR BOY AND THE THIEF** [–] [ ]

Jul 77. (7") *(PRT 5442)* **I'M BLOWIN' AWAY. / LUBA THE BARONESS** [ ] [–]

Nov 77. (7") *(PRT 5759)* <70009> **TIME RAG. / MIRACLES** [ ] [ ]

Jul 79. (lp/c) *(PRT/40 83474)* <35766> **HONEST LULLABY** [ ] [ ]
– Let your love flow / No woman, no cry / Light a light / The song at the end of the movie / Before the deluge / Honest lullaby / Michael / For Sasha / For all we know / Free at last. *(cd-iss. Feb97 on 'Columbia'; 473695-2)*

Feb 81. (lp/c) *(PRT/40 84790)* **EUROPEAN TOUR (live)** [ ] [–]
– The boxer / Don't cry for me Argentina / Gracias a la vida / The rose / For Sasha / Diamonds and rust / Soyuz druzyei / Cambodia / Kinder (sind so kleine hande) / Here's to you / Blowin' in the wind.

—— retired for several years, although she toured Europe again in '83

Goldcastle Ccapitol

May 88. (cd/c/lp) *(CD/TC+/VGC 1)* <71304> **RECENTLY** [ ] [ ]
– Brothers in arms / Recently / Asimbonanga / The Moon is a harsh mistress / James and the gang / Let us break bread together (freedom) / MLK / Do right woman, do right man / Biko. *(re-iss. Aug91 on 'Virgin' lp/c; OVED/+C 354) (cd re-iss. Dec03; same)*

Apr 89. (cd/c/lp) *(CD/TC+/VGC 9)* <71321> **DIAMONDS AND RUST IN THE BULLRING (live)** [ ] [ ]
– Diamonds and rust / (Ain't gotta let nobody) Turn me around / No woman, no cry / Famous blue raincoat / Swing low sweet chariot / Let it be / El preso numero nueve / Ilego contres Heridas / Txoria Txoria / Ellas danzan solas (cueca sola) / Gracias a la vida / No nos moveran. *(re-iss. Aug91 on 'Virgin' lp/c; OVED/+C 370)*

Nov 89. (cd/c/lp) *(CD/TC+/VGC 12)* <71324> **SPEAKING OF DREAMS** [ ] [ ]
– China / Warriors of the sun / Carrickfergus / Hand to mouth / Speaking of dreams / El Salvador / Rambler gambler – Whispering bells / Fairfax country / A mi manera. *(re-iss. Aug91 on 'Virgin' lp/c; OVED/+C 371) (cd re-iss. Dec03; same)*

—— now co-wrote with producers **WALLY WILSON** – (also) synthesizers / **KENNY GREENBERG** (also) guitars Other co-writers **KAREN O'CONNOR** or **PAT BUNCH.** Musicians:- **CHAD CROMWELL** – drums / **JERRY DOUGLAS** – various / **MARCOS SUZANO** – percussion / **EDGAR MEYER** – upright bass

Virgin Virgin

Jan 93. (cd/c) *(CD/TC 2705)* <86458> **PLAY ME BACKWARDS** [ ] Nov92 [ ]
– Play me backwards / Amsterdam / Isaac & Abraham / Stones in the road / Steal across the border / I'm with you / I'm with you (reprise) / Strange rivers / Through your hands / The dream song / Edge of glory. *(cd re-iss. Oct96 & Dec03 on 'Virgin-VIP'; CDVIP 164) (cd re-iss. Nov96 on 'Disky'; VI 87484-2)*

—— next feat. duets w/ JANIS IAN, MARY CHAPIN-CARPENTER, MARY BLACK . . .

Grapevine Capitol

Sep 95. (cd/c) *(GRA CD/MC 208)* <34989> **RING THEM BELLS (live)** [ ] [ ]
– Lily of the west / Sweet Sir Galahad / The band played Waltzing Matilda / Willie Moore / Swallow song / Don't make promises / Jesse / Ring the bells / Welcome me / Suzanne / You're ageing well / Pajarillo Barranqueno / Don't think twice it's all right / Diamonds and rust / The night they drove old Dixie down. *(re-iss. May99; same)*

May 99. (cd) *(GRACD 223)* <59357> **GONE FROM DANGER** [ ] Sep97 [ ]
– No mermaid / Reunion hill / Crack in the mirror / February / Fishing / If I wrote you / Lily / Who do you think I am / Mercy bound / Money for floods.

Sep 99. (cd-s) *(CDGPS 269)* **NO MERMAID / FUSHING / DIAMONDS AND RUST (with Mary-Chapin Carpenter)** [ ] [–]

Sanctuary Koch

Sep 03. (cd) *(SANCD 218)* <862-2> **DARK CHORDS ON A BIG GUITAR** [ ] [ ]
– Sleeper / In my time of need / Rosemary Moore / Caleb Meyer / Motherland / Wings / Rexroth's daughter / Elvis Presley blues / King's highway / Christmas in Washington.

– (selective) compilations, etc. –

on 'Vanguard' unless mentioned otherwise

Nov 63. (lp) *Squire;* <33001> **THE BEST OF JOAN BAEZ** (early '59 live Newport) [–] [45]

Jun 69. (lp) *(SVXL 100)* **JOAN BAEZ ON VANGUARD** [15] [–]

Dec 70. (d-lp) *<(VSD 6560-1)>* **THE FIRST 10 YEARS** [41] Nov70 [73]
<(cd-iss. Nov00; VCD 6560)>

Nov 72. (d-lp) *<(VSD 41-42)>* **THE JOAN BAEZ BALLAD BOOK** [ ] [ ]
(re-iss. Aug89 on 'Start' lp/c/cd; VFLP5/VFTC6/VFCD7 108)

Dec 93. (3xcd-box) *Virgin; (TPAK 30)* **THE COMPACT COLLECTION** [ ] [–]
– (RECENTLY / DIAMONDS AND RUST / SPEAKING OF DREAMS)

Apr 94. (3xcd-box) *(VCD 3125)* **RARE, LIVE AND CLASSIC 1958-1989** [ ] [–]

Apr 96. (d-cd) *A&M; (540 500-2)* **DIAMONDS (A JOAN BAEZ ANTHOLOGY)** [ ] [–]

Sep 98. (cd) *<(VCD 79512)>* **BAEZ SINGS DYLAN** [ ] [ ]

Jan 01. (cd) *Universal; (E 497440-2)* **UNIVERSAL MASTERS COLLECTION** [ ] [ ]

Jan 03. (cd) *Ariola; (610586)* **LIVE – EUROPE 1983** [ ] [–]

Mar 03. (cd) *Universal; (AA694 90418-2)* **20TH CENTURY MASTERS** [ ] [ ]

Sep 03. (4xcd-box) *A&M; (9860479)* **THE COMPLETE A&M RECORDINGS** [ ] [ ]

Ginger BAKER

Born: PETER BAKER, 19 Aug'39, Lewisham, London, playing the trumpet as his first instrument. Gaining drumming experience in the late 50's with jazz bands such as ACKER BILK, "GINGER" chose a new style when he joined BLUES INCORPORATED in 1962. Early the following year, he moved on to GRAHAM BOND ORGANISATION, although he subsequently left them mid-'66 to form CREAM with ERIC CLAPTON and JACK BRUCE. The thundering anchor holding down the band's psychedelic blues rock, the self-taught BAKER was also a pioneer of the dreaded drum solo. After their demise late '68, GINGER and ERIC formed BLIND FAITH (with STEVE WINWOOD and RIC GRECH), however, the supergroup split after releasing only one solitary album. Late in 1969, BAKER formed the AIRFORCE ensemble, releasing an eponymous set soon after which hit the UK Top 40 early in 1970. A second solo album followed later that year before he moved to Lagos, Nigeria, to buy land and build a 16-track studio. An album, 'STRATOVARIOUS' appeared in 1972, as well as a live set recorded with African star, FELA RANSOME KUTI. Taking time off to run his studio, he eventually hooked up with the GURVITZ brothers (PAUL and ADRIAN) to form the BAKER GURVITZ ARMY. This outfit released three jazz-rock efforts, one of which, the eponymous 1974 debut, almost made the UK Top 20. Not content with laying the groundwork for the world music boom of the 80's, the ever adventurous BAKER subsequently travelled to Italy where he ran a drum school in a mountain village! The mid-80's saw him tempted back into the musical slipstream, playing on PIL's 'ALBUM' in 1985 and working with leftfield guru, BILL LASWELL on a number of projects. More recently, this veritable grandmaster of rock drummers lent his inspired talents to the criminally underrated retro-rockers, MASTERS OF REALITY, most memorably and amusingly on the track 'T.U.S.A.'. The 90's have also seen BAKER continue to indulge his love of percussive based music, releasing a string of albums under the GINGER BAKER + AFRICAN FORCE moniker. He even found himself back in the Top 10 in the mid-90's, alongside JACK BRUCE and GARY MOORE. Going by the name of BBM, the trio scored with the 'Virgin' album, 'AROUND THE NEXT DREAM'. • **Covered:** SWEET WINE (Staple Singers) / TWELVE GATES OF THE CITY (Graham Bond) / STRAIGHT NO CHASER (Thelonius Monk) etc. • **Trivia:** He married in the mid-90's and took the surname his of wife, becoming GINGER LOUCKS-BAKER in the process.

Album rating: GINGER BAKER'S AIRFORCE (*5) / AIRFORCE II (*4) / STRATAVARIOUS (*4) / FELA RANSOME KUTI AND THE AFRICA '70 WITH GINGER BAKER (*5) / GINGER BAKER AT HIS BEST compilation (*6) / BAKER GURVITZ ARMY (*5) / ELYSIAN ENCOUNTER (*4) / HEARTS ON FIRE (*4) / 11 SIDES OF BAKER (*4) / FROM HUMBLE ORANGES (*4) / HORSES AND TREES (*5) / THE ALBUM (*4) / AFRICAN FORCE (*4) / PALANQUIN'S POLE (*4) / UNSEEN RAIN (*3) / GOING BACK HOME (*5) / FALLING OFF THE ROOF (*5) / COWARD OF THE COUNTY (*5)

GINGER BAKER'S AIRFORCE

with **GRAHAM BOND** – keyboards / **DENNY LAINE** – guitar / **RICK GRECH** – bass / **HAROLD McNAIR** – saxophone / **REMI KABAKA** – percussion / plus guests **STEVE WINWOOD, CHRIS WOOD, PHIL SEAMAN & BUD BEADLE**

Polydor — Atco

Feb 70. (d-lp) *(2662 001)* *<703>* **GINGER BAKER'S AIRFORCE (live)** — 37 — May70 33
– Da da man / Early in the morning / Don't care / Toad / Aiko biaye / Man of constant sorrow / Do what you like / Doin' it.

Mar 70. (7") *(56380)* *<6750>* **MAN OF CONSTANT SORROW. / DOIN' IT** — May70 85

— guests now were mainly African percussionists, vocalists and keyboard players.

Sep 70. (lp) *(2383 029)* *<SD 33-343>* **AIRFORCE II**
– Let me ride / Sweet wine / Do U no hu yor phrenz R? / We free kings / I don't want to go on without you / Toady / Twelve gates of the city.

May 71. (7"; GINGER BAKER'S DRUM CHOIR) *(2058 107)* **ATUNDE (WE ARE HERE). / (part 2)**

1972. (lp) *(2383 133)* *<7015>* **STRATAVARIOUS**
– Ariwo / Something nice / Ju Ju / Blood brothers / 69 coda.

— In 1971, he had moved to Akeja, Nigeria to buy land to build studio. He was augmented by FELA RANSOME KUTI and African musicians SALT.

Regal Zonophone — Signpost

1972. (lp) *(SLRZ 1023)* *<6134>* **FELA RANSOME-KUTI AND THE AFRICA '70 WITH GINGER BAKER LIVE! (live)**
– Let's start / Black man's cry / Ye ye de smell / Egbe mi o.

— BAKER retired for a while early 1973, but returned to form . . .

BAKER GURVITZ ARMY

with **ADRIAN GURVITZ** – guitar / **PAUL GURVITZ** – bass (both ex-GUN)

Vertigo — Janus

Dec 74. (lp) *(9103 201)* *<7015>* **BAKER GURVITZ ARMY** — 22
– Help me / Love is / Memory Lane / Inside of me / I wanna live again / Mad Jack / 4 Phil / Since beginning. *(re-iss. May77 on 'Mountain';)*

Mar 75. (7") *(6078 211)* **HELP ME. / I WANNA LIVE AGAIN**

— added **SNIPS** – vocals (ex-SHARKS) / **PETER LEMER** – keyboards (ex-SEVENTH WAVE)

Mountain — Atco

Aug 75. (7") *(TOP 2)* **SPACE MACHINE. / THE DREAMER**

Sep 75. (lp) *(TOPS 101)* *<123>* **ELYSIAN ENCOUNTER**
– People / The key / Time / The gambler / The dreamer / Remember / The artist / The hustler. *(cd-iss. Sep93 on 'Repertoire';)*

Oct 75. (7") *(TOP 4)* **THE GAMBLER. / TIME**

Nov 75. (7") **NIGHT PEOPLE. / ?** — -

— Trimmed slightly when PETER LEMER departed.

Apr 76. (7") *(TOP 10)* **TRACKS OF MY LIFE. / THE ARTIST**

May 76. (lp) *(TOPS 111)* *<36137>* **HEARTS ON FIRE**
– Hearts on fire / Neon lights / Smiling / Tracks of my life / Flying in and out of stardom / Dancing the night away / My mind is healing / Thirsty for the blues / Night people / Mystery.

Jun 76. (7") *(TOP 15)* **DANCING THE NIGHT AWAY. / NIGHT PEOPLE**

GINGER BAKER & FRIENDS

with loads of session people.

Mountain — Sire

Jan 77. (lp) *(TOPC 5005)* *<7532>* **ELEVEN SIDES OF BAKER**
– Ginger man / Candlestick maker / High life / Don Dorango / Little bird / N'kon kin' n'kon n'kon / Howlin' wolf / Ice cream dragon / Winner / Pampero / Don't stop the carnival.

Jan 77. (7") *(TOP 23)* **DON DORANGO. / CANDLESTICK MAKER** — -

— Retired again to breed ponies, but formed **ENERGY** in 1980 with **JOHN MIZAROLLI** – guitar / **MIKE DAVIS** – guitar / **HENRY THOMAS** – bass. In the early 80's, he joined ATOMIC ROOSTER briefly and HAWKWIND. In 1982, he emigrated to Italy with his 2nd wife where she ran a drama school.

GINGER BAKER & BAND

recorded 1982. **DOUG BROCKIE** – vocals, guitar / **KARL HILL** – bass, vocals

C.D.G. — not iss.

Jun 83. (c/lp) *(30+/INT 20303)* **FROM HUMBLE ORANGES** — - Italy -
– The eleventh hour / Too many apples / It / Under the Sun / On the road to granma's house / The land of Morder / This planet / Sore head in the morning blues / Wasting time / Lament.

— In 1985, he joined PUBLIC IMAGE LTD, recording 'ALBUM' with them. In 1986 with RAVI SHANKER and BILL LASWELL issued 'HORSES AND TREES' on 'Celluloid' lp/c/cd; *CELL/+C/CD 6126)*

Onsala Int — not iss.

Apr 87. (lp) *(ONS 2)* **GINGER BAKER IN CONCERT (live 1982)** — -
– Chemical blues / Perfect nation / Everything I say / Wheelchair dance festival / Lost in space / Where are you?

GINGER BAKER & AFRICAN FORCE

with **AMPOFO** – percussion, vocals / **ANSOU MANA BANGOURA** – perc., vocals / **FRANCIS MENSAH** – percussion / **JC COMMODORE** – percussion, vocals / **KAZDA** – co writers

I.T.M. — not iss.

1989. (lp/cd) *(ITM 0017/1417)* **AFRICAN FORCE** (rec'86) — -
– Brain damage / Sokoto / Ansumania / Aboa / African force. *(cd re-iss. Oct91; same) (cd re-iss. Jun01 on 'Thunderbolt'; CDTB 207)*

Apr 90. (cd/lp) *(ITM 1433/0033)* **PALANQUIN'S POLE** — -
– Go do / Brain damage / Ansumania / Palanquin's pole / Abyssinia-1.2.7. / Ginger's solo / Want come? go! *(cd re-iss. Mar00 on 'Thunderbolt'; CDTB 205)*

Oct 91. (cd; GINGER BAKER, SONNY SHARROCK & PETER BROTZMANN) *(ITM 1435)* **NO MATERIAL** — -

May 92. (cd; GINGER BAKER with COURTNEY PINE) *(ITM 1469)* **THE ALBUM** — -
– Sunshine of your love / Dream battle / Black audience / Nice – jam / Brain damage.

— now with **BILL LASWELL, JAH WOBBLE + NICK SKOPELTIS**

Axiom — not iss.

Feb 92. (cd) *(AXCD 3001)* **MIDDLE PASSAGE** — - German -
– Mektoub / Under black skies / Time be time / Altamont / Basil / South to the dust.

— next with **MIKE DAVIS** – guitar, vocals / **JOHN MIZAROLLI** – guitar / **HENRY THOMAS** – bass / **DAVID LENNOX** – keyboards

		Traditional Line	not iss.
Jun 92.	(cd) *(TL 1320)* **GINGER BAKER'S ENERGY** – Just like you / Lost your love my love / Don't be so serious / Countain on you / Help yourself / Natural thing / Waisting time / Menopause / Feel so blue / Motown / Natural thing.		–

— Having backed old friend JACK BRUCE on early 1994 live album 'CITIES', he became part of their trio BBM, alongside GARY MOORE. Their album 'AROUND THE NEXT DREAM' on 'Virgin' hit UK Top 10.

GINGER BAKER TRIO

— with **CHARLIE HAYDEN** – bass (of ORNETTE COLEMAN band) / **BILL FRISELL** – guitars (of NAKED CITY + POWER TOOLS)

		Atlantic	Atlantic
Dec 94.	(cd/c) *(<7567 82652-2/-4>)* **GOING BACK HOME** – Rambler / I Lu Kron / Straight, no chaser / Ramblin' / Ginger blues / Ain't emouchant / When we go / In the moment / Spiritual / East Timor.		
Dec 95.	(cd) *<7567 82900-2>* **FALLING OFF THE ROOF** – Falling off the roof / Amarillo, Barbados / Bemsha swing / Sunday at the hillcrest / Au Privave / Our Spanish love song / C.B.C. mimps / Skeleton / Vino vecchio / The day the sun come out / Taney County.	–	
Apr 99.	(cd; as GINGER BAKER and the DJQ2O with special guest JAMES CARTER) *(<7567 83168-2>)* **COWARD OF THE COUNTY** – Cyril Davies / Ginger Spice / Dangle the carrot / Megan showers / Jesus loves me / Coward of the county / Daylight / Jesus, I just want to go to sleep.		

– compilations, etc. –

1973.	(d-lp) *Polydor; (2659 023) / Atco; <3504>* **GINGER BAKER AT HIS BEST** *(re-iss. Feb76; same)*		
Jan 93.	(cd; by BAKER GURVITZ ARMY) *Traditional Line; (TL 1311)* **LIVE IN LONDON 1975 (live)**		–
Dec 99.	(cd; as GINGER BAKER & FELA KUTI) *Masterplan; (MP 42003)* **AFRICA**		–

Afrika BAMBAATAA

Born: KEVIN DONOVAN, 10 Apr'60, South Bronx, New York, USA. A former Black Spades gang member also known as KHAYAN AASIN, BAMBAATAA combined his street knowledge with a forward looking musical vision to create the Zulu Nation at the height of hip hop's 70's gestation period. A fraternal organisation designed to nurture the talents of young black rappers, DJ's and MC's, this collective promoted peace and racial harmony in an attempt to progress from the violence that characterised NY's gang life. BAMBAATAA was well qualified to head up such an ambitious project, his consummate DJ'ing skills and knowledge of popular music unsurpassed in his native city. Alongside contemporaries like GRANDMASTER FLASH, GRAND WIZARD THEODORE and KOOL HERC, the resourceful turntable maestro cut and pasted beats from a famously diverse array of source material including English punk groups like The CLASH and The SEX PISTOLS. Given this pivotal influence, then, the man's debut vinyl release arrived relatively late in the day, a 1980 double whammy of 'JAZZY SENSATION' and 'ZULU NATION THROWDOWN', two 12"ers cut by The JAZZY 5 and SOUL SONIC FORCE respectively, both crews under the aegis of the Zulu Nation and with BAMBAATAA as their driving creative force. It wasn't until the release of 1982's 'PLANET ROCK', however, that the name of AFRIKA BAMBAATAA became internationally synonymous with the cutting edge. In line with the developing hip hop trend, live backing musicians were dropped; in their place was a jaw-dropping synthesis of drum machine beats and pulsing electronica courtesy of KRAFTWERK's 'Trans Europe Express'. The record, only a minor hit at the time, remains one of the most pivotal releases of the last 20 years, providing a blueprint for the electro movement and the subsequent explosion of acid house, techno etc., through the pioneering work of producers Arthur Baker and John Robie. Inevitably perhaps, BAMBAATAA never really recovered from its seismic impact, coming close but never bettering it with a string of fine singles including the blistering follow-up SOUL SONIC FORCE single, 'LOOKING FOR THE PERFECT BEAT', and a couple of classic 1985 singles recorded under the TIME ZONE moniker, 'THE WILDSTYLE' and 'WORLD DESTRUCTION'. While the former utilised squelching synths, clipped depth-charge beats and samples of film dialogue to impressive effect, the latter was a link-up with ex-SEX PISTOL, JOHN LYDON in a cultural collision echoed years later with the LEFTFIELD/LYDON classic, 'Open Up'. Another collaboration, this time with fellow heavyweight, JAMES BROWN, failed to deliver, musically at least, on its promise of 'UNITY' in 1984. Album wise, BAMBAATAA released 'BEWARE (THE FUNK IS EVERYWHERE)' in 1986, as well as working with MATERIAL mainman, BILL LASWELL (who also contributed to the TIME ZONE releases) on the SHANGO project, a more straightforward soul/funk affair. With the emergence of sharp shooting young guns like PUBLIC ENEMY and LL COOL J, BAMBAATAA's profile dipped in the late 80's/early 90's and arguably, cheesy, Italian-produced house was hardly the best medium to win back lost street cred. Nevertheless, the big man from the Bronx remains a towering influence on undeground dance and hip hop, his occasional DJ'ing appearances received as something akin to the holy grail among the faithful. A mark of the man's respect among the dance cognoscenti was the 1992 release of 'DON'T STOP', a 'PLANET ROCK' remix project undertaken by the collective effort of electronic dons such as LFO, 808 STATE and ex-KRAFTWERK man, KARL BARTOS. BAMBAATAA's 90's reformation of the TIME ZONE wasn't quite so well received, a handful of singles and an album, 'WARLOCKS AND WITCHES, COMPUTER CHIPS, MICROCHIPS' (1996) released to relatively minimal interest.

Album rating: BEWARE (THE FUNK IS EVERYWHERE) (*6) / the PLANET ROCK various artists (*7) / THE LIGHT (*5) / THE DECADE OF DARKNESS 1990-2000 (*5) / WARLOCKS AND WITCHES, COMPUTER CHIPS, MICROCHIPS AND YOU (*4) / ZULU GROOVE (*5) / ELECTRO FUNK BREAKDOWN (*5)

AFRIKA BAMBAATAA and the SOUL SONIC FORCE

AFRIKA BAMBAATAA – DJ / with rappers, M.C. G.L.O.B.E. (JOHN B. MILLER), MR. BIGGS (ELLIS WILLIAMS) and POW WOW (ROBERT ALLEN) with D.J. JAZZY JAY

		Polydor	Tommy Boy
Aug 82.	(12") *(POSPX 497) <823>* **PLANET ROCK. / ('A'instrumental)** *(re-iss. Aug98 on 'Afrowax' 12"/cd-s; 12AWX/CDSAWX 1)*+ remix. *(re-iss. Feb99 on 'Tommy Boy'; TBV 341) (re-iss. Oct99 on 'Hot Classics'; HCL 2293)*	53	Jun82 48
Feb 83.	(7") *(POSP 561)* **LOOKING FOR THE PERFECT BEAT. / BONUS BEATS** (12"+=) *(POSPX 561)* – Bonus beats II / ('A'instrumental).		
		Tommy Boy	Tommy Boy
Feb 84.	(7") *(AFR 1)* **RENEGADES OF FUNK. / ('A'mix)**	30	
Aug 84.	(7"/ext-12"; AFRIKA BAMBAATAA & JAMES BROWN) *(AFR/+X 2)* **UNITY (PART 1 – THE THIRD COMING). / BECAUSE IT'S COMING**	49	
Oct 84.	(12") *(AFRX 3)* **FRANTIC SITUATION. / ('A'mix)**		

— in Jan'85, BAMBAATAA and JOHN LYDON (of PiL) featured on a second TIME ZONE (aka NICKY SKOPELITES and BILL LASWELL) single, 'WORLD DESTRUCTION', which hit the UK Top 50.

AFRIKA BAMBAATAA

WEA WEA

Aug 86. (12") *(U 8663T)* **BAMBAAATAA'S THEME (ASSAULT ON PRECINCT 13). / TENSION** ☐ ☐

Oct 86. (lp/c) *(253092-1/-4)* **BEWARE (THE FUNK IS EVERYWHERE)** ☐ ☐
– Funk jam party / Funk you / Bionic kats / What time is it? / Beware (the funk is everywhere) / Bambaataa's theme / Tension / Rock America / Kick out the jams.

AFRIKA BAMBAATAA & THE FAMILY

E.M.I. E.M.I.

Feb 88. (7") *(EM 41)* **RECKLESS. / MIND BODY AND SOUL** 17 –
(12"+=) *(12EM 41)* – ('A'-vocal Wildstyle mix).
(cd-s+=) *(CDEM 41)* – Recklessly (Soca chant zouk mix).
(12"+=) *(12EMXS 41)* – ('A'-Fon Force remix).
(above single featured UB40)

Mar 88. (cd/c/lp) *(CD/TC+/EMC 3545)* <C2-90157> **THE LIGHT** ☐ ☐
– The light / Reckless / Radical music, revolutionary dance / Something he can feel / Clean up your act / Zouk your body / World racial war / Shout it out / Sho nuff funky / All I want.

May 88. (7") *(EM 57)* **SHO NUFF FUNKY. / TELL ME WHEN YOU NEED IT AGAIN (vocal mix 1)** ☐ –
(12"+=) *(12EM 57)* – Tell me when you need it again (mix 2).
(12"+=) *(12EMX 57)* – Tell me when you need it again (mix 3).
(12"+=) *(12EMXS 57)* – ('A'-Funkin' all night mix).

Manhattan Manhattan

Oct 91. (7") *(MT 100)* **JUST GET UP AND DANCE. / ('A'mix)** 45 –

Oct 91. (cd/c) *(CD/TC MTL 1062)* <9777> **THE DECADE OF DARKNESS (1990-2000)** (compilation) ☐ ☐

AFRIKA BAMBAATAA PRESENTS TIME ZONE

Profile Profile

Apr 93. (12"/cd-s) *(PROF T/CD 389)* **TIME ZONE. / ('A'mixes)** ☐ ☐

Mar 94. (12"ep/cd-ep) *(PROF 409/+CD)* **WHAT'S THE NAME E.P.** ☐ ☐
– What's the name of this nation? Zulu! / Hold on, I'm coming / Ghost.

Nov 95. (12"/cd-s) *(PROF T/CD 442)* **THROW YOUR FUNKY HANDS UP. / ('A'mixes)** ☐ ☐

Feb 96. (cd)(c/d-lp) *(FILECD 464)(PRO 1464-4/-1)* **WARLOCKS AND WITCHES, COMPUTER CHIPS, MICROCHIPS AND YOU** ☐ ☐

ZYX ZYX

Aug 97. (cd-s) *(ZYX 86948)* **MIND CONTROL (mixes)** ☐ ☐

Hudson Vandam Celluloid

Dec 97. (cd) *(HVD 5103)* **ZULU GROOVE** ☐ Nov97 ☐
– World destruction / Shango message / Wild style / Zulu groove / Than you / Let's party down / Soca fever / World destruction.
(above was originally issued for 'Celluloid')

— In Jun'99, AFRIKA BAMBAATAA was credited on the WESTBAM single for 'Mute', AGHARTA – THE CITY OF SHAMBALLA'.

Dust It! Dust It!

Aug 99. (12"/cd-s) *(SPEC 130/+CD)* **ELECTRO FUNK EXPRESS (mixes)** ☐ ☐

Areeba Areeba

Sep 99. (12"; as AFRIKA BAMBAATAA & THE SOUL SONIC FORCE) *(ARET 004)* **WHO'S IN THE HOUSE (mixes; Doppelganger vocal / Scope Funktastic vocal / Doppelganger dub)** ☐ ☐

ZYX ZYX

Oct 99. (12") *(ZYX 91038)* **YOU ASK FOR THE MOON (mixes)** ☐ –
(above with KHAYAN & THe NEW WORLD POWER)

Jungle Sky Jungle Sky

Nov 99. (2x12"ep; Vs DJ SOULSLINGER) *(JSK 160)* **FIRE (remixes)** ☐ ☐

— in Aug'01, BAMBAATAA teamed up with PAUL OAKENFOLD to produce a UK Top 50 hit of 'PLANET ROCK'

– compilations, etc. –

Jul 87. (lp/c) *Blatant; (BLAT LP/MC 2)* **DEATH MIX THROWDOWN** ☐ –

Mar 88. (12") *E.M.I.; (12BAM 1)* **SHOUT IT OUT. / SHO NUFF FUNKY** ☐ –

Jul 91. (lp/cd) *Music Of Life; (SPOCK 3/+CD)* **HIP HOP FUNK DANCE CLASSICS VOL.1** ☐ ☐

Sep 92. (lp/cd; AFRIKA BAMBAATAA & THE UNIVERSAL ZULU NATION) *Music Of Life; (SPOCK 4/+CD)* **HIP HOP FUNK DANCE CLASSICS VOL.2** ☐ ☐

Jun 93. (cd/lp) *Music Of Life; (MOL CD/LP 30)* **HIP HOP FUNK DANCE CLASSICS VOL.3** ☐ ☐

Mar 99. (cd) *Tommy Boy; <(TBCD 1052)>* **DON'T STOP . . . PLANET ROCK** ☐ ☐

Mar 01. (cd; Various Artists) *D.M.C.; <85504>* **ELECTRO FUNK BREAKDOWN** – ☐

Apr 01. (d-lp/cd) *Tommy Boy; <(TB/+CD 1457)>* **LOOKING FOR THE PERFECT BEAT 1980-1985** ☐ ☐

BAND

Formed: 1967, by expatriate Canadians ROBBIE ROBERTSON, RICK DANKO, RICHARD MANUEL, LEVON HELM and GARTH HUDSON. Having previously backed up rockabilly singer RONNIE HAWKINS, the group recorded under the name The CANADIAN SQUIRES and later LEVON AND THE HAWKS. As The HAWKS, the group also backed BOB DYLAN on his 1965-66 world tour, HELM having fallen out with DYLAN at an earlier gig, the infamous Forest Hills concert where the folk messiah has "gone electric" much to the chagrin of his more purist fans. Following DYLAN's 1966 motorcycle accident and subsequent seclusion at Woodstock, the group also relocated to the area, HELM rejoining them. They then began work on a series of laid back, informal sessions with DYLAN which would later see the light of day as 'THE BASEMENT TAPES', released by DYLAN's label, 'Columbia', in 1975. A seminal set of experimental proto-country rock, the legendary recording sessions from which the album resulted saw The BAND developing their distinctive instrumental, vocal and songwriting dexterity which would mark out 'MUSIC FROM BIG PINK' (1968) as one of the pivotal debut releases of the decade. Named after the group's communal Woodstock home, it stood alongside 'Sweetheart Of The Rodeo' and 'John Wesley Harding' as a quietly confident display of back to basics musical integrity and an antidote to the psychedelic excesses of the previous year. The record highlighted the vocal diversity of HELM, DANKO and MANUEL both individually and collectively whether covering DYLAN material ('TEARS OF RAGE', 'I SHALL BE RELEASED') or tackling the compelling ROBERTSON / MANUEL penned originals. From the former's prudent guitar playing to the eclecticism of HUDSON's organ runs, the musicianship was flawless and while songs like 'THE WEIGHT' were deceptively simple, they possessed an air of strange grace. If this album introduced The BAND as major contenders, then their eponymous follow-up assured them of a place in rock history. A veritable distillation of classic American musical tradition, 'THE BAND' (1969) put rock into a bit of much needed perspective, its rich beauty a reminder of why people set words to song in the first place. Vivid narratives like 'THE NIGHT THEY DROVE OLD DIXIE DOWN' and 'KING HARVEST (HAS SURELY COME)' resonated as deeply as any Steinbeck novel yet no one could accuse ROBERTSON of misty eyed nostalgia; the characters and their attendant burdens that inhabit these songs were genuine, holding up a mirror to the struggles of modern society. By 'STAGE FRIGHT' (1970), ROBERTSON's songwriting prowess was becoming a little blunted. Much of the material centered around his on-the-road experiences and while the likes of 'THE SHAPE I'M IN' and the title track were enjoyable enough, there was nothing to match the depths of its predecessor. 'CAHOOTS' (1971) was even more bereft of fresh ideas, a VAN MORRISON collaboration, '4% PANTOMINE', one of the record's few saving graces. 'ROCK OF AGES' (1972) was a competent, if pointless, double live effort, embellished with horns courtesy of the ubiquitous ALLEN TOUSSAINT while 'MOONDOG MATINEE' (1973) was an even more inessential collection of rock'n'roll covers. 'NORTHERN LIGHTS – SOUTHERN CROSS' (1975) saw the verve (small V!) returning to ROBERTSON's songwriting while HUDSON's keyboard work came into its own. By the following year, however, they'd decided enough was enough, playing their farewell concert at San Francisco's Winterland ballroom on Thanksgiving Day. The event was recorded for posterity as 'THE LAST WALTZ', a triple album set that also served as a soundtrack for the rockumentary of the same name. With an all-star cast including the likes of NEIL YOUNG and JONI MITCHELL, the record was a spirited, poignant farewell to a group that had helped define an era. After a final album to fulfil contractual obligations, the rank 'ISLANDS' (1977), the various members went off to do their own thing and that should've been the end of it. Inevitably it wasn't, and while an initial comeback album attempt was dealt a severe blow when RICHARD MANUEL took his own life in 1986, The BAND did reform the following decade (minus ROBERTSON who knocked back an invitation to join). Without two of their mainstays, the group were always going to find it difficult and indeed, both their albums, 'JERICHO' (1994) and 'HIGH ON THE HOG' (1996) consisted largely of well below par cover material. 1998's 'JUBILATION' was a more worthwhile proposition, a solid, earthy set of largely self-penned songs which included a cover of Allen Toussaint's 'YOU SEE ME' and featured guest appearances from both ERIC CLAPTON and JOHN HIATT. Sadly, just over a year later, RICK DANKO was found dead in his New York home on the 10th of December, 1999. • **Covered:** WHEN I PAINT MY MASTERPIECE + FOREVER YOUNG + I MUST LOVE YOU TOO MUCH (Bob Dylan) / DON'T DO IT (Holland-Dozier-Holland) / LONG BLACK VEIL (Wilkin-Dill) / MYSTERY TRAIN (Elvis Presley) / THE GREAT PRETENDER (Platters) / SHE KNOWS (Procol Harum) / CRAZY MAMA (JJ Cale) / FREE YOUR MIND (D.Foster / T.McElroy) / WHERE SHOULD I ALWAYS BE (Bill Chaplin) / BACK TO MEMPHIS / STAND UP (B.Channel / R.Rector) / etc.

Album rating: MUSIC FROM BIG PINK (*8) / THE BAND (*10) / STAGE FRIGHT (*7) / CAHOOTS (*5) / ROCK OF AGES (*7) / MOONDOG MATINEE (*5) / NORTHERN LIGHTS – SOUTHERN CROSS (*6) / ISLANDS (*4) / THE LAST WALTZ with various artists (*7) / THE BEST OF THE BAND – ANTHOLOGY compilation (*7) / TO KINGDOM COME – THE DEFINITIVE COLLECTION compilation (*7) / JERICHO (*5) / LIVE AT WATKINS' GLEN live '73 (*6) / HIGH ON THE HOG (*2) / ACROSS THE GREAT DIVIDE boxed-set (*6) / JUBILATION (*5)

ROBBIE ROBERTSON (b. 4 Jul'44, Toronto, Canada) – guitar, vocals / **RICHARD MANUEL** (b. 3 Apr'45, Stratford, Canada) – piano, vocals, drums, sax / **RICK DANKO** (b. 9 Dec'43, Simcoe, Canada) – vocals, bass, violin, trombone / **GARTH HUDSON** (b. 2 Aug'37, London, Canada) – organ, saxophone, accordion / **LEVON HELM** (b.26 May'42, Marvel, AR) – drums, vocvals, mandolin, guitar

not iss. | Apex

1964. (7"; as CANADIAN SQUIRES) **UH-UH-UH. / LEAVE ME ALONE** [–] [ ]
<re-iss. 1965 on 'Ware'; >

Atlantic | Atco

Nov 65. (7"; as LEVON AND THE HAWKS) *(4054)* <6383> **THE STONES I THROW. / HE DON'T LOVE YOU AND HE'LL BREAK YOUR HEART** [ ] Mar65 [ ]

1968. (7"; as LEVON AND THE HAWKS) *<6625>* **GO GO LISA JANE. / HE DON'T LOVE YOU AND HE'LL BREAK YOUR HEART** [–] [ ]

Capitol | Capitol

Aug 68. (lp; stereo/mono) *(S+/ST <2955>)* **MUSIC FROM BIG PINK** [ ] [30]
– Tears of rage / To kingdom come / In a station / Caledonian mission / The weight / We can talk / Long black veil / Chest fever / Lonesome Suzie / This wheel's on fire / I shall be released. *(re-iss. Jun81 on 'Greenlight' lp/c; GO/TC-GO 2001) (cd-iss. May87; CDP 746 069-2) (lp re-iss. Apr99 on 'E.M.I.'; 499465-2) <(cd re-mast.Sep00 on 'E.M.I.'+=; 5 25390-2)>* – Yazoo street scandal / Tears of rage (alt.) / Katie's been gone / If I lose / Long distance operator / Lonesome Suzie (alt.) / Orange juice blues (blues for breakfast) / Key to the highway / Ferdinand the imposter. *(lp-iss.Jun01 on 'Simply Vinyl'; SVLP 338)*

Sep 68. (7") *(CL 15559) <2269>* **THE WEIGHT. / I SHALL BE RELEASED** [21] Aug68 [63]

Jan 70. (lp) *<(EST 132)>* **THE BAND** [25] Sep69 [9]
– Across the great divide / Rag mama rag / The night they drove old Dixie down / When you awake / Up on Cripple Creek / Whispering pines / Jemima surrender / Rockin' chair / Look out Cleveland / Jawbone / The unfaithful servant / King Harvest (has surely come). *(re-iss. Aug86 lp/c; EMS/TCEMS 1192) (cd-iss. Aug88 on 'E.M.I.'; CZ 70) (cd re-iss. Aug97 on 'E.M.I.' hit UK No.41; CDP 746493-2) <(cd re-mast.Sep00 +=; 5 25389-2)>* – Get up Jake / Rag mama rag (alt.) / The night they drove old Dixie down (alt.) / Up on Cripple Creek (alt.) / Whispering pines (alt.) / Jemima surrender (alt.) / King Harvest (has surely come) (alt.). *(lp re-iss. Jun01 on 'Simply Vinyl'; SVLP 326)*

Oct 69. (7") *(CL 15613) <2635>* **UP ON CRIPPLE CREEK. / THE NIGHT THEY DROVE OLD DIXIE DOWN** [ ] [25]

Feb 70. (7") *(CL 15629) <2705>* **RAG MAMA RAG. / THE UNFAITHFUL SERVANT** [16] [57]

Oct 70. (lp) *<(EASW 425)>* **STAGE FRIGHT** [15] Sep70 [5]
– Strawberry wine / Sleeping / Time to kill / Just another whistle stop / All la glory / The shape I'm in / The W.S. Walcott medicine show / Daniel and the sacred harp / Stage fright / The rumor. *(re-iss. Jun81 on 'Greenlight' lp/c; GO/TC-GO 2003) (cd-iss. Mar91; CZ 405) <(cd re-mast.Sep00 +=; 5 25395-2)>* – Daniel and the sacred harp (alt.) / Time to kill (alt.) / The W.S. Walcott medicine show (alt.) / Radio commercial.

Oct 70. (7") *<2870>* **TIME TO KILL. / THE SHAPE I'M IN** [–] [77]

Oct 70. (7") *(CL 15659)* **TIME TO KILL. / SLEEPING** [ ] [–]

Mar 71. (7") *(CL 15675)* **THE SHAPE I'M IN. / THE RUMOR** [ ] [–]

Oct 71. (lp) *<(EAST 651)>* **CAHOOTS** [41] [21]
– Life is a carnival / When I paint my masterpiece / Last of the blacksmiths / Where do we go from here? / 4% pantomime / Shoot out in Chinatown / The Moon struck one / Thinkin' out loud / Smoke signal / Volcano / The river hymn. *(re-iss. Jun81 on 'Greenlight' lp/c; GO/TC-GO 2015) (cd-iss. May89; CZ 138) <(cd re-mast.Sep00 +=; 5 25391-2)>* – Endless highway / When I paint my masterpiece (alt.) / Bessie Smith / Don't do it / Radio commercial.

Oct 71. (7") *(CL 15700) <3199>* **LIFE IS A CARNIVAL. / THE MOON STRUCK ONE** [ ] [72]

Dec 71. (7") *<3249>* **WHEN I PAINT MY MASTERPIECE. / WHERE DO WE GO FROM HERE?** [–] [ ]

Aug 72. (d-lp) *<(SABB 11045)>* **ROCK OF AGES (live)** [ ] [6]
– (introduction) / Don't do it / King harvest (has surely come) / Caledonia mission / Get up Jake / The W.S. Walcott medicine show / Stage fright / The night they drove all Dixie down / Across the great divide / This wheel's on fire / Rag mama rag / The weight / The shape I'm in / The unfaithful servant / Life is a carnival / The genetic method * / Chest fever / (I don't want to) Hang up my rock and roll shoes. *(re-iss. Jul83 on 'E.M.I.';) (re-iss. Apr87 – =*; CDP 746 617-2) <d-cd-iss. 1990 += *> <(d-cd re-iss. May01 +=; 530181-2)>* – Loving you is sweeter than ever / I shall be released / Up on Cripple Creek / The rumor / Rockin' chair / Time to kill / Down in the flood (with BOB DYLAN) / When I paint my masterpiece (with BOB DYLAN) / Don't ya tell Henry (with BOB DYLAN) / Like a rolling stone (with BOB DYLAN).

Nov 72. (7") *(CL 15737) <3433>* **DON'T DO IT (live). / RAG MAMA RAG (live)** [ ] Sep72 [34]

Feb 73. (7") *<3500>* **CALEDONIA MISSION. / (I DON'T WANT TO) HANG UP MY ROCK AND ROLL SHOES** [–] [ ]

Nov 73. (7") *(CL 15767) <3758>* **AIN'T GOT NO HOME. / GET UP JAKE** [ ] [73]

Dec 73. (lp) *<(ESW 11214)>* **MOONDOG MATINEE** [ ] Nov73 [28]
– Ain't got no home / Holy cow / Share your love / Mystery train / The Third Man theme / The promised land / The great pretender / I'm ready /

Saved / A change is gonna come. *(cd-iss. Jun98; 793592-2) <(cd re-iss. May01 on 'E.M.I.'+=; 5 25393-2)>* – Didn't it rain / Crying heart blues / Shakin' / What am I living for / Going back to Memphis / Endless highway.

— late '73, they renewed association with BOB DYLAN, helping out on album 'PLANET WAVES' and more so 'BEFORE THE FLOOD' a live album credited to BOB DYLAN / THE BAND. In '75 The BAND returned with brand new material.

Feb 74. (7") *<3828>* **THE THIRD MAN THEME. / THE W.S. WALCOTT MEDICINE SHOW** –

Dec 75. (lp) *<(ST 11440)>* **NORTHERN LIGHTS – SOUTHERN CROSS** 26
– Forbidden fruit / Hobo jungle / Ophelia / Acadian driftwood / Ring your bell / It makes no difference / Jupiter hollow / Rags and bones. *(cd-iss. Mar91; CZ 404) <(cd re-iss. May01 +=; 5 25394-2)>* – Twilight (early take) / Christmas must be tonight (alt.).

Feb 76. (7") *<4230>* **OPHELIA. / HOBO JUNGLE** – 62

Mar 76. (7") *(CL 15861)* **RING YOUR BELL. / FORBIDDEN FRUIT** –

Nov 76. (7") *<4316>* **TWILIGHT. / ACADIAN DRIFTWOOD** –

Apr 77. (lp) *<(EST 11602)>* **ISLANDS** Mar77 64
– Right as rain / Street walker / Let the night fall / Ain't that a lot of love / Christmas must be tonight / Islands / The saga of Pepote Rouge / Georgia on my mind / Knockin' lost John / Livin' in a dream. *(cd-iss. Mar91; CZ 406) (cd re-iss. May01 on 'E.M.I'+=; 525392-2)* – Twilight / Georgia on my mind (alt.).

Apr 77. (7") *<4361>* **GEORGIA ON MY MIND. / THE NIGHT THEY DROVE OLD DIXIE DOWN** –

Apr 77. (7") *(CL 15921)* **RIGHT AS RAIN. / KNOCKIN' LOST JOHN** –

— Joined by guests BOB DYLAN, NEIL YOUNG, RONNIE HAWKINS, JONI MITCHELL, ERIC CLAPTON, VAN MORRISON, NEIL DIAMOND, MUDDY WATERS, PAUL BUTTERFIELD, BOBBY CHARLES and DR. JOHN etc. Jams were from STEPHEN STILLS, RINGO STARR and RONNIE WOOD

Warners Warners

Apr 78. (t-lp) *(K 66076) <3WS 3146>* **THE LAST WALTZ** (live 25th Nov'76 – film soundtrack) 39 16
– Theme from the last waltz / Up on cripple creek / Who do you love / Helpless / Stage fright / Coyote / Dry your eyes / Such a night / It makes no difference / Mystery train / The shape I'm in / The night they drove old Dixie down / Mannish boy / Further on up the road / The shape I'm in / Down south in New Orleans / Ophelia / Tura lura lural (that's an Irish lullaby) / Caravan / Life is a carnival / Baby let me follow you down / I don't believe you (she acts like we never have met) / Forever young / I shall be released / The well / Evangeline / Out of the blue / The weight / The last waltz refrain / Theme from the last waltz (with orchestra). *(d-cd-iss. Jul88; K 266076) <(d-cd re-iss. Oct03 on 'Rhino'; 8122 73925-2)> <(4xcd-box iss.Apr02 on 'Rhino'+=; 8122 782782-3)>* – (extra tracks).

Jun 78. (7") *(K 17187)* **THEME FROM THE LAST WALTZ (live). / OUT OF THE BLUE (live)** –

Nov 78. (7") *<8592>* **OUT OF THE BLUE (live). / THE WELL (live)** –

— After their official split in 1978, HUDSON and MANUEL went into sessions. MANUEL hung himself 6 Mar'86, after a fit of depression. RICK DANKO and LEVON HELM went solo. In 1980, ROBBIE wrote score for film CARNY, before finally getting around to recording solo album in 1987.

— re-formed (now studio / earlier live) with **DANKO, HELM, HUDSON + JIM WEIDER** – bass / **RICHARD BELL** – piano / **RANDY CIARLANTE** – drums

Essential Pyramid

Feb 94. (cd/c) *(ESS CD/MC 199) <71564>* **JERICHO** Nov93
– Remedy / Blind Willie McTell / The caves of Jericho / Atlantic City / Too soon gone / Country boy / Move to Japan / Amazon (river of dreams) / Stuff you gotta watch / Same thing / Shine a light / Blues stay away from me.

Transatla. Rhino

Apr 96. (cd/c) *(TRA CD/MC 228) <R2/R4 72404>* **HIGH ON THE HOG**
– Stand up / Back to Memphis / Where I should always be / Free your mind / Forever young / The high price of love / Crazy mama / I must love you too much / She knows / Ramble jungle.

not iss. Platinum

Sep 98. (cd) *<161420>* **JUBILATION** –
– Book faded brown / Don't wait / Last train to Memphis / High cotton / Kentucky downpour / Bound by love / White cadillac (ode to Ronnie Hawkins) / If I should fail / Spirits of the dance / You see me / French girls (instrumental). *(UK-iss.Jun00 on 'River North'; 514 161420-2) (UK re-iss. Oct03 on 'Solo'; 221416)*

– compilations, etc. –

on 'Capitol' unless stated otherwise

Sep 76. (d-lp) *(ST 3927) <ST 11553>* **THE BEST OF THE BAND** Jul76 51
– Up on Cripple Creek / The shape I'm in / The weight / It makes no difference / Life is a carnival / Twilight / Tears of rage / Stage fright / Ophelia / ,The night they drove old Dixie down. *(re-iss. Jun82 on 'Fame' lp/c; FA/TC-FA 3016) (cd-iss. May87; CDP 746 070-2)*

Oct 76. (7") *(CL 115887)* **TWILIGHT. / THE WEIGHT** –

Jan 79. (d-lp) *(ESTSP 19) <SKBO 11856>* **ANTHOLOGY**
(cd-iss. May89; CZ 63)

Jul 84. (7") *EMI Gold; (G45 28)* **RAG MAMA RAG. / THE WEIGHT** –

Oct 89. (t-lp/d-c)(d-cd) *(EN/TCEN 5010)(CDS 792 169-2)* **TO KINGDOM COME – THE DEFINITIVE COLLECTION**

May 92. (cd) *Castle; (CCS CD/MC 333)* **THE COLLECTION** –
– Back to Memphis / Tears of rage / To kingdom come / Long black veil / Chest fever / The weight / I shall be released / Up on Cripple Creek / Loving you is sweeter than ever / Rag mama rag / The night they drove old Dixie down / Unfaithful servant / King Harvest (has surely come) / The shape I'm in / The W.S.Walcott medicine show / Daniel and the sacred harp / Stage fright / Don't do it (baby don't do it) / Life is a carnival / When I paint my masterpiece / 4% pantomine / The river hymn / Mystery train / Endless highway / Get up Jake / It makes no difference / Ophelia / Arcadian driftwood / Christmas must be tonight / The saga of Peopote rouge / Knockin' lost John.

Nov 94. (3xcd-box) *(CDBAND 1)* **ACROSS THE GREAT DIVIDE**

Apr 95. (cd) *(CDP 831742-2)* **LIVE AT WATKINS GLEN (live)** –
– Back to Memphis / Endless highway / I shall be released / Loving you is sweeter than ever / Too wet to work / Don't ya tell Henry / The rumour / Time to kill / Jam / Up on Cripple Creek.

Nov 96. (cd) *Disky; (DC 86716-2)* **THE WEIGHT** –

Aug 98. (cd) *E.M.I.; (495051-2)* **THE SHAPE I'M IN (THE VERY BEST OF THE BAND)** –
– The shape I'm in / Across the great divide / The night they drove old Dixie down / Stage fright / Rag mama rag / Ophelia / Up on Cripple Creek / Twilight / King Harvest (has surely come) / Life is a carnival / I shall be released / Tears of rage / Acadian driftwood / The weight / It makes no difference / Chest fever / Share your love with me / Don't do it (baby don't do it).

Feb 01. (cd) *Capitol; <(5 24941-2)>* **GREATEST HITS** Sep00
– The weight / Tears of rage / Chest fever / I shall be released / Up on Cripple Creek / The night they drove old Dixie down / Rag mama rag / King harvest (has surely come) / The shape I'm in / Stage fright / Time to kill / Life is a carnival / When I paint my masterpiece / Ain't got no home / It makes no difference / Ophelia / Acadian driftwood / The saga of Pepote Rouge.

Mar 02. (cd) *EMI Gold; (CDGOLD 1075)* **THE COLLECTION** (different) –

Oct 02. (cd) *Disky; (SI 905050)* **THE MOON STRUCK ONE** Dec02

Mar 03. (cd) *E.M.I.; (583268-2)* **THE ESSENTIAL BAND** –

□ BAND AID
(see under ⇒ BOOMTOWN RATS / Bob Geldof)

□ Thomas BANGALTER (see under ⇒ DAFT PUNK)

BANGLES

Formed: Los Angeles, California, USA . . . 1981 as The BANGS by sisters VICKI and DEBBI PETERSON alongside SUSANNA HOFFS, getting together after the siblings replied to an ad placed by the latter. After a one-off US indie 45, they became The BANGLES, added a bass player, ANNETTE ZILINSKAS and signed to Miles Copeland's

'IRS/Faulty' records in mid '82. An eponymous mini-set showed them to be a feisty garage-pop band whose sound was characterised by the harmonies of the PETERSON sisters and influenced by the likes of LOVE, GRASS ROOTS, The BYRDS, The BEATLES and The GO-GO's, an all-female quartet in the male dominated Paisley Underground. Replacing ZILINSKAS (who subsequently joined BLOOD ON THE SADDLE) with MICKI STEELE, the band secured a major label deal with 'CBS/Columbia' and breached the lower fringes of both the UK and US charts with debut album proper, 'ALL OVER THE PLACE' (1985). Although the rough edges had been smoothed out for public consumption, no hit singles were forthcoming and it would take the masterful pen of PRINCE to furnish the girls with a breakthrough track; 'MANIC MONDAY' was released in early '86, a MAMAS & PAPAS-esque tale of 9 to 5 frustration that quickly captured the popular imagination and climbed into the Top 3 on both sides of the Atlantic. 1986 proved to be The BANGLES' year, a follow-up album, 'DIFFERENT LIGHT', again achieving transatlantic Top 3 status and spawning a further minor hit in the melancholy reading of Jules Shear's 'IF SHE KNEW WHAT SHE WANTS' and a monster US No.1 in 'WALK LIKE AN EGYPTIAN'. To end the year, they were back in the Top 20 with a remix of 'WALKING DOWN YOUR STREET'. While only a solitary flop single, 'FOLLOW', appeared in '87, The BANGLES kickstarted their career in early '88 with a storming cover of Simon & Garfunkel's 'HAZY SHADE OF WINTER', cut for the soundtrack to cult 80's bratpack movie, 'Less Than Zero'. With seemingly no end to their pop ascendancy, The BANGLES again hired outside writers for the slick 'EVERYTHING' (1988), another massive Stateside success which spawned US Top 5, 'IN YOUR ROOM', as well as the band's syrupy calling card, 'ETERNAL FLAME', a transatlantic chart topper in early '89. With sex symbol HOFFS (who sang the latter unaccompanied) increasingly regarded as the band's focal point, tensions eventually split the band in 1990 as their run of hits stuttered to a halt. While HOFFS went on to a marginally successful solo career, the PETERSONS continued to work on the alternative/pop underground. Almost a decade and a half after they'd signed off, the band decided to reform and record 'DOLL REVOLUTION' (2003), as unremarkable a comeback as has been heard in recent years. Stodgy and weighed down by its ill-advised attempts at rootsy, bluesy rock, the record added little to the band's shiny pop legacy. • **Songwriters:** Mostly HOFFS collaborations, except GOING DOWN TO LIVERPOOL (Kimberley Rew – SOFT BOYS) / WALK LIKE AN EGYPTIAN (Liam Sternberg) / SEPTEMBER GURLS (Alex Chilton). HOFFS solo; BOYS KEEP SWINGING (David Bowie) + UNCONDITIONAL LOVE (Cyndi Lauper). • **Trivia:** SUSANNA HOFFS made film acting debut in 'The Allnighter' released 1987.

Album rating: ALL OVER THE PLACE (*6) / DIFFERENT LIGHT (*5) / EVERYTHING (*4) / BANGLES' GREATEST HITS compilation (*7) / ETERNAL FLAME – THE BEST OF . . . compilation (*7) / DOLL REVOLUTION (*5)

The BANGS

SUSANNA HOFFS (b.17 Jan'57, Newport Beach, Calif.) – vocals, rhythm guitar / **VICKI PETERSON** (b.11 Jan'58) – lead guitar, vocals (ex-The FANS) / **DEBBI PETERSON** (b.22 Aug'61) – drums, vocals (ex-The FANS)

not iss. Down Kitty

Dec 81. (7") *<BANG 1>* **GETTING OUT OF HAND. / CALL ON ME** [–] [ ]

The BANGLES

—— added **ANNETTE ZILINSKAS** – bass

not iss. Faulty-IRS

Jun 82. (m-lp) *<1302>* **THE BANGLES** [–] [ ]
– How is the air up there? / Mary Street / The real world / Want you / I'm in line.

—— **MICKI STEELE** (b.MICHAEL, 2 Jun'54) – bass, vocals (ex-RUNAWAYS, ex-SLOW CHILDREN) repl. ANNETTE who joined BLOOD ON THE SADDLE

C.B.S. Columbia.

Sep 84. (7") *(A 4527)* **HERO TAKES A FALL. / WHERE WERE YOU WHEN I NEEDED YOU** [ ] [ ]

Mar 85. (lp/c) *(CBS/40 26015) <39220>* **ALL OVER THE PLACE** [86] Jul84 [80]
– Hero takes a fall / Live / James / All about you / Dover beach / Tell me / Restless / Going down to Liverpool / He's got a secret / Silent treatment / More than meets the eye. *(re-iss. Oct86 lp/c/cd; 450091-1/-4/-2) (re-iss. Apr93 on 'Columbia' cd/c;)*

Mar 85. (7") *(A 4914)* **GOING DOWN TO LIVERPOOL. / DOVER BEACH** [56] [ ]
(12"+=) – *(TX 4914)* – The real world / I'm in line / How is the air up there?
(d7"+=) *(DA 4914)* – Hero takes a fall / Where were you when I needed you?

Jan 86. (7"/7"w-poster) *(A/QA 6796) <05757>* **MANIC MONDAY. / IN A DIFFERENT LIGHT** [2] [2]
(12"+=) *(TX 6796)* – Going down to Liverpool / Dover beach.

Mar 86. (lp/c/cd) *(CBS/40/CD 26659) <40039>* **DIFFERENT LIGHT** [3] Jan86 [2]
– Manic Monday / In a different light / Walking down your street / Walk like an Egyptian / Standing in the hallway / Return post / If she knew what she wants / Let it go / September gurls / Angels don't fall in love / September girls / Following / Not like you. *(re-iss. Mar90 cd/c/lp; 46558-2/-4/-1)*

Apr 86. (7"/7"sha-pic-d) *(A/WA 7062) <05886>* **IF SHE KNEW WHAT SHE WANTS. / ANGELS DON'T FALL IN LOVE** [31] [29]
(12"+=) *(TA 7062)* – Manic Monday (extended).
(d7"+=) *(DA 7062)* – Hero takes a fall (remix) / James.

Jul 86. (7") *(A 7255)* **GOING DOWN TO LIVERPOOL. / LET IT GO** [ ] [ ]
(12"+=) *(TA 7255)* – *Walking down your street – James (live medley).*

Sep 86. (7"/7"w-poster) *(650071-7/-0) <06257>* **WALK LIKE AN EGYPTIAN. / NOT LIKE YOU** [3] [1]
(12"+=) *(650071-6)* – ('A'dub version) / ('A'acappella).
(d7"+=) *(650071-8)* – Manic Monday / In a different light.

Dec 86. (7"/7"g-f/ext.12") *(BANGS/+G/T 1) <06674>* **WALKING DOWN YOUR STREET (remix). / RETURN POST** [16] [11]
(d7"+=) *(BANGS D1)* – Walk like an Egyptian / Not like you.

Apr 87. (7"/7"w-poster) *(BANGS/+Q 2)* **FOLLOWING. / DOVER BEACH** [55] [ ]
(12"+=/d7"+=) *(BANGS T/D 2)* – Bangles hit mix medley (Manic Monday – If she knew what she wants – Walking down your street – Going down to Liverpool – Walk like an Egyptian).

—— next 45 was a one-off for movie 'Less Than Zero' on 'Def Jam-CBS' label

Jan 88. (7"/7"pic-d) *(BANGS/+Q 3) <07630>* **HAZY SHADE OF WINTER. / (b-side by "Joan Jett & The Blackhearts")** [11] [2]
(12") *(BANGS T3)* – ('A'-Purple haze mix) / ('A'dub) / ('A'-Shady haze mix).
(cd-s++=) *(BANGS C3)* – (the 4 tracks) / Walk like an Egyptian.

Oct 88. (7"/7"w-poster) *(BANGS/+Q 4) <08090>* **IN YOUR ROOM. / BELL JAR** [35] [5]
(12"+=/12"pic-d+=/cd-s+=) *(BANGS T/P/C 4)* – Hazy shade of winter (remix).

Nov 88. (lp/c/cd) *(462977-1/-4/-2) <44056>* **EVERYTHING** [5] [15]
– In your room / Complicated girl / Bell jar / Something to believe in / Eternal flame / Be with you / Glitter years / I'll set you free / Watching the sky / Some dreams come true / Make a play for her now / Waiting for you / Crash and burn. *(re-iss. Apr93 on 'Columbia' cd/c;)*

Jan 89. (7") *(BANGS R5) <68533>* **ETERNAL FLAME. / WHAT I MEANT TO SAY** [1] [1]
(12"+=/cd-s+=) *(BANGS T/C 5)* – Walk like an Egyptian (dance mix).
(12") *(BANGS Q5)* – ('A'side) / Bangles hitmix.
(c-s) *(BANGS M5)* – ('A'side) / Going down to Liverpool / Hero takes a fall / James.

May 89. (7"/7"sha-pic-d/c-s) *(BANGS/+P/M 6) <68744>* **BE WITH YOU. / LET IT GO** [23] [30]
(12"+=/cd-s+=) *(BANGS T/C 6)* – In your room (extended).
(pic-cd-s+=) *(BANGS D6)* – Manic Monday (extended California mix).

Oct 89. (7") *(BANGS 7)* **I'LL SET YOU FREE. / WATCHING THE SKY** [74] [ ]
(12"+=/cd-s+=) *(BANGS T/C 7)* – Walking down your street (extended).

May 90. (cd/c/lp) *(466769-2/-4/-1) <46125>* **BANGLES' GREATEST HITS** (compilation) [4] [97]
– Hero takes a fall / Going down to Liverpool / Manic Monday / If she knew what she wants / Walk like an Egyptian / Walking down your street / Following / Hazy shade of winter / In your room / Eternal flame / Be with you / I'll set you free / Everything I wanted / Where were you when I needed you. *(re-iss. May95 + Dec95 on 'Columbia' cd/c; same)*

May 90. (7") *(BANGS 8)* **WALK LIKE AN EGYPTIAN (remix). / ('A'-Ozymandias remix)** [73] [ ]
(c-s+=/12"+=/cd-s+=) *(BANGS M/T/C 8)* – ('A'extended dance) / ('A'dub) / ('A'acappella).

— In the autumn of 1990 they disbanded; HOFFS went solo releasing two albums, 'WHEN YOU'RE A BOY' (1991) and 'SUSANNA HOFFS' (1996). The BANGLES were back in 2002

Liberty Koch

Mar 03. (cd) *(581510-2) <9515>* **DOLL REVOLUTION** [ ] Sep03 [ ]
– Tear off your own head (it's a doll revolution) / Stealing Rosemary / Something that you said / Ask me no questions / Rain song / Nickel Romeo / Ride the ride / I will take care of you / Here right now / Single by choice / Lost at sea / Song for a good son / Mixed messages / Between the two / Grateful.

Mar 03. (cd-s) *(BANGLES 003)* **SOMETHING THAT YOU SAID / GETTING OUT OF HAND / ETERNAL FLAME (acoustic)** [38] [–]

Jul 03. (cd-s) *(BANGLES 004)* **I WILL TAKE CARE OF YOU / TEAR OFF YOUR OWN HEAD (IT'S A DOLL REVOLUTION) / RIDE THE RIDE (acoustic)** [ ] [–]

– compilations, etc. –

Jul 98. (cd) *Columbia; <(480544-2)>* **THE DEFINITIVE COLLECTION** [ ] 1995 [ ]

Jul 98. (cd) *Sony; <65641>* **SUPER HITS** [–] [ ]
(UK-iss.Sep03 on 'Sony'; 502219-2)

Apr 99. (cd) *Columbia; (494469-2)* **THE BEST OF THE BANGLES** [ ] [ ]

Jul 01. (cd) *Sony TV; (SONYTV 121) <504169>* **ETERNAL FLAME – THE BEST OF THE BANGLES** [15] [ ]
– Manic Monday / Eternal flame / If she knew what she wants / Walk like an Egyptian / Walking down your street / Hero takes a fall / Going down to Liverpool / Following / Hazy shade of winter / In your room / Be with you / I'll set you free / Everything I wanted / Where were you when I needed you / My side of the bed / Bangles hit mix.

□ Tony BANKS / BANKSTATEMENT (see under ⇒ GENESIS)

BARCLAY JAMES HARVEST

Formed: Oldham, Lancashire, England . . . Autumn 1966 by art school students JOHN LEES and STUART WOLSTENHOLME. After their initial 45 on 'Parlophone', EMI subsequently found a new home for them on their aptly named 'Harvest' label. In 1970, their eponymous debut album was recorded with a full orchestra conducted by ROBERT GODFREY, their typically prog-rock sound proving a hit with the student fraternity. However their heavy use of mellotron proved none too popular with the critics of the day, who at times lambasted them for their neo-classical pretentions. In fact they were unfairly described by the music press as "the poor man's MOODY BLUES". Their 1971 follow-up 'ONCE AGAIN', featured what was to become their finest song, 'MOCKINGBIRD', a combination of both tender harmonies and quality instrumentation. They carried on in the same vein with two other albums 'BJH AND OTHER SHORT STORIES' and 'BABY JAMES HARVEST', leading to a contract with 'Polydor' in 1974. Finally gaining wide-scale recognition upon the release of their 4th album 'EVERYONE IS EVERYBODY ELSE', it remains a mystery to most why it didn't chart. By this stage their live appeal was such that 'Polydor' subsequently released a double live set, a piece of work that encompassed everything they'd been working towards during their career. Although Britain and the States had somehow ignored them, they won many converts in Europe, especially Germany, who were always interested in anything prog-rock or symphonic. With the onset of the "new wave" explosion, they were forced into the margins, although they retained a loyal family of fans. Of late – post-millennium – BJH split into two factions, one fronted by JOHN LEES ('THROUGH THE EYES OF JOHN LEE' 2000), the other by LES HOLROYD ('REVOLUTION DAYS' 2002). • **Trivia:** A CONCERT FOR THE PEOPLE was recorded near the Berlin Wall and was transmitted live on German TV and radio.

Album rating: BARCLAY JAMES HARVEST (*6) / ONCE AGAIN (*7) / BJH AND OTHER SHORT STORIES (*6) / BABY JAMES HARVEST (*6) / EVERYONE IS EVERYBODY ELSE (*8) / BARCLAY JAMES HARVEST LIVE (*8) / TIME HONOURED GHOSTS (*5) / OCTOBERON (*5) / GONE TO EARTH (*7) / LIVE TAPES (*4) / EYES OF THE UNIVERSE (*4) / TURN OF THE TIDE (*5) / A CONCERT FOR THE PEOPLE (BERLIN) (*4) / RING OF CHANGES (*5) / VICTIM OF CIRCUMSTANCE (*5) / FACE TO FACE (*4) / THE COMPACT BARCLAY JAMES HARVEST compilation (*8) / GLASNOST (*4) / WELCOME TO THE SHOW (*5) / CAUGHT IN THE LIGHT (*5) / RIVER OF DREAMS (*3) / REVIVAL LIVE: THROUGH THE EYES OF JOHN LEES (*4) / REVOLUTION DAYS (*3) / LIVE IN BOHN (*3)

STUART 'WOOLY' WOLSTENHOLME (b.15 Apr'47) – keyboards, vocals / **JOHN LEES** (b.13 Jan'48) – guitar, vocals, wind / **LES HOLROYD** (b.12 Mar'48, Bolton, England) – bass, vocals / **MELVIN PRITCHARD** (b.20 Jan'48) – drums

Parlophone Sire

Apr 68. (7") *(R 5693) <4105>* **EARLY MORNING. / MR. SUNSHINE** [ ] [ ]

Harvest Sire

Jun 69. (7") *(HAR 5003) <4112>* **BROTHER THRUSH. / POOR WAGES** [ ] [ ]

Jun 70. (lp) *(SHVL 770) <SES 97026>* **BARCLAY JAMES HARVEST** [ ] [ ]
– Taking some time on / Mother dear / The sun will never shine / When the world was waken / Good love child / The iron maiden / Dark now my sky. *(<cd re-mast.May02 on 'E.M.I.'+=; 538405-2>)* – Early morning / Mr. Sunshine / So tomorrow (BBC session) / Eden unobtainable (BBC session) / Night (BBC session) / Pools of blue (BBC session) / Need you oh so bad (BBC session) / Small time town (BBC session) / Dark now my sky (BBC session) / I can't go on without you / Eden unobtainable / Poor wages / Brother Thrush.

Aug 70. (7") *(HAR 5025)* **TAKING SOME TIME ON. / THE IRON MAIDEN** [ ] [–]

Feb 71. (lp) *(SHVL 788) <4904>* **ONCE AGAIN** [ ] [ ]
– She said / Happy old world / Song for dying / Galadriel / Mockingbird / Vanessa Simmons / Ball and chain / Lady loves. *(quad-lp Jul73; Q4SHVL 788) (re-iss. Jul83 on 'Fame' lp/c; FA/TCFA 3073) (cd-iss. Mar99 on 'Brimstone'; BRIM 002) (<cd re-mast.May02 on 'E.M.I.'+=; 538406-2>)* – Introduction – White sails (a seascape) / Too much on your plate / Happy old world (quad mix) / Vanessa Simmons (quad mix) / Ball and chain (quad mix).

Feb 71. (7") *(HAR 5034)* **MOCKINGBIRD. / VANESSA SIMMONS** [ ] [–]

Nov 71. (lp) *(SHVL 794) <5904>* **BJH AND OTHER SHORT STORIES** [ ] [ ]
– Ow / Harry's song / Ursula / Little lapwing / Song with no meaning / Blue John's blues / The poet / After the day. *(<cd re-mast.May02 on 'E.M.I.'+=; 538407-2>)* – Brave new world (demo) / She said (BBC session) / Galadriel (BBC session) / Ursula (the Swansea song) (BBC session) / Someone there you know (BBC session) / Medicine man (BBC session).

Apr 72. (7") *(HAR 5051)* **I'M OVER YOU. / CHILD OF MAN** [ ] [–]

Sep 72. (7"; as BOMBADIL) *(HAR 5056)* **BREATHLESS. / WHEN THE CITY SLEEPS** [ ] [–]
(re-iss. Mar75; HAR 5095)

Harvest Harvest

Oct 72. (7") *(HAR 5058)* <3501> **THANK YOU. / MEDICINE MAN**

Oct 72. (lp) *(SHSP 4023)* <11145> **BABY JAMES HARVEST** Feb73
– Crazy (over you) / Delph town morn / Summer soldier / Thank you / One hundred thousand smiles out / Moonwater. *(re-iss. May85 on 'E.M.I.' lp/c; ATAK/TC-ATAK 8) (re-iss. Mar87 on 'Fame' lp/c; FA/TC-FA 3172) (<cd re-mast.May02 on 'E.M.I.'+=; 538408-2>)* – Child of man / I'm over you / When the city sleeps / Breathless / Thank you (alt.) / Medicine man / Rock and roll woman / The joker / Child of man (BBC session) / Moonwater (2002 remix).

May 73. (7") *(HAR 5060)* **ROCK AND ROLL WOMAN. / THE JOKER**

Polydor Capitol

May 74. (7") *(2058 474)* **POOR BOY BLUES. / CRAZY CITY** –

Jun 74. (lp)(c) *(2383 286)(3170 186)* <PD 6508> **EVERYONE IS EVERYBODY ELSE**
– Child of the universe / Negative Earth / Paper wings / The great 1974 mining disaster / Crazy city / See me see you / Poor boy blues / Mill boys / For no one. *(re-iss. Aug83 lp/c; SPE LP/MC 11) (cd-iss. Nov87 & Feb92; 833 448-2) (cd re-mast.Jun03 +=; 065401-2)* – Child of the universe (alt.) / The great 1974 mining disaster (alt.) / Maestoso (a hymn in the roof of the world) / Negative earth (alt.) / Child of the universe (alt.).

Jul 74. (7") *<15104>* **CHILD OF THE UNIVERSE. / CRAZY CITY** –

Nov 74. (d-lp) *(2683 052)* **BARCLAY JAMES HARVEST – LIVE (live)** 40 –
– Summer soldier / Medicine man / Crazy city / After the day / The great 1974 mining disaster / Galadriel / Negative Earth / She said / Paper wings / For no one / Mockingbird. *(cd-iss. Jul91 on 'Connoisseur'; VSOPCD 164)*

Oct 75. (lp) *(2383 361)* <6617> **TIME HONOURED GHOSTS** 32
– In my life / Sweet Jesus / Titles / Jonathan / Beyond the grave / Song for you / Hymn for the children / Moon girl / One night. *(re-iss. Aug83 lp/c; SPE LP/MC 12) (cd-iss. Apr87 & Feb92; 831 543-2) (cd re-mast.Jun03 +=; 065400-2)* – Child of the universe.

Nov 75. (7") *(2058 660)* <15118> **TITLES. / SONG FOR YOU**

Polydor M.C.A.

Oct 76. (lp) *(2442 144)* <2234> **OCTOBERON** 19
– The world goes on / May day / Ra / Rock'n'roll star / Polk street rag / Believe in me / Suicide? *(re-iss. Aug83 lp/c; SPE LP/MC 13) (cd-iss. Jun84 & Feb92; 821 930-2) (cd re-mast.Jun03 +=; 065399-2)* – Rock'n'roll star (alt.) / Polk street rag (alt.) / Ra (alt.) / Rock'n'roll star (Top Of The Pops recording) / Suicide? (alt.).

Nov 76. (7") *<40690>* **POLK STREET RAG. / ROCK'N'ROLL STAR** –

Mar 77. (7"ep) *(2229 198)* **LIVE EP (live)** 49 –
– Rock'n'roll star / Medicine man (part 1 & 2).

Jul 77. (7") *(2058 904)* <40795> **HYMN. / OUR KID'S KID**

Sep 77. (lp)(c) *(2442 148)(3170 460)* <2302> **GONE TO EARTH** 30
– Hymn / Love is like a violin / Friend of mine / Poor man's Moody Blues / Hard hearted woman / Sea of tranquility / Spirit on the water / Leper's song / Taking me higher. *(cd-iss. Mar83; 800 092-2) (cd re-mast.Jun03 +=; 065398-2)* – Please give me one more chance (Lied) / Our kid's kid / Hymn / Friend of mine (single version) / Medicine man (live).

Mar 78. (7") *(2059 002)* **FRIEND OF MINE. / SUICIDE?**

Apr 78. (d-lp/d-c) *(PODV/+C 2001)* **LIVE TAPES (live)** –
– Child of the universe / Rock'n'roll star / Poor man's Moody Blues / Mockingbird / Hard hearted woman / One night / Take me higher / Suicide? / Crazy city / Jonathan / For no one / Polk street rag / Hymn. *(d-cd iss.Feb85 & Sep99; 821 523-2)*

Polydor Polydor

Sep 78. (lp/c) *(POLD/+C 5006)* <6173> **XII** 31
– Fantasy: Loving is easy / Berlin / Classics: A tale of two sixties / Turning in circles / Fact: The closed shop / In search of England / Sip of wine / Harbour / Science fiction: Nova Lepidoptera / Giving it up / Fiction: The streets of San Francisco. *(cd-iss. Jan85; 821 941-2) (cd re-mast.Jun03 +=; 065571-2)* – Berlin (single edit) / Loving is easy (single version) / Turning in circles (alt.) / Fact: The closed shop (alt.) / Nova Lepidoptera (instrumental).

Nov 78. (7",7"blue) *(POSP 012)* **LOVING IS EASY. / POLK STREET RAG** –

Jan 79. (7") **LOVING IS EASY. / TURNING IN CIRCLES** –

—— trimmed to a trio plus session men when WOLSTENHOLME went solo / **KEVIN McALEA** – keyboards (ex-BEES MAKE HONEY, ex-KATE BUSH)

Nov 79. (lp/c) *(POLD/+C 5029)* <6267> **EYES OF THE UNIVERSE**
– Love on the line / Alright get down boogie (Mu ala rusic) / The song they love to sing / Skin flicks / Sperratus / Capricorn / Play to the world. *(cd-iss. Jun84; 821 591-2)*

Dec 79. (7") *(POSP 97)* **LOVE ON THE LINE. / ALRIGHT GET DOWN BOOGIE (MU ALA RUSIC)** 63

Feb 80. (7") *(POSP 140)* **CAPRICORN. / BERLIN**

Nov 80. (7") *(POSP 195)* **LIFE IS FOR LIVING. / SHADES OF B. HILL** 61

May 81. (lp/c) *(POLD/+C 5040)* **TURN OF THE TIDE** 55 –
– Waiting on the borderline / How do you feel now / Back to the wall / Highway for fools / Echoes and shadows / Death of the city / I'm like a train / Doctor doctor / Life is for living / In memory of the martyrs. *(cd-iss. Mar83 & Feb92; 800 013-2)*

Jun 82. (lp/c) *(POLD/+C 5052)* **A CONCERT FOR THE PEOPLE (BERLIN)** 15 –
– Berlin / Loving is easy / Mockingbird / Sip of wine / Nova Lepidoptera / In memory of the martyrs / Life is for living / Child of the universe / Hymn. *(cd-iss. Mar83 & Feb92; 800 026-2)*

May 83. (lp/c)(cd) *(POLH/+C 3)(811 638-2)* **RING OF CHANGES** 36 –
– Fifties child / Looking from the outside / Teenage heart / High wire / Midnight drug / Waiting for the right time / Just a day away / Paradiso dos cavalos / Ring of changes. *(cd-iss. Feb92 cd/c; 811 638-2/-4)*

May 83. (7") *(POSP 585)* **JUST A DAY AWAY. / ROCK'N'ROLL LADY (live)** 68
(7"sha-pic-d) *(POPPX 585)* – ('A'side) / Looking from the outside.

Oct 83. (7") *(POSP 640)* **WAITING FOR THE RIGHT TIME. / BLOW ME DOWN**
(12"+=) *(POSPX 640)* – ('A'extended).

Mar 84. (7"/7"sha-pic-d) *(POSP/+P 674)* **VICTIMS OF CIRCUMSTANCE. / ('A'instrumental)**
(ext.12"+=) *(POSPX 674)* – Love on the line (live).

Apr 84. (lp/c)(cd) *(POLD/+C 5135)(817 950-2)* **VICTIMS OF CIRCUMSTANCE** 33 –
– Sideshow / Hold on / Rebel woman / Say you'll stay / For your love / Victim of circumstance / Inside my nightmare / Watching you / I've got a feeling.

Sep 84. (7") *(POSP 705)* **I'VE GOT A FEELING. / REBEL WOMAN**

Nov 86. (7") *(POSP 834)* **HE SAID LOVE. / ON THE WINGS OF LOVE**
(12"+=) *(POSPX 834)* – Hymn (live).

Feb 87. (lp/c)(cd) *(POLD/+C 5209)(831 483-2)* **FACE TO FACE** 65
– Prisoner of your love / He said love / Alone in the night / Turn the key / Guitar blues / African / Following me / All my life / Panic / Kiev. *(cd+=)* – On the wings of love.

Apr 88. (lp/c)(cd) *(POLD/+C 5219)(835 590-2)* **GLASNOST (live)**
– Berlin / Alone in the night / Hold on / African / On the wings of love / Poor man's Moody Blues / Love on the line / Medicine man / Kiev / Hymn / Turn the key / He said love.

Feb 90. (7"; as BJH) *(PO 67)* **CHEAP THE BULLET. / SHADOWS ON THE SKY** –
(12"+=) *(PZ 67)* – Berlin (live).
(cd-s+=) *(PZCD 67)* – Alone in the night (live) / Hold on (live).

Mar 90. (cd/c/lp; as BJH) *(841 751-2/-4/-1)* **WELCOME TO THE SHOW**
– The life you lead / Lady Macbeth / Cheap the bullet / Welcome to the show / John Lennon's guitar / African nights / Psychedelic child / Where do we go / If love is king / Halfway to freedom.

May 92. (7"/c-s) *(PO/+CS 208)* **STAND UP. / LIFE IS FOR LIVING (live)** –
(cd-s+=) *(PZCDB 208)* – Alone in the night / Poor man's Moody Blues (live).
(cd-s) *(PZCD 208)* – ('A'side) / John Lennon's guitar (live) / Play to the world (live) / ('A'extended).

Jun 93. (cd/c) *(519 303-2/-4)* **CAUGHT IN THE LIGHT**
– Who do we think we are? / Knoydart / Copii Romania / Back to Earth / Cold war / Forever yesterday / The great unknown / Spud-u-like / Silver wings / Once more / A matter of time / Ballad of Denshaw Mill.

1997. (cd) *(535576-2)* **RIVER OF DREAMS** – German –
– Back in the game / River of dreams / Yesterday's heroes / Children of the disappeared / Pools of tears / Do you believe in dreams / (Took me) So long / Mr. E / Three weeks to despair / The time of our lives.

Eagle — not iss.

Feb 99. (cd/c) *(EAG CD/MC 052)* **NEXUS** — –
– Festival! / The iron maiden / Brave new world / Hors d'oeuvre / Mocking bird / Sitting upon a shelf / Hymn / The devils that I keep / Titles / Float / Loving is easy / Star bright.

— **JOHN LEES** added **JEFF LEACH + KEVIN WHITEHEAD**

Apr 00. (cd) *(EAGCD 120)* **THROUGH THE EYES OF JOHN LEES: REVIVAL LIVE (live)** — –
– A devilish intro / She said / Festival! / For no one / The iron maiden / Hors d'Oeuvre / Mockingbird / Harbour / River of dreams / Poor man's Moody Blues / New song (old story) / Brave new world / Galadriel / Loving is easy / Star bright / Suicide / Brother Thrush / Mister E / Hymn.

— now **LES HOLROYD** with **MEL PRITCHARD** – percussion, drums / **JOHN "RABBIT" BUNDRICK** – keyboards / **STEVE PIGOTT** – keyboards / **MIKE BRYON HEHIR** – guitar

Musedia — not iss.

Feb 02. (cd) *(MREC 001)* **REVOLUTION DAYS** — –
– It's my life / Missing you / That was then . . . this is now / Prelude / January morning / Love on the line / Quiero el sol / Totally cool / Life is for living / Sleepy Sunday / Revolution day / Marlene (from the Berlin Suite). *(re-iss. Aug03 on 'Pure'; 2190101001-2)*

Pure — not iss.

Sep 03. (cd; as BARCLAY JAMES HARVEST featuring LES HOLROYD) *(2190102002-2)* **LIVE IN BOHN 30TH OCTOBER 2002 (live)** — –
– It's my life / Revolution day / Yesterday's heroes / Prelude / January morning / Rock'n'roll star / The song (they love to sing) / Life is for living / Marlene.

– compilations, etc. –

on 'Harvest' unless otherwise mentioned

Sep 72. (lp) *EMI Starline; (SRS 5126)* **EARLY MORNING ONWARDS** — –
– Early morning / Poor wages / Brother Thrush / Mr. Sunshine / Taking some time on / Mother dear / Mockingbird / Song with no meaning / I'm over you / Child of man / After the day. *(cd-iss. Mar99 on 'Brimstone'; BRIM 001)*

Mar 75. (7") *(HAR 5094)* **MOCKINGBIRD. / GALADRIEL** — –

Jan 77. (lp) *(SHSM 2013)* **THE BEST OF BARCLAY JAMES HARVEST** — –
(re-iss. Aug86 on 'E.M.I.' lp/c; ATAK/TC-ATAK 95)

Sep 79. (lp) *(SHSM 2023)* **THE BEST OF BARCLAY JAMES HARVEST VOL.2** — –

Feb 81. (lp) *(SHSM 2033)* **THE BEST OF BARCLAY JAMES HARVEST VOL.3** — –

Nov 85. (cd) *Polydor; (825 895-2)* **THE COMPACT STORY OF BARCLAY JAMES HARVEST**

Oct 87. (cd) *E.M.I.; (CDP 746 709-2)* **ANOTHER ARABLE PARABLE** — –

Dec 90. (cd/c) *Connoisseur; (VSOP CD/MC 140)* **ALONE WE FLY** — –
– Crazy city / For no one / Mockingbird / Hymn / Our kid's kid / Berlin / Loving is easy / Love on the line / Rock'n'roll lady / Shades of B Hill / Fifties child / Waiting for the right time / Blow me down / Sideshow / He said love / Guitar blues.

Mar 91. (d-cd/d-c/d-lp) *Harvest; (CD/TC+/EN 5014)* **THE HARVEST YEARS** — –

Jun 92. (cd) *Polydor; (513 587-2)* **THE BEST OF BARCLAY JAMES HARVEST** — –

Dec 92. (cd) *Beat Goes On; (BGOCD 152)* **BARCLAY JAMES HARVEST / ONCE AGAIN** — –
(re-iss. Oct95 on 'One Way'; OW 18456)

Dec 92. (cd) *Beat Goes On; (BGOCD 160)* **BJH & OTHER SHORT STORIES / BABY JAMES HARVEST** — –
(re-iss. Oct95 on 'One Way'; OW 18505)

May 93. (cd/c) *Spectrum; (550029-2/-4)* **SORCERERS & KEEPERS** — –

Feb 96. (4xcd-box) *EMI-Barclay; (CDBARCLAY 1)* **FOUR ORIGINALS** — –
– (first 4 albums)

Aug 96. (cd) *Connoisseur; (VSOPCD 228)* **ENDLESS DREAM** — –

Feb 97. (cd) *E.M.I.; (CTMCD 309)* **THE BEST OF BARCLAY JAMES JAMES HARVEST – THE CENTENARY COLLECTION** — –

Mar 97. (cd) *Disky; (DC 86721-2)* **MOCKINGBIRD** — –
(re-iss. Mar01 on 'Spectrum'; 544493-2)

Oct 00. (cd) *EMI Gold; (529237-2)* **THE COLLECTION** — –

Apr 01. (cd) *(529542-2)* **MOCKINGBIRD – THE BEST OF BARCLAY JAMES HARVEST** — –

Mar 02. (d-cd) *Snapper; (SMDCD 388)* **THROUGH THE EYES OF JOHN LEES / BRAVE NEW WORLD** — –

Apr 02. (d-cd) *(538980-2)* **BBC IN CONCERT 1972 (live)** — –

Mar 03. (d-cd) *E.M.I.; (<582345-2>)* **BABY JAMES HARVEST / ONCE AGAIN**

BARENAKED LADIES

Formed: Scarborough, Toronto, Canada . . . 1988 by songwriting college students ED ROBERTSON and STEVEN PAGE, both having cut their teeth in a RUSH covers band; JIM CREEGGAN, his brother ANDREW and TYLER STEWART later forming the complete line-up. This kooky and incredibly strange North American combo didn't reach the level of international success until 1998, and before then had never cultivated their talents outside their native Canada. The band began playing in colleges and dingy venues in the heart of Toronto's cosmopolitan scene, when, after a solid year of performing, they respectively discovered that they had created a huge local following. BARENAKED LADIES decided to take their sublime blend of pop/rock/rap/folk to eager crowds in Europe and the remainder of Canada before releasing the now cult debut EP 'THE YELLOW TAPE' (featuring 'BE MY YOKO ONO'). It climbed the charts on their home soil, becoming the first independent Canadian release to go gold! Following this minor ego boost, the group subsequently signed a contract with 'Reprise' records a year later, issuing the first album proper 'GORDON' (1992), which would see the BNL's earning a No.1 spot in the official Canadian charts. 'GORDON' fused structured melodies and graceful pop with 'Sgt. Pepper'-esque dizziness and a little touch of BRIAN WILSON psychedelic rock; it went on to stay a further 8 weeks at the top of the charts (bubbled under the US Top 100). Sophomore set, 'MAYBE YOU SHOULD DRIVE', wasn't released until 1994 and included top singles 'JANE' and the side splitting attempt at a love song, 'MY ALTERNATIVE GIRLFRIEND', both now standard BARENAKED LADIES traits. Having steadily climbed into the US Top 60, the group went on to score with their first Stateside hit 'THE OLD APARTMENT' in the Spring of '97 (taken from their patchy long-player of '96 'BORN ON A PIRATE SHIP'). Appearances on various talk shows, including 'Showbiz Today' and the 'David Letterman Show', helped the band receive international acclaim (with a televised New Year's party apparently reaching a drunken riotous plateau). By the release of their third studio album, 'ROCK SPECTACLE' (1997), the band were now reaching the mainstream by selling out dates across America and Europe. After a well deserved break, the BARENAKED LADIES embarked on what was to become their breakthrough instalment, 'STUNT' (1998), which was released to great critical and audience acclaim – of course its success arrived after smash hit single 'ONE WEEK'. The platter displayed an old-fashioned formula while using rimshot drums with nifty rap and a melodic break where lead singer CREEGGAN described life's little mishaps and misfortunes after a one-night stand. All in all, an entertaining single and equally good album where The BARENAKED LADIES had proved themselves to MOR audiences whilst suffering a post ironic chump-change. The group subsequently devoted a track to the 'Ed TV' soundtrack, and although their song was popular, it didn't help the film's chances at the box office. The lads subsequently roped in production maverick DON WAS for 2000's 'MAROON', a potentially very interesting combination that never quite lived up to its promise. Nevertheless, the 'LADIES' vital signs – irrepressible enthusiasm, crafty rhythmic trickery, offbeat humour and all round musical high jinks – were in rude health, a late 2001 compilation consolidating the impression that the Canadians have successfully perfected the experiment they began more than a decade ago. A new decade proper, and a new post-9/11 era made for the band's most thoughtful and less zany album to date, 'EVERYTHING TO EVERYONE' (2003). In its shrewdly aimed, smoothed-off lyrical barbs and topical subject matter there were definite signs of a preoccupation with weightier issues. The humour was still there for sure, although it was tempered by encroaching middle age and ocassionally even missing completely, as on the no messing 'WAR ON DRUGS'.

Album rating: GORDON (*7) / MAYBE YOU SHOULD DRIVE (*6) / BORN ON A PIRATE SHIP (*7) / ROCK SPECTACLE (*6) / STUNT (*5) / MAROON (*5) / DISC ONE 1991-2001: ALL THEIR GREATEST HITS compilation (*7) / EVERYTHING TO EVERYONE (*5)

ED ROBERTSON (b.25 Oct'70) – vocals, guitar / **STEVEN PAGE** (b.22 Jun'70) – guitar, vocals

not iss. own

1989. (c-ep) **BUCK NAKED** [–] [ ]

—— added **JIM CREEGGAN** (b.12 Feb'70) – bass, keyboards / **ANDREW CREEGGAN** (b. 4 Jul'71) – congas

1990. (c-ep) **BARENAKED LUNCH** [–] [ ]

—— added **TYLER STEWART** (b.21 Sep'67) – drums

1991. (c-ep) **THE YELLOW TAPE** [–] [ ]

Reprise Sire

Aug 92. (cd/c) *<7599 26956-2/-4>* **GORDON** [ ] [ ]
– Hello city / Enid / Grade 9 / Brian Wilson / Be my Yoko Ono / Wrap your arms around me / What a good boy / King of bedside manor / Box set / I love you / New kid on the block / Blame it on me / The flag / If I had $1,000,000 / Crazy.

Jul 93. (7"/c-s) *(W 0186/+C)* **IF I HAD $1,000,000. / GRADE 9** [ ] [ ]
(12"+=/cd-s+=) *(W 0186 T/CD)* – Crazy.

Aug 94. (cd/c) *<9362 45709-2/-4>* **MAYBE YOU SHOULD DRIVE** [57] [ ]
– A / Life, in a nutshell / Great provider / You will be waiting / Jane / Intermittently / These apples / Everything old is new again / Alternative girlfriend / Am I the only one? / Little tiny song / The wrong man was convicted.

Aug 94. (7"/c-s) *(W 0262/+C)* **JANE. / WHAT A GOOD BOY** [ ] [ ]
(cd-s+=) *(W 0262CD)* – Great provider (demo).

—— ANDREW departed and PAGE moved to lead vocals (**KEVIN HEARN** – keyboards; was to join on a part-time basis at first)

Jul 96. (c-s) *(W 0342C)* **IF I HAD $1,000,000 / TRUST ME** [ ] [ ]
(cd-s+=) *(W 0342CD)* – Shoe box.

Jul 96. (cd/c) *<9362 46128-2/-4>* **BORN ON A PIRATE SHIP** [ ] [ ]
– Stomach vs. heart / Straw hat and old dirty Hank / I know / This is where it ends / When I fall / I live with it every day / The old apartment / Call me calmly / Break your heart / Spider in my room / Same thing / Just a toy / In the drink / Shoe box.

Apr 97. (cd-s) *<17499>* **THE OLD APARTMENT / LOVERS IN A DANGEROUS TIME** [–] [88]

Oct 97. (cd-s) *<17290>* **BRIAN WILSON / BREAK YOUR HEART / BACK** [–] [68]

Oct 97. (cd/c) *<46393>* **ROCK SPECTACLE** [–] [86]
– Brian Wilson / Straw hat and old dirty Hank / Break your heart / Jane / When I fall / Hello city / What a good boy / The old apartment / Life, in a nutshell / These apples / If I had a $1,000,000.

Feb 99. (c-s/cd-s) *(W 468 C/CD) <17174>* **ONE WEEK / WHEN YOU DREAM (demo) / SHOEBOX (live)** [5] Sep98 [2]

Feb 99. (cd/c) *<9362 46963-2/-4>* **STUNT** [24] Jul98 [3]
– One week / It's all been done / Light up my room / I'll be that girl / Leave / Alcohol / Call and answer / In the car / Never is enough / Who needs sleep? / Told you so / Some fantastic (ivory and ivory) / When you dream. *(special d-cd Nov99 +=; 9362 47507-2)* – Brian Wilson (2000) / Old apartment (live) / Jane (live) / When I fall (live) / If I had $1,000,000 (live) / Straw hat and old dirty Hank (live) / Brian Wilson.

May 99. (c-s/cd-s) *(W 476 C/CD) <44602>* **IT'S ALL BEEN DONE / BRIAN WILSON (live) / THE OLD APARTMENT (live)** [28] Dec98 [44]

Jul 99. (c-s/cd-s) *(W 498 C/CD2) <44710>* **CALL AND ANSWER / IF I HAD $1,000,000 / JANE (live)** [52] Jun99 [ ]
(cd-s) *(W 498CD1)* – ('A'side) / One week (Big Beat mix) / One week (Paul's mix).

Nov 99. (c-s/cd-s) *(W 511 C/CD1)* **BRIAN WILSON (mixes; 2000 / album version / live from Rock Spectacle / instrumental)** [73] [–]

Sep 00. (cd/c) *<9362 47891-2/-4>* **MAROON** [64] [5]
– Too little too late / Never do anything / Pinch me / Go home / Falling for the first time / Conventioneers / Sell sell sell / The humour of the situation / Baby seat / Off the hook / Helicopters / Tonight is the night that I fell asleep at the wheel.

Nov 00. (c-s/cd-s) *(W 539 C/CD) <16827>* **PINCH ME / POWDER BLUE** [ ] Aug00 [25]

Apr 01. (c-s/cd-s) *(W 557 C/CD) <16774>* **TOO LITTLE TOO LATE / PINCH ME (Injeti remix)** [ ] Mar01 [86]

Nov 01. (cd) *<9362 48075-2>* **DISC ONE 1991-2001: ALL THEIR GREATEST HITS** (compilation) [ ] [38]
– The old apartment / Falling for the first time / Brian Wilson (live) / One week / Be my Yoko Ono / Alternative girlfriend / It's only me (the wizard of Magicland) / If I had $1,000,000 / Call and answer / Get in line / It's all been done / Jane / Lovers in a dangerous time / Pinch me / Shoebox / What a good boy / Too little too late / Enid / Thanks that was fun.

Sep 03. (cd-s) *<16537>* **ANOTHER POSTCARD (CHIMPS) / NEXT TIME (acoustic)** [–] [82]

Oct 03. (cd) *<48209>* **EVERYTHING TO EVERYONE** [–] [10]
– Celebrity / Maybe Katie / Another postcard / Next time / For you / Shopping / Testing 1, 2, 3 / Upside down / War on drugs / Aluminium / Unfinished / Second best / Take it outside / Have you seen my love?

Syd BARRETT

Born: ROGER KEITH BARRETT, 6 Jan'46, Cambridge, England. Earned the nickname SID (which he later changed to SYD), after regulars at the local Riverside Jazz Club found out his surname and christened him after an old drummer from the area, SID BARRET. SYD was talented enough to secure a place at the prestigious Camberwell Art School in 1963 and once in London, he teamed up with his old friend ROGER WATERS, who had asked him to join his band The SCREAMING ABDABS. At SYD's suggestion, the band renamed themselves PINK FLOYD after two Georgia bluesmen featured on an old record he owned. Turned onto LSD by a friend, he became fascinated by the mysteries of the Universe, even carrying around a Times Astronomical Atlas. This obsession would later inspire such FLOYD classics as 'ASTRONOMY DOMINE' and 'INTERSTELLAR OVERDRIVE'. The latter's main riff was famously derived from a chord pattern SYD worked out after hearing manager PETER JENNER attempting to hum LOVE's version of BURT BACHARACH's 'My Little Red Book'. The 1967 album 'THE PIPER AT THE GATES OF DAWN' on which these two tracks appeared, made the group and especially BARRETT, major league pop stars. This was something that did SYD's increasingly erratic mental health no good whatsoever. By the time of the album's release, he had moved into the infamous Cromwell Road flat in London, living on a daily diet of hallucinogenics and was beginning to develop a piercing stare, which would scare even the most hardened person in his company. At EMI's request, BARRETT recorded two further tracks, 'SCREAM THY LAST SCREAM' and 'VEGETABLE MAN', which were unsurprisingly rejected, EMI staff producer NORMAN SMITH dubbing them "lunatic ravings". His penultimate offering for FLOYD, 'APPLES AND ORANGES', flopped, and SYD's mental condition deteriorated further. After missing some shows and performances, WATERS eventually made it clear he was surplus to requirement. His last effort with PINK FLOYD, 'JUGBAND BLUES', appeared after his departure, on the second FLOYD album 'A SAUCERFUL OF SECRETS' (mid-68). It was his last poignant statement for FLOYD, a self-diagnosis of his encroaching schizophrenia. EMI (actually 'Harvest') still had enough confidence in SYD to offer him a solo deal, as he set about recording his debut, 'THE MADCAP LAUGHS'. Released early in 1970 after a laborious year in the studio, it featured drummer NICK MASON and other FLOYD-ians, thus its brief entry into the UK Top 40. Despite SYD being high on the tranquiliser Mandrax, the album had its moments, with the likes of 'OCTOPUS', 'DARK GLOBE', 'TERRAPIN', 'NO GOOD TRYIN' and 'LONG GONE', making up for the other lost-in-the-ether tracks. The hastily recorded 'BARRETT', released later the same year, used a band featuring DAVE GILMOUR (the friend who replaced him in PINK FLOYD), RICK WRIGHT and JERRY SHIRLEY, giving him some cohesion, and although it was more assured in depth, it lacked the fragility of its predecessor. The album was poorly received and SYD retreated to the cellar of his mother's home in Cambridge. He resurfaced in 1972 as part of the doomed STARS project (with TWINK & JACK MONK), before finally giving up music altogether. He never fully recovered from his debilitating mental illness and tragically, he's become almost blind due to diabetes related problems. Whether the drugs actually caused his decline or merely assisted it is something that will no doubt continue to be debated long into the future, although you can be sure SYD won't care to listen. A flawed genius whose legend and influence grows stronger with each passing year, SYD BARRETT was the whimsical child-like star, burning brightly in a kaleidoscope of technicolour sound, before dropping out into a haze of drug-induced psychosis. He has since been tributed and stylised by many, including TELEVISION PERSONALITIES, ROBYN HITCHCOCK and The LEGENDARY PINK DOTS. • **Trivia:** PINK FLOYD paid homage to SYD on their album SHINE ON YOU CRAZY DIAMOND track from album 'WISH YOU WERE HERE'. SYD attended these sessions but didn't contribute.

Album rating: THE MADCAP LAUGHS (*8) / BARRETT (*6) / OPEL collection (*6) / WOULDN'T YOU MISS ME – THE BEST OF SYD BARRETT compilation (*8)

SYD BARRETT – vocals, guitar; augmented by **DAVID GILMOUR + ROGER WATERS** with **MIKE RATLEDGE** – keyboards / **HUGH HOPPER** – bass / **ROBERT WYATT** – drums (all of SOFT MACHINE) plus **JOHN 'WILLIE' WATSON + JERRY SHIRLEY** – rhythm (latter of HUMBLE PIE)

Harvest Harvest

Oct 69. (7") *(HAR 5009)* **OCTOPUS. / GOLDEN HAIR**

Jan 70. (lp) *(SHVL 765) <SABB 11314>* **THE MADCAP LAUGHS** 40
– Terrapin / No good trying / Love you / No man's land / Dark globe / Here I go / Octopus / Golden Hair / Long gone / She took a long cold look / Feel / If it's in you / Late night. *(cd-iss. Oct87; CDP 746 607-2) (re-iss. cd Jun94; CDGO 2053) (re-iss. Feb97 on 'E.M.I.'; LPCENT 1) (lp re-iss. Jan01 on 'Simply Vinyl'; SVLP 289)*

— SYD retained GILMOUR, SHIRLEY + WILSON adding **RICK WRIGHT** – keyboards (of PINK FLOYD) and guest on one **VIC SAYWELL** – tuba

Nov 70. (lp) *(SHSP 4007)* **BARRETT** –
– Baby lemonade / Love song / Dominoes / It is obvious / Rats / Maisie / Gigolo aunt / Waving my arms in the air / Wined and dined / Wolfpack / Effervescing elephant / I never lied to you. *(cd-iss. May87; CDP 746 606-2) (re-iss. cd Jun94; CDGO 2054) (lp re-iss. Jan01 on 'Simply Vinyl'; SVLP 281)*

— his solo career ended and he formed short-lived STARS early in '72, with **TWINK** – drums (ex-PINK FAIRIES) + **JACK MONK** – bass (they made no recordings)

— In 1982, he was living with his mother having hung up guitar.

– compilations, others, etc. –

Sep 74. (d-lp) *Harvest; (SHDW 404)* **SYD BARRETT** –
– (THE MADCAP LAUGHS / BARRETT). *(d-cd-iss. Mar03; 582346-2)*

Jan 88. (12"ep) *Strange Fruit; (SFPS/+CD 043)* **THE PEEL SESSIONS (24.2.70)** –
– Terrapin / Gigolo aunt / Baby lemonade / Two of a kind / Effervescing elephant. *(cd re-iss. Sep95; same)*

Oct 88. (cd)(c/lp) *Harvest; (CDP 791 206-2)(TC+/SHSP 4126) / Capitol; <91206>* **OPEL** (recorded 68-70) Apr89
– Opel / Clowns and daggers (Octopus) / Rats / Golden hair (vocal) / Dollyrocker / Word song / Wined and dined / Swan Lee (Silas Lang) / Birdie hop / Let's split / Lanky (part 1) / Wouldn't you miss me / Golden hair (instrumental). *(re-iss. cd Jun94; CDGO 2055) (lp re-iss. Dec99 on 'Simply Vinyl'; SVLP 153)*

Apr 93. (3xcd-box) *E.M.I.; (SYDBOX 1)* **CRAZY DIAMOND – THE COMPLETE SYD BARRETT**
– (all 3 albums above)

Apr 94. (cd) *Cleopatra; (<CLEO 5771-2>)* **OCTOPUS – THE BEST OF SYD BARRETT** May92
– Octopus / Swan Lee (Silas Lang) / Baby lemonade / Late night / Wined and dined / Golden hair / Gigolo aunt / Wolfpack / It is obvious / Lanky (pt.1) / No good trying / Clowns and jugglers (Octopus) / Waving my arms in the air / Opel. *(re-iss. Jul01; CLP 2200CD)*

Apr 01. (cd) *Harvest; (532320-2)* **WOULDN'T YOU MISS ME – THE BEST OF SYD BARRETT**
– Octopus / Late night / Terrapin / Swan Lee / Wolfpack / Golden hair / Here I go / Long gone / No good trying / Opel / Baby lemonade / Gigolo aunt / Dominoes / Wouldn't you miss me / Wined and dined / Efferverscing elephant / Waving my arms in the air / I never lied to you / Love song / Two of a kind / Bob Dylan blues / Golden hair (instrumental).

BASEMENT JAXX

Formed: South London, England ... 1993 by producer & DJ duo SIMON RATCLIFFE and FELIX BUXTON. The pair met at a Thames party organised by the latter on a riverboat. After conversation, sparks flew between the two DJs and they promptly set up 'Atlantic Jaxx' records in the summer of 1994. The pair were astounded when their idol and key influence TONY HUMPHRIES played 'DA UNDERGROUND' (a song from their first EP with the same title) to near annihilation on his 'Mix-show' in 1995. Later the same year the group also released 'SAMBA MAGIC' on single and conscripted vocalist CORRINA JOSEPHS into the outfit. 1996 was spent doing remixes for The PET SHOP BOYS, 'LIL' MO YIN' and various other artists. The collective also released an eponymous EP, which saw the track 'FLY LIFE' reach the British Top 20 and go on to become a massive house anthem. Relentlessly being pursued by major labels, RATCLIFFE and BUXTON settled for imprint 'X.L.' (home of The PRODIGY), where the band went on to issue their first major album 'REMEDY' (1999). The obvious highlight was the rare 12" single, 'SAME OLD SHOW', a sampletastic "rude girl!" beatbox of a song that incorporated The Selector's 1980 hit 'On My Radio'. Two singles, 'RED ALERT' and the bass-breaking 'RENDEZ-VU', both became massive Ibiza and London house tracks, mixing styles as far apart as Chicago (drum'n'bass) to eclectic Latin disco-funk, the scope was undeniably wide. The pair of Brixton beatbreakers returned in the Summer of 2001 with an album to equal that of 'REMEDY', named after their now de-funked private nightclub 'ROOTY'. Not only was 'ROOTY' better in terms of music, production and eclecticness (check out the funky PRINCE grooves on 'SEXY FELINE MACHINE'), but the album also boasted fantastic singles 'ROMEO' and the macabre GARY NUMAN sampled 'WHERE'S YOUR HEAD AT?', which featured an equally wacked-out video starring some very scary monkeys. Other highlights included the KELE LA ROC fronted 'CRAZY GIRL', the Ibiza club floor-piece 'JUS 1 KISS' and the very laid bare 'BROKEN DREAMS', with its chilled, lounge-feel sweetness. It was inevitable that, due to the success of 'RED ALERT', the 'JAXX would spawn a whole host of hit singles, with both of the aforementioned reaching the Top 10 and the album crashing into the Top 5. 'KISH KASH' (2003) completed a home run of incredible records and even if it wasn't as groundbreaking as its predecessors, the very fact that they'd breathed life into that most difficult of music mediums – the dance long player – was surely an achievement in itself. The PRINCE influence was more notable than ever, while a raft of unlikely guest stars – from ME'SHELL NDEGEOCELLO to DIZZEE RASCAL to SIOUXSIE SIOUX – kept things interesting.

Album rating: ATLANTIC JAXX – A COMPILATION (*6) / REMEDY (*9) / ROOTY (*8) / KISH KASH (*7)

SIMON RATCLIFFE + FELIX BUXTON

Atlantic Jaxx unknown

Mar 96. (12"; by CORRINA JOSEPH) *(JAXX 005)* **I WANNA GET DOWN (WHEN U GET DOWN). /** [ ] [-]
Jun 96. (12"ep) *(JAXX 001)* **BASEMENT JAXX E.P. 1** [ ] [ ]
Jul 96. (12"ep) *(JAXX 002)* **BASEMENT JAXX E.P. 2** [ ] [ ]
– Be free / Deep jackin' / I'm thru with you / Dusk till dawn.
Jul 96. (12"ep) *(JAXX 003)* **SUMMER DAZE E.P.** [ ] [ ]
– Paradise / Phase 2 hi / Aprino jam / Samba magic.
Jul 96. (12"ep; by RATCLIFFE) *(JAXX 004)* **RATCLIFFE E.P.** [ ] [ ]
Jul 96. (12"ep) *(JAXX 006)* **BASEMENT JAXX E.P. 3** [ ] [ ]
– Daluma / Jus becuz / Fly life / Slide slide.
Nov 96. (12"; by HEARTISTS) *(JAXX 009)* **BELO HORIZONTI. /** [ ] [-]
(re-iss. Jul97 c-s/12"/cd-s; VCR C/T/D 23)
Feb 97. (12"ep) *(JAXX 008)* **SLEAZYCHEEKS E.P.** [ ] [ ]
– Ennao / Moradi / Get down, get horny / Jump / Stanley.
Mar 97. (12"ep) *(JAXX 010)* **URBAN HAZE E.P.** [ ] [ ]
– City people / Urban haze / Set yo' body free / Raw shit.

Multiply not iss.

May 97. (c-s/12"/cd-s) *(CA/12/CD MULTY 21)* **FLY LIFE (mixes)** [19] [-]
(12") *(12MULTY 21X)* – ('A'mixes).

Banana Krew not iss.

Aug 98. (12") *(001)* **SAME OLD SHOW. / AUTOMATIC** [ ] [-]

X.L. Astralwerks

Nov 98. (12") *(JAXL 001)* **RED ALERT. / YO-YO** [ ] [-]
Apr 99. (12")(cd-s) *(XLT 100)(XLS 100CD2) <6273>* **RED ALERT (mixes; Jaxx club / Eric Morillo & Harry Choo Choo Romero dub / Steve Gurley)** [5] Jul99 [ ]
(cd-s) *(XLS 100CD) <6274>* – ('A'side) / Razocaine / ('A'-Jaxx nite dub).
May 99. (cd/c/d-lp) *(XL CD/MC/LP 129) <6270>* **REMEDY** [4] Aug99 [ ]
– Rendez-vu / Yo-yo / Jump n' shout / U can't stop me / Jaxxalude / Red alert / Jazzalude / Always be there / Sneakalude / Same old show / Bingo bango / Gemilude / Stop 4 love / Don't give up / Being with U.
Jul 99. (c-s) *(XLC 110) <6281>* **RENDEZ-VU / MUSIC KEEPS ON PLAYIN' (Miracles mix of Red Alert)** [4] Oct99 [ ]
(12") *(XLT 110)* – All U crazies.
(cd-s) *(XLS 110CD)* – (some of above).
Oct 99. (c-s)(cd-s) *(XLC 116)(XLS 116CD)* **JUMP N' SHOUT / LA PHOTO / I BEG YOU** [12] [ ]
(12") *(XLT 116)* – ('A'side) / I Beg U / Boo slings dub.
Apr 00. (c-s) *(XLC 120)* **BINGO BANGO / (mix)** [13] [ ]
(12"+=)(cd-s+=) *(XLT 120)(XLS 120CD)* – Jump 'n' shout.
Jun 01. (c-s/12") *(XLC/XLT 132)* **ROMEO. / BONGOLOID / CAMBERWELL SKIES** [6] [ ]
(cd-s+=) *(XLS 132CD)* – ('A'mixes).
Jun 01. (cd/c/d-lp) *(XL CD/MC/LP 143) <10423>* **ROOTY** [5] [ ]
– Romeo / Breakaway / SFM / Kissalude / Jus 1 kiss / Broken dreams / I want U / Get me off / Where's your head at / Freakalude / Crazy girl / Do your thing / All I know.
Sep 01. (cd-s) *(XLS 136CD)* **JUS 1 KISS / TWILITE / JUS 1 KISS (Jaxx nite club) / JUS 1 KISS (video)** [23] [-]
(12")(cd-s) *(XLT 136)(XLS 136CD2)* – ('A'-extended) / ('A'-Sunship mix) / ('A'-Boris Dlugosch mix).
Nov 01. (cd-s) *(XLS 140CD)* **WHERE'S YOUR HEAD AT / (acoustic version)** [9] [-]
(12") *(XLT 140)* – ('A'extended) / ('A'-Stanton Warriors remix) / ('A'-Sounds Of Da Future mix).
Jun 02. (cd-s) *(XLS 146CD)* **GET ME OFF / DO YOUR THING (Jaxx Club remix) / BROKEN DREAMS (Los Amigos Invisibles mix)** [22] [-]
(12")(cd-s) *(XLT 146)(XLS 146CD2)* – ('A'-2002 club mix) / ('A'-Peaches remix) / ('A'-Superchumbo 'Supergetoff' remix).
Oct 03. (cd/lp) *(XLCD/XLLP 174) <93878>* **KISH KASH** [17] [ ]
– Good luck (with LISA KEKAULA) / Right here's the spot (with ME'SHELL NDEGEOCELLO) / Benjilude / Lucky star (with DIZZEE RASCAL) / Petrilude / Supersonic (with TOTLYN JACKSON) / Plug it in (with JC CHASEZ) / Cosmolude / If I ever recover / Cish cash (with SIOUXSIE SIOUX) / Tonight (with PHOEBE) / Hot 'n cold / Living room / Feels like home (with ME'SHELL NDEGEOCELLO).
Nov 03. (cd-s; by BASEMENT JAXX & DIZZEE RASCAL) *(XLS 172CD)* **LUCKY STAR / ('A'-Jaxx club remix) / ('A'-Dillinja remix)** [23] [-]
(12") *(XLT 172)* – ('A'-extended / Jaxxhouz dub / Jaxx club).
(12") *(XLR 172)* – ('A'-remixes; Dillinja / Dillinja dub).

– compilations, others, etc. –

Oct 97. (cd/d-lp) *Atlantic Jaxx; (JAXX CD/LP 001)* **ATLANTIC JAXX – A COMPILATION** [ ] [-]
– Intro / Be free / Smaba magic / CORRINA JOSEPH: Live your life / Fly life / Ennao / HEARTISTS: Belo horizonti / CORRINA JOSEPH: Lonely / Set yo' body free / CORRINA JOSEPH: Daluma / RATCLIFFE: Grapesoda / RONNIE RICHARDS: Missing you / Undaground.
Aug 99. (12") *Atlantic Jaxx; (JAXX 013)* **BETTA DAZE** [ ] [-]
Aug 02. (d12") *Atlantic Jaxx; (JAXL 009)* **DO YOUR THING (mixes)** [ ] [-]

☐ BASS-O-MATIC (see under ⇒ ORBIT, William)

BAUHAUS

Formed: Northampton, England . . . late 1978, by PETE MURPHY, DANIEL ASH, DAVID J and KEVIN HASKINS, initially calling themselves BAUHAUS 1919. Obtaining a one-off deal with indie label 'Small Wonder', they released an 8-minute epic 'BELA LUGOSI'S DEAD', backed with the infamous 'DARK ENTRIES', the latter track subsequently issued as a follow-up 45. A gender-bending but hard-edged collage of glam and punk influences shrouded in gothic horror posturing, BAUHAUS carved out their own inimitable niche in the early 80's post-new wave wasteland. After an album, 'IN THE FLAT FIELD' (1981) and a couple of singles (one a cover of T.Rex's 'TELEGRAM SAM') on '4 a.d.', the band signed to 'Beggars Banquet', scoring a Top 30 hit with debut set, 'MASK' (1981). Featuring the minor hit singles, 'KICK IN THE EYE' and 'THE PASSION OF LOVERS', the album remains their most consistent set. Still, the underground cred was called into question after MURPHY appeared in a TV ad for Maxell tapes later that year. More appropriate, perhaps, was the band's performance of 'BELA LUGOSI'S DEAD' for 1982 vampire film, 'The Hunger' starring the band's boyhood hero, DAVID BOWIE. In fact, it was one of BOWIE's classics, 'ZIGGY STARDUST', that gave BAUHAUS their commercial breakthrough, the single's Top 20 success seeing the accompanying album, THE SKY'S GONE OUT' make the UK Top 5. The droning affectations of 'SHE'S IN PARTIES' remains one of the band's most recognisable tracks while the swan song album, 'BURNING FROM THE INSIDE' (1983), saw BAUHAUS signing off on an unsettling, if creatively high point. MURPHY soon reappeared with MICK KARN of JAPAN in a new outfit, DALI'S CAR, although only one album, 'THE WAKING HOUR', surfaced in '84. The singer went on to release a string of albums, surprising many in Britain when he had a US Top 50 placing with 'DEEP', which contained the 1990 hit, 'CUTS YOU UP'. Meanwhile, the rest were enjoying success as LOVE AND ROCKETS (from earlier incarnation of TONES ON TAILS and DAVID J solo) and this trio also took America by storm having had a Top 3 smash, 'SO ALIVE' in '89. With current offshoots failing to sparkle during the rest of the 90's, BAUHAUS decided to officially re-form in mid 1998 for two concerts, which enabled their record label to cash-in on an accompanying best-of collection, 'CRACKLE'. The same year saw the release of LOVE AND ROCKETS' 'LIFT', a tired sounding affair which once more dabbled in electronica without any real direction or enthusiasm. MURPHY, meanwhile, fresh from the reunion, undertook a lengthy stint of solo touring which was eventually partly documented with 'ALIVE JUST FOR LOVE' (2001). A largely acoustic set with minimalist string accompaniment, the album was as intimate as MURPHY has ventured thus far, drawing on the choicest cuts from his growing solo back catalogue. 2002's 'DUST', meanwhile, was a long, patiently awaited studio set building on the exotic, ethnic influences apparent in his music as far back as the mid-90's. Together with collaborators MERCAN DEDE, MICHAEL BROOK, HUGH MARSH and JAMAALADEEN TACUMA, MURPHY sculpted his most absorbing work to date, entwining strands of Eastern spirituality, electronica and hypnotic percussion with his darkly constant muse. • **Covered:** THIRD UNCLE (Eno) / WAITING FOR THE MAN (Velvet Underground) / SEVERENCE (Dead Can Dance). PETER MURPHY solo, wrote with STREATHAM and covered; FINAL SOLUTION (Pere Ubu) / THE LIGHT POURS OUT OF ME (Magazine) / FUNTIME (Iggy Pop) / LOVE ME TENDER (Elvis Presley). LOVE AND ROCKETS covered BALL OF CONFUSION (Temptations) / BODY AND SOUL (trad). DAVID J covered 4 HOURS (ClockDva) / SHIP OF FOOLS (John Cale).

Album rating: IN THE FLAT FIELD (*5) / MASK (*6) / THE SKY'S GONE OUT (*6) / BURNING FROM THE INSIDE (*5) / BAUHAUS 1979-1983 compilation (*9) / CRACKLE collection (*6) / GOTHAM (*7)
Dali's Car: THE WAKING HOUR (*5) / Pete Murphy: SHOULD THE WORLD FAIL TO FALL APART (*5) / LOVE HYSTERIA (*5) / DEEP (*6) / CASCADE (*4) / WILD BIRDS 1985-1995 compilation (*7) / ALIVE: JUST FOR LOVE (*5) / DUST (*6) / Tones On Tails: NIGHT MUSIC compilation (*6) / Love And Rockets: SEVENTH DREAM OF TEENAGE HEAVEN (*6) / EXPRESS (*7) / EARTH SUN MOON (*7) / LOVE AND ROCKETS (*5) / HOT TRIP TO HEAVEN (*3) / SWEET F.A. (*3) / LIFT (*5) / SORTED! – THE BEST OF LOVE AND ROCKETS compilation (*6)

PETER MURPHY (b.11 Jul'57) – vocals / **DANIEL ASH** (b.31 Jul'57) – guitar, vocals / **DAVID J** (b. HASKINS, 24 Apr'57) – bass, vocals / **KEVIN HASKINS** (b.19 Jul'60) – drums, percussion

Small Wonder — not iss.

Aug 79. (12",12"white) *(TEENY 2)* **BELA LUGOSI'S DEAD. / BOYS / DARK ENTRIES** [ ] [–]
(re-dist.Mar81 & Mar82; same) (re-iss. Sep86 in various colours; same) (12"pic-d.1987; TEENY 2P) (re-iss. May88 & Jun98, c-s/cd-s; TEENY 2 C/CD)

Axis — not iss.

Jan 80. (7") *(AXIS 3)* **DARK ENTRIES. / UNTITLED** [ ] [–]
(re-iss. Feb80 on '4.a.d.'; AD 3) (some mispressed on 'Beggars Banquet'; BEG 37)

4.a.d. — not iss.

Jun 80. (7") *(AD 7)* **TERROR COUPLE KILL COLONEL. / SCOPES / TERROR COUPLE KILL COLONEL II** [ ] [–]
Oct 80. (lp) *(CAD 13)* **IN THE FLAT FIELD** [72] [–]
– Double dare / In the flat field / A god in an alcove / Dive / Spy in the cab / Small talk stinks / St. Vitus dance / Stigmata martyr / Nerves. *(cd-iss. Apr88 +=; CAD 13CD)* – Untitled. *(cd re-iss. Jul98; GAD 013CD)*
Oct 80. (7") *(AD 17)* **TELEGRAM SAM. / CROWDS** [ ] [–]
(12"+=) *(AD 17T)* – Rosegarden funeral of sores.

Beggars Banquet — A&M

Mar 81. (7"/12") *(BEG 54/+T)* **KICK IN THE EYE. / SATORI** [59] [–]
Jun 81. (7") *(BEG 59)* **THE PASSION OF LOVERS. / 1: 2: 3: 4:** [56] [–]
Oct 81. (lp/c) *(BEGA/BEGC 29)* **MASK** [30] [–]
– Hair of the dog / The passion of lovers / Of lillies and remains / Dancing / Hollow hills / Kick in the eye / Muscle in plastic / In fear of fear / Man with x-ray eyes / Mask. *(re-iss. Feb88 & Jul91 on 'Beggars Banquet-Lowdown' lp/c; BBL/+C 29) (cd-iss. Oct88 & Jul91 +=; BBL 29CD)* – Satori / Harry / Earwax / In fear of dub / Kick in the eye. *<US-iss.1995 on 'Atlantic'; 92576>*
Feb 82. (7"ep) *(BEG 74)* **SEARCHING FOR SATORI** [45] [–]
– Kick in the eye / Harry / Earwax.
(12"ep+=) *(BEG 74T)* – In fear of dub.
Jun 82. (7"/7"pic-d) *(BEG 79/+P)* **SPIRIT. / TERROR COUPLE KILL COLONEL (live)** [42] [–]
Sep 82. (7") *(BEG 83)* **ZIGGY STARDUST. / THIRD UNCLE (live)** [15] [–]
(12"+=) *(BEG 83T)* – Party of the first part / Waiting for the man.
Oct 82. (d-lp/d-c) *(BEGA/BEGC 42) / (BEGA/BEGC 38) <SP 4918>* **THE SKY'S GONE OUT / PRESS THE EJECT BUTTON AND GIVE ME THE TAPE (live)** [4] [ ]
– Third uncle / Silent hedges / In the night / Swing the heartache / Spirit / The three shadows (parts 1, 2, 3) / Silent hedges / All we ever wanted was everything / Exquisite corpse. *(re-iss. Feb88 & Jul91 on 'Beggars Banquet-Lowdown' lp/c; BBL/+C 42) (cd-iss. Oct88 & Jul91 +=; BBL 42CD)* – Ziggy Stardust / Watch that grandad go / Party of the first part / Spirit (extended). **PRESS THE EJECT BUTTON AND GIVE ME THE TAPE** – In the flat field / Rosegarden funeral of sores / Dancing / Man with the x-ray eyes / Bela Lugosi's dead / Spy in the cab / Kick in the eye / In fear of fear / Hollow hills / Stigmata martyr / Dark entries. *(re-iss. Feb88 & Jul91 on 'Beggars Banquet-Lowdown'; BBL/+C 38) (cd-iss. Oct88 & Jul91 +=; BBL 38CD)* – Terror couple kill colonel / Double dare / Waiting for the man / Hair of the dog / Of lillies and remains. *(free 7"ep with above; BH 1)* – SATORI IN PARIS (live)
Jan 83. (7") *(BEG 88)* **LAGARTIJA NICK. / PARANOIA! PARANOIA!** [44] [–]
(12"+=) *(BEG 88T)* – Watch that grandad go / In the flat field (live).
Mar 83. (7") *<2524>* **LAGARTIJA NICK. / ZIGGY STARDUST** [–] [ ]
Apr 83. (7"/7"pic-d) *(BEG 91/+P)* **SHE'S IN PARTIES. / DEPARTURE** [26] [ ]
(12"+=) *(BEG 91T)* – Here's the dub.
Jul 83. (lp/c) *(BEGA/BEGC 45) <3325>* **BURNING FROM THE INSIDE** [13] [ ]
– She's in parties / Antonin Artaud / King Volcano / Who killed Mr. Moonlight? / Slice of life / Honeymoon croon / Kingdom's coming / Burning from the inside / Hope. *(re-iss. Feb88 & Jul91 on 'Beggars Banquet-Lowdown' lp/c; BBL/+C 45) (cd-iss. Oct88 & Jul91 +=; BBL 45CD)* – Lagartija Nick / Departure / Here's the dub / The sanity assassin.

—— disbanded mid 1983. DAVID J. continued splinter solo venture before forming LOVE AND ROCKETS with DANIEL and KEVIN who had come from own outfit, TONES ON TAIL. MURPHY went solo (see below).

– compilations, others, etc. –

on 'Beggars Banquet' unless mentioned otherwise

Sep 83. (12"ep) *4 a.d.; (BAD 312)* **THE 4.A.D. SINGLES** [ ] [–]
– Dark entries / Terror couple kill colonel / Telegram Sam / Rosegarden full of sores / Crowds.
Oct 83. (12"ep) *(BEG 100E)* **THE SINGLES 1981-83** [52] [–]
– The passion of lovers / Kick in the eye / Spirit / Ziggy Stardust / Lagartija Nick / She's in parties. *(re-iss. Dec88 as 3"pic-cd; BBP 4CD)*
Nov 85. (d-lp/c) *(BEGA/BEGC 64)* **BAUHAUS 1979-1983** [36] [ ]
(d-cd-iss. Feb88; BEG 64CD) (re-iss. d-cd Sep95)
Jul 89. (d-lp/c)(d-cd) *(BEGA/BEGC 103)(BEGA 103CD) <9804>* **SWING THE HEARTACHE** (the BBC sessions) [ ] [ ]
(re-iss. 2xcd Sep95; BBL 64 CD1/CD2)
Aug 98. (cd) *(BEGL 2018CD)* **CRACKLE (live)** [ ] [ ]
– Double dare / In the flat field / Passion of lovers / Bela Lugosi's dead / Sanity assassin / She's in parties / Silent hedges / Hollow hills / Mask / Kick in the eye / Ziggy stardust / Dark entries / Terror couple kill colonel / Spirit / Burning from the inside / Crowds.

DALI'S CAR

were formed by **PETE MURPHY** – vocals / **MICK KARN** – bass, multi (ex-JAPAN) / **PAUL VINCENT LAWFORD** – rhythms

Paradox — Beggars Banquet

Oct 84. (7"/7"pic-d) *(DOX/+Y 1)* **THE JUDGEMENT IS THE MIRROR. / HIGH PLACES** [66] [–]
(12"+=) *(DOX 1-12)* – Lifelong moment.
Nov 84. (lp/c/cd) *(DOX LP/C/CD 1)* **THE WAKING HOUR** [84] [ ]
– Dali's car / His box / Cornwall stone / Artemis / Create and melt / Moonlife / The judgement is the mirror. *(re-iss. Jan89 on 'Beggars Banquet-Lowdown'; lp/c)(cd; BBL/+C 52)(BBL 52CD)*

PETER MURPHY

went solo, augmented by **JOHN McGEOGH** – guitar / **HOWARD HUGHES** – keyboards / **ROBERT SUAVE** – bass / **STEVE YOUNG** – rhythm prog. / **PLUG** – harmonica

Beggars Banquet | Beggars Banquet

Nov 85. (7") *(BEG 143)* **THE FINAL SOLUTION. / THE ANSWER'S CLEAR** [ ] [–]
(12"+=) *(BEG 143T)* – ('A'full version).
(12"pic-d+=) *(BEG 143TP)* – ('A'club mix).

Jun 86. (7"/12") *(BEG 162/+T)* **BLUE HEART. / CANVAS BEAUTY** [ ] [–]

Jul 86. (lp/c) *(BEGA/BEGC 69)* **SHOULD THE WORLD FAIL TO FALL APART** [82] [ ]
– Canvas beauity / The light pours out of me / Confessions / Should the world fail to fall apart / Never man / God . . . sends / Blue heart / The answer is clear / The final solution / Jemal. *(re-iss. Jul88 on 'Beggars Banquet-Lowdown' lp/c)(cd; BBL/+C 69)(BBL 69CD)*

Oct 86. (7") *(BEG 174)* **TALE OF THE TONGUE. / SHOULD THE WORLD FAIL TO FALL APART** [ ] [ ]
(12"+=) *(BEG 174T)* – ('A'-2nd version).

— **MURPHY** brought in **PAUL STATHAM** – co-composer, keyboards (ex-B-MOVIE) / **EDDIE BRACH** – bass / **PETER BONAS** – guitar / **TERL BRYANT** – drums

Feb 88. (7") *(BEG 207)* **ALL NIGHT LONG. / I'VE GOT A SECRET CAMERA** [ ] [–]
(12"+=) *(BEG 207T)* – Funtime (in cabaret).

Mar 88. (lp/c)(cd) *(BEGA/BEGC 92)(BEGA 92CD) <7634>* **LOVE HYSTERIA** [ ] [ ]
– All night long / His circle and hers meet / Dragnet drag / Socrates the python / Indigo eyes / Time has got nothing to do with it / Blind sublime / My last two weeks / Funtime. *(cd+=)* – I've got a miniature secret camera / Funtime (cabaret mix).

Mar 88. (7") *<8670>* **ALL NIGHT LONG. / FUNTIME (Cabaret mix)** [–] [ ]

Apr 88. (7"/7"box) *(BEG/+B 210)* **INDIGO EYES. / GOD SENDS (live)** [ ] [ ]
(12"+=) *(BEG 210T)* – Confessions (live).

Jun 88. (7") *<8707>* **INDIGO EYES. / MY LAST TWO WEEKS** [–] [ ]

Mar 90. (7") *(BEG 237) <9140>* **CUTS YOU UP. / STRANGE KIND OF LOVE** [ ] [55]
(12"+=/cd-s+=) *(BEG 237 T/CD)* – Roll call (reprise).

May 90. (cd)(c/lp) *(BEGA 107CD)(BEGC/BEGA 107) <9877>* **DEEP** [ ] [44]
– Deep ocean vast sea / Crystal waters / Marlene Dietrich's favourite poem / Seven veils / The line between the Devil's teeth (and that which cannot be repeated) / Cuts you up / A strange kind of love / Roll call. *(cd+=)* – Strange kind of love (alt.version).

Apr 92. (7") *(BEG 259)* **YOU'RE SO CLOSE. / THE SWEETEST DROP** [ ] [–]
(12"+=/cd-s+=) *(BEG 259 T/CD)* – Cuts you up (live) / All night long (live).

Apr 92. (cd)(c/lp) *(BEGA 123CD)(BEGC/BEGA 123) <66007>* **HOLY SMOKE** [ ] [ ]
– Keep me from harm / Kill the hate / You're so close / The sweetest drop / Low room / Let me love you / Our secret garden / Dream gone by / Hit song.

Jul 92. (7") *(BEG 261)* **HIT SONG. / SEVEN VEILS (live)** [ ] [–]
(12"+=/cd-s+=) *(BEG 261 T/CD)* – The line between the Devil's teeth (and that which cannot be repeated) (live).

Apr 95. (cd-ep) *(BBQ 52CD)* **THE SCARLET THING IN YOU / CRYSTAL WRISTS / WISH / DRAGNET DRAG (live)** [ ] [ ]

Apr 95. (cd/c) *(BBQ CD/MC 175) <92541>* **CASCADE** [ ] [ ]
– Mirror to my woman's mind / Subway / Gliding like a whale / Disappearing / Mercy rain / I'll fall with your knife / Scarlet thing in you / Sails wave goodbye / Wild birds flock to me / Huuvola / Cascade.

Mar 00. (cd) *(BBL 2019CD) <82019>* **WILD BIRDS 1985-1995** (compilation) [ ] Feb00 [ ]
– Cuts you up / Subway / The scarlet thing in you / Indigo eyes / Keep me from harm / Final solution / Deep ocean vast sea / A strange kind of love / Hit song / Huuvola / All night long / Dragnet drag / I'll fall with your knife / The sweetest drop / Roll call / Jemal (version 2).

— next with **PETER DiSTEFANO** – guitar (of PORNO FOR PYROS) / **HUGH MARSH** – violin

Metropolis | Metropolis

Aug 01. (d-cd) *(efa 17334-2) <213>* **ALIVE: JUST FOR LOVE (live)** [ ] Jul01 [ ]
– Cool cool breeze / All night long / Keep me from harm / Indigo eyes / Subway / I'll fall with your knife / Marlene Dietrich's favourite poem / A strange kind of love / My last two weeks / Big love of a tiny fool / Gliding like a whale / Cuts you up / Time has nothing to do with it / Angelic harmony / Who killed Mr. Moonlight / All we ever wanted was everything / Hope (midnight proposal) / Love me tender.

— **MERCAN DEDE** – multi; repl. DiSTEFANO

— added **JAMAALADEEN** – bass / + others

Apr 02. (cd) *(efa 17350-2) <238>* **DUST** [ ] [ ]
– Things to remember / Fake sparkle or golden dust? / No home without its sire / Just for love / Girlchild aglow / Your face / Jungle haze / My last two weeks / Subway (epilogue).

TONES ON TAILS

GLEN CAMPLING – vocals, bass, keyboards (roadie of BAUHAUS) / **DANIEL ASH** – guitar, vocals / **KEVIN HASKINS** – drums

4.a.d. | not iss.

Apr 82. (12"ep) *(BAD 203)* **A BIGGER SPLASH / COPPER. / MEANS OF ESCAPE / INSTRUMENTAL** [ ] [–]

Beggars Banquet | not iss.

Sep 82. (12") *(BEG 85T)* **THERE'S ONLY ONE. / NOW WE LUSTRE** [ ] [–]

Situation 2 | not iss.

May 83. (7") *(SIT 21)* **BURNING SKIES. / OK, THIS IS THE POPS** [ ] [–]
(12"+=) *(SIT 21T)* – When you're smiling / You, the night and the music.

— In 1983, they broke from BAUHAUS. ASH and HASKINS joined The JAZZ BUTCHER. TONES ON TAILS soon re-actified their line-up.

Beggars Banquet | not iss.

Mar 84. (7") *(BEG 106)* **PERFORMANCE. / SHAKES** [ ] [–]
(12"+=) *(BEG 106T)* – ('A'dub version).

Apr 84. (lp/c) *(BEGA/BEGC 51)* **POP** [ ] [ ]
– Performance / War / Lions / Happiness / The never never / Real life / Slender fungus / Movement of fear / Rain. *(re-iss. Oct88 & Jul91 on 'Beggars Banquet-Lowdown' lp/c)(cd; BBL/+C 51)(BBL 51CD) (cd-iss. Oct88 as 'NIGHT MUSIC' +=; BEGA 51CD)* – (rest of material).

May 84. (7") *(BEG 109)* **LIONS. / GO! (LET'S GO TO YA YA'S NOW)** [ ] [–]
(12",12"red) *(BEG 109T)* – ('A'side) / Go! (club mix).

Nov 84. (7"/12"blue) *(BEG 121/+T)* **CHRISTIAN SAYS. / TWIST** [ ] [ ]

— split from this name

Situation 2 | not iss.

Feb 85. (lp/c) *Situation 2; (SITU/SITC 12)* **TONES ON TAILS** (the singles compilation) [ ] [–]
(re-iss. Oct88 & Jul91 on 'Situation 2-Lowdown' lp/c; SITL/+C 12)

LOVE AND ROCKETS

ASH + **HASKINS** were joined by **DAVID J.** – vocals, bass, keyboards (also ex-BAUHAUS + a solo artist)

Beggars Banquet | Beggars Banquet

May 85. (7"/12") *(BEG 132/+T)* **BALL OF CONFUSION. / INSIDE THE OUTSIDE** [ ] [ ]

Sep 85. (7"/12") *(BEG 146/+T)* **IF THERE'S A HEAVEN ABOVE. / GOD AND MR. SMITH** [ ] [ ]

Oct 85. (lp/c) *(BEGA/BEGC 66) <85071>* **SEVENTH DREAM OF TEENAGE HEAVEN** [ ] [ ]
– If there's a Heaven above / A private future / 7th dream of teenage Heaven / Saudade / Haunted when the minutes drag / The dog-end of a day gone by / The game. *(cd-iss. May86; BEGA 66CD) (re-iss. Jan89 & Jul91 on 'Beggars Banquet-Lowdown' lp/c)(cd+=; BBL/+C 66)(BBL 66CD)* – Ball of confusion (USA mix) / God and Mr. Smith (Mars mix) / If there's a Heaven above (Canadian mix).

Beggars Banquet | Big Time

Jun 86. (12"m) *(BEG 163T)* **KUNDALINI EXPRESS. / LUCIFER SAM / HOLIDAY ON THE MOON** [ ] [ ]

Sep 86. (7"/12") *(BEG 166/+T)* **YIN AND YANG (THE FLOWERPOT MEN). / ANGELS AND DEVILS** [ ] [ ]

Sep 86. (lp/c) *(BEGA/BEGC 74) <6011>* **EXPRESS** [ ] [72]
– Kundalini express / It could be sunshine / Love me / All in my mind / Life in Laralay / Yin and Yang (the flowerpot men) / An American dream / All in my mind (acoustic version). *(cd-iss. Jan88; BEGA 74CD) (re-iss. Jan89 & Jul91 on 'Beggars Banquet-Lowdown' lp/c)(cd; BBL/+C 74)(BEGA 74CD) (cd re-mast.Sep01 +=; BBL 2031CD)* – Angels and devils / Holiday on the Moon / Lucifer Sam / B side (part 1) / B side (part

2) / Yin and Yang (the flowerpot man) / Ball of confusion (USA mix).

Sep 87. (lp/c)(cd) *(BEGA/BEGC 84)(BEGA 84CD) <6011>*
EARTH, SUN, MOON [ ] [64]
– The light / Mirror people / Welcome tomorrow / Here on Earth / Lazy / Waiting for the flood / Rainbird / Telephone is empty / Everybody wants to go to Heaven / The sun / Youth. *(re-iss. Jan89 & Jul91 on 'Beggars Banquet' lp/c)(cd+=; BBL/+C 84)(BBL 84CD)* – Mirror people (slow version).

Oct 87. (7"/12") *(BEG 186/+T)* **THE LIGHT. / MIRROR PEOPLE (slow version)** [ ] [ ]

Mar 88. (7") *(BEG 209)* **NO NEW TALE TO TELL. / EARTH, SUN, MOON** [ ] [ ]
(12"+=) *(BEG 209T)* – 7th dream of teenage Heaven.

May 88. (7") *(BEG 213)* **MIRROR PEOPLE. / DAVID LANFAIR** [ ] [ ]
(12"+=) *(BEG 213T)* – ('A'live version).

Aug 88. (7") *(BEG 217)* **LAZY. / THE DOG-END OF A DAY GONE BY** [ ] [ ]
(12"+=) *(BEG 217T)* – The purest blue.

Beggars Banquet | R.C.A.

Jan 89. (12"ep) *(BEG 224T)* **MOTORCYCLE / I FEEL SPEED. / BIKE / BIKEDANCE** [ ] [ ]

Jul 89. (7"/c-s/12") *(BEG 229/+C/T) <8956>* **SO ALIVE. / DREAMTIME** [ ] May89 [3]
(cd-s+=) *(BEG 229CD)* – Motorcycle / Bike. *(re-dist.Jan90)*

Sep 89. (lp/c)(cd) *(BEGA/BEGC 99)(BEGA 99CD) <9715>* **LOVE AND ROCKETS** [ ] [14]
– **** (Jungle law) / No big deal / The purest blue / Motorcycle / I feel speed / Bound for Hell / The teardrop collector / So alive / Rock and roll Babylon / No words no more. *<US cd re-iss. Dec02 +=; 82035>* – Bike / Bikedance / No big deal / Dreamtime / Wake up / Cuckoo land / The early worm / 1000 watts of your love / Bad monkey / Introduction (live) / 1000 watts of your love (live) / No words no more (live) / (interview live).

Oct 89. (7") *(BEG 234) <9045>* **NO BIG DEAL. / NO WORDS NO MORE** [ ] Sep89 [82]
(12"+=) *(BEG 234T)* – 100 watts of your love.

Beggars Banquet | American

Jul 94. (12"/cd-s) *(BBQ 36 T/CD)* **THIS HEAVEN / THIS HEAVEN (Secret Knowledge mix). / THIS HEAVEN (Lost In It) / THIS HEAVEN (Torched mix)** [ ] [–]

Sep 94. (12"/cd-s) *(BBQ 42 T/CD) <41690>* **BODY AND SOUL. / BODY AND SOUL (Secret Knowledge out of body mix) / BODY AND SOUL (Delta Lady Rebel Trouser mix)** [ ] [ ]
above featured **NATACHA ATLAS** – vocals (of TRANS-GLOBAL UNDERGROUND)

Sep 94. (cd/c/d-lp) *(BBQ CD/MC/LP 145) <45744>* **HOT TRIP TO HEAVEN** [ ] [ ]
– Body and soul (parts 1 & 2) / Ugly / Trip and glide / This Heaven / No worries / Hot trip to Heaven / Eclipse / Voodoo baby / Be the revolution / Set me free. *(re-iss. cd Sep95; BBL 145CD)*

Mar 96. (cd-ep; unreleased) *(BBQ 67CD)* **THE GLITTERING DARKNESS** [ ] [–]
– Sweet F.A. / The glittering darkness / Trip and glide / Ritual radio / Bad monkey.

Nov 97. (cd) *(BBL 180CD) <43058>* **SWEET F.A.** [ ] Mar96 [ ]
– Sweet F.A. / Judgement day / Use me / Fever / Sweet lover hangover / Pearl / Shelf life / Sad & beautiful world / Natacha / Words of a fool / Clean / Here come the comedown / Spiked / Sweet F.A. (reprise).

— added **DOUG DeANGELIS** – keyboards + **JILL CUNIFF** – guitar

not iss. | Red Ant

May 98. (cd-s) *<11901-3>* **RESURRECTION HEX (mixes) / LIFT / RESURRECTION HEX (mixes)** [–] [ ]
(12"/12") *<11901-4/-5>* – (above tracks).

Oct 98. (cd/c/lp) *<12314>* **LIFT** [–] [ ]
– Lift (Malibu mix) / R.I.P. 20 C. / Holy fool / Too much choice / Pink flamingo / Delicious ocean / Ghosts of the multiple feature / Bad for you / Resurrection hex / My drug / Deep deep down / Party's not over / Lift.

Nov 98. (12"/cd-s) *<15327>* **HOLY FOOL (mixes) / SO ALIVE** [–] [ ]

– compilations, etc. –

May 03. (cd) *Psychobaby; (<PBZ 1002-2>)* **SO ALIVE (live)** [ ] [ ]

Jun 03. (cd) *Beggars Banquet; (BBL 2036CD)* **SORTED! – THE BEST OF LOVE AND ROCKETS** [ ] [ ]
– Kundalini express / The dog-end of a day gone by / Mirror people '88 / Ball of confusion / Ying and Yang (the flowerpot man) / Holiday on the Moon / So alive / Holy fool / No new tale to tell / No big deal / Haunted when the minutes drag / It could be sunshine / Shelf life / Sweet love hangover / Saudade.

DANIEL ASH

Beggars Banquet | Beggars Banquet

Jun 91. (cd)(c/lp) *(BEGA 114CD)(BEGA/BEGC 114) <3014>*
COMING DOWN [ ] [ ]
– Blue moon / Coming down fast / Walk this way / Closer to you / Day tripper / This love / Blue angel / Me and my shadow / Candy darling / Sweet little liar / Not so fast / Coming down.

— Above features covers DAY TRIPPER (Beatles) / BLUE MOON (Rodgers / Hart) / ME AND MY SHADOW (Al Jolson/+).

Jun 91. (7") **WALK THIS WAY. / HEAVEN IS WAITING** [ ] [–]
(12") – ('A'side) / ('A'groovy vox) / ('A'groovy guitar).
(cd-s) – (all 4 tracks).

Apr 93. (12"ep/cd-ep) *(BBQ 9 T/CD)* **GET OUT OF CONTROL. / THE HEDONIST / GET OUT OF CONTROL (farewell mixes)** [ ] [ ]

May 93. (cd/c/lp) *(BBQ CD/MC/LP 129)* **FOOLISH THING DESIRE** [ ] [ ]
– Here she comes / Foolish thing desire / Bluebird / Dream machine / Get out of control / The void / Roll on / Here she comes again / The hedonist / Higher than this.

BAUHAUS

— re-formed for a live appearance

KK | Metropolis

Nov 99. (d-lp/d-cd) *(KK 200/+CD) <150>* **GOTHAM (live)** [ ] [ ]
– Double dare / In the flat field / A god in an alcove / In fear of fear / Hollow hills / Kick in the eye / Terror couple kill colonel / Silent hedges / Severence / Boys / She's in parties / The passion of lovers / Dark entries / Telegram Sam / Ziggy Stardust / Bela Lugosi's dead / All we ever wanted was everything / Spirit / Severence (studio version). *(re-iss. Mar02; same)*

☐ BBM (see under ⇒ BRUCE, Jack)

BEACH BOYS

Formed: Hawthorne, Los Angeles, California, USA ... 1961 by WILSON brothers BRIAN, DENNIS and CARL, who were soon joined by their cousin MIKE LOVE and neighbour AL JARDINE. They went through a series of cringe-inducing names before being individually christened The BEACH BOYS by a local DIY studio, who had released their first single 'SURFIN' on their small 'Candix' label. As sales of the record mushroomed, the band decided to keep the name. Murray Wilson, the brothers' tyrannical father, seized the opportunity to become their manager, producer and song publisher; not exactly a healthy combination and one which the band would come to regret when financial troubles dogged them throughout the next decade and beyond. For the moment however, on the surface at least, everything was hunky dory, the band riding the commercial crest of their surfing wave as they signed to 'Capitol' in 1962 and became the very essence of the sun-tanned, Californian dream. The hits came thick and fast with the prodigiously talented BRIAN writing most of the material. Songs like 'SURFIN SAFARI' and 'SURFIN U.S.A.' were effervescent feelgood anthems, their jaw dropping vocal harmonies framing images of surf, sea and beautiful girls. Early glimpses of BRIAN's penchant for introspection are evident on tracks like the poignant 'IN MY ROOM', co-written with GARY USHER, the first of many songwriters BRIAN would collaborate with during the course of his career. The execrable sentiments of songs like 'BE TRUE TO YOUR SCHOOL', were a result of a period of collaboration with lyricist ROGER CHRISTIAN, although this partnership also created livelier gems like 'LITTLE DEUCE COUPE' and 'I GET AROUND'. The latter song was probably the highlight of 'ALL SUMMER LONG', the 1964 album which saw the band make the leap from being primarily a singles act to creating consistent long players. By Christmas of that year, however, the strain of their horrendous recording/touring treadmill was too much for BRIAN and he suffered a series of nervous breakdowns. Producing and arranging 6 albums in just over 2 years as well as writing over 60 songs in the same period would've been too much for the hardiest of souls, let alone the painfully shy and sensitive BRIAN. This episode signalled the end of BRIAN's live commitment to the band, allowing him to concentrate solely on composing and recording. 'BEACH BOYS – TODAY' and 'SUMMER DAYS (AND SUMMER NIGHTS)' represented a career high with breathtaking material highlighting his preoccupation with achieving the perfect sound. BRIAN WILSON had become obsessed with outdoing The BEATLES who he saw as a threat, a paranoia that grew stronger after his first forays into the world of LSD. He first took the drug in the summer of '65 and it changed his approach to music, to his whole life in fact, with BRIAN later stating that his mind was opened and it scared the shit out of him. BRIAN then enlisted the unlikely help of erstwhile ad sloganeer Tony Asher to express the lyrical mood of these new pieces, and the result was 'PET SOUNDS'. Released in May '66, it still holds the coveted "best album of all-time" position among many critics, with fragile highlights being 'GOD ONLY KNOWS', 'WOULDN'T IT BE NICE' and 'CAROLINE NO', which perfectly evoked BRIAN's turbulent emotional state. Reportedly devastated at the album's lack of success in his home country (yes, it did hit Top 10) and feeling outdone by The BEATLES' 'Revolver' and DYLAN's 'Blonde On Blonde', he upped his drug use and vowed to go one better, dreaming of the ultimate studio masterpiece. Initially pencilled in for inclusion on 'PET SOUNDS' in its earliest incarnation, 'GOOD VIBRATIONS' was released in October that year and soon became their biggest ever selling single. With its pioneering use of the theramin and complex vocal arrangements, its success vindicated BRIAN's vision of grand sonic tapestries over the formulaic pop that other members (most notably MIKE LOVE and his father) wanted to churn out. Around this time, BRIAN began working on his masterpiece (with self-styled L.A. boho scenester/songwriter VAN DYKE PARKS), which had a working title of 'DUMB ANGEL', later changing to 'SMILE'. The sessions that resulted are the stuff of legend, with BRIAN's mental condition deteriorating rapidly under the weight of his own expectation. Among BRIAN's more whimsical foibles were having a box filled with sand so he could play piano barefoot "like on the beach, man" (Surf's Up, indeed). More worrying was the pathological superstition which saw him attempt to destroy tapes of the abandoned 'SMILE' album, although these did surface later on albums 'SMILEY SMILE', 'HEROES AND VILLAINS' and 'SURF'S UP'. From this point on, BRIAN retreated even further from the world at large and spent much of the following decade in bed. A string of average, occasionally good albums followed with DENNIS emerging as a fairly talented songwriter. Recorded after the band's acrimonious split with 'Capitol', 1971's 'SURF'S UP' was the highlight of this period with its 'SMILE'-era title track and spirited contributions from other band members. DENNIS WILSON's association with the infamous Charles Manson, albeit before he went on his killing spree in 1969, probably brought more attention than any music the band released at this time. With the exception of one outstanding BRIAN-penned song 'SAIL ON SAILOR' from the disappointing 'HOLLAND' set, much of the 70's material was creatively bland to say the least. On the 4th June 1973, their father died and eventually MIKE LOVE's brothers STAN and STEVE were removed from management after STEVE was found guilty of embezzling around $1 million. 1977's 'BEACH BOYS LOVE YOU' album saw BRIAN return to take the reins again for the first time in 10 years, and included some fine material. From here on in, The BEACH BOYS became nothing more than a nostalgic novelty act, living on past glories while producing stagnant albums for the over 40's. On the 28th December '83, tragedy struck when DENNIS drowned during a diving trip in Marina Del Ray. The band struggled on minus BRIAN who'd been sacked a year earlier. The band scored a surprise US No.1 hit in 1988 with the soppy 'KOKOMO', which was co-written with former MAMAS & THE PAPAS singer JOHN PHILLIPS. Meanwhile, BRIAN released a competent, not to mention long-awaited solo album under the guidance of his controversial therapist EUGENE LANDY. He even recorded a second album, which was strangely turned down by his new label 'Sire', despite garnering rave reviews from critics who'd heard the pre-release tapes. 1995 saw the release of BRIAN's 'I JUST WASN'T MADE FOR THESE TIMES', an album project combining re-working of older and rare material. A year later The BEACH BOYS scraped the barrel of banality when they did a nauseating run through of their 60's hit 'FUN, FUN, FUN' with STATUS QUO. This was surely the end of the sandy road for the once inspirational outfit; tragedy struck with the lung cancer death (on the 6th of February) of CARL. Remaining brother BRIAN carried on, his 'IMAGINATION' (1998) set receiving rave reviews from the "old fogey" brigade while reaching the Top 100 (Top 30 in Britain); he subsequently teamed up with BRIAN SETZER (ex-STRAY CATS) to record 'LITTLE DEUCE COUPE' for a V/A "save our beaches" benefit album, 'Music For Our Mother Ocean'. • **Covered:** THE TIMES THEY ARE A-CHANGIN' (Bob Dylan) / PAPA OOM MOW MOW (Rivingtons) / I CAN HEAR MUSIC (Ronettes) / BARBARA ANN (Regents) / LOUIE LOUIE (Kingsmen) / WHY DO FOOLS FALL IN LOVE? (Frankie Lymon & the Teenagers) / MONSTER MASH (Bobby Pickett) / JOHNNY B. GOODE (Chuck Berry) / DO YOU WANNA DANCE (Bobby Freeman) / YOU'VE GOT TO HIDE YOUR LOVE AWAY + I SHOULD HAVE KNOWN BETTER (Beatles) / ALLEY OOP (Hollywood Argyles) / BLUEBIRDS OVER THE MOUNTAIN (Ersel Hickey) / THEN I KISSED HER (Crystals) / COME GO WITH ME (Del-Vikings) / CALIFORNIA DREAMIN' (Mamas & The Papas) / THE WANDERER (Dion) / ROCK AND ROLL MUSIC (Chuck Berry) / BLUEBERRY HILL (Fats Domino) / MONA (Bo Diddley) / PEGGY SUE (Buddy Holly) / THE AIR THAT I BREATHE (Hollies) / HOT FUN IN THE SUMMERTIME (Sly & The Family Stone) / WALKING IN THE SAND (Shangri-la's) / UNDER THE BOARDWALK (Drifters) / etc.

Album rating: SURFIN' SAFARI (*4) / SURFIN' U.S.A. (*7) / SURFER GIRL (*5) / LITTLE DEUCE COUPE (*4) / SHUT DOWN VOL.2 (*6) / ALL SUMMER LONG (*7) / THE BEACH BOYS CONCERT (*4) / THE BEACH BOYS – TODAY! (*7) / SUMMER DAYS (AND SUMMER NIGHTS!!) (*7) / THE BEACH BOYS PARTY (*4) / PET SOUNDS (*10) / SMILEY SMILE (*7) / WILD HONEY (*6) / FRIENDS (*5) / 20/20 (*6) / SUNFLOWER (*7) / SURF'S UP (*7) / CARL AND THE PASSIONS: SO TOUGH (*4) / HOLLAND (*6) / THE BEACH BOYS IN CONCERT (*5) / ENDLESS SUMMER compilation (*8) / 15 BIG ONES (*5) / THE BEACH BOYS LOVE YOU (*5) / M.I.U. ALBUM (*5) / L.A. (LIGHT ALBUM) (*5) / KEEPIN' THE SUMMER ALIVE (*2) / THE BEACH BOYS (*4) / STILL CRUISIN' collection (*3) / SUMMER IN PARADISE (*2) / THE VERY BEST OF THE BEACH BOYS compilation (*9) / CLASSICS: SELECTED BY BRIAN WILSON compilation (*7) / Brian Wilson: BRIAN WILSON (*6) / I JUST WASN'T MADE FOR THOSE TIMES (*6) / IMAGINATION (*7)

BRIAN WILSON (b.20 Jun'42, Inglewood, California) – vocals, percussion / **CARL WILSON** (b.21 Dec'46) – guitar, vocals / **DENNIS WILSON** (b. 4 Dec'44) –

vocals, drums / **MIKE LOVE** (b.15 Mar'44, Baldwin Hills, California) – vocals / **AL JARDINE** (b. 3 Sep'42, Lima, Ohio) – vocals, guitar

not iss. | Candix

Dec 61. (7") *<301>* **SURFIN'. / LUAU** – |
Feb 62. (7") *<331>* **SURFIN'. / LUAU** – | 75

—— **DAVID MARKS** – vocals repl. JARDINE who became a dentist

Capitol | Capitol

Aug 62. (7") *(CL 15273) <4777>* **SURFIN' SAFARI. / 409** | 14 76

Nov 62. (lp) *<T 1808>* **SURFIN' SAFARI** – | 32
– Surfin' safari / County fair / Ten little indians / Chug-a-lug / Little girl (you're my Miss America) / 409 / Surfin' * / Heads you win – tails I lose / Summertime blues / Cuckoo clock * / Moon dawg / The shift. *(UK-iss.Apr63; SY 4572) (re-iss. Jun81 on Greenlight'; GO 2014)* – omitted *

Jan 63. (7") *(CL 15285) <4880>* **TEN LITTLE INDIANS. / COUNTY FAIR** | Nov62 49
(re-iss. Jun79; CL 16041)

Mar 63. (7") *(CL 15305) <4932>* **SURFIN' U.S.A.. / SHUT DOWN** 34 | 3 23
(re-iss. Jun79; CL 16042)

Apr 63. (lp; stereo/mono) *<S+/T 1890>* **SURFIN' U.S.A.** – | 2
– Surfin' U.S.A. / Farmer's daughter / Misirlou / Stoked / Lonely sea / Shut down / Noble surfer / Honky tonk / Lana / Surf jam / Let's go trippin' / Finders keepers. *(UK-iss.Aug65; same); hit No.17)*

—— **AL JARDINE** – vocals returned to repl. MARKS

Jul 63. (7") *<5009>* **SURFER GIRL. / LITTLE DEUCE COUPE** – | 7 15

Sep 63. (lp; stereo/mono) *<S+/T 1981>* **SURFER GIRL** – | 7
– Surfer girl / Catch a wave / Surfer Moon / South bay surfer / Rocking surfer / Little deuce Coupe / In my room / Hawaii / Surfer's rule / Our car club / Your summer dream / Boogie woogie. *(UK-iss.Mar67; same); hit No.13) (re-iss. Aug86 lp/c; EMS/TC-EMS 1175)*

Oct 63. (lp; stereo/mono) *<(S+/T 1998)>* **LITTLE DEUCE COUPE** | 4
– Little deuce Coupe / Ballad of ole' Betsy / Be true to your school / Car crazy cutie * / Cherry, cherry Coupe / 409 / Shut down / Spirit of America / Our car club * / No-go showboat / A young man is gone / Custom machine. *(re-iss. Jun81 on 'Greenlight'; GO 2025)* – omitted * *(re-iss. Aug86 lp/c; EMS/TC-EMS 1174)*

Nov 63. (7") *<5069>* **BE TRUE TO YOUR SCHOOL. / IN MY ROOM** – | 6 23

Dec 63. (7") *<5096>* **LITTLE SAINT NICK. / THE LORD'S PRAYER** – xmas |

Jan 64. (7"; as SURVIVORS) *<5102>* **PAMELA JEAN. / AFTER THE GAME** – |

Mar 64. (7") *(CL 15339) <5118>* **FUN, FUN, FUN. / WHY DO FOOLS FALL IN LOVE** | Feb64 5
(re-iss. Jun79; CL 16043)

Jul 64. (lp; stereo/mono) *<(S+/T 2027)>* **SHUT DOWN, VOLUME 2** | Apr64 13
– Fun, fun, fun / Don't worry baby / In the parkin' lot / "Cassius" Love vs "Sonny" Wilson / The warmth of the sun / This car of mine / Why do fools fall in love / Pom-pom play girl / Keep an eye on summer / Shut down (pt.II) / Louie louie / Denny's drum. *(re-iss. May89 on 'C5'; C5-535)*

—— Note:- 'SHUT DOWN' was a various artists surf US-lp issued Jul63 reaching No.7. It contained two BEACH BOYS tracks; 409 / Shut down.

Jun 64. (7") *(CL 15350) <5174>* **I GET AROUND. / DON'T WORRY BABY** 7 May64 | 1
(re-iss. Jun79; CL 16044)

Jul 64. (lp; stereo/mono) *<S+/T 2110>* **ALL SUMMER LONG** – | 4
– I get around / All summer long / Hushabye / Little Honda / We'll run away / Carl's big chance / Wendy / Do you remember? / Girls on the beach / Drive-in / Our favourite recording session / Don't back down. *(UK-iss.Jun65; same) (re-iss. Jul73 on 'Music For Pleasure'; MfP 50065) (re-iss. Aug86 lp/c; EMS/TC-EMS 1176)*

Oct 64. (7") *(CL 15361) <5245>* **WHEN I GROW UP (TO BE A MAN). / SHE KNOWS ME TOO WELL** 27 Aug64 | 9
(re-iss. Jun79; CL 16045)

Oct 64. (7"ep) *<R-5267>* **LITTLE HONDA / DON'T BACK DOWN. / WENDY / HUSHABYE** – | 65 44

Dec 64. (7") *<5312>* **THE MAN WITH ALL THE TOYS. / BLUE CHRISTMAS** – xmas |

Jan 65. (7") *(CL 15370) <5306>* **DANCE, DANCE, DANCE. / THE WARMTH OF THE SUN** 24 Oct64 | 8
(re-iss. Jun79; CL 16046)

Feb 65. (lp; stereo/mono) *<(S+/T 2198)>* **BEACH BOYS CONCERT (live)** | Nov64 1
– Fun, fun, fun / The little old lady from Pasadena / Little deuce Coupe / Long tall Texan / In my room / Monster mash / Let's go trippin' / Papa-oom-mow-mow / The wanderer / Hawaii / Graduation day / I get around / Johnny B. Goode. *(re-iss. Jun81 on 'Greenlight' lp/c; GO/TCGO 2005)*

—— **GLEN CAMPBELL** – vocals (on tour) repl. BRIAN who suffered breakdown. However BRIAN did stay as writer/producer (6th member)

Feb 65. (7") *<5372>* **DO YOU WANNA DANCE?. / PLEASE LET ME WONDER** – | 12 52

Mar 65. (7") *(CL 15384)* **ALL SUMMER LONG. / DO YOU WANNA DANCE?** | –
(re-iss. Jun79; CL 16047)

Mar 65. (lp; stereo/mono) *<(S+/T 2269)>* **THE BEACH BOYS TODAY!** – | 4
– Do you wanna dance? / Good to my baby / Don't hurt my little sister / When I grow up (to be a man) / Help me, Rhonda / Dance, dance, dance / Please let me wonder / I'm so young / Kiss me baby / She knows me too well / In the back of my mind / She knew me too well. *(UK-iss.Apr66; same); hit No.6) (re-iss. Jan72 as 'DO YOU WANNA DANCE' on 'Music For Pleasure'; MFP 5235)*

—— **BRUCE JOHNSTON** – vocals (ex-his combo) repl. GLEN CAMPBELL who went solo

May 65. (7") *(CL 15392) <5395>* **HELP ME, RHONDA. / KISS ME BABY** 27 Apr65 | 1
(re-iss. Jun79; CL 16048)

Jul 65. (lp; stereo/mono) *<(S+/T 2354)>* **SUMMER DAYS (AND SUMMER NIGHTS!!)** – | 2
– The girl from New York City / Amusements parks U.S.A. / Then I kissed her / Salt Lake City / Girl don't tell me / Help me Rhonda / Let him run wild / You're so good to me / Summer means new love / I'm bugged at my ol' man / And your dream comes true. *(UK-iss.Jul66; same); hit No.4) (re-iss. Jun78; CAPS 1023) (re-iss. Aug86 lp/c; EMS/TC-EMS 1178)*

Aug 65 (7") *(CL 15409) <5464>* **CALIFORNIA GIRLS. / LET HIM RUN WILD** 26 Jul65 | 3
(re-iss. Jun79; CL 16049)

Dec 65. (7") *(CL 15425) <5540>* **THE LITTLE GIRL I ONCE KNEW. / THERE'S NO OTHER (LIKE MY BABY)** | Nov65 20
(re-iss. Jun79; CL 16050)

Feb 66. (7") *(CL 15432) <5561>* **BARBARA ANN. / GIRL DON'T TELL ME** 3 Dec65 | 2
(re-iss. Jun79; CL 16051)

Feb 66. (lp; stereo/mono) *<(S+/T 2398)>* **BEACH BOYS' PARTY!** 3 Nov65 | 6
– Hully gully / I should have known better / Tell me why / Papa-oom-mow-mow / Mountain of love / You've got to hide your love away / Devoted to you / Alley oop / There's no other (like my baby) / I get around – Little deuce Coupe / The times they are a-changin' / Barbara Ann. *(re-iss. Aug86 lp/c; EMS/TC-EMS 1177)*

Apr 66. (7"; by BRIAN WILSON *(CL 15438) <5610>* **CAROLINE, NO. / SUMMER MEANS NEW LOVE** | Mar66 32

Apr 66. (7") *(CL 15441) <5602>* **SLOOP JOHN B. / YOU'RE SO GOOD TO ME** 2 Mar66 | 3
(re-iss. Jun79; CL 16052)

May 66. (lp; stereo/mono) *<(S+/T 2458)>* **PET SOUNDS** 2 | 10
– Wouldn't it be nice / You still believe in me / That's not me / Don't talk (put your head on my shoulder) / I'm waiting for the day / Let's go away for awhile / Sloop John B. / God only knows / I know there's no answer / Here today / I just wasn't made for these times / Pet sounds / Caroline, no. *(re-iss. Jun81 on 'Greenlight'; GO 2002) (re-iss. May82 on 'Fame'; FA 3018) (re-iss. Aug86 lp/c; EMS/TC-EMS 1179) <(cd-iss. Jun90; 7-48421)>* – Hang on to your ego / Trombone Dixie. *(re-iss. Nov93 on 'Fame' cd/c; CD/TC FA 3298)* – hit No.70 Sep95 & No.59 Aug02 – *(lp re-iss. Dec99 on 'Simply Vinyl'; SVLP 149) (cd re-iss. Sep00 mono; 527319-2)*

Jul 66. (7") *(CL 15459) <5706>* **GOD ONLY KNOWS. / WOULDN'T IT BE NICE** 2 | 39 8
(re-iss. Jun79; CL 16053)

Oct 66. (7") *<5676>* **GOOD VIBRATIONS. / LET'S GO AWAY FOR AWHILE** – | 1

Oct 66. (7") *(CL 15475)* **GOOD VIBRATIONS. / WENDY** 1 | –
(re-iss. Jun79; CL 16054)

Apr 67. (7") *(CL 15502)* **THEN I KISSED HER. / MOUNTAIN OF LOVE** [4] [–]
(re-iss. Jun79; CL 16055)

Capitol Brother

Aug 67. (7") *(CL 15510)* *<1001>* **HEROES AND VILLAINS. / YOU'RE WELCOME** [8] Jul67 [12]
(re-iss. Jun79; CL 16056)

Sep 67. (7"; BRIAN WILSON & MIKE LOVE) *(CL 15513)* *<1002>* **GETTIN' HUNGRY. / DEVOTED TO YOU** [ ] [ ]

Nov 67. (lp; stereo/mono) *<(S+/T 9001)>* **SMILEY SMILE** [9] Sep67 [41]
– Heroes and villains / Vegetables / Fall breaks and back to winter / She's goin' bald / Little pad / Good vibrations / With me tonight / Wind chimes / Gettin' hungry / Wonderful / Whistle in. *(cd-iss. Nov98 on 'Magic'; 497576-2)*

Capitol Capitol

Nov 67. (7") *(CL 15521)* *<2028>* **WILD HONEY. / WIND CHIMES** [29] [31]
(re-iss. Jun79; CL 16057)

Dec 67. (7") *<2068>* **DARLIN'. / HERE TODAY** [–] [19]

Jan 68. (7") *(CL 15527)* **DARLIN'. / COUNTRY AIR** [11] [–]
(re-iss. Jun79; CL 16058)

Mar 68. (lp; stereo/mono) *<(S+/T 2859)>* **WILD HONEY** [7] Dec67 [24]
– Wild honey / Aren't you glad / I was made to love her / Country air / A thing or two / Darlin' / I'd love just once to see you / Here comes the night / Let the wind blow / How she boogalooed it / Mama says.

May 68. (7") *(CL 15545)* *<2160>* **FRIENDS. / LITTLE BIRD** [25] [47]
(re-iss. Jun79; CL 16059)

Jul 68. (7") *(CL 15554)* *<2239>* **DO IT AGAIN. / WAKE THE WORLD** [1] [20]
(re-iss. Jun79; CL 16060)

Sep 68. (lp; stereo/mono) *<(S+/T 2895)>* **FRIENDS** [13] Jun68 [ ]
– Meant for you / Friends / Wake the world / Be here in the mornin' / When a man needs a woman / Passing by / Anna Lee, the healer / Little bird / Be still / Busy doing nothin' / Diamond head / Transcendental meditation.

Dec 68. (7") *(CL 15572)* *<2360>* **BLUEBIRDS OVER THE MOUNTAIN. / NEVER LEARN NOT TO LOVE** [33] [61]
(re-iss. Jun79; CL 16061)

Feb 69. (7") *(CL 15584)* *<2432>* **I CAN HEAR MUSIC. / ALL I WANT TO DO** [10] [24]
(re-iss. Jun79; CL 16062)

Feb 69. (lp) *<(EST 133)>* **20/20** [3] [68]
– Do it again / I can hear music / Bluebirds over the mountain / Be with me / All I want to do / The nearest faraway place / Cottonfields / I went to sleep / Time to get alone / Never learn not to love / Our prayer / Cabinessence.

Jun 69. (7") *(CL 15598)* *<2530>* **BREAK AWAY. / CELEBRATE THE NEWS** [6] [63]
(re-iss. Jun79; CL 16063)

Stateside Reprise

Feb 70. (7") *<0894>* **ADD SOME MUSIC TO YOUR DAY. / SUSIE CINCINNATTI** [–] [64]

Sep 70. (7") *<0929>* **SLIP ON THROUGH. / THIS WHOLE WORLD** [–] [ ]

Nov 70. (7") *(SS 2181)* *<0957>* **TEARS IN THE MORNING. / IT'S ABOUT TIME** [ ] [ ]

Nov 70. (lp) *(SSL 8251)* *<6382>* **SUNFLOWER** [29] Sep70 [ ]
– Slip on through / This whole world / Add some music to your day / Got to know the woman / Deirdre / It's about time / Tears in the morning / All I wanna do / Forever / Our sweet love / At my window / Cool, cool water. *(re-iss. Nov80 on 'Caribou'; 31773> – Cottonfields. (re-iss. Jul91 on 'Epic' cd/c; 467836-2/-4)*

Dec 70. (7"; by DENNIS WILSON & RUMBO) *(SS 2184)* **SOUND OF FREE. / LADY** [ ] [–]

Feb 71. (7") *<0998>* **COOL, COOL WATER. / FOREVER** [–] [ ]

Jun 71. (7") *(SS 2190)* *<1015>* **LONG PROMISED ROAD. / DEIRDRE** [ ] [ ]

Oct 71. (7") *<1047>* **LONG PROMISED ROAD. / TILL I DIE** [–] [89]

Nov 71. (7") *(SS 2194)* **DON'T GO NEAR THE WATER. / STUDENT DEMONSTRATION TIME** [ ] [ ]

Nov 71. (lp) *(SSL 10313)* *<6453>* **SURF'S UP** [15] Aug71 [29]
– Don't go near the water / Long promised road / Take a load off your feet / Disney girls (1957) / Student demonstration time / Feel flows / Lookin' at tomorrow / A day in the life of a tree / 'Til I die / Surf's up. *<re-iss. Nov80 on 'Caribou'; 31774> (re-iss. Jul91 on 'Epic' cd/c; 467835-2/-4)*

Nov 71. (7") *<1058>* **SURF'S UP. / DON'T GO NEAR THE WATER** [–] [ ]

— **BLONDIE CHAPLIN** – guitar repl. JOHNSTON who later went solo
added **RICKY FATAAR** – drums (DENNIS now just vocals)

Reprise Reprise

May 72. (7") *(K 14173)* *<1091>* **YOU NEED A MESS OF HELP TO STAND ALONE. / CUDDLE UP** [ ] [ ]

Jun 72. (d-lp) *(K 44184)* *<2083>* **CARL AND THE PASSIONS – SO TOUGH** [25] May72 [50]
– You need a mess of help to stand alone / Here she comes / He come down / Marcella / Hold on dear brother / Make it good / All this is that / Cuddle up. *(w/ 'PET SOUNDS') (re-iss. Jul91 on 'Epic' cd/c; 468349-2/-4)*

Aug 72. (7") *<1101>* **MARCELLA. / HOLD ON DEAD BROTHER** [–] [ ]

Jan 73. (lp) *(K 54008)* *<2118>* **HOLLAND** [20] [36]
– Sail on sailor / Steamboat / California saga (on my way to sunny Californ-i-a (medley):- Big surf – Beaks of eagles – California / The trader / Leaving this town / Only with you / Funky pretty. *(7"ep free-w/a) <2118>* **MOUNT VERNON AND FAIRWAY (A FAIRY TALE)** – Better get back in bed / Magic transistor radio / Mount Vernon and Fairway / I'm the pied piper / Radio King Dom. *(re-iss. Jul91 on 'Epic' cd/c; 467837-2/-4)*

Feb 73. (7") *<1138>* **SAIL ON SAILOR. / ONLY WITH YOU** [–] [79]

Feb 73. (7") *(K 14232)* **CALIFORNIA SAGA: CALIFORNIA. / SAIL ON SAILOR** [37] [–]

May 73. (7") *<1156>* **CALIFORNIA SAGA (ON MY WAY TO SUNNY CALIFORN-I-A). / FUNKY PRETTY** [–] [84]

Nov 73. (d-lp) *(K 84001)* *<6484>* **THE BEACH BOYS IN CONCERT (live)** [ ] [25]
– Sail on sailor / Sloop John B. / The trader / You still believe me / California girls / Darlin' / Marcella / Caroline, no / Leaving this town / Heroes and villains / We got love / Don't worry baby / Surfin' U.S.A. / Good vibrations / Fun, fun, fun / Funky pretty / Let the wind blow / Help me Rhonda / Surfer girl / Wouldn't it be nice. *(re-iss. Jun91 on 'Epic' cd/c; 468345-2/-4)*

Jul 74. (7") *<1310>* **I CAN HEAR MUSIC (live). / LET THE WIND BLOW (live)** [–] [ ]

Aug 74. (7"ep) *(K 14346)* **CALIFORNIA SAGA: CALIFORNIA / SAIL ON SAILOR. / MARCELLA / I'M THE PIED PIPER** [ ] [–]

— **JAMES GUERICO** – bass (on tour) repl. BLONDIE and RICKY /

— **DENNIS** returned to his drums

Jun 75. (7") *(K 14394)* *<1325>* **SAIL ON SAILOR. / ONLY WITH YOU** [ ] [49]

Dec 75. (7"w-drawn) *(K 14411)* *<1321>* **CHILD OF WINTER. / SUSIE CINCINNATI** [–] Dec74 [ ]

— **BRIAN** returned to live work

— After this point, The BEACH BOYS abandoned even the slightest attempt to push their own musical boundaries. Instead relying upon tired retreads of their earlier sound.

Jul 76. (7") *(K 14440)* *<1354>* **ROCK AND ROLL MUSIC. / THE T.M. SONG** [36] May76 [5]

Jul 76. (lp/c) *(K/K4 54079)* *<MSK 2251>* **15 BIG ONES** [31] [8]
– Rock and roll music / It's O.K. / Had to phone ya / Chapel of love / Everyone's in love with you / Talk to me / That same song / The T.M. song / Palisades park / Susie Cincinatti / A casual look / Blueberry Hill / Back home / In the still of the night / Just once in my life. *(re-iss. Jul91 on 'Epic' cd/c; 468346-2/-4)*

Aug 76. (7") *(K 14448)* *<1368>* **IT'S O.K. / HAD TO PHONE YA** [ ] [29]

Nov 76. (7") *<1375>* **SUSIE CINCINNATI. / EVERYONE'S IN LOVE WITH YOU** [–] [ ]

Apr 77. (7") *<1389>* **HONKIN' DOWN THE HIGHWAY. / SOLAR SYSTEM** [–] [ ]

Apr 77. (lp/c) *(K/K4 54079)* *<MSK 2258>* **THE BEACH BOYS LOVE YOU** [26] [53]
– Roller skating child / I'll bet he's nice / Airplane / Love is a woman / Johnny Carson / Let us go on this way / I wanna pick you up / Let's put our hearts together / Solar system / The night was so young / Ding dang / Mona / Honkin' down the highway / Good time. *(re-iss. Jun91 on 'Epic' cd/c; 468347-2/-4)*

Aug 77. (7"ep) *(K 14481)* **MONA / ROCK AND ROLL MUSIC. / SAIL ON SAILOR / MARCELLA** [ ] [–]

Sep 78. (lp/c) *(K/K4 54102)* *<MSK 2268>* **M.I.U. ALBUM** [ ] [ ]
– She's got rhythm / Come go with me / Hey little tomboy / Kona coast / Peggy Sue / Wontcha come out tonight / Sweet Sunday kinda love / Belles of Paris / Pitter patter / My Diane / Match point of your love / Winds of change. *(re-iss. Jul91 on 'Epic' cd/c; 468348-2/-4)*

Oct 78. (7") *(K 14489)* *<1394>* **PEGGY SUE. / HEY LITTLE TOMBOY** [ ] Aug78 [59]
Dec 78. (7") *(K 14494)* **KONA COAST. / SWEET SUNDAY KINDA LOVE** [ ] [-]

— **BRUCE JOHNSTON** – vocals, returned to add to DENNIS, CARL, AL, MIKE + BRIAN

Caribou Caribou

Mar 79. (7") *(CRB 7204)* *<9026>* **HERE COMES THE NIGHT. / BABY BLUE** [37] [44]
(12"blue+=) *(CRB 12-7204)* – ('A'-disco version).
Apr 79. (lp/c/pic-lp) *(CRB/40/11 86081)* *<35752>* **L.A. (LIGHT ALBUM)** [32] [100]
– Angel come home / Baby blue / Love surrounds me / Good timin' / Goin' south / Shortenin' bread / Lady Lynda / Sumahama / Full sail / Sumahama / Here comes the night. *(re-iss. Aug86; 4032806) (cd-iss. Jul89 on 'Pickwick'; 902127-2)*
May 79. (7") *<9029>* **GOOD TIMIN'. / LOVE SURROUNDS ME** [-] [40]
Jun 79. (7") *(CRB 7427)* *<9030>* **LADY LYNDA. / FULL SAIL** [6] [ ]
Aug 79. (7") *(CRB 7846)* **SUMAHAMA. / ANGEL COME HOME** [6] [ ]
Sep 79. (7") *<9031>* **SUMAHAMA. / IT'S A BEAUTIFUL DAY** [-] [ ]
Nov 79. (7") *(CRB 8055)* **GOOD TIMIN'. / GOIN' SOUTH** [ ] [-]
Mar 80. (7") *<9032>* **GOIN' ON. / ENDLESS HARMONY** [-] [83]
Mar 80. (7") *(CRB 8367)* **OH DARLING. / ENDLESS HARMONY** [ ] [-]
Mar 80. (lp) *(CRB 86109)* *<36283>* **KEEPIN' THE SUMMER ALIVE** [54] [75]
– Endless harmony / When girls get together / School day (ring! ring! goes the bell) / Sunshine / Santa Ana winds / Goin' on / Some of your love / Oh darlin' / Livin' with a heartache / Keepin' the summer alive. *(re-iss. Jun91 on 'Epic' cd/c; 468350-2/-4)*
Jun 80. (7") *(CRB 8663)* **KEEPIN' THE SUMMER ALIVE. / WHEN GIRLS GET TOGETHER** [ ] [-]
Jul 80. (7") *<9033>* **LIVING WITH A HEARTACHE. / SANTA ANA WINDS** [-] [ ]
Jul 80. (7") *(CRB 8633)* **SANTA ANA WINDS. / SUNSHINE** [ ] [-]

— **ADRIAN BAKER** – vocals (ex-solo) repl. CARL and BRUCE

— **CARL WILSON** returned after short solo career

Feb 82. (7") *(CRBA 2015)* *<02633>* **COME GO WITH ME. / DON'T GO NEAR THE WATER** [ ] Nov81 [18]

— Tragically on 28th Dec83, DENNIS drowned (see above). The other original 4 (BRIAN, CARL, AL and MIKE) carried on. Mar'85, ere credited on JULIO IGLESIAS single 'THE AIR THAT I BREATHE' *(CBS A 5009)*

May 85. (7") *(A 6324)* *<04913>* **GETCHA BACK. / MALE EGO** [ ] [26]
(12"+=) *(TA 6324)* – Here comes the night / Lady Lynda.
Jun 85. (lp/c/cd) *(CRB/40/CD 26378)* *<39946>* **THE BEACH BOYS** [60] [52]
– Getcha back / It's gettin' late / Crack at your love / Maybe I don't know / She believes in love again / California calling / Passing friend / I'm so lonely / Where I belong / I do love you / It's just a matter of time. *(cd+=)* – Male ego. *(re-iss. Ovt90 on 'C.B.S.' cd/c/lp; 467363-2/-4/-1)*
Jul 85. (7") *<05433>* **IT'S GETTIN' LATE. / IT'S O.K.** [-] [82]
Aug 85. (7") *(A 6471)* **PASSING FRIEND. / IT'S O.K.** [ ] [-]
Nov 85. (7") *<05624>* **SHE BELIEVES IN LOVE AGAIN. / IT'S JUST A MATTER OF TIME** [-] [ ]

Capitol Capitol

Jun 86. (7") *<5595>* **ROCK'N'ROLL TO THE RESCUE. / GOOD VIBRATIONS (live)** [-] [68]
Sep 86. (7") *(CL 425)* *<5630>* **CALIFORNIA DREAMIN'. / LADY LIBERTY** [ ] [57]
(12"+=) *(12CL 425)* – (Ballads medley).

— BRIAN now departed to go solo, the rest did one-off (Jul'87) with The FAT BOYS on their UK No.2 hit single 'WIPE OUT' *(Urban; URB 5)* Also hit No.12 in the US on 'Tin Pan'; *<885960>*

Nov 88. (7"/12") *(EKR 85/+T)* *<69385>* **KOKOMO. / TUTTI FRUTTI (by 'Little Richard')** [25] Aug88 [1]
above single was from the film 'Cocktail' on 'Elektra' label.
Aug 89. (7") *(CL 549)* *<44445>* **STILL CRUISIN'. / KOKOMO** [ ] [93]
(cd-s+=) *(CDCL 549)* – Rock'n'roll to the rescue (mix) / Lady Liberty.
(12"+=) *(12CL 549)* – Beach Boys Medley.
Jul 90. (c-s/cd-s) *<44475>* **SOMEWHERE NEAR JAPAN / KOKOMO** [-] [ ]

— **MIKE LOVE, CARL WILSON, AL JARDINE, BRUCE JOHNSTON** (now keyboards), **MELCHER** (keyboards + co-writer w/**LOVE**), **ADRIAN BAKER** (backing vocals), **KEITH WECHSLER** (keyboards / some drums), **CRAIG FALL** – guitar, keyboards / **ROD CLARK** – bass / **SAMMY MERENDINO** – drums / **VAN DYKE PARKS** – accordion, keyboards / **DANNY KORTCHMAR** – guitars / **JOEL PESKIN** – saxophone / **JOHN WESTON** – pedal steel

E.M.I. Brother

Jun 93. (cd/c) *(CD/TC EMD 1046)* *<727>* **SUMMER IN PARADISE** [ ] Aug92 [ ]
– Hot fun in the summertime / Surfin' / Slow summer dancin' (one summer night) / Strange things happen / Remember walking in the sand / Lahaina aloha / Under the boardwalk / Summer in Paradise forever. *(re-iss. cd May95 on 'Fame'; CDFA 3321)*

— guested on STATUS QUO's hit version of their 'FUN FUN FUN'.

not iss. Sub Pop

Jun 96. (7"m) *<SP 363>* **I JUST WASN'T MADE FOR THESE TIMES. / WOULDN'T IT BE NICE / HERE TODAY** [-] [ ]

– (selective) compilations, etc. –

on 'Capitol' unless stated otherwise

Oct 66. (lp; stereo/mono) *(S+/T 20856)* *<2545>* **THE BEST OF THE BEACH BOYS** [2] [8]
Oct 67. (lp; stereo/mono) *(S+/T 20956)* *<2706>* **THE BEST OF THE BEACH BOYS VOL.2** [3] Aug67 [50]
Nov 68. (lp; stereo/mono) *(S+/T 21142)* *<2905>* **THE BEST OF THE BEACH BOYS VOL.3** [8] Sep68 [ ]
May 70. (7") *(CL 15640)* *<2765>* **COTTONFIELDS. / THE NEAREST FARAWAY PLACE** [5] [ ]
Sep 70. (lp) *(T 21628)* **GREATEST HITS** [5] [-]
Aug 72. (lp) *(ST 21715)* *<11584>* **LIVE IN LONDON (live 1969)** [ ] Dec76 [75]
(re-iss. Sep77 on 'Music For Pleasure'; 50345)
Jul 74. (d-lp) *<2166>* **WILD HONEY / 20-20** [-] [50]
Aug 74. (7") *<3924>* **SURFIN' U.S.A. / THE WARMTH OF THE SUN** [-] [36]
Nov 74. (d-lp) *<(EA-ST 11307)>* **ENDLESS SUMMER** [ ] Jul74 [1]
(re-iss. Sep81 on 'Music For Pleasure'; MfP 50528) (cd-iss. Feb87 on 'E.M.I.'; CDP 746 467-2) (cd re-iss. May99; CDMFP 50528)
Apr 75. (d-lp) *(VMP 1007)* *<SVBB 11384>* **SPIRIT OF AMERICA** [ ] [8]
(cd-iss. Jun87; CDP7 746 618-2)
Oct 75. (lp) *Music For Pleasure; (MFP 50234) / Brother; <2223>* **GOOD VIBRATIONS – THE BEST OF BEACH BOYS** [ ] Jul75 [25]
Jun 76. (7") *(CL 15875)* **GOOD VIBRATIONS. / WOULDN'T IT BE NICE** [18] [-]
Jul 76. (lp/c) *E.M.I.; (EMTV/TC-EMTV 1)* **20 GOLDEN GREATS** [1] [ ]
(cd-iss. Nov87; CDEMTV 1) (re-iss. 1979 blue-lp; same) (re-iss. cd+c Sep94)
Aug 81. (7") *(CL 213)* *<5030>* **BEACH BOYS MEDLEY. / GOD ONLY KNOWS** [47] [12]
Jul 83. (d-lp) *(BBTV 1867193)* **THE VERY BEST OF THE BEACH BOYS** [1] [ ]
– Surfin' safari / Surfin' U.S.A. / Shut down / Little deuce Coupe / In my room / Fun, fun, fun / I get around / Don't worry baby / When I grow up (to be a man) / Wendy / Little Honda / Dance dance dance / All summer long / Do you wanna dance / Help me Rhonda / California girls / Little girl I once knew / Barbara Ann / You're so good to me / Then I kissed her / Sloop John B. / God only knows / Wouldn't it be nice / Here today / Good vibrations / Heroes and villains / Wild honey / Darlin' / Country air / Here comes the night / Friends / Do it again / Bluebirds over the mountain / I can hear music / Break away / Cottonfields.
Dec 84. (d-lp/d-c) *C.B.S.; (22178) / Caribou; <37445>* **TEN YEARS OF HARMONY (1970-1980)** [ ] Dec81 [ ]
Aug 86. (cd/c/d-lp) *(CD/TC+/EN 5005)* *<12396>* **MADE IN THE U.S.A.** [ ] Jul86 [96]
Jun 90. (7") *(CL 579)* **WOULDN'T IT BE NICE. / I GET AROUND** [58] [ ]
(12"+=/cd-s+=) *(12/CD CL 579)* – Medley of hits.
Jun 90. (cd)(c/d-lp) *(CDP7 94620-2)(TC+/EMTVD 51)* **SUMMER DREAMS** [2] [-]
Jun 90. (cd) *(CDP7 93691-2)* **SURFIN' SAFARI / SURFIN' U.S.A.** [ ] [ ]
(contains extra tracks) (c-iss.Jul91; C 493691)
Jun 90. (cd) *(CDP7 93692-2)* **SURFER GIRL / SHUT DOWN, VOLUME 2** [ ] [ ]

(contains extra tracks) (c-iss.Jul91; C 493692)
Jul 90. (cd) *(CDP7 93693-2)* **LITTLE DEUCE COUPE / ALL SUMMER LONG**
(contains extra tracks) (c-iss.Aug91; C 493693)
Aug 90. (cd) *(CDP7 93694-2)* **TODAY / SUMMER DAYS (AND SUMMER NIGHTS!!)**
(contains extra tracks) (c-iss.Aug91; C 493694)
Aug 90. (cd) *(CDP7 93695-2)* **BEACH BOYS' CONCERT / LIVE IN LONDON**
(contains extra tracks) (c-iss.Aug91; C 493695)
Aug 90. (cd) *(CDP7 93696-2)* **WILD HONEY / SMILEY SMILE**
(contains extra tracks) (c-iss.Aug91; C 493696)
Aug 90. (cd) *(CDP7 93697-2)* **FRIENDS / 20-20**
(contains extra tracks) (c-iss.Aug91; C 493697)
Aug 90. (cd) *(CDP7 93698-2)* **BEACH BOYS' PARTY / STACK O-TRACKS**
(contains extra tracks) (c-iss.Aug91; C 493698)
Jun 91. (7"/c-s) *E.M.I.; (EM/+C 1)* **DO IT AGAIN. / GOOD VIBRATIONS** 61
(cd-s+=) *(EMCT 1)* – Wouldn't it be nice.
Jul 93. (5xcd-box) *(CDS 789936-2)* **GOOD VIBRATIONS – 30 YEARS OF THE BEACH BOYS**
Jun 95. (d-cd/d-c) *E.M.I.; (CD/TC ESTVD 3)* **THE BEST OF THE BEACH BOYS** 26
Apr 96. (cd) *<29418>* **20 GOOD VIBRATIONS – THE GREATEST HITS** -
Oct 97. (4xcd-box) *(CDS 837662-2)* **THE PET SOUNDS SESSIONS** -
Jun 98. (cd/c) *E.M.I.; (495696-2/-4)* **GREATEST HITS** 28
Sep 98. (cd) *E.M.I.; (496391-2)* **ENDLESS HARMONY SOUNDTRACK** 56
Nov 98. (cd) *E.M.I.; <(4 95734-2>)* **ULTIMATE CHRISTMAS** Nov00 20
Jul 99. (cd) *Disky; (HR 85771-2)* **ORIGINAL GOLD**
Mar 00. (cd) *<21860>* **THE GREATEST HITS – VOLUME 1: 20 GOOD VIBRATIONS** - 95
Mar 00. (cd) *<20238>* **THE GREATEST HITS – VOLUME 2: 20 MORE GOOD VIBRATIONS** -
Jun 00. (cd) *(525000-2) <19707>* **THE BEST OF THE BEACH BOYS 1970-1986: THE BROTHER YEARS** Mar00 26
Jul 00. (cd) *Burning Airlines; (PILOT 062)* **STUDIO SESSIONS 1961-1962**
Aug 00. (cd) *<(525692-2)>* **SUNFLOWER / SURF'S UP**
Aug 00. (cd) *<(525694-2)>* **CARL AND THE PASSIONS – SO TOUGH / HOLLAND**
Sep 00. (cd) *<(527945-2)>* **15 BIG ONES / THE BEACH BOYS LOVE YOU**
Sep 00. (cd) *<(527948-2)>* **KEEPING THE SUMMER ALIVE / THE BEACH BOYS**
Sep 00. (cd) *<(527950-2)>* **M.I.U. / L.A. (LIGHT ALBUM)**
Apr 01. (cd) *<(531861-2)>* **BEACH BOYS CONCERT / LIVE IN LONDON 1969**
May 01. (d-cd) *<(531583-2)>* **HAWTHORNE, CA. – BIRTHPLACE OF A MUSICAL LEGACY (live)**
Jul 01. (cd/c) *(532615-2/-4)* **THE VERY BEST OF THE BEACH BOYS** 31
– Good vibrations / California girls / I get around / Wouldn't it be nice / Surfin' safari / Fun, fun, fun / Surfin' USA / Help me, Rhonda / Don't worry baby / When I grow up (to be a man) / Little deuce coupe / Dance, dance, dance / Little Honda / Do you wanna dance / Surfer girl / Then I kissed her / God only knows / Caroline, no / Sloop John B. / Barbara Ann / Heroes and villains / Do it again / Darlin' / Wild honey / Break away / Rock & roll music / I can hear music / Cottonfields / Lady Lynda / Kokomo.
Jul 02. (cd) *<(540087-2)>* **CLASSICS: SELECTED BY BRIAN WILSON**
– Surfer girl / The warmth of the sun / I get around / Don't worry baby / In my room / California girls / God only knows / Caroline, no / Good vibrations / Wonderful / Heroes and villains / Surf's up / Busy doin' nothin' / We're together again / Time to get alone / This whole world / Marcella / Sail on sailor / 'Til I die / California feelin'.
Aug 02. (cd) *Eagle; (EAGCD 155)* **LIVE AT KNEBWORTH 1980** -

BRIAN WILSON

Sire Sire

May 87. (7") *<28350>* **LET'S GO TO HEAVEN IN MY CAR. / TOO MUCH SUGAR** -
Jul 88. (lp/c)(cd) *(WX 157/+C)(925669-2) <25669>* **BRIAN WILSON** 54
– Love and mercy / Walkin' the line / Melt away / Baby let your hair grow long / Little children / One of the boys / There's so many / Night time / Let it shine / Rio Grande / Meet me in my dreams tonight. *(re-iss. cd Dec95; 7599 25669-2)*
Aug 88. (7") *(W 7814) <27814>* **LOVE AND MERCY. / HE COULDN'T GET HIS POOR OLD BODY TO MOVE**
(12"+=/3"cd-s+=) *(W 7814 T/CD)* – One for the boys.
Nov 88. (7") *(W 7787)* **NIGHT TIME. / ONE FOR THE BOYS** -
(12"+=/3"cd-s+=) *(W 7787 T/CD)* – Being with the one you love.
Feb 89. (7") *<27694>* **MELT AWAY. / BEING WITH THE ONE YOU LOVE** -

— with musicians **JIM KELTNER** – drums / **JAMES HUTCHINSON** – bass / **BENMONT TENCH** – keyboards / **MARK GOLDENBERG + WADDY WACHTEL** – guitar / **DAVID McMURRAY** – sax, flute

M.C.A. M.C.A.

Sep 95. (cd) *<(MCD 11270)>* **I JUST WASN'T MADE FOR THOSE TIMES** 59
– Meant for you / This whole world / Caroline, no / Let the wind blow / Love and mercy / Do it again / The warmth of the sun / Wonderful / Still I dream of it / Melt away / 'Til I die.

— A few months later, BRIAN teamed up with VAN DYKE PARKS (the main writer) on an album, 'ORANGE CRATE ART' for 'Warners' 9362 45427-2/-4.

R.C.A. Paladin-Giant

Jun 98. (cd) *(74321 57303-2) <24703>* **IMAGINATION** 30 88
– Your imagination / She says that she needs me / South American / Where has love been? / Keep an eye on summer / Dream angel / Cry / Lay down burden / Let him run wild / Sunshine / Happy days.

BEASTIE BOYS

Formed: Greenwich Village, New York, USA ... 1981 by ADAM YAUCH and MIKE DIAMOND. They recruited ADAM HOROWITZ to replace two others (KATE SCHELLENBACH and JOHN BERRY), and after two US indie releases they signed to 'Def Jam', the label run by The BEASTIE's friend and sometime DJ, RICK RUBIN. RUBIN paired with the BEASTIE BOYS was a match made in Heaven (or Hell, if you were unfortunate enough to own a Volkswagen) and the debut album 'LICENSED TO ILL' (1986) was the first real attempt to create a white, rock-centric take on of Afro-American Hip Hop. At turns hilarious and exhilarating, RUBIN and the BEASTIE's shared taste in classic metal was evident with samples from the likes of AC/DC and LED ZEPPELIN along with the theme tune from American TV show 'Mr. Ed'. With snotty rapping and riff-heavy rhymes, tracks like 'FIGHT FOR YOUR RIGHT (TO PARTY) and 'NO SLEEP TILL BROOKLYN' stormed the charts on both sides of the Atlantic, 'LICENSED TO ILL' becoming the fastest selling debut in Columbia's history. The record turned the band into a phenomenon and in 1987 they undertook a riotous headlining tour. Courting controversy wherever they played, the band were savaged by the press, a dispute with 'Def Jam' not helping matters any. Despite all the upheaval, by the release of 'PAUL'S BOUTIQUE' in 1989, the group's profile was negligible and the album was more or less passed over. A tragedy, as it remains one of hip hop's lost gems, a widescreen sampladelic collage produced by the ultra-hip DUST BROTHERS (US). Bypassing the obvious guitar riffs for samples of The BEATLES, CURTIS MAYFIELD and PINK FLOYD along with a kaleidoscopic array of cultural debris and hip references, the album was a funky tour de force. After another extended sabbatical during which the group relocated to California, the BEASTIE BOYS returned in 1992 with 'CHECK YOUR HEAD'. Hipness and attitude were still there in abundance but by now, the group were using live instrumentation. Despite veering from all out thrash to supple funk, the record was a success and only the BEASTIE BOYS could get away with a TED NUGENT collaboration ('THE BIZ VS THE NUGE'). 'ILL COMMUNICATION' (1994) developed this strategy to stunning effect. From the irresistible funk of 'SURE SHOT' and 'ROOT DOWN' to the laid back swing of 'GET IT TOGETHER' and 'FLUTE LOOP', this was the group's most mature and accomplished work to date. The hardcore was still there, 'TOUGH GUY' and 'HEART ATTACK MAN' but it was offset by the sombre strings of 'EUGENE'S LAMENT' and the mellow 'RICKY'S THEME'. A double A-side 'GET IT TOGETHER' and the screechingly brilliant 'SABOTAGE' (complete with entertaining cop-pastiche video) quite rightly returning them into the UK Top 20. From the artwork to the meditative feel of the music (well o.k., maybe not the punk numbers) it was no surprise that YAUCH had become a buddhist and the band subsequently played a high profile benefit for the oppressed nation of Tibet. Ever industrious, the group also started their own label and fanzine 'Grand Royal', signing the likes of LUSCIOUS JACKSON and the now "Big In Japan" BIS. Between development on their magnum-opus comeback (see below), The BEASTIE BOYS dabbled in more electronic/hardcore/instrumental tomfoolery via three mini-albums/EP's, 'ROOT DOWN' (1995), 'AGLIO E OLIO' (1995) and 'THE IN SOUND FROM WAY OUT!' (1996). 1998's 'INTERGALACTIC' single (along with bizarre Power-Rangers-esque video) led the way for the release of the eagerly-awaited 5th set proper, 'HELLO NASTY', an uncompromising, no-holds barred 23-track blinder. With reviews getting near perfect results it was inevitable that The BEASTIE's would have their first transatlantic chart-topper. The band had not lost their tongue-in-cheek attitude despite their recent shifts to a more harmonic religion. Such examples of this would be UK hit singles, 'BODY MOVIN' and 'REMOTE CONTROL', which would also turn up on double-CD anthology 'THE SOUNDS OF SCIENCE' (1999). Meanwhile, inbetween meditating and freestyling, ADAM HOROVITZ collaborated (from the East-Side of America) with the BEASTIE's live drummer AMERY SMITH on the West Coast to create an album of sheer lunacy under the mysterious guise of BS2000. An eponymous album was issued in 1997 on limited vinyl release through Grand Royal's website and immediately became an underground classic amongst the DJ's and The B-Boyz of Brooklyn. Mixing thrashing electronica with phat beats, cheesy hooks and throbbing bass, the set sat on the line between genius masterstroke and faltering mess. Imagine if Aldous Huxley and Albert Einstein had both taken mescaline and turned their mathematical theories into music. The side project returned three years later with the more musically accessible 'SIMPLY MORTIFIED' (2000). Much the same fare, but with distorted vocals, fantastic scratching and less songs, at least the passion was all there even if HOROVITZ's and SMITH's brains were somewhere else. Many would've liked to dismiss BS2000 as a sad joke or just another example of the BEASTIE's ever-increasing oddness – and perhaps it was, but that still didn't diminish the fact that it was as zany, as lo-fi and as nuts as anything to grace the underground indie scene that year. • **Songwriters:** Although they released few cover versions, they sampled many songs (see above). In 1992, they covered JIMMY JAMES (Jimi Hendrix) + TIME FOR LIVIN' (Stewart Frontline), also collaborating with NISHITA. • **Trivia:** ADAM HOROWITZ is the son of playwrite ISRAEL. HOROWITZ played a cameo role in TV serial 'The Equalizer' (circa '88).

Album rating: LICENSED TO 'ILL (*8) / PAUL'S BOUTIQUE (*7) / CHECK YOUR HEAD (*7) / ILL: COMMUNICATION (*9) / HELLO NASTY (*9) / THE SOUNDS OF SCIENCE compilation (*8) / BS 2000: BS 2000 (*5) / SIMPLY MORTIFIED (*7)

'MCA' ADAM YAUCH (b. 5 Aug'65, Brooklyn, New York) – vocals / **'MIKE D' MIKE DIAMOND** (b.20 Nov'66, New York) – vocals / **KATE SCHELLENBACH** (b. 5 Jan'66, New York City) – drums / **JOHN BERRY** – guitar

Ratcage Ratcage

Nov 82. (7"ep) <*(MOTR 21)*> **POLLY WOG STEW EP** [ ] [ ]
– B.E.A.S.T.I.E. boys / Transit cop / Jimi / Holy snappers / Riot fight / Ode to . . . / Michelle's farm / Egg raid on mojo. *(UK-iss.Apr88 12"/c-s; same) (re-iss. 12"ep/c-ep/cd-ep Feb93; same)*

—— **AD ROCK – ADAM HOROWITZ** (b.31 Oct'67, New York City) – vocals, guitar (ex-The YOUNG & THE USELESS) repl.BERRY + SCHELLENBACH (she later joined LUSCIOUS JACKSON)

Aug 83. (7") *<MOTR 26>* **COOKY PUSS. / BEASTIE REVOLUTION** [–] [ ]
(UK-iss.Jan85 + Jul87; MOTR 26 C/CD) (cd-ep-iss.Dec87; same) (re-issues +=) – Bonus batter / Cooky puss (censored version). *(re-iss. 12"ep/c-ep/cd-ep Feb93; same)*

—— added guest RICK RUBIN – scratcher, DJ

Def Jam Def Jam

Dec 85. (12"ep; w-drawn) *<002>* **ROCK HARD / BEASTIE GROOVE. / THE PARTY'S GETTING ROUGH / BEASTIE GROOVE (instrumental)** [–] [–]

Jan 86. (7"/12") *(A/TA 6686) <05683>* **SHE'S ON IT. / SLOW AND LOW** [ ] [ ]

May 86. (7"/12") *(A/TA 7055) <05864>* **HOLD IT NOW, HIT IT. / ACAPULCO (Hold it now, hit it acapella)** [ ] [ ]

Sep 86. (7") *(650 114-7)* **SHE'S ON IT. / SLOW AND LOW** [ ] [–]
(12"+=) *(650 114-6)* – Hold it now, hit it.

Nov 86. (7") *(650 169-7) <06341>* **IT'S THE NEW STYLE. / PAUL REVERE** [ ] [–]
(12"+=) *(650 169-6)* – ('A'&'B'instrumentals).
(d12"++=) *(650 169-8)* – Hold it now, hit it / Hold it now, hit it (Acapulco version) / Hold it now, hit it (instrumental).

Nov 86. (lp/c/cd) *(450 062-1/-4/-2) <40238>* **LICENSED TO 'ILL** [7] [1]
– Rhymin and stealin' / The new style / She's crafty / Posse in effect / Slow ride / Girls / (You gotta) Fight for your right (to party) / No sleep till Brooklyn / Paul Revere / Hold it now, hit it / Brass monkey / Slow and low / Time to get ill. *(re-iss. Nov89 on 'Capitol'; 460 949-1) (re-iss. Jun94 cd/c; 460 949-2/-4) (cd re-iss. Jul95 & Nov99; 527351-2)*

Dec 86. (7") *<06595>* **(YOU GOTTA) FIGHT FOR YOUR RIGHT (TO PARTY). / PAUL REVERE** [–] [7]

Feb 87. (7") *(650 418-7)* **(YOU GOTTA) FIGHT FOR YOUR RIGHT (TO PARTY). / TIME TO GET ILL** [11] [–]
(12"+=) *(650 418-6)* – No sleep till Brooklyn.

Apr 87. (7") *<06675>* **NO SLEEP TILL BROOKLYN. / SHE'S CRAFTY** [–] [ ]

May 87. (7"/7"sha-pic-d) *(BEAST/+P 1)* **NO SLEEP TILL BROOKLYN. / POSSE IN EFFECT** [14] [–]
(12"+=) *(BEASTT 1)* – Hold it now, hit it / Brass monkey.

Jul 87. (7"/7"s/7"s) *(BEAST/+B/D 2)* **SHE'S ON IT. / SLOW AND LOW** [10] [–]
(12"+=) *(BEASTT 2)* – Hold it now, hit it.

Sep 87. (7"/7"s/7"s/7"s/10"sha-pic-d) *(BEAST/+P/S/Q/W 3)* **GIRLS. / SHE'S CRAFTY** [34] [–]
(12"+=/12"s+=) *(BEASTT/+Q 3)* – Rock hard.

Mar 88. (7") *<07020>* **BRASS MONKEY. / POSSE IN EFFECT** [–] [48]

—— no more RICK RUBIN as DJ

Capitol Capitol

Jul 89. (7") *(CL 540) <44454>* **HEY LADIES. / SHAKE YOUR RUMP** [ ] [36]
(12"ep+=/cd-ep+=) *(12/CD CL 540)* **LOVE AMERICAN STYLE** – 33% God / Dis yourself in '89 (just do it). *(re-iss. Jul98 on 'Grand Royal'; GR 064)*

Jul 89. (cd/c/lp) *(DE/TC+/EST 2102) <91743>* **PAUL'S BOUTIQUE** [44] [14]
– To all the girls / Shake your rump / Johnny Ryall / Egg man / High plains drifter / The sound of science / 3-minute rule / Hey ladies / 5-piece chicken dinner / Looking down the barrel of a gun / Car thief / What comes around / Shadrach / Ask for Janice / B-boy bouillabaisse:- (a) 59 Chrystie Street, (b) Get on the mic, (c) Stop that train, (d) A year and a day, (e) Hello Brooklyn, (f) Dropping names, (g) Lay it on me, (h) Mike on the mic, (i) A.W.O.L.

Aug 89. (12"ep) *<Y 15523>* **AN EXCITING EVENING AT HOME WITH SHADRACH, MESHACH AND ABEDNEGO EP** [–] [ ]
– Shadrach / Caught in the middle of a 3-way mix / And what you give is what you get / Car thief / Some dumb cop gave me two tickets already / Your sister's def.

—— Trio now also on instruments; **MCA** – bass / **AD ROCK** – keyboards / **MIKE D** – drums

Apr 92. (c-s/7") *(TC+/CL 653)* **PASS THE MIC. / PROFESSOR BOOTY** [47] [ ]
(etched-12"+=/c-s+=) *(12CL/TCCLX 653)* – Time for livin' / Drunken Praying Mantis style.
(cd-s) *(CDCL 653)* – ('A'side) / Netty's girl / Something's got to give / ('A'-pt.2 – The skills to pay the bills).

May 92. (cd/c/d-lp) *(CD/TC+/EST 2171) <98938>* **CHECK YOUR HEAD** [ ] [10]
– Jimmy James / Funky boss / Pass the mic / Gratitude / Lighten up / Finger lickin' good / So what 'cha want / The biz .vs. the Nuge (with TED NUGENT) / Time for livin' / Something's got to give / The blue nun / Stand together / Pow / The maestro / Groove Holmes / Live at P.J.'s / Mark on the bus / Professor Booty / In 3's / Namaste. *(re-iss. Sep94; CDP 798938-2/-4) (d-lp re-iss. Nov98; GR 066)*

May 92. (12"ep/c-ep/cd-ep) *<Y/4Y/C2 15836>* **JIMMY JAMES / THE MAESTRO / JIMMY JAMES (album version) / BOOMIN' GRANNY / JIMMY JAMES (original) / DRINKIN' WINE** [–] [ ]

Jun 92. (12"ep/12"white-ep/c-ep) *(12CL 665)* **FROZEN METAL HEAD EP** [55] [–]
– Jimmy James / So what'cha want (All the way live freestyle version) / Jimmy James (original) / Drinkin' wine.
(cd-ep) *(CDCL 665)* – The blue nun *[repl. original]*

Jun 92. (cd-ep) *<15847>* **SO WHAT'CHA WANT (3 versions; including pt.2 – The Skills to pay the bills) / GROOVE HOLMES (2 versions)** [–] [93]

Dec 92. (12"ep/cd-ep) *<Y/C2 07777>* **GRATITUDE EP** [–] [ ]
– Gratitude / Stand together (live) / Finger lickin' good (remix) / Gratitude (live) / Honkey rink.

Capitol — Grand Royal

May 94. (cd/c/d-lp) *(CD/TC+/EST 2229) <28599>* **ILL: COMMUNICATION** [10] [1]
– Sure shot / Tough guy / Freak freak / Bobo on the corner / Root down / Sabotage / Get it together / Sabrosa / The update / Futterman's rule / Alright hear this / Eugene's lament / Flute loop / Do it / Rick's theme / Heart attack man / The scoop / Shambala / Bodhisattva vow / Transitions. *(lp re-iss. Apr97 on 'Grand Royal'; GR 006LP)*

Jul 94. (c-s/7"green) *(TC+/CL 716)* **GET IT TOGETHER. / SABOTAGE / DOPE LITTLE SONG** [19] [ ]
(10") *(10CL 716)* – (first 2 tracks) / ('A'-Buck Wild remix) / ('A'instrumental).
(cd-s) *(CDCL 716)* – (first 2 tracks) / ('A'-A.B.A. remix) / Resolution time.

Nov 94. (7"maroon) *(CL 726)* **SURE SHOT. / MULLET HEAD / SURE SHOT (Mario mix)** [27] [ ]
(10"+=) *(10CL 726)* – The vibes.
(cd-s+=) *(CDCLS 726)* – Son of neck bone.
(cd-s) *(CDCL 726)* – ('A'mixes:- Pruins – European B-Boy / Nardone / Large Professor / instrumental).

Jun 95. (m-cd/m-c/m-lp) *(CD/TC+/EST 2262) <33603>* **ROOT DOWN EP** (some live) [23] [50]
– Root down (free zone mix) / Root down / Root down (PP balloon mix) / Time to get ill / Heart attack man / The maestro / Sabrosa / Flute loop / Time for livin' / Something's got to give / So what'cha want. *(m-lp-iss.Apr97 on 'Grand Royal'; GR 018)*

Dec 95. (12"ep/cd-ep) *<GR 026/+CD>* **AGLIO E OLIO** (11 minutes of hardcore) [–] [ ]
– Brand new / Deal with me / Believe me / Nervous assistant / Square wave in unison / You catch a bad one / I can't think straight / I want some. *(UK-iss.Mar98; same)*

—— added guest co-writers **(MONEY) MARK RAMOS NISHITA** – claviers / **ERIC BOBO** – percussion / **EUGENE GORE** – violin

Mar 96. (cd/c) *(CD/TC EST 2281) <7243 8 33590-2/-4>* **THE IN SOUND FROM WAY OUT!** (instrumental) [45] [45]
– Groove Holmes / Sabrosa / Namaste / Pow / Son of neckbone / In 3's / Eugene's lament / Bobo on the corner / Shambala / Lighten up / Ricky's theme / Transitions / Drinkin' wine. *(lp re-iss. Jan99 on 'Grand Royal'; GRA 80013)*

Jun 98. (c-s) *(TCCL 803) <58705>* **INTERGALACTIC / HAIL SAGAN (Special K)** [5] Jul98 [28]
(cd-s+=) *(CDCL 803)* – ('A'-Prisoners Of Technology TMSI remix).
(10") *(10CL 803)* – ('A'side) / ('A'-Prisoners Of . . . remix).

Jul 98. (cd/c/d-lp) *(495723-2/-4/-1) <37716>* **HELLO NASTY** [1] [1]
– Super disco breakin' / The move / Remote control / Song for the man / Just a test / Body movin' / Intergalactic / Sneakin' out of hospital / Putting shame in your game / Flowin' prose / And me / Three MC's and one DJ / Can't, won't, don't stop / Song for Junior / I don't know / The negotiation Limerick file / Electrify / Picture this / Unite / Dedication / Dr. Lee PhD / Instant death.

Oct 98. (cd-s) *(CDCLS 809)* **BODY MOVIN' / (Mickey Finn mix) / DR. LEE phD (dub mix)** [15] [ ]
(cd-s) *(CDCL 809)* – ('A'side) / (Fatboy Slim remix) / (Peanut butter and jelly mix).
(12") *(12CL 809)* – ('A'side) / (Kut Masta Kurt remix) / (Erick Sermon remix) / (instrumental).
(re-iss. /re-mixed May99; GR 069/063)

May 99. (12"/cd-s) *(12CL/CDCLS 812)* **REMOTE CONTROL / THREE MC'S AND ONE DJ / THE NEGOTIATION LIMERICK FILE (Ganja Kru – or – the 41 Small Star remix)** [21] [ ]
(cd-s) *(CDCL 812)* – ('A'side) / Three MC's and one DJ (live video version) / Putting shame in your game (mix) / Three MC's and one DJ (enhanced video).

Aug 99. (12"ep) *<(GR 071)>* **SCIENTIST OF SOUND** [ ] [ ]
– Negotiation Limerick file (mixes) / Intergalactic / Three MC's and one DJ / Body movin' (mixes) / Putting shame in your game.

Nov 99. (d-cd/d-c) *(522940-2/-4) <22940>* **THE SOUNDS OF SCIENCE** (compilation) [36] [19]
– Beastie Boys / Slow and low / Shake your rump / Gratitude / Skills to pay the bills / Root down / Believe me / Sure shot / Body movin' / Boomin' granny / (You gotta) Fight for your right (to party) / Country Mike's theme / Pass the mic / Something's got to give / Bodhisattva vow / Sabrosa / Song for the man / Soba violence / Alive / Jimmy James / Three MC's and one DJ / Biz vs. the Nuge / Sabotage / Shadrach / Brass monkey / Time for livin' / Dub the mic / Benny and the jets / Negotion limerick file / I want some / She's on it / Son of neckbone / Get it together / Twenty questions / Remote control / Railroad blues / Live wire / So what'cha want / Netty's girl / Egg raid on mojo / Hey ladies / Intergalactic.

Dec 99. (10") *(10CL 818)* **ALIVE / START! / ALIVE (B.R.A. remix)** [28] [ ]
(cd-s+=) *(CDCLS 818)* – Start! (video).
(cd-s) *(CDCL 818)* – ('A'side) / You and me together / Big shot (live) / ('A'-video).

– compilations, etc. –

Feb 94. (cd/c) *Honey World; (CD/TC EST 2225) / Grand Royal; <89843>* **SOME OLD BULLSHIT** [ ] [46]
– (compilation of 1st 2 EP's) *(re-iss. Jan99; same)*

BS 2000

AD ROCK + AMERY SMITH

Grand Royal — Grand Royal

Aug 97. (lp) *<(GR 046)>* **BS2000** [ ] [ ]
– Nobody beats BS / Bubbles / No answer / Ajoqueso / O.J. / The real BS / Baby / Go get lifted / Cop suckers / Coco puff / Scorpio / Heaven / Computer pervert / We are BS 2000 / Go with the flow / Break dance / Thift king / Weep and chat / Oh right / Die roller blader / Shock / Dinner in five / Coffee drinker.

Nov 00. (7") *<(GR 092)>* **BUDDY. / BOOGIE BORED** [ ] [ ]
(cd-s+=) *<(GR 092CD)>* – Scrappy / Mr. Critic.

Feb 01. (cd/lp) *<(GR 093 CD/LP)>* **SIMPLY MORTIFIED** [ ] [ ]
– NY is good / Sick for a reason / It feels like / Yeah I like BS / Buddy / Better better / No matter what shade / To side to side / Extractions / Boogie bored / Wait a minute / New gouda / Save this for Davis / Scrappy / Me critic / Flossin' at Lawson / Dig deeper / Dilemma / In the basement / Dansk party / Mom song.

BEATLES

Formed: Liverpool, England ... by JOHN LENNON and PAUL McCARTNEY as schoolboy band The QUARRYMEN in 1957. GEORGE HARRISON joined up the following year, although they split late '59. They reformed in the Spring of 1960 as The SILVER BEATLES, adding PETE BEST and STU SUTCLIFFE. Dropping the SILVER part of their name, they employed manager Alan Williams, who secured them local gigs. Later that year, they toured Hamburg, West Germany, although they had to return when HARRISON was deported for being under eighteen. On the 21st of March '61, they debuted at Liverpool's 'Cavern Club', preceding another 3-month stint in Hamburg. While there, they recorded for 'Polydor' records, backing cabaret-type pop singer TONY SHERIDAN. (These recordings were later released, when the band were at the peak of their popularity). Around mid-'61, STU stayed in Hamburg to get married and study art. There, he was to tragically die of a brain haemorrhage on the 10th April of 1962. With PAUL now on bass and BRIAN EPSTEIN as their new manager, they laid down a demo for 'Decca', which was subsequently discarded by DICK ROWE. Instead he signed BRIAN POOLE & THE TREMELOES (!), although he soon found consolation when he contracted rivals-to-be The ROLLING STONES. Summer '62 brought sunshine when George Martin introduced them to EMI's 'Parlophone' label. During rehearsals BEST was fired and replaced by the more experienced drummer RINGO STARR. By the end of 1962 their debut single 'LOVE ME DO' was in the UK Top 20. The follow-up 'PLEASE PLEASE ME' (1963) reached No.2 and The BEATLES had arrived, their breezy, fresh-faced pop striking a chord in a music scene that was crying out for a band with the effortless charisma of the cheeky Scousers. More, their mop-topped, sharp-suited image (courtesy of BRIAN EPSTEIN) remains one of the most enduring impressions in the history of pop culture. And thus did that dog-eared cliche of a phenomenon, 'BEATLEMANIA' tighten its grip as the band toured above ROY ORBISON later that year to unprecedented scenes of teenage delirium. They also found time to knock out a debut album, 'PLEASE PLEASE ME' (1963), produced by their mentor George Martin and featuring a heady cocktail of live wig-outs ('I SAW HER STANDING THERE', 'TWIST AND SHOUT'etc.) and LENNON/McCARTNEY originals. This precocious songwriting partnership was entering its golden period as the band notched up an incredible string of No.1 singles in quick succession, 'FROM ME TO YOU' (1963), 'SHE LOVES YOU' (1963), 'I WANT TO HOLD YOUR HAND' (1963) and 'CAN'T BUY ME LOVE' (1964). The BEATLES finished 1963 in fine style; a No.1 follow-up album, 'WITH THE BEATLES', the biggest selling single in British history, 'SHE LOVES YOU' and a performance before the Queen Mother at the Royal Command Variety Performance. With British domination well under way, the band flew to America in February 1964, droves of hysterical fans greeting them upon their landing at New York's Kennedy Airport. They made a legendary appearance on the 'Ed Sullivan Show' and by April The BEATLES held the top five positions in the American Billboard singles charts (i.e. No.1:- CAN'T BUY ME LOVE, 2:- TWIST AND SHOUT, 3:- SHE LOVES YOU, 4:- I WANT TO HOLD YOUR HAND, 5:- PLEASE PLEASE ME). Flying high, that summer saw the release of The BEATLES' first movie and accompanying soundtrack, 'A HARD DAY'S NIGHT'. The band proved themselves as compelling on screen as on stage, and the film's revolutionary shooting technique created the blueprint for decades of rockumentaries to come. The same year also saw the release of the band's third album, 'BEATLES FOR SALE', a record which included some of the last genuine LENNON/McCARTNEY collaborations. Each were developing their own particular style and although all their songs continued to be credited as joint efforts, by the following year the pair seldom wrote together. 'HELP' (1965), a filmic follow-up to 'A HARD DAY'S NIGHT', featured some of LENNON and McCARTNEY's most focused songwriting to date (notably the title track and 'YESTERDAY') and was filmed at various locations around the globe. The BEATLES performed before a record number of fans at New York's Shea Stadium in August, the same month as 'HELP' was opened in the U.S. By this point The BEATLES were undoubtedly the biggest pop/rock band in the world, unique in their abilty to produce music that seemingly crossed all boundaries of age, race, class and gender. Even so, it was a shock to the rock world when the Queen announced in the summer of '65 that the band were each to receive an M.B.E.. It was almost unthinkable that bad boy rivals The ROLLING STONES would be given such a (dubious) honour, and while the two bands were poles apart musically, LSD and the burgeoning psychedelic culture brought them together briefly. 'RUBBER SOUL' (1965), written and recorded in just over a month, was the sound of The BEATLES in flux, shedding their clean cut image and interpreting the influence of BOB DYLAN's pioneering folk-rock experiments. Despite the transformation taking place, the sound was more fluid and assured, the songwriting more mature. LENNON's 'IN MY LIFE' was beautifully bittersweet while McCARTNEY almost equalled 'YESTERDAY' with 'MICHELLE' and the lilting 'NORWEGIAN WOOD' saw HARRISON's first forays into sitar work. The album was sandwiched between pioneering double A-sided singles 'DAY TRIPPER' / 'WE CAN WORK IT OUT' (1965) and 'PAPERBACK WRITER' / 'RAIN' (1966). 'RAIN' was the first overtly psychedelic BEATLES record, innovative in its use of rhythm and featuring an undulating LENNON vocal (a style much mimicked by many of todays crop of young bands). Its potential was fully realised on 'REVOLVER' (1966), oft cited as The BEATLES' pinnacle achievement and as one of the best albums ever made. McCARTNEY excelled himself with the string-cloaked melancholy of 'ELEANOR RIGBY', while HARRISON's biting 'TAXMAN' kicked off the album in strident style. But it was the psychedelic numbers which made most impact. 'SHE SAID SHE SAID' was a swirling piece of trip-pop, while 'TOMORROW NEVER KNOWS' remains one of the most bizarre and enigmatic songs in The BEATLES' canon. With a working title of 'THE VOID', the song was based on one of LENNON's first profound acid trips and was partly inspired by the ancient religious text beloved of hippies at the time, 'The Tibetan Book Of The Dead'. With a hypnotic drum sound that many have since tried and failed to recreate, backwards guitar that sounded like a flock of screeching pterodactyls and LENNON's mantra-like vocals, the record set a precedent in psychedelic rock. At this stage The BEATLES were already preoccupied with the possibilities of the recording studio and significantly, the band played their last gig in San Francisco's Candlestick Park the same month 'REVOLVER' was released. Ensconced in Abbey Road Studios, the band came up with the double A-side, 'PENNY LANE' / 'STRAWBERRY FIELDS FOREVER'. Released in February '67, the single's effects-laden innovation was a taster for The BEATLES' much heralded psychedelic concept album 'SGT. PEPPER'S LONELY HEARTS CLUB BAND'. Its release coinciding perfectly with the fabled 1967 'Summer Of Love', the record was a landmark in new studio technique. Utilising the (then) pioneering four-track recording process, the band painstakingly pieced together ornate pieces of sonic intricacy that set new standards. It contained many classics such as 'LUCY IN THE SKY WITH DIAMONDS' (wrongly thought by many to be about L.S.D.), 'SHE'S LEAVING HOME' and the never-ending 'A DAY IN THE LIFE', complete with prolonged intentionally stuck-in-the-groove outro. Fans and critics alike made it "their greatest album of all time", although many others thought it too overblown as well as over-produced. A month later, the anthemic 'ALL YOU NEED IS LOVE' gave them another No.1, helped no doubt by its simultaneous worldwide TV broadcast. The death of BRIAN EPSTEIN cast a shadow over the celebrations but the band moved on, filming/recording 'MAGICAL MYTERY TOUR' (1967). A trippy film and soundtrack inspired by KEN KESEY and his bunch of technicolour minstrels, it contained the infamous LENNON-penned surrealism of 'I AM THE WALRUS'. Screened on British TV on Boxing Day 1967, the film was almost universally panned. Unbowed, The BEATLES decamped to India for spiritual retreat with the Maharishi Mahesh Yogi, during which time they accumulated much of the material that would form the 'WHITE ALBUM'. Upon their return to English shores, they set about forming the 'Apple Corporation', which would handle all the business dealings of the band as well as functioning as a label for The BEATLES and likeminded talent. The first release was 'HEY JUDE' / 'REVOLUTION' (1968), the former a rousing torch song, the latter a stinging attack by LENNON on would-be radicals. Eventually released in November '68, 'THE BEATLES (White Album)' was a sprawling double set recorded in an environment of tension and breakdown of inter-band communications. Yet it contained some of The BEATLES finest songs, 'HARRISON's solemn 'WHILE MY GUITAR GENTLY WEEPS', LENNON's gorgeous 'DEAR PRUDENCE' and 'JULIA', a moving tribute to his mother. The album also included the cryptic genius of LENNON's 'HAPPINESS IS A WARM GUN' while 'REVOLUTION No.9' was The BEATLES at their most defiantly experimental. Nevertheless, the recording had strained relationships within the band to breaking point and the subsequent back to basics sessions in 1969 (eventually emerging as the 'LET IT BE' album) broke down in disarray. Incredibly, the band got it together one last time for 'ABBEY ROAD' (1969), a breathtaking sweep through the diverse styles of each of the songwriters. GEORGE HARRISON contributed two of his best tracks, 'SOMETHING' and the pastoral beauty of 'HERE COMES THE SUN'. McCARTNEY penned most of the medley which formed a sizeable chunk of the album and which included one of his most heartbreakingly lovely songs, 'GOLDEN SLUMBERS'. 'LET IT BE', eventually released in 1970 was hardly a fitting epitaph for The BEATLES, PHIL SPECTOR's production coming in for some flak. It did, however, contain such definitive BEATLES moments as the deeply reflective title track, the sleepy 'ACROSS THE UNIVERSE' and the beguiling 'THE LONG AND WINDING ROAD'. The BEATLES had officially split a couple of months before the album's release in April 1970, estranged amid personal rows and more serious business disagreements. LENNON, McCARTNEY and HARRISON all went on to respectable solo careers, although none of the subsequent recordings had quite the same impact as The BEATLES' material. Come the 90's, there was still a voracious market for anything BEATLES-related and fans were treated to successive live and outtakes sets, most of which topped the charts in both America and Britain. 1994's 'LIVE AT THE BBC was the first of these monster doubles, showcasing the band's early, rock'n'roll-influenced years with a slew of previously unissued material including many incendiary covers of both well known and more obscure songs. The three mid-90's volumes of 'ANTHOLOGY' meanwhile, trawled the archives for alternate takes, rough demos, live cuts and other odds 'n'sods, releasing them chronologically with each covering a distinct phase of the band's 60's career. Pick of the bunch was probably the third and final one, if for no other reason than the sheer experimentalism of their latter years and the inevitable, fascinating cast-offs which that produced (including acoustic demos from 'THE WHITE ALBUM' sessions and the semi-legendary stringless version of 'THE LONG AND WINDING ROAD'). The rather unnecessary '1' (2000) collected the complete sweep of the band's No.1 singles in both America and the States while 'LET IT BE . . .NAKED' (2003) offered an alternate take on the controversial original. While the record purported to be the finished article as originally envisioned, it certainly wasn't a warts'n'all release of the abandoned 'GET BACK' sessions and, in dispensing with the banter and asides of 'LET IT BE', sacrificed some of the original's spontaneity. In its favour was the inclusion of the aforementioned stringless ' . . .WINDING ROAD' and pre-SPECTOR versions of both 'ACROSS THE UNIVERSE' and 'I ME MINE' as well as a much better overall sound quality. Whether these and other minor differences warranted its release is another matter. Sadly, another chapter in the BEATLES saga drew to a close when GEORGE HARRISON finally succumbed to cancer on the 29th of November, 2001, a star-studded concert at London's Royal Albert Hall paying tribute to perhaps the greatest and most underrated Beatle of them all. The band remain one of the greatest cultural icons of the 20th Century with a back catalogue that even OASIS will never be able to match. • **Covered:** TWIST AND SHOUT (Isley Brothers) / A TASTE OF HONEY (Bobby Scott) / MONEY (Barrett Strong) / ROLL OVER BEETHOVEN + ROCK AND ROLL MUSIC (Chuck Berry) / YOU REALLY GOT A HOLD ON ME (Miracles) / PLEASE MR. POSTMAN (Marvelettes) / KANSAS CITY (Wilbert Harrison) / WORDS OF LOVE (Diamonds) / CHAINS (Cookies) / BABY IT'S YOU (Shirelles) / etc.

Album rating: PLEASE PLEASE ME (*8) / WITH THE BEATLES (*8) / A HARD DAY'S NIGHT (*8) / BEATLES FOR SALE (*7) / HELP! (*8) / RUBBER SOUL (*9) / REVOLVER (*10) / SGT. PEPPER'S LONELY HEARTS CLUB BAND (*10) / MAGICAL MYSTERY TOUR (*8) / THE BEATLES 'White Album' (*10) / YELLOW SUBMARINE (*5) / ABBEY ROAD (*9) / LET IT BE (*7) / THE BEATLES 1967-70 compilation (*10) / THE BEATLES 1962-66 compilation (*10) / LIVE AT THE BBC collection (*8) / 1 compilation (*10) / LET IT BE . . . NAKED (*6)

JOHN LENNON (b. JOHN WINSTON LENNON, 9 Oct'40) – vocals, rhythm guitar / **PAUL McCARTNEY** (b. JAMES PAUL McCARTNEY, 18 Jun'42) – vocals, guitar / **GEORGE HARRISON** (b.25 Feb'43) – vocals, lead guitar/ **STU SUTCLIFFE** (b. STUART, 23 Jun'40, Edinburgh, Scotland) – bass/ **PETE BEST** (b.1941) – drums

Polydor Decca

Jan 62. (7"; as TONY SHERIDAN & THE BEATLES) *(NH 66-833)* <*31382*> **MY BONNIE. / THE SAINTS** [ ] Apr62 [ ]
(re-iss. May63 hit UK No.48; same) (re-iss. Feb64; same) <US re-iss. Jan64 on 'M.G.M.'; K 13213>; hit No. 26) (above A-side was released Aug61 in Germany as TONY SHERIDAN & The BEAT BROTHERS)

— Were a quartet at the time, STU stayed in Germany, died 10 Apr'62 of brain haemorrhage. McCARTNEY now on bass and vocals.

— (Aug62) **RINGO STARR** (b.RICHARD STARKEY, 7 Jul'40) – drums (ex-RORY STORM & THE HURRICANES)repl. BEST

Parlophone not iss.

Oct 62. (7") *(R 4949)* **LOVE ME DO. / P.S. I LOVE YOU** [17] [–]
(re-iss. Feb63; same) <US-iss.Apr64 on 'Tollie'; 9008>; hit Nos. 1+10> *<US re-iss. Aug64 on 'Oldies'; 45 OL 151> <US re-iss. Oct65 on 'Capitol Starline'; 6062> (re-iss. Oct82; same); hit No.4) (re-iss. cd-s.1989) (re-iss. Oct92; same); hit No.53)*

Parlophone Vee Jay

Jan 63. (7") *(R 4983)* *<VJ 498>* **PLEASE PLEASE ME. / ASK ME WHY** [2] [ ]
(re-iss. Feb63; same) (re-iss. Jan83; same); hit 29) (re-iss. cd-s.1989)

Mar 63. (lp; mono)(lp; stereo) *(PMC 1202)(PCS 3042)* **PLEASE PLEASE ME** [1] [–]

– I saw her standing there / Misery / Anna (go to him) / Chains / Boys / Ask me why / Please please me / Love me do / P.S. I love you / Baby, it's you / Do you want to know a secret / A taste of honey / There's a place / Twist and shout. *(c-iss.1970's) (cd-iss. Feb87; CDP 746435-2); hit 32) (re-iss. Nov88 lp/c; PMC/TC-PMC 1202)*

Apr 63. (7") *(R 5015) <VJ 522>* **FROM ME TO YOU. / THANK YOU GIRL** 1 |
(re-iss. Apr83; same); hit No.40) (re-iss. cd-s.1989)

Jul 63. (lp) *<1062>* **INTRODUCING . . . THE BEATLES** – | Feb64 2
-(tracks nearly same as UK debut)

Aug 63. (7") *(R 5055) <Swan; S-4152>* **SHE LOVES YOU. / I'LL GET YOU** 1 | Sep63 1
(re-iss. Aug83; same); hit No.45) (re-iss. cd-s.1989)

Nov 63. (lp; mono)(lp; stereo) *(PMC 1206)(PCS 3042)* **WITH THE BEATLES** 1 | –
– It won't be long / All I've got to do / All my loving / Don't bother me / Little child / Till there was you / Please Mr. Postman / Roll over Beethoven / Hold me tight / You really got a hold on me / I wanna be your man / Roll over Beethoven / Devil in her heart / Not a second time / Money. *(c-iss.1970's) (cd-iss. Feb87; CDP 746436-2); hit No.40) (re-iss. Nov88 lp/c; PMC/TC-PMC 1206)*

Nov 63. (7") *(R 5084)* **I WANT TO HOLD YOUR HAND. / THIS BOY** 1 | –
(re-iss. Nov83; same); hit No.62) (re-iss. cd-s.1989)

Jan 64. (7") *<VJ 581>* **PLEASE PLEASE ME. / FROM ME TO YOU** – | 3
<US re-iss. Aug64 on 'Oldies'; 45 OL 150> <US re-iss. Oct65 on 'Capitol Starline'; 6063>

Parlophone | Capitol

Jan 64. (7") *<5112>* **I WANT TO HOLD YOUR HAND. / I SAW HER STANDING THERE** – | 1 / 14

Jan 64. (lp) *<2047>* **MEET THE BEATLES!** – | 1
– I want to hold your hand / I saw her standing there / This boy / It won't be long / All I've got to do / All my loving / Don't bother me / Little child / Till there was you / Hold me tight / I wanna be your man / Not a second time.

Mar 64. (7") *(R 5114) <5150>* **CAN'T BUY ME LOVE. / YOU CAN'T DO THAT** 1 | 1
(re-iss. Mar84; same); hit No.53) (re-iss. cd-s.1989)

Apr 64. (lp) *<2080>* **THE BEATLES' SECOND ALBUM** – | 1
– Roll over Beethoven / Thank you girl / You really got a hold on me / Devil in her heart / Money / You can't do that / Long tall Sally / I call your name / Please Mr. Postman / I'll get you / She loves you.

Jul 64. (7") *(R 5160)* **A HARD DAY'S NIGHT. / THINGS WE SAID TODAY** 1 | –
(re-iss. Jul84; same); hit No.52) (re-iss. cd-s.1989)

Jul 64. (7") *<5222>* **A HARD DAY'S NIGHT. / I SHOULD HAVE KNOWN BETTER** – | 1 / 53

Jul 64. (lp; mono)(lp; stereo) *(PMC 1230)(PCS 3058) <6366>* **A HARD DAY'S NIGHT (Soundtrack)** 1 | 1
– A hard day's night / I should have known better / If I fell / I'm happy just to dance with you / And I love her / Tell me why / Can't buy me love / Anytime at all / I'll cry instead / Things we said today / When I get home / You can't do that / I'll be back. *(re-iss. Jan71; same); hit 39) (cd-iss. Feb87; CDP 746437-2); hit No.30) (re-iss. Nov88 lp/c; PMC/TC-PMC 1230)*

Aug 64. (7") *<5234>* **I'LL CRY INSTEAD. / I'M HAPPY JUST TO DANCE WITH YOU** – | 25 / 95

Aug 64. (7") *<5235>* **AND I LOVE HER. / IF I FELL** – | 12 / 53

Sep 64. (7") *<5255>* **MATCHBOX. / SLOW DOWN** – | 17 / 25

Nov 64. (7") *(R 5200) <5327>* **I FEEL FINE. / SHE'S A WOMAN** 1 | 1 / 4
(re-iss. Nov84; same) ; hit No.65) (re-iss. cd-s.1989)

Dec 64. (lp; mono)(lp; stereo) *(PMC 1240)(PCS 3062)* **BEATLES FOR SALE** 1 | –
– No reply / I'm a loser / Baby's in black / Rock and roll music / I'll follow the sun / Mr. Moonlight / Medley: Kansas City – Hey hey hey hey / Eight days a week / Words of love / Honey don't / Every little thing / I don't want to spoil the party / What you're doing / Everybody's trying to be my baby. *(c-iss.1970's) (cd-iss. Feb87; CDP 746438-2); hit No.45) (re-iss. Nov88 lp/c; PMC/TC-PMC 1240)*

Jan 65. (lp) *<2228>* **BEATLES '65** – | 1
– (track listing near as above)

Feb 65. (7") *(5371>* **EIGHT DAYS A WEEK. / I DON'T WANT TO SPOIL THE PARTY** – | 1 / 39

Apr 65. (7") *(R 5265) <5407>* **TICKET TO RIDE. / YES IT IS** 1 | 1
(re-iss. Apr85; same); hit No.70) (re-iss. cd-s.1989)

Jul 65. (lp) *<2358>* **BEATLES VI** – | 1
– Kansas City / Eight days a week / You like me too much / Bad boy / I don't want to spoil the party / Words of love / What you're doing / Yes it is / Dizzy Miss Lizzy / Tell me what you see / Every little thing.

Jul 65. (7") *(R 5305) <5476>* **HELP!. / I'M DOWN** 1 | 1
(re-iss. Apr76; same); hit No.37) *(re-iss. Jul85; same) (re-iss. cd-s.1989)*

Jul 65. (lp; mono)(lp; stereo) *(PMC 1255)(PCS PCS 3071) <2386>* **HELP! (Soundtrack)** 1 | Aug65 1
– Help! / The night before / You've got to hide your love away / I need you / Another girl / You're going to lose that girl / Ticket to ride / Act naturally / It's only love / You like me too much / Tell me what you see / I've just seen a face / Yesterday / Dizzy Miss Lizzy. *(re-iss. Jul71 lp/c; same); hit No.33) (cd-iss. Apr87; CDP 746439-2); hit No.61) (re-iss. Nov88 lp/c; PMC/TC-PMC 1255)*

Sep 65. (7") *<5498>* **YESTERDAY. / ACT NATURALLY** – | 1

Dec 65. (7") *(R 5389) <5555>* **DAY TRIPPER. / WE CAN WORK IT OUT** 1 | 5 / 1
(re-iss. Dec85; same) (re-iss. cd-s.1989)

Dec 65. (lp; mono)(lp; stereo) *(PMC 1267)(PCS 3075) <2442>* **RUBBER SOUL** 1 | 1
– Drive my car / Norwegian wood (this bird has flown) / You won't see me / Nowhere man / Think for yourself / The word / Michelle / What goes on? / Girl / I'm looking through you / In my life / Wait / If I needed someone / Run for your life. *(c-iss.1970's) (cd-iss. Apr87; CDP 746440-2); hit UK No.60) (re-iss. Nov88 lp/c; PMC/TC-PMC 1267)*

Feb 66. (7") *<5587>* **NOWHERE MAN. / WHAT GOES ON** – | 3 / 81

Jun 66. (7") *(R 5452) <5651>* **PAPERBACK WRITER. / RAIN** 1 | 1 / 23
(re-iss. Mar76; same); hit No.23) (re-iss. Jun86; same) (re-iss. cd-s.1989)

Aug 66. (7") *(R 5493) <5715>* **YELLOW SUBMARINE. / ELEANOR RIGBY** 1 | 2 / 11
(re-iss. Aug86; same); hit No.63) (re-iss. cd-s.1989)

Aug 66. (lp; mono/stereo) *(PMC/PCS 7009) <2576>* **REVOLVER** 1 | 1
– Taxman / Love you to / I want to tell you / Eleanor Rigby / Here, there and everywhere / Good day sunshine / For no one / Got to get you into my life / I'm only sleeping / She said she said / And your bird can sing / Doctor Robert / Tomorrow never knows / Yellow submarine. *(c-iss.1970's) (cd-iss. Apr87; CDP 746441-2); hit UK No.55) (re-iss. Nov88 lp/c; PMC/TC-PMC 7009)*

Feb 67. (7") *(R 5570) <5810>* **PENNY LANE. / STRAWBERRY FIELDS FOREVER** 2 | 1 / 8
(re-iss. Mar76; same); hit No.32) (re-iss. Feb87; same); hit No.65) (re-iss. cd-s.1989)

Jun 67. (lp; mono/stereo) *(PMC/PCS 7027) <2653>* **SGT. PEPPER'S LONELY HEARTS CLUB BAND** 1 | 1
– Sgt.Pepper's lonely hearts club band / With a little help from my friends / Lucy in the sky with diamonds / Getting better / Fixing a hole / She's leaving home / Being for the benefit of Mr.Kite / Within you without you / When I'm sixty-four / Lovely Rita / Good morning, good morning / Sgt. Pepper's lonely hearts club band (reprise) / A day in the life. *(c-iss.1970's) (cd-iss. Jun87; CDP 746442-2); hit UK No.3) (re-iss. Nov88 lp/c; PMC/TC-PMC 7027) (re-iss. Jun92; same); hit UK No.6)*

Jul 67. (7") *(R 5620) <5964>* **ALL YOU NEED IS LOVE. / BABY YOU'RE A RICH MAN** 1 | 1 / 34
(re-iss. Jul87; same); hit No.47) (re-iss. cd-s.1989)

Nov 67. (7") *(R 5655) <2056>* **HELLO GOODBYE. / I AM THE WALRUS** 1 | 1 / 56
(re-iss. Nov87; same); hit No.63) (re-iss. cd-s.1989)

Dec 67. (d7"ep; stereo/mono) *(S+/MMT 1)* **MAGICAL MYSTERY TOUR** 2 | –
– Magical mystery tour / Your mother should know / Flying / Fool on the hill / Blue Jay way / I am the walrus.

Dec 67. (lp) *(imported) <2835>* **MAGICAL MYSTERY TOUR (Soundtrack)** 31 | 1
– (above UK-ep, plus 1967 singles) *(UK-iss.Oct76, cd-iss. Sep87; CDP 748 062-2); hit UK 52)*

Mar 68. (7") *(R 5675)* <2138> **LADY MADONNA. / THE INNER LIGHT** [1] [4] [96]
(re-iss. Mar88; same); hit No.67) (re-iss. cd-s.1989)

Apple Apple

Aug 68. (7") *(R 5722)* <2276> **HEY JUDE. / REVOLUTION** [1] [1] [12]
(re-iss. Mar76; same); hit No.12) (re-iss. Aug88; same); hit No.52) (re-iss. cd-s.1989)

Nov 68. (d-lp; mono/stereo) *(PMC/PCS 7067-8)* <101> **THE BEATLES (White Album)** [1] [1]
– Back in the U.S.S.R / Dear Prudence / Glass onion / Ob-la-di-ob-la-da / Wild honey pie / The continuing story of Bungalow Bill / While my guitar gently weeps / Happiness is a warm gun / Martha my dear / I'm so tired / Blackbird / Piggies / Rocky raccoon / Don't pass me by / Why don't we do it in the road / I will / Julia / Birthday / Yer blues / Mother nature's son / Everybody's got something to hide except me and my monkey / Sexy Sadie / Helter skelter / Long long long / Revolution 1 / Honey pie / Savoy truffle / Cry baby cry / Revolution 9 / Good night. *(re-iss. Sep78 white-lp; same) (cd-iss. Aug87; CDP CDS 746443-2); hit UK No.18) (re-iss. Nov88 lp/c; PCS/TCPCS 7067) (d-cd re-iss. Nov98; 496895-2)*

Jan 69. (lp; mono/stereo) *(PMC/PCS 7070)* <153> **YELLOW SUBMARINE (Soundtrack)** [4] [2]
– Yellow submarine / Only a northern song / All together now / Hey bulldog / It's all too much / All you need is love / Pepperland / Sea of time / Sea of holes / Sea of monsters / March of the Meanies / Pepperland laid waste / Yellow submarine in Pepperland. (with GEORGE MARTIN ORCHESTRA) *(re-iss. Aug87; CDP 746445-2); hit UK 60) (re-iss. Nov88 lp/c; PCS/TC-PCS 7070)*

Apr 69. (7"; by BEATLES with BILLY PRESTON) *(R 5777)* <2490> **GET BACK. / DON'T LET ME DOWN** [1] [1] [35]
(re-iss. Mar76; same); hit No.28) (re-iss. Apr89; same); hit 74) (re-iss. cd-s.1989)

May 69. (7") *(R 5786)* <2531> **THE BALLAD OF JOHN AND YOKO. / OLD BROWN SHOE** [1] [8]
(UK re-iss. May89) (re-iss. cd-s.1989)

Sep 69. (lp/c) *(PCS/TC-PCS 7088)* <383> **ABBEY ROAD** [1] [1]
– Come together / Maxwell's silver hammer / Something / Oh darling / Octopus's garden / I want you (she's so heavy) / Here comes the sun / Because / You never give me your money / Sun king / Mean Mr. Mustard / Polythene Pam / She came in through the bathroom window / Golden slumbers / Carry that weight / The end / Her majesty. *(UK re-iss. Oct87; CDP 746 446-2); hit No.30) (re-iss. Nov88 lp/c; PCS/TC-PCS 7088)*

Oct 69. (7") *(R 5814)* <2654> **SOMETHING. / COME TOGETHER** [4] [3] [1]
(UK re-iss. Oct89) (re-iss. cd-s.1989)

Mar 70. (7") *(R 5833)* <2764> **LET IT BE. / YOU KNOW MY NAME (LOOK UP THE NUMBER)** [2] [1]
(UK re-iss. Mar90) (re-iss. cd-s.1989)

May 70. (lp/c) *(PCS/TC-PCS 7096)* <34001> **LET IT BE** [1] [1]
– Two of us / Dig a pony / Across the universe / I me mine / Dig it / Let it be / Maggie Mae / I've got a feeling / The one after 909 / The long and winding road / For you blue / Get back. *(cd-iss. Oct87; CDP 746 447-2); hit No.50) (re-iss. Nov88 lp/c; PCS/TC-PCS 7096)*

May 70. (7") <2832> **THE LONG AND WINDING ROAD. / FOR YOU BLUE** [–] [1]

— officially disbanded April 1970 – all 4 had released, or were due to release, own albums. See **Paul McCARTNEY ⇒ , John LENNON ⇒ , George HARRISON ⇒ , Ringo STARR ⇒ .**

– (selective) compilations, etc. –

on 'Parlophone' UK / 'Capitol' US unless otherwise mentioned

Jul 63. (7"ep) *(GEP 8880)* **TWIST AND SHOUT** [2] [–]
– Twist and shout / A taste of honey / Do you want to know a secret / There's a place.

Sep 63. (7"ep) *(GEP 8882)* **THE BEATLES HITS** [14] [–]
– From me to you / Thank you girl / Please please me / Love me do.

Nov 63. (7"ep) *(GEP 8883)* **THE BEATLES (No.1)** [19] [–]
– I saw her standing there / Misery / Chains / Anna (go to him).

Jan 64. (7"; by TONY SHERIDAN & THE BEATLES) *Polydor; (NH 52-906)* **SWEET GEORGIA BROWN. / NOBODY'S CHILD** [ ] [–]

Feb 64. (7"ep) *(GEP GEP 8891)* **ALL MY LOVING** [12] [–]
– All my loving / Ask me why / Money / P.S. I love you.

Mar 64. (7"; by TONY SHERIDAN & THE BEATLES) *M.G.M.; <K 13227>* **WHY. / CRY FOR A SHADOW** [–] [88]

Mar 64. (7") *Tollie; <9001>* **TWIST AND SHOUT. / THERE'S A PLACE** [–] [2] [74]

Apr 64. (7") *Vee Jay; <VJ 587>* **DO YOU WANT TO KNOW A SECRET. / THANK YOU GIRL** [–] [2] [35]

May 64. (7") *Swan; <S-4182>* **SIE LIEBT DICH. / I'LL GET YOU** [–] [97]

May 64. (7"; by TONY SHERIDAN & THE BEATLES) *Polydor; (NH 52-317)* **AIN'T SHE SWEET. / IF YOU LOVE ME BABY** [29] [–]

Jun 64. (lp; by TONY SHERIDAN & THE BEATLES) *Polydor Special; (236 201)* **THE BEATLES' FIRST** [ ] [–]
(re-iss. Jun71 as THE EARLY YEARS on 'Contour') (re-iss. as 'THE FIRST ALBUM' cd+c May93 on 'Spectrum', credited to TONY SHERIDAN & THE BEATLES)

Jun 64. (7"; by TONY SHERIDAN & THE BEATLES) *Atco; <6302>* **SWEET GEORGIA BROWN. / TAKE OUT SOME INSURANCE ON ME BABY** [–] [ ]

Jun 64. (7"ep) *(GEP 8913)* **LONG TALL SALLY** [14] [–]
– Long tall Sally / I call your name / Slow down / Matchbox.

Jun 64. (7"ep) *<EAP 2121>* **FOUR BY THE BEATLES** [–] [92]
– All my loving / This boy / Roll over Beethoven / Please Mr.Postman.

Jul 64. (7"; by TONY SHERIDAN & THE BEATLES) *Atco; <6308>* **AIN'T SHE SWEET. / NOBODY'S CHILD** [–] [19]

Aug 64. (lp) *<2108>* **SOMETHING NEW** [–] [2]

Nov 64. (7"ep) *(GEP 8920)* **EXTRACTS FROM THE FILM 'A HARD DAY'S NIGHT'** [34] [–]
– I should have known better / If I fell / Tell me why / And I love her.

Dec 64. (7"ep) *(GEP 8924)* **EXTRACTS FROM THE ALBUM 'A HARD DAY'S NIGHT' 2** [ ] [–]
– Anytime at all / I'll cry instead / Things we said today / When I get home.

Dec 64. (lp) *<2222>* **THE BEATLES' STORY (narrative)** [–] [7]

Jul 66. (lp) *(2553>* **YESTERDAY . . . AND TODAY** [–] [1]

Dec 66. (lp) *(PMC/PCS 7016)* **A COLLECTION OF BEATLES OLDIES** [7] [–]
– She loves you / From me to you / We can work it out / Help! / Michelle / Yesterday / I feel fine / Yellow submarine / Can't buy me love / Bad boy / Day tripper / A hard day's night / Ticket to ride / Paperback writer / Eleanor Rigby / I want to hold your hand. *(re-iss. Oct83 on 'Fame' lp/c; FA/TC-FA 3081)*

Mar 70. (lp) *Apple; <385>* **HEY JUDE** [–] [2]
(UK-iss.May79 on 'Parlophone' lp/c; PCS/TC-PCS 7184)

Apr 73. (d-lp/d-c) *Apple; (PCSP/TC2-PCSP 717) <3403>* **THE BEATLES 1962-1966** [3] [3]
– Love me do / Please please me / She loves you / From me to you / She loves you / I want to hold your hand / All my loving / Can't buy me love / A hard day's night / And I love her / Eight days a week / I feel fine / Ticket to ride / Yesterday / Help! / You've got to hide your love away / We can work it out / Day tripper / Drive my car / Norwegian wood (this bird has flown) / Nowhere man / Michelle / In my life / Girl / Paperback writer / Eleanor Rigby / Yellow submarine. *(re-iss. Sep78 & Feb94 red-lp) (d-cd-iss. Jul91; CDPCSP 717) (re-iss. d-cd Sep93 on 'Apple-Parlophone'; same)* – hit UK No.3

Apr 73. (d-lp/d-c) *Apple; (PCSP/TC2-PCSP 718) <3404>* **THE BEATLES 1967-1970** [2] [1]
– Strawberry fields forever / Penny lane / Sgt. Pepper's lonely hearts club band / With a little help from my friends / Lucy in the sky with diamonds / A day in the life / All you need is love / I am the Walrus / Hello, goodbye / The fool on the hill / Magical mystery tour / Lady Madonna / Hey Jude / Revolution / Back in the U.S.S.R / While my guitar gently weeps / Ob-la-di, ob-la-da / Get back / Don't let me down / The ballad of John and Yoko / Old brown shoe / Here comes the sun / Come together / Something / Octopus's Garden / Let it be / Across the universe / The long and winding road. *(re-iss. Sep78 & Feb94 blue-lp) (d-cd-iss. Jul91; CDPCSP 718) (re-iss. d-cd Sep93 on 'Apple-Parlophone'; same)* – hit UK No.4

Mar 76. (7") *(R 6013)* **YESTERDAY. / I SHOULD HAVE KNOWN BETTER** [8] [–]

Jun 76. (lp/c) *(PCSP/TC-PCSP 719) <11537>* **ROCK'N'ROLL MUSIC** [11] [2]
(re-iss. Nov80 as . . . VOL.1 / . . . VOL.2 both on 'MfP')

Jun 76. (7") *<4274>* **GOT TO GET YOU INTO MY LIFE. / HELTER SKELTER** [–] [7]

Jul 76. (7") *(R 6016)* **BACK IN THE U.S.S.R. / TWIST AND SHOUT** [19] [–]

Aug 76. (d-lp) *Polydor; (2683 068)* **THE BEATLES TAPES (interviews)** [45] [–]

Nov 76. (7") *<4347>* **OB-LA-DI, OB-LA-DA. / JULIA** [–] [49]

May 77. (lp/c) *(EMTV/TC-EMTV 4) <11638>* **THE BEATLES AT THE HOLLYWOOD BOWL (live)** [1] [2]
(UK re-iss. Sep84 on 'MfP')

Dec 77. (d-lp/d-c) *(PCSP/TC-PCSP 721) <11711>* **LOVE SONGS** [7] [24]

Sep 78. (7") *(R 6022) <4612>* **SGT. PEPPER'S LONELY HEARTS CLUB BAND – WITH A LITTLE HELP FROM MY FRIENDS. / A DAY IN THE LIFE** [63] [71]

Nov 78. (14xlp-box) *(BBX 1)* **THE BEATLES COLLECTION** [ ] [ ]
– (all original albums boxed)

Oct 79. (lp/c) *(PCM/TC-PCM 1001) <12060>* **RARITIES** [71] Apr80 [21]

Nov 80. (lp/c) *(PCS/TC-PCS 7214)* **BEATLES BALLADS** [17] [ ]

Apr 82. (lp/c) *<12199>* **REEL MUSIC** [–] [19]

May 82. (7") *(R 6055) <5107>* **BEATLES MOVIE MEDLEY. / I'M HAPPY JUST TO DANCE WITH YOU** [10] Mar82 [12]
– ('A'medley); Magical Mystery Tour – All You Need Is Love – You've Got To Hide Your Love Away – I Should Have Known Better – A Hard Day's Night – Ticket To Ride – Get Back.

Oct 82. (d-lp/d-c) *(PCTC/TC-PCTC 260) <12245>* **20 GREATEST HITS** [10] [50]

Feb 88. (cd/c/d-lp) *E.M.I.; (CD/TC+/BPM 1)* **PAST MASTERS VOL.1** [49] [ ]

Feb 88. (cd/c/d-lp) *E.M.I.; (CD/TC+/BPM 2)* **PAST MASTERS VOL.2** [46] [ ]

Apr 92. (cd-epx14-box) *(CDBEP 14)* **THE BEATLES EP COLLECTION** [ ] [–]

Dec 94. (d-cd/d-c/d-lp) *Apple; (CD/TC+/PCSP 726)* **LIVE AT THE BBC (live)** [1] [3]
– Beatle greetings / From us to you / Riding on a bus / I got a woman / Too much monkey business / Keep your hands off my baby / I'll be on my way / Young blood / A shot of rhythm and blues / Sure to fall (in love with you) / Some other guy / Thank you girl / Sha la la la la! / Baby it's you / That's all right (mama) / Carol / Soldier of love / A little rhyme / Clarabella / I'm gonna sit right down and cry (over you) / Crying, waiting, hoping / Dear Wack! / You really got a hold on me / To know her is to love her / A taste of honey / Long tall Sally / I saw her standing there / The honeymoon song / Johnny B Goode / Memphis, Tennessee / Lucille / Can't buy me love / From Fluff to you / Till there was you // Crinsk Dee night / A hard day's night / Have a banana! / I wanna be your man / Just a rumour / Roll over Beethoven / All my loving / Things we said today / She's a woman / Sweet little sixteen / 1882! / Lonesome tears in my eyes / Nothin' shakin' / The hippy hippy shake / Glad all over / I just don't understand / So how come (no one loves me) / I feel fine / I'm a loser / Everybody's trying to be my baby / Rock and roll music / Ticket to ride / Dizzy Miss Lizzy / Medley: Kansas City – Hey! hey! hey! hey! / Set fire to that lot! / Matchbox / I forgot to remember to forget / Love these Goon shows! / I got to find my baby / Ooh! my soul / Ooh! my arms / Don't ever change / Slow down / Honey don't / Love me do.

Mar 95. (c-s/7") *Apple; (TC+/R 6406) <58348>* **BABY IT'S YOU / I'LL FOLLOW THE SUN** [7] [67]
(cd-s+=) *(CDR 6406)* – Devil in her heart / Boys.

Nov 95. (d-cd/d-c/t-lp) *Apple; (CD/TC+/PCSP 727) <34445>* **ANTHOLOGY 1** [2] [1]
– Free as a bird / Speech (by JOHN LENNON) / That'll be the day / In spite of all the danger / Sometimes I'd borrow (speech by PAUL McCARTNEY) / Hallelujah I love her so / You'll be mine / Cayenne / First of all (speech by PAUL) / My Bonnie (w/ TONY SHERIDAN) / Ain't she sweet / Cry for a shadow / Brian was a beautful guy (speech by JOHN) / Secured them an audition (speech by BRIAN EPSTEIN) / Searchin' / Three cool cats / The Sheik of Araby / Like dreamers do / Hello little girl / Well, the recording test (speech by BRIAN) / Besame mucho / Love me do / How do you do it? / Please please me / One after 909 (sequence) / One after 909 (complete) / Lend me your comb / I'll get you / We were performers (speech by JOHN) / I saw her standing there / From me to you / Money (that's what I want) / You really got a hold on me / Roll over Beethoven / She loves you / Till there was you (music man) / Twist and shout / This boy / I want to hold your hand / Boys, what I was thinking (speech by The BEATLES and MORECAMBE & WISE) / Moonlightbay (w/ MORECAMBE & WISE) / Can't buy me love / All my loving / You can't do that / And I love her / A hard day's night / I wanna be your man / Long tall Sally / Boys / Shout / I'll be back (take 2) / I'll be back (take 3) / You know what to do / No reply (demo) / Mr.Moonlight / Leave my kitten alone / No reply / Eight days a week (sequence) / Eight days a week (complete) / Kansas City – hey, hey, hey.
(below single was recently re-recorded from JOHN LENNON's 1977 cut)

Dec 95. (c-s/7") *Apple; (TC+/R 6422) <58497>* **FREE AS A BIRD. / CHRISTMAS TIME (IS HERE AGAIN)** [2] [6]
(cd-s+=) *(CDR 6422)* – I saw her standing there (take 9) / This boy (take 13).

Mar 96. (c-s/7") *Apple; (TC+/R 6425) <58544>* **REAL LOVE / BABY'S IN BLACK** [4] [11]
(cd-s+=) *(CDR 6425)* – Yellow submarine / Here, there and everywhere.

Mar 96. (d-cd/d-c/t-lp) *(CD/TC+/PCSP 728) <34448>* **ANTHOLOGY 2** [1] [1]
– Real love / Yes it is (version) / I'm down / You've got to hide your love away / If you've got trouble / That means a lot / Yesterday (take) / It's only love (take) / I feel fine / Ticket to ride / Yesterday (take) / Help! (version) / Everybody's trying to be my baby / Norwegian wood (this bird has flown) / I'm looking through you / 12-bar original / Tomorrow never knows / Got to get you into my life / And your bird can sing (version) / Taxman / Eleanor Rigby (strings only) / I'm only sleeping (rehearsal) / I'm only sleeping (take 1) / Rock & roll music / She's a woman / Strawberry fields forever (demo sequence) / Strawberry fields forever (take 1) / Strawberry fields forever (take 7 and edit piece) / Penny Lane (take) / A day in the life (version) / Good morning, good morning (version) / Only a Northern song / Being for the benefit of Mr. Kite (takes 1 & 2) / Being for the benefit of Mr. Kite (take 7) / Lucy in the sky with diamonds (take) / Within you, without you (instrumental) / Sgt. Pepper's lonely hearts club band (take) / You know my name (look up my number) / I am the walrus (version) / Fool on the hill (demo) / Your mother should know / Fool on the hill (take 4) / Hello, goodbye (version) / Lady Madonna (take) / Across the universe (alt. take).

Oct 96. (d-cd/d-c/t-lp) *(CD/TC+/PCSP 729) <46332>* **ANTHOLOGY 3** [4] [1]
– A beginning / Happiness is a warm gun / Helter skelter / Mean Mr. Mustard (take) / Polythene Pam / Glass onion (version) / Junk (take) / Piggies / Honey pie / Don't pass me by / Ob-la-di, ob-la-da / Good night (version) / Cry baby cry (version) / Blackbird / Sexy Sadie / While my guitar gently weeps / Hey Jude / Not guilty / Mother nature's son (take) / Glass onion (version) / Rocky racoon (take) / What's the new Mary Jane? / Step inside love / I'm so tired / I will / Why don't we do it in the road? (version) / Julia (take) / I've got a feeling (version) / She came in through the bathroom window / Dig a pony (version) / Two of us (take) / For you blue / Teddy boy / Medley: Rip it up – Shake, rattle and roll – Blue suede shoes / The long and winding road / Oh! darling (take) / All things must pass / Mailman, bring me no more blues / Get back / Old brown shoe / Octopus's garden / Maxwell's silver hammer (take) / Something / Come together (version) / Come and get it / Ain't she sweet / Because (version) / Let it be / I me mine / The end.

Sep 99. (cd/c/lp) *(<5 21481-2/-4/-1>)* **YELLOW SUBMARINE SONGTRACK** [8] [15]

Nov 00. (cd/c)(d-lp) *(529970-2/-4)(529325-1) <29325>* **1** [1] [1]
– Love me do / From me to you / She loves you / I want to hold your hand / Can't buy me love / A hard day's night / I feel fine / Eight days a week / Ticket to ride / Help! / Yesterday / Day tripper / We can work it out / Paperback writer / Yellow submarine / Eleanor Rigby / Penny Lane / All you need is love / Hello, goodbye / Lady Madonna / Hey Jude / Get back / The ballad of John and Yoko / Something / Come together / Let it be / The long and winding road.

Nov 01. (d-cd) *Bear Family; (<BCD 16447)* **BEATLES BOP – HAMBURG DAYS** [ ] [ ]

Nov 03. (cd)(lp) *(595713-2)(595438-0)* **LET IT BE . . . NAKED** [7] [ ]
– Get back / Dig a pony / For you blue / The long and winding road / Two of us / I've got a feelin / One after 909 / Don't let me down / I me mine / Across the universe / Let it be. *(cd w/ dvd+=)* – (fly on the wall outtakes). *(lp w/ free 7"+=)* – (interview).

□ BEATS INTERNATIONAL (see under ⇒ COOK, Norman)

BEAUTIFUL SOUTH

Formed: Hull, England . . . early 1989 by PAUL HEATON, DAVE HEMMINGWAY and DAVID ROTHERAY, who added SEAN WELCH and ex-HOUSEMARTINS roadie, DAVID STEED. They stuck with their 'Go! Discs' contract, the former two having been the integral part of STEED's employers. A debut single, 'SONG FOR WHOEVER' climbed to UK No.2, its parody of love song overload belying a bittersweet appeal which no amount of clever, ironic lyrics could detract from over the course of their career. With the addition of BRIANNA CORRIGAN, the bulk of the group's subsequent work would be characterised by the vocal trade-off's between her and HEATON, some of them priceless. Melody was everything with The BEAUTIFUL SOUTH and an irrepresible follow-up track, 'YOU KEEP IT ALL IN', made the UK Top 10. Both cuts were featured on their debut set, 'WELCOME TO THE BEAUTIFUL SOUTH' (1989), an impressive start which included the enduringly charming 'FROM UNDER THE COVERS' and a spine-tingling cover of 'I'LL SAIL THIS SHIP ALONE', HEATON's little-boy-lost vocals working miracles. Shrugging off the controversy of the cover art (a woman with a gun in her mouth), the band topped the charts the following year with the STEED / CORRIGAN duet, 'A LITTLE TIME', a classy follow-up album, 'CHOKE' (1990) also selling in bucketloads. The record marked out The BEAUTIFUL SOUTH as undisputed champions of chronicling everyday relationship breakdowns, although the set undoubtedly sold on the strength of their tunes rather than their lyrics. Previewed by the semi-tragic 'OLD RED EYES IS BACK', the occasionally brilliant '0898' (1992) album was a more bitterly realistic affair, the poignant small-time tragedy of 'BELL BOTTOMED TEAR' remaining one of their most emotionally jarring compositions to date. The record went Top 5, consolidating their position as mainstream pop mavericks. A fourth set, 'MIAOW' (1994), saw HEATON work with new recruit, JACQUELINE ABBOTT, a replacement for the solo bound CORRIGAN. The partnership worked equally well, HEATON developing as a songwriter, while also putting in a swooning cover of Fred Neil's 'EVERYBODY'S TALKIN''. The latter track was the record's biggest hit, although the band's popularity was confirmed as a greatest hits set, 'CARRY ON UP THE CHARTS' (1994), became one of the fastest selling albums in British history. They returned in suitably barbed style with 'BLUE IS THE COLOUR' (1996), another No.1 album which drew controversy with its Top 10 hit, 'DON'T MARRY HER', a slightly altered version provided for radio play. HEATON and ABBOTT teamed up exquisitely once again after yet another two-year spell, this time No.2 single 'PERFECT 10' from the chart-topping parent album, 'QUENCH' (1998), displayed the usual BEAUTIFUL SOUTH repartee. While critics continued to queue up in hope of writing off HEATON and Co, the band's comfy nook in the adult pop pantheon looked increasingly secure. Another day, another decade and another album; 'PAINTING IT RED' (2000) was business as usual for the group, their tried and tested formula of subversive pop skullduggery making few concessions to musical fashion. The infectious 'CLOSER THAN MOST' managed a Top 30 placing, its two follow-ups ('THE RIVER' and 'THE ROOT OF ALL EVIL') relatively poor Top 75 chart performances suggesting that The BEAUTIFUL SOUTH's brand of social comment may finally be redundant in the vacuum-packed, braindead wasteland that constitutes modern "pop". The creatively irrepressible HEATON got his solo career off to a decent start with 2002's 'FAT CHANCE', originally released under the BISCUIT BOY banner. Kitted-out with an up-to-the-minute production and armed with as much lyrical trickery as any BS fan could hope for, the album upated HEATON's standard musical context without sacrificing the charm. Highlights included 'MITCH', another perfectly observed HEATON-ROTHERAY classic, while the busybody-baiting 'IF' found its lyrical target with calculated precision. • **Songwriters:** HEATON and ROTHERAY, except GIRLFRIEND (Pebbles) / LOVE WARS (Womack & Womack) / ARTIFICIAL FLOWERS (Bobby Darin) / DREAM A LITTLE DREAM (Mamas & The Papas) / AIN'T NO SUNSHINE + LEAN ON ME + YOU JUST CAN'T SMILE IT AWAY (Bill Withers) / GOD BLESS THE CHILD (Billie Holiday) / I SOLD MY HEART TO THE JUNKMAN (LaBelle) / I STARTED A JOKE + YOU SHOULD BE DANCING (Bee Gees).

Album rating: WELCOME TO THE BEAUTIFUL SOUTH (*7) / CHOKE (*6) / 0898 (*6) / MIAOW (*6) / CARRY ON UP THE CHARTS compilation (*8) / BLUE IS THE COLOUR (*7) / QUENCH (*6) / PAINTING IT RED (*5) / SOLID BRONZE – GREAT HITS compilation (*8) / GAZE (*5) / Paul Heaton: FAT CHANCE (*4)

PAUL HEATON (b. 9 May'62, Bromborough, England) – guitar, vocals / **DAVE HEMMINGWAY** – keyboards (both ex-HOUSEMARTINS) / **DAVID ROTHERAY** (b. 9 Feb'??) – vocals, guitar / **SEAN WELCH** (b.12 Apr'??, Enfield, England) – bass / **DAVID STEED** (b.15 Oct'??, Huddersfield, England) – drums

Go! Discs Elektra

May 89. (7"/7"s/c-s) *(GOD/+P/MC 32)* **SONG FOR WHOEVER. / STRAIGHT IN AT 37** [2] [ ]
(12"+=/cd-s+=) *(GODX/GOCD 32)* – You and your big ideas.

— added **BRIANNA CORRIGAN** (b.County Antrim, Ireland) – vocals (ex-ANTHILL RUNAWAYS). She was to join full-time in 1990.

Sep 89. (7"/7"s/c-s) *(GOD/+P/MC 35)* **YOU KEEP IT ALL IN. / I LOVE YOU (BUT YOU'RE BORING)** [8] [ ]
(12"+=/cd-s+=) *(GODX/GOCD 35)* – You can't just smile it away / ('A'version).

Oct 89. (lp/c/cd) *(AGO LP/MC/CD 16) <60917>* **WELCOME TO THE BEAUTIFUL SOUTH** [2] [ ]
– Song for whoever / Have you ever been away? / From under the covers / I'll sail this ship alone / Girlfriend / You keep it all in / Woman in the wall / Oh Blackpool / Love is . . . / I love you (but you're boring). *(cd+=)* – Straight in at 37. *(cd re-iss. Aug98; 84208026)*

Nov 89. (7"/7"s/c-s) *(GOD/+P/MC 38)* **I'LL SAIL THIS SHIP ALONE. / BUT TILL THEN** [31] [–]
(12"+=/cd-s+=) *(GOD X/CD 38)* – ('A'orchestral version).
(7"white++=) *(GODT 38)* – ('A'-lp version).

Sep 90. (7"/7"s/c-s) *(GOD/+P/MC 47)* **A LITTLE TIME. / IN OTHER WORDS I HATE YOU** [1] [ ]
(12"+=/cd-s+=) *(GOD X/CD 47)* – What you see is what you get.

Oct 90. (cd/c/lp) *(828 233-2/-4/-1) <60985>* **CHOKE** [2] [ ]
– Tonight I fancy myself / My book / Let love speak up itself / Should've kept my eyes shut / I've come for my award / Lips / I think the answer's yes / A little time / Mother's pride / I hate you (but you're interesting) / The rising of Grafton Street. *(cd+=)* – What you see is what you get. *(re-iss. cd Apr93 & Aug98; same)*

Nov 90. (7"/7"s/c-s) *(GOD/+P/MC 48)* **MY BOOK. / BIG BEAUTIFUL SOUTH** [8] [–]
(12"+=/cd-s+=) *(GOD X/CD 48)* – Bigger doesn't mean better / Speak to me.

Mar 91. (7"/c-s) *(GOD/+MC 53)* **LET LOVE SPEAK UP ITSELF. / LOVE WARS** [51] [–]
(12"+=/cd-s+=) *(GOD X/CD 53)* – Danielle Steele / Headbutting husband.

Go! Discs Chameleon

Jan 92. (7"/c-s) *(GOD/+MC 66)* **OLD RED EYES IS BACK. / FLEET STREET B.C.** [22] [–]
(12"+=/cd-s+=) *(GOD X/CD 66)* – Diamonds.

Mar 92. (7"/c-s) *(GOD/+MC 71)* **WE ARE EACH OTHER. / HIS TIME RAN OUT** [30] [–]
(12"+=/cd-s+=) *(GOD X/CD 71)* – I started a joke.

Apr 92. (cd/c/lp) *(828 310-2/-4/-1) <61308>* **0898** [4] [ ]
– Old red eyes is back / We are each other / The rocking chair / We'll deal with you later / Domino man / 36D / Here it is again / Something that you said / I'm your No.1 fan / Bell bottomed tear / You play glockenspiel / I'll play drums / When I'm 84.

Jun 92. (7"/c-s) *(GOD/+MC 78)* **BELL BOTTOMED TEAR. / A THOUSAND LIES / THEY USED TO WEAR BLACK** [16] [–]
(cd-s+=) *(GODCD 78)* – You should be dancing (live) / Woman in the wall (live).

Sep 92. (7"/c-s/cd-s) *(GOD/+MC/CD 88)* **36D. / THROWING HIS SONG AWAY / TREVOR, YOU'RE BIZARRE!** [46] [–]
(cd-s) *(GOLCD 88)* – ('A'live) / From under the covers (live) / You keep it all in (live).

— **JACQUELINE ABBOTT** (b.1974) – vocals repl. CORRIGAN who went solo

Feb 94. (7"/c-s) *(GOD/+MC 110)* **GOOD AS GOLD. / LOVE ADJOURNED** [23] [–]

(cd-s+=) *(GODCD 110)* – Mini-correct.
(cd-s) *(GOLCD 110)* – ('A'side) / Frank and Delores / One man's rubbish.

Mar 94. (cd/c/lp) *(828 332-2/-4/-1)* *<41842>* **MIAOW** [6] [ ]
– Hold on to what / Good as gold (stupid as muck) / Especially for you / Everybody's talkin' / Prettiest eyes / Worthless lie / Hooligans don't fall in love / Hidden jukebox / Hole me close (underground) / Tattoo / Mini correct / Poppy.

May 94. (7"/c-s/cd-s) *(GOD/+MC/CD 113)* **EVERYBODY'S TALKIN'. / A WAY WITH THE BLUES / LET LOVE SPEAK UP ITSELF** [12] [–]
(cd-s) *(GOLCD 113)* – ('A'side) / Nearer to God / A piece of sky.

Aug 94. (7"/c-s/cd-s) *(GOD/+MC/CD 119)* **PRETTIEST EYES. / THE BEST WE CAN / SIZE** [37] [–]
(cd-s) *(GOLCD 19)* – ('A'side) / Why can't I / Missing her now.

Oct 94. (7"/c-s/cd-s) *(GOD/+MC/CD 122)* **ONE LAST LOVE SONG. / RIGHT MAN FOR THE JOB / JAVA** [14] [–]
(cd-s) *(GOLCD 122)* – ('A'side) / Mr. Obsession / You're only jealous.

Nov 94. (cd/c/lp) *(828 572-2/-4/-1)* **CARRY ON UP THE CHARTS – THE BEST OF THE BEAUTIFUL SOUTH** (compilation) [1] [–]
– Song for whoever / You keep it all in / I'll sail this ship alone / A little time / My book / Let love speak up itself / Old red eyes is back / We are each other / Bell bottomed tear / 36D / Good as gold (stupid as mud) / Everybody's talkin' / Prettiest eyes / One last love song.

Nov 95. (c-s/cd-s) *(GOD MC/CD 134)* **PRETENDERS TO THE THRONE. / VIRGIN / A LONG DAY IN THE FIELD** [18] [–]

Go! Discs Ark 21

Oct 96. (7"/c-s) *(GOD/+MC 155)* **ROTTERDAM. / A MINUTE'S SILENCE** [5] [–]
(cd-s+=) *(GODCD 155)* – Pollard.

Oct 96. (cd/c/lp) *(828 845-2/-4/-1)* *<810019>* **BLUE IS THE COLOUR** [1] [ ]
– Don't marry her / Little blue / Mirror / Blackbird on the wire / The sound of North America / Have fun / Liar's bar / Rotterdam / Foundations / Artificial flowers / One God / Alone.

Dec 96. (c-s) *(GODMC 158)* **DON'T MARRY HER / DREAM A LITTLE DREAM / GOD BLESS THE CHILD** [8] [–]
(cd-s) *(GODCD 158)* – ('A'side) / God bless the child / Without her.
(cd-s) *(GOLCD 158)* – ('A'side) / Dream a little dream / Les yeux ouverts.

Mar 97. (7"/c-s) *(582124-7/-4)* **BLACKBIRD ON THE WIRE. / LEAN ON ME** [23] [–]
(cd-s+=) *(582125-2)* – You just can't smile it away (live).
(cd-s) *(582197-2)* – ('A'live) / I'll sail this ship alone (live) / The sound of North America (live).

Mercury Mercury

Jun 97. (c-s) *(582238-4)* **LIAR'S BAR / THE OPENING OF A NEW BOOK / YOU'VE DONE NOTHING WRONG (live)** [43] [–]
(cd-s) *(582239-2)* – ('A'side) / Dumb / You've done nothing wrong (live).
(cd-s) *(582241-2)* – ('A'side) / The opening of a new book / Hold on to what? (live).

Sep 98. (c-s) *(566480-4)* **PERFECT 10 / IF** [2] [–]
(cd-s+=) *(566481-2)* – I'll sail this ship alone.
(cd-s) *(566483-2)* – ('A'side) / Loving arms (live) / One last love song.

Oct 98. (cd/c/lp) *(<538166-2/-4/-1>)* **QUENCH** [1] [ ]
– How long's a tear take to dry? / The lure of the sea / Big coin / Dumb / Perfect 10 / The slide / Look what I found in my beer / The table / Window shopping for blinds / Pockets / I may be ugly / Losing things / Your father and I.

Dec 98. (c-s) *(556752-4)* **DUMB / SUCK HARDER** [16] [–]
(cd-s+=) *(566753-2)* – Especially for you.
(cd-s) *(556755-2)* – ('A'side) / I sold my heart to the junkman / Blackbird on the wire.

Mar 99. (c-s) *(870820-4)* **HOW LONG'S A TEAR TAKE TO DRY? / ('A'remix)** [12] [–]
(cd-s+=) *(870821-2)* – Perfect 10 (acoustic).
(cd-s) *(870823-2)* – ('A'side) / Big coin (acoustic) / Rotterdam (acoustic).

Jun 99. (c-s) *(562165-4)* **THE TABLE / YOUR FATHER AND I (live)** [47] [–]
(cd-s+=) *(562165-2)* – Old red eyes is back (live).
(cd-s) *(562165-5)* – ('A'side) / Don't marry her (live) / Look what I found in my beer (live).

Mercury Ark 21

Sep 00. (c-s) *(562967-4)* **CLOSER THAN MOST / THE TABLE (acoustic)** [22] [–]
(cd-s+=) *(562967-2)* – Moths.
(cd-s) *(562968-2)* – ('A'side) / The state that I'm in / Blackbird on the wire (acoustic).

Oct 00. (cd/c/d-lp) *(548269-2/-4/-1)* *<810064>* **PAINTING IT RED** [2] [ ]
– Closer than most / Just checkin' / Hit parade / Masculine eclipse / 'Til you can't tuck it in / If we crawl / Tupperware queen / Half- hearted get (is second best) / The river / Baby please go / You can call me leisure / Final spark / 10,000 feet / Hot on the heels of heartbreak / The Mediterranean / A little piece of advice / Property quiz / Chicken wings.

Dec 00. (c-s) *(572755-4)* **THE RIVER / JUST CHECKIN' (remix)** [59] [–]
(cd-s+=) *(572755-2)* – Valentine's day wank.
(cd-s+=) *(572756-2)* – Little chef.

Nov 01. (cd-s) *(588870-2)* **THE ROOT OF ALL EVIL / FREE FOR ALL / PERFECT 10 (video)** [50] [–]
(cd-s) *(588871-2)* – ('A'side) / Chicken wings / Rotterdam (video).

Nov 01. (cd/c/d-lp) *(586444-2/-4/-1)* **SOLID BRONZE – GREAT HITS** (compilation) [10] [–]
– Rotterdam / Perfect 10 / Don't marry her / A little time / Everybody's talkin' / Good as gold / Dream a little dream / Song for whoever / Old red eyes is back / One last love song / Dumb / You keep it all in / How long's a tear take to dry? / Blackbird on the wire / Good as gold / Closer than most / The river / Pretenders to the throne / The root of all evil / Mediterranean (Morcheeba mix).

Mercury Mercury

Oct 03. (cd-s) *(9813038)* **JUST A FEW THINGS THAT I AIN'T / CHEAP / CARE AS YOU GO / ('A'-video)** [30] [–]
(cd-s) *(9813039)* – ('A'side) / The new fence / A long time coming.

Oct 03. (cd) *(<9865694>)* **GAZE** [14] Jan04 [ ]
– Pretty / Just a few things that I ain't / Sailing solo / Life vs. the lifeless / Get here / Let go with the flow / The gates / Angels and devils / 101% man / Half of him / Spit it all out / The last waltz.

Dec 03. (cd-s) *(9815083)* **LET GO WITH THE FLOW / SKOOL DAZE** [47] [–]
(cd-s) *(9815084)* – ('A'side) / Don't stop moving (live session) / Song for whoever (live session).

PAUL HEATON

with **MARTIN SLATTERY + SCOTT SHIELDS + DAVE ROTHERAY + DAMON BUTCHER**

Mercury Mercury

Jul 02. (cd-s) *(063987-2)* **THE PERFECT COUPLE / MITCH (Virgin radio session) / POEMS (demo)** [ ] [–]

Jul 02. (cd) *(<063045-2>)* **FAT CHANCE** [ ] Jan03 [ ]
– 10 lessons in love / Mitch / The perfect couple / Last day blues / Man's world / Barstool / Poems / If / Real blues / Proceed with care / Man girl boy woman.

☐ BE-BOP DELUXE (see under ⇒ NELSON, Bill)

BECK

Born: BECK HANSEN, 8 Jul'70, Los Angeles, California, USA. After absorbing the strains of primitive country blues artists like LEADBELLY and MISSISSIPPI JOHN HURT, along with the aural terrorism of hardcore noise, the 17-year old BECK relocated to New York in 1989 to try his hand on the post-punk East Village folk scene. Broke, he retired to L.A., setting himself up in the (now) trendy Silverlake district, playing low key gigs in local coffeehouses. Spotted by 'Bongload' owner TOM ROTHROCK, he was offered some studio time and the resulting sessions produced the 'LOSER' (1993) single. Caned by L.A.'s alternative radio stations, its popularity led to BECK signing with 'Geffen'. 'LOSER' (1994) in its re-issued, major label form went top 20 in both Britain and America, its slow burning hip hop blues turning the rosy cheeked BECK into an overnight slacker anti-hero. The 'MELLOW GOLD' (1994) album went some way towards crystallising BECK's skewed vision of a modern folk music that encapsulated roots blues, hip hop, country, noise-core and psychedelia. While the record went on to sell half a million copies, BECK's unique contract allowed him the option of recording for other labels. 'STEREOPATHIC SOUL MANURE' (1994) was a U.S. only release of rough early material on the small 'Flipside' label, while 'ONE FOOT IN THE GRAVE' (1995) was a mainly acoustic set released on CALVIN JOHNSON's 'K' records, its stark harmonica-driven title track remaining a highlight of the BECK live experience. Any dubious whispers of "one-hit wonder" were cast aside with the release of 1996's 'ODELAY', a record that topped many end of year polls and turned BECK into the music world's coolest hep cat. Garnering gushing praise from the dance, rock and hip hop communities alike, the album's effortless fusion of disparate styles was breathtaking. The cut'n'paste surrealism of the lyrics flourished imagery of a lucidness to match BOB DYLAN's 60's work and indeed, the gorgeously bittersweet 'JACKASS' used Dylan's 'IT'S ALL OVER NOW BABY BLUE' as a shimmering harmonic backdrop. The album segued smoothly from distortion and dissonance into downhome steel guitar hoedown, all the while retaining an irresistibly funky backbeat. For now, this pop auteur/wunderkid can do no wrong, his live experience is a dayglo potted history of American music and any readers who were lucky enough to catch his glorious set at the Chelmsford V97 festival, will know that BECK doesn't take too kindly to bottle throwing eunuchs! Towards the end of 1998, BECK found himself in the midst of another legal wrangle with label 'Geffen' when a dispute over who was to release his new 14-day recorded 'MUTATIONS' resulted in the label taking full control. The latter was subsequently released to critical acclaim due to Nigel Godrich's production of BECK's live direction. With less label fuss but with more media frenzy, the Lo-Fi loner issued his 4th 'Geffen' set, 'MIDNITE VULTURES' (1999), which proved to be a dark contrast between that and the aforementioned 'MUTATIONS'. After the strange kitsch-adelic sound of 'MIDNITE VULTURES', BECK reverted back to folksy troubadour mode once again complemented by producer Nigel Godrich. A wistful seventh album from the ever eclectic, robot-dancing HANSEN, 'SEA CHANGE' (2002) saw him revisiting the days of 'ONE FOOT IN THE GRAVE' and the Godrich produced no-fi album 'MUTATIONS'. With its gentle melodies and sombre, quasi-romantic overtones, BECK, as always, spiced up the mix by adding harpsicord, trombone, violins and pedal steel to give the set a swift breezy sound – like a psychedelic GRAM PARSONS. Well, he always has been really. • **Songwriters:** BECK writes most of his material, some with KARL STEPHENSON. 'LOSER' used a sample of DR.JOHN's 'I Walk On Guilded Splinters'. Covered: I'M SO GREEN (Can) / HALO OF GOLD (Moby Grape). • **Trivia:** The 'Geffen Rarities Vol.1' album of various artists, featured the BECK track, 'Bogusflow'.

Album rating: A WESTERN HARVEST FIELD BY MOONLIGHT (*4) / GOLDEN FEELINGS mini (*3) / MELLOW GOLD (*7) / STEREOPATHETIC SOULMANURE (*4) / ONE FOOT IN THE GRAVE (*6) / ODELAY (*9) / MUTATIONS (*7) / MIDNITE VULTURES (*8) / SEA CHANGE (*7)

BECK (HANSEN) – vocals, acoustic guitar with guests **RACHEL HADEN** – drums, vocals / **ANNA WARONKER** – bass, vocals / **PETRA HADEN** – violin, vocals / **MIKE BOITO** – organ / **DAVID HARTE** – drums / **ROB ZABRECKY** – bass

not iss. Flipside

1992. (ltd-7"blue-ep) *<FLIP 46>* **TO SEE THAT WOMAN OF MINE / MTV MAKES ME WANNA SMOKE CRACK. / (other side 2 tracks by BEAN)** [–] [ ]

not iss. Sonic Enemy

Jan 93. (c) *<none>* **GOLDEN FEELINGS** [–] [ ]
– The fucked up blues / Special people / Magic stationwagon / No money no honey / Trouble all my days / Bad energy / Schmoozer / Heartland feeling / Super golden black sunchild / Soul sucked dry / Feelings / Gettin home / Will I be ignored by the Lord / Bogus soul / Totally confused / Muthafukka / People gettin busy.

not iss. Bongload

1993. (ltd-12") *<BL 5>* **LOSER. / STEAL MY BODY HOME** [–] [ ]

1994. (ltd-7") *<BL 11>* **STEVE THREW UP. / MUTHERFUCKER / (CUPCAKE)** [–] [ ]
(both above UK-iss.Jan95; same) (cd-s iss.Dec97 & Oct00; BL 11CDS)

not iss. Fingerpaint

1994. (10"m-lp) *<FP 02>* **A WESTERN HARVEST FIELD BY MOONLIGHT** [–] [ ]
– Totally confused / Mayonaisse salad / Gettin' home / Blackfire choked our death / Feel like a piece of shit (mind control) / She is all (gimme something to eat) / Pinefresh / Lampshade / Feel like a piece of shit (crossover potential) / Mango (Vader rocks!) / Feel like a piece of shit (cheetoes time) / Styrofoam chicken (quality time). *<re-iss. Sep95; same> (UK cd-iss. Oct97 & May98; same)*

Geffen D.G.C.

Mar 94. (7"/c-s) *<DGC S7-19/CS-12 270>* **LOSER. / ALCOHOL** [–] [10]
(cd-s+=) *<DGCDM-21930>* – Corvette bumper / Soul suckin' jerk (reject) / Fume.

Mar 94. (7"/c-s) *(GFS/+C 67)* **LOSER. / ALCOHOL / FUME** [15] [–]
(cd-s) *(GFSTD 67)* – ('A'side) / Totally confused / Corvette bumper / MTV makes me want to smoke crack.

Mar 94. (cd/c/lp) *(GED/GEC/GEF 24634) <DGCD/DGC 24634>* **MELLOW GOLD** [41] [13]
– Loser / Pay no mind (snoozer) / Fuckin with my head (mountain dew rock) / Whiskeyclone, Hotel City 1997 / Soul suckin jerk / Truckdrivin neighbors downstairs (yellow sweat) / Sweet sunshine / Beercan / Steal my body home / Nitemare hippy girl / Motherfuker / Blackhole. *<lp-iss. on 'Bongload'(hidden track cd+=)* – Analog odyssey. *(lp re-iss. Apr97 & Sep99 & Jan01 on 'Bongload'; BL 12> (lp re-iss. Nov98 on 'Simply Vinyl'; SVLP 44)*

May 94. (cd-ep) *<DM-22000>* **BEERCAN / GOT NO MIND / ASSKIZZ POWERGRUDGE (PAYBACK '94) / TOTALLY CONFUSED / SPANKING ROOM / BONUS NOISE** [–] [ ]

May 94. (7"/c-s; w-drawn) *(GFS/+C 73)* **PAY NO MIND (SNOOZER). / SPECIAL PEOPLE** [–] [ ]
(12"+=/cd-s+=)<US cd-ep> *(GFST/+D 73)<GED 21911>* – Trouble all my days / Supergolden (sunchild).

—— BECK featured on Various Artists 'Mammoth' EP 'JABBERJAW: GOOD TO THE LAST DROP'. In the same year, with CHRIS BALLEW of The PRESIDENTS . . . and under the moniker of CASPAR AND MOLLUSK, they issued the single, 'TWIG'. He was also featured on below alongside CALVIN JOHNSON – vocals (ex-BEAT HAPPENING), SCOTT PLOUFF – drums / JAMES BERTRAM – bass / +2

not iss. K

Aug 94. (cd/c) *<(KLP 28 CD/C)>* **ONE FOOT IN THE GRAVE** [–] [ ]
– He's a mighty good leader / Sleeping bag / I get lonesome / Burnt orange peel / Cyanide breath mint / See water / Ziplock bag / Hollow log / Forcefield / Fourteen rivers fourteen floods / Asshole / I've seen the land beyond / Outcome / Girl dreams / Painted eyelids / Atmospheric conditions. *(UK-iss.Nov95; lp-iss.Jun97; KLP 28) (re-iss. Oct98; same)*

Nov 94. (7",7"brown) *<iPU 45>* **IT'S ALL IN YOUR MIND. / FEATHER IN YOUR CAP / WHISKEY CAN CAN** [–] [ ]
(UK-iss.Jan02; same as US)

D.G.C. D.G.C.

Jun 96. (c-s) *(GFSC 22156)* **WHERE IT'S AT / WHERE IT'S AT (Mario C & Mickey P remix)** [35] [61]
(cd-s+=)<US cd-ep> *(GFSTD 22156)<DGC CD-22214>* – Bonus beats.
(12"++=)<US 12"ep> *(GFST 22156)<DGC 12-22214>* – ('A'-U.N.K.L.E. remix).

Jun 96. (cd/c; as BECK!) *(GED/GEC 24908) <DGCD/DGC 24823>* **ODELAY** [18] [16]
– Devils haircut / Hotwax / Lord only knows / The new pollution / Derelict / Novacane / Jack-ass / Where it's at / Minus / Sissyneck / Readymade / High 5 (rock the catskills) / Ramshackle / Diskobox. *<lp-iss.Apr97 & Sep99 on 'Bongload'; BL 030LP> (lp-iss.Nov98 on 'Simply Vinyl'; SVLP 51)*

Nov 96. (7") *(GFSC 22183)* **DEVILS HAIRCUT. / LLOYD PRICE EXPRESS** [22] [94]
(cd-s)<US cd-ep> *(GFSTD 22183)<GED 22175>* – ('A'side) / Dark

and lovely (Dust Brothers remix) / American wasteland (Mickey P remix).
<US 12"ep++=> *<DGC 12-22222>* – Lloyd Price express / Clock.
(cd-s) *(GFSXD 22183)* – ('A'side) / ('A'-Noel Gallagher remix) / Groovy Sunday (Mike Simpson remix) / Trouble all my days.

Mar 97. (7") *(GFS 22205)* **THE NEW POLLUTION. / ELECTRIC MUSIC AND SUMMER PEOPLE** [14] [78]
(c-s) *(GFSC 22205)* – ('A'side) / Richard's hairpiece (Aphex Twin remix).
(cd-s)<US cd-ep> *(GFSTD 22205) <GED 22204>* – (all 3 tracks).
(cd-s)<US 12"ep> *(GFSTXD 22205) <DGC12 22300>* – ('A'side) / ('A'-Mario C & Mickey P remix) / Lemonade.
(rel.Europe 12" May97 on 'Play It Again Sam'; 22300)

May 97. (7") *(GFS 22253)* **SISSYNECK. / FEATHER IN YOUR CAP** [30] [ ]
(c-s) *(GFSC 22253)* – ('A'side) / The new pollution (remix by Mickey P).
(cd-s) *(GFSTD 22253)* – (all 3 tracks).

Aug 97. (d7"/cd-ep) *(GFS/+TD 22276) <22303>* **JACK-ASS (Butch Vig mix). / STRANGE INVITATION (orchestral version) / DEVIL GOT MY WOMAN // JACK-ASS (Lowrider mix). / BURRO / BROTHER** [ ] [-]

Aug 97. (12"ep) *<DGC12 22303>* **JACK-ASS / BURRO. / STRANGE INVITATION / BROTHER** [-] [97]

Oct 97. (7"/c-s) *(GFS/+C 22293)* **DEADWEIGHT / ERASE THE SUN** [23] [ ]
(cd-s+=) *(GFSTD 22293)* – SA-5.

—— BECK with **SMOKEY HORMEL** – guitar / **ROGER MANNING** – keyboards, percussion / **JUSTIN MELDAL JOHNSON** – bass / **JOEY WARONKER** – drums

Nov 98. (cd/c) *(GED/GEC 25184) <25309>* **MUTATIONS** [24] [13]
– Cold brains / Nobody's fault but my own / Lazy flies / Cancelled check / We live again / Tropicalia / Dead melodies / Bottle of blues / O Maria / Sing it again / Static / Diamond bollocks / Runners dial zero. *(lp/7"box-iss. on 'Bongload'; BL 39)*

Dec 98. (7"/c-s) *(GFS/+C 22365)* **TROPICALIA. / HALO OF GOLD** [39] [ ]
(cd-s+=) *(GFSTD 22365)* – Black balloon.

Oct 99. (7"pic-d/c-s) *(497181-7/-4)* **SEXX LAWS. / SALT IN THE WOUND** [27] [ ]
(cd-s+=) *(497181-2)* – ('A'-Wizeguyz mix).
(cd-s) *(497182-2)* – ('A'side) / This is my crew / ('A'-Malibu mix).

Nov 99. (cd/c) *<(490485-2/-4)>* **MIDNITE VULTURES** [19] [34]
– Sexx laws / Nicotine & gravy / Mixed bizness / Get real paid / Hollywood freaks / Peaches & cream / Broken train / Milk & honey / Beautiful way / Pressure zone / Debra. *(lp-iss.Mar00 on 'Bongload'; BL 46)*

Mar 00. (7") *(497312-7)* **MIXED BIZNESS. / DIRTY DIRTY** [34] [-]
(cd-s+=) *(497300-2)* – ('A'video).
(cd-s) *(497301-2)* – ('A'side) / Sexx laws (video).

Sep 02. (cd) *<(493393-2)>* **SEA CHANGE** [20] [8]
– The golden age / Paper tiger / Guess I'm doing fine / Lonesome tears / Lost cause / End of the day / It's all in your mind / Round the bend / Already dead / Sunday sun / Little one / Side of the road.

– compilations, etc. –

Apr 94. (cd) *Flipside; <FLIP 60>* **STEREOPATHETIC SOULMANURE** (home recordings '88-'93) [-] [ ]
– Pink noise (rock me Amadeus) / Rowboat / Thunder peel / Waitin' for a train / The spirit moves me / Crystal clear (beer) / No money no honey / 8.6.82 / Total soul future (eat it) / One foot in the grave / Aphid manure heist / Today has been a fucked up day / Rollins power sauce / Puttin it down / 11.6.45 / Cut 1/2 blues / Jagermeister pie / Ozzy / Dead wildcat / Satan gave me a taco / 8.4.82 / Tasergun / Modesto. *(UK-iss.Dec95 & Nov97 & Sep00 d-lp/cd; FLIP 660/+CD)*

Jeff BECK

Born: 24 Jun'44, Surrey, England. His solo career began in earnest at the start of '67, BECK having successfully filled the shoes of ERIC CLAPTON in The YARDBIRDS over the preceding two years. Under the wing of pop maestro MICKIE MOST, he scored an immediate UK hit with the anthemic 'HI HO SILVER LINING'. Two further commercial pop-rock numbers, 'TALLYMAN' and 'LOVE IS BLUE' signalled the end of BECK's brief chart liaison, also terminating his period with MOST. With blues-rock back in vogue, the axeman steered a course back into heavier territory, forming The JEFF BECK GROUP alongside old cohorts, ROD STEWART (vocals), RON WOOD (guitar), NICKY HOPKINS (piano) and MICKY WALLER (drums). The resulting two albums, 'TRUTH' (1968) and 'BECK-OLA' (1969), established BECK and co. as a major UK export across the Atlantic, both sets making the US Top 20. With ROD STEWART striking out his own, BECK turned to the unlikely source of hippy-dippy popster DONOVAN, who combined with the group on the summer '69 single, 'GOO GOO BARABAJAGAL'. In the early 70's, The JEFF BECK GROUP was re-modelled around newcomers COZY POWELL (drums) and BOBBY TENCH (vocals), the resulting two albums both making US Top 50 placings. With the country's top guitarist, ERIC CLAPTON, now partially sidelined, BECK took the opportunity to form his own supergroup, BECK, BOGART & APPICE. However, after only one album with the former VANILLA FUDGE heavyweights, BECK resumed a solo career. In the mid 70's he returned to form with the highly successful 'BLOW BY BLOW' opus, regarded by many as his finest hour. Along with many in the rock fraternity, BECK subsequently veered towards jazz-fusion, collaborating with JAN HAMMER on two albums, 'WIRED' (1976) and 'LIVE' (1977). After going to ground for a few years, BECK was 'THERE AND BACK' in the early 80's, although he spent the same amount of time recording his follow-up set, 'FLASH' (1985). This featured a belated reunion with old mucker, ROD STEWART, on the collaborative hit 45, 'PEOPLE GET READY'. After working with MICK JAGGER on his 1987 album, 'Primitive Cool', BECK returned in '89 with his 'GUITAR SHOP' project/album. In the early 90's, he collaborated (yet again!), this time with blues legend, BUDDY GUY, on a superb interpretation of the standard soul/blues classic, 'MUSTANG SALLY'. JEFF showcased yet another dimension to his talent when he recorded a 1993 GENE VINCENT tribute album, 'CRAZY LEGS', with his BIG TOWN PLAYBOYS. A six-year long wait resulted in 1999's 'WHO ELSE!', minor chart positions on both sides of the Atlantic reminding us that in some quarters the man has not been forgotten. Come the new millennium, BECK once again illustrated his instinctive ability to absorb outside influences and adapt his talents to the prevailing musical climate. Thus the digitised beats and bleeps of 'YOU HAD IT COMING' (2001) where the veteran guitarist places his six-string talents in a surprisingly effective contemporary setting. A departure from his familiar sound but an admirable attempt to get to grips with new technology. BECK upped the ante even further with 2003's 'JEFF', finishing what he started with producer Andy Wright. Immersing himself in cutting edge electronica, the guitarist pushed at the conceptual limits of conventional meets contemporary and in so doing, left most of his noodling peers for dust. Roping in the likes of APOLLO 440 and SPLATTERCELL (aka DAVID TORN), BECK grooved on the resulting electric sparks, tearing at the seams of his instrument and its potential. While the likes of 'J.B.'s BLUES' or at a push, the Delta meets drum and bass rollercoaster of 'HOT ROD HONEYMOON' was about as close as he came to his bluesy roots, few real fans could argue with the record's dizzying, feral dynamism. • **Songwriters:** BECK with covers being; HI HO SILVER LINING (Scott English & Larry Weiss) / TALLYMAN (Graham Gouldman) / ALL SHOOK UP + JAILHOUSE ROCK (Leiber – Stoller) / I'VE BEEN DRINKIN' (D.Tauber & J.Mercer) / I AIN'T SUPERSTITIOUS (Willie Dixon) / MORNING DEW (Tim Rose) / SUPERSTITIOUS + CAUSE WE'VE ENDED AS LOVERS (Stevie Wonder) / GREENSLEEVES (trad.) / OL' MAN RIVER ('Showboat' musical) / GOODBYE PORK PIE

HAT (Charlie Mingus) / SHE'S A WOMAN (Beatles) / STAR CYCLE (Jan Hammer) / WILD THING (Troggs) / etc. • **Trivia:** His song 'STAR CYCLE' (written by band members Hymas & Philips), became theme tune for 'The Tube' in 1983.

Album rating: TRUTH (*6) / BECK-OLA (*6) / ROUGH AND READY (*7) / BLOW BY BLOW (*6) / WIRED (*5) / JEFF BECK WITH THE JAN HAMMER GROUP LIVE (*4) / THERE AND BACK (*5) / FLASH (*4) / JEFF BECK'S GUITAR SHOP (*6) / THE BEST OF BECKOLOGY compilation (*7) / CRAZY LEGS (*4) / UP (*4) / WHO ELSE! (*5) / YOU HAD IT COMING (*5) / JEFF (*6)

JEFF BECK (solo) – vocals, lead guitar (ex-YARDBIRDS) with **JET HARRIS** – bass (ex-SHADOWS) / **VIV PRINCE** – drums (ex-PRETTY THINGS)

Columbia Epic

Mar 67. (7") *(DB 8151)* <10157> **HI-HO SILVER LINING. / BECK'S BOLERO** [14] [ ]

—— **RAY COOK** – drums repl. PRINCE

Jul 67. (7") *(DB 8227)* **TALLYMAN. / ROCK MY PLIMSOUL** [30] [–]

Feb 68. (7") *(DB 8359)* **LOVE IS BLUE. / I'VE BEEN DRINKING** [23] [–]

JEFF BECK GROUP

—— with **ROD STEWART** – vocals (also a solo artist, who sang on BECK's last 'B'side) / **RON WOOD** – bass (ex BIRDS) / **MICKY WALLER** (b. 6 Sep'44) – drums / **NICKY HOPKINS** – keyboards

Jul 68. (lp; stereo/mono) *(S+/CX 6293)* <26413> **TRUTH** [ ] [15]
– Shapes of things / Let me love you / Morning dew / You shook me / Ol' man river / Greensleeves / Rock my plimsoul / Beck's bolero / Blues de luxe / I ain't superstitious. *(re-iss. 1985 lp/c; ATAK/TC-ATAK 42) (re-iss. Jun86 on 'Fame' lp/c; FA/TC-FA 3155)*

—— **TONY NEWMAN** – drums repl. WALLER

—— (mid'69) The JEFF BECK GROUP teamed up with ⇒ DONOVAN, on their joint hit GOO GOO BARABAJAGAL (LOVE IS HOT). (see ⇒ DONOVAN)

Jul 69. (lp) *(SCX 6351)* <26478> **BECK-OLA** [39] [15]
– All shook up / Spanish boots / Girl from Mill Valley / Jailhouse rock / Plynth (water down the drain) / The hangman's knee / Rice pudding. *(re-iss. Jul85 on 'Capitol' lp/c; ED 260600-1/-4)*

Sep 69. (7"; w-drawn) *(DB 8590)* **PLYNTH (WATER DOWN THE DRAIN). / HANGMAN'S KNEE** [–] [–]

—— split (Sep'69) when ROD STEWART and RON WOOD joined The FACES.

JEFF BECK GROUP reformed (Apr'71) with **JEFF BECK** – guitar (only) plus **BOBBY TENCH** – vocals / **MAX MIDDLETON** – keyboards / **CLIVE CHAPMAN** – bass / **COZY POWELL** – drums (ex-BIG BERTHA, ex-ACE KEFFORD STAND, ex-SORCERORS)

Epic Epic

Oct 71. (lp/c) *(EPC/40 64619)* <30973> **ROUGH AND READY** [ ] [46]
– Got the feeling / Situation / Short business / Max's tune / I've been used / New ways – Train train / Jody. *(re-iss. Aug84 lp/c; EPC/40 32037) (quad-lp 1974; Q 64619) (cd-iss. 1990; 471047-2)*

Jan 72. (7") *(EPC 7720)* <10814> **GOT THE FEELING. / SITUATION** [ ] [ ]

Jul 72. (lp/c) *(EPC/40 64899)* <31331> **JEFF BECK GROUP** [ ] May72 [19]
– Ice cream cakes / Glad all over / Tonight I'll be staying here with you / Sugar cane / I can't give back the love I feel for you / Going down / I got to have a song / Highways / Definitely maybe. *(quad-lp 1974 on 'C.B.S.'; Q 31331) (cd-iss. 1990; 471047-2)*

Aug 72. (7") <10938> **DEFINITELY MAYBE. / HI HO SILVER LINING** [–] [ ]

—— Broke-up when COZY POWELL went solo & joined BEDLAM. Later to RAINBOW, etc. TENCH joined STREETWALKERS then VAN MORRISON. **JEFF** formed supergroup

BECK, BOGERT, APPICE

—— with **TIM BOGERT** – bass, vocals / **CARMINE APPICE** – drums (both ex-VANILLA FUDGE, etc.) plus **DUANE HITCHINS** – keyboards / **JIMMY GREENSPOON** – piano / **DANNY HUTTON** – vox

Mar 73. (7") *(EPC 1251)* **BLACK CAT MOAN. / LIVIN' ALONE** [ ] [–]

Apr 73. (7") <11027> **LADY. / OH TO LOVE YOU** [–] [ ]

Jul 73. (7") <10998> **I'M SO PROUD. / OH TO LOVE YOU** [–] [ ]

Apr 73. (lp/c) *(EPC/40 65455)* <32140> **BECK, BOGERT, APPICE** [28] [12]
– Black cat moan / Lady / Oh to love you / Superstition / Sweet sweet surrender / Why should I care / Love myself with you / Livin' alone / I'm so proud. *(re-iss. Sep84 lp/c; EPC/40 32491) (re-iss. Nov89 on 'Essential' lp/c/cd; ESS LP/MC/CD 011) (quad-lp 1975 on 'C.B.S.'; Q 65455)*

—— This trio, also released widely available (JAP-import Nov74 d-lp) LIVE IN JAPAN

JEFF BECK

—— group reformed as instrumental line-up, **BECK + MIDDLETON / PHILIP CHEN** – bass / **RICHARD BAILEY** – drums

Mar 75. (lp/c) *(EPC/40 69117)* <33409> **BLOW BY BLOW** [ ] [4]
– It doesn't really matter / You know what I mean / She's a woman / Constipated duck / Air blower / Scatterbrain / Cause we've ended as lovers / Thelonius / Freeway jam / Diamond dust. *(re-iss. Sep83 lp/c; EPC/40 32367) (re-iss. May94 & Nov95 & Sep99 cd/c; 469012-2/-4)*

May 75. (7") *(EPC 3334)* **SHE'S A WOMAN. / IT DOESN'T REALLY MATTER** [ ] [–]

Jun 75. (7") <50112> **CONSTIPATED DUCK. / YOU KNOW WHAT I MEAN** [–] [ ]

—— **JAN HAMMER** (b.1950, Prague, Czechoslavakia) – drums, synthesizer / **MICHAEL NARADA WALDEN** – keyboards, drums (both ex-MAHAVISHNU ORCHESTRA) / **WILBUR BASCOMBE** – bass (all 3 replaced CHEN)

Jul 76. (lp/c) *(EPC/40 86012)* <33849> **WIRED** [38] Jun76 [16]
– Led boots / Come dancing / Goodbye pork pie hat / Head for backstage pass / Blue wind / Sophie / Play with me / Love is green. *(re-iss. Mar82 lp/c; EPC/40 32067) (cd-iss. 1988; CD 86012)*

Aug 76. (7") <50276> **COME DANCING. / HEAD FOR BACKSTAGE PASS** [–] [ ]

—— (**BECK, HAMMER**) plus **TONY SMITH** – drums / **FERNANDO SAUNDERS** – bass / **STEVE KINDLER** – violin, synth.

Mar 77. (lp/c) *(EPC/40 86025)* <34433> **LIVE . . . WITH THE JAN HAMMER GROUP (live)** [ ] [23]
– Freeway jam / Earth (still our only home) / She's a woman / Full Moon boogie / Darkness – Earth in search of a sun / Scatterbrain / Blue wind. *(re-iss. Jun85 lp/c; EPC/40 32297)*

—— with **TONY HYMAS** – keyboards / **MO FOSTER** – bass / **SIMON PHILLIPS** – drums

Jul 80. (lp/c) *(EPC/40 83288)* <35684> **THERE AND BACK** [38] [21]
– Star cycle / Too much to lose / You never know / The pump / El Becko / The golden road / Space boogie / The final peace. *(re-iss. Aug84 lp/c; EPC/40 32197) (cd-iss. Jan89; CD 83288)*

Jul 80. (7") *(EPC 8806)* **THE FINAL PEACE. / SPACE BOOGIE** [ ] [–]

Aug 80. (7") <50914> **THE FINAL PEACE. / TOO MUCH TO LOSE** [–] [ ]

Feb 81. (12"ep) *(EPCA 1009)* **THE FINAL PEACE / SCATTERBRAIN. / TOO MUCH TO LOSE / LED BOOTS** [ ] [–]

—— retired from the studio for half a decade, before returning 1985 with **HAMMER, APPICE, HYMAS** and **JIMMY HALL** – vocals

Jun 85. (7") *(EPCA 6387)* <05416> **PEOPLE GET READY. / BACK ON THE STREET** [ ] [48]
(12"+=) *(TA 6387)* – You know, we know.
(above single featured ROD STEWART on vox)

Jul 85. (lp/c) *(EPC/40 26112)* <39483> **FLASH** [83] [39]
– Ambitious / Gets us all in the end / Escape / People get ready / Stop, look and listen / Get workin' / Ecstasy / Night after night / You know, we know. *(re-iss. Jan89; CD 26112) (re-iss. Mar94 on 'Pickwick' cd/c; 982838-2/-4)*

Sep 85. (7") <05595> **GETS US ALL IN THE END. / YOU KNOW, WE KNOW** [–] [ ]

Sep 85. (7") *(EPCA 6587)* **STOP, LOOK AND LISTEN. / YOU KNOW, WE KNOW** [ ] [–]
(12"+=) *(TA 6587)* – ('A'remix).

Mar 86. (7"/12") *(EPCA/TA 6981)* **AMBITIOUS. / ESCAPE** [ ] [ ]

Jul 86. (7") *(EPCA 7271)* **WILD THING. / GETS US ALL IN THE END** [ ] [ ]
(12"+=) *(TA 7271)* – Nighthawks.

—— In 1987, BECK went to session with MICK JAGGER on his 2nd album.

Oct 89. (lp/c/cd; JEFF BECK with TERRY BOZZIO & TONY HYMAS) *(463472-1/-4/-2)* <44313> **JEFF BECK'S GUITAR SHOP** [ ] [49]
– Guitar shop / Savoy / Behind the veil / Big block / Where were you / Stand on it / Day in the house / Two rivers / Sling shot.

Oct 89. (7") *(BECK 1)* **DAY IN THE HOUSE. / PEOPLE GET READY** [ ] [ ]
(cd-s+=) *(BECK 1CD)* – Cause we've ended as lovers / Blue wind.

(12") *(BECK 1T)* – ('A'side) / Guitar shop (guitar mix) / Cause we've ended as lovers.

—— In 1990, sessioned for JON BON JOVI on his BLAZE OF GLORY album.

—— In Sep'91 JEFF collaborated with BUDDY GUY on a single 'MUSTANG SALLY' on 'Silvertone'.

—— now with **MIKE SANCHEZ** – vocals, piano / **IAN JENNINGS** – bass, vocals / **ADRIAN UTLEY** – rhythm guitar / **CLIVE DENVER** – drums, vocals / **LEO GREEN** – tenor sax / **NICK HUNT** – baritone sax

Jun 93. (cd/c/lp; as JEFF BECK & THE BIG TOWN PLAYBOYS) *(473597-2/-4/-1)* <53562> **CRAZY LEGS** ☐ ☐
– Race with the devil / Cruisin' / Crazy legs / Double talkin' baby / Woman love / Lotta lovin' / Catman / Pink thunderbird / Baby blue / You better believe / Who slapped John? / Say mama / Red blue jeans and a pony tail / Five feet of lovin' / B-i-bickey-bi-bo-bo-go / Blues stay away from me / Pretty, pretty baby / Hold me, hug me, rock me.
(above was a tribute to GENE VINCENT & HIS BLUE CAPS)

—— 1999 with **TONY HYMAS** – keyboards, co-producer / **JENNIFER BATTEN** – guitars / **RANDY HOPE-TAYLOR – bass / STEVE ALEXANDER** – drums

Columbia Epic

Mar 99. (cd/c) *(493041-2/-4)* <67987> **WHO ELSE!** 74 99
– What mama said / Psycho Sam / Brush with the blues / Blast from the east / Space for the papa / Angel (footsteps) / THX138 / Hip-notica / Even odds / Declan / Another place. *(cd re-iss. Jan01; same)*

Epic Epic

Feb 01. (cd) *(501018-2)* <61625> **YOU HAD IT COMING** ☐ ☐
– Earthquake / Roy's toy / Dirty mind / Rollin' and tumblin' / Badia / Loose cannon / Rosebud / Left hook / Blackbird / Suspension.

—— 2003 with **HYMAS** plus **DEAN GARCIA** + **STEVE BARNEY** – rhythm

Aug 03. (cd) *(510820-2)* <86941> **JEFF** ☐ ☐
– So what / Plan B / Pork-u-pine / Seasons / Trouble man / Grease monkey / Hot rod honeymoon / Line dancing with monkeys / JB's blues / Pay me no mind / My thing / Bulgaria / Why Lord oh why?

– compilations, others, etc. –

1969. (lp) *Music For Pleasure; (MFP 5219)* **THE MOST OF JEFF BECK** ☐ –

Oct 72. (7"m) *RAK; (RR 3)* **HI HO SILVER LINING. / BECK'S BOLERO / ROCK MY PLIMSOUL** 14 –
(re-iss. Oct82 7"pic-d/12"; RRP/12RR 3) ; hit No.62.

Apr 73. (7"m; JEFF BECK AND ROD STEWART) *RAK; (RR 4)* **I'VE BEEN DRINKING. / MORNING DEW / GREENSLEEVES** ☐ –

Nov 77. (lp) *Embassy-CBS; (31546)* **GOT THE FEELING** ☐ –

Feb 83. (d-c) *Epic;* **BLOW BY BLOW / WIRED** ☐ –

May 85. (lp/c) *Fame; (FA 413125-1/-4)* **THE BEST OF JEFF BECK featuring ROD STEWART** ☐ –
(re-iss. Dec95 on 'Music For Pleasure' cd/c; CD/TC MFP 6202) <US cd-iss. Jul98 on 'E.M.I.'; 53595>

1985. (d-lp) *Epic; (EPC 461009-1)* **WIRED / FLASH** ☐ –

Sep 88. (cd) *E.M.I.; (CDP 746710-2)* **LATE 60's WITH ROD STEWART** ☐ –

May 89. (d-lp/d-c/d-cd) *That's Original; (TFO LP/MC/CD 19)* **JEFF BECK GROUP / ROUGH & READY** ☐ –

Feb 91. (cd)(c) *E.M.I.; (CZ 374)(TCEMS 1379)* **TRUTH / BECK-OLA** ☐ –

Feb 92. (7"/c-s; by JEFF BECK & ROD STEWART) *Epic; (657756-7/-4)* **PEOPLE GET READY. / TRAIN KEPT A ROLLIN'** 49 –
(cd-s) *(657756-2)* – ('A'side) / Cause we've ended as lovers / Where were you.
(cd-s) *(657756-5)* – ('A'side) / Train train / New ways.

Feb 92. (3xcd/3xc;box) *Epic; (469262-2/-4)* <48661> **BECKOLOGY** ☐ ☐
(re-iss. May94 & Apr98; same)

Mar 92. (cd/c/lp) *Epic; (471348-2/-4/-1)* <64689> **THE BEST OF BECKOLOGY** ☐ Aug95 ☐
– Heart full of soul (YARDBIRDS) / Shapes of things (YARDBIRDS) / Over under sideways down (YARDBIRDS) / Hi ho silver lining / Tallyman / Jailhouse rock / I've been drinking / I ain't superstitious / Superstition (BECK, BOGART & APPICE) / Cause we've ended as lovers / The pump / Star cycle (theme from 'The Tube') / People get ready (with ROD STEWART) / Wild thing / Where were you (w/ TERRY BOZZIO & TONY HYMAS) / Trouble in mind (TRIDENTS).

Mar 93. (3xcd-box) *Epic; (468802-2)* <64808> **FLASH / BLOW BY BLOW / THERE & BACK** ☐ Oct95 ☐

Jul 94. (cd) *Wisepack; (LECD 080)* **LEGENDS IN MUSIC** ☐ –

—— ('Wisepack' also issued another collection Aug95, with some tracks by ERIC CLAPTON; *LECDD 639*)

Oct 94. (cd) *Charly; (CDCD 1186)* **SHAPES OF THINGS** ☐ –

Oct 96. (cd) *EMI Gold; (CDGOLD 1060)* **THE BEST OF JEFF BECK** ☐ –

Apr 98. (cd) *Hallmark; (30858-2)* **GUITAR LEGENDS** ☐ –
(re-iss. Feb01 on 'EMI Plus'; 576228-2)

May 98. (cd) *EMI-Capitol;* <32983> **SHAPES OF THINGS** – ☐

Aug 99. (cd) *Dressed To Kill; (RECD 130)* **JEFF BECK** ☐ –

☐ BEEFEATERS (see under ⇒ BYRDS)

BEE GEES

Formed: By the GIBB brothers in Brisbane, Australia (where they had emigrated from Manchester, England) in 1958. The boys' inaugural performance had taken place three years previous at their dad's Manchester 'Blue Cats' residency where they played skiffle covers (yes, LONNIE DONEGAN had a lot to answer for!). The brothers continued to cut their teeth (quite, er, literally!?) in the parochial talent contests/amateur shows in their new hometown of Brisbane, going under name of the BROTHERS GIBB before abbreviating it to The BEE GEES. Interest in the talented schoolboy group was not long in coming and in 1959, DJ Bill Gates (no, not THE Bill Gates!) offered to manage the trio, promising them more lucrative gigs and air space. Becoming ever more adept at songwriting, the lads were subsequently signed to local label 'Leedon' where they released numerous 45's to moderate success. Realising that they were potentially big fish in the small Aussie music biz pond, they packed their bags and headed back to England in 1966. Ironically, as they made their plans to travel to the mother country, the title track from their album, 'SPICKS AND SPECKS', reached No.1 down under. However, their collective minds were made up and they settled in London, virtually unknown but totally confident of their ability to storm the world leading UK charts. Recruiting a drummer (COLIN PETERSON), bass player (VINCE MELOUNEY) and manager (the notorious ROBERT STIGWOOD), they secured a deal with 'Polydor' and released their debut British single, 'NEW YORK MINING DISASTER 1941' (suffixed in the USA with the chorus, "Have You Seen My Wife, Mr. Jones"). Their distinctive combination of good looks, vocal harmony and astute lyrics slotted in seamlessly with other contemporary Brit beat groups and the single soon went Top 20. Hot on its heels came further classic singles, 'TO LOVE SOMEBODY', 'MASSACHUSETTS' (a UK No.1), 'WORDS' and 'I'VE GOT TO GET A MESSAGE TO YOU'. On the album front, the lads also scored a number of successes culminating in Spring '69 with an obligatory pseudo-psychedelic (double!) album, 'ODESSA'. Around the same time, MAURICE tied the knot with diminutive Glasgow popster LULU while the latter album's release marked the departure of solo bound ROBIN. He made it in his own right later that year with the massive selling single, 'SAVED BY THE BELL' as the remaining MAURICE and BARRY retaliated chart-wise with 'DON'T FORGET TO REMEMBER ME'. As the decade drew to a close, it seemed that the once mighty BEE GEES were falling apart; not for the first time the brothers had surfed the big pop wave only to wipeout! Even after ROBIN's return in 1970, their moment seemed to have passed in the UK at least. However, their Stateside momentum continued, hits such as 'LONELY DAYS' and the No.1 'HOW

CAN YOU MEND A BROKEN HEART' keeping their name in the spotlight. The first years of the new decade found them quite possibly at their lowest creative ebb as the albums 'TRAFALGAR' (1972) and 'TO WHOM IT MAY CONCERN'(1973) sank without trace. Subsequently signing to Stigwood's new 'R.S.O.' label (also home of ERIC CLAPTON), The BEE GEES released 'LIFE IN A TIN CAN' (1973) to little response. Something different was needed to re-ignite the ol' Antipodean magic and the 1974 arrival of producer Arif Mardin for their 'MR. NATURAL' album marked a watershed in the brothers' career. Adopting a new dance-based sound, the icing on their funky rhythm-rich cake came in the form of the (then rare) falsetto harmonies, destined to become their trademark. Again guided by Mardin, they were on to a winner with 1975's 'MAIN COURSE'. Comeback single, 'JIVE TALKIN' deftly captured the essence of mid-70's funk and became a huge Stateside chart topper (Top 5 in Britain). 'NIGHTS ON BROADWAY' and er, 'FANNY (BE TENDER WITH MY LOVE)' repeated the formula as did the 'CHILDREN OF THE WORLD' album and its famous No.1 single, 'YOU SHOULD BE DANCING'. Yet again on the crest of a popular wave, their songs were much in demand by the disco/soul artists of the day including TAVARES and YVONNE ELLIMAN. They also ensured the success of a 1977 mid-budget movie entitled 'Saturday Night Fever' (which attempted to cash-in on the disco phenomenon) and an unknown young actor called John Travolta by penning a ditty or two for inclusion in its screenplay. One of the biggest grossing soundtracks of all-time, 'SATURDAY NIGHT FEVER', included THE "medallion man" anthem, 'STAYIN' ALIVE'. Never one to miss an opportunity, Stigwood lifted another two huge No.1 singles from the soundtrack, 'HOW DEEP IS YOUR LOVE' and 'NIGHT FEVER'. A rather bad career move in the form of the Stigwood-conceived musical version of the BEATLES' 'Sgt. Pepper' occupied them for much of the following year. In 1979, the album 'SPIRITS HAVING FLOWN' spawned three further US No.1's, 'TOO MUCH HEAVEN', 'TRAGEDY' and 'LOVE YOU INSIDE OUT', The BEE GEES continuing to flash their hairy chests as if Punk had never happened. Yet 1981's effort, 'LIVING EYES' surprisingly sank like a lead balloon, failing to break into either US or UK Top 40's. There were contributions to follow-up film 'STAYIN' ALIVE' but the disco medium was truly dead and the Brothers GIBB strategically withdrew to count their millions, do a bit of outside songwriting (for the likes of BARBRA STREISAND, DIONNE WARWICK, etc.) and ponder the next big thing. It was 1987 when they re-emerged on 'Warners' with 'ESP' and its hit single, 'YOU WIN AGAIN' although the storm clouds were gathering once again. Young brother, ANDY GIBB (who had a few hits in the latter half of '77) was found dead from a cocaine overdose. During the next four years, they released three fairly successful albums, 'ONE' (1989), 'HIGH CIVILIZATION' (1991) and 'SIZE ISN'T EVERYTHING' (1993). In 1997 the brothers became immortalised after their induction into the Rock'n'Roll Hall of Fame, releasing 'STILL WATERS' at the same time. In conclusion, there have been few more resilient bands through the last four decades. Just when they're considered dead and buried they reappear in a new and more commercial guise, always in command of melody, harmony and rhythm, with fingers and ears shrewdly on the pulse of musical fashion. 2001's transatlantic Top 20 success, 'THIS IS WHERE I CAME IN', saw them enter their fifth decade of recording with nary a hint of the jaded, faded listlessness that often permeates the umpteenth releases of certified rock dinosaurs. Nods to both the psych-pop era and their airbrushed heyday resist revelling in nostalgia, the brothers even making a passable stab at post-modern electronica. However, the BEE GEES were now two when MAURICE died (12th January, 2003) after receiving treatment for an intestinal blockage.

Album rating: BEE GEES' FIRST (*6) / HORIZONTAL (*6) / IDEA (*4) / ODESSA (*7) / THE BEST OF THE BEE GEES VOL.1 compilation (*8) / CUCUMBER CASTLE (*3) / TWO YEARS ON (*5) / TRAFALGAR (*4) / TO WHOM IT MAY CONCERN (*4) / LIFE IN A TIN CAN (*4) / THE BEST OF THE BEE GEES VOL.2 compilation (*7) / MR. NATURAL (*3) / MAIN COURSE (*7) / CHILDREN OF THE WORLD (*5) / BEE GEES GOLD VOL.1 compilation (*7) / HERE AT LAST . . . BEE GEES LIVE (*5) / SATURDAY NIGHT FEVER with Various Artists soundtrack (*8) / SPIRITS HAVING FLOWN (*6) / GREATEST compilation (*7) / LIVING EYES (*4) / STAYIN' ALIVE soundtrack (*4) / E.S.P. (*4) / ONE (*5) / HIGH CIVILIZATION (*3) / SIZE ISN'T EVERYTHING (*4) / STILL WATERS (*5) / THIS IS WHERE I CAME IN (*5) / THE RECORD – THEIR GREATEST HITS compilation (*7)

BARRY GIBB (b. 1 Sep'47, Manchester, England) – vocals, guitar / **MAURICE GIBB** (b.22 Dec'49, Isle Of Man) – vocals, bass / **ROBIN GIBB** (b.22 Dec'49, Isle Of Man) – vocals

Leedon | not iss.

Mar 63. (7") *(LK 346)* **THE BATTLE OF THE BLUE AND GREY. / THE THREE KISSES OF LOVE** – Austra –

Jun 63. (7") *(LK 412)* **TIMBER! / TAKE HOLD OF THAT STAR** – Austra –

Feb 64. (7") *(LK 534)* **DON'T SAY GOODBYE. / PEACE OF MIND** – Austra –

— in Jun'64, they backed JOHNNY DEVLIN on 'Festival' label single, 'BLUE SUEDE SHOES'. / 'WHOLE LOTTA SHAKIN' GOIN' ON'

Aug 64. (7") *(LK 696)* **CLAUSTROPHOBIA. / COULD IT BE** – Aussie –

Oct 64. (7") *(LK 745)* **TURN AROUND LOOK AT ME. / THEME FROM THE TRAVELS OF JAMIE McPHEETERS** – Aussie –

Dec 64. (7"; with TREVOR GORDON) *(LK 829* **HOUSE WITHOUT WINDOWS. / I'LL BE HAPPY** – Austra –

Apr 65. (7") *(LK 920)* **EVERY DAY I HAVE TO CRY. / YOU WOULDN'T KNOW IT** – Austra –

May 65. (7"; with TREVOR GORDON) *(LK 924)* **LITTLE MISS RHYTHM AND BLUES. / HERE I AM** – Austra –

Aug 65. (7") *(LK 1070)* **WINE AND WOMEN. / FOLLOW THE WIND** – Austra –

Nov 65. (7") *(LK 1150)* **I WAS A LOVER, A LEADER OF MEN. / AND THE CHILDREN LAUGHING** – Austra –

Nov 65. (lp) *(LL 31801)* **BARRY GIBB AND THE BEE GEES SING AND PLAY 14 BARRY GIBB SONGS** – Austra –
(re-iss. 1968 as 'BARRY GIBB AND THE BEE GEES' on 'Calendar', R 66241)

Mar 66. (7") *(LK 1282)* **CHERRY RED. / I WANT HOME** – Austra –

Spin | not iss.

Jun 66. (7") *(EK 1384)* **MONDAY'S RAIN. / ALL OF MY LIFE** – Austra –

Sep 66. (7") *(EK 1474)* **SPICKS AND SPECKS. / I AM THE WORLD** – Austra –

Nov 66. (lp) *(EL 32031)* **SPICKS AND SPECKS** – Austra –
(UK-iss.Sep93 on 'Remember' cd/c; RMB 7/4 5068)

Jan 67. (7") *(EK 1634)* **BORN A MAN. / BIG CHANCE** – –
(also iss.AUST. ep's THE BEE GEES (1964) / **WINE AND WOMEN** (1966) / **SPICKS AND SPECKS** (1967).

— added **VINCE MELOUNEY** (b. Australia) – guitar / **COLIN PETERSON** (b. Australia) – drums

Polydor | Atco

Feb 67. (7") *(56727)* **SPICKS AND SPECKS. / I AM THE WORLD** –

Apr 67. (7") *(56161) <6487>* **NEW YORK MINING DISASTER 1941. / I CAN'T SEE NOBODY** 12 May67 14
(above 'A'side was prefixed with 'HAVE YOU SEEN MY WIFE, MR. JONES')

Jun 67. (7") *(56178) <6503>* **TO LOVE SOMEBODY. / CLOSE ANOTHER DOOR** 41 Jul67 17

Jul 67. (lp; mono/stereo) *(582/583 012) <223>* **BEE GEES' FIRST** 8 Aug67 7
– Close another door / Craise Finton Kirk Royal Academy of Arts / Cucumber castle / Every Christian lion-hearted man will show you / Holiday / I can't see nobody / I close my eyes / In my own time / New York mining disaster 1941 / One minute woman / Please read me / Red chair / Fade away / To love somebody / Turn of the century. *(re-iss. Nov83 lp/c; SPE LP/MC 56) (cd-iss. 1985; 825220-2)*

Sep 67. (7") *(56192)* **MASSACHUSETTS. / BARKER OF THE F.O.** [1] [–]

Sep 67. (7") *<6521>* **HOLIDAY. / EVERY CHRISTIAN LION HEARTED MAN WILL SHOW YOU** [–] [16]

Nov 67. (7") *<6532>* **(THE LIGHTS WENT OUT IN) MASSACHUSETTS. / SIR GEOFFREY SAVED THE WORLD** [–] [11]

Nov 67. (7") *(56220)* **WORLD. / SIR GEOFFREY SAVED THE WORLD** [9] [–]

Jan 68. (7") *(56229) <6548>* **WORDS. / SINKING SHIPS** [8] [15]

Feb 68. (lp; mono/stereo) *(582/583 020) <233>* **HORIZONTAL** [16] [12]
– World / And the sun will shine / Lemons never forget / Really and sincerely / Birdie told me / With the sun in my eyes / Massachusetts / Harry Braff / Day time girl / The earnest of being George / Change is made / Horizontal. *(cd-iss. Feb90; 833659-2)*

Mar 68. (7") *(56242) <6570>* **JUMBO. / THE SINGER SANG HIS SONG** [25] [57]

Aug 68. (7") *(56273) <6603>* **I'VE GOTTA GET A MESSAGE TO YOU. / KITTY CAN** [1] [8]

Sep 68. (lp; mono/stereo) *(582/583 036) <253>* **IDEA** [4] Aug68 [17]
– Let there be love / In the summer of his years / Down to earth / I've gotta get a message to you / When the swallows fly / I started a joke / Swan song / Kitty can / Indian gin and whisky dry / Such a shame / I dea / I have decided to join the airforce / Kilburn Towers. *(cd-iss. Nov89; 833660-2)*

Dec 68. (7") *<6639>* **I STARTED A JOKE. / KILBURN TOWERS** [–] [6]

Feb 69. (7") *(56304) <6657>* **FIRST OF MAY. / LAMPLIGHT** [6] Mar69 [37]

Mar 69. (d-lp) *(582 049-050) <702>* **ODESSA** [10] Feb69 [20]
– Odessa (city on the Black Sea) / You'll never see my face again / Black diamond / Marley Purt drive / Edison / Melody fair / Give your best / Seven sea symphony with all nations (international anthem) * / Laugh in your face / Never say never again / First of May / The British opera. *(cd-iss. May85 – * track; 825451-2)*

— **BARRY + MAURICE** continue as a duo when ROBIN GIBB went solo (VINCE + COLIN also departed)

May 69. (7") *(56331) <6682>* **TOMORROW TOMORROW. / SUN IN THE MORNING** [23] [54]

Aug 69. (7") *(56343) <6702>* **DON'T FORGET TO REMEMBER. / THE LORD** [2] Sep69 [73]

Mar 70. (7") *<6741>* **IF ONLY I HAD MY MIND ON SOMETHING ELSE. / SWEETHEART** [–] [91]

Mar 70. (7") *(56377)* **I.O.I.O. / SWEETHEART** [49] [–]

May 70. (7") *<6752>* **I.O.I.O. / THEN YOU LEFT ME** [–] [94]

May 70. (lp) *(2383 010) <327>* **CUCUMBER CASTLE** (TV film soundtrack) [57] [94]
– If only I had my mind on something else / Then you left me / I was the child / Sweetheart / My thing / Turning tide / I.O.I.O. / I lay down and die / Bury me down the river / The chance of love / Don't forget to remember. *(cd-iss. Nov89; 833783-2)*

— **ROBIN** returned to make up the trio once again

Nov 70. (7") *(2001 104) 6795>* **LONELY DAYS. / MAN FOR ALL SEASONS** [33] [3]

Dec 70. (lp) *(2310 069) <353>* **TWO YEARS ON** [ ] Jan71 [32]
– Two years on / Portrait of Louise / Man for all seasons / Sincere relation / Back home / The first mistake I made / Lonely days / Alone again / Tell me why / Lay it on me / Every second, every minute / I'm weeping. *(cd-iss. Mar90; 833785-2)*

Jun 71. (7") *(2058 115) <6824>* **HOW CAN YOU MEND A BROKEN HEART. / COUNTRY WOMAN** [ ] [1]

— added **GEOFF BRIDGEFORD** – drums / **ALAN KENDALL** – lead guitar

Oct 71. (7") *<6847>* **DON'T WANNA LIVE INSIDE MYSELF. / WALKING BACK TO WATERLOO** [–] [53]

Nov 71. (lp) *(2383 052) <7003>* **TRAFALGAR** [ ] Sep71 [34]
– How can you mend a broken heart / Israel / The greatest man in the world / It's just the day / Remembering / Somebody stop the music / Trafalgar / Don't wanna live inside myself / When do I / Dearest / Lion in winter / Walking back to Waterloo. *(cd-iss. Mar90; 833786-2)*

Jan 72. (7") *(2058 185) <6871>* **MY WORLD. / ON TIME** [16] [16]

Jul 72. (7") *(2058 255) <6896>* **RUN TO ME. / ROAD TO ALASKA** [9] [16]

Oct 72. (lp) *(2383 139) <7012>* **TO WHOM IT MAY CONCERN** [ ] [35]
– Run to me / We lost the road / Never been alone / Paper mache, cabbages & kings / I can bring love / I held a party / Please don't turn out the lights / Sea of smiling faces / Bad bad dreams / You know it's for you / Alive / Road to Alaska / Sweet song of summer. *(cd-iss. Apr93; 833787-2)*

Nov 72. (7") *(2058 304) <6909>* **ALIVE. / PAPER MACHE, CABBAGES AND KINGS** [ ] [34]

R.S.O. R.S.O.

Mar 73. (7") *(2090 105) <401>* **SAW A NEW MORNING. / MY LIFE HAS BEEN A SONG** [ ] [94]

— now with **RIC GRECH** – bass / **SNEAKY PETE** – pedal steel / **JIM KELTNER** – drums / **JEROME RICHARDSON** – flute / **TOMMY MORGAN** – harmonica

Mar 73. (lp) *(2394 102; w-drawn) <870>* **LIFE IN A TIN CAN** [–] Jan73 [69]
– Saw a new morning / I don't wanna be the one / South Dakota morning / Living in Chicago / While I play / My life has been a song / Come home Johnny Bridie / Method to my madness. *(cd-iss. Apr93; 833788-2)*

Jun 73. (7") *(2090 111) <404>* **WOULDN'T I BE SOMEONE. / ELISA** [ ] [ ]

Mar 74. (7") *(2090 128) <408>* **MR. NATURAL. / IT DOESN'T MATTER MUCH TO ME** [ ] [93]

Jun 74. (7") *<410>* **THROW A PENNY. / I CAN'T LET YOU GO** [–] [ ]

Jul 74. (lp) *(2394 132) <4800>* **MR. NATURAL** [ ] Jun74 [ ]
– Charade / Throw a penny / Down the road / Voices / Give a hand take a hand / Dogs / Mr. Natural / Lost in your love / I can't let you go / Heavy breathing / Had a lot of love last night. *(cd-iss. Apr93; 833789-2)*

Aug 74. (7") *(2090 136) <501>* **CHARADE. / HEAVY BREATHING** [ ] [ ]

— back-up now from **ALAN KENDALL** – guitar / **BLUE WEAVER** – keyboards / **DENNIS BYRON** – drums

May 75. (7") *(2090 160) <510>* **JIVE TALKIN'. / WIND OF CHANGE** [5] [1]

Jun 75. (lp)(c) *(2394 150)(3216 050) <4807>* **MAIN COURSE** [ ] [14]
– Nights on Broadway / Jive talkin' / Winds of change / Songbird / Fanny (be tender with my love) / All this making love / Country lanes / Come on over / Edge of the universe / Baby as you turn away. *(re-iss. Aug84 lp/c; SPE LP/MC 111) (cd-iss. May88; 833790-2)*

Sep 75. (7") *(2090 171) <515>* **NIGHTS ON BROADWAY. / EDGE OF THE UNIVERSE** [ ] [7]

Jan 76. (7") *(2090 179) <519>* **FANNY (BE TENDER WITH MY LOVE). / COUNTRY LANES** [ ] Dec75 [12]

Jul 76. (7") *(2090 195) <853>* **YOU SHOULD BE DANCING. / SUBWAY** [5] [1]

Sep 76. (7") *(2090 207) <859>* **LOVE SO RIGHT. / YOU STEPPED INTO MY LIFE** [41] [3]

Oct 76. (lp) *(2394 169) <3003>* **CHILDREN OF THE WORLD** [ ] Sep76 [8]
– You should be dancing / You stepped into my life / Love so right / Lovers / Can't keep a good man down / Boogie child / Love me / Subway / The way it was / Children of the world. *(cd-iss. Nov89; 623658-2)*

Jan 77. (7") *<867>* **BOOGIE CHILD. / LOVERS** [–] [12]

Feb 77. (7") *(2090 224)* **CHILDREN OF THE WORLD. / BOOGIE CHILD** [ ] [–]

Jun 77. (d-lp)(d-c) *(2658 120)(3517 013) <3901>* **HERE AT LAST . . . BEE GEES . . . LIVE (live)** [ ] May77 [8]
– I've gotta get a message to you / Love so right / Edge of the universe / Come on over / Can't keep a good man down / New York mining disaster 1941 / Run to me / World / Holiday / I can't see nobody / I started a joke / Massachusetts / How can you mend a broken heart / To love somebody / You should be dancing / Boogie child / Down the road / Words / Winds of change / Nights on Broadway / Jive talkin' / Lonely days. *(re-iss. Oct84; 3517013)*

Jul 77. (7") *<880>* **EDGE OF THE UNIVERSE (live). / WORDS (live)** [–] [26]

Oct 77. (7") *(2090 259) <882>* **HOW DEEP IS YOUR LOVE. / CAN'T KEEP A GOOD MAN DOWN** [3] Sep77 [1]

Jan 78. (7") *(2090 267) <885>* **STAYIN' ALIVE. / Yvonne Elliman: IF I CAN'T HAVE YOU** [4] Dec77 [1]

Mar 78. (d-lp)(d-c) *(2658 123)(3517 014) <4001>* **SATURDAY NIGHT FEVER (soundtrack w/ Various Artists)** [1] Nov77 [1]
– Stayin' alive / How deep is your love / Night fever / More than a woman / If I can't have you (YVONNE ELLIMAN) / A fifth of Beethoven (WALTER MURPHY) / More than a woman (TAVARES) / Manhattan skyline (DAVID SHIRE) / Calypso breakdown (RALPH MacDONALD) / If I can't have you (YVONNE ELLIMAN) / Night on disco mountain (DAVID SHIRE) / Open sesame (KOOL & THE GANG) / Jive talkin' / You should be dancing / Boogie shoes (K.C. & THE SUNSHINE BAND) / Salsation (DAVID SHIRE) / K-Jee (M.F.S.B.) / Disco inferno (TRAMMPS). *(d-cd-iss. Nov83; 800068-2) (d-lp re-iss. Jan84; SPDLP 5) (d-cd re-iss. Oct95; 825389-2)*

Apr 78. (7") *(2090 272) <889>* **NIGHT FEVER. / DOWN THE ROAD (live)** [1] Jan78 [1]

Nov 78. (7") *(RSO 25) <913>* **TOO MUCH HEAVEN. / REST YOUR LOVE IN ME** 3 1

Feb 79. (7") *(RSO 27) <918>* **TRAGEDY. / UNTIL** 1 1

Feb 79. (lp/c) *(RSBG/TRSBG 1) <3041>* **SPIRITS HAVING FLOWN** 1 1
– Tragedy / Too much Heaven / Love you inside out / Reaching out / Search find stop (think again) / Spirits (having flown) / Living together / I'm satisfied / Until. *(re-iss. Sep83 lp/c; SPE LP/MC 48) (also iss.on US pic-lp) (cd-iss. Nov89; 827335-2)*

Apr 79. (7") *(RSO 31) <925>* **LOVE YOU INSIDE OUT. / I'M SATISFIED** 13 1

Nov 79. (d-lp/d-c) *(RSDX/+C 001) <4200>* **BEE GEES GREATEST** (compilation) 6 1
– Children of the world / Don't throw it all away / Fanny (be tender with my love) / How deep is your love / If I can't have you / Jive talkin' / Love me / Love so right / Love you inside out / More than a woman / Night fever / Nights on Broadway / Rest of your love on me / Spirits (having flown) / Stayin' alive / Too much Heaven / Tragedy / Wind of change / You should be dancing / You stepped into my life. *(cd-iss. 1983; 800071-2)*

Dec 79. (7") *(RSO 52)* **SPIRITS (HAVING FLOWN). / WINDS OF CHANGE** 16 –

— the trio were now augmented by many session people

Sep 81. (7") *(RSO 81) <1066>* **HE'S A LIAR. / (instrumental)** [ ] 30

Nov 81. (lp/c) *(RSBG/TRSBG 2) <3098>* **LIVING EYES** 73 41
– Living eyes / He's a liar / Paradise / Don't fall in love with me / Soldiers / I still love you / Wild flower / Nothing could be good / Cryin' every day / Be who you are. *(re-iss. Aug83 lp/c; SPE LP/MC 22) (cd-iss. Aug84; 813642-2)*

Nov 81. (7") *(RSO 85) <1067>* **LIVING EYES. / I STILL LOVE YOU** [ ] 45

Jul 83. (7") *(RSO 94) <813 713-7>* **THE WOMAN IN YOU. / STAYIN' ALIVE** [ ] May83 24
(12") *(RSOX 94)* – ('A'side) / Saturday night segue.

Jul 83. (lp/c) *(RSBG/TRSBG 3) <813269>* **STAYING ALIVE (soundtrack with Various Artists)** 14 6
– The woman in you / Love you too much / Breakout / Someone belonging to someone / Life goes on / Stayin' alive / Far from over (FRANK STALLONE) / Look out for number one (TOMMY FARAGHER) / Finding out the hard way (CYNTHIA RHODES) / Moody girl (FRANK STALLONE) / (We dance) So close to the fire (TOMMY FARAGHER) / I'm never gonna give you up (FRANK STALLONE & CYNTHIA RHODES).

Sep 83. (7") *(RSO 96) <815 235-7>* **SOMEONE BELONGING TO SOMEONE. / I LOVE YOU TOO MUCH** 49 Aug83 49
(12") *(RSOX 96)* – ('A'side) / Saturday night fever medley.

Warners Warners

Sep 87. (7"/c-s/12"/12"pic-d) *(W 8351/+C/T/TP) <28351>* **YOU WIN AGAIN. / BACKTAFUNK** 1 75

Sep 87. (lp/c)(cd) *(WX 83/+C)(925541-2) <25541>* **E.S.P.** 5 Oct87 96
– E.S.P. / You win again / Live or die / Giving up the ghost / The longest night / This is your life / Angela / Overnight / Crazy for your love / Backtafunk. *(re-iss. cd Feb95; same)*

Dec 87. (7") *(W 8139) <28139>* **E.S.P. / OVERNIGHT** 51 [ ]
(ext-12"+=) *(W 8139T)* – ('A'-Extra house vocals mix).

Feb 88. (7") *(W 7966)* **CRAZY FOR YOUR LOVE. / YOU WIN AGAIN** [ ] –
(12"+=) *(W 7966T)* – Giving up the ghost.

Mar 89. (7"/c-s) *(W 7523/+C)* **ORDINARY LIVES. / WING AND A PRAYER** 54 –
(12"+=/cd-s+=) *(W 7523 T/CD)* – ('A'extended).

Apr 89. (lp/c)(cd) *(WX 252/+C)(925887-2) <25887>* **ONE** 29 Aug89 68
– Ordinary lives / Bodyguard / Tears / Flesh and blood / House of shame / One / It's my neighbourhood / Tokyo nights / Wish you were here / Will you ever let him. *(re-iss. cd Feb95; same)*

Jun 89. (7"/c-s) *(W 2916/+C)* **ONE. / FLESH AND BLOOD** 71 –
(12"+=/cd-s+=) *(W 2916 T/CD)* – ('A'dance mix).

Jul 89. (7") *<22899>* **ONE. / WING AND A PRAYER** – 7

Nov 89. (7") *<22733>* **YOU WIN AGAIN. / WILL YOU EVER LET ME** – [ ]

Feb 91. (7"/c-s) *(W 0014/+C)* **SECRET LOVE. / TRUE CONFESSIONS** 5 [ ]
(12"+=/cd-s+=) *(W 0014 T/CD)* – Human sacrifice.

Mar 91. (cd)(lp/c) *(<7599 26530-2>)(WX 417/+C)* **HIGH CIVILIZATION** 24 [ ]
– High civilization / Secret love / When he's gone / Happy ever after / Party with no name / Ghost train / Dimensions / The only one / Human sacrifice / Evolution. *(re-iss. cd Feb95; same)*

May 91. (7"/c-s) **WHEN HE'S GONE. / MASSACHUSETTS (live)** [ ] –
(12"+=/cd-s+=) – You win again (live).

— now with **ALAN KENDALL + TIM CANSFIELD** – guitars / **GEORGE PERRY** – bass / **TIM MOORE** – keyboards / **TREVOR MURRELL** – drums / **LUIS JARDIM** – percussion / **ED CALLE** – sax / **GUSTAVO LEZCANO** – harmonica

Polydor Polydor

Aug 93. (7") *(PO 284) <859164>* **PAYING THE PRICE OF LOVE. / MY DESTINY** 23 Oct93 74
(cd-s+=) *(PZCD 284)* – (2-'A'mixes)

Sep 93. (cd/c) *(519945-2/-4) <521055>* **SIZE ISN'T EVERYTHING** 28 Oct93 [ ]
– Paying the price of love / Kiss of life / How to fall in love, pt.1 / Omega man / Haunted house / Heart like mine / Anything for you / Blue island / Above and beyond / For whom the bell tolls / Fallen angel / Decadence.

Nov 93. (cd-s) *(PZCD 299)* **FOR WHOM THE BELL TOLLS. / DECADENCE (YOU SHOULD BE DANCING)** 4 [ ]
(12"/c-s) – ('A'side) / Staying alive / Too much Heaven / Massachusetts.

Apr 94. (7"/c-s) *(PO/+CS 311)* **HOW TO FALL IN LOVE PART 1. / 855 7019** 30 [ ]
(cd-s+=) *(PZCD 311)* – Fallen angel.
(cd-s) *(PZDD 311)* – ('A'side) / I've gotta get a message to you / Tragedy / New York mining disaster 1941.

Feb 97. (c-s/cd-s) *(573527-4/-2)* **ALONE / CLOSER THAN CLOSE / RINGS AROUND THE MOON** 5 May97 28
(cd-s) *(573529-2)* – ('A'side) / How deep is your love / Words / I've gotta get a message to you.

Mar 97. (cd/c) *(<537302/-2/-4>)* **STILL WATERS** 2 May97 11
– Alone / I surrender / I could not love you more / Still waters (run deep) / My lover's prayer / With my eyes closed / Irresistible force / Closer than close / I will / Obsessions / Miracles happen / Smoke and mirrors.

Jun 97. (c-s) *(571220-4)* **I COULD NOT LOVE YOU MORE / (Brits medley)** 14 [ ]
(cd-s) *(571299-2)* – ('A'side) / Stayin' alive / Jive talkin'.
(cd-s) *(571223-2)* – ('A'side) / To love somebody / Love never dies.

Oct 97. (c-s/cd-s) *(571628-4/-2) <569218>* **STILL WATERS (RUN DEEP) / OBSESSIONS** 18 57
(cd-s) *(571885-2)* – ('A'side) / Night fever / More than a woman / You should be dancing.

Sep 98. (cd/c) *(<559220-2/-4>)* **LIVE ONE NIGHT ONLY (live)** 4 Nov98 72
– Intro – You should be dancing – Alone / Massachusetts / To love somebody / Words / Closer than close / Islands in the stream / Our love (don't throw it all away) / Night fever – More than a woman / Lonely days / New York mining disaster 1941 / I can't see nobody / And the sun will shine / Nights on Broadway / How can you mend a broken heart / Heartbreaker / Guilty / Immortality (BEE GEES & CELINE DION) / Tragedy / I started a joke / Grease / Jive talking / How deep is your love / Stayin' alive / You should be dancing. *(re-iss. Nov99; same)*

Mar 01. (c-s) *(587977-4)* **THIS IS WHERE I CAME IN / JUST IN CASE** 18 [ ]
(cd-s+=) *(587977-2)* – I will be there / ('A'-video).

Apr 01. (cd/c) *(<549458-2/-4>)* **THIS IS WHERE I CAME IN** 6 May01 16
– This is where I came in / She keeps on coming / Sacred trust / Wedding day / Man in the middle / Deja vu / Technicolour dreams / Walking on air / Loose talk costs lives / Embrace / The extra mile / Voice in the wilderness.

— sadly, on the 12th of January 2003, MAURICE died of a cardiac arrest while having an intestinal operation

– compilations, etc. –

Note; all below on 'Polydor' UK / 'Atco' US until stated otherwise

Nov 68. (lp) *(236 221) <264>* **RARE, PRECIOUS & BEAUTIFUL** [ ] 99

Oct 69. (lp) *(583063) <292>* **BEST OF THE BEE GEES** 7 Jul69 9
– Holiday / I've got to get a message to you / I can't see nobody / Words / I started a joke / Spicks and specks / First of May / World / Massachusetts / To love somebody / Every Christian lion hearted man will show you / New York mining disaster 1941. *(cd-iss. Mar87 on 'R.S.O.'; 831594-2)*

Mar 70. (lp) *(236 513) <321>* **RARE, PRECIOUS & BEAUTIFUL VOL.2** [ ] 100

Apr 70. (lp) *(236 556)* **RARE, PRECIOUS & BEAUTIFUL VOL.3** [ ] –

Jun 71. (lp) *(2447 012)* **MARLEY PURT DRIVE** (TV Film Soundtrack) [ ] –
– Odessa (city on the black sea) / You'll never see my face again / Black

diamond / Marley Purt drive / Edison / Melody fair / Suddenly / Whisper whisper.

Jun 73. (lp) *(234 106) / R.S.O.; <875>* **THE BEST OF THE BEE GEES, VOL.2** [ ] Jul73 [98]
(re-iss. Nov85; SPELP 90) (cd-iss. 1988 on 'R.S.O.'; 831960-2)

Nov 76. (lp) *R.S.O.; <3006>* **BEE GEES GOLD, VOLUME ONE** [–] [50]

Nov 90. (cd/c/lp) *(847339-2/-4/-1)* **THE VERY BEST OF THE BEE GEES** [8] [ ]
– You win again / How deep is your love / Night fever / Tragedy / Massachusetts / I've gotta get a message to you / You should be dancing / New York mining disaster 1941 / World / First of May / Don't forget to remember / Saved by the bell (ROBIN GIBB) / Run to me / Jive talkin' / More than a woman / Stayin' alive / Too much Heaven / Ordinary lives. *(cd+=/c+=)* – To love somebody / Nights on Broadway. *(re-iss. Mar97; same)* – hit UK No.6

Dec 90. (4xcd-box/4xc-box) *(843911-2/-4)* **TALES FROM THE BROTHERS GIBB: A HISTORY IN SONG 1967-1990** [ ] [ ]
(re-iss. Nov99; same)

Sep 00. (cd) *Platinum; (PLATCD 656)* **THE 60's COLLECTION** [ ] [–]

Oct 00. (cd) *Laserlight; (21441)* **FOLLOW THE WIND** [ ] [–]

Nov 01. (d-cd/d-c) *(589449-2/-4) <589400>* **THE RECORD – THEIR GREATEST HITS** [5] [49]
– Stayin' alive / How deep is your love / Night fever / More than a woman / Emotion / Too much heaven / Tragedy / Love you inside out / Guilty / Heartbreaker / Islands in the sun / You win again / One / Secret love / For who the bells toll / Alone / Immortality / This is where I came in / Spicks & specks.

Dec 02. (d-cd) *Thunderbolt; (CDTBD 008)* **EVER INCREASING CIRCLES / TOMORROW THE WORLD** [ ] [–]

Jun 03. (d-cd) *Black Box; (BB 202)* **SPICKS AND SPECKS** [ ] [–]

BELLE AND SEBASTIAN

Formed: Glasgow, Scotland ... early '96 by ex-choirboy/boxer!, STUART MURDOCH (the main songwriter) and ISOBEL CAMPBELL, who met and recruited additional members STUART DAVID, RICHARD COLBURN, STEVIE JACKSON and CHRIS GEDDES in a local cafe. They borrowed the group name from a popular 70's children's TV series (from France) about a young boy and his Pyrenees mountain dog. Two months into their career, the expanded outfit released a very limited (1000 copies) college financed album, 'TIGERMILK', which gained sufficient airplay on national radio to ensure encroaching cult status. By the end of the year (and now with 7th member, SARAH MARTIN) they had unleashed their second set, 'IF YOU'RE FEELING SINISTER', which went on to sell in excess of 15,000 copies and gained much respect from end of the year critic polls. Since then, BELLE AND SEBASTIAN have hit the singles chart three times with a series of highly desirable EP's, 'DOGS ON WHEELS', 'LAZY LINE PAINTER JANE' (with former THRUM larynx-basher MONICA QUEEN on excellent form) and culminating with their critically acclaimed Top 40 entry, '3.. 6.. 9 SECONDS OF LIGHT'. The fact that they've scaled such giddy heights of indie stardom with only a minimum of promotion and a handful of gigs speaks volumes for the quality of their vintage twee C-86-esque sound. By late summer '98, expectations for a new album had reached fever pitch, critics unanimously hailing 'THE BOY WITH THE ARAB STRAP' as one of the year's finest (sadly, too late for esteemed Mercury Prize) and helped ease it into the Top 20. Their by now trademark combination of fey vocals, killer hooklines and avant-pop experimentalism resulted in some of B&S's most infectious tracks to date. With the spirit of NICK DRAKE ghosting in and out of focus (especially on 'SLEEP THE CLOCK AROUND' and 'A SUMMER WASTING'), this troupe of Glaswegian revivalists succeeded in putting the 60's and 70's through an 80's filter, incredibly coming up with something quintessentially 90's! The uninitiated should head straight for the holy trinity of tracks opening side two wherein BELLE & SEBASTIAN do an "ARAB STRAP" so to speak, the "Bairn"-like narrative of 'A SPACE BOY DREAM' complementing the BOLAN-esque stomp of the title track and sandwiching the brassy, BOO RADLEYS (but don't let that put you off!) style 'DIRTY DREAM NUMBER TWO'. Fans eager to get a glimpse of these elusive Scots shysters in the flesh should keep their eyes peeled, actual gigs are woefully few and far between. Extra-curricular activities, meanwhile, included a US 'Sub Pop' 7" from STUART DAVID's spoken word/electro outfit, LOOPER (with also his wife, Wee KARN and his brother, RONNIE BLACK). They would continue as a unit early in 1999, releasing a debut album for 'Jeepster', while ISOBEL's side project, The GENTLE WAVES, also released a long-player on the same label. In July that year and due to demand from everybody bar possibly PETE WATERMAN and his STEPS (who were somewhat peeved about losing the recent Brit Newcomers award due to internet voting), BELLE & SEBASTIAN re-distributed their semi-quasi debut 'TIGERMILK'; this time it hit the UK Top 20. After a two-year recording gap, B&S confidently returned with their fourth studio outing, the sublime, if not translucent 'FOLD YOUR HANDS CHILD, YOU WALK LIKE A PEASANT'. From its flaky opener, 'I FOUGHT IN THE WAR', listeners could detect that this album would be pale in comparison to the aforementioned 'BOY WITH THE . . .'. It seemed that, since the band had apparently broken into the mainstream of America, that their sound was becoming more MOR, more tweaked, more . . . STUART MURDOCH. With that in mind, however, MURDOCH did allow other band members to take the artistic reins: JACKSON and CAMPBELL sang on more songs than usual, slightly thwarting the ever-impending NICK DRAKE references. It could be just that B&S, like many other artists, followed a pivotal record with one that was weaker. Or maybe the group had simply lost their edge. On the eve of the release for this album they started doing press interviews – something that was frowned upon during their earlier years. The band also covered uncharted territory by issuing the album 'STORYTELLING' (2002), the soundtrack to the Todd Solondz film of the same name. A bleak look into American suburbia, the movie was a follow-up to the highly controversial (and highly uncomfortable) work 'Happiness'. It eventually got edited so much by the producers that Solondz vowed never to make another movie again. Unfortunately, so was the B&S score, which didn't make the final cuts. And it's a shame really, because the group almost redeemed themselves by attempting to create proper film music. 'FREAK', 'FUCK THIS SHIT' and the humourously entitled 'BLACK AND WHITE UNITE' (believe it, you have to see the film to get the joke) all made for good soundtrack material. The only let down being the inclusion of 'sound-bites' from the film which were inter-spliced with the music. Unnecessary, and ultimately tiring, dialogue such as "Nigger, fuck me ..." was hardly worthy of 'Pulp Fiction' proportions. Still, an interesting enough album to accompany an interesting enough film. ISOBEL, meanwhile, collaborated with celebrated Falkirk-born avant-jazz man, BILL WELLS, on the album 'GHOST OF YESTERDAY' (a take on the legendary BILLIE HOLIDAY). Now signed to 'Rough Trade' records, B&S enlisted pop producer Trevor Horn to ride the faders, and while many thought it was the band committing indie suicide or selling out (more than they had already done), it was a blessing for MURDOCH and Co's camp. 'DEAR CATASTROPHE WAITRESS' (2003) re-instated BELLE & SEBASTIAN's indie cred, as well as harnessing new fans to the fore, much in the same way 'THE BOY WITH THE ARAB STRAP' had done five years previously. The songs were mostly uptempo numbers helmed by MURDOCH's keen ear for a good tune, with the band following tightly behind him incognito. Trevor Horn's production, while far from the nonsense pop of TATU and ABC, gave the B&S crowd the unthinkable – a straight up, clean and commercialy viable record. Strange, but rather beautiful.

Album rating: TIGERMILK (*8) / IF YOU'RE FEELING SINISTER (*8) / THE BOY WITH THE ARAB STRAP (*9) / FOLD YOUR HANDS CHILD, YOU WALK LIKE A PEASANT (*7) / STORYTELLING (*7) / DEAR CATASTROPHE WAITRESS (*7)

STUART MURDOCH (b. 1967) – vocals, acoustic guitar / **ISOBEL CAMPBELL** – cello, vocals / **STEVIE JACKSON** – guitars, vocals / **STUART DAVID** – bass / **RICHARD COLBURN** – drums / **CHRIS GEDDES** – piano

Electric Honey — not iss.

May 96. (lp) *(EHRLP 5)* **TIGERMILK** [ ] [–]
– The state I am in / Expectations / She's losing it / You're just a baby / Electronic renaissance / I could be dreaming / We rule the school / My wandering days are over / I don't love anyone / Mary Jo. *(re-iss. Jul99 on 'Jeepster' cd/c/lp; JPR CD/MC/LP 007)* – hit No.13

— added **SARAH MARTIN** – violin, saxophone / and also extra member **MICK COOKE** – trumpet

Jeepster — Enclave-Capitol

Nov 96. (cd/c/lp) *(JPR CD/MC/LP 001)* <56713> **IF YOU'RE FEELING SINISTER** [ ] Feb97 [ ]
– Stars of track and field / Seeing other people / Me and the Major / Like Dylan in the movies / The fox in the snow / Get me away from here, I'm dying / If you're feeling sinister / Mayfly / The boy done wrong again / Judy and the dream of horses.

May 97. (7") *(JPR7 001)* **DOG ON WHEELS. / THE STATE I AM IN (demo)** [59] [–]
(12"+=/cd-s+=) *(JPR 12/CDS 001)* – String bean Jean / Belle & Sebastian.

— guest on below, **MONICA QUEEN** – vocals (of THRUM)

Aug 97. (7") *(JPR7 002)* **LAZY LINE PAINTER JANE. / YOU MADE ME FORGET MY DREAMS** [41] [–]
(12"+=/cd-s+=) *(JPR 12/CDS 002)* – Photo Jenny / A century of Elvis.

Oct 97. (7"ep) *(JPR7 003)* **3.. 6.. 9 SECONDS OF LIGHT EP** [32] [–]
– A century of fakers / Le pastie de la bourgeoisie.
(12"ep+=/cd-ep+=) *(JPR 12/CDS 003)* – Beautiful / Put the book back on the shelf / *(hidden track-)* Songs for children.

— added guest **NEIL ROBERTSON** – bass

Jeepster — Matador

Sep 98. (cd/c) *(JPR CD/MC 003)* <OLE 311> **THE BOY WITH THE ARAB STRAP** [12] [ ]
– It could have been a brilliant career / Sleep the clock around / Is it wicked not to care? / Ease your feet in the sea / A summer wasting / Seymour Stein / A space boy dream / Dirty dream number two / The boy with the arab strap / Chickfactor / Simple things / The rollercoaster ride.

Dec 98. (12"ep/cd-ep) *(JPR 12/CDS 009)* **THIS IS JUST A MODERN ROCK SONG / I KNOW WHERE THE SUMMER GOES. / THE GATE / SLOW GRAFFITI** [–] -chart [–]
below featured the MAISONETTES

May 00. (7") *(JPR7 018)* **LEGAL MAN. / WINTER WOOSKIE** [15] [–]
(cd-s+=) *(JPRCDS 018)* <OLE 448> – Judy is a dick slap.
(12") *(JPR12 018)* – ('A'side) / Judy is a dick slap (extended).

Jun 00. (cd/md/lp) *(JPR CD/MD/LP 010)* <OLE 429> **FOLD YOUR HANDS CHILD, YOU WALK LIKE A PEASANT** [10] [80]
– I fought in a war / The model / Beyond the sunrise / Waiting for the moon to rise / Don't leave the light on baby / The wrong girl / The chalet lines / Nice day for a sulk / Woman's realm / Family tree / There's too much love.

— STUART DAVID left after the recording of above

Jun 01. (7") *(JPR7 022)* **JONATHAN DAVID. / THE LONELINESS OF A MIDDLE DISTANCE RUNNER** [31] [–]
(12"+=/cd-s+=) *(JPR 12/CD 022)* – Take your carriage clock and shove it.

Nov 01. (7") *(JPR7 023)* **I'M WAKING UP TO US. / I LOVE MY CAR** [39] [–]
(12"+=/cd-s+=) *(JPRCDS 023)* – Marx and Engels.

Jun 02. (cd/lp) *(JPR CD/LP 014)* <OLE 512> **STORYTELLING** [26] [ ]
– Fiction / Freak / Dialogue: Conan, early Letterman / Fuck this shit / Night walk / Dialogue: Jersey's where it's at / Black and white unite / Consuelo / Dialogue: Toby / Storytelling / Dialogue: Class rank / I don't want to play football / Consuelo leaving / Wandering alone / Dialogue: Mandingo cliche / Scooby driver / Fiction (reprise) / Big John Shaft.

Rough Trade — Rough Trade

Oct 03. (cd/d-lp) *(RTRADE CD/LP 080)* <83216> **DEAR CATASTROPHE WAITRESS** [21] [84]
– Step into my office, baby / Dear catastrophe waitress / If she wants me / Piazza, New York catcher / Asleep on a sunbeam / I'm a cuckoo / You don't send me / Wrapped up in books / Lord Anthony / If you find yourself caught in love / Roy Walker / Stay loose.

Nov 03. (7") *(RTRADES 128)* **STEP INTO MY OFFICE, BABY. / LOVE ON THE MARCH** [32] [–]
(cd-s+=) *(RTRADESCD 128)* – Desperation made a fool of me / Untitled.

– compilations, etc. –

Mar 00. (cd) *Jeepster; (JPRBOX 001) / Matador;* <*OLE 313*> **LAZY LINE PAINTER JANE** (the first 3 EP's) [ ] Oct00 [ ]

BELLY

Formed: Providence, Rhode Island, USA ... late '91 by ex-THROWING MUSES and BREEDERS co-leader TANYA DONELLY. Recruiting brothers, THOMAS and CHRIS GORMAN along with FRED ABONG, DONELLY set her pet project in motion with the 'SLOWDUST' EP in summer '92, BELLY remaining with '4 a.d.' (the label that had been home to both DONELLY's previous outfits). Produced by The PIXIES maestro, Gil Norton, the record introduced BELLY's hypnotic blend of provocative musings and strident, infectious indie-rock, a style which flowered on the follow-up EP, 'GEPETTO' (featuring a cover of The Flying Burrito Brothers' classic 'HOT BURRITO #2') and the hit single 'FEED THE TREE'. The debut album, 'STAR' narrowly missed the UK No.1 spot, DONELLY's little-girl-lost sweetness occasionally transforming into a fearsome howl. Similarly, DONELLY's lyrics were by turns twisted and twee, this delicate balance undoubtedly part of the band's appeal. Despite this incredible start, a second set, the Glyn Johns-produced, 'KING', took off in a rockier direction, losing some of the BELLY mystique in the process. Though the record made the UK Top 10, its relative critical and commercial failure eventually led to DONELLY splitting the group up and heading for a solo career. In 1997, her debut, 'LOVESONGS FOR UNDERDOGS', was released to minimal impact, although it did contain two minor hits, 'PRETTY DEEP' and 'THE BRIGHT LIGHT'. The long-awaited but aptly-titled follow-up, 'BEAUTYSLEEP' (2002), was a little stronger lyrically and featured a duet ('MOONBEAM MONKEY') with recently deceased MORPHINE vocalist MARK SANDMAN. • **Covered:** TRUST IN ME (Sherman – Sherman; for 'Jungle Book') / ARE YOU EXPERIENCED (Jimi Hendrix).

Album rating: STAR (*8) / KING (*7) / SWEET RIDE – THE BEST OF BELLY compilation (*7) / Tanya Donelly: LOVESONGS FOR UNDERDOGS (*5) / BEAUTYSLEEP (*6)

TANYA DONELLY (b.16 Jul'66, Newport, Rhode Island) – vocals, guitar / **THOMAS GORMAN** (b.20 May'66, Buffalo, N.Y.) – guitar **FRED ABONG** – bass / **CHRIS GORMAN** (b.29 Jul'67, Buffalo) – drums

4 a.d. — Sire

Jun 92. (12"ep/cd-ep) *(BAD 2009/+CD)* **SLOWDUST** [ ] [ ]
– Dusted / Slow dog / Dancing gold / Low red moon.

— **GAIL GREENWOOD** (b.10 Mar'60) – bass repl. FRED

Nov 92. (7") *(AD 2018)* **GEPETTO. / SEXY S** [ ] [ ]
(12"+=/cd-s+=) *(BAD 2018/+CD)* – Hot burrito #1 / Sweet ride.

Jan 93. (7"/c-s) *(AD/+C 3001)* **FEED THE TREE. / DREAM ON ME** [32] [–]
(12"+=/cd-s+=) *(BAD 3001/+CD)* – Trust in me / Star.

Jan 93. (cd)(lp/c) *(CAD 3002CD)(CAD/+C 3002)* <45187> **STAR** [2] [59]

– Someone to die for / Angel / Dusted / Every word / Gepetto / Witch / Slow dog / Low red moon / Feed the tree / Full Moon, empty heart / White belly / Untogether / Star / Sad dress / Stay. *(cd re-iss. Jul98; GAD 3002CD)*

Mar 93. (c-ep)(cd-ep) *(BADC 2018)(BADD 2018CD)* **GEPETTO (remix) / IT'S NOT UNUSUAL / STAR (demo)** [49] [ ]
(12"ep)(cd-ep) *(BADR 2018)(BAD 2018CD)* – ('A'side) / Hot burrito #1 / Sexy S / Sweet ride.

Feb 93. (cd-ep) *<941 547-2>* **LOW RED MOON / ARE YOU EXPERIENCED? / IT'S NOT UNUSUAL (3 mixes) / FULL MOON, EMPTY HEART (3 mixes)** [–] [ ]

Apr 93. (c-s) *<18570>* **FEED THE TREE / STAR** [–] [95]

Jan 95. (7"/c-s) *(AD/+C 5003)* **NOW THEY'LL SLEEP. / THIEF** [28] [ ]
(12"+=/cd-s+=) *(BAD 5003/+CD)* – Baby's arm / John Dark.

Feb 95. (cd)(lp/c) *(CAD 5004CD)(CAD/+C 5004) <45833>* **KING** [6] [57]
– Puberty / Seal my fate / Red / Silverfish / Super-connected / The bees / King / Now they'll sleep / Untitled and unsung / Lil' Ennio / Judas my heart. *(cd re-iss. Jul98; GAD 5004CD)*

Jul 95. (7"clear) *(AD 5007)* **SEAL MY FATE. / BROKEN / JUDAS MY HEART (live)** [35] [ ]
(cd-s) *(BAD 5007CD)* – ('A'-U.S. radio mix) / Spaceman / Diamond rib cage / Think about your troubles.
(cd-s) *(BADD 5007CD)* – ('A'live) / White belly (live) / Untitled and unsung (live) / The bees (live).

—— disbanded in July '96

– compilations, etc. –

Jul 02. (cd) *4 a.d.; (GAD 2211CD) / Rhino; <78246>* **SWEET RIDE – THE BEST OF BELLY** [ ] Jun02 [ ]
– Spaceman / Gepetto / Super-connected / Broken / Hot burrito #1 / Trust in me / Feed the tree / Dusted (live) / Seal my fate / Judas mon coeur / Are you experienced? / Thief / Full moon, empty heart / Now they'll sleep / Lilith / Slow dog / Dream on me / Sweet ride.

TANYA DONELLY

—— with **DEAN FISHER** + **WALLY GAGEL** – bass / **RICH GILBERT** – guitars / **STACY JONES** – guitar / + others

4 a.d. Warners

Nov 96. (d7"ep)(cd-ep) *(ADD 6018)(BAD 6018CD)* **SLIDING & DRIVING** [ ] [ ]
– Bum / Restless / Human / Swoon.

Aug 97. (7") *(AD 7007)* **PRETTY DEEP. / VANILLA (Wally's mix)** [55] [ ]
(cd-s) *(BAD 7007CD)* – ('A'side) / Spaghetti / Morna.
(cd-s) *(BADD 7007CD)* – ('A'side) / These days / Influenza.

Sep 97. (cd)(lp/c) *(CAD 7008CD)(CAD/+C 7008) <46495>* **LOVESONGS FOR UNDERDOGS** [ ] [ ]
– Pretty deep / The bright light / Landspeed song / Mysteries of the unexplained / Lantern / Acrobat / Breathe around you / Bum / Clipped / Goat girl / Manna / Swoon.

Nov 97. (7") *(AD 7012)* **THE BRIGHT LIGHT. / THE BRIGHT LIGHT (live)** [64] [–]
(cd-s) *(BAD 7012)* – ('A'side) / Bury my heart / How can you sleep.
(cd-s) *(BADD 7012)* – ('A'side) / Life on Sirius / Moon over Boston.

Nov 01. (cd-ep) *(BAD 2108CD)* **SLEEPWALK** [ ] [–]
– The storm / After your party (with BILL JANOVITZ) / Days of grace / Last rain.

Feb 02. (cd) *(CAD 2201CD) <72201>* **BEAUTYSLEEP** [ ] [ ]
– Life is but a dream / The storm / The night you saved my life / Keeping you / Moonbeam monkey / Wrap-around skirt / Another moment / Darkside / So much song / The wave / The shadow.

Pat BENATAR

Born: PATRICIA ANDRZEJEWSKI, 10 Jan'53, Brooklyn, New York, USA. In her late teens she married long-time boyfriend DENNIS BENATAR and moved to Richmond, Virginia. Returning to New York in the mid-70's, BENATAR turned her hand at the cabaret circuit, adopting a harder edged approach after meeting manager/mentor, RICK NEWMAN. In keeping with her new rock-chick image, PAT retained the (frankly, more rock'n'roll) BENATAR name after divorcing DENNIS in the early 80's. Signing a deal with 'Chrysalis', BENATAR had the soft metal/AOR thing down pat (ouch!) from the off, her debut album, 'IN THE HEAT OF THE NIGHT', eventually going platinum. Her undeniable vocal prowess almost made up for the weakness of the original material, BENATAR only really coming into her own singing other people's songs. She transformed SMOKIE's 'IF YOU THINK YOU KNOW HOW TO LOVE ME', into a sultry mood piece while JOHN MELLENCAMP's 'I NEED A LOVER' benefitted from her scuffed velvet tones. Boasting the likes of 'HIT ME WITH YOUR BEST SHOT' and 'TREAT ME RIGHT', the 'CRIMES OF PASSION' (1980) album was a million seller, establishing BENATAR as a major contender in the American market. Subsequent albums, 'PRECIOUS TIME' (1981) and 'GET NERVOUS' (1982), continued to sell in abundance despite a dearth of decent songs. Things picked up with 'LOVE IS A BATTLEFIELD', a brooding, catchy pop-rock number which gave BENATAR her biggest US hit single to date, the record reaching Top 5 in late '83. A year later, the singer released what was probably her finest moment in 'WE BELONG', a seductively melodic single which secured BENATAR her first substantial UK success. After moderate sales of the 'TROPICO' (1984) and 'SEVEN THE HARD WAY' (1985) albums, BENATAR took an extended break to look after her daughter. During this time, 'Chrysalis' released 'BEST SHOTS' (1987), a compilation that did surprisingly well in Britain (No.6) and saw BENATAR's subsequent 1988 album, 'WIDE AWAKE IN DREAMLAND', make the UK Top 20. That's not to say the record was any good, and it was clear her career was in decline. Subsequent efforts have sold poorly, BENATAR even chancing her arm with an ill-advised album of blues tracks, 'TRUE LOVE' (1991). After that album's critical and commercial panning, the singer returned to familiar if overly well-worn territory on 'GRAVITY'S RAINBOW' (1993), sounding as outdated as her previous record had sounded out of context. 'INNAMORATA' (1997) was more interesting, an acoustic-based set which at least payed BENATAR the favour of allowing space for her still impressive vocal chords. Unsurprisingly, it was also perhaps her most intimate record, showcasing a soulfulness missing on conveyor belt concert sets such as the one on which she shared the bill with longtime partner NEIL GIRALDO, 2002's 'LIVE: SUMMER VACATION TOUR SOUNDTRACK'. As cliched and pedestrian as its title suggested, the record was one for dedicated fans only, or at least those who were still keeping the faith. Which, judging by the creative stagnation of 'GO' (2003), her first new studio work of the new millennium, must've been increasingly difficult. • **Songwriters:** She collaborated with others, including CHINN / CHAPMAN plus her husband/producer (from 20th Feb'82) NEIL GERALDO. She also covered YOU BETTER RUN (Young Rascals) / PAYIN' THE COST TO BE THE BOSS (B.B. King) / HELTER SKELTER (Beatles) / IF YOU THINK YOU KNOW HOW TO LOVE ME (Smokie) / INVINCIBLE (Simon Climie). • **Trivia:** Her first 7" in US 1976 as "PAT BENETAR" was DAY GIG. / LAST SATURDAY on the 'Trace' label.

Album rating: IN THE HEAT OF THE NIGHT (*6) / CRIMES OF PASSION (*6) / PRECIOUS TIME (*4) / GET NERVOUS (*4) / LIVE FROM EARTH (*3) / TROPICO (*4) / SEVEN THE HARD WAY (*6) / WIDE AWAKE IN DREAMLAND (*4) / BEST SHOTS compilation (*7) / TRUE LOVE (*3) / GRAVITY'S RAINBOW (*3) / ALL FIRED UP: THE VERY BEST OF ... compilation (*6) / INNAMORATA (*4) / LIVE: SUMMER VACATION TOUR SOUNDTRACK with Neil Giraldo (*3) / GO (*3)

PAT BENATAR – vocals / **NEIL GERALDO** – keyboards (ex-DERRINGER) / **SCOTT ST. CLAIR SHEETS** – guitar / **ROGER CAPPS** – bass / **GLEN ALEXANDER HAMILTON** – drums

Chrysalis Chrysalis

Oct 79. (7") *(CHS 2373)* **IF YOU THINK YOU KNOW HOW TO LOVE ME. / SO SINCERE** [ ] [ ]

Dec 79. (lp/c) <*(CHR/ZCHR 1236)*> **IN THE HEAT OF THE NIGHT** [ ] Oct79 [12]
– Heartbreaker / I need a lover / If you think you know how to love me / In the heat of the night / My clone sleeps alone / We live for love / Rated X / Don't let it show / No you don't / So sincere. *(re-iss. Jun85 lp/c/cd; same/same/ACCD 1236)* – hit UK No.98 *(re-iss. Dec92 on 'Fame' cd/c; CD/TC FA 3286) (cd re-iss. Apr99 on 'DCC'; GZS 1056)*

Jan 80. (7") <*(CHS 2395)*> **HEARTBREAKER. / MY CLONE SLEEPS ALONE** [ ] Dec79 [23]

Mar 80. (7") <*2419*> **WE LIVE FOR LOVE. / SO SINCERE** [–] [27]

Apr 80. (7") *(CHS 2403)* **WE LIVE FOR LOVE. / I NEED A LOVER** [ ] [–]
(12"+=) *(CHS12 2403)* – If you think you know how to love me.

—— **MYRON GROOMBACHER** – drums; repl. HAMILTON

Jul 80. (7") <*2450*> **YOU BETTER RUN. / OUT-A-TOUCH** [–] [42]

Aug 80. (lp/c) <*(CHR/ZCHR 1275)*> **CRIMES OF PASSION** [ ] [2]
– Treat me right / You better run / Never wanna leave you / Hit me with your best shot / Hell is for children / Little paradise / I'm gonna follow you / Wuthering heights / Prisoner of love / Out-a-touch. *(cd-iss. Jun85; ACCD 1275)*

Sep 80. (7") <*2464*> **HIT ME WITH YOUR BEST SHOT. / PRISONER OF LOVE** [–] [9]

Nov 80. (7") *(CHS 2452)* **HIT ME WITH YOUR BEST SHOT. / YOU BETTER RUN** [ ] [–]
(7"red-ep+=) *(CHS 2474)* – Heartbreaker / We live for love.

Jan 81. (7") <*2487*> **TREAT ME RIGHT. / NEVER WANNA LEAVE YOU** [–] [18]

Jan 81. (7",7"clear) *(CHS 2511)* **TREAT ME RIGHT. / HELL IS FOR CHILDREN** [ ] [–]

Jul 81. (lp/c) <*(CHR/ZCHR 1346)*> **PRECIOUS TIME** [30] [1]
– Promises in the dark / Fire and ice / Just like me / Precious time / It's a tuff life / Take it anyway you want it / Evil genius / Hard to believe / Helter skelter. *(cd-iss. Jun85; ACCD 1346)*

Jul 81. (7"clear/7"pic-d) <*(CHS/+P 2529)*> **FIRE AND ICE. / HARD TO BELIEVE** [ ] [17]

Sep 81. (7") <*2555*> **PROMISES IN THE DARK. / EVIL GENIUS** [–] [38]

—— (Feb'82) **NEIL GERALDO** now on guitar / co-production.

Oct 82. (7",7"sha-pic-d/12"blue) *(CHS/+12 2662)* <*2647*><*03541*> **SHADOWS OF THE NIGHT. / THE VICTIM** [ ] [13]
(7"ep) *(CHS 2662)* – ('A'side) / Treat me right / Heartbreaker / Anxiety (get nervous).

Nov 82. (lp/pic-lp/c) *(CHR/PCHR/ZCHR 1386)* <*1396*> **GET NERVOUS** [73] [4]
– Shadows of the night / Looking for a stranger / Anxiety (get nervous) / Fight it out / The victim / Little too late / I'll do it / I want out / Tell it to her / Silent partner. *(cd-iss. Jun85; ACCD 1386)*

—— (Nov'82) **CHARLIE GIORDANO** – keyboards; repl. SHEETS

Jan 83. (7") <*03536*> **LITTLE TOO LATE. / FIGHT IT OUT** [–] [20]

Apr 83. (7") <*42688*> **LOOKING FOR A STRANGER. / I'LL DO IT** [–] [39]

Oct 83. (7"/7"pic-d/12") *(CHS/+P/12 2747)* <*42732*> **LOVE IS A BATTLEFIELD. / HELL IS FOR CHILDREN (live)** [49] Sep83 [5]

Oct 83. (lp/pic-lp/c) *(CHR/CHRP/ZCHR 1451)* <*41444*> **LIVE FROM EARTH (live)** [60] [13]
– Fire and ice / Lookin' for a stranger / I want out / We live for love / Hell is for children / Hit me with your best shot / Promises in the dark / Heartbreaker / Love is a battlefield * / Lipstick lies. *(* studio track) (cd-iss. Jun85; ACCD 1451)*

Oct 84. (7",7"pic-d) *(CHR 2821)* <*42826*> **WE BELONG. / SUBURBAN KING** [22] [5]
(12"+=) *(CHR12 2821)* – We live for love '85.

Nov 84. (lp/c) *(CHR/ZCHR 1471)* <*41471*> **TROPICO** [34] [14]
– Diamond field / We belong / Painted desert / Temporary heroes / Love in the ice age / Ooh ooh song / Outlaw blues / Suburban king / A crazy world like this / Takin' it back. *(cd-iss. Apr86; ACCD 1471)*

Jan 85. (7") <*42843*> **OOH OOH SONG. / LA CANCION OOH OOH** [–] [36]

Mar 85. (7"/12") *(PAT/+X 1)* **LOVE IS A BATTLEFIELD. / HERE'S MY HEART** [17] [–]

Jun 85. (7"/7"sha-pic-d) *(PAT/+P 2)* **SHADOWS OF THE NIGHT. / HIT ME WITH YOUR BEST SHOT** [50] [–]
(12"+=) *(PATX 2)* – Fire and ice.

—— **DONNIE NOSSOV** – bass repl. CAPPS
(below is the theme from the film 'The Legend Of Billie Jean')

Oct 85. (7") *(PAT 3)* <*42877*> **INVINCIBLE. / ('A'instrumental)** [53] Jun85 [10]
(12"+=) *(PATX 3)* – Promises in the dark / Heartbreaker.

Dec 85. (7"/12") *(PAT/+X 4)* <*42927*> **SEX AS A WEAPON. / RED VISION** [67] Nov85 [28]

Dec 85. (lp/c) *(CHR/ZCHR 1507)* <*41507*> **SEVEN THE HARD WAY** [69] [26]
– Sex as a weapon / Le bel age / Walking in the underground / Big life / Red vision / 7 rooms of gloom / Run between the raindrops / Invincible (theme from The Legend Of Billie Jean) / The art of letting go. *(cd-iss. Apr86; ACCD 1507)*

Feb 86. (7") <*42968*> **LE BEL AGE. / WALKING IN THE UNDERGROUND** [–] [54]

—— **FERNANDO SAUNDERS + FRANK LINX** – bass repl. NOSSOV

Jul 88. (7") *(PAT 5)* <*43268*> **ALL FIRED UP. / COOL ZERO** [19] [19]
(12"+=) *(PATX 5)* – Hit me with your best shot / Fire and ice / Just like me / Promises in the dark / Precious time.
(12"+=/cd-s+=) *(PAT XD/CD 5)* – ('A'-US version).

Jul 88. (lp/c/cd) *(CDL/ZCDL/CCD 1628)* <*41628*> **WIDE AWAKE IN DREAMLAND** [11] [28]
– All fired up / One love / Let's stay together / Don't walk away / Too long a soldier / Cool zero / Celebral man / Lift 'em on up / Suffer the little children / Wide awake in Dreamland. *(re-iss. cd Mar94; CD23CR 19)*

Sep 88. (7") *(PAT 6)* **DON'T WALK AWAY. / LIFT 'EM ON UP** [42] [ ]
(12"+=/cd-s+=) *(PAT X/CD 6)* – Hell is for children (live) / We live for love (special mix).

Dec 88. (7") *(PAT 7)* **ONE LOVE. / WIDE AWAKE IN DREAMLAND** [59] [ ]
(12"+=/12"pic-d+=) *(PATX/+P 7)* – Sex as a weapon.
(cd-s+=) *(PATCD 7)* – Love is a battlefield.

Apr 91. (cd/c/lp) *(CCD/ZCHR/CHR 1805)* <*21805*> **TRUE LOVE** [40] [37]
– Bloodshot eyes / Payin' the cost to be the boss / So long / I've got papers on you / I feel lucky / True love / The good life / Evening / I get evil / Don't happen no more. *(re-iss. Mar94 cd/c; same)*

Jun 91. (c-s/7") **PAYIN' THE COST TO BE THE BOSS. / TRUE LOVE** [ ] [–]
(12"+=/cd-s+=) – Evening.

Sep 93. (c-s) *(TCCHS 5001)* <*24839*> **SOMEBODY'S BABY. / ('A'- A-C mix)** [48] Aug97 [ ]
(cd-s+=) *(CDCHS 5001)* <*58001*> – Temptation / Promises in the dark (live).

Nov 93. (cd/c) *(CD/TC CHR 6054)* <*21982*> **GRAVITY'S RAINBOW** [ ] Jun93 [85]
– Pictures of a gone world / Everybody lay down / Somebody's baby / Ties that bind / You and I / Disconnected / Crazy / Everytime I fall back / Sanctuary / Rise (part 2) / Kingdom key / Tradin' down.

C.M.C. C.M.C.

Jun 97. (cd-s) <*87223*> **STRAWBERRY WINE (LIFE IS SWEET) / (version)** [–] [ ]

Sep 97. (cd) <*(06076 86216-2)*> **INNAMORATA** [ ] Jun97 [ ]
– (guitar intro) / Only love / River of love / I don't want to be your friend / Strawberry wine / Purgatory / At this time / Dirty little secrets / Angry / In these times / Innamorata / Gina's song. *(d-cd-iss. Oct98 as 'INNAMORATA 8/1/80' on 'SPV'; SPV 0852917-2)*

Gold Circle Gold Circle

Dec 01. (cd-s) <*58804*> **CHRISTMAS IN AMERICA / PLEASE COME HOME FOR CHRISTMAS / CHRISTMAS IN AMERICA (instrumental)** [–] [ ]

Jul 02. (cd; as PAT BENATAR / NEIL GIRALDO) *(GI 57500-2)* <*50024*> **LIVE: SUMMER VACATION TOUR SOUNDTRACK** [ ] Mar02 [ ]
– Treat me right / I need a lover / We live for love / Girl / I won't / We belong / Love is a battlefield / True love / Out of the ruins / Hell is for children / Heartbreaker / Please don't leave me / Promises in the dark / Hit me with your best shot / All fired up.

not iss. Bel Chiasso

Aug 03. (cd) <*79743*> **GO** [–] [ ]
– Go / Brave / I won't / Have it all / Sorry / Please don't leave me / Girl / Out of the ruins / In my dreams / Tell me / Brokenhearted.

– compilations, others, etc. –

—— on 'Chrysalis' unless mentioned otherwise

Dec 82. (d-c) *(ZCDP 108)* **IN THE HEAT OF THE NIGHT / CRIMES OF PASSION** ☐ –

Nov 87. (cd)(c/lp) *(CCD 1538)(Z+/PATV 1) <21715>* **BEST SHOTS** 6 Nov89 67
– Hit me with your best shot / Love is a battlefield / We belong / We live for love / Sex as a weapon / Invincible / Shadows of the night / Heartbreaker / Fire and ice / Treat me right / If you think you know how to love me / You better run. *(cd re-iss. Sep97; same)*

Apr 94. (cd/c) *(CD/TC CHR 6070)* **THE VERY BEST OF PAT BENATAR** ☐ ☐
– Heartbreaker / We live for love / Promises in the dark / Fire and ice / Ooh ooh song / Hit me with your best shot / Shadows of the night / Anxiety (get nervous) / I want out / Lipstick lies / Love is a battlefield / We belong / All fired up / Hell is for children / Invincible / Somebody's baby / Everybody lay down / True love.

Jan 95. (d-cd) *Chrysalis; <31094>* **ALL FIRED UP: THE VERY BEST OF PAT BENATAR** – ☐

Jul 98. (cd) *Ranch Life; <(CRANCH 6)>* **CONCERT CLASSICS** ☐ ☐

Sep 98. (cd) *Beat Goes On; (BGOCD 418)* **IN THE HEAT OF THE NIGHT / CRIMES OF PASSION** ☐ –

Nov 98. (cd) *Beat Goes On; (BGOCD 427)* **PRECIOUS TIME / GET NERVOUS** ☐ –

Mar 99. (cd) *Beat Goes On: (BGOCD 433)* **TROPICO / SEVEN THE HARD WAY** ☐ –

Mar 99. (cd) *E.M.I.; (CDP 852256-2)* **HEARTBREAKER** ☐ –

Jul 99. (cd) *King Biscuit; <88054>* **GREATEST HITS LIVE** – ☐
(UK+re-iss. Jun03; KNBS 40010B)>

Oct 99. (d-cd) *<99803>* **SYNCHRONISTIC WANDERINGS** – ☐

Sep 00. (cd; shared with BLONDIE) *Madacy; <3125>* **BACK TO BACK HITS** – ☐

Feb 01. (cd) *EMI Plus; <(576258-2)>* **THE DIVINE** ☐ Apr02 ☐

Oct 01. (cd) *EMI Gold; (535787-2)* **THE COLLECTION** ☐ –
<(re-iss. Apr02 on 'Disky'; SI 79405-2)>

Feb 02. (cd) *Disky; (SI 79217-2)* **PAT BENATAR** ☐ –

Jul 02. (cd) *E.M.I.; <539928>* **THE VERY BEST PAT BENATAR ALBUM EVER** – ☐

Jul 02. (cd) *Traditional Line; (TL 1349)* **LIVE AT ELECTRIC LADYLAND (live)** ☐ –

Oct 02. (cd) *Capitol; <41797>* **CLASSIC MASTERS** – ☐

Mar 03. (d-cd) *(581778-2)* **CRIMES OF PASSION / IN THE HEAT OF THE NIGHT** ☐ ☐

George BENSON

Born: 22 Mar'43, Pittsburgh, Pennsylvania, USA. Having played guitar since the age of eight (even performing on the radio as LITTLE GEORGIE BENSON), the talented wunderkid initially performed as an R&B vocalist before recording a handful of obscure sides for 'R.C.A.'. Turned on to jazz by the work of CHARLIE CHRISTIAN and WES MONTGOMERY, BENSON soon found himself plucked from obscurity by BROTHER JACK McDUFF (who introduced him to JOHN COLTRANE and MONTGOMERY himself amongst others) in the early 60's. 'THE NEW BOSS GUITAR OF GEORGE BENSON WITH THE BROTHER JACK McDUFF QUARTET' appeared in 1964 and now based in New York, BENSON was signed to 'Columbia' after being spotted by the legendary JOHN HAMMOND. Following a trio of albums for the label including the wittily titled double set, 'BENSON BURNER' (1966), the promising guitarist cut a one-off album for 'Verve' before signing to 'A&M' for a further trio of straightahead jazz albums. The new decade found him with producer Creed Taylor's 'C.T.I.' label where he cut a series of quirky fusion efforts with the likes of RON CARTER, BILLY COBHAM and Brazilian percussion wizard AIRTO MOREIRA, even cooking up versions of Jefferson Airplane's 'WHITE RABBIT' and The MAMAS AND THE PAPAS' 'California Dreamin'. Around the same time he also contributed to albums by the cream of the pioneering jazz artists like MILES DAVIS, HERBIE HANCOCK and FREDDIE HUBBARD. While BENSON scored a surprise UK Top 30 hit in 1975 with the 'SUPERSHIP' single (under the GEORGE 'BAD' BENSON moniker), he only really hit paydirt after signing to 'Warners' and opting for a new vocal-friendly R&B/funk-lite style. 'BREEZIN' (1976) introduced his new airbrushed MOR approach and promptly topped the US chart, helped along by the US Top 10 cover of Leon Russell's 'THIS MASQUERADE'. His success continued with the Top 10 'IN FLIGHT' (1977) album, the record upping the vocal ante and featuring a centrepiece cover of War's 'THE WORLD IS A GHETTO' while spawning a second UK Top 30 hit with an orchestrated cover of Eden Ahbez' 'NATURE BOY'. Instrumental prowess was showcased on a fine cover of Donny Hathaway's 'VALDEZ IN THE COUNTRY' yet it was the spirit of STEVIE WONDER that loomed largest over BENSON's new direction, from his vocal phrasing to the funky moog, clavinet and electric piano arrangements. By the release of 1980's QUINCY JONES-produced 'GIVE ME THE NIGHT' set, the impressively versatile BENSON had polished his vocal skills to perfection and the smooth boogie of the title track furnished him with the biggest and most enduring hit of his career (US Top 5) while the album itself made the No.3 position on both sides of the big pond. During the early-mid 80's his increasingly formulaic cocktail pop-soul was more successful in the UK with the 'IN YOUR EYES' (1983) album making the Top 5 and spawning a couple of major hits in 'LADY LOVE ME (ONE MORE TIME)' and the title track. With '20-20' (1985) and 'WHILE THE CITY SLEEPS . . .' (1986), the hits started to dry up and by the late 80's, BENSON had reverted back to his old swinging, guitar-toting jazz style for an album of standards, 'TENDERLY' (1989), working with old hands like CARTER and McCOY TYNER. Its success in the contemporary jazz market spurred him on for 1990's 'BIG BOSS BAND' (featuring the COUNT BASIE ORCHESTRA), while 1993's 'LOVE REMEMBERS' further reconfirmed his credentials. • **Songwriters:** Writes most of material collaborating with others noteably in 1980 producer QUINCY JONES and ROD TEMPERTON. He covered; ON BROADWAY (Drifters) / NATURE BOY + BEYOND THE SEA (Bobby Darin) / ALL BLUES (Miles Davis) / LOVE FOR SALE (Cole Porter) / THERE WILL NEVER BE ANOTHER YOU (Warren-Gordon) / LIL DARLIN' (Count Basie) / ABBEY ROAD album (Beatles) / LET'S DO IT AGAIN (Staple Singers) / etc. The 20-20 album featured songs specially written for him by The WOMACKS / GERRY GOFFIN / NEIL LARSON, STEVE LUKATHER, etc. • **Trivia:** He has guested on many artists' albums, including STEVIE WONDER (Songs In The Key Of Life) / MINNIE RIPERTON (Love Lies Forever) / CHAKA KHAN (Chaka).

Best/Latest CD compilation: THE GREATEST HITS OF . . . (*8)

GEORGE BENSON – vocals, guitar + sessions /with **JACK McDUFF** – organ / **RED HOLLOWAY** – tenor sax / **RONNIE BOYKINS** – bass / **MONTEGO JOE** – drums

not iss. Prestige

Aug 64. (lp) *<PR 7310>* **THE NEW BOSS GUITAR OF GEORGE BENSON WITH THE BROTHER JACK McDUFF QUARTET** – ☐
– Shadow dancers / The sweet Alice blues / I don't know / Just another Sunday / Will you still be mine? / Easy living / Rock-a-bye / My three sons.

not iss. Columbia

1966. (lp) *<CS 9325>* **IT'S UPTOWN** – ☐
– Clockwise / Summertime / Ain't that peculiar / Jaguar / Willow weep for me / A foggy day / Hello birdie / Bullfight / Stormy weather / Eternally / Myna bird blues. *(cd+c-iss.Jul93 as 'IT'S UPTOWN WITH THE GEORGE BENSON QUARTET' on 'Sony Collector's') (cd-iss. Dec94 on 'Columbia')*

1966. (lp) *<CS 9413>* **GEORGE BENSON COOKBOOK** – ☐
– The cooker / Benny's back / Bossa rocka / All of me / Big fat lady / Benson's river / Ready and able / The Borgia stick / Return of

the prodigal son / Jumpin' with the symphony Sid. *(cd-iss. Dec94 on 'Columbia')*

1966. (d-lp) *<CH 33569>* **BENSON BURNER** [–] [ ]
– Bayou / Hammond's bossa nova / Willow weep for me / Clabber biscuits / Chicken giblets / Mama wailer / Goodnight / The man from Toledo / My babe / Minor truth / Slow scene / Flamingo / Redwood city // The cooker / Return of the prodigal son / Push, push / Benson's rider / Doin' the thing / Bright eyes / Myna bird blues / What do you think / Peg-lrg Jack / Jaguar / Hello bride / Ain't that peculiar / Forevermore. *(UK-iss.Jan76 on 'CBS')*

1966. (7") **AIN'T THAT PECULIAR. / SUMMERTIME** [–] [ ]

1967. (7") **MAN FROM TOLEDO. / THE BORGIA STICK** [–] [ ]

1967. (lp) *<63533>* **WILLOW WEEP FOR ME** [–] [ ]
– Benson's river / Bayou / The Borgia stick / Return of the prodigal son / Bossa rocka / Farm boy / Willow weep for me / Myna bird blues / Bullfight / Hello birdie / Clockwise.

— with loads of sessioners.

A&M A&M

Oct 68. (lp) *<SP 3014>* **SHAPE OF THINGS TO COME** [–] [ ]
– Footin' it / Face it boy, it's over / Shapes of things to come / Chattanooga choo choo / Don't let me lose this dream / Shape of things that are and were / Last train to Clarksville. *(re-iss. 1976, cd-iss. Nov88)*

Nov 68. (7") **SHAPE OF THINGS TO COME. / CHATTANOOGA CHOO CHOO** [–] [ ]

Feb 69. (7") **DON'T LET ME LOSE THIS DREAM. / (pt. 2)** [–] [ ]

1969. (7") **MY WOMAN'S GOOD TO ME. / JACKIE ALL** [–] [ ]

1969. (7") **TELL IT LIKE IT IS. / MY CHERIE AMOUR** [–] [ ]

Aug 69. (lp) *<SP 3020>* **TELL IT LIKE IT IS** [–] [ ]
– Are you happy? / Water brother / Tell it like it is / Dontcha hear me callin' to ya / Jackie, all / Jama Joe / Land of a 1000 dances / My Cherie amour / My woman's good to me / Out in the cold again / Soul limbo.

1970. (7") **I GOT A WOMAN. / (pt. 2)** [–] [ ]

1970. (lp) **I GOT A WOMAN AND SOME BLUES** [ ] [ ]
– I got a woman / Out of the blues / Bluesadelic / Durham's turn / Good morning, blues / I worry 'bout you / Without her / She went a little bit farther / Goodbye, Columbus.

— next w / **CLARENCE PALMER** – organ / **RON CARTER** – bass / **JACK DeJOHNETTE** – drums / **MICHAEL CAMERSON + ALBERT NICHOLSON** – percussion

C.T.I. C.T.I.

Feb 71. (lp) *<CTI 6009>* **BEYOND THE BLUE HORIZON** [–] [ ]
– So what / The gentle rain / All clear / Ode to a Kudu / Somewhere in the east. *(re-iss. 1978)*

— next w / **CARTER / HERBIE HANCOCK** – piano / **BILLY COBHAM** – drums / **EARL KLUGH + JAY BERLINER** – guitar / **AIRTO MOREIRA** – percussion, vocals / **PHIL KRAUS** – vibes / **JOHN FROSK + ALAN RUBIN** – trumpet, flugelhorn / **JIM BUFFINGTON** – flugelhorn / **WAYNE ANDRE** – trombone / **PHIL BODNER** – flute, oboe / **GEORGE MARGE** – flute, clarinet, etc

Nov 71. (7") **WHITE RABBIT. /** [–] [ ]

Nov 71. (lp) *(CTI 6) <6015>* **WHITE RABBIT** [ ] [ ]
– White rabbit / The summer of '42 theme / Little train / California dreamin' / El mar. *(re-iss. Apr77) (cd-iss. Nov95 on 'Columbia')*

— next w / **CARTER, KLUGH, DeJOHNETTE / HAROLD MABERN** – piano / **GARY KING** – bass / **MOBLEU** – percussion

1973. (lp) *(CTI 20) <6033>* **BODY TALK** [ ] [ ]
– Dance / When love has grown / Plum / Body talk / Top of the world. *(re-iss. Feb84) (cd-iss. Dec86 on 'Musicdisc')*

— next w / **CARTER / KENNY BARRON** – piano / **PHIL UPCHURCH** – guitar, bass / **STEVE GADD** – drums + late 1971 wind section.

Jun 74. (lp) *<6045>* **BAD BENSON** [–] [78]
– Take five / Summer wishes, winter dreams / My Latin brother / No sooner said than done / Full compass / The changing world.

Sep 75. (7"; as GEORGE BAD BENSON) *(CTSP 002)* **SUPERSHIP. / MY LATIN BROTHER** [30] [ ]

— next 3 albums w / **PHIL UPCHURCH** – guitar / **RONNIE FOSTER + JORGE DALTO** – keyboards / **STANLEY BANKS** – bass / **HARVEY MASON** – drums / **RALPH McDONALD** – percussion

Warners Warners

May 76. (7") *<8209>* **THIS MASQUERADE. / LADY** [–] [10]

Aug 76. (lp/c) *(K 56199) <2919>* **BREEZIN'** [ ] Apr76 [1]
– Breezin' / This masquerade / Six to four / Affirmation / So this is love / Lady. *(re-iss. Jun89 lp/c/cd; same)*

Jul 76. (7") *(K 16796)* **BREEZIN'. / LADY** [ ] [–]

Oct 76. (7") *<8268>* **BREEZIN'. / SIX TO FOUR** [–] [63]

Nov 76. (7") *(K 16853)* **THIS MASQUERADE. / SIX TO FOUR** [ ] [–]

Jan 77. (lp/c) *(K/K4 56327) <2983>* **IN FLIGHT** [19] [9]
– Nature boy / The wind and I / The world is a ghetto / Gonna love you more / Valdez in the country / Everything must change. *(cd-iss. 1986; 2-56327)*

Apr 77. (7") *(K 16921)* **NATURE BOY. / THE WIND AND I** [26] [ ]

Jun 77. (7") *(K 16970) <8377>* **GONNA LOVE YOU MORE. / VALDEZ IN THE COUNTRY** [ ] [71]

Sep 77. (7") *(ARIST 133) <0251>* **THE GREATEST LOVE OF ALL. / Michael Masser: ALI'S THEME** [27] Jul77 [24]
(above issued on 'Arista' + from the movie 'The Greatest')

Jan 78. (d-lp/d-c) *(K/K4 66074) <3139>* **WEEKEND IN L.A. (live)** [47] [5]
– The greatest love of all / Down here on the ground / Ode to a Kudu / We as love / California p.m. / Lady blue / We all remember Wes / Windsong / On Broadway / It's all in the game / Weekend in L.A.

Mar 78. (7") *(K 17120) <8542>* **ON BROADWAY (live). / WE AS LOVE (live)** [ ] [7]

May 78. (7") *(K 17172)* **LADY BLUE (live). / DOWN HERE ON THE GROUND (live)** [ ] [ ]

Mar 79. (7") *(K 17333) <8759>* **LOVE BALLAD. / YOU'RE NEVER TOO FAR FROM ME** [29] Feb79 [18]

Apr 79. (d-lp/d-c) *(K/K4 66085) <3277>* **LIVIN' INSIDE YOUR LOVE** [24] Mar79 [7]
– Livin' inside your love / Hey girl / Nassau day / Soulful street / Prelude to fall / A change is gonna come / Love ballad / You're never too far from me / Love is a hurtin' thing / Welcome into my world / Before you go / Unchained melody. *(cd-iss. Jun89; K2 66085)*

Jun 79. (7") *(K 17409)* **UNCHAINED MELODY. / BEFORE YOU GO** [ ] [ ]

Sep 79. (7") *(K 17472)* **HEY GIRL. / WELCOME INTO MY WORLD** [ ] [ ]

Jun 80. (7") *<49505>* **GIVE ME THE NIGHT. / DINORAH, DINORAH** [–] [4]

Aug 80. (7") *(K 17673)* **GIVE ME THE NIGHT. / BREEZIN'** [7] [–]

Sep 80. (lp/c) *(K/K2 56823) <3453>* **GIVE ME THE NIGHT** [3] Aug80 [3]
– Love x love / Off Broadway / Moody's mood / Give me the night / What's on your mind / Dinorah, Dinorah / Love dance / Star of a story (x) / Midnight love affair / Turn out the lamplight. *(cd-iss. 1983; K2 56823)*

Sep 80. (7") *(K 17699)* **LOVE X LOVE. / OFF BROADWAY** [10] [–]

Oct 80. (7") *<49570>* **LOVE X LOVE. / LOVE DANCE** [–] [61]

Jan 81. (7"/12") *(W 17748/+T)* **WHAT'S ON YOUR MIND. / TURN OUT THE LAMPLIGHT** [45] [ ]

— in Aug'81, BENSON duetted with ARETHA FRANKLIN on her LOVE ALL THE HURT AWAY single which scraped into both UK + US Top 50 for 'Arista'.

Oct 81. (7") *(K 17877) <49846>* **TURN YOUR LOVE AROUND. / NATURE BOY** [29] [5]

Nov 81. (d-lp/c) *(K 66107) <3577>* **THE GEORGE BENSON COLLECTION** (compilation) [19] [14]
– Turn your love around / Love all the hurt away / Give me the night / Love ballad / Nature boy / Last train to Clarksville / Livin' inside your love / Never give up on a good thing / On Broadway / White rabbit / This masquerade / Here comes the Sun / Breezin' / Moody's mood for love (Moody's mood) / We got the love / The greatest love of all. *(c+=)* – Cast your fate to the wind. *(cd-iss. Jul88; K2 66107)*

Jan 82. (7"/12") *(K 17902/+T)* **NEVER GIVE UP ON A GOOD THING. / CALIFORNIA P.M.** [14] [–]

Feb 82. (7") *<5005>* **NEVER GIVE UP ON A GOOD THING. / LIVIN' INSIDE YOUR LOVE** [–] [52]

Apr 83. (7") *<29649>* **INSIDE LOVE (SO PERSONAL). / IN SEARCH OF A DREAM** [–] [43]

May 83. (7"/12") *(W 9614/+T)* **LADY LOVE ME (ONE MORE TIME). / IN SEARCH OF A DREAM** [11] [–]

Jun 83. (lp/c) *<(9 23744-1/-4)>* **IN YOUR EYES** [3] [27]
– Feel like making love / Inside love (so personal) / Lady love me (one more time) / Love will come again / In your eyes / Never too far to fall / Being with you / Use me / Late at night / In search of a dream. *(cd-iss. Jul88; 9 23744-2)*

Jul 83. (7"/12") *(W 9551/+T)* **FEEL LIKE MAKING LOVE. / USE ME** [28] [–]

Jul 83. (7") *<29563>* **LADY LOVE ME (ONE MORE TIME). / BEING WITH YOU** [–] [30]

Sep 83. (7") *(W 9487)* **IN YOUR EYES. / BEING WITH YOU** [7] [–]
(12"+=) *(W 9486)* – Weekend in L.A.

Dec 83. (7") *(W 9427)* **INSIDE LOVE (SO PERSONAL). / ON BROADWAY (live)** [57] [–]

(12"+=) *(W 9427T)* – Love will come again.
Mar 84. (7") *(W 9325)* **LATE AT NIGHT. / LOVE WILL COME AGAIN** [ ] [-]
(12"+=) *(W 9325)* – Welcome into my world.
Jan 85. (7"/12") *(W 9120/+T) <29120>* **20-20. / SHARK BITE** [29] Nov84 [48]
Jan 85. (lp/c/cd) *<(9 25178-1/-4/-2)>* **20-20** [9] [45]
– No one emotion / Please don't walk away / I just wanna hang around you / Nothing's gonna change my love for you / Beyond the sea (la mer) / 20-20 / New day / Hold me / Stand up / You are the love of my life.
Mar 85. (7") *(W 9014)* **BEYOND THE SEA (LA MER). / BREEZIN'** [60] [ ]
(12"+=) *(W 9014T)* – This masquerade.
Jul 85. (7"/12") *(W 8985/+T)* **I JUST WANNA HANG AROUND YOU. / YOU ARE THE LOVE OF MY LIFE** [ ] [ ]
Oct 85. (7"; as GEORGE BENSON & ROBERTA FLACK) *(W 8863)* **NO ONE EMOTION. / YOU ARE THE LOVE OF MY LIFE** [ ] [ ]
(12"+=) *(W 8863T)* – Affirmation.
Jul 86. (7"/12") *(W 8640/+T)* **KISSES IN THE MOONLIGHT. / OPEN YOUR EYES (instrumental)** [60] [ ]
Sep 86. (lp/c)(cd) *(WX 55/+C)<(9 25475-2)>* **WHILE THE CITY SLEEPS . . .** [13] [77]
– Shiver / Love is here tonight / Teaser / Secrets in the night / Too many times / Did you hear thunder / While the city sleeps . . . / Kisses in the moonlight. *(re-iss. cd Feb95)*
Nov 86. (7"/12") *(W 8523/+T)* **SHIVER. / LOVE IS HERE TONIGHT** [19] [ ]
Feb 87. (7"/12") *(W 8437/+T)* **TEASER. / DID YOU HEAR THE THUNDER** [45] [ ]
Jul 87. (lp/c/cd; GEORGE BENSON with EARL KLUGH) *(WX 91/+C)<(9 25580)>* **COLLABORATION** [47] [59]
– Mt. Airy road / Mimosa / Brazillian stomp / Dreamin' / Since you're gone / Collaboration / Jamaica. *(cd+=)* – Love theme from 'Romeo & Juliet'. *(re-iss. cd Feb95)*
Aug 87. (7"; with EARL KLUGH) **SINCE YOU'RE GONE / LOVE THEME FROM 'ROMEO & JULIET'** [-] [ ]
Aug 88. (7") *(W 7780)* **LET'S DO IT AGAIN. / LET'S GO** [56] [ ]
(12"+=) *(W 7780T)* – ('A'extended).
(12"+=) *(W 7780TX)* – ('A'instrumental).
(cd-s++=) *(W 7780CD)* – Shiver.
Aug 88. (lp/c)(cd) *(WX 160/+C)<(9 25705)>* **TWICE THE LOVE** [16] [76]
– Twice the love / Starting all over / Good habit / Everybody does it / Living on borrowed love / Let's do it again / Stephanie / Tender love / You're still my baby / Until you believe.
Oct 88. (7") *(W 7665)* **TWICE THE LOVE. / LOVE IS HERE TONIGHT** [ ] [ ]
(12") *(W 7665T)* – ('A'extended) / ('A'guitar love mix) / ('A'club).
(cd-s++=) *(W 7665CD)* – Breezin'.

— w / **CARTER** – bass / **McCOY TYNER** – piano / **LOUIS HAYES + AL FOSTER** – drums

Jul 89. (lp/c)(cd) *(WX 263/+C)<(9 25907-2)>* **TENDERLY** [52] [ ]
– You don't know what love is / Stella by starlight / Stardust / At the Mambo Inn / Here, there and everywhere / This is all I ask / Tenderly / I could write a book.

— w / **CARTER** – bass / **BARRY EASTMOND + RICHARD TEE + LOUIS HAYES + DAVID WITHUM** – keyboards / + a host of trumpeters & saxers incl. **RANDY BRECKER**

Oct 90. (cd/c/lp) *<(7599 26295-2/-4/-1)>* **BIG BOSS BAND** [ ] [ ]
– Without a song / Ready, now that you are / How do you keep the music playing / On Green Dolphin Street / Baby workout / I only have eyes for you / Portrait of Jennie / Walkin' my baby back home / Skylark / Basie's bag.
(above album featured The COUNT BASIE ORCHESTRA)
Jun 93. (cd/c) *<(7599 26685-2/-4)>* **LOVE REMEMBERS** [ ] [ ]
– I'll be good to you / Got to be there / My heart is dancing / Love of my life / Kiss and make up / Come into my world / Love remembers / Willing to fight / Somewhere island / Lovin' on borrowed time / Lost in love / Calling you.

— BENSON released a single with PATTI AUSTIN in August'92. 'I'LL KEEP YOUR DREAMS ALIVE' which hit UK No.68

— in Jul98, BENSON hit UK No.22 with MARY J BLIGE ('Seven Days')

G.R.P. G.R.P.
Jun 96. (cd/c) *<(GRP 9823-2/-4)>* **THAT'S RIGHT** [ ] [ ]
– That's right / Thinker / Marvin said / True blue / Holdin' on / Song for my brother / Johnnie Lee / Summer love / P park / Footprints in the sand / When love comes calling / Where are you now.
May 00. (cd) *(543840-2) <543586>* **ABSOLUTE BENSON** [ ] [ ]
– The ghetto / El barrio / Jazzenco / Deeper than you think / One on one / Hipping the hop / Lately / Come back baby / Medicine man.

– (selective) compilations, etc. –

Jul 76. (lp) *C.T.I.; <(CTI 6062)>* **GOOD KING BAD** [ ] Jun76 [51]
Sep 76. (lp) *A&M; <SP 3028>* **THE OTHER SIDE OF ABBEY ROAD** [ ] Jul76 [ ]
Nov 76. (lp; as GEORGE BENSON & JOE FARRELL) *C.T.I.; <6069>* **BENSON & FARRELL** [-] [100]
Jan 77. (lp) *C.T.I.; <6072>* **GEORGE BENSON IN CONCERT – CARNEGIE HALL (live)** [-] [ ]
Mar 82. (lp/c) *A&M; (A/C MID 115)* **THE BEST OF GEORGE BENSON** [ ] [-]
Jun 82. (lp) *C.T.I.; <66035>* **THE BEST OF GEORGE BENSON – THE EARLY YEARS** [-] [ ]
(cd-iss. Sep84; 8136 592)
Oct 82. (d-cd) *Warners; (K2 56199)* **BREEZIN' / IN FLIGHT** [ ] [ ]
Oct 85. (lp/c) *K-Tel; (NE1/CE2 308)* **THE LOVE SONGS** [1] [-]
Oct 91. (cd/c/lp) *Telstar; (STAR/STAC/TCD 2450)* **MIDNIGHT MOODS – THE LOVE COLLECTION** [25] [-]
Dec 92. (cd/c) *Columbia; (465405-2/-4)* **THE BEST OF GEORGE BENSON** [ ] [ ]
Dec 02. (d-cd) *Sony Jazz; (508932-2)* **BAD BENSON / BEYOND THE BLUE HORIZON** [ ] [ ]
Jun 03. (cd) *Rhino; (8122 73693-2) <78284>* **THE GREATEST HITS OF ALL – THE VERY BEST OF GEORGE BENSON** [4] Jul03 [ ]
– This masquerade / Breezin' / Greatest love of all / On Broadway (live) / Love ballad / Unchained melody / Give me the night / Love x love / Turn your love around / Love all the hurt away (with ARETHA FRANKLIN) / Never give up on a good thing / Being with you / Lady love me (one more time) / 20-20 / I just wanna hang around you / Kisses in the moonlight / Shiver / Let's do it again / Standing together.

Chuck BERRY

Born: CHARLES EDWARD ANDERSON BERRY, 18 Oct'26, St. Louis, Missouri, USA. Having learned the guitar while at school, BERRY had his first run-in with the law in his late teens, when he was sent to reform school for a 3-year stretch after being convicted of armed attempted robbery. Upon his release, he worked blue collar jobs by day, perfecting his playing and songwriting by night; BERRY's first professional combo (with pianist JOHNNIE JOHNSON and drummer EBBY HARDY) became a regular local attraction during the early to mid-50's with their upbeat blend of R&B/C&W. During a trip to Chicago ("home of the blues"), BERRY enjoyed an opportunistic encounter with the legendary MUDDY WATERS, who in turn, put him in touch with 'Chess' records. By the summer of '55, his first recording, 'MAYBELLENE' (an adaptation of an old country standard), was riding high in the US singles chart; this rock'n'roll template would be successfully utilised by BERRY right through to the end of the decade on such definitive R&B gems as 'TOO MUCH MONKEY BUSINESS', 'ROLL OVER BEETHOVEN', 'ROCK AND ROLL MUSIC', 'SWEET LITTLE SIXTEEN' and 'JOHNNY B. GOODE'. As well as inventing his inimitable stage party piece, the "duck-walk", BERRY injected a quintessentially Afro-American element of humour, wit and innuendo into the concept of pop music as teen rebellion, reclaiming the rock'n'roll crown from white pretenders such as BILL HALEY and ELVIS PRESLEY. However, the position of a famous black, anti-establishment star was a precarious one and BERRY fell foul of the authorities after employing a 14-year old Apache Indian as a hat-check girl in his nightclub. Unbeknown to BERRY, the girl had allegedly worked as a prostitute, and he was subsequently found guilty of contravening the 'Mann act' by bringing an under-age child across the Texas-Missouri border. In October '61, he was sentenced to jail for five years, although due to the judge's racist remarks, he was given a retrial. He was later successfully tried and sentenced to three years, although with good behaviour, he was out early in '64. While in jail, BERRY's work was being successfully reappraised with many British-invasion artists, including The BEATLES and The ROLLING STONES, covering his early material as a sizeable part of their repertoire. Inspired, "Crazy Legs" (as he was nicknamed) returned to the studio to record a new song, 'NADINE', the single becoming a Top 30 hit on both sides of the Atlantic. BERRY also set foot in Britain for the first time, wowing audiences with a further brace of recent hits including 'NO PARTICULAR PLACE TO GO' and 'YOU NEVER CAN TELL'. In June 1966, with flower-power just over the horizon, he signed to 'Mercury', although this ill-advised partnership proved commercially fruitless. In 1972, following a return to the 'Chess' label three years previous, he scored a UK No.1 novelty hit with the embarrassing 'MY DING-A-LING'. Its double entendre lyrical content sufficiently enraged morality pest, Mary Whitehouse, for her to press for a media ban. In June 1979, BERRY was again imprisoned (100 days this time) for tax evasion, although during this period he signed a deal with 'Atlantic'. Throughout the 80's, he continued to work sporadically, a docu-film 'HAIL! HAIL! ROCK'N'ROLL' being released early in '88, featuring footage from his 60th birthday concert (KEITH RICHARDS – his biggest fan – along with other star names formed his backing band at the time). BERRY subsequently retired from recording, choosing to live in his own amusement park in Wentzville, Missouri. He did, however, play live again in a November '89 revival concert alongside BO DIDDLEY, The COASTERS etc. The following month, more controversy surrounded him when it was claimed he had been videoing a ladies rest-room for immoral purposes! In June 1990, his house was raided by the drugs squad, who seized marijuana, guns and homemade pornography. He was later charged with possession of drugs and child abuse, although he was cleared of the latter and handed a fine and a 6-month suspended prison sentence for the drugs misdemeanour. Hail! hail!, rock'n'roll! right enough!

Best CD compilation: THE BEST OF CHUCK BERRY (*9)

CHUCK BERRY – vocals, guitar with **JOHNNIE JOHNSON** – piano / **JASPER THOMAS** – drums / **WILLIE DIXON** – bass / etc.

London Chess

Jul 55. (7") *<1604>* **MAYBELLENE. / WEE WEE HOURS** [-] [5]

Oct 55. (7") *<1610>* **THIRTY DAYS. / TOGETHER WE WILL ALWAYS BE** [-] [ ]

May 56. (7",78) *(HLU 8275) <1615>* **NO MONEY DOWN. / THE DOWNBOUND TRAIN** [ ] Feb56 [ ]

May 56. (7") *<1626>* **ROLL OVER BEETHOVEN. / DRIFTING HEART** [-] [29]
(UK-iss.May57 – 7",78; HLU 8428)

Aug 56. (7") *<1635>* **TOO MUCH MONKEY BUSINESS. / BROWN EYED HANDSOME MAN** [-] [ ]

Feb 57. (7",78) *(HLN 8375) <1645>* **YOU CAN'T CATCH ME. / HAVANA MOON** [ ] Nov56 [29]

Jun 57. (7",78) *(DB 3951) <1653>* **SCHOOL DAY (RING! RING! GOES THE BELL). / DEEP FEELING** [24] Mar57 [3]
(above was issued in UK on 'Columbia')

—— He retained **DIXON** and enlisted on most of 50's **FRED BELOW** – drums / **LAFAYETTE LEAKE** – piano

Jun 57. (7") *<1664>* **OH BABY DOLL / LA JAUNDA** [-] [57]

Dec 57. (7",78) *(HLM 8531) <1671>* **ROCK AND ROLL MUSIC. / BLUE FEELING** [ ] Sep57 [8]

1958. (lp) *<1426>* **AFTER SCHOOL SESSIONS** [-] [ ]
– School day / Deep feeling / Too much monkey business / Wee wee hours / Roly poly / No money down / Brown-eyed handsome man / Berry pickin' / Together we will always be / Havana Moon / Downbound train / Drifting heart.

Mar 58. (7",78) *(HLM 8585) <1683>* **SWEET LITTLE SIXTEEN. / REELIN' AND ROCKIN'** [16] Jan58 [2]

May 58. (7",78) *(HLM 8629) <1691>* **JOHNNY B. GOODE. / AROUND AND AROUND** [ ] Apr58 [8]

Aug 58. (7",78) *(HL 8677) <1697>* **BEAUTIFUL DELILAH. / VACATION TIME** [ ] Jun58 [81]

Oct 58. (7",78) *(HL 8712) <1700>* **CAROL. / HEY PEDRO** [ ] Aug58 [18]

Nov 58. (lp; stereo/mono) *(HA/+M 2132) <1432>* **ONE DOZEN BERRYS** [ ] [ ]
– Sweet little sixteen / Blue feeling / La juanda / Rockin' at the Philharmonic / Oh baby doll / Reelin' & rockin' / In-go / Rock and roll music / How you've changed / Low feeling / It don't take but a few minutes.

Dec 58. (7",78) *(HLM 8767) <1709>* **SWEET LITTLE ROCK AND ROLLER. / JOE JOE GUN** [ ] [47] Oct58 [83]

Dec 58. (7") *<1714>* **RUN RUDOLPH RUN. / MERRY CHRISTMAS BABY** [-] [69] [71]

Jan 59. (7") *<1716>* **ANTHONY BOY. / THAT'S MY DESIRE** [-] [60]

Apr 59. (7",78) *(HLM 8853) <1722>* **ALMOST GROWN. / LITTLE QUEENIE** [ ] [32] Mar59 [80]

Jul 59. (7",78) *(HLM 8921) <1729>* **BACK IN THE U.S.A. / MEMPHIS, TENNESSEE** [ ] Jun59 [37]

1959. (lp) *<1435>* **CHUCK BERRY IS ON TOP** [-] [ ]
– Almost grown / Carol / Maybellene / Sweet little rock and roller / Anthony boy / Johnny B. Goode / Little Queenie / Jo Jo Gunne / Roll over Beethoven / Around and around / Hey Pedro / Blues for Hawaiians. *(UK-iss.Oct87;) (re-iss. Oct94 cd/c;)*

Oct 59. (7") *<1737>* **CHILDHOOD SWEETHEART. / BROKEN ARROW** [-] [ ]

Mar 60. (7") *(HLM 9069) <1747>* **LET IT ROCK. / TOO POOPED TO POP** [ ] [64] Jan60 [42]

Apr 60. (7") *<1754>* **BYE BYE JOHNNY. / WORRIED LIFE BLUES** [-] [ ]

Jun 60. (7") *(HLM 9159)* **BYE BYE JOHNNY. / MAD LAD** [ ] [-]

Jun 60. (7") *<1763>* **MAD LAD. / I GOT TO FIND MY BABY** [-] [ ]

1960. (lp) *<1448>* **ROCKIN' AT THE HOPS** [-] [ ]
– Bye bye Johnny / Worried life blues / Down the road apiece / Confessin' the blues / Too pooped to pop ("Casey") / Mad lad / I got to find my baby / Betty Jean / Childhood sweetheart / Broken arrow / Driftin' blues / Let it rock. *(re-iss. +c.Aug87)*

Sep 60. (7") *<1767>* **JAGUAR AND THUNDERBIRD. / OUR LITTLE RENDEZVOUS** [-] [ ]

Pye Int. Chess

Sep 61. (7") *(7N 25100) <1779>* **I'M TALKIN' 'BOUT YOU. / LITTLE STAR** [ ] Feb61 [ ]

—— BERRY was convicted of an earlier crime of transporting a minor (14 year-old) across the border. He served two years in prison.

– early recordings, compilations, etc, while in prison –

Jun 62. (lp) *(NPL 28019) <1456>* **NEW JUKE BOX HITS** [ ] Nov61 [ ]
– I'm talking about you / Diploma for two / Thirteen question method / Away from you / Don't you lie to me / The way it was before / Little star / Route 66 / Sweet sixteen / Run around / Stop and listen / Rip it up.

May 63. (lp) *(NPL 28024) <1465>* **CHUCK BERRY** (compilation) <US-title 'CHUCK BERRY TWIST' different tracks> [12] 1962 [ ]
– Come back / Maybellene / Down the road apiece / Mad lad / School day (ring ring goes the bell) / Sweet little sixteen / Confessin' the blues / Back in the U.S.A. / Johnny B. Goode / Oh, baby doll / Come on / I got to find my baby / Betty Jean / Round and round / Almost grown. *(re-iss. US Dec63 as 'MORE CHUCK BERRY')(re-iss. 1984 on 'Audio Fidelity') (re-iss. Dec85 on 'Astan')*

Jul 63. (7") *(7N 25209) <1799>* **GO GO GO. / COME ON** [38] Jun61 [ ]

Aug 63. (7") *<1853>* **I'M TALKIN' 'BOUT YOU. / DIPLOMA FOR TWO** [-] [ ]

Oct 63. (lp) *(NPL 28027) <1480>* **CHUCK BERRY ON STAGE (fake live)** [6] Aug63 [29]
– Go go go / Memphis, Tennessee / Maybellene / Surfin' steel (blues for Hawaiians) / Rockin' on the railroad (let it rock) / Brown eyed handsome man (new version) / I still got the blues / Surfin' USA (sweet little sixteen) / Jaguar and thunderbird / I just want to make love to you / All aboard / Trick or treat / Man and the donkey / How high the moon.

Oct 63. (7") *<1866>* **MEMPHIS, TENNESSEE. / SWEET LITTLE SIXTEEN** –

Oct 63. (7") *(7N 25218)* **MEMPHIS, TENNESSEE. / LET IT ROCK** 6 –

Dec 63. (7") *(7N 25228)* **RUN RUDOLPH RUN. / JOHNNY B. GOODE** 36 –

—— Released from prison early '64. New recordings . . .

Feb 64. (7") *(7N 25236) <1883>* **NADINE (IS IT YOU?). / O RANGUTANG** 27 23

Apr 64. (7") *(7N 25242)* **NO PARTICULAR PLACE TO GO. / LIVERPOOL DRIVE** 3 –

May 64. (7") *<1898>* **NO PARTICULAR PLACE TO GO. / YOU TWO** – 10

May 64. (lp) *(NPL 28031)* **THE LATEST AND THE GREATEST** 8 –
– Nadine / Fraulein / Guitar boogie / Things I used to do / Don't you lie to me / Driftin' blues / Liverpool drive / No particular place to go / Lonely all the time (crazy arms) / Jaguar and Thunderbird / O rangutang / You two / Deep feeling / Bye bye Johnny.

Aug 64. (7") *(7N 25257) <1906>* **YOU NEVER CAN TELL. / BRENDA LEE** 23 Jul64 14

Sep 64. (lp) *(NPL 28039)* **YOU NEVER CAN TELL** 18 –
– You never can tell / Diploma for two / The little girl from Central / The way it was before / Around and around / Big Ben / Promised land / Back in the USA / Run around / Brenda Lee / Reeling and rockin' / Come on. *(re-iss. Dec67 on 'Marble Arch';)*

Oct 64. (7") *(7N 25271) <1912>* **LITTLE MARIE. / GO BOBBY SOXER** Sep64 54

—— Late in '64, he paired up with BO DIDDLEY to record single CHUCK'S BEAT. / BO'S BEAT; <1089> and album TWO GREAT GUITARS. They had already appeared together on 1963 EP's 'CHUCK AND BO' Volumes 1,2 & 3.

Dec 64. (lp) *<1488>* **ST. LOUIS TO LIVERPOOL (live)** –
– Little Marie / Our little rendezvous / No particular place to go / You two / Promised land / You never can tell / Go Bobby soxer / Things I used to do / Night beat / Liverpool drive / Merry Christmas baby / Brenda Lee. *(re-iss. Aug86)*

Jan 65. (7") *(7N 25285) <1916>* **THE PROMISED LAND. / THINGS I USED TO DO** 26

Chess Chess

Mar 65. (7") *(CRS 8006)* **LONELY SCHOOL DAYS. / I GOT A BOOKING** –

Mar 65. (lp) *(CRL 4005) <1495>* **CHUCK BERRY IN LONDON (live)**
– My little love light / She once was mine / After it's over / I got a booking / Night beat / His daughter Caroline / You came a long way from St. Louis / St. Louis blues / Jamaica farewell / Dead dad / Butterscotch / The song of my love / Why should we end this way / I want to be your driver.

May 65. (7") *(CRS 8012) <1926>* **DEAR DAD. / MY LITTLE LOVELIGHT** Mar65 95

Oct 65. (7") *<1943>* **IT WASN'T ME. / WELCOME BACK PRETTY BABY** –

Oct 65. (7") *(CRS 8022)* **IT WASN'T ME. / IT'S MY OWN BUSINESS** –

Nov 65. (lp) *(CRL 4506) <1498>* **FRESH BERRYS**
– It wasn't me / Run Joe / Everyday we rock and roll / One for my baby / Sad day long night * / It's my own business / Right off Rampart Street / Vaya con dios / Merrily we rock and roll / My Mustang Ford / Ain't that just like a woman / Wee hours blues. *<US version omitted * for 'Welcome back pretty baby'>*

Jul 66. (7") *(CRS 8037) <1963>* **RAMONA SAY YES. / LONELY SCHOOL DAYS** Jun66

Mercury Mercury

Dec 66. (7") *(MF 958) <72643>* **CLUB NITTY GRITTY. / LAUGH AND CRY** Nov66

Jul 67. (7") *(MF 994) <72680>* **BACK TO MEMPHIS. / I DO REALLY LOVE YOU** Jun67

Nov 67. (7") *<72748>* **FEELIN' IT. / IT HURTS ME TOO** –

Dec 67. (lp) *(SMCL 20110)* **IN MEMPHIS** –
– Back to Memphis / I do really love you / My heart will always belong to you / Ramblin' Rose / Sweet little rock and roller / Oh baby doll / Check me out / It hurts me too / Bring another drink / So long / Goodnight, well it's time to go.

Apr 68. (lp) *(MCL 20112) <SR 61138>* **LIVE AT THE FILLMORE AUDITORIUM (live)**
– Medley: Rockin' at the Fillmore – Everyday I have the blues / C.C. rider / Driftin' blues / Feelin' it / Flying home / Hoochie coochie man / It hurts me too / Fillmore blues / Wee baby James / Johnny B. Goode.

Oct 68. (7") *(MF 1057) <7840>* **ST. LOUIS TO FRISCO. / MA DEAR** Aug68

Nov 68. (lp) *<6463 015>* **FROM ST. LOUIS TO FRISCO** –
– St. Louis to Frisco / Ma dear / The love I lost / I love her, I love her / Little fox / Rock cradle rock / Soul rockin' / I can't believe / Misery / My tambourine / Oh captain / Mum's the word.

Aug 69. (7") *<72963>* **GOOD LOOKING WOMAN. / IT'S TOO DARK IN THERE** –

Nov 69. (lp) *<SMCL 20162>* **CONCERTO IN B. GOODE** –
– Good looking woman / My woman / It's too dark in there / Put her down / Concerto in 'B Goode'.

Chess Chess

Aug 70. (7") *<2090>* **TULANE. / HAVE MERCY JUDGE** –

Jan 71. (lp) *(6310 13) <1550>* **BACK HOME** 1970
– Tulane / Have mercy judge / Instrumental / Christmas / Gun / I'm a rocker / Flyin' home / Fish and chips / Some people.

1971. (lp) *(6310 115)* **SAN FRANCISCO DUES** –
– Oh Louisiana / Let's do our thing together / Your lick / Festival / Bound to lose / Bordeaux in my pirough / San Francisco dues / Viva rock and roll / My dream / Lonely school days (version 2).

Jun 72. (lp) *(6310 122)* **THE LONDON SESSIONS** 8 –
– Let's boogie / Mean old world / I will not let you go / London Berry blues / I love you / Reeling and rockin'(live) / My ding-a-ling (live) / Johnny B. Goode (live).

Aug 72. (7") *(6145 012)* **DOWN THE ROAD APIECE. / JOHNNY B. GOODE** –

Aug 72. (7") *<2131>* **MY DING-A-LING. / JOHNNY B. GOODE** – 1

Oct 72. (7") *(6145 019)* **MY DING-A-LING. / LET'S BOOGIE** 1 –

Dec 72. (7") *<2136>* **REELIN' AND ROCKIN' (live). / LET'S BOOGIE** – 27

Jan 73. (7") *(6145 020)* **REELIN' AND ROCKIN' (live). / I WILL NOT LET YOU GO** 18 –

Sep 73. (7") *<2140>* **BIO. / ROLL 'EM PETE** –

Oct 73. (lp) *(6499 650)* **BIO** –
– Bio / Hello little girl, goodbye / Woodpecker / Rain eyes / Aimlessly driftin' / Got it and gone / Talkin' about my buddy. *(re-iss. May88)*

Nov 73. (7") *(6145 027)* **SOUTH OF THE BORDER. / BIO** –

—— duets with daughter INGRID GIBSON on some tracks in 1975

Feb 75. (7") *<2169>* **SHAKE, RATTLE AND ROLL. / BABY WHAT YOU WANT ME TO DO** –

Mar 75. (7") *(6145 038)* **SHAKE, RATTLE AND ROLL. / I'M JUST A NAME** –

Apr 75. (lp) *(9109 101)* **CHUCK BERRY '75**
– Swanee river / I'm just a name / I just want to make love to you / Too late / South of the border / Hi-heel sneakers / You are my sunshine / My babe / Baby what you want me to do / A deuce / Shake, rattle and roll / Sue answer / Don't you to me.

—— on the 10th July '79, he was sentenced to four months in jail

Atlantic Atlantic

Aug 79. (7") *(K 11354) <7203>* **OH WHAT A THRILL. / CALIFORNIA**

Oct 79. (lp) *(50648) <SD 38118>* **ROCKIT** Aug79
– Move it / Oh what a thrill / I need you baby / If I were / House lights / I never thought / Havana moon / Pass away. *(re-iss. +cd.Nov88 on 'Magnum Force')*

—— virtually retired from the studio

– (selective) compilations, etc. –

on 'Chess' unless mentioned otherwise

May 64. (lp) *<1485>* **GREATEST HITS** – 34

May 72. (d-lp) *(6641 177) <LPS 1514D>* **GOLDEN DECADE VOL.1** 72

1973. (d-lp) *<2CH 60023>* **GOLDEN DECADE VOLUME 2** –

Jan 77. (lp) *(9288 690)* **MOTORVATIN'** (Greatest live) 7 –
(re-iss. Dec87 on 'Starblend'; SMT 009)

Jun 88. (d-lp/c/cd) *Castle; (CCS LP/MC/CD 194)* **THE COLLECTION** –
– Sweet little sixteen / Johnny B.Goode / Back in the U.S.A. / Maybellene / Too much monkey business / Rock and roll music / Reelin' and rockin' / No particular place to go / Roll over Beethoven / You never can tell / Nadine / Carol / School days / My ding-a-ling / Almost grown / Let it rock / Little Queenie / Promised land / Memphis Tennessee / Sweet little

rock'n'roller / Thirty days / Brown-eyed handsome man / Run Rudolph run / Merry Christmas baby.

Sep 89. (3xlp-box/3xc-box/3xcd-box) *M.C.A.,; (CH6/CHC4/CD 8001)* **CHESS BOX** ☐ ☐

Nov 89. (3xcd-box/3xc-box/3xlp-box) *Charly; (CD/TC+/BOX 256)* **CHUCK BERRY BOX SET** ☐ ☐

Nov 96. (cd/c) *M.C.A.; <(MCD/MCC 11560)>* **THE BEST OF CHUCK BERRY** ☐ ☐
– Roll over Beethoven / Sweet little sixteen / Johnny B Goode / You never can tell / You can't catch me / Downbound train / Too much monkey business / Havana moon / School days / Oh baby doll / Beautiful Delilah / Sweet little rock'n'roller / Anthony boy / Little Queenie / Almost grown / Let it rock / Back in the USA / Reelin' and rockin' / Around and around / Brown eyed handsome man / Maybelline / No particular place to go / Rock'n'roll / Run Rudolph run / Jo Jo Gunne / Carol / Confessin' the blues / Jaguar and Thunderbird / Down the road apiece / Thirty days / Merry Christmas baby / My ding-a-ling / I'm talking about you / Too pooped to pop / Bye bye Johnny / Promised land / Tulane / Come on / Nadine (is it you) / Memphis, Tennessee.

Dec 98. (cd) *Beat Goes On; (BGOCD 428)* **YOU NEVER CAN TELL / THE LATEST AND GREATEST** ☐ –

Aug 99. (cd) *Beat Goes On; (BGOCD 458)* **ONE DOZEN BERRYS / JUKE BOX HITS** ☐ –

BETA BAND

Formed: London, England ... 1994 by ex-patriate Scotsman, STEVE MASON, the St. Andrews-born singer meeting up with Edinburgh University students, decksman JOHN MacLEAN, drummer ROBIN JONES and GORDON ANDERSON on a train down to the capital. There they worked at various day jobs while sharing a flat in Shepherd's Bush, although ill-health forced ANDERSON to return home in August '96. Portsmouth-born RICHARD GREENTREE, formerly bassist of SINISTER FOOTWEAR would become part of the zany quartet in early '97 after being introduced through mutual friends, PUSHERMAN. Discovered and subsequently produced by THE VERVE's NICK McCABE (who saw some potential in their psychedelic transcendental dub malarky), they were signed to 'Regal' records. A pot-pourri of sound right enough (STONE ROSES or The MOONFLOWERS – remember them? – on a mantric mission!), the lads issued three EP's in the space of a year, 'CHAMPION VERSIONS', 'THE PATTY PATTY SOUND' and the excellent 'LOS AMIGOS DEL BETA BANDIDOS'. By popular demand (the vinyl was changing hands for upwards of £40 a time!) these were soon collected together on one shiny cd/album, simply titled 'THE THREE E.P.'S'. Lauded by the more discerning factions of the music press (the NME for one!), the bumbling art-rockers (by-passing the fashion stakes completely; safari suits, judo gear and horror of horrors, STEVE's "smart-arse" shell-suit being the disorder of the day) found themselves in the Top 40 by Autumn '98 with a long player that hung together surprisingly well. The sound of "baggy" ten years on, filtered through a kingsized bong, BETA standards such as 'DRY THE RAIN' ("It Will Be Alright"), 'INNER MEET ME', 'SHE'S THE ONE', 'DR. BAKER' and 'NEEDLES IN MY EYES' will surely come to be regarded as underground classics. To end the year, MASON moonlighted as KING BISCUIT TIME, releasing (to coincide with the latest edition of the band's zany in-house comic!) a bizarre EP of spaced-out drum'n'bass, '"SINGS" NELLY FOGGIT'S BLUES IN "ME AND THE PHARAOHS"'. With expectation and hype rife about the recording schedules and rumoured double-disc set of their debut set proper, the band were finally ready to promote 'THE BETA BAND' long-player in June '99. However, delays due to an objection from JIM STEINMAN (for the sample/use of his BONNIE TYLER – 'Total Eclipse Of The Heart' collaboration) and the band's post-release qualms that it was "fucking awful" contributed to complete bewilderment within the press and its readers. At the end of June, the album shot into the Top 20 despite poor reviews stating over-production was its downfall (or was it just plain arsing about?). Opening with the self-explanatory 'THE BETA BAND RAP' (which might've been handled better by the BONZO's in the 60's!) and finishing with the baffling 'THE COW'S WRONG', the album shocked fans who thought the quartet were perhaps a tad over-indulgent. On reflection though, The BETA BAND's original stage interpretations of the tracks could not be faulted. It's just a pity that critical cohorts like the MANICS were beginning to be proved right. As unfazed as ever, The BETA BAND shambled back into the fray with 'HOT SHOTS II' (2001; and a Top 20 hit!), the irony of the self-mocking title belying a half decent, occasionally brilliant set which certainly came closer to realising the promise of their early EP's. There was more focus, less sonic soup for the sake of it and more determined attempts at discernible songs. Which isn't to say they no longer walked that tightrope between endearingly wayward invention and rampant self-indulgence, the guiding hand of R&B producer C-Swing lending a contemporary edge to their urban meta-folk. • **Covered:** ONE (Nilsson). • **Trivia:** They guested on SPIRITUALIZED's 'Abbey Road' EP early '98.

Album rating: THE THREE E.P.'S (*9) / THE BETA BAND (*7) / HOT SHOTS 2 (*7)

STEVE MASON – vocals, percussion, drums, etc / **JOHN MacLEAN** – turntable, sampling / **RICHARD GREENTREE** – bass (ex-SINISTER FOOTWEAR) / **ROBIN JONES** – drums, percussion / GORDON ANDERSON departed before any recordings

Regal / Astralwerks

Jul 97. (12"ep) *(REG 16)* **CHAMPION VERSIONS** ☐ –
– Dry the rain / I know / B + A / Dogs got a bone.

Mar 98. (2x12"ep/cd-ep) *(REG 18/+CD)* **THE PATTY PATTY SOUND** ☐ –
– Inner meet me / The house song / The monolith / She's the one.

Jul 98. (cd-ep) *(REG 20CD)* **LOS AMIGOS DEL BETA BANDIDOS** ☐ –
– Push it out / It's over / Dr. Baker / Needles in my eyes.

Sep 98. (cd) *(7243 4 97385 2 2) <6252>* **THE THREE E.P.'S** (compilation) 35 ☐

Jun 99. (cd/d-lp) *(REG 30 CD/LP) <6268>* **THE BETA BAND** 18 ☐
– The Beta Band rap / It's not too beautiful / Simple boy / Round the bend / Dance o'er the border / Brokenupadingdong / Number 15 / Smiling / The hard one / The cow's wrong.

Jan 00. (12"/cd-s) *(REG 40/+CD)* **TO YOU ALONE. / SEQUINSIZER** ☐ –

Jul 01. (12"/cd-s) *(REG 60/+CD)* **BROKE. / WON / DANCE O'ER THE BORDER** 30 –

Jul 01. (d-lp/cd) *(REG 59/+CD) <10446>* **HOT SHOTS 2** 13 ☐
– Squares / Al Sharp / Humanbeing / Gone / Dragon / Broke / Quiet / Alleged / Life / Eclipse. *(bonus cd+=; REG 59CDL)* – Won.

Oct 01. (12"/cd-s) *(REG 65/+CD)* **HUMAN BEING. / UNKNOWN / THE HARD ONE** 57 –

Jan 02. (12"/cd-s) *(REG 69/+CD)* **SQUARES. / SQUARES (Bloah mix) / QUIET (acoustic – from 99X Atlanta session)** 42 –

KING BISCUIT TIME

aka **STEVE MASON** – vocals, etc

Regal / Astralwerks

Dec 98. (12"ep/cd-ep) *(REG 025/+CD)* **"SINGS" NELLY FOGGIT'S BLUES IN "ME AND THE PHARAOHS"** ☐ –
– Fatheriver / Niggling discrepancy / Little white / Eye o' the dug.

Jun 00. (12"ep/cd-ep) *(REG 049/+CD) <49657>* **NO STYLE EP** ☐ Jul00 ☐
– I walk the earth / Untitled / I love you / Time to get up.

☐ BETTER DAYS (see under ⇒ BUTTERFIELD, Paul)

☐ BEYONCE (see under ⇒ DESTINY'S CHILD)

B-52's

Formed: Athens, Georgia, USA . . . late '76, by KATE PIERSON, FRED SCHNEIDER, KEITH STRICKLAND, RICKY WILSON and his sister CINDY. After one self-financed 45 sold out its limited 2,000 copies, they drew the attention of Island's Chris Blackwell, who signed them after they played residency at Max's Kansas City late in 1978. They subsequently re-issued their 'ROCK LOBSTER' debut, the single making UK Top 40 lists the following year. Combining a kitsch image and sound which took in everything from rock'n'roll and 60's beat to new wave REZILLOS-style dual harmonies, The B-52's brightened up the increasingly dour late 70's/early 80's punk/pop scene. The marine madness of the classic 'ROCK LOBSTER' eventually made its way into the US charts in early 1980, by which time the eponymous '79 debut album had made UK Top 30. Even JOHN LENNON was a fan, the former BEATLES man surprisingly admitting that The B-52's were one of the groups who inspired him to start writing again. A strong follow-up set, 'WILD PLANET' (1980), made the Top 20 in both Britain and America, although critics weren't quite so enamoured with the more mannered 'MESOPOTAMIA' set (1982), produced by DAVID BYRNE of TALKING HEADS. The mid-80's were a bleak time for the band as RICKY finally died from AIDS on the 12th October, 1985, and the group struggled to capture the inspired creativity of their earlier period (fans were content in making 'ROCK LOBSTER' an even bigger UK hit than before). Signing a new deal with 'Reprise', The B-52's reunited with their roots on the 'BOUNCING OFF SATELLITES', an album which should have spawned a hit single, 'WIG'. DON WAS / NILE RODGERS-produced 'COSMIC THING' (1989), a remarkable comeback that showcased their alternative dancefloor smash, 'LOVE SHACK', the album becoming their most successful release to date, making the US Top 5. Trimmed to a trio of PIERSON, SCHNEIDER and STRICKLAND following the departure of CINDY in 1992, the group recorded another album in the classic B-52's style, 'GOOD STUFF', before setting to work on the soundtrack for the revamped 'Flintstones' movie. Something of a canny pairing, SCHNEIDER's nasal-voiced nonsense was a perfect backdrop for Fred and family's stone age adventures. • **Songwriters:** All mainly STRICKLAND or group compositions. PLANET CLAIRE (w/ Henry Mancini) • **Trivia:** In 1981, during lay-off, STRICKLAND, PIERSON and CINDY WILSON did one-off Japan venture as "MELON" with group The PLASTICS and ADRIAN BELEW. Late 1990, PIERSON contributed on singles by IGGY POP (Candy) and R.E.M. (Shiny Happy People).

Album rating: THE B-52's (*8) / WILD PLANET (*6) / PARTY MIX! remixes (*3) / MESOPOTAMIA mini (*4) / WHAMMY! (*5) / BOUNCING OFF THE SATELLITES (*4) / COSMIC THING (*7) / DANCE THIS MESS AROUND – THE BEST OF THE B-52's compilation (*9) / GOOD STUFF (*5) / TIME CAPSULE: SONGS FOR A FUTURE GENERATION compilation (*7) / NUDE ON THE MOON: THE B-52'S ANTHOLOGY double compilation (*7) / Fred Schneider: FRED SCHNEIDER AND THE SNAKE SOCIETY (*5) / JUST . . . FRED (*5)

KATE PIERSON (b.27 Apr'48, Weehawken, N.J.) – vocals, organ, bass / **CINDY WILSON** (b.28 Feb'57) – vocals, percussion, guitar / **RICKY WILSON** (b.19 Mar'53) – guitar / **FRED SCHNEIDER** (III) (b. 1 Jul'56, Newark, N.J.) – vocals, keyboards / **KEITH 'Julian' STRICKLAND** (b.26 Oct'53) – drums

not iss. — Boo-Fant

Nov 78. (7") *<DB-52>* **ROCK LOBSTER. / 52 GIRLS** [–] [ ]

Island — Warners

Jul 79. (7") *(WIP 6506)* **ROCK LOBSTER. / RUNNING AROUND** [37] [–]

Jul 79. (lp/c) *(WIP/ICT 9580) <3355>* **THE B-52's** [22] [59]
– Planet Claire / 52 girls / Dance this mess around / Rock lobster / Lava / There's a Moon in the sky (called the Moon) / Hero worship / 6060-842 / Downtown. *(lp w/free 7") (PSR 438)* – ROCK LOBSTER. / 52 GIRLS *(re-iss. May86; same) (cd-iss. Jan87; CID 9580) (re-iss. Jan94 + May94;)*

Sep 79. (7") *(WIP 6527)* **6060-842. / HERO WORSHIP** [ ] [ ]

Nov 79. (7"pic-d/7") *(P+/WIP 6551) <WBS 49212>* **PLANET CLAIRE. / THERE'S A MOON IN THE SKY (CALLED THE MOON)** [ ] May80 [ ]

Jan 80. (7") *<WBS 49173>* **ROCK LOBSTER. / 6060-842** [–] [56]

Jul 80. (7") *(WIP 6579)* **GIVE ME BACK MY MAN. / STROBE LIGHT** [61] [–]

Sep 80. (lp/c) *(ILPS/ICT 9622) <BSK 3471>* **WILD PLANET** [18] [18]
– Party out of bounds / Dirty back road / Runnin' around / Give me back my man / Private Idaho / Devil in my car / Quiche Lorraine / Strobe light / 53 miles west of Venus. *(cd-iss. May90; 842436-2)*

Oct 80. (7") *<WBS 49537>* **PRIVATE IDAHO. / PARTY OUT OF BOUNDS** [–] [74]

Nov 80. (7") *(WIP 6685)* **DIRTY BACK ROAD. / STROBE LIGHT** [ ] [–]

Jan 81. (7") *<WBS 49717>* **QUICHE LORRAINE. / LAVA** [–] [ ]

Jul 81. (m-lp/c) *(IPM/ICT 1001) <MINI 3596>* **THE PARTY MIX ALBUM** (remixes) [36] [55]
– Party out of bounds / Private Idaho / Give me back my man / Lava / Dance this mess around / 52 girls. *(cd-iss. May90; 846044-2)*

Aug 81. (7") *(WIP 6727)* **GIVE ME BACK MY MAN (Party mix). / PARTY OUT OF BOUNDS (version)** [ ] [–]

Feb 82. (m-lp/c) *(ISSP/ICT 4006) <3641>* **MESOPOTAMIA** [18] [35]
– Loveland / Deep sleep / Mesopotamia / Cake / Throw that beat in the garbage can / Nip it in the bud. *(cd-iss. May90; 846239-2) (cd re-iss. Aug01; IMCD 107)*

Mar 82. (7") *<50064>* **DEEP SLEEP. / NIP IT IN THE BUD** [–] [ ]

Jun 82. (7") *<29971>* **MESOPOTAMIA. / THROW THAT BEAT IN THE GARBAGE CAN** [–] [ ]

Apr 83. (7") *(IS 107)* **SONG FOR A FUTURE GENERATION. / ('A'instrumental)** [63] [–]
(12"+=) *(12IS 107)* – Planet Claire.
(d7"++=) *(ISD 107)* – There's a moon in the sky (called the moon).

May 83. (lp/c) *(ILPS 9759) <23819>* **WHAMMY!** [33] [29]
– Legal tender / Whammy kiss / Song for a future generation / Butterbean / Trism / Queen of Las Vegas / Don't worry / Big bird / Work that skirt. *(cd-iss. May90; 842445-2) (cd re-iss. Aug01; IMCD 109)*

Jul 83. (7") *<29579>* **LEGAL TENDER. / MOON 83** [–] [81]

Oct 83. (7") *<29561>* **SONG FOR A FUTURE GENERATION. / TREASON** [–] [ ]

— **RICKY** suffering from full blown AIDS, died 12 Oct'85.

May 86. (7"/7"sha-pic-d; rock/planet/lobster) *(BFT+/G/P/L 1)* **ROCK LOBSTER (new version). / PLANET CLAIRE** [12] [–]
(d7"+=) *(BFTD 1)* – Song for a future generation / 52 girls.
(12"+=) *(12BFT 1)* – Song for a future generation / Give me back my man.

— They carry on, augmented by session man **RALPH CARNEY** – guitar

Jun 87. (7"/7"pic-d) *(BFT/+P 2)* **WIG. / SUMMER OF LOVE** [ ] [ ]
(c-s+=/12+=) *(BFTD/12BFT 2)* – Song for a future generation.

Jul 87. (lp/c/cd) *(ILPS/ICT/CID 9871) <25504>* **BOUNCING OFF THE SATELLITES** [74] Sep86 [85]
– Summer of love / Girl from Ipanema goes to Greenland / Housework / Detour thru your mind / Wig / Theme for a nude beach / Ain't it a shame / Juicy jungle / Communicate / She brakes for rainbows. *(cd-iss. May90; 842480-2)*

Sep 87. (7") **SUMMER OF LOVE. / HOUSEWORK** [–] [ ]

— added on tour **PAT IRWIN** – keyboards / **ZACH ALFORD** – drums / **PHILIPPE SASSE** – (studio keyboards) / **SARA LEE** – bass (ex-GANG OF FOUR) (also studio)

Reprise — Reprise

Jul 89. (lp/c)(cd) *(WX 283/+C)(925854-2) <25854>* **COSMIC THING** [8] [4]
– Cosmic thing / Dry country / Deadbeat club / Love shack / Junebug / Roam / Bushfire / Channel Z / Topaz / Follow your blues.

Aug 89. (7") *<22817>* **LOVE SHACK. / CHANNEL Z** [–] [3]

Sep 89. (7") *(W 2831)* **CHANNEL Z (remix). / JUNEBUG** [61] [–]
(12")(cd-s) *(W 2831 T/CD)* – ('A'-Rock mix) / ('A'side) / ('A'dub mix). *(re-iss. Aug90;)*

Dec 89. (7") *<22667>* **ROAM. / BUSHFIRE** [–] [3]

Feb 90. (7"/7"g-f/7"pic-d/c-s/cd-s) *(W 9917/+X/P/C/CD)* **LOVE SHACK. / PLANET CLAIRE (live) / ROCK LOBSTER (live)** [2] [-]
(12") *(W 9917T)* – ('A'-Dany Rampling remix) / ('A'-Ben Grosse mix) / ('A'side).
Apr 90. (7") *<19938>* **DEADBEAT CLUB. / PLANET CLAIRE** [-] [30]
May 90. (7"/c-s/cd-s) *(W 9827/+C/CD)* **ROAM. / WHAMMY KISS (live) / DANCE THIS MESS AROUND (live)** [17] [-]
(12"/12"w-poster) *(W 9827T/+W)* – ('A'-Radio mix) / ('A'remix) / ('A'extended remix).
Sep 90. (7"/c-s) **DEADBEAT CLUB. / LOVE SHACK** [ ] [-]
(12"+=/cd-s+=) – B-52's megamix.

—— now trimmed to basic trio of **PIERSON, SCHNEIDER** – vox / + **STRICKLAND** – guitar with guest musicians **IRWIN / ALFORD / LEE /** plus **JEFF PORCARO + STERLING CAMPBELL** – drums / **DAVID McMURRAY** – sax / **JAMIE MULHOBERAC + RICHARD HILTON** – keyboards / **LENNY CASTRO** – percussion / **TRACY WORMWORTH** – bass

Jun 92. (7"/c-s) *(W 0109/+C)* *<18895>* **GOOD STUFF. / BAD INFLUENCE** [21] [28]
(12"+=/cd-s+=) *(W 0109 T/CD)* – Return to Dreamland.
(12") *(W 0109TX)* – (4-'A'mixes).
Jul 92. (cd/c/lp) *<(7599 26943-2/-4/-1)>* **GOOD STUFF** [8] [16]
– Tell it like it t-i-is / Hot pants explosion / Good stuff / Revolution Earth / Dreamland / Is that you Mo-Dean? / The world's green laughter / Vision of a kiss / Breezin' / Bad influence. *(re-iss. Feb95 cd/c; same)*
Sep 92. (7"/c-s) *(W 0130/+C)* **TELL IT LIKE IT T-I-IS. / THE WORLD'S GREEN LAUGHTER** [61] [ ]
(12"/cd-s) *(W 0130 T/CD)* – ('A'-4 other mixes).
Nov 92. (7"/c-s) *(W 0141/+C)* **IS THAT YOU MO-DEAN? / ('A'-Moby mix)** [ ] [ ]
(12"+=/cd-s+=) *(W 0141 T/CD)* *<40642-2>* – ('A'-2 other mixes) / Tell it like it t-i-is.
Feb 93. (7"/c-s) **HOT PANTS EXPLOSION. / LOVE SHACK** [ ] [ ]
(cd-s+=) – Channel Z / Roam.

—— **SCHNEIDER, PIERSON + STRICKLAND**

M.C.A. M.C.A.

Jun 94. (7"/c-s; BC-52's) *(MCS/+CS 1986)* *<54839>* **(MEET) THE FLINTSTONES. / ('A'-Barney's mix)** [3] May94 [33]
(cd-s+=) *(MCSTD 1986)* – (2-'A'mixes).
(above from that year's movie, 'The Flintstones')

– compilations, others, etc. –

Jun 90. (cd/c/lp) *Island; (ILPS/ICT/CID 9959)* **DANCE THIS MESS AROUND THE BEST OF THE B-52's** [36] [-]
– Party out of bounds / Devil in my car / Dirty back road / 6060-842 / Wig / Dance this mess around / Private Idaho / Rock lobster / Strobe light / Give me back my man / Song for a future generation / Planet Claire / 52 girls. *(cd+=)* – (2 extra mixes).
Feb 91. (cd) *Reprise; <26401>* **PARTY MIX! / MESOPOTAMIA** [-] [ ]
Nov 92. (d-cd) *Island; (ITSCD 1)* **THE B-52'S / WILD PLANET** [ ] [-]
Sep 95. (cd) *Spectrum; (551210-2)* **PLANET CLAIRE** [ ] [-]
Jul 98. (cd/c) *Reprise; (9362 46995-2/-4) <46920>* **TIME CAPSULE – SONGS FOR A FUTURE GENERATION** [ ] Jun98 [93]
– Planet Claire / 52 girls *[US-only]* / Rock lobster / Party out of bounds *[US-only]* / Strobelight *[US-only]* / Private Idaho / Quiche Lorraine (live) / Mesopotamia / Songs for a future generation *[US-only]* / Summer of love (original unreleased mix) / Channel Z / Deadbeat club / Love shack / Roam / Good stuff / Is that you Mo-Dean? / (Meet) The Flintstones *[UK-only]* / Debbie / Hallucinating Pluto.
Jan 99. (c-s) *Reprise; (W 0461C)* **LOVE SHACK '99 (mix) / (DJ Tonka remix)** [66] [-]
(cd-s+=) *(W 0461CD)* – ('A'-album mix).
Jan 02. (d-cd) *Rhino; <78357>* **NUDE ON THE MOON: THE B-52'S ANTHOLOGY** [-] [ ]
Aug 03. (3xcd-box) *Spectrum; (9808959)* **MESOPOTAMIA / PLANET CLAIRE / WHAMMY** [ ] [-]

FRED SCHNEIDER

solo, recorded 1984 and written with COTE

—— with various session people

Reprise Reprise

May 91. (cd/c/lp) *<(7559 26592-2/-4/-1)>* **FRED SCHNEIDER & THE SHAKE SOCIETY** [ ] [ ]
– Monster / Out the concrete / Summer in Hell / Orbit / I'm gonna haunt you / It's time to kiss / This planet's a mess / Wave / Boonga (the New Jersey caveman).
Jun 91. (cd-s) *<19262>* **MONSTER / SUMMER IN HELL** [-] [85]

—— next with **STEVE ALBINI** – producing backing from **DEADLY CUPCAKE, SHADOWY MEN ON A SHADOWY PLANET + SIX FINGER SATELLITE**

WEA WEA

Jun 96. (cd) *<(9362 46215-2)>* **JUST . . . FRED** [ ] [ ]
– Whip / Helicopter / Sugar in my hog / Bulldozer / Coconut / Center of the universe / Radioactive lady eyeball / Lick / Bad dream / Secret sharer / Stroke of genius.

BIG AUDIO DYNAMITE

Formed: London, England . . . 1984 by ex-CLASH guitarist/singer, MICK JONES, who was still under contract with 'C.B.S.' records. Amongst others, namely DAN DONOVAN, LEO WILLIAMS and GREG ROBERTS, he recruited film-maker/friend and non-musician DON LETTS. Although their 1985 debut 45, 'THE BOTTOM LINE', soon became a favourite, it narrowly missed out on a chart placing. However, the follow-up 'E=MC2', gave them a close brush with the Top 10 early the following year, resurrecting sales of the critically acclaimed but commercially disastrous album, 'THIS IS ...'. Mick's unique punk-ish vocals with the band's sound was not unlike a danceable CLASH. Indeed, the band were attempting to fashion a gleaming new hip-hop/electro/alternative rock hybrid, using the latter day CLASH sound as a springboard. The debut set was at least partially successful in this endeavour, standout cuts being the aforementioned 'E=MC2' and its follow-up Top 30 hit, 'MEDICINE SHOW'. A second set, 'NO.10 UPPING STREET' (1986) was even more ambitious, featuring contributions from JONES's former mucker, JOE STRUMMER. The following two years saw the band struggle as JONES survived a near fatal bout of pneumonia, the albums 'TIGHTEN UP VOL.88' (1988) and 'MEGATOP PHOENIX' (1989) brave attempts at further pushing back the boundaries between different genres, mixing up reggae, hip-hop and even country. However, by the end of the decade, the B.A.D. blueprint was being more successfully and inventively interpreted by a new wave of white kids armed with samples, drum machines and an attitude, enter EMF, JESUS JONES etc. The original line-up split at the turn of the decade although JONES recruited new players for BIG AUDIO DYNAMITE II, namely NICK HAWKINS, GARY STONEAGE and CHRIS KAVANAGH. The revamped B.A.D. recorded a further couple of critically and commercially underwhelming albums, 'KOOL-AID' (1990) and 'THE GLOBE' (1991), DJ ZONKA adding his turntable skills to the latter. Though JONES continued working under the B.A.D. name into the 90's, his output is largely confined to a cult following. • **Songwriters:** Mainly JONES and LETTS, with other members contributing. Covers: DUELLING BANJOS (Arthur Smith's theme from 'Deliverance' Soundtrack) / BATTLE OF NEW ORLEANS (trad). • **Trivia:** In 1991, JONES was credited on AZTEC CAMERA's Top 20 UK hit, 'GOOD MORNING BRITAIN'.

Album rating: THIS IS BIG AUDIO DYNAMITE (*7) / No.10 UPPING STREET (*6) / TIGHTEN UP, VOL.'88 (*4) / MEGATOP PHOENIX (*5) / THE GLOBE (*6) / HIGHER POWER (*4) / F-PUNK (*4) / GREATEST HITS compilation (*8)

MICK JONES (b.26 Jun'55) – vocals, guitar (ex-CLASH) / **DON LETTS** – effects, keyboards, vocals / **DAN DONOVAN** – keyboards / **LEO WILLIAMS** – bass / **GREG ROBERTS** – drums

C.B.S. Columbia

Sep 85. (7"/12") *(A/TA 6591)* **THE BOTTOM LINE. / B.A.D.** [ ] [ ]

Nov 85. (lp/c) *(CBS/40 26714)* *<40220>* **THIS IS BIG AUDIO DYNAMITE** [27] [ ]
– Medicine show / Sony / E=MC2 / The bottom line / Sudden impact / Stone Thames / B.A.D. / A party. *(cd-iss. Jun86; CD 26714)* *(re-iss. Nov88 lp/c/cd; 462 999-1/-4/-2)*

Mar 86. (7"/12") *(A/TA 6963)* **E=MC2. / THIS IS BIG AUDIO DYNAMITE** [11] [ ]
(d12"+=) *(QTA 6963)* – The bottom line (US remix) / B.A.D.

May 86. (7") *(A 7181)* **MEDICINE SHOW. / A PARTY** [29] [ ]
(12") *(TA 7181)* – ('A'extended) / ('B'dub).
(d12"+=) *(DTA 7181)* – E=MC2 (remix) / Albert Einstein meets the human beatbox.

Oct 86. (7") *(650147-7)* **C'MON EVERY BEATBOX. / BEDROCK CITY** [51] [ ]
(12"+=) *(650147-8)* – Beatbox's at dawn.
(with free one-sided-12"++=) *(XPR 1320)* – The bottom line (Rick Rubin remix).

Oct 86. (lp/c/cd) *(450137-1/-4/-2)* *<40445>* **No.10 UPPING STREET** [11] [ ]
– C'mon every beatbox / Beyond the pale / Limbo the law / Sambadrome / V thirteen / Ticket / Hollywood boulevard / Dial a hitman / Sightsee M.C! *(c+=/cd+=)* – Ice cool killer (dial a hitman-instrumental) / The big V (V thirteen – instrumental). *(re-iss. Oct89 lp/c; 463398-1/-4)*

Feb 87. (7") *(BAD 2)* **V THIRTEEN. / HOLLYWOOD BOULEVARD** [49] [ ]
(12"+=) *(BADT 2)* – ('B'club).

Jul 87. (12"m) *(BAADT 3)* **SIGHTSEE MC! (radio cut) / ANOTHER ONE RIDES THE BUS / SIGHTSEE MC! / SIGHTSEE – WEST LONDON** [ ] [–]

May 88. (7"/ext-12") *(BAAD/+T 4)* **JUST PLAY MUSIC. / MUCH WORSE** [51] [ ]
(12"+=/cd-s++) *(BAADQTA/CDBAAD 4)* – ('A'remix).

Jun 88. (lp/c/cd) *(461199-1/-4/-2)* *<44074>* **TIGHTEN UP VOL.'88** [33] [ ]
– Rock non stop (all night long) / Other 99 / Funny names / Applecart / Esquerita / Champagne / Mr. Walker said / The battle of All Saints Road, incorporating:- Battle of New Orleans – Duelling banjos / Hip neck and thigh / 2000 shoes / Tighten up vol.88 / Just play music. *(re-iss. Oct94 on 'Columbia' cd/c; 461199-2/-4)*

Jul 88. (7"/7"box) *(BAAD/+B 5)* **OTHER 99. / WHAT HAPPENED TO EDDIE?** [ ] [ ]
(12"/cd-s) *(BAADT/CDBAAD 5)* – ('A'extended) / Just play music (club mix).

Sep 89. (lp/c/cd) *(465790-1/-4/-2)* *<45212>* **MEGATOP PHOENIX** [26] [85]
– Start / Rewind / All mink and no manners / Union, Jack / Contact / Dragon town / Baby don't apologise / Is yours working yet? / Around the girls in 80 ways / James Brown / Everybody needs a holiday / Mick's a hippie burning / House arrest / The green lady / London Bridge / Stalag 123 / End.

Oct 89. (7") *(BAAD 6)* **CONTACT. / IN FULL EFFECT** [ ] [ ]
(12"+=/cd-s+=) *(BAADT/CDBAAD 6)* – Who beats / If I were John Carpenter.

BIG AUDIO DYNAMITE II

— were formed by **JONES + DONOVAN** (latter left mid'90) **NICK HAWKINS** (b. 3 Feb'65, Luton, England) – guitar / **GARY STONAGE** (b.24 Nov'62, Southampton, England) – bass / **CHRIS KAVANAGH** (b. 4 Jun'64, Woolwich, England) – drums (ex-SIGUE SIGUE SPUTNIK)all repl. others who formed SCREAMING TARGET in 1991

Oct 90. (cd/c/lp) *(467466-2/-4/-1)* **KOOL-AID** [55] [–]
– Change of atmosphere / Can't wait / Kickin' in / Innocent child / On one / Kool-aid / In my dreams / When the time comes.

Nov 90. (cd-s) *<74707>* **KOOL-AID EP** [–] [ ]

— added **DJ ZONKA** (b. MICHAEL CUSTANCE, 4 Jul'62) – DJ

Columbia Columbia

Jul 91. (cd/c/lp) *(467706-2/-4/-1)* *<46147>* **THE GLOBE** [63] [72]
– Rush / Can't wait (live) / I don't know / The globe / Innocent child / Green grass / Kool-aid / In my dreams / When the time comes / The tea party.

Jul 91. (7") *(657588-7)* *<74149>* **THE GLOBE (remix). / CITY LIGHTS** [ ] Jan92 [76]
('A'-Danny Rampling remix-12"+=) *(657588-6)* – ('A'dub mix) / ('A'instrumental) / ('A'-Orb ambient mix).
(cd-s+=) *(657588-2)* – ('A'-Danny Rampling dub).

Nov 91. (7"/c-s) *(657640-7/-4)* *<73987>* **RUSH. / (A3 version)** [ ] Sep91 [32]
(cd-s+=) *(657640-2)* – City lights (full version).
(12") *(657640-6)* – ('A'side) / ('A'-3 other mixes).
(above A-side was issued Feb'91 on other side of the CLASH single, 'Should I Stay Or Should I Go')

BIG AUDIO

— added **ANDRE SHAPPS** – keyboards

Nov 94. (c-s) *(661018-4)* **LOOKING FOR A SONG / MODERN STONEAGE BLUES** [68] [ ]
(12"+=/cd-s+=) *(661018-6/-2)* – ('A'-Zonka-Shapps early mix) / ('A'-Zonka-Shapps remix).
(cd-s) *(661018-5)* – ('A'extended) / ('A'-Zonka-Shapps Adventures In Space mix) / Medicine show (live) / Rush (live).

Nov 94. (cd/c/d-lp) *(477239-2/-4/-1)* *<53827>* **HIGHER POWER** [ ] [ ]
– Got to wake up / Harrow Road / Looking for a song / Some people / Slender Loris / Modern stoneage blues / Melancholy maybe / Over the rise / Why is it? / Moon / Lucan / Light up my life / Hope.

BIG AUDIO DYNAMITE

Radioactive not iss.

Jun 95. (c-s) *(RAXC 15)* **I TURNED OUT A PUNK / WHAT ABOUT LOVE** [ ] [–]
(cd-s+=) *(RAXTD 15)* – ('A'-Live fast, live fast mix).
(12") *(RAXT 15)* – ('A'side) / (A'-Live fast mix) / ('A'-Live fast instrumental) / ('A'-Feelin' lucky mix).

Jun 95. (cd/c) *(RAD/RAC 11280)* **F-PUNK** [ ] [–]
– I turned out a punk / Vitamin C / Psycho wing / Push those blues away / Gonna try / It's a jungle out there / Got to set her free / Get it all from my TV / Singapore / I can't go on like this / What about love?

— JONES and Co split soon after above

– compilations, etc. –

Nov 88. (d-cd) *C.B.S.; (CDBAD 241)* **THIS IS BIG AUDIO DYNAMITE / No.10 UPPING STREET** [ ] [–]

Sep 95. (cd/c) *Columbia; (481133-2/-4)* **PLANET B.A.D.** [ ] [–]
– The bottom line / E=MC2 / Medicine show / C'mon every beatbox / V thirteen / Sightsee MC! / Just play music / Other 99 / Contact / Free / Rush / The globe / Looking for a song / Harrow road (ska mix) / I turned out a punk.

BIG BLACK

Formed: Evanston, Illinois, USA ... 1982 by mainman STEVE ALBINI (vocals/guitar). The first official release, 'LUNGS' appeared later that year on local independent label, 'Ruthless', a six-track drum-machine driven EP that announced ALBINI's intent to take punk/hardcore into uncharted territory. Now with an expanded line-up numbering SANTIAGO DURANGO on guitar and JEFF PEZZATI on bass, the BIG BLACK trio unleashed two more 12"ep's/mini-lp's in the mid 80's, 'BULLDOZER' (1983) and 'RACER X' (1985), prior to the seminal 'IL DUCE' single in '86. Replacing PEZZATI with DAVE RILEY (aka LOVERING), they created a minor hardcore classic in 'ATOMIZER' (1986), its bleak examinations of small-town American despair a theme which would be echoed countless times by their grunge/industrial successors. With DURANGO off to study law, MERVIN BELLI came in for the inflammatory titled, 'SONGS ABOUT *!?KING', BIG BLACK giving their all on an album which they knew would be their last. However, they did bow out in uncharacteristic style with a double A-sided 45 covering Cheap Trick's 'HE'S A WHORE' and Kraftwerk's 'THE MODEL'. Taking his twisted vision to its warped conclusion, ALBINI formed the controversially named RAPEMAN with two former SCRATCH ACID players, DAVID WM. SIMS and REY

WASHAM. It wasn't just the name that provoked outrage, tracks such as 'HATED CHINEE', 'SUPERPUSSY' and 'KIM GORDON'S PANTIES' causing a fuss which possibly contributed to ALBINI abandoning the operation early in '89. Having already turned in classic productions for the likes of The PIXIES ('Surfer Rosa'), ALBINI, along with BUTCH VIG became one of the highest profile and most respected/hard working figures of the grunge era (credits include NIRVANA, TAD, PJ HARVEY, etc). ALBINI's other side project, SHELLAC, was first conceived in 1992 along with drummer TODD TRAINER although it only took vinyl form after BOB WESTON began working for STEVE in his Chicago studio. A sporadic string of singles ('URANUS', 'THE ADMIRAL' and 'THE RUDE GESTURE: A PICTORIAL HISTORY') emerged on 'Touch & Go', suggesting a natural progression from BIG BLACK in terms of blackboard-scraping guitar, painfully sardonic lyrics and general sonic terrorism. A debut album, 'AT ACTION PARK', appeared in late '94 although given ALBINI's hectic schedule it'd be a further four years before the slightly disappointing 'TERRAFORM' (1998) hit the shelves. After further singles, haphazard live appearances and the obligatory Peel Session, ALBINI & Co emerged blinking into the new millennium with '1000 HURTS' (2000). As raw, contrary and defiantly unconventional as ever, the record lurched along in the by now well established SHELLAC mould; unlikely to win over new fans but a rich source of perverse treats for diehards. • **Songwriters:** ALBINI and group compositions except; HEARTBEAT (Wire) / REMA REMA (Rema Rema) / Rapeman: JUST GOT PAID (ZZ Top).

Album rating: RACER-X mini (*5) / ATOMIZER (*7) / SONGS ABOUT *!?KING (*8) / PIGPILE live compilation (*7) / Rapeman: TWO NUNS AND A BLACK MULE (*7) / Shellac: AT ACTION PARK (*6) / TERRAFORM (*7) / 1000 HURTS (*8)

STEVE ALBINI – vocals, guitar

not iss. Ruthless

Nov 82. (12"ep) <RRBB 02> **LUNGS**
– Steelworker / Live in a hole / Dead Billy / I can be killed / Crack / R.I.P. *(UK-iss.Nov92 on 'Touch & Go'; TG 89)*

— added **SANTIAGO DURANGO** – guitar (ex-NAKED RAYGUN, ex-SILVER ABUSE) / **JEFF PEZZATI** – bass (ex-NAKED RAYGUN) / + on session 4th member **PAT BYRNE** – drums

Nov 83. (12"ep) <RRBB 07> **BULLDOZER**
– Cables / Pigeon kill / I'm a mess / Texas / Seth / Jump the climb. *(UK-iss.Nov92 on 'Touch & Go'; TG 90)*

Homestead Homestead

Apr 85. (m-lp) <(HMS 007)> **RACER-X** 1984
– Racer-x / Shotgun / The ugly American / Deep six / Sleep! / Big payback. *(re-iss. Nov92 on 'Touch & Go'; TG 91)*

Sep 86. (7") *(HMS 042)* **IL DUCE. / BIG MONEY** 1985
(re-iss. Nov92 on 'Touch & Go'; TG 96)

— **DAVE RILEY** (aka LOVERING) – bass (ex-SAVAGE BELIEFS) repl. PEZZATI / drum machine replaced BYRNE

Sep 86. (lp) <(HMS 43)> **ATOMIZER**
– Jordan, Minnesota / Passing complexion / Big money / Kerosene / Bad houses / Kerosene / Fists of love / Stinking drunk / Bazooka Joe / Strange things. *(re-iss. Nov86 on 'Blast First'; BFFP 11) (re-iss. Nov92 on 'Touch & Go' lp/cd; TG 93/+CD)*

Blast First Touch&Go

Jun 87. (12"ep/c-ep) *(BFFP 14/+C)* <TG 20> **HEADACHE** 1986
– My disco / Grinder / Ready men / Pete, king of all detectives.
(free 7"w.a./tracks on c-ep) *(TG 21)* – HEARTBEAT. / THINGS TO DO TODAY / I CAN'T BELIEVE *(UK re-iss. Nov92 on 'Touch & Go'; TG 20)*

— **MELVYN BELLI** – guitar; repl. DURANGO

Jul 87. (lp/c/cd) *(BFFP 19/+C/CD)* <TG 24/+C/CD> **SONGS ABOUT *!?KING**
– The power of independent trucking / The model / Bad penny / El doper / Precious thing / Columbian neck-tie / Kitty empire / Ergot / Kashmir S. Pulasiday / Fish fry / Pavement saw / Tiny, the king of the Jews / Bombastic intro. *(re-iss. Nov92 on 'Touch & Go' lp/cd +=; TG 24/+CD)* – He's A Whore.

Aug 87. (7") *(BFFP 24)* <TG 23> **HE'S A WHORE. / THE MODEL**
(re-iss. Nov92 on 'Touch & Go'; TG 23)

— Disbanded in 1988.

– compilations, etc. –

Mar 87. (lp) *Homestead; (HMS 044)* **THE HAMMER PARTY**
– (LUNGS + BULLDOZER) *(re-iss. Nov92 on 'Touch & Go' lp/cd +=; TG 92/+CD)* – RACER-X

Jun 87. (lp) *Not 2; (BUT 1)* **SOUND OF IMPACT (live bootleg)**
(re-iss. 1990)

Jan 88. (cd) *Blast First; (BFFP 23)* **THE RICH MAN'S EIGHT TRACK TAPE**
– (ATOMIZER + HEADACHE + HEARTBEAT) *(re-iss. Nov92 on 'Touch & Go'; TG 94CD)*

Oct 89. (lp/c/cd) *Blast First; (BFFP 49/+C/CD)* **BIG BLACK LIVE (live)**

Oct 92. (lp/cd) *Touch & Go;* <*(TG 81/+CD)*> **PIGPILE (live)**

RAPEMAN

— were formed by **ALBINI** with **DAVID WM. SIMS** – bass / **REY WASHAM** – drums (both ex-SCRATCH ACID, latter ex-BIG BOYS)

not iss. Fierce

1988. (7") <*none*> **HATED CHINEE. / MARMOSET**

Blast First Touch & Go

Nov 88. (12"ep) *(BFFP 27)* <*TG 34*> **BUDD (live) / SUPERPUSSY (live). / LOG BASS (live) / DUTCH COURAGE**

Dec 88. (lp/c/cd) *(BFFP 33/+C/CD)* <*TG 36/+C/CD*> **TWO NUNS AND BLACK MULE**
– Steak and black onions / Monobrow / Up beat / Cotition ignition mission / Kim Gordon's panties / Hated Chinee / Radar love wizard / Marmoset / Just got paid / Trouser minnow. *(cd+=)* – Budd / Superpussy / Log brass / Dutch courage.

Sub Pop Sub Pop

Aug 89. (7",7"clear) <*(SP 40)*> **INKI'S BUTT CRACK. / SONG NUMBER ONE**

— Had to split in Feb'89 due to the backlash against group name. SIMS returned to Austin, where he re-united with ex-SCRATCH ACID members to form JESUS LIZARD. They were produced by ALBINI who continued as a producer, noteably for others The PIXIES, The BREEDERS, NIRVANA, WEDDING PRESENT. ALBINI formed below in '93.

SHELLAC

STEVE ALBINI – guitar, vocals / **BOB WESTON** – bass (ex-VOLCANO SONS) / **TODD TRAINER** – drums (ex-RIFLE SPORT, etc)

Touch & Go Touch & Go

1993. (7"ep) <*TG 123*> **THE RUDE GESTURE: A PICTORIAL HISTORY EP**
– The guy who invented fire / Rambler song / Billiard player song.

1993. (7"ep) <*TG 124*> **URANUS EP**
– Doris / Wingwalker.

1994. (7"ep) **THE BIRD IS THE MOST POPULAR FINGER**
– XVI (aka Pull the cup) / The admiral.
(above issued on 'Drag City')

Oct 94. (lp/c/cd) <*(TG 141/+C/CD)*> **AT ACTION PARK** Sep94
– My black ass / Pull the cup / The admiral / Crow / Song of the minerals / A minute / The idea of north / Dog and pony show / Boche's dick / Il porno star.

1997. (cd) **THE FUTURIST** (10 movements)

May 98. (lp/cd) <*(TG 200/+CD)*> **TERRAFORM** Feb98
– Didn't we deserve a look at you the way you really are / This is a picture / Disgrace / Mouthpiece / Canada / Rush job / House full of garbage / Copper.

Jul 00. (lp/cd) <*(TG 211/+CD)*> **1000 HURTS**
– Prayer to God / Squirrel song / Mama Gina / Q.R.L. / Ghosts / Song against itself / Canaveral / New number order / Shoe song / Watch song.

BIG BROTHER & THE HOLDING CO.

Formed: San Francisco, California, USA . . . late '65 by SAM ANDREW, PETER ALBIN, DAVE ESKERSON and CHUCK JONES. Shortly after, the latter two were replaced by JAMES GURLEY and DAVID GETZ respectively. Through promoter CHET HELMS, they enlisted Texan JANIS JOPLIN, who had just turned down an opportunity to join The 13th FLOOR EVEVATORS. Signing to 'Mainstream' records in 1967, they turned in an excellent Monterey festival performance just prior to releasing their eponymous debut album. However, their blistering set caught the attention of 'Columbia', who subsequently released the 'CHEAP THRILLS' album, which hit No.1 in the States for 7 weeks in the fall of '68. This roughshod and at times ramshackle affair nevertheless captured the tremendous vocal talent of JOPLIN on soul-wrenching numbers such as 'PIECE OF MY HEART' (a Top 20 hit) and 'BALL AND CHAIN' (blues rock for acid heads). Her star rating outstripped her backing band at a rate of knots, and it was inevitable that she would take off for a solo career (see own entry). This all but killed any further success for BIG BROTHER, although they continued, releasing two further lacklustre albums in the early 70's. In 1987 however, GETZ, ANDREW, GURLEY and ALBIN recruited new singer MICHELLE BASTIAN for a series of low-key gigs. • **Note:** Nothing whatsoever to do with 80's outfit BIG BROTHER, who released 12" 'Adventures In Success'.

Album rating: BIG BROTHER AND THE HOLDING CO. (*5) / CHEAP THRILLS (*8) / BE A BROTHER (*3) / HOW HARD IT IS (*3) / CHEAPER THRILLS posthumous live (*4)

SAM ANDREW (b.18 Dec'41, Taft, California) – guitar, vocals / **PETE ALBIN** (b. 6 Jun'44) – bass, vocals / **JAMES GURLEY** (b.22 Dec'39, Detroit, Mich.) – guitar repl. DAVE ESKERSON (left Nov65) / **DAVID GETZ** (b.24 Jan'40, Brooklyn, N.Y.) – drums repl. CHUCK JONES (left Feb66) also on occasion / **ED BOGAS** – violin (left before Summer'66, to NEW RIDERS OF THE PURPLE SAGE)

— (Jun'66) added **JANIS JOPLIN** (b.19 Jan'43, Port Arthur, Texas) – vocals

Fontana / Mainstream

Jul 67. (7") <657> **BLIND MAN. / ALL IS LONELINESS** [–] [ ]

Sep 67. (7") <662> **DOWN ON ME. / CALL ON ME** [–] [ ]
<hit US No.43 in Aug'68> (UK-iss.Sep68 on 'London'; HLT 10226)

Nov 67. (lp; stereo/mono) *(S+/TL 5457)* <6099> **BIG BROTHER & THE HOLDING COMPANY** [ ] Aug67 [60]
– Bye bye baby / Easy rider / Intruder / Light is faster than sound / Call on me / Women is losers / Blind man / Down on me / Caterpillar / All is loneliness. *(re-iss. 1969 on 'London' mono/stereo; HA-T/SH-T 8377) <US re-iss. May71 on 'Columbia'; 30631>* – Coo Coo / The last mile. *(cd-iss. Apr93 as 'FIRST ALBUM' on 'Sony Europe';)*

Nov 67. (7") <666> **BYE BYE BABY. / INTRUDER** [–] [ ]

Dec 67. (7") *(TF 881)* **BYE BYE BABY. / ALL IS LONELINESS** [ ] [–]

Feb 68. (7") <675> **WOMEN IS LOSERS. / LIGHT IS FASTER THAN SOUND** [–] [ ]

C.B.S. / Columbia

Aug 68. (7") *(CBS 3683)* <44626> **PIECE OF MY HEART. / TURTLE BLUES** [ ] [12]

Sep 68. (lp) *(CBS 63392)* <PC 9700> **CHEAP THRILLS** [ ] Aug68 [1]
– Combination of the two / I need a man to love / Summertime / Piece of my heart / Turtle blues / O sweet Mary / Ball and chain. *<US re-iss. Mar81; > (cd-iss. Jan91 & Jun92 on 'Columbia'; CD 32004)*

— Folded late 1968. JANIS JOPLIN went solo, taking SAM ANDREW. In Aug69 GETZ and ALBIN re-formed BIG BROTHER & THE HOLDING COMPANY with **NICK GRAVENITES** – vocals / **MIKE PRENDERGAST** – guitar / **TED ASHBURTON** – piano

— soon split again, GETZ was also in NU BUGALOO EXPRESS.

— **GETZ, GURLEY, ALBIN, SAM ANDREW + NICK GRAVENITES** – vocals re-grouped **BIG BROTHER & THE HOLDING COMPANY** with **KATHI McDONALD** – vocals / **MIKE FINNEGAN** – keyboards / **DAVID SCHALLOCK** – guitar (both ex-NU BUGALOO EXPRESS)

Jan 71. (lp) *(CBS 64118)* <PC 30222> **BE A BROTHER** [ ] Nov70 [ ]
– Keep on / Joseph's coat / Home on the strange / Someday / Heartache people / Sunshine baby / Mr. Natural / Funkie Jim / I'll change your flat tire Merle / Be a brother. *<(cd-iss. Jul02 on 'Acadia'; ACA 8026)>*

Jan 71. (7") <45284> **KEEP ON. / HOME ON THE STRANGE** [–] [ ]

Aug 71. (lp) <KC 30738> **HOW HARD IT IS** [–] [ ]
– How hard it is / You've been talkin' 'bout me, baby / House on fire / Black widow spider / Last band on side one / Nu Boogaloo jam / Maui / Shine on / Buried alive in the blues / Promise her anything but give her Arpeggio. *<(cd-iss. Jul02 on 'Acacia'; ACA 8028)>*

Sep 71. (7") <45502> **NU BOOGALOO JAM. / BLACK WIDOW SPIDER** [–] [ ]

— Split Feb'72. ALBIN rejoined COUNTRY JOE (McDONALD) & THE FISH. He and GETZ were part of them in 1969. FINNEGAN played live with STEPHEN STILLS etc. GRAVENITES tried to revitalise ELECTRIC FLAG.

– compilations, etc. –

Nov 68. (7") *Mainstream;* <678> **COO COO. / THE LAST MILE** [–] [84]

Jan 84. (lp) *Edsel; (ED 135)* **CHEAPER THRILLS** (live 26th July '66) [ ] [–]
(cd-iss. Sep90; EDCD 135)

Apr 86. (lp) *Edsel; (ED 170)* **JOSEPH'S COAT** (best of 71's two albums) [ ] [–]

BIG COUNTRY

Formed: Dunfermline, Scotland . . . Autumn 1981 by STUART ADAMSON and BRUCE WATSON, following the former's departure from The SKIDS. They recruited brothers PETER (keyboards) and ALAN WISHART (bass) plus CLIVE PARKER (drums, ex-SPIZZ . . .) although by early 1982, the latter three had been replaced by the lynchpin rhythm section of MARK BRZEZICKI and TONY BUTLER. After they turned down a contract with 'Ensign', the band signed to 'Mercury-Phonogram' in Spring '82, soon moving to London where they began work on a debut set, 'THE CROSSING' (1983). Previewed by the classic singles, 'FIELDS OF FIRE' & 'IN A BIG COUNTRY', the album traversed the charts in both Britain and America, introducing the famous (and, in certain quarters, much maligned) 'bagpipe' twin-guitar sound. Very much in the Celtic, stir-the-blood tradition, 'THE CROSSING' was a call to arms in a posturing, terminally pretentious early 80's music scene, its expansive, soaring sound transporting even the most smog-bound city dweller to the Scottish highlands. ADAMSON somehow managed to sing from the heart without sounding earnest, the chiming lament, 'CHANCE', displaying the raw emotive power this band once harnassed. Despite their straightforward approach, BIG COUNTRY were initially lauded by the press, even making something of a fashion statement with their trademark check shirts. With follow-up set, 'STEELTOWN' (1984), ADAMSON's voice of conscience examined Scottish industrial and economic decay; despite the subject matter, tracks such as the rousing 'FLAME OF THE WEST' burned with hope and optimism. Though the record entered the British chart at No.1, its less immediate appeal failed to translate into further Stateside success. This is where BIG COUNTRY began to lose their vision; although subsequent releases like 'THE SEER' (1986) and 'PEACE IN OUR TIME' (1988) continued to chart high and feature some inspired moments, creatively the band were merely treading water. The fact that the track 'ONE GREAT THING' was used on a Tennent's lager advert only seemed to underline its more pedestrian qualities. Despite periods where the band came perilously close to splitting, BIG COUNTRY survived into the 90's, their albums never breaking the mould but eagerly received by the band's fiercely partisan fans. ADAMSON had always addressed social/political issues in a challenging and often sympathetic fashion, the band releasing a 1995 EP, 'NON!', in protest at France's nuclear testing programme. Signed to 'Transatlantic', however, the poor commercial showing of the band's last two albums, 'WHY THE LONG FACE?' (1995) and 'ECLECTIC' (1996), suggested that their appeal was waning. Late in 1999, and thought to be because of his alcohol problems, STUART moved to Nashville, Tennessee. There, he formed The RAPHAELS, a roots country-orientated outfit who released one set, 'SUPERNATURAL' (2001). Sadly, this was to be ADAMSON's last outing. For nearly two months the man went AWOL and was subsequently found dead in a Hawaiian hotel room on the 16th of December, 2001. Scotland, and indeed the world of music, would mourn the death of such an enigmatic figure. • **Songwriters:** Mostly ADAMSON / WATSON, except TRACKS OF MY TEARS (Smokey Robinson & The Miracles) / HONKY TONK WOMAN + RUBY TUESDAY (Rolling Stones) / AULD LANG SYNE (trad.) / ROCKIN' IN THE FREE WORLD (Neil Young) / FLY LIKE AN EAGLE (Steve Miller) / BLACK SKINNED BLUE EYED BOYS (Equals / Eddy Grant) / OH WELL (Fleetwood Mac) / (DON'T FEAR) THE REAPER (Blue Oyster Cult) / WOODSTOCK + BIG YELLOW TAXI (Joni Mitchell) / CRACKED ACTOR (David Bowie) / PARANOID (Black Sabbath) / SUMMERTIME (Gershwin – Du Bose Heyward) / ELEANOR RIGBY (Beatles) / SLING IT (Steve Harley) / I'M ON FIRE (Bruce Springsteen) / VICIOUS (Lou Reed) / I'M EIGHTEEN (Alice Cooper) / ON THE ROAD AGAIN (Canned Heat).

Album rating: THE CROSSING (*8) / STEELTOWN (*7) / THE SEER (*6) / PEACE IN OUR TIME (*4) / NO PLACE LIKE HOME (*5) / THE BUFFALO SKINNERS (*4) / WHY THE LONG FACE? (*4) / THROUGH A BIG COUNTRY – GREATEST HITS compilation (**8**) / ECLECTIC (*4) / DRIVING TO DAMASCUS (*4) / COME UP SCREAMING (*6)

STUART ADAMSON (b.11 Apr'58, Manchester, England) – vocals, lead guitar, synthesizer (ex-SKIDS) / **BRUCE WATSON** (b.11 Mar'61, Timmins, Ontario, Canada) – guitar (ex-DELINX) / **TONY BUTLER** (b. 3 Feb'57, London, England) – bass (ex-ON THE AIR) / **MARK BRZEZICKI** (b.21 Jun'57, Slough, England) – drums (ex-ON THE AIR); the latter two repl. Scots-born brothers PETER and ALAN WISHART

Mercury Mercury

Sep 82. (7") *(COUNT 1)* **HARVEST HOME. / BALCONY**
(12"+=)(12"clear+=) *(COUNT 12)(COUNX 1)* – Flag of nations (swimming).

Feb 83. (7") *(COUNT 2)* *<811450>* **FIELDS OF FIRE. / ANGLE PARK** 10 Jan84 52
(12"+=/12"clear+=) *(COUN T/X 2-12)* – ('A'-alternative mix).
(7"sha-pic-d+=) *(COUP 2)* – Harvest home.

May 83. (7") *(COUNT 3)* *<814467>* **IN A BIG COUNTRY. / ALL OF US** 17 Sep83 17
(12"+=) *(COUNT 3-12)* – ('A'-pure mix).
(12"++=) *(COUNT 313)* – Heart and soul.

Jun 83. (lp/c) *(MERH/+C 27)* *<812870>* **THE CROSSING** 3 Jul83 18
– In a big country / Inwards / Chance / 1,000 stars / The storm / Harvest home / Lost patrol / Close action / Fields of fire / Porrohman. *(c+=)* – (4 remixes). *(re-dist.Mar84 lp/c; MERS/+C 27) (cd-iss. 1986; 812 870-2)*

Aug 83. (7") *(COUNT 4)* **CHANCE. / TRACKS OF MY TEARS (live)** 9
(ext.12"+=)(ext.12"pic-d+=) *(COUNT 4-12)(COUP 4)* – The crossing.

Jan 84. (7") *(COUNT 5)* *<818834>* **WONDERLAND. / GIANT** 8 86
(12"+=) *(COUNT 5-12)* – ('A'extended).
(12"clear+=) *(COUNX 5)* – Lost patrol (live).
(d7"+=) *(COUNT 5-5)* – Lost patrol (live – parts one & two).

Apr 84 (m-lp) *<818835>* **WONDERLAND** – 65
– Wonderland / Angle park / The crossing / All fall together.

Sep 84. (7"/7"w-poster) *(MER/+P 175)* **EAST OF EDEN. / PRAIRIE ROSE.** 17
(12"+=/12"w-poster+=) *(MERX/+P 175)* – ('A'extended).

Oct 84. (lp/c) *(MERH/+C 49)* *<822831>* **STEELTOWN** 1 70
– Flame of the west / East of Eden / Steeltown / Where the rose is sown / Come back to me / Tall ships go / Girl with grey eyes / Rain dance / The great divide / Just a shadow. *(cd-iss. 1986; 822 831-2) (re-iss. May93 on 'Spectrum' cd/c;)*

Nov 84. (7") *(MER 185)* **WHERE THE ROSE IS SOWN. / BELIEF IN THE SMALL MAN** 29
(12"+=) *(MERX 185)* – ('A'extended remix) / Bass dance.
(d7"+=) *(MERD 185)* – Wonderland (live) / In a big country (live) / Auld Lang Syne (live).

Jan 85. (7") *(BCO 8)* **JUST A SHADOW. / WINTER SKY** 26
(12"+=) *(BCO 8-12)* – ('A'extended remix).

Apr 86. (7"/7"sha-pic-d) *(BIGC/+P 1)* **LOOK AWAY. / RESTLESS NATIVES** 7
(d7"+=) *(BIGCD 1)* – Margo's theme / Highland scenery.
(ext.12"+=) *(BIGCX 1-1)* – ('A'-Outlaw mix).
(12") *(BIG CX 1)* – ('A'extended) / Restless natives (soundtrack part one).

Jun 86. (7") *(BIGC 2)* **THE TEACHER. / HOME CAME THE ANGELS** 28
(12") *(BIGCX 2)* – ('A'-Mystery mix) / Restless natives (soundtrack part two).

Jul 86. (lp/c/cd) *(MERH/+C 87)(826 844-2)* *<826 844>* **THE SEER** 2 59
– Look away / The seer / The teacher / I walk the hill / Eiledon / One great thing / Hold the heart / Remembrance day / The red fox / The sailor. *(re-iss. cd Aug94 on 'Vertigo';)*

Sep 86. (7"/s7")('A'-Boston mix-12") *(BIGC/+G 3)(BIGCX 3-3)* **ONE GREAT THING. / SONG OF THE SOUTH** 19
(d7"+=) *(BIGCD 3)* – Porrohman (live) / Chance (live).
(d7"+=) *(BIGCE 3)* – Wonderland (live) / Inwards (live).
('A'-Big Baad Country mix.c-s+=) *(BIGCM 3)* – In a big country (pure mix) / Fields of fire (live).
('A'-Big Baad Country mix.12"+=) *(BIGCR 3)* – Look away (outlaw mix).

Nov 86. (7"/remix-12") *(BIGC/+X 4)* **HOLD THE HEART. / HONKY TONK WOMAN (live)** 55
(d12"+=) *(BIGCX 4-4)* – (interview parts one & two).

—— added on tour **JOSS PHILIP-GORSE** – keyboards

Mercury Reprise

Aug 88. (7") *(BIGC 5)* **KING OF EMOTION. / THE TRAVELLERS** 16
(12"+=) *(BIGC 5-12)* – Starred and Crossed.
(cd-s++=) *(BIGCD 5)* – Not waving but drowning.
(c-s+=) *(BIGMC 5)* – Starred and crossed / On the shore.

Sep 88. (7") **KING OF EMOTION. / IN A BIG COUNTRY** –

Sep 88. (lp/c)(cd) *(MERH/+C 130)(836 325-2)* *<25787>* **PEACE IN OUR TIME** 9
– King of emotion / Broken heart (thirteen valleys) / Thousand yard stare / From here to eternity / Everything I need / Peace in our time / Time for leaving / River of hope / In this place / I could be happy here. *(cd+=)* – The travellers.

Oct 88. (7") *(BIGC 6)* **BROKEN HEART (THIRTEEN VALLEYS). / SOAPY SOUTAR STRIKES BACK** 47
(12"+=/12"red+=) *(BIGC/+R 6-12)* – When a drum beats / On the shore.
(cd-s+=) *(BIGCD 6)* – Wonderland (12"mix).
(cd-s+=) *(BIGCDR 6)* – Made in Heaven / When a drum beats.

Jan 89. (7"/s7") *(BIGC/+P 7)* **PEACE IN OUR TIME. / PROMISED LAND** 39
(12"+=) *(BIGC 7-12)* – Over the border / The longest day.
(12"+=) *(BIGCR 7-12)* – In a big country (live) / Chance (live).
(cd-s+=) *(BIGCD 7)* – Chance / The longest day.

—— (Feb'90) **PAT AHERN – drums (ex-DAVE HOWARD SINGERS) repl. BRZEZICKI who joined PRETENDERS**

Apr 90. (7"/c-s) *(BIG C/MC 8)* **SAVE ME. / PASS ME BY** 41
(12"+=) *(BIGC 8-12)* – Dead on arrival.
(cd-s+=) *(BIGCD 8)* – World on fire.
(cd-s+=) *(BIGCD 8-12)* – Wonderland (live) / Thousand yard stare (live).

May 90. (cd/c/lp) *(846 022-2/-4/-1)* **THROUGH A BIG COUNTRY – GREATEST HITS** (compilation) 2 –
– Save me / In a big country / Fields of fire / Chance / Wonderland / Where the rose is sown / Just a shadow / Look away / King of emotion / East of Eden / One great thing / The teacher / Broken heart (thirteen valleys) / Peace in our time. *(c+=/cd+=)* – Eiledon / The seer / Harvest home. *(re-iss. Feb93 cd/c;)*

Jul 90. (7"/c-s) *(BIG C/MC 9)* **HEART OF THE WORLD. / BLACK SKINNED BLUE EYED BOYS** 50
(12"+=) *(BIGC 9-12)* – Broken heart (thirteen valleys) (acoustic) / Peace in our time (acoustic).
(cd-s+=) *(BIGCD 9)* – Restless Natives.

Vertigo not iss.

Aug 91. (7") *(BIC 1)* **REPUBLICAN PARTY REPTILE. / COMES A TIME / YOU, ME AND THE TRUTH** [37] [–]
(10"ep+=/12"ep+=) *(BIC T/X 1)* – Comes a time.
(cd-ep) *(BIGCD 1)* – ('A'side) / Freedom song / Kiss the girl goodbye / I'm only waiting.

Sep 91. (cd/c/lp) *(510230-2/-4/-1)* **NO PLACE LIKE HOME** [28] [–]
– We're not in Kansas / Republican party reptile / Dynamic lady / Keep on dreaming / Beautiful people / The hostage speaks / Beat the Devil / Heap of faith / Ships / Into the fire. *(cd+=)* – You, me and the truth / Comes a time. *(re-iss. Aug94; same)*

Oct 91. (7"/c-s) *(BIC/+C 2)* **BEAUTIFUL PEOPLE. / RETURN OF THE TWO HEADED KING** [72] [–]
(12"pic-d+=) *(BICX 2)* – Fly like an eagle.
(cd-s+=) *(BICCD 2)* – Rockin' in the free world (live).

—— **ADAMSON, BUTLER + WATSON** were joined by session men **SIMON PHILLIPS** – drums / **COLIN BERWICK** – keyboards

Compulsion Fox-RCA

Mar 93. (c-s/7") *(TC+/PULSS 4)* **ALONE. / NEVER TAKE YOUR PLACE** [24] [ ]
(12"pic-d+=) *(12PULSS 4)* – Winter sky / Look away.
(cd-s) *(CDPULSS 4)* – ('A'side) / Chance / Rockin' in the free world / Eastworld.

Mar 93. (cd/c/lp) *(CD/TC+/NOIS 2)* *<66294>* **THE BUFFALO SKINNERS** [25] Sep93 [ ]
– Alone / Seven waves / What are you working for / The one I love / Long way home / The selling of America / We're not in Kansas / Ships / All go together / Winding wind / Pink marshmallow moon / Chester's farm. *(re-iss. Sep94; same) (cd re-iss. May02 on 'EMI Gold'; 321988-2)*

Apr 93. (c-s/7") *(TC+/PULSS 6)* **SHIPS (WHERE WERE YOU). / OH WELL** [29] [ ]
(12"+=/cd-s+=) *(12/CD PULSS 6)* – (Don't fear) The reaper / Woodstock.
(cd-s+=) *(CDXPULSS 6)* – The buffalo skinners / Cracked actor / Paranoid.

Jun 94. (cd/c/lp) *(CD/TC+/NOIS 5)* **WITHOUT THE AID OF A SAFETY NET (live)** [35] [–]
– Harvest home / Peace in our time / Just a shadow / Broken heart (thirteen valleys) / The storm / Chance / Look away / Steeltown / Ships / Wonderland / What are you working for / Long way home / In a big country / Lost patrol. *(cd re-iss. Mar03 on 'Disky'; 76207-2)*

Transatla. Pure

May 95. (c-ep/cd-ep) *(TRAM/TRAX 1009)* **I'M NOT ASHAMED / ONE IN A MILLION (1st visit) / MONDAY TUESDAY GIRL / ('A'edit)** [69] [–]
(cd-ep) *(TRAX 1010)* – ('A'side) / Crazytimes / In a big country / Blue on a green planet.

Jun 95. (cd/c) *(TRA CD/MC/LP 109)* *<2200>* **WHY THE LONG FACE?** [48] [ ]
– You dreamer / Message of love / I'm not ashamed / ail into nothing / Thunder & lightning / Send you / One in a million / God's great mistake / Wild land in my heart / Thank you to the Moon / Far from me to you / Charlotte / Post nuclear talking blues / Blue on a green planet.

Aug 95. (12"ep/cd-ep) *(TRAT/TRAD 1012)* **YOU DREAMER EP** [ ] [–]
– You dreamer / Ice cream smile / Magic in your ice / Bianca.
(cd-ep) *(TRAX 1012)* – ('A'side) / I'm eighteen / Vicious / On the road again.

Nov 95. (cd-ep) *(TRAD 1013)* **NON!** [ ] [–]
– Post nuclear talking blues / Blue on a green planet / God's great mistake / All go together.
above was an action awareness record for Greenpeace.
below featured guests **BOBBY VALENTINO** – violin / **AARON EMERSON** – keyboards / **HOSSAM RAMZY + MOHAMMED TOUFIQ** – percussion / **CAROL LAULA + STEVE HARLEY + KYM MAZELLE** – vocals

Aug 96. (cd/c) *(TRA CD/MC 234)* **ECLECTIC** [41] [–]
– River of hope / King of emotion / Big yellow taxi / The buffalo skinners / Summertime / The night they drove old Dixie down / Eleanor Rigby / Winter sky / Sling it / I'm on fire / Where the rose is sown / Come back to me / Ruby Tuesday.

Track Record not iss.

Aug 99. (10"; BIG COUNTRY featuring EDDI READER) *(TRACK 0004C)* **FRAGILE THING. / I GET HURT / LOSERVILLE** [69] [–]
(cd-s) *(TRACK 0004A)* – (first & third tracks) / Dust on the road.
(cd-s) *(TRACK 0004B)* – (first two tracks) / John Wayne's dream.

Sep 99. (cd/c) *(TRK 1000 CD/CAS)* **DRIVING TO DAMASCUS** [ ] [–]
– Driving to Damascus / Dive in to me / See you / Perfect world / Somebody else / Fragile thing / The president slipped and fell / Devil in the eye / Trouble the waters / Bella / Your spirit to me / Grace. *(special cd+=; TRK 1000CDSP)* – Shattered cross / Too many ghosts.

Nov 99. (c-s) *(TRACK 0005C)* **SEE YOU / PERFECT WORLD** [ ] [–]
(cd-s+=) *(TRACK 0005A)* – This blood's for you.
(cd-s+=) *(TRACK 0005B)* – Camp Smedley's theme.

—— STUART ADAMSON retired for a while – late in '99

Oct 00. (d-cd) *(TRK 1003CD)* **COME UP SCREAMING (live)** [ ] [–]
– Harvest home / King of emotion / Driving to Damascus / John Wayne's dream / The storm / Where the rose is sown / Come back to me / Somebody else / Look away / You dreamer / Your spirit to me / The president slipped and fell / Drive in to me / Lost patrol / 13 valleys inwards / Wonderland / We're not in Kansas / Porroh man / Chance / In a big country / Fields of fire.

– compilations, etc. –

Aug 94. (cd) *Nighttracks; (CDNT 007)* **RADIO 1 SESSIONS** [ ] [–]
Aug 94. (cd) *Legends In Music; (LECD 043)* **BIG COUNTRY** [ ] [–]
Aug 95. (cd) *Spectrum; (550 879-2)* **IN A BIG COUNTRY** [ ] [–]
Oct 95. (cd) *Windsong; (WINCD 075)* **BBC LIVE IN CONCERT (live)** [ ] [–]
Mar 97. (cd) *Disky; (DC 87863-2)* **THE GREATEST HITS LIVE** [ ] [–]
May 00. (cd) *Snapper; (SMMCD 557)* **BRIGHTON ROCK** [ ] [–]
Mar 01. (cd) *Big Country Tracks; (<BCRTRK 001>)* **UNDERCOVER** (cover versions) [ ] May01 [ ]
Apr 01. (cd) *Big Country Tracks; (<BCRTRK 002>)* **RARITIES** [ ] May01 [ ]
Jun 01. (cd) *Big Country Tracks; (BCRTRK 003) / Cleopatra; <71146>* **ONE IN A MILLION** [ ] Jul01 [ ]
Aug 01. (cd) *Big Country Tracks; (<BCRTRK 005>)* **GREATEST 12" HITS VOL.1** [ ] Sep01 [ ]
Oct 01. (cd) *Universal; (E 586314-2)* **UNIVERSAL MASTERS COLLECTION** [ ] [–]
May 02. (d-cd) *Universal TV; (586989-2)* **GREATEST HITS** (BIG COUNTRY & The SKIDS) [71] [–]
Jul 02. (6xcd-s-box) *Track; (<TRKSP 001>)* **SINGLES COLLECTION** [ ] [ ]
Oct 02. (7xcd-s-box) *Track; (<TRKSP 002>)* **SINGLES COLLECTION VOL.2** [ ] [ ]
Jan 03. (cd) *Track; (<BCRTRK 006>)* **RARITIES VOL.3** [ ] [ ]
Mar 03. (cd) *Track; (TRK 1026CD)* **PEACE IN OUR TIME / NO PLACE LIKE HOME** [ ] [–]
Mar 03. (7xcd-s-box) *Track; (<TRKSP 003>)* **SINGLES COLLECTION VOL.3** [ ] [ ]
Jun 03. (7xcd-s-box) *Track; (<TRKSP 004>)* **SINGLES COLLECTION VOL.4** [ ] [ ]
Oct 03. (cd) *Spectrum; (063612-2)* **THE COLLECTION** [ ] [–]

RAPHAELS

ADAMSON plus **MARCUS HUMMON** – acoustic guitar / + others

Track Track

May 01. (cd) *(<TRK 0005CD>)* **SUPERNATURAL** [ ] Aug01 [ ]
– Supernatural / Simple man / Private battlefield / Old country, country / Learning to row / Shattered cross / Toujour aimez / My only crime / Stand up / Too many ghosts / Blue rose / Mexican trout / Life is a church.

—— ADAMSON was to die late 2001

☐ BIG STAR (see under ⇒ BOX TOPS)

☐ BIRTHDAY PARTY (see under ⇒ CAVE, Nick)

☐ BIZZY BONE
(see under ⇒ BONE THUGS-N-HARMONY)

BJORK

Born: BJORK GUDMUNDSDOTTIR, 21 Oct'65, Reykjavik, Iceland. Growing up in a creative communal family and something of a child prodigy, the strikingly unique BJORK enjoyed her first taste of the music business at the age of 11 when she impressed her teachers with her rendition of TINA CHARLES' No.1 'I LOVE TO LOVE', who in turn convinced a local radio station to play it. This led to her recording a self-titled album with many of Iceland's top musicians. It also included other covers; YOUR KISS IS SWEET (hit; Syreeta) / ALFUR UT UR HOL (FOOL ON THE HILL; Beatles) / CHRISTOPHER ROBIN (Melanie) / ALTA MIRA (Edgar Winter). BJORK graduated to her first band EXODUS, and in 1981 aged 14, she instigated another; TAPPI TIKARRASS, which meant 'Cork The Bitch's Arse'. In the next two years, the X-RAY SPEX-type outfit completed two albums 'BITID FAST I VITID' and 'MIRANDA'. She subsequently worked with KILLING JOKE theorists, JAZ COLEMAN and YOUTH, who had both fled to the frozen north in fear of a supposed impending apocalypse. In the interim, she guested for free-form jazz-rock duo STIFGRIM, who comprised of comedian/vocalist KRISTINN JON GUDMUNDSSON and guitarist STEINN SKAPTASON. They went down in the record books as one of over a hundred bands who took part in the longest ever continuous live performances (seven weeks!). She then spent two summer seasons playing synthesizer in a covers band named, CACTUS. In 1984, she teamed up with friends EINAR ORN BENEDIKTSSON (he of the legendary, erm, rapping "talent") and SIGTRYGGUR 'SIGGI' BALDERSSON to form KUKL ('Sorcery'), this FALL/BANSHEES influenced lot finding their way into Britain's earlobes (via the 'Crass' label) with two albums 'THE EYE' and 'HOLIDAYS IN EUROPE'. During this mid 80's period, she was also part of ROKHA ROKHA DRUM (as a drummer! and voice). They included lead vocalist JOHNNY TRIUMPH (b. SJON), who collaborated with BJORK's most famous and productive outfit The SUGARCUBES. Hooking up with BRAGI OLAFSSON, THOR ELDON (the father of BJORK's son, Sindri) and EINAR MELLAX, BJORK and Co. formed Iceland's first (and so far only) internationally renowned band. Signed to Derek Birkett's 'One Little Indian', the group had the critics frothing with their debut single, the sublime 'BIRTHDAY'. Like pop music from another planet, the song's reverberating bassline, celestial brass and ethereal production conspired to make this the aural equivalent of a particularly sensual massage. The track also introduced BJORK's inimitable vocals, a perversely melodic combination of wide-eyed child and Icelandic banshee. A further two slices of avant-garde strangeness, 'COLD SWEAT' and 'DEUS' followed into the UK Top 75 before a debut album, 'LIFE'S TOO GOOD', crashed into the Top 20 in Spring '88. An intoxicating blend of jazzy instrumentation, indie stylings and wilful weirdness, the album's success allowed the band to set up their own multi-media enterprise, 'Bad Taste Ltd.' back in Iceland. Though a follow-up, 'HERE TODAY, TOMORROW, NEXT WEEK' (1989) again made the UK Top 20, the critical reception was poor, particular vitriol reserved for EINER's (ORN) jarring vocal exhortations. After extensive touring the band headed back to Iceland to work on various outside jazz-styled projects, BJORK keeping her name in the music press via collaborative work with 808 STATE on their 'Ex:El' album. Then, in late '91, The SUGARCUBES bounced back with the celebratory avant-funk of 'HIT', the band putting in an unforgettable performance on Channel 4's 'The Word'. The accompanying album, 'STICK AROUND FOR JOY' (1992) saw the group back in critical favour, a brassy pot-pourri of spiked melody and faultless instrumental dexterity. To consolidate the new dancefloor-friendly direction, a set of remixes, 'IT'S-IT', was released in late '92, coinciding with the voluntary demise of The SUGARCUBES. It had been a short strange trip, but not as strange as BJORK's forthcoming rise to international pop superstardom. While she undoubtedly had a distinctive, beguiling charm, few would've predicted the massive critical and commercial achievements of her solo debut, entitled, er . . . 'DEBUT' actually. Released in summer '93, co-written with ex-SOUL II SOUL/MASSIVE ATTACK guru, NELLEE HOOPER and featuring such underrated talents as TALVIN SINGH and JHELISA ANDERSON, proceedings were dominated by pulsing, house-orientated material, although there was a fair smattering of off-the-wall BJORK oddities. Lauded by the indie and dance press alike, the album's kudos was further boosted by the success of the 'PLAY DEAD' single, a collaboration with soundtrack man, DAVID ARNOLD recorded for the movie, 'Young Americans'. A UK Top 3 success and a Mercury Music Prize nominee, 'DEBUT' turned BJORK into a household name, remixers clamouring to get to grips with her work. A true celebrity hobnobber, BJORK co-wrote the title track to MADONNA's 'Bedtime Stories' set, while 1995's follow-up album, 'POST', saw her working with everyone from TRICKY and SKUNK ANANSIE to The BRODSKY QUARTET and EVELYN GLENNIE! The latter two featured on the experimental/schizophrenic (delete according to taste) Top 5 hit, 'IT'S OH SO QUIET', an, ahem, 'adaptation' of Betty Hutton's 40's big band number which saw BJORK veer wildly from hushed reverence to shouting the rafters down in fine style. The song was characteristic of the album's more fragmented nature, a challenging listen but proof positive that the elfen firebrand wasn't content to rest on her laurels. The following year saw BJORK take up residence in the gossip columns rather than the charts, what with her highly publicised relationship with GOLDIE and her unfortunate fracas with a reporter at Bangkok airport (19th February '96). In September, an obsessed fan from Florida blew his brains out after sending a letter bomb to BJORK. Luckily neighbours contacted police after smelling his decomposed body and the bomb was averted, although unsurprisingly it caused her much distress. The stresses and strains of stardom formed the lyrical backbone for her acclaimed 1997 set, 'HOMOGENIC', a return to more electronic waters that was nevertheless more downbeat than dancefloor. One of the music world's more unpredictable stars, her maverick genius is sorely needed in a chart choked with indie loser clones. With a plethora of mixes behind her, BJORK looked set to be a film star, her part in the film, 'Dancer In The Dark' (alongside Catherine Deneuve) won her praise at Cannes 2000; she also wrote the score. With help from conductor/arranger Vincent Mendoza, she composed the musical fantasies of her doomed character, Selma (as full-set 'SELMASONGS'). Deliciously different from her studio albums, the soundtrack presented a forum for BJORK's more esoteric ideas, poignantly capturing the light, shade and emotional extremes of Selma's life. In contrast, the celestial calm of 'VESPERTINE' (2001) was located squarely inside the meditative confines of the author's immediate environment. A reclusive rhapsody to private contentment, the record's spectral choir, angelic harp and head-nodding beats (courtesy of MATMOS) weaved a suitably spiritual spell to accommodate BJORK's uncharacteristically restrained and subdued vocals. Listen for instance to its heart-rending and emotive hit singles, 'THE HIDDEN PLACE' and 'PAGAN POETRY', to find out exactly how much this little lady had progressed. • **Songwriters:** SUGARCUBES – all written by BJORK and EINAR, except TOP OF THE WORLD (Carpenters) / MOTORCYCLE MAMA (Sailcat). • **Trivia:** BJORK was married to THOR, although after they had a child, he soon married new SUGARCUBE, MAGGI. SIGGI and BRAGI were former brother-in-laws who were married to twin sisters. In 1989, they divorced and moved to Denmark to get married to each other!. The first openly gay marriage in rock/pop history.

Album rating: Tappi Tikarrass: MIRANDA (*4) / Kukl: THE EYE mini (*4) / HOLIDAYS IN EUROPE mini (*4) / Sugarcubes: LIFE'S BEEN GOOD (*9) / STICK AROUND FOR JOY (*8) / HERE TODAY, TOMORROW, NEXT WEEK (*8) / IT'S-IT remixes (*6) / THE GREAT CROSSOVER POTENTIAL compilation (*7) / Bjork: DEBUT (*9) / POST (*8) / TELEGRAM remixes (*7) / HOMOGENIC (*7) / SELMASONGS soundtrack (*7) / VESPERTINE (*7) / GREATEST HITS compilation (*9) / FAMILY TREE boxed collection (*6)

BJORK GUDMUNDSDOTTIR

Falkinn — not iss.

Dec 77. (lp/c) *(FA 006/+C)* **BJORK** [–] Icelan [–]
– Arabadrengurinn / Bukolla / Alta mira / Johannes Kjarvalv / Fusi Hreindyr / Himnafor / Oliver / Alfur ut ur hol / Musastiginn / Baenin.

TAPPI TiKARRASS

BJORK – vocals, keyboards, etc / **JAKOB MAGNUSSON** – bass (ex-EXODUS) / etc.

Spor — not iss.

Sep 81. (m-lp) *(SPOR 4)* **BITID FAST I VITID** [–] Icelan [–]

Gramm — not iss.

Aug 83. (lp) *(GRAMM 16)* **MIRANDA** [–] Icelan [–]

KUKL

BJORK – vocals, keyboards / **EINAR ORN BENEDIKTSSON** (b.29 Oct'62, Copenhagen, Denmark) – trumpet, vocals / **SIGTRYGGUR 'Siggi' BALDURSSON** (b. 2 Oct'62, Stavanger, Norway) – drums, percussion / **EINAR MELLAX** – keyboards

Gramm — not iss.

Sep 83. (7") *(GRAMM 17)* **SONGULL. / POKN FYRIR BYRJENDUR** [–] Icelan [–]

Crass — not iss.

Nov 84. (m-lp) *(1984-1)* **THE EYE** [ ] [–]
– Dismembered / Assassin / Anna. *(cd-iss. Mar97; 1984 2CD)*

Mar 86. (m-lp) *(Cat.No.4)* **HOLIDAYS IN EUROPE (THE NAUGHTY NOUGHT)** [ ] [–]
– (8 untitled tracks).

SUGARCUBES

BJORK, EINAR, EINAR + SIGGI recruited **THOR ELDON JONSON** (b. 2 Jun'62, Reykjavik) – guitar / **BRAGI OLAFSSON** (b.11 Aug'62, Reykjavik) – bass

One Little Indian — Elektra

Sep 87. (7") *(7TP 7)* **BIRTHDAY. / BIRTHDAY (Icelandic)** [65] [–]
(12"+=) *(12TP 7)* – Cat (Icelandic).
(cd-s;Dec87;++=) *(7TP 7CD)* – Motorcrash.

Feb 88. (7") *(7TP 9)* **COLD SWEAT. / DRAGON (Icelandic)** [56] [–]
(12"+=) *(12TP 9)* – Traitor (Icelandic).
(12"++=) *(L12TP 9)* – Birthday (demo).
(cd-s+=) *(7TP 9CD)* – Traitor (Icelandic) / Revolution.

Apr 88. (7") *(7TP 10)* **DEUS. / LUFTGITAR (Icelandic) (with JOHNNY TRIUMPH)** [51] [–]
(10"+=/12"+=) *(10TP/12TP 10)* – Organic prankster.
(cd-s+=) *(7TP 10CD)* – Night of steel (Icelandic).

Apr 88. (lp/c/cd/dat) *(TPLP/TPC/TPCD/DTPLP 5)* **LIFE'S TOO GOOD** [14] Jun 88 [54]
– Mama / Delicious demon / Birthday / Traitor / Blue eyed pop / Petrol / F***ing in rhythm and sorrow / Cold sweat / Deus / Sick for toys. *(cd+=)* – I want.

May 88. (12"ep)(cd-ep) **COLD SWEAT / COLD SWEAT (meat mix). / BIRTHDAY (Icelandic) / DELICIOUS DEMON / COLD SWEAT (instrumental)** [–] [ ]

—— **MARGRET 'Magga' ORNOLFSDOTTIR** (b.21 Nov'67, Reykjavik) – keyboards repl. MELLAX

Sep 88. (7") *(7TP 11)* **BIRTHDAY. / CHRISTMAS (with Jesus & Mary Chain)** [65] [–]
(12")(cd-s) *(12TP 11)(7TP 11CD)* – ('A'side) / Fucking in rhythm and sorrow (live) / Cowboy (live) / Cold sweat (live).
(12")(cd-s) *(12TP 11L)(7TP 11CDL)* – BIRTHDAY CHRISTMAS MIX: – Christmas eve – Christmas day / Christmas present / Petrol (live).
(US-green-ep title 'DELICIOUS DEMONS')

Dec 88. (c-s) **MOTORCRASH (live) / POLO** [–] [ ]
(12"+=)(3"cd-s+=) – Blue eyed pop.

Aug 89. (7"/c-s) *(26 TP7/+C)* **REGINA. / HOT MEAT** [55] [ ]
(7"ep+=) *(26 TP7L)* – Hey / Propeller vs jet.
(12"+=) *(26 TP12)* – Regina (Icelandic).
(cd-s+=) *(26 TP7CD)* – Hey / Regina (Icelandic).
(12") *(26 TP12L)* – ('A'-Propeller mix) / ('A'-Jet mix).

Oct 89. (lp/silver-lp/c)(cd) *(TPLP 15/+SP/C)(TPCD 15)* **HERE TODAY, TOMORROW, NEXT WEEK** [15] [70]
– Tidal wave / Regina / Speed is the key / Dream T.V. / Nail / Pump / Eat the menu / Bee / Dear plastic / Shoot him / Water / Day called Zero / Planet. *(cd+=)* – Hey / Dark disco! / Hot meat.

Feb 90. (7") *(32 TP7)* **PLANET. / PLANET (somersault version)** [ ] [ ]
(12"+=/cd-s+=) *(32 TP 12/7CD)* – Planet (Icelandic) / Cindy.

Dec 91. (7") *(62 TP7)* **HIT. / HIT (instrumental)** [17] [ ]
(12"+=) *(62 TP12)* – Theft.
(cd-s++=) *(62 TP7CD)* – Chihuahua (instrumental).
(12"+=) *(62 TP12L)* – Leash called love.

Feb 92. (lp/c/cd) *(TPLP 30/+C/CD)* **STICK AROUND FOR JOY** [16] [95]
– Gold / Hit / Leash called love / Lucky night / Happy nurse / I'm hungry / Walkabout / Hetero scum / Vitamin / Chihuahua.

Mar 92. (7"/c-s) *(72 TP7/+C)* **WALKABOUT (remix). / STONE DRILL (IN THE ROCK)** [ ] [ ]
(12"+=) *(72 TP12)* – Top of the world (live).
(cd-s++=) *(72 TP7CD)* – Bravo pop.

Aug 92. (12"ep) *(102 TP12)* **VITAMIN REMIXES** [ ] [–]
– ('A'-Babylon's Burnin mix) / ('A'-Earth dub) / ('A'-Laser dub in Hell mix) / ('A'-Decline of Rome part II & III) / ('A'-Meditation mix).
(cd-ep+=) *(102 TP7CD)* – ('A'-E mix).

Sep 92. (c-ep/12"ep/cd-ep) *(104 TP 7C/12/7CD)* **BIRTHDAY REMIX EP** [64] [ ]
– ('A'-Justin Robertson remix) / ('A'-Tommy D. dub mix) / ('A'-Jim & William Reid Christmas Eve mix) / ('A'original) / ('A'-Tommy D. 12" or dub mix) / ('A'-Justin Robertson dub) / ('A'-Jim & William Reid Christmas Day mix) / ('A'demo).
(cd-ep) *(104 TP7CDL)* – Birthday (Justin Robertson edit) / Birthday (Tommy D. edit) / Hit (Tony Humphries mix) / Mama (Mark Saunders mix).

Oct 92. (lp/c/cd/d-cd) *(TPLP 40/+C/CD/CDL)* <61426> **IT'S-IT** (remixes) [47] [ ]
– Birthday (Justin Robertson 12" mix) / Leash called love / Blue eyed pop / Motorcrash (Justin Robertson mix) / Planet / Gold (Todd Terry mix) / Water / Regina (Sugarcubes mix) / Mama (Mark Saunders mix) / Pump (Marius De Vries mix) / Hit (Tony Humphries sweet and low mix) / Birthday (Tommy D mix) / Coldsweat (DB/BP mix). *(cd w/ bonus cd)*

—— officially disbanded late 1992

– compilations, others, etc. –

all on 'One Little Indian' ('Elektra' US)

Apr 90. (11x12"box) *(TP BOX 1)* **12.11** (box set) [ ] [–]
Apr 90. (8x7"box) *(TP BOX 2)* **7.8** (box set) [ ] [–]
Apr 90. (6xcd-s-box) *(TP BOX 3)* **CD.6** [ ] [–]
Jul 98. (cd/c/lp) *(TPLP 333 CD/MC/LP)* <62102> **THE GREAT CROSSOVER POTENTIAL** [ ] [ ]
– Birthday / Cold sweat / Mama / Motor crash / Deus / Regina / Pump / Planet / Water / Hit / Vitamin / Walkabout / Gold / Chihuahua.

BJORK GUDMUNDSDOTTIR & TRIO GUDMUNDAR INGOLFSSONAR

Smekkleysa — not iss.

Oct 90. (lp/c/cd) *(SM 27/+C/CD)* **GLING-GLO** [–] Icelan [–]
– Gling-glo / Luktar-gvendur / Kata rokkar / Pabbi minn / Brestir og brak / Astartofrar / Bella simamaer / Litli tonlistarmadurinn / Pad sest ekki saetari mey / Bilavisur / Tondelevo / Eg veit ei hvad skal segja / I

dansi med per / Bornin vid tjornina / Ruby baby / I can't help loving that man.

BJORK

— solo, with **MARIUS DE VRIES, PAUL WALLER, MARTIN VIRGO + GARRY HUGHES** – keyboards / **NELLEE HOOPER** (co-writer of some), **LUIS JARDIM** (also bass) + **BRUCE SMITH** – drums, percussion / **JON MALLISON** – guitar / **TALVIN SINGH** – tabla / **CORKI HALE** – harp / **JHELISA ANDERSON** – backing vocals / **OLIVER LAKE, GARY BARNACLE, MIKE MOWER** – brass

One Little Indian — Elektra

Jun 93. (c-s) *(112 TP7C)* **HUMAN BEHAVIOUR / ATLANTIC** [36] [ ]
(12") *(112 TP12)* – ('A'-Underworld mix) / ('A'-Close to human mix) / ('A'-Dom T. mix).
(cd-s) *(112 TP7CD)* – ('A'side) / (above extras) / ('A'-Bassheads edit).

Jul 93. (cd/c/lp) *(TPLP 31 CD/C/L) <61468>* **DEBUT** [3] [61]
– Human behaviour / Crying / Venus as a boy / There's more to life than this recorded live at the Milk Bar toilets / Like someone in love / Big time sensuality / One day / Aeroplane / Come to me / Violently happy / The anchor song. *(re-iss. Nov93 cd/c; TPLP 31 CDX/CX)(+=)* – Play dead.

Aug 93. (7"/c-s) *(122 TP7/+C)* **VENUS AS A BOY. / ('A'-Dream mix)** [29] [ ]
(cd-s) *(122 TP7CD)* – ('A'side) / ('A'-Mykaell Riley mix) / There's more to life than this (non toilet mix) / Violently happy.
(cd-s) *(122 TP7CDL)* – ('A'side) / Stigdu mig / Anchor song (Black Dog mix) / I remember you.
(below single credited with DAVID ARNOLD and from the movie 'Young Americans', released on 'Island' records)

Oct 93. (7"/c-s) *(IS/CIS 573)* **PLAY DEAD. / ('A'-Tim Simenon remix)** [12] [ ]
(12"+=/cd-s+=) *(12IS/CID 573)* – ('A'-Tim Simenon mixes; Orchestral / 12" / Instrumental) / ('A'-Original film mix).

Nov 93. (c-s) *(132 TP7C)* **BIG TIME SENSUALITY / SiDASTA EG** [17] [–]
(cd-s+=) *(132 TP7CD)* – Gloria / Come to me (Black Dog Productions).
(12"/cd-s) *(132 TP 12/7CDL)* – ('A'-Dave Morales def radio mix) / ('A'-Fluke mixes) / ('A'-Justin Robertson – Lionrock Wigout & Prankster's Joyride mix) / ('A'-Dom T. mix).

Jan 94. (c-s) *<64561>* **BIG TIME SENSUALITY / THERE'S MORE TO LIFE THAN THIS** [–] [88]

— In Mar'94, BJORK was accused by SIMON FISHER (LOVEJOY) of not crediting him on 4 of her songs on her 'DEBUT' album.

Mar 94. (c-s) *(142 TP7C)* **VIOLENTLY HAPPY. / ('A'-Fluke mix)** [13] [ ]
(cd-s) *(142 TP7CD)* – ('A'side) / Anchor song (acoustic) / Come to me (acoustic) / Human behavior (acoustic).
(d-cd-s) *(142 TP7CDL)* – ('B'side) / ('A'-5 other mixes).

Sep 94. (cd/c) *(MUM CD/SC 59)* **BEST MIXES FROM THE ALBUM DEBUT (For All The People Who Don't Buy White Labels)** [ ] [–]
(above rel. on 'Mother')

Apr 95. (c-s) *(162 TP7C)* **ARMY OF ME / ('A'-ABA All-Stars mix)** [10] [ ]
(cd-s+=) *(162 TP7CD)* – You've been flirting again / Sweet intuition.
(cd-s+=) *(162 TP7CDL)* – ('A'-Massey mix) / ('A'-featuring SKUNK ANANSIE) / ('A'-ABA All-Stars instrumental).
(cd-s) *(162 TP7)* – ('A'side) / Cover me.

Jun 95. (cd/c/lp) *(TPLP 51 CD/C/L) <612740>* **POST** [2] [32]
– Army of me / Hyper-ballad / The modern things / It's oh so quiet / Enjoy / You've been flirting again / Isobel / Possibly maybe / I miss you / Cover me / Headphones. *(cd re-iss. Oct99; TPLP 51CD)*

Aug 95. (c-s/cd-s) *(172 TP7 C/CD)* **ISOBEL / CHARLENE (Black Dog mix) / I GO HUMBLE / VENUS AS A BOY (harpsicord version)** [23] [ ]
(cd-s) *(172 TP7CDL)* – ('A'side) / ('A'-Goldie mix) / ('A'-Eumir Deodato mix) / ('A'-Siggi mix).

Nov 95. (c-s) *(182 TP7C)* **IT'S OH SO QUIET / YOU'VE BEEN FLIRTING AGAIN (flat is a promise mix)** [4] [ ]
(cd-s+=) *(182 TP7CD)* – Hyper-ballad (Over the edge mix) / Sweet sweet intuition.
(cd-s) *(182 TP7CDL)* – ('A'side) / Hyper-ballad (Girl's blouse mix) / Hyper-ballad (with The Brodsky Quartet) / My spine (featuring Evelyn Glennie).

Feb 96. (c-s) *(192 TP7C)* **HYPER-BALLAD / HYPER-BALLAD (Robin Hood riding through the glen mix)** [8] [ ]
(cd-s+=) *(192 TP7CD)* – ('A'-The stomp remix) / ('A'-Fluke mix) / ('A'-Subtle abuse mix) / ('A'-Tee's freeze mix).
(cd-s) *(192 TP7CDL)* – ('A'side) / Isobel (the Carcass remix) / Cover me (Plaid mix) / ('A'-Towa Tei remix).

Oct 96. (cd-s) *(193 TP7CD)* **POSSIBLY MAYBE (mixes; Lucy / Calcutta Cyber Cafe / Dalas Austin)** [13] [ ]
(cd-s) *(193 TP7CDT)* – ('A'-Calcutta Cyber Cafe dub) / Cover me (Dillinja mix) / One day (Trevor Morais mix) / I miss you (Photek mix).
(cd-s) *(193 TP7CDL)* – ('A'live mix) / Big time sensuality (Plaid remix) / Visur vatnsenda-rosu / Hyper-ballad (live).

Nov 96. (cd/c/lp) *(TPLP 51 CDT/CT/T) <61897>* **TELEGRAM** (remixes) [ ] Jan97 [66]
(cd re-iss. Aug99; TPLP 51CDT)

Feb 97. (c-s) *(194 TP7C)* **I MISS YOU / I MISS YOU (Photek mix)** [36] [ ]
(cd-s) *(194 TP7CD)* – ('A'side) / ('A'-Dobie part 2) / ('A'Darren Emerson mix) / Karvel (Graham Massey mix).
(cd-s) *(194 TP7CDL)* – ('A'-Dobie part 1) / Hyperballad (LFO) Violently happy (live) / Headphones (Miko Vainio remix).

Sep 97. (cd-s) *(202 TP7CD)* **JOGA (mixes; album / Alec Empire / Alec Empire Digital Hardcore 1 & 2)** [ ] [ ]
(cd-s) *(202 TP7CDL)* – ('A'album mix) / Sod off / Immature (Bjork's version) / So broken.
(cd-s) *(202 TP7CDX)* – (mixes; Howie B. main / String & Vocal / Buzzwater) / All is full of love (original).

Sep 97. (lp/c/cd) *(TPLP 71/+C/CD) <62061>* **HOMOGENIC** [4] [28]
– Hunter / Joga / Unravel / Bachelorette / All neon like / 5 years / Immature / Alarm call / Pluto / All is full of love.

Dec 97. (c-s) *(212 TP7C)* **BACHELORETTE / ('A'-Howie "Spread" mix)** [21] [ ]
(cd-s+=) *(212 TP7CD)* – My snare / Scary.
(12") *(212 TP12P1)* – ('A'-Alec Empire remix) / ('B'side).
(12") *(212 TP12P2)* – ('A'-Mark Bell "Optimism" remix) / ('A'-Mark Bell "Zip" remix).
(cd-s) *(212 TP7CDL)* – (mixes; above + RZA / Grooverider / etc).

— In Aug'98. BJORK collaborated with FUNKSTORUNG on a single, 'ALL IS FULL OF LOVE', released on 'Fat Cat' cd-s; *CDFAT 022)*

Oct 98. (cd-s) *(222 TP7CD)* **HUNTER / ALL IS FULL OF LOVE (In Love With Funkstorung remix) / ('A'-U-Ziq remix)** [44] [ ]
(cd-s) *(222 TP7CDL)* – ('A'side) / ('A'-State Of Bengal mix) / ('A'-Skothus mix).
(cd-s) *(222 TP7CDX)* – ('A'-Moodswing mix) / So broken (DK Krust remix) / ('A'live).

Nov 98. (cd-s) *(232TP7CD)* **ALARM CALL (mixes; radio / Rhythmic Phonetics / Bjeck)** [33] [ ]
(cd-s) *(232 TP7CDL)* – (mixes; Potage du jour / French edit / French dub).
(cd-s) *(232 TP7CDX)* – (mixes; Phunk you / Gangsta / Locked).
(12") *(232 TP12P1)* – (mixes; Bjeck [Beck] / Rhythmic Phonetics [Matmos] / Speech therapy [Matmos]).
(12") *(232 TP12P2)* – (mixes; Enough is enough [Mark Bell] / Rise & shine [Mark Bell]) / All is full of love (Mark Bell mix).
(12") *(232 TP12P3)* – (mix; Reprosession [DJ Krust] / So broken (DJ Krush mix).
(12") *(232 TP12P4)* – (mixes; Alan Braxe & Ben Diamond [Stardust] / Teesmade dub [Swag] / Alan Braxe & Ben Diamond).
(12") *(232 TP12P5)* – (mixes; Andy Bradford & Mark Bell / album / Snooze button [Dom T] / (Moodswing [Mark Bell]).

Jun 99. (cd-s) *(242 TP7CD)* **ALL IS FULL OF LOVE (mixes; original / Funkstorung exclusive / strings)** [24] [ ]
(cd-s) *(242 TP7CDL)* – ('A'mixes; Howie B / Plaid / Guy Sigsworth).
(12") *(242 TP12)* – ('A'mixes; Mark Stent / Funkstorung exclusive / Mark Stent radio strings).
(12") *(242 TP12L)* – ('A'mixes; U-Ziq 7 minute / U-Ziq 1 minute / Funkstorung exclusive).

Sep 00. (lp/cd) *(TPLP 151/+CD) <62533>* **SELMASONGS: Music From The Motion Picture Dancer In The Dark** [34] [41]
– Overture / Cvalda / I've seen it all (with THOM YORKE) / Scatterheart / In the musicals / 107 steps / New world.

Aug 01. (cd-s) *(332 TP7CD)* **HIDDEN PLACE / GENEROUS PALMSTROKE / VERANDI** [21] [–]
(cd-s) *(332 TP7CDL)* – ('A'-acapella) / Mother heroic / Foot soldiers.

Aug 01. (d-lp/c/cd) *(TPLP 101/+C/CD) <62653>* **VESPERTINE** [8] [19]
– Hidden place / Cocoon / It's not up to you / Undo / Pagan poetry / Frosti / Aurora / An echo, a stain / Sun in my mouth / Heirloom / Harm of will / Unison.

Nov 01. (cd-s) *(352 TP7CD)* **PAGAN POETRY / DOMESTICA / BATABID (DVD)** 38 –
(cd-s) *(352 TP7CDL)* – ('A'side) / ('A'-Matthew Herbert mix) / Aurora (opiate mix).

Mar 02. (cd-s) *(332 TP7CD1)* **COCOON / PAGAN POETRY (new music box version) / SUN IN MY MOUTH (recomposed by ensemble)** 35 –
(cd-s) *(332 TP7CD2)* – ('A'-radio) / Aurora (new music box version) / Amphibian (DVD) / ('A'-video).

Nov 02. (d-lp/cd) *(TPLP 359/+CD)* <62787> **GREATEST HITS** (compilation) 53
– All is full of love / Hyperballad / Human behaviour / Joga / Bachelorette / Army of me / Pagan poetry / Big time sensuality (the Fluke minimix) / Venus as a boy / Hunter / Hidden place / Isobel / Possibly maybe / Play dead / It's in our hands.

Nov 02. (6xcd-box) *(TPLP 365CD)* <62815> **FAMILY TREE** (collection)
– Sidasta eg / Giora / Fuglar / Ammaeli / Mamma / Immature / Cover me / Generous palmstroke / Joga / Mother heroic / The modern things / Karvel / I go humble / Nature is ancient / Unravel / Cover me / Possibly maybe / The anchor song / Hunter / All neon like / I've seen it all / Bachelorette / Play dead / Venus as a boy / Hyperballad / You've been flirting again / Isobel / Joga / Unravel / Bachelorette / All is full of love / Scatterheart / I've seen it all (with THOM YORKE) / Pagan poetry / It's not up to you.

Nov 02. (cd-s) *(366 TP7CD1)* **IT'S IN OUR HANDS / COCOON (rectangled by ensemble) / HUMAN BEHAVIOUR (live)** 37 –
(cd-s) *(366 TP7CD2)* – ('A'side) / Matmos (mix) / Arcade (mix).

– others, etc. –

Aug 96. (12"ltd) *(193 TP12TD)* **POSSIBLY MAYBE (Talvin Singh mix). / I MISS YOU (Dobie mix)** –

Sep 96. (12"ltd) *(193 TP12DM)* **POSSIBLY MAYBE (LFO mix). / ENJOY (Dom T mix)** –

Oct 96. (12"ltd) *(193 TP12PT)* **BIG TIME SENSUALITY (Plaid mix). / ONE DAY (Trevor Morais mix)** –

Jun 97. (12"ltd) *(193 TP12PT)* **BIG TIME SENSUALITY. / ONE DAY** –

Jun 97. (12"ltd) *(193 TP12PD)* **I MISS YOU (Photek mix). / COVER ME (Dillinja mix)** –

Jun 97. (12"ltd) *(193 TP12GH)* **ISOBEL'S LONELY HEART (Goldie remix). / HYPERBALLAD (Robin Hood Riding Through The Glen mix)** –

Jun 97. (12"ltd) *(193 TP12MO)* **POSSIBLY MAYBE (Lucy mix – Mark Bell). / ENJOY (Further Over The Edge mix – Outkast)** –

Jun 97. (12"ltd) *(193 TP12TT)* **HYPERBALLAD (Towa Tei remix). / ENJOY (The Beats mix – Dom T)** –

Aug 98. (12"/cd-s; BJORK & FUNKSTORUNG) *Fat Cat; (12/CD FAT 022)* **ALL IS FULL OF LOVE (mixes)** –

Mar 00. (4xcd-box) *(252TP 7BOX)* **A COLLECTION OF SINGLES** –

☐ Frank BLACK (see under ⇒ PIXIES)

☐ BLACK BOX RECORDER (see under ⇒ AUTEURS)

BLACK CROWES

Formed: Atlanta, Georgia, USA . . . 1984 under the name MR CROWE'S GARDEN by the ROBINSON brothers, CHRIS and RICH (sons of STAN ROBINSON, who had a minor US hit in 1959 with 'Boom A Dip Dip'). By 1988, they'd adopted the BLACK CROWES moniker and assembled the line-up that would remain more or less stable throughout their career. Picked up by the ever eclectic RICK RUBIN, for his fledgling 'Def American' label, the band released their debut album in 1990 to almost universal acclaim. Taking its title from an old ELMORE JAMES song, the record was steeped in classic American musical tradition; a seamless mesh of hard-rock, blues, soul, country and R&B that drew inevitable comparisons with The FACES and The ROLLING STONES. Yet the BLACK CROWES were unmistakably American, Southern American in the tradition of The ALLMAN BROTHERS and LYNYRD SKYNYRD. The songwriting was simple but effective, while CHRIS ROBINSON's voice was a revelation, if a little wearing after prolonged exposure. This was feelgood music, genuine rough'n'ready soul music as opposed to the slick, neutered wallpaper that passes for much modern black soul. 'TWICE AS HARD', 'JEALOUS AGAIN', 'COULD'VE BEEN SO BLIND' and a rough hewn cover of OTIS REDDING's 'HARD TO HANDLE' sounded effortless, while ROBINSON put in a spine-tingling vocal performance on the emotive ballad, 'SHE TALKS TO ANGELS'. Live, the BLACK CROWES were naturally in their element and following the album's release, the band embarked on a punishing touring schedule, playing with everyone from DOGS D'AMOUR to ZZ TOP (in a well documented incident, the band were dropped from the ZZ TOP tour following CHRIS ROBINSON's criticisms of corporate sponsorship). With the permanent addition of keyboardist EDDIE HAWRYSCH to flesh out the sound, and replacing guitarist JEFF CEASE with MARC FORD (ex-BURNING TREE), the band cut 'THE SOUTHERN HARMONY AND MUSICAL COMPANION'. Released May 1992 (incredibly, recorded in just over a week), the album built on the solid blueprint of the debut. The band had amassed a sizeable following through their ceaseless live work and the album deservedly hit the top spot in America, No.2 in the UK. With the songwriting more assured and the arrangements more ambitious, The 'CROWES succeeded in carving out a musical identity distinct from their weighty musical influences. The addition of female backing singers added a richness to the sound and the record segued smoothly from the raucous R&B of opener 'STING ME' to the stoned melancholy of 'THORN IN MY PRIDE' and on to the darker, 'Midnight Rambler'-esque 'BLACK MOON CREEPING'. Just to make sure people knew where he was coming from (man), ROBINSON closed the set with a mellow, acoustic reading of BOB MARLEY's 'TIME WILL TELL'. Soon after the album's release, the band hit the road once more, a headlining spot at the 1994 Glastonbury Festival illustrating just how high the 'CROWES had flown. Released later that year amid a storm of controversy over the cover shot (Uncle Sam[antha] in a compromising position, you could say), 'AMORICA' was something of a disappointment. Perhaps the relentless touring was beginning to take its toll, as the record sounded claustrophobic and turgid, the pace rarely rising above a monotonous plod. The songs were also lacking in cohesion and focus, although moments of genius were still evident on the likes of 'A CONSPIRACY' and the single, 'WISER TIME'. The band continued to cut it live, getting further out both musically and image wise. While The 'CROWES had always been defiantly 70's in their choice of apparel, CHRIS ROBINSON, in particular, had graduated from a vaguely glam look to a latter day CHARLES MANSON-alike. This was the revenge of the 70's; oriental rugs, ragged denim flares, bare feet, hell, even a GRATEFUL DEAD t-shirt! Rambling organ solos were also de rigeur of course, but fans lucky enough to catch the band at their low-key London gigs at the tail end of '96/early '97, were treated to a stripped down, largely acoustic set. While completely clueless, mullet headed, rock bores voiced their disapproval, the Christ-like ROBINSON mesmerised the more discerning 'CROWES fans with sterling covers of BOB DYLAN, BYRDS and LITTLE FEAT material. The 1996 album, 'THREE SNAKES AND ONE CHARM' was also a return to form, encompassing a greater diversity of styles and adding a bit of SLY STONE-style funkiness to their ragged retro patchwork. Where the band go from here is anybody's guess although a drum'n'bass remix is unlikely. With bassist JOHNNY COLT and guitarist FORD both leaving within a few months of each other, things didn't look too good. However, all was well again by early '99 with the release of their fifth set, 'BY YOUR SIDE', a typical FACES-meets-'STONES effort that highlighted their best track for some time, 'KICKIN' MY HEART AROUND' (a minor hit from late the previous year). After a much-praised one nighter with 'ZEPPELIN's axe king JIMMY PAGE (an album, 'LIVE AT THE GREEK' was issued in 2000), The BLACK CROWES returned the following year with 'LIONS' on the 'V2' (Virgin/Branson) imprint. While the album notched up a respectable US Top 20 chart placing, the CROWES ultimately decided that they'd reached the end of the line with 2002's 'LIVE' documenting the ensuing farewell tour. Tight, raucous, and as close to the spirit of unpretentious rock'n'roll as you're likely to hear these days, the album was as fitting an epitaph as any given the 'CROWES' career-long commitment to the stage. If there was any criticism at all, it was the almost complete absence of covers, the reverence of which always made this band's readings of other people's songs worthwhile. • **Songwriters:** All written by ROBINSON brothers, except HARD TO HANDLE (Otis Redding) / RAINY DAY WOMAN NOS.12 & 35 + WHEN THE NIGHT COMES FALLING FROM THE SKY (Bob Dylan) / TIME WILL TELL (Bob Marley) / DREAMS (Allman Brothers). • **Trivia:** CHRIS and RICH's father STAN ROBINSON had a minor US hit in '59 with 'BOOM-A-DIP-DIP'. Chuck Leavell (ex-ALLMANS) produced and guested on the 1992 lp.

Album rating: SHAKE YOUR MONEY MAKER (*9) / THE SOUTHERN HARMONY AND MUSICAL COMPANION (*9) / AMORICA (*7) / THREE SNAKES AND ONE CHARM (*7) / SHO' NUFF: THE COMPLETE BLACK CROWES boxed set (*7) / BY YOUR SIDE (*7) / GREATEST HITS 1990-1999 – A TRIBUTE TO A WORK IN PROGRESS compilation (*8) / LIONS (*5) / LIVE (*5)

CHRIS ROBINSON (b.20 Dec'66) – vocals / **'Young' RICH ROBINSON** (b. RICHARD, 24 May'69) – guitar / **JEFF CEASE** (b.24 Jun'67, Nashville, USA) – guitar / **JOHNNY COLT** (b. 1 May'68, Cherry Point, New Connecticut) – bass (repl. 2 earlier) / **STEVE GORMAN** (b.17 Aug'65, Hopkinsville, Kentucky) – drums (repl. 5 earlier)

Def American | Def American

Mar 90. (cd/c/lp) *(842515-2/-4/-1)* *<24278>* **SHAKE YOUR MONEY MAKER** [ ] Oct89 [4]
– Twice as hard / Jealous again / Sister luck / Could I've been so blind / Hard to handle / Seeing things / Thick'n'thin / She talks to angels / Struttin' blues / Stare it cold. *(finally hit UK No.36 Aug91 – re-dist.Sep92) (re-iss. Dec94 on 'American-BMG' cd/c; 74321 24839-2/-4) (cd re-iss. Feb99 on 'Columbia'; 491790-2) (cd re-iss. Aug00; 499653-2)*

May 90. (7") *(DEFA 4)* *<19697>* **JEALOUS AGAIN. / THICK'N'THIN** [ ] Apr90 [75]
(12"+=/12"pic-d+=)(cd-s+=) (DEFA/+P 4-12)(DEFAC 4) – Waitin' guilty.

Aug 90. (7"/c-s) *(DEFA/+M 6)* *<19668>* **HARD TO HANDLE. / JEALOUS AGAIN (acoustic)** [45] Oct90 [45]
(12"+=/12"sha-pic-d+=) *(DEFA/+P 6-12)* – Twice as hard / Stare it cold (both live).
(cd-s+=) *(DEFAC 6)* – Twice as hard (remix).

Jan 91. (7"/c-s) *(DEFA/+M 7)* **TWICE AS HARD. / JEALOUS AGAIN (live)** [47] [–]
(12"+=)(cd-s+=) *(DEFA 7-12)(DEFAC 7)* – Jealous guy (live).
(12"pic-d+=) *(DEFAP 7-12)* – Could I've been so blind (live).

Mar 91. (c-s/7") *<19403>* **SHE TALKS TO ANGELS. / ('A'live video version)** [–] [30]

Jun 91. (7") *(DEFA 8)* **JEALOUS AGAIN. / SHE TALKS TO ANGELS** [70] [–]
(12"+=) *(DEFA 8-12)* – She talks to angels (live).
(cd-s++=) *(DEFAC 8)* – Could I've been so blind (live).
(12"pic-d) *(DEFAP 8-12)* – ('A'acoustic) / ('B'acoustic) / Waitin' guilty / Struttin' blues.

Jun 91. (7") *<19245>* **HARD TO HANDLE. / WAITIN' GUILTY** [–] [26]

Aug 91. (7") *(DEFA 10)* **HARD TO HANDLE. / SISTER LUCK (live)** [39] [–]
(cd-s+=) *(DEFCD 10)* – Sister Luck (live).
(7"sha-pic-d) *(DEFAP 10)* – Hard to handle / Stare it cold (live).
(12"+=) *(DEFA 10-12)* – Dreams (live).

Oct 91. (7") *(DEFA 13)* **SEEING THINGS. / COULD I'VE BEEN SO BLIND (live)** [72] [–]
(12"+=) *(DEFAG 13-12)* – She talks to angels (live) / Sister luck (live).
(cd-s) *(DEFAC 13)* – ('A'side) / Hard to handle / Jealous again / Twice as hard.

—— **MARK FORD** (b.13 Apr'66, Los Angeles, Calif.) – guitar (ex-BURNING TREE) repl. CEASE / added **EDDIE HAWRYSCH** – keyboards

Apr 92. (etched-7") *(DEFA 16)* *<18877>* **REMEDY / DARLING OF THE UNDERGROUND PRESS** [24] Jun92 [48]
(12"+=)(cd-s+=) *(DEFA 16-12)(DEFCD 16)* – Time will tell.

May 92. (cd/c/lp) *(512263-2/-4/-1)* *<26916>* **THE SOUTHERN HARMONY AND MUSICAL COMPANION** [2] [1]
– Sting me / Remedy / Thorn in my pride / Bad luck blue eyes goodbye / Sometime salvation / Hotel illness / Black moon creeping / No speak, no slave / My morning song / Time will tell. *(re-iss. Dec94 on 'American-BMG' cd/c; 74321 24840-2/-4) (cd re-iss. Feb99 on 'Columbia'; 491791-2) (cd re-iss. Aug01 on 'American'; 499654-2)*

Aug 92. (c-s,cd-s) *<18803>* **THORN IN MY PRIDE. / STING ME** [–] [80]

Sep 92. (7") *(DEFA 21)* **STING ME. / RAINY DAY WOMEN NOS.12 & 35** [42] [–]
(cd-s) *(DEFCD 21)* – ('A'side) / She talks to angels / Thorn in my pride / Darling of the underground press.

Nov 92. (7") *(DEFA 23)* **HOTEL ILLNESS. / NO SPEAK, NO SLAVE** [47] [–]
(12"clear) *(DEFX 23)* – ('A'side) / Words you throw away / Rainy day women Nos.12 & 35.
(cd-s) *(DEFCD 23)* – ('A'side) / Rainy day / (Chris interview).
(cd-s) *(DEFCB 23)* – ('A'side) / Words you throw away / (Rich interview).

Jun 93. (7"/cd-s) *(862202-7/-2)* **REMEDY. / HARD TO HANDLE** [ ] [–]
(12"+=/cd-s+=) *(862203-1/-2)* – Hotel illness / Jealous again.

—— added **EDDIE HARSCH** (b.27 May'57, Toronto, Ontario) – keyboards

American-BMG | American-BMG

Nov 94. (cd/c/lp) *(74321 23682-2/-4/-1)* *<43000>* **AMORICA** [8] [11]
– Gone / A conspiracy / High head blues / Cursed diamond / Non-fiction / She gave good sunflower / P.25 London / Ballad in urgency / Wiser time / Downtown money waster / Descending. *(cd+=/c+=)* – Tied up and swallowed. *(cd re-iss. Feb99 on 'Columbia'; 491792-2)*

Jan 95. (7"blue) *(74321 25849-7)* **HIGH HEAD BLUES. / A CONSPIRACY / REMEDY (live)** [25] [–]
(ext'B'live; 12"+=) *(74321 25849-6)* – Thick'n'thin (live).
(cd-s++=) *(74321 25849-2)* – ('A'extended).
('B'live-cd-s+=) *(74321 25849-5)* – P25 London (live).

Jul 95. (7") *(74321 27267-7)* **WISER TIME. / CHEVROLET** [34] [–]
('A'-Rock mix; cd-s+=) (74321 27267-2) – She talks to angels (acoustic).
(cd-s) *(74321 29827-2)* – ('A'acoustic) / Jealous again (acoustic) / Non fiction (acoustic) / Thorn in my pride (acoustic).

Jul 96. (10"pic-d/cd-s) *(74321 39857-1/-2)* **ONE MIRROR TOO MANY. / PIMPERS PARADISE / SOMEBODY'S ON YOUR CASE** [51] [–]

Jul 96. (cd/c) *(74321 38484-2/-4)* *<43082>* **THREE SNAKES AND ONE CHARM** [17] [15]
– Under a mountain / Good Friday / Nebakanezer / One mirror too many / Blackberry / Girl from a pawnshop / (Only) Halfway to everywhere / Bring on, bring on / How much for your wings? / Let me share the ride / Better when you're not alone / Evil eye. *(cd re-iss. Feb99 on 'Columbia'; 491793-2)*

—— COLT + FORD left; repl. by **SVEN PIPPEN** – bass (ex-MARY MY HOPE)

—— added touring guitarist **AUDLEY FREED** (ex-CRY OF LOVE)

Columbia | Columbia

Oct 98. (c-s) *(666666-4)* **KICKIN' MY HEART AROUND / IT MUST BE OVER** [55] [–]
(cd-s+=) *(666666-2)* – You don't have to go.
(cd-s+=) *(666666-5)* – Diamond ring (version).

Jan 99. (cd/c) *(491669-2/-4)* *<69361>* **BY YOUR SIDE** [34] [26]
– Go faster / Kickin' my heart around / By your side / Horsehead / Only a fool / Heavy / Welcome to the goodtimes / Go tell the congregation / Diamond ring / Then she said my name / Virtue and vice. *(cd re-iss. Aug01; same)*

Jul 99. (7"/cd-s) *<41902>* **ONLY A FOOL. / WHEN THE NIGHT COMES FALLING FROM THE SKY** [–] [ ]

Jun 00. (cd/c) *<63666>* **GREATEST HITS 1990-1999 – A TRIBUTE TO A WORK IN PROGRESS** (compilation) [–] [ ]
– Jealous again / Twice as hard / Hard to handle / She talks to angels / Remedy / Sting me / Thorn in my pride / Bad luck blue eyes goodbye / A conspiracy / Wiser time / Good Friday / Blackberry / Kickin' my heart around / Go faster / Only a fool / By your side. *(UK-iss.Mar02 on 'Universal'; 314 586789-2)*

—— In Jul'00, The BLACK CROWES were credited with JIMMY PAGE on a special 2CD-set, 'LIVE AT THE GREEK' (recorded late '99)

V2 V2

May 01. (cd) *(VVR 1015678) <27091>* **LIONS** [37] [20]
– Midnight from the inside out / Lickin' / Come on / No use lying / Losing my mind / Ozone mama / Greasy grass river / Soul singing / Miracle to me / Young man, old man / Cosmic friend / Cypress tree / Lay it all on me.

Jul 01. (cd-s) *(VVR 501657-3)* **SOUL SINGING / LOVE IS NOW / ALWAYS THE LAST TIME** [ ] [–]
(cd-s) *(VVR 501657-8)* – ('A'side) / Sleepyheads / ('A'live).

—— the band split after a farewell tour in 2001

Aug 02. (d-cd) *(VVR 102077-2) <27134>* **LIVE (live)** [ ] [ ]
– Midnight from the inside out / Sting me / Thick n thin / Greasy grass river / Sometimes salvation / Cursed diamond / Miracle to me / Wiser time / Girl from a pawnshop / Cosmic friend / Black moon creeping / High head blues / Title song / She talks to angels / Twice as hard / Lickin' / Soul singing / Hard to handle / Remedy.

– compilations, etc. –

Aug 98. (5xcd-box) *Columbia; (C5K 65741)* **SHO 'NUFF: THE COMPLETE BLACK CROWES** [ ] [ ]
(re-iss. Jun02; 586946-2)

Aug 00. (d-cd) *Columbia; (499857-2)* **AMORICA / THREE SNAKES AND ONE CHARM** [ ] [ ]

BLACK EYED PEAS

Formed: Los Angeles, California, USA . . . 1989 as ATBAN KLANN by breakdancers WILL.I.AM and APL.DE.AP. Despite being taken under the wing of EAZY-E and his 'Ruthless' set-up, the pair's debut album was shelved and their tenure with the company came to an end with the subsequent death of the NWA star. Expanding to a trio with the addition of TABOO, they renamed themselves The BLACK EYED PEAS and eventually secured a major label deal with 'Interscope'. The 'BEHIND THE FRONT' (1998) album presented BEP as peacenik rappers with a positive lyrical philosophy and organic, live instrumentation policy diametrically opposed to most hip hop players. Of course, such an approach was hardly unprecedented and the trio could trace a lineage back through the likes of DE LA SOUL, A TRIBE CALLED QUEST and DIGABLE PLANETS, and forward to the likes of The ROOTS and The FUGEES. Like The ROOTS, the 'PEAS used the flexibility of live backing to cover as many musical bases as took their creative whim, inviting the likes of MACY GRAY to guest alongside backing vocalist KIM HILL. 'BRIDGING THE GAP' (2000) was another earthy release out of step with hip hop's rampant materialism but all the better for it, inviting the likes of MOS DEF and LES NUBIANS to share in the good vibes. Those vibes finally translated into major crossover (though BEP have always been a crossover act by their very nature) success with 'ELEPHUNK' (2003) and its huge, staccato-sung single, 'SHUT UP' and its equally huge JUSTIN TIMBERLAKE collaboration, 'WHERE IS THE LOVE?' (a UK No.1 and Top 10 in America). There was as much effervescent experimentation as ever with the likes of TIPPA IRIE and even PAPA ROACH (though that might've been pushing it) guesting.

Album rating: BEHIND THE FRONT (*6) / BRIDGING THE GAP (*7) / ELEPHUNK (*7)

WILL.I.AM (b.15 Mar'75) – vocals, keyboards, percussion / **ALP.DE.AP** (b.28 Nov'74) – vocals, instruments / **TABOO** (b.14 Jul'75) – vocals / + session people

Interscope Interscope

Sep 98. (12") *(INT 95604)* **JOINTS & JAM (mixes)** [53] [–]
(cd-s+=) *(IND 95604)* – (mixes).

Sep 98. (cd) *<(IND 90152)>* **BEHIND THE FRONT** [ ] Jun98 [ ]
– Fallin' up / Clap your hands / Joints & jam / The way U make me feel / Movement / Karma / Be free / Say goodbye / Duet / Communication / What it is / Que dices? / A8 / Love won't wait / Head bobs / Positivity.

Apr 99. (12"/cd-s) *<97051>* **KARMA / ONE WAY / KARMA (mixes)** [–] [ ]

Aug 00. (12") *<497332>* **BEP EMPIRE (mixes)** [–] [ ]

Sep 00. (cd/d-lp) *<(490661-2/-1)>* **BRIDGING THE GAP** [ ] [67]
– BEP empire / Weekends (with ESTHERO) / Get original (with CHALI 2NA) / Hot (with CHALI 2NA) / Cali to New York (with DE LA SOUL & MAGIC) / Lil' Lil' / On my own (with LES NUBIAN & MOS DEF) / Release / Bridging the gaps / Go go / Rap song (with WYCLEF) / Bringing it back / Tell your mama come / Request + line (with MACY GRAY).

Oct 00. (12") *<497390>* **WEEKENDS. / (instrumental)** [–] [ ]

May 01. (12"/c-s; BLACK EYED PEAS featuring MACY GRAY) *<(497503-1/-4)>* **REQUEST + LINE. / (Track Masters remix)** [31] [63]
(cd-s+=) *(497503-2)* – Joints and jams / ('A'-video).

—— added **FERGIE** – vocals

Aug 03. (cd) *<(9860365)>* **ELEPHUNK** [4] Jun03 [26]
– Hands up / Labor day (it's a holiday) / Let's get retarded / Hey mama / Shut up / Smells like funk / Latin girls / Sexy / Fly away / The boogie that be / The APL song / Anxiety (with PAPA ROACH) / Where is the love? (with JUSTIN TIMERLAKE).
above album will hit UK No.3 in Jan'04

Sep 03. (12") *(9810997) <71411>* **WHERE IS THE LOVE? / SOMETHING FOR THAT ASS / WHERE IS THE LOVE? (instrumental)** [1] Jun03 [8]
(cd-s+=) *(9810996)* – ('A'-video).

Dec 03. (12") *(9814587)* **SHUT UP / TELL YOUR MAMA COME (live from House Of Blues, Chicago) / KARMA (live from House Of Blues, Chicago)** [2] NOv03 [ ]
(cd-s+=) *(9814501)* – ('A'-video).

BLACK FLAG

Formed: Hermosa Beach, California, USA . . . 1976 by GREG GINN and CHUCK DUKOWSKI. In 1977, their demo reached local indie label 'Bomp', who, after over half a year decided not to release BLACK FLAG's debut 45, 'NERVOUS BREAKDOWN'. Instead, GREG and CHUCK, with sound men MUGGER and SPOT, formed their own label, 'S.S.T.' (Solid State Tuners), issuing the aforesaid single in 1978. By the time BLACK FLAG's debut lp, 'DAMAGED', was released in 1981, the group had suffered label difficulties with 'MCA-Unicorn', who didn't like the outrageous content of the tracks. Numerous personnel changes had also occurred, mainly the substitution of KEITH MORRIS, with the harder looking and now legendary HENRY ROLLINS. SST took the major label to court and although the pivotal hardcore group won, they had to pay out a 6-figure sum. The influential label went on to help kickstart the careers of many hardcore/alternative acts such as HUSKER DU, MINUTEMEN, DINOSAUR JR, MEAT PUPPETS, etc. Meanwhile, BLACK FLAG (with GINN and ROLLINS at the helm), completed a series of near brilliant albums, ROLLINS even contributing a spoken word side on the half instrumental album, 'FAMILY MAN' (1984), a thing that he would do more when he took off on a successful solo venture that year. GINN and some new cohorts completed two more mid 80's sets, 'IN MY HEAD' and 'WHO'S GOT THE 10 1/2', before he too pursued a solo sojourn, although at first with instrumental punk-jazz fusion, GONE. BLACK FLAG were one of the first US acts to take DIY punk into hardcore, a hybrid sound that would later be revered by metal fans who had picked up on 90's US hardcore/punk groups like BAD RELIGION and OFFSPRING.

Album rating: DAMAGED (*8) / EVERYTHING WENT BLACK (*5) / THE FIRST FOUR YEARS (*7) compilation / MY WAR (*6) / FAMILY MAN (*4) / SLIP IT IN (*5) / LOOSE NUT (*5) / IN MY HEAD (*6) / WHO'S GOT THE 10 1/2 (*6) / WASTED . . . AGAIN (*7)

KEITH MORRIS – vocals / **GREG GINN** (b. 8 Jun'54) – guitar / **CHUCK DUKOWSKI** – bass / **BRIAN MIGDOL** – drums

not iss. S.S.T.

Oct 78. (7"ep) *<SST 001>* **NERVOUS BREAKDOWN. / FIX ME / I'VE HAD IT / WASTED** [-] □
<US 10"colrd-ep/12"ep/cd-ep iss.1990; same>

— **CHAVO PEDERAST** (aka RON REYES) – vocals (ex-RED CROSS) repl. KEITH who formed CIRCLE JERKS. **ROBO** – drums repl. MIGDOL

Mar 80. (12"ep) *<SST 003>* **JEALOUS AGAIN / REVENGE. / WHITE MINORITY / NO VALUES / YOU BET WE'VE GOT SOMETHING PERSONAL AGAINST YOU!** [-] □
(UK-iss.Mar83; same) <US 10"colrd-ep/12"ep/cd-ep iss.1990; same>

— **DEZ CADENA** – vocals, guitar (ex-RED CROSS) repl. REYES

Jan 81. (7"ep) *<SST 005>* **SIX PACK. / I'VE HEARD IT ALL BEFORE / AMERICAN WASTE** [-] □
(UK-iss.Dec81 on 'Alternative Tentacles'; VIRUS 9) <US 10"colrd-ep/12"/ep/cd-ep iss.1990; same>

— **HENRY ROLLINS** (b. HENRY GARFIELD, 13 Feb '61, Washington, D.C.) – vocals (ex-SOA) repl. CHUCK who formed WURM (with ED DANKY and SIMON SMALLWOOD (vocalist of DEAD HIPPIE) – one lp surfaced in '85, 'FEAST' <SST 041>. CHUCK later formed SWA and was part of OCTOBERFACTION

— group now **ROLLINS, GINN, CADENA** (now rhythm guitar only) + **ROBO**

S.S.T. S.S.T.

Nov 81. (lp) *<(SST 007)>* **DAMAGED** □ □
– Rise above / Spray paint / Six pack / What I see / TV party / Thirsty and miserable / Police story / Gimmie gimmie gimmie / Depression / Room 13 / Damaged II / No more / Padded cell / Life of pain / Damaged I.

— In the US, 'Posh Boy' issued '79 recording LOUIE LOUIE. / DAMAGED 1 *(PBS 13) (This was finally issued 10"coloured 1988 on 'SST' US) (re-iss. cd/c/lp Oct95; same)* LOUIE LOUIE was a KINGSMEN original.

— **BILL STEVENSON** + guest **EMIL** – drums repl. ROBO

1982. (7"ep) *<SST 012>* **TV PARTY. / I'VE GOT TO RUN / MY RULES** [-] □
<US 12"+cd-ep iss.1990; same>

— guest on half **DALE NIXON** – bass (actually GREG under pseudonym) repl. CADENA who formed DC3

Mar 84. (lp) *<(SST 023)>* **MY WAR** □ □
– My war / Can't decide / Beat my head agaist the wall / I love you / The swinging man / Forever time / Nothing left inside / Three nights / Scream. *(cd-iss. 1990; SST 023CD) (re-iss. cd/c/lp Oct95; same)*

— added **KIRA ROESSLER** – bass

Sep 84. (lp) *<(SST 026)>* **FAMILY MAN** □ □
– Family man / Salt on a slug / The pups are doggin' it / Let your fingers do the walking / Long lost dog of it / I won't stick any of you unless and until I can stick all of you / Hollywood diary / Armageddon man / Account for what? / Shred reading (rattus norvegicus) / No deposit, no return. *(cd-iss. 1990; SST 026CD) (re-iss. cd/c/lp Oct95; same)*

Oct 84. (12") *<(SST1 2001)>* **FAMILY MAN. / I WON'T STICK ANY OF YOU UNLESS AND UNTIL I CAN STICK ALL OF YOU** □ □

Dec 84. (lp) *<(SST 029)>* **SLIP IT IN** □ □
– Slip it in / Black coffee / Wound up / Rat's eyes / Obliteration / The bars / My ghetto / You're not evil. *(cd-iss. 1990; SST 029CD) (re-iss. cd/c/lp Oct95; same)*

Jan 85. (c) *<(SST 030)>* **LIVE '84 (live)** □ □
– The process of weeding out / My ghetto / Jealous again / I love you / Swinging man / Three nights / Nothing left inside / Black coffee. *(cd-iss. 1990; SST 030CD) (re-iss. cd/c/lp Oct95; same)*

Jun 85. (lp) *<(SST 035)>* **LOOSE NUT** □ □
– Loose nut / Bastard in love / Annihilate this week / Best one yet / Modern man / This is good / I'm the one / Sinking / Now she's black. *(cd-iss. 1990; SST 035CD) (re-iss. cd/c/lp Oct95; same)*

— trimmed to **GINN, KIRA + STEVENSON** when ROLLINS went solo

Sep 85. (m-lp) *<(SST 037)>* **THE PROCESS OF WEEDING OUT** □ □
– Your last affront / Screw the law / The process of weeding out / Southern rise. *(US 10"colrd/m-cd iss.1990)*

Nov 85. (lp) *<(SST 045)>* **IN MY HEAD** □ □
– Paralyzed / The crazy girl / Black love / Retired at 21 / Drinking and driving / White hot / In my head / Society's tease / It's all up to you / You let me down. *(cd-iss. 1990 +=; SST 045CD)* – Out of this world / I can see you. *(cd re-iss. Oct95; same)*

— **ANTHONY MARTINEZ** – drums; repl. STEVENSON who had already joined OCTOBERFACTION

May 86. (lp) *<(SST 060)>* **WHO'S GOT THE 10 1/2 (live in Portland 23/8/85)** □ □
– I'm the one / Loose nut / Bastard in love / Slip it in / This is good / Gimmie gimmie gimmie / Drinking and driving / Modern man / My war. *(cd-iss. 1990) (re-iss. cd/c/lp Oct95; same) (cd+=)* – Annihilate / Wasted / Sinking / Jam / Louie Louie / Best one yet.

— had already split earlier in '86. KIRA continued with DOS, alongside MIKE WATT of The MINUTEMEN. After playing bass on a one-off trio project/eponymous album in 1985 with TOM TROCCOLI'S DOG <SST 047> – solo artist GINN had also been part of TOM's own quintet, OCTOBERFACTION – he also teamed up with ANDREW WEISS to form instrumental group, GONE.

– compilations, others, etc. –

on 'S.S.T.' unless mentioned otherwise

Mar 83. (d-lp) *<(SST 015)>* **EVERYTHING WENT BLACK** (rare 78-81) □ □
(re-iss. Oct95 lp/c/cd; SST 015/+C/CD)

1984. (lp) *<SST 021>* **THE FIRST FOUR YEARS** [-] □
(UK-iss.Oct95 & Oct99 lp/c/cd; SST 021/+C/CD)

Dec 87. (lp/c/cd) *<(SST 166/+C/CD)>* **WASTED . . . AGAIN** □ □
– Wasted / TV party / Six pack / I don't care / I've had it / Jealous again / Slip it in / Annihilate this week / Loose nut / Gimme gimme / Louie Louie / Drinking and driving. *(re-iss. Oct95; same)*

Jun 93. (12"/c-s/cd-s) *(SST 226/+C/CD)* **I CAN SEE YOU** □ □

□ BLACK GRAPE (see under ⇒ HAPPY MONDAYS)

□ BLACKMORE'S RAINBOW (see under ⇒ RAINBOW)

BLACK REBEL MOTORCYCLE CLUB

Formed: San Francisco, California, USA . . . early 1999 by high school musicians ROBERT TURNER and PETER HAYES, eventually recruiting drummer NICK JAGO from the garage club scene around the city's Bay Area. If the film 'The Wild One' – from which BLACK REBEL MOTORCYCLE CLUB had grabbed their name – had been soundtracked by this particular group, all proverbial hell would have ensued. After extensively touring between San Francisco and L.A., the trio of leather-clad, brooding dirty rock'n'rollers decided to issue a self-produced demo of thirteen tracks, which finally wormed its way onto the A&R desk of 'Virgin' records. The group were signed in late 2000, and headed off on a tour with The DANDY WARHOLS across America, pulling in much praise and fanbase from the college circuit. They arrived on the shores of Britain just in time to feel the hype of the new garage revival (STROKES et al), and were thoroughly lauded by the NME and rock stars such as NOEL GALLAGHER and JIM REID. This was even before the debut album, 'B.R.M.C.' (2001) was released, so one can imagine the commotion when it turned out to be one of the finest rock'n'roll albums of the last decade. Fuzzy guitar, jiving chrouses, big hairy sweaty percussion – it had it all. The LP entered the Top 20 and they sold out an entire tour before going on the road with OASIS. Here's hoping BRMC aren't just a sparkle in the passing fads of popular music, but a continuous fiery flare . . .

Album rating: B.R.M.C. (*7) / TAKE THEM ON ON YOUR OWN (*)

PETER HAYES – vocals, guitar, bass, harmonica, keyboards / **ROBERT TURNER** – vocals, bass, guitar, keyboards / **NICK JAGO** – drums, percussion

		Virgin	Virgin
Feb 01.	(7"ep) **RED EYES AND TEARS / SCREAMING GUN. / AS SURE AS THE SUN / WHITE PALMS**	–	
Mar 01.	(7") **RIFLES. /**	–	
May 01.	(7") **LOVE BURNS. /**	–	
Oct 01.	(7") *(VUS 224)* **WHATEVER HAPPENED TO MY ROCK'N'ROLL (PUNK SONG). / RED EYES AND TEARS**		Nov01
	(cd-s+=) *(VUSCD 224)* – U.S. government / Fail-safe.		
Jan 02.	(cd) *(CDVUS 207)* <10045> **BLACK REBEL MOTORCYCLE CLUB**	25	Apr01
	– Love burns / Red eyes and tears / Whatever happened to my rock'n'roll (punk song) / Awake / White palms / As sure as the sun / Rifles / Too real / Spread your love / Head up high / Salvation. *(lp-iss.Jan02; VUSLP 207)*		
Jan 02.	(7") *(VUS 234)* **LOVE BURNS. / AT MY DOOR**	37	–
	(cd-s) *(VUSCD 234)* – ('A'side) / Screaming gun / Rifles.		
Jan 02.	(cd-ep) **SCREAMING GUN EP**	–	
	– Fail-safe / Down here / At my door / TV loop (down deep) / Screaming gun.		
May 02.	(7") *(VUS 245)* **SPREAD YOUR LOVE. / TONIGHT'S WITH YOU**	27	–
	(cd-s+=) *(VUSDX 245)* – Simple words.		
	(cd-s) *(VUSCD 245)* – ('A'side) / The weight is more / Loaded gun.		
Sep 02.	(7") *(VUS 257)* **WHATEVER HAPPENED TO MY ROVK'N'ROLL (PUNK SONG). / RIFLES (live)**	46	–
	(cd-s) *(VUSCD 257)* – ('A'side) / Shuffle your feet (XFM session) / ('A'-video).		
Aug 03.	(7") *(VUS 273)* **STOP. / HIGH – LOW**	19	–
	(cd-s+=) *(VUSCD 273)* – Take them on on your own.		
Aug 03.	(cd/d-lp) *(CDVUS/VUSLP 245)* <80095> **TAKE THEM ON ON YOUR OWN**	3	Sep03
	– Stop / Six barrel shotgun / We're all in love / In like the rose / Ha ha high babe / Generation / Shade of blue / U.S. government / And I'm aching / Suddenly / Rise or fall / Heart + soul.		
Nov 03.	(7") *(VUS 279)* **WE'RE ALL IN LOVE. / WAITING HERE**	45	–
	(cd-s+=) *(VUSCDX 279)* – Abstract dragon / ('A'-video).		

□ BLACK ROSE (see under ⇒ CHER)

BLACK SABBATH

Formed: Aston, Birmingham, England . . . early 1969 by TONY IOMMI, OZZY OSBOURNE, TERRY 'GEEZER' BUTLER and BILL WARD, out of the jazz fusion combo, EARTH (IOMMI had also filled in as JETHRO TULL guitarist for a few weeks). Taking the name, BLACK SABBATH from a horror film adapted from a Dennis Wheatley novel of the same name, they signed to 'Fontana' in late '69. After a flop single, 'EVIL WOMAN (DON'T PLAY YOUR GAMES WITH ME)', they were shunted to the more progressive 'Vertigo' label in early 1970. The inimitable SABBATH sound was stunningly defined on the opening title cut from the self-titled debut album, the record storming into the UK Top 10. Occult influenced, BLACK SABBATH fused IOMMI's deceptively basic, doom-laden guitar riffs with OZZY's (much-mimicked since) banshee shriek. Lyrically morbid, with futuristic/medieval themes, tracks like 'THE WIZARD' highlighting their tongue-in-cheek protest against God! The band then branded their name on the nation's musical consciousness with a Top 5 hit single!!! 'PARANOID', a skullcrushing but strangely melodic track which remains one of the most (in)famous metal songs of all time. Not surprisingly, the album of the same name (also in 1970!) bludgeoned its way straight to No.1, a metal classic rammed full of blinding tracks, not least the stop-start dynamics of 'WAR PIGS', the spiralling melancholy of 'IRON MAN' and the doom-driven 'FAIRIES WEAR BOOTS' ("and you gotta believe me!"). Their third set, 'MASTER OF REALITY' (1971), was another dark jewel in the SABBATH legend, softer tracks like 'EMBRYO' and 'ORCHID' sledgehammered into oblivion by mogadon monsters, 'CHILDREN OF THE GRAVE' and 'SWEET LEAF'. The last two years had witnessed SABBATH taking America by the throat, 'VOL. 4' in '72 loosening the grip somewhat, although it did boast a classic rock ballad, 'CHANGES'. Returning to more pseudo-satanic territory, 'SABBATH BLOODY SABBATH' was another milestone, its demonic credibility nevertheless diminished somewhat by the fact that the instrumental, 'FLUFF', was subsequently adopted by namesake Radio One DJ ALAN FREEMAN on his Saturday afternoon prog-rock show! Returning from a year-long sabbatical, the release of the largely disappointing sixth album, 'SABOTAGE', was indicative of the cracks appearing in the IOMMI/OSBOURNE relationship. However, the album did contain two brilliant opening salvos, 'HOLE IN THE SKY' and 'SYMPTOM OF THE UNIVERSE'. The beginning of the end came with the ill-advised experimentation of 'TECHNICAL ECSTASY' (1976), an album which led to OZZY's brief departure (his supernatural consumption of the demon drink was also a factor). However, a newly rehabilited OSBOURNE was back at the helm for 1978's 'NEVER SAY DIE', sales of which were boosted by a near UK Top 20 title track. In 1979, OZZY took off on a solo career, leaving behind IOMMI, BUTLER and WARD to pick up the pieces in LA (where the band had relocated). With a new manager, Don Arden, in tow, they finally recruited American, RONNIE JAMES DIO (from RAINBOW), after auditioning many would-be OZZY clones. This proved to be SABBATH's blackest period, pitch in fact, with the release of two mediocre albums in the early 80's, 'HEAVEN AND HELL' and 'MOB RULES'. Things went from bad to ridiculous in 1983, when DIO was substituted by another hard-rock frontman celebrity, IAN GILLAN, taken straight from the proverbial heart of DEEP PURPLE. The resulting, ironically-titled album, 'BORN AGAIN', was an exercise in heavy-metal cliche, although it still managed to hit the UK Top 5. The original SABBATH reunited on the 13th of July '85 for a rather disappointing one-off performance at the 'Live Aid' concert in Philadelphia. In 1986, IOMMI was in full control once more, even giving his name co-billing on the appalling, 'SEVENTH STAR' set. Astonishingly, SABBATH were given another chance by Miles Copeland's 'I.R.S.' records, IOMMI having found a new vocalist, TONY MARTIN, also securing the services of veteran drummer, COZY POWELL (ex-everyband) to boost the sales of their comeback album, 'HEADLESS CROSS' (1989). The 1990's saw IOMMI and group trying to relive past glories, the 1995 album 'FORBIDDEN' even including a vocal piece from US rapper, ICE-T. At the turn of 1997/8, IOMMI and OZZY had finally settled their differences, coming together in a much heralded SABBATH reunion, which will apparently result in a comeback album, 20 years too late for some! IOMMI finally released his first – eponymous – solo album in 2000, an all-star project that had the cream of the rock/metal world queuing up to work with the legendary riffmeister. Alongside OZZY himself, guest vocalists included HENRY ROLLINS, SKIN (of SKUNK ANANSIE), DAVE GROHL (NIRVANA/FOO FIGHTERS), PHIL ANSELMO (PANTERA), BILLY CORGAN – again! – (SMASHING PUMPKINS), IAN ASTBURY (CULT), PETER STEELE (TYPE O NEGATIVE), SERJ TANKIAN (SYSTEM OF A DOWN) and even BILLY IDOL while the likes of MATT CAMERON (PEARL JAM), BEN SHEPHERD (SOUNDGARDEN) and even BRIAN MAY (!!?!?) lent their musical talents. If not exactly a classic in the BLACK

SABBATH mould, the record was certainly diverse enough to offer most fans some value for money. • **Footnote:** Not a band for the easily-led and weak-minded, as the blame for teenage suicide attempts was always laid at their darkened door. Nevertheless, their influence on the worldwide metal scene is inestimable; as well as playing grunge before it was even invented, the likes of METALLICA et al, owe SABBATH a massive debt. • **Songwriters:** Mainly group compositions. Covered EVIL WOMAN (DON'T PLAY YOUR GAMES WITH ME) (Crow) / WARNING (Aynsley Dunbar).

Album rating: BLACK SABBATH (*8) / PARANOID (*9) / MASTER OF REALITY (*9) / VOLUME 4 (*8) / SABBATH BLOODY SABBATH (*8) / SABOTAGE (*7) / WE SOLD OUR SOULS FOR ROCK'N'ROLL compilation (*8) / TECHNICAL ECSTASY (*5) / NEVER SAY DIE (*5) / HEAVEN AND HELL (*7) / LIVE EVIL (*7) / BORN AGAIN (*5) / LIVE AT LAST (*4) / MOB RULES (*6) / LIVE EVIL (*7) / BORN AGAIN (*5) / SEVENTH STAR (*4) / THE ETERNAL IDOL (*4) / HEADLESS CROSS (*6) / BLACKEST SABBATH compliation (*7) / TYR (*5) / DEHUMANIZER (*5) / CROSS PURPOSES (*5) / FORBIDDEN (*4) / REUNION (*6) / THE BEST OF BLACK SABBATH compilation (*8) / Tony Iommi: IOMMI (*6)

OZZY OSBOURNE (b. JOHN, 3 Dec'48) – vocals / **TONY IOMMI** (b.19 Feb'48) – guitars / **TERRY 'GEEZER' BUTLER** (b.17 Jul'49) – bass / **BILL WARD** (b. 5 May'48) – drums

Fontana — not iss.

Jan 70. (7") *(TF 1067)* **EVIL WOMAN, DON'T PLAY YOUR GAMES WITH ME. / WICKED WORLD** [ ] [–]

Vertigo — Warners

Feb 70. (lp) *(VO 6)* *<1871>* **BLACK SABBATH** [8] Jul70 [23]
– Black Sabbath / The wizard / Behind the wall of sleep / N.I.B. / Evil woman, don't play your games with me / Sleeping village / Warning. *(re-iss. Jan74 on 'W.W.A.'; WWA 006) (re-iss. Jun80 + Nov85 on 'NEMS'; NEL 6002) (cd-iss. Dec86+=; NELCD 6002)* – Wicked world. *(cd/c re-iss. Oct96/Oct97 on 'Essential'; ESM CD/MC 301) (lp re-iss. Jan97 on 'Original Recordings'; ORRLP 004) (cd re-iss. Sep00 on 'Essential'; CMTCD 003)*

Mar 70. (7") *(V2)* **EVIL WOMAN (DON'T PLAY YOUR GAMES WITH ME). / WICKED WORLD** [ ] [–]

Aug 70. (7") *(6059 010)* *<7437>* **PARANOID. / THE WIZARD** [4] Nov70 [61]

Sep 70. (lp) *(6360 011)* *<1887>* **PARANOID** [1] Feb71 [12]
– War pigs / Paranoid / Planet Caravan / Iron man / Electric funeral / Hand of doom / Rat salad / Fairies wear boots. *(re-iss. Jan74 on 'W.W.A.'; WWA 007) (re-iss. Jun80 on 'NEMS'; NEL 6003); hit UK 54. (re-iss. Nov85 on 'NEMS' lp/pic-lp/c/cd; NEL/NEP/NELMC/NELCD 6003) (re-iss. Jun89 on 'Vertigo' lp/c/cd+=; 832701-1/-4/-2)* – Tomorrow's world (live). *(cd/c re-iss. Feb96/Oct97 on 'Essential'; ESM CD/MC 302) (cd re-iss. Sep00 on 'Essential'; CMTCD 004)* – hit No.63 Jul02

Aug 71. (lp) *(6360 050)* *<2562>* **MASTER OF REALITY** [5] [8]
– Sweet leaf / After forever / Embryo / Children of the grave / Orchid / Lord of this world / Solitude / Into the void. *(re-iss. Jan74 on 'W.W.A.'; WWA 008) (re-iss. Nov80 on 'NEMS'; NEL 6004) (re-iss. Nov85 on 'NEMS' lp/c/cd; NEL/+MC/CD 6004) (re-iss. cd Jun89 on 'Vertigo' lp/c/cd+=; 832707-1/-4/-2)* – Killing yourself to live (live). *(cd/c re-iss. Feb96/Oct97 on 'Essential'; ESM CD/MC 303) (cd re-iss. Sep00 on 'Essential'; CMTCD 005)*

Jan 72. (7") *<7530>* **IRON MAN. / ELECTRIC FUNERAL** [–] [52]
<re-iss. 1974; 7802>

Sep 72. (7") *(6059 061)* *<7625>* **TOMORROW'S DREAM. / LAGUNA SUNRISE** [ ] [ ]

Sep 72. (lp) *(6360 071)* *<2602>* **BLACK SABBATH VOL.4** [8] Oct72 [13]
– Wheels of confusion / Tomorrow's dream / Changes / FX / Supernaut / Snowblind / Cornucopia / Laguna sunrise / St. Vitus' dance / Under the sun. *(re-iss. Jan74 on 'W.W.A.'; WWA 009) (re-iss. Jun80 on 'NEMS'; NEL 6005) (c/cd-iss. 1988+=; NEL MC/CD 6005)* – Children of the grave (live). *(cd/c re-iss. Feb96/Oct97 on 'Essential'; ESM CD/MC 304) (cd re-iss. Sep00 on 'Essential'; MCTCD 006)*

W.W.A. — Warners

Oct 73. (7") *(WWS 002)* *<7764>* **SABBATH BLOODY SABBATH. / CHANGES** [ ] [ ]

Dec 73. (lp) *(WWA 005)* *<2695>* **SABBATH BLOODY SABBATH** [4] Jan74 [11]
– Sabbath bloody sabbath / A national acrobat / Fluff / Sabbra cadabra / Killing yourself to live / Who are you? / Looking for today / Spiral architect. *(w-drawn copies were on 'Vertigo'; 6360 115) (re-iss. Jun80 on 'NEMS'; NEL 6017) (re-iss. Nov85 c/cd; NEL MC/CD 6017) (re-iss. Jun89 on 'Vertigo' lp/c/cd+=; 832700-1/-4/-2)* – Cornucopia (live). *(cd/c re-iss. Feb96/Oct97 on 'Essential'; ESM CD/MC 305)*

N.E.M.S. — Warners

Sep 75. (lp) *(9119 001)* *<2822>* **SABOTAGE** [7] [28]
– Hole in the sky / Don't start (too late) / Symptom of the universe / Megalomania / Thrill of it all / Supertzar / Am I going insane (radio) / The writ. *(re-iss. Nov80 on 'NEMS'; NEL 6018) (re-iss. Nov85 c/cd; NEL MC/CD 6018) (re-iss. Jun89 on 'Vertigo' lp/c/cd+=; 832706-1/-4/-2)* – Sweat leaf (live). *(cd/c re-iss. Feb96/Oct97 on 'Essential'; ESM CD/MC 306)*

Feb 76. (d-lp) *(6641 335)* *<2923>* **WE SOLD OUR SOULS FOR ROCK'N'ROLL** (compilation) [35] [48]
– Black sabbath / The wizard / Warning / Paranoid / Wicked world / Tomorrow's dream / Fairies wear boots / Changes / Sweet leaf / Children of the grave / Sabbath bloody sabbath / Am I going insane (radio) / Laguna sunrise / Snowblind / N.I.B. *(re-iss. Nov80; NELD 101) (re-iss. Apr86 on 'Raw Power' d-lp/c/cd; RAW LP/TC/CD 017) (re-iss. Dec90 on 'Castle' cd/c/d-lp; CCS CD/MC/LP 249) (cd re-iss. Jan98 on 'Essential'; ESDCD 605)*

Feb 76. (7") *(6165 300)* **AM I GOING INSANE (RADIO). / HOLE IN THE SKY** [ ] [ ]

Vertigo — Warners

Oct 76. (lp) *(9102 750)* *<2969>* **TECHNICAL ECSTASY** [13] [51]
– Back street kids / You won't change me / It's alright / Gypsy / All moving parts (stand still) / Rock'n'roll doctor / She's gone / Dirty women. *(re-iss. Aug83 lp/c; PRICE/PRIMC 40) (cd-iss. Jun89; 838224-2) (cd/c re-iss. Jan96/Oct97 on 'Essential'; ESM CD/MC 328)*

Nov 76. (7") *<8315>* **IT'S ALRIGHT. / ROCK'N'ROLL DOCTOR** [–] [ ]

— Late '77 OZZY leaves and is briefly repl. by **DAVE WALKER** (ex-SAVOY BROWN) Early 1978 **OZZY** returned.

May 78. (7") *(SAB 001)* **NEVER SAY DIE. / SHE'S GONE** [21] [–]

Sep 78. (7",7"purple) *(SAB 002)* **HARD ROAD. / SYMPTOM OF THE UNIVERSE** [33] [–]

Oct 78. (lp) *(9102 751)* *<3186>* **NEVER SAY DIE!** [12] [69]
– Never say die / Johnny Blade / Juniors eyes / Hard road / Shock wave / Air dance / Over to you / Breakout / Swinging the chain. *(re-iss. May83 lp/c; PRICE/PRIMC 9) (re-iss. Sep93 on 'Spectrum' cd/c;) (cd/c re-iss. Jan96/Oct97 on 'Essential'; ESM CD/MC 329)*

— **RONNIE JAMES DIO** (b.1950, Cortland, N.J.) – vocals (ex-(RITCHIE BLACKMORE'S) RAINBOW, ex-ELF etc.) repl.OZZY who went solo.

Apr 80. (lp)(c) *(9102 752)(7231 402)* *<3372>* **HEAVEN AND HELL** [9] Jun80 [28]
– Neon knights / Children of the sea / Lady evil / Heaven and Hell / Wishing well / Die young / Walk away / Lonely is the word. *(re-iss. May83 lp/c; PRICE/PRIMC 10) (cd-iss. 1987; 830171-2) (re-iss. May93 on 'Spectrum' cd/c;) (cd/c re-iss. Jan96/Oct97 on 'Essential'; ESM CD/MC 330) (cd/c re-iss. Apr96 on 'Raw Power'; RAW CD/MC 104)*

Jun 80. (7") *(SAB 3)* **NEON KNIGHTS. / CHILDREN OF THE SEA** [22] [–]

Jul 80. (7") *<49549>* **LADY EVIL. / CHILDREN OF THE SEA** [–] [ ]

Nov 80. (7"/ext.12") *(SAB 4/+12)* **DIE YOUNG. / HEAVEN AND HELL (live)** [41] [–]

— **VINNIE APPICE** (b.Staten Island, N.Y.) – drums, percussion repl. WARD

Oct 81. (7"/12") *(SAB 5/+12)* **MOB RULES. / DIE YOUNG** [46] [–]

Nov 81. (lp/c) *(6302/7144 119)* *<3605>* **MOB RULES** [12] [29]
– Turn up the night / Voodoo / The sign of the southern cross / E5150 / The mob rules / Country girl / Slippin' away / Falling off the edge of the world / Over and over. *(re-iss. Jan85 lp/c; PRICE/PRIMC 77) (cd/c re-iss. Jan96/Oct97 on 'Essential'; ESM CD/MC 332)*

Feb 82. (7")(12"/12"pic-d) *(SAB 6)(SABP 6/+12)* **TURN UP THE NIGHT. / LONELY IS THE WORD** [37] [–]

Jan 83. (d-lp/d-c) *(SAB/+M 10)* *<23742>* **LIVE EVIL (live)** [13] [37]
– E5150 / Neon knights / N.I.B. / Children of the sea / Voodoo / Black sabbath / War pigs / Iron man / Mob rules / Heaven and Hell / The sign of the southern cross / Heaven and Hell (continued) / Paranoid / Children of the grave / Fluff. *(re-iss. Apr86 lp/c; PRID/+C 11) (cd/c re-iss. Apr96/Oct97 on 'Essential'; ESM CD/MC 333)*

— **IAN GILLAN** (b.19 Aug'45, Hounslow, England) – vocals (ex-DEEP PURPLE, ex-GILLAN) repl. RONNIE who formed DIO. **BILL WARD** – drums returned replacing VINNIE who also joined DIO. **BEV BEVAN** – drums (ex-ELECTRIC LIGHT ORCHESTRA) repl. BILL, only originals in band were IOMMI and BUTLER

Sep 83. (lp/c) *(VERL/+C 8)* *<23978>* **BORN AGAIN** [4] [39]
– Trashed / Stonehenge / Disturbing the priest / The dark / Zero the hero / Digital bitch / Born again / Hot line / Keep it warm. *(cd/c re-iss. Apr96/Oct97 on 'Essential'; ESM CD/MC 334)*

Oct 83. (7") *<29434>* **STONEHENGE. / THRASHED** [–] [ ]

— **DAVE DONATO** – vocals repl. GILLAN who rejoined DEEP PURPLE

— **TONY IOMMI** recruited **GLENN HUGHES** – vocals (ex-DEEP PURPLE, etc.) repl. DONATO / **DAVE SPITZ** (b. New York City) – bass repl. BUTLER / **ERIC SINGER** (b.Cleveland, Ohio) – drums repl. BEVAN / added **GEOFF NICHOLLS** (b.Birmingham) – keyboards (ex-QUARTZ) had toured '79.

Feb 86. (lp/c)(cd; as BLACK SABBATH featuring TONY IOMMI) *(VERH/+C 29)(826704-2) <25337>* **SEVENTH STAR** [27] [78]
– In for the kill / No stranger to love / Turn to stone / Sphinx (the guardian) / Seventh star / Danger zone / Heart like a wheel / Angry heart / In memory. *(cd/c re-iss. Apr96/Oct97 on 'Essential'; ESM CD/MC 335)*

— **TONY IOMMI** again added **BOB DAISLEY** – bass / **BEV BEVAN** – percussion / **TONY MARTIN** – vocals repl. HUGHES

Nov 87. (lp/c)(cd) *(VERH/+C 51)(832708-2) <25548>* **THE ETERNAL IDOL** [66] [ ]
– The shining / Ancient warrior / Hard life to love / Glory ride / Born to lose / Scarlet Pimpernel / Lost forever / The eternal idol. *(cd+=)* – Nightmare. *(cd/c re-iss. Apr96/Oct97 on 'Essential'; ESM CD/MC 336)*

— **IOMMI + MARTIN** recruited **COZY POWELL** – drums (ex-RAINBOW, ex-ELP) **LAURENCE COTTLE** – bass (on session)

I.R.S. I.R.S.

Apr 89. (7"/7"s) *(EIRS/+CB 107)* **HEADLESS CROSS. / CLOAK AND DAGGER** [62] [ ]
(12"+=/12"w-poster+=) *(EIRST/+PB 107)* – ('A'extended).

Apr 89. (lp/pic-lp/c/cd) *(EIRSA/+PD/C/CD 1002) <82002>* **HEADLESS CROSS** [31] [ ]
– The gates of Hell / Headless cross / Devil & daughter / When death calls / Kill in the spirit world / Call of the wild / Black moon / Nightwing. *(pic-lp+=)* – Cloak and dagger. *(re-iss. cd Apr94;) (cd re-iss. Aug99 on 'E.M.I.'; 521299-2)*

Jun 89. (one-sided; 7"/7"s/7"pic-d) *(EIRS/+B/PD 115)* **DEVIL AND DAUGHTER** [ ] [ ]
(12"+=) *(EIRST 115)* – (15 minute interview).

— **NEIL MURRAY** – bass (ex-VOW WOW, etc.) joined mid'89 repl.COTTLE

Aug 90. (lp/pic-lp/c/cd) *(EIRSA/+PD/C/CD 1038) <X2-13049>* **TYR** [24] [ ]
– Anno Mundi / The law maker / Jerusalem / The sabbath stones / The battle of Tyr / Odin's court / Valhalla / Feels good to me / Heaven in black. *(pic-lp+=)* – Paranoid (live) / Heaven and Hell (live). *(re-iss. cd Apr94) (cd re-iss. Aug99 on 'E.M.I.'; 521298-2)*

Sep 90. (7"/c-s) *(EIRS/C 148)* **FEELS GOOD TO ME. / PARANOID (live)** [ ] [ ]
(12"+=/cd-s+=) *(EIRS T/CD 148)* – Heaven and Hell (live).

— the 1981-83 line-up re-formed Oct91, **IOMMI, GEEZER, VINNIE** and **R.JAMES DIO**

I.R.S. Reprise

Jun 92. (lp/c/cd) *(EIRS A/C/CD 1064) <26965>* **DEHUMANIZER** [28] [44]
– Computer god / After all (the dead) / TV crimes / Letters from Earth / Masters of insanity / Time machine / Sins of the father / Too late / I / Buried alive. *(re-iss. cd Apr94 & Feb99; same)*

Jun 92. (7"pic-d) *(EIRSP 178)* **TV CRIMES. / LETTERS FROM EARTH** [33] [-]
(12"pic-d+=) *(12EIRSPD 178)* – Mob rules (live).
(cd-s+=) *(CDEIRS 178)* – Paranoid (live).
(cd-s+=) *(CDEIRSS 178)* – Heaven and Hell (live).

— **TONY MARTIN** returned on vocals to repl. DIO

— **BOBBY RONDINELLI** – drums (ex-RAINBOW) repl. APPICE

Feb 94. (cd/c/lp) *(EIRS CD/TC/LP 1067) <13222>* **CROSS PURPOSES** [41] [ ]
– I witness / Cross of thorns / Psychophobia / Virtual death / Immaculate deception / Dying for love / Back to Eden / The hand that rocks the cradle / Cardinal sin / Evil eye.

— The 1990 line-up was once again in force although COZY departed once again after below to be repl. by the returning RONDINELLI

I.R.S. Capitol

Jun 95. (cd/c) *(EIRS CD/TC 1072) <30620>* **FORBIDDEN** [71] [ ]
– The illusion of power / Get a grip / Can't get close enough / Shaking off the chains / I won't cry for you / Guilty as hell / Sick and tired / Rusty angels / Forbidden / Kiss of death.

— the original BLACK SABBATH reformed for live gigs

Epic Epic

Oct 98. (d-cd/d-c) *(491954-2/-4) <69115>* **REUNION (live late '97)** [41] [11]
– War pigs / Beyond the wall of sleep / N.I.B. / Fairies wear boots / Electric funeral / Sweet leaf / Spiral architect / Into the void / Snowblind / Sabbath bloody sabbath / Orchid – Lord of this world / Dirty women / Black sabbath / Iron man / Children of the grave / Paranoid / Psycho man (studio) / Selling my soul (studio). *(also d-cd; 491954-9)*

N.M.C. not iss.

Dec 99. (cd-ep) *(PILOT 49)* **BLACK MASS** [ ] [-]
– Paranoid / Black sabbath / Iron man / Blue suede shoes.

– compilations etc. –

on 'NEMS' / 'Warners' unless otherwise stated

Dec 77. (lp) *(NEL 6009)* **BLACK SABBATH'S GREATEST HITS** [ ] [ ]
(re-iss. Nov90 on 'Castle' lp/c/cd+=; CLA LP/MC/CD 200)

Aug 78. (7") *(NES 121)* **PARANOID. / SNOWBLIND** [ ] [-]

Jun 80. (lp) *(BS 001)* **LIVE AT LAST (live)** [5] [ ]
– Tomorrow's dream / Sweet leaf / Killing yourself to live / Cornucopia / Snowblind / Children of the grave / War pigs / Wicked world / Paranoid. *(cd-iss. Aug96 on 'Essential'; ESMCD 331) (<d-cd re-iss. Sep02 as 'PAST LIVES' on 'Sanctuary'+=; SANDP 138 / 84561>)* – Hand of doom / Hole in the sky / Symptom of the universe / Megalomania / Iron man / Black sabbath / N.I.B. / Behind the wall of sleep / Fairies wear boots.

Aug 80. (7") *(BSS 101)* **PARANOID. / SABBATH BLOODY SABBATH** [14] [-]

Aug 82. (7"pic-d) *(NEP 1)* **PARANOID. / IRON MAN** [ ] [ ]
(12"+=) *(12NEX 01)* – Fairies wear boots / War pigs.

Aug 85. (d-lp/c) *Castle; (CCS LP/MC 109)* **THE COLLECTION** [ ] [-]
(cd-iss. 1986; CCSCD 109)

Dec 85. (7xlp-box) *Castle; (BSBOX 01)* **BOXED SET** [ ] [-]
– (all albums with OZZY)

Jun 86. (12"ep) *That's Original; (TOF 101)* **CLASSIC CUTS FROM THE VAULTS** [ ] [-]
– Paranoid / War pigs / Iron man / Black sabbath.

Jun 88. (d-lp/d-c/d-cd) *That's Original; (TFO LP/MC/CD 10)* **SABBATH BLOODY SABBATH / BLACK SABBATH** [ ] [-]

Nov 88. (3"cd-ep) *Castle; (CD 3-5)* **BLACK SABBATH LIMITED EDITION** [ ] [-]
– Paranoid / Iron man / War pigs.

Dec 88. (6xcd-box) *Castle; (BSBCD 001)* **THE BLACK SABBATH CD COLLECTION** [ ] [-]

Mar 89. (cd-ep) *Old Gold; (OG 6129)* **PARANOID / ELECTRIC FUNERAL / SABBATH BLOODY SABBATH** [ ] [-]

Nov 89. (d-lp/c/cd) *Vertigo; (838 818-1/-4/-2)* **BLACKEST SABBATH** [ ] [ ]

Dec 89. (d-lp/d-c/cd) *Masterpiece; (TRK LP/MC/CD 103)* **BACKTRACKIN' (20th ANNIVERSARY EDITION)** [ ] [-]

Mar 90. (7") *Old Gold; (OG 9467)* **PARANOID. / IRON MAN** [ ] [-]

Oct 90. (cd/c/lp) *Castle; (CCS CD/MC/LP 199)* **THE BLACK SABBATH COLLECTION VOL.II** [ ] [-]

May 91. (3xcd/5xlp-box) *Essential; (ESB CD/LP 142)* **THE OZZY OSBOURNE YEARS** [ ] [-]
– (features first 6 albums)

Sep 94. (cd/c) *Spectrum; (550720-2/-4)* **IRON MAN** [ ] [-]

1995. (cd-box with video) *P.M.I.; (7243-8-30069-2)* **CROSS PURPOSES LIVE (live 1994)** [ ] [-]

Sep 95. (cd/c) *Raw Power; (RAW CD/MC 104)* **BETWEEN HEAVEN AND HELL (THE BEST OF BLACK SABBATH)** [ ] [-]

Nov 95. (3xcd-box) *E.M.I.; (CDOMB 014)* **THE ORIGINALS** [ ] [-]
– (HEADLESS CROSS / TYR / DEHUMANISER)

Apr 96. (cd/c) *Essential; (EIRS CD/TC 1076)* **THE SABBATH STONES** [ ] [-]

Nov 96. (4xcd-box) *Essential; (ESFCD 419)* **UNDER THE WHEELS OF CONFUSION** [ ] [-]

Oct 98. (3xcd-box) *Essential; (ESMBX 300)* **BLACK SABBATH / PARANOID / MASTER OF REALITY** [ ] [-]

Oct 98. (3xcd-box) *Essential; (ESMBX 301)* **TECHNICAL ECSTASY / NEVER SAY DIE / HEAVEN AND HELL** [ ] [-]

Jun 00. (d-cd/q-lp) *Raw Power; (RAW DD/LP 145)* **THE BEST OF BLACK SABBATH** [24] [-]

Sep 00. (6xcd-s-box) *Essential; (CMKBX 002)* **THE SINGLES BOX SET** [ ] [-]

TONY IOMMI

with **BILL WARD** plus guests vocalists (see below) + **MATT CAMERON** + **JOHN TEMPESTA** + **KENNY ARONOFF** – drums / **BEN SHEPHERD** + **LAURENCE COTTLE** – bass / **BRIAN MAY** – guitar

Priority Priority

Oct 00. (cd) *(CDPTY 207)* *<27857>* **IOMMI** [ ] [ ]
– Laughing man (in the devil mask) (with HENRY ROLLINS) / Meat (with SKIN) / Goodbye lament (with DAVE GROHL) / Time is mine (with PHIL ANSELMO) / Patterns (with SERJ TANKIAN) / Black oblivion (with BILLY CORGAN) / Flame on (with IAN ASTBURY) / Just say no to love (with PETER STEELE) / Who's fooling who (with OZZY OSBOURNE) / Into the night (with BILLY IDOL).

Mary J. BLIGE

Born: MARY JANE BLIGE, 11 Jan'71, Atlanta, Georgia, USA. Along with artists like MISSY ELLIOTT, FAITH EVANS and EVE, MARY J. BLIGE has become one of the most influential of modern day female R&B singers. Born in The Bronx, but raised in Savannah and Yonkers, BLIGE dropped out of high school and began playing truant in the local malls where she initially recorded a version of Anita Baker's 'CAUGHT UP IN THE RAPTURE' on a small, crude karaoke machine. However, it was this, possibly the cheapest demo imaginable, that sealed her fate as a rising artist when her father passed it on to 'Uptown' honcho Andre Harrell. He was so impressed, he signed BLIGE to sing back-up with little-known act FATHER MC SEAN COMBS (aka PUFF DADDY), a sometime assistant producer with the label. He became interested in the youngster's scorching talent and gained permission to produce a low-key album for BLIGE entitled 'WHAT'S THE 411?' (1991), a merge of hip-hop, soul and bubblegum pop that hit the US Top 10, and still hovering around even after the release of a remix version. She followed this up with another COMBS produced fare, 'MY LIFE' (1995), which featured a rougher, edgier sound and included more personal lyrics about her on-and-off relationship with K-CI HAILEY. The album did surprisingly well for a 'difficult' sophomore set, with critics hailing BLIGE as the ghetto version of ARETHA FRANKLIN. Record industry pressures were proving too taxing and BLIGE subsequently fell out with COMBS and the 'Uptown' imprint. She bounced back with two fantastic albums produced by JIMMY JAM and TERRY LEWIS, 1997's 'SHARE MY WORLD', a soul-orientated affair which peaked at No.1 in the Billboard charts. Fourth set 'MARY', which borrowed material from ELTON JOHN, LAURYN HILL and STEVIE WONDER, also hit the US Top 3 and was another to establish her in the now sympathetic British market. Inbetween writing songs for the likes of rising artists such as AALIYAH, BLIGE found time to record her sixth and best album 'NO MORE DRAMA' (2001), a soaring tribute to oppressed women everywhere. With her tongue firmly in her cheek, 'NO MORE DRAMA' exorcised the demons in her life, from her rough-and-tumble childhood, to her struggles with a revolving door of failed relationships, to her rise as a prominent and influential performer. BLIGE returned to the P. DIDDY fold with 'LOVE & LIFE' (2003), a fairly successful move which nevertheless failed to quite match the magic of their earlier collaborations. The mercurial voiced singer was on fine form throughout, spurred on by such esteemed company as JAY-Z, 50 CENT and METHOD MAN.

Album rating: WHAT'S THE 411? (*7) / WHAT'S THE 411? – REMIX ALBUM (*5) / MY LIFE (*6) / SHARE MY WORLD (*7) / THE TOUR (*5) / MARY (*7) / NO MORE DRAMA (*7) / DANCE FOR ME remixes (*5) / LOVE & LIFE (*6)

MARY J. BLIGE – vocals / with session people, etc

Uptown-MCA Uptown-MCA

Jun 92. (c-s,cd-s) *<54327>* **YOU REMIND ME / (instrumental)** [–] [29]
Aug 92. (cd/c) *<(UPT D/C 10681)>* **WHAT'S THE 411?** [ ] [6]
– Leave a message / Reminisce / Real love / You remind me / Intro talk / Sweet thing / Love no limit / I don't want to do anything / Slow down / My love / Changes I've been going through / What's the 411? *(re-dist.Mar93)* – hit No.53 *(cd re-iss. Jul96 on 'M.C.A.'; MCLD 19315)*
Nov 92. (c-s) *(MCSC 1721)* *<54455>* **REAL LOVE / (hip hop version)** [68] Aug92 [7]
(cd-s+=) *(MCSTD 1721)* – ('A'mixes).
Feb 93. (c-s) *(MCSC 1731)* *<54526>* **REMINISCE / (instrumental)** [31] Dec92 [57]
(12"+=/cd-s+=) *(MSCT/+D 1731)* –
Feb 93. (c-s,cd-s) *<54586>* **SWEET THING / SLOW DOWN** [–] [28]
May 93. (c-s,cd-s) *<54639>* **LOVE NO LIMIT / (instrumental)** [–] [44]
May 93. (c-s) *(MCSC 1770)* **YOU REMIND ME / (mix)** [48] [–]
(12"+=/cd-s+=) *(MCST/+D 1770)* – ('A'mixes).
Aug 93. (c-s) *(MCSC 1922)* **REAL LOVE (remix) / (version)** [26] [–]
(12"+=/cd-s+=) *(MCST/+D 1922)* – ('A'mixes).
Nov 93. (c-s) *(MCSC 1948)* *<54701>* **YOU DON'T HAVE TO WORRY / (remix with rap)** [36] Dec93 [63]
(12"+=/cd-s+=) *(MCST/+D 1948)* – (2-'A'mixes).
Dec 93. (cd/c) *<(UPT D/C 10942)>* **WHAT'S THE 411? REMIX** (remixes all but 2) [ ] [ ]
(cd re-iss. Oct96; MCLD 19338)
May 94. (c-s) *(MCSC 1972)* **MY LOVE / (mix)** [29] [–]
(cd-s+=/12"+=) *(MCS TD/X 1972)* – Reminisce.
(12") *(MCST 1972)* – On da street.
Nov 94. (c-s) *(MCSC 2033)* *<54927>* **BE HAPPY / (acappella)** [30] Oct94 [29]
(12"+=/cd-s+=) *(MCST/+D 2033)* – ('A'mixes).
(cd-s) *(MSCXD 2033)* – ('A'mixes).
Dec 94. (cd/c) *<(UPT D/C 11156)>* **MY LIFE** [59] [7]
– Intro / Mary Jane (all night long) / You bring me joy / Marvin interlude / I'm the only woman / K. Murray interlude / My life / You gotta believe / I never wanna live without you / I'm going down / My life interlude / Be with you / Mary's joint / Don't go / I love you / No one else / Be happy / (You make me feel like a) Natural woman. *(cd/c re-iss. Jan96 on 'M.C.A.'; MCD/MCC 11396)*
Apr 95. (c-s) *(MCSC 2053)* *<55008>* **I'M GOIN' DOWN / (mix)** [12] Mar95 [22]
(12"+=/cd-s+=) *(MCST/+D 2053)* – ('A'mixes).
Jun 95. (c-s,cd-s) *<55029>* **YOU BRING ME JOY / I LOVE YOU** [–] [57] [65]

— in summer '95, she featured with METHOD MAN (of WU TANG CLAN) on the hit single, 'I'LL BE THERE FOR YOU – YOU'RE ALL I NEED TO GET BY'

Sep 95. (c-s) *(MCSC 2088)* **MARY JANE (ALL NIGHT LONG) / (mix)** [17] [–]
(12"+=/cd-s+=) *(MCST/+D 2088)* – ('A'mixes).
Dec 95. (c-s) *(MCSC 2108)* *<55139>* **(YOU MAKE ME FEEL LIKE A) NATURAL WOMAN / (a Lost Boyz track)** [23] Oct95 [95]
(12"+=/cd-s+=) *(MCST/+D 2108)* – (other artist).
Mar 96. (7"/c-s) *(74321 35825-7/-4)* *<12957>* **NOT GON' CRY. / (other by Chaka Khan)** [39] Jan96 [2]
(cd-s+=) *(74321 35825-2)* – (other artist).
above from the movie, 'Waiting To Exhale' on 'Arista' records

— In Mar'97, she featured on JAY-Z's hit 'Can't Knock The Hustle'

Apr 97. (cd/c) *(MCD/MCC 11619)* *<11606>* **SHARE MY WORLD** [8] [1]
– Intro / I can love you / Love is all we need / Round and round / Share my world / (interlude) / Seven days / It's on / Thank you Lord (interlude) / Missing you / Everything / Keep your head / Can'y get you off my mind / Get to know you better / Searchin' / Our love / Not gon' cry / (You make me feel like a) Natural woman.
May 97. (c-s) *(MCSC 48053)* **LOVE IS ALL WE NEED / (mix)** [15] [–]
(12"+=/cd-s+=) *(MCST/+D 48053)* – ('A'mixes).
Jun 97. (12"/cd-s) *<5536-2/-3>* **I CAN LOVE YOU / LOVE IS ALL WE NEED (ALL WE NEED IS LOVE (remix)** [–] [28]
Aug 97. (c-s) *(MCSC 48059)* *<55354>* **EVERYTHING / (mix)** [6] [24]
(12"+=/cd-s+=) *(MCST/+D 48059)* – ('A'mixes).
Nov 97. (c-s) *(MCSC 48071)* **MISSING YOU / (mix)** [19] [ ]
(12"+=/cd-s+=) *(MCST/+D 48071)* – ('A'mixes).
Jul 98. (c-s; by MARY J. BLIGE & GEORGE BENSON) *(MCSC 48083)* **SEVEN DAYS / (mix)** [22] [ ]
(12"+=/cd-s+=) *(MCST/+D 48083)* – ('A'mixes).
Jul 98. (cd) *<(MCD 11848)>* **THE TOUR (live)** [ ] [21]
– Intro / Real love / You remind me / Reminische / Sweet thing / Mary Jane (all night long) / Love no limit / Summer madness / My life / You gotta believe / Slow down / Mary's joint / I'm the only woman / Share my world / I'm going down / Thank you Lord / I can love you / Keep your head /

Everything / Seven days / Not gon' cry / Missing you / Daydreaming / Misty blue.

— In Mar'99, MARY J duetted with GEORGE MICHAEL on the hit, 'AS'

Aug 99. (c-s) *(MCSC 40215)* *<radio cut>* **ALL THAT I CAN SAY / (mix)** [29] Jul99 [44]
(12"+=/cd-s+=) *(MCST/+D 40215)* – Beautiful.

Aug 99. (cd/c) *(MCD/MCC 11976)* *<11929>* **MARY** [5] [2]
– All that I can say / Sexy / Deep inside / Beautiful ones / I'm the love / As (with GEORGE MICHAEL) / Time / Memories / Don't waste your time / Not lookin' / Your child / No happy holidays / Love I never had / Give me you / Let no man put asunder / Give me you (Nino radio). *(re-iss. Apr00; 112255-2/-4)*

Nov 99. (12"/cd-s) *(MCST/+D 40224)* *<radio cut>* **DEEP INSIDE. / LET NO MAN PUT ASUNDER** [42] [63]
(cd-s) *(MCSTX 40224)* – ('A'side) / Sincerity (with NAS & DMX).

Apr 00. (c-s/cd-s) *(MCS C/TD 40230)* *<155708>* **GIVE ME YOU / (mixes)** [19] [68]
(cd-s) *(MCSTX 40230)* – ('A'side) / Sexy.

— in Oct'00, MARY J featured on WYCLEF JEAN's hit '911'

Aug 01. (cd) *<(112632-2)>* **NO MORE DRAMA** [4] [2]
– Love / Family affair / Steel away / Crazy games / PMS / No more drama / Keep it moving / Destiny / Where I've been (featuring EVE) / Beautiful day / Dance for me / Flying away / Never been / 2U / In the meantime / Forever no more (poem) / Testimony / Checkin' for me.

Sep 01. (c-s) *(MSC 40267)* *<155859>* **FAMILY AFFAIR / YOUR CHILD (Chunky Thompson's late nite mix)** [8] Jul01 [1]
(12"+=) *(MSCT 40267)* – ('A'mix).
(cd-s++=) *(MCSTD 40267)* – ('A'-video).

Jan 02. (cd-s; by MARY J. BLIGE & COMMON) *(MCSTD 40274)* **DANCE FOR ME (mixes)** [13] [ ]
(cd-s) *(MCSXD 40274)* – ('A'-mixes).
(12") *(MCDT 40274)* – ('A'mixes).

Apr 02. (c-s) *(MCSC 40281)* *<radio>* **NO MORE DRAMA / MARY JANE (ALL NIGHT LONG) (live)** [9] Dec01 [15]
(cd-s+=) *(MCSXD 40281)* – Everything.
(cd-s) *(MCSTD 40281)* – (mixes + video).

Aug 02. (c-s; MARY J. BLIGE & JA RULE) *(MCSC 40288)* **RAINY DAYZ / (extended)** [17] [ ]
(12"+=) *(MCST 40288)* – ('A'-Third Eye remix).
(cd-s+=) *(MCSTD 40288)* – ('A'video).
(cd-s) *(MCSXD 40288)* – ('A'side) / Let no man put asunder (Maurice J remix) / Sexy (with JUDAKISS).

Aug 02. (cd) *<(112959-2)>* **DANCE FOR ME** (remixes) [ ] Jul02 [76]

Geffen Geffen

Aug 03. (cd) *(9860700)* *<9560-2>* **LOVE & LIFE** [8] [1]
– Intro&life (with JAY-Z & P. DIDDY) / Don't go / When we / Not today (with EVE) / Finally we made it / Ooh! / Let me be the 1 (with 50 CENT) / Love @ first sight (with METHOD MAN) / Willing & waiting / Free / Friends / Press on / Feel like makin' love / It's a wrap / Message in our music / All my love / Special part of me / Ultimate relationship (a.m.). *(d-lp-iss/Sep03; 986061-2)* *(cd re-iss. Nov03 +=; 986134-5)* – Didn't mean / Whenever I say your name (with STING).

Sep 03. (12"; by MARY J. BLIGE & METHOD MAN) *(MCST 40338)* *<26043>* **LOVE @ FIRST SIGHT (mixes)** [18] Jul03 [22]
(cd-s+=) *(MCSTD 40338)* – Your child (Klymamma Griffin uptempo mix) / ('A'-video).

Nov 03. (12"/cd-s; by MARY J. BLIGE & EVE) *(MCST/+D 40349)* **NOT TODAY (mixes)** [40] [–]

— in Dec'03, MARY featured on STING's hit, 'Whenever I Say Your Name'

BLIND FAITH

Formed: London, England ... May '69 ... as supergroup of musicians ERIC CLAPTON, GINGER BAKER, STEVE WINWOOD and RIC GRECH. They introduced their accomplished style of roots blues at the BRIAN JONES memorial concert in Hyde Park, supporting The ROLLING STONES. Their first and only album recorded virtually live in the studio, was a massive seller on both sides of the Atlantic and included some stellar moments ('CAN'T FIND MY WAY HOME', 'PRESENCE OF THE LORD'). They subsequently undertook a promotional tour of the States that Autumn, although to the disappointment of many fans, the project was abruptly aborted. • **Songwriters:** CLAPTON and WINWOOD, with cover WELL ALL RIGHT (Buddy Holly). • **Trivia:** GINGER BAKER's 11 year-old daughter was controversially used posing topless on UK album sleeve. This was subsequently banned in the States.

Album rating: BLIND FAITH (*7)

STEVE WINWOOD (b.12 May'48, Birmingham, England) – vocals, keyboards (ex-TRAFFIC, ex-SPENCER DAVIS GROUP) / **ERIC CLAPTON** (b.30 Mar'45, Ripley, England) – guitar, vocals (ex-CREAM, ex-JOHN MAYALL . . . , ex-YARDBIRDS, etc) / **RIC GRECH** (b. 1 Nov'46, Bordeaux, France) – bass (ex-FAMILY) / **GINGER BAKER** (b.19 Aug'39, Lewisham, England) – drums (ex-CREAM, ex-GRAHAM BOND ORGANISATION, ex-BLUES INC.)

Polydor R.S.O.

Aug 69. (lp) *(583-059)* *<304>* **BLIND FAITH** [1] Jul69 [1]
– Had to cry today / Can't find my way home / Well all right / Presence of the Lord / Sea of joy / Do what you like. *<US re-iss. Feb77 on 'R.S.O.'; 3016>* *(re-iss. Nov77 on 'R.S.O.'; 2394 142)* *(re-iss. Aug83 on 'R.S.O.'; SPELP 14)* *(cd-iss. Apr86+=; 825 094-2)* *(cd re-iss. Sep95)* – Exchange and mart / Spending all my days. *(lp re-iss. Aug99 on 'Simply Vinyl'; SVLP 104)*

— Disbanded later 1969. GINGER BAKER formed AIRFORCE with STEVE WINWOOD. The latter returned to TRAFFIC before carving out a solo career. RIC GRECH went solo. As did ERIC CLAPTON who also formed DEREK & THE DOMINOES in 1970.

– compilations, others, etc. –

1977. (7") *R.S.O.;* *<873>* **CAN'T FIND MY WAY HOME. / PRESENCE OF THE LORD** [–] [ ]
Obviously no albums were released, although some BLIND FAITH tracks did surface on ERIC CLAPTON compilations, 'CROSSROADS' and 'THE HISTORY OF ERIC CLAPTON' (see ⇒)

BLIND MELON

Formed: Newport Beach, Los Angeles, California, USA . . . 1989 by West Point, Mississippi born BRAD SMITH and ROGER STEVENS. In the early 90's, they were joined by SHANNON HOON, CHRISTOPHER THORN and a little later, GLEN GRAHAM. After recording a widely circulated demo, the band were eventually picked up by 'Capitol'. While awaiting release of their self-titled debut, SHANNON (cousin of AXL ROSE) guested on the GUNS N' ROSES set, 'Use Your Illusion'. With MTV heralding their excellent 'NO RAIN' track, their debut album finally shot into the US Top 3 in 1993. A laid back 70's/GRATEFUL DEAD influenced affair, alternately jangly and funky, HOON's vocals weren't too dissimilar to AXL's. Following a disappointing second set, 'SOUP' (1995), HOON died of a drug overdose on the 21st October '95. Three years on and the sad death now behind them, THORN and SMITH re-united in the outfit LUMA, frontman CHRIS SHINN and veteran ex-PEARL JAM drummer DAVE KRUSEN were also part of the set-up on an internet-only EP in '99. Adding new singer CHRIS SHINN on vocals and guitar, the quartet became UNIFIED THEORY (an unsolved problem Einstein worked on before his death), releasing the eponymous 'UNIFIED THEORY', to sound reviews in August 2000. • **Covered:** JOHN SINCLAIR (John Lennon) / THE PUSHER (Steppenwolf).

Album rating: BLIND MELON (*6) / SOUP (*5) / NICO posthumous (*4) / Unified Theory: UNIFIED THEORY (*7)

SHANNON HOON (b. RICHARD SHANNON HOON, 26 Sep'67, Lafayette, Indiana) – vocals / **ROGER STEVENS** (b.31 Oct'70, West Point, Mis.) – guitar / **CHRISTOPHER THORN** (b.16 Dec'68, Dover, Pennsylvania) – guitar / **BRAD SMITH** (b.29 Sep'68, West Point) – bass / **GLEN GRAHAM** (b. 5 Dec'68, Columbus, Miss.) – drums

Capitol Capitol

Jun 93. (12"pic-d-ep/12"ep/cd-ep) *(12P/12/CD CL 687)* **TONES OF HOME / NO RAIN (live). / DRIVE (live) / SOAK THE SIN (live)** [62] [–]

Aug 93. (cd/c) *(CD/TC EST 2188)* *<96585>* **BLIND MELON** [53] [3]
– Soak the sin / Tones of home / I wonder / Paper scratcher / Dear ol' dad / Change / No rain / Deserted / Sleepy house / Holyman / Seed to a tree / Drive / Time. *(re-dist.Jul94 w/ free cd, hit UK 53)*

Aug 93. (c-s) *<44939>* **NO RAIN / NO RAIN (live) / SOAK THE SIN** [–] [20]

Dec 93. (c-s/7"yellow) *(TC+/CL 699)* **NO RAIN. / NO BIDNESS (live)** [17] [–]
(12"+=/cd-s+=) *(12/CD CL 699)* – I wonder.
(12"pic-d/pic-cd-s) *(12P/CDP CL 699)* – ('A'live) / Soak the sin / Paper scratcher / Deserted.

Jun 94. (c-s/7"green) *(TC+/CL 717)* **CHANGE. / PAPER SCRATCHER (acoustic)** [35] [–]
(12"pic-d/pic-cd-s) *(12/CDS CL 717)* – ('A'side) / No rain (live) / Candy says (live) / Time (live).

Jul 95. (cd-s) *(CDCL 755)* **GALAXIE / WILT / CAR SEAT (GOD'S PRESENTS)** [37] [–]
(12"+=) *(12CL 755)* – 2 x 4.
(cd-s) *(CDCLS 755)* – (first 2 tracks) / 2 x 4 / Change.

Aug 95. (cd/c) *(CD/TC EST 2261)* *<28732>* **SOUP** [48] [28]
– Galaxie / 2 x 4 / Vernie / Skinned / Toes across the floor / Walk / Dumptruck / Car seat (God's presents) / Wilt / The duke / St.Andrew's fall / New life / Mouthful of cavities / Lemonade.

—— On October 21st, '95, frontman SHANNON HOON died of drug overdose.

– compilations, etc. –

Feb 97. (cd) *Capitol; (CDEST 2291)* *<37451>* **NICO** [ ] [ ]
– Pusher / Hell / Soup / No rain / Soul one / John Sinclair / All that I need / Glitch / Life ain't so shitty / Swallowed / Oull / St. Andrew's hall / Letters from a porcupine.

UNIFIED THEORY

HOON + SMITH along with **CHRIS SHINN** – vocals, guitar / **DAVE KRUSEN** – guitar (ex-PEARL JAM, etc)

Universal Universal

Aug 00. (cd) *<(AA12 159275-2)>* **UNIFIED THEORY** [ ] [ ]
– Cessna / California / Instead of running / Wither / The sun will come / A.M. radio / Fin / Self medicate / Passive / Full flavor / Not dead / Keep on.

BLINK-182

Formed: Poway, nr. San Diego, California, USA ... 1992 by vocalist/guitarist TOM DELONGE, bassist MARK HOPPUS and drummer SCOTT RAYNOR. This post new cartoon punk outfit began when DELONGE and BARKER met in college. Soon, they were distributing their collection of demos (all which would later appear on 'BUDDHA' debut set) to A&R upstarts. Unfortunately their quest did not succeed, forcing our mangled, spiky-haired heroes to issue their second, self-financed set 'CHESHIRE CAT' (1995), whilst still under the name of BLINK. However, with pressures from an Irish group of the same name, the band re-emerged as BLINK-182 – the 182 in question, being the number of times Al Pacino said "fuck" in the movie, 'Scarface' – and issued the more successful 'DUDE RANCH' (1997). The album boasted college anthem 'DICK LIPS' which sent the boys quite literally on the road to semi-stardom via a little help from supportive peers GREEN DAY and NOFX. Major labels began to show interest, BLINK-182 (with new drummer TRAVIS BARKER) finally signing on the dotted line with 'M.C.A.' at the beginning of 1999. 'ENEMA OF THE STATE' (which featured porn actress Janine scantily clad in a nurse's uniform) surfaced in that summer and went on to achieve double platinum sales throughout America and Europe. Memorable single, 'WHAT'S MY AGE AGAIN?' (a catchy two minute punk/pop rant), saw the trio run naked through L.A. (in the video at least!) and earned them a cameo performance in "ironic" teen sex movie, 'American Pie'. No underlying message, it seemed that BLINK-182 were just out to drink, party and get nekid! Indeed, their next offering hinted as much. Forgetting the decidedly dismal 'THE MARK, TOM & TRAVIS SHOW' a year earlier, 'TAKE OFF YOUR PANTS AND JACKET' (2001), smashed in at No.1 in the US album charts and also broke into the UK Top 5, thanks to the hit single, 'THE ROCK SHOW'. In 2002, and with spare studio time in hand, TOM and TRAVIS (and producer JERRY FINN) formed side-project, BOXCAR RACER. Recruiting new kids on the block, guitarist DAVID KENNEDY and bassist ANTHONY CELESTINO, BLINK-182 surprised fans and critics alike with a more mature and darker sound on their eponymous album, issued in 2003. The riffs and teen-punk harmonies were still intact, but the band had created a richer atmosphere than on previous records. Think GREEN DAY's seminal 'Kerplunk', all twisted guitar hooks and downbeat lyrics of genuine angst and loss of self-control; example 'I MISS YOU'. Hell, even The Cure's ROBERT SMITH popped up to lend his vocals on the LP, and while it ain't no classic, it's still a departure from porn star covers and silly songs about masturbating and snot.

Album rating: BUDDHA (*5) / CHESHIRE CAT (*6) / DUDE RANCH (*7) / ENEMA OF THE STATE (*6) / THE MARK, TOM & TRAVIS SHOW (*4) / TAKE OFF YOUR PANTS AND JACKET (*6) / BLINK-182 (*7) / Boxcar Racer: BOXCAR RACER (*6)

TOM DELONGE (b.13 Dec'75) – vocals, guitar / **MARK HOPPUS** (b.15 Mar'72) – bass / **SCOTT RAYNOR** – drums

not iss. unknown

1993. (7"ep; as BLINK) **FLY SWATTER EP** [–] [ ]

not iss. Kung Fu

1994. (cd/lp) *<78765-2/-1>* **BUDDHA** [–] [ ]
– Carousel / T.V. / Strings / Fentoozler / Time / Romeo & Rebecca / 21 days / Sometimes / Degenerate / Point of view / My pet Sally / Reebok commercial / Toast and bananas / The girls next door / Don't. *(re-iss. Jan99 & Jul99; same)*

not iss. Rapido

Jun 96. (cd-ep) *<RAP 14>* **WASTING TIME – 1996 AUSTRALIAN TOUR EP** [–] [ ]
– Wasting time / Wrecked him / Lemmings / Enthused. *(UK-iss.Apr98; RAP 30)*

Grilled Cheese Grilled Cheese

Nov 96. (cd) *<(GRL 001)>* **CHESHIRE CAT** [ ] May95 [ ]
– Carousel / M + M's / Fentoozler / Touchdown boy / Strings / Peggy Sue / Sometimes / Does my breath smell? / Cacophony / T.V. / Toast and bananas / Wasting time / Romeo and Rebecca / Ben wah balls / Just about done / Depends. *(re-iss. Nov00 on 'M.C.A.'; 488136-2)*

Nov 96. (cd-s) *<(GRL 701)>* **THEY CAME TO CONQUER . . . URANUS** [ ] Dec95 [ ]
– Waggy / Wrecked him / Zulu.

May 97. (cd-ep) *<(CSGRL 004)>* **DICK LIPS EP** [ ] [ ]
– Dick lips / Apple shampoo / Wrecked him / Zulu.

Jul 97. (cd/lp) *<(CRGD/LPGRL 4)>* **DUDE RANCH** [ ] [67]
– Pathetic / Voyeur / Dammit / Boring / Dick lips / Waggy / Enthused / Untitled / Apple shampoo / Emo / Josie / A new hope / Degenerate / Lemmings / I'm sorry. *<(cd re-iss. Nov97 on 'M.C.A.'; MCD 11624)>*

Dec 97. (7") **DAMMIT. / DAMMIT (Growing Up edit)** [–] [ ]

—— **TRAVIS BARKER** (b.14 Nov'75) – drums (ex-AQUABATS, ex-PSYCHO BUTTERFLY) repl. SCOTT

Nov 98. (cd-ep) *<55513>* **JOSIE / WASTING TIME / CAROUSEL / I WON'T BE HOME FOR CHRISTMAS** [–] [ ]

Dec 98. (7") **I WON'T BE HOME FOR CHRISTMAS** [–] [–]

M.C.A. M.C.A.

Sep 99. (c-s) *(MCSC 40219)* *<radio cut>* **WHAT'S MY AGE AGAIN? / PATHETIC (live)** [38] Jul99 [59]
(cd-s+=) *<(MCSTD 40219)>* – Untitled (live).
(cd-s) *<(MCSXD 40219)>* – ('A'side) / Josie (live) / Aliens exist (live).

Oct 99. (cd) *(MCD 11950)* *<111950>* **ENEMA OF THE STATE** [15] Jun99 [9]

– Don't leave me / Adam's song / The party song / Wendy clear / Going away to college / Dysentery Gary / Aliens exist / All the small things / Mutt / Anthem / What's my age again? / Dumpweed.

Mar 00. (c-s) *(MCSC 40223)* *<155606>* **ALL THE SMALL THINGS DAMMIT (live)** 2 Nov99 6
(cd-s+=) *(MCSXD 40223)* – ('A'live) / ('A'-CD-Rom video).
(cd-s) *(MCSTD 40223)* – ('A'side) / Dumpweed (live) / What's my age again? (live).

Jun 00. (c-s) *(MCSC 40219)* **WHAT'S MY AGE AGAIN? / PATHETIC (live)** 17 –
(cd-s+=) *(MCSZD 40219)* – Untitled (live) / ('A'-CD-Rom).
(cd-s) *(MCSYD 40219)* – ('A'side) / Josie (live) / (interview on CD-Rom).

Nov 00. (cd) *<(112379-2)>* **THE MARK, TOM AND TRAVIS SHOW – THE ENEMA STRIKES BACK! (live)** 69 8
– Dumpweed / Don't leave me / Alines exist / Family reunion / Going away to college / What's my age again? / Dick lips / Blow job / Untitled / Voyeur / Pathetic / Adam's song / Peggy Sue / Wendy clear / Carousel / All the small things / Mutt / The country song / Dammit / Man overboard / (plus a whole bunch of funny shit in between).

Jun 01. (cd) *<(112627-2)>* **TAKE OFF YOUR PANTS AND JACKET** 4 1
– Anthem (part 2) / Online songs / First date / Happy holidays you bastard / Story of a lonely guy / The rock show / Stay together for the kids / Roller coaster / Reckless abandon / Everytime I look for you / Give me one good reason / Shut up / Please take me home / What went wrong / Time to break up / Fuck a dog / Man overboard (video).

Jul 01. (cd-s) *(MCSTD 40259)* *<radio cut>* **THE ROCK SHOW / TIME TO BREAK UP / MAN OVERBOARD** 14 71

Sep 01. (7") *(MCS 40264)* **FIRST DATE. / DON'T TELL ME IT'S OVER** 31 –
(cd-s+=) *(MCSTD 40264)* – Mother's day.

Nov 03. (cd) *(9861408)* *<133612>* **BLINK-182** 22 3
– Feeling this / Obvious / I miss you / Violence / Stockholm syndrome / Down / The fallen interlude / Go / Asthenia / Always / Easy target / All of this / Here's your letter / I'm lost without you. *(UK+=)* – Not now / Anthem (part 2 – live in Chicago) / Feeling this (video) / Obvious (video) / Down / The fallen interlude (video) / Violence (video).

Nov 03. (7"/cd-s) *(MCS/+TD 40347)* *<981409>* **FEELING THIS. / ROCK SHOW (live)** 15 Dec03 –

BOXCAR RACER

TOM DELONGE + TRAVIS BARKER plus **DAVID KENNEDY** – guitar / **ANTHONY CELESTINO** – bass

M.C.A. M.C.A.

May 02. (cd) *(112947-2)* *<112894-2>* **BOX CAR RACER** 27 12
– I feel so / All systems go / Watch the world / Tiny voices / Cat like thief / And I / Letters to God / My first punk song / Sorrow / There is / The end with you / Elevator / Instrumental.

Jun 02. (7") *(MCS 40290)* **I FEEL SO. / CAT LIKE THIEF** 41 –
(cd-s+=) *(MCSTD 40290)* – ('A'-guitar intro) / ('A'-video).

BLONDIE

Formed: New York City, New York, USA . . . August 1974 by former Playboy bunny girl, DEBBIE HARRY and boyfriend CHRIS STEIN. Other original members excluding female backing singers were sticksman, BILLY O'CONNOR (soon replaced by CLEM BURKE), bassist FRED SMITH (later of TELEVISION) and guitarist IVAN KRAL (later of PATTI SMITH GROUP). After line-up changes which saw the latter two replaced by GARY VALENTINE and JIMMY DESTRI respectively, the group soon found themselves supporting the likes of punk legend, IGGY POP. Subsequently hooking up with veteran producer, Richard Gottehrer, the group released their debut single, 'X-OFFENDER', on his 'Private Stock' label in late '76. This was followed up with a second track, 'IN THE FLESH', while the eponymous debut hit the shelves later that Spring. Trawling tacky 60's girly pop and sprucing it up with a healthy dose of punk muscle and attitude, BLONDIE laid the foundations for their swoonsomely infectious late 70's/early 80's hits. With HARRY as the peroxide Marilyn Monroe of new wave, BLONDIE almost immediately caught the eye of the UK scene, where a follow-up album, 'PLASTIC LETTERS', made the Top 10 in Spring '78. By this point BLONDIE had signed to 'Chrysalis' (who had reputedly bought the contract out for $500,000 in August of the previous year) and had replaced VALENTINE with FRANK INFANTE. A cover of Randy & The Rainbows 60's nugget, 'DENISE' (aka 'DENIS') almost topped the British charts, while another single pulled from the album, '(I'M ALWAYS TOUCHED BY YOUR) PRESENCE DEAR', made the Top 10. With the subsequent recruitment of bassist NIGEL HARRISON, INFANTE switched to rhythm guitar, the music taking on a whole new dimension with the seminal 'PARALLEL LINES' (1978). Produced by legendary pop picker, MIKE CHAPMAN, the album spawned a UK Top 5 in 'HANGING ON THE TELEPHONE', plus two No.1's with 'SUNDAY GIRL' and 'HEART OF GLASS'. The latter track's throbbing disco feel was further developed on fourth album, 'EAT TO THE BEAT', a set which featured yet another UK chart topper in the moody dancefloor classic, 'ATOMIC' (later famous for providing the aural backdrop to the disco scene in 'Trainspotting'). BLONDIE even teamed up with electro disco guru, GEORGIO MORODER, for 'CALL ME' (recorded for the soundtrack to 'American Gigolo'), the band's second transatlantic No.1. They repeated this feat with 'THE TIDE IS HIGH', a wonderfully dreamy cover of a track originally cut by reggae outfit, The PARAGONS, while also having a bash at hip hop with 'RAPTURE', their fourth US No.1. Both tracks were included on 1980's 'AUTOAMERICAN', an album which suggested BLONDIE were beginning to lose their musical curls. Although 'THE HUNTER' (1982) spawned a further British No.1 in 'ISLAND OF LOST SOULS', the album met with a less than rapturous reception, likewise their final tour. The band finally split in summer '82, STEIN forming his own 'Chrysalis'-backed label, 'Animal', before falling ill the following year. This put HARRY's solo career (begun rather noneventfully with 1981's BERNARD EDWARDS / NILE RODGERS collaborative set, 'KOO KOO') temporarily on the back burner, the singer re-emerging in late '86 with the UK Top 10, 'FRENCH KISSIN' IN THE U.S.A.'. The accompanying album, 'ROCKBIRD' made the Top 40 although 1989's 'DEF, DUMB AND BLONDE' was more successful, its shiny, poppy single 'I WANT THAT MAN' making the UK Top 20. If nothing else, she proved herself an adaptable stylist although much more interesting was a tongue in cheek duet with IGGY POP in 1990, 'WELL, DID YOU EVAH!'. Throughout her career, HARRY had also made the occasional venture into celluloid (see below). At the tender age of 53, but still looking every inch (or two) the ideal peroxide sex symbol, DEBBIE and her slightly younger crew of CHRIS, JIMMY and CLEM, re-formed BLONDIE for round the world tours. By early 1999, the band were topping the UK charts with the catchy 'MARIA', a song lifted from their aptly-titled Top 5 (US Top 40) parent album, 'NO EXIT'. A year later, BLONDIE opted for a quick follow-up, the 'greatest hits live' package 'LIVID' (2000) – I know I was. The aptly titled 'CURSE OF BLONDIE' (2003), meanwhile, was an altogether unnecessary addition to the band's revered catalogue, an ill-advised attempt to milk the renunion for more than it could conceivably have provided. Largely directionless and tired, HARRY would have done well to resurrect her solo career instead. • **Songwriters:** Most written by STEIN-HARRY except; HANGING ON THE TELEPHONE (Jack Lee; Nerves) / RING OF FIRE (Johnny Cash) / HEROES (David Bowie). • **Trivia:** DEBBIE HARRY filmography:- UNION CITY (1979) / ROADIE (1980) / VIDEODROME (1982) / HAIRSPRAY (1982) / Broadway play 'TEANECK TANZI: THE

VENUS FLYTRAP' (1983), which bombed after one night. She also appeared on 'The Muppet Show' circa 1980.

Album rating: BLONDIE (*6) / PLASTIC LETTERS (*7) / PARALLEL LINES (*8) / EAT TO THE BEAT (*6) / AUTOAMERICAN (*5) / THE BEST OF BLONDIE compilation (*9) / THE HUNTER (*4) / THE COMPLETE PICTURE – THE VERY BEST OF DEBORAH HARRY & BLONDIE compilation (*9) / BLONDE AND BEYOND compilation (*5) / NO EXIT (*6) / LIVID (*3) / THE CURSE OF BLONDIE (*4) / Debbie Harry: KOOKOO (*5) / ROCKBIRD (*6) / DEF, DUMB & BLONDE (*5) / DEBRAVATION (*4)

DEBBIE HARRY (b. 1 Jul'45, Miami, Florida) – vocals (ex-WIND IN THE WILLOWS) / **CHRIS STEIN** (b. 5 Jan'50, Brooklyn, New York) – guitar / **JIMMY DESTRI** (b.13 Apr'54) – keyboards (ex-KNICKERS) / **GARY VALENTINE** – bass / **CLEM BURKE** (b.CLEMENT, 24 Nov'55) – drums (ex-SWEET REVENGE)

Private Stock | Private Stock

Dec 76. (7") *<PVT 90>* **X OFFENDER. / IN THE SUN** [–] [ ]

Dec 76. (lp) *<PS 2023>* **BLONDIE** [–] [ ]
– X offender / Little girl lies / In the flesh / Look good in blue / In the sun / A shark in jet's clothing / Man overboard / Rip her to shreds / Rifle range / Kung Fu girls / The attack of the giant ants. *<re-iss. Feb77; PVLP 1017> (UK-iss.Dec77 on 'Chrysalis'; CHR 1165)* – (hit UK No.75 in Mar79) *(re-iss. Oct82 on 'Hallmark' lp/c; SHM/HSC 3119) (re-iss. Apr85 on 'M.F.P.' lp/c; MFP 41-5696-1/-4) (cd-iss. Sep94 on 'Chrysalis'; CDCHR 6081)*

Feb 77. (7") *<PVT 105>* **IN THE FLESH. / MAN OVERBOARD** [–] [ ]

May 77. (7") *(PVT 105)* **IN THE FLESH. / X OFFENDER** [ ] [–]

Chrysalis | Chrysalis

Nov 77. (7"m/12"m) *<CHS 2180/+12)* **RIP HER TO SHREDS. / IN THE FLESH / X OFFENDER** [ ] [–]
(re-iss. 12"m Dec81; same)

—— (Oct'77) **FRANK INFANTE** – bass (ex-WORLD WAR III) repl. VALENTINE

Feb 78. (7"m/12"m) *<(CHS 2180/+12)>* **DENIS. / CONTACT IN RED SQUARE / KUNG FU GIRLS** [2] [ ]
(re-iss. 12"white Dec81; same)

Feb 78. (lp/c) *<(CHR/ZCHR 1166)>* **PLASTIC LETTERS** [10] Feb78 [72]
– Fan mail / Denis / Bermuda Triangle blues (Flight 45) / Youth nabbed as sniper / Contact in Red Square / (I'm always touched by your) Presence, dear / I'm on E / I didn't have the nerve to say no / Love at the pier / No imagination / Kidnapper / Detroit 442 / Cautious lip. *(cd-iss. Sep94; CDCHR 6085)*

Apr 78. (7"m/12"m) *<(CHS/+12 2217)>* **(I'M ALWAYS TOUCHED BY YOUR) PRESENCE, DEAR. / POET'S PROBLEM / DETROIT 442** [10] [ ]
(re-iss. Dec81; same)

—— (Nov77 on recording of 2nd lp) added **NIGEL HARRISON** – bass (b.24 Apr'51, Stockport, England) now sextet with **INFANTE** – now on rhythm guitar

Aug 78. (7"yellow) *<(CHS 2204)>* **PICTURE THIS. / FADE AWAY (AND RADIATE)** [12] [ ]

Sep 78. (7") *<2251>* **I'M GONNA LOVE YOU TOO. / JUST GO AWAY** [–] [ ]

Sep 78. (lp/c) *<(CHR/ZCHR 1192)>* **PARALLEL LINES** [1] [6]
– Fade away (and radiate) / Hanging on the telephone / One way or another / Picture this / Pretty baby / I know but I don't know / 11:59 / Will anything happen / Sunday girl / Heart of glass / I'm gonna love you too / Just go away. *(re-iss. Nov83 on 'Fame' lp/c; FA/TCFA 3089-1/-4) (re-iss. Jul88 lp/c/cd; CDL/ZCDL/CCD 1192) (re-iss. Dec92 on 'Fame' cd/c; CD/TC FA 3282) (re-iss. Jul94 cd/c; CCD/ZCDL 1192)*

Nov 78. (7") *(CHS 2266)* **HANGING ON THE TELEPHONE. / WILL ANYTHING HAPPEN** [5] [–]

Nov 78. (7") *<CHS 2266>* **HANGING ON THE TELEPHONE / FADE AWAY AND RADIATE** [–] [ ]

Jan 79. (7") *(CHS 2275)* **HEART OF GLASS. / RIFLE RANGE** [1] [–]
(12"+=) – ('A'instrumental). *(re-iss. 12" Dec81; same)*

Feb 79. (7") *<CHS 2275>* **HEART OF GLASS. / 11:59** [–] [1]

May 79. (7") *(CHS 2320)* **SUNDAY GIRL. / I KNOW BUT I DON'T KNOW** [1] [–]
(12"+=) *(CHS/+12 2320)* – ('A' French version).
(re-iss. 12"clear Dec81; same)

May 79. (7") *<CHS 2336>* **ONE WAY OR ANOTHER. / JUST GO AWAY** [–] [24]

Sep 79. (7") *(CHS 2350)* **DREAMING. / SOUND ASLEEP** [2] [–]

Sep 79. (7") *<CHS 2379>* **DREAMING. / LIVING IN THE REAL WORLD** [–] [27]

Oct 79. (lp/c) *<(CHR/ZCHR 1225)>* **EAT TO THE BEAT** [1] [17]
– Dreaming / The hardest part / Union city blue / Shayla / Eat to the beat / Accidents never happen / Die young stay pretty Slow motion / / Atomic / Sound-a-sleep / Victor / Living in the real world. *(cd-iss. Jun87; CPCD 1225) (cd-iss. Nov92; CDCHR 1225)*

Nov 79. (7") *(CHS 2400)* **UNION CITY BLUE. / LIVING IN THE REAL WORLD** [13] [ ]

Jan 80. (7") *<CHS 2408>* **THE HARDEST PART. / SOUND-A-SLEEP** [–] [84]

Feb 80. (7") *<(CHS 2410)>* **ATOMIC. / DIE YOUNG STAY PRETTY** [1] May80 [39]
(12"+=) *(CHS12 2410)* – Heroes. *(re-iss. 12" Dec81; same)*

Apr 80. (7") *<(CHS 2414)>* **CALL ME. / ('A'instrumental)** [1] Feb80 [1]
(12"+=) *(CHS12 2414)* – ('A'-Spanish version).

Oct 80. (7") *<(CHS 2465)>* **THE TIDE IS HIGH. / SUZIE AND JEFFREY** [1] Nov80 [1]

Nov 80. (lp/c) *<(CDL/ZCDL 1290)>* **AUTOAMERICAN** [3] [7]
– Europa / Live it up / Here's looking at you / The tide is high / Angels on the balcony / Go through it / Do the dark / Rapture / Faces / Do the dark / T-Birds / Walk like me / Follow me. *(cd-iss. Sep94; CDCHR 6084)*

Jan 81. (7") *<(CHS 2485)>* **RAPTURE. / WALK LIKE ME** [5] [1]
(12") *(CHS12 2485)* – ('A'side) / Live it up.

Oct 81. (lp/c) *(CDLTV/ZCLTV 1) <1371>* **THE BEST OF BLONDIE** (compilation) [4] [30]
– Denis / The tide is high / In the flesh / Sunday girl / (I'm always touched by your) Presence dear / Dreaming / Hanging on the telephone / Rapture / Picture this / Union city blue / Call me / Atomic / Rip her to shreds / Heart of glass. *(cd-iss. Jan88; CCD 1371)*

Apr 82. (7"/7"pic-d) *<(CHS/+P 2608)>* **ISLAND OF LOST SOULS. / DRAGONFLY** [1] May82 [37]

May 82. (lp/c/pic-lp) *<(CDL/ZCDL/PCDL 1384)>* **THE HUNTER** [9] [33]
– Orchid club / Island of lost souls / Dragonfly / For your eyes only / The beast / War child / Little Caesar / Danceaway / (Can I) Find the right words (to say) / English boys / The hunter gets captured by the game. *(cd-iss. Sep94; CDCHR 6083)*

Jul 82. (7"/7"pic-d/12") *<(CHS/+P/12 2624)>* **WAR CHILD. / LITTLE CAESAR** [39] [ ]

—— (Aug'82) STEIN formed own 'Animal' label through 'Chrysalis'. CLEM BURKE joins EURYTHMICS and later RAMONES. He also teams up with HARRISON to form CHEQUERED PAST. A solo album, 'HEART ON THE WALL', was released by JIMMY DESTRI in 1982 and featured most of BLONDIE.

DEBBIE HARRY

solo, with **NILE RODGERS** and **BERNARD EDWARDS** on production, etc.

Chrysalis | Chrysalis

Jul 81. (7"/12") *<(CHS/+12 2526)>* **BACKFIRED. / MILITARY RAP** [32] [43]

Aug 81. (lp/c) *<(CHR/ZCCHR 1347)>* **KOO KOO** [6] [23]
– Jump jump / The jam was moving / Chrome / Under arrest / Inner city spillover / Surrender / Backfired / Now I know you / Military rap / Oasis. *(cd-iss. Sep94; CDCHR 6082)*

Sep 81. (7") *<(CHS 2554)>* **THE JAM WAS MOVING. / CHROME** [ ] [82]
(12"+=) *(CHS12 2554)* – Inner city spillover.

—— now worked with various session musicians.

Chrysalis | Geffen

Jan 84. (7") **RUSH RUSH. / DANCE DANCE DANCE** [–] [ ]

Jan 84. (7"/12") *(CHS/12CHS 2752)* **RUSH RUSH. / RUSH RUSH (dub)** [ ] [–]

Nov 86. (7") *(CHS 3066)* **FRENCH KISSIN' IN THE U.S.A. / ROCKBIRD** [8] [–]
('A'dance; 12"+=/12"pic-d+=) *(CHS12 3066/+B)* – ('A'dub version).

Nov 86. (7") *<28546>* **FRENCH KISSIN' IN THE U.S.A. / BUCKLE UP** [–] [57]

Nov 86. (lp/c/cd) *(CHR/ZCHR/CCD 1540) <24123>* **ROCKBIRD** [31] [97]
– I want you / French kissin' in the U.S.A. / Buckle up / In love with love / You got me in trouble / Free to fall / Rockbird / Secret life / Beyond the limit. *(cd re-iss. Sep94; CCD 1540)*

Feb 87. (7") *<(CHS 3093)>* **FREE TO FALL. / FEEL THE SPIN** [46] [ ]
(12"+=/12"pic-d+=) *(CHS12 3093/+B)* – Secret life.
(d7"+=) *(CHSD 3093)* – French kissin' in the U.S.A. / Rockbird.

Apr 87. (7") *(CHS 3128)* **IN LOVE WITH LOVE. / FEEL THE SPIN** [45] [–]

(12"+=/12"pic-d+=) *(CHS/+P 12-3128)* – French kissin' in the U.S.A. (French version).

Jun 87. (7") *<28476>* **IN LOVE WITH LOVE. / SECRET LIFE** [–] [70]

DEBORAH HARRY

— with **CHRIS STEIN** – guitar / **LEIGH FOXX** – bass / **TERRY BOZZIO** – drums / **TOMMY PRICE** – drums / **PHIL ASHLEY** – synthesizers / **STEVE GOLDSTEIN** – keyboards, etc.

Chrysalis Sire

Sep 89. (7"/c-s) *(CHS/+MC 3369)* **I WANT THAT MAN. / BIKE BOY** [13] [ ]
(12"pic-d+=/cd-s+=) *(CHS 12P/CD 3369)* – ('A'remix) / ('A'instrumental).

Oct 89. (lp/c/cd) *(CHR/ZCHR/CCD 1650) <25938>* **DEF, DUMB AND BLONDE** [12] [ ]
– I want that man / Lovelight / KIss it better / Bike boy * / Get your way / Maybe for sure / I'll never fall in love / Calmarie / Sweet and low / He is so / Bugeye / Comic books / Brite side / End of the run *. *(cd+=*) (cd re-iss. Sep94; CCD 1650)*

Nov 89. (7"/7"s) *(CHS/+PB 3452)* **BRITE SIDE. / BUGEYE** [59] [ ]
(12"+=/cd-s+=) *(CHS 12/CD 3452)* – In love with love.
('A'remix-cd-s++=) *(CHSCCD 3452)* – French kissin' in the U.S.A.

— Her touring group at time included **STEIN** and **FOXX** plus **SUZY DAVIS** – keyboards / **CARLA OLLA** – rhythm guitar / **JIMMY CLARK** – drums

Mar 90. (7"/7"s) *(CHS/+PB 3491)* **SWEET AND LOW. / LOVELIGHT** [57] [ ]
(12"/12"pic-d/cd-s) *(CHS 12/P12/CD 3491)* – (3-'A'mixes).

May 90. (7") *(CHS 3537)* **MAYBE FOR SURE. / GET YOUR WAY** [ ] [ ]
(12"+=/cd-s+=) *(12/CD CHS 3537)* – ('A'extended).
below featured on a Cole Porter tribute album, 'Red Hot & Blue'.

Dec 90. (7"/12"; by DEBORAH HARRY & IGGY POP) *(CHS/+12 3646)* **WELL DID YOU EVAH! / (b-side by The Thompson Twins)** [42] [ ]
(cd-s+=) *(CHSCD 3646)* – (track by 'Aztec Camera').

Jun 93. (c-s/7") *(TC+/CHS 4900)* **I CAN SEE CLEARLY. / STANDING IN MY WAY** [23] [ ]
(12"+=/cd-s+=) *(12/CD CHS 4900)* – Atomic / Heart of glass.
(cd-s+=) *(CDCHSS 4900)* – Call me / In love with love.

Jul 93. (cd/c/lp) *(CD/TC+/CHR 6033)* **DEBRAVATION** [24] [ ]
– I can see clearly / Stability / Strike me pink / Rain / Communion / Lip service / Mood ring / Dancing down the moon / Standing in my way / The fugitive / Dog star girl.

Sep 93. (c-s) *(TCCHS 5000)* **STRIKE ME PINK / 8 AND A HALF RHUMBA** [46] [ ]
(cd-s) *(CDCHS 5000)* – Dreaming.
(12"pic-d/cd-s) *(12CHSPD/CDCHSS 5000)* – ('A'side) / Sweet and low / On a breath.

BLONDIE

— re-formed in 1998 with **DEBBIE, CHRIS, CLEM + JIMMY**

Beyond-RCA Logic

Feb 99. (c-s) *(74321 64563-4) <78040>* **MARIA / MARIA (Soul Soultion mix)** [1] Mar99 [82]
(cd-s+=) *(74321 64563-2)* – Maria (Talvin Singh remix).
(cd-s) *(74321 63737-2)* – ('A'side) / In the flesh (live) / Screaming skin (live).

Feb 99. (cd/c) *(74321 64114-2/-4) <78003>* **NO EXIT** [3] [18]
– Screaming skin / Forgive & forget / Maria / No exit / Double take / Nothing is real but the girl / Boom boom in the zoom zoom room / Night wind sent / Under the gun / Out in the streets / Happy dog (for Caggy) / The dream's lost on me / Divine / Dig up the Congo. *(cd re-iss. Aug02 on 'Epic'+=; 501408-2)* – Hot shot / Rapture (live) / Heart of glass (live).

Jun 99. (c-s) *(74321 66948-4)* **NOTHING IS REAL BUT THE GIRL (Boilerhouse mix) / RIP HER TO SHREDS (live)** [26] [–]
(cd-s) *(74321 66380-2)* – ('A'side) / ('A'-Danny Tenaglia mix) / ('A'-Danny Tenaglia instradub).
(cd-s) *(74321 66947-2)* – ('A'-US radio mix) / Hanging on the telephone (live) / Shayla (live).

Nov 99. (cd-ep) *(74321 71653-2)* **NO EXIT / MARIA (J&B mix) / MARIA (Talvin Singh rhythmic mix) / NOTHING IS REAL BUT THE GIRL (Danny Tenaglia mix & his trance version)** [ ] [–]

Feb 00. (cd/c) *(501409-2)* **LIVID – THE GREATEST HITS LIVE (live)** [ ] [ ]
– Dreaming / Hanging on the telephone / Screaming skin / Atomic / Forgive and forget / The tide is high / Shayla / Sunday girl / Maria / Call me / Under the gun / Rapture / Rip her to shreds / X-offender / No exit / Heart of glass / One way or another.

Epic Sanctuary

Oct 03. (cd-s) *(674399-2)* **GOOD BOYS / MARIA (live) / RAPTURE (live) / GOOD BOYS (live)** [12] [–]
(cd-s) *(674399-5)* – ('A'side) / ('A'-Giorgio Moroder extended).
(12") *(674399-6)* – ('A'-Giorgio Moroder extended) / ('A'-Scissor Sisters' gyad byas myax mix) / ('A'-return to New York mix).

Oct 03. (cd) *(5119219)* **THE CURSE OF BLONDIE** [36] Apr04 [ ]
– Shake down / Good boys / Undone / Golden rod / Rules for living / Background melody (the only one) / Magic (Asaadoya Yunta) / End to end / Hello Joe / The tingler / Last one on the planet / Diamond bridge / Desire brings me back / Songs of love.

– compilations, others, etc. –

on 'Chrysalis' unless mentioned otherwise

Dec 82. (d-c) *(2CDP 101)* **EAT TO THE BEAT / AUTOAMERICAN** [ ] [–]

Feb 87. (7") *Old Gold; (OG 9672)* **DENIS. / PICTURE THIS** [ ] [–]

Feb 87. (7") *Old Gold; (OG 9674)* **SUNDAY GIRL. / HANGING ON THE TELEPHONE** [ ] [–]

Feb 87. (7") *Old Gold; (OG 9676)* **CALL ME. / UNION CITY BLUE** [ ] [–]

Feb 87. (7") *Old Gold; (OG 9678)* **HEART OF GLASS. / THE TIDE IS HIGH** [ ] [–]

Feb 87. (7") *Old Gold; (OG 9680)* **DREAMING. / ATOMIC** [ ] [–]

Nov 88. (7") *(CHS 3328)* **DENIS (remix). / RAPTURE (Teddy Riley remix)** [50] [–]
(12"+=/12"pic-d+=/cd-s+=) *(CHS/+12/12P/CD 3328)* – Heart of glass (remix) / Atomic (remix).

Dec 88. (lp/c/cd) *(CJB/ZCJB/CDJB 2)* **ONCE MORE INTO THE BLEACH (GREATEST HITS)** [50] [–]
– Denis / Heart of glass / Call me / Rapture / Rapture (bonus beats) / The tide is high / The jam was moving (DEBBIE HARRY) / In love with love (DEBBIE HARRY) / Rush rush (DEBBIE HARRY) / French kissin' in the U.S.A. (DEBBIE HARRY) / Feel the spin (DEBBIE HARRY) / Backfired (DEBBIE HARRY) / Sunday girl (French version).

Dec 88. (lp/c) *Star; (84026-1/-4)* **BLONDIE HIT COLLECTION** [ ] [–]

Feb 89. (7") *(CHS 3342)* **CALL ME. / CALL ME (version)** [61] [–]
(12"+=/cd-s+=) *(CHS 12/CD 3342)* – Backfired (DEBBIE HARRY).

Mar 91. (cd/c/d-lp) *(CCD/ZCHR/CHR 1817)* **THE COMPLETE PICTURE – THE VERY BEST OF DEBORAH HARRY & BLONDIE** [3] [ ]
– Heart of glass / I want that man / Call me / Sunday girl / French kissin' in the USA / Denis / Rapture / Brite side / (I'm always touched by your) Presence dear / Well, did you evah! / The tide is high / In love with love / Hanging on the telephone / Island of lost souls / Picture this / Dreaming / Sweet and low / Union city blue / Atomic / Rip her to shreds.

Jan 94. (cd/c) *(CD/TC CHR 6063)* **BLONDIE AND BEYOND – RARITIES AND ODDITIES** [ ] [–]

Aug 94. (c-s/12"/cd-s) *(12/ZC/CD CHS 5013)* **ATOMIC (re-mix). / ('A'mixes by Diddy & Alan Thompson)** [19] [–]
(cd-s) *(CDCHSS 5013)* – ('A'side) / Sunday girl (re-mix) / Union City blues (re-mix).

Nov 94. (d-cd) *(CDCHR 6089)* **THE PLATINUM COLLECTION** [ ] [–]

Jun 95. (12") *(12CHS 5023) HEART OF GLASS (re-mix). / CALL ME (re-mix)* [15] [ ]
(c-s) *(CDCHS 5023)* – ('A'side) / Rapture (re-mix) / Atomic (re-mix).
(cd-s+=) *(CDCHSS 5023)* – ('A'mixes).

Jul 95. (cd/c/d-lp) *(CD/TC+/CHR 6105)* **BEAUTIFUL – THE REMIX ALBUM** [25] [–]

Oct 95. (12"blue/cd-s) *(12/CD CHS 5027)* **UNION CITY BLUE (re-mix) / I FEEL LOVE (live)** [31] [–]
(cd-s) *(CDCHSS 5027)* – (other mixes by:- Diddy / The Burger Queens / OPM / Vinny Vero & Jammin' Hot).

Jul 98. (cd/c) *E.M.I.; (494996-2/-4)* **ATOMIC – THE VERY BEST OF . . .** [12] [ ]
(d-cd-iss. Feb99 +=; 499288-2) – ATOMIX

Jul 98. (c-s) *E.M.I.; (TCATOM 150)* **ATOMIC (1998 remix)** [ ] [–]
(12"+=/cd-s+=) *(12/CD ATOM 150)* – ('A'mixes).

Mar 99. (cd) *EMI Gold; (499421-2)* **THE ESSENTIAL COLLECTION** [ ] [–]

Jun 99. (cd) *E.M.I.; (521233-2)* **LIVE (live Philadelphia 1978 / Dallas 1980)** [ ] [–]

Oct 02. (cd) *E.M.I.; (543105-2)* **GREATEST HITS** [38] [ ]
– Dreaming / Call me / One way or another / Heart of glass / The tide is high / X-offender / Hanging on the telephone / Rip her to shreds / Rapture / Atomic / Picture this / In the flesh / Denis / I'm always touched by your presence dear / Union city blue / The hardest part / Island of lost souls / Sunday girl / Maria.

Sep 03. (d-cd) *(592228-2)* **BLONDIE / PLASTIC LETTERS** [ ] [–]

BLOODHOUND GANG

Formed: King Of Prussia, Pennsylvania, USA . . . 1994 by JIMMY ALI POP and DADDY LONG LEGS, along with LUPUS, SKIP O' POT2MUS and M.S.G. in tow. Not much can be said for these cheeky US punks who have so obviously ripped off quality comedic acts such as JERKY BOYS and BEASTIE BOYS (latter strictly 80's period only!). The BLOODHOUND GANG quite literally stamped on their peers' names, attempting to crush their credibility with sexual innuendos within nasty, juvenile rock. A topsy turvy blend of hip hop, metal, rap, quirky funk and a galaxy of fart jokes, the er . . . BG's signed to 'Columbia' after the minor success of the 'DINGLEBERRY HAZE' EP. The group issued the seminal classic 'USE YOUR FINGERS' (1995) and were subsequently dropped due to an abundance of irate listeners who even disliked their manic version of 'KIDS IN AMERICA'. However, once these pesky youths were knocked down, they arose to their feet once more, rebelling with the 'ONE FIERCE BEER COSTER' album (which was originally delivered through the small 'Republic' label). In 1996, David Geffen and his associates found some relative humour within the group, signing them and re-releasing the aforementioned set. The US hit album was heavily promoted with tongue-in-cheek single, 'KISS ME WHERE IT SMELLS FUNNY', its video apparently featured a bowler-hatted guy sprinting off to somewhere with a fish(!). This single sent giggling American teens ballistic in campuses everywhere and became the most alternative party tune since '(You've Gotta) Fight For Your Right (To Party)'. Echoes of KING MISSILE's frank and subtle-as-a-sledgehammer humour could be heard within the realms of the group's madness, although vaguely comparing such acts who were so diverse would be in itself insane. Later (in 1999), the band respectfully (not!) celebrated the female form with another long-player, 'HOORAY FOR BOOBIES', ahhem. To much critical lauding, it went on to win five Grammys and a whole host of international music awards, the best track being the hit single, 'THE BAD TOUCH'.

Album rating: USE YOUR FINGERS (*4) / ONE FIERCE BEER COASTER (*3) / HOORAY FOR BOOBIES (*8)

JIMMY POP ALI (b. M. BOWE) – vocals / **LUPUS** – guitar / **DADDY LONG LEGS** (b. JAMES FRANKS) – vocals / **M.S.G.** – vocals / **SKIP O' POT2MUS** – vocals

not iss. | Cheese Factory

Oct 94. (cd-ep) *<9401>* **DINGLEBERRY HAZE EP** [–] [ ]
– Go down / Cheese tidbit / Legend in my spare time / Neighbor invasion / Mama say / Rang dang / Earlameyer the butt pirate / One way / Record offer / Coo coo ca choo / Live at the Apollo. *<re-iss. 1999 on 'Interscope'; 90455>*

not iss. | TVT-Sony

May 95. (c-s/cd-s) *<7792-9/-8>* **MAMA SAY (mixes; original mess / hip hop / devil's food cake / I didn't get paid shit for this)** [–] [ ]

Jun 95. (cd/c) *<67225>* **USE YOUR FINGERS** [–] [ ]
– Rip Taylor is God / We are the knuckleheads / Legend in my spare time / B.H.G.P.S.A. / Mama say / Kids in America / You're pretty when I'm drunk / The evils of placenta hustling / One way / Shitty record offer / Go down / Earlameyer the butt pirate / No rest for the wicked / She ain't got no legs / We like meat / Coo coo ca choo / Rang dang / Nightmare at the Apollo – K.I.D.S. Incorporated. *(UK-iss.Feb98 on 'TVT-Sony'; same as US) (UK re-iss. Apr00 on 'Columbia'; 480703-2)*

—— **EVIL JARED** – bass / **SPANKY G** – drums / **Q-BALL** – DJ; repl. DADDY, M.S.G. + POT2MUS

not iss. | Republic

Dec 96. (lp) *<REP 26903-1>* **ONE FIERCE BEER COASTER** [–] [57]
– Kiss me where it smells funny / Lift your head up high (and blow your . . . .) / Fire water burn / I wish I was queer so I could get . . . . / Why's everybody always pickin' on me? / It's tricky / Asleep at the wheel / Shut up / Your only friends are make believe / Boom / Going nowhere slow / Reflections of Remoh. *<cd-iss. Sep97 on 'Geffen'; GED 25124> (UK lp-iss.Oct97 on 'Republic'; same as US)*

Geffen | Geffen

Aug 97. (c-s/12"/cd-s) *(GFS C/V/TD 22252)* **WHY'S EVERYBODY ALWAYS PICKIN' ON ME? (mixes; Honkus Maximus / Hemlock / Greek salad)** [56] [–]

Nov 97. (12") *<REP 9603-1>* **FIRE WATER BURN (Rudimental Jammy Jam). / FIRE WATER BURN (Jim Makin' Jamaican mix)** [ ] [ ]
(above on 'Republic', below on 'Bloodhound Gang')

Dec 97. (7") *<BHG 002>* **ONE CENSORED BEER COASTER** [ ] [ ]
– Yellow fever / The hidden track *[23 minutes long]*

Oct 99. (cd/c) *<(490455-2/-4)>* **HOORAY FOR BOOBIES** [ ] Sep99 [14]
– I hope you die / The inevitable return of the great white dope / Mama's boy / Three point one four / Mope / Yummy down on this / The ballad of Chasey Lain / R.S.V.P. / Magna cum nada / The bad touch / That cough came with a prize / Take the long way home / Hell yeah / Right turn Klyde / This is stupid / A lap dance is so much better when the stripper is crying / 10 coolest things about New Jersey / Along comes Mary. *(re-iss. Apr00 +=; 490457-2)* – (extra CD). – hit UK No.37

Mar 00. (c-s) *(497267-4)* **THE BAD TOUCH / WHY'S EVERYBODY KEEP PICKIN' ON ME** [4] [52]
(cd-s+=) *(497267-2)* – Boom / ('A'-CD-Rom video).
(cd-s) *(497268-2)* – ('A'side) / ('A'-The Eiffel 65 mix) / ('A'-The Rollergirl mix) / ('A'-God Lives Underwater mix).

Aug 00. (c-s) *(497380-4)* **THE BALLAD OF CHASEY LAIN / THE BALLAD OF CHASEY LAIN (Hot Snax mix)** [15] [–]
(cd-s) *(497381-2)* – ('A'side) / Mope (Pet Shop Boys mix) / The bad touch / The bad touch (uncensored video).
(cd-s) *(497382-2)* – ('A'version) / Mope (Pet Shop Boys mix) / The bad touch (Eiffel 65 extended) / ('A'-CD-Rom).

BLOOD, SWEAT & TEARS

Formed: New York, USA . . . late 1967 by BLUES PROJECT defectors, AL KOOPER and STEVE KATZ, together with rhythm section BOBBY COLOMBY and JIM FIELDER; FRED LIPSIUS subsequently joined on sax while original members were supplemented by a brass section of DICK HALLIGAN, RANDY BRECKER and JERRY WEISS. The first album (for 'Columbia') 'CHILD IS FATHER TO THE MAN' was released in early '68 to critical acclaim but only moderate commercial success. Internal strife caused KOOPER to leave soon after the record's release, his place taken by DAVID CLAYTON-THOMAS. BRECKER and WEISS also left, CHUCK WINFIELD and Brooklyn buddies JERRY HYMAN and LEW SOLOFF subsequently bolstering their ranks. Produced by JAMES GUERCIO, the eponymous second album was issued at the dawn of '69, a much more popular effort which hit the commercial bullseye, going triple platinum and winning a Grammy award; three hit singles, 'YOU'VE MADE ME SO VERY HAPPY', 'SPINNING WHEEL' plus 'AND WHEN I DIE', helped make it Album Of The Year. Although his powerful, soulful larynx perfectly complemented the brass-heavy jazz-pop sound, GUERCIO found CLAYTON-THOMAS' ego in the studio too much to take; the producer decided to quit while he was ahead, taking his skills to the more commercial (and less volatile) CHICAGO. With BST's lead vocalist beginning to dominate the outfit more and more, further friction was inevitable. However, the band began to court the media and became the critics' darlings for a short time (even appearing at Woodstock – much to the bemusement of the love children). The third album, 'BLOOD, SWEAT & TEARS 3' (1970) and 'B,S & T; 4 (1971), saw the band reconciled with KOOPER, although he returned in a production capacity. The winning formula continued, notably with the valedictory CLAYTON-THOMAS-penned 'GO DOWN GAMBLIN''. While DAVID's vocals helped win chart success, there were continual arguments over the band's musical direction (most of the members were classically-trained) which resulted in a huge bust-up in 1972. Exit one DAVID CLAYTON-THOMAS. He was almost immediately replaced on vocals by BOB DOYLE then JERRY FISHER, the subsequent domino effect seeing chaos reign supreme; different factions within the band had been pulling in different directions. Time for a Greatest Hits compilation perhaps?, 'BLOOD, SWEAT & TEARS GREATEST HITS' was issued in Spring '72 and went gold, peaking at 19 in the charts. Yet more musical chairs ensued when HENDERSON and HALLIGAN departed, the pair superseded by LOU MARINI JR and LARRY WILLIS respectively for subsequent albums, 'NEW BLOOD' (1972) and 'NO SWEAT' (1973). They were now however, losing their reputation as a crowd-pulling band, and even with CLAYTON-THOMAS' return, the writing was on the wall. Their ninth and final album for 'Columbia', 'MORE THAN EVER' (1976) was actually less good than ever in terms of the quality control; it was time for a parting of the ways. 'BRAND NEW DAY' (1977) – their first for 'A.B.C.' – continued the creative slump and failed (for the first time!) to break into the US Top 200. In truth, the once great BS&T was in its death throes, breathing its last as a backing section for CLAYTON-THOMAS' similarly expiring career. • **Songwriters:** Most by KOOPER until CLAYTON-THOMAS took over. Covered AND WHEN I DIE (Laura Nyro) / YOU'VE MADE ME SO VERY HAPPY (Brenda Holloway) / MORNING GLORY (Tim Buckley) / HI-DE-HO (Goffin-King) / GOT TO GET YOU INTO MY LIFE (Beatles) / etc.

Album rating: CHILD IS FATHER TO THE MAN (*7) / BLOOD, SWEAT & TEARS (*7) / BLOOD, SWEAT & TEARS 3 (*5) / B, S & T; 4 (*4) / BLOOD, SWEAT & TEARS GREATEST HITS compilation (*7) / NEW BLOOD (*3) / NO SWEAT (*3) / MIRROR IMAGE (*3) / NEW CITY (*3) / MORE THAN EVER (*3) / BRAND NEW DAY (*3) / NUCLEAR BLUES (*3) / CLASSIC . . . compilation (*6) / SMILING PHASES compilation (*5) / WHAT GOES UP: BEST OF . . . compilation (*7)

AL KOOPER (b. 5 Feb'44, Brooklyn, NY) – vocals, keyboards (ex-BLUES PROJECT, ex-BOB DYLAN Band) / **STEVE KATZ** (b. 9 May'45, New York City) – vocals, guitar (ex-BLUES PROJECT) / **RANDY BRECKER** (b.27 Nov'44, Philadelphia) – trumpet, flugelhorn / **JERRY WEISS** (b. 1 May'46, New York City) – trumpet, flugelhorn / **FRED LIPSIUS** (b.19 Nov'43, New York City) – alto sax, piano / **DICK HALLIGAN** (b.29 Aug'43, Troy, New York) – trombone, flute, keyboards / **JIM FIELDER** (b. 4 Oct'47, Dallas, Texas) – bass (ex-BUFFALO SPRINGFIELD) / **BOBBY COLOMBY** (b.20 Dec'44, New York City) – drums

C.B.S. Columbia

Jun 68. (lp) *(CBS 63296)* <9619> **CHILD IS FATHER TO THE MAN** [40] Apr68 [47]
– Overture / I love you more than you'll ever know / Morning glory / My days are numbered / Without her / Just one smile / Meagan's gypsy eyes / House in the country / I can't quit her / Somethin' goin' on / The modern adventures of Plato, Diogenes and Freud / So much love / Underture. *(re-iss. Jul77 as 'THE FIRST ALBUM' on 'Embassy-CBS'; CBS 31942) (cd-iss. 1988; 30DP 303) (cd re-iss. Nov95; CK 64214) (cd re-iss. Apr99 on 'Mobile Fidelity'; UDCD 742) <(cd re-iss. Oct00; 499823-2)<63987>*

Jun 68. (7") *(CBS 3563)* <44559> **I CAN'T QUIT HER. / HOUSE IN THE COUNTRY** [ ] [ ]

— (Mar'69) **DAVID CLAYTON-THOMAS** (b.DAVID THOMSETT, 13 Sep'41, Surrey, England, raised Canada) – vocals; repl. KOOPER who went solo

— **CHUCK WINFIELD** (b.5 Feb'43, Monessen, Pennsylvania) – trumpet, flugelhorn repl. BRECKER who later formed BRECKER BROTHERS. **LEW SOLOFF** (b.20 Feb'44, Brooklyn, New York) – trumpet, flugelhorn and **JERRY HYMAN** (b.19 May'47, New York) – trombone repl. WEISS

Apr 69. (lp) *(CBS 63504)* <9720> **BLOOD, SWEAT & TEARS** [15] Jan69 [1]
– Variations on a theme by Eric Satie (1st & 2nd movements) / Smiling phases / Sometimes in winter / More and more / And when I die / God bless the child / Spinning wheel / You've made me so very happy / Blues (part 2) / Variations on a theme by Eric Satie (reprise). *(re-iss. Dec88 on 'Beat Goes On' lp/cd; BGO LP/CD 28) <(cd re-iss. Oct00; 49982-2)<63986>*

Apr 69. (7") *(CBS 4116)* <44776> **YOU'VE MADE ME SO VERY HAPPY. / THE BLUES (part 2)** [35] Feb69 [2]

Jun 69. (7") *(CBS 4220)* <44871> **SPINNING WHEEL. / MORE AND MORE** [ ] May69 [2]

Dec 69. (7") *(CBS 4613)* <45008> **AND WHEN I DIE. / SOMETIMES IN WINTER** [ ] Oct69 [2]

Aug 70. (lp) *(CBS 64024)* <30090> **BLOOD, SWEAT & TEARS 3** [14] Jul70 [1]
– Hi-de-ho / The battle / Lucretia Mac Evil / Lucretia's reprise / Fire and rain / Lonesome Suzie / Symphony for the Devil – Sympathy for the Devil: Emergence – Evil's game; (a) Labyrinth, (b) Satan's dance, (c) The demand – Submergence / Contemplation – Return / He's a miner / Somethin' comin' on / 40,000 headman.

Aug 70. (7") *(CBS 5137)* <45204> **HI-DE-HO. / THE BATTLE** [ ] Jul70 [14]

Oct 70. (7") *(CBS 5220)* <45235> **LUCRETIA MAC EVIL. / LUCRETIA'S REPRISE** [ ] [29]

— **DAVID BARGERON** (b. 6 Sep'42, Massacusetts) – horns; repl. HYMAN

Jul 71. (lp) *(CBS 64355)* <30590> **B, S & T; 4** [ ] [10]
– Go down gamblin' / Cowboys and Indians / John The Baptist (holy John) / Redemption / Lisa, listen to me / Look to my heart / High on a mountain / Valentine's day / Take me in your arms (rock me a little while) / For my lady / Mama gets high / Look to my heart. *(cd-iss. Mar96 on 'Columbia'; CK 66422)*

Jul 71. (7") *(CBS 7417)* <45427> **GO DOWN GAMBLIN'. / VALENTINE'S DAY** [ ] [32]

Dec 71. (7") *(CBS 7578)* <45477> **LISA, LISTEN TO ME. / COWBOYS AND INDIANS** [ ] Oct71 [73]

Mar 72. (lp/c) *(CBS/40 64803)* <31170> **GREATEST HITS** (compilation) [ ] [19]
– You've made me so very happy / I can't quit her / Go down gamblin' / Hi-de-ho / Sometimes in winter / And when I die / Spinning wheel / Lisa, listen to me / I love you more than you'll ever know / Lucretia Mac Evil / God bless the child. *(re-iss. Jul83; CBS 32159) (cd-iss. Nov87; CD 64803) (quad-lp 1973; Q 64803) <US-quad; CQ 31170> <(cd-iss. Oct00 +=; 491547-2)* – So long Dixie / More and more.

— **JERRY FISHER** (b. 1943, Texas) – vocals; repl. BOBBY DOYLE who had repl. solo bound CLAYTON-THOMAS / **LOU MARINI Jr.** – saxophone; repl. LIPSIUS / **LARRY WILLIS** – keyboards; repl. HALLIGAN

Jul 72. (7") *(CBS 8267)* **SO LONG DIXIE. / KRAKBERGARNINGEN (CROWS FUNERAL)** [ ] [–]

Sep 72. (7") <45661> **SO LONG DIXIE. / ALONE** [–] [44]

Oct 72. (lp) *(CBS 65252)* <31780> **NEW BLOOD** [ ] [32]
– Down in the flood / Touch me / Alone / Velvet / I can't move no mountains / Over the hill / So long Dixie / Snow queen / Maiden voyage.

Nov 72. (7") *(CBS 1051)* **TOUCH ME. / VELVET** [ ] [–]

Dec 72. (7") <45755> **I CAN'T MOVE NO MOUNTAINS. / VELVET** [–] [ ]

May 73. (7") *(CBS 1519)* **BACK UP AGAINST THE WALL. / OVER THE HILL** [ ] [–]

Aug 73. (7") <45937> **ROLLER COASTER. / INNER CRISIS** [–] [ ]

Aug 73. (lp) *(CBS 65275)* <32180> **NO SWEAT** [ ] [72]
– Roller coaster / Save our ship / Django / Rosemary / Song for John / Almost sorry / Back up against the wall / Hip pickles / My old lady / Empty pages / Mary Miles / Inner crisis.

Oct 73. (7") <45965> **SAVE OUR SHIP. / SONG FOR JOHN** [–] [ ]

Nov 73. (7") *(CBS 1845)* **SAVE OUR SHIP. / INNER CRISIS** [ ] [–]

— **DAVID CLAYTON-THOMAS** returned to repl. JERRY LaCROIX who had briefly replaced KATZ (he was later to join AMERICAN FLYER)

— **TOM MALONE** – horns; repl. WINFIELD

Jun 74. (7") *(CBS 2462) TELL ME THAT I'M WRONG. / ROCK REPRISE* [ ] [83]

Sep 74. (lp) *(CBS 80153)* <32929> **MIRROR IMAGE** [ ] [ ]
– Tell me that I'm wrong / Look up to the sky / Love looks good on you (you're candy sweet) / Hold on to me / Thinking of you / Are you satisfied / Rock reprise / She's coming home.

Oct 74. (7") *(CBS 2594)* **LOVE LOOKS GOOD ON YOU. / ARE YOU SATISFIED** [ ] [–]

— **RON McCLURE** – bass; repl. FIELDER

— **BILL TILLMAN** – saxophone; repl. SOLOFF

Jun 75. (lp) *(CBS 80784) <33484>* **NEW CITY** [] May75 [47]
– Ride captain ride / Life / No show / I was a witness to a war / One room country shack / Applause / Yesterday's music / Naked man / Got to get you into my life / Takin' it home.

Jun 75. (7") *<10151>* **GOT TO GET YOU INTO MY LIFE. / NAKED MAN** [-] [62]

Sep 75. (7") *<10189>* **YESTERDAY'S MUSIC. / NO SHOW** [-] []

— **CLAYTON-THOMAS, COLOMBY, BARGERON, WILLIS, TILLMAN + McCLURE** brought in guests **PATTI AUSTIN / CHAKA KHAN** – vocals plus newcomers **MIKE STERN** – guitar / **DON ALIAS** – percussion / **STEVE KHAN** – guitar / **F.BUCHTELL** – trumpet

Aug 76. (lp) *(CBS 81465) <34233>* **MORE THAN EVER** [] Jul76 []
– They / I love you more than ever / Kathy Bell / Sweet Sadie the savior / Hollywood / You're the one / Heavy blue / Saved by the grace of your love.

Jan 77. (7") *<10400>* **YOU'RE THE ONE. / HEAVY BLUE** [-] []

— **DANNY TRIFAN** – bass repl. McCLURE / added **ROY McCURDY** – drums / **RANDY BERNSEN** – guitar repl. KHAN / **TONY KLATKA** – trumpet repl. ALIAS

A.B.C. A.B.C.

Nov 77. (lp) *(ABCL 5234) <1015>* **BRAND NEW DAY** [] []
– Somebody I trusted / Dreaming as one / Same old blues / Lady put out the light / Womanizer / Blue street / Gimme that wine / Rock & roll queen / Don't explain.

Nov 77. (7") *(ABC 4202)* **BLUE STREET. / PUT ON THE LIGHT** [] [-]

Jan 78. (7") *<12310>* **BLUE STREET. / SOMEBODY I TRUSTED** [-] []

— added **CHRIS ALBERT** – trumpet / **GREG HERBERT** – sax / **NEIL STUBENHAUS** – bass

— (1979) **CLAYTON-THOMAS** brought in new members **ROBERT PILTCH** – guitar / **RICHARD MARTINEZ** – keyboards / **BRUCE CASSIDY** – trumpet / **BOBBY ECONOMOU** – drums / **DAVID PILTCH** – bass / **EARL SEYMOUR** – sax, flute / **VERNON DORGE** – sax, flute

A.B.C. M.C.A.

Feb 80. (7") *<41198>* **NUCLEAR BLUES. / AGITATO** [-] []

Feb 80. (7"/12") *(MCA/+T 569)* **NUCLEAR BLUES. / I'LL DROWN IN MY OWN TEARS** [] [-]

Mar 80. (lp/c) *(MCF/+C 3061)* **NUCLEAR BLUES** [] [-]
– Agitato / Nuclear blues / Manic depression / I'll drown in my own tears / Fantasy stage / Spanish wine suite: La cantina – Spanish wine – Latin fire – The challenge – The duel – Amor – Spanish wine (reprise). *(re-iss. Sep89 on 'Big Time' lp/c; 221/211 5235)*

— BS&T broke-up in 1980, CLAYTON-THOMAS and COLOMBY did some reunion concerts and even re-formed with varied line-up in 1988

– compilations, etc. –

on 'CBS' UK 'Columbia' US unless mentioned otherwise

Mar 73. (7") *(CBS 1142)* **SPINNING WHEEL. / AND WHEN I DIE** [] [-]

1975. (7") *(13-33194)* **AND WHEN I DIE. / LUCRETIA MAC EVIL** [] [-]

Feb 76. (7") *(CBS 3947)* **YOU MADE ME SO VERY HAPPY. / SPINNING WHEEL** [] [-]
(re-iss. Jul84; A 4576)

Jul 78. (lp) *Hallmark; (SHM 963)* **BLOOD, SWEAT & TEARS** [] [-]

May 80. (lp/c) *(CBS/40 31824)* **CLASSIC BLOOD, SWEAT & TEARS** [] [-]

Nov 84. (lp/c) *Astan; (2/4 0140)* **THE CHALLENGE** [] [-]

Oct 85. (lp/c) *Platinum; (PLP/PMC 25)* **LATIN FIRE** [] [-]

May 91. (cd/c) *Elite; (ELITE 005 CD/MC)* **SMILING PHASES** [] [-]
– Smiling phases / More and more / Fire and rain / Lonesome Suzie / Somethin' comin' on / Cowboys and Indians / High on a mountain / Take me in your arms (rock me a little while) / Down in the flood / Touch me / Alone / Morning glory / Without her / Just one smile / Roller coaster / Rosemary / Back up against the wall / Velvet. *(re-iss. cd Sep93; same)*

Sep 93. (cd/c) *Castle; (CCS CD/MC 379)* **THE COLLECTION** [] [-]

Jan 96. (d-cd) *Columbia (481019-2) <64166>* **WHAT GOES UP (THE BEST OF BLOOD, SWEAT & TEARS)** [] Nov95 []
– I can't quit her / House in the country / I love you more than you'll ever know / You've made me so very happy / More and more / And when I die / Sometimes in winter / Smiling phases / Spinning wheel / God bless the child / Children of the wind / Hi-de-ho / Lucretia Mac Evil / He's a runner / Somethin' comin' on / 40,000 headman / Go down gamblin' / Mama gets high / Lisa, listen to me / Valentine's day / John the Baptist (Holy John) / So long Dixie / Snow queen / Maiden voyage / I can't move to the mountains / Time remembered / Roller coaster / Tell me that I'm wrong / Got to get you into my life / You're the one / Mean ole world (live).

Sep 99. (cd) *Mastertone; (MM 5104)* **HIP PICKLES** [] [-]

Jul 00. (cd) *Columbia; (498792-2) <65632>* **SUPER HITS** [] Jul98 []

May 01. (cd) *Sony Special; <32106>* **YOU'VE MADE ME SO VERY HAPPY** [-] []

Jul 03. (cd) *Columbia; (480546-2)* **THE DEFINITIVE COLLECTION** [] [-]

□ Mike BLOOMFIELD (see under ⇒ ELECTRIC FLAG)

BLUE NILE

Formed: Glasgow, Scotland ... 1981 by songwriter PAUL BUCHANAN, PAUL JOSEPH MOORE and ROBERT BELL. After a debut 45 on 'R.S.O.' (just prior to the label going belly up!), they were offered an unusual record contract by East Lothian label, 'Linn', the hi-fi manufacturer using their tape as a demo and subsequently being sufficiently impressed to sign the band up for their recently formed music business venture. After an initial single, 'STAY', in spring '84, the label issued the languorous debut album, 'A WALK ACROSS THE ROOFTOPS'. Garnering gushing reviews, this classic set of understated pop elegance created enough of a buzz for 'Virgin' to take over distribution. Its relatively lowly final chart position of No.80 belied the record's influence and impact, although it would be another five years before a follow-up as the trio locked themselves in the studio and diligently attempted to create another masterpiece. After a few false starts, they finally emerged in 1989 with 'HATS', a record which arguably topped their debut in the late night sophistication stakes, its moody atmospherics delicately caressed by PAUL BUCHANAN's silky croon (a singer who undoubtedly has the potential of being the next SINATRA). A UK Top 20 hit, the record's success saw The BLUE NILE leave their studio cocoon in the early 90's for a tour of America where they ended up working with such luminaries as ROBBIE ROBERTSON and RICKIE LEE JONES amongst others. Now signed to 'Warners', it looked as if The BLUE NILE were finally destined to leave cultdom behind with a third set, 'PEACE AT LAST' (1996). Another classy effort, again the trio enjoyed critical plaudits and modest chart success while simultaneously failing to corner the wider pop market. Rumours are they are about to release their fourth set in not too distant future (another 7-year itch!).

Album rating: A WALK ACROSS THE ROOFTOPS (*8) / HATS (*8) / PEACE AT LAST (*6)

PAUL BUCHANAN – vocals, guitar, synthesizer / **PAUL JOSEPH MOORE** – keyboards, synthesizer, etc. / **ROBERT BELL** – bass, synthesizer, etc.

R.S.O. not iss.

Oct 81. (7") *(RSO 84)* **I LOVE THIS LIFE. / SECOND ACT** [] [-]

— added guests **CALUM MALCOLM** – keyboards, vocals (ex-BADGER, ex-HEADBOYS) / **NIGEL THOMAS** – drums

Linn-Virgin A&M

Apr 84. (7"/12") *(LKS 1/+12)* **STAY. / SADDLE THE HORSES** [] 1985 []
(re-iss. Jan89 remixed 7"/12"/d7"+=; same/same/LKSD 1) – Tinseltown in the rain / Heatwave (instrumental).

Apr 84. (lp/c) *(LKH/+C 1)* **A WALK ACROSS THE ROOFTOPS** [80] 1985 []
– A walk across the rooftops / Tinseltown in the rain / From rags to riches / Stay / Easter parade / Heatwave / Automobile noise. *(cd-iss. Jan89; LKHCD 1)*

Jul 84. (7") *(LKS 2)* **TINSELTOWN IN THE RAIN. / HEATWAVE (instrumental)** [] [-]
('A'ext-12") *(LKS 2-12)* – Regret.

— now a basic trio plus session musicians.

Sep 89. (7") *(LKS 3)* **THE DOWNTOWN LIGHTS. / THE WIRES ARE DOWN** 67
(12"+=/3"cd-s+=) *(LKS 3-12/CD3)* – Halfway to Paradise (TV theme).

Oct 89. (lp/c/cd) *(LKH/+C/CD 2)* *<5284>* **HATS** 12
– Over the hillside / The downtown lights / Let's go out tonight / Headlights on the parade / From a late night train / Seven a.m. / Saturday night. *(re-iss. Apr92 on 'Virgin' cd/c; OVED CD/C 391)*

Sep 90. (7"/c-s) *(LKS/+C 4)* **HEADLIGHTS ON THE PARADE (Bob Clearmount mix). / ('A'-lp version)** 72
(12"+=/cd-s+=) *(LKS 4-12/CD4)* – Easter parade (with RICKIE LEE JONES).

Jan 91. (7"/c-s) *(LKS/+C 5)* **SATURDAY NIGHT. / ('A'version)** 50
(12"+=/cd-s+=) *(LKS 5-12/CD5)* – Seven a.m. (live in the U.S.) / or / Our lives.

Warners Warners

Jun 96. (cd/c/lp) *(<9362 45848-2/-4/-1>)* **PEACE AT LAST** 13
– Happiness / Tomorrow morning / Sentimental man / Love came down / Body and soul / Holy love / Family life / War is love / God bless you kid / Soon.

Sep 96. (c-ep/cd-ep) *(W 0373 C/CD2)* **HAPPINESS / NEW YORK MAN / WISH ME WELL** –
(cd-ep) *(W 0373CD1)* – ('A'side) / War is love / O Lolita.

BLUE OYSTER CULT

Formed: Long Island, New York, USA . . . 1970 as SOFT WHITE UNDERBELLY by BUCK DHARMA, ALLEN LANIER and AL BOUCHARD. They became STALK-FORREST GROUP and signed to 'Elektra', where they released one 45, 'WHAT IS QUICKSAND' / 'ARTHUR COMICS' <45693> but had an album rejected. In late 1971 they renamed themselves The BLUE OYSTER CULT, their manager/guru SANDY PEARLMAN securing them a recording contract with 'Columbia'. The first two albums, 'BLUE OYSTER CULT' (1972) and 'TYRANNY AND MEDITATION' (1973 and containing lyrics by producer Richard Meltzer) were sophisticated proto-metal classics, infusing the crunching guitar and rhythm with a keen sense of melody and keeping tight enough a rein on proceedings to avoid the hoary bombast that characterised other bands of their ilk. Lyrically the band peddled fairly cliched, if more intelligent than average, dark musings and with 1974's 'SECRET TREATIES', the music began to sound similarly predictable. Throughout the remainder of the 70's, the band gravitated to a cleaner cut hard rock sound, although the darkly shimmering 'DON'T FEAR THE REAPER' was a one-off return to their 60's psychedelic roots. The song gave the band a surprise Top 20 UK hit, and while they continued to enjoy minor chart successes with their subsequent releases, the quality of their output struggled to rise above stale cliche. • **Songwriters:** Group compositions, except CAREER OF EVIL (written by LANIER's one-time girlfriend PATTI SMITH) / BLACK BLADE (co-written with Michael Moorcock; ex-Hawkwind) / BETTY LOU'S GOT A NEW PAIR OF SHOES (Bobby Freeman) / KICK OUT THE JAMS (MC5) / WE GOTTA GET OUT OF THIS PLACE (Animals) / BORN TO BE WILD (Steppenwolf). • **Trivia:** AL BOUCHARD claimed he was the inspiration for the 1988 album, 'IMAGINOS'.

Album rating: BLUE OYSTER CULT (*6) / TYRANNY & MUTATION (*5) / SECRET TREATIES (*8) / ON YOUR FEET ON YOUR KNEES (*7) / AGENTS OF FORTUNE (*8) / SPECTRES (*5) / SOME ENCHANTED EVENING (*8) / MIRRORS (*5) / CULTOSAURUS ERECTUS (*4) / FIRE OF UNKNOWN ORIGIN (*6) / EXTRATERRESTRIAL LIVE (*3) / THE REVOLUTION BY NIGHT (*5) / CLUB NINJA (*4) / IMAGINOS (*6) / WORKSHOP OF THE TELESCOPES compilation (*7) / CULT CLASSICS (*3) / HEAVEN FORBID (*4) / BAD CHANNELS (*4) / CURSE OF THE HIDDEN MIRROR (*4) / A LONG DAY'S NIGHT (*6)

ERIC BLOOM – vocals, "stun" guitar / **BUCK DHARMA** (b.DONALD ROSIER) – lead guitar, vocals / **ALLEN LANIER** – rhythm guitar, keyboards / **JOE BOUCHARD** (b. 9 Nov'48, Watertown, N.Y.) – bass, vocals / **ALBERT BOUCHARD** (b.24 May'47, Watertown) – drums, vocals

not iss. Reichstag

1972. (7"ep) *<1106>* **LIVE BOOTLEG (live)** –
– In my mouth or on the ground / etc.

C.B.S. Columbia

1973. (lp) *(64904)* *<31063>* **BLUE OYSTER CULT** May72
– Transmaniacon MC / I'm on the lamb but I ain't no sheep / Then came the last days of May / Stairway to the stars / Before the kiss, a redcap / Screams / She's as beautiful as a foot / Cities on flame with rock and roll / Workshop of the telescopes / Redeemed. *(re-iss. Mar81; 32025) <(cd re-mast.Jun01 on 'Columbia'+=; 502234-2)<85482>* – Donovan's monkey (demo) / What is quicksand (demo) / A fact about sneakers (demo) / Betty Lou's got a new pair of shoes (demo).

1973. (7") *<45598>* **CITIES ON FLAME WITH ROCK AND ROLL. / BEFORE THE KISS, A REDCAP** –

1973. (7") *<45879>* **SCREAMING DIZ-BUSTERS. / HOT RAILS TO HELL** –

1974. (lp) *(65331)* *<32107>* **TYRANNY AND MUTATION** Mar74
– The red & the black / O.D.'d on life itself / Hot rails to Hell / 7 screaming diz-busters / Baby ice dog / Wings wetted down / Teen archer / Mistress of the salmon salt (quicklime girl). *(re-iss. 1981; 32056) <(cd re-mast.Jun01 on 'Columbia'+=; 502235-2)<85481>* – Cities on flame with rock & roll (live) / Buck's boogie / 7 screaming diz-busters (live) / O'D'd on life itself (live).

1974. (7") *<10046>* **CAREER OF EVIL. / DOMINANCE AND SUBMISSION** –

Sep 74. (lp) *(80103)* *<32858>* **SECRET TREATIES** Apr74 53
– Career of evil / Subhuman / Dominance and submission / ME 262 / Cagey cretins / Harvester of eyes / Flaming telepaths / Astronomy. *(re-iss. Mar82; 32055) <(cd re-mast.Jun01 on 'Columbia'+=; 502236-2)<85480>* – Boorman the chauffuer / Mommy / Mes dames sarat / Born to be wild / Career of evil.

Nov 75. (d-lp) *(88116)* *<33317>* **ON YOUR FEET OR ON YOUR KNEES (live)** Mar75 22
– Subhuman / Harvester of eyes / Hot rails to Hell / The red and the black / 7 screaming diz-busters / Buck's boogie / Then came the last days of May / Cities on flame / ME 262 / Before the kiss (a redcap) / I ain't got you / Born to be wild. *(re-iss. Sep87 lp/c; 460113-1/-4)*

Nov 75. (7") *<10169>* **BORN TO BE WILD (live). / (part 2)** –

Jun 76. (lp/c) *(CBS/40 81835)* *<34164>* **AGENTS OF FORTUNE** 26 29
– This ain't the summer of love / True confessions / (Don't fear) The reaper / E.T.I. (Extra Terrestrial Intelligence) / The revenge of Vera Gemini / Sinful love / Tattoo vampire / Morning final / Tenderloin / Debbie Denise. *(re-iss. Jul89; CDCBS 32221) (cd-iss. Jun94 on 'Sony'; 982732-2) (cd-iss. May95 & Jul99 on 'Columbia'; 468019-2) (lp re-iss. Oct97 on 'Simple Vinyl'; SVLP 2) <(cd re-mast.Jun01 on 'Columbia' +=; 502237-2)<85479>* – Fire of unknown origin (original) / Sally (demo) / (Don't fear) The reaper (demo) / Dance the night away (demo).

Jul 76. (7") *<10384>* **(DON'T FEAR) THE REAPER. / TATTOO VAMPIRE** – 12

Jul 76. (7") *(4483)* **(DON'T FEAR) THE REAPER. / R.U. READY 2 ROCK** –

Jan 77. (7") *<10560>* **DEBBIE DENISE. / THIS AIN'T THE SUMMER OF LOVE** –

Dec 77. (lp/c) *(CBS/40 86050)* *<35019>* **SPECTRES** 60 Nov77 43
– Godzilla / Golden age of leather / Death valley nights / Searchin' for Celine / Fireworks / R.U. ready 2 rock / Celestial the queen / Goin' through the motions / I love the night / Nosferatu. *(re-iss. Feb86 lp/c; CBS/40 32715) (cd-iss. Dec88; CDCBS 82371)*

Dec 77. (7") *(5689)* *<10659>* **GOING THROUGH THE MOTIONS. / SEARCHIN' FOR CELINE**

Feb 78. (7") *<10697>* **GODZILLA. / NOSFERATU** –

May 78. (7"/12") *(7/12 6333)* **(DON'T FEAR) THE REAPER. / R U READY 2 ROCK** 16 –
(re-iss. Jun84 on 'Old Gold'; OG 9398)

Jun 78. (7") *<10725>* **GODZILLA. / GODZILLA (live)** –

Aug 78. (7") *(6514)* **I LOVE THE NIGHT. / NOSFERATU** –

Sep 78. (lp) *(CBS/40 86074)* *<35563>* **SOME ENCHANTED EVENING (live)** 18 44
– R.U. ready 2 rock / E.T.I. (Extra Terrestrial Intelligence) / Astronomy / Kick out the jams / Godzilla / (Don't fear) The reaper / We gotta get out of this place. *(cd-iss. Jul97 on 'Columbia'; 487931-2)*

Oct 78. (7") *<10841>* **WE GOTTA GET OUT OF THIS PLACE. / E.T.I. (EXTRA TERRESTRIAL INTELLIGENCE)** [–] [ ]

Nov 78. (7") *(6909)* **WE GOTTA GET OUT OF THIS PLACE (live). / STAIRWAY TO THE STARS** [ ] [–]

Aug 79. (lp/c) *(CBS/40 86087) <36009>* **MIRRORS** [46] Jul79 [44]
– Dr. Music / The great sun jester / In thee / Mirrors / Moon crazy / The vigil / I am the storm / You're not the one (I was looking for) / Lonely teardrops.

Aug 79. (7"clear) *(7763)* **MIRRORS. / LONELY TEARDROPS** [ ] [–]

Sep 79. (7") *<11055>* **IN THEE. / LONELY TEARDROPS** [–] [74]

Oct 79. (7") *(8003)* **IN THEE. / THE VIGIL** [ ] [–]

Feb 80. (7") *<11145>* **YOU'RE NOT THE ONE (I WAS LOOKING FOR). / MOON CRAZY** [–] [ ]

Jul 80. (lp) *(86120) <36550>* **CULTOSAURUS ERECTUS** [12] [34]
– Black blade / Monsters / Divine wind / Deadline / Here's Johnny / The Marshall plan / Hungry boys / Fallen angel / Lips in the hills / Unknown tongue. *(cd-iss. Feb99 on 'Columbia'; 493420-2)*

Jul 80. (7") *<11401>* **HERE'S JOHNNY (THE MARSHALL PLAN). / DIVINE WIND** [–] [ ]

Jul 80. (7") *(8790)* **FALLEN ANGEL. / LIPS IN THE HILLS** [ ] [–]

Oct 80. (7") *(8986)* **DEADLINES. / MONSTERS** [ ] [–]

Jul 81. (lp) *(CBS 85137) <37389>* **FIRE OF UNKNOWN ORIGIN** [29] [24]
– Fire of unknown origin / Burnin' for you / Veteran of the psychic wars / Sole survivor / Heaven metal: the black and silver / Vengeance (the pact) / After dark / Joan Crawford / Don't turn your back. *<cd-iss. 1987; CK 85137>*

Aug 81. (7") *<02415>* **BURNIN' FOR YOU. / VENGEANCE (THE PACT)** [–] [40]

Sep 81. (7") *(A 1453)* **BURNIN' FOR YOU. / HEAVY METAL** [ ] [–]
(12"+=) *(A13 1453)* – The black & silver.

May 82. (d-lp) *(CBS 22203) <KF 37946>* **EXTRATERRESTRIAL LIVE (live)** [39] [29]
– Dominance and submission / Cities on flame / Dr. Music / The red and the black / Joan Crawford / Burnin' for you / Roadhouse blues / Black blade / Hot rails to Hell / Godzilla / Veteran of the psychic wars / E.T.I. (Extra Terrestrial Intelligence) / (Don't fear) the reaper.

Jun 82. (7") *<03137>* **BURNIN' FOR YOU (live). / (DON'T FEAR) THE REAPER (live)** [–] [ ]

— (late 1981) **RICK DOWNEY** – drums repl. ALBERT

Nov 83. (lp/c) *(CBS/40 25686) <38947>* **THE REVOLUTION BY NIGHT** [95] [93]
– Take me away / Eyes on fire / Shooting shark / Veins / Shadows of California / Feel the thunder / Let go / Dragon lady / Light years of love. *<cd-iss. Dec88; CK 38947>*

Nov 83. (7") *(A 3937)* **TAKE ME AWAY. / FEEL THE THUNDER** [ ] [–]
(12"+=) *(TA 3937)* – Burnin' for you / Dr. Music.

Feb 84. (7"/12") *(A/TA 4117) <04298>* **SHOOTING SHARK. / DRAGON LADY** [ ] [83]

May 84. (7") *<04436>* **TAKE ME AWAY. / LET GO** [–] [ ]

— **TONY ZVONCHEK** – keyboards (ex-ALDO NOVA) repl. LANIER

— **TOMMY PRICE** – drums repl. DOWNEY.

Oct 85. (7") *<05845>* **DANCIN' IN THE RUINS. / SHADOW WARRIOR** [–] [ ]

Dec 85. (lp/c/cd) *(CBS/40/CD 26775) <39979>* **CLUB NINJA** [ ] [63]
– White flags / Dancin' in the ruins / Rock not war / Perfect water / Spy in the house of the night / Beat 'em up / When the war comes / Shadow warrior / Madness to the method. *(cd-iss. Jun97 on 'Koch Int.'; 37943-2)*

Dec 85. (7") *(A 6779)* **WHITE FLAGS. / ROCK NOT WAR** [ ] [–]
(12"+=) *(TA 6779)* – Shooting shark.

Feb 86. (7") *<06199>* **PERFECT WATER. / SPY IN THE HOUSE OF NIGHT** [–] [ ]

— added **ALBERT BOUCHARD** – guitar, percussion, vocals
ALLEN LANIER – keyboards, returned to repl. TONY

Sep 88. (lp/c/cd) *(460036-1/-4/-2) <40618>* **IMAGINOS** [ ] Aug88 [ ]
– I am the one you warned me of / Les invisibles / In the presence of another world / Del Rio's song / The siege and investiture of Baron Von Frankenstein's castle at Weisseria / Astronomy (new version) / Magna of illusion. *(pic-lp Mar89; 460036-0)*

Oct 88. (7") *(652 985)* **ASTRONOMY. / MAGNA OF ILLUSION** [ ] [–]
(12"+=) *(652 985-8)* – ('A'-wild mix).
(12"+=/cd-s+=) *(652 985-6/-2)* – (Don't fear) The reaper.

— (early '89 tour) **JON ROGERS** – bass repl. JOE BOUCHARD / **CHUCK BURGI** – drums repl. RON RIDDLE who repl. RICK DOWNEY

Fragile Herald

Jun 94. (cd/c) *(CD/C FRL 003) <HER 008>* **CULT CLASSICS** (re-recorded best of) [ ] [ ]
– (Don't fear) The reaper / E.T.I. (Extra Terrestrial Intelligence) / Me 262 / This ain't the summer of love / Burnin' for you / O.D.'d on life itself / Flaming telepaths / Godzilla / Astronomy / Cities on fire with rock and roll / Harvester of eyes / Buck's boogie / (Don't fear) The reaper / Godzilla.

Jul 94. (c-s/7") *(TC+/FRS 1001)* **(DON'T FEAR) THE REAPER. / BURNIN' FOR YOU** [ ] [–]
(cd-s+=) *(CDFRS 1001)* – ('A'extended).
above were re-recordings of best known material.

— re-formed in '96 with **BLOOM, DHARMA + LANIER**

C.M.C. C.M.C.

Mar 98. (cd) *<(6076 86241-2)>* **HEAVEN FORBID** [ ] [ ]
– See you in black / Harvest moon / Power underneath despair / X-ray eyes / Hammer back / Damaged / Cold gay light of dawn / Real world / Live for me / Still burnin' / In thee.

Angel Air Angel Air

Nov 99. (cd) *<(SJPCD 046)>* **BAD CHANNELS (original soundtrack)** [ ] [ ]
– Demon kiss / Horsemen arrive / Joker: That's how it is – Jane Jane (the hurricane) / Fair game: Somewhere in the night – Blind faith / Synkotik sinfoney: Manic depresso – Mr. Cool / DMT: Myth of freedom – Touching myself again / Little old lady polka / Ukelaliens / Bad channels overture / Power station / Shadow / VU / Cosmos rules but lump controls / Battering ram / This dude is fucked / Pick up her feed / Spray that scumbag / Out of station / Tree full of owls / Cookie in bottle / Corky gets it / Eulogy for Corky / Spore bomb / Remodelling / Ginger snaps / The moon gets it. *(re-iss. Jun01; same)*

Sanctuary C.M.C.

Jun 01. (cd) *(SANCD 089) <86304>* **CURSE OF THE HIDDEN MIRROR** [ ] [ ]
– Dance on stilts / Showtime / Old gods return / Pocket / One step ahead of the Devil / I just like to be bad / Here comes that feeling / Out of the darkness / Stone of love / Eye of the hurricane / Good to feel hungry.

Sanctuary Sanctuary

Nov 02. (cd) *(SANCD 148) <86320>* **A LONG DAY'S NIGHT (live)** [ ] Sep02 [ ]
– Stairway to the stars / Burnin' for you / O.D.'d on lifestyle / Dance on stilts / Buck's boogie / Quicklime girl / Harvest moon / Last days of May / Cities on flame with rock & roll / Perfect water / Lips in the hills / Godzilla / (Don't fear) The reaper.

– compilations, others, etc. –

below on 'CBS'/ 'Columbia' unless otherwise mentioned

1984. (7") *(A 4584)* **(DON'T FEAR) THE REAPER. / I LOVE THE NIGHT** [ ] [–]

Apr 90. (cd/c/lp) *(465929-2/-4/-1) <44300>* **CAREER OF EVIL: THE METAL YEARS** [ ] [ ]
– Cities on flame / The red and the black / Hot rails to Hell / Dominance and submission / Seven screaming Diz-busters / M.E. 262 / E.T.I. (Extra Terrestrial Intelligence) / Beat 'em up / Black blade / The harvester of eyes / Flaming telepaths / Godzilla / (Don't fear) The reaper.

Jan 92. (cd/c) *Castle; (CLA CD/MC 269) / Gopaco; <149>* **LIVE 1976 (live)** [ ] 1994 [ ]

Jan 96. (d-cd) *(480949-2) <64163>* **WORKSHOP OF THE TELESCOPES** [ ] Sep95 [ ]
– Cities in flames with rock'n'roll / Transmaniacon MC / Before the kiss / Redcap / Stairway to the stairs / Buck's boogie / Workshop of the telescopes / Red and the black / 7 screaming dizbusters / Career of evil / Flaming telepaths / Astronomy / Subhuman / Harvester of eyes / M.E. 262 / Born to be wild / (Don't fear) The reaper / This ain't the summer of love / E.T.I. (Extra Terrestial Intelligence) / Godzilla / Goin' through the motions / Golden age of leather / Kick out the jams / We gotta get out of this place / In thee / Marshall plane / Veteran of the psychic wars / Burnin' for you / Dominance and submission / Take me away / Shooting shark / Dancin' in the ruins / Perfect water.

Jun 99. (cd) *Mobile Fidelity; (UDCD 738)* **BLUE OYSTER CULT / TYRANNY AND MUTATION** [ ] [–]

Feb 00. (cd) *Epic; (495243-2) / Columbia; <65918>* **THE BEST OF BLUE OYSTER CULT (DON'T FEAR THE REAPER)** [ ] [ ]

Jul 00. (cd) *Epic; (498791-2) / Sony; <65638>* **SUPER HITS** [ ] Jul98 [ ]

Aug 00. (d-cd) *S.P.V.; (SPV 31021910)* **HEAVEN FORBID / CULT CLASSICS** [ ] [–]
Jan 01. (d-cd) *Axe Killer; (AXE 306332CD)* **TYRANNY AND MUTATION / SECRET TREATIES** [ ] [–]
Sep 01. (d-cd) *Burning Airlines; <(PILOT 128)>* **TALES OF THE PSYCHIC WARS** [ ] [ ]
Mar 02. (d-lp) *Fruit Tree; <(FT 815LP)>* **TALES OF THE PSYCHIC WARS VOL.1** [ ] [ ]
Oct 02. (3xcd-box) *(509501-2)* **BLUE OYSTER CULT / SECRET TREATIES / AGENTS OF FORTUNE** [ ] [–]
Apr 03. (d-lp) *Fruit Tree; <(FT 820LP)>* **TALES OF THE PSYCHIC WARS VOL.2** [ ] [ ]

□ BLUESBREAKERS (see under ⇒ MAYALL, John)

□ BLUESOLOGY (see under ⇒ JOHN, Elton)

BLUETONES

Formed: Hounslow, London, England . . . 1994 by brothers MARK and SCOTT MORRISS, along with ADAM DEVLIN and ED CHESTERS. An indie band in the classic sense of the term, The BLUETONES stood somewhat apart and aloof from the Brit-pop class of '95. The previous year, they'd contributed the track, 'No.11', (later retitled 'BLUETONIC') to a 'Fierce Panda' compilation EP, 'Return To Splendour', before attracting attention from A&M's 'Superior Quality' label early in 1995. A struttingly assured live proposition, the initial buzz surrounding the band was almost tangible. It came as little surprise when a debut single, 'ARE YOU BLUE OR ARE YOU BLIND?' crashed into the charts at No.31, followed later in the long, hot summer of '95 by Top 20 hit, 'BLUETONIC'. A further series of gigs followed before the band narrowly missed the UK No.1 spot in early '96 with the 'SLIGHT RETURN' single. A classic slice of jangle-pop following the time-honoured lineage of The BYRDS, The SMITHS, The LA's and The STONE ROSES, MORRIS even donned a duffel coat(!) for the video, his nimble footed shuffle and boyish good looks generating talk of another IAN BROWN in the ascendant. The long awaited album, 'EXPECTING TO FLY' was released almost simultaneously, reaching the UK No.1 spot and eventually going platinum. Listeners expecting a series of breezy strumalongs were disappointed; the album's dense, evershifting sound rewarded repeated listening, classic rock references slipping in and out of focus but never revealing themselves fully. The catchy 'CUT SOME RUG' was the next single, making the Top 10 ahead of a new track, 'MARBLEHEAD JOHNSON' later that year. 1998's sophomore effort, 'RETURN TO THE LAST CHANCE SALOON' found the Londoners flirting with a bit of rootsy Americana, a sound that blended pleasantly if not spectacularly with their trademark indie rock. 'SOLOMON BITES THE WORM' and 'IF . . ..' both made the Top 20, the latter's title might well have got fans asking themselves questions such as what if . . . the BLUETONES finally made that classic album they've been promising for years. Unfortunately, 'SCIENCE & NATURE' (2000) wasn't to be that record. Instead, it was another set of fine if ultimately unremarkable trad-indie from a band who undoubtedly have the talent to do better. **• Covers:** DON'T STAND ME DOWN (Dexys Midnight Runners) / I WALKED ALL NIGHT (Hargus Robbins) / PRETTY BALLERINA (Left Banke) / THAT'S LIFE (Frank Sinatra) / WOMAN IN LOVE (Barbra Streisand) / SAIL ON SAILOR (Beach Boys) / BEAT ON THE BRAT (Ramones) / MOVE CLOSER (Phyllis Nelson).

Album rating: EXPECTING TO FLY (*8) / RETURN TO THE LAST CHANCE SALOON (*6) / SCIENCE & NATURE (*6) / THE SINGLES collection (*7) / LUXEMBOURG (*7)

MARK MORRISS – vocals / **ADAM DEVLIN** – guitars / **SCOTT MORRISS** – bass, vocals / **ED CHESTERS** – drums, percussion

Superior Polydor

Feb 95. (7"blue; mail-o) *(TONE 001)* **SLIGHT RETURN. / FOUNTAINHEAD** [–] [–]
Jun 95. (7") *(BLUE 001X)* **ARE YOU BLUE OR ARE YOU BLIND?. / STRING ALONG** [31] [–]
(12"+=/cd-s+=) *(BLUE 001 T/CD)* – Driftwood.
Oct 95. (7"/c-s) *(BLUE 002 X/MC)* **BLUETONIC. / GLAD TO SEE Y'BACK AGAIN?** [19] [–]
(12"+=/cd-s+=) *(BLUE 002 T/CD)* – Colorado beetle.
Dec 95. (cd-ep) *<1142>* **BLUETONES COMPANION** [–] [ ]
– Are you blue or are you blind? / String along / Driftwood / Bluetonic / Colorado beetle / Glad to see y' back again.

Superior A&M

Jan 96. (7"/c-s) *(BLUE 003 X/MC)* **SLIGHT RETURN. / DON'T STAND ME DOWN** [2] [–]
(cd-s+=) *(BLUE 003CD)* – Nae hair on't.
Feb 96. (cd/c/lp/s-lp) *(BLUECD/BLUEMC/BLUELP/BLUELPX 004) <540475>* **EXPECTING TO FLY** [1] [ ]
– Talking to Clarry / Bluetonic / Cut some rug / Things change / he fountainhead / Carnt be trusted / Slight return / Putting out fires / Vampire / A parting gesture / Time & again.
Apr 96. (7"/c-s) *(BLUE 005 X/MC)* **CUT SOME RUG. / CASTLE ROCK** [7] [–]
(cd-s+=) *(BLUE 005CD)* – The devil behind my smile.
Sep 96. (7"/c-s) *(BLUE 006 X/MC)* **MARBLEHEAD JOHNSON. / THE SIMPLE THINGS / NIFKIN'S BRIDGE** [7] [–]
(cd-s+=) *(BLUE 006CD)* – Are you blue or are you blind?
Feb 98. (7"/c-s) *(BLUE X/M 007)* **SOLOMON BITES THE WORM. / I WAS A TEENAGE JESUS** [10] [–]
(cd-s+=) *(BLUED 007)* – I walked all night.
Mar 98. (cd/c/lp) *(BLUE D/M/V 008) <LC 0485>* **RETURN TO THE LAST CHANCE SALOON** [10] [ ]
– Tone blooze / Unpainted Arizona / Solomon bites the worm / U.T.A. / 4-day weekend / Sleazy bed track / If . . . / The jub-jub bird / Sky will fall / Ames / Down at the reservoir / Heard you were dead / Broken starr. *(hidden track on cd+=)* – Woman done gone left me.
Apr 98. (7"/c-s) *(BLUE X/M 009)* **IF . . . / BLUE SHADOWS** [13] [ ]
(cd-s+=) *(BLUED 009)* – The watchman.
Jul 98. (7"/c-s) *(BLUE X/M 010)* **SLEAZY BED TRACK. / THE BALLAD OF MULDOON** [35] [–]
(cd-s+=) *(BLUED 010)* – Blue.

Superior Mercury

Feb 00. (c-s) *(BLUEM 012)* **KEEP THE HOME FIRES BURNING / PLEASE STOP TALKING** [13] [–]
(cd-s+=) *(BLUEDD 012)* – Be careful what you dream / ('A'video).
(cd-s) *(BLUED 012)* – ('A'side) / Armageddon (outta here) / Favourite son.
May 00. (c-s) *(BLUEM 013)* **AUTOPHILIA / IT'S A BOY** [18] [–]
(cd-s+=) *(BLUED 013)* – Thought you'd be taller.
(cd-s) *(BLUEDD 013)* – ('A'side) / Soup du jour / Vostok of love.
May 00. (cd/c/lp) *(BLUE CD/MC/LP 014) <7474>* **SCIENCE & NATURE** [7] [ ]
– Zorro / The last of the great navigators / Tiger Lily / Mudslide / One speed gearbox / Blood bubble / Autophilia / Keep the home fires burning / The basement song / Slack jaw / Emily's pine. *(cd+=)* – Keep the home fires burning (video) / Autophilia (video).
Mar 02. (7") *(BLUE 016)* **AFTER HOURS. / INGIMARSSON** [26] [–]
(cd-s) *(BLUED 016)* – ('A'side) / Groovy Roussos / Sail on sailor.
(cd-s) *(BLUEDD 016)* – ('A'side) / Reverse cowgirl / Woman in love.
Apr 02. (cd) *(BLUECD 017)* **THE SINGLES** (compilation) [14] [–]
– Are you blue or are you blind / Bluetonic / Slight return / Cut some drug / Marblehead Johnson / Solomon bites the worm / If . . . / Sleazy bed track / 4 day weekend / Keep the home fires burning / Autophilia or how I learned to stop worrying and love my car / Mudslide / After hours / Freeze dried pop (dumb it up) / Persuasion / Bluetones big score. *(d-cd+=; BLUEDD 017)* – After hours / Pretty ballerina / Blue / Blue shadows / That's life.
Apr 03. (7") *(BLUE 018S)* **FAST BOY. / LIQUID LIPS** [25] [–]
(cd-s+=) *(BLUE 018CDS)* – Beat on the brat.
(cd-s+=) *(BLUE 018CDS2)* – Move closer.
May 03. (cd/lp) *(BLUE 019 CD/LP)* **LUXEMBOURG** [49] [–]
– Here it comes again / Fast boy / Liquid lips / You're no fun anymore /

Big problem / I love the city / Never going nowhere / Little bear / Code blue / Turn it up.

Aug 03. (cd-s) *(BLUE 020CDS)* **NEVER GOING NOWHERE / SUFFER IN SILENCE / NEVER GOING NOWHERE (69 Corp vs. The Bluetones)** 40 –

(cd-s) *(BLUE 020CDS2)* – ('A'side) / Pram face / Choogie Monbassa.

□ BLUE VELVETS (see under ⇒ CREEDENCE CLEARWATER REVIVAL)

BLUR

Formed: Colchester, Essex, England . . . 1989 by DAMON ALBARN, GRAHAM COXON, ALEX JAMES and DAVE ROWNTREE. Initially they went under the moniker of SEYMOUR before opting for The GREAT WHITE HOPES. Finally settling with BLUR, they soon were on the books of David Balfe's 'Food' label, a subsidiary of Parlophone. There, they secured their first UK Top 50 entry with 'SHE'S SO HIGH', an early PINK FLOYD-influenced tune, that rode the coat-tails of the baggy brigade. With the ghost of SYD BARRETT even more pronounced, they created one of the more psychedelic singles of the era in 'THERE'S NO OTHER WAY', the record hitting Top 10 in '91. Another single, 'BANG', preceded their debut album, 'LEISURE', a record that received mixed reviews at the time. Still mainly a singles orientated outfit, they progressed dramatically with the much-improved, 'MODERN LIFE IS RUBBISH' (1993) album, which featured some classy tracks including the hits, 'FOR TOMORROW', 'CHEMICAL WORLD' and 'SUNDAY SUNDAY'. Although they had come on leaps and bounds creatively, this wasn't translated into sales. With the release of 'GIRLS AND BOYS', however, they embarked upon a commercial renaissance that saw the record become their biggest hit to date. It was the opening track on the critically approved 'PARKLIFE' album, which also spawned further hits, 'TO THE END' and the title track (co-sung with actor PHIL DANIELS). By this point they had evolved into a mod-ish indie-pop combo, ALBARN supplying the cockney barra-boy delivery over a musical backdrop that drew from the rich English pop heritage, once the domain of such luminaries as The SMALL FACES and The KINKS. The following year, 1995, saw them win the battle to the coveted No.1 spot with 'COUNTRY HOUSE', beating rivals OASIS who were sharpening their tongues for an onslaught of media slagging. However, BLUR lost ground in the credibility stakes, when their 'GREAT ESCAPE' album failed to impress the critics. OASIS, on the other hand, were scaling new heights with their 2nd album. 1997 marked a slight return to favour, both the single, 'BEETLEBUM', and their eponymous 5th album hitting pole position. With BLUR taking a slight sabbatical from the recording studio, GRAHAM COXON took the opportunity to release a respectable solo effort, 'THE SKY IS TOO HIGH', the BLUR factor and a few good reviews nearly carrying it into the Top 30. Having involved themselves with various remixers (including WILLIAM ORBIT, MOBY, THURSTON MOORE, ADRIAN SHERWOOD and JOHN McENTIRE on the once Japanese-only 'BUSTIN' & DRONIN') over the course of the last year or so, BLUR were seeing clearly once again. In March '99, the gospel-led 'TENDER' went straight to No.2 while the accompanying album, '13' (DAMON had recently split with ELASTICA's JUSTINE FRISCHMANN) topped the chart. Further singles, 'COFFEE & TV' (with COXON taking the lead) and 'NO DISTANCE LEFT TO RUN', only managed to reach the Top 20, it would seem BLUR (like possibly OASIS to come?) were beginning to falter slightly. A good time to release a greatest hits set then, 'BEST OF BLUR' (2000) – only a UK Top 3 – coming exactly a decade after the release of their debut single. The album charted Colchester's own pop idols through the various incarnations of their career with the conspicuous underrepresentation of 'MODERN LIFE . . .', their transitional but commercially flat 1993 effort. GRAHAM COXON also released his second solo effort, 'GOLDEN D', the same year, a spiky, DIY follow-up to his debut which found him revisiting Mission Of Burma's 'FAME AND FORTUNE' and 'THAT'S WHEN I REACH FOR MY REVOLVER'. The most pertinent millennial development in the BLUR camp, however, arguably came with the inception of GORILLAZ, the pop world's very first "virtual" dub/hip hop outfit. The brainchild of ALBARN and cartoonist JAMIE HEWLETT (creator of cult comic heroine 'Tank Girl', herself the inspiration for Lara Croft and a forerunner of the "girlpower" shenanigans), this cutting edge project also benefitted from the talents of CIBO MATTO's MIHO MATORI, hip hop beats merchant DAN 'THE AUTOMATOR' NAKAMURA, reggae bassist DAN JUNIOR and white funk veterans TINA WEYMOUTH and CHRIS FRANTZ (ex-TALKING HEADS, TOM TOM CLUB). As for the band "members", they were cute but dim lead singer 2-D (NOT based on DAMON as everyone thought), sinister, scowling guitarist MURDOC, b-boy RUSSEL and the mysterious, oriental NOODLE. GORILLAZ' debut EP, 'TOMORROW COMES TODAY' arrived in late 2000 while the seminal 'CLINT EASTWOOD' single was released the following year. A lurching slice of feelgood dub-hop which made the UK Top 5 and even the Italian Top 10, the track was a definite contender for single of the year. More importantly for a virtual band, the brilliantly inventive video brought the characters to life in a way that the eponymous 'GORILLAZ' (2001) album did not. Still, there were plenty of sterling pop thrills to be had amidst the occasionally unfocused dubscapes while ironically, perhaps, ALBARN's cockney leer sounded better in this environment than in the confines of BLUR. While the live shows may not quite have lived up to the hype, hits to the band's web site (www.gorillaz.com) dominate the EMI server's traffic. When BLUR did eventually get it together for the long awaited 'THINK TANK' (2003), the results were less than spectacular. Despite the presence of such savvy producers as FATBOY SLIM and WILLIAM ORBIT, the chilly, directionless experimentation of much of the album wasn't so much of a surprise given the acrimonious departure of COXON. ALBARN's recent dalliances with world music flitered through to a certain extent, with strings employed by a cast of North African musicians. Yet even this exotica wasn't enough to redeem the record, its emotionally barren soundscapes skewering the band's trademark pop aesthetic. Among the few high points was the UK Top 5 single, 'OUT OF TIME'. • **Covered:** MAGGIE MAY (Rod Stewart) / LAZY SUNDAY (Small Faces). • **Trivia:** DAMON's father, KEITH ALBARN, used to be the manager of 60's rock outfit, The SOFT MACHINE.

Album rating: LEISURE (*6) / MODERN LIFE IS RUBBISH (*8) / PARKLIFE (*9) / THE GREAT ESCAPE (*7) / BLUR (*8) / 13 (*6) / THE BEST OF BLUR compilation (*9) / THINK TANK (*5) / Gorillaz: GORILLAZ (*9) / G SIDES collection (*7)

DAMON ALBARN (b.23 Mar'68, Whitechapel, London) – vocals / **GRAHAM COXON** (b.12 Mar'69, Germany) – guitars / **ALEX JAMES** (b.21 Nov'68, Dorset, England) – bass, vocals / **DAVE ROWNTREE** (b. 8 Apr'63) – drums

Food-EMI S.B.K.

Oct 90. (c-s/7") *(TC+/FOOD 26)* **SHE'S SO HIGH. / I KNOW** 48 –

(12") *(12FOOD 26)* – ('A'-Definitive) / Sing / I know (extended).

(cd-s) *(CDFOOD 26)* – ('A'side) / I know (extended) / Down.

Apr 91. (c-s/7") *(TC+/FOOD 29)* **THERE'S NO OTHER WAY. / INERTIA** 8 –

(ext.12"+=/cd-s+=) *(12/CD FOOD 29)* – Mr.Briggs / I'm all over.

(12") *(12FOODX 20)* – ('A'remix). / Won't do it / Day upon day (live).

Jul 91. (c-s/7") *(TC+/FOOD 31)* **BANG. / LUMINOUS** 24 —
(ext.12"+=) *(12FOOD 31)* – Explain / Uncle Love.
(cd-s+=) *(CDFOOD 31)* – Explain / Beserk.

Aug 91. (cd/c/lp) *(FOOD CD/TC/LP 6)* <97880> **LEISURE** 7 —
– She's so high / Bang / Slow down / Repetition / Bad day / Sing / There's no other way / Fool / Come together / High cool / Birthday / Wear me down.

Dec 91, (c-s,cd-s) <07374> **THERE'S NO OTHER WAY / EXPLAIN** – 82

Mar 92. (c-s/7") *(TC+/FOOD 37)* **POPSCENE. / MACE** 32 —
(12"+=) *(12FOOD 37)* – I'm fine / Garden central.
(cd-s+=) *(CDFOOD 37)* – Badgeman Brown.

Apr 93. (c-s) *(TCFOOD 40)* **FOR TOMORROW. / INTO ANOTHER / HANGING OVER** 28 —
(12"+=) *(12FOOD 40)* – Peach.
(cd-s) *(CDFOOD 40)* – ('A'extended) / Peach / Bone bag.
(cd-s) *(CDSFOOD 40)* – ('A'side) / When the cows come home / Beachcoma / For tomorrow (acoustic).

May 93. (cd/c/lp) *(FOOD CD/TC/LP 9)* <89442> **MODERN LIFE IS RUBBISH** 15 —
– For tomorrow / Advert / Colin Zeal / Pressure on Julian / Star shaped / Blue jeans / Chemical world / Sunday Sunday / Oily water / Miss America / Villa Rosie / Coping / Turn it up / Resigned.

Jun 93. (7"red) *(FOODS 45)* **CHEMICAL WORLD. / MAGGIE MAY** 28 —
(12"/cd-s) *(12/CD FOOD 45)* – ('A'side) / Es Schmecht / Young and lovely / My ark.
(cd-s) *(CDFOODS 45)* – ('A'side) / Never clever (live) / Pressure on Julian (live) / Come together (live).

Oct 93. (7"yellow) *(FOODS 46)* **SUNDAY SUNDAY. / TELL ME, TELL ME** 26 —
(12") *(12FOODS 46)* – ('A'side) / Long legged / Mixed up.
(cd-s) *(CDFOODS 46)* – ('A'side) / Dizzy / Fried / Shimmer.
(cd-s) *(CDFOODX 46)* – ('A'side) / Daisy bell / Let's all go The Strand.

Mar 94. (7"/c-s) *(FOODS/TCFOOD 47)* **GIRLS AND BOYS. / MAGPIE / PEOPLE IN EUROPE** 5 –
(cd-s) *(CDFOOD 47)* – ('A'side) / People in Europe / Peter Panic.
(cd-s) *(CDFOODS 47)* – ('A'side) / Magpie / Anniversary waltz.

Apr 94. (cd/c/lp) *(FOOD CD/TC/LP 10)* <29194> **PARKLIFE** 1 Jun94 —
– Girls and boys / Tracy Jacks / End of a century / Park life / Bank holiday / Bad head / The debt collector / Far out / To the end / London loves / Trouble in the message centre / Clover over Dover / Magic America / Jubilee / This is a low / Lot 105.

May 94. (c-s) *(TCFOOD 50)* **TO THE END / GIRLS AND BOYS (Pet Shop Boys remix) / THREADNEEDLE STREET** 16 —
(12"/cd-s) *(12/CD FOOD 50)* – (1st 2 tracks; 2 versions of 2nd).
(cd-s) *(CDFOODS 50)* – ('A'side) / Threadneedle Street / Got yer.
(above featured LETITIA of STEREOLAB. Next with actor PHIL DANIELS.

Jun 94. (c-s,cd-s) <58155> **GIRLS AND BOYS / GIRLS AND BOYS (Pet Shop Boys radio mix) / MAGGIE MAY** – 59

Aug 94. (c-s/cd-s) *(TC/CDS FOOD 53)* **PARKLIFE. / SUPA SHOPPA / THEME FROM AN IMAGINARY FILM** 10 —
(12") *(12FOOD 53)* – (1st 2 tracks) / To the end (French version).
(cd-s) *(CDFOOD 53)* – (1st track) / Beard / To the end (French version).

Nov 94. (c-s/7") *(TCFOOD/FOODS 56)* **END OF A CENTURY. / RED NECKS** 19 —
(cd-s+=) *(CDFOOD 56)* – Alex's song.

Food Virgin

Aug 95. (c-s/7") *(TC+/FOOD 63)* **COUNTRY HOUSE. / ONE BORN EVERY MINUTE** 1 –
(cd-s+=) *(CDFOOD 63)* – To the end (with FRANCOISE HARDY).
(cd-ep) *(CDFOODS 63)* ('A'live) / Girls and boys (live) / Parklife (live) / For tomorrow (live).

Sep 95. (cd/c/lp) *(FOOD CD/MC/LP 14)* <40855> **THE GREAT ESCAPE** 1 —
– Stereotypes / Country house / Best days / Charmless man / Fade away / Top man / The universal / Mr. Robinson's quango / He thought of cars / It could be you / Ernold Same / Globe alone / Dan Abnormal / Entertain me / Yuko and Hiro.

Nov 95. (c-s) *(TCFOOD 69)* **THE UNIVERSAL / ENTERTAIN ME (the live it! remix)** 5 –
(cd-s+=) *(CDFOODS 69)* – Ultranol / No monsters in me.
(cd-ep) *(CDFOOD 69)* – ('A'live) / Mr. Robinson's quango (live) / It could be you (live) / Stereotypes (live).

Feb 96. (c-s/7") *(TC+/FOOD 73)* **STEREOTYPES. / THE MAN WHO LEFT HIMSELF / TAME** 7 –
(cd-s+=) *(CDFOOD 73)* – Ludwig.

Apr 96. (c-s/7") *(TC+/FOOD 77)* **CHARMLESS MAN. / THE HORRORS** 5 –
(cd-s+=) *(CDFOOD 77)* – A song / St. Louis.

— BLUR were joint winners (with rivals OASIS; NOEL) of the Ivor Novello Award for songwriter of the year.

May 96. (d-cd; ltd on 'EMI Japan') *(TOCP 8400)* **LIVE AT THE BUDOKAN (live)** – –

— ALEX JAMES helped to form one-off indie supergroup ME ME ME alongside JUSTIN WELCH (Elastica –), STEPHEN DUFFY and CHARLIE BLOOR. Had a UK Top 20 hit in Aug'96 with 'HANGING AROUND'.

Food Virgin

Jan 97. (7"red) *(FOOD 89)* **BEETLEBUM. / WOODPIGEON SONG** 1 –
(cd-s+=) *(CDFOODS 89)* – ('A'-Mario Caldato Jr mix) / Dancehall.
(cd-s) *(CDFOOD 89)* – ('A'side) / All your life / A spell for money.

Feb 97. (cd/c/lp) *(FOOD CD/TC/LP 19)* <42876> **BLUR** 1 61
– Beetlebum / Song 2 / Country sad ballad man / M.O.R. / On your own / Theme from retro / You're so great / Death of a party / Chinese bombs / I'm just a killer for your love / Look inside America / Strange news from another star / Movin' on / Essex dogs.

Apr 97. (7"purple) *(FOOD 93)* **SONG 2 / GET OUT OF THE CITIES** 2 –
(cd-s+=) *(CDFOODS 93)* – Polished stone.
(cd-s) *(CDFOOD 93)* – ('A'side) / Bustin' & dronin' / Country sad ballad man (live acoustic).

Jun 97. (7"white) *(FOOD 98)* **ON YOUR OWN. / POP SCENE (live) / SONG 2 (live)** 5 –
(cd-s+=) *(CDFOOD 98)* – On your own (live).
(cd-s) *(CDFOODS 98)* – ('A'side) / Chinese bombs (live) / Moving on (live) / M.O.R. (live).

Sep 97. (c-s/7"orange) *(TC+/FOOD 107)* **M.O.R. (Alan Moulder road version). / SWALLOWS IN THE HEATWAVE** 15 –
(cd-s+=) *(CDFOOD 107)* – Movin' on (William Orbit mix) / Beetlebum (Moby's minimal house mix).

Mar 98. (d-cd) *(TOCP 504445)* **BUSTIN' AND DRONIN'** — –

Mar 99. (c-s/7"blue) *(TC+/FOOD 117)* **TENDER. / ALL WE WANT** 2 –
(cd-s+=) *(CDFOOD 117)* – Mellow jam (short version).
(cd-s) *(CDFOODS 117)* – ('A'side) / French song (full version) / Song 2 (video).

Mar 99. (cd/c/d-lp) *(FOOD CD/MC/LP 29)* <99129> **13** 1 80
– Tender / Bugman / Coffee & TV / Swamp song / 1992 / B.L.U.R.E.M.I. / Battle / Mellow song / Trailerpark / Caramel / No distance left to run / Trimm trabb / Optigan 1.

Jun 99. (c-s) *(TCFOOD 122)* **COFFEE & TV / X-OFFENDER (Damon – Controls freaks bugman remix)** 11 –
(cd-s+=) *(CDFOOD 122)* – Coyote (Dave's bugman remix).
(12"++=) *(12FOOD 122)* – Trade stylee (Alex's bugman remix) / Metal hip slop (Graham's bugman remix).
(cd-s) *(CDFOODS 122)* – ('A'side) / (above 2).

Nov 99. (c-s) *(TCFOOD 123)* **NO DISTANCE LEFT TO RUN / BEAGLE 2 / SO YOU** 14 –
(cd-s) *(CDFOODS 123)* – ('A'side) / Battle (U.N.K.L.E. remix).
(cd-s) *(CDFOOD 123)* – ('A'side) / Tender (Cornelius mix).

Oct 00. (12") *(12FOOD 135)* **MUSIC IS MY RADAR. / BLACK BOOK** 10 —
(cd-s+=) *(CDFOOD 135)* – Headist / Into another (live).
(c-s+=) *(TCFOOD 135)* – She's so high.
(cd-s) *(CDFOODS 135)* – ('A'side) / She's so high / Seven days (live).

Oct 00. (cd/c/d-lp) *(FOOD CD/TC/LPD 33)* <50457> **BLUR: THE BEST OF** (compilation) 3 Nov00 —
– Beetlebum / Song 2 / There's no other way / The universal / Coffee & TV / Parklife / End of a century / No distance left to run / Tender / Girls and boys / Charmless man / She's so high / Country house / To the end / On your own / This is a low / For tomorrow (visit to Primrose Hill extended) / Music is my radar. *(d-cd+=; FOODCDS 33)* – LIVE: She's so high / Girls and boys / To the end / End of a century / Charmless man / Beetlebum / MOR / Tender / No distance left to run.

— now without COXON who continued with his own solo career

Apr 03. (7") *(R 6606)* **OUT OF TIME. / MONEY MAKES ME CRAZY (Marrakesh mix)** 5 –
(cd-s+=) *(CDRS 6606)* – Tune 2 / ('A'-video in Morocco).

May 03. (cd/d-lp) *(582997-2/-1)* *<84244>* **THINK TANK** [1] [ ]
– Ambulance / Out of time / Crazy beat / Good song / On the way to the club / Brothers and sisters / Caravan / We've got a file on you / Moroccan peoples revolutionary bowls club / Sweet song / Jets / Gene by gene / Battery in your leg. *(ltd-cd+=; 582997-0)* – Ambulance (live at MTV) / Crazy beat (live at MTV) / Caravan (live at MTV).

Jul 03. (7"red) *(R 6610)* **CRAZY BEAT. / THE OUTSIDER** [18] [–]
(cd-s+=) *(CDRS 6610)* – Don't be / ('A'-alt. video).

Oct 03. (7"red) *(R 6619)* **GOOD SONG. / MORRICONE** [22] [–]
(cd-s) *(CDRS 6619)* – ('A'side) / Me – White noise (alternate version).

– compilations, etc. –

all on 'Food' except where indicated

Sep 99. (cd-ep-box) *(BLURBOX 10)* **10th ANNIVERSARY BOX SET** [ ] [–]
– (all 22 hit singles)

Sep 03. (d-cd) *(592001-2)* **BLUR / 13** [ ] [–]

Sep 03. (d-cd) *(592002-2)* **PARKLIFE / MODERN LIFE IS RUBBISH** [ ] [–]

GORILLAZ

DAMON ALBARN – vocals (of DELTRON 3030) / **DAN "THE AUTOMATOR" NAKAMURA** – producer / **MIHO HATORI** – vocals (of CIBO MATTO) / **JAMIE HEWLETT** – visuals / plus **KID KOALA + DEL THA FUNKEE HOMOSAPIEN** – vocals / **2-D** – keyboards / **MURDOC** – bass / **RUSSEL** – drums / **NOODLE** – guitar / + **TINA WEYMOUTH** – vocals (ex-TALKING HEADS)

Parlophone Virgin

Nov 00. (12") *(12R 6545)* **TOMORROW COMES TODAY. / ROCK THE HOUSE / LATIN SIMONE** [ ] [–]
(cd-s+=) *(CDR 6545)* – ('A'-video).

Mar 01. (c-s) *(TCR 6552)* *<radio cut>* **CLINT EASTWOOD / CLINT EASTWOOD (Ed Case refix) / DRACULA** [4] Aug01 [57]
(cd-s+=) *(CDR 6552)* – ('A'CD-Rom).
(12") *(12R 6552)* – ('A'side) / ('A'-Ed Case refix full) / ('A'-Phil Life cypher version).

Mar 01. (cd/d-lp) *(531138-2/-1)* *<33748>* **GORILLAZ** [3] Jun00 [14]
– Re-hash / 5-4 / Tomorrow comes today / New genius (brother) / Clint Eastwood / Man research (clapper) / Punk / Sound check (gravity) / Double bass / Rock the house / 19-2000 / Latin Simone / Starshine / Slow country / M1 A1 / Clint Eastwood (Ed Case refix full version) / 19-2000 (soul child mix). *(cd+=)* – Dracula / Left hand Suzuki method.

—— in May'01, DAMON ALBARN & EINAR ORN BENEDIKTSSON released the soundtrack to '101 REYKJAVIK' for 'E.M.I.'; *(532989-2)*

Jun 01. (c-s) *(TCR 6559)* **19-2000 / HIP ALBATROSS** [6] [–]
(cd-s) *(CDR 6559)* – ('A'side) / ('A'-Soulchild remix) / Left hand Suzuki method.
(12"++=) *(12R 6559)* – ('A'-Wiseguys house of wisdom remix).

Oct 01. (c-s) *(TCR 6565)* **ROCK THE HOUSE / GHOST TRAIN** [18] [–]
(cd-s+=) *(CDR 6565)* – 19-2000 (video).
(cd-s) *(CDRS 6565)* – ('A'side) / Sounder / Faust / (making of the 'Rock The House' video).

Feb 02. (12") *(12R 6573)* **TOMORROW COMES TODAY. / TOMORROW (dub) / FILM MUSIC (mode remix)** [33] [–]
(cd-s) *(CDR 6573)* – ('A'side) / Film music / Tomorrow dub (Spacemonkeys mix) / ('A'-video).

Mar 02. (cd) *(536942-0)* *<11967>* **G SIDES** (compilation) [65] [84]
– 19/2000 (Soulchild mix) / Dracula / Rock the house / Sounder / Faust / Clint Eastwood (Phi life cypher version) / Ghost train / Hip albatross / Left hand Suzuki method / 12D3 / Clint Eastwood (video) / Rock the house (video).

—— In Aug'02, GORILLAZ feat. on SPACE MONKEYZ' hit, 'Lil' Dub Chefin'

BOARDS OF CANADA

Formed: Pentland Hills, nr. Edinburgh . . . 1995 by MICHAEL SANDISON and MARCUS EOIN. The group earned their acclaim after recording a ridiculous amount of tracks which became available on the now legendary 'TWOISM' mini-LP – limited to 100 copies and ever so collectable. Next up was for experimental electronica label 'Skam' who signed the pair in 1996. Hailed as 'Skam's greatest release to date, the 'HI SCORES' EP set the ball rolling for the team in 1996 (now worth over £500). Audiences couldn't get enough of its catchy but simple, A-B-C (or L.F.O.) synth formats and melodies. References were, of course, made to The APHEX TWIN and JEGA, however 'HI SCORES' had a better twisted back-beat to it than, say, RICHARD D. JAMES' cult 'ANALOGUE BUBBLEBATH VOL.1'. It fooled listeners into thinking the band were American by its sheer 1992 hip-hop nostalgia and chilled out beach party vibes. This impressive debut was quickly followed up in late 1996 by a series of tracks for 'UMV' and 'Slam/Musik Aus Strom' side project label 'Mask', with 1998 witnessing the unfettering of the excellent "difficult" third release, 'MUSIC HAS THE RIGHT TO CHILDREN'. Cool as well as deeply serene, the album (distributed by 'Warp' and 'Matador') intensified that early 90's Miami trip-hop identity and added in a little scratching and sampling for good measure. A prime example of this was the single out-take, and the most famous track you'll hear from the album, 'ROYGBIV', which sounded like the Terminator doing slow motion break dancing in a crowded Beverly Hills house party. 1999 saw the latest from BOC, a PEEL SESSIONS EP, another triumph from the Peel acres and an entry into the 'Matador' 10th anniversary collection, 'Everything Is Nice'. The duo finally returned with a two track EP, 'A BEAUTIFUL PLACE IN THE COUNTRY', towards the end of 2000. The single was an unexpected trip into the psychedelic shenanigans that were about to be, once again, explored by The BOARDS OF CANADA. In February 2002, their long-awaited sophomore album, 'GEOGADDI', was released to huge critical acclaim, which resulted in their first interview with the NME. For this they described the open Scottish wilderness as an inspiration for their hallucinogenic, spaced-out synth doodlings. They also declared that the meaning of their moniker was indeed (as older readers may recall!) lifted from an educational company whose films on science and nature had been shown while the pair had attended school. This reflected a lot of the new album; one track in question 'DANDELION' had a backwards moog drone accompanied by a man (actor Leslie Nielsen from 'Naked Gun' fame!) narrating a TV documentary about a diving team; this segued into the six and a half minute epic 'SUNSHINE RECORDER'. Track 16, 'THE DEVIL IN THE DETAILS', had a simple keyboard riff on a loop which played the insane shrills of a child and the voice of a distorted, disjointed telephone operator. 'GEODADDI' (a near Top 20 entry) was much darker and yet much more layered in terms of themes, music and ambience. For two guys living in the countryside this was quite a feat, a real slice of math-electronica that was both gentle and eerily sublime.

Album rating: TWOISM mini (*7) / HI SCORES mini (*7) / MUSIC HAS THE RIGHT TO CHILDREN (*9) / PEEL SESSIONS (*7) / GEOGADDI (*9)

MICHAEL SANDISON (b. 14 Jul'71) – electronics / **MARCUS EOIN** (b.27 May'73) – electronics

Music 70 not iss.

Aug 95. (ltd; m-lp) *(BOARD 1)* **TWOISM** [ ] [–]
– Sixtyniner / Directline / Iced cooly / Basefree / Twoism / Seeya later / Melissa juice / Smokes quantity. *(re-iss. Nov02 on 'Warp' m-lp/m-cd+=; WARP LP/CD 70)* – 1986 summer fire.

Skam not iss.

Dec 96. (m-lp) *(SKA 8)* **HIGH SCORES** [ ] [–]
– Hi scores / Turquoise hexagon sun / Nlogax / June 9th / Seeya later / Everything you do is a balloon. *(m-cd-iss. Nov02; SKA 8CD)*

Jan 98. (7") *(KMAS 1)* **AQUARIUS. / CHINOOK** [ ] [–]

Warp – Skam Matador

Mar 98. (10") *(WAP10 55)* **ROYGBIV. / TELEPHASIC WORKSHOP** [ ] [–]

Apr 98. (cd/d-lp) *(WARP CD/LP 55 – SKALD 1) <OLE 299-2/-1>*
MUSIC HAS THE RIGHT TO CHILDREN ☐ ☐
– Wildlife analysis / An eagle in your mind / The color of the fire / Telephasic workshop / Triangles & rhombuses / Sixtyten / Turquoise hexagon sun / Kaini industries / Bocuma / Roygbiv / Rue the whirl / Aquarius / Olson / Pete standing alone / Smokes quantity / Open the light / One very important thought. *(d-lp+=)* – Happy cycling.

Warp Warp

Jan 99. (cd-ep) *(<WAP 114CD>)* **PEEL SESSIONS** ☐ Mar99 ☐
– Aquarius (version 3) / Happy cycling / Olson (version 3).

Nov 00. (12"/cd-s) *(<WAP 144/+CD>)* **IN A BEAUTIFUL PLACE OUT IN THE COUNTRY EP** ☐ ☐
– Kid for today / Amo bishop Roden / In a beautiful place out in the country / Zoetrope.

Feb 02. (cd/t-lp) *(<WARP CD/LP 101>)* **GEOGADDI** 21 ☐
– Ready let's go / Music is math / Beware the friendly stranger / Gyroscope / Dandelion / Sunshine recorder / In the annexe / Julie and Candy / The smallest weird number / 1969 / Energy warning / The beach at Redpoint / Opening the mouth / Alpha and Omega / I saw drones / The devil in the details / A is to B as B is to C / Over the horizon radar / Dawn chorus / Diving station / You could feel the sky / Corsair / Magic window.

☐ BODY COUNT (see under ⇒ ICE-T)

Marc BOLAN

Born: MARC FELD, 30 Sep'47, London, England. He began his performing career under the improbable moniker of TOBY TYLER, before ditching it and signing to 'Decca'. After 3 flop singles, he enjoyed a brief stint with JOHN'S CHILDREN ('Desdemona') before teaming up in 1968 with bongo player STEVE PEREGRINE TOOK to form TYRANNOSAURUS REX. Far from the hoary, chest-beating proto-metal that name might imply, the band's sound was a folky melange of acoustic guitar, manic bongos and pop melodies. Unfortunately the band were victims of their era and prone to lyrical flights of fancy that often broke down into hippy cliche, just check out the title of their debut mid-68 album 'MY PEOPLE WERE FAIR AND HAD SKY IN THEIR HAIR . . . BUT NOW THEY'RE CONTENT TO WEAR STARS ON THEIR BROWS'. A bit of a hippy himself at the time, Radio One DJ JOHN PEEL championed their first single 'DEBORA', as well as material from their next 3 albums. They became a big draw on the underground circuit, helping the albums gain minor placings in the UK charts. MARC's ex-model features and effeminate charisma did no harm in making him an object of hippy chick lust, and it was about time the band had a sexier name to match. Just before the group became T.REX, TOOK was replaced by MICKEY FINN, as they gradually adopted an all-electric sound. The spanking new single 'RIDE A WHITE SWAN', nearly nailed the No.1 spot in October 1970 and made BOLAN a fully fledged pop idol. A jaunty little number with a stabbing guitar-line, it heralded the band's strident new sound, although it retained the quasi-mystical lyrical schtick. STEVE CURRY and BILL LEGEND were drafted in and the band notched up 8 consecutive Top 3 hits, including 4 UK chart-toppers. The celebratory 'HOT LOVE' and the timeless 'GET IT ON' both hit the top spot as did the 'ELECTRIC WARRIOR' album, displaying a welcome move to raunchier (but often equally silly) lyrics. BOLAN then set up his own label through EMI after 'JEEPSTER' was re-issued without his consent. He almost single handedly invented the "glam-rock" phenomenon, achieving the rare feat of being a rock idol and pop star at the same time. 'TELEGRAM SAM', 'METAL GURU' and the evergreen '20th CENTURY BOY' are still guaranteed to get you dusting down your 6" platforms a quarter of a century on. After the single 'THE GROOVER' was released in 1973 and after splitting with his wife JUNE CHILD, BOLAN brought in his new girlfriend GLORIA JONES to record 'TRUCK ON (TYKE)'. This was the first single by T.REX not to make the Top 10. His creativity was ebbing and he moved to America to record some lacklustre formulaic material in a variety of styles. Like early fan JOHN PEEL, BOLAN embraced the subsequent punk takeover and had a new deal with 'R.C.A.' before he met his untimely end on 16th September 1977. In yet another bizarre rock'n'roll death, his girlfriend crashed their car into a tree near Barnes Common, which soon became a shrine. Since his death, obsessive fans and curious observers alike have lapped up a stream of documentaries, greatest hits packages, tributes and re-issues (mostly on fan club label 'Marc On Wax'), which show no sign of abating.

• **Covers:** SUMMERTIME BLUES (Eddie Cochran) / DO YOU WANNA DANCE (Bobby Freeman) / DOCK OF THE BAY (Otis Redding) / TO KNOW HIM IS TO LOVE HIM (Teddy Bears) / RIP IT UP (Little Richard) / ENDLESS SLEEP (Joey Reynolds) / A TEENAGER IN LOVE (Dion).

Album rating: Tyrannosaurus Rex: MY PEOPLE WERE FAIR AND HAD SKY IN THE HAIR, BUT NOW THEY'RE CONTENT TO WEAR STARS ON THEIR BROWS (*6) / PROPHETS, SEERS AND SAGES, THE ANGEL OF THE AGES (*6) / UNICORN (*7) / A BEARD OF STARS (*6) / T.Rex: T.REX (*5) / ELECTRIC WARRIOR (*8) / THE SLIDER (*7) / TANX (*6) / ZINC ALLOY & THE HIDDEN RIDERS OF TOMORROW (*4) / BOLAN'S ZIP GUN (*4) / FUTURISTIC DRAGON (*5) / DANDY IN THE UNDERWORLD (*5) / THE ULTIMATE COLLECTION compilation (*9) / THE ESSENTIAL . . . compilation (*9)

MARC BOLAN

—— solo using session men

Decca not iss.

Nov 65. (7") *(F 12288)* **THE WIZARD. / BEYOND THE RISING SUN** ☐ –

Jun 66. (7") *(F 12413)* **THE THIRD DEGREE. / SAN FRANCISCO POET** ☐ –

Parlophone not iss.

Dec 66. (7") *(R 5539)* **HIPPY GUMBO. / MISFIT** ☐ –

—— BOLAN then joined JOHN'S CHILDREN before forming own band

TYRANNOSAURUS REX

MARC – vocals, guitars / **STEVE PEREGRINE TOOK** (b.28 Jul'49, London) – bongos, vocals

Regal Zonophone A&M

Apr 68. (7") *(RZ 3008)* **DEBORA. / CHILD STAR** 34 ☐

Jun 68. (lp; stereo/mono) *(S+/LRZ 1003)* **MY PEOPLE WERE FAIR AND HAD SKY IN THEIR HAIR . . . BUT NOW THEY'RE CONTENT TO WEAR STARS ON THEIR BROWS** 15 ☐
– Red hot mama / Scenesof / Child star / Strange orchestras / Chateau in Virginia Waters / Dwarfish trumpet blues / Mustang Ford / Afghan woman / Knight / Graceful fat shake / Weilder of words / Frowning Atahuallpa. *(re-iss. May85 on 'Sierra' lp/c; FEDB/CFEDB 5013) (cd-iss. Oct98 on 'Polydor'; 541009-2)*

Regal Zonophone Blue Thumb

Aug 68. (7") *(RZ 3011)* **ONE INCH ROCK. / SALAMANDA PALAGANDA** 28 ☐

Oct 68. (lp; stereo/mono) *(S+/LRZ 1005)* **PROPHETS, SEERS AND SAGES, THE ANGELS OF THE AGES** ☐ ☐
– Deboraarobed / Stacey grove / Wind quartets / Conesuala / Trelawny lawn / Aznagell the mage / The friends / Salamanda Palaganda / Our wonderful brownskin man / Oh Harley (the Saltimbanques) / Eastern spell / The travelling tragition / Juniper suction / Scenes of dynasty. *(re-iss. May85 on 'Sierra' lp/c; FEDB/CFEDB 5022) (cd-iss. Oct94 on 'Disky'; CUCD 10) (cd re-iss. Oct98 on 'Polydor'; 541010-2)*

Jan 69. (7") *(RZ 3016)* **PEWTER SUITOR. / WARLORD OF THE ROYAL CROCODILES** ☐ ☐

May 69. (lp; stereo/mono) *(S+/LRZ 1007)* **UNICORN** 12 ☐
– Chariots of silk / 'Pon a hill / The seal of seasons / The throat of winter / Cat black (the wizard's hat) / Stones of Avalon / She was born to be my

unicorn / Like a white star, tangled and far, Tulip that's what you are / Warlord of the royal crocodiles / Evenings of Damask / The sea beasts / Iscariot / Nijinsky hind / The pilgrim's tale / The misty coast of Albany / Romany soup. *(re-iss. May85 on 'Sierra' lp/c; FEDB/CFEDB 5024) (cd-iss. Oct94 on 'Disky'; CUCD 11) (cd re-iss. Oct98 on 'Polydor'; 541012-2)*

Jul 69. (7") *(RZ 3022)* **KING OF THE RUMBLING SPIRES. / DO YOU REMEMBER?** [44] [ ]

— **MICKEY FINN** (b. 3 Jan'47) – bongos, vocals repl. TOOK who joined PINK FAIRIES (He died Nov80)

Jan 70. (7") *(RZ 3025)* **BY THE LIGHT OF THE MAGICAL MOON. / FIND A LITTLE WOOD** [ ] [ ]

Mar 70. (lp) *(SLRZ 1013)* **A BEARD OF STARS** [21] [ ]
– Prelude / A day laye / The woodland bop / First heart mighty dawn dart / Pavillions of sun / Organ blues / By the light of the magical Moon / Wind cheetah / A beard of stars / Great horse / Dragon's ear / Lofty skies / Dove / Elemental child. *<US-import had free 7"; BLUE THING> (re-iss. May85 on 'Sierra' lp/c; FEDB/CFEDB 5035) (cd-iss. Oct98 on 'Polydor'; 541003-2)*

T. REX

Fly / Blue Thumb

Oct 70. (7"m) *(BUG 1) <121>* **RIDE A WHITE SWAN. / IS IT LOVE / SUMMERTIME BLUES** [2] Jan71 [76]

— added **STEVE CURRY** (b.21 May'47, Grimsby, England) – bass / **BILL LEGEND** (b. 8 May'44, Essex, England) – drums

Fly / Reprise

Dec 70. (lp/c) *(HIFLY/ZCFLY 2) <6440>* **T.REX** [13] Apr71 [ ]
– The children of Rarn / Jewel / The visit / Childe / The time of love is now / Diamond meadows / Root of star / Beltane walk / Is it love / One inch rock / Summer deep / Seagull woman / Sun eye / The wizard / The children of Rarn (reprise). *(re-iss. Mar78 + Oct81; same) (re-iss. May85 on 'Sierra' lp/c; FEDB/CFEDB 5010) (cd-iss. May92 on 'Castle';) (cd re-iss. Oct98 on 'Polydor'; 541011-2)*

Feb 71. (7"m) *(BUG 6)* **HOT LOVE. / WOODLAND ROCK / KING OF THE MOUNTAIN COMETH** [1] [–]

Apr 71. (7"m) *<1006>* **HOT LOVE. / ONE INCH ROCK / SEAGULL WOMAN** [–] [72]

Jul 71. (7"m) *(BUG 10)* **GET IT ON (BANG A GONG). / THERE WAS A TIME / RAW RAMP** [1] [–]

Sep 71. (lp/c) *(HIFLY/ZCFLY 6) <6466>* **ELECTRIC WARRIOR** [1] Oct71 [32]
– Mambo sun / Cosmic dancer / Jeepster / Monolith / Lean woman blues / Get it on (bang a gong) / Planet queen / Girl / The motivator / Life's a gas / Rip off. *(re-iss. Mar78 + Oct81; same) (cd-iss. May87 on 'Sierra; CDTR 2) (re-iss. Apr90 on 'Castle' c/cd+=; CLA MC/CD 180)* – Hot love / Deborah. *(cd re-iss. Oct98 on 'Polydor'; 541007-2) (lp re-iss. Sep99 on 'Simply Vinyl'; SVLP 117) (deluxe cd-iss. Sep01 on 'Polydor'+=; 493113-2)* – (work in progress tracks)

Nov 71. (7") *(BUG 16)* **JEEPSTER. / LIFE'S A GAS** [2] [–]

Dec 71. (7") *<1032>* **BANG A GONG (GET IT ON). / RAW RAMP** [–] [10]

E.M.I. / Reprise

Jan 72. (7"m) *(T REX 1) <1078>* **TELEGRAM SAM. / CADILLAC / BABY STRANGE** [1] Apr72 [67]
(re-iss. Mar82; same); hit No.69)

Feb 72. (7") *<1056>* **JEEPSTER. / RIP OFF** [–] [ ]

May 72. (lp/c) *(HIFLY/ZCFLY 8)* **BOLAN BOOGIE** (compilation) [1] [–]
– Get it on (bang a gong) / The king of the mountain cometh / She was born to be my unicorn / Dove / Woodland bop / Ride a white swan / Raw ramp / Jeepster / First heart mighty dawn dart / By the light of the magical Moon / Summertime blues / Hot love. *(re-iss. Mar78 & Oct81; same) (re-iss. Apr89 on 'Castle' lp/c/cd; CLA LP/MC/CD 145) (cd re-iss. Oct98 on 'Polydor'; 541006-2)*

May 72. (7"m) *(MARC 1) <1095>* **METAL GURU. / LADY / THUNDERWING** [1] [ ]

Jul 72. (lp/c) *(BLN/ 5001) <2095>* **THE SLIDER** [4] Aug72 [17]
– Metal guru / Mystic lady / Rock on / The slider / Baby boomerang / Spaceball ricochet / Buick MacKane / Telegram Sam / Rabbit fighter / Baby strange / Ballrooms of Mars / Chariot choogle / Main man. *(re-iss. Nov89 on 'Marc On Wax' lp/c/cd; MARC L/K/D 503) (cd re-iss. Jul94 on 'Edsel'; EDCD 390) (deluxe d-cd-iss. Jun02 on 'Edsel'+=;* **MEDCD 715)** – (alt. takes).

Jul 72. (7") *<1122>* **THE SLIDER. / ROCK ON** [–] [ ]

Sep 72. (7"m) *(MARC 2)* **CHILDREN OF THE REVOLUTION. / JITTERBUG LOVE / SUNKEN RAGS** [2] [ ]

Dec 72. (7") *(MARC 3)* **SOLID GOLD EASY ACTION. / BORN TO BOOGIE** [2] [ ]

Mar 73. (7") *(MARC 4)* **20th CENTURY BOY. / FREE ANGEL** [3] [ ]

Mar 73. (lp/c) *(BLN/ 5002) <2132>* **TANX** [4] [ ]
– Tenement lady / Rapids / Mister mister / Broken hearted blues / Shock rock / Country honey / Electric Slim and the factory man / Mad Donna / Born to boogie / Life is strange / The street and the babe shadow / Highway knees / Left hand Luke and the beggar boys. *(re-iss. Oct87 on 'Marc On Wax' lp/pic-lp/c/cd; RAP/+D/C/CD 504) (re-iss. Nov89 lp/c/cd; MARC L/K/D 504) (cd re-iss. Jul94 on 'Edsel'; EDCD 391) (cdluxe d-cd-iss. Aug02 +=; MEDCD 716)* – (alt. takes).

Jun 73. (7") *(MARC 5)* **THE GROOVER. / MIDNIGHT** [4] [–]

Jun 73. (7") **THE GROOVER. / BORN TO BOOGIE** [–] [ ]

— added **JACK GREEN** – guitar (plus 3 female backing singers incl. **GLORIA JONES**)

Nov 73. (7") *(MARC 6)* **TRUCK ON (TYKE). / SITTING HERE** [12] [–]

— (T.REX = FINN, CURRIE, GREEN, JONES – keyboards, vocals) / **DAVY LUTTON** – drums (ex-HEAVY JELLY), repl. LEGEND (2 more female singers)

Feb 74. (7"; as MARC BOLAN & T.REX) *(MARC 7)* **TEENAGE DREAM. / SATISFACTION PONY** [13] [ ]

Mar 74. (lp/c; as MARC BOLAN & T.REX) *(BNLA 7751)* **ZINC ALLOY AND THE EASY RIDERS OF TOMORROW** [12] [ ]
– Venus loon / Sound pit / Explosive mouth / Galaxy / Orange / Nameless wildness / Teenage dream / Liquid gang / Carsmile Smith & the old one / You've got to jive to stay alive – Spanish midnight / Interstellar soul / Painless persuasion and the meathawk / Immaculate / The avengers (superbad) / The leopards (featuring Gardinia and The Mighty Slug). *(re-iss. Oct87 on 'Marc On Wax' lp/pic-lp/c/cd; RAP/+D/C/CD 505) (re-iss. Nov89 lp/c/cd; MARC L/K/D 505) (cd re-iss. Jul94 on 'Edsel'; EDCD 392) (deluxe d-cd-iss. Jul02 +=; MEDCD 717)* – (alt. takes).

Jul 74. (7") *(MARC 8)* **LIGHT OF LOVE. / EXPLOSIVE MOUTH** [22] [–]

— added **DINO DINES** – keyboards

Nov 74. (7") *(MARC 9)* **ZIP GUN BOOGIE. / SPACE BOSS** [41] [–]

Feb 75. (lp/c) *(BNLA/ 7752)* **BOLAN'S ZIP GUN** [ ] [ ]
– Light of love / Solid baby / Precious star / Zip gun boogie / Token of my love / Think zine / 'Till dawn / Girl in the thunderbolt suit / I really love you baby / Golden belt. *(re-iss. Jul87 on 'Marc On Wax' lp/pic-lp/c/cd; RAP/+D/C/CD 506) (re-iss. Nov89 lp/c/cd; MARC L/K/D 506) (cd re-iss. Jul94 on 'Edsel'; EDCD 393) (deluxe d-cd-iss. Aug02 +=; MEDCD 718)* – (alt. takes).

— members FINN and GREEN departed. The latter to PRETTY THINGS. Now 5-piece comprising **BOLAN, JONES, CURRIE, LUTTON + DINES**

Jul 75. (7") *(MARC 10)* **NEW YORK CITY. / CHROME SITAR** [15] [–]

— next with **BILLY PRESTON** – keyboards

Oct 75. (7"m; as T.REX DISCO PARTY) *(MARC 11)* **DREAMY LADY. / DO YOU WANNA DANCE / DOCK OF THE BAY** [30] [–]

Feb 76. (lp/c) *(BLNA/ 5004)* **FUTURISTIC DRAGON** [50] [ ]
– Futuristic dragon / Jupiter lion / All alone / Chrome sitar / New York City / My little baby / Calling all destroyers / Theme for a dragon / Sensation boulevard / Ride my wheels / Dreamy lady / Dawn storm / Casual agent. *(re-iss. Oct87 on 'Marc On Wax' lp/pic-lp/c/cd; RAP/+D/C/CD 507) (re-iss. Nov89 lp/c/cd; MARC L/K/D 507) (cd re-iss. Jul94 on 'Edsel'; EDCD 394) (deluxe d-cd-iss. Jun02 +=; MEDCD 719)* – (alt. takes).

Feb 76. (7") *(MARC 13)* **LONDON BOYS. / SOLID BABY** [40] [–]

Jun 76. (7") *(MARC 14)* **I LOVE TO BOOGIE. / BABY BOOMERANG** [13] [–]

Sep 76. (7") *(MARC 15)* **LASER LOVE. / LIFE'S AN ELEVATOR** [41] [–]

Jan 77. (7"; by MARC BOLAN & GLORIA JONES) *(EMI 2572)* **TO KNOW HIM IS TO LOVE HIM. / CITY PORT** [ ] [–]

— now comprised BOLAN and DINES who brought in **MILLER ANDERSON** – guitar (ex-SAVOY BROWN) repl. GLORIA JONES who went solo / **HERBIE FLOWERS** – bass repl. CURRIE who went into sessions **TONY BRENNAN** – drums repl. LUTTON who joined WRECKLESS ERIC

Mar 77. (7") *(MARC 16)* **THE SOUL OF MY SUIT. / ALL ALONE** [42] [–]

Mar 77. (lp/c) *(BLNA 5005)* **DANDY IN THE UNDERWORLD** [26] [ ]
– Dandy in the underworld / Crimson moon / Universe / I'm a fool for you / I love to boogie / Visions of Domino / Jason B. Sad / Groove a little / Hang-ups / The soul of my suit / Pain and love / Teen riot structure. *(re-iss. Oct87 on 'Marc On Wax'; lp/pic-lp/c/cd; RAP/+D/C/CD 508) (re-iss. Nov89 lp/c/cd; MARC L/K/D 508) (cd re-iss.*

Jul94 on 'Edsel'; EDCD 395) (deluxe d-cd-iss. Jul02 +=; MEDCD 720) – (alt. takes).

May 77. (7") *(MARC 17)* **DANDY IN THE UNDERWORLD. / GROOVE A LITTLE** [ ] [–]

Aug 77. (7") *(MARC 18)* **CELEBRATE SUMMER. / RIDE MY WHEELS** [ ] [–]

—— On 16th Sep'77 MARC BOLAN died when his car driven by GLORIA hit a tree. ANDERSON joined SOUTHSIDE JOHNNY and FLOWERS formed SKY.

Apr 78. (7") *(MARC 19)* **CRIMSON MOON. / JASON B. SAD** [ ] [–]

– (selective) compilations, etc. –

on 'Fly' UK / 'Reprise' US unless mentioned otherwise.

Aug 71. (lp/c) *(TON/CTON 2)* **THE BEST OF T. REX** [21] [ ]

Mar 72. (d-lp/d-c) *(TOOFA/ZCTOF 3-4) / A&M; <3514>* **PROPHETS, SEERS AND SAGES, THE ANGELS OF THE AGES / MY PEOPLE WERE FAIR . . .** <US-title 'TYRANNOSAURUS REX – A BEGINNING'> [1] [ ]
(re-iss. Oct81; same)

Mar 72. (7"ep) *Magni Fly; (ECHO 102)* **DEBORA / ONE INCH ROCK. / WOODLAND BOP / SEAL OF SEASONS** [7] [ ]

Dec 72. (d-lp/d-c) *Cube; (TOOFA/ZCTOF 9-10)* **A BEARD OF STARS / UNICORN** [44] [ ]
(re-iss. Mar78 + Oct81; same) (re-iss. Sep88 on 'That's Original' d-lp/c/cd;) (re-iss. cd Oct94 on 'Disky';)

Sep 73. (7"; as BIG CARROT) *E.M.I.; (EMI 2047)* **BLACKJACK. / SQUINT EYE MANGLE** [ ] [–]

Nov 73. (lp/c) *E.M.I.; (BLN/ 5003)* **GREAT HITS** [32] [ ]

Jun 74. (lp; by MARC BOLAN) *Track; (2410 201)* **THE BEGINNING OF DOVES** [ ] [–]
(re-iss. Aug89 on 'Media Motion' lp/c/cd; MEDIA/+C/CD 2) (cd-iss. Oct91 on 'Receiver';)

Jun 74. (7"m; by MARC BOLAN) *Track; (2094 013)* **JASPER C. DEBUSSY. / HIPPY GUMBO / THE PERFUMED GARDEN OF GULLIVER SMITH** [ ] [–]

Jun 79. (lp/c) *E.M.I.; (NUT 5)* **SOLID GOLD T.REX** [51] [ ]
(re-iss. May82 on 'Fame' lp/c; FA/TC-FA 3005) (cd-iss. Feb99 on 'Repertoire'; RR 4800)

Mar 81. (12"pic-ep/12"clear-ep) *Rarn; (MBFS 001 C/P)* **THE RETURN OF THE ELECTRIC WARRIOR** [50] [–]
– Sing me a song / Endless sleep (extended) / The lilac hand of Menthol Dan. *(re-iss. 7"pic-d.Jul82;)*

Aug 81. (pic-lp; 2 diff) *Marc; (ABOLAN 1P)* **T.REX IN CONCERT (live)** [35] [–]

Sep 81. (7"/7"pic-d; by MARC BOLAN) *Cherry Red; (CHERRY/+P 29)* **YOU SCARE ME TO DEATH. / THE PERFUMED GARDEN OF GULLIVER SMITH** [51] [–]

Oct 81. (pic-lp/lp; by MARC BOLAN) *Cherry Red; (P+/ERED 20)* **YOU SCARE ME TO DEATH** [88] [–]
(re-iss. Nov94 on 'Emporio' cd/c; EMPR CD/MC 545)

Sep 83. (lp/c; by MARC BOLAN) *Marc On Wax; (MARC L/K 501)* **DANCE IN THE MIDNIGHT** [83] [–]
(re-iss. Apr85; same)

Apr 85. (d-lp/d-c; as MARC BOLAN & T.REX) *K-Tel; (NE/CE 1297)* **THE BEST OF THE 20th CENTURY BOY** [5] [–]
(cd-iss. Oct87; NCD 3325)

May 85. (7"ep) *Marc On Wax; (TANX 1)* **MEGAREX 1 (medley). / CHARIOT CHOOGLE / LIFE'S AN ELEVATOR** [72] [–]
(12"+=) *(12TANX 1)* – Solid baby.

May 87. (7"; as MARC BOLAN & T.REX) *Marc On Wax; (MARC 10)* **GET IT ON. / JEEPSTER** [54] [–]
(12"+=/c-s+=/cd-s+=) *(MARC B/C/CD 10)* – Cadillac.

Aug 87. (12"ep) *Strange Fruit; (SFPS 031)* **THE PEEL SESSIONS (27.10.70)** [ ] [–]
– Jewel / Ride a white swan / Elemental child / Sun eye. *(cd-ep-iss.Dec94; SFPSCD 031)*

Jun 91. (cd/c) *Music Club; (MC CD/TC 030)* **THE VERY BEST OF MARC BOLAN & T.REX** [ ] [–]
(gold-cd-iss. Mar96; MCCDSE 030)

Aug 91. (7"/c-s; as MARC BOLAN & T.REX) *Marc On Wax; (MARC/+C 501)* **20th CENTURY BOY. / MIDNIGHT / THE GROOVER** [13] [–]
(12"+=)(cd-s+=) – Telegram Sam.

Sep 91. (cd/c/lp; MARC BOLAN & T.REX) *Telstar; (TCD/STAC/STAR 2539)* **THE ULTIMATE COLLECTION** [4] [–]
– 20th century boy / Metal guru / I love to boogie / Debora / New York City / Telegram Sam / Hot love / Dreamy lady / One inch rock / The soul of my suit / London boys / Ride a white swan / Get it on / Light of love / Children of the revolution / Jeepster / Laser love / Zip gun boogie / The groover / King of the rumbling spires / Plateau skull / Truck on (Tyke) / Solid gold easy action / Teenage dream. *(cd has 4 extra above)*

Sep 95. (cd/c; as MARC BOLAN & T.REX) *Polygram TV; (525 961-2/-4)* **THE ESSENTIAL COLLECTION** [24] [–]
(re-iss. Oct00 on 'Universal TV'; same) – (hit UK No.34)

Mar 99. (cd) *Music Club; (MCCD 030)* **THE VERY BEST OF T.REX VOL.1** [ ] [–]

Mar 99. (cd) *Music Club; (MCCD 374)* **THE VERY BEST OF T.REX VOL.2** [ ] [–]

Apr 99. (4xcd-box) *Burning Airlines; (XPILOT 017)* **THE WARRIOR BOX SET** [ ] [–]
– (ELECTRIC WARRIOR SESSIONS / ELECTRIC BOOGIE / SPACEBALL / T.REX)

Sep 99. (d-cd) *Cleopatra; (CLP 577)* **T. REX CLASSICS** [ ] [–]

Sep 02. (cd) *Universal TV; (493432-2)* **THE ESSENTIAL COLLECTION (25th ANNIVERSARY EDITION)** [18] [–]
– 20th Century boy / Get it on / Telegram Sam / Ride a white swan / Jeepster / Hot love / Children of the revolution / Metal guru / I love to boogie / Debora (original full length version) / The groover / Truck on (tyke) / Teenage dream / New York City / King of the rumbling spires / By the light of the magical moon / Summertime blues / Cosmic dancer / Light of love / Dreamy lady / London boys / Laser love / One inch rock / Solid gold easy action. *(cd w/ dvd+=)* – (videos).

Graham BOND

Born: 28 Oct'37, Romford, Essex, England. Adopted as a child from a Dr. Barnardo's home, BOND cut his teeth in the late 50's as an alto sax player with The DON RENDELL QUINTET. In 1962, he replaced CYRIL DAVIES in BLUES INCORPORATED, an influential London-based R&B combo headed by ALEXIS KORNER; like many artists who'd pass through the band's ranks, BOND was a pioneer in his own right. Eager to implement his innovative use of the electric organ as a Blues tool, he formed his own outfit in 1963, The GRAHAM BOND ORGANISATION, taking JACK BRUCE and GINGER BAKER with him; future jazz guitar virtuoso JOHN McLAUGHLIN was also a short-lived early member. With the latter being quickly replaced by another time-served BLUES INCORPORATED man, DICK HECKSTALL-SMITH, the ORGANISATION cut a one-off 45 for 'Decca', 'LONG TALL SHORTY', before new manager, Robert Stigwood, helped them sign a deal with 'Columbia'. Early in 1965, the quartet showcased their hard-edged jazz-inspired R&B on their debut album, 'THE SOUND OF '65'. A second set, 'THERE'S A BOND BETWEEN US', appeared later the same year, again serving up a mixed platter of BOND originals and Blues standards with GRAHAM pioneering the soon-to-be ubiquitous mellotron. By '67, BOND's lack of commercial success had been compounded with the loss of both BRUCE and BAKER who'd soon make their mark as two-thirds of power trio supergroup, CREAM. A short stay in the USA – during which he issued the LP, 'LOVE IS THE LAW' – found him working with HARVEY MANDEL. Meanwhile, back in Britain, GB was finally hitting the Top 40, albeit with a set of early recordings 'SOLID BOND' (1970). After a brief call-up for GINGER BAKER's AIRFORCE, the restless wildman formed MAGICK with new like-minded wife DIANE STEWART; having initially dabbled in Eastern mystical influences in 1967, BOND became increasingly entrenched in the occult and even maintained he was the bastard son of the infamous Aleister Crowley. GRAHAM's latest incarnation delivered two 1971 albums, 'HOLY MAGICK' and 'WE PUT OUR MAGICK ON YOU', before his marriage and in turn the band fell apart. The following year, he collaborated with former CREAM lyricist PETE BROWN on a one-off album, 'TWO HEADS ARE BETTER THAN ONE'. BOND's final music venture came in the shape of MAGUS, a project put together with folkie CAROL ANNE PEGG. Again this ended in disarray and amid mounting financial difficulties, drug addiction and mental health problems, BOND was found dead under a London train on the 8th of May, 1974; mystery surrounds this as to whether it was suicide or a "cult" murder. It was a messy end for a man who has sometimes been referred to as The Godfather Of British R&B. • **Songwriters:** Self/group penned, except GOT MY MOJO WORKING (Muddy Waters) / WHAT'D I SAY (Ray Charles) / etc. • **Trivia:** BOND appeared on B-side of WHO single, 'Substitute' under the billing of The WHO ORCHESTRA (the track, 'Waltz For A Pig').

Album rating: THE SOUND OF '65 (*7) / THERE'S A BOND BETWEEN US (*6) / LOVE IS THE LAW (*4) / SOLID BOND compilation (*6) / Magick: HOLY MAGICK (*5) / WE PUT OUR MAGICK ON YOU (*5) / TWO HEADS ARE BETTER THAN ONE with Pete Brown (*5) / LIVE AT KLOOK'S KLEEK live collection (*5)

GRAHAM BOND ORGANISATION

GRAHAM BOND – vocals, organ (ex-BLUES INCORPORATED, ex-DUFFY POWER) / **DICK HECKSTALL-SMITH** – saxophone repl. guitarist JOHN McLAUGHLIN / **JACK BRUCE** – bass, vocals / **PETER 'GINGER' BAKER** – drums

Decca / not iss.

Jun 64. (7") *(F 11909)* **LONG TALL SHORTY. / LONG LEGGED BABY** [ ] [–]

Columbia / Ascot

Jan 65. (7") *(DB 7471)* **WADE IN THE WATER. / TAMMY** [ ] [–]

Mar 65. (lp) *(SX 1711)* **THE SOUND OF '65** [ ] [–]
– Hoochie coochie / Baby make love to me / Neighbour, neighbour / Early in the morning / Spanish blues / Oh baby / Little girl / I want you / Wade in the water / Got my mojo working / Train time / Baby, be good to me / Half a man / Tammy.

Mar 65. (7") *(DB 7528)* **TELL ME (I'M GONNA LOVE AGAIN). / LOVE COMES SHINING THROUGH** [ ] [–]

Jul 65. (7") *(DB 7647)* **LEASE ON LOVE. / MY HEART'S IN LITTLE PIECES** [ ] [–]

Nov 65. (lp) *(SX 1750)* **THERE'S A BOND BETWEEN US** [ ] [–]
– Who's afraid of Virgina Woolf / Hear me calling your name / The night time is the right time / Walkin' in the park / Last night / Baby it can't be true / What'd I say / Dick's instrumental / Don't let go / Keep-a-drivin' / Have you ever loved a woman / Camels and elephants.

— (Oct65) **NEIL HUBBARD** – guitar repl. BRUCE (to JOHN MAYALL and solo, then CREAM)

Feb 66. (7") *(DB 7838)* **ST. JAMES INFIRMARY. / SOUL TANGO** [ ] [–]

Apr 66. (7") *<2211>* **ST. JAMES INFIRMARY. / WADE IN THE WATER** [–] [ ]

— BOND retained HECKSTALL-SMITH and HUBBARD plus **JON HISEMAN** – drums repl. BAKER who (with BRUCE) formed CREAM

Page One / not iss.

Feb 67. (7") *(POF 014)* **YOU'VE GOT TO HAVE LOVE BABE. / I LOVE YOU** [ ] [–]

— Split Sep67, HECKSTALL-SMITH and HISEMAN joined JOHN MAYALL then COLOSSEUM. HUBBARD joined GREASE BAND then JUICY LUCY

GRAHAM BOND

— moved to the States & went solo, with **HARVEY MANDEL** – guitar / **HARVEY BROOKS** – bass / **EDDIE HOH** – drums

not iss. / Pulsar

1968. (lp) *<AR 10604>* **LOVE IS THE LAW** [–] [ ]
– Water, water / Oh shining on / Pictures in the fire / Baroque / Sisters and brothers / Stiffnecked chicken / Freaky beak / Walk onto me / Magic mojo / Brothers and sisters.

— (Dec69) returned to UK. He joined GINGER BAKER in AIRFORCE

Warners / Warners

Jan 70. (d-lp) *(WS 3001) <2555>* **SOLID BOND** (compilation 63-66) [40] [ ]
– Green onions / Springtime in the city / Can't stand it / The grass is greener / Doxy / Only sixteen / Last night / Long legged baby / Walkin' in the park / It's not goodbye / Neighbour neighbour / Ho ho country kicking blues.

Feb 70. (7") *(WB 8004) <7391>* **WALKING IN THE PARK. / SPRINGTIME IN THE CITY** [ ] [ ]

MAGICK

— were formed by **GRAHAM BOND** plus **DIANE STEWART** – vocals / **HENRY WILLIAMS** – guitar / **TERRY POOLE** – guitar / **STEVE GREGORY** – saxophone / **JOHN WEATHERS** – drums / **GASPER WILLIAMS** – percussion

Vertigo / Mercury

Feb 71. (lp) *(6360 021) <61327>* **HOLY MAGICK** [ ] [ ]
– Holy magick suite:- Meditation aumgn / The Qabalistic cross / The word of the Aeon / Invocation to the light / The pentagram ritual / The Qabablistic cross / Hymn of praise / Twelve gates to the city / The holy words Iao Saluco (these are the words) / Aquarius mantra (in Egyptian) / Enochian (Atlantean) call / Abrahadabra the word of the Aeon / Praise "city of light" / The Qabalistic cross aumgn / Return of Arthur / The magician / The judgement / An archangel Mikael. *(cd-iss. Aug91 on 'Repertoire'; REP 4106WP)*

Apr 71. (7") *(6059 042)* **WATER WATER. / TWELVE GATES TO THE CITY** [ ] [–]

Dec 71. (lp) *(6360 042)* **WE PUT OUR MAGICK ON YOU** [ ] [–]
– Forbidden fruit (part 1) / Moving towards the light / Ajama / Druid / I put my magick on you / Time to die / Hail Ra Haraknite / Forbidden fruit (part 2). *(re-iss. '74 on 'Philips'; SRMI 0612) (re-iss. Nov88 on 'Beat Goes On'; BGOLP 73) (cd-iss. Aug91 on 'Repertoire'; REP 4107WP)*

GRAHAM BOND & PETE BROWN

Chapter One / not iss.

Nov 72. (lp) *(CHSR 813)* **TWO HEADS ARE BETTER THAN ONE** [ ] [–]
– Lost tribe / Ig the pig / Oobati / Amazing grass / Scunthorpe crabmeat train sideways boogie shuffle stomp / C.F.D.T. (Colonel Fright's dancing terrapins) / Mass debate / Looking for time. *(cd-iss. Jul92 on 'See For Miles'+=; SEECD 345)* – Milk is turning sour in my shoes / Macumbe / The beginning / Aeroplane drinking man (Gladiator song) / Italian song / Spend my nights in armour / Fury of war / Magpie man / Drum roll / Swing song / Sailor's song / The ending.

Greenwich / not iss.

1972. (7"m) *(GSS 104)* **LOST TRIBE. / MACUMBE / MILK IS TURNING SOUR IN MY SHOES** [ ] [–]

— They also both recorded for soundtrack 'MALTAMOUR'. In 1973, BOND formed MAGUS with folk singer, CAROL ANNE PEGG. They split, and on the 8th of May '74 – after a bout of depression due to heroin addiction – he was found dead under a tube train in Finsbury.

– compilations etc. –

1964. (7"ep) *Decca;* **THE GRAHAM BOND ORGANISATION** [ ] [–]
– Hoochie coochie man / High healed sneakers / Little girl / Long legged baby / Strut around.

1971. (d-lp) *Philips; (6499 200-1)* **BOND IN AMERICA** [ ] [ ]

1972. (lp) *Philips; (6382 010)* **THIS IS GRAHAM BOND** [ ] [–]

Jan 77. (lp; by GRAHAM BOND ORGANISATION) *Charly; (CR 30198)* **THE BEGINNING OF JAZZ ROCK (live 1964)** [ ] [–]

Mar 88. (d-lp) *Edsel; (DED 254)* **THE SOUND OF '65 / THERE'S A BOND BETWEEN US** [ ] [–]
(cd-iss. Oct99 on 'Beat Goes On'; BGOCD 500)

Oct 88. (lp) *Decal; (LIK 47)* **LIVE AT KLOOKS KLEEK (live)** [ ] [–]
– Wade in the water ./ Big boss man / Early in the morning / Person to person blues / Spanish blues / Introduction by Dick Jordan / First time I met the blues / Stormy Monday / Train time / What'd I say. *(cd-iss. Dec97 on 'Charly'; CDGR 195) (lp re-iss. Jan02 on 'Get Back'; GET 609)*

Aug 98. (cd; shared with the ANIMALS) *Spalax; (14553)* **ROCK GENERATION** [ ] [–]

Nov 99. (cd) *Beat Goes On; (BGOCD 483)* **HOLY MAGICK / WE PUT OUR MAGICK ON YOU** [ ] [–]

BONE THUGS-N-HARMONY

Formed: Cleveland, Ohio, USA ... 1993 initially as BONE ENTERPRISE by KRAYZIE BONE (ANTHONY HENDERSON), LAYZIE BONE (STEVEN HOWSE), BIZZY BONE (CHARLES SCRUGGS), WISH BONE (BYRON McCANE) and FLESH-N-BONE (STANLEY HOWSE). It was quite a rare thing for a hip-hop group to emerge from a non-coastal region of America and still receive the success of a group such as BONE THUGS-N-HARMONY, who after being refused a record deal decided to take a risk and visit L.A. to audition for EAZY-E's own record label 'Ruthless'. They got the deal and issued the EP 'CREEPIN ON AH COME UP' (1993), which, to everyone's surprise entered the US Billboard charts at number 12 on the strength of the tracks 'THUGGISH RUGGISH BONES' and the bass-pounding 'FOR THE LOVE OF MONEY'. The group's rapping was fast, their production skills like a cross between East and West coast, ultimately to create what could've been termed as 'Mid-West Side' rap. After the initial sleeper hit of the first EP, the group issued their debut album, the semi-classic 'E 1999 ETERNAL', which featured the massive chart hit 'THA CROSSROADS' (samples courtesy of the ISLEYS), which peaked in the charts at No.1 for a consecutive eight weeks, earning BONE THUGS-N-HARMONY a Grammy award for 'Best Rap Performance'. The pressure was now on for America's new Hip-Hop darlings, especially for FLESH-N-BONE who left the band to release a solo album entitled 'T.H.U.G.S.' (1997). The other original members of the group indulged a vanity project entitled MO THUGS FAMILY, a weak excuse to collaborate with different artists including II TRUE, MT5 and FELECIA. The guise issued three sets, 'SCRIPTURES' (1997), 'CHAPTER II: FAMILY REUNION' (1998) and 'MO THUGS III: THE MOTHERSHIP' (2000) during the three years, but most of them were ignored outside of the BONE THUGS fan base. The group issued their long-awaited sophomore album 'ART OF WAR' in 1997. A double disc album, critics expressed how the group would have benefitted more if they had trimmed the album down. Fans on the other hand were pleased to have two discs of music, even if some tracks were unnecessary. The album spawned the single 'LOOK INTO MY EYES', which became a moderate hit, spending a few weeks in the US Top 10. After the lukewarm reponse towards the previous album, the band took a well-deserved break, each issuing solo albums and a 'Best Of . . .' album before making a return in the year 2000 with 'BTNHRESURRECTION'. With that album hitting US No.2, the band left less time before the release of a follow-up, 'THUG WORLD ORDER' (2002). Departing little from the BTNH recipe of macho raps and deft use of sampling, the record was business as usual although that very perfunctoriness made it difficult to ignore the sense that they'd rather have been working on solo projects.

Album rating: E 1999 ETERNAL (*7) / THE ART OF WAR (*4) / THE COLLECTION: VOLUME ONE compilation (*6) / BTNHRESURRECTION (*5) / THE COLLECTION: VOLUME TWO compilation (*5) / Bizzy Bone: HEAVEN'Z MOVIE (*5) / THE GIFT (*4) / Krayzie Bone: THUG MENTALITY 1999 (*5) / THUG ON DA LINE (*5) / L-Burna aka Layzie Bone: THUG BY NATURE (*5) / Bone Thugs-N-Harmony: THUG WORLD ORDER (*5)

KRAYZIE BONE (b. ANTHONY HENDERSON) – vocals / **LAYZIE BONE** (b. STEVEN HOWSE) – vocals / **BIZZY BONE** (b. CHARLES SCRUGGS) – vocals / **WISH BONE** (b. BYRON McCANE) – vocals / **FLESH-N-BONE** (b. STANLEY HOWSE) – vocals

Ruthless Ruthless

Jul 94. (m-cd/m-c) *<(88561-5526-2/-4)>* **CREEPIN ON AH COME UP** [ ] [12]
– Intro / Mr. Quija / Thuggish-ruggish-bone / No surrender / Down foe my thang / Creepin on ah come up / Foe tha love of $ / Moe cheese (instrumental).

Sep 94. (c-s,12") *<5527>* **THUGGISH-RUGGISH-BONE / ('A'instrumental)** [–] [22]

Feb 95. (c-ep,12"ep; BONE THUGS-N-HARMONY featuring EAZY-E) *<5540>* **FOE THA LOVE OF $ / MOE CHEESE. / THUGGISH RUGGISH BONE / MOE $** [–] [41]

Aug 95. (cd/c/lp) *(481038-2/-4/-1) <5539>* **E 1999 ETERNAL** [ ] Jul95 [1]
– De introduction / East 1999 eternal / Crept and we came down / Down 71 (the getaway) / Mr. Bill Collector / Budsmokers only / Tha crossroads / Me killa / Land of the heartless / No shorts, no losses / 1st of tha month / Budds lovaz / Die die die / Mr. Ouija 2 / Mo murda / Shots to the double glock. *(re-iss. Aug96 on 'Epic' cd/c hit UK No.39; 481038-6/-3)*

Oct 95. (12"/c-s) *(662517-6/-4) <6331>* **1ST OF THA MONTH. / ('A'radio edit with TRE) / DIE DIE DIE** [32] Aug95 [14]
(cd-s+=) *(662517-6-2)* – ('A'mixes).

Nov 95. (12",c-s,cd-s) *<6332>* **EAST 1999. / ('A'remix) / BUDDAH LOVAZ** [–] [62]

Jul 96. (cd-s) *(663550-2) <6335>* **THA CROSSROADS. / ('A'mixes)** [8] Apr96 [1]
(12"/c-s) *(663550-6/-4)* – Budsmokers only.

Oct 96. (c-s) *(663850-4)* **1ST OF THA MONTH / THUGGISH RUGGISH BONE** [15] [–]
(cd-s+=) *(663850-2)* – East 1999.
(cd-s+=) *(663850-5)* – Die, die, die.

Jan 97. (c-s) *(A 3982C)* **DAYZ OF OUR LIVEZ / (mix)** [37] [–]
(12"+=/cd-s+=) *(A 3982 T/CD)* – (mixes).
(above single on 'East West' & from the soundtrack 'Set It Off')

—— now without FLESH-N-BONE who released two albums, 'T.H.U.G.S. – TRUES HUMBLY UNITED GATHERIN' SOULS' (1996) and '5th DOG LET LOOSE' (2000)

(below single from the 'Batman & Robin' film)

Jul 97. (12"pic-d/c-s) *(664786-6/-4) <6343>* **LOOK INTO MY EYES. / ('A'mixes)** [16] Jun97 [4]
(cd-s+=) *(664786-2)* – Tha crossroads (U-neek mix) / 1st of tha month (edit).

Aug 97. (cd/c/lp) *(488080-2/-4/-1) <6340>* **THE ART OF WAR** [42] [1]
– Retaliation / Handle the vibe / Look into my eyes / Body rott / It's all mo'thug / Ready 4 war / Ain't nothin' changed / Clog up yo mind / Thug in me / Hardtimes / Mind of a souljah / If I could teach the world / Family tree / Mo thug / Thug luv / Hatin' nation / 7 sign / Wasteland warriors / Neighbourhood slang / U ain't Bone / Get cha thug on / All original / Blaze it / Let the law end / Whom die they lie / Friends / Evil Paradise / Mo thug family tree.

Oct 97. (c-s,cd-s) *<6344>* **IF I COULD TEACH THE WORLD / ('A'mixes)** [–] [27]

—— In Nov'98, BONE THUGS-N-HARMONY were on the US hit single, 'Ghetto Cowboy', by MO THUGS FAMILY (taken from August '98 album, 'SCRIPTURES VOL.2'; *489852-2)* see below

Mar 00. (cd/lp) *(496272-2/-1) <63581>* **BTNHRESURRECTION** [ ] [2]
– Show 'em / The righteous ones (featuring David's daughter) / 2 glocks / Battlezone / Ecstasy / Murder one / Souljahs marching / Servin' tha fiends / Resurrection (paper, paper) / Can't give it up / Weed song / Change the world / Don't worry / Mind on our money / No way out. *<US bonus+=>* – One night stand.

Epic Epic

Nov 02. (cd) *(508346-2) <86594>* **THUG WORLD ORDER** [ ] Oct03 [12]
– T.W.O. intro / Bone, bone, bone / Guess who's back (with LaREECE) / Home / What about us / Get up & get it (with 3LW & FELECIA) / Bad weed blues / All the way / (non-fiction words by Eazy-E) / Pump, pump / Set it straight / Money, money / Not my baby / Cleveland is the city / If I fall / A thug soldier conversation.

May 03. (cd-s; by BONE THUGS-N-HARMONY & PHIL COLLINS) *(673830-2)* **HOME / NOT DAT NIGGA / HOME (original extended) / HOME (video)** [19] [ ]
(cd-s) *(673830-5)* – ('A'side) / Tha crossroads (DJ Unique Mo Thug remix) / 1st of tha month (radio) / Tha crossroads (DJ Unique Mo Thug remix video).

– compilations, others, etc. –

Jul 95. (cd; as BONE ENTERPRISE) *Stoney Burke; <70020>* **FACES OF DEATH** [–] [ ]

Nov 98. (cd/c/lp) *(492857-2/-4/-1)* <69715> **THE COLLECTION VOLUME ONE** [ ] [32]
– Foe the love of $ / 1st of tha month / Shoot 'em up / Days of our livez / Breakdown / Notorious thugs (with NOTORIOUS B.I.G.) / BNK (with EAZY-E) / War (battlecry remix) (with HENRY ROLLINS) / Crossroads / Body rott / Thuggish ruggish bone / Fuck tha police / P.O.D. / If I could teach the world.

Nov 00. (cd) *(501143-2)* <85172> **THE COLLECTION VOLUME TWO** [ ] [41]
– C.L. and I.L. / Don't hate on me / Thug luv / Hook it up / 2 glocks (U-Neek's remix) / Look into my eyes (Atlantis remix) / All good / Weedman / Frontline warrior / Change the world (U-Neek's remix) / Can't give it up (Rock remix) / Ghetto cowboy. *(bonus+=)* – Sleepwalkers.

BIZZY BONE

not iss. Mo Thugs

Oct 98. (cd) <*1670*> **HEAVEN'Z MOVIE** [–] [3]
– Roll call / Thugz cry / Marchin' on Washington / Yes yes y'all / Menensky mobbin / Waitin' for warfare / Mr. Majesty II / Brain on drugs / On the freeway / Demons surround me / On fire / Nobody can stop me / Social studies.

not iss. A.M.C.

Mar 01. (cd) <*71150*> **THE GIFT** [–] [44]
– Schizophrenic / Don't be dumb / Whole wide world / Never grow / Muderah / Before I go / Be careful / Fried day / Voices in the head / Still thuggish ruggish / Don't doubt me / Time passing us by / Father / Jesus.

KRAYZIE BONE

Epic Mo Thugs

Apr 99. (d-cd) *(493113-2)* <*1671*> **THUG MENTALITY 1999** [ ] [4]
– (intro) / Heated heavy / Paper / (The messenger) / Payback iz a bitch (with BAM) / (Relay) Thugline / Dummy man (skit) / Dummy man / Thugz all ova da world (with TREACH) / Street people (with NIKO & DA BULLSHIT) / Pimpz thugz hustlaz & gangstaz / Da bullshit / Drama / World war / The war iz on (with SNOOP DOGG, KURUPT & LAYZIE BONE) / When I die (with FAT JOE, BIG PUNISHER & CUBAN LINK) / Thug alwayz (with BONE THUGS-N-HARMONY) / Thug mentality // Murda won't stop / Where my thugz at / Smokin' Budda / Knieght Rieduz (here we come) (with KNIEGHT RIEDUZ) / Try me / Theze dayz (with K-MONT, ASU & BAM) / Silent warrior / Shoot the club up / Silence (with GRAVEYARD SHIFT) / Look at you now / Won't ez up tonight / Sad song / I still believe (with MARIAH CAREY) / We starvin' / Smoke & burn (with UP IN CLOUDS) / Power (with THUG QUEEN) / That's the way / Armageddon (with SOULJAH BOY, MO HART, THUG QUEEN & FELICIA) / Murda Mo / Revolution (with The MARLEY BROTHERS).

Loud-Epic Ruthless

Sep 01. (cd) *(500587-2)* <85784> **THUG ON DA LINE** [ ] [27]
– Y'all don't know me / Ride the thug line / Can't hustle 4 ever / Talk to myself / A thugga' level / Da thugs / If they only knew / I don't give a fuck / Time after time / Ride if you like / If you a thug / Hard time hustlin' / Gemini / I don't know what / Rollin' up some mo' / Everybody wanna be thugs / Bloody murder (skit) / Kneight Riduz wuz here by Kneight Riduz / Ready for combat (skit) / Thug on da line.

L-BURNA A.K.A. LAYZIE BONE

Epic Ruthless

Mar 01. (cd) *(501197-2)* <85173> **THUG BY NATURE** [ ] [43]
– (Carole of the bones) / Battlefield / Connectin' the plots (with WC) / Fear no man / Time will tell (with DEKUMPOZED) / How long will it last / Deadly musical / There they go (with AARON HALL) / Still the greatest (with FLESH-N-BONE) / Make my day (with BABY S) / Lock-n-load / Up against the wall / Thug by nature / Smoke on / Listen / As the rain.

MO THUGS FAMILY

BONE THUGS-N-HARMONY + TRE, GRAVEYARD SHIFT, SOULJAH BOY, KEN DAWG + II TRU

Relativity Mo Thugs

Nov 96. (cd) <*1561*> **FAMILY SCRIPTURES** [–] [2]

Aug 98. (cd) *(489852-2)* <*1632*> **FAMILY SCRIPTURES CHAPTER II: FAMILY REUNION** [ ] Jun98 [25]

Jul 00. (cd) <*8111*> **LAYZIE BONE PRESENTS MO THUGS III: THE MOTHERSHIP** [–] [45]

— (also two US hits, 'GHETTO COWBOY' + 'TAKE YOUR TIME')

BON JOVI

Formed: Sayreville, New Jersey, USA . . . Spring '83, by JON BON JOVI and DAVID BRYAN, who duly recruited RICHIE SAMBORA, ALEC SUCH and TICO TORRES. Gaining a toehold on the music business ladder by helping out at his cousin's recording studio, JON found time to cut a rough demo of 'RUNAWAY', which subsequently gained radio play after being featured on a local various artists compilation. A line-up that would remain stable throughout BON JOVI's career was soon established and by the summer of 1983, the band had signed to a worldwide deal with 'Polygram'. The first two albums, 'BON JOVI' (1984) and '7800 DEGREES FAHRENHEIT' (1985) were generally derided by critics for their formulaic, glossy pop-metal content, yet the latter sold respectably, 'Polygram's marketing muscle and JON's pretty boy looks certainly not doing the band any harm. At this point, BON JOVI were just another name in an endless sea of wet-permed 'hair' bands on the hard-rock circuit and no one was quite expecting the splash that 'SLIPPERY WHEN WET' would make upon its release in 1986. Preceded by the squalling riff and anthemic chorus of 'YOU GIVE LOVE A BAD NAME', the album was heavy metal (in the broadest possible sense) for people who didn't like heavy metal (housewives, junior schoolgirls, construction workers, etc.). The next single taken from it was 'LIVIN' ON A PRAYER', a hard bitten tale of love on the breadline (rather ironic considering the moolah rolling into BON JOVI's coffers) that featured what must rank as one of the most bombastic choruses in the history of rock. Elsewhere on the record, the production loomed equally large and the songs were relentlessly hook-laden, with just enough edge to convince "real" rock fans that the band hadn't sold out. 'WANTED DEAD OR ALIVE' marked the beginning of JON's cowboy fantasies while 'I'D DIE FOR YOU' and 'NEVER SAY GOODBYE' were the obligatory 'sensitive' numbers. The album's success was partly down to the band hiring soft rock songsmith extrordinaire, DESMOND CHILD, whose unerringly catchy way with a tune saw the album going on to sell millions. BON JOVI were at the top of their career already, headlining the Monsters Of Rock shows in Britain and Europe. No doubt feeling more confident about his songwriting abilities, JON BON JOVI followed a more SPRINGSTEEN-esque direction on 'NEW JERSEY' (1988); more rock, less metal, while still retaining the spotless production and impeccable hooks. 'LIVING IN SIN', 'BLOOD ON BLOOD' (title taken from SPRINGSTEEN's 'HIGHWAY PATROLMAN', perchance?) and 'WILD IS THE WIND' were all reassuringly strident, the album again selling in mindboggling quantities. In many ways, JON BON JOVI is BON JOVI, so when JON-boy released his 'BLAZE OF GLORY' solo effort (a result of his acting role in 'YOUNG GUNS II'), it was a case of more of the same. When the band re-emerged in 1992 with 'KEEP THE FAITH', there was no question of the album failing to scale the heights of its predecessors. The songs were intact although the likes of 'I'LL SLEEP WHEN I'M DEAD' were verging on self-parody. Needless to say, a compilation, 'CROSSROADS', sold phenomenally with the subsequent studio album, 'THESE DAYS' also hitting No.1 in Britain. While the band continue to win the hearts of coffee table browsers the world over, most metal fans probably lost interest years ago. Something of a celeb these days with his short(er) hair, pseudo-trendy image and acting career, JON recently completed his own short film and accompanying soundtrack (he'd previously made his acting debut proper, in the 1996 film, 'Moonlight And Valentino'). In fact the man could do no wrong, going on to have further major chart success with his 'DESTINATION ANYWHERE' (1997) solo set and its UK Top 5 single, 'MIDNIGHT IN CHELSEA'. He even turned up on Chris Evans' TFI Friday with a rough'n'ready cover of Simon & Garfunkel's 'MRS. ROBINSON'. BON JOVI the band, meanwhile, returned in spring '99 with a one-off single, 'REAL LIFE', followed a year later by the 'CRUSH' album. The only surprises on offer – apart from the fact that JON BON seems immune to the ageing process – were that if anything, the band's sound was even more mainstream than before while previously undetectable influences of British 60's/70's pop/glam were apparent. As if to prove they could still rock it like a proverbial mother, the veterans released the 'ONE WILD NIGHT' live set in 2001. Unfortunately, they rocked out just a little too much on the self-conscious 'BOUNCE' (2002), its title something of a misnomer for so turgid an album. Unadvised forays into social commentary and an inexplicable absence of their trademark melodic gusto left something of an anaemic aftertaste. Almost as uninspired, or perhaps even more so, was 2003's 'THIS LEFT FEELS RIGHT', a rather pointless set of reworkings running the breadth of their career but failing to point the way to the future. Tastefully executed and designed to fit within the boundaries of their ageing audience's comfort zone, the songs nevertheless sounded glaringly out of context. • **Covered:** IT'S ONLY ROCK'N'ROLL (Rolling Stones) / WITH A LITTLE HELP FROM MY FRIENDS + HELTER SKELTER (Beatles) / I DON'T LIKE MONDAYS (Boomtown Rats) / ROCKIN' IN THE FREE WORLD (Neil Young) / HOUSE OF THE RISING SUN (trad). • **Miscellaneous:** April 1988 saw their manager DOC McGEE convicted for drug offences. He was sentenced to five years suspended, although he ended up doing community work. JON married his childhood sweetheart Dorothea Hurley on the 29th April '89. SAMBORA is married to actress Heather Locklear, while TORRES tied the knot with supermodel Eva Herzigova on the 7th of September '96.

Album rating: BON JOVI (*6) / 7800° FAHRENHEIT (*5) / SLIPPERY WHEN WET (*9) / NEW JERSEY (*7) / BLAZE OF GLORY solo (*5) / STRANGER IN THIS TOWN; Sambora solo (*6) / KEEP THE FAITH (*8) / CROSS ROAD – THE BEST OF BON JOVI compilation (*8) / (THESE DAYS) (*6) / DESTINATION ANYWHERE solo (*6) / CRUSH (*5) / ONE WILD NIGHT (*5) / BOUNCE (*4) / THIS LEFT FEELS RIGHT (*4)

JON BON JOVI (b. JOHN BONGIOVI, 2 Mar'62) – vocals, guitar / **RICHIE SAMBORA** (b.11 Jul'59, Woodbridge, N.J.) – lead guitar / **DAVID BRYAN** (b. DAVID BRYAN RASHBAUM, 7 Feb'62, New York City) – keyboards / **ALEC JOHN SUCH** (b.14 Nov'56, Yonkers, N.Y.) – bass (ex-PHANTON'S OPERA) / **TICO 'Tar Monster' TORRES** (b. HECTOR TORRES, 7 Oct'53, New York City) – drums (ex-FRANKIE & THE KNOCKOUTS)

Vertigo Mercury

Feb 84. (7") *<818309>* **RUNAWAY. / LOVE LIES** [–] [39]

Apr 84. (lp/c) *(VERL/+C 14) <814982>* **BON JOVI** [71] Feb84 [43]
– Runaway / Roulette / She don't know me / Shot through the heart / Love lies / Breakout / Burning for love / Come back / Get ready. *(cd-iss. Jul86; 814 982-2) (cd-enhanced.Oct98 & Sep00 on 'Jambco'; 538023-2)*

May 84. (7"/12") *(VER/+X 11)* **SHE DON'T KNOW ME. / BREAKOUT** [ ] [–]

May 84. (7") *<818958>* **SHE DON'T KNOW ME. / BURNING FOR LOVE** [–] [48]

Oct 84. (7") *(VER 14)* **RUNAWAY. / BREAKOUT (live)** [ ] [–]
(12"+=) *(VERX 14)* – Runaway (live).

Apr 85. (7") *<880736>* **ONLY LONELY. / ALWAYS RUN TO YOU** [–] [54]

May 85. (lp/c) *(VERL/+H 24) <824509>* **7800° FAHRENHEIT** [28] [37]
– In and out of love / The price of love / Only lonely / King of the mountain / Silent night / Tokyo road / The hardest part is the night / Always run to you / To the fire / Secret dreams. *(cd-iss. Jul86; 824 509-2) (cd-enhanced.Oct98 & Sep00 on 'Jambco'; 538026-2)*

May 85. (7"/7"pic-d) *(VER/+P 19)* **IN AND OUT OF LOVE. / ROULETTE (live)** [ ] [–]
(12"+=) *(VERX 19)* – Shot through the heart (live).

Jul 85. (7") *<880951>* **IN AND OUT OF LOVE. / BREAKOUT (Japanese live version)** [–] [69]

Jul 85. (7") *(VER 22)* **THE HARDEST PART IS THE NIGHT. / ALWAYS RUN TO YOU** [68] [–]
(12"+=) *(VERX 22)* – Tokyo Road (live).
(d7"++=) *(VERDP 22)* – Shot through the heart (live).
(12"red) *(VERXR 22)* – ('A'side) / Tokyo Road (live) / In and out of love (live).

Aug 86. (7"/10"sha-pic-d) *(VER/+P 26)* **YOU GIVE LOVE A BAD NAME. / LET IT ROCK** [14] [–]
(12"+=) *(VERX 26)* – Borderline.
(12"blue+=) *(VERXR 26)* – The hardest part is the night (live) / Burning for love (live).

Aug 86. (7") *<884953>* **YOU GIVE LOVE A BAD NAME. / RAISE YOUR HANDS** [–] [1]

Sep 86. (lp/c)(cd) *(VERH/+C 38)(<830 264-2>)* **SLIPPERY WHEN WET** [6] [1]
– Let it rock / You give love a bad name / Livin' on a prayer / Social disease / Wanted dead or alive / Raise your hands / Without love / I'd die for you / Never say goodbye / Wild in the streets. *(pic-lp Aug88; VERHP 38) (re-iss. Dec90; same); hit 46) (re-charted.Jun91 No.42, Sep92 re-issue) (cd-enhanced.Oct98 & Sep00 on 'Jambco'; 538025-2) (lp re-iss. Jun99 & Mar00 on 'Simply Vinyl'; SVLP 93)*

Oct 86. (7"/7"pic-d/7"w-patch) *(VER/+P/PA 28) <888184>* **LIVIN' ON A PRAYER. / WILD IN THE STREETS** [4] Dec86 [1]
(12"+=/12"green+=) *(VERX/+P 28)* – Edge of a broken heart.
(d12"+=) *(VERXG 28)* – Only lonely (live) / Runaway (live).

Mar 87. (7"/7"s) *(JOV/+S 1)* **WANTED DEAD OR ALIVE. / SHOT THROUGH THE HEART** [13] [–]
(12"+=) *(JOV 1-12)* – Social disease.
(12"silver++=) – *(JOVR 1-12)* – Get ready (live).

Mar 87. (7") *<888467>* **WANTED DEAD OR ALIVE. / I#D DIE FOR YOU** [–] [7]

Aug 87. (7") *(JOV 2)* **NEVER SAY GOODBYE. / RAISE YOUR HANDS** [21] [–]
(c-s+=) *(JOVC 2)* – ('A'acoustic).
(12"+=/12"yellow+=) *(JOV/+R 2-12)* – Wanted dead or alive (acoustic).

Sep 88. (7") *(JOV 3)* **BAD MEDICINE. / 99 IN THE SHADE** [17] [1]
(12"+=/cd-s+=) *(JOV 3-12/CD3)* – Lay your hands on me.
(12") *(JOVR 3-12)* – ('A'side) / You give love a bad name / Livin' on a prayer (live).

Sep 88. (lp/c)(cd) *(VERH/+C 62)(<836 345-2>)* **NEW JERSEY** [1] [1]
– Lay your hands on me / Bad medicine / Born to be my baby / Living in sin / Blood on blood / Stick to your guns / Homebound train / I'll be there for you / 99 in the shade / Love for sale / Wild is the wind / Ride cowboy ride. *(re-iss. Mar93 cd/c; same) (cd-enhanced.Oct98 & SEp00 on 'Jambco'; 538024-2)*

Nov 88. (7"/7"s) *(JOV/+S 4) <872156>* **BORN TO MY BABY. / LOVE FOR SALE** [22] [3]
(12"+=/12"g-f+=/12"pic-d+=) *(JOV/+R/P 4-12)* – Wanted dead or alive.
(cd-s+=) *(JOVCD 4)* – Runaway / Livin' on a prayer.

Apr 89. (7"/7"w-poster) *(JOV/+PB 5) <872564>* **I'LL BE THERE FOR YOU. / HOMEBOUND TRAIN** [18] Feb89 [1]
(12"+=) *(JOV 5-12)* – Wild in the streets (live).
(cd-s+=) *(JOVCD 5)* – Borderline / Edge of a broken heart.

May 89. (7") *<874452>* **LAY YOUR HANDS ON ME. / RUNAWAY (live)** [–] [7]

Aug 89. (7"/c-s)(7"red/7"white/7"blue) *(JOV/+MC 6)(JOVS 6 61/62/63)* **LAY YOUR HANDS ON ME. / BAD MEDICINE** [18] [–]
(10"pic-d+=) *(JOV 6-10)* – Blood on blood.
(12") *(JOVG 6-12)* – ('A'side) / Blood on blood (live) / Born to be my baby (acoustic).
(cd-s) *(JOVCD 6)* – ('A'side) / You give love a bad name / Let it rock.

Nov 89. (7"/c-s) *(JOV/+MC 7) <876070>* **LIVING IN SIN. / LOVE IS WAR** [35] Oct89 [9]
(12"+=/box-cd-s+=) *(JOV 7-12/CD7)* – Ride cowboy ride / Stick to your guns.
(12"white+=) *(JOVR 7-12)* **The boys are back in town.**

JON BON JOVI

Jul 90. (7") *(JBJ 1) <875896>* **BLAZE OF GLORY. / YOU REALLY GOT ME NOW (with LITTLE RICHARD)** 13 1
(12"+=/cd-s+=) *(JBJ T/CD 1)* – Blood money.

Aug 90. (cd/c/lp) *<(846473-2/-4/-1)>* **BLAZE OF GLORY – YOUNG GUNS II** 2 3
– Billy get your guns / Miracle / Blaze of glory / Blood money / Santa Fe / Justice in the barrel / Never say die / You really got me now / Bang a drum / Dyin' ain't much of a livin' / Guano City. *(re-iss. Apr95 cd/c;)*

Oct 90. (c-s) *<878392>* **MIRACLE / BLOOD MONEY** – 12

Nov 90. (7"/c-s) *(JBJ/+C 2)* **MIRACLE. / BANG A DRUM** 29 –
(12"+=/cd-s+=) *(JBJ T/CD 2)* – Dyin' ain't much of a livin' / (interview).

BON JOVI

Jambco Jambco

Oct 92. (7"/c-s) *(JOV/+MC 8) <864432>* **KEEP THE FAITH. / I WISH EVERYDAY COULD BE CHRISTMAS** 5 29
(cd-s+=) *(JOVCB 8)* – Living in sin.
(cd-s+=) *(JOVCA 8)* – Little bit of soul.

Nov 92. (cd/c/lp) *(514197-2/-4/-1) <514045>* **KEEP THE FAITH** 1 5
– I believe / Keep the faith / I'll sleep when I'm dead / In these arms / Bed of roses / If I was your mother / Dry country / Woman in love / Fear / I want you / Blame it on the love of rock'n'roll / Little bit of soul. *(d-cd-iss. Aug93; 518 019-2)* – (live versions). *(cd-enhanced.Oct98 & Sep00; 538034-2)*

Jan 93. (c-s) *<864852>* **BED OF ROSES / LAY YOUR HANDS ON ME (live)** – 10

Jan 93. (7"/c-s) *(JOV/+MC 9)* **BED OF ROSES. / STARTING ALL OVER AGAIN** 13 –
(12"+=) *(JOVT 9)* – Lay your hands on me (live).
(cd-s) *(JOVCD 9)* – ('A'side) / Lay your hands on me (live) / I'll be there for you (live) / Tokyo road (live).

May 93. (cd-s) *<862088>* **IN THESE ARMS / SAVE A PRAYER / IN THESE ARMS (live)** – 27

May 93. (7") *(JOV 10)* **IN THESE ARMS. / BED OF ROSES (acoustic)** 9 –
(cd-s) *(JOVCD 10)* – ('A'side) / Keep the faith (live) / In these arms (live).
(c-s) *(JOVMC 10)* – ('A'side) / Blaze of glory (acoustic).

Jul 93. (7"/c-s) *(JOV/+MC 11) <862428>* **I'LL SLEEP WHEN I'M DEAD. / NEVER SAY GOODBYE (live acoustic)** 17 97
(cd-s) *(JOVCD 11)* – ('A'side) / Blaze of glory / Wild in the streets (both live).
(cd-ep) **HITS LIVE EP** *(JOVD 11)* – ('A'side) / Blaze of glory / You give love a bad name / Bad medicine.

Sep 93. (7"/c-s) *(JOV/+MC 12)* **I BELIEVE (Clearmountain mix). / ('A'live)** 11 –
(cd-s) *(JOVCD 12)* – ('A'side) / Runaway (live) / Livin' on the prayer (live) / Wanted dead or alive ('HITS LIVE PART 2 EP').
(cd-s) *(JOVCB 12)* – ('A'side) / You give love a bad name (live) / Born to be my baby (live) / I'll sleep when I'm dead (live).

Mar 94. (7"/c-s) *(JOV/+MC 13)* **DRY COUNTY. / STRANGER IN THIS TOWN (live)** 9 –
(gold-cd-s+=) *(JOVBX 13)* – Blood money (live).
(cd-s) *(JOVCD 13)* – ('A'side) / It's only rock'n'roll (live) / Waltzing Matilda (live).

Sep 94. (c-s) *(JOVMC 14)* **ALWAYS. / THE BOYS ARE BACK IN TOWN** 2 –
(12"colrd) *(JOVT 14)* – ('A'side) / Prayer '94.
(cd-s) *(JOVCD)* – ('A'side) / ('A'mix) / Edge of a broken heart.

Sep 94. (cd-s) *<856227>* **ALWAYS / NEVER SAY GOODBYE / EDGE OF A BROKEN HEART** – 4

Oct 94. (cd/c/lp) *(522 936-2/-4/-1) <526013>* **CROSS ROAD – THE BEST OF BON JOVI** (compilation) 1 8
– Livin' on a prayer / Keep the faith / Someday I'll be Saturday night / Always / Wanted dead or alive / Lay your hands on me / You give love a bad name / Bed of roses / Blaze of glory / In these arms / Bad medicine / I'll be there for you / In and out of love / Runaway / Never say goodbye. *(cd-enhanced.Oct98; same)*

Dec 94. (7"pic-d/c-s) *(JOV P/MC 16)* **PLEASE COME HOME FOR CHRISTMAS / BACK DOOR SANTA** 7 –
(cd-s+=) *(JOVCD 16)* – I wish every day could be like Christmas.

Feb 95. (7"pic-d/c-s) *(JOV P/MC 15)* **SOMEDAY I'LL BE SATURDAY NIGHT. / GOOD GUYS DON'T ALWAYS WEAR WHITE (live)** 7 –
(cd-s+=) *(JOVCD 15)* – With a little help from my friends (live).
(cd-s+=) *(JOVDD 15)* – Always (live).

May 95. (c-s) *(JOVMC 17)* **THIS AIN'T A LOVE SONG. / LONELY AT THE TOP** 6 –
(cd-s+=) *(JOVCX 17)* – The end.
(cd-s) *(JOVCD 17)* – ('A'side) / When she comes / Wedding day / Prostitute.

May 95. (c-s) *<856227>* **THIS AIN'T A LOVE SONG / ALWAYS (live) / PROSTITUTE** – 14

Jun 95. (cd/c/d-lp) *(528 248-2/-4/-1) <528181>* **(THESE DAYS)** 1 9
– Hey God / Something for the pain / This ain't a love song / These days / Lie to me / Damned / My guitar lies bleeding in my arms / (It's hard) Letting you go / Hearts breaking even / Something to believe in / If that's what it takes / Diamond ring / All I want is everything / Bitter wine. *(re-iss. w/ free cd+=)* – (8 tracks). *(iss.w/ tour pack Jun96; 532 644-2) (cd-enhanced.Oct98; 538036-2)*

Sep 95. (c-s) *(JOVMC 18)* **SOMETHING FOR THE PAIN / THIS AIN'T A LOVE SONG** 8 –
(cd-s+=) *(JOVCX 18)* – I don't like Mondays.
(cd-s) *(JOVCD 18)* – ('A'side) / Living on a prayer / You give love a bad name / Wild in the streets.

Nov 95. (c-s) *(JOVMC 19) <852296>* **LIE TO ME / SOMETHING FOR THE PAIN (live)** 10 88 76
(cd-s+=) *(JOVCX 19)* – Always (live) / Keep the faith (live).
(cd-s) *(JOVCD 19)* – ('A'side) / Something for the pain / Hey God (live) / I'll sleep when I'm dead (live).

Feb 96. (c-s) *(JOVMC 20)* **THESE DAYS / 634-5789** 7 –
(cd-s+=) *(JOVCX 20)* – Rockin' in the free world (live) / (It's hard) Letting you go (live).
(cd-s) *(JOVCD 20)* – ('A'side) / Someday I'll be Saturday night / These days (live) / Helter skelter (live).

Jun 96. (c-s) *(JOVMC 21)* **HEY GOD / LIE TO ME (remix)** 13 –
(cd-s+=) *(JOVCX 21)* – House of the rising sun / Livin' on a prayer.
(cd-s) *(JOVCD 21)* – ('A'side) / The end / When she comes / ('A'live).

JON BON JOVI

— with **DAVID BRYAN** – keyboards / **KENNY ARONOFF** – drums / **ERIC BAZILIAN + DAVE STEWART**

Mercury Mercury

Jun 97. (c-s) *(MERMC 488)* **MIDNIGHT IN CHELSEA / MIDNIGHT IN CHELSEA (album version)** 4 –
(cd-s+=) *(MERCD 488)* – Sad song tonight / August 7th (acoustic).
(cd-s+=) *(MERCX 488)* – Drive / Every word was a piece of my heart.

Jun 97. (cd/c) *(536 011-2/-4) <534903>* **DESTINATION ANYWHERE** 2 31
– Queen of New Orleans / Janie, don't take your love to town / Midnight in Chelsea / Ugly / Staring at your window with a suitcase in my hand / Every word was a piece of my heart / It's just me / Destination anywhere / Learning how to fall / Naked / Little city / August 4, 4:15 / Cold hard heart. *(cd re-iss. Dec97 with bonus cd of live tracks; 536 758-2)* – Queen of New Orleans / Midnight in Chelsea / Destination anywhere / Ugly / It's just me / August 7, 4:15 / Jailbreak / Not fade away / Janie, don't take your love to town.

Aug 97. (c-s) *(MERMC 493)* **QUEEN OF NEW ORLEANS / MIDNIGHT IN CHELSEA (live)** 10 –
(cd-s+=) *(MERCD 493)* – ('A'album version) / Destination anywhere (live).
(cd-s) *(MERCX 493)* – ('A'side) / ('A'album version) / Every piece of my heart (acoustic) / Jailbreak (live).

Nov 97. (c-s) *(574986-4)* **JANIE, DON'T TAKE YOUR LOVE TO TOWN / TALK TO JESUS (demo)** 13 –
(cd-s+=) *(574987-2)* – Billy get your guns (live).
(cd-s) *(574989-2)* – ('A'album version) / Destination anywhere (MTV acoustic) / It's just me (MTV acoustic) / ('A'-MTV acoustic).

– (JOHN BONGIOVI) compilations, etc. –

Jul 97. (cd/c) *Masquerade; (MASQ CD/MC 1011)* **THE POWER STATION YEARS** (rec.1980-1983; remixed 1997)
(re-iss. Feb99; same)

Aug 97. (cd-ep) *Masquerade; (MASSCD 1001)* **MORE THAN WE BARGAINED FOR**

Nov 99. (cd) *Laserlight; (21490)* **JOHN BONGIOVI** –

BON JOVI

— same line-up

		Warners	Reprise
Mar 99.	(c-s) *(W 479C)* **REAL LIFE / KEEP THE FAITH (live)**	21	–
	(cd-s+=) *(W 479CD)* – Real life (instrumental).		
		Jambco	Jambco
May 00.	(c-s) *(562753-4)* **IT'S MY LIFE / HUSH**	3	33
	(cd-s+=) *(562752-2)* – You can't lose at love.		
	(cd-s) *(562768-2)* – ('A'side) / Temptation / I don't want to live forever / ('A'-CD-Rom).		
May 00.	(cd/c) *(54256-22/-14) <542474>* **CRUSH**	1	9
	– It's my life / Say it isn't so / Thank you for loving me / Two storey town / Next 100 years / Just older / Mystery train / Save the world / Captain Crash and the beauty queen from Mars / She's a mystery / I got the girl / One wild night.		
Aug 00.	(c-s) *(568898-4)* **SAY IT ISN'T SO / AIN'T NO CURE FOR LOVE (demo)**	10	–
	(cd-s+=) *(568897-2)* – Stay (demo).		
	(cd-s) *(568898-2)* – ('A'side) / Ordinary people (demo) / Welcome to the good times (demo).		
Nov 00.	(c-s) *(572730-4) <radio play>* **THANK YOU FOR LOVING ME / CAPTAIN CRASH AND THE BEAUTY QUEEN FROM MARS (live)**	12	57
	(cd-s+=) *(572730-2)* – Runaway (acoustic live).		
	(cd-s) *(572731-2)* – ('A'side) / Just older (live) / Born to be my baby (live).		
May 01.	(c-s) *(572949-4)* **ONE WILD NIGHT (2001 version) / LAY YOUR HANDS ON ME (live)**	10	–
	(cd-s+=) *(572949-2)* – I believe (live).		
	(cd-s) *(572950-2)* – ('A'side) / Hey God (live) / Tokyo road (live).		
May 01.	(cd) *<(548865-2)>* **ONE WILD NIGHT (live 1985-2001)**	2	20
	– It's my life / Livin' on a prayer / You give love a bad name / Keep the faith / Saturday night / Rockin' in the free world / Something to believe in / Wanted dead or alive / Runaway / In and out of love / I don't like Mondays / Just older / Something for the pain / Bad medicine / One wild night.		
		Mercury	Island
Sep 02.	(cd-s) *(063937-2)* **EVERYDAY / LUCKY (demo) / NO REGRETS (demo) / EVERYDAY (video)**	5	–
	(cd-s) *(063936-2)* – ('A'side) / Standing (demo) / Another reason to believe (demo) / (the making of Everyday – CD-ROM).		
Oct 02.	(cd/c) *(63395-2/-4) <063055>* **BOUNCE**	2	2
	– Undivided / Everyday / The distance / Joey / Misunderstood / All about lovin' you / Hook me up / Right side of wrong / Love me back to life / You had me from hello / Bounce / Open all night.		
Dec 02.	(c-s) *(63808-4)* **MISUNDERSTOOD / EVERYDAY (acoustic)**	21	–
	(cd-s+=) *(63815-2)* – Undivided (demo) / ('A'video).		
	(cd-s) *(63816-2)* – ('A'side) / Celluloid heroes (live) / Joey (demo).		
May 03.	(cd-s) *(980024-2)* **ALL ABOUT LOVIN' YOU / ALL ABOUT LOVIN' YOU (acoustic) / POSTCARD FROM THE WASTELAND (demo) / ALL ABOUT LOVIN' YOU (video)**	9	
Nov 03.	(cd) *(986139-2) <15400-2>* **THIS LEFT FEELS RIGHT (live acoustic)**	4	14
	– Wanted dead or alive / Livin' on a prayer (with OLIVIA D'ABO) / Bad medicine / It's my life / Lay your hands on me / You give love a bad name / Bed of roses / Everyday / Born to be my baby / Keep the faith / I'll be there for you / Always. *(special cd+=; 986138-9)* – Distance (live) / Joey (live).		

RICHIE SAMBORA

(solo with **BRYAN** + **TORRES** + **TONY LEVIN** – bass)

		Mercury	Mercury
Aug 91.	(7") *(MER 350) <868790>* **BALLAD OF YOUTH. / REST IN PEACE**	59	63
	(12"+=/cd-s+=) *(MER X/CD 350)* – The wind cries Mary.		
Sep 91.	(cd/c/lp) *(<848895-2/-4/-1>)* **STRANGER IN THIS TOWN**	20	36
	– Rest in peace / Church of desire / Stranger in this town / Ballad of youth / One light burning / Mr.Bluesman / Rosie / River of love / Father time / The answer. *(re-iss. Apr95 cd/c;)*		

— DAVID BRYAN also had solo album 'NETHERWORLD' (1992) for 'Moonstone'.

Feb 98.	(cd-s) *(568503-2)* **HARD TIMES COME EASY / MIDNIGHT RIDER – WANTED DEAD OR ALIVE (live) / WE ALL SLEEP ALONE (live) / BAD MEDICINE (live)**	37	
	(cd-s) *(568503-5)* – ('A'side) / Little help from my friends (live) / Stranger in this town (live) / I'll be there for you (live).		
Mar 98.	(cd/c) *<(536972-2/-4)>* **UNDISCOVERED SOUL**	24	
	– Made in America / Hard times come easy / Fallen from Graceland / If God was a woman / All that really matters / You're not alone / In it for love / Chained / Harlem rain / Who am I / Downside of love / Undiscovered soul.		
Jul 98.	(cd-s) *(566063-2)* **IN IT FOR LOVE / MADE IN AMERICA (German acoustic) / IN IT FOR LOVE (German acoustic)**	58	
	(cd-s) *(568825-2)* – ('A'side) / Livin' on a prayer (live at Ronnie Scott's) / I'll be there for you (live '91).		

□ BONNIE 'PRINCE' BILLY (see under ⇒ OLDHAM, Will)

BOOKER T. & THE M.G.'S

Formed: Memphis, Tennessee, USA ... 1962 when 'Stax' in-house musicians, BOOKER T. JONES, STEVE CROPPER, LEWIS STEINBERG (subsequently replaced with DONALD 'DUCK' DUNN) and AL JACKSON Jr. recorded a couple of instrumental tracks for label owner Jim Stewart. He duly released a single with 'BEHAVE YOURSELF' as the lead track; it was the B-side, however, 'GREEN ONIONS' which became a massive Top 3 US hit and a subsequent mod floor filler. This classic slice of lean, stinging R&B was a stunning showcase for the M.G.'s (Memphis Group) unique chemistry, JONES' organ stabbing and churning away over the taut rhythm section, while CROPPER snaked in with his wiry guitar playing. While continuing to work as part of the MAR-KEYS backing band in the early 60's, The M.G.'s also backed up a gamut of 'Stax' stars, not least the legendary OTIS REDDING, who himself had started out as a session player at the label. As the 60's progressed, the band's lock-tight R&B dance sound not only played a pivotal part in the emerging British mod culture but regularly saw them hit the American charts, especially towards the end of the decade when they scored with classics 'HIP HUG-HER', 'GROOVIN' and the Caribbean flavoured barnstormer, 'SOUL LIMBO'. The latter track hit the US Top 20 in late '68, while the album of the same name spawned another American Top 10 in 'HANG 'EM HIGH'. Like most of their albums, the record featured a fair smattering of finger-poppin' contemporary cover versions alongside the funky originals. The following year, they ventured into soundtrack work with 'UPTIGHT', a set which provided a rare UK Top 5 in 'TIME IS TIGHT'. As 'Stax' foundered in the early 70's, so The M.G.'s signed off after the 'McLEMORE AVENUE' (1970) set of 'Abbey Road' covers and the 'MELTING POT' (1971) album. While JONES married Priscilla Coolidge (sister of Rita) and recorded a number of albums with her, DUNN and JACKSON carried on as The M.G.'s for one further eponymous album in 1972. Like JONES, CROPPER had already co-written a string of soul classics and he subsequently went into production work. Tragically, JACKSON was not part of the intermittent BOOKER T. & THE M.G.'s reunions, having been shot dead by a burglar on 1st of October '75. The most recent incarnation of the group hooked up with NEIL YOUNG for a 1994 tour. • **Songwriters:** BOOKER T, except GROOVIN' (Young Rascals) / FOXY LADY (Jimi Hendrix) / THE HORSE (Jesse James) / LOVE CHILD (Richards-Sawyer-Taylor-Wilson) / SING A SIMPLE SONG (Pepper-Watt) / LADY MADONNA + MICHELLE (Beatles) / MRS.ROBINSON (Simon & Garfunkel) / THIS GUY'S IN LOVE WITH YOU (Bacharach-David) / LIGHT MY FIRE (Doors) / YOU'RE ALL I NEED TO GET BY (Ashford-Simpson) / IT'S YOUR THING (Isley Brothers) / and loads more.

• **Trivia:** SOUL LIMBO was/is used for theme tune to BBC TV's cricket coverage.

Album rating: GREEN ONIONS (*9) / MO' ONIONS (*7) / SOUL DRESSING (*7) / AND NOW! (*5) / IN THE CHRISTMAS SPIRIT (*3) / HIP HUG-HER (*5) / DOIN' OUR THING (*5) / SOUL LIMBO (*5) / UPTIGHT (*4) / THE BOOKER T. SET (*4) / McLEMORE AVENUE (*4) / MELTING POT (*4) / MEMPHIS SOUND (*4) / UNION EXTENDED (*4) / UNIVERSAL LANGUAGE (*3) / THE VERY BEST OF BOOKER T. & THE MG'S compilation (*7) / THAT'S THE WAY IT SHOULD BE (*3)

BOOKER T. JONES (b.12 Nov'44) – keyboards, multi (ex-MAR-KEYS) / **STEVE CROPPER** (b.21 Oct'41, Willow Springs, Missouri) – guitar (ex-MAR-KEYS) / **LEWIS STEINBERG** (b.13 Sep'33) – bass / **AL JACKSON Jr.** (b.27 Nov'35) – drums (ex-ROY MILTON BAND)

not iss. Volt

May 62. (7") *<102>* **BEHAVE YOURSELF. / GREEN ONIONS** [–] [ ]

London Stax

Sep 62. (7") *(HLK 9595) <STAX 127>* **GREEN ONIONS. / BEHAVE YOURSELF** [ ] Jul62 [3]

Nov 62. (lp) *<STAX 701>* **GREEN ONIONS** [–] [33]
– Green onions / Rinky-dink / I got a woman / Mo' onions / Twist and shout / Behave yourself / Stranger on the shore / Lonely avenue / One who really loves you / You can't sit down / A woman, a lover, a friend / Comin' home baby. *(UK-iss.Jul64; HA-K 8182)* – (hit No.11) *(re-iss. 1966 on 'Atlantic' mono/stereo; 587/588 033) (re-iss. Feb80 on 'Atlantic'; K 40072) (cd-iss. Jul91 & Dec94 on 'Atco'; 7567 82255-2)*

Feb 63. (7") *(HLK 9670) <STAX 131>* **JELLY BREAD. / AW' MERCY** [ ] Dec62 [82]

May 63. (7") *<STAX 134>* **HOME GROWN. / BIG TRAIN** [–] [ ]

Oct 63. (7") *(HLK 9784) <STAX 137>* **CHINESE CHECKERS. / PLUM NELLIE** [ ] Jul63 [78]
(re-iss. Jan68 on 'Stax'; 601 026)

Feb 64. (7") *<STAX 142>* **MO' ONIONS. / TIC-TAC-TOE** [–] [97]

—— **DONALD 'DUCK' DUNN** (b.24 Nov'41) – bass (ex-MAR-KEYS) repl. LEWIS

Jul 64. (7") *<STAX 153>* **SOUL DRESSING. / M.G. PARTY** [–] [95]

Aug 64. (lp) *<STAX 705>* **SOUL DRESSING** [–] [ ]
– Soul dressing / Tic-tac-toe / Big train / Jelly bread / Aw' mercy / Outrage / Night owl walk / Chinese checkers / Home grown / Mercy, mercy / Plum Nellie / Can't be still. *(UK-iss.1965 on 'Atlantic'; ATL 5027) (re-iss. 1967 on 'Atlantic'; 587 047) (cd-iss. May93 & Feb95 on 'Rhino-Atlantic'; 7567 82337-2)*

Sep 64. (7") *<STAX 161>* **CAN'T BE STILL. / TERRIBLE THING** [–] [ ]

Atlantic Stax

May 65. (7") *(AT 4033) <STAX 169>* **BOOT-LEG. / OUTRAGE** [ ] [58]

Jan 66. (7") *(AT 4063) <STAX 182>* **BE MY LADY. / RED BEANS & RICE** [ ] [ ]

Jun 66. (lp) *<STAX 711>* **AND NOW!** [–] [ ]
– My sweet potato / Jericho / No matter what shape / One mint julep / In the midnight hour / Summertime / Working in the coal mine / Don't mess up a good thing / Think / Taboo / Soul jam / Sentimental journey. *(UK-iss.1967; 589 002) (cd-iss. Aug93 on 'Rhino-Atlantic'; 8122 70297-2)*

Oct 66. (7") *(584 044) <1STAX 96>* **MY SWEET POTATO. / BOOKER LOO** [ ] Aug66 [85]

Dec 66. (7") *(584 060) <STAX 203>* **JINGLE BELLS. / WINTER WONDERLAND** [ ] [ ]

Dec 66. (lp) *<STAX 715>* **IN THE CHRISTMAS SPIRIT** (festive) [–] [ ]
(UK-iss.Nov68 as 'SOUL CHRISTMAS'; 589 013) (cd-iss. Aug93 & Dec95 on 'Rhino-Atlantic'; 7567 82338-2)

Mar 67. (7") *(584 088)* **GREEN ONIONS. / BOOT-LEG** [ ] [–]
(re-iss. Jun72; K 10109) – hit No.7 in Dec79 *(re-iss. 12" Apr80; K 10109T)*

Stax Stax

Apr 67. (7") *(601 009) <STAX 211>* **HIP HUG-HER. / SUMMERTIME** [ ] [37]

Jun 67. (lp) *<STAX 717>* **HIP HUG-HER** [–] [35]
– Hip hug-her / Soul sanction / Get ready / More / Double or nothing / Carnaby St. / Slim Jenkins' joint / Pigmy / Groovin' / Booker's motive / Sunny. *(cd-iss. Aug93 on 'Rhino-Atlantic'; 8122 71013-2)*

Aug 67. (lp; by MAR-KEYS & BOOKET T & THE MG'S) *<STAX 720>* **BACK TO BACK** (live) [–] [98]

Sep 67. (7") *(601 018) <STAX 224>* **SLIM JENKINS' PLACE. / GROOVIN'** [ ] [70] Jul67 [21]

May 68. (lp) *<STAX 724>* **DOIN' OUR THING** [–] [ ]
– I can dig it / Expressway (to your heart) / Doin' our thing / You don't love me / Never my love / The exodus song / The beat goes on / Ode to Billy Joe / Blue on green / You keep me hanging on / Let's go get stoned. *(UK-iss.1969 mono/stereo; 230/231 002) (cd-iss. Aug93 on 'Rhino-Atlantic'; 8122 70142-2)*

Oct 68. (7") *(STAX 102) <STAX 0001>* **SOUL LIMBO. / HEADS OR TAILS** [30] Jul68 [17]

Oct 68. (lp; stereo/mono) *(S+/XATS 1001) <STAX 2001>* **SOUL LIMBO** [ ] [ ]
– Be young, be foolish, be happy / La la means I love you / Hang 'em high / Willow weep for me / Over easy / Soul limbo / Eleanor Rigby / Heads or tails / (Sweet, sweet baby) Since you've been gone / Born under a bad sign / Foxy lady. *(re-iss. Feb88; SXE 009) (cd-iss. Apr90; CDSXE 009)*

Nov 68. (7") *<STAX 0013>* **HANG 'EM HIGH. / OVER EASY** [–] [9]
(re-iss. Sep87; STAX 813)

Mar 69. (7") *<STAX 0028>* **TIME IS TIGHT. / JOHNNY I LOVE YOU** [–] [6]

Apr 69. (7") *(STAX 119)* **TIME IS TIGHT. / HANG 'EM HIGH** [4] [–]

Apr 69. (lp; stereo/mono) *(S+/XATS 1005) <2006>* **UPTIGHT (Soundtrack)** [ ] Feb69 [98]
– Johnny, I love you / Cleveland now / Children, don't get weary / Tank's lament / Blues in the gutter / We've got Johnny Wells / Down at Ralph's joint / Deadwood Dick / Run tank run / Time is tight. *(re-iss. +cd.Jan90)*

Jul 69. (7") *(STAX 127) <STAX 0037>* **MRS. ROBINSON. / SOUL CLAP '69** [35] May69 [37]

Jul 69. (lp; stereo/mono) *(S+/XATS 1015) <STAX 2009>* **THE BOOKER T. SET** [ ] Jun69 [53]
– The horse / Love child / Sing a simple song / Lady Madonna / Mrs.Robinson / This guy's in love with you / Light my fire / Michelle / You're all I need to get by / I've never found a girl (to love me like you do) / It's your thing. *(re-iss. 1971; 2362 012) <re-iss. Dec86 on 'Mobile Fidelity Sound' lp/c; MFS/+5 8531> (re-iss. May90 cd/lp; CD+/SXE 026)*

Aug 69. (7") *<0049>* **SLUM BABY. / MEDITATION** [–] [88]

Nov 69. (7") *(STAX 136)* **THE HORSE. / SLUM BABY** [ ] [–]

May 70. (lp) *(SXATS 1031) <2027>* **McLEMORE AVENUE** [70] Apr70 [ ]
– Golden slumbers – Carry that weight – The end – Here comes the sun – Come together / Something / Because – You never give me your money / Sun king – Mean Mr. Mustard – Polythene Pam – She came in through the bathroom window – I want you – She's so heavy. *(re-iss. 1971; 2362 016) (re-iss. Dec88; SXE 016) (cd-iss. 1988 on 'Mobile Fidelity Sound'; MFCD 835)*

Jul 70. (7") *<0073>* **SOMETHING. / SUNDAY SERMON** [–] [76]

Sep 70. (7") *(STAX 152)* **SOMETHING. / DOWN AT RALPH'S JOINT** [ ] [–]

Mar 71. (lp) *(2325 030) <2035>* **MELTING POT** [ ] Feb71 [43]
– Melting pot / Back home / Chicken pox / Fuquawi / Kinda easy like / Hi ride / L.A. jazz song / Sunny Monday. *(re-iss. Jun76; STAX 1054) (cd-iss. Dec92 on 'Ace-Stax')*

Jun 71. (7") *(2025 026) <0082>* **MELTING POT. / KINDA EASY LIKE** [ ] Mar71 [45]

Sep 71. (7") *<0108>* **FUQUAWI. / JAMAICA THIS MORNING** [–] [ ]

—— May'71 they disbanded. JONES went solo and married singer PRISCILLA COOLIDGE (sister of RITA). He issued 3 albums with her 'BOOKER T. & PRISCILLA' / 'HOME GROWN' + 'CHRONICLES' (for 'A&M'), plus 'EVERGREEN' (for 'Epic' Feb75). CROPPER became workaholic session man and producer. DUNN and JACKSON continued as The MG's with newcomers **BOBBY MANUEL** – guitar / **CARSON WHITSETT** – keyboards. They issued a self-titled album and a few singles for 'Stax' in 1972.

—— On the 1st October 1975, AL JACKSON was shot dead by a burglar.

—— BOOKER T. & THE MG'S re-united (**BOOKER T., CROPPER and DUNN**) brought in **WILLIE HALL** (b. 8 Aug'50) – drums

Asylum Asylum

Mar 77. (lp) *(K 53057) <7E 1093>* **UNIVERSAL LANGUAGE** [ ] [ ]
– Sticky stuff / Grab bag / Space nuts / Love wheels / Motor cross / Last tango in Memphis / MG's salsa / Tie stick / Reincarnation.

Mar 77. (7") *<45392>* **STICKY STUFF. / TIE STICK** [–] [ ]

Jun 77. (7") *<45424>* **GRAB BAG. / REINCARNATION** [–] [ ]

—— Broke-up again. CROPPER and DUNN were in backing band that featured in the film 'The BLUES BROTHERS' in 1980. They continued to work on session/production.

—— BOOKER T went solo, releasing 3 albums for 'A&M'; 'TRY AND LOVE AGAIN' (Nov'78),'THE BEST OF YOU' (Feb'80) and 'I WANT YOU' (1981). Also issued a single, 'LET'S GO DANCING' in '79.

—— The BOOKER T TRIO released a cd-album, 'GO TELL IT TO THE MOUNTAIN' for 'Silkheart' (SHCD 114) Oct'92.

— JONES, CROPPER + DUNN recruited in 1992; **STEVE JORDAN** – drums who was replaced in 1994 by **STEVE POTTS** (b.12 Nov'53 – nephew of the late AL JACKSON).

Columbia Sony

Jun 94. (cd/c) *(474470-2/-4)* *<53307>* **THAT'S THE WAY IT SHOULD BE**
– Slip slidin' / Mo' greens / Gotta serve somebody / Let's wait awhile / That's the way it should be / Just my imagination (running away with me) / Camel ride / Have a heart / Cruisin' / I can't stand the rain / Sarasota sunset / I still haven't found what I'm looking for.

– compilations, others, etc. –

on 'Stax' unless mentioned otherwise

1963. (7"ep) *London; (REK 1367)* **R&B WITH BOOKER T** –
1964. (7"ep) *Atlantic; (AET 6002)* **R&B WITH BOOKER T VOL.2** –
Nov 68. (lp) *Atco; (228 015) / Atlantic; <8202>* **THE BEST OF BOOKER T. & THE MG'S**
– Green onions / Slim Jenkins' place / Hip hug-her / Soul dressing / Summertime / Bootleg / Jellybread / Tic-tac-toe / Can't be still / Groovin' / Mo' onions / Red beans and rice. *(re-iss. Jul84 on 'Atlantic' lp/c; K/K4 40072) (cd-iss. Apr87 on 'London'; FCE 60004) (cd re-iss. Jan93 on 'Atlantic'; 7567 81218-2)*
Dec 68. (7") *<STAX 236>* **SILVER BELLS. / WINTER SNOW** –
Nov 70. (lp) *(2362 002) <2033>* **GREATEST HITS**
(re-iss. Aug74; STX 1037)
1973. (d-lp) *Warners; (K 30042)* **STAR COLLECTION** –
Nov 74. (7"m) *(2025 207)* **TIME IS TIGHT. / BRING IT HOME TO ME / MY BABY SPECIALISES** –
Nov 75. (lp) *(STX 1037)* **MEMPHIS SOUND** –
Jan 76. (lp) *(STX 1045)* **UNION EXTENDED** (rare tracks) –
Jul 76. (7") *(STXS 2041)* **SOUL LIMBO. / MRS. ROBINSON** –
Nov 77. (7") *(STAX 1011)* **SOUL LIMBO. / SOUL CLAP '69** –
Nov 77. (7") *(STAX 2001)* **TIME IS TIGHT. / SOUL LIMBO** –
(re-iss. Sep85 on 'Old Gold'; OG 9530)
Dec 77. (12"ep) *Buddah-Pye; (BD 109)* **TIME IS TIGHT. / (3 other artists)** –
May 80. (lp; with The MARKEYS) *(STX 3007)* **TIME IS TIGHT** –
Mar 80. (7") *Atlantic; (K 11454)* **HIP HUG HER. / SLIM JENKINS' PLACE** –
Jun 80. (lp) *Hallmark; (SHM 3031)* **BOOKER T. & THE MG'S** –
Jan 85. (7") *Old Gold; (OG 9499)* **GREEN ONIONS. / CHINESE CHECKERS** –
Jun 87. (7") *(STAX 803)* **TIME IS TIGHT. / JOHNNY I LOVE YOU** –
Aug 87. (7"/7"pic-d/12") *(STA X/P/T 808)* **SOUL LIMBO. / HEADS OR TAILS** –
Apr 93. (cd) *(CDSX 46)* **THE BEST OF BOOKER T. & THE MG'S** (different) –
Apr 95. (cd) *(CDSXD 065)* **PLAY THE FLIP HITS** –
Nov 97. (12"; BOOKER T) *Junior Boys Own; (JBO 43)* **GROOVE ME (mixes; vocal mix / Bookstone dub / Swag's feeling alive / Swags 2x dub)** –
(12") *(JBO 43)* – (mixes; Farley & Heller's summer flava / original vocal – Benji's edit).
Nov 97. (12"; BOOKER T & TUFF JAM) *Fatt Boy; (FBOY 1)* **SWING LOW (mixes)** –
Oct 98. (3xcd-box) *Stax; (3SCD 4424)* **TIME IS TIGHT**
Oct 98. (cd) *Stax; (CDSXK 123)* **THE BEST OF BOOKER T. & THE MG'S**

BOOMTOWN RATS

Formed: Dun Laoghaire (near Dublin), Ireland . . . 1975 by former NME journalist BOB GELDOF, JOHNNIE FINGERS, GERRY COTT, PETE BRIQUETTE, GERRY ROBERTS and SIMON CROWE. Moving to London in late 1976, they signed to the newly formed 'Ensign' records. Though their music was rooted in R&B and they were more of a New Wave outfit than anything, The BOOMTOWN RATS were loosely affiliated with the burgeoning punk scene, at least initially. In the long, hot summer of '77, their debut single, 'LOOKIN' AFTER No.1' made the UK Top 20. This was closely followed by a similarly successful eponymous debut album and a second Top 20 hit, 'MARY OF THE 4th FORM'. With a lean sound lying somewhere between EDDIE & THE HOT RODS and The ROLLING STONES, The BOOMTOWN RATS were also a compelling live proposition, GELDOF's moody charisma helping to give the band a distinct identity. Major success came with 'A TONIC FOR THE TROOPS' (1978), this album spawning a number of hits including their first No.1 in the insistent 'RAT TRAP'. They scored a second number one and a massive worldwide hit with 'I DON'T LIKE MONDAYS', a stunningly effective, piano-driven belter inspired (if that's the appropriate word) by schoolgirl Brenda Spencer, who snipered/shot dead several of her school colleagues. The accompanying album, 'THE ART OF SURFACING' (1979) showed the 'RATS at the peak of their power, although subsequent albums increasingly followed a more mundane pop/rock direction and the band slowly faded from view, finally splitting in 1984. GELDOF's profile remained high, however, the Irishman helping to mastermind the mammoth undertaking that was LIVE AID. He and ULTRAVOX's MIDGE URE, assembled together all the major stars of the time to sing 'DO THEY KNOW IT'S CHRISTMAS', the resulting 45 making millions of pounds/dollars/etc for famine relief in Ethiopia. Not content with this, BOB and MIDGE reunited most of them again for the LIVE AID concert at Wembley Stadium on the 13th of July '85 (this was simultaneously broadcast over the Atlantic at JFK Stadium, Philadelphia). At the time, it amassed well over £10m, the money also being spread around other needy charities as well as Ethiopia (the total at the end of 1991 was over £100m). In June 1986, BOB was now Sir BOB GELDOF, after being knighted by the Queen and two months later he married long-time fiancee, PAULA YATES (TV presenter/writer/etc). She gave birth to FIFI TRIXIBELLE and in 1989, their second daughter, PEACHES, was born. During the latter half of a very busy decade for GELDOF, he managed to maintain a solo career, a hit single, 'THIS IS THE WORLD CALLING', was appropriate enough to become a Top 30 hit in 1986, while 1990's 'THE GREAT SONG OF INDIFFERENCE' went one step better. His backing band at the time, The VEGETARIANS OF LOVE, provided the title of the single's folky/cajun parent album, which also sold reasonably well. His last solo album, 'THE HAPPY CLUB' (1992), was something of a disappointment and Sir BOB virtually retired from the studio side of things to run his own Planet 24 company and The Big Breakfast on Channel 4. Paula was also part of the latter, although by 1995, she had opted to bed MICHAEL HUTCHENCE of INXS, citing BOB as the cause. BOB and Paula were subsequently divorced as the new couple became the media focal point (tragically, this was cut short when MICHAEL took his own life on the 22nd November, 1997 – see INXS). GELDOF was dealt yet another brutal blow when his tormented ex died from an overdose on the 17th September, 2000; BOB finally won custody of his children, and even their half-sister, daughter of Paula and Michael. Come the new millennium, busy BOB finally returned to the thing which fired his adult life in the first place: angry, questioning rock'n'roll music. There aren't many guys his age making records like 'SEX, AGE & DEATH' (2002), still railing against complacency and inertia with all the spastic energy of youth. Fittingly, GELDOF embraced contemporary studio trends rather than relying completely on conventional instruments, bringing a modern edge to the menace his muse has always possessed. • **Songwriters:** Most written by GELDOF except; BAREFOOTIN' (Robert Parker). GELDOF solo covered SUNNY AFTERNOON (Kinks). • **Trivia:** GELDOF starred in the feature films, 'The Wall' (1982) and 'Number One' (1984).

Album rating: THE BOOMTOWN RATS (*6) / A TONIC FOR THE TROOPS (*5) / THE FINE ART OF SURFACING (*5) / MONDO BONGO (*4) / V DEEP (*4) / IN THE LONG GRASS (*5) / Bob Geldof: DEEP IN THE HEART OF NOWHERE (*5) / THE VEGETARIANS OF LOVE (*5) / THE HAPPY CLUB (*4) / LOUDMOUTH – THE BEST OF THE BOOMTOWN RATS AND BOB GELDOF compilation (*8) / SEX, AGE & DEATH (*6)

BOB GELDOF (b. 5 Oct'54, Dublin, Ireland) – vocals / **JOHNNIE FINGERS** (b. JOHNNY MOYLETT) – keyboards, vocals / **GERRY COTT** – guitar / **PETE BRIQUETTE** (b. PATRICK CUSACK) – bass / **GERRY ROBERTS** – guitar, vocals / **SIMON CROWE** – drums, vocals

Ensign Mercury

Aug 77. (12"m) *(ENY 4)* **LOOKIN' AFTER No.1. / BORN TO BURN (live) / BAREFOOTIN' (live)** [11] [–]

Sep 77. (lp/c) *(ENVY/ENCAS 1) <SRM 1188>* **THE BOOMTOWN RATS** [18] [ ]
– Lookin' after No.1 / Neon heart / Joey's on the street again / Never bite the hand that feeds / Mary of the 4th form / (She gonna) Do you in / Close as you'll ever be / I can make it if you can / Kicks. *(re-iss. Dec83 on 'Mercury' lp/c; PRICE/PRIMC 57)*

Nov 77. (7") *(ENY 9)* **MARY OF THE 4th FORM. / DO THE RAT** [15] [–]

Ensign Columbia

Mar 78. (7") *(ENY 13)* **SHE'S SO MODERN. / LYING AGAIN** [12] [ ]

Jun 78. (7") *(ENY 14)* **LIKE CLOCKWORK. / HOW DO YOU DO?** [6] [ ]

Jul 78. (lp/c) *(ENVY/ENCAS 3) <35750>* **A TONIC FOR THE TROOPS** [8] [ ]
– Like clockwork / Blind date / (I never loved) Eva Braun / Living in an island / Don't believe what you read / She's so modern / Me and Howard Hughes / Can't stop * / (Watch out for) The normal people / Rat trap. *<US version repl.* with – Joey> (re-iss. Dec83 on 'Mercury' lp/c; PRICE/PRIMC 58)*

Oct 78. (7") *(ENY 16)* **RAT TRAP. / SO STRANGE** [1] [–]

Nov 78. (7") **RAT TRAP. / DO THE RAT** [–] [ ]

Jul 79. (7") *(ENY 30) <11117>* **I DON'T LIKE MONDAYS. / IT'S ALL THE RAGE** [1] Jan80 [73]

Oct 79. (lp/c) *(ENROX/ENCAS 11) <36248>* **THE FINE ART OF SURFACING** [7] [ ]
– Someone's looking at you / Diamond smiles / Wind chill factor (minus zero) / Having my picture taken / Sleep (Fingers' lullaby) / I don't like Mondays / Nothing happened today / Keep it up / Nice 'n' neat / When the night comes. *(re-iss. Nov84 on 'Mercury' lp/c; PRICE/PRIMC 73)*

Nov 79. (7") *(ENY 33)* **DIAMOND SMILES. / LATE LAST NIGHT** [13] [–]

Jan 80. (7",12") *(ENY 34)* **SOMEONE'S LOOKING AT YOU. / WHEN THE NIGHT COMES** [4] [–]

May 80. (7") *<11248>* **SOMEONE'S LOOKING AT YOU. / I DON'T LIKE MONDAYS (live)** [–] [ ]

Mercury Columbia

Nov 80. (7") *(BONGO 1)* **BANANA REPUBLIC. / MAN AT THE TOP** [3] [–]

Dec 80. (lp/c) *(6359/7150 042) <37062>* **MONDO BONGO** [6] [ ]
– Please don't go / The elephant's graveyard (guilty) / Banana republic / Fall down / Hurt hurts / Whitehall 1212 * / Mood mambo / Straight up / This is my room / Another piece of red / Under their thumb . . . is under my thumb / Go man go. *<US version repl. * with – Don't talk to me>*

Jan 81. (7") *(BONGO 2)* **THE ELEPHANT'S GRAVEYARD (GUILTY). / REAL DIFFERENT** [26] [–]

—— (Mar'81) trimmed to a quintet when GERRY COTT left to go solo

Nov 81. (7") *<60512>* **UP ALL NIGHT. / ANOTHER PIECE OF RED** [–] [ ]

Nov 81. (7") *(MER 87)* **NEVER IN A MILLION YEARS. / DON'T TALK TO ME** [62] [–]

Mar 82. (7"/12") *(MER/+X 91)* **HOUSE ON FIRE. / EUROPE LOOKED UGLY** [24] [–]

Mar 82. (lp/c) *(6359/7150 082)* **V DEEP** [64] [ ]
– Never in a million years / The bitter end / Talking in code / He watches it all / Storm breaks / Charmed lives / House on fire / Up all night / Skin on skin / Little death.

Jun 82. (7") *(MER 106)* **CHARMED LIVES. / NO HIDING PLACE** [ ] [–]
(d7"+=) *(MER 106-2)* – Nothing happened today (live) / Storm breaks (instrumental).
(12") *(MERX 106)* – ('A'side) / A storm breaks.

Aug 82. (7") *<03386>* **CHARMED LIVES. / NEVER IN A MILLION YEARS** [–] [ ]

Jan 84. (7") *(MER 154)* **TONIGHT. / PRECIOUS TIME** [73] [–]
(12"+=) *(MERX 154)* – Walking downtown.

May 84. (7") *(MER 163)* **DRAG ME DOWN. / AN ICICLE IN THE SUN** [50] [–]
(12"+=) *(MERX 163)* – Rat trap / She's so modern.

Nov 84. (7"pic-d) *(MER 179)* **DAVE. / HARD TIMES** [ ] [–]
(d7"+=) *(MER 179-2)* – I don't like Mondays / It's all the rage.
(12"+=) *(MERX 179)* – Banana republic (live) / Close as you'll ever be (live).

Dec 84. (lp/c) *(MERL/+C 38) <39335>* **IN THE LONG GRASS** [ ] [ ]
– A hold of me / Drag me down / Dave / Over again / Another sad story / Tonight / Hard times / Lucky / Icicle in the Sun / Up or down.

Feb 85. (7") *(MER 184)* **A HOLD OF ME. / NEVER IN A MILLION YEARS** [ ] [–]
(12"+=) *(MERX 184)* – Say hi to Mick.

Mar 85. (7") *<04892>* **ICICLE IN THE SUN. / RAIN** [–] [ ]

Jun 85. (7") *<05590>* **DRAG ME DOWN. / HARD TIMES** [–] [ ]

—— had already split late '84. FINGERS and CROWE formed GUNG HO. BOB GELDOF pieced together BAND/LIVE AID before going solo.

– compilations, others, etc. –

Dec 83. (6x7"box) *Mercury; (none)* **RAT PACK** (6 best of singles pack) [ ] [–]

Jan 88. (7") *Old Gold; (OG 9790)* **I DON'T LIKE MONDAYS. / RAT TRAP** [ ] [–]

BOB GELDOF

solo, with guests **DAVE STEWART, ERIC CLAPTON**, etc.

Mercury Atlantic

Oct 86. (7"/12") *(BOB/+X 101) <89341>* **THIS IS THE WORLD CALLING. / TALK ME UP** [25] [82]

Nov 86. (lp/c)(cd) *(BOB LP/MC 1)(830 607-2) <812687>* **DEEP IN THE HEART OF NOWHERE** [79] [ ]
– Love you like a rocket / In the pouring rain / This heartless night / Words from Heaven / Deep in the heart of nowhere / Night turns to day / I cry too / The beat of the night / When I was young / This is the world calling / August was a heavy month. *(cd+=)* – Pulled apart by horses / Good boys in the wrong / Truly true blue.

Jan 87. (7") *(BOB 102)* **LOVE YOU LIKE A ROCKET. / THIS IS THE WORLD CALLING** [61] [–]
(12"+=) *(BOBX 102)* – ('A'extended).
(cd-s+=) *(BOBCD 102)* – Pulled apart by horses / Truly true blue.

Mar 87. (7") *<89309>* **LOVE YOU LIKE A ROCKET. / PULLED APART BY HORSES** [–] [ ]

Jun 87. (7") *<89261>* **THE HEARTLESS NIGHT. / PULLED APART BY HORSES** [–] [ ]

Jun 87. (7") *(BOB 103)* **I CRY TOO. / LET'S GO** [ ] [ ]
(12"+=) *(BOBX 103)* – Night turns to day / Deep in the heart of nowhere.

—— He was now augmented by his **VEGETARIANS OF LOVE** backing band **GEOFF RICHARDSON** – viola, clarinet, etc. / **BOB LOVEDAY** – violin, bass, penny whistle / **PETE BRIQUETTE** – bass, keyboards / **PHIL PALMER** – guitars / **STEVE FLETCHER** – keyboard ALUN DUNN – accordion, organ / **RUPERT HINE** – keyboards, percussion, producer,

Jun 90. (7") *(BOB 104)* **THE GREAT SONG OF INDIFFERENCE. / HOTEL 75** [15] [ ]
(12"+=/cd-s+=) *(BOB X/CD 104)* – In the pouring rain.

Jul 90. (cd/c/lp) *(846 250-2/-4/-1) <82041-2/-4/-1>* **THE VEGETARIANS OF LOVE** [21] [ ]
– A gospel song / Love or something / Thinking Voyager 2 type things / The great song of indifference / Crucified me / Big romance stuff / The chains of pain / A rose at night / Let it go / No small wonder / Walking back to happiness / The end of the world. *(cd re-iss. Jun03; same)*

Aug 90. (7") *(BOB 105)* **LOVE OR SOMETHING. / OUT OF ORDER** [ ] [–]
(12"+=/cd-s+=) *(BOB X/CD 105)* – The great song of indifference (mix) / Friends for life / One of these girls.

Nov 90. (7") *(BOB 106)* **A GOSPEL SONG. / VEGETARIANS OF LOVE** [ ] [–]
(12"+=/cd-s+=) *(BOB X/CD 106)* – The warmest fire.

—— now with The HAPPY CLUBSTERS (same as last)

Vertigo Polygram

Jun 92. (7") *(BOB 107)* **ROOM 19 (SHA LA LA LA LEE). / HUGE BIRDLESS SILENCE** [ ] [-]
(cd-s+=) *(BOBCD 107)* – The great song of indifference / Sweat for you (BRIQUETTE & SHARKEY CO.).

Sep 92. (7") *(BOB 108)* **MY HIPPY ANGEL. / MAYBE HEAVEN** [ ] [-]
(cd-s+=) *(BOBCD 108)* – Love or something / ('A'extended).

Oct 92. (cd/c/lp) *(512 896-2/-4/-1)* *<519132>* **THE HAPPY CLUB** [ ] [ ]
– Room 19 (sha la la la lee) / Attitude chicken / The soft soil / A hole to fill / The song of the emergent nationalist / My hippy angel / The happy club / Like down on me / Too late God / Roads of Germany (after BD) / A sex thing / The house at the top of the world.

Apr 94. (7"/c-s) *(MER/+MC 85)* **CRAZY. / THE HAPPY CLUB** [65] [-]
(cd-s) *(MERCX 85)* – ('A'side) / Room 19 (sha la la la lee) (live) / The beat of the night (live) / Rat trap (live).
Note; below single by BOOMTOWN RATS (also compilation tracks *)

Jun 94. (7"colrd/c-s) *(VER/+MC 87)* **I DON'T LIKE MONDAYS. / BORN TO BURN / DO THE RAT** [38] [ ]
(cd-s) *(MERCD 87)* – ('A'side) / Looking after No.1 / Mary of the 4th form / She's so modern.
(cd-s) *(MERCX 87)* – ('A'side) / Rat trap / Someone's looking at you / Banana republic.

Jul 94. (cd/c) *(522 283-2/-4)* **LOUDMOUTH – THE BEST OF THE BOOMTOWN RATS & BOB GELDOF** (compilation) [10] [ ]
– I don't like Mondays * / This is the world calling / Rat trap * / The great song of indifference / Love or something / Banana republic * / Crazy / The elephant's graveyard (guilty) * / Someone's looking at you * / She's so modern * / House on fire * / The beat of the night / Diamond smiles * / Like clockwork * / Room 19 (sha la la la lee) / Mary of the 4th form * / Looking after No.1 *. *(* tracks by The BOOMTOWN RATS)*

Eagle Koch

Oct 01. (cd) *(EAGCD 187)* *<8415>* **SEX, AGE AND DEATH** [ ] Jun02 [ ]
– One for me / $6,000,000 loser / Pale white girls / The new routine / Mudslide / Mind in pocket / My birthday suit / Scream in vain / Inside your head / 10:15. *<US+=>* – Cool, blue and easy / The original Miss Jesus.

Jan 03. (cd-s) *(EAGXS 220)* **PALE WHITE GIRLS** [ ] [-]

BOO RADLEYS

Formed: Liverpool, England . . . 1988, by schoolmates SICE and MARTIN CARR. Another friend, TIM BROWN, was invited to join after teaching MARTIN how to play guitar. They took the group name from a weird character in the film, 'To Kill A Mockingbird'. The quartet was complete when they found drummer STEVE HEWITT. They worked hard on the Mersey gig circuit but no major deal was forthcoming. Come 1990, they finally found a home with small indie label, 'Action', who released their debut lp 'ICHABOD AND I'. On its merit, they were invited by the illustrious DJ John Peel to session for Radio 1. This led to a signing for 'Rough Trade', who issued 3 popular EP's between late 1990 & 91. They then moved to 'Creation', their psychedelic, BYRDS-influenced jangle-pop soon making them favourites of the music press (Singles Of The Week, etc). The release of 1992's 'EVERYTHING'S ALRIGHT FOREVER' and the following years' masterful 'GIANT STEPS' album infused their sugary pop with screeching guitars and jagged brass accompaniment. The latter secured them their first Top 20 placing, the tracks 'I HANG SUSPENDED', 'BARNEY (. . . AND ME)' and 'LAZARUS' being effervescent highlights. Early to rise in '95, they scored their first Top 10 hit with 'WAKE UP BOO!', taken from their similarly titled No.1 album. The single was subsequently spoiled after it was played to death as the theme tune for ITV's Breakfast TV. In 1996, SICE (aka EGGMAN) released a patchy solo album, while The BOO's returned with another slice (or SICE!) of nostalgic pop, 'C'MON KIDS'. After the album 'KINGSIZE' was released to some mixed reviews (towards the end of '98), the unhappy BOO's were quite literally treading water(beds) until their demise early the following year. • **Songwriters:** CARR lyrics / group music, except TRUE FAITH (New Order) / ALONE AGAIN OR (Love) / ONE OF US MUST KNOW (Bob Dylan) / THE QUEEN IS DEAD (Smiths). • **Trivia:** MERIEL BARHAM of The PALE SAINTS provided vocals on 2 tracks for GIANT STEPS album. ED BALL (ex-TV PERSONALITIES) often made guest appearances.

Album rating: ICHABOD AND I (*5) / EVERYTHING'S ALRIGHT FOREVER (*7) / GIANT STEPS (*9) / WAKE UP! (*8) / C'MON KIDS (*6) / KINGSIZE (*6) / Eggman: FIRST FRUITS (*5)

SICE (b. SIMON ROWBOTTOM, 18 Jun'69, Wallasey, England) – vocals, guitar / **MARTIN CARR** (b.29 Nov'68, Thurso, Scotland) – guitar / **TIM BROWN** (b.26 Feb'69, Wallasey) – bass / **STEVE DREWITT** (b. Northwich, England) – drums

Action not iss.

Jul 90. (lp) *(TAKE 4)* **ICHABOD AND I** [ ] [-]
– Eleanor everything / Bodenheim Jr. / Catweazle / Sweet salad birth / Hip clown rag / Walking 5th carnival / Kaleidoscope / Happens to us all.

— **ROB CIEKA** (b. 4 Aug'68, Birmingham, England) – drums repl. DREWITT to BREED

Rough Trade not iss.

Oct 90. (12"ep/cd-ep) *(RTT 241/+CD)* **KALEIDOSCOPE EP** [ ] [-]
– Kaleidoscope / How I feel / Aldous / Swansong.

Apr 91. (12"ep/cd-ep) *(R 201127-10/-13)* **EVERY HEAVEN EP** [ ] [-]
– The finest kiss / Tortoiseshell / Bluebird / Naomi.

Sep 91. (12"ep/cd-ep) *(R 275-0/-3)* **BOO UP! EP (Peel sessions)** [ ] [-]
– Everybird / Sometime soon she said / Foster's van / Song for up!

Dec 91. (cd) *(R 3012)* **LEARNING TO WALK** (compilation of above 3 EP's) [ ] [-]

Creation Columbia

Feb 92. (12"ep)(cd-ep) *(CRE 128T)CRESCD 124)***ADRENALIN EP** [ ] [-]
– Lazy day / Vegas / Feels like tomorrow / Whiplashed.

Mar 92. (cd/c/lp) *(CRE CD/MC/LP 120)* *<52912>* **EVERYTHING'S ALRIGHT FOREVER** [55] Aug92 [ ]
– Spaniard / Towards the light / Losing it (song for Abigail) / Memory babe / Skyscraper / I feel nothing / Room at the top / Does this hurt / Sparrow / Smile fades fast / Firesky / Song for the morning to sing / Lazy day / Paradise.

Jun 92. (7") *(CRE 128)* **BOO! FOREVER. / DOES THIS HURT** [67] [-]
(12"+=)(cd-s+=) *(CRE 128T)(CRESCD 128)* – Buffalo Bill / Sunfly II: Walking with the kings.

Nov 92. (7") *(CRE 137)* **LAZARUS. / LET ME BE YOUR FAITH** [76] [-]
(12"+=)(cd-s+=) *(CRE 137T)(CRESCD 137)* – At the sound of speed / Petroleum.

— added **STEVE KITCHEN** – trumpet, flugel horn / **JACKIE ROY** – clarinet / **LINDSAY JOHNSTON** – cello

Jul 93. (7") *(CRE 147)* **I HANG SUSPENDED. / RODNEY KING (St. Etienne mix)** [77] [-]
(12"+=)(cd-s+=) *(CRE 147T)(CRESCD 147)* – As bound a stomorrow / I will always ask where you have been though I know the answer.

Jul 93. (cd/c/d-lp) *(CRE CD/MC/LP 149)* *<53794>* **GIANT STEPS** [17] Aug93 [ ]
– I hang suspended / Upon 9th and Fairchild / Wish I was skinny / Leaves and sand / Butterfly McQueen / Rodney King (song for Lenny Bruce) / Thinking of ways / Barney (. . . and me) / Spun around / If you want it, take it / Best lose the fear / Take the time around / Lazarus / One is for / Run my way runway / I've lost the reason / The white noise revisited. *(cd re-iss. Aug98; same)*

Oct 93. (7"/c-s) *(CRE/+CD 169)* **WISH I WAS SKINNY. / PEACHY KEEN** [75] [-]
(12"+=)(cd-s+=) *(CRE 169T)(CRESCD 169)* – Furthur / Crow eye.

Feb 94. (7"/c-s) *(CRE/+CS 178)* **BARNEY (. . .AND ME). / ZOOM** [48] [-]
(12"+=)(cd-s+=) *(CRE 178T)(CRESCD 178)* – Tortoiseshell / Cracked lips, homesick.

May 94. (7") *(CRE 187)* **LAZARUS. / (I WANNA BE) TOUCHDOWN JESUS** [50] [-]
(12"+=) *(CRE 187T)* – ('A'-Secret Knowledge mix) / ('A'-Ultramarine radio mix).
(cd-s+=) *(CRESCD 187)* – ('A'acoustic) / ('A'-St. Etienne mix).

(cd-s) *(CRESCD 187X)* – ('A'-Secret Knowledge mix) / ('A'-Ultramarine mix) / ('A'-Augustus Pablo mix) / ('A'-12"mix).

Feb 95. (c-s) *(CRECS 191)* **WAKE UP BOO! / JANUS** [9] [–]
(cd-s+=) *(CRESCD 191)* – Blues for George Michael / Friendship song.
(12") *(CRE 191T)* – Wake up Boo!: Music for astronauts / Janus / Blues for George Michael.
(cd-s) *(CRESCD 191X)* – Wake up Boo!: Music for astronauts / ...And tomorrow the world / The history of Creation parts 17 & 36.

Mar 95. (cd/c/lp) *(CRE CD/MC/LP 179) <67249>* **WAKE UP!** [1] [ ]
– Wake up Boo! / Fairfax scene / It's Lulu / Joel / Find the answer within / Reaching out from here / Martin, Doom! it's 7 o'clock / Stuck on amber / Charles Bukowski is dead / 4am conversation / Twinside / Wilder. *(cd re-iss. Aug98; same)*

May 95. (c-s) *(CRECS 202)* **FIND THE ANSWER WITHIN / DON'T TAKE YOUR GUN TO TOWN** [37] [–]
(cd-s+=) *(CRESCD 202)* – Wallpaper.
(12"++=) *(CRE 202T)* – The only word I can find / Very together.
(cd-s) *(CRESCD 202X)* – ('A'-High Llamas mix) / The only word I can find / Very together.

Jul 95. (c-s) *(CRECS 211)* **IT'S LULU / THIS IS NOT ABOUT ME** [25] [–]
(cd-s+=) *(CRESCD 211)* – Reaching out from here (the High Llamas mix / Martin, doom! it's seven o'clock (Stereolab mix).
(cd-s) *(CRESCD 211X)* – ('A'side) / Joel (Justin Warfield mix) / Tambo / Donkey.

Sep 95. (c-s/7") *(C+/CRE 214)* **FROM THE BENCH AT BELVIDERE. / HI FALUTIN'** [24] [–]
(cd-s+=) *(CRESCD 214)* – Crushed / Nearly almost time.

Creation Mercury

Aug 96. (7") *(CRE 220)* **WHAT'S IN THE BOX? (SEE WHATCHA GOT). / BLOKE IN A DRESS** [25] [–]
(cd-s+=) *(CRESCD CRESCD 220)* – Flakes / ('A'-Kris Needs mix).
(cd-s) *(CRESCD 220X)* – ('A'side) / Atlantic / The absent boy / Annie and Marnie.

Sep 96. (cd/c)(d-lp) *(CRECD/CCRE 194)(CRELP 194L)* *<534256>* **C'MON KIDS** [20] [ ]
– C'mon kids / Meltin's worm / Melodies for the deaf / Get on the bus / Everything is sorrow / Bullfrog green / What's in the box? (see whatcha got) / Four saints / New Brighton promenade / Fortunate sons / Shelter / Ride the tiger / One last hurrah. *(lp w/ free 7")* SKYWALKER. / FRENCH CANADIAN BEAN SOUP

Oct 96. (7") *(CRE 236)* **C'MON KIDS. / SPION COP** [18] [–]
(cd-s+=) *(CRESCD 236)* – Too beautiful / Bullfrog green (ultra living mix).
• (cd-s) *(CRESCD 236X)* – ('A'side) / Nothing to do but scare myself / From the bench at Belvidere (Ultramarine mix) / Fortunate sons (Greg Hunter remix).

Jan 97. (7") *(CRE 248)* **RIDE THE TIGER. / VOTE YOU** [38] [–]
(cd-s+=) *(CRESCD 248)* – A part I know so well / Everything is sorrow (Grantby remix).
(cd-s) *(CRESCD 248X)* – ('A'side) / Roadie / Safe at home / C'mon kids (Mekon remix).

Creation Creation

Oct 98. (10") *(CRE 299X)* **FREE HUEY. / SPANISH LIZARDS** [54] [–]
(cd-s+=) *(CRESCD 299)* – ('A'-environmental science remix).
(cd-s) *(CRESCD 299X)* – ('A'side) / ('A'mixes).

Oct 98. (cd/d-lp)(c) *(CRE CD/LP 228)(CCRE 228)* **KINGSIZE** [62] [–]
– Blueroom in archway / The old newsstand at Hamilton Square / Free Huey / Monuments for a dead century / Heaven's at the bottom of this glass / Kingsize / High as monkeys / Eurostar / Adieu clo clo / Jimmy Webb is God / She is everywhere / Comb your hair / Song for the blueroom / The future is now.

— the band split early '99; CARR formed BRAVE CAPTAIN; SICE had already released a solo set as EGGMAN

☐ BOOTH AND THE BAD ANGEL (see under ⇒ JAMES)

BOSTON

Formed: 1975 . . . by technical whizz and sometime musical genius, TOM SCHOLZ, who had set-up his own basement studio in Boston, Massachusetts, USA. Signed to 'Epic' on the strength of some home-crafted demos, SCHOLZ assembled a crew of musician friends (BRAD DELP, BARRY GOUDREAU, FRAN SHEEHAN and JIM MASDEA) and set about creating his first opus. Quintessentially 70's yet one of the most enduring AOR tracks ever recorded, BOSTON's debut single, 'MORE THAN A FEELING', gave the band instant UK and US success upon its release in Christmas 1976. With its powerful twin lead guitar attack, softened with flawless harmonies, the song set a blueprint for the eponymous debut album. While the record contained nothing else quite as affecting, it was all well written stuff and highly listenable if you ignored the cliched lyrics. Inevitably, the album sold in its millions and the pressure was on to record a follow-up. Notoriously perfectionist in the studio, SCHOLZ was unhappy with a mere two years to craft 'DON'T LOOK BACK' (1978). While the title track was top drawer car-stereo material, the formula was sounding tired and the bulk of the album didn't lend itself to repeated listening. While SCHOLZ complained that its relatively disappointing sales (still in the millions!) were down to the record being released prematurely, it was, after all, the height of the punk explosion, when sleeve designs of intergalactic guitars wern't particularly appreciated by the kids (in Britain, at least). It was to be another seven years before BOSTON returned with a follow-up and during this period, SCHOLZ signed with 'M.C.A.', a legal battle with 'C.B.S.' ensuing. The boffin-like SCHOLZ also found time to invent the 'Rockman', a device that amplified guitar sound at low volume for home recording. 'THIRD STAGE' (1986) boasted another airbrushed space fantasy cover and another set of reliable melodic rock songs, 'AMANDA' reaching No.1 in the US singles chart, the album itself achieving a similar feat. Yet again it quickly sold over a million but the BOSTON concept reeked of staleness and after another interminably long lay-off, SCHOLZ/BOSTON came up with 'WALK ON' in 1994. Unsurprisingly, the album only made it to No.51 in the US chart; SCHOLZ had clearly tested his fans' patience once too often. After another interminable lay-off when most people had probably forgotten the band ever existed, BOSTON returned with 'CORPORATE AMERICA' (2002). Despite the implications of its title, the record was, as usual, more centered on SCHOLZ' painstakingly crafted, classic rock creations than topical analysis. There were few surprises here, except maybe that the man's creative trajectory is as uncannily straight as it ever was.

Album rating: BOSTON (*7) / DON'T LOOK BACK (*5) / THIRD STAGE (*5) / WALK ON (*4) / GREATEST HITS compilation (*7) / CORPORATE AMERICA (*5)

BRAD DELP (b.12 Jun'51) – vocals, guitar / **TOM SCHOLZ** (b.10 Mar'47, Toledo, Ohio) – guitar, keyboards, vocals / **BARRY GOUDREAU** (b.29 Nov'51) – guitar / **FRAN SHEENAN** (b.26 Mar'49) – bass / **SIB HASHIAN** (b.17 Aug'49) – drums; repl. debut lp session drummer JIM MASDEA

Epic Epic

Jan 77. (7") *(EPC 4658) <50266>* **MORE THAN A FEELING. / SMOKIN'** [22] Sep76 [5]

Jan 77. (lp/c) *(EPC/40 81611) <34188>* **BOSTON** [11] Sep76 [3]
– More than a feeling / Peace of mind / Foreplay – Long time / Rock & roll band / Smokin' / Hitch a ride / Something about you / Let me take you home tonight. *(re-iss. Mar81 lp/c; EPC/40 32038)* – hit UK 58) *(cd-iss. Mar87; CD 81611) (cd re-iss. Jul95; 480413-2) (lp re-iss. Oct97 on 'Simply Vinyl'; SVLP 4) (cd re-iss. Dec98; 4894129)*

Mar 77. (7") *(EPC 5043) <50329>* **LONG TIME. / LET ME TAKE YOU HOME TONIGHT** [ ] Jan77 [22]

Jun 77. (7") *(EPC 5288) <50381>* **PEACE OF MIND. / FOREPLAY** [ ] May77 [38]

Sep 78. (lp/c)<US-pic-lp> *(EPC/40 86057) <35050>* **DON'T LOOK BACK** [9] Aug78 [1]
– Don't look back / The journey / It's easy / A man I'll never be / Feelin' satisfied / Party / Used to bad news / Don't be afraid. *(re-iss. Jun81 lp/c; EPC/40 32048) (cd-iss. Mar87; CD 86057)*

Oct 78. (7") *(EPC 6653) <50590>* **DON'T LOOK BACK. / THE JOURNEY** [43] Aug78 [4]

Jan 79. (7") *(EPC 6837)* <50638> **A MAN I'LL NEVER BE. / DON'T BE AFRAID** [ ] Nov78 [31]

May 79. (7") *(EPC 7295)* <50677> **FEELIN' SATISFIED. / USED TO BAD NEWS** [ ] Mar79 [46]

— (broke up for a while, after 3rd album was shelved / not completed) BARRY GOUDREAU made solo album late '80 before in '82 forming ORION THE HUNTER. He was augmented by SCHOLZ and DELP. HASHIAN joined SAMMY HAGAR band.

— **BOSTON** re-grouped around **SCHOLZ + DELP** plus **GARY PIHL** – guitar and the returning **JIM MASDEA** – drums

M.C.A. M.C.A.

Oct 86. (7"/12") *(MCA/+S 1091)* <52756> **AMANDA. / MY DESTINATION** [ ] Sep86 [1]

Oct 86. (lp/c/cd) *(MCG/MCGC/DMCG 6017)* <6188> **THIRD STAGE** [37] [1]
– Amanda / We're ready / The launch: Countdown – Ignition – Third stage separation / Cool the engines / My Destination / A new world / To be a man / I think I like it / Can'tcha say (you believe in me) / Still in love / Hollyann. *(cd re-iss. Jun92; MCLD 19066)*

Nov 86. (7") <52985> **WE'RE READY. / THE LAUNCH: COUNTDOWN – IGNITION – THIRD STAGE SEPARATION** [–] [9]

Apr 87. (7") *(MCA 1150)* <53029> **CAN'TCHA SAY (YOU BELIEVE IN ME). / STILL IN LOVE** [ ] Mar87 [20]
(12"+=) *(MCAT 1150)* – Cool the engines.
(cd-s+=) *(DMCA 1150)* – The launch: Countdown – Ignition – Third stage separation.

— Early in '90 SCHOLZ (aka BOSTON) won $million lawsuit against CBS.

RTZ

— (RETURN TO ZERO) were formed by **BRAD + BARRY** with **BRIAN MAES** – keyboards / **TIM ARCHIBALD** – bass / **DAVID STEFANELLI** – drums

Giant Giant

Aug 91. (c-s,cd-s) <19273> **FACE THE MUSIC / RETURN TO ZERO** [–] [49]

Apr 92. (7") *(543918955-7)* <19051> **UNTIL YOUR LOVE COMES BACK AROUND. / EVERY DOOR IS OPEN** [ ] Jan92 [26]
(c-s+=)(12"+=/cd-s+=) *(543918955-4)(93624040-30/-42)* – Return to zero / ('A'extended).

Apr 92. (cd/c) <*(7599 24422-2/-4)*> **RETURN TO ZERO** [ ] Feb92 [ ]
– Face the music / There's another side / All you've got / This is my life / Rain down on me / Every door is open / Devil to pay / Until your love comes back around / Livin' for the rock'n'roll / Hard time (in the big house) / Return to zero.

May 92. (c-s,cd-s) <19112> **ALL YOU'VE GOT / LIVIN' FOR THE ROCK'N'ROLL** [–] [56]

BOSTON

— another comeback album with; **TOM SCHOLZ** – guitar, keyboards, bass, drums / **GARY 'PIHL'** – keyboards / **DAVID SIKES** – vocals, bass / **DOUG HOFFMAN** – drums / **FRAN COSMO + TOMMY FUNDERBURK** – vocals

M.C.A. M.C.A.

Jun 94. (cd/c) <*(MCD/MCC 10973)*> **WALK ON** [56] [7]
– I need your love / Surrender to me / Livin' for you / Walkin' at night / Walk on / Get organ-ized / Get reorgan-ized / Walk on (some more) / What's your name / Magdalene / We can make it.

Jul 94. (c-s) *(MCSC 1983)* <54803> **I NEED YOUR LOVE / WE CAN MAKE IT** [ ] Jun94 [51]
(cd-s+=) *(MCSTD 1983)* – The launch: The countdown – Ignition – Third stage separation.

— **CURLY SMITH** – drums; repl. HOFFMAN

not iss. Artemis

Aug 02. (cd) <*75114-2*> **CORPORATE AMERICA** [–] [42]
– I had a good time / Stare out your window / Corporate America / With you / Someone / Turn it off / Cryin' / Didn't mean to fall in love / You gave up on love / Livin' for you.

– compilations etc. –

Sep 79. (7"m) *Epic; (EPC 7888)* **DON'T LOOK BACK. / MORE THAN A FEELING / SMOKIN'** [ ] [–]

Apr 83. (7") *Old Gold; (OG 9299)* **MORE THAN A FEELING. / DON'T LOOK BACK** [ ] [–]

Aug 83. (d-c) *C.B.S.; (4022155)* **BOSTON / DON'T LOOK BACK** [ ] [–]

Aug 88. (3"cd-ep) *Epic;* <*34K 02355*> **MORE THAN A FEELING / FOREPLAY / LONG TIME** [–] [ ]

Jun 97. (cd/c) <*(484333-2/-4)*> **GREATEST HITS** [ ] [47]
– Tell me / Higher power / More than a feeling / Peace of mind / Don't look back / Cool the engines / Livin' for you / Feelin' satisfied / Party / Foreplay / Long time / Amanda / Rock/n'roll band / Smokin' / A man I'll never be / Star spangled banner / 4th of July reprise / Higher power.

David BOWIE

Born: DAVID ROBERT JONES, 8 Jan'47, Brixton, London. In 1964 he formed The KING BEES with schoolmate GEORGE UNDERWOOD but after one single they split when BOWIE joined The MANNISH BOYS. They also lasted half a year, DAVID going solo with backing from The LOWER THIRD. In early 1966, he became DAVID BOWIE and signed to 'Pye' although commercial success continued to elude him. After three years of trying, he finally charted with 'SPACE ODDITY', a classic that introduced his "MAJOR TOM" character. That year (1969) his father died, but he was compensated by the introduction to ANGIE, his future wife. Although he was regarded as one of the top newcomers to the rock/pop scene, it took him until 1972 to finally establish himself as *the* rock star. He formed his now famous backing band, The SPIDERS, and announced his bisexuality to the music press. The single, 'STARMAN', and parent album, 'ZIGGY STARDUST' (an archetype alter-ego), were to hit the UK top 10. By this stage he'd come a long way from being a 60's ANTHONY NEWLEY copyist, innovating a risqué, glam rock style and pioneering the 'feathercut', make-up for men and stage-mime (the latter being learnt from LINDSEY KEMP). Signed to 'R.C.A.', the company duly re-issued his past three albums which all broke into the UK charts and 'ALADDIN SANE' (1973) was the first of his many No.1 albums. 'DIAMOND DOGS' (1974) represented the finale of his futuristic concept work and bore the hit single, 'REBEL, REBEL', while the follow-up concert album, 'DAVID LIVE' (1974), documented the mammoth tour that followed. With 'YOUNG AMERICANS' in 1975, his music took a dramatic and not entirely well-received turn towards Philadelphia soul/disco. Nevertheless, the album hit No.2 in the UK and a collaborative single with JOHN LENNON, 'FAME', gave him a US No.1. BOWIE then made yet another about face; dallying briefly with themes of fascism and dictatorship, he recorded the stark 'STATION TO STATION' (1976) album, before relocating to Berlin with BRIAN ENO and continuing his move towards experimental/avant-garde rock. The resulting albums, 'LOW' and 'HEROES', both released in 1977, were fairly successful in the UK despite containing some of BOWIE's most uncommercial work to date. After a final album with ENO, BOWIE returned to more conventional rock, gaining another No.1 hit with his resurrection of Major Tom on 'ASHES TO ASHES' (1980). After a two and a half year hiatus, he returned with the NILE RODGERS-produced 'LET'S DANCE' album. A typically polished, 80's-sounding record, it featured the single 'CHINA GIRL', complete with controversial video (in 1977, BOWIE had originally collaborated on the track with IGGY POP for the wild man's 'The Idiot' album). The rest of BOWIE's 80's output was hardly essential and at the turn of the decade he set up the embarrassing TIN MACHINE project, a misguided attempt at a return to spontaneous rock'n'roll. Ignoring the critical barbs, he carried on with this set-up until 1991 but couldn't substantiate any major hits. The release of 'OUTSIDE' (1995), (a collaboration with his old mucker ENO) saw BOWIE back in critical favour, while 'EART HL ING' (1997) was an admirable attempt to incorporate cutting edge dance styles into his music, collaborating with drum 'n' bass don, A GUY CALLED GERALD. More recently and trying desperately to get his new material noticed by an ailing public (he was still excellent live), BOWIE delivered his final set towards the end of the 90's, 'HOURS . . .' – it had in fact been "years . . ." since his last great album. While 2002's 'HEATHEN' wasn't quite great, it was definitely getting there, a sure-footed beginning to a new decade which saw BOWIE revisiting his past in the shape of producer Tony Visconti. Although a fairly bold step for an artist of such tireless experimentation, the record was by no means a retreat into rose-tinted nostalgia. Visconti seemed to coax out the generous side to BOWIE's muse while utilising studio technology to achieve an authentic updating of the feel – if not quite the sound – of their 70's recordings. Also placing the record in a contemporary context were fairly radical reworkings of both Neil Young's 'I'VE BEEN WAITING FOR YOU' and early Pixies classic, 'CACTUS'. The partnership proved so successful in fact, that BOWIE and Visconti kept it going for 2003's 'REALITY', another very self-assured, if slightly more angular set which again featured some choice covers (Jonathan Richman's 'PABLO PICASSO' and George Harrison's 'TRY SOME, BUY SOME') and which suggested the veteran starman's retirement is more far off than ever. • **Songwriters:** He wrote all his own material even managing some for others (e.g. ALL THE YOUNG DUDES for (Mott The Hoople) / OH YOU PRETTY THINGS (Peter Noone) / THE MAN WHO SOLD THE WORLD / (Lulu) / PINK ROSE (Adrian Belew) / etc. He produced 'RCA' acts LOU REED (Transformer) / MICK RONSON (Slaughter on Tenth Avenue) / etc. BOWIE's cover album PIN-UPS featured SORROW (Merseys) / ROSALYN (Pretty Things) / HERE COMES THE NIGHT (Them) / SHAPES OF THINGS (Yardbirds) / FRIDAY ON MY MIND (Easybeats) / ANYWAY ANYHOW ANYWHERE + I CAN'T EXPLAIN (Who) / SEE EMILY PLAY (Pink Floyd) / WHERE HAVE ALL THE GOOD TIMES GONE (Kinks) / DON'T BRING ME DOWN + I WISH YOU WOULD (Pretty Things) / EVERYTHING'S ALRIGHT (Mojos) /. Other covers:- LET'S SPEND THE NIGHT TOGETHER (Rolling Stones) / KNOCK ON WOOD (Eddie Floyd) / ALABAMA SONG (Brecht-Weill) / DANCING IN THE STREET (Martha & The Vandellas). I FEEL FREE (Cream) / NITE FLIGHT (Scott Walker) / I KNOW IT'S GONNA HAPPEN SOMEDAY (Morrissey) / DON'T LET ME DOWN & DOWN (Tacha-Valmont) / THE SEEKER (Who). – TIN MACHINE :- He co-wrote with GABRELS except MAGGIE'S FARM (Bob Dylan) / WORKING CLASS HERO (John Lennon, who also co-wrote FAME for BOWIE in 1975) / IF THERE IS SOMETHING (Roxy Music). • **Trivia:** BOWIE'S acting career started in 1976 with the film 'THE MAN WHO FELL TO EARTH' and 'JUST A GIGOLO' (1978). After starring in stage production of ELEPHANT MAN in 1980, he returned to films THE HUNGER (1982) / MERRY XMAS MR. LAWRENCE (1983) / LABYRINTH (1986) / ABSOLUTE BEGINNERS (1986) / THE LAST TEMPTATION OF CHRIST (1989). In 1985, he was one of the major stars of LIVE AID concert, and co-sang on 'DANCIN' IN THE STREET' with MICK JAGGER.

Album rating: DAVID BOWIE (*4) / MAN OF WORDS, MAN OF MUSIC aka SPACE ODDITY (*6) / THE MAN WHO SOLD THE WORLD (*8) / HUNKY DORY (*9) / THE RISE AND FALL OF ZIGGY STARDUST . . . (*10) / ALADDIN SANE (*8) / BOWIE PIN-UPS (*5) / DIAMOND DOGS (*6) / DAVID LIVE (*5) / YOUNG AMERICANS (*6) / STATION TO STATION (*8) / LOW (*10) / HEROES (*9) / STAGE (*5) / LODGER (*4) / SCARY MONSTERS (AND SUPER CREEPS) (*8) / CHANGESONEBOWIE compilation (*10) / LET'S DANCE (*6) / TONIGHT (*4) / NEVER LET ME DOWN (*4) / CHANGESBOWIE compilation (*9) / Tin Machine: TIN MACHINE (*5) / TIN MACHINE II (*3) / OY, VEY BABY (*3) / David Bowie: BLACK TIE, WHITE NOISE (*5) / THE BUDDHA OF SUBURBIA soundtrack for TV (*5) / OUTSIDE (*6) / EART HL ING (*6) / HOURS . . . (*6) / HEATHEN (*7) / BEST OF BOWIE compilation (*8) / REALITY (*7)

DAVID BOWIE – vocals, acoustic guitar / with session people

Vocalion — not iss.

Jun 64. (7"; as DAVIE JONES with The KING BEES) *(Pop V 9221)* **LIZA JANE. / LOUIE LOUIE GO HOME** [ ] [–]
(re-iss. Sep78 on 'Decca'; F 13807)

Parlophone — not iss.

Mar 65. (7"; as The MANNISH BOYS) *(R 5250)* **I PITY THE FOOL. / TAKE MY TIP** [ ] [–]

Aug 65. (7"; as DAVY JONES) *(R 5315)* **YOU'VE GOT A HABIT OF LEAVING. / BABY LOVES THAT WAY** [ ] [–]

Pye — Warners

Jan 66. (7"; as DAVID BOWIE with The LOWER THIRD) *(7N 17020)* <5814> **CAN'T HELP THINKING ABOUT ME. / AND I SAID TO MYSELF** [ ] [ ]

Apr 66. (7") *(7N 17079)* **DO ANYTHING YOU SAY. / GOOD MORNING GIRL** [ ] [–]

Aug 66. (7") *(7N 17157)* **I DIG EVERYTHING. / I'M NOT LOSING SLEEP** [ ] [–]

Deram — Deram

Dec 66. (7") *(DM 107)* **RUBBER BAND. / THE LONDON BOYS** [ ] [–]

Feb 67. (7") <85009> **RUBBER BAND. / THERE IS A HAPY LAND** [–] [ ]

Apr 67. (7") *(DM 123)* **THE LAUGHING GNOME. / THE GOSPEL ACCORDING TO TONY DAY** [ ] [–]
(re-iss. Sep73; same); hit UK No.6 (re-iss. Jun82)

Jun 67. (lp; mono/stereo) *(DML/SML 1007)* **DAVID BOWIE** [ ] [–]
– Uncle Arthur / Sell me a coat / Rubber band / Love you till Tuesday There is a happy land / We are hungry men / When I live my dream / Little bombadier / Silly boy blue / Come and buy me toys / Join the gang / She's got medals / Maids of Bond Street / Please Mr. Gravedigger. *(re-iss. Nov69 on 'Philips'; SBL 7912) (re-iss. Aug84 lp/c; DOA 1) (cd-iss. Oct88; 800 087-2)*

Jul 67. (7") *(DM 135)* <85016> **LOVE YOU TILL TUESDAY. / DID YOU EVER HAVE A DREAM** [ ] [ ]

— (Jul68-Feb69) **BOWIE** formed FEATHERS with girlfriend **HERMOINE FARTHINGALE** + **JOHN HUTCHINSON** – bass. BOWIE went solo, recording solo album with session players **RICK WAKEMAN** – keyboards

Philips — Mercury

Jul 69. (7") *(BF 1801)* <72949> **SPACE ODDITY. / THE WILD EYED BOY FROM FREECLOUD** [5] [ ]

Nov 69. (lp) *(SBL 7912)* **DAVID BOWIE – MAN OF WORDS MAN OF MUSIC** [ ] [–]
– Space oddity / Unwashed and somewhat slightly dazed / Letter to Hermione / Cygnet committee / Janine / An occasional dream / The wild eyed boy from Freecloud / God knows I'm good / Memory of a free festival. *(re-iss. Nov72 as 'SPACE ODDITY' on 'RCA' lp/c; LSP/PK 4813) (hit No.17 UK + No.16 US; <ST 61246>) (re-iss. Oct84 on 'RCA' lp/c/cd; PL/PK/PD 84813) (re-iss. Apr90 on 'EMI' cd/c/lp; CD/TC+/EMC 3571) (+=)* – Conversation piece / Don't sit down. *(hit UK No.64) (cd re-iss. Sep97 on 'Premier-EMI'; CDP 791835-2)*

— **BOWIE** formed backing band **HYPE** with **TONY VISCONTI** – bass / **MICK RONSON** – guitar / **JOHN CAMBRIDGE** – drums

Mercury — Mercury

Mar 70. (7") *(MF 1135)* **THE PRETTIEST STAR. / CONVERSATION PIECE** [ ] [–]

— **MICK 'Woody' WOODMANSEY** – drums repl. CAMBRIDGE

Jun 70. (7") *(6052 026)* <73075> **MEMORY OF A FREE FESTIVAL (part 1). / (part 2)** [ ] [ ]

Jan 71. (7") *(6052 049)* **HOLY HOLY. / BLACK COUNTRY ROCK** [ ] [–]

Apr 71. (lp) *(6338 041)* <61325> **THE MAN WHO SOLD THE WORLD** [ ] [ ]
– The width of a circle / All the madmen / Black country rock / After all / Running gun blues / Saviour machine / She took me cold / The man who sold the world / The supermen. *(re-iss. Nov72 on 'RCA' lp/c; LSP/PK 4816) (hit No.26 UK) (re-iss. Apr83 on 'RCA' lp/c; INTS/INTK 5237) (hit UK 64) (re-iss. Oct84 on 'RCA Int.' lp/c/cd; NL/NK/PD 84654) (re-iss. Apr90 on 'EMI' cd/c/lp; CD/TC+/EMC 3573) (+=)* – Lightning frightening / Moonage daydream / Holy holy / Hang on to yourself. *(hit UK No.66) (cd re-iss. Sep97 on 'Premier-EMI'; CDP 791837-2)*

Jun 71. (7") <73175> **ALL THE MADMEN. /** [–] [ ]

— Became **SPIDERS FROM MARS (BOWIE, RONSON, WOODMANSEY), TREVOR BOULDER** – bass repl. VISCONTI

R.C.A. R.C.A.

Dec 71. (lp/c) *(SF/PK 8244) <AFL-1 4623>* **HUNKY DORY** [ ] [93]
– Changes / Oh! you pretty things / Eight line poem / Life on Mars? / Kooks / Quicksand / Fill your heart – Andy Warhol / Song for Bob Dylan / Queen bitch / The Bewlay Brothers. *(re-dist.Sep72 reached No.3 UK) (re-iss. Jan81 lp/c; INTS/INTK 5064) (hit No.32 UK) (pic-lp Apr84; BOPIC 2) (re-iss. Oct84 on 'RCA Int.' lp/c/cd; NL/NK/PD 83844) (re-iss. Apr90 on 'EMI' cd/c/lp; CD/TC+/EMC 3572) (+=)* – Bombers / The supermen (alt.) / Quicksand (demo) / The Bewlay Brothers (alt.). *(hit UK No.39) (cd re-iss. Sep97 on 'Premier-EMI'; LPCENT 21) (lp re-iss. Nov97 on 'E.M.I.'; CDP 791843-2)*

Jan 72. (7") *(RCA 2160) <74-0605>* **CHANGES. / ANDY WARHOL** [ ] Apr72 [66]
(re-iss. Dec74; same); reached No.41 UK

Apr 72. (7") *(RCA 2199) <74-0719>* **STARMAN. / SUFFRAGETTE CITY** [10] Jun72 [65]

Jun 72. (lp/c) *(SF/PK 8267) <AFL-1 4702>* **THE RISE AND FALL OF ZIGGY STARDUST AND THE SPIDERS FROM MARS** [5] [75]
– Five years / Soul love / Moonage daydream / Starman / It ain't easy / Lady Stardust / Star / Hang on to yourself / Ziggy Stardust / Suffragette city / Rock'n'roll suicide. *(re-iss. Jan81 lp/c; INTS/INTK 5063) (hit No.33 UK) (pic-lp Apr84; BOPIC 3) (re-iss. Oct84 on 'RCA Int.' lp/c/cd; NL/NK/PD 83843) (re-iss. Apr90 on 'EMI' cd+=/c+=/lp; CD/TC+/EMC 3577) <re-iss. Jun90 on 'Rykodisc'+=; 10134>; hit No.93.* – John, I'm only dancing (demo) / Velvet goldmine / Sweet head / Ziggy Stardust (demo) / Lady Stardust (demo). *(hit UK No.25) (re-iss. Feb97 on 'E.M.I.'; LPCENT 4)*

Sep 72. (7") *(RCA 2263)* **JOHN, I'M ONLY DANCING. / HANG ON TO YOURSELF** [12] [-]

Nov 72. (7") *(RCA 2302)* **THE JEAN GENIE. / ZIGGY STARDUST** [2] [-]

Nov 72. (7") *<74-0838>* **THE JEAN GENIE. / HANG ON TO YOURSELF** [-] [71]

Jan 73. (7") *<74-0876>* **SPACE ODDITY. / THE MAN WHO SOLD THE WORLD** [-] [15]

Apr 73. (7") *(RCA 2352)* **DRIVE-IN-SATURDAY. / ROUND AND ROUND** [3] [-]

— with guests **MIKE GARSON** – piano / **KEN FORDHAM** and **BUX** – saxophone, flute

Apr 73. (lp/c) *(RS/PK 1001) <AFL-1 4852>* **ALADDIN SANE** [1] May73 [17]
– Watch that man / Aladdin Sane (1913-1938-197?) / Drive-in Saturday / Panic in Detroit / Cracked actor / Time / The prettiest star / Let's spend the night together / The Jean genie / Lady grinning soul. *(re-iss. Feb81 on 'RCA Int.' lp/c; INTS/INTK 5067) (hit No.49 UK Feb82) (re-iss. Mar84 on 'RCA Int.' lp/c; NL/NK 83890) (pic-lp Apr84; BOPIC 1) (cd-iss. Jun85; PD 83890) (re-iss. Jul90 on 'EMI' cd/c/lp; CD/TC+/EMC 3579)(+=)* – (other rare tracks). *(hit UK No.43) (cd re-iss. Sep97 on 'Premier-EMI'; CDP 794768-2)*

Jun 73. (7") *<APBO 0001>* **TIME. / THE PRETTIEST STAR** [-] [ ]

Jun 73. (7") *(RCA 2316)* **LIFE ON MARS. / THE MAN WHO SOLD THE WORLD** [3] [-]

Aug 73. (7") *<APBO 0028>* **LET'S SPEND THE NIGHT TOGETHER. / LADY GRINNING SOUL** [-] [ ]

— **AYNSLEY DUNBAR** – drums repl. WOODY

Oct 73. (7") *(RCA 2424) <APBO 0160>* **SORROW. / AMSTERDAM** [3] Nov73 [ ]

Oct 73. (lp/c) *(RS/PK 1003) <AFL-1 0291>* **PIN-UPS** [1] [23]
– Rosalyn / Here comes the night / I wish you would / See Emily play / Everything's alright / I can't explain / Friday on my mind / Sorrow / Don't bring me down / Shapes of things / Anyway anyhow anywhere / Where have all the good times gone!. *(re-iss. Sep81 lp/c; RCA LP/K 3004) (re-iss. Apr83 on 'RCA Int.' lp/c; INTS/INTK 5236) (hit UK 57) (pic-lp Apr84; BOPIC 4) (re-iss. Jul90 on 'EMI' cd/c/lp; CD/TC+/EMC 3580) (hit No.52)*

— **DUNBAR** and **TONY NEWMAN** – drums / **HERBIE FLOWERS** – bass / **MIKE GARSON** – keyboards

Feb 74. (7") *(LPBO 5009)* **REBEL REBEL. / QUEEN BITCH** [5] [-]

Apr 74. (7") *(LPBO 5021)* **ROCK'N'ROLL SUICIDE. / QUICKSAND** [22] [-]

May 74. (7") *<APBO 0287>* **REBEL REBEL. / LADY GRINNING SOUL** [-] [64]

May 74. (lp/c; as BOWIE) *(<APL/APK 1-0576>)* **DIAMOND DOGS** [1] [ ]
– Future legend / Diamond dogs / Sweet thing / Candidate / Sweet thing (reprise) / Rebel rebel / Rock'n'roll with me / We are the dead / 1984 / Big brother (including 'Chant of the ever circling skeletal family'). *(re-iss. Feb81 on 'RCA Int.' lp/c; INTS/INTK 5068) (hit UK 60 in May83) (re-iss. Mar84 on 'RCA Int.' lp/c/cd; NL/NK/PD 83889) (pic-lp Apr84; BOPIC 5) (re-iss. Jun90 on 'E.M.I.' cd/c/lp; CD/TC+/EMC 3584) (+=)* – Dodo / Candidate. *(hit UK No.67)*

Jun 74. (7") *(<APBO 0293>)* **DIAMOND DOGS. / HOLY HOLY** [21] [ ]

— added **EARL SLICK** – guitar / **DAVID SANBORN** – saxophone

Sep 74. (7") *(RCA 2466)* **KNOCK ON WOOD (live). / PANIC IN DETROIT (live)** [10] [-]

Oct 74. (7") *<10026>* **1984 (live). / QUEEN BITCH** [-] [ ]

Nov 74. (d-lp/c) *(<APL/APK 2-0771>)* **DAVID LIVE (live at the Tower theatre Philadelphia '74)** [2] [8]
– 1984 / Rebel rebel / Moonage daydream / Sweet thing / Changes / Suffragette city / Aladdin Sane (1913-1938-197?) / All the young dudes / Cracked actor / Rock'n'roll with me / Watch that man / Knock on wood / Diamond dogs/ Big brother / The width of a circle / The Jean genie / Rock'n'roll suicide. *(re-iss. May84 lp/c; PL/PK 80771) (re-iss. Jun90 on 'EMI' cd/c/d-lp+=; CD/TC+/DBLD 1)* – (band intro) / Here today, gone tomorrow / Time. *(re-iss. d-cd Jun95 on 'EMI'; same)*

Dec 74. (7") *<10105>* **ROCK'N'ROLL WITH ME (live). / PANIC IN DETROIT (live)** [-] [ ]

— **ANDY NEWMARK** – drums / **WILLIE WEEKS** – bass / **CARLOS ALOMAR** – guitar / **EARL SLICK** – guitar / guests **LUTHER VANDROSS + JOHN LENNON** – backing vocals

Feb 75. (7") *(RCA 2523)* **YOUNG AMERICANS. / SUFFRAGETTE CITY** [18] [-]

Mar 75. (7") *<10152>* **YOUNG AMERICANS. / KNOCK ON WOOD (live)** [-] [28]

Mar 75. (lp/c) *(APL/APK 1-1006) <0998>* **YOUNG AMERICANS** [2] [9]
– Young Americans / Win / Fascination / Right / Somebody up there like me / Across the universe / Can you hear me / Fame. *(re-iss. Sep81 lp/c; RCA LP/K 3009) (re-iss. Oct84 lp/c/cd; PL/PK/PD 80998) (re-iss. Apr91 on 'E.M.I.' cd+=/c+=/lp; CD/TC+/EMD 1021)* – Who can I be now? / John, I'm only dancing (again) (1975) / It's gonna be me. *(hit UK No.54)*

Jul 75. (7") *(RCA 2579) <10320>* **FAME. / RIGHT** [17] Jun75 [1]

Sep 75. (7"m) *(RCA 2593)* **SPACE ODDITY. / CHANGES / VELVET GOLDMINE** [1] [-]

— retained **SLICK + ALOMAR**

— **GEORGE MURRAY** – bass + **DENNIS DAVIS** – drums repl. WEEKS + NEWMARK

Nov 75. (7") *(RCA 2640) <10441>* **GOLDEN YEARS. / CAN YOU HEAR ME** [8] [10]

Jan 76. (lp/c) *(<APL/APK 1-1327>)* **STATION TO STATION** [5] [3]
– Station to station / Golden years / Word on a wing / TVC 15 / Stay / Wild is the wind. *(re-iss. Sep81 lp/c; RCA LP/K 3013) (re-iss. Oct84 lp/c/cd; PL/PK/PD 81327) (re-iss. Apr91 on 'E.M.I.' cd/c/lp; CD/TC+/EMD 1020) (+=)* – Word on the wing (live) / Stay (live). *(hit UK No.57)*

May 76. (7") *(RCA 2682) <10664>* **TVC 15. / WE ARE THE DEAD** [33] [64]

Jun 76. (lp/c) *(RS/PK 1055) <1732>* **CHANGESONEBOWIE** (compilation) [2] [10]
– Space oddity / John, I'm only dancing / Changes / Ziggy Stardust / Suffragette city / The Jean genie / Diamond dogs / Rebel rebel / Young Americans / Fame / Golden years. *(re-iss. May84 lp/c/cd; PL/PK/PD 81732)*

Jul 76. (7") *(RCA 2726)* **SUFFRAGETTE CITY. / STAY** [ ] [-]

Aug 76. (7") *<10736>* **STAY. / WORD ON A WING** [-] [ ]

— now collaborated with **BRIAN ENO** – synthesizers

— **RICKY GARDINER** – guitar repl. SLICK

Jan 77. (lp/c) *(PL/PK 12030) <2030>* **LOW** [2] [11]
– Speed of life / Breaking glass / What in the world / Sound and vision / Always crashing in the same car / Be my wife / A new career in a new town / Warszawa / Art decade / Weeping wall / Subterraneans. *(re-iss. Dec80 on 'RCA Int.' lp/c; INTS/INTK 5065) ;hit UK 85 in Jun83) (re-iss. Mar84 on 'RCA Int.' lp/c/cd; NL/NK/PD 83856) (re-iss. Aug91 on 'E.M.I.' cd/c/lp; CD/TC+/EMD 1027) (+=)* – (bonus tracks). *(hit UK No.64)*

Feb 77. (7") *(PB 0905) <10905>* **SOUND AND VISION. / A NEW CAREER IN A NEW TOWN** [3] [69]

Jun 77. (7") *(PB 1017) <11017>* **BE MY WIFE. / SPEED OF LIFE** [ ] [ ]

— next guest **ROBERT FRIPP** – guitar who repl. RICKY GARDINER.

Oct 77. (7") *(PB 1121) <11121>* **HEROES. / V2-SCHNEIDER** [24] [ ]

Oct 77. (lp/c) *(PL/PK 12522) <2522>* **HEROES** [3] [35]
– Beauty and the beast / Joe the lion / Heroes / Sons of the silent age / Blackout / V-2 Schneider / Sense of doubt / Moss garden / Neukoln / Black out / The secret life of Arabia. *(re-iss. Dec80 lp/c; INTS/INTK 5066)*

(hit UK 75 in Jun83) (re-iss. Nov84 lp/c/cd; NL/NK/PD 83857) (re-iss. Apr91 on 'E.M.I.' cd/c/lp; CD/TC+/EMD 1025) (+=) – Joe the Lion (1991 remix) / Abolumajor.

Jan 78. (7") *(PB 1190) <11190>* **THE BEAUTY AND THE BEAST. / SENSE OF DOUBT** [39] [ ]

—— added **ADRIAN BELEW** – guitar / **SIMON HOUSE** – violin (ex-HIGH TIDE, ex-HAWKWIND) / **SEAN MAYES** – piano

Sep 78. (d-lp,yellow-d-lp/d-c) *(PL/PK 02913) <2913>* **STAGE (live)** [5] [44]
– Hang on to yourself / Ziggy Stardust / Five years / Soul love / Star / Station to station / Fame / TVC 15 / Warszawa / Speed of life / Art decade / Sense of doubt / Breaking glass / Heroes / What in the world / Blackout / Beauty and the beast. *(re-iss. Jul84 d-lp/cd; PL/PD 89002) (re-iss. Feb92 on 'EMI' d-cd/c; CD/TC EMD 1030)* – (bonus tracks).

Oct 78. (7"ep) *(BOW 1)* **BREAKING GLASS (live). / ZIGGY STARDUST (live) / ART DECADE (live)** [54] [–]

Apr 79. (7") *(BOW 2) <11585>* **BOYS KEEP SWINGING. / FANTASTIC VOYAGE** [7] [ ]

May 79. (lp/c) *(BOW LP/K 1) <3254>* **LODGER** [4] [20]
– Fantastic voyage / African night flight / Move on / Yassassin / Red sails / D.J. / Look back in anger / Boys keep swinging / Repetition / Red money. *(re-iss. May82 on 'RCA Int.' lp/c; INTS/INTK 5212) (re-iss. Mar84 on 'RCA Int.' lp/c/cd; NL/NK/PD 84234) (re-iss. Aug91 on 'E.M.I.' cd/c/lp; CD/TC+/EMD 1026)* – (2 tracks).

Jul 79. (7",7"green) *(BOW 3)* **D.J. / REPETITION** [29] [–]

Aug 79. (7") *<11661>* **D.J. / FANTASTIC VOYAGE** [–] [ ]

Oct 79. (7") *<11724>* **LOOK BACK IN ANGER. / REPITITION** [–] [ ]

Dec 79. (7"/ext.12") *(BOW 4/12-4)* **JOHN, I'M ONLY DANCING (AGAIN) (1975). / JOHN, I'M ONLY DANCING (1972)** [12] [–]

Jan 80. (7") *<11887>* **JOHN, I'M ONLY DANCING (1972). / JOE THE LION** [–] [ ]

Feb 80. (7") *(BOW 5)* **ALABAMA SONG. / SPACE ODDITY** [23] [ ]

—— guest **ROBERT FRIPP** – guitar repl. BRIAN ENO

Aug 80. (7") *(BOW 6)* **ASHES TO ASHES. / MOVE ON** [1] [–]

Sep 80. (7") *<12078>* **ASHES TO ASHES. / IT'S NO GAME** [–] [ ]

Sep 80. (lp/c) *(BOW LP/K 2) <3647>* **SCARY MONSTERS** [1] [12]
– It's no game (No.1) / Up the hill backwards / Scary monsters (and super creeps) / Ashes to ashes / Fashion / Teenage wildlife / Scream like a baby / Kingdom come / Because you're young / It's no game (No.2). *(re-iss. Oct84 lp/c/cd; PL/PK/PD 83647) (re-iss. Jun92 on 'EMI' cd/c; CD/TC EMD 1029) (+=)* – Space oddity / Panic in Detroit / Crystal Japan / Alabama song.

Oct 80. (7"/12") *(BOW/+T 7) <12134>* **FASHION. / SCREAM LIKE A BABY** [5] [70]

Jan 81. (7"/c-s) *(BOW/+C 8)* **SCARY MONSTERS (AND SUPER CREEPS). / BECAUSE YOU'RE YOUNG** [20] [–]

Mar 81. (7"/c-s) *(BOW/+C 9)* **UP THE HILL BACKWARDS. / CRYSTAL JAPAN** [32] [–]

—— (next single "UNDER PRESSURE" was a No.1 collaboration w/ "QUEEN")

Nov 81. (7"/12") *(BOW/+T 10)* **WILD IS THE WIND. / GOLDEN YEARS** [24] [–]

Nov 81. (lp/c) *(BOW LP/K 3) <4202>* **CHANGESTWOBOWIE** (compilation) [24] [68]
– Aladdin Sane / Oh you pretty things / Starman / 1984 / Ashes to ashes / Sound and vision / Fashion / Wild is the wind / John, I'm only dancing (again) (1975) / D.J. *(re-iss. May84 lp/c/cd; PL/PK/PD 84202)*

Feb 82. (7"ep) *(BOW 11)* **BAAL'S HYMN** [29] [–]
– Baal's hymn / Remembering Marie / Ballad of the adventurers / The drowned girl / The dirty song.

Apr 82. (7"/ext.12") *(MCA/+T 770) <52024>* **CAT PEOPLE (PUTTING OUT FIRE). / PAUL'S THEME (by GIORGIO MORODER)** [26] [67]

—— (above single taken from the feature film of the same name on 'MCA-UK' / 'Backstreet' US)

Nov 82. (7"/12"; by DAVID BOWIE & BING CROSBY) *(BOW/+T 12) <13400>* **PEACE ON EARTH – LITTLE DRUMMER BOY. / FANTASTIC VOYAGE** [3] [ ]
(cd-s iss.Oct02 on 'Oglio'+=; OGL 85001) – (video).

—— now with **NILE RODGERS** + **STEVIE RAY VAUGHAN** – guitar / **BERNARD EDWARDS** + **CARMINE ROJAS** – bass / **OMAR HAKIM** + **TONY THOMPSON** – drums / **SAMMY FIGUEROA** – percussion

EMI America | EMI America

Mar 83. (7"/12"/c-s) *(EA/12EA/45-TCEA 152) <8158>* **LET'S DANCE. / CAT PEOPLE (PUTTING OUT FIRE)** [1] [1]

Apr 83. (lp/pic-lp/c) *(AML/AMLP/TCAML 3029) <17093>* **LET'S DANCE** [1] [4]
– Modern love / China girl / Let's dance / China girl / Without you / Ricochet / Criminal world / Cat people (putting out fire) / Shake it. *(cd-iss. Jan84; CDP 7460022) (re-iss. cd Nov95 on 'Virgin American'; CDVUS 96) (cd re-iss. Jan98 on 'E.M.I.'; 493094-2)*

Jun 83. (7"/7"pic-d/12") *(EA/EAP/12EA 157) <8165>* **CHINA GIRL. / SHAKE IT** [2] [10]

Sep 83. (7"/12") *(EA/12EA 158) <8177>* **MODERN LOVE. / MODERN LOVE (live)** [2] [14]

Feb 84. (7") *<8190>* **WITHOUT YOU. / CRIMINAL WORLD** [–] [73]

—— retained **HAKIM, ROJAS, FIGUEROA** / brought back **ALOMAR** and recruited **DEREK BRAMBLE** – bass, snyths, etc.

Sep 84. (7"/12") *(EA/12EA 181) <8231>* **BLUE JEAN. / DANCING WITH THE BIG BOYS** [6] [8]

Sep 84. (lp/c)(cd) *(DB/TCDB 1)(CDP 746047-2) <17138>* **TONIGHT** [1] [11]
– Loving the alien / Don't look down / God only knows / Tonight / Neighbourhood threat / Blue Jean / Tumble and twirl / I keep forgetting / Dancing with the big boys. *(re-iss. cd Nov95 on 'Virgin American'; CDVUS 97) (cd re-iss. Jan 98 on 'E.M.I.'; 493102-2)*

Nov 84. (7") *(EA 187) <8246>* **TONIGHT. / TUMBLE AND TWIRL** [53] [53]
(12") *(12EA 187)* – ('A'vocal dance mix) / ('B'extended dance mix) / ('A'dub mix).

—— (next single, from the film "Falcon And The Snowman")

Jan 85. (7"/12"; by DAVID BOWIE with The PAT METHENY GROUP) *(EA 190) <8251>* **THIS IS NOT AMERICA. / ('A'instrumental by The PAT METHENY GROUP)** [14] [32]

May 85. (7"/7"pic-d) *(EA/+P 195) <8271>* **LOVING THE ALIEN. / DON'T LOOK DOWN** [19] [ ]
(ext.12"+=/ext.12"sha-pic-d+=) *(12EA/+P 195)* – ('A'extended dub mix).

Sep 85. (7"; by DAVID BOWIE & MICK JAGGER) *(EA 204) <8288>* **DANCING IN THE STREET (Clearmountain mix). / ('A'instrumental)** [1] [7]
(12") *(12EA 204)* – ('A'-Steve Thompson mix) / ('A'dub version) / ('A'edit).
(below single from 'Virgin' records film & album of the same name, cont. 3 BOWIE tracks, album reached No.19 UK)

Mar 86. (7"/7"sha-pic-d)(ext.12") *(VS/+S 838)(VS 838-12) <8308>* **ABSOLUTE BEGINNERS. / ('A'dub version)** [2] [53]
(re-iss. 3"cd-s Nov88; CDT 20)

—— (below single from the feature film "Labyrinth" which cont. 5 BOWIE tracks, album reached No.38 UK)

—— now with **ALOMAR, ROJAS** + **ERDAL KIZILCAY** – keyboards / **PHILIPPE SAISSE** – keyboards, etc. / **PETER FRAMPTON** – guitar

Jun 86. (7"/7"sha-pic-d) *(EA/+P 216) <8323>* **UNDERGROUND. / ('A'instrumental)** [21] [ ]
(ext.dance-12"+=) *(VS 906-12)* – ('A'dub).

—— (the next, was from animated film of the same name on 'Virgin')

Nov 86. (7"/7"sha-pic-d) *(VS/+S 906)* **WHEN THE WIND BLOWS. / ('A'instrumental)** [44] [–]
(12"+=) *(VS 906-12)* – ('A'dub).

Mar 87. (7"/7"red) *(EA/+X 230) <8380>* **DAY-IN DAY-OUT. / JULIE** [17] [21]
(ext.dance-12"+=/remix-12"+=)(ext.dance c-s+=) *(12EA/+X 230)(TCEA 230)* – ('A'extended dub).

Apr 87. (lp/c/cd) *(AMLS/TCAMLS/CDAMLS 3117) <17267>* **NEVER LET ME DOWN** [6] [34]
– Day-in day-out / Time will crawl / Beat of your drum / Never let me down / Zeroes / Glass spider / Shining star (makin' my love) / New York's in love / '87 and cry / Bang bang / Too dizzy. *(cd+=)* – Time will crawl (extended dance) / Never let me down (version) / Day-in day-out (Groucho mix).*(re-iss. cd Nov95 on 'Virgin American'; CDVUS 98) (cd re-iss. Jan98 on 'E.M.I.'; 493097-2)*

Jun 87. (7"/7"w-poster) *(EA/+P 237) <43020>* **TIME WILL CRAWL. / GIRLS** [33] [ ]
(12") *(12EA 237)* – ('A'extended dance mix) / ('A'version) / ('B'extended).
(12") *(12EAX 237)* – ('A'dance crew mix) / ('A'dub) / ('B'-Japanese version).

Aug 87. (7"/7"pic-d) *(EA/+P 239) <43031>* **NEVER LET ME DOWN. / '87 AND CRY** [34] [27]
(c-s+=) *(TCEA 239)* – Time will crawl (extended dance mix) / Day-in day-out (Groucho mix).
(ext.dance-12"+=) *(12EA 239)* – ('A'dub) / ('A'acappella).

TIN MACHINE

was the name of **BOWIE's** next project/band. **DAVID BOWIE** – vocals, saxophone / **REEVES GABRELS** – lead guitar / **TONY SALES** – bass / **HUNT SALES** – drums (both ex-IGGY POP, ex-TODD RUNDGREN RUNT)plus p/t member **KEVIN ARMSTRONG** – guitar

Manhattan Manhattan

May 89. (cd/c/lp) *(CD/MC+/MTLS 1044)* <91990> **TIN MACHINE** [3] [28]
– Heaven's in here / Tin machine / Prisoner of love / Crack city / I can't read / Under the god / Amazing / Working class hero / Bus stop / Pretty thing / Video crimes / Run * / Sacrifice yourself * / Baby can dance. *(cd+= *) (re-iss. cd Nov95 on 'Virgin American'; CDVUS 99)*

Jun 89. (7"/c-s) *(MT/TCMT 68)* **UNDER THE GOD. / SACRIFICE YOURSELF** [51] [ ]
(10"+=/12"+=/cd-s+=) *(10/12/CD MT 68)* – (the interview).

Aug 89. (7"/7"s/7"sha-pic-d/c-s) *(MT/MTG/MTPD/TCMT 73)* **TIN MACHINE. / MAGGIE'S FARM (live)** [48] [ ]
(12"+=) *(12MT 73)* – I can't read (live).
(cd-s++=) *(CDMT 73)* – Bus stop (live country version).

Oct 89. (7"/7"s/7"sha-pic-d/c-s) *(MT/MTS/MTPD/TCMT 76)* **PRISONER OF LOVE. / BABY CAN DANCE (live)** [ ] [ ]
(12"+=) *(12MT 76)* – Crack city (live).
(cd-s++=) *(CDMT 76)* – ('A'version).

London Victory

Aug 91. (7"/12") *(LON/+X 305)* **YOU BELONG IN ROCK'N'ROLL. / AMLAPURA** [33] [ ]
(pic-cd+=) *(LONCD 305)* – Stateside / Hammerhead.

Sep 91. (cd/c/lp) *(828 272-2/-4/-1)* <511216> **TIN MACHINE II** [23] [ ]
– Baby universal / One shot / You belong in rock'n'roll / If there is something / Amlapura / Betty wrong / You can't talk / Stateside / Shopping for girls / Big hurt / I'm sorry / Goodbye Mr. Ed / Hammerhead.

Oct 91. (7"/c-s) *(LON/+CS 310)* **BABY UNIVERSAL. / YOU BELONG IN ROCK'N'ROLL** [48] [ ]
(12") *(LONT 310)* – ('A'side) / A big hurt (live) / ('A'live).
(cd-s) *(LONCD 310)* – ('A'side) / Stateside (live) / If there is something (live) / Heaven's in here (live).

— In Feb'92, BOWIE's song 'SOUND AND VISION (remix)' was re-done with himself and 808 STATE on label 'Tommy Boy'.

Jul 92. (cd/c/lp) *(828 328-2/-4/-1)* <480004> **TIN MACHINE LIVE – OY VEY, BABY (live)** [ ] [ ]
– If there is something / Amazing / I can't read / Stateside / Under the god / Goodbye Mr. Ed / Heaven's in here / You belong in rock'n'roll.

DAVID BOWIE

(solo again) and starred in the film 'THE LINGUINI INCIDENT'.

Warners Warners

Aug 92. (7"/c-s) *(W 0127/+C)* **REAL COOL WORLD. / ('A'instrumental)** [53] [ ]
(12") *(W 0127T)* – ('A'club) / ('A'dub thing 1 & 2) / ('A'dub overture).
(cd-s+=) *(W 0127CD)* – (2 more 'A'mixes).

— with **NILE RODGERS** – guitar, co-producer / **DAVE RICHARDS + RICHARD HILTON + PHILIPPE SAISSE + RICHARD TEE** – keyboards / **BARRY CAMPBELL + JOHN REGAN** – bass / **PUGI BELL + STERLING CAMPBELL** – drums / **GERADO VELEZ** – percussion. Plus guests **MICK RONSON** – guitar / **LESTER BOWIE** – trumpet / **REEVES GABRELS** – guitar / **MIKE GARSON** – piano / **AL B.SURE!** – vocals / **WILD T.SPRINGER** – guitar

Savage-BMG Savage-BMG

Mar 93. (c-s) *(74321 139424)* **JUMP THEY SAY. / PALLAS ATHENA (Don't Stop Praying mix)** [9] [ ]
(cd-s+=) *(74321 139422)* – ('A'-Hard Hands mix) / ('A'-JAE-E remix).
(cd-s) *(74321 139432)* – ('A'-Brothers In Rhythm mix) / ('A'-Brothers In Rhythm instrumental) / ('A'-Leftfield vocal) / ('A'ext).
(12") *(74321 139424-1)* – ('A'-Hard Hands mix) / ('A'version) / ('A'-Leftfield 12" vocal) / ('A'-extended).

Apr 93. (cd/c/lp) *(<74321 13697-2/-4/-1>)* **BLACK TIE WHITE NOISE** [1] [39]
– The wedding / You've been around / I feel free / Black tie white noise / Jump they say / Nite flight / Pallas Athena / Miracle tonight / Don't let me down & down / Looking for Lester / I know it's gonna happen someday / The wedding song / Jump they say (alternate mix) / Lucy can't dance.

Jun 93. (7"/c-s) *(74321 14868-7/-4)* **BLACK TIE WHITE NOISE. / YOU'VE BEEN AROUND (Jack Dangers remix)** [36] [ ]
(cd-s+=) *(74321 14868-2)* – ('A'extended remix) / ('A'-Urban).
(12") *(74321 14868-1)* – ('A'extended) / ('A'trance mix) / ('A'version) / ('A'club mix with AL B.SURE!) / ('A'extended urban mix).

Oct 93. (7"/c-s) *(74321 16226-7/-4)* **MIRACLE TONIGHT. / LOOKING FOR LESTER** [40] [ ]
(cd-s+=) *(74321 16226-2)* – ('A'-Philly mix) / ('A'-Masereti mix).
(12") *(74321 16226-1)* – ('A'-Blunted mix) / ('A'-Make believe mix) / ('A'-Philly mix) / ('A'dance dub).

Nov 93. (7"/c-s) *(74321 17705-7/-4)* **BUDDHA OF SUBURBIA. / DEAD AGAINST IT** [35] [ ]
(cd-s+=) *(74321 17705-2)* – South horizon / ('A'-Lenny Kravitz rock mix).

Nov 93. (cd/c) *(74321 17004-2/-4)* **BUDDHA OF SUBURBIA (TV soundtrack)** [ ] [–]
– Buddah of suburbia / Sex and the church / South horizon / The mysteries / Bleed like a craze, dad / Strangers when we meet / Read against it / Untitled No.1 / Ian Fish / UK heir / Buddah of suburbia (featuring LENNY KRAVITZ).

— now with **ENO** – synthesizers, co-writer (on most) / **REEVES GABRELS / ERDAL KIZILCAY / MIKE GARSON / STERLING CAMPBELL / CARLOS ALOMAR / JOEY BARON / YOSSI FINE**

R.C.A. Virgin

Sep 95. (c-s/cd-s) *(74321 30703-4/-2)* **THE HEARTS FILTHY LESSON / I AM WITH NAME** [35] [–]
(cd-s+=) *(74321 30703-2)* – ('A'-Bowie mix) / ('A'-Trent Reznor alt.remix) / ('A'-Tony Maserati remix).
(12"pic-d) *(74321 30703-1)* – (5-'A'mixes; Bowie / alt. / Rubber / Simple text / Filthy).

Sep 95. (cd/c/d-lp) *(<74321 30702-2/-4/-1>)* **OUTSIDE** [8] [21]
– THE NATHAN ADLER DIARIES: A Hyper Cycle:- Leon takes us outside / Outside / The hearts filthy lesson / A small plot of land / segue – Baby Grace (a horrid cassette) / Hallo spaceboy / The motel / I have not been to Oxford Town / No control / segue – Algeria touchshriek / The voyeur of utter destruction (as beauty) / segue – Ramona A. Stone – I am with name / Wishful beginnings / We prick you / segue – Nathan Adler / Strangers when we meet.

Sep 95. (c-s) <38518> **THE HEARTS FILTHY LESSON / NOTHING TO BE DESIRED** [–] [92]

Nov 95. (7"/c-s) *(74321 32940-7/-4)* **STRANGERS WHEN WE MEET. / THE MAN WHO SOLD THE WORLD (live)** [39] [ ]
(cd-s+=) *(74321 32940-2)* – ('A'side again) / Get real.
(12") *(74321 32940-1)* – ('A'side) / The seeker / Hang ten high.

Feb 96. (7"pink/c-s) *(74321 35384-7/-4)* **HALLO SPACEBOY. / THE HEARTS FILTHY LESSON** [12] [ ]
(cd-s+=) *(74321 35384/-2)* – Moonage daydream (live) / Under pressure (live).
below a collaboration with A GUY CALLED GERALD. His main band:- REEVES GABRELS, MIKE GARSON + ZACHARY ALFORD + GAIL ANN DORSEY – vocals

Nov 96. (12"/cd-s) *(74321 39741-1/-2)* **TELLING LIES (mixes; Paradox / Feelgood / Adam F)** [ ] [–]

Jan 97. (12"/cd-s) *(74321 45207-1/-2)* **LITTLE WONDER. / TELLING LIES (Adam F mix)** [14] [ ]
(cd-s) *(74321 45208-2)* – ('A'mixes by Junior Vasquez & Danny Saber) / Jump they say (Leftfield mix).

Feb 97. (cd/c) *(<74321 44944-2/-4>)* **EART HL ING** [6] [39]
– Little wonder / Looking for satellites / Battle for Britain (the letter) / Seven years in Tibet / Dead man walking / Telling lies / Last thing you should do / I'm afraid of Americans / Law (earthlings on fire).

Apr 97. (12"/cd-s) *(74321 47584-1/-2)* **DEAD MAN WALKING. / TELLING LIES** [32] [ ]
(cd-s) *(74321 47585-2)* – ('A'mixes) / I'm deranged / Heart's filthy lesson.

Aug 97. (12"clear/cd-s) *(74321 51254-7/-2)* **SEVEN YEARS IN TIBET (mixes; Mandarin). / PALLAS ATHENA** [61] [ ]

Nov 97. (c-s,cd-s) <38618> **I'M AFRAID OF AMERICANS (versions V1, V2, V3 – with ICE CUBE, V4, V5, V6)** [–] [56]

Velvel not iss.

Feb 98. (cd-ep) *(ZYX 87578)* **I CAN'T READ (short & long version) / THIS IS NOT AMERICA** [73] [–]

Virgin Virgin

Sep 99. (c-s/cd-s) *(VSC/+DT 1753)* **THURSDAY'S CHILD / WE ALL GO THROUGH / NO ONE CALLS** [16] [–]
(cd-s) *(VSCDTX 1753)* – ('A'-Rock mix) / We shall all go to town / 1917 / ('A'-CD-Rom video).

Oct 99. (cd/c) *(CDV/TCV 2900)* <48157> **HOURS . . .** [5] [47]
– Thursday's child / Something in the air / Survive / If I'm dreaming my life / Seven / What's really happening? / The pretty things are going to hell / New angels of promise / Brilliant adventure / The dreamers.

— in Dec'99, BOWIE and QUEEN were back in the charts (UK No.14) with the remix of 'Under Pressure'

Jan 00. (cd-s) *(VSCDT 1767)* **SURVIVE / SURVIVE (Marius De Vries mix) / THE PRETTY THINGS ARE GOING TO HELL (from 'The Matrix')** [28] [ ]
(cd-s) *(VSCDX 1767)* – ('A'side) / Thursday's child (live) / Seven (live).

Jul 00. (cd-s) *(VSCDT 1776)* **SEVEN (mixes; Marius DeVries / Beck / demo)** [32] [ ]
(cd-s) *(VSCDX 1776)* – ('A'mix) / I'm afraid of Americans (Nine Inch Nails mix).
(cd-s) *(VSCDXX 1776)* – ('A'mix) / ('A'live) / Something in the air (live) / Pretty things are going to hell (live).

— in May'02, SCUMFROG feat. BOWIE on hit version of 'LOVING THE ALIEN'

I.S.O. – Columbia / I.S.O. – Columbia

Jun 02. (cd/lp) *(508222-2/-1)* <86630> **HEATHEN** [5] [14]
– Sunday / Cactus / Slip away / Slow burn / Afraid / I've been waiting for you / I would be your slave / I took a trip on a Gemini spaceship / 5.15 the angels have gone / Everyone says 'Hi' / A better future / Heathen (the rays). *(d-cd+=; 508222-9)* – Sunday (Moby remix) / Better future (air remix) / Conversation piece / Panic in Detroit (1979 recording).

Sep 02. (cd-s) *(673134-2)* **EVERYONE SAYS 'HI' / SAFE / WOOD JACKSON** [20] [–]
(cd-s) *(673134-5)* – ('A'side) / Baby loves that way / You've got a habit of leaving.
(cd-s) *(673134-3)* – ('A'side) / When the boys come marching home / The shadow man.

— in Jul'03, DAVID GUETTA vs BOWIE hit the UK Top 75 with 'JUST FOR ONE DAY (HEROES)'

Sep 03. (cd) *(512555-2)* <90576> **REALITY** [3] [29]
– New killer star / Pablo Picasso / Never get old / The loneliest guy / Looking for water / She'll drive the big car / Days / Fall dogs bombs the moon / Try some, buy some / Reality / Bring me the disco king.

Sep 03. (dvd-s) *(674279-9)* **NEW KILLER STAR (video) / REALITY / LOVE MISSILE F1-11** [ ] [–]

– compilations, etc. –

note; All below on 'RCA' unless otherwise mentioned

Mar 70. (lp; mono/stereo)(c) *Decca; (PA/SPA 58)(KCSP 58)* **THE WORLD OF DAVID BOWIE** [ ] [–]

May 75. (d-lp) *Decca; (DPA 3017-8) / London; <628-9>* **IMAGES 66-67** [ ] [ ]

Dec 80. (lp/c) *K-Tel; (NE/+C 1111)* **THE BEST OF DAVID BOWIE** [3] [–]

Apr 81. (lp/c) *Decca; (TAB/KTAB 17)* **ANOTHER FACE** [ ] [–]

Apr 81. (lp) *(BL 43606)* **CHRISTIANE F. – WIR KINDER VOM BAHNHOF ZOO (soundtrack)** [–] Europe [–]

Dec 82. (10x7"pic-d-singles) *(BOW 100)* **FASHIONS** [ ] [–]
– SPACE ODDITY / LIFE ON MARS / THE JEAN GENIE / REBEL REBEL / SOUND & VISION / DRIVE-IN SATURDAY / SORROW / GOLDEN YEARS / BOYS KEEP SWINGING / ASHES TO ASHES

Jan 83. (lp/c) *(PL/PK 45406)* **RARE** [34] [–]

Aug 83. (lp/c) *(BOW LP/K 004)* <4792> **GOLDEN YEARS (live recent)** [33] [99]

Aug 83. (lp) *Decca Rock Echoes; (TAB 71)* **A SECOND FACE** [ ] [–]

Oct 83. (d-lp/d-c) *(PL/PK 84862)* <4862> **ZIGGY STARDUST – THE MOTION PICTURE (live '73 film)** [17] [89]
(cd-iss. Sep92 on 'EMI'; CDP 780411-2)

Oct 83. (7") *(RCA 372)* <13660> **WHITE LIGHT WHITE HEAT (live). / CRACKED ACTOR (live)** [46] [ ]

Apr 84. (lp/c/cd) *(PL/PK/PD 84919)* <4919> **FAME AND FASHION (ALL TIME GREATEST HITS)** [40] [ ]

May 84. (lp/c) *Deram; (BOWIE/BOWMC 1)* **LOVE YOU TILL TUESDAY (soundtrack)** [53] [–]

Sep 89. (cd) *Rykodisc; <0120>* **SOUND + VISION** [–] [97]

Mar 90. (c-s/7") *EMI-USA; (TC+/FAME 90)* **FAME 90 (Gass mix). / ('A'-Queen Latifah's version)** [28] [ ]
(cd-s+=) *(CDFAME 90)* – ('A'house mix) / ('A'hip hop mix).
(12") *(12FAME 90)* – ('A'side) / ('A'house) / ('A'hip hop).
(7"pic-d) *(FAMEPD 90)* – ('A'side) / ('A'-bonus beats mix).

Apr 90. (cd/c/d-lp) *E.M.I.; (CD/TC+/DBTV 1) / Rykodisc; <20171>* **CHANGESBOWIE** [1] [39]
– Space oddity / John, I'm only dancing / Changes / Ziggy stardust / Suffragette city / The Jean genie / Diamond dogs / Rebel rebel / Young Americans / Fame ('90 remix) / Golden years / Heroes / Ashes to ashes / Fashion / Let's dance / China girl / Modern love / Blue Jean.

Nov 93. (d-cd/d-c/t-lp) *E.M.I.; (7243 828099-2/-4/-1)* **THE SINGLES COLLECTION** [9] [ ]
(re-iss. Nov95 d-cd/d-c/t-lp; CD/TC+/EM 1512)

May 94. (cd/c/d-lp) *Trident; (GY/+MC/LP 002)* **SANTA MONICA '72 (live)** [74] [–]

Oct 97. (cd/c) *E.M.I.; (821849-2/-4)* **THE BEST OF DAVID BOWIE 1969-1974** [13] [ ]

Apr 98. (cd/c) *E.M.I.; (494300-2/-4)* **THE BEST OF DAVID BOWIE 1974-1979** [39] [ ]

Sep 00. (3xcd-box) *E.M.I.; (528958-2) / Virgin; <28958>* **BOWIE AT THE BEEB – THE BEST OF THE BBC RECORDINGS 1968-1972** [7] [ ]

Nov 02. (d-cd) *E.M.I.; (539821-2)* **BEST OF BOWIE** [11] [ ]

BOWLING FOR SOUP

Formed: Wichita Falls, Texas, USA ... 1994 by frontman/songwriter JARET REDDICK and ERIK CHANDLER. Starting out as a hard touring covers/comedy act, BFS built up a grassroots following in the Texas backwaters before undertaking their first major, credit card-financed tour in 1997. Although they'd previously released a self-financed eponymous debut album in 1994, their first widely available records were 1998's 'TELL ME WHEN TO WHOA!' EP and 'ROCK ON HONOURABLE ONES!!!' long player, both issued on local indie label 'FFROE'. Yes, these guys loved their exclamation marks – not a great sign. Their debut for 'Jive', 'LET'S DO IT FOR JOHNNY!' (2000) brought yet more exclamation marks, "zany" humour and derivative punk-lite. By this point, CHRIS BURNEY and GARY WISEMAN (aka GARY WISEASS, titter titter) were also onboard and of course there was the obligatory Bryan Adams cover ('SUMMER OF '69'). 'DRUNK ENOUGH TO DANCE' went UK Top 20 in 2002; perhaps it should've been titled 'Drunk Enough To Listen'. • **Covered:** I RAN (SO FAR AWAY) (Flock Of Seagulls).

Album rating: ROCK ON HONORABLE ONES!!! (*4) / LET'S DO IT FOR JOHNNY! (*5) / DRUNK ENOUGH TO DANCE (*6)

JARET REDDICK – vocals, guitar / **CHRIS BURNEY** – guitar, vocals / **ERIK CHANDLER** – bass / unknown drummer

not iss. / F.F.R.O.E.

1998. (cd-ep) **TELL ME WHEN TO WHOA!** [–] [ ]
– Suckerpunch / Soho / You and me / Dance with you / Belgium / Everything / Andrew.

Jan 98. (cd) **ROCK ON HONORABLE ONES!!!** [–] [ ]
– 2113 / Scope / Valentino / Corndog / Cody / Belgium / Milo / Captain Hook / Ack!! / Thespian / Kool-aid / I don't know / Wisk / Ass man / Friday.

— **GARY WISEMAN** – drums; repl. original

Music For Nations / Jive-Zomba

Aug 00. (cd-s) *(CDKUT 182)* <26023> **THE BITCH SONG** [ ] [ ]

Aug 00. (cd) *(CDMFN 263)* <41707> **LET'S DO IT FOR JOHNNY!** [ ] May00 [ ]
– Suckerpunch / The bitch song / Pictures he drew / Dance with you / You and me / Scope / Valentino / Belgium / Andrew / Boulevard / Hang on / Summer of '69 / All figured out.

Aug 02. (c-s) *(TKUT 194)* <926036> **GIRL ALL THE BAD GUYS WANT / OTHER GIRLS (version)** [8] Sep02 [64]
(cd-s+=) *(CDKUT 194)* – Emily.
(cd-s) *(CDXKUT 194)* – ('A'side) / Greatest day (from the Britney movie 'Crossroads') / The bitch song (video).

Aug 02. (cd) *(CDMFN 282)* <41819> **DRUNK ENOUGH TO DANCE** [14] [ ]
– I don't wanna rock / Emily / Girl all the bad guys want / On and on (about you) / Surf Colorado / Life after Lisa / Where to begin / The last rock show / Self-centered / The hard way / Out the window / Cold shower Tuesdays / Running from your dad / Scaring

myself / She's got a boyfriend now / Last rock show / The greatest day.

Nov 02. (c-s/cd-s) *(T/CD KUT 198)* **EMILY / MILO** [67] [–]
(cd-s) *(CDXKUT 198)* – ('A'side) / Change my mind / Capt. Hook.

Aug 03. (cd-s) *(CDKUT 203)* **PUNK ROCK 101 / I RAN (SO FAR AWAY) / STAR SONG / ('A'-video)** [43] [–]

☐ BOXCAR RACER (see under ⇒ BLINK 182)

BOX TOPS

Formed: Memphis, Tennessee, USA . . . 1967 originally as RONNIE & THE DeVILLES. They signed to 'Bell' label offshoot 'Mala', and with the legendary DAN PENN and SPOONER OLDHAM writing/producing, the band soon topped the US chart with their debut 45, 'THE LETTER', which subsequently became a well covered standard for many artists. Throughout the 60's, they had a large number of hits, with CHILTON virtually taking over the reins just prior to their 1969 demise. CHILTON headed back to Memphis, where he hooked up with his old schoolfriend CHRIS BELL to form the hugely influential but desperately unlucky BIG STAR. The first two albums sounded like a rougher take on the pop sensibilities of The BEATLES and The BEACH BOYS, with the 1972 debut 'NO.1 RECORD', especially, having great commercial potential. Guitarist BELL acted as a foil for CHILTON's inspired outpourings and the album contained such acoustic gems as 'BALLAD OF EL GOODOO'. Despite garnering rave reviews, the album failed to sell, due almost wholly to the distribution problems of their label 'Ardent' (a 'Stax' offshoot). BELL left at the end of '72, after a fallout with CHILTON over live work, the upshot being that BIG STAR became CHILTON's "power-pop" baby. Generally thought to be his artistic peak, early '74's 'RADIO CITY' had a gloriously raw spontaneity, with 'SEPTEMBER GURLS' proving the pained highlight. Distribution problems continued to dog Ardent and as the record stiffed, BIG STAR gradually broke up. Although released under the BIG STAR moniker, 'BIG STAR'S THE THIRD ALBUM', later re-released as 'SISTER LOVERS', was more or less the work of CHILTON. A difficult album, although none the less rewarding, it showcased a vulnerable man exorcising his demons in haunting and deeply introspective songs. CHRIS BELL's similarly downbeat 'I AM THE COSMOS', was recorded just before his death in a car accident in 1978, and was posthumously released by 'Rykodisc' in the early 90's. In 1979, CHILTON re-surfaced after a quiet period in New York, where his makeshift band toured with the likes of TELEVISION and The CRAMPS, whom he went on to produce. That same year saw him record the folk-punk 'BANGKOK' single and 'FLIES ON SHERBET', a cult classic which featured a hotch-potch of inspired covers and CHILTON originals. In the 80's, he worked with TAV FALCO under the name The PANTHER BURNS before releasing a solo album 'HIGH PRIEST' in 1987, a fairly enjoyable romp through a patchwork of ragged styles. The praise lavished upon BIG STAR by the likes of PRIMAL SCREAM and TEENAGE FANCLUB, brought about a renaissance of sorts, and CHILTON re-formed the band in 1993. He also released a further solo album in 1995, 'A MAN CALLED DESTRUCTION'. Carrying on CHILTON's vintage R&B fixation was 2000's 'LOOSE SHOES AND TIGHT PUSSY' (er, 'SET' in the US). If the music had been as inspired as the title, it might have appealed to more than just CHILTON diehards. As it was, the man who once sneered through 'THE LETTER', seemed content to continue meandering along on other people's material. • **Covered:** CHILTON covered many incl. HIDE & SEEK (Big Joe Turner).

Album rating: THE LETTER – NEON RAINBOW (*5) / CRY LIKE A BABY (*5) / NON-STOP (*4) / DIMENSIONS (*4) / THE BEST OF THE BOX TOPS compilation (*6) / Big Star: #1 RECORD (*7) / RADIO CITY (*7) / SISTER LOVERS – THIRD ALBUM (*8) / Alex Chilton: LIKE FLIES ON SHERBET (*3) / BLACK LIST (*4) / 19 YEARS: A COLLECTION compilation (*7) / Big Star: COLUMBIA: LIVE AT MISSOURI UNIVERSITY (*4) / BIG STAR STORY compilation (*6) / Alex Chilton: CLICHES (*5) / A MAN CALLED DESTRUCTION (*3) / LOOSE SHOES AND TIGHT PUSSY (*4)

ALEX CHILTON (b.28 Dec'50) – vocals, guitar / **JOHN EVANS** – organ / **GARY TALLEY** (b.17 Aug'47) – guitar / **BILL CUNNINGHAM** (b.23 Jan'50) – bass, piano / **DANNY SMYTHE** – drums

Stateside Mala-Bell

Sep 67. (7") *(SS 2044)* *<565>* **THE LETTER. / HAPPY TIMES** [5] Jul67 [1]

Nov 67. (7") *(SS 2070)* *<580>* **NEON RAINBOW. / SHE KNOWS HOW** [ ] [24]

Jan 68. (lp; stereo/mono) *(S+/SL 10218)* *<6011>* **THE LETTER – NEON RAINBOW** [ ] Nov67 [87]
– The letter / She knows how / Trains & boats & planes / Break my mind / A whiter shade of pale / Everything I am / Neon rainbow / People make the world / I'm your puppet / Happy times / Gonna find somebody / I pray for rain. *<(cd-iss. Feb00 on 'Sundazed'+=; SC 6158)>* – Turn on a dream / The letter / Neon rainbow / Georgia farm boy.

Bell Mala

Mar 68. (7") *(BLL 1001)* *<593>* **CRY LIKE A BABY. / THE DOOR YOU CLOSED ON ME** [15] [2]

Apr 68. (lp; mono/stereo) *(M/S BLL 105)* *<6017>* **CRY LIKE A BABY** [ ] [59]
– Cry like a baby / Deep in Kentucky / I'm the one for you / Weeping Analeah / Every time / Fields of clover / Trouble with Sam / Lost / Good morning dear / 727 / You keep me hanging on / The door you closed to me. *<(cd-iss. Feb00 on 'Sundazed'+=; SC 6159)>* – Cry like a baby (mono) / The door you closed to me / You keep tightening up on me / Come on honey / Take me to your heart.

May 68. (7") *(BLL 1017)* *<12005>* **CHOO CHOO TRAIN. / FIELDS OF CLOVER** [ ] [26]

— **RICK ALLEN** (b.28 Jan'46, Little Rock, Arkansas) – organ, drums repl. EVANS **TOM BOGGS** (b.16 Jul'47, Wynn, Arkansas) – drums repl. SMYTHE (both return to college)

Sep 68. (7") *(BLL 1035)* *<12017>* **I MET HER IN CHURCH. / PEOPLE GONNA TALK** [ ] [37]

Oct 68. (lp; mono/stereo) *(M/S BLL 108)* *<6023>* **NON-STOP** [ ] [ ]
– Choo choo train / I'm movin' on / Sandman / She shot a hole in my soul / People gonna talk / I met her in church / Rock me baby / Rollin' in my sleep / I can dig it / Yesterday / Where's my mind / If I had let you in. *<(cd-iss. Feb00 on 'Sundazed'+=; SC 6160)>* – Let me go / Choo choo train (mono) / I met her in church (mono) / Got to hold on to you / Since I been gone.

Dec 68. (lp) *<6025>* **SUPER HITS** (compilation) [–] [45]
– The letter / Trains & boats & planes / Break my mind / A whiter shade of pale / She sot a hole in my soul / Neon rainbow / Cry like a baby / I'm your puppet / I met her in church / You keep me hanging on / Choo choo train. *(UK-iss.1970 mono/stereo; M/S BLL 129)*

Jan 69. (7") *(BLL 1045)* *<12035>* **SWEET CREAM LADIES, FORWARD MARCH. / SANDMAN** [ ] Dec68 [28]

Mar 69. (7") *(BLL 1063)* *<12038>* **I SHALL BE RELEASED. / I MUST BE THE DEVIL** [ ] [67]

— **JERRY RILEY** – guitar; repl. TALLEY

Jul 69. (7") *(BLL 1068)* *<12040>* **SOUL DEEP. / HAPPY SONG** [22] [18]

Oct 69. (7") *(BLL 1084)* *<12042>* **TURN ON A DREAM. / TOGETHER** [ ] [58]

Oct 69. (lp) *(SBLL 120)* *<6032>* **DIMENSIONS** [ ] Sep69 [77]
– Soul deep / I shall be released / Midnight angel / Together / I'll hold out my hand / I must be the Devil / Sweet cream ladies, forward march / The happy song / Ain't no way / Rock me baby. *<(cd-iss. Feb00 on 'Sundazed'+=; SC 6161)>* – King's highway / Soul deep / Sweet cream ladies, forward march / I see only sunshine / Lay your shine on me.

Jul 70. (7") *(BLL 1097)* *<865>* **YOU KEEP TIGHTENING UP ON ME. / COME ON HONEY** [ ] Mar70 [92]

— CHILTON (now the only original member), ALLEN, BOGGS and RILEY brought in **SWAIN SCHAEFER** – piano / **HAROLD CLOUD** – bass (both) repl. CUNNINGHAM

Sep 71. (lp) *(BELLS 149)* **BOX TOPS** [ ] [–]
– The letter / Cry like a baby / Soul deep / I'm movin' on / Lost / A whiter

shade of pale / Together / The happy song / Fields of clover / Weeping Analeah / I'll hold out my hand / I pray for rain.

– compilations, etc. –

Jan 73. (7") *London; (HLU 10402)* **SUGAR CREEK WOMAN. / IT'S ALL OVER** [ ] [–]
Jun 74. (lp) *Sound Superb; (SPR 90051)* **THE BEST OF THE BOX TOPS** [ ] [–]
May 78. (7") *Stiff; (BUY 28)* **CRY LIKE A BABY. / THE LETTER** [ ] [–]
Mar 82. (7") *J.B.; (JB 04)* **THE LETTER. / CRY LIKE A BABY** [ ] [–]
Jul 82. (7") *Old Gold; (OG 9116)* **THE LETTER. / CRY LIKE A BABY** [ ] [–]
Aug 82. (7"m) *Creole; (CR 178)* **THE LETTER. / (2 tracks by other artists)** [ ] [–]
Aug 82. (7"m) *Creole; (CR 179)* **CRY LIKE A BABY. / (2 tracks by other artists)** [ ] [–]
1988. (cd) *Warner Super Savers; (WSP 27611)* **THE ULTIMATE BOX TOPS** [ ] [–]
Nov 88. (lp) *Decal; (LIK 41)* **THE BEST OF THE BOX TOPS featuring ALEX CHILTON** [ ] [–]
– The letter / Neon rainbow / I pray for rain / The door you closed to me / Cry like a baby / Deep in Kentucky / Fields of clover / You keep me hangin' on / Choo choo train / I can dig it / Yesterday where's my mind / Soul deep / I shall be released / Together / I must be the Devil / Sweet cream ladies, forward march / Happy song.
Jun 89. (cd-ep) *Arista; (162071)* **THE LETTER / HAPPY TIMES / CRY LIKE A BABY / THE DOOR YOU CLOSED ON ME** [ ] [–]
Jun 99. (cd) *Camden-RCA; (74321 67452-2)* **SOUL DEEP (THE BEST OF THE BOX TOPS)** [ ] [–]
(lp-iss.Jun01 von 'Simply Vinyl'; SVLP 345)

BIG STAR

CHRIS BELL (b.12 Jan'51, Memphis) – vocals, guitar; repl. JOHN LIGHTMAN / plus **ALEX CHILTON / ANDY HUMMEL** (b.26 Jan'51) – bass / **JODY STEPHENS** (b. 4 Oct'52) – drums

not iss. Ardent

Apr 72. (lp) *<ADS 1501>* **#1 RECORD** [–] [ ]
– Feel / The ballad of El Goodo / In the street / Don't lie to me / Thirteen / The India song / When my baby's beside me / My life is right / Give me another chance / Try again / Watch the sunrise / St 100-6. *(re-iss. Nov86 & Jan90 on 'Big Beat' lp/c; WIK/+C 53) <(cd-iss. May02 on 'Akarma'; AK 028CD)>*
Apr 72. (7") *<2902>* **IN THE STREET. / WHEN MY BABY'S BESIDE ME** [–] [ ]
Jul 72. (7") *<2904>* **DON'T LIE TO ME. / WATCH THE SUNRISE** [–] [ ]

—— now trio when BELL left to go solo, He's killed in car crash 27th Dec'78.

Feb 74. (lp) *<ADS 2803>* **RADIO CITY** [–] [ ]
– O, my soul / Life is white / Way out west / What's going on / You got what you deserve / Mod Lang / Back of a car / Daisy glaze / She's a mover / September gurls / Morpha too – I'm in love with a girl. *(re-iss. Nov86 & Mar95 on 'Big Beat' lp/c; WIK/+C 54) <(cd-iss. May02 on 'Akarma'; AK 029)>*
Feb 74. (7") *<2909>* **O, MY SOUL. / MORPHATOO – I'M IN LOVE WITH A GIRL** [–] [ ]
May 74. (7") *<2912>* **SEPTEMBER GURLS. / MOD LANG** [–] [ ]
(UK-iss.Sep78 on 'Stax'; *STAX 504)*
1974. (7"; as BOX TOPS) *<0199>* **WILLOBEE AND DALE. / I'M GONNA BE ALRIGHT** [–] [ ]

—— ALEX CHILTON now sole BIG STAR with session people, incl. JODY STEPHENS + STEVE CROPPER. In 1975, after recording below album, they disbanded. It was finally released.

Aura P.V.C.

Jul 78. (lp) *(AUL 703) <7903>* **BIG STAR'S THE THIRD ALBUM** [ ] [ ]
– Stroke it Noel / For you / Kizza me / You can't have me / Nightime / Blue moon / Take care / Jesus Christ / Femme fatale / O Dana / Big black car / Holocaust / Kangaroo / Thank you friends. *(re-iss. 1987 on 'Dojo' lp/cd; DOJO LP/CD 55) <US re-iss. Nov87 lp/c/cd; PVC/+C/CD 8917> (UK cd-iss. Mar92 & Apr97 on 'Rykodisc'; RCD 10220) (cd re-iss. Oct94 on 'Line'; LICD 900492)*
Jul 78. (7") *(AUS 103)* **KIZZA ME. / DREAM LOVER** [ ] [–]
Dec 78. (7") *(AUS 107)* **JESUS CHRIST. / BIG BLACK CAR** [ ] [–]

ALEX CHILTON

went solo in 1977, with **RICHARD ROSEBROUGH** – drums / etc.

not iss. Ork

1977. (lp) *<81978>* **ONE DAY IN NEW YORK** [–] [ ]
1977. (12"ep) **SINGER NOT THE SONG** [–] [ ]

Aura Peabody

Feb 80. (lp) *(AUL 710)* **LIKE FLIES ON SHERBET** [ ] [–]
– Boogie shoes / My rival / Hey! little child / Hook or crook / I've had it / Rock hard / Girl after girl / Waltz across Texas / Alligator man / Like flies on sherbet. *(cd-iss. Sep92 on 'Great Expectations'+=;)* – No more the Moon shines on Lorena. *(cd re-iss. Oct94 on 'Line'; LICD 900486) (cd re-iss. Jan96 on 'Cooking Vinyl'; COOKCD 095) <(lp re-iss. Dec97 on 'Munster'; MR 137)>*
Jun 80. (7") *(AUS 117)* **HEY! LITTLE CHILD. / NO MORE THE MOON SHINES ON LORENA** [ ] [ ]

—— with **KNOX** – guitar / **MATTHEW SELIGMAN** – bass + **MORRIS WINDSOR** – drums

Line not iss.

1981. Line; (lp) *<OLLP 5081>* **BACH'S BOTTOM** (rec.1975) [–] German [–]
– Take me home / Make me like it / Everytime I close my eyes / All of the time / Oh baby I'm free / I'm so tired (parts 1 & 2) / Free again / Jesus Christ / The singer not the song / Summertime blues / Take me home again. *(cd-iss. Nov87; LICD 900091) (cd re-iss. Mar97 & Aug99 on 'Razor & Tie'; RE 2010)*
Jan 83. (lp) *(OLLP 5264)* **LIVE IN LONDON (live)** [ ] [ ]
– Bangkok / Tramp / In the street / Hey little child / Nightime / Rock hard / Alligator man / The letter / Train kept a rollin' / Kanga roo / My rival / Stranded on a dateless night / September gurls / No more the Moon shines on Lorena. *(cd-iss. May93 on 'Rev-Ola'; CREV 015CD)*

New Rose Big Time

Jul 85. (m-lp) *(ROSE 68)* **FEUDALIST TARTS** [–] France [–]
– Tee ni nee ni noo – Tip on in / Stuff / B-A-B-Y / Thank you John / Lost my job / Paradise. *(cd-iss. 1986 as 'STUFF'; ROSE 68CD)* – (with 10 extra tracks).
May 86. (7") *(NEW 068)* **NO SEX. / UNDERCRASS** [–] France [–]
(12"+=) *(NEW12 068)* – Wild kingdom.
(d7"+=) *(NEW 69)* – September gurls / I'm gonna make you mine (live Paris'85).
Nov 87. (7") *(NEW 96)* **MAKE A LITTLE MOVE. / LONELY WEEKENDS** [–] France [–]
Nov 87. (lp/c/cd) *(ROSE 130/+C/CD)* **HIGH PRIEST** [–] France [–]
– Take it off / Let me get close to you / Dalai Lama * / Volare / Thing for you / Forbidden love / Make a little love / Trouble don't last / Don't be a drag / Nobody's fool / Come by here / Raunchy / Junkyard * / Lonely weekends / Margie * / Rubber room *. *(cd+= *)*
Feb 88. (d7"-ltd) *(NEW 102)* **DALAI LAMA. / MARGIE / / JUNKYARD. / RUBBER ROOM** [–] France [–]
Jan 90. (m-lp/cd) *(ROSE 194/+CD)* **BLACKLIST** [–] France [–]
– Little GTO / Guantanamerika / Jailbait / Baby baby baby / Nice and easy does it / I will turn your money green.
(above cont.some covers). In 1992 CHILTON resurrected BIG STAR (see below).

New Rose Ardent

Feb 94. (cd) *(5481) <71606>* **CLICHES** [ ] [ ]
– My baby just cares for me / Time after time / All of you / Gavotte / Save your love for me / Lets get lost / Funny (but I still love you) / Frame for the blues / The Christmas song / There will never be another you / Somewhere along the way / What was.

Ruf not iss.

Jun 95. (cd) *(RRCD 90131-2)* **A MAN CALLED DESTRUCTION** [ ] [–]
– Sick and tired / Devil girl / Lies / It's your funeral / What's your sign girl / Il Ribelle / You don't have to go / Boplexity / New girl in school / You're lookin' good / Don't know anymore / Don't stop.

Shoeshine not iss.

Oct 96. (7") *(SHOE 005)* **MARGIE. / HIDE & SEEK** [ ] [–]

Axe Killer Bar/None

Oct 99. (cd) *(AXE 3052552CD) <110>* **LOOSE SHOES AND TIGHT PUSSY** <US title 'SET'> [ ] Feb00 [ ]
– Never found a girl / Lipstick traces / Hook me up / OOgum boogum / You's a viper / I remember mama / April in Paris / There will never be another you / Single again / You've got a booger bear under there / Shiny stockings / Goodnight my love. *<(10"lp-iss.Feb00 on 'Munster'; MR 174)> <(re-iss. Mar00 on 'Last Call'; 305255-2)>*

– compilations etc. –

Sep 85. (lp/cd) *Aura; (AURA 732)* **DOCUMENT** ☐ ☐-
– Kizza me / Downs / Holocaust / Big black car / Kangaroo / Dream lover / My rival / Hey little child / Hook or crook / Like flies on sherbet / Bangkok / September gurls / In the street.
Mar 86. (d-lp) *Fan Club; (FC 015)* **LOST DECADE (1969-77)** ☐- France ☐-
May 91. (cd/c) *Rhino; <R2/R4 70780>* **19 YEARS (1969-87)** ☐- ☐
Feb 92. (cd) *New Rose;* **ALEX CHILTON** ☐- French ☐-
Mar 96. (cd) *Rev-ola; (CREV 044CD)* **1970** ☐ ☐-
Mar 97. (cd) *Razor & Tie; (RE 2032)* **FEUDALISTIC TARTS / NO SEX** ☐ ☐-
Mar 97. (cd) *Razor & Tie; (RE 2033)* **HIGH PRIEST / BLACKLIST** ☐ ☐-
May 97. (d-cd) *Arcade; (302108-2)* **TOP 30** ☐ ☐-
Jan 03. (d-cd) *Castle; (CMRDD 645) / Earmark; <42019>* **LIKE FLIES ON SHERBET / LIVE IN LONDON** ☐ ☐

BIG STAR

re-formation with **CHILTON / JONATHAN BAUER** – guitar, vocals / **KEN STRINGFELLOW** – guitar, bass (ex-POSIES)

Zoo Zoo

Sep 93. (cd/c) *<(11060-2/-4)>* **LIVE AT MISSOURI UNIVERSITY (4.25.93) (live)** ☐ ☐
– In the street / Don't lie to me / When my baby's beside me / I am the cosmos / The ballad of El Goodo / Back of a car / Way out west / Daisy glaze / Baby strange / For you / Fool / September gurls / Thank you friends / Slut / Jeepster.

—— CHILTON teamed up with VEGA (from SUICIDE) and BEN VAUGHN on album 'CUBIST BLUES' for 'Last Call'; (7422466)

– compilations etc. –

Jul 78. (d-lp) *Stax; (SXSP 302)* **#1 RECORD / RADIO CITY** ☐ ☐
(cd-iss. Jun87 & Jan90 on 'Big Beat'; CDWIK 910) – (omits; In the street / St 100-6.
1988. (lp) *Line; (LILP 400509)* **BIG STAR'S BIGGEST** ☐- German ☐-
– The ballad of El Goodo / In the street / Don't lie to me / When my baby's beside me / Try again / Watch the sunrise / Life is white / What's goin' ahn / Back of a car / She's a mover / Way out west / September gurls / Jesus Christ / O'Dana / Holocaust / Kangaroo / Big black car / Thank you friends. *(UK cd-iss. Oct94; LICD 900509)*
Mar 92. (cd) *Rykodisc; (RCD 10221)* **BIG STAR LIVE (live)** ☐ ☐-
(re-iss. Apr97; same)
Mar 99. (cd) *Norton; <(CED 265)>* **NOBODY CAN DANCE** (live 1971 without BELL) ☐ ☐
Dec 99. (cd) *Big Beat; (CDWIKK 197)* **THE BEST OF BIG STAR** ☐ ☐-
Sep 03. (cd) *Rykodisc; <(RCD 10640)>* **BIG STAR STORY** ☐ ☐
– September gurls / Thank you friends / Don't lie to me / Ballad of El Goodo / Holocaust / I am the cosmos / In the street / You get what you deserve / Thirteen / You & your sister / Back of a car / Jesus Christ / Mod Lang / Baby strange / O Dana / Motel blues / Nightime / Hot thing.

BOY GEORGE

Born: GEORGE O'DOWD, 14 Jun'61, Eltham, Kent, England. Ironically the son of a boxing club manager, GEORGE became a familiar face on London's turn of the decade New Romantic scene, MALCOLM McLAREN even picking him out for a brief tenure in BOW WOW WOW (as LIEUTENANT LUSH) before the cross-dressing gender-bender formed his own outfit, IN PRAISE OF LEMMINGS alongside MIKEY CRAIG and JOHN SUEDE. Wisely, they soon opted for the moniker CULTURE CLUB instead as ex-DAMNED drummer JON MOSS was brought into the fold and ROY HAY replaced SUEDE. After having their demos turned down by 'E.M.I.', the group secured a contract with 'Virgin' in 1982 and proceeded to fire a couple of chart blanks in the shape of 'WHITE BOY' and 'I'M AFRAID OF ME'. Much more potent was 'DO YOU REALLY WANT TO HURT ME', a winning combination of white cod-reggae and candy-coated soul-pop that topped the UK chart and sold millions around the world. Decked out in flowing tunics and striking make-up, the dread-locked BOY GEORGE became an overnight sensation on the still fairly conservative MTV, beguiling fans by sheer force of his charisma and a lilting, sensual vocal style that transformed the often fairly average songs/arrangements. In retrospect, it's still surprising how big America was on CULTURE CLUB, almost putting second single, 'TIME (CLOCK OF THE HEART)' atop the chart at the tail end of '82 and affording a US issue of 'DO YOU REALLY..' the same treatment. The accompanying album, 'KISSING TO BE CLEVER' (1982) went Top 5 in the UK, Top 20 in America and CULTURE CLUB were ready to take on the world. The following year saw a slew of hits breach the Top 10 on both sides of the Atlantic, 'CHURCH OF THE POISON MIND', 'I'LL TUMBLE 4 YA' and the evergreen 'KARMA CHAMELEON', a transatlantic No.1. All three were lifted from sophomore effort, 'COLOUR BY NUMBERS' (1983), female backing vocalist HELEN TERRY adding an extra dimension to the established sound. After hitting such stratospheric peaks, however, the only way was down; as a sweetener for third album, 'WAKING UP WITH THE HOUSE ON FIRE' (1984), 'WAR SONG' left a sour taste in the mouth, at least for critics, who derided the sanctimonious inanity of its anti-war "message". Although both single and album made the No.2 position in the UK (they were already beginning to flag across the pond), a second single, 'THE MEDAL SONG', didn't even make the Top 30. The band's final two years were characterised by BOY GEORGE's worsening drug addiction and inter-band tension, their final album, 'FROM LUXURY TO HEARTACHE' (1986), drawing enthusiasm from only the most ardent of fans. The shit really hit the fan(s) later that summer when GEORGE's heroin problem had the tabloids sharpening their claws. He was easy prey, especially after being arrested for possession of cannabis. If that wasn't bad enough, keyboard player, MIKE RUDETSKI was found dead from a drugs overdose in GEORGE's house only days later. Amid the scandal, CULTURE CLUB officially split in Spring '87 with GEORGE pursuing a solo career. Although his first effort – a tame cover of 'EVERYTHING I OWN' – topped the chart, successive singles met with diminishing returns and the album, 'SOLD' (1987) barely scraped the Top 30. 'Virgin' kept the faith though, furnishing the man with his own label, 'More Protein'. This functioned as a platform for his new project, JESUS LOVES YOU, (re)born of GEORGE's newfound interest in the Hare Krishna religion. Surprisingly, perhaps, some of his most interesting compositions surfaced during this period, not least the acid-house influenced 'GENERATIONS OF LOVE' and the joyous 'BOW DOWN MISTER', which gave him a rare Top 30 hit in Spring '91. Having finally come to terms with his drug problem, GEORGE became increasingly focused on DJ'ing, making a name for himself on the burgeoning UK club scene. Save for a genius one-off cover of Dave Berry's 'THE CRYING GAME' (featured on the brilliant UK film of the same name) in 1992, it would be the mid-90's before the 34 year-old star released another solo album, 'Virgin' once again home for the largely ignored 'CHEAPNESS AND BEAUTY' (1995). Over the course of the next few years, GEORGE concentrated on DJ'ing and made his name as a top draw for many of the "superclubs", signing a lucrative deal with 'Ministry Of Sound' in Spring '96. A year on, his long drawn-out court battle with former "mate" KIRK BRANDON (ex-SPEAR OF DESTINY) came to an end when the judge dismissed BRANDON's objections to GEORGE's published comments regarding their former relationship. It was inevitable that GEORGE and his former CULTURE CLUB bandmates would make up, the lure of the lucre tempting the band to re-form in summer 1998 for massive sell-out concerts in Monte Carlo and America. A new single, 'I JUST WANNA BE LOVED', subsequently hit the UK Top 5 which prompted 'Virgin' to re-package their greatest hits in lieu of a flop new album, 'DON'T MIND IF I DO' (1999). • **Songwriters:** All written by GEORGE and HAY except STARMAN (David Bowie). GEORGE solo covered EVERYTHING I OWN (Bread; hit. Ken Boothe) / WHAT BECOMES OF THE BROKEN HEARTED (Jimmy Ruffin) / THE CRYING GAME (Dave Berry) / MY SWEET LORD (George Harrison) / FUNTIME (Iggy Pop) and co-wrote with DUST & THEWLIS. • **Trivia:** In 1988, BOY GEORGE protested about 'NO CLAUSE 28' law which the government used to ban homosexual literature. In 1989, he dueted with CONNIE FRANCIS on a version of Frank & Nancy Sinatra's 'Something Stupid'.

Album rating: Culture Club: KISSING TO BE CLEVER (*7) / COLOUR BY NUMBERS (*6) / WAKING UP WITH THE HOUSE ON FIRE (*5) / FROM LUXURY TO HEARTACHE (*4) / THIS TIME: THE FIRST 4 YEARS compilation (*7) / THE BEST OF CULTURE CLUB compilation (*6) / GREATEST MOMENTS compilation (*6) / DON'T MIND IF I DO (*5) / Boy George: SOLD (*4) / HIGH HAT (*3) / THE DEVIL IN SISTER GEORGE mini (*4) / CHEAPNESS AND BEAUTY (*3) / AT WORST . . . THE BEST OF BOY GEORGE & CULTURE CLUB compilation (*6) / Jesus Loves You: THE MARTYR MANTRAS (*4)

CULTURE CLUB

BOY GEORGE – vocals / **ROY HAY** (b.12 Aug'61) – guitar, keyboards (ex-RUSSIAN BOUQUET) repl. JOHN SUEDE / **MIKEY CRAIG** (b.15 Feb'60) – bass / **JON MOSS** (b.11 Sep'57) – drums, percussion (ex-EDGE, ex-DAMNED)

Virgin | Epic

May 82. (7"/12") *(VS 496/+12)* **WHITE BOY. / LOVE TWIST** [ ] [ ]

Jun 82. (7"/12") *(VS 509/+12)* **I'M AFRAID OF ME. / MURDER RAP TRAP** [ ] [ ]

Sep 82. (7"/7"pic-d) *(VS/+Y 518)* **DO YOU REALLY WANT TO HURT ME. / (dub version)** [1] [–]
(12"+=) *(VS 518-12)* – Love is cold (you were never so good).

Oct 82. (lp/c) *(V/TCV 2232)* *<38398>* **KISSING TO BE CLEVER** [5] Dec82 [14]
– White boy / You know I'm not crazy / I'll tumble 4 ya / Take control / Love twist / Boy boy (I'm the boy) / I'm afraid of me (remix) / White boys can't control it / Do you really want to hurt me. *(re-iss. 1987 lp/c; OVED/+C 209) (cd-iss. Jul87; CDV 2232) (cd re-iss. Oct96 on 'Virgin-VIP'; CDVIP 158)*

Nov 82. (7"/7"pic-d) *(VS/+Y 558)* **TIME (CLOCK OF THE HEART). / WHITE BOYS CAN'T CONTROL IT** [3] [–]
(12"+=) *(VS 558-12)* – Romance beyond the alphabet.

Nov 82. (7") *<03368>* **DO YOU REALLY WANT TO HURT ME. / YOU KNOW I'M NOT CRAZY** [–] [2]
(12") – ('A'side) / Love is cold (you were never no good).

Apr 83. (7") *<03796>* **TIME (CLOCK OF THE HEART). / ROMANCE BEYOND THE ALPHABET** [–] [2]

—— added guest vocalist **HELEN TERRY** in '83

Apr 83. (7"/7"pic-d) *(VS/+Y 571)* **CHURCH OF THE POISON MIND. / MAN SHAKE** [2] [–]
(12"+=) *(VS 571-12)* – Mystery boy.

Jun 83. (7") *<03912>* **I'LL TUMBLE 4 YA. / MYSTERY BOY** [–] [9]
(12"+=) - **Man shake.**

Sep 83. (7"/7"pic-d) *(VS/+Y 612)* *<04221>* **KARMA CHAMELEON. / THAT'S THE WAY** [1] Nov83 [1]
(12") *(VS 612-12)* – ('A'side) / I'll tumble 4 ya.

Oct 83. (7") *<04144>* **CHURCH OF THE POISONED MIND. / MYSTERY BOY** [–] [10]

Oct 83. (lp/c/cd/pic-lp) *(V/TCV/CDV/VP 2285)* *<39107>* **COLOUR BY NUMBERS** [1] [2]
– Karma chameleon / It's a miracle / Black money / Changing every day / That's the way (I'm only trying to help you) / Church of the poison mind / Miss me blind / Mister man / Stormkeeper * / Victims. *(c+=*/cd+=*) (re-iss. 1989 lp/c; OVED/+C 238) (cd re-iss. Feb92; CDV 2285) (cd re-iss. Dec98 on 'Virgin-VIP'; CDVIP 230)*

Nov 83. (7"/7"pic-d) *(VS/+Y 641)* **VICTIMS. / COLOUR BY NUMBERS** [3] [–]
(12"+=) *(VS 641-12)* – Romance revisited.

Feb 84. (7") *<04388>* **MISS ME BLIND. / COLOUR BY NUMBERS** [–] [5]

Mar 84. (7"/7"pic-d) *(VS/+Y 662)* *<04457>* **IT'S A MIRACLE. / LOVE TWIST (live)** [4] May84 [13]
(12"+=) *(VS 662-12)* – Miss me blind.

Sep 84. (7",7"red) *(VS 694)* *<04638>* **THE WAR SONG. / LA CANCION DE GUERRA** [2] [17]
(12"+=) *(VS 694-12)* – ('A'-Shriek mix).

Oct 84. (lp/c/cd/pic-lp) *(V/TCV/CDV/VP 2330)* *<39881>* **WAKING UP WITH THE HOUSE ON FIRE** [2] Nov84 [26]
– Dangerous man / The war song / Unfortunate thing / Crime time / Mistake No.3 / The dive / The medal song / Don't talk about it / Mannequin / Hello goodbye. *(re-iss. Jun88 lp/c; OVED/+C 184) (cd-iss. Aug98 on 'Virgin-VIP'; CDVIP 205)*

Nov 84. (7"/7"pic-d)(ext.12") *(VS/+Y 730)(VS 730-12)* **THE MEDAL SONG. / DON'T GO DOWN THAT STREET** [32] [–]

Nov 84. (7") *<04727>* **MISTAKE NO.3. / DON'T GO DOWN THAT STREET** [–] [33]

Mar 86. (7"/5"pic-d) *(VS/+X 845)* *<05847>* **MOVE AWAY. / SEXUALITY** [7] [12]
(12"+=) *(VS 845-12)* – ('A'-Tango dub remix).

Apr 86. (lp/c/cd) *(V/TC/CDV 2380)* *<40345>* **FROM LUXURY TO HEARTACHE** [10] [32]
– Move away / I pray / Work on me baby / Gusto blusto / Heaven's children / Thank God you woman / Reasons / Too bad / Come clean / Sexuality. *(c+=)* – Move away (remix) / Thank God you woman (remix). *(cd++=)* – Sexuality (remix). *(re-iss. 1989 lp/c; OVED/+C 251)*

May 86. (7"/7"pic-d)(12") *(VS/+Y 861)(VS 861-12)* **THANK GOD YOU WOMAN. / FROM LUXURY TO HEARTACHE** [31] [ ]

—— split in the Autumn of '86. MOSS formed HEARTBEAT UK while BOY GEORGE went solo

BOY GEORGE

—— solo although backed by WELL RED

Virgin | Virgin

Feb 87. (7") *(BOY 100)* **EVERYTHING I OWN. / USE ME** [1] [ ]
('A'-P.W. Botha mix; 12"+=) *(BOY 100-12)* – ('A'dub).

May 87. (7") *(BOY 101)* **KEEP ME IN MIND. / STATE OF LOVE** [29] [ ]
(ext; 12") *(BOY 101-12)* – I pray.
(c-s+=/12"pic-d+=) *(BOY C/Z 101-12)* – Everything I own.

Jun 87. (cd/c/lp) *(CD/TC+/V 2430)* *<90617>* **SOLD** [29] Jul87 [ ]
– Sold / I asked for love / Keep me in mind / Everything I own / Freedom / Just ain't enough / Where are you now? / Little ghost / Next time / We've got the right / To be reborn. *(cd re-iss. Aug98 on 'Virgin-VIP'; CDVIP 204)*

Jul 87. (7") *(BOY 102)* **SOLD. / ARE YOU TOO AFRAID** [24] [ ]
(12"+=/c-s+=) *(BOY/+C 102-12)* – Everything I own (go-go mix).

Nov 87. (7") *(BOY 103)* **TO BE REBORN. / WHERE ARE YOU NOW?** [13] [ ]
(12"+=) *(BOY 103-12)* –

Feb 88. (7") *(BOY 105)* *<99390>* **LIVE MY LIFE. / ('A'-Soul remix)** [62] Dec87 [40]
(12"+=) *(BOY 105-12)* – ('A'-Klub mix).
(12"+=) *(BOY 105-13)* – ('A'-Business mix) / ('A'-12"club).

Jun 88. (7") *(BOY 106)* **NO CLAUSE 28. / ('A'mix)** [57] [ ]
(ext; 12"+=/cd-s+=) *(BOY 106-12/CD 106)* – ('A'-beats mix).
(12"+=) *(BOY 106-13)* – ('A'-Emilio Pasquez space mix).

Sep 88. (7") *(BOY 107)* **DON'T CRY. / LEAVE IN LOVE** [ ] [ ]
(12"+=) *(BOY 107-12)* – ('A'&'B' versions).
(cd-s+=) *(BOYCD 107)* – ('A'&'B' versions) / A boy called Alice.

Feb 89. (7") *(BOY 108)* **DON'T TAKE MY MIND ON A TRIP. / GIRLFRIEND** [68] [ ]
(12"+=)(3"cd-s+=) *(BOY 108-12)(BOYCD 108)* – I go where I go.

Mar 89. (cd/c/lp) *(CD/TC+/V 2555)* *<91022>* **HIGH HAT** [ ] [ ]
– Don't cry / You are my heroin / I go where I go / Girl, with combination skin / Whisper / Something strange called love / I love you / Mama never knew / What becomes of the broken hearted. *(c+=/cd+=)* – American boys / Happy family.
(above was the withdrawn 'TENSE NERVOUS HEADACHE' set from last Oct)

—— BOY GEORGE then formed...

JESUS LOVES YOU

More Protein — not iss.

Nov 89. (7") *(PROT 2)* **AFTER THE LOVE. / ('A'version)** [68] [–]
(12"+=)(cd-s+=) *(PROT 2-12)(PROCD 2)* – ('A'version).

Jun 90. (7"/c-s) *(PRO T/C 5)* **GENERATIONS OF LOVE. / ('A'dub version)** [ ] [–]
(12"+=)(cd-s+=) *(PROT 5-12)(PROCD 5)* – ('A'-Sisters Of Mercy mix).

Nov 90. (7"/c-s) *(PRO T/C 7)* **ONE ON ONE. / ('A'-Massive mix)** [ ] [–]
(12"+=) *(PROT 7-12)* – Generations of love (90's mix).
(cd-s++=) *(PROCD 7)* – After the love.

Feb 91. (7"/c-s) *(PRO T/C 8)* **BOW DOWN MISTER. / LOVE HURTS** [27] [–]
(12"+=) *(PROT 8-12)* – ('A'mix).
(cd-s+=) *(PROCD 8)* – ('A'-different mix).

Apr 91. (cd/c/lp) *(CUM CD/TC/LP 1)* **THE MARTYR MANTRAS** [60] [–]
– Generations of love / One on one / Love's gonna let you down / After the love / I specialize in loneliness / No clause 28 / Love hurts / Siempre te amare / Too much love / Bow down mister. *(cd+=)* – Generations of love (90's mix).

May 91. (7") *(PROT 10)* **GENERATIONS OF LOVE. / ('A'mix)** [35] [–]
(12"+=) *(PROT 10-12)* – ('A'-Love dub mix).
(cd-s++=) *(PROCD 10)* – ('A'-different mixes).
(re-iss. 12" Aug96; PROT 115)

Sep 91. (7") **AFTER THE LOVE '91. / ('A'version)** [ ] [–]
(cd-s+=) – ('A'diff edit) / ('A'-10 glorious years mix).

BOY GEORGE

Spaghetti — S.B.K.

Sep 92. (7"/c-s) *(CIOA 6/+C)* **THE CRYING GAME. / I SPECIALIZE IN LONELINESS** [22] [–]
(12"+=/cd-s+=) – ('A'extended dance mix).

Feb 93. (c-s/cd-s) *<50437>* **THE CRYING GAME. / (the original Dave Berry version)** [–] [15]

Virgin — Virgin

Nov 92. (7"/c-s; by JESUS LOVES YOU) *(VS/+C 1449)* **SWEET TOXIC THING. / AM I LOSING CONTROL** [65] [ ]
(12"+=/cd-s+=) *(VST/VSCDX 1449)* – ('B'-Dizzy tequila mix) / Oh Lord.

— In Jun'93, GEORGE was credited on the UK hit single, 'More Than Likely' with PM DAWN

Mar 95. (7"/c-s) *(VS/+C 1538)* **FUNTIME. / GENOCIDE PEROXIDE** [45] [–]
(12"+=/cd-s+=) *(VST/VSCDG 1538)* – ('A'mixes).

May 95. (cd/c/lp) *(CD/TC+/V 2780)* **CHEAPNESS AND BEAUTY** [44] [ ]
– Funtime / Satans butterfly ball / Sad / God don't hold a grudge / Genocide peroxide / If I could fly / Same thing in reverse / Cheapness and beauty / Evil is so civilised / Blind man / Your love is what I am / Unfinished business / Il adore. *(cd re-iss. Aug98 on 'Virgin-VIP'; CDVIP 203)*

Jun 95. (c-s) *(VSC 1543)* **IL ADORE / THESE BOOTS ARE MADE FOR WALKING** [50] [ ]
(cd-s+=) *(VSCDX 1543)* – Sad / ('A'mixes).
(cd-s) *(VSCDD 1543)* – ('A'side) / Cheapness and beauty.

Sep 95. (c-s) *(VSC 1561)* **SAME THING IN REVERSE / ('A'-Evolution radio screamer mix)** [56] [ ]
(cd-s+=) *(VSCDT 1561)* – ('A'-Evolution brick in my hand mix) / ('A'-Clubzone).
(12") *(VST 1561)* – (2 'A'-Clubzone mixes) / (2 'A'-Evolution mixes).

More Protein — not iss.

Apr 96. (c-s) *(PROC 112)* **SAD / SATAN'S BUTTERFLY BALL** [ ] [–]
(cd-s+=/12"+=) *(PRO CD/T 112)* – ('A'+'B'mixes).

CULTURE CLUB

— re-formed original line-up for apparently one new song

Virgin — E.M.i.

Oct 98. (c-s/cd-s) *(VSC/+DT 1710)* **I JUST WANNA BE LOVED / DO YOU REALLY WANT TO HURT ME (mixes)** [4] [–]

Nov 98. (cd/c) *(CDVX/TCV 2865)* **GREATEST MOMENTS** (compilation) [21] [–]
– Do you really want to hurt me / Time (clock of the heart) / Church of the poisoned mind / Karma chameleon / Victims / I'll tumble 4 ya / It's a miracle / Miss me blind / Move away / Love is love / Everything I own / The crying game / I just wanna be loved / Generations of love (the Timewriter bootleg mix).

Jul 99. (c-s/cd-s) *(VSC/+DT 1736)* **YOUR KISSES ARE CHARITY / ('A'mixes)** [25] [–]
(cd-s) *(VSCDX 1736)* – ('A'side) / Do you really want to hurt me (Kinky Disco mix) / Time (clock of the heart) (Quivver's Amityville mix).

Nov 99. (c-s) *(VSC 1758)* **COLD SHOULDER / STARMAN** [43] [–]
(cd-s+=) *(VSCDT 1758)* – Your kisses are charity.

Nov 99. (cd/c) *(CDV/TCV 2887)* *<848666>* **DON'T MIND IF I DO** [64] [ ]
– I just wanna be loved / Cold shoulder / Maybe I'm a fool / Sign language / Mirror / Black comedy / Your kisses are charity / Weep for the child / See thru / Strange voodoo / Truth behind her smile / Fat cat / Confidence trick / Starman / Less than perfect.

– compilations, etc. –

Apr 87. (lp/c/cd) *Virgin; (VTV/VTVC/CDVTV 1)* **THIS TIME: THE FIRST FOUR YEARS** [8] [–]
– Do you really want to hurt me / Move away / I'll tumble 4 ya / Love is love / Victims / Karma chameleon / Church of the poison mind / Miss me blind / Time (clock of the heart) / It's a miracle / Black money / The war song. *(cd+=)* – I'll tumble 4 ya (US 12"remix) / Miss me blind (US 12"remix). *(c re-iss. Apr92; OVEDC 435)*

Nov 88. (7") *Old Gold; (OG 9816)* **DO YOU REALLY WANT TO HURT ME. / I'LL TUMBLE 4 YA** [ ] [–]
(Feb89; 12"+=; *OG 4101)* – Time (clock of the heart).

Nov 88. (7") *Old Gold; (OG 9822)* **KARMA CHAMELEON. / IT'S A MIRACLE** [ ] [–]
(Mar89; 12"+=) *(OG 4107)* – Miss me blind.

Nov 88. (7") *Old Gold; (OG 9832)* **CHURCH OF THE POISON MIND. / VICTIMS** [–] [ ]

Sep 89. (lp/c/cd) *VIP-Virgin; (VVIP/+C/D 102)* **THE BEST OF CULTURE CLUB** [ ] [–]
(re-iss. Oct94 cd/c; CD/TC VIP 102)

Sep 93. (cd/c/lp) *Virgin; (VT CD/TC/LP 19) / S.B.K.; <39014>* **AT WORST . . . THE BEST OF BOY GEORGE & CULTURE CLUB** [26] Nov93 [ ]
– CULTURE CLUB: Do you really want to hurt me / Time (clock of the heart) / Church of the poisoned mind / Karma chameleon / Victims / I'll tumble 4 ya / It's a miracle / Miss me blind / Move away / BOY GEORGE or JESUS LOVES YOU: Love is love / Love hurts / Everything I own / Don't cry / After the love / More than likely / The crying game / Generations of love (La la gone gaga mix) / Bow down mister (a small portion 28 polite mix) / Sweet toxic love (Deliverance mix).

Mar 94. (m-cd/m-lp) *Virgin; (VSCDG/VST 1490)* **THE DEVIL IN SISTER GEORGE EP** [26] [–]
– Miss me blind / Generations of love / Am I losing control / Love hurts / Everything I own.

May 94. (cd/c) *VIP-Virgin; (CD/TC VIP 116)* **COLLECT 12" MIXES PLUS** [ ] [–]

Jul 99. (d-cd) *Disky; (HR 85774-2)* **ORIGINAL GOLD** [ ] [–]

Sep 99. (cd; by BOY GEORGE) *Back Door; (BDCD 01)* **UNRECOUPABLE ONE MAN BANDIT 1996-1998** [ ] [–]

☐ BOYS NEXT DOOR (see under ⇒ CAVE, Nick)

Billy BRAGG

Born: STEVEN WILLIAM BRAGG, 20 Dec'57, Barking, Essex, England. Inspired by The CLASH, he formed Peterborough-based R&B/punk band, RIFF RAFF, in 1977. After releasing a string of indie 7" singles, (including the wonderfully titled 'I WANNA BE A COSMONAUT'), the band split in 1981, BILLY incredibly going off to join the army. Thankfully, a career in the military wasn't to be though, and he bought himself out after only 90 days. Complete with amplifier and guitar, he busked around Britain, finally furnished with some studio time in 1983 courtesy of 'Charisma' indie subsidiary, 'Utility'. The result was 'LIFE'S A RIOT WITH SPY VS SPY', and with the help and distribution of new label 'Go! Discs', the record finally hit the UK Top 30 in early '84. BRAGG's stark musical backdrop (for the most part, a roughly strummed electric guitar) and even starker vocals, belied a keen sense of melody and passionate, deeply humane lyrics. 'THE MILKMAN OF HUMAN KINDNESS' was a love song of the most compassionate variety which illustrated that BRAGG approached politics from a humanist perspective rather than a soapbox. After seeing firsthand how Thatcher had decimated mining communities, BRAGG's songs became more overtly political. 'BREWING UP WITH BILLY BRAGG' (1984) opened with the fierce 'IT SAYS HERE', but again the most affecting moments were to be found on heartfelt love songs like the wistful 'ST. SWITHIN'S DAY'. It would be another two years before he released a new album, in the interim taking time to make his Top Of The Pops debut and play a lead role in the 'Red Wedge' campaign. A well intentioned but ultimately hopeless initiative to persuade people to vote Labour, BRAGG toured alongside The STYLE COUNCIL, MADNESS, The COMMUNARDS and MORRISSEY. As the Conservatives romped home to another sickening victory, BRAGG licked his wounds and bounced back with a third album, 'TALKING WITH THE TAXMAN ABOUT POETRY' (1986). His most successful and accomplished release to date, the record spawned the classic single, 'LEVI STUBBS' TEARS' as well as the JOHNNY MARR collaboration, 'GREETINGS TO THE NEW BRUNETTE'. And of course, who could argue with the sentiments of 'HELP SAVE THE YOUTH OF AMERICA'?! Not content with saving our Transatlantic cousins, BRAGG also did his bit for kids back in Blighty. Recording a cover of 'SHE'S LEAVING HOME' with CARA TIVEY, BRAGG found himself at No.1 when the song was released as the B-side to WET WET WET's cover of 'WITH A LITTLE HELP FROM MY FRIENDS', the not inconsiderable proceeds going to the Childline charity. BRAGG's next album, 'WORKER'S PLAYTIME' (1988), saw a move away from the sparse accompaniment of old, while lyrically the record focused more on matters of the heart than the ballot box. 'THE INTERNATIONALE' (1990), meanwhile, was BRAGG's most political work to date, with the likes of 'NICARAGUITA' and 'THE RED FLAG'. On 'DON'T TRY THIS AT HOME' (1991), BRAGG enlisted a cast of musicians to flesh out the sound, a tactic that elicited mixed results. His stance with CND and anti-apartheid, anti-poll tax, etc, often saw him on wrong side of the law. For the 90's it looked as though he would become a bit more cosmopolitan but still ungagged. In 1998, BILLY and the alt-country group WILCO decided to do a tribute album dedicated to their dustbowl hero, WOODY GUTHRIE. 'MERMAID AVENUE' (a street in Coney Island where WOODY lived with his family in the late 40's and early 50's) was the title, the lyrics seemingly found in an attic while messers BRAGG and WILCO set them to tunes. From the bawdy, singalong raucousness of opener 'WALT WHITMAN'S NIECE' to the gorgeous, yawning back porch swing of 'CALIFORNIA STARS' and the desolate fragility of 'BIRDS AND SHIPS' (featuring a heart-stopping guest vocal by NATALIE MERCHANT), this ranked among the cream of both artists' back catalogues. While they each interpreted the material in their own way – BRAGG obviously coming closer to the mould of GUTHRIE's worldly, open hearted troubadour – both WILCO and BRAGG brought their own personality to bear on WOODY's words of wisdom. As well as being a great record in its own right – surely a contender for album of the year – this collection served to underline just how unceasingly prolific and inventive a songwriter GUTHRIE really was. The spirit of this work cut to the heart of popular music's foundations, no argument. Inevitably, 'MERMAID AVENUE VOL.2' (2000) couldn't quite match that high standard but was nevertheless an enjoyable companion piece to its predecessor. • **Covered:** WALK AWAY RENEE (Four Tops) / SHE'S LEAVING HOME + REVOLUTION (Beatles) / JEANE (Smiths) / SEVEN AND SEVEN IS (Love) / THERE IS POWER IN A UNION (trad.new words) / THINK AGAIN (Dick Gaughan) / CHILE YOUR WATERS RUN RED THROUGH SOWETO (B.Johnson Reagan) / TRAIN TRAIN (Z.Delfeur) / DOLPHINS (Fred Neil) / EVERYWHERE (Sid Griffin-Greg Trooper) / JERUSALEM (William Blake) / WHEN WILL I SEE YOU AGAIN (Three Degrees) / NEVER HAD NO ONE EVER (Smiths) / FEAR IS A MAN'S BEST FRIEND (John Cale)/ SHE SMILED SWEETLY (Rolling Stones) / A13, TRUNK ROAD TO THE SEA (Bobby Troup) / DRY BED (Woody Guthrie).

Album rating: LIFE'S A RIOT WITH SPY VS. SPY mini (*7) / BREWING UP WITH BILLY BRAGG (*8) / TALKING WITH THE TAXMAN ABOUT POETRY (*8) / BACK TO BASICS compilation (*7) / WORKERS PLAYTIME (*7) / THE INTERNATIONALE (*5) / DON'T TRY THIS AT HOME (*8) / WILLIAM BLOKE (*7) / BLOKE ON BLOKE (*6) / MERMAID AVENUE with Wilco (*8) / REACHING TO THE CONVERTED (MINDING THE GAPS) collection (*7) / MERMAID AVENUE VOL.II with Wilco (*6) / ENGLAND, HALF ENGLISH (*5) / MUST I PAINT YOU A PICTURE?: THE ESSENTIAL . . . compilation (*8)

RIFF RAFF

BILLY BRAGG – vocals, guitar and other members

		Chiswick	not iss.
May 78.	(7"ep) *(SW 34)* **I WANNA BE A COSMONAUT** – Cosmonaut / Romford girls / What's the latest? / Sweet as pie.		–
		Geezer	not iss.
Oct 80.	(7") *(GZ 1)* **EVERY GIRL AN ENGLISH ROSE. / U SHAPED HOUSE**		–
Oct 80.	(7") *(GZ 2)* **KITTEN. / FANTOCIDE**		–
Oct 80.	(7") *(GZ 3)* **LITTLE GIRLS KNOW. / SHE DON'T MATTER**		–
Oct 80.	(7") *(GZ 4)* **NEW HOME TOWN. / RICHARD**		–

BILLY BRAGG

		Utility	not iss.
Jun 83.	(m-lp) *(UTIL 1)* **LIFE'S A RIOT WITH SPY VS. SPY** – The milkman of human kindness / To have and have not / A new England / The man in the iron mask / The busy girl buys beauty / Lover's town revisited / Richard. *(re-iss. Jan84 on 'Go! Discs' lp/c; UTIL/+C 1) (cd-iss. Sep96 on 'Cooking Vinyl'; COOKCD 106)*	30	–

— added for back-up **KENNY CRADDOCK** – organ / **DAVE WOODHEAD** – trumpet

		Go! Discs	Elektra
Oct 84.	(lp/c) *(A/Z GOLP 4)* **BREWING UP WITH BILLY BRAGG** – It says here / Love gets dangerous / The myth of trust / From a Vauxhall Velox / The Saturday boy / Island of no return / St. Swithin's Day / Like soldiers do / This guitar says sorry / Strange things happen / A lover sings. *(cd-iss. Sep96 on 'Cooking Vinyl'; COOKCD 107)*	16	–
Feb 85.	(7") **ST. SWITHIN'S DAY. / A NEW ENGLAND**	–	Euro –
Mar 85.	(7"ep) *(AGOEP 1)* **BETWEEN THE WARS** – Between the wars / Which side are you on? / World turned upside down / It says here.	15	–
Dec 85.	(7"m) *(GOD 8)* **DAYS LIKE THESE. / I DON'T NEED THIS PRESSURE RON / SCHOLARSHIP IS THE ENEMY OF ROMANCE**	43	–

— + guests **JOHNNY MARR** – guitar / **KIRSTY MacCOLL** – b.vocals / **KENNY JONES** – drums, co-producer / **JOHN PORTER** – bass, co-producer / **SIMON MORTEON** – percussion / **BOBBY VALENTINO** – violin

Jun 86.	(7"m) *(GOD 12)* **LEVI STUBBS' TEARS. / THINK AGAIN / WALK AWAY RENEE** (12"+=) *(GODX 12)* – Between the wars (live).	29	–
Sep 86.	(lp/c) *(A/Z GOLP 6)* **TALKING WITH THE TAXMAN ABOUT POETRY** – Greetings to the new brunette / Train train / The marriage / Ideology / Levi Stubbs' tears / Honey, I'm a big boy now / There is power in a union / Help save the youth of America / Wishing the days away / The passion / The warmest room / The home front. *(cd-*	8	

iss. May87; AGOCD 6) (cd re-iss/Sep96 on 'Cooking Vinyl'; COOKCD 108)

Nov 86. (7"m) *(GOD 15)* **GREETINGS TO THE NEW BRUNETTE. / DEPORTEES / THE TATLER** | 58 | – |
(12"+=) *(GODX 15)* – Jeane / There is power in a union (instrumental).

— Oct'87, BRAGG is credited with OYSTER BAND backing **LEON ROSSELSON** on his single **BALLAD OF A SPYCATCHER** (Upside Down records)

— May'88, he's credited with **CARA TIVEY** on 45 **SHE'S LEAVING HOME** the B-side of **WET WET WET** – With A little Help From My Friends. This UK No.1 single issued on 'Childline' gave all proceeds to children's charity, with backing including his usual friends.

Go! Discs | Elektra

May 88. (12"ep/cd-ep) *(A/ZA GOLP 1) <960-787-2>* **HELP SAVE THE YOUTH OF AMERICA (LIVE AND DUBIOUS)** | | |
– Help save the youth of America / Think again / Chile your waters run red through Soweto / Days like these (DC mix) / To have and have not / There is power in a union (with The PATTERSONS).

Aug 88. (7"m) *(GOD 23)* **WAITING FOR THE GREAT LEAP FORWARD. / WISHING THE DAYS AWAY / SIN CITY** | 52 | – |

Sep 88. (lp/c/cd) *(AGOLP/ZGOLP/AGOCD 15) <60824>* **WORKER'S PLAYTIME** | 17 | |
– She's got a brand new spell / Must I paint you a picture / Tender comrade / The price I pay / Little timb-bomb / Rotting on demand / Valentine's day is over / Life with the lions / The only one / The short answer / Waiting for the great leap forward. *(cd re-iss. Sep96 on 'Cooking Vinyl'; COOKCD 109)*

Nov 88. (7") *(GOD 24)* **SHE'S GOT A BRAND NEW SPELL. / MUST I PAINT YOU A PICTURE** | | – |

— In Jul'89, BRAGG was credited on a NORMAN COOK Top 30 single 'Won't Talk About it'.

May 90. (m-lp/m-c/m-cd; on 'Utility') *(UTIL/+C/CD 011) <60960>* **THE INTERNATIONALE** | 34 | Jun90 |
– The internationale / I dreamed I saw Phil Ochs last night / The marching song of the convent battalions / Jerusalem / Nicaraguita / The red flag / My youngest son came home today.

— still holding on to **MARR, MacCOLL, TIVEY** (keyboards) and WOODHEAD plus **WIGGY** – guitar, bass / **J.F.T. HOOD** – drums / **AMANDA VINCENT** – keyboards / etc.

Jun 91. (7") *(GOD 56)* **SEXUALITY. / BAD PENNY** | 27 | – |
(12"+=/cd-s+=) *(GOD X/CD 56)* – (2 'A'mixes).

Aug 91. (7") *(GOD 60)* **YOU WOKE UP MY NEIGHBOURHOOD. / ONTARIO, QUEBEC AND ME** | 54 | – |
(12"+=/cd-s+=) *(GOD X/CD 60)* – Bread and circuses / Heart like a wheel. (above single 'A'featured **MICHAEL STIPE and PETER BUCK (R.E.M.)** with first 12"extra track with **NATALIE MERCHANT** (10,000 MANIACS) – also backing vocals

Sep 91. (cd/c/d-lp)(8x7"box) *(828279-2/-4/-1) <61121>* **DON'T TRY THIS AT HOME** | 8 | |
– Accident waiting to happen / Moving the goalposts / Everywhere / Cindy of a thousand lives / You woke up my neighbourhood / Trust / God's footballer / The few / Sexuality / Mother of the bride / Tank park salute / Dolphins / North sea bubble / Rumours of war / Wish you were here / Body of water. *(re-iss. Nov93 & Apr98 on 'Cooking Vinyl' lp/c/cd; COOK/+C/CD 062) (cd re-iss. Sep96; COOKCD 110)*

Feb 92. (7"ep) *(GOD 67)* **ACCIDENT WAITING TO HAPPEN (Red Star version) / SULK. / THE WARMEST ROOM (live) / REVOLUTION** | 33 | – |
(12"+=/cd-s+=) *(GOD X/CD 67)* – ('A'live version) / Levi Stubbs' tears / Valentine's day is over / North Sea bubble.

Cooking Vinyl | Elektra

Aug 96. (7"/c-s) *(FRY/+C 051)* **UPFIELD / THATCHERITES** | 46 | – |
(cd-s+=) *(FRYCD 051)* – Rule nor reason.

Sep 96. (lp/c/cd) *(COOK/+C/CD 100) <61935>* **WILLIAM BLOKE** | 16 | |
– From red to blue / Upfield / Everybody loves you babe / Sugardaddy / A Pict song / Brickbat / The space race is over / Northern industrial town / The fourteenth of February / King James version / Goalhanger.

May 97. (7") *(FRY 064)* **THE BOY DONE GOOD. / SUGARDADDY** | 55 | |
(cd-s+=) *(FRYCD 064)* – Just one victory / Qualifications.
(cd-s+=) *(FRYCDX 064)* – Never had no one ever / Run out of reasons.

Jun 97. (cd) *(COOKCD 127)* **BLOKE ON BLOKE** | 72 | – |
– The boy done good / Just one victory / Qualifications / Sugar daddy / Never had no one ever / Run out of seasons / Rule nor reason / Thatcherites.

BILLY BRAGG & WILCO

— **WILCO** were **JEFF TWEEDY** and Co

Elektra | Elektra

Jun 98. (cd/c) *(<7559 62204-2/-4>)* **MERMAID AVENUE** | 34 | 90 |
– Walt Whitman's niece / California stars / Way over yonder in the minor key / Birds and ships / Hoodoo voodoo / She came along to me / At my window sad and lonely / Ingrid Bergman / Christ for President / I guess I planted / One by one / Eisler on the go / Hesitating beauty / Another man's done gone / The unwelcome guest.

Nov 98. (7"/c-s) *(E 3798/+C)* **WAY OVER YONDER IN THE MINOR KEY. / MY THIRTY THOUSAND** | | – |
(cd-s+=) *(E 3798CD)* – Bug-eyed Jim.

May 00. (cd/c) *<(7559 62522-2/-4)>* **MERMAID AVENUE VOL.II** | 61 | 88 |
– Airline to Heaven / My flying saucer / Feed of man / Hot rod hotel / I was born / Secret of the sea / Stetson Kennedy / Remember the mountain bed / Blood of the lamb / Against th' law / All you fascists / Joe Dimaggio done it again / Meanest man / Black wind blowing / Someday some morning sometime.

BILLY BRAGG AND THE BLOKES

with **IAN McLAGAN** – keyboards, accordion / **MARTYN BARKER** – drums, percussion / **SIMON EDWARDS** – bass / **BEN MANDELSON** – bouzouki, mandolin, guitars / **DAVE WOODHEAD** – trumpet / **LU** – guitars

Cooking Vinyl | Elektra

Feb 02. (cd-s) *(FRYCD 120)* **ST. MONDAY / ENGLAND, HALF ENGLISH** | | – |

Mar 02. (lp/cd) *(COOK/+CD 222) <62743>* **ENGLAND, HALF ENGLISH** | 51 | |
– St. Monday / Jane Allen / Distant shore / England, half English / Npwa / Some days I see the point / Baby Faroukh / Take down the Union Jack / Another kind of Judy / He'll go down / Dreadbelly / Tears of my tracks.

May 02. (cd-s) *(FRYCD 131)* **TAKE DOWN THE UNION JACK / MYSTERY SHOES / ENGLAND, HALF ENGLISH (7" remix)** | 22 | – |
(cd-s) *(FRYCD 131X)* – ('A'-band version) / Yarra song / England, half English (12" remix).
(cd-s) *(FRYCD 131XX)* – ('A'side) / You pulled the carpet out / England, half English (ambient remix) / ('A'video).

– compilations, etc. –

May 87. (12"ep) *Strange Fruit; (SFPS 027)* **THE PEEL SESSIONS** | | – |
– A new England / Strange things happen / This guitar says sorry / Love gets dangerous / A13 trunk road to the sea / Fear . . . *(cd-iss. 1988; SFPSCD 027)*

Jun 87. (d-lp/d-c/cd) *Go! Discs; (AGOLP/ZGOLP/AGOCD 8)* **BACK TO BASICS** (best 83-85 material) | 37 | – |
(re-iss. Apr98 on 'Cooking Vinyl' d-lp/c/cd; COOK/+C/CD 060)

Feb 92. (cd/c/lp) *Strange Fruit; (SFR CD/MC/LP 117)* **THE PEEL SESSIONS ALBUM** | | – |
(cd with extra tracks)

Nov 93. (d-lp/c/cd) *Cooking Vinyl; (COOK/+C/CD 061)* **VICTIM OF GEOGRAPHY** | | – |
– Greetings to the new brunette / Train train / Marriage / Idealogy / Levi Stubbs' tears / Honey I'm a big boy now / There is a power in a union / Help save the youth of America / Wishing the days away / Passion / The warmest room / Home front / She's got a new spell / Must I paint you a picture / Tender comrade / The price I pay / Little time bomb / Rotting on demand / Valentine's day is over / Life with the lions / The only one / Short answer / Waiting for the great leap forward. *(re-iss. Apr98 cd/c; same)*

Aug 99. (cd/c/lp) *Cooking Vinyl; (COOK CD/MC/LP 186) / Rhino; <75962>* **REACHING TO THE CONVERTED (MINDING THE GAPS)** | 41 | |
– Shirley / Sulk / Accident waiting to happen / Boy done good / Heart like a wheel / Bad penny / Ontario Quebec and me / Walk away Renee / Rule nor reason / Days like these / Think again / Scholarship is the enemy of romance / Wishing the days away (ballad version) / Tatler / Jeane / She's leaving home.

Oct 03. (d-cd) *Cooking Vinyl; (COOKCD 266) / Rhino; <73993>* **MUST I PAINT YOU A PICTURE?: THE ESSENTIAL BILLY BRAGG** | 49 | |

– A new England / The man in the iron mask / The milkman of human kindness / To have and to have not / A lover sings / St. Swithin's Day / The Saturday boy / Between the wars / The world turned upside down / Levi Stubbs' tears / Walk away Renee / Greetings to the new brunette / There is power in a union / Help save the youth of America / The warmest room / Must I paint you a picture? / She's got a new spell / The price I pay / Valentine's Day is over / Waiting for the great leap forward / Sexuality / Cindy of a thousand lives / Moving the goalposts / Tank park salute / You woke up my neighbourhood / Accident waiting to happen (red stars version) / Sulk / Upfield / The fourteenth of February / Brickbat / The pace race is over / The boy done good / Ingrid Bergman (with WILCO) / WAy over yonder in the minor key (with WILCO) / My flying saucer (with WILCO) / All you fascists bound to lose (Blokes version) / NPWA / St. Monday / Some days I see the point / Take down the Union Jack (band version). *(ltd t-cd+=; COOKCD 266X)* – A13, trunk road to the sea / Fear is a man's best friend / Cold and bitter tears (live with TED HAWKINS) / Seven and seven is / When will I see you again / Rule nor reason (live) / Debris (live) / My bed (demo) / She smiled sweetly / Take down the Union Jack.

□ BRAINBOX (see under ⇒ FOCUS)

□ BRAIN DONOR (see under ⇒ COPE, Julian)

BREAD

Formed: Los Angeles, California, USA . . . late 1968 by DAVID GATES, JAMES GRIFFIN and ROB ROYER. GATES grew up in a musical family in Tulsa, Oklahoma learning piano, bass and guitar to a high standard by the time he reached high school. His composition, 'JO BABY', written about his girlfriend (and future wife) Jo Rita, was turned into a minor hit in '57 by CHUCK BERRY (who had visited Tulsa around that time). GATES was only sixteen at this point; by the time he was twenty he had recorded with LEON RUSSELL, moved to L.A. and established himself as a studio musician and producer. In this capacity he worked with a number of legends including ELVIS PRESLEY, MERLE HAGGARD and CAPTAIN BEEFHEART. Another band he produced were PLEASURE FAIRE whose members included ROB ROYER and JAMES GRIFFIN, who had already released his own solo record, 'SUMMER HOLIDAY'. He subsequently asked GATES to join the band and the trio signed to 'Elektra', changing their name to BREAD in the process. The first LP, 'BREAD' (1969) introduced their unique sound of melody-driven soft-rock ballads with a hint of American folk, one of the highlights being the gorgeous 'IT DON'T MATTER TO ME'. Enriched with strings, it became the only the track from their debut to hit the charts, making the US Top 10 the following year. Its belated success came on the back of 'MAKE IT WITH YOU', their chart-topping masterpiece and signature song taken from 'ON THE WATERS (1970). This album was an instant success and left them deeply embedded in the mainstream, the subsequent tour seeing new drummer MIKE BOTTS brought into the fold. The quartet went back to the studio to produce 'MANNA' (1971) and although its sales did not scale the dizzy heights of the previous effort, it did spawn their most recorded song (TELLY SAVALAS took it to No.1 in Britain), the slow ballad, 'IF'. A further single, 'MOTHER FREEDOM', barely dipped its toe into the charts, a poor attempt by the group to diversify into the rock territory stalked by bands like FREE. BREAD were back on form with two other Top 5 hits 'BABY I'M-A WANT YOU' (from the album of the same name) and 'EVERYTHING I OWN' (a two-times UK No.1, first for reggae star KEN BOOTHE and latterly for gay icon BOY GEORGE). The same year, the 'GUITAR MAN' album provided a further three Top 20 singles before the band split in 1973; internal difficulties between GATES and GRIFFIN over the former's songwriting domination of the group's hits caused the dissolution. However they did reunite in '76 for one more album, 'LOST WITHOUT YOUR LOVE' (1977), but even with the success of the Top 10 title track, the pair just couldn't bury the hatchet. Both went back to the pursuit of solo careers and unsurprisingly GATES had by far the most success of the two. He released two albums in between the BREAD years providing two hits with 'NEVER LET HER GO' and 'GOODBYE GIRL'. His only other hit, 'TOOK THE LAST TRAIN' came in '78 and although he continued to record into the '90s, he never managed to match the success he enjoyed with BREAD. • **Trivia:** GRIFFIN and ROYER (under pseudonyms) wrote 'FOR ALL WE KNOW', used in the film, 'Lovers And Other Strangers'; it subsequently became a hit for The CARPENTERS in 1971.

Best CD compilation(s): DAVID GATES & BREAD: ESSENTIALS (*8) / David Gates: THE DAVID GATES SONGBOOK – A LIFETIME OF MUSIC (*7)

DAVID GATES (b.11 Dec'40, Tulsa, Oklahoma, USA) - **vocals, keyboards / JAMES GRIFFIN** (b. Memphis) – guitar, keyboards, vocals / **ROB ROYER** – bass, vocals (ex-PLEASURE FAIRE) **JIM GORDON + RON EDGAR** – session drummers

Elektra Elektra

Oct 69. (7") *<(EKSN 45071)>* **DISMAL DAY. / LONDON BRIDGE** □ □

Nov 69. (lp) *<(EKS 74044)>* **BREAD** □ Oct69 □
– Dismal day / London Bridge / Could I / Look at me / Last time / Anyway you want me / Move over / Don't shut me down / You can't measure the cost / Family doctor / It don't matter to me / Friends & lovers. *(re-iss. Nov71; K 42029) (cd-iss. Jan96; 0349 73502-2)*

Feb 70. (7") *<(EKSN 45083)>* **MOVE OVER. / YOU CAN'T MEASURE THE COST** □ □

—— **MIKE BOTTS** (b. Sacramento) – drums (ex-WES MONTGOMERY) repl. session people

Jul 70. (7") *(2101 010) <45686>* **MAKE IT WITH YOU. / WHY DO YOU KEEP ME WAITING** 5 Jun70 1

Aug 70. (lp) *(2469 005) <EKS 74076>* **ON THE WATERS** 34 Jul70 12
– Why do you keep me waiting / Make it with you / Blue satin pillow / Look what you've done / I am what I am / Been too long on the road / I want you with me / Coming apart / Easy love / In the afterglow / Call on me / The other side of love. *(re-iss. Nov71; K 42050) (cd-iss. Jan96; 0349 73503-2)*

Oct 70. (7") *(2101 015) <EKSN 45701>* **IT DON'T MATTER TO ME. / CALL ON ME** □ Sep70 10

Feb 71. (7") *<(K 45711)>* **LET YOUR LOVE GO. / TOO MUCH LOVE** □ 28

May 71. (7") *(K 12014) <45720>* **IF. / TAKE COMFORT** □ Mar71 4

Jul 71. (lp) *<(EKS 74086)>* **MANNA** □ Mar71 21
– Let your love go / Take comfort / Too much love / If / Be kind to me / He's a good lad / She was my lady / Live in your love / What a change / I say again / Come again / Truckin'. *(re-iss. 1972; K 52001) (cd-iss. Jan96; 0349 73504-2)*

—— **LARRY KNECHTEL** (b. Bell, California) – guitar, multi (ex-DUANE EDDY) (also played piano on 'Bridge Over Troubled Water') repl. ROYER

Jul 71. (7") *<K 45740>* **MOTHER FREEDOM. / LIVE IN YOUR LOVE** – 37

Nov 71. (7") *(K 12033) <45751>* **BABY I'M A-WANT YOU. / TRUCKIN'** 14 Oct71 3

Mar 72. (7") *(K 12041) <45765>* **EVERYTHING I OWN. / I DON'T LIKE YOU** 32 Jan72 5

Mar 72. (lp/c) *(K/K4 42100) <75015>* **BABY I'M A-WANT YOU** 9 Jan72 3
– Baby I'm a-want you / Everything I own / Diary / Mother Freedom / Down on my knees / Nobody like you / Dream lady / Daughter / Games of magic / This isn't what the government / Just like yesterday / I don't love you. *(re-iss. Nov76; same)*

Apr 72. (7") *<45784>* **DIARY. / DOWN ON MY KNEES** – 15

Sep 72. (7") *(K 12066) <45803>* **THE GUITAR MAN. / JUST LIKE YESTERDAY** 16 Jul72 11

Nov 72. (lp/c) *(K/K4 52004) <75047>* **GUITAR MAN** □ 18
– The guitar man / Sweet surrender / Aubrey / Welcome to the music / Make it by yourself / Fancy dancer / Tecotote / Let me go / Yours for life / Picture in your mind / Don't tell me no / Didn't even know her name. *(re-iss. Nov76; same)*

Jan 73. (7") *(K 12075)* <45818> **SWEET SURRENDER. / MAKE IT BY YOURSELF** Nov72 15
Feb 73. (7") <45832> **AUBREY. / DIDN'T EVEN KNOW HER NAME** – 11
—— BREAD broke-up in May '73, BOTTS joined the LINDA RONSTADT band and KNECHTEL returned to sessions. GRIFFIN went solo (2 lp's 1974 & 1975)

DAVID GATES

—— solo, although not including his pre-BREAD stuff
Aug 73. (7") *(K 12114)* **CLOUDS. / I USE THE SOAP** Jul73 47
Oct 73. (lp/c) *(K/K4 42150)* <75066> **DAVID GATES – FIRST**
– Sail around the world / Sunday rider / I use the soap / Suite: Clouds – Rain / Help is on the way / Ann / Do you believe he's coming / Sight and sound / Lorilee. *(re-iss. Nov76; same) (cd-iss. Jan96; 7559 60610-2)*
Nov 73. (7") *(K 12126)* <45868> **SAIL AROUND THE WORLD. / HELP IS ON THE WAY** Oct73 50
May 74. (7") *(K 12162)* **SUITE: CLOUDS – RAIN. / (part 2)**
Jan 75. (7") *(K 12165)* <45223> **NEVER LET HER GO. / WATCH OUT** 29
May 75. (lp/c) *(K/K4 52012)* 1028> **NEVER LET HER GO** 32 Feb75
– Never let her go / Angel / Playin' on my guitar / Watch out / Part time love / Chain me / Light of my life / Someday / Greener days / Strangers. *(re-iss. Nov76; same)*
Jun 75. (7") *(K 12179)* **PART TIME LOVE. / SUNDAY RIDER**

BREAD

—— re-formed (see last line-up)
Dec 76. (7") *(K 12241)* <45365> **LOST WITHOUT YOUR LOVE. / CHANGE OF HEART** 27 Nov76 9
Jan 77. (lp/c) *(K/K4 52044)* 1094> **LOST WITHOUT YOUR LOVE** 17 26
– Hooked on you / She's the only one / Lost without your love / Change of heart / Belonging / Fly away / Lay your money down / The chosen one / Today the first day / Hold tight / Our lady of sorrow.
Mar 77. (7") *(K 12250)* **HOOKED ON YOU. / FLY AWAY** –
Apr 77. (7") <45389> **HOOKED ON YOU. / OUR LADY OF SORROW** – 60
—— split:- GRIFFIN soon teamed up with TERRY SYLVESTER (ex-The HOLLIES)

– compilations, etc. –

on 'Elektra' unless mentioned otherwise
Oct 72. (lp/c) *(K/K4 42115)* <75056> **THE BEST OF BREAD** 7 Mar73 2
– Make it with you / Everything I own / Diary / Baby I'm a-want you / It don't matter to me / Mother freedom / Down on my knees / Too much love / Let your love go / Look what you've done / Truckin'. *(re-iss. Nov76; same)*
May 73. (7"m) **IF. / IT DON'T MATTER TO ME / LET YOUR LOVE GO** –
Jun 74. (lp/c) *(K/K4 42161)* <1005> **THE BEST OF BREAD VOL.2** 48 May74 32
– Sweet surrender / Fancy dancer / The guitar man / Been too long on the coast / Friends and lovers / Aubrey / Daughter / Dream lady / Yours for life / Just like yesterday / He's a good lad / London Bridge. *(re-iss. Nov76; same)*
Aug 74. (7") *(K 12155)* **SWEET SURRENDER. / BEEN TOO LONG ON THE COAST** –
Jun 76. (7") *(K 12210)* **GUITAR MAN. / BABY I'M A-WANT YOU** –
Jun 76. (7") *(K 12221)* **MAKE IT WITH YOU. / EVERYTHING I OWN** –
(re-iss. Sep85 on 'Old Gold'; OG 9512)
Jun 76. (7") *(K 12222)* **IF. / SWEET SURRENDER** –
Oct 77. (lp/c) *(K/K4 52062)* **THE SOUND OF BREAD** 1 –
– Make it with you / Dismal day / London Bridge / Anyway you want me / Look what you've done / It don't matter to me / The last time / Let your love go / Truckin' / If / Baby I'm a-want you / Everything I own / Down on my knees / Aubrey / Diary / Sweet surrender / The guitar man / Fancy dancer / She's the only one / Lost without your love. *(cd-iss. Jan87 +=; K2 52062)* – Just like yesterday. *(lp re-iss. Oct97 on 'Simply Vinyl'; SVLP 5)*
Nov 83. (d-c) *(960 284-2)* **THE BEST OF BREAD VOL.1 & 2** –
Sep 85. (7") *Old Gold; (OG 9513)* **BABY I'M A-WANT YOU. / IF** –
Nov 87. (lp/c/cd) *Telstar; (STAR/STAC/TCD 2303)* **THE BREAD COLLECTION** –
Oct 88. (lp/c) *Hallmark; (SHM/HSC 3244)* **THE VERY BEST OF BREAD** –
(cd-is.Oct89 on 'Pickwick'+=) – (3 DAVID GATES tracks).
Aug 92. (cd) *Remember; (RMB 75063)* **LET YOUR LOVE GO** –
Sep 96. (cd/c; DAVID GATES & BREAD) <*(7559 61961-2/-4)*> **ESSENTIALS**
– Dismal day / Any way you want me / It don't matter to me / Make it with you / Look what you've done / I want you with me / Let your love go / Too much love / If / He's a good lad / Mother freedom / Baby I'm-a want you / Down on my knees / Everything I own / Diary / The guitar man / Aubrey / Sweet surrender / She's the only one / Lost without your love / Soap (I use the) / Ann / Never let her go / Goodbye girl. *(re-iss. Jun97; 9548 35408-2/-4)* – hit UK No.11

DAVID GATES

—— was solo again in 1978
Jan 78. (7") *(K 12276)* <45450> **GOODBYE GIRL. / SUNDAY RIDER** 15
Jul 78. (7") *(K 12307)* <45500> **TOOK THE LAST TRAIN. / ANN** 50 30
Jul 78. (lp/c) *(K/K4 52091)* <148> **GOODBYE GIRL** 28
– Goodbye girl / Took the last train / Overnight sensation / California lady / Ann / Drifter / He don't know how to love you / Sunday rider. *(cd-iss. Jan96; 7559 61172-2)*
Sep 78. (7") *(K 12318)* **NEVER LET HER GO. / LORILEE** –
Jan 80. (lp/c) *(K/K4 52206)* <251> **FALLING IN LOVE AGAIN**
– Can I call you / Where does the lovin' go / 20th century man / She was so young / Silky / Falling in love again / Starship ride / Chingo / Sweet desire.
Jan 80. (7") <46588> **WHERE DOES THE LOVIN' GO. / STARSHIP RIDE** – 46
Feb 80. (7") *(K 12423)* **FALLING IN LOVE AGAIN. / STARSHIP RIDE** –
Apr 80. (7") *(K 12439)* **WHERE DOES THE LOVIN' GO. / CHINGO** –

Arista Arista

Sep 81. (7") <0615> **TAKE ME NOW. / IT'S WHAT YOU SAY** – 62
Nov 81. (7") *(ARIST 446)* **COME HOME FOR CHRISTMAS. / IT'S WHAT YOU SAY**
Jan 82. (lp) *(SPART 1175)* <9563> **TAKE ME NOW** Nov81
– It's you / Take me now / She's a heartbreaker / This could be forever / Come home for Christmas / Still in love / Vanity / Nineteen on the Richter scale / Lady Valentine / It's what you say.
—— GATES went quiet for a long spell

Discovery Discovery

May 95. (cd) <*(1046 77012-2)*> **LOVE IS ALWAYS SEVENTEEN**
– Avenue of love / Love is always seventeen / Ordinary man / I will wait for you / Save this dance for me / No secrets in a small town / Heart, it's all over / I don't want to share your love / I can't find the words to say goodbye / Dear world / Thankin' you sweet baby James.

– (DAVID GATES) compilations, etc. –

1976. (7") *(K 12229)* **SUITE: CLOUDS – RAIN. / PART TIME LOVE** –
1976. (7") *(K 12230)* **AIL AROUND THE WORLD. / NEVER LET HER GO** –
1977. (lp) <6002> **THE DAVID GATES SONGBOOK** (early material) –
Sep 02. (cd) <*(0927 49140-2)*> **THE DAVID GATES SONGBOOK – A LIFETIME OF MUSIC** 11 Nov02
– Make it with you / Find me / Baby I'm-a want you / I can't play the songs / If / Love is always seventeen / It doesn't matter to me / The mustang / Everything I own / Mirror, mirror / Lost without your love / This could be forever / Aubrey / Sail around the world / Part-time lover / Sweet surrender / Goodbye girl / Never let her go / Diary / The guitar man.

☐ BREAKBEAT ERA (see under ⇒ SIZE, Roni)

BREEDERS

Formed: Boston, Massachusetts, USA ... 1989 by TANYA DONELLY (of THROWING MUSES) and KIM DEAL (of The PIXIES) as a side project to their respective musical careers, an opportunity to exercise their frustrated songwriting talent. Recruiting JOSEPHINE WIGGS (of PERFECT DISASTER) on bass and SHANNON DOUGHTY (of the late, great SLINT) on drums, the BREEDERS cut their debut outing, 'POD', in a matter of weeks. Released in May 1990, the album rapidly achieved cult status, even enjoying a hearty endorsement from one KURT COBAIN. Inevitably, the record was compared with The PIXIES by critics although in reality there was little in common between the two bands. Where The PIXIES were enigmatic and frenetic, The BREEDERS were deliberate, dark and intense. While the pace picked up with 'HELLBOUND', tracks like the opener, 'GLORIOUS' and 'IRIS' were more representative of the record as a whole and if their cover of LENNON's 'HAPPINESS IS A WARM GUN' didn't add much to the original, it sounded so BREEDERS-like within the context of the album that they could've conceivably penned it themselves. The group recorded a further EP, 'SAFARI' (1992), with the original line-up before DONELLY went off to work full-time with her own outfit, BELLY. Following The PIXIES' demise later that year, DEAL devoted all her energies to a BREEDERS follow-up album. Enlisting her sister KELLEY in place of the departed DONELLY, the band released the 'CANNONBALL' single in Autumn '93. With its undulating guitar riff and pneumatic rhythm section, the track became an alternative classic, tearing up indie dancefloors across the country. The subsequent album, 'LAST SPLASH', powered into the UK Top 5 upon its release the following month. While much of the set sounded less focused than the debut, it nevertheless contained another stellar guitar pop moment in 'DIVINE HAMMER', also released as a single. Although the album's sales topped the million mark, things went quiet on The BREEDERS front, save for a lone 10" EP in 1994. The following year, (KIM) DEAL did surface in the guise of The AMPS, releasing an album, 'PACER', on '4 a.d.'. A near decade long wait for a follow-up album was primed to erase expectations completely rather than build them up. For fans who hadn't grown out of barbed femme-punk in the meantime, 'TITLE TK' (2002) provided rich if not exactly cutting edge pickings. There was no 'CANNONBALL' this time around although there were moments of sparky, irreverent genius and hallucinatory hints of the sinister sensuality of old. If KIM DEAL sounded longer in both the tooth and throat, her lyrics were as impenetrably enthralling as ever, while sister KELLEY's slightly smoother vocals served as a intriguing foil. • **Songwriters:** KIM DEAL wrote bulk from 1992 onwards. • **Covered:** HAPPINESS IS A WARM GUN (Beatles / George Harrison) / LORD OF THE THIGHS (Aerosmith) / SO SAD ABOUT US (Who). The AMPS covered JUST LIKE A BRIAR (Tasties).

Album rating: POD (*7) / LAST SPLASH (*9) / TITLE TK (*7) / Amps: PACER (*6)

TANYA DONELLY (b.14 Jul'66, Newport, Rhode Island) – rhythm guitar, vocals (of THROWING MUSES) / **KIM DEAL** (b.10 Jun'61, Dayton, Ohio, USA) – guitar, vocals (of The PIXIES) / **JOSEPHINE WIGGS** (b.26 Feb'65, Letchworth, England) – bass, cello, vocals (of PERFECT DISASTER) / **SHANNON DOUGHTY** (aka MIKE HUNT) (b. BRITT WALFORD, Louisville, Kentucky) – drums (of SLINT) repl. NARCIZO and another from HUMAN SEXUAL RESPONSE

4 a.d. — Elektra

May 90. (cd)(lp/c) *(CAD 0006CD)(CAD/+C 0006)* <61331> **POD** [22] [ ]
– Glorious / Doe / Happiness is a warm gun / Oh! / Hellbound / When I was a painter / Fortunately gone / Iris / Opened / Only in 3's / Limehouse / Metal man.

— **DONELLY, KIM DEAL, JO WIGGS + JON MATLOCK** (of SPIRITUALIZED)

Apr 92. (12"ep/cd-ep) *(BAD 2003/+CD)* **SAFARI** [69] [ ]
– Safari / So sad about us / Do you love me now? / Don't call home.

— now **KIM** her sister **KELLEY DEAL** (b.10 Jun'61, Dayton) – guitar, vocals / **JO WIGGS** – bass, vox / **JIM MacPHERSON** (b.23 Jun'66, Dayton) – drums, vocals (ex-RAGING MANTRAS) / (DONELLY formed BELLY)

Aug 93. (12"ep/cd-ep) *(BAD 3011/+CD) <64566>* **CANNONBALL. / CRO-ALOHA / LORD OF THE THIGHS / 900** [40] Nov93 [44]

Sep 93. (cd)(lp/c) *(CAD 3014CD)(CAD/+C 3014) <61508>* **LAST SPLASH** [5] [33]
– New Year / Cannonball / Invisible man / No aloha / Roi / Do you love me now? / Flipside / I just wanna get along / Mad Lucas / Divine hammer / S.O.S./ Hag / Saints / Drivin' on 9 / Roi (reprise).

Oct 93. (7"clear/c-s) *(AD/+C 3017) <66260>* **DIVINE HAMMER. / HOVERIN'** [59] [ ]
(10"ep+=)(cd-ep+=) *(BADD 3017)(BAD 3017CD)* – I can't help it (if I'm still in love with you) / Do you love me now Jr (J. Mascis remix).

Jul 94. (10"ep) *(BADD 4012)* **HEAD TO TOE. / SHOCKER IN GLOOMTOWN / FREED PIG** [68] [-]
(cd-ep+=) *(BAD 4014CD)* – Saints.

AMPS

KIM DEAL / JIM MacPHERSON / NATHAN FARLEY + LUIS LERMA

4 a.d. — 4 a.d.

Oct 95. (12"ep/cd-ep) *(BAD 5015/+CD)* **TIPP CITY / JUST LIKE A BRIAR. / EMPTY GLASSES (Kim's basement 4 track version)** [61] [-]

Oct 95. (cd)(lp/c) *(CAD 5016CD)(CAD/+C 5016) <61623>* **PACER** [60] [ ]
– Pacer / Tipp city / I am decided / Mom's drunk / Bragging party / Hoverin' / First revival / Full on idle / Breaking the split screen barrier / Empty glasses / She's a girl / Dedicated. *(cd re-iss. Jul98; GAD 5016CD)*

BREEDERS

— new 1997 line-up, included **KIM DEAL + JIM MacPHERSON** plus **MICHAEL O'DEAN** – guitar / **NATE FARLEY** – guitar / **LOUIS NERMA** – bass / **CARRIE BRADLEY** – violin

— **TYLER TRENT** – drums; repl. MacPHERSON who later joined GUIDED BY VOICES

— 2001/2 line-up **KIM + KELLEY** with **RICHARD PRESLEY** – guitar (ex-FEAR) / **MANDO LOPEZ** – bass / **JOSE MEDELES** – drums

4 a.d. — Elektra

Mar 02. (10"ep) *(TAD 2203)* **OFF YOU. / LITTLE FURY / THE SHE** [ ] [-]
(cd-s iss.May02; TAD 2203CDP)

May 02. (lp/cd) *(CAD 2205/+CD) <62766>* **TITLE TK** [51] [ ]
– Little fury / London song / Off you / The she / Too alive / Son of three / Put on a side / Full on idle / Sinister Foxx / Forced to drive / T and T / Huffer.

Sep 02. (7") *(AD 2213)* **SON OF THREE. / BUFFY THEME** [72] [-]
(cd-s+=) *(BAD 2213CD)* – Safari (live).

Jacques BREL

Born: 8 Apr'29, Brussels, Belgium. Reared in a conservative middle-class environment, BREL went on to study law before entering the family business. He soon tired of a conventional lifestyle and instead relocated to Paris where he thought he'd try his hand at songwriting. Despite an awkward gait and buck-teeth, he soon graduated to performing his own compositions, appearing regularly at the Theatre Des Trois Baudets. BREL enthralled fans with a magnetic stage presence and a gift for dramaticism that helped define his vision of the doomed romantic, translating this to the wider record buying public with his first French hit, 'QUAND ON N'A QUE L'AMOUR'. Signed to 'Barclay' in France, BREL proceeded to release a string of singles which documented the dark underbelly of modern society in shrewdly observed style. A one-off album for 'C.B.S.', the self explanatory 'AMERICAN DEBUT' (1957), introduced BREL's literate genius to a whole new English speaking audience and influenced a host of future stars; while the likes of LEONARD COHEN would incorporate the spirit of BREL into his dark balladry, The KINGSTON TRIO interpreted him more literally, transforming 'LE MORIBUND' into the sentimental 'Seasons In The Sun' (later a UK hit for TERRY JACKS). British artists influenced by his work include SCOTT WALKER, DAVID BOWIE, RAY DAVIES, MARC ALMOND, MOMUS and The SENSATIONAL ALEX HARVEY BAND who covered 'NEXT' (a track centering on an army base brothel) as the title track to a 1973 album (mainman ALEX HARVEY had heard the track in a cult continental film, 'Jacques Brel Is Alive And Well And Living In Paris'). A hugely popular and hard working live performer, BREL had sold out both New York's Carnegie Hall and London's Royal Albert before giving up performing for good in the late 60's; he'd already stated his intention to boycott the USA after they became involved in the Vietnam war. He subseqently retired to French Polynesia from where he'd make sporadic recording trips back to Paris. Diagnosed with cancer in the mid-70's, BREL succumbed to the disease on the 10th of October 1978. Despite his dearth of either British or American chart success, he remains one of the last century's most influential songwriters.

Best Album: BREL (*8)

Best CD compilation: QUINZE ANS D'AMOUR (*8)

JACQUES BREL – vocals / with orchestra/session people

Barclay Columbia

1956. (7") **QUAND ON N'A QUE L'AMOUR. /** [–] French [–]
1957. (lp) *<AWS 324>* **AMERICAN DEBUT** [–] [ ]
1959. (lp) **LA VALSE A MILLE TEMPS** [–] French [–]
1962. (lp) **LES BOURGEOIS (live)** [–] French [–]

—— still signed to 'Barclay' in France

Fontana unknown

1962. (lp) *(SFJL 967)* **A L'OLYMPIA** [ ] [–]
(cd-iss. 1988 on 'Philips'; 814372-2)
1963. (lp) *(817004)* **LE PLAT PAYS** [–] French [–]
– Les bourgeois / Les paumes du petit matin / Le plat pays / Zangra / Une ile / Madeleine / Bruxelles / Chanson sans parole / Les biches / Caporal / Casse-pompom / La statue / Rosa. *(UK-iss.1970's on 'Barclay Logo-RCA'; 90015) (cd-iss. 1988 on 'Philips'; 817004-2)*
1964. (lp) **CES GENS-LA** [–] French [–]
– Ces gens-la / Jef / Jacky / Les bergers / Tango funebre / Fernand / Mathilde / L'age idiot / Frand'mere / Les desperes. *(UK-iss.1978 on 'Barclay Logo-RCA'; 90021) <US cd-iss. 1998 on 'Polydor'; 821594>*
1965. (lp) *(TL 5330)* **JACQUES BREL** (UK-iss.of 'LE PLAT PAYS') [ ] [–]
1965. (lp) *(TL 5391)* **JACQUES BREL, VOL.2** [ ] [–]
1966. (lp) **LES BONBONS** [–] French [–]
1967. (lp) *(STL 5429)* **JACQUES BREL '67** [ ] [–]
1968. (lp) **J'ARRIVE** [–] French [–]
(<US cd-iss. 1998 on 'Polydor'; 821595>

Barclay not iss.

Mar 73. (lp) *(80.470)* **NE ME QUITTE PAS** [ ] [–]
– Ne me quitte pas / Marieke / On n'oublie rien / Les flamandes / Les prenoms de Paris / Quand on n'a que l'amour / Les biches / Le prochain amour / Le moribund / La valse a mille temps / Je ne sais pas pourquoi. *(cd-iss. 1980's on 'Phonogram'; 813009-2) (cd re-iss. Jul90 on 'E.C.M.'; 813009-2)*
Nov 77. (lp) *(96010)* **BREL: LES MARQUISES** [–] French [–]
– Jaures / La ville s'endormait / Vieillir / Le bon dieu / Les f? / Orly / Les remparts de varsovie / Voir un ami pleurer / Knokke-le-zoute tango / Jojo / Le lion / Les marquises. *(cd-iss. 1984 on 'Phonogram'; 810537-2)*

—— JACQUES died of cancer on the 10th of October, 1978

– others, compilations, etc. –

Nov 79. (lp) *Barclay; (920492)* **LA CHANSON FRANCAISE** [–] French [–]
– J'aimais / Vasoul / Ces gens la / Amsterdam / Chanson des vieux amants / Les flamandes / Le plat pays / Quand on n' a l'amour / Les paumes du petit matin / Jef.
1980's. (lp) *Barclay Logo-RCA; (90016)* **LA CHANSON DES VIEUX AMANTS** [–] French [–]
– Mon enfance / Le cheval / Mon pere disait / La la la / Les coeurs tendres, du film "un idiot a Paris" / Files de . . . / Les bonbons 67 / La chanson des vieuz amants / A jeun / Le gaz.
1980's. (lp) *Barclay Logo-RCA; (90017)* **AMSTERDAM** [–] French [–]
– Amsterdam / Les timies / Le dernier repas / Les jardins du casino / Les vieux / Les bonbons / Au suivant / La fanette / Les bigotes / Les filles et les chiens / Les fenetres.
1980's. (lp) *Barclay Logo-RCA; (90018)* **VESOUL** [–] French [–]
– J'arrive / Vesoul / L'ostendaise / Je suis un soir d'ete / Regarde bien petit Comment tuer l'amant / de sa femme quand on a ete eleve comme moi dans la tradition / L'eclusier / Un enfant / La biere.
1980's. (lp) *Barclay Logo-RCA; (90019)* **LA FANETTE** [–] French [–]
– Mathilde / La fanette / Jef / Titine / Rosa / Jacky / Fernand / Zangra / Madeleine.
1980's. (lp) *Barclay Logo-RCA; (90020)* **LES VIEUX** [–] French [–]
– Les bonbons / Les vieux / La parlote / Le dernier repas / Titine / Au suivant / Les toros / La fanette / J'aimais / Les filles et les chiens / Les bigotes / Les fenetres. *(cd-iss. 1988 on 'Barclay'; 815989-2)*
Apr 83. (lp/c) *Philips; (6395/7206 216)* **MUSIC FOR THE MILLIONS** [–] French [–]
Aug 86. (d-lp) *Vanguard; (VS2LP 2779)* **BREL ALIVE IN PARIS** [ ] [ ]
Sep 86. (c) *Philips; (818359-4)* **JACQUES BREL** [–] French [–]
– Les prenoms de Paris / Clara / On n'oubile rien / Les singes / Madeleine / Les biches / Les paumes du petit matin / Zangra / La statue / Les bourgeois / Marieke / Ne me quitte pas / Le prochain amour / Le moribund / Au printemps / Le colombe / Les flamandes / L'Ivrogne / La valse a mille tempes / Mivre debout.
Feb 88. (cd/c) *Philips; (816458-2/-4)* **JACQUES BREL: MASTER SERIES** [–] French [–]
– Jaures / Ne me quitte pas / Les vieux / La quete / On n'oublie rien / Le plat pays / Mathilde / Les remparts de varsovie / Amsterdam / J'arive / Ces gens la / Jef / Vesoul / Au suivant / Madeleine / Les bourgeois.
Jan 89. (d-lp/c)(cd; Various Artists) *Silva Screen; (SD/CD 1000)(CGK 40817)* **JACQUES BREL IS ALIVE AND WELL AND LIVING IN PARIS** [ ] [ ]
1988. (cd) *Barclay; (810537-2)* **JAURES** [–] French [–]
1990's. (cd) *Vanguard; <79265>* **LE FORMIDABLE JACQUES BREL** [–] [ ]
Jun 92. (d-cd) *Verve; <816458-2>* **MASTER SERIE: JACQUES BREL** [–] [ ]
Nov 92. (cd) *Musicrama; <1668>* **QUINZE ANS D'AMOUR** [–] [ ]
– Grand Jacques (c'est trop facile) / Quand on n'a que l'amour / Valse a mille temps / Ne me quitte pas / Les flamandes / Le plat pays / Les bourgeois / Quete / Les vieux / Les bonbons / Jef / Mathilde / Au suivant / Chanson de Jacky / Ces gens-la / Mon enfance / Chanson des vieuz amants / J'arrive / Amsterdam.
Nov 92. (cd) *Alex; <3063>* **ORLY** [–] French [–]
Jul 93. (cd/c) *Duchesse; (CD3/MC2 52111)* **GREATEST HITS** [ ] [–]
Mar 96. (cd) *Isba; (5009)* **L'UNIVERS SYMPHONIQUE** [–] French [–]
1996. (d-cd) *Polygram; (531707)* **QUAND ON N'A QUE L'AMOUR** [–] French [–]
Oct 97. (cd) *Musicrama; <4015>* **AMSTERDAM** [–] [ ]
Jan 98. (cd) *Polygram; <521237-2>* **KNOKKE LIVE 1963 (live)** [–] [ ]
Jan 98. (cd) *Polydor; <839586-2>* **L'HOMME DE LA MANCHA (with JOAN DIENER)** [–] [ ]
Jan 98. (d-cd) *Polydor; <515753>* **MASTER SERIE** [–] [ ]
Jan 98. (cd) *Polydor; <845001>* **AMSTERDAM: THE BEST OF JACQUES BREL** [–] [ ]
Jan 98. (10xcd-box) *Polydor; <816719-2>* **GRAND JACQUES** [–] [ ]
– (GRAND JACQUES / LA VALSE A MILLE TEMPS / LES FLAMANDES / LE PLAT PAYS / JEF / J'ARRIVE / ORLY / BREL EN PUBLIC OLYMPIA 1961 / BREL EN PUBLIC 1964 / NE ME QUITTE PAS).
Jan 98. (cd) *<816720-2>* **JACQUES BREL 1: GRAND JACQUES** (rec.1955) [–] [ ]
– Haine / Grand Jacques (c'est trop facile) / Il pleut (les carreaux) / Diable (ca va) / Il nous faut regarder / C'est comme ca / Il peut pleuvoir / Fou du roi / Sur la place / S'll te faut / Bastille / Priere paienne / L'air de la betise / Qu'avons-nous fait, bonnes gens / Pardons / Saint Pierre / Pieds dans le ruisseau / Quand on n'a que l'amour / J'en appelle / Bourree du

celibataire / Heureux / Bles / Demain l'on se Marie (la chanson des vieux amants).

Jan 98. (cd) *<816721-2>* **JACQUES BREL 2: LA VALSE A MILLE TEMPS** (rec.1958) [-] [ ]
– Au printemps / Je ne sais pas / Dors ma mie bonsoir / Dites, si c'tait vrai (poeme) / Colonel / L'homme dans la cite / Lumiere jaillira / Voici / Litanies pour un retour / Seul / Dame patronnesse / La mort / La valse a mille temps / Je t'aime / Ne me quitte pas / Isabelle / Tendresse / Colombe.

Jan 98. (cd) *<816722-2>* **JACQUES BREL 3: LES FLAMANDES** (rec.1961) [-] [ ]
– Les flamandes / L'ivrogne / Marieke / Prochain amour / Vivre debout / Prenoms de Paris / Clara / On n'oublie rien / Singes / Voir / L'adventure / Moutons / Amants de coeur (the lovers) / Il neige sur Liege / Pourquoi faut-il que les hommes / Coeurs tendres / L'enfance / Chanson de Van Horst / Il y a / Foire.

Jan 98. (cd) *<816723-2>* **JACQUES BREL 4: LE PLAT PAYS** (rec.1963) [-] [ ]
– Le plat pays / Zangra / Caporal casse-pompon / La statue / Rosa / Les bourgeois / Madeleine / Les paumes du petit matin / Bruxelles / Chanson sans parole / Une ile / Le bigotes / Le vieux / Fenetres / Toros / Parlote / Filles et les chiens / La fanette / J'aimais / Bergers / Bonbons.

Jan 98. (cd) *<616724-2>* **JACQUES BREL 5: JEF** (rec.1964) [-] [ ]
– Jef / Tango funebre / Desespreres / L'age idiot / Mathilde / Au suivant / Titine / Quand maman reviendra / Dernier repas / Grand-mere / Fernand / Chanson de Jacky / Ces gens-la / La, la / Cheval / Mon enfance / Bonbons 67.

Jan 98. (cd) *<616725-2>* **JACQUES BREL 6: J'ARRIVE** (rec.1968) [-] [ ]
– Chanson des vieux amants / Jeun / Fils de / Mon pere disait / Gaz / L'ostendaise / Je suis un soir d'ete / Enfant / Comment tuer l'amant de sa femme quand o a / Vesoul / J'arrive / Biere / L'eclusier / Regarde bien petit / Quete / Mijn vlakke land (le plat pays) / De burgerij / Rosa / De nuttelozen van de nacht.

Jan 98. (cd) *<616726-2>* **JACQUES BREL 7: ORLY** (rec.1977) [-] [ ]
– Jaures / Ville s'endormait / Viellir / Bon dieu / Les f . . . / Orly / Remparts de varsovie / Voir un ami pleurer / Knokke-le-soute tango / JoJo / Le lion / Les marquises.

Jan 98. (cd) *<616727-2>* **JACQUES BREL 8: BREL EN PUBLIC OLYMPIA 1961 (live)** [-] [ ]
– Prenoms de Paris / Les bourgeois / Paumes du petit matin / Les Flamandes / La statue / Zangra / Marieke / Le biches / Madeleine / Singes / L'ivrogne / La valse a mille temps / Ne me quitte pas / Le moribund / Quand on n'a que l'amour.

Jan 98. (cd) *<616729-2>* **JACQUES BREL 9: BREL UN PUBLIC OLYMPIA 1964 (live)** [-] [ ]
– Amsterdam / Le timides / Dernier repas / Jardins du casino / Le vieux / Toros / Tango funebre / Le pat pays / Le bonbons / Mathilde / Les bigotes / Les bourgeois / Jef / Au suivant / Madeleine.

Jan 98. (cd) *<616729-2>* **JACQUES BREL 10: NE ME QUITTE PAS** (rec.1972) [-] [ ]
– Ne me quitte pas / Marieke / On n'oublie rien / Les Flamandes / Renoms de Paris / Quand on n'a que l'amour / Les biches / Prochain amour / Le moribund / Le valse a mille temps / Je ne sais pas pourquoi.

Apr 99. (cd) *Polygram; <559231-2>* **EN SCENES (ENREGISTREMENT INEDITS) (live)** [-] [ ]

Edie BRICKELL

Born: 10 Mar'66, Oak Cliff, Texas, USA. She joined Dallas group The NEW BOHEMIANS in 1985 after she drank enough to pluck up enough courage to venture on stage to front the band. As a group (alongside KENNY WITHROW, BRAD HOUSER, WES BURT-MARTIN, MATT CHAMBERLAIN and JOHN BUSH), they signed to Geffen records, recording a debut album, 'SHOOTING RUBBERBANDS AT THE STARS', with producer Pat Moran in Wales. This went platinum in the States, reaching Top 5, after the release of the single, 'WHAT I AM'. A soft-rock campus crooner, her voice/range was similar to that of RICKIE LEE JONES, JONI MITCHELL or even MELANIE. Though a follow-up 45, 'CIRCLE', failed to consolidate this success, the band were praised for their live work, touring with BOB DYLAN and generally becoming critical favourites. They further refined their loose, folky jazz/muso sound on 'GHOST OF A DOG' (1990), yet despite favourable reviews, the album's sales were disappointing. BRICKELL subsequently embarked upon a relationship with PAUL SIMON, marrying him in summer '92 and giving birth to his son later that year. By this point, the band had already split and BRICKELL worked on 'PICTURE PERFECT MORNING', a pared down solo set. Despite a few more star collaborations (including ART NEVILLE, DR. JOHN and BARRY WHITE!), the album was given a cool critical reception upon its 1994 release. 2002 saw the release of an inevitable if belated anthology, 'THE ULTIMATE COLLECTION', which actually had more material to draw from than might have been expected. Along with cuts from the two NEW BOHEMIANS albums was a cover of Bob Dylan's 'A HARD RAIN'S A-GONNA FALL' (from the 'Born on the 4th of July' soundtrack) as well as rare collaborations with the likes of JERRY GARCIA and ROB WASSERMAN. Most interesting were a handful of unreleased tracks credited to SLIP, an outfit apparently formed from the ashes of The NEW BOHEMIANS. Royalties came from a surprising direction, when, in 1999, former SPICE GIRL, EMMA BUNTON, featured on TIN TIN OUT'S hit version of 'WHAT I AM'. BRICKELL herself returned shortly after with 'VOLCANO' (2003), her first new material in almost a decade. Despite the time lapse, the singer was still in thrall to cryptic, playful acoustic nu-folk musings, resulting in enjoyable if occasionally fragmented listening. • **Songwriters:** EDIE wrote most of material, except some with WITHROW (and also BUSH). Covered; WALK ON THE WILD SIDE (Lou Reed) / THE EARLY DAY (John Williams). • **Trivia:** In Dec'89, EDIE and Co. collaborated on vinyl with SOUL II SOUL, recording their own composition 'CIRCLE'.

Album rating: SHOOTING RUBBERBANDS AT THE STARS (*7) / GHOST OF A DOG (*5) / PICTURE PERFECT MORNING (*4) / ULTIMATE COLLECTION compilation (*6) / VOLCANO (*5)

EDIE BRICKELL & THE NEW BOHEMIANS

EDIE BRICKELL – vocals, acoustic guitar / **KENNY WITHROW** (b.13 Apr'65) – guitar / **BRAD HOUSER** (b. 7 Sep'60) – bass / **WES BURT-MARTIN** (b.28 May'64) – guitar / **MATT CHAMBERLAIN** (b.17 Apr'67) – drums / **JOHN BUSH** – percussion / guests **WIX** – keyboards / (some by **BRENDAN ALY**)

Geffen Geffen

Sep 88. (lp/c)(cd) *(WX 215/+C)(924192-2) <24192>* **SHOOTING RUBBERBANDS AT THE STARS** [25] [4]
– What I am / Little Miss S. / Air of December / Love like we do / The wheel / Circle / Beat the time / She / Nothing / Now / Keep coming back. *(cd+=)* – I do. *(re-iss. Jan91 lp/c/cd; GEF/+C/D 24192) (cd re-iss. Mar95; GFLD 19268)*

Jan 89. (7"/7"box) *(GEF 49/+B)* **WHAT I AM. / I DO** [31] Nov88 [7]
(12"+=/cd-s+=) *(GEF 49 T/CD)* – Walk on the wild side.

Apr 89. (7") *(GEF 51) <27580>* **CIRCLE. / NOW** [74] Mar89 [48]
(12"+=/cd-s+=) *(GEF 51 T/CD)* – Plain Jane.

Nov 89. (7") *(GEF 61)* **LOVE LIKE WE DO. /** [ ] [-]

— Next 45, was from the film 'Born On The 4th Of July' on 'M.C.A.'

Mar 90. (7") *(MCA 1397)* **A HARD RAIN'S A-GONNA FALL. / THE EARLY DAY, MASSAPEQUA 1957** [ ] [ ]
(12"+=/cd-s+=) *(MCAT/DMCA 1397)* – ('A'version).

Nov 90. (cd)(lp/c) *<(7599 24304-2)>(WX 386/+C)* **GHOST OF A DOG** [63] [32]
– Mama help me / Black and blue / Carmelito / He said / Times like this / Ghost of a dog / 10,000 angels / Strings of love / Woyaha / Oak cliff bra / Stwisted / This eye. *(re-iss. May91 lp/c/cd; GEF/+C/D 24304) (cd re-iss. Mar95; GFLD 19269)*

Jan 91. (7"/c-s) **MAMA HELP ME. / OAK CLIFF BRA** [ ] [-]
(12"+=/cd-s+=) – What I am / Beat the time (live).

EDIE BRICKELL

— with **BILL DILLON, KENNY WITHROW, JOHN LEVENTHAL + BRIAN SOLTZ** – guitar / **TONY HALL, BAKIITHI KUMALO + BRAD HOUSER** –

bass / **SHAWN PELTON or WILLIE GREEN** – drums / + guests hubby **PAUL SIMON + ART NEVILLE**

Aug 94. (cd/c) *<(GED/GEC 24715)>* **PICTURE PERFECT MORNING** 59 68
– Tomorrow comes / Green / When the lights go down / Good times / Another woman's dream / Stay awhile / Hard times / Olivia / In the bath / Picture perfect morning / Lost in the moment. *(cd re-iss. Sep96; GFLD 19332)*

Sep 94. (c-s) *(GEFC 78) <19273>* **GOOD TIMES / PICTURE PERFECT MORNING** 40 60
(cd-s+=) *(GEFTD 78)* – Look out for me.
above featured BARRY WHITE on dual vocals! – HOUSER and CHAMBERLAIN formed their own eclectic funky jazz outfit, CRITTERS BUGGIN

— **BRICKELL** solo again with session people

not iss. / Cherry – Universal

Oct 03. (cd) *<00009630-2>* **VOLCANO** –
– Rush around / Oo la la / I'd be surprised / Songs we used to sing / Once in a blue moon / Volcano / More than friends / The messenger / The one who went away / Take a walk / Not saying goodbye / Came a long way / What would you do.

– compilations, etc. –

Apr 99. (cd) *M.C.A.; <25306>* **THE BEST OF** –

Sep 02. (cd) *Hip-O; <(AA314 541538-2)>* **ULTIMATE COLLECTION** Apr02
– What I am / Little Miss S. / Circle / A hard rain's a-gonna fall / Woyaho / Stwisted / Big day, little boat / Good times / Lost in the moment / Green / Like I do now (with CHRIS BOTTI) / Zillionaire (with JERRY GARCIA & ROB WASSERMAN) / Invisible man (by SLIP) / 1873 (Buffalo diary) (by SLIP) / Girl in a magazine (by SLIP) / Boys in the band / A little time / Vodka (with CARTER ALBRECHT) / Baby (with CARTER ALBRECHT).

□ BRIDGES (see under ⇒ A-HA)

BRINSLEY SCHWARZ

Formed: Tunbridge Wells, England . . . 1965 as the beat/psychedelic combo KIPPINGTON LODGE by SCHWARZ and NICK LOWE. After 5 flop singles between '67 & '69 (the first 'SHY BOY', should have been a hit), they renamed themselves in Autumn '69. They came under the wing of DAVID ROBINSON, former tour manager for JIMI HENDRIX, who now headed the Famepushers Agency. On 3rd April '70, he chartered a plane to fly 150 music journalists to New York to see them support VAN MORRISON at East Fillmore. This proved to be a six-figure sum disaster, due to an admittedly dodgy performance. Predictably, the press ignored their debut album for 'United Artists' and not surprisingly it bombed. Unbowed, they went off to take stock and write new material, resurfacing late in the year with follow-up 'DESPITE IT ALL'. The preceding single 'COUNTRY GIRL' was reminiscent of 'SWEETHEART OF THE RODEO'-era BYRDS and was as fine an example of country-rock as anything coming out of America at the time. Pioneers of the genre in the UK, the band went on to experiment with many other areas of American roots music, evidenced on their 1972 album, 'NERVOUS ON THE ROAD'. Their interest in the "down home" sound had deepened upon seeing American bar band EGGS OVER EASY playing at the Tally Ho club in London. The venue had become a focus for the burgeoning "pub rock" scene of which The BRINSLEY's would soon be such an integral part, along with acts such as BEES MAKE HONEY and DUCKS DELUXE. As well as digging the band's R&B boogie, BRINSLEY SCHWARZ were heavily influenced by EGGS OVER EASY's freewheeling attitude which didn't give a fig for the banks of Marshall stacks and sprawling concept albums which were de rigeur in the early 70's. The same back to basics spirit that inspired the BRINSLEY's to scale down the length of their songs and cut their hair, laid the foundations for the punk explosion later in the decade as well as breaking such important figures as ELVIS COSTELLO and JOE STRUMMER (101'ERS). For the moment though, the band had found a comfortable niche and the track 'HAPPY DOING WHAT WE'RE DOING', from the 'NERVOUS ON THE ROAD' set seemed to confirm this. Another two excellent albums followed, showcasing LOWE's comprehensive songwriting talent on such classic tracks as '(WHAT'S SO FUNNY 'BOUT) PEACE, LOVE AND UNDERSTANDING'. Ironically, no commercial breakthrough came and the band split amicably in 1975, with NICK LOWE going on to a successful solo career, while BRINSLEY and keyboard player BOB ANDREWS helped to form The RUMOUR (GRAHAM PARKER's backing band). • **Covered:** (The Beatles') I SHOULD HAVE KNOWN BETTER. / TELL ME WHY as 'The LIMELIGHT' in '75. • **Trivia:** In 1974, they were featured as The ELECTRICIANS (with DAVE EDMUNDS; their sometimes producer) in the film 'Stardust'.

Album rating: BRINSLEY SCHWARZ (*5) / DESPITE IT ALL (*5) / SILVER PISTOL (*7) / NERVOUS ON THE ROAD (*6) / PLEASE DON'T EVER CHANGE (*6) / THE NEW FAVOURITES OF BRINSLEY SCHWARZ (*7) / SURRENDER TO THE RHYTHM (THE BEST OF BRINSLEY SCHWARZ) compilation (*7)

KIPPINGTON LODGE

BRINSLEY SCHWARZ – guitar, sax / **NICK LOWE** (b.25 Mar'49, Woodbridge, England) – vocals, bass / **BARRY LANDERMAN** – organ / **PETE WHALE** – drums

Parlophone / Capitol

Oct 67. (7") *(R 5645)* **SHY BOY. / LADY ON A BICYCLE** –

Mar 68. (7") *(R 5677) <2236>* **RUMOURS. / AND SHE CRIED**
(above 4 tracks re-iss. Nov78.7"ep on 'EMI')

— **BOB ANDREWS** (b.20 Jun'49) – organ, vox repl. BARRY to VANITY FARE

Aug 68. (7") *(R 5717)* **TELL ME A STORY. / UNDERSTAND A WOMAN** –

Dec 68. (7") *(R 5750)* **TOMORROW TODAY. / TURN OUT THE LIGHT** –

May 69. (7") *(R 5776)* **IN MY LIFE. / I CAN SEE HER FACE** –

BRINSLEY SCHWARZ

— (**BRINSLEY, NICK + BOB**) recruited **BILLY RANKIN** – drums; to repl. PETE

U.A. / Capitol

Apr 70. (lp) *(UAS 29111) <SWBC 11869>* **BRINSLEY SCHWARZ**
– Hymn to me / Shining brightly / Rock & roll women / Lady constant / What do you suggest / Mayfly / Ballad of a has-been beauty queen. *(cd-iss. Feb94 on 'Repertoire'; REP 4421WY)*

May 70. (7") *(UP 35118)* **SHINING BRIGHTLY. / WHAT DO YOU SUGGEST** –

Jun 70. (7") *<3004>* **HYMN TO ME. / ROCK & ROLL WOMAN** –

Liberty / not iss.

Nov 70. (7") *(LBY 15419)* **COUNTRY GIRL. / FUNK ANGEL** –
(re-iss. 1972 on 'United Artists'; UP 35312)

Dec 70. (lp) *(LBG 83427)* **DESPITE IT ALL** –
– Country girl / The slow one / Funk angel / Piece of home / Love song / Starship / Ebury down / Old Jarrow.

— added **IAN GOMM** (b.17 Mar'47) – guitar, vocals

U.A. / U.A.

Oct 71. (lp) *(UAS 29217) <5566>* **SILVER PISTOL**
– Dry land / Merry go round / One more day / Nightingale / Silver pistol / The last time I was fooled / Unknown number / Range war / Egypt / Niki Hoeke speedway / Ju ju man / Rockin' chair. *(re-iss. Apr86 on 'Edsel'; ED 190) (cd-iss. Sep90; EDCD 190)*

Jan 72. (7") *<50915>* **SILVER PISTOL. / NIGHTINGALE** –

— Contributed 5 tracks to 'GREASY TRUCKERS' live lp, Apr72.

Sep 72. (lp) *(UAS 29374) <5647>* **NERVOUS ON THE ROAD**
– It's been so long / Happy doing what we're doing / Surrender to the

rhythm / Don't lose your grip on love / Nervous on the road (but can't stay at home) / Feel a little funky / I like it like that / Brand new you, brand new me / Home in my hand / Why, why, why, why, why. *(re-iss. Dec80 on 'Liberty'; LBR 1040) (cd-iss. Oct95 on 'Beat Goes On'; BGOCD 289) (cd re-iss. Nov02 on 'Repertoire'; REP 4941)*

Oct 72. (7") *<50976>* **NERVOUS ON THE ROAD. / HARRY DOING WHAT WE'RE DOING** [–] [ ]

May 73. (7"; as The HITTERS) *(UP 35530)* **THE HYPOCRITE. / THE VERSION** [ ] [–]

Aug 73. (7") *(UP 35588)* **SPEEDO. / I WORRY** [ ] [–]

Oct 73. (lp) *(UAS 29489)* **PLEASE DON'T EVER CHANGE** [ ] [–]
– Hooked on love / Why do we hurt the one we love? / I worry ('bout you baby) / Don't ever change / Home in my hand / Play that fast thing (one more time) / I won't make it without you / Down in Mexico / Speedo / Hypocrite (the version). *(re-iss. Jan88 on 'Edsel'; ED 237) (cd-iss. Sep90; EDCD 237)*

Mar 74. (7") *(UP 35642)* **I'VE CRIED MY LAST TEAR. / (IT'S GONNA BE A) BRINGDOWN** [ ] [–]

May 74. (7") *(UP 35700)* **(WHAT'S SO FUNNY 'BOUT) PEACE, LOVE AND UNDERSTANDING. / EVER SINCE YOU'RE GONE** [ ] [–]

Jul 74. (lp) *(UAS 29641)* **THE NEW FAVOURITES OF BRINSLEY SCHWARZ** [ ] [–]
– Peace, love and understanding / Ever since you're gone / Ugly things / I got the real thing / Look what's in your eye tonight / Now's the time / Small town, big city / Trying to live my life without you / I like you I don't love you / Down in the dive. *(re-iss. Aug80 on 'Liberty'; LBR 1033) (cd-iss. Nov02 on 'Repertoire'; REP 4942)*

Jan 75. (7") *(UP 35768)* **I LIKE YOU, I DON'T LOVE YOU. / EVERYBODY** [ ] [–]

Jan 75. (7"; as LIMELIGHT) *(UP 35779)* **I SHOULD HAVE KNOWN BETTER. / TELL ME WHY** [ ] [–]

Mar 75. (7") *(UP 35812)* **THERE'S A CLOUD IN MY HEART. / I GOT THE REAL THING** [ ] [–]

—— Disbanded Mar75. SCHWARZ and RANKIN joined DUCKS DELUXE, The former later joining with ANDREWS in GRAHAM PARKER & THE RUMOUR. IAN GOMM later went solo, as did NICK LOWE.

– compilations, others, etc. –

on 'United Artists' unless mentioned otherwise

Mar 74. (lp) *(USP 101)* **ORIGINAL GOLDEN GREATS** [ ] [–]

Jun 76. (7"m) *(UP 36409)* **COUNTRY GIRL. / HOOKED ON LOVE / SURRENDER TO THE RHYTHM** [ ] [–]

Jul 78. (lp) *(UAK 30177)* **FIFTEEN THOUGHTS OF BRINSLEY SCHWARZ** [ ] [–]

Sep 78. (7") *(UP 36466)* **PEACE, LOVE AND UNDERSTANDING. / I'VE CRIED MY LAST TEAR** [ ] [–]

1978. (7"ep; by KIPPINGTON LODGE) *E.M.I.; (NUT 2894)* **KIPPINGTON LODGE** [ ] [–]

May 88. (lp/c)(cd on 'Charly') *Decal; (LIK/TCLIK 22)(CDCHARLY 22)* **IT'S ALL OVER NOW** [ ] [–]

Jul 91. (cd/c/lp) *E.M.I.; (CD/TC+/EMS 1407)* **SURRENDER TO THE RHYTHM (THE BEST OF BRINSLEY SCHWARZ)** [ ] [–]
– Country girl / Surrender to the rhythm / Ugly things / Happy what we're doing / The look what's in your eyes / Last time I was fooled / Silver pistol / Nightingale / Hypocrite / Trying to live my life without you / I like it like that / Nervous on the road / Down in Mexico / I worry ('bout you baby) / Play that fast thing (one more time) / Don't lose your grip on love / Ju Ju man / Down in the dive / Home in my hand. *(cd re-iss. Jun00 on 'Liberty'; 796746-2)*

Jul 94. (cd) *Beat Goes On; (BGOCD 239)* **BRINSLEY SCHWARZ / DESPITE IT ALL** [ ] [–]

Dec 95. (cd) *Beat Goes On; (BGOCD 289)* **NERVOUS ON THE ROAD / THE NEW FAVOURITES OF . . .** [ ] [–]

Apr 98. (cd) *Edsel; (EDCD 546)* **HEN'S TEETH** [ ] [–]

Mar 00. (cd) *Beat Goes On; (<BGOCD 476>)* **ORIGINAL GOLDEN GREATS / FIFTEEN THOUGHTS OF BRINSLEY SCHWARZ** [ ] [ ]

Oct 01. (cd) *Hux; (<HUX 023>)* **WHAT'S SO FUNNY 'BOUT PEACE, LOVE AND UNDERSTANDING** [ ] [ ]

BRITISH SEA POWER

Formed: Brighton, England . . . late 2000 by YAN (guitar/vocals), NOBLE (guitar), WOOD (drums) and HAMILTON (bass/vocals). This eccentric quartet created ripples of interest with their JOY DIVISION-inspired indie-rock gigs and unusual stage aesthetics (large stuffed birds and matching military uniforms!). Releasing first single, 'FEAR OF DROWNING' on their own 'Golden Chariot' label in spring 2001, BSP also continued to run their own monthly club night, Club Sea Power, at Brighton venues The Lift and The Freebutt. After witnessing BRITISH SEA POWER in their natural environment, an impressed Geoff Travis of 'Rough Trade' promptly signed them up. Subsequently releasing two singles, 'REMEMBER ME' and 'THE SPIRIT OF ST. LOUIS', the lads continue to pay rock homage to British marine wildlife. BSP finally issued their long awaited debut album 'THE DECLINE OF . . .' in 2003, a brash, brooding exploration into what could only be described as a psychedelic mish-mash of pop and rock, set to melodic guitar hooks and well-read quasi romantic lyrics. A tough but rewarding listen, the group not only proved that, like their more accessible musical cousins The POSTAL SERVICE, they could successfully bring epic songscapes and tender melodics to the forum of indie rock. This album was crammed with great tracks, from the tense opener 'MEN TOGETHER TODAY', recalling NEW ORDER at their best, to the 13-minute acid-jam rock of 'LATELY' which sounded like YO LA TENGO on bad drugs. Elsewhere, spiky punk rock in the form of 'REMEMBER ME' and the thunderous 'FEAR OF DROWNING', which would make the late IAN CURTIS proud of his legacy. As for lyrics, it's not every day you hear a British indie band quote famous Russian poets and Czech philosophers, well, not unless your the MANICS, which, fortunatly BSP are not. The cheeky title is another quirk added to this strange and sometimes bewildering set, but unlike it suggests, BRITISH SEA POWER were not in decline at all, and that is what made it all the more of a celebrated experience.

Album rating: THE DECLINE OF BRITISH SEA POWER (*8)

YAN – vocals, guitar, keyboards / **M.J. NOBLE** – guitar / **HAMILTON** – bass, vocals / **WOOD** – drums

Golden Chariot — not iss.

Aug 01. (7") *(none)* **FEAR OF DROWNING. / A WOODEN HORSE** [ ] [–]

Rough Trade — Sanctuary

Dec 01. (7") *(RTRADES 032)* **REMEMBER ME. / A LOVELY DAY TOMORROW** [ ] [–]
(cd-s+=) *(RTRADESCD 032)* – Birdy.

Apr 02. (7") *(RTRADES 048)* **THE SPIRIT OF ST. LOUIS. / THE LONELY** [ ] [–]
(cd-s+=) *(RTRADESCD 048)* – No Red Indian.

Nov 02. (7") *(RTRADES 069)* **CHILDHOOD MEMORIES. / STRANGE COMMUNICATION** [ ] [–]
(cd-s+=) *(RTRADESCD 069)* – Beetroot fields.

Jun 03. (cd/lp) *(RTRADE CD/LP 090) <83214>* **THE DECLINE OF BRITISH SEA POWER** [54] Sep03 [ ]
– Men together today / Apologies to insect life / Favours in the beetroot fields / Something wicked / Remember me / Fear of drowning / The lonely / Carrion / Blackout / Lately / A wooden horse. *<US cd+=>* – Childhood memories / Heavenly waters.

Jun 03. (7") *(RTRADES 092)* **CARRION. / APOLOGIES TO INSECT LIFE** [36] [–]
(cd-s+=) *(RTRADESCD 092)* – Heavenly waters.
(cd-s) *(RTRADESCD 092X)* – ('A'-Ridgeway mix) / ('B'-Russian rock demo) / Albert's eyes.

Oct 03. (7") *(RTRADES 125)* **REMEMBER ME. / THE SCOTTISH WILDLIFE EXPERIENCE** [30] [–]
(cd-s) *(RTRADESCD 125)* – ('A'side) / Salty water / Good good boys.
(cd-s) *(RTRADESCD 126)* – ('A'side) / Moley & me / The smallest church in Sussex.

Ian BROWN

Born: 20 Feb'63, Ancoats, Manchester, England. Having hit the heights with the iconic STONE ROSES for nearly a decade, IAN was ready to hit out on his own. In early '98, the man launched his solo career (via a new deal with 'Polydor') by releasing the single, 'MY STAR', a taster from his debut album, 'UNFINISHED MONKEY BUSINESS', which also reached the Top 5. However, BROWN subsequently landed himself in deep water when he was charged with threatening behaviour on a flight between Paris and Manchester. Astonishingly sentenced to four months in prison at the end of October, the singer was released a couple of months early that Christmas eve. Back in circulation the following year, BROWN guested for 'Mo Wax' duo U.N.K.L.E. on the track, 'BE THERE'. Album No.2, 'GOLDEN GREATS', was completed and in the Top 20 towards the end of 1999. Previewed by the hit single, 'LOVE LIKE A FOUNTAIN', the set showed IAN (and co-writer DAVE McCRACKEN) venturing away from the staid and into every funkin' Rock genre under the sun. BROWN surfaced almost two years later with the brilliant orchestral driven single 'F.E.A.R.', in which he turned the letters of the word into a poetic acronym which resulted in a Top 20 hit. His third album proper, 'MUSIC OF THE SPHERES' was issued in October 2001 to almost unanimous critical acclaim and reinforced his self-confidence as an artist when it climbed into the Top 3. • **Covered:** BILLIE JEAN + THRILLER (Michael Jackson).

Album rating: UNFINISHED MONKEY BUSINESS (*6) / GOLDEN GREATS (*7) / MUSIC OF THE SPHERES (*7)

IAN BROWN on mostly all vocals/instruments except co-writers **AZIZ IBRAHIM** – guitars, etc / **SIMON MOORE** – drums / **NIGEL IPPINSON** – keyboards, bass / guests **MANI MOUNFIELD** + **NOEL GALLAGHER** + **DENISE JOHNSON** + co-writer/mixer **ROBBIE MADDIX**

Polydor Polydor

Jan 98. (7") *(571 987-7)* **MY STAR. / SEE THE DAWN** [5] [–]
(cd-s+=) *(571 987-2)* – Fourteen.

Feb 98. (cd/c/lp) *(539 565-2/-4/-1)* **UNFINISHED MONKEY BUSINESS** [4] [–]
– Intro under the paving stones: The beach / My star / Can't see me / Ice cold cube / Sunshine / Lions / Corpses in their mouths / What happened to ya part 1 / What happened to ya part 2 / Nah nah / Deep pile dreams / Unfinished monkey business.

Mar 98. (7") *(569 654-7)* **CORPSES. / JESUS ON THE MOVE / COME AGAIN (part one)** [14] [–]
(cd-s) *(569 657-2)* – (first 2 tracks) / Lions (with Denise).

Jun 98. (7") *(567 092-7)* **CAN'T SEE ME (Bacon & Quarmby remix). / CAN'T SEE ME (Bacon & Quarmby vocal dub)** [21] [–]
(cd-s+=) *(044 045-2)* – Under the paving stones: The beach (Gabriel's 13th dream remix) / ('A'video).
(cd-s) *(044 047-2)* – ('A'side) / ('A'-Harvey's invisible mix) / Come again part 2 / My star (CD-ROM video).
(12"++=) *(044 047-6)* – ('A'-Harvey's instrumental).

Oct 99. (7") *(561 516-7)* **LOVE LIKE A FOUNTAIN. / THE FISHERMAN** [23] [–]
(cd-s+=) *(561 516-2)* – ('A'-CD-Rom mix).
(cd-s) *(561 517-2)* – ('A'side) / ('A'-Stereo MC's mix) / ('A'-Aim mix).

Nov 99. (cd/c/lp) *(543 141-2/-4/-1)* <543720> **GOLDEN GREATS** [14] Feb00 [ ]
– Gettin' high / Love like a fountain / Free my way / Set my baby free / So many sisters / Golden gaze / Dolphins were monkeys / Neptune / First world / Babasonicos.

Feb 00. (7") *(561 637-7)* **DOLPHINS WERE MONKEYS. / CORPSES (live radio session)** [5] [–]
(cd-s) *(561 637-2)* – ('A'side) / Billie Jean / ('A'-Goldfinger mix) / ('A'-CD-Rom).
(cd-s) *(561 638-2)* – ('A'side) / ('A'-Unkle vs. South mix) / Love like a fountain (Andy Votel's remix).

Jun 00. (7") *(561 844-7)* **GOLDEN GAZE. / SUNSHINE (live radio session)** [29] [–]
(cd-s) *(561 844-2)* – ('A'side) / ('A'-Andy Gray remix) / Love like a fountain (Laj & Quakerman remix) / ('A'-CD-Rom).
(cd-s) *(561 845-2)* – ('A'side) / Thriller / ('A'-Sharktank's dirt it up remix).

Sep 01. (7") *(587 284-7)* **F.E.A.R. / (instrumental)** [13] [–]
(c-s) *(587 284-4)* – ('A'side) / ('A'-side with DANN).
(cd-s+=) *(587 284-2)* – Hear no see no speak no (extended) / ('A'video).

Oct 01. (cd/c) *(<589 126-2/-4>)* **MUSIC OF THE SPHERES** [3] [ ]
– F.E.A.R. / Stardust / The gravy train / Bubbles / Hear no see no / Northern lights / Whispers / El mundo pequeno / Forever and a day / Shadow of a saint.

Feb 02. (7") *(570538-7)* **WHISPERS. / EL MUNDO PEQUENO** [33] [–]
(cd-s) *(570538-2)* – ('A'side) / ('A'video) / Superstar / My star (remix).

Nov 02. (cd/d-lp) *(065927-2/-1)* **REMIXES OF THE SPHERES** (remixes) [ ] [–]

James BROWN

Born: 3 May'33 in Barnwell, South Carolina. At the age of five, BROWN moved to his Aunt's brothel in Augusta, Georgia, during which time he learned to play piano, drums and guitar. By the time he was nineteen, after a brief spell as a semi-pro boxer and a brief spell in jail, he had settled in Georgia and was a member of BOBBY BYRD's quartet, the GOSPEL STARLIGHTERS. A raw Southern gospel group, they subsequently evolved into a R&B outfit, in the process changing their name to the AVONS, then the FLAMES. The band performed R&B covers, among them an ORIOLES song, 'BABY PLEASE DON'T GO'. After some fine tuning, BROWN brought the "please" to the forefront, crafting the showstopping 'PLEASE, PLEASE, PLEASE'. On hearing the tune, LITTLE RICHARD, at the time Georgia's most celebrated black musician, told Brown to move to Macon, Georgia, where the song was cut at a local radio station under the band name the FAMOUS FLAMES, the prefix added coutesy of Richard's manager, Clint Brantly. Although the song was refused by a number of labels, when Ralph Bass of 'King' Records heard the tune, he immediately signed the group and the track was re-recorded at King's Ohio studio. The session proved to be more troublesome than expected, as the musical director and owner of the label couldn't come to grips with BROWN's unusual and now heavily influential writing style of hitting on the downbeat instead of the upbeat. Nevertheless, the track was eventually released on King's 'Federal' label in March '56, making No.5 on the Billboard R&B chart. It would be another three years before their next hit, the infectious 'TRY ME' reaching No.1 on the R&B chart and crucially creating enough money for BROWN to hire a backing band, the first quintet led by the tenor sax of J.C. DAVIS. It was during the end of the 50's, with the components all in place, that the band set about touring to sharpen their sound and BROWN's routines of knee-drops, flying splits and cochlea-piercing screams. Whilst BROWN continued to supply hits for 'King', he still hadn't hit the big time, subsequently trying to persuade the label to front the money for a live recorded performance. With 'King' not convinced that such a record would sell, BROWN decided to put up his own cash, coming up with one of the most successful live LP's of all time, the '63 killer 'LIVE AT THE APOLLO'. The record not only made it to No.2 on the Billboard album charts, it also had the knock-on effect of mammoth audience attendances, and in turn increased sales figures and the high profile that BROWN craved. This mushroomed to an even greater height when, in '65, he released the definitive funk single, 'PAPA'S GOT A BRAND NEW BAG', featuring a larger band led by the trumpet of LEWIS HAMLIN, in the process modifying his style from the gospel and blues structure to a more straight ahead approach. His singing was also reaching new heights of primordial intensity, fusing with a tight and oh-so-funky backing band. The middle to late 60's proved a purple patch for BROWN, with one classic single following another; 'IT'S A MAN'S WORLD' in '66, 'COLD SWEAT' in '67, 'SAY IT LOUD – I'M BLACK AND PROUD' in '68 and 'GET UP / I FEEL LIKE BEING A SEX MACHINE' in '70, his backing band including the likes of the PARKER brothers (MACEO and MELVIN) and older stalwarts like JIMMY NOLAN and ALPHONSO KELLUM on guitars. The early 70's saw the line-up constantly changing, PEE WEE ELLIS, BOOTSY COLLINS and PHELPS COLLINS the leading lights in the backing band dubbed first The PACEMAKERS, then latterly the now familiar J.B.'s, FRED WESLEY joining soon after to form the backbone of the band alongside MACEO. BROWN's '72 single, 'KING HEROIN' is often cited as the first rap record (although the waters are cloudy on this one), and he even made it to Zaire for the "Rumble In The Jungle", solidifying his status as Soul Brother Number One. He continued to tour the world throughout the '70s, simultaneously influencing popular music styles wherever he went, although the quality of his recordings became ever more infrequent set next to the standards he had already set, a prime example being the '79 offering 'TAKE A LOOK AT THOSE CAKES'. However, his spectacular cameo as the rocking reverend in the '80 cult classic film, 'The Blues Brothers' opened the gates to a whole new generation of fans, and as the Stars & Stripes clad special guest in 'Rocky IV', he stole the show whilst achieving yet another Top 10 hit with the cheesy 'LIVING IN AMERICA'. BROWN has had his problems with the law along the way, the most publicised event occurring in September '88, when he walked into an insurance seminar with a shotgun in an attempt to find out who had used his private toilet, the tale ending in a two-state police chase and two years in jail. Having amassed 98 entries on Billboard's Top 40 R&B singles chart over his career, earning the nickname 'the hardest working man in showbusiness', as well as being sampled by other musicians an estimated 4000 times, his journey from juvenile delinquent to the Godfather Of Soul bears all the hallmarks of greatness.

Album rating (selective): PLEASE, PLEASE, PLEASE (*6) / TRY ME! (*6) / LIVE AT THE APOLLO (*9) / PURE DYNAMITE! LIVE AT THE ROYAL (*6) / LIVE AT THE APOLLO, VOL.II (*7) / REVOLUTION OF THE MIND – LIVE AT THE APOLLO, VOL. III (*8) / THERE IT IS (*7) / THE PAYBACK (*7) / HELL (*7) / FUNKY PRESIDENT (*7) / THE BEST OF JAMES BROWN (THE GODFATHER OF SOUL) compilation (*9) / STAR TIME boxed set (*9) / THE GODFATHER (THE VERY BEST OF JAMES BROWN) compilation (*8) / THE NEXT STEP (*5)

JAMES BROWN & THE FAMOUS FLAMES

JAMES BROWN – vocals, multi / **BOBBY BYRD** – organ / **JOHNNY TERRY** - / **SYLVESTER KEELS** - / **NAFLOYD SCOTT** – guitar / **etc.**

not iss. Federal

Feb 56. (7") *<12258>* **PLEASE, PLEASE, PLEASE. / WHY DO YOU DO ME** –

May 56. (7") *<12264>* **I DON'T KNOW. / I FEEL THAT OLD FEELING COMING ON** –

Aug 56. (7") *<12277>* **NO, NO, NO, NO. / HOLD MY BABY'S HAND** –

Dec 56. (7") *<12289>* **JUST WON'T DO ME RIGHT. / LET'S MAKE IT** –

Jan 57. (7") *<12290>* **CHONNIE-ON-CHON. / I WON'T PLEAD NO MORE** –

Feb 57. (lp) *<610>* **PLEASE, PLEASE, PLEASE** –
– Please, please, please / Chonnie-on-chon / Hold my baby's hand / I feel that same old feeling coming on / Just won't do right / Baby cries over the ocean / I don't know / Tell me what I did wrong / Try me / That dood it / Begging, begging / I walked alone / No, no, no, no / That's when I lost my heart / Let's make it / Love or a game.

Mar 57. (7") *<12292>* **CAN'T BE THE SAME. / GONNA TRY** –

Jul 57. (7") *<12295>* **LOVE OR A GAME. / MESSING WITH THE BLUES** –

Nov 57. (7") *<12300>* **YOU'RE MINE, YOU'RE MINE. / I WALKED ALONE** –

Mar 58. (7") *<12311>* **THAT DOOD IT. / BABY CRIES OVER THE OCEAN** –

May 58. (7") *<12316>* **BEGGING, BEGGING. / THAT'S WHEN I LOST MY HEART** –

Nov 58. (7") *<12337>* **TRY ME. / TELL ME WHAT I DID WRONG** – 48

Apr 59. (7") *<12348>* **I WANT YOU SO BAD. / THERE MUST BE THE REASON** –

Jun 59. (7") *<12352>* **I'VE GOT TO CHANGE. / IT HURTS TO TELL YOU** –

Jul 59. (lp) *<635>* **TRY ME** –
– Try me / There must be a reason / Strange things happen / Messing with the blues / Why do you do me / I've got to cry / Fine old foxy self / I want you so bad / It was you / I've got to change / Can't be the same / It hurts to tell you / I won't plead no more / You're mine, you're mine / Gonna try / Don't let it happen to me.

Oct 59. (7") *<12361>* **GOOD GOOD LOVIN'. / DON'T LET IT HAPPEN TO ME** –

Dec 59. (7") *<12364>* **IT WAS YOU. / GOT TO CRY** –

—— Released MASHED POTATOES on 'Dade' label, as NAT KENDRICK & THE SWANS.

Feb 60. (lp) *<683>* **THINK** –
– Think / Good good lovin' / Wonder when you're coming home / I'll go crazy / This old heart / I know it's true / Bewildered / I'll never never let you go / You've got the power / If you want me / Baby, you're right / So long.

Mar 60. (7") *<12369>* **I'LL GO CRAZY. / I KNOW IT'S TRUE** –

Parlophone Federal

Jun 60. (7") *(R 4667) <12370>* **THINK. / YOU'VE GOT THE POWER** Apr60 33 86

Nov 60. (7") *(H 273) <12378>* **THIS OLD HEART. / WONDER WHEN YOU'RE GOING HOME** – Jul60 79
(above issued on 'Fontana' UK)

Parlophone King

Nov 60. (7") *<5423>* **THE BELLS. / AND I DO JUST WHAT I WANT** – 68

Jan 61. (7") *<5438>* **HOLD IT (instrumental). / THE SCRATCH (instrumental)** –

Feb 61. (7") *<5442>* **BEWILDERED. / IF YOU WANT ME** – 40

Apr 61. (7") *<5466>* **I DON'T MIND. / LOVE DON'T LOVE NOBODY** – 47

Jun 61. (7") *<5485>* **SUDS (instrumental). / STICKY (instrumental)** –

Aug 61. (7") *<5519>* **CROSSFIRING (instrumental). / NIGHT FLYING (instrumental)** –

Sep 61. (7") *<5524>* **BABY, YOU'RE RIGHT. / I'LL NEVER NEVER LET YOU GO** – 47

1961. (lp) *<743>* **THE AMAZING JAMES BROWN** –
– I love you, yes I do / Lost someone / You don't have to go / Dancin' little thing / The bells / Tell me what you're gonna do / So long / Just you and me / And I do just what I want / Come over here / I don't mind / Love don't love nobody.

Nov 61. (7") *<5547>* **I LOVE YOU, YES I DO. / JUST YOU AND ME DARLING** –

Jan 62. (7") *<5573>* **LOST SOMEONE. / CROSS FIRING (instrumental)** – 48

Jul 62. (7") *(R 4922) <5614>* **NIGHT TRAIN (instrumental). / WHY DOES EVERYTHING HAPPEN TO ME** Apr62 35
(re-iss. Dec64 on 'Sue'; WI 360)

Aug 62. (7") *(R 4952) <5657>* **SHOUT AND SHIMMY. / COME OVER HERE** 61

Sep 62. (7") *<5672>* **MASHED POTATOES U.S.A. / YOU DON'T HAVE TO GO** – 82

Nov 62. (7") *<5698>* **(CAN YOU) FEEL IT. / (part 2)** –

Dec 62. (7") *<5701>* **THREE HEARTS IN A TANGLE. / I'VE GOT MONEY** – 93

London King

Dec 62. (lp) *<826>* **LIVE AT THE APOLLO (live)** – 2
– I'll go crazy / Try me / Think / I don't mind / Lost someone (part 1 & 2) / Please, please, please / You've got the power / I found someone / Why do you do me like you do / I want you so bad / I love you yes I do /

Why does everything happen to me / Bewildered / Please don't go / Night train. *(UK-iss.Sep64; HA 8184) (re-iss. Aug75 on 'Polydor')* <*re-iss. Nov80 as 'LIVE AND LOWDOWN AT THE APOLLO, VOL.1' on 'Solid Smoke'; 8006*> *(re-iss. Sep73 on 'Polydor' lp/c; SPE LP/MC 46) (cd-iss. Jul90; 843479-2)*

Jan 63. (7") *<5710>* **EVERY BEAT OF MY HEART (instrumental). / LIKE A BABY** [–] [99]

Apr 63. (7") *(HL 9730) <5739>* **PRISONER OF LOVE. / CHOO CHOO (LOCOMOTION)** [ ] [18]

Jun 63. (7") *(HL 9775) <5767>* **THESE FOOLISH THINGS. / (CAN YOU) FEEL IT** [ ] [55]

Sep 63. (lp) *<851>* **PRISONER OF LOVE** [–] [73]
– Prisoner of love / Waiting in vain / Again / Lost someone / Bewildered / So long / Signed, sealed & delivered / Try me / (Can you) Feel it (pt.1) / How long darling / The thing in 'G'. *(re-iss. Nov83 on 'Polydor'; 8134 911)*

Oct 63. (7") *<5803>* **SIGNED, SEALED AND DELIVERED. / WAITING IN VAIN** [–] [77]

Jan 64. (7") *<5829>* **I'VE GOT TO CHANGE. / THE BELLS** [–] [ ]

Feb 64. (7") *<5842>* **OH BABY DON'T YOU WEEP. / (part 2)** [–] [23]

Mar 64. (7") *<5853>* **PLEASE, PLEASE, PLEASE. / IN THE WEE WEE HOURS** [–] [95]

— He signed to 'Smash' records in the US and was also retained by 'King'. In the UK, 'King' was licensed by 'London' until late '65. The releases on 'Smash' US were on 'Philips' UK, and marked *.

May 64. (7") *<1898> **CALEDONIA. / EVIL** [–] [95]

Jun 64. (7") *<5876>* **AGAIN. / HOW LONG DARLING** [–] [ ]

Jul 64. (lp) *(HA 8177) <883>* **PURE DYNAMITE! LIVE AT THE ROYAL (live)** [ ] Feb64 [10]
– Shout and shimmy / These foolish things / Signed, sealed and delivered / Like a baby / I'll never let you go / Please, please, please / Oh, baby, don't you weep / Good, good lovin'.

Jul 64. (7") *<5899>* **SO LONG. / DANCIN' LITTLE THING** [–] [ ]

Aug 64. (7") *<1908> **THE THINGS I USED TO DO. / OUT OF THE BLUE** [–] [99]

Sep 64. (7") *(BF 1368)*<1919>* **OUT OF SIGHT. / MAYBE THE LAST TIME** [ ] Aug64 [24]

Jun 64. (7") *<5922>* **TELL ME WHAT YOU'RE GONNA DO. / I DON'T CARE** [–] [ ]

Sep 64. (lp) *(BL 7630)*<67054>* **SHOWTIME (live)** [ ] May64 [61]

Sep 64. (lp) *Ember; (EMB 3357)* **TELL ME WHAT YOU'RE GONNA DO** [ ] [–]
– Just you and me darling / I love, yes I do / I don't mind / Come over here / The bells / Love don't love nobody / Dancin' little thing / Lost someone / And I do just what I want / So long / You don't have to go / Tell me what you're gonna do. *(cd-iss. Mar95 on 'Charly'; CPCD 8053)*

Oct 64. (7") *<5952>* **THINK. / TRY ME** [–] [ ]

Oct 64. (7") *<5956>* **FINE OLD FOXY SELF. / MEDLEY** [–] [ ]

Dec 64. (7") *(HL 9945) <5968>* **HAVE MERCY BABY. / JUST WON'T DO RIGHT** [ ] [92]

Mar 65. (7") *<1975> **DEVIL'S HIDEAWAY (instrumental). / WHO'S AFRAID OF VIRGINIA WOOLF (instrumental)** [–] [ ]

Apr 65. (lp) *(BL 7664)*<67057>* **GRITS AND SOUL (instrumental)** [ ] [ ]
– Grits / Tempted / There / After you're through / Devil's den / Who's afraid of Virginia Woolf / Infatuation / Wee wee / Mister hip / Headache.

Apr 65. (7") *<5995>* **THIS OLD HEART. / IT WAS YOU** [–] [ ]

Jul 65. (lp) *(HA 8231) <909>* **PLEASE, PLEASE, PLEASE** [ ] [ ]
– Try me / Please, please, please / I feel that old feeling coming on / That's when I lost my heart / Chonnie on chon / Hold my baby's hand / Tell me what I did wrong / Baby cries over the ocean / Begging, begging / No, no, no, no / That dood it / I don't know / I walked alone / Love or a game / Let's make it / Just won't do right. *(re-iss. Nov83; 2489 194)*

— His UK touring band 1965 **BOBBY BYRD, BOBBY BENNETT, JAMES CRAWFORD + LLOYD STALLWORTH**

Aug 65. (7") *(HL 9990) <5999>* **PAPA'S GOT A BRAND NEW BAG. / (part 2)** [25] Jul65 [8]

Sep 65. (lp) *<938>* **PAPA'S GOT A BRAND NEW BAG** [–] [26]
– Papa's got a brand new bag / Mashed potatoes U.S.A. / This old heart / Cross firing / Doin' the limbo / Baby, you're right / Love don't love nobody / Have mercy baby / And I do just what I want / I stay in the chapel every night / You don't have to go. *(UK-iss.Mar66; HA 8262) (re-iss. May67 on 'Pye International'; NPL 28099) (re-iss. Nov83 on 'Polydor'; 2489 195)*

Oct 65. (lp) *(HA 8240)* **JAMES BROWN AND HIS FAMOUS FLAMES TOUR THE U.S.A. (live)** [ ] [–]

Dec 65. (7") *(BF 1458)*<2008>* **TRY ME (instrumental) / PAPA'S GOT A BRAND NEW BAG (instrumental)** [ ] [63]

Dec 65. (lp) *(BL 7697)*<67072>* **JAMES BROWN PLAYS JAMES BROWN TODAY AND YESTERDAY** [ ] Nov65 [42]
– Papa's got a brand new bag / Oh baby don't you weep / Every beat of my heart / Out of sight / Sidewinder / Maybe the last time / Hold it / Song for my father.

Pye Int. King

Feb 66. (7") *(7N 25350) <6015>* **I GOT YOU (I FEEL GOOD). / I CAN'T HELP IT** [29] Nov65 [3]

Mar 66. (7") *<6020>* **LOST SOMEONE. / I'LL GO CRAZY** [–] Jan66 [94] [73]

Apr 66. (lp) *(NPL 29072) <946>* **I GOT YOU (I FEEL GOOD)** [ ] Jan66 [36]
– I got you (I feel good) / Good good lovin' / Lost someone / I can't help it / You've got the power / Night train / I've got money / Dancin' little thing / Three hearts in a tangle / Suds / Love don't love nobody.

Apr 66. (7") *(7N 25367) <6025>* **AIN'T THAT A GROOVE. / (part 2)** [ ] Feb66 [42]

Apr 66. (7") *<6029>* **PRISONER OF LOVE. / I'VE GOT TO CHANGE** [–] [ ]

May 66. (7") *<6032>* **COME OVER HERE. / TELL ME WHAT YOU'RE GONNA DO** [–] [ ]

Apr 66. (7") *(BF 1481)*<2028>* **NEW BREED (instrumental) / (part 2)** [ ] [ ]

May 66. (lp) *(BL 7718)*<67090>* **JAMES BROWN PLAYS NEW BREED** [ ] Apr66 [ ]
– New breed / Slow walk / Fat bag / Vanshelia / Jabo / Lost in the mood of changes / All about my girl / Hooks / Something else.

Jun 66. (7") *(7N 25371) <6035>* **IT'S A MAN'S MAN'S MAN'S WORLD. / IS IT YES OR IS IT NO?** [13] Apr66 [8]

Jun 66. (7") *<6037>* **JUST WON'T DO RIGHT. / I'VE GOT MONEY** [–] [ ]

Jun 66. (7") *<2042> **JAMES BROWN'S BOO-GA-LOO (instrumental) / LOST IN A MOOD OF CHANGES (instrumental)** [–] [ ]

Jul 66. (lp) *(NPL 28079) <985>* **IT'S A MAN'S, MAN'S, MAN'S WORLD** [ ] [90]
– It's a man's, man's, man's world / Is it yes or is it no? / Ain't that a groove (pt.1 & 2) / The scratch / Bewildered / The bells in the wee wee hours / Come over here / I don't mind / Just you and me / I love you, yes I do. *(re-iss. Nov83 on 'Polydor'; 2489 197)*

Jul 66. (7") *<6040>* **IT WAS YOU. / I DON'T CARE** [–] [ ]

Aug 66. (7") *<6044>* **THIS OLD HEART. / HOW LONG DARLING** [–] [ ]

Sep 66. (7") *(7N 25379) <6048>* **MONEY WON'T CHANGE YOU. / (pt.2)** [ ] Jul66 [53]

Nov 66. (7") *<6056>* **DON'T BE A DROP-OUT. / TELL ME THAT YOU LOVE ME** [–] [50]

Dec 66. (7") *<6064>* **THE CHRISTMAS SONG. / (pt.2)** [–] [ ]

Dec 66. (7") *<6065>* **SWEET LITTLE BABY BOY. / (pt.2)** [–] [ ]

Dec 66. (lp) *(NPL 28097)* **THE JAMES BROWN CHRISTMAS ALBUM** (festive songs) [ ] [–]

Dec 66. (7") *(7N 25411) <6071>* **BRING IT UP. / NOBODY KNOWS** [ ] [29]

Dec 66. (7") *<6072>* **LET'S MAKE CHRISTMAS MEAN SOMETHING THIS YEAR. / (pt.2)** [–] [ ]

Feb 67. (lp) *(NPL 28093)* **MIGHTY INSTRUMENTALS** [ ] [–]
– Papa's got a brand new bag (part 1) / Feel it / Hold it / Sticky / Scratch / James Brown's house party / Night train / Every beat of my heart / Cross firing / Suds / Doin' the limbo / Choo choo.

Mar 67. (7") *<2064> **LET'S GO GET STONED (instrumental) / OUR DAY WILL COME (instrumental)** [–] [ ]

Mar 67. (lp; stereo/mono) *(S+BL 7761)*<67084>* **HANDFUL OF SOUL** [ ] Nov66 [ ]
– Our day will come / Get loose / Oh Henry / Let's go get stoned / Hot mix / Hold on, I'm coming / King / When a man loves a woman / Message to Michael / 6345-789.

Apr 67. (7") *(7N 25418) <6086>* **KANSAS CITY. / STONE FOX (instrumental)** [ ] [55]

May 67. (lp) *(NPL 28103) <1016>* **SINGS RAW SOUL** [ ] Apr67 [88]
– Bring it up / Don't be a drop out / Till then / Tell me that you love me / Yours and mine / Money won't change you (part 1 & 2) / Only you / Let yourself go / The nearness of you / Nobody knows / Stone fox.

— In May '67, he issued 7" 'THINK' a collaboration with VICKI ANDERSON hit No.100 in the US.

Nov 67. (lp) *(NPL 28104) <1018>* **LIVE AT THE GARDEN (live)** [ ] Jun67 [41]
– Out of sight / Bring it up / Try me / Let yourself go / Hip bag '67 / Prisoner of love / It may be the last time / I got you / Ain't that a groove (parts 1 & 2) / Please, please, please / Bring it up.

Jul 67. (7") *(7N 25423) <6100>* **LET YOURSELF GO. / GOOD ROCKIN' TONIGHT** [ ] [46]

Jul 67. (lp) *(NPL 28100)* **MR. EXCITEMENT** (recordings from 1962) [ ] [–]
(re-iss. Nov83 on 'Polydor')

Jul 67. (7") **<2093>* **JIMMY MACK (instrumental) / WHAT DO YOU LIKE (instrumental)** [–] [ ]

—— In mid'67, he released 'I LOVE YOU PORGY'. / 'YOURS AND MINE' on 'Bethlehem' <3089>.

—— **ALFRED 'Pee-Wee' ELLIS** – brass; repl. JONES new **JIMMY NOLEN** – guitar / **CLYDE STUBBLEFIELD** – drums / **MACEO PARKER** – tenor sax / **ST. CLAIR PINCKNEY** – tenor sax / etc.

Sep 67. (7") *(7N 25430) <6110>* **COLD SWEAT. / (pt.2)** [ ] Jul67 [7]

Oct 67. (lp) *(658 043) <1020>* **COLD SWEAT** [ ] Sep67 [35]
– Cold sweat (pt.1 & 2) / Nature boy / Come rain or come shine / I love you Porgy / Back stabbin' / Fever / Mona Lisa / I want to be around / Good rockin' tonight / Stagger Lee / Kansas City. *(re-iss. Nov83 on 'Polydor')*

Oct 67. (7") *<6112>* **AMERICA IS MY HOME. / (part 2)** [–] [ ]
<hit US No.52 in May68>

Nov 67. (lp) *(582 703)* **THE JAMES BROWN SHOW (live)** [ ] [–]
– I'll go crazy / Try me / Think / I don't mind / Lost someone / Please, please, please / You've got the power / I found someone / Why do you do me / I want you so bad / I love you yes I do / Why does everything happen to me / Bewildered / Please don't go / Night train.

Nov 67. (7") *(7N 25441) <6122>* **GET IT TOGETHER. / (pt.2)** [ ] Oct67 [40]

Nov 67. (7") *<6133>* **FUNKY SOUL No.1 (instrumental) / THE SOUL OF J.B. (instrumental)** [–] [ ]

Nov 67. (7") *<6141>* **I GUESS I'LL HAVE TO CRY, CRY, CRY. / JUST PLAIN FUNK (instrumental)** [–] [ ]
<hit No.US 55 in Jul68>

Polydor King

Dec 67. (7") *(56740) <6144>* **I CAN'T STAND MYSELF (WHEN YOU TOUCH ME). / THERE WAS A TIME** [ ] [28] [36]

Mar 68. (lp) *(184 136) <1030>* **I CAN'T STAND MYSELF (WHEN YOU TOUCH ME)** [ ] [17]
– I can't stand myself (when you touch me) (part 1) / There was a time / Get it together (part 1) / Baby, baby, baby, baby / Time after time / The soul of J.B. (instrumental) / I can't stand myself (when you touch me) (part 2) / Get it together (part 2) / Why did you take your love away from me / Need your love so bad / You've got to change your mind / Fat Eddie *[US]* / Funky soul #1 *[UK]*.

Mar 68. (7"; with BOBBY BYRD) *<6151>* **YOU'VE GOT TO CHANGE YOUR MIND. / I'LL LOSE MY MIND** [–] [ ]

Mar 68. (7"; with VICKI ANDERSON) *<6152>* **YOU'VE GOT THE POWER. / WHAT THE WORLD NEEDS NOW IS LOVE** [–] [ ]

May 68. (7") *(56743) <6155>* **I GOT THE FEELIN'. / IF I RULED THE WORLD** [ ] Mar68 [6]

Apr 68. (lp) *(623 032)* **MR. DYNAMITE** [ ] [–]
– Money won't change you (part 1 & 2) / I don't mind / Doin' the limbo / I stay in the chapel every night / Scratch / Night train / I can't help it / Is it yes or is it no / Come over here / In the wee wee hours / Choo choo.

Apr 68. (7") *<6159>* **MAYBE GOOD, MAYBE BAD (instrumental). / (pt.2)** [–] [ ]

May 68. (7") *<6164>* **SHHHHHHHHH (FOR A LITTLE WHILE) (instrumental). / HERE I GO (instrumental)** [–] [ ]

May 68. (lp) *<1031>* **I GOT THE FEELIN'** [–] [ ]
– I got the feelin' / Maybe I'll understand – part 1 / You've got the power / Maybe good, maybe bad – part 1 / Shhhhhhh (for a little while) / Just plain funk / If I ruled the world / Maybe I'll understand – part 2 / Stone fox / It won't be me / Maybe good, maybe bad – part 2 / Here I go.

Jun 68. (7") *(56744) <6166>* **LICKING STICK, LICKING STICK. / (pt.2)** [ ] May68 [14]

JAMES BROWN

—— solo, but still with The FAMOUS FLAMES

Sep 68. (7") *(56752) <6187>* **SAY IT LOUD – I'M BLACK AND I'M PROUD. / (pt.2)** [ ] [10]

Sep 68. (d-lp) *<1022>* **LIVE AT THE APOLLO VOLUME 2 (live)** [–] [32]
– Introduction / Think / I want to be around / Thanks / That's life / Kansas City / Let yourself go / There was a time / I feel all right / Cold sweat / It may be the last time / I feel good / Prisoner of love / Out of sight / Try me / Bring it up / It's a man's man's world / Lost someone / Please, please, please. *(UK-iss.Jun69; 583 729/30) (re-iss. Jun70; 2612 005) (cd-iss. Dec88 on 'Polydor') (cd-iss. Jan 93)*

Nov 68. (7") *<6198>* **GOODBYE MY LOVE. / SHADES OF BROWN (instrumental)** [–] [31]

Nov 68. (7") *(BM 56540)* **THAT'S LIFE. / PLEASE, PLEASE, PLEASE** [ ] [–]

Dec 68. (7") *<6203>* **SANTA CLAUS GOES STRAIGHT TO THE GHETTO. / YOU KNOW IT (instrumental)** [–] [ ]

Dec 68. (7") *<6204>* **TIT FOR TAT (AIN'T NO TAKING BACK). / BELIEVERS SHALL ENJOY** [–] [86]

Dec 68. (7") *<6205>* **LET'S UNITE THE WHOLE WORLD AT CHRISTMAS. / IN THE MIDDLE (pt.1)** [–] [ ]

Jan 69. (7") *<6213>* **GIVE IT UP OR TURNIT A LOOSE. / I'LL LOSE MY MIND** [–] [15]

Jan 69. (lp) *(580 701)* **TURN IT LOOSE** [ ] [–]
– Give it up or turnit a loose / I'll lose my mind / I don't want nobody to give me tonight (open up the door, I'll get it myself) (parts 1 & 2).

Mar 69. (7") *<6216>* **ATTACK WITH THE NEWS. / SHADES OF BROWN (pt.2)** [–] [ ]

Mar 69. (7"; with MARVA WHITNEY) *<6218>* **YOU'VE GOT TO HAVE A JOB. / I'M TIRED, I'M TIRED, I'M TIRED** [–] [ ]

Mar 69. (7") *<6222>* **SOUL PROUD. / (pt.2)** [–] [ ]

Mar 69. (7") *<6223>* **YOU'VE GOT TO HAVE A MOTHER FOR ME. / (part 2)** [–] [ ]

Apr 69. (7") *<6224>* **I DON'T WANT NOBODY TO GIVE ME NOTHIN' (OPEN UP THE DOOR, I'LL GET IT MYSELF). / (pt.2)** [–] [20]

Apr 69. (lp) *<1047>* **SAY IT LOUD – I'M BLACK AND I'M PROUD** [–] [53]
– Say it loud I'm black and proud (parts 1 & 2) / I guess I'll have to cry, cry, cry / Goodbye my love (parts 1 & 2) / Shades of brown / Licking stick / I love you / Then you can tell me goodbye / Let them talk / Maybe I'll understand / I'll lose my mind. *(UK-iss.Sep69; 583 741)*

May 69. (7") *<6235>* **THE LITTLE GROOVE MAKER ME. / I'M SHOOK** [–] [ ]

May 69. (lp) *<1051>* **GETTIN' DOWN TO IT** [–] [99]
– Sunny / That's life / Strangers in the night / Willow weep for me / Cold sweat / There was a time / Chicago / For sentimental reasons / Time after time / All the way / It had to be you / Uncle. *(UK-iss.Jan70; 583 742)*

Jun 69. (7") *<6240>* **THE POPCORN (instrumental) / THE CHICKEN (instrumental)** [–] [30]

Jul 69. (7") *(56776) <6245>* **MOTHER POPCORN (YOU GOT TO HAVE A MOTHER FOR ME). / (pt.2)** [ ] Jun69 [11]

Aug 69. (7") *<6250>* **LOWDOWN POPCORN (instrumental) / TOP OF THE STACK (instrumental)** [–] [41]

Aug 69. (lp) *<1055>* **JAMES BROWN PLAYS AND DIRECTS THE POPCORN** [–] [40]
– The popcorn / Why am I treated so bad / In the middle / Soul pride / A new shift / Sudsy / The chicken / The chase. *(UK-iss.Mar70 as 'THE POPCORN'; 184 319)*

Sep 69. (7") *<6255>* **LET A MAN COME IN AND DO THE POPCORN PART ONE. / SOMETIME** [–] [21]

Sep 69. (7") *(56780) <6258>* **THE WORLD. / (pt.2)** [ ] [37]

Oct 69. (lp) *(583 768) <1063>* **IT'S A MOTHER** [ ] Sep69 [26]
– Mother popcorn (you got to have a mother for me) (parts 1 & 2) / Mashed potato popcorn (parts 1 & 2) / I'm shook / Popcorn with a feeling / Little groove maker me (parts 1 & 2) / Any day now (my wild beautiful bird) / If I ruled the world / You're still out of sight / Top of the stack.

Nov 69. (7") *<6273)* **I'M NOT DEMANDING. / (part 2)** [–] [ ]

Dec 69. (7") *<6275>* **PART TWO (LET A MAN COME IN AND DO THE POPCORN). / GETTIN' A LITTLE HIPPER (pt.1)** [–] [40]

Dec 69. (7") *<6277>* **IT'S CHRISTMAS TIME. / (pt.2)** [–] [ ]

Jan 70. (7") *(56787)* **THERE WAS A TIME. / I CAN'T STAND MYSELF (WHEN YOU TOUCH ME)** [ ] [–]

Jan 70. (7") *<6285>* **BROTHER RAPP. / (part 2)** [–] [ ]

Feb 70. (7") *<6290>* **FUNKY DRUMMER (instrumental) / (pt.2)** [–] [51]

Feb 70. (7") *<6292>* **IT'S A NEW DAY. / (pt.2)** [–] [32]

Feb 70. (lp) *<1092>* **AIN'T IT FUNKY** [–] [43]

– Ain't it funky now (parts 1 & 2) / Fat wood (parts 1 & 2) / Cold sweat / Give it up or turnit a loose / Nose job / Use your mother / After you done it. *(UK-iss.Aug70; 2343 010)*

Mar 70. (7") *(56793)* *<6280>* **AIN'T IT FUNKY NOW (instrumental). / (pt.2)** Nov69 24

Mar 70. (7") *<6300>* **TALKIN" LOUD AND SAYIN' NOTHIN'. / (part 2)** –

Apr 70. (7") *<6310>* **BROTHER RAPP (pt.1). / BEWILDERED** – 32

Jul 70. (7") *(2001 018)* **IT'S A NEW DAY. / GEORGIA ON MY MIND** –

Jul 70. (lp) *(2310 029)* *<1095>* **IT'S A NEW DAY SO LET A MAN COME IN**
– It's a new day so let a man come in / Do the popcorn / World / Georgia on my mind / It's a man's man's world / Give it up or turn it a loose / If I ruled the world / The man in the glass / I'm not demanding.

— (Also released lp SOUL ON TOP with The LOUIE BELLSON ORCHESTRA (Jul70) Released another duet 7" with VICKI ANDERSON – Let It Be Me.

— He breaks up The FAMOUS FLAMES to introduce his new band The JB's. They included **BOOTSY COLLINS, FRED WESLEY, BOBBY BYRD, JIMMY PARKER**, etc.

Sep 70. (7") *(2001 071)* *<6318>* **GET UP, I FEEL LIKE BEING A SEX MACHINE. / (pt.2)** 32 Jul70 15

— (released gospel 45, A MAN HAS TO GO BACK TO THE CROSSROADS on 'Bethlehem')

Sep 70. (7") *<6322>* **I'M NOT DEMANDING. / (part 2)** –

Nov 70. (7") *(2001 097)* *<6329>* **CALL ME SUPER BAD. / (pt.2)** – Sep70 13

Nov 70. (7") *<6339>* **HEY AMERICA (vocal). / (instrumental)** –

Dec 70. (d-lp) *(2625 004)* *<1115>* **SEX MACHINE (live)** Sep70 29
– Get up I feel like being a sex machine / Brother Rapp (parts 1 & 2) / Bewildered / I got the feelin' / Give it up or turn it a loose / I don't want nobody / To give me nothing / Licking stick / Lowdown / Popcorn / Spinning wheel / If I ruled the world / There was a time / It's a man's man's world / Please, please, please / I can't stand myself / Mother popcorn. *(cd-iss. Sep98; 517984-2)*

Dec 70. (7") *<6340>* **SANTA CLAUS IS DEFINITELY HERE TO STAY. / (instrumental)** –

Jan 71. (7") *<6347>* **GET UP, GET INTO IT, GET INVOLVED. / (pt.2)** – 34

Feb 71. (7") *<6359>* **TALKING LOUD AND SAYING NOTHING. / (pt.2)** –

Feb 71. (7") *<6366>* **SPINNING WHEEL (instrumental) / (part 2)** – 90

Mar 71. (7") *(2001 163)* *<6368>* **SOUL POWER. / (pt.2)** Feb71 29

May 71. (7") *(2001 190)* *<6363>* **I CRIED. / GET UP, GET INTO IT, GET INVOLVED** Feb71 50

May 71. (lp) *(2310 089)* *<1127>* **SUPER BAD** Jan71 61
– Superbad (parts 1 & 2) / Let it be me / Sometime a man has to go back to the crossroads / Giving out my juice / By the time I get to Phoenix.

— Most of his band except WESLEY, joined PARLIAMENT/FUNKADELIC.

Polydor People

Jun 71. (7") *<2500>* **ESCAPE-ISM. / (part 2)** – 35

Jul 71. (7") *(2001 213)* *<2501>* **HOT PANTS (SHE GOT TO USE WHAT SHE GOT, TO GET WHAT SHE WANTS). / (pt.2)** 15

Polydor Polydor

Sep 71. (lp) *(2425 086)* *<4054>* **HOT PANTS** Aug71 22
– Blues and pants / Can't stand it / Escape-ism (part 1) / Escape-ism (Part 2) / Hot pants (she got to use what she got to get what she wants) / Escape-ism. *(re-iss. Sep98 lp/cd; 517985-1/-2)*

Sep 71. (7") *(2001 223)* *<14088>* **MAKE IT FUNKY. / (pt.2)** 22

Oct 71. (7") *<14098>* **MY PART: MAKE IT FUNKY PART 3. / (other version)** – 68

Nov 71. (7") *(2066 153)* *<14100>* **I'M A GREEDY MAN. / (part 2)** 35

Feb 72. (d-lp) *(2659 011)* *<3003>* **REVOLUTION OF THE MIND – LIVE AT THE APOLLO, VOLUME III (live)** Dec71 39
– It's a new day so let a man come in and do the popcorn / Bewildered / Sex machine / Escape-ism / Make it funky / Try me / Fast medley: I can't stand myself – Mother popcorn – I got the feelin' / Give it up or turn it a loose / Call me Superbad / Get up, get into it, get involved (parts 1 & 2) / Soul power / Hot pants (she got to use what she got to get what she wants). *(cd-iss. Sep98; 517983-2)*

Feb 72. (7") *(2066 185)* *<14116>* **KING HEROIN. / THEME FROM KING HEROIN** 40

Apr 72. (7") *(2066 210)* *<14126>* **THERE IT IS. / (part 2)** 43

Jun 72. (7") *(2066 216)* *<14129>* **HONKY TONK. / (part 2)** 44

Aug 72. (7") *(2066 231)* *<14139>* **GET ON THE GOOD FOOT. / (part 2)** 18

Nov 72. (lp) *(2391 033)* *<5028>* **THERE IT IS** Jun72
– There it is (parts 1 & 2) / King heroin / I'm a greedy man (parts 1 & 2) / Who am I / Talkin' loud and sayin' nothing / Public enemy #1 (part 1) / Public enemy #1 (part 2) / I need help (I can't do it alone) / Never can say goodbye. *(re-iss. Sep98 lp/cd; 517986-1/-2)*

Nov 72. (7") *(2066 283)* *<14157>* **WHAT MY BABY NEEDS NOW IS A LITTLE MORE LOVIN'. / THIS GUY'S IN LOVE WITH YOU (with LYN COLLINS)** Dec72 56

Dec 72. (7") *(2066 285)* *<14153>* **I GOT A BAG OF MY OWN. / I KNOW IT'S TIME** Nov72 44

Dec 72. (7") *<14161>* **SANTA CLAUS GOES STRAIGHT TO THE GHETTO. / SWEET LITTLE BABY BOY** –

Jan 73. (7") *<14162>* **I GOT ANTS IN MY PANTS (AND I WANT TO DANCE). / (part 2)** – 27

Jan 73. (d-lp) *(2659 018)* *<3004>* **GET ON THE GOOD FOOT** Dec72 68
– Get on the good foot (parts 1 & 2) / The whole world needs liberation / Your love was good for me / Cold sweat / Recitation by Hank Ballard / I got a bag of my own / Nothing beats a try but a fail / Lost someone / Funky side of town / Please, please, please / Ain't it a groove / My part – Make it funky (parts 3 & 4) / Dirty Harry / I know it's a true. *(cd-iss. Mar99 on 'IMS-Universal'; E 523982-2)*

Mar 73. (7") *<14168>* **DOWN AND OUT IN NEW YORK CITY. / MAMA'S DEAD** – 50

Mar 73. (7") *<14169>* **LIKE IT IS, LIKE IT WAS. / THE BASS** –

May 73. (lp) *(2490 117)* *<6014>* **BLACK CAESAR (Soundtrack)** Feb73 31
– Down and out in New York city / Blind man can see it / Sportin' life / Dirty Harri / The boss / Make it good to yourself / Mama Feelgood / Mama's dead / White lightning (I mean moonshine) / Chase / Like it is, like it was. *(re-iss. Sep98 lp/cd; 517735-1/-2)*

May 73. (7") *(2066 329)* *<14177>* **THINK. / SOMETHING** 77
(above and below 2 different versions)

Jun 73. (7") *<14185>* **THINK. / SOMETHING** – 80

Jul 73. (7") *<14193>* **WOMAN. / (part 2)** –

Aug 73. (lp) *(2391 084)* *<6015>* **SLAUGHTER'S BIG RIP-OFF (Soundtrack)** Jul73 92
– Slaughter theme / Tryin' to get over / Transmographication / Happy for the poor / Brother Rapp / Big strong / Really, really, really / Sexy, sexy, sexy / To my brother / How long can I keep it up / People get up and drive your funky soul / King Slaughter / Straight ahead. *(cd-iss. Aug96; 3145 17136-2) (cd re-iss. Sep98; 517136-2)*

Aug 73. (7") *<14194>* **SEXY, SEXY, SEXY. / SLAUGHTER THEME** – 50

Sep 73. (7"; JAMES BROWN with LYN COLLINS) *<14199>* **LET IT BE ME. / IT'S ALL RIGHT** –

Oct 73. (7") *<14206>* **I'VE GOT A GOOD THING. / (part 2)** –

Nov 73. (7") *<14210>* **STONED(D) TO THE BONE. / (part 2)** – 58

Jan 74. (7") *(2066 411)* **STONE(D) TO THE BONE. / SEXY, SEXY, SEXY** –

Mar 74. (7") *<14223>* **THE PAYBACK. / (part 2)** – 26

Apr 74. (d-lp) *(2659 030)* *<3007>* **THE PAYBACK** Jan74 34
– The payback / Doing the best I can / Take some – leave some / Shoot your shot / Forever suffering / Time is running out fast / Stoned to the bone / Mind power. *(cd-iss. Sep98; 517137-2)*

Jun 74. (7") *(2066 485)* **MY THANG. / THE PAYBACK** –

Jul 74. (7") *<14244>* **MY THANG. / PUBLIC ENEMY #1** – 29

Sep 74. (7") *<14255>* **PAPA DON'T TAKE NO MESS. / (part 2)** – 31

Sep 74. (d-lp) *(2659 036)* *<9001>* **IT'S HELL** <US-title 'HELL'> Jul74 35
– Coldblooded / Hell / My thang / Savin' it and doin' it / Please, please, please / When the saints go marching in / These foolish things / Storming Monday / A man has to go back to the cross road before he finds himself / Sometime / I can't stand it / Lost someone / Don't tell a lie about me and I won't tell the truth about you / Papa don't take no mess. *(re-iss. Jul88)*

Jan 75. (7") *(2066 520)* *<14258>* **FUNKY PRESIDENT (PEOPLE IT'S BAD). / COLD BLOODED** Nov74 44

Feb 75. (7") *<14268>* **REALITY. / TWIST** – 80

Mar 75. (lp) *(2391 164)* *<6039>* **REALITY** Jan75 56
– Reality / Funky President (people it's bad) / Further on up the road / Check your body / Don't fence me in / All for one / I'm broken hearted / The twist / Who can I turn to.

Apr 75. (7") *<14270>* **SEX MACHINE (remix). / (part 2)** –

May 75. (lp) *(2391 175)* *<6042>* **SEX MACHINE TODAY**
– Sex machine (pt.1 & 2) / I feel good / Problems / Dead on it / Get up off of me / Deep in it.

Jun 75. (7") *<14279>* **DEAD ON IT. / (part 2)** –

Jul 75. (7") *<14281>* **HUSTLE!!! (DEAD ON IT). / (part 2)** –

Nov 75. (7") *<14295>* **SUPERBAD, SUPERSLICK. / (part 2)** [–] [ ]

Dec 75. (lp) *(2391 197) <6054>* **EVERYBODY'S DOIN' THE HUSTLE AND DEAD ON THE DOUBLE BUMP** [ ] Oct75 [ ]
– Hustle!!! (dead on it) / Papa's got a brand new bag / Your love / Turn on the heat and build some fire / Superbad, superslick / Calm & cool / Kansas City.

Jan 76. (7") *(2066 642) <14301>* **HOT (I NEED TO BE LOVED, LOVED, LOVED). / SUPERBAD, SUPERSLICK (part 1)** [ ] [ ]

Feb 76. (7") *<14303>* **DOOLEY'S JUNKYARD DOGS. / (part 2)** [–] [ ]

Feb 76. (7") *<14304>* **(I LOVE YOU) FOR SENTIMENTAL REASONS. / GOODNIGHT MY LOVE** [–] [ ]

Mar 76. (lp) *(2391 214)* **HOT** [ ] [–]
– Hot (I need to be loved, loved, loved) / so long / For sentimental reasons / Try me / The future shock of the world / woman / Most of all / Goodnight my love / Please, please, please. *(re-iss. Jul88; PD 6059)*

Jul 76. (7") *(2066 687) <14326>* **GET UP OFFA THAT THING. / RELEASE THE PRESSURE** [22] [45]

Sep 76. (lp) *(2391 228) <6071>* **GET UP OFFA THAT THING** [ ] Aug76 [ ]
– Get up offa that thing / Release the pressure / You took my heart / I refuse to lose / Can't take it with you / Home again / This feeling.

Nov 76. (7") *<14354>* **I REFUSE TO LOSE. / HOME AGAIN** [–] [ ]

Jan 77. (7") *(2066 763) <14360>* **BODYHEAT. / (part 2)** [36] [88]

Feb 77. (lp) *(2391 258) <6093>* **BODYHEAT** [ ] Jan77 [ ]
– Bodyheat / Woman / Kiss in '77 / I'm satisfied / What the world needs now is love / Wake up and give yourself a chance / Don't feel it. *(re-iss. Oct82 on 'Phoenix'; PHX 1025) (re-iss. Jul88; PD 6093)*

Jun 77. (7") *<14388>* **KISS IN '77. / WOMAN** [–] [ ]

Jul 77. (7") *(2066 834)* **HONKY TONK. / BROTHER RAPP** [ ] [–]

Sep 77. (7") *<14409>* **GIVE ME SOME SKIN. / PEOPLE WAKE UP AND LIVE** [–] [ ]

Sep 77. (lp) *(2391 300) <6111>* **MUTHA'S NATURE** [ ] [ ]
– Give me some skin / People who criticize / Have a happy day / Bessie / If you don't give a doggone about it / Summertime / People wake up and live / Take me higher and groove me.

Nov 77. (7") *<14433>* **TAKE ME HIGHER AND GROOVE ME. / SUMMERTIME (Martha & James)** [–] [ ]

Jan 78. (7") *<14438>* **IF YOU DON'T GIVE A DOGGONE ABOUT IT. / PEOPLE WHO CRITICIZE** [–] [ ]

—— His backing group, left for a while, but soon returned. JIMMY NOLAN was to die of a heart attack 18 Dec'83.

May 78. (7") *<14460>* **LOVE ME TENDER. / HAVE A HAPPY DAY** [–] [ ]

May 78. (lp) *(2391 342) <6140>* **JAM / 1980's** [ ] [ ]
– Jam / The spank / Nature / Eyesight / I never never never will forget.

Jun 78. (7") *(2066 915) <14465>* **EYESIGHT. / NEVER, NEVER, NEVER WILL FORGET** [ ] [ ]

Aug 78. (7") *<14487>* **LOVE ME TENDER. / THE SPANK** [–] [ ]

Oct 78. (7") *(2066 984) <14512>* **NATURE. / (part 2)** [ ] [ ]

Dec 78. (7") *<14522>* **FOR GOODNESS SAKES, LOOK AT THOSE CAKES. / (part 2)** [–] [ ]

Jan 79. (7") *(POSP 24)* **FOR GOODNESS SAKES, LOOK AT THOSE CAKES. / GET UP, I FEEL LIKE BEING A SEX MACHINE** [ ] [–]

Jan 79. (lp) *(2391 384) <6181>* **TAKE A LOOK AT THOSE CAKES** [ ] [ ]
– For goodness sakes, take a look at those cakes / A man understands / As long as I love you / Someone to talk about / Spring.

Apr 79. (7") *<14540>* **SOMEONE TO TALK ABOUT. / (part 2)** [–] [ ]

Jul 79. (7") *(POSP 68) <14557>* **IT'S TOO FUNKY IN HERE. / ARE WE REALLY DANCING** [ ] [ ]

Aug 79. (lp) *(2391 412) <6212>* **THE ORIGINAL DISCO MAN** [ ] [ ]
– It's too funky in here / Let the boogie do the rest / Still / The original disco man / Star generation / Women are something else.

Aug 79. (7") *<2005>* **STAR GENERATION. / WOMEN ARE SOMETHING ELSE** [–] [ ]

Sep 79. (7"/12") *(STEP/+X 2)* **STAR GENERATION. / LET THE BOOGIE DO THE REST** [ ] [–]

Nov 79. (7") *<2034>* **THE ORIGINAL DISCO MAN. / LET THE BOOGIE DO THE REST** [–] [ ]

Feb 80. (7") *(POSP 121) <2054>* **REGRETS. / STONE COLD DRAG** [ ] [ ]

Apr 80. (lp) *(2391 446) <6258>* **PEOPLE** [ ] [ ]
– Regrets / Don't stop the funk / That's sweet music / Let the funk flow / Stone cold drag / Are we really dancing / Sometimes that's all there is. *(re-iss. Jul88; PD 16258)*

May 80. (7") *<2078>* **LET THE FUNK FLOW. / SOMETIMES THAT'S ALL THERE IS** [–] [ ]

Aug 80. (7") *<2129>* **IT'S TOO FUNKY FOR ME IN HERE. / GET UP OFFA THAT THING** [–] [ ]

Oct 80. (d-lp) *(2683 085) <6290>* **JAMES BROWN . . . LIVE – HOT ON THE ONE (live)** [ ] Aug80 [ ]
– It's too funky in here / Gonna have a funky good time / Get up offa that thing / Bodyheat / I got the feelin' / Try me / Sex machine / It's a man's man's man's world / Get on the good foot / Papa's got a brand new bag / Please, please, please / Jam. *(cd-iss. Apr91; 847856-2)*

Oct 80. (7") *<2167>* **GIVE THE BASS PLAYER SOME. / (part 2)** [–] [ ]

R.C.A. — T.K.

Dec 80. (7"/12") *(RCA/+T 28) <1039>* **RAPP PAYBACK (WHERE IZ MOSES?). / (pt.2)** [39] [ ]

Dec 80. (lp) *(RCALP 5006) <5334>* **SOUL SYNDROME** [ ] [ ]
– Rapp payback / Mashed potatoes / Smokin' and drinkin' / Stay with me / Honky tonk. *(re-iss. Sep81 lp/c; RCA LP/K 3048)*

Feb 81. (7") *(RCA 44) <1042>* **STAY WITH ME. / SMOKIN' AND DRINKIN'** [ ] [ ]

May 81. (7") *(RCA 65)* **FUNKY MAN. / (part 2)** [ ] [ ]
(12"+=) *(RCAT 65)* – Mashed potatoes.

Polydor — not iss.

Apr 81. (lp) *(POLS 1029)* **THE THIRD COMING** [ ] [ ]
– Popcorn 80's / Give that bass player some / You're my only love / World cycle inc. / Superball / Superbad 80's / I go crazy.

Jun 81. (7") *(POSP 290)* **I GO CRAZY. / WORLD CYCLE INC.** [ ] [–]

Sonet — not iss.

Jun 83. (7"/12") *(SON/+L 2258)* **BRING IT ON . . . BRING IT ON. / NIGHT TIME IS THE RIGHT TIME** [45] [–]

Sep 83. (lp) *(SNTF 906)* **BRING IT ON** [ ] [–]
– Bring it on . . . bring it on / Today / You can't keep a good man down / Nighttime is the right time / Tennessee waltz / For your precious love.

—— In Aug'84, he teamed up with **AFRIKA BAMBAATAA** for one-off 7+12" UNITY (THE THIRD COMING) on 'Tommy Boy' (US No.49).

Scotti Bros — Scotti Bros

Jan 86. (7") *(A 6701) <05682>* **LIVING IN AMERICA. / Vince Di Cola: FAREWELL** [5] Dec85 [4]
(12"+=) *(TA 6701)* – ('B'extended).

—— (above from the film 'Rocky IV', and written by DAN HARTMAN)

Oct 86. (7") *(650059-7) <06275>* **GRAVITY. / GRAVITY (dub)** [65] [93]
(12") *(650059-6)* – ('A'side) / The big G (dig this myth).

Oct 86. (lp/c) *(SCT/40 57108) <40380>* **GRAVITY** [85] [ ]
– How do you stop / Turn me loose, I'm Dr.Feelgood / Living in America / Goliath / Repeat the beat (faith) / Return to me / Gravity. *(cd-iss. Mar87; CD 57108) (re-iss. Jul88; FZ 40380)*

Mar 87. (7") *<06568>* **HOW DO YOU STOP. / HOUSE OF ROCK** [–] [ ]

Apr 87. (7") *(JAMES 1)* **HOW DO YOU STOP. / REPEAT THE BEAT (FAITH)** [ ] [–]
(12"+=) *(JAMEST 1)* – Living in America.
(12"+=) *(JAMESQ 1)* – ('A'-House mix).

Jun 87. (7") *<07090>* **LET'S GET PERSONAL. / REPEAT THE BEAT** [–] [ ]

Urban-Polydor — Scotti Bros

May 88. (7") *<07783>* **I'M REAL. / TRIBUTE** [–] [ ]

May 88. (7") *(JSB 1)* **I'M REAL. / KEEP KEEPING** [31] [–]
(12"+=) *(JSBX 1)* – Tribute.
(cd-s++=) *(JSBCD 1)* – ('A'-Hype mix).

Jun 88. (lp/c)(cd) *(POLD/+C 5230)(834755-2) <44241>* **I'M REAL** [27] [96]
– Tribute / I'm real / Static / Time to get busy / She looks types a good / Keep keeping / Can't git enuf / It's your money / Godfather runnin' the joint.

Aug 88. (7") *(JSB 1) <07975>* **STATIC. / GODFATHER RUNNIN' THE JOINT** [ ] [ ]
(12"+=) *(JSBX 2)* – I'm real (US remix).
(cd-s++=) *(JSBCD 2)* – ('A'-Full Force mix).

Nov 88. (7") *<08088>* **TIME TO GET BUSY. / BUSY J.B.** [–] [ ]

Feb 89. (7") *<68559>* **IT'S YOUR MONEY. / YOU AND ME** [–] [ ]

—— He guested on ARETHA FRANKLIN single Nov88, 'GIMME YOUR LOVE'.

—— In Apr-May'88, JAMES and his wife ADRIANNE were arrested for possession of substances and guns. She also filed for divorce and pleaded not guilty. Later that year, after resisting arrest in a car chase, etc., he was sentenced to 6 years. He was released on parole on 27th Feb'91, but had to return until late 1993 to serve full sentence. In 1992, he was awarded a special grammy award, for his contribution to music. He appeared there with his wife, to sing finale.

Polydor Polydor

Jul 91. (cd/c/lp) *(510079-2/-4/-1)* **LOVE OVERDUE** [ ] [ ]
– (So tired of standing still we got to) Move on / Show me – dance, dance, dance / To the funk / Teardrops on your letter / Standing on higher ground / Later for dancing / You are my everything / It's time for love (put a little love).

Jul 91. (7") **(SO TIRED OF STANDING STILL WE GOT TO) MOVE ON / YOU ARE MY EVERYTHING** [ ] [–]
(12"+=) – ('A' extended).

Mar 93. (cd/c) *(514329-2/-4)* **UNIVERSAL JAMES** [ ] [ ]
– Can't get any harder / Just do it / Mine all mine / Watch me / Georgia-Lina / Show me your friends / Everybody's got a thang / How long / Make it funky 2000 / Moments.

Apr 93. (7"/c-s) *(PO/+CS 262)* **CAN'T GET ANY HARDER. / ('A'-O.B.C. mix)** [59] [ ]
(12"+=/cd-s+=) *(PZ/+CD 262)* – ('A'mixes).

Eagle Crash

Nov 98. (cd) *(EAGCD 054)* *<417081>* **I'M BACK** [ ] [ ]
– Can't stand it / Funk on ah roll / Kare / What it takes / Papa's got a brand new bag / Break away / Funk on ah roll / Lucky old sun / I don't hear no music / Every part of my heart / Eden / Peace in the world / Funk on ah roll / James on the loose.

Apr 99. (12"/cd-s) *(EAG 12/XS 073)* **FUNK ON AH ROLL / ('A'mix)** [40] [ ]
(cd-s) *(EAGXA 073)* – ('A'mixes).

C.N.R. Red Ink

Jun 03. (cd) *(2299999-2)* *<13943>* **THE NEXT STEP** [ ] Aug02 [ ]
– Automatic (remix) / Send her back to me (remix) / Motivation / Sunshine / Nothing but a jam / Baby you've got what it takes / It's time / Why did this happen to me / Good and natural / Killing is out, school is in.

– (selective) compilations, etc. –

on Polydor UK / King + Polydor (+'75) US, unless mentioned otherwise

Aug 72. (lp) *(2391 057)* *<5401>* **JAMES BROWN SOUL CLASSICS** [ ] [83]

May 75. (7") *<14270>* **SEX MACHINE (part 1). / (part 2)** [–] [61]

Feb 90. (cd/c/lp) *(841516-2/-4/-1)* **DUETS** [ ] [ ]

Jan 91. (d-cd) *(847258-2)* **MESSIN' WITH THE BLUES** (rare R&B/Blues) [ ] [ ]

May 91. (4xcd-box/4xc-box) *(849 108-2/-4)* **STAR TIME** [ ] [–]

Nov 91. (cd/c/lp) *(845 828-2/-4/-1)* **SEX MACHINE – THE VERY BEST OF JAMES BROWN** [19] [ ]
– (see K-Tel album except replacement of tracks marked * by:-) Night train / Out of sight / I'm a greedy man (pt.1) / Get up offa that thing / I'm real / It's too funky in here / Soul power (live).

Apr 85. (7") *Boiling Point; (FROG 1)* **FROGGY MIX. / (pt.2)** [50] [ ]
(12"+=) *(FROGX 1)* – (extra mixes).

Jun 85. (7") *(POSP 751)* **GET UP, I FEEL LIKE BEING A SEX MACHINE (pt.2). / PAPA'S GOT A BRAND NEW BAG** [47] [ ]
(12"+=) *(POSPX 751)* – Get up offa that thing (release the pressure) / Get on the good foot. *(re-iss. Feb86 hit UK-No.46)*

Apr 86. (7") *(POSP 783)* **SOUL POWER (pt.1). / IT'S A MAN'S, MAN'S, MAN'S WORLD** [ ] [ ]
(12"+=) *(POSPX 783)* – King Heroin / Don't tell it.

May 86. (d-lp) *Urban; (URB LP/DC 11)* **IN THE JUNGLE GROOVE** [ ] [ ]
(cd-iss. May88 on 'Polydor'; 829624-2)

Sep 87. (lp/c/cd) *K-Tel; (NE1/CE2/NCD3 376)* **THE BEST OF JAMES BROWN (THE GODFATHER OF SOUL)** [17] [–]
– Living in America /* Body heat / Hey America / Please, please, please / Hot pants (pt.1) / Think / I got you (I feel good) / Say it loud, I'm black and proud (pt.1) / Get up (I feel like being a) sex machine / Make it funky (pt.1) / Papa's got a brand new bag (pt.1) / Get on the good foot / * Gonna have a funky good time / Cold sweat / * Honky tonk / It's a man's man's man's world / * Gravity.

Jan 88. (7") *Urban; (URB 13)* **SHE'S THE ONE. / FUNKY PRESIDENT (PEOPLE IT'S BAD)** [45] [ ]
(12"+=) *(URBX 13)* – Funky drummer (edit) / Funky drummer (boms beat reprise).

Apr 88. (7") *Urban; (URB 17)* **THE PAYBACK MIX (pt.1). / GIVE IT UP OR TURNIT A LOOSE** [ ] [ ]
(12") *(URBX 17)* – ('A'side) / Keep on doing what you're doing but keep it funky / Stoned to the bone / Cold sweat.

— May'88 'A&M' released 'I GOT YOU (I FEEL GOOD)' hit UK 52, from the film 'Good Morning Vietnam', B-side by Martha Reeves & The Vandellas.

Oct 92. (7"; JAMES BROWN VS DAKEYNE) *F.B.I.; (FBI 9)* **I GOT YOU (I FEEL GOOD) (remix). / PROCESSED B'S** [72] [–]
(cd-s+=) *(FBICD 9)* – B-Funked.

Apr 02. (cd) *Universal TV; (589841-2)* **THE GODFATHER: THE VERY BEST OF JAMES BROWN** [30] [–]
– Papa's got a brand new bag / I got you (I feel good) / It's a man's man's man's world / Please please please / Think / Night train / Cold sweat / Give it up or turn it loose / Funky drummer (parts 1 & 2) / Get up I feel like being a sex machine / Soul power / Get on the good foot / Doing it to death / Get up offa that thing / I'm real / It's too funky in here / Living in America / Super bad / The boss / The payback mix.

Jackson BROWNE

Born: 9 Oct'48, Heidelberg, Germany. BROWNE's parents were actually American (father was in the Army) and the family subsequently moved back to Orange County, California. During the 60's, the budding singer/songwriter worked with the likes of TIM BUCKLEY, NITTY GRITTY DIRT BAND and even NICO, BROWNE later providing material for such luminaries as The BYRDS and LINDA RONSTADT. He duly signed a solo deal with 'Elektra', initially as a house writer, before being picked up by David Geffen's new 'Asylum' label in 1971. With the help of a number of high profile cover versions, 'DOCTOR MY EYES' (Jackson 5) / 'SHADOW DREAM SONG' (Tom Paxton), BROWNE's eponymous debut album hit the US Top 60. Featuring such ubiquitous L.A. session men as LELAND SKLAR and RUSS KUNKEL alongside such esteemed company as DAVID CROSBY, CLARENCE WHITE and SNEAKY PETE KLEINOW, the album established BROWNE at the forefront of the navel-gazing Californian singer/songwriter scene. His fragile melodies and bookish, confessional lyrics saw him adopted as a kind of genre figurehead, BROWNE garnering further kudos after co-penning the classic EAGLES track, 'TAKE IT EASY'. But while The EAGLES took that song's philosophy to its ultimate conclusion, BROWNE continued to analyse himself and his relationships on classic sets, 'FOR EVERYMAN' (1973) and 'LATE FOR THE SKY' (1974). Tragedy struck on 25th March 1976, when his wife, PHYLLIS, committed suicide, something that undoubtedly contributed to the bleak feel of 'THE PRETENDER' (1976), BROWNE's first album to make the US Top 10. The singer forged on nevertheless, releasing a further set, 'RUNNING ON EMPTY' (1978), which featured previously unreleased material and songs recorded on the road, notably a smash hit version of Maurice Williams & the Zodiacs' 'STAY'. His popularity had been steadily increasing as the decade wore on and BROWNE finally topped the American charts in summer 1980 with the 'HOLD OUT' album. The new decade saw BROWNE becoming increasingly politically active and outspoken on such controversial issues as nuclear power and US foreign policy. Inevitably, this was reflected in BROWNE's writing, the 'LAWYERS IN LOVE' set marking a move away from the personal towards the socially conscious. Subsequent politicised sets, 'LIVES IN THE BALANCE' (1986) and 'WORLD IN MOTION' (1989) were relative commercial failures, some sections of BROWNE's fanbase perhaps not impressed with his liberal convictions. With a star cast including DAVID CROSBY, JENNIFER WARNES, DON HENLEY and longtime collaborator, DAVID LINDLEY, BROWNE returned to more personal fare on 1993's 'I'M ALIVE'. While he might not enjoy the critical and commercial plaudits of his 70's heyday, the singer retains a loyal following, even in Britain, where he made a rare appearance, headlining the 1997 Cambridge Folk Festival. With his first album of the new millennium, 'THE NAKED RIDE HOME' (2002), the ageing songwriter was still picking apart the increasingly perilous state of his homeland, a subject which seems to propel his muse more effectively than most. Musically, there were no great surprises, in itself perhaps a relief given the ill-advised experimentation of some of his contemporaries.

Album rating: JACKSON BROWNE (*8) / FOR EVERYMAN (*7) / LATE FOR THE SKY (*8) / THE PRETENDER (*6) / RUNNING ON EMPTY (*6) / HOLD OUT (*4) / LAWYERS IN LOVE (*5) / LIVES IN THE BALANCE (*6) / WORLD IN MOTION (*4) / I'M ALIVE (*6) / LOOKING EAST (*5) / THE NEXT VOICE YOU HEAR – THE BEST OF JACKSON BROWNE compilation (*8) / THE NAKED RIDE HOME (*5)

JACKSON BROWNE – vocals, guitar, piano / with **CRAIG DOERGE** – keyboards / **LELAND SKLAR** – bass / **RUSS KUNKEL** – drums / **CLARENCE WHITE** – guitar / **DAVID CROSBY** – b.vocals

Asylum Asylum

Mar 72. (7") *(K 13043)* *<11004>* **DOCTOR MY EYES. / I'M LOOKING INTO YOU** [ ] Feb72 [8]

Apr 72. (lp) *(SYL 9002)* *<5051>* **JACKSON BROWNE** [ ] Mar72 [53]
– Jamaica say you will / A child in these hills / Song for Adam / Doctor my eyes / From Silver Lake / Something fine / Under the falling sky / Looking into you / Rock me on the water / My opening farewell. *(re-iss. Jun76 lp/c; K/K4 53022) (cd-iss. Jan87; K2 53022)*

Aug 72. (7") *(AYM 506)* *<11006>* **ROCK ME ON THE WATER. / SOMETHING FINE** [ ] Jul72 [48]

—— added **DAVID LINDLEY** – guitar, violin, etc. (ex-KALEIDOSCOPE)

Nov 73. (7") *(AYM 522)* *<11023>* **REDNECK FRIEND. / THE TIMES YOU'VE COME** [ ] Sep73 [85]

Dec 73. (lp/c) *(K/K4 43003)* *<5067>* **FOR EVERYMAN** [ ] Nov73 [43]
– Take it easy / Our lady of the well / Colors of the sun / I thought I was a child / These days / Redneck friend / The times you've come / Ready or not / Sing my songs to me / For everyman. *(cd-iss. Jan87; K2 43003)*

Apr 74. (7") *(AYM 526)* *<11030>* **TAKE IT EASY. / READY OR NOT** [ ] [ ]

—— retained **LINDLEY** and brought in **JAI WINDING** – keyboards / **DOUG HAYWOOD** – bass, vocals / **LARRY ZACK** – drums

Oct 74. (7") *<45227>* **WALKING SLOW. / BEFORE THE DELUGE** [–] [ ]

Nov 74. (7") *(AYM 535)* **WALKING SLOW. / THE LATE SHOW** [ ] [–]

Dec 74. (lp/c) *(SYL 9018)* *<EQ 1017>* **LATE FOR THE SKY** [ ] Oct74 [14]
– Late for the sky / Fountain of sorrow / Farther on / The late show / The road and the sky / For a dancer / Walking slow / Before the deluge. *(re-iss. Jun76 lp/c; K/K4 43007) (cd-iss. Jan87; K2 43007)*

Mar 75. (7") *(K 13022)* *<45242>* **FOUNTAIN OF SORROW. / THE LATE SHOW** [ ] [ ]

—— now with **KUNKEL, SKLAR, DOERGE and LINDLEY** plus **JEFF PORCARO** – drums / **JIM GORDON** – drums / **BOB GLAUB and CHUCK RAINEY** – bass / **ROY BITTAN and BILL PAYNE** – organ / **LUIS F.DAMIAN** – guitar / etc.

Nov 76. (lp/c) *(K/K4 53048)* *<7E 1079>* **THE PRETENDER** [26] [5]
– The fuse / Your bright baby blues / Linda Paloma / Here come those tears again / Daddy's tune / The only child / Daddy's tune / Sleep's dark and silent gate / The pretender. *(cd-iss. Jan87)*

Feb 77. (7") *(K 13073)* *<45379>* **HERE COME THOSE TEARS AGAIN. / LINDA PALOMA** [ ] [23]

Jul 77. (7") *(K 13086)* *<45399>* **THE PRETENDER. / DADDY'S TUNE** [ ] May77 [58]

Jan 78 (7") *(K 13105)* **YOU LOVE THE THUNDER. / COCAINE** [ ] [–]

Jan 78. (lp/c) *(K/K4 53070)* *<6E 113>* **RUNNING ON EMPTY** [28] [3]
– Running on empty / The road / Rosie / You love the thunder / Cocaine / Shaky town / Love needs a heart / Nothing but time / The load-out / Stay. *(cd-iss. Jan87; K2 53070)*

Mar 78. (7") *(K 13118)* *<45460>* **RUNNING ON EMPTY. / NOTHING BUT TIME** [ ] Feb78 [11]

Jun 78. (7") *(K 13128)* **STAY. / ROSIE** [12] [–]

Sep 78. (7") *<45485>* **STAY. / THE LOAD-OUT** [–] [20]

Nov 78. (7") *<45543>* **THE ROAD. / YOU LOVE THE THUNDER** [–] [ ]

Jul 80. (7") *(K 12466)* *<47003>* **BOULEVARD. / CALL IT A LOAN** [ ] [19]

Jul 80. (lp/c) *(K/K4 52226)* *<5E 511>* **HOLD OUT** [44] [1]
– Disco apocalypse / Hold out / That girl could sing / Boulevard / Of missing persons / Call it a loan / Hold on hold out. *(cd-iss. Jan87; K2 52226)*

Oct 80. (7") *(K 12479)* **DISCO APOCALYPSE. / BOULEVARD** [ ] [–]

Oct 80. (7") *<47036>* **THAT GIRL COULD SING. / OF MISSING PERSONS** [–] [22]

—— next single was from "Fast Times at Ridgemont High" Soundtrack featuring GRAHAM NASH + DAVID LINDLEY

Aug 82. (7") *(K 13185)* *<69982>* **SOMEBODY'S BABY. / THE CROW ON THE CRADLE** [ ] Jul82 [7]

—— **BROWNE** retained **KUNKEL, DOERGE, HAYWOOD, GLAUB / + RICK VITO** – guitar repl. LINDLEY

Elektra Asylum

Jul 83. (7") *(E 9826)* *<69826>* **LAWYERS IN LOVE. / SAY IT ISN'T TRUE** [ ] [13]
(with free 7") – TENDER IS THE NIGHT. / ON THE DAY

Aug 83. (lp/c) *<(960 268-1/-4)>* **LAWYERS IN LOVE** [37] [8]
– Lawyers in love / On the day / Cut it away / Downtown / Tender is the night / Knock on any door / For a rocker. *(cd-iss. Jul87; 960 268-2)*

Oct 83. (7") *(E 9791)* *<69791>* **TENDER IS THE NIGHT. / ON THE DAY** [ ] Sep83 [25]

Jan 84. (7") *<69764>* **FOR A ROCKER. / DOWNTOWN** [–] [45]

—— Late '85 / early in '86, JACKSON was credited on US Top 20 single 'You're A Friend Of Mine', with CLARENCE CLEMONS (ex-BRUCE SPRINGSTEEN). His girlfriend DARRYL HANNAH guested, backing vocals.

Feb 86. (lp/c)(cd) *(EKT 31/+C)<(960 457-2)>* **LIVES IN THE BALANCE** [36] [23]
– For America / Soldier of plenty / In the shape of a heart / Candy / Lawless avenues / Lives in the balance / Till I go down / Black and white.

Feb 86. (7"/7"sha-pic-d) *(EKR 35/+P)* *<69566>* **FOR AMERICA. / TILL I GO DOWN** [ ] [30]

Oct 86. (7"/7"sha-pic-d) *(EKR 42/+P)* *<69543>* **IN THE SHAPE OF A HEART. / VOICE OF AMERICA** [66] Jun86 [70]
(d7"+=) *(EKR 42)* – Running on empty / The pretender.

Jan 87. (7"/12") *(W 8698/+T)* **EGO MANIAC. / LOVE'S GONNA GET YOU** [ ] [–]
(above single on 'Warners')

Jun 89. (lp/c)(cd) *(EKT 50/+C)<(960 832-2)>* **WORLD IN MOTION** [39] [45]
– World in motion / Enough of the night / Chasing you into the light / How long / Anything can happen / When the stone begins to turn / The word justice / My personal revenge / I am a patriot / Lights and virtues. *(cd re-iss. Feb95; same)*

Jun 89. (7") *<69292>* **WORLD IN MOTION. / PERSONAL REVENGE** [–] [ ]

Oct 89. (7") *<69284>* **ANYTHING CAN HAPPEN. / LIGHTS AND VIRTUES** [–] [ ]

Jan 90. (7") *<69262>* **CHASING YOU INTO THE NIGHT. / HOW LONG** [–] [ ]

—— now with **DAVID LINDLEY, MARK GOLDENBERG, SCOTT THURSTON, MIKE CAMPBELL, WALLY WACHTEL** – guitars / **KEVIN McCORMICK** – bass / **BENMONT TENCH** – organ / **MAURICIO LEWAK** – drums / **LUIS CONTE + LENNY CASTRO** – percussion / plus guests **DAVID CROSBY / DON HENLEY / JENNIFER WARNES / SWEET PEA ATKINSON + SIR HARRY BOWENS**

Oct 93. (cd/c) *<(7559 61524-2/-4)>* **I'M ALIVE** [35] [40]
– I'm alive / My problem is you / Everywhere I go / I'll do anything / Miles away / Too many angels / Take this rain / Two of me, two of you / Sky blue and black / All good things.

Nov 93. (7"/c-s) *(EKR 176/+C)* **I'M ALIVE / TOO MANY ANGELS** [ ] [ ]
(cd-s) *(EKR 176CD)* – ('A'side) / Late for the sky / Running on empty / The pretender.

Jun 94. (7"/c-s) *(EKR 184/+C)* **EVERYWHERE I GO. / I'M ALIVE (live)** [67] [ ]
(cd-s+=) *(EKR 184CD2)* – The pretender (live) / Running on empty (live).
(cd-s) *(EKR 184CD1)* – ('A'side) / Take it easy / Doctor my eyes / In the shape of a heart.

Nov 94. (7"/c-s) *(EKR 193/+C)* **SKY BLUE AND BLACK. / TENDER IS THE NIGHT** [ ] [ ]
(12"+=/cd-s+=) *(EKR 193 T/CD)* – Everywhere I go.

— guests on below; BONNIE RAITT / RY COODER / DAVID CROSBY / DAVID LINDLEY / etc.

Feb 96. (cd/c) <(7559 61867-2/-4)> **LOOKING EAST** [47] [36]
– Looking east / The barricades of Heaven / Some bridges / Information wars / I'm the cat / Culver moon / Baby how long / Nino / Alive in the world / It is one.

Jul 96. (c-s/cd-s) *(EKR 221 C/CD)* **I'M THE CAT / BEFORE THE DELUGE** [ ] [ ]

Nov 97. (cd/c) <(7559 62111-2/-4)> **THE NEXT VOICE YOU HEAR – THE BEST OF JACKSON BROWNE** (compilation) [ ] Oct97 [47]
– Doctor my eyes / These days / Late for the sky / Fountain of sorrow / The pretender / Running on empty / Call it a loan / Somebody's baby / Tender is the night / Lives in the balance / In the shape of a heart / Sky blue and black / Barricades of Heaven / The rebel Jesus / The next voice you hear.

Oct 02. (cd) <(7559 62793-2)> **THE NAKED RIDE HOME** [53] Sep02 [36]
– The naked ride home / The night inside me / Casino nation / For taking the trouble / Never stop / Walking town / About my imagination / Sergio Leone / Don't you want me to be there / My stunning mystery companion.

– compilations, etc. –

on 'Asylum' unless mentioned otherwise

Sep 76. (7") *(K 13043)* **DOCTOR MY EYES. / TAKE IT EASY** [ ] [-]

Oct 82. (d-c) *(K4 62041)* **THE PRETENDER / LATE FOR THE SKY** [ ] [-]

Nov 83. (d-c) *(960 277-4)* **JACKSON BROWNE / RUNNING ON EMPTY** [ ] [-]

Jack BRUCE

Born: JOHN SYMON ASHER BRUCE, 14 May'43, Bishopbriggs. At 17 he won a scholarship to R.S.A. of music although the prodigiously talented teenager joined local band JIM McHARG'S SCOTSVILLE JAZZBAND, before moving to London and playing in BLUES INCORPORATED with ALEXIS KORNER. In 1963 he became a member of GRAHAM BOND ORGANISATION, joining JOHN MAYALL'S BLUESBREAKERS a couple of years later. He also released a one-off debut solo 45 around the same time and after a six month spell with MANFRED MANN, he made his greatest ever career move, co-forming legendary power trio, CREAM, alongside ERIC CLAPTON and GINGER BAKER. One of the greatest bass players of all time, his hard hitting style and booming vocals were an integral part of the CREAM sound, his technique mimicked by countless heavy rock bands in the years that followed. After the band's demise in late 1968, he went solo, remaining with 'Polydor'. Recorded with a backing band including DICK HECKSTALL-SMITH and CHRIS SPEDDING, his debut album, 'SONGS FOR A TAILOR' (1969) hit the UK Top 10 despite its ambitious, idiosyncratic blend of jazz-fusion (the track 'THEME FOR AN IMAGINARY WESTERN' subsequently becoming a hit for MOUNTAIN). This was his only commercial success though, and subsequent albums such as 'HARMONY ROW' (1971) and 'OUT OF THE STORM' (1974) failed to chart. Featuring MICK TAYLOR on guitar, the latter set was a more straightforward hard rock effort, while the 1977 set, 'HOW'S TRICKS' was recorded under the JACK BRUCE BAND moniker. 1980 saw him team up with DAVID SANCIOUS, DAVE CLEMPSON and BILLY COBHAM as JACK BRUCE & FRIENDS, releasing an album for 'Epic'. He then teamed up with another veteran guitarist, ROBIN TROWER, for an album on 'Chrysalis', although throughout much of the ensuing decade he focused on his drug and alcohol problems. The 90's saw BRUCE reunited with old mucker GINGER BAKER for the ethnic flavoured 'A QUESTION OF TIME', the pair subsequently forming BBM along with GARY MOORE and enjoying Top 10 success with 'AROUND THE NEXT DREAM'. Sadly for JACK, his son and member of the AFRO CELT SOUND SYSTEM died in October, 1997. In the summer of 2001, JACK was back with a fresh set of recordings, 'SHADOWS IN THE AIR' complemented by appearances by old chums CLAPTON, MOORE and DR. JOHN. 'MORE JACK THAN GOD' (2003), as well as possibly having the best title of his career, was one one of the best album's of his post-CREAM career. Collaborating with the likes of BERNIE WORRELL and VERNON REID (of LIVING COLOUR), BRUCE turned out a supple, insinuatingly effective set of songs fired by root-funk rhythms and Latin percussion, a recipe which was even applied to 'I FEEL FREE' with surpisingly impressive results. • **Trivia:** During 1970, he was also part of US jazz-rock outfit TONY WILLIAMS' LIFETIME, releasing album of same name.

Album rating: SONGS FOR A TAILOR (*8) / THINGS WE LIKE (*5) / HARMONY ROW (*6) / AT HIS BEST compilation (*6) / OUT OF THE STORM (*5) / HOW'S TRICKS (*5) / GREATEST HITS compilation (*6) / I'VE ALWAYS WANTED TO DO THIS (*5) / AUTOMATIC (*4) / A QUESTION OF TIME (*5) / SOMETHIN ELS (*5) / CITIES OF THE HEART (*5) / AROUND THE NEXT DREAM (*6; with BBM) / MONKJACK (*4) / SHADOWS IN THE AIR (*4) / JET SET JEWEL (*5) / ROPE LADDER TO THE MOON compilation (*7) / MORE JACK THAN GOD (*7)

JACK BRUCE – vocals, bass (ex-BLUES INCORPORATED, ex-GRAHAM BOND ORGANISATION) with session people

Polydor Atco

Dec 65. (7") *(BM 56036)* **I'M GETTIN' TIRED (OF DRINKING AND GAMBLING). / ROOTIN' TOOTIN'** [ ] [-]

— (see above for details between 1966 and 1968.) He brought in friends **JON HISEMAN** – drums / **DICK HECKSTALL-SMITH** – sax / **CHRIS SPEDDING** – guitar / etc.

Sep 69. (lp) *(583 058)* <33306> **SONGS FOR A TAILOR** [6] [55]
– Never tell your mother she's out of tune / Theme for an imaginary western / Tickets to water falls / Weird of Hermiston / Rope ladder to the Moon / The ministry of bag / He the Richmond / Boston ball game, 1967 / To Isengard / The clearout. *(re-iss. May84; 2459 360) (cd-iss. May88 & Apr97; 835 242-2) (cd re-mast.Apr03 +=; 065603-2)* – Ministry of bag (demo) / Weird of Hermiston (alt.) / The clearout (alt.) / Ministry of bag (alt.).

— **JOHN McLAUGHLIN** – guitar (solo artist) repl. SPEDDING

Jan 71. (lp) *(2343 033)* <33349> **THINGS WE LIKE** [ ] [ ]
– Over the cliff / Statues / Sam enchanted Dick (medley:- Sam's back / Rill's thrills) / Born to be blue / HCKHH blues / Ballad of Arthur / Things we like. *(re-iss. Apr71; 2310 070) (cd re-mast.Apr03 +=; 065604-2)* – Ageing Jack Bruce, three, from Scotland, England.

— retained some past musicians, bringing in **LARRY COYRELL** – guitar / **MIKE MANDEL** – keyboards / **MITCH MITCHELL** – drums

Sep 71. (lp) *(2310 107)* <33365> **HARMONY ROW** [ ] [ ]
– Can you follow? / Escape to the Royal wood (on ice) / You burned the tables on me / There's a forest / Morning story / Folk song / Smiles and grins / Post war / Letter of thanks / Victoria sage / The consul at sunset. *(<cd re-mast.Apr03 +=; 065605-2>)* – Green hills (aka Can you follow?) (instrumental) / You burned the tables on me (alt.) / Escape to the Royal Wood (on ice) (instrumental) / There's a forest (alt.) / Can you follow? (take 1).

Oct 71. (7") *(2058 153)* **THE CONSUL AT SUNSET. / LETTER OF THANKS** [ ] [ ]

— In 1972/73, he became part of WEST, BRUCE & LAING (see; MOUNTAIN) He also collaborated on lp ESCALATOR OVER THE HILL with PAUL HAINES and CARLA.

— now with **MICK TAYLOR** – guitar / **CARLA BLEY** – piano / **RONNIE LEAHY** – keyboards / **BRUCE GARY** – drums

R.S.O. R.S.O.

Oct 74. (7") *(2090 141)* **KEEP IT DOWN. / GOLDEN DAYS** [ ] [-]

Nov 74. (lp) *(2394 143)* <4805> **OUT OF THE STORM** [ ] [ ]
– Pieces of mind / Golden days / Running through our hands / Keep on wondering / Keep it down / Into the storm / One / Timeslip. *(cd re-mast.Apr03 +=; 065606-2)* – Keep it down (original) / Keep on wondering (original) / Into the storm (original) / Pieces of mind (original) / One (original).

— now with **SIMON PHILIPS** – drums / **HUGH BURNS** – guitar / **TONY HYMAS** – keyboards

Mar 77. (lp; as JACK BRUCE BAND) *(2394 180)* <1-3021>
HOW'S TRICKS ☐ ☐
– Without a word / Johnny B '77 / Times / Baby Jane / Lost inside a song / How's tricks / Madhouse / Waiting for the call / Outsiders / Something to live for. *(<cd re-mast.Apr03 +=; 065608-2>)* – Without a word (version) / Something to live for (version).

—— Friends: **DAVID SANCIOUS** – guitar, keyboards / **DAVE CLEMPSON** – guitar / **BILLY COBHAM** – drums

Epic Epic

Dec 80. (lp; as JACK BRUCE & FRIENDS) *(84672)* *<JE 36827>*
I'VE ALWAYS WANTED TO DO THIS ☐ ☐
– Hit and run / Running back / Facelift 318 / In this way / Mickey the fiddler / Dancing on air / Livin' without ja / Wind and the sea / Out to lunch / Bird alone.

—— In 1981 he teamed up with BILL LORDAN and ROBIN TROWER to release lp 'B.L.T.' Early the following year he and ROBIN TROWER released 'TRUCE' album on 'Chrysalis'; *CHR/ZCHR 1352).* He returned to solo work after below 45 was featured on TV car advert.

Virgin Virgin

Jun 86. (7"/12") *(VS 875/+12)* **I FEEL FREE. / MAKE LOVE** ☐ ☐

President Intercord

Jan 87. (lp/c) *(PTLS/PTLC 1082)* **AUTOMATIC** ☐ ☐
– A boogie / Uptown breakdown / Travelling child / New world / Make love (part 2) / Green and blue / The swarm / Encore / Automatic pilot.

—— next with **ANTON FIER** – drums (ex-PERE UBU) / **KENJI SUZUKI** – guitar

Epic Epic

Jan 88. (lp/c/cd; JACK BRUCE, ANTON FIER & KENJI SUZUKI) **INAZUMA SUPER SESSION – ABSOLUTELY LIVE (live)** ☐ ☐
– Generation breakdown / White room / Out into the field / Working harder / Sittin' on top of the world / Sunshine of your love / Crossroads / Spoonful – Beat of rock.

—— now with **VERNON REID, NICKY HOPKINS, ALLAN HOLDSWORTH, GINGER BAKER**

Jan 90. (cd/c/lp) *(465 692-2/-4/-1)* *<45729>* **A QUESTION OF TIME** ☐ ☐
– Life on Earth / Make love / No surrender! / Flying / Hey now princess / Blues you can't lose / Obsession / Kwela / Let me be / Only playing games / A question of time. *(re-iss. Feb91;)*

—— with **PETE BROWN** still lyricist / plus **ERIC CLAPTON** – lead guitar / **STUART ELLIOT** – drums / **PETER WIEHE** – rhythm guitar / **MAGGIE REILLY** – b.vocals / **CLEM CLEMPSON** – rhythm guitar, etc / **TRILOK GURTU** – percussion / and guests on 1 each **DICK HECKSTALL-SMITH + DAVID LIEBMAN** – saxophones

C.M.P. C.M.P.

Mar 93. (cd/c/lp) *(CMP CD/MC/LP 1001)* **SOMETHIN ELS** ☐ [–]
– Waiting on a word / Willpower / Ships in the night / Peace of the East / Close enough for love / G.B. dawn blues / Criminality / Childsong / F.M.

—— with **GARY MOORE** – guitar, vocals / **MAGGIE REILLY** – vocals / **GARY 'Mudbone' COOPER** – vocals, percussion / **CLEM CLEMPSON** – guitars / **DICK HECKSTALL-SMITH** -saxophone / **BERNIE WORRELL** – keyboards / **PETE BROWN** – vocals, percussion / **GINGER BAKER + SIMON PHILLIPS + GARY HUSBAND** – drums / **FRANCOIS GARNY** -bass / **MALCOLM BRUCE** – acoustic guitar, keyboards / **JONAS BRUCE** -keyboards / **ART THEMIN** – saxophone / **HENRY LOWTHER** -trumpet / **JOHN MUMFORD** -trombone / + **KIP HANRAHAN**

Mar 94. (d-cd/d-c) *(CMP CD/MC 1005)* **CITIES OF THE HEART (live)** ☐ ☐
– Can you follow? / Running thro' our hands / Over the cliff / Statues / First time I met the blues / Smiles & grins / Bird alone / Neighbor, neighbor / Born under a bad sign // Ships in the night / Never tell your mother she's out of tune / Theme for an imaginary western / Golden days / Life on Earth / NSU / Sitting on top of the world / Politician / Spoonful / Sunshine of your love. *(cd re-iss. Aug94 + Nov94 + Mar96 + Apr98; CMPCD 1005)*

BBM

(aka GINGER BAKER, JACK BRUCE & GARY MOORE) A near reformation of CREAM with MOORE taking the place of CLAPTON.

Virgin Capitol

Jun 94. (cd/c/lp) *(CD/TC+/V 2745)* *<39728>* **AROUND THE NEXT DREAM** [9] ☐
– Waiting in the wings / City of gold / Where in the world / Can't fool the blues / High cost of living / Glory days / Why does love (have to go wrong) / Naked flame / I wonder (why are you so mean to me?) / Wrong side of town.

Jul 94. (7"/c-s) *(VS/+C 1495)* **WHERE IN THE WORLD. / DANGER ZONE** [57] ☐
(cd-s+=) *(VSCDG 1495)* – The world keeps on turnin'.
(cd-s) *(VSCDX 1495)* – ('A'side) / Sittin' on top of the world / I wonder (why are you so mean to me?).

JACK BRUCE

Sep 95. (cd) *(CMPCD 1010)* **MONKJACK** ☐ [–]
– Third degree / The boy / Shouldn't we / David's harp / Know one blues / Time repairs / Laughing on music / Street / Folksong / Weird of Hermiston / Tightrope / The food / Immoral ninth.

Sanctuary Sanctuary

Jul 01. (cd) *(SANCD 84)* *<84511>* **SHADOWS IN THE AIR** ☐ ☐
– Out into the fields / 52nd Street / Heart quake / Boston ball game 1967 / This anger's a liar / Sunshine of your love / Directions home / Milonga / Dancing on air / Windowless rooms / Dark heart / Mr. Flesh / He the Richmond / White room / Surge.

Sep 03. (cd) *(SANCD 211)* *<84633>* **MORE JACK THAN GOD** ☐ Aug03 ☐
– So they invented race / Follow the fire / Kelly's blues / We're going wrong / Bizniz / Progress / I feel free / Ricin (daylight gathering) / The night that once was mine / Milonga too / Cold island / Uh, oh! / Politician / Lost in the city (jam mix).

– compilations, others, etc. –

on 'Polydor' UK unless mentioned otherwise

1974. (d-lp) *(2659 024) / R.S.O.; <PD 3505>* **AT HIS BEST** ☐ 1972 ☐
Nov 80. (d-lp)(d-c) *(2658 137)(3524 218)* **GREATEST HITS** ☐ ☐
Jul 89. (d-lp/c/cd) *(837 806-1/-4/-2)* **WILLPOWER** ☐ ☐
(cd re-iss. Apr95; same)
May 92. (cd/c) *Castle; (CCS CD/MC 326)* **THE COLLECTION** ☐ [–]
Nov 92. (cd; JACK BRUCE & FRIENDS) *Traditional Line; (TL 1324)* **LIVE AT THE BOTTOM LINE (live)** ☐ [–]
May 94. (cd; by DICK HECKSTALL-SMITH, JACK BRUCE & JOHN STEVENS) *Atonal; (EFA 11956-2)* **THIS THAT** ☐ [–]
Sep 95. (cd) *Windsong; (WINCD 076)* **BBC LIVE IN CONCERT** ☐ [–]
(re-iss. Jul98 on 'Strange Fruit'; SFRSCD 067)
Aug 96. (cd) *C.M.P.; (CMPCD 1013)* **THE COLLECTORS EDITION** ☐ [–]
(re-iss. May98; same)
Mar 98. (cd) *Strange Fruit; (WHISCD 010)* **LIVE ON THE TEST** ☐ [–]
Nov 99. (cd) *Ranch Life; (CRANCH 15)* **CONCERT CLASSICS** ☐ [–]
Sep 01. (d-cd) *Burning Airlines; (<PILOT 125>)* **DOING THIS . . . ON ICE! (live in 1980)** ☐ Oct01 ☐
Aug 02. (d-cd) *Superior; (SU 29501)* **JACK BRUCE AND FRIENDS IN CONCERT (live)** ☐ [–]
May 03. (d-cd; as JACK BRUCE BAND) *(<065607-2>)* **LIVE '75 (live at the Manchester Free Tade Hall)** ☐ ☐
May 03. (cd) *(<065609-2>)* **JET SET JEWEL** (shelved set from 1978) ☐ ☐
– The boy / Head in the sun / Neighbour, neighbour / Childsong / Jet set jewel / Please / Maybe it's dawn / Mickey the fiddler / She's moving on / The best is still to come.
Nov 03. (cd) *(065610-2)* *<650105>* **ROPE LADDER TO THE MOON: AN INTRODUCTION TO JACK BRUCE** ☐ ☐
– Never tell your mother she's out of tune / Rope ladder to the Moon / Weird of Hermiston / Theme from an imaginary western / Tickets to waterfalls / Things we like / Folk song / You burned the tables on me / Morning story / Running through our hands / Timeslip / One / Keep it down / How's tricks / Jet set level / Without a word / Jet set jewel.

☐ BS 2000 (see under ⇒ BEASTIE BOYS)

☐ B.T.O. (see under ⇒ BACHMAN-TURNER OVERDRIVE)

Tim BUCKLEY

Born: 14 Feb'47, Washington DC, USA. Signed to 'Elektra' in 1966 by FRANK ZAPPA manager HERB COHEN, who'd discovered him playing folk clubs around L.A. He recorded an eponymous debut with ZAPPA's musicians backing him up, before moving to New York where he was influenced by Greenwich Village troubadour FRED NEIL (whose 'DOLPHINS', he would later cover on 1973 album 'SEFRONIA'). 1967's 'GOODBYE AND HELLO', wore its influences on its sleeve but won critical plaudits for its cascading vocal versatility and meandering grace. Released a couple of years later, 'HAPPY / SAD's introspective intimations abandoned conventional song structures for abstract folk-jazz workouts. Despite their more experimental nature, the songs retained a tangible warmth of feeling, especially the lovely 'BUZZIN' FLY'. A frenetic period of creativity followed in 1970, with BUCKLEY releasing three albums in the space of a year. 'BLUE AFTERNOON' carried on in much the same vein while he took a further sidestep into improvisation with 'LORCA', culminating in the uncompromising 'STARSAILOR'. In true BUCKLEY fashion, he veered wildly into new territory with the sexually explicit 1972 album 'GREETINGS FROM L.A.', which exhibited an interest in black music. The doomed singer recorded two final rather patchy and self-indulgent albums before he died of an accidental drug overdose on 29th June '75. His poetic awareness and uncompromising efforts to push musical boundaries had taken him down a solitary path that bypassed commercial success and eventually led to disillusionment and death, although he left behind a musical legacy of shimmering beauty. In 1990, 'DREAM LETTER', an album of live material from 1968, was unearthed to critical acclaim and along with various other re-issues, has only served to feed the myth of one of rock's greatest enigmas. • **Covered:** SALLY GO ROUND THE ROSES (Jaynettes). • **Trivia:** His songs were later recorded by THIS MORTAL COIL (Song To The Siren + I Must Have Been Blind) and BLOOD, SWEAT & TEARS (Morning Glory).

Album rating: TIM BUCKLEY (*7) / GOODBYE & HELLO (*7) / HAPPY SAD (*7) / BLUE AFTERNOON (*7) / LORCA (*5) / STARSAILOR (*7) / GREETINGS FROM L.A. (*7) / SEFRONIA (*4) / LOOK AT THE FOOL (*4) / posthumous: BEST OF TIM BUCKLEY – 1983 US-import lp (*8) / DREAM LETTER – LIVE IN LONDON (*8) / LIVE AT THE TROUBADOUR 1969 (*5) / HONEYMAN (*5) / COPENHAGEN TAPES (*7) / MORNING GLORY – ANTHOLOGY double compilation (*9)

TIM BUCKLEY – vocals, guitar with **LEE UNDERWOOD** – guitar, keyboards / **BILLY MUNDI** – drums / **JIM FIELDER** – bass / **VAN DYKE PARKS** – piano / **JACK NITZSCHE** – string arrangements

Elektra Elektra

Nov 66. (7") <45606> **GRIEF IN MY SOUL. / WINGS** [–] [ ]

Dec 66. (lp; mono/stereo) *(EKL/EKS 4004)* <74004> **TIM BUCKLEY** [ ] Oct66 [ ]
– I can't see you / Wings / Song of the magician / Strange street affair under blue / Valentine melody / Aren't you the girl / Song slowly sung / It happens every time / Song for Jainie / Grief in my soul / She is / Understand your man. *<re-iss. Jul71 & Mar75; same> <cd-iss. 1990's; 61338>*

Jan 67. (7") *(EKSN 45008)* <45612> **AREN'T YOU THE GIRL. / STRANGE STREET AFFAIR UNDER BLUE** [ ] [ ]

—— BUCKLEY retained only UNDERWOOD, recruiting **CARTER C. COLLINS** – congas

Aug 67. (7") <45618> **LADY GIVE ME YOUR HEART. / ONCE UPON A TIME** [–] [ ]

Oct 67. (7") <45623> **MORNING GLORY. / ONCE I WAS** [–] [ ]

Nov 67. (7") *(EKSN 45018)* **MORNING GLORY. / KNIGHT-ERRANT** [ ] [–]

Dec 67. (lp; mono/stereo) *(EKL/EKS 318)* <7318> **GOODBYE AND HELLO** [ ] Oct67 [ ]
– No man can find the war / Carnival song / Pleasant street / Hallucinations / I never asked to be your mountain / Once I was / Phantasmagoria in two / Knight-Errant / Goodbye and hello / Morning glory. *(re-iss. Jul71; K 42070) (re-iss. Mar93 & Sep95 & Mar00 on 'Warners' cd/c; 7559 60896-2/-4)*

Jan 68. (7") *(EKSN 45023)* **ONCE I WAS. / PHANTASMAGORIA IN TWO** [ ] [–]

Mar 68. (7") *(EKSN 45031)* **WINGS. / I CAN'T SEE YOU** [ ] [ ]

—— added **JOHN MILLER** – acoustic & electric bass / **DAVID FREEDMAN** – vibes, percussion

Oct 68. (7") *(EKSN 45041)* **PLEASANT STREET. / CARNIVAL SONG** [ ] [ ]

Jul 69. (lp) *<(EKS 74045)>* **HAPPY – SAD** [ ] [81]
– Strange feeling / Buzzin' fly / Love from room 109 at the Islander (on Pacific Coast Highway) / Dream letter / Gypsy woman / Sing a song for you. *(re-iss. Jul71; K 42072) (cd-iss. Feb93; 7559 74045-2)*

—— added **JIMMY MADISON** – drums

Straight Straight

Feb 70. (7") *(S 4799)* **HAPPY TIME. / SO LONELY** [ ] [ ]

Feb 70. (lp) *<(STS 1060)>* **BLUE AFTERNOON** [ ] [ ]
– Happy time / Chase the blues away / I must have been blind / The river / So lonely / Cafe / Blue melody / Train. *<US re-iss. Jul71 on 'Warners'; WS 1842> <cd-iss. 1990's; 70356>*

—— BUCKLEY retained only UNDERWOOD and COLLINS, recruiting **JOHN BLAKIN** – bass

Elektra Elektra

Oct 70. (lp) *(2410 005) <EKS 74074>* **LORCA** [ ] [ ]
– Lorca / Anonymous proposition / I had a talk with a woman / Driftin' / Nobody walkin'. *<US re-iss. Jul71; K 42053> (re-iss. Mar75; same) <cd-iss. 1990's; 61339>*

—— BUCKLEY retained only UNDERWOOD and BALKIN, recruiting co-write **LARRY BECKETT / MAURI BAKET** – timpani / **BUZZ GARDNER + BUNK GARDNER** on wind and horns

Straight Straight

Jan 71. (lp) *<(STS 1064)>* **STARSAILOR** [ ] [ ]
– Come here woman / I woke up / Monterey / Moulin Rouge / Song to the siren / Jungle fire / Starsailor / The healing festival / Down by the borderline. *<US re-iss. Jul71 on 'Warners'; WS 1881> <cd-iss. 1991 on 'Rhino'; 70360>*

—— from now on BUCKLEY used loads of session people plus past friends.

Warners Warners

Oct 72. (7") *<7623>* **MOVE WITH ME. / NIGHTHAWKIN'** [–] [ ]

Oct 72. (lp) *(K 46176) <BS 2631>* **GREETINGS FROM L.A.** [ ] [ ]
– Move with me / Get on top / Sweet surrender / Nighthawkin' / Devil eyes / Hong Kong bar / Make it right. *<cd-iss. Jul89 on 'Disc Int.'; EN 73506> <(cd-iss. Feb96; 7599 27261-2)>*

Discreet-Warners Discreet-Warners

May 74. (lp) *(K 49201) <MS 2157>* **SEFRONIA** [ ] [ ]
– Dolphins / Honeyman / Because of you / Peanut man / Martha / Quicksand / I know I'd recognise your face / Stone in love / Sefronia – After Asklepiades, after Kafka / Sefronia – The King's chain / Sally go 'round the roses. *(re-iss. Oct89 on 'Edsel' lp/cd; ED/+CD 277) (cd re-iss. Feb97 on 'Manifesto'; PT 340701) (cd re-iss. Apr01 on 'Manifesto'; MFO 40701CD)*

May 74. (7") *<1187>* **STONE IN LOVE. / QUICKSAND** [–] [ ]

Jul 74. (7") *<1189>* **HONEYMAN. / DOLPHINS** [–] [ ]

Nov 74. (lp) *(K 59204) <DS 2201>* **LOOK AT THE FOOL** [ ] [ ]
– Look at the fool / Bring it on up / Helpless / Freeway blues / Tijuana moon / Ain't it peculiar / Who could deny you? / Mexicali voodoo / Down in the street / Wanda Lu. *(re-iss. Oct89 on 'Edsel' lp/cd; ED/+CD 294) (cd re-iss. Feb97 on 'Manifesto'; PT 340702) (cd re-iss. Apr01 on 'Manifesto'; MFO 40702CD)*

Nov 74. (7") *<1311>* **WANDA LU. / WHO COULD DENY YOU** [–] [ ]

—— TIM died on the 29th of June '75 (see biog.)

– compilations, etc. –

Sep 76. (7") *Elektra; (K 12223)* **MORNING GLORY. / ONCE I WAS** [ ] [ ]

Jun 90. (d-lp/d-cd) *Demon; (DFIEND/+CD 200) / Enigma; <73507>* **DREAM LETTER – LIVE IN LONDON 1968 (live)** [ ] May90 [ ]
– Introduction / Buzzin' fly / Phantasmagoria in two / Morning glory / Dolphins / I've been out walking / The earth is broken / Who do you love / Pleasant Street – You keep me hanging on / Love from room 109 – Strange

feelin' / Carnival song – Hi lily, hi lo / Hallucinations / Troubadour / Dream letter – Happy time / Wayfaring stranger – You got me runnin' / Once I was. *(d-cd re-iss. Feb97 on 'Manifesto'; PT 340703) (d-cd re-iss. Apr01 on 'Manifesto'; MFO 40703CD)*

Aug 91. (cd-ep) *Strange Fruit; (SFPSCD 082)* **THE PEEL SESSIONS** [ ] [-]
– Morning glory / Coming home to you / Sing a song for you / Hallucinations / Troubadour / Once I was.

Mar 94. (cd) *Demon; (EDCD 400) / Rhino; <71663>* **LIVE AT TROUBADOUR 1969 (live)** [ ] [ ]
– Strange feelin' / Venice mating call / I don't need it to rain / I had a talk with my woman / Gypsy woman / Blue melody / Chase the blues away / Driftin' / Nobody walkin'. *<(US+re-iss. May97 on 'Manifesto'; PT 340705) <(re-iss. Apr01 on 'Manifesto'; MFO 40705CD)>*

Aug 94. (cd) *Band Of Joy; (BOJCD 009)* **MORNING GLORY** [ ] [-]

Sep 95. (cd) *Edsel; (EDCD 450)* **HONEYMAN** (live 27th Nov'73) [ ] [-]
– Dolphins / Buzzin' fly / Get on top / Devil eyes / Pleasant Street / Sally, go 'round the roses / Stone in love / Honey man / Sweet surrender. *(re-iss. Apr01 on 'Manifesto'; MFO 40704CD)*

Jul 99. (cd) *Strange Fruit; (SFRSCD 084)* **ONCE I WAS** (the BBC sessions) [ ] [-]
– Dolphins / Honey man / Morning glory / Coming home to you (happy time) / Sing a song for you / Hallucinations – Troubadour / Once I was / I don't need it to rain. *(re-iss. Apr00 on 'Varese Sarabande'; 0302 061056-2) (lp-iss.Apr00 on 'Get Back'; TPM 205)*

Jul 00. (cd) *Pinnacle; (PLRCD 018)* **THE COPENHAGEN TAPES (live 1968)** [ ] [-]
– I don't need it to rain / Buzzin' fly / Strange feelin' / Gypsy woman.

Apr 01. (d-cd) *Rhino; <(8122 76722-2)>* **MORNING GLORY – THE ANTHOLOGY** [ ] Mar01 [ ]
– Wings / She is / Song slowly song / It happens every time / Aren't you the girl / Pleasant street / Hallucinations / No man can find the war / Once I was / Morning glory / Goodbye and hello / Buzzin' fly / Strange feelin' / Sing a song for you / Phantasmagoria in two (live) / I've been out walking (live) / Troubadour (live) / Happy time / Chase the blues away / I must have been blind / The river / So lonely / Blue melody / I had a talk with my woman (live) / Moulin Rouge / Song to the siren / Monterey / Sweet surrender / Hong Kong bar / Make it right / Sally go 'round the roses / Who could deny you / Song to the siren (from the 'Monkees' TV show).

May 01. (cd) *Maestro; <(MFO 40706CD)>* **THE DREAM BELONGS TO ME: RARE AND UNRELEASED RECORDINGS 1968-1973** [ ] [ ]

Oct 01. (cd) *Elektra; <(8122 73569-2)>* **TIM BUCKLEY / GOODBYE AND HELLO** [ ] [ ]

Jeff BUCKLEY

Born: 17 Nov'66, Orange County, California, USA. The offspring of the late, great TIM BUCKLEY, JEFF's chosen career as a musician, singer and songwriter was always destined to bear the heavy burden of his father's unique legacy (note: in this instance JEFF appears out of alphabetical sequence). To his credit, BUCKLEY Jnr. persevered at carving out a distinctive niche in the musical landscape of the early 90's, plugging away on the once legendary Greenwich Village scene of New York. Torch rather than tortured, JEFF utilised his inherited multi-octave vocal chords in ever more impressive and innovative fashion, both in tackling an eclectic variety of cover material (see below) and lavishly dramatic originals. Given his first British break in 1994, via 'LIVE AT THE SIN-E' EP (1992 in America) on the 'Big Cat' label, BUCKLEY was a surprise success at the grunge overload of Reading 1994. Coinciding with his appearance was the release of his major label ('Columbia') debut, 'GRACE', an emotionally raw and occasionally claustrophobic listen that gained almost unanimous praise from UK critics and enjoyed a brief residence in the Top 50. Tracks such as 'SO REAL', 'LAST GOODBYE' and 'DREAM LOVER', suggested a mercurial talent in the ascendant, although the lad had possibly listened to too much LED ZEPPELIN as a youth. Eventually resuming his recording career early in 1997 with TOM VERLAINE (ex-TELEVISION) at the controls, JEFF looked like making a severe dent in the rock mainstream with a follow-up to 'GRACE', although subsequent sessions proved problematic. Fate was to deal a cruel hand when, on the 29th of May '98, JEFF, like his father before him, was cut down in his prime; hardly a typical rock'n'roll death, the young singer was swept away by a powerful current while swimming in Memphis harbor. Exactly a year later, the half-finished project BUCKLEY had been working on at the time of his death was posthumously released as 'SKETCHES FOR MY SWEETHEART THE DRUNK'. A double CD partly curated by his mother, the UK Top 10 set gave an indication as to where JEFF was headed as well as serving as a convincing last word on the career of a man many considered a genius. Well, it wasn't quite the last word, that honour falling to 'MYSTERY WHITE BOY: LIVE '95-'96 (2000), a collection of live performances culled from the DAT recordings of his 'Grace' tour. Like the posthumous live recordings of his father, this record will no doubt be cherished by hardcore fans although its interest to the wider music buying public (outside the UK where it hit the Top 10) might well be more limited. • **Covers:** JE N'EN CONNAIS PAS LA FIN (Edith Piaf) / THE WAY YOUNG LOVERS DO (Van Morrison) / LILAC WINE (Elkie Brooks) / HALLELUJAH (Leonard Cohen) / KANGA ROO (Big Star) / KICK OUT THE JAMS (MC5) / YARD OF BLONDE GIRLS (Audrey Clark) / BACK IN N.Y.C. (Genesis) / SATISFIED MIND (J.Hayes & J.Rhodes).

Album rating: LIVE AT SIN-E mini (*6) / GRACE (*8) / SKETCHES FOR MY SWEETHEART THE DRUNK (*8) / MYSTERY WHITE BOY (*6) / LIVE A L'OLYMPIA (*5)

JEFF BUCKLEY – vocals, guitars, harmonium, organ, dulcimer / with **MICK GRONDAHL** – bass / **MATT JOHNSON** – drums, percussion / plus MICHAEL TIGHE – guitar / **GARLY LUCAS** – magicalguitarness

Big Cat / Columbia

Apr 94. (m-lp/m-cd) *(ABB 61/+CD) <77296>* **LIVE AT SIN-E (live)** [ ] [ ]
– Mojo pin / Eternal life / Je n'en connais pas la fin / The way young lovers do.

Columbia / Columbia

Aug 94. (cd/c/lp) *(475928-2/-4/-1) <57528>* **GRACE** [50] [ ]
– Mojo pin / Grace / Last goodbye / Lilac wine / So real / Hallelujah / Lover, you should've come over / Corpus christi Carol / Eternal life / Dream brother. *(lp re-iss. Jun99 on 'Simply Vinyl'; SVLP 77)*

May 95. (cd-s) *<475928>* **LAST GOODBYE / LAST GOODBYE (edit) / KANGA-ROO** [-] [ ]

May 95. (10"ep/cd-ep) *(662042-0/-2)* **LAST GOODBYE. / LOVER, YOU SHOULD'VE COME OVER (live) / TONGUE (live)** [54] [-]
(cd-ep) *(662042-5)* – ('A'side) / Dream brother (live) / So real (live).

1996. (m-cd) *<662155>* **LIVE FROM THE BATACLAN (live)** [-] [ ]
– Dream brother / The way young lovers do / Je n'en connais pas la fin / Hallelujah.

—— sadly, JEFF was to die in a drowning accident on the 29th of May '97

– posthumous releases, etc. –

May 98. (d-cd/d-c/d-lp) *(488661-2/-4/-1) <67228>* **SKETCHES FOR MY SWEETHEART THE DRUNK** [7] [64]
– The sky is a landfill / Everybody here wants you / Opened once / Nightmares by the sea / Yard of blonde girls / Witches' rave / Morning theft / Vancouver / You & I // Nightmares by the sea / New Year's prayer / Haven't you heard / I know we could be so happy baby (if we wanted to be) / Murder suicide meteor slave / Back in N.Y.C. / Gunshot glitter *[cd-only]*/ Demon John / Your flesh is so nice / Jewel box / Satisfied mind.

May 98. (cd-ep) *(665791-2)* **EVERYBODY HERE WANTS YOU / THOUSAND FOLD / ETERNAL LIFE (road version) / HALLELUJAH (live)** [43] [-]
(cd-ep) *(665791-5)* – ('A'side) / Lover, you should've come over (live and acoustic) / Tongue (live).

May 00. (cd/c/lp) *(497972-2/-4/-1) <69592>* **MYSTERY WHITE BOY – LIVE '95-'96** [8] [ ]

– Dream brother / I woke up in a strange place / Mojo pin / Lilac wine / What will you say / Last goodbye / Eternal life / Grace / Moodswing whiskey / The man that got away / Kanga-roo / Hallelujah – I know it's over. *(d-cd+=; 497972-9)* – That's all I ask / Lover, you should've come over / So real. *(cd re-iss. Apr02; same)*

Oct 01. (cd) *<(503204-9)>* **LIVE A L'OLYMPIA (live)** [ ] Jul01 [ ]
– Lover, you should have come over / Dream brother / Eternal life / Kick out the jams / Lilac wine / Grace / That's all I ask / Kashmir / Je n'en connais pas la fin / Hallelujah / What will you say (with ALIM QASIMOV).

Oct 02. (5xcd-s-box) *(501178-2) <87077>* **THE GRACE EP'S** [ ] Nov02 [ ]

Sep 03. (d-cd) *(512257-2) <89202>* **THE COMPLETE LIVE AT SIN-E** (adds extra tracks + monologue) [ ] [ ]

– others, etc. –

Oct 02. (cd; with GARY LUCAS) *Circus; (FYL 014)* **SONGS TO NO ONE 1991-1992** [ ] [-]

BUFFALO SPRINGFIELD

Formed: Los Angeles, California, USA . . . March '66. In a well-documented incident, STEPHEN STILLS and guitarist RICHIE FUREY were caught in a traffic jam on Sunset Strip, when by pure chance, STILLS recognised the driver of a black hearse, NEIL YOUNG. Along with bass player and fellow Canadian BRUCE PALMER, YOUNG had travelled down to Hollywood to try his luck in the fabled City of Angels. This fated get-together also led to another member being recruited, drummer DEWEY MARTIN. STILLS and YOUNG clashed right from the off, but it was essentially this tension that fuelled the band's creative spark in a JAGGERS/RICHARDS kind of fashion. Taking their name from a type of steamroller, and with the help of the SONNY & CHER management team of CHARLIE GREENE and BRIAN STONE, the band were signed to Atlantic offshoot 'Atco' in a matter of months. With the combined talent of STILLS and YOUNG's soaring harmonies and driving rhythm, the band often came on like a country-fied BEATLES, although their albums are notable for their striking stylistic diversity. The ambitiously eccentric, YOUNG-penned debut single, 'NOWADAYS CLANCY CAN'T EVEN SING', did nothing, while 'BURNED', the 2-minute pop thrill of a follow-up, fared equally badly. But then STILLS struck gold with the famous protest anthem 'FOR WHAT IT'S WORTH', released in the same month as the band's fine eponymous debut album. The song concerned itself with the previous summer's riots whereby a coterie of businessmen had threatened Sunset Strip's nightlife by proposing the building of a business district. Of course the students were none too happy, especially when 300 protesters were arrested. The song was duly adopted by rebels everywhere as a general mascot for fighting the good fight, and its vaguely psychedelic, menacing tone perfectly evoked the feelings of persecution felt by the emerging flower children. Throughout 1967, the band was rocked by internal squabbling with various members coming and going. An album, 'STAMPEDE', was recorded but never quite completed. It later surfaced as a bootleg and one track from it, 'DOWN TO THE WIRE', featuring an impassioned YOUNG vocal, was included on his, 'DECADE' (1976) compilation. YOUNG also missed the bands slot at the Monterey Pop Festival, DAVID CROSBY taking his place. Despite all this, the band completed a follow-up, 'BUFFALO SPRINGFIELD AGAIN', which was issued in late '67. Opinions on the album are mixed with some critics deeming it a classic of its time, others criticising its watered down production. The best moments are YOUNG's JACK NITZSCHE-arranged numbers, 'BROKEN ARROW' and 'EXPECTING TO FLY', the latter possessed a haunting, lysergic quality. STILL's compositions, 'BLUEBIRD' and 'ROCK AND ROLL WOMAN', lack the sophistication of YOUNG's surreal epics but are enjoyable none the less. The tension between YOUNG and STILLS eventually finished the band (DAVID CROSBY once commenting that they used their guitars as weapons, on stage and off!) with a final album, 'LAST TIME AROUND', released after the split. YOUNG contributed the fragile 'I AM A CHILD' and one other song before leaving the band early on during the sessions. YOUNG went on to an erratic, often mercurial career, while STILLS went off to help form CROSBY, STILLS and NASH (re-united with YOUNG in 1970). FURAY meanwhile, went off to join country rockers POCO. Along with The BYRDS and LOVE, BUFFALO SPRINGFIELD were one of the most influential, if somewhat short-lived bands to come out of L.A.

Album rating: BUFFALO SPRINGFIELD (*7) / BUFFALO SPRINGFIELD AGAIN (*9) / LAST TIME AROUND (*6) / THE BEST OF BUFFALO SPRINGFIELD . . . RETROSPECTIVE compilation (*8) / EXPECTING TO FLY compilation (*7)

STEPHEN STILLS (b. 3 Jan'45, Dallas, Texas) – lead guitar, vocals / **NEIL YOUNG** (b.12 Nov'45, Toronto, Canada) – lead guitar, vocals / **RICHIE FURAY** (b. 9 May'44, Dayton, Ohio) – vocals, guitar / **BRUCE PALMER** (b. 1944, Liverpool, Canada) – bass; repl. KEN KOBLUN / **DEWEY MARTIN** (b.30 Sep'42, Chesterfield, Canada) – drums (ex-DILLARDS)

Atlantic Atco

Oct 66. (7") *<6428>* **NOWADAYS CLANCY CAN'T EVEN SING. / GO AND SAY GOODBYE** [-] [ ]

Dec 66. (7"w-drawn) *<6452>* **BURNED. / EVERYBODY'S WRONG** [-] [ ]

Jan 67. (lp; stereo/mono) *(588/587 070) <SD+/33-200>* **BUFFALO SPRINGFIELD** [ ] Dec66 [ ]
– Don't scold me (*) / Go and say goodbye / Sit down I think I love you / Nowadays Clancy can't even sing / Everybody's wrong / Hot dusty roads / Flying on the ground / Burned / Do I have to come right out and say it? / Leave / Pay the price / Out of my mind. *<re-iss. Feb67 stereo/mono; SD+/33-200-A>* – For what it's worth (repl.track (*) ; hit US No.80> *(re-iss. 1971; K 30028) (cd-iss. Feb93; 7567 90389-2)*

Jan 67. (7") *(584 077) <6459>* **FOR WHAT IT'S WORTH. / DO I HAVE TO COME RIGHT OUT AND SAY IT?** [ ] [7]

— on stage **KEN KOBLUN** and **JIM FIELDER**, latter of The MOTHERS, repl. PALMER, although PALMER did return occasionally. / **DOUG HASTINGS** – guitar repl. YOUNG (also DAVID CROSBY guested at Monteray)

— **BOB WEST** – bass & CHARLIE CHIN – banjo deputise for above reshuffles

Jul 67. (7") *<6499>* **BLUEBIRD. / MR. SOUL** [-] [58]

— **STILLS, FURAY, MARTIN** and the returning **YOUNG** recruit **JIM MESSINA** (b. 5 Dec'47, Maywood, Calif.) – bass repl. FIELDER who joined BLOOD SWEAT & TEARS

Oct 67. (7") *(584 145) <6519>* **ROCK'N'ROLL WOMAN. / A CHILD'S CLAIM TO FAME** [ ] Sep67 [44]

Jan 68. (lp; stereo/mono) *(588/587 091) <SD+/33-226>* **BUFFALO SPRINGFIELD AGAIN** [ ] Nov67 [44]
– Mr. Soul / A child's claim to fame / Everydays / Expecting to fly / Bluebird / Hung upside down / Sad memory / Good time boy / Rock'n'roll woman / Broken arrow. *(re-iss. 1971; K 40014) (cd-iss. Jul88; 790-391-2)*

Feb 68. (7") *(584 165) <6545>* **EXPECTING TO FLY. / EVERYDAYS** [ ] Jan68 [98]

Jun 68. (7") *(584 189) <6572>* **UNO MUNDO. / MERRY-GO-ROUND** [ ] [ ]

Aug 68. (7") *<6602>* **KIND WOMAN. / SPECIAL CARE** [-] [ ]

— with original line-up they recorded another album, but they had split by May'68. MESSINA who had always been their sound recordist posthumously assembled line-up

Oct 68. (7") *<6615>* **ON THE WAY HOME. / FOUR DAYS GONE** [-] [82]

Dec 68. (lp) *(228 024) <SD33-256>* **LAST TIME AROUND** [ ] Aug68 [42]
– On the way home / It's so hard to wait / Pretty girl why / Four days gone / Carefree country day / Special care / The hour of not quite rain / Questions / I am a child / Merry-go-round / Uno mundo / Kind woman. *(re-iss. 1971; K 40077) (cd-iss. Mar94 on 'Atco'; 7567 90393-2)*

— After their split, NEIL YOUNG went solo and joined STEPHEN STILLS in CROSBY, STILLS NASH & YOUNG. FURAY formed POCO adding later

MESSINA. DEWEY MARTIN tried in vain to use BUFFALO SPRINGFIELD name.

– compilations, etc. –

on 'Atlantic' UK / 'Atco' US; unless otherwise mentioned

Mar 69. (lp) *(228 012)* *<SD33-283>* **RETROSPECTIVE – THE BEST OF BUFFALO SPRINGFIELD** Feb69 42
– For what it's worth / Mr. Soul / Sit down I think I love you / Kind woman / Bluebird / On the way home / Nowadays Clancy can't even sing / Broken arrow / Rock'n'roll woman / I am a child / Go and say goodbye / Expecting to fly. *(re-iss. 1971; K 40071) (cd-iss. Jul88; 790 417-2)*

Oct 69. (7") *Atco; (226 006)* **PRETTY GIRL WHY / QUESTIONS** –

Oct 70. (lp) *(K 2462 012)* **EXPECTING TO FLY** –

Oct 72. (7"ep) *(K 10237)* **BLUEBIRD / MR. SOUL. / ROCK'N'ROLL WOMAN / EXPECTING TO FLY** –

Dec 73. (d-lp) *(K 70001)* *<SD2 806>* **BUFFALO SPRINGFIELD**

Jul 01. (4xcd-box) *Rhino; <(8122 74324-2)>* **BOX SET**

—— some BUFFALO SPRINGFIELD live tracks appeared on NEIL YOUNG's compilation lp 'JOURNEY THROUGH THE PAST', and two on his 'DECADE' triple in '77.

BUFFALO TOM

Formed: Boston, Massachusetts, USA . . . 1986 by BILL JANOVITZ, CHRIS COLBOURN and TOM MAGINNIS. Signed to 'S.S.T.', the band debuted in summer '89 with an eponymous album of high octane melodic hardcore. Though drawing countless comparisons with DINOSAUR JR. (J. MASCIS produced them), the group ploughed on, developing their own unique sound and garnering critical praise for the impressive writing talents of JANOVITZ and COLBOURN. Somewhat akin to a grunge hybrid of HUSKER DU and VAN MORRISON, these soulful indie rockers signed to 'Beggars Banquet' subsidiary, 'Situation 2', for their follow-up set, 'BIRDBRAIN'. However, it was with the acclaimed 'LET ME COME OVER' (1992), that BUFFALO TOM's bruised beauty really began to resonate, the classic 'TAILLIGHTS FADE' warranting gushing but deserved praise from the music press. By taking their collective foot off the noise accelerator, the group had given the songs time to catch their breath and enjoy the scenery. This didn't translate into major sales, however, the record stalling just inside the UK Top 50. 'BIG RED LETTER DAY' (1993) went for a slicker sound, this approach paying off as the album became the first BUFFALO TOM record to make the Top 20. Released just prior to the band's 1995 Reading Festival appearance, 'SLEEPY EYED' proved that JANOVITZ and co. had the talent and ability to last the course, their sound noticeably more confident and mature. In fact, JANOVITZ was sufficiently sure of his talents to attempt a solo set in 1996, the rootsy 'LONESOME BILLY'. 'SMITTEN' (1998) was basically more of the same from the Boston crew, if a little more adventurous in the way of arrangements. JANOVITZ shone on the likes of the string-enhanced 'SCOTTISH WINDOWS' while fans of the BUFFALO mainman lapped up the stripped-bare beauty of his post-millennial solo set, 'UP HERE' (2001). • **Covers:** SHE BELONGS TO ME (Bob Dylan) / HEAVEN (Psychedelic Furs) / THE SPIDER AND THE FLY (Rolling Stones) / ALL TOMORROW'S PARTIES (Velvet Underground) / BLUE (Rain Parade) / WAH WAH (George Harrison) / CUPID COME (My Bloody Valentine) / HAWAIIAN BABY (Spinnanes) / GUIDING STAR (Teenage Fanclub).

Album rating: BUFFALO TOM (*6) / BIRDBRAIN (*6) / LET ME COME OVER (*9) / (BIG RED LETTER DAY) (*8) / SLEEPY EYED (*8) / SMITTEN (*7) / ASIDES FROM BUFFALO TOM compilation (*9) / BESIDES: A COLLECTION OF B-SIDES AND RARITIES compilation (*5) / Bill Janovitz: LONESOME BILLY (*5) / UP HERE (*6)

BILL JANOVITZ – vocals, guitar / **CHRIS COLBOURN** – bass / **TOM MAGINNIS** – drums

S.S.T. S.S.T.

Oct 89. (lp/c/cd) *<(SST/+C/CD 250)>* **BUFFALO TOM** Jul89
– Sunflower suit / The plank / Impossible / 500,000 warnings / The bus / Racine / In the attic / Flushing stars / Walk away / Reason why. *(cd re-iss. Apr92 on 'Megadisc'; MDC 7896) (re-iss. Oct92 on 'Beggars Banquet' lp/c/cd+=; BBQ LP/MC/CD 126)* – Blue / Deep in the ground.

Caff Corp not iss.

Feb 90. (7"ltd) *(CAFF 006)* **ENEMY (live). / DEEP IN THE GROUND** –

Megadisc Megadisc

Feb 90. (7") *(MD 5266)* **SUNFLOWER SUIT. / BLUE** – Dutch –

Jun 90. (12"/cd-s) *<(MD 12/C 5276)>* **CRAWL. / BLEEDING HEART / BLUE**

Situation 2 Beggars Banquet

Oct 90. (12"ep) *(SIT 71T)* **BIRDBRAIN. / REASON WHY (live acoustic) / HEAVEN (acoustic)** –

Oct 90. (cd)(c/lp) *(SITU 31CD)(SIT C/U 31) <2434-2/-4>* **BIRDBRAIN**
– Birdbrain / Skeleton key / Caress / Guy who is me / Enemy / Crawl / Fortune teller / Baby / Directive / Bleeding heart. *(cd+=)* – Heaven (acoustic) / Reason why (live acoustic). *(cd re-iss. Sep95 & Nov97 on 'Beggars Banquet'; BBL 31CD)*

May 91. (12"ep/cd-ep) *(SIT 77 T/CD)* **FORTUNE TELLER. / STYMIED (acoustic) / WAH WAH (live) / BUMBLE BEE** –

Situation 2 R.C.A.

Feb 92. (12"ep/cd-ep) *(SIT 86 T/CD)* **VELVET ROOF. / CRUTCH / SALLY BROWN / SHE BELONGS TO ME** –

Mar 92. (cd)(c/lp) *(SITU 36CD)(SIT C/U 36) <61105>* **LET ME COME OVER** 49
– Staples / Taillights fade / Mountains of your head / Mineral / Darl / Larry / Velvet roof / I'm not there / Stymied / Porchlight / Frozen lake / Saving grace. *(cd+=/c+=)* – Crutch. *(cd re-iss. Nov97 on 'Beggars Banquet'; BBL 36CD)*

May 92. (10"ep/12"ep/cd-ep) *(SIT 96 TT/T/CD)* **TAILLIGHTS FADE / BIRDBRAIN (live). / LARRY (live) / SKELETON KEY (live)**

Beggars Banquet Beggars Banquet

Oct 92. (7",7"green) *(BBQ 6)* **MINERAL. / SUNFLOWER SUIT** –
(cd-s+=) *(BBQ 6CD)* – Crawl / The bus.

Sep 93. (cd/c/lp) *(BBQ CD/MC/LP 142) <92292>* **(BIG RED LETTER DAY)** 17
– Sodajerk / I'm allowed / Tree house / Would not be denied / Latest monkey / My responsibility / Dry land / Torch singer / Late at night / Suppose / Anything that way. *(cd re-iss. Nov97; BBL 142CD)*

Sep 93. (12"ep/cd-ep) *(BBQ 20 T/CD)* **SODAJERK / WOULD NOT BE DENIED. / WITCHES / THE WAY BACK** –

Sep 93. (7") *<98366>* **SODAJERK. / WITCHES** –

Nov 93. (7") *(BBQ 25)* **TREE HOUSE. / LATE AT NIGHT (live acoustic)** –
(12"+=/cd-s+=) *(BBQ 25 T/CD)* – Let's make anything that way (live acoustic).

Beggars Banquet Atlantic

Apr 94. (12"ep/cd-ep) *(BBQ 30 T/CD)* **I'M ALLOWED. / FOR ALL TO SEE / BUTTERSCOTCH** –

Apr 94. (cd-ep) *<95942>* **I'M ALLOWED / BUTTERSCOTCH / ANYTHING THAT WAY (live acoustic) / LATE AT NIGHT (live acoustic)** –

Beggars Banquet East West

Jun 95. (10"ep/cd-ep) *(BBQ 49 TT/CD)* **SUMMER. / CLOUDS / DOES THIS MEAN YOU'RE NOT MY FRIEND?** –

Jul 95. (cd/c/lp) *(BBQ CD/MC/LP 177) <61782>* **SLEEPY EYED** 31
– Tangerine / Summer / Kitchen door / Rules / It's you / When you discover / Sunday night / Your stripes / Sparklers / Clobbered / Sundress / Twenty-points (the ballad of sexual dependency) / Souvenir / Crueler. *(cd re-iss. Nov97; BBL 177CD)*

Nov 95. (7"orange) *(BBQ 64)* **TANGERINE. / BREATHE** –
(cd-s+=) *(BBQ 64CD)* – The spider and the fly.

Beggars Banquet — Polydor

Sep 98. (7") *(BBQ 329)* **WISER (edit). / CUPID COME** [ ] [–]
(cd-s+=) *(BBQ 329CD)* – Hawaiian baby.

Sep 98. (cd/lp) *(BBQ CD/LP 205)* <557867> **SMITTEN** [ ] [ ]
– Rachael / Postcard / Knot it in / The bible / Scottish windows / White paint morning / Wiser / See to me / Register side / Do you in / Under milkwood / Walking wounded.

Feb 99. (cd-s) *(BT 2000CD)* **KNOT IN IT / RACHEL / POSTCARD (radio session)** [ ] [–]
(above issued on 'Megadisc', below issued on 'Ignition')

Oct 99. (7"/c-s/cd-s) *(IGN/+SMC/SCD 16)* **GOING UNDERGROUND. / Liam Gallagher & Steve Craddock: CARNATION** [6] [–]

Sep 00. (cd) *(BEGA 2028CD)* <82028> **ASIDES FROM BUFFALO TOM – THE BEST OF 1988-1999** (compilation) [ ] Aug00 [ ]
– Summer / Sodajerk / Taillights fade / Mineral / Kitchen door / Enemy / Sunflower suit / Tree house / Larry / Postcard / Tangerine / Rachael / I'm allowed / Birdbrain / Velvet roof / Going underground / Late at night / Wiser (single edit).

May 02. (cd) *(BBL 2033CD)* <82033> **BESIDES: A COLLECTION OF B-SIDES AND RARITIES** (compilation) [ ] [ ]
– Witches / For all to see / She belongs to me / Bumble bee / Never noticed / The way back / Sally Brown / Hawaiian baby / Butterscotch / Wah-wah / Anchors aweigh / Breathe / The spider and the fly / Clouds / Cupid come / Does this mean you're not my friend? / Guiding star / All tomorrow's parties.

BILL JANOVITZ

with **JOEY BURNS** – upright bass, vocals / **JOHN CONVERTINO** – drums / and guests CRAIG SCHUMACHER, HOWE GELB + NEIL HARRY

Beggars Banquet — Beggars Banquet

Dec 96. (cd/lp) *(BBQ CD/LP 186)* <80186> **LONESOME BILLY** [ ] Jan97 [ ]
– Girl's club / Think of all / Shoulder / Gaslight / Ghost in my piano / Strangers / My funny valentine / Peninsula / Talking to the Queen / Red balloon.

—— now with **PHIL AIKEN** – keyboards + **CHRIS TOPPIN** – vocals

Fire — Spin Art

Mar 02. (cd) *(FIRECD 76)* <SPIN 93> **UP HERE** [ ] Aug01 [ ]
– Atlantic / Best kept secret / Up here / Half a heart / Your stranger's face / Goodnight, whereever you are / Minneapolis / Like you do / Like shadows / Light in December / Long island.

☐ Eric BURDON (see under ⇒ ANIMALS)

☐ Tim BURGESS (see under ⇒ CHARLATANS)

Solomon BURKE

Born: 21 Mar'36, Philadelphia, Pennsylvania, USA. A low key but highly influential soul singer, SOLOMON BURKE brought all the grit, suffering and redemption of roots gospel and country to his chosen genre without ever really crossing over into the pop market like most of his contemporaries. Steeped in worship from an early age, he became something of a preaching prodigy, charged with his own gospel radio show at the age of only twelve. After cutting early sides for labels such as 'Apollo' and 'Singular', BURKE signed with 'Atlantic' in 1960, projecting his affinity gospel onto country, rock'n'roll and R&B. With only his second Atlantic single, 'JUST OUT OF REACH (OF MY TWO OPEN ARMS)', he helped integrate C&W as an underlying component of much Southern Soul, making the US Hot 100 into the bargain. This ability to distill the essential elements of different sounds, together with his strong, emotionally charged delivery and well turned out productions, rewarded him with a series of major R&B/minor pop hits over the early to mid-60's including 'CRY TO ME', 'IF YOU NEED ME', 'YOU'RE GOOD FOR ME', 'GOT TO GET YOU OFF MY MIND' and 'TONIGHT'S THE NIGHT'. As well as the influence on his contemporaries, these songs made an impression on rock artists like VAN MORRISON (who later namechecked BURKE on 1990's 'REAL REAL GONE') in his and the ROLLING STONES who covered the likes of 'CRY TO ME' and 'EVERYBODY NEEDS SOMEBODY TO LOVE'. By the end of the 60's, the singer had moved to 'Bell' where he scored another minor pop hit with a cover of John Fogerty's 'PROUD MARY', although the 70's found him bouncing between labels like 'Dunhill' and 'Chess' without much creative or commercial return. The early 80's meanwhile, saw BURKE revisiting his formative gospel years (even getting nominated for a Grammy with the 'TAKE ME, SHAKE ME' album) although he continued to record secular sets for roots labels like 'Rounder'. He also continued to tour, often in tandem with other classic 60's soul artists. While many critics drew a parallel with JOHNNY CASH's latter day artistic rebirth, it was difficult not to draw comparisons when 'DON'T GIVE UP ON ME' (2002) appeared unexpectedly in 2002. Produced by singer/songwriter JOE HENRY, the album finally provided BURKE with the optimum creative environment – not to mention quality material, supplied by heavyweight stars and longtime fans such as MORRISON, BOB DYLAN, TOM WAITS and ELVIS COSTELLO – in which to fully express the talent which had been untapped in recent decades. Spare, stripped down, with just enough organ accompaniment to bring out the man's gospel overtones, the record was pretty much a revelation for longtime fans, while BURKE's voice was as muscular and tender as ever if tempered by a grainy wisdom.

Album rating: SOLOMON BURKE'S GREATEST HITS compilation (*6) / IF YOU NEED ME (*5) / ROCK'N'SOUL (*5) / THE BEST OF SOLOMON BURKE compilation (*6) / KING SOLOMON (*5) / I WISH I KNEW (*4) / PROUD MARY (*5) / THE ELECTRONIC MAGNETISM (*5) / MUSIC TO MAKE LOVE BY (*3) / BACK TO MY ROOTS (*2) / SIDEWALKS, FENCES & WALLS (*6) / SOUL ALIVE! (*7) / A CHANGE IS GONNA COME (*6) / HOMELAND (*5) / THE DEFINITION OF SOUL (*5) / WE NEED A MIRACLE (*3) / NOT BY WATER, BUT FIRE THIS TIME (*4) / DON'T GIVE UP ON ME (*8)

SOLOMON BURKE – vocals / with session people, etc.

not iss. — Apollo

Dec 55. (7") <485> **CHRISTMAS PRESENTS. / WHEN I'M ALL ALONE** [–] [ ]

Feb 56. (7") <487> **I'M IN LOVE. / WHY DO ME THAT WAY** [–] [ ]

May 56. (7") <491> **I'M ALL ALONE. / TO THEE** [–] [ ]

Sep 56. (7") <500> **NO MAN WALKS ALONE. / WALKING IN A DREAM** [–] [ ]

Nov 56. (7") <505> **YOU CAN RUN BUT YOU CAN'T HIDE. / A PICTURE OF YOU** [–] [ ]

Apr 57. (7") <511> **I NEED YOU TONIGHT. / THIS IS IT** [–] [ ]

Jun 57. (7") <512> **FOR YOU AND YOU ALONE. / YOU ARE MY LOVE** [–] [ ]

Mar 58. (7") <522> **THEY ALWAYS SAY. / DON'T CRY** [–] [ ]

Aug 58. (7") <527> **MY HEART IS CHAPEL. / THIS IS IT** [–] [ ]

not iss. — Singular

Jun 59. (7") <1314> **DOODLE DEE DOO. / IT'S ALL RIGHT** [–] [ ]

Jul 60. (7") <1812> **THIS LITTLE RING. / I'M NOT AFRAID** [–] [ ]

London — Atlantic

Jun 61. (7") <2089> **KEEP THE MAGIC WORKING. / HOW MANY TIMES** [–] [ ]

Nov 61. (7") *(HLK 9454)* <2114> **JUST OUT OF REACH (OF MY TWO OPEN ARMS). / BE BOP GRANDMA** [ ] Sep61 [24]

Feb 62. (7") *(HLK 9512)* <2131> **CRY TO ME. / I ALMOST LOST MY MIND** [ ] Jan62 [44]

May 62. (7") *(HLK 9560)* <2147> **DOWN IN THE VALLEY. / I'M HANGING UP MY HEART FOR YOU** [ ] [71] [85]

Aug 62. (7") <2157> **I REALLY DON'T WANT TO KNOW. / TONIGHT MY HEART SHE IS CRYING (LOVE IS A BIRD)** [–] [93]

Jan 63. (7") *<2170>* **GO ON BACK TO HIM. / I SAID I WAS SORRY** [–] [ ]

Mar 63. (7") *<2180>* **WORDS. / HOME IN YOUR HEART** [–] [ ]

May 63. (7") *(HLK 9715) <2185>* **IF YOU NEED ME. / YOU CAN MAKE IT IF YOU TRY** [ ] Apr63 [37]

Jun 63. (lp) *<8075>* **IF YOU NEED ME** [–] [ ]
– If you need me / Words / Stupidity / Go on back to him / I said I was sorry / It's all right / Home in your heart / I really don't want to know / You can make it if you try / Send me some loving / This little ring / Tonight my heart she is crying. *(cd-iss. Jan97 on 'Sequel'; RSACD 860)*

Aug 63. (7") *(HLK 9763) <2196>* **CAN'T NOBODY LOVE YOU. / STUPIDITY** [ ] Jul63 [66]

Oct 63. (7") *<2205>* **YOU'RE GOOD FOR ME. / BEAUTIFUL BROWN EYES** [–] [49]

Feb 64. (7") *(HLK 9849) <2218>* **HE'LL HAVE TO GO. / ROCKIN' SOUL** [ ] Jan64 [51]

May 64. (7") *(HLK 9887) <2226>* **GOODBYE BABY (BABY GOODBYE). / SOMEONE TO LOVE ME** [ ] Apr64 [33]

Atlantic Atlantic

Aug 64. (7") *(AT 4004) <2241>* **EVERYBODY NEEDS SOMEBODY TO LOVE. / LOOKING FOR MY BABY** [ ] Jul64 [58]

Sep 64. (7") *<2254>* **YES I DO. / WON'T YOU GIVE HIM (ONE MORE CHANCE)** [–] [92]

Nov 64. (lp) *(ATL 5009)* **ROCK'N'SOUL** [ ] [–]
– Goodbye baby (goodbye baby) / Cry to me / Won't you give him (one more chance) / If you need me / Hard, ain't it hard? / Can't nobody love you / Just out of reach / You're good for me / You can't love them all / Someone to love me / Beautiful brown yes / He'll have to go. *(cd re-iss. Mar97 on 'Sequel'; RSACD 861)*

Dec 64. (7") *(AT 4014) <2259>* **THE PRICE. / MORE ROCKIN' SOUL** [ ] Nov64 [57]

Mar 65. (7") *(AT 4022) <2276>* **GOT TO GET YOU OFF MY MIND. / PEEPIN'** [ ] Feb65 [22]

Jun 65. (7") *(AT 4030) <2288>* **TONIGHT'S THE NIGHT. / MAGGIE'S FARM** [ ] May65 [28]

Sep 65. (7") *(AT 4044) <2299>* **SOMEONE IS WATCHING. / DANCE, DANCE, DANCE** [ ] Aug65 [89]

Dec 65. (7") *(AT 4061) <2308>* **ONLY LOVE (CAN SAVE ME NOW). / LITTLE GIRL THAT LOVES ME** [ ] Nov65 [94]

1966. (lp) *(588 016) <SD 8109>* **THE BEST OF SOLOMON BURKE** (compilation) [ ] Jul65 [ ]
– Got to get you off my mind / The price / Down in the valley / I'm hanging up my heart for you / If you need me / Just out of reach (of your two open arms) / Cry to me / Everybody needs somebody to love / Home in your heart / Tonight's the night / I really want to know / Words.

Feb 66. (7") *(AT 4073) <2314>* **BABY COME ON HOME. / (NO, NO, NO) CAN'T STOP LOVIN' YOU NOW** [ ] Dec65 [96]

May 66. (7") *<584 005) <2327>* **I FEEL A SIN COMING ON. / MOUNTAIN OF PRIDE** [ ] Mar66 [97]

May 66. (7") *<2345>* **LAWDY MISS CLAUDY. / SUDDENLY** [–] [ ]

Jun 66. (7") *<2349>* **KEEP LOOKIN'. / I DON'T WANT YOU NO MORE** [–] [ ]

Jul 66. (7") *(584 026)* **KEEP LOOKIN'. / SUDDENLY** [ ] [–]

Sep 66. (7") *<2359>* **WHEN SHE TOUCHES ME. / WOMAN HOW DO YOU MAKE ME LOVE YOU LIKE I DO** [–] [ ]

Nov 66. (7") *<2369>* **A TEAR FELL. / PRESENTS FOR CHRISTMAS** [–] [ ]

Mar 67. (7") *(584 100) <2378>* **KEEP A LIGHT IN THE WINDOW TILL I COME HOME. / TIME IS A THIEF** [ ] Feb67 [64]

Jul 67. (7") *(584 122) <2416>* **TAKE ME (JUST AS I AM). / I STAYED AWAY TOO LONG** [ ] Jun67 [49]

Oct 67. (7") *<2459>* **DETROIT CITY. / IT'S BEEN A CHANGE** [–] [ ]

Feb 68. (7") *<2483>* **PARTY PEOPLE. / NEED YOUR LOVE SO BAD** [–] [ ]

Apr 68. (lp) *(587 105) <8158>* **KING SOLOMON** [ ] [ ]
– It's been a change / Take me (just as I am) / Time is a thief / Keep a light in the window till I come home / Baby come on home / Detroit city / Someone is watching / Party people / When she touches me (nothing else matters) / Woman, how do you make me love you like I do / It's just a matter of time / Presents for Christmas. *(cd-iss. Mar97 on 'Sequel'+=; RSACD 862)* – Tonight's the night / Only love (can save me now) / I don't want you anymore / (No, no, no) I can't stop loving you now.

Jul 68. (7") *(584 191) <2507>* **I WISH I KNEW (HOW IT WOULD FEEL TO BE FREE). / IT'S JUST A MATTER OF TIME** [ ] Apr68 [68]

Aug 68. (7") *<2566>* **WHAT I'D SAY. / GET OUT OF MY LIFE WOMAN** [–] [ ]

Sep 68. (7") *(584 204)* **SAVE IT. / MEET ME IN CHURCH** [ ] [–]

Nov 68. (lp) *(588 177) <88185>* **I WISH I KNEW** [ ] [ ]
– I wish I knew (how it would feel to be free) / Get out of my life woman / Meet me in church / By the time I get to Phoenix / Then you can tell me goodbye / What'd I say / Since I met you baby / Save it / Shame on me / Why, why, why. *(cd-iss. Mar97 on 'Sequel'; RSACD 863)*

Bell Bell

Nov 68. (7") *(BLL 1047)* **UPTIGHT GOOD WOMAN. / I CAN'T STOP (NO NO NO)** [ ] [ ]

May 69. (7") *(BLL 1062) <783>* **PROUD MARY. / WHAT AM I LIVING FOR** [ ] Apr69 [45]

Jul 69. (7") *<806>* **THAT LUCKY OLD SUN. / HOW BIG A FOOL (CAN A FOOL BE)** [–] [ ]

Sep 69. (lp) *(SBLL 118) <6033>* **PROUD MARY** [ ] Jul69 [ ]
– Proud Mary / These arms of mine / I'll be doggone / How big a fool (can a fool be) / Don't wait too long / That lucky old sun / Uptight good woman / I can't stop / Please send me someone to love / What am I living for. <*(cd-iss. Jul00 on 'Sundazed'+=; SC 11079)*> – She thinks I still care / I'm gonna stay right here / Generation of revelations / In the ghetto / God knows I love you / The mighty Quinn / A change is gonna come.

Oct 69. (7") *<829>* **THE GENERATION OF REVELATION. / I'M GONNA STAY RIGHT HERE** [–] [ ]

Aug 70. (7") *<891>* **IN THE GHETTO. / GOD KNOWS I LOVE YOU** [–] [ ]

Polydor M.G.M.

Nov 70. (7") *<14185>* **FOR THE LOVE OF SUNSHINE. / LOOKIN' OUT MY BACK DOOR** [–] [ ]

Apr 71. (7") *<14221>* **THE ELECTRONIC MAGNETISM (THAT'S HEAVY, BABY). / BRIDGE OF LIFE** [–] [96]

Jul 71. (7") *<14279>* **J.C. I KNOW WHO YOU ARE. / THE THINGS LOVE WILL MAKE YOU DO** [–] [ ]

Nov 71. (7") *<14302>* **THE NIGHT THEY DROVE OLD DIXIE DOWN. / PSR 1983** [–] [ ]

Apr 72. (7") *<14353>* **LOVE'S STREET AND FOOL'S ROAD. / I GOT TO TELL IT** [–] [89]

Jun 72. (lp) *(2315 048)* **THE ELECTRONIC MAGNETISM** [ ] [ ]
– The electronic magnetism (that's heavy, baby) / Three psalms of Elton: Your song – Border song – Take me to the pilot / You can run but you can't hide / For the love of sunshine / Bridge of life / Together we'll light up the world / Stand / PSR 1983 / Lookin' out my back door / No man walks alone / J.C. / I know who you are.

Jun 72. (7") *<14402>* **WE'RE ALMOST HOME. / FIGHT BACK** [–] [ ]

Aug 72. (7") *<14425>* **GET UP AND DO SOMETHING FOR YOURSELF. / MISTY** [–] [ ]

May 73. (7") *<14571>* **SHANBALA. / LOVE THY NEIGHBOR** [–] [ ]

Nov 73. (7") *<14651>* **GEORGIA UP NORTH. / HERE COMES THE TRAIN** [–] [ ]

Anchor ABC-Dunhill

Apr 74. (7") *(ABC 4002) <4388>* **MIDNIGHT AND YOU. / I HAVE A DREAM** [ ] [ ]

May 74. (lp) *<50161>* **I HAVE A DREAM** [–] [ ]

Phonogram Chess

Mar 75. (7") *<2159>* **YOU AND YOUR BABY BLUES. / I'M LEAVING ON THAT LATE, LATE TRAIN** [–] [96]

Jun 75. (7") *<2171>* **LET ME WRAP MY ARMS AROUND YOU. / EVERLASTING LOVE** [–] [ ]

Jul 75. (lp) *(9109 102) <60042>* **MUSIC TO MAKE LOVE BY** [ ] [ ]
– Music to make love by (part 1) / Let me wrap my arms around you / Come rain or come shine / You and your baby blues / All the way / Thanks, I needed that / Everlasting love / Midnight and you / Music to make love by (part 2). *(cd-iss. May99; UMD 80558)*

1976. (7") *<401>* **I'LL NEVER STOP LOVING YOU. / DO RIGHT SONG** [–] [ ]

1977. (7") *<30003>* **I'M GOING BACK TO MY ROOTS. / LOVE'S PARADISE** [–] [ ]

1977. (lp) *<19002>* **BACK TO MY ROOTS** [–] [ ]

not iss. Amherst

1978. (7") *<736>* **PLEASE DON'T SAY GOODBYE TO ME. / SEE THAT GIRL** [–] [ ]

1978. (lp) *<AH 226>* **PLEASE DON'T SAY GOODBYE TO ME** [–] [ ]

not iss. Infinity

1979. (7") *<50046>* **SIDEWALKS FENCES AND WALLS. / BOO HOO HOO** –

1979. (lp) *<9024>* **SIDEWALKS, FENCES & WALLS** –
– Please don't say goodbye to me / Hold on! I'm comin' / Sidewalks, fences and walls / Boo hoo hoo (cra-cra-craya) / Lucky / Let your love flow #9 / The more I see that girl / Sweeter than sweetness / Please come back home to me.

not iss. Soultown

1981. (7") *<3001>* **BETTIN' IN AMERICA. / COWBOY HAT** –

not iss. Savoy

1981. (lp) *<SL 14660>* **LORD I NEED A MIRACLE RIGHT NOW** –
1982. (lp) *<SL 14679>* **INTO MY LIFE YOU CAME** –
Nov 82. (7") *<0002>* **SILENT NIGHT. / A CHRISTMAS PRAYER** –
1983. (lp) *<SL 14717>* **TAKE ME, SHAKE ME** (recorded live at Macon, GA) –
– Take me, shake me / Precious Lord, take my hand / Twelve gates to the city / I want Jesus to walk with me / You should be a witness / Peace in the valley / Praise him / Swing low, sweet chariot.
1984. (lp) *<SL 14738>* **THIS IS HIS SONG** –

not iss. Northern Earth

1985. (7") *<71442>* **MY AUNT MARGARITE. / GOD WE NEED A MIRACLE** –

Demon Rounder

1985. (d-lp) *(DFIEND 38) <ROU 2042-3>* **SOUL ALIVE! (live 1983 in Washington DC)** 1984
– Introduction: Everybody needs somebody to love / Medley: If you need me – Tonight's the night – You're good for me – I almost lost my mind – What am I living for – Just out of reach – I can't stop loving you – Down in the valley – Proud Mary / Tonight's the night – Beautiful brown eyes – Just a matter of time – Hold what you've got / He'll have to go / Cry to me / Monologue / (introduction to encore) / Medley: Meet me in church – The price / Words / Medley: You're good for me – Send me some lovin' / Medley: Gotta get you off my mind – Having a party – Amen. *(cd-iss. Aug90; FIENDCD 38) (d-cd re-iss. Nov02 on 'Rounder'; ROUCD 2167)*

Rounder Rounder

Nov 86. (7") *<4554>* **A CHANGE IS GONNA COME. / LET IT BE YOU AND ME** –
Dec 86. (lp/c/cd) *<(ROU/+C/CD 2053)>* **A CHANGE IS GONNA COME**
– Love buys love / Got to get myself some money / Let it be you and me / Love is all that matters / Don't tell me what a man won't do for a woman / A change is gonna come / Here we go again / It don't get no better than this / When a man loves a woman.
1987. (7") *<4557>* **LOVE BUYS LOVE. / (part 2)** –

Perfect not iss.

May 87. (12"m) *(PER12 9606)* **YOU SEND ME. / (2 parts)** –
Aug 88. (12"ep) *(PER12 8606)* **HOLD ON I'M COMING BACK / BOO HOO HOO. / SWEETER THAN SWEETNESS / PLEASE COME BACK HOME TO ME** –

Demon Manifesto

Aug 93. (cd) *(FIENDCD 737) <101>* **HOMELAND**
– Baby please don't cry / Try a little tenderness / I don't need nobody / Make it up to you / Stayin' away / Homeland / I'll be there / Love ain't no easy place to be / You're gonna love me / What I've got to do.

Pointblank Pointblank

Feb 97. (cd/c) *(VPB CD/TC 1075) <42557>* **THE DEFINITION OF SOUL**
– Why can't we come together / Your time to cry / Sweet spirit / You're the one / Just for you / Oooooo you / Everybody's got a game (with LITTLE RICHARD) / Today is your birthday / Use me, but leave my mind alone / It's so hard / Nobody but you.

not iss. Malaco

Jan 98. (cd) *<601>* **WE NEED A MIRACLE** –
– Twelve gates to the city / I believe in Jesus (I believe in God) / Never alone / Mother loves her children all the time / This little light of mine / Aunt Margarite / You should be a witness / Lord we need a miracle (right now) / I want Jesus to walk with me.

not iss. C.G.P.

Sep 99. (cd) *<GTR 237>* **NOT BY WATER, BUT FIRE THIS TIME** –
– Not by water, but fire this time / I'm trusting in him / Turn this thing around / He knows how much we can bear / Music box / In the midst of us / Mighty rushing wind / Thank you, Jesus . . . / The word of God / I'm blessed / How will I know? / Silent prayer / Praise him – Yes Lord / It's over.

—— released a canadian-only set, 'THE COMMITMENT' (2001)

Fat Possum Fat Possum

Jul 02. (cd) *(0358-2) <80358>* **DON'T GIVE UP ON ME**
– Don't give up on me / Fast train / Diamond in your mind / Flesh and blood / Soul searchin' / Only a dream / The judgement / Stepchild / The other side of the coin / None of us are free / Sit this one out. *(lp-iss.Dec02 on 'DBK Works'; DBK 104)*

Anti not iss.

Jan 03. (cd-s; as SOLOMON BURKE with The BLIND BOYS OF ALABAMA) *(1090-2)* **NONE OF US ARE FREE / DON'T GIVE UP ON ME (live) / I NEED A HOLIDAY** –

—— in Jul'03, SOLOMON featured on JUNKIE XL's minor UK hit, 'Catch Up To My Step'

– compilations (selective), etc. –

1962. (lp) *Apollo; <498>* **SOLOMON BURKE** –
1963. (lp) *London; (HA-K 8018)* **SOLOMON BURKE'S GREATEST HITS** –
– Down in the valley / I'm hanging up my heart for you / Cry to me / How many times / Baby (I wanna be loved) / Gotta travel on / Keep the magic working / I almost lost my mind / A tear fell / Be bop grandma / Looking for my baby / Just out of reach (of my two open arms). *(cd-iss. Jan97 on 'Sequel'; RSACD 859)*
1963. (7"ep) *London; (REK 1379)* **TONIGHT MY HEART SHE IS CRYING** –
1965. (7"ep) *Atlantic; (AET 6008)* **ROCK'N'SOUL** –
Aug 72. (7") *Pride; <1017>* **I CAN'T STOP LOVING YOU. / (part 2)** –
Nov 72. (7") *Pride; <1022>* **ALL I WANT FOR CHRISTMAS. / I CAN'T STOP LOVING YOU** –
Apr 73. (7") *Pride; <1028>* **MY PRAYER. / OOKIE BOOKIE MAN** –
Nov 73. (7") *Pride; <1038>* **SENTIMENTAL JOURNEY. / VAYA CON DIOS (with Lady Lee)** –
1981. (lp/c) *Charly; (CRB/TCCRB 1024)* **KING OF ROCK'N'SOUL / FROM THE HEART** –
1984. (lp/c) *Charly; (CRB/TCCRB 1075)* **CRY TO ME** –
Jul 87. (lp/c/cd) *International Voice; (IV/+MC/CD 21336)* **LOVE TRAP** –
1994. (cd) *Black Top; (CDBT 1108)* **LIVE AT THE HOUSE OF BLUES (live)** –
Jul 93. (d-cd) *Rhino; <(8122 70284-2)>* **HOME IN YOUR HEART: THE BEST OF SOLOMON BURKE**
May 98. (cd) *Rhino; <(8122 72972-2)>* **THE VERY BEST OF SOLOMON BURKE**
Apr 03. (cd) *Prestige; (CDSGP 0416)* **HOLD ON**
Sep 03. (cd) *Spectrum; (068714-2)* **THE COLLECTION** –

BURNING SPEAR

Formed: 1969, St. Anns, Jamaica. Mainman, WINSTON RODNEY, traced the path of 'the master of music' after a brief conversation with BOB MARLEY outside his nearby farm. Following MARLEY's advice to check out Studio One, the late 60's saw him record two classic LPs for the label, 'BURNING SPEAR', the superb eponymous debut, and 'ROCKING TIME', a true 'SPEAR classic, produced by Coxsone Dodd and featuring gritty keyboard sounds mixed with thumping bass lines and RODNEY's soaring vocals on extraordinary tracks such as 'SWELL HEADED', 'FOGGY ROAD' and the hypnotic title tune. BURNING SPEAR took his name from Jomo Kenyatta, Kenya's first head of state and an African freedom fighter; black history became synonymous with 'SPEAR after the release of his third album, 'MARCUS GARVEY', the first of eleven for 'Island/Mango'. He subsequently devoted a large part of his life and recordings to promoting the teachings of GARVEY – also born in St Anns – a prominent spokesman for self-determination and self-reliance for all of African descent; the leader became prominent for a time in America at the turn of the century before his message was distilled and to a large extent forgotten. The album dripped with quality, as did the next two offerings released between '75 and '76, 'GARVEY'S GHOST', a dub version of 'MARCUS GARVEY' and 'MAN IN THE HILLS'. 'SOCIAL LIVING', released in '78, continued this run of form with head-nodding aplenty and after some well received albums on the 'Heartbeat' label in the early and mid-'80s, 88's 'LIVE IN PARIS' set proved SPEAR's status as a true Reggae great. His concerts were always more of an event than just a live version of the album and this two disc recording became the quintessential SPEAR album, the recording featuring such outstanding tracks as 'MISTRESS MUSIC' and 'PEOPLE OF THE WORLD' as well as some early gems. 'MEK WE DWEET', the follow up to 'LIVE IN PARIS', recorded at the Tuff Gong studio in Kingston, continued SPEAR's lyrical message of social injustice but missed the groove of his earlier work. This was underlined in 1990 when 'MARCUS GARVEY' and 'GARVEY'S GHOST' were issued side by side on one CD in celebration of the 100th anniversary of GARVEY's birth. A recent return to form with 'APPOINTMENT WITH HIS MAJESTY' included a tribute to JERRY GARCIA, 'PLAY JERRY', and featured SPEAR's BURNING BAND in top form. Fusing his roots philosophy with dub and reggae over the past three decades, WINSTON RODNEY continues to educate through his positive music and inspirational lyrics.

Album rating (selective): MARCUS GARVEY (*8) / MAN IN THE HELLS (*7) / GARVEY'S GHOST (*6) / DRY AND HEAVY (*7) / SOCIAL LIVING (*7) / RESISTANCE (*7) / CHANT DOWN BABYLON: THE ISLAND ANTHOLOGY compilation (*8)

WINSTON RODNEY (b. 1 Mar'45, St.Ann's) – vocals / **RUPERT WILLINGTON** – vocals

released 2 unknown singles

— added **DELROY HINES** – vocals

Fab / not iss.

1970's. (7") **MARCUS GARVEY. /** [-] [-]
1970's. (7") **SLAVERY DAYS. /** [-] [-]
1970's. (7") **SWELL HEADED. /** [-] [-]
1970's. (lp) **BURNING SPEAR** [-] [-]
1970's. (7") *(FAB 240)* **FOGGY ROAD. / VERSION** [ ] [-]
1970's. (7") **ETHIOPIANS LIVE IT OUT. /** [-] [-]
1970's. (lp) **ROCKING TIME** [-] [-]
(UK-iss.Sep84 on 'Studio Worx'; SOL 1123)
above were imported into Britain having been recorded 1969-1971

— trio now with **EARL SMITH + TONY CHIN** – guitar / **ASTON BARRETT + ROBBIE SHAKESPEARE** – bass / **TYRONE DOWNIE + BERNARD HARVEY** – keyboards / **LEROY WALLACE** – drums / **HERMAN MARQUIS + RICHARD HALL** – saxes / **CARLTON SAMUELS** – flute / **VINCENT GORDON** – trombone

Island / not iss.

Dec 75. (lp) *(ILPS 9377)* **MARCUS GARVEY** [ ] [ ]
– Marcus Garvey / Slavery days / The invasion (a.k.a. Black wa-da-da) / Live good / Give me / Old Marcus Garvey / Tradition / Jordan river / Red, gold and green / Resting place. *(cd-iss. Aug87; CID 9377) (re-iss. Jan89 on 'Rita Marley Music'; RMM 1654)*
Jan 76. (7") *(WIP 6264)* **OLD MARCUS GARVEY. / TRADITION** [ ] [-]
Mar 76. (7") *(WIP 6294)* **I & I SURVIVE. / BLACK WA-DA-DA** [ ] [-]
Apr 76. (lp/c) *(ILPS/ZCI 9382)* **GARVEY'S GHOST** (dub versions) [ ] [-]
– The ghost / I & I survive / Black wa-dad-da / John Burns Shank / Brain food / Father – East of Jack / 2000 years / Dread river / Workshop / Reggaelation.

— **WINSTON RODNEY** now took BURNING SPEAR name (RUPERT + DELROY now not part of set-up)

Aug 76. (lp/c) *(ILPS/ZCI 9412)* **MAN IN THE HILLS** [ ] [-]
– Man in the hills / It's good / No more war / Black soul / The lion / People get ready / Children / Mother / Door peep / Groovy. *(cd-iss. Sep90 on 'Reggae Refreshers' RRCD 15)*
Oct 76. (7") *(WIP 6346)* **THE LION. / DOOR PEEP** [ ] [-]

— **WIRE LINDO** – keyboards repl. DOWNIE

Jul 77. (m-lp) *(MLPS 9431)* **DRY & HEAVY** [ ] [-]
– Any river / The sun / It's a long way around / I.W.I.N. / Throw down your arms / Dry & heavy / Wailing / Black disciples / Shout it out. *(cd-iss. Jul92 on 'Reggae Refreshers'; RRCD 40)*

— now with new line-ups from now on

Dec 77. (lp/c) *(ILPS/ZCI 9513)* **LIVE (live)** [ ] [-]
– Marcus Garvey / Slavery days / Black soul / The lion / Old Marcus Garvey / Man in the hills / Throw down your arms.

Stop / not iss.

Aug 78. (lp) *(1001)* **SOCIAL LIVING** [ ] [-]
– Marcus children suffer / Social living / Nyah Keith / Institution / Marcus Senior / Civilize reggae / Mister Garvey come / Marcus say jah no dead. *(re-iss. Jul80 on 'Island'; ILPS 9556) (re-iss. Oct94 on 'Blood & Fire' lp/cd; BAF LP/CD 4)*

Radic / not iss.

Apr 80. (lp/c) *(RDC/TC-RDC 2003)* **HAIL H.I.M.** [ ] [-]
– Hail H.I.M. / Columbus / Road foggy / Follow Marcus Garvey / Jah see and now / African teacher / African postman / Cry blood Africa / Jah a God raid. *(re-iss. Dec88; DSR 4422) (re-iss. Jun94 on 'Heartbeat' cd/c; HB CD/MC 145)*
May 82. (lp/c) *(RDC/TC-RDC 2004)* **FAROVER** [ ] [-]
– Farover / Greetings / Image / Rock / Education / She's mine / Message / O jah / Jah is my driver. *(re-iss. 1988 on 'Heartbeat' lp/c/cd; HB/+C/CD 11)*
Jun 82. (7") *(RIC 113)* **SHE'S MINE. / EDUCATION** [ ] [-]
Sep 82. (12"ep) *(12RIC 114)* **JAH IS MY DRIVER / DRIVER / DISTANCE / FAROVER DUB** [ ] [-]
Sep 83. (lp) *(RDC 1077681)* **THE FITTEST OF THE FITTEST** [ ] [-]
– 2000 years / For you / In Africa / Vision / Fire man / Bad to worse / Repatriation / The fittest of the fittest / Old boy Garvey. *(re-iss. 1988 on 'Heartbeat' lp/c/cd; HB/+C/CD 22)*

Heartbeat / Rounder

Sep 85. (cd) *(HB 33)* **RESISTANCE** [ ] [ ]
– Resistance / Mek we Yadd / Holy foundation / Queen of the mountain / The force / Jah say / We been there / Jah feeling / Love to you. *(re-iss. 1988 c/cd; HBC/+D 33)*

Greensleeves / Slash

Oct 86. (lp/cd) *(GREL/+CD 100)* <2606439> **PEOPLE OF THE WORLD** [ ] [-]
– We are going / This experience / Seville land / Who's the winner / Distant drum / People of the world / I'm not the worst / Built this city / No worry you'self / Little love song.

— BURNING SPEAR with **ANTHONY BRADSHAW** – guitar, vocals / **DEVON BRADSHAW** – vass / **NELSON MILLER** – drums / **LENFORD RICHARDS** – guitar / **ALVIN HAUGHTON** – percussion / **JENNIFER HILL** – saxophone / **NILDA RICHARDS** – trombone / **PAMELA FLEMING** – trumpet

Jun 88. (lp/cd) *(GREL/+CD 116)* **MISTRESS MUSIC** [ ] [ ]
– Tell the children / Leader / Woman I love you / One way / Negril / Mistress music / Love Garvey / Tell me tell me / Say you are in love / Fly me to the Moon.

Blue Moon / WEA

Sep 88. (7") *(BMS 608)* **TELL THE CHILDREN. /** [ ] [-]
Dec 88. (d-lp/c/cd) *(BM/+C/CD 120)* <925842-1/-4/-2> **LIVE IN PARIS: ZENITH (live)** [ ] [ ]
– Spear burning / We are going / The youth / New experience / African postman / Hapy day / Woman I love you / Queen of the mountain / Creation rebel / Mistress music / Built this city / The wilderness / Driver.

Mango / Mango

Jun 90. (cd/c/cd) *(DIDM/MCT/MLPS 1045)* **MEK WE DWEET** [ ] [ ]
– Mek we dweet / Garvey / Civilization / Elephants / My roots / Great man / African woman / Take a look / One people / Mek we dweet in dub.
Aug 91. (cd/c/lp) *(CIDM/MCT/MLPS 1089)* **JAH KINGDOM** [ ] [ ]
– Jah kingdom / Praise him / Come, come / World power / Tumble down / Call on Jah / Should I / When jah call / Thank you / Land of my birth / Estimated prophet.

Heartbeat / Heartbeat

Feb 93. (lp/c/cd) *(HB/+C/CD 119)* <617619> **THE WORLD SHOULD KNOW** [ ] [ ]
– The world should know / In a time like now / I stand strong / Identity / It's not a crime / Mi gi dem / Loving day / Sweeter

than chocolate / On the inside / Peace. *(cd re-iss. May96 on 'Declic'; 841212-2)*

Tribesman — not iss.

1994. (lp; BURNING SPEAR & FRED LOCKS) *(TMLP 1)* **12 THE HARD WAY** [ ] [–]

Apr 94. (12") *(TM 20)* **FREE THE WHOLE WIDE WORLD. / JAH NO DEAD** [ ] [–]

Declic — Declic

Sep 94. (cd/c/lp) *(50358-2/-4/-1)* **LIVE 1993 (live)** [ ] [ ]

Heartbeat — not iss.

Nov 95. (cd/c) *(40604-2/-4)* **RASTA BUSINESS** [ ] [ ]
– Africa / This man / Not stupid / Creation / Every other nation / Burning reggae / Rasta business / Old timer / Subject in school / Hello rastaman / Legal hustlers.

Nov 99. (lp) *(HBLP 211)* **AN APPOINTMENT WITH HIS MAJESTY** [ ] [ ]
– An appointment with his majesty / Play Jerry / Reggae physician / Music / African Jamaican / Loving you / My island / Don't sell out / Commercial develpment / Glory be to Jah / Clean it up / Come in peace.

– compilations, etc. –

Aug 79. (lp/c) *Island; (ILPS/ZCI 9567)* **HARDER THAN THE REST** [ ] [–]
– Marcus Garvey / Dry & heavy / Throw down your arms / Social living / The invasion / Black wa-dad-da / Slavery days / Old Marcus Garvey / Man in the hills / The sun / Civilize reggae.

Jul 85. (lp) *Island; (885083)* **REGGAE GREATS** [ ] [–]
(cd-iss. 1988 on 'Mango'; CIDRG 5) (cd re-iss. Jul89; IMCD 5)

Aug 87. (12") *Island; (12IS 332)* **MARCUS GARVEY. / TRADITION** [ ] [–]

Oct 87. (cd) *E.M.I.; (CDP 748 271-2)* **SELECTION** [ ] [–]
– The fittest of the fittest / Bad to worse / Road foggy / African teacher / She's mine / Fire man / Cry blood Africa / Jah a go raid / Message / Farover / Distance – Farover dub.

Jul 88. (lp) *World Records; (WRLP 102)* **MARCUS CHILDREN** [ ] [–]

Jan 89. (lp) *Rita Marley Music; (RMM 118)* **LIVING DUB VOL.1** [ ] [–]
(cd-iss. Jul93 on 'Heartbeat'; HBCD 131)

Jan 89. (lp) *Rita Marley Music; (RMM 1209)* **LIVING DUB VOL.2** [ ] [–]
(cd-iss. Sep93 on 'Heartbeat'; HBCD 132)

1989. (cd) *Island; (CIDD 9377)* **KEEP THE SPEAR BURNING** [ ] [–]

Nov 90. (cd/c) *Reggae Refreshers; (RR CD/CT 20)* **MARCUS GARVEY / GARVEY'S GHOST** [ ] [–]

Apr 92. (cd) *Sonic Sounds; (SONCD 0023)* **THE ORIGINAL BURNING SPEAR** [ ] [–]

Jan 95. (cd) *Heartbeat; (CDHB 175)* **LOVE AND PEACE (live)** [ ] [–]

Jul 96. (d-cd) *Island; (524190-2)* **CHANT DOWN BABYLON: THE ISLAND ANTHOLOGY** [ ] [–]

Nov 96. (cd) *Declic; (842 539-2)* **LIVING DUB VOL.3** [ ] [–]

Apr 99. (cd) *Declic; (B 1101-2)* **THE BEST OF BURNING SPEAR** [ ] [–]

Jun 99. (cd) *Musidisc; (12306-2)* **LIVING DUB VOL.4** [ ] [–]

□ JAKE BURNS & THE WHEEL
(see under ⇒ STIFF LITTLE FINGERS)

□ BURRITO BROTHERS
(see under ⇒ FLYING BURRITO BROTHERS)

BUSH

Formed: Kilburn, London, England ... 1992, as FUTURE PRIMITIVE, by the seasoned Brit team of singer and lyricist GAVIN ROSSDALE, guitarist NIGEL PULSFORD, bassist DAVE PARSONS (from TRANSVISION VAMP!) and drummer ROBIN GOODRIDGE. Virtually ignored outright in the capital, BUSH's luck changed after American label 'Trauma' got hold of a demo, their signature obviously worth its weight in gold to US A&R men looking for the British answer to the recently defunct grungesters, NIRVANA. They relocated to the States early '95, a highlight at this point playing New York's CBGB's. The following year, they issued their debut, 'SIXTEEN STONE', an album that garnered critical acclaim from more rockcentric quarters and massive US sales from all quarters. Finally hitting the Top 5, the set contained a handful of impressive NIRVANA-esque numbers, among them 'EVERYTHING ZEN', 'COMEDOWN' and 'TESTOSTERONE', tracks that were to break the band in the UK a year later. By the end of 1996, BUSH were burning a proverbial trail with their chart-topping follow-up, 'RAZORBLADE SUITCASE', an album that made the UK Top 5 early the next year. A string of British hit singles completed their rise to transatlantic fame, the Top 10 'SWALLOWED' being one of their more memorable efforts. Stepping a little into the world of electronica, BUSH delivered a remixed set, 'DECONSTRUCTED' (1997), although this recording (complete with help from TRICKY and GOLDIE) was only for the initiated. Towards the end of the millennium, BUSH were back to offer up their third album proper, 'THE SCIENCE OF THINGS' (1999), a Top 30 breaker in Britain and even bigger in the States. Two years on, ROSSDALE and Co were back to basics with album No.4, 'GOLDEN STATE' (2001), a rather disappointing set that failed to win any new fans. • **Covers:** REVOLUTION BLUES (Neil Young).

Album rating: SIXTEEN STONE (*7) / RAZORBLADE SUITCASE (*6) / DECONSTRUCTED (*5) / THE SCIENCE OF THINGS (*6) / GOLDEN STATE (*5)

GAVIN ROSSDALE (b.30 Oct'67, London) – vocals, guitar (ex-MIDNIGHT) / **NIGEL PULSFORD** (b.11 Apr'65, Newport, Wales) – guitar (ex-KING BLANK) / **DAVE PARSONS** (b. 2 Jul'66, Uxbridge, England) – bass (ex-TRANSVISION VAMP) / **ROBIN GOODRIDGE** (b.10 Sep'66, Crawley, England) – drums (ex-BEAUTIFUL PEOPLE)

Atlantic — Trauma

Apr 95. (c-s) *(A 8196C)* **EVERYTHING ZEN / BUD** [ ] [–]
(12"+=/cd-s+=) *(A 8196 T/CD)* – Monkey.

May 95. (cd/c/lp) *(<6544-92531-2/-4/-1>)* **SIXTEEN STONE** [ ] [4]
– Everything zen / Swim / Bomb / Little things / Comedown / Body / Machinehead / Testosterone / Monkey / Glycerine / Alien / X-girlfriend. *(re-iss. Jun96 on 'Interscope' cd/c; IND/INC 92531)* – w/ bonus cd; hit UK 42) *(cd re-iss. Nov01 on 'S.P.V.'; 0767287-2)*

Jul 95. (5"ltd/c-s) *(A 8160/+C)* **LITTLE THINGS. / X-GIRLFRIEND** [ ] [–]
(cd-s+=) *(A 8160CD)* – Swim.

Aug 95. (c-s) *<98134>* **COMEDOWN / TESTOSTERONE** [–] [30]

Dec 95. (c-s) *(A 8152C)* **COMEDOWN / REVOLUTION BLUES** [ ] [–]
(cd-s+=) *(A 8152CD)* – Testosterone.

Jan 96. (c-s) *<98088>* **GLYCERINE / SOLOMON'S BONES** [–] [28]

Interscope — Trauma

Apr 96. (c-s) *<98079>* **MACHINEHEAD / ALIEN (live)** [–] [43]

May 96. (10"ep) *(INV 95505)* **MACHINEHEAD. / COMEDOWN / SOLOMON'S BONES** [48] [–]
(cd-s) *(IND 95505)* – (first & third track) / Bud.
(cd-s) *(INDX 95505)* – (first & second track) / X-girlfriend.

Jan 97. (cd/c) *(<IND/INC 90091>)* **RAZORBLADE SUITCASE** [4] Nov96 [1]
– Personal Holloway / Greedy fly / Swallowed / Insect kin / Cold contagious / Tendency to start fires / Mouth / Straight no chaser / History / Synapse / Communicator / Bonedriven / Distant voices. *(d-lp-iss.Sep99 on 'Simply Vinyl'; SVLP 120) (cd re-iss. Nov01 on 'S.P.V.'; 0767286-2)*

Feb 97. (c-ep/cd-ep) *(INC/IND 95528)* **SWALLOWED / BROKEN TV. / GLYCERINE / IN A LONELY PLACE** [7] [–]
(cd-ep) *(INDX 95528)* – ('A'side) / ('A'-Toasted both sides) / Insect kin (live) / Cold contagious (16oz demo).

May 97. (c-s) *(INC 95536)* **GREEDY FLY / GREEDY FLY (album version)** [22] [–]
(cd-s+=) *(IND 95536)* – ('A'-16 oz demo).
(cd-s) *(INDX 95536)* – ('A'side) / Old / Insect kin (live) / Personal Holloway (live).

Nov 97. (c-s) *(INC 95553)* **BONEDRIVEN / SYNAPSE (Philip Steir remix)** [49] [–]
(cd-s+=) *(IND 95553)* – Personal Holloway (Soundclash Republic remix) / Straight no chaser.

(cd-s) *(INDX 95553)* – ('A'version) / ('A'-Beat Me Clever mix) / Everything zen (Derek DeLarge mix) / ('A'-Video cd-rom).

Nov 97. (cd) *(<IND 90161>)* **DECONSTRUCTED** [ ] [36]
– Everything zen (The lhasa fever mix) / Mouth (the stingray mix) / Swallowed (toasted both sides please – Goldie remix) / Synapse (my ghost in the bush of life remix) / History (Dub Pistols mix) / Personal Holloway (Fablo Paras Soundclash Republic mix) / Bonedriven (Mekon beat me clever mix) / Insect kin (Jack Dangers drum and bees mix) / Comedown (Lunatic calm mix) / Everything zen (Derek DeLarge mix) / In a lonely place (Tricky mix). *(re-iss. Nov01 on 'S.P.V.'; 0767284-2)*

Oct 99. (cd/c/lp) *<(490483-2/-4/-1)>* **THE SCIENCE OF THINGS** [28] [11]
– Warm machine / Jesus online / The chemicals between us / English fire / Spacetravel / 40 miles from the sun / Prizefighter / The disease of the dancing cats / Altered states / Dead meat / Letting the cables sleep / Mindchanger. *(cd re-iss. Nov01 on 'S.P.V.'; 0767285-2)*

Nov 99. (7"clear) *(497222-7) <album cut>* **THE CHEMICALS BETWEEN US. / HOMEBODY** [46] Sep99 [67]
(cd-s+=) *(497223-2)* – Letting the cables sleep (original demo).
(cd-s) *(497222-2)* – ('A'side) / ('A'-Supercollider remix) / ('A'-video).

Mar 00. (cd-s) *(497275-2)* **WARM MACHINE / SWALLOWED (live) / IN A LONELY PLACE (Tricky mix)** [45] [ ]
(cd-s) *(497276-2)* – ('A'side) / Greedy fly (live) / The chemicals between us (original demo).

May 00. (7") *(497336-7)* **LETTING THE CABLES SLEEP. / MOUTH (Stingray remix)** [51] [ ]
(cd-s+=) *(497336-2)* – ('A'-Apocalyptic version).
(cd-s) *(497335-2)* – ('A'side) / ('A'-Nightmares On Wax remix) / ('A'-original demo).

Atlantic Atlantic

Oct 01. (cd/c) *<(7567 83488-2/-4)>* **GOLDEN STATE** [53] [22]
– Solutions / Headful of ghosts / The people that we love / Superman / Fugitive / Hurricane / Inflatable / Reasons / Land of the living / My engine is with you / Out of this world / Float.

Nov 01. (c-s) *(AT 0116C)* **THE PEOPLE THAT WE LOVE / AMERICAN EYE** [ ] [–]
(cd-s+=) *(AT 0116CD)* – ('A'-Golden dub mix).

Kate BUSH

Born: CATHERINE BUSH, 30 Jul'58. Bexleyheath, Kent, England. In 1974, this child prodigy formed her own K.T.BUSH band with brother PADDY and future boyfriend DEL PALMER, having already stockpiled a sizeable number of songs. By summer '76, with help from DAVE GILMOUR (Pink Floyd), she had secured a development contract with EMI, subsequently setting to work on the songs which would make up her debut set. Things couldn't have got off to a better start in early '78 when the classic 'WUTHERING HEIGHTS' warbled its way to the top of the charts. The single announced the arrival of a distictively original talent, a swooping, soaring epic of a track which fully exhibited BUSH's stunning four-octave vocal range. The debut album, 'THE KICK INSIDE', followed into the Top 3 shortly after, the singer's ambitious, idiosyncratic brand of art-rock set to probing, intelligent and often fantastical lyrics. A second track, 'THE MAN WITH THE CHILD IN HIS EYES', also made the Top 10, while a hastily recorded follow-up album, 'LIONHEART' was released later that year. BUSH subsequently undertook her first and only tour, the experience proving so trying that she'd later keep her promotional work to a minimum. This freed her up to concentrate on lavish videos, characterised by her inspired eccentricity and imaginative choreography. Fuelled by the Top 5 success of the sassy 'BABOOSHKA', a third set, 'NEVER FOR EVER' (1980) became her first No.1 album, the record spawning further hits in 'ARMY DREAMERS' and the bizarre 'BREATHING'. The latter track's overtly experimental nature was carried over into her next album, 'THE DREAMING' (1982). Her first self-produced effort, the record's intricate inaccessiblity and conceptual weirdness tested even her most devoted fans. Although it made the UK Top 3, the record sold relatively poorly and BUSH retreated to her newly built, hi-tech home studio to create as near as she could get to a perfect album. She eventually emerged in summer '85 with the hypnotic grace of 'RUNNING UP THAT HILL', its foghorn-like synth refrain and mature, sensual vocals taking BUSH back into the Top 5 in the first time in five years and even giving her a rare US hit. The accompanying album, 'HOUNDS OF LOVE' (1985), was raved over by a wide cross section of critics, BUSH at her creative peak on a record which saw the singer rein in her more wayward tendencies and achieve a perfect balance of melody, drama and mystery. The album spawned a further two Top 20 hits in 'CLOUDBUSTING' and the title track while late in '86, she teamed up with hero PETER GABRIEL on the Top 10 hit, 'DON'T GIVE UP'. After this critical and commercial rebirth, BUSH returned in 1989 with 'THE SENSUAL WORLD', a markedly more reflective affair, its title track inspired by the Molly Bloom character in James Joyce's classic novel, 'Ulysses'. The record narrowly missed the No.1 spot and consolidated BUSH's position as the elder stateswoman of fiercely original femme-pop. Though her most recent album, 'THE RED SHOES' received a mixed critical reception, the singer remains a towering influence on today's more erm, wayward songstresses, step forward TORI AMOS. • **Covered:** ROCKET MAN + CANDLE IN THE WIND (Elton John) / I'M STILL WAITING (Diana Ross) / WHEN YOU WISH UPON A STAR (Walt Disney soundtrack). • **Trivia:** Her first major tour came in April'79, and although it was mildly successful, she only once appeared live again at 'The Secret Policeman's Third Ball' in 1987. Actor Donald Sutherland appeared in her video for 'CLOUDBUSTING' 45.

Album rating: THE KICK INSIDE (*7) / LIONHEART (*5) / NEVER FOR EVER (*6) / THE DREAMING (*6) / HOUNDS OF LOVE (*7) / THE WHOLE STORY compilation (*9) / THE SENSUAL WORLD (*7) / THE RED SHOES (*5)

KATE BUSH – vocals, keyboards with **PADDY BUSH** – mandolin, etc. / **DEL PALMER** – bass / **IAN BAIRNSON** – guitar / **DUNCAN MACKAY** – keyboards / **ANDREW POWELL** – keyboards / **STUART ELLIOTT** – drums / **DAVID PATON** – bass / **MORRIS PERT** – percussion / **BRIAN BATH** – guitar / + others (her backing musicians changed from time to time, see 2nd edition)

E.M.I. EMI America

Jan 78. (7") *(EMI 2719) <8003>* **WUTHERING HEIGHTS. / KITE** [1] [ ]

Feb 78. (lp/c) *(EMC/TC-EMC 3223) <11761>* **THE KICK INSIDE** [3] [ ]
– Moving / The saxophone song / Strange phenomena / Kite / The man with the child in his eyes / Wuthering heights / James and the cold gun / Feel it / Oh to be in love / L'amour looks something like you / Them heavy people / Room for the life / The kick inside. *(pic-lp 1979; EMPC 3223) (cd-iss. Jan84; CDP 746012-2) (re-iss. Oct88 on 'Fame' lp/c/cd; FA/TCFA/CDFA 3207) (re-iss. Sep94 cd/c; CD/TC EMS 1522)*

May 78. (7") *(EMI 2806) <8006>* **THE MAN WITH THE CHILD IN HIS EYES. / MOVING** [6] Feb79 [85]

Nov 78. (7") *(EMI 2887)* **HAMMER HORROR. / COFFEE HOMEGROUND** [44] [–]

Nov 78. (lp/c) *(EMA/TC-EMA 787) <1978>* **LIONHEART** [6] [ ]
– Symphony in blue / In search of Peter Pan (incl. When you wish upon a star) / Wow / Don't push your foot on the heartbrake / Oh England my lionheart / Fullhouse / In the warm room / Hammer horror / Kashka from Baghdad / Coffee homeground / Hammer horror. *(re-iss. Apr84 on 'Fame' lp/c; FA 41-3094-1/-4) (re-iss. Oct88 on 'Fame' lp/c/cd; FA/TCFA/CDFA 3094) (re-iss. Sep94 cd/c; CD/TC EMS 1523)*

Mar 79. (7") *(EMI 2911)* **WOW. / FULLHOUSE** [14] [–]

Sep 79. (d7"ep) *(MIEP 2991)* **KATE BUSH ON STAGE (live)** [10] [–]
– Them heavy people / Don't put you foot on the heartbrake / James and the cold gun / L'amour looks something like you.

Apr 80. (7") *(EMI 5058)* **BREATHING. / THE EMPTY BULLRING** [16] [–]

Jun 80. (7") *(EMI 5085)* **BABOOSHKA. / RAN TAN WALTZ** [5] [–]

Sep 80. (lp/c) *(EMA/TC-EMA 794)* **NEVER FOR EVER** [1] [ ]

– Babooshka / Delius / Blow away / All we ever look for / Egypt / The wedding list / Violin / The infant kiss / Night scented stock / Army dreamers / Breathing. *(re-iss. Sep82 lp/c; ATAK/TCATAK 91) (cd-iss. Mar87; CDP 746360-2) (cd-iss. Oct90; CDP 746360-2)*

Sep 80. (7"m) *(EMI 5106)* **ARMY DREAMERS. / DELIUS / PASSING THROUGH THE AIR** [16] [–]

Nov 80. (7") *(EMI 5121)* **DECEMBER WILL BE MAGIC AGAIN. / WARM AND SOOTHING** [29] [–]

Jul 81. (7") *(EMI 5201)* **SAT IN YOUR LAP. / LORD OF THE REEDY RIVER** [11] [–]

Jul 82. (7") *(EMI 5296)* **THE DREAMING. / DREAMTIME (instrumental)** [48] [–]

Sep 82. (lp/c) *(EMC/TC-EMC 3419)* *<17084>* **THE DREAMING** [3] [ ]
– Sat in your lap / There goes a tenner / Pull out the pin / Suspended in Gaffa / Leave it open / The dreaming / Night of the swallow Houdini / Get out of my house / All the love. *(cd-iss. Jan87; CDP 746361-2) (re-iss. Mar91 lp/c; ATAK/TCATAK 45) (cd-iss. Mar91; CDP 746361-2)*

Nov 82. (7") *(EMI 5350)* **THERE GOES A TENNER. / NE T'ENFUIS PAS** [ ] [ ]

Aug 85. (7") *(KB 1)* *<8285>* **RUNNING UP THAT HILL. / UNDER THE IVY** [3] [30]
(ext.12"+=) *(12KB 1)* – ('A'instrumental).

Sep 85. (lp/c)(cd) *(KAB/TC 1)(CDP 746164-2)* *<17171>* **HOUNDS OF LOVE** [1] [30]
– Running up that hill / Hounds of love / The big sky / Mother stands for comfort / Cloudbusting / And dream of sheep / Under ice / Waking the witch / Watching you without me / Jig of life / Hello Earth / The morning fog. *(cd+=)* – Cloudbusting (extended). *(re-iss. Oct90 lp/c; ATAK/TCATAK 157) (<cd-iss. Sep90; CDP 746164-2>) (cd re-iss. Jun97 +=; CDCNTAV 3)* (cd re-iss. Jan00 +=; *525239-2)* – Big sky (meteorogical mix) / Running up that hill (12" mix) / Be kind to my mistakes / Under the ivy / Burning bridge / My lagan love. *(lp re-iss. Jan01 on 'Simply Vinyl'; SVLP 290)*

Oct 85. (7") *(KB 2)* **CLOUDBUSTING. / BURNING BRIDGES** [20] [–]
('A'-Organon mix-12"+=) *(12KB 2)* – My Lagan Love.

Feb 86. (7") *(KB 3)* **HOUNDS OF LOVE. / HANDSOME CABIN BOY** [18] [–]
(12"+=) *(12KB 3)* – The alternative hounds of love / Jig of life.

May 86. (7"/7"pic-d) *(KB/+P 4)* **THE BIG SKY. / NOT THIS TIME** [37] [–]
(12"+=) *(12KB 4)* – The morning fog.

—— In Oct 86, she did a duet **DON'T GIVE UP** with **PETER GABRIEL** which hit for 'Geffen' UK No.9 / US No.72.

Nov 86. (7") *(KB 5)* **EXPERIMENT IV. / WUTHERING HEIGHTS (vocal)** [23] [–]
(12"+=) *(12KB 5)* – December will be magic again.

Nov 86. (lp/c)(cd) *(KBTV/TCKBTV 1)(CDP 746414-2)* *<17242>* **THE WHOLE STORY** (compilation) [1] [76]
– Wuthering heights / Cloudbusting / The man with the child in his eyes / Breathing / Wow / Hounds of love / Running up that hill / Army dreamers / Sat in your lap / Experiment IV / The dreaming / Babooshka. *(lp re-iss. Nov00 on 'Simply Vinyl'; SVLP 268)*

E.M.I. Columbia

Sep 89. (7"/c-s) *(EM/TCEM 102)* **THE SENSUAL WORLD. / WALK STRAIGHT DOWN THE MIDDLE** [12] [–]
(ext.12"+=/ext.cd-s+=) *(12/CD EM 102)* – ('A'instrumental).

Oct 89. (lp/c)(cd) *(EMD/TCEMD/CDEMD 1010)* *<44164>* **THE SENSUAL WORLD** [2] [43]
– The sensual world / Love and anger / The fog / Reaching out / Heads we're dancing / Deeper understanding / Between a man and a woman / Never be mine / Rocket's tail / This woman's work. *(cd+=)* – Walk straight down the middle.

Nov 89. (7"/7"pic-d) *(EM/TCEM 119)* **THIS WOMAN'S WORK. / BE KIND TO MY MISTAKES** [25] [–]
(12"+=/cd-s+=) *(12/CD EM 119)* – ('A'version) / I'm still waiting.

Mar 90. (7"/c-s) *(EM/TCEM 134)* **LOVE AND ANGER. / KEN** [38] [–]
(12"+=/cd-s+=) *(12/CD EM 134)* – The confrontation / Just one last look around the house before we go.

Apr 90. (7") *<73092>* **LOVE AND ANGER. / WALK STRAIGHT DOWN THE MIDDLE** [–] [ ]
(c-s+=) *<73098>* – This woman's work.

Nov 91. (7"/c-s) *(TRIBO/+C 2)* **ROCKET MAN (I THINK IT'S GOING TO BE A LONG LONG TIME). / CANDLE IN THE WIND** [12] [ ]
(12"+=/cd-s+=) *(TRIBOT 2)* – ('B'instrumental).
(above single on 'Mercury')

—— with **STUART ELLIOTT** – drums / **JOHN GIBLIN** – bass / **DANNY McINTOSH** – guitar / **GARY BROOKER** – hammond organ / **PADDY BUSH** + **COLIN LLOYD TUCKER** – vocals / **PAUL SPONG** + **STEVE SLOWER** – trumpet / **NEIL SIDWELL** – trombone / **NIGEL HITCHCOCK** – sax / **NIGEL KENNEDY** – violin / + guests **PRINCE** + **ERIC CLAPTON**

Sep 93. (7"/c-s) *(EM/TCEM 280)* **RUBBERBAND GIRL. / BIG STRIPEY LIE** [12] [–]
(12"pic-d+=/cd-s+=) *(12/CD EM 280)* – ('A'extended remix).

Nov 93. (cd/c/lp) *(CD/TC+/EMD 1047)* **THE RED SHOES** [2] [28]
– Rubberband girl / And so is love / Eat the music / Moments of pleasure / The song of Solomon / Lily / The red shoes / Top of the city / Constellation of the heart / Big stripey lie / Why should I love you? / You're the one.

Nov 93. (7"/c-s) *(EM/TCEM 297)* **MOMENTS OF PLEASURE. / SHOW A LITTLE DEVOTION** [26] [ ]
(12") *(12EM 297)* – ('A'side) / ('A'instrumental) / Home for Christmas.
(cd-s) *(CDEM 297)* – ('A'side) / December will be magic again / Experiment IV.

Dec 93. (c-s) *<77280>* **RUBBERBAND GIRL / THIS WOMAN'S WORK** [–] [88]

Apr 94. (7"/c-s) *(EMS/TCEM 316)* **THE RED SHOES. / YOU WANT ALCHEMY** [21] [ ]
(cd-s+=) *(CDEM 316)* – Cloudbusting (video mix) / This woman's work.
(cd-s) *(CDEMX 316)* – ('A'shoedance mix) / The big sky / Running up that hill.

—— In Jul 94, KATE partnered LARRY ADLER on 'Mercury' single 'THE MAN I LOVE'; *MER/+C/CD 408)*. It hit UK No.27, and was from his tribute album 'The Glory Of Gershwin'.

Nov 94. (7"pic-d/c-s) *(EMS/TCEMS 355)* **AND SO IS LOVE. / RUBBERBAND GIRL (U.S.mix)** [26] [ ]
(cd-s+=) *(CDEM 355)* – Eat the music (U.S. mix).

– compilations, others, etc. –

Jun 83. (m-lp) *EMI America; <19004>* **KATE BUSH** [–] [ ]

Oct 83. (7") *Old Gold; (OG 9380)* **WUTHERING HEIGHTS. / THE MAN WITH THE CHILD IN HIS EYES** [ ] [–]

Jan 84. (7"x13) *E.M.I.; (KBS 1)* **THE SINGLES FILE** [ ] [–]
– (all previous singles +) NE T'ENFUIS PAS. / UN BAISER D'ENFANT

Oct 90. (9xcd-box/8xc-box/8xlp-box) *(KBBX/+CD/C 1)* **THIS WOMAN'S WORK – ANTHOLOGY 1978-1990** [ ] [–]

Oct 92. (12"-box+cd) *(KB 2)* **NEVER FOREVER** [ ] [–]
(above issued w / free booklet & T-shirt)

Aug 94. (cd-vid) *E.M.I.; (SAV 4913063)* **LIVE AT HAMMERSMITH ODEON (live)** [ ] [–]
– (a complete history of all her songs, re-issuing albums)

Mar 03. (d-cd) *E.M.I.; (582364-2)* **THE DREAMING / LIONHEART** [ ] [–]

BUSTA RHYMES

Born: TREVOR SMITH, 20 May'72, Brooklyn, New York, USA. Growing up as a teenager in Long Island, NY (or Strong Island as it was known among the hip hop fraternity, subsequently immortalised in song by JVC FORCE), the young BUSTA RHYMES hooked up with MC's CUT MONITOR MILO, DINCO D and CHARLIE BROWN to form LEADERS OF THE NEW SCHOOL. A well established hotbed of talent, Long Island had already spawned the likes of PUBLIC ENEMY, RAKIM and EPMD. LEADERS OF THE NEW SCHOOL were next in line, 'Elektra' picking up BUSTA & Co when the frontman was barely out of school. Touting a distinctive rapping style influenced by his Jamaican background and the freestyle ethos of the genre's pioneers, RHYMES stamped his not inconsiderable personality firmly over the group's debut album, 'FUTURE WITHOUT A PAST' (1991). Although they only recorded one more long player before breaking up, 'T.I.M.E.' (1993), they left behind a couple of interesting collaborations, with funk godfather JAMES BROWN on 'CAN'T GET ANY HARDER' and A TRIBE CALLED QUEST on the freestyling classic, 'SCENARIO'. After working with various artists in the soul/R&B

field including the delectable MARY J. BLIGE, BUSTA RHYMES launched his solo career with the wild 'WOO-HAH!! GOT YOU ALL IN CHECK', making the US Top 10 and boosting sales of debut album, 'THE COMING' (1996). The man's finest moment, however, arguably arrived with the gloriously funky 'PUT YOUR HANDS WHERE MY EYES CAN SEE' leaving the cliched world of gangsta rap for dead and proving that less is more with a minimalist, shuffling rhythm, spooked-out rapping and a rivetting dayglo video. The accompanying album, 'WHEN DISASTER STRIKES' (1997) entered the US chart at No.3 and confirmed RHYMES' place among the new Hip Hop elite. The rapper wasted little time in consolidating his success, releasing a third set, 'EXTINCTION LEVEL EVENT – THE FINAL WORLD FRONT', a year later. As a singles artist he was more popular than ever, notching up another two sizeable Top 10 UK hits – 'GIMME SOME MORE' and 'WHAT'S IT GONNA BE?!' in 1999. This was no mean feat for a hardcore rapper, especially given the man's relentless creative output. The new millennium found him as busy as ever, still hanging on the theme of imminent chaos for humankind with 'ANARCHY' (2000). The following year also saw a compilation set ('TURN IT UP') and a fresh batch of tracks, 'GENESIS', an album which featured MARY J BLIGE, KELIS and P DIDDY (or PUFF DADDY to the uninitiated). Of all the guest spots, most memorable was KELIS' android vocal on 'WHAT IT IS', another RHYMES masterclass in sinewy, post-modern funk. A radical reworking of Public Enemy's 'SHUT 'EM DOWN', meanwhile, was as fresh as it was timely. The rap maverick was back in 2002 with 'IT AIN'T SAFE NO MORE', another swaggering trip through New York's post-9/11 musical landscape with RHYMES as guide, spitting out lyrics with the kind of eloquent fury few old hands can muster. Like its predecessor, the often ominous synth-cloaked production seemed tailor-made for BUSTA's post-millennial misgivings while the brilliant 'MAKE IT CLAP' ranked as his most compelling hit single of the new decade.

Album rating: THE COMING (*6) / WHEN DISASTER STRIKES (*7) / EXTINCTION LEVEL EVENT – THE FINAL WORLD FRONT (*7) / ANARCHY (*6) / TURN IT UP – THE VERY BEST OF . . . compilation (*8) / GENESIS (*6) / IT AIN'T SAFE NO MORE (*6)

BUSTA RHYMES – vocals / with various personnel

Elektra | Elektra

Mar 96. (cd/c/lp) *<(7559 61742-2/-4/-1)>* **THE COMING** [ ] [6]
– The coming / Do my thing / Abandon ship / Everything remains raw / Hot fudge – interlude / Flipmode squad meets the Def squad / Keep it movin' / End of the world / Finish line / Still shining / Ill vibe / It's a party / Woo-hah!! got you all in the check.

May 96. (c-s) *(EKR 220C) <64335>* **WOO-HAH!! GOT YOU ALL IN CHECK / EVERYTHING REMAINS RAW** [ ] Feb96 [8]
(12"+=/cd-s+=) *(EKR 220 T/CD)* – ('A'mix).

Jul 96. (c-s; BUSTA RHYMES featuring ZHANE) *<64268>* **IT'S A PARTY / ILL VIBE (with Q-TIP)** [–] [52]

Sep 96. (c-s; BUSTA RHYMES featuring ZHANE) *(EKR 226C) <64268>* **IT'S A PARTY / EVERYTHING REMAINS RAW** [23] [–]
(12"+=/cd-s+=) *(EKR 226 T/CD)* – ('A'mixes).

—— In Mar'97, BUSTA featured on B REAL UK Top 10 single, 'HIT EM HIGH (THE MONSTARS' ANTHEM)'.

Apr 97. (c-s) *(EKR 235C)* **DO MY THING / (DJ Scratch remix)** [39] [ ]
(12"+=/cd-s+=) *(EKR 235 T/CD)* – ('A'-Fila Brazillia mixes + instrumental).

Jul 97. (cd) *(7559 63992-2)* **FLIPMODE REMIXES** [ ] [ ]
– Woo-hah!! got you all in check / It's a party / Do my thing / Abandon ship.

Sep 97. (cd/c) *<(7559 62064-2/-4)>* **WHEN DISASTER STRIKES** [34] [3]
– (intro) / Whole world lookin' at me / Survival hungry / When disaster strikes / So hardcore / Get high tonight / Turn it up / Put your hands where my eyes can see / It's all good / There's not a problem my squad can't fix / We can take it outside / Rhymes galore / Thing we be doin' for money (parts 1 & 2) / One / Dangerous / Body rock / Get off my block / (outro).

Oct 97. (c-s) *(E 3900C)* **PUT YOUR HANDS WHERE MY EYES CAN SEE / ('A'mix)** [16] [ ]
(12"+=/cd-s+=) *(E 3900 T/CD)* – ('A'mixes).

Dec 97. (c-s) *(E 3877C) <64131>* **DANGEROUS / ('A'mix)** [32] [9]
(12"+=/cd-s+=) *(E 3877 T/CD)* – ('A'mixes).

—— In Mar'98, the BUSTA man featured with The NOTORIOUS B.I.G. on PUFF DADDY & THE FAMILY's Top 20 (US) hit, 'Victory'.

Apr 98. (c-s) *(E 3847C) <64104>* **TURN IT UP / FIRE IT UP** [2] [10]
(12"+=/cd-s+=) *(E 3847 T/CD)* – ('A'&'B'mixes).

Jun 98. (c-s/cd-s; BUSTA RHYMES featuring ERYKAH BADU) *(E 3833 C/CD1)* **ONE / FIRE IT UP / WOO HAH** [23] [ ]
(12"+=/cd-s+=) *(E 3833 T/CD2)* – ('A'side) / Rhymes galore.

Dec 98. (cd/c/lp) *<(7559 62211-2/-4/-1)>* **EXTINCTION LEVEL EVENT – THE FINAL WORLD FRONT** [65] [12]
– There's only one year left!!! (intro) / Everybody rise / Where we're about to take it / Extinction level event (the song of salvation) / Tear da roof off / Against all odds (with FLIPMODE SQUAD) / Just don't give it to me raw (what U asking 4) / Do it to death / Keepin' it tight / Gimme some more / Iz they wildin' wit' us or gettin' rowdy wit' us? (with MYSTIKAL) / A party goin' on over here / Do the bus a bus / Take it off / What's it gonna be?! (with JANET JACKSON) / Hot shit makin' ya bounce / What the fuck you want!! / This means war!! (with OZZY OSBOURNE) / The burial song (outro).

Jan 99. (c-s/12"/cd-s) *(E 3782 C/T/CD)* **GIMME SOME MORE. / DO IT LIKE NEVER BEFORE** [5] [ ]

Apr 99. (c-s/12"/cd-s; BUSTA RHYMES featuring JANET) *(E 3762 C/T/CD1) <64051>* **WHAT'S IT GONNA BE?! / TEAR DA ROOF OFF** [6] Mar99 [3]
(cd-s) *(E 3762CD2)* – ('A'mixes).

Jun 00. (cd/c/lp) *<(7559 62517-2/-4)>* **ANARCHY** [38] [4]
– The current state of anarchy – intro / Salute da gods!! / Enjoy da ride / We put it down for y'all / Bladow!! / Live it up / Fire / All night / Show me what you got / Get out!! / The heist / A trip out of town / How much we grew / Here we go again / We comin' through / C'mon all my niggaz, c'mon all my bitches / Make noise / Ready for war / Why we die / Anarchy / Outro.

Jul 00. (c-s/12"/cd-s) *(E 7075 C/T/CD)* **GET OUT / DO THE BUS A BUS / WHAT'S IT GONNA BE?! (featuring Janet Jackson)** [57] [ ]

Dec 00. (c-s/12"/cd-s) *(E 7136 C/T/CD)* **FIRE (mixes; original / KMG RMX radio / Gorch fonk RMX radio / original instrumental / KMG instrumental / Gorch fonk RMX instrumental)** [60] [ ]

—— in Jun'01, BUSTA featured on VIOLATOR's hit single, 'What It Is'

—— in Aug'01, the man featured on MOP's massive hit, 'Ante Up'

Sep 01. (cd) *<(8122 73559-2)>* **TURN IT UP – THE VERY BEST OF BUSTA RHYMES** (compilation) [44] [ ]
– Turn it up / Fire it up / Woo has got it all in check / Gimme some more / What's it gonna be (with JANET JACKSON) / Dangerous / It's a party (with ZHANE) / One (with ERYKAH BADU) / Hit 'em high (with B-REAL & COOLIO) / Do my thing / Do the bus a bus / The party is going on over here / Get out / Sobb story (with LEADERS OF THE NEW SCHOOL) / Scenario (with A TRIBE CALLED QUEST) / Dangerous (Soul Society mix) / Turn it up (Soul Society extended mix) / Fire (Gorch funk mix).

J – Arista | J – Arista

Dec 01. (cd/d-lp) *<(80813 20009-2)>* **GENESIS** [ ] Nov01 [7]
– (intro) / Everybody rise again / As I come back / Shut 'em down 2002 / Genesis / Betta stay up in your home (with RAH DIGGA) / We got what you want / Truck volume / Pass the courvoisier (with P. DIDDY) / Break ya neck / Bounce / Holla / Wife in-law / Ass on your shoulders / Make it hurt / What ii is (with KELIS) / There's only one (with MARY J. BLIGE) / You ain't fuckin' wit me / Match the name with the voice (with FLIPMODE SQUAD) / Bad dreams. *(re-dist.Mar02)* – hit No.58

Mar 02. (12"/cd-s) *(74321 92233-1/-2) <21061>* **BREAK YA NECK. / AS I COME BACK / BETTA STAY UP IN YOUR HOUSE** [11] Oct01 [26]

May 02. (c-s; by BUSTA RHYMES featuring P. DIDDY & PHARRELL) *(74321 93790-4) <21154>* **PASS THE COURVOISIER PART II / (version)** [16] Feb02 [11]
(12"+=/cd-s+=) *(74321 93790-1/-2)* – Shut 'em down 2002.

Nov 02. (cd) *(74321 98125-2) <020043>* **IT AIN'T SAFE NO MORE** [ ] [43]
– Intro / It ain't safe no more / What do you do when you're branded / Call the ambulance (with PHARRELL WILLIAMS & CHAD HUGO) / We goin' to do it to ya / What up / Turn me up some / Make it clap (with SPLIFF STAR) / Take it off – part 2 (with MEKA) / Taste it / Hey ladies / I know what you want (with MARIAH CAREY & FLIPMODE SQUAD) / Riot / Hop / Together (with RAH DIGGA) / Struttin' like a G.O.D. / The struggle will be lost (with CARL THOMAS) / Till it's gone.

Jan 03. (c-s; by BUSTA RHYMES & SPLIFF STAR) *(82876 50206-4) <21236>* **MAKE IT CLAP / (instrumental)** [16] Oct02 [46]
(12"+=/cd-s+=) *(82876 50206-1/-2)* – What do you do when you're branded.

May 03. (c-s; by BUSTA RHYMES with MARIAH CAREY & FLIPMODE SQUAD) *(82876 52829-4) <21258>* **I KNOW WHAT YOU WANT / CALL THE AMBULANCE (M.O.P. remix)** [3] Mar03 [3]
(12"+=/cd-s+=) *(82876 52829-1/-2)* – ('A'-instrumental).

Nov 03. (12"/cd-s; by BUSTA RHYMES & PHARRELL) *(82876 57251-1/-2) <54245>* **LIGHT YOUR ASS ON FIRE. / BLAZE OF GLORY / (instrumental)** [62] Aug03 [ ]

Bernard BUTLER

Born: 1 May'70, Stamford Hill, London, England. Temporarily putting aside his violin and piano, BUTLER took up guitar as a young teenager, idolizing JOHNNY MARR (of The SMITHS) in the mid-80's. In 1989, after an unsuccessful year at London's Queen Mary College, he answered an ad in the NME; it was to join SUEDE. His creative and imaginative songwriting helped the band and their chief wordsmith, BRETT ANDERSON reach the heady heights in the first half of the 90's, although a personality clash with the SUEDE mainman led BUTLER to seek out pastures new in the summer of '94. After a brief spell working with ALL ABOUT EVE singer JULIANNE REGAN, he began putting pen to paper once more in his new London abode (shared with wife, Elisa). He provided the song, 'YES', for the up and coming, flashily extravagant soul singer, DAVID McALMONT, thus the partnership McALMONT & BUTLER duly signed to Virgin offshoot, 'Hut'. A terrific follow-up single, 'YOU DO', gave the pair another UK Top 20 hit, while the accompanying album, 'THE SOUND OF . . .' became their swansong in late 1995; unfortunately they just couldn't stop backstabbing each other in the press. BERNARD subsequently worked with BRYAN FERRY, AIMEE MANN, EDWYN COLLINS, EDDI READER, NENEH CHERRY and made a substantial contribution to the BOOTH & THE BAD ANGEL project (aka TIM BOOTH of JAMES and ANGELO "Twin Peaks" BADALAMENTI). The following year (1997), BUTLER signed to 'Creation' and worked on his debut solo album, 'PEOPLE MOVE ON'. Released in the Spring of '98 and containing two Top 30 hits, 'STAY' and 'NOT ALONE', it knocked on the door of the Top 10 after receiving rave reviews. A largely acoustic affair the record saw BUTLER re-invent himself as a tortured balladeer, although the OTT production and ghosts of his more elaborate recent past seemed to haunt him. The esteemed guitarist went on to play the festival circuit, his axework outshining even the great MARR, especially his electric set at 'T In The Park'. Although it barely nudged the Top 50, 'FRIENDS AND LOVERS' (1999) offered further proof that BUTLER was a meticulous rock classicist. While there was nary a trace of the ruminating acoustica he'd so lovingly crafted on his debut, the album reflected BUTLER's genuine and convincing dedication to decadent 70's Brit-rock.

Album rating: PEOPLE MOVE ON (*6) / FRIENDS AND LOVERS (*5)

BERNARD BUTLER – vocals, guitar (ex-SUEDE, ex-McALMONT & BUTLER) / with **MAKOTO SAKAMOTO** – drums / and guests DENISE JOHNSON – backing vocals / NICK WOLLAGE – sax / EDWYN COLLINS – vocals / GEORGE SHILLING – cello / RICHARD BISSILL – French horn / & The Brilliant Strings conducted by BILLY McGEE: GINI BALL, JACKIE NORRIE, MARGARET ROSEBERRY, ANNE WOOD, ANNA HEMERY, SALLY HERBERT + ANNE STEPHENSON – violins / CHRIS PITISILLIDES + ELLEN BLAIR – viola / DINAH BEAMISH + SIAN BELL – cello

Creation Columbia

Jan 98. (7"/c-s) *(CRE/+CS 281)* **STAY. / HOTEL SPLENDIDE** [12] [–]
(cd-s+=) *(CRESCD 281)* – Sea.

Mar 98. (7"/c-s) *(CRE/+CS 289)* **NOT ALONE. / BYE BYE** [27] [–]
(cd-s+=) *(CRESCD 289)* – It's alright.

Apr 98. (cd/lp)(c) *(CRE CD/LP 221)(CCRE 221) <69332>* **PEOPLE MOVE ON** [11] [ ]
– Woman I know / You just know / People move on / A change of heart / Autograph / You light the fire / Not alone / When you grow / You've got what it takes / Stay / In vain / I'm tired. *(cd re-iss. Jan01; same)*

Jun 98. (7"/c-s) *(CRE/+CS 297)* **A CHANGE OF HEART. / MY DOMAIN** [45] [–]
(cd-s+=) *(CRESCD 297)* – More than I thought.

Oct 99. (7"/c-s/cd-s) *(CRE/+CS/SCD 324)* **YOU MUST GO ON. / (version)** [44] [–]

Oct 99. (cd/c/lp) *(CRECD/C-CRE/CRELP 248) <63651>* **FRIENDS AND LOVERS** [43] Feb00 [ ]
– Friends & lovers / I'd do it again if I could / Cocoon / Smile / You must go on / No easy way out / Everyone I know is falling apart / What happened to me / Let's go away / Precious / Has your mind got away? / You'll feel it when you're mine. *(cd re-iss. Jan01; same)*

Setanta Setanta

Jun 01. (cd-s; as BERNARD BUTLER & EDWYN COLLINS) *(SETCD 084) <1084>* **MESSAGE FOR JOJO / CAN'T DO THAT (THE HOOVER) / CLEAN** [ ] Jul02 [ ]
(12") *(SET 084T)* – ('A'-Trevor Jackson remix) / Can't do that (the hoover) (the Victorian Spaceman remix) / ('A'-radio edit).

— BERNARD is currently back working with BRETT ANDERSON

Paul BUTTERFIELD BLUES BAND

Formed: Chicago, Illinois, USA . . . 1963 by PAUL (born 17th December 1942, Chicago, Illinois, USA). He was a catalyst for the development of blues music played by white musicians in almost the same way that JOHN MAYALL was in Britain, although BUTTERFIELD held an advantage over MAYALL, in that he was able to sit in and play with HOWLIN' WOLF, MUDDY WATERS and LITTLE WALTER (with the latter taking on the role of mentor for the talented young harmonica player). BUTTERFIELD didn't have the greatest voice in the world but he was a formidable harpist, strictly following in the footsteps of LITTLE WALTER, JAMES COTTON, BIG WALTER HORTON and SONNY BOY WILLIAMSON and he was arguably the first white man to play blues with the same passion as the great black players. His first band was a quartet consisting of ex-HOWLIN' WOLF rhythm section, SAM LAY on drums and bassist JEROME ARNOLD (brother of harpist BILLY BOY ARNOLD), BUTTERFIELD and guitarist ELVIN BISHOP, but by the time they signed to 'Elektra' in 1965 the band had swelled to a sextet with the notable inclusion of MIKE BLOOMFIELD on lead guitar, who was to become a first class guitar hero. The debut album, 'THE PAUL BUTTERFIELD BLUES BAND' was released in 1966 and from the first bars of, 'BORN IN CHICAGO' it was clear that the band knew exactly what they were doing. They heavily covered ELMORE JAMES and LITTLE WALTER on the record and when LAY sang on their version of MUDDY WATERS', 'GOT MY MOJO WORKING' people thought that it was actually the great bluesman himself. On the second album, 'EAST WEST', ARNOLD was replaced by BILLY DAVENPORT and they went beyond the strict realms of blues by using compositions by CANNONBALL ADDERLEY, ALLEN TOUSSAINT and MONKEE-to-be, MIKE NESMITH, although the highlight was ROBERT JOHNSON's, 'WALKING BLUES'. BUTTERFIELD also contributed five tracks to an Elektra various artists album, 'What's Shakin', alongside LOVIN' SPOONFUL, ERIC CLAPTON, TOM RUSH and AL KOOPER. Supporting BOB DYLAN at the 1965 Newport Folk Festival, BUTTERFIELD and Co gained the infamous distinction of being the band who helped in DYLAN'S 'musical heresy' of going electric. BLOOMFIELD played on the first two albums which became high points for white blues in the sixties, although he quit in 1967 to form the psychedelic ELECTRIC FLAG. BUTTERFIELD, meanwhile, added a horn section and turned to soul, the band losing its direction with each successive album ('THE RESURRECTION OF PIGBOY CRABSHAW', 'IN MY OWN DREAMS', 'KEEP ON MOVING' and 'LIVE'). The low point came with the appalling 'LOVE MARCH' from the equally appalling 'KEEP ON MOVING', which he chose, for reasons only known to himself, to play at Woodstock in 1969. BUTTERFIELD started to play less and less harmonica and was turning more and more vocals on to other band members and it came as no surprise, and some relief, that he broke up the band in 1971 and moved to Woodstock. A retrospective 'BEST OF' was released in 1972 and specialist blues label Red Lightnin' produced 'AN OFFER YOU CAN'T REFUSE ', an album of early recordings, in the same year. In 1973, BUTTERFIELD formed BETTER DAYS and signed to BEARSVILLE Records for whom he recorded two poor albums before they split. Nothing was heard from BUTTERFIELD until 1976 when he made a guest appearance at The BAND'S farewell concert in San Francisco which was later documented in Martin Scorcese's film of the event, 'The Last Waltz'. (He duetted with LEVON HELM on 'Mystery Train', played harmonica for MUDDY WATERS on 'Mannish Boy' and was part of the all star cast on 'I Shall Be Released'). In 1981, BUTTERFIELD attempted a comeback by recording 'NORTH SOUTH' for Bearsville, although he fell ill with peritonitis (caused by his powerful harmonica playing) during the sessions, the album being delayed while he underwent two operations. He returned to live work after the release of the album although this failed to sell and he never regained his past popularity. In 1986, after a further lengthy recording silence, 'THE LEGENDARY PAUL BUTTERFIELD RIDES AGAIN' was released in America by 'Amherst' Records. BUTTERFIELD was found dead on the 4th of May 1987 in his North Hollywood flat. He found to his cost that it was easier to get into the blues than it was to get out, but his legacy remains and much of his catalogue is still available. • **Songwriters:** BUTTERFIELD and BISHOP except some covers. Time w / BETTER DAYS covered TOO MANY DRIVERS (Big Bill Broonzy) / NOBODY'S FAULT BUT MINE (trad; Nina Simone) / BORN UNDER A BAD SIGN (Booker T.) / HIGHWAY 28 (Dan Hicks) / RULE THE ROAD (Von Schmidt) / BABY PLEASE DON'T GO (Big Joe Williams) / IF YOU LIVE (Mose Allison). • **Trivia:** In 1965 they did back-up on record for BOB DYLAN, on manager Albert Grossman's recommendation. Album 'PIGBOY CRABSHAW' was actually ELVIN BISHOP's nick-name. BUZZ FIETON (a member in 1969) was later to resurface in US chart toppers Mr. Mister.

Album rating: PAUL BUTTERFIELD BLUES BAND (*7) / EAST-WEST (*8) / THE RESURRECTION OF PIGBOY CRABSHAW (*6) / IN MY OWN DREAM (*5) / KEEP ON MOVIN' (*4) / LIVE (*4) / SOMETIMES I JUST FEEL LIKE SMILIN' (*4) / OFFER YOU CAN'T REFUSE old material (*5) / GOLDEN BUTTER – THE BEST OF THE PAUL BUTTERFIELD BLUES BAND compilation (*6) / IT ALL COMES BACK (*4; by Better Days) / BETTER DAYS (*4; by Better Days) / PUT IT IN YOUR EAR (*4) / NORTH SOUTH (*4) / THE LEGENDARY PAUL BUTTERFIELD RIDES AGAIN (*4) / THE ORIGINAL LOST ELEKTRA SESSIONS exploitation (*7) / AN ANTHOLOGY – THE ELEKTRA YEARS double compilation (*8)

PAUL BUTTERFIELD (b.17 Dec'42) – vocals, harmonica (ex-MUDDY WATERS) / **MIKE BLOOMFIELD** (b.24 Jul'44) – slide guitar, lead guitar (ex-BOB DYLAN) / **ELVIN BISHOP** (b.21 Oct'42, Tulsa, Oklahoma) – guitar / **JEROME ARNOLD** – bass (ex-HOWLIN' WOLF) / **SAMMY LAY** – drums (ex-HOWLIN' WOLF)

London Elektra

1966. (7") *(HLZ 10100)* <45609> **COME ON IN. / I GOT A MIND TO GIVE UP LIVING** ☐ ☐

Elektra Elektra

May 66. (lp; mono/stereo) *<(EKL/EKS 7294)>* **THE PAUL BUTTERFIELD BLUES BAND** ☐ Oct65 ☐
– Born in Chicago / Shake your money-maker / Blues with a feeling / Thank you Mr. Poobah / I got my Mojo working / Mellow down easy / Screamin' / Our love is drifting / Mystery train / Last train / Look over yonders wall. *(re-iss. Feb71; K 42004) (re-iss. Mar85 on 'Edsel'; ED 150) (cd-iss. 1989 on 'WEA'; 960 647-2) <(re-iss. Mar93 & Dec94 & Sep95 cd/c; 7559 60647-2/-4)> <(lp re-iss. Oct01 on 'Sundazed'; SC 5095)>*

Oct 66. (7") *(EKSN 45007)* **ALL THESE BLUES. / NEVER SAY NO** ☐ –

— added **BARTY GOLDBERG** – guitar and **AL KOOPER** (b.5 Feb'44, Brooklyn, New York) – keyboards (ex-BOB DYLAN)

— **MARK NAFTALIN** – organ (appears on debut 8-tracks) repl. GOLDBERG and KOOPER who went solo & etc.

Dec 66. (lp; mono/stereo) *<(EKL/EKS 7315)>* **EAST – WEST** ☐ Aug66 65
– Walkin' blues / Get out of my life woman / I've got a mind to give up living / Work song / Never say no / Mary, Mary / Two trains running / All these blues / East west. *(re-iss. Feb71; K 22004) (re-iss. Feb87 on 'Edsel'; ED 212) (cd-iss. 1989 on 'WEA'; 960 751-2) <(re-iss. Sep95 on 'Warners' cd/c; 7559 60751-2/-4)> <(lp re-iss. Aug01 on 'Sundazed'; SC 5096)>*

— Recorded EP with JOHN MAYALL BLUESBREAKERS see ⇒

1967. (7") *(EKSN 45007)* **ALL THESE BLUES. / NEVER SAY NO** ☐ –

— **BILLY DAVENPORT** – drums repl. SAMMY LAY above now in 5-piece with **BUTTERFIELD, BISHOP, NAFTALIN** and **ARNOLD**

— then added brass section **GENE DINWIDDIE, DAVE SANBORN and KEITH JOHNSON / PHIL WILSON** – drums, vocals repl. DAVENPORT / **BUGSY MAUGH** – bass, vocals repl. ARNOLD

Nov 67. (7") *(EKSN 45020)* <45620> **RUN OUT OF TIME. / ONE MORE HEARTACHE** ☐ ☐

Feb 68. (lp; mono/stereo) *<EKL/EKS 74015>* **THE RESURRECTION OF PIGBOY CRABSHAW** ☐ Jan68 52
– One more heartache / Driftin' and driftin' / Pity the fool / Born under a bad sign / Run out of time / Double trouble / Drivin' wheel / Droppin' out / Tollin' bells. *(re-iss. 1971; K 42017) (re-iss. Feb89 on 'Edsel'; ED 301) <(re-iss. Jan03 on 'Sundazed'; SC 5097)>*

Apr 68. (7") *(EKSN 45047)* **GET YOURSELF TOGETHER. / MINE TO LOVE** ☐ –

— guest **AL KOOPER** – organ note; NAFTALIN aka NAFFY MARHAM

Sep 68. (lp) *(EKL 4025) <74025>* **IN MY OWN DREAM** ☐ Aug68 79
– Last hope's gone / Mine to love / Get yourself together / Just be with you / Morning blues / Drunk again / In my own dream. *(re-iss. 1971; K 42042) <(cd-iss. Apr02 on 'Wounded Bird'; WOU 4025)> <(lp re-iss. Jan03 on 'Sundazed'; SC 5098)>*

Nov 68. (7") *<45643>* **IN MY OWN DREAM. / GOT MY MOJO WORKING** – ☐

— **BUZZ FEITON** – guitar, organ, French horn, vocals repl. BISHOP who went solo

Sep 69. (7") *(EKSN 45069) <45658>* **WHERE DID MY BABY GO. / IN MY OWN DREAM** ☐ ☐

Nov 69. (lp) *<(EKS 74053)>* **KEEP ON MOVING** ☐ Oct69 ☐
– Love march / No amount of loving / Morning sunrise / Losing hand / Walking by myself / Except you / Love disease / Where did my baby go / All in a day / So far so good / Buddy's advice / Keep on moving. *(re-iss. 1971; K 42033) <(cd-iss. Apr02 on 'Wounded Bird'; WOU 4053)>*

Feb 70. (7") *(2101 012) <45692>* **LOVE MARCH. / LOVE DISEASE** ☐ ☐

— **BUTTERFIELD** retained **HARRIS** and **DINWIDDIE** and brought in **RALPH WALSH** – guitar GEORGE DAVIDSON – drums TREVOR LAWRENCE – brass

Feb 71. (d-lp) *<(EKD 2001)>* **LIVE (live)** Jan71 72
– Everything going to be alright / Love disease / The boxer / No amount of loving / Driftin' and driftin' / Intro the musicians / Number nine / I want to be with you / Born under a bad sign / Get together again / So far, so good.

— **DENNIS WHITTED** – drums repl. DAVIDSON augmented by guests **BOBBY HALL** – congos BIG BLACK – bongos with **CLYDIE KING, MERRY CLAYTON, VENETTA FIELDS & ONA DRAKE** – vocal harmonies

Sep 71. (lp) *(K 42095) <EKS 75013>* **SOMETIMES I JUST FEEL LIKE SMILIN'**
– Play on / 1000 ways / Pretty woman / Little piece of dying / Song for Lee / Trainman / Night child / Drowned in my own tears / Blind leading the blind.

— Disbanded late '71

Jun 72. (d-lp) *(K 62001) <7E 2005>* **GOLDEN BUTTER – THE BEST OF THE PAUL BUTTERFIELD BLUES BAND** (compilation) May72
– Born in Chicago / Shake your moneymaker / Mellow down easy / Our love is drifting / Mystery train / Look over yonders wall / East West / Walkin' blues / Get out of my life / Woman / Mary, Mary / Spoonful / One more mile, one more heartache / Last hope's gone / In my own dreams / Love march / Driftin' and driftin' / Blind leading the blind.

BETTER DAYS

were formed by **PAUL BUTTERFIELD** who recruited **GEOFF MULDAUR** – vocals, guitar, vibes (ex-JIM KWESKIN BAND) / **RONNIE BARRON** – keyboard, vocals, co-composer (ex-DR. JOHN) / **AMOS GARRETT** – guitar, bass (ex-JESSIE WINCHESTER BAND etc.) / **BILLY RICH** – bass / **CHRISTOPHER PARKER** – drums guests were **MARIA MULDAUR** – occ. violin & b.vocals / **DAVID SANDBORN** – horns / **BOBBY CHARLES** – b.vocals, co-composer, as was **DAVID WHITTED**

Bearsville Bearsville

Feb 73. (lp) *(K 45515) <BR 2119>* **BETTER DAYS** Jan73
– New walkin' blues / Please send me home to love / Broke my baby's heart / Baby please don't go / Nobody's fault but mine / Done a lot of wrong things / Buried alive in the blues / Rule the road / Highway 28. *(cd-iss. Feb93 on 'Rhino'; 8122 70877-2)*

Jan 74. (lp) *(K 45517) <BR 2170>* **IT ALL COMES BACK** Oct73
– It all comes back / Take your pleasure where you find it / Louisiana flood / Poor boy / If you live / It's getting harder to survive / Small town talk / Win or lose / Too many drivers. *(cd-iss. Feb93 on 'Rhino'; 8122 70880-2)*

— Split '74. GARRET joined MARIA MULDAUR and PARKER joined ARETHA FRANKLIN.

PAUL BUTTERFIELD

solo with sessioners

Feb 76. (lp) *(K 55509) <BR 6960>* **PUT IT IN YOUR EAR** Nov75
– You can run but you can't hide / (If I never sing) My song / The animal / Breadline / Ain't that a lot of love? / I don't wanna go / Day to day / Here I go again / The flame / Watch 'em tell a lie.

— PAUL then toured with LEVON HELM's ALL-STARS, before teaming up with RICK DANKO. He realeased another solo effort (below) augmented by MICHAEL TOLES – multi

not iss. Warners

1981. (lp) *<6995>* **NORTH SOUTH** –
– I get excited / Get some fun in your life / Footprints on the windshield / Upside down / Entch a train / Bread & Butterfield / Living in Memphis / Glow down / I let it go / Baby blue. *(UK cd-iss. Feb93 on 'Rhino'; 8122 70880-2)*

1981. (7") **LIVING IN MEMPHIS. / FOOTPRINTS ON THE WINDSHIELD** –

— went into session work in the 80's before making a come-back (below)

not iss. Amherst

1986. (lp/c/cd) *<AMH/+5/9 3305>* **THE LEGENDARY PAUL BUTTERFIELD RIDES AGAIN** –
– We stand a chance / Save me / Heart like a locomotive / Don't you hang me up / The wandering kind / Bad love / Mannish boy / The night ain't long enough / Changes.

— On 4th of May '87, BUTTERFIELD died of a long illness; peritonitis.

– compilations, etc.

1972. (lp; PAUL BUTTERFIELD & WALTER HORTON) *Red Lightnin'; (R 008)* **AN OFFER YOU CAN'T REFUSE** (recorded 1963) –
– Easy / Have a good time / Mean mistreater / In the mood / West side blues / Louise / Tin pan alley / Walter's boogie / Everything's gonna be alright / Last night / Loaded / One room country shack. *(re-iss. 1982; same)*

Jun 97. (cd) *Winner; <(WINNER 447)>* **EAST-WEST LIVE (live)** 1996

Oct 97. (d-cd) *Elektra; <62124>* **AN ANTHOLOGY – THE ELEKTRA YEARS** –
– Born in Chicago / Lovin' cup / One more mile / Off the wall / Come on in / Nut popper No.1 / Ain't no need to go no further / Born in Chicago / Shake your moneymaker / Blues with a feeling / Thank you Mr. Poobah / Our love is drifting / Mystery train / Mystery train / Last night / Walking blues / I got a mind to give up living / Work song / All these blues / East West / One more heartache / Double trouble / Last hope's gone / Come on in / Just to be with you / Get yourself together / In my own dream / Love march / Walking by myself / Love disease / Everything's gonna be alright / Driftin' and driftin' / Blind leading the blind / Song for Lee.

Sep 98. (cd) *Winner; <(WINNER 446)>* **STRAWBERRY JAM** 1996

Feb 00. (cd) *Essential; (ESMCD 833)* **THE BEST OF PAUL BUTTERFIELD** –

Apr 02. (cd) *Rhino; <(8122 73505-2)>* **THE ORIGINAL LOST ELEKTRA SESSIONS**

BUTTHOLE SURFERS

Formed: San Antonio, Texas, USA ... 1980 originally as The ASHTRAY BABY HEELS by ex-accountant GIBBY (son of US children's TV presenter "Mr. Peppermint") and PAUL LEARY, who met at Trinity College, San Antonio. By 1983, they had signed to JELLO BIAFRA's (Dead Kennedys) label, 'Alternative Tentacles'. Around the mid-80's, they gigged heavily in Britain due to lack of Stateside interest, and this, together with radio play from John Peel, helped them make it into the UK indie charts. Heavy psychedelia mixing noise, confusion and futuristic art-punk, the manic GIBBY, (complete with loudspeaker, etc), was always offensive and disturbing while their weird stage act included the nude dancer, KATHLEEN. She covered herself in green jello, while GIBBY simulated sex with her! GIBBY was well-known for other stage antics; pissing in plastic baseball bats ('piss wands') and anointing the audience at the front. There were other obscenities, too rude to print here (no need to mention President Carter's creamy briefcase). In 1987, they unleashed the brilliantly crazed 'LOCUST ABORTION TECHNICIAN', complete with a parody of BLACK SABBATH's 'SWEET LEAF', the humourously titled 'SWEAT LOAF'. Also deep inside its nightmarish musical grooves was their gem, 'TWENTY TWO GOING ON TWENTY THREE', a track that made John Peel's Festive 50. A longer sojourn in Britain culminated in some riotous, oversubscribed London gigs. The follow-up, 'HAIRWAY TO STEVEN' (another piss-take; this time of LED ZEPPELIN – Stairway To Heaven), deliberately left the tracks nameless (instead using obscene looking symbols) as a twisted tribute to ZEPPELIN's "untitled" symbols album. 1990 saw them shift to a more commercial sound with 'PIOUHGD' (which means "pissed-off" in Red Indian), which featured a re-working of DONOVAN's 'HURDY GURDY MAN'. Having signed to 'Capitol' in 1992, they were back to their abrasive sound of old with the JOHN PAUL JONES-produced album, 'INDEPENDENT WORM SALOON'. This, together with their previous effort, had given them their first taste of chart success in Britain, this being well surpassed in 1996 when 'ELECTRICLARRYLAND' hit the US Top 30. It was due, no doubt, to a surprise domestic hit with

'PEPPER', and probably their "fiery" guest appearance on American mock talk show, 'The LARRY Sanders Show' in '97. Abandoning their trademark psychedelic noise for crazy electronica, insane synth sound effects and dance/techno beats, Texas' very own masters of the punk revolution had always been a little off-kilter, but with their most recent album 'WEIRD REVOLUTION' (2001), the group seemed to have taken things beyond the realm of anything to date. Like the MELVINS before them, GIBBY HAYNES and his LSD army began experimenting with electronica on the late eighties side-project group The JACK OFFICERS, who made unlistenable computer music on some old Apple Macs. This had really the same slant; oodles of weirdness poured from the speakers as breakbeats tore the bass into shreads and HAYNES' distorted vocal loops were something not to be reckoned with. The album was not all experimental and avant garde, however, 'THE SHAME OF LIFE' proved that they still had an ounce of pop sensibility, although those who cringed at the BECK pisstake/ripoff that was 'PEPPER' found themselves cringing again. What was missing was the rock and punk edge that had made the 'SURFERS music so appealing in the first place; gone was LEARY's swirling guitar to be replaced by droning effects and fuzzy electronic noise that would've sounded more at home on NEIL YOUNG's disastrous 'Trans' LP. The BUTTHOLE SURFERS: great band, fantastic legacy, but this album was no more important than a computer generated fart in the wind. • **Songwriters:** GIBBY and co., except AMERICAN WOMAN (Guess Who) / THE ONE I LOVE (R.E.M.). P covered DANCING QUEEN (Abba).

Album rating: BROWN REASONS TO LIVE mini (*6) / PSYCHIC . . . POWERLESS . . . ANOTHER MAN'S SAC (*7) / REMBRANDT PUSSYHORSE (*7) / LOCUST ABORTION TECHNICIAN (*8) / HAIRWAY TO STEVEN (*7) / DOUBLE LIVE (*4) / PHIOHGD (*6) / INDEPENDENT WORM SALOON (*7) / ELECTRICLARRYLAND (*7) / WEIRD REVOLUTION (*5)

GIBBY HAYNES (b. GIBSON JEROME HAYNES, 1957) – vocals / **PAUL LEARY** (b.1958) – guitar / **KING COFFEY** – drums repl. ? / **ALAN ?** – bass

Alternative Tentacles / Alternative Tentacles

Apr 84. (m-lp) <(VIRUS 32)> **BUTTHOLE SURFERS** <'BROWN REASONS TO LIVE; US-title> [ ] 1983 [ ]
– The Shah sleeps in Lee Harvey's grave / Hey / Something / Bar-b-que / Pope / Wichita cathedral / Suicide / The legend of Anus Presley. *(re-iss. Sep93 as 'BROWN REASONS TO LIVE' brown-lp; same)*

Jan 85. (12"ep) <(VIRUS 39)> **LIVE PCPPEP (live)** [ ] [ ]
– Cowboy Bob / Bar-b-q pope / Dance of the cobras / The Shah sleeps in Lee Harvey's grave / Wichita cathedral / Hey / Something.

— **TERENCE** – bass repl. ALAN (?)

Fundam. / Touch & Go

Apr 85. (7") **LADY SNIFF. /** [-] [ ]

Jul 85. (lp) *(SAVE 5)* <TGLP 05> **PSYCHIC . . . POWERLESS . . . ANOTHER MAN'S SAC** [ ] [ ]
– Concubine / Eye of the chicken / Dum dum / Woly boly / Negro observer / Butthole surfer / Lady sniff / Cherub / Mexican caravan / Cowboy Bob / Gary Floyd. *(cd-iss. Jan88+=)* – CREAM CORN FROM THE SOCKET OF DAVIS *(cd re-iss. Jul99 on 'Latino Bugger'; LBV 003)*

— **MARK KRAMER** – bass (of SHOCKABILLY) repl. TREVOR who had repl. TERENCE

Oct 85. (12"ep) *(PRAY 69)* <TG 14> **CREAM CORN FROM THE SOCKET OF DAVIS** [ ] [ ]
– Moving to Florida / Comb – Lou Reed (two parter) / Tornados.

Red Rhino Europe / Touch & Go

Apr 86. (lp) *(RRELP 2)* <TGLP 8> **REMBRANDT PUSSYHORSE** [ ] [ ]
– Creep in the cellar / Sea ferring / American woman / Waiting for Jimmy to kick / Strangers die / Perry / Whirling hall of knives / Mark says alright / In the cellar. *(cd-iss. May88; RRECD 2) (cd re-iss. Jul99 on 'Latino Bugger'; LBV 004)*

— **JEFF 'TOOTER' PINKUS** – bass; repl. KRAMER who formed BONGWATER

Blast First / Touch & Go

Mar 87. (lp/c/cd) *(BFFP 15/+C/CD)* <TG 19/+C/CD> **LOCUST ABORTION TECHNICIAN** [ ] [ ]
– Sweat loaf / Graveyard 1 / Pittsburgh to Lebanon / Weber / Hay / Human cannonball / U.S.S.A. / Theoman / Kintz / Graveyard 2 / 22 going on 23 / The G-men. *(cd re-iss. Jul99 on 'Latino Bugger'; LBV 05)*

— added **THERESA NERVOSA (NAYLOR)** – 2nd drummer / **KATHLEEN** – naked dancer (above with GIBBY, PAUL, COFFEY and PINKUS)

Apr 88. (lp/cd) *(BFFP 29/+CD)* <TG 29/+CD> **HAIRWAY TO STEVEN** [ ] [ ]
– Hairway part 1 / Hairway part 2 / Hairway part 3 / Hairway part 4 / Hairway part 5 / Hairway part 6 / Hairway part 7 / Hairway part 8 / Hairway part 9. *(9 tracks marked rude symbols as titles) (cd re-iss. Jul99 on 'Latino Bugger'; LBV 06CD)*

Aug 89. (12"ep/10"ep/cd-ep) *(BFFP 41/+T/CD)* <TG 50> **WIDOWERMAKER** [ ] [ ]
– Helicopter / Bong song / 1401 / Booze tobacco.

— now without THERESA

Rough Trade / Rough Trade

Nov 90. (7") *(RT 240)* **THE HURDY GURDY MAN. / BARKING DOGS** [ ] [-]
(12"+=/cd-s+=) *(RTT 240/+CD)* – ('A'-Paul Leary remix).

Feb 91. (cd/c/lp) *(R 2081260-2/-4/-1)* <RTE R2601> **PIOUHGD** [68] [ ]
– Revolution part 1 / Revolution part 2 / Lonesome bulldog / Lonesome bulldog II / The hurdy gurdy man / Golden showers / Lonesome bulldog III / Blindman / No, I'm iron man / Something / P.S.Y. / Lonesome bulldog, IV. *(cd+=)* – Barking dogs. *<(cd-iss. Dec94 on 'Danceteria'; DAN 069CD)>*

— In Apr'92, GIBBY guested for MINISTRY on single 'Jesus Built My Hotrod'. PAUL LEARY had earlier issued a solo set, while DRAIN (COFFEY's outfit) delivered a further two albums.

Capitol / Capitol

Mar 93. (cd/c/lp) *(CD/TC+/EST 2192)* <98798> **INDEPENDENT WORM SALOON** [73] [ ]
– Who was in my room last night? / The wooden song / Tongue / Chewin' George Lucas' chocolate / Goofy's concern / Alcohol / Dog inside your body / Strawberry / Some dispute over t-shirt sales / Dancing fool / You don't know me / The annoying song / Dust devil / Leave me alone / Edgar / The ballad of naked man / Clean it up.

May 96. (cd/c/d-lp) *(CD/TC+/EST 2285)* <29842> **ELECTRICLARRYLAND** [ ] [31]
– Birds / Cough syrup / Pepper / Thermador / Ulcer breakout / Jingle of a dog's collar / TV star / My brother's wife / Ah ha / The Lord is a monkey / Let's talk about cars / L.A. / Space.

Sep 96. (7") *(CL 778)* **PEPPER. / HYBRID** [59] [-]
(cd-s+=) *(CDCL 778)* – Pepper (Butcha' Bros remix) / The Lord is a monkey.

— now with **HAYNES, LEARY + PINKUS**

not iss. / Hollywood

Aug 01. (cd) <162269> **WEIRD REVOLUTION** [-] [ ]
– The weird revolution / The shame of life / Dracula from Houston / Venus / Shit like that / Mexico / Intelligent guy / Get down / Jet fighter / The last astronaut / Yentel / They came in.

– compilations, others, etc. –

Jun 89. (d-lp/cd) *Latino Bugger; (LBV 01)* **DOUBLE LIVE (live)** [ ] [-]

Nov 94. (7"/7"pic-d) *Trance Syndicate; (TR 30/+PD)* **GOOD KING WENCENSLAUS. / THE LORD IS A MONKEY** [ ] [-]

Apr 95. (cd) *Trance Syndicate; <(TR 35CD)>* **THE HOLE TRUTH & NOTHING BUTT!** (early demos) [ ] [ ]

Jun 02. (d-lp/cd) *Latino Bugger; <(LBV 07/+CD)>* **HUMPTY DUMPTY L.S.D.** [ ] [ ]

BUZZCOCKS

Formed: Manchester, England . . . April 1976 by HOWARD DEVOTO and PETE SHELLEY who met at Bolton Institute Of Higher Education. Having recruited STEVE DIGGLE and JOHN MAHER, they played their first gig on the 20th of July '76 supporting the SEX PISTOLS. Early the following year, they released the first ever DIY punk "indie" 45 on 'New Hormones' in the form of the 'SPIRAL SCRATCH' EP. They then suffered a major bust up when frontman DEVOTO departed (to form MAGAZINE), although the rest carried on having signed to 'United Artists' on the strength of featuring on the now famous 'LIVE AT THE ROXY' Various artists compilation (with tracks 'Breakdown' and 'Love Battery'). By this time, SHELLEY had taken over vocal duties, while DIGGLE switched to guitar, having found a new bassist, GARTH SMITH. Early in 1978, they stormed the charts with the brooding love gem, 'WHAT DO I GET', a two-minute rush of bittersweet pop/punk angst which saw SHELLEY emerging as a strong frontman in his own right. The previous year's masturbating classic, 'ORGASM ADDICT', was too frenetic to allow SHELLEY's effeminate romance'n'roll stylings a look-in, although he blossomed on subsequent releases. A debut album, 'ANOTHER MUSIC IN A DIFFERENT KITCHEN' (1978), made the UK Top 20, while another SHELLEY-penned classic, 'EVER FALLEN IN LOVE (WITH SOMEONE YOU SHOULDN'T'VE?)', almost made the Top 10 later that year. With fervent support from Radio One DJ, John Peel, the band had squarely cornered the more accessible end of the punk market, although the 'LOVE BITES' album marked a move away from the short, sharp melodic shock which had become their trademark as songwriting duties were more democratically distributed. A final clutch of Top 30 hits, 'PROMISES' (their fifth hit in 1978), 'EVERYBODY'S HAPPY NOWADAYS' and 'HARMONY IN MY HEAD', saw the increasing influence of DIGGLE. 1979's 'A DIFFERENT KIND OF TENSION' saw SHELLEY's influence begin to dissipate and the album's mixed reviews signalled the band were running out of creative steam. After 'Liberty' took over their contract in 1980 and a further three 45's flopped, the BUZZCOCKS split, DIGGLE forming FLAG OF CONVENIENCE with MAHER. SHELLEY, meanwhile, went solo, making his debut in 1981 with the 'HOMOSAPIEN' album. Although the album made little commercial headway in Britain, the title track, bizarrely enough, topped the Australian charts. He released another two sets, 'XL-1' (1983) and 'HEAVEN AND THE SEA' (1986) to mild interest; far more newsworthy was the band's reformation in 1990 with a line-up of SHELLEY, DIGGLE, STEVE GARVEY and ex-SMITHS drummer, MIKE JOYCE. A comeback album, 'TRADE TEST TRANSMISSION' (1993) was lapped up by old punks and new converts alike, while a slightly modified line-up undertook a heartily received tour. A live set culled from the dates, 'FRENCH', was released in 1995, while a follow-up album, 'ALL SET' appeared a year later. The band's classic late 70's output remains one of the most influential bodies of work from the punk era, second only to perhaps the SEX PISTOLS. While 1999's 'MODERN' was a slightly turgid affair and never really troubled that legacy, it far outflanked the amateurish flailings of the young – largely American – bands who'd supposedly carry their flame. Much more satisfying was 2003's 'BUZZCOCKS', the eponymous title perhaps serving notice that the reformed band were, at the end of the day, the guardians of that classic buzzsaw sound and the only ones with the ability to carry it forward. That said, the record wasn't exactly a transformation although it did carry the weight that might be expected from these veterans, the resumption of the DEVOTO/SHELLEY writing partnership making things even more interesting. • **Covered:** HERE COMES THE NICE (Small Faces). • **Trivia:** In 1978, SHELLEY produced fun group, ALBERTO Y LOST TRIOS PARANOIAS.

Album rating: ANOTHER MUSIC IN A DIFFERENT KITCHEN (*9) / LOVE BITES (*7) / DIFFERENT KIND OF TENSION (*6) / SINGLES – GOING STEADY compilation (*9) / TRADE TEST TRANSMISSION (*5) / FRENCH (*4) / ALL SET (*5) / MODERN (*5) / BUZZCOCKS (*6) / Pete Shelley: SKY YEN (*4) / HOMOSAPIEN (*7) / XL-1 (*5) / HEAVEN AND THE SEA (*6)

HOWARD DEVOTO (b. HOWARD TROTTER, 1955) – vocals / **PETE SHELLEY** (b.PETER McNEISH, 17 Apr'55) – guitar, vocals / **STEVE DIGGLE** – bass, vocals / **JOHN MAHER** – drums

New Hormones | not iss.

Jan 77. (7"ep) *(ORG 1)* **SPIRAL SCRATCH** [ ] [–]
– Breakdown / Times up / Boredom / Friends of mine. *(re-iss. Aug79 credited as "BUZZCOCKS with HOWARD DEVOTO"; same); hit No.31) (re-iss. 1994 on 'Document' 12"ep/cd-ep)*

— (Mar'77) **GARTH SMITH** – bass; repl. DEVOTO who formed MAGAZINE **SHELLEY** now lead vocals, guitar / **DIGGLE** switched to guitar, vocals

U.A. | not iss.

Oct 77. (7") *(UP 36316)* **ORGASM ADDICT. / WHATEVER HAPPENED TO . . . ?** [ ] [–]

— **STEVE GARVEY** – bass repl. GARTH (on tour at first)

Jan 78. (7") *(UP 36348)* **WHAT DO I GET?. / OH SHIT** [37] [–]

U.A. | I.R.S.

Mar 78. (lp/c) *(UAG/TCK 30159)* **ANOTHER MUSIC IN A DIFFERENT KITCHEN** [15] [–]
– Fast cars / No reply / You tear me up / Get on our own / Love battery / 16 / I don't mind / Fiction romance / Autonomy / I need / Moving away from the pulsebeat. *(re-iss. Aug85 on 'Liberty' lp/c; ATAK/TC-ATAK 51) (re-iss. Jun87 on 'Fan Club' blue-lp; FC 021) (re-iss. May88 on 'Fame' lp/c/cd; FA/TC-FA/CD-FA 3199) (re-iss. cd Jul88 on 'E.M.I.'; CDP 790299-2) (cd re-iss. Jul96; PRDFCD 3) (cd re-iss. Aug01 on 'E.M.I.'+=; 534405-2)* – Orgasm addict / Whatever happened to? / What do I get / Oh shit.

Apr 78. (7") *(UP 36386)* **I DON'T MIND. / AUTONOMY** [55] [–]

Jul 78. (7") *(UP 36433)* **LOVE YOU MORE. / NOISE ANNOYS** [34] [–]

Sep 78. (7") *(UP 36455)* **EVER FALLEN IN LOVE (WITH SOMEONE YOU SHOULDN'T'VE?). / JUST LUST** [12] [–]

Sep 78. (lp/c) *(UAG/TCK 30197)* **LOVE BITES** [13] [–]
– Real world / Ever fallen in love with someone you shouldn't've / Operator's manuel / Nostalgia / Just lust / Sixteen again / Walking distance / Love is lies / Nothing left / E.S.P. / Late for the train. *(re-iss. Mar87 on 'Fame' lp/c; FA/TC-FA 3174) (re-iss. Jun87 on 'Fan Club' blue-lp; FC 022) (cd-iss. Jul88 on 'Fame'; CD-FA 3174) (cd re-iss. Jul96; PRDFCD 4) (cd re-iss. Aug01 on 'E.M.I.'+=)* – Love you more / Noise annoys / Promises / Lipstick.

Nov 78. (7") *(UP 36471)* **PROMISES. / LIPSTICK** [20] [–]

Mar 79. (7") *(UP 36499)* **EVERYBODY'S HAPPY NOWADAYS. / WHY CAN'T I TOUCH IT?** [29] [–]

Jul 79. (7") *(UP 36541)* **HARMONY IN MY HEAD. / SOMETHING'S GONE WRONG AGAIN** [32] [–]

Sep 79. (7") *(BP 316)* **YOU SAY YOU DON'T LOVE ME. / RAISON D'ETRE** [ ] [–]

Sep 79. (lp/c) *(UAG/TCK 30260)* *<SP 009>* **A DIFFERENT KIND OF TENSION** [26] [ ]
– Paradise / Sitting round at home / You say you don't love me / You know you can't help it / Mad mad Judy / Raison d'etre / I don't know what to do with my life / Money / Hollow inside / A different kind of tension / I believe / Radio Nine. *(initial copies cont. previous 45) (re-iss. Jun87 on 'Fan Club' blue-lp; FC 023) (cd-iss. Jul88 on 'E.M.I.'; CZ 93)*

Nov 79. (lp/c) *<010>* **SINGLES – GOING STEADY** (compilation) [–] [ ]
– Orgasm addict / What do I get / I don't mind / Love you more / Ever fallen in love with someone you shouldn't've / Promises / Everybody's happy nowadays / Harmony in my head / Whatever happened to . . . ? / Oh shit! / Autonomy / Noise annoys / Just luck / Lipstick / Why can't I touch it / Something's gone wrong again. *(UK-iss.Nov81 on 'Liberty' lp/c; LBR/TC-LBR 1043) (re-iss. Aug85 lp/c; ATAK/TC-ATAK 52) (cd-iss. Jun87 + Jun88 on 'E.M.I.'; CDP 746449-2) (re-iss. Sep90 cd/c/lp; CD/TC+/FA 3241) (cd re-iss. Aug01 on 'E.M.I.'+=; 534442-2)* – (extra tracks).

Feb 80. (7") *<IR 9010>* **I BELIEVE. / SOMETHING'S GONE WRONG AGAIN** [–] [ ]

Liberty | I.R.S.

Aug 80. (7") *(BP 365)* **WHY SHE'S A GIRL FROM THE CHAINSTORE. / ARE EVERYTHING** [61] [–]

Oct 80. (7") *(BP 371)* **STRANGE THING. / AIRWAVES DREAM** [ ] [–]

Nov 80. (7") *(BP 392)* **RUNNING FREE. / WHAT DO YOU KNOW** [ ] [–]

— (split Feb'81) **DIGGLE** went solo and formed FLAG OF CONVENIENCE, with MAHER

PETE SHELLEY

— augmented by **STEVE GARVEY** – bass / **JIM RUSSELL** – drums

Genetic-Island Arista

Aug 81. (7"/12") *(WIP/12WIP 6720)* **HOMOSAPIEN. / KEAT'S SONG** –

Sep 81. (lp/c) *(ILPS/ICT 9676)* **HOMOSAPIEN** Jun82
– Homosapien / Yesterday's here / I generate a feeling / Keat's song / Qu'est-ce que c'est que ca / I don't know what it is / Guess I must have been in love with myself / Pusher man / Just one of those affairs / It's hard enough knowing. *(re-iss. cd Sep94 on 'Grapevine'; GRACD 201) (cd re-iss. May98 on 'Razor & Tie'; RE 2126)*

Nov 81. (d7"/12") *(U/12 WIP 6740)* **I DON'T KNOW WHAT IT IS. / WITNESS THE CHANGE/ / IN LOVE WITH SOMEBODY ELSE. / MAXINE** –

Apr 82. (7"/12") *(WIP/12WIP 6720)* **HOMOSAPIEN. / LOVE IN VAIN** –

— **BARRY ADAMSON** – bass (ex-MAGAZINE, ex-BIRTHDAY PARTY) repl. GARVEY / added **MARTIN RUSHENT** – keyboards, producer

Island Arista

Feb 83. (7"/12") *(XX/+T 1)* **TELEPHONE OPERATOR. / MANY A TIME** 66 –

Apr 83. (lp) *(XL 1)* **XL-1** 42 Jul83
– Telephone operator / If you ask me (I won't say no) / What was Heaven? / You better than I know / Twilight / (Millions of people) No one like you / Many a time / I just wanna touch / You and I / XL-1 *. (c+= dub tracks) (track* = only playable on ZX Spectrum computer) *(re-iss. cd Sep94 on 'Grapevine'; GRACD 202)*

Immaculate not iss.

Nov 84. (7") *(IMMAC 1)* **NEVER AGAIN. / ONE ONE ONE** –
(12"+=) *(12IMMAC 1)* – Give it to me.

— **SHELLEY** brought in new **JOHN DOYLE** – drums / **MARK SANDERSON** – bass / **NORMAN FISCHER-JONES** – guitar / **GERARD COOKSON** – keyboards / **JIM GARDNER** – synth.

Mercury Mercury

Mar 86. (7"/12") *(MER/+X 215)* **WAITING FOR LOVE. / DESIGNER LAMPS** –

May 86. (7"/12") *(MER/+X 221)* **ON YOUR OWN. / PLEASE FORGIVE ME . . . BUT I CANNOT ENDURE IT ANY LONGER** –

Jun 86. (lp/c)(cd) *(MERH/+C 90)(830004-2)* **HEAVEN AND THE SEA**
– Never again / My dreams / Blue eyes / You can't take that away / No Moon . . . / Waiting for love / On your own / They're coming for you / I surrender / Life without reason / Need a minit.

Aug 86. (7"/12") *(MER/+X 225)* **BLUE EYES. / NELSON'S RIDDLE** –

Nov 86. (7"/12") *(MER/+X 234)* **I SURRENDER. / I NEED A MINUTE** –

— In 1988, **SHELLEY** formed **ZIP** with COOKSON and SANDERSON.

– his compilations, others, etc. –

Apr 80. (m-lp) *Groovy; (STP 2)* **SKY YEN** (rec.1974) –

Apr 89. (7"/12") *Immaculate; (IMMAC/12IMMAC 11)* **HOMOSAPIEN. PETE SHELLEY VS. POWER, WONDER AND LOVE / ('A'mix)** –
(3"cd-s+=) *(IMMACD 11)* – ('A'-Icon mix) / ('A'-shower mix).

BUZZCOCKS F.O.C.

— **DIGGLE, HAMMER + ANDY COUZENS** – guitar / **CHRIS GOODWIN** – drums

Thin Line not iss.

Jul 89. (12"/cd-s) *(THIN 003/+CD)* **TOMORROW'S SUNSET. / LIFE WITH THE LIONS / ('A'version)** –

BUZZCOCKS

— re-formed in 1990 **SHELLEY, DIGGLE, GARVEY** and **MIKE JOYCE** – drums (ex-SMITHS) repl. ANDY and CHRIS who formed The HIGH

Planet Pacific not iss.

Apr 91. (7"ep/12"ep/c-ep/cd-ep) **ALIVE TONIGHT** –
– Alive tonight / Successful street / Serious crime / Last to know.

— **JOHN MAHER** – drums returned to repl. MIKE who joined PIL.

— **TONY BARBER** – bass / **PHIL BARKER** – drums repl.GARVEY and MAHER

Essential Caroline

May 93. (7") *(ESS 2025)* **INNOCENT. / WHO'LL HELP ME TO FORGET** –
(12"+=/cd-s+=) *(ESS T/X 2025)* – Inside.

Jun 93. (cd/c/lp) *(ESM CD/MC/LP 389)* <1747> **TRADE TEST TRANSMISSION**
– Innocent / Smile / Palm of your hand / Last to know / Do it/ Who will help me to forget / Energy / Alive tonight / Inside / Isolation / Never gonna give it up / Crystal night / 369 / Chegga / It's unthinkable / Somewhere. *(reiss.cd Jul96; same)*

Aug 93. (12"/cd-s) *(ESS T/X 2031)* **DO IT. / TRASH AWAY / ALL OVER YOU** –

Apr 94. (12"/cd-s) **LIBERTINE ANGEL. / ROLL IT OVER / EXCERPT FROM PRISON RIOT HOSTAGE** –

Dojo I.R.S.

Nov 95. (cd) *(DOJOCD 237)* <36761> **FRENCH (live in Paris 12th April 1995)** Jan96
– I don't mind / Who'll help me to forget / Get on our own / Unthinkable / Strange thing / Energy / Breakdown / Innocent / Roll it over / Why she's a girl from the chainstore / Last to know? / Running free / Libertine angel / Why can't I touch it / Noise annoys / Isolation / Boredom / Do it / Harmony in my head / I believe.

I.R.S. I.R.S.

Apr 96. (cd) *(EIRSCD 1078)* <36962> **ALL SET**
– Totally from the heart / Without you / Give it to me / Your love / Point of no return / Hold me close / Kiss & tell / What am I supposed to do? / Some kind of wonderful / (What you) Mean to me / Playing for time / Pariah / Back with you.

Go Kart Go Kart

Mar 00. (lp/cd) *(<GK 058/+CD>)* **MODERN** Sep99
– Soul on a rock / Rendezvous / Speed of life / Thunder of hearts / Why compromise? / Don't let the car crash / Runaround / Doesn't mean anything / Phone / Under the sun / Turn of the screw / Sneaky / Stranger in your town / Choices.

— **SHELLEY + DIGGLE** with **TONY BARBER + HOWARD DeVOTO** (!)

Cherry Red Merge

Apr 03. (cd/lp) *(CD+/BRED 226) <MRG 227>* **BUZZCOCKS**
– Jerk / Keep on / Wake up call / Friends / Driving you insane / Morning after / Sick city sometimes / Stars / Certain move / Lester Sands / Up for the crack / Useless situation.

Damaged Goods not iss.

Apr 03. (7") *(DG 214)* **JERK. / DON'T COME HOME / OH SHIT (live)** –

– compilations, others, etc. –

Apr 87. (lp/c) *Weird Systems; (WS 021/+X1)* **TOTAL POP** –

Jan 88. (12"ep) *Strange Fruit; (SFPS 044)* **THE PEEL SESSIONS (7.9.77)** –
– Fast cars / What do I get / Moving away from the pulsebeat.

Oct 88. (c) *R.O.I.R.; (A 158)* **LEST WE FORGET (live)** –
(cd-iss. Nov94; RE 158CD)

Sep 89. (lp/cd) *Absolutely Free; (FREE LP/CD 002)* **LIVE AT THE ROXY CLUB, 2 APRIL 1977 (live)** –
(cd+=) – (1 extra track). *(re-iss. Jul90 & Jul93 on 'Receiver'; RR CD/LC/LP 131)*

Oct 89. (7"ep/12"ep/cd-ep) *E.M.I.; (EM/12EM/CDEM 104)* **THE FAB FOUR** –
– Ever fallen in love with someone you shouldn't've / Promises / Everybody's happy nowadays / Harmony in my head.

Nov 89. (4xlp/2xd-c/2xd-cd) *E.M.I.; (LP/TC/CD PROD 1)* **PRODUCT** –
– (cont. first 3 albums + 1 live and rare) *(re-iss. May95 cd; PRODUCT 1)*

Feb 90. (cd/lp) *Strange Fruit; (SFR CD/LP 104)* **THE PEEL SESSIONS ALBUM** –

Sep 91. (cd/c/d-lp) *E.M.I.; (CD/TC+/EM 1421)* **OPERATOR'S MANUAL (BUZZCOCKS BEST)** –

May 92. (cd) *EMI Gold; (CDGOLD 1029)* **ENTERTAINING FRIENDS LIVE AT THE HAMMERSMITH ODEON – MARCH 1979 (live)** –

Oct 92. (cd-s) *Old Gold; (OG 6182)* **EVER FALLEN IN LOVE WITH SOMEONE . . . / WHAT DO I GET / PROMISES** –

Apr 94. (cd) *E.M.I.; (CDPRDT 12)* **ANOTHER MUSIC IN A DIFFERENT KITCHEN / LOVE BITES** –

1995.	(7") *One Stop Music; (ONE 7001)* **NOISE ANNOYS. / ISOLATION (live)**		–
Jul 95.	(cd) *Dojo; (DLP 2)* **TIME'S UP**		–
	(re-iss. Mar00 on 'The Grey Area'; SCRATCH 2/+CD)		
Nov 95.	(cd-s) *Old Gold; (12623 6332-2)* **EVER FALLEN IN LOVE WITH SOMEONE YOU SHOULDN'T HAVE FALLEN IN LOVE WITH / PROMISES**		–
Jun 97.	(cd) *EMI Gold; (CDGOLD 2073)* **CHRONOLOGY**		–
Sep 97.	(cd) *EMI Gold; (CDGOLD 1093)* **I DON'T MIND**		–
Oct 98.	(cd) *E.M.I.; (497771-2)* **THE BBC SESSIONS**		–
Jun 99.	(cd) *Almafame; (<YEAAH 1>)* **PARIS ENCORE DU PAIN**		
Sep 99.	(d-cd) *E.M.I.; (521767-2)* **MODERN / A DIFFERENT KIND**		–
Jul 00.	(d-cd) *Burning Airlines; (PILOT 078)* **BEATING HEARTS (LIVE IN MANCHESTER 1978)**		–
	(d-lp-iss.Feb01 on 'Get Back'; GET 74)		
Jul 01.	(cd) *Castle Pie; (PIESD 259)* **LIVE IN PARIS (live)**		–
Sep 01.	(d-lp) *Get Back; (GET 80)* **SMALL SONGS WITH BIG HEARTS**		–
Nov 01.	(cd) *Dressed To Kill; (MIDRO 805)* **ORGASM ADDICTS**		–
Apr 02.	(cd) *EMI Gold; (538464-2)* **FINEST (EVER FALLEN IN LOVE)**		–
Jun 02.	(cd) *N.M.C.; (SJLTD 01)* **NOISE ANNOYS – MANCHESTER APOLLO 1978 (live)**		–
Jun 02.	(cd) *N.M.C.; (SJLTD 02)* **LIVE TENSION – RAINBOW THEATRE, LONDON, 09/11/79)**		–
Jul 02.	(lp) *Get Back; (GET 92)* **FAST CARS**		–
Mar 03.	(d-cd) *E.M.I.; (582350-2)* **ANOTHER MUSIC IN ANOTHER KITCHEN / LOVE BITES** – (with extra tracks).		–
May 03.	(14xcd-box) *E.M.I.; (551824-2)* **INVENTORY**		–

BYRDS

Formed: Los Angeles, California, USA ... 1964 as The JETSET by JIM McGUINN, GENE CLARK and DAVID CROSBY. All three had come from folky backgrounds, McGUINN having toured with The CHAD MITCHELL TRIO as a teenager and CLARK already having proved an accomplished songwriter with The NEW CHRISTY MINSTRELS. CROSBY, meanwhile was an ambitious singer/songwriter who'd performed with LES BAXTER'S BALLADEERS. The JETSET recorded a one-off flop single for 'Elektra', 'PLEASE LET ME LOVE YOU', under the pseudonym of The BEEFEATERS. Later the same year, they recruited expert bluegrass player CHRIS HILLMAN, previously of The HILLMEN, who'd incorporated his instrumental dexterity on the mandolin into his bass playing. Drummer MICHAEL CLARKE, with his chiselled, BRIAN JONES-esque looks, completed the line-up, initially playing on cardboard boxes when the band were too hard-up to afford a real drum-kit! Profoundly influenced by The BEATLES, they soon changed their name to The BYRDS (the mis-spelling a tribute to their heroes), and set about realising their vision of marrying the fab four's electric energy to the folk music which was their stock in trade. With the help of long-time manager JIM DICKSON and the unlikely recommendation of MILES DAVIS, the band signed to 'Columbia'. At the insistence of DICKSON and producer TERRY MELCHER, the reluctant BYRDS eventually agreed to re-work their earlier demo of 'MR. TAMBOURINE MAN' (this and other demos later surfaced on 'PREFLYTE'). It was a canny decision which did nothing less than change the course of pop/rock history. The resulting song's unforgettable euphoric rush charged DYLAN's lyrics with a youthful romanticism, encapsulating in 3 minutes, what it was to be young and have the world at your feet. It soon hit No.1 on both sides of the Atlantic and it still sounds as fresh today as it did then, a timeless slice of hypnotic, bittersweet pop with McGUINN's delivery forging an affecting DYLAN / LENNON hybrid. Much has since been made of the fact that only one BYRD, McGUINN, actually played on the record, with MELCHER hiring session musicians like LEON RUSSELL, LARRY KNECHTAL and HAL BLAINE. However, any doubts about The BYRDS' ability as a band were dispelled with the self-titled debut album, a folk-rock classic. It was a case of more of the same really, with the band turning in a dazzling string of DYLAN covers, making the songs distinctly their own. 'CHIMES OF FREEDOM' was a ringing, hippy call to arms, fuelled by a starry-eyed optimism and they even managed to transform the Welsh mining disaster ballad 'BELLS OF RHYMNEY', into an effervescent swirl. GENE CLARK was the band's chief songwriter at this stage, contributing the classic BEATLES-esque originals 'FEEL A WHOLE LOT BETTER', 'I KNEW I'D WANT YOU' and 'HERE WITHOUT YOU'. In the summer of '65, they played a residency at Ciro's nightclub on Sunset Strip, often cited as the origin of the L.A. hippy movement (described by The L.A. Times as being frequented by people who looked like they'd been dragged from Sherwood Forest!). They were back at No.1 by the end of 1965, when they managed to transform PETE SEEGER's Book Of Ecclesiastes-adaptation 'TURN! TURN! TURN!' into a classic pop record, a miracle of biblical proportions. Very early the next year, the second album boasted two more DYLAN covers, an uninspiring update of 'THE TIMES THEY ARE A-CHANGIN' and 'LAY DOWN YOUR WEARY TUNE', apparently the song that finally persuaded DYLAN that The BYRDS were doing something above and beyond mere imitation. McGUINN contributed two songs, one of which was his tribute to the assassinated JOHN F. KENNEDY, 'HE WAS A FRIEND OF MINE', while CLARK offered three originals, including the classic 'SET YOU FREE THIS TIME'. Recorded the previous January, 'EIGHT MILES HIGH' pioneered psychedelic rock, predating the efforts of The BEATLES, The BEACH BOYS and the San Franciscan bands. The JOHN COLTRANE-inspired track was promptly vetoed by radio stations on its spring '66 release, amid allegations that the song was an explicit account of an LSD trip. After the completion of the third album 'FIFTH DIMENSION', CLARK departed, citing his paranoia-fuelled fear of flying and CROSBY's digs regarding his tambourine playing. The new album heralded a move away from sparkling pop to a more complex, ambitious and intelligent sound. Influenced heavily by Indian sitar player RAVI SHANKAR, and modal jazz, the record didn't fulfil the promise of the preceding single but still contained some memorable moments. McGUINN's 'MR SPACEMAN' hinted at the country sound the band would later embrace. Just prior to releasing the fourth album, 'YOUNGER THAN YESTERDAY', the band issued 'SO YOU WANT TO BE A ROCK'N'ROLL STAR', a sarcastic reaction to manufactured bands by a group that had fallen out of favour with the Hollywood set. The album was an assorted bag of styles, with HILLMAN emerging as a talented songwriter on the likes of 'TIME BETWEEN' and 'THOUGHTS AND WORDS', while CROSBY had his finest moment with the haunting 'EVERYBODY'S BEEN BURNED'. Despite the melange of styles, the album predated 'SGT PEPPER', once again proving that The BYRDS were ahead of their time. By the time of 'THE NOTORIOUS BYRD BROTHERS' in 1968, CROSBY's dictatorial manner had led to his ejection from the band, along with MICHAEL CLARKE. A contender for the The BYRDS best album, the record was again stylistically diverse but included possibly the band's finest moment in the GOFFIN/KING number, 'GOIN' BACK' (later a hit for DUSTY SPRINGFIELD). Its wistful musings on the passage from childhood to maturity were set against a backdrop of heavenly harmonies and celestial pedal steel while 'WASN'T BORN TO FOLLOW' (another GERRY GOFFIN-

CAROLE KING cover), was a triumphant clarion call of phased, psychedelic country. With the addition of GRAM PARSONS and HILLMAN's cousin KEVIN KELLEY, the band steered radically away from the studio-enhanced sound of 'NOTORIOUS', straight into the heart of country, once again staying one step ahead of their peers and foreshadowing the country-rock boom of the early 70's. 'SWEETHEART OF THE RODEO', with its purist sound, confounded the hippies and despite playing a show at the Grand Ole Opry, and even, God forbid, cutting their hair! for the occasion, the country crowd remained suspicious of their druggy image, thereby ensuring little commercial success. Released in '68, PARSONS was the driving force behind the album, contributing beautiful songs like 'HICKORY WIND' and 'ONE HUNDRED YEARS FROM NOW', which sat majestically alongside covers of LOUVIN BROTHERS and DYLAN material. The gypsy-like PARSONS soon left, taking HILLMAN with him to form The FLYING BURRITO BROTHERS. McGUINN (who'd now changed his name to ROGER, following his immersion in the Indonesian religion, Subud) recruited country guitar maestro CLARENCE WHITE along with a cast of other musicians. The albums that followed were inconsistent, although they contained a few BYRDS classics and highlighted WHITE's virtuoso guitar playing. 'DR BYRDS & MR HYDE', featured the ironic stab at the country establishment, 'DRUG STORE TRUCK DRIVING MAN', while 'BALLAD OF EASY RIDER's gentle meandering title track was a minor classic. The half live/half studio set, 'UNTITLED', from 1970, included an impassioned performance from WHITE on 'LOVER ON THE BAYOU' and a lovely version of LOWELL GEORGE's 'TRUCK STOP GIRL'. Probably the strongest set of the latter day BYRDS, it also included the single 'CHESTNUT MARE', and the evocative McGUINN and JACQUES LEVY song 'ALL THE THINGS'. Much of McGUINN's songs during this period came from the abandoned 'Gene Tryp' project which he had begun with New York psychologist LEVY to chart the history of American music. The last few albums weren't quite as ambitious in their scope, but 'BYRDMANIAX' and 'FARTHER ALONG' were enjoyable despite having the weight of such an illustrious career on their shoulders. McGUINN did the right thing and called it a day at last in mid-72, later joining up with the original BYRDS for an uninspired album a year later. Two of the BYRDS most talented members died in separate incidents in the early 70's, CLARENCE WHITE killed by a drunken driver, GRAM PARSONS from a heroin overdose. CROSBY survived a descent into free-base cocaine addiction and a liver transplant to record songs in Nashville with McGUINN and HILLMAN in 1990. A proposed tour never happened but the tracks are included on the wonderful 'Columbia' boxed set released the same year. More recently, McGUINN was sighted running through some old numbers on 'Later With Jools (Holland)' in true troubadour style. An endless list of artists and bands (TOM PETTY, R.E.M., LONG RYDERS, SMITHS, PRIMAL SCREAM, RIDE, etc), have kept alive the spirit of The BYRDS in their own particular style, while the band's own recordings remain timeless treasures.

Album rating: MR. TAMBOURINE MAN (*8) / TURN! TURN! TURN! (*8) / FIFTH DIMENSION (*6) / YOUNGER THAN YESTERDAY (*8) / THE BYRDS' GREATEST HITS compilation (*10) / THE NOTORIOUS BYRD BROTHERS (*9) / SWEETHEART OF THE RODEO (*8) / DR. BYRDS & MR. HYDE (*5) / BALLAD OF EASY RIDER (*5) / UNTITLED (*6) / BYRDMANIAX (*4) / GREATEST HITS VOL.2 compilation (*8) / FARTHER ALONG (*4) / THE BYRDS (*4) / THE VERY BEST OF THE BYRDS compilation (*8) / Roger McGuinn: ROGER McGUINN (*6) / PEACE ON YOU (*5) / ROGER McGUINN & HIS BAND (*5) / CARDIFF ROSE (*7) / THUNDERBYRD (*5) / McGUINN, CLARK & HILLMAN (*6) / CITY (*4) / MEAN STREETS with Chris Hillman (*3) / BACK FROM RIO (*6) / BORN TO ROCK'N'ROLL compilation (*7) / LIVE FROM MARS (*5)

GENE CLARK (b. HAROLD EUGENE CLARK, 17 Nov'41, Tipton, Missouri, USA) – vocals, tambourine / **JIM McGUINN** (b.JAMES JOSEPH McGUINN, 13 Jul'42, Chicago, Illinois, USA) – guitar, vocals / **DAVID CROSBY** (b.DAVID VAN CORTLAND, 14 Aug'41, L.A.) – guitar, vocals

Pye Inter. Elektra

Nov 64. (7"; as BEEFEATERS) *(7N 25277)* <45013> **PLEASE LET ME LOVE YOU. / DON'T BE LONG** Sep64

— added **CHRIS HILLMAN** (b. 4 Dec'42, L.A.) – bass, vocals (ex-HILLMEN) / **MICHAEL CLARKE** (b. 3 Jun'43, New York City) – drums

C.B.S. Columbia

Jun 65. (7") *(201765)* <43271> **MR. TAMBOURINE MAN. / I KNEW I'D WANT YOU** 1 May65 1

Aug 65. (7") *(201796)* <43332> **ALL I REALLY WANT TO DO. / I'LL FEEL A WHOLE LOT BETTER** 4 Jul65 40

Aug 65. (lp; stereo/mono) *(S+/BPG 62571)* <9172> **MR. TAMBOURINE MAN** 7 Jun65 6
– Mr. Tambourine man / I'll feel a whole lot better / Spanish Harlem incident / You won't have to cry / Here without you / The bells of Rhymney / All I really want to do / I knew I'd want you / It's no use / Don't doubt yourself, babe / Chimes of freedom / We'll meet again. *(re-iss. Jul77; CBS/40 31503) <(cd re-mast.May96 on 'Columbia'+=; 483705-2)<64845>* – She has a way * / I'll feel a whole lot better / It's no use / You won't have to cry / All I really want to do / You and me (instrumental) *. *(lp re-iss. Jul98 on 'Simply Vinyl'; SVLP 32) <(lp re-iss. Jun99 on 'Sundazed'+= *; SCLP 5057)>*

Oct 65. (7") *(202008)* <43424> **TURN! TURN! TURN!. / SHE DON'T CARE ABOUT TIME** 26 1

Feb 66. (7") *(202037)* <43501> **SET YOU FREE THIS TIME. / IT WON'T BE WRONG** 79 63

Mar 66. (lp; stereo/mono) *(S+/SPG 62652)* <9254> **TURN! TURN! TURN!** 11 Dec65 17
– Turn! Turn! Turn! (to everything there is a season) / It won't be wrong / Set you free this time / Lay down your weary tune / He was a friend of mine / The world turns all around her / Satisfied mind / If you're gone / The times they are a-changin' / Wait and see / Oh! Susannah. *(re-iss. Jul77; CBS/40 31526) <(cd re-mast.May96 on 'Columbia'+=; 483706-2)<64846>* – The day walk (never before) / She don't care about time (mono) * / The times they are a-changin' (mono) * / It's all over now, baby blue (version 1) / She don't care about time (version 1) / The world turns all around her (alt.) / Stranger in a strange land (instrumental) *. *(lp re-iss. Nov98 on 'Simply Vinyl'; SVLP 27) <(lp re-iss. Jun99 on 'Sundazed'+= *; SCLP 5058)>*

— trimmed to a quartet when GENE CLARK went solo

Apr 66. (7") *(202067)* <43578> **EIGHT MILES HIGH. / WHY?** 24 14

Jul 66. (7") *(202259)* <43702> **5D (FIFTH DIMENSION). / CAPTAIN SOUL** 44

Sep 66. (lp; stereo/mono) *(S+/BPG 62783)* <9349> **FIFTH DIMENSION** 27 Aug66 24
– 5D (Fifth Dimension) / Wild mountain thyme / Mr. Spaceman / I see you / What's happening?!?! / I come and stand at every door / Eight miles high / Hey Joe / John Riley / Captain Soul / 2-4-2 Foxtrot (the Lear jet song). *(re-iss. Jul83 lp/c; CBS/40 32284) <(cd re-mast.May96 on 'Columbia'+=; 483707-2)<64847>* – Why? / I know my rider (I know you rider) * / Psychodrama city / Eight miles high (alt.) * / Why? * / John Riley (instrumental). *(lp re-iss. Nov98 on 'Simply Vinyl'; SVLP 47) <(lp re-iss. Jun99 on 'Sundazed'+= *; SCLP 5059)>*

Oct 66. (7") *(202295)* <43766> **MR. SPACEMAN. / WHAT'S HAPPENING?!?!** Sep66 36

Feb 67. (7") *(202559)* <43987> **SO YOU WANT TO BE A ROCK'N'ROLL STAR. / EVERYBODY'S BEEN BURNED** Jan67 29

Apr 67. (lp; stereo/mono) *(S+/BPG 62988)* <9442> **YOUNGER THAN YESTERDAY** 37 Mar67 24
– So you want to be a rock'n'roll star / Have you seen her face / C.T.A. – 102 / Renaissance fair / Time between / Everybody's been burned / Thoughts and words / Mind gardens / My back pages / The girl with no name / Why? *(re-iss. Mar87 on 'Edsel' cd/c/lp; CD/C+/ED 227) (cd re-mast.May96 on 'Columbia'+=; 483708-2)<64848>* – It happens each day * / Don't make waves * / My back pages / Mind gardens / Lady friend / Old John Robertson. *(lp re-iss. Oct97 on 'Simply Vinyl'; SVLP 7) <(lp re-iss. Jun99 on 'Sundazed'+= *; SUNLP 5060)>*

May 67. (7") *(2648)* <44054> **MY BACK PAGES. / RENAISSANCE FAIR** Mar67 30

Jun 67. (7") *<44157>* **HAVE YOU SEEN HER FACE. / DON'T MAKE WAVES** - 74

Sep 67. (7") *<44230>* **LADY FRIEND. / OLD JOHN ROBERTSON** – 82
Sep 67. (7") *(2924)* **LADY FRIEND. / DON'T MAKE WAVES** –
Oct 67. (lp; stereo/mono) *(S+/BPG 63107) <9516>* **THE BYRDS' GREATEST HITS** (compilation) Aug67 6
– Mr. Tambourine man / I'll feel a whole lot better / Bells of rhymney / Turn! turn! turn! / All I really want to do / Chimes of freedom / Eight miles high / Mr.Spaceman / 5D (Fifth Dimension) / So you want to be a rock'n'roll star / My back pages. *(re-iss. Jan84; CBS/40 32068) (cd-iss. Jun89; CD 32068) (cd re-mast.Feb91; 467843-2) (cd re-mast.May96 on 'Columbia'; 483705-2)*

— **GENE CLARK** – guitar, vocals returned to repl. DAVID who formed CROSBY, STILLS and NASH (JIM also changed name to ROGER McGUINN)

Dec 67. (7") *(3093) <44362>* **GOIN' BACK. / CHANGE IS NOW** Nov67 89
(re-iss. Jun77; 5300)
Now a trio of **McGUINN, HILLMAN and CLARKE** (GENE continued solo career)
Apr 68. (lp; stereo/mono) *(S+/BPG 63169) <9575>* **THE NOTORIOUS BYRD BROTHERS** 12 Jan68 47
– Artificial energy / Goin' back / Natural harmony / Draft morning / Wasn't born to follow / Get to you / Change is now / Old John Robertson / Tribal gathering / Dolphin's smile / Space odyssey. *(re-iss. Aug88 on 'Edsel' cd/lp; CD+/ED 262) <(cd re-iss. Mar97 on 'Columbia'+=; 486751-2)<65151* – Moog raga (instrumental) / Bound to fall (instrumental) / Triad / Goin' back / Draft morning / Universal mind decoder (instrumental). *(lp re-iss. Oct97 on 'Simply Vinyl'; SVLP 6)*

— **KEVIN KELLEY** (b.1945, California) – drums (ex-RISING SONS) repl. MICHAEL who joined DILLARD & CLARK. Also added **GRAM PARSONS** (b.INGRAM CECIL CONNOR III, 5 Nov'46, Winterhaven, Florida) – guitar, vocals, keyboards (ex-INTERNATIONAL SUBMARINE BAND) / guests on album – **SNEAKY PETE** – pedal steel guitar / **DOUG DILLARD** – banjo

May 68. (7") *(3411) <44499>* **YOU AIN'T GOING NOWHERE. / ARTIFICIAL ENERGY** 45 74
Sep 68. (lp) *(63353) <9670>* **SWEETHEART OF THE RODEO** Aug68 77
– You ain't going nowhere / I am a pilgrim / The Christian life / You're still on my mind / Pretty Boy Floyd / You don't miss your water / Hickory wind / One hundred years from now / Blue Canadian Rockies / Life in prison / Nothing was delivered. *(re-iss. Jun87 on 'Edsel' cd/lp; CD+/ED 234) <(cd re-iss. Mar97 on 'Columbia'+=; 486752-2)<65150>* – You got a reputation / Lazy days / Pretty Polly The Christian life (Gram Parsons vocal) / Life in prison (alt.) / You're still on my mind (alt.) / One hundred years from now (Gram Parsons vocal) / All I have are memories (instrumental). *(lp re-iss. Nov98 on 'Simply Vinyl'; SVLP 57) (cd re-iss. Oct99 on 'Columbia'; MILLEN 6) <(d-cd iss.Sep03 on 'Columbia'+=; 510921-2)<505473>* – (bonus cd of alt. takes).
Oct 68. (7") *(3752) <44643>* **PRETTY BOY FLOYD. / I AM A PILGRIM**

— **CARLOS BERNAL** – guitar played on US tour replacing GRAM who joined FLYING BURRITO BROTHERS alongside HILLMAN and SNEAKY PETE. Soon McGUINN recruited entirely new members **CLARENCE WHITE** (b. 6 Jun'44, Lewiston, Maine, USA) – guitar, vocals (ex-NASHVILLE WEST) repl. BERNAL / **GENE PARSONS** (b. 9 Apr'44) – drums, vocals (ex-NASHVILLE WEST) repl. KELLEY / **JOHN YORK** – bass, vocals repl. HILLMAN

Mar 69. (7") *(4055) <44746>* **BAD NIGHT AT THE WHISKEY. / DRUG STORE TRUCK DRIVIN' MAN**
Apr 69. (lp) *(63545) <9755>* **DR. BYRDS AND MR. HYDE** 15 Mar69
– This wheel's on fire / Old blue / Your gentle way of loving me / Child of the universe / Nashville West / Drug store truck drivin' man / King Apathy III / Candy / Bad night at the Whiskey / My back pages – B.J. blues – Baby what you want me to do. *(cd-iss. Aug91 on 'Beat Goes On'; BGOCD 107) <(cd re-mast.Mar97 & Jul03 on 'Columbia'+=; 486753-2)<65113>* – Stanley's song / Lay lady lay / This wheel's on fire / My back pages – B.J. blues – Baby what you want me to do (alt.) / Nashville west (alt.). *(lp re-iss. Feb99 on 'Simply Vinyl'; SVLP 70)*
Jun 69. (7") *(4284) <44868>* **LAY LADY LAY. / OLD BLUE**
Sep 69. (7") *(4572)* **WASN'T BORN TO FOLLOW. / CHILD OF THE UNIVERSE** –
Oct 69. (7") *<44990>* **THE BALLAD OF EASY RIDER. / WASN'T BORN TO FOLLOW** – 5
Jan 70. (lp) *(63795) <9942>* **BALLAD OF EASY RIDER** 41 Dec69 36
– Ballad of Easy Rider / Fido / Oil in my lamp / Tulsa County / Jack Tarr the sailor / Jesus is just alright / It's all over now, baby blue / There must be someone / Gunga Din / Deportee (plane wreck at Los Gatos) / Armstrong, Aldrin and Collins. *<(cd re-mast.Mar97 & Jul03 on 'Columbia'+=; 486751-2)<65114>* – Way beyond the sun / Mae Jean goes to Hollywood / Oil in my lamp (alt.) / Tulsa County (alt.) / Fiddler a dram (moog experiment) / Ballad of easy rider (long version) / Build it up (instrumental).
Feb 70. (7") *(4753) <45071>* **JESUS IS JUST ALRIGHT. / IT'S ALL OVER NOW, BABY BLUE** 97

— **SKIP BATTIN** (b. 2 Feb'34, Gallipolis, Ohio) – bass; repl. YORK

Nov 70. (d-lp) *(66253) <30127>* **UNTITLED (1/2 live)** 11 Oct70 40
– Lover of the bayou / Positively 4th Street / Nashville West / So you want to be a rock'n'roll star / Mr. Tambourine man / Mr. Spaceman / Eight miles high // Chestnut mare / Truck stop girl / All the things / Yesterday's train / Hungry planet / Just a season / Take a whiff (on me) / You all look alike / Welcome back home. *<(d-cd re-mast.Feb00 on 'Columbia'+=; 495077-2)<65847>* – All the things / Yesterday's train / Lover of the bayou / Kathleen's song / White's lightning (part 2) / Willin' / You ain't goin' nowhere (live) / Old Blue (live) / It's alright, ma (I'm only bleeding) (live) / Ballad of easy rider (live) / My back pages (live) / Take a whiff on me (live) / Jesus is just alright (live) / This wheel's on fire (live). *(3xlp-set-iss.JUn02 on 'Simply Vinyl'+=; SVLP 381)*
Dec 70. (7") *(5322) <45259>* **CHESTNUT MARE. / JUST A SEASON** 19
May 71. (7") *(7253)* **I TRUST (EVERYTHING'S GONNA WORK OUT FINE). / THIS IS MY DESTINY** –
Aug 71. (lp) *(64389) <30640>* **BIRDMANIAX** Jul71 46
– Glory, glory / Pale blue / I trust / Tunnel of love / Citizen Kane / I wanna grow up to be a politician / Absolute happiness / Green apple quick step / My destiny / Kathleen's song / Jamaica say you will. *(cd-iss. Sep90 on 'Line'; CLCD 900930) <(cd re-mast.Feb00 on 'Columbia'+=; 495079-2)<65848>* – Just like a woman / Pale blue (alt.) / Think I'm gonna feel better.
Oct 71. (7") *(7501) <45440>* **GLORY, GLORY. / CITIZEN KANE**
Oct 71. (lp) *(64650) <31795>* **THE BYRDS' GREATEST HITS VOLUME 2** (compilation) <US title 'THE BEST OF THE BYRDS (GREATEST HITS, VOLUME II'> Dec72
– The ballad of Easy rider / Jesus is just alright / Chestnut mare / You ain't goin' nowhere / I am a pilgrim / Goin' back / I trust / Lay lady lay / Wasn't born to follow / The times they are a-changin' / Drug store truck drivin' man / Get to you.
Jan 72. (lp) *(64676) <31050>* **FARTHER ALONG** Dec71
– Tiffany queen / Get down your line / Farther along / B.B. class road / Bugler / America's great national pastime / Antique Sandy / Precious Kate / So fine / Lazy waters / Bristol steam convention blues. *<(cd re-mast.Feb00 on 'Columbia'+=; 495078-2)<65849>* – Lost my drivin' wheel / Born to rock & roll / Bag full of money / Bristol steam convention blues (alt.).
Jan 72. (7") *(7712) <45514>* **AMERICA'S GREAT NATIONAL PASTIME. / FARTHER ALONG**

— They split mid '72, SKIP joined NEW RIDERS OF THE PURPLE SAGE. CLARENCE WHITE was killed in a road accident 14 Jul'73. / **JOHN GUERRIN** – drums (session men) took over briefly when reforming

— McGUINN then re-formed the original **"BYRDS"** Himself, **CROSBY, CLARK, HILLMAN + CLARKE**

Asylum Asylum
Apr 73. (lp) *(SYLA 8754) <5058>* **THE BYRDS** 31 Mar73 20
– Full circle / Sweet Mary / Changing heart / For free / Born to rock'n'roll / Things will be better / Cowgirl in the sand / Long live the King / Borrowing time / Laughing / (See the sky) about to rain. *(cd-iss. Feb93 on 'Warners; 7559 60955-2)*
May 73. (7") *(AYM 516)* **THINGS WILL BE BETTER. / FOR FREE** –
Jun 73. (7") *(AYM 517) <11016>* **FULL CIRCLE. / LONG LIVE THE KING** Apr73
Jul 73. (7") *<11019>* **COWGIRL IN THE SAND. / LONG LIVE THE KING** –

— McGUINN, HILLMAN and CLARK all went solo, later teaming up together on album. CROSBY re-formed CROSBY, STILL and NASH. Sadly, MICHAEL CLARKE was to die of liver failure 19th December '93.

– compilations, etc. –

On 'CBS' / 'Columbia' unless mentioned otherwise.
Feb 66. (7"ep) *(EP 6069)* **THE TIMES ARE A-CHANGING** 15 –
Oct 66. (7"ep) *(EP 6077)* **EIGHT MILES HIGH** 18 –
Aug 69. (lp) *Together; <ST-T 1001>* **PREFLYTE (demo recordings of '64)** –
<re-iss. 1973 on 'Columbia'; C 32183> (UK-iss.Sep73 on 'Bumble'; GEXP 8001)
Dec 69. (lp) *Together; <ST-T 1019>* **EARLY L.A.** –

May 73. (d-lp) *(68242)* **THE HISTORY OF THE BYRDS** [47] [–]
– Mr. Tambourine man / Turn! turn! turn! / She don't care about time / Wild mountain thyme / Eight miles high / Mr.Spaceman / 5D (Fifth Dimension) / So you want to be a rock'n'roll star / Time between / My back pages / Lady friend / Goin' back / Old John Robertson / Wasn't born to follow / You ain't goin' nowhere / Hickory wind / Nashville West / Drug store truck drivin' man / Gunga Din / Jesus is just alright / The ballad of Easy Rider / Chestnut mare / Yesterday's train / Just a season / Citizen Kane / Jamaica say you will / Tiffany queen / America's great national pastime. *(re-iss. Sep87 d-lp/c; 460115-1/-4)*

Feb 80. (lp/c) *(CBS/40 31795)* **THE BYRDS PLAY DYLAN** [ ] [ ]
(cd-iss. Apr94 & Feb96 on 'Sony'; 476757-2)

Aug 80. (lp/c) *(CBS/40 31851)* **THE ORIGINAL SINGLES 1965-1967** [ ] [ ]
(re-iss. Nov81 lp/c; CBS/40 32069)

Feb 82. (lp/c) *(CBS/40 32103)* **THE ORIGINAL SINGLES 1967-1969** [ ] [ ]

Feb 91. (cd/c) *Raven; (RV CD/CA 10)* **FULL FLYTE 1965-1970** [ ] [–]

Jul 91. (3xcd-box) *Columbia; (468338-2)* **MR. TAMBOURINE MAN / TURN! TURN! TURN! / YOUNGER THAN YESTERDAY** [ ] [–]

Mar 93. (cd/c) *Columbia; (471665-2/-4) <32644>* **20 ESSENTIAL TRACKS FROM THE BOXED SET: 1965-1990** [ ] [ ]

Jun 97. (d-cd) *Columbia; (487995-2)* **THE VERY BEST OF THE BYRDS** [ ] [–]
– Mr. Tambourine man / All I really want to do / Chimes of freedom / I'll feel a whole lot better / Turn! turn! turn! (there is a season) / The times they are a-changin' / The world turns all around her / It won't be wrong / He was a friend of mine / Eight miles high / 5D (Fifth dimension) / Mr. Spaceman / So you want to be a rock & roll star / My back pages / Renaissance fair / Goin' back / Wasn't born to follow / Dolphin's smile / You ain't goin' nowhere / One hundred years from now / You're still on my mind / Hickory wind / Ballad of easy rider / Jesus is just alright / It's all over now, baby blue / Lay lady lay / Chestnut mare. *(d-lp-iss.Apr02 on 'Simply Vinyl'; SVLP 375)*

Jun 00. (lp) *Sundazed; <(SCLP 5061)>* **SANCTUARY** [ ] [ ]

Nov 00. (lp) *Sundazed; <(SCLP 5065)>* **SANCTUARY II** [ ] [ ]

Dec 01. (lp) *Sundazed; <(SCLP 5066)>* **SANCTUARY III** [ ] [ ]

Oct 02. (3xcd-box) *Columbia; (509502-2)* **YOUNGER THAN YESTERDAY / THE NOTORIOUS BYRD BROTHERS / SWEETHEART OF THE RODEO** [ ] [–]

Nov 02. (cd-ep) *Magic; (3930244)* **SET YOU FREE THIS TIME / THE TIMES THEY ARE A-CHANGIN' / IT WON'T BE WRONG / OH SUSANNA** [ ] [–]

Jul 03. (cd) *(495080-2)* **FILMORE WEST 1969** [ ] [ ]

Sep 03. (cd) *(512778-2)* **MOJO PRESENTS . . . THE BYRDS** [ ] [ ]

ROGER McGUINN

C.B.S. Columbia

Jun 73. (7") *<45931>* **DRAGGIN'. / TIME CUBE** [–] [ ]

Jun 73. (lp) *(CBS 65274) <31946>* **ROGER McGUINN** [ ] [ ]
– I'm so restless / My new woman / Lost my drivin' wheel / Draggin' / Time cube / Bag full of money / Hanoi Hannah / Stone / Heave away / M'Linda / The water is wide. *(re-iss. Jul88 on 'Edsel'; ED 281) (cd-iss. Feb91; EDCD 281)*

Jul 74. (7") *<10019>* **SAME OLD SOUND. / GATE OF HORN** [–] [ ]

Sep 74. (lp) *(CBS 80171) <32956>* **PEACE ON YOU** [ ] [92]
– Peace on you / Without you / Going to the country / One more time / Same old sound / Do what you want to / Together / Better change / Gate of horn / Lady.

Sep 74. (7") *(2649) <10044>* **PEACE ON YOU. / WITHOUT YOU** [ ] [ ]

—— his band; **GREG ATTAWAY / STEVE LOVE / DAVID LOVELACE**

Jul 75. (lp; as ROGER McGUINN & BAND) *(CBS 80877) <33541>* **ROGER McGUINN AND BAND** [ ] Jun75 [ ]
– Somebody loves you / Knockin' on Heaven's door / Bull Dog / Painted lady / Lover of the bayou / Lisa / Circle song/ So long / Easy does it / Born to rock and roll.

Jul 75. (7"; as ROGER McGUINN & BAND) *<10181>* **SOMEBODY LOVES YOU / EASY DOES IT** [–] [ ]

Oct 75. (7"; as ROGER McGUINN & BAND) *<10201>* **LOVER OF THE BAYOU. / EASY DOES IT** [–] [ ]

Jun 76. (7") *<10385>* **TAKE ME AWAY. / FRIEND** [–] [ ]

Jun 76. (lp) *(CBS 81369) <34154>* **CARDIFF ROSE** [ ] [ ]
– Jolly Roger / Take me away / Rock and roll time / Partners in crime / Friend / Up to me / Round table / Prettly Polly / Dream land.

May 77. (lp) *(CBS 81883) <34656>* **THUNDERBYRD** [ ] [ ]
– All night long / It's gone / Dixie highway / American girl / We can do it all over again / Why, baby why / I'm not lonely anymore / Golden loom / Russian Hill.

May 77. (7") *(5231)* **AMERICAN GIRL. / RUSSIAN HILL** [ ] [–]

May 77. (7") *(10543>* **AMERICAN GIRL. / I'M NOT LONELY ANYMORE** [–] [ ]

McGUINN, CLARK & HILLMAN

—— (nearly a BYRDS reformation; ROGER, GENE & CHRIS)

Capitol Capitol

Feb 79. (7") *(CL 16065)* **SURRENDER TO ME. / BYE BYE BABY** [ ] [–]

Feb 79. (lp/c) *<(EST/TC-EST 11910)>* **McGUINN, CLARK & HILLMAN** [ ] [39]
– Long long time / Little mama / Don't you write her off / Sad boy / Surrender to me / Backstage pass / Stopping traffic / Feeling higher / Release me girl / Bye bye baby. *(cd-iss. Feb99 on 'E.M.I.'; CDP 796355-2)*

Apr 79. (7") *(CL 16077) <4693>* **DON'T YOU WRITE HER OFF. / SAD BOY** [ ] Mar79 [33]

Jun 79. (7") *<4739>* **SURRENDER TO ME. / LITTLE MAMA** [–] [ ]

Sep 79. (7") *<4763>* **BYE BYE BABY. / BACKSTAGE PASS** [–] [ ]

Jan 80. (lp; by ROGER McGUINN and CHRIS HILLMAN featuring GENE CLARK) *<(EST/TC-EST 12043)>* **CITY** [ ] [ ]
– Who taught the night / One more chance / Won't let you down / Street talk / City / Skate date / Givin' herself away / Let me down easy / Deeper in / Painter fire.

Feb 80. (7") *<4821>* **STREET TALK. / ONE MORE CHANCE** [–] [ ]

Apr 80. (7") *<4855>* **CITY. / DEEPER IN** [–] [ ]

McGUINN / HILLMAN

Mar 81. (lp/c) *<(EST/TC-EST 12108)>* **McGUINN / HILLMAN – MEAN STREETS** [ ] [ ]
– Mean streets / Entertainment / Soul shoes / Between you and me / Angel / Ain't no money / Love me tonight / King for a night / A secret side of you / Turn your radio on. *(cd-iss. Feb91;)*

Mar 81. (7") *(4952>* **TURN YOUR RADIO ON. / MAKING MOVIES** [–] [ ]

May 81. (7") *<4973>* **LOVE ME TONIGHT. / KING FOR A NIGHT** [–] [ ]

not iss. Universal

1983. (7") *<66006>* **YOU AIN'T GOIN' NOWHERE. / DON'T YOU HEAR JERUSALEM MOAN** [–] [ ]

ROGER McGUINN

—— used session people **STAN LYNCH** – drums / **GEORGE HAWKINS** – bass / **DAVID COLE** – acoustic guitar / **JOHN JORGENSEN** – guitar / **BELMONT TENCH** – keyboards / **MICHAEL THOMPSON** – acoustic guitar

Arista Arista

Feb 91. (cd/c/lp) *(261/411/211 348) <8648>* **BACK FROM RIO** [ ] Jan91 [44]
– Someone to love / Car phone / You bowed down / Suddenly blue / The trees are all gone / king of the hill / Without your love / The time has come / Your love is a gold mine / If we never meet again.

Feb 91. (7") **KING OF THE HILL. / YOUR LOVE IS A GOLD MINE** [ ] [ ]
(cd-s+=) – The time has come.

Polydor Hollywood

Jan 97. (cd) *<(162090-2)>* **LIVE FROM MARS (live)** [ ] Nov96 [ ]
– Heartbreak hotel / Daddy roll 'em / Gate of Horn / Chestnut mare / Bells of rhymney / Turn! turn! turn! (to everything there is a season) / Beach ball / Wild mountain thyme / You showed me / Mr. Tambourine man (acoustic) / Mr. Tambourine man (electric) / Mr. Spaceman / Eight miles high / So you want to be a rock & roll star / King of the hill / May the road rise / Fireworks / May the road rise.

– compilations, etc. –

Mar 92. (cd/c) *Columbia; (471269-2/-4) <CK/CT 47494>* **BORN TO ROCK AND ROLL** [ ] [ ]

Dec 92. (cd; McGUINN / CLARK / HILLMAN) *Edsel; (EDCD 358)* **RETURN FLYTE** [ ] [–]

Jun 93. (cd) *Edsel; (EDCD 373)* **RETURN FLIGHT VOL.2** [ ] [ ]

Feb 97. (d-cd; McGUIIN, HILLMAN & CLARK) *Strange Fruit (SFRCD 001)* **3 BYRDS LAND IN LONDON** [ ] [–]

Aug 01. (cd) *Appleseed; <(APRCD 1046)>* **TREASURES FROM THE FOLK DEN** (original mp3 recordings) [ ] [ ]

☐ David BYRNE (see under ⇒ TALKING HEADS)

☐ BYSTANDERS (see under ⇒ MAN)

The CLASH

CABARET VOLTAIRE

Formed: Sheffield, England . . . 1973 by STEPHEN MALLINDER, RICHARD H. KIRK and CHRIS WATSON, naming themselves after the experimental Parisian Dadaist performances of pre-20's France. A farcical 1975 debut gig saw them using a backing tape of a steamhammer while KIRK played clarinet; his jacket was also covered in fairy lights (!), the whole set up not going down with a rioting audience who proceeded to beat him up! Inspired by the likes of CAN and BRIAN ENO, the CABS contributed two songs (one of them, 'BAADER MEINHOF', was nearly chosen as a debut 45!) to a 1978 various artists double EP, 'A FACTORY SAMPLER', before they signed to Geoff Travis's new independent operation, 'Rough Trade'. Later that year, the trio issued their debut release, 'EXTENDED PLAY', a four track EP that included their industrial mangling of The Velvet Underground's 'HERE SHE COMES NOW'. A classic follow-up, 'NAG NAG NAG', fused electronic sound with the yobbish rush of adrenaline-fuelled punk to devastating effect. 1979 also saw the release of their debut long-player, 'MIX-UP', a pivotal experimental affair which, although marking out new territory, was a challenging listen end to end. The early years of the following decade found CABARET VOLTAIRE ploughing their own idiosyncratic furrow over the course of three studio albums (two live events were also issued), namely 'THE VOICE OF AMERICA' (1980), 'RED MECCA' (1981) and '2 X 45' (1982), before WATSON's departure left MALLINDER and KIRK as a duo. In 1983, they were sought out by Virgin off-shoot, 'Some Bizzare', their avant-garde inaccessibility now taking on a more commercial hue with 'THE CRACKDOWN', an album which nearly took them into the UK Top 30. Incorporating elements of Eastern exotica, the record was also more dancefloor friendly than anything they had recorded to date; tracks such as 'JUST FASCINATION', '24-24', 'ANIMATION' and 'WHY KILL TIME (WHEN YOU CAN KILL YOUSELF)', were lent the rhythmic expertise of SOFT CELL's DAVE BALL (later of The GRID). Ironically, the more overtly pop approach of SOFT CELL and their ilk (DEPECHE MODE, HUMAN LEAGUE and OMD) led to the more adventurous CABS being squeezed out of the market. They did, however, maintain a loyal if not massive following who stuck by them through a series of lesser mid-80's albums, 'MICRO-PHONIES' (1984), 'THE COVENANT, THE SWORD AND THE ARM OF THE LORD' (1985) and 'CODE' (1987), the latter set their first for 'Parlophone'. Since 1983, both MALLINDER and KIRK had moonlighted in various side projects, the former releasing a solo album, 'POW-WOW', the latter far more prolific in his output with 'BLACK JESUS VOICE' (1986) the pick of the bunch. The late 80's house scene, meanwhile, saw CABARET VOLTAIRE cited as a prominent influence on many of the genre's prime movers; the result was a creative renaissance of sorts which led to a remix by PETE WATERMAN (!) for the 'KEEP ON' single, while house producer, MARSHALL JEFFERSON, took controls on the comeback set, 'GROOVY, LAID BACK AND NASTY' (1990). Despite this uncharacteristic dalliance with the mainstream, the CABS slipped back into semi-obscurity with their former Belgian label, 'Les Disques Du Crepescule' releasing a handful of low profile sets, 'BODY AND SOUL' (1991), 'PERCUSSION FORCE' (1991), 'INTERNATIONAL LANGUAGE' (1993) and 'THE CONVERSATION' (1994).

Album rating: MIX-UP (*5) / THE VOICE OF AMERICA (*4) / RED MECCA (*7) / 2x45 (*7) / JOHNNY YES NO soundtrack (*3) / THE CRACKDOWN (*8) / MICRO-PHONIES (*6) / DRINKING GASOLINE (*6) / THE COVENANT, THE SWORD & THE ARM (*6) / CODE (*7) / GROOVY, LAIDBACK & NASTY (*6) / THE LIVING LEGENDS compilation (*9) / THE GOLDEN MOMENTS OF CABARET VOLTAIRE compilation (*7) / LISTEN UP WITH CABARET VOLTAIRE compilation (*7) / COLOURS (*5) / PLASTICITY (*5) / Stephen Mallinder: POW WOW (*6) / Richard H. Kirk: BLACK JESUS VOICE (*6)

STEPHEN MALLINDER – vocals, bass, electronics, percussion, trumpet, piano / **RICHARD H. KIRK** – guitar, vocals, synthesizer, bongos, piano / **CHRISTOPHER R. WATSON** – electronics, tapes

(issued cassette 25 copies LIMITED EDITION in 1976 on own label)

Rough Trade | not iss.

Nov 78. (7"ep) *(RT 003)* **EXTENDED PLAY** | | –
– Talkover / Here she comes now / Do the Mussolini – headkick / The set up.

Jun 79. (7") *(RT 018)* **"NAG NAG NAG." / IS THAT ME (FINDING SOMEONE AT THE DOOR AGAIN)?** | | –

Oct 79. (lp) *(ROUGH 4)* **MIX-UP** | | –
– Kurlian photograph / No escape / 4th shot / Heaven and Hell / Eyeless sight (live) / Photophobia / On every other street / Expect nothing / Capsules. *(re-iss. Sep90 on 'Mute' lp/cd; CABS 8/+CD)*

Dec 79. (7") *(RT 035)* **SILENT COMMAND. / The Soundtrack 'CHANCE VERSUS CAUSALITY'** | | –

— added guest **MARK TATTERSALL** – drums

Jan 80. (lp) *(ROUGH 7)* **LIVE AT THE Y.M.C.A. 27.10.79 (live)** | | –
– Untitled / On every other street / Nag nag nag / The set up / Havoc / Expect nothing / Here she comes now / No escape / Baader Meinhof. *(re-iss. Jun90 on 'Mute' lp/cd; CABS 4/+CD)*

— now with guests **JOHN CLAYTON** – percussion / **JANE** – tapes

Mar 80. (12"ep) *(RT 038)* **THREE MANTRAS** | | –
– Eastern mantra / Western mantra. *(re-iss. Jun90 on 'Mute' m-lp/cd; CABS 7/+CD)*

— with guest **HAYDN BOYES-WESTON** – drums (ex-2.3) (also on debut lp)

Jul 80. (lp) *(ROUGH 11)* **THE VOICE OF AMERICA** | | –
– The voice of America / Damage is done / Partially submerged / Kneel to the boss / Premonition / This is entertainment / If the shadows could march? / Stay out of it / Obsession / News from nowhere / Messages received. *(re-iss. Jun90 on 'Mute' lp/cd; CABS 2/+CD)*

Nov 80. (7") *(RT 060)* **SECONDS TOO LATE. / CONTROL ADDICT** | | –

Jul 81. (12"ep) *(TWI 018)* **3 CREPUSCULE TRACKS** | – | Belg. | –
– Sluggin' fer Jesus (Pt.1) / Your agent man / Sluggin' fer Jesus (Pt.2). (above released on 'Crepuscule')

— **NICK ALLDAY** – drums (ex-GRAPH) repl. HAYDN

Aug 81. (lp) *(ROUGH 27)* **RED MECCA** | | –
– Touch of evil / Sly doubt / Landslide / A thousand ways / Red mask / Split

second feling / Black mask / Spread the virus / A touch of evil (reprise). *(re-iss. Jun90 on 'Mute' lp/cd; CABS 3/+CD)*

Sep 81. (lp) *(COPY 002)* **LIVE AT THE LYCEUM (live)** [ ] [-]
– Taxi music / Seconds too late / Your agent man / Split second feeling / Sluggin' fer Jesus (Pt.1) / Kneel to the bass / Obsession / A thousand ways. *(re-iss. Sep90 on 'Mute' lp/cd; CABS 13/+CD)*

Nov 81. (7") *(RT 095)* **JAZZ THE GLASS. / BURNT TO THE GROUND** [ ] [-]

Dec 81. (12") *(RT 096)* **EDDIE'S OUT. / WALLS OF JERICHO** [ ] [-]
(limited copies contained last 7" free) (below on 'Solidarity')

Mar 82. (12"ep; by PRESSURE COMPANY) *(SOLID 1)* **LIVE IN SHEFFIELD 19th JANUARY 1982 (live)** [ ] [-]
– War of nerves / Wait & shuffle / Get out of my face / Vitrions China (paradox).

— **ALAN FISH** – drums, percussion (of HULA) repl. **ALLDAY** / guest **ERIC RANDOM** – guitar (also a solo artist)

Jun 82. (2x12"lp) *(ROUGH 42)* **2 x 45** [98] [-]
– Breathe deep / Yashar / Protection / War of nerves (T.E.S.) / Wait and shuffle / Get out of my face. *(re-iss. Sep90 on 'Mute' lp/cd; CABS 9/+CD)*

Nov 82. (lp) *(RTD 1)* **HAI! (live)** [-] German [-]
– Walls of Kyoto / 3 days monk / Yashar (version) / Over and over / Diskono / Taxi music (version). *(re-iss. Sep90 on 'Mute' lp/cd; CABS 11/+CD)*

— trimmed to a duo (**MALLINDER** + **KIRK**) when WATSON departed. Retained **ALAN FISH** and brought in **DAVE BALL** – keyboards (of SOFT CELL)

Feb 83. (12") *(TWI 020)* **FOOLS GAME (SLUGGIN' FER JESUS Pt.3). / GUT LEVEL** [-] Belg. [-]
(above released on 'Crepuscule')

Some Bizzare – Virgin / not iss.

Jul 83. (7") *(CVS 1)* **JUST FASCINATION. / EMPTY WALLS** [ ] [-]
(12") *(CVS 1-12)* – ('A'side) / The crackdown.

Aug 83. (lp/c) *(CV/TCV 1)* **THE CRACKDOWN** [31] [-]
– 24-24 / In the shadows / Talking time / Animation / Over and over / Just fascination / Why kill time (when you can kill yourself) / Haiti / Crackdown. *(free 12"w/ above + on c+cd)* – MOSCOW / BADGE OF EVIL. / DISKONO / DOUBLE VISION *(cd-iss. 1984; CDCV 1) (re-iss. Aug86 lp/c; OVED/+C 156)*

Nov 83. (lp) *(DVR 1)* **JOHNNY YESNO** (1982 video) [ ] [-]
– Taxi music / Hallucination sequence / DT's / Cold turkey / The quarry (in the wilderness) / Title sequence / Taxi music dub. *(re-iss. Sep90 on 'Mute' lp/cd; CABS 10/+CD)*
(above released on 'DoubleVision')

Dec 83. (7"/ext.12") *(CVS 2/+12)* **THE DREAM TICKET. / SAFETY ZONE** [ ] [-]

Sep 84. (7"/ext.12") *(CVS 3/+12)* **SENSORIA. / CUT THE DAMN CAMERA** [ ] [-]

Nov 84. (lp/c/cd) *(CV/TCV/CVCD 2)* **MICRO-PHONIES** [69] [-]
– Do right / The operative / Digital rasta / Spies in the wires / Theme from Earthshaker / James Brown / Slammer / Blue heat / Sensoria. *(cd+=)* – Blue heat (extended) / Sensoria (extended). *(re-iss. Sep91 on 'Virgin'; cd/c; same)*

Jan 85. (7"/12") *(CVS 4/+12)* **JAMES BROWN. / BAD SELF (part 1)** [ ] [-]

Jun 85. (2x12"/c) *(CVM/TCVM 1)* **DRINKING GASOLINE** [71] [-]
– Kino / Sleepwalking / Big funk / Ghost talk. *(re-iss. Sep91 on 'Virgin'; same)*

Sep 85. (7") *(CVS 5)* **I WANT YOU. / DRINK YOUR POISON** [ ] [-]
(12") *(CVS 5-12)* – ('A'side) / Drink your poison, C.O.M.A.

Oct 85. (lp/c/cd) *(CV/TCV/CDCV 3)* **THE COVENANT, THE SWORD AND THE ARM OF THE LORD** [57] [-]
– L21st / I want you / Hell's home / Kickback / The arm of the Lord / Warm / Golden halos / Motion rotation / Whip blow / The web. *(cd+=)* – Sleepwalking / Big funk *(re-iss. Sep91 on 'Virgin'; same)*

— guest **DEE BOYLE** – drums (of CHAAK) repl. FISH

DoubleVision / not iss.

Jun 86. (12"ep) *(DVR-DVRP 21)* **THE DRAIN TRAIN** [ ] [-]
– Shakedown (the whole thing) / Menace / Electro-motive.
(w/ free-12") – SHAKEDOWN (The Whole Thing). / SHAKEDOWN (dub).

Parlophone / Manhattan

Jul 87. (7") *(R 6157)* **DON'T ARGUE. / DON'T ARGUE (WHO'S ARGUING)** [69] [-]
(12") *(12R 6157)* – ('A'extended) / ('A'-Hate & Destroy mix).
(12") *(12RX 6157)* – ('A'dance mix) / ('A'dub).

Sep 87. (7") *(R 6166)* **HERE TO GO. / HERE TO GO (dub)** [ ] [ ]
(12") *(12R 6166)* – ('A'extended mix) / ('A'-Space dub mix).
(12") *(12RX 6166)* – ('A'-Linn drum mix) / ('A'-Eleven Eleven mix).

Oct 87. (lp/c/cd) *(PCS/TCPCS/CDPCS 7312)* <46999> **CODE** [ ] [ ]
– Don't argue / Sex, money, freaks / Thank you America / Here to go / Trouble (won't stop) / White car / No one here / Life slips by / Code. (cd+=) – Here to go (little dub) / Hey hey.

Oct 89. (7") *(RS 6227)* **HYPNOTISED (Daniel Miller mix). / ('A'-Gerald's vocal mix)** [66] [-]
(12") *(12RS 6227)* – ('A'-Fon Force mix) / ('A'-Fon Force dub) / ('A'-Daniel Miller dub mix) / ('A'-Robert Gordon mix).
(cd-s) *(CDCDR 6227)* – ('A'-Fon Force mix) / ('A'-Gerald's vocal mix).
(12") *(12RX 6227)* – (cd tracks) / ('A'-A Guy Called Gerald's music mix) / ('A'-Western Works mix).

Mar 90. (7") *(R 6250)* **KEEP ON. / KEEP ON (Les dub)** [55] [-]
(12") *(12R 6250)* – ('A'-Sweet Exorcist mix) / ('A'-Sleazy Dog mix) / ('A'-Mayday mix).
(cd-s) – ('A'-western works mix) / ('A'club mix).

Jun 90. (cd/c/lp) *(CD/TC+/PCS 7338)* <92249> **GROOVY, LAIDBACK AND NASTY** [ ] [ ]
– Searchin' / Hypnotised / Minute by minute / Runaway / Keep on (I got this feeling) / Magic / Time beats / Easy life. *(free 12"ep w/ above)* **GROOVY, LAIDBACK AND NASTY** (remixes) – Runaway / Magic / Searchin' / Rescue me (city lights) * / Easy life. *(cd+= *)*

Jul 90. (7") *(R 6261)* **EASY LIFE. / ('A'-Robert Gordon mix)** [61] [ ]
(12") *(12R 6261)* – ('A'side) / Fluid / Positive I.D.
(cd-s) *(CDR 6261)* – ('A'side) / ('A'-Jive Turkey mix) / Fluid.
(12") *(12RX 6261)* – ('A'vocal) / ('A'-Strange mix) / ('A'-Very strange mixes by Robert Gordon and Fon Force).

Crepescule / not iss.

Feb 91. (12") *(TWI 948)* **WHAT IS REAL. / ('A'-Virtual reality mix)** [ ] [-]
(cd-s+=) *(TWI 948-2)* – Legacy of a computer.

Mar 91. (lp/cd) *(TWI 944/+2)* **BODY AND SOUL** [ ] [-]
– No resistance / Shout / Happy / Decoy / Bad chemistry / Vibration / What is real / Western land. *(cd+=)* – What is real (dreamtime mix).

Jul 91. (m-lp/cd) *(TWI 951/+2)* **PERCUSSION FORCE** [ ] [-]
– Don't walk away / Keep on pushin' / Don't walk away (Robert Gordon mix) / Dynamic zone / Jazz the computer (part 1) / Keep on pushin' (version). *(cd+=)* – T.Phunk / Don't walk away (version) / Jazz the computer part 2.

Plastex / Instinct

Oct 91. (m-lp) *(EXL 001)* <93> **COLOURS** [ ] [ ]
– Colours (original style mix) / Alright / Smooth / Colours (thunder mix) / Wildlife / Colours (club mix) / Ex.

Oct 92. (d-lp/c/cd) *(EXL/+C/CD 003)* <255> **PLASTICITY** [ ] [ ]
– Low cool / Soul vine (70 billion people) / Resonator /Inside the electronic revolution / From another source / Deep time / Back to Brazilia / Neuron factory / Delmas 19 / Cooled out / Invisible generation / Soulenoid (scream at the right time). *(cd re-iss. Mar96 on 'Crepescule'; TWI 975-2)*

Jun 93. (cd) *(EXLCD 004)* <264> **INTERNATIONAL LANGUAGE** [ ] [-]
– Everything is true / Radical chic / Taxi mutant / Let it come down / Afterglow / The rest / Millenium / Belly of the beast (back in Babylon) / Other world.

Apollo-R&S / Instinct

Jul 94. (q-lp/d-cd) *(AMB 4934/+CD)* <273> **THE CONVERSATION** [ ] [ ]
– Exterminating angel (intro) / Brutal but clean / The message / Let's start / Night rider / Night rider / I think / The heat / Harmonic parallel / Project 80 (parts 1-4) / Exterminating angel (outro).

— disbanded soon after above

– compilations, others, etc. –

1981. (c) *Industrial; (IRC 35)* **74-76** [ ] [-]
(cd-iss. Jun92 on 'Grey Area-Mute'; CABS 15CD)

Feb 88. (lp/cd) *Crepuscule; (TWI 749/+2)* **8 CREPESCULE TRACKS** [-] Belgium [-]
(cd re-iss. Mar96; same)

Jul 83. (12") *Factory Benelux; (FBN 25)* **YASHAR (5.00). / YASHAR (7.20)** [-] Belgium [-]

Nov 87. (cd) *Rough Trade; (RUFCD 6001)* **THE GOLDEN MOMENTS OF CABARET VOLTAIRE** [ ] [-]
– Do the Mussolini (Head Kick) / Nag nag nag / Photophobia / Expect nothing / Seconds Too late / This is entertainment / Obsession / Sluggin for Jesus / Landslide / Red mask / Get out of my face.
(below releases on 'Mute' unless otherwise mentioned)

May 90. (cd-ep) *(CABS 1CD)* **"NAG NAG NAG." / YASHAR / YASHAR (John Robie remixes)**

Jun 90. (lp/c/cd) *(CABS 5/+C/CD)* **LISTEN UP WITH CABARET VOLTAIRE** (rare demos)

Jun 90. (d-lp/c/cd) *(CABS 6/+C/CD)* **THE LIVING LEGENDS . . . CABARET VOLTAIRE** (the singles)
– Do the Mussolini (head kick) / Talk over / Here she comes now / The set up / Nag, nag, nag / Silent command / Jazz the glass / Walls of Jericho / Seconds too late / Eddie's out / Burnt to the ground / Extract from : Chance Verses Casuality / Control addict / Is that me (finding someone at the door again).

Jun 90. (c) *(CABS 2C)* **LIVE AT THE LYCEUM / THE VOICE OF AMERICA**

Jun 90. (c) *(CABS 7C)* **THE DRAIN TRAIN / THREE MANTRAS**

Jun 90. (c) *(CABS 8C)* **MIX-UP / LIVE AT THE Y.M.C.A.**

Jun 90. (c) *(CABS 10C)* **2 x 45 / JOHNNY YESNO**

Jun 90. (c) *(CABS 11C)* **HAI! / RED MECCA**

Apr 92. (12"ep/cd-ep) *Virgin; (CVT 5)* **I WANT YOU hardcore hell) / KINO 4. / I WANT YOU (808 heaven mix) / KINO 5**
– (Altern 8 remixes / Western re-works '92)

May 92. (d-lp/cd)(c) *Virgin; (CV/+CD 4)(TCV 4)* **TECHNOLOGY** (remixes late 70's & early 80's)

Oct 00. (cd) *Burning Airlines; (<PILOT 039>)* **RADIATION (BBC SESSIONS)**
(lp-iss.Sep01 on 'Get Back'; GET 82)

Apr 01. (cd) *E.M.I.; (532573-2)* **REMIXED**

Nov 01. (3xcd-box) *Virgin; (CVBOX 1)* **CONFORM TO DEFORM – THE VIRGIN YEARS**

Dec 01. (cd) *Virgin; (CVCD 5) / Superfecto; <1>* **THE ORIGINAL SOUND OF SHEFFIELD – THE BEST OF THE VIRGIN/EMI YEARS**

Oct 02. (12") *Nova Mute; (12NOMU 103)* **NAG NAG NAG. / NAG NAG NAG (R.H. Kirk 4 remix)**
(12") *(L12NOMU 103)* – ('A'-Tiga & Zyntherius radio version) / ('A'Akufen's karaoke slam mix).
(cd-s) *(CDNOMU 103)* – (all of the above).

Oct 02. (cd) *The Grey Area; (CABS 16CD) / Mute; <9190>* **THE ORIGINAL SOUND OF SHEFFIELD – THE BEST OF CABARET VOLTAIRE 1978-1982**
– Do the Mussolini (headkick) / Set up / Baader Meinhof / Nag nag nag / Silent command / No escape / This is entertainment /Obsession / Seconds too late / Split second feeling / Spread the virus / Yashar / Wait and shuffle / Loosen the clamp.

Jan 03. (cd) *Cherry Red; (<CDMRED 220>)* **LIVE AT THE HACIENDA 1983-1986 (live)** Feb03

Jun 03. (3xcd-box) *The Grey Area; (CABS 17CD) / Mute; <9211>* **METHODOLOGY '74/'78. ATTIC TAPES!**

☐ CACTUS (see under ⇒ VANILLA FUDGE)

J.J. CALE

Born: JEAN-JACQUES CALE, 5 Dec'38, Oklahoma, U.S.A. After a childhood spent immersing himself in the blues and rockabilly, CALE's first foray into the music business was as a country player in Nashville. When this came to little, CALE followed the bright lights and Tulsa musical compadres RUSSELL BRIDGES (aka LEON RUSSELL), CARL RADLE (later of DEREK & THE DOMINOES) and JIMMY KARSTEIN to L.A. where he worked as an engineer for 'Liberty' records. Around this time he was also performing solo in L.A. clubs, releasing a one-off single for the label, 'OUTSIDE LOOKING IN' in summer 66. CALE's most sought after artefact from this period, however, is his pseudo-psychedelic project, 'A TRIP DOWN SUNSET STRIP', recorded under the moniker of The LEATHERCOATED MINDS. One track left over from this session was eventually revamped and released as 'AFTER MIDNIGHT', a slow burning piano blues groove which was pivotal in getting CALE's career off the ground. Subsequently covered by ERIC CLAPTON (who had heard the track through DELANEY & BONNIE) in 1970, the single's success (and a little encouragement from producer Audie Ashworth) spurred on CALE (now eking out a living back in TULSA after another ill-fated period in Nashville) to write a whole album's worth of songs. The result was 'NATURALLY' (1972), a back porch blend of country, blues, rockabilly and R&B which would serve the singer well over more than 30 years as a recording artist. Released on LEON RUSSELL's 'Shelter' records, the set included a re-recorded 'AFTER MIDNIGHT' as well as such CALE staples as 'CALL ME THE BREEZE' (later covered by LYNYRD SKYNYRD), 'MAGNOLIA' (later covered by POCO and JOSE FELICIANO) and the languorous 'CRAZY MAMA' (CALE's US Top 30 hit). The record also introduced CALE's trademark vocal style, a tersely minimalist, often barely audible drawl which complemented the unadorned music perfectly; interestingly, CALE's insistence that his voice be mixed down was drawn from his conviction that this would draw the listener in. Maybe there was something in this, most of CALE's albums pulsing with a subtly hypnotic power that was hard to resist. A follow-up set, 'REALLY' (1973), was more upbeat, recorded in various studios including Muscle Shoals where CALE cut the moody, horn-embellished R&B of 'LIES'. 'OKIE' (1974) was a more organic affair, with several of the tracks recorded at CALE's house. The singer subseqently moved to Nashville where he and ASHWORTH set up a studio in the producer's house, recording most of the material which would make up the excellent 'TROUBADOUR' (1976) album. It became his first album to chart in the UK (Top 60) while the brassy swing of 'HEY BABY' enjoyed a brief tenure in the US Hot 100. The set also included the brooding road fever of 'TRAVELIN' LIGHT' (arguably one of CALE's finest moments, positively frenetic against the bulk of his work!) and his most famous track, 'COCAINE', covered, of course, to much success by ERIC CLAPTON. Yet again, CALE could've taken the bit between his teeth and made a shot at the big time on the back of the single's success; instead, he chose to spend the proceeds on building a studio in his Nashville home. '5' (1979) became CALE's highest charting album to date, making the UK Top 40, though you could hardly call this reticent studiophile a pop star. Shunning most publicity at any opportunity, it's just as well that it often took an interpretation by another artist for CALE's songs to gain radio airplay. Nevertheless, in the early 80's, he signed a major label deal with 'Phonogram International', releasing 'GRASSHOPPER' (1982) and '#8' (1983); though they both sold fairly well in Britain, CALE was apparently unhappy and asked to be released from his contract. He then retired from the music business for the bulk of the 80's and his hardly prolific recording rate slowed to nought. CALE eventually returned at the end of the decade with 'TRAVEL-LOG', courtesy of a new deal with 'Silvertone' (who'd also taken on JOHN LEE HOOKER). The mid-90's saw him again throw in his lot with a major label, this time 'Virgin', who released 'CLOSER TO YOU' in summer '94. 'Phonogram', meanwhile, issued a long overdue overview of CALE's career in 1997; entitled 'ANYWAY THE WIND BLOWS', the record is worth picking up for the previously unissued tracks alone, especially the neon-lit desert psych-out (no, seriously!) of 'DURANGO'. • **Trivia:** MARK KNOPFLER and RICHARD THOMPSON guested on his '#8' album in 1983.

Album rating: NATURALLY (*7) / REALLY (*5) / OKIE (*5) / TROUBADOUR (*7) / 5 (*4) / SHADES (*4) / GRASSHOPPER (*4) / #8 (*4) TRAVEL-LOG (*7) / NUMBER 10 (*6) / CLOSER TO YOU (*4) / GUITAR MAN (*5) / ANYWAY THE WIND BLOWS – THE ANTHOLOGY compilation (*8)

J.J. CALE – vocals, guitar, piano; with loads of session musicians (too numerous to mention)

Liberty Liberty

Jun 66. (7") <(LIB 55881)> **OUTSIDE LOOKIN' IN. / IN OUR TIME** [ ] Apr66 [ ]
Dec 66. (7") <LIB 55931> **AFTER MIDNIGHT. / SLOW MOTION** [–] [ ]

— In 1967, CALE and LEON RUSSELL formed The LEATHERCOATED MINDS who issued one lp, 'A TRIP DOWN SUNSET STRIP' for 'Fontana'; (STL 5412)

A&M Shelter

Oct 71. (7") *<7306>* **CRAZY MAMA. / MAGNOLIA** [–] [ ]
Jan 72. (lp) *(AMLS 68105) <8098>* **NATURALLY** [ ] [51]
– Call me the breeze / Call the doctor / Don't go to strangers / Woman I love / Magnolia / Clyde / Crazy mama / Nowhere to run / After midnight / River runs deep / Bringing it back / Crying eyes. *(re-iss. Apr76 on 'Island'; ISA 5003) (re-iss. Aug83 on 'Mercury' lp/c; PRICE/PRIMC 25) (cd-iss. Jan87 on 'Mercury'; 830 042-2) (lp re-iss/Dec98 on 'Vivante'; VPLP 002)*
Jan 72. (7") *<7314>* **CRAZY MAMA. / DON'T GO TO STRANGERS** [–] [22]
Aug 72. (7") *(AMS 7022) <7321>* **AFTER MIDNIGHT. / CRAZY MAMA** [ ] May72 [42]
Jan 73. (7") *(AMS 7042) <7326>* **LIES. / RIDING HOME** [ ] Oct72 [42]
Jan 73. (lp) *(AMLS 68157) <8912>* **REALLY** [ ] Dec72 [92]
– Lies / Everything will be alright / I'll kiss the world goodbye / Changes / Right down here / If you're ever in Oklahoma / Ridin' home / Going down / Soulin' / Playin' in the streets / Mo Jo / Louisiana women. *(re-iss. Apr76 on 'Island'; ISA 5002) (re-iss. Aug83 on 'Mercury' lp/c; PRICE/PRIMC 26) (cd-iss. May90 & Feb03 on 'Mercury'; 810 314-2)*
May 73. (7") *<7332>* **GOING DOWN. / LOISIANA WOMEN** [–] [ ]
Jun 74. (7") *(AMS 7018)* **CAJUN MOON. / STARBOUND** [ ] [–]
Jun 74. (lp) *(AMLS 68261) <2107>* **OKIE** [ ] [ ]
– Crying / I'll be there (if you ever want me) / Everlovin' woman / Cajun moon / I'd like to love you baby / Starbound / Rock and roll records / The old man and me / Everlovin' woman / Cajun Moon / I'd like to love you baby / Anyway the wind blows / Precious memories / Okie / I got the same old blues. *(re-iss. Apr76 on 'Island'; ISA 5004) (re-iss. Aug83 on 'Mercury' lp/c; PRICE/PRIMC 34) (cd-iss. May90 on 'Mercury'; 842 102-2)*
Aug 74. (7") *<40290>* **I'LL BE THERE (IF YOU EVER WANT ME). / PRECIOUS MEMORIES** [–] [ ]
Mar 75. (7") *<40366>* **I GOT THE SAME OLD BLUES. / ROCK AND ROLL RECORDS** [–] [ ]

Island Shelter

Sep 76. (lp) *(ISA 5011) <52002>* **TROUBADOUR** [53] [84]
– Hey baby / Travelin' light / You got something / Ride me high / Hold on / Cocaine / I'm a gypsy man / The woman that got away / Super blue / Let me do it to you / Cherry / You got me on so bad. *(re-iss. Aug83 on 'Mercury' lp/c; PRICE/PRIMC 35) (cd-iss. Oct83 on 'Mercury'; 800 001-2)*
Oct 76. (7") *(WIP 6339)* **HEY BABY. / MAGNOLIA** [ ] [–]
Dec 76. (7") *<62002>* **HEY BABY. / COCAINE** [–] [96]
Jan 77. (7") *(WIP 6366)* **TRAVELIN' LIGHT. / COCAINE** [ ] [–]
Feb 78. (7") *(WIP 6434)* **I'M A GYPSY MAN. / CHERRY** [ ] [–]

Island M.C.A.

Jun 79. (7") *(WIP 6479)* **KATY KOOL LADY. / JUAREZ BLUES** [ ] [–]
Jul 79. (lp) *(ISA 5018) <3163>* **5** [40] [ ]
– Thirteen days / Boilin' point / I'll make love to you anytime / Don't cry sister / Too much for me / A sensitive kind / Friday / Lou-Easy-Ann / Let's go to Tahiti / Katy kool lady / Fate of a fool / Mona. *(with free 7"; JJ-1)* – KATY KOOL LADY. / JUAN AND MARIA JUAREZ BLUES *(re-iss. May90; 810 313-2)*
Aug 79. (7") *(WIP 6521)* **KATY KOOL LADY. / JUAN AND MARIA JUAREZ BLUES** [ ] [–]
Feb 81. (lp) *(ISA 5021) <5158>* **SHADES** [44] [ ]
– Carry on / Deep dark dungeon / Wish I had not said that / Pack my jack / If you leave her / Mama don't / Runaround / What do you expect / Love has been gone / Cloudy day. *(cd-iss. Oct83 on 'Mercury'; 800 105-2) (re-iss. May84 on 'Mercury' lp/c; PRICE/PRIMC 65)*
Feb 81. (7") *<51095>* **CARRY ON. / DEEP DARK DUNGEON** [–] [ ]
Mar 81. (7") *(WIP 6696)* **CARRY ON. / CLOUDY DAY** [ ] [–]
May 81. (7") *(WIP 6697)* **MAMA DON'T. / WHAT DO YOU EXPECT** [ ] [–]

Island Mercury

Jan 82. (7") *<76145>* **DEVIL IN DISGUISE. / DRIFTER'S WIFE** [–] [ ]
Mar 82. (lp/c) *(ISA 5022) <SRM1 4038>* **GRASSHOPPER** [36] [ ]
– City girls / Devil in disguise / One step ahead of the blues / You keep me hangin' on / Downtown L.A. / Can't live here / Grasshopper / Drifters wife / Don't wait / A thing going on / Nobody but you / Mississippi river / Does your mama like to reggae / Dr.Jive. *(cd-iss. Oct83 on 'Mercury'; 800 038-2) (re-iss. Nov84 on 'Mercury' lp/c; PRICE/PRIMC 74)*
Mar 82. (7") *(WIP 6775)* **CITY GIRLS. / ONE STEP AHEAD OF THE BLUES** [ ] [–]

Mercury Mercury

Sep 83. (lp/c) *(MERL/+C 22) <811 152>* **#8** [47] [ ]
– Money talks / Losers / Hard times / Reality / Takin' care of business / People lie / Unemployment / Trouble in the city / Teardrops in my tequila / Livin' here too. *(cd-iss. 1984; 811 152-2)*
Sep 83. (7") *(MER 146)* **TEARDROPS IN MY TEQUILA. / AFTER MIDNIGHT** [ ] [–]
(12"+=) *(MERX 146)* – Cocaine.
Jun 84. (lp/c) *(814 401-1/-4)* **LA FEMME DE MON POTE** [–] French [–]
– Bringing it back / City girls / Mons (5) / Right down here / The woman that got away / Ride me high / Starbound (okie) / You keep me hangin' on / Super blue / Magnolia.
(above album was Soundtrack to French film MY BEST FRIEND'S GIRL)

— CALE retired from music business, writing only score for German film 50/50 around mid-1986. Below album took 5 years to record using backing band **TIM DRUMMOND + DOUG BELL** – bass / **JIM KARSTEIN** – drums, percussion / **JIM KELTNER** – drums, percussion, organ / **CHRISTINE LAKELAND** – guitar, organ, vocals / **SPOONER OLDHAM** – keyboards / **JAY MITTHAUER** – drums guests on * HOYT AXTON + JAMES BURTON

Silvertone Silvertone

Oct 89. (7") *(ORE 12)* **SHANGHAID. / ARTIFICIAL PARADISE** [ ] [–]
(cd-s+=) *(ORE 12CD)* – Hang ups.
Oct 89. (lp/c/cd) *(ORE LP/C/CD 507) <1306>* **TRAVEL-LOG** [ ] Mar90 [ ]
– Shanghaid / Hold on baby / No time / Lady luck / Disadvantage / Lean on me / End of the line / New Orleans / Tijuana / That kind of thing / Who's talking / Change your mind / Humdinger / River boat song. *(re-iss. Apr94 cd/c; same)*
Aug 92. (lp/c/cd) *(ORE/+C/CD 523) <41586>* **NUMBER 10** [58] Nov92 [ ]
– Lonesome train / Digital blues / Feeling in love / Artificial paradise / Passion / Take out some insurance / Jailer / Low rider / Traces / She's in love / Shady grove / Roll on mama. *(re-iss. Apr95 cd/c; same))*
Aug 92. (7") **LONESOME TRAIN. / LOW RIDER** [ ] [ ]
(cd-s+=) – Passion.

— During this period, he produced JOHN PAUL HAMMOND's albums 'Got Love If You Want It' and 'Trouble No More'.

Virgin Virgin

Jun 94. (cd/c) *(CDV/TCV 2746) <39610>* **CLOSER TO YOU** [ ] [ ]
– Long way home / Sho-biz blues / Slower baby / Devil's nurse / Like you used to / Borrowed time / Rose in the garden / Brown dirt / Hard love / Ain't love funny / Closer to you / Steve's song.
Apr 96. (cd) *(CDVIR 48) <41480>* **GUITAR MAN** [ ] [ ]
– Death in the wilderness / It's hard to tell / Days go by / Low down / This town / Guitar man / If I had a rocket / Perfect woman / Old Blue / The doctor told me / Miss of St. Louie / Nobody knows.

– compilations, etc. –

May 77. (7") *Island; (WIP 6393)* **AFTER MIDNIGHT. / BRINGING IT BACK** [ ] [–]
Jun 84. (lp/c)(cd) *Mercury; (MERL/+C 42)(818 633-2)* **SPECIAL EDITION** [ ] [–]
– Cocaine / Don't wait / Magnolia / Devil in disguise / A sensitive kind / Carry on / After midnight / Money talks / Call me the breeze / Lies / City girls / Cajun moon / Don't cry sister / Crazy mama.
May 88. (d-lp) *Mercury; (830 179-1)* **NATURALLY / OKIE** [ ] [–]
Jul 88. (lp/c) *Knight; (KNLP/KNMC 10006)* **NIGHTRIDING** [ ] [–]
May 97. (cd) *Universal; (E 534754-2)* **THE VERY BEST OF J.J. CALE** [ ] [–]
Jun 97. (d-cd) *Mercury; <(532901-2)>* **ANYWAY THE WIND BLOWS: THE ANTHOLOGY** [ ] [ ]
– Call me the breeze / Crazy mama / Magnolia / After midnight / Lies / Changes / If you're ever in Oklahoma / Midnight in Memphis / Cajun moon / Rock & roll records / Anyway the wind blows / Crying / Everlovin' woman / I got the same old blues / Woke up this morning / Cocaine / The woman that got away / Ride me high / Hey baby / Durangoc (live) / I'll make love to you anytime / Don't cry sister / Thirteen days / Things ain't simple (live) / Sensitive kind / Carry on / Runaround (live) / Mama don't (live) / City girls (live) / Devil in disguise / You keep me hangin' on / Downtown L.A. / A thing going on / Don't wait / Wish I had me a dollar (live) / Money talks / Hard times / People lie / Unemployment / Trouble in the city / Santa Cruz / Shanghaid / Change your mind / New

Orleans / Humdinger / Lonesome train / Jailer / Artificial paradise / Long way home / Closer to you.

Jan 00. (cd) *Universal; (E 542227-2)* **MASTERS COLLECTION** [ ] [–]

May 01. (cd) *Virgin; (CDVIR 1390) / Narada; <5064-2>* **J.J. CALE LIVE (live 1990-1996)** [ ] [ ]

Jul 02. (cd) *Mercury; <586761>* **THE BEST OF J.J. CALE – THE MILLENNIUM COLLECTION** [–] [ ]

John CALE

Born: 9 Mar'42, Garnant, Carmarthen, Wales. He studied classical piano and later viola at London's Guildhall School Of Music. As an 8 year old schoolboy prodigy, he'd already composed music for the BBC. In 1963, he moved to New York on a scholarship, and under JOHN CAGE and LaMONTE YOUNG's tuition, he experimented with avant-garde music. In 1965, he met LOU REED, and formed the legendary VELVET UNDERGROUND, CALE's wailing viola and white noise experimentation meshing with REED's pop sensibilities and dark lyrics to create their distinctive sound. After being fired by the band in 1968, he went solo, releasing a couple of albums for 'Columbia'. His debut in 1970 'VINTAGE VIOLENCE', saw him exhibiting a more traditional side to his enigmatic persona, with gentle folky songs. A collaboration entitled 'CHURCH OF ANTHRAX', with minimalist composer TERRY RILEY, followed in 1971. CALE continued the trend towards his baroque'n'roll roots with 'ACADEMY OF PERIL', before returning once more to the songwriter format of his first album. With LITTLE FEAT members LOWELL GEORGE and RICHIE HAYWARD among his backing band, he cut the classic 'PARIS 1919', which infused his melancholic songwriting with a disturbing unease. This was the template for much of CALE's 70's output with 1974's 'FEAR' also introducing a more aggressive element. 'HELEN OF TROY' (1975), featured a version of 'HEARTBREAK HOTEL' guaranteed to send a shiver up anyone's spine, although the album was generally disappointing overall. In 1976, he cemented his reputation by producing the legendary PATTI SMITH album, 'HORSES', having previously worked on the classic blast of primal noise that was THE STOOGES first album. His career went into a bit of a slump in the latter half of the 70's, and after an infamous incident in which he allegedly beheaded a chicken onstage (!), he had a brief dalliance with the New York punk scene. He regained his footing with 1982's 'MUSIC FOR A NEW SOCIETY', an intelligent, minimalistic affair. The mid-80's saw him sign to British label 'Beggars Banquet', and release the more mainstream 'ARTIFICIAL INTELLIGENCE'. 'WORDS FOR THE DYING', released in 1989, was a return to the classical field which included a collaboration with BRIAN ENO. They also teamed up on the sparse 'WRONG WAY UP' from 1990. 'SONGS FOR DRELLA' (a tribute to mentor ANDY WARHOL), saw CALE hook up once more with his old sparring partner LOU REED, together producing an album that outshone CALE's more recent solo outings. He and REED re-united with the others in VELVET UNDERGROUND for live work which resulted in the comeback album 'LIVE MCMXCIII'. A year later, another collaboration, this time with BOB NEUWIRTH, was largly ignored by the public. Throughout his career, he also sessioned for others, including ENO, and produced MODERN LOVERS (JONATHAN RICHMAN), SQUEEZE, etc. CALE's first record of the new millennium, 'HOBOSAPIENS' (2003), was also his most adventurous for more than a decade. With ENO returning the guest favours alongside a host of hired hands, the album was alive with spontaneous creativity and freewheeling imagination. Embracing contemporary musical trends and technology, CALE gave free reign to a muse that only seems to have become even more literate, erudite and waggish with age.

Album rating: VINTAGE VIOLENCE (*5) / CHURCH OF ANTHRAX with Terry Riley (*5) / THE ACADEMY IN PERIL (*5) / PARIS 1919 (*8) / FEAR (*7) / SLOW DAZZLE (*6) / HELEN OF TROY (*5) / GUTS compilation (*7) / SABOTAGE – LIVE (*4) / HONI SOIT (*4) / MUSIC FOR A NEW SOCIETY (*6) / CARIBBEAN SUNSET (*4) / COMES ALIVE (*4) / ARTIFICIAL INTELLIGENCE (*5) / WORDS FOR THE DYING (*6) / SONGS FOR DRELLA with Lou Reed (*7) / WRONG WAY UP with Eno (*7) / EVEN COWGIRLS GET THE BLUES live collection (*5) / FRAGMENTS OF A RAINY SEASON (*7) / LAST DAYS ON EARTH with Bob Neuwirth (*5) / SEDUCING DOWN THE DOOR a collection (*7) / PARIS S'EVEILLE ... (*5) / 23 SOLO PIECES FOR LA NAISSANCE DE L'AMOUR (*5) / THE ISLAND YEARS compilation (*7) / WALKING ON LOCUSTS (*4) / EAT/KISS: MUSIC FOR THE FILMS OF ANDY WARHOL (*5) / NICO (*5) / HOBOSAPIENS (*8)

JOHN CALE – vocals, viola, keyboards, bass, guitar (with session people)

C.B.S. Columbia

Nov 70. (7") *<45154>* **FAIRWEATHER FRIEND. / CLEO** [–] [ ]

Dec 70. (lp) *(64256) <CS 1037>* **VINTAGE VIOLENCE** [ ] [ ]
– Hello there / Gideon's bible / Adelaide / Big white cloud / Cleo / Please / Charlemange / Bring it on up / Amsterdam / Ghost story / Fairweather friend. *(re-iss. May87 on 'Edsel' lp/cd; ED/+CD 230) (cd-iss. Sep94 on 'Columbia'; 477356-2) (<cd re-iss. Jul03 on 'Legacy'+=; 499945-2>)* – Fairweather friend (alt.) / Wall.

Jan 71. (7") *<45266>* **GIDEON'S BIBLE. / BIG WHITE CLOUD** [–] [ ]

Apr 71. (lp; JOHN CALE & TERRY RILEY) *(64259) <CS 30131>* **CHURCH OF ANTHRAX** [ ] [ ]
– Church of anthrax / The hall of mirrors in the palace at Versailles / The soul of Patrick Lee / Ides of March / The protege. *(cd-iss. Oct93 on 'Sony Europe';) (cd re-iss. Mar96 on 'Columbia'; 476640-2)*

Reprise Reprise

Apr 72. (lp) *(K 44212) <MS 2079>* **ACADEMY IN PERIL** [ ] [ ]
– The philosopher / Brahms / Legs Larry at Television Centre / Academy in peril / Intro: days of steam / 3 orchestral pieces: (a) Faust, (b) The balance, (c) Capt. Morgan's lament / King Harry / John Milton. *(re-iss. Apr86 on 'Edsel'; XED 182) (cd-iss. Apr89; EDCD 182) (cd-iss. Oct93 on 'Warners'; 7599 26930-2)*

May 72. (7") *<1108>* **DAYS OF STEAM. / LEGS LARRY AT TELEVISION CENTER** [–] [ ]

Mar 73. (lp) *(K 44239) <MS 2131>* **PARIS 1919** [ ] [ ]
– Child's Christmas in Wales / Hanky panky nohow / The endless plain of fortune / Andalucia / Macbeth / Paris 1919 / Graham Greene / Half past France / Antartica starts here. *(cd-iss. Oct93 on 'Warners'; 7599 25926-2)*

— Around this time he contributed to album 'JUNE 1st, 1974' on 'Island' with others ENO, NICO, KEVIN AYERS. *(ILPS 9291)*

— now with **ENO** – synth / **PHIL MANZANERA** – guitar / **ARCHIE LEGGAT** – bass / **FRED SMITH** – drums guest on below 'A'side **JUDY NYLON** – vocals

Island A&M

Jul 74. (7") *(WIP 6202)* **THE MAN WHO COULDN'T AFFORD TO ORGY. / SYLVIA SAID** [ ] [–]

Sep 74. (lp) *(ILPS 9301)* **FEAR** [ ] [–]
– Fear is a man's best friend / Buffalo ballet / Barracuda / Emily / Ship of fools / Gun / The man who couldn't afford to orgy / You know more than I know / Momamma scuba. *(re-iss. Aug91 cd)(c; IMCD 140)(ICM 9301)*

— with **CHRIS SPEDDING** + **PHIL MANZANERA** – guitar / **PAT DONALDSON** – bass / **TIMI DONALD** + **GERRY CONWAY** – drums / **ENO** – synthesizer / **CHRIS THOMAS** – violin, electric piano

Apr 75. (lp) *(ILPS 9317)* **SLOW DAZZLE** [ ] [–]
– Mr. Wilson / Taking it all away / Dirty ass rock'n'roll / Darling I need you / Rollaroll / Heartbreak hotel / Ski patrol / I'm not the loving kind / Guts / The jeweller. *(cd-iss. Jun88; CID 9317) (re-iss. cd Aug94; IMCD 202) (cd re-iss. Jun03; 846069-2)*

— **PHIL COLLINS** – drums; repl. CONWAY, MANZANERA + THOMAS.

Nov 75. (lp) *(ILPS 9350)* **HELEN OF TROY** [ ] [–]
– My Maria / Helen of Troy / China sea / Engine / Save us / Cable Hogue / I keep a close watch / Pablo Picasso / Leaving it up to you * / Baby what you want me to do? / Sudden death. *(some copies repl.* by)* – Coral Moon'. *(cd-iss. Apr94; IMCD 177)*

Feb 77. (lp) *(ILPS 9459)* **GUTS** (compilation) [ ] [–]
– Guts / Mary Lou / Helen of Troy / Pablo Picasso / Leaving it up to you /

Fear is a man's best friend / Gun / Dirty ass rock 'n' roll / Heartbreak hotel. *(cd-iss. Aug94; IMCD 203)*

— with **RITCHIE FLIEGLER** – lead guitar / **BRUCE BRODY** – mogg synthesizer / **JIMMY BAIN** – bass / **KEVIN CURRIE** – drums

Illegal / not iss.

Sep 77. (7"ep) *(ILL 003)* **ANIMAL JUSTICE** [ ] [–]
– Chicken shit / Memphis / Hedda Gabbler.

— with **MARK AARON** – guitar / **JOE BIDWELL** – keyboards / **GEORGE SCOTT** – bass / **DOUG BROWN** – drums / **DEERFRANCE** – vocals

not iss. / Spy

Dec 79. (lp) *<SP 004>* **SABOTAGE (live)** [–] [ ]
– Mercenaries (ready for war) / Baby you know / Evidence / Dr.Mudd / Walkin' the dog / Captain Hook / Only time will tell / Sabotage / Chorale. *(UK cd-iss. Apr01 on 'Doesel Motor'+=; MOTORCD 1002)* – Chickenshift / Memphis / Hedda Gabler / Rosegarden full of sores.

not iss. / I.R.S.

1980. (7") *<9008>* **MERCENARIES (READY FOR WAR). / ROSEGARDEN FUNERAL OF SORES** [–] [ ]

— with **STURGIS NIKIDES** – guitar, vocals / **JIM GOODWIN** – keyboards, synth. / **PETER MUNY** – bass / **ROBERT MEDECI** – drums

A&M / A&M

Mar 81. (lp) *(AMLH 64849)* **HONI SOIT** [ ] [ ]
– Dead or alive / Strange times in Casablanca / Fighter pilot / Wilson Joliet / Streets of Laredo / Honi soit (la premiere Lecon de Francaise) / Riverbank / Russian roulette / Magic & lies. *(cd-iss. Jul94; CDMID 1936)*

Apr 81. (7") *(AMS 8130)* **DEAD OR ALIVE. / HONI SOIT** [ ] [ ]

— now w/ **ALAN LANIER** – keyboards / **D. J. YOUNG** – guitar / **DAVID LICHTENSTEIN** – drums / **JOHN WONDERLING** / **MIKE McCLINTOCK** / **ROBERT ELK**

Ze-Island / Passport

Aug 82. (lp/c) *(ILPS/ICT 7019) <PB 6019>* **MUSIC FOR A NEW SOCIETY** [ ] [ ]
– Taking your life in your hands / Thoughtless kind / Sanities / If you were still around / Close watch / Mama's song / Broken bird / Chinese envoy / Changes made / Damn life / Rise, Sam and Rimsky Korsakov. *(cd-iss. Mar94 on 'Yellow Moon'; YMCD 003)*

Apr 83. (7") *(IS 113)* **I KEEP A CLOSE WATCH. / CLOSE WATCH (instrumental)** [ ] [ ]

— **ANDY HEERMANS** – bass, vocals repl. LANIER

Ze-Island / Ze-Island

Jun 83. (lp/c) *(<ILPS/ICT 7024>)* **CARIBBEAN SUNSET** [ ] [ ]
– Hungry for love / Experiment number 1 / Model Beirut recital / Caribbean sunset / Praetorian underground / Magazines / Where there's a will / The hunt / Villa Albani.

Aug 84. (7") *(IS 197)* **OOH LA LA. / MAGAZINES** [ ] [–]

Sep 84. (lp/c) *(ILPS/ICT 7026) <8402>* **JOHN CALE COMES ALIVE (live)** [ ] [ ]
– Ooh la la / Evidence / Dead or alive / Chinese envoy / Leaving it up to you / Dr. Mudd / Waiting for the man / Heartbreak hotel / Fear / Never give up on you.

— with **DAVID YOUNG** – guitar / **JAMES YOUNG** – keyboards / **GRAHAM DOWDALL** – percussion

Beggars Banquet / P.V.C.

Jul 85. (7"/12") *(BEG 145/+T)* **DYING ON THE VINE. / EVERYTIME THE DOGS BARK** [ ] [–]

Nov 85. (lp/c) *(BEG A/C 68) <PVC 8947>* **ARTIFICIAL INTELLIGENCE** [ ] [ ]
– Everytime the dogs bark / Dying on the vine / The sleeper / Vigilante lover / Chinese takeaway (Hong Kong 1997) (medley) / Song of the valley / Fade away tomorrow / Black rose / Satellite walk. *(re-iss. Jan89 on 'Lowdown-Beggars Banquet' lp/c; BBL/+C 68) (cd-iss. Mar96; BBL 68CD)*

Nov 85. (12"m) *(BEG 153T)* **SATELLITE WALK. / DYING ON THE VINE / CRASH COURSE IN HARMONICS** [ ] [–]

— now w/ **BRIAN ENO** – synthesizers, keyboards / **NEIL CATCHPOLE** – viola, violin / choir

Land / Warners

Oct 89. (lp/c/cd) *(LAND/+C/CD 009) <26024>* **WORDS FOR THE DYING** [ ] [ ]
– The Falkland suite:- Introduction-There was a saviour – Interlude 1 / On a wedding anniversary – Interlude II – Lie still, sleep becalmed – Do not go gentle into that good night / Songs without words 1 & 2 / The soul of Carmen Miranda. *(re-iss. cd Oct95 & Aug99 on 'All Saints'; ASCD 009)*

— Apr'90, CALE & Lou REED⇒, collaborated on Andy Warhol tribute album SONGS FOR DRELLA. On 'Warners' records lp/c//cd *WX 345/+C //7599 26140-2*. It was CALE's first excursion into the Top 30.

— Oct'90, he teamed up with ENO on the album 'WRONG WAY UP' on 'Land'

Delabel / not iss.

Nov 91. (cd) **PARIS S'EVEILLE, SUIVI D'AUTRES COMPOSITIONS** [–] France [–]
– Paris S'eveille, suivi d'autres / Sanctus (four etudes for electronic orchestra) / Animals at night / The cowboy laughs at round-up / Primary motive 1) Factory speech, 2) Strategy session, 3) Closing titles / Antartica starts here / Booker T. (by VELVET UNDERGROUND) *(UK-iss.Mar93 on 'Crepuscule'; TWI 952-2) (re-iss. Nov95 on 'Yellow Moon'; YMCD 007)*

Crepuscule / not iss.

Nov 93. (cd) *(TWI 9542)* **23 SOLO PIECES FOR LA NAISSANCE DE L'AMOUR** [ ] [–]
– La naissance de l'amour / If you love me no more / And if I love you still / Judith / Converging themes / Opposites attract / I will do it, I will keep it / Keep it to yourself / Walk towards the sea / Unquiet heart / Waking up to love / Mysterious relief / Never been so hapy / Beyond expectations / Conversations in the garden / La naissance de l'amour II / Secret dialogue / Roma / On the dark side / La naissance de l'amour III / Eye to eye / Maria's car crash and hotel rooms / La naissance de l'amour IV. *(re-iss. Nov95 on 'Yellow Moon'; YMCD 007)*

M.C.A. / M.C.A.

May 94. (cd; JOHN CALE / BOB NEUWIRTH) *(11037)* **LAST DAY ON EARTH (soundtrack)** [ ] [ ]
– Overture- a) A tourist, b) A contract, c) A prisoner / Cafe Shabu / Pastoral angst / Who's in charge? / Short of time / Angel of death / Paradise Nevada / Old China / Ocean life / Instrumental / Modern world / Streets come alive / Secrets / Maps of the world / Broken hearts / The high and the mighty road.

Hannibal / Hannibal

Sep 96. (cd) *(<HNCD 1395>)* **WALKING ON LOCUSTS** [ ] [ ]
– Dancing undercover / Set me free / So what / Crazy Egypt / So much for love / Tell me why / Indistinct notion of cool / Secret corrida / Circus / Gatorville and points east / Some friends / Entre nous.

Jun 97. (cd) *(<HNCD 1407>)* **EAT / KISS – MUSIC FOR THE FILMS OF ANDY WARHOL** [ ] [ ]
– KISS:- Infinite guitar, quartet / Frozen warning, Jimmy, metal-violin solo – Daid Tiye (backing vocal) / B.J., quartet, Moe / Violin solo – Todd, Tiye, quartet / Harpsichord, infinite guitar / Quartet, Moe – Harpsichord, Tiye – percussion / Quartet, cello solo – Dawn, harpsichord / B.J., quartet, electric piano / B.J., quartet, electric piano / Quartet solo / Solo Tiye, strings // EAT:- B.J., 12-string guitar intro – David / Reading from 'Melanethon' (Swedenborg) / Todd solo, 12-string, Moe / Piano, B.J.

Erato / Erato

Nov 98. (cd; with ED WUBBE / ICE NINE) *(<3984 22122-2>)* **NICO** [ ] [ ]
– intro / New York underground / Night club theme / Modelling / Out of China / Death camp / Ari sleepy / Iceberg / Jim / Iceberg / Espana / Nibelungen.

E.M.I. / E.M.I.

May 03. (cd-ep) *(CDEM 621)* **5 TRACKS** [ ] [–]
– Verses / Waiting for blonde / Chums of dumpty / E is missing / Wilderness approaching.

Oct 03. (cd) *<(591711-2)>* **HOBOSAPIENS** [ ] Nov03 [ ]
– Zen / Reading my mind / Things / Look horizon / Magritte / Archimedes / Caravan / Bicycle / Twilight zone / Letter from abroad / Things X / Over her head / Set me free.

Oct 03. (12") *(12EM 628)* **BICYCLE. / LOOK HORIZON** [ ] [–]

Oct 03. (12") *(12EM 629)* **THINGS. / THINGS X** [ ] [–]

– compilations, etc. –

Jul 91. (c) *Danceteria; (DANCD 113)* **EVEN COWBOYS GET THE BLUES (live 1978-79 at CBGB's)** [ ] [ ]
(cd-iss. Jun97; same)

Oct 92. (cd) *Hannibal; (HNCD 1372)* **FRAGMENTS OF A RAINY SEASON (live)** [ ] [–]

Oct 92. (cd) *Traditional Line; (TL 001326)* **BROKEN HEARTS LIVE 1984-1992 (live)** [ ] [–]

Jul 94. (d-cd) *Rhino; <R2 71685>* **SEDUCING DOWN THE DOOR: A JOHN CALE COLLECTION** [–] [ ]

Sep 96. (d-cd) *Island; (524235-2)* **THE ISLAND YEARS ANTHOLOGY** [ ] [–]

Feb 99. (cd) *Island; (IMCD 259)* **CLOSE WATCH (AN INTRODUCTION TO JOHN CALE)** [ ] [ ]

– Paris 1919 / Mr. Wilson / Leaving it up to you / Dying on the vine / Guts / Heartbreak hotel / Ship of fools / Cable hogue / Gun / Riverbank / Child's Christmas in Wales / Fear is a man's best friend / If you were still around / Wilson Joilet / I keep a close watch.

May 00. (cd) *Table Of The Elements;* <*(TOECD 74)*> **INSIDE THE DREAM SYNDICATE VOL.1: DAY OF NIAGARA** [ ] [ ]

Apr 01. (cd) *Table Of The Elements; (TOECD 75)* **SUN BLINDNESS MUSIC** [ ] [–]

Dec 01. (cd) *Table Of The Elements;* <*(TOECD 79)*> **INSIDE THE DREAM SYNDICATE VOL.2: DREAM INTERPRETATION** [ ] [ ]

Dec 01. (cd) *Table Of The Elements;* <*(TOECD 80)*> **INSIDE THE DREAM SYNSICATE VOL.3: STAINLESS STEEL GAMELAN** [ ] [ ]

Jan 03. (cd) *Les Disques . . .; (TWI 1008)* **ANTARTIDA** (soundtrack from 1995) [ ] [–]

Jan 03. (cd) *Les Disques . . .; (TWI 1023)* **THE UNKNOWN** [ ] [–]

Jan 03. (cd) *Les Disques . . .; (TWI 1028)* **N'OUBLIE PAS QUE TU VAS MOURIR** (soundtrack) [ ] [–]

Jan 03. (cd) *Les Disques . . .; (TWI 1083)* **LE VENT DE LA NUIT** [ ] [–]

CALEXICO

Formed: California, USA . . . 1990 by JOEY BURNS and JOHN CONVERTINO. CALEXICO had always been known as the obscure offshoot band to HOWE GELB's masters of alt country, GIANT SAND. True, both BURNS and CONVERTINO have enjoyed success in GELB's weird, tumbling desert band, but CALEXICO had moved from "backing band" with their third album proper, 'HOT RAIL'. It all began when BURNS met session musician CONVERTINO in L.A. At that point, he was touring with GIANT SAND and invited CONVERTINO to accompany the band on their European tour. After the tour had ended, the duo moved to Tucson, Arizona and began playing and collecting weird instruments from a down-town store Chicago Music. A group was formed, FRIENDS OF DEAN MARTINEZ and the strange musical instruments were put to good use: harps, accordions, marimba and vibraphone were all added to the mix of jazzy lounge music, which, in turn, was so bad it was sheer brilliant. But the band were to split after a disagreement with founder BILL ELM. Session work followed, and BURNS and CONVERTINO were beginning to build a strong musical prowess. They finally put plan into action in 1996, recording and issuing the lo-fi porch soundtrack 'SPOKE' (issued on the German label 'Haus Musik'), which caught the attention of 'Touch & Go' records. 'THE BLACK LIGHT', arguably their best work, was unfettered in 1998 to widespread critical acclaim. It was hard to categorise CALEXICO's music: a strange amalgamation of blues, post-rock, surf music, Portuguese/Mexican Mariachi fused with MORRICONE's sweeping soundtracks. Basically, it sounded like CALEXICO's (a small railway town on the Californian/Mexican border) national anthem, if it were to have one. The same energy could be heard on the follow-up, 'HOT RAIL' (2000). Much the same record (almost like a Part 2), but slightly inferior, the set again treated us to the Desert experience with singles 'BALLAD OF CABLE HOGUE' and 'SERVICE AND REPAIR' to boot. The group were still faithful to GELB, however, appearing on albums 'Chore Of Enchantment' (in 2000) and 'Confluence' (in 2001). Meanwhile, CONVERTINO and BURNS moonlighted with yet another outfit, ABBC, along with Parisians GABRIEL NAIM AMOR and THOMAS BELHOM. Their collaborative work, 'TETE A TETE, was released towards the end 2000 – think eerie westerns and experimental textured jazz. CALEXICO's fourth album came in the form of 'FEAST OF WIRE' (2003), a dark follow-up to the aforementioned 'HOT RAIL'. Sticking along the same lines (no pun intended), the CONVERTINO and BURNS partnership had seemed to restrain itself, with the songs either cut short or lacking in the epic intensity of some of their earlier work. Tracks such as 'DUB LATINO' and 'QUATTRO (WORDS DRIFT IN)' all had that sparse desert drift to them, but essentially it seemed as if the band had remade the same album three times over, as the template for 1998's 'BLACK LIGHT' was much different from that of the whispered acoustic affair 'SPOKE'. But then again music fans were not complaining – CALEXICO keep doing their thing, whilst we quite happily swing.
• **Covered:** CHANEL NO.5 (Mark Eitzel) / CLOTHES OF SAND (Nick Drake) / TULSA TELEPHONE BOOK (Tom T. Hall) / DRIVING ON 9 (Minutemen) / SUNDOWN, SUNDOWN (Lee Hazlewood) / CASEY'S LAST RIDE (Kris Kristofferson) / ALONE AGAIN OR (Love).

Album rating: "SPOKE" (*7) / THE BLACK LIGHT (*8) / HOT RAIL (*8) / EVEN MY SURE THINGS FALL THROUGH collection (*4) / FEAST OF WIRE (*7) / ABBC: TETE A TETE (*6)

JOEY BURNS – vocals, guitar, bass, cello, accordion, organ (of GIANT SAND) / **JOHN COVERTINO** – drums, vibes, organ, marimba, percussion, accordion (of GIANT SAND) / **TASHA BUNDY** – drums

not iss. — All City

1996. (7") <*ALLCITY 2*> **LAQUER. / DRAPE** [–] [ ]
(UK-iss.Oct97 on 'All City'; same)

not iss. — Wabana

1996. (7") <*ORE 004*> **SPARK. / THE RIDE** [–] [ ]

—— guests **BRIDGET KEATING** – violin / **DAVID COFFMAN** – guitar

Quarter Stick — Quarter Stick

Sep 97. (cd) <*(QS 51CD)*> **"SPOKE"** [ ] Aug97 [ ]
– Low expectations / Mind the gap / Mazurra / Sanchez / Haul / Slag / Paper route / Glimpse / Navy cut / Spokes / Scout / Point Vicente / Wash / Ice cream jeep / Windjammer / Mazurka / Removed / Hitch / Stinging nettle. *(re-iss. May00; same)*

—— **NICK LUCA** – Spanish guitar; repl. COFFMAN

—— + guests **HOWE GELB** + **NEIL HARRY** + **GABRIEL LANDIN**

City Slang — Quarter Stick

Oct 98. (cd/d-lp) *(efa 08707-2/-1)* <*QS 54CD*> **THE BLACK LIGHT** [ ] May98 [ ]
– Gypsy's curse / Fake fur / Ride (part II) / Where water flows / The black light / Sideshow / Chach / Missing / Minas de cobre (for better metal) / Over your shoulder / Vinegaroon / Trigger / Sprawl / Stray / Old man waltz / Bloodflow / Frontera.

Oct 98. (cd-s) *(08713-2)* **STRAY / LAQUER / DRAPE** [ ] [–]

Apr 99. (7"/cd-s) *(08719-7/-2)* **THE RIDE (PART II). / MINAS DE COBRE (mixes; extend-o-mix / Spatial / acoustic)** [ ] [–]

—— they also issued a few concert/gig ltd-CD's 'ROAD MAP' (1999) and 'TRAVELALL' (2000); 'AEROCALEXICO' (2001) and 'SCRAPING' (2000) followed

—— **JOHN** + **JOEY** with **NICK LUCA** – guitar / **RUBEN MORENO** + **MARTIN WENK** – trumpets / **MADELEINE SOSIN** – violin / etc

Apr 00. (7") *(20154-7)* **BALLAD OF CABLE HOGUE. / CRYSTAL FRONTIER** [ ] [–]
(cd-s+=) *(20154-2)* – Hard hat.

May 00. (cd/lp) *(20153-2/-1)* <*2006-2*> **HOT RAIL** [57] [ ]
– El picador / Ballad of Cable Hogue / Ritual road map / Fade / Untitled III / Sonic wind / Muleta / Mid-town / Service and repair / Untitled II / Drenched / 16 track scratch / Tree avisos / Hot rail.

Sep 00. (cd-s) *(20167-2)* **SERVICE AND REPAIR / CROOKED ROAD AND THE BRIAR / BANDERILLA** [ ] [–]

Mar 01. (d7"ep) *(20173-7)* **CRYSTAL FRONTIER / CHANEL #5. / CROOKED ROAD AND THE BRIAR / BANDERILLA** [ ] [–]
(cd-s) *(20173-2)* – (first 2 tracks) / ('A'-widescreen mix) / ('A'-acoustic).
(12") *(20173-6)* – ('A'-widescreen mix) / ('A'-buscemi remix) / Untitled 3 (virus style mix).

Feb 03. (cd/lp) *(20213-2/-1)* <*QS 78*> **FEAST OF WIRE** [71] [ ]
– Sunken waltz / Quattro (world drifts in) / Stucco / Black heart / Pepita / Not even Stevie Nicks . . . / Close behind / Woven birds / The book and the canal / Attack el robot! attack! / Across the wire / Dub Latina / Guero Canelo / Whipping the horse's eyes / Crumble / No doze. *(ltd d-cd+=; 593147-0)* – Alone again or / Woven birds

(Cinematic Orchestra mix) / Convict pool / Woven birds (stratus mix).

Apr 03. (cd-s) *(20215-2)* **QUATTRO (WORLD DRIFTS IN) / PRASKOVIA / PAMPA** ☐ –

Jul 03. (12") *(20223-6)* **ALONE AGAIN OR. / WOVEN BIRDS (Cinematic Orchestra mix) / WOVEN BIRDS (Stratus mix)** ☐ –
(cd-s+=) *(20223-2)* – Convict pool.

– compilations, etc. –

May 01. (cd) *QuarterStick; <QS 67>* **EVEN MY SURE THINGS FALL THROUGH** – ☐
– Sonic wind (instrumental) / Crystal frontier / Untitled III / Chanel No.5 / Banderilla / Crooked road and the briar / Crystal frontier / Hard hat / Crystal frontier / Ballad of Cable Hogue / The black light.

ABBC

CONVERTINO + BURNS with **GABRIEL NAIM AMOR** – guitar, violin + **THOMAS BELHOM** – percussion, etc.

Wabana Wabana

Nov 00. (cd/lp) *<(ORE 24/+CD)>* **TETE A TETE** ☐ ☐
– La valse des 24 heures / Elevator baby / En route to the blanchisserie / Mobile home / Orange trees in the yard / Gilbert / Pluie sans nuages / The wrestler's masque / Je voudrais me rappeller / Le savon se dissout dans la rigole. *(re-iss. Jul01 on 'Cargo' cd/lp; CAR 031 CD/LP)*

Easy Tiger! not iss.

Apr 01. (7") *(MUSE 009)* **GILBERT. / BUTTERFLY MOUTH** ☐ –

☐ Randy CALIFORNIA (see under ⇒ SPIRIT)

Terry CALLIER

Born: 24 May'45, Chicago, Illinois, USA. A vocalist of astonishing gifts, CALLIER initially emerged on the US troubadour scene of the mid-60's (although one 'Chess' single, 'LOOK AT ME NOW' appeared in '63) with the belated 1968 release of 'THE NEW FOLK SOUND OF TERRY CALLIER'. Over the years, the sound in question has been variously described as soul-folk, folk-jazz, soul-jazz, hell, even operatic-soul! While a lazy comparison could be made with fellow Afro-American songsmith, RICHIE HAVENS, CALLIER remains an oddity, until very recently a criminally overlooked oddity at that. While the man achieved a nominal amount of fame via the apocalyptic rumblings of his debut set, subsequent early 70's releases languished in obscurity despite moments of stellar inspiration. If CALLIER had a theme tune, it'd surely be 'ORDINARY JOE', ironically the most charismatic slice of sun-kissed, blue-eyed soul this side of STEVIE WONDER. A highlight of 1972's 'OCCASIONAL RAIN' album alongside the downcast beauty of 'GOLDEN CIRCLE', it remains a mystery as to why these songs failed to capture the imagination of the record buying public first time round. No doubt part of the problem was marketing, there really is no classification for the likes of 'YOU GOIN' MISS YOUR CANDYMAN' (from 1973's 'WHAT COLOR IS LOVE'), the kind of sparse, foreboding harangue in which CALLIER really comes into his own. After a further extended break, the ochre-voiced singer returned for another ill-fated crack at success, this time signed to 'Elektra'. The albums 'FIRE ON ICE' (1978) and 'TURN YOU TO LOVE' (1979) signalled the end of CALLIER's recording career, his small but loyal band of fans left with a relatively slim legacy as he turned his hand to computer programming (no kidding!) for most of the next 15 years. Perhaps this was a blessing in disguise, given the amount of musical abortions churned out in the 80's; whatever, CALLIER was eventually rehabilitated from being the sole preserve of chin-stroking jazz buffs/soul weekender types after a collaboration with nu-folk chanteuse BETH ORTON. Released in late '97, 'THE BEST BIT' EP featured goose-bump duets on a cover of Tim Buckley's 'DOLPHINS' and a revamped 'LEAN ON ME' (a track originally recorded for 'OCCASIONAL RAIN'), its success encouraging CALLIER to plough ahead with a whole new album of original material for the 'Talking Loud' label. The result was 'TIMEPEACE', one of '98's warmest, most stress-defying and altogether most satisfyingly contented albums, the sound of a man who quietly knew all along that his talent was too strong to be kept down indefinitely. CALLIER's rich, sage tones against BETH ORTON's girlish folkiness may not be everyone's cup of tea, but their double act was arguably one of the highlights of the man's long overdue '98 tour, an event that was almost akin to the second coming among his more enthusiastic fans. If 1999's 'LIFETIME' wasn't quite up to the standard of its predecessor, it was still touched by its author's low-key genius, something which shone like a beacon on 'ALIVE' (2001), a gig recored at London's Jazz Cafe. There's perhaps no more natural an environment for CALLIER and together with sidemen BOSCO DE OLIVEIRA and GARY PLUMLEY, he weaved a magical spell over a rapt and often ecstatic audience, combing his back catalogue as well as mining more recent work and covering Curtis Mayfield's 'PEOPLE GET READY' with more empathy than any artist save perhaps Mayfield himself. With 'SPEAK YOUR PEACE' (2002), meanwhile, CALLIER reached an artistic peak unamatched since the resumption of his career, and maybe in his career as a whole. In JEAN-PAUL 'BLUEY' MAUNICK and 4 HERO's MARC MAC (TERRY had already guested on 4 HERO's 2001 set, 'Creating Patterns'), the venerated singer-songwriter had found sympathetic, perceptive collaborators who were able to inhabit and furnish the unique musical space he occupies with such easy grace and clarity of vision. Highlights included the duet with longtime admirer PAUL WELLER, 'BROTHER TO BROTHER', and a transcendent cover of Isley-Jasper-Isley's 'CARAVAN OF LOVE'. 2003's 'TOTAL RECALL' employed the same team on an album of remixed makeovers and covers, complete with spoken word interludes by the man himself.

Album rating (selective): THE NEW FOLK SOUND OF TERRY CALLIER (*7) / OCCASIONAL RAIN (*7) / ESSENTIAL (THE VERY BEST OF TERRY CALLIER) compilation (*8) / TIMEPEACE (*7) / LIFETIME (*7) / ALIVE (*7) / SPEAK YOUR PEACE (*7) / TOTAL RECALL remixes (*5)

TERRY CALLIER – vocals, guitar (with various session people)

not iss. Chess

1963. (7") **LOOK AT ME NOW. /** – ☐

not iss. Prestige

1968. (lp) *<PR 7383>* **THE NEW FOLK SOUND OF TERRY CALLIER** – ☐
– 900 miles / Oh dear, what can the matter be / Johnny be gay if you can / Cotton eyed Joe / It's about time / Promenade in green / Spin spin spin / I'm a drifter. *(UK-iss.Nov95 & Mar98 on 'Beat Goes Public' cd/lp; CD+/BGPM 1101) <lp re-iss. Jan03; same> <(cd re-iss. Jul03; CDBGPM 156)>*

not iss. Cadet

1968. (7") *<5623>* **LOOK AT ME NOW. / YOU GOIN' MISS YOUR CANDY MAN** – ☐

1972. (lp) *<CA 50007>* **OCCASIONAL RAIN** – ☐
– Segue #1 – Go ahead on / Ordinary Joe / Golden circle / Segue #5 – Go head on / Trance on Sedgewick Street / Do you finally need a friend / Segue #4 – Go head on / Sweet Edie-D / Occasional rain / Segue #2 – Go head on / Blues for Marcus / Lean on me / Last segue – Go head on. *<(cd re-iss. Oct99 on 'Universal'; 380512-2)>*

1972. (7") *<5692>* **ORDINARY JOE. / GOLDEN CIRCLE OF YOUR LOVE** – ☐

1973. (lp) *<CA 50019>* **WHAT COLOR IS LOVE** – ☐
– Dancing girl / What color is love / You goin' miss your candyman / Just as long as we're in love / Ho tsing mee (a song of the sun) / I'd rather be

with you / You don't care. <*(cd-iss. Jun98 on 'Universal'; UMD 80510)*> <*(cd re-iss. Oct99 on 'Universal'; 380510-2)*>

1973. (7") <*5697*> **I JUST CAN'T HELP MYSELF (I DON'T WANT NOBODY ELSE). / GOTTA GET CLOSER TO YOU** [–] [ ]

1973. (lp) <*CA 50041*> **I JUST CAN'T HELP MYSELF** [–] [ ]
– (I just can't help myself) I don't want nobody else / Brown-eyed lady / Gotta get closer to you / Satin doll / Until tomorrow / Alley-wind song / Can't catch the trane / Bowlin' green. <*(cd re-iss. Oct99 on 'Universal'; 380511-2)*>

Elektra Elektra

Aug 78. (lp) *(K 52096)* <*6E-143*> **FIRE ON ICE** [ ] [ ]
– Be a believer / Holdin' on to your love / Street fever / I been doin' alright / Butterfly / Disco in the sky / African violet / Love to love / Martin St. Martin. <*(re+cd-iss. Jan01; 7559 62604-2/-1)*>

Oct 78. (7") <*45527*> **STREET FEVER. / BUTTERFLY** [–] [ ]

Jul 79. (7") *(K 12372)* <*46054*> **SIGN OF THE TIMES. / OCCASIONAL RAIN** [ ] [ ]

Nov 79. (lp) *(K 52140)* <*6E-189*> **TURN YOU TO LOVE** [ ] [ ]
– Sign of the times / Pyramids of love / Turn you to love / Do it again / Ordinary Joe / Occasional rain / Still water / You and me / Mother's love. *(re-iss. May85; same)* <*(cd+re-iss. Jan01; 7559 62603-2/-1)*>

not iss. Erect

1982. (12") <*ERD 1214*> **I DON'T WANT TO SEE MYSELF (WITHOUT YOU). / IF I COULD MAKE YOU (CHANGE YOUR MIND)** [–] [ ]
(UK-iss.Jul90 on 'Acid Jazz'; JAZID 27T)

—— In 1997, TERRY was involved with two collaborations, 'Religion & Politics' with URBAN SPECIES and 'Best Bit' EP with BETH ORTON.

Talkin' Loud Verve

Feb 98. (cd/lp) *(539 249-2/-1)* <*537137*> **TIMEPEACE** [ ] [ ]
– Ride suite ride (intro) / Lazarus man / Keep your heart right / Java sparrow / People get ready – Brotherly love / Love theme from Spartacus / No more blues / Timepeace / Following your footprints / C'est la vie / Coyote moon / Aka New York Al / Traitor to the race. <*(cd re-iss. Oct99; same)*>

May 98. (cd-s) *(TLCD 32)* **LOVE THEME FROM SPARTACUS / KEEP YOUR HEART RIGHT / AFRICAN VIOLET (live) / WHAT COLOR IS LOVE? (live)** [57] [–]
(12"/cd-s) *(TLX/TLDD 32)* – ('A'side) / ('A'-Zero 7 mix) / ('A'-4 Hero mix) / Roy Stepper's delight / ('A'-Aqua mental mix).

Sep 99. (cd/lp) *(543 054-2/-4)* <*547728*> **LIFETIME** [ ] [ ]
– When my lady danced / Sunset boulevard / Holdin' on / When the music is gone / Where a lark is singing / 4 miles / Love can do (with BETH ORTON) / Fix the blame / I don't want to see myself (without you) / Nobody but yourself / Comin' up from Babylon / Lifetime.

Oct 99. (7") *(LOUD 7)* **HOLDIN' ON. / WHEN THE LADY DANCED** [ ] [–]

Nov 99. (2x12"/cd-ep) *(TL X/CD 52)* **I DON'T WANT TO SEE MYSELF (WITHOUT YOU) EP** [ ] [–]
– Kings of tomorrow (vocal) / Kings of tomorrow (dub) / Heller & Farley Saturday in Chicago mix / Heller & Farley full groove mix / Mikey Benn vocal / Mikey Benn dub / I don't want to see myself (without you) (original) / I waited for you.

Mr. Bongo Mr. Bongo

Mar 01. (cd/lp) <*(MRB CD/LP 019)*> **ALIVE (live)** [ ] [ ]
– Ordinary Joe / Step into the light / Lazarus man / Lament for the late ad / African violet / You goin' miss your candyman / What color is love / Dancing girl / People get ready / I don't want to see myself (without you).

May 02. (cd/lp) <*(MRB CD/LP 023)*> **SPEAK YOUR PEACE** [ ] [ ]
– Monuments of Mars / Running around / Darker than a shadow / Turn this mutha / Caravan of love / Sierra Leone / Speak your peace / Tokyo moon / We are not alone / Just my imagination (running away with me) / Imagine a nation / Chelsea blue / Got to get it all straightened out.

Nov 02. (12"/cd-s) *(MRB 12/CDS 018)* **RUNNING AROUND. / RUNNING AROUND (fug beats radio) / MONUMENTS OF MARS (Hopper mix)** [ ] [–]

Oct 03. (cd/lp) <*(MRB CD/LP 031)*> **TOTAL RECALL** (remixes) [ ] Dec03 [ ]

– compilations, etc. –

Apr 94. (cd/d-lp) *Charly; (CD+/ARC 514)* **THE VERY BEST OF TERRY CALLIER ON CADET** [ ] [ ]

1996. (cd) *Premonition; <PREM 739-2>* **T.C. IN D.C. (live in 1982 with ERIC HOCHBERG & PENN McGEE)** [–] [ ]

Apr 98. (cd/d-lp) *M.C.A.; <(MCD/MCA 11781)>* **ESSENTIAL (THE VERY BEST OF TERRY CALLIER)** [ ] [ ]
– Ordinary Joe / Gotta get closer to you / Lover (where have you gone) / Just as lobg as we're in love / Baby take your time / Occasional rain / Dancing girl / Look at me now / You were just foolin' me / I just can't help myself / Sail away / Colour me free / Soulful clown / City side and country / I'd rather be with you / You don't care / Blues. *(cd re-iss. Oct99; 11781-2)*

Apr 98. (cd) *Premonition; (7669 178740-2)* **FIRST LIGHT** [ ] [ ]
– Ordinary Joe / If I could make you mine / Can't catch the train / Golden circle / Lean on me / Gravy waltz / Alley wind song / Naomi / Trick all your time away / Blues for Marcus / 900 miles / Occasional rain.

CALLING

Formed: San Fernando Valley, Los Angeles, California, USA ... mid-90's by ALEX BAND and AARON KAMIN. While their first loose aggregate stepped out as GENERATION GAP, the addition of more permanent members SEAN WOOLSTENHULME, BILLY MOHLER and NATE WOOD found them renaming themselves The CALLING. Having earlier signed a development deal with 'R.C.A.', the group finally released their debut album, 'CAMINO PALMERO', in 2001. Yet more made to measure post-post-post-grunge floundering, the record added a big fat zero to the advancement of rock music, indistinguishable as it was from any number of faceless US acts peddling similar aural drudgery. Having already been issued on the soundtrack to the equally pedestrian Coyote Ugly movie, the melodramatic 'WHEREVER YOU WILL GO' made the US Top 5 in 2002, while the aforementioned album went platinum.

Album rating: CAMINO PALMERO (*4)

ALEX BAND (b. 8 Jun'81) – vocals / **AARON KAMIN** (b. 10 Aug'77) – guitar / **SEAN WOOLSTENHULME** (b. 1 Mar'81, Gilbert, Arizona) – guitar, vocals / **BILLY MOHLER** (b.22 Feb'75) – bass / **NATE WOOD** (b. 3 Oct'79) – drums

B.M.G. R.C.A.

Jul 01. (cd) <*07863 67885-2*> **CAMINO PALMERO** [–] [ ]
– Unstoppable / Nothing's changed / Wherever you will go / Could it be any harder / Final answer / Adrienne / We're forgiven / Things don't always turn out that way / Just that good / Thank you / Stigmatized. *(UK-iss.Mar02; 74321 91610-2)*; hit No.12 Jun02; having hit US No.36 a few months earlier)

Jun 02. (c-s) *(74321 94765-4)* **WHEREVER YOU WILL GO / NOTHING'S CHANGED** [3] Mar02 [5]
(cd-s+=) *(74321 94765-2)* <*83663*> – Lost.
(the import hit UK No.64 a week earlier!)

Oct 02. (c-s) *(74321 96835-4)* **ADRIENNE / ('A'-acoustic version)** [18] [–]
(cd-s+=) *(74321 96835-2)* – Lost / ('A'-video).

—— (Jun-Oct'02) now down to just ALEX + AARON; SEAN joined LIFEHOUSE

CAMEL

Formed: London, England ... 1972 by R&B veteran PETE BARDENS, plus ex-backing band of PHILIP GOODHAND-TAIT; DOUG FERGUSON, ANDY WARD and ANDY LATIMER. Their first recording, 'GOD OF LIGHT REVISITED – PARTS ONE, TWO, THREE', featured on one side of a various double album, 'Greasy Truckers – Live At Dingwalls'. The following year, they issued their eponymous debut on 'M.C.A.', before moving to 'Deram' for the follow-up, 'MIRAGE' (1974). CAMEL really came into their own with their conceptual interpretation of Paul Gallico's 'THE SNOW GOOSE'. A Top 30 breakthrough, it was dominated by excellent instrumental pieces which perfectly translated Gallico's children's story into a prog-rock framework. However, Gallico served a writ against the group for copyright infringement. Unbowed, CAMEL came up with yet another successful album, 'MOONMADNESS', this time utilising vocals which took them a stage further in their musical development. Another Top 20 album followed in 1977, 'RAIN DANCES', a softer, more conventional affair, as was the 1978 studio follow-up, 'BREATHLESS'. Although they retained a loyal fan-base within the college fraternity, the onset of more hip sounds (i.e. punk & new wave) effectively swept them under the carpet. They disbanded in '84, but re-formed seven years later. Their comeback album, 'DUST AND DREAMS' (1992), was inspired by John Steinbeck's book, 'The Grapes Of Wrath', while CAMEL's (virtually down to friends of LATIMER and COLIN BASS – a member since '79) 1996 effort, 'HARBOUR OF KINGS', was Irish folk inspired.

Album rating: CAMEL (*4) / MIRAGE (*5) / THE SNOW GOOSE (*8) / MOONMADNESS (*6) / RAIN DANCES (*6) / BREATHLESS (*5) / I CAN SEE YOUR HOUSE FROM HERE (*6) / NUDE (*6) / THE SINGLE FACTOR (*4) / STATIONARY TRAVELLER (*5) / PRESSURE POINTS – CAMEL LIVE (*4) / DUST AND DREAMS (*5) / NEVER LET GO (*4) / ECHOES – THE RETROSPECTIVE compilation (*7) / HARBOUR OF TEARS (*4) / COMING OF AGE (*4) / A NOD AND A WINK (*5)

PETER BARDENS – keyboards, vocals (ex-THEM, ex-solo, ex-SHOTGUN EXPRESS) / **ANDY LATIMER** – vocals, guitar / **DOUG FERGUSON** – bass / **ANDY WARD** – drums, percussion

M.C.A. / not iss.

Nov 72. (7") *(MU 1177)* **NEVER LET GO. / CURIOSITY** – –

Dec 73. (lp) *(MUPS 477)* **CAMEL** –
– Slow yourself down / Mystic queen / Six ate / Separation / Never let go / Curiosity / Arubaluba. *(re-iss. 1974; MCF 2065) (re-iss. Aug81 lp/c; MCL/+C 1601) (re-iss. Nov82 on 'Fame' lp/c; FA/TCFA 3054) (cd-iss. Jul93 on 'Camel Prod.'; CP 002CD) (cd re-mast.Jun02 on 'Deram'+=; 882925-2)* – Never let go (single version) / Homage to the god of light (live at the Marquee Club 29 Oct 1974).

Deram / Janus

1974. (lp) *(SML 1107)* *<7009>* **MIRAGE**
– Freefall / Supertwister / Nimrodel: – The procession – The white rider / Earthrise / Lady fantasy: – Encounter – Smiles for you – Lady fantasy. *(cd-iss. Jun89; 820 613-2) (cd re-mast.Jun02 +=; 882929-2)* – Supertwister (live at the Marquee) / Mystic queen (live at the Marquee) / Arubaluba (live at the Marquee) / Lady fantasy: Encounter – Smiles for you – Lady fantasy (alt. take).

Decca / Janus

May 75. (lp/c) *(SKLR/KSKC 5207)* *<7016>* **THE SNOW GOOSE** 22
– The great marsh – Rhayader – Rhayader goes to town – Sanctuary – Fritha – The snow goose – Friendship – Migration – Rhayader alone / Flight of the snow goose – Preparation – Dunkirk – Epitaph – Fritha alone – La princesse Perdue – The great marsh. *(re-iss. Nov76; same) (cd-iss. Jul88; 800 080-2) (cd re-mast.Jun02 on 'Deram'+=; 882930-2)* – Flight of the snow goose (single edit) / Rhayader (single edit) / Flight of the snow goose (alt. take) / Rhayader goes to town (live at the Marquee) / The snow goose – Freefall (live at the Marquee).

May 75. (7") *(FR 13581)* **FLIGHT OF THE SNOW GOOSE. / RHAYADER** –

Sep 75. (7") *(FR 13603)* **THE SNOW GOOSE. / FREEFALL** –

Apr 76. (lp/c) *(TXSR/KTXCR 115)* *<7024>* **MOONMADNESS** 15
– Aristillus / Song within a song / Chord change / Spirit of the water / Another night / Air born / Lunar sea. *(cd-iss. 1983 & Jul89; 810 879-2) (cd re-mast.Jun02 on 'Deram'+=; 882931-2)* – Another night (single version) / Spirit of the water (demo) / Song within a song (live at the Hammersmith Odeon) / Lunar sea (live at the Hammersmith Odeon) / Preparation – Dunkirk (live at the Hammersmith Odeon) / Air born (live at the Hammersmith Odeon).

Jun 76. (7") *(FR 13656)* *<262>* **ANOTHER NIGHT. / LUNAR SEA**

— **RICHARD SINCLAIR** – bass (ex-CARAVAN) repl. FERGUSON

Sep 77. (lp/c) *(TXSR/KTXCR 124)* *<7035>* **RAIN DANCES** 20
– First light / Metrognome / Tell me / Highways of the sun / Unevensong / One of these days I'll get an early night / Elke / Skylines / Rain dances. *(cd-iss. Dec91 on 'London'+=; 820 725-2)* – Highways of the sun (single edit).

Sep 77. (7") *(FR 13729)* **HIGHWAYS OF THE SUN. / TELL ME** –

— added **MEL COLLINS** – saxophone (ex-KING CRIMSON etc.) / **DAVE SINCLAIR** – keyboards (ex-CARAVAN etc.)

Apr 78. (d-lp/d-c) *(DBCR/KBC 7-8)* **A LIVE RECORD (live)** –
– First light * / Metrognome / Unevensong * / Skylines / Song within a song / Lunar sea / Raindances * / Never let go / Chord changes * / Ligging at Louis' / Lady fantasy: Encounter – Smiles for you – Lady fantasy / (spoken introduction) – The great marsh – Rhayader – Rhayader goes to town – Sanctuary – Fritha – The snow goose – Friendship – Migration – Rhayader alone / Flight of the snow goose: – Preparation – Dunkirk – Epitaph – Fritha alone – La princesse Perdue – The great marsh / The white rider * / Another night *. *(d-cd-iss. Jul93 on 'Deram'; 844122-2) (<d-cd re-mast.Jun02 +=*; 882928-2)*

Decca / Arista

Sep 78. (lp/c) *(TXSR/KTXSR 132)* *<4206>* **BREATHLESS** 26
– Breathless / Echoes / Wing and a prayer / Down on the farm / Starlight ride / Summer lightning / You make me smile / The sleeper / Rainbow's end. *(re-iss. Aug92 on 'Deram' cd/c; 820 726-2/-4)*

— **COLIN BASS** – bass, vocals repl. RICHARD who later rejoined CARAVAN / **KIT WATKINS** – keyboards, flute repl. PETER who went solo then LATIMER, WARD

Sep 79. (lp/c) *(TXSR/KTXSR 137)* *<4254>* **I CAN SEE YOUR HOUSE FROM HERE** 45
– Wait / Your love is no stronger than mine / Eye of the storm / Who are we / Survival / Hymn to her / Neon magic / Remote romance. *(cd-iss. Jan89 & Oct93 on 'London'; 820 614-2)*

Oct 79. (7") *(FR 13871)* **YOUR LOVE IS NO STRONGER THAN MINE. / NEON MAGIC** –

Feb 80. (7") *(FR 13879)* **REMOTE ROMANCE. / RAINBOW'S END / TELL ME** –

— **DUNCAN MACKAY** – keyboards (ex-COCKNEY REBEL) repl. KIT

Jan 81. (lp/c) *(SKL/KSKC 5323)* **NUDE** 36 –
– City life / Nude / Drafted / Docks / Beached / Landscapes / Changing places / Pomp and circumstance / Please come home / Reflections / Captures / The homecoming / Lies / The last farewell / The birthday cake / Nude's return. *(cd-iss. 1987; 810 880-2)*

— **JAN SCHELHAAS** – keyboards (ex-CARAVAN) repl. MACKAY who joined BUDGIE

Decca / Passport

May 82. (lp/c) *(SKL/KSKC 5328)* *<PB 6013>* **THE SINGLE FACTOR** 57
– No easy answer / You are the one / Heroes / Selva / Manic / Lullaby / Sasquatch / Camelogue / Today's goodbye / A heart's desire / End piece. *(cd-iss. 1983 & May94; 800 081-2)*

— **PAUL BURGESS** – drums, percussion repl. WARD (who joined MARILLION)

Mar 84. (lp/c)(cd) *(SKL/KSKC 5334)(820 020-2)* **STATIONARY TRAVELLER** 57 –
– Pressure points / Refugee / Copos / Cloak and dagger man / Stationary traveller / West Berlin / Fingertips / Missing / Afterwords / Long goodbyes. *(cd re-iss. Jul89; same)*

Mar 84. (7"/12") *(CAMEL/CAMEX 1)* **CLOAK AND DAGGER MAN. / PRESSURE POINTS** –

— **LATIMER, BASS + BURGESS** with returning guests **MEL COLLINS & PETER BARDENS** brought in **TOM SCHERPENZEEL** – keyboards / **RICHIE CLOSE** – keyboards + **CHRIS RAINBOW** – vocals, keyboards

Nov 84. (lp/c)(cd) *(SKL/KSKC 5338)(823 812-2)* **PRESSURE POINTS – CAMEL LIVE** (live 11th May'84) –
– West Berlin / Pressure points / Drafted / Captured / Lies / Rhayader goes to town / Sasquatch / Fingertips / Rhayader / Wait. *(cd re-iss. 1987 on 'London'; 820 166-2)*

— CAMEL disbanded in '84 but re-formed again in 1991

Camel / not iss.

Sep 92. (cd/c) *(CP 001 CD/C)* **DUST AND DREAMS** –
– Dust bowl / Go west / Dusted out / Mother road / Needles / Rose of Sharon / End of the line / Storm clouds / Cotton camp / Broken ranks / Sheet rain / Whispers / Little rivers and little Rose / Hopeless anger / Whispers in the rain. *(cd re-iss. Jul93; same)*

Nov 93. (d-cd) *(CP 004CD)* **NEVER LET GO (live '92)** –
– Never let go / Earthrise / Rhyader / Rhayader goes to town / Spirit of the water / Unevensong / Echoes / Ice / City life / Drafted // Dust bowl / Go west / Dusted out / Mother road / Needles / Rose of Sharon / Milk n' honey / End of the line / Storm clouds / Cotton camp / Broken banks / Sheet rain / Whispers / Little rivers and little rose / Hopeless anger / Whispers in the rain / Sasquatch / Lady fantasy.

— **LATIMER + BASS / + MICKEY SIMMONDS** – keyboards / **DAVID PATON** – bass, vocals / **MAE McKENNA** – a capella vocal / **JOHN XEPOLEAS** – drums / **NEIL PANTON** – oboe, soprano sax, harmonium / **JOHN BURTON** – french horn / **BARRY PHILLIPS** – cello / **KAREN BENTLEY** – violin / **ANITA STONEHAM** – violin

Jan 96. (cd) *(CP-006CD)* **HARBOUR OF TEARS** [ ] [-]
– Irish air / Irish air (instrumental reprise) / Harbour of tears / Cobh / Send home the slates / Under the moon / Watching the bobbins / Generations / Eyes of Ireland / Running from paradise / End of the day / Coming of age / The hour candle (a song for my father).

— **LATIMER + BASS** recruited **FOSS PATTERSON** – keyboards, vocals / **DAVE STEWART** – drums, percussion, octapad

Apr 98. (d-cd) *(<CP 008CD>)* **COMING OF AGE (live)** [ ] Oct99 [ ]
– Lunar sea / Hymn to her / Rhayader / Rhayader goes to town / Preparation / Dunkirk / Drafted / Docks / Beached / Spirit of the water / Ice / Sasquatch // Milk 'n honey / Mother road / Needles / Rose of Sharon / Irish air / Irish air (reprise) / Harbour of tears / Cobh / Send home the slates / Under the moon / Watching the Bobbins / Eyes of Ireland / Running from Paradise / End of the day / Coming of age / The hour candle.

Jul 02. (cd) *(<CO 013CD>)* **A NOD AND A WINK** [ ] Aug02 [ ]
– A nod and a wink / Simple pleasures / A boy's life / Fox hill / The miller's tale / Squigely fair / For today.

– compilations etc. –

Sep 81. (lp/c) *Decca; (SKL/KSKC 5325)* **CHAMELEON** [ ] [-]

Nov 85. (d-lp/c/cd) *Castle; (CCS LP/MC/CD 116)* **THE COLLECTION** [ ] [-]
– Aristilus / Freefall / Supertwister / Spirit of the water / Lunar sea / The white rider / Earthrise / Song within a song / Rhayader – Rhayader goes to town – Migration – Rhayader alone – La princesse Perdue – The great marsh / Drafted / Captured / Sasquatch / Rain dances / Highways of the sun / First light.

May 91. (cd/c) *Elite; (2334)* **LANDSCAPE** [ ] [-]

Jul 93. (cd) *Camel Prod.; (<CP 003CD>)* **CAMEL ON THE ROAD 1972 (live)** [ ] Aug92 [ ]

— In July '94, PETE BARDENS released cd 'BIG SKY' for 'H.T.D.'.

Nov 94. (d-cd) *Deram; (<8 44340-2>)* **ECHOES – THE RETROSPECTIVE** [ ] Jul93 [ ]
– Never let go / Free fall / Lady fantasy: Encounter – Smiles for you – Lady fantasy / Rhayader / Rhayader goes to town / Song within a song / Air born / Lunar sea / Unevensong / Tell me / Elke / Skylines / Breathless / Echoes / The sleeper / Your love is stranger than mine / Hymn to her / Ice / Drafted / Lies / Sasquatch / You are the one / Refugee / West Berlin / Mother road / Whispers in the rain.

Jan 95. (cd) *Camel Prod.; (<CP 005CD>)* **CAMEL ON THE ROAD 1982 (live)** [ ] Oct94 [ ]

Mar 97. (cd) *Camel Prod.; (<CP 007CD>)* **CAMEL ON THE ROAD 1981 (live)** [ ] Jun97 [ ]

Jan 01. (cd) *Camel Prod.; (<CP 010CD>)* **GODS OF LIGHT '73-'75 (live)** [ ] Sep00 [ ]

Oct 01. (cd) *Camel Prod.; (<CP 011CD>)* **THE PARIS COLLECTION** [ ] [ ]

Oct 01. (d-cd) *Decca; (882995-2)* **LUNAR SEA: AN ANTHOLOGY 1973-1985** [ ] [-]

☐ Ali CAMPBELL (see under ⇒ UB40)

CAN

Formed: Cologne, Germany ... 1968 initially as INNER SPACE by HOLGER CZUKAY and IRMIN SCHMIDT. MICHAEL KAROLI and JAKI LIEBEZEIT were soon recruited along with DAVID JOHNSON and black American vocalist MALCOLM MOONEY. Later that year, JOHNSON bailed out prior to their debut album, 'MONSTER MOVIE' (1970). Having studied under KARL-HEINZ STOCKHAUSEN, CZUKAY and SCHMIDT (who were also influenced by JOHN CAGE, TERRY RILEY and The VELVET UNDERGROUND) pioneered their own take on avant-garde minimalism, creating a hypnotic, free-form sound, relentless in its intensity. The album included a 20-minute piece, 'YOU DOO RIGHT', extracted from a marathon improv-session and highlighting the very real dementia of MOONEY's ravings. He suffered a nervous breakdown soon after and was subsequently replaced by the Japanese 'vocalist' DAMO SUZUKI prior to recording 'SOUNDTRACKS'. More improvised beauty was evidenced on their next set, the German Top 40 classic, 'TAGO MAGO' (1971), a sprawling double-set that featured two of their more hypnotic tracks, 'HALLELUWAH' and 'MUSHROOM'. On their next two releases, 'EGE BAMYASI' and 'FUTURE DAYS', CAN explored even more ritualistic textures alongside SUZUKI's partly-spoken tri-lingual ramblings. SUZUKI subsequently returned to Japan to become a Jehovah's Witness, after a final gig at the 1973 Edinburgh Festival. Vocal duties were now shared by KAROLI and SCHMIDT on the more percussive 'SOON OVER BABALUMA' album (1974). They signed to Richard Branson's innovative 'Virgin' label the following year, 'LANDED' being a prime example of British-influenced avant-garde rock. In 1976, they surprised many by having a Top 30 hit, 'I WANT MORE', penned by PINK FLOYD's DAVID GILMOUR. With the addition of ROSKO GEE and sessionman REEBOP KWAKU BAAH, they moved in a more African/reggae influenced direction; CZUKAY having already withdrawn from most of the proceedings. Their final efforts were of little significance, the 1979 album interesting only for its re-hash of Offenbach's 'CAN-CAN', which had previously been released as a single. KAROLI, SCHMIDT and CZUKAY all continued in the 80's as solo artists, the latter teaming up once again with LIEBEZEIT (and JAH WOBBLE) on the 1982 album 'FULL CIRCLE'. The original line-up reformed in 1986 for an album, 'RITE TIME', but the record lacked the inspiration and originality that characterised CAN's earlier work. The band remain highly regarded, cited as a major influence by artists as diverse as CARL CRAIG and PRIMAL SCREAM. Even The FALL paid homage to them by crediting a song as 'I AM DAMO SUZUKI'. A plethora of post-CAN work (mainly from CZUKAY) appeared from time to time, although their legacy was always from the experimental 70's. More recently (on the 17th of November, 2001), the death of MICHAEL KAROLI filtered through to the media. He would be sadly missed by his great friend CZUKAY.

Album rating: MONSTER MOVIE (*7) / SOUNDTRACKS (*6) / TAGO MAGO (*7) / EGE BAMYASI (*7) / FUTURE DAYS (*7) / LIMITED EDITION collection (*6) / SOON OVER BABALUMA (*6) / LANDED (*5) / FLOW MOTION (*5) / UNLIMITED EDITION collection (*5) / SAW DELIGHT (*6) / CANNIBALISM compilation (*7) / OUT OF REACH (*3) / CAN (*4) / DELAY 1968 exploitation (*5) / RITE TIME (*5) / CANNIBALISM II compilation (*6) / CANNIBALISM III compilation (*5) / ANTHOLOGY 1968-1993 compilation (*8) / Holger Czukay: CANAXIS 5 with Rolf Dammers (*7) / MOVIES (*7) / ON THE WAY TO THE PEAK OF NORMAL (*5) / FULL CIRCLE (*5) / DER OSTEN IST ROT (*5) / ROME REMAINS ROME (*7) / RADIO WAVE SURFER (*4) / MOVING PICTURES (*5) / GOOD MORNING STORY (*5) / LA LUNA (*5) / Michael Karoli with Polly Estes; DELUGE (*7) / Jaki Liebezeit: PHANTOM BAND (*5) / FREEDOM OF SPEECH (*5) / NOWHERE (*5) / Irmin Schmidt: FILM MUSIK (*5) / TOY PLANET (*5) / FILM MUSIK VOL.2 (*5) / FILM MUSIK VOL.3 & 4 (*5) / MUSIC AT DUSK (*5) / IMPOSSIBLE HOLIDAYS (*5)

IRMIN SCHMIDT (b.29 May'37, Berlin, Germany) – keyboards / **HOLGER CZUKAY** (b.24 Mar'38, Danzig, Germany) – bass, electronics / **DAVID JOHNSON** – flute / **MICHAEL KAROLI** (b.29 Apr'48, Straubing, Germany) – guitar, violin / **JAKI LIEBEZEIT** (b.26 May'38, nr.Dresden, Germany) – drums / **MALCOLM MOONEY** – vocals

Music Factory not iss.

Nov 68. (7"; by IRMIN SCHMIDT) **KAMA SUTRA. /** [-] German [-]

— Now a quintet when JOHNSON departed (below issued Germany Aug'69)

U.A. U.A.

May 70. (lp) *(UAS 29094)* **MONSTER MOVIE** [ ] [-]
– Father cannot yell / Mary, Mary so contrary / You doo right / Outside my door. *(cd-iss. Jun89 on 'Spoon-Mute'; SPOONCD 004)*

— **KENJI 'DAMO' SUZUKI** (b.16 Jan'50, Japan) – vocals repl.MOONEY who suffered a nervous breakdown

Sep 70. Liberty; (7") **SOUL DESERT. / SHE BRINGS THE RAIN** – German –

Sep 71. (lp) *(UAS 29283)* **SOUNDTRACKS** –
– Deadlock / Tango whiskyman / Deadlock (instrumental) / Don't turn the light on, leave me alone / Soul desert / Mother sky / She brings the rain. *(cd-iss. Jun89 on 'Spoon-Mute'; SPOONCD 005)*

1971. (7") **TURTLES HAVE SHORT LEGS. / HALLELUWAH (edit)** – German –

1971. (7") **SPOON. / SHIKAKO MARU TEN** – German –

Feb 72. (d-lp) *(UAD 60009-10)* **TAGO MAGO** –
– Paperhouse / Mushroom / Oh yeah / Halleluwah / Aumgn / Peking O / Bring me coffee or tea. *(cd-iss. Jul89 on 'Spoon-Mute'; SPOONCD 006-007)*

Nov 72. (lp) *(UAS 29414)* <063> **EGE BAMYASI**
– Pinch / Sing swan song / One more night / Vitamin C / Soup / I'm so green / Spoon. *(cd-iss. Jun89 on 'Spoon-Mute'; SPOONCD 008)*

Feb 73. (7") *(UP 35506)* **SPOON. / I'M SO GREEN** –

Jun 73. (lp) *(UAS 29505)* <213> **FUTURE DAYS**
– Future days / Spray / Moonshake / Bel Air. *(cd-iss. Jun89 on 'Spoon-Mute'; SPOONCD 009)*

Oct 73. (7") *(UP 35596)* <446> **MOONSHAKE. / FUTURE DAYS (edit)**

— trimmed to a quartet when DAMO SUZUKI left to become a Jehovah's Witness. Now **SCHMIDT / KAROLI** (shared vocals) **CZUKAY + LIEBEZEIT**

Nov 74. (lp) *(UAG 29673)* <343> **SOON OVER BABALUMA**
– Dizzy dizzy / Come sta, la luna / Splash / Chain reaction / Quantum physics. *(cd-iss. Jun89 on 'Spoon-Mute'; SPOONCD 010)*

Dec 74. (7") *(UP 35749)* **DIZZY DIZZY. / SPLASH** –

Virgin Polydor

Sep 75. (lp) *(V 2041)* **LANDED**
– Full moon on the highway / Half past one / Hunters and collectors / Vernal equinox / Red hot Indians / Unfinished. *(cd-iss. Jun87; CDV 2041) (re-iss. Aug88; OVED 194)*

— approx Mar76, tried two vocalists one a Malayan, the other **MICHAEL COUSINS** (English). added **DAVID GILMOUR** – guest/composer (3) b.vocals of PINK FLOYD

Jul 76. (7") *(VS 153)* **I WANT MORE. / . . . AND MORE** 26

Oct 76. (lp) *(V 2071)* **FLOW MOTION**
– I want more / Cascade waltz / Laugh till you cry . . . live till you die / . . .And more / Babylonian pearl / Smoke (E.F.S. No.59) / Flow motion. *(cd-iss. Jun87; CDV 2071) (re-iss. Aug88; OVED 88)*

Nov 76. (7") *(VS 166)* **SILENT NIGHT. / CASCADE WALTZ** –

— added **ROSKO GEE** – bass + **REEBOP KWAKU BAAH** (b. Konongo, Ghana) – percussion (both ex-TRAFFIC) (HOLGER now synths., samplers)

Mar 77. (lp) *(V 2079)* **SAW DELIGHT**
– Don't say no / Sunshine day and night / Call me / Animal waves / Fly by night. *(cd-iss. Jun87; CDV 2079) (re-iss. Aug88; OVED 195)*

Apr 77. (7") *(VS 172)* **DON'T SAY NO. / RETURN** –

— HOLGER went on a few holidays (& solo). The rest of the band below (**SCHMIDT, KAROLI, LIEBEZEIT, BAAH & GEE**) recorded album.

Lightning Peters Int.

Jun 78. (7") *(LIG 545)* **CAN-CAN. / CAN BE** –

Jul 78. (lp) *(LIP 4)* <9024> **OUT OF REACH**
– Serpentine / Pauper's daughter and I / November / Seven days awake / Give me no roses / Like Inobe God / One more day. *(re-iss. Jun86 on 'Thunderbolt'; THBL 025) (cd-iss. Nov88; CDTB 025) (cd re-iss. May99 on 'MagMid'; MM 030)*

Laser not iss.

Jul 79. (lp) *(LASL 2)* **CAN** –
– All gates open / Safe / Sunday jam / Sodom / Aspectacle / E.F.S. No.99: "can can" / Ping pong / Can be. *(re-iss. Feb85 as 'INNER SPACE' on 'Thunderbolt'; THBL 020) (cd-iss. Jun87; THBL 020)*

— had already split late '78. JAKI formed PHANTOM BAND and collaborated with HOLGER. IRMIN went solo and formed BRUNO SPOERRI. MICHAEL in '84 went solo. All their releases were mainly German only. **CAN** re-formed 1969 line-up 20 years on.

Mercury not iss.

Oct 89. (lp/c/cd) *(838 883-1/-4/-2)* **RITE TIME** –
-On the beautiful side of a romance / The without law man / Below this level (patient's song) / Movin' right along / Like a new world / Hoolah hoolah / Give the drummer some / In the distance lies the future. *(cd-iss. Oct94 on 'Spoon-Mute'; SPOONCD 029)*

White Label not iss.

Sep 90. (cd)(c)(lp) **FISHERMAN'S FRIEND REMIXES** –

– compilations, others, etc. –

on 'United Artists' unless otherwise mentioned

Aug 74. (lp) *(USP 103)* **LIMITED EDITION** –

May 76. (d-lp) *Caroline; (CAD 3001)* **UNLIMITED EDITION** –

Nov 76. (lp) *Sunset; (SLS 50400)* **OPENER** (71-74 material) –

Oct 78. (d-lp) *(UDM 105-6)* **CANNIBALISM** –

May 81. (7") *Virgin; (VS 422) / Polydor;* **I WANT MORE. / . . . AND MORE**
(12"+=) *(VS 422-12)* – Silent night.

1981. (lp) *(SPOON 012)* **DELAY 1968** – German –
– Butterfly / Pnoom / 19th century man / Thief / Man named Joe / Uphill / Little star of Bethlehem. *(cd-iss. Jun89 on 'Spoon-Mute'; SPOONCD 012)*

Oct 81. (lp) *Virgin; (OVED 3)* **INCANDESCENCE** –

1982. (c) *Pure Freude; (PF 23)* **ONLYOU** – German –

Mar 83. (12"ep) *Cherry Red; (12CHERRY 57)* **MOONSHAKE. / TURTLES HAVE SHORT LEGS / ONE MORE NIGHT** –

Jan 85. (c) *Tago Mago; (TM 4755)* **PREHISTORIC FUTURE** – France –

Jun 91. (cd) *Spoon-Mute; (SPOONCD 23-24)* **UNLIMITED EDITION** (new collection) –

Nov 92. (cd) *Spoon-Mute; (SPOONCD 021)* **CANNIBALISM II** –
– Uphill / Pnoom / Connection / Mother Upduff / Little star / T.V. spot / Doko E. / Turtles have short legs / Shikaku maru ten / Gomorrha / Blue bag / Red hot Indians / Half past one / Flow motion / Smoke / I want more . . .and more / Laugh till you cry / Aspectacle animal waves / Sunshine day and night / E.F.S. No.7 / Melting away.

Oct 94. (cd) *Spoon-Mute; (SPOONCD 3031)* **ANTHOLOGY 1968-1993** –

Feb 95. (cd) *Spoon-Mute; (SPOONCD 022)* **CANNIBALISM III** –
– (solo work 1979-1991 from CZUKAY, SCHMIDT, LIEBEZEIT & KAROLI)

Oct 95. (cd) *Strange Fruit; (SFRCD 135)* **LIVE AT THE BBC (Peel sessions)** –

May 97. (t-lp/d-cd) *Grey Area; (SPOON/+CD 39-40)* **SACRILEGE** –

Mar 99. (d-cd+video+book) *Spoon-Mute; (SPOON 041)* **CAN BOX**

Sep 99. (d-cd) *Spoon-Mute; (SPOON 042/043)* **CAN LIVE (live)**

CANNED HEAT

Formed: 1966, Los Angeles, California, USA by ALAN WILSON and BOB HITE. WILSON, nicknamed 'BLIND OWL' because of his thick-lensed glasses, was already a renowned harmonica player and had accompanied SON HOUSE on his album, 'FATHER OF FOLK BLUES'. He met HITE (known as 'THE BEAR' due to his massive 300 pound frame) in 1965 and they soon discovered a shared passion for blues archives (WILSON had studied music at Boston University and did a thesis on blues music while HITE had a collection of blues 78s that numbered in the thousands). They were joined by FRANK COOK on drums and HENRY 'SUNFLOWER' VESTINE, a former member of The MOTHERS OF INVENTION, on guitar. Taking their name from TOMMY JOHNSON, 'CANNED HEAT BLUES' they completed the line-up with the addition of LARRY 'THE MOLE' TAYLOR who was a session bass player with CHUCK BERRY, JERRY LEE LEWIS and The MONKEES. CANNED HEAT's eponymous debut album was released in 1967 and showed some promise, although it only offered copies of 12-bar standards such as, 'ROLLIN' AND TUMBLIN'', 'DUST MY BROOM' and 'BULLFROG BLUES'. Later the same year they performed with distinction at the Monterey Festival, while things got even better with the arrival of new drummer ALFREDO FITO and the subsequent release of the second album, 'BOOGIE WITH CANNED HEAT' in 1968. This was an impressive selection which included, 'FRIED HOCKEY BOOGIE' (a song destined to become a concert favourite) and the hypnotic 'ON THE ROAD AGAIN' (originally recorded by The MEMPHIS JUG BAND in the early Twenties) which gave them a UK Top 10 and US Top 20 hit single. For the next album, 'LIVIN' THE BLUES', WILSON adapted a HENRY THOMAS song, 'BULLDOZE BLUES', by keeping the tune and rewriting the lyric, the result being 'GOIN' UP THE COUNTRY', which highlighted WILSON's trademark falsetto (seemingly taken from SKIP JAMES) and gave them a UK and US Top 20 hit as well as being one of the highlights of the Woodstock movie. Their newfound chart status allowed them to bully their record company, 'Liberty', into giving ALBERT COLLINS a deal with their subsidiary, 'Imperial'. CANNED HEAT recorded a further four albums between 1969-70 including a self financed collaboration with JOHN LEE HOOKER (which gave HOOKER his first chart album). For 'HALLELUJAH', guitarist HARVEY MANDEL replaced HENRY VESTINE who could no longer work with LARRY TAYLOR. They enjoyed further UK hits with a cover of WILBERT HARRISON's, 'LET'S WORK TOGETHER', which reached number 2, and the cajun-like, 'SUGAR BEE' (originally by CLEVELAND CROCHET) but they were shocked by the suicide of ALAN WILSON, whose body was found in HITE'S backyard on the 3rd of September 1970. His death brought about a major reshuffle with TAYLOR and MANDEL going to JOHN MAYALL's BLUESBREAKERS, VESTINE returning and ANTONIO DE LA BARREDA becoming the new bassist. The new line-up completed one album, 'HISTORICAL FIGURES AND ANCIENT HEADS', before BOB HITE's brother RICHARD, replaced BARREDA for the 1973 release, 'THE NEW AGE'. Throughout the next decade, HITE tried to keep the band going although he was unable to get a permanent record deal. A new impetus came with 'HUMAN CONDITION' but the years of struggle took their toll on HITE, who collapsed and died after a gig on the 5th of April 1981. The band's name lived on with TAYLOR and DE LA PARRA recruiting new guitarists JAMES THORNBURY and JUNIOR WATSON and they still tour today although their line-up is constantly changing. The band were still cranking it out come the end of the 90's: while 'BOOGIE 2000' (1999) suggested there was precious little pre-millennial tension in the CANNED HEAT camp (although the music could've done with some), the record was admittedly better than 1996's dismal 'CANNED HEAT BLUES BAND'. 'FRIENDS IN THE CAN' (2003), meanwhile, found the likes of WALTER TROUT, TAJ MAHAL and even the late JOHN LEE HOOKER guesting (the latter on 'LITTLE WHEEL', resurrected from sessions for the late, great bluesman's 1989 album, 'The Healer'), contributing to an infectiously upbeat vibe missing on many oldsters' sets. • **Songwriters:** HITE and WILSON, except ROLLIN' AND TUMBLIN' (Muddy Waters) / WOOLY BULLY (Sam The Sham & The Pharoahs) / SUGAR BEE (Cleveland Crotchet) / BULLDOZE BLUES (Henry Thomas). • **Trivia:** 'Blind Owl' WILSON was so-called due to his bespectacled eyes.

Album rating: CANNED HEAT (*6) / BOOGIE WITH CANNED HEAT (*6) / LIVIN' THE BLUES (*6) / HALLELUJAH (*7) / CANNED HEAT '70 CONCERT (*4) / CANNED HEAT COOKBOOK compilation (*9) / FUTURE BLUES (*5) / HOOKER 'N' HEAT with John Lee Hooker (*5) / HISTORICAL FIGURES AND ANCIENT HEADS (*5) / NEW AGE (*3) / ONE MORE RIVER TO CROSS (*3) / LIVE AT TOPANGA CORRAL (*3) / THE HUMAN CONDITION (*4) / KINGS OF THE BOOGIE (*4) / THE BOOGIE ASSAULT – LIVE IN AUSTRALIA (*3) / RE-HEATED (*3) / INTERNAL COMBUSTION (*4) / UNCANNED – THE BEST OF CANNED HEAT compilation (*8) / BLUES BAND (*2) / BOOGIE 2000 (*3) / LIVE IN OZ (*4) / FRIENDS IN THE CAN (*5)

BOB 'THE BEAR' HITE (b.26 Feb'45, Torrance, California) – vocals, harmonica / **AL 'BLIND OWL' WILSON** (b. 4 Jul'43, Boston, Mass.) – vocals, guitar, harmonica / **HENRY VESTINE** (b.25 Dec'44, Washington, D.C.) – guitar (ex-MOTHERS OF../ ZAPPA) / **LARRY TAYLOR** (b.SAMUEL TAYLOR, 26 Jun'42, Brooklyn, N.Y.) – bass repl. MARK ANDES who had repl. STUART BROTMAN (to KALEIDOSCOPE) / **FRANK COOK** – drums

Liberty Liberty

Aug 67. (lp; mono/stereo) *(LBL/LBS 83059)* <7526> **CANNED HEAT** [ ] [76]
– Rollin' and tumblin' / Bullfrog blues / Evil is going on / Goin' down slow / Catfish blues / Dust my broom / Help me / Big road blues / The story of my life / The road song / Rich woman. *(re-iss. Feb73 as 'ROLLIN' & TUMBLIN'' on 'Sunset'; SLS 50321) (re-iss. Jun89 on 'See for Miles'; SEE 268) (cd-iss. Aug90; SEECD 268)*

Jan 68. (7") *(LBF 150)* <55979> **ROLLIN' AND TUMBLIN'. / BULLFROG BLUES** [ ] [ ]

— **FITO 'ADOLPHO' DE LA PARRA** (b. 3 Feb'46, Mexico City, Mexico) – drums (ex-BLUESBERRY JAM) repl. COOK

Mar 68. (7") <56005> **EVIL WOMAN. / THE WORLD IS A JUDGE** [–] [ ]

May 68. (7") *(LBF 15090)* **ON THE ROAD AGAIN. / THE WORLD IN A JUG** [8] [–]
(re-iss. Sep75 on 'United Artists'; UP 36001)

Jun 68. (lp; mono/stereo) *(LBL/LBS 83103)* <7541> **BOOGIE WITH CANNED HEAT** [5] Feb68 [16]
– Evil woman / My crime / On the road again / World in a jug / Turpentine moan / Whiskey headed woman No.2 / Amphetamine Annie / An owl song / Marie Laveau / Fried hockey boogie. *(re-iss. Feb86 on 'See for Miles'; SEE 62) (cd-iss. Feb90; SEECD 62)*

Jul 68. (7") <56038> **ON THE ROAD AGAIN. / BOOGIE MUSIC** [–] [16]

Nov 68. (7") *(LBF 15169)* <56077> **GOING UP THE COUNTRY. / ONE KIND FAVOUR** [19] [11]

Dec 68. (d-lp) *(LDS 84001)* <27200> **LIVING THE BLUES** [ ] [18]
– Pony blues / My mistake / Sandy's blues / Going up the country / Walking by myself / Boogie music / One kind favour / Parthenogenesis:- Nebulosity – Rollin' and tumblin' – Five owls – Bear wires – Snooky flowers – Sunflower power – Ragi Kafi – Icebag – Childhood's / Refried the boogie (part 1 – live) / Refried the boogie (part 2 – live). *(re-iss. Jul87 on 'See for Miles' lp; SEE 97) (cd-iss. Feb90; SEECD 97) (re-iss. May99 on 'Akarma' d-cd/d-lp; AK 051 CD/LP)*

Apr 69. (7") *(LBF 15200)* <56097> **TIME WAS. / LOW DOWN** [ ] Mar69 [67]

— **HARVEY MANDEL** (b.11 Mar'45, Detroit, Mich.) – guitar (+ solo artist) repl. VESTINE

Aug 69. (lp) *(LBS 83239)* <7618> **HALLELUJAH** [ ] [37]
– Same all over / Change my ways / Canned Heat / Sic 'em pigs / I'm her man / Time was / Do not enter / Big fat / Huautla / Get off my back / Down in the gutter, but free. *(re-iss. Feb89 on 'See for Miles'; SEE 248) (cd-iss. Aug90; SEECD 248)*

Sep 69. (7") *(LBF 15255)* **POOR MAN. / SIC 'EM PIGS** [ ] [ ]

Dec 69. (7") <56140> **CHANGE MY WAYS. / GET OFF MY BACK** [–] [ ]

Jan 70. (lp) *(LBS 83303)* <11000> **CANNED HEAT COOKBOOK** (compilation) [8] Nov69 [86]
– Bullfrog blues / Rollin' and tumblin' / Going up the country / Time was / Boogie music / On the road again / Same all over / Sic 'em pigs / Fried hockey boogie / I will wait for you. *(re-iss. Nov75 on 'Sunset'; SLS 50377)*

Jan 70. (7") *(LBF 15302)* <56151> **LET'S WORK TOGETHER. / I'M HER MAN** [2] Sep70 [26]

Jun 70. (7") *(LBF 15350)* **SUGAR BEE. / SHAKE IT AND BREAK IT** [49] [–]

Jun 70. (lp) *(LBS 83333)* <5509> **CANNED HEAT '70 CONCERT (live in Europe)** [15] Jul71 [ ]
– That's all right mama / Bring it on home / Pulling hair blues / Back out on the road – On the road again / London blues / Let's work together / Goodbye for now. *(re-iss. Oct88 as '70: LIVE IN EUROPE' on 'Beat Goes On'; BGOLP 12) (cd-iss. Sep89; BGOCD 12)*

— **ANTONIO DE LA BARREDA** (aka TONY OLAV) – bass repl. LARRY TAYLOR

Sep 70. (7") *(LBF 15395)* **FUTURE BLUES. / SKAT** [ ] [–]

Sep 70. (lp) *(LBS 83364)* <11002> **FUTURE BLUES** [27] [59]
– Sugar bee / Shake it and break it / That's all right mama / My time ain't long / Scat / Let's work together / London blues / So sad (the world's in a tangle) / Future blues. *(re-iss. Jul89 on 'Beat Goes On' lp/cd; BGO LP/CD 49)*

— On 3rd Sep70, **AL WILSON** suffering depression died of drug o/d. He appeared on the releases below until stated.

Dec 70. (7") *(LBF 15429)* **CHRISTMAS BLUES. / DO NOT ENTER** [ ] [–]

Jan 71. (7") *(LBF 15439)* **WOOLY BULLY. / MY TIME AIN'T LONG** [ ] [ ]

— **HENRY VESTINE** – guitar returned to repl. MANDEL who returned to JOHN MAYALL (next with veteran US blues legend)

Mar 71. (d-lp; by CANNED HEAT / JOHN LEE HOOKER)
(LPS 103-4) <35002> **HOOKER'N'HEAT** Feb71 73
– Messin' with the Hook / The feelin' is gone / Send me your pillow / Sittin' here thinkin' / Meet me in the bottom / Altmonia blues / Drifter / You talk too much / Burning Hell / Bottle up and go / The world today / I got my eyes on you / Whiskey and wimmen' / Just you and me / Let's make it / Peavine / Boogie chillen No.2. *<re-iss. Oct71 on 'United Artists'; 9955> (re-iss. Sep88 as lp 'THE BEST OF HOOKER'N'HEAT' on 'See for Miles'; SEE 234) (cd-iss. Aug89 as 'HOOKER'N'HEAT (THE BEST OF PLUS)'; SEECD 234)*

— **JOEL SCOTT HILL** – guitar, vocals finally repl. AL WILSON, now alongside **HITE, BARREDA, PARRA and VESTINE**

U.A. U.A.

Mar 71. (7"; CANNED HEAT & JOHN LEE HOOKER)
<50779> **LET'S MAKE IT. / WHISKEY AND WIMMEN** –
Sep 71. (7") *(UP 35279) <50831>* **LONG WAY FROM L.A.. / HILL'S STOMP**

— **LITTLE RICHARD** – piano, vocals guested on next album

Mar 72. (lp) *(UAG 29304) <5557>* **HISTORICAL FIGURES AND ANCIENT HEADS** Feb72 87
– Sneakin' around / Hill's stomp / Rockin' with the king / I don't care what you tell me / Long way from L.A. / Cherokee dance / That's all right / Utah. *(re-iss. Aug90 on 'Beat Goes On' cd/lp; BGO CD/LP 83)*
Apr 72. (7") *(UP 35348) <50892>* **ROCKIN' WITH THE KING. / I DON'T CARE WHAT YOU TELL ME** Mar72 88
Jul 72. (7") *<50927>* **CHEROKEE DANCE. / SNEAKIN' AROUND** –

— **RICHARD HITE** – bass (BOB's brother) (ex-POPPA HOP) repl. BARREDA / added **JAMES SHANE** – guitar / **ED BEYER** – keyboards

Jun 73. (7") *(UP 35562)* **KEEP IT CLEAN. / YOU CAN RUN, BUT YOU SURE CAN'T HIDE** –
Sep 73. (lp) *(UAS 29455) <049F>* **NEW AGE**
– Keep it clean / Harley Davidson blues / Don't deceive me / You can run, but you sure can't hide / Rock and roll music / Lookin' for my rainbow / Framed / Election blues / So long wrong *(cd-iss. May91 on 'Beat Goes On'; BGOCD 85)*
Sep 73. (7") *<167>* **LOOKIN' FOR MY RAINBOW. / ROCK AND ROLL MUSIC** –
Nov 73. (7") *<243>* **HARLEY DAVIDSON BLUES. /** –

Atlantic Atlantic

Feb 74. (7") *(K 10420) <3010>* **ONE MORE RIVER TO CROSS. / HIGHWAY 401**
Mar 74. (lp) *(K 50026) <SD 7289>* **ONE MORE RIVER TO CROSS**
– L.A. town / I need someone / Bagful of boogie / I'm a hog for you baby / You am what I am / Shake rattle & roll / Bright times are comin' / Highway 401 / We remember Fats.
Jan 75. (7") *<3236>* **THE HARDER THEY COME. / ROCK 'N' ROLL SHOW** –

— **RICHARD HITE + FITO DE LA PARRA** took over control of band when BOB & HENRY got stoned. ED BAYER also departed. Recruited **CHRIS MORGAN** – guitar / **GENE TAYLOR** – keyboards (both ex-POPPA HOP)

Sonet Takoma

Dec 78. (lp) *(SNTF 783) <7066>* **THE HUMAN CONDITION**
– Strut my stuff / Hot money / House of blue lights / Just got to be there / You just got the rock / Human condition / She's lookin' good / Open up your backdoor / Wrapped up.

— (later in 70's) **BOB HITE** returned (he was to die of heart attack 4th Apr81)

— re-united + re-formed with **FITO, VESTINE,** and **TAYLOR** and others, **RAUL E. RODRIGUEZ + F.M. HALEY.**

not iss. Destiny

1982. (lp) *<10007>* **KINGS OF THE BOOGIE** –
– Kings of the boogie / Stoned bad street fighting man / So fine / You just can't get close to me / Hell's just on down the road / I was wrong / Little crystal / Dog house blues / Sleepy hollow baby / Chicken shack. *<re-iss. 1981 as 'DOG HOUSE BLUES' on 'Rhino'; > (re-iss. Oct85 on 'Platinum' lp/c; PLP/PMC 20)*

not iss. A.L.A.

1984. (12"ep) *<1996>* **THE HEAT BROS '84** –

— **JAMES THORNBERRY** – slide guitar, vocals, harmonica repl. VESTINE.

Bedrock not iss.

Dec 87. (blue-lp) *(BEDLP 5)* **THE BOOGIE ASSAULT (LIVE IN AUSTRALIA)**
– Kings of the boogie / Stoned bad street fighting man / So fine / You just can't get close to me / Hell's just on down the road / I was wrong / Little crystal / Dog house blues / Sleepy hollow baby / Chicken shack. *(cd-iss. Mar89; BEDLP 5CD)*

not iss. Chameleon

1990. (cd) *<SPV 858805>* **REHEATED** –
– Looking for the party / Driftin' / I'm watching you / Bullfrog blues / Hucklebuck / Mercury blues / Gunstreet girl / I love to rock and roll / So fine (Betty Jean) / Take me to the river / Red headed woman / Built for comfort. *(UK-iss.Mar96 on 'SPV'; same)*

— new line-up; **VESTINE / DE LA PARRA / THORNBURY / + JUNIOR WATSON** – guitar, vocals / **RON SHUMAKE** – bass, vocals

Aim Topic

Sep 93. (cd)(c) *(AIM CD/C 1033)* **BURNIN' (live in Australia 1990)**
– Let's work together / Gamblin' woman / Hucklebuck / Sunnyland / Rollin' and tumblin' / Nitwit / Gunstreet girl / One way out / J.J. jump / Mercury blues.

— **TAYLOR + MANDEL** returned

Aim River Road

Jul 95. (cd) *(AIM 1044)* **INTERNAL COMBUSTION**
– I used to be bad / John Lee Hooker boogie / Remember Woodstock / (You'll have to) Come and get it / The heat in me is up / It' hot / Vision of you / Nothing at all / 24 hours / Gamblin' woman / I might be tempted. *(re-iss. Jan96 on 'Connoisseur'; FPCCD 01)*

— **ROBERT LUCAS** – (new) vocals; repl. TAYLOR + MANDEL

not iss. A&M

1996. (cd) *<161416>* **BLUES BAND** –
– Stranger / Quiet woman / Iron horse / Jr.'s shuffle / Creole queen / Keep it to yourself / Boogie music / Going up the country / See these tears / One kind favor / Oh baby / Gorgo boogie.

Ruf Ruf

Sep 99. (cd) *<(RUF 1041)>* **BOOGIE 2000**
– Wait and see / Last man who'll ever have to sing the blues / World of make believe / Dark clouds / Searchin' for my baby / I got loaded / Too much goddyup (not enough whoa) / She split / 2000 reasons (Y2K blues) / Road to Rio / Can I come home / I'm so tired.
Feb 03. (cd) *(MYSCD 148)* **LIVE IN OZ featuring WALTER TROUT (live)** –
– One the road again / Amphetamine Annie / Going up the country / Let's work together / Kings of the boogie / Refried hockey boogie / Hell's on down the line / Chicken shack boogie / So long.
(above issued on 'Mystic') (next with various blues guests)
May 03. (cd) *<(RUF 1066)>* **FRIENDS IN THE CAN**
– Same old games / Bad trouble / Black coffee / Getaway / It don't matter / Let's work together / 1, 2, 3, here we go again / That fat cat / Home to you / Never get out of these blues alive / Little wheel / Let's work together / Geataway.

– compilations, etc. –

Jan 70. (lp) *Pye International; (NSPL 28129) / Janus; <3009>* **VINTAGE HEAT**
Jun 70. (7") *Pye International; (7N 25513)* **SPOONFUL. / BIG ROAD BLUES** –
1973. (lp; with CLARENCE GATEMOUTH BROWN) *Barclay; (80603)* **GATE'S ON HEAT** – France –
Jul 75. (lp; with MEMPHIS SLIM) *Barclay; (80607)* **MEMPHIS HEAT** – France –
Nov 76. (7"ep) *United Artists; (REM 407)* **REMEMBER CANNED HEAT** –
– On the road again / Let's work together / Going up the country.
Nov 76. (lp) *D.J.M.; (DJB 26072) / Wand; <WDS 693>* **LIVE AT TOPANGA CORRAL (live)** 1971
May 84. (7") *EMI-Golden; (G45 24)* **ON THE ROAD AGAIN. / LET'S WORK TOGETHER**
1987. (d-lp) *Rhino; <RNDA 71105>* **INFINITE BOOGIE** –
Feb 88. (lp)(cd) *Rhino; <RNLP 801><RNCD 75776>* **HOOKER 'N' HEAT VOL.2** –
Aug 89. (7") *E.M.I.; (EM 100)* **LET'S WORK TOGETHER. / GOIN' UP THE COUNTRY** –
(12"+=) *(12EM 100)* – Rollin' and tumblin'.
(cd-s+=) *(CDEM 100)* – Amphetamine Annie.
Sep 89. (lp/c)(cd) *E.M.I.; (GO/TC-GO 2026)(CDP 793114-2)* **LET'S WORK TOGETHER (THE BEST OF CANNED HEAT)**

– On the road again / Bullfrog blues / Rollin' and tumblin' / Amphetamine / Annie / Fried hockey boogie / Sic 'em pigs / Poor Moon / Let's work together / Going up the country / Boogie music / Same all over / Time was / Sugar bee / Rockin' with the king / That's alright mama / My time ain't long.

Apr 90. (d-lp)(cd) *Bear Family; (BTS 964410)(BTCD 9779 409)* **LIVE AT THE TURKU ROCK FESTIVAL (live in Finland)** [–] German [–]

Feb 92. (cd) *Thunderbolt; (CDTB 130)* **STRAIGHT AHEAD** [ ] [–] *(re-iss. Apr97; same)*

Oct 92. (cd) *Carlton; (SMS 053)* **ROCK LEGENDS VOL.1** [ ] [–]

Nov 92. (3xcd-box) *Liberty; (CANNED 780275-2)* **THE BIG HEAT** [ ] [–]

Jul 93. (cd) *Charly; (CCCD 1104)* **LIVE** [ ] [–]

Aug 94. (d-cd) *E.M.I.; (CDEM 15431)* **UNCANNED (THE BEST OF CANNED HEAT)** [ ] [ ]

Feb 95. (cd) *In-Akustik; (INAK 8804)* **BOOGIE UP THE COUNTRY (live in West Germany 1987)** [ ] [–]

Feb 95. (cd) *B.A.M.; (KLMCD 015)* **PEARLS OF THE PAST VOL.2 – CANNED HEAT** [ ] [–]

Feb 96. (cd) *Prestige; (CSGSP 079)* **BIG ROAD BLUES** [ ] [–]

Feb 97. (cd) *EMI Gold; (CDGOLD 1076)* **ON THE ROAD AGAIN** [ ] [–]

May 97. (cd) *Disky; (DC 87865-2)* **THE BEST OF CANNED HEAT** [ ] [–]

Mar 99. (cd) *Start; (SRH 806)* **ON THE ROAD AGAIN** [ ] [–]

☐ Jerry CANTRELL (see under ⇒ ALICE IN CHAINS)

CAPTAIN BEEFHEART

Born: DON VAN VLIET, 15 Jan'41, Glendale, Los Angeles, California, USA. Started out as a child-prodigy sculptor who, between the ages of five and thirteen, had his clay animals featured on a weekly TV show hosted by Portuguese sculptor Augustino Rodriguez. An opportunity to develop his art skills were halted when his parents declined a scholarship on his behalf to study art in Europe, preferring instead to move to Lancaster in the Mojave desert. There, he met FRANK ZAPPA at the local high school, setting up a few local bands while ZAPPA started to write a script for a B-movie 'CAPTAIN BEEFHEART MEETS THE GRUNT PEOPLE'. When FRANK went to Los Angeles to form The MOTHERS OF INVENTION, DON adopted the name CAPTAIN BEEFHEART and set about recruiting The MAGIC BAND. They signed to 'A&M' in 1964, releasing their version of BO DIDDLEY's 'DIDDY WAH DIDDY', which sold enough copies to encourage the label to buy studio time for an album. When completed, president Jerry Moss rejected the tapes, citing it too strange and anti-commercial. Undaunted, VAN VLIET and a new set of musicians, including RY COODER, re-recorded most of these masters, the album 'SAFE AS MILK' finally surfacing in 1967 on the 'Buddah' label. This was a masterpiece of its time, full of BEEFHEART on a HOWLIN' WOLF-style trip; the great tracks being 'ELECTRICITY', 'ABBA ZABA', 'AUTUMN CHILD' & 'ZIG ZAG WANDERER'. However, RY COODER departed for safer pastures when VAN VLIET/BEEFHEART left the stage halfway through their set at the 1967 Monterey Pop Festival, leaving the band to play to a bewildered but carefree hippy audience. BEEFHEART often showed signs of outlandish behaviour which split the band up as much as his personality. Late in 1968, they recorded another album, 'MIRROR MAN', although this was shelved until his popularity had grown in the early 70's. However, one album did appear that year, 'STRICTLY PERSONAL', which BEEFHEART slammed for its radical remix by producer BOB KRASNOW. This riled him so much that he signed a new contract with old friend ZAPPA who gave him complete artistic control on his new 'Straight' label. Having written about 30 songs in a day, BEEFHEART took his new bunch of weirdo musicians (ANTENNAE JIMMY SEMENS, DRUMBO, ART TRIPP III, ZOOT HORN ROLLO and THE MASCARA SNAKE) to rehearse in a house which was close-by an old friend JIMMY CARL BLACK (drummer for ZAPPA). They stayed there for a full eight months, only one of them at a time venturing out if the band was in need of food & drink, etc. This was VAN VLIET's tyrannical way of keeping the band tight, so as to establish virtuoso musicianship while he got on with the weird vocals. The resulting album (a double!) 'TROUT MASK REPLICA' was handed to ZAPPA, much to his surprise, after four and a half hours in the studio. When released at the turn of the decade, it was initially given the thumbs down by many critics and fans. Those hardy enough to give it a few tolerant spins, however, were convinced of its genius. The record surprisingly nearly made the UK Top 20, having been played to death on John Peel's Radio 1 night-time show. Its virtual insanity was literally not of this world, utilising the complex structures of jazz legend ORNETTE COLEMAN; the best tracks to break through – to the sane among us, were 'THE BLIMP', 'PENA', 'DALI'S CAR', 'ELLA GURU' & 'OLD FART AT PLAY'. It has since become regarded as a classic, although it should never be played to someone not of your generation. He returned a thank-you to ZAPPA, when he sang a track, 'WILLIE THE WIMP', on his 'Hot Rats' album, although their friendship was fraying with every meeting, two egos too big for one room. In 1970, he settled down to a more conventional avant-garde Delta-blues album 'LICK MY DECALS OFF, BABY' (compared that is, to their last). It was another excellent set; combing through the depths of his unearthly roots to find tracks such as 'DOCTOR DARK', 'I LOVE YOU, YOU BIG DUMMY' and the title track. 1972 saw another great album 'THE SPOTLIGHT KID', featuring the delights of 'CLICK CLACK', 'I'M GONNA BOOGLARIZE YOU BABY' & 'WHEN IT GROWS IT STACKS'. Their next, 'CLEAR SPOT' covered new territory on softer tracks like 'TOO MUCH TIME' & 'MY HEAD IS MY ONLY HOUSE UNLESS IT RAINS', tempting the MAGIC BAND to bail out and form their own outfit, MALLARD. The album did, however, include another powerful BEEFHEART special in the shape of 'BIG EYED BEANS FROM VENUS'. In 1974, with a new line-up, he signed to UK's 'Virgin' label but his work at this point, especially on the albums 'UNCONDITIONALLY GUARANTEED' & 'BLUEJEANS & MOONBEAMS', were just above average. He tried to escape yet another restrictive deal; it was said he would sign anything, and teamed up with his old pal FRANK ZAPPA and The MOTHERS. Their collaboration, 'BONGO FURY', set the ball rolling for a litigation battle between him and 'Virgin' UK, resulting in another deal!, this time with 'Warner Brothers' for the 1978 album 'SHINY BEAST (BAT CHAIN PULLER)', a marked return to form on some tracks. Virgin won the rights to this album, which gained a UK release in early 1980. Two other records surfaced in the next two years; 'DOC AT RADAR STATION' and the considerably better 'ICE CREAM FOR CROW', the latter containing the excellent title track, his final epitaph. He retired from the music business and set up home with his wife JAN at a trailer park in the Mojave desert. Still an avid sculptor and painter, with the help of fan Julian Schnabel, he began exhibiting his primitive canvases which made him more money than his records ever did. In the mid-80's, a host of young British indie acts including STUMP, McKENZIES, The SHRUBS, etc, took on the mantle of the BEEFHEART sound. Always asked if he would return, BEEFHEART has repeatedly refused to get back on the bandwagon (having fallen into ill-health, both physically and mentally, a return to the recording studio is unlikely to say the least). A remarkable figure of his time, DON VAN VLIET exemplified the glory of not worrying about the exploitation of the music industry, only happy with his own, and of course the MAGIC BAND's work. Let's just hope he's around for several more years to enjoy whatever he creates. • **Trivia:** He also covered Jack Nitzsche's 'HARD WORKIN' MAN' on the 1978 film 'Blue Collar', which starred Harvey Keitel.

Album rating: SAFE AS MILK (*10) / STRICTLY PERSONAL (*6) / TROUT MASK REPLICA (*10) / LICK MY DECALS OFF, BABY (*8) / MIRROR MAN earlier recording (*7) / THE SPOTLIGHT KID (*8) / CLEAR SPOT (*8) / UNCONDITIONALLY GUARANTEED (*6) / BLUEJEANS & MOONBEAMS (*9) / BONGO FURY; with Frank Zappa (*5) / SHINY BEAST (BAT CHAIN PULLER) (*6) / DOC AT RADAR STATION (*6) / ICE CREAM FOR CROW (*7) / THE LEGENDARY A&M SESSIONS mini of early stuff (*5) / I MAY BE HUNGRY BUT I SURE AIN'T WEIRD collection (*6) / A CARROT IS AS CLOSE AS A RABBIT GETS TO A DIAMOND compilation (*8) / GROW FINS boxed set (*8) / MERSEYTROUT – LIVE IN LIVERPOOL 1980 (*7)

CAPTAIN BEEFHEART & HIS MAGIC BAND

DON VAN VLIET – vocals, harmonica, occasional guitar, wind instruments / **ALEX ST. CLAIRE SNOUFFER** – guitar / **DOUG MOON** – guitar / **JERRY HANDLEY** – bass / **PAUL BLAKELY** – drums

A&M A&M

1966. (7") *<794>* **DIDDY WAH DIDDY. / WHO DO YOU THINK YOU'RE FOOLING** [–] [ ]

1966. (7") *<818>* **MOONCHILD. / FRYING PAN** [–] [ ]

1968. (7") *(AMS 726)* **MOONCHILD. / WHO DO YOU THINK YOU'RE FOOLING** [ ] [–]

—— **JOHN FRENCH** (DRUMBO) – drums; repl. BLAKELY (MOON also departed) / **RY COODER** guested on 2 tracks below

Pye Inter Kama Sutra

Jan 68. (7") *(7N 25443)* **YELLOW BRICK ROAD. / ABBA ZABA** [ ] [–]

Feb 68. (lp) *(NPL 28110) <BDS 5001>* **SAFE AS MILK** [ ] Nov67 [ ]
– Sure 'nuff 'n yes I do / Zig zag wanderer / Call on me / Dropout boogie / I'm glad / Electricity / Yellow brick road / Abba zaba / Plastic factory / Where there's woman / Plastic factory / Grown so ugly / Autumn child. *(re-iss. 1968 on 'Marble Arch' 2 tracks less; MAL 1117) (re-iss. 1970 on 'Buddha' stereo; 623 171) (re-iss. Jan82 on 'P.R.T.'; NCP 1004) (re-iss. Jul85 on 'Buddah' lp/c; 252260-1/-4) (cd-iss. May91 on 'Castle'; CLACD 234) (cd re-mast.Sep99 on 'Buddha-RCA'+=; 74321 89175-2)* – Safe as milk (take 5) / On tomorrow / Big black baby / Flower pot / Dirty blue Gene / Trust us (take 9) / Korn ring finger. *(lp re-iss. Sep99 on 'Simply Vinyl'; SVLP 122)*

—— **JEFF COTTON** (ANTENNAE JIMMY SEMENS) – guitar; repl. COODER who went solo (HERB BERMANN co-contributed several songs)

Liberty Blue Thumb

Dec 68. (lp; mono/stereo) *(LBL/LBS 83172) <BTS 1>* **STRICTLY PERSONAL** [ ] Oct68 [ ]
– Ah feel like ahcid / Safe as milk / Trust us / Son of Mirror Man – Mere man / On tomorrow / Beatle bones 'n' smokin' stones / Gimme dat harp boy / Kandy korn. *(re-iss. Nov79 lp/c; LBR/TCR 1006) (cd-iss. Aug94 on 'E.M.I.'; CZ 529) (lp re-iss. Dec99 on 'Simply Vinyl'; SVLP 157)*

—— **The CAPTAIN** retained **DRUMBO** and **ANTANNAE** plus new members **ZOOT HORN ROLLO** (b.BILL HARKLEROAD) – brass, narrator, guitar, flute / **ROCKETTE NORTON** (b.MARK BOSTON) – bass, narrator / **THE MASCARA SNAKE** (b.VICTOR HAYDEN) – clarinet / guest **DOUG MOON** returned

Straight Straight

Nov 69. (d-lp) *(STS 1053) <RS 2027>* **TROUT MASK REPLICA** [21] [ ]
– Frownland / The dust blows forward 'n dust blows back / Dachau blues / Ella guru / Hair pie: bake 1 / Moonlight on Vermont / Hair pie: bake 2 / Pena / Well / When big Joan sets up / Fallin' ditch / Sugar 'n spikes / Ant man bee / Pachuco cadaver / Bills corpse / Sweet sweet bulbs / Neon meate dream of an octafish / China pig / My human gets me blues / Dali's car / Orange claw hammer / Wild life / She's too much for my mirror / Hobo chang ba / The blimp (mousetrap replica) / Steal softly thru snow / Old fart at play / Veteran's day poppy. *(re-iss. May75 on 'Reprise'; K 64026) (re-iss. cd Sep94 & Jul00 on 'WEA'; K 927196-2)*

—— **ED MARIMBA** (ART TRIPP) – marimba (ex-MOTHERS OF INVENTION) repl. THE MASCARA SNAKE

Jan 71. (lp) *(STS 1063) <RS 6240>* **LICK MY DECALS OFF, BABY** [20] [ ]
– Lick my decals off, baby / Doctor Dark / I love you, you big dummy / Peon / Bellerin' plain / Woe-is-uh-me-bop / Japan in a dishpan / I wanna find a woman that'll hold my big toe till I have a go / Petrified forest / One rose that I mean / The Buggy boogie woogie / The Smithsonian Institute blues (or the big dig) / Space-age couple / The clouds are full of wine (not whiskey or rye) / Flash Gordon's ape. *(re-iss. Jul73 on 'Reprise') <US cd-iss. 1990 on 'Enigma'; >*

CAPTAIN BEEFHEART

—— **THE WINGED EEL FINGERLING** (r.n. ELLIOT INGBER) – guitar, etc. (ex-MOTHERS etc.) repl. SEMENS who had already formed MU

Reprise Reprise

Jan 72. (7") *<1068>* **CLICK CLACK. / I'M GONNA BOOGLARIZE YOU BABY** [–] [ ]

Feb 72. (lp) *(K 44162) <RS 2050>* **THE SPOTLIGHT KID** [44] [ ]
– I'm gonna booglarize you baby / White jam / Blabber 'n smoke / When it blows its stacks / Alice in Blunderland / The spotlight kid / Click clack / Grow fins / There ain't no Santa Claus on the evenin' stage / Glider.

CAPTAIN BEEFHEART and the MAGIC BAND

—— **ROY 'OREJON' ESTRADA** – bass (ex-LITTLE FEAT, ex-MOTHERS OF INVENTION) repl. INGBER / augmented by backing vocals The **BLACKBERRIES / RUSS TITELMAN** – guitar (guested, as he did on "Safe as Milk")

Nov 72. (lp) *(K 54007) <MS 2115>* **CLEAR SPOT** [ ] [ ]
– Low yo yo stuff / Nowadays a woman's gotta hit a man / Too much time / Circumstances / My head is my only house unless it rains / Sun zoom sparks / Clear spot / Crazy little thing / Long neck bottles / Her eyes are a blue million miles / Big eyed beans from Venus / Golden birdies.

Mar 73. (7") *(K 14233) <1133>* **TOO MUCH TIME. / MY HEAD IS MY ONLY HOUSE UNLESS IT RAINS** [ ] [ ]

—— **ALEX SAINT CLAIRE** – guitar; returned to repl. ROY

—— added **MARK MARCELLINO** – keyboards

Virgin Mercury

Apr 74. (lp) *(V 2015) <SRM1 709>* **UNCONDITIONALLY GUARANTEED** [ ] [ ]
– Upon the my-o-my / Sugar bowl / New electric ride / Magic be / Happy love song / Full moon, hot sun / I got love on my mind / This is the day / Lazy music / Peaches. *(re-iss. Aug82 + Aug85 on 'Fame' lp/c; FA/TCFA 3034) (re-iss. Aug88; OVED 66) (cd-iss. Jun88; CDV 2015)*

Apr 74. (7") *(VS 110)* **UPON THE MY-O-MY. / MAGIC BE** [ ] [–]

Apr 74. (7") *<73494>* **UPON THE MY-O-MY. / I GOT LOVE ON MY MIND** [–] [ ]

—— **IRA INGBER** – bass; repl. SAINT CLAIRE / added new session men **MARK GIBBONS** – keyboards / **MICHAEL SMOTHERMAN** – keyboards, vocals / **JIMMY CARAVAN** – keyboards / **DEAN SMITH** – guitar / **BOB WEST** – bass / **GENE PELLO** – drums / **TY GRIMS** – percussion

Nov 74. (lp) *(V 2123) <SRM1 1018>* **BLUEJEANS & MOONBEAMS** [ ] [ ]
– Party of special things do / Same old blues / Observatory crest / Pompadour swamp / Captain's holiday / Rock'n'roll's evil doll / Further than we've gone / Twist ah luck / Bluejeans and moonbeams. *(re-iss. Mar84; OVED 19) (cd-iss. Jun88; CDV 2023)*

—— Late '75 **BEEFHEART** collaborated with **FRANK ZAPPA** on **"BONGO FURY"** album. This was a near live album with 2 studio tracks.

—— His new touring band featured past members **ELLIOT, INGBER** and **JOHN FRENCH** plus **DENNY WHALLEY** – slide guitar / **BRUCE FOWLER** – trombone (both on bongos)

—— His '76 band were **DRUMBO, WHALLEY, JEFF MORRIS TEPPER** – slide guitar, guitar + **JOHN THOMAS** – piano (they recorded first sessions for the next album)

—— **ERIC DREW FELDMAN** – synthesizer; repl. THOMAS / **ROBERT ARTHUR WILLIAMS** – drums; repl. DRUMBO / **RICHARD REDUS** – slide guitar, guitars. accordion, fretless bass; repl. WHALLEY / **ART TRIPP III** – marimba, percussion; returned from MALLARD **BRUCE LAMBOURNE FOWLER** also returned

Virgin Warners

Feb 80. (lp) *(V 2149) <BSK 3256>* **SHINY BEAST (BAT CHAIN PULLER)** [ ] 1979 [ ]
– The floppy boot stomp / Tropical hot dog night / Ice rose / Harry Irene / You know you're a man / Bat chain puller / When I see mommy I feel like

a mummy / Owed t'Alex / Candle mambo / Love lies / Suction prints / Apes-ma. *(re-iss. Aug88; OVED 67) (cd-iss. Jun87; CDV 2149)*

—— **GARY LUCAS** – french horn, guitar (on 1); repl. REDUS

—— **DRUMBO (JOHN FRENCH)** also returned

Virgin Virgin

Aug 80. (lp) *(V 2172) <13148>* **DOC AT RADAR STATION**
– Hot head / Ashtray heart / A carrot is as close as a rabbit gets to a diamond / Run paint run run / Sue Egypt / Brickbats / Dirty blue Gene / Best batch yet / Telephone / Flavor bud living / Sheriff of Hong Kong / Making love to a vampire with a monkey on my knee. *(re-iss. Aug88; OVED 68) (cd-iss. Jun88; CDV 2172)*

—— The CAPTAIN brought in **RICHARD 'MIDNIGHT HAT SIZE' SNYDER** – guitar, bass, marimba, viola / **CLIFF R. MARTINEZ** – drums, percussion, etc / to add to **TEPPER** + **LUCAS** FELDMAN remained a guest

Aug 82. (12") *(VS 534-12) <03190>* **LIGHT REFLECTED OFF THE OCEANS OF THE MOON. / ICE CREAM FOR CROW** –

Sep 82. (lp) *(V 2237)* **ICE CREAM FOR CROW** 90 –
– Ice cream for crow / The host the ghost the most holy-o / Semi-multicoloured caucasian / Hey Garland, I dig your tweed coat / Evening bell / Cardboard cutout sundown / The past sure is tense / Ink mathematics / The witch doctor life / "81" poop hatch / The thousandth and tenth day of the human totem pole / Skeleton makes good. *(re-iss. Aug88; OVED 121) (cd-iss. Apr88; CDV 2237) <US cd-iss. 1990 on 'Caroline'; CAROL 1632-2>*

—— BEEFHEART retired from the music business to concentrate on painting/sculpting in his recently bought Mojave desert home.

– compilations etc. –

Jul 70. (lp) *Buddah; (2349 002)* **DROPOUT BOOGIE** –
(a re-iss. of "SAFE AS MILK" 2 tracks less)

May 71. (lp) *Buddah; (2365 002) <BDS 5077>* **MIRROR MAN** (rec.1967; not one night in 1965 as stated on sleeve!) 49
– Tarotplane / Kandy korn / 25th century Quaker / Mirror man. *(re-iss. May82 on 'P.R.T.'; NCP 1006) (re-iss. Apr86 on 'Edsel'; ED 184) (cd-iss. May91 on 'Castle'; CLACD 235) (cd re-iss. Sep99 as 'THE MIRROR MAN SESSIONS' on 'Buddha-RCA'+=; 74321 69174-2)* – Trust us (take 6) / Safe as milk (take 12) / Beatle bones n' smokin' stones / Moody Liz (take 8) / Gimme dat harp boy. *(lp re-iss. Nov99 on 'Simply Vinyl'; SVLP 143)*

1975. (lp) *WRMB;* **WHAT'S ALL THIS BOOGA-BOOGA MUSIC (live)** –

Aug 76. (d-lp) *Reprise; (K 84006)* **TWO ORIGINALS OF . . .**
– (LICK MY DECALS OFF, BABY / THE SPOTLIGHT KID)

Nov 77. (d-lp/d-c) *Pye; (FILD/ZCFILD 008)* **THE CAPTAIN BEEFHEART FILE** (first 2-lp's) –

1978. (d-lp) *Impossible;* **EASY TEETH** –

Jan 78. (7") *Buddah; (BDS 466)* **SURE 'NUFF 'N' YES I DO. / ELECTRICITY** –

May 78. (7") *M.C.A.; (MCA 366)* **HARD WORKIN' MAN (by Jack Nitzsche featuring Captain Beefheart). / Coke Machine (by Jack Nitzsche)** –
above also features RY COODER – on guitar

1978. (7"pic-ep) *Virgin; (SIXPACK 1)* **SIX-PACK / SIX TRACK** –
– Sugar bowl / Same old blues / Upon the my-o-my / Magic be / Rock'n'roll's evil doll / New electric ride.

Jul 83. (10"lp/c) *P.R.T.; (DOW/ZCDOW 15)* **MUSIC IN SEA MINOR** –

Jul 84. (lp/pic-lp) *Design; (PIL/+P 4)* **TOP SECRET** –

Oct 84. (m-lp) *A&M; (AMY 226)* **THE LEGENDARY SESSIONS** –
– Diddy wah diddy / Who do you think you're fooling / Moonchild / Frying pan / Here I am, I always am. *(re-iss. Oct86 on 'Edsel'; BLIMP 902) (cd-iss. Mar92; BLIMPCD 902)*

Jun 88. (d-lp/c/d-cd) *That's Original; (TFO LP/MC/CD 11)* **SAFE AS MILK / MIRROR MAN** –
(re-iss. d-cd.May91 on 'Castle')

Feb 91. (d-cd) *Reprise; (7599 26249-2)* **THE SPOTLIGHT KID / CLEAR SPOT** –

Jul 91. (cd) *The Collection; (ORO 146)* **ZIG ZAG WANDERER** –
(re-iss. Nov96 & Oct98 on 'Wooded Hill'; HILLCD 6)

Jun 92. (cd) *Sequel; (NEXCD 215)* **I MAY BE HUNGRY BUT I SURE AIN'T WEIRD – THE ALTERNATIVE CAPTAIN BEEFHEART** –

Jun 93. (cd) *Virgin Universal; (CDVM 9028) <88303-2>* **A CARROT IS AS CLOSE AS A RABBIT GETS TO A DIAMOND**
– Sugar bowl / The past sure is tense / Happy love song / The floppy boot stomp / Bluejeans and moonbeams / Run paint run run / This is the day / Tropical hot dog night / Observatory crest / The host the ghost the most holy o / Harry Irene / I got love on my mind / Pompadour swamp / Love lies / Sheriff of Hong Kong / Further than we've gone / Candle mambo / Light reflected off the oceans of the Moon / A carrot is as close as a rabbit gets to a diamond.

Nov 93. (cd) *Movieplay Gold; (MPG 74025)* **LONDON 1974 (live)** –

Jan 98. (cd) *Camden-RCA; (74321 55846-2)* **ELECTRICITY** –

Nov 98. (7") *Table Of Elements; <(TOE 759)>* **SPITBALL SCALPED UH BABY. /**

Nov 98. (cd+book) *Sonic Book; (SB 1)* **PEARLS BEFORE SWINE** (poems, paintings, aphorisms & discography) –

May 99. (5xcd-box) *Revenant; (REV 210)* **GROW FINS** (rarities 1965-1982)

May 99. (d-lp) *Xeric; <(XERLP 96)>* **GROW FINS VOL.1 – JUST GOT BACK FROM THE CITY 1965-1967 / ELECTRICITY 1968**

Sep 99. (d-lp) *Xeric; <(XERLP 97)>* **GROW FINS VOL.2 – THE TROUT MASK REPLICA HOUSE SESSIONS 1969**

Oct 00. (cd) *Ozit; <(BF 4003)>* **MERSEYTROUT – LIVE IN LIVERPOOL 1980** (rec. 29 October 1980)
– Toaster (bass solo) / Nowadays a woman's gotta hit a man / Abba zabba / Hothead / Dirty blue Jean / Best batch yet / One man sentence (poem) / Safe as milk / Flavour bud living / Her eyes are a blue million miles / One red rose that I mean / Doctor Dark / Bat chain puller / My human gets me blues / Sugar 'n' spikes / Veterans' day poppy / Dropout boogie / Sheriff of Hong Kong / Kandy korn / Suction prints / Big eyed beans from Venus.

May 01. (d-lp) *Table Of Elements; <(TOELP 52)>* **GROW FINS VOL.3**

CARAVAN

Formed: Canterbury, Kent, England . . . mid 1967. Stalwarts of that well-documented scene, PYE HASTINGS, RICHARD COUGHLAN and the unrelated! DAVE and RICHARD SINCLAIR soon evolved into CARAVAN. They had all stemmed from The WILDE FLOWERS, a pioneering band that'd seen SOFT MACHINE luminaries ROBERT WYATT, KEVIN AYERS and HUGH HOPPER pass through its ranks. From 1961, messrs from the Simon Langton private school, GRAHAM FLIGHT (the original singer before AYERS took over in '65), BRIAN HOPPER, HUGH HOPPER, RICHARD SINCLAIR and ROBERT WYATT all established themselves locally as a decent covers band; they did write several themselves. By early 1967, only BRIAN was to remain from the original WILDE FLOWERS line-up, recent acquisitions being the aforementioned COUGHLAN, HASTINGS, DAVE SINCLAIR and bassist DAVE LAWRENCE, although the latter and BRIAN duly quit the music scene as they evolved into CARAVAN. As SOFT MACHINE developed its distinctive psychedelic jazz-rock, CARAVAN's eponymous debut album, released in 1968 on 'Verve', highlighted the band's wistful melody and extended workouts that scuplted moods rather than songs. They signed to 'Decca', releasing 'IF I COULD DO IT ALL OVER AGAIN, I'D DO IT ALL OVER YOU' in 1970. The albums unfortunate title belied a quality set of melancholy prog-rock that extended the ideas of their debut. 1971 saw the band release 'IN THE LAND OF THE GREY AND PINK', probably their best effort, once again featuring the Hammond organ that was CARAVAN's trademark. A series of line-up changes began with DAVE SINCLAIR leaving for ROBERT WYATT'S MATCHING MOLE, the band relacing him with STEVE MILLER (alas, not he of 'The Joker' fame) for the 'WATERLOO LILY' album.

MILLER's stay was brief, as he and RICHARD SINCLAIR took off to form HATFIELD & THE NORTH. By the next album, 1973's 'FOR GIRLS WHO GROW PLUMP IN THE NIGHT', they recruited new line-up (see below) plus the returning DAVE SINCLAIR. The original sleeve artwork was knocked back by the record company for its depiction of a pregnant naked woman. The record was released amid an extended period of live work, the group recording an album on tour with the New Symphonia. The even more unfortunately titled 'CUNNING STUNTS' album displayed a distinct lack of any material even remotely stunning, the band becoming a bit bogged-down in the prog-rock quagmire. However it did breach the UK Top 50 in 1975, setting the scene for another unworthy follow-up, 'BLIND DOG AT ST. DUNSTANS'. The onset of Punk obviously did nothing for their cause, although PYE bravely struggled on with a series of half-baked albums, struggled in vain to capture the mellow CARAVAN vibe of old. The four originals reconvened for 1982's 'BACK TO FRONT' and then signed off until the early 90's when neo-psychedelic crusty bands like OZRIC TENTACLES, wearing their influences proudly, led to a bit of a CARAVAN renaissance. Various members under various monikers recorded 'CARAVAN OF DREAMS' (1992) and 'THE BATTLE OF HASTINGS' (1995).

Album rating: CARAVAN (*5) / IF I COULD DO IT ALL OVER AGAIN, I'D DO IT OVER YOU (*6) / IN THE LAND OF GREY AND PINK (*8) / WATERLOO LILY (*6) / FOR GIRLS WHO GROW PLUMP IN THE NIGHT (*7) / CARAVAN AND THE NEW SINFONIA (*4) / CUNNING STUNTS (*6) / BLIND DOG AT ST. DUNSTANS (*5) / CANTERBURY TALES – THE BEST OF CARAVAN compilation (*8) / BETTER BY FAR (*4) / THE ALBUM (*4) / BACK TO FRONT (*4) / LIVE 1990 (*4) / COOL WATER (*4) / BATTLE OF HASTINGS (*5) / RICHARD SINCLAIR'S CARAVAN OF DREAMS (*4) / AN EVENING OF MAGIC (*4) / ALL OVER YOU (*4) / CANTERBURY COMES TO LONDON (*6) / ALL OVER YOU . . . TOO (*4)

RICHARD SINCLAIR (b. 6 Jun'48) – vocals, bass, guitar (ex-WILDE FLOWERS) / **PYE HASTINGS** (b.21 Jan'47, Scotland) – guitar, vocals (ex-WILDE FLOWERS) / **RICHARD COUGHLAN** (b. 2 Sep'47, Herne Bay, England) – drums, percussion (ex-WILDE FLOWERS) / **DAVID SINCLAIR** (b.24 Nov'47, Herne Bay) – keyboards, vocals with guests **JIMMY HASTINGS** – flute, arrangements / **BRIAN HOPPER** – horns

Verve — Verve Folk

Oct 68. (lp; stereo/mono) *(S+/VLP 6011)* **CARAVAN** ☐ [–]
– Place of my own / Ride / Policeman / Love song with flute / Cecil runs / Magic man / Grandma's lawn / Where but for Caravan would I be. *(re-iss. Jun72 & 1979 on 'M.G.M.'; 2353 058) (cd-iss. Sep96 on 'H.T.D.'; HTDCD 65)*

Jan 69. (7") *(VS 1518) <5102>* **PLACE OF MY OWN. / RIDE** ☐ ☐

Decca — London

Sep 70. (7") *(F 13063)* **IF I COULD DO IT ALL OVER AGAIN, I'D DO IT ALL OVER YOU. / HELLO HELLO** ☐ [–]

Sep 70. (lp) *(SKL 5052) <PS 582>* **IF I COULD DO IT ALL OVER AGAIN, I'D DO IT ALL OVER YOU** ☐ ☐
– If I could do it all over again, I'd do it all over you / And I wish I were stoned / Don't worry / As I feel I die / With an ear to the ground I can make it: Martinian – Only Cox – Reprise / Hello, hello / Asforteri / Can't be long now – Francoise – For Richard – Warlock / Limits. *(cd-iss. Jan89 on 'London'; 820 521-2) (re-iss. c Jul93; 820 521-4) (re-iss. Apr96 on 'H.T.D.' cd/c; HTD CD/MC 57) (cd re-rec.Apr97+=; HTDCD 57L) (cd re-mast.Feb01 on 'Deram'; 882968-2)*

Feb 71. (7") *(F 23125) <20065>* **LOVE TO LOVE YOU (AND TONIGHT PIGS WILL FLY). / GOLF GIRL** ☐ ☐

— added part-timers **JIMMY HASTINGS** – flute, tenor sax, piccolo / **DAVID GRINSTEAD** – cannon, bell and wind

Deram — London

May 71. (lp) *(SDL-R 1) <PS 593>* **IN THE LAND OF GREY AND PINK** ☐ ☐
– Golf girl / Winter wine / Love to love you (and tonight pigs will fly) / In the land of grey and pink / Nine feet underground: Nigel blows a tune – Love's a friend – Make it 76 – Dance of the seven paper hankies – Hold grandad by the nose – Honest I did! – Disassociation – 100% proof. *(cd-iss. Apr89; 820 520-2) (re-iss. c Jul93; 820 520-4) (cd re-mast.Feb01 on 'Deram'; 882983-2)*

— **STEVE MILLER** – keyboards (ex-DYBLE, COXHILL & THE MILLER BROTHERS') repl. DAVID who joined ROBERT WYATT'S MATCHING MOLE / with guests **JIMMY HASTINGS, LOL COXHILL** – saxophone / **MIKE COTTON** – trumpet / **PHIL MILLER** – guitar

Apr 72. (lp) *(SDL 8) <PS 615>* **WATERLOO LILY** ☐ ☐
– Waterloo Lily / Nothing at all – It's coming soon / Songs and signs / Aristocracy / The love in your eye / To catch me a brother / Subsultus – Debouchement – Tilbury kecks / The world is yours. *(cd-iss. Jul90; 820 919-2) (re-iss. c Jul93; 820 919-4) (cd re-mast.Feb01 on 'Deram'; 882982-2)*

— **DEREK AUSTIN** – keyboards repl. STEVE MILLER who formed DELIVERY / **STUART EVANS** – bass repl. RICHARD SINCLAIR who joined HATFIELD & THE NORTH added **PETER GEOFFREY RICHARDSON** – electric viola to founders **HASTINGS & COUGHLAN. DAVE HASTINGS** returned to repl. AUSTIN /

JOHN G. PERRY – bass, vocals (ex-SPREADEAGLE) repl. EVANS

Oct 73. (lp) *(SDL 12) <PS 627>* **FOR GIRLS WHO GROW PLUMP IN THE NIGHT** ☐ ☐
– Memory Lain, Hugh / Headloss / Hoedown / Surprise, surprise / E'Thlu Thlu / The dog, the dog, he's at it again / Be all right / Chance of a lifetime / L'auberge du sanglier / A hunting we shall go / Pengola / Backwards / A hunting we shall go (reprise). *(cd-iss. Aug91; 820 971-2) (re-iss. c Jul93; 820 971-4) (cd re-mast.Feb01 on 'Deram'; 882980-2)*

Nov 73. (7") *<20080>* **HEADLOSS. /** ☐ [–]

— **MARTYN FORD** – conducted orchestra **SIMON JEFFES** – arranger

Apr 74. (lp) *(SKLR 1110) <PS 650>* **CARAVAN AND THE NEW SYMPHONIA (LIVE AT DRURY LANE) (live)** ☐ ☐
– (introduction) / Mirror of the day / The love in your eye / Virgin on the ridiculous / For Richard. *(re-iss. Jun92 cd/c; 844 125-2/-4) (cd re-mast.Feb01 on 'Deram'; 882969-2)*

— **MIKE WEDGWOOD** – bass (ex-CURVED AIR) repl. PERRY (to QUANTUM JUMP)

Decca — B.T.M.

Aug 75. (lp) *(SKLR 5210) <BTM 5000>* **CUNNING STUNTS** [50] ☐
– The show of your lives / Stuck in a hole / Lover / No back stage pass / Welcome the day / The Dabsong conshirtoe:- The mad Dabsong – Ben Karratt rides again – Pro's and con's / Wraiks and ladders – Sneakin' out the bare square – All sorts of unmentionable things / The fear and loathing in Tollington Park rag. *(re-iss. Apr93 on 'Deram' cd/c; 844 126-2/-4) (cd re-iss. Sep94 on 'Repertoire'; REP 4494) (cd re-iss. Jan96 on 'H.T.D.'; HTDCD 52) (cd re-mast.Feb01 on 'Dream'; 882981-2)*

Sep 75. (7") *(FR 13599)* **STUCK IN A HOLE. / LOVER** ☐ ☐

— **JAN SCHELHAAS** – keyboards (ex-GARY MOORE) repl. DAVID SINCLAIR

B.T.M. — Arista

Apr 76. (lp) *(BTM 1007) <4088>* **BLIND DOG AT ST. DUNSTANS** [53] ☐
– Here I am / Chiefs and Indians / A very smelly, grubby little oik / Bobbing wide / Come on back / A very smelly, grubby little oik (reprise) / Jack and Jill / CAn you hear me / All the way (with John Wayne's single-handed liberation of Paris). *(cd-iss. Sep94 on 'Repertoire'; REP 4501) (cd re-iss. May96 on 'H.T.D.'; HTDCD 60)*

Jul 76. (7") *(SBT 104)* **ALL THE WAY (WITH JOHN WAYNE'S SINGLE-HANDED LIBERATION OF PARIS). / CHIEFS AND INDIANS** ☐ ☐

— **DEK MESSECAR** – bass (ex-DARRYL WAY'S WOLF) repl. WEDGEWOOD who went solo (above now alongside **HASTINGS, COUGHLAN, RICHARDSON** and **SCHELHAAS**)

Arista — Arista

May 77. (7") *(ARIST 110)* **BETTER BY FAR. / SILVER STRINGS** ☐ ☐

Aug 77. (lp/c) *(SPARTY/TCARTY 1008) <AB 4134>* **BETTER BY FAR** ☐ ☐
– Feelin' alright / Behind you / Better by far / Silver strings / The last unicorn / Give me more / Man in the car / Let it shine / Nightmare.

— **DAVE SINCLAIR** – keyboards returned from CAMEL (tour) to repl. DEK. Now a quartet when JAN joined CAMEL in '79

Kingdom — not iss.

Oct 80. (7") *(KV 8009)* **HEARTBREAKER. / IT'S NEVER TOO LATE** ☐ [–]

Oct 80. (lp/c) *(KVL/+X 9003)* **THE ALBUM** ☐ [–]
– Heartbreaker / Corner of my eye / Watcha gonna tell me / Piano player / Make yourself at home / Golden mile / Bright shiny day / Piano player / Clera blue sky / Keepin' up de fences. *(re-iss. 1983 lp/c; KVL/CKVL 9003) (cd-iss. Aug92; CDKVL 9003)*

Mar 81. (7") *(KV 8014)* **KEEPIN' UP DE FENCES. / GOLDEN MILE** ☐ [–]

— **RICHARD SINCLAIR** – vocals, bass returned from CAMEL, joined all founders, repl. RICHARDSON who went into sessions etc.
also added **MEL COLLINS** – saxophone (ex-KING CRIMSON, etc., etc.,)

Jun 82. (lp) *(KVS 5011)* **BACK TO FRONT** [ ] [–]
– Back to Herne Bay front / Betcha wanna take it all / Hold on hold on / A.A. man / Videos of Hollywood / Sally don't change it / All aboard / Taken my breath away / Proper job / Back to front. *(cd-iss. Aug92; CDKVS 5011)*

— disbanded but re-formed briefly in 1990 . . . In 1992, they became . . .

RICHARD SINCLAIR'S CARAVAN OF DREAMS

with also **DAVE SINCLAIR + JIMMY HASTINGS** / plus **ANDY WARD** (ex-CAMEL)

H.T.D. not iss.

Jul 92. (cd/c) *(HTD CD/MC 7)* **CARAVAN OF DREAMS** [ ] [–]
– Going for a song / Cruising / Only the brave / Plan it Earth / Heather / Keep.

Jan 94. (d-cd) *(HTDCD 17)* **AN EVENING OF MAGIC (live)** [ ] [–]
– In the land of grey and pink / Only the brave – Plan it Earth / Share it / Videos / Heather / Going for a song / O Caroline / Nine feet underground / Felafel shuffle / Keep on caring / Cruising / Emily / Halfway between Heaven and Earth – It didn't matter anyway / Golf girl.

RICHARD SINCLAIR

R.S.S. not iss.

Jul 94. (cd) *(RSSCD 001)* **R.S.V.P.** [ ] [–]
– What's rattlin' / My sweet darlin' / Videos / Barefoot / Outback in Canterbury / Over from Dover / Out of the shadows / Where are they now? / Bamboo / What in the world.

— In Jun'00, SINCLAIR collaborated with HUGH HOPPER on the album, 'SOMEWHERE IN FRANCE' *(Voiceprint; VP 133CD)*

CARAVAN

— the originals **HASTINGS, DAVE SINCLAIR + COUGHLAN** were back in 1990 + in 1994/5 with also **GEOFF RICHARDSON** – violin

Mar 93. (cd) *(<NINETY 2>)* **LIVE 1990 (live)** [ ] Nov95 [ ]
– Headloss / Videos of Hollywood / Nine feet underground / If I could do it all over again / Winter wine / In the land of grey and pink / For Richard. *(re-iss. Oct98; same)*

H.T.D. H.T.D.

Apr 94. (cd) *(HTDCD 18)* **COOL WATER** [ ] [–]
– Cool water / Just the way you are / Tuesday is rock and roll nite / The crack of the willow / Ansaphone / Cold fright / Side by side / You woke me up in one of those / To the land of my fathers / Poor Molly / Send reinforcements. *(re-iss. Mar98; same)*

Oct 95. (cd/lp) *(<HTD CD/LP 41>)* **THE BATTLE OF HASTINGS** [ ] [ ]
– It's a sad, sad affair / Somewhere in your heart / Cold as ice / Liar / Don't want love / Travelling ways / This time / If it wasn't for ego / It's not real / Wendy wants another 6" mole / I know why you're laughing.

Apr 96. (cd/c) *H.T.D.; (HTD CD/MC 57)* **ALL OVER YOU** (re-recorded) [ ] [–]
– If I could do it all over again, I'd do it over you / Place of my own / The love in your eye – To catch me a brother / In the land of grey and pink / Golf girl / Disassociation (nine feet underground) / Hello, hello / Asforteri 25 / For Richard: Can't be long now – Francoise / Memory lain Hugh / Headloss / Be all right – Chance of a lifetime / If I could do it all over again I'd do it over you 2 (single mix). *(cd re-recorded Apr97; HTDCD 57L)*

— added **JIM LEVERTON** – bass (ex-SAVOY BROWN, ex-FAT MATTRESS, ex-JUICY LUCY) + **DOUG BOYLE** – guitar

H.T.D. Transatla.

Nov 97. (cd) *(HTDCD 79)* *<TRACD 302>* **CANTERBURY COMES TO LONDON (live at The Astoria)** [ ] Apr99 [ ]
– Memory lain Hugh / Headloss / Nine feet underground / The dog, the dog, he's at it again / Cold as ice / Somewhere in your heart / I know why you're laughing / Liar / For Richard / Golf girl.

Sep 99. (cd) *(HTDCD 102)* *<TRACD 325>* **ALL OVER YOU . . . TOO** [ ] [ ]
– Hoedown / A very smelly grubby little oik / Bobbing wide / The dog, the dog, he's at it again (version) / Stuck in a hole / Ride / Nightmare / C'thlu thlu / Bobbing wide (reprise). *(re-iss. Feb00 on 'Transatlantic'; TRACD 325)*

– compilations etc. –

Nov 76. (d-lp) *Decca; (DKLR 81-82)* **CANTERBURY TALES – THE BEST OF CARAVAN** [ ] [–]
– If I could do it all over again I'd do it all over you / Aristocracy / Can't be long now – Francoise – For Richard – Warlock / Nine feet underground: Nigel blows a tune – Love's a friend – Make it 76 – Dance of the seven paper hankies – Hold grandad by the nose – Honest I do – Disassociation – 100 proof / Golf girl / Hoedown / The love in your eye / Subsultus – Debouchement – Tilbury kecks / Memory Laine, Hugh / Headloss / Virgin on the ridiculous / The dog, the dog, he's at it again.

1978. (lp) *London; <50011>* **THE BEST OF CARAVAN** [–] [ ]
(UK-iss.Sep87 on 'C5' lp/c; C5/+K 505) (cd-iss. 1990 & Apr93; C5CD 505X)

Jul 81. (lp) *Rock Roots; (TAB 23)* **THE SHOW OF OUR LIVES** [ ] [–]
(<cd-iss. Oct98 on 'Mooncrest'; CRESTCD 036>)

Sep 84. (lp) *Kingdom; (KVC 6003)* **THE CANTERBURY COLLECTION** ('80-'82 material) [ ] [–]
(cd-iss. Jan87; CDKVL 9028)

Apr 85. (lp) *See For Miles; (SEE 46)* **AND I WISH I WERE STONED, DON'T WORRY** [ ] [–]

May 91. (cd/c) *Elite; (ELITE 002 PCD/PMC)* **SONGS AND SIGNS** [ ] [–]
(originally only available in 1979 on German 'Decca'; 623668)

Aug 91. (cd/c) *Elite; (ELITE 017 CDP/MCP)* **WITH AN EAR TO THE GROUND** [ ] [–]

Oct 91. (cd) *Windsong; (WINCD 003)* **IN CONCERT (live)** [ ] [–]

Code 90 Code 90

Nov 94. (cd) *Deram; (515 524-2)* **ANTHOLOGY** [ ] [–]

Nov 94. (cd; by WILDE FLOWERS) *Voiceprint; (VP 123CD)* **THE WILDE FLOWERS** (rec.1965-67) [ ] [–]
– Impotence / Those words they say / Memories / Don't try to change me / Parchman farm / Almost grown / She's gone / Slow walkin' talk / He's bad for you / It's what I feel (a certain kind) / Memories (instrumental) / Never leave me / Time after time / Just where I want / No game when you lose / Impotence / Why do you care / The pieman cometh / Summer spirit / She loves to hurt / The big show / Memories. *(re-iss. Sep96 on 'Blueprint'; BP 123CD)*

Feb 98. (cd) *Mooncrest; (<CRESTCD 029>)* **TRAVELLING MAN** [ ] Mar98 [ ]

Feb 98. (cd) *Hux; (HUXCD 002)* **SONGS FOR OBLIVION FISHERMEN** [ ] [–]

Apr 98. (cd) *Strange Fruit; (SFRSCD 058)* **LIVE IN CONCERT** [ ] [–]

Nov 98. (cd) *Hux; (HUX 013)* **ETHER WAY – THE PEEL SESSIONS 1975-1977** [ ] [–]

Nov 98. (cd) *Voiceprint; (VP 201CD)* **CANTERBURIED SOUNDS VOL.1** (Various CARAVAN-esque solo/rare material) [ ] [–]

Nov 98. (cd) *Voiceprint; (VP 202CD)* **CANTERBURIED SOUNDS VOL.2** [ ] [–]

Nov 98. (cd) *Voiceprint; (VP 203CD)* **CANTERBURIED SOUNDS VOL.3** [ ] [–]

Nov 98. (cd) *Voiceprint; (VP 204CD)* **CANTERBURIED SOUNDS VOL.4** [ ] [–]

May 99. (cd) *H.T.D.; (HTDCD 96)* **SURPRISE SUPPLIES** [ ] [–]
(re-iss. Mar02 on 'Talking Elephant'; TECD 039)

Sep 99. (cd) *Delta; (470087)* **HEADLOSS** [ ] [–]

Nov 99. (d-cd) *Deram; (515522-2)* **CARAVAN – ANTHOLOGY** [ ] [–]

Jul 00. (d-cd) *Decca; (524755-2)* **WHERE BUT FOR CARAVAN WOULD I (AN ANTHOLOGY)** [ ] [–]

Oct 00. (cd) *H.T.D.; (<HTDCD 114>)* **THE H.T.D. YEARS** [ ] [ ]

Jul 01. (d-cd) *Castle; (CMDDD 276) / SAnctuary; <81186>* **TRAVELLING WAYS: THE H.T.D. ANTHOLOGY** [ ] [ ]

Feb 02. (cd) *Decca; (<882902-2>)* **LIVE AT FAIRFIELD HALLS, 1974 (live)** [ ] [ ]

Feb 03. (cd) *Classic Rock Legends; (<CRP 1013>)* **A NIGHT'S TALE** [ ] [ ]

Mar 03. (cd) *Classic Rock Legends; (<CRP 1049>)* **LIVE IN NOTTINGHAM** [ ] [ ]

Apr 03. (cd) *R.S.K.; (MLP 03CD)* **LIVE UK TOUR 1975 (live)** [ ] [–]

Jul 03. (cd) *Classic Rock Legends; (<CRL 1096>)* **NOWHERE TO HIDE** [ ] [ ]

Aug 03. (cd) *Classic Rock Legends; (<CRL 1097>)* **WITH STRINGS ATTACHED** [ ] [ ]

CARDIGANS

Formed: Jonkoping, Sweden ... October 1992 by songwriters PETER SVENSSON and MAGNUS SVENINGSSON, along with LARS-OLAF JOHANSSON, BENGT LAGERBERG and cutesy bombshell, NINA PERSSON. Despite the fact the band's founding members came from a heavy-metal background, The CARDIGANS' sound leaned more towards fragile, angelic indie-pop drawing on the melodic traditions of fellow Swedes, ABBA and UK pop ironists BEAUTIFUL SOUTH as well as French 60's pop (especially FRANCOISE HARDY's Burt Bacharach period). They initially released an album in Sweden before signing to 'Polydor' UK and in 1995/96, scored minor successes with 'CARNIVAL', 'SICK & TIRED' and 'RISE & SHINE', all stemming from their UK debut album, 'LIFE' (1995). In the late summer of '96, they peaked critically with the starry-eyed 'LOVEFOOL', a near Top 20 hit first time around and an even bigger success upon its re-issue in conjunction with the 'Romeo & Juliet' soundtrack in 1997. The song was a standout track on their acclaimed follow-up set, 'THE FIRST BAND ON THE MOON', although the band no doubt came to regard it as something of an albatross round their necks. Presumably a reaction to being filed under Scando-pop, the more deliberately experimental 'GRAN TURISMO' (1998) saw the band sacrifice some of their charm for instant "alternative" appeal. PERSSON's subsequent activities included fruitful collaborations with TOM JONES and DAVID ARNOLD, while in 2001 she resurfaced with a new outfit, A CAMP. Together with SHUDDER TO THINK's NATHAN LARSON and augmented and produced by MARK LINKOUS (of SPARKLEHORSE fame), their eponymous set was an alt-countrified pot-pourri of pleasant cuts including a cover of Paul Westerberg's 'ROCK'N'ROLL GHOST'. It was a markedly different CARDIGANS which belatedly emerged in 2003 with 'LONG GONE BEFORE DAYLIGHT', a muted, sombre affair bereft of the exuberance of their best work but lacking the gravitas to make this brand of gloomy confessional hit home. • **Covered:** SABBATH BLOODY SABBATH + IRON MAN (Black Sabbath) / MR. CROWLEY (Ozzy Osbourne) / BOYS ARE BACK IN TOWN (Thin Lizzy).

Album rating: EMMERDALE (*6) / LIFE (*8) / FIRST BAND ON THE MOON (*7) / GRAN TURISMO (*6) / LONG GONE BEFORE DAYLIGHT (*5) / A Camp: A CAMP (*7)

NINA PERSSON (b. Karlskoga, Sweden) – vocals / **PETER SVENSSON** – guitar / **MAGNUS SVENINGSSON** – bass / **LARS-OLAF JOHANSSON** – keyboards / **BENGT LAGERBERG** – drums, flute

Trampolene — not iss.

Feb 94. (cd) *(TRACD 1501)* **EMMERDALE** [–] Sweden [–]
– Sick & tired / Black letter day / In the afternoon / Over the water / After all . . . / Cloudy sky / Our space / Rise and shine / Celia inside / Sabbath bloody sabbath / Seems hard / The last song. *(UK-iss.Jan97 on 'Stockholm' cd/c; 523215-2/-4) (re-iss. May99; same)*

May 94. (cd-s) *(TRACDS 501)* **RISE & SHINE / AFTER ALL** [–] Sweden [–]

Aug 94. (cd-s) *(TRACDS 502)* **BLACK LETTER DAY / I FIGURED OUT** [–] Sweden [–]

Sep 94. (cd-s) *(TRACDS 503)* **SICK & TIRED / PLAIN PARADE / LAIKA / POOH SONG** [–] Sweden [–]

Stockholm – Polydor — Minty Fresh

Nov 94. (7"/c-s) *(PO/+CS 336)* **SICK & TIRED. / PLAIN PARADE** [ ] [–]
(cd-s) *(PZCD 336)* – ('A'side) / Pooh song / The boys are back in town / Carnival (Puck version).

May 95. (7"/c-s) *(PO/+CS 345)* **CARNIVAL. / MR. CROWLEY (live)** [72] [–]
(cd-s+=) *(PZCD 345)* – Emmerdale.
(re-iss. Nov95, hit No.35; same)

Jun 95. (cd/c/lp) *(523556-2/-4/-1) <MF 15>* **LIFE** [58] [ ]
– Carnival / Gordon's garden party / Daddy's car / Sick & tired / Tomorrow / Rise & shine / Beautiful one / Travelling with Charley / Fine / Celia inside / Hey! get out of my way / After all. *(cd re-iss. May99; same) (lp re-iss. Sep99 on 'Simply Vinyl'; SVLP 114)*

Sep 95. (c-s) *(577311-4)* **SICK & TIRED / PLAIN PARADE** [34] [ ]
(cd-s+=) *(577311-2)* – Laika / Pooh song.

Feb 96. (7"/c-s) *(577824-7/-4)* **RISE & SHINE. / PIKE BUBBLES** [29] [ ]
(cd-s+=) *(577825-2)* – Cocktail party bloody cocktail party.

Stockholm – Polydor — Mercury

Sep 96. (7"white/c-s) *(575528-7/-4)* **LOVEFOOL. / NASTY SUNNY BEAM** [21] [ ]
(cd-s+=) *(575295-2)* – Iron man (first try).

Sep 96. (cd/c/lp) *(<533117-2/-4/-1>)* **FIRST BAND ON THE MOON** [18] [35]
– Your new cuckoo / Been it / Heartbreaker / Happy meal II / Never recover / Step on me / Lovefool / Loser / Iron man / The great divide / Choke. *(cd re-iss. May99; same*

Nov 96. (7"brown/c-s) *(575966-7/-4)* **BEEN IT. / BEEN IT (radio)** [56] [ ]
(cd-s+=) *(575966-2)* – Blah blah blah / Losers (first try).
below was featured on the film 'Romeo & Juliet'

Apr 97. (c-s) *(571050-4)* **LOVEFOOL / ('A'-Todd Terry remix)** [2] [ ]
(cd-s+=) *(571050-2)* – ('A'-Todd Terry's frozen sun mix).
(cd-s) *(571051-2)* – ('A'side) / Sick & tired (live) / Carnival (live) / Rise & shine (live).

Aug 97. (7"/c-s) *(571633-7/-4)* **YOUR NEW CUCKOO. / LOVEFOOL (radio)** [35] [ ]
(cd-s+=) *(571633-2)* – I figured out (demo '93) / After all (demo '93).
(cd-s) *(571661-2)* – ('A'radio) / ('A'-Hyper disco mix) / ('A'-Super stereo mix).

Oct 98. (c-s) *(567988-4)* **MY FAVOURITE GAME / LOVEFOOL (live)** [14] [ ]
(cd-s+=) *(567991-2)* – ('A'-Wubbledub mix).
(cd-s) *(567989-2)* – ('A'side) / War / Sick and tired (live).

Oct 98. (cd/c) *(<559081-2/-4>)* **GRAN TURISMO** [8] [ ]
– Paralyzed / Erase – Rewind / Explode / Starter / Hanging around / Higher / Marvel hill / My favourite game / Do you believe / Junk of the hearts / Nil.

Feb 99. (c-s) *(563535-4)* **ERASE – REWIND / MY FAVOURITE GAME** [7] [ ]
(cd-s+=) *(563533-2)* – Explode (remixed) / ('B'-CD-Rom).
(cd-s) *(563535-2)* – ('A'side) / ('A'mixes; Cut La Roc vocal mix & Naid remix).

Jul 99. (c-s) *(561268-4)* **HANGING AROUND / MY FAVOURITE GAME (acoustic radio session)** [17] [–]
(cd-s) *(561268-2)* – ('A'side) / Erase – Rewind (CD-Rom video; banned directors cut).
(cd-s) *(561269-2)* – ('A'side) / My favourite game (Rollo from Faithless remix) / ('A'-CD-Rom video).

— The CARDIGANS backed TOM JONES on a collaborative single, 'Burning Down The House'. In April 2000, NINA PERSSON & DAVID ARNOLD hit UK No.49 with the single 'THEME FROM RANDALL & HOPKIRK (DECEASED)'

Mar 03. (c-s) *(065723-4)* **FOR WHAT IT'S WORTH / DAS MODEL / THE ROAD** [31] [–]
(cd-s+=) *(065723-2)* – ('A'-video).

Mar 03. (cd)(lp) *(<38109-2>)(E 67101-1)* **LONG GONE BEFORE DAYLIGHT** [47] [ ]
– Communication / You're the storm / Good horse / And thewn you kissed me / Couldn't care less / Please sister / For what it's worth / Lead me into the night / Live and learn / Feathers and down / 03.45: no sleep. *(cd+=)* – Hold me / If there is a chance.

Jul 03. (cd-s) *(980967-3)* **YOU'RE THE STORM / HOLD ME / YOU'RE THE STORM (Sandkvie session) / YOU'RE THE STORM (video)** [74] [–]

– compilations, etc. –

May 97. (10xcd-ep-box) *Border; (CARDSIN 1)* **THE COMPLETE SINGLES COLLECTION** [ ] [–]

— there is also a Various Artists tribute album *(TR 012CD)*

A CAMP

NINA PERSSON / + NATHAN LARSON – instruments (of SHUDDER TO THINK) / with **MARK LINKOUS** + guests, etc.

Polydor Universal

Aug 01. (7"/cd-s) *(15216-7/-2)* **I CAN BUY YOU. / ANGEL OF SADNESS / CHARLIE CHARLIE** [46] [–]

Sep 01. (cd) *(014851-2) <415594>* **A CAMP** [ ] [ ]
– Frequent flyer / I can buy you / Angel of sadness / Such a bad comedown / Song for the leftovers / Walking the cow / Hard as a stone / Algebra / Silent night / The same old song / The oddness of the Lord / Rock'n'roll ghost / The bluest eyes in Texas / Elephant.

☐ Belinda CARLISLE (see under ⇒ GO-GO'S)

CARS

Formed: Boston, Massachusetts, USA . . . 1976 by BENJAMIN ORR, GREG HAWKES and ELLIOT EASTON who started out touring as CAP 'N' SWING. Manager Fred Davis was successful in getting a demo of 'JUST WHAT I NEEDED' playlisted on US radio and they duly signed to 'Elektra', having added RIC OCASEK and DAVID ROBINSON. The track was released simultaneously with their eponymous 1978 debut album, an American new wave milestone which also caught the attention of UK hipsters eager for something a bit easier on the ear than British punk. Taking 70's Anglo art-rock as base material, The CARS combined synthesized cool with an American classic rock sensibility. This recipe was realised in irresistibly infectious style with 'MY BEST FRIEND'S GIRL', a UK Top 3 hit later that year. On subsequent albums however, the band's predeliction for moody experimentation saw the singles dry up. Though 'CANDY-O' (1979), 'PANORAMA' (1980) and 'SHAKE IT UP' (1981), all reached the US Top 10, they spawned only a couple of major hits in the former's 'LET'S GO' and the latter's title track while further success in Britain had faltered completely. After a two year break, however (during which time, OCASEK released a solo set, 'BEATITUDE' – 1983), the band returned with the commercially revved-up 'HEARTBEAT CITY' (1984). Motoring squarely for the AOR market, the group scored a sizeable Top 5 transatlantic hit with the polished atmospherics of the ORR-penned 'DRIVE'. The song would later become forever linked with images of famine-plagued Ethiopia after it was used as part of a Live Aid documentary. The album itself made the Top 5 and provided a further two major Stateside hits in 'YOU MIGHT THINK' and 'MAGIC'. After a mid-80's break during which the various members pursued solo projects, The CARS spluttered to a halt with the poorly received 'DOOR TO DOOR' in 1987. OCASEK reappeared from time to time in the following years, mainly in connection with his production work. Sadly, on October 3rd, 2000, founder member BENJAMIN ORR died of cancer. • **Songwriters:** All written by OCASEK, ORR and EASTON, except THINK IT OVER and MAYBE BABY (Buddy Holly).

Album rating: THE CARS (*7) / CANDY-O (*5) / PANORAMA (*4) / SHAKE IT UP (*5) / HEARTBEAT CITY (*7) / THE CARS' GREATEST HITS compilation (*7) / DOOR TO DOOR (*3) / JUST WHAT I NEEDED – ANTHOLOGY compilation (*7) / Ric Ocasek: BEATITUDE (*4) / THIS SIDE OF PARADISE (*4) / FIREBALL ZONE (*4) / QUICK CHANGE WORLD (*4) / TROUBLIZING (*3) / Elliott Easton: CHANGE NO CHANGE (*4) / Benjamin Orr: THE LACE (*4) / Greg Hawkes: NIAGARA FALLS (*3)

RIC OCASEK (b. RICHARD OTCASEK, 23 Mar'49, Baltimore, Maryland) – vocals, guitar / **BENJAMIN ORR** (b. ORZECHOWSKI, in Cleveland, Ohio) – vocals, bass / **ELLIOT EASTON** (b. ELLIOT STEINBERG, 18 Dec'53, Brooklyn, N.Y.) – guitar / **GREG HAWKES** – keyboards, saxophone (ex-MILKWOOD, with ORR and OCASEK) / **DAVID ROBINSON** – drums (ex-The POP, ex-DMZ, ex-MODERN LOVERS)

Elektra Elektra

Aug 78. (7") *<45491>* **JUST WHAT I NEEDED. / I'M IN TOUCH WITH YOUR WORLD** [–] [27]

Aug 78. (lp/c) *(K/K4 52088) <135>* **THE CARS** [29] Jun78 [18]
– Good times roll / My best friend's girl / Just what I needed / I'm in touch with your world / Don't cha stop / You're all I've got tonight / Bye bye love / Moving in stereo / All mixed up. *(cd-iss. Jan84; 252 088)*

Oct 78. (7"pic-d) *(K 12301)* **MY BEST FRIEND'S GIRL. / MOVING IN STEREO** [3] [–]

Oct 78. (7") *<45537>* **MY BEST FRIEND'S GIRL. / DON'T CHA STOP** [–] [35]

Jan 79. (7"pic-d) *(K 12312)* **JUST WHAT I NEEDED. / I'M IN TOUCH WITH YOUR WORLD** [17] [–]

May 79. (7") *(K 12352) <46014>* **GOOD TIMES ROLL. / ALL MIXED UP** [ ] Mar79 [41]

Jun 79. (lp/c) *(K/K4 52088) <507>* **CANDY-O** [30] [3]
– Let's go / Since I held you / It's all can do / Double life / Shoo be doo / Candy-O / Nightspots / You can't hold on too long / Lust for kicks / Got a lot on my head / Dangerous type. *(cd-iss. Jan84; 252 148)*

Jul 79. (7"pic-d) *(K 12371) <46063>* **LET'S GO. / THAT'S IT** [51] Jun79 [14]

Sep 79. (7"pic-d) *(K 12385)* **DOUBLE LIFE. / COME AROUND** [ ] [–]

Oct 79. (7") *<46546>* **IT'S ALL I CAN DO. / GOT A LOT ON MY HEAD** [–] [41]

Jan 80. (7") *<46580>* **DOUBLE LIFE. / CANDY-O** [–] [ ]

Jan 80. (7") *(K 12416)* **IT'S ALL I CAN DO. / CANDY-O** [ ] [–]

Sep 80. (lp/c) *(K/K4 52240) <514>* **PANORAMA** [ ] [5]
– Panorama / Touch and go / Gimme some slack / Don't tell me no / Getting through / Misfit kid / Down boys / You wear those eyes / Running to you / Up and down. *(cd-iss. 1986; 252 240)*

Sep 80. (7") *<47039>* **TOUCH AND GO. / DOWN BOYS** [ ] [37]

Jan 81. (7") *<47080>* **DON'T TELL ME NO. / DON'T GO TO PIECES** [–] [ ]

Mar 81. (7") *<47101>* **GIMME SOME SLACK. / DON'T GO TO PIECES** [–] [ ]

Nov 81. (lp/c) *(K/K4 52330) <567>* **SHAKE IT UP** [ ] [9]
– Since you're gone / Shake it up / I'm not the one / Victim of love / Cruiser / A dream away / This could be love / Think it over / Maybe baby. *(cd-iss. 1986; 252 330)*

Nov 81. 7"pic-d) *(K 12583) <47250>* **SHAKE IT UP. / CRUISER** [ ] [4]

Mar 82. (7") *<47433>* **SINCE YOU'RE GONE. / THINK IT OVER** [–] [41]

May 82. (7") *(K 13177)* **SINCE YOU'RE GONE. / MAYBE BABY** [37] [–]

Jun 82. (7") *<47479>* **THIS COULD BE LOVE. / VICTIM OF LOVE** [–] [ ]

Aug 82. (7") *(K 13187)* **THINK IT OVER. / I'M NOT THE ONE** [ ] [–]

Mar 84. (7") *<69744>* **YOU MIGHT THINK. / HEARTBEAT CITY** [–] [7]

Mar 84. (lp/c) *(960 296-1/-4) <60296>* **HEARTBEAT CITY** [25] [3]
– Hello again / Magic / Stranger eyes / It's not the night / I refuse / Looking for love / Drive / You might think / Why can't I have you / Heartbeat city. *<cd-iss. Jul84>*

Apr 84. (7") *(E 9741)* **WHY CAN'T I HAVE YOU. / JACKIE** [ ] [–]

May 84. (7") *<69724>* **MAGIC. / I REFUSE** [–] [12]

Sep 84. (7"/12") *(E 9706/+T) <69706>* **DRIVE. / STRANGER EYES** [5] Jul84 [3]
(re-iss. Jul85; hit UK No.4)

Oct 84. (7") *<69681>* **HELLO AGAIN. / ('A'dub)** [–] [20]

Nov 84. (7") *(E 9718)* **YOU MIGHT THINK. / I REFUSE** [ ] [–]
(12"+=) *(E 9710T)* – Let's go.

Jan 85. (7") *<69657>* **WHY CAN'T I HAVE YOU. / HEARTBEAT CITY** [–] [33]
(12"+=) *(E 9741T)* – Hello again (remix) / Moving in stereo.

Sep 85. (7") *(EKR 3)* **HEARTBEAT CITY. / WHY CAN'T I HAVE YOU** [ ] [–]
(12"+=) *(EKR 3T)* – Chemistry / Hello again.

Oct 85. (7") *<69589>* **TONIGHT SHE COMES. / JUST WHAT I NEEDED** [–] [7]

Nov 85. (7"pic-d) *(EKR 30)* **TONIGHT SHE COMES. / BREAKAWAY** [ ] [–]
(12"+=) *(EKR 30T)* – Just what I needed.

Nov 85. (lp/c)(cd) *(EKT 25/+C)(960 464-2) <60464>* **THE CARS' GREATEST HITS** (compilation) [27] [12]

– Just what I needed / Since you're gone / You might think / Good times roll / Touch and go / Drive / Tonight she comes / My best friend's girl / Heartbeat city / Let's go / Magic / Shake it up. *(c+=/cd+=)* – I'm not the one.

Jan 86. (7") *<69569>* **I'M NOT THE ONE. / HEARTBEAT CITY** [–] [32]

Mar 86. (7") *(EKR 38)* **I'M NOT THE ONE (remix). / SINCE YOU'RE GONE** [ ] [–]

(12"+=) *(EKR 38T)* – Shake it up.

Sep 87. (7") *(EKR 63) <69446>* **YOU ARE THE GIRL. / TA TA WAYO WAYO** [ ] Aug87 [17]

(12"+=/12"pic-d+=) *(EKR 63T/+P)* – Tonight she comes.

Sep 87. (lp/c)(cd) *(EKT 42/+C)(960 747-2) <60747>* **DOOR TO DOOR** [72] [26]

– Leave or stay / You are the girl / Double trouble / Fine line / Everything you say / Ta ta wayo wayo / Strap me in / Coming up you / Wound up on you / Go away / Door to door.

Nov 87. (7") *<69427>* **STRAP ME IN. / DOOR TO DOOR** [–] [85]

Jan 88. (7") *<69432>* **COMING UP YOU. / DOUBLE TROUBLE** [–] [74]

— disbanded early 1988. OCASEK married Paulina Porizkova (23 Aug'89) while continuing his solo career; ORR and EASTON also released solo sets

– compilations, etc. –

Jan 96. (d-cd) *Elektra; (0349 73506-2)* **JUST WHAT I NEEDED – ANTHOLOGY** [ ] [ ]

May 99. (d-cd) *Rhino Deluxe; <(8122 75700-2)>* **THE CARS** [ ] [ ]

CARTER THE UNSTOPPABLE SEX MACHINE

Formed: Streatham, South London, England ... 1988 by FRUITBAT (LES CARTER) and JIM BOB (JIM MORRISON). They had both been in early 80's outfit The BALLPOINTS, and after a lengthy period with real jobs, they formed the group JAMIE WEDNESDAY in 1984; signing to 'Rough Trade' subsidiary label 'Pink', they released two singles before disbanding in early '87. The following year they became CARTER THE UNSTOPPABLE SEX MACHINE, debuting that summer with 'SHELTERED LIFE', railing against shady landlords. It was the first in a memorable, if occasionally grating series of DIY agit-pop/punk singles which characterised an era of British indie music; "baggy" had died a lingering death and "grunge" was lumbering over the horizon, a time when all kinds of sub-standard ephemera made the cover of the NME. CARTER were at least entertaining, an undulatingly melodic follow-up single, 'SHERIFF FATMAN', unlucky not to chart (it later became their first Top 30 hit when re-released in the summer of '91). By this point, CARTER mania had firmly gripped the student nation and you couldn't go to any gig without seeing the ubiquitous '30 SOMETHING' baseball shirt. The 1991 album of the same name followed on from the sample-happy drum-machine-driven crusty pop of the debut, '101 DAMNATIONS' (1990), and provided a further controversial hit in the anti-army brutality rant, 'BLOODSPORTS FOR ALL'. The chirpy cockney duo (now signed to 'Chrysalis') topped off their annus glorious with a riotous headlining slot at the Reading Festival. There was some grief, however, as the ever vigilant ROLLING STONES legal team made explicit their concern over 'AFTER THE WATERSHED's none too subtle lift from JAGGER and Co.'s 'RUBY TUESDAY'. Following a Christmas re-issue of 'RUBBISH' (featuring one of their inimitable cover versions on the b-side, The Pet Shop Boys' 'RENT' coming in for the CARTER treatment this time around), the group returned in Spring '92 with one of their finest singles, 'THE ONLY LIVING BOY IN NEW CROSS'. A third set, ironically titled '1992 – THE LOVE ALBUM' topped the UK chart, another round of witty punning and HALF MAN HALF BISCUIT style humour. With the advent of American underground domination however, CARTER sounded increasingly tame, subsequent albums 'POST HISTORIC MONSTERS' and 'WORRY BOMB' entering the Top 10 but not hanging around. After a mid-90's split, the band, now signed to indie label, 'Cooking Vinyl', returned in 1997 and 1998 with the largely ignored 'A WORLD WITHOUT DAVE' and 'I BLAME THE GOVERNMENT'. JIM MORRISON virtually went solo in '99 resurfacing with his own JIM'S SUPER STEREOWORLD and signing to 'Fierce Panda'. After two DIY singles, 'BONKERS IN THE NUT' and 'COULD U B THE 1 I WAITED 4', he finally issued a debut. Pomp-punk and the kitchen sink also best described a follow-up mini-set in 2002, 'IN A BIG FLASH CAR ON A SATURDAY NIGHT'; it was a marked improvement on JIM and FRUITBAT's alter-ego collaboration, WHO'S THE DADDY NOW?, which resulted in a one-off single in 2001, 'THE BEEPER SONG'.
• **Covered:** RANDY SCOUSE GIT (Monkees) / EVERYBODY'S HAPPY NOWADAYS (Buzzcocks) / BEDSITTER (Soft Cell) / THIS IS HOW IT FEELS (Inspiral Carpets) / PANIC (Smiths) / MANNEQUIN (Wire) / KING ROCKER (Generation X) / DOWN IN THE TUBE STATION AT MIDNIGHT (Jam) / ANOTHER BRICK IN THE WALL (Pink Floyd) / THE IMPOSSIBLE DREAM (Mitch Leigh – Joe Darion) / HIT (Sugarcubes) / SPEEED KING (These Animal Men) / SILVER DREAM MACHINE (David Essex).
• **Trivia:** Surprisingly it was JONATHAN KING who gave them tabloid exposure in his 'Sun' column.

Album rating: 101 DAMNATIONS (*9) / 30 SOMETHING (*8) / 1992 – THE LOVE ALBUM (*7) / POST-HISTORIC MONSTERS (*8) / STARRY EYED AND BOLLOCK NAKED (A COLLECTION OF B-SIDES) (*6) / WORRY BOMB (*5) / STRAW DONKEYS – THE SINGLES compilation (*6) / A WORLD WITHOUT DAVE mini (*5) / I BLAME THE GOVERNMENT (*4) / LIVE! (*5) / SESSIONS collection (*5) / Jim's Super Stereoworld: JIM'S SUPER STEREOWORLD (*6) / IN A BIG FLASH CAR ON A SATURDAY NIGHT mini (*5)

JAMIE WEDNESDAY

JIM 'Jim Bob' MORRISON (b.22 Nov'60) – vocals, acoustic guitar / **LES 'Fruitbat' CARTER** (b.12 Feb'58) – bass / **LINDSEY HENRY** – trumpet / **SIMON LOWE** – brass / **DEAS LEGGETT** – drums

Pink / not iss.

Nov 85. (12"ep) *(PINKY 6)* **VOTE FOR LOVE / THE WALL. / WHITE HORSES / BUTTONS AND BOWS** [ ] [–]

May 86. (12"ep) *(PINKY 10)* **WE THREE KINGS OF ORIENT AREN'T. / LAST NIGHT I HAD THE STRANGEST DREAM / I THINK I'LL THROW A PARTY FOR MYSELF** [ ] [–]

— disbanded Feb'87

CARTER THE UNSTOPPABLE SEX MACHINE

— was duo formed by **JIM BOB & FRUITBAT** who now both played guitar with back-up of tape machines & JIM BOB – vocals

Big Cat / Chrysalis

Aug 88. (12"m) *(BBA 03)* **SHELTERED LIFE. / IS THIS THE ONLY WAY THROUGH TO YOU? / GRANNY FARMING IN THE U.K.** [ ] [–]

(re-iss. Jun94 on 'Southern' cd-ep; 18620-2)

Nov 89. (12"ep) *(ABB 100T)* **SHERIFF FATMAN / R.S.P.C.E.. / TWIN-TUB WITH GUITAR / EVERYBODY'S HAPPY NOWADAYS** [ ] [–]

Jan 90. (lp/c/cd) *(ABB/+C/CD 101) <21881>* **101 DAMNATIONS** [ ] [ ]

– A perfect day to drop the bomb / Midnight on the murder mile / The road to Domestos / An all-American sport / 24 minutes to Tulsa Hill /

Good grief / Charlie Brown / Everytime a churchbell rings / Good grief / Sheriff Fatman / G.I. blues. *(re-dist.Sep91; same); hit No.29)*

May 90. (12"/cd-s) *(ABB 102 T/CD)* **RUBBISH. / RENT / ALTERNATIVE ALF GARNET** [ ] [–]

Oct 90. (export; m-lp/m-cd) *(ABB 103X/+CD)* **HANDBUILT FOR PERVERTS** [–] [–]

Rough Trade not iss.

Oct 90. (7") *(RT 242)* **ANYTIME, ANYPLACE, ANYWHERE. / RE-EDUCATING RITA** [ ] [–]
(12"+=/cd-s+=) *(RTT 242/+CD)* – Alternative title / Randy sarf git.

Jan 91. (7"/c-s) *(R 2011 268-7/-6)* **BLOODSPORTS FOR ALL. / 2001: A CLOCKWORK ORANGE** [48] [–]
(12"+=/cd-s+=) *(R 2011 268-0/-3)* – Bedsitter.

Feb 91. (cd/c/lp) *(RT 2011 270-2/-4/-1)* <21884> **30 SOMETHING** [8] [ ]
– Surfin' USM / My second to last will and testament / Anytime anyplace anywhere / Prince in a pauper's grave / Shopper's paradise / Billy's smart circus / Bloodsport for all / Sealed with a Glasgow kiss / Say it with flowers / Falling on a bruise / The final comedown. *<US-iss.Aug91 on 'Chrysalis'; same as US> (re-iss. Jan92 on 'Chrysalis' cd/c/lp; CCD/ZCHR/CHR 1897); hit UK 21) (re-iss. Feb95; same as US)*

Chrysalis Chrysalis

Jun 91. (7") *(USM 1)* **SHERIFF FATMAN. / R.S.P.C.E.** [23] [ ]
(c-s+=/12"+=/cd-s+=) *(USM X/XMS/CD 1)* – Twin-tub with guitar / Everybody's happy nowadays.

Oct 91. (7"/c-s) *(USM/+XMC 2)* **AFTER THE WATERSHED. / THE 90's REVIVAL / A NATION OF SHOPLIFTERS** [11] [–]
(12"+=/cd-s+=) *(USM X/CD 2)* – This is how it feels.

Dec 91. (7"/c-s) *(USM/+XMC 3)* **RUBBISH. / ALTERNATIVE ALF GARNER** [14] [–]
(12"+=/cd-s+=) *(USM X/CD 3)* – Rent.

Apr 92. (7"/c-s/12"/cd-s) *(USM/+XMC/X/CD 4)* **THE ONLY LIVING BOY IN NEW CROSS. / WATCHING THE BIG APPLE TURN / PANIC** [7] [–]

May 92. (cd/c/lp) *(CCD/ZCHR/CHR 1946)* <21946> **1992 – THE LOVE ALBUM** [1] [ ]
– 1993 / Is wrestling fixed? / The only living boy in New Cross / Suppose you gave a funeral and nobody came / England / Do re mi, so far so good / Look mum, no hands / While you were out / Skywest and crooked / The impossible dream. *(re-iss. Mar94 & Feb95 cd/c;)*

Jun 92. (7"/c-s/12"/cd-s) *(USM/+XMC/X/CD 5)* **DO RE MI, SO FAR SO GOOD / MANNEQUIN. / KING ROCKER / DOWN IN THE TUBE-STATION AT MIDNIGHT** [22] [–]

Nov 92. (7"/c-s/12"/cd-s) *(USM/+XMC/X/CD 6)* **THE IMPOSSIBLE DREAM / TURN ON, TUNE IN AND SWITCH OFF / WHEN THESAURUSES RULED THE WORLD / BRING ON THE GIRLS** [21] [–]

Aug 93. (7"/c-s) *(USM/+XMC 7)* **LEAN ON ME I WON'T FALL OVER. / HIT** [16] [–]
(12"+=/cd-s+=) *(12/CD USM 7)* – Always the bridesmaid never the bride.

Sep 93. (cd/c/lp) *(CD/TC+/CHR 7090)* **POST HISTORIC MONSTERS** [5] [–]
– 2 million years B.C. / The music that nobody likes / Mid day crisis / Cheer up, it might never happen / Stuff the jubilee! / A bachelor for Baden Powell / Spoilsports personality of the year / Suicide isn't painless / Being here / Evil / Sing fat lady sing / Travis / Lean on me I won't fall over / Lenny and Terence / Under the thumb and over the Moon. *(re-iss. Feb95; same)*

Oct 93. (7"/c-s) *(USM/+XMC 8)* **LENNY AND TERENCE. / HER SONG** [40] [–]
(12"+=/cd-s+=) *(12/CD USM 8)* – Commercial fucking suicide (part 1) / Stuff the jubilee (1977).

Mar 94. (c-s/7") *(TC+/USM 10)* **GLAM ROCK COPS. / LEAN ON ME (I WON'T FALL OVER) (by The FAMILY CAT)** [24] [–]
(12"+=/cd-s+=) *(12USM/CDUSMS 10)* – ('A'-GRID mixes).
(cd-s) *(CDUSM 10)* – ('A'side) / Bloodsports for all (by SULTANS OF PING F.C.) / Lenny and Terence (by BLADE) / Falling on a bruise (by PUBLIC WORKS).

Mar 94. (cd/c/lp) *(CD/TC+/CHR 6069)* **STARRY EYED AND BOLLOCK NAKED (A COLLECTION OF B-SIDES)** (compilation) [22] [–]
– Is this the only way to get through to you? / Granny farming in the UK / R.S.P.C.E. / Twin tub with guitar / Alternative Alf Garnett / Re educating Rita / 2001: A clockwork orange / The 90's revival / A nation of shoplifters / Watching the big apple turn over / Turn on, tune in and switch off / When Thesauruses ruled the Earth / Bring on the girls! / Always the bridesmaid never the bride / Her song / Commercial f**king suicide / Stuff the jubilee (1977) / Glam rock cops. *(re-iss. Feb95 & Sep98; same)*

— added **WEZ BOYNTON** – drums (ex-RESQUE)

Nov 94. (c-s/7") *(TC+/USM 11)* **LET'S GET TATTOOS. / ESPECIALLY 4 U** [30] [–]
(cd-s+=) *(CDUSMS 11)* – Speed king / Silver dream machine.
(cd-s) *(CDUSM 11)* – ('A'side) / Turbulence / King for a day.

Jan 95. (c-s/7"colrd) *(TC+/USM 12)* **THE YOUNG OFFENDER'S MUM. / TROUBLE** [34] [–]
(cd-s+=) *(CDUSMS 12)* – This one's for me.
(cd-s) *(CDUSM 12)* – ('A'side) / Rubbish (live) / Suicide isn't painless (live) / Falling on a bruise (live).

Feb 95. (cd/c/d-lp) *(CD/TC+/CHR 6096)* **WORRY BOMB** [9] [–]
– Cheap'n'cheesy / Airplane food – airplane fest food / The young offender's mum / Gas (man) / The life and soul of the party dies / My defeatest attitude / Worry bomb / Senile delinquent / Me and Mr.Jones / Let's get tattoos / Going straight / God, Saint Peter and the guardian angel / The only looney left in town / Ceasefire. *(d-cd+=) (CDCHRX 6096)* **DOMA SPORTOVA . . . LIVE IN ZAGREB, 20/5/94** – Alternative Alf Garnett / Do re me so far so good / A bachelor pad for Baden Powell / Re-educating Rita / The only living boy in New Cross / Lean on me I won't fall over / Granny farming in the U.K. / Travis / Sing fat lady sing / Lenny and Terence / Commercial fucking suicide part 1.

Sep 95. (c-s/7"red) *(TC+/USM 13)* **BORN ON THE 5th OF NOVEMBER. / D.I.V.O.R.C.E.F.G.** [35] [–]
(cd-s) *(CDUSM 13)* – ('A'side) / Tomorrow when you die / The aftertaste of Paradise / Airplane food.

Oct 95. (cd/c/lp) *(CD/TC+/CHR 6110)* **STRAW DONKEY . . . THE SINGLES** (compilation) [37] [–]
– A sheltered life / Sheriff Fatman / Rubbish / Antime anyplace anywhere / Bloodsport for all / After the watershed (early learning the hard way) / The only living boy in New Cross / Do re mi, so far so good / The impossible dream / Lean on me (I won't fall over) / Lenny and Terence / Glam rock cops / Let's get tattoos / The young offender's mum / Born on the 5th of November. *(cd re-iss. Sep97; same)*

— CARTER split for around a year after above

Cooking Vinyl Cooking Vinyl

Mar 97. (m-lp/m-cd) *(<COOK/+CD 120>)* **A WORLD WITHOUT DAVE** [73] Apr97 [ ]
– Broken down in broken town / A world without Dave / Before the war / Nowhere fast / Johnny Cash / And God created Brixton. *(cd+=)* – Stand up and be counted / Negative equity / Road rage.

Cooking Vinyl True North

Jan 98. (cd) *(COOKCD 136)* <TN 163> **I BLAME THE GOVERNMENT** [ ] Sep98 [ ]
– The wrong place at the wrong time / 23:59 end of the world / Sunshine / The undertaker and the hippy protest singer / Sweetheart sugar baby / Growing old disgracefully / The man who bought the world winning the war / I blame the government / Citizen's band radio / Psycho Bill / Closedown / Girls can keep a secret.

Feb 99. (cd) *(COOKCD 149)* **LIVE! (live)** [ ] [–]
– 24 minutes from Tulse Hill / Rubbish / Do re mi (so far so good) / Anytime anyplace anywhere / A prince in a pauper's grave / A perfect day to drop the bomb / Say it with flowers / Rent / Cheer up it might never happen / The taking of Peckham 123 / Lenny and Terence (with JAMES ATKIN) / Suicide isn't painless / Growing old disgracefully / Elvis lives and Carterbreakamerica / Airplane food / Let's get tattoos / The model.

– compilations, etc. –

Oct 98. (cd) *Cooking Vinyl; (COOKCD 165)* **SESSIONS** (BBC 1991, 1994, 1997) [ ] [–]
– Sheriff Fatman / A prince in pauper's grave / Sealed with a Glasgow kiss / A sheltered life / Alternative Alf Garnett / Re-educating Rita / Commercial flippin' suicide / Granny farming in the UK / Johnny Cash / Nowhere fast / Girls can keep a secret.

☐ Caitlin CARY (see under ⇒ WHISKEYTOWN)

Johnny CASH

Born: 26 Feb'32, Kingsland, Arkansas, USA (where a statue of "The Man in Black" now stands). The third of seven children born to poor sharecropper parents, Ray and Annie Cash, JOHNNY attended Dyess High School in Arkansas and won his first talent contest at age seventeen. In 1950, he joined the Air Force and served overseas in Germany, being discharged in 1954 as a staff sergeant (his other pre-musical jobs included salesman, assembly line worker and margarine factory operative). Young CASH, however, was destined for greater things; the birth of Rock'n'Roll, or more correctly its rockabilly predecessor, was the perfect vehicle for his budding singing and songwriting talents. After initially playing in a combo called the TENNESSEE TWO (later the TENNESSEE THREE), he was subsequently spotted and signed by Sam Phillips for his influential 'Sun' record label in 1955 as a fellow stable-mate to rockers ROY ORBISON, JERRY LEE LEWIS, CARL PERKINS and a little-known truck driver named ELVIS PRESLEY (CASH, PERKINS, LEWIS and PRESLEY were to become known as "The Million Dollar Quartet"). While the others took the rock road, CASH churned out a string of country-influenced hit singles and albums ('BIG RIVER', 'I WALK THE LINE', 'RING OF FIRE', 'SAN QUENTIN' and 'FOLSOM PRISON' being typical of his slow western, macho, half-spoken/half-sung drawl) between 1955 and 1968, his rising fame running parallel with a notorious reputation offstage as a violent, hot-headed heavy boozer and pill-popper. As his career soared, so his personal life disintegrated, ending in divorce after a stormy marriage to first wife, Vivien Liberto. Along with the infamous Folsom Prison and San Quentin Prison live albums (Grammy award winners both), this image established his blue-collar following and consolidated his position as the champion of the underdog in America. He rapidly established himself as the hottest property in country music, selling over fifty million records and even outselling the Beatles in America for a time. He married June Carter in 1968, erstwhile member of the legendary all-singing CARTER FAMILY. Her calming influence on him was to prove a major factor in the style and quality of his later recordings. As the decade turned, he became involved in TV, hosting The Johnny Cash Show and bringing many cult names, (BOB DYLAN, NEIL YOUNG, HANK WILLIAMS Jnr. et al.) to a wider audience. CASH, influenced by his new wife, turned to religion around this time, making a film 'Gospel Road', while various religious organisations and charities benefitted from the newly converted wild man of country. He continued to tour non-stop during the 70's and 80's, including shows for Vietnam draftees and tours behind the then Iron Curtain. Two books were published, 'Man in Black' in 1975 and 'Man in White' in 1987. The 80's also saw him becoming a member of "outlaw" country band, The HIGHWAYMEN alongside KRIS KRISTOFFERSON, WAYLON JENNINGS and WILLIE NELSON, with whom he toured the world to sellout concerts and more recording success. The 90's, meanwhile, saw CASH resurrected as an alternative hero (via a guest track – 'THE WANDERER' – on U2's 1993 album, 'Zooropa') by Rick Rubin and his 'American' label, who released comeback set, 'AMERICAN RECORDINGS' (1994). He garnered even more critical kudos with 1996's 'UNCHAINED', wherein he even had a crack at Soundgarden's 'RUSTY CAGE' and Beck's 'ROWBOAT'. His compositions are still covered by today's up-and-coming artists while his frequent appearances on MTV have kept his popularity high, despite failing health and a less rigourous tour schedule. He's now the head of a family of five, the most famous of whom is ROSANNE CASH, a minor C&W star in her own right. He has been inducted into all of music's four Halls of Fame: Songwriters (1989), Rock'n'Roll (1992) and, of course, Country Music (1980) and Rockabilly (1994), a unique achievement among his peers as is his grand total of seven Grammys, three multi-platinum albums ('FOLSOM PRISON', 'SAN QUENTIN' and 'GREATEST HITS') and 130 (yes 130!) hits on the Billboard charts. On a more depressing note, CASH has had to contend with ongoing health problems over the last few years and has recently been diagnosed with Parkinson's disease, having to abandon a US show midway through. The man in black made a startling comeback with his album 'AMERICAN 3: SOLITARY MAN' (2000), a sort of half covers album and a musician's jamboree all in one. CASH not only covered such classics as Tom Petty's 'I WON'T BACK DOWN' and U2's 'THE ONE', but he also did a fantastic job at recreating PALACE man and fellow crooner Will Oldham's 'I SEE A DARKNESS', to much heightened effect. MERLE HAGGARD, the Bluegrass legend popped in to lend his voice to the CASH penned 'I'M LEAVING NOW' and he basically transformed his own 'FIELD OF DIAMONDS IN THE SKY' from jangling country to a heart-felt holler. But it's the lonesome guitar and theatrical piano trills on Nick Cave's 'MERCY SEAT' that really put things in perspective; when CASH sings, " . . .and I'm not afraid to die", you know he really feels it, shining a whole new light on the meaning behind the track. And perhaps that was the biggest compliment you could pay such a revered figure as CASH: each song he covered came into its own through his extraordinary talent and minimalistic guitar playing – not to mention RICK RUBIN's 'Live' production. That is the kind of power that JOHNNY CASH's music will always command. And so to the last chapter of his critical rebirth and sadly, the last chapter of his life. 'AMERICAN IV: THE MAN COMES AROUND' (2002) continued with the strategy of edifying contemporary songs with a lifetime's worth of hard-won experience. Again, the ones which worked best were the ones least likely to succeed on paper, such as Nine Inch Nails' 'HURT' and Depeche Mode's 'PERSONAL JESUS'. Released as a double-A single, the songs made the UK Top 40, while the compelling, revelatory video was nominated at the MTV video music awards. JOHNNY CASH finally succumbed to his ongoing health problems on the 12th of September 2003, at the age of 71, just four months after his wife. Few recording artists pushed their creative boundaries as long and as hard as JOHNNY CASH, while even fewer – if any – managed to sustain that achievement (and – for what it's worth – confound and impress contemporary critics) right up until their final days, and for that we should be grateful. • **Songwriters:** CASH penned except; THE WAYS OF A WOMAN IN LOVE (Charlie Rich) / RING OF FIRE (Merle Haggard & June Carter) / IT AIN'T ME BABE + WANTED MAN (Bob Dylan) / A BOY NAMED SUE (Shel Silverstein) / IF I WERE A CARPENTER (Tim Hardin) / SUNDAY MORNING COMING DOWN (Kris Kristopherson) / JOHNNY 99 (Bruce Springsteen) / DADDY SANG BASS (Carl Perkins) / THE HIGHWAYMAN (Jimmy Webb) / BIRD ON A WIRE (Leonard Cohen) / THIRTEEN (Glen Danzig) / THE BEAST IN ME (Nick Lowe) / THE MAN WHO COULDN'T CRY (Loudon Wainwright III). The 1964 album BITTER TEARS was written by PETER LA FARGE. • **Trivia:** In 1969, he guested on BOB DYLAN's 'Nashville Skyline' lp track, 'THE GIRL FROM NORTH COUNTRY'.

Album rating (selective): RIDE THIS TRAIN (*7) / I WALK THE LINE (*7) / AT FOLSOM PRISON (*8) / AT SAN QUENTIN (*7) / ONE PIECE AT A TIME (*6) / THE MAN IN BLACK – THE DEFINITIVE JOHNNY CASH compilation (*8) / THE MYSTERY OF LIFE (*6) / AMERICAN RECORDINGS (*7) / UNCHAINED (*7) / AMERICAN III: SOLITARY MAN (*6) / AMERICAN

IV: THE MAN COMES AROUND (*5) / MAN IN BLACK – THE VERY BEST OF . . . double compilation (*8)

JOHNNY CASH – vocals, guitar / with various backers

London Sun

Jun 55. (7",78) <221> **CRY! CRY! CRY! / HEY PORTER** –
(UK-iss.Oct70 on 'Sun'; 6094 005)

Jan 56. (7",78) <232> **FOLSOM PRISON BLUES. / SO DOGGONE LONESOME** –

Jan 57. (7",78) *(HL 8358)* <241> **I WALK THE LINE. / GET RHYTHM** Aug56 17

Jun 57. (7",78) *(HLS 8427)* <258> **TRAIN OF THOUGHT. / THERE YOU GO** Nov56

Aug 57. (7",78) *(HLS 8461)* <266> **NEXT IN LINE. / DON'T MAKE ME GO** Jun57 99

Oct 57. (lp) *<SLP 1220>* **JOHNNY CASH WITH HIS HOT & BLUE GUITAR** –
– The rock island line / I heard that lonesome whistle blow / Country boy / If the good Lord's willing and the creeks don't rise / Cry cry cry / Remember me / I'm so doggone lonesome / I was there when it happened / I walk the line / The wreck of the old 97 / Folsom Prison blues / Doin' my time. *(UK-iss.Feb81 on 'Charly'; CRM 2013)*

Dec 57. (7",78) *(HLS 8514)* <279> **HOME OF THE BLUES. / GIVE MY LOVE TO ROSE** Sep57 88

Apr 58. (7",78) *(HLS 8586)* <283> **BALLAD OF A TEENAGE QUEEN. / BIG RIVER** Jan58 14

Jul 58. (7",78) *(HLS 8656)* <295> **GUESS THINGS HAPPEN THAT WAY. / COME IN STRANGER** 11
May58 66

Oct 58. (7",78) *(HLS 8709)* <302> **THE WAYS OF A WOMAN IN LOVE. / YOU'RE THE NEAREST THING TO HEAVEN** Aug58 24

Philips Columbia

Nov 58. (7",78) *(PB 874)* <41251> **ALL OVER AGAIN. / WHAT DO I CARE** 38
Sep58 52

—— In Dec'58, 'Sun' and CASH had their first of a number of Top 100 successes with 'IT'S JUST ABOUT TIME'.

Jan 59. (7",78) *(PB 897)* <41313> **DON'T TAKE YOUR GUNS TO TOWN. / I STILL MISS SOMEONE** 32

Jan 59. (lp) *(BBL 7298)* <1253> **THE FABULOUS JOHNNY CASH** 19
– Run softly, blue river / Frankie's man, Johnny / That's all over / The troubadour / One more ride/ That's enough / I still miss someone / Don't take your guns to town / I'd rather die young / Pickin' time / Shepherd of my heart / Supper-time. *(UK re-iss. Jun62 on 'C.B.S.'; 62042)*

May 59. (7",78) *(PB 928)* <41371> **FRANKIE'S MAN, JOHNNY. / YOU DREAMER YOU** Apr59 57

Sep 59. (7",78) *(PB 953)* <41427> **I GOT STRIPES. / FIVE FEET HIGH AND RISING** 43
76

—— recruited new drummer **W.S.HOLLAND** who stayed for next 30 years.

Dec 59. (7",78) *(PB 979)* <41481> **THE LITTLE DRUMMER BOY. / I'LL REMEMBER YOU** 63

Jan 60. (lp) *(BBL 7353)* <CS 8148> **SONGS OF OUR SOIL**
– Drink to me / Five feet high and rising / Man on the hill / Hank and Joe and me / Clementine / Don't step on mother's roses / Great speckled bird / I want to go home / Caretaker / Old Apache squaw / My grandfather's clock / It could happen to you.

Apr 60. (7") *(PB 1017)* <41618> **SEASONS OF MY HEART. / SMILING BILL McCALL**

Jun 60. (lp) *(BBL 7373)* <CS 8522> **HYMNS BY JOHNNY CASH**
– It was Jesus / I saw a man / Are all the children in / The old account / Lead me gently home / Swing low, sweet chariot / Snow in his hair / Lead me, father / I called him / These things shall pass / He'll be a friend / God will.

Jul 60. (7") <41707> **SECOND HONEYMOON. / HONKY-TONK GIRL** –

Oct 60. (7") *(PB 1075)* <41804> **GOING TO MEMPHIS. / LOADING COAL**

Oct 60. (lp) *(BBL 7358)* <CS 8254> **NOW THERE WAS A SONG**
– Seasons of my heart / I couldn't keep from crying / I feel better all over / My shoes keep walking back to you / Time changes everything / I'd just be a fool enough (to fall) / Why do you punish me / Transfusion blues / I will miss you when you go / I'm so lonesome, I could cry / Just one more / Honky-tonk girl. *(re-iss. May62 on 'C.B.S.'; 62028) (cd-iss. Feb95;)*

Dec 60. (lp) *(BBL 7417)* <CS 8255> **RIDE THIS TRAIN**
– Loading coal / Slow rider / Lumberjack / Dorraine of Ponchartrain / Going to Memphis / When papa played the dobro / Boss Jack / Old Doc Brown. *(re-iss. May62 on 'C.B.S.'; 62575)*

Jan 61. (7") <41920> **LOCOMOTIVE MAN. / GIRL IN SASKATOON** –

May 61. (7") *(PB 1148)* <41995> **THE REBEL – JOHNNY YUMA. / FORTY SHADES OF GREEN**

Nov 61. (7") *(PB 1200)* <42147> **TENNESSEE FLAT-TOP BOX. / TALL MEN** Sep61 84

Jan 62. (7") <42301> **THE BIG BATTLE. / WHEN I'VE LEARNED** –

May 62. (7") <42425> **IN THE JAILHOUSE NOW. / LITTLE AT A TIME** –

Aug 62. (7") <42512> **BONANZA! / PICK A BALE O' COTTON** – 94

Nov 62. (7"; JOHNNY CASH with The CARTER FAMILY) <42615> **WERE YOU THERE (WHEN THEY CRUCIFIED MY LORD). / (THERE'LL BE) PEACE IN THE VALLEY (FOR ME)** –

C.B.S. Columbia

Mar 63. (7") <42665> **BUSTED. / SEND A PICTURE OF MOTHER** –

May 63. (lp) *(BPG 62119)* <8730> **BLOOD, SWEAT AND TEARS** Mar63 80
– The legend of John Henry's hammer / Tell him I'm gone / Another man done gone / Busted / Casey Jones / Nine pound hammer / Chain gang / Waiting for a train / Roughneck. *(cd-iss. Feb95;)*

Jul 63. (7") *(AAG 159)* <42788> **RING OF FIRE. / I'D STILL BE THERE** May63 17

Oct 63. (lp; stereo/mono) *(S+/BPG 62171)* <8853> **RING OF FIRE – THE BEST OF JOHNNY CASH** (compilation) Jul63 26
– Ring of fire / I'd still be there / What do I care / I still miss someone / Forty shades of green / Were you there (when they crucified my Lord) / The rebel – Johnny Yuma / Bonanza / The big battle / Remember the Alamo / Tennessee flat-top box / (There'll be) Peace in the valley (for me).

Nov 63. (7") *(AAG 173)* <42880> **THE MATADOR. / STILL IN TOWN** Oct63 44

Nov 63. (lp; stereo/mono) *(S+/BPG 62284)* **THE CHRISTMAS SPIRIT** (festive) –

Feb 64. (7") <42964> **UNDERSTAND YOUR MAN. / DARK AS A DUNGEON** – 35

Sep 64. (lp; stereo/mono) *(S+/BPG 62371)* <8990> **I WALK THE LINE** (new versions of old recordings) 53
– I walk the line / Bad news / Folsom Prison blues / Give my love to Rose / Hey Porter / I still miss someone / Understand your man / Wreck of old '97 / Still in town / Goodbye, little darlin' / Big river / Troublesome waters.

Dec 64. (7") <43058> **BAD NEWS. / THE BALLAD OF IRA HAYES** –

Jan 65. (lp; stereo/mono) *(S+/BPG 62463)* <9048> **BITTER TEARS (BALLADS OF THE AMERICAN INDIAN)** 47
– As long as the grass shall grow / Apache tears / Custer / The talking leaves / The ballad of Ira Hayes / Drums / White girl / The vanishing race. *(cd-iss. Feb95;)*

Mar 65. (7") *(201741)* <43206> **ORANGE BLOSSOM SPECIAL. / ALL OF GOD'S CHILDREN AIN'T FREE** Feb65 80

Apr 65. (lp; stereo/mono) *(S+/BPG 62501)* <9109> **ORANGE BLOSSOM SPECIAL** Mar65 49
– Orange blossom special / The long black veil / It ain't me babe / The wall / Don't think twice, it's alright / You wild Colorado / Mama, you've been on my mind / When it's springtime in Alaska (it's forty below) / All of God's children ain't free / Danny boy / Wildwood flower / Amen.

May 65. (7") *(201760)* <43145> **IT AIN'T ME BABE. / TIME AND TIME AGAIN** 28 Oct64 58

Jun 65. (7") <43313> **STREETS OF LAREDO. / MISTER GARFIELD** –

Aug 65. (7") *(210809)* **RING OF FIRE. / STREETS OF LAREDO** –

Sep 65. (7") <43342> **THE SONS OF KATIE ELDER. / CERTAIN KINDA HURTIN'** –

Nov 65. (7") <43420> **PICKIN' TIME. / HAPPY TO BE WITH YOU** –

Mar 66. (7") *(202046)* <43496> **THE ONE ON THE RIGHT IS ON THE LEFT. / COTTON PICKIN' HANDS** Feb66 46

Jul 66. (7") *(202256)* <43673> **EVERYBODY LOVES A NUT. / AUSTIN PRISON** 96

Jul 66. (lp; stereo/mono) *(S+/BPG 62717) <9292>* **EVERYBODY LOVES A NUT** [28] [88]
– Everybody loves a nut / The one on the right is on the left / A cup of coffee / The bug that tried to crawl around the world / The singing star's queen / Austin Prison / Dirty old egg – Sucking dog / Take me home / Please don't play / Red river valley / Boa constrictor / Joe Bean.

Oct 66. (7") *<43763>* **BOA CONSTRICTOR. / BOTTOM OF A MOUNTAIN** [–] [ ]

Nov 66. (lp; stereo/mono) *(S+/BPG 62760)* **HAPPINESS IS YOU** [ ] [–]
– Happiness is you / Guess things happen that way / Ancient history / You comb her hair / She came from the mountains / For lovin' me / No one will ever know / Is this my destiny / A wound time can't erase / Happy to be with you / Wabash cannonball.

Jan 67. (7") *(202546) <43921>* **YOU BEAT ALL I EVER SAW. / PUT THE SUGAR TO BED** [ ] [ ]

Mar 67. (lp; stereo/mono) *(S+/BPG 62972)* **FROM SEA TO SHINING SEA** [ ] [–]
– From sea to shining sea / Whirl anmd the suck / Call daddy from the mine / The frozen four-hundred-pound fair-to-middlin' cotton picker / The walls of a prison / The masterpiece / You and Tennessee / Another song to sing / The flint arrowhead / Cisco Clifton's fillin' station / Shrimpin' sailin' / From sea to shining sea (reprise). *(hit No.40 in May68)*

Jul 67. (7"; with JUNE CARTER) *<44011>* **JACKSON. / PACK UP YOUR SORROWS** [–] [ ]

Sep 67. (lp; stereo/mono) *(S+/BPG 63062) <9478>* **JOHNNY CASH'S GREATEST HITS, VOLUME 1** (compilation) [ ] Jul67 [82]
– Jackson (with JUNE CARTER) / I walk the line / Understand your man / Orange blossom special / The one on the right is on the left / Ring of fire / It ain't me babe / The balad of Ira Hayes / The rebel – Johnny Yuma / Five feet high and rising / Don't take your guns to town. *(UK hit No.23 Dec69) (cd+c.iss.Nov93 on 'Sony Europe')*

Sep 67. (7"; with JUNE CARTER) *<44158>* **YOU'LL BE ALRIGHT. / LONG-LEGGED GUITAR-PICKIN' MAN** [–] [ ]

Nov 67. (lp; stereo/mono) *(S+/BPG 63105) <9528>* **CARRYIN' ON WITH JOHNNY CASH & JUNE CARTER** [ ] Sep67 [ ]
– Long-legged guitar pickin' man / Shantytown / It ain't me babe / Fast boat to Sydney / Pack up your sorrows / I got a woman / Jackson / Oh, what a good thing we had / You'll be all right / No, no, no / What'd I say.

Nov 67. (7") *<44288>* **RED VELVET. / THE WIND CHANGES** [–] [ ]

Jan 68. (7") *<44373>* **ROSANNA'S GOING WILD. / ROLL CALL** [–] [91]

Feb 68. (7") *(CBS 3268)* **ROSANNA'S GOING WILD. / LONG-LEGGED GUITAR-PICKIN' MAN (with JUNE CARTER)** [ ] [–]

Apr 68. (7") *(CBS 3433)* **A CERTAIN KIND OF HURTIN'. / ANOTHER SONG TO SING** [ ] [–]

Jun 68. (7") *(CBS 3549) <44513>* **FOLSOM PRISON BLUES (live). / THE FOLK SINGER** [ ] May68 [32]

Jun 68. (lp) *(CBS 63308) <9639>* **JOHNNY CASH AT FOLSOM PRISON (live prison gig)** [ ] [13]
– Folsom prison blues / Dark as a dungeon / I still miss someone / Cocaine blues / 25 minutes to go / Orange blossom special / The long black veil / Send a picture of mother / The wall / Dirty old egg sucking dog / Flushed from the bathroom of your heart / Jackson (with JUNE CARTER) / Give my love to Rose / I got stripes / Green green grass of home / Greystone chapel. *(cd/c-iss.Jan95 on 'Success';)*

Jan 69. (7") *(CBS 3878) <44689>* **DADDY SANG BASS. / HE TURNED THE WATER INTO WINE** [ ] Dec68 [42]

May 69. (lp) *(CBS 63428) <KC 9726>* **THE HOLY LAND** [ ] Feb69 [54]
– Prologue / Land of Israel / A mother's love / This is Nazareth / Nazareth town of Canaan / He turned the water into wine / My wife June at the sea of Galilee / Beautiful words / Our guide Jacob at Mount Tabor / The ten commandments / Daddy sang bass / At the wailing wall / Come to the wailing wall / In Bethlehem / In garden of Gethsemane / The fourth man / On the Via Dolorosa / Church of the holy / Sepulchre / At Calvary / God is not dead.

—— CASH guested on BOB DYLAN's country 1969 album 'Nashville Skyline'.

—— In Jun'69, he also began own self-titled TV show, with The CARTER FAMILY, CARL PERKINS, etc.

—— **BOB WOTTON** – guitar repl. LUTHER who died in a house fire.

Aug 69. (lp) *(CBS 63629) <CS 9827>* **JOHNNY CASH AT SAN QUENTIN (live prison gig)** [2] Jun69 [1]
– Wanted man / Wreck of the old 97 / I walk the line / Darling companion / Starkville city jail / San Quentin / A boy named Sue / Peace in the valley / Folsom prison blues. *(cd-iss. Mar94 on 'Sony Collectors')*

Aug 69. (7") *(CBS 4460) <44944>* **A BOY NAMED SUE. / SAN QUENTIN** [4] Jul69 [2]

Dec 69. (7") *(CBS 4638) <45020>* **BLISTERED. / SEE RUBY FALL** [ ] [50] Nov69 [75]

Feb 70. (7"; with JUNE CARTER) *<45064>* **IF I WERE A CARPENTER. / 'CAUSE I LOVE YOU** [–] [36]

Feb 70. (lp) *(CBS 63796) <9943>* **HELLO, I'M JOHNNY CASH** [6] [6]
– Southwind / The Devil to pay / Cause I love you / See Ruby fall / If I were a carpenter / To beat the Devil / Blistered / Wrinkled, crinkled, wadded dollar bill / I've got a thing about trains / Jesus was a carpenter.

May 70. (7") *(CBS 4934) <45134>* **WHAT IS TRUTH. / SING A TRAVELLING SONG** [21] Apr70 [19]

Aug 70. (d-lp) *(CBS 66237) <29>* **THE WORLD OF JOHNNY CASH** (compilation) [5] May70 [54]
– I still miss someone / Pickin' time / My shoes keep walking back to you / I want to go home / I feel better all over / I'm so lonesome I could cry / Supper-time / In them old cotton fields back home / Delia's gone / One more ride / Accidentally on purpose / In the jailhouse now / I gorgot more than you'll ever know / Casey Jones / Frankie's man, Johnny / The legend of John Henry's hammer / When papa played the dobro / Busted / Sing it pretty, Sue / Waiting for a train.

Aug 70. (7") *<45211>* **SUNDAY MORNING COMING DOWN. / I'M GONNA TRY TO BE THAT WAY** [–] [46]

Oct 70. (7") *(CBS 5252)* **25 MINUTES TO GO. / I'M GONNA TRY TO BE THAT WAY** [ ] [–]

Dec 70. (lp) *(CBS 64089) <30100>* **THE JOHNNY CASH SHOW (live)** [18] Nov70 [44]
– Sunday morning coming down / Come along and ride this train (medley): Six days on the road – There ain't no easy run – The sailor on a concrete sea / These hands / I'm gonna try to be that way / Come along and ride this train (medley): Mississippi Delta land – Detroit City – Uncloudy day – No setting sun – Mississippi Delta land / Here was a man (dialogue).

Jan 71. (7") *(CBS 5364) <45269>* **FLESH AND BLOOD. / THIS SIDE OF THE LAW** [ ] Dec70 [54]

Mar 71. (lp) *(CBS 70087)* **LITTLE FAUSS AND BIG HALSY (soundtrack)** [ ] [–]
– Rollin' free / The ballad of Little Fauss and Big Halsy / The ballad of Little Fauss and Big Halsy (instrumental) / 7:06 union / The little man / The little man (instrumental) / Wanted man / Rollin' free (instrumental) / True love is greater than friendship / Movin'.

Apr 71. (7") *(CBS 7122) <45339>* **MAN IN BLACK. / LITTLE BIT OF YESTERDAY** [ ] Mar71 [58]

Jun 71. (7"ep) *(CBSEP 9155)* **THE BALLAD OF LITTLE FAUSS & BIG HALSY** [ ] [–]

Jun 71. (7") *(CBS 7300) <45393>* **SINGING IN VIETNAM TALKING BLUES. / YOU'VE GOT A NEW LIGHT SHINING** [ ] [ ]

Sep 71. (lp) *(CBS 64331) <30550>* **THE MAN IN BLACK** [18] Jun71 [56]
– The preacher said Jesus said / Orphan of the road / You've got a new light shining in your eyes / If not for love / The man in black / Singin' in Vietnam talkin' blues / Ned Kelly / Look for me / Dear Mrs. / I talk to Jesus every day. *(included a duet with evangelist BILLY GRAHAM)*

Sep 71. (7"; with JUNE CARTER) *<45431>* **I'LL BE LOVING YOU. / NO NEED TO WORRY** [–] [ ]

Oct 71. (lp) *<30887>* **THE JOHNNY CASH COLLECTION (HIS GREATEST HITS, VOLUME II)** (compilation) [–] [94]

Nov 71. (7") *<45460>* **I PROMISE YOU. / PAPA WAS A GOOD MAN** [–] [ ]

—— early '72, he appeared in the film, 'A Gunfight' and TV's 'Colombo'

Mar 72. (7") *(CBS 7797) <45534>* **A THING CALLED LOVE. / DADDY** [4] [ ]

May 72. (lp) *(CBS 64898) <31332>* **A THING CALLED LOVE** [8] [ ]
– Kate / Melva's wine / A thing called love / I promise you / Papa was a good man / Tear stained letter / Mississippi sand / Daddy / Arkansas lovin' man / The miracle man. *(re-iss. Dec85;)*

Jun 72. (7") *(CBS 8036) <45590>* **KATE. / THE MIRACLE MAN** [ ] May72 [75]

Aug 72. (7"; with JUNE CARTER) *<45631>* **IF I HAD A HAMMER. / I GOTTA BOY** [–] [ ]

Oct 72. (7") *<45660>* **COUNTRY TRASH. / ONEY** [–] [ ]

Nov 72. (lp) *(CBS 65163) <31645>* **JOHNNY CASH: AMERICA (A 200-YEAR SALUTE IN STORY AND SONG)** [ ] [ ]
– (Opening dialogue) / Paul Revere / Begin West movement / The road to Kaintuck / To the shining mountains / The battle of New Orleans /

Southwestward / Remember the Alamo / Opening the west / Lorena / The Gettysburg address / The west / Big foot / Like a young colt / Mister Garfield / A proud land / The big battle / On wheels and wings / Come take a trip in my airship / Reaching for the stars / These are my people.

Dec 72. (7"; with others) <45679> **THE WORLD NEEDS A MELODY. / A BIRD WITH BROKEN WINGS CAN'T FLY** –

Mar 73. (7") *(CBS 1115)* <45740> **ANY OLD WIND THAT BLOWS. / KENTUCKY STRAIGHT** Feb73

Apr 73. (lp) *(CBS 65431)* <32091> **ANY OLD WIND THAT BLOWS** Feb73
– Any old wind that blows / Kentucky Straight / The loving gift / The good Earth / Best friend / Oney / The ballad of Annie Palmer / Too little, too late / If I had a hammer / Country trash / Welcome back Jesus.

Jun 73. (7"; with JUNE CARTER) <45758> **HELP ME MAKE IT THROUGH THE NIGHT. / A LOVING GIFT** –

Jun 73. (d-lp) *(CBS 68243)* **THE GOSPEL ROAD** (religious & narrations) –

Aug 73. (7") *(CBS 1490)* <45786> **CHILDREN. / LAST SUPPER**

Oct 73. (7"; with The CARTER FAMILY) <45890> **BALLAD OF BARBARA. / PRAISE THE LORD AND PASS THE SOUP** –

Oct 73. (lp) *(CBS 65689)* <32443> **JOHNNY CASH AND HIS WOMAN**
– The color of love / Saturday night in Hickman County / Allegheny / Life has it's ups and downs / Matthew 24 (is knocking at the door) / The city of New Orleans / Tony / The pine tree / We're for love / Godshine.

Oct 73. (7"; with JUNE CARTER CASH) <45929> **ALLEGHENY. / WE'RE FOR LOVE** –

Nov 73. (7"; with MOTHER MAYBELLE CARTER) <45938> **DIAMONDS IN THE ROUGH. / PICK THE WILDWOOD FLOWERS** –

Dec 73. (7"; with JUNE CARTER CASH) *(CBS 1994)* **JACKSON. / WE'RE FOR LOVE** –

Dec 73. (7") <45979> **CHRISTMAS AS I KNEW IT. / THAT CHRISTMAS FEELING (with TOMMY CASH)** –

Feb 74. (7") <45997> **JACOB GREEN. / ORLEANS PARISH PRISON** –

Apr 74. (7") <46028> **RAGGED OLD FLAG. / DON'T GO NEAR THE WATER** –

May 74. (lp) *(CBS 80113)* <32917> **RAGGED OLD FLAG**
– Ragged old flag / Don't go near the water / All I do is drive / Southern comfort / King of the hill / Pie in the sky / Lonesome to the bone / While I've got it on my mind / Good morning friend / I'm a worried man / Please don't let me out / What on Earth (will you do for Heaven's sake).

Jun 74. (7") *(CBS 2396)* **SOUTHERN COMFORT. / DON'T GO NEAR THE WATER** –

Aug 74. (7") <10011> **CRYSTAL CHANDELIERS & BURGANDY. / THE JUNKIE AND THE JUICEHEAD (MINUS ME)** –

Oct 74. (7"; with ROSIE NIX) <10048> **FATHER AND DAUGHTER. / DON'T TAKE YOUR GUNS TO TOWN** –

Oct 74. (lp) *(CBS 80348)* <33086> **THE JUNKIE AND THE JUICEHEAD MINUS ME**
– The junkie and the juicehead (minus me) / Don't take your guns to town / Broken freedom song / I do believe / Ole slewfoot / Keep on the sunny side / Father and daughter (father and son) / Crystal chandeliers and burgandy / Friendly gates / Bily & Rex & Oral & Bob / Jesus / Lay back with my woman.

Jan 75. (7") *(CBS 2900)* <10066> **THE LADY CAME FROM BALTIMORE. / LONESOME TO THE BONE**

May 75. (7") <10116> **MY OLD KENTUCKY HOME. / HARD TIMES COMIN'** –

May 75. (lp) *(CBS 80634)* <33370> **JOHN R. CASH**
– My old Kentucky home (turpentine and dandelion wine) / Hard times comin' / The lady came from Baltimore / Lonesome to the bone / The night they drove old Dixie down / Clean your own tables / Jesus was our saviour (cotton was our king) / Reason to believe / Cocaine Carolina / Smokey factory blues.

Aug 75. (7") *(CBS 3499)* **SMOKEY FACTORY BLUES. / CLEAN YOUR OWN TABLES** –

Nov 75. (lp) *(CBS 81012)* <34193> **LOOK AT THEM BEANS**
– Texas 1947 / What have you got / Planned tonight, Diana / Look at them beans / No charge / I hardly ever sing / Beer drinking songs / Down the road I go / I never met a man like you before / All round cowboy / Gone / Down at Drippin' Springs.

Nov 75. (7") <10177> **LOOK AT THEM BEANS. / ALL AROUND COWBOY** –

Jan 76. (7") <10237> **TEXAS 1947. / I HARDLY EVER SING BEER DRINKING SONGS** –

Mar 76. (7") *(CBS 4096)* <10279> **STRAWBERRY CAKE. / I GOT STRIPES**

Mar 76. (lp) *(CBS 81211)* <34088> **STRAWBERRY CAKE (live)**
– Big river / Doin' my time / I still miss / Someone / I got stripes / Medley: Church in the wildwood – Lonesone valley / Strawberry cake / Rock Island Line / Navajo / Destination / Victoria Station / The fourth man.

May 76. (7"; with The TENNESSEE THREE) *(CBS 4287)* <10321> **ONE PIECE AT A TIME. / GO ON BLUES** 32 Apr76 29

Jun 76. (lp; with The TENNESSEE THREE) *(CBS 81416)* <34193> **ONE PIECE AT A TIME** 49
– Let there be country / One piece at a time / In a young girl's mind / Mountain lady / Michigan city howdy do / Sold out of flagpoles / Committed to Parkview / Daughter of a railroad man / Love has lost again / Go on blues. *(re-iss. Mar81 lp/c; CBS/40 32016)*

Jul 76. (7") <10381> **MOUNTAIN LADY. / SOLD OUT OF FLAGPOLES** –

Sep 76. (7") <10424> **RIDIN' ON THE COTTON BELT. / IT'S ALL OVER** –

Nov 76. (7"; with JUNE CARTER CASH) <10436> **FAR SIDE BANKS OF JORDAN. / OLD TIME FEELING** –

Feb 77. (lp) *(CBS 81566)* <34314> **THE LAST GUNFIGHTER BALLAD**
– I will dance with you / The last gunfighter ballad / Far side banks of Jordan (with JUNE CARTER CASH) / Ridin' on the cotton belt / Give it away / You're so close to me / City jail / Cindy / I love you / Ballad of Barbara / That silver haired daddy of mine.

Apr 77. (7") *(CBS 5107)* <10483> **THE LAST GUNFIGHTER BALLAD. / CITY JAIL**

Aug 77. (lp) *(CBS 82156)* <34833> **THE RAMBLER**
– Hit the road and go / If it wasn't for the Wabash River / Lady / After the ball / No earthly good / A Wednesday car / My cowboy's last ride / Calilou.

Sep 77. (7") *(CBS 5564)* <10587> **LADY. / HIT THE ROAD AND GO**

Dec 77. (7") <10623> **CALILOU. / AFTER THE BALL** –

Apr 78. (7") <10681> **I WOULD LIKE TO SEE YOU AGAIN. / LATELY** –

Apr 78. (lp) *(CBS 82676)* <35313> **I WOULD LIKE TO SEE YOU AGAIN**
– I would like to see you again / Lately / I wish I was crazy again / Who's Gene Autrey / Hurt so bad / I don't think I could take you back again / Abner Brown / After taxes / There ain't no good / Chain gang / That's the way it is / I'm alright now.

Jun 78. (7"; by JOHNNY CASH & WAYLON JENNINGS) *(CBS 6401)* <10742> **THERE AIN'T NO GOOD CHAIN GANG. / I WISH I WAS CRAZY AGAIN**

Sep 78. (7") <10817> **GONE GIRL. / I'M ALRIGHT NOW** –

Jan 79. (7") <10855> **IT'LL BE HER. / IT COMES AND GOES** –

Mar 79. (7") *(CBS 7153)* <10888> **I WILL ROCK AND ROLL WITH YOU. / A SONG FOR THE LIFE**

Apr 79. (lp/c) *(CBS/40 83323)* <35646> **GONE GIRL**
– Gone girl / I will rock and roll with you / Diplomat / No expectations / It comes and goes / It'll be her / Gambler / Cajun born / You and me / A song for the life.

Sep 79. (lp/c) *(CBS/40 83757)* <36086> **SILVER**
– The L&N don't stop here anymore / Lonesome to the bone / Bull rider / I'll say it's true (with GEORGE JONES) / Ghost riders in the sky / Cocaine blues / Muddy waters / West Canterbury / Subdivision blues / Lately I been leanin' towards the blues / I'm gonna sit on the porch and pick my old guitar.

Oct 79. (7") <10961> **GHOST RIDERS IN THE SKY. / I'M GONNA SIT ON THE PORCH AND PICK MY OLD GUITAR** –

Dec 79. (7") <11103> **I'LL SAY IT'S TRUE. / COCAINE BLUES** –

Mar 80. (7") <11237> **BULL RIDER. / LONESOME TO THE BONE** –

Mar 80. (lp/c) *(CBS/40 84132)* **A BELIEVER SINGS THE TRUTH** –
– Wings in the morning / Gospel boogie (a wonderful time up there) / Over the next hill / He's alive / I've got Jesus in my soul / When he comes / I was there when it happened (so I guess I ought to know) / I'm a new born man / There are strange things happening every day / Children go where I send thee / I'm just an old chunk of coal (but I'll be a diamond someday) / Lay me down in Dixie / Don't take everybody for your friend /

You'll get yours, I'll get mine / O come angel band / This train is bound for glory / I'm gonna try to be that way / What on earth (will you do for Heaven's sake) / That's enough / The greatest cowboy of them all.

Oct 80. (7"; with MARTY ROBBINS) *<11283>* **SONG OF THE PATRIOT. / SHE'S A GO-ER**

Dec 80. (lp/c) *(CBS/40 84607) <36779>* **ROCKABILLY BLUES**
– Cold lonesome morning / Without love / W.O.M.A.N. / The cowboy who started the fight / The 20th century is almost over / Rockabilly blues (Texas 1955) / The last time / She's a go-er / It ain't nothin' new babe / One way rider.

Dec 80. (7") *<11340>* **COLD LONESOME MORNING. / THE COWBOY WHO STARTED TO FIGHT**

Feb 81. (7") *<11399>* **THE LAST TIME. / ROCKABILLY BLUES (TEXAS 1965)**

Apr 81. (7") *<11424>* **WITHOUT LOVE. / IT AIN'T NOTHIN' NEW BABE**

Jun 81. (lp/c) *(CBS/40 84990) <37179>* **THE BARON**
– The baron / Mobile boy / Magnolia blossoms / I learned the hard way / A ceiling, four walls and a floor / Hey hey train / The reverend Mr.Black / The blues keep gettin' bluer / Chattanooga city limit sign / Thanks to you / The greatest love affair.

Oct 81. (7") *(A 1155) <60516>* **THE BARON. / I WILL DANCE WITH YOU**

Jan 82. (7") *<02189>* **MOBILE BOY. / THE HARD WAY**

Mar 82. (7") *<02669>* **THE REVEREND MR. BLACK. / CHATTANOOGA CITY LIMIT SIGN**

May 82. (lp/c; by JOHNNY CASH, JERRY LEE LEWIS & CARL PERKINS) *(CBS/40 85609)* **THE SURVIVORS** Mar82
– Get rhythm / I forgot to remember to forget / Goin' down the road feeling bad / That silver haired daddy of mine / Matchbox / I'll fly away / Whole lotta shakin' goin' on / Rockin' my life away / Blue suede shoes / There will be peace in the valley for me / Will the circle be unbroken / I saw the light. *(re-iss. Sep85 on 'Hallmark')*

Nov 82. (7") *<03058>* **I'VE BEEN TO GEORGIA ON A FAST TRAIN. / SING A SONG**

Nov 82. (lp/c) *(CBS/40 85881) <38094>* **THE ADVENTURES OF JOHNNY CASH**
– I've been to Georgia on a fast train / John's fair weather friends / Paradise / we must believe in magic / Only love / Good old American guest / I'll cross over Jordan some day / Sing a song / Ain't gonna hobo no more.

Jan 83. (7") *<03317>* **AIN'T GONNA HOBO NO MORE. / JOHN'S FAIR WEATHER FRIENDS**

Apr 83. (7") *<03524>* **I'LL CROSS OVER JORDAN SOME DAY. / WE MUST BELIEVE IN MAGIC**

Oct 83. (7"; with JUNE CARTER) *<04060>* **BRAND NEW DANCE. / I'M RAGGED BUT I'M RIGHT**

Oct 83. (7"; with JUNE CARTER) *(A 3804)* **JOHNNY 99. / BRAND NEW DANCE**

Nov 83. (lp/c) *(CBS/40 25471)* **JOHNNY 99**
– Highway patrolman / That's the truth / God bless Robert E.Lee / New cut road / Johnny 99 / Ballad of the ark / Joshua gone to Barbados / Girl from the canyon / Brand new dance / I'm ragged but I'm right.

Jan 84. (7") *<04227>* **JOHNNY 99. / NEW CUT ROAD**

Apr 84. (7") *<04428>* **THAT'S THE TRUTH. / JOSHUA GONE TO BARBADOS**

Oct 84. (7") *(A 4722) <04513>* **CHICKEN IN BLACK. / BATTLE OF NASHVILLE**

The HIGHWAYMAN

— were formed by country stars **JOHNNY CASH, WAYLON JENNINGS, WILLIE NELSON & KRIS KRISTOFFERSON** (same label)

Aug 85. (7") *<04881>* **THE HIGHWAYMAN. / THE HUMAN CONDITION**

Sep 85. (lp/c) *(CBS/40 26466) <40056>* **THE HIGHWAYMAN** May85 92
– The highwayman / The last cowboy song / Jim, I wore a tie today / Big river / Committed to Parkview / Desperados waiting for the train / Deportees (plane wreck at Los Gatos) / Welfare line / Against the wind / The twentieth century is almost over. *(cd-iss. 1987; CD 26466) (cd re-iss. Apr90; 902296-2)*

Apr 90. (cd/c/lp; as WILLIE NELSON, JOHNNY CASH, WAYLON JENNINGS & KRIS KRISTOFFERSON) *(466652-2/-4/-1) <45240>* **THE HIGHWAYMAN 2** Mar90 79
– Silver stallion / Born and raised in black and white / Two stories wide / We're all in the corner / American remains / Anthem '84 / Angels love bad men / Songs that made a difference / Living legend / Texas. *(d-cd-iss. Oct93 on 'Sony Europe' incl. 1985 lp)*

Apr 90. (7") *<73233>* **SILVER STALLION. / AMERICAN DREAMS**

Jun 90. (7") *<73381>* **BORN AND RAISED IN BLACK AND WHITE. / TEXAS**
(above singles were credited as the second album)

JOHNNY CASH

— had continued with solo career

Oct 85. (7") *<05594>* **DESPERADOES WAITING FOR A TRAIN. / THE TWENTIETH CENTURY IS ALMOST OVER**

Dec 85. (7") *<05672>* **I'M LEAVING NOW. / EASY STREET**

Dec 85. (lp/c) *(CBS/40 26689)* **RAINBOW**
– I'm leaving now / Here comes that rainbow again / They're all the same to me / Easy street / Have you ever seen the rain / You beat all I ever saw / Unwed fathers / Love me like you used to / Casey's last ride / Borderline (a musical whodunit).

Jun 86. (lp/c; JOHNNY CASH & WAYLON JENNINGS) *(CBS/40 26922)* **HEROES**
– Folks out on the road / I'm never gonna roam again / American by birth / Field of diamonds / Heroes / Even cowgirls get the blues / Love is the way / The ballad of forty dollars / I'll always love you in my own crazy way / One too many mornings. *(cd-iss. Nov93 on 'Sony';)*

Jun 86. (7"; by JOHNNY CASH & WAYLON JENNINGS) *<05896>* **AMERICAN BY BIRTH. / EVEN COWGIRLS GET THE BLUES**

Sep 86. (7"; by JOHNNY CASH & WAYLON JENNINGS) *<06287>* **THE BALLAD OF FORTY DOLLARS. / FIELD OF DIAMONDS**

Mercury Mercury

May 87. (lp/c)(cd) *(MERH/+C 108)<(832031-2)>* **JOHNNY CASH IS COMING TO TOWN**
– The big light / The ballad of Barbra / I'd rather have you / Let him roll / The night Hank Williams came to town / Sixteen tons / Letters from home / W.Lee O'Daniel and the light crust dough boys / Heavy metal (don't mean rock'n'roll to me) / My ship will sail.

Aug 87. (7"; JOHNNY CASH & WAYLON JENNINGS) *(MER 225) <888459-7>* **THE NIGHT HANK WILLIAMS CAME TO TOWN. / I'D RATHER HAVE YOU**

Jan 88. (7") *<888719-7>* **THE BALLAD OF BARBRA. / SIXTEEN TONS**

May 88. (7") *<MER 263)* **THE BIG LIGHT. / SIXTEEN TONS**

— next feat. daughter and son **ROSANNE + JOHN** plus other guests **HANK WILLIAMS JR., PAUL McCARTNEY, EMMYLOU HARRIS, WAYLON JENNINGS** and **The EVERLY's**

Oct 88. (lp/c/cd) *<(834778-1/-4/-2)>* **WATER FROM THE WELLS OF HOME**
– As long as I live / Ballad of a teenage queen / Last of the drifters / Where did we go right / Call me the breeze / That ole wheel / Sweeter than the flowers / Ballad of Robb MacDunn / New moon over Jamaica.

Nov 88. (7") *<874562-7>* **THAT OLE WHEEL. / THE LAST OF THE DRIFTERS** Jan89

Feb 89. (7") *<872420-7>* **BALLAD OF A TEENAGE QUEEN. / GET RHYTHM** Oct88

Feb 90. (cd/c/lp) *<(842155-2/-4/-1)>* **BOOM CHICKABOOM**
– A backstage pass / Farmer's almanac / Family bible / I love you, I love you / Monteagle mountain / Cat's in the cradle / Don't go near the water / Harley / Hidden shame / That's one you owe me.

Feb 90. (7") *<875626-7>* **CAT'S IN THE CRADLE. / I LOVE YOU, I LOVE YOU**

Mar 91. (cd/c/lp) *<(848051-2/-4/-1)>* **THE MYSTERY OF LIFE**
– The greatest cowboy of them all / I'm an easy rider / The mystery of life / Hey porter / Beans for breakfast / Goin' by the book / Wanted man / I'll go somewhere and sing my songs again / The hobo song / The angel and the badman.

Apr 91. (7") **THE MYSTERY OF LIFE. / I'M AN EASY RIDER**
(cd-s+=) – Veterans' day.

Spirit Of America Spirit Of America

Oct 93. (cd/c) **IT AIN'T ME BABE**

American American

Oct 94. (cd/c) *(74321 23685-2/-4) <45520>* **AMERICAN RECORDINGS** May94
– Delia's gone / Let the train blow the whistle / The beast in me / Drive on / Why me / Thirteen / Oh bury me nought / Bird on a wire / Tennessee stud / Down there by the train / Like a soldier / The man who couldn't cry.

Nov 96. (cd/c) *(74321 39742-2) <43097>* **UNCHAINED** [ ] [ ]
– Rowboat / Sea of heartbreak / Rusty cage / One rose / Country boy / Memories are made of this / Spiritual / Kneeling drunkard's plea / Southern accents / Mean eyed cat / Meet me in Heaven / I never picked cotton / Unchained / I've been elsewhere.

Jun 98. (cd/c; by JOHNNY CASH & WILLIE NELSON) *(491531-2/-4) <69416>* **VH1 STORYTELLERS (live)** [ ] [ ]
– Ghost riders in the sky / Worried man / Family bible / Don't take your guns to town / Funny how time slips away / Flesh and blood / Crazy / Unchained / Night life / Drive on / Me and Paul / I still miss someone / Always on my mind / Folsom prison blues / On the road again.

Oct 00. (cd) *(500986-2) <69691>* **AMERICAN III: SOLITARY MAN** [ ] [88]
– I won't back down / Solitary man / That lucky old sun (just rolls around heaven all day) / One / Nobody / I see a darkness / The mercy seat / Would you lay with me (in a field of stones) / Field of diamonds / Before my time / Country trash / Mary of the wild moor / I'm leavin' now / Wayfaring stranger.

Lost Highway Universal

Nov 02. (cd)(d-lp) *<(063339-2)><(63336-1)>* **AMERICAN IV: THE MAN COMES AROUND** [ ] [22]
– The man comes around / Hurt / Give my love to Rose / Bridge over troubled water (with FIONA APPLE) / I hung my head / The first time ever I saw your face / Personal Jesus / In my life / Sam Hall / Danny boy / Desperado (with DON HENLEY) / I'm so lonesome I could cry (with NICK CAVE) / The streets of Laredo / Tear stained letter / We'll meet again.

Apr 03. (cd-s) *(77998-2)* **HURT / PERSONAL JESUS / WICHITA LINEMAN / HURT (video)** [42] [–]
(re-iss. Nov03; same) – hit No.39

— sadly, JOHNNY was to die on the 12th September 2003

– (selective) compilations, etc. –

Jan 59. (7",78) *London; (HLS 8789) / Sun; <309>* **IT'S JUST ABOUT TIME. / I JUST THOUGHT YOU'D LIKE TO KNOW** [ ] [47] Dec58 [85]

Aug 59. (7",78) *London; (HLS 8928) / Sun; <321>* **KATY TOO. / I FORGOT TO REMEMBER TO FORGET** [ ] Jul59 [66]

Mar 60. (7") *London; (HLS 9070) / Sun; <334>* **STRAIGHT A'S IN LOVE. / I LOVE YOU BECAUSE** [ ] [84]

Sep 60. (7") *London; (HLS 9182) / Sun; <343>* **DOWN THE STREET TO 301. / THE STORY OF A BROKEN HEART** [ ] Jul60 [85]

Mar 61. (7") *London; (HLS 9314) / Sun; <355>* **OH LONESOME ME. / LIFE GOES ON** [ ] Dec60 [93]

Jun 68. (lp) *C.B.S.; (CBS 63316)* **OLD GOLDEN THROAT** [37] [–]
(re-iss. Sep82 on 'Bear Family'; BF 15072)

Jul 69. (lp) *C.B.S.; (CBS 63521)* **MORE OF OLD GOLDEN THROAT** [ ] [–]
(re-iss. Sep82 on 'Bear Family'; BFX 15073)

Nov 69. (7") *Sun; <1103>* **GET RHYTHM. / HEY PORTER** [–] [60]

Feb 70. (7") *Sun; <1111>* **ROCK ISLAND LINE. / NEXT IN LINE** [–] [93]

Dec 70. (lp) *Sun; (6467 001) <100>* **ORIGINAL GOLDEN HITS, VOLUME 1** [ ] Sep69 [95]

Dec 70. (lp) *Sun; (6467 007) <101>* **ORIGINAL GOLDEN HITS, VOLUME 2** [ ] Sep69 [98]

Nov 71. (lp) *Hallmark; (SHM 739)* **JOHNNY CASH** [43] [–]

Sep 72. (d-lp) *C.B.S.; (67201)* **STAR PORTRAIT** [16] [–]

Oct 76. (lp) *C.B.S.; (10000)* **THE BEST OF JOHNNY CASH** [48] [–]

Jun 78. (lp/c) *C.B.S.; (CBS/40 10009)* **ITCHY FEET – 20 FOOT TAPPIN' GREATS** [36] [–]
– Folsom prison blues / I walk the line / Ring of fire / Forty shades of green / I still miss someone / There ain't no good chain gang / Busted / Twenty five minutes to go / Orange blossom special / It ain't me babe / A boy named Sue / San Quentin / Don't take your guns to town / The one on the right is on the left / Jackson / Hey porter / Daddy sang bass / I got stripes / A thing called love / One piece at a time. *(cd-iss. Oct94 on 'Columbia'; 477504-2) (re-iss. Apr95 on 'Columbia'; 468116-2/-4)*

Aug 94. (cd/c) *Columbia; (MOOD CD/C 35)* **THE MAN IN BLACK – THE DEFINITIVE COLLECTION** [15] [–]
– Ring of fire / I walk the line / Get rhythm (live) / It ain't me babe / I still miss someone / (Ghost) Riders in the sky / The baron / Sunday morning coming down / Daddy sang bass / Jackson (with JUNE CARTER) / One piece at a time / Orange blossom special / Folsom prison blues (live) / San Quentin (live) / A boy named Sue (live) / A thing called love / Don't take your guns to town / Wanted man / Big river / Without love / No expectations / Highway patrolman / Singin' in Vietnam talkin' blues / Man in black.

Jul 99. (cd) *Columbia; (494896-2)* **THE FABULOUS / THE SONGS OF OUR SOUL** [ ] [ ]

Aug 99. (d-cd) *Snapper; (SMDCD 213)* **THE ESSENTIAL SUN COLLECTION** [ ] [–]

Feb 02. (d-cd) *Sony; (506345-2) <503023>* **MAN IN BLACK – THE VERY BEST OF JOHNNY CASH** [39] Sep01 [ ]

Eva CASSIDY

Born: 2 Feb'63, Oxon Hill, Maryland, USA; raised in Washington. EVA's undeniable talent evolved through the eclectic music scene that thrived locally around the inns and clubs close to her home, but, her main musical influence was that of her father Hugh Cassidy who taught her to play guitar at the tender age of nine. Sadly, EVA's talent wasn't fully recognized until after her tragic death from cancer on the 2nd of November, 1996. It was difficult for the rigidly defined American music industry to pigeonhole EVA's music as her style ranged through jazz, blues, roots (folk/country) and soul. She used her interpretive intuition transforming numbers that had been written and recorded by other people (i.e. 'OVER THE RAINBOW' by Judy Garland and 'FIELDS OF GOLD' by Sting). EVA began to experiment with the former track in 1984, although success was a long time coming and was only achieved in its final form late in 1996; the year she passed away. The unassuming lady released two records during her life time. The first was a duet with Washington's underrated CHUCK BROWN entitled 'THE OTHER SIDE', which was recorded in 1992 and heavily influenced by music from the nostalgic 30's and 40's ('GOD BLESS THE CHILD' and 'FEVER' are two prime examples). EVA, reluctant to be in the limelight, withdrew occasionally and stepped back into the world of art, another field in which she was very gifted. Another four albums were released after EVA's premature death, the first of note being 'SONGBIRD' (1998) which was popularised in Britain thanks initially to BBC Radio 2. It steadily climbed both the US and UK charts and finally peaked at No.1 early in 2001, going platinum in the process. In fact, in the first three months of 2001, EVA outsold every single artist in the world, apart from DIDO. 'LIVE AT BLUES ALLEY' (her only set released while she was alive) also made it to the top around this time. She was even rated No.21 in a list of top female voices of all-time in a poll commissioned by the BBC. It was indeed a pity and a crying shame that EVA's sweet voice was dismissed when she was alive. It's probably fair to say that CASSIDY's musical offcuts and dust-gathering early recordings are more compelling than the average artist's prime studio material. Which explains the release of 'IMAGINE' (2002) and 'AMERICAN TUNE' (2003), two odds and sods collections of songs unearthed by her various band members. Eschewing quality control for emotional impact, the songs run the gamut from impromtu live recordings to studio offcuts, with more than enough rough diamonds to please besotted fans and casual listeners alike. Highlights among the many covers strewn across both sets include a rootsy rendering of Sandy Denny's 'WHO KNOWS WHERE THE TIME GOES', and an understated interpretation of the Paul Simon title song on the latter.

Album rating: LIVE AT BLUES ALLEY (*8) / EVA BY HEART (*8) / SONGBIRD collection (*9) / THE OTHER SIDE with Chuck Brown (*5) / TIME AFTER TIME (*6) / NO BOUNDARIES (*4) / IMAGINE (*7) / AMERICAN TUNE (*5)

EVA CASSIDY – vocals, guitar / with session band

not iss. — Eva Music

1996. (cd) *<2263>* **LIVE AT BLUES ALLEY (live)** [–] [ ]
– Cheek to cheek / Stormy Monday / Bridge over troubled water / Fine and mellow / People get ready / Blue skies / Tall trees in Georgia / Fields of gold / Autumn leaves / Honeysuckle rose / Take me to the river / What a wonderful world / Oh, I has I a golden thread. *<(re-iss. Sep97 – UK Oct99 – on 'Blix Street'; G2 10046)> <US re-dist.May01>* – hit No.2

—— EVA died on the 2nd of November, 1996

– posthumous releases, collections, etc. –

not iss. — Liason

1997. (cd) *<110296>* **EVA BY HEART** [–] [ ]
– I know you by heart / Time is a healer / Wayfaring stranger / Wade in the water / Blues in the night / Songbird / Need your love so bad (with CHUCK BROWN) / Say goodbye / Nightbird / Waly, Waly / How can I keep from singing? / Dark end of the street. *<(re-iss. Sep97 – UK Jun99 – on 'Blix Street'; G2 10047)>*

Blix Street — Blix Street

Jul 98. (cd) *<(G2 10045)>* **SONGBIRD** [ ] May98 [ ]
– Fields of gold / Wade in the water / Autumn leaves / Wayfaring stranger / Songbird / Time is a healer / I know you by heart / People get ready / Oh, I had a golden thread / Over the rainbow. *(UK re-dist.Jan01; same)* – hit No.1 *<US re-dist.Mar01; same>* – hit No.1

Jun 99. (cd; by EVA CASSIDY & CHUCK BROWN) *<(G2 10066)>* **THE OTHER SIDE** [ ] [ ]
– Let the good times roll / Fever / You don't know me / I could have told you so / Gee baby ain't I good to you / I'll go crazy / You don't know what love is / Drown in my own tears / God bless the child / Red top / Dark end of the street / Shadow of your smile / Over the rainbow / You've changed.

May 00. (cd/c) *<(G2/G4 10073)>* **TIME AFTER TIME** [52] [ ]
– Kathy's song / The ltter / Wayfaring stranger / Fever / Time after time / I wish I was a single girl again / Easy street dreams / Gas station mountain home / Ain't no sunshine / Anniversary song / Woodstock / Way beyond the blue. *(re-dist.Feb01)* – hit UK No.25

Jul 00. (cd-s) *(HIT 18)* **TIME AFTER TIME / SONGBIRD / WHAT A WONDERFUL WORLD** [ ] [ ]

Apr 01. (cd-s) *(HIT 16)* **OVER THE RAINBOW. / DARK END OF THE STREET** [42] [–]

Sep 01. (cd-s) *(HIT 20)* **ANNIVERSARY SONG / SAY GOODBYE** [ ] [–]

Oct 01. (cd) *Brunswick; (BICD 1005) / Renata; <1>* **NO BOUNDARIES** [ ] Sep01 [ ]
– Emotional step (extended) / The waiting is over / You are / A natural woman (you make me feel like) / Little children / I've got this feeling / When it's too late / On the inside / Emotional step (radio edit) / Natural woman (traditional) / Little children (reflection).

Aug 02. (cd) *<(G2 10075)>* **IMAGINE** [1] [32]
– It doesn't matter anymore / Fever / Who knows where the time goes? / You've changed / Imagine / Still not ready / Early morning rain / Tennessee waltz / I can only be me / Danny boy.

Nov 02. (cd-s) *(HIT 24)* **IMAGINE / EARLY MORNING RAIN ? TIME AFTER TIME** [ ] [–]

Feb 03. (cd-s) *(HIT 25)* **IT DOESN'T MATTER ANYMORE / YOU'VE CHANGED / EASY STREET DREAM** [ ] [–]

Aug 03. (cd) *<(G2 10079)>* **AMERICAN TUNE (live)** [1] [ ]
– Drowning in the sea of love / True colours / The water is wide / Hallelujah I love him so (studio) / God bless the child / Dark eyed Molly / American tune / It don't mean a thing (if it ain't got that swing) / Yesterday (studio) / You take my breath away.

Sep 03. (cd-s) *(HIT 27)* **YOU TAKE MY BREATH AWAY / OVER THE RAINBOW (video)** [54] [–]

CAST

Formed: Liverpool, England ... 1994 by ex-LA'S guitarist JOHN POWER, alongside KEITH O'NEIL, LIAM TYSON and PETER WILKINSON. Bassist POWER had become increasingly disillusioned with The LA'S interminable absence from the music scene, taking his future into his own hands and developing his 60's influenced songwriting within a more solid framework. Fortuitously, POWERS' strident, melodic sound was perfectly in tune with the emerging retro fixated Brit-pop sound and, with the influential backing of OASIS, CAST crashed into the Top 20 in the summer of '95 with 'FINETIME'. Surfing on a wave of frothy powerchords and an irrepressibly buoyant melody, 'ALRIGHT' followed soon after, the track becoming something of a theme tune and a definitive highlight of their debut set, 'ALL CHANGE'. Released later that Autumn, the album divided the critics, some raving over its immaculate melodic appeal, some deriding its workmanlike adherence to "classic songwriting". Whatever, there was no doubting POWER's ear for a tune, and the sublime 'SANDSTORM' gave the band a further Top 10 hit in early '96. CAST's solid style inevitably translated well to the live arena and they built up a rabid following of beany-topped fans, the same constituency of check-shirted "lads" who frequented OASIS and OCEAN COLOUR SCENE gigs. In Autumn '96, the group scored their first Top 5 with 'FLYING', a lilting new track which further showcased their mastery of BEATLES-esque pop dynamics. However, the critics were just dying to sink their claws into this resolutely untrendy outfit, with the fine 'MOTHER NATURE CALLS' (1997) unfairly receiving mixed reviews. Detractors rounded on POWER's spiritually-enhanced muse and mystical leanings but there was no arguing with the life-affirming power inherent in songs like 'GLIDING STAR', another Top 10 smash in summer '97. Influenced by the WHO on a 'Magic Bus'-type thing (with production from GIL NORTON and string accompaniment courtesy of DAVID ARNOLD) POWER and Co retro-fied their way back into the charts with 'BEAT MAMA'. A hook-line festival-friendly tune, it previewed their third Top 10 album, 'MAGIC HOUR' (1999), yet another to gain the support from both the Indie and Modern Rock factions. Unfortunately, when they arrived back with a fourth set, 'BEETROOT' (2001), CAST were no longer in vogue – or for that matter in the album charts. POWER eventually resurfaced in 2003 with his John Leckie-produced solo debut, 'HAPPENING FOR LOVE'. Again, the scouse 60's evangelist came a critical cropper on his woolly lyrics, unfortunately detracting from the ringing fervour of his delivery and the inherent soundness of the songs themselves.

Album rating: ALL CHANGE (*7) / MOTHER NATURE CALLS (*6) / MAGIC HOUR (*5) / BEETROOT (*4) / John Power: HAPPENING FOR LOVE (*4)

JOHN POWER (b.14 Sep'67) – vocals, guitar (ex-LA'S) / **LIAM TYSON** (b. 7 Feb'69) – guitar / **PETER WILKINSON** (b. 9 May'69) – bass (ex-SHACK) / **KEITH O'NEIL** (b.18 Feb'69) – drums

Polydor — Polydor

Jul 95. (7"green/c-s/cd-s) *(579 506-7/-4/-2)* **FINETIME. / BETTER MAN / SATELLITES** [17] [–]

Sep 95. (7"blue/c-s/cd-s) *(579 926-7/-4/-2)* **ALRIGHT. / FOLLOW ME DOWN / MEET ME** [13] [–]

Oct 95. (cd/c/d-lp) *(529 312-2/-4/-1)* **ALL CHANGE** [7] [ ]
– Alright / Promised land / Sandstorm / Mankind / Tell it like it is / Four walls / Finetime / Back of my mind / Walkaway / Reflections / History / Two of a kind.

Jan 96. (7"orange/c-s) *(577 872-7/-4)* **SANDSTORM. / HOURGLASS / BACK OF MY MIND (live)** [8] [–]
(cd-s+=/tin-cd-s+=) *(577 873/903-2)* – Alright (live).

Mar 96. (7"clear/c-s) *(576 284-7/-4)* **WALKAWAY. / FULFILL / FINETIME (acoustic)** [9] [–]
(cd-s) *(576 285-2)* – (first 2 tracks) / Mother.

Oct 96. (7"/c-s) *(575 476-7/-4)* **FLYING. / BETWEEN THE EYES / FOR SO LONG** [4] [–]
(pic-cd-s+=) *(575 477-2)* – Walkaway.

Mar 97. (7"/c-s) *(573 648-7/-4)* **FREE ME. / COME ON EVERYBODY / CANTER** [7] [–]
(cd-s+=) *(573 649-2)* – ('A'acoustic).
(cd-s) *(573 651-2)* – ('A'side) / Release my soul / Dancing on the flames.

Apr 97. (cd/c/lp) *(537 567-2/-4/-1)* **MOTHER NATURE CALLS** [3] [ ]
– Free me / On the run / Live the dream / Soul tied / She sun shines / I'm so lonely / The mad hatter / Mirror me / Guiding star / Never gonna tell you

what to do (revolution) / Dance of the stars. *(special edition d-cd Nov97; 539681-2)*

Jun 97. (7") *(571 172-7)* **GUIDING STAR. / OUT OF THE BLUE** [9] [–]
(c-s+=) *(571 172-4)* – Keep it alive.
(cd-s+=) *(571 173-2)* – Free me (live) / Mirror me (live).
(cd-s) *(571 295-2)* – ('A'side) / Keep it alive / Redemption song (live) / ('A'acoustic).

Sep 97. (c-s) *(571 500-4)* <6025> **LIVE THE DREAM / HOLD ON / FLOW** [7] Apr98 [ ]
(cd-s) *(571 501-2)* – (first 2 tracks) / Effectomatic who / ('A'acoustic).
(cd-s) *(571 685-2)* – (first & third tracks) / On the run.

Nov 97. (c-s) *(569 256-4)* **I'M SO LONELY / THINGS YOU MAKE ME DO / THEME FROM** [14] [–]
(cd-s) *(569 057-2)* – (first 2 tracks) / Never gonna tell you / History.
(cd-s) *(569 059-2)* – (tracks 1 & 3) / History.

Apr 99. (c-s) *(563592-4)* **BEAT MAMA / GET ON YOU / HOEDOWN** [9] [–]
(cd-s) *(563593-2)* – (first 2 tracks) / 3 nines are 28.
(cd-s) *(563595-2)* – (first & third tracks) / Whiskey song.

May 99. (cd/c/d-lp) *(547176-2/-4/-1)* **MAGIC HOUR** [6] [ ]
– Beat mama / Compared to you / She falls / Dreamer / Magic hour / Company man / Alien / Higher / Chasing the day / The feeling remains / Burn the light / Hideaway.

Jul 99. (c-s) *(561227-4)* **MAGIC HOUR / ALLBRIGHT** [28] [–]
(cd-s) *(561227-2)* – ('A'side) / Gypsy song / I never wanna lose you.
(cd-s) *(561228-2)* – ('A'side) / Beat mama / What you gonna do.

Jul 01. (c-s) *(587175-4)* **DESERT DROUGHT / COBWEBS** [45] [–]
(cd-s+=) *(587175-2)* – ('A'-Deserts dry mouth mix) / ('A'video).
(cd-s) *(587176-2)* – ('A'side) / Curtains (purple curtains mix) / ('A'-Solomon remix).

Jul 01. (cd/lp) *(589096-2/-1)* **BEETROOT** [ ] [–]
– Desert drought / Heal me / Curtains / Kingdoms and crowns / Giving it all away / Lose myself / I never can say / High wire / Meditations / Jetstream / U-turn / Universal grinding wheel / Engaged.

JOHN POWER

with **MARTYN CAMPBELL** – bass / **PAUL MAGUIRE** – drums

Eagle | not iss.

Jun 03. (cd) *(EAGCD 249)* **HAPPENING FOR LOVE** [ ] [–]
– Electrify / Paradise / Everyday folk / Small farm / TNT / Songbird / Mariner / Happening for love / Change for tomorrow / Viva / Island.

CATATONIA

Formed: Cardiff, Wales . . . 1991 by songwriters MARK ROBERTS and PAUL JONES, who had both been part of 'Ankst' label outfit, Y CRYFF. Having found OWEN POWELL from The CRUMB BLOWERS and sultry blonde singer, CERYS MATTHEWS, they set about taking their style of Welsh accented hooks to the alternative indie scene. However, things did not get off to a flying start, when the group offended the label's strict Welsh-only language policy and were moved on to another leek-biased label, 'Crai', where they released two singles in 1993/94. In the summer of '94, Geoff Travis's 'Rough Trade Singles Club' label issued 'WHALE', Travis subsequently grabbing them for his 'Blanco Y Negro'. 1996 became a shining year for them with four hit singles and a well-received album, the Stephen Street-produced 'WAY BEYOUND BLUE' denting the Top 40. Much was anticipated for a glorious 1998 after they hit the Top 40 in late '97 with 'I AM THE MOB'. All predictions came true as CERYS and Co stormed the Top 3 as early as January that year with the X-Files inspired 'MULDER AND SCULLY'. This was only one of the many successes (others being 'ROAD RAGE', 'STRANGE GLUE' and 'GAME ON') taken from their acclaimed chart-topping album, 'INTERNATIONAL VELVET', although indie sex symbol CERYS would also team up with SPACE for the tongue-in-cheek romantic duet, 'The Ballad Of Tom Jones'. Never far away from the limelight and with the help of producer TOMMY D., CATATONIA returned in Spring '99 via Top 10 smash, 'DEAD FROM THE WAIST DOWN'. The highest of three hits (the other two being 'LONDINIUM' and 'KARAOKE QUEEN') taken from their follow-up No.1 album, 'EQUALLY CURSED AND BLESSED', the 5-piece indie-pop outfit were going into the 21st Century on a high note. With an incredible amount of hits under their belts, a hectic touring schedule, press and PR hounding the group constantly, it seemed like things were beginning to erode within CATATONIA. Singer and indie 'babe' MATTHEWS admitted to the press that she had had a breakdown during the group's pandemonious year. The result was the very disappointing 'PAPER SCISSORS STONE' (2001), a cynical, alter-ego version of the album that set their names in stone, 'INTERNATIONAL . . .'. Missing was the sweet pop charm and charisma of MATTHEWS' throaty vocals and in its place was the rancid leftovers of a band gone awry. The album was treated nonchalantly by the press, however fans of the group re-emerged to show their support as the album sauntered its way into the Top 20 (as well as single 'STONE BY STONE'). It was to be a sad departure from the music scene, as CATATONIA officially called it a day in September 2001. That said, few post-split solo albums have sounded as re-energised or as charismatic as 'COCK-A-HOOP' (2003), CERYS' hymn to the joys of kicking her bad habits and the delights of musical carte-blanche. While CATATONIA diehards may have turned their noses up at the rootsy sense of musical and spiritual rebirth, MATTHEWS still sings like no-one else, especially when she's belting out the likes of the Roger Cook & Hugh Cornwell-penned 'CHARDONNAY' or the Handsome Family's goth-country classic, 'WEIGHTLESS AGAIN'.
• **Covered:** Cerys:- FIFTEEN MINUTES (Kirsty MacColl) / IF I WAS WITH A WOMAN (Ian Dury).

Album rating: THE SUBLIME MAGIC OF CATATONIA European compilation or THE CRAI EP'S (*7) / WAY BEYOND BLUE (*7) / INTERNATIONAL VELVET (*8) / EQUALLY CURSED AND BLESSED (*6) / PAPER SCISSORS STONE (*5) / GREATEST CATATONIA HITS compilation (*8) / Cerys Matthews: COCKAHOOP (*7)

CERYS MATTHEWS (b.11 Apr'69) – vocals / **MARK ROBERTS** (b. 3 Nov'69, Colwyn Bay, Wales) – guitar (ex-Y CYRFF) / **OWEN POWELL** (b. 9 Jul'67, Cambridge, England) – guitar (ex-CRUMB BLOWERS) / **PAUL JONES** (b. 5 Apr'60, Colwyn Bay) – bass (ex-Y CYRFF) / **ALED RICHARDS** (b. 5 Jul'69, Llanelli, Carmarthen, Wales) – drums

Crai | not iss.

Sep 93. (c-ep)(cd-ep) *(C 039L)(CD 039B)* **FOR TINKERBELL EP** [ ] [–]
– For Tinkerbell / New mercurial heights / Dimbran / Sweet Catatonia / Gyda Gwen – New mercurial heights (Welsh mix).

Jun 94. (c-s)(cd-s) *(C 042L)(CD 042B)* **HOOKED. / FALL BESIDE HER / DIFRYCHEULYD (SNAIL AMBITION)** [ ] [–]
(above 2 re-iss. together Dec98; CRAI 064)

Rough Trade Sing. Club | not iss.

Aug 94. (7") *(45rev 33)* **WHALE. / YOU CAN** [ ] [–]

Nursery | not iss.

Feb 95. (7"red) *(NYS 12L)* **BLEED. / THIS BOY CAN'T SWIM** [ ] [–]
(cd-s+=) *(NYSCD 12)* – Painful.

Nov 95. (cd) *(NYSCD 12X)* **THE SUBLIME MAGIC OF CATATONIA** (compilation) [–] Europe [–]
– Bleed / This boy can't swim / Painful / Dream on / Whale / You can / Hooked / Fall beside her / Difrycheulyd (Snail ambition). *(hidden track +=)* – Cariadon ffol.

Blanco Y Negro | Atlantic

Dec 95. (7"white; mail-o) *(SAM 1746)* **BLOW THE MILLENNIUM BLOW. / BEAUTIFUL SAILOR** [–] [–]

Jan 96. (7"/c-s) *(NEG 85/+C)* **SWEET CATATONIA. / TOURIST** [61] [–]
(cd-s) *(NEG 85CD)* – ('A'side) / Acapulco gold / Cut you inside (demo).

Apr 96. (7"yellow) *(NEGAT 88X)* **LOST CAT. / TO AND FRO** [41] [–]

(c-s/cd-s) *(NEGAT 88 CAS/CD1)* – ('A'side) / All girls are fly / Indigo blind.
(cd-s) *(NEG 88CD2)* – ('A'side) / Sweet Catatonia (live – Mark Radcliffe 1FM session) / Whale (live – Mark Radcliffe 1FM session).

Sep 96. (7") *(NEG 93)* **YOU'VE GOT A LOT TO ANSWER FOR. / DO YOU BELIEVE IN ME?** [35] [–]
(cd-s+=) *(NEG 93CD1)* – Dimbran.
(cd-s) *(NEG 93CD2)* – ('A'side) / You can / All girls are fly.
(c-s) *(NEG 93CAS)* – ('A'side) / Blow the millennium blow (Splott remix).

Sep 96. (cd/c/lp) *(0630 16305-2/-4/-1)* **WAY BEYOND BLUE** [40] [–]
– Lost cat / Sweet Catatonia / Some half baked / Ideal called wonderful / You've got a lot to answer for / Infantile / Dream on. *(lp w/free 7"/cd w/hidden track)* – Gyda Gwen. *(lp re-iss. Jun99; same)*

Nov 96. (7"red) *(NEG 97)* **BLEED. / DO YOU BELIEVE IN ME? (live – Reading Festival 1FM)** [46] [–]
(cd-s+=) *(NEG 97CD2)* – Bleed (live evening session 1FM).
(cd-s) *(NEG 97CD1)* – ('A'side) / Way beyond blue (live – Mark Radcliffe 1FM session) / Painful (live – Reading Festival 1FM).
(c-s) *(NEG 97CASS)* – ('A'side) / Way beyond blue (live – Mark Radckiffe 1FM session) / Bleed (live – evening session 1FM).

Oct 97. (7"orange/c-s) *(NEG 107/+CASS)* **I AM THE MOB. / JUMP OR BE SANE** [40] [–]
(cd-s+=) *(NEG 107CD)* – My selfish Gene / ('A'-Luca Brasi mix).

Jan 98. (7"blue/c-s) *(NEG 109/+CASS)* **MULDER AND SCULLY. / NO STONE UNTURNED** [3] [–]
(cd-s+=) *(NEG 109CD)* – Mantra for the lost / ('A'-The Ex-files).

Feb 98. (cd/c/lp) *(<3984 20834-2/-4/-1>)* **INTERNATIONAL VELVET** [1] [ ]
– Mulder and Scully / Game on / I am the mob / Road rage / Johnny come lately / Goldfish and paracetamol / International velvet / Why I can't stand one night stands / Part of the furniture / Don't need the sunshine / Strange glue / My selfish gene. *(lp w/ free 12"radio sessions)* – International velvet / No stione unturned / Murder & Scully / Strange glue.

—— Feb'98:- CERYS featured on a SPACE hit, 'The Ballad Of Tom Jones'

Apr 98. (7"yellow/c-s) *(NEG 112/+CASS)* **ROAD RAGE. / I'M CURED** [5] [–]
(cd-s+=) *(NEG 112CD)* – Blow the millennium (pt.2) / ('A'-Ghia).

Blanco Y Negro | Imprint

Jul 98. (7"red/c-s) *(NEG 113/+CASS)* **STRANGE GLUE. / THAT'S ALL FOLKS** [11] [ ]
(cd-s+=) *(NEG 113CD)* – Road rage (live).

Oct 98. (7"green/c-s) *(NEG 114/+CASS)* **GAME ON. / STRANGE GLUE (live acoustic)** [33] [–]
(cd-s+=) *(NEG 114CD)* – Mulder and Scully (live in Newport).

Mar 99. (7"orange/c-s) *(NEG 115/+C)* **DEAD FROM THE WAIST DOWN. / BRANDING A MOUNTAIN** [7] [–]
(cd-s+=) *(NEG 115CD)* – Bad bad boy.

Apr 99. (cd/lp) *(3984 27094-2/-4/-1) <83294>* **EQUALLY CURSED & BLESSED** [1] Mar00 [ ]
– Dead from the waist down / Londinium / She's a millionaire / Storm the palace / Karaoke queen / Bulimic beats / Shoot the messenger / Postscript / Valarian unwanted / Nothing hurts / Dazed beautiful and bruised.

Jul 99. (7"/c-s) *(NEG 117/+C)* **LONDINIUM. / INTERCONTINENTAL** [20] [–]
(cd-s+=) *(NEG 117CD)* – Apathy revolution.

Nov 99. (7"/c-s) *(NEG 119/+C)* **KARAOKE QUEEN. / DON'T WANNA TALK ABOUT IT** [36] [–]
(cd-s+=) *(NEG 119CD)* – All girls are fly (da-be).

Jul 01. (7"/c-s) *(NEG 134/+C)* **STONE BY STONE. / LONG TIME LONELY** [19] [–]
(cd-s+=) *(NEG 134CD)* – Apple core (full extended mix).

Aug 01. (cd/c/lp) *(8573 88848-2/-4/-1)* **PAPER SCISSORS STONE** [6] [–]
– Godspeed / Immediate circle / Fuel / What it is / Stone by stone / Mother of misogyny / Is everybody here on drugs / Imaginary friends / Shore leave / Apple core / Beautiful loser / Blues song / Village idiot / Arabian derby.

—— the band split a month later

– compilations, etc. –

Sep 02. (cd) *Blanco Y Negro; (0927 49193-2)* **GREATEST CATATONIA HITS** [24] [ ]
– Mulder & Scully / The ballad of Tom Jones / Strange glue / Road rage / Stone by stone / Londinium / Game on / Dead from the waste down / You've got a lot to answer for / Baby, it's cold outside / Karaoke queen / Lost cat / I am the mob / Sweet Catatonia / Bleed. *(d-cd+=; 0927 49194-2)* – Do you believe in me / The mother of misogyny / Indigo blind / Godspeed / Imaginary friend / Way beyond blue / Dream on / Whale / Branding a mountain / Acapulco gold. *(hidden track+=)* – All girls are fly / Blues song.

CERYS MATTHEWS

with a number of session people

Blanco Y Negro | not iss.

May 03. (cd) *(2564 60306-2)* **COCKAHOOP** [30] [–]
– Chardonnay / Caught in the middle / La bague / Weightless again / Only a fool / Ocean / Arglwydd dyma fi / If you're looking for love / The good in goodbye / Gypsy songs / All my trials.

Jul 03. (cd-s) *(NEG 147CD1)* **CAUGHT IN THE MIDDLE / BANJO MOON / CHILLI WINDS** [47] [–]
(cd-s) *(NEG 147CD2)* – ('A'side) / Il est midi / Four cotton dresses.

☐ CATCH (see under ⇒ EURYTHMICS)

Nick CAVE

Born: NICHOLAS EDWARD CAVE, 22 Sep'57, Warracknabeal, Australia. He was the main man behind punk/power-pop outfit, The BOYS NEXT DOOR, completing the band with neighbours MICK HARVEY, TRACY PEW and PHIL CALVERT. Formed in Caulfield, Melbourne in late '77, they issued a one-off version of Nancy Sinatra's 'THESE BOOTS WERE MADE FOR WALKING', before they added a fifth member, ROWLAND S. HOWARD. After an album, 'DOOR, DOOR', was released on 'Mushroom' records in 1979, they came to England as The BIRTHDAY PARTY, taking their name from a Harold Pinter play. The band were subsequently snapped up by IVO on the (then) new indie label '4 a.d.', after a recent 'HEE-HAW' EP was given some night time airing by John Peel. About as extreme as any music ever released by the label, The BIRTHDAY PARTY were more a wake than a celebration, albeit one with more than its fair share of black humour. Their first UK album, 'PRAYERS ON FIRE' (1981), featured such enduringly sharp material as 'ZOO MUSIC GIRL', 'CRY', 'CAPERS' and 'NICK THE STRIPPER', although for many obsessive fans and critics alike, 'RELEASE THE BATS' remains the definitive track. Issued in summer '81, the single was a gothic slice of avant-garde that took over the territory once belonging to the likes of PERE UBU and The POP GROUP. Later that year, TRACY PEW was jailed for drunk driving, a revolving cast of BARRY ADAMSON, CHRIS WALSH and HARRY HOWARD deputising for him on tour. Live, The BIRTHDAY PARTY were even more unhinged than on vinyl, their demented stage show setting them apart from the masses of up and coming goth-rock acts around at the time. While TRACY was behind bars, NICK, ROWLAND and MICK teamed up as The TUFF MONKS with fellow Australians, The GO-BETWEENS on a one-off 45, 'AFTER THE FIREWORKS'. A further album, 'JUNKYARD' (which hit UK Top 75 in 1982), assured The BIRTHDAY PARTY's position as cult favourites among those who favoured black as a fashion statement. Later that year, ROWLAND hooked up with mistress of soft-porn new wave, LYDIA LUNCH, for a cover of Lee Hazlewood & Nancy Sinatra's 'SOME VELVET MORNING', while The BIRTHDAY PARTY were trimmed to a quartet for 'THE BAD SEED' EP. Released in early '83, the set included the incendiary 'SONNY'S BURNING', arguably the group's finest track. Having moved to Berlin to escape the pressures of critical adulation, the party was finally over after the appropriately titled 'MUTINY' EP. CAVE, who at the time also lived in London, played a few low-key gigs in '83 backed by The CAVEMEN who subsequently became

The BAD SEEDS. Including a couple of his cronies from the BIRTHDAY PARTY days, MICK HARVEY and BLIXA BARGELD (also a member of cheery industrial types, EINSTURZENDE NEUBAUTEN), the initial line-up also boasted ex-MAGAZINE man, BARRY ADAMSON, who stayed with the band for the first four albums. Released on 'Mute' (whom CAVE was still contracted to), the debut long player, 'FROM HER TO ETERNITY' (1984), introduced CAVE's preoccupation with the ELVIS myth on a cover of 'IN THE GHETTO', an obsession indulged in greater depth on 'THE FIRSTBORN IS DEAD' (1985). The spit and thrash of the BIRTHDAY PARTY had now been replaced with a skeletal, funereal musical backing to accompany CAVE's ominous crooning. Part hellfire preacher, part damned sinner, CAVE's tales of murder most foul and general debauchery were almost always set in a context (real or implied) of Old Testament morality. Yep, this crazy cat's got that old-time religion, his songs steeped in the shadowy blues of the Mississippi Delta and the lure of his namesake, Old Nick himself. While 'KICKING AGAINST THE PRICKS' (1986), an album of covers, saw the likes of 'BLACK BETTY' and 'BY THE TIME I GET TO PHOENIX', falling under CAVE's dark spell like lambs to the slaughter, the singer came into his own on 'YOUR FUNERAL . . . MY TRIAL' later that year. Rich in dark, dense imagery, the compelling narratives of crime and punishment were further developed on 'TENDER PREY' (1988). In the couple of years preceding the next BAD SEEDS release, CAVE published his first novel, 'AND THE ASS SAW THE ANGEL', and appeared in the film, 'GHOSTS OF THE CIVIL DEAD', as well as scoring the soundtrack (along with HARVEY and BARGELD). Largely acoustic, 'THE GOOD SON' (1990) saw CAVE and his BAD SEEDS return in moodily intense style, grandiose string arrangements complementing CAVE's sombre intonations. 'HENRY'S DREAM' (1992) was somewhat more menacing with the chilling 'JACK THE RIPPER', although 'STRAIGHT TO YOU' found CAVE applying his vocal intensity in lovelorn ballad mode with impressive results. Further musings on the nature of love pervaded 'LET LOVE IN' (1994), although the apocalyptic antipode was back on familiar blood-stained ground with 'MURDER BALLADS' a couple of years later. Against a minimal musical backdrop, CAVE recounted tales of a lyrical savagery that made his earlier work read like nursery rhymes. As well as a duet with POLLY HARVEY, the record saw an unlikely, but interesting pairing with KYLIE MINOGUE (!) on 'WHERE THE WILD ROSES GROW'. In comparison, 'THE BOATMAN'S CALL' (1997) was almost evangelical, an opus that seemed to find NICK as at peace with himself and the world as he's ever been. That's not to say this was a happy record, far from it, as CAVE reflected on the redemptive power of love, and the pain of love lost. Mooted by many critics as his best work to date, it was certainly his most accessible and possessed an atmosphere of meditative grace that set it apart from much of his previous output. In a music world of MTV mediocrity, CAVE's dark, defiantly individual stance is somehow comforting, though you wouldn't necessarily want to meet the man down a dark alley late at night. Later in 1997, CAVE was rumoured to be working on a blues covers album with TIM ROSE, while he was also set to star alongside Ewan Bremner in the film, 'Rhinoceros Hunting In Budapest'. A second volume of 'King Ink' hit the book shops in March '98 although more publicity was generated via the release of a long-overdue NICK CAVE & THE BAD SEEDS best of compilation. With 'NO MORE SHALL WE PART' (2003), CAVE confirmed his position as one of popular music's truly great, visionary singer/songwriters. Although it lacked the peaceful, redemptive power of 'THE BOATMAN'S CALL', the record's hollow-eyed laments achieved a dignified grace which most writers can only dream about. Nor was the man's almost biblical narrative intensity confined to first-person pleas and ruminations; with the likes of 'GOD IS IN THE HOUSE', CAVE painted perhaps one of the most vivid portraits of small town America yet committed to disc. Perhaps one of the most revelatory CAVE moments of recent years came with a South Bank Show retrospective; the sequence with the late NINA SIMONE – featuring an uncharacteristically star-struck looking NICK – was a poignant highlight. While some critics pointed to a fall in standards with 'NOCTURAMA' (2003), CAVE had merely decided to diversify his approach and stir things up a bit, both musically and on the production front. Thus the limpid balladry of 'STILL IN LOVE' and 'ROCK OF GIBRALTAR' had their seething, polar opposites in the anarchic (if hilarious) 'DEAD MAN IN MY BED' and the epic 'BABE, I'M ON FIRE', perhaps more accurately reflecting both CAVE's career trajectory and his artistic impulse. • **Covered:** RUNNING SCARED (Roy Orbison) / BLACK BETTY (Ram Jam) / BY THE TIME I GET TO PHOENIX (Jim Webb) / MUDDY WATER (Johnny Rivers) / HEY JOE (Jimi Hendrix) / ALL TOMORROW'S PARTIES (Velvet Underground) / THE CARNIVAL IS OVER (Seekers) / SOMETHING'S GOTTEN HOLD OF MY HEART (Gene Pitney) / HELPLESS (Neil Young) / WHAT A WONDERFUL WORLD (Ray Charles) / etc. mainly from his covers album KICKING AGAINST THE PRICKS.

Album rating: Boys Next Door: DOOR DOOR (*6) / Birthday Party: PRAYERS ON FIRE (*8) / DRUNK ON THE POPE'S BLOOD (*6) / JUNKYARD (*6) / HITS compilation (*8) / LIVE 1981-1982 collection (*7) / Nick Cave & The Bad Seeds: FROM HER TO ETERNITY (*7) / THE FIRSTBORN IS DEAD (*8) / KICKING AGAINST THE PRICKS (*6) / YOUR FUNERAL . . . MY TRIAL (*6) / TENDER PREY (*6) / THE GHOST OF THE CIVIL DEAD soundtrack (*5) / THE GOOD SON (*8) / HENRY'S DREAM (*8) / LIVE SEEDS (*6) / LET LOVE IN (*8) / MURDER BALLADS (*7) / THE BOATMAN'S CALL (*9) / THE BEST OF NICK CAVE & THE BAD SEEDS compilation (*9) / NO MORE SHALL WE PART (*7) / NOCTURAMA (*6)

BOYS NEXT DOOR

NICK CAVE – vocals / **MICK HARVEY** (b.29 Sep'58, Rochester, Australia) – guitar / **TRACY PEW** – bass / **PHIL CALVERT** – drums

Suicide not iss.

May 78. (7") *(103140)* **THESE BOOTS ARE MADE FOR WALKING. / BOY HERO** – Austra –

—— (Dec'78) added **ROWLAND S. HOWARD** (b.24 Oct'59, Melbourne) – guitar (ex-YOUNG CHARLATANS)

Mushroom not iss.

May 79. (7") *(K 7492)* **SHIVERS. / DIVE POSITION** – Austra –

May 79. (lp) *(L 36931)* **DOOR, DOOR** – Austra –
– The nightwatchman / Brave exhibitions / Friends of my world / The voice / Roman Roman / Somebody's watching / After a fashion / Dive position / I mistake myself / Shivers. *(Australian cd-iss. 1987; D 19227) (cd-iss. Mar93 on 'Grey Area-Mute';)*

Missing Link not iss.

Dec 79. (12"ep) *(MLEP-3)* **HEE-HAW** – Austra –
– Catholic skin / The red clock / Faint heart / The hair shirt / Death by drowning. *(Australia re-iss. Dec83; credited as BIRTHDAY PARTY; ING 008)*

Feb 80. (7"gig freebie) *(MLS 16)* **HAPPY BIRTHDAY. / THE RIDDLE HOUSE** – Austra –

BIRTHDAY PARTY

—— (same line-up & label)

Jul 80. (7") *(MLS 18)* **MR. CLARINET. / HAPPY BIRTHDAY** – Austra –

Nov 80. (lp) *(LINK 7)* **THE FIRST ALBUM** (originally credited to BOYS NEXT DOOR) – Austra –
– Mr. clarinet / Hats on wrong / The hair shirt / Guilt parade / Riddle house / The friend catcher / Waving my arms / The red clock / Cat man / Happy birthday.

(below Australian releases only are with different label mentioned)

4.a.d. not iss.

Oct 80. (7"m) *(AD 12)* **THE FRIEND CATCHER. / WAVING MY ARMS / CATMAN** [ ] [–]

Apr 81. (lp) *(CAD 104)* **PRAYERS ON FIRE** [ ] [–]
– Zoo music girl / Cry / Capers / Nick the stripper / Ho-ho / Figure of fun / King Ink / A dead song / Yard / Dull day / Just you and me. *(cd-iss. Apr88+=; CAD 104CD)* – Blundertown / Kathy's kisses.

Jun 81. Missing Link; (12"m) *(MSD 479)* **NICK THE STRIPPER. / BLUNDER TOWN / KATHY'S KISSES** [–] Austra [–]

Aug 81. (7") *(AD 111)* **RELEASE THE BATS. / BLAST OFF** [ ] [–]

Oct 81. (7") *(AD 114)* **MR. CLARINET. / HAPPY BIRTHDAY** [ ] [–]

Feb 82. (m-lp) *(JAD 202)* **DRUNK ON THE POPE'S BLOOD (live)** [ ] [–]
– (Sometimes) Pleasure heads must burn / King Ink / Zoo music girl / Loose / LYDIA LUNCH:- The Agony Is The Ecstasy.

— (Dec81) while **TRACY PEW** was in jail for drunk driving he was replaced on tour only by either BARRY ADAMSON, CHRIS WALSH or **HARRY HOWARD**

May 82. (lp) *(CAD 207)* **JUNKYARD** [73] [–]
– She's hit / Dead Joe / Dim locator / Hamlet (pow-pow-pow) / Several sins / Big-Jesus-trash-can / Kiss me back / 6" gold blade / Kewpie doll / Junkyard. *(cd-iss. Apr88+=; CAD 207CD)* – Dead Joe (version) / Release the bats / Blast off.

— In Sep'82, ROLAND S. HOWARD did duet with LYDIA LUNCH on 12" 'Some Velvet Morning. / I Fell In Love With A Ghost'; *BAD 210)*

Nov 82. Missing Link; (7") *(MLS 32)* **NICK THE STRIPPER. / BLUNDERTOWN** [–] Austra [–]

— Now quartet when **CALVERT** joined **PSYCHEDELIC FURS**. (HARVEY now drums)

Feb 83. (12"ep) *(BAD 301)* **THE BAD SEED** [ ] [–]
– Sonny's burning / Wild world / Fears of gun / Deep in the woods.

— **JEFFREY WEGENER** – drums (ex-LAUGHING CLOWNS) repl. HARVEY Also **BLIXA BARGELD** – guitar (of EINSTURZENDE NEUBAUTEN) repl. absent HOWARD

Mute not iss.

Nov 83. (12"ep) *(12MUTE 29)* **MUTINY!** [ ] [–]
– Jennifer's veil / Mutiny in Heaven / Swampland / Say a spell.

— Disbanded Autumn 1983. TRACY joined The SAINTS. (He was later to die late '86 of epileptic fit aged 28). ROWLAND HOWARD formed CRIME & THE CITY SOLUTION. NICK CAVE went solo, forming his BAD SEEDS taking with him MICK HARVEY.

– compilations, etc. – (all mostly UK)

on '4 a.d.' unless otherwise stated

Jun 83. (12"ep) *(BAD 307)* **THE BIRTHDAY PARTY EP** [ ] [–]
– Release the bats / Blast off / The friend catcher / Mr. Clarinet / Happy birthday.

Apr 85. (d-lp) *Missing Link; (ING 009)* **IT'S STILL LIVING (live)** [–] Austra [–]

Dec 85. (lp) *Missing Link; (LINK 22)* **A COLLECTION – BEST AND RAREST** [–] Austra [–]

Feb 87. (12"ep) *Strange Fruit; (SFPS 020)* **THE PEEL SESSION** (21.4.81) [ ] [–]
– Release the bats / Rowland around in that stuff / (Sometimes) Pleasure heads must burn / Loose. *(re-iss. Aug88 cd-ep; SFPSCD 020)*

Oct 88. (12"ep/cd-ep) *Strange Fruit; (SFPS/+CD 058)* **THE PEEL SESSIONS** (2.12.81) [ ] [–]
– Big-Jesus-trash-can / She's hit / Bully bones / 6" gold blade.

Aug 89. (cd) *(CAD 301CD)* **MUTINY / THE BAD SEED** [ ] [–]

Aug 89. (cd) *(CAD 307CD)* **HEE-HAW** [ ] [–]
– (contains tracks from THE BIRTHDAY PARTY lp)

Oct 92. (d-lp/cd)(c) *(DAD 2016/+CD)(DADC 2016)* **HITS** [ ] 1998 [ ]
– The friend catcher / Happy birthday / Mr. Clarinet / Nick the stripper / Zoo music girl / King Ink / Release the bats / Blast off / She's hit / 6" Gold blade / Hamlet (pow, pow, pow) / Dead Joe / Junkyard / Big-Jesus-Trash-Can / Wild world / Sonny's burning / Deep in the woods / Swampland / Jennifer's veil / Mutiny in Heaven.

Jul 99. (cd) *(CAD 9005CD)* **LIVE 1981-1982 (live)** [ ] [ ]

NICK CAVE & THE BAD SEEDS

— **NICK CAVE** – vocals / **MICK HARVEY** – guitar, keyboards / **BLIXA BARGELD** (b.12 Jan'59, Berlin, Germany) – guitar (of EINSTURZENDE NEUBAUTEN) / **BARRY ADAMSON** (b. 1 Jun'58, Manchester, England) – bass, guitar (ex-MAGAZINE, ex-PETE SHELLEY) / **HUGO RACE** – drums

Mute Restless

Jun 84. (7") *(MUTE 32)* **IN THE GHETTO. / THE MOON IS IN THE GUTTER** [ ] [–]

— added **ANITA LANE** – synthesizers (ex-solo artist)

Jun 84. (lp) *(STUMM 17)* *<71435>* **FROM HER TO ETERNITY** [40] [ ]
– Avalanche / Cabin fever / Well of misery / From her to eternity / Wings of flies / Saint Huck / A box for black Paul. *(cd-iss. 1987+=; CDSTUMM 17)* – In the ghetto / The Moon is in the gutter / From her to eternity (1987).

— **THOMAS WYDLER** (b. 9 Oct'59, Zurich, Switzerland) – drums (ex-DIE HAUT) repl. HUGO + ANITA

Mute Homestead

Jun 85. (lp/c) *(STUMM/CSTUMM 21)* *<HMS 026>* **THE FIRSTBORN IS DEAD** [53] [ ]
– Tupelo / Say goodbye to the little girl tree / Train long suffering / Black crow king / Knockin' on Joe / Wanted man / Blind Lemon Jefferson. *(cd-iss. Apr88; CDSTUMM 21)*

Jul 85. (7") *(7MUTE 38)* **TUPELO. / THE SIX STRINGS THAT DREW BLOOD** [ ] [–]

Jun 86. (7") *(7MUTE 47)* **THE SINGER. / RUNNING SCARED** [ ] [–]
(12"+=) *(12MUTE 47)* – Black Betty.

Aug 86. (cd/c/lp) *(CD/C+/STUMM 28)* *<HMS 065>* **KICKING AGAINST THE PRICKS** [89] [ ]
– Muddy water / I'm gonna kill that woman / Sleeping Annaleah / Long black veil / Hey Joe / The singer / Black Betty * / Running scared * / All tomorrow's parties / By the time I get to Phoenix / The hammer song / Something's gotten hold of my heart / Jesus met the woman at the well / The carnival is over. *(cd+= *)*

Nov 86. (cd/c/lp) *(CD/C+/STUMM 34)* *<HMS 073>* **YOUR FUNERAL . . . MY TRIAL** [ ] [ ]
– Sad waters / The Carny / Your funeral . . . my trial / Stranger than kindness / Jack's shadow / Hard on for love / She fell away / Long time man. *(cd+=)* – Scum.

— **CAVE** retained **HARVEY, BARGELD** and **WYDLER,** bringing in **ROLAND WOLF** – bass / **KID CONGO POWERS** (b. BRIAN TRISTAN, 27 Mar'61, La Puente, Calif.) – guitar (ex-CRAMPS, ex-GUN CLUB)

Mute Mute-Elektra

May 88. (7") *(MUTE 52)* **THE MERCY SEAT. / NEW DAY** [ ] [–]
(12"+=) *(12MUTE 52)* – ('A'video mix).
(cd-s+=) *(CDMUTE 52)* – From her to eternity (film version) / Tupelo (version).

Sep 88. (cd/c/lp) *(CD/C+STUMM 52)* *<75401>* **TENDER PREY** [67] [ ]
– The mercy seat / Up jumped the Devil / Deanna / Watching Alice / Mercy / City of refuge / Slowly goes the night / Sunday's slave / Sugar, sugar, sugar / New morning. *(cd+=)* – The mercy seat (video mix). *(free-12"ep.w/above)* **AND THE ASS SAW THE ANGEL** (narration/book) – One Autumn / Animal static / Mah sanctum / Lamentation.

Sep 88. (12") *(12MUTE 86)* **DEANNA. / THE GIRL AT THE BOTTOM OF MY GLASS** [ ] [–]

Mar 89. (cd/c/lp; NICK CAVE – MICK HARVEY – BLIXA BARGELD) *(<CD/C+/IONIC 3>)* **GHOSTS . . . OF THE CIVIL DEAD** (Soundtrack w/ dialogue) [ ] [ ]
– The news / Introduction – A prison in the desert / David Hale – I've been a prison guard since I was 18 years old / Glover – I was 16 when they put me in prison / David Hale – you're danglin' us like a bunch of meat on a hook / Pop mix / Glover – we were united once / David Hale – the day of the murders / Lilly's theme ("A touch of warmth") / Maynard mix / David Hale – what I'm tellin' is the truth / Outro – The free world / Glover – one man released so they can imprison the rest of the world.

— (now a 5-piece, without WOLF)

Mar 90. (12"/cd-s/7") *(12/CD+/MUTE 108)* **THE SHIP SONG. / THE TRAIN SONG** [ ] [–]

Apr 90. (cd/c/lp) *(CD/C+/STUMM 76)* *<60988>* **THE GOOD SON** [47] Oct90 [ ]
– Foi na cruz / The good son / Sorrow's child / The weeping song / The ship song / The hammer song / Lament / The witness song / Lucy. *(w/-7"/cd-s)* **THE MERCY SEAT / CITY OF REFUGE / DEANNA (all acoustic)**

Sep 90. (12"/7") *(12+/MUTE 118)* **THE WEEPING SONG. / COCKS 'N' ASSES** [ ] [–]
(cd-s+=) *(12/CD MUTE 118)* – Helpless / (some with hidden track).

— **CONWAY SAVAGE** (b.27 Jul'60, Foster, Australia) – keyboards + **MARTYN P. CASEY** – 10 Jul'60, Chesterfield, England) – bass (ex-TRIFFIDS) repl. KID CONGO

Mar 92. (7") *(MUTE 140)* **STRAIGHT TO YOU. / JACK THE RIPPER (acoustic)** [68] [–]
(12"+=/cd-s+=) *(12/CD MUTE 140)* – Blue bird.

Apr 92. (cd/c/lp) *(CD/C+/STUMM 92) <61323>* **HENRY'S DREAM** 29 May92
– Papa won't leave you Henry / I had a dream, Joe / Straight to you / Brother, my cup is empty / Christina the astonishing / When I first came to town / John Finn's wife / Loom of the land / Jack the ripper.

Aug 92. (7") *(LMUTE 147)* **I HAD A DREAM, JOE. / THE GOOD SON (live)** –
(12"/cd-s) *(12/CD MUTE 147)* – ('A'side) / The Carny (live) / The mercy seat (live) / The ship song (live).

Nov 92. (c-s/7"; by NICK CAVE & SHANE MacGOWAN) *(C+/MUTE 151)* **WHAT A WONDERFUL WORLD. / A RAINY NIGHT IN SOHO** 72 –
(7") *(MUTE 151D)* – ('A'side / Lucy (by SHANE MacGOWAN).
(12"/cd-s) *(12/CD MUTE 151)* – (all 3 tracks).

Sep 93. (cd) *(CDMUTE 122) <61554>* **LIVE SEEDS (live)** 67
– Mercy seat / Deanna / The ship song / Papa won't leave you Henry / Plain gold ring / John Finn's wife / Tupelo / Brother my cup is empty / The weeping song / Jack the ripper / The good son / From her to eternity. *(re-iss. Sep96; LCDSTUMM 122)*

Mar 94. (12/cd-s/7"silver) *(12/CD+/MUTE 160)* **DO YOU LOVE ME? / CASSIEL'S SONG / SAIL AWAY** 68 –

Apr 94. (cd/c/lp) *(CD/C+/STUMM 123) <61645>* **LET LOVE IN** 12
– Do you love me? / Nobody's baby now / Loverman / Jangling Jack / Red right hand / I let love in / Thirsty dog / Ain't gonna rain anymore / Lay me low / Do you love me? (part 2).

— **JAMES JOHNSON** – guitar (of GALLON DRUNK) repl. on tour only BLIXA

Jul 94. (7"pic-d) *(MUTE 169)* **LOVERMAN. / (I'LL LOVE YOU) TILL THE END OF THE WORLD** –
(12"/cd-s) *(12/CD MUTE 169)* – ('A'side) / B side.

Oct 94. (7"red) *(MUTE 172)* **RED RIGHT HAND. / THAT'S WHAT JAZZ IS TO ME** –
(cd-s+=) *(CDMUTE 172)* – Where the action is.

Oct 95. (c-s/7"; NICK CAVE & THE BAD SEEDS featuring KYLIE MINOGUE) *(C+/MUTE 185)* **WHERE THE WILD ROSES GROW. / THE BALLAD OF ROBERT MOORE & BETTY COLTRANE** 11 –
(cd-s+=) *(CDMUTE 185)* – The willow garden.

Feb 96. (cd/c/lp) *(CD/C+/STUMM 138) <46195>* **MURDER BALLADS** 8
– Song of joy / Stagger Lee / Henry Lee / Lovely creature / Where the wild roses grow (featuring KYLIE MINOGUE) / The curse of Millhaven / The kindness of strangers / Crow Jane / O'Malley's bar / Death is not the end.

Feb 96. (7"; by NICK CAVE & PJ HARVEY) *(MUTE 189)* **HENRY LEE. / KING KONG KITCHEE KITCHEE KI-MI-O** 36 –
(c-s+=/cd-s+=) *(C/CD MUTE 189)* – Knoxville girl.

— <most UK singles were given a US release in 1996>

— JOHNSON was repl. by **JIM SCLAVUNOS + WARREN ELLIS**

Feb 97. (7") *(MUTE 192)* **INTO MY ARMS. / LITTLE EMPTY BOAT** 53 –
(cd-s+=) *(CDMUTE 192)* – Right now I'm a-roaming.

Mar 97. (cd/c) *(CD/C+/STUMM 142) <46530>* **THE BOATMAN'S CALL** 22
– Into my arms / Lime tree harbour / People ain't no good / Brompton oratory / There is a kingdom / (Are you) The one that I've been waiting for? / Where do we go now but nowhere? / West country girl / Black hair / Idiot prayer / Far from me / Green eyes.

May 97. (7") *(MUTE 206)* **(ARE YOU) THE ONE THAT I'VE BEEN WAITING FOR? / COME INTO MY SLEEP** 67 –
(cd-s+=) *(CDMUTE 206)* – Black hair (band version) / Babe, I got you bad.

May 98. (cd/c/d-lp) *(CD/C+/MUTEL 004) <46960>* **THE BEST OF NICK CAVE & THE BAD SEEDS** (compilation) 11
– Deanna / Red right hand / Straight to you / Tupelo / Nobody's baby now / Stranger than kindness / Into my arms / (Are you) The one that I've been waiting for? / The Carny / Do you love me? / The mercy seat / Henry Lee (feat. PJ HARVEY) / The weeping song / The ship song / Where the wild roses grow (feat. KYLIE MINOGUE) / For her to eternity. *(special d-cd; LCDMUTEL 004)* **LIVE AT THE ROYAL ALBERT HALL** – Stranger than kindness / The ship song / Let love in / Brompton oratory / Red right hand / Lime tree arbour / The weeping song / Henry Lee / Where the wild roses grow / Deanna / Straight to you / Tupelo / Nobody's baby now / Into my arms / (Are you) The one that I've been waiting for? / The Carny / Do you love me? / The mercy seat / From her to eternity.

Mar 01. (10"/cd-s) *(10/CD MUTE 249)* **AS I SAT SADLY BY HER SIDE. / LITTLE JANEY'S GONE / GOOD GOOD DAY** 42 –

Apr 01. (cd/c/d-lp) *(CD/C+/STUMM 164) <48039>* **NO MORE SHALL WE PART** 15
– As I sat sadly by her side / And no more shall we part / Hallelujah / Love letter / Fifteen feet of pure white snow / God is in the house / Oh my Lord / Sweetheart come / The sorrowful wife / We came along this road / Gates to the garden / Darker with the day. *(special cd+=; LCDSTUMM 164)* – Bless his ever loving heart / Grief came riding.

May 01. (10") *(10MUTE 262)* **FIFTEEN FEET OF PURE WHITE SNOW. / GOD IS IN THE HOUSE (westside session) / AND NO MORE SHALL WE PART (westside session)** 52 –
(cd-s) *(CDMUTE 262)* – (first 2 tracks) / We came along this road (westside session).

Mute Anti

Feb 03. (cd/lp) *(CD+/STUMM 207) <86668>* **NOCTURAMA** 20
– Wonderful life / He wants you / Right out of your hand / Bring it on / Dead man in my bed / Still in love / There is a town / Rock of Gibraltar / She passed by my window / Babe, I'm on fire.

Feb 03. (10") *(10MUTE 265)* **BRING IT ON. / SHOOT ME DOWN / SWING LOW** 58 –
(cd-s+=) *(CDMUTE 265)* – ('A'-video).

Jun 03. (10"/cd-s) *(10/CD MUTE 290)* **HE WANTS YOU / BABE, I'M ON FIRE. / LITTLE GHOST SONG / EVERYTHING MUST CONVERGE** –

Sep 03. (7") *(MUTE 318)* **ROCK OF GIBRALTAR. / NOCTURAMA** –

Harry CHAPIN

Born: 7 Dec'42, Greenwich Village, New York City, USA. Son of a big band drummer, he played in Brooklyn Heights Boys' Choir before forming a trio with his brothers, TOM and STEPHEN. Becoming a documentary film maker in the 60's, he directed the Oscar-nominated 'Legendary Champions' in 1968 before forming his own backing group and signing for 'Elektra' in 1971. His narrative folk-rock style served him well over the early-mid 70's period, CHAPIN's debut set, 'HEADS AND TALES' (1972) enjoying an extended residency in the American charts following the Top 30 success of the 'TAXI' single. CHAPIN later became something of a mini-star when radio staple, 'W-O-L-D' (about a morning DJ) hit the Top 40 on both sides of the Atlantic in 1974. In the space of a few months he released a fourth set, 'VERITIES & BALDERDASH', his most commercially successful to date. The album's appeal was considerably sweetened with the inclusion of 'CAT'S IN THE CRADLE', a treatise on injustice which became CHAPIN's only No.1 single (and a big hit for snotty metallers, UGLY KID JOE). The following year, CHAPIN concentrated on his anti-hunger initiatives, becoming a tireless social activist whose lobbying drew more recognition than his subsequent musical output. He continued to play more than his fair share of benefit concerts, although tragically he was killed in a car crash (on the 16th July 1981), travelling to just such a gig. Ironically, CHAPIN had made a brief return from commercial oblivion the previous year with the 'SEQUEL' single (billed, funnily enough, as a sequel to 'TAXI'), which almost made the American Top 20. • **Trivia:** His younger brother TOM CHAPIN released an album in 1988 for 'Flying Fish'; 'LET ME BACK INTO YOUR LIFE'.

Album rating: HEAD & TALES (*6) / SNIPER AND OTHER LOVE SONGS (*4) / SHORT STORIES (*5) / VERITIES & BALDERDASH (*7) / PORTRAIT GALLERY (*5) / GREATEST STORIES – LIVE (*4) / ON THE ROAD TO KINGDOM COME (*4) / DANCE BAND ON THE TITANIC (*5) / LIVING ROOM SUITE (*4) / LEGENDS OF THE LOST AND FOUND – NEW GREATEST STORIES LIVE (*4) / SEQUEL (*5) / ANTHOLOGY compilation (*7) / THE LAST PROTEST SINGER posthumous (*4) / STORY OF A LIFE: THE HARRY CHAPIN BOX collection (*7)

HARRY CHAPIN – vocals, guitar, with **RON PALMER** – guitar / **TIM SCOTT** – cello / **JOHN WALLACE** – bass / **STEVE CHAPIN** – keyboards / **RUSS KUNKEL** – drums, percussion

Elektra Elektra

Feb 72. (7") *<45-770>* **TAXI. / EMPTY** [–] [24]

Mar 72. (lp) *(K 42107) <75023>* **HEADS & TALES** [ ] [60]
– Could you put your light on, please / Greyhound / Everybody's lonely / Sometime, somewhere wife / Empty / Taxi / Any old kind of day / Dogtown / Same sad singer. *<cd-iss. 1993; 2-75023>*

Jul 72. (7") *(K 12060) <45-792>* **COULD YOU PUT YOUR LIGHT ON, PLEASE. / ANY OLD KIND OF DAY** [ ] [ ]

Oct 72. (7") *<45-811>* **SUNDAY MORNING SUNSHINE. / BURNING HERSELF** [–] [75]

Oct 72. (lp) *(K 42125) <75042>* **SNIPER AND OTHER LOVE SONGS** [ ] [ ]
– Sunday morning sunshine / Sniper / And the baby never cries / Burning herself / Barefoot boy / Better place to be (parts 1 & 2)/ Circle / Woman child / Winter song. *<(cd-iss. Jun02 on 'Wounded Bird'; WOU 504-2)>*

Jan 73. (7") *<45-828>* **BETTER PLACE TO BE. / WINTER SONG** [–] [ ]

— **MICHAEL MASTERS** – cello / **PAUL LEKA** – keyboards / **JIM CHAPIN** – drums, repl. SCOTT, brother STEVE CHAPIN + KUNKEL

Apr 74. (lp) *(K 42155) <75065>* **SHORT STORIES** [ ] Dec73 [61]
– Short stories / W-O-L-D / Song for myself / Song man / Changes / They call her easy / Mr. Tanner / Mail order Annie / There's a lot of lonely people tonight / Old College Avenue. *<cd-iss. 2003 on 'Rhino'; 76106>*

Apr 74. (7") *(K 12133) <45-874>* **W-O-L-D. / SHORT STORIES** [34] Dec73 [36]

May 74. (7") *<45-893>* **OLD COLLEGE AVENUE. / WHAT MADE AMERICA FAMOUS** [–] [ ]

— **STEVE CHAPIN** returned and added **ALLAN SCHWARTZBERG** – drums

Sep 74. (7") *<45-203>* **CAT'S IN THE CRADLE. / VACANCY** [–] [1]

Sep 74. (lp) *(K 52007) <1012>* **VERITIES & BALDERDASH** [ ] [4]
– Cat's in the cradle / I wanna learn a love song / Shooting star / 30,000 pounds of bananas / She sings songs without words / What made America famous / Vacancy / Halfway to Heaven / Six-string orchestra. *<cd-iss. 1993; 2-1012>*

Oct 74. (7") *(K 12157) CAT'S IN THE CRADLE. / SHOOTING STAR* [ ] [–]

Mar 75. (7") *(K 12173) <45-236>* **I WANNA LEARN A LOVE SONG. / SHE SINGS SONGS WITHOUT WORDS** [ ] Feb75 [44]

Jul 75. (7") *(K 12184) <45-264>* **DREAMS GO BY. / SANDY** [ ] [ ]

Nov 75. (lp) *(K 52023) <1041>* **PORTRAIT GALLERY** [ ] Sep75 [53]
– Dreams go by / Tangled up puppet / Star tripper / Babysitter / Someone keeps calling my name / The rock / Sandy / Dirt gets under the fingernails / Bummer / Stop singing those sad songs. *<cd-iss. 1993; 60602>*

Jan 76. (7") *(K 12194) <45-285>* **TANGLED UP PUPPET. / DIRT GETS UNDER THE FINGERNAILS** [ ] [ ]

Mar 76. (7") *<45-304>* **THE ROCK. / STAR TRIPPER** [–] [ ]

— **HOWIE FIELDS** – drums + **DOUG WALKER** – guitar were added

Apr 76. (d-lp) *(K 62017) <2009>* **GREATEST STORIES – LIVE (live)** [ ] [48]
– Dreams go by / W.O.L.D. / Saturday morning / I wanna learn a love song / Mr.Tanner / Better place to be / Let time go lightly / Cat's in the cradle / Taxi / Circle / 30,000 pounds of bananas / She is always seventeen / Love is just another word / The shortest story. *<(cd-iss. Jun89; 7559 60630-2)>*

Jun 76. (7") *<45-327>* **BETTER PLACE TO BE (live). / (part 2) (live)** [–] [86]

Aug 76. (7") *(K 12211)* **BETTER PLACE TO BE (live). / TAXI (live)** [ ] [–]

— now w/ **WALKER, WALLACE, FIELDS, S. CHAPIN + RON EVANUIK**

Oct 76. (lp/c) *(K/K4 52040) <1082>* **ON THE ROAD TO KINGDOM COME** [ ] [87]
– On the road to kingdom come / The parade's still passing by / The mayor of Candor lied / Laugh man / Corey's coming / If my Mary was here / Fall in love with him / Caroline / Roll down the river. *<cd-iss. 1993; 60613>*

Jan 77. (7") *<45-368>* **IF MY MARY WAS HERE. / COREY'S COMING** [–] [ ]

— **KIM SCHOLES** – cello, repl. EVANUIK

Sep 77. (7") *<45-426>* **DANCE BAND ON THE TITANIC. / I WONDER WHAT HAPPENED TO HIM** [–] [ ]

Sep 77. (d-lp) *(K 62021) <301>* **DANCE BAND ON THE TITANIC** [ ] [58]
– Dance band on the Titanic / Why people should stay the same / My old lady / We grew up a little bit / Bluesman / Country dreams / I do it for you, Jane / I wonder what happened to him / Paint a picture of yourself (Michael) / Mismatch / Merceneries / Manhood / One light in a dark valley (an imitation spiritual) / There was only one choice. *<cd-iss. 1993; 60549>*

Oct 77. (7") *(K 12271)* **DANCE BAND ON THE TITANIC. / (part 2)** [ ] [–]

May 78. (7") *<45-445>* **MY OLD LADY. / I'D DO IT FOR YOU, JANE** [–] [ ]

Jun 78. (lp/c) *(K/K4 52089) <142>* **LIVING ROOM SUITE** [ ] [ ]
– Dancin' boy / If you want to feel / Poor damned fool / I wonder what happened to this world / Jenny / It seems you only love me when it rains / Why do little girls / Flowers are red / Somebody said. *<cd-iss. 1993; 60528>*

Aug 78. (7") *(K 12308) <45-497>* **IF YOU WANT TO FEEL. / I WONDER WHAT WOULD HAPPEN TO THE WORLD** [ ] [ ]

May 79. (7") *(K 12361)* **FLOWERS ARE RED. / WHY DO LITTLE GIRLS** [ ] [–]

— w/ **WALLACE, WALKER, FIELDS, S. CHAPIN + SCHOLES**

Nov 79. (d-lp) *(K 62026) <703>* **LEGENDS OF THE LOST AND FOUND – NEW GREATEST STORIES LIVE (live)** [ ] Oct79 [ ]
– Stranger with the melodies / Copper / The day they closed the factory down / Pretzel man / Old folkie / Get on with it / We were three / Odd job man / Legends of the lost and found / You are the only song / Mail order Annie / Tangled up puppet / Poor damned fool / Corey's coming / If my Mary were here / Flowers are red.

Nov 79. (7") *<45-524>* **FLOWERS ARE RED. / JENNY** [–] [ ]

— **YVONNE CABLE** – cello; repl. SCHOLES

Boardwalk Boardwalk

Oct 80. (7") *(FWS 1) <5700>* **SEQUEL. / I FINALLY FOUND IT SANDY** [ ] [23]

Epic Boardwalk

Apr 81. (7") *(EPCA 1168) <5705>* **REMEMBER WHEN THE MUSIC. / NORTH WEST 222** [ ] [ ]

May 81. (lp) *(EPC 84996)* **SEQUEL** [ ] Oct80 [58]
– Sequel / I miss America / Story of a life / Remember when the music / Up on the shelf / Salt and pepper / God babe, you've been good for me / Northwest 222 / I finally found it Sandy / Remember when the music (reprise).

Aug 81. (7") *<119>* **STORY OF A LIFE. / SALT AND PEPPER** [–] [ ]

— HARRY was killed in a motor crash on 16th July 1981

– compilations, etc. –

on 'Elektra' unless mentioned otherwise

Jun 76. (7") *(K 12224)* **W.O.L.D. / CAT'S IN THE CRADLE** [ ] [–]

Nov 85. (lp/c) *(EKT 16/+C)* **ANTHOLOGY** [ ] [–]
– W.O.L.D. / Any old kind of day / Cat's in the cradle / 30,000 pounds of bananas / Taxi / She is always seventeen / Sunday morning sunshine / I wanna learn a love song / Better place to be / Song man.

1989. (7") *Old Gold; (OG 9907)* **CAT'S IN THE CRADLE. / W.O.L.D.** [ ] [–]

1989. (lp/c/cd) *Sequel; (NEX LP/MC/CD 101) / D.C.C.; <41>* **THE LAST PROTEST SINGER** [ ] [ ]
– Last of the protest singers / November rains / Basic protest song / Last stand / Sounds like America to me / Word wizard / Anthem / A quiet little love affair / I don't want to be president / Silly little girl / You only own the light.

May 98. (d-cd) *Velvel; <(VEL 47401)>* **THE BOTTOM LINE – ENCORE COLLECTION (live January 1981)** [ ] Mar98 [ ]

Nov 99. (3xcd-box) *Rhino; <(8122 75875-2)>* **STORY OF A LIFE – THE HARRY CHAPIN BOX** [ ] Oct99 [ ]

Aug 01. (cd) *Rhino; <(8122 74344-2)>* **VH1 BEHIND THE MUSIC – THE HARRY CHAPIN COLLECTION** [ ] [ ]

Jul 02. (cd) *Rhino; <8122 76061>* **THE ESSENTIALS** [–] [ ]

□ Roger CHAPMAN (see under ⇒ FAMILY)

Tracy CHAPMAN

Born: 20 Mar'64, Cleveland, Ohio, USA. A budding singer/songwriter from childhood, CHAPMAN's break came while attending Medford University (Tufts) where she met Brian Koppelman, son of industry bigwig, Charles. Through this valuable contact, CHAPMAN secured a manager in Elliot Roberts and a deal with 'Elektra', an eponymous debut album following in Spring '88.

Critically acclaimed upon release, its sparse, grainy yet soulful and cathartic nu-folk sketched vivid portraits of everyday suffering shot through with the desire for individual freedom and the redemptive power of love. Although the record's initial release was fairly low-key, CHAPMAN landed a support slot with 10,000 MANIACS and the rave reviews continued, so far, so good; what really kicked off her career, however, was a show-stopping performance at the Nelson Mandela 70th birthday concert in London, an event beamed around the globe via satellite. Sales of her debut went into overdrive, the album eventually topping both the UK and US charts, while 'FAST CAR' raced up the singles chart. A cliche perhaps, but CHAPMAN had literally become an international superstar almost overnight, her success especially surprising bearing in mind she was a young black woman singing about issues many people would rather ignore. She subsequently undertook a high profile Amnesty International tour, a strong follow-up set, 'CROSSROADS' (1989) giving her another UK No.1. Some felt the album had been a bit hastily recorded, the record inevitably failing to scale the commercial heights of its predecessor; while CHAPMAN was an articulate, observant voice for the dispossessed, she was also a singer who shied away from the showbiz limelight. It would be another three years before 'MATTERS OF THE HEART' (1992), a competent effort which nevertheless brought criticisms of water treading. Although CHAPMAN's profile had diminished considerably by the mid-90's, a fourth set, 'NEW BEGINNING' made the US Top 5, while 'GIVE ME ONE REASON' became her highest charting single to date. The new millennium saw TRACY's first album for four years, 'TELLING STORIES' (2000), a US Top 40 set and a return to basics courtesy of co-producer David Kershenbaum. With the John Parish-produced 'LET IT RAIN' (2002), CHAPMAN continued in her own quietly effective way, playing to her own committed band of fans and ceding little if any ground to contemporary trends of whatever genre. • **Covered:** trad song HOUSE OF THE RISING SUN (Glenn Yarborough) / GET UP STAND UP (Bob Marley).

Album rating: TRACY CHAPMAN (*9) / CROSSROADS (*5) / MATTERS OF THE HEART (*4) / NEW BEGINNING (*5) / TELLING STORIES (*6) / COLLECTION compilation (*8) / LET IT RAIN (*5)

TRACY CHAPMAN – vocals, acoustic guitar / with **JACK HOLDER** – guitar, organ / **LARRY KLEIN** – bass / **DENNY FONGHEISER** – drums

Apr 88. (lp/c)(cd) *(EKT 44/+C)<(K 960774-2)>* **TRACY CHAPMAN** [1] [1]
– Talkin' bout a revolution / Fast car / Across the lines / Behind the wall / Baby can I hold you / Mountains o' things / She's got her ticket / Why? / For my lover / If not now . . . / For you.

May 88. (7") *(EKR 73) <69412>* **FAST CAR. / FOR YOU** [5] [6]
(12"+=) *(EKR 73T)* – Behind the wall.

Aug 88. (7"/12") *(EKR 78/+T)* **TALKIN' BOUT A REVOLUTION. / IF NOT NOW . . .** [ ] [–]
(cd-s+=) *(EKR 78CD)* – She's got her ticket.

Sep 88. (7") *<69383>* **TALKIN' BOUT A REVOLUTION. / BEHIND THE WALL** [–] [75]

Oct 88. (7") *<69356>* **BABY CAN I HOLD YOU. / IF NOT NOW . . .** [–] [48]

Nov 88. (7") *(EKR 82)* **BABY CAN I HOLD YOU. / ACROSS THE LINES** [ ] [–]
(12"+=/cd-s+=) *(EKR 82 T/CD)* – Mountain o' things.

Sep 89. (7"/c-s) *(EKR 95/+C) <69273>* **CROSSROADS. / BORN TO FIGHT** [61] [90]
(12"+=) *(EKR 95T)* – Fast car.
(cd-s+=) *(EKR 95CD)* – Mountain o' things (live).

Oct 89. (lp/c)(cd) *(EKT 61/+C)<(K 960888-2)>* **CROSSROADS** [1] [9]
– Crossroads / Bridges / Freedom now / Material world / Be careful of my heart / Subcity / Born to fight / A hundred years / This time / All that you have is your soul.

Feb 90. (7") *(EKR 107)* **ALL THAT YOU HAVE IS YOUR SOUL. / SUBCITY** [ ] [–]
(12"+=) *(EKR 107T)* – Freedom now.

Feb 90. (7") **ALL THAT YOU HAVE IS YOUR SOUL. / MATERIAL WORLD** [–] [ ]

Apr 92. (7"/c-s) **BANG BANG BANG. / WOMAN'S WORK** [ ] [ ]
(12"+=/cd-s+=) – House of the rising Sun.

May 92. (cd)(lp/c) *<(7559 61215-2)>(EKT 98/+C)* **MATTERS OF THE HEART** [19] [ ]
– Bang bang bang / So / I used to be a sailor / The love that you had / Woman's work / These are the things / Short supply / Dreaming on a world / Open arms / Matters of the heart. *(re-iss. cd+c Nov93)*

Jul 92. (7"/c-s) **DREAMING ON A WORLD. / WOMAN'S WORK** [ ] [ ]
(cd-s+=) – ('A'extended) / House of the rising Sun.

Nov 95. (cd/c) *<(7559 61850-2/-4)>* **NEW BEGINNING** [ ] [4]
– Heaven's here on Earth / New beginning / Smoke and ashes / Cold feet / At this point in my life / the promise / The rape of the world / Tell it like it is / Give me one reason / Remember the tin man / I'm ready.

Mar 96. (c-s) *<64346>* **GIVE ME ONE REASON. / THE RAPE OF THE WORLD** [–] [3]

May 96. (cd-s) *(EKR 222CD)* **GIVE ME ONE REASON / THE RAPE OF THE WORLD / HOUSE OF THE RISING SUN** [ ] [–]

Mar 97. (c-s) *(E 3969C)* **GIVE ME ONE REASON / FAST CAR** [ ] [ ]
(cd-s+=) *(E 3969CD)* – Talking 'bout a revolution.

Feb 00. (cd/c) *<(7559 62478-2/-4)>* **TELLING STORIES** [ ] [33]
– Telling stories / Less than strangers / Speak the word / IT's ok / Wedding song / Unsung psalm / Nothing yet / Paper and ink / Devotion / The only one / First try. *(d-cd-iss. May00 +=; 7559 62541-2)* – live:- Fast car / Talkin' 'bout a revolution / Three little birds / House of the rising sun / Mountains o' things / Behind the wall / Baby can I hold you.

Oct 02. (cd-s) *(E 7335CD)* **YOU'RE THE ONE / I AM YOURS** [ ] [–]

Oct 02. (cd) *<(7559 62836-2)>* **LET IT RAIN** [36] [25]
– Let it rain / Another sun / You're the one / In the dark / Almost / Hard wired / Say hallelujah / Broken / Happy / Goodbye / I am yours / Over in love (instrumental). *<(d-cd-iss. Mar03 +=; 7559 62861-2)>* – live:- You're the one / Give me one reason / Talkin' 'bout a revolution / I am yours / Get up stand up.

– compilations, etc. –

Sep 01. (cd/c) *Elektra; <(7559 62700-2/-4)>* **COLLECTION** [3] [ ]
– Fast car / Subcity / Baby can I hold you / The promise / I'm ready / Crossroads / Bang bang bang / Telling stories / Smoke and ashes / Speak the word / Wedding song / Open arms / Give me one reason / Talkin' 'bout a revolution / She's got her ticket / All that you have is your soul.

CHARLATANS (UK)

Formed: Northwich, Cheshire, England . . . late 1989 by MARTIN BLUNT, ROB COLLINS, JON BROOKES and JON BAKER. They soon found a frontman in singer TIM BURGESS and after a few attempts at getting a record deal, they set up their own 'Dead Dead Good' label. Early in 1990, they scored a massive indie hit with the 'INDIAN ROPE' single. Following the explosion of the "Madchester" scene, the label was taken over by the Beggars Banquet subsidiary, 'Situation 2', for whom they recorded their first Top 10 hit, 'THE ONLY ONE I KNOW'. Another hammond-driven classic, 'THEN', preceded a late summer chart topping debut album, 'SOME FRIENDLY'. A relatively quiet year followed, during which MARTIN BLUNT nearly retired due to severe depression. However, it was actually BAKER who departed after playing at London's Royal Albert Hall. Come 1992, MARK COLLINS (ex-WALTONES) was drafted in and things looked brighter when the single, 'WEIRDO', gave them another Top 20 hit. Their second album, however, ('BETWEEN 10TH AND 11TH'), was given the thumbs down by the music press, hence its failure to secure a respectable chart placing. This was not the only setback that year, as ROB COLLINS was charged with aiding and abetting an armed robbery. A year later, although maintaining his innocence, he was sentenced to several months in jail, later being released in early 1994 on good behaviour. 'CAN'T GET OUT OF BED', saw them return in fine style, and was lifted from the Top 10 album 'UP TO OUR HIPS'. TIM then moonlighted on singles by SAINT ETIENNE and The CHEMICAL BROTHERS, before the group were back to their best on the eponymous 1995 album. From its retro cover art, to the 'Sympathy For The Devil'-style single, 'JUST WHEN YOU'RE THINKIN' THINGS OVER', the album was an obvious homage to The ROLLING STONES. Tragically, on 23rd of July '96, ROB COLLINS was killed when his car spun off a road in Wales. The coroners report concluded that he was the driver and also that he had twice the legal amount of alcohol in his blood. They had just recorded their fifth album, 'TELLIN' STORIES', preceded by their biggest hit singles to date, 'ONE TO ANOTHER' and 'NORTH COUNTRY BOY'. With The CHARLATANS momentum seemingly unstoppable while every other 'baggy' band fell by the wayside, BURGESS and Co celebrated their longevity with a career retrospective, 'MELTING POT' (1998). With newboy TONY ROGERS finally getting his chance to perform in the place of COLLINS and with the group signing a major deal via 'M.C.A.', The CHARLATANS were ready to take their place back in indie-rock – albeit minus a few hundred thousand admittedly stolen by their accountant, Trevor Williams. Their sixth album, 'US AND US ONLY' (1999), was a test of sorts, its subsequent No.2 peak position in the UK charts an indication that they were still wanted by their ageing fanbase; the STONE ROSES, THE VERVE and OASIS, where were they now? Seven albums and still going strong, The CHARLATANS set out their stall for the 21st century with Top 3 set, 'WONDERLAND' (2001). This time around BURGESS was wielding a bit of soulpower, reaching for the skies with a hitherto unheard falsetto on hit singles such as 'LOVE IS THE KEY' and 'A MAN NEEDS TO BE TOLD'. The grooves were also slicker and sexier, hints of CURTIS MAYFIELD's funkier moments revealing themselves on the latter especially. Frontman TIM BURGESS branched out on his own in 2003 to record the brilliantly diverse solo album 'I BELIEVE IN THE SPIRIT'. Sounding nothing like his usual band, the album, laced with sugary pop melodies, strange waltzes and finely executed keyboards, you would be forgiven for thinking that you were listening to early TIM BUCKLEY fused with DONOVAN. It is just a shame, however, that The CHARLATANS never reached such a high standard of music, which makes you wonder: is it worth BURGESS going back when he's got such a good thing going? • **Songwriters:** Group compositions except; I FEEL MUCH BETTER ROLLING OVER (Small Faces). On their eponymous 1995 album, the track 'HERE COMES A SOUL SAVER' featured a guitar riff remarkably similar to that of PINK FLOYD's 'Fearless' (from 'Meddle' 1971).

Album rating: SOME FRIENDLY (*8) / BETWEEN 10th & 11th (*5) / UP TO OUR HIPS (*7) / THE CHARLATANS (*8) / TELLIN' STORIES (*8) / MELTING POT compilation (*8) / US AND US ONLY (*7) / WONDERLAND (*5) / LIVE IT LIKE YOU LOVE IT – THE BEST OF THE CHARLATANS LIVE collection (*6) / Tim Burgess: I BELIEVE (*6)

TIM BURGESS (b.30 May'68) – vocals (ex-ELECTRIC CRAYONS) repl. BAZ KETTLEY / **ROB COLLINS** (b.23 Feb'63) – organ / **JON BAKER** (b.1969) – guitar / **JON BROOKS** (b.1969) – drums / **MARTIN BLUNT** (b.1965) – bass (ex-MAKIN' TIME, ex-TOO MUCH TEXAS w / TIM)

Dead Dead Good | not iss.

Feb 90. (7") *(GOOD ONE SEVEN)* **INDIAN ROPE. / WHO WANTS TO KNOW** [89] [–]
(12"+=) *(GOOD ONE TWELVE)* – You can talk to me. *(re-iss. Jul91 12"/cd-s; GOOD 1 T/CD, hit No.57) (re-iss. cd-s Oct96)*

Situation 2 | Beggars Banquet

May 90. (7") *(SIT 70)* **THE ONLY ONE I KNOW. / EVERYTHING CHANGED** [9] [ ]
(12"+=) *(SIT 70T)* – Imperial 109.
(cd-s++=) *(SIT 70CD)* – You can talk to me.

Sep 90. (7"/c-s) *(SIT 74/+C)* **THEN. / TAURUS MOANER** [12] [ ]
(12"+=/cd-s+=) *(SIT 74 T/CD)* – ('A'-alternate take) / ('B'instrumental).

Oct 90. (lp/c/cd/s-lp) *(SITU 30/+MC/CD/R)* <2411> **SOME FRIENDLY** [1] [73]
– You're not very well / White shirt / Opportunity / Then / 109 pt.2 / Polar bear / Believe you me / Flower / Sonic / Sproston Green. *(cd+=)* – The only one I know. *(cd re-iss. Sep95 on 'Beggars Banquet'; BBL 30CD)*

Feb 91. (7"/c-s) *(SIT 76/+CS)* **OVER RISING. / WAY UP THERE** [15] [ ]
(12"/c-s+=/cd-s+=) *(SIT 76 T/TC/CD)* – Happen to die / Opportunity Three (re-work).

— **MARK COLLINS** – guitar (ex-WALTONES, ex-CANDLESTICK PARK) repl. BAKER

Oct 91. (7"/c-s) *(SIT 84/+C)* **ME IN TIME. / OCCUPATION H. MONSTER** [28] [ ]
(12"+=/cd-s+=) *(SIT 84 T/CD)* – Subtitle.

Feb 92. (7"/c-s) *(SIT 88/+C)* **WEIRDO. / THEME FROM 'THE WISH'** [19] [–]
(12"+=/cd-s+=) *(SIT 88 T/CD)* – Sproston Green (U.S. remix) / ('A'-alternate take).

Mar 92. (lp/c/cd) *(SITU 37/+MC/CD)* <61108> **BETWEEN 10th AND 11th** [21] [ ]
– I don't want to see the lights / Ignition / Page one / Tremelo song / The end of everything etc / Subtitle / Can't even be bothered / Weirdo / Chewing gum weekend / (No one) Not even the rain. *(re-iss. cd Sep95 on 'Beggars Banquet'; BBL 37CD)*

Jun 92. (c-s) *(SIT 97C)* **TREMELO SONG (alternate take) / THEN (live) / CHEWING GUM WEEKEND (live) / TREMELO SONG** [44] [ ]
(12") *(SIT 97T)* – Happen to die (unedited) repl. last version.
(cd-s) *(SIT 97CD1)* – ('A'side) / Happen to die (unedited) / Normality swing (demo).
(cd-s) *(SIT 97CD2)* – ('A'live April '92) / Then (live) / Chewing gum weekend (live).

— ROB COLLINS was imprisoned in Sep'93 for taking part in a robbery. (see above) He had already recorded below while awaiting trial, and was free just in time to feature on Top Of The Pops.

Beggars Banquet | Beggars Banquet

Jan 94. (7"/c-s) *(BBQ 27/+C)* **CAN'T GET OUT OF BED. / WITHDRAWN** [24] [–]
(12"+=/cd-s+=) *(BBQ 27 T/CD)* – Out.

Mar 94. (cd-ep) *(BBQ 31CD)* **I NEVER WANT AN EASY LIFE IF ME AND HE WERE EVER TO GET THERE / ONLY A BOHO / SUBTERRAINEAN / CAN'T GET OUT OF BED (demo)** [38] [–]

Mar 94. (cd/c/lp) *(BBQ CD/MC/LP 147)* <92352> **UP TO OUR HIPS** [8] [ ]
– Come in number 21 / I never want an easy life / If me and he were ever to get there / Can't get out of bed / Feel flows / Autograph / Jesus hairdo / Up to our hips / Patrol / Another rider up in flames / Inside – looking out. *(re-iss. cd Sep95; BBL 147CD)*

Jun 94. (c-s) *(BBQ 32C)* **JESUS HAIRDO / PATROL (Dust Brothers mix)** [48] [–]
(12"+=) *(BBQ 32T)* – Feel flows (the carpet kiss mix).
(cd-s+=) *(BBQ 32CD1)* – Stir it up / Feel flows (Van Basten mix).
(cd-s) *(BBQ 32CD2)* – ('A'side) / I never want an easy life / Another rider up in flames / Up to our hips (BBC Radio 1 live sessions).

Dec 94. (7"/c-s) *(BBQ 44/+C)* **CRASHIN' IN. / BACK ROOM WINDOW** [31] [–]
(12"+=/cd-s+=) *(BBQ 44 T/CD)* – Green flashing eyes.

May 95. (7"/c-s) *(BBQ 55/+C)* **JUST LOOKIN'. / BULLET COMES** [32] [–]
(cd-s+=) *(BBQ 55CD)* – Floor nine.

Aug 95. (c-s) *(BBQ 60C)* **JUST WHEN YOU'RE THINKIN' THINGS OVER / FRINCK / YOUR SKIES ARE MINE** [12] [–]
(cd-s+=) *(BBQ 60CD)* – Chemical risk (toothache remix).
(12") *(BBQ 60T)* – (first 2 tracks) / Chemical risk dub (toothache remix) / Nine acre dust (Dust Brothers mix).

Aug 95. (cd/c/d-lp) *(BBQ CD/MC/LP 174)* <92602> **THE CHARLATANS** [1] [ ]
– Nine acre court / Feeling holy / Just lookin' / Crashin' in / Bullet comes / Here comes a soul saver / Just when you're thinkin' things over / Tell everyone / Toothache / No fiction / See it through / Thank you. *(d-lp+=)* – Chemical risk (toothache remix).

— On 23rd July '96, ROB COLLINS was killed in a car crash (see above).

Aug 96. (7"/c-s/cd-s) *(BBQ 301/+C/CD)* **ONE TO ANOTHER. / TWO OF US / REPUTATION** [3] [–]

— **MARTIN DUFFY** – keyboards (of PRIMAL SCREAM) augmented

Beggars Banquet | M.C.A.

Mar 97. (7"/c-s/cd-s) *(BBQ 309/+C/CD)* **NORTH COUNTRY BOY. / AREA 51 / DON'T NEED A GUN** [4] [–]

Apr 97. (cd/c/lp) *(BBQ CD/MC/LP 190)* <11622> **TELLIN' STORIES** [1] [ ]
– With no shoes / North country boy / Tellin' stories / One to another / You're a big girl now / How can you leave us / Area 51 / How high / Only teethin' / Get on it / Rob's theme / Two of us / Reputation.

Jun 97. (7"/c-s) *(BBQ 312/+C)* **HOW HIGH. / DOWN WITH THE MOOK** [6] [–]
(cd-s+=) *(BBQ 312CD)* – Title fight.

Oct 97. (7") *(BBQ 318)* **TELLIN' STORIES. / KEEP IT TO YOURSELF** [16] [–]
(c-s+=) *(BBQ 318C)* – Thank you (live).
(cd-s++=) *(BBQ 318CD)* – Clean up kid.

Beggars Banquet | Beggars Banquet

Feb 98. (cd/c/lp) *(BBQ CD/MC/LP 198)* <80198> **MELTING POT** (compilation) [4] [ ]
– The only one I know / Then / Opportunity three / Over rising / Sproston Green (U.S. version) / Weirdo / Theme from the wish / Patrol (The Chemical Brothers mix) / Can't get out of bed / I never want an easy life if me & he were ever to get there / Jesus hairdo / Crashin' in / Just lookin' / Here comes a soul saver / Just when you're thinkin' things over / One to another / North country boy. *(cd re-iss. May02; same)*

— (1997) **TONY RODGERS** was now the replacement for ROB

M.C.A. | Universal

Oct 99. (7") *(MCS 40220)* **FOREVER. / WHEN YOUR SHIP COMES IN** [12] [–]
(c-s/cd-s+=) *(MCS C/TD 40220)* – Great place to leave.
(cd-s) *(MCSXD 40220)* – ('A'side) / Sleepy little sunshine boy / ('A'-CD enhanced).

Oct 99. (cd/c/lp) *(MCD/MCC/MCA 60069)* <112058> **US AND US ONLY** [2] [ ]
– Forever / Good witch, bad witch / Impossible / The blonde waltz / A house is not a home / Senses / My beautiful friend / I don't care where you live / The blind stagger / Good witch, bad witch / Watching you.

Dec 99. (7") *(MCS 40225)* **MY BEAUTIFUL FRIEND. / SCORCHED** [31] [–]
(c-s/cd-s+=) *(MCS C/TD 40225)* – Your precious love.
(cd-s) *(MCSXD 40225)* – ('A'mixes + CD-enhanced).

May 00. (7"/cd-s) *(MCS/+XD 40231)* **IMPOSSIBLE. / YOU GOT IT I WANT IT** [15] [–]
(c-s/cd-s) *(MCS C/TD 40231)* – ('A'side) / Don't go giving it up / ('A'-video).

Aug 01. (7") *(7") (MCS 40262)* **LOVE IS THE KEY. / VIVA LA SOCIALE** [16] [–]
(cd-s+=) *(MCSTD 40262)* – It's about time.

Sep 01. (cd/d-lp) *(MCD/MCA 60076)* <014910> **WONDERLAND** [2] [ ]
– You're so pretty – we're so pretty / Judas / Love is the key / A man needs to be told / I just can't get over losing you / The bell and the butterfly / And if I fall / Wake up / Is it in you? / Ballad of the band. *(d-lp+=)* – Right on / Love to you.

Nov 01. (7") *(MCS 40271)* **A MAN NEEDS TO BE TOLD. / SHOTGUN** [31] [–]
(cd-s+=) *(MCSTD 40271)* – Ballad of the band (Ianocce remix).
(cd-s) *(MCSXD 40271)* – ('A'side) / All I desire / Love is the key (live) / ('A'-video).

Apr 02. (12") *(MCST 40283)* **YOU'RE SO PRETTY – WE'RE SO PRETTY. / ('A'-Lo Fidelity Allstars) / SILLY THING** [ ] [–]
(cd-s) *(MCSTD 40283)* – ('A'side) / ('A'-Lo Fidelity Allstars) / Room 118.

Jul 02. (cd) *(MCD 60080)* <64169-2> **LIVE IT LIKE YOU LOVE IT – THE BEST OF THE CHARLATANS LIVE (live)** [40] Oct02 [ ]
– Love is the key / Judas / Tellin' stories / The man needs to be told / One to another / The only one I know / Impossible / North country boy / You're so pretty – we're so pretty / Weirdo (with JOHNNY MARR) / How high / Forever / And if I fall / Sproston green.

– compilations, etc. –

May 02. (cd) *Beggars Banquet; (BEGL 2032CD)* **SONGS FROM THE OTHER SIDE** (B-sides) [55] [–]

TIM BURGESS

with various band members

P.I.A.S. | not iss.

Sep 03. (7") *(PIASB 109-7)* **I BELIEVE IN THE SPIRIT. / WHO THE CAP FIT** [44] [–]
(cd-s+=) *(PIASB 109CD)* – I believe in the West Coast.

Sep 03. (cd/lp) *(PIASB 099 CD/LP)* **I BELIEVE** [38] [–]
– I believe in the spirit / Held in straps / Only a boy / We all need love / Oh my corazon / Be my baby / Years ago / Say yes / Spend the night / Po' boy soul / All I ever do.

Nov 03. (7") *(PIASB 119-7)* **ONLY A BOY. / ROUGH TIME** [54] [–]
(cd-s+=) *(PIASB 119CD)* – Wait til the sun shines Irie.

Ray CHARLES

Born: RAY CHARLES ROBINSON, 23 Sep'30, Albany, Georgia, USA. While encouraged to take up the piano at an early age after his family moved to Greenville, Florida, the young ROBINSON was afflicted by glaucoma (after witnessing the death of his brother) at the age of seven and subsequently went blind. Using Braille, he studied composition at the St. Augustine School for the Deaf and the Blind as well as learning instruments such as organ and saxophone. The troubles continued to pile up, however, as both his mother and father died before he reached the age of sixteen. Leaving school, he survived by playing in various dance bands around Florida before saving enough money to move to Seattle. As R.C. ROBINSON he began playing with The McSON TRIO (alongside guitarist GOSSADY McGHEE and bassist MILTON GARRAD) before signing to Jack Lauderdale's 'Downbeat' label in 1949. To avoid confusion with boxer Sugar Ray Robinson, he began recording as RAY CHARLES (accompanied by The MAXIM TRIO) and released his debut single, 'CONFESSION BLUES', the same year; a further two singles followed before the label was taken over by 'Swingtime'. Subsequently working with JOHNNY MOORE'S THREE BLAZERS, CHARLES continued cutting sides in the 'sepia Sinatra' style of singers such as NAT 'KING' COLE and CHARLES BROWN. 1951's 'BABY LET ME HOLD YOUR HAND' and 'KISS-A-ME BABY' marked his first couple of R&B Top 10 hits, during which time he embarked on a national tour with blues man LOWELL FULSON. Starting out as a sideman, CHARLES soon advanced to musical director and the experience put him in good stead for a subsequent stint in New Orleans with GUITAR SLIM. He both arranged and played piano on SLIM's million-selling 1954 hit for 'Specialty', 'The Things That I Used To Do', CHARLES duly incorporating a more organic, gospel-influenced style into his own recordings. Adding alto sax and a quartet of horn players, the singer signed to 'Atlantic' and perfected his thrilling marriage of earthy, hollering gospel and raw R&B with 1955's 'I'VE GOT A WOMAN'. The track narrowly missed top spot on the R&B chart and initiated a string of such hits wherein CHARLES alchemised various black music styles in what amounted to a blueprint for 60's soul. His first brush with the pop chart came in summer '59 with the classic 'WHAT'D I SAY', a raucous combination of gospel, jump-blues and rock'n'roll that made him a national star overnight. A cover of Hank Snow's 'I'M MOVIN' ON' followed into the Top 40 while 'THE GENIUS OF RAY CHARLES' (1960) album made the Top 20, its combination of sentimental balladry and big-band ebullience setting the tone for many of his future recordings. 1960 was also the year he moved to 'ABC Paramount', thrashing out a deal whereby he was given far more creative control as well as full ownership of the mastertapes (virtually unheard of in those days). Things got off to a great start with a stunning US No.1 cover of pop standard, 'GEORGIA ON MY MIND', while female backing singers, The RAELETTES, spiced up CHARLES' rasp on 'HIT THE ROAD JACK' (another No.1) and a rollicking 'UNCHAIN MY HEART'. 1962 saw him recording a set of duets with BETTY CARTER as well as making a shock move into country with the No.1 album, 'MODERN SOUNDS IN COUNTRY AND WESTERN MUSIC'. Having already cut a number of straight jazz albums at 'Atlantic', CHARLES proved there were few boundaries to his eclectic talent with unique interpretations of country standards like Don Gibson's 'I CAN'T STOP LOVING YOU' (a transatlantic No.1) and Hank Williams' 'HEY GOOD LOOKIN''. 1963's brassy Top 5 remake of Harlan Howard's 'BUSTED' proved uncannily prophetic as CHARLES was arrested for possession of heroin two years later; though he took a year out to fight his addiction, he was back in court on a second drugs rap in 1967, the judge refraining from handing out a prison sentence but fining him heavily and putting him on four years probation. By the time he'd formed his own label, 'Tangerine' (through which he released material by other artists as well as his own), in the mid-late 60's his sound was increasingly catering to the MOR market though he could still come up with funky little gems like the 1969 collaboration with JIMMY LEWIS, 'IF IT WASN'T FOR BAD LUCK' and 1971's instrumental 'BOOTY BUTT'. He also cut a couple of notable albums during the 70's, the black consciousness-centred (CHARLES was a vocal supporter of the civil rights movement and its leader, Martin Luther King) 'A MESSAGE FROM THE PEOPLE' (1972) and 1975's 'RENAISSANCE'. 1976, meanwhile, found him recording a pop interpretation of 'PORGY AND BESS' with CLEO LAINE, CHARLES going on to cut unlikely recordings with everyone from CLINT EASTWOOD! (a track from the film 'Any Which Way You Can) and BILLY JOEL to INXS. An early 80's move to 'Columbia' saw him attempt a fully fledged transformation into country on 'WISH YOU WERE HERE TONIGHT' (1983) and 'FRIENDSHIP' (1984), the latter an album of collaborations with the likes of JOHNNY CASH, MERLE HAGGARD and WILLIE NELSON. If critics weren't too enamoured with these efforts, CHARLES certainly didn't redeem himself with 1985's Xmas set, 'THE SPIRIT OF CHRISTMAS'. Nevertheless, he won a grammy for his 1990 duet with CHAKA KHAN, 'I'LL BE GOOD TO YOU' (from QUINCY JONES' 'Back On The Block' album) while he endeared himself to a whole new generation of American youth with a series of ads for Diet Pepsi. While it undoubtedly seems his glory days are behind him, RAY CHARLES remains one of the true giants and founding fathers of modern music, his part in the development of soul especially, beyond question. His versatility and eclecticism remain unparalleled with his influence apparent in the vocal style of everyone from STEVIE WONDER to VAN MORRISON and JOE COCKER. • **Songwriters:** RAY wrote most of material, although at times lending from others, i.e.- LET THE GOOD TIMES ROLL (Shirley & Lee) / GEORGIA ON MY MIND (Hoagy Carmichael) / HIT THE ROAD JACK (Percy Mayfield) / YOU ARE MY SUNSHINE (Jimmie Davis) / YOUR CHEATIN' HEART + TAKE THESE CHAINS FROM MY HEART (Hank Williams) / THAT LUCKY OLD SUN (?) / MAKIN' WHOOPEE (?) / CRY (Johnny Ray) / I'M A FOOL TO CARE (Joe Barry) / TOGETHER AGAIN (Buck Owens) / ELEANOR RIGBY + YESTERDAY (Beatles) / WHAT AM I LIVING FOR? (Chuck Willis) / LOOK WHAT THEY'VE DONE TO MY SONG, MA? (Melanie) / LIVING FOR THE CITY (Stevie Wonder) / etc.

• **Miscellaneous:** Many didn't know at the time, but RAY was married to gospel singer DELLA REESE for 22 years, until they divorced late 1977. Also note that The Ray Charles Singers – who had US hits in the 60's – were in fact conducter Charles Ray Offenberg and not RAY himself.

Best CD compilation: THE DEFINITIVE . . . (*8)

RAY CHARLES – vocals, piano / **GISADY McGHEE** – guitar / **MILTON GARRAD** – bass

		not iss.	Downbeat
1949.	(78; as the MAXIM TRIO) *<171>* **CONFESSION BLUES. / I LOVE YOU, I LOVE YOU**	–	
1949.	(78) *<178>* **BLUES BEFORE SUNRISE. / HOW LONG BLUES**	–	
1949.	(78) *<179>* **A SENTIMENTAL BLUES. / YOU'LL NEVER MISS THE WATER**	–	

		not iss.	Swingtime
1949.	(78; as the MAXIM TRIO) *<211>* **ALONE IN THIS CITY. / CAN ANYONE ASK FOR MORE**	–	
1949.	(78; as the MAXIM TRIO) *<212>* **LET'S HAVE A BALL. / ROCKIN' CHAIR BLUES**	–	
1949.	(78) *<213>* **IF I GIVE YOU MY LOVE. / unknown**	–	
1950.	(78) *<215>* **I'VE HAD MY FUN. / SITTIN' ON TOP OF THE WORLD**	–	
1950.	(78) *<216>* **AIN'T THAT FINE. / DON'T PUT YOUR DREAMS ALL IN ONE BASKET**	–	
1950.	(78) *<217>* **SEE SEE RIDER. / WHAT HAVE I DONE**	–	
1950.	(78) *<218>* **HONEY, HONEY. / SHE'S ON THE BALL**	–	
1950.	(78) *<228>* **LATE IN THE EVENING BLUES. / TH' EGO SONG**	–	
1950.	(78) *<229>* **I'LL DO ANYTHING BUT WORK. / SOMEDAY**	–	
1951.	(78) *<249>* **ALL TO MYSELF. / I WONDER WHO'S KISSING HER NOW**	–	
1951.	(7",78) *<250>* **BABY, LET ME HOLD YOUR HAND. / (I'M JUST A) LONELY BOY**	–	
1952.	(7",78) *<274>* **KISS-A-ME BABY (ALL NIGHT LONG). / I'M GLAD FOR YOUR SAKE**	–	
1952.	(7") *<276>* **CHANGEABLE WOMAN BLUES. / MOONRISE**	–	
1952.	(7",78) *<297>* **HEY, NOW. / BABY WON'T YOU PLEASE COME HOME**	–	
1952.	(7",78) *<300>* **GUITAR BLUES. / BABY LET ME HEAR YOU CALL MY NAME** *<re-iss. 1952 on 'Sittin-In-With'; 641>*	–	

—— **RAY** added sax / + **4 other horn players** / + **DAVID NEWMAN** – saxophone

		not iss.	Atlantic
Jun 52.	(7") *<976>* **ROLL WITH MY BABY. / THE MIDNIGHT HOUR**	–	
1953.	(7") *<984>* **THE SUN'S GONNA SHINE AGAIN. / JUMPIN' IN THE MORNING**	–	
1953.	(7") *<999>* **MESS AROUND. / FUNNY (BUT I STILL LOVE YOU)**	–	
1953.	(7") *<1008>* **HEARTBREAKER. / FEELIN' SAD**	–	
1954.	(7") *<1021>* **IT SHOULD'VE BEEN ME. / SINNER'S PRAYER**	–	
1954.	(7") *<1037>* **DON'T YOU KNOW (BABY?). / LOSING HAND**	–	
1954.	(7") *<1050>* **I'VE GOT A WOMAN. / COME BACK BABY**	–	
1955.	(7") *<1063>* **THIS LITTLE GIRL OF MINE. / A FOOL FOR YOU**	–	
1955.	(7") *<1076>* **BLACKJACK. / GREENBACKS**	–	
1956.	(7") *<1085>* **I'LL DROWN IN MY OWN TEARS. / MARY ANN**	–	
1956.	(7") *<1096>* **HALLELUJAH, I LOVE HER SO. / WHAT WOULD I DO WITHOUT YOU?**	–	
1956.	(7") *<1108>* **LONELY AVENUE. / LEAVE MY WOMAN ALONE**	–	
1957.	(7") *<1124>* **AIN'T THAT LOVE. / I WANT TO KNOW**	–	
1957.	(7") *<1143>* **IT'S ALL RIGHT. / GET ON THE RIGHT TRACK BABY**	–	

Jul 57. (lp) *<8006>* **RAY CHARLES SINGS** –
– Ain't that love / I'll drown in my own tears / Come back baby / Sinner's prayer / Funny / Losing hand / A fool for you / Hallelujah I love her so / Mess around / This little girl of mine / Mary Ann / Greenbacks / Don't you know / I got a woman. *<UK-iss.Mar67 as 'HALLELUJAH, I LOVE HER SO'; 587 056>*

Oct 57. (7") *<1154>* **SWANEE RIVER ROCK (TALKIN' 'BOUT THAT RIVER). / I WANT A LITTLE GIRL** – 34

1957. (lp) *<1259>* **THE GREAT RAY CHARLES** –
– The Ray / My melancholy baby / Black coffee / There's no you / Doodlin' / Sweet sixteen bars / I surrender dear / Undecided. *(UK-iss.Nov58 on 'London-Jazz'; LTZK 15134)*

1958. (7") *<1172>* **TALKIN' 'BOUT YOU. / THAT'S ENOUGH** –

1958. (lp) *<1289>* **RAY CHARLES AT NEWPORT (live)**
– The right time / In a little Spanish town / I got a woman / Blues waltz / Hot rod / Talkin' 'bout you / Sherry / A fool for you. *(UK-iss.Mar59 on 'London-Jazz'; LTZK 15149) (re-iss. Feb69 & Mar73 on 'Atlantic')*

1958. (lp; as RAY CHARLES & MILT JACKSON) *<1279>* **SOUL BROTHERS** –
– How long blues / Cosmic Ray / The genius after hours / Charlesville / Bags of blues / 'Deed I do / Blue funk / Soul brothers / Bags' guitar blues / Soul meeting / Hallelujah I love her so / Blue genius / X-Ray blues / Love on my mind. *(UK-iss.Feb59 on 'London-Jazz'; LTZK 15146) <re-iss. 1961 as 'SOUL MEETING'; 1360> (UK-iss.Mar64 on 'London' mono/stereo; HAK/SHK 8045) (re-iss. 1973 & Jul76 on 'Atlantic') (d-cd-iss. May93)*

1958. (7") *<1180>* **YES INDEED. / I HAD A DREAM** –

1958. (lp) *<8025>* **YES INDEED!** –
– What would I do without you / It's all right / I want to know / Yes indeed / Got on the right track baby / Talkin' 'bout you / Swanee River rock / Lonely Avenue / Blackjack / The sun's gonna shine again / I had a dream / I want a little girl / Heartbreaker / Leave my woman alone. *(UK-iss.Mar59 on 'London'; HAE 2168) (re-iss. 1968 on 'Atlantic')*

1958. (7") *<1196>* **YOU BE MY BABY. / MY BONNIE** –

London Atlantic

Dec 58. (7",78) *(HLE 8768) <2006>* **ROCKHOUSE (part 1). / ROCKHOUSE (part 2)** 79

Feb 59. (7") *<2010>* **(THE NIGHT TIME IS) THE RIGHT TIME. / TELL ALL THE WORLD ABOUT YOU** – 95

May 59. (7") *<2022>* **THAT'S ENOUGH. / TELL ME, HOW YOU FEEL?** –

Jul 59. (7",78) *(HLE 8917) <2031>* **WHAT'D I SAY (part 1). / WHAT'D I SAY (part 2)** Jun59 6

Aug 59. (lp) *<8029>* **WHAT'D I SAY** –
– What'd I say (part 1&2) / Jumping in the mornin' / You be my baby / Tell me how you feel / What kind of man are you / Rock house (part 1&2) / Roll with my baby / Tell all the world about you / My Bonnie / That's enough. *(UK-iss.Mar60 on 'London'; HAE 2226) <US re-iss. Aug61, hit No.20> (re-iss. Oct69)*

Dec 59. (7",78) *(HLE 9009) <2043>* **I'M MOVIN' ON. / I BELIEVE TO MY SOUL** Oct59 40

Feb 60. (7") *(HLE 9058) <2047>* **LET THE GOOD TIMES ROLL. / DON'T LET THE SUN CATCH YOU CRYIN'** 78
Jan60 95

Feb 60. (lp) *<1312>* **THE GENIUS OF RAY CHARLES** – 17
– Let the good times roll / It had to be you / Alexander's ragtime band / Two years of torture / When your lover has gone / 'Deed I do / Just for a thrill / You won't let me go / Tell me you'll wait for me / Don't let the sun catch you cryin' / Am I blue? / Come rain or come shine. *(UK-iss.May60 on 'London'Jazz'; LTZK 15190) (cd-iss. Aug93)*

H.M.V. ABC Paramount

1960. (7") *<10081>* **WHO YOU GONNA LOVE? / MY BABY (I LOVE HER, YES I DO)** –

Aug 60. (7") *(POP 774) <10118>* **STICKS AND STONES. / WORRIED LIFE BLUES** Jun60 40

Oct 60. (lp) *(CLP 1387) <335>* **THE GENIUS HITS THE ROAD** Sep60 9
– Alabama bound / Georgia on my mind / Basin Street blues / Mississippi mud / Moonlight in Vermont / New York's my home / California, here I come / Moon over Miami / Deep in the heart of Texas / Carry me back to Old Virginny / Blue Hawaii / Chattanooga choo choo.

Oct 60. (7",78) *(POP 792) <10135>* **GEORGIA ON MY MIND. / CARRY ME BACK TO OLD VIRGINNY** 24 Sep60 1

Feb 61. (7") *(POP 825) <10164>* **RUBY. / HARDHEARTED HANNAH** 28
Nov60 55

May 61. (7") *(POP 838) <10141>* **THEM THAT GOT. / I WONDER** Jan61 58

H.M.V. Impulse!

Jun 61. (7") *<202>* **I'VE GOT NEWS FOR YOU. / I'M GONNA MOVE TO THE OUTSKIRTS OF TOWN** – 66
84

Jul 61. (7") *(POP 862) <200>* **ONE MINT JULEP. / LET'S GO** Feb61 8

Sep 61. (lp) *(CLP 1449) <355>* **DEDICATED TO YOU** Feb61 11
– Hardhearted Hannah / Nancy / Margie / Ruby / Rosetta / Stella by starlight / Cherry / Josephine / Candy / Marie / Diane / Sweet Georgia Brown.

Nov 61. (lp) *(CLP 1475) <2>* **GENUIS + SOUL = JAZZ** Mar61 4
– From the heart / I've got news for you / Moanin' / Let's go / One mint julep / I'm gonna move to the outskirts of town / Stompi' room only / Mister C / Strike up the band / Birth of the blues. *(re-iss. +c+cd.Sep89 on 'Essential') (re-iss. cd Jul95 on 'Actual Jazz')*

H.M.V. ABC Paramount

Oct 61. (7") *(POP 935) <10244>* **HIT THE ROAD JACK. / THE DANGER ZONE** 6 Sep61 1

Jan 62. (7") *(POP 969) <10244>* **UNCHAIN MY HEART. / BUT ON THE OTHER HAND BABY** 9
Nov61 72

Feb 62. (7"; by RAY CHARLES & BETTY CARTER) *<10298>* **BABY IT'S COLD OUTSIDE. / WE'LL BE TOGETHER AGAIN** – 91

Mar 62. (lp; by RAY CHARLES and BETTY CARTER) *(CLP 1520) <385>* **RAY CHARLES AND BETTY CARTER** Sep61 52
– Everytime we say goodbye / You and I / Intro; Goodbye / We'll be together again / People will say we're in love / Cocktails for two / Side by side / Baby it's cold outside / Together / For all we know / It takes twoo to tango / Alone together. *(re-iss. c+cd.Nov89 on 'Essential')*

Apr 62. (7") *(POP 1017) <10314>* **HIDE NOR HAIR. / AT THE CLUB** 20
Mar62 44

May 62. (lp) *(CLP 1580) <410>* **MODERN SOUNDS IN COUNTRY AND WESTERN MUSIC** 6 Apr62 1
– Bye bye love / You don't know me / Half as much / I love you so much it hurts / Just a little lovin' / Born to lose / Worried mind / It makes no difference now / You win again / Careless love / I can't stop loving you / Hey, good lookin'.

May 62. (7") *(POP 1034) <10330>* **I CAN'T STOP LOVING YOU. / BORN TO LOSE** 1 1
Apr62 41

Sep 62. (7") *(POP 1064) <10345>* **YOU DON'T KNOW ME. / CARELESS LOVE** 9 2
Jul62 60

Nov 62. (7") *(POP 1099) <10375>* **YOUR CHEATING HEART. / YOU ARE MY SUNSHINE** 13 29
7

Feb 63. (lp) *(CLP 1613) <435>* **MODERN SOUNDS IN COUNTRY AND WESTERN MUSIC VOL.2** 15 Oct62 2
– You are my sunshine / No letter today / Someday (you'll want me to want you)/ Don't tell me your troubles / Midnight / Oh, lonesome me / Take these chains from my heart / Your cheating heart / I'll never stand in your way / Making believe / Teardrops in my heart / Hang your head in shame.

Mar 63. (7") *(POP 1133) <10405>* **DON'T SET ME FREE. / THE BRIGHTEST SMILE IN TOWN** 37 20
Feb63 92

Apr 63. (lp) *(CLP 1626) <415>* **RAY CHARLES' GREATEST HITS** (compilation of hits) 16 Aug62 5

May 63. (7") *(POP 1161) <10435>* **TAKE THESE CHAINS FROM MY HEART. / NO LETTER TODAY** 5 Apr63 8

Jul 63. (7") *(POP 1202) <10453>* **NO ONE. / WITHOUT LOVE (THERE IS NOTHING)** 35 21
Jun63 29

Oct 63. (7") *(POP 1221) <10481>* **BUSTED. / MAKE BELIEVE** 21 Aug63 4

Oct 63. (lp) *(CLP 1678) <465>* **INGREDIENTS IN A RECIPE FOR SOUL** Aug63 9
– Busted / Where can I go / Born to the blue / That lucky old sun / Ol' man river / In the evening / A stranger in town / Ol' man time / Over the rainbow / You'll never walk alone. *(cd-iss. Jun95 on 'Personality') (re-iss. cd Jul95 on 'Actual Jazz')*

Jan 64. (7") *<10509>* **THAT LUCKY OLD SUN. / OL' MAN TIME** – 20

Jan 64. (7") *(POP 1251) THAT LUCKY OLD SUN. / MISSISSIPPI MUD* [ ] [–]

Mar 64. (7") *(POP 1272) <10530>* **BABY, DON'T YOU CRY. / MY HEART CRIES FOR YOU** [ ] [39]
Feb64 [38]

May 64. (lp) *(CLP 1728) <480>* **SWEET AND SOUR TEARS** [ ] Mar64 [9]
– Cry / Guess I'll hang my tears out to dry / A tear fell / No one to cry to / You've got me crying again / After my laughter came tears / Teardrops from my eyes / Don't cry baby / Cry me a river / Baby, don't you cry / Willow weep for me / I cried for you.

Jun 64. (7") *(POP 1315) <10557>* **MY BABY DON'T DIG ME. / SOMETHING'S WRONG** [ ] May64 [51]

Sep 64. (7") *(POP 1333) <10571>* **NO ONE TO CRY TO. / A TEAR FELL** [38] [50]
Jul64 [55]

Nov 64. (lp) *(CLP 1728) <495>* **HAVE A SMILE WITH ME** [ ] Aug64 [36]
– Smack dab in the middle / Feudin' and fightin' / Two ton Tessie / I never see Maggie alone / Move it on over / Ma (she's making eyes at me) / The thing / The man with the weird beard / The naughty lady of Shady Lane / Who cares (for me).

Nov 64. (7") *(POP 1350) <10588>* **SMACK DAB IN THE MIDDLE. / I WAKE UP CRYING** [ ] Sep64 [52]

Dec 64. (7") *<10609>* **MAKIN' WHOOPEE. / (instrumental)** [–] [46]

Jan 65. (7") *(POP 1383)* **MAKIN' WHOOPEE. / MOVE IT ON OVER** [42] [–]

Mar 65. (7") *(POP 1392) <10615>* **CRY. / TEARDROPS FROM MY EYES** [ ] [58]

Apr 65. (7") *(POP 1414)* **LIGHT OUT OF DARKNESS. / PLEASE FORGIVE & FORGET** [ ] [–]

Apr 65. (lp) *(CLP 1872) <500>* **RAY CHARLES LIVE IN CONCERT (live)** [ ] Feb65 [80]
– Opening (introduction) / Swing a little taste / I gotta woman / Margie / You don't know me / Hide nor hair / Baby, don't you cry / Makin' whoopee / Hallelujah I love her so / Don't set me free / What'd I say / Finale. *(cd-iss. Aug93)*

Apr 65. (7") *<10649>* **I GOTTA WOMAN (part 1). / I GOTTA WOMAN (part 2)** [–] [79]

May 65. (7") *<10663>* **WITHOUT A SONG (part 1) / WITHOUT A SONG (part 2)** [–] [ ]

Jul 65. (7") *(POP 1437)* **I GOTTA WOMAN. / WITHOUT A SONG** [ ] [–]

Aug 65. (7") *(POP 1457) <10700>* **I'M A FOOL TO CARE. / LOVE'S GONNA LIVE HERE** [ ] Jul65 [84]

Oct 65. (7") *(POP 1484) <10720>* **THE CINCINNATI KID. / THAT'S ALL I AM TO YOU** [ ] [ ]

Oct 65. (lp) *(CLP 1914) <520>* **COUNTRY AND WESTERN MEETS RHYTHM & BLUES** [ ] Aug65 [ ]
– Together again / I like to hear it sometime / I've got a tiger by the tail / Please forgive and forget / I don't care / Next door to the blues / Blue moon of Kentucky / Light out of darkness / Maybe it's nothing at all / All night long / Don't let her know / Watch it baby.

Dec 65. (7") *(POP 1502) <10739>* **CRYING TIME. / WHEN MY DREAMBOAT COMES HOME** [ ] [6]

Apr 66. (7") *(POP 1519) <10785>* **TOGETHER AGAIN. / YOU'RE JUST ABOUT TO LOSE YOUR CLOWN** [48] [19]
Mar66 [91]

May 66. (lp; mono/stereo) *(CLP/CSD 3533) <544>* **CRYING TIME** [ ] Mar66 [15]
– Crying time / No use crying / Let's go get stoned / Going down slow / Peace of mind / Tears / Drifting blues / We don't see eye to eye / You're in for a big surprise / You're just about to lose your crown / Don't you think I ought to know / You've got a problem.

H.M.V. ABC-TRC

Jun 66. (7") *(POP 1537) <10808>* **LET'S GO GET STONED. / THE TRAIN** [ ] May66 [31]

Sep 66. (7") *(POP 1551) <10840>* **I CHOSE TO SING THE BLUES. / HOPELESSLY** [ ] Aug66 [32]

Nov 66. (lp; mono/stereo) *(CLP/CSD 3574) <550>* **RAY'S MOODS** [ ] Sep66 [52]
– What-cha doing in there (I wanna know) / Please say you're fooling / By the light of the silvery Moon / You don't understand / Maybe it's because of love / Chitlins with candied yams / Granny wasn't grinning that day / She's lonesome again / Sentimental journey / A born loser / It's a man's world / A girl I used to know.

Nov 66. (7") *(POP 1556) <10865>* **PLEASE SAY YOU'RE FOOLING. / I DON'T NEED NO DOCTOR** [ ] [64]
[72]

— some of the above singles were cred. to RAY CHARLES & HIS ORCHESTRA

Mar 67. (7") *<10901>* **I WANT TO TALK ABOUT YOU. / PLEASE SAY YOU'RE FOOLING** [–] [98]

Apr 67. (7") *(POP 1589)* **YOU WIN AGAIN. / BYE BYE BYE** [ ] [–]

Jun 67. (7") *(POP 1595) <10938>* **HERE WE GO AGAIN. / SOMEBODY OUGHT TO WRITE A BOOK ABOUT IT** [38] May67 [15]

Sep 67. (lp; mono/stereo) *(CLP/CSD 3630) <595>* **RAY CHARLES INVITES YOU TO LISTEN** [ ] Jul67 [76]
– She's funny that way (I got a woman crazy for me) / How deep is the ocean (how high is the sky) / You made me love you (I didn't wanna do it) / Yesterday / I'll be seeing you / Here we go again / All for you / Love walked in / Gee, baby ain't I good to you / People.

Sep 67. (7") *(POP 1607) <10970>* **IN THE HEAT OF THE NIGHT. / SOMETHING'S GOT TO CHANGE** [ ] Aug67 [33]

Stateside ABC-TRC

Dec 67. (7") *(SS 2071) <11009>* **YESTERDAY. / NEVER HAD ENOUGH OF NOTHING YET** [44] Nov67 [25]

Mar 68. (7") *(SS 2099) <11045>* **THAT'S A LIE. / GO ON HOME** [ ] Feb68 [64]

Jul 68. (7") *(SS 2120) <11090>* **ELEANOR RIGBY. / UNDERSTANDING** [36] [35]
May68 [46]

Nov 68. (7") *(SS 2132) <11133>* **SWEET YOUNG THING LIKE YOU. / LISTEN, THEY'RE PLAYING OUR SONG** [ ] [83]
Aug68 [92]

Jan 69. (7"; as RAY CHARLES & JIMMY LEWIS) *<11170>* **IF IT WASN'T FOR BAD LUCK. / WHEN I STOP DREAMING** [–] [77]

Feb 69. (lp; stereo/mono) *(S+/SL 10269) <625>* **A PORTRAIT OF RAY** [ ] Apr68 [51]
– Eleanor Rigby / Am I blue / Never say naw / Sun died / Yesterday / When I stop dreaming / I won't leave / Sweet young thing like you / Bright lights and you girl / Understanding.

Mar 69. (7") *<11193>* **I'LL BE YOUR SERVANT. / I DIDN'T KNOW WHAT TIME IT WAS** [–] [ ]

May 69. (7") *<11213>* **LET ME LOVE YOU. / I'M SATISFIED** [–] [94]

Jul 69. (lp; stereo/mono) *(S+/SL 10281) <675>* **I'M ALL YOURS – BABY!** [ ] Mar69 [ ]
– Yours / I didn't know what the time was / Love is here to stay / Memories of you / Till the end of time / I had the craziest dream / Someday / Indian love call / I dream of you (more than you dream I do) / Gloomy Sunday

Sep 69. (7") *(SS 2155) <11239>* **WE CAN MAKE IT. / I CAN'T STOP LOVING YOU BABY** [ ] [ ]

Nov 69. (7") *<11251>* **CLAUDIE MAE. / SOMEONE TO WATCH OVER ME** [–] [ ]

Feb 70. (lp; stereo/mono) *(S+/SL 10293) <695>* **DOING HIS THING** [ ] Jul69 [ ]
– The same thing that can make you laugh (can make you cry) / Finders keepers, losers weepers / You ought to change your ways / Baby please / Come and get it / We can make it / I'm ready / That thing called love / If it wasn't for bad luck / I told you so.

Feb 70. (7") *<11259>* **LAUGHIN' AND CLOWNIN'. / THAT THING CALLED LOVE** [–] [98]

Tangerine Tangerine

May 71. (7"; as RAY CHARLES ORCHESTRA) *(6121 001)* *<1015>* **BOOTY BUTT (instrumental). / ZIG ZAG (instrumental)** [ ] Mar71 [36]

Jul 71. (lp) *(6495 001) <1512>* **MY KIND OF JAZZ** (instrumental) [ ] Jul70 [ ]
– Golden boy / Booty butt / This here / I remember Clifford / Sidewinder / Bluesette / Pas-se-o-ne blues / Zig zag / Senior blues.

Probe ABC-Tangerine

Oct 70. (7") *(SS 2170) <11271>* **TILL I CAN'T TAKE IT ANYMORE. / IF YOU WERE MINE** [ ] Sep70 [41]

Nov 70. (lp) *(SPB 1015) <707>* **LOVE COUNTRY STYLE** [ ] Aug70 [ ]
– f you were mine / Ring of fire / Your love is so doggone good / Don't change on me / Till I can't take it anymore / You've still got a place in my heart / I keep it hid / Sweet memories / Good morning dear / Show me the sunshine.

Mar 71. (7") *(PRO 524) <11219>* **DON'T CHANGE ON ME. / SWEET MEMORIES** [ ] [36]

Jul 71. (lp) *(SPB 1039) <726>* **VOLCANIC ACTION OF MY SOUL** [ ] May71 [52]
– See you then / What am I living for / Feel so bad / The long and winding road / The three bells / All I ever need is you / Wichita lineman / Something / I may be wrong (but I think you're wonderful) / Down in the valley.

Aug 71. (7") *<11308>* **FEEL SO BAD. / YOUR LOVE IS SO DOGGONE GOOD** [–] [68]

Oct 71. (7") *(PRO 539)* **THE LONG AND WINDING ROAD. / WICHITA LINEMAN** [ ] [–]

Dec 71. (7") *<11317>* **WHAT AM I LIVING FOR. / TIRED OF MY TEARS** [–] [54]

Jun 72. (7") *(PRO 566) <11329>* **LOOK WHAT THEY'VE DONE TO MY SONG, MA. / AMERICA THE BEAUTIFUL** [ ] [65]

Sep 72. (lp) *(SPB 1060) <755>* **A MESSAGE FROM THE PEOPLE** [ ] Apr72 [52]
– Lift every voice and sing / Seems like I gotta do wrong / Heaven help us all / There'll be no peace without all men as one / Hey mister / What have they done to my song, ma / Abraham, Martin and John / Take me home, country roads / Every Saturday night / America the beautiful.

Aug 72. (7") *<11337>* **HEY MISTER. / THERE'LL BE NO PEACE WITHOUT ALL MEN AS ONE** [–] [ ]

Jan 73. (7") *<11344>* **EVERY SATURDAY NIGHT. / TAKE ME HOME, COUNTRY ROADS** [–] [ ]

Feb 73. (lp) *(SPB 1066) <765>* **THROUGH THE EYES OF LOVE** [ ] Nov72 [ ]
– My first night alone without you / I can make it thru the days (but oh those lonely nights) / Someone to watch over me / A perfect love / If you wouldn't be my lady / You leave me breathless / Never ending song of love / Rainy night in Georgia.

May 73. (7") *<11351>* **I CAN MAKE IT THRU THE DAYS (BUT OH THOSE LONELY NIGHTS). / RING OF FIRE** [–] [81]

London Crossover

Nov 73. (7") *(HLU 10432) <973>* **COME LIVE WITH ME. / EVERYBODY SING** [ ] [82]

Jan 74. (7") *<974>* **LOUISE. / SOMEBODY** [–] [ ]

Apr 74. (lp) *(SHU 8467) <9000>* **COME LIVE WITH ME** [ ] Jan74 [ ]
– Till there was you / If you go away / It takes so little time / Somebody / Come live with me / Problems, problems / Louise / Where was he / Everybody sing.

Aug 75. (lp) *(SHU 8485) <9005>* **RENAISSANCE** [ ] Jun75 [ ]
– Living for the city / Then I'll be home / My God and I / We're gonna make it / For mama / Sunshine / Bein' green / Sail away.

Sep 75. (7") *<981>* **LIVING FOR THE CITY. / THEN I'LL BE HOME** [–] [91]

Sep 75. (7") *(HLU 10505)* **LIVING FOR THE CITY. / FOR MAMA** [ ] [–]

Jan 76. (7") *<985>* **AMERICA THE BEAUTIFUL. / SUNSHINE** [–] [ ]

London R.C.A.

Oct 76. (7"; by RAY CHARLES & CLEO LAINE) *(HLU 10541) <PB 10800>* **OH LAWD, I'M ON MY WAY. / OH BESS, WHERE'S MY BESS?** [ ] [ ]

Dec 76. (d-lp; by RAY CHARLES & CLEO LAINE) *(D 31-32) <1831>* **PORGY AND BESS** [ ] Nov76 [ ]
– Summertime (instrumental) / Summertime / My man's gone now / A woman is a sometimes thing / They pass by singing / What you want wild Bess / I got plenty o' nothin' (instrumental) / I got plenty o' nothing / Buzzard song / Bess, you is a woman / Oh doctor Jesus / Crab man's call / Here come de honey man / Strawberry woman's call / It ain't necessarily so (instrumental) / It ain't necessarily so / There's a boat dat's leaving for New York (instrumental) / There's a boat dat's leaving for New York / Oh Bess, oh where's my Bess? / Oh lawd I'm on my way.

London Atlantic

Jul 77. (7") *(HLU 10554)* **I CAN SEE CLEARLY NOW. / LET IT BE** [ ] [–]

Nov 77. (7") *<3443>* **I CAN SEE CLEARLY NOW. / ANONYMOUS LOVE** [–] [ ]

Jan 78. (lp) *(SHU 8509) <19142>* **TRUE TO LIFE** [ ] Nov77 [78]
– I can see clearly now / The jealous kind / Oh what a beautiful morning / How long has this been goin' on / Be my love / Anonymous love / Heavenly music / Game number nine / Let it be.

1978. (7") *<3473>* **A PEACE THAT WE NEVER COULD ENJOY. / GAME NUMBER NINE** [–] [ ]

1978. (7") *<3527>* **YOU FORGET YOUR MEMORY. / RIDING THUMB** [–] [ ]

Nov 78. (lp/c) *(SHU/KSACU1 8519) <19199>* **LOVE AND PEACE** [ ] [ ]
– Take off that dress / She knows / You 20th century fox / Riding thumb / We had it all / A peace that we never could enjoy / No achievement showing / Is there anyone out there / Give the poor man a break.

Dec 78. (7") *<3549>* **CHRISTMAS TIME. / THERE'LL BE NO PEACE WITHOUT ALL MEN AS ONE** [–] [ ]

Aug 79. (7") *<3611>* **SOME ENCHANTED EVENING. / YOU 20TH CENTURY FOX** [–] [ ]

Sep 79. (lp/c) *(SHU/KSAC1 8537) <19251>* **AIN'T IT SO** [ ] [ ]
– Some enchanted evening / Blues in the night / Just because / What'll I do / One of these days / Love me or set me free / Drift away / Love me tonight.

Nov 79. (7") *<3634>* **LOVE ME OR SET ME FREE. / JUST BECAUSE** [–] [ ]

Oct 80. (7"; by RAY CHARLES & CLINT EASTWOOD) *<49608>* **BEERS TO YOU (w/CLINT EASTWOOD). / COTTON-EYED CLINT (by the TEXAS OPERA COMPANY)** [–] [ ]
(above from the movie 'Any Which Way You Can' on 'Warners')

Dec 80. (7") *(HL 10579) <3762>* **COMPARED TO WHAT. / NOW THAT WE'VE FOUND EACH OTHER** [ ] [ ]

— in Oct'80, he issued SHAKE YOUR TALL FEATHER. / MINNIE THE MOOCHER with "CAB CALLOWAY")

C.B.S. Columbia

Mar 83. (7") *<03429>* **STRING BEAN. / BORN TO LOVE ME** [–] [ ]

Mar 83. (lp) *(CBS/40 25065) <38293>* **WISH YOU WERE HERE TONIGHT?** [ ] [ ]
– 3/4 times / Ain't your memory got no pride at all / I don't want no stranger sleepin' in my bed / Born to love me / Let your love flow / Shakin' your head / String bean / I Wish you were here tonight? / You've got the longest leaving act / You feel good all over. *(cd-iss. Apr90 on 'Pickwick')*

May 83. (7") *(CBS 3407)* **I WISH YOU WERE HERE TONIGHT. / YOU FEEL GOOD ALL OVER** [ ] [–]

1983. (7") *<03810>* **YOU FEEL GOOD ALL OVER. / 3/4 TIME** [–] [ ]

1983. (7") *<04083>* **AIN'T YOUR MEMORY GOT NO PRIDE AT ALL. / I DON'T WANT NO STRANGERS SLEEPING IN MY BED** [–] [ ]

1983. (7"; as RAY CHARLES with GEORGE JONES & CHET ATKINS) *<04297>* **I WISH YOU WERE HERE TONIGHT. / WE DIDN'T SEE A THING** [–] [ ]

1984. (7") *<04420>* **DO I EVER CROSS YOUR MIND. / THEY CALL IT LOVE** [–] [ ]

Jul 84. (lp/c) *(CBS/40 25764) <38990>* **DO I EVER CROSS YOUR MIND** [ ] [ ]
– I had it all / Do I ever cross your mind / Woman sensuous woman / Then I'll be over you / Lay around and love on you / Love of my life / They call it love / If I were you / Workin' man's woman / I was on Georgia time.

1984. (7") *<04500>* **WOMAN, SENSUOUS WOMAN. / I WAS ON GEORGIA TIME** [–] [ ]

Oct 84. (lp/c) *(CBS/40 26060) <39415>* **FRIENDSHIP** [ ] [75]
– Two old cats like us / This old heart / We didn't see a thing / Who cares / Rock and roll shoes / Friendship / It ain't gonna worry my mind / Little hotel room / Crazy old soldier / Seven Spanish angels.

1984. (7"; by RAY CHARLES with B.J. THOMAS) *<04531>* **ROCK AND ROLL SHOES. / THEN I'LL BE OVER YOU** [–] [ ]

Mar 85. (7"; by RAY CHARLES with WILLIE NELSON) *(CBS 4991) <04715>* **SEVEN SPANISH ANGELS. / WHO CARES (with JANE FRICKIE)** [ ] [ ]

1985. (7"; by RAY CHARLES with MICKEY GILLEY) *<04860>* **IT AIN'T GONNA WORRY MY MIND. / CRAZY OLD SOLDIER (with JOHNNY CASH)** [–] [ ]

1985. (7"; by RAY CHARLES with HANK WILLIAMS JR.) *<05575>* **TWO OLD CATS LIKE US. / LITTLE HOTEL ROOM (with MERLE HAGGARD)** [–] [ ]

Dec 85. (lp/c) *(CBS/40 26562) <40125>* **THE SPIRIT OF CHRISTMAS** [ ] [ ]
– What child is this / Little drummer boy / Santa Claus is coming to town / This time of the year / Rudolph the red-nosed reindeer / That spirit of Christmas / All I want for Christmas / Christmas in my heart / Winter wonderland / Christmas time.

Aug 86. (7") *<06172>* **THE PAGES OF MY MIND. / SLIP AWAY** [–] [ ]

Aug 86. (lp/c) *(CBS/40 26856) <40338>* **FROM THE PAGES OF MY MIND** [ ] [ ]
– The pages of my mind / Slip away / Anybody wit the blues / Class reunion / Caught a touch of your love / A little bit of Heaven / Dixie Moon / Over and over (again) / Beaucoup love / Love is worth the pain.

Nov 86. (7") *<06370>* **DIXIE MOON. / A LITTLE BIT OF HEAVEN** [–] [ ]

—— RAY was credited on BILLY JOEL's 'Baby Grand' 45 (Apr'87), then semi-retired from the music biz but continued acting mainly on 'Moonlighting' and 'St. Elsewhere'.

Sep 88. (lp/c/cd) *(461183-1/-4/-2) <40703>* **JUST BETWEEN US** [ ] [ ]
– Nothing like a hundred miles / I wish I'd never loved you at all / Too hard to love you / Now I don't believe that anymore / Let's call the whole thing off / Stranger in my own hometown / Over the top / I'd walk a little more for you / If that's what cha want / Save the bones for Henry Jones.

—— In the early 90's, he featured on QUINCY JONES + CHAKA KHAN's hit, 'I'll Be Good To You'.

WEA Warners

Oct 90. (cd/c/lp) *<2-/4-/1-26343>* **WOULD YOU BELIEVE?** [–] [ ]
– I'll take care of you / Your love keeps me satisfied / Ellie, my love / I can't get enough / Let's get back to where we left off / Child support, alimony / Fresh out of tears / Living without you / Where're the stairs? / Leave him!

Mar 93. (c-s) *<18611>* **A SONG FOR YOU / I CAN'T GET ENOUGH** [–] [ ]

Mar 93. (cd/c) *<(7599 26735-2/-4)>* **MY WORLD** [ ] [ ]
– My world / A song for you / None of us are free / So help me God / Let me take over / One drop of love / If I could / Love has a mind of its own / I'll be there / Still crazy after all these years.

—— BILLY PRESTON featured on keyboards

—— In Nov'93, RAY teamed up with INXS on their hit 'Please (You Got That . . .)'

Qwest Qwest

Feb 96. (cd) *<(9362 46107-2)>* **STRONG LOVE AFFAIR** [ ] Jan96 [ ]
– All she wants to do is love me / Say no more / No time to waste time / Angelina / Tell me what you want me to do / Strong love affair / Everybody's handsome child / Out of my life / The fever / Separate ways / I need a good woman bad / If you give me your heart.

XIII Bis Crossover

Nov 02. (cd) *(640281-2) <4000>* **THANKS FOR BRINGING LOVE AROUND AGAIN** [ ] Apr02 [ ]
– What'd I say (new version) / Can you love me like that / How did you feel the morning after / I love you more than I ever have / Really got a hold on me / Thanks for bringing love around again / Save your lovin' just for me / I just can't get enough of you / Ensemble / New Orleans / Mr. Creole / Mother.

– (selective) compilations, etc. –

Nov 60. (lp) *London; (HAK 2284) / Atlantic; <8039>* **RAY CHARLES IN PERSON (live)** [ ] Jul60 [13]
(re-iss. Apr69 on 'Atlantic') (below re-iss. Jan68)

Dec 60. (7") *London; (HLK 9251) / Atlantic; <2084>* **COME RAIN OR COME SHINE. / TELL ME YOU'LL WAIT FOR ME** [ ] [83]

Nov 61. (lp) *Atlantic; <8054>* **DO THE TWIST!** [–] [11]

Aug 62. (d-lp) *Atlantic; <900>* **THE RAY CHARLES STORY** [–] [14]

Mar 62. (lp) *London-Jazz; (LTZK 15238) / Atlantic; <8052>* **THE GENIUS SINGS THE BLUES** [ ] Nov61 [73]

Feb 63. (lp) *London; (HAK 8035) / Atlantic; <1369>* **THE GENIUS AFTER HOURS** [ ] Aug61 [49]

Mar 67. (d-lp) *ABC Paramount; <590>* **A MAN AND HIS SOUL** [–] [77]

Sep 68. (lp; stereo/mono) *Stateside; (S+/SL 10241)* **GREATEST HITS VOL.2** [24] [–]

Aug 80. (lp) *London; (RAYTV 1)* **HEART TO HEART – 20 RAY CHARLES' HOTTEST HITS** [29] [–]

Mar 90. (cd/c/lp) *Arcade; (RCL D/C/P 101)* **THE COLLECTION** [36] [–]
– Your cheatin' heart / Hit the road Jack / Georgia on my mind / Unchain my heart / One mint julep / Take these chains from my heart / I can't stop loving you / Busted / You are my sunshine / Making whoopee / Let's go get stoned / My heart cries for you / Feel so bad / The lucky old Sun / Smack dab in the middle / Crying time / If it wasn't for bad luck / In the heat of the night / Eleanor Rigby / Born to lose / No one / Hard hearted / Hannah / Yesterday.

Mar 93. (d-cd/d-c) *Arcade; (ARC 9464-2/-4)* **THE LIVING LEGEND** [48] [–]

Sep 98. (cd) *Atlantic; (7567 80865-2)* **AT NEWPORT** (remastered) [ ] [ ]

Aug 01. (d-cd/d-c) *Warner-ESP; <(8122 73556-2/-4)>* **THE DEFINITIVE RAY CHARLES** [13] [ ]

CHEAP TRICK

Formed: Rockford, Illinois, USA . . . 1972 by main writer RICK NIELSEN and TOM PETERSSON, who were part of The GRIM REAPERS prior to becoming FUSE. This brief early period only produced one self-titled album, before they enlisted the help of THOM MOONEY and ROBERT 'STEWKEY' ANTONI, fresh from (TODD RUNDGREN's) NAZZ. In 1972, they changed their moniker yet again, this time to The SICK MAN OF EUROPE, recruiting BUN E. CARLOS in place of the departing MOONEY. This primitive incarnation of CHEAP TRICK also saw the inclusion of new vocalist RANDY 'XENO' HOGAN, although after two years of steady touring he was replaced by ROBIN ZANDER. With the classic line-up now in place, the band secured a deal with 'Epic', releasing their eponymous debut album early in '77. Coming at a time of musical turbulence (new wave/punk had just arrived), the album failed to excite an interest from either critics or rock fans. More marketable was the band's highly original image, ZANDER and PETERSSEN the good-lookers, while CARLOS was the joker in the pack with his Tweedle-Dee/Dum attire (i.e. baseball cap, bow-tie and all-round eccentricity). Tours supporting KISS and QUEEN helped promote the band's off-the-wall appeal to a wider audience, the follow-up, 'IN COLOR' (also in '77) gaining healthy sales and a US Top 75 placing. The album featured the excellent 45, 'I WANT YOU TO WANT ME', a flop first time around, although a live equivalent subsequently made the US Top 10 in 1979. Following on from the success of their third studio album, 'HEAVEN TONIGHT' (1978), their harder-edged live set, 'AT BUDOKAN' turned their popularity in Japan into even greater commercial heights in America. The record struck platinum, hitting Top 5 in the process and making them virtual overnight international stars over the ensuing decade. Another Top 10'er, 'DREAM POLICE' (1979), consolidated their newfound fame, although this was nearly wrecked when The BEATLES-influenced CHEAP TRICK worked with the legendary GEORGE MARTIN on the album, 'ALL SHOOK UP'. PETERSSEN felt the strain and bailed out before their next album, 'ONE ON ONE' (1982), which had seen JON BRANDT come in as a replacement for the temporary PETE COMITA. In 1983, they employed the services of TODD RUNDGREN (who didn't!?) on their album of that year, 'NEXT POSITION PLEASE', which was a relative flop compared to the lofty chart heights of its predecessors. After a near return to form with the 1985 album, 'STANDING ON THE EDGE', they trawled a creative and commercial trough with 'THE DOCTOR'. Drastic measures were needed; PETERSSEN returned and the group drafted in outside writers to make 1988's 'LAP OF LUXURY' their most successful album of the decade. Of course, this was due in no small part to CHEAP TRICK achieving their first singles chart topper, 'THE FLAME'. Their AOR formula was utilised once more on their 1990 'BUSTED', although this was to be their last taste of major chart action for some time. The 1994 'Warner Brothers' set, 'WOKE UP WITH A MONSTER' saw the band attempting to recapture their heady 70's sound. Three years later, after a one-off for the seminal cult-indie label, 'Sub Pop', CHEAP TRICK released an eponymous set which dented the US Top 100. Come the end of the decade the band were in retrospective mood for a small series of residencies in various US cities, airing one of their first three albums in whole each night. A novel idea, and one which provided the material for 1999's 'MUSIC FOR HANGOVERS', a spirited live effort which offered few surprises but revealed an enthusiasm undimmed by the passing years. Longtime fans also lapped up 'SILVER' (2001), another live affair recorded at a special 25th anniversary homecoming show. In contrast to its predecessor, the record featured more obscure treats while the likes of SMASHING PUMPKINS' BILLY CORGAN and SLASH added a dash of celebrity appeal. • **Covered:** AIN'T THAT A SHAME (Fats Domino) / DON'T BE CRUEL (Elvis Presley) / DANCING THE NIGHT AWAY (Motors) / SPEAK NOW (Terry Reid) / MONEY (Barrett Strong) / MAGICAL MYSTERY TOUR (Beatles).

Album rating: CHEAP TRICK (*7) / IN COLOR (*6) / HEAVEN TONIGHT (*7) / AT BUDOKAN (*7) / DREAM POLICE (*5) / ALL SHOOK UP (*4) / ONE ON ONE (*5) / NEXT POSITION PLEASE (*4) / STANDING ON THE EDGE (*5) / THE DOCTOR (*3) / LAP OF LUXURY (*5) / BUSTED (*4) / THE GREATEST HITS compilation (*6) / BUDOKAN II early live (*5) / WOKE UP WITH A MONSTER (*4) / CHEAP TRICK on 'Red Ant' 1997 (*4) / Robin Zander: ROBIN ZANDER (*6)

FUSE

RICK NIELSEN (b.22 Dec'46, Rockford)– guitar / **JOE SUNBERG** – vocals / **CRAIG MYERS** – guitar / **TOM PETERSSON** (b. 9 May'50) – bass / **CHIP GREENMAN** – drums

not iss. Epic

Jul 68. (7") <5-10514> **HOUND DOG. / CRUISIN' FOR BURGERS** [–] [ ]
<originally-iss.Jun68 as GRIM REAPERS on 'Smack'; >

Jul 69. (lp) <26502> **FUSE** [–] [ ]
– Across the skies / Permanent rresident / Show me / To your health / In a window / 4-4 3-4 / Mystery ship / Sad day. *<cd-iss. 2001 on 'Rewind'+=; 55018>* – Hound dog / Cruisin' for burgers.

—— split soon after above **NIELSEN** and **PETERSSON** teamed up invariably as NAZZ and FUSE with ex-NAZZ members **ROBERT 'STEWKEY' ANTONI** – vocals / **THOM MOONEY** – drums

—— In '72 they became **The SICK MAN OF EUROPE** and moved to Philadelphia / **BUN E. CARLOS** (b.BRAD CARLSON, 12 Jun'51) – drums (ex-PAGANS) repl. MOONEY / **XENO** (r.n. RANDY HOGAN) – vocals repl. STEWKEY / **RICK SZELUGA** – bass repl. PETERSSON for a short while, until they became in '73 . . .

CHEAP TRICK

NIELSEN, PETERSSON, CARLOS and **XENO)**

—— Oct74 **ROBIN ZANDER** (b.23 Jan'53, Loves Park, Illinois) – vocals, guitar (ex-TOONS) repl. XENO who joined STRAIGHT UP

Epic Epic

Mar 77. (7") *<50375>* **OH CANDY. / DADDY SHOULD HAVE STAYED IN HIGH SCHOOL** [–] [ ]

Mar 77. (lp) *(EPC 81917) <34400>* **CHEAP TRICK** [ ] Jan77 [ ]
– Hot love / Speak now or forever hold your peace / He's a whore / Mandocello / The ballad of T.V. violence (I'm not the only boy) / Elo kiddies / Daddy should have stayed in high school / Taxman, Mr Thief / Cry cry / Oh Candy. *(re-iss. Nov81 lp/c; EPC/40 32070) <cd-iss. Jun88 on 'Collector's Choice'; EK 34400> (cd re-iss. Jul97; 487933-2) (cd re-iss. Oct98 on 'Columbia'; 491229-2)*

Nov 77. (7") *(EPC 5701) <50435>* **I WANT YOU TO WANT ME. / OH BOY (instrumental)** [ ] [ ]
(re-iss. Mar78; same)

Nov 77. (lp/c) *(EPC/40 82214) <34884>* **IN COLOR** [ ] Aug77 [73]
– Hello there / Big eyes / Downed / I want you to want me / You're all talk / Oh Caroline / Clock strikes ten / Southern girls / Come on, come on / So good to see you. *<cd-iss. Jun88 on 'Collector's Choice'; EK 34844> (cd-iss. Oct93 on 'Sony Europe'; 982833-2) (cd re-iss. Oct98 on 'Columbia'; 491230-2)*

Nov 77. (7") *<50485>* **SOUTHERN GIRLS. / YOU'RE ALL TALK** [–] [ ]

Mar 78. (7") *(EPC 6199)* **SO GOOD TO SEE YOU. / YOU'RE ALL TALK** [ ] [–]

May 78. (7") *(EPC 6394) <50570>* **SURRENDER. / AUF WIEDERSEHEN** [ ] [62]

May 78. (lp/c) *(EPC/40 82679) <35312>* **HEAVEN TONIGHT** [ ] [48]
– Surrender / On top of the world / California man / High roller / Auf wiedersehen / Takin' me back / On the radio / Heaven tonight / Stiff competition / How are you / Oh Claire. *(cd-iss. Sep93 on 'Sony Europe'; 982993-2) (cd re-iss. Oct98; 491231-2)*

Jul 78. (7") *(EPC 6427)* **CALIFORNIA MAN. / STIFF COMPETITION** [ ] [–]

Aug 78. (7") *<50625>* **CALIFORNIA MAN. / I WANT YOU TO WANT ME** [–] [ ]

Feb 79. (lp,yellow-lp/c) *(EPC/40 86083) <35795>* **AT BUDOKAN (live)** [29] [4]
– Hello there / Come on, come on / Look out / Big eyes / Need your love / Ain't that a shame / I want you to want me / Surrender / Goodnight now / Clock strikes ten. *(re-iss. as d-lp.Nov81' EPC 32595) (cd-iss. Feb86; CDEPC 86083) (re-iss. Jul91 on 'Essential' cd/c; ESS CD/MC 949)*

Feb 79. (7"; w-drawn) *(EPC 7144) <50814>* **VOICES (live). / SURRENDER (live)** [ ] Nov79 [32]

Mar 79. (7",7"orange) *(EPC 7258) <50680>* **I WANT YOU TO WANT ME (live). / CLOCK STRIKES TEN (live)** [29] [7]

Jul 79. (7") *(EPC 7724)* **SURRENDER (live). / AUF WIEDERSEHEN (live)** [ ] [–]

Sep 79. (7") *(EPC 7839) <50743>* **AIN'T THAT A SHAME (live). / ELO KIDDIES** [ ] Jul79 [35]

Sep 79. (lp/pic-lp/c) *(EPC/11/40 83522) <35773>* **DREAM POLICE** [41] [6]
– Dream police / Way of the world / The house is rockin' (with domestic problems) / Gonna raise Hell / I'll be with you tonight / Voices / Writing on the wall / I know what I want / Need your love.

Oct 79. (7") *(EPC 7880) <50744>* **DREAM POLICE. / HEAVEN TONIGHT** [ ] Sep79 [26]

Jan 80. (7") *(EPC 8114)* **WAY OF THE WORLD. / OH CANDY** [73] [–]

Mar 80. (7"ep) *(EPC 8335)* **I'LL BE WITH YOU TONIGHT. / HE'S A WHORE / SO GOOD TO SEE YOU** [ ] [–]

Apr 80. (7") *<50887>* **EVERYTHING WORKS IF YOU LET IT. / WAY OF THE WORLD** [–] [44]

Jul 80. (7") *(EPC 8755)* **EVERYTHING WORKS IF YOU LET IT. / HEAVEN TONIGHT** [ ] [–]

Oct 80. (7") *(EPC 9071) <50942>* **STOP THIS GAME. / WHO D'KING** [ ] [48]

Oct 80. (lp/c) *(EPC/40 86124) <36498>* **ALL SHOOK UP** [ ] [24]
– Stop this game / Just got back / Baby loves to rock / Can't stop it but I'm gonna try / World's greatest lover / High Priest of rhythmic noise / Love comes a-tumblin' down / I love you honey but I hate your friends / Go for the throat (use your own imagination) / Who d'king. *<cd-iss. Jun88 on 'Collector's Choice'; EK 36498>*

Jan 81. (7") *(EPC 9502)* **WORLD'S GREATEST LOVER. / HIGH PRIEST OF RHYTHMIC NOISE** [ ] [ ]

—— **PETE COMITA** (b. Italy) – bass repl. PETERSSON who formed own group with his wife

Aug 81. (7") *<47187>* **REACH OUT. / I MUST BE DREAMING** [–] [ ]

—— (above single from the film 'Heavy Metal'. issued on 'Full Moon-Asylum') now alongside **NIELSEN** (some bass), **ZANDER + CARLOS**

—— (late '81) **JON BRANT** (b.20 Feb'54) – bass (on three songs) repl. COMITA

May 82. (7") *(EPCA 2406) <02968>* **IF YOU WANT MY LOVE. / FOUR LETTER WORD** [57] [45]

May 82. (lp,red-lp/pic-lp/c) *(EPC/11/40 85740) <38021>* **ONE ON ONE** [95] [39]
– I want you / One on one / If you want my love / Oo la la la / Lookin' out for number one / She's tight / Time is runnin' / Saturday at midnight / Love's got a hold on me / I want be man / Four letter word. *(re-iss. Jun85; EPC 32654)*

Sep 82. (7") *<03233>* **SHE'S TIGHT. / ALL I REALLY WANT TO DO** [–] [65]

Aug 83. (7") *<04078>* **DANCING THE NIGHT AWAY. / DON'T MAKE OUR LOVE A CRIME** [–] [ ]

Sep 83. (lp/c) *(EPC/40 25490) <38794>* **NEXT POSITION PLEASE** [ ] [61]
– I can't take it / Borderline / I don't love her anymore / Next position please / Younger girls / Dancing the night away / 3-D / You say jump / Y.O.Y.O.Y. / Won't take no for an answer / Heaven's falling / Invaders of the heart. *<US c+=/cd+=>* – You take too much / Don't make our love a crime.

Sep 83. (12"ep) *(EPCTA 3743)* **DANCING THE NIGHT AWAY / AIN'T THAT A SHAME. / I WANT YOU TO WANT ME / SURRENDER** [ ] [–]

Nov 83. (7") *<04216>* **I CAN'T TAKE IT. / YOU TALK TOO MUCH** [–] [ ]

Feb 84. (7") *<29723>* **SPRING BREAK. / GET READY** [–] [ ]
(above from the film 'Spring Break', issued on 'Warner Bros')
(below issued on 'Pasha' US)

1984. (7") *<04392>* **UP THE CREEK. / (other artist)** –

Sep 85. (7") *(A 6390) <05431>* **TONIGHT IT'S YOU. / WILD WOMEN** Jul85 44
(12"+=) *(EPCTX 6390)* – I want you to want me / If you want my love.

Oct 85. (lp/c) *(EPC/40 26374) <39592>* **STANDING ON THE EDGE** Aug85 35
– Little sister / Tonight it's you / She's got motion / Love comes / How about you / Standing on the edge / This time around / Rock all night / Cover girl / Wild wild women.

Jun 86. (7") *<06137>* **MIGHTY WINGS. / (other artist)** –

Nov 86. (lp/c) *(EPC/40 57087) <40405>* **THE DOCTOR** Oct86
– It's up to you / Rearview mirror romance / The doctor / Are you lonely tonight / Name of the game / Kiss me red / Take me to the top / Good girls go to heaven (bad girls go everywhere) / Man-u-lip-u-later / It's only love. *(cd-iss. May87; CDEPC 57087)*

Nov 86. (7") *<06540>* **IT'S ONLY LOVE. / NAME OF THE GAME** –

—— TOM PETERSSON – bass, vocals returned to repl. BRANT

May 88. (7"/7"sha-pic-d) *(651466-7/-0) <07745>* **THE FLAME. / THROUGH THE NIGHT** Apr88 1
(12"+=/cd-s+=) *(EPC 651466-6/-2)* – I want you to want me / If you want my love. *<re-iss. Dec88; 73792>*

May 88. (lp/c/cd) *(460782-1/-4/-2) <40922>* **LAP OF LUXURY** 18
– Let go / No mercy/ The flame / Space / Never had a lot to lose / Don't be cruel / Wrong side of love / All we need is a dream / Ghost town / All wound up. *(re-iss. cd Oct93 on 'Sony Europe'; 982839-2)*

Aug 88. (7"/7"sha-pic-d) *(652896-7/-0) <07965>* **DON'T BE CRUEL. / I KNOW WHAT I WANT** Jul88 4
(12"+=/cd-s+=) *(652896-6/-2)* – California man / Ain't that a shame.
(3"cd-s+=) *(653005-3)* – Dream police / Way of the world.

Oct 88. (7"/c-s) *<08097>* **GHOST TOWN. / WRONG SIDE OF LOVE** – 33

Jan 89. (7"/c-s) *<68563>* **NEVER HAD A LOT TO LOSE. / ALL WE NEED IS A DREAM** – 75

—— In Feb89, ZANDER dueted with Heart's ANN WILSON on US Top 10 single 'SURRENDER TO ME'.

Aug 90. (7"/c-s) *(656148-7/-4) <73444>* **CAN'T STOP FALLIN' INTO LOVE. / YOU DRIVE, I'LL STEER** Jul90 12
(12"+=/cd-s+=) *(656148-6/-2)* – The flame.

Sep 90. (cd/c/lp) *(466876-2/-4/-1) <46013>* **BUSTED** Jul90 48
– Back 'n blue / I can't understand it / Wherever would I be / If you need me / Can't stop falling into love / Busted / Walk away / You drive, I'll steer / When you need someone / Had to make you mine / Rock'n'roll tonight.

Sep 90. (7"/c-s; w-drawn) *<73566>* **IF YOU NEED ME. / BIG BANG** –

Oct 90. (7"/c-s) *<73580>* **WHEREVER WOULD I BE. / BUSTED** – 50

Oct 91. (cd/c) *(469086-2/-4) <48681)* **THE GREATEST HITS** (compilation)
– Magical mystery tour / Dream police / Don't be cruel / Tonight it's you / She's tight / I want you to want me (live) / If you want my love / Ain't that a shame / Surrender / The flame / I can't take it / Can't stop fallin' into love / Voices *(re-iss. May94; same)*

—— ROBIN ZANDER issued an eponymous solo set in '93

Warners Warners

Mar 94. (cd/c) *<(9362 45425-2/-4)>* **WOKE UP WITH A MONSTER**
– My gang / Woke up with a monster / You're all I wanna do / Never run out of love / Didn't know I had it / Ride the pony / Girlfriends / Let her go / Tell me everything / Cry baby / Love me for a minute.

Sub Pop Sub Pop

Mar 97. (7") *<(SP 393)>* **BABY TALK. / BRONTOSAURUS**

Red Ant Red Ant

Jun 97. (cd-ep) *<(RAAX 1001)>* **SAY GOODBYE / YEAH YEAH / VOICES (live) / SURRENDER (live)**

Jun 97. (cd) *<(RAACD 002)>* **CHEAP TRICK** Apr97 99
– Anytime / Hard to tell / Carnival game / Shelter / You let a lotta people down / Baby no more / Yeah yeah / Say goodbye / Wrong all along / Eight miles low / It all comes back to you.

Cheap Trick Cheap Trick

Jul 99. (cd) *<(CTU 20001)>* **MUSIC FOR HANGOVERS (live)** Jun99
– Oh Claire / Surrender / Hot love / I can't take it / I want you to want me / Taxman, Mr. Thief / Mandocello / Oh Caroline / How are you? / If you want my love / Dream police / So good to see you / The ballad of TV violence (I'm not the . . .) / Gonna raise hell.

not iss. J.V.C.

Feb 01. (d-cd) *<2001>* **SILVER (live August 28, 1999)** – Japan –
– Ain't that a shame / I want you to want me / Oh, Candy / That 70's song / Voices / If you want my love / She's tight / Can't stop fallin' into love / Gonna raise hell / I can't take it / It all comes back to you / Tonight it's you / Time will let you know / World's greatest lover / The flame / Stop this game / Dream police / I know what I want / Woke up with a monster / Never had a lot to lose / You're all talk / I'm losin' you / Hard to tell / Oh Claire / Surrender / Just got back / Day tripper / Who d'king.

– compilations etc. –

Apr 80. (10"m-lp) *Epic; <36453>* **FOUND ALL THE PARTS (rare '76-'79)** – 39
– Day tripper (live) / Can't hold on / Such a good girl / Take me I'm yours.

Oct 91. (cd/c) *Castle; (CCS CD/MC 309)* **THE COLLECTION** –

Feb 94. (cd) *Epic; <EK 53308>* **BUDOKAN II (live)** –

Aug 96. (4xcd-box) *Columbia; <(E4K 649384)>* **SEX, AMERICA, CHEAP TRICK**
(re-iss. Oct01 on 'Sony'; 504493-2)>

May 98. (d-cd) *Columbia; (489650-2) <65527>* **AT THE BUDOKAN – THE COMPLETE CONCERT** Apr98

Nov 98. (cd) *Sony; <2820>* **DON'T BE CRUEL** –

Sep 00. (cd) *Epic; (499660-2)* **CHEAP TRICK / IN COLOR** –

Oct 00. (cd) *Epic; (499677-2) <66015>* **THE AUTHORISED GREATEST HITS**

CHEMICAL BROTHERS

Formed: North London, England . . . 1989 by DJ's ED SIMONS and TOM ROWLANDS (the latter had been part of 'Deconstruction' act, ARIEL, who released one single, 'ROLLERCOASTER'). The pair had met at Manchester University, and, discovering a shared love of techno and classic hip hop, they set about creating their own club night, 'NAKED UNDER LEATHER'. The logical next step was to cut their own record and with 'SONG TO THE SIREN', they successfully blended their myriad influences into an abrasive chunk of freak-beat techno. Wildly impressed, 'Junior Boys Own' maestro ANDY WEATHERALL released the single in early 1993, the more discerning underground D.J.'s of the time caning the track at club nights across the country. The record was credited to The DUST BROTHERS, the name SIMONS and ROWLANDS assumed for their DJ work. Later the same year, they released the 'Fourteenth Century Sky' EP which included the definitive 'CHEMICAL BEATS'. 'MY MERCURY MOUTH' from the 1994 EP of the same name was equally impressive and by this point the DUST BROTHERS had become one of the hippest name-drops among the dance cognoscenti. Their seminal reworking of SAINT ETIENNE's 'Like A Motorway', together with a DJ spot on PRIMAL SCREAM's 1994 tour further increased their profile and it wasn't long before the major record labels came sniffing round. Signing to 'Virgin', they released 'LEAVE HOME' in 1995, following it up with the top ten debut album, 'EXIT PLANET DUST'. The duo were now trading under the moniker of The CHEMICAL BROTHERS following objections from The DUST BROTHERS (U.S), a highly rated hip hop production team (Responsible for the BEASTIE BOYS' classic, 'Paul's Boutique'). For the most part, the debut was an unrelenting, exhilarating, rollercoaster ride of breakbeat techno, only letting up on 'ALIVE: ALONE' (featuring a BETH ORTON vocal) and the TIM BURGESS (of CHARLATANS fame) collaboration, 'LIFE IS SWEET'. The 'LOOPS OF FURY EP' was as uncompromising as the title suggests while the 'SETTING SUN' (featuring NOEL GALLAGHER on vocals) single gave the CHEMICALS' their first No.1 later that year. The track featured a 'TOMORROW NEVER KNOWS'-style rhythm pattern, the follow-up album, 'DIG YOUR

OWN HOLE' (1997), similarly psychedelic in its reach. Using samples from 60's theramin pioneers LOTHAR AND THE HAND PEOPLE, and featuring a guest spot from MERCURY REV's JONATHAN DONOHUE, the album was more thrillingly diverse than the debut. With a mindbending live show, universal critical acclaim and even a burgeoning Stateside career, The CHEMICAL BROTHERS could do no wrong. After initiating their own record label, 'Freestyle Dust' (which released DJ-styled set, 'BROTHER'S GONNA WORK IT OUT'), ROWLANDS and SIMONS were back with a third album, 'SURRENDER' (1999). Featuring guest vocals by NOEL GALLAGHER (on Top 10 hit, 'LET FOREVER BE'), BERNARD SUMNER (on 'OUT OF CONTROL'), BOBBY GILLESPIE (on 'UNDER THE INFLUENCE'), HOPE SANDOVAL (on 'ASLEEP FROM DAY') and JONATHAN DONAHUE (on 'DREAM ON'), the album crashed into the charts at No.1 and even cracked America by making the Top 40. Following in the back to basics vein of the 'MUSIC RESPONSE' EP, 2002's 'COME WITH US' was the sound of The 'BROTHERS stepping off the celebrity podium. Or at least stepping off long enough to concoct the kind of heavy duty science which made them so great in the first place. While the by now predictable guest slots from the likes of BETH ORTON and RICHARD ASHCROFT threatened to dilute the album's overall impact, the sonic momentum of tracks such as 'GALAXY BOUNCE' and 'IT BEGAN IN AFRIKA' carried it off blindingly. More interesting was the FLAMING LIPS collaboration featured on 'SINGLES 93-03' (2003), a collection which could've been more sympathetically curated. • **Songwriters:** ROWLANDS-SIMONS except samples of Blake Baxters 'Brothers Gonna Work It Out' on 'LEAVE HOME'. Borrowed SWALLOW's; 'Peekaboo' & 'Follow Me Down'.

Album rating: EXIT PLANET DUST (*9) / DIG YOUR OWN HOLE (*9) / SURRENDER (*8) / COME WITH US (*7) / SINGLES 93-03 compilation (*8)

DUST BROTHERS

TOM ROWLANDS (b.11 Jan'71, Kingston upon Thames, Surrey, England) – keyboards / **ED SIMONS** (b. 9 Jun'70, Oxford, England) – synthesizers, etc

Junior Boys Own | not iss.

1993. (12") *(JBO 10)* **SONG TO THE SIREN. / SONG TO THE SIREN (Sabres Of Paradise mixes)** [ ] [–]

1993. (12"ep) *(COLLECT 004)* **FOURTEENTH CENTURY SKY EP** [ ] [–]
– Chemical beats / One too many mornings / Dope coil / Her jazz.
(above issued on 'Boys Own')

May 94. (12"ep) *(JBO 20)* **MY MERCURY MOUTH EP** [ ] [–]
– My mercury mouth / If you kling to me I'll klong to you / Dust-up beats.

CHEMICAL BROTHERS

TOM ROWLANDS + **ED SIMONS** with voices by **TIM BURGESS** (CHARLATANS) + **BETH ORTON** (solo artist)

Virgin | AstralWerks

Jun 95. (12") *(CHEMST 1) <6167>* **LEAVE HOME (Sabres Of Paradise mix). / LET ME IN MATE** [17] Sep95 [ ]
(12") *(CHEMSTX 1)* – ('A'-Underworld mixes).
(cd-s) *(CHEMSD 1)* – (all above except 'Let Me In Mate')

Jun 95. (cd/c/d-lp) *(XDUST CD/MC/LP 1) <6157>* **EXIT PLANET DUST** [9] Aug95 [ ]
– Leave home / In dust we trust / Song to he siren / Three little birdies down beats / Fuck up beats / Chemical beats / Chico's groove / One too many mornings / Life is sweet / Playground for a wedgeless firm / Alive alone.

Aug 95. (12") *(CHEMSD 2)* **LIFE IS SWEET. / ('A'-Daft Punk remix) / ('A'-remix 1) / ('A'-remix 2)** [25] [–]
(cd-s) *(CHEMSD 2)* – ('A'-remix 1, repl.by) Leave home (terror drums).
(cd-s) *(CHEMSDX 2)* – ('A'remix 1) / If you kling to me I'll klong to you / Chico's groove (mix 2).

Jan 96. (12"ep/cd-ep) *(CHEMS T/D 3) <6174>* **LOOPS OF FURY EP** [13] [ ]
– Chemical beats (Dave Clarke remix) / Loops of fury / (The best part of) Breaking up / Get up on it like this.

Oct 96. (c-s/12"/cd-s) *(CHEMS C/T/D 4) <6187>* **SETTING SUN. / ('A'extended & instrumental mixes) / BUZZ TRACKS** [1] Jan97 [80]
above featured NOEL GALLAGHER (Oasis) on vocals/ co-writer

Mar 97. (12"/cd-s) *(CHEMS T/D 5) <6195>* **BLOCK ROCKIN' BEATS. / PRESCRIPTION BEATS / MORNING LEMON** [1] [ ]
(cd-s) *(CHEMSDX 5)* – ('A'mixes).

Apr 97. (cd/c/d-lp) *(XDUST CD/MC/LP 2) <6180>* **DIG YOUR OWN HOLE** [1] [14]
– Block rockin' beats / Dig your own hole / Elektrobank / Piku / Setting sun / It doesn't matter / Don't stop the rock / Get up on it like this / Lost in the k-hole / Where do I begin / The private psychedelic reel.

Sep 97. (12") *(CHEMST 6) <6204>* **ELEKTROBANK. / NOT ANOTHER DRUGSTORE / ('A'-Dust Brothers remix)** [17] [ ]
(cd-s+=) *(CHEMSD 6)* – Don't stop the rock (electronic version).
(cd-s+=) *(CHEMSDX 6)* – These seats are made for breakin'.

Dec 97. (ltd;12"/cd-s) *(CHEMS T/DX 7)* **THE PRIVATE PSYCHEDELIC REEL. / SETTING SON (live)** [ ] [–]

Sep 98. (cd/c) *(XDUST CDX 101) <6243>* **BROTHER'S GONNA WORK IT OUT: A DJ REMIX ALBUM** [7] [95]

May 99. (c-s/12"/cd-s) *(CHEMS C/D/T 8)* **HEY BOY HEY GIRL. / FLASHBACK / SCALE** [3] [ ]

Jun 99. (cd/c/lp) *(XDUST CD/MC/LP 4) <47610>* **SURRENDER** [1] [32]
– Music: response / Under the influence / Out of control / Orange wedge / Let forever be / The sunshine underground / Asleep from day / Got glint? / Hey boy hey girl / Surrender / Dream on.

Aug 99. (7"/c-s) *(CHEMS LH/C 9)* **LET FOREVER BE. / ('A'-album version)** [9] [ ]
(12"/cd-s) *(CHEMS T/D 9)* – ('A'side) / Diamond sky / Studio K.

Oct 99. (c-s/cd-s) *(CHEMS C/D 10)* **OUT OF CONTROL / POWER MOVE / OUT OF CONTROL (Sasha remix)** [21] [ ]
(12") *(CHEMST 10)* – ('A'mixes).

Nov 00. (cd-ep) *<VIR 38751>* **MUSIC: RESPONSE EP** [–] [ ]
– Music: response / Freak of the week / Enjoyed / Music: response / Music: response / Out of control / Got glint?

Sep 01. (c-s) *(CHEMSC 12) <ASW 38798>* **IT BEGAN IN AFRIKA / IT BEGAN IN AFRIKA (extended)** [8] Oct01 [ ]
(12"+=/cd-s+=) *(CHEMS T/D 12)* – Hot acid rhythm 1.

Jan 02. (12") *(CHEMST 14)* **STAR GUITAR. / STAR GUITAR (Pete Heller expanded)** [8] [–]
(cd-s) *(CHEMSD 14)* – ('A'-edit) / Base 6.

Jan 02. (cd/d-lp) *(XDUST CD/LP 5) <11682>* **COME WITH US** [1] [32]
– Come with us / It began in Afrika / Galaxy bounce / Star guitar / Hoops / My elastic eye / The state we're in (with BETH ORTON) / Denmark / Pioneer skies / The test (with RICHARD ASHCROFT). *(extra cd; XDUSTCDX 5)*

Apr 02. (12") *(CHEMST 15)* **COME WITH US. / H.I.A.** [14] [–]
(cd-s) *(CHEMSD 15)* – ('A'edit) / The test (edit) / ('A'-Fatboy Slim remix).

Sep 03. (12"; by CHEMICAL BROTHERS / FLAMING LIPS) *(CHEMST 18)* **THE GOLDEN PATH. / NUDE NIGHT** [17] [–]
(cd-s+=) *(CHEMSD 18)* – ('A'-Ewan Pearson extended vocal mix).

Sep 03. (cd/4xlp) *(XDUST CD/LP 6) <93142>* **SINGLES 93-03** (compilation) [9] [ ]
– Song to the siren / Chemical beats / Leave home / Setting sun (with NOEL GALLAGHER) / Block rockin' beats / The private psychedelic reel / Hey boy hey girl / Let forever be / Out of control / Star guitar / The test / Get yourself high / The golden path (with FLAMING LIPS). *(d-cd+=; XDUSTCDX 6)* – Not another drugstore (Planet Nine remix with ONE INCH PUNCH) / The duke / If you kling to me I'll klong to you / Otter rock / Morning lemon / Galaxy bounce / Loops of fury / Delik / Elektrobank (live from the Roxy NYC November 1996) / Under the influence (mix 2) / Piku playground (live).

– collections, etc. –

Oct 02. (d-cd) *Freestyle Dust; (812901-2)* **DIG YOUR OWN HOLE / EXIT PLANET DUST** [ ] [–]

CHER

Born: CHERILYN SARKASIAN LA PIER, 20 May'46, El Centro, California, USA. Relocating to L.A. in her late teens, the would-be actress fell in with SONNY BONO and had her first taste of the music business singing backup on PHIL SPECTOR sessions, the production maestro subsequently issuing her BEATLES tribute, 'RINGO I LOVE YOU' on his own 'Annette' label in 1964. She married BONO the same year and the pair proceeded to cut a handful of unsuccessful duets as CAESAR & CLEO for the small 'Vault' imprint. Playing alongside British invasion acts like The DAVE CLARK FIVE and HERMAN'S HERMITS, the duo were eventually picked up by 'Reprise' for a couple of singles, 'JUST YOU' and 'BABY DON'T GO'. These flopped upon initial release and the couple (renamed SONNY and CHER) moved on to 'Atco' where they hit paydirt in summer '65 with 'I GOT YOU BABE', a transatlantic No.1 marrying the cutesy pop appeal of the SPECTOR era to the new folk-rock sensibility of hip Hollywood. Decked out in garish hippie garb, the incongruous couple became the love generation darlings of Sunset Strip and 'Imperial' signed up CHER for a solo deal. Although her debut (as CHERILYN), 'DREAM BABY' had stiffed earlier in the year, her cover of Bob Dylan's 'ALL I REALLY WANT TO DO' competed with The BYRDS' version of the same song that summer while her Top 20 (Top 10 UK) album of the same name featured yet more DYLAN material. Meanwhile, the SONNY & CHER album, 'LOOK AT US' (1965) narrowly missed the US No.1 spot and over the course of the ensuing decade or so, CHER attempted (not always successfully) to maintain a solo career in tandem with her SONNY partnership. Her predeliction for cringeing puns was revealed with 'THE SONNY SIDE OF CHER' (1966), an album that spawned one of her biggest solo hits (transatlantic No.3), 'BANG BANG (MY BABY SHOT ME DOWN). 1966-67 proved rockier but CHER was back in the Top 10 in 1968 with 'YOU BETTER SIT DOWN KIDS'. This signalled the end of her tenure with 'Imperial' and she moved on to 'Atco' for a commercially bleak couple of years before her early-mid 70's revival. Her success with SONNY followed the same pattern and after 1967's 'THE BEAT GOES ON', it'd be a further four years before the duo racked up another Top 10 hit with 'ALL I EVER NEED IS YOU'. By this point both had signed to 'Kapp' ('M.C.A.' in Britain), churning out rubbish like 'A COWBOY'S WORK IS NEVER DONE'. The latter proved to be their last Top 10 hit and after a final couple of singles on 'Warners', the couple ended both their creative and marital partnership, divorcing on the 26th of June 1974. CHER's solo career, meanwhile, had been rekindled with a 1971 US No.1 hit, 'GYPSYS, TRAMPS & THIEVES', her charismatic half-Cherokee identity melodramatically stamped over further No.1's, 'HALF-BREED' and 'DARK LADY'. A matter of days after her divorce from BONO she married GREG ALLMAN with whom she recorded the execrable 'ALLMAN AND WOMAN: TWO THE HARD WAY' (1977). Her critical stock was hardly improved with her opportunistic disco effort, 'TAKE ME HOME' (1979) although it did put her back in the US Top 10. Newly signed to decadent disco/KISS stronghold, 'Casablanca', CHER followed up with an attempt at heavy rock/metal the following year with the 'BLACK ROSE' album (also billed as BLACK ROSE). By this point she'd divorced ALLMAN and was dating ex-STEVE MILLER BAND guitarist, LES DUDEK, who both played on and produced the latter set. Unsurprisingly it sank without trace and CHER moved on once more to 'Columbia' where she cut one album, 'I PARALYZE'(!), before turning her attention to film work. Although she was a veteran of the TV chat show (having hosted both a SONNY & CHER and solo version in the 60's/70's), a Broadway appearance in Robert Altman's 'Come Back To The Five And Dime, Jimmy Dean, Jimmy Dean' led to roles in 80's movies like 'Silkwood', 'Mask', 'Witches Of Eastwick', 'Moonstruck' (for which she netted an Oscar) and 'Suspect'. With her profile sufficiently raised, the mainstream late 80's resurgence of soft rock/AOR/metal was a perfect vehicle for CHER's commercial comeback; newly signed to 'Geffen', she hit the Top 10 in 1987 with "power-ballad", 'I FOUND SOMEONE'. A US Top 10 duet with PETER CETERA, 'AFTER ALL', spurred on the success of 1989's 'HEART OF STONE' album and its US Top 3 hit, 'IF I COULD TURN BACK TIME'. More tortuous Top 10 torch balladry followed with 'JUST LIKE JESSE JAMES' although CHER saved her most cloying material 'til last; taken from the film, 'Mermaids' (in which she starred), 'THE SHOOP SHOOP SONG (IT'S IN HIS KISS)' gave CHER her first solo UK No.1 in 1991. Tacked onto the 'LOVE HURTS' (1991) album, the song's massive popularity even pushed the album itself to No.1 and CHER enjoyed a British popularity previously unwitnessed. A 1992 greatest hits set gave her another UK No.1 while a reworking of 'I GOT YOU BABE' with the inimitable BEAVIS & BUTT-HEAD proved she at least had a sense of humour under all the histrionics. She was back at No.1 again in 1995 alongside CHRISSIE HYNDE, NENEH CHERRY and ERIC CLAPTON with the Comic Relief charity song, 'LOVE CAN BUILD A BRIDGE'. A year later, her comeback set, 'IT'S A MAN'S WORLD', stalled at No.10 and faired even worse in the States. Tragedy was to strike early in '98 (January 5th) when her ex-husband and recently elected politician SONNY BONO died instantly after hitting a tree during a skiing trip. Later that year, CHER was to gain some consolation when she scored a massive best-selling UK No.1 with 'BELIEVE' (later to do the same in America). If Christmas 1999's greatest hits set didn't convince you then 'LIVING PROOF' (2001) was indeed, er, living proof that the evergreen CHER has got more than a little music biz mileage left in her yet. She may have a few years on MADONNA but the club-friendly grooves confirmed her newest incarnation as dance-pop diva. • **Covered:** BLOWIN' IN THE WIND + LIKE A ROLLING STONE (Bob Dylan) / ALFIE (hit: Cilla Black) / SONNY (Bobby Hebb) / DARK LADY (Johnny Durill) / GYPSYS, TRAMPS AND THIEVES (Robert Stone) / HALF-BREED (Mary Dean & Al Capps) / NEEDLES AND PINS (Searchers) / IT'S NOT UNUSUAL (hit; Tom Jones) / TWELTH OF NEVER (Johnny Mathis) / ELUSIVE BUTTERFLY (Bob Lind) / UNTIL IT'S TIME FOR YOU TO GO (Elvis Presley) / CATCH THE WIND (Donovan) / PIED PIPER (Crispan St. Peters) / YOU DON'T HAVE TO SAY YO LOVE ME (Dusty Springfield) / GIRL FROM IPANEMA (Stan Getz) / OUR DAY WILL COME (Ruby & The Romantics) / OLD MAN RIVER (Paul Robeson) / I WALK ON GILDED SPLINTERS (Dr.John) / FOR WHAT IT'S IT'S WORTH (Buffalo Springfield) / BABY I LOVE YOU (Ronettes) / LOVE HURTS (Everly Brothers) / I FOUND SOMEONE (Michael Bolton-Mark Mangold) / WE ALL SLEEP ALONE (Bon Jovi-Child) / OH NO NOT MY BABY (Goffin-King) / THE SHOOP SHOOP SONG (IT'S IN HIS KISS) (Rudy Clark) / Around this time in the 90's, DESMOND CHILD & DIANE WARREN wrote her material. HEART OF STONE (was originally written for BUCKS FIZZ! by Pete Sinfield & Andy Hill). • **Trivia:** In 1981, CHER dueted with MEAT LOAF on his 'Dead Ringer For Love' single. She appeared with SONNY on many TV specials in the 60's/70's.

Best CD compilation: THE VERY BEST OF CHER (*8)

CHER – vocals (with session people; no band at this time)

Liberty | Imperial

Mar 65. (7"; as CHERILYN) <66081> **DREAM BABY. / STAN QUETZEL** [–] [ ]

Jun 65. (7") <(LIB 66114)> **ALL I REALLY WANT TO DO. / I'M GONNA LOVE YOU** [9] [15]

Sep 65. (lp; stereo/mono) *(S+/LBY 3058)* <12292> **ALL I REALLY WANT TO DO** [7] [16]
– All I really want to do / I go to sleep / Needles and pins / Don't think twice / She thinks I still care / Dream baby / The bells of Rhymney / Girl don't come / See see rider / Come and stay with me / Cry myself to sleep / Blowin' in the wind.

Oct 65. (7") <(LIB 66136)> **WHERE DO YOU GO. / SEE SEE RIDER** [ ] [25]

Mar 66. (7") <(LIB 66160)> **BANG BANG (MY BABY SHOT ME DOWN). / OUR DAY WILL COME** [3] [2]

May 66. (lp; stereo/mono) *(S+/LBY 3072)* <12301> **THE SONNY SIDE OF CHER** [11] Apr66 [26]
– Bang bang (my baby shot me down) / Elusive butterfly / Where do you go / Our day will come / The girl from Ipanema / It's not unusual / Like a rolling stone / Time / Come to your window / Old man river / Milord / A young girl (une enfante).

Jul 66. (7") <LIB 66192> **ALFIE. / SHE'S NO BETTER THAN ME** [–] [32]

Aug 66. (7") *(LIB 12034)* **I FEEL SOMETHING IN THE AIR. / COME TO YOUR WINDOW** [43] [–]

Sep 66. (7") *(LIB 12038)* **SUNNY. / SHE'S NO BETTER THAN ME** [32] [–]

Oct 66. (lp; stereo/mono) *(S+/LBY 3081)* <12320> **CHER** [ ] Sep66 [59]
– Sunny / Twelth of never / You don't have to say you love me / I feel something in the air (magic in the air) / Will you love me tomorrow / Until it's time for you to go / Cruel war / Catch the wind / Pied piper / Homeward bound / I want you / Alfie.

Nov 66. (7") *(LIB 12038)* **MAMA (WHEN MY DOLLIES HAVE BABIES). / BEHIND THE DOOR** [ ] [–]

Nov 66. (7") <66217> **BEHIND THE DOOR. / MAGIC IN THE AIR** [–] [97]

Feb 67. (7") <66223> **DREAM BABY. / MAMA (WHEN MY DOLLIES HAVE BABIES)** [–] [ ]

Aug 67. (7") <66252> **HEY JOE. / OUR DAY WILL COME** [–] [94]

Oct 67. (7") <66261> **YOU BETTER SIT DOWN KIDS. / MAMA (WHEN MY DOLLIES HAVE BABIES)** [–] [9]

Dec 67. (lp; stereo/mono) *(LBS/LBL 83051)* <12358> **WITH LOVE – CHER** [47] Nov67 [ ]
– You better sit down, kids / But I can't love you more / Hey Joe / Mama (when my dollies have babies) / Behind the door / Sing for your supper / Look at me / There but for fortune / I will wait for you / The times they are a-changin'.

Feb 68. (7") *(LBF 15038)* **YOU BETTER SIT DOWN KIDS. / ELUSIVE BUTTERFLY** [ ] [9]

Jun 68. (7") <66282> **THE CLICK SONG NUMBER ONE. / BUT I CAN"T LOVE YOU MORE** [–] [ ]

Jul 68. (lp; stereo/mono) *(LBS/LBL 83156)* <12373> **BACKSTAGE** [ ] [ ]
– Go now / Carnival (manha de carnaval) (cancion de orfeo) / It all adds up now / Reason to believe / Masters of war / Do you believe in magic / I wasn't ready / A house is not a home / Take me for a little while / The impossible dream (the quest) / The click song number one / Song called children.

Sep 68. (7") <66307> **TAKE ME FOR A LITTLE WHILE. / SONG CALLED CHILDREN** [–] [ ]

Atlantic | Atco

Feb 69. (7") <6658> **YOURS UNTIL TOMORROW. / THOUGHT OF LOVING YOU** [–] [ ]

Apr 69. (7") <6684> **CHASTITY'S SONG. / WALK ON GILDED SPLINTERS** [–] [ ]

Jun 69. (7") *(584 278)* **WALK ON GILDED SPLINTERS. / TONIGHT I'LL BE STAYING HERE WITH YOU** [ ] [–]

Jul 69. (lp; mono/stereo) *(226/228 036)* <SD33 298> **3614 JACKSON HIGHWAY** [ ] [ ]
– For what it's worth / (Just enough to keep me) Hangin' on / (Sittin' on) The dock of the bay / Tonight I'll be staying here with you / I threw it all away / Walk on guilded splinters / Lay baby lay / Please don't tell me / Cry like a baby / Do right woman, do right man / Save the children.

Atco | Atco

Sep 69. (7") *(226 003)* <6704> **FOR WHAT IT'S WORTH. / (JUST ENOUGH TO KEEP ME) HANGIN' ON** [ ] [ ]

Nov 69. (7") <6713> **YOU MADE ME SO VERY HAPPY. / FIRST TIME** [–] [ ]

Jun 70. (7") <6793> **SUPERSTAR. / FIRST TIME** [–] [ ]

Feb 71. (7") <6868> **LAY LADY LAY. / (JUST ENOUGH TO KEEP ME) HANGIN' ON** [–] [ ]

M.C.A. | Kapp

May 71. (7") *(MU 1137)* <2134> **CLASSIFIED 1A. / DON'T PUT IT ON ME** [ ] [ ]

Sep 71. (7") *(MU 1142)* <2146> **GYPSYS, TRAMPS AND THIEVES. / HE'LL NEVER KNOW** [4] [1]

Nov 71. (lp) *(MUPS 438)* <3649> **CHER** <US-title 'GYPSYS, TRAMPS & THIEVES'> [ ] [16]
– The way of love / Gypsys, tramps and thieves / He'll never know / Fire and rain / When you find out where you're goin' let me know / He ain't heavy, he's my brother / I hate to sleep alone / I'm in the middle / Touch and go / One honest man. *(re-iss. Aug81 on 'Music For Pleasure';)*

Jan 72. (7") <2158> **THE WAY OF LOVE. / DON'T PUT IT ON ME** [–] [7]

Feb 72. (7") *(MU 1148)* **THE WAY OF LOVE. / FIRE AND RAIN** [ ] [–]

Jun 72. (7") *(MU 1158)* <2171> **LIVING IN A HOUSE DIVIDED. / ONE HONEST MAN** [ ] May72 [22]

Aug 72. (lp) *(MUPS 459)* <5514> **FOXY LADY** [ ] Jul72 [43]
– Living in a house divided / It might as well stay Monday (from now on) / Song for you / Down, down, down / Don't try to close a rose / The first time / Let me down easy / If I knew then / Don't hide your love / Never been to Spain

Nov 72. (7") *(MU 1168)* <2184> **DON'T HIDE YOUR LOVE. / THE FIRST TIME** [ ] Sep72 [46]

M.C.A. | M.C.A.

May 73. (lp) *(MUPS 484)* <2101> **BITTERSWEET WHITE LIGHT** [ ] Apr73 [ ]
– By myself / I got it bad and that ain't good / Am I blue / How long has this been going on / The man I love / Jolson medley: Sonny boy – My mammy – Rock-a-bye your baby with a Dixie melody / More than you know / Why was I born / The man that got away.

Jun 73. (7") *(MU 1196)* <40039> **AM I BLUE. / HOW LONG WAS THIS BEEN GOING ON** [ ] May73 [ ]

Aug 73. (7") *(MU 1215)* <40102> **HALF-BREED. / MELODY** [ ] Jul73 [1]

Oct 73. (lp) *(MCF 2501)* <2104> **HALF-BREED** [ ] Sep73 [28]
– My love / Two people clinging to a thread / Half-breed / The greatest song I ever heard / How can you mend a broken heart / Carousel man / David's song / Melody / The long and winding road / This God-forsaken day / Ruby Jean & Billie Lee. *<US = last track repl. by>* – Chastity sun.

Jan 74. (7") *(MCA 101)* <40161> **DARK LADY. / TWO PEOPLE CLINGING TO A THREAD** [36] [1]

May 74. (7") *(MCA 140)* <40245> **TRAIN OF THOUGHT. / DIXIE GIRL** [ ] [27]

Jun 74. (lp) *(MCF 2559)* <2113> **DARK LADY** [ ] May74 [69]
– Train of thought / I saw a man and he danced with his wife / Make the man love me / Just what I've been lookin' for / Dark lady / Miss Subway of 1952 / Dixie girl / Rescue me / What'll I do (from The Great Gatsby) / Apples don't fall from the tree.

Aug 74. (7") *(MCA 152)* <40273> **I SAW A MAN AND HE DANCED WITH HIS WIFE. / I HATE TO SLEEP ALONE** [ ] [42]

Apr 75. (7") *(MCA 188)* **RESCUE ME. / DIXIE GIRL** [ ] [–]

Warners | Warners

May 75. (lp) *(K 56111)* <2850> **STARS** [ ] [ ]
– Love enough / Bell bottom blues / These days / Mr. Soul / Just this one time / Geronimo's Cadillac / The bigger they come the harder they fall / Love hurts / Rock and roll doctor / Stars.

Jun 75. (7") <8096> **GERONIMO'S CADILLAC. / THESE DAYS** [–] [ ]

Phil Spector Int. | Warner Spector

Jul 75. (7"; CHER & NILSSON) *(2010 006)* <402> **A LOVE LIKE YOURS (DON'T COME KNOCKING EVERY DAY). / (JUST ENOUGH TO KEEP ME) HANGIN' ON** [ ] Apr75 [ ]

Mar 76. (7") *(2010 013)* <400> **A WOMAN'S STORY. / BABY I LOVE YOU** [ ] Feb75 [ ]

Oct 76. (7") <8263> **LONG DISTANCE LOVE AFFAIR. / BORROWED TIME** [–] [ ]

Oct 76. (lp) *(K 56292)* <BS 2898> **I'D RATHER BELIEVE IN YOU** [ ] [ ]
– Long distance love affair / I'd rather believe in you / I know (you don't love me) / Silver wings and golden rings / Flashback / It's a cryin' shame / Early morning strangers / Knock on wood / Spring / Borrowed time.

Jan 77. (7") *<8311>* **PIRATE. / SEND THE MAN OVER** [–] [93]
Apr 77. (lp) *(K 56401) <3046>* **CHERISHED** [ ] [ ]
– Pirate / He was beautiful / War paint and soft feathers / Love the devil out of ya / She loves to hear the music / L.A. plane / Again / Dixie / Send the man over / Thunderstorm.
May 77. (7") *(8366>* **WAR PAINT AND SOFT FEATHERS. / SEND THE MAN OVER** [–] [ ]

— CHER collaborated with husband GREGG ALLMAN late '77 on lp, 'TWO THE HARD WAY' and the single, 'LOVE ME' / 'MOVE ME'.

Casablanca Casablanca

Mar 79. (7") *(CAN 147) <965>* **TAKE ME HOME. / MY SONG (TOO FAR GONE)** [ ] Feb79 [8]
Apr 79. (lp/c) *(CAL/ACCAN 2047) <7133>* **TAKE ME HOME** [ ] Feb79 [25]
– Take me home / Wasn't it good / Say the word / Happy was the day we met / Git down (guitar groupie) / Pain in my heart / Let this be a lesson to you / It's too late to love me now / My song (too far gone).
Jul 79. (7") *(CAN 156) <987>* **WASN'T IT GOOD. / IT'S TOO LATE TO LOVE ME NOW** [ ] May79 [49]
(12") *(CANL 156)* – ('A'side) / Take me home.
Oct 79. (7"/12") *(CAN/+L 164) <2208>* **HELL ON WHEELS. / GIT DOWN (GUITAR GROUPIE)** [ ] Sep79 [59]
Mar 80. (lp) *<(NBLP 7184)>* **PRISONER** [ ] Oct79 [ ]
– Prisoner / Holdin' out for love / Shoppin' / Boys and girls / Mirror image / Hell on wheels / Holy smoke / Outrageous.
Mar 80. (7") *(CAN 185)* **IT'S TOO LATE TO LEAVE ME NOW. / SHOPPIN'** [ ] [–]
Mar 80. (7") *<2228>* **HOLDING OUT FOR LOVE. / BOYS AND GIRLS** [–] [ ]
Mar 82. (7") *(CAN 1009)* **HOLDIN' OUT FOR LOVE. / OUTRAGEOUS** [ ] [–]

BLACK ROSE

— **CHER** with boyfriend at the time **LES DUDEK** – guitar (ex-STEVE MILLER BAND) / **MIKE FINNEGAN** – keyboards, vocals / **GARY FURGASON** – drums / **TREY THOMPSON** – bass / **RON RITCHOTTE** – guitar

Casablanca Casablanca

Nov 80. (7") *<2296>* **YOUNG AND PRETTY. / TAKE IT FROM THE BOYS** [–] [ ]
Nov 80. (lp) *<(NBLP 7234)>* **BLACK ROSE** [ ] [ ]
– Never should've started / Julie / Take it from the boys / We all fly home / 88 degrees / You know it / Young and pretty / Fast company.
Feb 81. (7") *<2312>* **NEVER SHOULD'VE STARTED. / YOUNG AND PRETTY** [–] [ ]

— lack of success led the group to part

CHER

— went solo again (with various session people)

C.B.S. Columbia

Mar 82. (7") *(CBS 2227) <02850>* **RUDY. / DO I EVER CROSS YOUR MIND** [ ] [ ]
Aug 82. (7") *(CBS 2609) <03150>* **I PARALYZE. / WALK WITH ME** [ ] [ ]
Nov 82. (lp/c) *<(CBS/40 85850)>* **I PARALYZE** [ ] [ ]
– Rudy / Games / I paralyze / When the love is gone / Say what's on your mind / Back on the street again / Walks with me / The book of love / Do I ever cross your mind. *(cd-iss. Jun99 on 'Varese Sarabande'; VSD 6039)*

— CHER turned to acting (full-time) and subsequently appeared in many films (see above Filmography); she was back in the charts in '87

Geffen Geffen

Oct 87. (7"/7"pic-d) *(GEF 31/+P) <28191>* **I FOUND SOMEONE. / DANGEROUS TIMES** [5] [10]
(12"+=/12"pic-d+=) *(GEF 31T/+P)* – ('A'version).
Dec 87. (lp/c)(cd) *(WX 132/+C)(924164-2) <24164>* **CHER** [26] Nov87 [32]
– I found someone / We all sleep alone / Bang bang (my baby shot me down) / Main man / Give our love a fightin' chance / Perfection / Dangerous times / Skin deep / Working girl / Hard enough getting over you. *(re-iss. Jan91 lp/c/cd; GEF/+C/D 24164) (re-iss. Mar93 cd/c; GFL D/C 24164) (cd re-iss. Nov96; GED 24164)*
Apr 88. (7") *(GEF 35) <27986>* **WE ALL SLEEP ALONE (remix). / WORKING GIRL** [47] [14]
(12"+=/12"pic-d+=/3"cd-s+=) *(GEF 35 T/TP/CD)* – I found someone.
Sep 88. (7") *(GEF 44) <27894>* **SKIN DEEP. / PERFECTION** [ ] Jul88 [79]
(ext-12"+=/cd-s+=) *(GEF 44 T/CD)* – ('A'dub version).
Dec 88. (7") *<27742>* **MAIN MAN. / HARD ENOUGH GETTING OVER YOU** [–] [ ]
May 89. (7"/c-s; by CHER & PETER CETERA) *(GEF 52/+C) <27529>* **AFTER ALL. / DANGEROUS TIMES** [ ] Mar89 [6]
(12"+=/cd-s+=) *(GEF 52 T/CD)* – I found someone / Main man.
Jul 89. (lp/c)(cd) *(WX 262/+C)(924239-2) <24239>* **HEART OF STONE** [7] [10]
– If I could turn back time / Just like Jesse James / You wouldn't know love / Heart of stone / Still in love with you / Love on a rooftop / Emotional fire / All because of you / Does anybody really fall in love anymore? / Starting over / Kiss to kiss / After all. *(re-iss. Jan91 lp/c/cd; GEF/+C/D 24239)*
Jul 89. (7"/c-s) *(GEF 59/+C) <22886>* **IF I COULD TURN BACK TIME. / SOME GUYS** [6] [3]
(12"+=) *(GEF 59T)* – Kiss to kiss.
(cd-s+=) *(GEF 59CD)* – ('A'remix) / ('A'rock guitar mix) / I found someone.
Jan 90. (7"/c-s) *(GEF 69/+C) <22844>* **JUST LIKE JESSE JAMES. / STARTING OVER** [11] Oct89 [8]
(12"+=/cd-s+=) *(GEF 69 T/CD)* – I found someone.
Mar 90. (7"/c-s) *(GEF 75/+C) <19953>* **HEART OF STONE. / ALL BECAUSE OF YOU** [43] Feb90 [20]
(12"+=/cd-s+=) *(GEF 75 T/CD)* – Working girl.
Jul 90. (7"/c-s) *(GEF 77/+C)* **YOU WOULDN'T KNOW LOVE. / KISS TO KISS** [55] [–]
(12"+=) *(GEF 77T)* – Bang bang / Heart of stone.
(7"ep/cd-ep) *(GEF 77 D/CD)* – ('A'side) / If I could turn back time / I found someone / We all sleep alone (remix).
Oct 90. (7"/c-s) **BABY I'M YOURS. / (IT'S BEEN) HARD ENOUGH GETTING OVER YOU** [ ] [–]
(12"+=/cd-s+=) – Just like Jesse James.
Nov 90. (7") *<19659>* **THE SHOOP SHOOP SONG (IT'S IN HIS KISS). / LOVE ON A ROOFTOP** [–] [33]
Apr 91. (7"/c-s) *(656673-7/-4)* **THE SHOOP SHOOP SONG (IT'S IN HIS KISS). / BABY I'M YOURS** [1] [–]
(12"+=/cd-s+=) *(656673-6/-2)* – We all sleep alone.
(above single from the film 'Mermaids' and released on 'Epic')
Jun 91. (lp/c/cd) *<(GEF/+C/CD 24427)>* **LOVE HURTS** [1] [48]
– Save up all your tears / Love hurts / Love and understanding / Fires of Eden / I'll never stop loving you / The shoop shoop song (it's in his kiss) / One small step / A world without heroes / Could've been you / When love calls your name / When lovers become strangers / Who you gonna believe. *(cd re-iss. Mar95; GFLD 19266)*
Jul 91. (7"/c-s) *(GFS 5/+C) <19023>* **LOVE AND UNDERSTANDING. / TRAIL OF BROKEN HEARTS** [10] Jun91 [17]
(12"+=/cd-s+=) *(GFS 5 T/CD)* – If I could turn back time.
Sep 91. (7"/c-s) *(GFS 11/+C) <19105>* **SAVE UP ALL YOUR TEARS. / A WORLD WITHOUT HEROES** [37] [37]
(12"+=/cd-s+=) *(GFS 11 T/CD)* – Love and understanding.
Nov 91. (7"/c-s) *(GFS 16/+C)* **LOVE HURTS. / ONE SMALL STEP** [43] [ ]
(12"+=/cd-s+=) *(GFS 16 T/CD)* – Just like Jesse James.
Mar 92. (7"/7"pic-d/c-s) *(GFS 19/+P/C)* **COULD'VE BEEN YOU. / LOVE AND UNDERSTANDING** [31] [ ]
(12"sha-pic-d+=/cd-s+=) *(GFS 19 T/CD)* – Save up all your tears.
Nov 92. (cd/c/d-lp) *<(GED/GEC/GEF 24439)>* **GREATEST HITS 1965-92** (compilation) [1] [ ]
– Oh no not my baby / Whenever you're near / Many rivers to cross (live) / Love and understanding / Save up all your tears / The shoop shoop song (it's in his kiss) / If I could turn back time / Just like Jesse James / Heart of stone / I found someone / We all sleep alone / Bang bang (my baby shot me down) (with SONNY) / Dead ringer for love (with MEAT LOAF) / Dark lady / Gypsys, tramps and thieves / I got you babe (with SONNY).
Nov 92. (7"/c-s) *(GFS 29/+C)* **OH NO NOT MY BABY. / LOVE HURTS** [33] [ ]
(cd-s+=) *(GFS 29TD)* – Love on a rooftop / Main man.
Jan 93. (7"/c-s) *(GFS 31/+C)* **MANY RIVERS TO CROSS. / WHO YOU GONNA BELIEVE** [37] [ ]
(cd-s+=) *(GFS 31TD)* –
Feb 93. (7"/c-s) *(GFS 32/+C)* **WHENEVER YOU'RE NEAR. / COULD'VE BEEN YOU** [72] [ ]
(12"pic-d+=/cd-s+=) *(GFS 32 TP/TD)* – You wouldn't know love / I'll never stop loving you.
Jan 94. (c-s/cd-s; by CHER with BEAVIS & BUTT-HEAD) *(GFS C/TD 64)* **I GOT YOU BABE. / Sonny & Cher: I GOT YOU BABE** [35] [ ]

— BEAVIS & BUTT-HEAD; cult TV cartoon characters who have already carved up a lot of parental hysteria by their use of foul language and violence.

In March '95 – alongside CHRISSIE HYNDE, NENEH CHERRY and ERIC CLAPTON – she hit UK No.1 with charity Comic Relief song 'LOVE CAN BUILD A BRIDGE'.

WEA Reprise

Oct 95. (c-s) *(WEA 021C)* **WALKING IN MEMPHIS / THE FALL** [11] [ ]
(cd-s+=) *(WEA 021CD1)* – Angels running.
(cd-s) *(WEA 021CD2)* – ('A'-Shut up and dance instrumental) / ('A'mixes).

Nov 95. (cd/c) *(0630 12670-2/-4)* <46179> **IT'S A MAN'S WORLD** [28] [64]
– Walking in Memphis / Not enough love in the world / One by one / I wouldn't treat a dog (the way you treated me) / Angels running / Paradise is here / I'm blowin' away / Don't come around tonite / What about the moonlight / The same mistake / The gunman / The sun ain't gonna shine anymore / Shape of things to come / It's a man's, man's, man's world.

Jan 96. (c-s) *(WEA 032C)* **ONE BY ONE / WALKING IN MEMPHIS (mix)** [7] [–]
(12"+=/cd-s+=) *(WEA 032 T/CD)* – It's a man's world.

Apr 96. (c-s) *(WEA 032C)* **NOT ENOUGH LOVE IN THE WORLD / ONE BY ONE (Sam Ward mix)** [31] [ ]
(cd-s) *(WEA 032CD)* – ('A'side) / One by one (Jr. Vasquez mixes).

Jun 96. (c-s) <17695> **ONE BY ONE / I WOULDN'T TREAT A DOG (THE WAY YOU TREATED ME)** [–] [52]

Jul 96. (c-s) *(WEA 071C)* **THE SUN AIN'T GONNA SHINE ANYMORE / PARADISE IS HERE** [26] [ ]
(cd-s) *(WEA 071CD)* – Not enough love in the world (mix).

WEA Warners

Oct 98. (c-s/cd-s) *(WEA 175 C/CD)* <44576> **BELIEVE / ('A'mixes; Phat 'n' phunky / Club 69 phunk club / Almighty definitive)** [1] [1]
(12"+=/cd-s+=) *(WEA 175 T/CD2)* – ('A'mixes; Xenomania Mad Tim.. Club 69 future anthem / Grips heartbroken / + 3 dub).

Oct 98. (cd/c) *(3984 25319-2/-4)* <47121> **BELIEVE** [8] [4]
– Believe / The power / Runaway / All or nothing / Strong enough / Dov'e l'amore / Takin' back my heart / Taxi taxi / Love is the groove / We all sleep alone.

Feb 99. (c-s) *(WEA 201C)* <44644> **STRONG ENOUGH / ('A'mix)** [5] May99 [57]
(cd-s) *(WEA 201CD1)* – ('A'mixes; Club 69 / Pumpin' Dolls vocal epic / male / Club 69 phunk).
(cd-s) *(WEA 201CD2)* – ('A'mixes; Marc Andrews / Pumpin' Dolls cashmere / D-Bop melt / Club 69 phuture / Pumpin' Dolls radio).
(12") *(WEA 201T)* – ('A'mixes; some of above).

Jun 99. (c-s) *(WEA 212C)* **ALL OR NOTHING / STRONG ENOUGH (club)** [12] [–]
(cd-s+=) *(WEA 212CD1)* – ('A'-almighty mixes).
(cd-s) *(WEA 212CD2)* – ('A'-K-Klass mixes).

Oct 99. (c-s) *(WEA 230C)* **DOV'E L'AMORE / ('A'mix)** [21] [–]
(cd-s) *(WEA 230CD1)* – ('A'mixes).
(cd-s) *(WEA 230CD2)* – ('A'mixes).
(12") *(WEA 230T)* – ('A'mixes).

Nov 99. (cd/c) *(8573 80420-2/-4)* <24509> **GREATEST HITS** <US-title 'IF I COULD TURN BACK TIME – CHER'S GREATEST HITS'> (compilation) [7] Aug99 [57]
– Love and understanding / Save up all your tears / The shoop shoop song (it's in his kiss) / After all / If I could turn back time / Just like Jesse James / Heart of stone / I found someone / We all sleep alone / Bang bang / Take me home / Dark lady / Half-breed / The way of love / The way of love / Gypsys, tramps and thieves / I got you babe.

Nov 01. (c-s/cd-s) *(WEA 337 C/CD)* **THE MUSIC'S NO GOOD WITHOUT YOU / (extended) / DOV'A L'AMORE (Emilio Estefan Jr. extended)** [8] [ ]
(cd-s) *(WEA 337CDX)* – ('A'-extended radio) / ('A'-almighty 12" mix) / All or nothing (Danny Tenaglia international mix).

Nov 01. (cd/c) <(0927 42463-2/-4)> **LIVING PROOF** [46] Feb02 [ ]
– The music's no good without you / Alive again / This is a song for the lonely / Different kind of love song / Rain rain / Love so high / Body to body heart to heart / Love is a lonely place without you / Real love / Love one another / You take it all / When the money's gone.

WEA Rhino

Nov 03. (cd) *(5046 68586-2)* <R2 73852> **THE VERY BEST OF CHER** (compilation) [38] Apr03 [4]
– Believe / If I could turn back time / Save up all your tears / Walking in Memphis / Shoop shoop song (it's in his kiss) / Love and understanding / I found someone / Just like Jesse James / One by one / Love can build a bridge (with CHRISSIE HYNDE & NENEH CHERRY) / Strong enough / All or nothing / A different kind of love song / Heart of stone / Music's no good without you / Dov'e l'amore (Emilio Estefan Jr. extended mix) / Gypsies, tramps and thieves / The beat goes on (SONNY & CHER) / I got you babe (SONNY & CHER) / All I really want to do / Bang bang (my baby shot me down) (original version).
(above album will hit No.17 in Jan'04)

– (selective) compilations, etc. –

Nov 68. (lp) *Liberty; (LBS 83105) / Imperial;* <12406> **CHER'S GOLDEN GREATS** [ ] [ ]
Jan 72. (d-lp) *United Artists;* <88> **CHER SUPERPAK** [–] [92]
Nov 75. (lp) *Sunset; (SLS 50378)* **GOLDEN HITS** [ ] [–]
Oct 72. (d-lp) *United Artists;* <94> **CHER SUPERPAK, VOL.II** [–] [95]
May 93. (cd/c) *Spectrum; (550038-2/-4)* **TAKE ME HOME / PRISONER** [ ] [–]
Apr 93. (cd) *Movieplay Gold; (MPG 74017)* **GYPSYS, TRAMPS & THIEVES** [ ] [–]
Jul 93. (cd/c) *M.C.A.; (MCL D/C 19208)* **CHER / FOXY LADY** [ ] [–]
Jul 93. (cd/c) *M.C.A.; (MCL D/C 19209)* **HALF BREED / DARK LADY** [ ] [–]
Nov 95. (3xcd-box) *CDOMB 005)* **ALL I REALLY WANT TO DO / SONNY SIDE OF CHER / CHER** [ ] [–]
Jan 96. (cd) *Disky; (SE 86567-2)* **YOU BETTER SIT DOWN KIDS** [ ] [–]
Apr 96. (cd) *Universal; (AA314 532320-2)* **THE CASABLANCA YEARS** [ ] [ ]
Sep 96. (cd) *E.M.I.; (CDP 792773-2)* **BANG BANG (MY BABY SHOT ME DOWN)** [ ] [–]
Nov 98. (cd) *Spectrum; (550038-2)* **TAKE ME HOME / PRISONER** [ ] [–]
Feb 99. (cd) *Magic; (497941-2)* **SUNNY** [ ] [–]
Apr 99. (cd) *E.M.I.; (499900-2)* **THE BEST OF CHER** [ ] [–]
Dec 99. (cd) *Magic; (523511-2)* **WITH LOVE** [ ] [–]
Jan 00. (cd) *Universal; (E 490528-2)* **UNIVERSAL MASTERS COLLECTION** [ ] [ ]
Sep 00. (cd) *Universal; (AAMCAD 11899)* **BITTERSWEET: THE LOVE SONGS** [ ] [ ]
Dec 00. (cd) *Disky; (BA 86022-2)* **BASIC ORIGINAL HITS** [ ] [–]
Feb 01. (cd) *M.C.A.; (MCBD 19511)* **GYPSIES TRAMPS AND THIEVES: THE BEST OF CHER** [ ] [ ]
Feb 01. (cd) *EMI Plus; (5761410)* **THE STORY** [ ] [ ]
Feb 01. (cd) *Raven; (RVCD 108)* **BEHIND THE DOOR 1964-1974** [ ] [ ]
Oct 02. (cd) *Disky; (GO 79348-2)* **ALL I REALLY WANT TO DO** [ ] [–]
Feb 03. (cd) *M.C.A.; (MCBD 19524)* **BLUE: ALL TIME GREAT LOVE SONGS** [ ] [ ]
Mar 03. (cd) *Universal; (AA881 12154-2)* **20THE CENTURY MASTERS** [ ] [ ]
Aug 03. (3xcd-box) *Spectrum; (9809420)* **THE CASABLANCA YEARS / LOVE SONGS / CHER** [ ] [ ]

SONNY & CHER

not iss. Vault

1963. (7"; as CAESAR & CLEO) <909> **THE LETTER. / SPRING FEVER** [–] [ ]
<re-iss. Oct65 as SONNY & CHER; 916> – hit No.75 *(UK-iss.Oct65 on 'Vocalion'; VL 9247)*

Reprise Reprise

1964. (7"; as CAESAR & CLEO) <0308> **LOVE IS STRANGE. / DO YOU WANT TO DANCE** [–] [ ]
1964. (7") <0309> **BABY DON'T GO. / LOVE IS STRANGE** [–] [ ]
Feb 65. (7") *(R 20309)* **BABY DON'T GO. / WALKING THE QUETZEL** [ ] [–]

Atlantic Atco

Oct 64. (7") <6345> **JUST YOU. / SING C'EST LA VIE** [–] [ ]
<re-iss. Aug65> – hit No.20
Jul 65. (7") *(AT 4035)* <6359> **I GOT YOU BABE. / IT'S GONNA RAIN** [1] [1]

—— In Aug'65, SONNY had his first solo hit with 'LAUGH AT ME' which hit US No.10 and UK No.9 – the re-issue of 'BABY DON'T GO' also hit US No.8 at the same time. A month later, CHER contributed vocals to BONNIE + THE TREASURES 7", 'Home Of The Brave'

Oct 65. (7") *(AT 4047)* <6381> **BUT YOU'RE MINE. / HELLO** [17] [15]
Oct 65. (lp; mono/stereo) *(ATL/STL 5036)* <177> **LOOK AT US** [7] Aug65 [2]

– I got you babe / Unchained melody / Then he kissed me / Sing c'est la vie / It's gonna rain / 500 miles / Just you / The letter / Let it be me / You don't love me / You've really got a hold on me / Why don't they let us fall in love. *<(cd-iss. Jul98 on 'Sundazed'; SC 6139)>*

Feb 66. (7") *(AT 4069)* *<6395>* **WHAT NOW MY LOVE. / I LOOK FOR YOU** 13 Jan66 16

Jun 66. (7") *(584 018)* *<6420>* **HAVE I STAYED TOO LONG. / LEAVE ME BE** 42 49

May 66. (lp; mono/stereo) *(587/588 006)* *<183>* **THE WONDROUS WORLD OF SONNY & CHER** 15 Apr66 34
– Summertime / Tell him / I'm leaving it all up to you / But you're mine / Bring it on home to me baby / Set me free / What now my love / Leave me be / I look for you / Laugh at me / Turn around / So fine. *<(cd-iss. Jul98 on 'Sundazed'; SC 6140)>*

Sep 66. (7") *(584 040)* *<6440>* **LITTLE MAN. / MONDAY** 4 21

Nov 66. (7") *<6449>* **LIVING FOR YOU. / LOVE DON'T COME** – 87

Nov 66. (7") *(584 057)* **LIVING FOR YOU. / TURN AROUND** 44 –

Jan 67. (7") *(584 078)* *<6461>* **THE BEAT GOES ON. / LOVE DON'T COME** 29 6

Apr 67. (lp; mono/stereo) *(587/588 052)* *<203>* **IN CASE YOU'RE IN LOVE** Mar66 45
– The beat goes on / Groovy kind of love / You baby / Monday / Love don't come / Podunk / Little man / We'll sing in the sunshine / Misty roses / Stand by me / Living for you / Cheryl's goin' home. *<(cd-iss. Jul98 on 'Sundazed'; SC 6141)>*

May 67. (7") *(584 110)* *<6480>* **A BEAUTIFUL STORY. / PODUNK** Apr67 53

May 67. (lp) *<214>* **GOOD TIMES (soundtrack)** – 73
– I got you babe / It's the little things / Good times / Trust me / Don't talk to strangers / I'm gonna love you / Just a name / I got you babe.

Aug 67. (7") *(584 129)* *<6486>* **PLASTIC MAN. / IT'S THE LITTLE THINGS** Jun67 74

Sep 67. (7") *<6507>* **IT'S THE LITTLE THINGS. / DON'T TALK TO STRANGERS** – 50

Dec 67. (7") *(584 162)* *<6541>* **GOOD COMBINATION. / YOU AND ME** 56

Feb 68. (7") *(584 168)* *<6555>* **CIRCUS. / Sonny Bono: I WOULD MARRY YOU TODAY**

Sep 68. (7") *(584 215)* *<6605>* **YOU GOTTA HAVE A THING OF YOUR OWN. / I GOT YOU BABE**

1969. (7") *<6683>* **YOU'RE A FRIEND OF MINE. / I WOULD MARRY YOU TODAY** –

Atco Atco

Jul 70. (7") *(2091 021)* *<6758>* **GET IT TOGETHER. / HOLD YOU TIGHTER**

M.C.A. Kapp

Jun 71. (7") *(MU 1139)* *<2141>* **REAL PEOPLE. / SOMEBODY**

Oct 71. (lp) *(MUPS 435)* *<3654>* **SONNY AND CHER LIVE (live)** Sep71 35
– What now my love / The beat goes on / Once in a lifetime / More today than yesterday / Gotta get you into my life / Someday (you'll want me to want you) / Danny boy / Laugh at me / Something / Hey Jude / I got you babe.

Nov 71. (7") *(MU 1145)* *<2151>* **ALL I EVER NEED IS YOU. / I GOT YOU BABE (live)** 8 Oct71 7

Jun 72. (lp) *(MUPS 452)* *<3660>* **ALL I EVER NEED IS YOU** Feb72 14
– All I ever need is you / Here comes that rainy day feeling / More today than yesterday / Crystal clear / Muddy waters / United we stand / A cowboy's work is never done / I love what you did with the love I gave you / You better sit down kids / We'll watch the sun coming up / Somebody.

Apr 72. (7") *(MU 1154)* *<2163>* **A COWBOY'S WORK IS NEVER DONE. / SOMEBODY** Feb72 8

Aug 72. (7") *(MU 1164)* *<2176>* **WHEN YOU SAY LOVE. / CRYSTAL CLEAR – MUDDY WATERS** Jul72 32

M.C.A. M.C.A.

Feb 73. (lp) *(MCF 3672)* *<2101>* **MAMA WAS A ROCK AND ROLL SINGER, PAPA USED TO WRITE ALL HER SONGS** Jun73
– It never rains in Southern California / I believe in you / I can see clearly now / Rhythm of your heartbeat / Mama was a rock and roll singer, papa used to write all her songs (parts 1 & 2) / By love I mean / Brother Love's travelling salvation show / You know darn well / The greatest show on Earth / Listen to the music.

Apr 73. (7") *(MU 1194)* *<40026>* **MAMA WAS A ROCK AND ROLL SINGER, PAPA USED TO WRITE ALL HER SONGS. / (part 2)** Mar73 77

Jul 73. (7") *(MUS 1211)* *<40083>* **THE GREATEST SHOW ON EARTH. / YOU KNOW DARN WELL I DO**

May 74. (d-lp) *(MCSP 257)* *<8004>* **LIVE IN LAS VEGAS VOL.2 (live)** Dec73
– All I ever need is you / I can see clearly now / You've got a friend / Where you lead / You'd better sit down kids / A cowboy's work is never done / I got you babe / Gypsies, tramps and thieves / Brother Love's travelling salvation show / You and I / Superstar / Bang bang (my baby shot me down).

— they decided to end partnership as they separated and divorced on 26th June 1974 (see biography above). Professionally they did re-unite in 1976-77 on US TV 'SONNY & CHER SHOW' again

not iss. Warners

1977. (7") *<8341>* **YOU'RE NOT RIGHT FOR ME. / WRONG NUMBER** –

– (selective) compilations, etc. –

on 'Atlantic' UK, 'Atco' US unless mentioned otherwise

Aug 65. (7") *Reprise;* *<0392>* **BABY DON'T GO. / WALKIN' THE QUETZAL (or) LOVE IS STRANGE** – 8

Oct 65. (lp; with Various Artists) *Reprise;* *<6177>* **BABY DON'T GO** – 69

Oct 67. (lp) *(588 083)* *<33219>* **THE BEST OF SONNY & CHER** Aug67 23
– The beat goes on / What now my love / I got you babe / Little man / Just you / Let it be me / A beautiful story / It's the little things / But you're mine / Sing c'est la vie / Laugh at me / Living for you. *(re-iss. Aug72 lp/c; K/K4 40012)*

1975. (lp) *<11000>* **THE BEAT GOES ON – THE BEST OF SONNY & CHER** –
(cd-iss. Jun93 on 'Atco'; 7567 91796-2)

Dec 90. (cd/c/lp) *W.E.A.;* *(9548 30152-2/-4/-1)* **THE SONNY & CHER COLLECTION**

May 93. (7"/c-s) *Epic;* *(659240-7/-4)* **I GOT YOU BABE. / (Beavis & Butt-head intro)** 66 –
(cd-s+=) *(659240-2)* – (Beavis & Butt-head outro).

Mar 03. (cd) *Universal;* *(E 118231-2)* **THE HIT SINGLES COLLECTION**

Feb 02. (d-cd) *BR Music;* *(BS 8124-2)* **THE SINGLES PLUS**

Neneh CHERRY

Born: NENEH MARIANN KARLSSON, 10 March '64, Stockholm, Sweden. Raised and educated by her Swedish mother and stepfather DON CHERRY (the famous jazz trumpeter) in Manhattan, New York, her early influences were inevitably jazz luminaries such as ORNETTE COLEMAN. In 1981, she moved to London, augmenting The SLITS before joining Bristolian avant-garde indie-jazz collective, RIP, RIG & PANIC. They made three albums, 'GOD' (1981), 'I AM COLD' (1982) and 'ATTITUDE' (1983), before she left to form FLOAT UP CP. In 1986, CHERRY guested on THE THE's 'Slow Train To Dawn' (from the 'Infected' album). The same year, she met CAMERON McVEY (aka BOOGA BEAR) and together they started a writing partnership, launching her solo career in 1988, with McVEY as producer/musician. A revamped version of an old MORGAN-McVEY (mid-80's outfit of whom CAMERON formed one half alongside JAMIE MORGAN) track, 'BUFFALO STANCE' took CHERRY into the charts for the first time, the British and American Top 5 no less. A fresh 'n' funky lesson in street suss hip-hop, punctuated by CHERRY's cockney wide girl interludes, the record was a taster (along with the evocative 'MANCHILD', another Top 5 smash) for her acclaimed debut set, 'RAW LIKE SUSHI' (1989). Drawing on her avant-rock background and love of jazz, soul, pop and R&B, CHERRY had created an intelligent, sensual and uniquely feminine take on a male-dominated genre. CHERRY was already a mother of two and on tracks like 'INNER CITY MAMA', she displayed a lyrical maturity missing in much modern soul/R&B. Her feminist credibility was already rock solid, CHERRY having appeared on Top Of The Pops in a lycra bodysuit while heavily pregnant. In 1990, she covered Cole Porter's 'I'VE GOT YOU UNDER MY SKIN', for the 'Red, Hot + Blue' charity album, subsequently moving back to Sweden with new husband, McVEY and beginning work on a follow-up set. 'HOMEBREW' eventually appeared in 1992, a less immediate record which struggled to make the Top 30. Nevertheless, CHERRY was back in the UK Top 3 with the spine-tingling YOUSSOU N'DOUR collaboration, '7 SECONDS', possibly her most powerful vocal performance to date. Another piece of teamwork, this time with CHER, CHRISSIE HYNDE and ERIC CLAPTON on Comic Relief charity single, 'LOVE CAN BUILD A BRIDGE' saw her top the British singles chart. The following year, CHERRY signed to the hip 'Virgin' subsidiary, 'Hut', scoring her first solo Top 10 in years with 'WOMAN'. An accompanying album, 'MAN' (1996) made the Top 20, expanding her established lyrical themes and proving that she could still cut the proverbial mustard. • **Covered:** TROUBLE MAN (Marvin Gaye) / GOLDEN RING (S.Douglas-J.Skeete). Sampled BORN TO BE WILD (Steppenwolf) / FOR THE LOVE OF MONEY (O'Jays) / SUGAR FREE (Juicy).

Album rating: RAW LIKE SUSHI (*6) / HOMEBREW (*5) / MAN (*5)

NENEH CHERRY – vocals / **CAMERON McVEY** – keyboards / etc

Circa | Virgin

Nov 88. (7") *(YR 21)* *<99231>* **BUFFALO STANCE. / ('A'-Electro ski mix)** [3] Mar89 [3]
(12"+=) *(YRTX 21)* – ('A'-Scratchappela mix).
(3"cd-s++=) *(YRCD 21)* – ('A'-Give me a muthaf**kin' break beat).
(12"+=) *(YRT 21)* – ('A'instrumental).

May 89. (7"/c-s) *(YR/+C 30)* **MANCHILD. / ('A'version)** [5] [–]
(12"+=/3"cd-s+=) *(YR T/CD 30)* – ('A'versions).
(12"+=) *(YRTX 30)* – Buffalo stance.

Jun 89. (c/lp/cd) *(CIRC/+A/D 8)* *<91252>* **RAW LIKE SUSHI** [2] [40]
– Buffalo stance * / Manchild * / Kisses on the wind / Inna city mama / The next generation / Love ghetto / Heart * / Phoney ladies / Outre risqué locomotive / So here I come. *(cd+=)* – My bitch / (tracks marked * = extra remixes).

Aug 89. (7"/c-s) *(YR/+C 33)* *<99183>* **KISSES ON THE WIND. / BUFFALO BLUES** [20] Jul89 [8]
(12"+=/3"cd-s+=) *(TR T/CD 33)* – ('A'extended).
(12") *(TRTX 33)* – ('A'mixes).

Nov 89. (c-s) *<99153>* **HEART / PHONY LADIES** [–] [73]

Dec 89. (7"/c-s) *(YR/+C 42)* **INNA CITY MAMA. / THE NEXT GENERATION** [34] [–]
(12"+=) *(YRT 42)* – Kisses on the wind.
(cd-s++=) *(YRCD 42)* – So here I come.
(12") *(YRTX 42)* – ('A'mixes).

Sep 90. (7"/c-s) *(YR/+C 53)* **I'VE GOT YOU UNDER MY SKIN. / ('A'version)** [25] [–]
(12"+=/cd-s+=) *(YR T/CD 53)* – ('A'-long version).
(12") *(YRTX 53)* – ('A'-different mix).

Sep 92. (7"/c-s) *(YR/+C 83)* **MONEY LOVE. / TWISTED** [23] [ ]
(ext;12"+=/cd-s+=) *(YR T/CD 83)* – ('A'-Paul Oakenfield) / ('A'-Perfecto mix).

— Below album featured guests GURU from GANGSTARR / J$ / MICHAEL STIPE

Oct 92. (c/cd/lp) *(CIRC/+A/D 25)* *<86516>* **HOMEBREW** [27] [ ]
– Sassy / Money love / Move with me / I ain't gone under yet / Twisted / Buddy X / Somedays / Trout / Peace in mind / Red paint. *(re-iss. Jul93; same)*

Mar 93. (c-s) *<12648>* **BUDDY X / MOVE WITH ME** [–] [43]

Jun 93. (7"/c-s) *(YR/+C 98)* *<12648>* **BUDDY X (What's Up Mix) / BUDDY X (Falcon & Fabian Remix)** [35] [–]
(12"+=/cd-s+=) *(YR T/CD 98)* – (4 other 'A' mixes).

— In May '94, she was credited on UK Top 3 single '7 SECONDS' with YOUSSOU N'DOUR (Columbia; 660508-2/-4). In Mar '95, alongside CHER, CHRISSIE HYNDE and ERIC CLAPTON, she hit No.1 UK with Comic Relief charity song 'LOVE CAN BUILD A BRIDGE'.

Hut | not iss.

Jul 96. (c-s) *(HUTC 70)* **WOMAN / HAD YOU IN ME** [9] [–]
(cd-s+=) *(HUTCD 70)* – Heart throbs / Telephone pole.
(cd-s) *(HUTDX 70)* – ('A'mixes).

Sep 96. (cd/c) *(CDHUT/HUTMC 38)* **MAN** [16] [–]
– Woman / Feel it / Hornbeam / Trouble man / Golden ring / 7 seconds / Kootchi / Beastiality / Carry me / Together now / Everything. *<US-iss.1998 on 'E.M.I.'; 41981>*

Dec 96. (c-s) *(HUTC 75)* **KOOTCHI / CRACK BABY** [38] [–]
(cd-s+=) *(HUTCD 75)* – ('A'mix) / Somedays.
(cd-s) *(HUTDG 75)* – ('A'mixes).

Feb 97. (c-s) *(HUTC 79)* **FEEL IT / I WANNA KNOW** [68] [ ]
(cd-s+=) *(HUTCD 79)* – Trout / Devotion.
(cd-s) *(HUTDX 79)* – ('A'mixes).

— In Nov'99, 'BUDDY X' was given ('99) duet treatment by DREEM TEAM VS. NENEH CHERRY, hitting UK No.15

CHIC

Formed: New York City, New York, USA . . . 1972 as The BIG APPLE BAND by NILE RODGERS, BERNARD EDWARDS and TONY THOMPSON. They worked together sessioning for disco acts (i.e. NEW YORK CITY's hit 'I'm Doin' Fine' and CAROL DOUGLAS) before forming CHIC in 1976. They added singer NORMA JEAN WRIGHT who had previously cut a solo album with CHIC at the controls. CHIC were finally signed by 'Atlantic', after the company president at the time got an earful of their demo. Late in 1977, 'DANCE DANCE DANCE (YOWSAH YOWSAH YOWSAH)' hit the charts, eventually peaking at No.6 on both sides of the Atlantic. With a change of vocalists (LUCI MARTIN replacing NORMA) the following year, they issued 'LE FREAK', which gave them their first US No.1. It also introduced their instantly recognisable funky bass/guitar interplay which would go on to influence not only the disco scene but many British pop acts of the 80's. In 1979, RODGERS and EDWARDS produced another disco act, SISTER SLEDGE, presiding over their two classic dancefloor hits, 'He's The Greatest Dancer' and 'We Are Family'. Later in the year, CHIC had their second No.1 with 'GOOD TIMES', its insistent bassline "borrowed" by The SUGARHILL GANG for 1980's 'Rapper's Delight'; the group were subsequently collared for plagiarism and ordered to pay the due royalties. Meanwhile, offers poured in for production work from the likes of DIANA ROSS ('Diana'), DEBBIE HARRY ('Koo Koo') and DAVID BOWIE ('Let's Dance'), the growing demand for the seemingly invincible RODGERS-EDWARDS team contributing to the break-up of the band (RODGERS joined The HONEYDRIPPERS with former LED ZEPPELIN legends, PLANT and PAGE).

Album rating: CHIC (*7) / C'EST CHIC (*5) / RISQUE (*8) / LES PLUS GRANDS SUCCES DE CHIC compilation (*6) / REAL PEOPLE (*5) / TAKE IT OFF (*4) / TONGUE IN CHIC (*5) / BELIEVER (*4) / DANCE DANCE DANCE – THE BEST OF CHIC compilation (*8) / CHIC-ISM (*4)

NILE RODGERS (b.19 Sep'52, New York) – guitar / **BERNARD EDWARDS** (b.31 Oct'52, Greenville, New Connecticut) – bass / **TONY THOMPSON** – drums / **ALFA ANDERSON** (b. 7 Sep'46) + **NORMA JEAN WRIGHT** – vocals

Atlantic | Atlantic

Nov 77. (7") *(K 11038)* *<3435>* **DANCE DANCE DANCE (YOWSAH YOWSAH YOWSAH). / SAO PAULO** [6] Oct77 [6]

Feb 78. (lp/c) *(K/K4 50441)* *<19153>* **CHIC** [ ] Nov77 [27]
– Dance dance dance (yowsah yowsah yowsah) / Sao paulo / You can get by / Everybody dance / Est ce que c'est Chic / Falling in love with you / Strike up the band. *(cd-iss. Nov93; 7567 80407-2)*

Mar 78. (7") *(K 11097)* *<3469>* **EVERYBODY DANCE. / YOU CAN GET BY** [9] [38]

— **LUCI MARTIN** (b.10 Jan'55) – vocals repl. NORMA JEAN WRIGHT

Nov 78. (7") *(K 11209)* *<3519>* **LE FREAK. / SAVIOR FAIRE** [7] Oct78 [1]

(12"+=) *(K 11209)* – Chic (everybody say).
Dec 78. (lp/c) *(K/K4 50565)* <19209> **C'EST CHIC** 2 Nov78 4
– Chic cheer / Le freak / I want your love / Happy man / Dance dance dance / Savoir faire / At last I am free / Sometimes you win / Funny bone / Everybody dance. *(cd-iss. Nov93; 7567 81552-2)*
Feb 79. (7") *(K 11245)* <3557> **I WANT YOUR LOVE. / FUNNY BONE** 4 7
(12") *(K 11245T)* – ('A'side) / Chic cheer / Le freak.
Jun 79. (7") *(K 11310)* <3584> **GOOD TIMES. / A WARM SUMMER NIGHT** 5 1
Aug 79. (lp/c) *(K/K4 50634)* <16003> **RISQUE** 29 5
– Good times / A warm summer night / My feet keep dancing / My forbidden lover / Can't stand to love you / Will you cry when you hear this song / What about me. *(cd-iss. Nov93; 7567 80406-2)*
Sep 79. (7") **MY FORBIDDEN LOVER. / WHAT ABOUT ME** 15 43
Nov 79. (7") *(K 11415)* <3638> **MY FEET KEEP DANCING. / WILL YOU CRY WHEN YOU HEAR THIS SONG** 21
Dec 79. (lp/c) *(K/K4 50686)* <16011> **(LES PLUS GRANDS SUCCES DE CHIC –) GREATEST HITS** (compilation) 30 88
– Le freak / I want your love / Dance dance dance (yowsah yowsah yowsah) / Everybody dance / My forbidden lover / Good times / My feet keep dancing.
Jul 80. (7") *(K 11539)* <3665> **REBELS ARE WE. / OPEN UP** 61
Jul 80. (lp/c) *(K/K4 50711)* <16016> **REAL PEOPLE** 30
– Real people / Rebels are we / You can't do it alone / Chip off the old block / I got protection / Open up / 26. *(cd-iss. Jan96; 7567 80420-2)*
Sep 80. (7") *(K 11617)* **26. / CHIP OFF THE OLD BLOCK** –
Nov 80. (7") <3768> **REAL PEOPLE. / CHIP OFF THE OLD BLOCK** – 79
Nov 81. (lp/c) *(K/K4 50845)* <19323> **TAKE IT OFF**
– Flashback / Take it off / Just out of reach / Telling lies / Stage fright / So fine / Baby doll / Your love is cancelled / Burn hard / Would you be my baby. *(cd-iss. Jan96; 7567 80421-2)*
Jun 82. (7") <4032> **SOUP FOR ONE. / BURN HARD** – 80
(above was the title track from the film for which NILE & RODGERS wrote soundtrack released 'Mirage')
Nov 82. (lp) *(780 031-1)* <80031> **TONGUE IN CHIC**
– Hangin' / I feel your love comin' on / When you love someone / Chic (everybody say) / Hey fool / Sharing love / City lights. *(cd-iss. Jan96; 7567 80031-2)*
Jan 83. (7"/12") *(A 9898/+T)* **HANGIN'. / CITY LIGHTS** 64 –
Jan 83. (7") <89954> **HANGIN'. / CHIC (EVERYBODY SAY)** –
Dec 83. (lp) *(780 107-1)* <80107> **BELIEVER**
– Believer / You are beautiful / Take a closer look / Give me the lovin' / Show me your light / You got some love for me / In love with music / Party everybody. *(cd-iss. Jan96; 7567 80107-2)*
Dec 83. (7") <89725> **YOU GOT SOME LOVE FOR ME. / GIVE ME THE LOVIN'** –

— Early in 1983, they had already split. EDWARDS and THOMPSON later joined The POWER STATION with ROBERT PALMER and members of DURAN DURAN.

NILE RODGERS

went solo, also augmented by EDWARDS and THOMPSON

Mirage-WEA Mirage-WEA

Feb 83. (lp/c) *(B 0073)* **ADVENTURES IN THE LAND OF THE GOOD GROOVE**
– The land of the good groove / Yum yum / Beat / Get her crazy / It's all in your hands / Rock bottom / My love song for you / Most down.
Mar 83. (7") *(U 9911)* **THE LAND OF GOOD GROOVE. / MY LOVE SONG FOR YOU**
May 83. (7") *(U 9918)* **YUM YUM. / GET HER CRAZY**

— After spell with The HONEYDRIPPERS (see LED ZEPPELIN), he continued solo.

Warners Warners

Jun 85. (lp/c) *(925290-1/-4)* **B-MOVIE MATINEE**
– Groove master / Let's go out tonight / Same wavelength / Plan number 9 / State your mind / Face in the window / Doll squad.
Jun 85. (7"/12") *(W/WT 9049)* **LET'S GO OUT TONIGHT. / DOLL SQUAD**
Jan 86. (12") *(WT 8921)* **STATE OF MIND. / STAY OUT OF THE LIGHT**

— In 1986, RODGERS formed The OUTLOUD with PHILLIPE SAISSE + FELICIA COLLINS. Made one eponymous album that year.

CHIC

— reformed 1991; **STERLING CAMPBELL** – drums repl. THOMPSON / + new vocalists **SYLVER LOGAN SHARP + JENN THOMAS**

W.E.A. W.E.A.

Jan 92. (7"/c-s) *(W 0083/+C)* **CHIC MYSTIQUE. / ('A'-Lovely without rap mix)** 48
(12"+=) *(W 0083T)* – ('A'-4 a.m. mix) / ('A'-Lovely mix).
(cd-s++=) *(W 0083CD)* – ('A'extended) / ('A'acappella mix).
Mar 92. (cd)(lp/c) *<(7599 26394-2)>(WX 463/+C)* **CHIC-ISM**
– Chic mystique / Your love / Jusagroove / Something you can feel / One and only one / Doin' that thing to me / Chicism / In it to win it / My love's for real / Take my love / High / M.M.F.T.C.F. *(cd re-iss. Feb95; same)*
May 92. (7") *(W)* **YOUR LOVE. / ('A'mix)**
(12"+=/cd-s+=) *(W)* – ('A'extended).

— On the 18 April '96, BERNARD EDWARDS died of unknown causes.

– compilations, others, etc. –

on 'Atlantic' unless mentioned otherwise

Nov 84. (7") *(A 9604)* **CHIC CHEERS. / SAVOIR FAIRE**
(12"+=) *(TA 9604)* – Dance, dance, dance (yowsah, yowsah, yowsah).
Sep 87. (7"/12") *(A/AT 9198)* **JACK LE FREAK. / SAVOIR FAIRE** 19
Nov 87. (lp/c/cd; shared with SISTER SLEDGE) *Telstar; (STAR/STAC/TCD 2319)* **FREAK OUT** 72 –
Jul 90. (7"/c-s) *East West; (A 7949)* **MEGACHIC (Chic Medley). / LE FREAK** 58 –
(12"+=/cd-s+=) *(A 7949 T/CD)* – ('A'edit).
Aug 90. (cd/c/lp) *East West; (2292 41750-2/-4/-1)* **MEGACHIC (THE BEST OF CHIC VOL.1)**
Jul 91. (cd/c/d-lp; shared with ROSE ROYCE) *Dino; (DIN CD/MC/TV 23)* **THEIR GREATEST HITS – SIDE BY SIDE** –
Nov 91. (cd/c) <82333-2/-4> **DANCE DANCE DANCE – THE BEST OF CHIC** –
Jun 93. (cd) <(8122 71086-2)> **THE BEST OF CHIC – VOL.2** Nov92

CHICAGO

Formed: Chicago, Illinois, USA ... 1966 by WALTER PARAZAIDER, LEE LOUGHNANE, TERRY KATH, DANNY SERAPHINE, JAMES PANKOW and ROBERT LAMM. Originally named CHICAGO TRANSIT AUTHORITY by manager and producer JAMES WILLIAM GUERCIO, the group were the first US pop-rock band to include a horn section and were nearly the most successful American act of all time (running pretty close behind THE BEACH BOYS of course). After the recruitment of bassist, vocalist and organ player PETER CETERA, the group redirected themselves to Hollywood where they signed a permanant contract with 'Columbia' records, albeit shortening their name to CHICAGO. The band issued their debut album, 'CHICAGO TRANSIT AUTHORITY' (1969), stunning critics with their fusion of jazz, rock'n'roll and good-old spirited R&B and selling an awesome two million copies in the process. Like the proverbial domino effect, this marked the beginning of a string of unforgettable albums which all bore the CHICAGO logo and were simply titled in the numerical order that they were released in (i.e. 'CHICAGO 2' 'CHICAGO 3', need I go on!?). The band churned out a number of hit singles during the 70's, culminating with the smoochiest and bed-cert 'IF YOU LEAVE ME NOW' (1976) being the most prominent of the bunch. Penned by bassist CETERA himself, the song displayed all of the romantic codes, with slow vocals and a memorable horn section, which, in itself, proved CHICAGO's talent to drive a song into new heights. The track became a bestselling hit, earning a top spot in the American Billboard charts and going double gold – even more success which was added to the band's ever growing CV. Afterwards, the troupe became familiar with swooping ballads, which the majority of their audience seemed to like, although one would argue that they had peaked with their prolific earlier works. CHICAGO had now run into their teens ('CHICAGO 13', 'CHICAGO 14', aarrgghh!) in the late '70's/early 80's after the release of the disappointing 'HOT STREETS' (1978) – er, working title '12'. It was around about this point when the band slowly began to deteriorate: they left the side of their long-term manager GUERICO just before the accidental and tragic death of guitarist/vocalist TERRY KATH. However, things weren't that bad, the 'CHICAGO 16' (1982) set selling over a million copies and the single 'HARD TO SAY I'M SORRY' entering the Top 5 on both sides of the Atlantic. The band continued to flaunt their dizzy orchestrations and trademark jazzy textures with 'CHICAGO 17' and 'CHIGAGO 18', although a few live albums were a bit beyond the pale. The group subsequently retired in the early '90's, although they issued a Big Band-style CD-disc in 1995 and a Christmas CD in '98. • **Songwriters:** LAMM wrote lyrics, KATH and group the music. Covered I'M A MAN (Spencer Davis Group). • **Trivia:** 80's newcomer JASON SCHEFF was son of Elvis Presley's bassman JERRY.

Album rating: CHICAGO TRANSIT AUTHORITY (*7) / CHICAGO II (*6) / CHICAGO III (*5) / CHICAGO AT CARNEGIE HALL (*3) / CHICAGO V (*5) / CHICAGO VI (*5) / CHICAGO VII (*5) / CHICAGO VIII (*5) / CHICAGO IX – CHICAGO'S GREATEST HITS compilation (*6) / CHICAGO X (*4) / CHICAGO XI (*4) / HOT STREETS (*4) / CHICAGO 13 (*3) / CHICAGO XIV (*3) / CHICAGO – GREATEST HITS VOLUME II compilation (*5) / CHICAGO 16 (*4) / CHICAGO 17 (*4) / CHICAGO 18 (*4) / CHICAGO 19 (*4) / GREATEST HITS 1982-1989 compilation (*5) / TWENTY 1 (*4) / NIGHT AND DAY (*2) / HEART OF CHICAGO 1967-97 compilation (*7) / THE CHICAGO STORY . . . compilation (*8)

ROBERT LAMM (b.13 Oct'44, Brooklyn, N.Y.) – vocals, keyboards / **TERRY KATH** (b.31 Jan'46) – vocals, guitar / **PETER CETERA** (b.13 Sep'44) – vocals, bass / **DAN SERAPHINE** (b.28 Aug'48) – drums / **LEE LOUGHNANE** (b.21 Oct'46) – trumpet, vocals / **JAMES PANKOW** (b.20 Aug'47) – trombone / **WALTER PARAZAIDER** (b.14 Mar'48) – reeds

C.B.S. Columbia

Sep 69. (d-lp; as CHICAGO TRANSIT AUTHORITY) *(CBS 66221) <8>* **CHICAGO TRANSIT AUTHORITY** [9] May69 [17]
– (introduction) / Does anybody really know what time it is? / Beginnings / Questions 67 and 68 / Listen / Poem 58 / Free form guitar / South California purples / I'm a man / (prologue, August 29, 1968) / Someday / Liberation. *(re-iss. Sep87) (cd-iss. Oct93 on 'Sony Europe') (re-iss. cd+c Jun94 on 'Columbia'; 474788-2/-4) <(cd re-mast.Jul02 on 'Rhino'; 8122 76171-2)>*

Jul 69. (7") *(CBS 4381) <44909>* **QUESTIONS 67 AND 68. / LISTEN** [ ] [71]

Nov 69. (7") *<45011>* **BEGINNINGS. / POEM 58** [–] [ ]

Dec 69. (7") *(CBS 4715)* **I'M A MAN. / DOES ANYBODY REALLY KNOW WHAT THE TIME IS?** [8] [–]

Mar 70. (d-lp) *(CBS 66233) <24>* **CHICAGO II** [6] Feb70 [4]
– Movin' in / The road / Poem for the people / In the country / Wake up sunshine (ballet for a girl in Buchannon) / Make me smile / So much to say, so much to give / Anxiety's moment / West Virginia fantasies / Colour my world / To be free / Now more than ever / Fancy colours / 25 or 6 to 4 / (prelude) / A.M. mourning / P.M. mourning / Memories of love / It better end soon (movements 1-4) / Where do we go from here? *(cd-iss. Oct93 on 'Sony Europe') <(cd re-mast.Jul02 on 'Rhino'+=; 8122 76172-2)>* – Make me smile / 25 or 6 to 4.

Apr 70. (7") *(CBS 4919) <45127>* **MAKE ME SMILE. / COLOUR MY WORLD** [ ] [9]

Jul 70. (7") *(CBS 5076) <45194>* **25 OR 6 TO 4. / WHERE DO WE GO FROM HERE?** [7] [4]

Nov 70. (7") *<45264>* **DOES ANYBODY REALLY KNOW WHAT THE TIME IS? / LISTEN** [–] [7]

Mar 71. (7") *(CBS 7061) <45331>* **FREE. / FREE COUNTRY** [ ] Feb71 [20]

Mar 71. (d-lp) *(CBS 66260) <30110>* **CHICAGO III** [31] Jan71 [2]
– Sing a mean tune kid / Loneliness is just a word / What else can I say / I don't want your money / Flight 602 / Motorboat to Mars / Free / Free country / At the sunrise / Happy 'cause I'm going home / Mother / Lowdown / A hard risin' morning without breakfast / Off to work / Fallin' out / Morning blues again / When all the laughter dies in sorrow / Canon / Once upon a time . . . / Progress? / The approaching storm / Man vs. man: The end. *(cd-iss. Oct93 on 'Sony Europe') <(cd re-mast.Jul02 on 'Rhino'; 8122 76173-2)>*

May 71. (7") *(CBS 7218) <45370>* **LOWDOWN. / LONELINESS IS JUST A WORD** [ ] [35]

Jul 71. (7") *(CBS 7348) <45417>* **BEGINNINGS. / COLOUR MY WORLD** [ ] Jun71 [7]

Nov 71. (q-lp) *(CBS 66405) <30865>* **LIVE AT CARNEGIE HALL – IV (live 5-10 April '71)** [ ] [3]
– In the country / Fancy colours / Does anybody really know what time it is? (free form intro) / Does anybody really know what time it is? / South California purples / Questions 67 and 68 / Sing a mean tune kid / Beginnings / It better end soon (5 movements) / Introduction / Mother / Lowdown / Flight 602 / Motorboat to Mars / Where do we go from here? / I don't want your money / Happy 'cause I'm going home / Wake up sunshine (ballet for a girl in Buchannon) / Make me smile / So much to say, so much to give / Anxiety's moment / West Virginia fantasies / Colour my world / To be free / Free / Now more than ever / A song for Richard and his friends / 25 or 6 to 4 / I'm a man. *(cd-iss. Apr89; CD 66405)*

Jan 72. (7") *<45467>* **QUESTIONS 67 AND 68 (live). / I'M A MAN (live)** [–] [ ]

Aug 72. (7") *(CBS 8331) <45657>* **SATURDAY IN THE PARK. / ALMA MATER** [ ] [3]

Sep 72. (lp) *(CBS 69018) <31102>* **CHICAGO V** [24] Jul72 [1]
– Saturday in the park / A hit by Varese / All is well / Now that you've gone / Dialogue (part 1 & 2) / While the city sleeps / State of the union / Goodbye / Alma mater. *(cd-iss. May88; CD 69018) (cd-iss. Nov93 on 'Pickwick'; 983301-2) <(cd re-mast.Aug02 on 'Rhino'+=; 8122 76175-2)>* – A song for Richard and his friends / Mississippi delta city blues / Dialogue (part 1 & 2) – single version.

Nov 72. (7") *(CBS 847?) <45717>* **DIALOGUE (part I & II). / NOW THAT YOU'VE GONE** [ ] Oct72 [24]

Aug 73. (7") *(CBS 1653) <45880>* **FEELIN' STRONGER EVERY DAY. / JENNY** [ ] Jun73 [10]

Aug 73. (lp) *(CBS 69041) <32400>* **CHICAGO VI** [ ] Jul73 [1]
– Critic's choice / Just you 'n' me / Darlin' dear / Jenny / What's this world comin' to / Something in this city changes people / Hollywood / Jenny / In terms of two / Rediscovery / Feelin' stronger every day. *(cd-iss. May88; 69041) <(cd re-mast.Aug02 on 'Rhino'; 8122 76176-2)>* – Beyond all our sorrows (by TERRY KATH) / Tired of being alone (with AL GREEN).

Sep 73. (7") *<45933>* **JUST YOU 'N' ME. / CRITIC'S CHOICE** [–] [4]

Oct 73. (7") *(CBS 1819)* **JUST YOU 'N' ME. / FEELIN' STRONGER EVERY DAY** [ ] [–]

Apr 74. (7") *(CBS 2245) <46020>* **(I'VE BEEN) SEARCHIN' SO LONG. / BYBLOS** [ ] Mar74 [9]

May 74. (d-lp/c) *(CBS/40 88015) <32810>* **CHICAGO VII** [ ] Mar74 [1]
– Prelude to Aire / Aire / Devil's sweet / Italian from New York / Hanky panky / Life saver / Happy man / (I've been) Searchin' so long / Mongonucleosis / Song of the evergreens / Byblos / Wishing you were here / Call on me / Women don't want to love me / Skinny boy. *(cd-iss. May88; CK 32810) <(cd re-mast.Jan03 on 'Rhino'+=; 8122 76177-2)>* – Byblos (rehearsal).

Jun 74. (7") *<46062>* **CALL ON ME. / PRELUDE TO AIRE** [–] [6]

Oct 74. (7") *(CBS 2468)* **CALL ON ME. / AIRE** [ ] [–]

Oct 74. (7") *<10049>* **WISHING YOU WERE HERE. / LIFE SAVER** [–] [11]

Dec 74. (7") *(CBS 2510)* **WISHING YOU WERE HERE. / SONG OF THE EVERGREENS** [ ] [–]

Apr 75. (7") *(CBS 3103) <10092>* **HARRY TRUMAN. / TILL WE MEET AGAIN** [ ] Feb75 [13]

Apr 75. (lp/c) *(CBS/40 80348) <33100>* **CHICAGO VIII** [ ] [1]
– Anyway you want / Brand new love affair (part I & II) / Never been in love before / Hideaway / Till we meet again / Harry Truman / Oh, thank you great spirit / Long time no see / Ain't it blue / Old days. *<(cd re-mast.Jan03 on 'Rhino'+=; 8122 76178-2)>* – Sixth sense / Bright eyes / Satin doll (live).

Jun 75. (7") *(CBS 3335) <10131>* **OLD DAYS. / HIDEAWAY** [ ] Apr75 [5]

Oct 75. (7") *(CBS 3745) <10185>* **NEVER BEEN IN LOVE BEFORE. / (part 2)** [ ] Aug75 [ ]

Oct 75. (7") *<10200>* **BRAND NEW LOVE AFFAIR. / HIDEAWAY** [–] [61]

Nov 75. (lp/c) *(CBS/40 69187) <33900>* **CHICAGO IX – CHICAGO'S GREATEST HITS** (compilation) [ ] [1]
– 25 or 6 to 4 / Does anybody really know what time it is? / Colour my world / Just you 'n' me / Saturday in the park / Feelin' stronger every day /

Make me smile / Wishing you were here / Call on me / (I've been) Searchin' so long / Beginnings. *(re-iss. Nov84 lp/c; CBS/40 32535) (cd-iss. Jul87; CD 69187) (re-iss. Mar91 cd/c; CD/40 32535)*

Jul 76. (7") *(CBS 4458) <10360>* **ANOTHER RAINY DAY IN NEW YORK. / HOPE FOR LOVE** — Jun76 32

Jul 76. (lp/c) *(CBS/40 86010) <34200>* **CHICAGO X** — 21 Jun76 3
– Once or twice / You are on my mind / Skin tight / If you leave me now / Together again / Another rainy day in New York City / Mama mama / Scrapbook / Gently I'll wake you / You get it up / Hope for love. *(cd-iss. May88; CD 86010) <(cd re-mast.Mar03 on 'Rhino'+=; 8122 76179-2)>* – I'd rather be rich / Your love's an attitude.

Sep 76. (7") *(CBS 4603) <10390>* **IF YOU LEAVE ME NOW. / TOGETHER AGAIN** — 1 Aug76 1

Feb 77. (7") *<10523>* **YOU ARE ON MY MIND. / GENTLY I'LL WAKE YOU** — – 49

Sep 77. (lp/c) *(CBS/40 86031) <34860>* **CHICAGO XI** — 6
– Mississippi Delta queen blues / Baby, what a big surprise / Policeman / Till the end of time / Take me back to Chicago / Vote for me / Takin' it on uptown / This time / The inner struggles of a man / (prelude) / Little one. *(cd-iss. May88; CD 86031) <(cd re-mast.Mar03 on 'Rhino'+=; 8122 76180-2)>* – Wish I could fly / Paris.

Oct 77. (7") *(CBS 5672) <10620>* **BABY, WHAT A BIG SURPRISE. / TAKIN' IT ON UPTOWN** — 41 Sep77 4

Jan 78. (7") *(CBS 5924) <10737>* **TAKE ME BACK TO CHICAGO. / POLICEMAN** — May78 63

Mar 78. (7") *(CBS 6174) <10683>* **LITTLE ONE. / TILL THE END OF TIME** — Feb78 44

—— On the 23rd of January '78, TERRY KATH died after accidentally shooting himself in the head. Later in year, he was repl. by **DONNIE DACUS** – guitar (ex-STEPHEN STILLS)

Sep 78. (lp/c) *(CBS/40 86069) <35512>* **HOT STREETS** — 12
– Alive again / The greatest love on earth / Little Miss Lovin' / Hot streets / Take a chance / Gone long gone / Ain't it time / Love was new / No tell lover / Show me the way. *(re-iss. Mar94 on 'Pickwick'; 982942-2) <(cd re-mast.Apr03 on 'Rhino'+=; 8122 76181-2)>* – Love was new (alt. vocal).

Oct 78. (7") *(CBS 6787) <10845>* **ALIVE AGAIN. / LOVE WAS NEW** — 14

Mar 79. (7") *(CBS 7050) <10879>* **NO TELL LOVER. / TAKE A CHANCE** — Dec78 14

Apr 79. (7") *<10935>* **GONE LONG GONE. / THE GREATEST LOVE ON EARTH** — – 73

Aug 79. (7") *(CBS 7822) <11061>* **MUST HAVE BEEN CRAZY. / CLOSER TO YOU** — 83

Sep 79. (lp/c) *(CBS/40 86093) <36105>* **CHICAGO 13 – STREET PLAYER** — Aug79 21
– Street player / Mama take / Must have been crazy / Window dreamin' / Paradise alley / Aloha mama / Reruns / Loser with a broken heart / Life is what it is / Run away. *<(cd re-mast.Apr03 on 'Rhino'+=; 8122 76182-2)>* – Closer to you / Street player (dance mix).

Oct 79. (7") *(CBS 7991)* **MAMA TAKE. / WINDOW DREAMIN'** — –

Apr 80. (7") *(CBS 8040) <11138>* **STREET PLAYER. / WINDOW DREAMIN'**

—— **CHRIS PINNICK** – guitar; repl. DACUS

Aug 80. (7") *(CBS 8921) <11341>* **SONG FOR YOU. / I'D RATHER BE RICH** — Jul80

Aug 80. (7") *<11345>* **THUNDER AND LIGHTNING. / I'D RATHER BE RICH** — – 56

Sep 80. (lp/c) *(CBS/40 86118) <36517>* **CHICAGO XIV** — Aug80 71
– Manipulation / Upon arrival / Song for you / Where did the lovin' go / Birthday boy / Hold on / Overnight cafe / Thunder and lightning / I'd rather be rich / The American dream. *(re-iss. Dec92 cd/c on 'Sony Collectors'; 982834-2/-4) <(cd re-mast.Apr03 on 'Rhino'+=; 8122 76183-2)>* – Doin' business / Live it up / Soldier of fortune.

Dec 81. (lp/c) *(CBS/40 85444) <37682>* **CHICAGO – GREATEST HITS, VOLUME II** (compilation)
– Baby, what a big surprise / Dialogue (part 1 & 2) / No tell lover / Alive again / Old days / If you leave me now / Questions 67 and 68 / Happy man / Gone long gone / Take me back to Chicago.

—— added **BILL CHAMPLIN** – vocals, bass, guitar (ex-SONS OF CHAMPLIN)

Full Moon — Full Moon

Jun 82. (lp/c) *(K/K4 99235) <23689>* **CHICAGO 16** — 44 9
– What you're missing / Waiting for you to decide / Bad advice / Chains / Hard to say I'm sorry / Get away / Follow me / Sonny think twice / Rescue you / What can I say / Love me tomorrow. *(cd-iss. 1983; 299235)*

Aug 82. (7") *(K 79301) <29979>* **HARD TO SAY I'M SORRY. / SONNY THINK TWICE** — 4 Jun82 1

Nov 82. (7") *(K 79338) <29911>* **LOVE ME TOMORROW. / BAD ADVICE** — Sep82 22

Jan 83. (7") *<29798>* **WHAT YOU'RE MISSING. / RESCUE YOU** — – 81

Full Moon – Warners — Full Moon – Warners

Jun 84. (7") *(W 9306) <29306>* **STAY THE NIGHT. / ONLY YOU** — Apr84 16

Jun 84. (lp/c/cd) *(925060-1/-4/-2) <25060>* **CHICAGO 17** — May84 4
– Stay the night / We can stop the hurtin' / Hard habit to break / Only you / Remember the feeling / Along comes a woman / You're the inspiration / Please hold on / Prima Donna / Once in a lifetime. *(hit No.24 in Dec84)*

Oct 84. (7"/12") *(W 9214/+T) <29214>* **HARD HABIT TO BREAK. / REMEMBER THE FEELING** — 8 Aug84 3

Nov 84. (7") *<29126>* **YOU'RE THE INSPIRATION. / ONCE IN A LIFETIME** — – 3

Jan 85. (7") *(W 9126)* **YOU'RE THE INSPIRATION. / LOVE ME TOMORROW** — 14 –
(12"+=) *(W 9126T)* – Once in a lifetime.

Apr 85. (7"/12") *(W 9082/+T) <29082>* **ALONG COMES A WOMAN. / WE CAN STOP THE HURTIN'** — Feb85 14

—— **JERRY SCHEFF** – bass; repl. CETERA who went solo

Oct 86. (7") *(W 8628) <28628>* **25 OR 6 TO 4 (remix). / ONE MORE DAY** — Aug86 48
(12"+=) *(W 8628T)* – Hard habit to break.

Oct 86. (lp/c)(cd) *(WX 61/+C)(925714-2) <25714>* **CHICAGO 18** — 35
– Niagara Falls / Forever / If she would have been faithful . . . / 25 or 6 to 4 / Will you still love me? / Over and over / It's alright / Nothin's gonna stop us now / I believe / One more day. *(cd re-iss. Feb93; same)*

Nov 86. (7") *<28512>* **WILL YOU STILL LOVE ME? / 25 OR 6 TO 4** — – 3

Feb 87. (7") *(W 8439)* **WILL YOU STILL LOVE ME? / FOREVER** — –
(12"+=) *(W 8439T)* – Hard habit to break.

Jul 87. (7") *<28283>* **NIAGARA FALLS. / I BELIEVE** — – 91

Oct 87. (7") *(W 8424) <28424>* **IF SHE WOULD HAVE BEEN FAITHFUL . . . / FOREVER** — Mar87 17
(12"+=) *(W 8424T)* – 25 or 6 to 4.

Warners — Reprise

Jun 88. (lp/c)(cd) *(WX 161/+C)(925714-2) <25714>* **CHICAGO 19** — 43
– Heart in pieces / I don't want to live without your love / I stand up / We can last forever / Come in from the night / Look away / What kind of man would I be? / Runaround / You're not alone / Victorious.

Aug 88. (7"/c-s) *(W 7855/+C) <27855>* **I DON'T WANNA LIVE WITHOUT YOUR LOVE. / I STAND UP** — May88 3
(12"+=) *(W 7855T)* – 25 or 6 to 4.
(cd-s+=) *(W 7855CD)* – Will you still love me?

Sep 88. (7"/c-s) *(W 7766/+C) <27766>* **LOOK AWAY. / COME IN FROM THE NIGHT** — 1
(12"+=/cd-s+=) *(W 7766 T/CD)* – 25 or 6 to 4.

Jan 89. (7") *<27757>* **YOU'RE NOT ALONE. / IT'S ALRIGHT** — – 10

May 89. (7") *<22985>* **WE CAN LAST FOREVER. / ONE MORE DAY** — – 55

Oct 89. (cd)(lp/c) *(K 926107-2)(WX 328/+C) <26080>* **THE HEART OF CHICAGO** <US title 'GREATEST HITS 1982-1989'> (compilation) — 9 Nov89 37
– If you leave me now / Baby, what a big surprise / Where did the lovin go / Take me back to Chicago / Hard to say I'm sorry / Love me tomorrow / Hard habit to break / Only you / You're the inspiration / Along comes a woman / Remember the feeling / If she would have been faithful . . . *(c+=/cd+=)* – Will you still love me? / What kind of man would I be? / Look away. *(re-iss. Feb94; same)* – hit UK No.6

Feb 90. (7") *(W 2741) <22741>* **WHAT KIND OF MAN WOULD I BE? / 25 OR 6 TO 4** — Nov89 5
(12"+=/cd-s+=) *(W 2741 T/CD)* – You're the inspiration / Hard to say I'm sorry.

Jul 90. (7") *<19679>* **HEARTS IN TROUBLE. / (B-side by Hans Zimmer)** — 75
(12"+=/cd-s+=) – (track by other artist).
(above on 'D.G.C.' in the US)

—— trimmed when SERAPHINE departed Aug'90

Jan 91. (c-s) *<19466>* **CHASIN' THE WIND / ONLY TIME CAN HEAL THE WOUNDED** — – 39

Feb 91. (cd/c/lp) *<(7599 26391-2/-4/-1)>* **TWENTY 1** [ ] [66]
– Explain to my heart / If it were you / You come to my senses / Somebody somewhere / What does it take / One from the heart / Chasin' the wind / God save the Queen / Man to woman / Only time can heal the wounded / Who do you love / Holdin' on.

Giant-RCA Giant-RCA

Jun 95. (cd) *(74321 26767-2) <24615>* **NIGHT AND DAY** [ ] [90]
– Moonlight serenade / Night and day / Chicago (from 'The Joker Is Wild') / Sing, sing, sing / Dream a little dream / Goody goody / Sophisticated lady / Don't get around much anymore / String of pearls / Take the 'A' train / Caravan / In the mood / Blues in the night. *(re-iss. Sep97; same)*

not iss. Chicago

Nov 98. (cd) *<3035>* **CHICAGO 25 – THE CHRISTMAS ALBUM** (festive) [–] [47]
– Little drummer boy / God rest ye merry gentlemen / Have yourself a merry little Christmas / The Christmas song / O come all ye faithful / Child's prayer / Felix Navidad / Santa Claus is coming to town / Christmas time is here / Let it snow! let it snow! let it snow! / What child is this / White Christmas / Silent night / One little candle. *<(UK+re-iss. Nov02 on 'Rhino'+=; 8122 76199-2)>*

Oct 99. (cd) *<3026>* **CHICAGO 26 – LIVE (live)** [–] [ ]
– Ballet for a girl in Buchannon / (I've been) Searchin' so long / Mongonucleosis / Hard habit to break / Call on me / Feelin' stronger every day / Just you 'n' me / Beginnings / Hard to day I'm sorry – Get away / 25 0r 6 to 4 / Back to you / If I should ever lose you / (Your love keeps lifting me) Higher and higher.

not iss. Rhino

Oct 03. (cd) *<8122 73892-2>* **WHAT'S IT GONNA BE, SANTA? – CHICAGO CHRISTMAS** (festive) [–] [ ]

– compilations, etc. –

on 'C.B.S.' / 'Columbia' unless stated otherwise

Apr 73. (7") *(CBS 1167)* **25 OR 6 TO 4. / MAKE ME SMILE** [ ] [–]
(re-iss. 1975; 13-33193) (re-iss. Mar76; 3961)

1975. (7") *(13-33197)* **DOES ANYBODY REALLY KNOW WHAT THE TIME IS? / FREE** [ ] [–]

1975. (7") *(13-33201)* **BEGINNINGS. / QUESTIONS 67 AND 68** [ ] [–]

1975. (7") *(13-33210)* **COLOUR MY WORLD. / I'M A MAN** [ ] [–]

1975. (7") *(13-33241)* **SATURDAY IN THE PARK. / DIALOGUE** [ ] [–]

Aug 75. (7") *(CBS 2815)* **WISHING YOU WERE HERE. / LIFE SAVER** [ ] [–]

Jan 77. (7") *(CBS 4940)* **WISHING YOU WERE HERE. / GENTLY I'LL WAKE YOU** [ ] [–]

Mar 79. (7") *(CBS 7079)* **I'M A MAN. / 25 OR 6 TO 4** [ ] [–]

Nov 82. (lp/c) *TV; (TVA/TVC 6)* **LOVE SONGS** [42] [–]

Nov 82. (7") *(A 2939)* **IF YOU LEAVE ME NOW. / 25 OR 6 TO 4** [ ] [ ]

Nov 82. (lp/c) *(CBS/40 25133)* **IF YOU LEAVE ME NOW** [ ] [–]
(re-iss. Apr86; CBS/40 32391) (cd-iss. Dec89; CD 32391)

Jan 83. (c-ep) *(40 3064)* **GREATEST ORIGINAL HITS** [ ] [–]
– If you leave me now / 25 or 6 to 4 / Baby, what a big surprise / Wishing you were here.

Dec 83. (lp) *Meteor; (MTLP 1003)* **BEGINNINGS** [ ] [–]
(re-iss. Jan85 on 'Topline' lp/c; TOP/KTOP 116) (cd-iss. Feb93 on 'Charly'; CDCD 1034)

Jul 84. (pic-lp) *Design; (PIXLP 2)* **TORONTO ROCK'N'ROLL REVIVAL (live)** [ ] [–]
(cd-iss. Jul91 as 'LIVE IN TORONTO' on 'Thunderbolt'; CDTB 103) (cd re-iss. Mar99 as 'LIVE IN TORONTO' on 'MagMid'; MM 021)

Apr 86. (lp/c) *Showcase; (SHLP/SHTC 121)* **CHICAGO LIVE (live)** [ ] [–]
(cd-iss. Dec88 on 'Spectrum'; SPEC 85019)

Aug 88. (3"cd-s) *<38K 33193>* **25 OR 6 TO 4. / MAKE ME SMILE** [–] [ ]

Feb 89. (lp) *Crusader; (RMB 5649)* **THE BEST OF CHICAGO** [ ] [–]

May 89. (lp/c/cd) *That's Original; (TFO LP/MC/CD 18)* **THE COLLECTION** [ ] [–]
– (CHIGAGO XIII / STREET PLAYER)

Jul 91. (3xcd-box) *(468332-2)* **IF YOU LEAVE ME NOW / CHICAGO V / CHICAGO X** [ ] [–]

Apr 93. (cd) *Pulsar;* **I'M A MAN & OTHER GREAT HITS LIVE (live)** [ ] [–]
(re-iss. Jul97 on 'Hallmark' cd/c; 30565-2/-4)

May 94. (4xcd-box/4xc-box) *Columbia-Legacy; (469209-2/-4)* **GROUP PORTRAIT** [ ] [ ]

Jun 94. (cd) *Javelin; (HADCD 172)* **IN CONCERT (live)** [ ] [–]

Aug 94. (cd) *Wisepack; (LECD 075)* **LEGENDS IN MUSIC – CHICAGO** [ ] [–]

Sep 94. (cd/c) *Prestige; (CDS/CASS GP 0126)* **25 OR 6 TO 4** [ ] [–]

Sep 96. (cd) *Experience; (EXP 006)* **CHICAGO** [ ] [–]

Mar 98. (cd) *Eagle; (EABCD 088)* **THE MASTERS** [ ] [–]

Feb 99. (cd/c) *Warner ESP; <(9362 46554-2/-4)>* **THE HEART OF CHICAGO 1967-1997** [21] May97 [55]
– You're the inspiration / If you leave me now / Make me smile / Hard habit to break / Saturday in the park / Wishing you were here / The only one / Colour my world / Look away / Here in my heart / Just you 'n' me / Does anyone really know what time it is / Will you still love me / Beginnings / Hard to say I'm sorry / Get away.

May 99. (d-cd) *Collection; (KBOX 234)* **CHICAGO** [ ] [–]

Sep 02. (cd)<d-cd> *Rhino; (8122 73630-2) <83016>* **THE CHICAGO STORY: COMPLETE GREATEST HITS** [11] Feb03 [ ]
– If you leave me now / Hard to say I'm sorry / You're the inspiration / Hard habit to break / Will you still love me? / Baby what a big surprise / Look away / What kind of man would I be? / I don't wanna live without your love / Love me tomorrow / Just you 'n' me *[US-only]* / Happy man *[US-only]* / You're not alone / Chasin' the wind *[US-only]* / Wishing you were here *[US-only]* / No tell lover *[US-only]* / (I've been) Searchin' so long *[US-only]* / Colour my world / You come to my senses / We can last forever *[US-only]* / 25 or 6 to 4 / Saturday in the park / Questions 67 and 68 *[US-only]* / I'm a man / Stay the night / Only you *[US-only]* / Dialogue pts.1 & 2 *[US-only]* / Old days *[US-only]* / Beginnings *[US-only]* / Lowdown *[US-only]* / Another rainy day in New York City *[US-only]* / Call on me *[US-only]* / Feelin' stronger every day *[US-only]* / Take me back to Chicago / Sing, sing, sing *[US-only]* / Along comes a woman / Does anybody really know what time it is? *[US-only]* / Make me smile *[US-only]* / Street player *[US-only]*.

Sep 03. (5xcd-box+dvd) *<(8122 73704-2)>* **THE BOX** [ ] Jul03 [ ]

☐ Alex CHILTON (see under ⇒ BOX TOPS)

CHUMBAWAMBA

Formed: Burnley / Barnsley, Yorkshire, England ... 1980 by vegan sextet, ALICE NUTTER, BOFF, LOU, MAVIS, HARRY and DANBERT NOBACON, who shacked up in a Leeds commune. In 1982, they appeared as SKIN DISEASE on a single 'BACK ON THE STREETS', and toured as CHUMBAWAMBA a year later with CRASS, while releasing three cassettes independently. In 1985/86, they caused a little controversy by issuing records arguing the merits of the BAND/LIVE AID charity causes. Needless to say, these were banned from radio airplay. More publicity surrounded them around this time, when they poured red paint over The CLASH, after the one-time punks arrived in Leeds for their 'Busking Britain Tour'. 1987's 'NEVER MIND THE BALLOTS: HERE'S THE REST OF YOUR LIFE', meanwhile, berated all parties in the forthcoming general election although obviously the Tories came in for the most disdain, 'MR HESELTINE MEETS HIS PUBLIC'. The same year, CHUMBAWAMBA railed against tabloid hypocrisy when they released 'LET IT BE' under the moniker of SCAB AID. Perhaps as a reaction to yet another Conservative victory, the band released an album of traditional folk protest songs, 'ENGLISH REBEL SONGS 1381-1914' (1988), their MADDY PRIOR (Steeleye Span) meets CRASS sound rising with ease to the challenge. Discovering the subversive possibilities in the emerging rave culture, the band turned in the dancefloor-friendly 'SLAP!' in summer 1990, although it took a pair-up with agit-hip hoppers CREDIT TO THE NATION for CHUMBAWAMBA to finally get their message across to a wider audience. Now signed to 'One Little Indian', the track in question, 'ENOUGH IS ENOUGH', gave the band a minor UK chart hit. Its call to challenge the rise of right-wing activism was echoed in a similarly successful follow-up, 'TIMEBOMB'. The attendant album, 'ANARCHY', made the British Top 30. Unimaginable ten years earlier, the once crustie band signed to conglomorate, 'E.M.I.' in the mid-90's, obviously deciding to subvert the pop world from within (a likely story!). Not only did they come pretty damn close with the annoyingly infectious 'TUBTHUMPING' (a No.2 UK hit!), but they broke the normally impenetrable American market. The accompanying album, 'TUBTHUMPER' (1997) made the US Top 5 (having earlier made UK Top 20), proving that patience is a virtue, even for those committed to radical social change. Love them or loathe them (and there's never usually any waverers!), CHUMBAWAMBA are now something of an institution, their newfound pop/MTV-friendly sound ushering in a new era of chart topping protest, er, possibly . . . The faux anarchs were back in 2000 with a US album 'WYSIWYG' (What You See Is What You Get), a rambling, disjointed effort which saw no-one in particular pay attention. After the release of compilation 'UNEASY LISTENING' (2000), CHUMBAWAMBA issued the pretty dismal 'READYMADES' (2002), an album full of songs but not much soul. • **Songwriters:** Group, except some traditional Hungarian folk tunes. Also sampled JOHN LENNON (Imagine), ELVIS, ALTERNATIVE TV, GANG OF FOUR, CRASS, FALL, X-RAY SPEX, STIFF LITTLE FINGERS, DAGMAR KRAUSE and GERSHWIN!. The lp tracks on 'ENGLISH REBEL SONGS' were all traditional. Covered on 'JESUS H CHRIST'; ALRIGHT NOW (Free) / MONEY, MONEY, MONEY (Abba) / SOLID GOLD EASY ACTION (T.Rex) / HEY YOU GET OFF MY CLOUD (Rolling Stones) / STAIRWAY TO HEAVEN (Led Zeppelin) / BIGMOUTH STRIKES AGAIN (Smiths) / I SHOULD BE SO LUCKY (Kylie Minogue) / MANNEQUIN (Wire) / HUNCHBACK OF NOTRE DAME (Frantic Elevators; Mick Hucknall) / NEW YORK MINING DISASTER 1941 (Bee Gees). • **Trivia:** In 1982, track 'THREE YEARS LATER' appeared on 'Crass' label album 'BULLSHIT DETECTOR 2'. ALICE NUTTER was named after a 17th century witch. DANBERT NOBACON released a single before he joined them, which featured a picture of his utensil on the cover!. 'NEVER SAY DI' single (proceeds to charity) was surprisingly in support of Princess Diana, as they were anti-royalists. 'BEHAVE!' was a tribute ha!, about 'The Hit Man And Her' (aka PETE WATERMAN & MICHAELA).

Album rating: PICTURES OF STARVING CHILDREN SELL RECORDS: CHARITY, LIES AND TRADITION (*7) / NEVER MIND THE BALLOTS: HERE'S THE REST OF YOUR LIFE (*7) / ENGLISH REBEL SONGS 1381-1914 mini (*5) / SLAP! (*6) / SHHH (*8) / ANARCHY (*9) / SHOWBUSINESS! CHUMBAWAMBA LIVE (*5) / SWINGIN' WITH RAYMOND (*5) / TUBTHUMPER (*6) / UNEASY LISTENING compilation (*7) / WYSIWYG (*6) / READYMADES (*7)

ALICE NUTTER – vocals / **BOFF** (b. BILLY McCOID) – guitar, vocals, clarinet / **LOU** (b. LOUISE MARY WATTS) – vocals, guitar / **MAVE DILLAN** – bass, trumpet, French horn / **HARRY** (b. DARREN HAMER) – drums / **DANBERT NOBACON** (b. ALAN WHALEY) – vocals / with **SIMON COMMONKNOWLEDGE** – keyboards, accordion, piano

—— (released 3 cassettes before the mid-80's)

Agit Prop | not iss.

Sep 85. (7"ep) *(AGIT 001)* **REVOLUTION EP** [ ] [–]
– Unity / Stagnation / Natural response / Adversity.

Apr 86. (7") *(AGIT 002)* **WE ARE THE WORLD. / A STATE OF MIND** [ ] [–]

—— In '86, they issued DESTROY FASCISM as The ANTIDOTE; alongside The EX

Oct 86. (lp) *(PROP 001)* **PICTURES OF STARVING CHILDREN SELL RECORDS: CHARITY, LIES AND TRADITION** [ ] [–]
– (prologue) / How to get your band on television / British colonialism and the BBC – Flickering pictures hypnotise / Commercial break / Unilever / More whitewashing / . . . An interlude. Beginning to take it back / Dutiful servants and political masters / Coca- colanisation / . . . And in a nutshell "food aid is our most powerful weapon" / Invasion.

Jul 87. (lp) *(PROP 002)* **NEVER MIND THE BALLOTS: HERE'S THE REST OF YOUR LIFE** [ ] [–]
– Always tell the voter what the voter wants to hear / Come on baby (let's do the revolution) / The wasteland / Today's sermon / Ah-men / Mr. Heseltine meets his public / The candidates find common ground / Here's the rest of your life.

—— under the name SCAB AID, they issued 'Let It Be' on the 'Scum' label.

Jul 88. (7") *(AGIT 003)* **FIGHT THE ALTON BILL. / SMASH CLAUSE 29!** [ ] [–]

Oct 88. (10"m-lp) *(PROP 003)* **ENGLISH REBEL SONGS 1381-1914** [ ] [–]
– The Cutty wren / The diggers song / Colliers march / The triumph of General Ludd / Chartist anthem / Song of the times / Smashing of the van / World turned upside down / Poverty knock / Idris strike song / Hanging on the old barbed wire / The Cutty wren (reprise). *(re-iss. Feb93 lp/cd; PROP 3/+CD) (re-iss. Feb95 on 'One Little Indian' lp/c/cd; TPLP 64/+C/CD) <US cd-iss. Jun98 on 'Imprint'; 8769>*

—— In Dec'89; they appeared on 'Agit Prop' Various Artists (SPORTCHESTRA) lp '101 SONGS ABOUT SPORT' *PROP 004)*. Another Various 'THIS SPORTING LIFE' was iss.Aug'90.

—— added **DUNST** (b. DUNSTON BRUCE) – vocals, percussion, soprano sax / **COBIE** – live sound / + others

Jul 90. (cd/lp) *(CD+/PROP 7)* **SLAP!** [ ] [–]
– Ulrike / Tiananmen Square / Cartrouble / Chase PC's flee attack by own dog / Rubens has been shot! / I never gave up: Rappoport's testament / Slap! / That's how grateful we are / Meinhof. *(re-iss. Feb95 & Jan99 on 'One Little Indian' lp/c/cd; TPLP 65/+C/CD)*

—— In Mar'91, CHUMBAWAMBA AND OTHER SUBVERSIVES released 7"; GREATEST HITS for 'Peasant Revolt'. At the same time ALICE and LOUISE (I think?) as The PASSION KILLERS released mail-order EP 'FOUR WAR IS SHIT SONGS' featuring tracks 'Shipbuilding', 'Reuters' + 2 for 'Rugger Bugger' records.

—— added **MATTY** (MC FUSION / MATTHEW HANSON) – vocals (of CREDIT TO THE NATION) / **NEIL FERGUSON** – guitar, keyboards / **GEOFF SLAPHEAD** – fiddle / **HOWARD STOREY** – vocals

Jan 92. (12"ep/cd-ep) *(AGIT 5)* **I NEVER GAVE UP** [ ] [–]
– (Rondo mix) / (Cass mix) / Laughing nevere stopped (mix). *(re-iss. Jul94 on 'Southern'; 18521-1/-2)*

Mar 92. (cd/c/lp) *(001)* **JESUS H CHRIST** [–] w-drawn [–]
(above was to have been issued on 'Tragic Flop')

Jun 92. (cd/c/lp) *(CD/TC+/PROP 11)* **SHHH** [ ] [–]
– Shhh / Big mouth strikes again / Nothing that's new / Behave! / Snip snip snip / Look! no strings! / Happiness is just a chant away / Pop star kidnap / Sometimes plunder / You can't trust anyone nowadays / Stitch that. *(re-iss. Nov94 & Sep97 on 'Southern' cd/c/lp; 18515-2/-4/-1)*

Jul 92. (7") *(none)* **NEVER SAY DI. / FOR THE LOVE OF A PRINCESS** [–] [–]
(above was actually a hoax & never quite made it to recording stage)

Nov 92. (12"/cd-s) *(AGIT 666/+CD)* **SOMEONE'S ALWAYS TELLING YOU HOW TO BEHAVE! / (2-'A'mixes by PAPA BRITTLE)** [ ] [–]

One Little Indian | E.M.I.

Sep 93. (12"ep/c-ep/cd-ep; CHUMBAWAMBA & CREDIT TO THE NATION) *(79 TP 7C/12/7CD)* **ENOUGH IS ENOUGH. / HEAR NO BULLSHIT (on fire mix) / THE DAY THE NAZI DIED (1993 mix)** [56] [–]

Nov 93. (12"ep/c-ep/cd-ep) *(89 TP 12/7C/7CD)* **TIMEBOMB. / TECHNO THE BOMB / THE WORLD TURNED UPSIDE DOWN** [59] [–]

May 94. (lp/c/cd) *(TPLP 46/+C/CD) <40903>* **ANARCHY** [29] Jun98 [ ]
– Give the anarchist a cigarette / Timebomb / Homophobia / On being pushed / Heaven – Hell / Love me / Georgina / Doh! / Blackpool rock / This year's thing / Mouthful of shit / Never do what you are told / Bad dog / Enough is enough / Rage.

May 94. (12"ep/c-ep/cd-ep) *(119 TP 12/7C/7CD)* **HOMOPHOBIA (with The SISTERS OF PERPETUAL INDULGENCE). / MORALITY PLAY IN THREE ACTS / ('A'acappella mix) / SONG FOR DEREK JARMEN** [ ] [ ]
(cd-ep) *(119 TP7CDL)* – ('A'side) / Enough is enough (with CREDIT TO THE NATION) / The day the Nazi died (with CREDIT TO THE NATION) / Morality play in three acts.

Mar 95. (lp/c/cd) *(TPLP 56/+C/CD)* **SHOWBUSINESS! CHUMBAWAMBA LIVE (live)** [ ] [–]
– Never do what you are told / I never gave up / Give the anarchist a cigarette / Heaven-Hell / That's how grateful we are / Homophobia / Morality play in three acts / Bad dog / Stitch that / Mouthful of shit / The day the Nazi died / Timebomb (Jimmy Echo vocal) / Slag aid.

Oct 95. (7"/c-s) *(139 TP7/+C)* **UGH! YOUR UGLY HOUSES! / THIS GIRL** [ ] [–]
(cd-s+=) *(139 TPCD)* – Mannequin / Hunchback of Notre Dame.

Oct 95. (d-lp/c/d-cd) *(TPLP 66/+C/CD)* **SWINGIN' WITH RAYMOND** [70] [ ]
– This girl / Never let go / Just look at me now / Not the girl I used to be / The morning after (the night before) / Love can knock you over / All mixed up / This dress kills / Salome (let's twist again) / Oxymoron / Waiting, shouting / Hey you! outside now! / Ugh! your ugly houses!

E.M.I. Republic

Aug 97. (c-s) *(TCEM 486)* *<56146>* **TUBTHUMPING / (Buttthumping mix) / (Danny Boy mix)** [2] [6]
(cd-s+=) *(CDEM 486)* – ('A'-Mawr mix: Pablo & Lawrie) / ('A'-Timeshard mix) / ('A'-Gunshot mix).
(7"red) *(EM 486)* – ('A'side) / Farewell to the Crown (featuring The OYSTER BAND) / Football song ("Shit ground, no fans").

Sep 97. (cd/c) *(CD/TC EMC 3773)* *<53099>* **TUBTHUMPER** [19] [3]
– Tubthumping / Amnesia / Drip drip drip / Big issue / Good ship lifestyle / One by one / Outsider / Creepy crawling / Mary Mary / Small town / I want more / Scapegoat. *(re-iss. Jun98 cd+=/c+=; 495238-2/-4)* – Top of the world (ole, ole, ole).

Jan 98. (c-s) *(TCEM 498)* **AMNESIA / AMNESIA (Zion Train 359 Amherst Road mix) / TUBTHUMPING (Escape From New York mix)** [10] [ ]
(cd-s) *(CDEM 498)* – (first 2 tracks) / ('A'-Done Lying Down mix) / ('A'-Jimmy Echo version) / ('A'-Decontrol mix).
(cd-s) *(CDEMS 498)* – (first & third tracks) / Tubthumping (original) / Tubthumping (Tin Tin Out mix).

May 98. (c-s) *(TCEM 511)* **TOP OF THE WORLD (OLE, OLE, OLE) / I'M A WINNER BABY / STRIKE! (Barnsley 3, Man Utd 2 mix)** [21] [–]
(cd-s) *(CDEM 511)* – (first 2 tracks) / The best is yet to come (acoustic) / The best is yet to come.

Feb 99. (cd) *(499231-2)* **UNEASY LISTENING** (compilation) [ ] [–]
– . . .And in a nutshell / Mouthful of shit / Behave / Timebomb / Morality play in three acts / Enough is enough / On being pushed / Hanging on the old barbed wire / Ugh! your ugly houses! / Look! no strings! / Big mouth strikes again / This girl / Smash clause 29! / Georgina / Waiting, shouting / Song of the mother in debt . . . / On the day the Nazi died / Give the anarchist a cigarette / Nothing knocks me over / We don't go to God's house anymore.

Apr 99. (cd-s; with NEGATIVLAND) *<(SEELAND 020CD)>* **THE ABC'S OF ANARCHISM / SMELLY WATER / c. IS FOR STUPID (ABC remix by DJ Dr.J Land)** [ ] [–]
(above issued on 'Seeland')

Mar 00. (c-s/cd-s) *(TC/CD EMS 563)* **SHE'S GOT ALL THE FRIENDS MONEY CAN BUY / LEST WE FORGET / PASSENGER LIST FOR DOOMED FLIGHT No.1721** [ ] [–]
(cd-s) *(CDEM 563)* – ('A'mixes).

Apr 00. (cd) *(525584-2)* *<157521>* **WYSIWYG** [ ] [ ]
– I'm with stupid / Shake baby shake / Pass it along / Hey hey we're the junkies / The health & the happiness show / I'm coming out / I'm in trouble again / Social dogma / www.dot / New York mining disaster 1941 / I not sorry, I was having fun / Jesus in Vegas / The standing still / She's got all the friends money can buy / Ladies for compassionate lynching / Celebration, Florida / Moses with a gun / The physical impossibilty of death in the mind of Jerry Springer / Smart bomb / Knickers / Lie lie lie lie / Dumbing down.

Mutt Republic

Aug 02. (cd) *(MUTTCD 001)* *<018071>* **READYMADES** [ ] Jun02 [ ]
– Salt fare, North Sea / Jacob's ladder / All in vain / Home with me / If it is to be, it is up to me / Don't try this at home / Song for Len Shackleton / Without rhyme or reason (the killing of Harry Stanley) / Don't pass go / One way or the other / When I'm bad / Sewing up crap / After Shelley.

Sep 02. (cd-s) *(MUTTCDS 088)* **HOME WITH ME** [ ] [–]

– compilations, others, etc. –

Feb 92. (lp/cd) *Agit Prop; (PROP 4)* **FIRST 2** [ ] [–]
– (as said 1st 2 albums, originally Aug89 as '100 SONGS ABOUT SPORT'; *PROP 004) (re-iss. Feb95 on 'One Little Indian' d-lp/c/cd; TPLP 63/+C/CD)*

Apr 96. (cd+book) *One Little Indian; (EYE 1)* **PORTRAITS OF ANARCHISTS** [ ] [–]

Jan 99. (cd) *One Little Indian; (TPLP 65CD)* **LOVE / HATE** [ ] [–]

☐ CINERAMA (see under ⇒ WEDDING PRESENT)

☐ CITY (see under ⇒ KING, Carole)

Eric CLAPTON

Born: ERIC PATRICK CLAPP, March 30th 1945, Ripley, Surrey, England. Brought up by his grandparents, CLAPTON later attended Kingston Art College where he studied stained glass design. Heavily influenced by ROBERT JOHNSON, B.B. KING and BUDDY GUY, CLAPTON was a self taught musician (he had been given a £14 guitar by his grandparents on his 14th birthday) and began playing with TOM McGUINNESS in his first band, The ROOSTERS, in January 1963. Eight months later, they left The ROOSTERS and joined CASEY JONES AND THE ENGINEERS, although this didn't last long and CLAPTON's first big break came in October 1963 when he was asked to replace TOP TOPHAM in The YARDBIRDS. The latter act had just taken over from The ROLLING STONES as the resident band at the Crawdaddy Club in Richmond; CLAPTON, nicknamed "Slowhand" by the band's manager, GIORGIO GOMELSKY, quickly outshone the singer, KEITH RELF, and became the principal focal point of the group, although he left them on the eve of their chart success in 1965, complaining that their music had become too commercial. CLAPTON had recorded only one album with The YARDBIRDS but his potential shone out on 'FIVE LONG YEARS' and 'SMOKESTACK LIGHTNING'. The highlight of the album, entitled, 'FIVE LIVE YARDBIRDS', was a rendition of Chuck Berry's 'TOO MUCH MONKEY BUSINESS'. He then joined JOHN MAYALL's BLUESBREAKERS in April 1965 and around this time the famous, although unsubstantiated phrase, 'CLAPTON IS GOD' was coined. Again, he only recorded one album although it was to be the spark for the blues boom of the sixties. That album was 'BLUESBREAKERS WITH ERIC CLAPTON', recorded over one weekend with no track laid down in more than one take. He left THE BLUESBREAKERS in 1966 and immediately formed CREAM with GINGER BAKER and JACK BRUCE. CREAM broke up in November 1968 and CLAPTON played on the GEORGE HARRISON-penned BEATLES track, 'While My Guitar Gently Weeps' (under the name, L'ANGELO MYSTERIOSO), and also contributed to HARRISON's solo album, 'WONDERWALL MUSIC'. CLAPTON subsequently formed BLIND FAITH with BAKER, STEVE WINWOOD and RIC GRECH, and although they topped the charts on both sides of the Atlantic with their eponymous debut set, they couldn't cope with the high pressure expected of a "supergroup", and broke up in 1970. He was still only 24 but fame had taken its toll and he retreated into the ranks of DELANEY & BONNIE AND FRIENDS from which he formed his own, equally laid back DEREK AND THE DOMINOES. By this time CLAPTON was actively trying to shun publicity and even refused to have his name on the cover of the classic album, 'LAYLA AND OTHER ASSORTED LOVE SONGS'. Meanwhile, his debut solo lp was recorded in Los Angeles in 1970; issued shortly after, it reached the UK and US Top 20. The following year, the second DEREK AND THE DOMINOES album was scrapped due to the band's worsening drugs problem and they decided to call it a day. CLAPTON went into seclusion, only coming out for the occasional charity performance (including the Concert For Bangladesh). Ironically, 'LAYLA' (a song written about GEORGE HARRISON's wife PATTI), gave the now defunct DEREK AND THE DOMINOES a belated Top 10 hit in the UK in 1972. PETE TOWNSHEND, concerned for his friend's health, persuaded CLAPTON to take part in an all-star comeback concert in 1973 at London's Rainbow Theatre with RON WOOD, STEVE WINWOOD, JIM CAPALDI and many others. The performance was recorded and the resulting album, 'ERIC CLAPTON'S RAINBOW CONCERT' reached a respectable Top 20 slot on both sides of the Atlantic. The success of the project and the album did not, however, convince CLAPTON to step back into the limelight and he retreated once more. The guitarist underwent a course of electronically adapted acupuncture in 1974, eventually got rid of the habit and told record boss, Robert Stigwood, that he was ready to come back. TOM DOWD was brought in as producer although CLAPTON had only two songs in mind, 'PLEASE BE WITH ME' by Charles Scott Boyer and his own, 'GIVE ME STRENGTH'. A new band was assembled with CARL RADLE, JAMIE OLDAKER, DICK SIMS, GEORGE TERRY and YVONNE ELLIMAN and MARCY LEVY (LEVY would later resurface as MARCELLA DETROIT in SHAKESPEAR'S SISTER). In August 1974, the first single from the comeback sessions, a brilliant version of Bob Marley's 'I SHOT THE SHERIFF', was released and reached an unexpected UK number 9; many observers speculated that he was ill-advised in trying to cross over music boundaries. Later the same month, the accompanying album, '461 OCEAN BOULEVARD' (named after the address of the recording studio), was released to UK Top 3 success. His long guitar solos had now been trimmed down in line with his more basic approach to songwriting, apparent on subsequent hit album, 'THERE'S ONE IN EVERY CROWD' (1975); his version of 'SWING LOW SWEET CHARIOT' reached UK Top 20. In August of the same year, he hit the charts with yet another cover, Bob Dylan's 'KNOCKIN'ON HEAVEN'S DOOR', while the live album, 'E.C. WAS HERE', kept his profile high. During this period, GEORGE TERRY was taking on most of the lead guitar work as CLAPTON was still reluctant to be in the forefront. In September 1976, 'NO REASON TO CRY' reached UK Top 10, its credibility factor enhanced by the talents of BOB DYLAN & THE BAND. CLAPTON reciprocated by performing 'FURTHER ON UP THE ROAD' (with new band member, SERGIO PASTORA, on percussion) at THE BAND's 'LAST WALTZ' farewell concert. 'SLOWHAND' released in 1977, was only kept off the US top spot by 'Saturday Night Fever', while the painfully sentimental single, 'WONDERFUL TONIGHT' (the second song written for PATTI) reached Top 20; other highlights were JJ Cale's 'COCAINE' and John Martyn's 'MAY YOU NEVER'. The following year's 'BACKLESS' followed in much the same head-nodding vein, CLAPTON obviously remaining oblivious to the energy and attitude of the burgeoning punk scene. In March 1979, he decided to embark on a world tour with an all-new UK band consisting of ALBERT LEE, CHRIS STAINTON, DAVE MARKEE and HENRY SPINETTI. The veteran troupe recorded live tracks at the Budokan in Japan (the resulting album, 'JUST ONE NIGHT' was a transatlantic Top 5 success the following year), and during the tour, CLAPTON finally married his long time love, PATTI. The 70's had not been an easy time for CLAPTON and his disciples, his heroin addiction subsequently replaced by a copious intake of cognac. In May 1980, ex-PROCOL HARUM stalwart, GARY BROOKER, replaced STAINTON for a British tour, although later in the month, CLAPTON was saddened to hear that his former bass player, CARL RADLE, had died of chronic kidney disease. CLAPTON wasn't in the best of health himself, the guitarist admitted to hospital in Minnesota during his 1980 tour of America with doctors estimating that he would have had under an hour to live had his ulcer burst. With his health restored, and with the revitalisation of the adult rock market (beginning with the early 80's introduction of the Compact Disc), CLAPTON re-emerged as a revered elder statesman of rock, although he had a further setback when he was hospitalised in April 1981 after a car accident. He recovered from this and went on to contribute to PHIL COLLINS' debut album (beginning a long standing friendship/working relationship) and also returned to live work by performing with JEFF BECK at 'The Secret Policeman's Other Ball'. CLAPTON's last album for 'R.S.O.', 'ANOTHER TICKET', reached the UK Top 20, although success was limited in the States; later that year he decided to form his own 'Duck' Records. The following year he released 'MONEY AND CIGARETTES', the album (featuring RY COODER and ALBERT LEE amongst others) seeing him back in the Top 20 on both sides of the Atlantic. In between numerous charity concerts, "God" managed to record his next album, 'BEHIND THE SUN' (1985), the Top 10 (US Top 40) set being produced by PHIL COLLINS, TED TEMPLEMAN and RUSS TITELMAN. Later that year, CLAPTON ventured into TV soundtrack work, co-writing the Ivor Novello award winning 'EDGE OF DARKNESS' theme with MICHAEL KAMEN. By this point, CLAPTON was in his slick, Armani suit-wearing period, his polished follow-up, 'AUGUST' (again produced by COLLINS), contained the semi-classic tracks, 'BEHIND THE MASK' and the TINA TURNER duet 'TEARING US APART'. In 1987 he began his first series of concerts at the Royal Albert Hall, London (they would become an annual event and by 1990, he had built up to 18 consecutive nights). Towards the end of the decade, CLAPTON completed the score for the Mickey Rourke-starring film, 'Homeboy', while his next album proper, 'JOURNEYMAN' (1989; Top 5), found CLAPTON rediscovering his guitar. Tragedy was to rear its ugly head again in 1990, when, on August the 27th, three members of his entourage died along with STEVIE RAY VAUGHAN in a helicopter crash following a concert in East Troy, Wisconsin. In 1991, at his annual Albert Hall residency (now up to a staggering 24 shows; the performances would subsequently be released as concert set, '24 NIGHTS'), he decided to split each show into five segments – a four piece band, a second four piece band with different percussion, a nine piece band, a blues band with guitarists ALBERT COLLINS, ROBERT CRAY, BUDDY GUY and JIMMIE VAUGHAN, and a nine piece band with orchestra conducted by MICHAEL KAMEN. Incredibly, CLAPTON underwent further emotional trauma, when in March that year, his 4-year old son, CONOR, died after falling out of a skyscraper window. Not surprisingly, CLAPTON shunned the world for some time, only reappearing in September on BUDDY GUY's first album for over a decade, 'Damn Right I've Got The Blues'. A live version of 'WONDERFUL TONIGHT' (from the '24 NIGHTS' set) reached the UK Top 30 and rounded off a year of highs and lows to match any that he'd faced previously. 1992 began with a recording of an 'MTV UNPLUGGED' show, and, backed by NATHAN EAST, ANDY FAIRWEATHER LOW, RAY COOPER and CHUCK LEAVELL, he performed new material, 'THE CIRCUS LEFT TOWN' and 'TEARS IN HEAVEN' along with standards including a drastically pared down version of 'LAYLA'. The resulting album went on to be the most successful of his career (UK No.2 and US No.1), although he allegedly didn't even want it released! It also showed CLAPTON's return to his blues roots with Big Bill Broozny's 'HEY HEY', a stunning version of Robert Johnson's

'MALTED MILK' and Muddy Waters' 'ROLLIN AND TUMBLIN'. However, it was the aforementioned heart-rending tribute to his son, 'TEARS IN HEAVEN' (lyrics by Will Jennings) that stole the show, CLAPTON's voice wracked with the pain of his bereavement (the song subsequently won him another Ivor Novello award). Following on from more film soundtrack work (i.e. 'Lethal Weapon 3' and 'Rush'), his 1994 album, 'FROM THE CRADLE', saw him completely back to his blues roots with standards like Willie Dixon's 'GROANIN THE BLUES' and Lowell Fulson's 'RECONSIDER BABY'. Although the brilliant 'MOTHERLESS CHILD' lingered in the lower regions of the charts, he finally scored his first No.1 single backing CHRISSIE HYNDE, CHER and NENEH CHERRY on the 1995 Childline single, 'LOVE CAN BUILD A BRIDGE'. CLAPTON continued to tour, play charity gigs and had even taken to giving interviews (something he wasn't exactly noted for in the past). 1998's 'PILGRIM' was an elegiac, often intensely personal set of reflections on his journey through life, the death of his son understandably still permeating his muse. The album also inaugurated his production/writing partnership with Simon Climie (once of 80's pop act CLIMIE FISHER), a pairing that remained in place – at least in terms of production – for 'RIDING WITH THE KING' (2000). A collaboration with legend B.B. KING, the record's enjoyable if predictable run-through of blues favourites provided a bit of light relief for fans and quite possibly a modicum of release and catharsis for CLAPTON himself. The guitarist continued to look to the past with 'REPTILE' (2001), his first solo studio set of the new decade. The sleeve featured CLAPTON as a grinning youngster while many of the songs were interpretations of R&B hits from his youth such as Ray Charles' 'COME BACK BABY' and John Greer's 'GOT YOU ON MY MIND'. He also paid tribute to one of his major latter day influences with a reading of 'TRAVELIN' LIGHT', one of J.J. Cale's most atmospheric 70's efforts. With his umpteenth live set, 'ONE MORE CAR, ONE MORE RIDER' (2002), it was difficult to avoid the impression that CLAPTON seems content to motor along comfortably in the middle of the road, wary of ratcheting up his muse a few gears. Long time favourites like 'KEY TO THE HIGHWAY' and 'BELL BOTTOM BLUES' made for pleasant enough listening, but fans must be tired waiting on a set which finally fires on all cylinders. • **Covered:** AFTER MIDNIGHT + I'LL MAKE LOVE TO YOU ANYTIME (J.J. Cale) / SWING LOW SWEET CHARIOT (spiritual/gospel trad.) / WILLIE AND THE HAND JIVE + CRAZY COUNTRY HOP (Johnny Otis) / HAVE YOU EVER LOVED A WOMAN (Billy Myles) / NOBODY KNOWS YOU WHEN YOU'RE DOWN AND OUT (Jimmy Cox) / KEY TO THE HIGHWAY (Sager/Broonzy) / KNOCK ON WOOD (Eddie Floyd) / BEHIND THE MASK (Michael Jackson co-wrote w/others; covered by Yellow Magic Orchestra) / WATCH YOURSELF (Buddy Guy) / WORRIED LIFE BLUES (Mecio Merryweather) / HOODOO MAN (Sonny Boy Williamson) / HOUND DOG (hit; Elvis Presley) / DOUBLE TROUBLE (Otis Rush) / SIGN LANGUAGE (Bob Dylan) / FLOATING BRIDGE and EVERYBODY OUGHTA (Sleepy John Estes) / LEAD ME ON (Womack/Womack) / BEFORE YOU ACCUSE ME (Bo Diddley) / RUNNING ON FAITH + PRETENDING (. . . Williams) / RUN SO FAR (Wilbert Harrison) / DON'T KNOW WHICH WAY TO GO (Willie Dixon) / etc. • **Trivia:** In 1966 (with JACK BRUCE, PAUL JONES, STEVE WINWOOD and PETE YORK), CLAPTON briefly formed The POWERHOUSE, who recorded three songs for 'Elektra' compilation, 'WHAT'S SHAKIN'.

Album rating: ERIC CLAPTON (*7) / LAYLA AND OTHER ASSORTED LOVE SONGS; Derek & The Dominoes (*9) / THE RAINBOW CONCERT (*5) / IN CONCERT; Derek & The Dominoes (*5) / 461 OCEAN BOULEVARD (*8) / THERE'S ONE IN EVERY CROWD (*5) / E.C. WAS HERE (*5) / NO REASON TO CRY (*6) / SLOWHAND (*7) / BACKLESS (*6) / JUST ONE NIGHT (*3) / ANOTHER TICKET (*6) / TIME PIECES: BEST OF ERIC CLAPTON compilation (*7) / MONEY AND CIGARETTES (*6) / TIME PIECES II: LIVE IN THE 70'S collection (*6) / BEHIND THE SUN (*5) / AUGUST (*6) / CROSSROADS compilation (*9) / JOURNEYMAN (*7) / 24 NIGHTS (*4) / UNPLUGGED (*7) / FROM THE CRADLE (*6) / THE CREAM OF ERIC CLAPTON collection (*7) / CROSSROADS 2: LIVE IN THE 70's collection (*6) / PILGRIM (*5) / REPTILE (*6) / ONE MORE CAR, ONE MORE RIDER (*4)

ERIC CLAPTON – vocals, guitar (ex-DELANEY & BONNIE, ex-BLIND FAITH ex-CREAM, ex-JOHN MAYALL'S BLUESBREAKERS, ex-YARDBIRDS, etc) featured his **DOMINOES** musicians plus **STEPHEN STILLS** – guitar

Polydor Atco

Aug 70. (lp) *(2383 021)* <329> **ERIC CLAPTON** — 17 Jul70 13
– Slunky / Bad boy / Lonesome and a long way from home / After midnight / Easy now / Blues power / Bottle of red wine / Lovin' you lovin' me / I've told you for the last time / I don't know why / Let it rain. *(re-iss. Nov82 & Feb83)*

— In Oct 70, CLAPTON guested on KING CURTIS single 'TEASIN'. / 'SOULIN'

Nov 70. (7") *(2001 096)* <6784> **AFTER MIDNIGHT. / EASY NOW** — Oct70 18

DEREK AND THE DOMINOES

ERIC CLAPTON – vox, guitar with **BOBBY WHITLOCK** – keyboards, vocals / **CARL RADLE** – bass / **JIM GORDON** – drums **/ and guest DUANE ALLMAN** – guitar

Sep 70. (7"w-drawn) *(2058 057)* **TELL THE TRUTH. / ROLL IT OVER** — – –

Dec 70. (7") *(2058 130)* <6809> **LAYLA. / BELL BOTTOM BLUES** — –

Jan 71. (d-lp) *(2625 005)* <SD2 704> **LAYLA & OTHER ASSORTED LOVE SONGS** — Nov70 16
– I looked away / Bell bottom blues / Keep on growing / Nobody knows you when you're down and out / I am yours / Anyday / Key to the highway / Tell the truth / Why does love got to be so sad? / Have you ever loved a woman / Little wing / It's too late / Layla / Thorn tree in the garden. *(re-iss. Aug74 & Nov77; 2671 110) (re-iss. Jan84; SPDLP 1) (cd-iss. Mar91; 823277-2) (LAYLA REMASTERED – 20th ANNIVERSARY EDITION d-cd/d-c; 847083-2/-4)*

Feb 71. (7") <6803> **BELL BOTTOM BLUES. / KEEP ON GROWING** — – 91

Mar 71. (7") <6809> **LAYLA. / I AM YOURS** — – 51
<re-iss. Apr72; 15040> – hit No.10

Jul 72. (7") *(2058 130)* **LAYLA. / I AM YOURS** — 7 –

— split Spring '71 but left behind posthumous album below, etc

R.S.O. Polydor

Sep 72. (7") <15049> **LET IT RAIN. / EASY NOW** — – 48

Mar 73. (d-lp) *(2659 020)* <28800> **DEREK AND THE DOMINOES – IN CONCERT (live)** — 36 Jan73 20
– Why does love got to be so sad? / Got to get better in a little while / Let it rain / Presence of the Lord / Tell the truth / Bottle of red wine / Roll it over / Blues power / Have you ever loved a woman. *(d-cd-iss. Jan94; 831416-2)*

Apr 73. (7") *(2090 104)* **WHY DOES LOVE GOT TO BE SO SAD? (live). / PRESENCE OF THE LORD (live)** — –

Jun 73. (7") <15056> **BELL BOTTOM BLUES. / LITTLE WING** — – Feb73 78

— In '71 ERIC had virtually retired into session work. He appeared in GEORGE HARRISON's Bangla Desh concert, 1st Aug'71.

ERIC CLAPTON

returned for a one-off concert at the Rainbow, 13Jan73 with **PETE TOWNSHEND** – guitar / **RON WOOD** – guitar / **STEVE WINWOOD** – keyboards / **JIMMY KARSTEIN & JIM CAPALDI** – drums / **REE BOP** – percussion / **RIC GRECH** – bass

Polydor R.S.O.

Sep 73. (lp) *(2479 116)* <877> **THE RAINBOW CONCERT** — 19 18
– Badge / Roll it over / Presence of the Lord / Pearly queen / After midnight / Little wing. *(re-iss. Aug83 on 'R.S.O.' lp/c; SPE LP/MC 23) (cd-iss. 1988; 831 320-2) (re-iss. May95 cd/c; 527472-2/-4)*

Oct 73. (7") <400> **PRESENCE OF THE LORD (live). / WHY DOES LOVE GOT TO BE SO BAD?** — –

— **ERIC CLAPTON** went solo again with **GEORGE TERRY** – guitar (ex-sessions) / **CARL RADDLE** – bass (ex-DEREK AND THE DOMINOES, ex-DELANEY & BONNIE) / **DICK SIMS** – keyboards (ex-BOB SEGER) / **JAMIE OLDAKER** – drums (ex-BOB SEGER) / **MARCY LEVY** – b.vocals (ex-BOB SEGER) / **YVONNE ELLIMAN**

R.S.O. R.S.O.

Jul 74. (7") *(2090 132)* *<409>* **I SHOT THE SHERRIF. / GIVE ME STRENGTH** [9] [1]

Aug 74. (lp/c) *(2479/ 116)* *<4801>* **461 OCEAN BOULEVARD** [3] Jul74 [1]
– Motherless children / Give me strength / Willie and the hand jive / Get ready / I shot the sheriff / I can't hold out / Please be with me / Steady rollin' man / Mainline Florida. *(re-iss. Aug83 lp/c; SPE LP/TC 24) (cd-iss. Nov89; 839 874-2)*

Oct 74. (7") *(2090 139)* *<503>* **WILLIE AND THE HAND JIVE. / MAINLINE FLORIDA** [ ] [26]

— added **MARCY LEVY** – vocals, tambourine

Apr 75. (7") *(2058 560)* *<509>* **SWING LOW SWEET CHARIOT. / PRETTY BLUE EYES** [19] [ ]

Apr 75. (lp/c) *(2479/ 132)* *<4806>* **THERE'S ONE IN EVERY CROWD** [15] [21]
– We've been told (Jesus' coming soon) / Swing low sweet chariot / Little Rachel / Don't blame me / The sky is crying / Singing the blues / Better make it through today / Pretty blue eyes / High / Opposites. *(re-iss. Mar85 lp/c; SPE LP/MC 92) (cd-iss. Nov86; 829 649-2)*

Aug 75. (7") *(2090 166)* *<513>* **KNOCKIN' ON HEAVEN'S DOOR. / SOMEONE LIKE YOU** [38] [ ]

Sep 75. (lp/c) *(2479 179)* *<4809>* **E.C. WAS HERE (live)** [14] [20]
– Have you ever loved a woman / Presence of the Lord / Drifting blues / Can't find my way home / Ramblin' on my mind / Further on up the road. *(re-iss. Aug83 lp/c; SPE LP/MC 21) (cd-iss. Jul92; 831519-2)*

— added **SERGIO PASTORA** – percussion (ex-BOB SEGER)

Aug 76. (lp/c) *(2479 179)* *<3801>* **NO REASON TO CRY** [8] Sep76 [15]
– Beautiful thing / Carnival / Sign language / County jail blues / All our past times / Hello old friend / Double trouble / Innocent times / Hungry / Black summer rain. *(re-iss. Aug83 lp/c; SPE LP/MC 2) (cd-iss. Dec86; 813 582-2)*

Oct 76. (7") *(2090 208)* *<861>* **HELLO OLD FRIEND. / ALL OUT PAST TIMES** [ ] [24]

Feb 77. (7") *(2090 284)* *<868>* **CARNIVAL. / HUNGRY** [ ] [ ]

— augmented by five piece when ELLIMAN then PASTORA both went solo

Nov 77. (7") *(2090 294)* *<886>* **LAY DOWN SALLY. / COCAINE** [39] [3]

Nov 77. (lp/c) *(2479 201)* *<3030>* **SLOWHAND** [23] [2]
– Cocaine / Wonderful tonight / Lay down Sally / Next time you see her / We're all the way / The core / May you never / Mean old Frisco / Peaches and diesel. *(re-iss. Aug83 lp/c)(cd; SPE LP/MC 25)(823 276-2)*

Mar 78. (7") *(2090 275)* *<895>* **WONDERFUL TONIGHT. / PEACHES AND DIESEL** [ ] May78 [16]

— **ERIC CLAPTON & HIS BAND**

ERIC now backed up only by **SIMS, OLDAKER** and **RADLE** when MARCY LEVY went solo and GEORGE TERRY went into sessions.

Sep 78. (7") *(RSO 21)* *<910>* **PROMISES. / WATCH OUT FOR LUCY** [37] [9] [40]

Nov 78. (lp/c) *(RSD/TRSD 5001)* *<3039>* **BACKLESS** [18] [8]
– Walk out in the rain / Watch out for Lucy / I'll make love to you anytime / Roll it / Tell me that you love me / If I don't be there by morning / Early in the morning / Promises / Golden ring / Tulsa time. *(re-iss. Aug83 lp/c; SPE LP/MC 1) (cd-iss. Jan89; 813 581-2)*

Mar 79. (7") *<928>* **TULSA TIME. / COCAINE** [–] [ ]

Mar 79. (7") *(RSO 24)* **IF I DON'T GET THERE BY MORNING. / TULSA TIME** [ ] [–]

— added **ALBERT LEE** – guitar (ex-solo artist, etc.) to complete new band, **DAVE MARKEE** – bass repl.CARL / **HENRY SPINETTI drums** repl. JAMIE

May 80. (d-lp/d-c) *(RSDX/+C 2)* *<4202>* **JUST ONE NIGHT (live at Budokhan)** [3] [2]
– Tulsa time / Early in the morning / Lay down Sally / Wonderful tonight / If I don't be there by morning / Worried life blues / All our past times / After midnight / Double trouble / Setting me up / Blues power / Ramblin' on my mind / Cocaine / Farther on up the road. *(d-cd-iss. Nov88; 800 093-2)*

Jul 80. (7") *<1039>* **TULSA TIME (live). / COCAINE (live)** [ ] Jun80 [30]

Oct 80. (7") *<1051>* **BLUES POWER (live). / EARLY IN THE MORNING (live)** [–] [76]

— **GARY BROOKER & CHRIS STAINTON** – keyboards repl. DICK

Feb 81. (7") *(RSO 74)* *<1060>* **I CAN'T STAND IT. / BLACK ROSE** [ ] [10]

Feb 81. (lp/c) *(RSD/TRSD 5008)* *<3095>* **ANOTHER TICKET** [18] Mar81 [7]
– Something special / Black rose / Blow wind blow / Another ticket / I can't stand it / Hold me Lord / Floating bridge / Catch me if you can / Rita Mae. *(re-iss. Apr84 lp/c; SPE LP/MC 67) (cd-iss. Feb87; 827 579-2)*

Apr 81. (7") *(RSO 75)* *<1064>* **ANOTHER TICKET. / RITA MAE** [ ] [78]

— **ERIC CLAPTON** retained **LEE** and recruited **RY COODER, ROGER HAWKINS, DONALD 'DUCK' DUNN** plus backing vocalists **JOHN SAMBATAO** and **CHUCK KIRKPATRICK**

Duck-Warners Duck-Warners

Feb 83. (7") *(W 9780)* *<29780>* **I'VE GOT A ROCK'N'ROLL HEART. / MAN OVERBOARD** [ ] Jan83 [18]
(12"+=) *(W 9780T)* – Everybody oughta make a change.

Feb 83. (lp/c) *(W 3773/+4)* *<23773>* **MONEY AND CIGARETTES** [13] [16]
– Everybody outta make a change / The shape you're in / Ain't going down / I've got a rock'n'roll heart / Man overboard / Pretty girl / Man in love / Crosscut saw / Slow down Linda / Crazy country hop. *(cd-iss. 1984; 923 773-2) (cd re-iss. Feb95;)*

Apr 83. (7"/7"pic-d) *(W 9701/+P)* **THE SHAPE YOU'RE IN. / CROSSCUT SAW** [75] [ ]
(12"+=) *(W 9701T)* – Pretty girl.

May 83. (7") *(W 9651)* **SLOW DOWN LINDA. / CRAZY COUNTRY HOP** [ ] [ ]
(12"+=) *(W 9651T)* – The shape you're in.

— **CLAPTON** put together a new band. **TIM RENWICK** – guitar (ex-SUTHERLAND BROTHERS & QUIVER) / **CHRIS STAINTON** – keyboards (ex-solo, ex-JOE COCKER) / **DONALD 'DUCK' DUNN** – bass (ex-BOOKER T. AND THE M.G.'s) / **JAMIE OLDAKER** – drums (returned) **MARCY LEVY** (returned) **& SHAUN MURPHY** – backing vocals

Mar 85. (7") *(W 9069)* *<29081>* **FOREVER MAN. / TOO BAD** [51] [26]
(12"+=) *(W 9069T)* – Something's happening.

Mar 85. (lp/c/cd) *(925166-1/-4/-2)* *<25166>* **BEHIND THE SUN** [8] [34]
– She's waiting / See what love can do / Same old blues / Knock on wood / Something's happening / Forever man / It all depends / Tangled in love / Never make you cry / Just like a prisoner / Behind the sun. *(re-iss. cd Feb95;)*

May 85. (7") *<28986>* **SEE WHAT LOVE CAN DO. / SHE'S WAITING** [–] [89]

Jul 85. (7") *(W 8954)* **SHE'S WAITING. / JAILBAIT** [ ] [–]

Dec 85. (7"; by ERIC CLAPTON & MICHAEL KAMEN) *(RESL 178)* **EDGE OF DARKNESS. / SHOOT OUT** [65] [–]
(c-s)(12") *(Z/12 RSL 178)* – ('A'side) / Escape from North Moor. *(re-iss. cd-ep.Feb89; CDRSL 178)*
(above from TV series 'Edge Of Darkness' on 'BBC' records)

Nov 86. (lp/c)(cd) *(WX 71/+C)(925476-2)* *<25476>* **AUGUST** [3] Dec86 [37]
– It's in the way that you use it / Run / Tearing us apart / Bad influence / Hung up on your love / Take a chance / Hold on / Miss you / Holy mother / Behind the mask. *(cd+=)* – Grand illusion. *(re-iss. cd Feb95;)*

Jan 87. (7") *(W 8461)* **BEHIND THE MASK. / GRAND ILLUSION** [15] [ ]
(12"+=) *(W 8461T)* – Wanna make love to you.
(d7"+=) *(W 8461F)* – White room (live) / Crossroads (live).

Mar 87. (7") *(W 8397)* **IT'S IN THE WAY THAT YOU USE IT. / BAD INFLUENCE** [ ] [ ]
(d7+=/12"+=) *(W 8397 8397 F/T)* – Old ways / Pretty girl.

— **GREG PHILLINGANES** also joined

Jun 87. (7"; by ERIC CLAPTON & TINA TURNER) *(W 8299)* **TEARING US APART. / HOLD ON** [56] [ ]
(12"+=) *(W 8299T)* – Run.

Nov 87. (7") *(W 8141)* **HOLY MOTHER. / TANGLED IN LOVE** [ ] [ ]
(12"+=) *(W 8141T)* – Behind the mask / Forever man.

— now backed in concert by BUCKWHEAT ZYDECO

Feb 89. (cd/c/lp) *(CD/TC+/V 2741)* *<2574>* **HOMEBOY (Soundtrack w/ others on 'Virgin' records UK)** [ ] [ ]
– Travelling east / Johnny / Call me if you need me (MAGIC SAM) / Bridge / Pretty baby (J.B. HUTTO & THE NEW HAWKS) / Dixie / Ruby's loft / I want to love you baby (PEGGY SCOTT / JO JO BENSON) / Bike ride / Ruby / Living in the real world (The BRAKES) / Final flight / Dixie / Homeboy. *(cd+=)* – Country bikin' / Party / Training / Chase.

— now with **ALAN CLARKE, ROBERT CRAY, GEORGE HARRISON, PHIL COLLINS,** etc

Nov 89. (7") *<22732>* **PRETENDING. / BEFORE YOU ACCUSE ME** [–] [55]

Nov 89. (lp)(c/cd) *(WX 322)(926074-4/-2) <26074>* **JOURNEYMAN** [3] [16]
– Pretending / Anything for your love / Bad love / Running on faith / Hard times / Hound dog / No alibis / Run so far / Old love / Breaking point / Lead me on / Before you accuse me.

Jan 90. (7") *(W 2644)* **BAD LOVE. / BEFORE YOU ACCUSE ME** [ ] [–]
(c-s/12"/cd-s) *(W 2644 C/T/CD)* – ('A'side) / Badge (live) / Let it rain (live).

Mar 90. (7") *<19980>* **BAD LOVE. / HARD TIMES** [–] [88]

Mar 90. (7"/7"box/c-s) *(W 9981/+B/C)* **NO ALIBIS. / RUNNING ON FAITH** [53] [ ]
(12"+=) *(W 9981T)* – Behind the mask (live) / Cocaine (live).
(cd-s+=) *(W 9981CD)* – No alibis (live) / Cocaine (live).

Jun 90. (7") *(W 9970)* **PRETENDING. / HARD TIMES** [ ] [–]
(12"+=) *(W 9970T)* – Knock on wood.
(cd-s++=) *(W 9970CD)* – Behind the sun.

— with **ALAN CLARKE** – keyboards / **NATHAN EAST** – bass / **STEVE FERRONE** – drums / **PHIL PALMER** – guitar / **RAY COOPER** – guitar / **RICHARD TEE** – piano / **CRAIG PHILLINGAMES** – keyboards, synths. and The NATIONAL PHILHARMONIC ORCHESTRA.

Oct 91. (d-cd)(d-lp/d-c) *(7599 <26420-2>)(WX 373/+C)* **24 NIGHTS (live)** [17] [38]
– Badge / Running on faith / White room / Sunshine of your love / Watch yourself / Have you ever loved a woman / Worried life blues / Hoodoo man / Pretending / Bad love / Old love / Wonderful tonight / Bell bottom blues / Hard times / Edge of darkness.

Nov 91. (7") *(W 0069)* **WONDERFUL TONIGHT (live). / EDGE OF DARKNESS (live)** [30] [–]
(c-s/12"/cd-s) *(W 0069 C/T/CD)* – ('A'side) / Layla (band version) / Cocaine.

Jan 92. (cd) *(7599 <26794-2>)* **RUSH (Soundtrack)** [ ] [24]
– Tears in Heaven / Will Gaines / Tracks and lines / Realization / New recruit / Preludia fugue / Kristen and Jim / Help me up / Cold turkey / Don't know which way to go. *(re-iss. cd Feb95;)*

— **CHUCK LEAVELL** – keyboards (ex-ALLMANS) repl. CRAIG and RICHARD / **ANDY FAIRWEATHER-LOW** – guitar (ex-AMEN CORNER, ex-solo) repl. PHIL backing singers **KATIE KISSOON + TESSA MILES**

Jan 92. (7"/c-s) *(W 0081/+C)* **TEARS IN HEAVEN. / WHITE ROOM (live)** [5] [–]
(12"+=/cd-s+=) *(W 0081 T/CD)* – Tracks & lines / Bad love (live).

Jan 92. (c-s) *<19038>* **TEARS IN HEAVEN / TRACKS AND LINES** [–] [2]

— In Jul'92, ERIC teamed up with ELTON JOHN on single 'RUNAWAY TRAIN'. A month later, STING was his co-collaborator on another hit 'IT'S PROBABLY ME'.

Sep 92. (7"/c-s) *(W 0134/+C)* **LAYLA (live acoustic). / TEARS IN HEAVEN (live acoustic)** [45] [–]
(cd-s+=) *(W 0134CD)* – (MTV unplugged interview).

Sep 92. (c-s) *<18787>* **LAYLA (live acoustic) / SIGNE (live acoustic)** [–] [12]

Sep 92. (cd)(lp/c) *(9362 <45024-2>)(WX 480/+C)* **UNPLUGGED (live acoustic)** [2] [1]
– Signe / Before you accuse me / Hey hey / Tears in Heaven / Lonely stranger / Nobody knows when you're down & out / Layla / Running on faith / Walkin' blues / Alberta / San Francisco Bay blues / Malted milk / Old love / Rollin' & tumblin'.

Sep 94. (cd/c/lp) *(9362 <45737-2/-4/-1>)* **FROM THE CRADLE** [1] [1]
– Third degree / Hoochie coochie man / Standin' round cryin' / Groanin' the blues / Blues before sunrise / Reconsider baby / Five long years / I'm tore down / How long blues / Goin' away baby / Blues leave me alone / Sinner's prayer / Motherless child / It hurts me too / Someday after a while.

Oct 94. (c-s) *(W 0271C)* **MOTHERLESS CHILD. / DRIFTIN'** [63] [ ]
(12"+=/cd-s+=) *(W 0271CD)* – County jail blues / 32-20 blues.

— In Mar'95, alongside CHER, CHRISSIE HYNDE and NENEH CHERRY, he hit UK No.1 with charity Comic Relief single 'LOVE CAN BUILD A BRIDGE'.

Jul 96. (c-s) *(W 0358C) <17621>* **CHANGE THE WORLD / DANNY BOY** [18] [5]
(cd-s+=) *(W 0358CD)* – ('A'instrumental).

Mar 98. (cd/c) *(<9362 46577-2/-4>)* **PILGRIM** [6] [4]
– My father's eyes / River of tears / Pilgrim / Broken hearted / One chance / Circus / Goin' down slow / Fall like rain / Born in time / Sick and tired / Needs his woman / She's gone / You were there / Inside of me.

Mar 98. (c-s) *(W 0443C)* **MY FATHER'S EYES / THEME FROM A MOVIE THAT NEVER HAPPENED** [33] [–]
(cd-s+=) *(W 0443CD)* – Inside of me.

Jun 98. (c-s) *(W 0447C)* **CIRCUS / TEARS IN HEAVEN** [39] [–]
(cd-s+=) *(W 0447CDX)* – Wonderful tonight / Edge of darkness.
(cd-s) *(W 0447CD)* – ('A'side) / Behind the mask / Bad love / Tearing us apart.

Nov 98. (c-s) *(W 456C)* **PILGRIM / NEED HIS WOMAN** [ ] [–]
(cd-s+=) *(W 456CD)* – ('A'mix).

Oct 99. (c-s/cd-s) *(W 508 C/CD)* **BLUE EYES BLUE / CIRCUS / OLD LOVE** [ ] [–]
(cd-s+=) *(W 508CDX)* – Tearing us apart.

Oct 99. (cd/c) *(9362 47564-2/-4) <47553>* **CLAPTON CHRONICLES – THE BEST OF ERIC CLAPTON** (compilation) [6] [20]
– Blue eyes blue / Change the world / My father's eyes / Tears in Heaven / Layla / Pretending / Bad love / Before you accuse me (take a look at yourself) / It's in the way that you use it / Forever man / Running on faith / She's waiting / River of tears / I get lost / Wonderful tonight.

— in Jun'00, ERIC collaborated with B.B. KING on the hit album, 'RIDING WITH THE KING'

Mar 01. (cd/c/d-lp) *(<9362 47966-2/-4>)* **REPTILE** [7] [5]
– Reptile / Got you on my mind / Travelin' light / Believe in life / Come back baby / Broken down / Find myself / I ain't gonna stand for it / I want a little girl / Second nature / Don't let me be lonely tonight / Modern girl / Superman inside / Son and Sylvia.

Nov 02. (d-cd) *(<9362 48397-2>)* **ONE MORE CAR, ONE MORE RIDER: LIVE ON TOUR 2001** [69] [43]
– Key to the highway / Reptile / Got you on my mind / Tears in Heaven / Bell bottom blues / Change the world / My father's eyes / River of tears / Goin' down slow / She's gone / I want a little girl / Badge / (I'm your) Hoochie coochie man / Have you ever loved a woman / Cocaine / Wonderful tonight / Layla / Wonderful tonight / Layla / Sunshine of your love / Over the rainbow.

– compilations, etc. –

issued 'Polydor' UK / 'Atco' US, unless mentioned otherwise.

Aug 72. (lp) *(2659 012) <803>* **THE HISTORY OF ERIC CLAPTON** [20] Apr72 [6]

Feb 73. (lp) *(5526>* **CLAPTON** [–] [67]

Apr 73. (lp) *(2659 025) <3503>* **AT HIS BEST** [ ] Oct72 [87]

1970. (7"; by ERIC CLAPTON & KING CURTIS) **TEASIN'. / SOULIN'** [–] [ ]

now 'R.S.O.' UK+US until mentioned

Jun 81. (lp/c) *Decca; (TAB/KTAB 21)* **STEPPIN' OUT (live)** [ ] [–]

Jan 82. (7"/12") *(RSO/+X 87)* **LAYLA (Derek & The Dominoes). / WONDERFUL TONIGHT** [4] [ ]

Mar 82. (7") *(RSO 88)* **I SHOT THE SHERIFF. / COCAINE** [64] [ ]
(12"+=) *(RSOX 88)* – Knockin' on Heaven's door (live).

Apr 82. (lp/c) *(RSD/TRSD 5010) <3099>* **TIME PIECES – THE BEST OF ERIC CLAPTON** [20] [ ]
(cd-iss. 1984; 800 014-2) (re-iss. Nov88 & Apr95; same)

Aug 82. (d-c) *(3524 229)* **SLOWHAND / BACKLESS** [ ] [ ]

Nov 82. (t-lp-set) *(BOX 3)* **461 OCEAN BOULEVARD / BACKLESS / SLOWHAND** [ ] [ ]

May 83. (lp/c) *(RSD/TRSD 502)* **TIME PIECES VOL.II – 'LIVE' IN THE SEVENTIES** [ ] [ ]
(cd-iss. 1985; 811 835-2)

Jun 83. (d-c) *(TWOMC 6)* **461 OCEAN BOULEVARD / ANOTHER TICKET** [ ] [–]

Apr 84. (7") *(RSO 98)* **WONDERFUL TONIGHT. / COCAINE** [ ] [ ]

May 84. (d-lp/d-c) *Starblend; (ERIC/ERIK 1)* **BACK TRACKIN'** [29] [–]
– I shot the sheriff / Knockin' on Heaven's door / Lay down Sally / Promises / Swing low sweet chariot / Wonderful tonight / Sunshine of your love (CREAM) / Tales of brave Ulysses (CREAM) / Badge (CREAM) / Little wing (DEREK & THE DOMINOES) / Layla (DEREK & THE DOMINOES) / Cocaine / Strange brew (CREAM) / Spoonful (CREAM) / Let it rain / Have you ever loved a woman? (DEREK & THE DOMINOES) / Presence of the Lord (BLIND FAITH) / Crossroads (CREAM) / Roll it over (DEREK & THE DOMINOES live) / Can't find my way home (live) / Blues power (live) / Further on up the road (live). *(re-iss. Feb85 on 'Polydor' d-cd; 821 937-2) (re-iss. cd Feb91;)*

Jul 84 (7") *Old Gold; (OG 9422)* **LAYLA (Derek & the Dominoes) / ONLY YOU KNOW AND I KNOW** [ ] [–]

Nov 84. (lp/c) *Astan; <2/4 0118>* **TOO MUCH MONKEY BUSINESS** [–] [ ]

Mar 86. (lp/c) *Thunderbolt; (THB L/C 013)* **SURVIVOR** [ ] [–]
(cd-iss. Mar88; CDTB 013)

Mar 86. (7") *Old Gold; (OG 9586)* **I SHOT THE SHERIFF. / KNOCKIN' ON HEAVEN'S DOOR** [ ] [–]

Apr 86. (lp/c) *Arcade; (ADAH/+C 428)* **GREATEST HITS** – –

Aug 87. (7") *Polydor; (POSP 881)* **WONDERFUL TONIGHT. / I SHOT THE SHERIFF**
(12"+=) *(POSPX 881)* – Layla (full version).
(cd-s+=) *(POCD 881)* – Swing low sweet chariot.

Sep 87. (d-lp/c)(cd) *Polydor; (ECTV/+C 1)(833 519-2)* **THE CREAM OF ERIC CLAPTON** 9 –
(re-charted Sep92, hit UK No.49) (re-iss. Mar94 cd/c; 521881-2/-4) <US re-iss. Mar95; >; hit No.80)

Apr 88. (d-lp/c/cd) *Castle; (CCS LP/CS/CD 162)* **THE EARLY CLAPTON COLLECTION** –

Apr 88. (6xlp/4xc/4xcd) *(<835 261-1/-4/-2>)* **CROSSROADS** 34
(above features all his work of past 25 years) (YARDBIRDS to solo)

May 88. (lp/c) *Big Time; (22/21 15515)* **FIVE LONG YEARS** –

Jul 88. (7") *Polydor; (PO 8)* **AFTER MIDNIGHT. / I CAN'T STAND IT**
(12"+=) *(PZ 8)* – What you doing today.
(cd-s++=) *(PZCD 8)* – Sunshine of your love (CREAM).

Feb 89. (c) *Venus; (VENUMC 4)* **THE MAGIC OF ERIC CLAPTON** –
(re-iss. Jun93 on 'Royal Collection' cd/c; RC 83/82 107)

Oct 90. (cd/c) *O.N.N.; (ONN 73 CD/MC)* **THE FIRST TIME I MET THE BLUES** –

Nov 90. (4xcd/3xc; DEREK & THE DOMINOES) *Polydor; (847 083-2/-4)* **THE LAYLA SESSIONS (Derek & The Dominoes)**

Jul 91. (7") *Polydor;* **LAYLA. (Edit) / BELL BOTTOM BLUES**

Nov 91. (cd/c/d-lp) *Polydor;* **THE BEST OF ERIC CLAPTON (with CREAM)**
(re-iss. Jul93 cd/c;)

Jul 92. (cd) *Koch Int.; (TL 1322)* **BLUES YOU CAN'T LOOSE** –

Apr 93. (cd) *Pulsar; (PULS 201)* **MISTER SLOWHAND** –

Dec 93. (cd) *Immediate; (CSL 6040)* **THE EARLY YEARS** –

Mar 94. (d-cd; DEREK & THE DOMINOES) *Polydor; (521 682-2)* **LIVE AT FILLMORE (live)**
(re-iss. Sep95; same)

Aug 94. (cd) *Charly; (CDCD 1174)* **BEGINNINGS** –

Nov 95. (3xcd-box) *Polydor;* **SLOWHAND / 461 OCEAN BOULEVARD / THERE'S ONE IN EVERY CROWD**

Mar 96. (4xcd-box) *Polydor; (529 305-2)* **CROSSROADS 2 (LIVE IN THE SEVENTIES)** –

Apr 96. (cd/c) *Hallmark; (30300-2/-4)* **BLUES POWER** –
(re-iss. Apr98; same)

Oct 98. (10"lp/cd) *Get Back; (GET 540/+CD)* **FROM YARDBIRDS TO BLUESBREAKERS** –

May 99. (d-cd) *Collection; (KBOX 235)* **ERIC CLAPTON** –

May 99. (3xcd-box) *Dressed To Kill; (REDTK 124)* **CLAPTON, PAGE & BECK** –

Jun 99. (d-cd/d-c) *(<547178-2/-4>)* **BLUES** 52 52

Feb 00. (cd/c) *Castle Pulse; (PLS CD/MC 103)* **STRICTLY THE BLUES** –

Oct 00. (d-cd) *Universal; (E 539049-2)* **461 OCEAN BOULEVARD / SLOWHAND** –
(also see under CREAM)

Gene CLARK

Born: HAROLD EUGENE CLARK, 17 Nov'41, Tipton, Missouri, USA. Born into a large farming family, GENE grew up listening to country, bluegrass and rockabilly before taking up the guitar and learning to write songs as he entered his teens. Plucked from obscurity in Kansas by The NEW CHRISTY MINSTRELS' RANDY SPARKS, CLARK left college to sing with the folk outfit that also unleashed KENNY ROGERS and JOHN DENVER on an unsuspecting world. In the event, he only appeared on two albums before his concept of music was turned upside down upon hearing The BEATLES. Deciding that this was the future of music, he quit the MINSTRELS and headed to L.A. where he figured he'd meet some musicians who felt the same way. He figured correct and was soon bringing the house down at Ciro's nightclub alongside JIM (later ROGER) McGUINN, DAVID CROSBY and MICHAEL CLARKE. Calling themselves The BYRDS, they represented an American folk-rock teen sensation equivalent to The BEATLES. What's more, CLARK had penned one of the best songs on their debut album, namely 'I'LL FEEL A WHOLE LOT BETTER'. While the band rapidly became one of the biggest in the world, CLARK's innate fear of flying quickly became a major problem. That, coupled with a dispute over publishing royalties and GENE's increasing alienation from the endless round of touring and interviews led to his eventual departure in February 1966. This despite being the band's most prolific, versatile and accomplished songwriter (he'd also co-written the groundbreaking 'EIGHT MILES HIGH') as well as their most imposing stage presence. A debut solo single, the orchestrated 'ECHOES', emerged in December while CLARK wasted little time in assembling a formidable team of session players for his impressive proto-country rock album, 'GENE CLARK WITH THE GODSIN BROTHERS' (1967). Alongside bluegrass singers, VERN and REX GODSIN, the album boasted the talents of GLEN CAMPBELL, CLARENCE WHITE, DOUG DILLARD and LEON RUSSELL as well as BYRDS, CHRIS HILLMAN and MICHAEL CLARKE yet its release date clashed with The BYRDS' 'Younger Than Yesterday' and it sank without trace; both were issued on 'C.B.S.'. The harpsichord orchestration of mooted follow-up single, 'THE FRENCH GIRL', wasn't heard until 1991 when it was belatedly included on a repackaged version of CLARK's debut album, confusingly titled 'ECHOES'. GENE duly decided he was unhappy with this musical direction and a follow-up album was abandoned. Instead, the singer signed a solo deal with 'A&M' and a further round of sessions came to nothing. Present at those sessions, however, was DOUG DILLARD and by Autumn '67, the pair's musical partnership had resulted in 'THE FANTASTIC EXPEDITION OF DILLARD & CLARK'. A pioneering fusion of bluegrass and harmony-rich country-rock, the album featured guitarist BERNIE LEADON, who'd go on to work within a similar musical format with The EAGLES. 'THROUGH THE MORNING, THROUGH THE NIGHT' (1969) continued in a similar vein albeit with a profusion of covers. Restless due to his lack of commercial success, CLARK enlisted the original BYRDS line-up to back him up on a one-off 1970 single, 'ONE IN A HUNDRED'. This was followed by a brief period with the FLYING BURRITO BROTHERS before he began work on a new solo set with guitarist JESSE ED DAVIS. The result was the eponymous 'GENE CLARK' (1971; usually referred to as 'WHITE LIGHT'), a sparser, more affecting DYLAN-influenced affair that drew rave reviews in both the States and Europe; GENE's vocals, especially, were more immediate and intimate. After contributing material to the soundtrack for a Dennis Hopper movie, 'The American Dreamer', CLARK began work on the 'ROADMASTER' album; yet again the sessions were abandoned before completion although a version surfaced in Holland (where, bizarrely enough, CLARK has a huge fanbase) on the 'Ariola' label. Following an ill-fated BYRDS reunion, CLARK cut 'NO OTHER' (1974) for 'Asylum'. Certainly his most talked about album – if only for its back cover shot of a fully made-up GENE in glam-rock image shock – it marked the most daringly experimental work of his career, combining state of the art studio techniques, trippy sound effects and female backing vocals with his trademark country-rock. Again, with national touring out of the question due to GENE's fear of flying, the record was destined for cult classic status. Following a further solo album on 'R.S.O.', 'TWO SIDES TO EVERY STORY' (1977), he again hooked up with ex-BYRDS McGUINN and HILLMAN for a couple of unremarkable albums on 'Capitol'. The 80's, meanwhile, found him working with the likes of The LONG RYDERS and TEXTONES singer, CARLA OLSON, with whom he cut a fine album of duets, 'SO REBELLIOUS A LOVER' (1987). By the release of 'SILHOUETTED IN LIGHT' (1992), a CLARK/OLSON live set, GENE had already passed away, dying of natural causes on the 24th of May '91. Held back by personal fears and natural modesty, CLARK never reaped the commercial rewards he deserved yet his rich, emotive songs attract ever more devotees with each passing year while his spirit lives on in the work of many young alt-country bands.

Album rating: GENE CLARK WITH THE GODSIN BROTHERS (*6) / THE FANTASTIC EXPEDITION OF DILLARD & CLARK or ECHOES (*7) / THROUGH THE MORNING, THROUGH THE NIGHT by Dillard & Clark (*5) / GENE CLARK (WHITE LIGHT) (*7) / ROADMASTER (*7) / NO OTHER (*8) / TWO SIDES TO EVERY STORY (*4) / FIREBYRD (*4) / SO REBELLIOUS A LOVER with Carla Olson (*5) / SILHOUETTED IN LIGHT (*5) / AMERICAN DREAMER compilation (*7) / FLYING HIGH compilation (*8)

GENE CLARK – vocals, guitar / with The **GODSIN BROTHERS (REX + VERN** – both guitars + vocals)

C.B.S. Columbia

Apr 67. (lp) *(CBS 62934)* **GENE CLARK WITH THE GODSIN BROTHERS**
– Echoes / Think I'm gonna feel better / Tried so hard / Is yours mine / Keep on pushing / I found you / So you say you lost your baby / Elevator operator * / The same one / Couldn't believe her / Needing someone. *<US remixed & re-iss. 1972 as 'EARLY L.A. SESSIONS' extra track *> (re-iss. May88 on 'Edsel'; ED 263) (re-iss. 1991 original) (CBS-Epic re-issued it as 'ECHOES' in 1991+= & Sep97+=; 488224-2)* – (6 extra BYRDS tracks). *(cd-iss. Jun97 on 'Edsel'; EDCD 529) <(lp re-iss. Jun00 on 'Sundazed'; SCLP 5062)>*

1967. (7") *(202523) <43903>* **ECHOES. / I FOUND YOU**

1967. (7") **SO YOU SAY YOU LOST YOUR BABY. / IS YOURS MINE** –

— CLARK briefly re-joined The BYRDS in October '67

— In Aug68, **GENE CLARK** and occasional ex-BYRD; **DOUG DILLARD** – banjo formed . . .

DILLARD & CLARK

— with also **MICHAEL CLARKE** – drums (ex-BYRDS) / **DON BECK** – pedal steel / **BERNIE LEADON** – guitar, vocals / **DAVID JACKSON** – bass (both ex-HEARTS & FLOWERS)

A&M A&M

Oct 68. (lp) *(AMLS 939) <SP 4158>* **THE FANTASTIC EXPEDITION OF DILLARD & CLARK**
– Out on the side / She darkened the sun / Don't come rollin' / Train leaves here this mornin' / With care from somewhere / The radio song / Git it on brother (git in line brother) / In the plan / Something's wrong / Why not your baby / Lyin' down the middle / Don't be cruel. *(cd-iss. Jun90 on 'Demon'; FIENDCD 62)*

Nov 68. (7") **OUT ON THE SIDE. / TRAIN LEAVES HERE THIS MORNIN'** –

Feb 69. (7") **LYIN' DOWN THE MIDDLE. / DON'T BE CRUEL** –

May 69. (7") **WHY NOT YOUR BABY. / THE RADIO SONG** –

— (Jan69) **JON CORNEAL** – drums (ex-FLYING BURRITO BROTHERS) repl. MICHAEL CLARKE who joined FLYING BURITTO BROTHERS / **DONNA WASHBURN** – guitar, vocals repl. BECK

— (May69) **BYRON BERLINE** – fiddle repl. LEADON to FLYING BURRITO BROTHERS

Sep 69. (lp) *(AML 966) <SP 4203>* **THROUGH THE MORNING, THROUGH THE NIGHT**
– No longer a sweetheart of mine / Through the morning, through the night / Rocky top / So sad / Corner street bar / I bowed my head and cried holy / Kansas city southern / Four walls / Polly / Roll in my sweet baby's arms / Don't let me down. *(cd-iss. Jan91 on 'Edsel'; EDCD 195)*

Nov 69. (7") **ROCKY TOP. / DON'T LET ME DOWN** –

— DOUG DILLARD continued with other solo albums & The DILLARDS

GENE CLARK

— after a rest period he continued solo

A&M A&M

1971. (lp) *(64297) <SP 4292>* **GENE CLARK (WHITE LIGHT)**
– The virgin / With tomorrow / White light / Because of you / One in a hundred / Spanish guitar / Where my love lies asleep / Tears of rage / 1975. *<US cd-iss. 1990's; D32Y 3530> (cd re-iss. Jul02 as 'WHITE LIGHT' +=; 493209-2)>* – Because of you / Stand by me / Ship of the Lord / Opening day / Winter in.

Ariola not iss.

Dec 72. (lp) *(27897)* **ROADMASTER** – Dutch –
– She's the kind of girl / One in a hundred / Here tonight / Full circle song / In a misty morning / Rough and rocky / Roadmaster / I really don't want to know / I remember the railroad / She don't care about time / Shooting star. *(UK-iss.1988 on 'Edsel'; ED 198) (cd-iss. Jun90; EDCD 198)*

Asylum Asylum

Jan 75. (lp) *(SYL 9020) <1016>* **NO OTHER** Oct74
– Life's greatest fool / Silver raven / No other / Strength of strings / From a silver phial / Some misunderstanding / The true one / Lady of the north. *(re-iss. 1988 on 'Edsel'; ED 299) (cd-iss. Sep94 on 'Line'; LECD 9008890) <(cd re-iss. Sep02 on 'Collector's Choice'; CCM 0314-2)> <(cd re-mast.Aug03 on 'Rhino'+=; 8122 73701-2)>* – Train leaves here this morning / Life's greatest fool / (alt.) / Silver raven (demo) / No other (demo) / From a silver phial (demo) / Some misunderstanding (demo) / Lady of the north (demo).

Jan 75. (7") *(AYM 536)* **NO OTHER. / THE TRUE ONE**

Mar 75. (7") *(AYM 540) <45222>* **LIFE'S GREATEST FOOL. / FROM A SILVER PHIAL**

Polydor R.S.O.

Mar 77. (lp) *(2394 176) <3011>* **TWO SIDES TO EVERY STORY**
– Home run king / Lonely Saturday / In the pines / Kansas city southern / Silent crusade / Give my love to Maria / Sister moon / Mary Lou / Hear the wind / Past address.

1977. (7") *<876>* **HOME RUN KING. / LONELY SATURDAY** –

Spindrift Takoma

1984. (lp) *(SPIN 122) <TAK 7112>* **FIREBYRD**
– Mr. Tambourine man / Something about you / Rain song / Rodeo rider / Vanessa / If you could read my mind / Feel a whole lot better / Made for love / Blue raven. *(cd-iss. Jul95 as 'THIS BIRD HAS FLOWN' on 'Edsel'+=; EDCD 436)* – C'est la Bonne Rue / Dixie flyer / All I want. *(cd-iss. Dec97 on 'Spindrift'; SPINCD 122) (cd re-iss. Mar98 on 'Movieplay Gold'; MPG 74053)*

— other solo (import) releases below **CARLA** – vocals of TEXTONES)

Demon Razor&Tie

Apr 87. (lp; by GENE CLARK & CARLA OLSON) *(FIEND 89) <RE 1992>* **SO REBELLIOUS A LOVER**
– The drifter / Gypsy rider / Every angel in heaven / Del gato / Deportee / Fair and tender ladies / Almost Saturday night / I'm your toy / Are we still making love / Why did you leave me today / Don't it make you want to go home. *(cd-iss. Aug87+=; FIENDCD 89)* – Lover's turnaround.

— GENE CLARK died of natural causes on 24th May '91

Mar 92. (cd/c) *(FIEND CD/CASS 710)* **SILHOUETTED IN LIGHT (live in concert with CARLA OLSON)** –
– Your fire burning / Number one is to survive / Love wins again / Fair and tender ladies / Photograph / Set you free this time / Last thing on my mind / Gypsy rider / Train leaves here this morning / Almost Saturday night / Delgato / Feel a whole lot better / She don't care about time / Speed of the sound of loneliness / Will the circle be unbroken.

– posthumous releases, etc. –

Mar 93. (cd) *Raven; (RVCD 21)* **AMERICAN DREAMER 1964-1974** –
– I feel a whole lot better / Set you free this time / She don't care about time / Echoes / So you say you lost your baby / Radio song / With care from someone / Out on the side / The train leaves here this morning / Something's wrong / Through the morning, through the night / She's the kind of girl / One in a hundred / Here tonight / Virgin / With tomorrow / White light / Spanish guitar / American dreamer / Outlaw song / Full circle / From a silver phial / Silver raven.

Sep 98. (d-cd) *A&M; <(540725-2)>* **FLYING HIGH**
– You showed me / Feel a whole lot better / Set you free this time / She don't care about time / Tried so hard / So you say you lost your baby / French girl / Los Angeles / I pity the poor immigrant / That's alright for me / The train leaves here this morning / Why not your baby / Radio song / Git it on brother / Something's wrong / Stone must be the wall / No longer a sweetheart of mine / Through the morning through the night / Kansas

City southern / Polly / Dark hollow / One in a hundred / She's the kind of girl.

Jul 01. (cd) *Evangeline; <(GEL 4030)>* **GYPSY ANGEL: THE GENE CLARK DEMOS 1983-1990**

Sep 03. (cd) *Delta Deluxe; <(4723839)>* **UNDER THE SILVERY MOON**

□ Vince CLARKE & Paul QUINN (see under ⇒ YAZOO)

□ Vince CLARKE & Martyn WARE (see under ⇒ ERASURE)

Dave CLARK FIVE

Formed: Tottenham, London, England ... 1958 by singing drummer DAVE CLARK and original bass player, CHRIS WALSH. After a series of personnel changes, CLARK finally settled on a line-up of MIKE SMITH, LENNY DAVIDSON, RICK HUXLEY and DENNY PAYTON. Following a couple of early instrumental efforts for the 'Piccadilly' label, the band signed to 'Columbia' in 1963 and debuted that Spring with 'THE MULBERRY BUSH'. The raucous 'DO YOU LOVE ME' followed later that year and became their first UK success while third single, 'GLAD ALL OVER', knocked The BEATLES off the No.1 spot and saw the DC5 briefly touted as a serious challenge to the Fab Four. While that prediction may have been a bit wild, the band's booming, big-production sound and stomping R&B beat provided ample ammunition for a sustained chart assault during the British Invasion of the US charts; 'BITS AND PIECES' was a transatlantic Top 5 in early '64 while 'CAN'T YOU SEE THAT SHE'S MINE' and 'BECAUSE' both made the American Top 5 later that summer. Their US profile was so successful they appeared on the Ed Sullivan show more times than any other English band and even released a US live set, 'AMERICAN TOUR' (1964). What distinguished them from many of their peers was their self-determination; most of the songs were self-penned while CLARK handled both the production and management. As a unit, then, they sounded more cohesive and this perhaps explains their relative longevity with regards to the short-lived beat-pop era. Summer '65 saw another US/UK Top 5 with 'CATCH US IF YOU CAN', lifted from the soundtrack of the obligatory group film; they'd already made their acting debut the previous year with 'Get Yourself A College Girl'. Later that year they scored their first (and only) US No.1 with a cover of Bobby Day's 'OVER AND OVER'. While the hits increasingly became thinner on the ground (and dried up completely in the States by 1968) during the psychedelic revolution of the late 60's, the DC5 scored the occasional UK Top 10 right up until 1970 when they hit with a cover of The Youngbloods' 'EVERYBODY GET TOGETHER'. By the release of a final single in summer '71, 'WON'T YOU BE MY LADY', the group had already disbanded. CLARK and SMITH continued to record for 'Columbia' as DAVE CLARK & FRIENDS although even this was abandoned in 1973. CLARK subsequently undertook session work etc. although he was back in the spotlight in 1986 having written and produced the hit musical, 'Time' (featuring a host of superstars including CLIFF RICHARD, FREDDIE MERCURY, DIONNE WARWICK, LEO SAYER and STEVIE WONDER). The man was back again in 1990 with a 50's revival set, 'IT'S ONLY ROCK'N'ROLL'. • **Songwriters:** CLARK and vocalist MIKE SMITH. Covered (singles only); THE MULBURY BUSH (nursery rhyme) / DO YOU LOVE ME (Contours) / I LIKE IT LIKE THAT (Chris Kenner) / OVER AND OVER (Bobby Day) / YOU GOT WHAT IT TAKES (Marv Johnson) / YOU MUST HAVE BEEN A BEAUTIFUL BABY (Bobby Darin) / EVERYBODY KNOWS (Les Reed & Barry Mason) / RED BALLOON (Raymond Froggatt) / PUT A LITTLE LOVE IN YOUR HEART (Jackie DeShannon) / BRING IT ON HOME TO ME (Sam Cooke) / PARADISE (Amen Corner) / GOOD OLD ROCK'N'ROLL (Cat Mother & The All-Night Newsboys) / DRAGGIN' THE LINE (Tommy James) / SWEET CITY WOMAN (Stampeders) / SOUTHERN MAN (Neil Young) / etc.

Best CD compilation: 25 THUMPING HITS (*7)

DAVE CLARK (b.15 Dec'42, Tottenham, London, England) – drums, vocals / **MIKE SMITH** (b.12 Dec'43, Edmunton, London) – vocals, keyboards / **LENNY DAVIDSON** (b.30 May'44, Enfield, London) – guitar, vocals / **RICK HUXLEY** (b. 5 Aug'42, Dartford, Kent, England) – bass, vocals / **DENNY PAYTON** (b. 8 Aug'43, Walthamstow, London) – saxophone, etc.

Ember | not iss.

Aug 62. (7") *(EMBS 156)* **CHAQUITA. / IN YOUR HEART** [ ] [–]
<US re-iss. May64 on 'Jubilee'; 5476>

Piccadilly | Laurie

Jun 62. (7") *(7N 35088) <3188>* **FIRST LOVE. / I WALK THE LINE** [ ] Jul63 [ ]
<US re-iss. & flipped over; Mar64 on 'Rust'; 5078>

Dec 62. (7") *(7N 35500)* **I KNEW IT ALL THE TIME. / THAT'S WHAT I SAID** [ ] [–]
<US re-iss. May64 on 'Congress'; 212>; hit No.53

Columbia | Epic

Mar 63. (7") *(DB 7011)* **THE MULBURRY BUSH. / CHAQUITA** [ ] [–]

Sep 63. (7") *(DB 7112)* **DO YOU LOVE ME. / DOO-DAH** [30] [–]

Nov 63. (7") *(DB 7154) <9656>* **GLAD ALL OVER. / I KNOW YOU** [1] Jan64 [6]

Feb 64. (7") *(DB 7210) <9671>* **BITS AND PIECES. / ALL OF THE TIME** [2] Mar64 [4]

Apr 64. (7") *<9678>* **DO YOU LOVE ME. / CHAQUITA** [–] [11]

Apr 64. (lp) *<BN 26093>* **GLAD ALL OVER** [–] [3]
– Glad all over / All of the time / Stay / Chaquita / Do you love me / Bits and pieces / I know you / No time to lose / Doo dah / Time / She's all mine.

Apr 64. (lp) *(33SX 1598)* **A SESSION WITH THE DAVE CLARK FIVE** [3] [–]
– Can't you see that she's mine / I need you, I love you / I love you no more / Rumble / Funny / On Broadway / Zip-a-dee-doo-dah / Can I trust you / Forever and a day / Theme without a name / She's all mine / Time.
(re-iss. '68 on 'Music For Pleasure';)

May 64. (7") *(DB 7291)* **CAN'T YOU SEE THAT SHE'S MINE. / BECAUSE** [10] [–]

Jun 64. (7") *<9692>* **CAN'T YOU SEE THAT SHE'S MINE. / NO TIME TO LOSE** [–] [4]

Jun 64. (lp) *<BN 26104>* **THE DAVE CLARK FIVE RETURN!** [–] [5]
– Can't you see that she's mine / I need you, I love you / I love you, no more / Rumble / Funny / Zip-a-dee-doo-dah / Can I trust you / Forever and a day / Theme without a name / On Broadway.

Jul 64. (7") *<9704>* **BECAUSE. / THEME WITHOUT A NAME** [–] [3]

Aug 64. (7") *(DB 7335)* **THINKING OF YOU BABY. / WHENEVER YOU'RE AROUND** [26] [–]

Aug 64. (lp) *<BN 26117>* **AMERICAN TOUR (live)** [–] [11]
– Because / Who does he thinks he is / Move on / Whenever you're around / I want you still / Long ago / Come on over / Blue Monday / Sometimes / Any time you want love / I cried over you / Ol' soul.

Sep 64. (7") *<9722>* **EVERYBODY KNOWS (I STILL LOVE YOU). / OL' SOL** [–] [15]

Oct 64. (7") *(DB 7377) <9739>* **ANYWAY YOU WANT IT. / CRYING OVER YOU** [25] Nov64 [14]

Dec 64. (lp) *<BN 26128>* **COAST TO COAST** [–] [6]
– Any way you want it / Give me love / I can't stand it / I'm left without you / Say you want me / Everybody knows (I still love you) / Crying over you / Say you want me / When / Don't you know me / It's not true.

Jan 65. (7") *(DB 7453)* **EVERYBODY KNOWS. / SAY YOU WANT ME** [37] [–]

Jan 65. (7") *<9763>* **COME HOME. / YOUR TURN TO CRY** [–] [14]

Mar 65. (7") *(DB 7503)* **REELIN' AND ROCKIN'. / LITTLE BITTY PRETTY ONE** [24] [–]

Apr 65. (7") *<9786>* **REELIN' AND ROCKIN'. / I'M THINKING** [–] [23]

May 65. (7") *(DB 7580)* **COME HOME. / MIGHTY GOOD LOVING** [16] [–]

Apr 65. (lp) *<BN 26139>* **WEEKEND IN LONDON** [–] [24]
– Come home / We'll be running / Blue suede shoes / Hurting inside / I'll never know / 'Til the right one comes along / I'm thinking / Your turn to cry / Little bitty pretty one / Remember, it's me / Mighty good loving.

Jun 65. (7") *<9811>* **I LIKE IT LIKE THAT. / HURTING INSIDE** [–] [7]

Jul 65. (7") *(DB 7625) <9833>* **CATCH US IF YOU CAN. / ON THE MOVE** [5] Aug65 [4]

Aug 65. (lp) *(SX 1756) <BN 26162>* **CATCH US IF YOU CAN (Soundtrack)** <US-title 'HAVING A WILD WEEKEND'> [8] [15]
– Catch us if you can / On the move / If you come back / Long ago / Any time you want love / I can't stand it / Your turn to cry / Hurtin' inside / Don't be taken in / Don't you realize / I cried over you / Sweet memories.

Nov 65. (7") *(DB 7744) <9863>* **OVER AND OVER. / I'LL BE YOURS** [45] [1]

Nov 65. (lp) *<BN 26178>* **I LIKE IT LIKE THAT** [–] [32]
– I like it like that / Pumping / I need love / Maybe it's you / That's how long our love will last / A little bit of love / I'll be yours my love / Please love me / Goodbye my friends / I am on my own / She's loving girl / You know you're lying.

Jan 66. (7") *<9882>* **AT THE SCENE. / I MISS YOU** [–] [18]

Mar 66. (7") *(DB 7863) <10004>* **TRY TOO HARD. / ALL NIGHT LONG** [ ] [12]

May 66. (7"<US flipped over>) *(DB 7909) <10031>* **LOOK BEFORE YOU LEAP. / PLEASE TELL ME WHY** [50] Jun66 [28]

Jun 66. (lp) *<BN 26198>* **TRY TOO HARD** [–] [77]
– Try too hard / Today / I never will / Looking in / Ever since you've been away / Somebody find a new love / I really love you / It don't feel good / Scared of falling in love / I know.

Aug 66. (7") *<10053>* **SATISFIED WITH YOU. / DON'T LET ME DOWN** [–] [50]

Sep 66. (lp) *<BN 26212>* **SATISFIED WITH YOU** [–] [ ]
– Satisfied with you / Go on / Do you still love me / I meant you / Look before you leap / Please tell me why / You never listen / I still need you / It'll only hurt for a little while / Good lovin'.

Oct 66. (7") *(DB 8028)* **NINETEEN DAYS. / I NEED LOVE** [ ] [–]

Oct 66. (7") *<10076>* **NINETEEN DAYS. / SITTING HERE BABY** [–] [48]

Jan 67. (7") *<10114>* **I'VE GOT TO HAVE A REASON. / GOOD TIME WOMAN** [–] [44]

Mar 67. (7") *(DB 8152)* **YOU GOT WHAT IT TAKES. / SITTING HERE BABY** [28] [–]

Mar 67. (7") *<10144>* **YOU GOT WHAT IT TAKES. / DOCTOR RHYTHM** [–] [7]

Apr 67. (lp) *<BN 26236>* **5 BY 5 = GO!** [–] [ ]
– Just a little bit now / Maze of love / Return my love / Best day's work / Who do you think you're talking to / Got love if you want it / Red ballooon / Please stay / Devoted to me / 3406 / Away from the noises / When I am alone / I still need you / No one can break a heart like you.

May 67. (7") *(DB 8194)* **TABATHA TWITCHIT. / MAN IN A PIN-STRIPED SUIT** [ ] [–]

Jun 67. (7") *<10179>* **YOU MUST HAVE BEEN A BEAUTIFUL BABY. / THE MAN IN THE PIN-STRIPED SUIT** [–] [35]

Aug 67. (7") *<10209>* **A LITTLE BIT NOW. / YOU DON'T PLAY ME AROUND** [–] [67]

Aug 67. (lp) *<BN 26312>* **YOU GOT WHAT IT TAKES** [–] [ ]
– You've got what it takes / I've got to have a reason / You won't play me around / Thinkin' of you baby / Lovin' so good / Doctor Rhythm / Play with me / Let me be / Blueberry Hill / Tabatha twitchit.

Oct 67. (7") *<10244>* **RED AND BLUE. / CONCENTRATION BABY** [–] [89]

Nov 67. (7") *(DB 8286)* **EVERYBODY KNOWS. / CONCENTRATION BABY** [2] [–]

Dec 67. (7") *<10265>* **EVERYBODY KNOWS. / INSIDE AND OUT** [–] [43]

Feb 68. (lp) *(SX 6207) <BN 26354>* **EVERYBODY KNOWS** [ ] [ ]
– Everybody knows / Little bit now / At the place / Inside and out / Red and blue / You must have been a beautiful baby / Good love is hard to find / Lost in his dreams / Hold on tight / I'll do the best I can / Concentration baby.

Feb 68. (7") *(DB 8342)* **NO ONE CAN BREAK A HEART LIKE YOU. / YOU DON'T WANT MY LOVIN'** [28] [–]

May 68. (7") *<10325>* **PLEASE STAY. / FORGET** [–] [ ]

Sep 68. (7") *(DB 8465) <10375>* **THE RED BALLOON. / MAZE OF LOVE** [7] [ ]

Nov 68. (7") *(DB 8505)* **LIVE IN THE SKY. / CHILDREN** [38] [–]

Feb 69. (7") *(DB 8545)* **THE MULBERRY TREE. / SMALL TALK** [ ] [–]

Mar 69. (lp) *(SX 6309)* **5 BY 5 1964-69: 14 TITLES BY DAVE CLARK FIVE** (compilation) [ ] [–]

May 69. (7") *<10474>* **(IF) PARADISE (WAS HALF AS NICE). / 34-06** [–] [ ]

Jul 69. (7") *<10509>* **IF SOMEBODY LOVES YOU. / BEST DAY'S WORK** [–] [ ]

Oct 69. (7") *(DB 8624)* **PUT A LITTLE LOVE IN YOUR HEART. / 34-06** [31] [–]

Dec 69. (7") *<10547>* **BRING IT ON HOME TO ME. / DARLING I LOVE YOU** [–] [ ]

Dec 69. (7") *(DB 8638)* **GOOD OLD ROCK'N'ROLL MEDLEY: Good Old Rock'n'roll – Sweet Little Sixteen – Long Tall Sally – / Whole Lotta Shakin' Goin' On. / GOOD OLD ROCK'N'ROLL MEDLEY part 2: Blue Suede Shoes – Lucille – Reelin' And Rockin' – Memphis Tennessee** [7] [–]

Feb 70. (7") *(DB 8660)* **EVERYBODY GET TOGETHER / DARLING I LOVE YOU** [8] [–]

Apr 70. (7") *(DB 8681)* **JULIA. / FIVE BY FIVE** [ ] [–]

Jun 70. (7") *(DB 8689)* **HERE COMES SUMMER. / BREAK DOWN AND CRY** [44] [–]
(re-iss. Jun75 on 'EMI')

Sep 70. (7") *<10635>* **HERE COMES SUMMER. / FIVE BY FIVE** [–] [ ]

Oct 70. (7") *(DB 8724) <10684>* **MORE GOOD OLD ROCK'N'ROLL MEDLEY:- Rock And Roll Music – Blueberry Hill – Good Golly Miss Molly – My Blue Heaven. / MORE GOOD OLD ROCK'N'ROLL MEDLEY part 2:- Keep A Knockin' – Loving You – One Night – Lawdy Miss Clawdy** [34] [ ]

Dec 70. (7") *(DB 8749) <10704>* **SOUTHERN MAN. / IF YOU WANNA SEE ME CRY** [ ] [ ]

Dec 70. (lp) *(SCX 6437)* **IF SOMEBODY LOVES YOU** [ ] [–]
– If somebody loves you / It ain't what you do / Live in the sky / Five by five / Here comes summer / How do you get to Heaven / Everybody get together / Julia / Break down and cry / I'm on my own / Red and blue / If you wanna see me cry / Worried time / Darling I love you.

Jun 71. (7") *(DB 8791) <10768>* **WON'T YOU BE MY LADY. / INTO YOUR LIFE** [ ] [ ]

— They had already officially disbanded.

DAVE CLARK & FRIENDS

DAVE CLARK & MIKE SMITH

Columbia Epic

Oct 71. (7") *(DB 8834)* **ONE EYED, BLUES SUITED, GUN TOTIN' MAN. / DRAGGIN' THE LINE** [ ] [–]

Feb 72. (7") *(DB 8862)* **THINK OF ME. / RIGHT OR WRONG** [ ] [–]

Jun 72. (7") *(8907) <10894>* **RUB IT IN. / I'M SORRY BABY** [ ] [ ]
(re-iss. Aug74 on 'E.M.I.'; EMI 2205)

Sep 72. (lp) *(SCX 6494)* **DAVE CLARK & FRIENDS** [ ] [–]
– Southern man / Bring it on home to me / Signs / Won't you be my lady / The time has come / If you've got a little love to give / Officer McKirk / (If) Paradise (is half as nice) / Draggin' the line / Think of me / One-eyed, blue-suited, gun-totin' man / Right or wrong / I don't know / Put a little love in your heart.

E.M.I. not iss.

Mar 73. (7") *(EMI 2013)* **SWEET CITY WOMAN. / LOVE COMES BUT ONCE** [ ] [–]

Oct 73. (7") *(EMI 2082)* **SHA-NA-NA. / I DON'T KNOW** [ ] [–]

— CLARK ended musical career, and concentrated on his business. In 1986 he co-wrote musical TIME, which featured many superstars including CLIFF RICHARD, FREDDIE MERCURY, DIONNE WARWICK, LEO SAYER, STEVIE WONDER, etc. DAVID CASSIDY replaced CLIFF in the lead role.

May 86. (d-lp/d-c) **DAVE CLARK'S TIME – THE ALBUM** [21] [–]
– (various artists album)

Mooncrest not iss.

Nov 90. (cd/c/lp; DAVE CLARK) **IT'S ONLY ROCK'N'ROLL** [ ] [–]

– (selective) compilations, etc. –

on 'Columbia' UK 'Epic' US unless otherwise stated

Jan 64. (7"ep) *(SEG 8289)* **THE DAVE CLARK FIVE** [28] [–]
– I know you / Poison Ivy / Twist and shout / No time to lose.

Mar 66. (lp) *(BN 26185)* **DAVE CLARK FIVE'S GREATEST HITS** [–] [9]
– Over and over / Everybody knows (I still love you) / Can't you see that she's mine / Bits and pieces / I like it like that / Catch us if you can / Because / Any way you want it / Do you love me / Glad all over.

Feb 77. (d-lp) *Polydor; (POLTV 7)* **25 THUMPING GREAT HITS** [7] [–]
– Glad all over / Do you love me? / Bits and pieces / Can't you see that's she's mine / Catch us if you can / Because / Over and over / Reelin' and rockin' / You got what it takes / Everybody knows / Good old rock'n'roll / Sweet little sixteen / Long tall Sally / Chantilly lace / Whole lotta shakin' goin' on / Blue suede shoes / Wild weekend / Here comes summer / Live in the sky / Red balloon / Come home / Sweet city woman / Sha-na-na / Put a little love in your heart / Everybody get together.

Apr 93. (cd/c/d-lp) *E.M.I.; (CD/TC+/EMTV 75) / Hollywood;* **GLAD ALL OVER AGAIN** <US title 'THE HISTORY OF . . .'> [28] [ ]

Apr 93. (12"ep/c-ep/cd-ep) *E.M.I.; (12/TC/CD EMCT 8)* **GLAD ALL OVER EP** [37] [–]

Jan 02. (d-cd) *Collectors; (HOL 1482-2)* **THE HISTORY OF THE DAVE CLARK FIVE** [ ] [ ]

CLASH

Formed: London, England . . . early '76, by MICK JONES, PAUL SIMONON, JOE STRUMMER (ex-101'ers) and TERRY CHIMES (future PIL member, KEITH LEVENE, also had a brief spell). After a riotous tour supporting the SEX PISTOLS, their manager, BERNIE RHODES, attained a deal with major label big boys 'C.B.S.' in early '77 and subsequently unleashed the two minute classic, 'WHITE RIOT'. A driving chantalong stomp, the record smashed into the UK Top 40 and announced the arrival of a band whose influence and impact was second only to the 'PISTOLS. In contrast to LYDON and Co., The CLASH manipulated the energy of punk as a means of political protest and musical experimentation. 'THE CLASH' (1977) was a blinding statement of intent, a finely balanced masterwork of infectious hooklines and raging conviction. 'I'M SO BORED WITH THE U.S.A.' and 'CAREER OPPORTUNITIES' railed against inertia, while a cover of Junior Murvin's 'POLICE AND THIEVES' was the first of many sporadic forays into dub reggae. The album went Top 20, lauded by many critics as the definitive punk set, while a further two classic singles (not on the album), 'CLASH CITY ROCKERS' and 'WHITE MAN IN HAMMERSMITH PALAIS' made the Top 40 (the latter addressing the issue of racism, a subject never far from the band's agenda). CBS (and no doubt the band themselves) were keen to break America, subsequently enlisting the production services of BLUE OYSTER CULT guru, SANDY PERLMAN for follow-up set, 'GIVE 'EM ENOUGH ROPE' (1978). The album's more rock-based, less frenetic approach met with some criticism and despite the label's best efforts, the record just failed to crack the American Top 100. It had, however, made No.2 in Britain and spawned the band's first Top 20 hit in 'TOMMY GUN'. The CLASH subsequently set out to tour the States, while British fans lapped up 'THE COST OF LIVING' EP and its incendiary cover of Sonny Curtis's 'I FOUGHT THE LAW'. Finally, in late '79, The CLASH delivered their marathon masterwork, 'LONDON CALLING'. Overseen by seasoned producer, Guy Stevens, the double set showed The CLASH at an assured creative peak, from the anthemic echo of the title track to the brooding 'GUNS OF BRIXTON'. A UK Top 10'er, it finally cracked the States (Top 30), its universal acclaim spurred them on to ever more ambitious endeavours. After the plangent dub of the 'BANKROBBER' and 'THE CALL-UP' singles, the band unleashed the sprawling, triple vinyl set, 'SANDINISTA!' in December 1980. The record's wildly experimental material met with critical pasting, the bulk of the album's tracks failing to withstand repeated listening. Its relatively poor sales (still at single vinyl price!) forced a back to basics rethink for 'COMBAT ROCK' (1982). Although the record was a healthy seller, it sounded laboured; ironically, it became The CLASH's biggest selling album in America, where the 'ROCK THE CASBAH' single made the Top 10. Drummer TOPPER HEADON was already long gone by this point and was replaced by CHIMES, who had left after the 1977 debut; JONES too, was kicked out the following year. The band stumbled on for a further album, 'CUT THE CRAP' in 1985, before finally disbanding the following month. While JONES enjoyed mid-80's success with BIG AUDIO DYNAMITE, STRUMMER embarked on a low key solo career before working with his pal SHANE MacGOWAN in The POGUES. The CLASH fever gripped the nation again in 1991 when 'SHOULD I STAY OR SHOULD I GO' (a Top 20 hit in 1983), hit the top of the charts after being used in a Levi jeans advert (what else!?). A best of double set, 'THE STORY OF THE CLASH VOL.1', flew off the shelves and rumours were rife of a CLASH reunion (unceremoniously quashed by STRUMMER). Come the late 90's, STRUMMER was back from music biz oblivion fronting his own band, The MESCALEROS. Debut set, 'ROCK ART & THE X-RAY STYLE' (1999) ran a gamut of genres without really asserting STRUMMER's personality on any of them. 'GLOBAL A GO-GO' (2001) was significantly more focused and cohesive, the former CLASH man casting his witty, worldly wise perspective over a series of ventures into off-kilter world-beat. Tragically, JOE was to die of heart failure at his home in Somerset on the 22nd of December, 2002. 'STREETCORE' (2003) was STRUMMER's final musical will and testament, reverting back to his roots with a searing vengeance, resurrecting the dub-rock perfected by the CLASH. Railing against the world's downward spiral with all the outrage and wisdom of a seasoned campaigner, the likes of 'COMA GIRL' and 'GET DOWN MOSES' burned with the kind of righteous fury only the likes of STRUMMER could ignite. Among the record's few mellower moments, 'LONG SHADOW' courted a country-roots vibe while an emotional rendition of Bob Marley's 'REDEMPTION SONG' and a reworked version of Bobby Charles' 'Before I Grow Too Old' (retitled 'SILVER AND GOLD') offered solace in the face of so much corruption and chaos. Its greatest tragedy was also its driving force, STRUMMER, who still had so much left to say and the sharp, focused artistic faculties to say it. • **Covered:** PRESSURE DROP (Maytals) / POLICE ON MY BACK (Equals) / ARMAGIDEON TIME (Willie Williams) / JUNCO PARTNER + ENGLISH CIVIL WAR (unknown trad) / EVERY LITTLE BIT HURTS (Ed Cobb) / BRAND NEW CADILLAC (Vince Taylor). • **Trivia:** Early in 1980, the band featured live in the docu-film 'Rude Boy' about a fictionalised CLASH roadie. JOE STRUMMER went into acting 1986 (Straight To Hell) / 1989 (Lost In Space).

Album rating: THE CLASH (*10) / GIVE 'EM ENOUGH ROPE (*8) / LONDON CALLING (*9) / SANDINISTA! (*7) / COMBAT ROCK (*6) / CUT THE CRAP (*4) / THE STORY OF THE CLASH, VOL.1 compilation (*9) / CLASH ON BROADWAY (*7) / SUPER BLACK MARKET CLASH (*7) / FROM HERE TO ETERNITY live collection (*8) / THE ESSENTIAL CLASH compilation (*9) / Joe Strummer: EARTHQUAKE WEATHER (*5) / Joe Strummer & The Mescaleros: ROCK ART AND THE X-RAY STYLE (*5) / GLOBAL A GO-GO (*6) / STREETCORE (*7)

JOE STRUMMER (b. JOHN GRAHAM MELLOR, 21 Aug'52, Ankara, Turkey / raised London) – vocals, guitar (ex-101'ers) / **PAUL SIMONON** (b.15 Dec'55, Brixton, England) – bass, vocals / **MICK JONES** (b. MICHAEL JONES, 26 Jun'55) – guitar, vocals / **TORY CRIMES** (b. TERRY CHIMES, 25 Jan'55) – drums

C.B.S. Epic

Mar 77. (7") *(S-CBS 5058)* **WHITE RIOT. / 1977** [38] [–]

Apr 77. (lp/c) *(CBS/40 82000)* **THE CLASH** [12] [–]
– Janie Jones / Remote control / I'm so bored with the U.S.A. / White riot / Hate and war / What's my name / Deny / London's burning / Career oportunities / Cheat / Protex blue / Police and thieves / 48 hours / Garage land. *<US-iss.Aug79 on 'Epic'; 36060> (tracks differed & contained free 7")* – GROOVY TIMES. / GATES OF THE WEST *(this lp version UK-iss.Jan91 on cd) (re-iss. Nov82 lp/c; CBS/40 32232) (cd-iss. Apr89 on 'Columbia'; CD 32232) (cd re-iss. Aug91 on 'Columbia'; 468783-2) (cd re-iss. Oct99 on 'Columbia' cd/lp; 495344-2/-1; US version; 495345-2/-1) (lp re-iss. Oct99 on 'Simply Vinyl'; SVLP 131)*

— (Jan'77) (NICKY) **TOPPER HEADON** (b.30 May'55, Bromley, Kent, England) – drums; repl. CHIMES who later joined COWBOYS INTERNATIONAL and GENERATION X

May 77. (7") *(S-CBS 5293)* **REMOTE CONTROL. / LONDON'S BURNING (live)** [ ] [–]

Sep 77. (7") *(S-CBS 5664)* **COMPLETE CONTROL. / THE CITY OF THE DEAD** [28] [–]

Feb 78. (7") *(S-CBS 5834)* **CLASH CITY ROCKERS. / JAIL GUITAR DOORS** [35] [–]

Jun 78. (7") *(S-CBS 6383)* **(WHITE MAN) IN HAMMERSMITH PALAIS. / THE PRISONER** [32] [–]

Nov 78. (lp/c) *(CBS/40 82431)* *<35543>* **GIVE 'EM ENOUGH ROPE** [2] Feb79 [ ]
– Safe European home / English civil war / Tommy gun / Julie's been working for the drug squad / Guns on the roof / Drug-stabbing time / Stay free / Cheapstakes / All the young punks (new boots and contracts). *(re-iss. 1984 lp/c; CBS/40 32444) (cd-iss. Jan91; CD 32444) (re-iss. Oct99 on 'Columbia' cd/lp; 495346-2/-1)*

Nov 78. (7") *(S-CBS 6788)* **TOMMY GUN. / 1, 2, CRUSH ON YOU** [19] [–]

Feb 79. (7") *(S-CBS 7082)* **ENGLISH CIVIL WAR. / PRESSURE DROP** [25] [–]

May 79. (7"ep) *(S-CBS 7324)* **THE COST OF LIVING** [22] [–]
– I fought the law / Groovy times / Gates of the west / Capital radio.

Jul 79. (7") *<50738>* **I FOUGHT THE LAW. / (WHITE MAN) IN HAMMERSMITH PALAIS** [–] [ ]

— added on tour MICKEY GALLAGHER – keyboards (ex-IAN DURY)

Dec 79. (7") *(S-CBS 8087)* **LONDON CALLING. / ARMAGIDEON TIME** [11] [–]
(12"+=) *(CBS12 8087)* – Justice tonight (version) / Kick it over (version).

Dec 79. (d-lp/c) *(CLASH/+C 3)* *<36328>* **LONDON CALLING** [9] Jan80 [27]
– London calling / Brand new Cadillac / Jimmy Jazz / Hateful / Rudie can't fail / Wrong 'em boyo / Death or glory / Koka Kola / The card cheat / Spanish bombs / The right profile / Lost in the supermarket / The guns of Brixton / Lover's rock / Four horsemen / I'm not down / Revolution rock / Train in vain. *(re-iss. Feb88 on 'Columbia' d-lp/c; 460114-1/-4) (cd-iss. Apr89 on 'Columbia'; 460114-2) (re-iss. Oct99 on 'Columbia' cd/d-lp; 495347-2/-1) (d-lp re-iss. Oct99 on 'Simply Vinyl'; SVLP 133)*

Mar 80. (7") *<50851>* **TRAIN IN VAIN (STAND BY ME). / LONDON CALLING** [–] [27]

Aug 80. (7") *(S-CBS 8323)* **BANKROBBER. / Mickey Dread: ROCKERS GALORE . . . UK TOUR** [12] [–]

Nov 80. (7") *(S-CBS 9339)* **THE CALL-UP. / STOP THE WORLD** [40] [–]

Nov 80. (10"m-lp) *<36846>* **BLACK MARKET CLASH** [–] [74]
– Time is tight / Capital radio / Bankrobber / Pressure drop / The prisoner / City of the dead / Justice tonight – kick it over (version). *(UK-iss.Sep91 on 'Columbia' cd/c; 468763-2/-4)*

Dec 80. (t-lp/d-c) *(CBS/40 FSLN 1)* *<37037>* **SANDINISTA!** [19] [24]
– The magnificent seven / Hitsville U.K. / Junco partner / Ivan meets G.I. Joe / The leader / Something about England / Rebel waltz / Look here / The crooked beat / Somebody got murdered / One more time / One more dub / Lightning strikes (not once but twice) / Up in Heaven (not only here) / Corner soul / Let's go crazy / If music could talk / The sound of the sinners / Police on my back / Midnight log / The equaliser / The call up / Washington bullets / Broadway / Lose this skin / Charlie don't surf / Mensforth Hill / Junkie slip / Kingston advice / The street parade / Version city / Living in fame / Silicone on sapphire / Version pardner / Career opportunites (version) / Shepherds delight. *(d-cd-iss. Apr89 on 'Columbia'; 463364-2) (re-iss. Oct99 on 'Columbia' d-cd/d-lp; 495348-2/-1)*

Jan 81. (7") *(S-CBS 9480)* **HITSVILLE U.K. / RADIO ONE** [56] [–]

Feb 81. (7") *<51013>* **HITSVILLE U.K. / POLICE ON MY BACK** [–] [ ]

Apr 81. (12"ep) *<02036>* **THE CALL-UP / THE COOL-OUT. / THE MAGNIFICENT SEVEN / THE MAGNIFICENT DANCE** [–] [ ]

Apr 81. (7"/12") *(A/+12 1133)* **THE MAGNIFICENT SEVEN. / THE MAGNIFICENT DANCE** [34] [–]

Nov 81. (7") *(A 1797)* **THIS IS RADIO CLASH. / RADIO CLASH** [47] [–]
(12"+=) *(A12 1797)* – Outside broadcast / Radio 5.

— **TERRY CHIMES** returned to repl. HEADON who later went solo (signed to 'Mercury', released a couple of singles – 'DRUMMIN' MAN', LEAVE IT TO LUCK' and 'I'LL GIVE YOU EVERYTHING' – all from the 1986 album, 'WAKING UP', which featured 60's soul singer, JIMMY HELMS)

Apr 82. (7") *(A 2309)* **KNOW YOUR RIGHTS. / FIRST NIGHT BACK IN LONDON** [43] [–]

May 82. (lp/c) *(CBS/40 FMLN 2)* *<37689>* **COMBAT ROCK** [2] [7]
– Know your rights / Car jamming / Should I stay or should I go / Rock the Casbah / Red angel dragnet / Straight to Hell / Overpowered by funk / Atom tan / Sean Flynn / Ghetto defendant / Inoculated city / Death is a star. *(re-iss. Nov86 lp/c; CBS/40 32787) (cd-iss. Jan91 on 'Columbia'; CD 32787) (re-iss. Oct99 on 'Columbia' cd/lp; 495349-2/-1) (lp re-iss. Oct99 on 'Simply Vinyl'; SVLP 132)*

May 82. (7") *<03006>* **SHOULD I STAY OR SHOULD I GO. / INNOCULATED CITY** [–] [ ]

Jun 82. (7"/7"pic-d) *(A/+11 2479)* *<03245>* **ROCK THE CASBAH. / LONG TIME JERK** [30] Sep82 [8]
(12") *(A12 2479)* – ('A'side) / Mustapha dance.

Jul 82. (7") *<03061>* **SHOULD I STAY OR SHOULD I GO. / FIRST NIGHT BACK IN LONDON** [–] [45]

Sep 82. (7"/7"pic-d/12") *(A/+11/12 2646)* **SHOULD I STAY OR SHOULD I GO. / STRAIGHT TO HELL** [17] [–]

Feb 83. (7") *<03547>* **SHOULD I STAY OR SHOULD I GO? / COOL CONFUSION** [–] [50]

— (Feb83-Jan84) **STRUMMER & SIMONON** brought in new musicians **PETE HOWARD** – drums (ex-COLD FISH),repl. CHIMES who later joined HANOI ROCKS / **NICK SHEPHERD** – guitar (ex-CORTINAS) + **VINCE WHITE** – guitar; repl. JONES who formed BIG AUDIO DYNAMITE

Sep 85. (7") *(A 6122)* **THIS IS ENGLAND. / DO IT NOW** [24] [–]
(12"+=) *(A12 6122)* – Sex mad roar.

Nov 85. (lp/c) *(CBS/40 26601)* *<40017>* **CUT THE CRAP** [16] [88]
– Dictator / Dirty punk / We are The Clash / Are you red.. Y / Cool under heat / Movers and shakers / This is England / Three card trick / Play to win / Fingerpoppin' / North and south / Life is wild. *(cd-iss. Apr89 on 'Columbia'; CD 465110-2) (cd-iss. Dec92 on 'Columbia';)*

— disbanded Dec'85 and STRUMMER went solo (see below). SHEPHERD formed HEAD. In the early 90's, SIMONON formed HAVANA 3 A.M. who comprised NIGEL DIXON (ex-WHIRLWIND), GARY MYRICK and TRAVIS WILLIAMS. Signing to 'I.R.S.', they released only one 50's style eponymous rock album in 1991 before splitting their quiffs.

– compilations, others, etc. –

on 'C.B.S.' unless mentioned otherwise

Nov 82. (c-ep) *(A40 2907)* **COMPLETE CONTROL / LONDON CALLING / BANKROBBER / CLASH CITY ROCKERS** [ ] [–]

Sep 86. (c-ep) *(450 123-4)* **THE 12" TAPE** [ ] [–]
– London calling / The magnificent dance / This is Radio Clash / Rock the Casbah / This is England. *(cd-iss. Nov92 on 'Columbia'; 450123-2)*

Mar 88. (7") *(CLASH 1)* **I FOUGHT THE LAW. / THE CITY OF THE DEAD / 1977** [29] [–]
(12"+=/cd-s+=) *(CLASH T/C 1)* – Police on my back / 48 hours.

Mar 88. (d-lp/c/cd) *(460244-1/-4/-2)* *<44035>* **THE STORY OF THE CLASH** [7] [ ]
– The magnificent seven / Rock the Casbah / This is Radio Clash / Should I stay or should I go / Straight to Hell / Armagideon time / Clampdown / Train in vain / Guns of Brixton / I fought the law / Somebody got murdered / Lost in the supermarket / Bank robber / White man in Hammersmith Palais / London's burning / Janie Jones / Tommy gun / Complete control / Capital radio / White riot / Career opportunities / Clash city rockers / Safe European home / Stay free / London calling / Spanish bombs / English civil war / Police and thieves. *(re-iss. Mar91 as THE STORY OF THE CLASH VOL.1, on 'Columbia'; same)* – (hit UK 13) *(re-iss. Oct95 on 'Columbia'; same) (re-iss. Oct99 on 'Columbia' cd/d-lp; 495351-2/-4)*

Apr 88. (7"/7"box) *(CLASH/+B 2)* **LONDON CALLING. / BRAND NEW CADILLAC** [46] [–]
(12"+=) *(CLASHT 2)* – Rudie can't fail.
(cd-s+=) *(CLASHC 2)* – The street parade.

Jul 90. (7"/c-s) *(656072-7/-4)* **RETURN TO BRIXTON (remix). / ('A'-SW2 mix)** [57] [–]
(12"+=/cd-s+=) *(656072-6/-2)* – The guns of Brixton.

Feb 91. (7"/c-s) *Columbia; (656667-7/-4)* **SHOULD I STAY OR SHOULD I GO. / B.A.D. II: Rush** [1] [–]
(12"+=/cd-s+=) *(656667-6/-2)* – ('B'dance mix) / Protex blue.
(cd-s) *(656667-5)* – ('A'side) / London calling / Train in vain / I fought the law.

Apr 91. (7"/c-s) *Columbia; (656814-7/-4)* **ROCK THE CASBAH. / MUSTAPHA DANCE** [15] [–]
(12"+=/cd-s+=) *(656814-6/-2)* – The magnificent dance / This is Radio Clash.
(cd-s) *(656814-5)* – ('A'side) / Tommy gun / (White man) In Hammersmith Palais / Straight to Hell.

Jun 91. (7"/c-s) *Columbia; (656946-7/-4)* **LONDON CALLING. / BRAND NEW CADILLAC** [64] [ ]
(12"+=) *(656946-6)* – Return to Brixton (remix).
(cd-s++=) *(656946-2)* – The call-up.

Oct 91. (7"/c-s) *Columbia; (656-7/-4)* **TRAIN IN VAIN (STAND BY ME). / THE RIGHT PROFILE** [ ] [–]
(cd-s+=) *(656-2)* – Groovy times / Gates to the west.
(pic-cd-s+=) *(656-5)* – ('A'remix) / Death or glory.

Nov 91. (cd/c) *Columbia; (468946-2/-4)* **THE SINGLES COLLECTION** [68] [ ]

Nov 93. (cd/d-lp) *Columbia; (474546-2) <63895>* **SUPER BLACK MARKET CLASH** [ ] [ ]
(re-iss. Oct99 cd/d-lp; 495352-2/-1)

May 94. (3xcd-box/3xc-box) *Columbia; (469308-2/-4)* **THE CLASH ON BROADWAY** [ ] [ ]
(re-iss. Feb00 on 'Legacy'; 497453-2)

Oct 99. (cd/c/d-lp) *Columbia; (496183-2/-4/-1) <65747>* **FROM HERE TO ETERNITY (live)** [13] [ ]
– Complete control / London's burning / What's my name / Clash city rockers / Career opportunities / White man in Hammersmith Palais / Capitol radio / City of the dead / I fought the law / London calling / Armagideon time / Train in vain / Guns of Brixton / The magnificent seven / Know your rights / Should I stay or should I go / Straight to Hell. *(cd re-iss. Dec01; same)*

Oct 02. (3xcd-box) *Epic; (509662-2)* **THE CLASH (US version) / LONDON CALLING / COMBAT ROCK** [ ] [ ]

Oct 02. (12") *Columbia; (VJAY 26)* **ROCK THE CASBAH. / THE MAGNIFICENT SEVEN** [ ] [–]

Mar 03. (d-cd) *Sony TV; (510998-2) <89056>* **THE ESSENTIAL CLASH** [18] [99]
– White riot / 1977 / London's burning / Complete control / Clash city rockers / I'm so bored with the U.S.A. / Career opportunities / Hate and war / Cheat / Police and thieves / Janie Jones / Garageland / Capital Radio One / White man in Hammersmith Palais / English civil war / Tommy gun / Safe European home / Julie's been working for the drug squad / Stay free / Groovy times / I fought the law / London calling / Guns of Brixton / Clampdown / Rudie can't fail / Lost in the supermarket / Jimmy Jazz / Train in vain / Bankrobber / The magnificent seven / Ivan meets GI Joe / Stop the world / Somebody got murdered / Street parade / Broadway / This is Radio Clash / Ghetto defendant / Rock the casbah / Straight to hell / Should I stay or should I go / This is England.

— The CLASH also appeared under different guises for singles below

May 83. (12"; FUTURA 2000 with The Clash) *Celluloid; (CYZ 104)* **ESCAPADES OF FUTURA 2000** [ ] [–]

Dec 83. (7"; JANIE JONES & THE LASH) *Big Beat; (NS 91)* **HOUSE OF THE JU-JU QUEEN. / SEX MACHINE** [ ] [–]

— They can also be heard on TYMON DOGG's 45; 'Lose This Skin' (May80)

JOE STRUMMER

C.B.S. / Epic

Oct 86. (7"/12") *(A/TA 7244)* **LOVE KILLS. / DUM DUM CLUB** [69] [–]

Virgin / Virgin

Feb 88. (cd/c/lp) *(CD/TC+/V 2497) <90686>* **WALKER (Soundtrack)** [ ] [ ]
– Filibustero / Omotepe / Sandstorm / Machete / Viperland / Nica libre / Latin romance / The brooding side of madness / Tennessee rain / Smash everything / Tropic of no return / The unknown immortal / Musket waltz.

Epic / Epic

Jun 88. (7"/7"s) *(TRASH/+P 1)* **TRASH CITY. / THEME FROM A PERMANENT RECORD** [ ] [–]
(12"+=/pic-cd-s+=) *(TRASH T/C 1)* – Nerfititi rock.

— STRUMMER was augmented by new band **JACK IRONS** – drums (of RED HOT CHILI PEPPERS) **ZANDON SCHLOSS** – guitar (ex-CIRCLE JERKS) / **RONNIE MARSHALL** – bass (of TONE LOC)

Aug 89. (7"/c-s) *(STRUM/+M 1)* **GANGSTERVILLE. / JEWELLERS AND BUMS** [ ] [–]
(7"ep+=) *(STRUME 1)* – Passport to Detroit / Punk rock blues.
(12"+=/cd-s+=) *(STRUM T/C 1)* – Don't tango with my django.

Sep 89. (lp/c/cd) *(465347-1/-4/-2) <45372>* **EARTHQUAKE WEATHER** [58] [ ]
– Gangsterville / King of the bayou / Island hopping / Slant six / Dizzy's goatee / Shouting street / Boogie with your children / Leopardskin limousines / Sikorsky parts / Jewellers and bums / Highway on zero street / Ride your donkey / Passport to Detroit / Sleepwalk.

Oct 89. (7") *(STRUM 2)* **ISLAND HOPPING. / CHOLO VEST** [ ] [–]
(12"+=/cd-s+=/7"ep+=) *(STRUM T/C/E 2)* – Mango street / Baby o' boogie.

— STRUMMER joined The POGUES on tour, deputising when SHANE McGOWAN was under the bottle. At the start of 1992, he had begun writing with them, so who knows? At least it will quell the dogged persistent rumours of a CLASH reformation.

JOE STRUMMER & THE MESCALEROS

— **STRUMMER** with **RICHARD NORRIS** – keyboards / **GED DYSON** – drums / **SCOTT SHIELDS** – bass / **ANTHONY GENN** – strings

Mercury / Epitaph

Aug 99. (12"/cd-s) *(MER/+CD 523)* **YALLA YALLA. / X-RAY STYLE / TIME AND THE TIDE** [ ] [–]

Oct 99. (cd/c/lp) *(546654-2/-4/-1) <80424>* **ROCK ART & THE X-RAY STYLE** [71] [ ]
– Tony Adams / Sandpaper blues / X-ray style / Techno D-day / The road to rock'n'roll / Nitcomb / Diggin' the new / Forbidden city / Yalla yalla / Willesden to Cricklewood.

— **STRUMMER, SHIELDS + GENN** recruited **MARTIN SLATTERY** – bass, flute, synthesizers, etc + **TYMON DOGG** – guitars, etc.

Hellcat / Hellcat

Jul 01. (7") *(1057-7)* **JOHNNY APPLESEED. / COOL 'N OUT** [ ] [–]

Jul 01. (cd/lp) *(<8 0440-2/-1>)* **GLOBAL A GO-GO** [68] [ ]
– Johnny Appleseed / Cool 'n' out / Global a go-go / Bhindi bhagee / Gamma ray / Mega bottle ride / Shaktar Donetsk / Mondo bongo / Bummed out city / At the border, guy / Minstrel boy.

— on 22 Dec'02, JOE died of a heart attack

Oct 03. (7") *(1137-7)* **COMA GIRL. / YALLA YALLA (live)** [33] [–]
(cd-s+=) *(1136-2)* – Blitzkrieg bop (live).
(cd-s) *(1135-2)* – ('A'side) / Harder they come (live) / Rudi, a message to you (live).

Oct 03. (cd/lp) *(0454-2/-1) <80454>* **STREETCORE** [50] [ ]
– Coma girl / Get down Moses / Long shadow / Arms aloft / Ramshackle day parade / Redemption song / All in a day / Burnin' streets / Midnight jam / Silver and gold.

Dec 03. (7"pic-d) *(1149-7)* **REDEMPTION SONG. / ARMS ALOFT / JUNCO PARTNER (live)** [46] [ ]
(cd-s) *(1148-2)* – (first 2 tracks) / Armageddon time (live).
(cd-s) *(1147-2)* – (first 2 tracks) / Pressure drop (live).

□ Adam CLAYTON & Larry MULLEN (see under ⇒ U2)

Jimmy CLIFF

Born: JAMES CHAMBERS, 1 Apr'48, St. Catherine, Jamaica, his earliest musical influences stemmed from Trinidad, the birthplace of Calypso. However, by the time JIMMY left home for Kingston in '62, his real interest lay in the imported sounds of boogie and blues from the States. As the boogie sound blended with calypso, mento and Jamaican folk music, so "Ska" was born. CLIFF cut his first track at Federal studio (owned at the time by the dominant force in

Jamaican recording, Ken Khouri) for Count Boysie's sound system, who, in turn, would air the track at dances. The single was never released, although after a few more attempts with various systems, 'HURRICANE HATTIE' delivered CLIFF's first hit, produced by Leslie Kong, who at the time had little knowledge of the music business, but plenty of money to hire the best musicians on the islands, and was to be involved in CLIFF's finest work. By '63, CLIFF had his second hit with 'MISS JAMAICA', going on to score with 'MY LUCKY DAY' and 'MISS UNIVERSE', although he was barely earning a decent living. A brief attempt to break "Ska" in the States led to CLIFF meeting Chris Blackwell (head of 'Island' records), who persuaded him to try his luck in England, CLIFF moving over in '65. The trip to America had opened the singer's eyes to soul music, this influence subsequently coming to the fore in both his gigs and recordings of the mid-'60s. After a couple of near misses with Island, the album, 'HARD ROAD TO TRAVEL', was released in '67, amongst the tracks a poppy version of Procol Harum's 'WHITER SHADE OF PALE'. During this period, he built up a strong fanbase in Britain without the hits and cash to go with it; unsurprisingly, his spirits were low, made apparent in his classic track, 'MANY RIVERS TO CROSS', which he wrote in '68. A trip to Brazil the same year to attend an international song contest saw CLIFF pulling off a hit in the country with 'WATERFALL', as well as inspiring him to write 'WONDERFUL WORLD, BEAUTIFUL PEOPLE'. On the way back from Brazil, CLIFF stopped off in Jamaica for the first time since '65, recording material for his subsequent debut LP for Trojan, 'JIMMY CLIFF', and catching up with the sounds of rock-steady and reggae, the new style coming to the fore on the LP. Released in England at a time when Trojan scored the majority of their hits, the LP proved the pinnacle of CLIFF's recording career, listing 'MANY RIVERS TO CROSS' and the sublime 'USE WHAT I GOT', as well as the melancholy sounds of a rare ballad, 'COME INTO MY LIFE'. After the international success of 'WONDERFUL WORLD, BEAUTIFUL PEOPLE', CLIFF recorded the inspired protest song, 'VIETNAM', although the major success he craved continued to evade him with the record being rejected for US release as it was considered "too upbeat". 'WILD WORLD', penned by CAT STEVENS, gave CLIFF a glimmer of success, in the meantime producing DESMOND DEKKER's 'You Can Get It If You Really Want' and The PIONEERS' hit 'Let Your Yeah Be Yeah', before launching his second set, the unforgettable 'ANOTHER CYCLE' in '71. Superstar status was eventually achieved through an unforseen medium; film. 'THE HARDER THEY COME' not only starred CLIFF but used four of his songs, including the title track, as well as the infectious 'YOU CAN GET IT IF YOU REALLY WANT'. Incredibly, when 'THE HARDER THEY COME' was released in '72, it failed to chart, CLIFF becoming disillusioned with Island and moving to 'E.M.I.' in '73. From this point onwards, his output failed to match the high standards he had previously set for himself, his style shifting away from the reggae sound that had formed the basis of his fame. • **Trivia:** In 1985, he wrote 'TRAPPED' for BRUCE SPRINGSTEEN, who sang it on the charity album, 'USA FOR AFRICA'.

Album rating: JIMMY CLIFF (*6) / WONDERFUL WORLD, BEAUTIFUL PEOPLE (*7) / HARD ROAD TO TRAVEL (*5) / ANOTHER CYCLE (*6) / THE HARDER THEY COME (*9) / UNLIMITED (*5) / STRUGGLING MAN (*5) / THE BEST OF JIMMY CLIFF compilation (*7) / BRAVE WARRIOR (*5) / FOLLOW MY MIND (*4) / GIVE THANX (*4) / OH JAMAICA (*4) / I AM THE LIVING (*4) / GIVE THE PEOPLE WHAT THEY WANT (*4) / HOUSE OF EXILE (*4) / SPECIAL (*4) / THE POWER AND THE GLORY (*5) / CAN'T GET ENOUGH OF IT (*4) / CLIFF HANGER (*4) / SENSE OF DIRECTION (*5) / HANG FIRE (*5) / IMAGES (*5) / SAVE OUR PLANET EARTH (*4) / BREAKOUT (*5) / THE COOL RUNNER LIVE IN LONDON (*3)

JIMMY CLIFF – vocals / with various session people

Date	Release	UK	US
		Blue Beat	not iss.
1962.	(7"; JIMMY CLIFF with CAVALIERS COMBO) *(BB 78)* **I'M SORRY. / The BLUE BEATS with RED PRICE: Roarin'**		–
		Island	not iss.
1962.	(7") *(WI 012)* **HURRICANE HATTY. / DEAREST BEVERLEY**		–
1962.	(7") *(WI 016)* **MISS JAMAICA. / GOLD DIGGER**		–
1962.	(7") *(WI 025)* **SINCE LATELY. / I'M FREE**		–
1963.	(7") *(WI 062)* **MY LUCKY DAY. / ONE EYED JACKS**		–
1963.	(7") *(WI 070)* **KING OF KINGS. / Sir Percy: OH YEAH**		–
1963.	(7") *(WI 112)* **MISS UNIVERSE. / THE PRODIGAL**		–
		Black Swan	not iss.
1963.	(7") *(WI 403)* **THE MAN. / YOU ARE NEVER TOO OLD**		–
		Stateside	not iss.
Sep 64.	(7") *(SS 342)* **ONE EYED JACKS. / KING OF KINGS**		–
		Fontana	not iss.
Jan 66.	(7") *(TF 641)* **CALL ON ME. / PRIDE AND PASSION**		–
		Island	not iss.
Feb 67.	(7") *(WIP 6004)* **AIM AND AMBITION. / GIVE AND TAKE**		–
May 67.	(7") *(WIP 6011)* **I GOT A FEELING. / HARD ROAD TO TRAVEL**		–
Oct 67.	(7") *(WIP 6024)* **THAT'S THE WAY LIFE GOES. / THANK YOU**		–
Jan 68.	(lp) *(ILP 962)* **HARD ROAD TO TRAVEL** – Reward / Let's dance / Can't get enough of it / I've got a feeling / All I know about you / Give and take / Pride and passion / Searchin' for my baby / Hard road to travel / A whiter shade of pale / Call on me / Aim and ambition.		–
Jun 68.	(7"; JACKIE EDWARDS & JIMMY CLIFF) *(WIP 6036)* **SET ME FREE. / HERE I COME**		–
Jul 68.	(7") *(WIP 6039)* **WATERFALL. / REWARD**		–
		Trojan	A&M
Oct 69.	(7") *(TR 690)* **WONDERFUL WORLD, BEAUTIFUL PEOPLE. / HARD ROAD TO TRAVEL**	6	–
Nov 69.	(7") *<1146>* **WONDERFUL WORLD, BEAUTIFUL PEOPLE. / WATERFALL**	–	25
Dec 69.	(lp) *(TRLS 16) <4251>* **JIMMY CLIFF** <US-title 'WONDERFUL WORLD'> – Many rivers to cross / Vietnam / My ancestors / Hard road to travel / Hello sunshine / Wonderful world, beautiful people / Sufferin' in the land / Use what I got / That's the way it goes / Come into my life. *(re-iss. 1983 lp/c; TRLS/ZCTRLS 16) (cd-iss. Mar94 on 'Trojan'; CDTRL 16)*		
Jan 70.	(7") *(TR 7722)* **VIETNAM. / SHE DOES IT RIGHT**	46	–
Feb 70.	(7") *<1167>* **COME INTO MY LIFE. / VIETNAM**	–	89
Mar 70.	(7") *(TR 7745)* **SUFFERING. / COME INTO MY LIFE**		–
May 70.	(7") *(TR 7767) <1201>* **YOU CAN GET IT IF YOU REALLY WANT. / BE AWARE**		
		Island	A&M
Jul 70.	(7") *(WIP 6087)* **WILD WORLD. / BE AWARE**	8	–
Nov 70.	(7") *(WIP 6097)* **SYNTHETIC WORLD. / I GO TO PIECES**		–
Feb 71.	(7") *(WIP 6103)* **GOODBYE YESTERDAY. / BREAKDOWN**		–
May 71.	(7") *<1270>* **GOODBYE YESTERDAY. / LET'S SEIZE THE TIME**	–	
Aug 71.	(7") *(WIP 6110)* **SITTING IN LIMBO. / THE BIGGER THEY COME**		–
Sep 71.	(lp) *(ILPS 9159)* **ANOTHER CYCLE** – Take a look at yourself / Please tell me why / Rap / Opportunity only knocks once / My friend's wife / Another cycle / Sitting in limbo / Oh, how I miss you / Inside out, upside down / One thing is over.		–

— In 1972, he appeared and contributed some tracks to 'THE HARDER THEY COME' film soundtrack on 'Island'. In US, it was released early 1975. *(cd-iss. Sep86) (cd-re-iss. Oct90 on 'Mango')*

Date	Release	UK	US
Jul 72.	(7") *(WIP 6132)* **TRAPPED. / STRUGGLIN' MAN**		–
Oct 72.	(7") *(WIP 6139)* **THE HARDER THEY COME. / MANY RIVERS TO CROSS**		
		E.M.I.	Reprise
May 73.	(7") *<1177>* **BORN TO WIN. / BLACK QUEEN**	–	

Jul 73. (7") *(EMI 2042)* **OH MY LOVE. / OH JAMAICA** [ ] [ ]

Aug 73. (lp) *(EMA 757)* <2147> **UNLIMITED** [ ] [ ]
– Under the Sun, Moon and stars / Fundamental reggay / World of peace / Black queen / Be true / Oh Jamaica / Commercialization / The price of peace / On my life / I see the light / Rip off / Poor slave / Born to win. *(re-iss. Oct90 lp/c/cd; CDTRJ/ZCTRJ/TRJC 100)*

Oct 73. (7") *(EMI 2065)* **FUNDAMENTAL REGGAY. / THE MONEY VERSION** [ ] [–]

May 74. (7") *(EMI 2160)* **LOOK WHAT YOU DONE TO MY LIFE. / I'VE BEEN DEAD 400 YEARS** [ ] [–]

Jun 74. (lp) *(ILPS 9235)* **STRUGGLING MAN** [ ] [–]
– Struggling man / When you're young / Better days are coming / Sooner or later / Those good old days / Can't stop worrying, can't stop loving you / Let's seize the time / I can't live without you / Going back west / Come on people.

Jul 74. (7") *(EMI 2189)* **MONEY WON'T SAVE YOU. / YOU CAN'T BE WRONG AND GET IT RIGHT** [ ] [–]

Nov 74. (7") *(EMI 2244)* **DON'T LET IT DIE. / ACTIONS SPEAK LOUDER THAN WORDS** [ ] [–]

Dec 74. (lp) *(EMC 3035)* <2188> **HOUSE OF EXILE** <US-title 'MUSIC MAKER'> [ ] [ ]
– Brother / I want to know / House of exile / Foolish pride / No.1 rip-off man / Long time no see / Music maker / My love is solid as a rock / You can't be wrong and get it right / Look what you do to my life, devil woman / Money won't save you / I've been dead 400 years. *(cd-iss. Dec95 on 'EMI Europe')*

Dec 74. (7") <1315> **MUSIC MAKER. / YOU CAN'T BE WRONG AND GET RIGHT** [–] [ ]

1975. (lp) *(EMC 3078)* **BRAVE WARRIOR** [ ] [–]
– My people / Bandwagon / Every tub / Don't let it die / Actions speak louder than words / A million teardrops / Brave warrior / Save a little loving / My people (reprise).

Sep 75. (7") *(EMI 2346)* **OH JAMAICA. / MILLION TEARDROPS** [ ] [–]

Reprise Reprise

Nov 75. (lp) *(K 54061)* <2218> **FOLLOW MY MIND** [ ] [ ]
– Look at the mountains / The news / I'm gonna live, I'm gonna love / Going mad / Dear mother / Who feels it, knows it / Remake the world / No woman no cry / Wahjahka man / Hypocrite / If I follow my mind / You're the only one. *(cd-iss. Jan96; 7599 26311-2)*

Apr 76. (7") K 14423) **LOOK AT MY MOUNTAINS. / NO WOMAN NO CRY** [ ] [–]

1976. (lp) *(K 54086)* <2256> **LIVE IN CONCERT (live)** [ ] [ ]
– You can get it if you really want / Vietnam / Fountain of life / Many rivers to cross / Wonderful world, beautiful people / Under the Sun, Moon and stars / Wild world / Sitting in limbo / Struggling man / The harder they come. *(cd-iss. Feb92 on 'WEA'; 759927232-2)*

1976. (7") <1383> **HARDER THEY COME (live). / VIETNAM (live)** [–] [ ]

Warners Warners

1978. (lp) *(K 56558)* <3240> **GIVE THANX** [ ] [ ]
– Bongo man / Stand up and fight back / She is a woman / You left me standing by the door / Footprints / Medley in Afrika / Wanted man / Lonely street / Love I need / Universal love (beyond the boundaries).

Jan 79. (7") *(K 17295)* **STAND UP AND FIGHT BACK. / FOOTPRINTS** [ ] [ ]

Jun 80. (7") *(K 79135)* **ALL THE STRENGTH WE GOT. / LOVE AGAIN** [ ] [ ]

Jul 80. (lp) *(K 99089)* <5153> **I AM THE LIVING** [ ] [ ]
– I am the living / Another summer / All the strength we got / It's the beginning of the end / Gone clear / Love again / Morning train / Satan's kingdom. *(cd-iss. Jan96; 0630 12991-2)*

Oct 80. (7") *(K 79182)* **ANOTHER SUMMER. / SATAN'S KINGDOM** [ ] [–]

Jan 81. (7") **ANOTHER SUMMER. / IT'S THE BEGINNING OF THE END** [–] [ ]

Sep 81. (lp) *(K 99160)* <5153> **GIVE THE PEOPLE WHAT THEY WANT** [ ] [ ]
– Son of man / Give the people what they want / Experience / Shelter of your love / Majority rule / Let's turn the tables / Material world / World in trap / What are you doing with your life / My philosophy. *(cd-iss. Jan96; 9031 74825-2)*

Sep 81. (7") **MY PHILOSOPHY. / SHELTER OF YOUR LOVE** [–] [ ]

— 1982 with backing group ONENESS

C.B.S. Columbia

Jul 82. (7") *(A 2605)* **ROOTS RADICAL. / RUB-A-DUB PARTNER** [ ] [–]

Jul 82. (7") **PEACE OFFICER. / SPECIAL** [–] [ ]

Jul 82. (lp/c) *(CBS/40 85878)* **SPECIAL** [ ] [–]
– Special / Love is all / Peace officer / Treat the youths right / Keep on dancing / Rub-a-dub partner / Roots radical / Love heights / Originator / Rock children / Where there is love.

Sep 82. (7") *(A 2825)* **SPECIAL. / KEEP ON DANCING (dub)** [ ] [–]

Jan 83. (7") *(A 3037)* **LOVE IS ALL. / ORIGINATOR / ROOTS RADICAL** [ ] [–]

Oct 83. (7") *(A 3849)* **REGGAE NIGHTS. / LOVE HEIGHTS** [ ] [–]
(12"+=) *(TA 3849)* – ('A'instrumental).

Oct 83. (lp/c) *(CBS/40 25761)* **THE POWER AND THE GLORY** [ ] [ ]
– We all are one / Sunshine in the music / Reggae nights / Piece of the pie / American dream / Roots woman / Love solution / The power and the glory / Journey. *(cd-iss. 1988; CD 25761)*

Jan 84. (7") <04335> **WE ALL ARE ONE. / ROOTS WOMAN** [–] [ ]

Jan 84. (7") *(A 4056)* **WE ARE ALL ONE. / NO APOLOGY** [ ] [–]
(12"+=) *(TA 4056)* – Piece of the pie.

Aug 84. (7") *(A 4636)* **REGGAE MOVEMENT. / TREAT THE YOUTHS RIGHT** [ ] [–]
(12"+=) *(TA 4636)* – ('A'dub movement).

Jul 85. (7") *(A 6370)* <05396> **HOTSHOT. / MODERN WORLD** [ ] [ ]
(12"+=) *(TA 6370)* – Reggae night / ('A'instrumental).

Aug 85. (lp/c/cd) *(CBS/40/CD 26528)* **CLIFF HANGER** [ ] [ ]
– Hitting with music / American sweet / Arrival / Brown eyes / Reggae street / Hot shot / Sunrise / Dead and awake / Now and forever / Nuclear war. *(cd re-iss. Feb97 on 'Columbia'; 471220-2)*

Aug 85. (7") <05716> **AMERICAN SWEET. / REGGAE MOVEMENT** [–] [ ]

1986. (7"; with ELVIS COSTELLO & THE ATTRACTIONS) <06135> **7-DAY WEEKEND. / BRIGHTEST STAR** [–] [ ]

1986. (7") <06235> **CLUB PARADISE. / THIRD WORLD PEOPLE** [–] [ ]

— In 1986, JIMMY starred in the film 'Club Paradise' on soundtrack.

Mar 88. (lp/c/cd) *(460139-1/-4/-2)* **HANGING FIRE** [ ] [ ]
– Love me love me / Hanging fire / Girls and cars / She was so right for me / It's time / Reggae down Babylon / Hold tight (eye for an eye) / Soar like an angel.

Mar 88. (7") **LOVE ME LOVE ME. / SUNSHINE IN THE MUSIC** [–] [ ]

not iss. Cliff

Oct 89. (lp/c/cd) <3312-1/-4/-2> **IMAGES** [–] [ ]
– Turning point / Rebel in me / First love / Everliving love / Trapped / Pressure / Image of the beast / Save our Planet Earth / No justice / Johnny too bad / Dance reggae dance / The grass is greener.

Musidisc not iss.

Oct 90. (cd/c/lp) *(10655-2/-4/-1)* **SAVE OUR PLANET EARTH** [ ] [–]
– Turning point / Rebel in me / First love / Everliving love / Trapped / Pressure / Image of the beast / Save our Planet Earth / No justice / Johnny too bad.

Columbia Chaos

Mar 94. (7"/c-s) *(660 198-7/-4)* <77207> **I CAN SEE CLEARLY NOW. / (track by Tony Rebel)** [23] Oct93 [18]
(cd-s+=) *(660 198-2)* – (track by other artist).
(above from the film 'Cool Runnings')

not iss. Island

May 98. (cd) <524471> **HIGHER AND HIGHER** [–] [ ]
– Higher and higher / You can get it if you really want / Wonderful world / Many rivers to cross / I can see clearly now / Soul mate / Ashe music / Crime / Save our planet earth / Rebel in me / Bob yu did yu job / Melody tempo harmony. *(UK-iss.Mar03 on 'Universal'; E 524258-2)*

not iss. Eureka

Jun 99. (cd) <970236> **HUMANATARIAN** [–] [ ]
– Humanitarian / Rise up / Giants / Come up to my love / How long / Let's jam / Keep the family / Drifters / The hill / I walk with love / I'm in all / Humanitarian (slow). <*bonus* +=> – Ob-la-di, ob-la-da / You've got a friend.

– (selective) compilations, etc. –

note; on 'Island' unless mentioned otherwise

Mar 76. (lp) *(ICD 6)* **THE BEST OF JIMMY CLIFF** ☐ -
– Hard road to travel / Sooner or later / Sufferin' in the land / Keep your eye on the sparrow / Struggling man / Wild world / Vietnam / Another cycle / Wonderful world, beautiful people / The harder they come / Let your yeah be yeah / Synthetic world / I'm no immigrant / Give and take / Many rivers to cross / Going back west / Sitting in limbo / Come into my life / You can get it if you really want / Goodbye yesterday. *(cd-iss. 1988 on 'Mango'; CICD 6) (cd re-iss. Mar96 on 'Reggae Refreshers'; RRCD 50)*

Feb 87. (lp) *See For Miles; (SEE 83)* **FUNDAMENTAL REGGAY** ☐ -
(cd-iss. Jan91 +=; SEECD 83) – (extra tracks).

Jun 94. (d-cd) *Trojan; (CDTRL 342)* **MANY RIVERS TO CROSS** ☐ -

Aug 99. (cd) *Castle Pie; PIESCD 027)* **WONDERFUL WORLD BEAUTIFUL PEOPLE** ☐ -

May 01. (cd) *Music Club; (MCCD 458)* **YOU CAN GET IT IF YOU REALLY WANT: THE BEST OF JIMMY CLIFF** ☐ -

Aug 03. (cd) *EMI Gold; (591557-2)* **THE E.M.I. YEARS 1973-1975** ☐ -

Aug 03. (cd) *Columbia; <(511386-2)>* **SUNSHINE IN THE MUSIC** ☐ ☐

☐ CLINTON (see under ⇒ CORNERSHOP)

George CLINTON

Born:22 Jul'40, Kannapolis, North Carolina, USA. Raised in Newark, New Jersey, CLINTON's love of doo-wop inspired him to form The PARLIAMENTS. They released a couple of singles in 1955, before moving to Detroit and recording for 'Gordy (Tamla Motown)' in 1962. The band made little progress, although GEORGE wrote songs for Motown artists such as The JACKSON 5 and DIANA ROSS. In 1965, unsuccessful in their attempts to land a deal, they issued a one-off 45, 'THAT WAS MY GIRL', for 'Golden World'. In 1967, he created the earliest incarnations of his future psychedelic image and added new musicians such as EDDIE HAZEL and BERNIE WORRELL. Signing to 'Revilot' in the States, they then hit Top 20 with single '(I WANNA) TESTIFY'. After a series of flops, he was stopped temporarily by Motown writers HOLLAND-DOZIER-HOLLAND from using PARLIAMENT'S name. Meanwhile, CLINTON was being heavily influenced by The MC5, JIMI HENDRIX, SLY & THE FAMILY STONE, the primal throb of The STOOGES and radical politics, not to mention a hefty dose of LSD. By the late 60's, his group had evolved into FUNKADELIC and signed to 'Westbound'. The eponymous debut album of 1970 set the scene with its marriage of skintight rhythm, slow burning vocals and searing psychedelic guitar freakouts. Meanwhile, CLINTON had been given back the rights to The PARLIAMENTS moniker, changing it simply to PARLIAMENT, and signing to 'Invictus'. More or less the same line-up that'd recorded 'FUNKADELIC', worked on 'OSMIUM', PARLIAMENT's 1971 debut. While this album was more in keeping with the free range psychedelia of FUNKADELIC, PARLIAMENT became a vehicle for the more groove-orientated instalments in the P-FUNK saga. The 'PARLIAFUNKADELICAMENT THANG' effect was akin to a mind-bending 60's trip put through the blender of 70's excess with a soundtrack that combined soul, blues, gospel, psychedelic rock, sex and politics to create P-FUNK. Over the coming years the collective would grow into a large musical corporation which featured over 35 members, releasing such classic albums as FUNKADELIC's 'MAGGOT BRAIN' (1971) and 'COSMIC SLOP' (1973), while PARLIAMENT's first two dancefloor friendly albums, 'UP FOR THE DOWN STROKE' (1974) and 'CHOCOLATE CITY' (1975), set the scene for the landmark 'MOTHERSHIP CONNECTION', an interstellar concept piece from the inner galaxy of CLINTON's fevered mind. His re-definition of the black man's past and sci-fi vision of the future was underpinned by the precocious instrumental precision of former JB's trio BOOTSY COLLINS, BERNIE WORRELL and FRED WESLEY. CLINTON furthered his conceptual reach with 1977's 'FUNKENTELECHY VS THE PLACEBO SYNDROME', in which he presented his ideas of the Man keeping the kids oppressed through material dependency. In the meantime, FUNKADELIC had signed to 'Warners' and 1978's anthemic celebration of P-Funk, 'ONE NATION UNDER A GROOVE,' saw them reach a commercial and artistic peak, having already hit the US Top 30 two years previously with 'TEAR THE ROOF OFF THE SUCKER'. By the turn of the decade, there were so many side projects taking up the creative energy of the P-FUNK posse (BOOTSY'S RUBBER BAND, PARLET, HORNY HORNS, etc), that both PARLIAMENT and FUNKADELIC fizzled out, the latter releasing the last decent effort in 1981's 'ELECTRIC SPANKING OF WAR BABIES'. CLINTON went on to a solo career, offering the excellent 'COMPUTER GAMES' album and accompanying canine madness of the 'ATOMIC DOG' single. In the 90's, the ageing, dayglo warrior guested on records by PRIMAL SCREAM and ICE CUBE, as well as playing to sold out shows worldwide with The P-FUNK ALLSTARS. CLINTON's unswerving belief in the power of the funk to set people free (in every sense) lends his music a delirious, hedonistic quality, which, together with his synthesis of disparate musical styles and technology, is an ever present influence on a diverse range of artists, not least the P-FUNK sampling hip-hop community. • **Covered:** SUNSHINE OF YOUR LOVE (Cream). • **Trivia:** In 1985, he collaborated with THOMAS DOLBY on 'DOLBY'S CUBE' single 'May The Cube Be With You'. Note: – An entirely different George Clinton surprised us with 'ABC' release 'Please Don't Run From Me'.

Album rating: Parliament: OSMIUM (*5) / UP FOR THE DOWN STROKE (*6) / CHOCOLATE CITY (*6) / MOTHERSHIP CONNECTION (*8) / CLONES OF DR. FUNKENSTEIN (*7) / LIVE – P FUNK EARTH TOUR (*6) / FUNKENTELECHY VS. THE PLACEBO SYNDROME (*8) / MOTOR BOOTY AFFAIR (*7) / GLORYHALLASTOOPID (*6) / TROMBIPULATION (*5) / GREATEST HITS (THE BOMB) compilation (*7) / TEAR THE ROOF OFF compilation (*8) / DOPE DOGS (*6) / THE BEST OF PARLIAMENT: GIVE UP THE FUNK compilation (*9) / Funkadelic: FUNKADELIC (*7) / FREE YOUR MIND . . . AND YOUR ASS WILL FOLLOW (*6) / MAGGOT BRAIN (*8) / AMERICA EATS ITS YOUNG (*6) / COSMIC SLOP (*7) / STANDING ON THE EDGE OF GETTING IT ON (*6) / LET'S TAKE IT TO THE STAGE (*7) / FUNKADELIC'S GREATEST HITS compilation (*6) / TALES OF KIDD FUNKADELIC (*6) / HARDCORE JOLLIES (*6) / ONE NATION UNDER A GROOVE (*8) / UNCLE JAM WANTS YOU (*6) / THE ELECTRIC SPANKING OF WAR BABIES (*7) / MUSIC FOR YOUR MOTHER compilation (*8) / George Clinton: COMPUTER GAMES (*6) / YOU SHOULDN'T-NUF BIT FISH (*6) / SOME OF MY BEST FRIENDS ARE JOKES (*7) / R&B SKELETONS IN THE CLOSET (*7) / THE CINDERELLA THEORY (*6) / HEY MAN . . . SMELL MY FINGER (*6) / THE AWESOME POWER OF A FULLY OPERATIONAL MOTHERSHIP (*5) / GREATEST FUNKIN' HITS (*6)

The PARLIAMENTS

GEORGE CLINTON – vox / **CHARLES BUTCH DAVIS** – vocals / **CALVIN SIMON** – vocals repl. GENE BOYKIN / **ROBERT LAMBERT** – vocals repl. HERBIE JENKINS / **GRADY THOMAS** – vocals repl. DANNY MITCHELL

not iss. Hull-/Apt

May 59. (7") *<25036>* **POOR WILLIE. / PARTY BOYS** - ☐

— **JOHNNY MURRAY** repl. LAMBERT

not iss. Flip

1959. (7") *<100>* **LONELY ISLAND. / (YOU MAKE ME WANNA) CRY** - ☐

not iss. Symbol

1961. (7") *<917>* **I'LL GET YOU YET. / YOU'RE CUTE** - ☐

not iss. U.S.A.

1961. (7") *<719>* **MY ONLY LOVE. / TO BE ALONE** –

— Spent 4 years writing for Motown . . . then sign to (see below)

— **CLARENCE 'Fuzzy' HASKINS** – vocals repl. JOHNNY MURRAY + CALVIN SIMON **RAYMOND DAVIS** – vocals repl. BUTCH DAVIS

not iss. Golden World

1966. (7") *<46>* **HEART TROUBLE. / THAT WAS MY GIRL** –

— added **EDDIE HAZEL** – lead guitar / **TAWL ROSS** – rhythm guitar / **BILLY NELSON** – bass / **MICKEY ATKINS** – organ (on some) / **TIKI FULWOOD** – drums

not iss. Revilot

Jun 67. (7") *<207>* **(I WANNA) TESTIFY. / I CAN FEEL THE ICE MELTING** – 20

Sep 67. (7") *<211>* **ALL YOUR GOODIES ARE GONE (THE LOSER'S SEAT). / DON'T BE SORE AT ME** – 80

Nov 67. (7") *<214>* **THE GOOSE (THAT LAID THE GOLDEN EGG). / LITTLE MAN** –

Jan 68. (7") *<217>* **LOOK AT WHAT I ALMOST MISSED. / WHAT YOU BEEN GROWING** –

Nov 68. (7") *<228>* **A NEW DAY BEGINS. / I'LL WAIT** –
<re-iss. Jan69 on 'Atco'; 6675>; hit No.44>

— 12 years later, this song was to give CLINTON rights to group name.

not iss. Funkedelic

1969. (7"; ROSE WILLIAMS with GEORGE CLINTON & FUNKADELICS) *<6709>* **WHATEVER MAKES MY BABY FEEL GOOD. / ('A'instrumental)** –

FUNKADELIC

— **CLINTON** + **RAYMOND DAVIS** – vocals / **CLARENCE 'Fuzzy' HASKINS** – vocals / **EDDIE HAZEL** – lead guitar / **TAWL ROSS** – rhythm guitar / **TKI FULTON** – drums / **MICKEY ATKINS** – some organ

BERNIE WORRELL – keyboards repl. ATKINS

Pye Int. Westbound

1969. (7") *<148>* **MUSIC FOR MY MOTHER. / ('A'instrumental)** –

Sep 69. (7") *<150>* **I'LL BET YOU. / QUALIFY AND SATISFY** – 63

Apr 70. (7") *(7N 25519) <158>* **I GOT A THING, YOU GOT A THING, EVERYBODY'S GOT A THING. / FISH, CHIPS & SWEAT** Feb70 80

Sep 70. (lp) *(NSPL 28137) <2000>* **FUNKADELIC** Mar70
– Mommy, what's a Funkadelic? / I'll bet you / Music for my mother / I got a thing, you got a thing, everybody's got a thing / Good old music / Quality and satisfaction / What is soul?. *(re-iss. Aug89 on 'Westbound' lp/c/cd; SEW/SEWC/CDSEW 010)*

Dec 70. (7") *<167>* **I WANNA KNOW IF IT'S GOOD TO YOU. / ('A'instrumental)** – 81

1971. (lp) *(NSPL 28137) <2001>* **FREE YOUR MIND . . . AND YOUR ASS WILL FOLLOW** Oct70 92
– Free your mind and your ass will follow / Friday night, August 14th / Funky dollar bill / I wanna know if it's good to you / Some more / Eulogy and light. *(re-iss. Feb90 on 'Westbound' lp/c/cd; SEW/SEWC/CDSEW 012)*

Apr 71. (7") *(7N 25548) <175>* **YOU & YOUR FOLKS, ME & MINE. / FUNKY DOLLAR BILL** Feb71 91

PARLIAMENT

(i.e. **CLINTON & FUNKADELIC** musicians) + **R.DAVIS / G.THOMAS / F.HASKINS / C.SIMON**

Invictus Invictus

Dec 70. (7") *<9077>* **I CALL MY BABY PUSSYCAT. / LITTLE OLE COUNTRY BOY** –
(UK-iss.Dec84 on 'H.D.H.'; HDH 457)

Feb 71. (7") *<9091>* **RED HOT MAMA. / LITTLE OLE COUNTRY BOY** –

Jul 71. (lp) *(SVT 1004) <7302>* **OSMIUM** Dec70
– The breakdown / Call my baby Pussycat / Little ole country boy / Moonshine Heather / Oh Lord – why Lord – prayer / Red hot mama / My automobile / Nothing before me but thang / Funky woman / Come on in out of the rain / The silent boatman. *(re-iss. Feb90 as 'RHENIUM' on 'H.D.H.' cd/c/lp; HDH CD/MC/LP 008)* – (extra tracks) *(cd-iss. Jul93;)*

Jul 71. (7") *(INV 513)* **LIVIN' THE LIFE. / THE SILENT BOATMAN** –

Jul 71. (7") *<9095>* **THE BREAKDOWN. / LITTLE OLE COUNTRY BOY** –

Sep 71. (7") *<9123>* **COME IN OUT OF THE RAIN. / LITTLE OLE COUNTRY BOY**

FUNKADELIC

Now without NELSON + ROSS. Replaced by **GARY SHIDER** – guitar

Westbound Westbound

Sep 71. (7") *<185>* **CAN YOU GET TO THAT. / BACK IN OUR MINDS** – 93

Sep 71. (lp) *(6310 200) <2007>* **MAGGOT BRAIN** Aug71
– Maggot brain / Can you get to that / Hit it and quit it / You and your folks, me and mine / Super stupid / Back in our minds / Wars of armageddon. *(re-iss. Aug89 lp/c/cd; SEW/SEWC/CDSEW 002)*

— added **WILLIAM BOOTSY COLLINS** – bass / **CATFISH COLLINS** – guitar / **FRANKIE 'Kash' WADDY** – drums (all of The J.B.'s, ex-JAMES BROWN)

Jul 72. (d-lp) *<2020>* **AMERICA EATS IT'S YOUNG** –
– You hit the nail on the head / If you don't like the effects / Don't produce the cause / Everybody is going to make it this time / A joyful process / We hurt too / Loose booty / Philmore / I call my baby Pussycat / America eats its young / Biological speculation / That was my girl / Balance / Miss Lucifer's love / Wake up. *(UK cd-iss. Jul90 cd/c/lp; CDSEWD/SEWC2/SEW2 029)*

1972. (7") *<197>* **I MISS MY BABY. / BABY I OWE YOU SOMETHING GOOD** –

1972. (7") *<198>* **HIT AND QUIT IT. / A WHOLE LOT OF BS** –

1973. (7") *<205>* **LOOSE BOOTY. / A JOYFUL PROCESS** –

Jul 73. (lp) *<2022>* **COSMIC SLOP** –
– Happy dug out / You can't miss what you can't measure / March to the witches castle / Let's make it last / Cosmic slop / No compute (alias spit don't make no babies) / Broken heart / Trash a go-go / Can't stand the strain. *(UK-iss.Feb91 cd/c/lp; CDSEW/SEWC/SEWA 035)*

1973. (7") *<218>* **COSMIC SLOP. / YOU DON'T LIKE THE EFFECTS, DON'T PRODUCE THE CAUSE** –

— added **FRED WESLEY & MACEO PARKER** – horns (both of J.B.'s)

Nov 74. (lp) *<1001>* **STANDING ON THE VERGE OF GETTING IT ON** – Sep74
– Red hot mama / Alice in my fantasies / I'll stay / Sexy ways / Standing on the verge of getting it on / Jimmy's got a little bit of bitch in him / Good thoughts, bad thoughts. *(re-iss. Aug91 cd/c/lp; CDSEW/SEWC/SEWA 040)*

Nov 74. (7") *<224>* **(STANDING) ON THE VERGE OF GETTING IT ON. / JIMMY'S GOT A LITTLE BIT OF BITCH IN HIM** –

1975. (7") *<5000>* **RED HOT MAMA. / VITAL JUICES** –

1975. (lp) *<1004>* **FUNKADELIC'S GREATEST HITS** (compilation) – Jul74

20th Century Westbound

Jun 75. (lp) *(215>* **LET'S TAKE IT TO THE STAGE** –
– Good to your earhole / Better by the pound / Be my beach / No head no backstage pass / Let's take it to the stage / Get off your ass and jam / Baby I owe you something good / Stuffs & things / The song is familiar / Atmosphere. *(UK re-iss. Mar92 cd/c/lp; CDSEW/SEWC/SEWA 044)*

Oct 75. (7") *<5014>* **BETTER BY THE POUND. / STUFFS AND THINGS** – 99

Jan 76. (7") *<5026>* **LET'S TAKE IT TO THE STAGE. / BIOLOGICAL SPECULATION** –

— **MIKE HAMPTON** – guitar repl. EDDIE HAZEL who went solo

1976. (lp) *<227>* **TALES OF KIDD FUNKADELIC** –
– Butt to butt resuscitation / Let's take it to the people / Undisco kid / Take your dead ass home / I'm never gonna tell it / Takes of Kidd Funkadelic / How do yeaw view you. *(UK re-iss. Mar93 cd/lp; CDSEW/SEWA 054)*

1976. (7") *<5029>* **UNDISCO KIDD. / HOW DO YEAW VIEW YOU** –

— After one more compilation 'THE BEST OF FUNKADELIC EARLY YEARS, VOL.1' in 1977, COLLINS continued with BOOTSY'S RUBBER BAND. Also leaving were HASKINS, SIMON and DAVIS who were to form own FUNKADELIC in the early 80's. They and 'Lax' label issued album CONNECTIONS AND DISCONNECTIONS (without CLINTON).

— Meanwhile in the mid-70's,

PARLIAMENT

(**CLINTON, etc.**) were signed to . . .

Casablanca Casablanca

Dec 74. (7") *<0003>* **THE GOOSE (pt.1). / (pt.2)** [–] [ ]

Dec 74. (lp) *(CAL 2011) <7002>* **UP FOR THE DOWN STROKE** [ ] Aug74 [ ]
– Up for the down stroke / Testify / The goose / I can move you (if you let me) / I just got back / All your goodies are gone / Whatever makes baby feel good / Presence of a brain. *(re-iss. May77 & Nov78; same)*

Feb 75. (7") *(CBX 505) <0013>* **UP FOR THE DOWN STROKE. / PRESENCE OF A BRAIN** [ ] Aug74 [63]

Feb 75. (7") *<811>* **TESTIFY. / I CAN MOVE YOU (IF YOU LET ME)** [–] [ ]

May 75. (7") *<831>* **CHOCOLATE CITY. / ('A'long version)** [–] [94]

Jun 75. (lp) *(CAL 2012) <7014>* **CHOCOLATE CITY** [ ] Apr75 [91]
– Chocolate city / Ride on / Together / Side effects / What comes funky / Let me be / If it don't fit (don't force it) / Misjudged you / Big footin'. *(re-iss. May77; same)*

Nov 75. (7") *<843>* **RIDE ON. / BIG FOOTIN'** [–] [ ]

Jun 76. (7") *<852>* **P. FUNK (WANTS TO GET FUNKED UP). / NIGHT OF THE THUMPASORUS PEOPLES** [–] [ ]

Jun 76. (lp) *(CAL 2013) <7022>* **MOTHERSHIP CONNECTION** [ ] Feb76 [13]
– P. Funk (wants to get funked up) / Mothership connection (star child) / Unfunky UFO / Supergroovalisticprosifunkstication (the thumps bump) / Handcuffs / Tear the roof off the sucker (give up the funk) / Night of the thumpasorus people. *(re-iss. May77; same) (re-iss. Aug87; 824 502-1/-4)*

Jun 76. (7") *(CBX 518) <856>* **TEAR THE ROOF OFF THE SUCKER (GIVE UP THE FUNK). / P. FUNK (WANTS TO GET FUNKED UP)** [ ] May76 [15]

1976. (7") *<864>* **STAR CHILD. / SUPERGROOVALISTICPROSIFUNKSTACATION (THE THUMPS BUMB)** [–] [ ]

Oct 76. (7",12") *<871>* **DO THAT STUFF. / HANDCUFFS** [–] [ ]

May 77. (lp) *(CAL 2001) <7034>* **THE CLONES OF DR. FUNKENSTEIN** [ ] Oct76 [20]
– Prelude / Gamin' on ya / Dr. Funkenstein / Children of productions / Gettin' to know you / Do that stuff / Everything is on the one / I've been watching you (move your sexy body) / Funkin' for fun. *(re-iss. Feb91 cd/c/lp; 842620-2)*

Jan 77. (7") *<875>* **DR. FUNKENSTEIN. / CHILDREN OF PRODUCTION** [–] [ ]

May 77. (7"m) *(CAN 103)* **TEAR THE ROOF OFF THE SUCKER (GIVE UP THE FUNK). / DR. FUNKENSTEIN / P. FUNK (WANTS TO GET FUNKED UP)** [ ] [–]

Jun 77. (d-lp) *(CALD 5002) <7053>* **PARLIAMENT LIVE – P.FUNK EARTH TOUR (live)** [ ] May77 [29]
– P. Funk (wants to get funked up) / Dr. Funkenstein's supergroovalisticprosi-funkstication / Medley: (a) Let's take it to the stage, (b) Take your dead ass home, (c) Say som'n nasty / Do that stuff / The landing (of the holy mothership) / The undisco Kidd (the girl is bad) / Children of production / Mothership connection (star child) / Swing down, sweet chariot / This is the way we funk with you (featuring Mike Hampton; lead snare) / Dr. Funkenstein / Gamin' on you / Tear the roof off the sucker medley:- (a) Give up the funk (tear the roof off the sucker) (b) Get off your ass and jam / Night of the thumpasorus people / Fantasy is reality.

1977. (7") *<892>* **FANTASY IS REALITY. / THE LANDING (OF THE HOLY MOTHERSHIP)** [–] [ ]

Dec 77. (lp) *(CALN 2021) <7084>* **FUNKENTELECHY VS. THE PLACEBO SYNDROME** [ ] [13]
– Bop gun (endangered species) / Sir Nose D'voidoffunk / Pay attention B-3M / Wizard of finance / Funkentelechy / Placebo syndrome / Flash light.

Jan 78. (7") *(CAN 115) <900>* **BOP GUN (ENDANGERED SPECIES). / I'VE BEEN WATCHING YOU (MOVE YOUR SEXY BODY)** [ ] Nov77 [ ]
(12"+=) *(CANL 115)* – Do that stuff. *<US-12" has 2 'A'mixes>*

Apr 78. (7") *(CAN 123) <909>* **FLASH LIGHT. / SWING LOW, SWEET CHARIOT (live)** [ ] Feb78 [16]
(US-12") *<same>* – (2 'A'mixes).

1978. (7") *<921>* **FUNKENTELECHY (part 1). / (part 2)** [–] [ ]

— Early '78, other PARLIAMENT / FUNKADELIC off-shoots "PARLET" (vocalists MALLIA FRANKLIN, JEANETTE WASHINGTON and SHIRLEY HAYDEN) released album 'THE PLEASURE PRINCIPLE'. Another album 'INVASIONS OF THE BODY SNATCHERS' was further issued Jul 79. "The BRIDES OF FUNKENSTEIN" (vocalists LYNN MABRY and DAWN SILVA) released album 'FUNK OR WALK' on 'Atlantic' late 1978.

FUNKADELIC

meanwhile had reappeared signing to . . .

Warners Warners

1977. (7") *<8309>* **COMIN' ROUND THE MOUNTAIN. / IF YOU GOT FUNK, YOU GOT STYLE** [–] [ ]

Feb 78. (lp) *(K 56299) <2973>* **HARDCORE JOLLIES** [ ] Nov77 [96]
– Osmosis phase one / Comin' round the mountain / Smokey / If you got funk, you got style / Hardcore jollies / Terribitus phase two / Sould mate / Cosmic slop / You scared the lovin' outta me / Adolescent funk. *(re-iss. Jul93 on 'Charly' cd/lp; CDGR/LPGR 101)*

Feb 78. (7") *<8367>* **SMOKEY. / SOUL MATE** [–] [ ]

— add **JEROME BRAILEY** – drums (who had joined PARLIAMENT mid '76) / **WALTER 'JUNIE' MORRISON** – keyboards (ex-OHIO PLAYERS)

Nov 78. (7"/12") *(K 17246/+T) <8618>* **ONE NATION UNDER A GROOVE (part 1). / (part 2)** [9] Oct78 [28]

Dec 78. (lp) *(K 56539) <3209>* **ONE NATION UNDER A GROOVE** [56] Sep78 [16]
– One nation under a groove / Groovallegience / Who says a funk band can't play rock / Promentalashitbackwashipsychosisenema squad / Into you / Cholly (funk getting ready to roll) / Lunchmeat and phobia / P.E.squad / Doodoo chasers / Maggot brain. *(re-iss. Jul93 on 'Charly' cd/lp; CDGR/LPGR 100)*

Apr 79. (7") *(K 17321) <8735>* **CHOLLY (FUNK GETTING READY TO ROLL). / INTO YOU** [ ] [ ]
(US-12") *<same>* – (2-'A'mixes).

— drummer BRAILEY left to form own group MUTINY.

Oct 79. (lp) *(K 56712) <3371>* **UNCLE JAM WANTS YOU** [ ] [18]
– Freak of the week / (Not just) Knee deep / Uncle Jam / Field manoeuvres / Cholly wants to go to California / Foot soldiers. *(re-iss. Jun93 on 'Charly' cd/lp; CDGR/LPGR 103)*

Jan 80. (7") *(K 17494) <49040>* **(NOT JUST) KNEE DEEP. / (part 2)** [ ] Oct79 [77]

1980. (7") *<49117>* **UNCLE JAM. / (part 2)** [–] [ ]

Aug 81. (7"/12") *(K 17786/+T) <49667>* **THE ELECTRIC SPANKING OF WAR BABIES. / THE ELECTRIC SPANKING (instrumental)** [ ] [ ]

Apr 81. (lp) *(K 56874) <3482>* **THE ELECTRIC SPANKING OF WAR BABIES** [ ] [ ]
– The electric spanking of war babies / Electrocuties / Funk gets stronger / Brettino's bounce / She loves you / Shockwaves / Oh, I / Laka-prick. *(re-iss. Jun93 on 'Charly' cd/lp; CDGR/LPGR 102)*

1981. (7") *<49807>* **SHOCKWAVES. / BRETTINO'S BOUNCE** [–] [ ]

— (above featured CLINTON's long-time friend SLY STONE)

— The FUNKADELIC project had now been abandoned, due to splinter band.

PARLIAMENT

were still around simultaneously with FUNKADELIC and continued throughout the 80's.

Casablanca Casablanca

Dec 78. (7") *(CAN 136) <950>* **AQUA BOOGIE (A PSYCHO ALPHADISCOBETABIOQUADOLOOP). / (YOU'RE A FISH AND I'M A) WATER SIGN** [ ] [89]

Dec 78. (lp/pic-lp) *(CAL N/H 2043) <7125>* **MOTOR-BOOTY AFFAIR** [ ] [23]
– Mr. Wiggles / Rumpopsteelskin / (You're a fish and I'm a) Water sign / Aqua boogie (a psychoalphadiscobetabioquadoloop) / One of those funky things / Liquid sunshine / Motor-booty affair / Deep. *(re-iss. Feb91 cd/c/lp; 842621-2)*

1979. (7") *<976>* **RUMPOFSTEELSKIN. / LIQUID SUNSHINE** [–] [ ]

Jul 79. (7"/12") *(CAN/+L 154)* **DEEP. / FLASH LIGHT** [ ] [–]

Dec 79. (lp) *<(NBLP 7195)>* **GLORYHALLASTOOPID – OR PIN THE TALE ON THE FUNKY** [–] [44]
– Party people / Big bang theory / Freeze (sizzaleenmean) / Colour me funky / Theme from the black hole / May we bang you / Gloryhallastoopid (or pin the tale on the funky).

Jan 80. (12") *(CANL 188)* **THEME FROM THE BLACK HOLE. / THE BIG BANG THEORY** [ ] [–]

Apr 80. (7") <(NR 2222)> **PARTY PEOPLE. / PARTY PEOPLE (reprise)** Dec79
(12") – ('A'side) / Tear the roof off the sucker (give up the funk) / Flash light.

1980. (7") <2235> **THEME FROM THE BLACK HOLE. / (YOU'RE A FISH AND I'M A) WATER SIGN** –

Apr 81. (7"/12") *(CAN/+L 223)* <2250> **AGONY OF DE FEET. / THE FREEZE (SIZZALEENMEAN)**

Apr 81. (lp) <(NBLP 7249)> **TROMBIPULATION** Jan81 **61**
– Trombipulation / crush it / Long way round / Agony of de feet / Now doo review / Let's play house / Body language / Peck-a-groove. *(cd-iss. Feb91; 842623-2)*

— PARLIAMENT were also defunkt, leaving behind a few exploitation releases

1981. (12") <NBD 20235> **CRUSH IT. / BODY LANGUAGE** –

GEORGE CLINTON

(solo) with numerous session people and **BOOTSY COLLINS / FRED WESLEY**

— another GEORGE CLINTON issued 1979 single 'Please Don't Run From Me'

Capitol Capitol

Nov 82. (lp/c) <(EST/TCEST 12246)> **COMPUTER GAMES** **40**
– Get dressed / Man's best friend / Loopzilla / Pot sharing tots / Computer games / Atomic dog / Free alterations / One fun at a time. *(re-iss. May95 on 'MCI' cd/c; MUS CD/MC 511) (cd-iss. Apr97 on 'E.M.I.'; REPLAYCD 45)*

Nov 82. (7") *(CL 271)* <5160> **LOOPZILLA. / POT SHARING TOTS** **57**
(12"+=) *(12CL 271)* – ('A'-broadcast version).
(US-12") <8538> – (2-'A'versions).

Feb 83. (7")(12") *(CL 280)* <5201><8556> **ATOMIC DOG. / MAN'S BEST FRIEND**
(12"+=) *(12CL 280)* <8544> – ('A'instrumental).

1983. (7") <5222> **GET DRESSED. / FREE ALTERATIONS** –

Dec 83. (7"/12") *(CL 319)* <5296><8572> **NUBIAN NUT. / FREE ALTERATIONS**
(12") <9039> – (2-'A'versions).

Jan 84. (lp/c) <(EST/TCEST 12308)> **YOU SHOULDN'T NUF BIT FISH** Dec83
– Nubian nut / Quickie / Last dance / Silly millameter / Stingy / You shouldn't – Nuf bit fish. *(cd-iss. Sep91 on 'E.M.I.'; CZ 469)*

1984. (7")(12") <5324><8580> **QUICKIE. / LAST DANCE** –

1984. (7")(ext-12") <5332><9065> **LAST DANCE. / LAST DANCE (version)** –

Jul 85. (7") *(CL 365)* <5473> **DOUBLE OH-OH. / BANGLADESH**
(12") <8642> – (2-'A'versions).

Sep 85. (lp/c) *(CLINT/TC-CLINT 1)* <12417> **SOME OF MY BEST JOKES ARE FRIENDS** Aug85
– Some of my best jokes are friends / Double oh-oh / Bulletproof / Pleasures of exhaustion (do it till I drop) / Bodyguard / Bangladesh / Thrashin' / Some of my best jokes are friends – reprise.

Dec 85. (7")(12") <5504><8653> **BULLETPROOF. / SILLY MILLAMETER** –

Apr 86. (7") *(CL 402)* **DO FRIES GO WITH THAT SHAKE. / PLEASURES OF EXHAUSTION (DO IT TILL I DROP)** **57**
(UK-12"+=) *(12CL 402)* – Scratch medley.
(US-12") <15219> – (2-'A'versions).

— Did he release IRON EAGLE (Soundtrack) album around this time?

May 86. (7") <5602> **HEY GOOD LOOKIN'. / ('A'mix)** –
(12"+=) <15263> – ('A'extended).

May 86. (lp) <12481> **R&B SKELETONS (IN THE CLOSET)** –
– Hey good looking / Do fries go with that shake / Mix master suite – Startin' from scratch – Counter irritant – Nothing left to burn – Electric Pygmies – Intense – Cool Joe – R&B Skeleton (in the closet). *(UK cd-iss. Sep91 on 'E.M.I.'; CZ 470)*

1986. (7") <5642> **R&B SKELETONS IN THE CLOSET. / NUBIAN NUT** –

1987. (lp) <12534> **THE BEST OF GEORGE CLINTON & THE MOTHERSHIP CONNECTION LIVE FROM HOUSTON (live)** –
– Atomic dog / R&B skeletons (in the closet) / Quickie / Do fries go with that shake / Hey good lookin' / Double oh-oh / Nubian nut / Last dance.

Paisley Park Paisley Park

Jul 89. (7"/12") *(W 7557/+T)* <27557> **WHY SHOULD I DOG U OUT (part 1). / (part 2)**

Aug 89. (lp/c/cd) *(K 925994-1/-4/-2)* <25994> **THE CINDERELLA THEORY**
– Airbound / Tweakin' / The Cinderella theory / Why should I dog you out? / Serious slammin' / There I go again / (She's got it) Goin' on / The banana boat song / French kiss / Rita bewitched / Kredit-Kard / Airbound (reprise).

1989. (7") <22190> **TWEAKIN'. / FRENCH KISS** –
(12") <21337> – ('A'side) / Hysterical / ('A'remix).

Oct 93. (cd/c) *(7599 25518-2/-4)* **HEY MAN, SMELL MY FINGER**
– Martial law / Paint the White House black / Way up / Dis beat disrupts / Get satisfied / Hollywood / Rhythm and rhyme / The big pump / If true love / High in my hello / Maximumisness / Kickback / The flag was still there / Martial law (hey man . . . smell my finger) (single version). *(re-iss. Mar95 on 'New Power Generation' cd/c; NPG 6053-2/-4)*

— CLINTON guested for PRIMAL SCREAM on their early 1994 album 'GIVE OUT BUT DON'T GIVE UP'. To start the second half of '94, he featured on ICE CUBE single 'BOP GUN (ONE NATION) ', a re-indition of his old FUNKADELIC number.

Essential Rykodisc

Feb 95. (cd) *(ESSCD 280)* **FIFTH OF FUNK**
– Flatman and Robin / Count Funkula (I didn't know that funk was loaded) / Thumparella (Oh Kay) / Eyes of a dreamer / I found you / Ice melting in your heart / Clone ranger / Who do you love / Up up up and away / Can't get over losing you / Rat kissed the cat / Too tight for light / Every little bit hurts. *(re-iss. Apr97; ESMCD 490)*

P-FUNK ALL STARS

— another CLINTON aggregation

not iss. Hump

1982. (7") <1> **HYDRAULIC PUMP. / (part 2)** –

1982. (7") <3> **ONE OF THOSE SUMMERS. / IT'S TOO FUNKY IN HERE** –

not iss. CBS

1983. (7") <04032> **GENERATOR POP. / (part 2)** –

not iss. Uncle Jam

1983. (lp) <39168> **URBAN DANCEFLOOR GUERRILLAS** –

Westbound Westbound

Oct 90. (d-cd/d-c/d-lp) *(CDSEW2/SEWC2/SEW2 031)* **P-FUNK ALL STARS LIVE (live at The Beverly Theater 1983)**

Jun 95. (cd/lp) *(CD+/SEWD 097)* **HYDRAULIC FUNK** (early material) –
– Pump up and down / Pumpin' it up / Copy cat / Throw your hand up in the air / Generator pop / Acupuncture / One of those summers / Catch a keeper / Pumpin' you is so easy / Generator pop (mix).

GEORGE CLINTON & THE P-FUNK ALL STARS

Hot Hands Hot Hands

Apr 95. (12"/cd-s) *(12/CD HOTH 1)* **FOLLOW THE LEADER. / ('A'-D&S radio mix) / ('A'-Kool az phuk mix)**

May 95. (cd/c) *(HOTH CD/CD/MC/LP 1)* **DOPE DOGS** Mar95
– Dog star (fly on) / U.S. custom coast guard dope dog / Some next shit / Just say ding (databoy) / Help Scottie, help (I'm tweaking and I can't beam up!) / Pepe (the pill popper) / Back against the wall / Fifi / All sons of bitches / Sick 'em / I ain't the lady (he ain't the tramp) / Pack of wild dogs / Tales that wag the dog / My dog.

MJJ-Epic MJJ-Epic

May 96. (c-s) *(663321-4)* **IF ANYBODY GETS FUNKED UP (IT'S GONNA BE YOU) (Colin Wolfe mix) / (album mix)**
(12"+=/cd-s+=) *(663321-6/-2)* – ('A'-Colin Wolfe instrumental).

Jun 96. (cd/c/lp) *(483833-2/-4/-1)* **T.A.P.O.A.F.O.M.**
– If anybody gets funked up (it's gonna be you) / Summer swim / Funky kind (gonna knock it down) / Mathematics / Hard as steel / New spaceship / Underground angel / Let's get funky / Flatman and Bobbin / Sloppy seconds / Rock the party / Get your funk on / T.A.P.O.A.F.O.M. (fly away).

— also P-FUNK singles on UK 'Frontline' in 1995; 'P-FUNK ERA' & 'RETURN OF THE GANGSTA'

Premier Capitol

Mar 97. (d-lp/cd) *(PRMD/+CD 20)* <33911> **THE GREATEST FUNKIN' HITS** (remixes) Oct96

– (GEORGE CLINTON compilations) –

Aug 92. (cd/c/lp; Various) *Essential; (ESS CD/MC/LP 185)* **GEORGE CLINTON FAMILY SERIES – VOL.1** [ ] [–]
(cd re-iss. Jul96; ESMCD 383)

Jan 93. (cd/c/lp; Various) *Essential; (ESS CD/MC/LP 189)* **GEORGE CLINTON FAMILY SERIES – VOL.2** [ ] [–]
(cd re-iss. Jul96; ESMCD 384)

Feb 93. (cd/lp) *Music Of Life; (MOL CD/LP 026)* **SAMPLE SOME OF DISC, SAMPLE SOME OF DAT** [ ] [–]
(re-iss. Nov94 cd/lp; MOL CD/LP 36)

Jun 93. (cd/c/lp; Various) *Essential; (ESS CD/MC/LP 190)* **GEORGE CLINTON FAMILY SERIES PART 3 – P IS THE FUNK** [ ] [–]
(cd re-iss. Jul96; ESMCD 385)

Sep 93. (cd/c/lp; Various) *Essential; (ESS CD/MC/LP 198)* **GEORGE CLINTON FAMILY SERIES – VOL.4** [ ] [–]

Oct 93. (cd/lp) *Music For Life; (MOL CD/LP 33)* **SAMPLE SOME OF DISC, SAMPLE SOME OF DAT, VOL.II** [ ] [–]

– (PARLIAMENT) compilations –

Sep 86. (lp/c) *Club; (JAB B/C 18)* **UNCUT FUNK – THE BOMB (THE BEST OF PARLIAMENT)** [ ] [–]

May 93. (d-cd) *Mercury; (514417-2)* **TEAR THE ROOF OFF: 1974-80** [ ] [ ]
(re-iss. Sep95; same)

Oct 94. (cd; PARLIAMENTS) *Goldmine; (GSCD 052)* **I WANNA TESTIFY** [ ] [ ]

Sep 95. (cd) *Mercury; (526995-2)* **GIVE UP THE FUNK** [ ] [–]

Jun 97. (cd) *Deepbeats; (DEEPMO 23)* **PARLIAMENT – THE EARLY YEARS** [ ] [–]

– (FUNKADELIC) compilations, etc –

1989. (12") *M.C.A.; <23953>* **BY THE WAY OF THE DRUM. / ('A'edit) / ('A'instrumental)** [–] [ ]

Aug 90. (4xpic-cd-box) *Westbound; (WBOXPD 1)* **FUNKADELIC PICTURE DISC BOX SET** [ ] [–]

Oct 92. (d-cd/d-c/d-lp) *Westbound; (CDSEW/SEWC/SEW 2055)* **MUSIC FOR YOUR MOTHER (the singles)** [ ] [ ]

Mar 94. (4xpic-cd-box) *Westbound; (WBOXPD 5)* **PICTURE DISC BOXED SET VOLUME 2** [ ] [ ]
– (COSMIC SLOP / TALES OF KIDD FUNKADELIC / LET'S TAKE IT TO THE STAGE / STANDING ON THE VERGE OF GETTING IT ON)

Mar 94. (cd/lp) *Charly; (CDGR/LPGR 104)* **THE BEST OF FUNKADELIC 1976-1981** [ ] [–]
(cd re-iss. Mar01 on 'Snapper'; SNAP 001CD)

Nov 94. (cd) *Charly; (CPCD 8064)* **HARDCORE FUNK JAM** [ ] [–]

Oct 94. (4xcd-box) *Sequel; (NEFCD 273)* **PARLIAMENT / FUNKADELIC LIVE (live)** [ ] [–]

Apr 96. (c-s/12"/cd-s) *Charly; (MC/12/CD NATION 1)* **ONE NATION UNDER A GROOVE** [ ] [–]

Apr 96. (cd) *Westbound; (CDSEWD 108)* **FUNKADELIC LIVE (live Rochester 1971)** [ ] [ ]

May 97. (cd/c) *Southbound; (CD+/SEWD 115)* **FINEST** [ ] [ ]

Sep 97. (cd) *Music Club; (MCCD 307)* **ULTIMATE FUNKADELIC** [ ] [–]

Mar 98. (d-cd) *Charly; (CPCD 83062)* **THE VERY BEST OF FUNKADELIC** [ ] [ ]

Sep 99. (cd) *Delta; (47004)* **FUNK GETS STRONGER** [ ] [–]

Aug 00. (cd) *Metro; (METRCD 025)* **ORIGINAL COSMIC FUNK CREW** [ ] [–]

Jan 02. (4xcd-box) *Snapper; (SNAB 909CD)* **THE COMPLETE RECORDINGS 1976-1981** [ ] [ ]

☐ COAL PORTERS (see under ⇒ LONG RYDERS)

Eddie COCHRAN

Born: EDWARD RAY COCHRAN, 3 Oct'38, Oklahoma City, Oklahoma. Raised in Albert Lea, Minnesota, he later moved with his Irish parents to Bell Gardens, Los Angeles in 1951. Four years later, the young, self-taught guitarist EDDIE formed The COCHRANS with his hillbilly friend, HANK COCHRAN (no relation), the pair soon securing a deal with 'Ekko'. Songwriter JERRY CAPEHEART joined the duo early in 1956 for a single 'WALKIN' STICK BOOGIE', although HANK subsequently moved to Nashville after CAPEHEART became EDDIE's new writing partner (and later manager). Although their first collaboration, 'SKINNY JIM', flopped, CAPEHEART negotiated a deal with 'Liberty', who, in turn, released his major label debut, 'SITTIN' IN THE BALCONY'. Boosted by a cameo role in the rock'n'roll movie, 'The Girl Can't Help It' (performing 'TWENTY FLIGHT ROCK'), the single became a Top 20 hit in the Spring of '57. After a couple of flops and minor hits during the next year, he finally recorded a commercial follow-up in 'SUMMERTIME BLUES', a lip-curling, deceptively simple, all-time classic, which introduced COCHRAN the leather-clad, rebellious rocker to hordes of screaming female fans. Rock'n'roll's answer to James Dean, he eventually followed up with two more attitude-stoked nuggets, 'C'MON EVERYBODY' and 'SOMETHIN' ELSE'; twenty years on, the SEX PISTOLS – with SID VICIOUS at the helm – resurrected these hits in appropriately snotty punk style. In the interim, COCHRAN took part in the Alan Freed / Hal Roach film, 'Go, Johnny Go!', although he had to withdraw from a winter tour alongside his famous friend, BUDDY HOLLY. The tour in question was the ill-fated jaunt that claimed the lives of not just HOLLY, but RICHIE VALENS and BIG BOPPER, all three dying when their plane crashed in February '59. Early the following year, on the strength of his UK success (he was now a bigger star in Britain than he was in the States!), COCHRAN toured around England with co-headliner, GENE VINCENT, for a few months. Having accepted an extension to stay for further shows, he invited girlfriend, SHARON SHEELEY, to come over for her birthday. However, on the 17th of April 1960, COCHRAN, SHEELEY and VINCENT were involved in a car crash, when their London cab skidded off the road. While SHEELEY and VINCENT suffered a few broken bones, EDDIE COCHRAN died after being propelled through the windscreen. A month later, the poignantly titled 'THREE STEPS TO HEAVEN' hit the top of the British charts while criminally ignored in his native America. A plethora of material was posthumously issued, most selling well enough to again hit the UK charts; nearly four decades on, his best songs still retain a primal power which successive generations of musicians have strived to capture. To think that EDDIE was only twenty-one when he died, one can only speculate as to what heights he might have scaled. • **Songwriters:** As said above plus covers: SITTIN' IN THE BALCONY (Johnny Dee) / SOMETHIN' ELSE + LONELY (c.Sharon Sheeley) / HALLELUJAH I LOVE HER SO (Ray Charles) / MY WAY (Paul Anka) / WEEKEND (Post-Post) / CUT ACROSS SHORTY (Wilkin-Walker) / NERVOUS BREAKDOWN (. . . Roccuzzo) / etc.

Best CD compilation: LEGENDARY MASTERS (*9)

COCHRAN BROTHERS

EDDIE – guitar, vocals / **HANK COCHRAN** (no relation) – vocals, guitar / with **CONNIE 'GUMBO' SMITH** – bass / **HAROLD HENSLEY** – fiddle

not iss. Ekko

Jul 55. (7",78) <1003> **MR. FIDDLE. / TWO BLUE SINGIN' STARS** [–] [ ]

Nov 55. (7",78) <1005> **GUILTY CONSCIENCE. / YOUR TOMORROW MAY NEVER COME** [–] [ ]

— (next 7", in Feb'56 **WALKIN' STICK BOOGIE. / ROLLIN'** was credited to **JERRY CAPEHEART with The COCHRAN BROTHERS** on 'Cash' records.

Jun 56. (7",78) <3001> **TIRED AND SLEEPY. / FOOL'S PARADISE** [–] [ ]

EDDIE COCHRAN

not iss. Crest

Oct 56. (7",78) *<1026>* **SKINNY JIM. / HALF LOVED** [–] [ ]

London Liberty

Apr 57. (7",78) *(HLU 8386)* **20 FLIGHT ROCK. / DARK LONELY STREET** [ ] [–]

Jul 57. (7",78) *(HLU 8433) <55056>* **SITTIN' IN THE BALCONY. / DARK LONELY STREET** [ ] Mar57 [18]

Jun 57. (7",78) *<55070>* **MEAN WHILE I'M MAD. / ONE KISS** [–] [ ]

Aug 57. (7",78) *<55087>* **DRIVE IN-SHOW. / AM I BLUE** [–] [82]

Nov 57. (7",78) *<55112>* **20 FLIGHT ROCK. / CRADLE BABY** [–] [ ]

Jan 58. (7",78) *<55123>* **JEANIE, JEANIE, JEANIE. / POCKET FULL OF HEARTACHES** [–] [94]

Apr 58. (7",78) *<55138>* **PRETTY GIRL. / THERESA** [–] [ ]

Aug 58. (lp) *(HA-U 2093)* **SINGIN' TO MY BABY** [ ] [–]
– Sittin' in the balcony / Completely sweet / Undying love / I'm alone because I love you / Lovin' time / Proud of you / Am I blue / Twenty flight rock / Drive-in show / Mean when I'm mad / Stockin's 'n' shoes / Tell me why / Have I told you lately that I love you / Cradle baby / One kiss. *(re-dist.Jul60, hit UK No.19) (re-iss. Sep63 on 'Liberty'; LBY 1158)* – hit No.20 *(re-iss. Nov68 on 'Liberty' mono/stereo; LBL/LBS 83152)*

Sep 58. (7",78) *(HLU 8702) <55144>* **SUMMERTIME BLUES. / LOVE AGAIN** [18] Aug58 [8]

Jan 59. (7",78) *(HLU 8792) <55166>* **C'MON EVERYBODY. / DON'T EVER LET ME GO** [6] Dec58 [35]
(re-iss. Mar84 on 'United Artists'; UP 603)

— Augmented by **The KELLY FOUR: JIM STIVERS** – piano / **MIKE HENDERSON** – sax / **DAVE SCHRIEBER** – bass / **GENE RIDGIO** – drums

Jun 59. (7",78) *(HLU 8880) <55177>* **TEENAGE HEAVEN. / I REMEMBER** [ ] Jan59 [99]

Sep 59. (7",78) *(HLU 8944) <55203>* **SOMETHIN' ELSE. / BOLL WEEVIL SONG** [22] Aug59 [58]
(re-iss. Sep79 on 'United Artists'; UP 36521)

Jan 60. (7",78) *(HLW 9022) <55217>* **HALLELUJAH I LOVE HER SO. / LITTLE ANGEL** [22] Dec59 [ ]
Tragedy struck on the 17th of April 1960 when EDDIE was killed (see above). Below release was already recorded and due out.

May 60. (7",78) *(HLG 9115) <55242>* **THREE STEPS TO HEAVEN. / CUT ACROSS SHORTY** [1] [ ]

– (selective) compilations, etc. –

on 'Liberty' unless mentioned otherwise

Sep 60. (lp) *London; (HAG 2267)* **THE EDDIE COCHRAN MEMORIAL ALBUM** [9] [–]
– C'mon everybody / Three steps to Heaven / Cut across Shorty / Jeannie, Jeannie, Jeannie / Pocketful of hearts / Hallelujah, I love her so / Don't ever let me go / Summertime blues / Teresa / Somethin' else / Pretty girl / Teenage heaven / Boll Weevil song / I remember. *(re-iss. Apr63 on 'Liberty'; LBY 1127)* – hit No.11 *(re-iss. Apr68 on 'Liberty' mono/stereo; LBL/LBS 83009)*

Sep 60. (7") *London; (HLG 9196) / Liberty; <55278>* **SWEETIE PIE. / LONELY** [38] [ ]
(above was flipped over after 3 weeks and hit UK No.41)

Jun 61. (7") *London; (HLG 9362)* **WEEKEND. / CHERISHED MEMORIES** [15] [–]

Nov 61. (7") *London; (HLG 9460)* **JEANNIE, JEANNIE, JEANNIE. / POCKETFUL OF HEARTS** [31] [–]

Dec 62. (lp) *(LBY 1109)* **CHERISHED MEMORIES** [15] [–]
– Cherished memories / I've waited so long / Never / Skinny Jim / Half loved / Weekend / Nervous breakdown / Let's go together / Rock and roll blues / Dark lonely street / Pink pegged slacks / That's my desire / Sweetie pie / Think of me. *(re-iss. Nov68 mono/stereo; LBL/LBS 83072E) (re-iss. Feb72 on 'Sunset'; SLS 50289) (re-iss. Sep83 lp/c; LBR/TC-LBR 182701-1/-4)*

Apr 63. (7") *(LIB 10088)* **MY WAY. / ROCK AND ROLL BLUES** [23] [–]

Apr 68. (7") *(LBF 15071)* **SUMMERTIME BLUES. / LET'S GET TOGETHER** [34] [–]

Aug 68. (7") *(LBF 15109)* **MILK COW BLUES. / SOMETHIN' ELSE** [ ] [–]

Apr 70. (lp) *(LBS 83337)* **THE VERY BEST OF EDDIE COCHRAN (10th ANNIVERSARY ALBUM)** [34] [–]

Aug 70. (7") *(LBF 15366)* **C'MON EVERYBODY. / MEAN WHEN I'M MAD** [ ] [–]

Nov 70. (lp) *Sunset; (SLS 50155)* **C'MON EVERYBODY** [ ] [–]
(re-iss. Mar88 on 'Liberty' cd/c/lp with extra tracks; CD/TC+/ECR 1) – hit UK No.53

Apr 75. (lp) *United Artists; (UAG 29760) <LA 428E>* **THE VERY BEST OF EDDIE COCHRAN (15th ANNIVERSARY ALBUM)** [ ] [ ]
(re-iss. May82 on 'Fame' lp/c; FA/TC-FA 3019) (cd-iss. May90; CDFA 3019)

Aug 79. (lp/c) *United Artists; (UAK/TCK 30244)* **THE EDDIE COCHRAN SINGLES ALBUM** [39] [–]

Jan 88. (7") *(EDDIE 501)* **C'MON EVERYBODY. / DON'T EVER LET ME GO** [14] [–]
(12"+=/cd-s+=) *(12/CD EDDIE 501)* – Skinny Jim / Jeannie, Jeannie, Jeannie.

Mar 91. (4xcd-box) *(CDECB 1)* **THE EDDIE COCHRAN BOX SET** [ ] [–]

Oct 97. (cd) *Music Club; (MCCD 318)* **RARE 'N' ROCKIN': 28 GEMS FROM THE GOLDEN AGE OF ROCK'N'ROLL** [ ] [–]

Feb 98. (cd) *Disky; (TO 86095-2)* **THE ORIGINAL** [ ] [ ]

Apr 98. (cd) *Razor & Tie; (RE 2162-2)* **SOMETHIN' ELSE: THE FINE LOOKIN' HITS OF EDDIE COCHRAN** [ ] [ ]

Oct 99. (cd) *Rockstar; (RSRCD 011)* **ROCKIN' IT COUNTRY STYLE: THE LEGENDARY CHUCK FOREMAN RECORDINGS 1953-1955** [ ] [ ]

Oct 99. (cd; with GENE VINCENT) *Rockstar; (RSRCD 016)* **TOWN HALL PARTY 1958-1959** [ ] [ ]

Sep 00. (cd; with GENE VINCENT) *Rockstar; (RSRCD 018)* **ROCK'N'ROLL MEMORIES** [ ] [ ]

Feb 01. (cd) *E.M.I.; (5761430)* **THE STORY** [ ] [ ]

Jul 01. (cd) *E.M.I.; (533631-2)* **TWELVE OF HIS BIGGEST HITS – NEVER TO BE FORGOTTEN** [ ] [ ]

Joe COCKER

Born: JOHN ROBERT COCKER, 20 May'44, Sheffield, England. COCKER's first musical influence was RAY CHARLES, after hearing the track 'What'd I Say', also taking in the blues sounds of LIGHTNIN' HOPKINS, MUDDY WATERS and JOHN LEE HOOKER. Pipefitter by day and pub singer by night, his band, VANCE ARNOLD & THE AVENGERS were signed to 'Decca' in '65, cutting the BEATLES cover, 'I'LL CRY INSTEAD'. Although the single failed to achieve any real success, COCKER gave it a second bash in '67, making a demo tape for the influential Denny Cordell, the producer of Procol Harum's 'A WHITER SHADE OF PALE'. This proved a shrewd move, his subsequent single (cut by Cordell), 'MARJORINE', leading to a deal with A&M. '68 saw COCKER catapulted to fame with a cover of the Beatles' 'WITH A LITTLE HELP FROM MY FRIENDS', featuring JIMMY PAGE on guitar. Reaching No.1 in Britain, the song showcased COCKER's powerful, gravel-throated voice and his ability to make a song his own. With heavyweight fame looming large, COCKER hired manager Dee Anthony, who promptly booked him for gigs in America with his group, the GREASE BAND, and in '69, the Cordell produced album, 'WITH A LITTLE HELP FROM MY FRIENDS' was issued, featuring the talents of STEVE WINWOOD and MATTHEW FISHER, amonst others. The set received critical and commercial acclaim, featuring an inspired version of Dylan's 'I SHALL BE RELEASED' as well as the spell-binding rendition of Traffic's 'FEELIN ALRIGHT', the next single to be lifted from the album. With the festival scene buzzing, JOE and the GREASE BAND appeared in America on a series of five gigs, the last being the Woodstock Music and Arts Fair in Bethal, New York, where his full-on performance of 'WITH A LITTLE HELP . . .' summed up the mood of the weekend. His second long-player, 'JOE COCKER!', produced a Top 10 in the UK with a LEON RUSSELL-penned 'DELTA LADY', the album characterised by COCKER's primordial, blasting vocals. Dismantling the GREASE BAND in 1970 after a hectic two years on the road, his next outfit was assembled a matter of weeks later for a few gigs he had forgotten about. The MAD DOGS band, made up of LEON RUSSELL and a full horn section from the recently disbanded DELANEY & BONNIE & FRIENDS, almost immediately created a hit with 'THE LETTER', a cover of the Box Tops' 1967 pop hit. A live recording, 70's 'MAD DOGS AND ENGLISHMEN' (recorded at Fillmore during the tour of the same name), solidified COCKER's fame, the album rocketing to No.2 on the Billboard chart and the tour being released as a film, premiering at Cannes in '71. Ironically, the tour left COCKER a wreck and led to his withdrawal from the music business. A half-hearted comeback in '72 saw the release of 'JOE COCKER' (without the exclamation mark, which is exactly what it was) while another comeback set in May '74, 'I CAN STAND A LITTLE RAIN' was equally disastrous. Although 'YOU ARE SO BEAUTIFUL' (taken from that album) charted in March '75, the personal turmoil continued, painfully illustrated by John Belushi's hilarious impersonation of COCKER on Saturday Night Live. The rest of the 70's saw the release of a string of lacklustre albums and an end to his relationship with 'A&M'. COCKER subsequently signed to 'Elektra / Asylum' in '78, before moving to 'Island' in '82, his first release for the label, 'SHEFFIELD STEEL', borrowing the talents of SLY & ROBBIE to lukewarm effect. The comeback that had threatened to happen with the release of the album actually came a year later with 'UP WHERE WE BELONG', a duet sung with JENNIFER WARNES and the love theme to the movie, 'An Officer And A Gentleman'. COCKER was on the move again in '84, signing to 'Capitol', where he released six albums, appealing largely to the AOR market, while the '90s saw JOE teaming up with BRYAN ADAMS before rehashing his two most celebrated recordings, 'WITH A LITTLE HELP . . .' and 'FEELIN' ALRIGHT' for the commercial re-run of Woodstock '94. Now with Sony's '550' label, he continues to tour the globe and confound the critics with his durability – a new set, 'NO ORDINARY WORLD' was released towards the end of 1999. On the evidence of the 'RESPECT YOURSELF' (2002), COCKER's soulful rasp seemed to be continuing to mature like a fine malt, smoky, peaty and designed to put hairs on your chest. Sure, he still went over the top from time to time, inflating songs to bursting point, but on the likes of Randy Newman's 'EVERYTIME IT RAINS', COCKER proved he still has one of the most durable voices in the business. • **Songwriters:** Pens some with band (GREASE BAND) member CHRIS STAINTON. Covers:- SHE CAME IN THROUGH THE BATHROOM WINDOW + YOU'VE GOT TO HIDE YOUR LOVE AWAY (Beatles) / YOU ARE SO BEAUTIFUL (Billy Preston-Jim Price) / JUST LIKE A WOMAN + I SHALL BE RELEASED + WATCHING THE RIVER FLOW (Bob Dylan) / DON'T LET ME BE MISUNDERSTOOD (Nina Simone) / DARLING BE HOME SOON (Lovin' Spoonful) / BIRD ON THE WIRE + I'M YOUR MAN (Leonard Cohen) / HONKY TONK WOMEN (Rolling Stones) / I'VE BEEN LOVING YOU TOO LONG (Otis Redding) / GIVE PEACE A CHANCE (John Lennon) / ST.JAMES INFIRMARY (Graham Bond) / LAWDY MISS CLAWDY (Little Richard) / MANY RIVERS TO CROSS (Jimmy Cliff) / I HEARD IT THROUGH THE GRAPEVINE (Barrett Strong) / TALKING BACK TO THE NIGHT (Steve Winwood) / INNER CITY BLUES (Marvin Gaye) / UNCHAIN MY HEART (Ray Charles) / UP WHERE WE BELONG (Buffy Sainte Marie-Will Jennings-Jack Nitzchse) / DON'T LET THE SUN GO DOWN ON ME (Elton John) / CAN'T FIND MY WAY HOME (Blind Faith) / THE MOON IS A HARSH MISTRESS (Jimmy Webb) / FIVE WOMEN (Prince) / TWO WRONGS DON'T MAKE A RIGHT (Bendith-Schwartz) / TEMPTED (Squeeze) / I STILL CAN'T BELIEVE IT'S TRUE (. . . Cadd) / LET THE HEALING BEGIN (Tony Joe White) / HAVE A LITTLE FAITH IN ME (John Hiatt) / THE SIMPLE THINGS (Shanks-Neigher-Roy) / SUMMER IN THE CITY (Lovin' Spoonful) / THE GREAT DIVIDE (J.D. Souther) / HIGHWAY HIGHWAY (Steven Allen Davis) / TOO COOL (G.Sutton-K.Fleming) / SOUL TIME (Will Jennings-Frankie Miller) / OUT OF THE BLUE (Robbie Robertson) / HELL AND HIGHWATER (John Miles) / STANDING KNEE DEEP IN A RIVER (Bob McDill-Dickey Lee-Bucky Jones) / TAKE ME HOME (Kipner-Capek-Jordan) / and many more.

Album rating: WITH A LITTLE HELP FROM MY FRIENDS (*7) / JOE COCKER! (*7) / MAD DOGS AND ENGLISHMEN (*7) / COCKER HAPPY early stuff (*5) / SOMETHING TO SAY (*4) / I CAN STAND A LITTLE RAIN (*5) / JAMAICA SAY YOU WILL (*3) / STINGRAY (*5) / LUXURY YOU CAN AFFORD (*5) / SHEFFIELD STEEL (*5) / A CIVILIZED MAN (*4) / COCKER (*4) / UNCHAIN MY HEART (*5) / ONE NIGHT OF SIN (*3) / JOE COCKER LIVE! (*4) / NIGHT CALLS (*4) / THE LEGEND: THE ESSENTIAL COLLECTION compilation (*7) / HAVE A LITTLE FAITH (*5) / ORGANIC (*5) / ACROSS FROM MIDNIGHT (*5) / NO ORDINARY WORLD (*4) / RESPECT YOURSELF (*4)

JOE COCKER – vocals, (touring band JOE COCKER'S BIG BLUES) with **DAVE HOPPER** – guitar / **VERNON NASH** – piano / **DAVE GREEN** – bass / **DAVE MEMMOT** – drums Record company used session men instead incl. **BIG JIM SULLIVAN** – guitar

Decca   not iss.

Oct 64. (7") *(F 11974)* **I'LL CRY INSTEAD. / PRECIOUS WORDS** [ ] [–]

—— He formed **The GREASE BAND** in '67 retaining **NASH** and **MEMMOTT** and recruited **CHRIS STAINTON** – bass, and **FRANK MYLES** – guitar. But once again opted for session musicians incl. **CLEM CATTINI** – drums / **J. PAGE & A. LEE** – guitar. Although STAINTON did appear. (JIMMY PAGE also appeared on next 45)

Regal Zonophone   A&M

Sep 68. (7") *(RZ 3006) <928>* **MARJORINE. / THE NEW AGE OF LILY** [48] [ ]

—— **JOE COCKER & THE GREASE BAND** with **STAINTON** brought in new guys **TOMMY EYRE** – keyboards / **MICKEY GEE** – guitar / **TOMMY REILLY** – drums

Sep 68. (7") *(RZ 3013) <991>* **WITH A LITTLE HELP FROM MY FRIENDS. / SOMETHING'S COMING ON** [1] Nov68 [68]

—— **MENRY McCULLOCH** – guitar repl. MICKEY GEE (he later joined SHAKIN' STEVENS) **KENNY SLADE** – drums repl. REILLY Plus of course a huge selection of session people

May 69. (lp) *(SLRZ 1006) <AM 4182>* **WITH A LITTLE HELP FROM MY FRIENDS** [ ] [35]
– Feeling alright / Bye bye blackbird / Change in Louise / Marjorine / Just like a woman / Do I still figure in your life / Sandpaper Cadillac / Don't let me be misunderstood / With a little help from my friends / I shall be released. *(re-iss. Oct81 on 'Cube' lp/c; TOOFA/ZCTOF 1) (cd-iss. 1988 on 'Cube'; 846316) (re-iss. Feb90 on 'Castle' cd/c; CLA CD/MC 172) (cd re-iss. Oct98 on 'Polydor'; 393106-2)*

Jun 69. (7") *<1063>* **FEELING ALRIGHT. / SANDPAPER CADILLAC** [–] [69]
<re-iss. Dec71, hit No.33>

—— **JOE'S GREASE BAND** retained **STAINTON** – now keyboards and **McCULLOCH ALAN SPENNER** – bass repl. TOMMY EYRE who joines AYNSLEY DUNBAR, etc.

BRUCE ROWLANDS – drums repl. KENNY SLADE who went into sessions

Sep 69. (7") *(RZ 3024) <1112>* **DELTA LADY. / SHE'S GOOD TO ME** [10] [69]

Nov 69. (lp) *(SLRZ 1011) <AM 4224>* **JOE COCKER!** [ ] [11]
– Dear landlord / Bird on the wire / Lawdy Miss Clawdy / She came in through the bathroom window / Hitchcock railway / That's your business now / Something / Delta lady / Hello little friend / Darling be home soon. *(re-iss. May91 on 'Castle' cd/c; CLA CD/MC 238) (cd re-iss. Oct98 on 'Polydor'; 394224-2)*

Dec 69. (7") *<1147>* **SHE CAME IN THROUGH THE BATHROOM WINDOW. / CHANGE IN LOUISE** [–] [30]

Jun 70. (7") *(RZ 3027)* *<1174>* **THE LETTER. / SPACE CAPTAIN** [39] Apr70 [7]

—— Early '70, he retained **STAINTON** and assembled his **MAD DOGS AND ENGLISHMEN** entourage which included **LEON RUSSELL & THE SHELTER PEOPLE** – guitar, piano / **DON PRESTON** – guitar CARL RADLE – bass / **BOBBY KEYS** – sax / **JIM PRICE** – trumpet / **JIM KELTNER** – drums plus even more session people, over 10, which was documented on film in '71.

A&M A&M

Sep 70. (d-lp) *(<AMLD 6002>)* **MAD DOGS & ENGLISHMEN (live)** [16] [2]
– (introduction) / Honky tonk women / Sticks and stones / Cry me a river / Bird on the wire / Feeling alright / Superstar / Let's go get stoned / Blue medley: I'll drown in my own tears – When something is wrong with my baby – I've been loving you too long / Girl from North Country / Give peace a chance / She came in through the bathroom window / Space captain / The letter / Delta lady. *(re-iss. 1983 d-lp/d-c; AMLS/CDM 6002) (cd-iss. 1988; CDA 6002) <US d-cd-iss. Jan86 on 'Mobile Fidelity'; MFCD 2-824> (cd re-iss. Jan97; 396002-2) (cd re-iss. Oct98 on 'Polydor'; 540698-2) (cd re-iss. Dec98 on 'Mobile Fidelity'; UDCD 736)*

Fly A&M

Oct 70. (7") *(BUG 3)* *<1200>* **CRY ME A RIVER (live). / GIVE PEACE A CHANCE (live)** [ ] [11]

Apr 71. (lp) *(HIFLY 3)* **COCKER HAPPY** (older material) [ ] [–]
– Hitchcock railway / She came in through the bathroom window / Marjorine / She's good to me / Hello little friend / With a little help from my friends / Delta lady / Darlin' be home soon / Do I still figure in your life / Feeling alright / Something's coming on / The letter. *(re-iss. May85 on 'Sierra' lp/c; FEDB/CFEDB 5011) (cd-iss. Oct94 on 'Disky'; CUCD 01)*

—— JOE retained **STAINTON** and some of his past session men

May 71. (7") *(BUG 9)* *<1258>* **HIGH TIME WE WENT. / BLACK EYED BLUES** [ ] [22]

—— now with the CHRIS STAINTON BAND" (a 12-piece) retaining **KEYS, PRICE** and **KELTNER.** (also had loads of session men)

Aug 72. (7") *(BUG 25)* *<1370>* **MIDNIGHT RIDER. / WOMAN TO WOMAN** [ ] [27] [56]

Dec 72. (lp) *(HIFLY 13)* *<AM 4368>* **SOMETHING TO SAY** <US-title 'JOE COCKER'> [ ] [30]
– Pardon me sir / High time we went / She don't mind / Black eyed blues / Something to say / Midnight rider / Do right woman / Woman to woman / St. James infirmary blues. *(cd-iss. Oct98 on 'Polydor'; 394368-2)*

Feb 73. (7") *(BUG 28)* **PARDON ME SIR. / SHE DON'T MIND** [ ] [–]

Feb 73. (7") *<1407>* **PARDON ME SIR. / ST. JAMES INFIRMARY BLUES** [–] [51]

—— now (complete new line-up) **STAINTON** joined TUNDRA / **HENRY McCULLOCH** – guitar / **MICK WEAVER** (aka WYNDER K. FROG) – keyboards / **BUFFALO GELBER** – bass / **JIMMY KARSTEIN** – drums

Jun 74. (7") *(BUG 47)* *<1539>* **PUT OUT THE LIGHT. / IF I LOVE YOU** [ ] [46]

Aug 74. (lp/c) *(HIFLY/ZCFLY 18)* *<AM 3633>* **I CAN STAND A LITTLE RAIN** [ ] [11]
– Put out the light / I can stand a little rain / I get mad / Sing me a song / The moon is a harsh mistress / Don't forget me / You are so beautiful / It's a sin when you love somebody / Performance / Guilty. *(re-iss. Apr89 on 'Castle' lp/c/cd; CLA LP/MC/CD 144) (cd re-iss. Oct98 on 'Polydor'; 393175-2)*

Dec 74. (7") *(BUG 57)* **YOU ARE SO BEAUTIFUL. / I GET MAD** [ ] [–]

Dec 74. (7") *<1641>* **YOU ARE SO BEAUTIFUL. / IT'S A SIN WHEN YOU LOVE SOMEBODY** [–] [5]

—— He then formed **JOE COCKER & The COCK'N'BULL BAND** with **WEAVER** plus **ALBERT LEE** – guitar / **PETER GAVIN** – drums / **ANDY DENNO** – bass

JOE COCKER retained **LEE, GAVIN** plus touring band **RICHARD TEE** – keyboards / **GORDON EDWARDS** – bass / **CORNELL DUPREE** – guitar / **KENNY SLADE** – percussion and three girl backing singers

Jul 75. (7") *<1749>* **I THINK IT'S GONNA RAIN TODAY. / OH MAMA** [–] [ ]

Aug 75. (lp/c) *(HIFLY/ZCFLY 20)* *<AM 4529>* **JAMAICA SAY YOU WILL** [ ] [42]
– (That's what I like) In my woman / Where am I now / I think it's going to rain today / Forgive me now / Oh mama / Lucinda / If I love you / Jamaica say you will / It's all over but the shoutin' / Jack-a-diamonds. *(cd-iss. Oct98 on 'Polydor'; 394529-2)*

Oct 75. (7") *(BUG 61)* **IT'S ALL OVER BUT THE SHOUTIN'. / SANDPAPER CADILLAC** [ ] [–]

Oct 75. (7") *<1758>* **JAMAICA SAY YOU WILL. / IT'S ALL OVER BUT THE SHOUTIN'** [–] [ ]

—— **JOE COCKER & STUFF** retained **TEE, EDWARDS** and **DUPREE** added **ERIC GALE** – guitar repl. LEE who went solo **STEVE GADD drums** repl. GAVIN

A&M A&M

Apr 76. (7") *<1805>* **THE MAN IN ME. / (part 2)** [–] [ ]

Apr 76. (lp/c) *(AMLH/CAM 64574)* *<AM 4574>* **STINGRAY** [ ] [70]
– The jealous kind / I broke down / You came along / Catfish / Moon dew / The man in me / She is my lady / Worrier / Born thru indifference with you / A song for you. *(cd-iss. Oct98 on 'Polydor'; 394574-2)*

Jul 76. (7") *(AMS 7243)* *<1830>* **THE JEALOUS KIND. / YOU CAME ALONG** [ ] [ ]

Sep 76. (7") *(AMS 7257)* *<1855>* **I BROKE DOWN. / YOU CAME ALONG** [ ] [ ]

—— JOE then joined **KOKOMO** for a month late '76 (no recordings). Took a long time off from studio & stage. Returned with a host of session people

Asylum Asylum

Sep 78. (7") *<45540>* **FUN TIME. / WATCHING THE RIVER FLOW** [–] [ ]

Sep 78. (lp/c) *(K/K4 53087)* *<6E 145>* **LUXURY YOU CAN AFFORD** [ ] [76]
– Fun time / Watching the river flow / Boogie baby / A white shade of pale / I can't say no / Southern lady / I know (you don't want me no more) / What you did to me last night / Lady put the light out / Wasted years / I heard it through the grapevine. *(cd-iss. Jan96 on 'WEA'; 7559 60821-2)*

Sep 78. (7") *(K 13138)* **FUN TIME. / I CAN'T SAY NO** [ ] [–]

Jan 79. (7") *(K 13148)* **A WHITER SHADE OF PALE. / WATCHING THE RIVER FLOW** [ ] [ ]

—— In Sep'81, JOE was credited on a single 'I'm So Glad I'm Standing Here Today' and guested on 'Standing Still' by the CRUSADERS.

JOE COCKER returned to solo work '82, (first w/ SLY DUNBAR + ROBBIE SHAKESPEARE)

Island Island

Jun 82. (7"/12") *(WIP/12WIP 6708)* **SWEET LITTLE WOMAN. / LOOK WHAT YOU'VE DONE** [ ] [ ]

Jul 82. (lp/c) *(ILPS/ICT 9700)* *<9750>* **SHEFFIELD STEEL** [ ] [ ]
– Look what you've done / Shocked / Sweet little woman / Seven days / Marie / Ruby Lee / Many rivers to cross / So good so right / Talking back to the night / Just like always. *(cd-iss. Jul92; IMCD 149) (cd re-mast.Oct02 +=; 063152-2)* – Sweet little woman (12" mix) / Look what you've done (12" mix) / Right in the middle of falling in love / Inner city blues.

Aug 82. (7") *(WIP 6802)* **MANY RIVERS TO CROSS. / TALKING BACK TO THE NIGHT** [ ] [ ]

below from the film 'An Officer and a Gentleman'

Jan 83. (7"; JOE COCKER & JENNIFER WARNES) *(WIP 6830)* *<99996>* **UP WHERE WE BELONG. / SWEET LITTLE WOMAN** [7] Aug82 [1]

Jun 83. (7") *(IS 115)* **THROW IT AWAY. / EASY RIDER** [ ] [–]

Capitol Capitol

Jun 84. (7") *(CL 333)* *<5338>* **CIVILIZED MAN. / A GIRL LIKE YOU** [ ] [ ]

Jun 84. (lp/c)(cd) *(EJ 240139-1/-4)(CDP 746038-2)* *<12335>* **CIVILIZED MAN** [100] May84 [ ]
– Civilized / There goes my baby / Come on in / Tempted / Long drag off a cigarette / I love the night / Crazy in love / A girl like you / Hold on (I feel our love is changing) / Even a fool would let go. *(re-iss. Jul88 lp/c; ATAK/TC-ATAK 115) (cd re-iss. Apr92; EJ 240139-2)*

Aug 84. (7") *<5390>* **CRAZY IN LOVE. / COME ON IN** [–] [ ]

Nov 84. (7") *(CL 347)* *<5412>* **EDGE OF A DREAM (from the film 'Teachers'). / TEMPTED** [ ] Oct84 [69]

Feb 86. (7") *<5557>* **SHELTER ME. / TELL ME THERE'S A WAY** [–] [91]

Mar 86. (7") *(CL 362)* **SHELTER ME. / ONE MORE TIME** [ ] [–]
(12"+=) *(12CL 362)* – If you have love, give me some.

Apr 86. (lp/c)(cd) *(EST/TC-EST 2009)(CDP 746268-2)* *<12394>* **COCKER** [ ] [50]
– Shelter / A to Z / Don't you love me anymore / Living without your love / Don't drink the water / You can leave your hat on / Heart of the matter / Inner city blues / Love is on a fade / Heaven. *(re-iss. Oct89 on 'Fame' cd/c/lp; CD/TC+/FA 3227) (re-iss. Jul94; CDEST 2009)*

May 86. (7"/12") *(CL/12CL 404)* **DON'T YOU LOVE ME ANYMORE. / TELL ME THERE'S WAY** [ ] [–]

May 86. (7") *<5626>* **DON'T YOU LOVE ME ANYMORE. / DON'T DRINK THE WATER** [–] [ ]

Jun 86. (7"/12") *(CL/12CL 413)* **YOU CAN LEAVE YOUR HAT ON. / LONG DRAG OFF THE CIGARETTE** [ ] [–]

Oct 87. (7") *(CL 465)* **UNCHAIN MY HEART. / THE ONE** [46] [–]
(12") *(12CL 465)* – ('A'side) / ('A'-Rock mix) / The one.
(cd-s+=) *(CDCL 465)* – ('A'dance mix) / You can leave your hat on.

Oct 87. (7") *<44072>* **UNCHAIN MY HEART. / SATISFIED** [–] [ ]

Oct 87. (cd/c/lp) *(CD/TC+/EST 2045) <48285>* **UNCHAIN MY HEART** [ ] [89]
– Unchain my heart / Two wrongs (don't make a right) / I stand in wonder / The river's rising / Isolation / All our tomorrows / A woman loves a man / Trust in me / The one / Satisfied. *(re-iss. Jun89; CDP 748285-2) (cd re-iss. Aug92; CDEST 2045)*

Dec 87. (7") *<44101>* **TWO WRONGS (DON'T MAKE A RIGHT). / ISOLATION** [–] [ ]

Dec 87. (7"/12") *(MCA/+S 129) <53077>* **LOVE LIVES ON. / ON MY WAY TO YOU** [ ] [ ]
(above from the movie, 'Bigfoot & The Hendersons' – US title 'Harry & The Hendersons', on 'M.C.A.')

May 88. (7") *(CL 493)* **DON'T YOU LOVE ME NO MORE. / ALL OUR TOMORROWS** [ ] [–]
(12"+=) *(12CL 493)* – Tell me there's a way.
(cd-s++=) *(CDCL 493)* – With a little help from my friends.

Jul 89. (cd/c/lp) *(CD/TC+/EST 2098) <92861>* **ONE NIGHT OF SIN** [ ] [52]
– When the night comes / I will live for you / I've got to use my imagination / Letting go / Just to keep from drowning / The unforgiven * / Another mind gone / Fever / You know it's gonna hurt / Bad bad sign / I'm your man / One night of sin. *(cd+= *) (cd re-iss. Mar94; same)*

Oct 89. (c-s,cd-s) *<44437>* **WHEN THE NIGHT COMES. / ONE NIGHT OF SIN** [–] [11]

Nov 89. (7") *(CL 535)* **WHEN THE NIGHT COMES. / RUBY LEE** [65] [–]
(12"+=/cd-s+=) *(12/CD CL 535)* – ('A'extended).

—— **JOE COCKER BAND** is **DERIC DYER** – sax, keys, perc. / **STEVE HOLLEY** – drums / **PHIL GRANDE** – lead guitar / **JEFF LEVINE** – keyboards / **KEITH MACK** – rhythm guitar / **CHRIS STAINTON** – keyboards / **T.M. STEVENS** – bass, vocals / **DOREEN CHANTER** – vocals / **MAXINE GREEN** – vocals / **CRYSTAL TALIEFERO** – vocals, percussion / **The MEMPHIS HORNS:- WAYNE JACKSON, ANDREW LOVE, GARY GAZAWAY**

Jun 90. (cd/c/d-lp) *(CD/TC+/ESTSP 25) <93416>* **JOE COCKER LIVE (live)** [ ] [95]
– Feeling alright? / Shelter me / Hitchcock railway / Up where we belong / You can leave your hat on / Guilty / When the night comes / Unchain my heart / With a little help from my friends / You are so beautiful / The letter / She came in through the bathroom window / High time we went / What are you doing with a fool like me (studio) / Living in the promise land (studio).

May 90. (c-s,cd-s) *<44543>* **WHAT ARE YOU DOING WITH A FOOL LIKE ME? / ANOTHER MIND GONE** [–] [96]
(studio:- **KENNY RICHARDS** – drums / **EARL SLICK** – guitar / **BASHARI JOHNSON** – percussion, b.vocals – **TAWATHA AGEE, VANEESE THOMAS & FONZI THORNTON.**)

Capitol / Alliance

Oct 91. (cd/c/lp) *(CD/TC+/ESTU 2167) <97801>* **NIGHT CALLS** [25] Jul92 [ ]
– Love is alive / Little bit of love / Please no more / There's a storm coming / You've got to hide your love away / I can hear the river / Don't let the Sun go down on me / Night calls / Five women / Can't find my way home / Not too young to die of a broken heart / Out of the rain.

Oct 91. (c-s/7") **NIGHT CALLS. / OUT OF THE RAIN** [ ] [–]
(12"+=/cd-s+=) – Not too young to die of a broken heart.

Mar 92. (c-s/7") *(TC+/CL 645)* **(ALL I KNOW) FEELS LIKE FOREVER. / WHEN THE NIGHT COMES** [25] [–]
(cd-s+=) *(CDCL 645)* – Up where we belong / With a little help from my friends.

May 92. (c-s/7") *(TC+/CL 657)* **NOW THAT THE MAGIC HAS GONE. / FIVE WOMEN** [28] [–]
(12"+=/cd-s+=) *(12/CD CL 657)* – Two wrongs don't make a right / The letter.

Jun 92. (c-s/7") *(TC+/CL 664)* **UNCHAIN MY HEART. / YOU CAN LEAVE YOUR HAT ON** [17] [–]
(12"+=/cd-s+=) *(12/CD CL 664)* – The one / ('A'-Rock mix).

Nov 92. (c-s/7") *(TC+/CL 674)* **WHEN THE NIGHT COMES. / YOU'VE GOT TO HIDE YOUR LOVE AWAY** [61] [ ]
(cd-s+=) *(CDCL 674)* – Tempted / I still can't believe it's true.
(cd-s) *(CDCLS 674)* – ('A'side) / The Moon is a harsh mistress / I'm your man / She came in through the bathroom window.

—— now w / **JACK BRUNO** – drums / **BOB FEIT** + **TONY JOE WHITE** + **TIM PIERCE** – guitar / **CHRIS STAINTON** – keyboards / **LENNY CASTRO** – percussion / **C.J. VANSTON** – organ

Capitol / 550 Music

Aug 94. (c-s) *(TCCL 722)* **THE SIMPLE THINGS / SUMMER IN THE CITY** [17] [–]
(cd-s+=) *(CDCL 722)* – With a little help from my friends (live).
(cd-s) *(CDCLS 722)* – ('A'side) / Angeline / My strongest weakness.

Sep 94. (cd/c/lp) *(CD/TC+/EST 2233) <66460>* **HAVE A LITTLE FAITH** [9] [ ]
– Let the healing begin / Have a little faith in me / The simple things / Summer in the city / The great divide / Highway highway / Too cool / Soul time / Out of the blue / Angeline / Hell and highwater / Standing knee deep in a river / Take me home.

Oct 94. (c-s/cd-s) *(TC/CD CL 729)* **TAKE ME HOME. (featuring BEKKA BRAMBLETT) / TEMPTED / UNCHAIN MY HEART (90's version)** [41] [–]
(cd-s) *(CDCLS 729)* – ('A'side) / Up where we belong / You can leave your hat on.

Dec 94. (c-s/cd-s) *(TC/CD CL 727)* **LET THE HEALING BEGIN / SUMMER IN THE CITY (2-mixes)** [32] [–]
(cd-s) *(CDCLS 727)* – ('A'side) / You are so beautiful (live) / The letter (live).

Sep 95. (c-s) *(TCCL 744)* **HAVE A LITTLE FAITH / THE SIMPLE THINGS (live) / LET THE HEALING BEGIN (live)** [67] [–]
(cd-s) *(CDCLS 744)* – ('A'side) / Summer in the city (live) / Angeline (live).

Oct 96. (c-s) *(TCCL 779)* **DON'T LET ME BE MISUNDERSTOOD / SOMETHING / HIGH LONESOME BLUE** [53] [–]
(cd-s) *(CDCLS 779)* – ('A'side) / Human touch / Anybody seen my girl.

Oct 96. (cd/c/lp) *(CD/TC+/ESTD 6) <67880>* **ORGANIC** [49] [ ]
– Into the mystic / Bye bye blackbird / Delta lady / Heartful of rain / Don't let me be misunderstood / Many rivers to cross / High lonesome blue / Sail away / You and I / Darlin' be home soon / Dignity / You can leave your hat on / You are so beautiful / Can't find my way home.

Capitol / C.M.C.

Aug 97. (c-s) *(TCCL 793)* **COULD YOU BE LOVED / THAT'S THE WAY HER LOVE IS** [ ] [–]
(cd-s+=) *(CDCLS 793)* – ('A'-Catania mix) / Summer in the city.

Sep 97. (cd/c/lp) *(CD/TC+/EST 2301) <86245>* **ACROSS FROM MIDNIGHT** [ ] [ ]
– Tonight / Could you be loved / That's all I need to know / N'oubliez jamais / What do I tell my heart / Wayward soul / Loving you tonight / Across from midnight / What do you say / Last one to know / That's the way love is / Need your love so bad.

Parlophone / Red Ink

Oct 99. (cd-s) *(CDR 6526)* **DIFFERENT ROADS / YOU CAN LEAVE YOUR HAT ON (live) / WHEN THE NIGHT COMES (live)** [ ] [–]

Oct 99. (cd/c) *(523091-2/-4) <13601>* **NO ORDINARY WORLD** [63] Aug00 [ ]
– First we take Manhattan / Different roads / My father's son / While you see a chance / She believes in me / No ordinary world / Where would I be now / Ain't gonna cry again / Soul rising / Naked without you / Love to lean on / On my way home. *<US+=>* – Lied to me / Love made me a promise.

May 02. (cd-s) *(CDR 6579)* **NEVER TEAR US APART / YOU ARE SO BEAUTIFUL (live) / YOU CAN LEAVE YOUR HAT ON (live)** [ ] [–]

Jun 02. (cd) *(539643-2) <59480>* **RESPECT YOURSELF** [51] Jul02 [ ]
– You can have my heart / Love not war / You took it so hard / Never tear us apart / This is your life / Respect yourself / I'm listening now / Leave a light on / It's only love / Every time it rains / Midnight without you.

– (selective) compilations, etc. –

Apr 72. (d-lp) *Cube; (TOOFA 1-2)* **WITH A LITTLE HELP FROM MY FRIENDS / JOE COCKER!** [29] [–]

Mar 88. (d-lp/c/d-cd) *That's Original; (TFO LP/MC/CD 4)* **JAMAICA SAY YOU WILL / COCKER HAPPY** [ ] [–]
(d-cd.iss-Sep91)

Feb 92. (3xcd-box) *Castle; (CLABX 902)* **3 ORIGINALS** [ ] [–]
– (COCKER HAPPY / SOMETHING TO SAY / WITH A LITTLE HELP FROM MY FRIENDS)

Jun 92. (cd/c) *Polygram TV; (515411-2/-4)* **THE LEGEND** [4] [–]
– Up where we belong (with JENNIFER WARNES) / With a little help from my friends / Delta lady / The letter / She came in through the bathroom window / A whiter shade of pale / Love the one you're with (live) / You are so beautiful / Let it be / Just like a woman / Many rivers to cross / Talking back to the night / Fun time / I heard it through the grapevine / Please give peace a chance (live) / Don't let me be misunderstood / Honky tonk woman (live) / Cry me a river (live).

Dec 95. (4xcd-box) *A&M; (540236-2)* **THE LONG VOYAGE HOME** [ ] [–]

Mar 97. (3xcd-box) *E.M.I.; (CDOMB 024)* **CIVILIZED MAN / COCKER / UNCHAIN MY HEART** [ ] [–]

Jul 97. (cd; JOE COCKER & THE GREASE BAND) *Strange Fruit; (SFRSCD 036)* **ON AIR** [ ] [–]

Feb 99. (cd/c) *Parlophone; (497719-2/-4) / Mushroom; <33120>* **THE BEST OF JOE COCKER** [24] [ ]
– Unchain my heart / You can leave your hat on / When the night comes / Now that the magic has gone / Shelter me / Many rivers to cross / Feels like forever / Night calls / Tempted / Summer in the city / Have a little faith in me / Don't let me be misunderstood / One night of sin / You've got to hide your love away / You are so beautiful / Let the healing begin / Civilized man.

Apr 00. (cd) *Voiceprint; (VP 214CD)* **VANCE ARCHER & THE AVENGERS LIVE** [ ] [ ]

Mar 03. (d-cd) *Capitol; <(582351-2)>* **CIVILIZED MAN / ONE NIGHT OF SIN** [ ] [ ]

□ COCKNEY REBEL (see under ⇒ HARLEY, Steve)

COCTEAU TWINS

Formed: Grangemouth, Scotland . . . late 1981 when the (then) trio of ELIZABETH FRASER, ROBIN GUTHRIE and WILL HEGGIE visited London to hand DJ John Peel a demo tape. He booked them for sessions on his Radio One night time show and they subsequently signed to IVO WATT-RUSSELL's indie label, '4 a.d.'. The COCTEAUS' debut offering, 'GARLANDS', was hastily recorded, hitting the shops just over a week later and giving a hint of things to come with an interesting fusion of monochromatic rhythms, textured guitar distortion and sampling technology. Resisting many offers from the majors, they were back in the studio again for 1983's 'LULLABIES' EP and 'HEAD OVER HEELS' album. A mesmerising collage of irridescent guitar soundscapes and sheets of feedback perforated with FRASER's unintelligible but highly emotive warbling, the latter record was a blueprint for the best of The COCTEAU TWINS work. After a support slot to OMD, WILL HEGGIE departed, making the long trip back north to set up his own outfit, LOWLIFE. Around the same time ROBIN and LIZ hit No.1 in the indie charts when guesting for 'IVO/4 a.d.' ensemble, THIS MORTAL COIL on 'SONG TO THE SIREN'; it was mistakenly thought by many to be a COCTEAU TWINS off-shoot, rather than IVO's project. That idea was laid to rest after the album, 'IT'LL END IN TEARS', was issued in '84. Meanwhile, The COCTEAU TWINS were back with another blissed out masterpiece, 'TREASURE', introducing newcomer, SIMON RAYMONDE on bass and seeing LIZ explore hitherto uncharted vocal territory in a fascinating, enigmatic and occasionally unsettling language that communicated everything and nothing. It also marked their first taste of Top 30 success although they surpassed this with 1986's more inscrutably minimalist Top 10 effort, 'VICTORIALAND'. An abortive film project collaboration with HAROLD BUDD was issued at the end of the year as they headed towards an increasingly "New Age"-style sound. Two more classics, 'BLUE BELL KNOLL' and 'HEAVEN OR LAS VEGAS' were released over the next half decade, both finding a home in the US charts for 'Capitol' records. In 1992, they finally succumbed to signing for 'Fontana' in the UK, leading to a comeback album, 'FOUR CALENDAR CAFE' in '93. Many longtime fans were disappointed with what was surely the duo's most accessible, grounded album to date yet devoid of much of the mystery that made their earlier work so alluring. The following year saw LIZ guest on FUTURE SOUND OF LONDON's ambient venture, 'Lifeforms'; she would subsequently go on to perform on MASSIVE ATTACK's 'Teardrops' single in '98. After another 3-year hiatus, FRASER and GUTHRIE returned with 'MILK & KISSES' (1996), a typically COCTEAU-esque affair that moved some critics to suggest the band were treading water. ROBIN resurfaced towards the end of 2000 via VIOLET INDIANA. His working partner on this collaboration was former MONO diva, SIOBHAN DE MARE, a slightly less ethereal vocalist than FRASER, witnessed on their debut EP, 'CHOKE'. The material on the EP, and especially on the debut album 'ROULETTE' (2001), evoked a laid-back GALAXIE 500-esque wig-out with GUTHRIE's instrumentation quite similar to the spacey hypnotics of TRANSIENT WAVES or PIANO MAGIC. DE MARE's whispering vocals on 'ROULETTE' were awesome and she did manage to completely re-invent her voice on the stand-out track 'SUNDANCE' where she soars while GUTHRIE's guitar spirals out of control. The pair issued a single 'KILLER EYES' at the end of 2001, which featured some fantastic B-sides such as the sparse 'STORM' and the free-jazz influenced 'SAFE WORLD'. GUTHRIE's debut solo album, 'IMPERIAL' (2003), meanwhile, returned to the impressionistic soundscapes formerly expored by the COCTEAU's, swathing his guitar playing in miasmic effects and only occasionally grounding himself with the most basic of percussive structures.
• **Trivia:** ROBIN has produced many '4.a.d.' outfits in addition to The GUN CLUB (1987). An item for some time, LIZ and ROBIN became parents in 1989. Early in 1991, LIZ was surprisingly but not undeservedly nominated for Best Female Vocalist at the 'Brit' awards.

Album rating: GARLANDS (*7) / HEAD OVER HEELS (*8) / TREASURE (*9) / VICTORIALAND (*8) / THE MOON AND THE MELODIES with Harold Budd (*5) / THE PINK OPAQUE compilation (*8) / BLUE BELL KNOLL (*7) / HEAVEN OR LAS VEGAS (*7) / FOUR CALENDAR CAFE (*6) / MILK & KISSES (*7) / THE BBC SESSIONS collection (*7) / STARS AND TOPSOIL compilation (*9) / Violet Indiana: ROULETTE (*7) / Robin Guthrie: IMPERIAL (*6)

ELIZABETH FRASER (b.29 Aug'63) – vocals / **ROBIN GUTHRIE** (b. 4 Jan'62) – guitar, drum programming, keyboards / **WILL HEGGIE** – bass

4 a.d. | not iss.

Jul 82. (lp) *(CAD 211)* **GARLANDS** [ ] [–]
– Blood bitch / Wax and wane / But I'm not / Blind dumb deaf / Grail overfloweth / Shallow than halo / The hollow men / Garlands. *(c-iss.Apr84 +=; CADC 211)* – Dear heart / Blind dumb deaf / Hearsay please / Hazel. *(cd-iss. 1986 ++=; CAD 211CD)* – Speak no evil / Perhaps some other acorn. *<US cd-iss. 1991 on 'Alliance'; 96415>*

Sep 82. (12"ep) *(BAD 213)* **LULLABIES** [ ] [–]
– It's all but an ark lark / Alas dies laughing / Feathers-Oar-Blades.

Mar 83. (7") *(AD 303)* **PEPPERMINT PIG. / LAUGH LINES** [ ] [–]
(12"+=) *(BAD 303)* – Hazel.

—— Trimmed to a duo when HEGGIE left to form LOWLIFE

Oct 83. (lp) *(CAD 313)* **HEAD OVER HEELS** [51] [–]
– When mama was moth / Sugar hiccup / In our anglehood / Glass candle grenades / Multifoiled / In the gold dust rush / The tinderbox (of a heart) / My love paramour / Musette and drums / Five ten fiftyfold. *(c-iss.Apr84 +=; CADC 313) (cd-iss. 1986 +=; CAD 313CD)* – SUNBURST AND SNOWBLIND EP *<US cd-iss. 1991 on 'Alliance'; 96416>*

Oct 83. (12"ep) *(BAD 314)* **SUNBURST AND SNOWBLIND** [ ] [–]
– Sugar hiccup / From the flagstones / Because of whirl-Jack / Hitherto.

—— added **SIMON RAYMONDE** (b. 3 Apr'62, London, England) – bass, keyboards, guitar (ex-DROWNING CRAZE)

Apr 84. (7") *(AD 405)* **PEARLY DEWDROPS DROP. / PEPPER-TREE** [29] [–]
(12"+=) *(BAD 405)* – The spangle maker.

Nov 84. (lp/c) *(CAD/+C 412)* **TREASURE** [29] [–]

– Ivo / Lorelei / Beatrix / Persephone / Pandora – for Cindy / Amelia / Aloysius / Cicely / Otterley / Donimo. *(cd-iss. 1986; CAD 412CD)* *<US cd-iss. 1991 on 'Alliance'; 96418>*

Mar 85. (7") *(AD 501)* **AIKEA-GUINEA. / KOOKABURRA** [41] [–]
(12"+=) *(BAD 501)* – Rococo / Quiquose.

Nov 85. (12"ep) *(BAD 510)* **TINY DYNAMITE** [52] [–]
– Pink orange red / Ribbed and veined / Sultitan Itan / Plain tiger.

Nov 85. (12"ep) *(BAD 511)* **ECHOES IN A SHALLOW BAY** [65] [–]
– Great spangled fritillary / Melonella / Pale clouded white / Eggs and their shells *(cd-iss. Oct86 +=; BAD 510/511)* – TINY DYNAMITE

—— **RICHARD THOMAS** – saxophone, bass (of DIF JUZ) repl. SIMON who fell ill

Apr 86. (lp/c)(cd) *(CAD/+C 602)(CAD 602CD)* **VICTORIALAND** [10] [ ]
– Lazy calm / Fluffy tufts / Throughout the dark months of April and May / Whales tales / Oomingmak / Little Spacey / Feet-like fins / How to bring a blush to the snow / The thinner the air. *<US cd-iss. 1991 on 'Alliance'; 96417>*

—— **SIMON RAYMONDE** returned repl.temp. RICHARD (back to DIF JUZ)

Oct 86. (7") *(AD 610)* **LOVE'S EASY TEARS. / THOSE EYES, THAT MOUTH** [53] [–]
(12"+=) *(BAD 610)* – Sigh's smell of farewell.

—— next was a one-off collaboration with label new signing **HAROLD BUDD** – piano

4 a.d. Relativity

Nov 86. (lp/c)(cd; by HAROLD BUDD, ELIZABETH FRASER, ROBIN GUTHRIE, SIMON RAYMONDE) *(CAD/+C 611)(CAD 611CD)* *<8143>* **THE MOON AND THE MELODIES** [46] [ ]
– Sea, swallow me / Memory gongs / Why do you love me? / Eyes are mosaics / She will destroy you / The ghost has no home / Bloody and blunt / Ooze out and away, one how.

4 a.d. Capitol

Sep 88. (lp/c/dat)(cd) *(CAD/+C/T 807)(CAD 807CD)* *<90892>* **BLUE BELL KNOLL** [15] [ ]
– Blue bell knoll / Athol-brose / Carolyn's fingers / For Phoebe still a baby / The itchy glowbo blow / Cico buff / Suckling the mender / Spooning good singing gum / A kissed out red floatboat / Ella megablast burls forever.

Oct 88. (7") **CAROLYN'S FINGERS. / BLUE BELL KNOLL** [–] [ ]

—— In Apr'90, LIZ was heard on Ian McCulloch's (ex-ECHO & THE BUNNYMEN) 'Candleland' single.

Aug 90. (7"/c-s) *(AD 0011/+C)* **ICEBLINK LUCK. / MIZAKE THE MIZAN** [38] [–]
(12"+=/cd-s+=) *(AD 0011 T/CD)* – Watchiar.

Sep 90. (cd)(lp/c) *(CAD 0012CD)(CAD/+C 0012)* *<C2/C1/C4 93669>* **HEAVEN OR LAS VEGAS** [7] [99]
– Cherry coloured funk / Pitch the baby / Iceblink luck / Fifty-fifty clown / Heaven or Las Vegas / I wear your ring / Fotzepolitic / Wolf in the breast / Road, river and rail / Frou-frou foxes in midsummer fires.

—— on U.S. tour, augmented by **MITSUO TATE** + **BEN BLAKEMAN** – guitars

Fontana Capitol

Sep 93. (7"/c-s) *(CT/+C 1)* **EVANGELINE. / MUD AND LARK** [34] [–]
(12"pic-d+=/cd-s+=) *(CT X/CD 1)* – Summer-blink.

Oct 93. (cd/c/lp) *(518259-2/-4/-1)* *<C2/C4/C1 99375>* **FOUR CALENDAR CAFE** [13] [78]
– Know who you are ate every age / Evangeline / Blue beard / Theft and wandering around lost / Oil of angels / Squeeze-wax / My truth / Essence / Summerhead / Pur.

Dec 93. (cd-s) *(COCCD 1)* **WINTER WONDERLAND. / FROSTY THE SNOWMAN** [58] [–]
(above festive tracks, deleted after a week in UK Top 60)

Feb 94. (7"/c-s) *(CT/+C 2)* **BLUEBEARD. / THREE SWEPT** [33] [ ]
(12"+=) *(CTX 2)* – Ice-pulse.
(cd-s++=) *(CTCD 2)* – ('A'acoustic).

Sep 95. (7"/7"/cd-ep) *(CCT//CTT/CTCD 3)* *<30548>* **TWINLIGHTS** [59] Dec95 [ ]
– Rilkean heart / Golden-vein // Pink orange red / Half-gifts.

Oct 95. (12"ep/cd-ep) *(CT X/CD 4)* *<36240>* **OTHERNESS** (An Ambient EP) [59] Dec95 [ ]
– Feet like fins / Seekers who are lovers / Violaine / Cherry coloured funk.

Mar 96. (cd-ep) *(CTCD 5)* **TISHBITE / PRIMITIVE HEART / FLOCK OF SOUL** [34] [–]
(12"ep/cd-ep) *(CT X/DDD 5)* – (title track) / Round / An Elan.

Apr 96. (cd/c/lp) *(514 501-2/4/-1)* *<37049-2/-4/-1>* **MILK & KISSES** [17] [99]
– Violaine / Serpent skirt / Tishbite / Half-gifts / Calfskin smack / Rilkean heart / Ups / Eperdu / Treasure hiding / Seekers who are lovers. *(also ltd.cd; 532 363-2)*

Jul 96. (12") *(CTX 6)* **VIOLAINE. / ALICE** [56] [–]
(cd-s+=) *(CTDD 6)* – Circling girl.
(cd-s) *(CTCD 6)* – ('A'side) / Tranquil eye / Smile.

—— towards the end of 2000, GUTHRIE worked as the duo VIOLET INDIANA (alongside SIOBHAN DE MARE, ex-MONO), releasing the 'CHOKE' EP for his 'Bella Union' imprint

– compilations, others, etc. –

Dec 85. (cd) *4 a.d.; (CAD 513CD) / Relativity;* *<ENC 8040>* **THE PINK OPAQUE** [ ] Sep85 [ ]
– The spangle maker / Millimillenary / Wax and wane / Hitherto / Pearly-dewdrops' drops (12" Version) / From the flagstones / Aikea-Guinea / Lorelei / Pepper-tree / Musette and drums.

Nov 91. (10xcd-ep-box) *Capitol; (CTBOX 1)* **THE SINGLES COLLECTION** [ ] [–]
– (above featured previous 9 singles + new 1) (sold separately Mar92)

Sep 99. (d-cd) *Bella Union; (BELLACD 14)* **THE BBC SESSIONS** [ ] [ ]

Oct 00. (cd) *4 a.d.; (CAD2K 019CD)* *<370019>* **STARS AND TOPSOIL 1982-1990** [ ] [ ]
– Blind dumb deaf / Sugar hiccup / My love paramour / Pearly dewdrops drop / Lorelei / Pandora / Aikea guinea / Pink orange red / Pale clouded white / Lazy calm / Thinner the air / Orange appled / Cico buff / Carolyn's fingers / Fifty fifty clown / Iceblink luck / Heaven or Las Vegas / Watchiar.

VIOLET INDIANA

ROBIN GUTHRIE – guitars, etc. / **SIOBHAN DE MARE** – vocals (ex-MONO)

Bella Union Instinct

Nov 00. (cd-ep) *(BELLACD 22)* **CHOKE EP** [ ] [–]
– Purr la perla / Busted / Silent / Torn up.

Apr 01. (cd) *(BELLACD 24)* *<571>* **ROULETTE** [ ] May01 [ ]
– Air kissing / Busted / Sundance / Powder river / Little echo / Angel / Poison gorgeous / Hiding / Rage days / Liar / Feline or famine / Killer eyes.

May 01. (cd-ep) *(BELLACD 26)* **KILLER EYES EP** [ ] [–]
– Killer eyes / Storm / Safe word / Killer eyes (CD-Rom).

Oct 01. (cd-ep) *(BELLACD 28)* **SPECIAL EP** [ ] [–]
– Jailbird / Poppy / Sky / Chapter 3.

ROBIN GUTHRIE

Bella Union Bella Union

Mar 03. (cd) *(BELLACD 48)* *<69969>* **IMPERIAL** [ ] [ ]
– Imperial / Freefall / Thunderbird road / Tera / Crossing the line / Into Stressa / Music for labour / Falling from grace / Elemental / Drift.

Leonard COHEN

Born: 21 Sep'34, Montreal, Canada. Emerging from the tail end of the beatnik scene in the early 60's, COHEN was nearing his mid thirties and had already published several volumes of poetry as well as two novels when he came to record his debut album, 'SONGS OF LEONARD COHEN'. Released in 1968, the record is still regarded by many as his finest work and includes two of his best loved and well known songs in 'SUZANNE' and 'SISTERS OF MERCY'. Musically, the album was sparse, fragile acoustic guitar accompanying COHEN's highly distinctive, tortured sliver of a voice. All ravaged sophistication and doomed romance, COHEN was inevitably compared with the likes of JACQUES BREL, although the richness of the imagery he employed immediately set him apart. While the seemingly self-pitying, bedsit-friendly image saw him panned and parodied by critics, he found an appreciative audience among disillusioned hippies as the singer/songwriter movement began to gather strength. Always more popular in Britain and

Europe than America, his debut album reached No.13 in the UK charts. The follow-up, 'SONGS FROM A ROOM' (1969) was almost as good, another opus cloaked in a melancholic intensity and an aching sense of loss, boasting such timeless COHEN fare as 'BIRD ON A WIRE', 'THE PARTISAN' and 'LADY MIDNIGHT'. The record reached No.2 in Britain and COHEN set off for Europe on an extensive round of touring that included an appearance at the Isle Of Wight festival in 1970. Following the release of 'SONGS OF LOVE AND HATE' (1971), the singer embarked on another sojourn to foreign shores, even playing for Israeli soldiers at various military bases, an experience that informed a large part of the lyrical themes on 'NEW SKIN FOR THE OLD CEREMONY' (1974). It was to be another three years before the next studio release and in the interim, 'Columbia' issued a fairly representative best of package. Upon its release, 'DEATH OF A LADIES MAN' (1977) was met with puzzlement and derision, COHEN's subtle, quasi-mystical lyricism suffocated under a typically high powered PHIL SPECTOR production. Vocal in his embarrassment over the album, COHEN returned to more complementary arrangements and structures on 'RECENT SONGS' (1979). The early 80's saw COHEN concentrate on poetry and prose, even making a film, 'I Am A Hotel', in 1983. Returning to the music scene in 1985 with 'VARIOUS POSITIONS', COHEN still had a cult audience in Europe, one that mushroomed with the release of 'I'M YOUR MAN' in 1988. As a purveyor of effortlessly cool urban existentialism on the likes of 'FIRST WE TAKE MANHATTAN', COHEN attracted a new generation of disaffected music fans. It seems he was also held in high regard by the younger generation of fellow artists who showed their appreciation with a 1991 tribute album, 'I'M YOUR FAN'. Among those interpreting COHEN's finer moments (with mixed results) were NICK CAVE, R.E.M., IAN McCULLOCH and The PIXIES. 'THE FUTURE' (1992) saw COHEN achieve his biggest commercial success since the 70's; although never the most prolific of artists, the record was his sole studio release of the 90's. As he came out of the monastery and down from the mountain, COHEN must have still thought it was the 1980's judging by the use of synth and programming on his subsequent album, the boringly-titled 'TEN NEW SONGS' (2001). Aided by long-time collaborator SHARON ROBINSON (who co-wrote 'EVERYBODY KNOWS' on the album 'I'M YOUR MAN' and scoops all of the musical and production credits here), COHEN still managed to uphold his poetic visions and bedsit romanticism. The songs (there's ten of them, you know) still had that "LEONARD COHEN afterworld" that KURT COBAIN sang about, but musically the set disappoints. 'A THOUSAND KISSES DEEP' re-vamps Robert Frost's classic poem 'Stopping By The Woods On A Snowy Evening" and COHEN's deep, almost whispering vocals in 'HERE IT IS' was indeed spine-tingling. • **Covered:** ALWAYS (Irving Berlin) / THE PARTISAN (A.Marly/ H.Zaret-Bernard) / BE FOR REAL (Frederick Knight). • **Trivia:** His long-time dual backing singer and solo artist JENNIFER WARNES released album 'FAMOUS BLUE RAINCOAT' which contained all songs written by COHEN.

Album rating: THE SONGS OF LEONARD COHEN (*8) / SONGS FROM A ROOM (*6) / SONGS OF LOVE AND HATE (*6) / LIVE SONGS (*4) / NEW SKIN FOR THE OLD CEREMONY (*5) / GREATEST HITS compilation (*9) / DEATH OF A LADIES' MAN (*4) / RECENT SONGS (*5) / VARIOUS POSITIONS (*5) / I'M YOUR MAN (*7) / THE FUTURE (*7) / COHEN LIVE (*4) / TEN NEW SONGS (*6) / THE ESSENTIAL double compilation (*9)

LEONARD COHEN – vocals, guitar (with various session people)

C.B.S. Columbia

Feb 68. (lp) *(CBS 63241) <9533>* **SONGS OF LEONARD COHEN** [13] [83]
– Suzanne / Master song / Winter lady / The stranger song / Sisters of mercy / So long, Marianne / Hey, that's no way to say goodbye / Stories of the street / Teachers / One of us cannot be wrong. *(re-iss. Nov91;)*

Apr 68. (7") *<44439>* **SUZANNE. / HEY, THAT'S NO WAY TO SAY GOODBYE** [–] [ ]

May 68. (7") *(CBS 3337)* **SUZANNE. / SO LONG, MARIANNE** [ ] [–]

Apr 69. (lp) *(CBS 63587) <9767>* **SONGS FROM A ROOM** [2] [63]
– Bird on the wire / Story of Isaac / Bunch of lonesome heroes / The partisan / Seems so long ago, Nancy / Old revolution / The butcher / You know who I am / Lady midnight / Tonight will be fine. *(re-iss. Nov81; CBS 32074) (cd-iss. Feb88; CDCBS 63587) (re-iss. cd Jun90; CD 32074)*

May 69. (7") *(CBS 4245) <44827>* **BIRD ON THE WIRE. / SEEMS SO LONG AGO, NANCY** [ ] [ ]

Mar 71. (lp) *(CBS 69004) <30103>* **SONGS OF LOVE AND HATE** [4] [ ]
– Avalanche / Last year's man / Dress rehearsal rag / Diamonds in the mine / Love call you by your first name / Famous blue raincoat / Sing another song / Boys / Joan of Arc. *(re-iss. Sep82 lp/c; CBS/40 32219) (re-iss. Jun94 on 'Columbia' cd/c; 476799-2/-4)*

Jul 71. (7") *(CBS 7292)* **JOAN OF ARC. / DIAMONDS IN THE MINE** [ ] [–]

Jul 72. (7"ep) *(CBS 9162)* **McCABE & MRS. MILLER** [ ] [–]
– Sisters of mercy / Winter lady / The stranger song.

— w / **RON CORNELIUS** – guitar / **BOB JOHNSTON** – organ, guitar, harmonica / **CHARLIE DANIELS** – bass, fiddle / **ELKIN FOWLER** – banjo, guitar / **JENNIFER WARNES** – vocals / **PETER MARSHALL** – bass / **DAVID O'CONNOR** – guitar

Apr 73. (lp) *(CBS 65224) <31724>* **LIVE SONGS (live)** [ ] [ ]
– (minute prologue) / Passing through / You know who I am / Bird on the wire / Nancy / Improvisation / Story of Isaac / Please don't pass me by (a disgrace) / Tonight will be fine / Queen Victoria. *(re-iss. Mar84 lp/c; CBS/40 32272) (cd-iss. May88; CDCBS 65224)*

Apr 73. (7") *<45852>* **NANCY (live). / PASSING THROUGH (live)** [–] [ ]

Jul 74. (7") *(CBS 2494)* **BIRD ON THE WIRE (live). / TONIGHT WILL BE FINE (live)** [ ] [ ]

— now w/ loads of sessioners

Aug 74. (lp) *(CBS 69087) <33167>* **NEW SKIN FOR THE OLD CEREMONY** [24] [ ]
– Is this what you wanted / Chelsea hotel No.2 / Lover lover lover / Field Commander Cohen / Why don't you try / There is a war / A singer must die / I tried to leave you / Who by fire / Take this longing / Leaving Green sleeves. *(c-iss.Jun86; CBS40 32660) (cd-iss. Jun88; CDCBS 69087) (cd re-iss. Apr96; CD 32660)*

Nov 74. (7") *(CBS 2699)* **LOVER LOVER LOVER. / WHO BY FIRE** [ ] [ ]

Nov 75. (lp) *(CBS 69161) <34077>* **GREATEST HITS** (compilation) [ ] [ ]
– Suzanne / Sisters of mercy / So long, Marianne / Bird on the wire / Lady Midnight / The partisan / Hey, that's no way to say goodbye / Famous blue raincoat / Last year's man / Chelsea hotel No.2 / Who by fire / Take this longing. *(re-iss. Apr85 lp/c; CBS/40 32644) (cd-iss. Jun88; CDCBS 69161); hit UK No.99) (re-iss. cd Jun89; CDCBS 32644)*

Nov 77. (lp/c) *(CBS/40 86042) <3125>* **DEATH OF A LADIES MAN** [35] [ ]
– True love leaves no traces / Iodine / Paper thin hotel / Memories / I left a woman waiting / Don't go home with your hard-on / Fingerprints / Death of a ladies man. *(cd-iss. Jun88; CDCBS 86042) (re-iss. cd May95; CD 86042)*

Dec 77. (7") *(CBS 5882)* **MEMORIES. / DON'T GO HOME WITH YOUR HARD-ON** [ ] [ ]

Mar 78. (7") *(CBS 6095)* **TRUE LOVE LEAVES NO TRACES. / I LEFT A WOMAN WAITING** [ ] [ ]

Sep 79. (lp/c) *(CBS/40 86097) <36364>* **RECENT SONGS** [ ] [ ]
– The guests / Humbled in love / The window / Came so far for beauty / The lost Canadian (un Canadien errant) / The traitor / Our lady of solitude / The gypsy's wife / The smokey life / The ballad of absent mare. *(cd-iss. Jun88; CDCBS 86097) <US cd-iss. May88; CK 36264> (re-iss. cd.Dec93 on 'Sony Europe';) (re-iss. May94 on 'Columbia' cd/c; 474750-2/-4)*

C.B.S. Passport

Feb 85. (lp/c) *(CBS/40 26222) <6045>* **VARIOUS POSITIONS** [52] [ ]
– Dance me to the end of love / Come back to you / The law / Night comes on / Hallelujah / The captain / Hunter's lullaby / Heart with no companion / If it be your will. *(cd-iss. May87; CDCBS 26222) (re-iss. Oct89 lp/c; 465 569-1/-4)*

Feb 85. (7") *(A 6052)* **DANCE ME TO THE END OF LOVE. / THE LAW** [ ] [–]

C.B.S. / Columbia

Jan 88. (7") *(651 352-7)* **FIRST WE TAKE MANHATTAN. / SISTERS OF MERCY** [ ] [–]
(12"+=/cd-s+=) *(651 352-6/-2)* – Bird on the wire / Suzanne.

Feb 88. (lp/c/cd) *(460642-1/-4/-2)* *<44191>* **I'M YOUR MAN** [48] [ ]
– First we take Manhattan / Ain't no cure for love / Everybody knows / I'm your man / Take this waltz / Jazz police / I can't forget / Tower of song. *(re-iss. Jul90 lp/c; same) (re-iss. cd Dec95; 460642-9)*

May 88. (7") *(651 599-7)* **AIN'T NO CURE FOR LOVE. / JAZZ POLICE** [ ] [ ]
(12"+=/cd-s+=) *(651 599-6/-2)* – Hey that's no way to say goodbye / So long, Marianne.

Columbia / Columbia

Nov 92. (cd/c/lp) *(472498-2/-4/-1)* *<53226>* **THE FUTURE** [36] [ ]
– The future / Waiting for the miracle / Be for real / Closing time / Anthem / Democracy / Light as the breeze / Always / Tacoma trailer. *(d-cd-iss. Feb93; 472498-2D)* – SONGS OF LEONARD COHEN

May 93. (cd-ep) *(658942-2)* **CLOSING TIME / FIRST WE TAKE MANHATTAN / FAMOUS BLUE RAINCOAT / WINTER LADY** [ ] [–]

Jul 94. (cd) *(477171-2)* *<66327>* **COHEN LIVE (live)** [ ] [ ]
– Dance me to the end of love / Bird on the wire / Everybody knows / Joan Of Arc / There is a war / Sisters of mercy / Hallelujah / I'm your man / Who by fire / One of us cannot be wrong / If it be your will / Heart with no companion / Suzanne. *(cd re-iss. Jan99; same)*

Oct 01. (cd) *(501202-2)* *<85953>* **TEN NEW SONGS** [26] [ ]
– In my secret life / A thousand kisses deep / That don't make it junk / Here it is / Love itself / By the rivers dark / Alexandra leaving / You have loved enough / Boogie street / The land of plenty.

– compilations, others, etc. –

on 'CBS' (later 'Columbia') UK / 'Columbia' US unless stated.

Mar 73. (7") *(CBS 8353)* **SUZANNE. / BIRD ON THE WIRE** [ ] [ ]

May 76. (7") *(CBS 4306)* **SUZANNE. / TAKE THIS LONGING** [ ] [ ]

Aug 83. (7"ep/c-ep) *Pickwick; (7SR/7SC 5022)* **SCOOP 33** [ ] [–]
– Suzanne / Hey, that's no way to say goodbye / Joan of Arc / Bird on the wire / Paper thin hotel / Lady midnight.

May 88. (cd) *<CK 34077>* **THE BEST OF LEONARD COHEN** [–] [ ]
(UK-iss.Oct94; 32644)

Apr 90. (cd) *Collectors Choice; (902 297-2)* **SO LONG, MARIANNE** [ ] [–]
(re-iss. Nov93; same) (re-iss. Dec95 on 'Columbia' cd/c; 460500-2/-4)

Sep 92. (d-cd) *(461012-2)* **NEW SKIN FOR THE OLD CEREMONY / SONGS FROM A ROOM** [ ] [ ]

Oct 92. (3xcd-box) *(472268-2)* **SONGS FROM A ROOM / VARIOUS POSITIONS / I'M YOUR MAN** [ ] [ ]

Oct 93. (3xcd-box) *(474146-2)* **SONGS OF LEONARD COHEN / SONGS OF LOVE & HATE / LIVE SONGS** [ ] [ ]

Feb 95. (d-cd) *(478480-2)* **SONGS FROM A ROOM / SONGS OF LOVE & HATE** [ ] [–]

Sep 01. (3xcd-box) *(499919-2)* **SONGS OF LEONARD COHEN / SONGS OF LOVE AND HATE / NEW SKIN FOR THE OLD CEREMONY** [ ] [ ]

Sep 01. (3xcd-box) *(504558-9)* **DEATH OF A LADIES MAN / RECENT SONGS / THE FUTURE** [ ] [ ]

Jan 03. (d-cd) *Sony TV; (497995-2)* *<86884>* **THE ESSENTIAL** [70] Oct02 [ ]
– Suzanne / The stranger song / Sisters of mercy / Hey, that's no way to say goodbye / So long, Marianne / Bird on a wire / The partisan / Famous blue raincoat / Chelsea hotel No.2 / Take this longing / Who by fire / The guests / Hallelujah / If it be your will / Night comes on / I'm your man / Everybody knows / Tower of song / Ain't no cure for love / Take this waltz / First we take Manhattan / Dance me to the end of love (live) / The future / Democracy / Waiting for the miracle / Closing time / Anthem / In my secret life / Alexandra leaving / A thousand kisses deep / Love itself.

COLDPLAY

Formed: London, England … early 1998 by CHRIS MARTIN and PHIL HARVEY, the latter would become their manager/ financer/ 5th member after CHRIS found new pals/musicians – JON BUCKLAND, Edinburgh-born GUY BERRYMAN and WILL CHAMPION – while at university. These VERVE inspired mellow-ites issued a limited pressing of 500 copies of their self-financed debut, 'THE SAFETY' EP. After interest from 'Fierce Panda' (who released their single 'BROTHERS AND SISTERS'), the group looked set to conquer the indie charts with their new style of JEFF BUCKLEY-esque melancholia. 'BLUE ROOM' EP (1999) – and their first for 'Parlophone' – featured the classy Chris Alison-produced track 'HIGH SPEED', a dreamy "psychefeelia" song; touching, moody and soft, oh so soft! Supporting tortured HEAD brothers SHACK, enabled the band to delve further into the twisted world of moving rock and reach deeper into the minds of fans who had not yet overcome the departure of Brit pop. Come in Mr. ASHCROFT … your time is up! A second single, 'SHIVER', was their first to break into the UK Top 40, however, this would be well surpassed when summer 2000 follow-up, 'YELLOW', slid into the Top 5. The album, 'PARACHUTES' (2000), received rave reviews from all and sundry and shot into the UK charts at No.1 – it would subsequently touch American hearts and souls not long after. Warm, melancholy and passionate were a few select words to describe this Mercury Prize nomination which also featured a further Top 10 hit and Virgin playlist fave, 'TROUBLE'. The boys were back on top form (and No.1) in 2002, come the release of their second full-length album, 'A RUSH OF BLOOD TO THE HEAD'. It displayed all of the same qualities of the first, although the songs seemed to sit with the listener longer. An example of this was the single 'IN MY PLACE', a poignant but uplifting track that showed-off MARTIN's voice well, not to mention the rest of the group's excellent musicianship. The album glided from one song to the next, like a paper aeroplane in the breeze. At times, sounding almost identical to old ECHO AND THE BUNNYMEN, MARTIN must've taken notes from the old post-New Wave romantics, as at the end of 2002 he began dating a certain actress named Gwyneth Paltrow. Turn on the TV and you will probably hear some commercial or cult programme use 'THE SCIENTIST' as a theme – the world was indeed progressing and COLDPLAY were winning Grammys.

Album rating: PARACHUTES (*9) / A RUSH OF BLOOD TO THE HEAD (*9)

CHRIS MARTIN – vocals, piano / **JON BUCKLAND** – guitar / **GUY BERRYMAN** (b. Scotland) – bass / **WILL CHAMPION** – drums

own label / not iss.

Apr 98. (7"ep) *(none)* **THE SAFETY ep** [ ] [–]
– Bigger stronger / No more keeping my feet on the ground / Such a rush.

Fierce Panda / not iss.

Apr 99. (7") *(NING 068)* **BROTHERS AND SISTERS. / EASY TO PIECES** [ ] [–]
(cd-s+=) *(NING 068CD)* – Only superstition.

Parlophone / Capitol

Oct 99. (12"ep/cd-ep) *(12R/CDR 6528)* **BLUE ROOM EP** [ ] [–]
– Bigger stronger / Don't panic / See you soon / High speed / Such a rush.

Mar 00. (7") *(R 6536)* **SHIVER. / FOR YOU** [35] [–]
(cd-s+=) *(CDR 6536)* – Careful where you stand.

Jun 00. (c-s/7") *(TC+/R 6538)* *<radio cut>* **YELLOW. / HELP IS ROUND THE CORNER** [4] Feb01 [48]
(cd-s+=) *(CDR 6538)* – No more keeping my feet on the ground.

Jul 00. (cd/c/lp) *(527783-2/-4/-1)* *<30162>* **PARACHUTES** [1] Dec00 [51]
– Don't panic / Shiver / Spies / Sparks / Yellow / Trouble / Parachutes / High speed / We never change / Everything's not lost.

Oct 00. (c-s/cd-s/7") *(TC/CD+/R 6549)* **TROUBLE. / BROTHERS AND SISTERS / SHIVER (Jo Whiley lunchtime social)** [10] [–]

Aug 02. (c-ep/12"ep/cd-ep) *(TCR/12R/CDR 6579)* **IN MY PLACE / ONE I LOVE / I BLOOM BLAUM** [2] [–]

Aug 02. (cd/c/lp) *(5405-4-2/-4/-1)* *<40504>* **A RUSH OF BLOOD TO THE HEAD** [1] [5]
– Politik / In my place / God put a smile upon your face / The scientist / Clocks / Daylight / Green eyes / Warning sign / A whisper / A rush of blood to the head / Amsterdam.

Nov 02. (7") *(R 6588)* **THE SCIENTIST. / 1.36 (featuring Tim Wheeler & Simon Pegg)** [10] [–]
(cd-s+=) *(CDR 6588)* – I ran away.

— In Feb'03, CHRIS MARTIN was credited on RON SEXSMITH's single, 'Gold In Them Hills'

Mar 03. (7") *(R 6594)* **CLOCKS. / CRESTS OF WAVES** 9 –
(cd-s+=) *(CDR 6594)* – Animals.

Jun 03. (cd-s) *<52608>* **CLOCKS / YELLOW** – 29

Lloyd COLE

Born: 31 Jan'61, Buxton, England. In summer of '83, COLE and BLAIR COWAN formed LLOYD COLE & THE COMMOTIONS after a meeting at Glasgow University. They subsequently recruited some fellow students, NEIL CLARK, LAWRENCE DONEGAN (son of LONNIE) and STEPHEN IRVINE, signing with 'Polydor' and scoring almost immediately with the classic 'PERFECT SKIN' single, a Top 30 hit in Spring '84. This was followed up by 'FOREST FIRE' and by the time the band's seminal debut set, 'RATTLESNAKES' was released later that Autumn, the critics were already fawning over the group's subtle, intelligent retro pop/rock. They scored extra points for the intellectual ruminations and name dropping in the lyrics, COLE's languorous croon a model of detached cool inevitably drawing comparisons with LOU REED. An auspicious start to their career, the album sold well enough to guarantee a Top 20 placing for the following year's 'BRAND NEW FRIEND' single. More readily endearing, the track's lilting pop melancholy was characteristic of the general mood on 'EASY PIECES' (1985), although the blackly humourous 'LOST WEEKEND' upped the tempo and provided the band with another Top 20 hit. By this point, COLE and his COMMOTIONS, had graduated from being the darlings of the college circuit to achieve considerable crossover success and the future looked good. A third set, 'MAINSTREAM' (1987), sounded lacklustre in comparison, only 'SEAN PENN BLUES' partly recovering the sly wit of old. After a further flop EP and a relatively successful best of compilation, the band went their separate ways. COLE embarked on a solo career, taking COWAN and relocating to New York, where he recruited ex-LOU REED players, ROBERT QUINE and FRED MAHER. The resulting album, 'LLOYD COLE' (1990) achieved a respectable chart placing but a muted critical reception, despite some genuinely evocative moments. Subsequent sets, the more buoyant 'DON'T GET WEIRD ON ME BABE' (1991) and 'BAD VIBES' (1993) rather unfairly met a similar fate. 1995's 'LOVE STORY', on the other hand, saw something of a belated critical comeback, the classy single, 'LIKE LOVERS DO', COLE's biggest hit in years, with the singer proving that a midnight shadow and artful lyrics still had a place in the pop jungle. After an extended period of legal hassles with 'Mercury', COLE emerged with a new band, The NEGATIVES, and an eponymous millennial album released on French-based indie label, 'XIII Bis'. While the song, by and large, remained the same, highlights such as 'PAST IMPERFECT' (a suitably askance view of his 80's heyday) suggested the ageing intellectual wasn't quite ready to don his dad-rock slippers. All of which made the release of 'PLASTIC WOOD' (2001) perhaps a little less surprising than it might have been. For the first time in his career, COLE abandoned the rock format, confounding expectations with a whole album's worth of ambient electronica. While he resisted singing, he couldn't quite give up his acoustic strumming or his penchant for winsome melody, factors which only served to enhance the music's enchanting ebb and flow. In complete contrast, 'ETC.' (2001), released around the same time, gathered together odds and sods from the vaults. More familiar territory then, but of an unexpectedly high quality for cutting room floor material. Sympathetic covers of Karen Black's 'MEMPHIS' and Bob Dylan's 'YOU'RE A BIG GIRL NOW' hinted at an as yet untapped talent for interpretation. 2003's 'MUSIC IN A FOREIGN LANGUAGE' kept up the momentum, if that's not too strong a word for a record so fragile and reflective. A cover of Nick Cave's 'PEOPLE AIN'T NO GOOD' spoke volumes of COLE's creative trajectory: he's certainly got more in common now with old Nick than he ever did in the 80's, from a songwriting point of view at least. COLE has eased himself into the role of world weary, wisely cynical yet lovelorn balladeer as seemingly inevitably as CAVE has. Yet while the Australian still rocks out on occasion, COLE keeps it contantly low-key, ruminating on life as only a man of his pedigree can. • **Covered:** GLORY (Television) / MYSTERY TRAIN (Elvis Presley) / I DON'T BELIEVE YOU + IF YOU GOTTA GO, GO NOW (Bob Dylan) / CHILDREN OF THE REVOLUTION (T.Rex). • **Trivia:** 60's chanteuse/singer, SANDIE SHAW, had minor UK chart hit in 1986 with their 'ARE YOU READY TO BE HEARTBROKEN?'.

Album rating: RATTLESNAKES (*7) / EASY PIECES (*6) / MAINSTREAM (*5) / 1984-1989 compilation (*7) / LLOYD COLE (*5) / DON'T GET WEIRD ON ME, BABE (*5) / BAD VIBES (*4) / LOVE STORY (*5) / THE COLLECTION compilation (*7) / THE NEGATIVES (*6) / PLASTIC WOOD (*6) / ETC. (*6) n/ MUSIC IN A FOREIGN LANGUAGE (*6)

LLOYD COLE & THE COMMOTIONS

LLOYD COLE (b.31 Jan'61, Derbyshire, England) – vocals, guitar / **NEIL CLARK** (b. 3 Jul'55) – guitar / **BLAIR COWAN** – keyboards, vocals / **LAWRENCE DONEGAN** (b.13 Jul'61) – bass (ex-BLUEBELLS) / **STEPHEN IRVINE** (b.16 Dec'59) – drums

Polydor Geffen

Apr 84. (7") *(COLE 1)* **PERFECT SKIN. / THE SEA AND THE SAND** 26
(12"+=) *(COLEX 1)* – You will never be so good.

Aug 84. (7"/7"g-f) *(COLE/+G 2)* **FOREST FIRE. / ANDY'S BABY** 41
(12"+=) *(COLEX 2)* – Glory.

Oct 84. (lp/c)(cd) *(LCLP/LCMC 1)(823 683-2) <24064>* **RATTLESNAKES** 13
– Perfect skin / Speedboat / Rattlesnakes / Down on Mission Street / Forest fire / Charlotte Street / 2CV / Four flights up / Patience / Are you ready to be heartbroken? *(cd+=)* – The sea and the sand / You will never be no good / Sweetness / Andy's babies. *(cd re-iss. Jan92; same)*

Oct 84. (7") *(COLE 3)* **RATTLESNAKES. / SWEETNESS** 65
(12"+=) *(COLEX 3)* – Four flights up.

Aug 85. (7") *(COLE 4)* **BRAND NEW FRIEND. / HER LAST FLING** 19
(12"+=) *(COLEX 4)* – Speedboat (live) / 2CV (live).

Oct 85. (7"/10") *(COLE/+T 5)* **LOST WEEKEND. / BIG WORLD** 17
(12"+=) *(COLEX 5)* – Never ends.

Nov 85. (lp/c)(cd) *(LCLP/LCMC 2)(827 670-2) <24093>* **EASY PIECES** 5
– Rich / Why I love country music / Pretty gone / Grace / Cut me down / Brand new friend / Lost weekend / James / Minor characters / Perfect blue. *(c+=)* – Her last fling / Big world. *(cd++=)* – Never ends. *(cd re-iss. Jan92; same) (re-iss. May93 on 'Spectrum' cd/c; 550035-2/-4)*

Jan 86. (7") *(COLE 6)* **CUT ME DOWN (remix). / ARE YOU READY TO BE HEARTBROKEN? (live)** 38
(12"+=) *(COLEX 6)* – Forest fire (live).
(d7"++=) *(COLEG 6)* – Perfect blue (instrumental).

— trimmed to a studio quartet when COWAN became part-time (gigs only)

Polydor Capitol

Sep 87. (7") *(COLE 7)* **MY BAG. / JESUS SAID** 46 –
('A'dance-12"+=/cd-s+=) *(COL EX/CD 7)* – Perfect skin.

Oct 87. (lp/c)(cd) *(LCLP/LCMC 3)(833 691-2) <90893>* **MAINSTREAM** 9
– My bag / From the hip / 29 / Mainstream / Jennifer she said / Mister malcontent / Sean Penn blues / Big snake / Hey Rusty / These days.

Oct 87. (7") *<44253>* **MY BAG. / LOVE YOUR WIFE** –

Jan 88. (7"/7"g-f) *(COLE/+G 8)* **JENNIFER SHE SAID. / PERFECT BLUE** 31
(12"+=) *(COLEX 8)* – Mystery train (live) / I don't believe you (live).
(cd-s+=) *(COLCD 8)* – My bag (mix).

Apr 88. (7"ep/ext-12"ep/cd-ep) *(COL E/EX/CD 9)* **FROM THE HIP** 59
– From the hip / Please / Lonely mile / Love you wife.

Mar 89. (lp/c/cd) *(837 736-1/-4/-2)* <92223> **1984-1989** (compilation) 14 Jun89
– Perfect skin / Are you ready to be heartbroken? / Forest fire / You will never be so good / Rattlesnakes / Perfect blue / Brand new friend / Cut me down / Lost weekend / Her last fling / Mr. Malcontent / My bag / Jennifer she said / From the hip.

Apr 89. (7") *(COLE 10)* **FOREST FIRE ('89 remix). / PERFECT BLUE**
(12"+=/cd-s+=) – ('A'&'B'extended).

— DONEGAN left and subsequently became a journalist. The group folded in the Spring of '89.

LLOYD COLE

— solo with **BLAIR COWAN** – keyboards / **DARYLL SWEET** – bass / **ROBEDRT QUINE** – guitar / **FRED MAHER** – drums, etc / **NICKY HOLLAND + PARKER DU LANY** – backing vocals / (on tour; **DAN McCARROLL** repl. MAHER / **DAVID BALL** repl. SWEET)

Polydor Capitol

Jan 90. (7"/c-s) *(COL E/CS 11)* **NO BLUE SKIES. / SHELLY I DO** 42 –
(10"+=/12"+=/cd-s+=) *(COL ET/EX/CD 11)* – Wild orphan.

Feb 90. (cd/c/lp) *(841 907-2/-4/-1)* <92751> **LLOYD COLE** 11
– Don't look back / What do you know about love? / Loveless / No blue skies / Sweetheart / To the church / Downtown / A long way down / Ice cream girl / I hate to see you baby doing that shift / Undressed / Waterline / Mercy killing. *(cd re-iss. Apr95;)*

Mar 90. (7"/c-s) *(COL E/CS 12)* **DON'T LOOK BACK. / BLAME MARY JANE** 59 –
(10"+=/12"+=/cd-s+=) *(COL ET/EX/CD 12)* – Witching hour.

Oct 90. (7"/c-s) *(COL E/CS 13)* **DOWNTOWN. / A LONG WAY DOWN (live)** –
(12"+=/cd-s+=) *(COL EX/CD 13)* – Sweetheart (live).

— COLE now with **COWAN + CLARK**

Aug 91. (7"/c-s) *(COL E/CS 14)* **SHE'S A GIRL AND I'M A MAN. / WEIRD ON ME** 55 –
(12"+=/cd-s+=) *(COL EX/CD 14)* – Children of the revolution.

Sep 91. (cd/c/lp) *(511093-2/-4/-1)* <96077> **DON'T GET WEIRD ON ME BABE** 21
-Butterfly / Theme for her / Margo's waltz / Half of everything / Man enough / What he doesn't know / Tell your sister / Weeping wine / To the lions / Pay for it / The one you never had / She's a girl and I'm a man.

Oct 91. (7"/c-s) *(COL E/CS 15)* **WEEPING WINE. / TELL YOUR SISTER** –
(12"+=/cd-s+=) *(COL EX/CD 15)* – Somewhere out in the east.

Mar 92. (7"/c-s) *(COL E/CS 16)* **BUTTERFLY. / JENNIFER SHE SAID** –
(12"+=/cd-s+=) *(COL EX/CD 16)* – ('A'-The Planet Anne Charlotte mix).

Fontana Rykodisc

Sep 93. (7"/c-s) *(VIBE 1/+C)* **SO YOU'D LIKE TO SAVE THE WORLD. / VICIOUS** 72 –
(cd-s+=) *(VIBED 1)* – Mystic lady.
(cd-s) *(VIBES 1)* – ('A'side) / For your pleasure for your company / 4 M.B.

Oct 93. (cd/c/lp) *(518318-2/-4/-1)* <10306> **BAD VIBES** 38 Jan94
– Morning is broken / So you'd like to save the world / Holier than thou / Love you so what / Wild mushrooms / My way to you / Too much of a good thing / Fall together / Mister Wrong / Seen the future / Can't get arrested. *(cd re-iss. Aug01; same)*

Nov 93. (7"/c-s) *(VIBE 2/+C)* **MORNING IS BROKEN. / RADIO CITY MUSIC HALL** –
(cd-s+=) *(VIBED 2)* – Radio City music hall / Eat your greens.
(cd-s+=) *(VIBES 2)* – The slider / Mannish girl.
above album w/ **ADAM PETERS, ANN CHARLOTTE VENGSGAARD, JOHN MICCO, JOHN CARRUTHERS, NEIL CLARK, MATTHEW SWEET, DAN McCARROLL, ANTON FIER, CURTIS WATTS, FRED MAHER, DANA VLCEK, Lightning BOB HOFFNAR + PETER MARK**

Sep 95. (cd-s) *(LCCD 1)* **LIKE LOVERS DO / TRAFFIC / FOREST FIRE** 24 –
(cd-s) *(LCDD 1)* – ('A'side) / I will not leave you alone / Rattlesnakes.
(cd-s) *(LCDC 1)* – ('A'side) / Brand new baby blues (demo) / Perfect skin.

Sep 95. (cd/c) *(528529-2/-4)* <10327> **LOVE STORY** 27
– Trigger happy / Sentimental fool / I didn't know that you cared / Love ruins everything / Baby / Be there / The June bride / Like lovers do / Happy for you / Traffic / Let's get lost / For crying out loud.

Nov 95. (c-s) *(LCMCC 2)* **SENTIMENTAL FOOL / BRAND NEW FRIEND** 73
(cd-s+=) *(LCCD 2)* – Lost weekend / Cut me down.
(cd-s) *(LCDD 2)* – ('A'side) / Most of the time / Millionaire / Sold.

Jan 96. (c-s/cd-s) *(LCCMC/LCCD 3)* **BABY / MY BAG / JENNIFER SHE SAID / FROM THE HIP**
(cd-s) *(LCDD 3)* – ('A'side) / The steady slowing down of the heart / Like lovers do.

Mercury not iss.

Sep 98. (c-s) *(MERMC 511)* **THAT BOY / IF YOU GOTTA GO, GO NOW** –
(cd-s+=) *(MERCD 511)* – Tie me down.
(cd-s) *(MERDD 511)* – ('A'side) / Rain on the parade / Missing.

XIII Bis What Are?

Jun 01. (cd; as LLOYD COLE & THE NEGATIVES) *(15548-2)* <60445> **THE NEGATIVES** Nov00
– Past imperfect / Impossible girl / No more love songs / What's wrong with this picture / Man on the verge / Negative attitude / Vin ordinaire / Never felt so cold / Too much E / Tried to rock / That boy / I'm gone. *(UK-only+=)* – Artificial tears.

XIII Bis Megaworld

Nov 01. (cd) <13900-2> **PLASTIC WOOD** (rec.1999-2000) –
– Omni 7th / Sim trees / 4-train / Velvet / Headlights / Dry ice / Plastic wood / After before and after / B-mushroom / Out time / On ice / The beach / Glass jar / Manhattan chase / Park west / Afterthought / Post script / Machinist.

Nov 01. (cd) *(05712)* <13901-2> **ETC.** (demos from late 90's)
– Backwoods / Old enough to know better / Another lover / 39 down / Sunburst / Memphis / You're a big girl now / Alright people / Santa Cruz / Love like this can't last / Went to Woodstock / Fool you are (demo) / Weakness / Backwoods (reprise).

Sanctuary Sanctuary

Jun 03. (cd-s) *(SANXD 198)* **NO MORE SAD SONGS** –

Jun 03. (cd) *(SANCD 182)* <59018> **MUSIC IN A FOREIGN LANGUAGE** Jul03
– Music in a foreign language / My other life / Late night, early town / Cutting out / No more love songs / Today I'm not so sure / My alibi / People ain't no good / Brazil / Shelf life.

Oct 03. (cd-s) *(SANXD 225)* **CUTTING OUT** –

– compilations, etc. –

Jan 91. (cd/c) *Polydor; (847733-2/-4)* **RATTLESNAKES / EASY PIECES** –

Jan 99. (cd/c) *Universal TV; (538104-2/-4)* **THE COLLECTION** 24 –
– Are you ready to be heartbroken? / Perfect skin / Forest fire / Rattlesnakes / Brand new friend / Lost weekend / My bag / Jennifer she said / No blue skies / Don't look back / Downtown / Undressed / She's a girl and I'm a man / Butterfly / So you'd like to save the world / My way to you / Like lovers do / Baby / Fool you are / That boy.

Mar 01. (cd) *Spectrum; (549605-2)* **AN INTRODUCTION TO LLOYD COLE & THE COMMOTIONS** –

☐ Allen COLLINS BAND (see under ⇒ LYNYRD SKYNYRD)

Edwyn COLLINS

Born: 23 Aug'59, Edinburgh, Scotland. COLLINS formed ORANGE JUICE in Glasgow, Scotland . . . 1977 initially as the NU-SONICS with JAMES KIRK, STEPHEN DALY and ALAN DUNCAN, who was subsequently replaced by DAVID McCLYMONT. In 1979, ORANGE JUICE signed to local indie label 'Postcard', the hub of the burgeoning Glasgow indie scene masterminded by ALAN HORNE. In contrast to the post-punk miserabilism coming out of England, ORANGE JUICE were purveyors of studiedly naive, wide-eyed indie pop as best sampled on the brace of early 45's, 'FALLING AND

LAUGHING', 'BLUE BOY', 'SIMPLY THRILLED HONEY' and 'POOR OLD SOUL' (later collected on 1993's retrospective, 'THE HEATHER'S ON FIRE'). They subsequently signed to 'Polydor' in 1981, releasing a debut album, 'YOU CAN'T HIDE YOUR LOVE FOREVER', early the following year. Though some of their die-hard fans inevitably accused them of selling out, the set almost made the UK Top 20, its charming guitar pop auguring well for the future. The band suffered internal ruction soon after the album's release, however, MALCOLM ROSS and ZEKE MANYIKA replacing KIRK and DALY respectively. The Nigerian-born MANYIKA injected a newfound rhythmic thrust into the follow-up album, 'RIP IT UP' (1982), the clipped funk of the title track providing the band with their only Top 40 hit, albeit a sizeable one. Despite this belated success, further tensions reduced the band to a duo of COLLINS and MANYIKA who recorded an impressive mini-set, 'TEXAS FEVER' (1984) under the production auspices of reggae veteran, DENNIS BOVELL. Later that year saw the release of swansong set, 'THE ORANGE JUICE – THE THIRD ALBUM', a far more introspective affair which found COLLINS at a low ebb. The singer had already released a cover of The Velvet Underground's 'PALE BLUE EYES', with PAUL QUINN and subsequently embarked on a solo career which remained low key for the ensuing decade. Initially signed to ALAN McGEE's "side" label, 'Elevation', his first two solo singles flopped and as the label went belly-up, COLLINS opted for 'Demon' records. He finally issued a long-awaited album, 'HOPE AND DESPAIR' in summer '89. An eclectic, rootsy affair borne of COLLINS' troubled wilderness years, the record was hailed by the same critics who so vehemently supported ORANGE JUICE. Yet despite the praise, it seemed COLLINS was destined for cult appeal; a second 'Demon' set, 'HELLBENT ON COMPROMISE' (1990) failed to lift his profile and COLLINS went to ground. Well, not completely, the singer honing his production skills for indie outfits such as A HOUSE and The ROCKINGBIRDS. The throaty-voxed singer finally re-emerged in 1994 with 'GORGEOUS GEORGE', the record he'd been threatening to make for years. Recorded on classic studio equipment, the record's organic feel coupled with COLLIN's mordant cynicism and razor sharp songwriting resulted in a massive worldwide hit, 'A GIRL LIKE YOU'. With its crunching, NEIL YOUNG-like riffing and infectious delivery, the record was initially released in Europe and Australia before eventually hitting the Top 5 in the UK a year on. Though 1997's 'THE MAGIC PIPER' (from the album 'I'M NOT FOLLOWING YOU') didn't quite match this commercial feat, COLLINS remains one of Scotland's most accomplished songwriters with a reliable line in caustic wit. In 2002, his brand of humour was taken a step further via the release of 'DOCTOR SYNTAX', an album which saw COLLINS, for the first time, use beats and samples courtesy of SEBASTIAN LEWSLEY. The set comprised COLLINS' trademark guitar-led love songs, but with an edgier, personalised production. 'THE BEATLES' was obviously a direct ode to his peers, although 'SPLITTING UP' exemplified COLLINS' songwriting abilities by ten. '20 YEARS TOO LATE' employed a retro-electro-synth feel accompanied by some strange rapping never before encountered on an EDWYN COLLINS record.

• **Songwriters:** ORANGE JUICE: most written by COLLINS, some with MANYIKA. Note that KIRK was the writer of FELICITY, and ROSS provided PUNCH DRUNK. • **Covered:** L.O.V.E. (Al Green), while COLLINS solo tried his hand at MY GIRL HAS GONE (Smokey Robinson) + TIME OF THE PREACHER (Willie Nelson) / WON'T TURN BACK (Vic Godard).

Album rating: Orange Juice: YOU CAN'T HIDE YOUR LOVE FOREVER (*7) / RIP IT UP (*6) / TEXAS FEVER mini (*5) / THE ORANGE JUICE (*5) / THE ESTEEMED ORANGE JUICE (THE VERY BEST OF ORANGE JUICE) compilation (*9) / Edwyn Collins: HOPE AND DESPAIR (*6) / HELLBENT ON COMPROMISE (*6) / GORGEOUS GEORGE (*8) / I'M NOT FOLLOWING YOU (*6) / DOCTOR SYNTAX (*6) / A CASUAL INTRODUCTION 1981-2001 compilation (*8)

ORANGE JUICE

EDWYN COLLINS – vocals, guitar, occasional violin / **JAMES KIRK** – guitar, vocals / **DAVID McCLYMONT** – bass, synths; repl. ALAN DUNCAN / **STEPHEN DALY** – drums

Postcard / not iss.

Feb 80. (7") *(80-1)* **FALLING AND LAUGHING. / MOSCOW** [ ] [–]
(free 7"flexi) *(LYN 7609)* – FELICITY (live).

Aug 80. (7") *(80-2)* **BLUE BOY. / LOVE SICK** [ ] [–]

Dec 80. (7") *(80-6)* **SIMPLY THRILLED HONEY. / BREAKFAST TIME** [ ] [–]

Mar 81. (7") *(81-2)* **POOR OLD SOUL. / (part 2)** [ ] [–]

Jun 81. (7"; w-drawn) *(81-6)* **WAN LIGHT. / YOU OLD ECCENTRIC** [–] [–]

Polydor / Polydor

Oct 81. (7") *(POSP 357)* **L.O.V.E. LOVE. / INTUITION TOLD ME PT.2** [65] [–]
(12"+=) *(POSPX 357)* – Moscow.

Jan 82. (7") *(POSP 386)* **FELICITY. / IN A NUTSHELL** [63] [–]
(12"+=) *(POSPX 386)* – You old eccentric.

Feb 82. (lp/c) *(POLS/+C 1057)* **YOU CAN'T HIDE YOUR LOVE FOREVER** [21] [ ]
– Falling and laughing / Untitled melody / Wan light / Tender object / Dying day / L.O.V.E. love / Intuition told me (part 1) / Upwards and onwards / Satellite city / Three cheers for our side / Consolation prize / Felicity / In a nutshell.

—— **MALCOLM ROSS** – guitar (ex-JOSEF K) + **ZEKE MANYIKA** (b. Nigeria) – percussion, vocals, synths; repl. KIRK DALY who subsequently formed MEMPHIS, releasing only one single for 'Swamplands', 'YOU SUPPLY THE ROSES', early 1985

Jul 82. (7"/10") *(POSP/+T 470)* **TWO HEARTS TOGETHER. / HOKOYO** [60] [–]

Oct 82. (7") *(POSP 522)* **I CAN'T HELP MYSELF. / TONGUES BEGIN TO WAG** [42] [ ]
(12"+=) *(POSPX 522)* – Barbeque.

Nov 82. (lp/c) *(POLS/+C 1076)* **RIP IT UP** [39] [ ]
– Rip it up / Breakfast time / A million pleading faces / Mud in your eye / Turn away / I can't help myself / Flesh of my flesh / Louise Louise / Hokoyo / Tenter hook. *(cd-iss. Jul89; 839768-2)*

Feb 83. (7") *(POSP 547)* **RIP IT UP (remix). / SNAKE CHARMER** [8] [ ]
(some w/ live c-s+=) – The Felicity Flexi Session: The formative years – Simply thrilled honey / Botswana / Time to develop / Blue boy.
(d7"+=) *(POSPD 547)* – Sad lament / Lovesick.
(12") *(POSPX 547)* – ('A'side) / Sad lament / ('A'long version).

May 83. (7"/7"pic-d/ext.12") *(OJ/OJP/OJX 4)* **FLESH OF MY FLESH. / LORD JOHN WHITE AND THE BOTTLENECK TRAIN** [41] [–]

—— basically now a duo of **COLLINS** + **MANYIKA** with session people replacing ROSS (who joined AZTEC CAMERA) and McCLYMONT (to The MOODISTS)

Feb 84. (7") *(OJ 5)* **BRIDGE. / OUT FOR THE COUNT** [67] [–]
(free 7"flexi w/ above) *(JUICE 1)* – Poor old soul (live).
(12"+=) *(OJX 5)* – ('A'-Summer '83 mix).

Feb 84. (m-lp/c) *(OJM LP/MC 1)* **TEXAS FEVER** [34] [–]
– Bridge / Craziest feeling / Punch drunk / The day I went down to Texas / A place in my heart / A sad feeling. *(cd-iss. Mar98 +=; 539982-2)* – Leaner period / Out for the count / Move yourself.

Apr 84. (7") *(OJ 6)* **WHAT PRESENCE?! / A PLACE IN MY HEART (dub)** [47] [ ]
(free c-s w/ above) *(OJC 6)* – In a nutshell (live) / Simply thrilled honey (live) / Dying day (live).
(12"+=) *(OJX 6)* – ('A'extended).

Oct 84. (7") *(OJ 7)* **LEAN PERIOD. / BURY MY HEAD IN MY HANDS** [74] [–]
(free 7"flexi w/ above) *(JUICE 3)* – Rip it up / What presence?!
(12"+=) *(OJX 7)* – ('A'extended).

Nov 84. (lp/c) *(OJ LP/MC 1)* **THE ORANGE JUICE – THE THIRD ALBUM** [ ] [–]
– Get while the goings good / Salmon fishing in New York / I guess I'm just a little sensitive / Burning desire / The artisan / Lean period / What

presence?! / Out for the count / All that mattered / Seacharger. *(re-iss. Aug86 lp/c; SPE LP/MC 102) (c+=remixes)* – I can't help myself / Rip it up / Love struck / Flesh of my flesh / Out for the count / What presence?! / Lean period.

— disbanded after above album; MANYIKA went solo, as did EDWYN COLLINS. He'd already (in Aug'84) hit UK No.72 with PAUL QUINN on 7"/12" 'PALE BLUES EYES' (a Velvet Underground cover) released on 'Swamplands'.

– compilations, others, etc. –

Jul 85. (lp/c) *Polydor; (OJ LP/MC 3)* **IN A NUTSHELL** [ ] [–]
– Falling and laughing / Poor old soul (live) / L.O.V.E. / In a nutshell / Felicity / I can't help myself / Hokoyo / Rip it up / Flesh of my flesh / A place in my heart / Bridge / Out for the count / The artisans / What presence?! *(w/free 7"flexi)* – Felicity.

Jan 91. (cd/c) *Polydor; (847 727-2/-4)* **THE ORANGE JUICE / YOU CAN'T HIDE YOUR LOVE FOREVER** [ ] [–]

Jul 92. (cd) *Polydor; (513618)* **THE VERY BEST OF ORANGE JUICE (THE ESTEEMED ORANGE JUICE)** [ ] Oct95 [ ]
– Falling and laughing / Consolation prize (live) / Old encentric / L.O.V.E. love / Felicity / In a nutshell / Rip it up / I can't help myself / Flesh of my flesh / Tenterhook / Bridge / The day I went down to Texas / Punch drunk / A place in my heart / A sad lament / Lean period / I guess I'm just a little too sensitive / The artisans / Salmon fishing in New York / What presence?! / Out for the count. *(re-iss. cd Sep95; same)* – (extra track).

Jul 92. (lp/c/cd) *Postcard; (DUBH 922/+MC/CD)* **OSTRICH CHURCHYARD (live in Glasgow)** [ ] [–]
– Louise Louise / Three cheers for our side / To put it in a nutshell / Satellite city / Consolation prize / Holiday hymn / Intuition told me (parts 1 & 2) / Wan light / Dying day / Texas fever / Tender object. *(cd+=/c+=)* – Falling and laughing / Lovesick / Poor old soul / You old eccentric. *(cd re-iss. Oct95; DUBH 954CD)*

May 93. (7") *Postcard; (DUBH 934)* **BLUEBOY. / LOVESICK** [ ] [–]
(cd-s+=) *(DUBH 934CD)* – Poor old soul (French version) / Poor old soul (instrumental).

Jul 93. (lp/cd) *Postcard; (DUBH 932/+CD)* **THE HEATHER'S ON FIRE** [ ] [–]
– Falling and laughing / Moscow / Moscow Olympics / Blue boy / Love sick / Simply thrilled honey / Breakfast time / Poor old soul / Poor old soul pt.2 / Felicity / Upwards and onwards / Dying day / Holiday hymn. *(re-iss. cd Oct95; DUBH 955CD)*

EDWYN COLLINS

solo, with **DENNIS BOVELL, MALCOLM ROSS, ALEX GRAY + CHRIS TAYLOR**

Elevation | not iss.

May 87. (7") *(ACID 4)* **DON'T SHILLY SHALLY. / IF EVER YOU'RE READY** [ ] [–]
(12"+=) *(ACID 4T)* – Queer fish.

Elevation | not iss.

Nov 87. (7") *(ACID 6)* **MY BELOVED GIRL. / CLOUDS (FOGGING UP MY MIND)** [ ] [–]
(12"+=) *(ACID 6T)* – My (long time) beloved girl.
(7"box+=) *(ACID 6B)* – 50 shades of blue (acoustic) / What's the big idea.

— now with **BERNARD CLARKE** – keyboards / **DENNIS BOVELL** – bass / **DAVE RUFFY** – drums

Demon | not iss.

Jun 89. (lp/c/cd) *(FIEND/+C/CD 144)* **HOPE AND DESPAIR** [ ] [–]
– Coffee table song / 50 shades of blue / You're better than you know / Pushing it to the back of my mind / The wheels of love / Darling, they want it all / The beginning of the end / The measure of the man / Testing time / Let me put my arms around you / The wide eyed child in me / Ghost of a chance. *(c+=/cd+=)* – If ever you're ready. *(re-iss. cd Sep95)*

Jul 89. (7") *(D 1064)* **THE COFFEE TABLE SONG. / JUDAS IN BLUE JEANS** [ ] [–]
(12"+=) *(D 1064T)* – Out there.

Oct 89. (7") *(D 1065)* **50 SHADES OF BLUE (new mix). / IF EVER YOU'RE READY** [ ] [–]
(12") *(D 1065T)* – ('A'extended) / Kindred spirit / Just call her name / Ain't that always the way.
(cd-s) *(D 1065CD)* – ('A'side) / Judas in blue jeans / Kindred spirit / Just call her name.

Oct 90. (lp/c/cd) *(FIEND/+C/CD 195)* **HELLBENT ON COMPROMISE** [ ] [–]
– Means to an end / You poor deluded fool / It might as well be you / Take care of yourself / Graciously / Someone else besides / My girl has gone / Everything and more / What's the big idea? / Hellbent medley:- Time of the preacher – Long time gone. *(re-iss. cd Oct95; same)*

— now with **STEVEN SKINNER** – guitar / **PHIL THORNALLEY** – bass / **PAUL COOK** – drums

Setanta | Bar None

Aug 94. (cd/c/lp) *(SET CD/MC/LP 014) <058>* **GEORGEOUS GEORGE** [ ] Sep95 [ ]
– The campaign for real rock / A girl like you / Low expectations / Out of this world / If you could love me / North of Heaven / Georgeous George / It's right in front of you / Make me feel again / You got it all / Subsidence / Occupy your mind. *(re-iss. Jul95, hit UK No.8)*

Oct 94. (c-ep) *(ZOP 001C)* **EXPRESSLY EP** [42] [–]
– A girl like you / A girl like you (Macrame remix by Youth).
(cd-ep+=) *(ZOP 001CD1)* – Out of this world (I hear a new world) (St.Etienne remix) / Occupy your mind.
(cd-ep) *(ZOP 001CD2)* – ('A'side) / Don't shilly shally (Spotters'86 demo) / Something's brewing / Bring it on back.

Mar 95. (12"ep) *(ZOP 002CD1)* **IF YOU COULD LOVE ME (radio edit). / IN A BROKEN DREAM / INSIDER DEALING / ('A'-MC Esher mix)** [ ] [ ]
(cd-ep) *(ZOP 002CD1)* – (first 3 tracks) / Hope and despair.
(cd-ep) *(ZOP 002CD2)* – ('A'side) / If ever you're ready / Come to your senses / A girl like you (the Victoria Spaceman mix).

Jun 95. (7") *(ZOP 0037)* **A GIRL LIKE YOU. / YOU'RE ON YOUR OWN** [4] [–]
(c-s+=) *(ZOP 003C)* – If you could love me (acoustic version).
(cd-s++=) *(ZOP 003CD)* – Don't shilly shally (Spotters '86 demo).

Oct 95. (c-s) *<58-1234>* **A GIRL LIKE YOU / IF YOU COULD LOVE ME** [–] [32]
(above used on the film 'Empire Records')

Feb 96. (c-s) *(ZOP 004C)* **KEEP ON BURNING / IF YOU COULD LOVE ME (IN TIME AND SPACE)** [45] [–]
(cd-s+=) *(ZOP 004CD1)* – Lava lamp / The campaign for real rock.
(cd-s) *(ZOP 004CD2)* – Won't turn back / You've grown a beard / A girl like you (live) / White room.

Setanta | Sony

Jul 97. (12") *(SET 041T)* **THE MAGIC PIPER. / A GIRL LIKE YOU (Makrame mix) / WELWYN GARDEN CITY** [32] [–]
(cd-s) *(SETCDA 041)* – ('A'side) / More than you bargained for / Red menace / It takes a little time.
(cd-s) *(SETCDB 041)* – ('A'side) / Who is it? / Who is it? (halterbacked by the Victorian spaceman / Welwyn Garden City.

Sep 97. (cd/c/lp) *(SET CD/MC/LP 039) <68716>* **I'M NOT FOLLOWING YOU** [55] Oct97 [ ]
– It's a steal / The magic piper (of love) / Seventies night / No one waved goodbye / Downer / Keep on burning / Running away with myself / Country rock / For the rest of my life / Superficial cat / Adidas world / I'm not following you.

Oct 97. (7") *(SET 045)* **ADIDAS WORLD. / HIGH FASHION** [71] [–]
(cd-s+=) *(SETCDA 045)* – Mr. Bojangles / Talking 'bout the times.
(cd-s) *(SETCDB 045)* – ('A'side) / Episode 3 / Episode 5 / Episode 10 (no, no, no Adidas – Adilated by . . .).

Nov 97. (d12") *(ZOPPR 005)* **I HEAR A NEW WORLD** [ ] [–]
– (mixes; Red Snapper / Deadly Avenger Supershine / Red Snapper vocal / DOWNER (James Lavelle mix) // THE MAGIC PIPER (the Wiseguys sniper mix) / ADIDAS WORLD (adilated by Sebastian Lawsely) / DOWNER (James Lavelle vocal).

— in Apr'01, EDWYN collaborated with BERNARD BUTLER on the 'Setanta' single 'MESSAGE FOR JOJO'

Apr 02. (cd) *(SETCD 098)* **DOCTOR SYNTAX** [ ] [–]
– Never felt like this / Should've done that / Mine is at / No idea / The Beathes / Back to the back room / Splitting up / Johnny Teardrop / 20 years too late / It's a funny thing / Calling on you.

Sep 02. (cd-s) *(SETCD 112)* **JOHNNY TEARDROP / NEVER FELT LIKE THIS / POSTER** [ ] [–]

Oct 02. (cd) *(SETCD 113)* **A CASUAL INTRODUCTION 1981-2001** (compilation) [ ] [–]
– A girl like you / What presence? (ORANGE JUICE) / Magic piper (of love) / Rip it up (ORANGE JUICE) / A sad lament (ORANGE JUICE) / Witch queen of New Orleans / Johnny teardrop / Gorgeous George / Ghost of a chance / Campaign for real rock / Hope and despair / Falling and laughing (ORANGE JUICE) / Keep on burning / Adidas world / Felicity (ORANGE JUICE) / Tenterhook (ORANGE JUICE) / Witchcraft / Graciously.

Judy COLLINS

Born: 1 May'39, Denver, Colorado, USA. Her father encouraged her to follow a musical career and by the age of ten, JUDY was studying piano with female composer Antonia Brica. A career as a concert pianist was well within her grasp (having performed Mozart upon her live debut at the age of thirteen) but the then revolutionary music of WOODY GUTHRIE began to turn her head and she soon deserted the piano for the more portable (and trendy) guitar. By the age of sixteen she was wowing them in the Colorado folk scene and had her sights set on Greenwich Village in New York City. Arriving there in 1961, she was immediately signed by Elektra's Jac Holzman who was impressed by her crystal-pure vocals and recognised her innate talent for sympathetic interpretation of trad folk material. Her relationship with the label was to endure over three decades while her recordings brought the raw material of such composers as BOB DYLAN, LEONARD COHEN, JONI MITCHELL, SANDY DENNY and many others to a professional polish. Like many 60's artists, she began to experiment with different types of music and her repertoire expanded to encompass material by cult European composers like BRECHT, WEILL and JACQUES BREL. She also moved towards stage and film work which she adopted with the same enthusiasm as her music career. Having already released a string of critically acclaimed albums, her 1966 set, 'IN MY LIFE', highlighted her increasing diversity while 'WILDFLOWERS' marked her first foray into singer/songwriting and featured arrangements by classic ragtime producer, JOSHUA RIFKIN. The latter album also saw her break into the US Top 5 for the first time while spawning a rare hit single in the shape of Joni Mitchell's 'BOTH SIDES NOW'. Late 1970, meanwhile, saw COLLINS score the biggest hit single (US Top 5/UK Top 20) of her career with an unaccompanied version of 'AMAZING GRACE', the track lifted from 'WHALES AND NIGHTINGALES' (1971). The following year's retrospective, 'COLOURS OF THE DAY' made the US Top 40 and it's a mark of JUDY's popularity that this record still sells in considerable numbers; apparently it's ex-President Bill Clinton's fave album and he even named his daughter after the Joni Mitchell cover, 'CHELSEA MORNING'. COLLINS extended her vocal reach even further in 1975 with a Top 10 reading of the Stephen Sondheim Broadway weepie, 'SEND IN THE CLOWNS'. The accompanying album, 'JUDITH', confirmed her increasing tendency toward contemporary ballads in the form of both cover material and her own compositions. Throughout the remainder of the 70's and on into the 80's she continued to record and sell albums to her loyal following in respectable amounts although the chart hits faded. At the dawn of the 90's she released 'FIRES OF EDEN' (1991) which relied more heavily on her own songs than many previous collections had done and included classic track, 'THE BLIZZARD'. COLLINS fulfilled a lifelong ambition by releasing an album of BOB DYLAN compositions the following year and in 1995 completed a project entitled 'SHAMELESS', also publishing a book of the same name later that year. As she moved into her sixties her appetite for work hardly abated, with punishing concert tours and TV/stage work still featuring prominently in her busy schedule. COLLINS' commitment to the underprivileged continues unswervingly, the singer undertaking anti-landmine tours as a UNICEF representative in the former Yugoslavia. Her autobiography, 'Singing Lessons' was released in 1999 to critical and popular acclaim while she continues to explore new avenues in music with 'BOTH SIDES NOW – CLASSIC BROADWAY', a Broadway hits album.

• **Songwriters:** Wrote songs/lyrics herself and many covers by BOB DYLAN, LEONARD COHEN, JONI MITCHELL, The BYRDS, etc. Others included; WHO KNOWS WHERE THE TIME GOES (Sandy Denny) / IN MY LIFE (Beatles) / CATS IN THE CRADLE (Harry Chapin) / FROM A DISTANCE (Julie Gold) / WIND BENEATH MY WINGS (Henley/Silbar) / I PITY THE POOR IMMIGRANT (Bob Dylan) / THE AIR THAT I BREATHE (Hollies). • **Trivia:** Her 1969 boyfriend, STEPHEN STILLS, wrote a song inspired by her 'SUITE: JUDY BLUE EYES'. ROGER McGUINN played on her third album.

Album rating: A MAID OF CONSTANT SORROW (6) / GOLDEN APPLES OF THE SUN (*6) / JUDY COLLINS #3 (*6) / THE JUDY COLLINS CONCERT (*4) / JUDY COLLINS' FIFTH ALBUM (*6) / IN MY LIFE (*7) / WILDFLOWERS (*7) / WHO KNOWS WHERE THE TIME GOES (*6) / RECOLLECTIONS compilation (*7) / WHALES & NIGHTINGALES (*6) / LIVING (*5) / COLORS OF THE DAY – THE BEST OF JUDY COLLINS compilation (*7) / TRUE STORIES AND OTHER DREAMS (*6) / JUDITH (*6) / BREAD & ROSES (*6) / SO EARLY IN THE SPRING, THE FIRST 15 YEARS compilation (*8) / HARD TIMES FOR LOVERS (*4) / RUNNING FOR MY LIFE (*4) / TIME OF OUR LIVES (*4) / HOME AGAIN (*4) / TRUST YOUR HEART (*4) / SANITY AND GRACE (*4) / FIRES OF EDEN (*5) / JUDY SINGS DYLAN . . . JUST LIKE A WOMAN (*4) / COME REJOICE . . . A JUDY COLLINS CHRISTMAS (*4) / SHAMELESS (*5) / BOTH SIDES NOW – CLASSIC BROADWAY (*5)

JUDY COLLINS – vocals, acoustic guitar (with session people)

not iss. | Elektra

Oct 61. (lp) *<EKS 7209>* **A MAID OF CONSTANT SORROW** [–] [ ]
– A maid of constant sorrow / The prickle bush / Wild mountain thyme / Tim Evans / Sailor's life / Bold Fenian men / Wars of Germany / O daddy be gay / I know where I'm going / John Riley / Pretty Savo / The rising of the moon. *(UK-iss.1965 on 'Elektra'; EKL 209) (re-iss. 1975; K 52032)*

Jul 62. (lp) *<EKS 7222>* **GOLDEN APPLES OF THE SUN** [–] [ ]
– Golden apples of the sun / Bonnie ship the Diamond / Little brown dog / Twelve gates to the city / Christ child lullaby / Great Selchie of Shule Skerry / Tell me who I'll marry / Fannerio / Crow on the cradle / Lark in the morning / Sing hallelujah / Shule Aaron.

Mar 64. (lp) *<EKS 7243>* **#3** [–] [ ]
– Anathea / Bullgine run / Farewell / Hey, Nelly, Nelly / Ten o'clock all is well / The dove / Masters of war / In the hills of Shiloh / The bells of Rhymney / Deportee / Come away Melinda / Turn turn turn.

1964. (7") **TURN TURN TURN. / FAREWELL** [–] [ ]

Oct 64. (lp) *<EKS 7280>* **IN CONCERT – TOWN HALL (live)** [–] [ ]
– Winter sky / That was the last thing on my mind / Tear down the walls / Bonnie boy is young / Me & my uncle / Wild ripping water / The lonesome death of Hattie Carroll / My ramblin' boy / Redwinged blackbird / Coal tattoo / Cruel mother / Bottle of wine / Medgar Evers lullaby / Hey, Nelly, Nelly.

London | Elektra

Sep 65. (lp) *<EKS 7300>* **JUDY COLLINS' FIFTH ALBUM** [–] [69]
– Pack up your sorrows / The coming of the roads / So early, early in the Spring / Tomorrow is a long time / Daddy you've been on my mind / Thirsty boots / Mr. Tambourine man / Lord Gregory / In the heat of the summer / Early morning rain / Carry it on / It isn't nice.

Mar 66. (7") *(HLZ 10029)* **I'LL KEEP IT WITH MINE. / THIRSTY BOOTS** [ ] [ ]

Dec 66. (lp) *<EKS 7320>* **IN MY LIFE** [ ] [46]
– Tom Thumb's blues / Hard lovin' loser / Pirate Jenny / Suzanne / La Colombe / Marat / Sade / I think it's going to rain today / Sunny Goodge Street / Liverpool lullaby / Dress rehearsal rag / In my life. *(UK-iss.1971; K 42009)*

Jan 67. (7") **HARD LOVIN' LOSER. / I THINK IT'S GOING TO RAIN TODAY** [–] [ ]

Jan 67. (7") *(EKSN 45011)* **HARD LOVIN' LOSER. / IN MY LIFE** [ ] [–]

Elektra | Elektra

Jan 68. (lp) *<(EKS 74012)>* **WILDFLOWERS** [ ] [5]
– Both sides now / Michael from the mountains / Since you asked / Sisters of mercy / A ballata of Francesco Landini / Lasso di Donna / La chanson des vieux amants (the song of old lovers) / Sky fell / Albatross / Hey that's no way to say goodbye. *(re-iss. May87 lp/cd; K/K2 42014)*

Oct 68. (7") *<45639>* **BOTH SIDES NOW. / WHO KNOWS WHERE THE TIME GOES** [–] [8]

Nov 68. (7") *(EKSN 45043)* **BOTH SIDES NOW. / HEY THAT'S NO WAY TO SAY GOODBYE** [ ] [–]

(re-prom.Jan70) – hit No.14 *(re-iss. Oct73; K 12005) (re-iss. Sep76; K 12225)*

Dec 68. (lp) <*(EKS 74033)*> **WHO KNOWS WHERE THE TIMES GOES** [ ] [29]
– Hello, hurray / Story of Isaac / My father / Someday soon / Who knows where the time goes / I pity the poor immigrant / The first boy I loved / Bird on the wire / Pretty Polly. *(cd-iss. Feb93 & Mar95)*

Feb 69. (7") *(EKSN 45053)* <45649> **SOMEDAY SOON. / MY FATHER** [ ] Jan69 [55]

Oct 69. (7") *(EKSN 45073)* <45657> **CHELSEA MORNING. / PRETTY POLLY** [ ] Jul69 [78]

Nov 69. (7") <45680> **TURN! TURN! TURN! – TO EVERYTHING THERE IS A SEASON. / PACK UP YOUR SORROWS** [–] [69]

Dec 69. (7") *(EKSN 45077)* **TURN! TURN! TURN! / MR. TAMBOURINE MAN** [ ] [–]

Jan 70. (7") **PACK UP YOUR SORROWS. / TURN! TURN! TURN!** [–] [ ]

Nov 70. (7") *(2101 020)* **AMAZING GRACE. / I PITY THE POOR IMMIGRANT** [5] [–]

Nov 70. (7") <45709> **AMAZING GRACE. / NIGHTINGALE** [–] [15]

—— back into UK Top 40 Sep71, In Apr72 dented UK Top 20, re-iss. Nov76)

Jan 71. (lp) *(K 42059)* <75010> **WHALES & NIGHTINGALES** [37] Nov70 [17]
– Farewell to Tarwathie / Song for David / Sons of / The patriot game / Oh had I a golden thread / Prothalmum / Gene's song / Time passes slowly / Maricke / Nightingale I / Nightingale II / Simple gifts / Amazing Grace.

Nov 71. (7") *(K 12035)* <45755> **OPEN THE DOOR (SONG FOR JUDITH). / INNISFREE** [ ] [90]

Jan 72. (lp) *(K 42102)* <75014> **LIVING** (part live) [ ] Nov71 [64]
– Joan of Arc / Four strong winds / Vietnam love song / Innisfree / Open the door (song for Judith) / All things are quite silent / Easy times / Chelsea morning / Famous blue raincoat / Just like Tom Thumb's blues.

Feb 73. (7") *(K 12089)* <45831> **COOK WITH HONEY. / SO BEGINS THE TASK** [ ] [32]

Mar 73. (lp) *(K 42132)* <75053> **TRUE STORIES & OTHER DREAMS** [ ] Feb72 [27]
– Che / Song for Martin / Cook with honey / So begins the task / Fisherman song / Dealer (done and losin') / The secret gardens / Holly Ann / The hostage song.

1973. (7") **THE SECRET GARDENS. / THE HOSTAGE** [–] [ ]

May 75. (7") *(K 12177)* <45253> **SEND IN THE CLOWNS. / HOUSES** [6] Jun75 [36]
<*US re-prom.Sep77*> – hit No.19

May 75. (lp/c) *(K/K4 52019)* <1032> **JUDITH** [7] Apr75 [17]
– Born to the breed / Send in the clowns / The Moon is a harsh mistress / Angel spread your wings / Houses / The loving of the game / Song for Duke / Salt of the earth / Brother can you spare a dime / City of New Orleans / I'll be seeing you / Pirate ships. *(cd-iss. 1983; K2 52019)*

Jul 75. (7") *(K 12181)* **I'LL BE SEEING YOU. / BORN TO THE BREED** [ ] [–]

Sep 75. (7") *(K 12189)* **SALT OF THE EARTH. / SONG FOR DUKE** [ ] [–]

Sep 76. (lp/c) *(K/K4 52039)* <1076> **BREAD & ROSES** [ ] [25]
– Bread and roses / Everything must change / Special delivery / Out of control / Plegaria del labrador / Come down in time / Spanish is the loving tongue / I didn't know about you / Take this longing / Love hurts / Marjorie / King David.

Oct 76. (7") **BREAD AND ROSES. / OUT OF CONTROL** [–] [ ]

Nov 76. (7") *(K 12239)* **BREAD AND ROSES. / KING DAVID** [ ] [–]

Feb 77. (7") **SPECIAL DELIVERY. / EVERYTHING MUST CHANGE** [–] [ ]

May 77. (7") **BORN TO THE BREED. / SPECIAL DELIVERY** [–] [ ]

Mar 79. (7") **DOROTHY. / WHERE OR WHEN** [–] [ ]

Mar 79. (lp/c) *(K/K4 52121)* *<6E 171>* **HARD TIMES FOR LOVERS** [ ] [54]
– Hard times for lovers / Marie / Happy end / Desperado / I remember sky / Theme from 'The Promise' (I'll never say goodbye) / Starmaker / Dorothy / Theme from 'The Ice Castle' (Through the eyes of love) / Where or when. *(cd-iss. Oct94; 7599 60536-2)*

Mar 79. (7") *(K 12343)* <46020> **HARD TIMES FOR LOVERS. / HAPPY END** [ ] [66]

May 80. (lp/c) *(K/K4 52205)* *<6E 253>* **RUNNING FOR MY LIFE** [ ] [ ]
– Running for my life / Bright morning star / Green Finch & Linnet bird / Marieke / Pretty woman / Almost free / I could really show you around / I've done enough dying for today / Anyone would love you / Rainbow connection / This is the day.

May 80. (7") **BRIGHT MORNING STAR. / ALMOST FREE** [–] [ ]

Jul 80. (7") **THE RAINBOW CONNECTION. / RUNNING FOR MY LIFE** [–] [ ]

Jan 82. (7") **MEMORY. / THE LIFE YOU DREAM** [–] [ ]

Mar 82. (lp/c) *(K/K4 52347)* *<E 60001>* **THE TIME OF OUR LIVES** [ ] [ ]
– Great expectations / The rest of your life / Grandaddy / It's gonna be one of those nights / Memory / Sun son / Mama mama / Drink a round to Ireland / Don't say goodbye love. *<(cd-iss. Nov00; 7559 60001-2)>*

May 82. (7") *(K 13180)* **GREAT EXPECTATIONS. / MEMORY** [ ] [–]

1982. (7") **MAMA MAMA. / IT'S GONNA BE ONE OF THOSE NIGHTS** [–] [ ]

Nov 84. (7"; JUDY COLLINS with T.G. SHEPHERD) **HOME AGAIN. / DREAM ON** [–] [ ]

Jan 85. (lp) *<(9 60304-1)>* **HOME AGAIN** [ ] Nov84 [ ]
– Only you / Sweetheart on parade / Everybody works in China / Yellow kimono (Tokyo time) / From where I stand / Home again / Shoot first / Don't say love / Dream on / The best is yet to come.

Feb 85. (7") **ONLY YOU. /** [–] [ ]

Goldcastle Goldcastle

Nov 88. (cd/c/lp) *<(CD/TC+/VGC 7)>* **TRUST YOUR HEART** [ ] Nov87 [ ]
– Amazing Grace / Trust your heart / Jerusalem / Day by day / The life you dream / The rose / Moonfall / Morning has broken / When a child is born / When you wish upon a star. *(re-iss. Aug91 on 'Virgin' lp/c; OVED/+C 372)*

Jun 89. (cd/c/lp) *<(CD/TC+/VGC 11)>* **SANITY AND GRACE (live)** [ ] [ ]
– History / Wind beneath my wings / Lovin' and leavin' / From a distance / Sanity and grace / daughters of time / Cats in the cradle / Pretty Polly / Born to the breed. *(re-iss. Aug91 on 'Virgin' lp/c; OVED/+C 373)*

Columbia Columbia

Feb 91. (cd/c/lp) *(467373-2/-4/-1)* **FIRES OF EDEN** [ ] [ ]
– The blizzard / Fortune of soldiers / Test of time / Fires of Eden / Home before dark / The air that I breathe / City of cities / Dreaming / Queen of the night / From a distance / The blizzard – reprise.

—— next album covers by BOB DYLAN

Geffen Geffen

Mar 94. (cd) *<(GED 24612)>* **JUDY SINGS DYLAN . . . JUST LIKE A WOMAN** [ ] [ ]
– Like a rolling stone / It's all over now, baby blue / Simple twist of fate / Sweetheart like you / Gotta serve somebody / Dark eyes / Love minus zero – No limit / Just like a woman / I believe in you / With God on our side / Bob Dylan's dream.

– compilations, etc. –

on 'Elektra' unless mentioned otherwise

Nov 69. (lp) *(K 42035)* <74055> **RECOLLECTIONS (THE BEST OF JUDY COLLINS)** [ ] Sep69 [29]
<(cd-iss. Nov00; 7559 61350-2)>

1972. (7") **SUZANNE. / SOMEDAY SOON** [–] [ ]

1972. (7") **IN MY LIFE. / SUNNY GOODGE STREET** [–] [ ]

May 72. (lp) *<75030>* **COLORS OF THE DAY – THE BEST OF JUDY COLLINS** [–] [37]
– Somebody soon / Since you've asked / Both sides now / Sons of Susan / Farewell / Tarwathie / Who knows where the time goes / Sunny Goodge Street / My father always promised / Albatross / In my life. *(UK cd-iss. Feb92; 7559 60681-2)*

Jul 72. (lp/c) *(K/K4 42110)* **AMAZING GRACE – THE BEST OF JUDY COLLINS** [ ] [–]
(cd-iss. Jun85; K2 42110) (cd re-iss. Sep95;)

Aug 77. (d-lp) *(K 62019)* *<6002>* **SO EARLY IN THE SPRING: THE FIRST 15 YEARS** [ ] Jul77 [42]
– Pretty Polly / So early, early in the spring / Pretty Saro / Golden apples of the sun / Bonnie ship the diamond / Farewell to Tarwathie / The hostage / La Colombe / Coal tattoo / Carry it on / Bread and roses / The Marat-Sade / Special delivery / The lovin' of the game / Both sides now / Marieke / Send in the clowns / Bird on the wire / Since you've asked / Born to the breed / My father / Holly Ann / Houses / Secret gardens.

1977. (lp/c) *(K 62006)* **MOST BEAUTIFUL SONGS OF . . .** [ ] [ ]

Aug 77. (7"ep) *(K 12270)* **AMAZING GRACE / SEND IN THE CLOWNS. / HOSTAGE / BOTH SIDES NOW** [ ] [–]

Jul 81. (7") *(K 12534)* **AMAZING GRACE. / BOTH SIDES NOW** [ ] [ ]

Oct 82. (lp/c) *Hallmark; (SHM/HSC 3061)* **BOTH SIDES NOW** [ ] [–]

Sep 85. (7") *Old Gold; (OG 9516)* **AMAZING GRACE. / SEND IN THE CLOWNS** [ ] [–]

Dec 85. (lp/c) *Telstar; (STAR/STAC/TCD 2265)* **AMAZING GRACE** [34] [–]
(re-iss. cd/c Mar93 on 'Pickwick'; 9548 31616-2/-4)

Jun 92.	(c/cd) *Laserlight; (79/15 451)* **WIND BENEATH MY WINGS**		–
Oct 95.	(cd) *Vanguard; <(VCD 77013)>* **LIVE AT NEWPORT 1959-1966 (live)**		
Dec 97.	(d-cd) *<(7559 62104-2)>* **FOREVER – AN ANTHOLOGY**		
Oct 99.	(cd) *Disky; (SI 24864-2)* **SEND IN THE CLOWNS**		
Sep 01.	(cd) *Rhino; <(8122 74374-2)>* **THE VERY BEST OF JUDY COLLINS**		
Oct 01.	(cd) *Rhino; <(8122 73560-2)>* **A MAID OF CONSTANT SORROW / GOLDEN APPLES OF THE SUN**		
Oct 02.	(cd) *Delta; (4716364)* **LIVE AT WOLF TRAP (live)**		
Oct 02.	(cd) *Delta; (4716566)* **ALL ON A WINTRY NIGHT (live)**		
Mar 03.	(cd) *Delta; (4716970)* **SHAMELESS**		

Phil COLLINS

Born: 31 Jan'51, London, England. COLLINS began his career with FLAMING YOUTH before joining art-prog rockers, GENESIS, replacing JOHN MAYHEW on the drum stool for the 1970 album, 'Trespass'. His impeccable playing anchored the GENESIS sound over their early mid-70's, PETER GABRIEL fronted peak on such classic sets as 'Nursery Cryme' (1971), 'Foxtrot' (1972) and 'Selling England By The Pound' (1973). With GABRIEL subsequently leaving after the epic 'Lamb Lies Down On Broadway' (1974), COLLINS was promoted from drummer to frontman in one fell swoop when auditions proved fruitless. Proving that he was more than capable of filling GABRIEL's hallowed shoes, COLLINS successfully steered the band through the rocky patch of late 70's punk and beyond. Mirroring his band's move into glossy MOR with the 'DUKE' (1980) album, COLLINS' solo career came ready made for the heart of the mainstream pop/rock crossover market. Trailed by overweight radio favourite 'IN THE AIR TONIGHT', 'FACE VALUE' (1981) was a transatlantic million seller and a British No.1 to boot. Here was a man who truly polarised opinion from the start, his ubiquitous smugness and increasingly sterile pop making him a favourite target for critics. Yet his breezy melodies, cheeky chappy demeanour and soul-lite hollering made him hugely popular as the cult of the 80's coffee-table star took hold. A second set, 'HELLO, I MUST BE GOING' (1982) was another massive seller, again blessed with an insidiously catchy No.1 single in the form of 'YOU CAN'T HURRY LOVE' (originally a 60's hit for The SUPREMES). A string of subsequent singles failed to make any commercial impression and for a while it looked like COLLINS' career was faltering. Any such doubts were cast aside with the hugely successful ballad, 'AGAINST ALL ODDS (TAKE A LOOK AT ME NOW)'. While many detractors would've preferred an empty space, COLLINS inhabitated the American No.1 spot for a good few weeks with this soundtrack piece which subsequently won a Grammy. He was back again early the following year with the pop/funk of 'SUSSIDIO' and his biggest album to date in 'NO JACKET REQUIRED' (1985). This was the set that really broke America, the record selling faster than Michael Jackson's 'Thriller'; its success was boosted by a further two US No.1's, the American release of 'SUSSIDIO' and the slushy ballad, 'ONE MORE NIGHT'. Seemingly unable to get enough of the man, the Americans secured a LIVE AID performance and put him back astride the US charts with the STEPHEN BISHOP-penned 'SEPARATE LIVES', a collaborative ballad with MARILYN MARTIN (he had earlier struck big time with a duet with PHILIP BAILEY on 'EASY LOVER'). Having acted as a child, COLLINS procured the star part in the film 'Buster' (1988) as well as contributing several songs to the soundtrack. One of these was a nauseous cover of The Mindbenders' 'GROOVY KIND OF LOVE', while the asinine 'TWO HEARTS' (co-written with LAMONT DOZIER) gave him another US peak position. A transatlantic No.1 (what else?!), COLLINS' fourth studio set, ' . . . BUT SERIOUSLY' (1989) was a lame attempt at addressing more serious issues . Many people found 'ANOTHER DAY IN PARADISE' downright offensive, COLLINS masquerading as a friend of the street dwellers, although the man did contribute a lot of his earnings to this and certain charities (was 'I WISH IT WOULD RAIN DOWN' Pink Floyd's 'Wish You Were Here' Part 2, or what?). He continued in inimitably goal-getting fashion throughout the 90's, eventually leaving GENESIS in the mid-90's. Having released 'BOTH SIDES' in '93, he returned in 1996 with, 'DANCE INTO THE LIGHT', his first album for the unfortunately named new label, 'Face Value'. The accompanying single, 'WEAR MY HAT', was another to trigger mass deja vu in the listening public, PAUL SIMON's 'You Can Call Me Al' strangely coming to mind this time around. Rock on though, PHIL, GENESIS are missing you badly. After various musical distractions and side alleys including a fleeting and unlikely appearance alongside LIL' KIM on her cover of 'IN THE AIR TONITE', 2002's 'TESTIFY' was back to monotonous business for COLLINS, a tired set of songs with even more well-worn themes. • **Covered:** ALWAYS (Irving Berlin) / THE TIMES THEY ARE A-CHANGIN' (Bob Dylan).

Album rating: FACE VALUE (*8) / HELLO, I MUST BE GOING! (*6) / NO JACKET REQUIRED (*7) / . . . BUT SERIOUSLY (*5) / SERIOUS HITS . . . LIVE! (*4) / BOTH SIDES (*5) / DANCE INTO THE NIGHT (*4) / . . .HITS compilation (*8) / A HOT NIGHT IN PARIS (*4) / TARZAN soundtrack with Mark Mancina (*6) / TESTIFY (*5)

PHIL COLLINS – vocals, piano, drums, etc (with session people)

		Virgin	Atlantic
Jan 81.	(7") *(VSK 102) <3824>* **IN THE AIR TONIGHT. / THE ROOF IS LEAKING** *(re-iss. & remixed Jun88; same); hit UK No.4.*	2	May81 19
Feb 81.	(lp/c) *(V/TCV 2185) <16029>* **FACE VALUE** – In the air tonight / This must be love / Behind the lines / The roof is leaking / Droned / Hand in hand / I missed again / You know what I mean / I'm not moving / If leaving me is easy / Tomorrow never knows / Thunder and lightning. *(cd-iss. Jun88; CDV 2185)*	1	7
Mar 81.	(7"/12") *(VS 402/+12) <3790>* **I MISSED AGAIN. / I'M NOT MOVING**	14	19
May 81.	(7") *(VS 423)* **IF LEAVING ME IS EASY. / DRAWING BOARD: IN THE AIR TONIGHT – I MISSED AGAIN – IF LEAVING ME IS EASY (demo versions)**	17	–
Oct 82.	(7"/7"pic-d) *(VS/+Y 524)* **THRU' THESE WALLS. / DO YOU KNOW, DO YOU CARE**	56	–
Nov 82.	(lp/c) *(V/TCV 2252) <80035>* **HELLO, I MUST BE GOING!** – I don't care anymore / I cannot believe it's true / Like China / Do you know, do you care? / You can't hurry love / It don't matter to me / Thru' these walls / Don't let him steal your love away / The west side / Why can't it wait 'til morning. *(cd-iss. Jun88; CDV 2252) (re-iss. Jun91;)*	2	8
Nov 82.	(7"/7"pic-d) *(VS/+Y 531)* **YOU CAN'T HURRY LOVE. / I CANNOT BELIEVE IT'S TRUE** (12"+=) *(VST 531)* – Oddball. *(cd-iss. 1988; CDT 1)*	1	–
Nov 82.	(7") *<89933>* **YOU CAN'T HURRY LOVE. / DO YOU KNOW, DO YOU CARE**	–	10
Mar 83.	(7") *(VS 572)* **DON'T LET HIM STEAL YOUR HEART AWAY. / THUNDER AND LIGHTNING** (12") *(VS 572-12)* – ('A'side) / And so to f . . . (live).	45	–
Feb 83.	(7") *<89877>* **I DON'T CARE ANYMORE. / THE WEST SIDE**	–	39
May 83.	(7") *(VS 603)* **WHY CAN'T IT WAIT 'TIL MORNING. / LIKE CHINA**		–
May 83.	(7") *<89864>* **I CANNOT BELIEVE IT'S TRUE. / THRU THESE WALLS**	–	79
Feb 84.	(7") *<89700>* **AGAINST ALL ODDS (TAKE A LOK AT ME NOW). / (b-side by Larry Carlton)**	–	1

Mar 84. (7"/7"pic-d) *(VS/+Y 674)* **AGAINST ALL ODDS. / MAKING A BIG MISTAKE (by Mike Rutherford)** [2] [–]
(above from the film of the same name)

May 84. (7") *<89668>* **WALK THROUGH THE FIRE. / MAKING A BIG MISTAKE (by Mike Rutherford)** [–] [ ]

Jan 85. (7") *(VS 736)* **SUSSUDIO. / THE MAN WITH THE HORN** [12] [–]
(12"+=/12"pic-d+=) *(VS/+Y 736-12)* – ('A'extended).

Feb 85. (lp/c/cd) *(V/TCV/CDV 2345) <81240>* **NO JACKET REQUIRED** [1] [1]
– Sussudio / Only you know and I know / Long long way to go / Don't want to know / One more night / Don't lose my number / Who said I would / Doesn't anybody stay together anymore? / Inside out / Take me home. (cd+=) – We said hello, goodbye.

Feb 85. (7") *<89588>* **ONE MORE NIGHT. / THE MAN WITH THE HORN** [–] [1]

—— Mar'85 saw him duet with **PHIL BAILEY (ex-EARTH, WIND & FIRE)** on single **EASY LOVER** which hit UK No.1 & US No.2 (Nov84)

Apr 85. (7"/7"sha-pic-d) *(VS/+S 755)* **ONE MORE NIGHT. / I LIKE THE WAY** [4] [–]
(12"+=) *(VS 755-12)* – ('A'extended).

Apr 85. (7") *<89560>* **SUSSIDIO. / I LIKE THE WAY** [–] [1]

Jul 85. (7") *(VS 777)* **TAKE ME HOME. / WE SAID HELLO, GOODBYE** [19] [–]
(w/ free 7"+=) *(VS 674)* – Against all odds / Making a big mistake.
(12"+=) *(VS 777-12)* – ('A'extended).

Jul 85. (7") *<89536>* **DON'T LOSE MY NUMBER. / WE SAID HELLO GOODBYE** [–] [4]

Sep 85. (7"; by PHIL COLLINS & MARILYN MARTIN) *<89498>* **SEPARATE LIVES. / I DON'T WANNA KNOW** [–] [1]

Nov 85. (7"/7"white/ 7";2-interlocking pic-discs; by PHIL COLLINS & MARILYN MARTIN) *(VS/+S/SD 818)* **SEPARATE LIVES. / ONLY YOU KNOW AND I KNOW** [4] [–]

Mar 86. (7") *<89472>* **TAKE ME HOME. / ONLY YOU KNOW AND I KNOW** [–] [7]

Aug 88. (7"/12"/12"g-f) *(VS/+T/TG 1117) <89017>* **GROOVY KIND OF LOVE. / BIG NOISE (instrumental)** [1] [1]
(cd-s+=) *(VSCD 1117)* – Will you still be waiting.

—— (above & below singles were from the film 'BUSTER', in which he starred and contributed some tracks to soundtrack released Sep88)

Nov 88. (7") *(VS 1141) <88980>* **TWO HEARTS. / THE ROBBERY (excerpt by Anne Dudley)** [6] [1]
(12"/cd-s) *(VS T/CD 1141)* – ('A'side) / ('B'extended).

Nov 89. (7"/12") *(VS/+T 1234) <88774>* **ANOTHER DAY IN PARADISE. / HEAT ON THE STREET** [2] [1]
(c-s+=/3"cd-s+=) *(VSC/VSCD 1234)* – Saturday night and Sunday morning.

Nov 89. (lp/c/cd) *(V/TCV/CDV 2620) <82050>* **. . . BUT SERIOUSLY** [1] [1]
– Hang in long enough / That's just the way it is / Do you remember? / Something happened on the way to Heaven / Colours / I wish it would rain down / Another day in Paradise / Heat on the street / All of my life / Saturday night and Sunday morning / Father to son / Find a way to my heart.

Jan 90. (7") *(VS 1240)* **I WISH IT WOULD RAIN DOWN. / HOMELESS (ANOTHER DAY IN PARADISE) (demo)** [7] [–]
(12"+=/12"s+=/3"cd-s+=) *(VS T/TX/CD 1240)* – You've been in love just (that little bit too long).

Jan 90. (7") *<88738>* **I WISH IT WOULD RAIN DOWN. / YOU'VE BEEN IN LOVE JUST (THAT LITTLE BIT TOO LONG)** [–] [3]

Apr 90. (7") *<87955>* **DO YOU REMEMBER?. / I WISH IT WOULD RAIN DOWN** [–] [4]

Apr 90. (7"/7"s/c-s) *(VS/+P/C 1251)* **SOMETHING HAPPENED ON THE WAY TO HEAVEN. / RAIN DOWN (demo)** [15] [–]
(12"+=/cd-s+=) *(VS T/CD 1251)* – ('A'remix).

Jul 90. (7"/c-s) *(VS/+C 1277)* **THAT'S JUST THE WAY IT IS. / BROADWAY CHORUS (SOMETHING HAPPENED ON THE WAY TO HEAVEN)** [26] [–]
(12"+=/cd-s+=) *(VS T/CD 1277)* – In the air tonight (extended).

Jul 90. (7") *<87885>* **SOMETHING HAPPENED ON THE WAY TO HEAVEN. / LIONEL (DO YOU REMEMBER? – DEMO)** [–] [4]

Sep 90. (7"/c-s) *(VS/+C 1300)* **HANG IN LONG ENOUGH. / AROUND THE WORLD IN 80 PRESETS** [34] [–]
(cd-s+=) *(VSCD 1300)* – ('A'-12"mix).
(pic-cd-s) *(VSCDX 1300)* – ('A'side) / That's how I feel / ('A'dub).
(12") *(VST 1300)* – ('A'side) / ('A'dub) / ('A'-12"mix).

Nov 90. (c-s) *<87800>* **HANG IN LONG ENOUGH. / SEPARATE LIVES (live)** [–] [23]

—— live with **LELAND SKLAR** – bass / **CHESTER THOMPSON** – drums / **DARYL STUERMER** – guitar / **BRAD COLE** – keyboards / **BRIDGETTE BRYANT, ARNOLD McCULLER and FRED WHITE** – backing vocals. plus **DON MYRICK** – alto sax / **LUI LUI** – trombone / **RAHMLEE MICHAEL DAVIS** – trumpet / **HARRY KIM** – trumpet.

Nov 90. (cd/c/lp) *(PC CD/TC/LP 1) <82157>* **SERIOUS HITS . . .LIVE! (live)** [2] [11]
– Something happened on the way to Heaven / Against all odds (take a look at me now) / Who said I would / One more night / Don't lose my number / Another day in Paradise / Do you remember? / Separate lives / In the air tonight / You can't hurry love / Two hearts / Sussidio / Groovy kind of love / Easy lover / Take me home.

Nov 90. (7"/c-s) *(VS/+C 1305)* **DO YOU REMEMBER? (live). / AGAINST THE ODDS (live)** [57] [–]
(12"+=) *(VST 1305)* – Doesn't anyone stay together anymore (live).
(cd-s++=) *(VSCDT 1305)* – The roof is leaking (live).
(cd-s) *(VSCDG 1305)* – ('A'side) / Doesn't anyone stay together anymore (live) / The roof is leaking (live).

Jan 91. (promo-cd-s) *<PR-3758>* **WHO SAID I WOULD (live)** [–] [73]

—— In May 93, PHIL was credited on DAVID CROSBY'S Top 50 hit 'Hero'.

Oct 93. (7"/c-s) *(VS/+C 1500) <87299>* **BOTH SIDES OF THE STORY. / ALWAYS (live)** [7] [25]
(cd-s+=) *(VSCDT 1500)* – Both sides of the demo.
(cd-s++=) *(VSCDG 1500)* – Rad Dudeski.

Nov 93. (cd/c/lp) *(CD/TC+/V 2800) <82550>* **BOTH SIDES** [1] [13]
– Both sides of the story / Can't turn back the years / Everyday / I've forgotten everything / We're sons of our fathers / Can't find my way / Survivors / We fly so close / There's a place for us / We wait and wonder / Please come out tonight.

Jan 94. (7"/c-s) *(VS/+C 1505) <87300>* **EVERYDAY. / DON'T CALL ME ASHLEY** [15] [24]
(cd-s+=) *(VSCDT 1505)* – ('A'demo).
(cd-s+=) *(VSCDG 1505)* – Doesn't anybody stay together anymore (live).

Apr 94. (7"/c-s) *(VS/+C 1510)* **WE WAIT AND WE WONDER. / HERO (with DAVID CROSBY)** [45] [–]
(cd-s+=) *(VSCDX 1510)* – For a friend.
(cd-s) *(VSCDG 1510)* – ('A'side) / Take me with you / Stevie's blues – There's a place for us (instrumental).

—— now not a GENESIS member, having announced departure early '96.

East West / Atlantic

Sep 96. (c-s) *(EW 066C) <87043>* **DANCE INTO THE LIGHT / TAKE ME DOWN** [9] [45]
(cd-s+=) *(EW 066CD)* – It's over (demo).

Oct 96. (cd/c) *(0630 16000-2/-4) <82949>* **DANCE INTO THE LIGHT** [4] [23]
– Dance into the light / That's what you said / Lorenzo / Just another story / Love police / Wear my hat / It's in your eyes / Oughta know by now / Take me down / The same moon / River so wide / No matter who / The times they are a-changin'.

Dec 96. (c-s) *(EW 076C) <87016>* **IT'S IN YOUR EYES / DON'T WANT TO GO** [30] Jan97 [77]
(cd-s+=) *(EW 076CD1)* – Always (live).
(cd-s) *(EW 076CD2)* – ('A'side) / Easy lover (live) / Separate lives (live).

Jul 97. (c-s) *(EW 113C)* **WEAR MY HAT / (edited hat dance mix)** [43] [–]
(cd-s+=) *(EW 113CD)* – (hat dance mix) / (wear my dub).

Oct 98. (cd/c) *(CDV/TCV 2870) <83139>* **. . .HITS** (compilation) [1] [18]
– Another day in paradise / True colours / Easy lover / You can't hurry love / Two hearts / I wish it would rain down / Against all odds (take a look at me now) / Something happened on the way to Heaven / Separate lives / Both sides of the story / One more night / Sussidio / Dance into the light / A groovy kind of love / In the air tonight / Take me home.

Oct 98. (c-s/cd-s) *(VSC/+DT 1715)* **TRUE COLOURS / IN THE AIR TONIGHT / I MISSED AGAIN** [26] [ ]
(cd-s) *(VSCDG 1715)* – ('A'side) / Don't lose my number / Take me home.

—— next with **GEORGE DUKE + BRAD COLE** – piano / **DARYL STUERMER** – guitar / **GERALD ALBRIGHT** – alto sax / **JAMES CARTER** – tenor sax

WEA WEA

May 99. (cd/c; the PHIL COLLINS BIG BAND) *(3984 27221-2/-4)* <83198> **A HOT NIGHT IN PARIS** [ ] Jul99 [ ]
– Sussudio / That's all / Invisible touch / Hold on my heart / Chips and salsa / I don't care anymore / Milestones / Against all odds / Pick up the pieces / Los endos suite.

Disney US Disney UK

Oct 99. (cd/c; by PHIL COLLINS & MARK MANCINA) *(010247-2/-4 DNY)* <8 60645> **TARZAN** [ ] May99 [5]
– Two worlds / You'll be in my heart (w/ GLENN CLOSE) / Son of man / Trashin' the camp (ROSIE O'DONNELL) / Strangers like me / Two worlds (reprise) / Trashin' the camp (w/ 'N SYNC) / You'll be in my heart / Two worlds / A wonderous place / Moves like an ape, looks like a man / The gorillas / One family / Two worlds (finale).

Nov 99. (c-s/cd-s) *(010073 9/5 DNY)* <860025> **YOU'LL BE IN MY HEART / (version) / TRASHIN' THE CAMP** [17] Jun99 [21]

— In Sep'01, PHIL featured on LIL' KIM's hit mix of 'In The Air Tonite'

East West Atlantic

Nov 02. (cd-s) *(EW 254CD)* <49327> **CAN'T STOP LOVING YOU / HIGH FLYING ANGEL / SUSSUDIO** [28] [76]

Nov 02. (cd) *(5046 61484-2)* <83563> **TESTIFY** [15] [30]
– Wake up call / Come with me / Testify / Don't get me started / Swing low / It's not too late / This love this heart / Driving me crazy / The least you can do / Can't stop loving you / Through my eyes / You touch my heart.

— in May'03, PHIL featured on the BONE THUGS-N-HARMONY hit, 'Home'

Nov 03. (cd-s) *(DISNEY 001)* **LOOK THROUGH MY EYES / (instrumental) / TRANSFORMATION (Bulgarian Women's Choir)** [61] [–]
(above taken from the Disney animation, 'BROTHER BEAR', a collaborative effort/album from PHIL COLLINS & MARK MENCINA)

– compilations, others, etc. –

Jan 88. (cd)<US-lp/cd) *Virgin; (CDEP 4)* **12 INCHERS** [ ] [ ]
– (12" remixed extended versions of 6 hits)

Ry COODER

Born: RYLAND COODER, 15 Mar'47, Los Angeles, California, USA. He sessioned for the likes of JACKIE DE SHANNON and TAJ MAHAL, before moving on to CAPTAIN BEEFHEART in 1967. He nearly replaced BRIAN JONES in The ROLLING STONES, although he chose to only guest on their 'Let It Bleed' album, contributing searing bottleneck slide work to a number of songs, most effectively on the classic title track. By the time COODER was offered a solo deal by 'Reprise' in 1970, he was already one of the most adaptable, respected and gifted guitarists in the world, equally adept at playing other instruments such as the banjo and mandolin. Guesting on LITTLE FEAT's eponymous 1970 debut, COODER released his own self-titled solo set the following year. An impressive start, the record was largely made up of cover material, including an abrasive cover of Woody Guthrie's 'DO RE MI', a mandolin rendition of Sleepy John Este's 'GOIN' TO BROWNSVILLE' and a brilliantly drawling version of Randy Newman's biting 'OLD KENTUCKY HOME'. A follow-up long-player, 'INTO THE PURPLE VALLEY' (1972) was a more stripped down affair, highlighting his slide work, most notably on another Woody Guthrie number, 'VIGILANTE MAN'. Subsequent albums, 'BOOMER'S STORY' (1972) and PARADISE AND LUNCH' (1974), covered similar territory, jazz pianist EARL HINES guesting on the latter. It was 1978's 'CHICKEN SKIN MUSIC', that had the critics in rapture, however, its Hawaiian slack guitar and Tex-Mex stylings lent genuine authenticity by the contributions of star players GABBY PAHINUI and FLACO JIMENEZ together with the gospel vocals of BOBBY KING. These collaborations with respected players in the field of world music were a blueprint for much of COODER's subsequent output. In the meantime, he dabbled in ragtime and vaudeville with 'JAZZ' (1978), while 1979's 'BOP TILL YOU DROP' signalled a move away from traditional music to rock'n'roll and R&B. The latter album also saw COODER make a rare entry into the UK Top 40, something he only repeated with 1982's 'THE SLIDE AREA'. During the 80's, COODER moved sideways into soundtrack work, his atmospheric slide work fitting the bill for a number of Hollywood studios. Having already worked on 'Performance' in the late 60's, COODER proceeded to turn in impressive scores including 'THE LONG RIDERS' (1980), 'THE BORDER' (1982), 'JOHHNY HANDSOME' (1989) and most famously (and effectively) 'PARIS, TEXAS' (1985). The 90's saw the irrepressible guitarist team up with Indian musician, VISHANA MOHAN BHATT, for 'A MEETING BY THE RIVER' (1993), a magical, hypnotic fusion of Delta blues and Eastern classical/folk. Another groundbreaking set was released the following year in 'TALKING TIMBUKTU' (1994), a Grammy winning piece upon which COODER sparred with African guitarist ALI FARKA TOURE. The greatest critical praise, however, was probably reserved for the celebrated 'BUENA VISTA SOCIAL CLUB' (1997), a benchmark recording which saw COODER jam with some of Cuba's oldest (we're talking in their 80's and 90's here!) and most accomplished musicians. Contemporary music's most talented curator was back in 2003 with another imaginatively conceived collaboration, this time in tandem with Cuban guitar maestro MANUEL GALBAN. A strange beast, 'MAMBO SINUENDO' was a largely instrumental amalgam of classic mambo and vintage easy listening sophistication, all sown up with hints of the Hawaiian, slack-keyed whinny which COODER has proved himself so adept at in the past. • **Covered:** VIGILANTE MAN (Woody Guthrie) / GET RHYTHM (Johnny Cash) / HE'LL HAVE TO GO (hit; Jim Reeves) / LITTLE SISTER (Pomus-Shuman) / 13 QUESTION METHOD (Chuck Berry) / MONEY HONEY (hit; Drifters) / STAND BY ME (Ben E. King) / IT'S ALL OVER NOW (Bobby Womack) / GOODNIGHT IRENE (Leadbelly) / NEED A WOMAN (Bob Dylan) / BLUE SUEDE SHOES (Carl Perkins) / ALL SHOOK UP (Elvis Presley) / and loads more. The JAZZ album had early 1940's covers, etc. • **Trivia:** He also wrote score for 1980 film SOUTHERN COMFORT which sadly was not issued on soundtrack.

Album rating: RY COODER (*6) / INTO THE PURPLE VALLEY (*7) / BOOMER'S STORY (*7) / PARADISE AND LUNCH (*7) / CHICKEN SKIN MUSIC (*8) / SHOWTIME (*5) / JAZZ (*6) / BOP TILL YOU DROP (*5) / BORDERLINE (*6) / THE LONG RIDERS soundtrack (*4) / THE BORDER soundtrack (*5) / RY COODER LIVE (*5) / THE SLIDE AREA (*4) / PARIS, TEXAS soundtrack (*7) / ALAMO BAY soundtrack (*5) / WHY DON'T YOU TRY ME TONIGHT compilation (*7) / BLUE CITY soundtrack (*4) / CROSSROADS soundtrack (*4) / GET RHYTHM (*5) / JOHNNY HANDSOME soundtrack (*5) / TRESPASS soundtrack (*5) / A MEETING BY THE RIVER with V.M. Bhatt (*5) / TALKING TIMBUKTU with Ali Farka Toure (*8) / GERONIMO soundtrack (*5) / MUSIC BY RY COODER compilation/soundtracks (*7) / THE BEST OF RY COODER compilation (*8) / BEUNA VISTA SOCIAL CLUB by Buena Vista Social Club (*8) / MAMBO SINUENDO with Manuel Galban (*7)

RY COODER – vocals, guitar (ex-CAPTAIN BEEFHEART & HIS MAGIC BAND) plus session people too numerous to mention

Reprise Reprise

Oct 70. (7") <0910> **GOIN' TO BROWNSVILLE. / AVAILABLE SPACE** [–] [ ]

Dec 70. (7") <0940> **ALIMONY. / PIGMEAT** [–] [ ]

Jan 71. (lp) *(K 44093)* <RSLP 6402> **RY COODER** [ ] Dec70 [ ]
– Alimony / France chance / One meat ball / Do re mi / Old Kentucky home (turpentine & dandelion wine) / How can a poor man stand such times and live? / Available space / Pig meat / Police dog blues / Goin' to Brownsville / Dark is the night. *(cd-iss. May95 on 'Warners'; 7599-27510-2)*

May 71. (7") *(RS 23497)* **HOW CAN A POOR MAN STAND SUCH TIMES AND LIVE. / GOIN' TO BROWNSVILLE** [ ] [–]

Feb 72. (7") <1009> **ON A MONDAY. / DARK IS THE NIGHT** [–] [ ]

Feb 72. (lp) *(K 44142)* <2052> **INTO THE PURPLE VALLEY** [ ] [ ]
– How can you keep on moving / Billy the kid / Money honey / F.D.R. in

Trinidad / Teardrops will fall / Denomination blues / On a Monday / Hey porter / Great dreams from heaven / Taxes on the farmer feeds us all / Vigilante man. *(cd-iss. 1988; K2 44142)*

Feb 72. (7") *(K 14151)* **MONEY HONEY. / ON A MONDAY** [ ] [-]

Apr 72. (7") *<1071>* **MONEY MONEY. / BILLY THE KID** [-] [ ]

Oct 72. (7") *<1167>* **BOOMER'S STORY. / BILLY THE KID** [-] [ ]

Nov 72. (lp) *(K 44224) <2117>* **BOOMER'S STORY** [ ] [ ]
– Boomer's story / Cherry ball blues / Crow black children / Axe sweet mama / Maria Elena / Dark end of the street / Rally 'round the flag / Comin' in on a wing and a prayer / President Kennedy / Good morning Mr. Railroad man. *(cd-iss. Jan93 on 'WEA'; 7599 26398-2)*

May 74. (lp) *(K 44260) <2179>* **PARADISE AND LUNCH** [ ] [ ]
– Tamp 'em up solid / Tattler / Married man's a fool / Jesus on the mainline / It's all over now / Fool about a cigarette – Feelin' good / If walls could talk / Mexican divorce / Ditty wa ditty. *(cd-iss. 1988; K2 44260)*

— next with **FLACO JIMENEZ** – accordion / **GABBY PAHINUI** – steel guitar / **BOBBY KING** – gospel vocals

Oct 76. (lp/c) *(K/K4 54083) <2254>* **CHICKEN SKIN MUSIC** [ ] [ ]
– The bourgeois blues / I got mine / Always lift him up / He'll have to go / Smack dab in the middle / Stand by me / Yellow roses / Chloe / Goodnight Irene. *(cd-iss. 1988; 254083)*

Mar 77. (7") *(K 14457)* **HE'LL HAVE TO GO. / THE BOURGEOIS BLUES** [ ] [-]

Warners Warners

Aug 77. (lp/c) *(K/K4 56386) <3059>* **SHOW TIME (live)** [ ] [ ]
– School is out / Alimony / Jesus on the mainline / ark end of the street / Viva sequin – Do re mi / Volver, volver / How can a poor man stand such times and live? / Smack dab in the middle. *(cd-iss. Nov93; 7599 27319-2)*

Aug 77. (7") *<8384>* **SCHOOL IS OUT (live). / JESUS ON THE MAINLINE (live)** [-] [ ]

Jun 78. (lp/c) *(K/K4 56488) <3197>* **JAZZ** [ ] [ ]
– Face to face I shall meet him / Davenport blues / In a mist / Big bad Bill is sweet William now / Happy meeting in glory / We shall be happy / Nobody / Shine / Flashes / Dream / Pearls / Tia Juana. *(cd-iss. 1988; K2 25688)*

Jun 79. (7") *<49055>* **LITTLE SISTER. / DOWN IN HOLLYWOOD** [-] [ ]

Aug 79. (lp/c) *(K/K4 56691) <3358>* **BOP TILL YOU DROP** [36] [62]
– Little sister / Go home girl / The very thing that makes you rich (makes me poor) / I think it's gonna work out fine / Down in Hollywood / Look at granny run run / Trouble, you can't fool me / Don't mess up a good thing / I can't win. *(cd-iss. 1983; K2 56691)*

Aug 79. (7") *(K 17460)* **LITTLE SISTER. / GO HOME GIRL** [ ] [-]

Oct 79. (7") *<49081>* **THE VERY THING THAT MAKES YOU RICH (MAKES ME POOR). / LITTLE SISTER** [-] [ ]

Jun 80. (lp) *(K 56826) <3448>* **THE LONG RIDERS (Soundtrack)** [ ] [ ]
– (main title) The long riders / I'm a good old rebel / Seneca square dance / Archie's funeral (hold to God's unchanging hand) / I always knew that you were the one / Rally 'round the flag / Wildwood boys / Better things to talkabout / My grandfather / Cole Younger polka / Escape from Northfield / Leaving Missouri / Jesse James.

Oct 80. (lp/c) *(K/K4 56864) <3489>* **BORDERLINE** [35] Jan81 [43]
– 634-5789 / Speedo / Why don't you try me / Down in the Boondocks / Johnny Porter / The way we make a broken heart / Crazy 'bout an automobile (every woman I know) / The girls from Texas / Borderline / Never make a move too soon. *(cd-iss. 1988; 25686-2)*

Oct 80. (7") *<49677>* **BORDERLINE. / THE GIRLS FROM TEXAS** [-] [ ]

Oct 80. (7") *(K 17713)* **634-5789. / THE GIRLS FROM TEXAS** [ ] [-]

Dec 80. (7") **CRAZY 'BOUT AN AUTOMOBILE. / BORDERLINE** [-] [ ]

Aug 81. (7") *(K 17844)* **CRAZY 'BOUT AN AUTOMOBILE (EVERY WOMAN I KNOW). / THE VERY THING THAT MAKES YOU RICH (MAKES ME POOR)** [ ] [-]
(12"+=) *(K 17844T)* – If walls could talk / Look at granny run run.

— In March '82, he contributed tracks to 'THE BORDER' soundtrack, which was issued on 'M.C.A.' (MCF 3133) / 'Backstreet' US

Apr 82. (lp/c) *(K/K4 56976) <3651>* **THE SLIDE AREA** [18] [ ]
– UFO has landed in the ghetto / I need a woman / Gypsy woman / Blue suede shoes / Mama, don't treat your daughter mean / I'm drinking again / Which came first / That's the way love turned out for me. *(cd-iss. Jul88; K2 56976)*

May 82. (d7") *(K 17952)* **GYSPY WOMAN. / ALIMONY** [ ] [-]
(with free 7") *(SAM 149)* – TEARDROPS WILL FALL / IT'S ALL OVER NOW

Feb 85. (lp) *(925270-1) <25270>* **PARIS, TEXAS (Soundtrack)** [ ] [ ]
– Paris, Texas / Brothers / Nothing out there / Cancion Mixteca / No safety zone / Houston in two seconds / She's leaving the bank / On the couch / I knew these people / Dark was the night. *<(cd-iss. May01; 9362 48088-2)>*

Aug 85. (lp) *(25311) <SLASH 3>* **MUSIC FROM ALAMO BAY (Soundtrack)** [ ] [ ]
– Theme from Alamo Bay / Gooks on main street / Klan meeting / Too close / Sailfish evening / The last stand / Glory / Search and destroy / Quatro vicios.
(above issued on 'London' UK / 'Slash' US)

Mar 86. (lp/c)(cd) *(WX 37/+C)(40864-2)* **WHY DON'T YOU TRY ME TONIGHT (THE BEST OF RY COODER)** (compilation) [ ] [-]
– How can a poor man stand such times and live? / Available space / Money honey / Tattler / He'll have to go / Smack dab in the middle / Dark end of the street / Down in Hollywood / Little sister / I think it's gonna work out fine / Crazy 'bout an automobile (every woman I know) / 634-5789 / Why don't you try me tonight.

Jul 86. (lp) *(925386-1) <25386>* **BLUE CITY (Soundtrack)** [ ] [ ]
– Blue city down / Elevation 13 foot / True believers – Marianne / Nice bike / Greenhouse / Billy and Annie / Pops and 'timer – Tell me something slick / Blue city / Don't take your guns to town / A leader of men / Not even Key West.

Jul 86. (7") **BILLY AND ANNIE. / TELL ME SOMETHING SLICK** [-] [ ]

Jul 86. (7") *<28723>* **CROSSROADS. / FEEL IT (BAD BLUES)** [-] [ ]

Jul 86. (lp) *(925399-1) <25399>* **CROSSROADS** [ ] May86 [85]
– Crossroads / Down in Mississippi / Cotton needs pickin' / Viola Lee blues / See you in Hell, blind boy / Walkin' away blues / Nitty gritty Mississippi / He made a woman out of me / Feelin' bad blues / Somebody's callin' my name / Willie Brown blues.

Dec 87. (lp/c)(cd) *(WX 121/+C)(925639-2) <25639>* **GET RHYTHM** [75] Nov87 [ ]
– Get rhythm / Low-commotion / Going back to Okinawa / 13 question method / Women will rule the world / All shook up / I can tell by the way you smell / Across the borderline / Let's have a ball.

Jan 88. (7") **GET RHYTHM. / GOING BACK TO OKINAWA** [-] [ ]

Apr 88. (7") **ALL SHOOK UP. / GET YOUR LIES STRAIGHT** [-] [ ]

Apr 88. (7"/10") *(WB/WTE 8107)* **GET RHYTHM. / GET YOUR LIES STRAIGHT** [ ] [-]
(12"+=/3"cd-s+=) *(WT/WCD 8107)* – Down in Hollywood.

Oct 89. (lp/c)(cd) *(WX 307/+C)<(K 925886-2)>* **JOHNNY HANDSOME (Soundtrack)** [ ] [ ]
– Main theme / I can't walk this time – The prestige / Angola / Clip joint rhumba / Sad story / Fountain walk / Cajun metal / First week at work / Greasy oysters / Smells like money / Sunny's tune / I like your eyes / Adios Donna / Cruising wife Rafe / How's my face / End theme. *(re-iss. cd Feb95; same)*

— In 1991, he recorded Soundtrack for Robin Williams film 'PECOS BILL'. He also teamed up with NICK LOWE, JOHN HIATT and JIM KELTNER in band LITTLE VILLAGE. In 1992, he and DAVID LINDLEY were part of The PAHINUI BROTHERS who released Aug'92 eponymous album for 'Private'.

WEA Sire

Jan 93. (cd/c) *<(6362 45220-2/-4)>* **TRESPASS** (soundtrack w/ other artists) [ ] [82]
– Video drive-by / Trespass / East St.Louis toodle-oo / Orgil Bros. / Goose and lucky / You think it's on now / Solid gold / Heroin / Totally boxed in / Give 'm cops / Lucy in the trunk / We're rich / King of the street / Party lights. *(re-iss. Feb95;)*

— **RY** – bottle neck guitar; with **VISHWA MOHAN BHATT** – mohan vina / **JOACHIM COODER** (his 14 year old son) / **SUKHVINDER** – tabla

Topic Water Lily

Apr 93. (cd; RY COODER & V.M. BHATT) *(WLACS 029)* **A MEETING BY THE RIVER** [ ] [ ]
– A meeting by the river / Longing / Ganges Delta blues / Isa Lei. *(re-iss. Aug98; same)*

— in Mar'94, COODER collaborated with ALI FARKA TOURE on the 'World Circuit' album, 'TALKING TIMBUKTU'

— now **COODER** with **ELIADES OCHOA** – vocals, guitar / **COMPAY SEGUNDO** – vocals, guitar / **IBRAHIM FERRER** – vocals / **RUBEN GONZALEZ** – piano

World Circuit Nonesuch

Jun 97. (cd; as the BUENA VISTA SOCIAL CLUB) *(WCD 050) <79478>* **THE BUENA VISTA SOCIAL CLUB** [44] [80]
– Chan chan / De camino a la vereda / El cuarto de tula / Pueblo nuevo /

Dos gardenias / Y tu que has hecho? / Viente anos / El carretero / Candela / Amor de loca juventud / Orgullecida / Murmullo / Buena Vista social club / La bayamesa. *(lp-iss.Dec98 on 'Rock The House'; RTH 79468)*

Nonesuch Nonesuch

Jan 03. (cd; by RY COODER & MANUEL GALBAN) <*(7559 79691-2)*> **MAMBO SINUENDO** [40] [52]
– Drume negrita / Monte adentro / Los twangueros / Patricia / Caballo viejo / Mambo sinuendo / Bodas de oro / Echale salsita / La luna en tu Mirada / Secret love / Bolero sonambulo / Maria la lo.

– compilations, etc. –

May 93. (cd; by The RISING SONS featuring RY COODER & TAJ MAHAL) *Columbia; (472865-2)* **THE RISING SONS** [ ] [ ]

1994. (cd) *Reprise;* <*45599*> **RIVER RESCUE: THE VERY BEST OF . . .** [–] [ ]

Jun 95. (d-cd) *WEA;* <*(9362 45987-2)*> **MUSIC BY RY COODER** [ ] [ ]

Norman COOK

Born: QUENTIN COOK, 31 Jul'63, London, England. Following the demise of sunny agit-prop popsters, The HOUSEMARTINS, bassist COOK returned to his Brighton base and pursued his interest in the burgeoning dance culture. Already a budding DJ by the time HEATON & Co. split, the future man of many pseudonyms initially began recording club orientated music under his own name. Signed to 'Go! Beat', the dance arm of his previous band's now defunct label, 'Go! Discs', COOK enjoyed his debut hit via a collaboration with labelmate BILLY BRAGG on 'WON'T TALK ABOUT IT'. After a further minor solo hit, COOK initiated the BEATS INTERNATIONAL project with the classic 'DUB BE GOOD TO ME' single. Splicing the bassline from The CLASH's 'Guns Of Brixton' with the S.O.S BAND's 'Just Be Good To Me' proved a masterstroke, LINDY LAYTON's (soon to be a solo star in her own right) teasing, girlish vocal the icing on a vinyl cake which furnished COOK with a massive selling No.1 record in 1990. Also on board for the new venture were LESTER NOEL, keyboardist ANDY BOUCHER and percussionist LUKE CRESSWELL, the attendant Top 20 album 'LET THEM EAT BINGO' (1990) in addition finding COOK collaborating with a diverse cast of names including hip hop'ers DOUBLE TROUBLE and ex-DAMNED man, CAPTAIN SENSIBLE. A follow-up single revamping 'WON'T TALK..' with LAYTON on vocals made the Top 10 while the album's pot-pourri of rhythmic styles provided a further minor single in the innovative 'BURUNDI BLUES'. 1991's follow-up album, 'EXCURSION ON THE VERSION' followed in a more dub-centric vein, evidenced by the 'ECHO CHAMBER' single. A willingness to experiment was nevertheless the record's enduring characteristic, with further attempts at COOK-style soul and hip-hop. Although he failed to repeat the success of the debut single, his kudos as a remixer and producer were now firmly established. By 1992, BEATS INTERNATIONAL had run its natural course and COOK secured a new outlet for his rapidly improving songwriting talents through FREAK POWER, a more conventional band comprising bonafide musicians and dealing in sounds of a decidedly acid-jazzy persuasion. Signed to 'Island' subsidiary, '4th & Broadway', the tongue-in-cheek, smokily laid-back grooves of the group's debut single, 'TURN ON, TUNE IN, COP OUT' furnished them with a minor Top 30 hit upon its initial release in 1993. A highlight of the fine album, 'DRIVE-THRU BOOTY' (1995) alongside rump-shaking follow-up single, 'RUSH', the track was subsequently used on a Levi's 501 commercial, becoming one of '95's biggest hits. Like many other acts given the Levi's treatment, however, it eventually proved to be the kiss of death for the outfit, a second album, 'MORE OF EVERYTHING FOR EVERYBODY' (1997) failing to chart and subsequent releases flopping amid drug-related touring problems. By this point, however, the industrious COOK had already notched up a series of massive club smashes under his PIZZAMAN alias, many of his anthemic house monsters crossing over into the pop charts with 'TRIPPIN' ON SUNSHINE' becoming a Top 20 hit second time around in Spring '96. Concurrent with the rise of The CHEMICAL BROTHERS, The Heavenly Social club and all things "Big Beat", the chameleon-like COOK then turned his hand to some block rockin' beats and came up with one of 1997's most critically acclaimed albums, 'BETTER LIVING THROUGH CHEMISTRY'. Released under the FATBOY SLIM moniker and preceded by a clutch of blistering breakbeat 12"ers including 'SANTA CRUZ' (featured on the seminal 'BRIT HOP AND AMYL HOUSE' compilation) and 'EVERYBODY LOVES A 303', the record proved to be COOK's most cohesive and thrilling dalliance with dance music to date. A year later, FATBOY SLIM's 'ROCKAFELLER SKANK' (a take-off from a FALL tune) was racing up the charts and even broke this unusual set-up into the American Hot 100. Incredibly, COOK almost made No.1 yet again with a follow-up FATBOY SLIM album, 'YOU'VE COME A LONG WAY, BABY', possibly his most contagious, outrageous release to date. However, it was 'PRAISE YOU' indeed, after the single of that name topped the UK chart early in 1999 and eventually gave him a US Top 40 entry later in the year. COOK subsequently married "hyper" TV presenter/radio DJ, Zoe Ball, ah! showbiz couples, aren't they just worth reading about every day in the tabloids. MR. NORMAN COOK followed up his breakthrough masterpiece with a cross-over mix of dance, big beat techno, soul, funk, jive and R&B that he cleverly titled 'HALFWAY BETWEEN THE GUTTER AND THE STARS' (2001), a blistering brew that begins with a cheesy piece of funk narration and never ceases to quieten until the final 'SONG FOR SHELTER'. In retrospect, it's fair to say that 'HALFWAY . . .' was a much more accomplished album than 'YOU'VE COME A LONG WAY BABY'; the JIM MORRISON-sampled 'BIRD OF PREY' is truly excellent, with its trance-enducing drone imitating MORRISON's baritone vocals perfectly. Elsewhere on the album, 'YA MAMA' cooks up some seriously hard-hitting techno dance (with a psychotic and disturbingly insane video to go along with it), while 'WEAPON OF CHOICE' was just an excuse to watch Chrisopher Walken dance around a hotel lobby for four-and-half minutes. MACY GRAY lent her vocals to 'DEMONS' and 'LOVE LIFE', wailing along with COOK's funked-out Trip-Hop. So, the ex-HOUSEMARTINS' bassist had indeed come a long way! • **Songwriters:** COOK, and some with ASHLEY SLATER in FREAK POWER. Covered RUNNING AWAY (Sly & The Family Stone).

Album rating: Beats International: LET THEM EAT BINGO (*6) / EXCURSION OF THE VERSION (*4) / Freak Power: DRIVE THRU BOOTY (*5) / MORE OF EVERYTHING FOR EVERYBODY (*4) / Fatboy Slim: BETTER LIVING THROUGH CHEMISTRY (*8) / YOU'VE COME A LONG WAY, BABY (*8) / HALFWAY BETWEEN THE GUTTER AND THE STARS (*7)

NORMAN COOK – multi (solo) with various people

Go! Discs Elektra

Jun 89. (7"/c-s; NORMAN COOK featuring BILLY BRAGG. / NORMAN COOK featuring MC WILDSKI) *(GOD/+MC 33)* **WON'T TALK ABOUT IT. / BLAME IT ON THE BASSLINE** [29] [ ]
(12"+=/cd-s+=) *(GOD X/CD 33)* – Blame it on the bonus beats / Blame it on the acappella.
(12"+=) *(GODXR 33)* – Blame it on the bonus beats / ('B'dub).

Oct 89. (7"/c-s; NORMAN COOK featuring LESTER) *(GOD/+MC 37)* **FOR SPACIOUS LIES. / FOR SPACIOUS LIES (dance mix) / THE INVASION OF THE ESTATE AGENTS** [48] [ ]
(12"+=/cd-s+=) *(GOD X/CD 37)* – For spacious ballad.

BEATS INTERNATIONAL

NORMAN COOK with **LINDY LAYTON & LESTER NOEL** – vocals / **ANDY BOUCHER** – keyboards / **LUKE CRESSWELL** – percussion

Feb 90. (7"/c-s; BEATS INTERNATIONAL featuring LINDY LAYTON) *(GOD/+MC 39)* <64970> **DUB BE GOOD TO ME. / THE INVASION OF THE ESTATE AGENTS** [1] Mar90 [76]
(12"+=/cd-s+=) *(GOD X/CD 39)* – Just be good to me (acappella) / The invasion of the freestyle – Discuss.
(12") *(GODXR 39)* – ('A'-Smith & Mighty mix) / Before I go too dub / ('A'-Norman Cook's excursion on the version) / ('A'-Smith & Mighty mellow mix).

Mar 90. (cd/c/lp) *(842 196-2/-4/-1)* <60921> **LET THEM EAT BINGO** [17] [ ]
– Burundi blues / Dub be good to me / Before I grow too old / The ragged trousered percussionists / For spacious lies / Blame it on the bassline / Won't talk about it / Dance to the drummer's beat / Babies makin' babies (stoop rap) / The whole world's down on me / Tribute to King Tubby. *(some lp's cont. 12"ep)* – BINGO BEATS *(cd+=)* – For spacious lies.

May 90. (7"/c-s) *(GOD/+MC 43)* <64948> **WON'T TALK ABOUT IT. / BEATS INTERNATIONAL THEME** [9] Aug90 [76]
(12"+=/cd-s+=) *(GOD X/CD 43)* – ('A'extended).
(12") *(GODXR 43)* – ('A'-Frankie Foncett mix) / ('A'-Chad Jackson mix) / (bonus beats).

Sep 90. (7"/c-s) *(GOD/+MC 45)* **BURUNDI BLUES. / THEME FROM THE DEERSTALKER** [51] [–]
(12"+=/cd-s+=) *(GOD X/CD 45)* – Burundi dub.
(12") *(GODXR 45)* – ('A'-Boilerhouse mix) / ('A'-Boilerhouse guitar & vocal mix) / ('A'-Traditional version).

Feb 91. (7"/c-s) *(GOD/+MC 51)* **ECHO CHAMBER. / INCH BY INCH** [60] [–]
(12"+=) *(GODX 51)* – Daddy Freddy's echo chamber.
(cd-s++=) *(GODCD 51)* – ('A'-extended).
(12") *(GODXR 51)* – ('A'-Boilerhouse mix) / ('A'-instrumental) / ('A'-Boilerhouse instrumental).

Sep 91. (7"/c-s) *(GOD/+MC 59)* **THE SUN DOESN'T SHINE. / WAKE THE DEAD** [66] [–]
(12"+=/cd-s+=) *(GOD X/CD 59)* – Crazy for you / ('A'-extended).

Oct 91. (cd/c/lp) *(828 290-2/-4/-1)* **EXCURSION OF THE VERSION** [ ] [ ]
– Brand new beat / Change your mind / Love is green / Echo chamber / The sun doesn't shine / Herman / Three foot skank / No more Mr. Nice guy / Eyes on the prize / Ten long years / In the ghetto. *(cd+=/c+=)* – Come home.

Nov 91. (7"/c-s) *(GOD/+MC 64)* **IN THE GHETTO (version one). / OH, THAT'S DEEP** [44] [–]
(12"+=/cd-s+=) *(GOD X/CD 64)* – (version two) / (version three).

FREAK POWER

NORMAN COOK – guitar, vox / **ASHLEY SLATER** – vocals, trombone / **CYRIL McCAMMON** – keyboards, vox / **DALE DAVIES** – bass / **PETE ECKFORD** – percussion / **JIM CARMICHAEL** – drums

Fourth & Broadway | Fourth & Broadway

Oct 93. (7"/c-s) *(BRW/BRCA 284)* **TURN ON, TUNE IN, COP OUT. / GETTING OVER THE HUMP** [29] [ ]
(12"+=/cd-s+=) *(12BRW/BRCD 284)* – (2-'A'mixes).

Feb 94. (7"/c-s) *(BRW/BRCA 291)* **RUSH. / PARTY TILL WE PART** [62] [ ]
(12"+=/cd-s+=) *(12BRW/BRCD 291)* – (2-'A'mixes).

Oct 94. (c-s/12"/cd-s) *(BRCA/12BRW/BRCD 298)* **GET IN TOUCH / (Colonel Kurtz mix) / CHEW THE BONE / (uptight vocal mix)** [ ] [–]

Mar 95. (7"/c-s) *(BRW/BRCA 317)* **TURN ON, TUNE IN, COP OUT. / GETTING OVER THE HUMP** [3] [ ]
(12"+=) *(12BRW 317)* – (2-'A'mixes).
(cd-s++=) *(BRCD 317)* – ('A'mix).

Apr 95. (cd/lp) *(BRCD/BRLP 606)* **DRIVE-THRU BOOTY** [11] [ ]
– Moonbeam woman / Turn on, tune in, cop out / Get in touch / Freak power / Running away / Change my mind / What it is? / Waiting for the story to end / Rush / Big time / The whip. *(re-iss. Oct95 d-cd+=/d-lp+=; BRCDX/BRLPX 606)* – IN DUB

May 96. (c-s) *(BRCA 331)* **NEW DIRECTION / ('A'-Fila Brazillia mix)** [60] [–]
(12"+=/cd-s+=) *(12BRW/BRCD 331)* – ('A'mixes incl. Way out west).

Jun 96. (cd/c/lp) *(BRCD/BRCA/BRLP 619)* **MORE OF EVERYTHING FOR EVERYBODY** [ ] [ ]

Aug 96. (c-s) *(BRCA 335)* **CAN YOU FEEL IT / ('A'-Matty's mix)** [ ] [–]
(12"+=/cd-s+=) *(12BRW/BRCD 335)* – ('A'mixes; Todd's rubber room + Bass bin twins mix).

Southern | not iss.

Dec 97. (12") *(ECB 14)* **NO WAY. / ('A'mixes)** [ ] [–]

DeConstruct | not iss.

Apr 98. (c-s) *(74321 57857-4)* **NO WAY / ('A'-Norman Cook's dub mix)** [29] [ ]
(12"+=/cd-s+=) *(74321 57857-1/-2)* – ('A'mixes; full + Dee Jay Delite).

PIZZAMAN

— aka **NORMAN COOK** with various members

Loaded | not iss.

Apr 94. (12") *(12LOAD 8)* **BABY LOOP. / SANS BATEAUX** [ ] [–]

Aug 94. (7") *(LOAD 16)* **TRIPPIN' ON SUNSHINE. / ('A'-Play boy's mixing thing)** [33] [–]
(12"+=/cd-s+=) *(LOAD 16 12/CD)* – ('A'mixes; Californian sunshine / Play boy's fully loaded).

Jun 95. (c-s) *(CALOAD 24)* **SEX ON THE STREETS / SEX ON THE STREETS (Play boy's fully loaded dub)** [24] [–]
(12"+=/cd-s+=) *(12/CD LOAD 24)* – ('A'mixes; Goodfello's / Red Jerry / Wildchild 0703 dub).
(re-entered the chart Jan96 and hit No.23)

Nov 95. (c-s) *(CALOAD 29)* **HAPPINESS / ('A'club mix)** [19] [–]
(12"+=/cd-s+=) *(12/CD LOAD 29)* – ('A'mixes; club / Euro).

May 96. (c-s) *(CALOAD 32)* **TRIPPIN' ON SUNSHINE / ('A'mixes; Impulsion big pizza II / Biff And Memphis)** [18] [ ]
(12"+=/cd-s+=) *(12/CD LOAD 32)* – ('A'-Californian mix).

Sep 96. (c-s) *(CALOAD 39)* **HELLO HONKY TONKS (ROCK YOUR BODY) / ('A'-Pizzaman mix)** [41] [ ]
(12"+=/cd-s+=) *(12/CD LOAD 39)* – ('A'mixes; Cotton club).

Jul 97. (c-s) *(MCRODEO 956)* **GOTTAMAN / (Distant drum mix)** [ ] [–]
(12") *(RODEO 956-12)* – ('A'-Pizzaman) / (Distant drum mix).
(cd-s+=) *(CDRODEO 956)* – ('A'-Gregario mix).

FATBOY SLIM

aka **NORMAN COOK** with the Skint crew, etc

Skint | Astralwerks

Mar 96. (12") *(SKINT 1)* **SANTA CRUZ / THE WEEKEND BONUS BEATS. / THE WEEKEND STARTS HERE / NEAL CASSADY STARTS HERE** [ ] [–]

Mar 96. (12"/cd-s) *(SKINT 6/+CD)* **EVERYBODY LOVES A 303. / LINCOLN MEMORIAL / WE REALLY WANT TO SEE THOSE FINGERS** [ ] [–]

Sep 96. (12"/cd-s) *(SKINT 12/+CD)* **PUNK TO FUNK. / KNUF OT KNUP / BIG BEAT SOUFFLE** [ ] [–]

Apr 97. (12"/cd-s) *(SKINT 19/+CD)* **GOING OUT OF MY HEAD. / MICHAEL JACKSON / NEXT TO NOTHING** [57] [–]

Oct 97. (12"/cd-s) *(SKINT 31/+CD)* **EVERYBODY NEEDS A 303 / (original 12"). / EVERYBODY LOVES A CARNIVAL / NEAL CASSADY STARTS HERE** [34] [–]
(cd-s) *(SKINT 31XCD)* – Everybody loves a carnival / Everybody loves a filter / Es paradis / Where you're at.

Nov 97. (cd/c/d-lp) *(BRASSIC 2 CD/MC/LP)* **BETTER LIVING THROUGH CHEMISTRY** [ ] [ ]
– Song for Lindy / Santa Cruz / Going out of my head / The weekend starts here / Everybody needs a 303 / Give the po' man a break / 10th & Crenshaw / First down / Punk to funk / The sound of Milwaukee. *(d-lp+=)* – Michael Jackson / Next to nothing.

Jun 98. (c-s) *(SKINT 35MC)* <6 6242> **THE ROCKAFELLER SKANK / THE ROCKAFELLER SKANK (long version)** [6] Nov98 [76]
(12"+=/cd-s+=) *(SKINT 35/+CD)* – Always read the label / Tweakers delight.

Jul 98. (cd/c; FATBOY SLIM mixes Various Artists) *(BRASSIC 9 CD/MC)* **ON THE FLOOR AT THE BIG BEAT BOUTIQUE** [ ] [–]
<US-iss.Apr00; 49130>

Oct 98. (c-s) *(SKINT 39MC)* **GANGSTER TRIPPIN' / THE WORLD WENT DOWN** [3] [ ]
(12"+=/cd-s+=) *(SKINT 39/+CD)* – Jack it up (DJ Delite).

Oct 98. (cd/c/d-lp) *(BRASSIC 11 CD/MC/LP)* *<ASW 66247>*
YOU'VE COME A LONG WAY, BABY [1] [34]
– Right here, right now / The Rockafeller skank / In Heaven / Gangster tripping / Build it up – Tear it down / Kalifornia / Soul surfing / You're not from Brighton / Praise you / Love island / Acid 8000.

Jan 99. (c-s) *(SKINT 42MC)* *<66254>* **PRAISE YOU / THE ROCKAFELLER SKANK (Mulder's Urban takeover remix)** [1] Feb99 [36]
(12"+=/cd-s+=) *(SKINT 42/+CD)* – Sho nuff.

Apr 99. (c-s) *(SKINT 46MC)* **RIGHT HERE, RIGHT NOW / DON'T FORGET YOUR TEETH** [2] [ ]
(12"+=/cd-s+=) *(SKINT 46/+CD)* – Praise you (original).

—— FATBOY SLIM was also credited on FREDDY FRESH's hit, 'Badder Badder Schwing'

Oct 00. (c-s) *(SKINT 58MC)* **SUNSET (BIRD OF PREY) / MY GAME** [9] [ ]
(12"+=/cd-s+=) *(SKINT 58/+CD)* – ('A'-Darren Emerson remix).

Nov 00. (cd/c/d-lp) *(BRASSIC 20 CD/MC/LP)* *<50460>*
HALFWAY BETWEEN THE GUTTER AND THE STARS [8] [51]
– Talking bout my baby / Star 69 / Sunset (bird of prey) / Love life (feat. MACY GRAY) / Ya mama / Mad flava / Retox (feat. ASHLEY SLATER) / Weapon of choice (feat. BOOTSY COLLINS) / Drop the hate / Demons (feat. MACY GRAY) / Song for shelter (feat. ROLAND CLARK & ROGER SANCHEZ).

Jan 01. (c-s; by FATBOY SLIM & MACY GRAY) *(SKINT 60MC)* **DEMONS** [16] [–]
(12"+=/cd-s+=) *(SKINT 60/+CD)* – ('A'mixes).

Apr 01. (c-s) *(SKINT 64MC)* **STAR 69 / (Timo Mass remix)** [10] [–]
(12"+=/cd-s+=) *(SKINT 64/+CD)* – ('A'-X-Press 2 remix).

Sep 01. (c-s) *(12"/cd-s) (SKINT 71/+CD)* **YA MAMA. / SONG FOR SHELTER** [30] [–]
(cd-s) *(SKINT 71XCD)* – ('A'mixes).

Jan 02. (12") *(FAT 18)* **RETOX (remixes)** [73] [–]

– compilations, others, etc. –

Mar 00. (cd) *Hip-O; <564787>* **THE FATBOY SLIM / NORMAN COOK COLLECTION** [–] [ ]

Sam COOKE

Born: SAMUEL COOK, 22 Jan'31, Clarksdale, Mississippi, USA. The son of a Baptist minister, SAM was steeped in gospel from his earliest days, singing in the church choir before graduating to bonafide gospel groups in his teens. In 1951 he became lead tenor with The SOUL STIRRERS, achieving widespread critical acclaim within the gospel community for his stunning interpretations of traditional hymns and self-penned material like 'TOUCH THE HEM OF HIS GARMENT'. The outfit signed to Art Rupe's L.A.-based 'Specialty' label (also home to JOE LIGGINS, PERCY MAYFIELD and most famously, LITTLE RICHARD) where they cut a string of singles throughout the early 50's. In 1956, SAM made a move into the pop market with a debut solo track, 'LOVEABLE', released under the alias DALE COOK so as not to offend his gospel fanbase. Following another handful of singles and an album, 'TWO SIDES OF SAM COOKE' (1957), the singer's ongoing wish to become a fully fledged secular star brought him to a final showdown with Rupe who was strongly opposed to any transformation. 'Specialty' producer Bumps Blackwell had backed COOKE all the way and in 1957, Rupe washed his hands of both of them. Armed with the freshly penned 'YOU SEND ME', the pair signed with Hollywood label, 'Keen' and duly took the track to the top of the US chart. While Rupe was quite possibly kicking himself, the yearning ballad made COOKE a star overnight, his clean-cut good looks, sophisticated phrasing and luminous delivery endearing him to a massive youth-orientated audience that held more than its fair share of teenage girls. A string of Top 20/Top 30 hits followed in an overtly pop vein, COOKE and Bumps adapting to the demise of straightahead R&B with airy romantic singles like 'WIN YOUR LOVE FOR ME', 'LOVE YOU MOST OF ALL' and the brilliant 'WONDERFUL WORLD', actually written as a joint effort between future biz moguls Lou Adler (under the pseudonym Barbara Campbell) and Herb Alpert. COOKE was also savvy enough to start his own label, 'SAR', publishing arm, 'Kags Music' and even film company, 'SAR Pictures'; together with his manager, JW Alexander, COOKE helped initiate the careers of future stars like BOBBY WOMACK and BILLY PRESTON. While SAR's output remained on the grittier side of R&B, COOKE's 1960 signing to 'R.C.A.' saw the singer veer towards a supper club, orchestrated easy listening style courtesy of in-house producers like Hugo Peretti and Luigi Creatore. Even so, COOKE still managed to get back to his roots on hits like 'TWISTIN' THE NIGHT AWAY' (a UK/US Top 10 in 1962), the sublime 'BRING IT ON HOME TO ME' (featuring a wonderful call-and-response section with former PILGRIM TRAVELLER, LOU RAWLS) and the 1963 Top 20 cover of Willie Dixon's 'LITTLE RED ROOSTER'. The latter track appeared on 'NIGHT BEAT' (1963), one of his better albums of the period featuring COOKE in hollering blues mode. 1963 was also the proposed year of release for 'LIVE AT THE HARLEM SQUARE CLUB', a gritty concert set recorded at a show on the infamous chitlin' circuit. The record never saw the light of day until the mid-80's with COOKE's paymasters eager to cater to his newfound white MOR audience instead. The record couldn't have been in starker contrast to 'AT THE COPA' (1965), a live set recorded the previous summer during SAM's residency at New York's swish 'Copacabana' nightclub. Tragically, COOKE wasn't around to see its release; on 11th December 1964, he was shot dead by motel manageress, Bertha Franklin, who maintained she acted in self defence after the singer had allegedly raped 22-year old Elisa Boyer. The controversial nature of the case has since fuelled countless rumours that COOKE's death was set up as a result of vested interests and rivalry in the music business. Whatever the truth, his shockingly premature demise was a body blow for soul music and the whole black community; 1965's posthumous Top 10 single, 'A CHANGE IS GONNA COME' was a poignant reminder of COOKE's commitment to ending racial segregation. One of the singer's closest friends and admirers, CASSIUS CLAY (aka MOHAMMED ALI), once described COOKE as "the world's greatest rock'n'roll singer . . .". Few would disagree. • **Songwriters:** COOKE wrote mostly all material, except SEND ME SOME LOVIN' (Little Richard) / LIITLE RED ROOSTER (Willie Dixon) / etc.
Best CD collection: PORTRAIT OF A LEGEND (*8)

SAM COOKE – vocals (with various session people)

not iss. Specialty

1956. (7",78; as DALE COOK) *<596>* **LOVEABLE. / FOREVER** [–] [ ]

1956. (7",78) *<619>* **I'LL COME RUNNING BACK TO YOU. / FOREVER** [–] [ ]
<re-iss. Dec57> – hit No.18 B-side No.60

1957. (7",78) *<627>* **THAT'S ALL I NEED TO KNOW. / I DON'T WANT TO CRY** [–] [ ]
(UK-iss.May58 on 'London'; HLU 8615)

1957. (7",78) *<667>* **I NEED YOU NOW. / HAPPY IN LOVE** [–] [ ]

1957. (lp) *<2116>* **TWO SIDES OF SAM COOKE** [–] [ ]
– The last mile of the way / Touch the hem of his garment / Jesus gave

me water / Were you there / Pilgrim of sorrow / He's my guide / I'll come running back to you / I don't want to cry / Loveable / That's all I need to know / Forever / Happy in love.

London | Keen

1957. (7",78) *<3-4002>* **(I LOVE YOU FOR) SENTIMENTAL REASONS. / DESIRE ME** [–] [ ]
<re-iss. Dec57> – hit No.17 + B-side No.47

1957. (7",78) *<3-4009>* **LONELY ISLAND. / YOU WERE MADE FOR ME** [–] [ ]
<re-iss. Mar58> – hit No.26 + B-side No.27

—— next with the BUMPS BLACKWELL ORCHESTRA

Jan 58. (7",78) *(HLU 8506) <3-4013>* **YOU SEND ME. / SUMMERTIME** [29] [1] Oct57 [81]

H.M.V. | Keen

Mar 58. (lp) *(CLP 1261) <A-2001>* **SAM COOKE** [ ] [ ]
– You send me / The lonesome road / Tammy / Ol' man river / Moonlight in Vermont / Canadian sunset / Summertime / Around the world / Ain't misbehavin' / The bells of St. Mary's / So long / Danny boy / That lucky old sun. *(cd-iss. Dec93 on 'Entertainers')*

May 58. (7",78) *<3-2005>* **ALL OF MY LIFE. / STEALING KISSES** [ ] [ ]

Jul 58. (7",78) *<3-2006>* **WIN YOUR LOVE FOR ME. / LOVE SONG FROM "HOUSEBOAT" (ALMOST IN YOUR ARMS)** [–] [22]

Nov 58. (7",78) *<3-2008>* **LOVE YOU MOST OF ALL. / BLUE MOON** [–] [26]

Nov 58. (lp) *(CLP 1273) <A-2003>* **ENCORE** [ ] [ ]
– When I fall in love / I cover the waterfront / My foolish heart / Today I sing the blues / The gypsy / It's the talk of the town / Oh look at me now / Someday (You'll want me to want you) / Along the Navajo Trail / Running wild / Ac-cent-tchu-aet the positive / Mary, Mary Lou.

Feb 59. (7",78) *(POP 568)* **LOVE YOU MOST OF ALL. / WIN YOUR LOVE FOR ME** [ ] [–]

May 59. (7",78) *(POP 610) <3-2018>* **EVERYBODY LIKES TO CHA CHA CHA. / LITTLE THINGS YOU DO** [ ] Mar59 [31]

Aug 59. (7",78) *(POP 642) <3-2022>* **ONLY SIXTEEN. / LET'S GO STEADY AGAIN** [23] Jun59 [28]

Sep 59. (7") *<8-2101>* **SUMMERTIME. / (part 2)** [–] [ ]

Nov 59. (lp) *<A-2004>* **TRIBUTE TO THE LADY – BILLIE HOLIDAY** [–] [ ]

Dec 59. (7") *(POP 675) <8-2105>* **THERE, I'VE SAID IT AGAIN. / ONE HOUR AHEAD OF THE POSSE** [ ] Nov59 [81]

Feb 60. (7") *<8-2111>* **'TAIN'T NOBODY'S BIZNESS (IF I DO). / NO ONE** [–] [ ]

Feb 60. (lp) *<8-6101>* **HIT KIT** [–] [ ]

—— now orchestration by his new 'R.C.A.' producers HUGO & LUIGI

R.C.A. | RCA Victor

—— some 45's/lp's were still being issued by 'Keen' ('H.M.V.' UK)

May 60. (7") *(RCA 1184) <47-7701>* **TEENAGE SONATA. / IF YOU WERE THE ONLY GIRL** [ ] Mar60 [50]

May 60. (7") *<47-7730>* **YOU UNDERSTAND ME. / I BELONG TO YOUR HEART** [–] [ ]

Jun 60. (7"; on 'Keen') *(POP 754) <8-2112>* **WONDERFUL WORLD. / ALONG THE NAVAJO TRAIL** [27] May60 [12]

Jun 60. (7"; on 'Keen') *<8-2117>* **WITH YOU. / I THANK GOD** [–] [ ]

Jun 60. (lp; on 'Keen') *<8-6103>* **I THANK GOD** [–] [ ]

Sep 60. (7") *(RCA 1202) <47-7783>* **CHAIN GANG. / I FALL IN LOVE EVERY DAY** [9] Aug60 [2]

Oct 60. (7"; on 'Keen') *<8-2118>* **STEAL AWAY. / SO GLAMOUROUS** [–] [ ]

Nov 60. (lp; on 'Keen') *<8-6106>* **THE WONDERFUL WORLD OF SAM COOKE** [–] [ ]
– Wonderful world / Desire me / Summertime / Almost in your arms / That's heaven to me / No one / With you / Blue moon / Stealing kisses / You were made for me / There, I've said it again / I thank God. *(UK-iss.1966 on 'Immediate'; IMLP 002)*

Dec 60. (7"; on 'Keen') *<8-2122>* **MARY, MARY LOU. / EEE-YI-EEE-YI-OH** [–] [ ]

Jan 61. (7") *(RCA 1221) <47-7816>* **SAD MOOD. / LOVE ME** [ ] Nov60 [29]

Feb 61. (lp) *(RD 27190) <LPM 2221>* **COOKE'S TOUR** [ ] Nov60 [ ]
– Faraway places / Under Paris skies / South of the border / Bali Ha'I / The coffee song / Arrivederci Roma / London by night / Jamaica farewell / Galway bay / Sweet Leilani / The Japenese farewell song / The house I live in.

Apr 61. (7") *(RCA 1230) <47-7853>* **THAT'S IT – I QUIT – I'M MOVIN' ON. / WHAT DO YOU SAY** [ ] Feb61 [31]

Apr 61. (lp) *(RD 27215) <LPM 2236>* **HITS OF THE 50's** [ ] Jan61 [ ]
– Hey there / Mona Lisa / Too young / The great pretender / You, you, you / Unchained melody / The wayward wind / Secret love / The song from Moulin Rouge / I'm walking behind you / Cry / Venus. *(cd-iss. Jun95; 74321 26056-2)*

Jul 61. (7") *(RCA 1242) <47-7883>* **CUPID. / FAREWELL, MY DARLING** [7] May61 [17]
(re-iss. 1969; RCA 1817)

Sep 61. (7") *(RCA 1260) <47-7927>* **FEEL IT. / IT'S ALL RIGHT** [ ] [56] [93]

Oct 61. (lp) *(RD 27222) <LPM 2293>* **SWING LOW** [ ] Aug61 [ ]
– Swing low, sweet chariot / I'm just a country boy / They call the wind Maria / Twilight on the trail / If I had you / Chain gang / Grandfather's clock / I dream of Jeanie with the light brown hair / Long, long ago / Pray / You belong to me / Goin' home.

Feb 62. (lp) *(RD 27245) <LPM 2392>* **MY KIND OF BLUES** [ ] Dec61 [ ]
– Don't get around much anymore / Little girl blue / Nobody knows you when you're down and out / Out in the cold again / But not for me / Exactly like you / I'm just a lucky so and so / Since I met you baby / Baby, won't you please come home / Trouble in mind / You're always on my mind / The song is ended.

Feb 62. (7") *(RCA 1277) <47-7983>* **TWISTIN' THE NIGHT AWAY. / ONE MORE TIME** [6] Jan62 [9]

Jun 62. (lp) *(RD 27263) <LPM 2555>* **TWISTIN' THE NIGHT AWAY** [ ] [72]
– Twistin' the night away / Sugar dumpling / Twistin' in the kitchen with Dinah / Somebody's gonna miss me / A whole lotta woman / The twist / Twistin' in the old town tonight / Movin' and a-groovin' / Camptown twist / Somebody have mercy / Soothe me / That's it – I quit – I'm movin' on.

Jul 62. (7") *(RCA 1296) <47-8036>* **BRING IT ON HOME TO ME. / HAVING A PARTY** [ ] [13] May62 [17]

Oct 62. (7") *(RCA 1310) <47-8088>* **NOTHING CAN CHANGE THIS LOVE. / SOMEBODY HAVE MERCY** [ ] [12] Sep62 [70]

Oct 62. (lp) *<lpm 2625>* **THE BEST OF SAM COOKE** (compilation) [–] [22]
– You send me / Only sixteen / Everybody loves to cha cha cha / For sentimental reasons / Wonderful world / Summertime / Chain gang / Twistin' the night away / Sad mood / Having a party / Bring it on home to me.

Jan 63. (7") *(RCA 1327) <47-8129>* **SEND ME SOME LOVIN'. / BABY, BABY, BABY** [ ] [13] [60]

Mar 63. (lp; mono/stereo) *(RD/SF 7539) <LPM/LSP 2673>* **MR. SOUL** [ ] [94]
– I wish you love / Willow weep for me / Chains of love / Smoke rings / All the way / Send me some lovin' / Cry me a river / Driftin' blues / (I love you for) Sentimental reasons / Nothing can change this love / Little girl / These foolish things. *(re-iss. Jul80 on 'RCA Int.'; INTS/INTK 5024)*

May 63. (7") *(RCA 1341) <47-8164>* **ANOTHER SATURDAY NIGHT. / LOVE WILL FIND A WAY** [23] Apr63 [10]

Aug 63. (7") *(RCA 1361) <47-8215>* **FRANKIE AND JOHNNY. / COOL TRAIN** [30] Jul63 [11]

Sep 63. (lp; mono/stereo) *(RD/SF 7583) <LPM/LSP 2709>* **NIGHT BEAT** [ ] [62]
– Nobody knows the trouble I've seen / Lost and lookin' / Mean old world / Please don't drive me away / I lost everything / Get yourself another fool / Little red rooster / Laughin' and clownin' / Trouble blues / You gotta move / Fool's paradise / Shake, rattle and roll. *(cd-iss. Sep95 on 'London'; 528567-2)*

Oct 63. (7") *<47-8247>* **LITTLE RED ROOSTER. / YOU GOTTA MOVE** [–] [11]

Nov 63. (7") *(RCA 1367)* **LITTLE RED ROOSTER. / SHAKE RATTLE AND ROLL** [ ] [–]

Feb 64. (7") *(RCA 1386) <47-8299>* **GOOD NEWS. / BASIN STREET BLUES** [ ] Jan64 [11]

May 64. (lp; mono/stereo) *(RD/SF 7635) <LPM/LSP 2899>* **AIN'T THAT GOOD NEWS** [ ] Mar64 [34]
– Ain't that good news / Meet me at Mary's place / Good times / Rome wasn't built in a day / Another Saturday night / Tennessee waltz / change is gonna come / Falling in love / Home / Sittin' in the sun / No second time / The riddle song.

Jun 64. (7") *(RCA 1405)* <47-8368> **GOOD TIMES. / TENNESSEE WALTZ** [ ] [11] [35]

Oct 64. (7") <47-8426> **COUSIN OF MINE. / THAT'S WHERE IT'S AT** [–] [31] [93]

Jan 65. (lp; mono/stereo) *(RD/SF 7674)* <LPM/LSP 2970> **SAM COOKE AT THE COPA (live)** [ ] Oct64 [29]
– (opening introduction) / The best things in life are free / Bill Bailey / Nobody knows you when you're down and out / Frankie and Johnny / Medley: Try a little tenderness – (I love you) For sentimental reasons – You send me / If I had a hammer / When I fall in love / This little light of mine / Blowin' in the wind / Tennessee waltz.

—— on 11th of December '64, COOKE was shot dead (see biography)

– posthumous, exploitation, etc. –

Jan 65. (7") *(RCA 1436)* <47-8486> **SHAKE. / A CHANGE IS GONNA COME** [ ] [7] [31]

Feb 65. (lp; mono/stereo) *(RD/SF 7730)* <LPM/LSP 3367> **SHAKE** [ ] [44]
– Shake / Yeah man / Win your love for me / Love you most of all / Meet me at Mary's place / I've got the whole world shakin' / A change is gonna come / I'm in the mood for love / I'm just a country boy / You're nobody 'til somebody loves you / Comes love / Ease my troublin' mind.

Apr 65. (7") *(RCA 1452)* <47-8539> **IT'S GOT THE WHOLE WORLD SHAKIN'. / (SOMEBODY) EASE MY TROUBLIN' MIND** [ ] Mar65 [41]

May 65. (7") <47-8586> **WHEN A BOY FALLS IN LOVE. / THE PIPER** [–] [52]

Jul 65. (lp; mono/stereo) <LMP/LSP 3373> **THE BEST OF SAM COOKE VOLUME 2** (compilation) [–] [ ]
– Frankie and Johnny / That's where it's at / Shake / Baby, baby, baby / Another Saturday night / Little red rooster / Good news / Cousin of mine / Tennessee waltz / A change is gonna come / Basin Street blues / Love will find a way.

Sep 65. (7") *(RCA 1476)* <47-8631> **SUGAR DUMPLING. / BRIDGE OF TEARS** [ ] Jul65 [32]

Jan 66. (lp; mono/stereo) *(RD/SF 7764)* <LPM/LSP 3435> **TRY A LITTLE LOVE** [ ] Oct65 [ ]
– Try a little love / Don't cry on my shoulder / Bridge of tears / I fall in love every day / You're always on my mind / Almost in your arms / When a boy falls in love / To each his own / Tammy / The gypsy / The little things you do / You send me.

Feb 66. (7") <47-8751> **FEEL IT. / THAT'S ALL** [–] [95]

Apr 66. (7") <47-8803> **LET'S GO STEADY AGAIN. / TROUBLE BLUES** [–] [97]

Oct 66. (lp; mono/stereo) <LPM/LSP 3517> **THE UNFORGETTABLE SAM COOKE** [–] [ ]
– I'm gonna forget about you / Sugar dumpling / I ain't gonna cheat on you no more / Soothe me / With you / One more time / Feel it / Wonderful world / It's all right / A whole lotta woman / No one / That's all.

Dec 66. (7") <47-8934> **MEET ME AT MARY'S PLACE. / IF I HAD A HAMMER** [–] [ ]

– (selective) compilations, etc. –

Feb 86. (7") *R.C.A.; (PB 49871)* **WONDERFUL WORLD. / CHAIN GANG** [2] [–]
(12"+=) *(PT 49872)* – Cupid / A change is gonna come.

Apr 86. (d-lp/d-c/d-cd) *R.C.A.; (PL/PK/PD 87127)* <7127> **THE MAN AND HIS MUSIC** [8] Mar86 [ ]
– Meet me at Mary's place / Good times / Shake / Sad mood / Bring it on home to me / That's where it's at / That's heaven to me / Touch the hem of his garment / You send me / I'll come running back to you / Win your love for me / Wonderful world / Cupid / Just for you / Chain gang / Only sixteen / When a boy falls in love / Rome wasn't built in a day / Everybody loves to cha cha cha / Nothing can change this love / Love will find a way / Another Saturday night / Having a party / Twistin' the night away / Somebody have mercy / Good news / Soothe me / A change is gonna come.

Apr 86. (7") *(RCA 49849)* **ANOTHER SATURDAY NIGHT. / LITTLE RED ROOSTER** [75] [–]
(12"+=) *(PT 49850)* – Frankie and Johnny.

Oct 03. (cd) *Universal; (9807446) / Abko;* <92642> **PORTRAIT OF A LEGEND 1951-1964** [30] Jul03 [ ]
– Touch the hem of his garment / Lovable / You send me / Only sixteen / (I love you) For sentimental reasons / Just for you / Win your love (for me) / Everybody loves to cha cha cha / I'll come running back to you / You were made for me / Sad mood / Cupid / Wonderful world / Chain gang / Summertime / Little red rooster / Bring it on home to me / Nothing can change this love / Sugar dumpling / (Ain't that) Good news / Meet me at Mary's place / Twistin' the night away / Shake / Tennessee waltz / Another Saturday night / Good times / Having a party / That's where it's at / A change is gonna come / Jesus gave me water.

Alice COOPER

Formed: Initially as a group by VINCENT FURNIER (son of a preacher), Phoenix, Arizona . . . 1965 as The EARWIGS. Together with his partners in musical crime, GLEN BUXTON, MICHAEL BRUCE, DENNIS DUNAWAY and NEAL SMITH, FURNIER relocated to L.A., becoming The SPIDERS and enjoying healthy airplay for their debut single, 'DON"T BLOW YOUR MIND', released on the local 'Santa Cruz' label. After another low key single and a brief name change to NAZZ, the band adopted the improbable moniker of ALICE COOPER (a 17th Century witch, apparently), signing to FRANK ZAPPA's 'Straight' records. Turgid, clumsy cod-psychedelia, the debut album, 'PRETTIES FOR YOU' (1969) didn't bode well, while 'EASY ACTION' (1970) fared little better. Moving to Detroit in 1970, the band were inspired by the Motor City madness of MC5 and The STOOGES, tightening up their sound and developing their theatrical shock tactics. FURNIER simultaneously used the band name for his ghoulish, androgynous alter-ego, infamously embellishing the band's stage show with all manner of sick trickery: simulated hangings, mangled baby dolls, a live snake, mmm . . . nice. Signing to 'Warners' and drafting in BOB EZRIN on production, the band actually started writing material to match the effectiveness of their live shows. This wasn't gloomy, horror soundtrack minimalism, however, it was freewheeling, revved-up rock'n'roll, often with more than a touch of tongue-in-cheek humour. While 'KILLER' probably stands as COOPER's peak achievement, with the hilarious 'UNDER MY WHEELS' and the classic 'BE MY LOVER', the band really hit big with 'SCHOOL'S OUT' (1972). The title track was an irrepressible blast of adolescent-style attitude that made the UK No.1 spot and propelled the album to the upper reaches of the charts on both sides of the Atlantic. The 'ELECTED' single was another hit and the accompanying 'BILLION DOLLAR BABIES' (1973) album made UK and US No.1. 'MUSCLE OF LOVE' (1974) didn't fare quite so well and cracks were beginning to show in the songwriting armoury. COOPER subsequently sacked the rest of the band in the Summer of '74, hiring a cast of musicians that had previously backed up LOU REED. 'WELCOME TO MY NIGHTMARE' (1975; complete with eerie narration by the legendary VINCENT PRICE) was the last great vintage COOPER effort, a macabre concept album that spawned the hit single, 'ONLY WOMEN BLEED'. In contrast to his superfreak, anti-hero stage character, offstage COOPER was becoming something of a celebrity, hobnobbing with the Hollywood elite and even hosting his own TV show, wherein the band shamelessly retrod past glories. By the end of the decade, his musical output had degenerated into AOR mush and he spent time in rehab for alcohol addiction. His early 80's work was hardly inspiring and even after a new deal with 'M.C.A.', the subsequent albums, 'CONSTRICTOR' and 'RAISE YOUR FIST AND YELL' failed to resurrect the (unclean) spirit of old. The latter did contain the anthemic 'FREEDOM' and the records were an attempt at the heady rock'n'roll of yore, COOPER even resuming the schlock shock for the subsequent tour. However, it was only with the help of hair-rock writer, DESMOND CHILD, that ALICE once again became a major player on the metal scene, the 'POISON' single seeing COOPER return to the Top 10 for the first time since his 70's heyday. The accompanying album, 'TRASH', fared almost as well, although it sounded about as menacing as BON JOVI. 'HEY STOOPID' (1989) consolidated COOPER's newfound success, as did 'THE LAST TEMPTATION' (1994). Things went quiet on the recording for a while, although the pro-am golfer COOPER continued to pop up in places where you'd least expect him, 'Wayne's World' (1992 movie), US chat shows etc. With appearances from the likes of ROB ZOMBIE and SLASH, 1997's 'A FISTFUL OF ALICE' album was one of the man's better live efforts while 'BRUTAL PLANET' (2000) finally found the grandaddy of gore back in the studio. More streetwise than schlock, the album delivered a sharp poke in the eye to those who'd already written him off for the umpteenth time. With the millennial 'DRAGONTOWN' (2001), COOPER proved that middle age hasn't mellowed him just yet. A half decent attempt at teaching the young upstarts a thing or two about being bad, COOPER proved that, lyrically at least, he still has few challengers when it comes to twisted humour. No prizes for guessing the subject matter of 'DISGRACELAND', a PRESLEY "tribute" that doesn't quite match The CRAMPS' 'A Date With Elvis' but tries hard. 'EYES OF ALICE COOPER' (2003) marked a return to the man's natural environs of sleazy hard-rock, leaving behind his half-realised attempts at getting hip to nu-metal. Lyrically, he was still outsmarting almost any other writer in his peergroup (and most of the young bucks as well), with pinpoint portraits like 'MAN OF THE YEAR'; COOPER could also be seen opposite wee Ronnie Corbett in a TV ad for Sky. • **Songwriters:** ALICE wrote / co-wrote with band most of material, also using producer BOB EZRIN. DICK WAGNER to BERNIE TAUPIN also contributed in the 70's. On 'CONSTRICTOR' album, ALICE co-wrote with ROBERTS, some with KELLY and WEGENER. Collaborated with DESMOND CHILD in '89 and JACK PONTI, VIC PEPE, BOB PFEIFER in 1991. Covered:- SUN ARISE (trad.; a Rolf Harris hit) / SEVEN AND SEVEN IS (Love) / FIRE (Jimi Hendrix). • **Trivia:** Film cameo appearances have been:- DIARY OF A HOUSEWIFE (1970) / SGT. PEPPER'S LONELY HEARTS CLUB BAND (1978) / ROADIE (1980) / PRINCE OF DARKNESS (1987) / FREDDIE'S DEAD: THE FINAL NIGHTMARE (1991' he also acted!). In 1975 he sang 'I'M FLASH' on the Various Artists concept album 'FLASH FEARLESS VS.THE ZORG WOMEN Pts.5 & 6'.

Album rating: PRETTIES FOR YOU (*5) / EASY ACTION (*5) / LOVE IT TO DEATH (*8) / KILLER (*8) / SCHOOL'S OUT (*7) / BILLION DOLLAR BABIES (*8) / MUSCLE OF LOVE (*6) / WELCOME TO MY NIGHTMARE (*8) / ALICE COOPER GOES TO HELL (*6) / LACE AND WHISKEY (*5) / THE ALICE COOPER SHOW (*6) / FROM THE INSIDE (*6) / FLUSH THE FASHION (*6) / SPECIAL FORCES (*6) / ZIPPER CATCHES SKIN (*6) / DA DA (*6) / CONSTRICTOR (*5) / RAISE YOUR FIST AND YELL (*5) / TRASH (*5) / HEY STOOPID (*5) / BEAST OF ALICE COOPER compilation (*8) / THE LAST TEMPTATION (*5) / CLASSICKS compilation (*8) / A FISTFUL OF ALICE (*5) / BRUTAL PLANET (*6) / THE DEFINITIVE compilation (*8) / DRAGONTOWN (*5) / THE EYES OF ALICE COOPER (*5)

The SPIDERS

ALICE COOPER (b.VINCENT DAMON FURNIER, 4 Feb'48, Detroit) – vocals / **GLEN BUXTON** (b.17 Jun'47, Washington DC) – lead guitar / **MICHAEL BRUCE** (b.21 Nov'48, California) – rhythm guitar, keyboards / **DENNIS DUNAWAY** (b.15 Mar'46, California) – bass / **NEAL SMITH** (b.10 Jan'48, Washington DC) – drums

not iss. — Santa Cruz

1967. (7") *<SCR 10.003>* **DON'T BLOW YOUR MIND. / NO PRICE TAG** [–] [ ]

not iss. — Very

1967. (7") *<001>* **WONDER WHO'S LOVING HER NOW. / LAY DOWN AND DIE, GOODBYE** [–] [ ]

ALICE COOPER

Straight — Straight

Dec 69. (lp) *<(STS 1051)>* **PRETTIES FOR YOU** [ ] Jun69 [ ]
– Titanic overture / 10 minutes before the worm / Sing low sweet cheerio / Today Mueller / Living / Fields of regret / No longer umpire / Levity ball / B.B. on Mars / Reflected / Apple bush / Earwigs to eternity / Changing, arranging.

Jan 70. (7") *<101>* **LIVING. / REFLECTED** [–] [ ]

Jun 70. (lp) *<(STS 1061)>* **EASY ACTION** [ ] [ ]
– Mr. and Misdemeaner / Shoe salesman / Still no air / Below your means / Return of the spiders / Laughing at me / Refridgerator heaven / Beautiful flyaway / Lay down and die, goodbye.

Jun 70. (7") *<7141>* **CAUGHT IN A DREAM. / EIGHTEEN** [–] [ ]

Nov 70. (7") *<7398>* **RETURN OF THE SPIDERS. / SHOE SALESMAN** [–] [ ]

Straight — Warners

Apr 71. (7") *(S 7209) <7499>* **EIGHTEEN. / IS IT MY BODY** [ ] Feb71 [21]

Jun 71. (lp) *(STS 1065) <1883>* **LOVE IT TO DEATH** [ ] Mar71 [35]
– Caught in a dream / Eighteen / Long way to go / Black Juju / Is it my body / Hallowed be my name / Second coming / Ballad of Dwight Fry / Sun arise. *(re-iss. Dec71 on 'Warners' lp/c; K/K4 46177)* – hit UK No.28 in Sep'72.

Warners — Warners

Jun 71. (7") *(7490>* **CAUGHT IN A DREAM. / HALLOWED BE THY NAME** [–] [94]

Dec 71. (7") *(K 16127) <7529>* **UNDER MY WHEELS. / DESPERADO** [ ] [59]
(re-iss. Aug74; same)

Dec 71. (lp/c) *(K/K4 56005) <2567>* **KILLER** [27] Nov71 [21]
– Under my wheels / Be my lover / Halo of flies / Desperado / You drive me nervous / Yeah yeah yeah / Dead babies / Killer. *(cd-iss. Sep89 on 'WEA'; 927255-2)*

Jan 72. (7") *<7568>* **BE MY LOVER. / YEAH YEAH YEAH** [–] [49]

Feb 72. (7") *(K 16154)* **BE MY LOVER. / YOU DRIVE ME NERVOUS** [ ] [–]

Jul 72. (7") *(K 16188) <7596>* **SCHOOL'S OUT. / GUTTER CAT** [1] May72 [7]

Jul 72. (lp/c) *(K/K4 56007) <2623>* **SCHOOL'S OUT** [4] Jun72 [2]
– School's out / Luney tune / Gutter cat vs. the jets / Street fight / Blue Turk / My stars / Public animal No.9 / Alma mater / Grande finale. *(cd-iss. Sep89 on 'WEA'; 927260-2)*

Oct 72. (7") *(K 16214) <7631>* **ELECTED. / LUNEY TUNE** [4] [26]

Feb 73. (7") *(K 16248) <7673>* **HELLO HURRAY. / GENERATION LANDSLIDE** [6] Jan73 [35]

Mar 73. (lp/c) *(K/K4 56013) <2685>* **BILLION DOLLAR BABIES** [1] [1]
– Hello hurray / Raped and freezin' / Elected / Billion dollar babies / Unfinished sweet / No more Mr. Nice guy / Generation landslide / Sick things / Mary Ann / I love the dead. *(cd-iss. Jan93 on 'WEA'; 7599 27269-2) (d-cd-iss. Mar01; 8122 79791-2)* – (with extra tracks).

Apr 73. (7") *(K 16262) <7691>* **NO MORE MR. NICE GUY. / RAPED AND FREEZIN'** [10] [25]

Jul 73. (7") *<7724>* **BILLION DOLLAR BABIES. / MARY ANN** [–] [57]

Jan 74. (lp/c) *(K/K4 56018) <2748>* **MUSCLE OF LOVE** [34] Dec73 [10]
– Muscle of love / Woman machine / Hard hearted Alice / Man with the golden gun / Big apple dreamin' (hippo) / Never been sold before / Working up a sweat / Crazy little child / Teenage lament '74. *(cd-iss. Nov99; 7599 26226-2)*

Jan 74. (7") *(K 16345) <7762>* **TEENAGE LAMENT '74. / HARD HEARTED ALICE** [12] Dec73 [48]

Mar 74. (7") *<7783>* **MUSCLE OF LOVE. / CRAZY LITTLE CHILD** [–] [ ]

Jun 74. (7") *<8023>* **MUSCLE OF LOVE. / I'M EIGHTEEN** [–] [ ]

Sep 74. (lp/c) *(K/K4 56043) <2803>* **ALICE COOPER'S GREATEST HITS** (compilation) [ ] Aug74 [8]
– I'm eighteen / Is it my body / Desperado / Under my wheels / Be my lover / School's out / Hello hurray / Elected / No more Mr. Nice guy / Billion dollar babies / Teenage lament '74 / Muscle of love. *(cd-iss. Jun89; K2 56045)*

— **ALICE** sacked rest of band, who became BILLION DOLLAR BABIES. He brought in **DICK WAGNER** – guitar, vocals / **STEVE** (DEACON) **HUNTER** – guitars / **PRAKASH JOHN** – bass / **PENTII 'Whitey' GLAN** – drums / **JOSEF CHIROWSKI** – drums (all ex-LOU REED band)

Anchor Atlantic

Feb 75. (7") *(1012) <3280>* **DEPARTMENT OF YOUTH. / COLD ETHYL** [ ] [–]

Mar 75. (lp/c) *(ANC L/K 2011) <18130>* **WELCOME TO MY NIGHTMARE** [19] [5]
– Welcome to my nightmare / Devil's food / The black widow / Some folks / Only women bleed / Department of youth / Cold Ethyl / Years ago / Steven / The awakening / Escape. *<cd-iss. Sep87 on 'Atlantic'; SD 19157>*

Apr 75. (7") *<3254>* **ONLY WOMEN BLEED. / COLD ETHYL** [–] [12]

Jun 75. (7") *(1018)* **ONLY WOMEN BLEED. / DEVIL'S FOOD** [ ] [–]

Aug 75. (7") *<3280>* **DEPARTMENT OF YOUTH. / SOME FOLKS** [–] [67]

Oct 75. (7") *<3298>* **WELCOME TO MY NIGHTMARE. / COLD ETHYL** [–] [45]

Nov 75. (7") *(1025)* **WELCOME TO MY NIGHTMARE. / BLACK WIDOW** [ ] [–]

Warners Warners

Jun 76. (lp/c) *(K/K4 56171) <2896>* **ALICE COOPER GOES TO HELL** [23] [27]
– Go to Hell / You gotta dance / I'm the coolest / Didn't we meet / I never cry / Give the kid a break / Guilty / Wake me gently / Wish you were here / I'm always chasing rainbows / Going home. *(cd-iss. May94; 7599 27299-2)*

Jun 76. (7") *(K 16792) <8228>* **I NEVER CRY. / GO TO HELL** [ ] [12]

Apr 77. (7") *<8349>* **YOU AND ME. / IT'S HOT TONIGHT** [–] [9]

Apr 77. (7") *(K 16935)* **(NO MORE) LOVE AT YOUR CONVENIENCE. / IT'S HOT TONIGHT** [44] [–]

May 77. (lp/c) *(K/K4 56365) <3027>* **LACE AND WHISKEY** [33] [42]
– It's hot tonight / Lace and whiskey / Road rats / Damned if you do / You and me / King of the silver screen / Ubangi stomp / (No more) Love at your convenience / I never wrote those songs / My God.

Jul 77. (7") *(K 16984)* **YOU AND ME. / MY GOD** [ ] [–]

Jul 77. (7") *<8448>* **(NO MORE) LOVE AT YOUR CONVENIENCE. / I NEVER WROTE THOSE SONGS** [–] [ ]

— **FRED MANDEL** – keyboards repl. JOSEF

Dec 77. (lp/c) *(K/K4 56439) <3138>* **THE ALICE COOPER SHOW (live)** [ ] [ ]
– Under my wheels / I'm eighteen / Only women / Sick things / Is it my body / I never cry / Billion dollar babies / Devil's food – The black widow / You and me / a. I love the dead – b. Go to hell – c. Wish you were here / School's out.

— **Alice COOPER** now basically a solo artist with session people, which retaining **MANDEL, DAVEY JOHNSTONE** – guitar (ex-ELTON JOHN) / **MARK VOLMAN + HOWARD KAYLAN** – backing vocals (ex-TURTLES)

Dec 78. (7") *(K 17270) <8695>* **HOW YOU GONNA SEE ME NOW. / NO TRICKS** [61] Oct78 [12]

Dec 78. (lp/c) *(K/K4 56577) <3263>* **FROM THE INSIDE** [68] [60]
– From the inside / Wish I were born in Beverly Hills / The quiet room / Nurse Rozetta / Millie and Billie / Serious / How you gonna see me now / For Veronica's sake / Jacknife Johnny / Inmates (we're all crazy). *(cd-iss. Jun99; 7599 26064-2)*

Jan 79. (7") *<8760>* **FROM THE INSIDE. / NURSE ROZETTA** [–] [ ]

above w / **JOHN LO PRESTI** – bass / **DENNIS CONWAY** – drums

May 80. (lp/c) *(K/K4 56805) <3436>* **FLUSH THE FASHION** [56] [44]
– Talk talk / Clones (we're all) / Pain / Leather boots / Aspirin damage / Nuclear infected / Grim facts / Model citizen / Dance yourself to death / Headlines. *(cd-iss. Jun99; 7599 26229-2)*

Jun 80. (7") *(K 17598) <49204>* **CLONES (WE'RE ALL). / MODEL CITIZEN** [ ] May80 [40]

Sep 80. (7") *<49526>* **DANCE YOURSELF TO DEATH. / TALK TALK** [–] [ ]

— now w / **MIKE PINERA + DAVEY JOHNSTONE** – guitar / **DUANE HITCHINGS** – keyboards / **ERIC SCOTT** – bass / **CRAIG KRAMPF** – drums

Sep 81. (7") *<49780>* **WHO DO YOU THINK WE ARE. / YOU WANT IT, YOU GOT IT** [–] [ ]

Sep 81. (lp/c) *(K/K4 56927) <3581>* **SPECIAL FORCES** [96] [ ]
– Who do you think we are / Seven and seven is / Prettiest cop in the block / Don't talk old to me / Generation landslide '81 / Skeletons in the closet / You want it, you got it / You look good in rags / You're a movie / Vicious rumours. *(cd-iss. Jun99; 7599 26230-2)*

Feb 82. (7") *(K 17924) <49848>* **SEVEN AND SEVEN IS (live). / GENERATION LANDSLIDE '81 (live)** [62] [ ]

May 82. (7"/7"pic-d) *(K 17940/+M)* **FOR BRITAIN ONLY. / UNDER MY WHEELS (live)** [66] [–]
(12"+=) *(K 17940T)* – Who do you think we are (live) / Model citizen (live).

— now w / **MIKE PINERA + DAVEY JOHNSTONE** – guitar / **DUANE HITCHINGS** – keyboards / **ERIC SCOTT** – bass / **CRAIG KRAMPF** – drums

Oct 82. (7") *<29928>* **I LIKE GIRLS. / ZORRO'S ASCENT** [–] [ ]

Oct 82. (lp/c) *(K/K4 57021) <23719-1/-4>* **ZIPPER CATCHES SKIN** [ ] [ ]
– Zorro's ascent / Make that money (Scrooge's song) / I am the future / No baloney homosapiens / Adaptable (anything for you) / I like girls / Remarkably insincere / Tag, you're it / I better be good / I'm alive (that was the day my dead pet returned to save my life). *(cd-iss. Jun99; 7599 23719-2)*

— **COOPER + WAGNER** re-united w / **EZRIN + PRAKASH** and recruited **GRAHAN SHAW** – synth / **JOHN ANDERSON + RICHARD KOLINGA** – drums

Mar 83. (7") *(K 15004)* **I AM THE FUTURE (remix). / ZORRO'S ASCENT** [ ] [–]

Mar 83. (7") *<29828>* **I AM THE FUTURE (remix). / TAG, YOU'RE IT** [–] [ ]

Nov 83. (lp/c) *(923969-1/-4) <23969-1/-4>* **DA DA** [93] [ ]
– Da da / Enough's enough / Former Lee Warner / No man's land / Dyslexia / Scarlet and Sheba / I love America / Fresh blood / Pass the gun around. *(cd-iss. Jun99; 7599 23969-2)*

Nov 83. (12"m) *(ALICE 1T)* **I LOVE AMERICA. / FRESH BLOOD / PASS THE GUN AROUND** [ ] [ ]

— band now consisted of **KANE ROBERTS** (b.16 Jan'59) – guitar, vocals / **DAVID ROSENBERG** – drums / **PAUL DELPH** – keyboards, vocals / **DONNIE KISSELBACK** – bass, vocals / **KIP WINGER**

M.C.A. M.C.A.

Oct 86. (7") *(MCA 1090) <52904>* **HE'S BACK (THE MAN BEHIND THE MASK). / BILLION DOLLAR BABIES** [61] [ ]
(12"+=) *(MCAT 1090)* – I'm eighteen.

Oct 86. (lp/c) *(MCF/+C 3341) <5761>* **CONSTRICTOR** [41] [59]
– Teenage Frankenstein / Give it up / Thrill my gorilla / Life and death of the party / Simple disobedience / The world needs guts / Trick bag / Crawlin' / The great American success story / He's back (the man behind the mask).

Apr 87. (7") *(MCA 1113)* **TEENAGE FRANKENSTEIN. / SCHOOL'S OUT (live)** [ ] [–]
(12"+=) *(MCAT 1113)* – Only women bleed.

— **KEN K. MARY** – drums repl.ROSENBERG / **PAUL HOROWITZ** – keyboards, repl. DELPH + KISSELBACH.

Oct 87. (lp/pic-lp/c) *(MCF/+P/C 3392) <42091>* **RAISE YOUR FIST AND YELL** [48] [73]
– Freedom / Lock me up / Give the radio back / Step on you / Not that kind of love / Prince of darkness / Time to kill / Chop, chop, chop / Gail / Roses on white lace. *(cd-iss. May88; DMCF 3392)*

Mar 88. (7") *(MCA 1241) <53212>* **FREEDOM. / TIME TO KILL** [50] [ ]
(12"+=/12"s+=) *(MCA T/X 1241)* – School's out (live).

— retained **KIP WINGER** bringing in guests **JON BON JOVI, RICHIE SAMBORA** plus **JOE PERRY, TOM HAMILTON, JOEY KRAMER** etc.

— **COOPER + WAGNER** re-united w / **EZRIN + PRAKASH** and recruited **GRAHAN SHAW** – synth / **JOHN ANDERSON + RICHARD KOLINGA** – drums

Epic Epic

1988. (7") *<08114>* **I GOT A LINE ON YOU. / LIVIN' ON THE EDGE** [–] [ ]

Jul 89. (7") *(655061-7) <68958>* **POISON. / TRASH** [2] Sep89 [7]
(12"+=) *(655061-8)* – The ballad of Dwight Fry.
(cd-s++=) *(655061-2)* – I got a line on you (live).
(12"+=) *(655061-9)* – Cold Ethyl (live).

Aug 89. (lp/c/cd) *(465130-1/-4/-2) <45137>* **TRASH** [2] [20]
– Poison / Spark in the dark / House of fire / Why trust you / Only my heart talkin' / Bed of nails / This maniac's in love with you / Trash / Hell is living without you / I'm your gun. *(re-iss. Sep93 cd/c; same)*

Sep 89. (7"/7"green/7"red/7"blue/c-s) *(ALICE/+G/R/B/M 3)* **BED OF NAILS. / I'M YOUR GUN** [38] [–]
(12"+=/12"w-poster/12"pic-d+=) *(ALICE T/Q/P 3)* – Go to Hell (live).
(cd-s++=) *(ALICEC 3)* – Only women bleed (live).

Dec 89. (7"/7"sha-pic-d/c-s) *(ALICE/+P/M 4)* **HOUSE OF FIRE. / THIS MANIAC'S IN LOVE WITH YOU** [65] [–]
(12"+=/cd-s+=) *(ALICE T/C 4)* – Billion dollar babies (live) / Under my wheels (live).

(7"sha-pic-d) *(ALICEX 4)* – ('A'side) / POISON (live).
(12"pic-d+=/12"w-poster+=) *(ALICE S/Q 4)* – Spark in the dark (live) / Under my wheels (live).

Jan 90. (c-s) *<73085>* **HOUSE OF FIRE / BALLAD OF DWIGHT FRY** [–] [56]

Apr 90. (cd-s) *<73268>* **ONLY MY HEART TALKIN'. / UNDER MY WHEELS (live)** [–] [89]

— (Mar'90) touring band **PETE FRIEZZEN** – guitar / **AL PITRELLI** – guitar / **TOMMY CARADONNA** – bass / **DEREK SHERINIAN** – keyboards / **JONATHAN MOVER** – drums

— (1991 sessions) **STEVE VAI, JOE SATRIANI, STEF BURNS** (on tour), **VINNIE MOORE, MICK MARS, SLASH** – guitars / **HUGH McDONALD, NIKKI SIXX** – bass / **MICKEY CURRY** – drums / **ROBERT SALLEY, JOHN WEBSTER** – keyboards / **STEVE CROES** – synclaiver

Jun 91. (7"/c-s) *(656983-7/-4)* **HEY STOOPID. / WIND-UP TOY** [21] [–]
(12"+=/12"pic-d+=/cd-s+=) *(656983-6/-8/-9)* – It rained all night.

Jun 91. (cd/c/lp) *(468416-2/-4/-1) <46786>* **HEY STOOPID** [4] [47]
– Hey stoopid / Love's a loaded gun / Snakebite / Burning our bed / Dangerous tonight / Might as well be on Mars / Feed me Frankenstein / Hurricane years / Little by little / Die for you / Dirty dreams / Wind-up toy. *(cd re-iss. Mar96; same)*

Jul 91. (cd-s) *<73845>* **HEY STOOPID. / IT RAINED ALL NIGHT** [–] [78]

Sep 91. (7"/c-s) *(657438-7/-4)* **LOVE'S A LOADED GUN. / FIRE** [38] [ ]
(12"+=/12"pic-d+=/sha-pic-cd-s+=) *(657438-6/-8/-9)* – Eighteen (live '91).

Jun 92. (7"/c-s) *(658092-7/-4)* **FEED MY FRANKENSTEIN. / BURNING OUR BED** [27] [ ]
(12"pic-d+=/cd-s+=) *(658092-6/-2)* – Poison / Only my heart talkin'.
(cd-s+=) *(658092-5)* – Hey stoopid / Bed of nails.

— w / **STEF BURNS** – guitar, vocals / **GREG SMITH** – bass, vocals / **DEREK SHERINIAN** – keyboards, vocals / **DAVID VOSIKKINEN** – drums

May 94. (c-s) *(660347-4)* **LOST IN AMERICA. / HEY STOOPID (live)** [22] [ ]
(12"pic-d+=/pic-cd-s+=) *(660347-2)* – Billion dollar babies (live) / No more Mr.Nice Guy (live).

Jun 94. (cd/c/lp) *(476594-2/-4/-1) <52771>* **THE LAST TEMPTATION** (w /free comic) [6] [68]
– Sideshow / Nothing's free / Lost in America / Bad place alone / You're my temptation / Stolen prayer / Unholy war / Lullaby / It's me / Cleansed by fire.

Jul 94. (c-s) *(660563-4)* **IT'S ME. / BAD PLACE ALONE** [34] [ ]
(12"pic-d+=/pic-cd-s+=) *(660563-2)* – Poison / Sick things.

Oct 95. (cd/c) *(480845-2/-4) <67219>* **CLASSICKS** (compilation) [ ] [ ]
– Poison / Hey stoopid / Feed my Frankenstein / Love's a loaded gun / Stolen prayer / House of fire / Lost in America / It's me / Under my wheels (live) / Billion dollar babies (live) / I'm eighteen (live) / No more Mr. Nice guy (live) / Only women bleed (live) / School's out (live) / Fire.

— now with **REB BEACH** – guitar / **RYAN ROXIE** – guitar / **PAUL TAYLOR** – keyboards / **TODD JENSEN** – bass / **JIMMT DeGRASSO** – drums / guests; SAMMY HAGAR, BOB ZOMBIE + SLASH

E.M.I. Capitol

Jun 97. (cd) *(CTM CD/MC 331) <33080>* **A FISTFUL OF ALICE (live)** [ ] [ ]
– School's out / Under my wheels / I'm eighteen / Desperado / Lost in America / Teenage lament '74 / I never cry / Poison / No more Mr. Nice guy / Welcome to my nightmare / Only women bleed / Feed my Frankenstein / Elected / Is anyone home? (studio).

Eagle Spitfire

Jun 00. (cd) *(EAGCD 115) <15038>* **BRUTAL PLANET** [38] [ ]
– Brutal planet / Wicked young man / Sanctuary / Blow me a kiss / Eat some more / Pick up the bones / Pessi-mystic / Gimme / It's the little – things / Take it like a woman / Cold machines.

Aug 00. (cd-s) *(EAGXS 157)* **GIMME / BRUTAL PLANET / GIMME (CD-Rom video)** [ ] [–]

Oct 01. (cd) *(EAGCD 181) <15200>* **DRAGONTOWN** [ ] Sep01 [ ]
– Triggerman / Deeper / Dragontown / Sex, death and money / Fantasy man / Somewhere in the jungle / Dusgraceland / Sister Sara / Every woman has a name / I just wanna be God / It's much too late / The sentinel.

— now with **RYAN ROXIE** – guitar / **ERIC DOVER** – guitar / **ERIC SINGER** – drums / **CHUCK GARRIC** – bass / **TED ANDREADIS** – percussion, keyboards / **SCOTT GILMAN** – clarinet, sax / **WAYNE KRAMER** – guitar

Spitfire Eagle Red

Sep 03. (cd) *(SPIT 090) <20028>* **THE EYES OF ALICE COOPER** [ ] [ ]
– What do you want from me? / Between high school & old school / Man of the year / Novocaine / Bye bye, baby / Be with you awhile / Detroit city / Spirits rebellious / This house is haunted / Love should never feel like this / The song that didn't rhyme / I'm so angry / Backyard brawl. *(lp-iss.Oct03 on '5160'; 5160 018)*

– compilations, others, etc. –

on 'Warners' unless otherwise stated

Mar 73. (7") **BE MY LOVER. / UNDER MY WHEELS** [–] [ ]

Jun 73. (d-lp) *(K 66021)* **SCHOOLDAYS** (1st-2 lp's) [ ] [ ]

Feb 75. (7"ep) *(K 16409)* **SCHOOL'S OUT / NO MORE MR.NICE GUY. / BILLION DOLLAR BABIES / ELECTED** [ ] [–]

Feb 76. (7") *(K 16287)* **SCHOOL'S OUT. / ELECTED** [ ] [–]
(re-iss. Dec80; same) (re-iss. Sep85 on 'Old Gold'; OG 9519)

Dec 77. (7"ep/12"ep) *Anchor; (ANE 7/12 001)* **DEPARTMENT OF YOUTH EP** [ ] [–]
– Department of youth / Welcome to my nightmare / Black widow / Only women bleed.

1978. (7") **I'M EIGHTEEN. / SCHOOL'S OUT** [–] [ ]

Apr 84. (pic-lp) *Design; (PXLP 3)* **ROCK'N'ROLL REVIVAL: TORONTO LIVE '69 (live)** [ ] [–]
(re-iss. Apr86 as 'FREAKOUT SONG' on 'Showcase'; SHLP 115)

Apr 87. (m-lp/c) *Thunderbolt; (THBM/+C 005)* **LADIES MAN (live'69)** [ ] [–]
(cd-iss. Aug88; CDTHBM 005) (re-iss cd.Jun91; same) (cd re-iss. Aug98 on 'MagMid'; MM 011)

Dec 89. (lp/c)(cd) *W.E.A.; (WX 331/+C)(241781-2)* **THE BEAST OF ALICE COOPER** [ ] [ ]
– School's out / Under my wheels / Billion dollar babies / Be my lover / Desperado / Is it my body? / Only women bleed / Elected / I'm eighteen / Hello hurray / No more Mr. Nice guy / Teenage lament '74 / Muscle of love / Department of youth.

Jul 90. (cd-box) *Enigma; (773 362-2)* **PRETTIES FOR YOU** [ ] [–]

Jul 90. (cd-box) *Enigma; (773 391-2)* **EASY ACTION** [ ] [–]

May 92. (lp/cd) *Edsel; (NEST/+CD 903)* **LIVE AT THE WHISKEY A GO GO, 1969 (live)** [ ] [–]

Oct 92. (cd) *Pickwick; (SMA 054)* **ROCK LEGENDS VOL.2** [ ] [–]

Apr 93. (cd) *Pulsar; (PULS 010)* **NOBODY LIKES ME** [ ] [–]

Sep 94. (cd) *Wisepack; (LECD 085)* **LEGENDS IN MUSIC** [ ] [–]

Jul 97. (cd) *Going For A Song; (GFS 071)* **ALICE COOPER** [ ] [–]

May 98. (cd) *Dressed To Kill; (DRESS 603)* **SNORTING ANTHRAX** [ ] [–]

Jun 98. (cd) *Raven; (RVCD 69)* **FREEDOM FOR FRANKENSTEIN: HITS AND PIECES 1984-1994** [ ] [ ]

Apr 99. (4xcd-box) *Rhino; <(8122 75680-2)>* **THE LIFE AND CRIMES OF ALICE COOPER** [ ] [ ]

Jul 00. (cd) *Epic; (498788-2)* **SUPER HITS** [ ] [–]

Feb 01. (cd/c) *Warners; <(8122 73534-2/-4)>* **THE DEFINITIVE ALICE COOPER** [33] [ ]
– I'm eighteen / Desperado / Under my wheels / Halo of flies / School's out / Elected / Hello hooray / Generation landslide / No more Mr. Nice Guy / Billion dollar babies / Teenage lament '74 / Muscle of love / Only women bleed / Welcome to my nightmare / Department of love / I never cry / You and me / How you gonna see me now / From the inside / Poison / Hey stoopid.

Oct 01. (4xcd-box) *Rhino; <(8122 73573-2)<* **THE LIFE AND CRIMES OF ALICE COOPER** [ ] [ ]

Aug 03. (cd) *Epic; (511385-2)* **HELL IS** [ ] [–]

COOPER TEMPLE CLAUSE

Formed: Reading, England . . . 1999 by vocalist BEN GAUTREY, TOM BELLAMY, DAN FISHER, DIDZ, KIERAN MAHON and JOHN HARPER. Like a mad hybrid between KULA SHAKER and GAY DAD, The COOPER TEMPLE CLAUSE were rocking out in a bad/good way, while slyly winking at their newly composed fanbase. We can imagine it: six geezers (with deliberately 'ironic' mullet hair-cuts) from Reading, playing trash glam Brit-rock and being crowned as NME darlings. Yet for a band that were supposed to be christening a new type of Brit-rock, The COOPER TEMPLE CLAUSE's debut EP 'THE HARDWARE' (in March 2001) recycled the old GAY DAD, WARM JETS, DANDY WARHOLS vibe that simply made them look like stringent copycats. However, after the guitar strumming pop-rock double-A single 'FILM-MAKER' / 'BEEN TRAINING DOGS' (a Top 20 hit early 2002), CTC came of age through their debut UK Top 30 album 'SEE THIS THROUGH AND LEAVE'. Featuring hit-to-be, 'WHO NEEDS ENEMIES?', the album was relentless to the end; if you were sick of OASIS and the Brit-rock crew, this was for you. The COOPER TEMPLE CLAUSE were back with their sophomore album 'KICK UP THE FIRE AND LET THE FLAMES BREAK LOOSE' (2003). Much of the same mix of rock and experimental programmed beats as seen on their debut, the band had a winner in the explosive, emotionally raw single 'THE SAME MISTAKES' (with a great video to boot). Elsewhere the album was as ferocious as the title suggested, making the 'CLAUSE one of the most exciting British bands in the post-RADIOHEAD slump.

Album rating: SEE THIS THROUGH AND LEAVE (*7) / KICK UP THE FIRE AND LET THE FLAMES BREAK LOOSE (*7)

BEN GAUTREY – vocals / **DAN FISHER** – guitar / **TOM BELLAMY** – guitar, effects / **KIERAN MAHON** – keyboards / **DIDZ HAMMOND** – bass / **JON HARPER** – drums

		Morning-BMG	BMG Inter..
Mar 01.	(d7"ep; 1 white) *(MORNING 2)* **THE HARDWARE EP**		–
	– The Devil walks in the sand / Solitude / Way out west / Sister soul.		
May 01.	(cd-ep) *(MORNING 5)* **THE WARFARE EP**		–
	– Panzer attack / I'll still write / Mansell.		
	(d7"ep; 1 white+=) *(MORNING 6)* – Panzer attack (acoustic).		
Sep 01.	(7") *(MORNING 11)* **LET'S KILL MUSIC. / GIRL INK AGE**	41	–
	(cd-s) *(MORNING 9)* – ('A'side) / Panzer attack (Dirty Sanchez remix) / ('A'-video).		
	(cd-s) *(MORNING 10)* – ('A'side) / My darling (nasty angel) / ('A'-Dirty Sanchez remix).		
Dec 01.	(cd-ep) *<29903>* **THE HARDWARE EP + THE WARFARE EP**	–	
Jan 02.	(7"/cd-s) *(MORNING 17/15)* **FILM-MAKER. / BEEN TRAINING DOGS**	20	–
	(cd-s+=) *(MORNING 16)* – Safe enough distance away.		
Feb 02.	(cd/d-lp) *(MORNING 18/20) <92034>* **SEE THIS THROUGH AND LEAVE**	27	
	– Did you miss me? / Film-maker / Panzer attack / Who needs enemies? / Amber / Digital observations / Let's kill music / 555-4823 / Been training dogs / The lake / Murder song. *(d-cd-iss. +=; MORNING 19)* – The Devil walks in the sand / Way out west / I'll still write / Panzer attack (live) / Let's kill music (live) / Film-maker (video) / Let's kill music (video) / Been training dogs (live).		
May 02.	(cd-s) *(MORNING 23)* **WHO NEEDS ENEMIES? / BEFORE THE MOOR / ONE QUICK FIX**	22	–
	(cd-s) *(MORNING 24)* – ('A'side) / Lapitu (bedtime story) / Not quite enough.		
	(cd-s) *(MORNING 25)* – ('A'side) / Jesus, you smoke too / ('A'-enhanced video).		
Sep 03.	(7") *(MORNING 32)* **PROMISES PROMISES. / OUR EYES ARE BRIGHT**	19	–
	(cd-s) *(MORNING 30)* – ('A'side) / On off on / I know.		
Sep 03.	(cd/d-lp) *(MORNING 33/34) <59573>* **KICK UP THE FIRE AND LET THE FLAMES BREAK LOOSE**	5	Feb04
	– The same mistakes / Promises promises / New toys / Talking to a brick wall / Into my arms / Blind pilots / A.I.M. / Music box / In your prime / Written apology. *(dvd+=; MORNING 36)* – (videos).		
Nov 03.	(7") *(MORNING 40)* **BLIND PILOTS. / HABIT OF A LIFETIME**	37	–
	(cd-s) *(MORNING 38)* – ('A'side) / Derelict / I want you to think I could be / ('A'-x-rated video).		

Julian COPE

Born: 21 Oct'57, Deri, Caerphilly, Wales, although he was raised in Liverpool, England. His first foray into the music business was with The CRUCIAL THREE, alongside IAN McCULLOCH and PETE WYLIE. During the Autumn of '78, COPE formed The TEARDROP EXPLODES (originally named A SHALLOW MADNESS), with MICK FINKLER and PAUL SIMPSON. In late '78, a deal was inked with local UK indie label, 'Zoo', and after three critically acclaimed singles, they transferred to the major label, 'Mercury,' in July 1980. Keyboard-biased TEARDROP EXPLODES were mostly influenced by 60's pop psychedelia, COPE sounding distinctly like a modern, post-new wave SCOTT WALKER. Their first hit came about via 'WHEN I DREAM', a classic lifted from their classic album, Top 30 'KILIMANJARO' (1980); early in 1981, they cashed-in when 'REWARD' delivered them a Top tenner. 'TREASON', the next 45, didn't emulate this feat, although it still managed a Top 20 placing. Their second album, 'WILDER' (1981), was another commercial success, although it lacked the bite of its predecessor. A few minor hits followed over the next year and a bit, but it was clear JULIAN was gearing up for a solo career. Remaining with 'Mercury' records, he released two albums in 1984, 'WORLD SHUT YOUR MOUTH' and 'FRIED', both receiving a lukewarm response from the music press. On-stage antics such as cutting his stomach (IGGY POP-like) and singing perched on a high pole, saw him develop a weird new character; often he perfomed through his alter-ego (SQWUBBSY a seven foot giant). COPE subsequently signed for 'Island' in 1985, leaving behind the unissued (until 1990) 'SKELLINGTON' LP. Around the same time he suffered a marriage break-up and drug problems, although he re-married in 1986. Re-emerging triumphantly in 1986, he charted with the Top 20 hit 45, 'WORLD SHUT YOUR MOUTH' (curiously enough, the song wasn't included on the 1984 album of the same name). The single was a taster for the following year's comeback album 'SAINT JULIAN', a record which almost gave him his first solo top ten hit. A disappointing pop album, 'MY NATION UNDERGROUND', dealt his street cred a bitter blow and he retreated somewhat with two (meant for mail-order) 1990 albums, the aforementioned 'SKELLINGTON' and 'DROOLIAN'. He returned in fine fashion a year later with the splendid double-set, 'PEGGY SUICIDE', a record that targeted pollution and even the dreadful Tory poll tax (something he protested against vehemently). In 1992, he brought back his old influences (CAN, FAUST, "Kraut-rock") with 'JEHOVAKILL'. Creatively, the album was an admirable effort although it bombed both commercially and critically. This was his last for 'Island', who dropped him unceremoniously after he recorded the 'RITE' CD-album for German release. In 1994, he signed with 'Echo' and returned with three varying albums, 'AUTOGEDDON' (1994), '20 MOTHERS' (1995) and 'INTERPRETER' (1996). With a much needed direction change, COPE opted to form a fresh post-millennium outfit, BLOOD DONOR (along loyal sidekick, THIGHPAULSANDRA). Their album 'LOVE, PEACE & FUCK' (2001), was Krautrock centered around lyrics inspired by Celtic, Viking and Druid folklore. • **Songwriters:** COPE penned except; READ IT IN BOOKS (co-with; Ian McCulloch). He wrote all material, except NON-ALIGNMENT PACT (Pere Ubu) / COPE covered FREE YOUR MIND AND YOUR ASS WILL FOLLOW (Funkadelic) / ARE YOU HUNG UP? (Mothers Of Invention). • **Trivia:** The album DROOLIAN, was released as part of a campaign to free from jail ROKY ERICKSON (ex-13th FLOOR ELEVATORS). In '90, COPE took part in the Anti-Poll tax march from Brixton to Trafalgar Square.

Album rating: Teardrop Explodes: KILIMANJARO (*9) / WILDER (*7) / EVERYBODY WANTS TO SHAG THE TEARDROP EXPLODES posthumous (*7) / PIANO (*6) / THE GREATEST HIT compilation (*7) / Julian Cope:

Album rating: WORLD SHUT YOUR MOUTH (*7) / FRIED (*7) / SAINT JULIAN (*7) / MY NATION UNDERGROUND (*8) / SKELLINGTON (*7) / DROOLIAN (*7) / PEGGY SUICIDE (*8) / JEHOVAHKILL (*5) / AUTOGEDDON (*6) / 20 MOTHERS (*8) / INTERPRETER (*5) / FLOORED GENIUS: THE BEST OF JULIAN COPE & THE TEARDROP EXPLODES 1979-1991 compilation (*8) / FLOORED GENIUS, VOL.2 (1983-91) compilation (*7) / Brain Donor: LOVE, PEACE & FUCK (*6)

TEARDROP EXPLODES

JULIAN COPE – vocals, bass / **PAUL SIMPSON** – keyboards / **MICK FINKLER** – guitar / **GARY DWYER** – drums

Zoo — not iss.

Feb 79. (7"m) *(CAGE 003)* **SLEEPING GAS. / CAMERA CAMERA / KIRBY WORKERS' DREAM FADES** [ ] [–]

— **GERARD QUINN** – keyboards; repl. SIMPSON who formed WILD SWANS

May 79. (7") *(CAGE 005)* **BOUNCING BABIES. / ALL I AM IS LOVING YOU** [ ] [–]

— **DAVID BALFE** – keyboards (ex-LORI & THE CHAMELEONS, ex-BIG IN JAPAN, ex-THOSE NAUGHTY LUMPS) repl. QUINN who joined The WILD SWANS

Mar 80. (7") *(CAGE 008)* **TREASON (IT'S JUST A STORY). / READ IT IN BOOKS** [ ] [–]

— **ALAN GILL** – guitar (ex-DALEK I) repl. FINKLER now (COPE, DWYER, BALFE + GILL)

Mercury — Mercury

Sep 80. (7") *(TEAR 1)* **WHEN I DREAM. / KILIMANJARO** [47] [–]

Oct 80. (lp) *(6359 035) <4016>* **KILIMANJARO** [24] [ ]
– Ha ha I'm drowning / Sleeping gas / Treason (it's just a story) / Second head / Poppies in the field / Went crazy / Brave boys keep their promises / Bouncing babies / Books / Thief of Baghdad / When I dream. *(re-iss. Mar81 lp/c +=; 6359/7150 035)* – Reward. *(re-iss. Jul84 lp/c; PRICE/PRIMC 59) (re-iss. May89 & Jan96 lp/c/cd; 836 897-1/-4/-2) (cd re-mast.Nov00 ++=; 548322-2)* – Kilimanjaro / Strange house in the snow / Use me / Traison / Sleeping gas (live).

(below trumpet by RAY MARTINEZ)

Jan 81. (7") *(TEAR 2)* **REWARD. / STRANGE HOUSE IN THE SNOW** [6] [–]

Apr 81. (7") *(TEAR 3)* **TREASON (IT'S JUST A STORY). / USE ME** [18] [–]
(12"+=) *(TEAR 3-12)* – Traison (c'est juste une histoire).

Jun 81. (7") *(TEAR 4)* **POPPIES IN THE FIELD. / HA HA I'M DROWNING** [ ] [–]
(d7"+=) *(TEAR 44)* – Bouncing babies / Read it in books.

— **TROY TATE** – guitar, vocals (ex-INDEX, ex-SHAKE) repl. GILL

Sep 81. (7") *(TEAR 5)* **PASSIONATE FRIEND. / CHRIST VS. WARHOL** [25] [–]

— on session/gigs **ALFIE ALGIUS** (b. Malta) – bass / **JEFF HAMMER** – keyboards

Nov 81. (lp/c) *(6359/7150 056) <4035>* **WILDER** [29] [ ]
– Bent out of shape / Colours fly away / Seven views of Jerusalem / Pure joy / Falling down around me / The culture bunker / Passionate friend / Tiny children / Like Leila Khaled said / . . .And the fighting takes over / The great dominions. *(re-iss. Jun87 lp/c; PRICE/PRIMC 112) (re-iss. May89 & Jan96 lp/c/cd; 836 896-1/-4/-2) (cd re-mast.Nov00 +=; 548284-2)* – Window shopping for a new crown of thorns / East of the equator / Rachael built a steamboat / You disappear from view / Suffocate / Ouch monkeys / Soft enough for you / The in-psychlopedia.

Nov 81. (7") *(TEAR 6)* **COLOURS FLY AWAY. / WINDOW SHOPPING FOR A NEW CROWN OF THORNS** [54] [–]
(12"+=) *(TEAR 6-12)* – East of the equator.

— **DAVID BALFE** returned

— **RON FRANCOIS** – bass (ex-SINCEROS) repl. guests

Jun 82. (7"/7"g-f) *(TEAR 7/+G)* **TINY CHILDREN. / RACHAEL BUILT A STEAMBOAT** [44] [–]
(12"+=) *(TEAR 7-12)* – Sleeping gas (live).

— now trio of **COPE, DWYER + BALFE** plus session man **FRANCOIS**

— TROY TATE went solo and joined FASHION

Mar 83. (7") *(TEAR 8)* **YOU DISAPPEAR FROM VIEW. / SUFFOCATE** [41] [–]
(d7"+=/12"+=) *(TEAR 88/8-12)* – Soft enough for you / Ouch monkeys / The in-psychlopedia.

— disbanded early '83; BALFE went into producing films and music; JULIAN COPE went solo augmented by DWYER

– compilations, others, etc. –

Jun 85. (7") *Mercury; (TEAR 9)* **REWARD (remix). / TREASON (IT'S JUST A STORY)** [ ] [–]
(12"+=) *(TEAR 9-12)* – Strange house in the snow / Use me.

Jan 90. (7") *Fontana; (DROP 1)* **SERIOUS DANGER. / SLEEPING GAS** [ ] [–]
(12"+=)(c-s+=/cd-s+=) *(DROP 1-12)(DRO MC/CD 1)* – Seven views of Jerusalem.

Mar 90. (cd/c/lp) *Fontana; (842 439-2/-4/-1)* **EVERYBODY WANTS TO SHAG THE TEARDROP EXPLODES** (long lost 3rd album) [72] [–]
– Ouch monkey's / Serious danger / Metranil Vavin / Count to ten and run forever / In-psychlopaedia / Soft enough for you / You disappear from view / The challenger / Not only my friend / Sex / Terrorist / Strange house in the snow.

Apr 90. (7") *Fontana; (DROP 2)* **COUNT TO TEN AND RUN FOR COVER. / REWARD** [ ] [–]
(12"+=)(cd-s+=) *(DROP 2-12)(DROCD 2)* – Poppies / Khaled said.

Nov 90. (cd/c/lp) *Document; (DCD/DMC/DLP 004)* **PIANO** (early material) [ ] [–]
– Sleeping gas / Camera camera / Kirkby workers dream fades / Bouncing babies / All I am is loving you / Treason / Books / Take a chance / When I dream / Kwalo Klobinsky's lullaby.

Dec 93. (cd/lp) *Windsong; (<WIN CD/LP 050>)* **BBC LIVE IN CONCERT (live)** [ ] Jan95 [ ]

Aug 95. (d-cd) *Mercury; (528601-2)* **WILDER / KILIMANJARO** [ ] [–]

Oct 01. (cd) *Mercury; (586391-2)* **THE GREATEST HIT – THE BEST OF THE TEARDROP EXPLODES** [ ] [–]
– Reward / Passionate friend / Treason (it's just a story) / Ha ha I'm drowning / The culture bunker / Colours fly away / Sleeping gas / Suffocate / When I dream / Tiny children / . . .And the fighting takes over / The in-psychlopedia / Christ vs. Warhol / You disappear from view / The great dominions.

Aug 02. (cd) *Spectrum; (544616-2)* **THE COLLECTION** [ ] [–]

JULIAN COPE

JULIAN COPE – vocals, guitar, keyboards / with **GARY DWYER** / **STEVE CREASE + ANDREW EDGE** – drums / **STEPHEN LOWELL** – lead guitar / **RON FRANCOIS** – bass / **KATE ST. JOHN** – oboe

Mercury — not iss.

Nov 83. (7") *(COPE 1)* **SUNSHINE PLAYROOM. / HEY HIGH CLASS BUTCHER** [64] [–]
(12"+=) *(COPE 1-12)* – Wreck my car / Eat the poor.

Feb 84. (lp/c) *(MERL/+C 37)* **WORLD SHUT YOUR MOUTH** [40] [–]
– Bandy's first jump / Metranil Vavin / Strasbourg / An elegant chaos / Quizmaster / Kolly Kibber's birthday / Sunshine playroom / Head hang low / Pussy face / The greatness and perfection of love / Lunatic and fire pistol. *(cd-iss. 1986; 818 365-2)*

Mar 84. (7") *(MER 155)* **THE GREATNESS AND PERFECTION OF LOVE. / 24a VELOCITY CRESCENT** [52] [–]
(12"+=) *(MERX 155)* – Pussyface.

Nov 84. (lp/c) *(MERL/+C 48)* **FRIED** [87] [–]
– Reynard the fox / Bill Drummond said / Laughing boy / Me singing / Sunspots / Me singing / Bloody Assizes / Search party / O king of chaos / Holy love / Torpedo. *(cd-iss. 1986; 822 832-2) (cd re-iss. Sep98 +=; 532370-2)* – I went on a chourney / Mik mak mok / Land of fear.

Feb 85. (7") *(MER 182)* **SUNSPOTS. / I WENT ON A CHOURNEY** [ ] [–]
(d7"+=) *(MER 182-2)* – Mik mak mok / Land of fear.

— **COPE** recruited Americans **DONALD ROSS SKINNER** – guitar / **JAMES ELLER** – bass / **DOUBLE DE HARRISON** – keyboards / **CHRIS WHITTEN** – drums

Island — Island

Sep 86. (7") *(IS 290) <99479>* **WORLD SHUT YOUR MOUTH. / UMPTEENTH UNNATURAL BLUES** [19] Feb87 [84]
(d7"+=) *(ISB 290)* – ('A'-Trouble Funk remix) / Transportation.

(c-s+=) *(CIS 290)* – I've got levitation / Non-alignment pact.
(12"++=) *(12IS 290)* – (all extra above).

Jan 87. (7") *(IS 305)* **TRAMPOLENE. / DISASTER** [ ] [–]
(7"ep+=/12"ep+=) *(ISW/12IS 305)* – Mock Turtle / Warwick the kingmaker.

Feb 87. (m-lp) <90560> **JULIAN COPE** [–] [ ]
– World shut your mouth / Transportation / Umpteenth unnatural blues / Non-alignment pact / I've got levitation.

Mar 87. (lp/c/cd) *(ILPS/ICT/CID 9861)* <90571> **SAINT JULIAN** [11] [ ]
– Trampolene / Shot down / Eve's volcano (covered in sin) / Spacehopper / Planet ride / Trampolene / World shut your mouth / Saint Julian / Pulsar NX / Space hopper / Screaming secrets / A crack in the clouds. *(re-iss. Aug91 cd)(c; IMCD 137)(ICM 2023)*

Apr 87. (7") *(IS 318)* **EVE'S VOLCANO (COVERED IN SIN). / ALMOST BEAUTIFUL CHILD** [ ] [–]
(12"+=) *(12IS 318)* – Pulsar NX (live) / Shot down (live).
(12"+=) *(12ISX 318)* – Spacehopper – Annexe / ('B'side; pt.II).
(cd-s++=) *(CID 318)* – (all 3 extra above).

—— **DAVE PALMER** – drums (studio) / **MIKE JOYCE** – drums (tour) repl. WHITTEN / added **RON FAIR** – keyboards / **ROOSTER COSBY** – percussion, some drums

Sep 88. (7") *(IS 380)* **CHARLOTTE ANNE. / CHRISTMAS MOURNING** [35] [–]
(12"+=/12"pic-d+=/pic-cd-s+=) *(12IS/12ISP/CIDP 380)* – Books / A question of temptation.

Oct 88. (lp/c/cd) *(ILPS/ICT/CID 9918)* <91025> **MY NATION UNDERGROUND** [42] [ ]
– 5 o'clock world / Vegetation / Charlotte Anne / My nation underground / China doll / Someone like me / Easter everywhere / I'm not losing sleep / The great white hoax. *(re-iss. Aug91 cd)(c; IMCD 138)(ICM 9918)*

Nov 88. (7") *(IS 399)* **5 O'CLOCK WORLD. / S.P.Q.R.** [42] [–]
(10"+=/12"+=/pic-cd-s+=) *(10IS/12IS/CIDP 399)* – Reynard in Tokyo (extended live).

Jun 89. (7") *(IS 406)* **CHINA DOLL. / CRAZY FARM ANIMAL** [53] [–]
(10"+=/10"pic-d+=/12"+=) *(10IS/10ISP/12IS 406)* – Desi.
(cd-s++=) *(CID 406)* – Rail on.

—— **COPE** retained **SKINNER & COSBY** plus **J.D. HASSINGER** – drums / **TIM** – keyboards / **BRAN** – bass (both of Guernsey)

Jan 91. (7"/c-s) *(IS/CIS 483)* **BEAUTIFUL LOVE. / PORT OF SAINTS** [32] [–]
(12"+=/cd-s+=) *(12IS/CID 483)* – Love L.U.V. / Unisex cathedral.
(12"pink+=) *(12ISX 483)* – Love L.U.V. / Dragonfly.

Mar 91. (cd/c/d-lp) *(CID/ICT/ILPSD 9977)* <848338-2/-4> **PEGGY SUICIDE** [23] [ ]
– Pristeen / Double vegetation / East easy rider / Promised land / Hanging out & hung up on the line / Safesurfer / If you loved me at all / Drive, she said / Soldier blue / You . . . / Not raving but drowning / Head / Leperskin / Beautiful love / Uptight / Western Front 1992 CE / Hung up & hanging out to dry / The American Lite / Las Vegas basement. *(cd re-iss. Aug94 & Apr02; IMCD 188)*

Apr 91. (7"/c-s) *(IS/CIS 492)* **EAST EASY RIDER. / BUTTERFLY E** [51] [–]
(12"+=/cd-s+=) *(12IS/CID 492)* – Almost live / Little donkey.
(12"pic-d+=) *(12ISX 492)* – Easty Risin' / Ravebury stones.

Jul 91. (7"/c-s) *(IS/CIS 497)* **HEAD. / BAGGED – OUT KEN** [57] [–]
(12"+=/cd-s+=) *(12IS/CID 497)* – Straw dogs / Animals at all.

Oct 92. (7"/c-s) *(IS/CIS 545)* **FEAR LOVES THE SPACE. / SIZEWELL B.** [42] [–]
(12"pic-d+=) *(12ISX 545)* – I have always been here before / Gogmagog.

Oct 92. (cd/c/d-lp) *(<514052-2/-4/-1>)* **JEHOVAHKILL** [20] Dec92 [ ]
– Soul desert / No harder shoulder to cry on / Akhenaten / The mystery trend / Upwards at 45° / Cut my friends down / Necropolis / Slow rider / Gimme back my flag / Poet is priest / Julian H Cope / The subtle energies commission / Fa-fa-fa-fine / Fear loves this place / Peggy Suicide is missing. *(cd re-iss. Aug94; IMCD 189)*

—— Next was last in the 90's album trilogy about pollution. Its theme this time was the car, (coincidentally he had just passed his driving test). It featured usual musicians.

Echo — American

Jul 94. (cd/c/lp) *(ECH CD/MC/LP 001)* <45705> **AUTOGEDDON** [16] Aug94 [ ]
– Autogeddon blues / Madmax / Don't call me Mark Chapman / I gotta walk / Ain't no gettin' round gettin' round / Paranormal in the West Country (medley): i) Paranormal pt.1, ii) Archdrude's roadtrip. iii) Kar-ma-kanik / Ain't but the one way / S.t.a.r.c.a.r. *(cd re-iss. Mar99; same)*

Aug 95. (7"yellow/c-s) *(ECS/+MC 11)* **TRY TRY TRY. / WESSEXY** [24] [–]
(cd-s+=) *(ECSCD 11)* – Baby, let's play vet / Don't jump me, mother.

Aug 95. (cd/c/d-lp) *(ECH CD/MC/LP 005)* **20 MOTHERS** [20] [–]
– Wheelbarrow man / I wandered lonely as a child / Try try try / Stone circles 'n' you / Queen – Mother / I'm your daddy / Highway to the sun / 1995 / By the light of the Silbury moon / Adam and Eve hit the road / Just like Pooh Bear / Girl-call / Greedhead detector / Don't take roots / Senile get / The lonely guy / Cryingbabiessleeplessnights / Leli B. / Road of dreams / When I walk through the land of fear.

Echo — Cooking Vinyl

Jul 96. (7"white-ep/cd-ep) *(ECS/+CDX 022)* **I COME FROM ANOTHER PLANET, BABY. / HOW DO I UNDERSTAND MY MOTORMAN? / IF I COULD DO IT ALL OVER AGAIN, I'D DO IT OVER YOU** [34] [–]
(cd-s) *(ECSCD 022)* – Ambulance: Weesex post-ambient therapy.

Sep 96. (7"white) *(ECS 025)* **PLANETARY SIT-IN. / CUMMER IN SUMMERTIME / TORCH** [34] [–]
(cd-s) *(ECSCX 025)* – ('A'-Radio sit-in mixes).

Oct 96. (cd/c/lp) *(ECH CD/MC/LP 12)* <9007> **INTERPRETER** [39] Feb97 [ ]
– I come from another planet, baby / I've got my TV and my pills / Planetary sit-in / Since I lost my head, it's awl-right / Cheap new age fix / Battle for the trees / Arthur / Spacerock with me / Re-directed male / Maid of constant sorrow / Loveboat / Dust.

—— look out for 'DISCOVER ODIN: JULIAN COPE AT THE BRITISH MUSEUM' a partly spoken-word CD on 'Head Heritage' released in US 2001

BRAIN DONOR

—— aka **JULIAN COPE** with **THIGHPAULSANDRA** – synths

Impresario — not iss.

Apr 01. (7"/cd-s) *(IMP/+CD 007)* **SHE SAW ME COMING. / SHAMAN UFO** [ ] [–]

Jul 01. (7"/cd-s) *(IMP/+CD 009)* **GET OFF YOUR PRETTY FACE. / WHO WILL ENTERTAIN YOUR MORON** [ ] [–]

Sep 01. (cd/lp) *IMPODD CD/LP 001)* **LOVE, PEACE & FUCK** [ ] [–]
– She saw me coming / Get off your pretty face / Pagan dawn / Odin's gift to his mother (theme from speed kills) / Hairy music / U-know! – You take the credit / Laghnasad / She's gotta have it. *(lp re-iss. Jul02; same)*

– (COPE) compilations, others, etc. –

Feb 85. (7"; as RABBI JOSEPH GORDON) *Bam Caruso; (NRICO 30)* **COMPETITION. / BELIEF IN HIM** [ ] [–]

May 90. (cd/lp) *Copeco-Zippo; (JUCD/JULP 89)* **SKELLINGTON** (1985 lost lp) [ ] [–]
– Doomed / Beaver / Me & Jimmy Jones / Robert Mitchum / Out of my mind on dope and speed / Don't crash here / Everything playing at once / Little donkey / Great white wonder / Incredibly ugly girl / No how, no why, no way, no where, no when / Comin' soon.

Jul 90. (cd/lp) *Mofo-Zippo; (MOFOCO CD/LP 90)* **DROOLIAN** [ ] [–]

Jul 92. (c-s/7") *Island; (C+/IS 534)* **WORLD SHUT YOUR MOUTH (remix). / DOOMED** [44] [–]
(12"+=/cd-s+=) *(12/CD IS 534)* – Reynard the fox / The elevators / Levitation.

Aug 92. (cd/c/d-lp) *Island; (CID/ICT/ILPSD 8000)* <512788> **FLOORED GENIUS – THE BEST OF JULIAN COPE AND THE TEARDROP EXPLODES 1981-1991** [22] Oct92 [ ]
– Reward / Treason / Sleeping gas / Bouncing babies / Passionate friend / The great dominions (; all TEARDROP EXPLODES) / The greatness & perfection of love / An elegant chaos / Sunspots / Reynard the fox / World shut your mouth / Trampolene / Spacehopper / Charlotte Anne / China doll / Out of my mind on dope & speed / Jellypop perky Jean / Beautiful love / East easy rider / Safesurfer.

Nov 92. (d-cd) *Island; (ITSCD 11)* **SAINT JULIAN / MY NATION UNDERGROUND** [ ] [–]

Nov 93. (cd/lp) *Nighttracks; (CD/LP NT 003) / Dutch East India; <DEI 8124>* **BEST OF THE BBC SESSIONS 1983-91 (FLOORED GENIUS VOL.2)** [ ] Feb94 [ ]
– The greatness and perfection of love / Head hang low / Hey, hey high class butcher / Sunspots / Me singing / Hobby / 24a Velocity Crescent / Laughing boy / O king of chaos / Reynard the fox / Pulsar / Crazy farm animal / Christmas mourning / Planet rider: transmitting / Soul medley: Free your mind and your ass will follow – Are you hung up? / You think it's love / Double vegetation. *(cd re-iss. May98 on 'Strange Fruit'; SFRSCD 61)*

Jun 97. (cd) *Island; (IMCD 251)* **THE FOLLOWERS OF SAINT JULIAN** [ ] [–]

Feb 99. (cd) *Island; (IMCD 260)* <524636> **LEPER SKIN (AN INTRODUCTION TO JULIAN COPE)** [ ] May99 [ ]
– Shot down / World shut your mouth / Trampolene / Planet ride / Transporting / Books / Charlotte Anne / Crazy farm animal / Hanging out and hung up on the line / Soul desert / The mystery trend / Pristeen / Double vegetation / Upwards at 45 degrees / Safesurfer.
Sep 01. (cd) *Spectrum; (544586-2)* **THE COLLECTION** [ ] [–]

CORAL

Formed: Hoylake, Wirral, England ... 1996 by neighbourhood friends JAMES SKELLY, IAN SKELLY, PAUL DUFFY, LEE SOUTHALL, BILL RYDER-JONES and finally NICK POWER on organ. Picking up where The LA'S left off, fellow scousers, The CORAL unleashed their Mersey-flavoured debut single 'SHADOWS FALL' in 2001 and were, instantly, hailed by NME as the best new band in England. 'THE OLDEST PATH' EP was released in the same year, as hype surrounding the band began to reach fever pitch. The momentum was carried into 2002 which saw the release of the 'SKELETON KEY' EP and also their self-titled UK Top 5 debut album. A joyous, neo-psychedelic record, the eponymous 'THE CORAL', established the group as natural successors to the long line of great Liverpudlian bands and, no, that does not include SPACE. Exactly a year on, summer 2003 produced yet another fantastic set of songs via their sophomore set, 'MAGIC AND MEDICINE'. Featuring major UK hits, 'DON'T THINK YOU'RE THE FIRST' and 'PASS IT ON', the sextet came of age, recreating a feel for the past (LOVE, The LA's, etc.) while still having twelve feet firmly set in the present/future.

Album rating: THE CORAL (*8) / MAGIC AND MEDICINE (*8)

JAMES SKELLY – vocals, guitar / **LEE SOUTHALL** – guitar, vocals / **NICK POWER** – organ / **BILL RYDER-JONES** – guitar, trumpet / **PAUL DUFFY** – bass, saxophone / **IAN SKELLY** – drums

Deltasonic not iss.

Jul 01. (cd-ep) *(DLTCD 1)* **SHADOWS FALL EP** [ ] [–]
– Shadows fall / The ballad of Simon Diamond / A sparrow's song.
Dec 01. (cd-ep) *(DLTCD 3)* **THE OLDEST PATH EP** [ ] [–]
– The oldest path / God knows / Short balled / Flys.

Deltasonic Sony

Apr 02. (cd-ep) *(672522-2)* <87023> **SKELETON KEY EP** [ ] [ ]
– Skeleton key / Dressed like a cow / Darkness / Sheriff John Brown / Skeleton key (video). *<US-only+=>* – The oldest path.
Jul 02. (7"m) *(DLT 005)* **GOODBYE. / GOOD FORTUNE / TRAVELLING CIRCUS** [21] [–]
(cd-s+=) *(DLTCD 005)* – ('A'-CD rom).
(cd-s) *(DLTCD2 005)* – ('A'side) / Dressed like a cow (live) / Goodbye (live) / The Coral mini movie (video).
Jul 02. (cd/lp) *(DLT CD/LP 006)* <508478> **THE CORAL** [5] Feb03 [ ]
– Spanish man / I remember when / Shadows fall / Dreaming of you / Simon Diamond / Goodbye / Waiting for the heartaches / Skeleton key / Wildfire / Badman / Calenders and clocks. *(lp+=)* – Simian technology. *(hidden cd track+=)* – Time travel.
Oct 02. (7"m) *(DLT 008)* **DREAMING OF YOU. / ANSWER ME / FOLLOW THE SUN** [13] [–]
(cd-s+=) *(DLTCD 008)* – ('A'-video).
(cd-s) *(DLTCD2 008)* – ('A'side) / Sweet Sue / Another turn in the lock / ('A'-acoustic video version).
Mar 03. (7") *(DLT 010)* **DON'T THINK YOU'RE THE FIRST. / SEE THROUGH BERGERAC** [10] [–]
(cd-s+=) *(DLTCDC 010)* – Witchcraft / ('A'-video).
(cd-s) *(DLTCDC2 010)* – ('A'side) / Tiger lily / Teenage machine age.
Jul 03. (7") *(DLT 013)* **PASS IT ON. / SHADOWS FALL (acoustic)** [5] [–]
(cd-s+=) *(DLTCD 013)* – Run run.
Jul 03. (cd/lp) *(DLT CD/LP 014)* <512560> **MAGIC AND MEDICINE** [5] Sep03 [ ]
– In the forest / Don't think you're the first / Liezah / Talkin' gypsy market blues / Secret kiss / Milkwood blues / Bill McCai / Eskimo lament / Careless hands / Pass it on / All of our love / Confessions of A.D.D.D.
Oct 03. (7") *(DLT 015)* **SECRET KISS. / GOD KNOWS (new mix)** [25] [–]
(cd-s+=) *(DLTCD2 015)* – Not the girl.
(cd-s) *(DLTCD 015)* – ('A'side) / Who's that knockin' / See my love / ('A'video).
Nov 03. (7"pic-d) *(DLT 017)* **BILL McCAI. / BOY AT THE WINDOW** [23] [–]
(cd-s+=) *(DLTCD 017)* – Nosferatu / ('A'-video).
(cd-s) *(DLTCD2 017)* – ('A'side) / When good times go bad / From a leaf to a tree.

□ Chris CORNELL (see under ⇒ SOUNDGARDEN)

CORNERSHOP

Formed: Preston, England ... 1987, evolving from GENERAL HAVOC by Asian songwriting brothers, TJINDER and AVTAR SINGH. They first came to attention of the music press late in 1992, when they publicly derided MORRISSEY for his alleged racist leanings. Already signed to the up and coming 'Wiiija' label, they delivered their debut EP, 'IN THE DAYS OF FORD CORTINA', in a blaze of publicity. Described as JESUS & MARY CHAIN with sitars, the unconventional Sikh/white thrash fusion was entertaining if hardly professional. Inevitably the initial press hype soon backfired on them, although they struggled on through a clutch of patchy albums including 'HOLD ON IT HURTS' (1994) and 'WOMAN'S GOTTA HAVE IT' (1995). Major alterations were subsequently carried out on the 'SHOP, after which TJINDER re-opened for business in 1997 with the sonic nirvana of 'WHEN I WAS BORN FOR THE 7th TIME'. A surprise Top 40 success, well worthy of merit with its consummate blend of hip hop, Indian folk, country and indie funk, the album spawned the classic 'BRIMFUL OF ASHA' (a ltd-edition original release, it went on to hit the top of the charts in early '98). The record also featured a suitably exotic version of the Beatles' 'NORWEGIAN WOOD (THIS BIRD HAS FLOWN)', while 'CANDYMAN' took elements from LARRY CORYELL's 'The Opening'. CORNERSHOP subsequently toured the States and Europe for almost a year after the album's release. Mentally and physically exhausted, the irate TJINDER SINGH and his equally worn associate BEN AYRES hibernated in a South London studio, preparing their off-shoot band CLINTON's debut album (following a back-catalogue of three 12" singles over four years). Released on their own 'Meccico' imprint (through 'Hut'), 'DISCO AND THE HALFWAY TO DISCONTENT' (1999), didn't exactly sound like the kind of record that was made by two men who were on the verge of musical breakdown. Opening track, 'PEOPLE POWER IN THE DISCO HOUR', made the speakers pound like a nomadic tribesman beating from the inside. Other tracks dabbled in sitar techniques, that for once, didn't sound like some mystical KULA SHAKER thing! The theme of disco ran throughout the set, occasionally taking inspiration from their dub reggae peers, proving that CLINTON had, most definitely, danced those blues away! CORNERSHOP returned in glorious style in 2002, courtesy of album 'HANDCREAM FOR A GENERATION'. The set featured the single 'LESSONS LEARNED FROM ROCKY 1 TO ROCKY 3', a brilliantly funky, fuzz disco tune which reinstated the band's status and had the fans all dancing at the same time. Although the set wasn't just a loose collection of modern disco-rock, it also delved deeply into psychedelia and even, sometimes, Brit pop (OASIS bassist PAUL McGUIGAN made a feted appearance).

While managing to meld styles from Eastern and Western music, CORNERSHOP also played with the formula which made 'BRIMFUL . . .' so special in the first place; catchy choruses and even catchier instrumental hooks.

Album rating: HOLD ON IT HURTS (*5) / WOMAN'S GOTTA HAVE IT (*5) / WHEN I WAS BORN FOR THE 7th TIME (*9) / HANDCREAM FOR A GENERATION (*7) / Clinton: DISCO AND THE HALFWAY TO DISCONTENT (*8)

TJINDER SINGH (b. 8 Feb'68, New Cross, Wolverhampton, England) – guitar / **AVTAR SINGH** (b.11 May'65, Punjab, India) – bass, vocals / **DAVID CHAMBERS** (b.1969, Lincoln, England) – drums / **ANTHONY SAFFERY** – sitar / **NEIL MILNER** – tapes

Chapati Heat — not iss.

Dec 91. (7"ep; as the GENERAL HAVOC) *(BIRD 1)* **FAST JASPAL EP** ☐ –
– Moonshine / Vacuum cleaner / Another cup of tea, Arch Deacon?

— **BEN AYRES** (b. BENEDICT, 30 Apr'68, St John's, Canada) – guitar, vocals; repl. ANTHONY + NEIL

Wiiija — Merge

Jan 93. (7"ep; some colrd) *(WIJ 019V)* **IN THE DAYS OF FORD CORTINA EP** ☐ –
– Waterlogged / Moonshine / Kawasaki (more heat than chapati) / Hanif Kureishi scene.

Apr 93. (10"ep) *(WIJ 22V)* **LOCK STOCK & DOUBLE-BARREL** ☐ –
– England's dreaming / Trip easy / Summer fun in a beat up Datsun / Breaking every rule language English.
(cd-ep+=) *(WIJ 22CD)* – (hidden track).

Jul 93. (m-cd) *(WAKEUP 001)* **ELVIS SEX-CHANGE** ☐ –
– (above 2 EP's)

Jan 94. (7"ep/cd-ep) *(WIJ 29 V/CD)* **READERS' WIVES EP** ☐ –
– Readers' wives / Inside Rani (short version) / Tandoori chicken.

Jan 94. (cd/c/lp) *(WIJ 030 CD/C/V)* <MRG 74> **HOLD ON IT HURTS** ☐ Jan95 ☐
– Jason Donovan – Tessa Sanderson / Kalluri's radio / Readers' wives / Change / Inside Rani (long version) / Born disco; died heavy metal / Counteraction / Where d'u get your information / Tera mera pyar / You always said my language would get me into trouble. *(lp w/ free 7")* – BORN DISCO; DIED HEAVY METAL (disco mix). / ENGLAND'S DREAMING

Mar 94. (7"ep/cd-ep) *(WIJ 033 V/CD)* **BORN DISCO; DIED HEAVY METAL. / THE SAFETY OF OBJECTS / REHOUSED** ☐ –

Apr 94. (7") *(XPI 24)* **SEETAR MAN. / (track by Blood Sausage)** ☐ –
(above issued on 'Clawfist')

— CHAMBERS departed before below album

Wiiija — Luaka Bop – Warners

Apr 95. (7"etched) *(LTD 004)* **6 A.M. JULLANDAR SHERE** ☐ –

May 95. (cd/lp) *(WIJ 045 CD/V)* <46018> **WOMAN'S GOTTA HAVE IT** ☐ ☐
– 6 a.m. Jullandar shere / Hong Kong book of Kung Fu / Roof rack / My dancing days are done / Call all destroyer / Camp orange / Never leave yourself (vocal overload mix) / Jamsimran king / Wog / Looking for a way in / 7.20 a.m. Jullander shere.

Aug 95. (7") *(CIP 101)* **MY DANCING DAYS ARE DONE. / Prohibition: I AM NOT A FISH** – French –
(above issued on French label, 'Bruit Distordu')

Feb 96. (12"ep/cd-ep) *(WIJ 048 V/CD)* **6 A.M. JULLANDAR SHERE: The Grid & Star Liner mixes** ☐ –
– (Jeh Jeh mix) / (All Fetters Loose mix) / (original).

— AVTAR departed around 1995/96, leaving **TJINDER + BEN** to recruit **PETER BENGRY** – percussion / **ANTHONY SAFFREY** – sitar, harmonium, keyboards (returned) / **NICK SIMMS** – drums, tambourine

Jun 96. (12"ep) *(WIJ 049V)* <43648> **W.O.G. – THE U.S. WESTERN ORIENTAL MIXES** ☐ ☐
– (original) / (Freaky's) / (Witchman's Assimilation) / Freaky's Acid DJ) / (Witchman's extended beats).

Dec 96. (12"etched) *(ROOT 011)* **BUTTER THE SOUL** ☐ –
(above released on 'Art Bus')

Jun 97. (7") *(WIJ 70)* **GOOD SHIPS. / FUNKY DAYS ARE BACK AGAIN** ☐ –
(12"+=/cd-s+=) *(WIJ 70 T/CD)* – ('A'-Intro – instrumental / 'B'extended beats mix).

Aug 97. (7") *(WIJ 75)* **BRIMFUL OF ASHA. / EASY WINNERS (part 1)** 60 –
(cd-s+=) *(WIJ 75CD)* – Rehoused / ('A'-Sofa Surfers mix).
(cd-s) *(WIJ 75CDX)* – ('A'side) / Easy winners (part 2) / Counteraction / ('A'-Mucho Macho mix).
(12") *(WIJ 75T)* – ('A'side) / It's Indian tobacco my friend.

Sep 97. (cd/c/d-lp) *(WIJ CD/MC/LP 1065)* <46576> **WHEN I WAS BORN FOR THE 7th TIME** 17 ☐
– Sleep on the left side / Brimful of Asha / Butter the soul / Chocolat / We're in yr corner / Funky days are back again / What is happening? / When the light appears boy / Coming up / Good shit / Good to be on the road back home again / It's Indian tobacco my friend / Candyman / State troopers / Norwegian wood (this bird has flown).

Nov 97. (12"etched) *(ROOT 014T)* **BRIMFUL OF ASHA (Norman Cook remix)** ☐ –

Feb 98. (7"/c-s) *(WIJ 81/+MC)* **BRIMFUL OF ASHA. / ('A'-Norman Cook remix)** 1 ☐
(12"+=) *(ROOT 014T)* – ('A'-Norman Cook extended).
(cd-s++=) *(WIJ 81CD)* – U47S.

May 98. (c-s) *(WIJ 80C)* <44524> **SLEEP ON THE LEFT SIDE / ('A'-Les Rhythms Digitales mix)** 23 ☐
(12"+=/cd-s+=) *(WIJ 80 T/CD)* – ('A'-Ashley Beadle mix) / ('A'-Ashley Beadle extended).

Nov 98. (12"ltd) *(WIJ 093T)* **CANDYMAN (mixes; Rob Swift vocal & instrumental / Schizoid Man / Uptight Vienna)** ☐ –

— added **PAUL McGUIGAN** – bass (ex-OASIS)

Wiiija — V2

Feb 02. (12") *(ROOT 22)* **LESSONS LEARNED FROM ROCKY I TO ROCKY III** ☐ –
(12") *(ROOT 23)* – ('A'mixes).

Mar 02. (7") *(WIJ 129)* <27741> **LESSONS LEARNED FROM ROCKY I TO ROCKY III. / RETURNING FROM THE WRECKAGE** 37 May02 ☐
(cd-s+=) *(WIJ 129CD)* – ('A'-Osymyso mix).
(cd-s) *(WIJ 129CD2)* – ('A'-mixes; Cowcube / Midfield General instrumental / DEtroit Grand Pubahs).

Apr 02. (cd/lp) *(WIJ CD/LP 1115)* <27126> **HANDCREAM FOR A GENERATION** 30 ☐
– Heavy soup (with OTIS CLAY) / Staging the plaguing of the raised platform / Music plus 1 / Lessons learned from Rocky I to Rocky III / Wogs will walk / Motion the 11 / People power / Sounds super recordings / The London radar / Spectral mornings (with NOEL GALLAGHER) / Slip the drummer one / Heavy soup (outro).

Aug 02. (7") *(WIJ 130)* **STAGING. / GREEN P'S** ☐ –
(cd-s+=) *(WIJ 130CD)* – Lessons learned from Rocky I to Rocky III (video).
(cd-s) *(WIJ 130CD2)* – ('A'-Super Jaws mix) / Straight aces / Motion the 11 (Guigsy's mix).

CLINTON

— alter-ego of **TJINDER + BEN**

Wiiija — not iss.

Dec 94. (etched-12") *(JJAR 001)* **JAM JAR (Marv Johnson mix) / EVERYBODY KNOWS THAT THE MOST IMPORTANT PEOPLE SPEAK FIRST** ☐ –

Sep 95. (etched-12") *(ROOT 010)* **SUPERLOOSE! (Bobby Austin mix) / FINANCIAL HEADACHE** ☐ –

Apr 97. (12") *(ROOT 012)* **SUPERLOOSE! (Automator Hot Vox mix). / SUPERLOOSE! (Automator instrumental)** ☐ –

Mar 99. (7") *(ROOT 013)* **DAVID D. CHAMBERS. / INSTRUMENTAL / VOCAL** ☐ –

Hut — Astralwerks

Aug 99. (12"/cd-s) *(HUT T/CD 116)* **BUTTONED DOWN DISCO. / ('A'-Scratch perverts boil in the bag mix) / ('A'-Fila Brazillia disco frisco mix)** ☐ –

Sep 99. (cd/c/lp) *(CDHUT/HUTMC/HUTLP 56)* <ASW 48792-2> **DISCO AND THE HALFWAY TO DISCONTENT** ☐ Feb00 ☐
– People power in the disco hour / Saturday night and dancing / Buttoned down disco / Hip-hop bricks / Electric ice cream (Miami jammies) / G.T. road / Hot for May sound / Sing hosana / Mr. President / Giddian di rani / Before the fizz is gone / Welcome to Tokyo Otis Clay. <US+=> – David D. Chambers / Fila Brazillia disco Frisco mix.

Apr 00. (12"/cd-s) *(HUT T/CD 125)* <38700> **PEOPLE POWER IN THE DISCO (mixes; Wiseguys / Los Amigos Invisibles / Romanthony)** ☐ Feb00 ☐

Elvis COSTELLO

Born: DECLAN McMANUS, 25 Aug'55, Liverpool, England. The son of a jazz bandleader, he grew up listening to the sounds of the day; the BEATLES (he was a member of their fanclub), the KINKS, the WHO and the sounds of Motown were all to instil in him a love of rock'n'roll and help shape his own musical style. Dividing his time between playing clubs at night and working as a computer operator during working hours (the strain on his eyes leading to the wearing of his now trademark glasses), he subsequently moved to London in 1974 to become frontman and songwriter for a country-rock group called Flip City. Flogging his demos far and wide, the newly formed 'Stiff' label duly took on his talent, McMANUS changing his name to ELVIS COSTELLO; 'Elvis', a challenge to the rock establishment, and 'Costello', his mother's maiden name. While at Stiff he met his long time collaborators NICK LOWE and Jake Rivera, who would in turn become producer and manager to COSTELLO. His first album was recorded in 24 hours, backed by CLOVER, a country and western bar band with a certain HUEY LEWIS at the helm (although he did not participate in the sessions). After little success with the first two singles, 'ALISON' and 'LESS THAN ZERO', the man resorted to playing outside a CBS Records international convention taking place at the Hilton in London. Although arrested, the stunt worked, and in '77 his first album, 'MY AIM IS TRUE' was released by 'Columbia' (US), stand out tracks including the aforementioned singles and 'WATCHING THE DETECTIVES'. Produced by LOWE, the record was hailed as one of the finest debuts in rock history, blending the Stiff sound of punk and new wave with COSTELLO's cynical observations on life. Voted Album of the Year in Rolling Stone's annual poll, COSTELLO toured the States with his newly assembled backing band, The ATTRACTIONS. America got its first taste of COSTELLO's independent stance when his appearance on Saturday Night Live turned into a scathing attack on the media. His next two albums, 'THIS YEARS MODEL' and 'ARMED FORCES' (originally titled Emotional Fascism) were to prove an artistic peak, as well as being commercially successful, the latter charting in the Top 10. Released in 1980, 'GET HAPPY' abandoned the new wave sound for a more 60's Motown approach. With 20 songs on the original LP (and 10 more on the CD reissue), it proved COSTELLO was in prime songwriting mode, the record swiftly followed by his fifth set, 'TRUST' (1981), sounding as captivating and twisted as its predecessor was fast and loose. In between these two sets was the Nashville covers album, 'ALMOST BLUE' more a curiosity than a stand out success. 'IMPERIAL BEDROOM', released in '82, is often cited as COSTELLO's best album, and was produced by the Beatles engineer, Geoff Emerick (who would later go on to produce the '96 effort 'ALL THIS USELESS BEAUTY'). Not surprisingly then, it was compared to the masterpieces of the BEATLES and the BEACH BOYS, and included such fan favourites as 'MAN OUT OF TIME' and 'THE LONG HONEYMOON'. 'PUNCH THE CLOCK', released in '83, and featuring CHET BAKER on the track 'SHIPBUILDING', was less ambitious than the previous album, while 'GOODBYE CRUEL WORLD', released the following year, was his worst record by some margin, starting out as an attempt at folk-rock, but ending up as an example of the '80s sound gone wrong. By this time, a split had developed between COSTELLO and the ATTRACTIONS, and 'KING OF AMERICA' was the penultimate album recorded with this combination until 'BRUTAL YOUTH' in '94. With backing from The CONFEDERATES and co-production by T-BONE BURNETT, it featured a mixture of country and folk with a fair splattering of rockabilly with varied success. 'BLOOD & CHOCOLATE' (1986) was notable both for the return of NICK LOWE as producer and the man's split from the ATTRACTIONS. With LOWE at the helm, the record was far removed from his '84 effort, featuring a nastier, meatier version of 'THIS YEARS MODEL' plus 'POISONED ROSE', the latter track boasting the bass playing of the legendary jazz bassist RAY BROWN. Subsequently signing to 'Warner Brothers', his first release was the darkly comic and commercially successful 'SPIKE' (1989), its considerable sales due largely to the hit single, 'VERONICA', although it also featured songs of genuine outrage such as 'TRAMP THE DIRT DOWN' and 'LET HIM DANGLE'. The next few years saw COSTELLO become more adventurous in an attempt to break away from the past, symbolised by a change of image. 'MIGHTY LIKE A ROSE' remains arguably his most underrated album, while the follow up, 'THE JULIET LETTERS' (featuring The Brodsky Quartet), mixed pop with chamber music to commercial failure but critical praise. 'BRUTAL YOUTH' in '94 saw the reunion of COSTELLO and the ATTRACTIONS (dubbed the Distractions) and included one of the most beautiful recordings of his career in 'ROCKING HORSE ROAD', while the follow up, 'ALL THIS USELESS BEAUTY', was the ATTRACTIONS' swansong and inexplicably a commercial failure. Collaborations outside of his albums for 'Columbia' and 'Warners' are numerous, COSTELLO winning a BAFTA with RICHARD HARVEY for the soundtrack to 'G.B.H.' and also contributing the track, 'MY MOOD SWINGS' to the Cohen Brothers film, 'The Big Lebowski'. Perhaps the most intriguing partnership never to see the light of day, save for three releases as obscure B-Sides, was his collaboration with country legend, GEORGE JONES, singing 'non-country' songs such as Hoagy Carmichael's 'MY RESISTANCE IS LOW' and Bruce Springsteen's 'BRILLIANT SURPRISE'. A collaboration was released at the back end of '98 featuring an album's worth of COSTELLO and BURT BACHARACH material, 'PAINTED FROM MEMORY', together again after the magnificent 'God Give Me Strength' (which was originally recorded on the 'Grace Of My Heart' soundtrack). A subsequent tribute album of COSTELLO's songs by the likes of JOHNNY CASH, JUNE TABOR, NICK LOWE and ROBERT WYATT demonstrated both the man's musical versatility and the songwriting skills which have made him such an integral part of the last 25 years of popular music. Solo once again, ELVIS COSTELLO was back in chart land courtesy of stripped-down, bare-bones set, 'WHEN I WAS CRUEL' (2002). Possibly short of production techniques, once provided by Mitchell Froom or Marc Ribot, the record still managed to encompass all of ELVIS's songwriting craft. It was exactly that craft which COSTELLO strived to chisel and refine with 'NORTH' (2003), yet another career diversion in which the restless songwriter looked once again to the fields of classical, easy listening and jazz for his inspiration (he had recently found a new love in jazz singer DIANA KRALL having split with CAIT O'RIORDON after 16 years of marriage). The result was a hushed set of elegant balladry and restrained, sophisticated pop, perhaps the most "adult"-sounding set of songs he's yet come up with. • **Songwriters:** All penned by COSTELLO, bar NEAT NEAT NEAT (Damned) / I CAN'T STAND UP FOR FALLING DOWN (Sam & Dave) / SWEET DREAMS (Patsy Cline) / A GOOD YEAR FOR THE ROSES (Jerry Chestnut) / DON'T LET ME BE MISUNDERSTOOD (Nina Simone) / I WANNA BE LOVED (Farnell Jenkins) / THE UGLY THINGS (Nick Lowe) / YOU'RE NO GOOD (Swinging Blue Jeans) / FULL FORCE GALE (Van Morrison) / YOU'VE GOT TO

HIDE YOUR LOVE AWAY (Beatles) / STEP INSIDE LOVE (Cilla Black) / STICKS & STONES (Ray Charles) / FROM HEAD TO TOE (Smokey Robinson) / CONGRATULATIONS (Paul Simon) / STRANGE (Screaming Jay Hawkins) / HIDDEN CHARMS (Willie Dixon) / REMOVE THIS DOUBT (Supremes) / I THREW IT ALL AWAY (Bob Dylan) / LEAVE MY KITTEN ALONE (Little Willie John) / EVERYBODY'S CRYIN' MERCY (Mose Allison) / I'VE BEEN WRONG BEFORE (Randy Newman) / BAMA LAMA BAMA LOO (Little Richard) / MUST YOU THROW DIRT IN MY FACE (Louvin Bros.) / POURING WATER ON A DROWNING MAN (James Carr) / THE VERY THOUGHT OF YOU (Ray Noble) / PAYDAY (Jesse Winchester) / PLEASE STAY (Bacharach-David) / RUNNING OUT OF FOOLS (Jerry Ragavoy) / DAYS (Kinks) / SHE (hit; Charles Aznavour) / etc. • **Trivia:** He has also produced The SPECIALS (1979) / SQUEEZE (1981) / POGUES (1985).

Album rating: MY AIM IS TRUE (*9) / THIS YEAR'S MODEL (*9) / ARMED FORCES (*9) / GET HAPPY!! (*8) / TRUST (*8) / ALMOST BLUE (*5) / IMPERIAL BEDROOM (*8) / PUNCH THE CLOCK (*7) / GOODBYE CRUEL WORLD (*5) / KING OF AMERICA (*7) / BLOOD & CHOCOLATE (*7) / OUT OF OUR IDIOT collection (*5) / SPIKE (*5) / MIGHTY LIKE A ROSE (*5) / THE JULIET LETTERS with Brodsky Quartet (*5) / BRUTAL YOUTH (*6) / KOJAK VARIETY (*4) / ALL THIS USELESS BEAUTY (*5) / EXTREME HONEY compilation (*6) / PAINTED FROM MEMORY with Burt Bacharach (*5) / THE SWEETEST PUNCH re-working (*4) / THE VERY BEST OF ELVIS COSTELLO & THE ATTRACTIONS compilation (*8) / WHEN I WAS CRUEL (*5) / NORTH (*6)

ELVIS COSTELLO

(solo) – vocals, guitar with backing band The **SHAMROCKS,** (alias CLOVER) / **JOHN McFEE** – guitar / **ALEX CALL** – guitar, vocals / **SEAN HOPPER** – keyboards / **JOHN CIAMBOTTI** – bass / **MICHAEL SHINE** – drums

Stiff / Columbia

Mar 77. (7") *(BUY 11)* **LESS THAN ZERO. / RADIO SWEETHEART** [ ] [–]

May 77. (7") *(BUY 14)* **ALISON. / WELCOME TO THE WORKING WEEK** [ ] [ ]

Jun 77. (7") *<3-10641>* **ALISON. / MIRACLE MAN** [–] [ ]

Jul 77. (7") *(BUY 15)* **(THE ANGELS WANNA WEAR MY) RED SHOES. / MYSTERY DANCE** [ ] [–]

Jul 77. (lp/c) *(SEEZ/ZSEEZ 3) <JC 35037>* **MY AIM IS TRUE** [14] Nov77 [32]
– Welcome to the working week / Miracle man / No dancing / Blame it on Cain / Alison / Sneaky feelings / (The angels wanna wear my) Red shoes / Less than zero / Mystery dance / Pay it back / I'm not angry / Waiting for the end of the world. *<re-iss. US Mar78 +=> (AL 35037>* – Watching the detectives. *(re-iss. Jul86 on 'Imp' lp/c/cd; FIEND/+CASS/CD 13) (re-mast.Mar93 & Aug99 on 'Demon'++=; DPAM 1)* – Radio sweetheart / Stranger in the house / Imagination (is a powerful deceiver) / Mystery dance / Cheap reward / Jump up / Wave a white flag / Blame it on Cain / Poison moon. *(d-cd iss.Sep01 on 'Demon' MANUS 101)*

ELVIS COSTELLO & THE ATTRACTIONS

— **STEVE NIEVE** (b.NASON)– keyboards repl. HOPPER to HUEY LEWIS & THE NEWS **BRUCE THOMAS** – bass, vocals (ex-QUIVER)repl. CIAMBOTTI, CALL + McFEE / **PETE THOMAS** (b.9 Aug'54, Sheffield, England)– drums (ex-CILLI WILLI, ex-WILKO JOHNSON)repl. SHINE

Oct 77. (7"m) *(BUY 20)* **WATCHING THE DETECTIVES. / BLAME IT ON CAIN (live) / MYSTERY DANCE (live)** [15] [–]

Nov 77. (7" *<3-10705>* **WATCHING THE DETECTIVES. / ALISON** [–] [ ]

Radar / Columbia

Mar 78. (7") *(ADA 3)* **(I DON'T WANT TO GO TO) CHELSEA. / YOU BELONG TO ME** [16] [–]

Mar 78. (lp/c) *(XX LP/C 11) <35331>* **THIS YEAR'S MODEL** [4] [30]
– No action / This year's girl / The beat / Pump it up / Little Triggers / You belong to me / Hand in hand / (I don't want to go to) Chelsea * / Lip service / Living in Paradise / Lipstick vogue / Night rally *. *(free-7"w/ above) (SAM 83)* – STRANGER IN THE HOUSE. / NEAT NEAT NEAT *<tracks * repl. by* 'Radio Radio' *on US version> (re-iss. May80 on 'F-Beat'; XXLP 4) (re-iss. Apr84 on 'Imp'; FIEND/+CASS 18) (cd-iss. Jan86; FIENDCD 18) (re-mast.Mar93 & Aug99 on 'Demon'++=; DPAM 2)* – Big tears / Crawling to the USA / Running out of angels / Green shirt / Big boys.

May 78. (7") *(ADA 10)* **PUMP IT UP. / BIG TEARS** [24] [–]

Jul 78. (7") *<3-10762>* **THIS YEAR'S GIRL. / BIG TEARS** [–] [ ]

Oct 78. (7") *(ADA 24)* **RADIO RADIO. / TINY STEPS** [29] [ ]

Jan 79. (lp/c) *(RAD/RAC 14) <35709>* **ARMED FORCES** [2] [10]
– Accidents will happen / Senior service / Oliver's army / Big boys / Green shirt / Party girl / Goon squad / Busy bodies / Sunday's best * / Moods for moderns / Chemistry class / Two little Hitlers. *(free 7"w/ above) (SAM 90) <AE 71171>* LIVE AT HOLLYWOOD HIGH EP:- Accidents Will Happen / Alison / Watching The Detectives. *<track * repl. by* '(What's So Funny 'Bout) Peace, Love And Understanding' *on US version + re-issue> (re-iss. May80 on 'F-Beat'; XXLP 5) (re-iss. Apr84 on 'Imp' lp/c; FIEND/+CASS 21) (cd-iss. Jan86; FIENDCD 21) (re-mast.Mar93 & Aug99 on 'Demon'+=; DPAM 3)* – My funny valentine / Tiny steps / Clean money / Talking in the dark / Wednesday week / (above EP). *(d-cd re-iss. Oct02 on 'Demon'+=; MANUS 103)* – (live tracks).

Feb 79. (7") *(ADA 31)* **OLIVER'S ARMY. / MY FUNNY VALENTINE** [2] [ ]

May 79. (7"m) *(ADA 35)* **ACCIDENTS WILL HAPPEN. / TALKING IN THE DARK / WEDNESDAY WEEK** [28] [ ]

ELVIS COSTELLO

solo, but still used ATTRACTIONS

F-Beat / Columbia

Feb 80. (7") *(XX 1)* **I CAN'T STAND UP FOR FALLING DOWN. / GIRLS TALK** [4] [ ]

Feb 80. (lp/c) *(XX LP/C 1) <36347>* **GET HAPPY!!** [2] [11]
– Love for tender / Opportunity / The imposter / Secondary modern / King Horse / Possession / Man called Uncle / Clowntime is over / New Amsterdam / High fidelity / I can't stand up for falling down / Black and white world / Five years in reverse / B movie / Motel matches / Human touch / Beaten to the punch / Temptation / I stand accused / Riot act. *(re-iss. Apr84 on 'Imp' lp/c; FIEND/+CASS 24) (cd-iss. Jan86; FIENDCD 24) (re-mast.May94 & Aug99 on 'Demon'+=; DPAM 5)* – Girls talk / Clowntime is over No.2 / Getting mighty crowded So young / Just a memory / Hoover factory / Ghost train / Dr. Luther's assistant / Black & white world / Riot act.

Apr 80. (7") *(XX 3)* **HIGH FIDELITY. / GETTING MIGHTY CROWDED** [30] [ ]
(12"+=) *(XX 3T)* – Clowntime is over (version 2).

Jun 80. (7") *(XX5)* **NEW AMSTERDAM. / DR. LUTHER'S ASSISTANT** [36] [ ]
(7"ep+=) *(XX 5E)* – Ghost train / Just a memory.

ELVIS COSTELLO & THE ATTRACTIONS

(same line-up)

Dec 80. (7"m) *(XX 12)* **CLUBLAND. / CLEAN MONEY / HOOVER FACTORY** [60] [ ]

Jan 81. (lp/c) *(XX LP/C 11) <37051>* **TRUST** [9] [28]
– Clubland / Lovers walk / You'll never be a man / Pretty words / Strict time / Luxembourg / Watch your step / New lace sleeves / From a whisper to a scream / Different finger / White knuckles / Shot with his own gun / Fish 'n' chip paper / Big sister's clothes. *(re-iss. Apr84 on 'Imp'; lp/c; FIEND/+CASS 30) (cd-iss. Jan86; FIENDCD 30) (re-mast.May94 & Aug99 on 'Demon'+=; DPAM 6)* – Black sails in the sunset / Big sister / Sad about girls / Twenty-five to twelve / Love for sale / Weeper's dream / Gloomy Sunday / Boy with a problem / Seconds of pleasure.

Feb 81. (7") *(XX 14)* **FROM A WHISPER TO A SCREAM. / LUXEMBOURG** [ ] [ ]

Sep 81. (7") *(XX 17)* **GOOD YEAR FOR THE ROSES. / YOUR ANGEL STEPS OUT OF HEAVEN** [6] [ ]

Oct 81. (lp/c) *(XX LP/C 13) <37562>* **ALMOST BLUE** [7] [50]
– Why don't you love me (like you used to do) / Sweet dreams / Sucess / I'm your toy / Tonight the bottle let me down / Brown to blue / Good year for the roses / Sittin' and thinkin' / Colour of the blues / Too far gone / Honey hush / How much I lied. *(re-iss. Apr84 on 'Imp' lp/c; FIEND/+CASS 33) (cd-iss. Jan86; FIENDCD 33) (re-mast.Oct94 & Aug99 on 'Demon'+=; DPAM 7)* – He's got you (live) / Cry cry (live) / There won't be me anymore (live) / Sittin' and thinkin' (live) / Honey hush (live) / Psycho (live) / Your angel steps out of Heaven / Darling, you know I wouldn't lie / My shoes keep walking back to you / Tears before bedtime / I'm your toy (live).

Dec 81. (7") *(XX 19)* **SWEET DREAMS. / PSYCHO (live)** [42] [ ]

Apr 82. (7"m) *(XX 21)* **I'M YOUR TOY (live). / CRY CRY CRY / WONDERING** [51] [ ]
(12"ep) *(XX 21T)* – ('A'side) / My shoes keep walking back to you / Blues keep calling / Honky tonk girl. (w/ The ROYAL PHILHARMONIC)

Jun 82. (7"m) *(XX 26)* **YOU LITTLE FOOL. / BIG SISTER / THE STAMPING GROUND (The Emotional Toothpaste)** [52] [ ]

Jul 82. (lp/c) *(XX LP/C 17) <38157>* **IMPERIAL BEDROOM** [6] [30]
– Beyond belief / Tears before bedtime / Shabby doll / The long honeymoon / Man out of time / Almost blue / . . .And in every home / The loved ones / Human hands / Kid about it / Little savage / Boy with a problem / Pidgin English / You little fool / Town cryer. *(re-iss. Apr84 on 'Imp' lp/c; FIEND/+CASS 36) (cd-iss. Jan86; FIENDCD 36) (re-mast.Oct94 & Aug99 on 'Demon'+=; DPAM 8)* – From head to toe / The world of broken hearts / Night time / Really mystified / I turn around / Seconds of pleasure / The stamping ground / Shabby doll / Imperial bedroom. *(d-cd iss.Oct02 on 'Demon'+=; MANUS 108)* – (alt. & live tracks).

Jul 82. (7") *(XX 28)* **MAN OUT OF TIME. / TOWN CRYER (alt.take)** [58] [–]

Jul 82. (7") *<CNR 03269>* **MAN OUT OF TIME. / (one-side)** [–] [ ]
(12"+=) *(XX 28T)* – Imperial bedroom.

Sep 82. (7") *(XX 30)* **FROM HEAD TO TOE. / THE WORLD OF BROKEN HEARTS** [43] [ ]
(below from the film 'Party Party' and released on 'A&M')

Nov 82. (7") *(AMS 8267)* **PARTY PARTY. / IMPERIAL BEDROOM** [48] [ ]
(below ELVIS as "The IMPOSTER" and issued on 'Imp-Demon')

May 83. (7") *(IMP 001)* **PILLS AND SOAP. / ('A'extended)** [16] [ ]

Jul 83. (7") *(XX 32) <04045>* **EVERYDAY I WRITE THE BOOK. / HEATHEN TOWN** [28] [36]
(12"+=) *(XX 32T) <44-04115>* – Night time.

Jul 83. (lp/c) *(XX LP/C 19) <38897>* **PUNCH THE CLOCK** [3] [24]
– Let them all talk / Everyday I write the book / The greatest thing / The element within her / Love went mad / Shipbuilding / T.K.O. (boxing day) / Charm school / The invisible man / Mouth almighty / King of thieves / Pills and soap / The world and his wife. *(re-iss. Sep84 lp/c/cd; ZL/ZK/ZD 70026) (re-iss. Jan88 on 'Demon' lp/c/cd; FIEND/+CASS/CD 72) (re-mast.Feb95 & Aug99 on 'Demon'+=; DPAM 9)* – Heathen town / The flirting kind / Walking on thin ice / Town where time stood still / Shatterproof / The world and his wife (live) / Everyday I write the book (live).

Sep 83. (7"/ext.12") *(XX 33/+T) <04266>* **LET THEM ALL TALK. / KEEP IT CONFIDENTIAL** [59] [ ]
(below also as "The IMPOSTER" and issued on 'Imp')

Apr 84. (7") *(TRUCE 1)* **PEACE IN OUR TIME. / WITHERED AND DEAD** [48] [ ]

Jun 84. (7") *(XX 35) <05625>* **I WANNA BE LOVED. / TURNING THE TOWN RED** [25] [ ]
(12"+=) *(XX 35T)* – ('A'extended smoochy'n'runny mix).
(12"+=) *(XX 35Z)* – ('A'discotheque version).

Jun 84. (lp/c) *(ZL/ZK 70317) <39429>* **GOODBYE CRUEL WORLD** [10] [35]
– The only flame in town / Home truth / Room with no number / Inch by inch / Worthless thing / Love field / I wanna be loved / The comedians / Joe Porterhouse / Sour milk cow blues / The great unknown / The deportees club / Peace in our time. *(cd-iss. Mar86; ZD 70317) (re-iss. Jan88 on 'Demon' lp/c/cd; FIEND/+CASS/CD 75) (cd re-mast.Feb95 & Aug99 on 'Demon'+=; DPAM 10)* – Turning the town red / Baby it's you / Get yourself another fool / I hope you're happy now / The only flame in town (live) / Worthless thing (live) / Motel matches (live) / Sleepless nights (live) / Deportee.

Aug 84. (7"/'A'disco-12") *(XX 37/+T) <04502>* **THE ONLY FLAME IN TOWN. / THE COMEDIANS** [71] Jul84 [56]
('A'disco-12"+=) *(XX 37Z) <44-05081>* – Pump it up (1984 dance mix).

—— (In May'85, guested on JOHN HIATT single 'Living A Little')
(below as The COWARD BROTHERS (w/ T-BONE BURNETT) + issued on 'Imp')

Jul 85. (7") *(IMP 006)* **THE PEOPLE'S LIMOUSINE. / THEY'LL NEVER TAKE THEIR LOVE FROM ME** [ ] [ ]

The COSTELLO SHOW

featuring The ATTRACTIONS and The CONFEDERATES
Zadded **JAMES BURTON** – guitar / **MITCHELL FROOM** – keyboards / **JERRY SCHEFF** – bass / **JIM KELTNER** – drums / **RON TUTT** – drums (i.e. The CONFEDERATES)

F-Beat Columbia

Jan 86. (7") *(ZB 40555) <05809>* **DON'T LET ME BE MISUNDERSTOOD. / BABY'S GOT A BRAND NEW HAIRDO** [33] [ ]
(12"+=) *(ZT 40556)* – Get yourself another fool.

Feb 86. (lp/c/cd) *(ZL/ZK/ZD 70946) <40173>* **KING OF AMERICA** [11] [39]
– Brilliant mistake / Lovable / Our little angel / Don't let me be misunderstood / Glitter gulch / Indoor fireworks / Little palaces / I'll wear it proudly / American without tears / Eisenhower blues / Poisoned rose / The big light / Jack of all parades / Suit of lights / Sleep of the just. *(re-iss. Jan88 on 'Demon' lp/c/cd; FIEND/+CASS/CD 78) (re-mast.Jul95 & Aug99 on 'Demon' cd+=/d-lp+=; DPAM/+LP 11)* – LIVE ON BROADWAY – Coward Brothers:- The people's limousine / They'll never take her love from me / Suffering face / Shoes without heels / King of confidence.

ELVIS COSTELLO & THE ATTRACTIONS

ELVIS, BRUCE, STEVE & PETE plus guest **NICK LOWE** – guitar

Imp-Demon Columbia

Aug 86. (7") *(IMP 007) <06326>* **TOKYO STORM WARNING. / (part 2)** [73] [ ]
(12"+=) *(IMP 007T)* – Black sails in the sunset.

Sep 86. (lp/c/cd) *(FIEND/+CASS/CD 80) <40518>* **BLOOD & CHOCOLATE** [16] [84]
– Uncomplicated / I hope you're happy now / Tokyo storm warning / Home is anywhere you hang your head / I want you / Honey are you straight or are you blind? / Blue chair / Battered old bird / Crimes of Paris / Poor Napoleon / Next time around. *(cd re-mast.Sep95 & Aug99 on 'Demon'+=; DPAM 12)* – Seven day weekend / Forgive her anything / Blue chair / Baby's got a brand new hairdo / American without tears No.2 / A town called big nothing (really big nothing). *(cd w/ bonus interview disc) (d-cd iss.Feb02 on 'Demon' +=; MANUS 112) <US-iss on 'Rhino'; 78355>* – Leave my kitten alone / New rhythm method / Forgive her anything / Crimes of Paris / Uncomplicated / Battered old bird / Seven day weekend / Blue chair / Baby's got a brand new hairdo (live) / American without tears No.2 / All these things / Pouring water on a drowning man / Running out of fools / Tell me right now / Lonely blue boy.

Nov 86. (7") *(IMP 008)* **I WANT YOU. / (part 2)** [ ] [ ]
(12"+=) *(IMP 008T)* – I hope you say you're happy.

Demon Columbia

Jan 87. (7") *(D 1047)* **BLUE CHAIR. / AMERICA WITHOUT TEARS NO.2 (Twilight version)** [ ] [ ]
(12"+=) *(D 1047T)* – Shoes without heels.

May 87. (7"/12") *(D 1052/+T)* **A TOWN CALLED BIG NOTHING. / RETURN TO BIG NOTHING** [ ] [–]
(above as "McMANUS GANG" featuring SY RICHARDSON)

ELVIS COSTELLO

solo, with mostly **FROOM, KELTNER, PETE THOMAS** (2), **MICHAEL BLAIR** – percussion / **MARC RIBOT** – guitar / **JERRY MAROTTA** – drums / **PAUL McCARTNEY, ROGER McGUINN, CAIT O'RIORDAN, T-BONE BURNETT, CHRISSIE HYNDE** on 1 or 2, plus The DIRTY DOZEN BRASS BAND (GREGORY DAVIS, EFREM TOWNS, ROGER LEWIS, KEVIN HARRIS, KIRK JOSEPH, C. JOSEPH, plus loads more)

Warners Warners

Feb 89. (lp/c)(cd) *(WX 238/+C)(925848-2) <25848>* **SPIKE** [5] [32]
– . . .This town . . . / Let him dangle / Deep dark truthful mirror / Veronica / God's comic / Chewing gum / Tramp the dirt town / Stalin Malone / Satellite / Pads, paws and claws / Baby plays around / Miss Macbeth / Any king's shilling / Coal train robberies * / Last boat leaving. *(cd+= *) (<d-cd iss.Sep01 on 'Rhino'+=; 8122 74286-2>)* – demos:- Miss Macbeth / This town / Deep dark truthful mirror / Coal train robberies / Satellite / Pads, paws and claws / Let him dangle / Veronica / Tramp the dirt down / Baby plays around / Put your big toe in the milk of human kindness / Last boat leaving / Ugly things / You're no good / Point of no return / Room nobody lives in / Stalin Malone (vocal version).

Feb 89. (7") *(W 7558) <22981>* **VERONICA. / YOU'RE NO GOOD** [31] [19]
(12"+=/12"poster+=/cd-s+=/pic-cd-s) *(W 7558 T/TW/CD/CDX)* – The room nobody lives in / Coal train robberies.

May 89. (7"ep/10"ep) *(W 2949/+TE)* **BABY PLAYS AROUND / POISONED ROSE. / ALMOST BLUE / MY FUNNY VALENTINE** [65] [ ]
(c-ep/12"ep/cd-ep) *(W 2949 C/T/CD)* – (2nd track repl. by) Point of no return.

Apr 91. (7"/c-s) *(W 0025/+C)* **THE OTHER SIDE OF SUMMER. / COULDN'T CALL IT UNEXPECTED #4** [43] [ ]
(12"+=/cd-s+=) *(W 0025 T/CD)* – The ugly things.

May 91. (lp/c/cd) *(WX 419/+C/CD)* <26575> **MIGHTY LIKE A ROSE** [5] [55]
– The other side of summer / How to be dumb / All grown up / Invasion hit parade / Harpers bizarre / Hurry down doomsday (the bugs are taking over) / After the fall / Georgie and her rival / So like Candy / Interlude: Couldn't call it unexpected #2 / Playboy to a man / Sweet pear / Broken / Couldn't call it unexpected #4. *(re-iss. cd Feb95; 7599 26675-2) (<d-cd-iss. Nov02 on 'Rhino'+=;8122 78189-2>)* – Mischievous ghost / St. Stephen's day murders / The other side of summer / Deep dark truthful mirror / Hurry down doomsday / All growing up / Georgia and her rival / Forgive her anything / It started to come to me / I still miss someone / The last town I painted / Put your big toe in the milk of human kindness / Invasion hit parade / Just another mystery train / Broken.

— in Jul'91, ELVIS COSTELLO & RICHARD HARVEY issued the TV soundtrack for 'G.B.H.'; they later teamed up for 'JAKE'S PROGRESS'

Oct 91. (7") *(W 0068)* **SO LIKE CANDY. / VERONICA (demo)** [ ] [ ]
(12"+=/cd-s+=) *(W 0068 T/CD)* – Couldn't call it unexpected (live) / Hurry down doomsday (the blues are taking over).

— In 1992, he wrote material for WENDY JAMES (Transvision Vamp)

ELVIS COSTELLO / THE BRODSKY QUARTET

with **MICHAEL THOMAS + IAN BELTON** – violins / **PAUL CASSIDY** – viola / **JACQUELINE THOMAS** – violincello (all co-wrote music with him)

Jan 93. (cd/c) *(<9362 45180-2/-4>)* **THE JULIET LETTERS** [18] [ ]
– Deliver us / For other eyes / Swine / Expert rites / Dead letter / I almost had a weakness / Why? / Who do you think you are? / Taking my life in your hands / This offer is unrepeatable / Dear sweet filthy world / The letter home / Jacksons, Monk and Rowe / This sad burlesque / Romeo's seance / I thought I'd write to Juliet / Last post / The first to leave / Damnation's cellar / The birds will still be singing. *(cd re-iss. Dec96; same)*

Feb 93. (c-s) *(W 0159)* **JACKSONS, MONK AND ROWE / THIS SAD BURLESQUE** [ ] [-]
(cd-s+=) *(W 0159CDX)* – (interviews).

Elvis COSTELLO

Mar 94. (7"/c-s) *(W 0234/+C)* **SULKY GIRL. / A DRUNKEN MAN'S PRAISE OF SOBRIETY** [22] [ ]
(cd-s+=) *(W 0234CD)* – Idiophone / ('A'album version).

Mar 94. (cd/c) *(<9362 45535-2/-4>)* **BRUTAL YOUTH** [2] [34]
– Pony St. / Kinder murder / 13 steps lead down / This is Hell / Clown strike / You tripped at every step / Still too soon to know / 20% amnesia / Sulky girl / London's brilliant parade / My science fiction twin / Rocking horse road / Just about glad / All the rage / Favourite hour. *(<d-cd iss.Feb02 on 'Rhino'+=; 8122 78390-2)>* – This is Hell (alt.) / Idiophone / Abandon words / Poisoned letter / A drunken man's praise of sobriety / Pony St. / Just about glad / Clown strike / Rocking horse road (demo) / 13 steps lead down (demo) / All the rage (demo) / Sulky girl (demo) / You tripped at every step (alt.)

Apr 94. (7"/c-s) *(W 0245/+C)* **13 STEPS LEAD DOWN. / DO YOU KNOW WHAT I'M SAYING?** [59] [ ]
(cd-s) *(W 0245CD)* – ('A'side) / Puppet girl / Basement kiss / We despise you.

Jul 94. (7"/c-s) *(W 0251/+C)* **YOU TRIPPED AT EVERY STEP. / YOU'VE GOT TO HIDE YOUR LOVE AWAY** [ ] [ ]
(cd-s+=) *(W 0251CD)* – Step inside love / Sticks & stones.

Nov 94. (c-s) *(W 0270C)* **LONDON'S BRILLIANT PARADE / LONDON'S BRILLIANT** [48] [ ]
(12"+=) *(W 0270T)* – My resistance is low / Congratulations.
(cd-s) *(W 270CD1)* – ('A'side) / Sweet dreams / The loved ones / From head to toe.
(cd-s) *(W 270CD2)* – ('A'side) / New Amsterdam / Beyond belief / Shipbuilding.

May 95. (cd/c) *(<9362 45903-2/-4>)* **KOJAK VARIETY** [21] [ ]
– Strange / Hidden charms / Remove this doubt / I threw it all way / Leave my kitten alone / Everybody's cryin' mercy / I've been wrong before / Bama lama bama loo / Must you throw dirt in my face / Pouring water on a drowning man / The very thought of you / Payday / Please stay / Running out of fools / Days. *(cd re-iss. Dec96; same)*

Aug 95. (cd; by ELVIS COSTELLO & BILL FRISELL) *(<9362 46073-2>)* **DEEP DEAD BLUE** [ ] Nov95 [ ]
– Weird nightmare / Love field / Shamed into love / Gigi / Poor Napoleon / Baby plays around / Deep dead blue.

ELVIS COSTELLO & THE ATTRACTIONS

Apr 96. (c-s) *(W 0348C)* **IT'S TIME / LIFE SHRINKS** [58] [ ]
(cd-s+=) *(W 0348CD)* – Brilliant disguise.

May 96. (cd/c) *(<9362 46198-2/-4>)* **ALL THIS USELESS BEAUTY** [28] [53]
– The other end of the telescope / Little atoms / All this useless beauty / Complicated shadows / Why can't a man stand alone / Distorted angel / Shallow grave / Poor fractured atlas. *(cd re-iss. Jul00; same) (<d-cd iss.Sep01 on 'Rhino'+=; 8122 74284-2>)*Starting to come with me / You bowed down / It's time / I want to vanish / Almost ideal eyes / My dark life (with BRIAN ENO) / The day is done (with FAIRFIELD FOUR) / What do I do now / The bridge I burned / demos:- It's time / Complicated shadows / You bowed down / Mistress and maid / Distorted angel / The world's greatest optimist / The only flame in town / The comedians (demo) / Days take care of everything / Hidden shame / Why can't a man stand alone.

Jul 96. (cd-s) *(W 0364CD)* **LITTLE ATOMS / WHY CAN'T A MAN STAND ALONE / ALMOST IDEAL EYES / JUST ABOUT GLAD** [ ] [ ]

Jul 96. (cd-s) *(W 0365CD)* **THE OTHER END OF THE TELESCOPE / ALMOST IDEAL EYES / BASEMENT KISS (live) / COMPLICATED SHADOWS (demo)** [ ] [ ]

Jul 96. (cd-s) *(W 0366CD)* **DISTORTED ANGEL / ALMOST IDEAL EYES / LITTLE ATOMS (DJ Food mix) / Lush: ALL THIS USELESS BEAUTY** [ ] [ ]

Jul 96. (cd-s) *(W 0367CD)* **ALL THIS USELESS BEAUTY / ALMOST IDEAL EYES / Sleeper: THE OTHER END OF THE TELESCOPE / DISTORTED ANGEL (Tricky mix)** [ ] [ ]

ELVIS COSTELLO with BURT BACHARACH

Mercury Mercury

Sep 98. (cd/c) *(<538002-2/-4>)* **PAINTED FROM MEMORY** [32] [78]
– In the darkest place / Toledo / I still have that other girl / This house is empty now / Tears at the birthday party / Such unlikely lovers / My thief / Long division / Painted from memory / The sweetest punch / What's her name today? / God give me strength. *(special iss.Apr99; 546165-2)*

Apr 99. (cd-s) *(870965-2)* **TOLEDO / TEARS AT THE BIRTHDAY PARTY (live) / INCH BY INCH (live)** [72] [ ]
(cd-s) *(870967-2)* – ('A'side) / Such unlikely lovers (live) / Baby plays around (live).

Jul 99. (c-s) *(MERMC 521)* **SHE / THE HOUSE IS EMPTY NOW** [19] [ ]
(cd-s+=) *(MERDD 521)* – What's her name today.
(cd-s) *(MERCD 521)* – ('A'side) / Painted from memory / Sweetest punch.

Sep 99. (cd; ELVIS COSTELLO / BURT BACHARACH / BILL FRISELL) *(<559865-2>)* **THE SWEETEST PUNCH** (re-workings of above) [ ] [ ]

ELVIS COSTELLO

Mercury Mercury

Apr 02. (7") *(582887-7)* **TEAR OFF YOUR OWN HEAD (IT'S A DOLL'S REVOLUTION). / WHEN I WAS CRUEL** [58] [-]
(cd-s) *(582887-2)* – ('A'side) / The Imposter vs. the floodtide (dust and petals) / Revolution doll.

Apr 02. (cd)(d-lp) *(<586 829-2>)(586 775-1)* **WHEN I WAS CRUEL** [17] [20]
– 45 / Spooky girlfriend / Tear off your own head (it's a doll's revolution) / When I was cruel No.2 / Soul for hire / 15 petals / Tart / Dust 2 . . . / Dissolve / Alibi / . . .Dust / Daddy can I turn this? / My little blue window / Episode of blonde / Radio silence. *(d-cd iss.Sep02 +=; 63894-2)* – Smile (New York sudio version) / When I was cruel (studio) / 15 petals (live) / Spooky girlfriend (live) / Honeyhouse (Imposter mix) / Watching the detectives / My funny valentine (live) / Dust (live) / Uncomplicated (live) / Smile (live).

Sep 02. (7") *(063915-7)* **45. / MY MOOD SWINGS** [ ] [-]
(cd-s+=) *(063915-2)* – Peroxide side (blunt cut).

Deutsche Grammophon Deutsche Grammophon

Sep 03. (cd) *(9809165)* <99902> **NORTH** [44] [57]
– You left me in the dark / Someone took the words away / When did I stop dreaming? / You turned to me / Fallen / When it sings / Still / Let me tell you about her / Can you be true? / When green eyes turn blue / I'm in the mood again.

– compilations, others, etc. –

Mar 80. (c) *F-Beat; (XXC 6)* **TEN BLOODY MARYS & TEN HOW'S YOUR FATHERS** □ –
– Clean money / Girls talk / Talking in the dark / Radio sweetheart / Big tears / Crawling to the USA / Just a memory / Watching the detectives / Stranger in the house / Clowntime is over (N.2) / Getting mighty crowded / Hoover factory / Tiny steps / (What's so funny 'bout) Peace, love and understanding / Dr. Luther's assistant / Radio radio / Black and white world (No.2) / Wednesday week / My funny valentine / Ghost train. *(re-iss. Apr84 on 'Imp' lp/c; FIEND/+CASS 27) (cd-iss. Jan86; FIENDCD 27) (re-iss. cd Mar93; FIENDCD 27X)*

Oct 80. (lp) *Columbia; <JC 36839>* **TAKING LIBERTIES** – 28
(virtually 'TEN BLOODY MARYS')

Apr 85. (lp/c/cd) *Telstar; (STAR/STAC/TCD 2247)* **THE BEST OF ELVIS COSTELLO – THE MAN** 8 –
– Watching the detectives / Oliver's army / Alison / Accidents will happen / Pump it up / High fidelity / Pills and soap (THE IMPOSTER) / (I don't want to go to) Chelsea / New lace sleeves / A good year for the roses / I can't stand up for falling down / Clubland / Beyond belief / New Amsterdam / Green shirt / Everyday I write the book / I wanna be loved / Shipbuilding (THE IMPOSTER). *(re-iss. May86 on 'Imp' lp/c/cd; FIEND/+CASS/CD 52) (re-iss. cd Mar93 on 'Demon'; FIENDCD 52X)*

Apr 85. (7",7"green) *F-Beat; (ZB 40086)* **GREEN SHIRT. / BEYOND BELIEF** 68 –
(12"+=,12"green+=) *(ZT 40086)* – ('A'extended).
(d7"+=) *(ZB 40085-7)* – Oliver's army / A good year for the roses.
(Nov85; d7"+=) *(same)* – The people's limousine / They'll never take her love away from me.

Nov 85. (12"ep) *Stiff; (BUYIT 239)* **WATCHING THE DETECTIVES / RADIO SWEETHEART. / LESS THAN ZERO / ALISON** □ –

Oct 87. (lp/c/cd; under various pseudonyms) *Demon; (<FIEND/+CASS/CD 67>)* **OUT OF OUR IDIOT** □ □
– Seven day weekend / Turning the town red / Heathen town / The people's limousine / So young / American without tears No.2 / Get yourself another fool / Walking on thin ice / Blue chair / Baby it's you / From head to toe / Shoes without heels / Baby's got a brand new hairdo / The flirting kind / Black sails in the sunset / Imperial bedroom / The stamping ground / Little goody two shoes / Withered and died / A town called big nothing / Big sister. *(re-iss. cd Mar93; FIENDCD 67X)*

Oct 89. (d-lp/c/d-cd/dat) *Demon; (D-)FIEND CASS/CD/DAT 160)* **GIRLS, GIRLS, GIRLS** 67 –
– Watching the detectives / I hope you're happy now / This year's girl / Lover's walk / Pump it up / Strict time / Temptation / (I don't want to go to) Chelsea / High fidelity / Lovable / Mystery dance / Big tears / Uncomplicated / Lipstick vogue / Man out of time / Brilliant mistake / New lace sleeves / Accidents will happen / Beyond belief / Black and white world / Green shirt / The loved ones / New Amsterdam / Red shoes / King horse / Big sister's clothes // Alison / Men called uncle / Party girl / Shabby doll / Motel matches / Tiny steps / Almost blue / Riot act / Loved filed / Possession / Poisoned rose / Indoor fireworks / I want you / Oliver's army / Pills and soap / Sunday's best / Watch your step / Less than zero / Clubland / Tokyo storm warning / Shipbuilding. *(d-cd iss.Sep96 & Oct99; same)*

Nov 89. (c) *Demon; (FIENDCASS 161)* **GIRLS, GIRLS, GIRLS, VOL.2** (see above) □ –

Nov 93. (4xcd-box) *Demon; (DPAM BOX1)* **THE FIRST 2 1/2 YEARS** □ –
– (MY AIM IS TRUE / THIS YEAR'S MODEL / ARMED FORCES / LIVE AT EL MOCAMBO).

Nov 94. (cd/c/lp) *Demon; (DPAM CD/MC/LP 13) / Rykodisc; <40203>* **THE VERY BEST OF ELVIS COSTELLO** 57 Oct94 □
– Alison / Watching the detectives / (I don't want to go to) Chelsea / Pump it up / Radio, radio / (What's so funny 'bout) Peace, love and understanding / Oliver's army / Accidents will happen / I can't stand up for falling down / New Amsterdam / High fidelity / Clubland / Watch your step / Good year for the roses / Beyond belief / Man out of time / Everyday I write the book / Shipbuilding / Love field / Brilliant mistake / Indoor fireworks / I want you. *(cd re-iss. Oct99; same)*

Oct 97. (cd) *Warners; (9362 46801-2)* **EXTREME HONEY: THE VERY BEST OF THE WARNER BROS. YEARS** □ □
– The bridge I burned / Veronica / Sulky girl / So like candy / 13 steps lead down / All this useless beauty / My dark life / Other side of summer / Kinder murder / Deep dark truthful mirror / Hurry down doomsday (the bugs are taking over) / Poor fractured atlas / Birds will still be singing / London's brilliant parade / Tramp the dirt down / Couldn't call it unexpected, No.4 / I want to vanish / All the rage.

Aug 99. (d-cd/d-c) *Universal TV; (546490-2/-4)* **THE VERY BEST OF ELVIS COSTELLO** 4 –
– (What's so funny 'bout) Peace, love and understanding / Oliver's army / Watching the detectives / Alison / (I don't want to go to) Chelsea / Accidents will happen / Pump it up / I can't stand up for falling down / Radio, radio / Clubland / Good year for the roses / Man out of time / I wanna be loved / Everyday I write the book / Brilliant mistake / The other side of summer / Tokyo storm warning / Sulky girl / So like candy / Veronica / She / Big tears / Beyond belief / Lipstick vogue / Green shirt / Pills and soap / Tramp the dirt down / Shipbuilding / High fidelity / New lace sleeves / (The angels wanna wear my) Red shoes / Talking in the dark / New Amsterdam / I hope you're happy now / Riot act / My funny valentine / Indoor fireworks / Almost blue / I want you / God give me strength / That day is done / I want to vanish.

— his first 4 singles were also re-issued together around 1980 and could be found on 'Stiff' 10-pack Nos.11-20).

— The ATTRACTIONS released two singles and an album (Aug80) 'MAD ABOUT THE WRONG BOY' on 'F-Beat'.

□ John COUGAR
(see under ⇒ MELLENCAMP, John Cougar)

COUNTING CROWS

Formed: Bay Area, San Francisco, California, USA ... August '91 out of early 90's outfit, SORDID HUMOR (along with TOM BARNES on vocals and guitar plus bassist JIM GORDON). 'CROWS vocalist/songwriter ADAM DURITZ and guitarist DAVID BRYSON (on production only) had both been members of this folky outfit, 'Capricorn' releasing the album 'LIGHT MUSIC FOR DYING PEOPLE' after they were famous. The COUNTING CROWS' success was mainly due to 'MR JONES', a highly melodic slice of laid-back rock that was caned by both MTV and radio, resulting in the T-BONE BURNETT-produced album, 'AUGUST AND EVERYTHING AFTER' (1993), selling by the million. The record (which featured MARIA McKEE on backing vocals) was a professional, coffee table-friendly package of Roots rock that at times came across like a more polished JAYHAWKS. Two further singles, 'ROUND HERE' and 'RAIN KING' were issued, although they failed to dent the Top 40, by which time BEN MIZE had been drafted in to replace BOWMAN. Their long-awaited GIL NORTON-produced sophomore set, 'RECOVERING OF THE SATELLITES' (1996), disappointed no one and duly climbed to No.1 (UK Top 5), minor British hits such as 'ANGEL OF THE SILENCES', 'A LONG DECEMBER' and 'DAYLIGHT FADING', obvious highlights. A tad ambitious was their next album (a double live set!), 'ACROSS THE WIRE' (1998), all the best tunes were there of course although it was only a moderate seller peaking at No.19 in the US chart. That three year long wait for a studio album was up in November '99, 'THIS DESERT LIFE' finally making it to the shelves and returning the reclusive COUNTING CROWS to the Top 10. Something of a departure from their downbeat recent efforts, 'HARD CANDY' (2002) was a bold, robust, meticulously crafted pop record. Rootsy, lovelorn, with the sad-eyed soul of an ageing poet, but a pop record nonetheless. DURITZ offered up his hard-won wisdom more engagingly than on previous outings while the dense weave of instrumentation added to an atmosphere of careworn joy. With its unconventional sequencing and inclusion of some filler, 'FILMS ABOUT GHOSTS: THE BEST OF' (2003) wasn't a great best of, although casual fans could find all the hits including the UK Top 20 cover of Joni Mitchell's 'BIG YELLOW TAXI'. • **Songwriters:** DURITZ; some w /BRYSON, except ROUND

HERE (Himalyans) / THE GHOST IN YOU (Psychedelic Furs) / OOH LA LA (Faces) / FRIEND OF THE DEVIL (Grateful Dead) / YOU AIN'T GOIN' NOWHERE (Bob Dylan) / START AGAIN (Teenage Fanclub) / RETURN OF THE GREVIOUS ANGEL (Gram Parsons) / etc.

Album rating: AUGUST AND EVERYTHING AFTER (*8) / RECOVERING THE SATELLITES (*7) / ACROSS THE WIRE – ALIVE IN NEW YORK (*6) / THIS DESERT LIFE (*7) / HARD CANDY (*7) / FILMS ABOUT GHOSTS: THE BEST OF . . . compilation (*8)

ADAM DURITZ (b. 1 Aug'64, Baltimore, Maryland) – vocals, piano, harmonica / **DAVID BRYSON** (b. 5 Nov'61) – guitar, vocals / **DAN VICKREY** (b.26 Aug'66, Walnut Creek, Calif.) – guitar / **MATT MALLEY** (b. 4 Jul'63) – bass, vocals / **CHARLIE GILLINGHAM** (b.12 Jan'60, Torrance, Calif.) – piano, organ, accordion, chamberlain, vocals / **STEVE BOWMAN** (b.14 Jan'67) – drums, vocals

Geffen Geffen

Oct 93. (cd/c) *<(GED/GEC 24528)>* **AUGUST AND EVERYTHING AFTER** [16] [4]
– Round here / Omaha / Mr. Jones / Perfect blue buildings / Anna begins / Time and time again / Rain king / Sullivan Street / Ghost train / Raining in Baltimore / A murder of one.

Apr 94. (7"/c-s) *(GFS/+C 69)* **MR. JONES. / RAINING IN BALTIMORE** [28] [–]
(cd-s+=) *(GFSTD 69)* – Rain king / ('A'acoustic).

Jun 94. (7"/c-s) *(GFS/+C 74)* **ROUND HERE. / GHOST TRAIN** [70] [–]
(cd-s+=) *(GFSTD 74)* – The ghost in you (live).

Oct 94. (c-s) *(GFSC 82)* **RAIN KING / A MURDER OF ONE** [49] [ ]
(cd-s+=) *(GFSTD 82)* – Mr. Jones (acoustic live).

— **BEN MIZE** (b. 2 Feb'71) – drums, vocals; repl. BOWMAN

Oct 96. (c-s) *(GFSC 22182)* **ANGEL OF THE SILENCES / ROUND HERE (live)** [41] [–]
(cd-s+=) *(GFSTD 22182)* – Recovering the satellites.

Oct 96. (cd/c) *<(GED/GEC 24975)>* **RECOVERING OF THE SATELLITES** [4] [1]
– Catapult / Angel of the silences / Daylight fading / Goodnight Elisabeth / Children in bloom / Have you seen me lately? / Miller's angels / Another horsedreamer's blues / Recovering the satellites / Monkey / Mercury / A long December / Walkaways.

Dec 96. (c-s) *(GFSC 22190)* **A LONG DECEMBER. / GHOST TRAIN (live)** [62] [–]
(cd-s+=) *(GFSTD 22190)* – Sullivan Street (live).

May 97. (c-s) *(GFSC 22247)* **DAYLIGHT FADING / DAYLIGHT FADING (live)** [54] [–]
(cd-s+=) *(GFSTD 22247)* – Rain king (live).
(cd-s) *(GFSXD 22247)* – ('A'side) / Time and time again (live) / Miller's angels (demo).

Dec 97. (cd-s) *(GFSTD 21910)* **A LONG DECEMBER / GHOST TRAIN (live)** [68] [–]
(cd-s) *(GFSXD 21910)* – Sullivan Street (live).

Jul 98. (d-cd) *<(GED 25226)>* **ACROSS THE WIRE – LIVE IN NEW YORK** (VH1 storytellers // MTV live from the 10 spot) [27] [19]
– Round here / Have you seen me lately? / Angels of the silences / Catapult / Mr. Jones / Rain king / Mercury / Ghost train / Anna begins // Recovering the satellites / Angels of the silences / Rain king / Sullivan Street / Children in bloom / Have you seen me lately? / Raining in Baltimore / Round here / I'm not sleeping / A murder of one / A long December / Walkaways.

— disc 1 rec. live at Chelsea Studios, New York, August 12, 1997 // disc 2 rec. live at Hammersmith Ballroom, New York, November 6th, 1997

Oct 99. (cd-s) *(497188-2) <album cut>* **HANGINAROUND / MERCURY / GOODNIGHT ELIZABETH** [46] [28]
(cd-s) *(497184-2)* – ('A'side) / Baby I'm a big star / Omaha.

Nov 99. (cd/c) *<(490415-2/-4)>* **THIS DESERT LIFE** [19] [8]
– Hanginaround / Mrs. Potter's lullaby / Amy hit the atmosphere / Four days / All my friends / High life / Colorblind / I wish I was a girl / Speedway / St. Robinson in his Cadillac dream. *(lp-iss.Mar03 on 'Universal'; AA69490415-1)*

Jun 02. (c-s) *(497741-4)* **AMERICAN GIRLS / START AGAIN** [33] [ ]
(cd-s+=) *(497745-2)* – Someday / ('A'-video).
(cd-s) *(497740-2)* – ('A'side) / Blues run the game / Mercy.

Jul 02. (cd) *<(493366-2)>* **HARD CANDY** [9] [5]
– Hard candy / American girls / Good time / If I could give all my love (Richard Manuel is dead) / Goodnight L.A. / Butterfly in reverse / Miami / New frontier / Carriage / Black and blue / Why should you come when I call? / Up all night (Frankie Miller goes to Hollywood) / Holiday in Spain. *(UK re-iss. Jan03 +=; 493560-2)(hit No.40)* – 4 white stallions / You ain't going nowhere / Big yellow taxi.

Feb 03. (c-s; by COUNTING CROWS & VANESSA CARLTON) *(497831-4)* **BIG YELLOW TAXI / AMERICAN GIRLS (live acoustic)** [16] [–]
(cd-s) *(497849-2)* – ('A'side) / If I could give all my love (Richard Manuel is dead) (live acoustic) / Hard candy (live acoustic) / ('A'-video).
(cd-s) *(497830-2)* – ('A'side) / Amie / Miami (live acoustic).

Jun 03. (cd-s) *(980683-0)* **IF I COULD GIVE ALL MY LOVE / BIG YELLOW TAXI (live) / Ooh la la (live)** [50] [–]
(cd-s) *(980683-1)* – ('A'side) / Long December (live) / Return of the grevious angel.

Nov 03. (cd) *(986179-0) <00016761-2>* **FILMS ABOUT GHOSTS: THE BEST OF . . .** (compilation) [–] [32]
– Angels of the silences / Round here / Rain king / A long December / Hanginaround / Mrs. Potter's lullaby / Mr. Jones / Recovering the satellites / American girls / Big yellow taxi / Omaha / Friend of the Devil / Einstein on the beach (for an eggman) / Anna begins / Holiday in Spain / She don't want nobody near.
(above album will hit UK No.15 when released in Jan'04)

☐ COUNTRY JOE AND THE FISH
(see under ⇒ McDONALD, Country Joe)

☐ COVERDALE PAGE (see under ⇒ WHITESNAKE)

☐ Sarah CRACKNELL (see under ⇒ SAINT ETIENNE)

CRADLE OF FILTH

Formed: Suffolk, England . . . 1991 by gothic grave robbers fronted by former journalist, DANI DAVEY. Influenced by the Scandinavian black-metal scene, the group nevertheless carved out their own inimitably gothic-punk-orchestral English sound. Their 1994 debut, 'THE PRINCIPLE OF EVIL MADE FLESH' had distinct gothic overtones, although bludgeoning death-metal was their stock-in-trade. Another set, 'VEMPIRE' (1996), was quickly succeeded by their first for 'Music For Nations', 'DUSK . . . AND HER EMBRACE', although CRADLE OF FILTH garnered more attention for their controversial promo-shoots and "masturbating-nun" T-shirts. 1998 satanism and sex always on the agenda, DANI was the focal point since his awakening from the grave in '96. A TV documentary was made for BBC2, the band a tad uncomfortable when a devoted fan's mum followed them around in her camper van. However, 'CRUELTY AND THE BEAST' (1998), saw COF in the UK Top 50, Europe – especially Scandinavia – having already succumbed to their majesty. Towards the end of the decade, the Suffolk Satan botherers threw yet more filth at our pop kids with the release of home video, 'PANDAEMONAEON', the featured music also released separately as a mini-set, 'FROM THE CRADLE TO ENSLAVE'. Alongside such interestingly titled fare as 'OF DARK BLOOD AND F**KING' was an unlikely rendition of The Misfits' 'DEATH COMES RIPPING'. A new full length album, 'MIDIAN', arrived in late 2000, chock full of the usual tortuous vocals, brain-melting riffs, ridiculously symphonic keyboards and general gothic-tinged heathenry – bliss. On new imprint, 'Abra Cadavar', COF delivered yet another brief UK Top 75 entry, 'BITTER SUITES TO SUCCUBI' (2001), a sort-of odds'n'sods collection; a further two exploitation sets, 'LOVECRAFT AND WITCH HEARTS' and 'LIVE BAIT FOR THE DEAD' (both 2002) filled in time before the long-awaited 'DAMNATION AND A DAY' (2003). Incredibly, the band managed to secure a major label deal with 'Sony', using the increased budget to procure themselves the services of a full orchestra and choir. • **Covered:** DEATH COMES RIPPING

(Misfits) / SLEEPLESS (Anathema) / FOR THOSE WHO DIED (SABBAT) / BLACK METAL (Venom) / SODOMY AND LUST (Sodom) / HELL AWAITS (Slayer) / HALLOWED BE THY NAME (Iron Maiden) / NO TIME TO CRY (Sisters Of Mercy) / THE FIRE STILL BURNS (Twisted Sister).

Album rating: THE PRINCIPLE OF EVIL MADE FLESH (*5) / DUSK AND HER VEMPIRE – OR DARK FAIRYTALES IN PHALLUSTEIN (*5) / DUSK . . . AND HER EMBRACE (*6) / CRUELTY AND THE BEAST (*6) / FROM THE CRADLE TO ENSLAVE mini (*4) / MIDIAN (*6) / BITTER SUITES TO SUCCUBI collection (*6) / LOVECRAFT AND WITCH HEARTS compilation (*7) / LIVE BAIT FOR THE DEAD collection (*4) / DAMNATION AND A DAY (*6) / December Moon: SOURCE OF ORIGIN (*6)

DANI DAVEY – vocals / **DAMIEN GREGORI** – keyboards / **STUART ANSTIS** – guitar / **GIAN PYRES** – guitar / **ROBIN EAGLESTONE** – bass / **NICHOLAS BARKER** – drums

Cacophonous Cacophonous

Mar 94. (cd/lp,blue-lp) *(<NIHL 1 CD/LP>)* **THE PRINCIPLE OF EVIL MADE FLESH** [ ] [ ]
– Darkness our bride (jugular wedding) / The principle of evil made flesh / The forest whispers my name / Iscariot / The black goddess rises / One final graven kiss / A crescendo of passion bleeding / To Eve the art of witchcraft / Of mist and midnight skies / In secret love we drown / A dream of wolves in the snow / Summer dying fast. *(re-iss. Jul98; same) <US re-iss. Feb00; same>*

—— STUART now took the name **JARED DEMETER** for next recording

Apr 96. (cd/lp) *(<NIHL 6/+LP>)* **VEMPIRE – OR DARK FAIRYTALES IN PHALLUSTEIN** [ ] [ ]
– Ebony dressed for sunset / Forest whispers my name / Queen of winter throned / Nocturnal supremacy / She mourns a lengthening shadow / Rape and ruin of angels (hosanas in extremis). *(re-iss. Jul98; same)*

Music For Nations Fierce

Nov 96. (cd/c/lp) *(CD/T+/MFN 208) <11096>* **DUSK . . . AND HER EMBRACE** [ ] Jan97 [ ]
– Human inspired to nightmare / Heaven from asunder / Funeral in Carpathia / Gothic romance / Malice through the looking glass / Duske and her embrace / Graveyard moonlight / Beauty sleeps in Sodom / Haunted shores. *(sha-cd-iss. Mar97 +=; CDMFNC 208)* – Hell awaits / Camilia's masque. *(other cd; CDMFNX 208)* – Nocturnal supremacy '96.

—— **LES 'LECTOR' SMITH** – keyboards; repl. DAMIEN GREGORI who departed mid-97

May 98. (cd/c/lp) *(CD/T+/MFN 242) <11128>* **CRUELTY AND THE BEAST** [48] [ ]
– Once upon atrocity / Thirteen autumns and a widow / Cruelty beneath thee orchids / Beneath the howling stars / Venus in fear / Desire in violent overture / The twisted nails of faith / Bathory aria: Benighted like Usher / Portrait of the dead countess / Lustmord and wargasm (the lick of carnivorous winds). *(other cd+=; CDMFNX 242)* – (bonus tracks).

—— **STUART SMITH** – guitar; repl. PYRES

Music For Nations Metal Blade

Nov 99. (m-cd) *(CDMFN 254) <14301>* **FROM THE CRADLE TO ENSLAVE** [ ] Dec99 [ ]
– From the cradle to enslave / Of dark blood and fucking / Death comes ripping / Sleepless / Perverts church (from the cradle to deprave) / Funeral in Carpathia (be quick or be dead version).

—— STUART had now departed; he subsequently formed APHELION, releasing 'APHELION I-VI' mini-set in March '01

Music For Nations Koch

Oct 00. (cd/lp) *(CD+/MFN 666) <8219>* **MIDIAN** [63] Nov00 [ ]
– At the gates of Midian / Cthulhu dawn / Saffron's curse / Death magick for adepts / Lord abortion / Amor e morta / Creatures that kissed in cold mirrors / Her ghost in the fog / Satanic mantra / Tearing the veil from grace / Tortured soul asylum.

Epic Red Ink

Mar 03. (dvd-s) *(673554-9)* **BABYLON A.D. (SO GLAD FOR THE MADNESS)** [35] [–]

Mar 03. (cd) *(510963-2) <71423>* **DAMNATION AND A DAY** [44] [ ]
– FANTASIA DOWN:- A bruise upon the silent nation / A promise of fever / Hurt and virtue / An enemy led the tempest / PARADISE LOST:- Damned in any language / Better to reign in Hell / Serpent tongue / Carrion / SEWER SIDE UP:- The mordent liquor of tears / Presents from the poisoned hearted / Doberman pharaoh / Babylon A.D. (so glad for the madness) / THE SCENTED GARDEN:- A scarlet witch lit the season / Mannequin / Thank God for the suffering / The smoke of her burning / End of daze.

– compilations, etc. –

Jun 01. (cd) *AbraCadaver; <(CDF 001CD)>* **BITTER SUITES TO SUCCUBI** [63] [ ]
– Dinner at deviant's place / All hope in eclipse / Born in a burial gown / Suicide and other comforts / Black goddess II Ebon Nemesis (2001 version) / Principle of evil made flesh (2001 version) / No time to cry / Born in a burial gown (video).

May 02. (d-cd) *Music For Nations; (CDMFN 285) / Koch; <8412>* **LOVECRAFT AND WITCH HEARTS** [ ] Jun02 [ ]
– Creatures that kissed in cold mirrors / Dusk and her embrace / Beneath the howling stars / Her ghost in the fog / Funeral in Carpathia / The twisted nails of faith / From the cradle to enslave / Saffron's curse / Malice through the looking glass / Cruelty brought thee orchids / Lord Abortion / Once upon atrocity / Thirteen autumns and a widow / For those who died / Sodomy and lust / Twisting further nails / Amor E morte / Carmilla's masque / Lustmord and wargasm II / Dawn of eternity / Of dark blood and fucking / Dance macabre / Hell awaits / Hallowed be thy name.

Aug 02. (d-cd) *AbraCadaver; (<CDF 006CD>)* **LIVE BAIT FOR THE DEAD (live)** [ ] Sep02 [ ]
– Intro: The ceremony opens / Lord Abortion / Ebony pressed for sunset / The forest whispers my name / Cthulhu dawn / Dusk and her embrace / The principle of evil made flesh / Cruelty brought thee orchids / Her ghost in the fog / Summer dying fast / Interlude: Creatures that kissed in cold mirrors / From the cradle to enslave / Queen of winter, throned / Born in a burial gown / No time to cry / Funeral in Carpathia / Deleted scenes of a snuff princess / Scorched earth erotica (original demo) / Nocturnal supremacy / From the cradle to enslave (under marshall remix) / The fire still burns.

CRAMPS

Formed: New York City, New York, USA . . . 1975 by LUX INTERIOR and POISON IVY, who recruited fellow weirdos BRYAN GREGORY and PAM 'BALAM' GREGORY (the latter was replaced by MIRIAM LINNA, who in turn was superseded by NICK KNOX). The trashiest, sleaziest 50's throwbacks to ever besmirch the good name of rock'n'roll, The CRAMPS took the genre's inherit debauchery to its thrilling (and often hilarious) conclusion. Crawling from the mire of CBGB's punk scene like the proverbial Swamp Thing in one of their beloved B-movies, The CRAMPS started as they meant to go on, initiating their vinyl career in 1978 with an obscure cover, 'THE WAY I WALK'. The single was backed with a riotous mangling of The Trashmen's 'SURFIN' BIRD', as close to a theme tune as the band came. A follow-up, 'HUMAN FLY', introduced LUX's impressive capacity for disturbingly accurate animal (and insect!) noises, its voodoo surf twang and creeping tempo scarier than the frontman's skintight leotard. Subsequently signed to Miles Copeland's 'I.R.S.' label, The CRAMPS set up shop in Sun Studios, Memphis (where else?!) with producer ALEX CHILTON at the production helm, working on the material for their acclaimed debut set, 'SONGS THE LORD TAUGHT US' (1980). Featuring such bad taste gems as 'GARBAGEMAN' (more animal noises!), 'I WAS A TEENAGE WEREWOLF' and 'STRYCHNINE', the record further boosted the band's cult following. The departure of GREGORY after the 'DRUG TRAIN' single was the first in a long series of line-up changes through which IVY (the sexiest thing in stockings!) and INTERIOR were the only constants. With KID CONGO POWERS as a replacement, the band cut the less convincing 'PSYCHEDELIC JUNGLE' (1981), their final release for Copeland whom they later sued. A short spell with the French 'New Rose' label and then 'Big Beat' saw the release of the live mini 'SMELL OF FEMALE' (1983). This went at least some way to capturing the cheap thrills of a CRAMPS gig, though readers are advised to experience the real thing; if the primeval spirit of raw rock'n'roll doesn't move you, then the sight of a grown man in a leather thong and and high heels just might! INTERIOR had always modelled himself on a kind of ELVIS-from-the-crypt and in 1986, The CRAMPS met their maker, so to speak, on the classic 'A DATE WITH ELVIS'. The likes of 'THE HOT PEARL SNATCH', 'CAN YOUR PUSSY DO THE DOG?' and 'WHAT'S INSIDE A GIRL?', need no further explanation save that THE KING was no doubt turning in his grave. Though this marked a creative and commercial peak of sorts, The CRAMPS continued to think up the best song titles in the Western World over a string of late 80's/90's albums, including 'STAY SICK' (1990), 'LOOK MOM, NO HEAD' (1991; essential if only for the IGGY POP collaboration, 'MINISKIRT BLUES'), 'FLAME JOB' (1994) and 'BIG BEAT FROM BADSVILLE' (1997). Though they've hardly pushed back the boundaries of music, The CRAMPS are arguably even more essential now than in their heyday, if only to remind the current crop of indie dullards what it REALLY means to play "The Devil's Music". Now in their fifties (well, LUX, at any rate), the CRAMPS showed no signs of ageing gracefully with their first album of new material in over five years, 'FIENDS OF DOPE ISLAND' (2003). The most interesting titles of the album, and perhaps the year, had to be 'PAPA SATAN SANG LOUIE' and 'ELVIS FUCKS CHRIST', as good an indicator as any of the band's reliably static musical development.

• **Songwriters:** Most written by LUX and IVY except SURFIN' BIRD (Trashmen) / FEVER (Little Willie John) / THE WAY I WALK (Robert Gordon) / GREEN DOOR (Jim Lowe) / SHE SAID (Hasil Adkins) / JAILHOUSE ROCK (Elvis Presley) / MULESKINNER BLUES (Fendermen) / PSYCHOTIC REACTION (Count Five) / LONESOME TOWN (Ricky Nelson) / HARD WORKIN' MAN (Jack Nitzche) / HITSVILLE 29 B.C. (Turnbow) / WHEN I GET THE BLUES (Larry Mize) / HOW COME YOU DO ME? (...Joiner) / STRANGE LOVE (...West) / BLUES BLUES BLUES (...Thompson) / TRAPPED LOVE (Kohler-Fana) / SINNERS (Freddie & The Hitchhikers) / ROUTE 66 (Bobby Troup) / etc.

• **Trivia:** Their fan club was surprisingly based in Grangemouth, Scotland (wee Marty fi the Nash ran it!)

Album rating: SONGS THE LORD TAUGHT US (*7) / PSYCHEDELIC JUNGLE (*7) / OFF THE BONE compilation (*8) / SMELL OF FEMALE (*6) / A DATE WITH ELVIS (*7) / STAY SICK (*6) / LOOK MOM, NO HEAD! (*5) / FLAMEJOB (*6) / BIG BEAT FROM BADSVILLE (*5) / FIENDS OF DOPE ISLAND (*5)

LUX INTERIOR (b. ERICK LEE PURKHISER, 21 Oct'46, Akron, Ohio) – vocals / **POISON IVY RORSCHACH** (b. KIRSTY MARLANA WALLACE, 1954, Sacramento, Calif.) – guitar / **BRYAN GREGORY** (b. Detroit, Mich.) – guitar / **NICK KNOX** (b. NICHOLAS STEPHANOFF) – drums repl. MIRIAM LINNA (later to The ZANTEES & The A-BONES) who had repl. PAM 'BALAM' GREGORY

not iss. / Vengeance

Apr 78. (7") <666> **THE WAY I WALK. / SURFIN' BIRD** – [ ]

Nov 78. (7") <668> **HUMAN FLY. / DOMINO** – [ ]

Illegal / I.R.S.

Jun 79. (12"ep) *(ILS 12-013)* **GRAVEST HITS** [ ] –
– Human fly / The way I walk / Domino / Surfin' bird / Lonesome town. *(re-iss. Sep82 – 7"blue-ep / re-iss. Mar83- 7"red-ep; same)*

Mar 80. (7") *(ILS 0017)* **FEVER. / GARBAGEMAN** [ ] –

Apr 80. (lp) *(ILP 005)* *<SP 007>* **SONGS THE LORD TAUGHT US** [ ] [ ]
– TV set / Rock on the Moon / Garbageman / I was a teenage werewolf / Sunglasses after dark / The mad daddy / Mystery plane / Zombie dance / What's behind the mask / Strychnine / I'm cramped / Tear it up / Fever. *(cd-iss. Jul98 on 'E.M.I.'; 493836-2)*

May 80. (7") *<IR 9014>* **DRUG TRAIN. / GARAGEMAN** – [ ]

Jul 80. (7"m) *(ILS 021)* **DRUG TRAIN. / LOVE ME / I CAN HARDLY STAND IT** [ ] –

— **KID CONGO POWERS** (b. BRIAN TRISTAN, 27 Mar'61, La Puente, Calif.) – guitar; repl. JULIEN BOND, who had repl. GREGORY for two months mid 1980 (BRYAN was to die on 10th January, 2001)

I.R.S. / I.R.S.

May 81. (7"yellow) *(PFS 1003)* *<IR 9021>* **GOO GOO MUCK. / SHE SAID** [ ] Aug81 [ ]

May 81. (lp) *<(SP 70016)>* **PSYCHEDELIC JUNGLE** [ ] Jul81 [ ]
– Green fuzz / Goo goo muck / Rockin' bones / Voodoo idol / Primitive / Caveman / The crusher / Don't eat stuff off the sidewalk / Can't find my mind / Jungle hop / The natives are restless / Under the wires / Beautiful gardens / Green door. *(cd-iss. Sep98 on 'E.M.I.'; 496504-2)*

Oct 81. (12"m) *(PFSX 1008)* **THE CRUSHER. / SAVE IT / NEW KIND OF KICK** [ ] –

— (LUX, IVY & NICK were joined by **IKE KNOX** (Nick's cousin) – guitar; repl. KID CONGO who returned to GUN CLUB (appeared on live tracks 83-84)

Big Beat / not iss.

Nov 83. (red-m-lp) *(NED 6)* **SMELL OF FEMALE (live)** 74 –
– Faster pussycat / I ain't nuthin' but a gorehound / Psychotic reaction / The most exhalted potentate of love / You got good taste / Call of the wig hat. *(pic-lp Jun84; NEDP 6) (re-iss. Feb91 cd+=/c+=; CDWIKM/WIKMC 95)* – Beautiful gardens / She said / Surfin' dead. *(lp re-mast.Nov01 on 'Vengeance'; VENG 670)*

— (signed to below label in France)

New Rose / New Rose

Mar 84. (7"/7"pic-d) *(NEW 28/+P)* **FASTER PUSSYCAT. / YOU GOT GOOD TASTE** – French –

Mar 84. (7"colrd;various) *(NEW 33)* **I AIN'T NUTHIN' BUT A GOREHOUND. / WEEKEND ON MARS** – French –

— **CANDY FUR** (DEL-MAR) – guitar; repl. IKE

Big Beat / not iss.

Nov 85. (7"orange) *(NS 110)* **CAN YOUR PUSSY DO THE DOG? / BLUE MOON BABY** 68 –
(12"blue+=) *(NST 110)* – Georgia Lee Brown.

Feb 86. (blue-lp/c/cd) *(WIKA/WIKC/CDWIK 46)* **A DATE WITH ELVIS** 34 –
– How far can too far go / The hot pearl snatch / People ain't too good / What's inside a girl? / Can your pussy do the dog? / Kizmiaz / Cornfed dames / Chicken / (Hot pool of) Woman need / Aloha from Hell / It's just that song. *<US-iss.1994 on 'Capitol'; 73579> (lp re-mast.Nov01 on 'Vengeance'; VENG 671)*

May 86. (7") *(NS 115)* **WHAT'S INSIDE A GIRL? / GET OFF THE ROAD** [ ] –
(12"+=) *(NST 115)* – Give me a woman.
(Mar87; cd-s++=) *(CRAMP 1)* – Scene / Heart of darkness.

Enigma / Enigma

Jan 90. (7"/7"sha-pic-d/c-s) *(ENV/+PD/TC 17)* **BIKINI GIRLS WITH MACHINE GUNS. / JACKYARD BACKOFF** 35 [ ]
(12"+=/cd-s+=) *(12ENV/ENVCD 17)* – Her love rubbed off.

Feb 90. (cd/c/lp) *(CDENV/TCENV/ENVLP 1001)* *<73543>* **STAY SICK** 62 [ ]
– Bop pills / Goddam rock'n'roll / Bikini girls with machine guns / All women are bad / Creature from the black leather lagoon / Shortenini' bread / Daisy's up your butterfly / Everything goes / Journey to the centre of a girl / Mama oo pow pow / Saddle up a buzz buzz / Muleskinner blues. *(cd+=)* – Her love rubbed off. *(pic-lp Nov90; ENVLPPD 101) (re-iss. Feb94 cd/lp; CD+/WIKD 126) (lp re-mast.Nov01 on 'Vengeance'; VENG 672)*

Apr 90. (7"/c-s) *(ENV/+TC 19)* **ALL WOMEN ARE BAD. / TEENAGE RAGE (live)** [ ] –
(12"+=/12"pic-d+=/cd-s+=) *(12ENV/12ENVPD/ENVCD 19)* – King of the drapes (live) / High school hellcats (live).

Aug 90. (7") *(ENV 22)* **CREATURE FROM THE BLACK LEATHER LAGOON. / JAILHOUSE ROCK** [ ] –
(12"+=/12"pic-d+=/cd-s+=) *(12ENV/12ENVPD/CDENV 22)* – Beat out my love.

Sep 90. (cd-ep) *<773617-2>* **CREATURE FROM THE BLACK LEATHER LAGOON / JAILHOUSE ROCK / JACKYARD BACKOFF / BEAT OUT MY LOVE / HER LOVE RUBBED OFF** – [ ]

— **LUX & IVY** were joined by **SLIM CHANCE** – guitar (ex-PANTHER BURNS) / **JIM SCLAVUNOS** – drums

Big Beat / Restless

Sep 91. (7") *(NST 135)* **EYEBALL IN MY MARTINI. / WILDER WILDER FASTER FASTER** [ ] –
(12"+=/cd-s+=) *(12/CD NST 135)* – Wilder wilder faster faster.

Sep 91. (cd/c/lp) *(CDWIK/WIKDC/WIKAD 101)* *<72586>* **LOOK MOM, NO HEAD!** [ ] [ ]
– Dames, booze, chains and boots / Two headed sex change / Blow up your mind / Hard workin' man / Miniskirt blues / Alligator stomp / I wanna

get in your pants Bend over, I'll drive / Don't get funny with me / Eyeball in my Martini / Hipsville 29 B.C. / When I get the blues (the strangeness in me). *(also pic-lp/pic-cd; WIKDP/CDWIKD 101) (lp re-mast.Nov01 on 'Vengeance'; VENG 673)*

— **NICKY ALEXANDER** – drums (ex-WEIRDOS); repl. JIM

Sep 92. (cd-ep) *(CDNST 136)* **BLUES FIX EP** [ ] [–]
– Hard workin' man / It's mighty crazy / Jelly roll rock / Shombalor.

— **HARRY DRUMDINI** – drums; repl. NICKY

Creation / Medicine – Warners

Oct 94. (7") *(CRE 180)* **ULTRA TWIST! / CONFESSIONS OF A PSYCHO CAT** [ ] [–]
(12"+=)(cd-s+=) *(CRE 180T)(CRESCD 180)* – No club love wolf.

Oct 94. (cd/c/lp) *(CRECD/C-CRE/CRELP 170)* <24592> **FLAMEJOB** [ ] [ ]
– Mean machine / Ultra twist / Let's get f*cked up / Nest of the cuckoo bird / I'm customized / Sado country auto show / Naked girl falling down the stairs / How come you do me? / Inside out and upside down (with you) / Trapped love / Swing the big eyed rabbit / Strange love / Blues blues blues / Sinners / Route 66 (get your kicks on). *(cd re-iss. Jan01; same)*

Feb 95. (7") *(CRE 196)* **NAKED GIRL FALLING DOWN THE STAIRS. / LET'S GET F*CKED UP** [ ] [–]
(cd-s+=) *(CRESCD 196)* – Surfin' bird.

Epitaph / Epitaph

Oct 97. (cd/c/lp) *<(6516-2/-4/-1)>* **BIG BEAT FROM BADSVILLE** [ ] [ ]
– Cramp stomp / God monster / It thing hard on / Like a bad girl should / Sheena's in a goth gang / Queen of pain / Monkey with your tail / Devil behind that bush / Super goo / Hypno sex ray / Burn she devil, burn / Wet nightmare / Badass bug / Haulass hyena. *(lp re-mast.Nov01 on 'Vengeance'; VENG 674)*

Dec 97. (7") *(6527-7)* **LIKE A BAD GIRL SHOULD. / WET NIGHTMARE** [ ] [–]
(cd-s+=) *(6527-2)* – I walked all night.

Vengeance / Vengeance

Mar 03. (7") *(VENG676)* **BIG BLACK WITCHCRAFT ROCK. / BUTCHER PETE** [ ] [–]

Apr 03. (lp/cd) *<(VENG 675/+CD)>* **FIENDS OF DOPE ISLAND** [ ] [ ]
– Big black witchcraft rock / Papa Satan sang Louie / Hang up / Fissure of Rolando / Dr. Fucker M.D. (Musical Deviant) / Dopefiend boogie / Taboo / Elvis fucking Christ! / She's got balls / Oowee baby / Mojo man from Mars / Color me black / Wrong way ticket.

– compilations, others, etc. –

May 83. (lp) *Illegal; (ILP 012) / I.R.S.; <SP 70042>* **OFF THE BONE** <US-title 'BAD MUSIC FOR BAD PEOPLE'> [44] Feb84 [ ]
– Human fly / The way I walk / Domino / Surfin' bird / Lonesome town / Garbageman / Fever / Drug train / Love me / I can't hardly stand it / Goo goo muck / She said / The crusher / Save it / New kind of kick. *(cd-iss. Jan87; ILPCD 012) (cd re-iss. 1992 on 'Castle'+=;)* – Uranium Rock / Good taste (live). *(cd re-iss. Apr98 on 'E.M.I.'; 493837-2) (lp re-iss. May01 on 'Simply Vinyl'; SVLP 327)*

1984. (4x7"box) *New Rose;* **I AIN'T NUTHIN' BUT A GOREHOUND. / WEEKEND ON MARS // FASTER PUSSYCAT. / YOU GOT GOOD TASTE // CALL OF THE WIG HAT. / THE MOST EXHALTED POTENTATE OF LOVE // PSYCHOTIC REACTION. / (one sided)** [–] French [–]
(all 4 either blue/white/black/green)

May 86. (7") *New Rose; (NEW 71)* **KIZMIAZ. / GET OFF THE ROAD** [–] [–]
(12"+=) *(NEW 70)* – Give me a woman.

Nov 87. (lp) *Vengeance;* **ROCKIN' AND REELIN' IN AUCKLAND, NEW ZEALAND (live)** [–] [ ]
(UK cd-iss. Sep94 on 'Big Beat'; CDWIKD 132) (lp re-mast.Nov01 on 'Vengeance'; VENG 669)

Sep 00. (3xcd-box) *EMI; (528345-2)* **SONGS THE LORD TAUGHT US / OFF THE BONE / PSYCHEDELIC JUNGLE** [ ] [–]

CRANBERRIES

Formed: Limerick, Ireland . . . 1990 initially as covers band The CRANBERRY SAW US (corny, or what!) by brothers NOEL and MIKE HOGAN, plus FERGAL LAWLER. The inclusion of singer DOLORES O'RIORDAN, saw the release the following year of an independent single, 'UNCERTAIN'. The quartet returned to the studio late in '91, subsequently resurfacing on the 'Island' label with 'DREAMS', 'LINGER' and 'PUT ME DOWN'. These tracks were featured on 1993's glorious debut album, 'EVERYBODY ELSE IS DOING IT, SO WHY CAN'T WE', which went on to sell a million in America (a year later it went platinum in Britain). An indie style major outfit, initially described as The Irish SUNDAYS, The CRANBERRIES were distinguished by DOLORES' heavily accented vocals, endearing naive and girlish one minute, howling banshee-style the next. An acquired taste, definitely, but one which millions seemingly, erm, acquired, drawn in no doubt by their canny way with a romantic Celtic melody. After their slow beginnings, The CRANBERRIES were now hot property, the UK music press finally recognised their unique talent. Confusingly for newly acquainted fans, a follow-up album, 'NO NEED TO ARGUE' hit the shops the same year ('94), previewed by the grunge like 'ZOMBIE', a "loud" single (in every sense of the word), which made the UK Top 20. Incredibly, the track became a massive international hit for rave outfit, AMY, who took it back into the UK Top 20 in 1995. A third set, 'TO THE FAITHFUL DEPARTED' (1996) saw the band enlisting gloss-rock producer, Bruce Fairbairn, in what was surely a move to further dominate the American market. Songs about Bosnia, John Lennon etc, didn't prevent it from cleaning up commercially once more, although most critics were unimpressed. If the CRANBERRIES thought they were harshly treated by the press on this occasion, they hadn't dreamt of the stick they would endure for next record, 'BURY THE HATCHET' (1999). Although its initial sales were once again promising both in the UK and US, the album quickly tailed off into the proverbial oblivion (six feet under it would seem); surely babe DOLORES and her melancholic muckers couldn't get away with this sort of thing again. The appropriately titled 'WAKE UP AND SMELL THE COFFEE' (2001) tried hard to recover lost ground, even to the extent of renewing their production partnership with Stephen Street. Yet despite valiant attempts at trimming the musical flab, the album weighed in at a gross Top 50 in the US and an even more disheartening No.61 placing in the UK. • **Songwriters:** DOLORES and NOEL, except (THEY LONG TO BE) CLOSE TO YOU (Carpenters) / GO YOUR OWN WAY (Fleetwood Mac). • **Trivia:** They supported MOOSE in the summer of '91, DOLORES guesting on their 1992 album, 'XYZ'.

Album rating: EVERYBODY ELSE IS DOING IT, SO WHY CAN'T WE (*8) / NO NEED TO ARGUE (*7) / TO THE FAITHFUL DEPARTED (*4) / BURY THE HATCHET (*4) / WAKE UP AND SMELL THE COFFEE (*4) / STARS: THE BEST OF 1992-2002 compilation (*7)

DOLORES O'RIORDAN (b. 6 Sep'71) – vocals, acoustic guitar / **NOEL HOGAN** (b.25 Dec'71) – guitar / **MIKE HOGAN** (b.29 Apr'73) – bass / **FERGAL LAWLER** (b. 4 Mar'71) – drums

Xerica / not iss.

Oct 91. (12"ep) *(XER 14T)* **UNCERTAIN / NOTHING LEFT AT ALL. / PATHETIC SENSES / THEM** [ ] [–]

Island / Island

Sep 92. (7") *(IS 548)* **DREAMS. / WHAT YOU WERE** [ ] [–]
(12"+=/cd-s+=) *(12IS/CID 548)* – Liar.

Feb 93. (c-s/7") *(C+/IS 556)* **LINGER. / REASON** [74] [–]
(12"/cd-s) *(12IS/CID 556)* – ('A'side) / How (radical mix).

Mar 93. (cd/c/lp) *(CID/ICT/ILPS 8003) <514156>* **EVERYBODY ELSE IS DOING IT, SO WHY CAN'T WE?** 64 18
– I still do / Dreams / Sunday / Pretty / Waltzing black / Not sorry / Linger / Wanted / Still can't . . . / I will always / How / Put me down. *(re-dist.Nov93; same) (re-iss. Mar94, hit UK No.1)*

Oct 93. (c-s) *<862800>* **LINGER / HOW** – 8

Jan 94. (c-s/7") *(C+/IS 559)* **LINGER. / PRETTY (live)** 14 –
(10"+=/cd-s+=) *(10IS/CID 559)* – Waltzing black (live) / I still do (live).

Apr 94. (c-s/7") *(C+/IS 594) <864436>* **DREAMS. / WHAT YOU WERE** 27 Mar94 42
(cd-s+=) *(CID 594)* – Liar.
(cd-s) *(CIDX 594)* – ('A'live) / Liar (live) / Not sorry (live) / Wanted (live).

—— Jun'94; DOLORES featured on JAH WOBBLE's hit 'The Sun Does Rise'.

Sep 94. (c-s/7") *(C+/IS 600)* **ZOMBIE. / AWAY** 14 –
(cd-s+=) *(CID 600)* – I don't need.
(cd-s) *(CIDX 600)* – ('A'extended) / Waltzing black (live) / Linger (live).

Oct 94. (cd/c/lp) *(CIS/ICT/ILPS 8029) <524050>* **NO NEED TO ARGUE** 2 6
– Ode to my family / I can't be with you / 21 / Zombie / Empty / Everything I said / The icicle melts / Disappointment / Ridiculous thoughts / Dreaming my dreams / Yeats' grave / Daffodil lament / No need to argue.

Nov 94. (c-s/7") *(C+/IS 601)* **ODE TO MY FAMILY. / SO COLD IN IRELAND** 29 –
(cd-s+=) *(CID 601)* – No need to argue / Dreaming my dreams.
(cd-s) *(CIDX 601)* – ('A'live) / Dreams (live) / Ridiculous thoughts (live) / Zombie (live).

Feb 95. (c-s/7") *(C+/IS 605)* **I CAN'T BE WITH YOU. / (THEY LONG TO BE) CLOSE TO YOU** 23 –
(cd-s+=) *(CID 605)* – Empty (BBC session).
(cd-s) *(CIDX 605)* – ('A'-BBC session) / Zombie (acoustic) / Daffodil lament (live).

Jul 95. (c-s/7") *(C+/IS 616)* **RIDICULOUS THOUGHTS. / LINGER** 20 –
(cd-s+=) *(CID 616)* – Twenty one (live) / Ridiculous thoughts (live).

Apr 96. (c-s) *(CIS 633)* **SALVATION / I'M STILL REMEMBERING** 13 –
(cd-s+=) *(CID 633)* – I just shot John Lennon.

May 96. (cd/c/colrd-lp) *(CID/ICT/ILPS 8048) <524234>* **TO THE FAITHFUL DEPARTED** 2 4
– Hollywood / Salvation / When you're gone / Free to decide / War child / Forever yellow skies / The rebels / I just shot John Lennon / Electric blue / I'm still remembering / Will you remember? / Joe / Bosnia.

Jul 96. (c-s) *(CIS 637)* **FREE TO DECIDE / CORDELL** 33 –
(cd-s+=) *(CID 637)* – The picture I view.
(cd-s) *(CIDX 637)* – ('A'side) / Salvation (live) / Bosnia.

Nov 96. (c-s) *<854802>* **FREE TO DECIDE / WHEN YOU'RE GONE** – 22

Apr 99. (c-s) *(572568-4)* **PROMISES / SWEETEST THING** 13
(cd-s+=) *(572591-2)* – Linger (live).
(cd-s) *(572593-2)* – ('A'side) / Dreams (live) / Promises (live).

Apr 99. (cd/c/d-lp) *(524644-2/-4/-1) <524611>* **BURY THE HATCHET** 7 13
– Animal instinct / Loud and clear / Promises / You and me / Just my imagination / Shattered / Desperate Andy / Saving grace / Copycat / What's on my mind / Delileh / Fee fi fo / Dying in the sun. *(d-cd iss.Apr00 +=; 542507-2)* – Sorry son / Baby blues / The sweetest thing / Woman without pride / Such a shame / Papparazzi on mopeds // Promises (live) / Animal instinct (live) / Loud and clear (live) / You and me (live) / Shattered (live) / Desperate Andy (live) / Delilah (live).

Jul 99. (c-s/cd-s) *(56219 1-4/7-2)* **ANIMAL INSTINCT / PAPARAZZI ON MOPEDS** 54
(cd-s) *(562198-2)* – ('A'side) / Ode to my family (live) / Baby blues / Salvation (live).

Oct 99. (c-s) *(562412-4)* **JUST MY IMAGINATION / GOD TO BE WITH YOU**
(cd-s+=) *(562414-2)* – Zombie (live).
(cd-s) *(562415-2)* – ('A'side) / Such a shame / Promises (live).

M.C.A. M.C.A.

Oct 01. (cd-s) *(MCSTD 42070)* **ANALYSE / ANALYSE (oceanic) / I CAN'T BE WITH YOU (live)** –

Oct 01. (cd) *(112706-2) <112739>* **WAKE UP AND SMELL THE COFFEE** 61 46
– Never grow old / Analyse / Time is ticking out / Dying inside / This is the day / The concept / Wake up and smell the coffee / Pretty eyes / I really hope / Every morning / Do you know / Carry on / Chocolate Brown. *(UK+=)* – In the ghetto / Dreams (live) / Promises (live).

Sep 02. (cd) *(063386-2) <063277>* **STARS: THE BEST OF 1992-2002** (compilation) 20
– Dreams / Linger / Zombie / Ode to my family / I can't be with you / Ridiculous thoughts / Salvation / Free to decide / When you're gone / Hollywood / Promises / Animal instinct / Just my imagination / You and me / Analyse / Time is ticking out / This is the day / Daffodil lament / New New York / Stars. *(d-cd+=; 063354-2)* – Zombie (live) / Ode to my family (live) / Animal instinct (live) / Salvation (live) / Daffodil lament (live) / Zombie (video).

– compilations, etc. –

Nov 95. (d-cd) **EVERYBODY ELSE IS DOING IT, SO WHY CAN'T WE? / NO NEED TO ARGUE**

Apr 02. (4xcd-box) *Island; (<586707-2>)* **TREASURE BOX**

Robert CRAY

Born: 1 Aug'53, Columbus, Georgia, USA. A long time admirer of ALBERT COLLINS, CRAY formed his first band ONE WAY STREET, in high school (where, incidentally, COLLINS performed), graduating to support the legendary bluesman on his future forays in the area. He subsequently met bass player, RICHARD COUSINS, in 1973, both of them serving a two year apprenticeship with COLLINS and later stepping out independently to form what was to become The ROBERT CRAY BAND, featuring CRAY (guitar and vocals), COUSINS (bass), PETER BOE (keyboards) and DAVID OLSON (drums). Their debut album, 'WHO'S BEEN TALKIN' was cut during constant touring throughout the US in 1978 and showed CRAY'S clean cut style of blues and soul, owing much to ALBERT COLLINS and PETER GREEN, (with the influence of JIMI HENDRIX showing on the faster numbers). Although the record was, initially shelved for two years, it was eventually issued in the US by the short lived 'Tomato' label (whose licence was picked up by 'Atlantic' and by 'Charly' Records in the UK). He recorded 'BAD INFLUENCE' in 1983 (with ERIC CLAPTON – who held CRAY in high regard – guesting) the record released on 'Hightone' in the US and 'Demon' in Britain (it would take 4 years to chart!). The album showed that his talent as a songwriter was flourishing and as a result there were only two covers although, one of them, 'GOT TO MAKE A COMEBACK', by EDDIE FLOYD, is one of the highlights. In 1984, The ROBERT CRAY BAND completed their first European tour to critical acclaim and in 1985, had their first chart entry with 'FALSE ACCUSATIONS', the set topping the UK Independent chart and reaching number 68 in the national album chart. In the US meanwhile, it won the 'Best Blues Album' award from the National Association of Independent Record Distributors, although it only reached number 141 in the charts. The album featured such enduring tracks as, 'PLAYIN' IN THE DIRT', 'THE LAST TIME (I GET BURNED LIKE THIS)', 'PAYIN' FOR IT NOW' and 'SONNY', a classic CRAY set. A collaboration with ALBERT COLLINS and JOHNNY COPELAND followed in the form of 'SHOWDOWN' and he subsequently signed to 'Mercury' Records where he began work on his debut album, 'STRONG PERSUADER'. During 1986 he played 170 gigs, including his seventh Euro tour since 1984, building on his increasing reputation in the UK. In October, he joined KEITH RICHARDS, ERIC CLAPTON and others on stage in St. Louis for CHUCK BERRY's 60th birthday concert, later featured in the film 'HAIL HAIL ROCK N ROLL'. One month later, he won a record six Handy awards at America's 7th National Blues ceremony. CRAY's first stadium tour started in May 1987 as support to HUEY LEWIS AND THE NEWS, just as 'BAD INFLUENCE', originally released in 1983, charted in the US. April 1987 saw the outstanding 'STRONG

PERSUADER' at 13 in the US charts, becoming the first blues album to crack the Top 20 since 1972. Lyrically he was improving all the time, his guitar was as crisp as ever and the album went on to sell over a million copies. The single from the album, 'SMOKING GUN' (although there were better tracks on the album), was to be his breakthrough, reaching 22 in the US and as his fame spread, he was invited to back ERIC CLAPTON on a month long tour of the States. His next single, 'RIGHT NEXT DOOR (BECAUSE OF ME)', didn't fare so well at home, although it did give him his first single hit in the UK, reaching number 50. He was back touring with ERIC CLAPTON again in November (this time in Japan) and it was clear that a great friendship was forming. The following year, 1988, he won the Grammy for 'Best Contemporary Blues Recording' on 'STRONG PERSUADER', and recorded his next album, 'DON'T BE AFRAID OF THE DARK', in Los Angeles with DAVID SANBORN guesting on saxophone. The record was his most successful to date (number 13 in the UK and number 32 in the US) although the title track, released as a single, failed to make any significant impact. He won his second Grammy for 'DON'T BE AFRAID OF THE DARK' and went on to guest on ERIC CLAPTON'S 'JOURNEYMAN' while being on the bill at CLAPTON's eighteen show marathon at the Albert Hall. His sixth album, 'MIDNIGHT STROLL', an altogether tougher album, recorded with a new line-up, reached UK number 19 and US number 51. In 1991, he was selected to present HOWLIN' WOLF's induction trophy to the WOLF's widow, Lilly Burnett, at the sixth annual Rock & Roll Hall of Fame Awards. Later that year, he took part in the Newport Jazz Festival with B.B. KING and JOHN LEE HOOKER, which led to him playing on HOOKER'S album 'MR. LUCKY'. He took the stage in Seville, Spain as part of a five concert series, 'Guitar Legends' to celebrate Expo 92 and later joined BOZ SCAGGS, JOHNNY RIVERS and The DOOBIE BROTHERS with MICHAEL McDONALD to celebrate the 25th anniversary of The MEMPHIS HORNS in Memphis. CRAY'S next two albums seemed to show a slide in his chart status with the bland 'I WAS WARNED' reaching UK number 29 and US 103, while 'SHAME AND A SIN', although showing some signs of the earlier spark, peaked at only 48 and 143 in the UK and US respectively. His 1995 album, 'SOME RAINY MORNING' left you wondering whether he was looking forwards or backwards, CRAY obviously suffering a lack of direction. Although his chart success may be waning he will always have the respect of the public and his fellow performers by virtue of the unassuming way he goes about his business. With 'SWEET POTATO PIE' (1997), CRAY initiated a not so subtle change in direction, from slick blues to equally slick but sympathetically rendered Southern soul. It was a refreshing change, not only for CRAY but for the US blues scene in general, with the Grammy-scooping guitarist delving deeper into a classic Memphis groove on 1999's 'TAKE YOUR SHOES OFF'. While he never surrendered his blues licks completely, he moulded his playing around arrangements and rhythms which harked back to the glory days of Stax/Volt without sounding painfully derivative. Thus we got covers of Mack Rice's '24-7 MAN' and Solomon Burke's 'WON'T YOU GIVE HIM (ONE MORE CHANCE), whereas in the past, the reading of Willie Dixon's 'TOLLIN' BELLS' would've sufficed. Rice again gets the CRAY treatment ('LOVE SICKNESS') on 'SHOULDA BEEN HOME' (2001), another richly satisfying stew of blues-baked soul food with the emphasis on hurtin', heartbreakin' lyrical fare and downtempo testifying. Save for his soulful embrace of the late 90's, CRAY has never really been one for experimentation although 'TIME WILL TELL' (2003) certainly took more artistic risks than usual. The addition of strings and even sitar were unprecedented if slightly out of context, while attempts at tackling political themes (notably on lead track 'SURVIVOR') were commendable if not entirely convincing. Much more welcome were the horns of SLY STONE veterans CYNTHIA ROBINSON and JERRY MARTINI, on 'YOUR PAL'. • **Songwriters:** Mostly CRAY compositions with group collaborations. 1992 producer DENNIS WALKER wrote most with CRAY or PUGH. The same album saw CRAY co-write with BOZ SCAGGS and STEVE CROPPER on 'A PICTURE OF A BROKEN HEART' & 'ON THE ROAD DOWN' respectively. Covered; GOT TO MAKE A COMEBACK (Eddie Floyd) / DON'T TOUCH ME (Johnny 'Guitar' Watson) / TOO MANY COOKS (Willie Dixon) / YOU'RE GONNA NEED ME (Albert King) / SAVE IT (Bordleaux Bryant) / TRICK OR TREAT (Otis Redding) / etc. • **Trivia:** In 1980 he and band appeared in the film 'Animal House' as OTIS DAY's house group.

Album rating: WHO'S BEEN TALKIN' (*5) / BAD INFLUENCE (*7) / FALSE ACCUSATIONS (*6) /STRONG PERSUADER (*6) / DON'T BE AFRAID OF THE DARK (*7) / MIDNIGHT STROLL (*7) / I WAS WARNED (*5) / SHAME + A SIN (*5) / SOME RAINY MORNING (*5) / SWEET POTATO PIE (*6) / HEAVY PICKS compilation (*7) / SHOULDA BEEN HOME (*7) / TIME WILL TELL (*5)

ROBERT CRAY BAND

ROBERT CRAY – vocals, guitar / **RICHARD COUSINS** – bass / **DAVE OLSON** – drums / also **MIKE VANNICE** – sax, keyboards / **WARREN RAND** – sax / **CURTIS SALADO** – (guest) harmonica

not iss. Tomato

1980. (lp) *<7041>* **WHO'S BEEN TALKIN'** [-] [ ]
– Too many cooks / The score / The welfare (turns its back on you) / That's what I'll do / I'd rather be a wino / Who's been talkin' / Sleeping in the ground / I'm gonna forget about you / Nice as a fool can be / If you're thinkin' what I'm thinkin'. *(UK cd-iss. Oct86 on 'Charly'; CDCHARLY 28) (re-iss. Oct87 on 'Charly-R&B' lp/c; CRB/TC-CRB 1140) <US-re-iss. May88 lp/c/cd; 269 601-1/-4/-2> (re-iss. Oct88 on 'Charly' cd/c/lp; CD/TC+/CLM 101) (re-iss. Apr92 as 'THE SCORE' on 'Charly' cd/c; CDBM/TCBM 16)*

— retained **COUSINS, OLSON + SALADO**

Demon Hightone

Mar 84. (lp) *(FIEND 23) <H 8001>* **BAD INFLUENCE** [ ] Nov83 [ ]
– Phone booth / The grinder / Got to make a comeback / So many women, so little time / Where do I go from here / Waiting for a train / March on / Don't touch me / No big deal. *<cd-iss. Feb87; HCD 8001> (re-iss. Jul87 lp/c/cd+=; FIEND/+CASS/CD 23)* – I got loaded / Share what you've got, Keep what you need. *(cd re-iss. Apr96 on 'Hightone'; HCD 8001)*

— **PETER BOE** – keyboards, vocals repl. SALADO, VANNICE + RAND

Oct 85. (lp/c) *(FIEND/+CASS 43) <H 8005>* **FALSE ACCUSATIONS** [68] [ ]
– Porch light / Change of heart, change of mind (S.O.F.T.) / She's gone / Playin' in the dirt / I've slipped her mind / False accusations / The last time (I get burned like this) / Payin' for it now / Sonny. *(cd-iss. 1986; FIENDCD 43) (cd re-iss. Apr96 on 'Hightone'; HCD 8005)*

Nov 85. (12"ep) *(D 1038T)* **CHANGE OF HEART, CHANGE OF MIND (soft) / I GOT LOADED. / PHONE BOOTH / BAD INFLUENCE** [ ] [ ]

— In Nov'85, an album, 'SHOWDOWN!' with ALBERT COLLINS and JOHNNY COPELAND was released by 'Sonet' (SNTF 954)

Mercury Mercury

Oct 86. (7") *(CRAY 1)* **I GUESS I SHOWED HER. / DIVIDED HEART** [ ] [ ]
(12"+=) *(CRAY 1-12)* – Got to be a comeback / Share what you've got, keep what you need.

Nov 86. (lp/c)(cd) *(MERH/+C 97)<(830568-2)>* **STRONG PERSUADER** [34] [13]
– Smoking gun / I guess I showed her / Right next door (because of me) / Nothin' but a woman / Still around / More than I can stand / Foul play / I wonder / Fantasized / New blood.

Feb 87. (7") *(CRAY 2) <888343>* **SMOKING GUN. / FANTASIZED** [ ] [22]
(12"+=) *(CRAY 2-12)* – Divided heart.

May 87. (7") *(CRAY 3) <888327>* **RIGHT NEXT DOOR (BECAUSE OF ME). / NEW BLOOD** [50] [80]
(12"+=) *(CRAY 3-12)* – Share what you've got, keep what you need.
(10"+=) *(CRAY 3-10)* – I wonder / Smoking gun.

Aug 87. (7") *(CRAY 4)* **NOTHIN' BUT A WOMAN. / I WONDER**
(12"+=) *(CRAY 4-12)* – Still around / New blood.
(10"+=) *(CRAY 4-10)* – Right next door (because of me).

Aug 88. (7") *(CRAY 5) <870569>* **DON'T BE AFRAID OF THE DARK. / AT LAST** 74
(12"+=) *(CRAY 5-12)* – Without a trace.
(cd-s++=) *(CRACD 5)* – Smoking gun.

Aug 88. (lp/c)(cd) *(MERH/+C 129)<(834923-2)>* **DON'T BE AFRAID OF THE DARK** 13 32
– Don't be afraid of the dark / Don't you even care? / Your secret's safe with me / I can't go home / Night patrol / Acting this way / Gotta change the rules / Across the line / At last / Laugh out loud.

Oct 88. (7") *(CRAY 6)* **NIGHT PATROL. / MORE THAN I CAN STAND**
(12"+=) *(CRAY 6-12)* – Divided heart.
(cd-s++=) *(CRACD 6)* – I wonder.

Jan 89. (7") *(CRAY 7)* **ACTING THIS WAY. / LAUGH OUT LOUD**
(12"+=) *(CRAY 7-12)* – ('A'-Guitar version).
(cd-s++=) *(CRACD 7)* – Smoking gun.

ROBERT CRAY

— solo, retained only **COUSINS** plus **JIMMY PUGH** – keyboards / **KEVIN HAYES** – drums, percussion / **TIM KAIHATSU** – guitar / & The MEMPHIS HORNS: **WAYNE JACKSON** – trumpet, trombone / **ANDREW LOVE** – tenor saxophone (credited later as **ROBERT CRAY BAND with The MEMPHIS HORNS**)

Aug 90. (12"ep/cd-ep) **THE FORECAST (CALLS FOR PAIN) / HOLDIN' COURT. / LABOUR OF LOVE / MIDNIGHT STROLL**

Sep 90. (cd/c/lp) *<(846652-2/-4/-1)>* **MIDNIGHT STROLL** 19 51
– The forecast (calls for pain) / These things / My problem / Labour of love / Bouncin' back / Consequences / The things you do to me / Wall around time / Move a mountain / Midnight stroll. *(cd+=)* – Holdin' court. *(re-iss. Mar93 cd/c; same)*

Jan 91. (7") **CONSEQUENCES. / SMOKING GUN**
(12"+=/cd-s+=) – Right next door (because of me).

— **KARL SEVAREID** – bass; repl. COUSINS

Aug 92. (cd/c/lp) *<(512721-2/-4/-1)>* **I WAS WARNED** 29
– Just a loser / I'm a good man / I was warned / The price I pay / Won the battle / On the road down / A whole lotta pride / A picture of a broken heart / He don't live here anymore / Our last time. *(cd re-iss. Apr95; same)*

— **EDWARD MANION** – saxophone + **MARK PENDER** – trumpet; repl. horn section

Oct 93. (cd/c) *<(518517-2/-4)>* **SHAME + A SIN** 48
– 1040 blues / Some pain, some shame / I shiver / You're gonna need me / Don't break this ring / Stay go / Leave well enough alone / Passing by / I'm just lucky that way / Well I lied / Up and down.

Nov 93. (7"/c-s) **I HATE TAXES. / SMOKING GUN**
(cd-s+=) – 1040 blues / Right next door.

— with **PUGH / SEVAREID / HAYES**

May 95. (cd/c) *<(526928-2/-4)>* **SOME RAINY MORNING** 63
– Moan / I'll go on / Steppin' out / Never mattered much / Tell the landlord / Little boy big / Enough for me / Jealous love / Will you think of me / Holdin' on / Love well spent.

— Apr'96, he returned to the UK chart (at 65) augmenting JOHN LEE HOOKER on his single 'BABY LEE'.

May 97. (cd/c) *(534698-2/-4)* **SWEET POTATO PIE**
– Nothing against you / Do that for me / Back home / Save it / The one in the middle / Little birds / Trick or treat / Simple things / Jealous minds / Not bad for love / I can't quit.

Indigo Indigo

Feb 99. (cd) *(IGOXCD 516)* **IN CONCERT (live)**
– Chicken (intro) / That will never do / I've gotta take a chance / One more kiss / I'm so satisfied / A Collins (intro) / Don't lose your cool / Angel of mercy / That ain't the way to do it / I don't want you cuttin' my hair / Don't want no woman / Watch me baby / Collins' instrumental jam / Albert's alley.

Rykodisc Rykodisc

Apr 99. (cd/c) *<(RCD/RAC 10479)>* **TAKE YOUR SHOES OFF**
– Love gone to waste / That wasn't me / All the way / There's nothing wrong / 24-7 man / Pardon / Let me know / It's all gone / Won't you give him one more chance / Living proof / What about me / Tollin' bells.

May 01. (cd) *<(RCD 10611)>* **SHOULDA BEEN HOME**
– Baby's arms / Already gone / Anytime / Love sickness / I'm afraid / No one special / Out of Eden / Cry for me baby / Far away / Renew blues / Help me forget / The 12 year old boy.

Sanctuary Sanctuary

Jul 03. (cd) *(SANCD 194) <84613>* **TIME WILL TELL**
– Survivor / Up in the sky / Back door slam / I didn't know / You pal / Lotta lovin' / What you need (good man) / Spare some love? / Distant shore / Time makes two.

– compilations, others, etc. –

Jan 92. (cd/c/lp) *Tomato-Rhino; (269653-2/-4/-1)* **TOO MANY COOKS** (1978 session)

Jun 97. (cd/c) *Hallmark; (30664-2/-4)* **NEW BLUES** –

Dec 99. (cd) *Mercury; <(546557-2)>* **HEAVY PICKS: THE ROBERT CRAY BAND COLLECTION** Nov99

CRAZY HORSE

Formed: California, USA . . . 1962 as DANNY & THE MEMORIES by DANNY WHITTEN, BILLY TALBOT and RALPH MOLINA. After recording one 45 for 'Valiant', they finally settled for The ROCKETS moniker in 1967. Releasing an eponymous album early the following year, the group subsequently attracted the attention of NEIL YOUNG who procured them as a credited backing band on his early solo sets, 'Everybody Knows This Is Nowhere' (1969) and 'After The Goldrush' (1970). Signing to 'Reprise' in their own right, CRAZY HORSE delivered an eponymous solo album early in 1971. Featuring such West Coast luminaries as JACK NITZCHE, NILS LOFGREN, RY COODER and BARRY GUILBEAU and deservedly receiving rave reviews, the record alternated hard-bitten, country-ish rockers with desolate, lovelorn ballads; WHITTEN's tortured 'I DON'T WANT TO TALK ABOUT IT' was subsequently covered by everyone from ROD STEWART to EVERYTHING BUT THE GIRL, taking on an added poignancy following his untimely, fatal heroin overdose on the 18th November 1972. At the time of his death, WHITTEN had already been replaced as frontman by GREG LEROY, who had made his debut earlier that year on the album, 'LOOSE'; others new members numbered JOHN BLANTON and GEORGE WHITSELL, who deputised for producer, NITZSCHE. Nevertheless, the shock of WHITTEN's death eventually led to the group's break-up, although a final album, 'CRAZY HORSE AT CROOKED CREEK' appeared on 'Epic' records early in '73. YOUNG had also been affected by WHITTEN's death and the same year gathered together TALBOT and MOLINA (alongside new guitarist, FRANK SAMPEDRO) to record the compelling 'Tonight's The Night' album, a tribute of sorts to both WHITTEN and BRUCE BERRY (their roadie who had met a similar fate). Upon its belated 1975 release, the record was credited to NEIL YOUNG & CRAZY HORSE, the core of TALBOT, MOLINA and SAMPEDRO remaining at YOUNG's side from that point on (although the singer alternated with solo material) and working their gritty magic on such classic albums as 'Zuma' (1975), 'Rust Never Sleeps' (1979), 'Ragged Glory' (1990) and 'Weld' (1991). CRAZY HORSE themselves went back into the studio in the late 70's to record 'CRAZY MOON', a follow-up to the debut finally worth the name. With SAMPEDRO a worthy successor to WHITTEN, the likes of 'GOING DOWN AGAIN' (on which SAMPEDRO, in retrospect, sounds uncannily like NOEL GALLAGHER! – apparently a CRAZY HORSE fan) as soulful as anything on the debut. In 1993/94, CRAZY HORSE hooked up with another one of their admirers, ex-ICICLE WORKS frontman, IAN McNABB, on his Mercury-nominated set, 'Head Like A Rock'.

Album rating: CRAZY HORSE (*8) / LOOSE (*5) / CRAZY HORSE AT CROOKED CREEK (*5) / CRAZY MOON (*6)

DANNY & THE MEMORIES

DANNY WHITTEN (b. Los Angeles) – vocals, guitar / **BILLY TALBOT** (b. New York) – bass / **RALPH MOLINA** (b. Puerto Rica) – drums

not iss. Valiant

1964. (7") *<6049>* **CAN'T HELP LOVIN' THAT GIRL OF MINE. / DON'T GO** [–] [ ]
<re-iss. 1965; 705>

— Later in 1965, they were backing band to EDDIE HODGES on single 'LOVE MINUS ZERO – NO LIMIT' on 'Stateside' UK / 'Aurora' US.

The ROCKETS

with guests **LEON WHITSELL** – guitar, vocals / **GEORGE WHITSELL** – guitar, vocals / **BOBBY NOTKOFF** – violin

not iss. White Whale

Mar 68. (7") *<270>* **HOLE IN MY POCKET. / LET ME GO** [–] [ ]
Mar 68. (lp) *<WWS 7116>* **THE ROCKETS** [–] [ ]
– Hole in my pocket / Won't you say you'll stay / Mr. Chips / It's a mistake / Let me go / Try my patience / I won't always be around / Pill's blues / Stretch your skin / Eraser. *(UK cd-iss. May97 on 'Edsel'; EDCD 520)*

CRAZY HORSE

WHITTEN, TALBOT & MOLINA plus **JACK NITZSCHE** – keyboards, with **NILS LOFGREN** – guitar / **RY COODER** – steel guitar / **BOB GUILBEAU** – fiddle

Reprise Reprise

Feb 71. (7"w/drawn) **DOWNTOWN. / CROW JANE LADY** [–] [ ]
Apr 71. (lp) *(<RSLP 6438>)* **CRAZY HORSE** [ ] Feb71 [84]
– Gone dead train / Dance, dance, dance / Look at all the things / Beggars day / I don't want to talk about it / Downtown / Carolay / Dirty, dirty / Nobody / I'll get by / Crow Jane lady. *(re-iss. Mar86 on 'Edsel'; ED 175) <cd-iss. Apr94; 7599 268-8-2)>*
Apr 71. (7") *(RS 23503)* **DANCE, DANCE, DANCE. / LOOK AT ALL THE THINGS** [ ] [–]
1971. (7") *<1025>* **DANCE, DANCE, DANCE. / CAROLAY** [–] [ ]
1971. (7") *<1046>* **DIRTY, DIRTY. / BEGGARS DAY** [–] [ ]

— **GREG LEROY** – guitar, vocals repl. WHITTEN (He later died, see above) **JOHN BLANTON** – keyboards / **GEORGE WHITSELL** – guitar repl. NITZSCHE (producer)

Apr 72. (lp) *(K 44171) <MS 2059>* **LOOSE** [ ] Jan 72 [ ]
– Hit and run / Try / One thing I love / Move / All alone now / All the little things / Fair weather friend / You won't miss me / Going home / I don't believe it / Kind of woman / One sided love / And she won't even blow smoke in my direction.
Apr 72. (7") *(K 14159) <1075>* **ALL ALONE NOW. / ONE THING I LOVE** [ ] [ ]

— **RICK CURTIS** – guitar, vocals repl. WHITSELL. **MICHAEL CURTIS** – keyboards, guitar repl. BLANTON

Epic Epic

Jan 73. (lp) *(EPC 65223) <KE 31710>* **CRAZY HORSE AT CROOKED CREEK** [ ] [ ]
– Rock and roll band / Love is gone / We ride / Outside lookin' in / Don't keep me burning / Vehicle / Your song / Lady soul / Don't look back / 85 El Paso's. *<(cd-iss. Jun03 on 'Wounded Bird'; WOU 1710)>*
Feb 73. (7") *<10925>* **ROCK AND ROLL BAND. / OUTSIDE LOOKIN' IN** [–] [ ]
Jun 73. (7") *(EPC 1121)* **WE RIDE. / OUTSIDE LOOKING IN** [ ] [–]

— CRAZY HORSE now concentrated on working with NEIL YOUNG

— **FRANK SAMPEDRO** – guitar, vox had now been recruited by TALBOT and MOLINA. CRAZY HORSE re-united for another studio album.

R.C.A. R.C.A.

Apr 79. (lp) *(PL 13054) <AFL1-3054>* **CRAZY MOON** [ ] Nov78 [ ]
– She's hot / Going down again / Lost and lonely / Dancin' lady / End of the line / New Orleans / Love don't come easy / Downhill / Too late now / That day / Thunder & lightning. *(cd-iss. Apr98 on 'Camden-BMG'; 74321 578212) (cd re-iss. Aug00 on 'One Way'; OW 34485)*

— as a trio they continued to augment NEIL YOUNG well into the 90's.

— **SONNY MONE + MATT PUICCI** – guitars, vocals repl. MOLINA

World Service Curb

Nov 89. (lp/cd) *(SERV 009/+CD) <77707>* **LEFT FOR DEAD** [ ] [ ]
– Left for dead / Child of war / You and I / Mountain man / I could never lose your love / In the middle / If I ever do / World of love / Show a little faith.

— In 1993/94, the best known trio (TALBOT, MOLINA & SAMPEDRO), worked with IAN McNABB (ex-ICICLE WORKS)

CREAM

Formed: London, England . . . mid '66 as the first ever supergroup, by ERIC CLAPTON, GINGER BAKER and JACK BRUCE, who'd all cut their teeth with top-flight R&B outfits earlier in the decade. This fine pedigree led to Robert Stigwood signing them to his newly-founded 'Reaction' label, after their lauded debut at The National Jazz & Blues Festival in Windsor on the 3rd of July '66. Their initial 45, 'WRAPPING PAPER', gave them the first of many Top 40 hits, a track that didn't inspire much critical praise. To end the year, they issued a debut album, 'FRESH CREAM', lifting from it the breezy psychedelic single, 'I FEEL FREE', a number which united BRUCE and poet/lyricist PETE BROWN in a new songwriting partnership. It also gave CREAM their biggest hit to date, reaching No.11 in the UK. Alongside original material, the album featured updated blues standards, 'SPOONFUL' (Willie Dixon), 'ROLLIN' & TUMBLIN' (Muddy Waters) and 'I'M SO GLAD' (Skip James). Over the course of the next six months, they became increasingly influenced by the pioneering psychedelic blues of JIMI HENDRIX. This was much in evidence on the next 45, 'STRANGE BREW', a slow-burning piece of sinister psych-blues. One of the highlights of their second album, 'DISRAELI GEARS', this record also featured such enduring CREAM classics as, 'SUNSHINE OF YOUR LOVE' (a US-only Top 5 hit), 'TALES OF BRAVE ULYSSES' & 'WORLD OF PAIN'. In fact every track was fantastic and the album remains an essential purchase for any self-respecting record collector. Their third set, 'WHEELS OF FIRE', recorded in San Francisco and New York, consisted of two records – one studio, one live. The former featured an ominous cover of BOOKER T's 'BORN UNDER A BAD SIGN', while the live disc included a definitive re-working of ROBERT JOHNSON's 'CROSSROADS'. However, the album (which was soon split into two single lp's) failed to garner the same critical praise as its predecessor, pandering too heavily to commerciality. They played their farewell tour in November '68, culminating in a legendary sell-out show on the 26th at The Royal Albert Hall. They were already in the US Top 10 with the GEORGE HARRISON and CLAPTON-penned 'WHITE ROOM', the song later becoming a fitting epitaph after it was given a UK release in early '69. All went on to high-profile solo careers, the most obvious being ERIC 'God' CLAPTON.

Album rating: FRESH CREAM (*6) / DISRAELI GEARS (*9) / WHEELS OF FIRE (*8) / GOODBYE (*5) / THE BEST OF CREAM compilation (*7) / LIVE CREAM collection (*5) / LIVE CREAM VOL.2 collection (*5) / HEAVY CREAM compilation (*6) / STRANGE BREW – THE VERY BEST OF CREAM compilation (*9)

ERIC CLAPTON (b. ERIC PATRICK CLAPP, 30 May'45, Ripley, Surrey, England) – guitar, vocals (ex-YARDBIRDS, ex-JOHN MAYALL'S BLUESBREAKERS) / **JACK BRUCE** (b. JOHN BRUCE, 14 May'43, Glasgow, Scotland) – vocals, bass (ex-GRAHAM BOND, ex-JOHN MAYALL'S BLUESBREAKERS, ex-MANFRED MANN) / **GINGER BAKER** (b. PETER BAKER, 19 Aug'39, Lewisham, London, England) – drums (ex-GRAHAM BOND ORGANISATION, ex-ALEXIS KORNER'S BLUES INCORPORATED)

Reaction Atco

Oct 66. (7") *(591 007)* **WRAPPING PAPER. / CAT'S SQUIRREL** [34] [–]

Dec 66. (lp; mono/stereo) *(593/594 001)* *<33206>* **FRESH CREAM** [6] [39]
– N.S.U. / Sleepy time time / Dreaming / Sweet wine / Spoonful / Cat's squirrel / Four until late / Rollin' and tumblin' / I'm so glad / Toad. *(re-iss. Feb69; stereo); reached No.7 UK. (re-iss Oct70 as 'FULL CREAM'; 2447 010) (re-iss. Mar75 as 'CREAM' on 'Polydor'+=; 2384 067); 2 tracks) (cd-iss. Jan84+=; 827 576-2)* – Wrapping paper / The coffee song. *(cd re-iss. Mar98; 531810-2) (lp re-iss. Aug99 on 'Simply Vinyl'; SVLP 106)*

Dec 66. (7") *(591 011)* *<6462>* **I FEEL FREE. / N.S.U.** [11] [ ]

Jun 67. (7") *(591 015)* *<6488>* **STRANGE BREW. / TALES OF BRAVE ULYSSES** [17] [ ]

Nov 67. (7") *<6522>* **SPOONFUL. / (part 2)** [–] [ ]

Nov 67. (lp; mono/stereo) *(593/594 003)* *<33232>* **DISRAELI GEARS** [5] [4]
– Strange brew / Sunshine of your love / World of pain / Dance the night away / Blue condition / Tales of brave Ulysses / S.W.L.A.B.R. / We're going wrong / Outside woman blues / Take it back / Mother's lament. *<US re-iss. Feb77 on 'R.S.O.'; 3010> (re-iss. Nov77 on 'R.S.O.'; 239 412-2) (cd-iss. Jan84 on 'Track'; 823 636-2) (cd re-iss. Mar98; 531811-2) (lp re-iss. Jun99 on 'Simply Vinyl'; SVLP 87)*

Polydor Atco

Jan 68. (7") *<6544>* **SUNSHINE OF YOUR LOVE. / S.W.L.A.B.R.** [–] [5]
(UK-iss.Sep68; 56286); hit No.25)

May 68. (7") *(56258)* *<6575>* **ANYONE FOR TENNIS. / PRESSED RAT AND WARTHOG** [40] [64]

— **FELIX PAPPALARDI** – producer, instruments guested as 4th p/t member

Aug 68. (d-lp; mono/stereo) *(582/583 031-2)* *<2-700>* **WHEELS OF FIRE** [3] Jul68 [1]
(re-iss. 1972; 2612 001) <US re-iss. Feb77 on 'R.S.O.'; 3802> (re-iss. Jan84 on 'R.S.O.'; 3216 036) (cd-iss. Jan84; 8254 142) (cd re-iss. Feb89; 827 658-2) (cd re-iss. Mar98; 531812-2) (d-lp re-iss. Apr00 on 'Simply Vinyl'; SVLP 202)

Aug 68. (lp; mono/stereo) *(582/583 033)* **WHEELS OF FIRE – IN THE STUDIO** [7] [–]
– White room / Sitting on top of the world / Passing the time / As you said / Pressed rat and warthog / Politician / Those were the days / Born under a bad sign / Deserted cities of the heart. *(re-iss. Nov77 on 'R.S.O.'; 2394 136)*

Aug 68. (lp; mono/stereo) *(582/583 040)* **WHEELS OF FIRE – LIVE AT THE FILLMORE (live)** [ ] [–]
– Crossroads / Spoonful / Traintime / Toad. *(re-iss. Nov77 on 'R.S.O.'; 2394 137)*

Jan 69. (7") *(65300)* *<6617>* **WHITE ROOM. / THOSE WERE THE DAYS** [28] Sep68 [6]

— They split around mid-'68. The rest of their releases were posthumous and CLAPTON went solo after forming BLIND FAITH with BAKER. He also went solo. JACK BRUCE went solo, etc.

– compilations, others, etc. –

either 'Polydor' in UK and 'Atco' in the US

Jan 69. (7") *<6646>* **CROSSROADS. / PASSING THE TIME** [–] [28]

Mar 69. (lp) *(583 053)* *<7001>* **GOODBYE** [1] [2]
– I'm so glad (live) / Politician (live) / Sitting on top of the world (live) / Badge / Doing that scrapyard thing / What a bringdown. *(re-iss. Nov77 & Aug84 on 'R.S.O.'; 2394 178) (cd-iss. Jan84.+=; 823 660-2)* – Anyone for tennis. *(cd re-iss. Mar98; 531815-2) (lp re-iss. May00 on 'Simply Vinyl'; SVLP 211)*

Apr 69. (7") *(56315)* *<6668>* **BADGE. / WHAT A BRINGDOWN** [18] Mar69 [60]
(re-iss. Oct72; 2058 285)

Nov 69. (lp) *(583 060)* *<291>* **BEST OF CREAM** [6] Jul69 [3]
– Sunshine of your love / Badge / Crossroads / White room / Swlabr / Born under a bad sign / Tales of brave Ulysses / Strange brew / I feel free. *(re-iss. Nov77 on 'R.S.O.'; 3216 031) (re-iss. Apr86 on 'Arcade'; ADAH 429)*

Jun 70. (lp) *(2383 016)* *<33-328>* **LIVE CREAM (live)** [4] Apr70 [15]
– N.S.U. / Sleepy time time / Lawdy mama / Sweet wine / Rollin' and tumblin'. *(re-iss. Nov77 & Mar85 on 'R.S.O.' lp/c; SPE LP/MC 93) (cd-iss. May88; 827 577-2) (cd re-iss. Mar98; 531816-2)*

Jun 72. (lp) *(2383 119)* *<7005>* **LIVE CREAM VOL.2** [15] Mar72 [27]
– Deserted cities of the heart / White room / Politician / Tales of brave Ulysses / Sunshine of your love / Steppin' out. *(re-iss. Nov77 on 'R.S.O.';) (cd-iss. May88; 823 661-2) (cd re-iss. Mar98; 531817-2)*

Apr 73. (d-lp) *(2659 022)* *<3502>* **HEAVY CREAM** [ ] Oct72 [ ]

Nov 92. (cd) *I.T.M.; (ITM 960002)* **THE ALTERNATIVE ALBUM** [ ] [–]
(re-iss. Jan97 & Dec99 on 'Masterplan'; MP 42009)

Feb 95. (cd/c) *(523 752-2/-4)* **THE VERY BEST OF CREAM** [ ] [ ]
– White room / I feel free / Tales of brave Ulysses / I'm so glad / Toad / Sunshine of your love / Strange brew / N.S.U. / Born under a bad sign / Badge / Crossroads.

Sep 97. (4xcd-box) *(539000-2)* **THOSE WERE THE DAYS** [ ] [ ]

Apr 03. (cd) *(76048-2)* **AT THE BBC** [ ] [ ]

CREATION

Formed: Middlesex, England . . . 1961 as (5-piece!) MARK FOUR by KENNY PICKETT, JACK JONES and EDDIE PHILLIPS. Under the guidance of manager ROBERT STIGWOOD they released a couple of flop singles for 'Mercury'. Following a further two stiffs for 'Decca' and 'Fontana' respectively, they changed their line-up in mid-66 and became The CREATION. They also employed new manager TONY STRATTON-SMITH who found American producer SHEL TALMY and a new label, 'Planet'. Things started looking up when the group unleashed 2 superb 45's in 1966, 'MAKING TIME' and 'PAINTER MAN', both hitting the UK Top 50 (aided by alleged chart hyping from TONY). The former marked their finest moment, a blistering combination of searing R&B and psychedelia while the latter hit No.1 in Germany. When they moved to 'Polydor' in 1967, however, they ran out of steam and split the year after. Unfortunately their only LP release had been in Germany, where they had found some degree of success. In 1996, The CREATION were back on song with a fresh set, 'POWER SURGE', released for who else, 'Creation' records. • **Trivia:** PHILLIPS was the first person to play guitar with a violin bow, a feat later achieved by JIMMY PAGE of LED ZEPPELIN. • **Songwriters:** PICKETT or PHILLIPS plus covers:- ROCK AROUND THE CLOCK (Bill Haley) / TRY IT BABY (Marvin Gaye) / LIKE A ROLLING STONE (Bob Dylan) / BONY MORONIE (Larry Williams) / HEY JOE (hit; Jimi Hendrix). • **Trivia:** In 1970, PICKETT co-wrote UK No.1 hit 'Grandad' for CLIVE DUNN (Dad's Army) with HERBIE FLOWERS. PICKETT was later to write 'TEACHER TEACHER' for DAVE EDMUNDS, before he co-wrote some more songs with BILLY BREMNER. **Legacy:** PAINTER MAN was a 1979 UK Top 10 hit for BONEY M, while much later The GODFATHERS (in 1990) and RIDE (in 1994) covered HOW DOES IT FEEL TO FEEL. Many have been inspired by them including TELEVISION PERSONALITIES / TIMES / BIFF BANG POW and the label 'Creation'.

Album rating: HOW DOES IT FEEL TO FEEL compilation (*8) / POWER SURGE (*7)

MARK FOUR

KENNY PICKETT (b. 3 Sep'47, Ware, England) – vocals / **EDDIE PHILLIPS** (b.EDWIN, 15 Aug'45, Leytonstone, England) – lead guitar / **MICK THOMPSON** – rhythm guitar / **JOHN DALTON** – bass / **JACK JONES** (b. 8 Nov'44, Northampton, England) – drums

Mercury not iss.

May 64. (7") *(MF 815)* **ROCK AROUND THE CLOCK. / SLOW DOWN** [ ] [–]

Aug 64. (7") *(MF 825)* **TRY IT BABY. / CRAZY COUNTRY HOP** [ ] [–]

Decca not iss.

Aug 65. (7") *(F 12204)* **HURT ME IF YOU WILL. / I'M LEAVING** [ ] [–]

Fontana not iss.

Feb 66. (7") *(TF 664)* **WORK ALL DAY (SLEEP ALL NIGHT). / GOING DOWN FAST** [ ] [–]

— Split after final gig on 6th June 1966. DALTON joined The KINKS.

CREATION

BOB GARNER – bass (ex-TONY SHERIDAN BAND) repl. THOMPSON

Planet Planet

Jun 66. (7") *(<PLF 116>)* **MAKING TIME. / TRY AND STOP ME** [49] [ ]

Oct 66. (7") *(<PLF 119>)* **PAINTER MAN. / BIFF BANG POW** [36] [ ]

KIM GARDNER – bass (ex-BIRDS) repl. GARNER

Polydor Decca

Jun 67. (7") *(56177)* **IF I STAY TOO LONG. / NIGHTMARES** [ ] [ ]

Oct 67. (7") *(56207)* **LIFE IS JUST BEGINNING. / THROUGH MY EYES** [ ] [–]

Nov 67. (7") *<32227>* **HOW DOES IT FEEL TO FEEL. / LIFE IS JUST BEGINNING** [–] [ ]

Jan 68. (7") *(56230)* **HOW DOES IT FEEL TO FEEL. / TOM TOM** [ ] [–]

RON WOOD – guitar (ex-BIRDS) repl. DIGGER who had briefly repl. PICKETT. **PICKETT** returned to repl. PHILLIPS + GARDNER

May 68. (7") *(56246)* **MIDWAY DOWN. / THE GIRLS ARE NAKED** [ ] [–]

— Disbanded soon after above. PICKETT continued to write for SHEL TALMY and he also became road manager for LED ZEPPELIN in America. RON WOOD joined The FACES and later became a member of The ROLLING STONES. GARDNER co-formed ASHTON, GARDNER & DYKE who had a 1970 Top 3 hit with 'RESURRECTION SHUFFLE'. He later formed BADGER. JACK JONES drifted into cabaret session work.

— CREATION re-formed in the mid-80's with **PHILLIPS, PICKETT, NOBBY DALTON** – bass (ex-KINKS) + **MICK AVORY** – drums (ex-KINKS).

Jet not iss.

Apr 87. (7") *(JET 7-047)* **A SPIRIT CALLED LOVE. / MAKING TIME** [ ] [–]

(12"+=) *(JET 12-047)* – Mumbo jumbo.

— **PHILLIPS**, etc, without PICKETT formed pub band CUCKOOS NEST. In 1994, The CREATION re-formed with **PICKETT, JONES + PHILLIPS**

Creation Rykodisc

Jul 94. (7") *(CRE 200)* **CREATION. / SHOCK HORROR** [ ] [–]

(cd-s+=) *(CRECD 200)* – Power surge.

Mar 96. (cd/lp) *(CRE CD/LP 176)* **POWER SURGE** [ ] [ ]

– Creation / Power surge / Someone's gonna bleed / Shock horror / That's how I found love / Killing song / Nobody wants to know / City life / English language / Free men live forever / Ghost division / O+N.

— on the 10th Jan'97, KENNY PICKETT died of a heart attack at his home

– compilations, etc. –

Sep 73. (lp) *Charisma; (CS 8)* **CREATION '66-67** [ ] [–]

Oct 73. (7") *Charisma; (CB 213)* **MAKING TIME. / PAINTER MAN** [ ] [–]

(re-iss. Nov77 on 'Raw'; RAW 4)

Sep 82. (lp) *Edsel; (ED 106)* **HOW DOES IT FEEL TO FEEL** [ ] [–]

– How does it feel to feel / Life is just beginning / Through my eyes / Ostrich man / I am the walker / Tom Tom / The girls are naked / Painter man / Try and stop me / Biff bang pow / Making time / Cool jerk / For all that I am / Nightmares / Midway down / Can I join your band?. *(cd-iss. Aug90; EDCD 106)* – Uncle Bert / Like a rolling stone / If I stay too long / Hey Joe. *(lp re-iss. Feb00 on 'Get Back'; GET 519)*

1983. (lp) *Eva; (12005)* **THE MARK FOUR / THE CREATION** [ ] [–]

(cd-iss. 1992 & Jul99; EVAB 16)

May 84. (7") *Edsel; (E 5006)* **MAKING TIME. / UNCLE BERT** [ ] [–]

1985. (7"ep; by MARK FOUR) *Bam Caruso; (OPRA 037)* **LIVE AT THE BEAT SCENE CLUB** [ ] [–]

– Hurt me if you will / Got my mojo working / That's how strong my love is.

Apr 93. (m-lp) *Edsel; (NESTCD 904)* **PAINTER MAN** [ ] [–]

Oct 93. (cd/lp) *Cohesion; (COCRD/COCRL 1)* **LAY THE GHOST (live)** [ ] [–]

Apr 98. (cd) *Diablo; (DIAB 857)* **OUR MUSIC IS RED WITH PURPLE FLASHES** [ ] [–]

Oct 98. (cd) *Retroactive; (RECD 9002)* **MAKING TIME – CREATION VOL.1** [ ] [–]

(re-iss. Jun00; SD 8937)

Oct 98. (cd) *Retroactive; (RECD 9003)* **BIFF BANG POW – CREATION VOL.2** [ ] [–]

(re-iss. Jun00; SD 8936)

Mar 99. (cd) *Repertoire; (REP 4735)* **WE ARE THE PAINTERMEN** [ ] [–]

Feb 00. (lp) *Get Back; (GET 518)* **THE SINGLES COLLECTION** [ ] [–]

Jul 02. (cd) *Repertoire; (REP 4736)* **THE BEST OF THE CREATION** [ ] [–]

☐ CREATURES (see under ⇒ SIOUXSIE & THE BANSHEES)

CREED

Formed: Tallahassee, Florida, USA ... 1994 by singer SCOTT STAPP and guitarist MARK TREMONTI, who hooked up with rhythm section BRIAN MARSHALL and SCOTT PHILLIPS. Another band to emerge from the post-Grunge scene, although EDDIE VEDDER and LAYNE STALEY have no fears here about their mantle being taken by these lads. A year or two into their career, CREED released a self-financed debut set, 'MY OWN PRISON', which sold its initial batch and made major labels take note. 'Epic' (through subsidiary 'Wind-Up') finally won the battle for their signatures early in '97 and with a new producer, Ron St. Germain, remixed and re-issued the album later in the year. "Grunge was not dead!" was the claim of their teen-metal followers, although CREED themselves denied they were part of that genre and were just a basic rock'n'roll band – basic being the key word. 'MY OWN PRISON' started a steady rise up the American charts finally peaking at No.22 a year later, although Britain had to wait until early '99 to get its first taste of million-sellers CREED. By which point, Grunge had certainly been well and truly buried. Meanwhile, back in the States, the glum-rockers were just about to serve up a second helping in the shape of 'HUMAN CLAY' (1999) – a difficult second album indeed that nevertheless topped the chart. Proving that earnestness will indeed get you everywhere, CREED were back with another helping of stadium dirge in the form of 'WEATHERED' (2001). Indicating that their inimitably American rawk might be twisting the arm of angst-ridden Brit youth, the record nudged into the UK Top 50, while, of course, cleaning up in the States (No.1). • **Covered:** I'M EIGHTEEN (Alice Cooper) / RIDERS ON THE STORM (Doors). • **Note:** not to be confused with mid-90's act who issued 12" singles on 'Rectory'.

Album rating: MY OWN PRISON (*6) / HUMAN CLAY (*5) / WEATHERED (*4)

SCOTT STAPP – vocals / **MARK TREMONTI** – guitar, vocals / **BRIAN MARSHALL** – bass / **SCOTT PHILLIPS** – drums

Wind Up-Epic Wind Up-Epic

Oct 97. (cd) *<13049>* **MY OWN PRISON** [–] [22]

– Torn / Ode / My own prison / Pity for a dime / In America / Illusion / Unforgiven / Sister / What's this life for / One. *<US originally iss.1997 on 'Blue Collar'; 5066> (UK-iss.Feb99 on 'Wind-Up – Epic'; 493072)*

Feb 99. (-) *<radio cut>* **ONE** [–] [70]

Sep 99. (cd/c) *(495027-2/-4) <13053>* **HUMAN CLAY** [ ] [1]

– Are you ready / What if / Beautiful / Say I / Wrong way / Faceless man / Never die / With arms wide open / Higher / Wash away those years / Inside us all. *(re-dist.Jan01)* – hit UK No.29

Jan 00. (7"/cd-s) *(668315-7/-2) <radio cut>* **HIGHER / I'M EIGHTEEN / ROADSIDE BLUES (live)** [47] Aug99 [7]

Jan 01. (7"claret) *(670695-7) <album cut>* **WITH ARMS WIDE OPEN. / WITH ARMS WIDE OPEN (acoustic)** [13] Mar00 [1]

(c-s+=) *(670695-4)* – Wash away those tears.

(cd-s+=) *(670695-2)* – ('A'-new version / Strings / CD-ROM).

Sep 01. (7") *(671064-7)* **HIGHER. / I'M EIGHTEEN** [64] [–]

(c-s) *(671064-4)* – ('A'side) / To whom it may concern.

(cd-s) *(671064-2)* – ('A'side) / Is this the end / Roadhouse blues (live).

Nov 01. (cd) *(504979-2) <13075>* **WEATHERED** [44] [1]

– Bullets / Freedom fighter / Who's got my back? / Signs / One last breath / My sacrifice / Stand here with me / Weathered / Hide / Don't stop dancing / Lullaby.

Mar 02. (7") *(672316-7)* *<radio>* **MY SACRIFICE. / RIDERS ON THE STORM (with Robbie Kreiger)** 18 Oct01 4
(cd-s+=) *(672316-2)* – With arms wide open (strings version) / ('A'-video).

Jul 02. (cd-s) *(672826-2)* **ONE LAST BREATH / BULLETS / I'M EIGHTEEN / ('A'video)** 47 –

Sep 02. (cd-s) *<672984>* **ONE LAST BREATH / IS THIS THE END / MY OWN PRISON / ONE LAST BREATH (dub)** – 6

CREEDENCE CLEARWATER REVIVAL

Formed: El Cerrito, California, USA . . . late 1959 as school group The BLUE VELVETS by JOHN FOGERTY, STU COOK and DOUG CLIFFORD. JOHN soon invited other multi-instrumentalist and brother TOM. After one 45 on a local label, they became The GOLLIWOGS in 1964 and signed to label 'Fantasy' where TOM was working as a clerk. The 'BROWN EYED GIRL' single was a moderate success although subsequent releases stiffed. Following DOUG and JOHN's compulsory spell in the forces (no hippy draft dodging for these guys!) the group became CREEDENCE CLEARWATER REVIVAL, releasing their debut single, an inspired cover of 'SUZIE Q,' in September '68. A top 20 hit, it was closely followed by another cover, SCREAMIN' JAY HAWKINS' 'I PUT A SPELL ON YOU' (1968) and a self-titled debut album the following year. Despite hailing from Berkeley in California, CREEDENCE, or at least JOHN FOGERTY lived and breathed a Southern fantasy of "Backwood Bayous", "Cajun Queens" and "Hoodoos" (eh?!). This was swamp R&B of the rootsiest pedigree, utilising a simple but stunningly effective hybrid of raw rock'n'roll, country and blues. FOGERTY's voice was an instrument in its own right, a life-affirming bellow that equalled MARVIN GAYE and OTIS REDDING for soulfulness and if his early classics fail to send a shiver up your spine, it'd be an idea to check your pulse. The man was also blessed with the ability to write insanely catchy songs which were nevertheless steeped in Southern authenticity. 'PROUD MARY' / 'BORN ON THE BAYOU' (1969) was the first in an avalanche of hits that saw CREEDENCE become one of the world's biggest selling bands during their heyday of '69-70. The classic 'GREEN RIVER' (1969) spawned perhaps their best known track, the apocalyptic swamp-pop of 'BAD MOON RISING' as well as the poignant country soul of 'LODI' and the blistering title track. 'DOWN ON THE CORNER' (1970) kept up the run of hit singles while 'WILLY AND THE POOR BOYS' (1970) remains the definitive CCR album. From the passionate politicism of 'FORTUNATE SON' to the desolate strangeness of 'EFFIGY', the album ran the gamut of the band's influences. There was no stopping the prolific FOGERTY at this point and a mere six months later the band released 'COSMO'S FACTORY' (1970). Coming within a whisker of its predecessor, the album produced the top ten hits 'TRAVELLIN' MAN' (1970), 'UP AROUND THE BEND' (1970) and 'LONG AS I CAN SEE THE LIGHT' (1970) as well as their driving cover of MARVIN GAYE's 'I HEARD IT THROUGH THE GRAPEVINE'. While 'PENDULUM' (1971) was slated as a disappointment, it nevertheless held nuggets like the gorgeous 'HAVE YOU EVER SEEN THE RAIN' and the rousing 'HEY TONIGHT'. By this point, however, internal disputes were rife and TOM left for a solo career a month after the album's release. Pared down to a trio, CCR cut a final studio album, 'MARDI GRAS' (1971) before splitting in 1973. JOHN released his first solo outing the same year, a collection of purist country under the BLUE RIDGE RANGERS moniker, following it up with 'JOHN FOGERTY' in 1975. While the album contained the FOGERTY classics, 'ROCKIN' ALL OVER THE WORLD' and 'ALMOST SATURDAY NIGHT', and his voice was still incredible, his earlier songwriting sharpness sounded blunted. Retreating to a farm for a life of rural bliss with his family, it was 10 years before FOGERTY returned with 'CENTERFIELD' (1985). Although it sold two million copies, the album was again slightly disappointing and led to FOGERTY gaining a place in the history books for being possibly the only artist ever to be sued (by 'Fantasy' owner SAUL ZAENTZ) for plagiarising his own material. 'EYE OF THE ZOMBIE' (1986) was average while 'BLUE MOON SWAMP' (1997) was hardly worth waiting a decade for. Despite being the driving force behind a band that has influenced artists as diverse as SONIC YOUTH, HANOI ROCKS and STATUS QUO (!), it seems increasingly unlikely that FOGERTY is going to come up with something that does his legend justice. • **Covered:** SUZIE Q (Dale Hawkins) / OOBY DOOBY (Roy Orbison) / HELLO MARY LOU (Ricky Nelson) / etc. • **Miscellaneous:** TOM FOGERTY was to die of tuberculosis on the 6th September '90.

Album rating: CREEDENCE CLEARWATER REVIVAL (*5) / BAYOU COUNTRY (*6) / GREEN RIVER (*8) / WILLY AND THE POOR BOYS (*9) / COSMO'S FACTORY (*7) / PENDULUM (*6) / MARDI GRAS (*4) / CREEDENCE GOLD compilation (*8) / MORE CREEDENCE GOLD compilation (*7) / LIVE IN EUROPE (*4) / THE ROYAL ALBERT HALL CONCERT (*4) / THE COLLECTION double compilation (*9) / John Fogerty: THE BLUE RIDGE RANGERS (*5) / JOHN FOGERTY (*4) / CENTERFIELD (*7) / EYE OF THE ZOMBIE (*4) / BLUE MOON SWAMP (*7)

The BLUE VELVETS

JOHN FOGERTY (b.28 May'45, Berkeley, Calif.)– vocals, guitar / **TOM FOGERTY** (b. 9 Nov'41, Berkeley)– rhythm guitar, piano / **STU COOK** (b.25 Apr'45, Portland, Calif.)– bass / **DOUG 'COSMO' CLIFFORD** (b.24 Apr'45, Palo Alto, Calif.)- **drums**

not iss. Orkhestra

1962. (7") *<1010>* **HAVE YOU EVER BEEN LONELY. / BONITA** –

The GOLLIWOGS

same line-up (TOM sang lead on first)

not iss. Fantasy

Nov 64. (7") *<590>* **DON'T TELL ME NO LIES. / LITTLE GIRL** –

Jun 65. (7") *<597>* **YOU CAME WALKING. / WHERE YOU BEEN** –

Aug 65. (7") *<599>* **YOU CAN'T BE TRUE. / YOU GOT NOTHIN' ON ME** –

Vocalion Scorpio

Jan 66. (7") *(VF 9266)* *<404>* **BROWN-EYED GIRL. / YOU BETTER BE CAREFUL**

Mar 66. (7") *(VF 9283)* *<405>* **FRAGILE CHILD. / FIGHT FIRE**

Dec 66. (7") *<408>* **WALKING ON THE WATER. / YOU BETTER GET IT** –

Nov 67. (7") *<412>* **PORTERVILLE. / CALL IT PRETENDING** –
(above single was soon later credited to below group name) *(also, a compilation album of some singles above was released in '74 on 'Fantasy')*

CREEDENCE CLEARWATER REVIVAL

same line-up

Liberty Fantasy

Sep 68. (7") *<616>* **SUZIE Q. (part 1). / SUZIE Q. (part 2)** – 11

Nov 68. (7") *<617>* **I PUT A SPELL ON YOU. / WALK ON THE WATER** –

Apr 69. (lp) *(LBS 83259) <8382>* **CREEDENCE CLEARWATER REVIVAL** Jul68 52
– I put a spell on you / Suzie Q. / The working man / Ninety-nine and a half (won't do) / Get down woman / Porterville / Gloomy / Walk on the water. *(re-iss. Mar73 on 'Fantasy'; FT 506) (re-iss. Jul84 on 'Fantasy' lp/c; FAS LP/K 5002) (re-iss. Aug87 on 'Fantasy' lp/c/cd; FACE/FACC/CDFE 501)*

May 69. (7") *(LBF 15223) <619>* **PROUD MARY. / BORN ON THE BAYOU** 8 Jan69 2

Jun 69. (lp) *(LBS 83261) <8387>* **BAYOU COUNTRY** Feb69 7
– Born on the bayou / Bootleg / Graveyard train / Good golly Miss Molly / Penthouse pauper / Keep on chooglin' / Proud Mary. *(hit UK No.62 in May'70) (re-iss. Mar73 on 'Fantasy'; FT 507) (re-iss. Jul84 on 'Fantasy' lp/c; FAS LP/K 5003) (re-iss. Aug87 on 'Fantasy' lp/c/cd; FACE/FACC/CDFE 502)*

Aug 69. (7") *(LBF 15230) <622>* **BAD MOON RISING. / LODI** 1 2 May69 52

Nov 69. (7") *(LBF 15250) <625>* **GREEN RIVER. / COMMOTION** 19 2 Jul69 30

Dec 69. (lp) *(LBS 83273) <8393>* **GREEN RIVER** 20 Sep69 1
– Green river / Commotion / Tombstone shadow / Wrote a song for everyone / Bad moon rising / Lodi / Cross-tie walker / Sinister purpose / Lodi / Wrote a song for everyone / Night time is the right time. *(re-iss. Mar73 on 'Fantasy'; FT 504) (re-iss. Jul84 on 'Fantasy' lp/c; FAS LP/K 5004) (re-iss. Aug87 on 'Fantasy' lp/c/cd; FACE/FACC/CDFE 503)*

Feb 70. (7") *(LBF 15283) <634>* **DOWN ON THE CORNER. / FORTUNATE SON** 31 Oct 69 3 14

Mar 70. (lp) *(LBS 83338) <8397>* **WILLY AND THE POOR BOYS** 10 Dec69 3
– Down on the corner / It came out of the sky / Cotton fields / Poor boy shuffle / Feelin' blue / Fortunate son / Don't look now (it ain't you or me) / The midnight special / Side of the road / Effigy. *(re-iss. Mar73 on 'Fantasy'; FT 503) (re-iss. Jul84 on 'Fantasy' lp/c; FAS LP/K 5005) (re-iss. Aug87 on 'Fantasy' lp/c/cd; FACE/FACC/CDFE 504)*

Mar 70. (7") *(LBF 15310) <637>* **TRAVELIN' BAND. / WHO'LL STOP THE RAIN** 8 Jan70 2

Jun 70. (7") *(LBF 15354) <641>* **UP AROUND THE BEND. / RUN THROUGH THE JUNGLE** 3 Apr70 4

Aug 70. (7") *(LBF 15384) <645>* **LONG AS I CAN SEE THE LIGHT. / LOOKIN' OUT MY BACK DOOR** 20 B-side 2

Sep 70. (lp) *(LBS 83388) <8402>* **COSMO'S FACTORY** 1 Jul70 1
– Ramble tamble / Before you accuse me / Travelin' band / Ooby dooby / Lookin' out my back door / Run through the jungle / Up around the bend / My baby left me / Who'll stop the rain / I heard it through the grapevine / Long as I can see the light. *(re-iss. Mar73 on 'Fantasy'; FT 502) (re-iss. Jul84 lp/c; FAS LP/K 506) (re-iss. Aug87 on 'Fantasy' lp/c/cd; FACE/FACC/CDFE 505)*

Jan 71. (lp) *(LBG 83400) <8410>* **PENDULUM** 23 Dec70 5
– Pagan baby / Sailor's lament / Chameleon / Have you ever seen the rain / (Wish I could) Hideaway / Born to move / Hey tonight / It's just a thought / Molina / Rude awakening No.2. *(re-iss. Mar73 on 'Fantasy'; FT 508) (re-iss. Jul84 on 'Fantasy' lp/c; FAS LP/K 5007) (re-iss. Nov89 on 'Fantasy' lp/c/cd; FACE/FACC/CDFE 512) (cd re-iss. Jan99 on 'Akarma'; 8410)*

Mar 71. (7") *(LBF 15440) <655>* **HAVE YOU EVER SEEN THE RAIN. / HEY TONIGHT** 36 Jan71 8
(re-iss. Apr71 on 'United Artists'; UP 35210)

— now a trio when TOM FOGERTY departed to go solo (Feb'71)

U.A. Fantasy

Jul 71. (7") *(UP 35261) <665>* **SWEET HITCH-HIKER. / DOOR TO DOOR** 36 6

Fantasy Fantasy

Apr 72. (7") *<676>* **SOMEDAY NEVER COMES. / TEARIN' UP THE COUNTRY** – 25

Jul 72. (lp) *<(FAN 9404)>* **MARDI GRAS** Apr72 12
– Lookin' for a reason / Take it like a friend / Need someone to hold / Tearin' up the country / Hello Mary Lou / Someday never comes / What are you gonna do / Hello Mary Lou / Door to door / Sweet hitch-hiker. *(re-iss. Mar73; FT 505) (re-iss. Jul84 lp/c; FAS LP/K 5008) (re-iss. Nov89 lp/c/cd; FACE/FACC/CDFE 513)*

— split Oct'72

– compilations etc. –

on 'Fantasy' unless mentioned otherwise

Dec 72. (7") *(FRC 101)* **BORN ON THE BAYOU. / I PUT A SPELL ON YOU** –

Jan 73. (lp) *(501) <9418>* **CREEDENCE GOLD** Nov72 15
– Proud Mary / Down on the corner / Bad Moon rising / I heard it through the grapevine / Midnight special / Have you ever seen the rain / Born on the bayou / Suzie Q. *(cd-iss. Sep91; CDFE 515)*

Mar 73. (7") *(FRC 104)* **IT CAME OUT OF THE SKY. / SIDE O' THE ROAD** –

Sep 73. (lp) *(512) <9430>* **MORE CREEDENCE GOLD** Jul73 61
– Hey tonight / Run through the jungle / Fortunate son / Bootleg / Lookin' out my back door / Molina / Who'll stop the rain / Sweet hitch-hiker / Good golly Miss Molly / I put a spell on you / Don't look now / Lodi / Porterville / Up around the bend. *(cd-iss. Sep91; CDFE 516)*

May 74. (d-lp) *(520) <FCCR 1>* **LIVE IN EUROPE (live 1971)** Nov73
– Born on the bayou / Green river / It came out of the sky / Door to door / Travellin' band / Fortunate son / Porterville / Up around the bend / Suzie Q / Commotion / Lodi. *(re-iss. Feb90 lp/c/cd; FACE/FACC/CDFE 514)*

Mar 76. (d-lp) *(528) <FCCR 2>* **CHRONICLE (THE 20 GREATEST HITS)** Feb76 100
– Suzie Q. / I put a spell on you / Proud Mary / Bad Moon rising / Lodi / Green river / Commotion / Down on the corner / Fortunate son / Travellin' band / Who'll stop the rain / Up around the bend / Run through the jungle / Lookin' out my back door / Long as I can see the light / Have you ever seen the rain? / Hey tonight / Sweet hitch-hiker / Someday never comes. *(cd-iss. Jun87 on 'Polydor'+=; 821 742-2)* – I heard it through the grapevine.

Mar 76. (7") *(FTC 128) <759>* **I HEARD IT THROUGH THE GRAPEVINE. / GOOD GOLLY MISS MOLLY** Dec75 43

Jul 77. (7"m) *(FTC 142)* **BAD MOON RISING. / PROUD MARY / GREEN RIVER** –

Nov 78. (7"m) *(FTC 164)* **WHO'LL STOP THE RAIN. / PROUD MARY / HEY TONIGHT** –

Jun 79. (lp) *(FT 558)* **GREATEST HITS (20 GOLDEN)** 35

Jul 79. (7") *(FRC 178)* **I HEARD IT THROUGH THE GRAPEVINE. / John Fogerty: ROCKIN' ALL OVER THE WORLD** –
(12") *(12FTC 178)* – ('A'side) / Keep on chooglin' (extended).

1979. (7") *<908>* **COMMOTION. / TOMBSTONE SHADOW** –

1979. (7") *<917>* **BAD MOON RISING. / MEDLEY U.S.A.** –

1979. (7") *<920>* **LODI. / COTTON FIELDS** –

1979. (7") *<957>* **I HEARD IT THROUGH THE GRAPEVINE – UP AROUND THE BEND (medley). / PROUD MARY – LODI (medley)** –

Feb 81. (lp/c) *Music For Pleasure-Fantasy; <(MPF/+5 4501)>* **LIVE AT THE ROYAL ALBERT HALL (live)** <US-title 'THE CONCERT'> Dec80 62
(re-iss. Jul89 as 'THE CONCERT' on 'Fantasy' lp/c/cd; FACE/FACC/CDFE 511)

Aug 81. (7") *Golden Grooves; (GOLD 521)* **PROUD MARY. / UP AROUND THE BEND** –

Oct 81. (7") *Golden Grooves; (GOLD 530)* **BAD MOON RISING. / GOOD GOLLY MISS MOLLY** –

Feb 82. (lp/c) *Music For Pleasure-Fantasy; (MPF/+5 4500)* **THE HITS ALBUM** –

Sep 85. (7") *Old Gold; (OG 9569)* **BAD MOON RISING. / LONG AS I SEE THE LIGHT** –

Sep 85. (7") *Old Gold; (OG 9570)* **PROUD MARY. / TRAVELLIN' BAND** –

Oct 85. (d-lp/c) *Impression; (IMD P/K 3)* **THE CREEDENCE COLLECTION** 68 –

Jun 87. (cd) *<(CDCCR 3)>* **CHRONICLE VOL.2**

May 88. (cd) *Arcade; (01279161)* **THE COMPLETE HITS ALBUM VOL.1** –

May 88. (cd) *Arcade; (01279261)* **THE COMPLETE HITS ALBUM VOL.2** –

Jun 88. (7") *Ace; (NS 124)* **BAD MOON RISING. / HAVE YOU EVER SEEN THE RAIN?** –
(12"+=) *(NST 124)* – Keep on chooglin'.

Jun 88. (lp/c/cd) *(FACE/FACC/FAX 509)* **THE BEST OF – VOLUME 1**

Aug 88. (lp/c) *(FACE/FACC 510)* **THE BEST OF – VOLUME 2**

Dec 88. (cd) *<8029 852-2>* **CHOOGLIN'** –
(UK-iss.Nov92; CDFE 517)

Apr 92. (7") *Epic; (658004-7)* **BAD MOON RISING. / AS LONG AS I CAN SEE THE LIGHT** 71 –
(cd-s+=) *(658004-2)* –

Dec 92. (cd) *(CDFE 518)* **CREEDENCE COUNTRY**

Aug 95. (cd-s) *Old Gold; (OG 6306)* **TRAVELLIN' BAND. / WHO'LL STOP THE RAIN** –

Sep 95. (cd-s) *Old Gold; (12623 6326-2)* **UP AROUND THE BEND / RUN THROUGH THE JUNGLE** [ ] [–]

BLUE RIDGE RANGERS

— was JOHN FOGERTY's first total solo venture

Fantasy Fantasy

Dec 72. (7") *<689>* **JAMBALAYA (ON THE BAYOU). / WORKING ON A BUILDING** [–] [16]

Apr 73. (lp) *(F 1511) <9415>* **BLUE RIDGE RANGERS** [ ] [47]
– Blue ridge mountain blues / Somewhere listening (for my name) / You're the reason / Jambalaya (on the bayou) / She thinks I still care / California blues (blue yodel #4) / Workin' on a building / Please help me I'm falling / Have thine own way, Lord / I ain't never / Hearts of stone / Today I started loving you. *<re-iss. Aug86; 1061150> (re-iss. Sep87 lp/c/cd; FACE/FACC/CDFA 506)*

May 73. (7") *(FRC 105) <700>* **HEARTS OF STONE. / SOMEWHERE LISTENING (FOR MY NAME)** [ ] Mar73 [37]

Oct 73. (7") *(FRC 110) <710>* **BACK IN THE HILLS. / YOU DON'T OWN ME** [ ] Jul73 [ ]

JOHN FOGERTY

solo, plays / sings everything

Fantasy Fantasy

Mar 74. (7") *(FTC 111) <717>* **COMING DOWN THE ROAD. / RICOCHET** [ ] [ ]

Fantasy Asylum

Sep 75. (7") *(FTC 119) <45274>* **ROCKIN' ALL OVER THE WORLD. / THE WALL** [ ] [27]

Oct 75. (lp) *(FT 526) <1046>* **JOHN FOGERTY** [ ] [78]
– Rockin' all over the world / You rascal you / The wall / Travelin' high / Lonely teardrops / Almost Saturday night / Where the river flows / Sea cruise / Dream – Song / Flyin' away. *(re-iss. Sep87 lp/c/cd; FACE/FACC/CDFE 507)*

Dec 75. (7") *<45291>* **ALMOST SATURDAY NIGHT. / SEA CRUISE** [–] [78]

May 76. (7") *(FTC 133) <45309>* **YOU GOT THE MAGIC. / EVIL THING** [ ] [87]

— JOHN FOGERTY returned after 9 years complete with new session people

Warners Warners

Feb 85. (7") *(W 9100) <29100>* **THE OLD MAN DOWN THE ROAD. / BIG TRAIN (FROM MEMPHIS)** [ ] Dec84 [10]

Feb 85. (lp/c/cd) *(925203-1/-4/-2) <25203>* **CENTERFIELD** [48] Jan85 [1]
– The old man down the road / Rock and roll girls / Big train (from Memphis) / I saw it on T.V. / Mr. Greed / Searchlight / Centerfield / I can't help myself / Zant Kant danz. *(cd re-iss. Nov93; same)*

Jun 85. (7") *(W 9053) <29053>* **ROCK AND ROLL GIRLS. / CENTERFIELD** [ ] [20]
Mar85 [44]

— now with **JOHN ROBINSON** – drums / **NEIL STUBENHAUS** – bass

Oct 86. (lp/c/cd) *(925449-1/-4/-2) <25449>* **EYE OF THE ZOMBIE** [44] [26]
– Goin' back home / Eye of the zombie / Headlines / Knockin' on your door / Change in the weather / Violence is golden / Wasn't that a woman / Soda pop / Sail away.

Oct 86. (7") *(W 8657) <28657>* **EYE OF THE ZOMBIE. / I CONFESS (with Bobby King)** [ ] [81]
(12"+=) *(W 8657T)* – I can't help myself.

Dec 86. (7") *<28535>* **CHANGE IN THE WEATHER. / MY TOOT TOOT** [–] [ ]

— returned after another 10 years in the proverbial wilderness

Warners Warners

Jun 97. (cd/c) *<(9362 45426-2/-4)>* **BLUE MOON SWAMP** [ ] May97 [37]
– Southern streamline / Hot rod heart / Blueboy / Hundred and ten in the shade / Rattlesnake highway / Bring it down to Jelly Roll / Walking in a hurricane / Swamp river days / Rambunctions boy / Joy of my life / Blue moon nights / Bad bad boy.

Oct 97. (cd-d) *<17283>* **BLUEBOY / BAD BAD BOY** [–] [ ]

— his live band were basically **KENNY ARONOFF** – drums / **BOB GLAUB** – bass / **MIKE CANIPE** – guitar

Jun 98. (cd) *<(9362 46908-2)>* **PREMONITION (live)** [ ] [29]
– Born on the bayou / Green river / Susie Q. / I put a spell on you / Who'll stop the rain / Premonition / Almost Saturday night / Rockin' all over the world / Joy of my life / Down on the corner / Centerfield / Swamp river days / Hot rod heart / The old man down the road / Bad moon rising / Fortunate son / Proud Mary / Travelin' band.

☐ Peter CRISS (see under ⇒ KISS)

Jim CROCE

Born: 10 Jan'43, Philadelphia, Pennsylvania, USA, although he moved to New York in 1967 with his wife INGRID. He'd already started playing guitar by the early 60's, forced to adapt his guitar-picking technique after suffering a broken finger; this was sustained during one of his many jobs which also included broadcasting a university campus folk/blues radio show in 1963. Signing to 'Capitol, he and his spouse cut a one-off album, 'APPROACHING DAY' (1968), before returning to Pennsylvania. A soft-rock acoustic singer/songwriter/guitarist in the JAMES TAYLOR mould, CROCE (who was driving trucks in his spare time to make ends meet) would subsequently sign to 'A.B.C.' with the help of an old college mate turned record producer, Tommy West. His debut solo set, 'YOU DON'T MESS AROUND WITH JIM' (1972), began a steady ascent of the US chart, finally peaking at No.1 thanks to the success of its title track and 'OPERATOR (THAT'S NOT THE WAY IT FEELS)'. Concentrating on streetwise subject matter and accompanied by the distinctive lead acoustic guitar of MAURY MUEHLIESEN, CROCE's unique, laid back approach was further developed on the man's 1973 sophomore set, 'LIFE AND TIMES'. This was preceded by what was to become CROCE's signature tune, 'BAD, BAD LEROY BROWN', a surprise but worthy No.1 in America which sadly went unnoticed in Britain. CROCE was obviously on the brink of a huge career with a cover of the latter song soon-to-be recorded by no less a personage than Ol' Blue Eyes himself, FRANK SINATRA, the ultimate songwriting acclaim. This popularity was largely achieved on the back of a punishing touring schedule which was ultimately to cost him and his guitarist their lives as they flew all over the states promoting their work. On September the 20th, 1973, JIM and MAURY's charter plane crashed after take-off, killing them both along with four other passengers. He was survived by his wife and child, Adrian, whose baby pic appears on the inner cover of top-selling posthumous compilation album, 'PHOTOGRAPHS AND MEMORIES' (1974); Adrian is now a recording artist in his own right. One can only speculate as to whether JC's easy-going style would have survived the 70's. All the signs were that he would have probably broadened out into a mainstream lyric writer. • **Songwriters:** CROCE except, SALON SALOON (Maury Meuhleisen) / THURSDAY (S.Joseph) / I GOT A NAME (Fox-Gimbel) / CHAIN GANG (Sam Cooke) / HE DON'T LOVE YOU (Impressions) / SEARCHIN' (Coasters) / OLD MAN RIVER (Kern-Hammerstein) / etc.

Album rating: APPROACHING DAY (*4) / YOU DON'T MESS AROUND WITH JIM (*6) / LIFE AND TIMES (*6) / I GOT A NAME posthumous (*6) / PHOTOGRAPHS AND MEMORIES – HIS GREATEST HITS compilation (*6) / THE VERY BEST OF JIM CROCE compilation (*7)

INGRID & JIM CROCE

JIM CROCE – vocals, acoustic guitar / with **INGRID** (b.27 Apr'47) – vocals, acoustic guitar

not iss. Capitol

Jan 69. (lp) *<ST 315>* **APPROACHING DAY** [–] [ ]
– Age / Spin spin spin / I am who I am / What do people do / Another day, another town / Vespers / Big wheel / Just another day / The next man that I marry / What the hell / The man that is me. *(UK-iss.1977 as 'ANOTHER*

DAY' on 'Pickwick'; PWK 3332) (cd-iss. May96 as 'BOMBS OVER PUERTO RICO' on 'Bear Family'; BCD 15894)

— in 1970, JIM guested on MAURY MUEHLIESEN's debut album 'Gingerbread'

JIM CROCE

— JIM now used session players

Vertigo A.B.C.

Apr 72. (lp) *(6360 700) <356>* **YOU DON'T MESS AROUND WITH JIM** [ ] [1]
– You don't mess around with Jim / Tomorrow's gonna be a brighter day / New York's not my home / Hard time losin' man / A long time ago / Walkin' back to Georgia / Operator (that's not the way it feels) / Time in a bottle / Rapid Roy (the stock car boy) / Box 10 / Photographs and memories / Hey tomorrow.

Jul 72. (7") *(6000 069) <11328>* **YOU DON'T MESS AROUND WITH JIM. / PHOTOGRAPHS AND MEMORIES** [ ] Jun72 [8]

Oct 72. (7") *(6073 251) <11335>* **OPERATOR (THAT'S NOT THE WAY IT FEELS). / RAPID ROY (THE STOCK CAR BOY)** [ ] [17]

Jan 73. (7") *<11346>* **ONE LESS SET OF FOOTSTEPS. / IT DOESN'T HAVE TO BE THAT WAY** [-] [37]

Apr 73. (7") *<11359>* **BAD, BAD LEROY BROWN. / A GOOD TIME MAN LIKE ME AIN'T GO NO BUSINESS (SINGIN' THE BLUES)** [-] [1]

Jul 73. (lp) *(6360 701) <769>* **LIFE AND TIMES** [ ] Feb73 [7]
– One less set of footsteps / Roller derby queen / Dreamin' again / Careful man / Alabama rain / A good time man like me ain't got no business (singin' the blues) / Next time, this time / Bad, bad Leroy Brown / These dreams / Speedball Tucker / It doesn't have to be that way. *(re-iss. Nov76; same)*

May 73. (7") *(6073 258)* **BAD, BAD LEROY BROWN. / ROLLER DERBY QUEEN** [ ] [-]

Nov 73. (7") *(6073 260) <11389>* **I GOT A NAME. / ALABAMA RAIN** [ ] Sep73 [10]

— JIM was killed on the 20th of September '73 when his chartered plane crashed on take-off. His guitarist MAURY MUEHLIESEN was also to die.

– compilations, others. etc. –

Nov 73. (7") *A.B.C.; (11405>* **TIME IN A BOTTLE. / HARD TIME LOSIN' MAN** [-] [1]

Dec 73. (7") *A.B.C.; <11413>* **IT DOESN'T HAVE TO BE THAT WAY. / ROLLER DERBY QUEEN** [-] [64]

Feb 74. (7") *Vertigo; (6073 272)* **TIME IN A BOTTLE. / HEY TOMORROW** [ ] [-]

Apr 74. (lp) *Vertigo; (6360 703) / A.B.C.; <797>* **I GOT A NAME** [ ] Dec73 [2]
– I got a name / Lover's cross / Five short minutes / Ages / Workin' at the carwash blues / I'll have to say I love you in a song / Salon and saloon / Thursday / Top hat bar and grill / Recently / The hard way / Every time.

Mar 74. (7") *A.B.C.; <11424>* **I'LL HAVE TO SAY I LOVE YOU IN A SONG. / SALON AND SALOON** [-] [9]

May 74. (7") *A.B.C.; <11447>* **WORKIN' AT THE CAR WASH BLUES. / THURSDAY** [-] [32]
<re-iss. 1970's; 12015>

Sep 74. (lp) *A.B.C.; <835>* **PHOTOGRAPHS AND MEMORIES – HIS GREATEST HITS** [-] [2]
– Bad, bad Leroy Brown / Operator (that's not the way it feels) / Photographs and memories / Rapid Roy (the stock car boy) / Time in a bottle / New York's not my home / Workin' at the car wash blues / I got a name / I'll have to say I love you in a song / You don't mess around with Jim / Lover's cross / One less set of footsteps / These dreams. *(UK-iss.Jul77 on 'Lifesong'; LSLP 5000) (re-iss. Jun88 on 'Castle' lp/c/cd; CLA LP/MC/CD 119) (cd re-iss. Apr99 on 'Essential'; ESMCD 699)*

Apr 75. (7") *Philips; (6072 278)* **BAD, BAD LEROY BROWN. / I GOT A NAME** [ ] [-]

Jun 75. (7") *Philips; (6073 280)* **I'LL HAVE TO SAY I LOVE YOU IN A SONG. / WORKIN' AT THE CAR WASH BLUES** [ ] [-]

Sep 75. (7") *Philips; (6073 281)* **LOVER'S CROSS. / SPEEDBALL TUCKER** [ ] [-]

Oct 75. (d-lp) *Lifesong; <LSDP 900>* **THE FACES I'VE BEEN** (early recordings from 1961-1971) [-] [87]
– This land is your land / Greenback dollar / Pig's song / Gunga Din / Sun come up / Big fat woman / Charlie Green play the slide trombone / Railroads and riverboats / Railroad song / The way we used to / Maybe tomorrow / Stone walls / I remember Mary / Country girl / Which way are you going / King's song / Mississippi lady / Chain gang medley: Chain gang – He don't love you – Searchin' / Old man river / Carmella / South Philly / Cars and dates / Chrome and clubs / The Chinese / Trucks and ups / The army. *(UK-iss.Jul77; same as US)*

Dec 75. (7") *Lifesong; <45001>* **CHAIN GANG MEDLEY: CHAIN GANG – HE DON'T LOVE YOU – SEARCHIN'. / STONE WALLS** [-] [63]

1976. (7") *Lifesong; <45005>* **MISSISSIPPI LADY. / MAYBE TOMORROW** [-] [ ]

1970's. (7") *Golddiggers; <1005>* **YOU DON'T MESS AROUND WITH JIM. / LOVER'S CROSS** [-] [ ]

Jan 77. (7") *Lifesong; (ELS 3500)* **I'LL HAVE TO SAY I LOVE YOU IN A SONG. / PHOTOGRAPHS AND MEMORIES** [ ] [-]

Feb 77. (lp) *Lifesong; <6007>* **TIME IN A BOTTLE: JIM CROCE'S GREATEST LOVE SONGS** [-] [ ]
(re-iss. Sep86 on 'Castle' lp/c/cd; CLA LP/MC/CD 117) (cd re-iss. Apr99 on 'Essential'; ESMCD 697)

1979. (lp) *Lifesong; <35571>* **BAD, BAD LEROY BROWN: JIM CROCE'S GREATEST CHARACTER SONGS** [-] [ ]

Mar 80. (c) *K-Tel; (CE 2059)* **HIS GREATEST HITS** [ ] [-]

Sep 86. (lp/c/cd) *Castle; (CLA LP/MC/CD 118)* **DOWN THE HIGHWAY** [ ] [-]
(cd re-iss. Apr99 on 'Essential'; ESMCD 698)

Dec 86. (d-lp/c/cd) *Castle; (CCS LP/MC/CD 154)* **THE JIM CROCE COLLECTION** [ ] [-]
– Time in a bottle / Operator (that's not the way it feels) / Salon saloon / Alabama rain / Dreamin' again / It doesn't have to be that way / I'll have to say I love you in a song / Lover's cross / Thursday / These dreams / A long time ago / Photographs and memories / I got a name / Mississippi lady / New York's not my home / Chain gang medley:- Chain gang – He don't love you – Searchin' / You don't mess around with Jim / Old man river / Which way are you goin' / Bad, bad Leroy Brown / Walkin' back to Georgia / Box 10 / Speedball Tucker / Rapid Roy (the stock car boy).

May 88. (d-lp/d-c) *Commander; (80044 1-2)* **JIM CROCE SONGBOOK** [ ] [-]

May 88. (lp/c/cd) *Commander; (3/6/9 9010)* **GREATEST HITS** [ ] [-]

1988. (cd) *Roadrunner; (RR34 9841)* **THE LEGEND OF JIM CROCE** [ ] [-]

Feb 90. (cd/c/lp) *Essential; (ESS CD/MC/LP 020)* **THE FINAL TOUR (live)** [ ] [-]
(cd re-iss. May94 on 'Castle'; CLACD 341) (cd re-iss. Apr99 on 'Essential'; ESMCD 700)

Nov 92. (d-cd) *Essential; (ESDCD 188)* **50th ANNIVERSARY COLLECTION** [ ] [-]

Oct 94. (cd) *Woodford Music; (WMCD 5703)* **SIMPLY THE BEST** [ ] [-]

May 97. (cd) *Music Club; (MCCD 295)* **THE BEST OF JIM CROCE** [ ] [-]

May 97. (d-cd) *Snapper; (SMDCD 102)* **BAD, BAD LEROY BROWN – THE DEFINITIVE JIM CROCE** [ ] [-]

Mar 98. (cd/c) *Castle Select; (SEL CD/MC 505)* **THE VERY BEST OF JIM CROCE** [ ] [-]

Feb 99. (d-cd) *Castle Select; (SELDD 558)* **TIME IN A BOTTLE – THE DEFINITIVE COLLECTION** [ ] [-]

Oct 99. (cd) *Castle Pie; (PIESCD 137)* **THE COLLECTION** [ ] [-]

Jul 01. (cd) *EMI Plus; (576261-2)* **SINGER / SONGWRITER** [ ] [-]

Jun 03. (cd) *Disky; (SI 79517-2)* **THE VERY BEST OF JIM CROCE** [ ] [-]

Jan 03. (d-cd) *BR Music; (BS 80402)* **THE COMPLETE COLLECTION** [ ] [-]

Jun 03. (d-cd) *Disky; (HR 905593)* **ORIGINAL GOLD** [ ] [-]

CROSBY, STILLS, NASH (& YOUNG)

Formed: Los Angeles, California, USA ... Summer 1968 as a superband trio (DAVID) CROSBY, (STEPHEN) STILLS and (GRAHAM) NASH. Their eponymous first offering was released in Summer '69 and soon broke into the US Top 10. Featuring the distinctive songwriting talent of each member respectively on

'GUINNEVERE', 'SUITE: JUDY BLUE EYES' and 'MARRAKESH EXPRESS', the album introduced the close harmonising that would come to characterise the band. Later that year the trio recruited NEIL YOUNG (ex-BUFFALO SPRINGFIELD) who'd played an electric set on their mid-'69 gigs and who'd already embarked on his successful solo career. The newly augmented line-up played Woodstock as well as supporting The ROLLING STONES at their ill-fated Altamont concert which, ironically, saw the dreams of the Woodstock generation shatter. Nevertheless the band were adopted as hippy flagbearers and after lifting the coveted 'Best Newcomers' award at The Grammys, they released their magnum opus, 'DEJA VU' (1970). With YOUNG contributing the achingly gorgeous 'HELPLESS' and the sublime 'COUNTRY GIRL' suite, his intensity, both vocal and instrumental was a towering influence although STILLS offered a powerful cover of JONI MITCHELL's 'WOODSTOCK'. NASH's 'TEACH YOUR CHILDREN' and 'OUR HOUSE' were slighter in comparison but rounded out the record perfectly. Blighted by ego problems with drug habits to match, the band split the same month as YOUNG's ominous 'OHIO' single was released, an inspired protest against the killing of four students by the National Guard during an anti-war demo at Kent State University. The patchy, posthumous live album 'FOUR-WAY STREET' (1971) was hardly a fitting epitaph although predictably it sold in bucketloads. While YOUNG continued with his mercurial solo career, STILLS released a follow-up to his well-received debut solo album and later recorded with the country-inflected MANASSAS. CROSBY and NASH, meanwhile, worked as a duo, releasing their eponymous debut in 1972. Minus STILLS and YOUNG, the record was pleasant if hardly essential, lacking the tension that had made CSN&Y so compelling. The inevitable reunion took place in 1974 and the biggest personality clash in rock toured the world to ecstatic audiences although the band couldn't keep it together long enough to record anything concrete in the studio (the fact that YOUNG travelled in his own tourbus didn't bode too well). STILLS and YOUNG recorded the 'LONG MAY YOU RUN' album in 1976 which boasted the wistful charm of the title track and the exquisite 'FONTAINEBLEU' but was otherwise fairly lacklustre. The following year CROSBY, STILLS and NASH reformed and recorded the million selling 'CSN', again another inoffensive collection which lacked the focus YOUNG had brought to the group in the past. Indeed, while CSN were touring their particular brand of polite folk-Pop, YOUNG was interpreting punk with his 'LIVE RUST' and 'RUST NEVER SLEEPS' albums, outstripping CSN creatively and commercially. 'DAYLIGHT AGAIN' (1982) spawned the American singles 'WASTED ON THE WAY' and 'SOUTHERN CROSS' while the band split later the same year as CROSBY was sentenced to five years for drugs and firearms offences. In the event, he was allowed to attend a rehabilitation program as an alternative which he later reneged on and did actually serve some time during the mid-80's. Out on bail, he appeared live with STILLS, NASH and YOUNG at Live Aid and the quartet made a long-awaited second album in 1988, 'AMERICAN DREAM'. Although it eclipsed most of the YOUNG-less CSN material, it was hardly the masterpiece people had waited almost two decades for. The standout track was CROSBY's 'COMPASS', a song borne of his drug-induced hardships. NEIL YOUNG subsequently refused to tour the record and that, more or less, was that. CSN continued unbowed, even after CROSBY underwent a liver transplant following the release of the 'AFTER THE STORM' (1994) album. With YOUNG now almost in the 30th year of a solo career which showed no sign of letting up (even if his recent output has been under par), it didn't appear likely that he would ever re-unite with his old sparring partners. However, the er, 'LOOKING FORWARD' (1999) set (was it?) heralded the one-off return of CSN&Y. NASH was also back in his own right with 2002's 'SONGS FOR SURVIVORS', one of the better releases to come from the CSN&Y camp over the last decade. Unassuming and largely acoustic, the record showcased a voice which has weathered nicely with the years, furnishing the harmonies with a warm, burnished veneer. CROSBY supplied guest vocals while veteran drummer RUSS KUNKEL played, co-produced and co-wrote opener 'DIRTY LITTLE SECRET'. • **Songwriters:** All 4 took a hand individually and later together in all songs. Also covered; WOODSTOCK (Joni Mitchell) / DEAR MR. FANTASY (Traffic) / and a few more.

Album rating: CROSBY, STILLS & NASH (*8) / DEJA VU (*9; & Young) / FOUR-WAY STREET (*7; & Young) / SO FAR compilation (*7; & Young) / CSN (*7) / REPLAY compilation (*7) / DAYLIGHT AGAIN (*6) / ALLIES (*5) / AMERICAN DREAM (*5; & Young) / LIVE IT UP (*4) / AFTER THE STORM (*4) / LOOKING FORWARD (*4; & Young) / David Crosby: IF I COULD ONLY REMEMBER MY NAME (*8) / GRAHAM NASH & DAVID CROSBY (*5; with Graham Nash) / WIND ON THE WATER (*5; with Graham Nash) / WHISTLING DOWN THE WIRE (*4; with Graham Nash) / CROSBY/NASH LIVE (*4; with Graham Nash) / THE BEST OF CROSBY/NASH compilation (*5; with Graham Nash) / OH YES I CAN (*5) / THOUSAND ROADS (*5) / IT'S ALL COMING BACK TO ME NOW (*4) / Stephen Stills: STEPHEN STILLS (*8) / STEPHEN STILLS 2 (*6) / MANASSAS (*6) / DOWN THE ROAD (*4; with Manassas) / STILLS (*5) / STEPHEN STILLS LIVE (*4) / ILLEGAL STILLS (*5) / LONG MAY YOU RUN (*5; as Stills-Young Band) / STILL STILLS – THE BEST OF STEPHEN STILLS compilation (*6) / THOROUGHFARE GAP (*3) / RIGHT BY YOU (*5) / STILLS ALONE (*5) / TURN BACK THE PAGES compilation (*6) / Graham Nash: SONGS FOR BEGINNERS (*7) / WILD TALES (*5) / EARTH AND SKY (*4) / INNOCENT EYES (*4) / SONGS FOR SURVIVORS (*5)

CROSBY, STILLS & NASH

DAVID CROSBY (b. DAVID VAN CORTLAND, 14 Aug'41, Los Angeles, Calif.) – vocals, guitar (ex-BYRDS) / **STEPHEN STILLS** (b. 3 Jan'45, Dallas, Texas)– vocals, guitar, bass, keyboards (ex-BUFFALO SPRINGFIELD) / **GRAHAM NASH** (b. 2 Feb'42, Blackpool, England)– vocals, guitar (ex-HOLLIES)
with **DALLAS TAYLOR** – drums

Atlantic Atlantic

Jun 69. (lp) *(588 189) <8229>* **CROSBY, STILLS & NASH** 25 6
– Suite: Judy blue eyes / Marrakesh express / Guinnevere / You don't have to cry / Pre-road downs / Wooden ships / Lady of the island / Helplessly hoping / Long time gone / 49 bye-byes. *(re-iss. 1972; K 40033) (cd-iss. Jul87; K2 40033)*

Jul 69. (7") *(584 283) <2652>* **MARRAKESH EXPRESS. / HELPLESSLY HOPING** 17 28

Oct 69. (7") *(584 304) <2676>* **SUITE: JUDY BLUE EYES. / LONG TIME GONE** [ ] Sep69 21

CROSBY, STILLS, NASH & YOUNG

— added **NEIL YOUNG** (b.12 Nov'45, Toronto, Canada) – guitar, vocals (ex-BUFFALO SPRINGFIELD) also **GREG REEVES** – bass

Mar 70. (lp) *(2401 001) <7200>* **DEJA VU** 5 1
– Carry on / Teach your children / Almost cut my hair / Helpless / Woodstock / Deja vu / Our house / 4 + 20 / Country girl: Whiskey boot hill – Down, down, down – Country girl / Everybody I love you. *(re-iss. 1972 lp/c; K/K4 50001) (cd-iss. May87; K2 50001)*

Apr 70. (7") *(2091 002)* **TEACH YOUR CHILDREN. / COUNTRY GIRL** [ ] –

May 70. (7") *(2091 010) <2723>* **WOODSTOCK. / HELPLESS** [ ] Mar70 11

May 70. (7") *<2735>* **TEACH YOUR CHILDREN. / CARRY ON** – 16

Aug 70. (7") *(2091 023) <2740>* **OHIO. / FIND THE COST OF FREEDOM** [ ] Jun70 14

Nov 70. (7") *(2091 039) <2760>* **OUR HOUSE. / DEJA VU** [ ] Sep70 30

— (May'70) **CALVIN 'FUZZY' SAMUELS** – bass repl. REEVES **JOHN BARBATA** – drums (ex-TURTLES) repl. TAYLOR

— (Aug'70) split before release of posthumous album below with last line-up

Apr 71. (d-lp) *(2657 007) <2-902>* **FOUR-WAY STREET (live)** 5 1
– On the way home / Teach your children / Triad / The Lee shore / Chicago / Right between the eyes / Cowgirl in the sand / Don't let it bring

you down / 49 bye-byes / Love the one you're with / Pre-road downs / Long time gone / Southern man / Ohio / Carry on / Find the cost of freedom. *(re-iss. 1972 lp/c; K/K4 60003) (cd-iss. Jul87; K2 60003) (d-cd re-iss. Aug92)*

— Their solo recordings, excluding NEIL YOUNG's, are below

STEPHEN STILLS

— - vocals, guitar with **STEPHEN FROMHOLTZ** – guitar / **PAUL HARRIS** – keyboards / **DALLAS TAYLOR** – drums / **CALVIN SAMUELS** – bass / plus Memphis Horns

Atlantic Atlantic

Nov 70. (lp) *(2401 004)* *<7202>* **STEPHEN STILLS** [30] [3]
– Love the one you're with / Do for the others / Church (part of someone) / Old times, good times / Go back home / Sit yourself down / To a flame / Black queen / Cheroke / We are not helpless. *(cd-iss. Oct95; 7567 82809-2)*

Dec 70. (7") *(2091 046)* *<2778>* **LOVE THE ONE YOU'RE WITH. / TO A FLAME** [37] [14]

May 71. (7") *(2091 069)* *<2790>* **SIT YOURSELF DOWN. / WE ARE NOT HELPLESS** [ ] Mar71 [37]

Jul 71. (lp) *(2401 013)* *<7206>* **STEPHEN STILLS 2** [22] [8]
– Change partners / Nothin' to do but today / Fishes and scorpions / Sugar babe / Know you got to run / Open secret / Relaxing town / Singin' call / Ecology song / Word game / Marianne / Bluebird revisited. *(re-iss. 1978;) (cd-iss. 1991; 7567-82389-2)*

Jul 71. (7") *(2091 117)* *<2806>* **CHANGE PARTNERS. / RELAXING TOWN** [ ] Jun71 [43]

Sep 71. (7") *(2091 141)* *<2820>* **MARIANNE. / NOTHIN' TO DO BUT TODAY** [ ] Aug71 [42]

STEPHEN STILLS & MANASSAS

STILLS retained **SAMUELS, HARRIS** and **TAYLOR,** brought in **CHRIS HILLMAN** – guitar, vocals / **AL PERKINS** – steel guitar, guitar / **JOE LALA** – percussion / **KENNY PASSARELLI** – bass (ex-JOE WALSH) repl. SAMUELS

Atlantic Atlantic

May 72. (d-lp/c) *(K/K4 60021)* *<2-903>* **MANASSAS** [30] Apr72 [4]
– Fallen eagle / Jesus gave love away for free / Colorado / So begins the task / Hide to the deep / Don't look at my shadow / It doesn't matter / Johnny's garden / Bound to fall / How far / Move around / The love gangster / Song of love / Rock'n'roll crazies – Cuban bluegrass / Jet set (sigh) / Anyway / Both of us (bound to lose) / What to do / Right now / The treasure (take one) / Blues man. *(cd-iss. Feb93 & Oct95; 7567 82808-2)*

May 72. (7") *<2876>* **IT DOESN'T MATTER. / ROCK'N'ROLL CRAZIES – CUBAN BLUEGRASS** [–] [61]

Aug 72. (7") *(K 10147)* **IT DOESN'T MATTER. / FALLEN ANGEL** [ ] [–]

Nov 72. (7") *<2888>* **ROCK'N'ROLL CRAZIES. / COLORADO** [–] [92]

May 73. (lp/c) *(K/K4 40440)* *<7250>* **DOWN THE ROAD** [33] [26]
– Isn't it about time / Lies / Pensamiento / So many times / Business on the street / Do you remember the Americans / Down the road / City junkies / Guaguanco de Vero / Rollin' my stone. *(cd-iss. Nov93; 7567 81424-2)*

May 73. (7") *(K 10306)* *<2959>* **ISN'T IT ABOUT TIME. / SO MANY TIMES** [ ] Apr73 [56]

Jul 73. (7") *(K 10340)* *<2917>* **GUAGUANCO DE VERO. / DOWN THE ROAD** [ ] Feb73 [ ]

— (Sep73) **HARRIS, PERKINS and HILLMAN joined SOUTHERN HILLMAN FURAY BAND. STEPHEN STILLS** formed his own band, retaining **PASSARELLI** and **LALA** plus **DONNIE DACUS** – guitar / **JERRY AIELLO** – keyboards / **HUSS KUNKEL** – drums

CROSBY, STILLS NASH & YOUNG

— (May'74) re-formed, mainly for concerts. Augmented by **TIM DRUMMOND** – bass / **RUSS KUNKEL** – drums / **JOE LALA** – percussion

STEPHEN STILLS

— went solo again (Feb75) with new band **LALA, DACUS, AIELLO** plus **GEORGE PERRY** – bass / **RONNIE ZIEGLER** – drums

C.B.S. Columbia

Jun 75. (lp/c) *(69146)* *<33575>* **STILLS** [31] [19]
– Turn back the pages / My favorite changes / My angel / In the way / Love story / To mama Christopher and the old man / First things first / New mama / As I come of age / Shuffle just as bad / Cold cold world / Myth of Sisyphus.

Jul 75. (7") *(3497)* *<10179>* **TURN BACK THE PAGES. / SHUFFLE JUST AS BAD** [ ] [84]

— added **RICK ROBERTS** – guitar, vocals (of FIREFALL)

Apr 76. (7") *<10369>* **BUYIN' TIME. / SOLDIER** [–] [ ]

May 76. (lp/c) *(81330)* *<34148>* **ILLEGAL STILLS** [54] [30]
– Buyin' time / Midnight in Paris / Different tongues / Closer to you / Soldier / The loner / Stateline blues / No me nieges / Ring of love / Circlin'.

Jul 76. (7") *(4416)* **THE LONER. / STATELINE BLUES** [ ] [–]

STILLS-YOUNG BAND

STEPHEN STILLS – vocals, guitar / **NEIL YOUNG** – vocals, guitar with **AIELLO, PERRY, VITALE + LALA**

Reprise Reprise

Sep 76. (7") *(K 14446)* *<1365>* **LONG MAY YOU RUN. / 12:8 BLUES** [ ] [ ]

Oct 76. (lp/c) *(K/K4 54081)* *<2253>* **LONG MAY YOU RUN** [12] [26]
– Long may you run / Make love to you / Midnight on the bay / Black coral / Ocean girl / Let it shine / 12/8 blues (all the same) / Fontainebleau / Guardian angel. *(cd-iss. Jul93; K2 54081)*

Dec 76. (7") *<1370>* **MIDNIGHT ON THE BAY. / BLACK CORAL** [–] [ ]

— CROSBY, STILLS & NASH re-formed in '77 (see further on for more solo STILLS)

DAVID CROSBY

with loads of session people, too numerous to mention.

Atlantic Atlantic

Feb 71. (lp) *(2401 005)* *<SD 7203>* **IF I COULD ONLY REMEMBER MY NAME** [12] [12]
– Music is love / Cowboy movie / Tamalpais High (at about 3) / Laughing / What are their names / Traction in the rain / Song with no name (tree with no leaves) / Orleans / I'd swear there was somebody here. *(re-iss. 1972 lp/c; K/K4 40320) (cd-iss. Nov93; 56781415-2)*

Apr 71. (7") *<2792>* **MUSIC IS LOVE. / LAUGHING** [–] [95]

Jul 71. (7") *<2809>* **ORLEANS. / TRACTION IN THE RAIN** [–] [ ]

GRAHAM NASH & DAVID CROSBY

duo (DAVID & GRAHAM) with more sessioners and left over GRATEFUL DEAD members which were included on DAVID's debut solo album.

May 72. (lp/c) *(K/K4 50011)* *<7220>* **GRAHAM NASH & DAVID CROSBY** [13] Apr72 [4]
– Southbound train / Whole cloth / Black notes / Strangers room / Where will I be / Page 43 / Frozen smiles / Games / Girl to be on my mind / The wall song / Immigration man.

May 72. (7") *<2873>* **IMMIGRATION MAN. / WHOLE CLOTH** [–] [36]

Jul 72. (7") **SOUTHBOUND TRAIN. / WHOLE CLOTH** [ ] [–]

Jul 72. (7") *<2892>* **SOUTHBOUND TRAIN. / THE WALL SONG** [–] [99]

— after CROSBY, STILLS, NASH & YOUNG reunion May74-Feb75

— resurrected partnership, with steady band members **CRAIG DOERGE** – keyboards / **LEE SKLAR + TIM DRUMMOND** – bass / **DANNY KOOTCH & RUSS KUNKEL** – drums / **DAVID LINDLEY** – guitar, violin.

Polydor A.B.C.

Jan 76. (lp) *(2310 428)* *<902>* **WIND ON THE WATER** [ ] Oct75 [6]
– Carry me / Mama lion / Bittersweet / Take the money and run / Naked in the rain / Love work out / Low down payment / Cowboy of dreams / Homeward through the haze / Fieldworker / To the last whale. *(cd-iss. Nov91 on 'Thunderbolt'; CDTB 128) (cd re-iss. Mar97 on 'Nectar'; NTMCD 550)*

Nov 75. (7") *(2001 615)* *<12140>* **CARRY ME. / MAMA LION** [ ] [52]

Mar 76. (7") *<12165>* **TAKE THE MONEY AND RUN. / BITTERSWEET** [–] [ ]

May 76. (7") *(2001 660)* *<12185>* **LOVE WORK OUT. / BITTERSWEET** [ ] [ ]

Jul 76. (lp) *(2319 468)* *<956>* **WHISTLING DOWN THE WIRE** [ ] [26]
– Spotlight / Broken bird / Time after time / Dancer / Mutiny / J.B.'s blues / Marguerita / Taken at all / Foolish man / Out of the darkness.

Aug 76. (7") **OUT OF THE DARKNESS. / LOVE WORK OUT** [ ] [–]

Aug 76. (7") *<12199>* **OUT OF THE DARKNESS. / BROKEN BIRD** [–] [89]

Oct 76. (7") *<12217>* **SPOTLIGHT. / FOOLISH MAN** [–] [ ]

—— CROSBY STILLS & NASH re-formed '77 (see further on)

GRAHAM NASH

solo using C,S & N past members plus GRATEFUL DEAD main men

Atlantic Atlantic

Jun 71. (lp) *(2401 011) <SD 7204>* **SONGS FOR BEGINNERS** [13] [15]
– Military madness / Better days / Wounded bird / I used to be a king / Be yourself / Simple man / Man in the mirror / There's only one / Sleep song / Chicago / We can change the world. *<(cd-iss. Feb93; 7567 81416-2)> (cd re-iss. Feb00; 72042)*

Jun 71. (7") *(2091 096) <2804>* **CHICAGO. / SIMPLE MAN** [ ] May71 [35]

Aug 71. (7") *<2827>* **MILITARY MADNESS. / SLEEP SONG** [–] [73]

Sep 71. (7") *(2091 135)* **MILITARY MADNESS. / I USED TO BE A KING** [ ] [–]

Nov 71. (7") *<2840>* **I USED TO BE A KING. / WOUNDED BIRD** [–] [ ]

Nov 73. (7") *<2990>* **PRISON SONG. / HEY YOU (LOOKING AT HTE MOON)** [–] [ ]

Mar 74. (lp/c) *(K/K4 50025) <SD 7288>* **WILD TALES** [ ] Dec73 [34]
– Wild tales / Hey you (looking at the Moon) / Prison song / You'll never be the same / And so it goes / Oh! Camil (the winter soldier) / I miss you / On the line / Another sleep song.

Mar 74. (7") *(K 10425)* **ON THE LINE. / I MISS YOU** [ ] [–]

Aug 74. (7") *(K 10470)* **GRAVE CONCERN. / ANOTHER SLEEP SONG** [ ] [–]

—— GRAHAM rejoined below and had more solo releases later.

CROSBY, STILLS & NASH

reformed in '77, with various session men.

Atlantic Atlantic

Jun 77. (lp/c) *(K 50369) <19104>* **CSN** [23] [2]
– Shadow captain / See the changes / Carried away / Fair game / Anything at all / Cathedral / Dark star / Just a song before I go / Cold rain / In my dreams / I give you give blind.

Jun 77. (7") *(K 10947) <3401>* **JUST A SONG BEFORE I GO. / DARK STAR** [ ] May77 [7]

Oct 77. (7") *(K 11024) <3432>* **FAIR GAME. / ANYTHING AT ALL** [ ] Sep77 [43]

Dec 77. (7") *<3453>* **CARRIED AWAY. / I GIVE YOU GIVE BLIND** [–] [ ]

STEPHEN STILLS

more solo releases with session people & his tour band **DALLAS TAYLOR** – drums / **GEORGE PERRY** – bass / **MIKE FINNEGAN** – keyboards / **JERRY TOLMAN & BONNIE BRAMLETT** – b.vocals

C.B.S. Columbia

Sep 78. (7") *(6662) <10804>* **CAN'T GET NO BOOTY. / LOWDOWN** [ ] [ ]

Oct 78. (lp) *(82859) <35380>* **THOROUGHFARE GAP** [ ] [83]
– You can't dance alone / Thoroughfare gap / We will go / Beaucoup yumbo / What's the game / Midnight rider / Woman Lleva / Lowdown / Not fade away / Can't get no booty.

Nov 78. (7") *<10872>* **THOROUGHFARE GAP. / LOWDOWN** [–] [ ]

GRAHAM NASH

solo, with usual and past session people + CROSBY, STILLS & YOUNG

Capitol Capitol

Jan 80. (7") *<4812>* **IN THE 80'S. / T.V. GUIDE** [–] [ ]

Mar 80. (7") *<4849>* **OUT ON THE ISLAND. / HELICOPTER SONG** [–] [ ]

Mar 80. (lp) *(12014)* **EARTH & SKY** [ ] [ ]
– Earth & sky / Love has come / Out on the island / Skychild / Helicopter song / Barrel of pain / T.V. guide / It's alright / Magical child / In the 80's.

May 80. (7") *<4879>* **EARTH & SKY. / MAGICAL CHILD** [–] [ ]

CROSBY, STILLS & NASH

re-formed mid '82, with session men

Atlantic Atlantic

Jul 82. (lp/c) *(K/K4 50896) <19360>* **DAYLIGHT AGAIN** [ ] [8]
– Turn your back on love / Wasted on the way / Southern cross / Into the darkness / Delta / Since I met you / Too much love to hide / Song for Susan / You are alive / Might as well have a good time / Daylight again. *(cd-iss. Oct94; 7567 82672-2)*

Nov 82. (7") *(K 11747) <4058>* **WASTED ON THE WAY. / DELTA** [ ] Jul82 [9]

Nov 82. (7") *(K 11749) <89969>* **SOUTHERN CROSS. / INTO THE DARKNESS** [ ] Sep82 [18]

Jan 83. (7") *<89888>* **TOO MUCH LOVE TO HIDE. / SONG FOR SUSAN** [–] [69]

Jun 83. (lp) *(78-0075-1) <80075>* **ALLIES (live)** [ ] [43]
– War games / Raise a voice / Turn your back on love / Barrel of pain / Shadow captain / Dark star / Blackbird / He played real good for free / Wasted on my way / For what it's worth. *(cd-iss. 1984; 780 075-2)*

Jul 83. (7") *(A 9818) <89812>* **WAR GAMES (live). / SHADOW CAPTAIN (live)** [ ] Jun83 [45]
(12") *(A 9818T)* – ('A'side) / Dark Star (live) / Keep your . . .

Sep 83. (7") *<89775>* **RAISE A VOICE (live). / FOR WHAT IT'S WORTH (live)** [–] [ ]

—— split Aug'82, when CROSBY was sentenced to 5 years for drugs. He got leniency, when he agreed to rehabilitate himself in a drug hospital Dec'84.

STEPHEN STILLS

solo again (2nd single featured WALTER FINNEGAN)

W.E.A. Atlantic

Aug 84. (7") *<89633>* **STRANGER. / NO HIDING PLACE** [–] [61]

Sep 84. (lp/c) *(780 177-1) <80177>* **RIGHT BY YOU** [ ] Aug84 [75]
– 50/50 / Stranger / Flaming heart / Love again / No problem / Can't let go / Grey to green / Only love can break your heart / No hiding place / Right by you. *(cd-iss. Nov93; 7567 80177-2)*

Oct 84. (7") *<89611>* **CAN'T LET GO. / GREY TO GREEN** [–] [67]
(above as STEPHEN STILLS featuring MICHAEL FINNIGAN)

Dec 84. (7") *<89597>* **ONLY LOVE CAN BREAK YOUR HEART. / LOVE AGAIN** [–] [ ]

not iss. Vision

Sep 91. (cd/c/lp) *<3323>* **STILLS ALONE** [–] [ ]
– Isn't it so / Everybody's talkin' / Just isn't like you / In my life / Ballad of Hollis Brown / Singin call / The right girl / Blind fiddler medley / Amazonia / Treetop flyer.

– compilations, etc. –

Apr 03. (cd) *Columbia; (507881-2)* **TURN BACK THE PAGES – THE BEST OF STEPHEN STILLS** [ ] [–]

Nov 03. (cd) *Raven; <(RVCD 179)>* **TURNIN' BACK THE PAGES – THE COLUMBIA RECORDINGS 1975-1978** [ ] [ ]

GRAHAM NASH

solo, he had rejoined The HOLLIES between Sep81-Apr83

Atlantic Atlantic

Apr 86. (7") *(A 9434) <89434>* **INNOCENT EYES. / I GOT A ROCK** [ ] [84]

Apr 86. (lp/c) *(781-633-1/-4) <81633>* **INNOCENT EYES** [ ] [ ]
– See you in Prague / Keep away from me / Innocent eyes / Chippin' away / Over the wall / Don't listen to the rumours / Sad eyes / Newday / Glass and steel / I got a rock.

Jul 86. (7") *<89396>* **SAD EYES. / NEWDAY** [–] [ ]

Oct 86. (7") *<89373>* **CHIPPIN' AWAY. / NEWDAY** [–] [ ]

CROSBY, STILLS, NASH & YOUNG

re-formed yet again

Atlantic Atlantic

Nov 88. (7") *<88966>* **GOT IT MADE. / THIS OLD HOUSE** [–] [69]

Nov 88. (lp/c)(cd) *(WX 233/+C)(781 886-2) <81888>* **AMERICAN DREAM** [ ] [16]
– American dream / Got it made / Name of love / Don't say goodbye / This old house / Nighttime for the generals / Shadowland / Drivin' thunder / Clear blue skies / That girl / Compass / Soldiers of peace / Feel your love / Night song.

Jan 89. (7") *(A 9003) <88966>* **AMERICAN DREAM. / COMPASS** [55] [ ]
(12"+=) *(A 9003T)* – Soldiers of peace.
(12"g-f++=) *(A 9003TX)* – Ohio.

DAVID CROSBY

solo again

A&M A&M

Feb 89. (lp/c/cd) *<(AMA/AMC/CDA 5232)>* **OH YES I CAN**
– Drive my car / Melody / Monkey and the underdog / In the wide ruin / Tracks in the dust / Drop down mama / Lady of the harbour / Distances / Flying man / Oh yes I can / My country 'tis of thee.

Feb 89. (7") *(AM 500)* **DRIVE MY CAR. / TRACKS IN THE DUST**
(12"+=) *(AMY 500)* – Flying men.

Apr 89. (7"/12") *(AM/+Y 502)* **LADY OF THE HARBOR. / DROP DOWN MAMA**

— with band **LELAND SKLAR** – bass / **RUSSELL KUNKEL + JEFF PORCARO** – drums / **CRAIG DOERGE** – keyboards / **ANDY FAIRWEATHER-LOWE** – guitar / **DEAN PARKS** – guitar, flute / **BERNIE LEADON** – acoustic guitar / **C.J. VANSTON** – keyboards / with many guests **JACKSON BROWNE + DON WAS** plus outside writers + on session **PHIL COLLINS, JONI MITCHELL, MARC COHN, JIMMY WEBB, PAUL BRADY, STEPHEN BISHOP, JOHN HIATT, BONNIE HAYES + NOEL BRAZIL.**

Atlantic Atlantic

May 93. (7"/c-s; by DAVID CROSBY featuring PHIL COLLINS) *<87360>* **HERO. / COVERAGE** 44
(cd-s+=) – Fare thee well.

Jun 93. (cd/c) *<(7567 82484-2/-4)>* **THOUSAND ROADS**
– Hero / Too young to die / Old soldier / Through your hands / Yvette in English / Thousand roads / Columbus / Helpless heart / Coverage / Natalie.

Mar 95. (cd/c) *<(7567 82620-2/-4)>* **IT'S ALL COMING BACK TO ME NOW (live '93)**
– In my dreams / Rusty and blue / Hero / Till it shines on you / 1000 roads / Cowboy movie / Almosy cut my hair / Deja vu / Long time gone / Wooden ships.

Sams Sams

Sep 98. (cd) *(145)* **CPR**

CROSBY, STILLS & NASH

with **JOE VITALE** – drums, organ, synth bass / **LELAND SKLAR** – bass / **CRAIG DOERGE** – keyboards / **MIKE LANDAU** – guitar / **MIKE FISHER** – percussion

East West Atlantic

Jun 90. (cd/c/lp) *<(7567 82101-2/-4/-1)>* **LIVE IT UP** 57
– Live it up / If anybody had a heart / Tomboy / Haven't we lost enough / Yours and mine / (Got to keep) Open / Straight line / House of broken dreams / Arrows / After the dolphin.

Jul 90. (7") *<87909>* **LIVE IT UP. / CHUCK'S LAMENT** –

Aug 94. (cd/c) *<(7567 82654-2/-4)>* **AFTER THE STORM** 98
– Only waiting for you / Find a dream / Camera / Unequal love / Till it shines / It won't go away / These empty days / In my life / Street to lean on / Bad boyz / After the storm / Panama.

CROSBY, STILLS, NASH & YOUNG

Nov 99. (cd/c) *<(9362 47436-2/-4)>* **LOOKING FORWARD** 54 26
– Faith in me / Looking forward / Stand and be counted / Heartland / Seen enough / Slowpoke / Dream for him / No tears left / Out of control / Someday soon / Queen of them all / Sanibel.

– their compilations etc. –

on 'Atlantic' unless mentioned otherwise

Aug 74. (lp/c) *(K/K4 50023) <18100>* **SO FAR – THE BEST OF . . .** 25 1
– Woodstock / Marrakesh express / You don't have to cry / Teach your children / Love the one you're with / Almost cut my hair / Wooden ships / Dark star / Helpless / Chicago – We can change the world / Cathedral / 4 + 20 / Our house / Change partners / Just a song before I go / Ohio / Wasted on the way / Southern cross / Suite: Judy blue eyes / Carry on – Questions / Horses through a rainstorm / Johnny's garden / Guinnevere / Helplessly hoping / The Lee Shore / Taken it all / Shadow captain / As I come of age / Drive my car / Dear Mr. Fantasy / In my dreams / Yours and mine / Haven't we lost enough? / After the dolphin / Find the cost of freedom. *(cd-iss. Jan87; K2 50023) (cd re-iss. Oct94; 7567 82648-2)*

Oct 75. (d-lp) *(K 60063)* **TWO ORIGINALS OF STEPHEN STILLS (1st 2 lp's)** –

Dec 75. (lp) *(K 50214) <18156>* **STEPHEN STILLS – LIVE (live)**

Jan 77. (lp) *(K 50327) <18201>* **STEPHEN STILLS – THE BEST OF STEPHEN STILLS**
– Love the one you're with / It doesn't matter / We are not helpless / Marianne / Bound to fall / Isn't it about time / Change partners / Go back home / Johnny's garden / Rock and roll crazies – Cuban bluegrass / Sit yourself down.

Nov 77. (lp; CROSBY & NASH) *Polydor; (2310 565) / A.B.C.; <1042>* **LIVE (live)** 52

Jan 79. (lp; CROSBY & NASH) *Polydor; (2310 626) / A.B.C.; <1102>* **THE BEST OF CROSBY & NASH** Oct78
(re-iss. Nov80)

Nov 80. (lp/c) *Atlantic; (K/K4 50766) <16026>* **REPLAY** Sep80
– Carry on / Marrakesh express / Just a song before I go / First things first / Shadow captain / To the last whale / Love the one you're with / Pre-road downs / Change partners / I give you give blind / Cathedral. *(cd-iss. Oct94; 7567 82648-2)*

Dec 91. (d-cd/d-c) *(7567 80487-2/-4)* **CARRY ON**

Dec 91. (4xcd-box/4xc-box) *East West; (7567 82319-2/-4)* **THE BEST OF CROSBY, STILLS & NASH** –

Feb 92. (7"/c-s) *East West;* **OUR HOUSE. / MARRAKESH EXPRESS**
(12"+=/cd-s+=) – Carry on / Dear Mr. Fantasy (STEPHEN STILLS / GRAHAM NASH).
(above A-side was re-actified on a famous building society TV ad)

GRAHAM NASH

not iss. Artemis

Jul 02. (cd) *<751130>* **SONGS FOR SURVIVORS** –
– Dirty little secret / Blizzard of lies / Lost another one / The Chelsea hotel / I'll be there for you / Nothing in the world / Where love lies tonight / Pavanne / Liar's nightmare / Come with me. *(UK-dvda-iss.Jul03; 69286010929-2)*

□ CROSS (see under ⇒ QUEEN)

Sheryl CROW

Born: 11 Feb'62, Kennett, Missouri, USA. She left university after studying classical music before subsequently relocating to St. Louis. In the mid-80's, SHERYL set off to L.A. and finally cut her teeth as SHIRLEY CROW on MICHAEL JACKSON's 1988 'Bad' tour. The singer/songwriter then earned her crust by singing back-up for ROD STEWART, DON HENLEY and JOE COCKER. With ambitions of becoming a solo singer, she handed a demo tape to producer, Hugh Padgham, who, with a recommendation from STING, got her signed to 'A&M' in '91. An album of unproductive songs was shelved but with the help of a second producer, Bill Bottrill, she emerged late in 1993 with debut set, 'TUESDAY NIGHT MUSIC CLUB'. Although it didn't sell immediately, it became a deserved smash a year later after a support slot to the re-formed EAGLES and a well-received appearance at WOODSTOCK II. Suddenly her album turned gold and a single, 'ALL I WANNA DO', almost hit No.1. Its easy-going swing was characteristic of the album as a whole and the singer's EDIE BRICKELL / ROSIE VELA-esque narratives translated into further hits with 'CAN'T CRY ANYMORE' and the evocative 'RUN BABY RUN'. Now as much of a female role model as ALANIS MORISSETTE, SHERYL scored a second UK Top 10 with 'IF IT MAKES YOU HAPPY'. Arguably her finest moment to date, the song had a gritty passion missing from her earlier work and the rootsier, harder hitting sound indicated the direction of the new album. Simply titled, 'SHERYL CROW' (1996), the record saw her paying homage to her musical heroes, primarily The ROLLING STONES but also BOB DYLAN. A second transatlantic success, the album spawned further hits in 'EVERYDAY IS A WINDING

ROAD', 'HARD TO MAKE A STAND' and 'A CHANGE WOULD DO YOU GOOD'. Yet despite the promise of the first single, the bulk of the album sounded as though she was merely going through the motions, especially on the lacklustre 'A CHANGE . . .'. A crowd-buoying performance at a mud caked Glastonbury Festival proved she's made of sterner stuff than her glossy image might suggest. SHERYL undoubtably has the potential, it's just a shame she doesn't harness it more often. By the time her third album, 'THE GLOBE SESSIONS' (1998) was issued, SHERYL CROW had a hard time maintaining her rockier, rootsy edge while also trying to take the album in a different direction. Songs such as 'THERE GOES THE NEIGHBORHOOD' displayed CROW's usual pop rock motif, albeit with jangling STONES-like guitars used to almost overkill. Standout tracks on the album came from her ability to create beautiful and unrestrained ballads; 'RIVERWIDE' was a lush, sweeping track that oozed Celtic overtones, while 'MISSISSIPPI', an actual outtake from Dylan's 'TIME OUT OF MIND', was perhaps the strongest song on the whole set. CROW took her show on the road one year later and most memorably performed her final concert of the year at Central Park, as the live album 'SHERYL CROW AND FRIENDS: LIVE IN CENTRAL PARK' (1999) testified. KEITH RICHARDS, CHRISSIE HYNDE, ERIC CLAPTON and The DIXIE CHICKS all participated, although it didn't translate as well on record. With 2002's 'C'MON C'MON', it seemed as if the singer had finally hit upon the right balance of roots revival, pop nous, confident writing and rock star guts which she had always seemed capable of. The rest of the album carried on where hit single 'SOAK UP THE SUN' left off, the sound of an artist in her element at last. • **Songwriters:** Writes lyrics mainly / songs by BILL BOTTRELL or BAERWALD-GILBERT-McLEOD, etc. except I'M GONNA BE A WHEEL SOMEDAY (Fats Domino) / D'YER MAKER (Led Zeppelin) / MISSISSIPPI (Bob Dylan) / THE FIRST CUT IS THE DEEPEST (Cat Stevens). • **Trivia:** The track, 'HUNDREDS OF TEARS', featured on 'Pointbreak' movie soundtrack. Another two, 'STRONG ENOUGH' and 'NO ONE SAID IT WOULD BE EASY', were heard in the 1994 film 'Kalifornia'.

Album rating: TUESDAY NIGHT MUSIC CLUB (*7) / SHERYL CROW (*8) / THE GLOBE SESSIONS (*6) / . . . AND FRIENDS: LIVE AT CENTRAL PARK (*5) / C'MON, C'MON (*7) / THE VERY BEST OF SHERYL CROW compilation (*7)

SHERYL CROW – vocals + sessioners incl. BILL BOTTRILL

A&M A&M

Sep 93. (7"/c-s) *(580 380-7/-4)* **RUN, BABY, RUN. / ALL BY MYSELF** [ ] [ ]
(cd-s+=) *(580 381-2)* – The na-na song / Reach around jerk.

Oct 93. (cd/c) *(540 126-2/-4) <0126>* **TUESDAY NIGHT MUSIC CLUB** [68] [3]
– Run, baby, run / Leaving Las Vegas / Strong enough / Can't cry anymore / Solidify / The na-na song / No one said it would be easy / What I can do for you / All I wanna do / We do what we can / I shall believe. *<re-dist.US Feb94> (re-dist.Sep94; hit UK No.22 + No.8 early '95) (re-iss. cd May95; 540 368-2)* – (w/ free cd '6 TRACK LIVE MINI-ALBUM'; *540 126-18)*

Feb 94. (7"/c-s) *(580 462-7/-4)* **WHAT I CAN DO FOR YOU. / VOLVO COWGIRL 99** [ ] [ ]
(cd-s+=) *(580 463-2)* – ('A'version) / I shall believe.

Apr 94. (7"/c-s) *(580 568-7/-4)* **RUN, BABY, RUN. / LEAVING LAS VEGAS (acoustic)** [ ] [ ]
(cd-s+=) *(580 569-2)* – All by myself / Reach around jerk.

Apr 94. (c-s) *<0582>* **LEAVING LAS VEGAS / THE NA-NA SONG** [–] [60]

Jun 94. (7"/c-s) *(580 644-7/-4)* **LEAVING LAS VEGAS. / LEAVING LAS VEGAS (live)** [66] [–]
(cd-s) *(580 645-2)* – ('A'side) / I shall believe (live) / What I can do for you (live).
(cd-s) *(580 647-2)* – ('A'side) / No one said it would be easy (live) / The na-na song (live).

Oct 94. (7"/c-s) *(580 842-7/-4) <0702>* **ALL I WANNA DO (remix). / SOLIDIFY** [5] Jul94 [2]
(cd-s+=) *(580 843-2)* – I'm gonna be a wheel someday.
(cd-s) *(580 845-2)* – ('A'acoustic live) / Run, baby, run (acoustic live) / Leaving Las Vegas (acoustic live).

Dec 94. (c-s) *<0798>* **STRONG ENOUGH / WHAT I CAN DO FOR YOU** [–] [5]

Jan 95. (7"/c-s) *(580 918-7/-4)* **STRONG ENOUGH. / NO ONE SAID IT WOULD BE EASY** [33] [–]
(cd-s+=) *(580 919-2)* – All I wanna do (live).
(cd-s) *(580 921-2)* – ('A'side) / All by myself / ('A'live) / Reach around jerk.

May 95. (c-s/cd-s) *(581 055-4/-2)* **CAN'T CRY ANYMORE / ALL I WANNA DO / STRONG ENOUGH (US version) / WE DO WHAT WE CAN** [33] [–]
(cd-ep) *(581 057-2)* – ('A'side) / What I can do for you (live) / No one said it would be easy (live) / I shall believe (live).

Jun 95. (c-s) *<0798>* **CAN'T CRY ANYMORE / WE DO WHAT WE CAN** [–] [36]

Jul 95. (c-s) *(581 146-4)* **RUN, BABY, RUN / LEAVING LAS VEGAS** [24] [–]
(cd-s) *(581 147-2)* – ('A'side) / Can't cry anymore (live) / Reach around jerk (live) / I shall believe (live).
(cd-s) *(581 149-2)* – ('A'side) / Strong enough (live) / No one said it would be easy (live) / The na-na song (live).

Oct 95. (c-s) *(581 220-4)* **WHAT I CAN DO FOR YOU / LEAVING LAS VEGAS (live)** [43] [–]
(cd-s) *(581 221-2)* – ('A'side) / D'yer maker / I'm gonna be a wheel someday / No one said it would be easy.
(cd-s) *(581 229-2)* – ('A'live) / All I wanna do (live) / Strong enough (live) / Can't cry anymore (live).

Sep 96. (c-s) *<1874>* **IF IT MAKES YOU HAPPY / KEEP ON GROWING** [–] [10]

Sep 96. (7") *(581 902-7)* **IF IT MAKES YOU HAPPY. / ALL I WANNA DO** [9] [–]
(c-s+=/cd-s+=) *(581 903-4/-2)* – Run, baby, run / Leaving Las Vegas.
(cd-s) *(581 885-2)* – ('A'side) / On the outside / Keep on growing / The book.

Oct 96. (cd/c) *(540 590-2/-4) <540587>* **SHERYL CROW** [5] [6]
– Maybe angels / A change / Home / Sweet Rosalyn / If it makes you happy / Redemption day / Hard to make a stand / Everyday is a winding road / Love is a good thing / Oh Marie / Superstar / The book / Ordinary morning / Free man. *(d-cd-iss. Nov97; 540719-2)*

Nov 96. (c-s/cd-s) *(582 021-4/-2)* **EVERYDAY IS A WINDING ROAD / STRONG ENOUGH / CAN'T CRY ANYMORE / WHAT I CAN DO FOR YOU** [12] Mar97 [11]
(cd-s) *(582 023-2)* – ('A'side) / If it makes you happy (live BBC) / All I wanna do (live BBC) / Run, baby, run (live BBC).

Mar 97. (c-s/cd-s) *(582 147-4/-2)* **HARD TO MAKE A STAND / HARD TO MAKE A STAND (alt.) / HARD TO MAKE A STAND (live) / IN NEED** [22] [ ]
(cd-s) *(582 149-2)* – ('A'side) / Sad sad world / No one said it would be easy (live) / If it makes you happy (live).

Jul 97. (c-s) *(582 217-4)* **A CHANGE WOULD DO YOU GOOD / EVERYDAY IS A WINDING ROAD (live) / CAN'T CRY ANYMORE (live) / LEAVING LAS VEGAS (live)** [8] [ ]
(cd-s) *(582 271-2)* – (first 2 tracks) / If it makes you happy / Hard to make a stand.
(cd-s) *(582 209-2)* – ('A'track) / Hard to make a stand (live) / On the outside (live) / ('A'live).

Oct 97. (cd-s) *(582399-2)* **HOME / STRONG ENOUGH / SWEET ROSALYN / I SHALL BELIEVE** [25] [ ]
(cd-s) *(582401-2)* – ('A'side) / Hard to make a stand / Can't cry anymore / Redemption day.

Dec 97. (c-s) *(582456-4)* **TOMORROW NEVER DIES / ORDINARY MORNING** [12] [ ]
(cd-s+=) *(582457-2)* – The book / No one said it would be easy.
(cd-rom) *(044067-2)* – ('A'mixes + CD-Rom).

Aug 98. (c-s) *(582761-4/-2) <radio play>* **MY FAVOURITE MISTAKE / SUBWAY RIDE / CRASH & BURN** [9] [20]
(cd-s) *(582763-2)* – ('A'side) / In need (new remix) / Carolina.

Sep 98. (cd/c) *(540974-2/-4) <540959>* **THE GLOBE SESSIONS** [2] [5]
– My favourite mistake / There goes the neighbourhood / Riverwide / It don't hurt / Maybe that's something / Am I getting through (part I & II) / Anything but down / The difficult kind / Mississippi / Members only / Crash & burn / Resuscitation. *(special d-cd Mar99 +=; 541025-2)* – A change would do you good / Riverwide / It don't hurt / Strong enough /

The difficult kind / Everyday is a winding road.

Nov 98. (c-s) *(582806-4)* **THERE GOES THE NEIGHBOURHOOD / STRAIGHT TO THE MOON** 19 [ ]
(cd-s+=) *(582807-2)* – My favourite mistake (live).
(cd-s) *(582809-2)* – ('A'live) / You always get your way / Hard to make a stand (live).

Feb 99. (c-s) *(582826-4)* <*radio cut*> **ANYTHING BUT DOWN / RUN BABY RUN (live)** 19 Mar99 49
(cd-s+=) *(582829-2)* – Riverwide (live).
(cd-s) *(582827-2)* – ('A'side) / Leaving Las Vegas (live) / Mississippi (live).

Aug 99. (c-s) *(667888-4)* **SWEET CHILD O' MINE / (pop mix)** 30 –
(cd-s) *(667888-2)* – ('A'side) / If it makes you happy / A change would do you good / ('A'-CD-Rom).
(above issued on 'Columbia')

Dec 99. (cd/c) <*(490574-2/-4)*> **SHERYL CROW AND FRIENDS LIVE FROM CENTRAL PARK (live)** [ ] [ ]
– Everyday is a winding road / My favourite mistake / Leaving Las Vegas / Strong enough (w/ DIXIE CHICKS) / It don't hurt / A change would do you good / Gold dust woman (w/ STEVIE NICKS) / If it makes you happy (w/ CHRISSIE HYNDE) / All I wanna do / Happy (w/ KEITH RICHARDS & CHRISSIE HYNDE) / The difficult kind (w/ SARAH McLACHLAN) / White room / There goes the neighbourhood / Tombstone blues (w/ KEITH RICHARDS & DIXIE CHICKS).

Apr 02. (c-s) *(497705-4)* **SOAK UP THE SUN / EVERYDAY IS A WINDING ROAD / IF IT MAKES YOU HAPPY** 16 17
(cd-s) *(497704-2)* – ('A'side) / Chances are / You're not the one / ('A'-video).
(cd-s) *(497705-2)* – ('A'side) / My favourite mistake (live) / A change would do you good (live).

Apr 02. (cd) <*(493262-2)*> **C'MON, C'MON** 2 2
– Steve McQueen / Soak up the sun / You're an original / Safe and sound / C'mon, c'mon / It's so easy / Over you / Lucky kid / Diamond road / It's only love / Abilene / Hole in my pocket / Weather channel. *(UK+=)* – Missing / I want you.

Jun 02. (c-s) *(497742-4)* **STEVE McQUEEN / IF IT MAKES YOU HAPPY (live)** 44 –
(cd-s+=) *(497742-2)* – My favourite mistake (live).

Oct 03. (cd) *(986109-2)* <*152102*> **THE VERY BEST OF SHERYL CROW** (compilation) 2 Nov03 2
– All I wanna do / Soak up the sun / My favourite mistake / The first cut is the deepest / Everyday is a winding road / Leaving Las Vegas / Strong enough / Light in your eyes / If it makes you happy / The difficult kind / Picture (with KID ROCK) / Steve McQueen / A change would do you good / Home / There goes the neighbourhood / I shall believe / Let's get free.

Oct 03. (cd-s) *(9813556)* **THE FIRST CUT IS THE DEEPEST / EVERYDAY IS A WINDING ROAD (live at Central Park) / MY FAVOURITE MISTAKE (live at Central Park)** 37 17

CROWDED HOUSE

Formed: New Zealand . . . virtually as SPLIT ENDS in October '72 by TIM FINN and PHIL JUDD. They slightly altered their name to SPLIT ENZ, stylising their own brand of tongue-in-cheek pop, inspired no doubt, by SPARKS and ROXY MUSIC. In fact, PHIL MANZANERA, guitarist of the latter, produced and remixed their 'SECOND THOUGHTS' album in 1976. They were subsequently joined by TIM's brother NEIL, as a replacement for chief songwriter, JUDD. With TIM's more melodic sensibilities increasingly to the fore, the band enjoyed some belated success with the 'TRUE COLOURS' (1980) album. A single, 'I GOT YOU', even hit the British Top 20, topping the Australian charts for over two months. Despite their pop charm, the band's latter day albums such as 'TIME AND TIDE' (1982) and 'CONFLICTING EMOTIONS' (1984) sold relatively poorly outside Australia/NZ. They finally split for good in 1985, with NEIL forming CROWDED HOUSE alongside PAUL HESTER and NICK SEYMOUR. Relocating to L.A., the band signed to 'Capitol' and enjoyed massive Stateside success with their eponymous debut album in 1986/87. Taking the popcraft of SPLIT ENZ and injecting it with an aching melody, NEIL FINN proved himself an exquisite songwriter. The standout track was the bittersweet 'DON'T DREAM IT'S OVER' (later a UK hit for PAUL YOUNG), while other near misses were 'SOMETHING SO STRONG' and 'WORLD WHERE YOU LIVE'. Yet they couldn't repeat the formula on follow-up, 'TEMPLE OF LOW MEN' (1988), the album just scraping into the American Top 40 and failing miserably in Britain. There was only one thing for it, TIM had to return; with his additional songwriting and harmony vocals, 'WOODFACE' (1991) was a near masterpiece. If 'WEATHER WITH YOU' was perhaps a little sugary and 'CHOCOLATE CAKE' a mite leaden, there was no denying the swoonsome beauty of 'FALL AT YOUR FEET' and the almost spiritual reverence of 'FOUR SEASONS IN ONE DAY'. The trademark offbeat humour was still bubbling under the surface, rising to the top on the likes of 'THERE GOES GOD'. Although the set was slow to pick up, it deservedly spent more than two years in the British charts, although incredibly it failed to take off in the States. An unlikely pairing with former KILLING JOKE bassist/dance guru, YOUTH, led to CROWDED HOUSE's most experimental, profound and possibly finest effort in 'TOGETHER ALONE' (1993). Recorded at Kare Kare (a remote coastal area in their native New Zealand), the album was shrouded in an atmosphere of mystical calm and resolve, even on the rockier tracks such as 'LOCKED OUT'. 'DISTANT SUN' was a glorious burst of life-affirming, semi-acoustic melody, although it was the hypnotic grace of 'FINGERS OF LOVE' and 'PRIVATE UNIVERSE' which really carried the essence of this masterpiece. Enjoying another extended residence in the UK charts and spawning another string of hit singles, few could have predicted it would be the band's swansong. Yet after a further bout of touring and a UK No.1 compilation, 'RECURRING DREAM' (1996), the band announced a split amid tearful farewell shows. TIM FINN (husband of actress, Greta Scacchi), who had combined a solo career that encompassed a handful of albums (the last of which was the UK Top 30 'BEFORE AND AFTER' in 1993), formed one-off trio, ALT, with ANDY WHITE and LIAM O'MAONLAI. The FINN brothers were awarded OBE's for their services to New Zealand's music industry. With 'SAY IT IS SO' (2000), TIM FINN completed another chapter in his long but frustratingly sporadic solo career. Not that it wasn't worth waiting for, especially with the tantalising prospect of the pop songsmith having decamped to Nashville. Unsurprisingly, the record's homespun atmospherics and oblique lyrics preclude any CROWDED HOUSE polish. Instead, FINN was revealed as having matured into a singer/songwriter of considerable depth, alive to the possibility that less is, more often than not, more. In an unprecedented burst of solo creativity, the CROWDED HOUSE founder released another fine set, 'FEEDING THE GODS', in 2001, the same year his brother NEIL got in on the act with 'ONE NIL', his own solo follow-up to 1998's Top 5 (UK) 'TRY WHISTLING THIS'. While that album was all about realising experimental, if still unerringly melodic, ideas extraneous to the CROWDED HOUSE formula, the Top 20 'ONE NIL' stuck to the singing/songwriting tools of his trade. No surprises then, but a solid effort with guest appearances by the likes of SHERYL CROW and LISA GERMANO. • **Songwriters:** NEIL FINN penned except MR. TAMBOURINE MAN (Bob Dylan) + EIGHT MILES HIGH + SO YOU WANT TO BE A ROCK'N'ROLL STAR (Byrds). SPLIT ENZ; either NEIL or TIM. • **Trivia:** SIX MONTHS IN A LEAKY BOAT was banned by the BBC in 1982, due to the Argentian / Falklands conflict. NICK is the brother of HUNTER + COLLECTORS' frontman, MARK SEYMOUR.

Album rating: Split Enz: MENTAL NOTES (*6) / SECOND THOUGHTS (*5) / DIZRHYTHMIA (*7) / FRENZY (*5) / TRUE COLOURS (*7) / WAIATA (*5) / TIME AND TIDE (*6) / SEE YA 'ROUND (*4) / HISTORY NEVER REPEATS compilation (*7) / Crowded House: CROWDED HOUSE (*5) / TEMPLE OF LOW MEN (*6) / WOODFACE (*8) / TOGETHER ALONE (*7) / RECURRING DREAM – THE VERY BEST OF CROWDED HOUSE compilation (*9) / AFTERGLOW collection (*6) / Tim Finn: ESCAPADE (*5) / BIG CANOE (*5) / TIM FINN (*7) / BEFORE AND AFTER (*6) / SAY IT IS SO (*6) / FEEDING THE GODS (*5) / ALTITUDE (*6; with Alt:= with Andy White & Liam O'Maonlai) / FINN (*5; as Finn:= Tim & Neil) / Neil Finn: TRY WHISTLING THIS (*6) / ONE NIL (*6) / 7 WORLDS COLLIDE (*5)

SPLIT ENZ

TIM FINN (b. BRIAN TIMOTHY FINN, 25 Jun'52, Te Awamutu, New Zealand) – vocals, piano / **PHIL JUDD** – vocals, guitar / **JONATHAN CHUNN** – bass / **MILES GOLDING** – violin / **MICHAEL HOWARD** – drums

Vertigo — not iss.

Apr 73. (7"; as SPLIT ENDS) **FOR YOU. /** — –

—— **EDDIE RAYNOR** – keyboards repl. MILES / **WALLY WILKINSON** – guitar + **NOEL CROMBIE** – percussion repl. HOWARD

Mushroom — not iss.

Jun 75. (lp) *(L 35588)* **MENTAL NOTES** – Austra –
– Late last night / Walking down a road / Titus / Lovey dovey / Sweet dreams / Stranger than fiction / Time for a change / Matinee idyll / The woman who loves you / Mental notes. *(UK-iss.Aug76 on 'Chrysalis' lp/c; CHR/ZCHR 1131)*

Jun 75. (7") **TITUS. /** – Austra –

Sep 75. (7") **LOVEY DOVEY. /** – Austra –

May 76. (lp) *(L 35981)* **SECOND THOUGHTS** (re-mixes of debut) – Austra –

—— **NEIL FINN** (b.27 May'58, Te Awamutu, New Zealand) – vocals, guitar repl. JUDD / JON and drummer EMLYN CROWTHER were repl. by Englishmen **NIGEL GRIGGS** (b.18 Aug'49) – bass / **MALCOLM GREEN** (b.25 Jan'53) – drums / **ROBERT GILLIE** – saxophone
(next iss. Australia; May77 on 'Mushroom')

Chrysalis — Mushroom

Nov 76. (7") *(CHS 2120)* **LATE LAST NIGHT. / WALKING DOWN THE ROAD**

Feb 77. (7") *(CHS 2131)* **ANOTHER GREAT DIVIDE. / STRANGER THAN FICTION** — –

Oct 77. (7") *(CHS 2170)* **MY MISTAKE. / CROSSWORDS**
(12"+=) *(CHS 2170-12)* – The woman who loves you.

Oct 77. (lp/c) *(CHR/ZCHR 1145)* **DIZRHYTHMIA**
– Bold as brass / My mistake / Parrot fashion love / Sugar and spice / Without a doubt / Crosswords / Charley / Nice to know / Jambouree. *(Aus-iss.; 36347)*

—— JUDD re-joined but quit again, while GILLIE also quit

Mushroom — not iss.

1978. (lp) *(L 36921)* **FRENZY** – Austra –
– I see red / Give it a whirl / Master plan / Famous plan / Hermit McDermitt / Stuff and nonsense / Marooned / Frenzy / The roughest toughest game in the world / She got body she got soul / Betty / Abu Dhabi / Mind over matter.

—— now without WILKINSON

Illegal — not iss.

Nov 79. (7"m) *(ILS 0019)* **I SEE RED. / GIVE IT A WHIRL / HERMIT McDERMITT** — –

—— Issued earlier in Australia

—— Initial A&M material iss.Australia 1979 'Mushroom'.

A&M — A&M

Aug 80. (lp/c) *(AMLH/CAM 64822)* <4822> **TRUE COLOURS** 42 40
– Shark attack / I got you / What's the matter with you / I hope I never / Nobody takes me seriously / Missing persons / Poor boy / How can I resist her / The choral sea. *(cd-iss. 1988; CDA 3235) (re-iss. Oct92 cd/c; CD/C MID 130)*

Aug 80. (7") *(AMS 7546)* <2252> **I GOT YOU. / DOUBLE HAPPY** 12 53

Nov 80. (7") *(AMS 7574)* **NOBODY TAKES ME SERIOUSLY. / THE CHORAL SEA** — –

Jan 81. (7") *(AMS 8101)* **POOR BOY. / MISSING PERSON**

Jan 81. (7") <2285> **I HOPE I NEVER. / THE CHORAL SEA** –

Mar 81. (7") <2293> **NOBODY TAKES ME SERIOUSLY. / WHAT'S THE MATTER WITH YOU** –

Mar 81. (lp/c) *(AMLH/CAM 64848)* <4848> **WAIATA** — May81 45
– Hard act to follow / One step ahead / I don't wanna dance / Iris / Whale / Clumsby / History never repeats / Walking through the ruins / Ships / Ghost girl / Albert of India.

Apr 81. (7"m) *(AMS 8128)* **HISTORY NEVER REPEATS. / SHARK ATTACK / WHAT'S THE MATTER WITH YOU** 63 –

Jun 81. (7") *(AMS 8146)* <2339> **ONE STEP AHEAD. / IN THE WARS**

—— MALCOLM GREEN left and NOEL now on drums

Apr 82. (7") *(AMS 8216)* <2411> **SIX MONTHS IN A LEAKY BOAT. / MAKE SOME SENSE OF IT**

Apr 82. (lp/c) *(AMLH/CAM 64894)* <4894> **TIME AND TIDE** 71 58
– Dirty creature / Giant heartbeat / Hello Sandy Allen / Never ceases to amaze me / Lost for words / Small world / Take a walk / Pioneer / Six months in a leaky boat / Haul away / Log cabin fever / Make some sense of it.

Aug 84. (7") *(AMS 203)* <2652> **MESSAGE TO THE GIRL. / BON VOYAGE (KIAKATIA)**

Aug 84. (lp/c) *(AMLH/CAM 64963)* <4963> **CONFLICTING EMOTIONS** — Jul84
– Strait old line / Bullett brain and cactus head / Message to my girl / Working up an appetite / Our day / No mischief / The devil you know / I wake up every night / Conflicting emotions / Bon voyage. *(cd-iss. 1988)*

—— Now a quartet (**EDDIE RAYNOR, NEIL FINN, NIGEL GRIGGS + NOEL CROMBIE**) when TIM FINN married actress Greta Saatchi and went solo

Jan 85. (m-lp) **SEE YA 'ROUND (live)** – NZ –
– Breakin' my back / I walk away / Doctor love / One mouth is fed / Years go by / Voices / The lost cat / Adz / This is massive / Kia kaha / Ninnie knees up.

—— disbanded 1985; NEIL formed CROWDED HOUSE, which later included TIM. A year later, PHIL JUDD, NOEL CROMBIE, NIGEL GRIGGS and MICHAEL DEN ELZEN formed their own outfit, SCHNELL FENSTER, who released two quirky-funk/jazz sets, 'SOUND OF TREES' (1988) and 'OK ALRIGHT A HUH OH YEAH' (1991).

– compilations, etc. –

Dec 80. (lp) *Chrysalis; (CHR 1329)* **BEGINNING OF THE ENZ** — –

Sep 87. (d-lp) *Concept; (CCQ 050)* **COLLECTION: 1973-1984 . . . THE BEST OF SPLIT ENZ** – Austra –

Oct 92. (cd) *Chrysalis; (CDMID 175)* **HISTORY NEVER REPEATS (THE BEST OF SPLIT ENZ)**
– I got you / Hard act to follow / Six months in a leaky boat / What's the matter with you / One step ahead / I see red / Message to my girl / History never repeats / I hope I never / Dirty creature / Poor boy.

Feb 94. (cd/c) *Chrysalis; (CD/TC CHR 6059)* **THE BEST OF SPLIT ENZ**

Apr 95. (cd) *Mushroom; (D 98010)* **ANNIVERSARY** — –

CROWDED HOUSE

NEIL FINN – vocals, guitar, piano / **NICK SEYMOUR** (b. 9 Dec'58, Benella, Australia) – bass / **PAUL HESTER** (b. 8 Jan'59, Melbourne) – drums, vocals with many guests **TIM PIERCE** – guitar / **MITCHELL FROOM** – keyboards, producer / **JOE SATRIANI** – b.vox / **JORGE BERMUDEZ** – percussion etc.

Capitol — Capitol

Aug 86. (7") *(CL 416)* **WORLD WHERE YOU LIVE. / THAT'S WHAT I CALL LOVE**
(ext.12"+=) *(12CL 416)* – Can't carry on.
(ext.c-s+=/ext.cd-s+=) *(TC/CD CL 416)* – Something so strong / Don't dream it's over.

Mar 87. (7") *(CL 438)* <5614> **DON'T DREAM IT'S OVER. / THAT'S WHAT I CALL LOVE** 27 Jan87 2
(c-s+=/12"+=) *(TC/12 CL 438)* – ('A'extended).

Mar 87. (7") <5634> **LOVE YOU 'TIL I DIE. / MEAN TO ME** –

Mar 87. (lp/c)(cd) *(EST/TC-EST 2016)(CDP 746693-2)* <12485> **CROWDED HOUSE** — Aug86 12
– World where you live / Now we're getting somewhere / Don't dream it's over / Mean to me / Love you 'til the day I die / Something so strong / Hole in the river / I walk away / Tombstone / That's what I call love. *(cd+=)* – Can't carry on. *(re-iss. Mar94 cd/c; same)*

Jun 87. (7") *(CL 456)* <5695> **SOMETHING SO STRONG. / I WALK AWAY** — Apr87 7
(12"+=) *(12CL 456)* – Don't dream it's over (live).

Aug 87. (7") *<44033>* **WORLD WHERE YOU LIVE. / HOLE IN THE RIVER** [–] [65]

Nov 87. (7") *<44083>* **NOW WE'RE GETTING SOMEWHERE. / TOMBSTONE** [–] [ ]

Jun 88. (7") *(CL 498) <44164>* **BETTER BE HOME SOON. / KILL EYE** [ ] [42]
(12"+=/cd-s+=) *(12/CD CL 498)* – Don't dream it's over (live).

Jul 88. (lp/c)(cd) *(EST/TC-EST 2064)(CDP 748763-2) <48763>* **TEMPLE OF LOW MEN** [ ] [40]
– I feel possessed / Kill eye / Into temptation / Mansion in the slums / When you come / Never be the same / Love this life / Sister madly / In the lowlands / Better be home soon.

Aug 88. (7") *<44226>* **INTO TEMPTATION. / BETTER BE HOME SOON** [–] [ ]

Aug 88. (7") *(CL 509)* **SISTER MADLY. / MANSION IN THE SLUMS** [ ] [ ]
(12"+=/cd-s+=) *(12/CD CL 509)* – Something so strong (live).

Nov 88. (12"ep) *<44406>* **I FEEL POSSESSED. /** [–] [ ]

—— added **TIM FINN** – vocals, piano, keyboards

Jun 91. (cd)(c/lp) *(CDP 793559-2)(TC+/EST 2144) <93559>* **WOODFACE** [34] [83]
– Chocolate cake / It's only natural / Fall at your feet / Tall trees / Four seasons in one day / Weather with you / Whispers and moans / There goes God / Fame is / All I ask / As sure as I am / Italian plastic / She goes on / How will you go. *(album hit UK No.6 in Feb92)*

Jun 91. (c-s/7") *(TC+/CL 618)* **CHOCOLATE CAKE. / AS SURE AS I AM** [69] [ ]
(12"+=/cd-s+=) *(12/CD CL 618)* – Anyone can tell.

Oct 91. (c-s) *<44747>* **FALL AT YOUR FEET / WHISPERS AND MOANS** [–] [75]

Oct 91. (c-s/7") *(TC+/CL 626)* **FALL AT YOUR FEET. / DON'T DREAM IT'S OVER** [17] [–]
(cd-s+=) *(CDCL 626)* – Sister madly / Better be home soon.
(cd-s) *(CDCLX 626)* – ('A'side) / Six months in a leaky boat (live) / Now we're getting somewhere (live) / Something so strong (lp version).

—— reverted to a trio again, when TIM departed Autumn '91. He was replaced on tour in 1993 by US session keyboard player **MARK HART** (b. 2 Jul'53, Fort Scott, Kansas)

Feb 92. (c-s/7") *(TC+/CL 643)* **WEATHER WITH YOU. / INTO TEMPTATION** [7] [ ]
(cd-s) *(CDCL 643)* – ('A'side) / Mr. Tambourine man (live) / Eight miles high (live) / So you want to be a rock'n'roll star (live).
(cd-s) *(CDCLS 643)* – ('A'side) / Fall at your feet (live) / When you come (live) / Walking on the spot (live).

Jun 92. (c-s/7") *(TC+/CL 655)* **FOUR SEASONS IN ONE DAY. / THERE GOES GOD** [26] [ ]
(cd-s) *(CDCL 655)* – ('A'side) / Dr. Livingstone (live) / Recurring dream (live) / Anyone can tell (live).
(cd-s) *(CDCLS 655)* – ('A'side) / Weather with you (live) / Italian plastic (live) / Message to my girl (live).

Sep 92. (c-s/7") *(TC+/CL 661)* **IT'S ONLY NATURAL. / CHOCOLATE CAKE** [24] [ ]
(cd-s+=) *(CDCL 661)* – Medley:- It's only natural – Six months in a leaky boat – Hole in the river / The burglar's song.

Sep 93. (c-s/7") *(TC+/CL 697)* **DISTANT SUN. / WALKING ON THE SPOT** [19] [ ]
(cd-s+=) *(CDCL 697)* – Throw your arms around me (live) / One step ahead (live).
(cd-s) *(CDCLS 697)* – ('A'side) / This is massive (live) / When you come (live).

Oct 93. (cd/c/lp) *(CD/TC+/EST-U 2215) <27048>* **TOGETHER ALONE** [4] [73]
– Kare Kare / In my command / Nails in my feet / Black & white boy / Fingers of love / Pineapple head / Locked out / Private universe / Walking on the spot / Distant sun / Catherine wheels / Skin feeling / Together alone.

Nov 93. (c-s/7") *(TC+/CL 701)* **NAILS IN MY FEET. / ZEN ROXY** [22] [ ]
(cd-s+=) *(CDCL 701)* – Don't dream it's over (live).

Feb 94. (c-s) *(TCCL 707)* **LOCKED OUT. / DISTANT SUN (live)** [12] [ ]
(cd-s+=) *(CDCL 707)* – Hole in the river (live) / Sister Madly (live).
(10"+=) *(10CL 707)* – Private universe (live) / Fall at your feet (live).
(cd-s) *(CDCLS 707)* – ('A'side) / Private universe (live) / Fall at your feet (live) / Better be home soon (live).

Jun 94. (c-s) *(TCCL 715)* **FINGERS OF LOVE (live). / NAILS IN MY FEET (live)** [25] [ ]
(cd-s) *(CDCL 715)* – ('A'side) / Skin feeling / Kare Kare (live) / In my command (live).
(10") *(10CL 715)* – ('A'side) / Love u till the day I die (live) / Whispers and moans (live) / It's only natural (live).
(cd-s) *(CDCLS 715)* – ('A'side) / Catherine wheels / Pineapple head (live) / Something so strong (live).

Sep 94. (c-s) *(TCCL 723)* **PINEAPPLE HEAD (live). / WEATHER WITH YOU** [27] [ ]
(10"+=/cd-s+=) *(10/CD CL 723)* – Don't dream it's over / Together alone.

—— NEIL and TIM were awarded O.B.E.'s in Queen's birthday honours.

Jun 96. (c-s) *(TCCL 774)* **INSTINCT / RECURRING DREAM** [12] [ ]
(cd-s+=) *(CDCL 774)* – Weather with you (live) / Chocolate cake (live).
(cd-s) *(CDCLS 774)* – ('A'side) / World where you live (live) / In the lowlands (live) / Into temptation (live).

Jun 96. (cd/c/lp) *(CD/TC+/EST 2283) <38250>* **RECURRING DREAM – THE VERY BEST OF CROWDED HOUSE** (compilation) [1] [ ]
– Weather with you / World where you live / Fall at your feet / Locked out / Don't dream it's over / Into temptation / Pineapple head / When you come / Private universe / Not the girl you think you are / Instinct / I feel possessed / Four seasons in one day / It's only natural / Distant sun / Something so strong / Mean to me / Better be home soon / Everything is good for you. *(cd w/extra live-cd; CDESTX 2283)* – There goes God / Newcastle jam / Love u till the day I die / Hole in the river / Pineapple head / Private universe / How will you go / Left hand / Whispers and moans / Kill eye / Fingers of love / Don't dream it's over / When you come / Sister madly / In my command.

Aug 96. (c-s) *(TCCL 776)* **NOT THE GIRL YOU THINK YOU ARE. / BETTER BE HOME SOON (live)** [20] [ ]
(cd-s+=) *(CDCL 776)* – Private universe (live) / Fingers of love (live).
(cd-s) *(CDCLS 776)* – ('A'side) / Instinct (live) / Distant sun (live) / Fall at your feet (live).

Oct 96. (7") *(CL 780)* **DON'T DREAM IT'S OVER. / WEATHER WITH YOU (live)** [25] [ ]
(cd-s+=) *(CDCLS 780)* – Into temptation (live) / Locked out (live).
(cd-s) *(CDCL 780)* – ('A'side) / Four seasons in one day (live) / In my command (live) / Pineapple head (live).

—— they were now no longer, having disbanded June '96

– compilations, etc. –

Nov 95. (3xcd-box) *E.M.I.; (CDOMB 001)* **CROWDED HOUSE / TEMPLE OF LOW MEN / WOODFACE** [ ] [ ]

Feb 00. (cd) *Capitol; (533722-2) <650011>* **AFTERGLOW** (leftovers) [18] [ ]
– I am in love / Sacred cow / You can touch / Help is coming / I love you Dawn / Dr. Livingstone / My telly's gone bung / Private universe / Lester / Anyone can tell / Recurring dream / Left hand / Time immemorial.

May 02. (cd) *EMI Gold; (538945-2)* **IT'S ONLY NATURAL – THE COLLECTION** [ ] [–]

Jun 03. (cd) *Capitol; <82678>* **CLASSIC MASTERS** [–] [ ]

Sep 03. (d-cd) *Capitol; (592024-2)* **CROWDED HOUSE / WOODFACE** [ ] [–]

TIM FINN

—— (solo with some SPLIT ENZ members)

Epic A&M

Nov 83. (7") *<2572>* **GRAND ADVENTURE. / THROUGH THE YEARS** [–] [ ]

Nov 83. (7") *(A 3932)* **FRACTION TOO MUCH FRICTION. / BELOW THE PAST** [ ] Apr84 [ ]

Jan 84. (7") *<2597>* **MADE MY DAY. / GRAND ADVENTURE** [–] [ ]

Jun 84. (lp/c) *(EPC/40 25812) <4972>* **ESCAPADE** [ ] Sep83 [ ]
– Fraction too much friction / Staring at the embers / Through the years / Not for nothing / In a minor key / Made my day / Wait and see / Below the belt / I only want to know / Growing pains. *(cd-iss. Oct93 on 'Sony Europe';) (re-iss. Jun94 cd/c; 474610-2/-4)*

Virgin Virgin

Mar 86. (7") *(VS 849)* **NO THUNDER NO FIRE NO CAR. / SEARCHING FOR THE STREETS** [ ] [–]

Apr 86. (lp/c/cd) *(V/TCV/CDV 2369) <90879>* **THE BIG CANOE** [ ] [ ]
– Are we one or are we two? / Searching the streets / Hole in my heart / Spiritual hung / Don't bury my heart / Timmy / So into wine / Hyacinth / Big canoe. *(re-iss. cd Mar94; OVED 221)*

Jun 86. (7"/12") *(VS 866/+12)* **CARVE YOU IN MARBLE. / HOLE IN MY HEART** [ ] [–]

Capitol Capitol

Apr 89. (lp/c/cd) *(EST/TC-EST/CD-EST 2088)* <48735> **TIM FINN** [ ] [ ]
– Young mountain / Not even close / How'm I gonna sleep / Parihaka / Tears inside / Birds swim fish fly / Suicide on Downing Street / Show a little mercy / Crescendo / Been there, done that. *(re-iss. Oct92; same)*

Jul 89. (7") *(CL 542)* <44339> **HOW'M I GONNA SLEEP. / CRUEL BLACK CROW** [ ] [ ]
(12"+=/cd-s+=) *(12/CD CL 542)* – Six months in a leaky boat.

— with **RICHARD THOMPSON / ANDY WHITE / LIAM O'MAONLAI**

Jun 93. (c-s) *(659248-4)* **PERSUASION. / STRANGENESS AND CHARM (version)** [43] [ ]
(cd-s) *(659248-2)* – ('A'side) / Parihaka / Secret heart / ('A'acoustic).
(cd-s) *(659248-5)* – ('A'side) / Six months in a leaky boat (live) / Not even close (live) / Protected (live).

Jun 93. (cd/c) *(CD/TC EST 2202)* <94904> **BEFORE AND AFTER** [29] [ ]
– Hit the ground running / Protected / In love with it all / Persuasion / Many's the time (in Dublin) / Funny way / Can't do both / In your sway / Strangness in charm / Always never now / Walk you home / I found it *(cd re-iss. Sep94; same)*

Sep 93. (c-s) *(TCCL 694)* **HIT THE GROUND RUNNING. / NO MORE TEARS** [50] [ ]
(cd-s+=) *(CDCL 694)* – Not made of stone / You've changed.
(cd-s) *(CDCLS 694)* – ('A'side) / Walk you home (live) / Charlie (live w / PHIL MANZANERA) / ('A'live).

ALT

TIM FINN / + **ANDY WHITE** – vocals, guitar (former solo artist) / **LIAM O'MAONLAI** – vocals, guitar (ex-HOTHOUSE FLOWERS). ALT (ANDY, LIAM & TIM) recorded in Australia, although initiated in Dublin.

Parlophone Cooking Vinyl

Jun 95. (cd/c) *(CD/TC PCS 7377)* <9001> **ALTITUDE** [67] Oct95 [ ]
– We're all men / Penelope tree / When the winter comes / Favourite girl / Swim / The refugee tree / What you've done / Second swim / Girlfriend guru / Mandala / I decided to fly / The day you were born / Halfway round the world.

FINN

TIM + NEIL duo

Parlophone not iss.

Oct 95. (c-s) *(TCR 6417)* **SUFFER NEVER / WEATHER WITH YOU (demo)** [29] [–]
(cd-s+=) *(CDRS 6417)* – Prodigal son (demo) / Catherine wheel (demo).
(cd-s) *(CDR 6417)* – ('A'side) / Strangeness and charm (demo) / In love with it all (demo) / Four seasons in one day.

Oct 95. (cd/c) *(CD/TC FINN 1)* **FINN** [15] [–]
– Only talking sense / Eyes of the world / Mood swinging man / Last day of June / Suffer never / Angels heap / Niwhai / Where is my soul / Bullets in my hairdo / Paradise ((wherever you are) / Kiss the road of Rarotonga.

Nov 95. (c-s/cd-s) *(TCR/CDR 6421)* **ANGELS HEAP / IT'S ONLY NATURAL (demo) / CHOCOLATE CAKE (demo)** [41] [–]
(cd-s) *(CDRS 6421)* – ('A'side) / There goes God (demo) / How will you go (demo).

— in '96, TIM collaborated with ANNA PACQUIN on a children's project EP, 'MAGNIFICENT NOSE & OTHER STORIES'

NEIL FINN

— with augmentation from a host of musicians on a few tracks each

Jun 98. (c-s) *(TCR 6495)* **SHE WILL HAVE HER WAY / ASTRO** [26] [ ]
(cd-s+=) *(CDRS 6495)* – 808 song.
(c-s) *(CDR 6495)* – ('A'side) / Faster than light / Identical twin.

Jun 98. (cd/c/lp) *(72434 95139-2/-4/-1)* <69372> **TRY WHISTLING THIS** [5] [ ]
– Last one standing / Souvenir / King tide / Try whistling this / She will have her way / Sinner / Twisty bass / Loose tongue / Truth / Astro / Dream date / Faster than light / Addicted.

Oct 98. (c-s/cd-s) *(TCR/CDRS 6505)* **SINNER / TOKYO / SHE COMES SCATTERED** [39] [–]
(cd-s) *(CDR 6505)* – ('A'live) / Not the girl you think you are (live) / Last one standing (live).

Mar 01. (cd-s) *(CDR 6557)* **WHEREVER YOU ARE / DRIVING ME MAD (web) / THE LAST TO KNOW (web)** [32] [–]
(cd-s) *(CDRS 6557)* – ('A'side) / Underestimated / Now I get it.

Apr 01. (cd) *(532039-2)* <532112> **ONE NIL** [14] Mar01 [ ]
– The climber / Rest of the day off / Hole in the ice / Wherever you are / Last to know / Don't ask why / Secret god / Turn and run / Elastic heart / Anytime / Driving me mad / Into the sunset.

Jun 01. (cd-s) *(CDRS 6560)* **THE LAST TO KNOW / TRY WHISTLING THIS (live) / DISTANT SUN (live)** [ ] [–]
(cd-s) *(CDR 6560)* – ('A'live) / Loose tongue (live) / Not the girl you think you are (live).

Sep 01. (cd-s) *(CDR 6563)* **HOLE IN THE ICE / LOOSE TONGUE (live) / NOT THE GIRL YOU THINK YOU ARE (live)** [43] [–]
(cd-s) *(CDRS 6563)* – ('A'live) / Try whistling this (live) / Distant sun (live) / ('A'video).

— Friends below:- JOHNNY MARR, ED O'BRIEN, EDDIE VEDDER, LISA GERMANO, SEBASTIAN STEINBERG, PHIL SELWAY, PAUL JEFFREY, etc.

Parlophone Nettwerk

Nov 01. (cd; by NEIL FINN & FRIENDS) *(536645-2)* <30258> **7 WORLDS COLLIDE (live at the St. James)** [ ] Feb02 [ ]
– Anytime / Take a walk / The climber / Loose tongue / Down on the corner / There is a light that never goes out / Paper doll / Turn and run / Angels heap / Edible flowers / Stuff and nonsense / I see red / She will have her way / Parting ways / Weather with you / Paradise (wherever you are) / Don't dream it's over.

Apr 02. (cd) <30265> **ONE ALL** (remixes) [–] [ ]

TIM FINN

Frenz Of The Enz not iss.

Jun 99. (cd-ep) **FAR OUT** [–] NewZ [–]
– Roadtrip / Currents / Need to be right / Death of a popular song / Some dumb reason.

Hypertension What Are?

Dec 00. (cd) *(HYP 0202)* <60039> **SAY IT IS SO** [ ] Feb00 [ ]
– Underwater mountain / Shiver / Good together / Roadtrip / Currents / Need to be right / Twinkle / Big wave rider / Death of a popular song / Some dumb reason / Rest.

Sep 01. (cd) <60052> **FEEDING THE GODS** [–] [ ]
– Songline / I'll never know / Subway dreaming / Say it is so / What you've done / Sawdust and splinters / Dead man / Commonplace / Waiting for your moment / Party was you / Incognito in California.

□ CRUNT (see under ⇒ BABES IN TOYLAND)

CULT

Formed: Bradford, England . . . 1982 as the SOUTHERN DEATH CULT for whom IAN ASTBURY (then going under the name IAN LINDSAY) took on vocal duties. Having spent time in Canada as a kid, ASTBURY had been profoundly influenced by Native American culture and problems soon arose when the singer felt his pseudo hippy/Red Indian philosophy was being compromised by the band set-up. The group split the following year, ASTBURY keeping the name but shortening it to DEATH CULT. Relocating to London, ASTBURY duly recruited a new band (all seasoned hands on the post-punk circuit) and released an eponymous, 4-track 12" single. The band released a further solitary single, 'GOD'S ZOO', before trimming the name further to The CULT. While the band's music still betrayed slight indie/goth tendencies, they were eager to lose the 'gothic' tag. 'DREAMTIME' (1984) sounded confused and directionless, and it wasn't until 'LOVE', the following year, that the band fashioned some kind of distinct identity. Veering from the cascading bombast of the classic singles, 'RAIN' and 'SHE

SELLS SANCTUARY' to the mystic schtick of 'BROTHER WOLF, SISTER MOON', the album semi-successfully ploughed a deeper retro furrow than the myriad BYRDS clones of the day. ASTBURY's flowing locks were also something of an anomaly for an 'alternative' band in those dark 80's days, and the band were derided in some areas of the music press. The CULT's response was to throw caution to the wind and do what they'd probably always secretly dreamed of doing, writing massive, anthemic heavy rock songs. With metal guru RICK RUBIN at the production helm, DUFFY's guitar was pushed way up in the mix and the sound generally tightened. The result: any fans clinging to gothic pretensions were aghast while Kerrang readers loved it. Possibly The CULT's finest moment, it spawned the booty-shaking singles 'LOVE REMOVAL MACHINE', 'LI'L DEVIL' and 'WILDFLOWER', hell, it even had a cover of 'BORN TO BE WILD'! 'SONIC TEMPLE' (1989) was another heavy rock effort, if a bit more grandiose in its reach, featuring their tribute to doomed 60's child, EDIE SEDGEWICK, 'EDIE (CIAO BABY)'. This album saw The CULT finally gain major success in America, the US 'big rock' sound evident in the record's grooves. Line-up changes had dogged The CULT throughout their career and by 1991, ASTBURY and DUFFY were the only remaining members from the original line-up. That year's album, 'CEREMONY', sounded somewhat listless, although it was a relative success. 1993 saw a No.1 compilation album, 'PURE CULT' selling like hotcakes, although people weren't quite so eager to shell out for '94's 'THE CULT' album. Their glory days were clearly over, the band remaining a cult (!) phenomenon. In 1996, ASTBURY was in full flight again, fronting a new rock outfit, The HOLY BARBARIANS, although the album, 'CREAM' didn't shift many copies. The ageing rock warrior finally released a bonafide solo album in the shape of 1999's 'SPIRIT/LIGHT/SPEED', enlisting former MASTERS OF REALITY man, CHRIS GOSS, on guitar and production duties. While the lyrical sentiments and mystic overtones remained the same – check out the Che Guevara-style sleeve – the music made a concerted effort to get hip with some pre-millennial industrial angst. When the long awaited new CULT album, 'BEYOND GOOD AND EVIL' finally arrived in summer 2001, it came as little surprise that the new noised-up approach remained intact. Save for a few nods to their classic late 80's/early 90's heyday, the band embraced the harsher sonic climate of post-metal with DUFFY giving it laldy on the distortion pedal. Having said that, oldtime CULT fans were placated to a certain degree with the reliable ASTBURY wail and an obvious reluctance to completely forego the killer hooks which made them so compelling in the first place. Of late, ASTBURY was fronting a revitalised DOORS (OF THE 21st CENTURY) on major global concerts. • **Songwriters:** From '83 onwards, all by ASTBURY / DUFFY. Covered WILD THING (Troggs) / LOUIE LOUIE (Kingsmen) / CONQUISTADOR (Theatre Of Hate) / FAITH HEALER (Alex Harvey).

Album rating: SOUTHERN DEATH CULT (*6; as the Southern Death Cult) / DREAMTIME (*7) / LOVE (*8) / ELECTRIC (*6) / SONIC TEMPLE (*8) / CEREMONY (*6) / PURE CULT compilation (*7) / THE CULT (*5) / BEYOND GOOD AND EVIL (*6) / Holy Barbarians: CREAM (*6) / Ian Astbury: SPIRIT/LIGHT/SPEED (*5)

SOUTHERN DEATH CULT

IAN LINDSAY (b. ASTBURY, 14 May'62, Heswell, Cheshire, England)– vocals / **BUZZ BURROWS** – guitar / **BARRY JEPSON** – bass / **AKY (NAWAZ QUERESHI)** – drums

Situation2 | not iss.

Dec 82. (7") *(SIT 19)* **FATMAN. / MOYA** [ ] [–]
(12"+=) *(SIT 19T)* – The girl.

Beggars Banquet | not iss.

Jun 83. (lp) *(BEGA 46)* **SOUTHERN DEATH CULT** [43] [–]
– All glory / Fatman / Today / False faces / The crypt / Crow / Faith / Vivisection / Apache / Moya. *(re-iss. Jul88 lp/c/cd; BBL/+C 46/+CD) (cd re-iss. Sep96; BBL 2009CD)*

— (Apr'83) (as BUZZ, AKY and BARRY formed GETTING THE FEAR)

DEATH CULT

with now **IAN ASTBURY** recruited new people– BILLY DUFFY (b.12 May'61)– lead guitar (ex-THEATRE OF HATE, ex-NOSEBLEEDS) / **JAMIE STUART** – bass (ex-RITUAL, ex-CRISIS) / **RAY MONDO** (r.n.SMITH)– drums (ex-RITUAL)

Situation2 | not iss.

Jul 83. (12"ep) *(SIT 23T)* **BROTHERS GRIMM / HORSE NATION. / GHOST DANCE / CHRISTIANS** [ ] [–]

— **NIGEL PRESTON** – drums (ex-SEX GANG CHILDREN) repl. MONDO

Nov 83. (7"/12") *(SIT 29/+T)* **GOD'S ZOO. / GOD'S ZOO (THESE TIMES)** [ ] [ ]
(re-iss. Nov88)

CULT

— (same line-up)

Situation2 | not iss.

May 84. (7") *(SIT 33)* **SPIRITWALKER. / A FLOWER IN THE DESERT** [ ] [–]
(12"+=) *(SIT 33T)* – Bone rag.

Beggars Banquet | Sire

Aug 84. (lp/c) *(BEG A/C 57)* **DREAMTIME** [21] [ ]
– Horse nation / Spiritwalker / 83rd dream / Butterflies / Go west (crazy spinning circles) / Gimmick / A flower in the desert / Dreamtime / Rider in the snow / Bad medicine waltz. *(free live-lp w/ above, also on c)* **DREAMTIME AT THE LYCEUM** *(CULT 1)* – 83rd dream / God's zoo / Bad medicine / A flower in the desert / Dreamtime / Christians / Horse nation / Bone rag / Ghost dance / Moya. *(pic-lp iss.Dec84; BEGA 57P) (re-iss. Oct88 lp/c/cd; BBL/+C 57/+CD)* – Bone rag / Sea and sky / Resurrection Joe.

Sep 84. (7"/7"poster) *(BEG 115/+P)* **GO WEST. / SEA AND SKY** [ ] [–]
(12"+=) *(BEG 115T)* – Brothers Grimm (live).

Dec 84. (7") *(BEG 122)* **RESURRECTION JOE. / ('A'-Hep cat mix)** [74] [–]
(12"+=) *(BEG 122T)* – ('A'extended).

May 85. (7") *(BEG 135)* **SHE SELLS SANCTUARY. / NO.13** [15] [–]
(12"+=) *(BEG 135T)* – The snake.
(12") *(BEG 135TP)* – ('A'-Howling mix) / Assault on sanctuary.
(c-s) *(BEG 135C)* – ('A'extended) / ('A'-Howling mix) / The snake / Assault on sanctuary.

Jul 85. (7") *<28820>* **SHE SELLS SANCTUARY. / LITTLE FACE** [–] [ ]

— **MARK BRZEZICKI** – drums (of BIG COUNTRY) deputised repl. PRESTON

Sep 85. (7") *(BEG 147)* **RAIN. / LITTLE FACE** [17] [–]
(12"+=) *(BEG 147T)* – (Here comes the) Rain.

Oct 85. (lp/c)(cd) *(BEGA/BEGC 65)(BEGA 65CD) <25359>* **LOVE** [4] [87]
– Nirvana / Big neon gliter / Love / Brother Wolf, Sister Moon / Rain / The phoenix / The hollow man / Revolution / She sells sanctuary / Black angel. *(cd+=)* – Judith / Little face. *(cd re-iss. Apr97; BBL 65)*

— **LES WARNER** (b.13 Feb'61) – drums (ex-JOHNNY THUNDERS, etc) repl. MARK

Nov 85. (7") *(BEG 152)* **REVOLUTION. / ALL SOULS AVENUE** [30] [–]
(d7"+=/c-s+=/12"+=) *(BEG D/C/T 152)* – Judith / Sunrise.

Feb 87. (7") *(BEG 182)* **LOVE REMOVAL MACHINE. / WOLF CHILD'S BLUES** [18] [–]
(12"+=) *(BEG 182T)* – ('A'extended).
(d7"+=) *(BEG 182D)* – Conquistador / Groove Co.
(c-s++=) *(BEG 182C)* – (all above).

Apr 87. (lp/c)(cd) *(BEGA/BEGC 80)(BEGA 80CD) <25555>* **ELECTRIC** [4] [38]
– Wild flower / Peace dog / Lil' devil / Aphrodisiac jacket / Electric ocean / Bad fun / King contrary man / Love removal machine / Born to be wild / Outlaw / Memphis hip shake. *(gold-pic-lp Aug87; BEGA 80G) (cd re-iss. Apr97; BBL 80CD)*

Apr 87. (7") *(BEG 188)* **LIL' DEVIL. / ZAP CITY** [11] [–]
(12"+=) *(BEG 188T)* – She sells sanctuary (live) / Bonebag (live).
(d12"+=/c-s+=) *(BEG 188 TD/C)* – She sells sanctuary (live) / The phoenix (live) / Wild thing . . .Louie Louie (live).
(cd-s+=) *(BEG 188CD)* – Love removal machine (live) / The phoenix (live) / She sells sanctuary (live).

May 87. (7") *<29290>* **LIL' DEVIL. / MEMPHIS HIPSHAKE** [–] [ ]

Aug 87. (7"/7"pic-d) *(BEG 195/+P) <28213>* **WILD FLOWER. / LOVE TROOPER** [24] [ ]
(12"+=) *(BEG 195T)* – ('A'extended rock mix).
(c-s++=) *(BEG 195C)* – Horse nation (live).
(d7"+=) *(BEG 195D)* – Outlaw (live) / Horse nation (live).
(cd-s+=) *(BEG 195CD)* – (all 5 above) / She sells sanctuary (live).
(12") *(BEG 195TR)* – ('A'ext.) / ('A'-Guitar dub) / ('B'side).

— **MICKEY CURRY** – (on session) drums repl. WARNER + KID CHAOS

Mar 89. (7"/c-s) *(BEG 228/+C) <27543>* **FIRE WOMAN. / AUTOMATIC BLUES** [15] May89 [46]
(12"+=/3"cd-s+=) *(BEG 228 T/CD)* – Messin' up the blues.
(12") *(BEG 228TR)* – ('A'-L.A. rock mix) / ('A'-N.Y.C. rock mix).

Apr 89. (lp/c)(cd) *(BEGA/BEGC 98)(BEGA 98CD) <25871>* **SONIC TEMPLE** [3] [10]
– Sun king / Fire woman / American horse / Edie (ciao baby) / Sweet soul sister / Soul asylum / New York City / Automatic blues / Soldier blue / Wake up time for freedom. *(c+=/cd+=)* – Medicine train. *(cd re-iss. Apr97; BBL 98CD)*

— **ASTBURY, DUFFY + STUART** were joined by **MATT SORUM** – drums / **MARK TAYLOR** – keyboards (on tour)

Jun 89. (7"/7"gf/c-s) *(BEG 230/+G/C)* **EDIE (CIAO BABY). / BLEEDING HEART GRAFFITI** [32] [–]
(pic-cd+=) *(BEG 230CP)* – Lil' devil (live) / Love removal machine (live).
(12"/12"poster) *(BEG 230 T/TP)* – ('A'side) / Medicine train / Love removal machine (live).
(3"cd-s) *(BEG 230CD)* – ('A'side) / Love removal machine (live) / Revolution (live).

Sep 89. (7") *<22873>* **EDIE (CIAO BABY). / LOVE REMOVAL MACHINE** [–] [93]

Nov 89. (7"/c-s) *(BEG 235/+C)* **SUN KING. / EDIE (CIAO BABY)** [39] [–]
(12"+=/12"hologram+=) *(BEG 235T/+H)* – She sells sanctuary.
(cd-s++=) *(BEG 235CD)* – ('A'extended).

Feb 90. (7"/c-s) *(BEG 241/+C)* **SWEET SOUL SISTER. / THE RIVER** [42] [–]
(12"gf+=) *(BEG 241TG)* – American horse (live).
(cd-s+=) *(BEG 241CG)* – Soul asylum (live).
(cd-s) *(BEG 241CD)* – ('A'rock mix) / American horse (live) / ('A'live).
(12") *(BEG 241TR)* – ('A'rock's mix) / Soul asylum (live).
(12") *(BEG 241TP)* – ('A'rock's mix) / ('A'side) / ('A'live).

Mar 90. (c-s) *<19926>* **SWEET SOUL SISTER. / SOLDIER BLUE** [–] [ ]

— (Apr-Oct90) **MARK MORRIS** – bass (ex-BALAAM AND THE ANGEL) repl. STUART

— (1991) **ASTBURY and DUFFY** brought in **CHARLIE DRAYTON** – bass / **MICKEY CURRY** – drums / **RICHIE ZITO** – keyboards, producer / **BELMONT TENCH** – piano, mellotron / **TOMMY FUNDERBUCK** – backing vocals

Sep 91. (7"/c-s) *(BEG 255/+C)* **WILD HEARTED SON. / INDIAN** [40] [–]
('A'ext.12"+=) *(BEG 255T)* – Red Jesus.
(cd-s++=) *(BEG 255CD)* – ('A'extended version).

Sep 91. (cd)(c/lp) *(BEGA 122CD)(BEGC/BEGA 122) <26673>* **CEREMONY** [9] [25]
– Ceremony / Wild hearted son / Earth mofo / White / If / Full tilt / Heart of soul / Bangkok rain / Indian / Sweet salvation / Wonderland.

Feb 92. (7"/c-s) *(BEG 260/+C)* **HEART OF SOUL. / EARTH MOFO** [51] [–]
(12"+=/cd-s+=) *(BEG 260 T/CD)* – Edie (ciao baby) (acoustic) / Heart of soul (acoustic).

Beggars Banquet | Alex

Jan 93. (12"ep) *(BEG 263T)* **SANCTUARY 1993 MIXES** [15] [–]
– She sells sanctuary / ('A'-Dog Star Rising) / ('A'-Slutnostic mix) / ('A'-Sundance mix).
(cd-ep) *(BEG 263CD2)* – ('A'live) repl. above original.
(cd-ep) *(BEG 263CD1)* – (first 2 tracks) / ('A'-Phlegmatic mix) / ('A'-Flusteresqueish mix).

Feb 93. (d-lp/c)(cd/4x12") *(BEGA/BEGC 130)(BEGA 130 CD/B) <3246>* **PURE CULT** compilation) [1] [ ]
– She sells sanctuary / Fire woman / Lil' devil / Spiritwalker / The witch / Revolution / Wild hearted Sun / Love removal machine / Rain / Edie (ciao baby) / Heart of soul / Love / Wildflower / Go west / Ressurection Joe / Sun king / Sweet soul ister / Earth mofo. *(d-lp w/ other d-lp)* LIVE AT THE MARQUEE '91 *(cd re-iss. Jun00; BEGA 2026CD)*

— **ASTBURY + DUFFY** now with **CRAIG ADAMS** (b. 4 Apr'62, Otley, England) – bass (ex-MISSION, ex-SISTERS OF MERCY) + **SCOTT GARRETT** (b.14 Mar'66, Washington, D.C.) – drums

Sep 94. (c-s) *(BBQ 40C)* **COMING DOWN. / ('A'remix)** [50] [–]
(12"+=/cd-s+=) *(BBQ 40 T/CD)* – Gone.

Oct 94. (cd/c/lp) *(BBQ CD/MC/LP 164) <45673>* **THE CULT** [21] [69]
– Gone / Coming down / Real grrrl / Black Sun / Naturally high / Joy / Star / Sacred life / Be free / Universal you / Emperor's new horse / Saints are down. *(cd re-iss. Apr97; BBL 164CD)*

Dec 94. (c-s) *(BBQ 45C)* **STAR. / BREATHING OUT** [65] [–]
(12"+=/cd-s+=) *(BBQ 45 T/CD)* – The witch (extended).

— In Apr'95, they cancelled tour, due to new guitarist JAMES STEVENSON returning to the re-formed GENE LOVES JEZEBEL.

HOLY BARBARIANS

— **IAN ASTBURY** plus **PATRICK SUGG** – guitar, vocals (ex-LUCIFER WONG) / **SCOTT GARRETT** – drums / **MATT GARRETT** – bass

Beggars Banquet | Warners

Apr 96. (7") *(BBQ 65)* **SPACE JUNKIE. / DOLLY BIRD** [ ] [–]
(cd-s+=) *(BBQ 65CD)* – Hate you.

May 96. (cd/c/lp) *(BBQ CD/MC/LP 182) <46223>* **CREAM** [ ] [ ]
– Brothers fights / Dolly bird / Cream / Blind / Opium / Space junkie / She / You are there / Magick Christian / Bodhisattva.

IAN ASTBURY

— with **WITCHMAN (JOHN ROOME) + CHRIS GOSS**

Jun 00. (7") *(BBQ 344)* **HIGH TIME AMPLIFIER. / TYGER** [ ] [–]
(cd-s+=) *(BBQ 344CD)* – ('A'-Witchman mix).

Jul 00. (cd/lp) *(BBQ CD/LP 208) <80208>* **SPIRIT/LIGHT/SPEED** [ ] [ ]
– Back on Earth / High time amplifier / Devil's mouth / Tonight (illuminated) / Metaphysical pistol / The witch (SLT return) / It's over / El che – Wild like a horse / Tyger / Shambala (R.F.L.).

CULT

— re-formed with **ASTBURY + DUFFY + SORUM**

Atlantic | Atlantic

Jun 01. (cd/c) *(<7567 83440-2/-4>)* **BEYOND GOOD AND EVIL** [69] [37]
– War (the process) / The saint / Rise / Take the power / Breathe / Nico / American gothic / Ashes and ghosts / Shape the sky / Speed of light / True believers / My bridges burn.

– compilations, others, etc. –

all on 'Beggars Banquet'

Dec 88. (pic-cd-ep) *(BBP 1CD)* **THE MANOR SESSIONS** [ ] [–]

Dec 89. (pic-cd-ep) *(BBP 2CD)* **THE LOVE MIXES** [ ] [ ]

Dec 89. (pic-cd-ep) *(BBP 3CD)* **THE ELECTRIC MIXES** [ ] [ ]

Aug 91. (pic-cd-ep) *(BBP 6CD)* **SPIRITWALKER / A FLOWER IN THE DESERT / BONE BAG / GO WEST / SEA AND SKY / BROTHERS GRIMM (live)** [–] [–]

Aug 91. (pic-cd-ep) *(BBP 7CD)* **RESURRECTION JOE / SHE SELLS SANCTUARY / THE SNAKE / NO.13 / ASSAULT ON SANCTUARY / RESURRECTION JOE (Hep Cat mix)** [–] [–]

Aug 91. (pic-cd-ep) *(BBP 8CD)* **RAIN / LITTLE FACE / REVOLUTION / ALL SOULS AVENUE / JUDITH / SUNRISE** [–] [–]

Aug 91. (pic-cd-ep) *(BBP 9CD)* **LOVE REMOVAL MACHINE / CONQUISTADOR / GROOVE CO. / ZAP CITY / LOVE TROOPER / WOLF CHILD'S BLUES / LIL' DEVIL** [–] [–]

Aug 91. (pic-cd-ep) *(BBP 10CD)* **WILD FLOWER / WILD FLOWER (guitar dub) / HORSE NATION (live) / OUTLAW (live) / SHE SELLS SANCTUARY (live) / BONE BAG (live) / PHOENIX (live) / WILD THING . . . LOUIE LOUIE** [–] [–]

Aug 91. (pic-cd-ep) *(BBP 11CD)* **FIRE WOMAN / AUTOMATIC BLUES / MESSIN' UP THE BLUES / EDIE)CIAO BABY) / BLEEDING HEART GRAFFITI / SUN KING / FIRE WOMAN (L.A. rock mix) / FIRE WOMAN (N.Y.C. rock mix)** – –

Aug 91. (pic-cd-ep) *(BBP 12CD)* **SWEET SOUL SISTER / THE RIVER / LOVE REMOVAL MACHINE (live) / LIL' DEVIL (live) / REVOLUTION (live) / SWEET SOUL SISTER (live) / AMERICAN HORSE (live) / SOUL ASYLUM (live) / SWEET SOUL SISTER (Rock's mix)** – –

Aug 91. (10x pic-cd-ep) *(CBOX 1)* **SINGLES COLLECTION 1984-1990** –
– (all above)

Jun 92. (video w/free cd-ep) **FAITH HEALER / FULL TILT (live) / LOVE REMOVAL MACHINE (live)**

Sep 96. (cd; as DEATH CULT) *(BBL 2008CD)* **GHOST DANCE**

Nov 00. (6xcd-box) *(RCBOX 1CD) <82030>* **RARE CULT**

Nov 00. (cd) *(BBL 2029CD) <82029>* **THE BEST OF RARE CULT**

☐ CULTURE CLUB (see under ⇒ BOY GEORGE)

CURE

Formed: Crawley, Sussex, England ... 1976 initially as The EASY CURE by ROBERT SMITH, LAWRENCE TOLHURST and MICHAEL DEMPSEY. In 1978, following a brief liaison with the small 'Hansa' label the previous year, the band recorded a one-off '45, 'KILLING AN ARAB', for indie operation, 'Small Wonder'. Although actually inspired by classic Albert Camus novel, 'The Outsider', the track was met with its fair share of controversy upon its early '79 re-release by Chris Parry's new 'Fiction' imprint. A subsequent debut album, 'THREE IMAGINARY BOYS' (1979) remains among The CURE's finest work, their strangely accessible post-punk snippets lent an air of suppressed melancholy by SMITH's plangent whine. The record almost scraped into the Top 40, while the pop brilliance of accompanying single, 'BOYS DON'T CRY', saw The CURE lauded as one of the UK's most promising young bands. With SIMON GALLUP replacing DEMPSEY (who joined The ASSOCIATES), the group again drew critical plaudits for the insidious 'JUMPING SOMEONE ELSE'S TRAIN'. A track railing against fashion victims, The CURE carved out their own solitary path over the course of the next three albums. Claustrophobic is normally the favoured critical bon mot in getting to grips with The CURE's sound and few would argue that the spiralling disorientation of 'A FOREST' was easy listening. SMITH and CO.'s first Top 40 hit, the track previewed follow-up set, 'SEVENTEEN SECONDS' (1980), an album which took them into the UK Top 20 despite its gloomy sound. Revered by the more pasty faced among the group's fanbase, 'FAITH' (1981) and 'PORNOGRAPHY' (1982) ploughed a similarly grim furrow, although the latter set went Top 10. Internal feuding subsequently led to the departure of GALLUP, SMITH and TOLHURST taking charge and effecting a bit of a stylistic departure on the more flippantly pop-friendly 'LET'S GO TO BED' (not before you take that eyeliner off, BOB) single. Finally, in summer of the following year, The CURE scored a long awaited breakthrough hit with 'THE WALK', the track narrowly missing the Top 10. Nevertheless, SMITH was simultaneously busying himself with SIOUXSIE AND THE BANSHEES, contributing guitar to their Top 5 cover of The Beatles' 'Dear Prudence' and playing on the 'Hyaena' album as well as hooking up with BANSHEES man, STEVE SEVERIN, for side project, The GLOVE. Meanwhile, the flouncing 'LOVECATS' single introduced the group to a whole new audience, a song with an alarmingly high irritability factor that still gets played to death by radio. With SMITH back on board in a full-time capacity by Spring '84, The CURE again managed to take their skewered pop vision into the pop charts with 'THE CATERPILLAR', a track lifted from bizarre new album, 'THE TOP' (1984). More line-up changes occurred prior to the recording of the band's breakthrough set, 'HEAD ON THE DOOR' (1985), including the return of SIMON GALLUP. Trailed by the classic 'IN BETWEEN DAYS', the record spawned a further major hit in the glockenspiel weirdness of 'CLOSE TO ME', its breathy claustrophobia segueing into a sassy, brassy finale. The track was also accompanied by a celebrated video (directed by long standing associate Tim Pope), featuring the whole band, erm, playing inside a wardrobe (honestly!). A subsequent two year lull was punctuated by an impressive singles retrospective, 'STANDING ON A BEACH' (1986), before the band returned with the sprawling 'KISS ME, KISS ME KISS ME' (1987) double set. Hardly an easy ride, the record showcased the many strange faces of The CURE and more, incredibly making the US Top 40 where they'd slowly been building up a cult following. This time around there was no stellar pop to liven up the Stock, Aitken & Waterman-clogged Top 10 although the record did spawn a trio of minor hits in 'WHY CAN'T I BE YOU', 'CATCH' and 'JUST LIKE HEAVEN'. The latter track was later privy to a genius fuzz-pop mangling courtesy of DINOSAUR JR., an interpretation that reportedly impressed SMITH no end. The CURE were now a formidable commercial proposition on both sides of the Atlantic, which probably explains why the ponderous 'DISINTEGRATION' (1989) album made the UK Top 3 and the 'LOVESONG' single almost topped the American Hot 100. The turn of the decade saw major upheaval as TOLHURST finally bailed out after clashing with SMITH, a pared down line up of SMITH, GALLUP, PORL THOMPSON, BORIS WILLIAMS and PERRY BAMONTE seeing the group through most of the following decade. A remix album, 'MIXED UP', appeared in 1990, its sensual dancefloor appeal illustrating just how adaptable the band's music was, bearing in mind that SMITH and Co. were sometimes dismissed as whimsical, goth-pop throwbacks. New material finally arrived in Spring '92 with the 'WISH' album, the huge hit 'FRIDAY I'M IN LOVE' following in their occasional tradition of jangling dreaminess. The album itself became The CURE's first UK No.1, missing the top of the American charts by a whisker; the band were now sufficiently world dominating that they could almost get away with two double live albums, 'SHOW' and 'PARIS', released simultaneously in late '93. The remainder of the decade saw the band's profile at its lowest since their shadowy beginnings, a low-key 1996 set, 'WILD MOOD SWINGS' their sole studio output in almost five years. While that album flirted with pop stylings, The CURE resorted to navel-gazing type with 'BLOODFLOWERS' (2000), presented as the third and final part of a trilogy that already featured 'PORNOGRAPHY' and 'DISINTEGRATION'. While the record undoubtedly qualified as classic CURE, there were few glimpses of the maverick streak which made their mid-period work so interesting. • **Songwriters:** Group compositions, except covers of FOXY LADY + PURPLE HAZE (Jimi Hendrix), HELLO I LOVE YOU (Doors). • **Trivia:** SMITH married childhood sweetheart Mary Poole on the 13th of August '88.

Album rating: THREE IMAGINARY BOYS (*8) / BOYS DON'T CRY exploitation (*7) / SEVENTEEN SECONDS (*6) / FAITH (*6) / PORNOGRAPHY (*6) / JAPANESE WHISPERS mini (*6) / THE TOP (*7) / CONCERT: LIVE (*5) / THE HEAD ON THE DOOR (*7) / STANDING ON THE BEACH / STARING AT THE SEA: THE SINGLES compilation (*9) / KISS ME, KISS ME, KISS ME (*7) / DISINTEGRATION (*8) / MIXED UP (*4) / WISH (*6) / PARIS (*4) / SHOW (*4) / WILD MOOD SWINGS (*5) / GALORE – THE SINGLES 1987-1997 compilation (*6) / BLOODFLOWERS (*6) / GREATEST HITS compilation (*8)

ROBERT SMITH (b.21 Apr'59, Blackpool, England) – vocals, lead guitar / **LAWRENCE TOLHURST** (b. 3 Feb'59) – drums, keyboards / **MICHAEL DEMPSEY** – bass

Small Wonder | not iss.

Aug 78. (7") *(SMALL 11)* **KILLING AN ARAB. / 10.15 SATURDAY NIGHT** [ ] [–]

Fiction | not iss.

Jan 79. (7") *(FICS 001)* **KILLING AN ARAB. / 10.15 SATURDAY NIGHT** [ ] [–]

May 79. (lp/c) *(FIX/+C 1)* **THREE IMAGINARY BOYS** [44] [–]
– 10.15 Saturday night / Accuracy / Grinding halt / Another day / Object / Subway song / Foxy lady / Meat hook / So what / Fire in Cairo / It's not you / Three imaginary boys. *(cd-iss. Apr90; 827 686-2)*

May 79. (7") *(FICS 002)* **BOYS DON'T CRY. / PLASTIC PASSION** [ ] [–]

— **SIMON GALLUP** (b. 1 Jun'60, Surrey, England) – bass, keyboards (ex-MAG-SPYS, ex-LOCKJAW) repl. DEMPSEY who joined The ASSOCIATES

Oct 79. (7") *(FICS 005)* **JUMPING SOMEONE ELSE'S TRAIN. / I'M COLD** [ ] [–]

— added **MATHIEU HARTLEY** – keyboards, synthesizers

Nov 79. (7") *(FICS 006)* **I'M A CULT HERO (as "CULT HERO"). / I DIG YOU** [ ] [–]

— (on above they backed FRANK BELL)

Mar 80. (7"/ext.12") *(FICS/+X 10)* **A FOREST. / ANOTHER JOURNEY BY TRAIN** [31] [–]

Apr 80. (lp/c) *(FIX/+C 004)* **SEVENTEEN SECONDS** [20] [–]
– A reflection / Play for today / Secrets / In your house / Three . . . / The final sound / A forest / M / At night / Seventen seconds. *(cd-iss. Jan86; 825 354-2)*

— reverted to trio of **SMITH, TOLHURST & GALLUP** when HARTLEY left to form CRY.

Mar 81. (7"/ext.12") *(FICS/+X 12)* **PRIMARY. / DESCENT** [43] [–]

Fiction | P.V.C.

Apr 81. (lp/c) *(FIX/+C 6)* *<2383 605>* **FAITH** [14] [ ]
– The holy hour / Primary / Other voices / All cats are grey / The funeral party / Doubt / The drowning man / Faith. *(cd-iss. Jan86; 827 687-2) (c+=)* **CARNAGE VISORS** (film soundtrack)

Oct 81. (7") *(FICS 14)* **CHARLOTTE SOMETIMES. / SPLINTERED IN HER HEAD** [44] [–]
(12"+=) *(FICSX 14)* – Faith (live).

Fiction | A&M

Apr 82. (lp/c) *(FIX D/C 7)* *<4902>* **PORNOGRAPHY** [8] [ ]
– One hundred years / A short term effect / The hanging garden / Siamese twins / The figurehead / A strange day / Cold / Pornography. *(cd-iss. Jan86; 827 688-2)*

Jul 82. (7") *(FICS 15)* **THE HANGING GARDEN. / KILLING AN ARAB (live)** [34] [–]
(d7"+=) *(FICG 15)* – One hundred years (live) / A forest (live).

— **STEVE GOULDING** – bass repl. GALLUP who later joined FOOLS DANCE. (LOL now keyboards)

Nov 82. (7"/ext.12") *(FICS/+X 17)* **LET'S GO TO BED. / JUST ONE KISS** [44] [–]

— trimmed to duo of **SMITH + TOLHURST**

Jul 83. (7"/7"pic-d) *(FICS/+P 18)* **THE WALK. / THE DREAM** [12] [–]
(12"+=) *(FICXT 18)* *<23928>* – The upstairs room / Lament.
(free 12"w/ free 12") *(FICSX 17)* – Let's go to bed / Just one kiss.

— added **PHIL THORNALLEY** – bass / **ANDY ANDERSON-drums** (ex-BRILLIANT)

Oct 83. (7"/7"pic-d) *(FICS/+P 19)* **THE LOVECATS. / SPEAK MY LANGUAGE** [7] [–]
(ext.12"+=) *(FICSX 19)* – Mr. Pink eyes.

Dec 83. (m-lp/c) *(FIXM/+C 8)* *<25076>* **JAPANESE WHISPERS** [26] [ ]
– Let's go to bed / The dream / Just one kiss / The upstair's room / The walk / Speak my language / Lament / The lovecats. *(cd-iss. Apr87; 817 470-2)*

Mar 84. (7"/7"pic-d) *(FICS/+P 20)* **THE CATERPILLAR. / HAPPY THE MAN** [14] [–]
(12"+=) *(FICSX 20)* – Throw your foot.

Apr 84. (lp/c)(cd) *(FIXS/+C 9)(821 136-2)* *<25086>* **THE TOP** [10] [ ]
– Shake dog shake / Birdmad girl / Wailing wall / Give me it / Dressing up / The caterpillar / Piggy in the mirror / The empty world / Bananafishbones / The top.

— added **PORL THOMPSON** (b.8 Nov'57, London, England) – guitar, saxophone, keyboards (a member in '77)

Oct 84. (lp/d-c)(cd) *(FIXH/+C 10)(823 682-2)* **CONCERT – THE CURE LIVE (live)** [26] [–]
– Shake dog shake / Primary / Charlotte sometimes / The hanging garden / Give me it / The walk / One hundred years / A forest / 10.15 Saturday night / Killing an Arab. *(d-c+=)* **CURIOSITY: CURE ANOMALIES 1977-1984** – Heroin face / Boys don't cry / Subway song / At night / In your house / The drowning man / Other voices / The funeral party / All mine / Forever.

— **SIMON GALLUP** returned to repl. PORL. **BORIS WILLIAMS** (b.24 Apr'57, Versailles, France) – drums (ex-THOMPSON TWINS) repl. ANDERSON who joined JEFFREY LEE PIERCE (of The GUN CLUB)

Fiction | Elektra

Jul 85. (7") *(FICS 22)* **IN BETWEEN DAYS. / EXPLODING BODY** [15] [–]
(12"+=) *(FICSX 22)* – A few hours after this.

Aug 85. (lp/c)(cd) *(FIXH/+C 11)(827 231-2)* *<60435>* **THE HEAD ON THE DOOR** [7] [59]
– In between days / Kyoto song / The blood / Six different ways / Push / The baby screams / Close to me / A night like this / Screw / Sinking.

Sep 85. (7"/7"poster) *(FICS/+G 23)* **CLOSE TO ME (remix). / A MAN INSIDE MY MOUTH** [24] [–]
(12"+=) *(FICSX 23)* – Stop dead.
(10"++=) *(FICST 23)* – New day.

Jan 86. (7") *<69604>* **IN BETWEEN DAYS. / STOP DEAD** [–] [99]

Mar 86. (7") *<69551>* **CLOSE TO ME. / SINKING** [–] [ ]

Apr 86. (7") *(FICS 24)* **BOYS DON'T CRY (new mix). / PILLBOX BLUES** [22] [–]
(club-12"+=) *(FICSX 24)* – Do the Hansa.

May 86. (lp/d-c)(cd) *(FIXH/+C 12)(829 239-2)* *<60477>* **STANDING ON THE BEACH / STARING AT THE SEA** (compilation of A's & B's) [4] [48]
– Killing an Arab / Boys don't cry / Jumping someone else's train / A forest / Primary / Charlotte sometimes / The hanging garden / Let's go to bed / The walk / The lovecats / The caterpillar / In between days / Close to me. *(cd+=)* – 10.15 Saturday night / Play for today / Other voices / A night like this. *(re-iss. Feb91; same)*

Apr 87. (7"/ext.12") *(FICS/+X 25)* *<69474>* **WHY CAN'T I BE YOU? / A JAPANESE DREAM** [21] Jun87 [54]
(d7"+=) *(FIGSG 25)* – Six different ways (live) / Push (live).

May 87. (d-lp/c)(cd) *(FIXH/+C 13)(832 130-2)* *<60737>* **KISS ME KISS ME KISS ME** [6] [35]
– The kiss / Catch / Torture / If only tonight we could sleep / Why can't I be you? / How beautiful you are / Snakepit / Hey you / Just like heaven / All I want / Hot hot hot!!! / One more time / Like cockatoos / Icing sugar / The perfect girl / A thousand hours / Shiver and shake / Fight. *(pic-lp.Dec87; FIXP 13) (free-ltd.12"orange / or green,w/cd) – A Japanese dream / Breathe / Chain of flowers / Sugar girl / Snow in summer / Icing sugar (remix).*

— added on tour **ROBERT O'CONNELL** – keyboards (ex-PSYCHEDELIC FURS)

Jul 87. (7"/7"clear) *(FICS/+P 26)* **CATCH. / BREATHE** [27] [ ]
(c-s+=/12"+=) *(FICS C/X 26)* – A chain of flowers.
(7"ep+=) *(FICSE 26)* – Kyoto song (live) / A night like this (live).

Oct 87. (7",7"white/ 7"pic-d) *(FICS/+P 27)* **JUST LIKE HEAVEN. / SNOW IN SUMMER** [29] [–]
(12"+=/cd-s+=) *(FICSX/FIXCD 27)* – Sugar girl.

Oct 87. (7") *<69443>* **JUST LIKE HEAVEN. / BREATHE** [–] [40]

Feb 88. (12"/cd-s) *(FICSX/FIXCD 28)* *<69424>* **HOT HOT HOT!!! (extended remix). / HOT HOT HOT!!! (remix) / HEY YOU!!! (extended remix)** [45] [65]

Apr 89. (7"/7"gf/ 7"clear) *(FICS/+G/P 29)* **LULLABY (remix). / BABBLE** [5] [–]
(ext.12"+=/ext.12"pink+=) *(FIC SX/VX 29)* – Out of mind. (3"cd-s++=) *(FICCD 29)* – ('A'extended).

May 89. (lp/c)(cd) *(FIXH/+C 14)(839 353-2)* *<60855>* **DISINTEGRATION** [3] [12]
– Plainsong / Pictures of you / Closedown / Lovesong / Lullaby / Fascination street / Prayers for rain / The same deep water as you / Disintegration / Untitled. *(cd+=)* – Last dance / Homesick. *(pic-lp Apr90; FIXHP 14)*

May 89. (7") *<69300>* **FASCINATION STREET. / BABBLE** [–] [46]

Aug 89. (7"/7"box/c-s) *(FIC S/SG/CD 30)* *<69280>* **LOVESONG. / 2 LATE** [18] [2]
(ext.12"+=) *(FICSX 30)* – Fear of ghosts.
(cd-s++=)(cd-vid++=) *(FICCD 30)(081398-2)* – ('A'-12"mix).

Nov 89. (c-s) *<69249>* **LULLABY / HOMESICK** [–] [74]

— (Mar'89) reverted to a quintet when TOLHURST left **SMITH, GALLUP, THOMPSON, WILLIAMS + PERRY BAMONTE** (b. 6 Sep'60, London, England) – keyboards

Mar 90. (7"/7"green/c-s) *(FIC A/PA/CA 34)* **PICTURES OF YOU (remix). /** 24 71
(ext.12"+=/ext.12"green+=/cd-s+=) *(FICXA/FIXPA/FICDA 34)* – Fascination Street (live).
(7"/7"purple/c-s) *(FIC B/PB/CB 34) <64974>* – PICTURES OF YOU (remix). / PRAYERS FOR RAIN (live)
(12"+=/12"purple+=/cd-s+=) *(FICXB/FIXPB/FICDB 34)* – Disintigration (live).

— (W.H. Smith's released ENTREAT (May90) a live EP, which featured the 5 tracks +=) – Closedown / Homesick / Untitled.

Sep 90. (7"/c-s) *(FIC S/CS 35)* **NEVER ENOUGH. / HAROLD AND JOE** 13 Oct90 72
(12"+=/cd-s+=/pic-cd-s+=) *(FICSX/FICCD/FICDP 35)* – Let's go to bed (milk mix).

Oct 90. (7"/c-s) *(FIC S/CS 36) <64911>* **CLOSE TO ME (closet remix). / JUST LIKE HEAVEN (dizzy mix)** 13 Jan91 97
(12"+=/cd-s+=) *(FIC SX/CD 36)* – Primary (red mix).
(cd-s+=) *(FICDR 36)* – Why can't I be you? (extended).

Nov 90. (cd)(d-lp/c) *(847 009-2)(FIXH/+C 18) <60978>* **MIXED UP** (remix album) 8 14
– Lullaby (extended mix) / Close to me (closer mix) / Fascination Street (extended mix) / The walk (everything mix) / Lovesong (extended mix) / A forest (tree mix) / Pictures of you (extended dub mix) / Hot hot hot!!! (extended mix) / The caterpillar (flicker mix) / Inbetween days (shiver mix) / Never enough (big mix).

Apr 91. (cd)(lp/c) *(843 359-2)(FIXH/+C 17)* **ENTREAT (live)** 10
– (finally nationally released; see above)

Mar 92. (7"/c-s) *(FIC S/CS 39) <64766>* **HIGH. / THIS TWILIGHT GARDEN** 8 42
('A'-Higher mix-12"+=) *(FICSX 39)* – Play.
(cd-s+=) *(FICCD 39)* – (all above).

Apr 92. (12"clear) *(FICSX 41)* **HIGH (trip mix). / OPEN (fix mix)** 44 43
(cd-s) *(FICCD 41)* – (see last cd-s for 4 tracks).

Apr 92. (cd)(d-lp/c) *(513 261-2)(FIXH/+C 20) <61309>* **WISH** 1 2
– Open / High / Apart / From the edge of the deep green sea / Wendy time / Doing the unstuck / Friday I'm in love / Trust / A letter to Elise / Cut / To wish impossible things / End.

May 92. (7"/c-s) *(FIC S/CS 42) <64742>* **FRIDAY I'M IN LOVE. / HALO** 6 18
('A'-Strangelove mix-12"colrd+=) *(FICSX 42)* – Scared as you.
(cd-s+=) *(FICCD 42)* – (all above).

Oct 92. (7"/c-s) *(FIC S/CS 46)* **A LETTER TO ELISE. / THE BIG HAND** 28
(Blue mix-12"+=) *(FICSX 46)* – A foolish arrangement.
(cd-s+) *(FICCD 46)* – (all above).

Sep 93. (d-cd/d-c/d-lp) *(FIX CD/MC/LP 25) <61551>* **SHOW (live)** 29 42
– Tape / Open / High / Pictures of you / Lullaby / Just like Heaven / Fascination Street / A night like this / Trust / Doing the unstuck / The walk / Let's go to bed / Friday I'm in love / In between days / From the edge of the deep green sea / Never enough / Cut / End.

— PORL departed after the above.

Oct 93. (cd/c/d-lp) *(FIX CD/MC/LP 26) <61552>* **PARIS (live)** 56
– The figurehead / One hundred years / At night / Play for today / Apart / In your house / Lovesong / Catch / A letter to Elise / Dressing up / Charlotte sometimes / Close to me.

Apr 96. (c-s) *(576468-4)* **THE 13TH (swing radio mix) / IT USED TO BE ME** 15 –
(cd-s+=) *(576469-2)* – ('A'-Killer bee mix).
(cd-s) *(576493-2)* – ('A'-Two chord cool mix) / Ocean / Adonais.

Apr 96. (c-s) *<64292>* **THE 13TH / ADONAIS** – 44

May 96. (cd/c/lp) *(FIX CD/MC/LP 28) <61744>* **WILD MOOD SWINGS** 9 12
– Want / Club America / This is a lie / The 13th / Strange attraction / Mint car / Jupiter crash / Round & round & round / Gone! / Numb / Trap / Treasure / Bare.

Jun 96. (c-s) *(FICCS 52) <64275>* **MINT CAR / HOME** 31 58
(cd-s+=) *(FICCD 52)* – ('A'-buskers mix).
(cd-s) *(FISCD 52)* – ('A'-electric mix) / Waiting / A pink dream.

Nov 96. (c-s) *(FICCS 53)* **GONE! / THIS IS A LIE (ambient mix)** 60
(cd-s+=) *(FICD 53)* – Strange attraction (strange mix) / The 13th (feels good mix).

Nov 97. (cd/c/lp) *(FIX CD/MC/LP 30) <62117>* **GALORE – THE SINGLES 1987-1997** (compilation) 37 32
– Why can't I be you / Catch / Just like Heaven / Hot, hot, hot / Lullaby / Fascination Street / Love song / Pictures of you / Never enough / Close to me / High / Friday I'm in love / Letter to Elise / The 13th / Mint car / Strange attraction / Gone / Wrong number.

Nov 97. (c-s) *(FICMC 54)* **WRONG NUMBER / ('A'-radio mix mix)** 62 –
(12"/cd-s+=) *(FIC SX/D 54)* – ('A'mixes).

Feb 00. (d-lp/cd) *(FIX/+CD 31) <62236>* **BLOODFLOWERS** 14 16
– Out of this world / Watching me fall / Where the birds always sing / Maybe someday / The last day of summer / There is no if . . . / The loudest sound / 39 / Bloodflowers.

Oct 01. (cd-s) *(587389-2)* **CUT HERE / SIGNAL TO NOISE / CUT HERE (missing mix) / CUT HERE (video)** 54 –

Nov 01. (cd) *(589435-2) <62726>* **GREATEST HITS** (compilation) 33 58
– Boys don't cry / A forest / Let's go to bed / The walk *[US-only]* / The lovecats / Caterpillar *[UK-only]* / Inbetween days / Close to me / Why can't I be you? / Just like Heaven / Lullaby / Lovesong / Pictures of you *[UK-only]* / Never enough / High / Friday I'm in love / Mint car / Wrong number / Cut here / Just say yes. *(d-cd-iss. +=; 589434-2)* – (acoustic versions).

– compilations, etc. –

Aug 83. (lp/c) *Fiction; (SPE LP/MC 26) / P.V.C.; <7916>* **BOYS DON'T CRY** 71 Aug80
– Boys don't cry / Plastic passion / 10.15 Saturday night / Accuracy / Object * / Jumping someone else's train / Subway song / Killing an Arab / Fire in Cairo / Another day / Grinding halt / World war * / Three imaginary boys. *(cd-iss. Nov86; 815 011-2) (w/ out tracks * +=)* – So what.

May 86. (7") *P.V.C.;* **BOYS DON'T CRY. / LET'S GO TO BED** –

May 88. (12"ep/cd-ep) *Strange Fruit; (SFPS/+CD 050)* **PEEL SESSIONS** –
– Killing an Arab / Boys don't cry / 10:15 Saturday night / Fire in Cairo.

Oct 88. (vid-cd) *Fiction; (080184-2)* **WHY CAN'T I BE YOU (video) / JAPANESE DREAM / HEY YOU / WHY CAN'T I BE YOU** –

Oct 88. (vid-cd) *Fiction; (080182-2)* **IN BETWEEN DAYS (video) / SIX DIFFERENT WAYS (live) / PUSH (live)** –

Oct 88. (vid-cd) *Fiction; (080186-2)* **CATCH (video) / CATCH / BREATHE / A CHAIN OF FLOWERS / ICING SUGAR (new mix)** –

CYPRESS HILL

Formed: Los Angeles, California, USA . . . 1988 by DJ MUGGS, B-REAL and SEN DOG. In the early 90's, after signing to US 'Columbia' label through their own 'Ruffhouse' label, the hard-core rappers cracked the Top 40 with their eponymous debut. The album contained the single, 'I COULD JUST KILL A MAN', alongside the dirty, trippy narcotica of tracks like 'ULTRAVIOLET DREAMS' and 'SOMETHING FOR THE BLUNTED'. With B-REAL's sneering intonation and the bass-heavy production, CYPRESS HILL were instantly recognisable. Tireless advocators of marijuana use (and legalisation), most of the band's music was so claustrophobically heavy it sounded like they'd been stoned since birth. Influenced by the infamous 'Rodney King' incident in L.A., the follow-up album, 'BLACK SUNDAY' (1993) took a decidedly darker turn, gangsta-like bravado ('LICK A SHOT', 'COCK THE HAMMER', 'A TO THE K') interspersing the trademark homages to hash. 'INSANE IN THE BRAIN' (1993) was the first in a string of U.K. hit singles and the band consolidated their success in Britain by playing at a number of predominantly white rock festivals, proving their crossover appeal. 'CYPRESS HILL III (TEMPLES OF BOOM)' (1996) upped the gangsta ante with such subtle fare as 'KILLAFORNIA' and 'KILLA HILL NIGGAS' although the hopelessly stoned vibe was still sufficiently alive and kicking (or head bowed and nodding) to satisfy fans. The subsequent departure of SEN DOG hit CYPRESS HILL hard and although they attempted to regroup with replacement BARRON RICKS, 'IV' (1998) was the closest they'd yet come to self-parody. Their UK stock nevertheless remained high, hovering around the Top 20 with 'TEQUILA SUNRISE' and a RUN DMC-style JASON NEVINS revamp of 'INSANE IN THE BRAIN'. CYPRESS HILL also followed the ailing East Coast rappers in their unadvised stab at rap-metal hokum, devoting one whole side of 'SKULL & BONES' (2000) to such time wasting. Needless to say LIMP BIZKIT were involved; when, oh, when are any of these bands going to realise that it's been done before (years ago) and sounded so much better the first time. While the return of SEN DOG had revitalised their dope-induced sonic doomscapes, the trio's rock fetishism was encapsulated with 'LIVE AT THE FILLMORE' (2000). From the cover art to the riffed-up reinvention of their classic early 90's material, the album oozed testosterone. Sure, it was high adrenaline stuff, thrilling enough in its own way but lacking in the spooked-out paranoia which defined their sound. 'STONED RAIDERS' (2001) doggedly continued with the riff-rap albeit with occasionally more playful results. Much more easy to digest were MUGGS' two chapters of '. . .PRESENTS THE SOUL ASSASSINS', released in 1997 and 2000 respectively. Left to his own devices, the quicksilver producer created a vapourous, filmic epic with walk-on parts from the great and the good of hip hop: WYCLEF JEAN, KRS-ONE, DR DRE, RZA and MOBB DEEP amongst others. While the follow-up wasn't graced with quite as much talent, MUGGS' haunted, twilight-zone musical vision once again hypnotized and confounded in equal measure. As did his detour into sweeping, cinematic electronica, 2003's 'DUST'. While guests GREG DULLI and JOSH TODD were plucked from the confines of alternative rock, their presence fleshed out MUGGS' ambitious soundscapes amid careening string parts and distended synth washes. • **Songwriters:** Group penned. WE AIN'T GOIN' OUT LIKE THAT sampled; THE WIZARD (Black Sabbath) / WHEN THE SH-- GOES DOWN sampled; DEEP GULLY (Outlaw Blues Band) / LIL' PUTOS sampled; ODE TO BILLY JOE (Bobbie Gentry) / etc. • **Trivia:** MUGGS also produced HOUSE OF PAIN, BEASTIE BOYS and ICE CUBE.

Album rating: CYPRESS HILL (*9) / BLACK SUNDAY (*8) / CYPRESS HILL III – TEMPLES OF BOOM (*6) / IV (*6) / SKULL & BONES (*7) / LIVE AT THE FILLMORE (*5) / STONED RAIDERS (*7) / Muggs: PRESENTS THE SOUL ASSASSINS, CHAPTER I (*6) / MUGGS PRESENTS THE SOUL ASSASSINS, CHAPTER II (*5) / DUST (*7)

B-REAL (b. LOUIS FREESE, 2 Jun'70) – vocals (ex-DVX) / **SEN DOG** (b. SENEN REYES, 20 Nov'65, Cuba) – vocals (ex-DVX) / **DJ MUGGS** (b. LAWRENCE MUGGERUD, 28 Jan'68, Queens, N.Y.) – DJ, producer (ex-7A3)

Ruffhouse Ruffhouse

Jan 92. (cd/c/lp) *(468893-2/-4/-1)* *<47889>* **CYPRESS HILL** Nov91 31
– Pigs / How I could just kill a man / Hand on the pump / Hole in the head / Ultraviolet dreams / Light another / The phuncky feel one / Break it up / Real estate / Stoned is the way of the walk / Psycobetabuckdown / Something for the blunted / Latin lingo / The funky Cypress Hill shit / Tres equis / Born to get busy. *(cd re-iss. May94 & Feb97; same) (lp re-iss. Jan00 on 'Simply Vinyl'; SVLP 170)*

Feb 92. (7") *<73930>* **HOW I COULD JUST KILL A MAN. / THE PHUNKY FEEL ONE** – 77 94

Apr 92. (c-s) *<74105>* **HAND ON THE PUMP / REAL ESTATE** –
(cd-s) *<74332>* – ('A'-Mugg's Blunted mix) / ('A'extended mix) / ('A'-instrumental) / Hand on the glock.

Jun 92. (12"ep/cd-ep) *<74478>* **LATIN LINGO (Prince Paul mix) / STONED IS THE WAY OF THE WALK (reprise) / HAND ON THE GLOCK** –

Jul 93. (c-s) *<77135>* **INSANE IN THE BRAIN / STONED IS THE WAY OF THE WALK** – 19

Jul 93. (c-s) *(659533-4)* **INSANE IN THE BRAIN (radio version). / WHEN THE SH-- GOES DOWN (radio version)** 32 –
(12"+=/cd-s+=) *(659533-6/-2)* – ('A'instrumental).
(re-iss. May00; same)

Jul 93. (cd/c/lp) *(474075-2/-4/-1)* *<53931>* **BLACK SUNDAY** 13 1
– I wanna get high / I ain't goin' out like that / Insane in the brain / When the sh-- goes down / Lick a shot / Cock the hammer / Interlude / Lil' putos / Legalize it / Hits from the bong / What go around come around, kid / A to the K / Hand on the glock / Break 'em off some.

Sep 93. (c-s) *(659670-8)* **WHEN THE SH-- GOES DOWN (extended). / LATIN LINGO / HOW COULD I JUST KILL A MAN (the Killer mix)** 19 –
(12"+=/cd-s+=) *(659670-6/-2)* – ('A'instrumental) / The phunky feel one (extended).

Dec 93. (c-s) *(659690-4)* *<77307>* **I AIN'T GOIN' OUT LIKE THAT. / HITS FROM THE BONG** 15 65
(12"+=/cd-s+=) *(659690-6/-2)* – When the sh-- goes down (Diamond D mix).
(re-iss. May00; same)

Feb 94. (c-s) *(660176-4)* **INSANE IN THE BRAIN. / STONED IS THE WAY OF THE WALK** 21 –
(12"+=) *(660176-6)* – Latin lingo (Prince Paul mix).
(cd-s) *(660176-2)* – ('A'side) / Something for the blunted.
(re-iss. May00; same)

Apr 94. (c-s) *(660319-4)* **LICK A SHOT (Baka Boys remix). / I WANNA GET HIGH** 20
(12"+=/cd-s+=) *(660319-6/-2)* – Scooby Doo.
(re-iss. May00; same)

Sep 95. (c-s) *(662354-4)* *<78042>* **THROW YOUR SET IN THE AIR / KILLA HILL NIGGAS** 15 45
(12"+=/cd-s+=) *(662354-6/-2)* – ('A'-Slow roll remix) / ('B'instrumental).
(re-iss. May00; same)

Oct 95. (cd/c/d-lp) *(478127-2/-4/-1)* *<66991>* **CYPRESS HILL III / TEMPLES OF BOOM** 11 3
– Spark another owl / Throw your set in the air / Stoned raiders / Illusions / Killa hill niggas / Boom biddy bye bye / No rest for the wicked / Make a move / Killafornia / Funk freakers / Locotes / Red light visions / Strictly hip hop / Let it rain / Everybody must get stoned. *(d-cd+=/t-lp+=; 478127-9/-0)* – DJ MUGGS BUDDHA MIX:- Hole in the head – How could I just kill a man – Insane in the brain – Stoned is the way of the walk – Hits from the bong – Hand on the pump – Real estate – I wanna get high. *(cd re-iss. Jan99; same)*

Feb 96. (12"ep) *(662905-6)* **ILLUSIONS / THROW YOUR SET IN THE AIR (radio version). / ILLUSIONS (harpsicord mix) / ILLUSIONS (harpsicord instrumental)** 23
(cd-ep) *(662905-2)* – ('A'mixes).
(re-iss. May00; same)

—— SEN DOG went solo (DOGWOOD) and was repl. by DJ SCANDALOUS

Jun 96. (c-s) *<78339>* **BOOM BIDDY BYE BYE / ('A'version)** – 87

Aug 96. (m-cd/m-c/m-lp) *(485230-2/-4/-1)* *<67780>* **UNRELEASED & REVAMPED EP** 29 21
– Boom biddy bye bye (Fugees remix) / Throw your hands in the air / Intellectual dons (featuring Call O Da Wild) / Hand on the pump (Muggs' blunted mix) / Whatta you know / Hits from the bong (T-Ray's mix) / Illusions (Q-Tip remix) / Latin lingo (Prince Paul mix) / When the ship goes down (Diamond D remix).

—— **MUGGS** and **B-REAL** recruited **BARON** – rapper / **ERIC BOBO** – percussion

Sep 98. (12"/cd-s) *(666493-6/-2)* **TEQUILA SUNRISE (mixes' radio / clean / radio edit featuring Fat Joe / Spanish)** 23
(cd-s) *(666493-5)* – ('A'side) / Champions (featuring PMD) / Can you handle this.
(re-iss. May00; same)

Oct 98. (cd/c/lp) *(491604-2/-4/-1)* *<69037>* **IV** 25 11
– Looking through the eye of a pig / Checkmate / From the window of my room / Prelude to a come up (featuring Mc EIHT) / Riot starter / Audio X (featuring BARRON RICKS) / Steel magnolia (featuring BARRON RICKS) / I remember that freak bitch (from the club) (featuring BARRON RICKS – interlude part 2) / (Goin' all out) Nothin' to lose / Tequila sunrise (featuring BARRON RICKS) / Dead men tell no tales / Feature presentation (featuring BARRON RICKS) / Chance infinite / Dr. Greenthumb / 16 men till there's no men left / High times / Clash of the Titans / Lightning strikes. *(cd re-iss. Aug01; same)*

Mar 99. (c-s/cd-s) *(667120-4/-2)* <79024> **DR. GREENTHUMB (clean radio mix) / DR. GREENTHUMB (Fun Lovin' Criminals clean remix)** 34 Sep98 70
(12") *(667120-2)* – ('A'-version) / ('A'-Fun Lovin' Criminals instrumental remix) / ('A'-Fun Lovin' Criminals remix).
(re-iss. May00; same)
Jun 99. (c-s; JASON NEVINS vs CYPRESS HILL) *(INCRL 17MC)* **INSANE IN THE BRAIN / ('A'mix)** 19 ☐
(cd-s) *(INCRL 17CD)* – ('A'mixes).
(cd-s) *(INCRL 17CDX)* – ('A'mixes).
(above issued on 'Incredible')

— **SEN DOG** returned to repl. BARRON
Apr 00. (c-s) *(669264-4)* **RAP SUPERSTAR / ROCK SUPERSTAR** 13 ☐
(cd-s) *(669264-2)* – ('A'side) / ('A'instrumental) / Loco en el cocoa (Insane In The Brain).
(cd-s+=) *(669264-5)* – ('B'side) / Checkmate (Hang 'Em High remix) / Fistful.
Apr 00. (cd/c) *(495183-2/-8/-4)* <69990> **SKULL & BONES** 6 May00 5
– Intro / Another victory / Rap superstar / Cuban necktie / What U want from me / Stank ass hoe / Highlife / Certified bomb / Can I get a hit / We live this shit / Worldwide / Rock superstar. *(d-cd; 495183-2)* – Valley of chrome / Get out of my head / Can't get the best of me / Man / Dust.
Sep 00. (c-s) *(669789-4)* **CAN'T GET THE BEST OF ME / HIGHLIFE** 35 ☐
(cd-s+=) *(669789-2)* – Do you know who I am / ('A'-CD-ROM).
(cd-s) *(669789-5)* – ('A'side) / Highlife (Fredwreck mix) / Rap superstar ((Alchemist remix).
Dec 00. (cd/c) *(500558-2/-4)* <85184> **LIVE AT THE FILLMORE (live)** ☐ ☐
– Hand on the pump / Real estate / How I could just kill a man / Insane in the brain / Pigs / Looking through the eye of a pig / Cock the hammer / Checkmate / Can't get the best of me / Lick a shot / A to the K / I ain't goin' out like that / I wanna get high / Stoned is the way of the walk / Hits from the bong / Riot starter / (Rock) Superstar.
Nov 01. (c-s) *(672166-4)* **TROUBLE / LOWRIDER (explicit) / TROUBLE (explicit)** 33 ☐
(cd-s) *(672166-2)* – (first 2 tracks) / Rock superstar.
(cd-s) *(672166-5)* – (first 2 tracks) / Jack you back (live).
Dec 01. (cd/c/lp) *(504171-2/-4/-1)* <85740> **STONED RAIDERS** 71 64
– (intro) / Trouble / Kronologik (with KURUPT) / Southland killers (with MC REN & KING TEE) / Bitter / Amplified / It ain't easy / Memories / Psychodelic vision / Red meth & B (with REDMAN & METHOD MAN) / Lowrider / Catastrophe / L.I.F.E. (with KOCANE) / Here is something you can't understand (with KURUPT).

– compilations, etc. –

on 'Ruffhouse' unless mentioned otherwise
May 00. (3xcd-box) *(498283-2)* **CYPRESS HILL / BLACK SUNDAY / TEMPLES OF BOOM** ☐ ☐
(re-iss. Nov00 & Sep01; same)
May 00. (cd) *(496287-2)* **LOS GRANDES EXITOS EN ESPANOL** ☐ ☐

MUGGS

not iss. Columbia
Feb 97. (12"; with The SOUL ASSASSINS featuring DR. DRE & B REAL) <78518> **PUPPET MASTER. / (version)** – ☐
Mar 97. (cd/lp) <66820> **MUGGS PRESENTS THE SOUL ASSASSINS, CHAPTER I** ☐ 20
– The time has come / Puppet master (DR. DRE & B REAL) / Decisions, decisions (GOODIE MOB) / Third world (RZA & GENIUS GZA) / Battle of 2001 (CYPRESS HILL) / Devil in a blue dress (LA THE DARKMAN) / Heavy weights (MC EIHT) / Move ahead (KRS-ONE) / It could happen to you (MOBB DEEP) / Life is tragic (INFAMOUS MOBB) / New York undercover (CALL O' DA WILD) / John 3:16 (WYCLEF FROM THE REFUGEE CAMP).

Ruff Life Ruff Life
Oct 00. (cd/d-lp) <(RLCD/RLLP 02)> **MUGGS PRESENTS THE SOUL ASSASSINS, CHAPTER II** ☐ ☐
– Real life (KOOL G. RAP) / We will survive (G.O.D. PT.III) / You better believe it (XZIBIT & KING LEE) / When the fat lady sings (GZA) / This some 'n to (GOODIE MOB) / Armageddon (interlude) (KURUPT) / Victory or defeat (HOSTYLE OF SCREWBALL) / Heart of the assassin (CHACE INFINITE, KRONDON & PHENAM aka DON KRISIS) / Suckers are hidin' (DILATED PEOPLES) / When the pain inflict (KURUPT & ROSCOE) / Don't trip (CYPRESS HILL & JESSIE MOSS) / Razor to your throat (EVERLAST) / Millennium thrust (SELF-SCIENTIFIC).

Anti Anti
Mar 03. (cd) <(6636-2)> **DUST** ☐ ☐
– I know / Rain / Niente / Morta / Faded / Chasing shadows / Tears / Cloudy days / Fat city / Believer / Gone for good / Blip / Dead flowers / Far away.
May 03. (cd-s) *(ANTI 1117-2)* **RAIN** ☐ ☐

BOB DYLAN

☐ Chuck D (see under ⇒ PUBLIC ENEMY)

DAFT PUNK

Formed: Paris, France … 1992 originally as DARLING, by THOMAS BANGALTER (his father was the man behind such disco gems as 'CUBA' by The GIBSON BROTHERS and 'D.I.S.C.O.' by OTTOWAN) and GUY-MANUEL DE HOMEM CHRISTO. The duo had one track included on a STEREOLAB-compiled various artists album, described as "Daft Punk" by one daft critic. The lads were then daft enough to adopt this moniker as a full-time concern, releasing a clutch of 12"ers in the mid 90's on the Scottish dance label, 'Soma'. The grunge disco classic, 'DA FUNK', was a massive underground club hit, creating a buzz that eventually led to a major label signing race. 'Virgin' subsequently came out on top (oo er!), securing the pleasure of releasing their soon-to-be widely acclaimed debut long player, 'HOMEWORK'. Issued in early '97, it hit the UK Top 10 as well as surprisingly breaking new ground in the States on the back of the minimalist 70's trance-funk oddity 'AROUND THE WORLD', which was their second UK Top 10 smash. While 1977 was the year of punk, 1997 was most definitely the year of DAFT PUNK, the duo wowing fans at sold out venues and bulging festival dance tents up and down the country. Come 1998, BANGALTER was riding even higher in the charts with the irresistible disco-house shimmy of STARDUST's 'MUSIC SOUNDS BETTER WITH YOU'. This served as a taster for DP's first single of the new millennium, 'ONE MORE TIME', a digi-pop classic featuring a treated vocal by NY garage star, ROMANTHONY. The accompanying album, 'DISCOVERY' (2001), confirmed DAFT PUNK's maturation from acid-house pranksters to masters of seamlessly updated electro-pop cum 70's/80's retro chic, drawing inspiration from the obvious (GIORGIO MORODER, The BUGGLES) to the not so obvious (STEVE MILLER, VANGELIS).

Album rating: HOMEWORK (*8) / DISCOVERY (*7)

THOMAS BANGALTER (b. 3 Jan'75) – electronics / **GUY-MANUEL DE HOMEM CHRISTO** (b. 8 Feb'74) – electronics

		UK		US
		Soma		not iss.
Apr 94.	(12"ep) *(SOMA 014)* **NEW WAVE EP** – French teen / New wave / Alive (the new wave finale) / +1 .			–
May 95.	(12"ep) *(SOMA 025)* **DA FUNK / DA FUNK (version) / MUSIQUE**			–
		Virgin		Virgin
Jan 97.	(cd/c/d-lp) *(CD/TC+/V 2821)* **HOMEWORK** – Daftendirekt / Wdpk 83.7 fm / Revolution 909 / Da funk / Phoenix / Fresh / Around the world / Rollin' & scratchin' / Teachers / High fidelity / Rock'n roll / Oh yeah / Burnin' / Indo silver club / Alive / Funk Ad.	8	Mar97	
Feb 97.	(7"/c-s) *(VS LH/C 1625)* **DA FUNK. / MUSIQUE** (12"+=/cd-s+=) *(VS T/CD 1625)* – ('A'original).	7		
Apr 97.	(7"/c-s) *(VS LH/C 1633)* <8950116-2> **AROUND THE WORLD. / TEACHERS** (12"+=/cd-s+=) *(VS T/CD 1633)* – ('A'-Motorbass remix).	5	Aug97	61
Sep 97.	(c-s/cd-s) *(VS C/CD 1649)* **BURNIN' / (mixes by Slam & Ian Pooley)** (12"+=) *(VST 1649)* – ('A'remixes by DJ Sneak).	30		
Feb 98.	(c-s/12"/cd-s) *(VS C/T/CDT 1682)* **REVOLUTION 909. / ('A'-Roger Sanchez mix) / ('A'-acappella)**	47		
Nov 00.	(c-s/cd-s) *(VSC/+DT 1791)* <38758> **ONE MORE TIME / (radio mix)** (12") *(VST 1791)* – ('A'mixes).	2	Jan01	61
Mar 01.	(cd/c/d-lp) *(CDVX/TCV/VX 2940)* <49606> **DISCOVERY** – One more time / Aerodynamic / Digital love / Harder, better, faster, stronger / Crescendolls / Nightvision / Superheroes / High life / Something about us / Voyager / Veridis quo / Short circuit / Face to face / Too long.	2		44
Mar 01.	(12") *(VST 1799)* **AERODYNAMIC. / AERODYNAMITE**			–
Jun 01.	(c-s/cd-s) *(VSC/+DT 1810)* **DIGITAL LOVE (mixes)** (12") *(VST 1810)* – ('A'side) / Digital dub.	14		
Nov 01.	(12"/cd-s) *(VST/VSCDT 1822)* **HARDER, BETTER, FASTER, STRONGER. / (mixes; Breakers break / Pete Heller's stylus)** (12") *(VSTX 1822)* – ('A'-Neptunes remix) / Aerodynamic (Slum Village remix).	25		

– compilations, etc. –

on 'Virgin' / US 'Astralwerks' unless mentioned otherwise

		UK		US
Oct 01.	(cd/lp) *(CD+/V 2952)* <11139> **ALIVE 1997 (live)**		Nov01	
Oct 01.	(d-cd) *(810847-2)* **DISCOVERY / HOMEWORK**			–

THOMAS BANGALTER

		UK		US
		Roule		Virgin
Mar 97.	(12"ep) *(ROULE 301ST)* **TRAX ON DA ROCKS EP** – Trax on da rocks / Roule boule / What to do / Outrun / Ventura. *(re-iss. Jan02; same)*			–
Mar 97.	(12") *(ROULE 302ST)* **SPINAL SCRATCH. / SPINAL BEATS** *(re-iss. May98 & Jan02; same)*			–
Nov 97.	(12"; as THOMAS BANGALTER & ALAN BRAXE) *(ROULE 303)* **VELOCITY EP**			–
Jul 98.	(12"; as STARDUST) *(ROULE 305ST)* <38651> **MUSIC SOUNDS BETTER WITH YOU (club mix). / ('A'-Bob Sinclair remix)** *(re-dist.Aug98 on 'Virgin'; DINSD 175)* – hit UK No.2 above with **ALAN 'BRAXE' QUEME + BENJAMIN 'DIAMOND' COHEN**	55	Sep98	62
Oct 98.	(12"ep) *(ROULE 306ST)* **TRACKS ON DA ROCKS VOL.2** – Club soda / Extra dry / Shuffle / Colossus / Turbo. *(re-iss. Jan02; same)*			
Jul 00.	(12"; as THOMAS BANGALTER & DJ FALCON) *(ROULE 309-12)* **TOGETHER. / OUTRAGE** *(re-iss. Jan02; same)*			–
Dec 02.	(12"; by THOMAS BANGALTER & DJ FALCON) **SO MUCH LOVE TO GIVE**	71		–

Dick DALE

Born: RICHARD MONSOUR, 4 May'37, Boston, Massachusetts, USA. The son of a Lebanese emigrant, DALE formed the DEL-TONES in 1960 and attempted to replicate in sound the visceral thrill of riding whitewater surf. While acts such as

Seattle's VENTURES had precipitated the craze for tremelo-soaked instrumental music, it was in sunny Southern California that the surf guitar sound would be pioneered. Chiefly by DALE, who was duly christened 'The Pied Piper of Balboa Beach'. Although he had competition in the likes of The BELAIRS, DALE's demon staccato runs electrified audiences while his association with the Fender guitar company allowed him to road-test new equipment. Following the success of his Top 60 debut single, 'LET'S GO TRIPPIN' (widely acknowledged as the first bonafide surf track) in 1961, DALE introduced Fender's new reverb unit on the landmark 'MISIRLOU' the following year. If you didn't already know, you'd never guess that the track had been adapted from a 1940's Greek pop song such was DALE's breakneck, finger-blurring ferocity on his stratocaster (amplified, of course, all the way to 11). Backed up by pummelling drums and bleating sax, the overall effect was intoxicating, inspiring countless imitators (the BEACH BOYS of course, putting their own slant on the surf craze). Drawing on his Middle Eastern heritage, DALE would subsequently incorporate various strands of world music into his studio experiments, making him an unlikely ambassador of global musical unity years before the likes of PAUL SIMON and PETER GABRIEL. A debut album, 'SURFER'S CHOICE' also emerged in 1962 and spawned a further reverb-crazed single, 'SURFBEAT', towards the end of the year. Subsequently snapped up by 'Capitol', DALE released a string of albums including 'KING OF THE SURF GUITAR' (1963), 'CHECKERED FLAG' (1963) and 'MR. ELIMINATOR' (1964), the latter two concentrating on the subsequent hot-rod/dragster craze (alongside the likes of The SCRAMBLERS and RONNIE & THE DAYTONAS). Although DALE preferred his L.A. beach stronghold to touring, a young JIMI HENDRIX – who was stationed at the local San Pedro airbase – was apparently lucky enough to catch his live show on a regular basis. It's fair to say that America went surf mad in the early 60's, the craze becoming so all-pervasive that even JAMES BROWN and ALBERT KING got in on the action! Needless to say, it also burned out just as fast and following 'SUMMER SURF' (1965), DALE bowed out of the spotlight. He next surfaced on vinyl in 1987 with a collaborative (alongside the late STEVIE RAY VAUGHAN) cover of the Chantay's classic 'PIPELINE' for the soundtrack to retro surf film, 'Back To The Beach'. In 1994 – having been invited a year previous – a whole new generation of landlocked kids were treated to the joys of aural surfing when DALE's 'MISERLOU' was used over the opening sequence of Quentin Tarantino's 'Pulp Fiction'. The resulting resurge in interest saw DALE back in the studio for a trio of mid-90's albums – 'TRIBAL THUNDER' (1993), 'UNKNOWN TERRITORY' (1994) and 'CALLING UP SPIRITS' (1996) – and, at long last, a UK tour!

Best CD compilation: KING OF THE SURF GUITAR: THE BEST OF . . . (*8)

DICK DALE and the DEL-TONES

DICK DALE – guitar / with the DEL-TONES

not iss. — Del-Tone

Aug 59. (7") *<5012>* **OOH-WHEE-MARIE. / BREAKING HEART** –

Nov 59. (7") *<5013>* **STOP TEASIN'. / WITHOUT YOUR LOVE** –

Aug 60. (7") *<5014>* **JESSIE PEARL. / ST. LOUIS BLUES** –

Nov 60. (7"; by DICK DALE) *<106>* **THE FAIREST OF THEM ALL. / WE'LL NEVER HEAR THE END OF IT** –

— <above issued on 'Cupid'> *<re-iss. 1963 on 'Saturn'; 401> <re-iss. 1963 on 'Yes'; 7014> <re-iss. 1963 on 'Concert Hall'; 371>*

May 61. (7") *<5016>* **OOH-WHEE-MARIE. / WITHOUT YOUR LOVE** –

Oct 61. (7") *<5017>* **LET'S GO TRIPPIN'. / DEL-TONE ROCK** – 60

Mar 62. (7") *<5018>* **SHAKE N' STOMP. / JUNGLE FEVER** –

May 62. (7") *<5019>* **MISIRLOU. / EIGHT TILL MIDNIGHT** –

Nov 62. (7") *<5020>* **SURF BEAT. / PEPPERMINT MAN** –

Jan 63. (7") *<5028>* **A RUN FOR LIFE. / LOVIN' ON MY BRAIN** –

DICK DALE and his DEL-TONES

Capitol — Capitol

Jan 63. (7") *<4939>* **MISERLOU. / EIGHT TILL MIDNIGHT** –

Mar 63. (lp) *<(DT 1886)>* **SURFERS' CHOICE** Jan63

– Surf beat / Sloop John B. / Take it off / Night owl / Fanny Mae / Miserlou twist / Peppermint twist / Surfing drums / Shake n' stomp / Lovey dovey / Death of a gremmie / Let's go trippin'. *<orig.rel.Nov62 on 'Del-Tone'; LPM 1001>*

Mar 63. (7") *(CL 15296) <4940>* **SURF BEAT. / PEPPERMINT MAN**

Jun 63. (7") *<4963>* **KING OF THE SURF GUITARS. / HAVA NAGILA** –

Jun 63. (lp) *<(ST 1930)>* **KING OF THE SURF GUITAR**

– King of the surf guitars / The lonesome road / Kansas City / Dick Dale stomp / What'd I say / Greenback dollar / Hava nagila / You are my sunshine / Mexico / Break time / Riders in the sky / If I never get to Heaven.

Jul 63. (7") *<5010>* **SECRET SURFIN' SPOT. / SURFIN' AND A-SWINGIN'** –

Oct 63. (7") *(CL 15320) <5048>* **THE SCAVENGER. / WILD IDEAS** 98

Nov 63. (lp) *<ST 2002>* **CHECKERED FLAG** –

– The scavenger / Surf buggy / Hot rod racer / Mag wheels / Big black cad / Ho-dad machine / Grudge run / Motion / 426 – super stock / The wedge / It will grow on you / Night rider.

Dec 63. (7"; as DICK DALE) *<5098>* **THE WEDGE. / NIGHT RIDER** –

Mar 64. (7") *<5140>* **THE VICTOR. / MR. ELIMINATOR** –

Mar 64. (lp) *<ST 2053>* **MR. ELIMINATOR** –

– Mr. Eliminator / 50 miles to go / Flashing eyes / Taco wagon / The squirrel / The victor / Blond in the 406 / Firing up / My X-Ke / Nitro fuel / Hot rod alley.

Jun 64. (7") **<5187> GRUDGE RUN. / WILD, WILD MUSTANG** –

Jul 64. (lp) *<ST 2111>* **SUMMER SURF** –

– Summer surf / Feel so good / Surfin' / Spanish kiss / Star of David / Banzai washout / Glory wave / Surfin' rebel / Never on Sunday / Mama's gone surfin' / Tidal wave / Thunder wave.

(some w/ free 7" by Jerry Cole & His Spacemen)

Aug 64. (7") *<5225>* **GLORY WAVE. / NEVER ON SUNDAY** –

Nov 64. (7") *<5290>* **WHO CAN HE BE? / OH MARIE** –

Feb 65. (7") *<5389>* **LET'S GO TRIPPIN' '65. / WATUSI JO** –

Mar 65. (lp) *<ST 2293>* **ROCK OUT WITH DICK DALE AND HIS DEL-TONES – LIVE AT CIRO'S (live)** –

– Peter Gunn / Money honey / Angry generation / Summertime blues / Blowin' in the wind / Don't stop now (movin' and a-groovin') / Let's go trippin' '65 / Bony Moronie / Watusi Jo / Money / What'd I say.

DICK DALE

— with various session people

not iss. — Cougar

Jan 67. (7") *<C-711>* **RAMBLIN' MAN. / YOU'RE HURTIN' NOW** –

May 67. (7") *<C-712>* **TACO WAGON. / SPANISH KISS** –

not iss. — Accent

1967. (lp) *<3536>* **COAST TO COAST** –

1968. (7") *<1243>* **EYES OF A CHILD. / JUST A WAITIN'** –

not iss. — Balboa

1983. (lp) *<BR 1001>* **THE TIGERS LOOSE 'KING OF THE SURF GUITAR'** –

– Peter Gunn / The wedge / Pick and play / Summertime blues / House of the rising sun / Miserlou / Let's go trippin' / Lovey dovey / Firing up / Something on your mind / King of the surf guitar / Jessie Pearl.

not iss. — Columbia

1987. (7") *<07340>* **PIPELINE. / (other by Stevie Ray Vaughan)** –

— band:- **PRAIRE PRINCE** – drums (ex-TUBES) / **RON EGLIT** – bass / **SCOTT MATTHEWS** – drums / **VINCE WELNICK** – keyboards not iss. Hightone

May 93. (cd/c) *<HCD/HC 8046>* **TRIBAL THUNDER** [-] [ ]
– Nitro / New victor / Esperanza / Shredded heat / Trail of tears / Caravan / Eliminator / Speardance / Hot links: Caterpillar crawl – Rumble / Long ride / Tribal thunder. *(UK-iss.Mar95; same as US)*

Jun 94. (cd/c) *<HCD/HC 8055>* **UNKNOWN TERRITORY** [-] [ ]
– Scalped / Mexico / F groove / Terry Dicktyl / Take it or leave it / Ghost riders in the sky / Fish taco / California sun / Maria Elena / Hava nagila / The beast / Unknown territory / Ring of fire. *(UK-iss.Mar95; same as US)*

Beggars Banquet Beggars Banquet

May 96. (cd/lp) *(BBQ CD/LP 184)* *<80184>* **CALLING UP SPIRITS** [ ] [ ]
– Nitrus / The wedge Paradiso / The pit / Fever / Doom box / Catamount / The window / Calling up spirits / Temple of Gizeh / Bandito / Third stone from the sun / Peppermint man / Gypsy fire. *(cd re-iss. Aug98; BBL 184CD)*

– compilations, others, etc. –

1975. (lp) *GNP-Crescendo; <GNPS 2095>* **GREATEST HITS** [-] [ ]
– Misirlou / Surf beat / Sloop John B. / King of the surf guitar / The wedge / Those memories of you / Let's go trippin' / The victor / Peppermint man / Get back the feelin' / Peter Gunn. *(UK-iss.1988; same)*

1975. (7") *GNP-Crescendo; <804>* **LET'S GO TRIPPIN'. / THOSE MEMORIES OF YOU** [-] [ ]

Jun 88. (lp) *Rhino; <(RNLP 70074)>* **KING OF THE SURF GUITAR: THE BEST OF DICK DALE & THE DEL-TONES** [ ] 1986 [ ]
– Let's go trippin' / Shake n' stomp / Miserlou / Peppermint man / Surf beat / Take it off / King of the surf guitar / Hava nagila / Riders in the sky / The wedge / Night rider / Mr. Eliminator / The victor / Taco wagon / Tidal wave / Banzai washout / One double one oh! / Pipeline. *<(cd-iss. Aug89; R2 70074)>*

Oct 88. (7") *Pulchwave; (PSC 666)* **PICK AND PLAY. / THE WEDGE** [ ] [-]
(12"+=/3"cd-s) *(12PSC/PSCD 666)* – Hava nagila / King of the surf guitar (remix).

Jun 97. (d-cd) *Rhino; <72631>* **BETTER SHRED THAN DEAD: THE DICK DALE ANTHOLOGY** (1959-1995) [-] [ ]

Jul 00. (cd/lp) *GNP Crescendo; <(GNPD/GNPS 2095)>* **GREATEST HITS 1961-1976** [ ] [ ]

Sep 01. (lp) *Surf; (SURF 4950)* **RARITIES** [ ] [-]

Nov 01. (cd) *Sindrome; <8964>* **SPACIAL DISORIENTATION** [-] [ ]

☐ DALI'S CAR (see under ⇒ BAUHAUS)

☐ Roger DALTREY (see under ⇒ WHO)

DAMNED

Formed: London, England ... May 1976 by BRIAN JAMES and RAT SCABIES who soon found The CAPTAIN and former undertaker, DAVE VANIAN. Signed to new UK indie label, 'Stiff', by JAKE RIVERA, they released the classic track, 'NEW ROSE', produced by stablemate, NICK LOWE. The DAMNED became the first "New Wave Punks" to release and chart with an album, namely the enduring 'DAMNED DAMNED DAMNED' (1977). One of the classic punk debuts, the album pogo'd and thrashed its way through a frenetic set of three-chord wonders, LOWE's garden shed production underlining the riotous pandemonium. The band had also broken into the Top 40, although ironically enough, prolonged chart success would come later in the 80's when The DAMNED had changed almost beyond recognition. Live, the band were also one of the major attractions on the London scene; with VANIAN's proto-goth affectations, SENSIBLE's beret-topped antics and SCABIES' demented-drummer persona all competing against each other, The DAMNED were indeed a motley crew. Their musical assault was bolstered later that year by a second guitarist, LU EDMONDS, who debuted on the flaccid 'MUSIC FOR PLEASURE' (1977). The album was universally derided and SCABIES soon left for pastures new. Although future CULTURE CLUB man, JOHN MOSS was drafted in briefly as a replacement, the band splintered early the following year. After a period of solo work, VANIAN, SENSIBLE and SCABIES regrouped as The DAMNED early in '79 and emerged rejuvenated into the UK Top 20 via the impressive 'LOVE SONG'. With ALGY WARD completing the line-up, the band scored a second chart hit with 'SMASH IT UP', releasing their lauded 'MACHINE GUN ETIQUETTE' album later that year. Sure, they were still as swift and deadly as the title might suggest, but somehow they'd acquired a mastery of pop dynamics; a third single, 'I JUST CAN'T BE HAPPY TODAY', was the closest they'd yet come to a rock-solid tune. PAUL GRAY replaced WARD for 1980's 'UNTITLED (THE BLACK ALBUM)', an even more surprising, ambitious double set which flew in the face of punk convention with its rampant experimentalism. The poppy 'STRAWBERRIES' (1982) marked the last stand of CAPTAIN SENSIBLE, who'd scored with the annoying 'HAPPY TALK' earlier that summer, the first fruits of his solo deal with 'A&M'. VANIAN and SCABIES lumbered on with new members ROMAN JUGG and BRYN MERRICK, suprisingly enough enjoying major chart success with a string of overtly commercial, pseudo-goth rockers, the biggest of which, a cover of BARRY RYAN's 'ELOISE', made the Top 3. 'PHANTASMAGORIA' (1985) became their biggest selling album to date, catering to a whole new generation of fans. Most critics were agreed, however, that it paled in comparison to their earlier work, the DAMNED finally fading in the late 80's. For any interested parties, the band periodically get together with an amorphous line-up for all-dayers and one-off gigs; old punks never die, they just tour with The DAMNED. With the horsemen of the apocalypse holding fire just yet, The DAMNED made an unlikely return from the recording grave with 'GRAVE DISORDER' (2001). Boasting a line-up of VANIAN and SENSIBLE alongside newcomers PATRICIA MORRISON, MONTY OXY MORON and PINCH, the interminably resurrected rockers trawled familiar, if never exactly predictable, musical and lyrical territory with customary disregard for current trends. • **Songwriters:** Most written by JAMES, until he left, when group took over. Covered:- HELP! (Beatles) / I FEEL ALRIGHT (Stooges / Iggy Pop) / JET BOY JET GIRL (New York Dolls) / CITADEL (Rolling Stones) / ELOISE (Paul & Barry Ryan) / WHITE RABBIT (Jefferson Airplane) / ALONE AGAIN OR (Love) / WILD THING (Troggs) / LET THERE BE RATS (aka DRUMS) (Sandy Nelson). • **Trivia:** NICK MASON (Pink Floyd drummer) produced disappointing 2nd album MUSIC FOR PLEASURE. CAPTAIN SENSIBLE had UK-No.1 in 1982 with (Rogers-Hammerstein's) HAPPY TALK, and although briefly, became a top disco/pop act abroad.

Album rating: DAMNED DAMNED DAMNED (*8) / MUSIC FOR PLEASURE (*5) / MACHINE GUN ETIQUETTE (*7) / BLACK ALBUM (*6) / BEST OF THE DAMNED compilation (*8) / STRAWBERRIES (*5) / PHANTASMAGORIA (*5) / ANYTHING (*3) THE LIGHT AT THE END OF THE TUNNEL compilation (*7) / FINAL DAMNATION exploitation (*4) / I'M ALRIGHT JACK AND THE BEANSTALK (*4) / GRAVE DISORDER (*5)

DAVE VANIAN (b. DAVE LETTS) – vocals / **BRIAN JAMES** (b. BRIAN ROBERTSON) – guitar (ex-LONDON S.S.) / **CAPTAIN SENSIBLE** (b. RAY BURNS, 23 Apr'55) – bass, vocals / **RAT SCABIES** (b. CHRIS MILLER, 30 Jul'57) – drums (ex-LONDON S.S.)

Stiff Frontier

Nov 76. (7") *(BUY 6)* **NEW ROSE. / HELP!** [ ] [-]

Feb 77. (7") *(BUY 10)* **NEAT NEAT NEAT. / STAB YOR BACK / SINGALONGASCABIES** [ ] [-]

Feb 77. (lp) *(SEEZ 1)* **DAMNED DAMNED DAMNED** [36] Apr77 [ ]
– Neat neat neat / Fan club / I fall / Born to kill / Stab yor back / Feel the pain / New rose / Fish / See her tonite / 1 of the 2 / So messed up / I

feel alright. *(re-iss. Apr87 on 'Demon' lp/c/cd; FIEND/+CASS/CD 91) (pic-lp 1988; PFIEND 91) (<cd re-iss. Nov97 on 'Frontier'; 31033-2>) (cd re-iss. Aug00 on 'Edsel'; EDCD 677)*

— added (ROBERT) **LU EDMUNDS** – guitar

Sep 77. (7") *(BUY 18)* **PROBLEM CHILD. / YOU TAKE MY MONEY** [ ] [–]

Nov 77. (lp) *(SEEZ 5)* **MUSIC FOR PLEASURE** [ ] [ ]
– Problem child / Don't cry wolf / One way love / Politics / Stretcher case / Idiot box / You take my money / Alone / Your eyes / Creep (you can't fool me) / You know. *(re-iss. Apr88 on 'Demon' lp/c/cd; FIEND/+CASS/CD 108)*

Dec 77. (7",7"purple) *(BUY 24)* **DON'T CRY WOLF. / ONE WAY LOVE** [ ] [–]

— **DAVE BERK** – drums (ex-JOHNNY MOPED) repl. SCABIES who formed various bands

— **JOHN MOSS** – drums replaced BERK. They split Feb 78. VANIAN joined DOCTORS OF MADNESS. SENSIBLE formed SOFTIES then KING. EDMUNDS & MOSS formed THE EDGE. MOSS later joined ADAM & THE ANTS then CULTURE CLUB. EDMUNDS became part of ATHLETICO SPIZZ 80, The MEKONS, SHRIEKBACK, PIL. etc. BRIAN JAMES formed TANZ DER YOUTH, who released one single, 'I'M SORRY I'M SORRY' for 'Radar', before going solo the following year (1979) to issue his version of 'AIN'T THAT A SHAME'. He subsequently formed another punk supergroup, The HELLIONS, issuing one 1981 single for 'Illegal', 'WHY WHY WHY', before he jointly formed The LORDS OF THE NEW CHURCH. The DAMNED re-formed in Autumn '78 as The **DOOMED** with LEMMY of MOTORHEAD on bass. (1 gig) **HENRY BADOWSKI** – bass (ex-CHELSEA) replaced LEMMY. The group reverted to name The **DAMNED** with originals VANIAN, SENSIBLE (now guitar & keyboards) and **SCABIES**

— **ALGY WARD** – bass (ex-SAINTS) replaced BADOWSKI who went solo

Chiswick Roadrunner

Apr 79. (7",7"red) *(CHIS 112)* **LOVE SONG. / NOISE NOISE NOISE / SUICIDE** [20] [–]
(re-iss. 7"blue Feb82 on 'Big Beat'; NS 75)

Oct 79. (7") *(CHIS 116)* **SMASH IT UP. / BURGLAR** [35] [–]
(re-iss. 7"red Mar82 on 'Big Beat'; NS 76)

Nov 79. (lp) *(CWK 3011)* **MACHINE GUN ETIQUETTE** [31] Dec79 [ ]
– Love song / Machine gun etiquette / I just can't be happy today / Melody Lee / Anti-Pope / These hands / Plan 9 channel 7 / Noise noise noise / Looking at you / Smash it up (parts 1 & 2). *(re-iss. Jun85 on 'Ace' lp/c; DAM/+MC 3) (cd-iss. 1986 +=; CDWIK 905)* – Ballroom blitz / Suicide / Rabid (over you) / White rabbit.

Nov 79. (7") *(CHIS 120)* **I JUST CAN'T BE HAPPY TODAY. / BALLROOM BLITZ / TURKEY SONG** [46] [–]

— **PAUL GRAY** – bass, vocals (ex-EDDIE AND THE HOT RODS) repl. WARD who formed TANK

Jun 80. (7";w-drawn) *(CHIS 130)* **WHITE RABBIT. / RABID (OVER YOU) / SEAGULLS** [ ] [–]

Sep 80. (7"m/12"m) *(CHIS/+12 135)* **THE HISTORY OF THE WORLD (part 1). / I BELIEVE THE IMPOSSIBLE / SUGAR AND SPITE** [ ] [–]

Nov 80. (d-lp) *(CWK 3015)* **UNTITLED** (THE BLACK ALBUM) (1/2 studio, 1/4 live, 1/4 concept) [29] [–]
– Wait for the blackout / Lively arts / Silly kids games / Drinking about my baby / Hit and miss / Doctor Jekyll and Mr. Hyde / 13th floor vendetta / Twisted nerve / Sick of this and that / History of the world (part 1) / Therapy // Curtain call / live side:- Love song / Second time around / Smash it up (parts 1 & 2) / New rose / I just can't be happy today / Plan 9 Channel 7. *(re-iss. Aug82 on 'Ace' as one-lp/d-c; DAM/+MC 3) (c-iss.Jun85; TCWIK 3015) (cd-iss. Mar90; CDWIK 906)* – (omits live tracks)

Nov 80. (7"m) *(CHIS 139)* **THERE AINT NO SANITY CLAUS. / HIT OR MISS / LOOKING AT YOU (live)** [ ] [–]

N.E.M.S. not iss.

Nov 81. (d7"ep) *(TRY 1)* **FRIDAY THE 13th** [50] [–]
– Disco man / The limit club / Citadel / Billy bad breaks.

Bronze not iss.

Jul 82. (7"m/7"pic-d) *(BRO/+P 149)* **LOVELY MONEY. / LOVELY MONEY (disco) / I THINK I'M WONDERFUL** [42] [–]

Sep 82. (7"ep) *(BRO 156)* **DOZEN GIRLS. / TAKE THAT / MINE'S A LARGE ONE, LANDLORD / TORTURE ME** [ ] [–]

Oct 82. (lp/c) *(BRON 542)* **STRAWBERRIES** [15] [–]
– Ignite / Generals / Stranger on the town / Dozen girls / The dog / Gun fury / Pleasure and the pain / Life goes on / Bad time for Bonzo / Under the floor again / Don't bother me. *(re-iss. Mar86 on 'Legacy' red-lp/c; LLM/+K 3000) (re-iss. Dec86 on 'Dojo' lp/cd; DOJO LP/CD 46) (cd re-iss. Nov92 on 'Dojo'; DOJOCD 46) (cd-iss. Apr94 on 'Cleopatra'; CLEO 1029-2) (cd re-iss. Mar97 on 'Essential'; ESMCD 473) (cd re-iss. JUn01 on 'Castle'; CMRCD 246)*

Nov 82. (7"m) *(BRO 159)* **GENERALS. / DISGUISE / CITADEL ZOMBIES** [ ] [–]

Damned not iss.

Nov 83. (pic-lp/lp) *(P+/DAMU 2)* **LIVE IN NEWCASTLE (live)** [–] mail-o [–]
(cd-iss. Jan94 on 'Receiver'; RRCD 181)

Plus One not iss.

May 84. (7"colrd/7"pic-d) *(DAMNED 1/+P)* **THANKS FOR THE NIGHT. / NASTY** [ ] [–]
(re-iss. 12"-ltd.1985 +=; DAMNED 1T) – Do the blitz.

— **VANIAN** and **SCABIES** recruited new guys **ROMAN JUGG** (b. Barry, Wales) – guitar, keyboards / who replaced the CAPTAIN who carried on with solo career. **BRYN MERRICK** (b. Barry, Wales) – bass; repl. GRAY

M.C.A. Off Beat

Mar 85. (7"/7"pic-d/'A'-Spic'n'Spec mix-12") *(GRIM/+P/T 1)* **GRIMLY FIENDISH. / EDWARD THE BEAR** [21] [–]
(12"white+=) *(GRIMX 1)* – ('A'-Bad Trip mix).

Jun 85. (7") *(GRIM 2)* **SHADOW OF LOVE. / NIGHTSHIFT** [25] [ ]
('A'-Ten Inches Of Hell mix-10"+=) *(GRIMX 2)* – Would you.
(12"+=) *(GRIMT 2)* – Would you.
(d7"+=) *(GRIMY 2)* – Let there be Rats / Wiped out.

Jul 85. (lp/c/pic-lp/white-lp/blue-lp) *(MCF/+C/P/W/B 3275)* **PHANTASMAGORIA** [11] [ ]
– Street of dreams / Shadow of love / There'll come a day / Sanctum sanctorium / Is it a dream / Grimly fiendish / Edward the bear / The eighth day / Trojans. *(free 7" w.a.)* I JUST CAN'T BE HAPPY TODAY *(re-iss. 1986; same)* – (contains free 12"blue ELOISE) *(cd-iss. Aug89; DMCL 1887)*

Sep 85. (7") *(GRIM 3)* **IS IT A DREAM (Wild West End mix) / STREET OF DREAMS (live)** [34] [ ]
(12"+=) *(GRIMT 3)* – Curtain call (live) / Pretty vacant (live) / Wild thing (live).

Jan 86. (7") *(GRIM 4)* **ELOISE. / TEMPTATION** [3] [ ]
(12"blue+=/'A'-No Sleep Until Wednesday mix-12") *(GRIM T/X 4)* – Beat girl.

Nov 86. (7") *(GRIM 5)* **ANYTHING. / THE YEAR OF THE JACKAL** [32] [ ]
(10"blue+=,10"yellow+=) *(GRIMX 5)* – ('A'mixes).
(12"+=) *(GRIMT 5)* – Thanks for the night.

Nov 86. (lp/c/cd) *(MCG/MCGC/DMCG 6015)* *<5966>* **ANYTHING** [40] [ ]
– Anything / Alone again or / The portrait / Restless / In dulce decorum / Gigolo / The girl goes down / Tightrope walk / Psychomania.

Feb 87. (7"colrd/12"clear) *(GRIM/+T 6)* **GIGOLO. / THE PORTRAIT** [29] [–]

Apr 87. (7") *(GRIM 7)* **ALONE AGAIN OR. / IN DULCE DECORUM** [27] [–]
(12"+=) *(GRIMT 7)* – Psychomania.
(d7"++=) *(DGRIM 7)* – Eloise.

Nov 87. (7") *(GRIM 8)* **IN DULCE DECORUM. / PSYCHOMANIA** [72] [–]
(12"+=) *(GRIMT 8)* – ('A'dub).

— disbanded in the late 80's (ROMAN + BRYN formed The MISSING MEN) although re-union gigs were forthcoming

Essential Restless

Aug 89. (green-lp) *(ESCLP 008)* *<72385>* **FINAL DAMNATION** (live '88 reunion) [ ] [ ]
– See her tonite / Neat neat neat / Born to kill / I fall / Fan club / Fish / Help / New rose / I feel alright / I just can't be happy today / Wait for the blackout / Melody Lee / Noise noise noise / Love song / Smash it up (parts 1 & 2) / Looking at you / The last time. *(cd-iss. Apr94 on 'Castle'; CLACD 338) (cd re-iss. Jun01 on 'Castle'; CMRCD 247)*

— **VANIAN + SCABIES** re-formed er, **The DAMNED** alongside **ALAN LEE SHAW** – guitar (ex-RINGS, ex-MANIACS), **KRIS DOLLIMORE** – guitar (ex-GODFATHERS) + **MOOSE** – bass (ex-NEW MODEL ARMY)

Seadog not iss.

Dec 96. (lp) *(SEALLP 102)* **I'M ALRIGHT JACK AND THE BEANSTALK** [ ] [–]
– I need a life / Testify / Shut it / Tailspin / Not of this earth / Running man / My desire / Never could believe / Heaven . . . can take your lies / Shadow to fall / No more tears / Prokofiev. *(re-iss. Apr97 on 'The Record Label' cd/c; MOCDR/MOMC 1) (cd re-iss. Sep02 on 'Castle'+=; CMRCD 543)* – BBC sessions:- Testify / I need a life /

Never could believe / Neat neat neat. <US cd-iss. Oct02 on 'Sanctuary'; 81231>

— the real DAMNED re-formed in 2001 with **VANIAN, SENSIBLE,** plus **PATRICIA MORRISON** – bass (ex-SISTERS OF MERCY) / **MONTY OXY MORON** – keyboards / **PINCH** – drums (ex-ENGLISH DOGS)

Nitro Nitro

Aug 01. (cd/lp) *(<15844-2/-1>)* **GRAVE DISORDER**
– Democracy / Song.com / Thrill kill / She / Looking for action / Would you be so hot (if you weren't dead?) / Absinthe / Amen / Neverland / 'Til the end of time / Obscene. *<US+=>* – W / Beauty of the beast.

– compilations, etc. –

1981. (4x7"box) *Stiff; (GRAB 2)* **FOUR PACK** [-]
– (NEW ROSE / NEAT NEAT NEAT / PROBLEM CHILD / DON'T CRY WOLF)

Nov 81. (lp/c) *Ace; (DAM/+C 1)* **THE BEST OF THE DAMNED** [43] [-]
– New rose / Neat neat neat / I just can't be happy today / Jet boy jet girl / Hit or miss / There ain't no sanity claus / Smash it up (parts 1 & 2) / Plan 9 channel 7 / Rabid (over you) / Wait for the blackout / History of the world (part 1). *(cd-iss. Oct87; CDDAM 1)*

May 82. (7"/7"pic-d) *Big Beat; (NS/+P 77)* **WAIT FOR THE BLACKOUT. / Captain Sensible & The Softies: JET BOY, JET GIRL** [-]

Oct 82. (7"green) *Big Beat; (NS 80)* **LIVELY ARTS. / TEENAGE DREAM** [-]
(10"+=) *(NST 80)* – I'm so bored.

Nov 82. (lp) *Ace; (NED 1)* **LIVE SHEPPERTON 1980 (live)** [-]
– Love song / Second time around / I just can't be happy today / Melody Lee / Help / Neat neat neat / Looking at you / Smash it up (parts 1 & 2) / New rose / Plan 9 channel 7. *(also iss.Nov82 on 'Big Beat'; WIKM 27) (c-iss.Jun85; WIKC 27) (cd-iss. Jun88; CDWIKM 27)*

Nov 85. (12"ep) *Stiff; (BUYIT 238)* **NEW ROSE / NEAT NEAT NEAT. / STRETCHER CASE / SICK OF BEING SICK** [-]

Jan 86. (lp/c/cd) *Dojo; (DOJO LP/TC/CD 21)* **DAMNED BUT NOT FORGOTTEN** [-]
(cd re-iss. Nov92; same) (cd re-iss. Feb97 on 'Essential'; ESMCD 472) (cd re-iss. Jun01 on 'Castle'; CMRCD 245)

Jun 86. (12"ep) *Strange Fruit; (SFPS 002)* **THE PEEL SESSIONS** (10.5.77) [-]
– Sick of being sick / Stretcher case / Feel the pain / Fan club. *(c-ep.1987; SFPSC 002) (cd-ep.May88; SFPSCD 002)*

Jul 86. (blue-m-lp) *Stiff; (GET 4)* **THE CAPTAIN'S BIRTHDAY PARTY – LIVE AT THE ROUNDHOUSE** [-]
(cd-iss. Nov91 on 'Demon'; VEXCD 7)

Jul 87. (12"ep) *Strange Fruit; (SFPS 040)* **THE PEEL SESSIONS (30.11.76)** [-]
– Stab yor back / Neat neat neat / New rose / So messed up / I fall.

Oct 87. (cd/lp) *I.D.; (C+/NOSE 18)* **MINDLESS, DIRECTIONLESS, ENEMY (live)** [-]
(re-iss. Jun89 cd/c/lp; CDOSE/KOSE/NOSE 18X)

Dec 87. (d-lp) *M.C.A.; (MCSP 312)* **THE LIGHT AT THE END OF THE TUNNEL** [87] [-]
(d-cd-iss. Apr92; MCLDD 19007)

Jun 88. (lp/c) *Big Beat; (WIK/+C 80)* **THE LONG LOST WEEKEND: BEST OF VOL.1/2** [-]

1990. (cd) *Marble Arch; (cd)* **THE DAMNED LIVE (live)** [-]

Dec 90. (cd/c/d-lp) *Castle; (CCS CD/MC/LP 278)* **THE COLLECTION** [-]

Jan 91. (12"blue-ep) *Deltic; (DELT 7T)* **FUN FACTORY ('82). / Captain Sensible: FREEDOM / PASTIES / A RIOT ON EASTBOURNE PIER** [-]

Jun 91. (cd/colrd-lp) *Receiver; (RR CD/LP 159)* **BALLROOM BLITZ – LIVE AT THE LYCEUM (live)** [-]

Dec 91. (cd) *Dojo; (DOJOCD 65)* **TOTALLY DAMNED (live + rare)** [-]

Jan 92. (cd) *Street Link; (AOK 101)* **ALTERNATIVE CHARTBUSTERS** [-]

Feb 92. (clear-lp) *Receiver; (RRLP 159)* **LIVE AT THE LYCEUM (live)** [-]

Aug 92. (cd) *Connoisseur; (VSOPCD 174)* **THE MCA SINGLES A'S & B'S** [-]

Sep 92. (cd) *Demon; (VEXCD 12)* **SKIP OFF SCHOOL TO SEE THE DAMNED (THE STIFF SINGLES A'S & B'S)** [-]

May 93. (cd) *Receiver; (RRCD 179)* **SCHOOL BULLIES** [-]

Jul 93. (cd) *Success; (550 747-2)* **THE DAMNED: FROM THE BEGINNING** [-]

Nov 93. (cd) *Strange Fruit; (SFRSCD 070)* **SESSIONS OF THE DAMNED** [-]

Jun 94. (cd/c) *M.C.I.; (MUS CD/MC 017)* **ETERNALLY DAMNED – THE VERY BEST OF THE DAMNED** [-]

Dec 94. (cd) *Cleopatra; (CLEO 7139-2)* **TALES FROM THE DAMNED** [-]

May 95. (cd) *Spectrum; (550 747-2)* **FROM THE BEGINNING** [-]

Sep 95. (cd/c) *Emporio; (EMPR CD/MC 592)* **NOISE – THE BEST OF: LIVE** [-]

Jun 96. (cd) *Nighttracks; (CDNT 011)* **THE BBC RADIO 1 SESSIONS** [-]

Oct 96. (cd) *Cleopatra; (CLP 9804)* **FIENDISH SHADOWS** [-]

Feb 97. (3xcd-box) *Demon; (FBOOK 14)* **NEAT NEAT NEAT** [-]

Mar 97. (cd) *Cleopatra; (CLP 9960)* **THE CHAOS YEARS** [-]

May 97. (d-cd) *Snapper; (SMDCD 143)* **BORN TO KILL** [-]

Jun 97. (lp) *Cleopatra; (CLP 9782)* **SHUT IT** [-]

Nov 97. (7") *Skinnies Cut; (AVL 1077)* **PROKOFIEV. /** [-]

Nov 97. (7") *Marble Orchard; (MOS 2)* **TOUR SINGLE. /** [-]

Jul 98. (cd) *Strange Fruit; (SFRSCD 070)* **THE SESSIONS OF THE DAMNED** [-]

Oct 98. (7") *Musical Tragedy; (MT 418)* **PRETTY VACANT. / DISCO MAN** [-]

Jun 99. (t-cd) *Cleopatra; (CLP 542)* **THE DAMNED BOX SET** [-]

Dec 99. (cd) *Chiswick; (CDWIKK 198)* **MARVELLOUS: THE BEST OF THE DAMNED** [-]

Dec 99. (cd) *Musical Tragedies; (efa 12354-2) / Sudden Death; <5>* **MOLTEN LAGER (live)** Sep00

Jun 00. (d-cd) *Essential; (ESACD 901)* **ANTHOLOGY**

Oct 01. (d-cd) *Castle; (CMDDD 357)* **LIVE ANTHOLOGY**
– (BALLROOM BLITZ / LIVE IN NEWCASTLE / SCHOOL BULLIES)

☐ DAMN YANKEES (see under ⇒ NUGENT, Ted)

☐ DANCING HOOD (see under ⇒ SPARKLEHORSE)

☐ Evan DANDO (see under ⇒ LEMONHEADS)

DANDY WARHOLS

Formed: Portland, Oregon, USA . . . mid 90's by buzzed-up guys, COURTNEY TAYLOR and PETER HOLMSTROM, who, with rhythm section, ERIC HEDFORD and feisty babe, ZIA McCABE, emerged from their recording basement in 1996. After a one-off double mini-CD, the harmony-fuelled psychedelia of 'DANDYS RULE OK', they inked a deal with 'Capitol', although they riled their bosses by failing to deliver on a promised set of songs; exposure in the Rolling Stone was subsequently mis-timed. Unsurprisingly the band gave themselves a proverbial kick up the ass and rose from their drug ashes with a fine set of songs, two of which ('EVERYDAY SHOULD BE A HOLIDAY' and 'NOT IF YOU WERE THE LAST JUNKIE ON EARTH') were UK Top 30 singles and preceded their Top 20 album, ' . . .THE DANDY WARHOLS COME DOWN' (1998). Spending just over a year in the studio – HEDFORD being replaced by BRENT DeBOER – The DANDY WARHOLS emerged with the most accomplished set to date, 'THIRTEEN TALES FROM URBAN BOHEMIA' (2000). It took a little while for audiences to catch on to its excellent pop sensibilities, as the album didn't really become a hit for the band until their notoriously catchy single 'BOHEMIAN LIKE YOU' (virtually ignored on its initial release) was used to great effect in a mobile phone ad. Surprisingly, on its second outing, the song crashed into the UK Top 5 and suddenly people had forgotten that The DANDY WARHOLS were perhaps the coolest band around. The final outcome of the set was more focused on creating an atmosphere, or a feeling instead of ten drugged-up love songs and three great singles (as was the case on 'COME DOWN'). Hippy cowboy anthem 'GET OFF' served as proverbial candy for the ear, while 'COUNTRY LEVER' and the strange musings on 'HORSE PILLS' really set the tone for one of the fullest and freshest albums of the year. After the massive success of 'BOHEMIAN LIKE YOU', the band followed it up quickly (almost too quickly) with a disappointing set in the same vein as 'COME DOWN', but a tad less ambitious. With DURAN DURAN's NICK RHODES manning the engineering desk, and PETER LOEW replacing HOLMSTROM on guitar, the DANDY's started to dabble in electronic machinery such as synths, drum machines and a whole host of other gadgets. What it really displayed was a lost sense of irony on the band's part; from the empty, drug-inspired downers that have always plagued their albums to the speedball cocktails of throbbing pop-rock such as 'THE DANDY WARHOLS LOVE ALMOST EVERYONE', even down to the VELVETS/WARHOL pastiche of the banana cover by feted artist Ron English. • **Covers:** THE WRECK OF THE EDMUND FITZGERALD (Gordon Lightfoot) / FREE FOR ALL (Ted Nugent) / HELLS BELLS (Ac/Dc) / EIGHT DAYS A WEEK (Beatles) / CALL ME (Blondie) / RELAX (Frankie Goes To Hollywood) / THE JEAN GENIE (David Bowie) / etc.

Album rating: DANDYS RULE OK (*6) / . . .THE DANDY WARHOLS COME DOWN (*7) / THIRTEEN TALES FROM URBAN BOHEMIA (*8) / WELCOME TO THE MONKEY HOUSE (*6)

COURTNEY TAYLOR(-TAYLOR) – vocals, guitar / **PETER HOLMSTROM** – guitar / **ERIC HEDFORD** – drums / **ZIA McCABE** – bass, keyboards

Tim/Kerr Tim/Kerr

Sep 95. (cd-s) *<TK 0088>* **THE LITTLE DRUMMER BOY / DICK / (IT DOESN'T TAKE A GENIUS)** [–] [ ]

Dec 95. (2xm-cd) *<(TK95CD 0091)>* **DANDYS RULE OK** [ ] [ ]
– Introduction by young Tom / Dandy Warhol's T.V. theme song / Ride / Best friend / Not your bottle / (Tony, this song is called) Lou Weed / Nothin' to do / Coffee and tea wrecks / Genius / Dick / Just try / Nothing (lifestyle of a tortured artist for sale) / Grunge Betty / Prelude – It's a fast-driving rave-up with the Dandy Warhols sixteen minutes – Finale // Little drummer boy / Dick / (It doesn't take a) Genius / Untitled. *(re-iss. Sep98 on 'Capitol'; 496409-2) (re-iss. Sep00 on 'Dandy'; DR 001)*

Jan 96. (pic-d-cd) *<(TK 95PD 104)>* **RIDE / WE LOVE YOU DICK** [ ] [ ]

Capitol Capitol

Feb 98. (c-s/7"purple) *(TC+/CL 797)* **EVERYDAY SHOULD BE A HOLIDAY. / ONE (ULTRA LAM WHITE BOY)** [29] [–]
(cd-s+=) *(CDCL 797)* – Head.

Apr 98. (7") *(CL 800)* **NOT IF YOU WERE THE LAST JUNKIE ON EARTH. / GENIUS (live)** [13] [–]
(cd-s+=) *(CDCLS 800)* – Ride (live).
(cd-s) *(CDCL 800)* – ('A'side) / ('A'live) / It's a fast drivin' rave up with the Dandy Warhols sixteen minutes (live).

May 98. (cd/c) *<(8 36505-2/-4)>* **. . .THE DANDY WARHOLS COME DOWN** [16] [ ]
– Be-in / Boys better / Minnesoter / Orange / I love you / Not if you were the last junkie on earth / Every day should be a holiday / Good morning / Whipping tree / Green / Cool as Kim Deal / Hard on for Jesus / Pete International airport / The creep out. *(d-lp iss.Mar98 on 'Tim/Kerr'; TK 1671)*

Jul 98. (7") *(CL 805)* **BOYS BETTER. / NOTHIN' TO DO** [36] [–]
(cd-s+=) *(CDCL 805)* – Grunge Betty.
(cd-s) *(CDCLS 805)* – ('A'side) / The wreck of the Edmund Fitzgerald / Free for all.

— **BRENT DeBOER** – drums, vocals; repl. HEDFORD

May 00. (7") *(CL 821)* **GET OFF. / PHONE CALL** [38] [–]
(cd-s+=) *(CDCLS 821)* – White gold.
(cd-s) *(CDCL 821)* – ('A'side) / Not if you were the last junkie on earth (live) / I love you (live).

Jun 00. (cd) *(857787-2)* *<CDP 5778>* **THIRTEEN TALES FROM URBAN BOHEMIA** [51] Aug00 [ ]
– Godless / Mohammed / Nietzsche / Country leaver / Solid / Horse pills / Get off / Sleep / Cool scene / Bohemian like you / Retarded / Shakin' / Big Indian / The gospel. *(d-lp iss.Oct00; SCZ 787) (re-iss. Nov01; same)* – hit UK No.32

Aug 00. (7") *(CL 823)* **BOHEMIAN LIKE YOU. / HELLS BELLS** [42] [–]
(cd-s+=) *(CDCLS 823)* – Lance.
(cd-s) *(CDCL 823)* – ('A'side) / Retarded / Dub song.

Jul 01. (12"/cd-s) *(12CL/CDCL 829)* **GODLESS / ('A'-Massive Attack remix / dub / instrumental)** [66] [–]

Oct 01. (c-s) *(TCCL 829)* **BOHEMIAN LIKE YOU / HELLS BELLS / LANCE** [5] [–]
(cd-s) *(CDCL 829)* – ('A'side) / Retarded / Dub song.

Mar 02. (c-s) *(TCCL 835)* **GET OFF / STARS (acoustic)** [34] [–]
(cd-s+=) *(CDCL 835)* – Eight days a week (acoustic) / ('A'-video).

— **PETER LOEW** – guitar; repl. HOLMSTROM

May 03. (7"yellow) *(CL 843)* **WE USED TO BE FRIENDS. / MINNESOTER (thee slayer hippie mix)** [18] [–]
(cd-s) *(CDCL 843)* – Call me / Relax.

May 03. (cd/lp) *(590123-2/-1)* *<84368>* **WELCOME TO THE MONKEY HOUSE** [20] [ ]
– Welcome to the monkey house / We used to be friends / Plan A / Dope (wonderful you) / I am a scientist / I am over it / The Dandy Warhols love almost everyone / Insincere because I / You were the last high / Heavenly / I am sound / Hit rock bottom / (You come in) Burned.

Jul 03. (7"white) *(CL 845)* **YOU WERE THE LAST HIGH. / WE USED TO BE FRIENDS (Kenn Richards mix)** [34] [–]
(cd-s) *(CDCL 845)* – ('A'side) / We used to be friends (Coates & Stiles mix) / Everyday should be a holiday (Tony Lash mix).
(cd-s) *(CDCLX 845)* – ('A'side) / Sun / Dye.

Nov 03. (7"blue) *(CL 851)* **PLAN A. / THE JEAN GENIE** [66] [–]
(cd-s+=) *(CDCL 851)* – You were the last high (Dirty Vegas dub) / ('A'-video).

– compilations, etc. –

Oct 02. (d-cd) *E.M.I.; (541130-2)* **DANDY'S RULE OK / THIRTEEN TALES FROM URBAN BOHEMIA** [ ] [–]

☐ DANNY & THE MEMORIES
(see under ⇒ CRAZY HORSE)

Terence Trent D'ARBY

Born: TERENCE TRENT DARBY, 15 Mar'62, New York City, New York, USA. After being raised in Manhattan, he moved to East Orange, Chicago with preacher father. After enlisting in the army in 1980, he was based in Germany (took up boxing), where in 1982 he joined funk band, TOUCH. After some recordings, he left for London in 1984, where, after two years making demos, etc, he signed to 'C.B.S.' with the help of manager, Klaus Pieter 'KP' Schleinitz. With a promotional push on UK TV Channel 4's 'The Tube', he hit chart land immediately with 'IF YOU LET ME STAY', followed soon by an acclaimed debut MARTYN WARE-produced album, 'INTRODUCING THE HARDLINE ACCORDING TO . . .'. A funk/soul romantic who fashioned himself between PRINCE, STEVIE WONDER and SMOKEY ROBINSON, his debut set ran the gamut of modern R&B, from the smouldering 'SIGN YOUR NAME' to the itchy funk of 'WISHING WELL', a US No.1. The flipside of D'ARBY's good looks and electric charisma was a penchant of not being the most modest of chaps, his attitude not always appealing to everyone. This, together with a wilfully experimental and commercially suicidal follow-up set, 'NEITHER FLESH NOR FISH' (1989), saw D'ARBY's career lose momentum in the late 80's/early 90's. Virtually written off, D'ARBY came storming back in 1993 with 'SYMPHONY OR DAMN', a record that was still stamped with pretentiousness yet redeemed by a breathtaking stylistic diversity and poise that squarely challenged LENNY KRAVITZ. A Top 5 hit with four UK singles, the album put D'ARBY back on track. Although 1995's heavier 'TTD'S VIBRATOR' wasn't quite so successful or alluring, it's safe to say that D'ARBYs chameleon, seer-like musical vision has still to be fully realised. • **Covered:** HEARTBREAK HOTEL (Elvis Presley) / UNDER MY THUMB and JUMPIN' JACK FLASH (Rolling Stones) / WONDERFUL WORLD (Sam Cooke).

Album rating: INTRODUCING THE HARDLINE ACCORDING TO . . . (*7) / NEITHER FISH NOR FLESH (*3) / SYMPHONY OR DAMN (*5) / TTD'S VIBRATOR (*5)

C.B.S. Columbia

Feb 87. (7"/7"s) *(TRENT/+Q 1) <07398>* **IF YOU LET ME STAY. / LOVING YOU IS ANOTHER WORD FOR LONELY** 7 Oct87 68
(12"w-free 12"+=) *(TRENTT 1)* – ('A'-Hardline mix).

Jun 87. (7"/7"s) *(TRENT/+G 2) <07675>* **WISHING WELL. / ELEVATORS AND HEARTS** 4 Jan88 1
(12"+=) *(TRENTT 2)* – ('A'mix).
(12"+=) *(TRENTQ 2)* – Wonderful world.

Jul 87. (lp/c/cd) *(450911-1/-4/-2) <40964>* **INTRODUCING THE HARDLINE ACCORDING TO TERENCE TRENT D'ARBY** 1 Oct87 4
– If you all get to Heaven / If you let me stay / Wishing well / I'll never turn my back on you / Dance little sister / Seven more days / Let's go forward / Rain / Sign your name / As yet untitled / Who's loving you?. *(pic-lp.Dec87; 450911-0) (re-iss. May95 cd/c; same)*

Sep 87. (7"/7"s) *(TRENT/+Q 3) <08023>* **DANCE LITTLE SISTER. / (part 2)** 20 Aug88 30
(12"+=) *(TRENTT 3)* – Sunday jam (one woman man).
(c-s+=) *(TRENTC 3)* – Heartbreak hotel.

Dec 87. (7"/7"s) *(TRENT/+Q 4) <07911>* **SIGN YOUR NAME. / GREASY CHICKEN (live)** 2 May88 4
(12"+=/12"pic-d+=) *(TRENT T/P 4)* – Under my thumb (live) / Jumpin' Jack Flash (live).
(10"+=) *(TRENTG 4)* – Rain (remix) / If you all get to Heaven (remix).
(cd-s-pic+=) *(TRENTC 4)* – Dance little sister.

Oct 89. (lp/c/cd) *(465809-1/-4/-2) <45351>* **NEITHER FLESH NOR FISH** 12 Nov89 61
– Declaration / Neither flesh nor fish / I have faith in these desolate times / It feels so good to love someone like you / I'll be alright / Billy don't fall / This side of love / You will pay tomorrow / Roly Poly / I don't want to bring your gods down / And I need to be with someone tonight.

Nov 89. (7"/c-s) *(TRENT/+M 5)* **THIS SIDE OF LOVE. / SAD SONG FOR SISTER SARAH**
(12"+=/12"s) *(TRENT T/Q 5)* – Sign your name (live).
(cd-s+=/pic-cd-s+=) *(TRENT C/P 5)* – Seven more days.

Jan 90. (7"/7"pic-d) *(TRENT/+E 6)* **TO KNOW SOMEONE DEEPLY IS TO LOVE SOMEONE SOFTLY. / LOOSE VARIATIONS ON A DEAD MAN'S VIBE IN CM** 55
(12"+=/cd-s+=) *(TRENT T/C 6)* – ('A'mix) / Rain (live).

— now with **TIM PIERCE** – guitar / **NEIL STUBENHAUSEN or KEVIN WYATT** – bass plus various guests

Columbia Columbia

Apr 93. (c-s) *(659 073-4)* **DO YOU LOVE ME LIKE YOU SAY? / READ MY LIPS (I DIG YOUR SCENE) / PERFUMED PAVILLION (THE MOTION OF MY MEMORIES)** 14
(cd-s+=) *(659 073-2)* – ('A'original).
(cd-s) *(659 073-5)* – ('A'side) / Wishing well / If you let me stay / To know someone is to love someone.
(12"/cd-s) *(659 073-6)* – (3 'A'mixes) / Read my lips (I dig your scene).

May 93. (cd/c/lp) *(473 561-2/-4/-1) <53616>* **SYMPHONY OR DAMN** 4
– PART I – CONFRONTATION; Welcome to my monasteryo / She kissed me / Do you love me like you say? / Baby let me share my love / Delicate / Neon messiah / Penelope please / Wet your lips / Turn the page.
– PART II – RECONCILIATION; Castilian blue / "T.I.T.S." – "F & J" / Are you happy? / Succumb to me / I still love you / Seasons / Let her down easy. *(re-iss. Sep96 cd/c; same)*

Jun 93. (7"/c-s) *(659 331-7/-4)* **DELICATE. / SHE'S MY BABY** 14 –
(cd-s+=) *(659 331-2)* – Dance little sister (extended) / Survivor.

Aug 93. (c-s) *<77128>* **DELICATE / SHE KISSED ME** – 74

Sep 93. (7"/c-s) *(659 592-7/-4)* **SHE KISSED ME. / DO YOU LOVE ME LIKE YOU SAY? (Masters At Work 12" Mix)** 16
(12"+=/cd-s+=) *(659 592-6/-2)* – (2-'B'mixes).

Nov 93. (7"white/c-s) *(659 864-7/-4)* **LET HER DOWN EASY. / TURN THE PAGE** 18
(12"+=) *(659 864-6)* – Do you love me like you say?
(cd-s) *(659 864-2)* – ('A'side) / Sign your name / Delicate.

— with **LOUIS METOYER** – guitar / **KEVIN WYATT** – bass / **EPHEN THEARD (STEVO)** – drums / etc.

Mar 95. (c-s) *(661 423-4)* **HOLDING ON TO YOU / ANGELS FLY BECAUSE** 20
(cd-s+=) *(661 423-2)* – Your love is indecipherable / Epilog.
(cd-s) *(661 423-5)* – ('A'side) / Sign your name / Delicate / To know someone deeply is to know someone softly.

Apr 95. (cd/c) *(478 505-2/-4) <67070>* **TTD'S VIBRATOR** 11
– Vibrator / Supermodel sandwich / Holding on to you / Read my lips (I dig your scene) / Undeniably / We don't have that much time together / C.Y.F.M.L.A.Y.? / If you go before me / Surrender / TTD's recuring dream / Supermodel sandwich w/cheese / Resurrection / It's been said.

Aug 95. (c-s) *(662 258-4)* **VIBRATOR / SURRENDER (Brooklyn mix)** 57
(cd-s+=) *(662 258-2)* – Surrender (MK mix) / I realy want you.
(cd-s) *(662 258-5)* – ('A'side) / Do you love me like you say? / She kissed me / Attracted to you.

– others, etc. –

Sep 89. (7"; as The INCREDIBLE E.G. O'REILLY) *Polydor; (EGOR 1)* **THE BIRTH OF MAUDIE. / AN CHUILEANN** –

TOUCH

(featuring **TERENCE TRENT D'ARBY** – vocals) **MIKE WILLIAMS, MARK BURTON** – guitar / **FRANK 'Babyface' ITT** – bass / **STEFAN LUPP** – keyboards / **DETLEF VOGEL** – guitar / **BENNY BRACIN** – drums

Aug 89. (lp/cd) *(839 303-1/-2)* **TOUCH** (early works rec.'83) – German –
– I want to know (international lady) / Eggs and coffee / Don't call me up / Long way / Weekends / Passion / Immaterial / Somebody else / Get up and run / Cross my heart.

DARKNESS

Formed: Norfolk, England . . . late 90's as EMPIRE by brothers JUSTIN and DAN HAWKINS, Scotsman FRANKIE POULLAIN (who claimed to be five years younger to the press!) and ED GRAHAM. The revenge of 80's hair-metal in all its spandex-clad, critic-baiting, monster hook glory, The DARKNESS were perhaps an inevitable cultural blip on an otherwise insufferably uber-cool and irony-saturated music scene. That they emerged from the ruins of a bonafide prog rock outfit (the EMPIRE mentioned above) only made their unselfconsciously unfashionable stance all the more er.. unselfconsciously unfashionable. With JUSTIN HAWKINS famously taking up the vacant lead singer role after a show-stopping karaoke performance of Queen's 'BOHEMIAN RHAPSODY', the band's championing of flamboyance over fakery seemed written in the cards. Or, in more heavy metal terms, glimpsed in the crystal ball. A series of London gigs allowed JUSTIN all the exposure he needed to prove that good old rock'n'roll props like skintight strides, acrobatic stage antics and ridiculous falsetto squealing were what the kids really wanted. A sneering music press be damned, The DARKNESS released their debut EP, 'I BELIEVE IN A THING CALLED LOVE', on indie label, 'Must Destroy Music', in summer 2002. Support slots with the likes of DEF LEPPARD and DEEP PURPLE followed before single 'KEEP YOUR HANDS OFF MY WOMAN', edged into the UK Top 50 early the following year. The hype only accelerated as 'Atlantic' signed them up. A further single, 'GROWING ON ME', just missed the Top 10 while debut album, 'PERMISSION TO LAND' (2003), hit UK No.1 soon afterwards. From its disturbingly BOSTON-esque sleeve to its meaty power ballads and cod-metal lyrics, the album could've been plucked ripe from the late 70's or the 80's. It was unreconstructed for sure, utterly decadent, certainly, but there was also an undercurrent of humour (if stopping short of irony) and more importantly, a killer instinct for huge melodies and chest-beating choruses. In other words, it wasn't rocket science; and in these days of regulation post-rock glumness, maybe that was a blessing. Towards the end of 2003, a re-release of ' . . .A THING CALLED LOVE' and the festive-baiting, 'CHRISTMAS TIME (DON'T LET THE BELLS END)' both narrowly missed the No.1 spot – we had finally seen the light.

Album rating: PERMISSION TO LAND (*8)

JUSTIN HAWKINS – vocals, guitar, synthesizer / **DAN HAWKINS** – guitar / **FRANKIE POULLAIN** (b. FRANCIS GILES PATTERSON, 15 Apr'67, Edinburgh, Scotland) – bass / **ED GRAHAM** – drums

Must Destroy | Atlantic

Aug 02. (cd-ep) *(DUSTY 001CD)* **I BELIEVE IN A THING CALLED LOVE EP** [ ] [–]
– I believe in a thing called love / Love on the rocks with no ice / Love is only a feeling.

Feb 03. (7") *(DESTROYER 6)* **GET YOUR HANDS OFF MY WOMAN. / THE BEST OF ME** [43] [–]
(cd-s+=) *(DUSTY 006CD)* – ('A'-Profane version).

Jun 03. (7") *(DESTROYER 10)* **GROWING ON ME. / HOW DARE YOU CALL THIS LOVE?** [11] [–]
(cd-s+=) *(DUSTY 010CD)* – Bareback.

Jul 03. (cd/lp) *(5046 67452-2/-1)* <60817> **PERMISSION TO LAND** [1] Aug03 [ ]
– Black shuck / Get your hands off my woman / Growing on me / I believe in a thing called love / Love is only a feeling / Givin' up / Stuck in a rut / Friday night / Love on the rocks with no ice / Holding my own.

— the album would rise to No.39 in the US early 2004

Sep 03. (7"pic-d/cd-s) *(DARK 01/+CD)* **I BELIEVE IN A THING CALLED LOVE. / MAKIN' OUT / PHYSICAL SEX** [2] [–]

Dec 03. (7"sha-pic-d/cd-s) *(DARK 02/+CD)* **CHRISTMAS TIME (DON'T LET THE BELLS ENDS). / I LOVE YOU 5 TIMES** [2] [–]

DASHBOARD CONFESSIONAL

Formed: Boca Raton, Florida, USA . . . 2000 by singer, songwriter, and driving force CHRISTOPHER CARRABA. CARRABA had fronted bands like the VACANT ANDIES and FURTHER SEEMS FOREVER, but found the solo process to be more receptive and gainful to the material he was writing. As DASHBOARD CONFESSIONAL he released debut LP, 'THE SWISS ARMY ROMANCE', in late 2000 on 'Drive-Thru' records. A solid first effort, it contained finely composed indie acoustic songs like 'LIVING IN YOUR LETTERS', although there wasn't much to distinguish it from similar indie releases. In 2001, now on 'Vagrant' records, he released the 'DROWNING' EP, and second full-set, 'THE PLACES YOU HAVE COME TO FEAR THE MOST'. CARRABA's heartfelt musings occasionally weighed heavy with naivety, but then they did appear to target the teen market. 'SCREAMING INFIDELITIES' became a Modern Rock hit, adopted by many US indie/pop kids. In a busy (and successful) year for DASHBOARD CONFESSIONAL, CARRABA also hit the road, firstly a joint tour with the WEAKERTHANS, then as part of the 'Vagrant Across America' tour with labelmates including HOT ROD CIRCUIT. Maintaining the momentum, the melancholic 'SO IMPOSSIBLE' EP was released in late 2001, and DASHBOARD CONFESSIONAL became a duo with the recruitment of SUNNY DAY REAL ESTATE's DAN HOERNER. With CARRABA's largely acoustic ditties being tailor made for MTV's 'UNPLUGGED', it came as no big surprise when DASHBOARD CONFESSIONAL made their contribution to the veteran series in 2002. With the Gil Norton-produced 'A MARK, A MISSION, A BRAND, A SCAR' (2003), meanwhile, CARRABA took his unashamedly teenage-orientated angst-odyssey to new artistic heights, with Norton coaxing out the most accessible aspects of the lad's painfully sensitive songwriting. Unsurprisingly, it was a recipe for critical and commercial success, coming within a hair's breadth of the US No.1 position.

Album rating: THE SWISS ARMY ROMANCE (*5) / THE PLACES YOU HAVE COME TO FEAR THE MOST (*6) / MTV UNPLUGGED (*5) / A MARK A MISSION A BRAND A SCAR (*8)

CHRISTOPHER CARRABA – vocals, guitars, etc. (ex-FURTHER SEEMS FOREVER)

not iss. | Drive-Thru

Nov 00. (cd) *<DRIVETHRU 22CD>* **THE SWISS ARMY ROMANCE** [–] [ ]
– Screaming infidelities / The sharp hint of new tears / Living in your letters / The Swiss Army romance / Turpentine chaser / A plain morning / Age six racer / Again I go unnoticed / Ender will save us all / Shirts and gloves / (untitled). *(UK-iss.Jul01; same as US) <(re-iss. Apr03 on 'Vagrant'+=; VR 380CD)>* – Hold on / This is a forgery.

not iss. | Fiddler

Mar 01. (cd-ep) *<12>* **THE DROWNING EP** [–] [ ]
– Drowning / Anyone anyone? / For Justin.

Vagrant | Vagrant

Mar 01. (cd) *<(VR 354CD)>* **THE PLACES YOU HAVE COME TO FEAR THE MOST** [ ] [ ]
– The brilliant dance / Screaming infidelities / The best deceptions / This ruined puzzle / Saints and sailors / The good fight / Standard lines / Again I go unnoticed / The places you have come to fear the most / This bitter pill. *(re-iss. Mar02 on 'B-Unique'; BUN 018) (re-iss. Aug02 on 'Universal'; 910354-2)*

— added **DAVE HOERNER** – guitar (of SUNNY DAY REAL ESTATE)

Dec 01. (cd-ep) *<VR 362>* **SO IMPOSSIBLE** [–] [ ]
– For you to notice . . . / So impossible / Remember to breathe / Hands down. *(UK-iss.Mar03; same as US)*

Apr 02. (cd-ep) *<36>* **SUMMER KISSES EP** [–] [ ]
– Living in your letters / The sharp hint of new tears / Turpentine chaser / Ender will save us all.

— <above issued on 'Eulogy'>

— **CARRABA** added **DAN BONEBRAKE** – bass / **MIKE MARSH** – drums

Dec 02. (cd) *<(VR 378CD)>* **MTV UNPLUGGED (live)** [ ] [ ]
– Swiss army romance / The best deceptions / Remember to breathe / The good fight / The sharp hint of new tears / So impossible / The places you have come to fear the most / Turpentine chaser / Living in your letters / For you to notice / The brilliant dance / Screaming infidelities / Saints and sailors / Again I go unnoticed / Hands down. *<(re-iss. Apr03 += w/dvd; 493692-0)*

— **SCOTT SCHOENBECK** – bass; repl. DAN

Jul 03. (cd) *<(VR 385CD)>* **A MARK A MISSION A BRAND A SCAR** [ ] [ ]
– Hands down / Rapid hope loss / As lovers go / Carry this picture / Bend and not break / Ghost of a good thing / Am I missing / Morning calls / Carve your heart out yourself / So beautiful / Hey girl / If you can't leave it be, might as well make it bleed / Several ways to die trying. *<(re-iss. Aug03 on 'Universal'+=; 9810554-2)>* – This old wound / The end of an anchor. *<hit US No.2> <(re-iss. Nov03 on 'Universal' w/ dvd+=; 9810554)*

Universal | Universal

Nov 03. (7") *(9813791)* **HANDS DOWN. / I DO** [60] [–]
(cd-s+=) *(9813790)* – Saints and sailors (MTV unplugged version) / ('A'-video).

DATSUNS

Formed: Cambridge, New Zealand . . . 1997 by DOLF DE DATSUN, CHRISTIAN LIVINGSTONE, PHIL SOMERVELL and MATT OSMENT, calling themselves The TRINKETS and dominating the college rock scene until their mighty rise in 2002. Winning battle of the bands competitions in and around Cambridge, the four-piece garage rock collective issued minor singles on their own 'Hell Squad' imprint, before embarking on a whirlwind tour of Australia, which ultimately gave them the confidence to venture into the cut-throat world of the British music scene. They were in luck, however, thanks to the garage rock revival of The WHITE STRIPES et al, and were hailed by many a music rag as "the best new band since the last best new band" (joke). 'Virgin' offshoot label 'V2' stepped in and offered The DATSUNS – whose live performances got almost as messy as . . . TRAIL OF DEAD's – a record contract, thrusting the floppy-haired foursome into the limelight. A single 'I'M IN LOVE' was issued in 2002 and made John Peel's revolving playlist, not to mention an addition on his 'Live At Fabric' compilation. The group successfully lived up to the hype by releasing their self-titled debut at the close of the year.

Album rating: THE DATSUNS (*8)

DOLF DE DATSUN – vocals, bass / **CHRISTIAN LIVINGSTONE** – guitar, vocals / **PHIL SOMERVELL** – guitar, vocals / **MATT OSMENT** – drums

		Hellsquad	not iss.
2000.	(ltd-7") *(HS 002)* **SUPER GYRATION! / HOOTCHIE MAMA**		–
2001.	(7"purple) *(HS 003)* **FINK FOR THE MAN. / TRANSISTOR**		–
May 02.	(7") *(HS 005)* **LADY. / MF FROM HELL**		–
Sep 02.	(ltd-7") *(HS 007)* **IN LOVE. / LITTLE BRUISE**	– tour	–
Sep 02.	(ltd-7") *(HS 008)* **SITTIN' PRETTY. / THE TERRIBLE POWER**	– tour	–
		V2	V2
Sep 02.	(7") *(VVR 502095-3)* **IN LOVE. / LITTLE BRUISE**	25	–
	(cd-s) *(VVR 502095-3)* – ('A'side) / Supergyration.		
Oct 02.	(cd) *(VVR 102096-2)* *<63881 27149>* **THE DATSUNS** – Sittin' pretty / MF from Hell / Lady / Harmonic generator / What would I know / At your touch / Fink for the man / In love / You build me up / Freeze sucker. *(lp-iss. on 'Sweet Nothing'; SNLP 019)*	17 Feb03	
Feb 03.	(7") *(VVR 502122-7)* **HARMONIC GENERATOR. / FREEZE SUCKER**	33	–
	(cd-s) *(VVR 502122-3)* – ('A'side) / Transistor / O woe is me / ('A'-video).		
	(cd-s) *(VVR 502122-8)* – ('A'side) / Sittin' pretty (live session) / Fink for the man (live session).		
Aug 03.	(cd-s) *(VVR 502175-3)* **MF FROM HELL / AIN'T GOT TIME FOR LOVE / IN LOVE (toe rag demo)**	55	–
	(cd-s) *(VVR 502175-8)* – ('A'live) / What would I know (live) / At your touch (SBN session) / ('A'-video).		

☐ Dave DAVIES (see under ⇒ KINKS)

Miles DAVIS

Born: 25 May 1926, Alton, Illinois, USA, but raised in East St. Louis. The single most influential black musician (and certainly jazz musician) ever, next to JAMES BROWN, DAVIS began playing trumpet professionally in the early 40's. In 1944, after a period with bandleader BILLY ECKSTINE, he moved with his new wife to New York, where he briefly attended the Juilliard School Of Music before joining singer, RUBBERLEGS WILLIAMS. Around the same time, DAVIS also recorded and performed with his roommate/mentor, saxophonist CHARLIE PARKER. DAVIS subsequently assembled his own 9-piece ensemble, dubbed The TUBA BAND, which included saxophonists GERRY MULLIGAN and LEE KONITZ. They issued a number of radical 78's (singles), which were later (in 1957) compiled on seminal jazz work, 'THE BIRTH OF THE COOL'. After initially being influenced by bop pioneers such as PARKER and DIZZY GILLESPIE, DAVIS was now beginning to develop his own languid, downbeat style. Through the early to mid-50's, with revolving personnel, DAVIS worked sporadically due to his heroin addiction, although his reputation as the hippest cat on the jazz block continued to spread. In 1955, after a bout of illness, he formed his now famous MILES DAVIS QUINTET, a groundbreaking formation that numbered JOHN COLTRANE, RED GARLAND, PAUL CHAMBERS and PHILLY JOE JONES. This relatively stable line-up recorded a string of albums including 'WORKIN'', 'STEAMIN'' and 'COOKIN'', while "the man with the horn" subsequently signed for 'Columbia' and put together a new band consisting of JIMMY COBB, BILL EVANS and CANNONBALL ADDERLEY amongst an ever changing cast of others. This period saw the release of the seminal 'KIND OF BLUE' (1959), an album which revolutionised jazz with its substitution of conventional chord structures for modal improvisation. In collaboration with arranger GIL EVANS, DAVIS also recorded career best works in Gershwin's 'PORGY AND BESS' (1959) and the hauntingly beautiful 'SKETCHES OF SPAIN' (1960). In 1963, he formed a new combo of young musicians, namely HERBIE HANCOCK, RON CARTER, TONY WILLIAMS and WAYNE SHORTER; this line-up produced enough brilliant performances to enthuse a new beatnik buying public, giving the unfashionable trumpet a new lease of life and an unlikely US chart position for the 'SEVEN STEPS TO HEAVEN' set. Five years later, DAVIS shocked both the jazz and rock fraternities, when, like DYLAN, he introduced electric instrumentation into a traditionally acoustic genre with the 'MILES IN THE SKY' album; in other words, DAVIS pioneered jazz-rock fusion. Other new talent to emerge during this transitional period, were JOHN McLAUGHLIN, JOE ZAWINUL and CHICK COREA to name but a few. Their following two albums, 'IN A SILENT WAY' (1969) and the double-set, 'BITCHES' BREW' (1970), saw them universally peaking, both critically and commercially (the latter hit the US Top 40, his only effort ever to do so!). Augmented on the second of these by keyboard wizard, LARRY YOUNG (who had replaced HANCOCK), DAVIS and Co. had created a work of genre-defying genius that explored the outermost limits of jazz, a mission that SUN RA had set out upon some years earlier. After the release of two further, wildly experimental concert sets, 'LIVE AT FILLMORE' (1971) and 'LIVE EVIL' (1972), DAVIS survived a serious car crash and became increasingly more reclusive, shying away from the mainstream music business. Up until 1975 however, DAVIS continued recording, moving further away from jazz and into electronic funk with albums, 'ON THE CORNER' (1973), 'GET UP WITH IT' (1974) and 'AGHARTA' (1975); the latter set was his last for five years. In the early 80's, his return was heralded with the comeback album, 'THE MAN WITH THE HORN' (1981); a decidedly more commercial affair, it helped the infamously volatile DAVIS reach a new plateau of middleground popularity. In 1986, he broke a 27-year partnership with 'Columbia' after signing with 'Warner Brothers', his umpteenth album, 'TUTU' delivering his smooth interpretation of Scritti Politti's 'PERFECT WAY', having previously challenged his long-standing fans with an elevator-friendly version of Cyndi Lauper's 'TIME AFTER TIME'. Although he continued recording, DAVIS increasingly devoted more of his time to his second love, art. Sadly, just as his recording career might have taken off once more, he died on the 27th of December 1991 after contracting AIDS some years earlier. • **Trivia:** In 1982, he married actress CICELY TYSON.

Album rating (selective): BIRTH OF THE COOL (*9) / WORKIN' / STEAMIN' / COOKIN' / RELAXIN' (all *6) / SKETCHES OF SPAIN (*8) / KIND OF BLUE (*10) / MILESTONES (*8) / SOMEDAY MY PRINCE WILL COME (*7) / E.S.P. (*7) / MILES SMILES (*9) / NEFERTITI (*6) / MILES IN THE SKY (*6) / FILLES DE KILIMANJARO (*7) / IN A SILENT WAY (*7) / BITCHES' BREW (*8) / A TRIBUTE TO JACK JOHNSON (*8) / ON THE CORNER (*7) / PANGAEA (*6) / THE MAN WITH THE HORN (*6) / WE WANT MILES (*6) / STAR PEOPLE (*6) / DECOY (*5) / YOU'RE UNDER ARREST (*6) / AURA (*5) / TUTU (*7) / MUSIC FROM SIESTA (*5) / LIVE AROUND THE WORLD (*6) / AMANDLA (*6) / HOT SPOT (*5) / DINGO (*5) / DOO-BOP (*5) / MILES & QUINCY LIVE AT MONTREUX (*6)

(1948) **MILES DAVIS** – trumpet / **GIL EVANS, GERRY MULLIGAN, LEE KONITZ, JOHN LEWIS, JOHNNY CARISI, GUNTHER SCHULLER, SANDY SIEGELSTEIN** – saxophones / **JAY JAY JOHNSON** – trombone / **JOHN 'Bill' BARBER** – tuba / **MAX ROACH** (or) **KENNY CLARKE** – drums / with on some **JUNIOR COLLINS** – French horn / **MIKE ZWERIN.**

Capitol Capitol

1950. (78) *(CL 13249)* **BUDO. / MOVE**
1950. (78) *(CL 13255)* **BOPLICITY. / ISRAEL**
1950. (78) *(CL 13429)* **VENUS DE MILO. / DARN THAT DREAM**
1950. (lp) *<DT 1974>* **BIRTH OF THE COOL** –
– Move / Jeru / Moon dreams / Venus De Milo / Budo / Deception / Godchild / Boplicity / Rocker / Israel / Rouge.

— (May52 with) **JOHNSON + CLARKE** plus **JACKIE McLEAN** – alto sax / **GIL COGGINS** – piano / **OSCAR PETTIFORD** – bass

not iss. Blue Note

Oct 51. (lp) *<6525>* **DIG** –
– Dig / It's only a paper moon / Dental / Bluing / Out of the blue. *(UK-iss.1958 on 'Esquire'; 32-062)*
May 52. (lp) **MILES DAVIS VOL.1** –
– How deep is the ocean / Dear old Stockholm / Chance it / Yesterdays / Donna / Woody 'n you.

— (Apr53) **PERCY HEATH** – bass repl. PETTIFORD / **ART BLAKEY** – drums repl. CLARKE / **JIMMY HEATH** – tenor sax repl. McLEAN
Tracks recorded: – Tempes fugit / Kelo / Enigma / Ray's idea / C.T.A. / I waited for you.
Sep 53. (lp) **AT LAST! MILES DAVIS AND THE LIGHTHOUSE ALL STARS** –

— (Mar54) **HORACE SILVER** – piano repl. JIMMY, JAY JAY + GIL
Mar 54. (lp) **MILES DAVIS VOL. 2** –
Tracks recorded: – Take-off / Weirdo / Well you needn't / The leap / Lazy Susan / It never entered my mind.
They also recorded tracks: – Four / Old Devil Moon / Blue haze.

— He formed The MILES DAVIS QUARTET earlier (May53) with **PERCY HEATH** – bass **JOHN LEWIS** – piano / **MAX ROACH** – drums with guest **CHARLIE MINGUS** – piano (1)
Albums issued at this time:- BAGS GROOVE / . . . & HORNS / MILES DAVIS Tracks recorded: – When lights are low / Tune up / Miles ahead / Smooch.

— The first incarnation of **MILES DAVIS QUINTET** appeared with **MILES, HORACE, PERCY, KENNY CLARKE** plus **DAVEY SCHILDKRAUT** – alto sax

MILES DAVIS ALL-STARS

— were **CLARKE, JOHNSON, SILVER, PERCY HEATH & LUCKY THOMPSON**

not iss. Prestige

Apr 54. (lp) *<7078>* **WALKIN'** –
– Walkin' / Blues 'n' boogie / Solar / You don't know what love is / Love me or leave me. *(UK-iss.1960 on 'Esquire'; 32-098) (cd-iss. Aug93 + Nov93 on 'Jazz Hour')*

— (Jun55) **MILES** – trumpet + **RED GARLAND** – piano / **PHILLY JOE JONES** – drums / **OSCAR PETTIFORD** – bass
1955. (lp) *<7007>* **THE MUSING OF MILES** –
– I didn't / Will you still be mine? / Green haze / I see your face before me / A night in Tunisia / A gal in Calico. *(UK-iss.1950's on 'Esquire'; 32-012) (re-iss. Jun84)*

— (Nov55) **JOHN COLTRANE** – tenor sax + **PAUL CHAMBERS** – bass repl. OSCAR

MILES DAVIS QUINTET

Nov 55. (lp) *<7014>* **MILES** –
– Just squeeze me / There is no greater love / How am I to know? / S'posin' / The theme / Stablemates.
(above 2 albums issued as 'MILES' in 1958)
Oct 56. (lp) *<7094>* **COOKIN' (live)** –
– If I were a bell / Stella by starlight / Walkin' / Miles. *(UK-iss.1958 on 'Esquire'; 32-048)*
1958. (lp) *<7129>* **RELAXIN' WITH THE MILES DAVIS QUINTET** –
– You're my everything / I could write a book / Cleo / It could happen to you / Woodyn' you. *(UK-iss.195 on 'Esquire'; 32-068)*
1958. (lp) *<7166>* **WORKIN' WITH THE MILES DAVIS QUINTET** –
– It never entered my mind / Four / In your own sweet way / The theme (take 1 + 2) / Treme's blues / Ahmad's blues / Half Nelson. *(UK-iss.1960 on 'Esquire'; 32-108)*
1958. (lp) *<7200>* **STEAMIN' WITH THE MILES DAVIS QUINTET** –
– Surrey with the fringe on top / Salt peanuts / Something I dreamed last night / Diane / Well you needn't / When I fall in love. *(UK-iss.1961 on 'Esquire'; 32-138)*
1959. (lp) *<7540>* **ODYSSEY** –
– Dr. Jackie / Bitty ditty / Minor march / Change.
1959. (lp) *<7650>* **MODERN JAZZ GIANTS** –
– Bag's groove – take 1 & 2 / Bemsha swing – take 1 & 2 / Swing spring.
1959. (lp) *<7744>* **CONCEPTION** –
1959. (lp) *<7847>* **OLEO** –
– Oleo / Doxy / Airegin / But not for me – take 1 & 2 / Vierd blues / In our own sweet way / No line.

— **BILL EVANS** – piano + **JIMMY COBB** – drums repl. GARLAND + JONES / added **CANNONBALL ADDERLEY** – alto sax

Fontana Prestige

May 57. (lp) *(TFL 5007) <7822>* **MILES AHEAD**
– Springsville / Maids of Cadiz / Duke / My ship / Miles ahead / Blues for Pablo / New rhumba / Meaning of the blues / Lament / I don't wanna be kissed.

Fontana Columbia

Apr 58. (lp) *(TFL 5035) <9428>* **MILESTONES**
– Doctor Jekyll / Sid's ahead / Two bass hits / Miles / Billy Boy / Straight no chaser. *(cd-iss. 1992)*

— added on below lp **JOHN COLTRANE** – tenor sax
May 59. (lp) *(STFL 513) <8163>* **KIND OF BLUE**
– So what / Freddie Freeloader / Blue in green / All blues / Flamenco sketches. *(cd-iss. Apr97 on 'Columbia-Legacy'+=; CK 64935)* – Flamenco sketches (alternate mix). *(cd re-iss. Oct99; MILEN 101) (re-dist.Apr01; same)* – hit No.70
Nov 59. (lp) *(TFL 5056) <8085>* **PORGY AND BESS**
– The buzzard song / Bess, you is my woman / Gone, gone, gone, gone / Summertime / Bess, oh where's my Bess / Prayer / Objector Jesus / Fisherman / Strawberry and Devil crab / My man's gone now / It ain't necessarily so / Here comes de honey man / I love you Porgy / There's a boat that's leaving soon for New York. *(re-iss. Sep82) (re-iss. +cd.Feb88)*
Jan 60. (7") *<42069>* **IT AIN'T NECESSARILY SO. / I LOVES YOU PORGY** –
(above + below lp's credited arranger GIL EVANS ORCHESTRA)
1960. (7") *(JAZ 100)* **BUDO. / TADD'S DELIGHT**
above issued on 'Philips' at this time.

C.B.S. Columbia

Apr 60. (lp) *(CBS 62327) <8271>* **SKETCHES OF SPAIN**
– Concerto de Aranjuez / Will o' the wisp / The pan piper / Saeta / Solea. *(re-iss. Mar81 + Apr88, cd-iss. Dec85 + Apr92)*

— In Autumn 1960, **SONNY STITT** – saxophone repl. COLTRANE in Sweden. Later in the year **SAM RIVERS** then **WAYNE SHORTER** repl. SONNY
Sep 61. (d-lp) *<820>* **IN PERSON (AT THE BLACKHAWK)** – 68
– Fran-dance / So what / Cleo / If I were a bell / Neo / Round midnight. *cd-iss. Jun 93 on 'Giants of Jazz')*

— **HANK MOBLEY** – saxophone repl. COLTRANE
Mar 62. (lp) *(TFL 5172) <8456>* **SOMEDAY MY PRINCE WILL COME**
– Someday my prince will come / Old folks / Pfrancing / Drad-dog /

Teo / I thought about you. *(re-iss. 1964 on 'C.B.S.'; 62104) (re-iss. Jul75 on 'Code-CBS') (cd-iss. Jan86 + Apr92)*

Sep 62. (lp) *<8612>* **MILES DAVIS AT CARNEGIE HALL 1961 (live)** – 59
– So what / Spring is here / No blues / Cleo / Someday my prince will come / The meaning of the blues / Lament / New rhumba. *(cd-iss. Apr93 on 'Sony Europe')*

Oct 62. (7") *<42583>* **NEW RHUMBA. / SLOW SAMBA** –

Dec 62. (lp) *(CBS 62323) <8649>* **ROUND ABOUT MIDNIGHT**
– Round about midnight / Ah leucha / All of you / Bye bye blackbird / Tadd's delight / Dear old Stockholm. *(cd-iss. Apr92)*
(above recorded 1956)

— now with **HERBIE HANCOCK** – piano / **TONY WILLIAMS** – drums / **RON CARTER** – bass / **GEORGE COLEMAN** – tenor sax

Sep 63. (lp; stereo/mono) *(S+/BPG 62170) <8851>* **SEVEN STEPS TO HEAVEN** 62
– Basin street blues / Seven steps to Heaven / I fall in love too easily / So near so far / Baby won't you please come home / Joshun. *(re-iss. Jul75 on 'Code-CBS')*

Oct 63. (7") *<42853>* **SEVEN STEPS TO HEAVEN. / THE DEVIL MAY CARE** –

Apr 64. (lp; stereo/mono) *(S+/BPG 62213) <8906>* **QUIET NIGHTS** 93
– Once upon a summertime / Aos pes da cruz / Song No.1 / Wait till you see her / Corrovado / Summer night. *(re-iss. Jul75 on 'Code-CBS') (cd-iss. Jul89)*

1964. (lp; stereo/mono – MILES DAVIS & THELONIUS MONK) *(S+/BPG 62389) <8978>* **MILES AND MONK AT NEWPORT**
– Ah-leu-cha / Straight, no chaser / Fran-dance / Two bass hit / Nutty / Blue Monk. *(re-iss. Jul75 on 'Code-CBS')*

Sep 64. (lp; stereo/mono) *(S+/BPG 62390) <8983>* **DAVIS IN EUROPE (live)**
– Untitled medley:- Agitation / Footprints / Round midnight / No blues / Masqualero / All of you. *(re-iss. Jul75 on 'Code-CBS')*

— Line-up now **DAVIS, WILLIAMS, HANCOCK, CARTER + SHORTER**

Apr 65. (lp; stereo/mono) *(S+/BPG 62510) <9106>* **MY FUNNY VALENTINE: MILES DAVIS LIVE IN CONCERT (live)**
– My funny valentine / All of you / Stella by starlight / All blues / I thought about you. *(UK-iss.Jul75 on 'Code-CBS') (cd-iss. May87 on 'CBS')*

Jan 66. (lp; stereo/mono) *(S+/BPG 62577) <9150>* **E.S.P.**
– E.S.P. / Eighty one / Little one / R.J. / Agitation / Iris / Mood. *(re-iss. Jul75 on 'Code-CBS') (cd-iss. Apr92)*

— credited his QUINTET, (**SHORTER** repl. COLEMAN)

1967. (lp; stereo/mono) *(S+/BPG 62933) <9401>* **MILES SMILES**
– Orbits / Circle / Footprints / Dolores / Freedom jazz dance / Ginger bread boy. *(re-iss. Aug75 on 'Code-CBS')*

1968. (lp; stereo/mono) *(S+/BPG 63097) <9532>* **THE SORCERER**
– Prince of darkness / Vonetta / Limbo / Masquealero / Pee wee / The sorcerer. *(re-iss. Aug76) (re-iss. Jul87) (re-iss. cd Sep93)*

1968. (lp) *(CBS 63248) <9594>* **NEFERTITI**
– Nefertiti / Fall / Hand jive / Madness / Riot / Pinocchio. *(re-iss. Aug76) (cd-iss. Apr92)*

Nov 68. (lp) *(CBS 63352) <9628>* **MILES IN THE SKY**
– Stuff / Paraphernalia / Black comedy / Country son. *(re-iss. Aug75 on 'Code-CBS')*

1969. (lp) *(CBS 63551) <9750>* **FILLES DE KILIMANJARO**
– Frelon burn (Brown hornet) / Tout de suite / Petits machins (little stuff) / Filles de Kilimanjaro (girls of . . .) / Mademoiselle Mabry. *(cd-iss. Apr92)*

MILES DAVIS

— with past members **HERBIE HANCOCK** – electric piano / **WAYNE SHORTER** – soprano sax / **TONY WILLIAMS** – drums. New:- **DAVE HOLLAND** – bass repl. CARTER / **CHICK COREA** – electric piano / **JOSEF ZAWINUL** – electric piano & organ / **JOHN McLAUGHLIN** – guitar

Aug 69. (lp) *(CBS 63630) <9875>* **IN A SILENT WAY** Jul69
– Ssh-Peaceful / In a silent way / It's about that time.

1970. (7") *<45090>* **GREAT EXPECTATIONS. / LITTLE BLUE FROG** –

— **LARRY YOUNG** – electric piano repl. HANCOCK who cont. solo work / **JACK DeJOHNETTE + LENNY WHITE** – drums repl. WILLIAMS who formed his LIFETIME / added **JIM RILEY** – percussion / **HARVEY BROOKS** – Fender bass / **BENNIE MAUPIN** – clarinet

Jun 70. (d-lp) *(CBS 66236) <26>* **BITCHES BREW** 71 May70 35
– Pharoah's dance / Bitches brew / Spanish key / John McLaughlin / Miles runs the voodoo down / Sanctuary. *(re-iss. Sep87, d-cd-iss. Apr92)*

Jul 70. (7") *(CBS 7104) <45171>* **MILES RUNS THE VOODOO DOWN. / SPANISH KEY**

Jan 71. (d-lp) *(CBS 66257) <30038>* **MILES DAVIS AT FILLMORE (live)** Nov70
– Wednesday Miles / Thursday Miles / Friday Miles / Saturday Miles. *(re-iss. Jul75 on 'Code-CBS')*

Feb 71. (7") *<45327>* **SATURDAY MILES. / FRIDAY MILES** –

— Other members at this time **BILLY COBHAM** – percussion / **KEITH JARRETT** – keyboards

May 71. (lp) *(CBS 70089) <30455>* **A TRIBUTE TO JACK JOHNSON (Soundtrack)** Apr71
– Right off / Yesternow. *(re-imported Jan76) (cd-iss. Sep93)*

May 71. (7") *<45350>* **RIGHT OFF. / (part 2)** –

Dec 71. (d-lp) *(CBS 67219) <30954>* **LIVE-EVIL**
– Sivod / Little church / Medley: Gemini-Double image / What I say / Nem um talvez / Selim / Funky tonk / Inamorata.

Sep 72. (7") *<45709>* **MOLESTER. / (part 2)** –

Nov 72. (7") *<45822>* **VOTE FOR MILES. / (part 2)** –

Nov 72. (lp) *(CBS 65246) <31906>* **ON THE CORNER**
– On the corner / New York girl / Thinkin' one thing and doin' another / Vote for Miles / Black satin / One and one / Helen Butte / Mr. Freedom X. *(re-iss. Jan87) (re-iss. Dec88 on 'B.G.O.', cd-iss. Apr92) (re-iss. cd Feb94 on 'Sony')*

Apr 73. (d-lp) *(CBS 68222)* **IN CONCERT (live)** –

Jun 74. (d-lp) *(CBS 88024) <32866>* **BIG FUN**
– Go ahead, John / Lonely fire / Great expectations / Mulher Laranja / Ife.

Jun 74. (7") *<45946>* **BIG FUN. / HOLLYWOOD** –

Oct 74. (7") *<46074>* **GREAT EXPECTATIONS. / GO AHEAD JOHN** –

Jan 75. (d-lp) *(CBS 88092) <33236>* **GET UP WITH IT**
– He loved him madly / Maiysha / Honky tonk / Rated X / Calypso frelimo / Red China blues / Mtume / Billy Preston.

Jan 75. (7") *<10110>* **RED CHINA BLUES. / MAIYSHA** –

Nov 75. (d-lp) *(CBS 88159) <33967>* **AGHARTA (live)**
– Prelude (pt.1 & 2) / Maiysha / Interlude / Theme from Jack Johnson. *(re-iss. Jan87) (re-iss. d-cd Sep93)*

Jun 76. (d-lp) *(36AP 178990)* **PANGAEA (live)** – Japan –
-Zimbabwe (parts 1-3). *(d-cd-iss. Sep93 on 'Warners')*
In the mid-70's, he suffered from injuries sustained in a car crash. He recuperated, with record co. issuing some recordings/out-takes.

Apr 77. (lp) *<34396>* **WATER BABIES** (rec.'68-69) –
– Water babies / Capricorn / Sweet pea / Two-faced / Dual Mr. Tillman Anthony. *(re-iss. Jul86)*

Nov 77. (lp) *(CBS 82100)* **PARIS FESTIVAL INTERNATIONAL (live)** –
– Rifftide / Good bait / Don't blame me / Lady bird / Wah'hoo / Allen's alley / Embraceable you / Ornithology / All the things you are.

Jan 80. (d-lp) *(CBS 88471)* **CIRCLE IN THE ROUND** (recorded 1955-70) –
– Two bars hit / Love for sale / Blues No.2 / Circle in the round / Ted's bag / Side car 1 + 2 / Splash / Sanctuary / Guinnevere. *(re-iss. May82) (re-iss. cd Sep93)*

— DAVIS returned tour/studio with **MARCUS MILLER** – bass / **MIKE STERN** – guitar / **BILL EVANS** – soprano + tenor sax / **AL FOSTER** – drums / **MINO CINELU** – percussion

Jul 81. (7") *<02467>* **FAT TIME. / SHORT** –

Jul 81. (lp) *(CBS 84708) <36790>* **THE MAN WITH THE HORN** 53
– Fat time / Back seat Betty / Short / Aida / The man with the horn / Urasula. *(cd-iss. 1983)(re-iss. cd Sep93)*

Jun 82. (d-lp) *(CBS 88579) <38005>* **WE WANT MILES (live Boston/Tokyo)** May82
– Jean Pierre / Back seat Betty / Fast track / My man's gone now / Kix. *(re-iss. cd Sep93)*

— added **JOHN SCOFIELD** – electric guitar / **TOM BARNEY** – electric bass

May 83. (7") *<03605>* **STAR ON CICELY. / IT GETS BETTER** –

May 83. (lp) *(CBS 25395) <38657>* **STAR PEOPLE**
– Come get it / It gets better / Speak / Star people / U'il / Star on Cicely. *(cd-iss. May87) (re-iss. cd Sep93)*

— **DARYLL 'The Munch' JONES** – electric bass repl. MILLER to SCRITTI POLITTI / **ROBERT IRVING III** – synthesizers, co-composer repl. MIKE

STERN + TOM BARNEY / **BRANFORD MARSALIS** shared sax duties with **EVANS**

Jun 84. (7") *<04564>* **DECOY. / CODE M.D.** [–] [ ]

Jun 84. (lp/c/cd) *(CBS/40/CD 25951)* **DECOY** [ ] [ ]
– Decoy / Robot 415 / Code M.D. / Freaky Deaky / What it is / That's right / That's what happened. *(re-iss. cd Sep93)*

— **VINCE WILBURN JR.** – drums + **STEVE THORNTON** – percussion repl. CINELU / **BOB BERG** – soprano sax repl. MARSALIS + EVANS / guest on 2 tracks **JOHN McLAUGHLIN** – guitar

May 85. (7"/12") *(A/TA 4871) <04829>* **TIME AFTER TIME. / KATIA** [ ] [ ]

Jun 85. (lp/c) *(CBS/40 26447) <40023>* **YOU'RE UNDER ARREST** [88] May85 [ ]
– One phone call – Street scenes / Human nature / Intro: MD1 – Something's on your mind- MD2 / Ms. Morrisine / Katia prelude / Katia / Time after time / You're under arrest medley: Jean Pierre – You're under arrest – Then there were none. *(cd-iss. May87; CD 26447) (re-iss. cd Sep93)*

— **MILES DAVIS** now with basic line-up of **MILLER, GEORGE DUKE** – multi / **PAULINHO DA COSTA** – synthesizers / plus **JASON MILES** – synth.prog. / **ADAM HOLZMAN** – synth.prog. / **STEVE REID** – percusson / **OMAR HAKIM** – drums, perc / etc.

Warners Warners

Oct 86. (lp/c/cd) *(925490-1/-4/-2) <25490>* **TUTU** [74] [ ]
– Tutu / Tomaas / Portia / Splatch / Backyard ritual / Perfect way / Don't lose your mind / Full Nelson.

Jan 87. (7") *<28501>* **TUTU. / PORTIA** [–] [ ]

Mar 87. (7") *<28406>* **FULL NELSON. / TOMAAS** [–] [ ]

May 87. (7") *<28309>* **BACKYARD RITUAL. / TOMAAS** [–] [ ]

Feb 88. (lp/c/cd) *(925655-1/-4/-2) <25655>* **SIESTA (Soundtrack)** [ ] [ ]
– Lost in Madrid (pt.1): Siesta – Kitt's kiss / Lost in Madrid (part 2): / Theme for Augustine – Wind – Seduction – Kiss / Submission / Lost in Madrid (pt.3): Conchita – Lament / Lost in Madrid (pt.4): Rat dance – The call / Claire – Lost in Madrid (pt.5): Afterglow / Los Feliz.
In 1988, he appeared on albums by JONI MITCHELL and SCRITTI POLITTI.

— Next included loads of musicians, including **MILLER, DUKE, CINELU, MILES, FOSTER, DA COSTA, HAKIM, KENNY GARRETT** – soprano sax / **DON ALIAS** – percussion

May 89. (lp/c)(cd) *(WX 250/+C)(925873-2) <25873>* **AMANDLA** [49] [ ]
– Catembe / Cobra / Big time / Hannibal / Jo Jo / Amandla / Jilli / Mr. Pastorius.

— due to heroin addiction, MILES lost his battle against AIDS on the 28th September '91. He had already contributed to the 'DINGO' <(7599 26438-2)> soundtrack with MICHAEL LEGRAND.

— next was a collaboration with **EAZY MO BEE** – rapper, writer

May 92. (cd/c/lp) *<7599 26938-2/-4/-1>* **DOO-BOP** [ ] [ ]
– Mystery / The doo-bop song / Chocolate chip / High speed chase / Blow / Sonya / Fantasy / Duke Booty / Mystery (reprise).

– (selective) compilations, etc. –

1957. (lp) *Capitol; <DT 1974>* **BIRTH OF THE COOL** [–] [ ]
– Move / Jeru / Moon dreams / Venus De Milo / Budo / Decepetion / Godchild / Boplicity / Rocker / Israel / Rouge. *(UK-iss.Jul78 on 'Capitol'; CAPS 1024) (cd-iss. Apr90+=; CDP 792 862-2)* – Darn that dream. *(cd-iss. Mar95 on 'Blue Note')*

1976. (d-lp) *(68606)* **LIVE AT THE PLUGGED NICKEL** [ ] [ ]
(re-iss. Dec82)

May 76. (d-lp) *(88138)* **CLASSICS** [ ] [ ]

Dec 80. (12xlp-box) *Prestige; (P 012)* **CHRONICLE – THE COMPLETE PRESTIGE RECORDINGS 1951-1956** [ ] [ ]
(re-iss. Jun92 as 8xcd-box)

Jul 95. (cd) *Le Jazz; (LEJAZZCD 45)* **AT THE ROYAL ROOST 1948, AT BIRDLAND 1950/1, 1953** [ ] [–]

Jul 95. (8xcd-box) *Sony Jazz; (CXK 66955)* **LIVE AT PLUGGED NICKEL 1965** [ ] [–]

Oct 95. (cd) *Sony Jazz; (481434-2)* **HIGHLIGHTS FROM THE PLUGGED NICKEL** [ ] [–]

Oct 95. (5xcd-box) *Sony Jazz; (CXK 67397)* **THE COMPLETE COLUMBIA STUDIO SESSIONS (with GIL EVANS)** [ ] [ ]

Nov 95. (3xcd-box) *Blue Note; (CDOMB 007)* **BIRTH OF THE COOL / VOLUME 1 / VOLUME 3** [ ] [–]

Dec 95. (cd) *Music De-Luxe; (MSCD 19)* **COOL** [ ] [–]

Sep 96. (cd/c) *Sony; (SONYTV 17 CD/MC)* **THE VERY BEST OF** [64] [ ]

Nov 96. (8xcd-box) *Prestige; (PCD 0122)* **THE COMPLETE PRESTIGE RECORDINGS: CHRONICLE 1051-1965** [ ] [ ]

Jun 98. (cd) *Capitol Jazz; <(494550-2)>* **THE COMPLETE BIRTH OF THE COOL** [ ] [ ]

Apr 00. (6xcd-box) *Sony Jazz; (C6K 65833)* **THE COMPLETE COLUMBIA RECORDINGS** (with JOHN COLTRANE) [ ] [ ]

May 00. (cd) *Giants Of Jazz; (CD 53350)* **FROM BE-BOP TO COOL** [ ] [ ]

Aug 02. (20xcd-box) *W.S.M.; <(0927 41836-2)>* **THE COMPLETE MILES DAVID AT MONTREUX** [ ] [ ]

Mar 03. (cd) *E.M.I.; (582202-2)* **THE ESSENTIAL MILES DAVIS** [ ] [ ]

Sep 03. (5xcd-box) *Sony Jazz; (CSK 86395)* **THE COMPLETE JACK JOHNSON SESSIONS** [ ] [ ]

Spencer DAVIS GROUP

Formed: Birmingham, England . . . August 1963, DAVIS meeting PETER YORK and the WINWOOD brothers STEVE and MUFF at a local jazz club. It was soon apparent that the veterans (in the early 20's), were being overshadowed by the precocious 15-year old multi-talented STEVE. After a year on the circuit, they signed to 'Fontana' records with the aid of 'Island' owner CHRIS BLACKWELL, who had recommended the act. Their early 45's failed to distinguish them from the R&B pack (having only achieved minor placings) and it was only with the release of JACKIE EDWARDS' 'KEEP ON RUNNING' that the band exploded onto the scene. It topped the chart for one week in January 1966, a year that also saw the rejuvenation of 'THE FIRST LP' (which hit Top 10), a follow-up 45, 'SOMEBODY HELP ME' (another No.1) and STEVE's first self-penned hit, 'WHEN I COME HOME'. A prolific period for the band, they ended the year on a high, having scored with another Top 10 album and their third slice of genius, 'GIMME SOME LOVIN' (denied pole position by The Four Tops' 'Reach Out I'll Be There'). Still only 17, STEVE's 'Motown'-influenced vocal talent increasingly began to outlive the basic R&B backing the rest of the band were providing. Breaking away from the group, he took a more psychedelic approach with his new outfit, TRAFFIC. SPENCER DAVIS soldiered on with a new line-up, but it was clear the spark had been extinguished and the hits soon dried up. • **Other covers:** DIMPLES (John Lee Hooker) / EVERY LITTLE BIT HURTS (Brenda Holloway) / etc. • **Trivia:** Late in 1967, they made a small cameo appearance in the film 'HERE WE GO ROUND THE MULBERRY BUSH'.

Best CD compilation: EIGHT GIGS A WEEK: THE STEVE WINWOOD YEARS (*7)

SPENCER DAVIS (b.17 Jul'41, Swansea, Wales) – guitar, vocals, harmonica (ex-SAINTS) / **STEVE WINWOOD** (b.12 May'48, Birmingham) – vocals, keyboards, guitar / **MUFF WINWOOD** (b.MERVYN, 14 Jun'43) – bass, vocals / **PETER YORK** (b.15 Aug'42, Middlesborough, England) – drums

Fontana Fontana

Aug 64. (7") *(TF 471)* **DIMPLES. / SITTIN' AND THINKIN'** [ ] [–]

Oct 64. (7") *(TF 499) <1960>* **I CAN'T STAND IT. / MIDNIGHT TRAIN** [47] Mar65 [ ]

Jan 65. (7") *(TF 530)* **EVERY LITTLE BIT HURTS. / IT HURTS ME SO** [41] [–]

May 65. (7") *(TF 571)* **STRONG LOVE. / THIS HAMMER** [44] [–]

Jul 65. (lp) *(TL 5242)* **THEIR FIRST LP** (hit-Jan66) [6] [–]
– My babe / Dimples / Searchin' / Every little bit hurts / I'm blue (gong gong song) / Sittin' and thinkin' / I can't stand it / Here right now / Jump back / It's gonna work out fine / Midnight train / It hurts me so. *(re-iss. 1968 as 'EVERY LITTLE BIT HURTS' on 'Wing'; WL 1165)*

Fontana Atco

Nov 65. (7") *(TF 632) <6400>* **KEEP ON RUNNING. / HIGH TIME BABY** [1] [76]

Jan 66. (lp) *(TL 5295)* **THE SECOND ALBUM** [2] [–]

– Look away / Keep on running / This hammer / Georgia on my mind / Please do something / Let me down easy / Strong love / I washed my hands in muddy water / Since I met you baby / You must believe me / Hey darling / Watch your step.

Mar 66. (7") *(TF 679)* *<6416>* **SOMEBODY HELP ME. / STEVIE'S BLUES** [1] [ ]

Aug 66. (7") *(TF 739)* **WHEN I COME HOME. / TRAMPOLINE** [12] [–]

Sep 66. (lp) *(TL 5359)* **AUTUMN '66** [4] [–]
– Together till the end of time / Take this hurt off me / Nobody knows you when you're down and out / Midnight special / When a man loves a woman / When I come home / Mean woman blues / Dust my blues / On the green light / Neighbour, neighbour / High time baby / Somebody help me.

Fontana U.A.

Oct 66. (7") *(TF 762)* *<50108>* **GIMME SOME LOVING. / BLUES IN F** [2] Jan67 [7]
(above 'A'side was different remix in the States)

Jan 67. (7") *(TF 785)* *<50144>* **I'M A MAN. / CAN'T GET ENOUGH OF IT** [9] Mar67 [10]

Mar 67. (lp; mono/stereo) *<UAL3/UAS6 578>* **GIMME SOME LOVIN'** [–] [54]
– Gimme some lovin' / Keep on running / This hammer (the hammer song) / Nobody knows you when you're down and out / When I come home / It hurts me so / Somebody help me / Midnight special / Here right now / Trampoline / Sittin' and thinkin' / Goodbye Stevie. *<(cd-iss. Jul01 on 'Sundazed'+=; SC 11103)>* – Jump back / It's gonna work out fine / I'm blue (gong gong song) / I'm getting better / She put the hurt on me / Blues in F / High time baby / Drown in my tears.

Jun 67. (7") *<50162>* **SOMEBODY HELP ME. / ON THE GREEN LIGHT** [–] [47]

— **EDDIE HARDIN** (b. EDWARD HARDING, 19 Feb'49) – organ, vocals replaced STEVE who joined TRAFFIC and later BLIND FAITH then solo. / **PHIL SAWYER** (b.8 Mar'47) – lead guitar replaced MUFF who became A&R man, / also **CHARLIE McCRACKEN** – bass (guest)

Jul 67. (lp; mono/stereo) *<UAL3/UAS6 589>* **I'M A MAN** [–] [83]
– I'm a man / Every little bit hurts / Searchin' / I can't stand it / Dimples / Look away / Georgia on my mind / My babe / I can't get enough of it / On the green light / Stevie's blues / Midnight train. *<(cd-iss. Jul01 on 'Sundazed'+=; SC 11104)>* – Watch your step / You must believe me / Strong love / Hey darling / Waltz for Lumumba / Please do something / Let me down easy / Stevie's groove.

Jul 67. (7") *(TF 854)* *<50202>* **TIME SELLER. / DON'T WANT YOU NO MORE** [30] [100]

U.A. U.A.

Dec 67. (7") *(UP 1203)* **MR. SECOND CLASS. / SANITY INSPECTOR** [35] [–]

Dec 67. (7") *<50286>* **AFTER TEA. / LOOKING BACK** [–] [ ]

Mar 68. (7") *(UP 2213)* **AFTER TEA. / MOONSHINE** [ ] [–]

Apr 68. (lp; stereo/mono) *(S+/ULP 1192)* **WITH THEIR NEW FACE ON** [ ] [–]
– With his new face on / Mr. Second class / Alec in transitland / Sanity inspector / Feel your way / Morning sun / Moonshine / Don't want you no more / Time seller / Stop me, I'm fallin'. *(cd-iss. Nov97 on 'Repertoire'+=; REP 4648)* – After tea / Aquarius der wassermann / Let the sunshine / Feel your way / I'm lost / Pools winner / Morning sun.

— (Nov'68) **DEE MURRAY** – bass / **NIGEL OLSSON** – drums repl. HARDIN & YORK who formed self named duo.

1969. (lp) *<UAS 6691>* **HEAVIES** [–] [ ]
– Please do something / Waltz for lum umba / I'm blue (gong gong song) / Hey darling / Mean woman blues / Watch your step / Drown in my own tears / Together til' the end of time / Take this hurt off me / Back into my life again.

— (signed to 'Date-Columbia' and copies of album 'LETTERS FROM EDITH' surfaced; US title 'FUNKY')

— split mid '69. MURRAY and OLSSON joined ELTON JOHN's Band.

1971. (lp; by SPENCER DAVIS & PETER JAMESON) *(UAS 29177)* **IT'S BEEN SO LONG** [ ] [ ]
– It's been so long / Crystal river / One hundred years ago / Balkan blues / Brother can you make up your mind / Mountain lick / Jav's tune / King of her / It's too late now.

1972. (lp; by SPENCER DAVIS) *(UAS 29361)* **MOUSETRAP** [ ] [ ]
– Rainy season / Listen to the rhythm / What can I be / Tried / Easy rider / Tumbledown tenement row / Sunday walk in the rain / I washed my hands in muddy water / Sailor's lament / Hollywood Joe / In the hills of Tennessee / Ella speed.

1972. (7"; by SPENCER DAVIS) *<50922>* **LISTEN TO THE RHYTHM. / SUNDAY WALK IN THE RAIN** [–] [ ]

1972. (7"; by SPENCER DAVIS) *<50993>* **RAINY SEASON. / TUMBLE-DOWN TENEMENT ROW** [–] [ ]

— now group re-united w / **HARDIN, YORK, FENWICK + CHARLIE McCRACKEN** – bass

Vertigo Vertigo

Mar 73. (7") *(6059 076)* **CATCH YOU ON THE REBOB. / THE EDGE** [ ] [–]

May 73. (lp) *(6360 088)* **GLUGGO** [ ] [–]
– Catch you on the Moon / Don't it let it bring you down / Alone / Today Gluggo, tomorrow the world / Feeling rude / Legal eagle shuffle / Trouble in mind / Mr.Operator / Tumbledown tenement row.

May 73. (7") *<110>* **DON'T LET IT BRING YOU DOWN. / TODAY GLUGGO, TOMORROW THE WORLD** [–] [ ]

Jun 73. (7") *(6059 082)* **MR. OPERATOR. / TOUCHING CLOTH** [ ] [–]

Oct 73. (7") *(6059 087)* *<112>* **LIVIN' IN A BACK STREET. / SURE NEED A HELPING HAND** [ ] [ ]

Jun 74. (lp) *(6360 105)* **LIVIN' IN A BACK STREET** [ ] [ ]
– Living in a backstreet / One night / Hanging around / No reason / Fasted thing / On four wheels / Backstreet boys / Another day / Sure need a helping hand / We can give it a try / Let's have a party. *(cd-iss. Nov97 on 'Repertoire'; REP 4682)*

— SPENCER retired from solo work until 1983.

Allegience not iss.

Apr 84. (lp/c) *(ALE/+C 5603)* **CROSSFIRE** [ ] [–]
– Blood runs hot / Don't want you no more / Love is on a roll / Crossfire / Private number / Just a gigolo / Careless love / A pretty girl is like a melody / When the day is done / Hush-a-bye. *(cd-iss. Dec92 as 'NOW' on 'Kenwest'; SPCD 352)*

May 84. (7"; by SPENCER DAVIS & DUSTY SPRINGFIELD) *(ALES 3)* **PRIVATE NUMBER. / DON'T WANT YOU NO MORE** [ ] [–]

— SPENCER became an executive at Island records in the mid 70's. In mid-80's, **SPENCER DAVIS BAND** reformed with others **DON KIRKPATRICK, EDDIE TREE** – guitars / **RICK SERATTE** – keys / **CHARLIE HARRISON** – bass / **BRYAN HITT** – drums (ex-WANG CHUNG)

In Akustik not iss.

1988. (cd; as SPENCER DAVIS with PETE YORK & COLIN HODGKINSON) *(INAK 8410)* **LIVE TOGETHER** (rec.1984) [ ] [–]
– Keep on running / Midnight special / Walking blue / Mistakes / Sliding delta / I'm a man / Crossfire / Blood runs hot / Trouble in mind / Somebody help me / Don't leave me / Tulsa time / Gimme some lovin' / Muddy waters. *(re-iss. Mar95 & Jul00; same)*

1988. (cd) *(INAK 8590CD)* **24 HOURS – LIVE IN GERMANY** (rec.1985) [ ] [–]
– Twenty four hours / Lady cop / Sensitive kind / The Moon is a harsh mistress / On the green line / Pockey way / I'll take your love / Don't want you no more / Strong love / Route 66 / Easy rider / Knock on your door / Spiral times. *(re-iss. Mar95 & Jul00; same)*

– (selective) compilations, etc. –

Mar 68. (lp; mono/stereo) *Island; (ILP/+S 9070)* **THE BEST OF THE SPENCER DAVIS GROUP FEATURING STEVIE WINWOOD** [ ] [–]
(re-iss. Oct86; same) (cd-iss. May88; CID 9070) (re-iss. cd Mar93; IMCD 151)

Mar 68. (lp) *United Artists; <UAS 6641>* **SPENCER DAVIS' GREATEST HITS** [–] [ ]

1971. (lp) *Date; <4021>* **FUNKY** (US shelved LP) [–] [ ]
– I met a woman / Letter from Edith / Raintree river / What a way to die / Funky / Magical day / I guess I'm wasting my time / Poor misguided woman / And the gods came down / New Jersey turnpike. *(cd-iss. Jul02 on 'Angel Air'+=; SJPCD 021)* – With their new face on / Time seller / Feel your way / Taking out time / Mr. Second class / After tea / Groove extra / Moonshine / The girls song / Aquarius – Let the sunshine in / Dust my blues (live).

Jun 94. (cd) *R.P.M.; (RPMCD 127)* **TAKING OUT TIME 1967-69** [ ] [–]

Jun 95. (cd) *R.P.M.; (RPMCD 150)* **CATCH YOU ON THE REBOP – LIVE IN EUROPE 1973** [ ] [–]

Mar 96. (d-cd) *Island Chronicles; (CRNCD 5)* **EIGHT GIGS A WEEK – THE STEVE WINWOOD YEARS** [ ] [–]

Jun 99. (d-cd) *Eagle; (EDMCD 88)* **THE MASTERS** [ ] [–]

Jan 00. (cd) *Universal; (E 546252-2)* **UNIVERSAL MASTERS COLLECTION**
Aug 00. (cd) *R.P.M.; (RPM 207)* **MOJO RHYTHMS & MIDNIGHT BLUES – THE LIVE ALBUM VOL.1: SESSIONS 1965-1968**
Nov 00. (cd) *R.P.M.; (RPM 216)* **MOJO RHYTHMS & MIDNIGHT BLUES – THE LIVE ALBUM VOL.2: SHOWS 1965-1968**
May 02. (cd+cd-rom) *R.P.M.; (RPM 508)* **TIME SELLER**
Nov 02. (cd) *Purple; (PUR 329)* **LIVE IN EUROPE 1973**
Feb 03. (cd) *R.P.M.; (RPM 188)* **MULBURRY BUSH**
Mar 03. (cd) *Spectrum; (544974-2)* **THE COLLECTION**

☐ John DEACON (see under ⇒ QUEEN)

DEACON BLUE

Formed: Glasgow, Scotland ... 1985 by former remedial teacher, RICKY ROSS, who recruited JAMES PRIME, GRAEME KELLING, EWEN VERNAL and DOUGIE VIPOND: by sheer accident/inspiration, ROSS invited girlfriend, LORRAINE to sing/accompany his vocals and she soon became the sixth member. Subsequently signed to 'C.B.S.' by their manager, MUFF WINWOOD (ex-SPENCER DAVIS GROUP), the band released their debut single, 'DIGNITY', in Spring '87. A tale of working class pride, the song reflected DEACON BLUE's inherent politicism (although they were hardly The REDSKINS) while the slightly jazzy pop/rock dynamics of the music came as little surprise bearing in mind the group took their name from a STEELY DAN song. The debut album, 'RAINTOWN', followed a few months later, a promising set of soulful Celtic pop which suggested a more solid, less flighty PREFAB SPROUT. The melancholy ebb and flow of 'CHOCOLATE GIRL' was DEACON BLUE at their laidback best, the track a minor hit in summer '88 following similar low-key chart success for a re-issued 'DIGNITY' and 'WHEN WILL YOU (MAKE MY TELEPHONE RING)'. It was the anthemic 'REAL GONE KID', however, which took the band from the fringes of the Scottish scene into the hearts of the mainstream pop market, the song's infectious keyboard hook and girly harmonies seeing it reach the Top 10 in October '88. Trailed by the Top 20 success of 'WAGES DAY', a second album, 'WHEN THE WORLD KNOWS YOUR NAME', topped the UK album charts the following Spring; perhaps they'd been afflicted by SIMPLE MINDS syndrome, as the cool subtletly which had characterised their first release was replaced with a heavy dose of stadium-friendly bombast. Presumably as a reaction to such critical rumblings, DEACON BLUE opted to release an EP of BACHARACH & DAVID covers in summer '90, its Top 5 success closely followed by a B-sides/rarities affair, 'OOH LAS VEGAS' (1990). A follow-up proper, 'FELLOW HOODLUMS' (1991), was another major success although it failed to convince their detractors, and roping in dance bod production duo, Paul Oakenfold/Steve Osbourne, for 'WHATEVER YOU SAY, SAY NOTHING' (1993), smacked of desperation. A split finally came the following year, DEACON BLUE bowing out with a No.1 greatest hits set, and fittingly, with a third-time-lucky success for the superior 'DIGNITY'. While VIPOND went on to be a presenter on STV and Radio Scotland, ROSS worked with ex-STEELY DAN sessioner, JEFF 'SKUNK' BAXTER amongst others on a debut solo set, 'WHAT YOU ARE' (1996) – (ROSS also played 'T In The Park' that year). He issued his slightly disappointing solo album 'THIS IS THE LIFE' in 2002, which sounded almost exactly like DEACON's earlier works, although with a modern spin. Who would've thought such a pop icon could've been so heavily influenced by OASIS? Well, the evidence was all there; 'THREATENING RAIN' and 'RODEO BOY' all cranked up the stadium rock guitars, matched with accompanying pianos and BEATLES-esque riffs. Opener 'NORTHERN SOUL' drifted into the rest of the album, hiding like a musical chameleon behind ROSS's mournful ballads and playful pop tinkerings. • **Songwriters:** All written by ROSS, except covers ANGELIOU (Van Morrison) / TRAMPOLENE (Julian Cope) / I'M DOWN (Beatles).

Album rating: RAINTOWN (*7) / WHEN THE WORLD KNOWS YOUR NAME (*7) / OOH LAS VEGAS collection (*6) / FELLOW HOODLUMS (*5) / WHATVER YOU SAY, SAY NOTHING (*5) / OUR TOWN – THE GREATEST HITS compilation (**8**) / WALKING BACK HOME (*4) / THE VERY BEST OF DEACON BLUE double compilation (*8) / Ricky Ross: WHAT YOU ARE (*5) / THIS IS THE LIFE (*5)

RICKY ROSS (b.22 Dec'57, Dundee) – vocals / **JAMES PRIME** (b. 3 Nov'60, Kilmarnock) – keyboards (ex-ALTERED IMAGES) / **GRAEME KELLING** (b. 4 Apr'57, Paisley) – guitar / **EWEN VERNAL** (b.27 Feb'64, Glasgow) – bass, keyboard bass / **DOUGIE VIPOND** (b.15 Oct'66, Johnstone) – drums, percussion / **LORRAINE McINTOSH** (b.13 May'64, Glasgow) – vocals

C.B.S. Columbia

Mar 87. (7") *(DEAC 1) <07755>* **DIGNITY. / RICHES**
(with free c-s+=) – (excerpts 'RAINTOWN' lp)
(12"+=) *(DEAC T1)* – Ribbons and bows.

May 87. (lp/c/cd) *(450549-1/-4/-2)* **RAINTOWN** –
– Born in a storm / Raintown / Ragman / He looks like Spencer Tracy now / Loaded / When will you (make my telephone ring) / Chocolate girl / Dignity / The very thing / Love's great fears / Town to be blamed. *(re-dist.Feb88; same); hit UK No.14) (re-packaged Aug88 free with above lp+c)* **RICHES** *(XPR 1361)* – Which side are you on / King of the western world * / Riches * / Angeliou / Just like boys / Raintown / Church / Suffering / Shifting sand / Ribbons and bows / Dignity. *(cd+= *) (re-iss. Jul98 cd/c; 450549-2/-4)*

Jun 87. (7") *(DEAC 2)* **LOADED. / LONG DISTANCE FROM ACROSS THE ROAD** –
(c-s+=/ext.12"+=) *(DEAC C/T 2)* – Which side of the world are you on / Kings of the western world.

Aug 87. (7") *(DEAC 3)* **WHEN WILL YOU (MAKE MY TELEPHONE RING). / CHURCH** –
(12"+=) *(DEAC T3)* – A town to be blamed (live) / Angeliou (live).

Jan 88. (7") *(DEAC 4)* **DIGNITY. / SUFFERING** 31 –
(10"+=) *(DEAC Q4)* – Shifting sand.
(cd-s++=) *(CDDEAC 4)* – Just like boys.
(7"ep+=) *(DEAC EP4)* – Ronnie Spector / Raintown (piano).
(ext.12"+=) *(DEAC T4)* – Ronnie Spector / Just like boys.

Mar 88. (7"/7"box) *(DEAC 5)* **WHEN WILL YOU (MAKE MY TELEPHONE RING). / THAT BRILLIANT FEELING** 34 –
(12"+=/cd-s+=/pic-cd-s+=) *(DEACT/CDDEAC/CPDEAC 5)* – Punch and Judy man / Disneyworld.

Apr 88. (7") *<07954>* **WHEN WILL YOU (MAKE MY TELEPHONE RING). / TOWN TO BE BLAMED** –

Jul 88. (7") *(DEAC 6)* **CHOCOLATE GIRL. / S.H.A.R.O.N.** 43 –
(12"+=) *(DEAC T6)* – Love's great fears (live) / Dignity (live).
(7"ep+=/cd-s+=) *(DEACEP/CDDEAC 6)* – The very thing / Love's great fears.

Oct 88. (7") *(DEAC 7) <068944>* **REAL GONE KID. / LITTLE LINCOLN** 8
(12"+=/12"w-poster+=) *(DEAC/+Q T7)* – ('A'extended).
(7"ep+=/cd-s+=) *(DEACEP/CDDEAC 7)* – Born again / It's not funny anymore.

Feb 89. (7"/s7") *(DEAC/+Q 8)* **WAGES DAY. / TAKE ME TO THE PLACE** 18 –
(12"+=) *(DEAC T8)* – ('A'extended).
(7"ep+=/cd-s+=) *(DEACEP/CDDEAC 8)* – Take the saints away / Trampolene.

Apr 89. (lp/c/cd) *(463321-1/-4/-2)* **WHEN THE WORLD KNOWS YOUR NAME** 1 –
– Queen of the New Year / Wages day / Real gone kid / Love and regret / Circus lights / This changing light / Fergus sings the blues / Sad loved girl / The world is hit by lightning / Silhouette / One hundred things / Your constant heart / Orphans. *(re-iss. Jul98 cd/c; 463321-2/-4)*

May 89. (7"/7"box) *(DEAC/+B 9)* **FERGUS SINGS THE BLUES. / LONG WINDOW TO LOVE** 14 –
(12"+=/12"g-f+=) *(DEAC/+G T9)* – ('A'extended).

(ext.c-ep+=) *(DEAC C9)* – London A to Z.
(10"+=/cd-ep+=) *(DEAC QT/CD DEAC 9)* – London A to Z / Back here in Beano land.

Sep 89. (7"/c-s) *(DEAC/+M 10)* **LOVE AND REGRET. / DOWN IN THE FLOOD** [28] [–]
(cd-s+=) *(CDDEAC 10)* – Undeveloped heart / ('A'extended).
(ext.12"+=) *(DEAC T10)* – Undeveloped heart.
(10"/cd-s) *(DEAC QT/CD DEAC 10)* – ('A'live) / Spanish moon – Down in the flood (live) / Dark end of the street (live) / When will you (make my telephone ring) (live).

Dec 89. (7"/c-s) *(DEAC/+M 11)* **QUEEN OF THE NEW YEAR. / MY AMERICA** [21] [–]
(12"+=) *(DEACT 11)* – ('A'extended) / Circus lights (acoustic).
(7"ep+=/cd-ep+=) *(DEAC EP/CD DEAC 11)* – Sad loved girl (extended) / Las Vegas.
(c-s/12") *(DEAC QM/DEAC QT 11)* – ('A'live) / Chocolate girl (live) / Undeveloped heart (live) / A town to be blamed (live).

Aug 90. (7"ep/12"ep/cd-ep) *(DEAC/+T/CD 12)* **FOUR BACHARACH AND DAVID SONGS** [2] [–]
– I'll never fall in love again / The look of love / Message to Michael / Are you there (with another girl).

Sep 90. (d-cd/c/d-lp) *(467 242-2/-4/-1)* **OOH LAS VEGAS** (B-sides, sessions) [3] [–]
– Disneyworld / Ronnie Spector / My America / S.H.A.R.O.N. / Undeveloped heart / Souvenirs / Born again / Down in the flood / Back here in Beanoland / Love you say / Let your hearts be troubled/ / Gentle teardrops / Little Lincoln / That country / Is it cold beneath the hill? / Circus lights / Trampolene / Las Vegas / Killing the blues / Long window to love / Christine / Take me to the place / Don't let the teardrops start.

Columbia Columbia

May 91. (7"/c-s) *(656 893-7/-4)* **YOUR SWAYING ARMS. / FOURTEEN YEARS** [23] [–]
(cd-s+=) *(656 893-2)* – Faifley.
(12"++=) *(656 893-6)* – ('A'extended).
(10") *(656 893-0)* – ('A'-12"alternative mix) / ('A'-Drumapella mix) / ('A'-7"mix) / ('A'-dub mix).

Jun 91. (cd/c/lp) *(468 550-2/-4/-1)* **FELLOW HOODLUMS** [2] [–]
– James Joyce soles / Fellow hoodlums / Your swaying arms / Cover from the sky / The day that Jackie jumped the jail / The wildness / A brighter star than you will shine / Twist and shout / Closing time / Goodnight Jamsie / I will see you tomorrow / One day I'll go walking. *(cd/md re-iss. Aug98;* **468550-2/-3)**

Jul 91. (7"/c-s) *(657 302-7/-4)* **TWIST & SHOUT. / GOOD** [10] [–]
(12"+=) *(657 302-6)* – ('A'extended) / I'm down.
(cd-s+=) *(657 302-2)* – Golden bells.

Oct 91. (7"/c-s) *(657 502-7/-4)* **CLOSING TIME. / I WAS LIKE THAT** [42] [ ]
(cd-s+=) *(657 502-2)* – Into the good night.
(12"++=) *(657 502-6)* – Friends of Billy the bear.

Dec 91. (7"/c-s) *(657 673-7/-4)* **COVER FROM THE SKY. / WHAT DO YOU WANT THE GIRL TO DO / CHRISTMAS (BABY PLEASE COME HOME)** [31] [–]
(12"+=) *(657 673-6)* – Real gone kid / Loaded / One hundred things.
(cd-s+=) *(657 673-2)* – Wild mountain thyme / Silhouette / I'll never fall in love again.

Columbia Sony

Nov 92. (7"/c-s) *(658 786-7/-4)* **YOUR TOWN. / ALMOST BEAUTIFUL** [14] [–]
(cd-s+=) *(658 786-2)* – I've been making such a fool.
(12") *(658 786-6)* – ('A'-Perfecto mix) / ('A'extended).

Feb 93. (7"/c-s) *(658 973-2/-4)* **WILL WE BE LOVERS. / SLEEPER** [31] [ ]
(cd-s+=) *(658 973-2)* – Paint it red.
(12") *(658 973-6)* – ('A'side) / (4 other A-mixes).

Mar 93. (cd/c/lp) *(473 527-2/-4/-1)* **WHATEVER YOU SAY, SAY NOTHING** [4] [–]
– Your town / Only tender love / Peace and jobs and freedom / Hang your head / Bethlehem's gate / Last night I Dreamed of Henry Thomas / Will we be lovers / Fall so freely down / Cut lip / All over the world. *(cd/md re-iss. Jan99; 473527-2/-3)*

Apr 93. (7"/c-s) *(659 184-7/-4)* **ONLY TENDER LOVE. / RICHES** [22] [–]
(cd-s+=) *(659 184-2)* – Which side are you on? / Shifting sand.
(12") *(659 184-6)* – ('A'side) / Pimp talking / Cracks you up.
(cd-s) *(659 184-5) – (above 3) / Your town (Perfecto mix).*

Jul 93. (c-ep/cd-ep) *(659 460-4/-2)* **HANG YOUR HEAD EP** [21] [–]
– Hang your head – freedom train (live) / Here on the wind / Indigo sky.
(cd-ep) *(659 460-5)* – (1st track) / Ribbons & bows / Just like boys / Church.

Mar 94. (7"/c-s) *(660 222-7/-4)* **I WAS RIGHT AND YOU WERE WRONG. / MEXICAN RAIN** [32] [–]
(cd-s+=) *(660 222-2)* – Goin' back / Wages day.
(cd-s) *(660 222-5)* – ('A'extended) / Kings of the western world / Suffering / Raintown (piano version).

Apr 94. (cd/c/d-lp) *(476 642-2/-4/-1)* **OUR TOWN – THE GREATEST HITS** (compilation) [1] [–]
– Dignity / Wages day / Real gone kid / Your swaying arms / Fergus sings the blues / I was right and you were wrong / Chocolate girl / I'll never fall in love again / When will you (make my telephone ring) / Twist and shout / Your town / Queen of the New Year / Only tender love / Cover from the sky / Love and regrets / Will we be lovers / Loaded / Bound to love / Still in the mood. *(d-lp+=)* – Beautiful stranger. *(cd/md re-iss. Aug00; 476642-2/-3)*

May 94. (7"/c-s) *(6604485-7/-4)* **DIGNITY. / BEAUTIFUL STRANGER** [20] [–]
(cd-s+=) *(660448-2)* – Waves of sorrow / Bethlehem's gate.
(cd-s) *(660448-5)* – ('A'side) / Fergus sings the blues (live) / Loaded (live) / Chocolate girl (live).

—— disbanded after above release and ROSS went solo. VIPOND had already secured a regular spot on a Scottish sporty TV programme (Sportscene, etc) and joined the SWISS FAMILY ORBISON along with KIT CLARK (ex-DANNY WILSON), EWEN joined the BRIAN KELLOCK TRIO, TOMMY SMITH and the NIGEL CLARK QUINTET.

RICKY ROSS

—— - vocals, guitar, piano; with **JEFF 'Skunk' BAXTER** – guitars / **MARK HARRIS** – bass / **SCOTT CRAGO** – drums / + other guests

Columbia Sony

May 96. (c-s/cd-s) *(663 135-4/-2)* **RADIO ON / DARK WEATHER / JOE / MY FRIEND TONIGHT** [35] [–]
(cd-s) *(663 135-5)* – ('A'side) / Death work song / Never always / Always alone.

Jun 96. (cd/c) *(483998-2/-4)* **WHAT YOU ARE** [36] [–]
– Good evening Philadelphia / Icarus / Cold Easter / What you are / Radio on / When sinners fall / Jack Singer / The lovers / Wake up and dream / Rosie Gordon lies so still / Promise you rain / Love isn't hard it's strong.

Jul 96. (c-s) *(663 533-4)* **GOOD EVENING PHILADELPHIA / ('A'live)** [58] [–]
(cd-s) *(663 533-5)* – ('A'side) / Radio on (live) / Icarus (live) / Rosie Gordon lies so still (demo).
(cd-s) *(663 533-2)* – ('A'side) / In the pines / The river is wide / Shake some action.

Internationale not iss.

Oct 97. (cd) *(INTER 001)* **NEW RECORDING** [ ] [–]
– My only tie / Blue horse / The further north you go / The undeveloped heart / Cresswell Street / I love you / Earth a little lighter / I'm sure Buddy would know / Here's singer / On the line / Ash Wednesday.

Mar 98. (cd-ep) *(INTER 002)* **THE UNDEVELOPED HEART EP** [ ] [–]
– The undeveloped heart ('98 remix) / Ghost / Wake up and dream / Passing through / Only love remains.

DEACON BLUE

—— re-formed with the original members

Columbia not iss.

Oct 99. (cd/c) *(496380-2/-4)* **WALKING BACK HOME** (old & new songs) [39] [–]
– Love hurts / Jesus do your hands still feel the rain / The very thing / The day that Jackie jumped the jail / Love and regret / Christmas and Glasgow / The wildness / When you are young / Love's great fears / Chocolate girl / Plastic shoes / A brighter star than you will shine / Beautiful stranger / All I want / When will you (make my telephone ring) / Walking back home / I'll never fall in love again.

Papillion not iss.

Apr 01. (cd-s) *(BTFLYS 0011)* **EVERYTIME YOU SLEEP / HEY CRAIG / WHEN YOU WERE A BOY YOU WERE A BEAUTIFUL BOY** [64] [–]
(cd-s) *(BTFLYX 0011)* – ('A'side) / Twist and shout (live) / Cover from the sky (live)

Apr 01. (cd) *(BTFLYCD 0014)* **HOMESICK** [59] [–]
– Rae / Out there / This train will take you anywhere / Everytime you sleep / Now that you're here / Silver lake / A is for astronaut / You lie so beautifully still / Homesick / Even higher ground / I am born.

Jun 01. (cd-s) *(BTFLYS 0018)* **A IS FOR ASTRONAUT / PEACE AND JOBS AND FREEDOM (live) / TOWN TO BE BLAMED (live)** ☐ ☐-

– compilations, etc. –

on 'Columbia' unless mentioned otherwise

Feb 97. (cd) *(487147-2)* **RICHES AND MORE** ☐ ☐-

Sep 00. (d-cd) *(499927-2)* **RAINTOWN / WHEN THE WORLD KNOWS YOUR NAME** ☐ ☐-
(re-iss. Dec02; same)

Nov 01. (d-cd) *(504978-2)* **THE VERY BEST OF DEACON BLUE** ☐ ☐-

RICKY ROSS

Papillion not iss.

Apr 02. (cd) *(BTFLYCD 0021)* **THIS IS THE LIFE** ☐ ☐-
– Northern soul / London comes alive / Rodeo boy / Angel and Mercedes / I sing about you / Nothing cures that / This is the life / Threatening rain / Starring love / Hippy girl / My girl going to town / Looking for my own Lone Ranger / Way to work.

DEAD CAN DANCE

Formed: Melbourne, Australia . . . 1981 by multi-instrumentalist, BRENDAN PERRY (ex-MARCHING GIRLS) and vocalist, LISA GERRARD, both of Anglo-Irish parentage. After initially immersing himself in the punk scene, PERRY became increasingly intrigued by the possibilities offered by electronic music, subsequently hooking up with GERRARD and two other early members, PAUL ERIKSON and SIMON MONROE. With a solitary homeland recording (very limited for 'Fast Forward' cassette mag) to their name, PERRY and GERRARD decided to take DEAD CAN DANCE to London where they fitted in perfectly among the avant-garde hopefuls at up and coming indie label, '4 a.d.'. At pains to point out that their name symbolised the energy inherent in apparently lifeless matter rather than the goth connotations many assumed, DEAD CAN DANCE were soon mesmerising critics and fans alike with their otherworldly synthesis of classical, ethnic and electronic music. An eponymous debut album emerged in 1984 and although its noisy dissonance only hinted at the sculpted aesthetics to come, highlights included 'A PASSAGE IN TIME', 'THE TRIAL' and 'THE FATAL IMPACT'. However, with a costly 15-piece ensemble in tow, they only selected a few venues for concerts and never toured consistently. 1985's 'SPLEEN AND IDEAL' was a more atmospheric, darkly intoxicating affair, introducing more varied instrumental textures and the wailing Middle Eastern, OFRA HAZA-style vocals of GERRARD on such compulsive tracks as 'THE CARDINAL SIN', 'MESMERISM' and every monk's favourite, 'DE PROFUNDIS (OUT OF THE DEPTHS OF SORROW)'. 'WITHIN THE REALM OF A DYING SUN' (1987) moved towards classical territory with a cast of violin, viola, etc, while 'SERPENT'S EGG' (1988) tackled medieval folk styles of Eastern Europe. PERRY and GERRARD moved even further into the past (or rather brought the past into the future) with their exploration of Renaissance era music – both spiritual and secular – on 1990's 'AION'. The early 90's found PERRY and GERRARD working on a variety of side projects including scoring music for a production of 'Oedipus Rex' and the soundtrack to the movie, 'Baraka'. DEAD CAN DANCE briefly emerged from the realm of cult obscurity and into the Top 50 (also hovered under the US Top 100) in 1993 with their seventh album, 'INTO THE LABYRINTH'. LISA went on to release a few solo outings, one under the pseudonym of ELIJAH'S MANTLE, while DEAD CAN DANCE managed to capture the mystical allure of their studio work on live set, 'TOWARD THE WITHIN' (1994). With 1995's 'SPIRITCHASER', DEAD CAN DANCE nearly cracked the UK Top 40 while making the US Top 75, a mark of burgeoning popular appeal for a band who were already almost universally respected among fellow artists across the musical spectrum. DEAD CAN DANCE had been keeping uncharacteristically quiet, although LISA GERRARD (who'd debuted solo in 1995 with 'THE MIRROR POOL') released a collaborative set with PETER BOURKE (of SOMA) entitled 'DUALITY' (1998). Towards the end of the decade and with DCD now defunct, it would be BRENDAN's turn to go single-handed. 'EYE OF THE HUNTER' was a marked shift from his earlier goth-meets-baroque style rock in that he chose to virtually mimic his idols, SCOTT WALKER ('ARCHANGEL' & 'SATURDAY'S CHILD) and TIM BUCKLEY ('I MUST HAVE BEEN BLIND' – didn't he do this for '4ad' conglomerate THIS MORTAL COIL). However, the seriousness of his intentions came across quite well, although the world of opera might be getting ready for a new recruit – perhaps not! Inevitably perhaps, GERRARD's talent found a welcoming home in the world of film soundtracks, more specifically Ridley Scott's much praised 'Gladiator'. Co-writing with Hans Zimmer, the former DCD songstress was instrumental in shaping the film's wide ranging score; three years later '4 a.d.' released the score to the movie 'WHALE RIDER'. • **Songwriters:** GERRARD / PERRY (some w/ others and some trad folk samples). • **Trivia:** They also can be heard on '4 a.d.' amalgam THIS MORTAL COIL and also featured two tracks on various lp, 'Lonely As An Eyesore'.

Album rating: DEAD CAN DANCE (*7) / SPLEEN AND IDEAL (*6) / WITHIN THE REALM OF A DYING SUN (*8) / THE SERPENT'S EGG (*7) / AION (*8) / A PASSAGE IN TIME compilation (*8) / INTO THE LABYRINTH (*7) / TOWARD THE WITHIN (*6) / SPIRITCHASER (*6) / WAKE – BEST OF . . . compilation (*7) / Lisa Gerrard: THE MIRROR POOL (*6) / DUALITY with Peter Bourke (*6) / GLADIATOR with Hans Zimmer (*7) / WHALE RIDER (*5) / Brendan Perry: EYE OF THE HUNTER (*6)

BRENDAN PERRY – multi-instrumentalist, vocals (ex-SCAVENGERS, ex-MARCHING GIRLS) / **LISA GERRARD** – vocals, percussion / **PETER ULRICH** – percussion, drums, tapes with **JAMES PINKER** – timpani, mixer / **SIMON RODGER** – trombone; plus **MARTIN McCARRICK** + **GUY FERGUSON** – cello / **CAROLYN LOSTIN** – violin / **RICHARD AVISON** – trombone / **TONY AYERS** – timpani / **ANDREW NUTTER** – soprano vox

4 a.d. Rough Trade

Feb 84. (lp) *(CAD 404)* **DEAD CAN DANCE** ☐ ☐-
– The fatal impact / The trial / Frontier / Fortune / Ocean / East of Eden / Threshold / A passage in time / Wild in the woods / Musica eternal. *(cd-iss. Feb87; CAD 404CD)* – (includes below EP). *<US-iss.1994 on '4 a.d.-Reprise' cd,c; 45546>*

Sep 84. (12"ep) *(BAD 408)* **GARDEN OF ARCANE DELIGHTS** ☐ ☐-
– Carnival of light / In power we entrust the love advocated / The arcane / Flowers of the sea.

Nov 85. (lp/c)(cd) *(CAD/+C 512)(CAD 512CD)* **SPLEEN AND IDEAL** ☐ ☐-
– De profundis (out of the depths of sorrow) / Ascension / Circum radiant dawn / The cardinal sin / Mesmerism / Enigma of the absolute / Advent / Avatar / Indoctrination (a design for living). *(cd+=)* – This tide. *<US-iss.1994 on '4 a.d.-Reprise' cd,c; 45547>*

—— now a basic duo of **BRENDAN** + **LISA** when ULRICH departed (SIMON + JAMES formed HEAVENLY BODIES). Retained **FERGUSON** + **AVISON** and recruited **ALISON HARLING** + **EMLYN SINGLETON** – violin / **PIERO GASPARINI** – viola / **TONY GAMMAGE** + **MARK GERRARD** (bother) – trumpet / **RUTH WATSON** – oboe, bass trombone / **JOHN** + **PETER SINGLETON** – trombone / **ANDREW CAXTON** – tuba, bass trombone

Jul 87. (lp/c)(cd) *(CAD/+C 705)(CAD 705CD)* **WITHIN THE REALM OF A DYING SUN** ☐ ☐-
– Anywhere out of the world / Windfall / In the wake of adversity / Xavier / Dawn of the iconoclast / Cantara / Summoning of the muse / Persephone (the gathering of flowers). *<US-iss.1994 on '4 a.d.-Reprise' cd,c; 45577>*

— **LISA + BRENDAN** brought in **DAVID NAVARRO SUST** (retained **ALISON + TONY**), new **REBECCA JACKSON** – violin / **SARAH BUCKLEY + ANDREW BEESLEY** – violas

Oct 88. (lp/c)(cd) *(CAD/+C 808)(CAD 808CD)* **THE SERPENT'S EGG** ☐ ☐-
– The host of Seraphim / Orbis de Ignis / Severance / Chant of the Paladin / The writing on my father's hand / Echolalia / In the kingdom of the blind, the one-eyed are kings / Song of Sophia / Mother tongue / Ullysses. *<US-ss.1994 on '4 a.d.-Reprise' cd,c; 45576>*

Jul 90. (cd)(lp/c) *(CAD 0007CD)(CAD/+C 0007)* **AION** ☐ ☐-
– The arrival and the reunion / Saltarello / Mephisto / The song of the Sibyl / Fortune presents gifts not according to the book / As the bell rings the maypole spins / The end of words / Black sun / Wilderness / The promised womb / The garden of Zephirus / Radharc. *<US-iss.1994 on '4 a.d.-Reprise' cd,c; 45575>*

Sep 93. (cd)(c)(d-lp) *(CAD 3013CD)(CADC 3013)(DAD 3013) <45384>* **INTO THE LABYRINTH** 47 ☐
– Yulunga (spirit dance) / The ubiquitous Mr. Lovegrove / The wind that shakes the barley / The carnival is over / Ariadne / Saldek / Towards the within / Tell me about the forest (you once called home) / The spider's Stratagem / Emmeleia / How fortunate the man with none. *(d-lp+=)* – Bird / Spirit.

Oct 94. (cd)(d-lp/c) *(DAD 4015CD)(DAD/+C 4015) <45769>* **TOWARD THE WITHIN** ☐ ☐
– Rakim / Persian love song / Desert song / Yulunga (spirit dance) / Piece for solo flute / The wind that shakes the barley / I am stretched on your grave / I can see now / American dreaming / Cantara / Oman / Song of the Sibyl / Tristan / Sanveen / Don't fade away.

Jun 96. (c/cd)(d-lp) *(CAD 6008/+CD)(DAD 6008) <46230>* **SPIRITCHASER** 43 75
– Nierika / Song of the stars / Indus / Song of the dispossessed / Dedicaci outr / The snake and the Moon / Song of the Nile / Devorzhum.

– compilations, etc. –

Oct 91. (cd)(c) *4 a.d.; (CAD 1010CD)(CADC 1010) / Rykodisc; <RCD2/RACS 0215>* **A PASSAGE IN TIME** (part compilation) ☐ ☐
– Salterello / Song of Sophia / Ullyses / Cantara / The garden of Zephirus / Enigma of the absolute / Wilderness / The host of Seraphim / Anywhere out of the world / The writing on my father's hand / Severance / The song of the Sibyl (traditional version; Catalan 16th Century) / Fortune presents gifts not according to the book / In the kingdom of the blind the one-eyed are kings / Bird / Spirit.

Dec 91. (cd) *Emperion; (IMP 008)* **THE HIDDEN TREASURES** (out-takes, live, rare) ☐ ☐-
– Awakening / Reached from above / In power we entrust the love advocated / To the shore / Alone / Pray for dawn / Lartomento / The night we were lost / Lyndra / Isabella / Tune for Sheba / Cyndrill / The serpent's army / They don't even cry / Eyeless in Gaza / The endless longing of sea doves.

Nov 01. (3xcd-box) *Rhino; <(DCDBOX 1)>* **DEAD CAN DANCE 1981-1998** ☐ ☐

May 03. (d-cd) *4 a.d.; (DAD 2303CD) <72303>* **WAKE: THE BEST OF . . .** ☐ ☐

LISA GERRARD

— with The VICTORIAN PHILHARMONIC ORCHESTRA. She had worked on the scores for 'Oedipus Rex' and 'Baraku', while sidelining with ELIJAH'S MANTLE.

Aug 95. (cd)(c) *(CAD 5009CD)(CADC 5009) <45916>* **THE MIRROR POOL** ☐ ☐
– Violina: The last embrace / La Bas: Song of the drowned / Persian love song: The silver gun / Sanvean: I am your shadow / The rite / Ajhon / Glorafin / Majhnavea's music box / Largo / Werd / Laurelei / Celon / Ventelas / Swans / Nilleshna / Gloradin. *(cd re-iss. Jul98; GAD 5009CD)*

— next a collaboration with **PETER BOURKE** (of SOMA)

Apr 98. (cd; by LISA GERRARD & PETER BOURKE) *(CAD 8004CD) <46854>* **DUALITY** ☐ ☐
– Shadow magnet / Tempest / Forest veil / The comforter / The unfolding / Pilgrimage of lost children / The human game / The circulation of shadows / Sacrifice / Nadir (synchronicity).

— in May'00, HANS ZIMMER & LISA GERRARD collaborated on the soundtrack to hit (& UK No.17 / US No.66) chart album of 'GLADIATOR'

Jul 03. (cd) *(CAD 2304CD) <72304>* **WHALE RIDER** (soundtrack) ☐ Jun03 ☐
– Paikea legend / Journey away / Rejection / Biking home / Ancestors / Suitcase / Pai calls the whales / Reiputa / Disappointed / They came to die / Pai theme / Paikea's whale / Empty water / Waka in the sky / Go forward.

BRENDAN PERRY

with various musicians

Oct 99. (lp/cd) *(<CAD 9015/+CD>)* **EYE OF THE TIGER** ☐ ☐
– Saturday's child / Voyage of bran / Medusa / Sloth / I must have been blind / The captive heart / Death will be my bride / Archangel.

DEAD KENNEDYS

Formed: San Francisco, California, USA . . . early 1978 by JELLO BIAFRA and EAST BAY RAY, who recruited KLAUS FLOURIDE, TED and briefly, the mysterious 6025. Inspired by British punk rock, BIAFRA formed The DEAD KENNEDYS primarily as a vehicle for his raging, razor-sharp satire of America and everything it stood for. Public enemy #1 from the off, major labels steered well clear of the band, BIAFRA and Co. subsequently forming their own label, the legendary 'Alternative Tentacles', releasing 'CALIFORNIA UBER ALLES' as their debut 45 in late '79. A scathing critique of California governor, Jerry Brown, the record introduced the singer's near-hysterical vocal undulations set against a pulverising punk/hardcore musical backdrop. Released on the independent 'Fast' imprint in Britain, the record's initial batch of copies sold like proverbial hotcakes. The 1980 follow-up, 'HOLIDAY IN CAMBODIA' (released on Miles Copeland's 'Faulty' label; 'Cherry Red' in the UK), remains The DEAD KENNEDYS' most viciously realised moment, a dark, twisting diatribe on American middle-class liberal trendies. Later in the year, the group kept up their aural assault with a debut album, 'FRESH FRUIT FOR ROTTING VEGETABLES', an unexpected Top 40 entry in the seemingly "Punk Is Dead" Britain, which contained the aforesaid 45's plus perennial favourites, 'LET'S LYNCH THE LANDLORD', 'DRUG ME' and the forthcoming UK hit, 'KILL THE POOR'. The record also offered a glimpse of BIAFRA's reassuringly twisted sense of humour in such surreal cuts as 'STEALING PEOPLE'S MAIL' and 'VIVA LAS VEGAS' (the latter was a hit for Elvis!). In 1981, drummer D.H. PELIGRO replaced TED, making his debut on the bluntly-titled 'TOO DRUNK TO FUCK', the only UK Top 40 charting single in musical history (up to that point!) to utilise the "f***" word. Once again mocking the inherent hypocrisy of corporate America, The DEAD KENNEDYS released a frenetic 10" mini-set, 'IN GOD WE TRUST INC.' (1981), highlights being the self-explanatory 'NAZI PUNKS FUCK OFF' (a US-only single) and a deadpan version of 'RAWHIDE'. The band then took a brief hiatus, busying themselves with an 'Alternative Tentacles' compilation of promising unsigned American bands, entitled 'Let Them Eat Jellybeans'. That same year (1982), the group released their second album proper, 'PLASTIC SURGERY DISASTERS'; issued on 'Statik' in the UK, it featured the singles 'BLEED FOR ME' and 'HALLOWEEN'. Spending the ensuing few years touring, the band resurfaced in 1985 with 'FRANKENCHRIST', an album that finally saw BIAFRA's upstanding enemies closing in (ie. the PMRC, the US government, etc) due to the album's free "penis landscape" poster by Swiss artist H.R. Giger. Although BIAFRA and Co. (including some senior label staff) were tried in court for distributing harmful material to minors (a revised obscenity law), the case was subsequently thrown out after a hung jury. Nevertheless, the cost of the trial effectively put the band out of business, The DEAD KENNEDYS poignantly-titled finale, 'BEDTIME FOR DEMOCRACY' being issued late in 1986. Although

KLAUS and RAY followed low-key solo careers, the ever-prolific BIAFRA vociferously protested against his treatment on spoken-word sets, 'NO MORE COCOONS' (1987) and 'THE HIGH PRIEST OF HARMFUL MATTER' (1989). He subsequently collaborated with a wide range of hardcore/industrial acts such as D.O.A., NO MEANS NO and TUMOR CIRCUS, although it was with LARD (a project with MINISTRY mainmen, AL JOURGENSEN and PAUL BARKER) that BIAFRA really came into his own. A late 80's mini-set, 'THE POWER OF LARD' preceded a full-length album, 'THE LAST TEMPTATION OF LARD', a minor UK hit early in 1990. This demented set included such hilarious BIAFRA monologues as 'CAN GOD FILL TEETH?' and even a rendition of Napolean XIV's 'THEY'RE COMING TO TAKE ME AWAY'. In 1994, he hooked up with another likeminded soul in hillbilly punk, MOJO NIXON, releasing one album, 'PRAIRIE HOME INVASION' (the title possibly a parody of an ICE-T album). BIAFRA continues to work at 'Alternative Tentacles', supplying the country with suitably deranged hardcore and occasionally taking time out for other projects, most recently a second LARD set, 'PURE CHEWING SATISFACTION' (1997). • **Trivia:** In 1979, BIAFRA stood in the elections for Mayor of San Francisco (he came 4th!).

Album rating: FRESH FRUIT FOR ROTTING VEGETABLES (*9) / IN GOD WE TRUST INC. mini (*5) / PLASTIC SURGERY DISASTERS (*6) / FRANKENCHRIST (*6) / BEDTIME FOR DEMOCRACY (*5) / GIVE ME CONVENIENCE OR GIVE ME DEATH compilation (*8) / Jello Biafra: NO MORE COCOONS spoken (*5) / HIGH PRIEST OF HARMFUL MATTER spoken (*5) / THE LAST TEMPTATION OF LARD with Lard (*6) / THE LAST SCREAM OF THE MISSING NEIGHBORS with D.O.A. (*6) / THE SKY IS FALLING AND I WANT MY MOMMY with No Means No (*5) / I BLOW MINDS FOR A LIVING (*6) / HIGH VOLTAGE CONSPIRACY FOR RADICAL FREEDOM with Tumor Circus (*5) / PRAIRIE HOME INVASION with Mojo Nixon (*6) / BEYOND THE VALLEY OF THE GIFT POLICE (*5) / PURE CHEWING SATISFACTION with Lard (*5) / BECOME THE MEDIA (*4) / IF EVOLUTION IS OUTLAWED, ONLY OUTLAWS WILL EVOLVE compilation (*6) / MACHINE GUN IN THE CLOWN'S HAND (*3)

JELLO BIAFRA (b. ERIC BOUCHER, 17 Jun'58, Boulder, Colorado) – vocals / **EAST BAY RAY** (b. RAY GLASSER, Castro Valley, California) – guitar, (synthesisers-later 80's) / **KLAUS FLUORIDE** (b. Detroit, Michigan) – bass, vocals / **BRUCE SLESINGER** (aka TED) – drums

Fast — Alternative Tentacles

Oct 79. (7") *(FAST 12)* <AT 95-41> **CALIFORNIA UBER ALLES. / MAN WITH THE DOGS**

Cherry Red — Faulty-IRS

Jun 80. (7")12" *(CHERRY/12CHERRY 13)* <IR 9016> **HOLIDAY IN CAMBODIA. / POLICE TRUCK**
(re-iss. 7"/cd-s Jun88 & Mar95; same)

Sep 80. (lp) *(B-RED 10)* <SP 70014> **FRESH FRUIT FOR ROTTING VEGETABLES** 33 Nov80
– Kill the poor / Forward to death / When ya get drafted / Let's lynch the landlord / Drug me / Your emotions / Chemical warfare / California uber alles / I kill children / Stealing people's mail / Funland at the beach / Ill in my head / Holiday in Cambodia / Viva Las Vegas. *(cd-iss. Nov87 & Mar95 & Sep01; CDBRED 10) (d-cd-iss. Sep01 +=; CDSBRED 155)* – (bonus tracks).

Oct 80. (7") *(CHERRY 16)* **KILL THE POOR. / IN SIGHT** 49 –
(re-iss. Nov87 & Mar95; CDCHERRY 16)

—— **D.H. PELIGRO** (b. DARREN, East St.Louis, Illinois) – drums; repl. BRUCE/TED

Cherry Red — Alternative Tentacles

May 81. (7"/12") *(CHERRY/12CHERRY 24)* <VIRUS 2> **TOO DRUNK TO FUCK. / THE PREY** 36
(re-iss. May88 & Mar95 cd-s; CDCHERRY 24)

Statik — Alternative Tentacles

Nov 81. (10"ep) *(STATEP 2)* <VIRUS 5> **IN GOD WE TRUST INC.**
– Religious vomit / Moral majority / Kepone factory / Dog bite / Nazi punks fuck off / We've got a bigger problem now / Rawhide. *<US c-ep+=; VIRUS 5C>* – Too drunk to fuck / The prey / Holiday in Cambodia. *(re-iss. Jun92 cd-ep; STATEP 2CD)*

Dec 81. (7") <VIRUS 6> **NAZI PUNKS FUCK OFF. / MORAL MAJORITY** –

Jul 82. (7"/12") *(STAT/+12 22)* <VIRUS 23> **BLEED FOR ME. / LIFE SENTENCE**
(cd-s Jun92; STAT 22CD)

Nov 82. (lp) *(STATLP 11)* **PLASTIC SURGERY DISASTERS** –
– Government flu / Terminal preppie / Trust your mechanic / Well paid scientist / Buzzbomb / Forest fire / Halloween / Winnebago warrior / Riot / Bleed for me / I am the owl / Dead end / Moon over Marin. *(re-iss. Oct85; same) (cd-iss. Nov86 & Jun92 & Jun98 +=; same)* – IN GOD WE TRUST INC. *(cd re-iss. Feb01 on 'Decay'+=; DKS 6/9CD)* – IN GOD WE TRUST INC.

Nov 82. (7"/12") *(STAT/+12 27)* <VIRUS 28> **HALLOWEEN. / SATURDAY NIGHT HOLOCAUST**
(cd-s Jun92; STAT 27CD)

—— meanwhile KLAUS and EAST BAY released solo singles (see below)

Alternative Tentacles — Alternative Tentacles

May 82. (12"; KLAUS FLUORIDE) <(VIRUS 12)> **SHORTNING BREAD. / DROWNING COWBOY**

Jun 84. (7"; EAST BAY RAY) <(VIRUS 34)> **TROUBLE IN TOWN. / POISON HEART**
(12 re-iss. Apr89 on 'New Rose' France; GMO 40)

Aug 84. (12"ep; KLAUS FLUORIDE) **CHA CHA CHA WITH MR. FLUORIDE** –
– Ghost riders / etc.

Dec 85. (lp) <(VIRUS 45)> **FRANKENCHRIST**
– Soup is good food / Hellnation / This could be anywhere (this could be everywhere) / A growing boy needs his lunch / Chicken farm / Macho-rama (invasion of the beef-patrol) / Goons of Hazzard / At my job / M.T.V. – Get off the air / Stars and stripes of corruption. *(cd-iss. 1986 & Jun98; VIRUS 45CD) (cd re-iss. Feb01 on 'Decay'; DKS 11CD)*

Dec 86. (lp/c/cd) <(VIRUS 50/+C/CD)> **BEDTIME FOR DEMOCRACY**
– Take this job and shove it / Hop with the jet set / Dear Abby / Rambozo the clown / Fleshdunce / The great wall / Shrink / Triumph of the swill / I spy / Macho insecurity / Cesspools in Eden / One-way ticket to Pluto / Do the slag / Gone with the wind / A commercial / Anarchy for sale / Chickenshit conformist / Where do ya draw the line / Potshot heard round the world / D.M.S.O. / Lie detector. *(cd re-iss. Jun98; same) (cd re-iss. Feb01 on 'Decay'; DKS 12CD)*

—— split December '86 when RAY departed (he subsequently turned up in SKRAPYARD). KLAUS FLUORIDE went solo, releasing albums 'BECAUSE I SAY SO' (1988) and 'THE LIGHT IS FLICKERING' (1991) and forming acoustic outfit FIVE YEAR PLAN

– compilations, etc. –

on 'Alternative Tentacles' unless mentioned otherwise

Jun 87. (lp/cd) <(VIRUS 57/+CD)> **GIVE ME CONVENIENCE OR GIVE ME DEATH** 84
– Police truck / Too drunk to f*** / California uber alles / Man with the dogs / In sight / Life sentence / A child and his lawnmower / Holiday in Cambodia / Night of the living rednecks / I fought the law / Saturday night holocaust / Pull my strings / Short songs / Straight A's / Kinky sex makes the world go round / The prey. *(cd+=/free flexi-disc)* – BUZZBOMB FROM PASADENA *(cd re-iss. Feb01 on 'Decay'; DKS 13CD)*

Jun 93. (7"ep) *Subterranean; (SUB 24)* **NAZI PUNKS **** OFF / ARYANISMS. / ('A'live) / CONTEMPTUOUS** –
(re-iss. Dec97 & Jul00; same)

Feb 01. (cd) *Decay; (DKS 14CD) / Manifesto; <42905>* **MUTINY ON THE BAY (live)** Apr01

☐ DEATH CULT (see under ⇒ CULT)

DEATH IN VEGAS

Formed: London, England . . . mid 90's by the production duo of RICHARD FEARLESS and STEVE HELLIER. The former was a public schoolboy and subsequently studied graphic design (and indie-rock for homework!) at art college before getting his act together at the Joy club. By the time DIV came to release distorted breakbeat singles like 'OPIUM SHUFFLE' (as DEAD ELVIS) and

'DIRT', FEARLESS was already a respected DJ at the capital's superhip Heavenly Social club (where The Chemical Brothers also made their name). After the underground success of their early releases, DIV became much in demand remixers for major labels desperate for a bit of street cred. After the techno-noir of their acclaimed debut album, 'DEAD ELVIS' (1997), the re-issues of 'DIRT' and 'ROCCO' managed Top 75 placings. Just prior to these, they had covered a BEAT hit, 'TWIST AND CRAWL', which featured RANKING ROGER of all guests(!). With the older and wiser TIM HOLMES (engineer on their debut LP) now in place of HELLIER, higher profile vocal contributors such as BOBBY GILLESPIE (of PRIMAL SCREAM), JIM REID (of the Jesus & Mary Chain), DOT ALLISON (ex-ONE DOVE) and IGGY POP were called upon – Scotland 3, the USA 1, you could say. 'THE CONTINO SESSIONS' – a name taken from the basement of their Clerkenwell (East London) studios – was unleashed in September '99, rave reviews from every music tabloid creating a stir for the dance-cum-goth album. A UK Top 20 pacesetter, the record and its pieces of 12"-only wonderments (i.e. 'DIRGE', 'NEPTUNE CITY' and 'AISHA') were crafted into shape like NEU! meeting FELT meeting the VELVET UNDERGROUND; a classic! Three years down the line, and with a bit of a middle Eastern feel, DEATH IN VEGAS issued the sometimes sublime and sometimes clumsy third effort 'SCORPIO RISING' (2002, lifted from experimental film maker Kenneth Anger's movie of the same name). A hotpotch of electronica, psychedelia and rock, the duo, as on 'THE CONTINO . . .' hauled in a eclectic bunch of guests ranging from the obvious – DOT ALLISON, MAZZY STAR – to the surprising – LIAM GALLAGHER, PAUL WELLER. What emerged was an interesting listen infusing instrumentals with more fuller, rounded songs. DR. SUBRANIAM lended his talented hand, playing, what sounds like, a sitar on the floaty windblown instrumental 'HELP YOURSELF', while SUSAN DILLANE of WOODBINE added some (s)ex-factor with her deep and wheezy vocals on the tracks '23 LIES' and 'GIRLS'. But its ADULT's NICOLA KUPERUS' stern headmistresss-esque vocals on single 'HANDS AROUND MY THROAT' that brought that all too familiar menace to the DIV mix.

Album rating: DEAD ELVIS (*8) / THE CONTINO SESSIONS (*9) / SCORPIO RISING (*7)

RICHARD FEARLESS (b. MAGUIRE, 1972, Zambia, Africa) – DJ, samples / **STEVE HELLIER** – producer / with guest **ANDY VISSER** – flute, sax (also on album)

Concrete Time Bomb

May 95. (12"; as DEAD ELVIS) *(HARD 6-12)* **OPIUM SHUFFLE (mixes)** [ ] [–]

— with guests **ANTHONY ANDERSON** – guitar / **MAT FLINT** – bass (both also on album)

Nov 95. (ltd-10") *(HARD 8-10)* **REMATERIALISED (dub mixes)** [ ] [–]

— bass by **NICK 'AVIN IT** (also on album)

Apr 96. (12") *(HARD 9-12)* **DIRT. / GBH (the original king stuffing) / GBH LIVE (the original king stuffing)** [ ] [–]
(10") *(HARD 9-10)* – Rematerialised dub 1 2 3 / GBH dub 1 2.

Oct 96. (12"/cd-s) *(HARD 14-12)* **ROCCO (dub) / ROCCO (Dave Clarke mix) / ROCCO (sing for a drink mix)** [ ] [–]
(cd-s+=) *(HARD 14CD)* – ('A'-drvrsiz edit).

Feb 97. (12") *(HARD 23-12)* **REKKIT (full mix). / I SPY** [ ] [–]
(cd-s+=) *(HARD 23CD)* – ('A'-radio mix) / ('A'-greetings from Lino Square).
(12") *(HARD 23-12X)* – Death by a thousand cuts (remixes by Two Lone Swordsmen; greetings from Lino Square / effective machine / short jacking / vega sintro).

— other guests **SELAH** – vocals / **SEAMUS BEAGHAN** – hammond organ / **TIM WELLER** – drums / **JONATHAN HAINES** – strings / **PAUL RUTHERFORD** – trombone

Mar 97. (cd/d-lp) *(HARD 22 LPCD/LP12)* <43511> **DEAD ELVIS** [52] Sep97 [ ]
– All that glitters / Opium shuffle / GBH / Dirt / Rocco / Rekkit / I spy / 68 balcony. *(cd+=)* – Amber / Rematerialised / 68 balcony / Sly.

Apr 97. (12") *(HARD 26-12)* **TWIST AND CRAWL (featuring RANKING ROGER). / TWIST AND CRAWL (dub version) / OPIUM SHUFFLE (Monkey Mafia mix)** [ ] [–]
(cd-s+=) *(HARD 26CD)* – Opium shuffle (album version).

Jul 97. (12") *(HARD 27-12)* <47520> **DIRT (mixes; Slayer / original album / Mullet) / ROCCO (Dave Clarke mix)** [61] [ ]
(cd-s+=) *(HARD 27CD)* – ('A'Slayer edit).

Oct 97. (12"ep/cd-ep) *(HARD 29-12/-CD)* **ROCCO / DR. CLEAN. / CITY RUB / CLAIMING MARILYN** [51] [–]
(cd-s) *(HARD 29CDX)* – ('A'-album version) / City rub (Tim's rub) / ('A'-Dave Clarke remix).

— **TIM HOLMES** (the engineer) repl. HELLIER

Jul 99. (ltd-12") *(HARD 39-12)* **DIRGE. / LUTHER'S FUNK** [—] [–]

Sep 99. (cd/c/d-lp) *(HARD 41 CD/MC/LP)* <43521> **THE CONTINO SESSIONS** [19] [ ]
– Dirge (with DOT ALLISON) / Soul auctioneer (with BOBBY GILLESPIE) / Death threat / Flying / Aisha (with IGGY POP) / Lever street / Aladdin's story / Broken little sister (with JIM REID) / Neptune city.

Oct 99. (ltd-12") *(YAWNING 1)* **BLOOD YAWNING** [ ] [–]

Nov 99. (12"/cd-s) *(HARD 40 12/CD)* **NEPTUNE CITY. / BLOOD YAWNING** [—] [ ]

Jan 00. (cd-s) *(HARD 43CD1)* **AISHA / FLYING (live) / LUTHER'S FUNK** [9] [–]
(12") *(HARD 43-12)* – ('A'side) / ('A'-Trevor Jackson nightclubbing instrumental mix) / ('A'-Trevor Jackson nightclubbing mix).
(cd-s) *(HARD 43CD2)* – ('A'edit) / ('A'-Trevor Jackson nightclubbing mix) / Neptune city (Two lone Swordsmen Concrete funk mix) / ('A'-video).

Apr 00. (12"/cd-s) *(HARD 44 12/CD1)* **DIRGE (mixes)** [24] [–]
(cd-s) *(HARD 44CD2)* – ('A'side) / Death threat (live) / Dirge (video).

Jul 00. (10") *(HARD 45-10)* **ONE MORE TIME (mixes)** [ ] [–]

Jul 02. (d12") *(HARD 51-12)* **LEATHER GIRLS. / NATJA** [ ] [–]

Sep 02. (cd-s) *(HARD 48CD)* **HANDS AROUND MY THROAT (mixes: U.X.B. + For The Throat)** [36] [–]
(cd-s) *(HARD 48CD2)* – (mixes).
(12") *(HARD 49-12)* – (mixes).

Sep 02. (d-lp/cd) *(HARD 53-1/CD1)* <95460> **SCORPIO RISING** [19] [ ]
– Leather / Girls / Hands around my throat / 23 lies / Scorpio rising / Killing smile / Natja / So you say you lost your baby / Diving horses / Help yourself. *(w/ enhanced video)*

Dec 02. (cd-s; by DEATH IN VEGAS with LIAM GALLAGHER) *(HARD 54CD1)* **SCORPIO RISING (mixes; album / The Polyphonic Spree / Scientist)** [14] [–]
(cd-s+=) *(HARD 54CD2)* – (mixes; Live XFM@Ulu / Scientist dub).
(12") *(HARD 54-12)* – (mixes).

DEEP PURPLE

Formed: London, England . . . 1968 intially as ROUNDABOUT, by former Searchers sticksman, CHRIS CURTIS. He duly recruited classically-trained organist, JON LORD and guitar maestro, RITCHIE BLACKMORE, who was living in Germany at the time. By Spring of that year, the band had become DEEP PURPLE with NICK SIMPER on bass and ROD EVANS on vocals. Their debut single, a cover of JOE SOUTH's 'HUSH', reached the US Top 5 and the band were subsequently furnished with a three album contract, signing with 'Tentagramme' in America (a label run by US comedian Bill Cosby!), 'Parlophone'in Britain. This line-up (known as Mk.I in DEEP PURPLE parlance) recorded three albums, 'SHADES OF DEEP PURPLE' (1968), 'BOOK OF TALIESYN' (1969) and the eponymous 'DEEP PURPLE' (1969), littered with chugging, proto-metal covers of the era's pop hits a la VANILLA FUDGE. Following the collapse of 'Tentagramme', the band signed with

'Warners', drafting in IAN GILLAN and ROGER GLOVER (both ex-EPISODE SIX) to replace EVANS and SIMPER respectively. The revamped line-up's first release was the pseudo-classical drivel of the live 'CONCERTO FOR GROUP AND ORCHESTRA WITH THE ROYAL PHILHARMONIC ORCHESTRA' (1970). Thankfully, after the record failed to sell in any great quantity, common sense prevailed and BLACKMORE steered the group in a heavier direction. 'IN ROCK', released later the same year, announced the arrival of a major contender in the heavyweight arena alongside the likes of BLACK SABBATH and LED ZEPPELIN. Preceded by the lumbering 'BLACK NIGHT' (No.2 in the UK) single, the album was dinosaur rock before the phrase was even coined; the pummelling rhythm section of GLOVER and PAICE driving the beast ever onward while BLACKMORE's razor sharp guitar solos clawed mercilessly at LORD's shuddering organ. 'CHILD IN TIME' was the ballad, the full range of GILLAN's talent on show as he progressed from mellow musings to his trademark glass-shattering shriek. While 'FIREBALL' (1971) was competent, if lacking in the songs department, 'MACHINE HEAD' (1972) was the DEEP PURPLE tour de force, the classic album from the classic Mk.II line-up. Cuts like 'HIGHWAY STAR' and 'SPACE TRUCKIN' were relentless, high-octane metal riff-athons which became staples in the DP live set for years to come. 'SMOKE ON THE WATER' probably stands as the band's most famous track, its classic three chord bludgeon and tale of disaster averted, reaching No.4 in America upon its release as a single a year later. This further boosted 'MACHINE HEAD's sales into the millions, DEEP PURPLE now firmly established as a world class act. The band also had a stellar live reputation, the concert double set, 'MADE IN JAPAN' (1972), going on to achieve cult status among metal afficiondos and earning the group a place in the Guinness Book Of Records as loudest band, woaargh!! As the heavy touring and recording schedule ground on, the beast began to stumble, however, recording a further, fairly lacklustre album, 'WHO DO WE THINK WE ARE' (1973), before disintegrating later that summer among constant in-fighting and personality clashes. BLACKMORE, LORD and PAICE remained, enlisting future WHITESNAKE vocalist DAVID COVERDALE on vocals and GLENN HUGHES (ex-TRAPEZE) in place of GLOVER to create DEEP PURPLE Mk.III. 'BURN' (1974) and 'STORMBRINGER' (1974) were characterised by COVERDALE's bluesy voice, although the new boy and BLACKMORE were not exactly fond of each other, the latter eventually quitting in 1975. His replacement was semi-legendary guitarist TOMMY BOLIN, who graced 'COME TASTE THE BAND' (1975). Less than a year later, however, DEEP PURPLE were no more, the behemoth finally going belly up after the perils of rock'n'roll had finally taken their toll. While BOLIN overdosed on heroin, of the remaining members, GLENN HUGHES reformed TRAPEZE while COVERDALE formed WHITESNAKE. BLACKMORE, meanwhile, had not been simply sitting around stuffing cucumbers down his pants and turning his amp up to 11, he had formed the rather grandiose-sounding RITCHIE BLACKMORE'S RAINBOW. The other key member of DEEP PURPLE, IAN GILLAN, had also been equally prolific during the 70's, initially with the IAN GILLAN BAND. A revamped DEEP PURPLE is where the paths of messrs. BLACKMORE, GILLAN, GLOVER, LORD and PAICE (the latter two had dabbled in solo and group work throughout the 70's – see discography) crossed once more. While the comeback album, 'PERFECT STRANGERS' (1984), was welcomed by fans, it became clear that the ever-dominant BLACKMORE was being as dominant as ever. After another relatively successful studio effort, 'HOUSE OF BLUE LIGHT' (1987), and a live album, GILLAN was given the order of the boot. Typically incestuous, DEEP PURPLE then recruited ex-RAINBOW man, JOE LYNN TURNER, for the awful 'SLAVES AND MASTERS' (1990) album. In an increasingly absurd round of musical chairs, GILLAN was then reinstated, consequently clashing once more with BLACKMORE who eventually stomped off to reform RAINBOW. DEEP PURPLE lumbered on, recruiting STEVE MORSE for their 1996 album, 'PURPENDICULAR'. 'ABANDON' (1998) was another to disappoint their ever faithful support who were literally growing old and grey waiting for them to retire. If The ROLLING STONES are still rolling, some might say, what's to stop DEEP PURPLE? Well, considering The 'STONES have had around three line-up changes in their whole career while DEEP PURPLE have almost managed the same number for each album, the future doesn't look particularly promising. Following on from the conceit of 1971's 'CONCERTO FOR GROUP AND ORCHESTRA', DP decided to bring the dreaded rock-meets-classical concept into the 21st Century. 'LIVE AT THE ROYAL ALBERT HALL' (2000) found the lads backed up by the London Symphony Orchestra, dredging up past classics and rendering them so far out of context it was hard to ascertain exactly who this album was aimed at. Nevertheless, guest appearances by the likes of RONNIE JAMES DIO and strangely, SAM BROWN, made for at least minor diversions from the muddled ambitions of the main programme. On a completely different note, in all senses of the term, 'BANANAS' (2003), was a back-to-the-roots kind of affair, or at least it would have been if DEEP PURPLE had started out sounding this relaxed. Less bombast, self indulgence and ego made for one of the better DP sets of recent years with a really quite surprising suppleness to the blues-boogie on offer. The absence of LORD wasn't felt too badly either, with veteran DON AIREY doing a fine job and earning a couple of writing credits on the better tracks. • **Songwriters:** Mk.I:-Mostly BLACKMORE / EVANS / LORD. Mk.II:- Group. Mk.III:- BLACKMORE / COVERDALE, adding at times LORD and PAICE. Mk.IV:- Permutate any two of COVERDALE, BOLIN or HUGHES. Covered HUSH (Joe South) / WE CAN WORK IT OUT + HELP (Beatles) / KENTUCKY WOMAN (Neil Diamond) / RIVER DEEP MOUNTAIN HIGH (Ike & Tina Turner) / HEY JOE (Jimi Hendrix) / I'M SO GLAD (Cream). • **Trivia:** To obtain charity monies for the Armenian earthquake disaster late 1989, BLACKMORE, GILLAN and others (i.e. BRUCE DICKINSON, ROBERT PLANT, BRIAN MAY etc.) contributed to Top 40 new version of SMOKE ON THE WATER.

Album rating: SHADES OF DEEP PURPLE (*5) / THE BOOK OF TALIESYN (*4) / DEEP PURPLE (*4) / CONCERTO FOR GROUP AND ORCHESTRA (*1) / IN ROCK (*8) / FIREBALL (*7) / MACHINE HEAD (*9) / MADE IN JAPAN (*8) / WHO DO WE THINK WE ARE (*6) / BURN (*7) / STORMBRINGER (*5) / COME TASTE THE BAND (*6) / DEEPEST PURPLE compilation (*9) / PERFECT STRANGERS (*6) / HOUSE OF BLUE LIGHT (*5) / NOBODY'S PERFECT (*5) / SLAVES AND MASTERS (*4) / COME HELL OR HIGH WATER (*7) / PURPENDICULAR (*5) / ABANDON (*4) / LIVE AT THE ROYAL ALBERT HALL (*5) / BANANAS (*5)

RITCHIE BLACKMORE (b.14 Apr'45, Weston-Super-Mare, Avon, England) – guitar (ex-MANDRAKE ROOT, ex-OUTLAWS, ex-SCREAMING LORD SUTCH, etc.) / **JON LORD** (b.9 Jun'41, Leicester, England) – keyboards (ex-FLOWERPOT MEN) / **NICK SIMPER** (b. 1946, Southall, London) – bass (ex-JOHNNY KIDD & PIRATES) / **ROD EVANS** (b.19 Jan'45, Edinburgh, Scotland) – vocals (ex-MAZE, ex-M.I.FIVE) / **IAN PAICE** (b.29 Jun'48, Nottingham, England) – drums (ex-MAZE, ex-M.I.FIVE)

		Parlophone	Tetragramme
Jun 68.	(7") *(R 5708)* <1503> **HUSH. / ONE MORE RAINY DAY**		4
Sep 68.	(lp) *(PCS 7055)* <102> **SHADES OF DEEP PURPLE**		24

– And the address / Hush / One more rainy day / (prelude) Happiness – I'm so glad / Mandrake root / Help / Love help me / Hey Joe. *(re-iss. Feb77 on 'EMI Harvest'; SHSM 2016) (cd-iss. Mar89; CZ 170) (cd-iss. Feb95 on 'Fame'; CDFA 3314) (lp re-iss. Nov97 on 'E.M.I.'; LPCENT 25) (cd re-mast.Feb00 on 'Liberty'; 498336-2)*

Nov 68. (7") *<1508>* **KENTUCKY WOMAN. / HARD ROAD** [–] [38]
Nov 68. (7") *(R 5745)* **KENTUCKY WOMAN. / WRING THAT NECK** [ ] [–]
Jan 69. (7") *<1514>* **RIVER DEEP – MOUNTAIN HIGH. / LISTEN, LEARN, READ ON** [–] [53]
Feb 69. (7") *(R 5763)* **EMMARETTA. / WRING THAT NECK** [ ] [–]
Apr 69. (7") *<1519>* **EMMARETTA. / THE BIRD HAS FLOWN** [–] [ ]

Harvest Tetragramme

Jun 69. (lp/c) *(SHVL/TC-SHVL 751) <107>* **BOOK OF TALIESYN** [ ] Jan69 [54]
– Listen, learn, read on / Wring that neck / Kentucky woman / Shield / a) Exposition – b) We can work it out / The shield / Anthem / River deep, mountain high. *(re-iss. Jun85 on 'EMI';) (cd-iss. Aug89; CDP 792408-2) (cd re-iss. Feb96 on 'Premier'; CZ 171) (cd re-mast.Feb00 on 'Liberty'; 521608-2)*
Nov 69. (lp) *(SHVL 759) <119>* **DEEP PURPLE** [ ] Jul69 [ ]
– Chasing shadows / Blind / Lalena: (a) Faultline, (b) The painter / Why didn't Rosemary? / The bird has flown / April. *(re-iss. Jun85 on 'EMI';) (cd-iss. Mar89; CZ 172) (re-iss. cd May95 on 'Fame'; CDFA 3317) (cd re-mast.Feb00 on 'Liberty'; 521597-2)*

— (In Jun'69 below two were used on session for 'HALLELUJAH'. They became regular members after the recording of 'DEEP PURPLE' album.) / **IAN GILLAN** (b.19 Aug'45, Hounslow, London) – vocals (ex-EPISODE SIX) replaced EVANS who joined CAPTAIN BEYOND. / **ROGER GLOVER** (b.30 Nov'45, Brecon, Wales) – bass (ex-EPISODE SIX) replaced SIMPER who later formed WARHORSE

Jul 69. (7") *(HAR 5006) <1537>* **HALLELUJAH (I AM THE PREACHER). / APRIL (part 1)** [ ] [ ]

Harvest Warners

Jan 70. (lp/c) *(SHVL/TC-SHVL 767) <1860>* **CONCERTO FOR GROUP AND ORCHESTRA WITH THE ROYAL PHILHARMONIC ORCHESTRA (live)** [26] May70 [ ]
– First Movement: Moderato – Allegro / Second Movement: Andante (part 1) – Andante conclusion / Third Movement: Vivace – Presto. *(cd-iss. Aug90 on 'E.M.I.'+=; CZ 342)* – Wring that neck / Child in time.
Jun 70. (7") *(HAR 5020)* **BLACK NIGHT. / SPEED KING** [2] [–]
Jun 70. (lp/c) *(SHVL/TC-SHVL 777) <1877>* **DEEP PURPLE IN ROCK** [4] Sep70 [ ]
– Speed king / Blood sucker / Child in time / Flight of the rat / Into the fire / Living wreck / Hard lovin' man. *(re-iss. May82 on 'Fame' lp/c; FA/TC-FA 3011) (cd-iss. Apr88; CDFA 3011) (pic-lp.Jun85; EJ 2603430) (purple-lp iss.1995 on 'E.M.I.'; 7243-8-34019-8) (with free-lp)* – Black night / Speed king (piano version) / Cry free (Roger Glover remix) / Jam stew / Flight of the rat (Roger Glover remix) / Speed king (Roger Glover remix) / Black night (Roger Glover remix).
Jul 70. (7") *<7405>* **BLACK NIGHT. / INTO THE FIRE** [–] [66]
Feb 71. (7") *(HAR 5033) <7493>* **STRANGE KIND OF WOMAN. / I'M ALONE** [6] [ ]
Sep 71. (lp/c) *(SHVL/TC-SHVL 793) <2564>* **FIREBALL** [1] Aug71 [32]
– Fireball / No no no / Demon's eye / Anyone's daughter / The mule / Fools / No one came. *(re-iss. Mar84 on 'Fame' lp/c; FA/TC-FA 41-3093-1/-4) (re-iss. Aug87 lp/c; ATAK/TC-ATAK 105) (re-iss. Oct87 on 'E.M.I.' lp/c; EMS/TC-EMS 1255) (cd-iss. Jan88 on 'E.M.I.'; CZ 30) (pic-lp.Jun85 on 'E.M.I.'; EJ 2403440) (lp re-iss. 1996 on 'E.M.I.'; 7243-8-53711-0) (with free lp)* – Strange kind of woman (remix '96) / I'm alone / Freedom (session out-take) / Slow train (session out-take) / Midnight in Moscow – Robin Hood – William Tell – Fireball (the noise abatement) / Backwards piano / No one came (remix '96).
Oct 71. (7") *(HAR 5045)* **FIREBALL. / DEMON'S EYE** [15] [–]
Nov 71. (7") *<7528>* **FIREBALL. / I'M ALONE** [–] [ ]

Purple Warners

Mar 72. (7") *(PUR 102) <7572>* **NEVER BEFORE. / WHEN A BLIND MAN CRIES** [35] [ ]
Apr 72. (lp/c) *(TPSA/TC-TPSA 7504) <2607>* **MACHINE HEAD** [1] [7]
– Highway star / Maybe I'm a Leo / Pictures of home / Never before / Smoke on the water / Lazy / Space truckin'. *(re-iss. Jun85 on 'E.M.I.' lp/c; ATAK/TC-ATAK 39) (re-iss. Oct86 on 'Fame' lp/c; FA/TC-FA 3158) (cd-iss. Mar87 on 'E.M.I.'; CZ 83) (cd re-iss. Mar89; CDFA 3158) (re-iss. Sep97 on 'E.M.I.' d-cd/d-lp; CD+/DEEPP 3)*
Jun 72. (7") *<7595>* **LAZY. / WHEN A BLIND MAN CRIES** [–] [ ]
Oct 72. (7") *<7634>* **HIGHWAY STAR. / (part 2)** [–] [ ]
Dec 72. (d-lp/d-c) *(TPSP/TC2-TPSP 351) <2701>* **MADE IN JAPAN (live)** [16] Apr73 [6]
– Highway star / Child in time / Smoke on the water / The mule / Strange kind of woman / Lazy / Space truckin'. *(cd-iss. Sep88 on 'E.M.I.'; CDTPS 351) (re-iss. Oct92 on 'Fame' cd/c; CD/TC FA 3268) (re-iss. Jan98 on 'E.M.I.' cd/lp; 857864-2/-4)* – hit No.73
Feb 73. (lp/c) *(TPSA/TC-TPSA 7508) <2678>* **WHO DO YOU THINK WE ARE!** [4] Jan73 [15]
– Woman from Tokyo / Mary Long / Super trouper / Smooth dancer / Rat bat blue / Place in line / Our lady. *(re-iss. Jun85 on 'E.M.I.' lp/c; ATAK/TC-ATAK 127) (cd-iss. Oct87 on 'E.M.I.'; CZ 6) (cd re-iss. Dec94 on 'Fame'; CDFA 3311) (cd re-iss. Jul00 on 'E.M.I.'+=; 521607-2)* – (the 1999 remixes).
Apr 73. (7") *<7672>* **WOMAN FROM TOKYO. / SUPER TROUPER** [–] [80]
May 73. (7") *<7710>* **SMOKE ON THE WATER. / (part 2)** [–] [4]
Sep 73. (7") *<7737>* **WOMAN FROM TOKYO. / SUPER TROOPER** [–] [60]

— **BLACKMORE, LORD** and **PAICE** brought in new members / **DAVID COVERDALE** (b.22 Sep'49, Saltburn-by-the-sea, Cleveland, England) – vocals replaced GILLAN who later formed own band. / **GLENN HUGHES** (b.Penkridge, England) – bass (ex-TRAPEZE) repl. GLOVER who became top producer.

Feb 74. (lp/c) *(TPS/TC-TPS 3505) <2766>* **BURN** [3] [9]
– Burn / Might just take your life / Lay down stay down / Sail away / You fool no one / What's goin' on here / Mistreated / "A" 200. *(re-iss. Mar84 on 'E.M.I.' lp/c; ATAK/TC-ATAK 11) (cd-iss. Jul89; CZ 203)*
Mar 74. (7") *(PUR 117) <7784>* **MIGHT JUST TAKE YOUR LIFE. / CORONARIAS REDIG** [ ] [91]
May 74. (7") *<7809>* **BURN. / CORONARIAS REDIG** [–] [ ]
Nov 74. (lp/c) *(TPS/TC-TPS 3508) <2832>* **STORMBRINGER** [6] [20]
– Stormbringer / Love don't mean a thing / Holy man / Hold on / Lady double dealer / You can't do it right (with the one you love) / High ball shooter / The gypsy / Soldier of fortune. *(re-iss. Jun85 on 'E.M.I.' lp/c; ATAK/TC-ATAK 70) (cd-iss. Oct88 on 'E.M.I.'; CZ 142)*
Nov 74. (7") *<8049>* **HIGH BALL SHOOTER. / YOU CAN'T DO IT RIGHT** [–] [ ]
Jan 75. (7") *<8069>* **STORMBRINGER. / LOVE DON'T MEAN A THING** [–] [ ]

— **TOMMY BOLIN** (b.1951, Sioux City, Iowa, USA) – guitar (ex-JAMES GANG, ex-ZEPHYR) repl. BLACKMORE who formed RAINBOW. (see further below)

Oct 75. (lp/c) *(TPSA/TC-TPSA 7515) <2895>* **COME TASTE THE BAND** [19] [43]
– Comin' home / Lady luck / Gettin' together / Dealer / I need love / Drifter / Love child / This time around – Owed to the 'G' / You keep on moving. *(re-iss. Jun85 on 'E.M.I.' lp/c;) (cd-iss. Jul90 on 'E.M.I.'; CZ 343) (cd re-iss. Jul95 on 'Fame'; CDFA 3318)*
Mar 76. (7") *(PUR 130)* **YOU KEEP ON MOVING. / LOVE CHILD** [ ] [–]
Mar 76. (7") *<8182>* **GETTIN' TIGHTER. / LOVE CHILD** [–] [ ]
Nov 76. (lp/c) *(TPSA/TC-TPSA 7517) <2995>* **MADE IN EUROPE (live)** <US title 'DEEP PURPLE LIVE'> [12] [ ]
– Burn / Mistreated (interpolating 'Rock me baby') / Lady double dealer / You fool no one / Stormbringer. *(cd-iss. Jul90 on 'E.M.I.'; CZ 344)*

— split Spring 76, TOMMY BOLIN went solo. He died (of an overdose) 4th Dec'76. HUGHES reformed TRAPEZE. COVERDALE formed WHITESNAKE, he was later joined by LORD and PAICE, after they had been in PAICE, ASHTON and LORD. Remarkably **DEEP PURPLE** reformed 8 years later with early 70's line-up. **GILLAN, BLACKMORE, LORD, PAICE** and **GLOVER.**

Polydor Mercury

Nov 84. (lp/pic-lp/c) *(POLH/+P/C 16) <824003>* **PERFECT STRANGERS** [5] [17]
– Knocking at your back door / Under the gun / Nobody's home / Mean streak / Perfect strangers / A gypsy's kiss / Wasted sunsets / Hungry daze. *(c+=)* – Not responsible. *(re-iss. Mar91 cd/c/lp; 823777-2/-4/-1) (cd re-mast.Aug99; 546045-2)*
Jan 85. (7"/7"pic-d) *(POSP/+P 719)* **PERFECT STRANGERS. / SON OF ALERIK** [48] Mar85 [ ]
(12"+=) *(POSPX 719)* – Wasted sunsets / Hungry daze.
Jun 85. (7"/12") *(POSP/+X 749) <880477>* **KNOCKING AT YOUR BACK DOOR. / PERFECT STRANGERS** [68] Jan85 [61]
Jan 87. (lp/c)(cd) *(POLH/+C 32)(<831318-2>)* **THE HOUSE OF BLUE LIGHT** [10] [34]
– Bad attitude / The unwritten law / Call of the wild / Mad dog / Black and white / Hard lovin' woman / The Spanish archer / Strangeways / Mitzi Dupree / Dead or alive. *(re-iss. Mar91 lp/c; 831318-1/-4) (cd re-mast.Aug99; 546162-2)*

Jan 87. (7"/7"pic-d) *(POSP/+P 843)* **CALL OF THE WILD. / STRANGEWAYS** [ ] [ ]
(12") *(POSPX 843)* – ('A'side) / ('B'-long version).

Jun 88. (7") *(PO 4)* **HUSH (live). / DEAD OR ALIVE (live)** [62] [ ]
(12"+=/cd-s+=) *(PZ/+CD 4)* – Bad attitude (live).

Jun 88. (d-lp/d-c)(cd) *(PODV/+C 10)(<835897-2>)* **NOBODY'S PERFECT (live)** [38] [ ]
– Highway star / Strange kind of woman / Perfect strangers / Hard lovin' woman / Knocking at your back door / Child in time / Lazy / Black night / Woman from Tokyo / Smoke on the water / Hush. *(d-lp has extra tracks) (re-iss. Mar91 d-lp/d-c; 835897-1/-4) (cd re-mast.Aug99; 546128-2)*

— **JOE LYNN TURNER** – vocals (ex-RAINBOW, ex-YNGWIE MALMSTEEN'S RISING FORCE) repl. GILLAN who continued solo.

R.C.A. R.C.A.

Oct 90. (7") <c-s> *(PB 49247)* *<2703>* **KING OF DREAMS. / FIRE IN THE BASEMENT** [70] [ ]
(12"+=/cd-s+=) *(PT/PD 49248)* – ('A'-album version).

Nov 90. (cd/c/lp) *(PD/PK/PL 90535)* *<2421>* **SLAVES AND MASTERS** [45] [87]
– King of dreams / The cut runs deep / Fire in the basement / Truth hurts / Breakfast in bed / Love conquers all / Fortuneteller / Too much is not enough / Wicked ways. *(re-iss. cd Apr94; 74321 18719-2)*

Feb 91. (7"/c-s) *(PB/PK 49225)* **LOVE CONQUERS ALL. / TRUTH HURTS** [57] [ ]
(12"+=)(12"pic-d+=)(cd-s+=) *(PT 49212)(PT 49224)(PD 49226)* – Slow down sister.

— early 70s line-up again after TURNER was sacked.

R.C.A. Giant

Jul 93. (cd/c/lp) *(74321 15240-2/-4/-1)* *<24517>* **THE BATTLE RAGES ON** [21] [ ]
– The battle rages on / Lick it up / Anya / Talk about love / Time to kill / Ramshackle man / A twist in the tale / Nasty piece of work / Solitaire / One man's meat. *(re-iss. cd Oct95; same)*

Arista Arista

Nov 94. (cd/c/d-lp) *(<74321 23416-2/-4/-1>)* **COME HELL OR HIGH WATER (live mid-93)** [ ] [ ]
– Highway star / Black night / Twist in the tail / Perfect strangers / Anyone's daughter / Child in time / Anya / Speed king / Smoke on the water.

— **STEVE MORSE** – guitar (ex-DIXIE DREGS) repl. JOE SATRIANI who repl. BLACKMORE on European tour late '93-mid '94

R.C.A. C.M.C.

Feb 96. (cd/c) *(74321 33802-2/-4)* *<86201>* **PURPENDICULAR** [58] [ ]
– Vavoom: Ted the mechanic / Loosen my strings / Soon forgotten / Sometimes I feel like screaming / Cascades: I'm not your lover / The aviator / Rosa's cantina / A castle full of rascals / A touch away / Hey Cisco / Somebody stole my guitar / The purpendicular waltz.

May 98. (cd) *(495306-2)* *<86250>* **ABANDON** [ ] [ ]
– Any fule kno that / Almost human / Don't make me happy / Seventh heaven / Watching the sky / Fingers to the bone / Jack Ruby / She was / Whatsername / 69 / Evil Louie / Bludsucker.

— next with The LONDON SYMPHONY ORCHESTRA

Eagle Spitfire

Jan 00. (d-cd) *(EDGCD 124)* *<15068>* **LIVE AT THE ROYAL ALBERT HALL (live 1999)** [ ] Feb00 [ ]
– Pictured within / Wait a while / Sitting in a dream / Love is all / Via Miami / That's why God is singing the blues / Take it off the top / Hard road (wring that neck) / Pictures of home / Concerto for group and orchestra / Ted the mechanic / Watching the sky / Sometimes I feel like screaming / Smoke on the water.

— **DON AIREY** – keyboards (ex-RAINBOW) repl. LORD

Capitol Sanctuary

Aug 03. (cd) *(591049-2)* *<86351>* **BANANAS** [ ] Sep03 [ ]
– House of pain / Sun goes down / Haunted / Razzle dazzle / Silver tongue / Walk on / Pictures of innocence / I got your number / Never a word / Bananas / Doing it tonight / Contact lost.

– compilations, exploitation releases, etc. –

Sep 72. (d-lp) *Warners; <2644>* **PURPLE PASSAGES** [–] [57]

Oct 72. (7") *Warners;* **HUSH. / KENTUCKY WOMAN** [–] [ ]

1972. (lp) *Citation; <CTN 18010>* **THE BEST OF DEEP PURPLE** [–] [ ]

Jun 75. (lp/c) *Purple; (TPSM/TC-TPSM 2002)* **24 CARAT PURPLE (1970-73)** [14] [–]
– Woman from Tokyo / Fireball / Strange kind of woman / Never before / Black night / Speed king / Smoke on the water / Child in time. *(re-iss. Sep85 on 'Fame' lp/c; FA41 3132-1/-4) (cd-iss. Oct87; CDFA 3132)*

Mar 77. (7"m,7"purple) *Purple; (PUR 132)* **SMOKE ON THE WATER. / CHILD IN TIME / WOMAN FROM TOKYO** [21] [ ]

Sep 77. (7"ep) *Purple; (PUR 135)* **NEW LIVE & RARE** [31] [ ]
– Black night (live) / Painted horse / When a blind man cries.

Jan 78. (lp/c) *Purple; (TPS 3510)* **POWERHOUSE** (early 70's line-up) [ ] [–]

Sep 78. (7"ep) *Purple; (PUR 137)* **NEW LIVE & RARE VOL.2** [45] [ ]
– Burn (edit) / Coronarias redig / Mistreated (live).

Oct 78. (lp/c) *Harvest; (SHSM 2026)* **THE SINGLES A's & B's** [ ] [–]
(re-iss. Nov88 on 'Fame' cd/c/lp; CD/TC+/FA 3212) (cd-iss. Jan93 on 'E.M.I.'; TCEMC 3658)

Apr 79. (lp/c) *Purple; (TPS/TC-TPS 3514)* **THE MARK II PURPLE SINGLES** [24] [ ]

Apr 79. (7"/12") *Harvest; (HAR 5178)* **BLACK NIGHT. / STRANGE KIND OF WOMAN** [ ] [ ]

Jul 80. (lp/c) *E.M.I.; (EMTV/TC-EMTV 25) / Warners; <3486>* **DEEPEST PURPLE** [1] Oct80 [ ]
– Black night / Speed king / Fireball / Strange kind of woman / Child in time / Woman from Tokyo / Highway star / Space truckin' / Burn / Demon's eye / Stormbringer / Smoke on the water. *(cd-iss. Aug84; CDP 746032-2) (re-iss. 1989 lp/c; ATAK/TC-ATAK 138) (re-iss. Jul90 on 'Fame' cd/c/lp; CD/TC+/FA 3239) (cd re-iss. Aug00 on 'Harvest'; CDP 746032-2)*

Jul 80. (7") *Harvest; (HAR 5210)* **BLACK NIGHT. / SPEED KING (live)** [43] [–]

Oct 80. (7"ep) *Harvest; (SHEP 101)* **NEW LIVE & RARE VOL.3** [48] [ ]
– Smoke on the water (live) / The bird has flown / Grabsplatter.

Dec 80. (lp/c) *Harvest; (SHDW 412)* **IN CONCERT 1970-1972 (live)** [30] [ ]
– Speed king / Wring that neck / Child in time / Mandrake root / Highway star / Strange kind of woman / Lazy / Never before / Space truckin' / Lucille. *(cd-iss. May92;)*

Aug 82. (lp/c) *Harvest; (SHSP/TC-SHSP 4124)* **DEEP PURPLE LIVE IN LONDON (live '74)** [23] [ ]
– Burn / Might just take your life / Lay down, stay down / Mistreated / Smoke on the water / You fool no one.

Jun 85. (d-lp/d-c) *Harvest; (PUR/TC-PUR 1)* **THE ANTHOLOGY** [50] [ ]
(d-cd iss.Mar91 on 'E.M.I.'; CDEM 1374)

Nov 87. (lp/c/cd) *Telstar; (STAR/STAC/TCD 2312)* **THE BEST OF DEEP PURPLE** [ ] [–]

Oct 88. (d-lp/d-c/d-cd) *Connoisseur; (DPVSOP LP/MC/CD 125)* **SCANDINAVIAN NIGHTS (live)** [ ] [–]
(d-cd re-iss. Aug99; same)

Mar 91. (d-cd/d-c/t-lp) *E.M.I.; (CD/TC+/EM 5013)* **THE ANTHOLOGY** [ ] [ ]

Aug 91. (d-cd/d-c/d-lp) *Connoisseur; (DPVSOP CD/MC/LP 163)* **IN THE ABSENCE OF PINK (KNEBWORTH '85 live)** [ ] [–]

Sep 91. (cd/c/lp) *Polgram TV; (845534-2/-4/-1)* **PURPLE RAINBOWS** [ ] [–]
– (all work including RAINBOW, GILLAN, WHITESNAKE, etc.)

Apr 92. (cd/c) *Polygram; (511438-2/-4)* **KNOCKING AT YOUR BACK DOOR** [ ] [–]

May 93. (cd/c) *Spectrum; (550027-2/-4)* **PROGRESSION** [ ] [–]

Jul 93. (cd) *Connoisseur; (VSOPCD 187)* **THE DEEP PURPLE FAMILY ALBUM** (associated releases) [ ] [–]

Nov 93. (3xcd-box) *E.M.I.; (CDEM 1510)* **LIVE IN JAPAN (live)** [ ] [–]

May 95. (d-cd) *Connoisseur; (DPVSOPCD 217)* **ON THE WINGS OF A RUSSIAN FOXBAT – LIVE IN CALIFORNIA 1976** [ ] [–]

Jun 95. (12"/cd-s) *E.M.I.; (CD/12 EM 382)* **BLACK NIGHT (remix). / SPEED KING (remix)** [66] [–]

Sep 95. (cd) *Spectrum; (551339-2)* **CHILD IN TIME** [ ] [–]

Nov 95. (3xcd-box) *E.M.I.; (CDOMB 002)* **BOOK OF TALIESYN / SHADES OF DEEP PURPLE / DEEP PURPLE IN CONCERT** [ ] [–]

May 96. (cd) *Premier; (PRMUCD 2)* **CALIFORNIA JAMMING** [ ] [–]

Jul 96. (3xcd-box) *Connoisseur; (DPVSOPCD 230)* **THE FINAL CONCERTS (live)** [ ] [–]

Feb 97. (cd) *EMI Gold; (CDGOLD 1060) / Disky; <DC 878642>* **THE COLLECTION** | | Mar97

Jun 97. (d-cd) *E.M.I.; (CDEM 1615)* **LIVE AT THE OLYMPIA (live)**

Jul 98. (cd) *Camden; (74321 59737-2)* **PURPLEXED** | | -

Oct 98. (cd/c/d-lp) *E.M.I.; (496807-2/-4/-1)* **THE VERY BEST OF** | 39 |

– Hush / Black night / Speed king / Child in time / Strange kind of woman / Fireball / Demon's eye / Smoke on the water / Highway star / When a blind man cries / Never before / Woman from Tokyo / Burn / Stormbringer / You keep on moving / Perfect strangers / Ted the mechanic / Any fule know that. *(d-cd-iss. ; 496808-2)*

Nov 98. (4xcd-box) *Connoisseur; (DPBOX 400)* **ON THE ROAD (live)** | | -

Jan 00. (d-cd) *Eagle; (EDGCD 124) / Spitfire; <15068>* **LIVE AT THE ROYAL ALBERT HALL with The London Symphony Orchestra**

Feb 00. (cd) *Liberty; (495635-2)* **IN PROFILE** | | -

Apr 00. (cd) *Spectrum; (544204-2)* **UNDER THE GUN** | | -

Apr 00. (cd) *Purple; (PUR 303)* **DAYS MAY COME AND DAYS MAY GO (THE CALIFORNIA REHEARSALS JUNE 1975)**

Sep 00. (3xcd-box) *E.M.I.; 528344-2)* **SHADES OF / BOOK OF TALIESYN / DEEP PURPLE** | | -

Sep 00. (cd) *EMI Gold; (528512-2)* **ANTHEMS** | | -

DEF LEPPARD

Formed: Sheffield, England . . . 1977 as ATOMIC MASS by RICK SAVAGE, PETE WILLIS and TONY KENNING. Frontman JOE ELLIOT came into the picture not long after and the band adopted the name DEAF LEOPARD, soon altering it to the more rock'n'roll DEF LEPPARD. Additional guitarist STEVE CLARK joined in time for the band's first gigs in July 1978, while FRANK NOON replaced KENNING on drums prior to the band recording their first single. With finance provided by ELLIOT's father, the group issued a debut EP on their own label, 'Bludgeon Riffola', entitled 'GETCHA ROCKS OFF' (was the young BOBBY GILLESPIE a fan, perchance?). Later that year (1979), with RICK ALLEN taking up permanent residence on the drum stool, and following tours supporting AC/DC etc., the band were signed to 'Vertigo'. This prompted a move to London and in 1980, their debut album, 'ON THROUGH THE NIGHT', broke the UK Top 20 although it would be America that would initially embrace the band. They were certainly metal, albeit metal of the most easy listening variety and while the critics hated them, their growing army of fans lapped up their every release. Although 'HIGH 'N' DRY' (1981) marked the beginning of their association with MUTT LANGE and was far more assured in terms of songwriting, DEF LEPPARD's big break came with 1983's 'PYROMANIA'. Legendary for its use of all manner of studio special effects and state-of-the-art technology, the record revolutionised heavy metal and became the benchmark by which subsequent 80's albums were measured. Yet it wasn't a case (as it so often is) of studio flash masking a dearth of genuine talent, DEF LEPPARD were actually capable of turning out finely crafted songs over the course of a whole album. Highly melodic and relentlessly hook-laden, the Americans loved 'PYROMANIA' and its attendant singles, 'PHOTOGRAPH', and 'ROCK OF AGES', the album selling over 7 million copies. Tragedy struck, however, when RICK ALLEN lost his arm in a car crash on New Year's Eve 1984. A true metal warrior, ALLEN soldiered bravely on using a customised drum kit with programmable drum pads and foot pedals. Bearing in mind ALLEN's accident and the band's perfectionist nature, four years wasn't too long to wait for a new album, and for the majority of fans the delay was well worth it. A melodic rock tour de force, the album finally broke the band in their home country with three of its attendant singles reaching the UK Top 10, 'LOVE BITES' giving the band their first No.1. Similarly successful across the Atlantic and worldwide, the album sold a staggering amount, DEF LEPPARD staking their claim as the biggest heavy metal act on the planet. Ironically, just as the group were entering the big league, tragedy struck again as STEVE CLARK was found dead in January 1991 after a prolonged drink/drugs binge. The band recruited elder statesman of rock, VIVIAN CAMPBELL, as a replacement and began work on the 'ADRENALIZE' (1992) album. While the likes of single, 'LET'S GET ROCKED' bordered on the cringeworthy (if only for the awful title), the album's glossy pop-metal once again pulled in the punters in their millions. The next few years saw the release of a B-sides/rareties affair, 'RETRO ACTIVE' (1993) and greatest hits collection, 'VAULT' (1995). A new studio set, 'SLANG', eventually graced the racks in 1996, showcasing a more modern sound (ELLIOT had even traded in his poodle mane for a relatively trendy bobbed haircut). A record executive's wet dream, DEF LEPPARD remain radio friendly unit shifters in the true sense of the phrase. Very much a product of their era, and that era being hair metal's late 80's pre-grunge heyday, DEF LEPPARD seemed something of an anachronism come the dawn of the new millennium. Especially with a record as true to form as 'EUPHORIA' (1999), as musuclar and as charismatic a set as the band have recorded yet completely out of sync with trends in music in general and in the rock/metal world especially. While the likes of BON JOVI seem to be able to adapt much more easily, Sheffield's veterans looked to be either unwilling or unable to do so. 'X' (2002) didn't exactly remedy the situation, with the band sounding more and more like candidates for a safe, unchallenging musical middle age. • **Songwriters:** Group compositions, except ONLY AFTER DARK (Mick Ronson) / ACTION (Sweet) / YOU CAN'T ALWAYS GET WHAT YOU WANT (Rolling Stones) / LITTLE WING (Jimi Hendrix) / ELECTED + UNDER MY WHEELS (Alice Cooper) / ZIGGY STARDUST + REBEL REBEL (David Bowie) / NOW I'M HERE (Queen) / STAY WITH ME (Rod Stewart & The Faces) / 'CAUSE WE ENDED AS LOVERS + LED BOOTS (Jeff Beck). Roadie STUMPUS MAXIMUS covered; PLEASE RELEASE ME (Engelbert Humperdinck).

Album rating: ON THROUGH THE NIGHT (*5) / HIGH 'N' DRY (*6) / PYROMANIA (*7) / HYSTERIA (*7) / ADRENALIZE (*6) / RETROACTIVE compilation (*5) / VAULT 1980-1995 – DEF LEPPARD'S GREATEST HITS compilation (*8) / SLANG (*5) / EUPHORIA (*6) / X (*4)

JOE ELLIOT (b. 1 Aug'59) – vocals / **PETE WILLIS** – lead guitar / **STEVE CLARK** (b.23 Apr'60) – guitar / **RICK SAVAGE** (b. 2 Dec'60) – bass / **FRANK NOON** – drums

Bludgeon Riffola | not iss.

Jan 79. (7"ep) *(SRT-CUS 232)* **THE DEF LEPPARD EP** | | -

– Ride into the sun / Getcha rocks off / The overture.

Feb 79. (7"m) *(MSB 001)* **RIDE INTO THE SUN / GETCHA ROCKS OFF / THE OVERTURE** | | -

—— **RICK ALLEN** (b. 1 Nov'63) – drums; repl. FRANK who later joined LIONHEART, then WAYSTED

Vertigo | Mercury

Aug 79. (7"m) *(6059 240)* **GETCHA ROCKS OFF. / RIDE INTO THE SUN / THE OVERTURE** | | -

Nov 79. (7") *(6059 247)* **WASTED. / HELLO AMERICA** | 61 |

Feb 80. (7") *(LEPP 1)* **HELLO AMERICA. / GOOD MORNING FREEDOM** | 45 |

Mar 80. (lp)(c) *(9102 040)(7231 028) <3828>* **ON THROUGH THE NIGHT** | 15 | 51

– Rock brigade / Hello America / Sorrow is a woman / It could be you / Satellite / When the walls come tumblin' down / Wasted / Rocks off / It don't matter / Answer to the master / Overture. *(re-iss. Jan89 lp/c/cd; 822533-1/-4/-2)*

Jun 80. (7") *<76064>* **ROCK BRIGADE. / WHEN THE WALLS COME TUMBLIN' DOWN** – [ ]

Jul 81. (lp/c) *(6359/7150 045) <4021>* **HIGH 'N' DRY** 26 38
– High 'n' dry (Saturday night) / You got me runnin' / Let it go / Another hit and run / Lady Strange / Mirror, mirror (look into my eyes) / No no no / Bringin' on the heartbreak / Switch 625. *<US re-iss. May84 +=; 818836>* – Bringin' on the heartbreak (remix) / Me and my wine. *(re-iss. Jan89 lp/c/cd+=; 818836-1/-4/-2)* – You got me runnin' (remix) / Me and my wine.

Aug 81. (7") *(LEPP 2) <76120>* **LET IT GO. / SWITCH 625** [ ] [ ]

Jan 82. (7") *(LEPP 3)* **BRINGIN' ON THE HEARTACHE (remix). / ME AND MY WINE** [ ] –
(12"+=) *(LEPP 3-12)* – You got me runnin'.

—— **PHIL COLLEN** (b. 8 Dec'57) – lead guitar (ex-GIRL) repl. PETE

Jan 83. (7") *(VER 5) <811215>* **PHOTOGRAPH. / BRINGIN' ON THE HEARTBREAK** 66 –
(12"+=) *(VERX 5)* – Mirror, Mirror (look into my eyes).

Feb 83. (7") *<811215>* **PHOTOGRAPH. / ACTION! NOT WORDS** – 12

Mar 83. (lp/c) *(VERS/+C 2) <810308>* **PYROMANIA** 18 Jan83 2
– Rock! rock! (till you drop) / Photograph / Stagefright / Too late for love / Die hard the hunter / Foolin around / Rock of ages / Comin' under fire / Action! not words / Billy's got a gun. *(cd-iss. 1988; 810308-2)*

Jun 83. (7") *<812604>* **ROCK OF AGES. / BILLY'S GOT A GUN** – 16

Aug 83. (7"/7"s/7"sha-pic-d/12") *(VER/+Q/P/X 6)* **ROCK OF AGES. / ACTION! NOT WORDS** 41 –

Aug 83. (7") *<814178>* **FOOLIN'. / COMIN' UNDER FIRE** – 28

Nov 83. (7") *(VER 8) <814178>* **FOOLIN'. / TOO LATE FOR LOVE** [ ] –
(12"+=) *(VERX 8)* – High'n'dry.

Jun 84. (7") *<818779>* **BRINGIN' ON THE HEARTBREAK (remix). / ME AND MY WINE** – 61

Aug 85. (7"/7"g-f) *(VER/+G 9)* **PHOTOGRAPH. / BRINGIN' ON THE HEARTBREAK** [ ] –
(12"+=) *(VERX 9)* – Mirror, mirror.

—— Remained a 5-piece although RICK ALLEN lost an arm in a car crash (31st December '84). He now used a specially adapted programmable drum pads and foot pedals.

Jul 87. (7") *(LEP 1)* **ANIMAL. / TEAR IT DOWN** 6 –
(12"+=/12"red+=) *(LEP X/C 1)* – ('A'extended).
(cd-s++=) *(LEPCD 1)* – Women.

Aug 87. (lp/pic-lp/c)(cd) *(HYS LP/PD/MC 1)(<830675>)* **HYSTERIA** 2 1
– Women / Rocket / Animal / Love bites / Pour some sugar on me / Armageddon it / Gods of war / Don't shoot shotgun / Run riot / Hysteria / Excitable / Love and affection. *(cd+=)* – I can't let you be a memory.

Aug 87. (7") *<888757>* **WOMEN. / TEAR IT DOWN** – 80

Sep 87. (7"/7"sha-pic-d/c-s) *(LEP/+S/MC 2)* **POUR SOME SUGAR ON ME. / I WANNA BE YOUR HERO** 18 –
(12"+=) *(LEPX 2)* – ('A'extended mix).

Oct 87. (7") *<888832>* **ANIMAL. / I WANNA BE YOUR HERO** – 19

Nov 87. (7"/7"s/c-s) *(LEP/+S/MC 3) <870004>* **HYSTERIA. / RIDE INTO THE SUN ('87 version)** 26 Jan88 10
(12"+=/12"s+=) *(LEPX 3/+13)* – Love and affection (live).
(cd-s++=) *(LEPCD 3)* – I wanna be your hero.

Apr 88. (7") *<870298>* **POUR SOME SUGAR ON ME. / RING OF FIRE** – 2

Apr 88. (7"/7"s) *(LEP/+P 4)* **ARMAGEDDON IT! (The Atomic mix). / RING OF FIRE** 20 –
(12"+=/12"s+=) *(LEPX/+B 4)* – ('A'version).
(pic-cd-s++=) *(LEPCD 4)* – Animal / Pour some sugar on me.

Jul 88. (7"g-f) *(LEPG 5) <870402>* **LOVE BITES. / BILLY'S GOT A GUN (live)** 11 1
(12"+=/12"box+=/cd-s+=) *(LEP X/XB/CD 5)* – Excitable (orgasmic mix).

Nov 88. (7") *<870692>* **ARMAGEDDON IT. / RELEASE ME (STUMPUS MAXIMUS & THE GOOD OL' BOYS)** – 3

Jan 89. (7"/7"s) *(LEP/+C 6)* **ROCKET. / RELEASE ME (STUMPUS MAXIMUS & THE GOOD OL' BOYS)** 15 –
('A'-Lunar mix; 12"+=/12"s+=/12"pic-d+=/cd-s+=) *(LEP X/XC/XP/CD 6)* – Rock of ages (live).

Feb 89. (7") *<872614>* **ROCKET. / WOMEN (live)** – 12

—— STEVE CLARK was found dead on the 8th of January '91 after drinking/drugs session. Replaced by **VIVIAN CAMPBELL** (b.25 Aug'62, Belfast, N.Ireland) – guitar (ex-DIO, ex-WHITESNAKE, ex-SHADOWKING)

Mar 92. (7"/c-s) *(DEF/+MC 7) <866568>* **LET'S GET ROCKED. / ONLY AFTER DARK** 2 15
(12"pic-d+=) *(DEFXP 7)* – Too late for love (live).
(pic-cd-s+=) *(DEFCD 7)* – Women (live).

Apr 92. (cd/c/lp) *(510978-2/-4/-1) <512185>* **ADRENALIZE** 1 1
– Let's get rocked / Heaven is / Make love like a man / Tonight / White lightning / Stand up (kick love into motion) / Personal property / Have you ever needed someone so bad / I wanna touch you / Tear it down. *(pic-lp iss.Dec92, w / 2 extra tracks; 510978-0) (lp re-iss. Nov99 on 'Simply Vinyl'; SVLP 148)*

Jun 92. (7"/c-s) *(LEP/+MC 7) <864038>* **MAKE LOVE LIKE A MAN. / MISS YOU IN A HEARTBEAT** 12 36
(12"+=) *(LEPXP 7)* – Two steps behind (acoustic).
(cd-s++=) *(LEPCD 5)* – Action.

Aug 92. (c-s) *<864136>* **HAVE YOU EVER NEEDED SOMEONE SO BAD / ELECTED (live)** – 12

Sep 92. (7"/c-s) *(LEP/+MC 8)* **HAVE YOU EVER NEEDED SOMEONE SO BAD. / FROM THE INSIDE** 16 –
(12"pic-d+=) *(LEPXP 8)* – You can't always get what you want.
(cd-s++=) *(LEPCD 8)* – Little wing.

Dec 92. (c-s) *<864604>* **STAND UP (KICK LOVE INTO MOTION) / FROM THE INSIDE (THE ACOUSTIC HIPPIES FROM HELL)** – 34

Jan 93. (7"etched/c-s) *(LEP/+MC 9)* **HEAVEN IS. / SHE'S TOO TOUGH** 13 –
(pic-cd-s+=) *(LEPCD 9)* – Let's get rocked (live) / Elected (live).
(12"pic-d) *(LEPX 9)* – ('A'side) / Let's get rocked (live) / Tokyo road (live).

Mar 93. (c-s) *<862016>* **TONIGHT / SHE'S TOO TOUGH** – 62

Apr 93. (7"/c-s) *(LEP/+MC 10)* **TONIGHT. / NOW I'M HERE (live)** 34 –
(12"pic-d+=) *(LEPX 10)* – Hysteria (live).
(cd-s+=) *(LEPCD 10)* – Photograph (live).
(cd-s) *(LEPCB 10)* – ('A'side) / Pour some sugar on me / ('A'demo).

Sep 93. (7"/c-s) *(LEP/+MC 12) <77116>* **TWO STEPS BEHIND. / TONIGHT (acoustic demo)** 32 12
(cd-s+=) *(LEPCD 12)* – S.M.C.

—— <above single from the film 'Last Action Hero' on 'Columbia' US>

Oct 93. (cd/c/lp) *(<518305-2/-4/-1>)* **RETRO ACTIVE** 6 9
– Desert song / Fractured love / Two steps behind (acoustic) / Only after dark / Action / She's too tough / Miss you in a heartbeat (acoustic) / Only after dark (acoustic) / Ride into the sun / From the inside / Ring of fire / I wanna be your hero / Miss you in a heartbeat / Two steps behind.

Nov 93. (c-s,cd-s) *<858080>* **MISS YOU IN A HEARTBEAT (acoustic version) / LET'S GET ROCKED (live)** – 39

Jan 94. (7"/c-s) *(LEP/+MC 13)* **ACTION. / MISS YOU IN A HEARTBEAT (demo)** 14 –
(cd-s+=) *(LEPCD 13)* – She's too tough (demo).
(cd-s+=) *(LEPCX 13)* – Two steps behind (demo) / Love bites (live).

Oct 95. (c-s) *(LEPMC 14)* **WHEN LOVE & HATE COLLIDE / POUR SOME SUGAR ON ME (remix)** 2 –
(cd-s+=) *(LEPCD 14)* – Armageddon it! (remix).
(cd-s++=) *(LEPDD 14)* – ('A'demo).
(cd-s) *(LEP 14)* – ('A'side) / Rocket (remix) / Excitable (remix).
(cd-s) *(LEP 14)* – ('A'side) / Excitable (remix) / ('A'demo).

Oct 95. (cd/c/lp) *(528656-2/-4/-1) <528815>* **VAULT 1980-1995 DEF LEPPARD GREATEST HITS** (compilation) 3 15
– Pour some sugar on me / Photograph / Love bites / Let's get rocked / Two steps behind / Animal / Heaven is / Rocket / When love & hate collide / Action / Make love like a man / Armageddon it / Have you ever needed someone / So bad / Rock of ages / Hysteria / Bringin' on the heartbreak. *(cd w/free cd)* – LIVE AT DON VALLEY, SHEFFIELD

Nov 95. (c-s) *<852424>* **WHEN LOVE AND HATE COLLIDE / CAN'T KEEP AWAY FROM THE FLAME** – 58

Apr 96. (c-s) *(LEPMC 15)* **SLANG / ANIMAL (live acoustic)** 17 –
(cd-s+=) *(LEPCD 15)* – Ziggy Stardust (live acoustic) / Pour some sugar on me (live acoustic).
(cd-s) *(LEPDD 15)* – ('A'side) / Can't keep the flame away / When love and hate collide (strings and piano version).

May 96. (cd/c/lp) *(<532486-2/-4/-1>)* **SLANG** 5 14
– Truth / Turn to dust / Slang / All I want is everything / Work it out / Breathe a sigh / Deliver me / Gift of flesh / Blood runs cold / Where does love go when it dies / Pearl of euphoria. *(cd w/ free cd rec. live in Singapore)* – Armageddon it / Two steps behind / From the inside / Animal / When love & hate collide / Pour some sugar on me.

Jun 96. (c-s) *(LEPMC 16)* **WORK IT OUT / TWO STEPS BEHIND** 22 –
(cd-s+=) *(LEPCD 16)* – Move with me slowly.

(cd-s) *(LEPDD 16)* – ('A'side) / ('A'demo) / Truth?

Sep 96. (c-s) *(LEPMC 17)* **ALL I WANT IS EVERYTHING / WHEN SATURDAY COMES** [38] [–]
(cd-s+=) *(LEPCD 17)* – Jimmy's theme / ('A'radio edit).
(cd-s) *(LEPDD 17)* – ('A'side) / 'Cause we ended as lovers / Led boots / ('A'radio edit).

Nov 96. (c-s) *(578838-4)* **BREATHE A SIGH / ROCK! ROCK! (TILL YOU DROP)** [43] [–]
(cd-s+=) *(578839-2)* – Deliver me (live) / Slang (live).
(cd-s) *(578841-2)* – ('A'side) / Another hit and run (live) / All I want is everything (live) / Work it out (live).

Jun 99. (cd/c) *(<546 244-2/212-4>)* **EUPHORIA** [11] [11]
– Demolition man / Promises / Back in your face / Goodbye / All night / Paper sun / It's only love / 21st century sha la la girl / To be alive / Disintigrate / Guilty / Day after day / Kings of oblivion.

Jul 99. (c-s) *(562136-4)* **PROMISES / BACK IN YOUR FACE – GOODBYE – ALL NIGHT (excerpts)** [41] [ ]
(cd-s+=) *(562137-2)* – Under my wheels.
(cd-s) *(562136-2)* – ('A'side) / World's collide / Immortal.

Sep 99. (c-s) *(562288-4)* **GOODBYE / IMMORTAL** [ ] [ ]
(cd-s+=) *(562288-2)* – Burnout.
(cd-s) *(562289-2)* – ('A'side) / Who do you love? / When love and hate collide.

Aug 02. (cd-s) *(063969-2)* **NOW / LET ME BE THE ONE (acoustic) / SNIPPETS / ('A'-video)** [23] [–]
(cd-s) *(063968-2)* – ('A'side) / Stay with me / Rebel rebel.
(cd-s) *(063967-2)* – ('A'side) / Pour some sugar on me (live) / Let's get rocked (live).

Aug 02. (cd) *(<063120-2>)* **X** [14] [11]
– Now / Unbelievable / You're so beautiful / Everyday / Long long way to go / Four letter word / Torn to shreds / Love don't lie / Gravity / Cry / Girl like you / Let me be the one / Scar.

Apr 03. (cd-s) *(9800024)* **LONG LONG WAY TO GO / 10 TIMES BIGGAR THAN LOVE / NOW (acoustic) / ('A'-video)** [40] [–]

DEFTONES

Formed: Sacramento, California, USA . . . 1989, by magnetic frontman CHINO MORENO, plus STEPHEN CARPENTER, CHI CHENG and ABE CUNNINGHAM. One of the more promising acts to have signed to MADONNA's 'Maverick' label (through 'Warners'), DEFTONES released their debut album, 'ADRENALINE' in 1995. Like a gonzoid cross between JONATHAN DAVIS (KORN) and ZACK DE LA ROCHA, CHINO's incendiary live presence helped the group build up a loyal following. By the release of their next set, 'AROUND THE FUR' (1997), their post-metal noise had reached fruition, from the sonic assault of the album's opener, 'MY OWN SUMMER (SHOVE IT)' to 'HEADUP' (a collaboration with Sepultura's MAX CAVALERA). After much soul searching and turmoil, the veteran – at least in terms of today's high turnover music scene – Cali noise abusers returned with that difficult third album, 'WHITE PONY' (2000). Older and wiser if no more content with his lot, the perennially pissed off MORENO reflects on his lost youth in 'TEENAGER' while TOOL frontman MAYNARD JAMES KEENAN joins the fray on the poignant 'PASSENGER'. Leaving the rap-metal posturing to the young pretenders, DEFTONES took their foot off the gas while still maintaining a head of steam. With its stark, eponymous title and skull adorned cover, 2003's 'DEFTONES' suggested a statement of intent recorded to claim back territory lost during their lengthy sabbatical. MORENO certainly sounded more aggrieved than ever, and the band had rarely played with so much feral aggression, although it was tempting to lament possibilities opened up on 'WHITE PONY' and left unexplored here. Perhaps MORENO had exhausted his more abstruse creative impulses on the TEAM SLEEP project, a collaboration with DJ CROOK and guitarist TOM WILKINSON. • **Covered:** THE CHAUFFEUR (Duran Duran) / TO HAVE AND TO HOLD (Depeche Mode).

Album rating: ADRENALINE (*9) / AROUND THE FUR (*8) / WHITE PONY (*6) / BACK TO SCHOOL (MINI MAGGIT) (*6) / DEFTONES (*5)

CHINO MORENO – vocals / **STEPHEN CARPENTER** – guitar / **CHI CHENG** – bass, vocals / **ABE CUNNINGHAM** – drums

Maverick Maverick

Oct 95. (cd/c) *<9362 46054-2/-4>* **ADRENALINE** [ ] [ ]
– Bored / Minus blindfold / One weak / Nosebleed / Lifter / Root / 7 words / Birthmark / Engine No.9 / Fireal.

Nov 97. (cd/c) *<9362 46810-2/-4>* **AROUND THE FUR** [56] [29]
– My own summer (shove it) / Lhabia / Mascara / Around the fur / Be quiet and drive / Lotion / Dai the flu / Headup / MX.

Mar 98. (7"/c-s) *(W 0432/+C)* **MY OWN SUMMER (SHOVE IT). / ROOT (live)** [29] [ ]
(cd-s+=) *(W 0432CD)* – Nosebleed (live) / Lifter (live).
(cd-s) *(W 0432CDX)* – ('A'side) / Lotion (live) / Fireal swords (live) / Bored (live).

Jun 98. (7") *(W 0445)* **BE QUIET AND DRIVE (FAR AWAY). / ('A'acoustic)** [50] [ ]
(cd-s+=) *(W 0445CD)* – Birthmark (live).
(cd-s) *(W 0445CDX)* – ('A'side) / Engine No.9 (live) / Teething (live).

Jun 00. (cd/lp) *<9362 47799-2/-1>* **WHITE PONY** [13] [3]
– Fleticeria / Digital bath / Elite / RX queen / Street carp / Teenager / Knife party / Korea / Passenger / Change (in the house of flies) / Pink maggit. *<US-iss.+=>* – The boy's republic.

Aug 00. (cd-s) *(W 531CDX)* **CHANGE (IN THE HOUSE OF FLIES) / (+ 2 similar versions)** [53] [–]

Mar 01. (m-cd) *<9362 48082-2>* **BACK TO SCHOOL (MINI MAGGIT)** [35] [ ]
– Back to school (mini maggit) / Falticeira (live) / Back to school (live) / Nosebleed (live) / Teething (live) / Change (in the house of flies) (live acoustic) / Pink maggit / White pony EPK (short version).

May 03. (7") *(W 605)* **MINERVA. / SINATRA** [15] [–]
(cd-s+=) *(W 605CD)* – Sleep walk.

May 03. (cd) *(9362 48391-2)* *<48350>* **DEFTONES** [7] [2]
– Hexagram / Needles and pins / Minerva / Good morning beautiful / Deathblow / When girls telephone boys / Battle-axe / Lucky you / Bloody cape / Anniversary of an uninteresting event / Moana.

Sep 03. (7") *(W 623)* **HEXAGRAM. / BLOODY CAPE** [68] Dec03 [ ]
(cd-s+=) *(W 623CD)* *<42666>* – Lovers / ('A'-video).

DEL AMITRI

Formed: Glasgow, Scotland . . . 1983 by singer/songwriter JUSTIN CURRIE and IAIN HARVIE, who recruited additional musicians BRYAN TOLLAND and PAUL TYAGI prior to recording their debut single, 'SENSE SICKNESS', for independent label, 'No Strings'. Emerging in the golden era of Scots indie when 'Postcard' was the hippest namedrop on the block, the group's early, acoustic-orientated approach brought inevitable comparisons with ORANGE JUICE and their ilk, while CURRIE's subtly sardonic lyrics marked him out as an aspiring wordsmith. A punishing round of gigging, including a number of prestigious support slots, slowly raised DEL AMITRI's profile and subsequently attracted the interest of 'Chrysalis' records. Signed to a major label deal, the band made their album debut in Spring '85 with 'DEL AMITRI', a competent set which showcased the band's intelligent folk pop/rock. The initial press reaction was encouraging and the future looked bright prior to a subsequent dispute with the company leaving them label-less. Lending new meaning to the term "grassroots following", DEL AMITRI's loyal band of US fans were pivotal in the success of their ensuing American tour, promoting gigs and providing an accommodation alternative to the dreaded tour van. The success of the jaunt led to another major label venture, this time around with 'A&M', who were far more successful in getting DEL AMITRI's career off the ground. Throughout the interim "wilderness"

years, CURRIE had been carefully honing his writing skills, the more mature approach paying off when the 'KISS THIS THING GOODBYE' single made the UK Top 60. Released at the same time, a belated follow-up album, 'WAKING HOURS' (1989), eventually made the British Top 10 following the success of 'NOTHING EVER HAPPENS'. A world-weary diatribe on societal inertia, the track's earthy sound – if not its tone of barely concealed bitterness – was characteristic of the more accessible path DEL AMITRI were now cultivating. With his legendary sideburns and windswept good looks, CURRIE also became something of an unlikely early 90's sex symbol, the shag candidate for the more discerning female prior to EVAN DANDO cornering the market with his flowing locks. Whatever, CURRIE was certainly the group's focal point and many fans no doubt scarcely noticed that new boys DAVID CUMMINGS (a replacement for MICK SLAVEN, who himself had succeeded TOLLAND on the previous set) and BRIAN McDERMOTT had been recruited for a third set, 'CHANGE EVERYTHING' (1992). More polished and chart-friendly than any DEL AMITRI release to date, the record narrowly missed the UK No.1 spot, its immaculately crafted (yet often verging on bland) MOR spawning another major hit in 'ALWAYS THE LAST TO KNOW' and a further trio of fairly minor chart encounters with 'BE MY DOWNFALL', 'JUST LIKE A MAN' and 'WHEN YOU WERE YOUNG'. A fourth set, 'TWISTED' (1995), hardly broke new ground, although it did spawn a US Top 10 in 'ROLL TO ME'; that DEL AMITRI appealed to the American market was hardly surprising, their reliably safe, inoffensive coffee-table roots rock ideal fodder for FM radio. Never being the trendiest of bands, DEL AMITRI never really suffered a backlash, carving out their own little niche with relative success almost guaranteed. In 2002, the group issued the eagerly awaited set 'CAN YOU DO ME GOOD?', which featured the single 'JUST BEFORE YOU LEAVE', a light and breezy soul number that reflected the mood of the album. Tracks such as 'OUT FALLS THE PAST' and 'CASH AND PRIZES' hadn't lost 'AMITRI their melodic appeal, synonymous with the outfit's earlier works, although the album as a whole disappointed.
• **Songwriters:** CURRIE – HARVIE composed except covers; DON'T CRY NO TEARS (Neil Young) / BYE BYE PRIDE (Go-Betweens) / CINDY INCIDENTLY (Faces). • **Trivia:** DEL AMITRI means 'from the womb' in Greek.

Album rating: DEL AMITRI (*6) / WAKING HOURS (*8) / CHANGE EVERYTHING (*7) / TWISTED (*6) / SOME OTHER SUCKER'S PARADE (*5) / HATFUL OF RAIN – THE BEST OF DEL AMITRI compilation (**8**) / CAN YOU DO ME GOOD? (*6)

JUSTIN CURRIE (b.11 Dec'64) – vocals, bass, acoustic guitar / **IAIN HARVIE** (b.19 May'62) – guitar / **BRYAN TOLLAND** – guitar / **PAUL TYAGIS** – drums, percussion

No Strings — not iss.

Aug 83. (7") *(NOSP 1)* **SENSE SICKNESS. / THE DIFFERENCE IS** [ ] [–]

Chrysalis — Chrysalis

May 85. (lp/c) *(CHR/ZCHR 1499)* **DEL AMITRI** [ ] [ ]
– Heard through a wall / Hammering heart / Former owner / Sticks and stones girl / Deceive yourself (in ignorant Heaven) / I was here / Crows in a wheatfield / Keepers / Ceasefire / Breaking bread. *(cd-iss. Dec90; CCD 1499)*

Jul 85. (7") *(CHS 2859)* **STICKS AND STONES GIRL. / THIS KING IS POOR** [ ] [–]
(12"+=) *(CHS12 2859)* – The difference is.

Oct 85. (7") *(CHS 2925)* **HAMMERING HEART. / LINES RUNNING NORTH** [ ] [–]
(12"+=) *(CHS12 2925)* – Brown eyed girl.

—— **MICK SLAVEN** – guitar (ex-BOURGIE BOURGIE) repl. TOLLAND / sessions from **ANDY ALSTON** – keyboards / **ROBERT CAIRNS** – violin / **BLAIR COWAN** – accordion / **STEPHEN IRVINE** – drums / **JULIAN DAWSON** – harmonica / **JAMES O'MALLEY** – bass / **CAROLINE LEVELLE** – cello / **WILL MOWAT** – seq, keyboards

A&M — A&M

Jul 89. (7") *(AM 515)* **KISS THIS THING GOODBYE. / NO HOLDING ON** [59] [ ]
(12"+=/3"cd-s+=) *(AMY/CDEE 515)* – Slowly, it's coming back.

Jul 89. (lp/c/cd) *(AMA/AMC/CDA 9006)* <5287> **WAKING HOURS** [ ] Feb90 [95]
– Kiss this thing goodbye / Opposite view / Move away Jimmy Blue / Stone cold sober / You're gone / When I want you / This side of the morning / Empty / Hatful of rain / Nothing ever happens. *(re-dist.Feb90 hit UK No.6; same) (re-iss. Mar95 cd/c; same)*

Oct 89. (7") *(AM 527)* **STONE COLD SOBER. / THE RETURN OF MAGGIE BROWN** [ ] [ ]
(12"+=/3"cd-s+=) *(AMY/CDEE 527)* – Talk it to death.

Jan 90. (7"/c-s) *(AM/+MC 536)* **NOTHING EVER HAPPENS. / SO MANY SOULS TO CHANGE** [11] [ ]
(12"+=/cd-s+=) *(AMY/CDEE 536)* – Don't I look like the kind of guy you used to hate? / Evidence.

Mar 90. (7"/7"g-f/c-s) *(AM/+S/MC 551)* **KISS THIS THING GOODBYE. / NO HOLDING ON** [43] [–]
(10"+=/12"+=/cd-s+=) *(10AMX/AMY/AMCD 551)* – Slowly, it's coming back.

Apr 90. (c-s) <1485> **KISS THIS THING GOODBYE. / THE RETURN OF MAGGIE BROWN** [–] [35]

Jun 90. (7"/c-s) *(AM/+MC 555)* **MOVE AWAY JIMMY BLUE. / ANOTHER LETTER HOME** [36] [ ]
(12"+=) *(AMX 555)* – April the first / This side of the morning (live).
(12"+=/cd-s+=) *(AM Y/CD 555)* – April the first / More than you'd ever know.

Oct 90. (7"/c-s) *(AM/+MC 589)* **SPIT IN THE RAIN. / SCARED TO LIVE** [21] [ ]
(12"+=) *(AMY 589)* – The return of Maggie Brown.
(10"++=/cd-s++=) *(AM X/CD 589)* – Talk it to death.

—— **DAVID CUMMINGS** – guitar repl. SLAVEN / **BRIAN McDERMOTT** – drums (who guested on last) repl. TYGANI

Apr 92. (7"/c-s) *(AM/+MC 870)* <1604> **ALWAYS THE LAST TO KNOW. / LEARN TO CRY** [13] [–]
(cd-s+=) *(AMCD 870)* – Angel on the roof / The whole world is quiet.

Jun 92. (cd/c/lp) *(395385-2/-4/-1)* <5385> **CHANGE EVERYTHING** [2] [ ]
– Be my downfall / Just like a man / When you were young / Surface of the Moon / I won't take the blame / The first rule of love / The ones that you love lead you nowhere / Always the last to know / To last a lifetime / As soon as the tide comes in / Behind the fool / Sometimes I just have to say your name. *(re-iss. cd/c Mar95; same)*

Jun 92. (7"/c-s) *(AM/+MC 884)* **BE MY DOWNFALL. / WHISKEY REMORSE** [30] [–]
(10"+=/cd-s+=) *(AM X/CD 884)* – Lighten up the load / The heart is a bad design.

Jul 92. (c-s) <1604> **ALWAYS THE LAST TO KNOW / BE MY DOWNFALL** [–] [30]

Sep 92. (7"/c-s) *(AM/+MC 0057)* **JUST LIKE A MAN. / SPIT IN THE RAIN (remix)** [25] [ ]
(cd-s+=) *(AMCDR 0057)* – I won't to take the blame (acoustic) / Scared to live.
(cd-s) *(AMCD 0057)* – ('A'side) / Don't cry no tears / Bye bye pride / Cindy incidentally.

Jan 93. (7"/c-s) *(AM/+MC 0132)* **WHEN YOU WERE YOUNG. / LONG JOURNEY HOME THE ONES THAT YOU LOVE LEAD YOU NOWHERE** [20] [ ]
(cd-s+=) *(AMCDR 0132)* – The verb to do / Kestral road.
(cd-s) *(AMCD 0132)* – ('A'side) / The ones that you love lead you nowhere (live) / Kiss this thing goodbye (live) / Hatful of rain (live).

Feb 95. (c-s) *(580 959-4)* **HERE AND NOW / LONG WAY DOWN** [21] [ ]
(10"+=) *(580 969-1)* – Someone else will / Queen of false alarms.
(cd-s+=) *(580 959-2)* – Queen of false alarms / Crashing down.
(cd-s) *(580 969-2)* – ('A'side) / Always the last to know (live) / When I want you (live) / Stone cold sober (live).

Feb 95. (cd/c/lp) *(540 311-2/-4/-1)* <0311> **TWISTED** [3] [ ]
– Food for songs / Start with me / Here and now / One thing left to do / Tell her this / Being somebody else / Roll to me / Crashing down / It might as well be you / Never enough / It's never too late to be alone / Driving with the brakes on. *(re-iss. d-cd Aug95; 540396-2)*

Apr 95. (7"/c-s) *(581 004-7/-4)* **DRIVING WITH THE BRAKES ON. / LIFE BY MISTAKE** [18] [ ]
(cd-s+=) *(581 005-2)* – A little luck / In the meantime.
(cd-s) *(581 007-2)* – ('A'side) / Nothing ever happens / Kiss this thing goodbye / Always the last to know.

Jun 95. (c-s) *(581 128-4)* **ROLL TO ME / IN THE FRAME** 22 –
(cd-s+=) *(581 129-2)* – Food for songs (acoustic) / One thing left to do (acoustic).
(cd-s) *(581 131-2)* – ('A'side) / Spit in the rain / Stone cold sober (remix) / Move away Jimmy Blue.
Jun 95. (c-s) <*1114*> **ROLL TO ME / LONG WAY DOWN** – 10
Oct 95. (c-s) *(581 214-4)* **TELL HER THIS / A BETTER MAN** 32 –
(cd-s+=) *(581 215-2)* – The last love song / When you were young.
(cd-s) *(518 217-2)* – ('A'side) / Whiskey remorse / Fred Partington's daughter / Learn to cry.
Jun 97. (c-s) *(582 252-4)* **NOT WHERE IT'S AT / SLEEP INSTEAD OF TEARDROPS** 21 –
(cd-s+=) *(582 253-2)* – Spair pair of laces / Before the evening steals the afternoon.
(cd-s+=) *(582 255-2)* – A grimace not a smile / Low friends in high places.
Jul 97. (cd/c/lp) *(540 705-2/-4/-1)* **SOME OTHER SUCKER'S PARADE** 6 –
– Not where it's at / Some other sucker's parade / Won't make it better / What I think she sees / Medicine / High times / Mother nature's writing / No family man / Cruel light of day / Funny way to win / Through all that nothing / Life is full / Lucky guy / Make it always be too late. *(cd re-iss. Jun03; same)*

—— In Sep'97, 'MEDICINE' was due for release but withdrawn; see below single for corresponding b-sides; 582365-2/582367-2/582569-2.

Nov 97. (cd-s) *(582 433-2)* **SOME OTHER SUCKER'S PARADE / DRIVING WITH THE BRAKES ON (live) / MOVE AWAY JIMMY BLUE (live) / THE ONES THAT YOU LOVE LEAD YOU NOWHERE (live)** 46 –
(cd-s) *(582 435-2)* – ('A'side) / Roll to me (live) / Here & now (live) / Hatful of rain (live).
(cd-s) *(582 437-2)* – ('A'side) / ('A'live) / Always the last to know (live) / Stone cold sober (live).
Jun 98. (c-s/cd-s) *(582 705-4/-2)* **DON'T COME HOME TOO SOON / THREE LITTLE WORDS / PAPER THIN / DON'T COME HOME TOO SOON (instrumental)** 15 –
(cd-s) *(582 707-2)* – ('A'side) / Nothing ever happens / Kiss this thing goodbye / Always the last to know.
Aug 98. (c-s) *(566 347-4)* **CRY TO BE FOUND / CANNED LAUGHTER** 40 –
(cd-s+=) *(566 347-2)* – One step at a time.
(cd-s) *(566 349-2)* – ('A'side) / Being somebody else (live) / Not where it's at.
Sep 98. (cd/c) *(<540 940-2/-4>)* **HATFUL OF RAIN – THE BEST OF DEL AMITRI** (compilation) 5
– Cry to be found / Roll to me / Kiss this thing goodbye / Not where it's at / Nothing ever happens / Always the last to know / Here & now / Just like a man / Spit in the rain / When we were young / Driving with the brakes on / Stone cold sober / Tell her this / Move away Jimmy Blue / Be my downfall / Some other sucker's parade / Don't come home too soon. *(d-cd includes* **LOUSY WITH LOVE – THE B-SIDES***; 540 941-2)* – Scared to live / The return of Maggie Brown / In the frame / Sleep instead of teardrops / Long journey home / Paper thin / The last love song / Verb to do / In the meantime / Long way down / Whiskey remorse / Before the evening steals the afternoon / So many souls to change.

Mercury not iss.

Apr 02. (c-s) *(497696-4)* **JUST BEFORE YOU LEAVE / I'M AN UNBELIEVER** 37 –
(cd-s+=) *(497697-2)* – You love me.
(cd-s) *(497696-2)* – ('A'side) / Septic jubilee / Belong belong / ('A'-video).
Apr 02. (cd/c) *(493216-2/-4)* **CAN YOU DO ME GOOD?** 30 –
– Just before you leave / Cash and prizes / Drunk in a band / One more last hurrah / Buttons on my cloths / Baby, it's me / Wash her away / Last cheap shot at the dream / Out falls the past / She's passing this way / Jesus saves / Just getting by.

DE LA SOUL

Formed: Amityville, Long Island, New York, USA ... 1987 by DAVID JOLICOEUR (TRUGOY THE DOVE), KELVIN MERCER (POSDNOUS) & VINCENT MASON (PACEMASTER MASE). They quickly set about writing their soon-to-be critically acclaimed cross-Atlantic debut album, '3 FEET HIGH AND RISING', which made the Top 30 in the Spring of '89. Psychedelic hip-hop rappers, influenced a little by the mid 80's urban scene, they dressed mostly in baggy sportswear, infusing their lyrics with a pseudo flower-power, visionary attitude, termed as 'daisy-age'. These hip hop gypsies sampled everything from JAMES BROWN (again!) to STEELY DAN, the latter on debut hit 'ME MYSELF AND I'. Produced by STETSASONIC's PRINCE PAUL, it featured cameos from A TRIBE CALLED QUEST, JUNGLE BROTHERS (their inspiration) and QUEEN LATIFAH. Their much-anticipated but disappointing 1991 follow-up, 'DE LA SOUL IS DEAD,' accurately predicted their fate. Nevertheless, the album sold respectably and on reflection, many critics acknowledged that it contained some disturbing but poignant messages. On '93's 'BUHLOONE MINDSTATE', DE LA SOUL were back on top form once again, firing subtly subversive broadsides at the white middle class ruling system. Following 1996's 'STAKES IS HIGH', the trio took an extended break before coming back with the first installment in a proposed trio of albums billed as 'ART OFFICIAL INTELLIGENCE'. Unfortunately, this first volume, 'MOSAIC THUMP' (2000), proved as weak as the pun of the series' title. Like many old school crews, DE LA SOUL have obviously found it difficult to square their refined sensibilities with the more aggressive climate of current day hip hop. Despite the contributions of JAYDEE and BUSTA RHYMES amongst others, DE LA SOUL's attempts at sounding contemporary sound forced at best. Not so the second volume in the series, 'AIO: BIONIX' (2001), a belated return to form revelling in the kind of irreverent playfulness they seemed to have consigned to history more than a decade ago. Catalysed by producer Dave West's winning sonic backdrop, the veteran trio turned in some of the best lyrical smarts since their celebrated debut.

Album rating: 3 FEET HIGH AND RISING (*9) / DE LA SOUL IS DEAD (*6) / BUHLOONE MINDSTATE (*6) / STAKES IS HIGH (*7) / ART OFFICIAL INTELLIGENCE: MOSAIC THUMP (*7) / AOI: BIONIX (*6) / THE BEST OF DE LA SOUL or TIMELESS: THE SINGLES COLLECTION compilation (*7)

TRUGOY THE DOVE (b. DAVID JOLICOEUR, 21 Sep'68, Brooklyn) – vocals / **POSDNOUS** (b. KELVIN MERCER, 17 Aug'69, Bronx) – vocals / **PACEMASTER MASE** (b. VINCENT MASON, 24 Mar'70, Brooklyn) – DJ

Tommy Boy Tommy Boy

Jul 88. (7") **PLUG TUNIN'. / FREEDOM OF SPEAK** –
Oct 88. (7") <*(TB 917)*> **JENIFA (TAUGHT ME). /**

Big Life Tommy Boy

Mar 89. (lp/c/cd) *(DLS LP/MC/CD 1)* <*TB/+C/CD 1019*> **3 FEET HIGH AND RISING** 13 24
– Intro / The magic number / Change in speak / Cool breeze on the rocks / Can you kep a secret / Jenifa (taught me) / Ghetto thang / Transmitting live from Mars / Eye know / Take it off / A little bit of soap / Tread water / Say no go / Do as De La does / Plug tunin' / De La orgee / Buddy / Description / Me myself and I / This is a recording for living in a fulltime era I can do anything / D.A.I.S.Y. age / Potholes in my lawn. *(cd re-iss. Jan96; DLSCD 1) (cd re-iss. Jun97 +=; TBCD 1019)* – Plug tunin' (12"mix). *(re-iss. Sep99, hit UK No.17)*
Mar 89. (7") *(BLR 7)* <*7926*> **ME MYSELF AND I. / BRAIN WASHED FOLLOWER** 22 Feb89 34
(12"+=) *(BLR 7T)* – Ain't hip to be labelled a hippie / What's more. *(re-iss. Sep99 on 'B.C.M.'; BCM 14232)*
(cd-s+=) *(BLR 7CD)* – Ain't hip to be labelled a hippie / ('A'version).
(12"+=) *(BLR 7R)* – ('A'remixes).
Jun 89. (7"/7"pic-d) *(BLR 10/+P)* **SAY NO GO. / THEY DON'T KNOW THAT THE SOUL DON'T GO FOR THAT** 18
(12"+=/cd-s+=) *(BLR 10 T/CD)* – ('A'versions).

(12"+=) *(BLR 10R)* – ('A'remixes). *(re-iss. Sep99 on 'B.C.M.'; BCM 12295)*

Sep 89. (7"/7"pic-d/c-s) *(BLR 13/+P/C)* **EYE KNOW. / THE MACK DADDY ON THE LEFT** [14] [ ]
(12"+=/cd-s+=) *(BLR 13 T/CD)* – ('A'versions).

Dec 89. (7"/c-s) *(BLR 14/+MC)* **THE MAGIC NUMBER. / BUDDY** [7] [ ]
(12"+=/cd-s+=) *(BLR 14 T/CD)* – Ghetto thang.
(12"+=) *(BLR 14R)* – ('A'remixes). *(re-iss. Sep99 on 'B.C.M.'; BCM 12387)*

—— In Mar'90, DE LA SOUL were credited on QUEEN LATIFAH's UK Top 20 single 'MAMA GAVE BIRTH TO THE SOUL CHILDREN' *(Gee Street; GEE 26)*

Apr 91. (7"/c-s) *(BLR 42/+MC)* **RING RING RING (HA HA HEY). / PILES AND PILES OF DEMO TAPES BI DA MILES** [10] [ ]
(12") *(BLR 42T)* – ('A'extended) / Afro connection of a mis / ('A'-sax version).
(cd-s+=) *(BLR 42CD)* – ('A'-party mix).

May 91. (cd/c/d-lp) *(BLR CD/MC/LP 8)* *<TB/+C/CD 1029>* **DE LA SOUL IS DEAD** [7] [26]
– Intro / Oodles of O's / Talkin' bout hey love / Pease porridge / (skit 1) / Johnny's dead aka Vincent Mason (live from the BK lounge) / A roller skating jam named 'Saturdays' (disco fever edit) / WRMS' dedication to the bitty / Bitties in the BK lounge / (skit 2) / Let, let me in / Rap de rap show / Millie pulled a pistol on Santa / (skit 3) / Pass the plugs / Ring ring ring (ha ha hey) / WRMS: Cat's in control / (skit 4) / Shwingalokate / Fanatic of the B word / Keepin' the faith / (skit 5). *(cd re-iss. Jan96; DLSCD 8)*

Jul 91. (7"/c-s) *(BLR 55/+MC)* **A ROLLER SKATING JAM CALLED 'SATURDAYS'. / WHAT YOUR LIFE CAN TRULY BE** [22] [ ]
(12"+=/cd-s+=) *(BLR 55 T/CD)* – ('A'-disco mix) / Who's skatin'.

Nov 91. (7"/c-s) *(BLR 64/+MC)* **KEEPIN' THE FAITH (remix). / ('A'instrumental)** [50] [ ]
(12"+=) *(BLR 64T)* – Roller skating jam called 'Saturdays' / Ring ring ring (ha ha hey).
(cd-s) *(BLR 64CD)* – (2 'A'versions) / ('A'instrumental) / ('A' funky mix).

Sep 93. (7"/c-s) *(BLR/+C 103)* *<7586>* **BREAKADAWN. / EN FOCUS (vocal version)** [39] [76]
(12"+=/cd-s+=) *(BLR T/CD 103)* – ('A'mixes).

Oct 93. (cd/c/lp) *(BLR CD/MC/LP 25)* *<1063>* **BUHLOONE MIND STATE** [37] Sep93 [40]
– Intro / Eye patch / En focus / Patti Dooke / I be blowin' / Long Island wildin' / Ego trippin' / Paul Revere / Three days later / Area / I am I be / In the woods / Breakadawn / Dave has a problem . . . seriously / Stone age / Lonely days.

—— In Mar'94. they teamed up with TEENAGE FANCLUB on the single 'FALLIN' *(Epic 660262-4/-2)*. From the rap-rock film 'Judgement Night'.

Nov 95. (12"/cd-s) *(BLR T/D 132)* **ME MYSELF & I (radio mix) / AIN'T HIP TO BE LABELED A HIPPIE (vocal) / ME MYSELF AND I (instrumental). / WHAT'S MORE / ME MYSELF AND I (oblapos mode) / BRAIN WASHED FOLLOWER (vocal) / ME MYSELF AND I (oblapos instrumental)** [ ] [–]

Tommy Boy Tommy Boy

Jun 96. (c-s) *(TBC 7730)* **STAKES IS HIGH / ('A'-UK clean version)** [55] [ ]
(cd-s) *<(TBCD 7730)>* – ('A'side) / ('A'extended) / ('A'-DJ original) / The bizness.
(12") *(TBV 7730)* – ('A'extended) / ('A'-DJ original) / ('A'-album version) / ('A'-acapella).

Jul 96. (cd/c/d-lp) *<(TB CD/C/V 1149)>* **STAKES IS HIGH** [42] [13]
– Intro / Supa emcees / The bizness (featuring COMMON SENSE) / Wonce again Long Island / Dinninit / Brakes / Dog eat dog / Baby baby baby ooh baby / Long Island degrees / Betta listen / Itsoweezee (featuring HOT) / 4 more (featuring ZHANE) / Big brother beat (featuring MOS DEF) / Down syndrome / Pony ride (featuring TRUTH ENOLA) / Stakes is high / Sunshine. *(cd re-iss. Feb97; same)*

Mar 97. (c-ep/12"ep/cd-ep) *(TB C/V/CD 7779)* **4 MORE / BABY BABY BABY BABY OOH BABY. / ITZSOWEEZEE / SWEET DREAMS** [52] [ ]

Jul 00. (12"/cd-s; by DE LA SOUL featuring REDMAN) *(TBV/TBCD 2102/+A)* **OOOH. / WORDS AND VERBS** [29] [ ]
(cd-s) *(TBCD 2102B)* – ('A'side) / So good.

Aug 00. (cd/d-lp) *(TBCD/TBV 1348)* *<1361>* **ART OFFICIAL INTELLIGENCE: MOSAIC THUMP** [22] [9]
– Spitkicker.com – Say R / U can do (life) / My writes (with RASH / J-RO OF THA LIKS / XZIBIT) / Oooh. (with REDMAN) / Thru ya city (with DV ALIAS KHRIST) / I.C. y'all (with BUSTA RHYMES) / View / Set the mood (with INDEED) / All good (with CHAKA KHAN) / Declaration / Squat! (with MIKE D & AD ROCK) / Words from the chief rocker (with BUSY BEE) / With me / Copa (cabanga) / Foolin' / The art of getting jumped / U don't wanna B.D.S. (with FREDDIE FOX).

Oct 00. (12"/cd-s; by DE LA SOUL featuring CHAKA KHAN) *(TBV/TBCD 2154/+A)* *<2178>* **ALL GOOD / (MJ Cole mix) / (original instrumental)** [33] [96]
(cd-s) *(TBCD 2154B)* – ('A'mixes).

Dec 01. (cd/lp) *<(TBCD/TBV 1362)>* **AOI: BIONIX** [ ] [ ]
– Intro / Bionix / Baby phat (featuring DEVIN THE DUDE + ELIZABETH "YUMMY" BINGHAM) / Simply / Simply havin / Held down / Reverend Do Good #1 / Watch out (with JOSE "PERICO" HERNANDEZ) / Special (with ELIZABETH "YUMMY" BINGHAM) / Reverend Do Good #2 / The sauce (with PHILLY BLACK & SMILES PATRON) / Am I worth you? / Pawn star (with SHELL COUNCIL & JASON SPEARS) / What we do (for love) (with SOULSTICE, CLAUDIA & SLICK RICK) / Reverend Do Good #3 / Peer pressure (with B-REAL) / It's American / Trying people.

Feb 02. (12"/; as DE LA SOUL featuring DEVIN THE DUDE & ELIZABETH "YUMMY" BINGHAM) *(TBV 2395)* **BABY PHAT / (instrumental)** [55] [–]
(cd-s+=) *(TBCD 2395A)* – Watch out (clean + instrumental).
(cd-s) *(TBCD 2395B)* – ('A'side) / Watch out / All good? (can 7 supermarket mix).

– compilations, etc. –

May 03. (cd) *Rhino; <73860>* **TIMELESS: THE SINGLES COLLECTION** [–] [ ]

Jun 03. (cd/d-lp) *Warners; (8122 73665-2/-1)* **THE BEST OF DE LA SOUL** [17] [–]
– Me myself and I / Say no go / Eye know / Magic number / Potholes in my lawn (12" vocal version) / Buddy (with JUNGLE BROTHERS, Q-TIP & PHIFE) / Ring ring ring (ha ha hey) / Roller skating jam named Saturdays / Keepin' the faith / Breakadawn / Stakes is high / 4 more (with ZHANE) / Oooh (with REDMAN) / All good (with CHAKA KHAN) / Thru ya city (with DV ALIAS KHRIST) / Baby phat (with DEVIN THE DUDE & ELIZABETH "YUMMY" BINGHAM) / Watch out.

DELGADOS

Formed: Glasgow, Scotland . . . late 1994 by ex-university graduates, ALUN WOODWARD, EMMA POLLOCK, STEWART HENDERSON and PAUL SAVAGE. Not only did they kickstart Scotland's flagging (nae, virtually dead) indie scene, they did it by initiating their own imprint, 'Chemikal Underground'. The label's debut, 'MONICA WEBSTER', was greatly received by the music press and of course, who else? DJ John Peel, their angular guitar reminiscent of PAVEMENT, although ALUN and EMMA's twee vocal touches called to mind BELLE & SEBASTIAN. Single after single continued to impress until the excellent debut album, 'DOMESTIQUES', surfaced in late '96. Their "difficult" second album, 'PELOTON' (1998), managed to crack the UK Top 60, spurred on by indie hits, 'PULL THE WIRES FROM THE WALL' and 'THE WEAKER ARGUMENT DEFEATS THE STRONGER'. But perhaps it was their third and most accomplished set, 'The GREAT EASTERN' (named after a shelter in Glasgow's East end) which secured the group's ever growing reputation. For one, the album itself had not one weak point among the ten-or-so tracks, which segued like needle into thread. The DELGADOS owe much of this feat to the whistling flutes, assortment of horns and ambiguous use of orchestration which popped up throughout the set's dizzying array of songs. Stand out tracks (and, boy, did they really stand out!) included 'AMERICAN TRILOGY', 'AYE TODAY' and the frail accompaniment of closing number, 'MAKE YOUR MOVE'. Although the album failed to crack the mainstream, it did reach the minor regions of the charts, as did aforementioned single 'AMERICAN TRILOGY'. So, God bless the much dismissed DELGADOS – where would ARAB STRAP, MOGWAI and now majors-tempted BIS be without them and their seminal label?! • **Covers:** THE DIRGE (New Bad Things) / SACRE CHARLEMAGNE (France Gall) / A VERY CELLULAR SONG (Incredible String Band) / HOW CAN WE HANG ON TO A DREAM? (Tim Hardin) / MR BLUE SKY (Electric Light Orchestra).

Album rating: DOMESTIQUES (*9) / PELOTON (*8) / THE GREAT EASTERN (*8) / HATE (*8)

ALUN WOODWARD – vocals, guitar / **EMMA POLLOCK** – vocals, guitar / **STEWART HENDERSON** – bass / **PAUL SAVAGE** – drums

Chemikal U/ground — March

Jul 95. (7") *(chem 001)* **MONICA WEBSTER. / BRAND NEW CAR** [ ] [–]

Aug 95. (7"ep/cd-ep) *(SCAN/+CS 07)* **THE LAZARWALKER EP** [ ] [–]
– Primary alternative / Lazarwalker / Buttonhole / Blackwell.
(above iss. on 'Radarscope') (below iss. on 'Boa'; B-side alter-ego)

Dec 95. (ltd-7") *(HISS 4)* **LIQUIDATION GIRL. / Van Impe: unknown** [ ] [–]

Dec 95. (7"; various artists) *<che 47>* **I've Only Just Started To Breathe** [ ] [–]

Mar 96. (7"ep/cd-ep) *(chem 004/+cd)* **CINECENTRE. / THIRTEEN GLIDING PRINCIPLES / M. EMULATOR** [ ] [–]

Aug 96. (7"ep/cd-ep) *(chem 006/+cd)* **UNDER CANVAS / EEN TELF. / BEAR CLUB / STRATHCONA** [ ] [–]

Oct 96. (7") *(100gm 18)* **BOOKER T JONES. / (other track by URUSEI YATSURA)** [–] Japan [–]
– Booker T Jones / (other track by URUSEI YATSURA).
(above on Japanese '100 Guitar Mania' via 'Stolen Ecstasy' series)

Oct 96. (7"ep/cd-ep) *(chem 008/+cd)* **SUCROSE / CHALK. / EUROSPRINT / THE DIRGE** [ ] [–]

Nov 96. (lp/cd) *(chem 009/+CD) <MAR 027>* **DOMESTIQUES** [ ] [ ]
– Under canvas under wraps / Leaning on a cane / Strathcona slung / Tempered; not tamed / One more question / Big business in Europe / Falling & landing / Akumulator / Sucrose / Pinky / Friendly conventions / Smaller mammals / 4th channel / d'Estus morte.

Jun 97. (7") *(LISS 20)* **SACRE CHARLEMAGNE. / (other by The NEW BAD THINGS)** [ ] [–]
(above release on 'Lissys')

Mar 98. (d7"/cd-s) *(chem 022/+cd)* **EVERYTHING GOES AROUND THE WATER. / BLACKPOOL / THE DROWNED AND THE SAVED** [ ] [–]

May 98. (7") *(chem 023)* **PULL THE WIRES FROM THE WALL. / MAURON CHANSON** [69] [–]
(cd-s+=) *(chem 023cd)* – Mark the day.

Jun 98. (cd) *(chem 024cd)* **PELOTON** [56] [–]
– Everything goes around the water / The arcane model / The actress / Clarinet / Pull the wires from the wall / Repeat failure / And so the talking stopped / Don't stop / Blackpool / Russian orthodox / The weaker argument defeats the stronger.

Sep 98. (7") *(chem 029)* **THE WEAKER ARGUMENT DEFEATS THE STRONGER. / A VERY CELLULAR SONG** [ ] [–]
(cd-s+=) *(chem 029cd)* – The actress – Irian Jaya remix.

Chemikal U/ground — Beggars Banquet

Apr 00. (lp/cd) *(chem 040/+cd) <81021>* **THE GREAT EASTERN** [72] May00 [ ]
– The past that suits you best / Accused of stealing / American trilogy / Reasons for silence / Thirteen gliding principles / No danger / Aye today / Witness / Knowing when to run / Make your move.

May 00. (7") *(chem 039)* **AMERICAN TRILOGY. / EUPHORIA HEIGHTS** [61] [–]
(cd-s+=) *(chem 039cd)* – How can we hang on to a dream?
(cd-s+=) *(chem 039cdx)* – ('A'-CD rom) / Make your move.

Sep 00. (7") *(chem 044)* **NO DANGER. / THE CHOICES YOU'VE MADE** [ ] [–]
(cd-s+=) *(chem 044cd)* – Don't sleep.

Mantra — Mantra

Sep 02. (7") *(MNT 75)* **COMING IN FROM THE COLD. / COALMAN** [ ] [–]
(cd-s+=) *(MNT 75CD)* – Crutches.

Oct 02. (cd/lp) *(MNT CD/LP 1031) <81034>* **HATE** [57] Jan03 [ ]
– The light before we land / All you need is hate / Woke from dreaming / The drowning years / Coming in from the cold / Child killers / Favours / All rise / Never look at the sun / If this is a plan. *<US cd+=>* – Coalman / Mad drums / Coming in from the cold (video).

Feb 03. (7") *(MNT 79)* **ALL YOU NEED IS HATE. / MAD DRUMS** [72] [–]
(cd-s+=) *(MNT 79CD)* – Mr Blue Sky.

– compilations, etc. –

Sep 97. (cd) *Strange Fruit; (SFRSCD 037)* **BBC SESSIONS** [ ] [–]
– Primary alternative / I've only just started to breathe / Lazarwalker / Indian fables / Under canvas under wraps / Sucrose / Teen elf / Thirteen gliding principles / Friendly conventions / Tempered; not tamed / Falling and landing. *(re-iss. May00; same)*

Sandy DENNY

Born: ALEXANDRA ELENE MacLEAN DENNY, 6 Jan'47, Wimbledon, London, England. From playing guitar and piano from an early age, SANDY, as she would be known all her life, grew up listening to the sounds of her father's collection of classical, jazz and traditional Scottish folk music, before finding her own taste in the sound of 60's pop/folk, especially BOB DYLAN. After a brush with nursing and attending Kensington Art College, she started singing regularly in the folk clubs of London, where she met JOHN RENBOURN and ALEX CAMPBELL. An invitation in late '66 from CAMPBELL to join a folk session for the BBC World Service show, A Cellarfull Of Folk, led to her first recordings on the LP's 'ALEX CAMPBELL AND FRIENDS' and 'SANDY AND JOHNNY'. With a regular spot at The Troubadour, she was heard by DAVE COUSINS of The STRAWBS. Joining the band soon afterwards, she recorded 'SANDY DENNY & THE STRAWBS' in '67 featuring 'WHO KNOWS WHERE THE TIME GOES', one of DENNY's most powerful songs. Meanwhile, through gigs around London's folk scene, she had formulated friendships with DANNY THOMPSON of PENTANGLE fame, and the founder of 'Witchseason' records, JOE BOYD, as well as earning herself a strong reputation as one of the best folk singers in the country. When JUDY DYBLE left FAIRPORT CONVENTION, featuring a young RICHARD THOMPSON, in '68, DENNY auditioned and made an immediate impact, her classy singing and mercurial personality bringing out the best in the musicians around her. 'What We Did On Our Holidays', SANDY's first album with FAIRPORT, was full of highlights, including DENNY's song 'FOTHERINGAY', and a crystal clear rendition of 'SHE MOVES THROUGH THE FAIR'. Whilst rehearsing for their second album, SANDY met TREVOR LUCAS, an Australian singer/songwriter and member of the band ECLECTION. After the two bands shared a bill in Birmingham, she left with him instead of returning to London with FAIRPORT. It proved a fortuitous move, as FAIRPORT's journey ended in tragedy, a crash taking the life of drummer, MARTIN LAMBLE. This event led to a re-think of the band's repertoire, and in the meantime the songs recorded before the crash were compiled by BOYD to form the album, 'UNHALFBRICKING', featuring a re-recording of 'WHO KNOWS WHERE THE TIME GOES' and 'AUTOPSY'. DENNY's vocals throughout the album are stunning, her voice matured and yet containing a purity that is strangely compelling to the listener. After the inclusion of DAVE SWARBRICK on violin, FAIRPORT's next album, 'Liege And Lief', proved groundbreaking, but soon after, SANDY was to leave the band to form FOTHERINGAY, with ex-ECLECTION members, including her husband-to-be TREVOR LUCAS, and recording their only album, simply titled 'FOTHERINGAY', as well as recording a duet with ROBERT PLANT, 'THE BATTLE OF EVERMORE', on 'LED ZEPPELIN IV'. Although the album and the group were well-received by fans, the band dispersed after a misunderstanding between BOYD and DENNY, RICHARD THOMPSON going on to produce SANDY's first of four solo albums, the haphazard 'THE NORTH STAR GRASSMAN AND THE RAVEN'. Her second solo album, 'SANDY' was produced by BOYD, and is her stand-out album, especially her mesmerising singing on 'THE QUIET JOYS OF BROTHERHOOD'. The LP did not live up to expected sales figures, but did earn her many new fans, including DYLAN, FRANK ZAPPA, and PETE TOWNSHEND, who cast her as the nurse in 'Tommy'. After touring America in the Spring of '73, she completed her third solo set, 'LIKE AN OLD FASHIONED WALTZ', a fine example of her timeless singing, and her first album without a trace of folk. During this period, SANDY performed the shows of her life, and married long-time partner, LUCAS, with THOMPSON as best man. By '74, she had returned to FAIRPORT, the line-up having included her husband since '73. The atmosphere within the band was strained as FAIRPORT and DENNY attempted to gel their by now different styles, yet the GLYN JOHNS produced album, 'Rising For The Moon', turned out to be a triumph, SANDY's 'ONE MORE CHANCE' bringing together exceptional instrumental work with singing unprecedented in DENNY's recording career, her voice full of maturity yet also possessing a fragility that gives a real urgency to the song, written as a plea for peace. Although her work kept improving, her career failed to fully take off, and after 'Rising . . .' failed to be the commercial success it should have been, FAIRPORT were dropped by 'Island', and the band drifted apart. '77 saw her final solo offering, 'RENDEZVOUS', including an unfortunate rendition of 'CANDLE IN THE WIND' and a hint of reggae on 'GOLDDUST'. It did have its fine moments with 'ONE WAY DONKEY RIDE' and 'I'M A DREAMER', but its sales were poor, and DENNY's contract expired at 'Island'. It was to be her final recording. In April '78, SANDY fell down a flight of stairs at a friend's home, lapsing into a coma which led to her death from a brain haemorrhage on the 21st of that month. • **Covered:** TOMORROW IS A LONG TIME (Bob Dylan) / LET'S JUMP THE BROOMSTICK (Brenda Lee) / SILVER THREADS AND GOLDEN NEEDLES (Springfields). FOTHERINGAY covered; TOO MUCH OF NOTHING (Bob Dylan).

Album rating: THE NORTH STAR GRASSMAN AND THE RAVENS (*6) / SANDY (*7) / LIKE AN OLD FASHIONED WALTZ (*5) / RENDEZVOUS (*6) / THE BEST OF SANDY DENNY compilation (*7)

SANDY DENNY – vocals (with below artists **JOHNNY SILVO & ALEX CAMPBELL**) (below a compilation of 'ALEX CAMPBELL & FRIENDS' and 'SANDY & JOHNNY' albums '67)

Saga / not iss.

1970. (lp) *(EROS 8153)* **SANDY DENNY** [ ] [–]
– This train / 3:10 to Yuma / Pretty Polly / You never wanted me / Milk and honey / My ramblin' boy / The last thing on my mind / Make me a pallet on your floor / The false bride / Been on the road so long. *(re-iss. 1978 as 'THE ORIGINAL SANDY DENNY' on 'Mooncrest'; CREST 28) (cd-iss. Feb91 cd/c; CREST CD/MC 002)*

FOTHERINGAY

SANDY DENNY – vocals (ex-FAIRPORT CONVENTION, ex-STRAWBS) plus **JERRY DONAHUE** – guitar, vocals / **TREVOR LUCAS** – guitar, vocals (ex-ECLECTION) / **GERRY CONWAY** – drums (ex-ECLECTION) / **PAT DONALDSON** – bass

Island / A&M

Jun 70. (lp) *(ILPS 9125) <4269>* **FOTHERINGAY** [18] [ ]
– Nothing more / The sea / The ballad of Ned Kelly / Peace in the end / Winter winds / The way I feel / The pond down the stream / Too much of nothing / Banks of the Nile. *(re-iss. Jul87 on 'Hannibal' lp/c; HNB L/C 4426) (cd-iss. May89; HNCD 4426)*

Jul 70. (7") *(WIP 6085)* **PEACE IN THE END. / WINTER WINDS** [ ] [–]

Aug 70. (7") *<1223>* **THE BALLAD OF NED KELLY. / THE SEA** [–] [ ]

Split early '71. CONWAY, DONALDSON and DONAHUE then backed MICK GREENWOOD with the latter joining LUCAS (now a producer) to FAIRPORTS.

SANDY DENNY

Island / A&M

Sep 71. (lp) *(ILPS 9165) <4317>* **THE NORTH STAR GRASSMAN AND THE RAVENS** [31] [ ]
– Late November / Black waterside / The sea captain / Down in the flood / John the gun / Next time around / The optimist / Let's jump the broomstick / Wretched Wilbur / The north star grassman and the ravens / Crazy lady blues. *(re-iss. Nov86; ILPM 9165) (re-iss. May89 on 'Carthage' lp/c; CGLP/CGC 4429) (re-iss. Aug91 cd)(c; IMCD 133)(ICM 9165)*

Feb 72. (7") *<1331>* **CRAZY LADY BLUES. / LET'S JUMP THE BROOMSTICK** [–] [ ]

Sep 72. (7"ep) *(WIP 6141)* **HERE IN SILENCE. / MAN OF IRON (soundtrack from 'Pass Of Arms' film)** [ ] [–]

Sep 72. (lp) *(ILPS 9207) <4371>* **SANDY** [ ] [ ]
– It'll take a long time / Sweet Rosemary / For nobody to hear / Tomorrow is a long time / Quiet joys of brotherhood / Bushes and friars / The lady / Listen listen / It sets me wild / The music weaver. *(re-iss. Aug91 cd)(c; IMCD 132)(ICM 9207)*

Sep 72. (7") *(WIP 6142) <1410>* **LISTEN LISTEN. / TOMORROW IS A LONG TIME** [ ] [ ]

Nov 73. (7") *(WIP 6176)* **WHISPERING GRASS. / FRIENDS** [ ] [–]

Jun 74. (lp) *(ILPS 9258) <9340>* **LIKE AN OLD FASHIONED WALTZ** [ ] [ ]
– Solo / Whispering grass / Like an old fashioned waltz / Friends / Carnival / Dark of the night / At the end of the day / Until the real thing comes along / No end. *(re-iss. May88 & Jun96 on 'Carthage'; CGLP 4425) (cd-iss. Nov88 & May95; CGC 4425)*

—— SANDY had returned to FAIRPORT CONVENTION between Mar74-Jan76 and after a years rest she was back with solo work in '77.

May 77. (lp) *(ILPS 9433)* **RENDEZVOUS** [ ] [–]
– I wish I was a fool for you / Gold dust / Candle in the wind / Take me away / One way donkey ride / I'm a dreamer / All our days / Silver threads and golden needles / No more sad refrains. *(re-iss. Jan87 on 'Hannibal' lp/c; HNBL/HNBC 4423) (cd-iss. Jan89 +=; HNCD 4423)* – Full moon.

—— tragically SANDY died on the 21st April '78

– compilations, others, etc. –

1973. (lp; by SANDY DENNY & THE STRAWBS) *Hallmark; (SHM 813)* **ALL OUR OWN WORK** [ ] [–]
(re-iss. Jul91 on 'Hannibal' cd/c; HNCD/HNBC 1361)

1978. (7") *Mooncrest; (MOON 54)* **MAKE ME A PALLET ON YOUR FLOOR. / THIS TRAIN** [ ] [–]

Jan 86. (4xlp-box) *Hannibal; (SDSP 1)* **WHO KNOWS WHERE THE TIME GOES?** [ ] [–]
– (best material from 1967-1977, including live, out-takes, demos, and group work with STRAWBS, FAIRPORT CONVENTION, FOTHERINGAY, & The BUNCH) *(re-iss. May89 & Nov91; HNBX 5301)*

Aug 87. (lp) *Island; (SDC/CDSC 100)* **THE BEST OF SANDY DENNY** [ ] [ ]
– Listen, listen / One way donkey ride / It'll take a long time / Farewell, farewell / Tam Lin / The pond and the stream / Late November / The sea / Banks of the Nile / Next time around / For shame of doing wrong / Stranger to himself / I'm a dreamer / Who knows where the time goes? *(re-iss. Sep89 on 'Hannibal' cd/c; HNCD/HNBC 1328) (re-iss. Mar96 cd)(c; IMCD 217)(ICM 2084)*

Jul 95. (cd) *Special Delivery; (SPDCD 1052) / Raven; <46>* **THE ATTIC TRACKS 1972-1984 (with TREVOR LUCAS & FRIENDS)** [ ] Feb97 [ ]

May 98. (cd) *Island; (IMCD 252) <524493>* **GOLD DUST: LIVE AT THE ROYALTY (live)** [ ] Jun98 [ ]

May 99. (cd) *Island; (IMCD 253) / Polygram; <524511>* **LISTEN LISTEN: AN INTRODUCTION TO SANDY DENNY** [ ] Apr00 [ ]

Aug 00. (d-cd) *Island; (CRNCD 7) / A&M; <542747>* **NO MORE SAD REFRAINS: THE ANTHOLOGY**
Oct 02. (cd) *Universal; <063314>* **THE BEST OF SANDY DENNY: THE MILLENNIUM COLLECTION** – –
Mar 03. (cd) *Disky; (SI 905319)* **HERITAGE** –

DEPECHE MODE

Formed: Basildon, Essex, England . . . 1976 by VINCE CLARKE, MARTIN GORE and ANDY FLETCHER while still at school. The line-up was completed by frontman DAVE GAHAN, and by 1980 they had adopted the DEPECHE MODE moniker, immersing themselves in the London 'New Romantic' scene which spawned the likes of SPANDAU BALLET and VISAGE. After gigging around the capital and having a track, 'PHOTOGRAPHIC', included on the 'Some Bizzare Album' various artists collection, the band were picked up by the fledgling 'Mute' label. While their debut single, 'DREAMING OF ME', scraped the lower regions of the chart in 1981, a follow-up, 'NEW LIFE', almost made the Top 10. Dominated by synthesizers and drum machines, yet retaining a keen sense of melody, the band initially took their cue from KRAFTWERK. As evidenced on their insanely catchy Top 10 breakthrough, 'JUST CAN'T GET ENOUGH' (the first of 24 consecutive Top 30 hits), their lyrics weren't quite as enigmatic as their Teutonic heroes, although they improved with time. The success of the single (which no doubt still gets played ten times a night in French discos!) paved the way for the debut album, 'SPEAK AND SPELL' (1981), a promising collection of catchy synth-pop fare which made the UK Top 10. Chief songwriter VINCE CLARKE quit shortly after, going on to pastures new with YAZOO and then ERASURE, GORE taking up the pensmith chores for the follow-up album, 'A BROKEN FRAME' (1982). Shortly after its release, ALAN WILDER, who had previously toured with the band, was recruited as a full time replacement for CLARKE. Like its predecessor, 'CONSTRUCTION TIME AGAIN' (1983) failed to make any significant leap forward from the debut, musically at least, although it did contain the classic 'EVERYTHING COUNTS', GAHAN's voice summoning up as much portentous doom as he could muster. While the 'PEOPLE ARE PEOPLE' single gave the band valuable exposure in America, their real breakthrough came with 1984's 'SOME GREAT REWARD'. Featuring the likes of 'BLASPHEMOUS RUMOURS' and 'MASTER AND SERVANT", the album was palpably darker, the music more satisfyingly varied. 'BLACK CELEBRATION' (1986) was deliberately darker still, much of the material creeping along at a funereal pace. 'MUSIC FOR THE MASSES' (1987) was the band's biggest Stateside success to date, the material for the live album, '101' (1989) coming from the American leg of their 1988 sell-out world tour. 'VIOLATOR' (1990) was heralded as DEPECHE MODE's best work since 'SOME GREAT REWARD', spawning two of their better singles in 'PERSONAL JESUS' and the uncharacteristically emotional 'ENJOY THE SILENCE'. Never the warmest sounding band, with 'SONGS OF FAITH AND DEVOTION' (1993) their clinical sound was softened somewhat with a move towards more rock-centric territory. That's not to say the music was soft, at least not on the single, 'I FEEL YOU', a dirty great guitar riff grinding away relentlessly. Elsewhere, the album had something of a transcendent, redemptive quality about it on such powerful tracks as 'MERCY IN YOU' and 'ONE CARESS'. The record gave the band their first No.1, UK and US, although some longtime fans were understandably miffed at the band's new direction. The mid-90's brought the most turbulent period in the band's long career as GAHAN reportedly attempted suicide amid his battle with drug addiction. Add to that the departure of WILDER (who went to work on solo project RECOIL) and it seemed DEPECHE MODE had reached the end of the line. If nothing else, though, this band are doggedly determined, GAHAN beating his drug problem and enlisting BOMB THE BASS guru TIM SIMENON to help create an enticingly different sound on 1997's 'ULTRA'. No doubt overjoyed that their heroes had been resurrected, the group's staunch fanbase ensured the album would once again top the UK chart. The record was also a blueprint of sorts for 'EXCITER' (2001), maverick production touches supplied this time around by LFO man, MARK BELL. GAHAN's ongoing singing tuition reaped darkly alluring rewards, drawing the listener in to a late-night vigil of brooding acoustica and stained velour romance. This singular atmosphere was carried over, to some extent, with 2003's 'PAPER MONSTERS', GAHAN's tentative solo debut. Unsurprisingly, much of the subject matter concerned the man's not so distant descent into personal chaos, with the likes of 'HIDDEN HOUSES' making emotionally brave attempts to work through his experiences with a clear pen rather than burying it all in metaphor. GORE, meanwhile, had actually beaten GAHAN's release schedule by a few months, making his own solo debut with 'COUNTERFEIT 2' (2003). A belated follow-up to his 1989 mini-set, the album found GORE tackling a range of material with more reverance than originality although the selection was interesting enough in its own right. • **Covered:** ROUTE 66 (Chuck Berry) / MARTIN L. GORE's covered NEVER TURN YOUR BACK ON MOTHER EARTH (Sparks) / MOTHERLESS CHILD (John Lennon) / COMPULSION (Joe Crow) / IN A MANNER OF SPEAKING (Tuxedomoon) / GONE GONE GONE (Comsat Angels) / SMILE IN THE CROWD (Durutti Column) / COMING BACK TO YOU (Leonard Cohen) / IN MY TIME OF DYING (trad.) / STARDUST (David Essex) / I CAST A LONESOME SHADOW (Russwurm – Thompson) / IN MY OTHER WORLD (Julee Cruise) / LOVERMAN (Nick Cave) / BY THIS RIVER (Eno & Cluster) / LOST IN THE STARS (Anderson – Weill) / DAS LIED VOM EINSAMEN MADCHEN (Gilbert – Heymann) / TINY GIRLS (Iggy Pop) / CANDY SAYS (Lou Reed).

Album rating: SPEAK & SPELL (*6) / A BROKEN FRAME (*6) / CONSTRUCTION TIME AGAIN (*7) / SOME GREAT REWARD (*7) / THE SINGLES 1981-1985 compilation (*9) / BLACK CELEBRATION (*8) / MUSIC FOR THE MASSES (*7) / 101 (*5) / VIOLATOR (*7) / SONGS OF FAITH & DEVOTION (*7) / SONGS OF LOVE & DEVOTION LIVE (*3) / ULTRA (*6) / THE SINGLES 86>98 compilation (*7) / EXCITER (*6) / Martin L. Gore: COUNTERFEIT mini (*4) / COUNTERFEIT 2 (*5) / Dave Gahan: PAPER MONSTERS (*6)

VINCE CLARKE (b. 3 Jul'60, South Woodford, England) – keyboards, synthesiser / **DAVID GAHAN** (b. 9 May'62, Epping, England) – vocals / **MARTIN GORE** (b.23 Jul'61) – keyboards, synthesizer, vocals / **ANDY FLETCHER** (b. 8 Jul'61, Nottingham, England) – guitar, synthesiser, drum machine

Mute Sire

Mar 81. (7") *(MUTE 013)* **DREAMING OF ME. / ICE MACHINE** 57
Jun 81. (7") *(MUTE 014)* **NEW LIFE. / SHOUT!** 11
(12") *(12MUTE 014)* – ('A'extended) / ('B'-Rio mix).
Sep 81. (7") *(MUTE 016)* **JUST CAN'T GET ENOUGH. / ANY SECOND NOW** 8 –
(12") *(12MUTE 016)* – ('A'-Schizo mix) / ('B'-altered).
Oct 81. (lp/c) *(STUMM/CSTUMM 5) <3642>* **SPEAK & SPELL** 10
– New life / Just can't get enough / I sometimes I wish I was dead / Puppets / Boys say go / No disco / What's your name / Photographic / Tora! Tora! Tora! / Big Muff / Any second now. *(cd-iss. Apr88 +=; CDSTUMM 5)* – Dreaming of me / New life (extended) / Shout! (Rio mix) / Any second now (altered mix).
Nov 81. (7") **JUST CAN'T GET ENOUGH. / TORA! TORA! TORA!** –

— **ALAN WILDER** (b. 1 Jun'59, London, England) – electronics (ex-HITMEN) repl. VINCE who formed YAZOO

Jan 82. (7"/ext.12") *(MUTE/12MUTE 018)* **SEE YOU. / NOW, THIS IS FUN** [6] Aug82 [ ]

Apr 82. (7") *(MUTE 022)* **THE MEANING OF LOVE. / OBERKORN (IT'S A SMALL TOWN)** [12] [ ]
(12") *(12MUTE 022)* – ('A'extended) / ('B'-Fairly odd mix).

Aug 82. (7") *(7BONG 1)* **LEAVE IN SILENCE. / EXCERPT FROM MY SECRET GARDEN** [18] [ ]
(ext.12"+=) *(12BONG 1)* – ('A'quieter version).

Sep 82. (lp/c) *(STUMM/CSTUMM 9)* <23751> **A BROKEN FRAME** [8] [ ]
– Leave in silence / My secret garden / Monument / Nothing to fear / See you / Satellite / The meaning of love / A photograph of you / Shouldn't have done that / The sun and the rainfall. *(cd-iss. Jul88; CDSTUMM 13)*

Feb 83. (7"/ext.12") *(7/12 BONG 2)* **GET THE BALANCE RIGHT. / THE GREAT OUTDOORS** [13] [ ]
(12") *(L12BONG 2)* – ('A'side) / My secret garden (live) / See you (live) / Satellite (live) / Tora! Tora! Tora! (live).

Jul 83. (7") *(7BONG 3)* **EVERYTHING COUNTS. / WORK HARD** [6] [ ]
(12") *(12BONG 3)* – ('A'-larger amounts) / ('B'-East End mix).
(12") *(L12BONG 3)* – ('A'side) / Boys say go (live) / New life (live) / Nothing to fear (live) / The meaning of love (live).

Aug 83. (lp/c) *(STUMM/CSTUMM 13)* **CONSTRUCTION TIME AGAIN** [6] [–]
– Love in itself / More than a party / Pipeline / Everything counts / Two minute warning / Shame / The landscape is changing / Told you so / And then . . . *(cd-iss. Jul88; CDSTUMM 13)*

Sep 83. (7") *(BONG 4)* **LOVE IN ITSELF. / FOOLS** [21] [ ]
(12") *(12BONG 4)* – Love in itself (3) / (4) / Fools (bigger).
(12") *(L12BONG 4)* – ('A'side) / Just can't get enough (live) / Photograph (live) / A photograph of you (live) / Shout! (live).

Mar 84. (7") *(7BONG 5)* <29221> **PEOPLE ARE PEOPLE. / IN YOUR MEMORY** [4] May85 [13]
(12"+=) *(L12BONG 5)* – ('A'-On-U-Sound remix).
(12") *(12BONG 5)* – ('A'different mix) / ('B'-Slik mix).

Jul 84. (lp) <25124> **PEOPLE ARE PEOPLE** [–] [71]
– People are people / Everything counts / Get the balance right / Love in itself / Now this is fun / Leave in silence / Told you so / Work hard.

Aug 84. (7") *(7BONG 6)* <28918> **MASTER AND SERVANT. / SET ME FREE (RENOVATE ME)** [9] Aug85 [ ]
('A'-Slavery whip mix-12"+=) *(12BONG 6)* – ('A'voxless).
('A'-On-U-Sound mix-12"+=) *(L12BONG 6)* – Are people people?.

Sep 84. (lp/c) *(STUMM/CSTUMM 19)* <25194> **SOME GREAT REWARD** [5] Jan85 [51]
– Something to do / Lie to me / People are people / It doesn't matter / Stories of old / Somebody / Master and servant / If you want to / Blasphemous rumours. *(cd-iss. Sep87; CDSTUMM 19)*

Nov 84. (7") *(7BONG 7)* **BLASPHEMOUS RUMOURS. / SOMEBODY** [16] [ ]
(7"ep+=) *(7BONG 7E)* – Told you so (live) / Everything counts (live).
(12"+=) *(12BONG 7)* – Ice machine / Two minute warning / Everything counts (live).

May 85. (7"/remix-12") *(7/12 BONG 8)* **SHAKE THE DISEASE. / FLEXIBLE** [18] [ ]
(12") *(L12BONG 8)* – Edit the shake / Master and servant (live) / Flexible (deportation mix) / Something to do (metal mix).

Sep 85. (7"/remix-12") *(7/12 BONG 9)* **IT'S CALLED A HEART. / FLY ON THE WINDSCREEN** [18] [ ]
(ext.d12"+=) *(D12BONG 9)* – ('A'-slow mix) / ('A'-death mix).

Oct 85. (lp/c) *(MUTEL/CMUTEL 1)* <25346> **THE SINGLES 1981-1985** (compilation) <US-title 'CATCHING UP WITH DEPECHE MODE'> [6] [ ]
– People are people / Master and servant / It's called a heart / Just can't get enough / See you / Shake the disease / Everything counts / New life / Blasphemous rumours / Leave in silence / Get the balance right / Love in itself / Dreaming of me. *(c+=)* – (2 extra). *(cd-iss. Sep87; CDMUTEL 1)*

Feb 86. (7") *(7BONG 10)* **STRIPPED. / BUT NOT TONIGHT** [15] [ ]
(ext.12"+=) *(12BONG 10)* – Breathing in fumes / Fly on the windscreen (quiet mix) / Black day.

Mar 86. (lp/c) *(STUMM/CSTUMM 26)* <25429> **BLACK CELEBRATION** [4] [90]
– Black celebration / Fly on the windscreen – final / A question of tlust / Sometimes / It doesn't matter two / A question of time / Stripped / Here is the house / World full of nothing / Dressed in black / New dress. *(cd-iss. Sep87+=; CDSTUMM 26)* – But not tonight / Breathing in fumes / Black day.

Apr 86. (7") *(7BONG 11)* **A QUESTION OF LUST. / CHRISTMAS ISLAND** [28] [ ]
(free c-s. w/7") *(CBONG 11)* – ('A'-Flood mix) / If you want (live) / Shame (live) / Blasphemous rumours (live).
(ext.12"+=) *(12BONG 11)* – It doesn't matter (instrumental) / People are people (live) / A question of lust (minimal).

Aug 86. (7") *(7BONG 12)* **A QUESTION OF TIME. / BLACK CELEBRATION** [17] [ ]
(ext.12"+=) *(12BONG 12)* – Stripped (live) / Something to do (live).
(12") *(L12BONG 12)* – ('A'-Newtown mix) / ('A'live) / ('B'-Black tulip mix) / More than a party (live).

Apr 87. (7") *(7BONG 13)* <28366> **STRANGELOVE. / PIMPF** [16] [76]
('A'-Maximix-12"+=) *(12BONG 13)* – ('A'Midimix).
(cd-s++=) *(CDBONG 13)* – Agent orange.
('A'-Blind mix-12"+=) *(L12BONG 13)* – ('A'-Pain mix) / Agent orange.

Aug 87. (7") *(7BONG 14)* <28189> **NEVER LET ME DOWN AGAIN. / PLEASURE, LITTLE PLEASURE** [22] [63]
(12"/c-s) *(12/C BONG 14)* – ('A'-split mix) / ('B'-glitter mix) / ('A'-aggro mix).
(cd-s++=) *(CDBONG 14)* – To have and to hold (Spanish taster).
(12") *(L12BONG 14)* – ('A'-Tsangarides mix) / ('B'-join mix) / To have and to hold (Spanish taster).

Sep 87. (cd/d-c/lp,clear-lp) *(CD/C+/STUMM 47)* <25614> **MUSIC FOR THE MASSES** [10] [35]
– Never let me down again / The things you said / Strangelove / Sacred / Little 15 / Behind the wheel / I want you now / To have to hold / Nothing / Pimpf. *(cd+=)* – Agent orange / Never let me down again (aggro mix) / To have and to hold (Spanish) / Pleasure the treasure (glitter mix). *(d-c+=)* – BLACK CELEBRATION (album)

Dec 87. (7") *(7BONG 15)* <27991> **BEHIND THE WHEEL. / ROUTE 66** [21] [61]
(c-s+=/cd-s+=) *(C/CD BONG 15)* – ('A'-Shep Pettibone mix) / ('A'-lp version).
(12") *(12BONG 15)* – ('A'-Shep Pettibone mix) / ('B'-Beatmasters mix).
(12") *(L12BONG 15)* – ('A'-Beatmasters mix) / ('B'-Casualty mix).

May 88. (7"import) *(LITTLE 15)* **LITTLE 15. /** [60] [ ]

Sep 88. (7") <27777> **STRANGELOVE. / NOTHING** [–] [50]

Feb 89. (7") *(7BONG 16)* **EVERYTHING COUNTS (live). / NOTHING (live)** [22] [ ]
(12"+=/cd-s+=) *(12/CD BONG 16)* – Sacred (live) / A question of lust (live).
(remix-cd-s) *(CDLBONG 16)* – Strangelove (remix).
(3"cd-s) *(LCDBONG 16)* – ('A'-Tim Simenon & M. Saunders remix) / ('B'-Justin Strauss remix) / Strangelove (Tim Simenon & M. Saunders remix).
(12") *(L12BONG 16)* - **('A'-Bomb The Bass mix) / ('B'-Hijack mix).**
(10") *(10BONG 16)* – ('A'-Absolute mix) / ('B'-US mix) / ('A'-1983 mix).

Mar 89. (d-cd/d-c/d-lp) *(CD/C+/STUMM 101)* <25853> **101 (live)** [5] [45]
– Pimpf / Behind the wheel / Strangelove / Sacred * / Something to do / Blasphemous rumours / Stripped / Somebody / Things you said / Black generation / Shake the disease / Nothing * / Pleasure little treasure / People are people / A question of time / Never let me down again / A question of lust * / Master and servant / Just can't get enough / Everything counts *. *(c+=*/cd+=*)*

Aug 89. (7")<US-c-s> *(BONG 17)* <19941> **PERSONAL JESUS. / DANGEROUS** [13] Nov89 [28]
(7"g-f+=/12"+=/c-s+=/cd-s+=) *(G/12/C/CD BONG 17)* – ('A'acoustic mix).
('A'pump mix-3"cd-s) *(LCDBONG 17)* – ('A'-Telephone stomp mix).

Feb 90. (c-s/7") *(C+/BONG 18)* <19885> **ENJOY THE SILENCE. / MEMPHISTO** [6] Mar90 [8]
(cd-s+=) *(LCDBONG 18)* – ('A'-Bassline):- Bassline / Harmonium / Rikki Tick Tick / Memphesto.
(etched-12"/3"cd-s) *(XL12/XLCD BONG 18)* – ('A'-The quad: Final mix).

Mar 90. (cd/c/lp) *(CD/C+/STUMM 64)* <26081> **VIOLATOR** [2] [7]
– World in my eyes / Sweetest perfection / Personal Jesus / Halo / Waiting for the night / Enjoy the silence / Policy of truth / Blue dress / Clean.

May 90. (c-s/7") *(C+/BONG 19)* <19842> **POLICY OF TRUTH. / KALEID (remix)** [16] Aug90 [15]
('A'-Trancentral mix; 12"+=/cd-s+=) *(LCDBONG 19)* – ('A'-Pavlov's dub mix).

Sep 90. (12"/cd-s/7") *(12/CD+/BONG 20)* <19580> **WORLD IN MY EYES. / HAPPIEST GIRL / SEA OF SIN** [17] Nov90 [52]
(12") *(L12BONG 20)* – (first 2 tracks) / ('A'remix).
(c-s+=)(cd-s+=) *(CDLBONG 20)* – Meaning of love / Somebody.

Feb 93. (c-s/7") *(C+/BONG 21)* <18600> **I FEEL YOU. / ONE CARESS** [8] [37]
(12"+=)(cd-s+=) *(12/CD BONG 21)* – ('A'-Throb mix) / ('A'-Babylon mix).
(12"/cd-s) *(12L/CDL BONG 21)* – ('A'side) / ('A'swamp mix) / ('A'-Renegade Soundwave mix) / ('A'-Helmut mix).

Mar 93. (cd/c/lp) *(CD/C+/STUMM 106)* <45243> **SONGS OF FAITH AND DEVOTION** [1] [1]
– I feel you / Walking in my shoes / Condemnation / Mercy in you / Judas / In your room / Get right with me / Rush / One caress / Higher love. *(live version of album iss.Dec93; same)*

May 93. (7"/c-s) *(7/C BONG 22)* <18506> **WALKING IN MY SHOES. / MY JOY** [14] [69]
(12"+=/cd-s+=) *(12/CD BONG 22)* – ('A'-Grungy Gonads mix).
(ext;12"/cd-s) *(L12/LCD BONG 22)* – ('A'-Random Carpet mix) / ('A'-Anandamidic mix) / ('A'-Mark Stent 12" Ambient Whale mix).

Sep 93. (7"/c-s) *(7/C BONG 23)* **CONDEMNATION. / DEATH'S DOOR (jazz mix)** [9] [ ]
(cd-s+=) *(CDBONG 23)* – Rush (spiritual mix) / Rush (amylnitrate mix).
(12"+=) *(12BONG 23)* – Rush (mixes).
(12"/cd-s) *(L12/LCD 23)* – ('A'live) / Personal Jesus (live) / Enjoy the silence (live) / Halo (live).

Dec 93. (cd) <45505> **SONGS OF FAITH AND DEVOTION – LIVE (live)** [–] [ ]

Jan 94. (c-s) *(CBONG 24)* **IN YOUR ROOM (Zephyr mix) / HIGHER LOVE (Adrenaline mix)** [8] [ ]
('A'-Jeep Rock mix; cd-s+=) *(XLCDBONG 24)* – ('A'-Apex mix).
(12"++=) *(12BONG 24)* – ('A'-extended Zephyr mix).
(cd-s) *(CDBONG 24)* – ('A'-Zephyr mix) / ('A'extended Zephyr mix) / Never let me down again / Death's door.
(cd-s) *(LCDBONG 24)* – ('A'side) / Policy of truth / World in my eyes / Fly on the windscreen (final).
(12"++=) *(L12BONG 24)* – Never let me down again / Death's door.

— ANDREW FLETCHER departed to take over groups' business affairs.

— On the 17th August '95, GAHAN was thought by the music press to have attempted suicide by cutting at his wrists after his wife left him. His record company however said this had been an accident and was over-hyped by the media.

Feb 97. (cd-s) *(12BONG 25)* <17409> **BARREL OF A GUN / PAINKILLER / ('A'-Underworld soft mix) / ('A'-One Inch Punch mix)** [4] [47]
(12") *(L12BONG 25)* – ('A'-One Inch Punch mix) / ('A'-United mix) / Painkiller (Plastikman mix) / Painkiller.
(cd-s) *(LCDBONG 25)* – ('A'-Underworld hard mix) / ('A'-United mix) / Painkiller (Plastikman mix).
(12") *(12BONG 25)* – ('A'-Underworld hard mix) / ('A'-3 Phase mix) / ('A'-One Inch Punch mix) / ('A'-United mix).

Apr 97. (c-s) *(CBONG 26)* <43845> **IT'S NO GOOD / SLOWBLOW** [5] [38]
(cd-s+=) *(CDBONG 26)* – ('A'-Bass bounce mix) / ('A'-Speedy J mix).
('A'-Hardfloor mix; cd-s+=) *(LCDBONG 26)* – ('A'-Andrea Parker mix) / ('A'-Motor bass mix).
(12") *(12BONG 26)* – ('A'-Hardfloor mix) / ('A'-Speedy J mix) / ('A'-Motor bass mix) / ('A'-Andrea Parker mix) / ('A'-Dom T mix).

Apr 97. (cd/c/lp) *(CD/C+/Stumm 148)* <46522> **ULTRA** [1] [5]
– Barrel of a gun / The love thieves / Home / It's no good / Uselink / Useless / Sister of night / Jazz thieves / Freestate / The bottom line / Insight.

Jun 97. (c-s) *(CBONG 27)* <17314> **HOME / IT'S NO GOOD** [23] Nov97 [88]
('A'-Grantby mix; cd-s+=) *(LCDBONG 27)* – ('A'-Jedi Knights remix: Drowning in time) / Barrel of a gun.
(12") *(12BONG 27)* – ('A'-Jedi Knights remix: Drowning in time) / ('A'-Grantby mix) / ('A'-Air around the golf remix) / ('A'-LFO mix).
(cd-s) *(CDBONG 27)* – ('A'side) / ('A'-LFO mix) / ('A'-The Noodles and the damage done mix).

Oct 97. (cd-s) *(CDBONG 28)* **USELESS / ('A'-Escape From Wherever parts 1&2) / ('A'-Cosmic Blues mix) / BARREL OF A GUN (video)** [28] [ ]
(12") *(12BONG 28)* – ('A'-The Kruder & Dorfmeister session) / ('A'-CJ Bolland funky sub mix) / ('A-Air 20 mix).
(cd-s) *(LCDBONG 28)* – ('A'-CJ Bolland ultrasonar mix) / ('A'-The Kruder & Dorfmaister session) / ('A'live) / It's no good (CD-rom).

Sep 98. (cd-s) *(CDBONG 29)* <44546> **ONLY WHEN I LOSE MYSELF / SURRENDER / HEADSTAR** [17] [61]
(12"/cd-s) *(12/LCD BONG 29)* – ('A'-Subsonic legacy remix) / ('A'-Dan The Automator remix) / Headstar (Luke Slater remix).
(12") *(L12BONG 29)* – ('A'remixes) / Painkiller / Surrender.
(cd-s+=) *(XLCDBONG 29)* – World in my eyes.

Sep 98. (d-cd/c/3x12") *(CD/C+/MUTEL 5)* <47110> **THE SINGLES 86>98** (compilation) [5] Oct98 [38]
– Stripped / A question of lust / A question of time / Strangelove / Never let me down again / Behind the wheel / Personal Jesus / Enjoy the silence / Policy of truth / World in my eyes / I feel you / Walking in my shoes / Condemnation / In your room / Barrel of a gun / It's no good / Home / Useless / Only when I lose myself / Little 15 / Everything counts (live).

Apr 01. (cd-s) *(CDBONG 30)* <44982> **DREAM ON / DREAM ON (Easy Tiger Bertrand Burgalat mix) / DREAM ON (A.S. Dragon version)** [6] [85]
(12") *(12BONG 30)* – ('A'-Bushwacka tough guy mix) / ('A'-Dave Clarke remix) / ('A'-Bushwacka blunt mix).
(cd-s) *(LCDBONG 30)* – ('A'-Bushwacka tough guy mix) / ('A'-Dave Clarke acoustic) / ('A'-Octagon Man mix) / ('A'-Kid 606 mix).

May 01. (cd/c/lp) *(CD/C+/STUMM 190)* <47960> **EXCITER** [9] [8]
– Dream on / Shine / The sweetest condition / When the body speaks / The dead of night / Lovetheme / Freelove / Comatose / I feel loved / Breathe / Easy tiger / I am you / Goodnight lovers.

Jul 01. (cd-s) *(CDBONG 31)* **I FEEL LOVED / DIRT / I FEEL LOVED (extended instrumental)** [12] [–]
(12"+=/cd-s+=) *(12/LCD BONG 31)* – ('A'-Tenaglia's labour of love mix) / ('A'-Thomas Brickman mix) / ('A'-Chamber's remix).

Nov 01. (cd-s) *(CDBONG 32)* **FREELOVE / ZENSTATION / STEREONERD** [19] [–]
(12") *(12BONG 32)* – (first & third tracks) / ('A'-Console remix) / ('A'-DJ Muggs remix) / ('A'versions).
(cd-s) *(CDLBONG 32)* – ('A'versions).

Feb 02. (12"/cd-s) *(12/CD BONG 33)* **GOODNIGHT LOVERS / WHEN THE BODY SPEAKS (acoustic). / THE DEAD OF NIGHT (Electronicat remix) / GOODNIGHT LOVERS (isan falling leaf mix)** [ ] [–]

– compilations, others –

on 'Mute' unless otherwise mentioned

Nov 91. (6xcd-ep-box) *(DMBX 1CD)* **SINGLES BOX SET** [ ] [–]
Nov 91. (6xcd-ep-box) *(DMBX 2CD)* **SINGLES BOX SET** [ ] [–]
Nov 91. (6xcd-ep-box) *(DMBX 3CD)* **SINGLES BOX SET** [ ] [–]

MARTIN L. GORE

Mute Sire

Jun 89. (m-cd/m-c/m-lp) *(CD/C+/STUMM 67)* <25980> **COUNTERFEIT** [51] [ ]
– Smile in the crowd / Never turn your back on Mother Earth / Gone / Motherless child / Compulsion / In a manner of speaking.

Mute Reprise

Apr 03. (cd-s) *(CDMUTE 296)* **STARDUST / I CAST A LONESOME SHADOW (Stewart Walker remix) / LIFE IS STRANGE** [44] [–]
(12") *(12MUTE 296)* – ('A'-Atom remix) / ('A'-Atom instrumental) / I cast a lonesome shadow (Stewart Walker instrumental).

Apr 03. (cd/lp) *(CD+/STUMM 214)* <48469> **COUNTERFEIT VOL.2** [ ] [ ]
– In my time of dying / Stardust / I cast a lonesome shadow / In my other world / Loverman / By this river / Oh my love / Das lied vom einsamen madchen / Tiny girls / Candy says.

DAVE GAHAN

with various backing

Mute Reprise

May 03. (cd-s) *(CDMUTE 294)* <WB 42620> **DIRTY STICKY FLOORS / STAND UP / MAYBE** [18] Jul03 [ ]
(cd-s) *(LCDMUTE 294)* – ('A'mixes).
(12") *(12MUTE 294)* – ('A'-Junkie XL vocal) / ('A'-Junkie XL dub).
(12") *(L12MUTE 294)* – ('A'-Lexicon Avenue vocal) / ('A'-silencerz remix).

Jun 03. (cd/lp) *(CD+/STUMM 216)* <48471> **PAPER MONSTERS** [36] [ ]
– Dirty sticky floors / Hold on / A little piece / Bottle living / Black and blue again / Stay / I need you / Bitter apple / Hidden houses / Goodbye.

Aug 03. (cd-s) *(CDMUTE 301)* **I NEED YOU / CLOSER / BREATHE** [27] [–]
(cd-s) *(LCDMUTE 301)* – ('A'-Ladytronic detoxxmix) / ('A'-Gabriel & Dresden unplugged mix) / ('A'-Jay's summer dub).
(12") *(12MUTE 301)* – ('A'-Gabriel & Dresden unplugged) / ('A'-Jay's summer dub).

(12") *(L12MUTE 301)* – ('A'-Ladtronic detoxxmix) / ('A'-Ladytron detoxxmix intrumental).

Oct 03. (cd-s) *(CDMUTE 310)* **BOTTLE LIVING / HOLD ON / BOTTLE LIVING (Tomcraft vocal)** 36 –
(cd-s) *(LCDMUTE 310)* – ('A'-Machinehead lyric mix) / ('A'-Raumschmiere vocal mix) / Hidden houses (Alexander Kowalski remix).
(cd-s) *<42671-2>* – (all tracks above).

☐ DEREK & THE DOMINOES
(see under ⇒ CLAPTON, Eric)

☐ DESERT SESSIONS
(see under ⇒ QUEENS OF THE STONE AGE)

DESTINY'S CHILD

Formed: Houston, Texas, USA … 1990 by MATTHEW KNOWLES, joining together his daughter BEYONCe KNOWLES, his niece KELENDRIA (KELLY) ROWLAND with wannabes LaTAVIA ROBERSON and LeTOYA LUCKETT. Their musical campaign began in 1990 when MATTHEW brought together his dream, all-girl R&B group, naming them DESTINY'S CHILD and entering them into talent concerts, et al. It took eight years for the group to finally get some recognition, however, and it came in the form of 'KILLING TIME', an individual track featured on the soundtrack to 1997's WILL SMITH smash movie 'Men In Black'. After this introduction the group were signed to giants 'Columbia' and attracted the attention of producer and FUGEES casualty WYCLEF JEAN. He helped co-produce their debut self-titled album in 1998 and also featured on the hit single 'NO, NO, NO, (PART 2)'. The group proceeded to tour with WYCLEF, gaining a vast following in the process. The single 'BILLS, BILLS, BILLS' hit No.1 in the US and was subsequently followed by sophomore album 'WRITING'S ON THE WALL' (1999). But as the band were heading for mega-stardom, tensions were rising within the group over the amount of leeway and attention given to KNOWLES' siblings BEYONCe and KELLY. Just as the single 'SAY MY NAME' was fast becoming the biggest seller of the year, ROBERSON and LUCKETT departed from the group in early 2000, filing a lawsuit against KNOWLES and the remainder of DESTINY'S CHILD. This didn't distract the main man one bit, as he quickly recruited teenagers FARRAH FRANKLIN and MICHELLE WILLIAMS who made their first appearance on the video for 'SAY MY NAME'. But all was not well with eighteen-year-old FRANKLIN; she left the group five months after her addition to begin work on a solo album. The trio then issued their massive smash hit 'INDEPENDENT WOMEN PART 1', to accompany the modern movie version of 'Charlie's Angels'. No.1 follow-up, 'SURVIVOR' (very reminiscent of COOLIO's 'Gangster's Paradise') and the egotistical, vocally histrionic 'BOOTYLICIOUS' (also a #1), were both taken from the trio's third and most successful album 'SURVIVOR' (2001). Following in the wake of that album's huge success, WILLIAMS was surprisingly the first to emerge with a solo set. Perhaps even more surprising was the fact that 'HEART TO YOURS' (2002) was – to all intents and purposes – a gospel album even if the sound wasn't too far removed from contemporary R&B. The young diva even bravely tried her hand at a duet with gospel grand dame SHIRLEY CAESAR, on 'STEAL AWAY TO JESUS'. Concerns of a more secular nature occupied BEYONCe on her own debut turn, 'DANGEROUSLY IN LOVE' (2003). Fresh from her role in Mike Myers' latest Austin Powers instalment, the R&B wunderkind swept the floor with the competition as the album topped both the UK and US charts and 'CRAZY IN LOVE' fuelled a million bootylicious fantasies. Which just leaves KELLY ROWLAND, whose 'SIMPLY DEEP' (2003) followed a similar blueprint to her bandmates, a Top 20 US hit powered by her NELLY duet, 'DILEMMA'.

Album rating: DESTINY'S CHILD (*6) / THE WRITING'S ON THE WALL (*6) / SURVIVOR (*7) / THIS IS A REMIX (*6) / Michelle Williams: HEART TO YOURS (*5) / Beyonce: DANGEROUSLY IN LOVE (*7) / Kelly Rowland: SIMPLY DEEP (*5)

BEYONCe KNOWLES (b. 4 Sep'81) – vocals / **LaTAVIA ROBERSON** (b. 1 Nov'81) – vocals / **LeTOYA LUCKETT** (b.11 Mar'81) – vocals / **KELENDRIA ROWLAND** (b.11 Feb'81) – vocals

Columbia Columbia

Mar 98. (c-s) *(665659-4) <78618>* **NO, NO, NO / (part 2)** 5 Nov97 3
(cd-s+=) *(665659-2)* – ('A'-without rap + instrumental).

Mar 98. (cd/c) *(488535-2/-4) <67728>* **DESTINY'S CHILD** 45 Feb98 67
– Second nature / No, no, no – part 2 (with WYCLEF JEAN) / With me – part 1 (with JERMAINE DUPRI) / Tell me / Bridges / No, no, no – part 1 / With me – part 2 (with MASTER P) / Show me the way / Killing time / Illusion (with WYCLEF JEAN & PRAS) / Birthday / Sail on / My time has come (dedicated to Andrea Tillman) / Know that. *(re-iss. Oct99; same) (cd re-iss. Aug01 extended; 488535-9)*

— In Mar'98, DESTINY'S CHILD hit the US charts with 'Just Be Straight With Me' alongside SILKK THE SHOCKER and others

Jul 98. (c-s) *(666147-4)* **WITH ME / (instrumental)** 19 –
(cd-s+=) *(666147-2)* – (versions).

— In Nov'98, the girls featured on MATTHEW MARSDEN's UK Top 30 hit, 'She's Gone'

Jan 99. (c-s; as DESTINY'S CHILD featuring TIMBALAND) *(666491-4)* **GET ON THE BUS / (mix)** 24 –
(cd-s+=) *(666491-2)* – (mixes).

Jul 99. (c-s/cd-s) *(667690-4/-2) <radio cut>* **BILLS, BILLS, BILLS / excerpts:- BUG A BOO / SO GOOD / NOW THAT SHE'S GONE** 6 May99 81
(cd-s) *(667690-5)* – ('A'side) / (instrumental) / (3 versions).

Jul 99. (cd/c/lp) *(494394-2/-4/-1) <69870>* **THE WRITING'S ON THE WALL** 12 5
– Intro / So good / Bills, bills, bills / Bugaboo / Confessing / Temptation / Now that she's gone / Where'd you go / Hey ladies / If you leave / Jumpin', jumpin' / Say my name / She can't love you / Stay / Sweet sixteen / Amazing grace. *(d-cd-iss. Nov00 +=; 494394-9)* – Get on the bus / Independent women parts 1 & 2 / Eight days of Christmas / No, no, no (Wyclef remix). *(cd re-iss. Aug02; same)*

Oct 99. (c-s/cd-s) *(668188-4/-2) <radio cut>* **BUG A BOO / (mixes)** 9 Sep99 33
(cd-s) *(668188-2)* – ('A'side) / Bills, bills, bills (mix) / So good.

Mar 00. (c-s/cd-s) *(669188-4/-2) <79342>* **SAY MY NAME / (Timbaland remix)** 3 Dec99 1
(cd-s) *(669188-5)* – ('A'mixes).

— now without LaTAVIA + LeTOYA who were repl. by **MICHELLE WILLIAMS + FARRAH FRANKLIN** (the latter departed after 5 months)

Jul 00. (c-s/cd-s) *(669629-4/-2) <79446>* **JUMPIN', JUMPIN' / UPSIDE DOWN** 5 May00 3
(cd-s) *(669629-2)* – ('A'side) / Say my name / Bills, bills, bills.

Nov 00. (c-s) *(670593-4) <79493>* **INDEPENDENT WOMEN PART 1 / INDEPENDENT WOMEN** 1 Sep00 1
(cd-s+=) *(670593-2)* – ('A'side) / ('A'-Victor Calderone mix) / ('A'-Maurice radio mix).
(12"/cd-s) *(670593-6/-5)* – ('A'mix) / Independent women part 2 / Say my name (Timbaland mix) / So good.

Apr 01. (c-s) *(671173-4) <radio cut>* **SURVIVOR / SURVIVOR (Maurice's soul survivor remix)** 1 Mar01 2
(cd-s/12") *(671173-2/-6)* – ('A'side) / ('A'-Azza'z soul remix) / ('A'-Victor Calderone remix).
(cd-s) *(671173-5)* – ('A'-full vocal remix) / Independent women (live at the Brits) / So good (Maurice's soul remix).

May 01. (cd/c/lp) *(501783-2/-4/-1) <61083>* **SURVIVOR** 1 1
– Independent women part 1 / Survivor / Bootylicious / Nasty girl / Fancy / Apple pie a la mode / Sexy daddy / Perfect man / Independent women part 2 / Happy face / Dance with me / My heart still beats / Emotion / Brown eyes / Dangerously in love / Story of beauty / Gospel medley (dedicated to Andretta Tillman) / Outro (DC-3).

Jul 01. (c-s) *(671738-4) <79622>* **BOOTYLICIOUS / BOOTYLICIOUS (M&J Jelly mix)** [2] May01 [1]
(cd-s) *(671738-2)* – ('A'side) / ('A'-Ed Case refix) / BEYONCe & WYCLEF JEAN: Cards never lie / ('A'video).
(12") *(671738-6)* – ('A'side) / ('A'-Ed Case refix) / ('A'-Rocwilder remix).

Nov 01. (c-s) *(672111-4) <79672>* **EMOTION / EMOTION (Victor Calderone remix)** [3] Sep01 [10]
(cd-s) *(672111-2)* – ('A'side) / 8 days of Christmas / ('A'-Maurice Joshua remix) / ('A'-video).
(cd-s) *(672111-5)* – ('A'-Neptunes remix) / Bootylicious (Rocwilder & Missy Elliott remix) / Survivor (Jameson remix) / Bootylicious (Rocwilder & Missy Elliott remix video).

Nov 01. (cd) *(504170-2) <86098>* **8 DAYS OF CHRISTMAS** (festive) [ ] [59]

Mar 02. (cd/d-lp) *(507627-2/-1) <86431>* **THIS IS A REMIX** (remixes) [25] [29]

MICHELLE WILLIAMS

Columbia Columbia

May 02. (cd) *(508243-2) <86432>* **HEART TO YOURS** [ ] Apr02 [57]
– Heart to yours / Heard a word / So glad (with MARY MARY) / Sun will shine again / Better place (9.11) / Change the world / Everything / You care for me (with ISAAC CARREE & LOWELL PYE) / Steal away to Jesus (with SHIRLEY CAESAR) / Rock with me / Gospel medley (with DESTINY'S CHILD) / Heaven (with CARL THOMAS).

BEYONCE

Columbia Sony

Jul 02. (c-s; as BEYONCE KNOWLES) *(672982-4)* **WORK IT OUT / (Nu Groove electric mix)** [7] [–]
(cd-s+=) *(672982-2)* – ('A'-Azra's soul mix).
(12"+=) *(672982-6)* – ('A'-Maurice's Nu Soul mix).

Jun 03. (cd) *(509395-2) <86386>* **DANGEROUSLY IN LOVE** [1] [1]
– Crazy in love (with JAY-Z) / Naughty girl / Baby boy (with SEAN PAUL) / Hip hop star (with BIG BOI & SLEEPY BROWN) / Be with you / Me, myself & I / Yes / Signs (with MISSY ELLIOTT) / Speechless / That's how you like it (with JAY-Z) / The closer I get to you (with LUTHER VANDROSS) / Dangerously in love 2 – Interlude / Gift from Virgo / Work it out *[UK-only]* / '03 Bonnie & Clyde (with JAY-Z) *[UK-only]* / Daddy.

Jun 03. (cd-s; by BEYONCE & JAY-Z) *(674067-2)* **CRAZY IN LOVE (mixes)** [1] [1]
(cd-s+=/12"+=) *(647067-5/-6)* – ('A'-mixes).

Oct 03. (cd-s; by BEYONCE & SEAN PAUL) *(674408-2) <76867>* **BABY BOY / SUMMERTIME (with GHOSTFACE KILLAH)** [2] [1]
(12"+=) *(647067-6)* – ('A'-Maurice's Nu Soul mix).
(cd-s) *(647067-5)* – ('A'mixes; Junior Vasquez) / Crush (with SOLANGE).

KELLY ROWLAND

Columbia Columbia

Jan 03. (cd-s) *(673518-2) <673212>* **STOLE (mixes)** [2] Oct02 [27]
(12"/cd-s) *(673518-6-5)* – ('A'mixes).
—— (the single hit No.57 on import late 2002)

Feb 03. (cd) *(509604-2) <86516>* **SIMPLY DEEP** [1] [12]
– Stole / Dilemma (with NELLY) / Haven't told you / Can't nobody / Love-Hate / Simply deep (with SOLANGE KNOWLES) / (Love lives in) Strange places / Obsession / Heaven / Past 12 / Everytime you walk out that door / Train on a track / Beyond imagination / Make you wanna stay (with JOE BUDDEN).

Apr 03. (c-s) *(673814-4) <79839>* **CAN'T NOBODY / (mix with Jakk Frost)** [5] Feb03 [97]
(12"+=) *(673814-6)* – ('A'-hip hop mix).
(cd-s+=) *(673814-2)* – (mixes + video).

Aug 03. (cd-s) *(674215-2)* **TRAIN ON A TRACK / (HR Crump remix) / EMOTION (live) / (video)** [20] [–]
(cd-s) *(674215-5)* – ('A'side) / ('A'-CED solo & Ron G mix).

DEVO

Formed: Akron, Ohio, USA ... 1972 by two sets of brothers, MARK and BOB MOTHERSBAUGH together with GERALD and BOB CASALE (drummer, ALAN MYERS completed the line-up). From the early 70's, they had been known as The DE-EVOLUTION BAND, before sensibly abbreviating the name to DEVO. This bunch of lab-coated weirdos (taking up The RESIDENTS terminally skewed vision) issued two obscure 45's on their own indie label, 'Booji Boy', which were heavily imported into Britain through leading indie outlet, 'Stiff,' late in 1977. Early the following year, both the double A-sided 'MONGOLOID' / 'JOCKO HOMO' and a hilarious electro-fied rendition of The Rolling Stones' '(I CAN'T GET NO) SATISFACTION', were repressed due to popular demand, the singles subsequently becoming minor chart entries. After a third classic, 'BE STIFF' also hit UK Top 75, the flowerpot-headed, potato-faced futurists secured a deal with 'Virgin' ('Warners' in the US) and continued to inject a quirky humour into the po-faced New Wave movement with a fourth hit, 'COME BACK JONEE'. A debut album, inspiringly titled 'Q: ARE WE NOT MEN? A: WE ARE DEVO!' (produced by BRIAN ENO, who else!?), was released a month later to a confused but appreciative audience who helped propel the record into the Top 20 (Top 100 US). However, their follow-up set, 'DUTY NOW FOR THE FUTURE' (1979), suffered a slight backlash, the novelty wearing thin without the impact of a hit single. 1980's 'FREEDOM OF CHOICE' would have suffered a similar fate, but for a freak US Top 20 single, 'WHIP IT'. The rest of their 80's output lacked their early wit, although America embraced such albums as 'DEV-O LIVE' (1981), 'NEW TRADITIONALISTS' (1981), 'OH NO, IT'S DEVO' (1982) and 'SHOUT' (1984). Having disbanded in the middle of the decade, DEVO (with new drummer, DAVID KENDRICK) reformed in 1988, signing to 'Enigma' and releasing one non-event of an album after another. Their days of inspired innovation now behind them, the legacy of DEVO was nevertheless plundered to unusual effect when SOUNDGARDEN, SUPERCHUNK and even ROBERT PALMER!!! covered their 1980 classic, 'GIRL U WANT'.
• **Songwriters:** GERALD and MARK wrote most of material, SECRET AGENT MAN (Johnny Rivers) / ARE U EXPERIENCED (Jimi Hendrix) / WORKING IN A COALMINE (Lee Dorsey).
• **Trivia:** In 1982, DEVO had contributed services to choreographer TONI BASIL on her debut solo album 'WORD OF MOUTH'. In the late 70's, MARK had appeared on HUGH CORNWALL (of The STRANGLERS) and ROBERT WILLIAMS collaboration 'Nosferatu'.

Album rating: Q: ARE WE NOT MEN? A: WE ARE DEVO! (*8) / DUTY NOW FOR THE FUTURE (*7) / FREEDOM OF CHOICE (*7) / DEV-O LIVE mini (*2) / NEW TRADITIONALISTS (*6) / OH NO! IT'S DEVO (*6) / SHOUT (*4) / E-Z LISTENING DISC collection (*4) / TOTAL DEVO (*4) / NOW IT CAN BE TOLD (DEVO AT THE PALACE 12/9/88) live (*5) / SMOOTH NOODLE MAPS (*4) / HARDCORE DEVO, VOL.1 compilation (*6) / THE GREATEST HITS compilation (*7) / HARDCORE DEVO, VOL.2 compilation (*5) / DEVO LIVE: THE MONGOLOID YEARS compilation (*4) / HOT POTATOES: THE BEST OF DEVO compilation (*8)

BOB MOTHERSBAUGH – vocals, guitar / **MARK MOTHERSBAUGH** – keyboards, synthesizers / **BOB CASALE** – guitar / **JERRY CASALE** – bass, vocals / **ALAN MYERS** – drums repl. JIM MOTHERSBAUGH

Stiff Booji Boy

Feb 78. (7") *(DEV 1) <7033-14>* **MONGOLOID. / JOCKO HOMO** [62] 1977 [ ]

Apr 78. (7")(12") *(DEV 2)(BOY 1)* **(I CAN'T GET ME NO) SATISFACTION. / SLOPPY (I SAW MY BABY GETTING)** [41] 1977 [ ]
<re-iss. 1978 on 'Bomp'; 72843>

Stiff / not iss.

Jul 78. (7"clear,7"lemon) *(BOY 2)* **BE STIFF. / SOCIAL FOOLS** [71] [–]

Virgin / Warners

Aug 78. (7"grey) *(VS 223)* **COME BACK JONEE. / SOCIAL FOOLS** [60] [–]

Sep 78. (lp/c) *(V/TCV 2106)* *<3239>* **Q: ARE WE NOT MEN? A: WE ARE DEVO!** [12] [78]
– Uncontrollable urge / (I can't get no) Satisfaction / Praying hands / Space junk / Mongoloid / Jocko homo / Too much paranoias / Gut feeling – (slap your mammy) / Come back Jonee / Sloppy (I saw my baby getting) / Shrivel-up. *(w/free flexi-7"; VDJ 27) (pic-lp; VP 2106) (re-iss. Mar84 lp/c; OVED/+C 37)*

Jan 79. (7") *<WB 8745>* **COME BACK JONEE. / PRAYING HANDS** [–] [ ]

Jun 79. (7") *(VS 265)* **THE DAY MY BABY GAVE ME A SURPRIZE. / PENETRATION IN THE CENTREFOLD** [ ] [–]

Jun 79. (lp/c) *(V/TCV 2125)* *<3337>* **DUTY NOW FOR THE FUTURE** [49] [73]
– Devo corporate anthem / Clockout / Timing X / Wiggly world / Blockhead / Strange pursuit / S.I.B. (Swelling Itching Brain) / Triumph of the will / The day my baby gave me a surprize / Pink pussycat / Secret agent man / Smart patrol – Mr. DNA / Red eye. *(re-iss. Mar84 lp/c; OVED/+C 38)*

Jul 79. (7") *<WBS 49028>* **SECRET AGENT MAN. / RED EYE EXPRESS** [–] [ ]

Aug 79. (7") *(VS 280)* **SECRET AGENT MAN. / SOO BAWLS** [ ] [–]

May 80. (7") *(VS 350)* **GIRL U WANT. / TURN AROUND** [ ] [–]

May 80. (lp/c) *(V/TCV 2162)* *<3435>* **FREEDOM OF CHOICE** [47] [22]
– Girl u want / It's not right / Whip it / Snowball / Ton o' luv / Freedom of choice / Gates of steel / Cold war / Don't you know / That's Pep! / Mr. B's ballroom / Planet Earth. *(re-iss. Mar84 lp/c; OVED/+C 39)*

Jul 80. (7") *<WBS 49524>* **GIRL U WANT. / MR. B'S BALLROOM** [–] [ ]

Aug 80. (7") *<WBS 49550>* **WHIP IT. / TURN AROUND** [–] [14]

Nov 80. (7") *(VS 383)* **WHIP IT. / SNOWBALL** [51] [–]
(12"+=) *(VS 383-12)* – Gates of steel.

Nov 80. (7") *<WBS 49621>* **FREEDOM OF CHOICE. / SNOWBALL** [–] [ ]

Mar 81. (7") *<WBS 49711>* **GATES OF STEEL. / BE STIFF (live)** [–] [ ]

May 81. (m-lp/m-c) *(OVED 1)* *<3548>* **DEV-O LIVE (live)** [ ] Apr81 [49]
– Freedom of choice (theme song) / Whip it / Girl u want / Gates of steel / Be stiff / Planet Earth.

Jun 81. (7") *<WBS >* **THROUGH BEING COOL. / GOING UNDER** [–] [ ]

Aug 81. (7") *(VS 450)* **THROUGH BEING COOL. / RACE OF DOOM** [ ] [–]

Aug 81. (lp/c) *(V/TCV 2191)* *<3595>* **NEW TRADITIONALISTS** [50] [24]
– Through being cool / Jerkin' back 'n' forth / Pity you / Soft things / Going under / Race of doom / Love without anger / The super thing / Beautiful world / Enough said. *(re-iss. Aug87 lp/c; OVED/+C 73)*

Aug 81. (7") *<WBS 47204>* **WORKING IN A COALMINE. / PLANET EARTH** [–] [ ]
<above issued on 'Full Moon' US>

Oct 81. (7") *(VS 457)* **WORKING IN A COALMINE. / ENOUGH SAID** [ ] [–]

Oct 81. (7") *<WBS 49834>* **BEAUTIFUL WORLD. / ENOUGH SAID** [–] [ ]

Jan 82. (7") *(VS 470)* **BEAUTIFUL WORLD. / THE SUPER THING** [ ] [–]

Mar 82. (7") *<WBS 50010>* **JERKIN' BACK 'N' FORTH. / MECHA MANIA BOY** [–] [ ]

Oct 82. (7")*<US-7"/12">* *(VS 536)* *<WBS 29931/29906>* **PEEK-A-BOO. / FIND OUT** [ ] [ ]

Oct 82. (lp/c) *(V/TCV 2241)* *<23741>* **OH NO! IT'S DEVO!** [ ] [47]
– Time out for fun / Peek-a-boo / Out of synch / Explosions / That's good / Patterns / Big mess / Speed racer / What I must do / I desire / Deep sleep. *(re-iss. Aug88 lp/c; OVED/+C 122)*

Jan 83. (7") *<WBS 29811>* **THAT'S GOOD. / WHAT MUST I DO** [–] [ ]

Jun 83. (7"/12") *(MCA/+T 822)* *<52215>* **THEME FROM DOCTOR DETROIT. / (track by James Brown)** [ ] May83 [59]
(above issued on 'M.C.A.' UK / 'Backstreet' US>

Warners / Warners

Oct 84. (7") *<29133>* **ARE YOU EXPERIENCED?. / GROWING PAINS** [–] [ ]

Oct 84. (lp/c) *(925 097-1/-4)* *<25097>* **SHOUT!** [ ] [83]
– Shout / The satisfied mind / Don't rescue me / The 4th dimension / C'mon / Here to go / Jurisdiction of love / Puppet boy / Please please / Are you experienced?

Mar 85. (7") *(W 9119)* **SHOUT. / C'MON** [ ] [–]
(d7"+=) *(W 9119F)* – Mongoloid / Jocko homo.

—— **DAVID KENDRICK** – drums; repl. MYERS

Enigma / Enigma

Jul 88. (lp/c/cd) *(ENVLP/TCENV/CDENV 503)* *<73303>* **TOTAL DEVO** [ ] Jun88 [ ]
– Baby doll / Disco dancer / Some things never change / Plain truth / Happy guy / Don't be cruel / I'd cry if you died / Agitated / Man turned inside out / Blow up. *(cd re-iss. Mar95 on 'Restless'; 72756-2)*

Jul 89. (3 sided-lp/cd) *(ENVLP/CDENV 532)* **NOW IT CAN BE TOLD (DEVO AT THE PALACE 12/9/88) (live)** [ ] [ ]
(cd re-iss. Mar95 on 'Restless'; REST 72755-2)

Oct 90. (7") **POST-POST MODERN MAN. / WHIP IT (live)** [ ] [ ]
(12"+=) – ('A'-Ultra post mix).
(cd-s++=) – Baby doll (mix).

Oct 90. (cd/c/lp) *(CDENV/TVENV/ENVLP 1006)* *<73526>* **SMOOTH NOODLE MAPS** [ ] Jun90 [ ]
– Stuck in a loop / Post-post modern man / When we do it / Spin the wheel / Morning dew / A chance is gonna cum / The big picture / Pink jazz trancers / Devo has feelings too / Jimmy / Danghaus. *(re-iss. cd Mar95 on 'Restless'; REST 72757-2)*

– compilations, etc. –

Jan 79. (m-lp) *Stiff; (ODD 1)* **BE STIFF** (first 3 singles) [ ] [–]

May 83. (12"ep) *Virgin; (VS 594-12)* **COME BACK JONEE. / WHIP IT / + 2** [ ] [–]

Aug 87. (cd) *Rykodisc; <RCD2 0031>* **E-Z LISTENING DISC** [–] [ ]
(UK-iss.Nov91; same as US)

Oct 90. (cd) *Fan Club; (FC 065) / Rykodisc; <RCD/RLP 10188>* **HARDCORE DEVO, VOL.1** (demos 74-77) [ ] Aug90 [ ]
(re-iss. c Mar94 on 'New Rose'; 422105)

Dec 90. (cd) *Warners; <26449>* **THE GREATEST HITS** [–] [ ]

Dec 90. (cd) *Warners; <26450>* **THE REST: GREATEST MISSES** [–] [ ]

Dec 91. (cd) *Rykodisc; <(RCD 20208)>* **HARDCORE DEVO, VOL.2: 1974-1977** [ ] Aug91 [ ]
(re-iss. c Mar94; RACS 0208)

Oct 92. (cd) *Rykodisc; <(RCD 20209)>* **DEVO LIVE: THE MONGOLOID YEARS (live)** [ ] [ ]

Jun 93. (cd) *Virgin; (CDV 2106)* **Q: ARE WE NOT MEN? A: WE ARE DEVO / DEV-O LIVE** [ ] [ ]

Jun 93. (cd) *Virgin; (CDV 2125)* **DUTY NOW FOR THE FUTURE / NEW TRADITIONALISTS** [ ] [ ]

Jun 93. (cd) *Virgin; (CDV 2241)* **OH NO! IT'S DEVO / FREEDOM OF CHOICE** [ ] [ ]

Sep 93. (cd/c) *Virgin; (CDVM/TCVM 9016)* **HOT POTATOES: THE BEST OF DEVO** [ ] [–]
– Jocko homo / Mongoloid / Satisfaction (I can't get me no) / Whip it / Girl u want / Freedom of choice / Peek-a-boo / Thru being cool / That's good / Working in a coalmine / Devo corporate anthem / Be stiff / Gates of steel / Come back Jonee / Secret agent man / The day my baby gave me a surprise / Beautiful world / Big mess / Whip it (HMS & M remix). *(lp-iss.Apr01 on 'Simply Vinyl'; SVLP 320)*

Oct 94. (3xcd-box) *Virgin; (TPAK 38)* **THE COMPACT COLLECTION** [ ] [–]
– (Q: ARE WE NOT MEN / DUTY NOW FOR THE FUTURE / OH NO IT'S DEVO!)

Aug 96. (cd-rom) *Discovery: <none>* **ADVENTURES OF SMART PATROL** [–] [ ]

May 00. (d-cd) *Rhino; <(8122 75967-2)>* **PIONEERS WHO GOT SCALPED: THE ANTHOLOGY** [ ] [ ]

Apr 02. (cd) *Rhino; <76037>* **THE ESSENTIALS** [–] [ ]

□ Howard DEVOTO (see under ⇒ MAGAZINE)

DEXYS MIDNIGHT RUNNERS

Formed: Birmingham, England ... July '78 by ex-KILLJOYS members, KEVIN ROWLAND and AL ARCHER, taking the name from pep pill, 'dexedrine'. With a cast of players including PETE SAUNDERS, PETE WILLIAMS, BOBBY JUNIOR (soon replaced with ANDY 'STOKER' GROWCOTT) and the brass section of Scottish-born "Big" JIM PATTERSON, J.B. BLYTE and STEVE 'BABYFACE' SPOONER, the band set out to emulate their heroes of the mid-60's soul scene. After a minor debut hit with 'DANCE STANCE' (and the replacement of SAUNDERS with ex-MERTON PARKAS/future STYLE COUNCIL man, MICK TALBOT), a brilliant tribute to one such hero, 'GENO' (Washington), saw DEXYS topping the UK charts in Spring 1980. A third single, 'THERE THERE MY DEAR', was issued later that summer, with a debut album, 'SEARCHING FOR THE YOUNG SOUL REBELS', following into the Top 10. Sporting an image inspired by Martin Scorcese's classic 'Mean Streets' movie (i.e. New York dockers) and coupling it with their idiosyncratic 80's take on classic soul, DEXY's were initially the toast of the UK music press. There was dissension in the ranks, however, the bulk of the band leaving in early '81 to form BUREAU; with ROWLAND and PATERSON the only remaining members, they bolstered the line-up with new recruits, BILLY ADAMS, MICKEY BILLINGHAM, PAUL SPEARE, BRIAN MAURICE, SEB SHELTON and STEVE WYNNE. The resulting single, 'SHOW ME', hit the Top 20 later that summer, although a follow-up, 'LIARS A TO E', failed to chart and the group retired to reconsider their approach. Augmenting the group with The EMERALD EXPRESS (that is, fiddlers HELEN O'HARA, STEVE BRENNAN and ROGER MacDUFF), DEXYS re-emerged in Spring '82 with a revamped Irish folk/soul hybrid (not too dissimilar to 'His Band And The Street Choir'-era VAN MORRISON, a rousing cover of Van The Man's 'JACKIE WILSON SAID' making the Top 5 later that year) and a suitably dishevelled gypsy/romantic vagabond image. 'THE CELTIC SOUL BROTHERS' introduced this new approach and although the track just missed the Top 40, a classic follow-up, 'COME ON EILEEN', was a massive transatlantic No.1 smash; not only were DEXYS big news again in Britain, they'd cracked America (albeit briefly) and the subsequent album, 'TOO-RYE-AY (1982) was the most successful of their career. Yet again, however, the line-up splintered and the momentum faltered, the brass section of PATTERSON, MAURICE and SPEAR departing in summer '82. It would be a further three years before the release of 'DON'T STAND ME DOWN', a considerably lower-key effort which enjoyed only a brief sojourn in the charts. A solitary hit single, 'BECAUSE OF YOU' (used as a theme for TV sitcom, 'Brush Strokes') followed in 1986, before DEXYS were consigned to history and ROWLAND faded into musical folklore. Despite his revered talent, the maverick Celtic minstrel had only release one solo set, 'THE WANDERER' in 10 years, with live performances a rarity. However in early 1997, ROWLAND inked a deal with 'Creation' records and finally came up with some new material (including the wearing of kinky lingerie!) for his er, cumback covers set, 'MY BEAUTY' (1999). Actually, apart from his embarrassing OTT attire, the album might've done quite well, although only the appropriately titled 'I CAN'T TELL THE BOTTOM FROM THE TOP' made it worthwhile

• **Songwriters:** All penned by ROWLAND, except BURNING DOWN THE WALLS OF HEARTACHE (Johnny Johnson & The Bandwagon) / ONE WAY LOVE (Russell-Meade) / SOUL FINGER (Bar-Kays).

Album rating: SEARCHING FOR THE YOUNG SOUL REBELS (*8) / TOO-RYE-AYE (*7) / DON'T STAND ME DOWN (*5) / THE VERY BEST OF DEXYS MIDNIGHT RUNNERS compilation (*8) / Kevin Rowland: THE WANDERER (*4) / MY BEAUTY (*5) / Dexys Midnight Runners: LET'S MAKE THIS PRECIOUS compilation (*7)

KEVIN ROWLAND – vocals, guitar (b.17 Aug'53, Wolverhampton, England) (ex-KILLJOYS, as **KEVIN ROLAND) / AL ARCHER** – guitar, vocals (ex-KILLJOYS) / **PETE SAUNDERS** – keyboards / **PETE WILLIAMS** – bass, vocals / **JIMMY PATTERSON** (b. Scotland) – trombone / **J.B. BLYTE** – tenor, saxophone / **STEVE 'BABYFACE' SPOONER** – alto sax / **ANDY 'STOKER' GROWCOTT** – drums; repl. BOBBY JUNIOR

Parlophone — not iss.

Nov 79. (7") *(R 6028)* **DANCE STANCE. / I'M JUST LOOKING** — 40 — –

—— **MICK TALBOT** – keyboards (ex-MERTON PARKAS) repl. SAUNDERS

Mar 80. (7") *(R 6033)* **GENO. / BREAKING DOWN THE WALLS OF HEARTACHE** — 1 — –

Jun 80. (7") *(R 6038)* **THERE THERE MY DEAR. / THE HORSE** — 7 — –

Jul 80. (lp/c) *(PCS/TCPCS 7213)* **SEARCHING FOR THE YOUNG SOUL REBELS** — 6 — –
– Burn it down / Tell me when my light turns green / The teams that meet in caffs / I'm just looking / Geno / Seven days too long / I couldn't help it if I tried / Thankfully not living in Yorkshire, it doesn't apply / Keep it / Love (pt.1) / There, there my dear. *(re-iss. 1982 on 'Fame' lp/c;) (cd-iss. Jan88; CZ 31) (lp re-iss. Dec99 on 'Simply Vinyl'; SVLP 154) (cd re-mast.Sep00 on 'E.M.I.'+=; 525600-0)* – Geno (video) / There, there my dear (video).

Nov 80. (7") *(R 6042)* **KEEP IT PART TWO . / ONE WAY LOVE** — — –

Mar 81. (7") *(R 6046)* **PLAN B. / SOUL FINGER** — 58 — –

—— **ROWLAND + PATERSON** recruited new guys **BILLY ADAMS** – guitar / **MICKEY BILLINGHAM** – keyboards / **PAUL SPEARE** – tenor sax / **BRIAN MAURICE** – alto sax / **SEB SHELTON** – drums (ex-SECRET AFFAIR) / **STEVE WYNNE** – bass (replaced ARCHER, GROWCOTT and TALBOT who formed BUREAU)

Mercury — Mercury

Jun 81. (7") *(DEXYS 6)* **SHOW ME. / SOON** — 16 —

Nov 81. (7") *(DEXYS 7)* **LIARS A TO E. / . . . AND YES, WE MUST REMAIN THE WILDHEARTED OUTSIDERS** — —

—— retained **ADAMS, SHELTON, PATTERSON / + GIORGIO KILKENNY** – bass repl. WYNNE

DEXYS MIDNIGHT RUNNERS & The EMERALD EXPRESS

—— added **HELEN O'HARA** – violin, vocals repl. BILLINGHAM / **STEVE BRENNAN** – violin / **ROGER MacDUFF** – violin

Mar 82. (7") *(DEXYS 8)* **THE CELTIC SOUL BROTHERS. / LOVE (part 2)** — 45 —

Jun 82. (7") *(DEXYS 9) <76189>* **COME ON EILEEN. / DUBIOUS** — 1 — Jan83 — 1
(12"+=) *(DEXYS 9-12)* – Liars A to E (remix).

Jul 82. (lp/c) *(MERS/+C 8) <4069>* **TOO-RYE-AY** — 2 — Feb83 — 14
– The Celtic soul brothers / Let's make this precious / All in all / Jackie Wilson said (I'm in Heaven when you smile) / Old / Plan B – I'll show you / Liars A to E / Until I believe in my soul / Come on Eileen. *(cd-iss. Jan83; 810054-2) (re-iss. Jul86 lp/c; PRICE/PRIMC 89) (cd re-mast.Mar96; 514839-2) (cd re-iss. Aug00 +=; 542961-2)* – The Celtic soul brothers (video) / Come on Eileen (video).

KEVIN ROWLAND & DEXYS MIDNIGHT RUNNERS

—— PATTERSON left June '82, MAURICE and SPEARE left July '82

Sep 82. (7") *(DEXYS 10)* **JACKIE WILSON SAID. / LET'S MAKE THIS PRECIOUS** — 5 —
(12"+=) *(DEXYS 10-12)* – T.S.O.P.

Nov 82. (7") *(DEXYS 11)* **LET'S GET THIS STRAIGHT FROM THE START. / OLD (live)** — 17 —
(12"+=) *(DEXYS 11-12)* – Respect (live).

Mar 83. (7"/7"s) *(DEXY S/P 12) <811142>* **THE CELTIC SOUL BROTHERS. / REMINISCE PART ONE** — 20 — May83 — 86
(12"+=) *(DEXYS 12-12)* – Show me.

DEXYS MIDNIGHT RUNNERS

—— line-up **ROWLAND, O'HARA & ADAMS / JIMMY PATTERSON** – trombone (returned) + new part-time sessioners / **NICKY GATFIELD** – saxophone / **JULIAN LITTMAN** – mandolin / **JOHN EDWARDS** – bass / **TOMMY EVANS** – steel guitar / **TIM DANCY** – drums / **ROBERT NOBLE** – keyboards, synth / and special guest star **VINCENT CRANE** – piano (ex-ATOMIC ROOSTER)

Sep 85. (lp/c)(cd) *(MERH/+C 56)(822989-2)* **DON'T STAND ME DOWN** 22 –
– The occasional flicker / This is what she's like / Knowledge of beauty / One of those things / Reminisce part two / Listen to this / The waltz. *(cd+=)* – This is what she's like (instrumental). *(cd re-iss. Jun97 on 'Creation'; CRECD 154) (cd re-iss. Feb03 on 'E.M.I.'; 530803-2)*

Nov 85. (7") *(DEXYS 13)* **THIS IS WHAT SHE'S LIKE. / ('A'instrumental)** –
(12"+=) *(DEXYS 13-12)* – Reminisce (part 1).
(10") *(DEXYS 13-10)* – ('A'side) / Marguerita time.
(d7"++=) *(DEXYD 13)* – ('A'&'B'versions).

Oct 86. (7") *(BRUSH 1)* **BECAUSE OF YOU. / KATHLEEN MAVOUREEN** 13 –
(12"+=) *(BRUSH 1-12)* – Sometimes theme.

KEVIN ROWLAND

Mercury not iss.

Apr 88. (7") *(DEXYS 14)* **WALK AWAY. / EVEN WHEN I HOLD YOU** –
(12"+=/12"box+=) *(DEXY S/B 14-12)* – ('A'version) / The way you look tonight.
(cd-s+=) *(DEXCD 14)* – The way you look tonight / Because of you.

Jun 88. (lp/c)(cd) *(MERH/+C 121)(834488-2)* **THE WANDERER** –
– Young man / Walk away / You'll be the one for me / Heartaches by the number / I am a wanderer / Tonight / When you walk alone / Age can't wither you / I want / Remember me.

Jul 88. (7") *(ROW 1)* **TONIGHT. / KEVIN ROWLAND'S BAND** –
(12"+=) *(ROW 1T)* – Come on Eileen.

Oct 88. (7") *(ROW 2)* **YOUNG MAN. / ONE WAY TICKET TO PALOOKAHVILLE** –
(12"+=) *(ROW 2-12)* – Jackie Wilson said (I'm in heaven when you smile).
(cd-s++=) *(ROWCD 2)* – Show me.

Creation not iss.

Sep 99. (c-s/cd-s) *(CRE CS/SCD 332)* **CONCRETE AND CLAY / I CAN'T TELL THE BOTTOM FROM THE TOP** –

Oct 99. (cd) *(CRECD 216)* **MY BEAUTY** –
– The greatest love of all / Rag doll / Concrete and clay / Daydream believer / This guy's in love with you / The long and winding road / It's getting better / I can't tell the bottom from the top / Labelled with love (I'll stay with my dreams) / Reflections of my life / You'll never walk alone.

– DEXYS compilations, others, etc. –

Mar 83. (lp) *E.M.I.; (EMS 1007)* **GENO** 79
(re-iss. Oct87 lp/c; ATAK/TC-ATAK 72) (cd-iss. Jun88 on 'Fame'; CDFA 3189)

Mar 84. (7") *EMI Gold; (G 455)* **DANCE STANCE. / THERE THERE MY DEAR** –

1989. (cd-video) *Mercury; (080 628-2)* **COME ON EILEEN / THE CELTIC SOUL BROTHERS / JACKIE WILSON SAID (I'M IN HEAVEN WHEN YOU SMILE) / LIARS TO E** –

Mar 90. (7") *Old Gold; (OG 9900)* **COME ON EILEEN. / JACKIE WILSON SAID (I'M IN HEAVEN WHEN YOU SMILE)** –

Sep 92. (cd-s) *Old Gold; (126238342-2)* **GENO / THERE THERE MY DEAR / DANCE STANCE** –

Jun 91. (cd/c/lp) *Mercury; (846460-2/-4/-1)* **THE VERY BEST OF DEXYS MIDNIGHT RUNNERS** 12
– Come on Eileen / Jackie Wilson said (I'm in heaven when you smile) / Let's get this straight (from the start) / Because of you / Show me / The Celtic soul brothers (more, please, thank you) / Liars a to e / One way love / Old / Geno / There there my dear / Breakin' down the walls of heartache / Dance stance / Plan b / Keep it / I'm just looking / Soon / This is what she's like / Soul finger. (cd+=) – (5 extra tracks) *(re-iss. Jul92)*

Jun 91. (7") *Mercury;* **COME ON EILEEN. / BECAUSE OF YOU** –
(12"+=/cd-s+=) – Let's get this straight (from the start).

May 93. (cd/c) *Spectrum; (550 003-2/-4)* **BECAUSE OF YOU** –

Nov 93. (cd) *Windsong; (WINCD 047)* **BBC RADIO 1 LIVE IN CONCERT – NEWCASTLE (live)** –

Jul 95. (cd) *Nighttracks; (CDNT 009)* **1980-1982 – THE RADIO SESSIONS** –

Aug 95. (d-cd) *Mercury; (528608-2)* **TOO RYE AYE / DON'T STAND ME DOWN** –

May 96. (cd) *Premier; (PRMUCD 1)* **IT WAS LIKE THIS** –

Sep 03. (cd-s) *E.M.I.; (CDDEXYS 2003)* **MANHOOD / MANHOOD (radio) / REMINISCE (part two) / I'LL STAY FOREVER MY LOVE** –

Sep 03. (cd) *E.M.I.; (592680-2)* **LET'S MAKE THIS PRECIOUS – THE BEST OF DEXYS MIDNIGHT RUNNERS** 75 –
– Geno / The Celtic soul brothers (more please thank you) / Come on Eileen / Jackie Wilson said (I'm in Heaven when you smile) / Manhood / Because of you / I love you / Show me / There, there my dear / Tell me when my light turns green / Breaking down the walls of heartache / Plan B / Let's get this straight (from the start) / This is what she's like / Let's make this precious / My national pride / Until I believe in my soul / My life in New England.

Neil DIAMOND

Born: NOAH KAMINSKY, 24 Jan'41, Brooklyn, New York, USA. By the time he'd graduated from Brooklyn's Erasmus high school and embarked upon a degree at New York University, DIAMOND had already begun writing and recording. As one-half of the duo NEIL & JACK (with Jack Parker), he released a couple of early singles on the small 'Duel' label before cutting a one-off solo track for 'Columbia' in 1963. Upon dropping out of university he began working full-time as a staff writer for various publishers, providing material for the likes of CLIFF RICHARD, JAY & THE AMERICANS and most successfully, The MONKEES, for whom he wrote the 1967 US No.1, 'I'M A BELIEVER'. A year previous, DIAMOND had signed a new recording contract with 'Bang' records and had already scored a Top 10 hit with 'CHERRY, CHERRY' following on from the minor chart success of his definitive 'SOLITARY MAN'. A string of moderate Jeff Barry/Ellie Greenwich-produced hits ensued over the next two years including the classics, 'GIRL, YOU'LL BE A WOMAN SOON' and 'KENTUCKY WOMAN'. Wrapping his ominous baritone around hook-driven, rootsy pop-rock, DIAMOND had created a songwriting formula that was irresistibly populist yet enduring, his success encouraging him to push for full creative control and make it as a credible singer/songriter in his own right. 'Uni' subsequently offered him the deal he was looking for and despite the relative failure of the experimental 'VELVET GLOVES AND SPIT' (1968) album, the hits began rolling in at the turn of the decade as the anthemic 'SWEET CAROLINE' became his biggest hit to date (US Top 5) in summer '69. The accompanying album, 'TOUCHING YOU TOUCHING ME' (1970), established his credentials/ambitions with a tasteful selection of covers from the likes of FRED NEIL and JONI MITCHELL while also spawning a second major hit in 'HOLLY HOLY'. Later that year he scored his first US No.1 (UK No.3) with 'CRACKLIN' ROSIE', a highlight of the 'TAPROOT MANUSCRIPT' (1971) set wherein he even attempted an ambitious suite, 'THE AFRICAN TRILOGY'. Despite his wish to be recognised as a "serious" singer/songwriter, DIAMOND just couldn't help penning gloriously catchy, future karaoke classics like 'I AM . . . I SAID' (transatlantic Top 5) and 'SONG SUNG BLUE' (US No.1) while late 1973's 'HOT AUGUST NIGHT' live set captured his lavish showmanship on vinyl and cemented his superstar status. 'Columbia' were so impressed they stumped up five million dollars for his record-breaking signing later that year, their investment paying off as the 'JONATHAN LIVINGSTON SEAGULL' (1974) soundtrack ended up coining in more cash than the film itself. The BAND's ROBBIE ROBERTSON lent DIAMOND a modicum of street cred by producing 1976's 'BEAUTIFUL NOISE', a concept effort based on NEIL's formative years as a Brill Building protoge. Even through the punk era, DIAMOND kept racking up the hits, scoring another US No.1 in 1978 via the BARBRA STREISAND duet, 'YOU DON'T BRING ME FLOWERS'. The album of the same name also spawned another karaoke fave in the shape of country-tinged singalong, 'FOREVER IN BLUE JEANS' (Top 20), cheesy MOR maybe but great stuff all the same. Surprisingly perhaps, the man's biggest success was yet to come, arriving in the shape of his soundtrack to a remake of 1920's movie, 'The Jazz Singer' in which DIAMOND himself starred alongside Laurence Olivier. Released in late 1980, the record went multi-platinum and spawned three US Top 10 singles, 'LOVE ON THE ROCKS', 'HELLO AGAIN' and 'AMERICA'. The polished balladry of 'HEARTLIGHT' (1982) brought further success in the States with its title track becoming an MOR radio staple. Despite a surprise Top 10 placing in the UK, 'PRIMITIVE' (1984) found DIAMOND treading water if not drowning in a stagnant pond of romantic mush. 'HEADED FOR THE FUTURE' (1986) attempted to bring him up to date without much success while 'HOT AUGUST NIGHT II' (1987) was a pale reflection of its predecessor. Signing to 'Columbia' at the dawn of the 90's, DIAMOND revisited the era of the 60's songwriter with the critically mauled 'ON THE ROOF – SONGS OF THE BRILL BUILDING' (1993). More successful was 'TENNESSEE MOON' (1996), DIAMOND's Nashville record. Essentially a singles artist, the man's various greatest hits sets are a worthy addition to even the hippest of record collections and while the likes of UB40 have covered his work to great success in the past, alt-rockers URGE OVERKILL demonstrated his kitsch appeal to brilliant effect with their 'Pulp Fiction' performance of 'GIRL, YOU'LL BE A WOMAN SOON'. DIAMOND had his own shot at celluloid interpretation on 1998's 'AS TIME GOES BY – THE MOVIE ALBUM', labouring over the likes of 'UNCHAINED MELODY' and 'MOON RIVER'. Into the new millennium, DIAMOND decided to reconfirm his identity as a singer/songwriter with 'THREE CHORD OPERA' (2001), his first album of wholly original, self-penned material in over 30 years. • **Covered:** NEW ORLEANS (Gary U.S. Bonds) / UNTIL IT'S TIME FOR YOU TO GO (Buffy Sainte-Marie) / HE AIN'T HEAVY, HE'S MY BROTHER (Hollies) / HEARTLIGHT + FRONT PAGE STORY (Bacharach/Bayer-Sager) / I'M ALIVE (co-with David Foster) / MORNING HAS BROKEN (Cat Stevens) / etc, etc, etc

Album rating: JUST FOR YOU (*5) / VELVET GLOVES AND SPIT (*5) / TOUCHING YOU, TOUCHING ME (*6) / TAPROOT MANUSCRIPT (*6) / STONES (*4) / MOODS (*5) / HOT AUGUST NIGHT (*7) / DOUBLE GOLD compilation (*7) / RAINBOW collection (*5) / JONATHAN LIVINGSTON SEAGULL (*6) / HIS 12 GREATEST HITS compilation (*8) / SERENADE (*4) / BEAUTIFUL NOISE (*6) / LOVE AT THE GREEK (*4) / I'M GLAD YOU'RE HERE WITH ME TONIGHT (*4) / YOU DON'T BRING ME FLOWERS (*5) / SEPTEMBER MORN (*4) / THE JAZZ SINGER (*6) / ON THE WAY TO THE SKY (*3) / 12 GREATEST HITS, VOL.II compilation (*6) / HEARTLIGHT (*3) / PRIMITIVE (*3) / HEADED FOR THE FUTURE (*3) / HOT AUGUST NIGHT II (*4) / THE BEST YEARS OF OUR LIVES (*5) / LOVESCAPE (*3) / THE GREATEST HITS 1966-1992 compilation (*8) / THE CHRISTMAS ALBUM (*2) / UP ON THE ROOF – SONGS FROM THE BRILL BUILDING (*4) / LIVE IN AMERICA (*4) / TENNESSEE MOON (*4) / AS TIME GOES BY – THE MOVIE ALBUM (*3) / THREE CHORD OPERA (*5) / THE ESSENTIAL . . . compilation (*8)

NEIL DIAMOND – vocals, acoustic guitar / **JACK PACKER** – vocals, acoustic guitar

not iss. | Duel

1960. (7"; as NEIL & JACK) *<508>* **YOU ARE MY LOVE AT LAST. / WHAT WILL I DO** [–] [ ]

1961. (7"; as NEIL & JACK) **I'M AFRAID. / TILL YOU'VE TRIED LOVE** [–] [ ]

—— NEIL now used various session people

not iss. | Columbia

1963. (7") *<42809>* **CLOWN TOWN. / AT NIGHT** [–] [ ]

—— He then began writing for JAY & THE AMERICANS, CLIFF RICHARD and later The MONKEES. He returned to the studio early 1966.

London | Bang

May 66. (7") *(HLZ 10049) <519>* **SOLITARY MAN. / DO IT** [ ] [55]

Sep 66. (7") *(HLZ 10072) <528>* **CHERRY, CHERRY. / I'LL COME RUNNING** [ ] Aug66 [6]

Nov 66. (7") *(HLZ 10092) <536>* **I GOT THE FEELIN' (OH NO NO). / THE BOAT THAT I ROW** [ ] [16]

Jan 67. (lp; mono/stereo) *(HAZ 8307) <BLP/+S 214>* **THE FEEL OF NEIL DIAMOND** [ ] Oct66 [ ]
– Solitary man / Red rubber ball / La bamba / Do it / Hanky panky / Monday Monday / New Orleans / Someday baby / I got the feelin' / I'll come running / Love to love / Cherry, Cherry.

Feb 67. (7") *(HLZ 10111) <540>* **YOU GOT TO ME. / SOMEDAY BABY** [ ] Jan67 [18]

Apr 67. (7") *(HLZ 10126) <542>* **GIRL, YOU'LL BE A WOMAN SOON. / YOU'LL FORGET** [ ] [10]

Jul 67. (7") *(HLZ 10151) <547>* **I THANK THE LORD FOR THE NIGHT. / LONG WAY HOME** [ ] [13]

Sep 67. (lp; mono/stereo) *<BLP/+S 217>* **JUST FOR YOU** [–] [80]
– Girl, you'll be a woman soon / The long way home / Red red wine / You'll forget / The boat that I row / Cherry, Cherry / I'm a believer / Shilo / You got to me / Solitary man / Thank the Lord for the night time.

Nov 67. (7") *(HLZ 10161) <551>* **KENTUCKY WOMAN. / THE TIME IS NOW** [ ] Oct67 [22]

Jan 68. (7") *(HLZ 10177) <554>* **NEW ORLEANS. / HANKY PANKY** [ ] Dec67 [51]

Apr 68. (7") *(HLZ 10187) <556>* **RED RED WINE. / RED RUBBER BALL** [ ] [62]

Uni | Uni

May 68. (7") *(UN 503) <55065>* **BROOKLYN ROADS. / HOLIDAY INN BLUES** [ ] [58]

M.C.A. | Uni

Jun 68. (lp) *(MUPS 365) <73030>* **VELVET GLOVES AND SPIT** [ ] [ ]
– Two-bit manchild / A modern day version of love / Honey dripping times / The pot smoker's song / Brooklyn roads / Shilo / Sunday sun / Holiday inn blues / Practically newborn / Knackerffeng / Merry-go-round. *(re-iss. 1970 on 'Uni'; UNLS 106) (re-iss. 1974; MCF 2512) (re-iss. Feb82 lp/c; MCL/+C 1640) (re-iss. Apr92 cd/c; MCL D/C 1904-2/-4)*

Jul 68. (7") *(MU 1033) <55075>* **TWO-BIT MANCHILD. / BROAD OLD WOMAN (9 a.m. INSANITY)** [ ] [66]

Sep 68. (7") *<55084>* **SUNDAY SUN. / HONEY DRIPPING TIMES** [–] [68]

Apr 69. (7") *(MU 1070) <55109>* **BROTHER LOVE'S TRAVELLING SALVATION SHOW. / A MODERN DAY VERSION OF LOVE** [ ] Mar69 [22]

Apr 69. (lp) *(MUPS 382) <73047>* **BROTHER LOVE'S TRAVELLING SALVATION SHOW** [ ] Mar69 [82]
– Brother Love's travelling salvation show / Dig in / River runs, newgrown plums / Juliet / Long gone / And the grass won't pay you no mind / Memphis street / Glory road / Deep in the morning / If I ever knew your name / You're so sweet horseflies keep hanging round your face / Hurtin' / You don't come easy. *(re-iss. 1970 on 'Uni'+=; UNLS 107)* – Sweet Caroline. *(re-iss. 1974; MCF 2536)*

Jul 69. (7") *(MU 198) <55136>* **SWEET CAROLINE (GOOD TIMES NEVER SEEMED SO GOOD). / DIG IN** [ ] [4]

Uni | Uni

Nov 69. (7") *(UN 512) <55175>* **HOLLY HOLY. / HURTIN' YOU DON'T COME EASY** [ ] Oct69 [6]

Jan 70. (lp) *(UNLS 110) <73071>* **TOUCHING YOU TOUCHING ME** [ ] Dec69 [30]
– Sweet Caroline (good times never seemed so good) / Until it's time for you to go / Everybody's talkin' / Mr. Bojangles / Smokey lady / Holly holy / Both sides now / And the singer sings his song / Ain't no way / New York boy.

Feb 70. (7") *<55204>* **UNTIL IT'S TIME FOR YOU TO GO. / AND THE SINGER SINGS HIS SONG** [–] [53]

May 70. (7") *(UN 522) <55224>* **SOOLAIMON (AFRICAN TRILOGY II). / AND THE GRASS WON'T PAY YOU NO MIND** [ ] [30]

Aug 70. (7") *(UN 529) <55250>* **CRACKLIN' ROSIE. / LORDY** [3] [1]
(re-iss. Feb74 on 'M.C.A.'; MCA 113)

Sep 70. (lp) *(UNLS 116) <73084>* **GOLD (live at Troubador)** [23] [10]
– Lordy / Both sides now / Solitary man / Holly holy / Cherry, cherry / Kentucky woman / Sweet Caroline / Thank the Lord for the night time / And the singer sings his songs / Brother Love's travelling salvation show. *(re-iss. 1974 on 'M.C.A.'; MCF 2515) (re-iss. Oct87 on 'Music For Pleasure'; MFP 5815)*

Nov 70. (7") *<55264>* **HE AIN'T HEAVY HE'S MY BROTHER. / FREE LIFE** [–] [20]

Feb 71. (7") *(UNS 531)* **SWEET CAROLINE. / BROTHER LOVE'S TRAVELLING SALVATION SHOW** [8] [–]
(re-iss. Jan74 on 'M.C.A.'; MCA 106)

Mar 71. (lp) *(UNLS 117) <73092>* **TAPROOT MANUSCRIPT** [19] Nov70 [13]
– Cracklin' Rosie / Free life / Coldwater morning / Done too soon / He ain't heavy he's my brother / The African trilogy (a folk ballet: I am the lion / Madrigal / Soolamain / Missa / African smile / Childsong (reprise). *(re-iss. 1974 on 'M.C.A.'; MCF 2509) (re-iss. Sep86 lp/c; MCL/+C 1707) (cd-iss. 1987 on 'M.C.A.'; DIDX 273) (cd re-iss. Aug92; MCLD 19119)*

Apr 71. (7") *(UN 532) <55278>* **I AM . . . I SAID. / DONE TOO SOON** [4] [4]
Mar71 [65]

Nov 71. (7") *(UN 536) <55310>* **STONES. / CRUNCHY GRANOLA SUITE** [ ] [14]

Nov 71. (lp) *(UNLS 121) <93106>* **STONES** [18] [11]
– I am . . . I said / The last thing on my mind / Husbands and wives / Chelsea morning / Crunchy granola suite / Stones / If you go away / Suzanne / I think it's going to rain today / I am . . . I said (reprise). *(re-iss. 1974 on 'M.C.A.'; MCF 2530) (cd-iss. Aug90; DMCL 1908) (cd re-iss. Apr92; MCLD 19118)*

Apr 72. (7") *(UN 538) <55326>* **SONG SUNG BLUE. / GITCHY GOOMY** [14] [1]

Jul 72. (lp) *(UNLS 128) <93136>* **MOODS** [7] [5]
– Walk on water / Song sung blue / Porcupine pie / High rolling man / Canta libre / Captain Sunshine / Play me / Gitchy goomy / Theme / Prelude in E major / Morningside. *(cd-iss. 1985 on 'M.C.A.'; DMCA 115) (cd re-iss. Jul87 on 'M.C.A.'; CDCAD 31061) (cd re-iss. 1988 on 'M.C.A.'; DIDX 272) (re-iss. Sep91 on 'M.C.A.' cd/c; DMCL/MCLC 1759) (re-iss. Apr92 on 'M.C.A.' cd/c; MCL D/C 19043)*

Aug 72. (7") *(UNS 546) <55346>* **PLAY ME. / PORCUPINE PIE** [ ] [11]

Nov 72. (7") *(UNS 551) <55352>* **WALK ON WATER. / HIGH ROLLING MAN** [ ] [17]

Uni M.C.A.

Mar 73. (7") *(UNS 556) <40017>* **CHERRY CHERRY (live). / MORNINGSIDE** [ ] [31]

Dec 73. (d-lp) *(ULD 1-2) <2-8000>* **HOT AUGUST NIGHT (live)** [32] Dec72 [5]
– Prologue / Crunchy granola suite / Done too soon / Dialogue / Solitary man / Cherry cherry / Sweet Caroline / Porcupine pie / You're so sweet / Red red wine / Soggy pretzels / And the grass won't pay you no mind / Shilo / Girl you'll be a woman soon / Play me / Canta libre / Morningside / Song sung blue / Cracklin' Rosie / Holly holy / I am . . . I said / Soolamain / Brother Love's travelling salvation show / Encore. *(re-iss. 1975 on 'M.C.A.'; MCSP 255)*

C.B.S. Columbia

Nov 73. (7") *(CBS 1843) <45942>* **BE. / FLIGHT OF THE GULL** [ ] [ ]

Jan 74. (lp/c) *(CBS/40 69047) <KS 32550>* **JONATHAN LIVINGSTON SEAGULL (Film Soundtrack)** [35] Nov73 [2]
– Prologue / Be / Flight of the gull / Dear father / Skybird / Lonely looking sky / The odyssey: Be – Lonely looking sky – Dear father / Anthem / Be / Skybird / Dear father / Be. *(cd-iss. 1986)*

Apr 74. (7") *(CBS 2191) <45998>* **SKYBIRD. / LONELY LOOKING SKY** [ ] Feb74 [75]

Oct 74. (lp/c) *(CBS/40 69067) <PC 32919>* **SERENADE** [11] [3]
– I've been this way before / Rosemary's wine / Lady Magdalene / The last Picasso / Longfellow serenade / Yes I will / Reggae strut / The gift of song. *(re-iss. Jun81; CBS 32050) (cd-iss. May87; CD 69067) (re-iss. Sep89 on 'Pickwick' lp/c/cd; 982195-1/-4/-2) (re-iss. Dec95 on 'Columbia' cd/c; 465012-2/-4)*

Nov 74. (7") *(CBS 2769) <10043>* **LONGFELLOW SERENADE. / ROSEMARY'S WINE** [ ] [5]

Feb 75. (7") *(CBS 3058) <10084>* **I'VE BEEN THIS WAY BEFORE. / REGGAE STRUT** [ ] [34]

Jun 75. (7") *(CBS 3350) <10138>* **THE LAST PICASSO. / THE GIFT OF SONG** [ ] [ ]

Jun 76. (7") *(CBS 4398) <10366>* **IF YOU KNOW WHAT I MEAN. / STREET LIFE** [35] [11]

Jul 76. (lp/c) *(CBS/40 86004) <PC 33935>* **BEAUTIFUL NOISE** [10] [4]
– Beautiful noise / Stargazer / Lady oh / Don't think . . . feel / Surviving the life / If you know what I mean / Street life / Home is a wounded heart / Jungletime / Signs / Dry your eyes. *(re-iss. Apr87 lp/c; 450452-1/-4) (cd-iss. May87; CD 86004) (re-iss. Mar91; 450452-2)*

Sep 76. (7") *<10405>* **DON'T THINK . . . FEEL. / HOME IS A WOUNDED HEART** [–] [43]

Sep 76. (7") *(CBS 4601)* **BEAUTIFUL NOISE. / HOME IS A WOUNDED HEART** [13] [–]

Feb 77. (d-lp/d-c) *(CBS/40 95001) <34402>* **LOVE AT THE GREEK (live)** [3] [8]
– Street life / Kentucky woman / Sweet Caroline (good times never seem so good) / The last Picasso / Longfellow serenade / Beautiful noise / Lady-oh / Stargazer / If you know what I mean / Surviving the life / Glory road / Song sung blue / Holly holy / Brother Love's travelling salvation show / Jonathan Livingstone Seagull / Be / Dear father / Lonely looking sky / Sanctus / Skybird / Be (encore) / I've been this way before. *(cd-iss. May87) (re-iss. cd+c Apr93 on 'Columbia')*

Dec 76. (7") *<10452>* **BEAUTIFUL NOISE. / SIGNS** [–] [ ]

Mar 77. (7") *(CBS 5115)* **STARGAZER (live). / STREET LIFE (live)** [ ] [–]

Jun 77. (7") *(CBS 5350)* **I'VE BEEN THIS WAY BEFORE (live). / SURVIVING THE LIFE (live)** [ ] [–]

Jul 77. (7") *(CBS 5440)* **DON'T THINK . . . FEEL. / SIGNS** [ ] [–]

Dec 77. (7") *(CBS 5869) <10657>* **DESIREE. / ONCE IN A WHILE** [39] [16]

Dec 77. (lp/c) *(CBS/40 86044) <34990>* **I'M GLAD YOU'RE HERE WITH ME TONIGHT** [16] [6]
– God only knows / Let me take you in my arms / Once in a while / Let the little boy sing / I'm glad you're here with me tonight / Lament in D minor / Dance of the sabres / Desiree / As if / Free man in Paris. *(cd-iss. May87; CD 86044) (re-iss. Oct90 cd/c/lp; CD/40CBS 32395)*

Feb 78. (7") *(CBS 6064)* **GOD ONLY KNOWS. / ONCE IN A WHILE** [ ] [–]

Mar 78. (7") *<10720>* **I'M GLAD YOU'RE HERE WITH ME TONIGHT. / DANCE OF SABRES** [–] [ ]

Apr 78. (7") *(CBS 6288)* **I'M GLAD YOU'RE HERE WITH ME TONIGHT. / AS IF** [ ] [–]

Sep 78. (7") *(CBS 6207)* **LET ME TAKE YOU IN MY ARMS. / AS IF** [ ] [–]

Nov 78. (7"; NEIL DIAMOND & BARBRA STREISAND) *(CBS 6803) <10840>* **YOU DON'T BRING ME FLOWERS. / (instrumental)** [5] [1]

Dec 78. (lp/c) *(CBS/40 86077) <35625>* **YOU DON'T BRING ME FLOWERS** [15] [4]
– The American popular song / Forever in blue jeans / Remember me / You've got your troubles / You don't bring me flowers / The dancing bumble-bee-bumble boogie / Mothers and daughters, fathers and sons / Memphis flyer / Say maybe / Diamond girls. *(cd-iss. May87; CD 86077) (re-iss. Aug91 on 'Columbia' cd/c; 468782-2/-4)*

Feb 79. (7") *(CBS 7047) <10897>* **FOREVER IN BLUE JEANS. / REMEMBER ME** [16] [20]

May 79. (7") *<10945>* **SAY MAYBE. / DIAMOND GIRLS** [–] [55]

May 79. (7") *(CBS 7408)* **THE AMERICAN POPULAR SONG. / DIAMOND GIRLS** [ ] [–]

Jan 80. (7") *(CBS 8130) <11175>* **SEPTEMBER MORN. / I'M A BELIEVER** [ ] [17]

Jan 80. (lp/c) *(CBS/40 86096) <36121>* **SEPTEMBER MORN** [14] Dec79 [10]
– September morn / Mama don't know / That kind / Jazz time / The good Lord loves you / Dancing in the street / The shelter of your arms / I'm a believer / The sun ain't gonna shine anymore / Stagger Lee. *(cd-iss. May87; CD 86096) (cd re-iss. Feb97 on 'Columbia'; 484455-2)*

Mar 80. (7") *<11232>* **THE GOOD LORD LOVES YOU. / JAZZ TIME** [–] [67]

Mar 80. (7") *(CBS 8322)* **DANCING IN THE STREET. / JAZZ TIME** [ ] [–]

Capitol Capitol

Oct 80. (7") *(CL 16173) <4939>* **LOVE ON THE ROCKS. / ACAPULCO** [17] [2]

Nov 80. (lp/c) *<(EAST/TCEAST 12120)>* **THE JAZZ SINGER (soundtrack)** [14] [3]
– America / Adon o lume / You baby / Love on the rocks / Amazed and

confused / The Robert E. Lee / Summer love / Hello again / Acapulco / Hey Louise / Songs of life / Jerusalem / Kol ridre / My name is Yussef (theme) / America (reprise). *(cd-iss. Jul84; CDEAST 12120) (re-iss. Jul98 on 'Columbia' cd/c; 483927-2/-4)*

Jan 81. (7") *(CL 16176) <4960>* **HELLO AGAIN. / AMAZED AND CONFUSED** [51] [6]

Apr 81. (7") *(CL 16197) <4994>* **AMERICA. / SONGS OF LIFE** [ ] [8]

C.B.S. Columbia

Oct 81. (lp/c) *(CBS/40 85343) <37628>* **ON THE WAY TO THE SKY** [39] [17]
– Yesterday's songs / On the way to the sky / Right by you / Only you / Save me / Be mine / The drifter / Fear of the market place / Rainy day song / Guitar Heaven / Love burns. *(cd-iss. Jul87; CD 85343)*

Nov 81. (7") *(CBS 1755) <02604>* **YESTERDAY'S SONGS. / GUITAR HEAVEN** [ ] [11]

Jan 82. (7") *(CBS 2033)* **RAINY DAY SONGS. / BE MINE TONIGHT** [ ] [–]

Feb 82. (7") *<02712>* **ON THE WAY TO THE SKY. / SAVE ME** [–] [27]

Jun 82. (7") *(CBS 2580) <02928>* **BE MINE TONIGHT. / RIGHT BY YOU** [ ] [35]

Sep 82. (7") *(CBS 2814) <03219>* **HEARTLIGHT. / YOU DON'T KNOW ME** [47] [5]

Oct 82. (lp/c) *(CBS/40 25073) <38359>* **HEARTLIGHT** [43] [9]
– Heartlight / I'm alive / I'm guilty / Hurricane / Lost amongst the stars / A fool for you / In enserada / Star flight / Front page story / Comin' home / First you have to say you love me. *(cd-iss. May87; CD 25073) (re-iss. cd Mar94 on 'Sony'; 982835-2)*

Jan 83. (7") *(CBS 3050)* **FRONT PAGE STORY. / LOVE AMONG THE STARS** [ ] [–]

Feb 83. (7") *<03503>* **I'M ALIVE. / LOST AMONGST THE STARS** [–] [35]

Apr 83. (7") *<03801>* **FRONT PAGE STORY. / I'M GUILTY** [–] [65]

Jul 84. (7") *(CBS 4458) <04541>* **TURN AROUND. / BROOKLYN ON A SATURDAY NIGHT** [ ] [62]

Aug 84. (lp/c) *(CBS/40 86036) <39199>* **PRIMITIVE** [7] [35]
– Turn around / Primitive / Fire on the tracks / Brooklyn on a Saturday night / Sleep with me tonight / Crazy / My time with you / Love's own song / It's a trip (go for the moon) / You make it feel like Christmas / One by one. *(cd-iss. May87; CD 86036) (re-iss. Aug91 on 'Sony' cd/c; 982636-2/-4)*

Sep 84. (7") *(CBS 4673)* **PRIMITIVE. / IT'S A TRIP** [ ] [–]

Sep 84. (7") *<04646>* **SLEEP WITH ME TONIGHT. / ONE BY ONE** [–] [ ]

Nov 84. (7") *<04719>* **YOU MAKE IT FEEL LIKE CHRISTMAS. / CRAZY** [–] [ ]

Nov 84. (7") *(CBS 4888)* **YOU MAKE IT FEEL LIKE CHRISTMAS. / ONE BY ONE** [ ] [–]

May 86. (7") *<05889>* **HEADED FOR THE FUTURE. / ANGEL** [–] [53]

May 86. (lp/c/cd) *(CBS/40/CD 26952) <40368>* **HEADED FOR THE FUTURE** [36] [20]
– Headed for the future / The man you need / I'll see you in the radio (Laura / Stand up for love / It should have been me / Lost in Hollywood / The story of my life / Angel / Me beside you / Love doesn't live here anymore. *(cd re-iss. Feb98 on 'Columbia'; 489453-2)*

Jul 86. (7"/12") *(A/TA 7225)* **STAND UP FOR LOVE. / THE STORY OF MY LIFE** [ ] [–]

Jul 86. (7") *<06136>* **THE STORY OF MY LIFE. / LOVE DOESN'T LIVE HERE ANYMORE** [–] [ ]

Nov 87. (7"/cd-s) *(651201-7/-2) <07614>* **I DREAMED A DREAM. / SWEET CAROLINE** [ ] [ ]

Dec 87. (d-lp/c/cd) *(460406-1/-4/-2) <40990>* **HOT AUGUST NIGHT II (live)** [74] Nov87 [59]
– Song of the whales (fanfare) / Headed for the future / September morn / Thank the Lord for the night time / Cherry cherry / Sweet Caroline / Hello again / Love on the rocks / America / Forever in blue jeans / You don't bring me flowers / I dreamed a dream / Back in L.A. / Song sung blue / Crackling Rosie / I am . . . I said / Holly holy / Soolamain / Brother Love's travelling salvation show / Heartlight. *(re-iss. Sep93 on 'Columbia')*

Jan 88. (7") *<07751>* **CHERRY CHERRY (live). / AMERICA (live)** [–] [ ]

Feb 89. (lp/c/cd) *(463201-1/-4/-2) <45025>* **THE BEST YEARS OF OUR LIVES** [42] Jan89 [46]
– The best years of our lives / Hard times for young lovers / This time / Everything's gonna be fine / Hooked on a memory of you / Take care of me / Baby can I hold you / Carmelita's eyes / Courtin' disaster / If I couldn't see you again / Long hard climb.

May 89. (7") *<08514>* **THIS TIME. / IF I COULDN'T SEE YOU AGAIN** [–] [ ]

May 89. (7"/c-s) *(654518-7/-4)* **THIS TIME. / BABY CAN I HOLD YOU** [ ] [–]
(12"+=) *(654518-6)* – Hooked on the morning of you.
(cd-s+=) *(654518-2)* – Beautiful noise / If you know what I mean.

Sep 89. (7") *<08741>* **THE BEST YEARS OF OUR LIVES. / CARMELITA'S EYES** [–] [ ]

Columbia Columbia

Oct 91. (cd/c/lp) *(468890-2/-4/-1) <48610>* **LOVESCAPE** [36] Sep91 [44]
– If there were no dreams / Mountains of love / Don't turn around / Someone who believes in you / When you miss your love / Fortune of the night / One hand, one heart / Hooked on the memory of you / Wish everything was alright / The way / Sweet L.A. days / All I really need is you / Lonely lady 17 / I feel you / Common ground. *(cd re-iss. Apr99; 468890-2)*

Jun 92. (cd/c/d-lp) *(471502/-2/-4) <52703>* **THE GREATEST HITS 1966-1992** (compilation) [1] May92 [90]
– Solitary man / Cherry, Cherry / I get the feelin' (oh no, no) / Thank you Lord for the night time / Girl, you'll be a woman soon / Kentucky woman / Shilo / You got to me / Brooklyn roads / Red, red wine / I'm a believer / Sweet Caroline / Soolaimon / Cracklin' Rose / Song sung blue / lay me / Holly holy / Morningside / Crunchy granola suite/ / Brother Love's travelling salvation show / I am . . . I said / Be / Longfellow serenade / Beautiful noise / If you know what I mean / Desiree / September morn / You don't bring me flowers (w / BARBRA STREISAND) / Forever in blue jeans / Hello America / Love on the rocks / Yesterday's songs / Heartlight / Headed for the future / Heartbreak Hotel (w / KIM CARNES) / All I really need is you. *(re-iss. Aug98; same)*

Nov 92. (7"/c-s) *(658826-7/-4)* **MORNING HAS BROKEN. / SANTA CLAUS IS COMING TO TOWN** [36] [ ]
(cd-s) *(658826-2)* – ('A'side) / Happy xmas (war is over) / Silver bells / Love on the rocks.

Nov 92. (cd/c/lp) *(472410-2/-4/-1) <52914>* **THE CHRISTMAS ALBUM** [50] [8]
– O come o come Emmanuel / We three kings of Orient are / Silent night / Little drummer boy / Santa Claus is coming to town / Christmas song / Morning has broken / Happy Xmas (war is over) / White Christmas / God rest ye merry gentlemen / Jingle bells rock / Hark the herald angels sing / Silver bells / You make it feel like Christmas / Holy night.

Sep 93. (cd/c/lp) *(474356-2/-4/-1) <57529>* **ON THE ROOF – SONGS FROM THE BRILL BUILDING** [28] [28]
– You've lost that lovin' feelin' (duet with DOLLY PARTON) / Up on the roof / Love potion number nine / Will you love me tomorrow/ Don't be cruel / Do wah diddy diddy (with MARY'S DANISH) / I (who have nothing) / Do you know the way to San Jose? / Don't make me over / River deep mountain high / A groovy kind of love / Spanish Harlem / Sweets for my sweet / Happy birthday sweet sixteen / Ten lonely guys / Save the last dance for me.

Aug 94. (d-cd/d-c) *(477211-2/-4) <66321>* **LIVE IN AMERICA (live)** [ ] [93]
– America / Hello again / Kentucky woman / You got to me / Cherry cherry / I'm a believer / Sweet Caroline / Love on the rocks / Hooked on the memory of you (with LINDA PRESS) / Lady oh / Beautiful noise / Play me / Up on the roof / You've lost that lovin' feelin' (with RAVEN KANE) / River deep, mountain high / I (who have nothing) / Missa / Soolaimon / Holly holy / And the grass won't pay you no mind / You don't bring me flowers (with RAVEN KANE) / September morn / Havah nagilah / Solitary man / Red red wine / Song sung blue / Forever in blue jeans / Heartlight / Cracklin' Rose / I am . . .I said / Crunchy Granola suite / Brother Love's traveling salvation show.

Nov 94. (cd/c) *(477598-2/-4) <66465>* **THE CHRISTMAS ALBUM VOLUME II** [ ] [51]
– Joy to the world / Mary's boy child / Deck the halls / We wish you a merry Christmas / Winter wonderland / Have yourself a merry little Christmas / I'll be home for Christmas / Rudolph the red nosed reindeer / Sleigh ride / Candlelight carol / Away in a manger / O come all ye faithful (adesta Fidells) / O little town of Bethlehem / Angels we have heard on high / The first noel / Hallelujah chorus.

Feb 96. (cd/c) *(481378-2/-4) <67382>* **TENNESSEE MOON** [12] [14]
– Tennessee moon / One good love / Shame / A matter of love / Marry me / Deep inside of you / Gold don't rush / Like you do / Can anybody hear me / Win the world / No limit / Reminisce for a while / Kentucky woman / If I lost my way / Everybody / Talking optimist blues (good day today) / Open wide these prison doors / Blue highway. *(cd re-iss. Jan99; same)*

Nov 98. (d-cd/d-c) *(491655-2/-4) <69540>* **AS TIME GOES BY – THE MOVIE ALBUM** 68 31
– As time goes by / Secret love / Unchained melody / Can you feel the love tonight / The way you look / Love with the proper stranger / Puttin' on the Ritz / When you wish upon a star / Windmills of your mind / Ebb tide / True love / My heart will go on / The look of love / Can't help falling in love / Ruby / I've got you under my skin / One for my baby / And I love her / Moon river / In the still of the night / As time goes by (reprise).

Sep 01. (cd) *(502493-2) <85500>* **THREE CHORD OPERA** 49 Jul01 15
– I haven't played this song in years / Don't look down / I believe in happy endings / At the movies / Midnight dream / You are the best part of me / Baby let's drive / My special someone / A mission of love / Elijah's song / Leave a little room for God / Turn down the lights.

– (selective) compilations, etc. –

1968. (7") *Bang; <561>* **SHILO. / LA BAMBA** –
<re-iss. Jan70; 575> – hit No.24

Jul 68. (lp) *Bang; <219>* **NEIL DIAMOND'S GREATEST HITS** – 100

Jul 70. (7") *Bang; <578>* **SOLITARY MAN. / THE TIME IS NOW** – 21

Sep 70. (lp) *Bang; <221>* **SHILO** – 52

Dec 70. (7") *Bang; <580>* **DO IT! / HANKY PANKY** – 36

Feb 71. (lp) *Bang; <224>* **DO IT!** – 100

Jun 71. (7") *President; (PT 342) / Bang; <586>* **I'M A BELIEVER. / CROOKED STREET** 51

Jan 73. (d-lp) *Bang; <227>* **DOUBLE GOLD** – 36

Aug 73. (7") *London; (HLM 10427) / Bang; <703>* **THE LONG WAY HOME. / MONDAY, MONDAY** 91

Aug 73. (7") *M.C.A.; <40092>* **THE LAST THING ON MY MIND. / CANTA LIBRE** – 56

Feb 74. (lp/c) *M.C.A.; (MCF/+C 2529) <2103>* **RAINBOW** 39 Dec73 35

Jun 74. (lp/c) *M.C.A.; (MCF/+C 2550) <2106>* **HIS 12 GREATEST HITS** 13 May74 29
(cd-iss. May87; DMCA 114)

Nov 78. (lp/c) *M.C.A.; (MCTV 2)* **20 GOLDEN GREATS** 2 –
(re-iss. Feb91 cd/c; D+/MCTV 2) (re-iss. May96 cd/c; MCD/MCC 11452)

Jan 81. (lp/c) *M.C.A.; (MCF/+C 3092)* **LOVE SONGS** 43
(re-iss. Apr97 cd/c; MCB D/C 19525)

Jun 82. (lp/c) *C.B.S.; (CBS/40 85844) / Columbia; <38068>* **12 GREATEST HITS VOLUME 2** 32 May82 48
(cd-iss. May87; CD 85844)

Dec 83. (lp) *K-Tel; (NE 1262)* **THE VERY BEST OF NEIL DIAMOND** 33 –

Aug 93. (3xcd-box) *Columbia; (474143-2)* **I'M GLAD YOU'RE HERE WITH ME TONIGHT / BEAUTIFUL NOISE / YOU DON'T SEND ME FLOWERS**

Jul 96. (d-cd) *M.C.A.; (MCD 33005)* **SWEET CAROLINE / MOODS**

Aug 96. (cd/c) *Sony TV – MCA; (MOOD CD/C 45)* **THE ULTIMATE COLLECTION** 5 –

Oct 96. (3xcd-box) *Columbia; (C3K 65013)* **IN MY LIFETIME** –

Nov 97. (3xcd-box) *Columbia; (488676-2)* **BEAUTIFUL NOISE / JONATHAN LIVINGSTONE SEAGULL / THE JAZZ SINGER** –

Sep 00. (cd) *Universal; (AA88 112119-2)* **THE NEIL DIAMOND COLLECTION**

Mar 02. (d-cd) *Sony TV; (501066-2) / Legacy; <85681>* **THE ESSENTIAL . . .** 11 Dec01 90
– Solitary man / Cherry cherry / I got the feelin' (oh no no) / Kentucky woman / Girl, you'll be a woman soon / You got to me / Red red wine / Thank the Lord for the night time / I'm a believer / Sweet Caroline / Song sung blue / Holly holy / I am I said / Crackin' Rosie / Play me (live) / Morningside (live) / Crunchy granola suite (live) / Brooklyn roads (live) / Soolaimon (live) / America / Hello again / Love on the rocks / Captain Sunshine (live) / He ain't heavy (he's my brother) / Yes I will / Lady Magdalene (live) / Shilo (live) / Brother Love's travelling salvation show (live) / If you know what I mean / Beautiful noise / You don't bring me flowers (with BARBRA STREISAND) / Desiree / Forever in blue jeans / September morn / I've been this way before / Yesterday's songs / Heartlight / Headed for the future / You are the best part of me.

Apr 02. (3xcd-box) *M.C.A.; (112824-2)* **PLAY ME: THE COMPLETE UNI STUDIO RECORDINGS**

Mar 03. (cd) *Universal; (AAMCAD 11947)* **20TH CENTURY MASTERS**

Mar 03. (d-cd) *Universal; (AAMCAD 211050-2)* **GLORY ROAD**

Bo DIDDLEY

Born: OTHA ELLAS BATES, 30 Dec'28, McComb, Missouri, USA. As a toddler, he was given the surname, McDANIEL, after he was adopted by his mother's cousin, Mrs. Gussie McDaniel. In the early 50's, BO DIDDLEY (named after a one-stringed African guitar) gave up a promising boxing career, moving in 1955 from Chicago street busking to sign for 'Checker' records. His debut recording, 'BO DIDDLEY', sold well enough in R&B circles to give him his first break later in the year on the 'Ed Sullivan Show'. Its flip side, 'I'M A MAN', also became a standard for many 60's beat combos (The WHO, YARDBIRDS, MANFRED MANN and especially The ROLLING STONES), and although DIDDLEY initially failed to score a Billboard Hot 100 hit, the bulk of his output was later embraced by countless rock acts. Songs such as 'BRING IT TO JEROME', 'DIDDY WAH DIDDY', 'WHO DO YOU LOVE' and 'MONA', followed a tried and tested formula which saw the "boss" man fusing R&B and rock'n'roll in drivingly rhythmic style (much like his recording companion, CHUCK BERRY). His umpteenth attempt at commercial success was finally rewarded with a belated minor US hit 45, 'CRACKIN UP' in the summer of '59. This was almost immediately followed by an even bigger hit, 'SAY MAN', which saw BO flaunt his quick witted humour in a taunting match with maracas man, JEROME. DIDDLEY continued in the same fashion throughout the early 60's, scoring low-key hits with 'ROAD RUNNER' and 'YOU CAN'T JUDGE A BOOK BY THE COVER', the momentum of the British beat boom seeing three DIDDLEY long-players ('BO DIDDLEY', ' . . . IS A GUNSLINGER' and ' . . . RIDES AGAIN') gaining a full UK release and subsequent Top 20 success in the Autumn of '63. His fourth album to grace the charts, 'BO DIDDLEY'S BEACH PARTY', surfaced early the following year, although this period represented the pinnacle of his career and as the white R&B/rock bands took over, DIDDLEY and his ilk were consigned to the margins. Save for a lone Top 40 excursion in 1965 with 'HEY GOOD LOOKIN', DIDDLEY had to settle for cult status in the decades to come, although he was a guest of The CLASH in 1979.

Best CD compilation: HIS BEST (CHESS 50th ANNIVERSARY COLLECTION) (*8)

BO DIDDLEY – vocals, guitar

London Checker

Jun 55. (7",78) *<814>* **BO DIDDLEY. / I'M A MAN** –
<re-iss. Dec61; 997>

—— **BILLY BOY ARNOLD** – harmonica / **JEROME GREEN** – bass, maracas, etc. / **FRANK KIRKLAND** – drums / guest **OTIS SPANN** – piano

Jun 56. (7",78) *<819>* **DIDDLEY DADDY. / SHE'S FINE, SHE'S MINE** –

Jun 56. (7"ep) *(RE-U 1054)* **RHYTHM & BLUES WITH BO DIDDLEY** –
– (above 4 tracks).

Sep 56. (7",78) *<827>* **BRING IT TO JEROME. / PRETTY THING** –

Dec 56. (7",78) *<832>* **DIDDY WAH DIDDY. / I'M LOOKING FOR A WOMAN** –

Mar 57. (7",78) *<842>* **WHO DO YOU LOVE. / IN BAD** –

Jul 57. (7",78) *<850>* **COPS AND ROBBERS. / DOWN HOME SPECIAL** –

Oct 57. (7",78) *<860>* **HEY! BO DIDDLEY. / MONA** –

Feb 58. (7",78) *<878>* **SAY! (BOSS MAN). / BEFORE YOU ACCUSE ME** –

Jun 58. (7",78) *<896>* **HUSH YOUR MOUTH. / DEAREST DARLING** –

Nov 58. (7",78) *<907>* **WILLIE AND LILLIE. / LET'S MEET THE MONSTER** –

Feb 59. (lp) *(HA-M 2230) <1436>* **GO BO DIDDLEY** Oct58

– Crackin' up / I'm sorry / Bo's guitar / Willie and Lillie / You don't love me (you don't care) / Say! (boss man) / The great grandfather / Oh, yea! / Don't let it go / Little girl / Dearest darling / The clock struck twelve.

Feb 59. (7",78) *<914>* **I'M SORRY. / OH YEA!** [–] [ ]

Aug 59. (7",78) *(HLM 8913) <924>* **CRACKIN' UP. / THE GREAT GRANDFATHER** [ ] Jun59 [62]

Nov 59. (7",78) *(HLM 8975) <931>* **SAY MAN. / THE CLOCK STRIKES TWELVE** [ ] Oct59 [20]

Jan 60. (7") *(HLM 9035) <936>* **SAY MAN, BACK AGAIN. / SHE'S ALRIGHT** [ ] [ ]

Apr 60. (7") *(HLM 9112) <942>* **ROAD RUNNER. / MY STORY** [ ] [75]

Jun 60. (7") *<951>* **CRAWDADDY. / WALKIN' AND TACKIN'** [–] [ ]

Nov 60. (7") *<965>* **GUNSLINGER. / SIGNIFYING BLUES** [–] [ ]

Mar 61. (7") *<976>* **NOT GUILTY. / AZTEC** [–] [ ]

Jun 61. (7") *<985>* **CALL ME. / PILLS** [–] [ ]

—— added half-sister **THE DUCHESS** – guitar

Sep 61. (lp) *<2977>* **BO DIDDLEY IS A GUNSLINGER** [–] [ ]
– Gunslinger / Ride on Josephine / Doing the craw-daddy / Cadillac / Somewhere / Whoa mule / Sixteen tons / Cheyenne / No more lovin' / Diddling. *(UK-iss.Nov63 on 'Pye Jazz'; NJL 33)* – hit No.20

Pye Int. Checker

Oct 62. (7") *(7N 25165) <1019>* **YOU CAN'T JUDGE A BOOK BY THE COVER. / I CAN TELL** [ ] Jul62 [48]
(UK re-iss. Sep63; 7N 25216)

Nov 62. (lp) *<2984>* **BO DIDDLEY** [–] [ ]
– You can't judge a book by the cover / Mama don't allow no twistin' / Mr. Khruschev / Sad sack / You all green / Diddling / Who may your lover be / Babes in the wood / Bo's bounce / Bo's twist / I can tell / Give me a break. *(UK-iss.Nov63; NPL 28026)* – hit No.11 *(re-iss. Apr87) (cd-iss. Dec86)*

May 63. (lp) *(NPL 28025) <2992>* **HEY! BO DIDDLEY** [ ] [ ]
– Mess around / Somebody's crying / Hong Kong / Can I go home with you / I'm going home / Rhyme song / Cracklin' / Rockin' on. *(cd-iss. May94 on 'Charly')*

Jun 63. (7") *(7N 25193)* **WHO DO YOU LOVE?. / THE TWISTER** [ ] [–]

Jul 63. (7") *(7N 25210)* **BO DIDDLEY. / DETOUR** [ ] [–]

Sep 63. (7") *(7N 25217)* **PRETTY THING. / ROAD RUNNER** [34] [–]

Oct 63. (7") *<1045>* **GREATEST LOVER IN THE WORLD. / SURFER'S LOVE CALL** [–] [ ]

Nov 63. (lp) *(NPL 28029)* **BO DIDDLEY RIDES AGAIN** [19] [–]
– Bring it to Jerome / Cops and robbers / Mumblin' guitar / Oh, yea! / You don't love me / Down home special / Bo Diddley is loose / Help out / Call me (Bo's blues) / Don't let it go / Nursery rhyme / Dearest darling. *(cd-iss. Feb94 on 'See For Miles')*

Nov 63. (7") *(7N 25227)* **BO DIDDLEY IS A LOVER. / DOIN' THE JAGUAR** [ ] [–]

Jan 64. (lp) *(NPL 28032)* **BO DIDDLEY'S BEACH PARTY** [13] [ ]
– Memphis / Gunslinger / Hey Bo Diddley / Old Smokey / Bo Diddley's dog / I'm all right / Mr.Custer / Bo's waltz / What's buggin' you / Roadrunner. *(re-iss. 1989)*

Feb 64. (7") *(7N 25235) <1058>* **MEMPHIS. / MONKEY DIDDLE** [ ] [ ]

May 64. (7") *(7N 25243)* **MONA. / GIMME GIMME** [ ] [–]

Jun 64. (lp) *(NPL 28034) <2976>* **IN THE SPOTLIGHT** [ ] [ ]
– Gimme, gimme / Not guilty / Scuttle bug / Say, man / Let me in / Hong Kong / Mississippi / Craw-dad / Bo's a lumber Jack / Walkin' and talkin' / I need you, baby / You're looking good / She's alright.

Aug 64. (7") *(7N 25258) <1083>* **MAMA KEEP YOUR BIG MOUTH SHUT. / JO-ANN** [ ] [ ]

1964. (lp) *<2988>* **ROADRUNNER** [–] [ ]
– Bo Diddley / I'm a man / Pretty thing / Who do you love / Mona (I need you baby) / Say man / Hush your mouth / Road runner / You can't judge a book by looking at the cover / Cops and robbers / Hey Bo Diddley / Crackin' up / Diddley daddy / Bring it to Jerome. *(UK-iss.Jul84 on 'Black Lion') (cd-iss. Nov89 on 'Instant-Charly')*

Chess Checker

Mar 65. (7") *(CRS 8000) <1098>* **HEY GOOD LOOKIN'. / YOU AIN'T BAD (AS YOU CLAIM TO BE)** [39] [ ]

Mar 65. (lp) *(CRL 4002) <2992>* **HEY GOOD LOOKIN'** [ ] [ ]
– Mess around / Somebody's crying / King Kong / Can I go home with you / I'm going home / Rhyme song / Crackin' / Rockin' on. *(re-iss. Aug86 on 'Magnum Force') (re-iss. +cd.May88 on 'Jazz Life')*

May 65. (7") *(CRS 8014)* **SOMEBODY BEAT ME. / MUSH MOUTH MILLIE** [ ] [–]

Sep 65. (7") *(CRS 8021)* **LET THE KIDS DANCE. / LET ME PASS** [ ] [–]

Sep 65. (lp) *(CRL 4507)* **LET ME PASS** [ ] [–]
– Let me pass / Stop my monkey / Greasy spoon / Tonight is ours / Root hoot / Stinkey / Hey red riding hood / Let the kids dance / He's so mad / Soul food / Corn bread / Somebody beat me / 500% more man / Mama, keep your big mouth shut / We're gonna get married / Easy *(cd-iss. Feb94 on 'See For Miles')*

Nov 65. (7") *<1223>* **500% MORE MAN. / LET THE KIDS DANCE** [–] [ ]

Dec 65. (7") *(CRS 8026)* **500% MORE MAN. / STOP MY MONKEY** [ ] [–]

Jan 66. (lp) *<2996>* **500% MORE MAN** [–] [ ]
– 500% more man / Let me pass / Stop my monkey / Greasy spoon / Tonight is ours / Root hoot / Hey Red Riding Hood / Let the kids dance / He's so mad / Soul food / Corn bread / Somebody beat me.

—— JEROME and The DUCHESS left his band

Apr 66. (7") *<1142>* **WE'RE GONNA GET MARRIED. / DO THE FROG** [–] [ ]

Jun 66. (7") *(CRS 8036)* **WE'RE GONNA GET MARRIED. / EASY** [ ] [–]

Jan 67. (lp) *(CRL 4525) <3001>* **THE ORIGINATOR** [ ] [ ]
– Pills / Jo Ann / Two flies / Yakky doodle / What do you know about love / Lazy woman / You ain't bad / Love you baby / Limbo / Background to a music / Puttentang / Africa speaks.

May 67. (7") *(CRS 8053) <1158>* **OOH BABY. / BACK TO SCHOOL** [ ] Jan67 [88]

Feb 68. (7") *(CRS 8057) <1168>* **WRECKING MY LOVE LIFE. / BOO-GA-LOO BEFORE YOU GO** [ ] [ ]

Jun 68. (7") *(CRS 8078) <1200>* **ANOTHER SUGAR DADDY. / I'M HIGH AGAIN** [ ] [ ]

Mar 69. (lp; with MUDDY WATERS & LITTLE MILTON) *(CRL 4529) <3010>* **SUPERBLUES** [ ] [ ]
– Long distance call / Who do you love? / I'm a man / Bo Diddley / You can't a book by the cover / I just want to make love to you / My babe / You don't love me.

Apr 69. (7") *(CRS 8088) <1213>* **BO DIDDLEY '69. / SOUL TRAIN** [ ] [ ]

Feb 70. (7") *<1238>* **THE SHAPE I'M IN. / POLLUTION** [–] [ ]

—— BO virtually retired from business, but released comebacks below. He surfaced periodically on live work.

Chess Chess

Oct 71. (lp) *<50001>* **ANOTHER DIMENSION** [–] [ ]
– The shape I'm in / I love you more than you'll ever know / Pollution / Bad moon rising / Down on the corner / Said shut up woman / Bad side of the moon / Lodi / Go for broke.

1972. (7") *<2117>* **I SAID SHUT UP WOMAN. / I LOVE YOU MORE THAN YOU'LL EVER KNOW** [–] [ ]

1972. (7") *<2129>* **BO DIDDLEY-ITIS. / INFATUATION** [–] [ ]

1972. (7") *<2134>* **HUSBAND-IN-LAW. / BO-JAM** [–] [ ]

1973. (7") *<2142>* **DON'T WANT NO LYIN' WOMAN. / MAKE A HIT RECORD** [–] [ ]

1973. (d-lp) *(6467 304) <60005>* **GOT ANOTHER BAG OF TRICKS** (compilation) [ ] [ ]

R.C.A. R.C.A.

Apr 76. (7") *<10618>* **DRAG ON. / NOT FADE AWAY** [–] [ ]

Magnum Force not iss.

Apr 86. (lp) *(MFM 021)* **HEY . . . BO DIDDLEY IN CONCERT** (with MAINSQUEEZE) [ ] [–]
– Intro – Bo Diddley vamp / Doctor Jeckyll / Everleen / I don't know where I've been / You can't judge a book by the cover / Road runner / I'm a man / Bubble Bo Diddley.

New Rose not iss.

Jun 84. (7") **AIN'T IT GOOD TO BE FREE. / BO DIDDLEY PUT THE ROCK IN ROCK'N'ROLL** [ ] French [–]

Jun 84. (lp) *(ROSE 34)* **AIN'T IT GOOD TO BE FREE** [ ] [–]
– Bo Diddley / Bo Diddley put the rock in rock'n'roll / Gotta be a change / I don't want your welfare / Mona, where's your sister / Stabilize yourself / I don't know where I've been / I ain't gonna force it on you / Evil woman / Let the fox talk. *(re-iss. +cd.Feb88)*

Sep 89. (lp/c/cd) *(ROSE 188/+C/CD)* **LIVING LEGEND** [ ] [–]
– Turbo Diddley 2000 / R.U. serious? / Jeanette Jeanette / I broke the chain / Bo-pop quake / The best / I'll lick yo' face / U killed it / Going home to McComb.

– (selective) compilations, etc. –

Jul 73. (lp) *London; (6499 476)* **THE LONDON BO DIDDLEY SESSIONS**
(cd-iss. Jun90 on 'Chess'; CHD 9296)
May 82. (lp/c) *Chess; (CXMD 4003)* **CHESS MASTERS VOLUME 1**
(re-iss. Mar88 on 'Stylus' lp/c/cd; SMR/SMC/SMD 849)
May 83. (lp/c) *Chess; (CXMD 4009)* **CHESS MASTERS VOLUME 2**
Nov 89. (2xcd/2xc/2xlp;box) *(CD/TC+/BOX 257)* **BO DIDDLEY BOX SET** – –
Nov 93. (12xcd-box) *Charly; (CDREDBOX 8)* **BO DIDDLEY: THE CHESS YEARS** – –
Jul 95. (cd) *Beat Goes On; (BGOCD 287)* **HEY! BO DIDDLEY / BO DIDDLEY**
Aug 95. (cd) *Triple X; (TX 51161CD)* **THE MIGHTY BO DIDDLEY** – –
Aug 97. (cd) *Chess-MCA; (MCD 09373)* **HIS BEST**
Oct 98. (cd) *Beat Goes On; (BGOCD 424)* **IN THE SPOTLIGHT / BO DIDDLEY RIDES AGAIN**
Sep 00. (cd) *Spectrum; (544348-2)* **THE ESSENTIAL BO DIDDLEY** – –
Jul 01. (cd) *Universal; <(E 112244-2)>* **THE UNIVERSAL MASTERS COLLECTION**

DIDO

Born: FLORIAN CLOUD DE BOUNEVIALLE ARMSTRONG, 25 Dec'71, London, England, daughter of a poet mother and publisher father. DIDO (nicknamed after a woman who killed herself in ancient literature!) showed her musical prowess at an early age, entering the highly esteemed Guildhall School of Music in London at the age of six. By the time she was ten she was already proficient in the violin, piano and recorder. As she came into her teenage years she began to tour with classical musicians while simultaneously singing with local pop groups, something the youngster had discovered a love and talent for by the age of 16. Soon after in 1995 her older brother, ROLLO, renowned DJ and producer, invited her to sing with his dance/trip-hop outfit, FAITHLESS, on their debut album, 'REVERENCE' (1996) released the following year. The album's success in dance circles gave DIDO some attention, and she subsequently toured with FAITHLESS for the next two years while taking time out to write her own material. These demos were heard by revered 'Arista' boss/producer, Clive Davis, who signed DIDO to the label in 1997. This led to the release of her long-awaited debut album, 'NO ANGEL' (1999), two years later. This album was probably best considered as a dance album in the chill-out vein; combining a mix of mid-tempo dance beats with more acoustic stylings, with the lush overlay of DIDO's vocals, quite reminiscent of her contempoary BETH ORTON. It was a highly regarded piece on its release, but gained real commercial success when rapper EMINEM used the song, 'THANKYOU' as the backing to his massive selling hit, 'STAN' in 2000. The record buying public's interest in the original led to 'THANKYOU' being released the following year. Worldwide sales of this and the aforementioned 'NO ANGEL' set, gave DIDO the recognition she deserved. The most famous coffee table chanteuse in music was back in 2003 with platinum-selling 'LIFE FOR RENT', a set which stylistically varied little from its predecessor. Impeccably produced and tastefully executed with just enough personality to insinuate itself into your subconscious, the album – like the debut – represented the pinnacle of cultured adult pop.

Album rating: NO ANGEL (*8) / LIFE FOR RENT (*7)

DIDO – vocals (ex-FAITHLESS) / with session people

Arista Arista

Jun 99. (cd/c) *(74321 80268-2/-4) <19025>* **NO ANGEL** May00 4
– Here with me / Hunter / Don't think of me / My lover's gone / All you want / Thankyou / Honesty OK / Slide / Isobel / I'm no angel / My life / Take my hand. *(re-iss. Oct00; same)* – hit UK No.50 *(cd re-iss. Jan01; 74321 83274-2)* – hit UK No.1
Feb 01. (c-s) *(74321 83273-4)* **HERE WITH ME / HERE WITH ME (Lukas Burton mix)** 4 –
(cd-s+=) *(74321 83273-2)* – ('A'-chillin' with the family mix) / ('A'-Parks & Wilson homeyard dub).
May 01. (c-s) *(74321 85304-4) <13922>* **THANKYOU / THANKYOU (deep dish mix)** 3 Jan01 3
(cd-s+=) *(74321 85304-2)* – ('A'-skinny mix).
(12") *(74321 85304-1)* – ('A'side) / ('A'-deep dish dub).
Sep 01. (cd-s) *(74321 88545-2)* **HUNTER / HUNTER (MJ Cole) / TAKE MY HAND (Rollo & Sister Bliss remix)** 17 –
(cd-s) *(74321 88572-2)* – ('A'side) / ('A'-FK/EK vocal) / Take my hand (Brothers In Rhythm remix).
(12") *(74321 88418-1)* – ('A'mixes).

—— in Apr'02, DIDO feat. on the FAITHLESS single, 'ONE STEP TOO FAR'

Sep 03. (cd-s) *(82876 54602-2) <radio>* **WHITE FLAG / PARIS / WHITE FLAG (Ronin mix)** 2 18
(12") *(82876 54602-1)* – ('A'-Beginerz remix) / ('A'-Idjut Boys remix).
Sep 03. (cd/c) *(82876 54598-2/-4) <50137>* **LIFE FOR RENT** 1 4
– White flag / Stoned / Life for rent / Mary's in India / See you when you're 40 / Don't leave home / Who makes you feel / Sand in my shoes / Do you have a little time / This land is mine / See the sun.
Dec 03. (cd-s) *(82876 57946-2)* **LIFE FOR RENT / (live acoustic) / (Skinny 4 rent remix)** 8 –
(cd-s) *(82876 57947-2)* – ('A'side) / Stoned (spiritchaser remix) / ('A'-video).

□ DIFFORD & TILBROOK (see under ⇒ SQUEEZE)

Ani DiFRANCO

Born: 23 Sep'70, Buffalo, New York, USA. Having learned to sing and play guitar at an early age, DiFRANCO began playing professionally after a move to the centre of New York. As fiercely independent and enterprising as she was talented, DiFRANCO set up her own 'Righteous Babe' imprint for the release of her eponymous debut album. Issued in 1990 as an American-only release, the album had originally been on sale at live shows before demand soon outstripped supply and necessitated a larger operation. Featuring the cream of the apparently massive catalogue of songs she'd built up throughout her teens, the record's intimate acoustic confessionals went down a storm with both militant lesbians and straight down the line folk/rock fans. Openly bisexual herself, the tattooed, pierced and shaven-headed DiFRANCO steadily built up a diehard following of kindred spirits through a punishing tour schedule. 1991's 'NOT SO SOFT' was another bare bones acoustic affair dealing in heartfelt sexual politics although it wasn't until the release of the more instrumentally rich 'IMPERFECTLY' (1992) and 'PUDDLE DIVE' (1993), that DiFRANCO began to draw attention from major labels. Standing by her DIY ethos, she released her most widely acknowledged album to date in 'OUT OF RANGE' (1994). Again embellishing her rhythmic acoustic guitar playing with eclectic instrumental textures, the record set the scene for her breakthrough opus, 'NOT A PRETTY GIRL'. With girl power very much on the agenda in the mid-90's, DiFRANCO finally gained recognition as one of America's foremost female commentators alongside the likes of LIZ PHAIR, HEATHER NOVA, etc. The one-woman powerhouse also finally clinched a UK deal with 'Cooking Vinyl', while 1996's acclaimed 'DILATE' gave DiFRANCO her first Top 100 US chart placing.

Following on from 1997's well received double set, 'LIVING IN CLIP', she scored her biggest success to date with near Top 20 US album, 'LITTLE PLASTIC CASTLES' (1998). 1999 proved a busy year for DiFRANCO as she released both the solo set, 'UP UP UP UP UP UP' and a collaborative effort with UTAH PHILLIPS entitled 'FELLOW WORKERS'. While the latter was an alt-folk history of the beleaguered US working class, ANI was back on familiar, if unerringly downcast and mercilessly self-critical, territory with 'TO THE TEETH', her third long player of 1999. Yet however much the singer seems to exorcise her demons through music, it seems there are more waiting in the wings. 'REVELLING: RECKONING' (2001) found DiFRANCO's self-confession and apocalyptic worldview as uncompromising as ever, proving that integrity, at least, is not a quality she's lacking. 'SO MUCH SHOUTING, SO MUCH LAUGHTER' (2002), meanwhile, documented the singer's live career in the first two years of the new decade, a double set like its 1997 predecessor. Split roughly into two thematic segments, the first disc rounded up longtime concert favourites while the second homed in on her more gender-centred pieces. Judging by the enthusiasm of the various crowds, the fact that DiFRANCO's studio albums have become increasingly uneven hardly matters given the passion she seemingly still puts in to each and every performance. While 'EVOLVE' (2003) didn't exactly lack that passion and definitely benefitted from more adventurous arrangements, she again stretched herself just a little too thin in places, overreaching the intended impact. That said, the epic 'SERPENTINE' almost succeeded in its lofty ambitions, an agit-folk tour-de-force which concentrated recurring themes in her writing.

Album rating: ANI DiFRANCO (*6) / NOT SO SOFT (*6) / IMPERFECTLY (*7) / PUDDLE DIVE (*7) / LIKE I SAID – SONGS 1990-1991 compilation (*7) / OUT OF RANGE (*7) / NOT A PRETTY GIRL (*8) / DILATE (*7) / MORE JOY, LESS SHAME (*5) / THE PAST DIDN'T GO ANYWHERE with Utah Phillips (*5) / LIVING IN CLIP (*8) / LITTLE PLASTIC CASTLE (*7) / UP UP UP UP UP UP (*6) / FELLOW WORKERS with Utah Phillips (*5) / TO THE TEETH (*6) / REVELLING – RECKONING (*7) / SO MUCH SHOUTING, SO MUCH LAUGHTER (*6) / EVOLVE (*5)

ANI DiFRANCO – vocals, guitar

Haven / Righteous Babe

Nov 89. (cd) <*RBR 001CD*> **ANI DiFRANCO** [-] [ ]
– Both hands / Talk to me now / Slant / Work you way out / Dog coffee / Lost woman song / Pale purple / Rush hour / Fire door / The story / Every angle / Out of habit / Letting the telephone ring / Egos like hairdos. *(UK-iss.Jul95; same) (re-iss. Jun97 on 'Cooking VInyl'; COOKCD 112)* <*(re-iss. Mar02; same)*>

1991. (cd) <*RBR 002CD*> **NOT SO SOFT** [-] [ ]
– Anticipate / Rockabye / She says / Make me stay / On every corner / Small world / Not so soft / Roll with it / Itch / Gratitude / Whole night / The next big thing / Brief bus stop / Looking at the holes. *(UK-iss.Sep97 on 'Cooking Vinyl'; COOKCD 133)* <*(re-iss. Mar02; same)*>

1992. (cd) <*RBD 003CD*> **IMPERFECTLY** [-] [ ]
– What if no one's watching / Fixing her hair / In or out / Every state line / Circle of light / If it isn't her / Good, bad, ugly / I'm no heroine / Coming up / Make them apologize / Waiting song / Served faithfully / Imperfectly. *(UK-iss.Jul95 & Mar02; same)*

Jul 93. (cd/c) *(HAVEN CD/MC 002)* <*RBR 004 CD/C*> **PUDDLE DIVE** [ ] [ ]
– Names and dates and times / Anyday / 4th of July / Willing to fight / Egos like hairdos / Back around / Blood in the boardroom / Born a lion / My IQ / Used to you / Pick yer nose / God's country. *(re-iss. Jan95 & Mar02; same)*

Jul 94. (cd) <*(RBR 005CD)*> **LIKE I SAID: SONGS 1990-1991** (re-recorded early tracks) [ ] [ ]
– Anticipate / Rockabye / Not so soft / Roll with it / Work your way out / Fire door / Gratitude / Whole night / Both hands / She says / Rush hour / Out of habit / Lost woman song / Talk to me now / Slant. <*(re-iss. Mar02; same)*>

Haven / Righteous Babe

Jan 95. (cd/c) *(HAVEN CD/MC 3)* <*RBR 006CD*> **OUT OF RANGE** [ ] Jul94 [ ]
– Buildings and bridges / Out of range / Letter to a John / Hell yeah / How have you been / Overlap / Face up and sing / Falling is like this / Out of range / You had time / If he tries anything / Diner. <*(cd re-iss. Mar02; same)*>

Righteous Babe / Righteous Babe

Nov 95. (cd) <*(RBR 007CD)*> **NOT A PRETTY GIRL** [ ] Jul95 [ ]
– Worthy / Tiptoe / Cradle and all / Shy / Sorry I am / Light of some kind / Not a pretty girl / The million you never made / Hour follows hour / 32 flavors / Asking too much / This bouquet / Crime for crime. *(UK-iss.Jan97 on 'Cooking Vinyl'; COOKCD 113)* <*(re-iss. Mar02; same)*>

Cooking Vinyl / Righteous Babe

Jul 96. (cd) *(COOKCD 103)* <*RBR 008CD*> **DILATE** [ ] May96 [87]
– Untouchable face / Outta me, onto you / Superhero / Dilate / Amazing grace / Napoleon / Shameless / Done wrong / Going down / Adam and Eve / Joyful girl. <*(re-iss. Mar02; same)*>

Dec 96. (m-cd) *(COOKCD 119)* <*RBR 010CD*> **MORE JOY, LESS SHAME** [ ] [ ]
– Joyful girl / Joyful girl / Joyful girl / Joyful girl / Shameless / Both hands. <*(re-iss. Mar02; same)*>

Jan 97. (cd-s) *(FRYCD 049)* **OUTTA ME ONTO YOU / SHY** [ ] [ ]

Apr 97. (cd; UTAH PHILLIPS & ANI DiFRANCO) *(COOKCD 124)* <*RBR 009CD*> **THE PAST DIDN'T GO ANYWHERE** [ ] Oct96 [ ]
– Bridges / Nevada City, California /Korea / Anarchy / Candidacy / Bum on the road / Enormously wealthy / Mess with people / Natural resources / Heroes / Half a ghost town / Holding on.

Jun 97. (d-cd) *(COOKCD 122)* <*RBR 011CD*> **LIVING IN CLIP (live)** [ ] Apr97 [ ]
– Whatever / Wherever / Gravel / Willing to fight / Shy / Joyful girl / Hide and seek / Napoleon / I'm no heroine / Amazing grace / Anitipate / Tiptoe / Sorry I am / Diner – Slant / 32 flavors / Out of range / Untouchable face / Shameless / Distracted / Adam and Eve / Fire door / Both hands / Out of habit / Every state line / Not so soft / Travel tips / Wrong with me / In or out / We're all gonna blow / Letter to a John / Overleaf. <*(re-iss. Mar02; same)*>

Feb 98. (cd) *(COOKCD 140)* <*RBR 012CD*> **LITTLE PLASTIC CASTLE** [ ] [22]
– Little plastic castle / Fuel / Gravel / As is / Two little girls / Deep dish / Loom / Pixie / Swan dive / Glass house / Independence day / Pulse.

Jan 99. (cd) *(COOKCD 173)* <*RBR 013CD*> **UP UP UP UP UP UP** [ ] [29]
– Tis of thee / Virtue / Come away from it / Jukebox / Angel food / Angry anymore / Everest / Up up up up up up / Know now then / Trickle down / Hat shaped hat. <*(re-iss. Mar02; same)*>

Mar 99. (cd-s) *(FRYCD 079)* **NOT ANGRY ANYMORE / (mixes; album / extended)** [ ] [-]

May 99. (cd; ANI DiFRANCO & UTAH PHILLIPS) <*RBR 015CD*> **FELLOW WORKERS** [-] [ ]
– Joe Hill (instrumental) / Stupid's song / The most dangerous woman / Stupid's pledge / Direct action / Pie in the sky / Shoot or stab them / Lawrence / Bread and roses / Why come? / Unless you are free / I will not obey / The long memory / The silence that is me / Joe Hill / The saw-playing musician / Dump the bosses / The internationale.

Nov 99. (cd) *(COOKCD 190)* <*RBR 017CD*> **TO THE TEETH** [ ] [76]
– To the teeth / Soft shoulder / Wish I may / Freak show / Going once / Hello Birmingham / Back back back / Swing / Carry you around / Cloud blood / Arrivals gate / Providence / I know this bar. <*(re-iss. Mar02; same)*>

Righteous Babe / Righteous Babe

Jul 00. (cd-ep) *(74873 17020-2)* <*RBR-CD 20*> **SWING SET** [ ] [ ]
– Swing (radio set) / Swing (album version) / To the teeth (shoot-out remix) / Do re me (live) / When I'm gone / Hurricane.

Apr 01. (d-cd) <*(RBRCD 024)*> **REVELLING / RECKONING** [ ] [50]
– Ain't that the way / O.K. / Garden of simple / Tamburitza lingua / Marrow / Heartbreak even / Harvest / Kazoointoit / Whatall is nice / What how when where (why whoo) / Fierce flawless / Rock paper scissors / Beautiful night / Your next bold move / This box contains . . . / Reckoning / So what / Prison prism / Imagine that / Flood waters / Grey / Subdivision / Old old song / Sick of me / Don't nobody know / School night / That was my love / Revelling / In here.

Sep 02. (d-cd) <*(RBR 029)*> **SO MUCH SHOUTING, SO MUCH LAUGHTER (live)** [ ] [32]
– Swan dive / Letter to a John – Tamburitza lingua / Grey / Cradle and all / Whatall is nice / What how when where (why who) / To the teeth / Revelling / Napoleon / Shrug / Welcome to: / Comes a time / Ain't that the way / Dilate / Gratitude / Rock paper scissors / 32 flavors / Loom – Pulse /

Not a pretty girl / Self evident / Reckoning / My I.Q. / Jukebox / You had time.

Mar 03. (cd) *<(RBR 030)>* **EVOLVE** [ ] [30]
– Promised land / In the way / Icarus / Slide / O my my / Evolve / Shrug / Phase / Here for now / Second intermission / Serpentine / Welcome to:

– compilations, etc. –

Nov 94. (cd) *Tradition & Moderne; (T&M 105)* **WOMEN IN (E)MOTION FESTIVAL** [ ] [–]
<US-iss.Jun98 on 'Imprint'; 28376>

☐ DILLARD & CLARK (see under ⇒ CLARK, Gene)

☐ DIM STARS (see under ⇒ HELL, Richard)

DINOSAUR JR.

Formed: Amherst, Massachusetts, USA . . . 1983 by J. MASCIS. Initially recording hardcore punk under the DEEP WOUND moniker, the band recruited PATRICK MURPHY and metamorphosed into DINOSAUR. Their self-titled debut album appeared in 1985, a raw blueprint for their distinctive candy-coated noise rock that was good enough to secure an American tour support slot with SONIC YOUTH. After protestations from aging West Coast rockers DINOSAUR, J.MASCIS' crew added the JR. to their name. Subsequently recording one album for 'SST', 'YOU'RE LIVING ALL OVER ME' (1987), the band further developed their melodic distortion although it was the 'FREAK SCENE' (1988) single, their debut for 'Blast First', which saw DINOSAUR JR. pressed to the cardigan-clad bosoms of the nation's pre-baggy indie kids. A wildly exhilarating piece of pristine pop replete with copious amounts of intoxicating noise pollution, MASCIS' go-on-impress-me vocals epitomised the word slacker when that dubious cliche was still gestating in some hack's subconscious. The follow-up album, 'BUG' (1988) was arguably the band's finest moment, perfectly crafted pop spiked with scathing slivers of guitar squall. BARLOW departed soon after the album's release, going off to form SEBADOH while MASCIS' mob came up with a wonderfully skewed cover of The CURE's 'JUST LIKE HEAVEN'. DON FLEMING (of GUMBALL fame) and JAY SPIEGEL featured on DINOSAUR JR.'s major label debut for 'WEA' subsidiary 'Blanco Y Negro', 'THE WAGON' (1991). Another slice of cascading noise-pop, the single raised expectations for the follow-up album 'GREEN MIND' (1991). More or less a MASCIS solo album, it failed to live up to its promise although by the release of 1993's 'WHERE YOU BEEN', MASCIS had found a permanent bassist in MIKE JOHNSON. Their most successful album to date, DINOSAUR JR. at last reaped some rewards from the grunge scene they'd played a major role in creating. With both JOHNSON and MASCIS releasing solo albums in 1996, the latter finally re-emerged late 2000 with the KEVIN SHIELDS-produced 'MORE LIGHT' (issued under J. MASCIS & THE FOG billing). Anyone expecting some kind of artistic rebirth or millennial rejuvenation was to be sorely disappointed as J delivered another set of ragged, tumbledown fuzz-pop. The slacker's slacker, MASCIS makes music that seemingly hangs together by only the seared threads of his own beleaguered vocal chords and he isn't likely to change anytime soon. Not on 'FEEL SO FREE' (2002) anyhow, an album again billed to J MASCIS + THE FOG wherein MASCIS, if anything, loosened things up even further. There was certainly less noise for noise's sake as J signalled a move towards a more groove-orientated sound right from the opening bar of 'FREEDOM'. Perhaps it was no coincidence that the word "free" cropped up more than once throughout this record and it was difficult to avoid the impression that the ageing indie-rocker was perhaps shedding some excess sonic skin. • **Songwriters:** MASCIS wrote all, except LOTTA LOVE (Neil Young) / QUICKSAND (David Bowie) / I FEEL A WHOLE LOT BETTER (Byrds) / GOIN' BLIND (Kiss) / HOT BURRITO 2 (Gram Parsons). J. MASCIS solo:- EVERY MOTHER'S SON (Lynyrd Skynyrd) / THE BOY WITH THE THORN IN HIS SIDE (Smiths) / ON THE RUN (Wipers) / ANTICIPATION (Carly Simon) / LEAVING ON A JET PLANE (John Denver). MIKE JOHNSON solo:- SECOND LOVERS SONG (Lynyrd Skynyrd) / LOVE AND OTHER CRIMES (Lee Hazlewood) / IF YOU'RE GONE (Gene Clark). • **Trivia:** In Jun'91, MASCIS moonlighted as a drummer with Boston satanic hard-core group UPSIDE DOWN CROSS, who made one self-titled album Autumn '91 on 'Taang!'. He also wrote songs and made a cameo appearance in the 1992 film, 'Gas, Food, Lodging'.

Album rating: DINOSAUR (*6) / YOU'RE LIVING ALL OVER ME mini (*7) / BUG (*8) / GREEN MIND (*7) / WHERE YOU BEEN (*8) / WITHOUT A SOUND (*5) / HAND IT OVER (*7) / J. Mascis: MARTIN AND ME (*6) / J. Mascis & The Fog: MORE LIGHT (*6) / FREE SO FREE (*7)

LOU BARLOW (b.17 Jul'66, Northampton, Mass.) – guitar / **J. MASCIS** (b. JOSEPH, 10 Dec'65) – drums / **CHARLIE NAKAJIMA** – vocals / **SCOTT HELLAND** – bass

not iss. Radiobeat

Dec 83. (7"ep; as DEEP WOUND) <RB 002> **I SAW IT** [–] [ ]
– I saw it / Sisters / In my room / Don't need / Lou's anxiety song / Video prick / Sick of fun / Deep wound / Dead babies.

— **J. MASCIS** – vocals, guitar, percussion / **LOU BARLOW** – bass, ukelele, vocals / added **MURPH** (b. EMMETT "PATRICK" MURPHY, 21 Dec'64) – drums (ex-ALL WHITE JURY)

not iss. Homestead

Jun 85. (lp; as DINOSAUR) *<HMS 015>* **DINOSAUR** [–] [ ]
– Forget the swan / Cats in a bowl / The leper / Does it float / Pointless / Repulsion / Gargoyle / Several lips / Mountain man / Quest / Bulbs of passion.

Mar 86. (7"; as DINOSAUR) *<HMS 032>* **REPULSION. / BULBS OF PASSION** [–] [ ]
(UK-iss.Apr97; same)

S.S.T. S.S.T.

Mar 87. (12"ep) *<SST 152>* **DINOSAUR JR.** [–] [ ]
– Little fury things / In a jar / Show me the way. *(cd-ep iss.Dec88; SSTCD 152)*

Jul 87. (m-lp/c) *<(SST/+C 130)>* **YOU'RE LIVING ALL OVER ME** [ ] [ ]
– Little fury things / Kracked / Sludgefeast / The lung / Raisans / Tarpit / In a jar / Lose / Poledo / Show me the way. *(cd-iss. Oct95; same)*

Blast First S.S.T.

Sep 88. (7") *(BFFP 30)* **FREAK SCENE. / KEEP THE GLOVE** [ ] [ ]
(US-iss.7",7"green; SST 220)

Oct 88. (lp/c/cd) *(BFFP 31/+C/CD)* *<SST/+C/CD 216>* **BUG** [ ] [ ]
– Freak scene / No bones / They always come / Yeah we know / Let it ride / Pond song / Budge / The post / Don't. *(cd re-iss. Feb99; SST 216CD)*

— **DONNA BIDDELL** – bass (ex-SCREAMING TREES) repl. BARLOW who formed SEBADOH

Apr 89. (7"/etched-12"/cd-s) *(BFFP 47 S/T/CD)* *<SST 244>* **JUST LIKE HEAVEN. / THROW DOWN / CHUNKS (A Last Rights Tune)** [78] Feb 90 [ ]
(US version 12"ep+=/c-ep+=/cd-ep+=) (SST/+C/CD 244) – Freak scene / Keep the glove.

— DONNA left and was repl. by **DON FLEMING** – guitar + **JAY SPIEGEL** – drums (both B.A.L.L.)

Glitterhouse Sub Pop

Jun 90. (7"/7"white) *(GR 0097)* *<SP 68>* **THE WAGON. / BETTER THAN GONE** [ ] [ ]

— In Oct 90, J.MASCIS and other ex-DINOSAUR JR member FLEMING + SPIEGEL, made an album 'RAKE' as VELVET MONKEYS (aka B.A.L.L. + friends).

Blanco Y Negro — Sire

Jan 91. (7"/c-s) *(NEG 48/+C)* **THE WAGON. / THE LITTLE BABY** [49] [–]
(12"+=/cd-s+=) *(NEG 48 T/CD)* – Pebbles + weeds / Quicksand.

Feb 91. (lp/c/cd) *(BYN 24/+C/CD)* <26479> **GREEN MIND** [36] [ ]
– The wagon / Puke + cry / Blowing it / I live for that look / Flying cloud / How'd you pin that one on me / Water / Muck / Thumb / Green mind.

Aug 91. (7"/c-s) *(NEG 52/+C)* **WHATEVER'S COOL WITH ME. / SIDEWAYS** [ ] [–]
(12"+=/cd-s+=) *(NEG 52 T/CD)* – Thumb (live) / Keep the glove (live).

—— **MASCIS + MURPH** introduced new member **MIKE JOHNSON** (b.27 Aug'65, Grant's Pass, Oregon, USA) – bass (ex-MARK LANEGAN, ex-GEORGE LANE, ex-SNAKEPIT)

Nov 92. (7") *(NEG 60)* **GET ME. / HOT BURRITO #2** [44] [–]
(c-s+=/12"+=/cd-s+=) *(NEG 60 C/T/CD)* – Qwest (live).

Jan 93. (7") *(NEG 61)* **START CHOPPIN'. / TURNIP FARM** [20] [–]
(10"+=/12"+=/cd-s+=) *(NEG 61 TEP/T/CD)* – Forget it.

Feb 93. (lp/c/cd) *(BYN 28/+C/CD)* <45108> **WHERE YOU BEEN?** [10] [50]
– Out there / Start choppin' / What else is new? / On the way / Not the same / Get me / Drawerings / Hide / Goin' home / I ain't sayin'.

Jun 93. (7"/c-s/12") *(NEG 63/+C/T)* **OUT THERE. / KEEBLIN' (live) / KRACKED (live)** [44] [ ]
(10"+=) *(NEG 63TE)* – Post.
(cd-s++=) *(NEG 63CD)* – Quest (live).
(cd-s) *(NEG 63CDX)* – ('A'side) / Get me / Severed lips / Thumb (radio sessions).

—— now without MURPH

Aug 94. (7"/c-s) *(NEG 74/+C)* **FEEL THE PAIN. / GET OUT OF THIS** [25] [ ]
(10"etched+=/cd-s+=) *(NEG 74 TE/CD)* – Repulsion (acoustic).

Sep 94. (cd/c/lp) *(4509 96933-2/-4/-1)* <45719> **WITHOUT A SOUND** [24] [44]
– Feel the pain / I don't think so / Yeah right / Outta hand / Grab it / Even you / Mind glow / Get out of this / On the brink / Seemed like the thing to do / Over your shoulder.

Feb 95. (7"green/c-s) *(NEG 77 X/C)* **I DON'T THINK SO. / GET ME (live)** [67] [ ]
(cd-s+=) *(NEG 77CD)* – What else is new? / Sludge.

Mar 97. (c-s/12"/cd-s) *(NEG 103 C/T/CD)* **TAKE A RUN AT THE SUN. / DON'T YOU THINK IT'S TIME / THE PICKLE SONG** [53] [ ]

Mar 97. (cd/c/lp) *(0630 18312-2/-4/-1)* <46506> **HAND IT OVER** [ ] [ ]
– Take a run at the sun / Never bought it / Nothin's goin' on / I'm insane / Can't we move this alone / Sure not over you / Loaded / Mick / I know yer insane / Gettin' rough / Gotta know.

Trade 2 — not iss.

Sep 97. (7") *(TRDSC 009)* **I'M INSANE. / I MISUNDERSTOOD** [ ] [–]

– compilations, etc. –

Aug 91. (10"m-lp) *S.S.T.; (SST 275)* **FOSSILS** [–] [ ]
– Little fury things / In a jar / Show me the way / Freak scene / Keep the glove / Just like heaven / Throw down / Chunks. *<(cd-iss. +UK May93 & Oct96; SST 276CD)>*

Feb 99. (cd) *Strange Fruit; (SFRSCD 078)* **THE BBC SESSIONS** [ ] [–]
– Raisins / Does it float / Leper / Bulbs of passion / Keep the glove / In a jar / Get me / Keeblin / Budge / No bones.

J. MASCIS

WEA — Warners

May 96. (cd/c) <(46177)> **MARTIN + ME** [ ] Apr96 [ ]
– Thumb / So what else is new / Get me / Blowin' it / Repulsion / Goin' home / The boy with the thorn in his side / Not you again / On the run / Keeblin / Flying cloud / Anticipation / Drawerings / Every mother's son.

J MASCIS + THE FOG

with guest **KEVIN SHIELDS**

City Slang — Artemis

Sep 00. (cd-s) *(20171-2)* **WHERE'D YOU GO / CAN I TELL U STORIES / TOO HARD** [ ] [–]

Oct 00. (cd/lp) *(20168-2/-1)* <76665> **MORE LIGHT** [ ] [ ]
– Same day / Waistin' / Where'd you go / Back before you go / Grand me to you / Anmaring / All the girls / I not fine / Can I take this on / Does the kiss fit / More light.

Jun 01. (cd-s) *(97745)* **WAISTIN' / LEAVING ON A JET PLANE** [ ] [–]

City Slang — Ultimatum

Oct 02. (cd/lp) *(20205-2/-1)* <76685> **FREE SO FREE** [ ] [ ]
– Freedom / If that's how its gotta be / Set us free / Bobbin / Free so free / Tell the truth / Someone said / Everybody lets me down / Say the word / Outside. *(UK re-iss. Jan03 on 'Ultimatum'; ULT 685LP)*

– (MASCIS) compilations, etc. –

Aug 03. (cd) *Strange Fruit; (SFRSCD 122)* **THE BBC SESSIONS** [ ] [–]

DION

Born: DION DiMUCCI, 18 Jul'39, The Bronx, New York, USA. Exercising his boyhood tonsils on street corners with fellow Italian-American Doo-Wop devotees, DION had his first taste of professional performing after being picked to appear on the Teen Club TV show in Philadelphia. In 1957, he formed DION & THE TIMBERLAINES, who, after one flop single, became DION & THE BELMONTS. The following year, the group notched up their first US hit when 'I WONDER WHY' made the Top 30. Chart regulars from then on in, the clean-cut DION and crew amassed several further hits including their finest two minutes, 'A TEENAGER IN LOVE', an angst-ridden schoolyard anthem that furnished them with their first Top 5 US hit and a new line in designer college sweat shirts. DION was lucky just to be able to enjoy his success; a few months previous (3rd February, 1959), he narrowly escaped death after declining a ride on the doomed charter plane that killed BUDDY HOLLY, RITCHIE VALENS and BIG BOPPER. Towards the end of 1960, DION, on the advice of his manager, embarked on a successful solo career that spawned two US million sellers, 'RUNAROUND SUE' and 'THE WANDERER' (also major hits in the UK). Although his run of success continued with 'LOVERS WHO WANDER', 'LITTLE DIANE', 'LOVE CAME TO ME' and 'RUBY BABY' (the latter his first effort for new label, 'Columbia'), privately DION was battling with a drugs problem. Like many teen idols of the day, his career took a bit of a battering with the onslaught of the British Invasion during 1964. He subsequently moved through roots-blues before reinventing himself as a mellow folk-protest singer in 1968 with the US Top 5 tribute single, 'ABRAHAM, MARTIN AND JOHN' (a big UK hit for MARVIN GAYE a few years later); he finally kicked his habit into touch the same year. After a further series of misguided cover versions (including 'PURPLE HAZE'!), DION & THE BELMONTS re-formed for a one-off special on the 2nd June, 1972, at Madison Square Garden; the 'REUNION' album quickly followed. For the remainder of the 70's and on into the 80's, DION lingered in the commercial wilderness and subsequently converted to Christianity. However, in 1989, the man returned in fine style with a harder-edged rock'n'roll set, 'YO FRANKIE', masterminded by producer DAVE EDMUNDS. • **Songwriters:** Penned some of own material, except several by ERNIE MARESCA. The group worked in the late 1950's with writers DOC POMUS and MORT SHUMAN. Covered; WHERE OR WHEN (Rodgers & Hart) / WHEN YOU WISH UPON A STAR (?) / IN THE STILL OF THE NIGHT (Cole Porter). DION solo covered RUBY BABY + DRIP DROP (Leiber-Stoller) / COME GO WITH ME (Del Vikings) / I'M YOUR HOOCHIE COOCHIE MAN (Muddy Waters) / JOHNNY B. GOODE (Chuck Berry) / SPOONFUL (Willie Dixon) / ABRAHAM, MARTIN & JOHN (Dick

Holler) / PURPLE HAZE (Jimi Hendrix) / FROM BOTH SIDES NOW (Joni Mitchell) / AND THE NIGHT STOOD STILL (Diane Warren) / SAN DIEGO SERENADE (Tom Waits) / etc. • **Trivia:** DION was featured on the sleeve of the BEATLES' 'Sgt. Pepper' album.

Best Albums: BORN TO BE WITH YOU (*8) / YO FRANKIE (*7)

Best CD compilation: THE BEST OF DION & THE BELMONTS (*7)

DION & THE BELMONTS

DION DiMUCCI – lead vocals / **CARLO MASTRANGELO** (b. 5 Oct'39) – vocals / **FRED MILANO** (b.26 Aug'40) – vocals / **ANGELO D'ALEO** (b. 3 Feb'41) – vocals

not iss. Mohawk

1957. (7",78; as DION & THE TIMBERLAINES) <105> **THE CHOSEN FEW. / OUT IN COLORADO** [–] [ ]
<re-iss. 1957 on 'Jubilee'; 5294>

1957. (7",78; as The BELMONTS) <106> **TEEN-AGE CLEMENTINE. / SANTA MARGUERITA** [–] [ ]

1958. (7",78) <107> **WE WENT AWAY. / TAG ALONG** [–] [ ]

London Laurie

Jul 58. (7",78) *(HL 8646)* <3013> **I WONDER WHY. / TEEN ANGEL** [ ] May58 [22]

Oct 58. (7",78) *(HL 8718)* <3015> **NO ONE KNOWS. / I CAN'T GO ON (ROSALIE)** [ ] Aug58 [19]

Feb 59. (7",78) *(HL 8799)* <3021> **DON'T PITY ME. / JUST YOU** [ ] Dec58 [40]

Jun 59. (7",78) *(HLU 8874)* <3027> **A TEENAGER IN LOVE. / I'VE CRIED BEFORE** [28] Apr59 [5]

Oct 59. (lp) *(HA-U 2194)* *<LLP 2002>* **PRESENTING DION & THE BELMONTS** [ ] [ ]
– I wonder why / Teen angel / Where or when / You better not do that / Just you / I got the blues / Don't pity me / A teenager in love / Wonderful girl / Funny feeling / I've cried before / That's my desire / No one knows / I can't go on (Rosalie). *(UK-iss.1984 on 'Ace'; CH 107) (cd-iss. 1989; CDCHM 107)*

—— now a trio when D'ALEO was conscripted to US navy

Nov 59. (7",78) *(7N 25038)* <3035> **EVERY LITTLE THING I DO. / A LOVER'S PRAYER** [ ] [48] Sep59 [73]
(above single on 'Pye Int.' UK)

Jan 60. (7",78) *(HLU 9030)* <3044> **WHERE OR WHEN. / THAT'S MY DESIRE** [ ] Dec59 [3]

Top Rank Laurie

Apr 60. (7") <3052> **WHEN YOU WISH UPON A STAR. / WONDERFUL GIRL** [–] [30]

May 60. (7") *(JAR 368)* **WHEN YOU WISH UPON A STAR. / MY PRIVATE JOY** [ ] [–]

Jul 60. (7") <3059> **IN THE STILL OF THE NIGHT. / A FUNNY FEELING** [–] [38]

Sep 60. (7") *(JAR 503)* **IN THE STILL OF THE NIGHT. / SWINGING ON A STAR** [ ] [–]

Dec 60. (lp; with others) *(25-027)* **THE TOPPERMOST – VOL.1** [ ] [–]
– When you wish upon a star / In the still of the night / My private joy / My day begins with you / Swinging on a star / All the things you are / Paper moon / In other words / I'm through with love / When the red, red robin / September song.

DION

—— went solo; The BELMONTS signed to 'Sabina' and issued their own 45's

Nov 60. (7") *(JAR 521)* <3070> **LONELY TEENAGER. / LITTLE MISS BLUE** [47] [12] Oct60 [96]

Nov 60. (lp) *<LLP 2004>* **ALONE WITH DION** [–] [ ]
– Lonely teenager / After the dance / P.S. I love you / Save the last dance for me / Little Miss Blue / Havin' fun / Close your eyes / Fools rush in / My one and only love / North east end of the corner / One for my baby / Then I'll be tired of you. *(re-iss. 1985 on 'Ace'; CH 115)*

Feb 61. (7") *(JAR 545)* <3081> **HAVIN' FUN. / NORTH-EAST END OF THE CORNER** [ ] [42]

Apr 61. (7") <3090> **KISSIN' GAME. / HEAVEN HELP ME** [–] [82]

May 61. (lp; as DION & THE BELMONTS) *<LLP 2006>* **WISH UPON A STAR** (collection) [–] [ ]
– When you wish upon a star / In the still of the night / A lover's prayer / My private joy / My day / Swinging on a star / All the things you are / It's only a paper moon / In other words / I'm through with love / When the red, red robin comes bob, bob bobbin' along / September song. *(re-iss. 1985 on 'Ace'; CH 138)*

Jul 61. (7") <3101> **SOMEBODY NOBODY WANTS. / COULD SOMEBODY TAKE MY PLACE TONIGHT** [–] [ ]

Oct 61. (7") *(JAR 586)* <3110> **RUNAROUND SUE. / RUNAWAY GIRL** [11] Sep61 [1]
(re-iss. Aug76 on 'Philips') (re-iss. Aug82 on 'EMI Gold')

Dec 61. (lp) *(CLP 1539)* *<LLP 2009>* **RUNAROUND SUE** [ ] Nov61 [11]
– Runaround Sue / Somebody wants me / Dream lover / Life is but a dream / The wanderer / Runaway girl / I'm gonna make it somehow / The majestic / Could somebody take my place tonight / Little star / Lonely world / In the still of the night / Kansas City / Take good care of my baby. *(re-iss. 1985 on 'Ace'; CH 148) (cd-iss. Aug89; CDCHM 148)*

H.M.V. Laurie

Feb 62. (7") *(POP 971)* <3115> **THE WANDERER. / THE MAJESTIC** [10] [2] Nov61 [36]

May 62. (7") *(POP 1020)* <3123> **LOVERS WHO WANDER. / (I WAS) BORN TO CRY** [ ] [3] Apr62 [42]

Stateside Laurie

Aug 62. (7") *(SS 115)* <3134> **LITTLE DIANE. / LOST FOR SURE** [ ] Jul62 [8]

Aug 62. (lp) *(SL 10034)* *<LLP 2009>* **LOVERS WHO WANDER** [ ] Jul62 [8]
– Lovers who wander / Come go with me / King without a queen / So long friend / Twist / Little Diane / Mi muchacha / Stagger Lee / Shout / Tonight, tonight / Born to cry / Queen of the hop / Candy man / Sandy / Lost for sure / Love came to me. *(UK-iss.Jan86 on 'Ace'; CH 163)*

Nov 62. (7") *(SS 139)* <3145> **LOVE CAME TO ME. / LITTLE GIRL** [ ] [10]

C.B.S. Columbia

Jan 63. (7") *(AAG 133)* <42662> **RUBY BABY. / HE'LL ONLY HURT YOU** [ ] [2]

Mar 63. (lp; stereo/mono) *(S+/BPG 62137)* *<CS 8810>* **RUBY BABY** [ ] [20]
– Ruby baby / The end of the world / Go away little girl / Gonna make it alone / Fever / My mammy / Will love ever come my way / The loneliest man in the world / You made me love you (I didn't want to do it) / He'll only hurt you / You're nobody 'til somebody loves you / Unloved, unwanted me.

May 63. (7") *(AAG 145)* <42776> **THIS LITTLE GIRL. / THE LONELIEST MAN IN THE WORLD** [ ] Apr63 [21]

Jul 63. (7") *(AAG 161)* <42810> **BE CAREFUL OF STONES THAT YOU THROW. / I CAN'T BELIEVE (THAT YOU DON'T LOVE ME ANYMORE)** [ ] [31]

DION DiMUCCI

Sep 63. (7") *(AAG 169)* <42852> **DONNA THE PRIMA DONNA. / YOU'RE MINE** [ ] [6]

Sep 63. (lp; stereo/mono) *(S+/BPG 62203)* *<CS 8907>* **DONNA THE PRIMA DONNA** [ ] [ ]
– Donna the prima donna / Can't we be sweethearts / Sweet, sweet baby / This little girl of mine / Flim flam / Troubled man / This little girl / Oh happy days / You're mine / Donna / I can't believe (that you don't love me anymore) / Be careful of stones that you throw.

Nov 63. (7") *(AAG 177)* <42917> **DRIP DROP. / NO ONE'S WAITING FOR ME** [ ] [6]

Mar 64. (7") *(AAG 188)* <42977> **I'M YOUR HOOCHIE COOCHIE MAN. / THE ROAD I'M ON (GLORIA)** [ ] [ ]

1964. (lp; as DION & THE BELMONTS) *<LLP 2016>* **TOGETHER WITH THE BELMONTS** [–] [ ]
– We belong together / Every little thing I do / Meant to be / Come take a walk with me / Tag along / Teen angel / Such a long way / We went away / I can't go on / That's how I need you / Will you love me still / Faith.

Oct 64. (7") *(AAG 224)* <43096> **JOHHNY B. GOODE. / CHICAGO BLUES** [ ] [71]

Mar 65. (7") *(201728)* <43213> **SWEET SWEET BABY. / UNLOVED, UNWANTED ME** [ ] [ ]

Jun 65. (7"; as DION) *(201780)* <43293> **SPOONFUL. / KICKIN' CHILD** [ ] [ ]

—— In 1966, he formed folk-pop outfit

DION & THE WANDERERS

1966. (7") *<43423>* **YOU MOVE ME BABE. / TOMORROW WON'T BRING THE RAIN** [–] [ ]

1966. (7") *<43483>* **TIME IN MY HEART FOR YOU. / WAKE UP BABY** [–] [ ]

1966. (7") *<43692>* **SO MUCH YOUNGER. / TWO TON FEATHER** [–] [ ]

DION & THE BELMONTS

— (see last line-up)

H.M.V. — ABC Paramount

Nov 66. (7") *(POP 1565) <10868>* **BERIMBAU (MY GIRL). / THE MONTH OF MAY** [ ] [ ]

Mar 67. (7") *(POP 1585) <10896>* **MOVIN' MAN. / FOR BOBBIE** [ ] [ ]

May 67. (lp) *(CLP 3618) NANCS 599>* **TOGETHER AGAIN** [ ] [ ]
– Movin' man / Berimbau / Come to my side / All I wanna do / But not for me / New York town / Loserville / For Bobbie / Jump back baby / Baby you've been on my mind / My girl / The month of May. *(re-iss. 1969 on 'B&C'; CAS 1002)*

DION

— solo

not iss. — Columbia

1968. (lp) *<CS 9773>* **WONDER WHERE I'M BOUND** [–] [ ]
– I can't help but wonder where I'm bound / It's all over now, baby blue / A Sunday kind of love / Knowing I won't go back there / 900 miles / Now / Southern train / The seventh son / Farewell / Wake up baby / Baby, please don't go.

London — Laurie

Nov 68. (7") *(HLP 10229) <3463>* **ABRAHAM, MARTIN AND JOHN. / DADDY ROLLIN'** [ ] Oct68 [4]
(re-iss. Mar75 on 'UK Decca')

Dec 68. (lp; mono/stereo) *(HA-P/SH-P 8390) <SLP 2047>* **DION** [ ] [ ]
– Abraham, Martin and John / Purple haze / Tomorrow is a long time / Everybody's talkin' / Sonny boy / The dolphins / He looks a lot like me / Sun fun song / From both sides now / Sisters of mercy / Loving you is sweeter than ever. *(re-iss. Feb87 as 'ABRAHAM, MARTIN & JOHN' on 'Ace'; CH 204)*

Feb 69. (7") *<3478>* **PURPLE HAZE. / THE DOLPHINS** [–] [63]

Apr 69. (7") *<3495>* **FROM BOTH SIDES NOW. / SUN FUN SONG** [–] [91]

Warners — Warners

Jun 69. (7") *<3504>* **LOVING YOU IS SWEETER THAN EVER. / HE LOOKS A LOT LIKE ME** [–] [ ]

Jun 69. (7") *(HLP 10277)* **BOTH SIDES NOW. / SONNY BOY** [ ] [–]

Jan 70. (7") *<(WB 7356)>* **IF WE ONLY HAVE LOVE. / NATURAL MAN** [ ] [ ]

Jul 70. (lp) *<(WS 1826)>* **SIT DOWN OLD FRIEND** [ ] [ ]
– Natural man / I don't believe my race is run / Jammed up blues / Little pink pony / You can't judge a book by the cover / If we only have love / Sweet pea / Just a little girl / Let go, let God / King con man / Sit down old friend.

Aug 70. (7") *<(WB 7401)>* **YOUR OWN BACK YARD. / SIT DOWN OLD FRIEND** [ ] [75]

Apr 71. (7") *<WB 7469>* **CLOSE TO IT ALL. / LET IT BE** [ ] [ ]

Apr 71. (7") *(WB 6120)* **CLOSE TO IT ALL. / WINDOWS** [ ] [–]

Apr 71. (lp) *<(WS 1872)>* **YOU'RE NOT ALONE** [ ] [ ]
– Close to it all / Sunniland / Windows / The visitor / Peaceful place / Let it be / The stuff I got / Blackbird / Josie / Attraction works better than promotion.

Jun 71. (7") *<7491>* **JOSIE. / SUNNILAND** [–] [ ]

Jul 71. (7") *(K 16100)* **SUNNILAND. / PEACEFUL PLACE** [ ] [–]

Dec 71. (lp) *(K 46122) <WS 1945>* **SANCTUARY (some live)** [ ] [ ]
– Sunshine lady / Sanctuary / Willigo / Harmony sound / Gotta get up / Please be my friend / Take a little time / The wanderer / Abraham, Martin and John / Almond joy / Ruby baby / Brand new morning.

May 72. (7") *(K 16132) <7537>* **SANCTUARY. / BRAND NEW MORNING** [ ] [ ]

Nov 72. (lp) *(K 46199) <WS 2642>* **SUITE FOR LATE SUMMER** [ ] [ ]
– Seagull / Wedding song / Jennifer knew / It all fits together / To dream tomorrow / Didn't you change / Tennessee Madonna / Traveler in the rain / Running close behind you.

Nov 72. (7") *<7663>* **RUNNING CLOSE BEHIND YOU. / SEAGULL** [–] [ ]

— On 2nd of Jun'72 DION re-united with The BELMONTS for a live one-off

Feb 73. (lp) *(K 46208) <2664>* **REUNION (live at Madison Square Garden)** [ ] [ ]
– The wanderer / No one knows / I wonder why / Teenager in love / Ruby baby / That's my desire / Drip drop / Where or when / Runaround Sue / Little Diane.

1973. (7") *<7704>* **DOCTOR ROCK AND ROLL. / SUNSHINE LADY** [–] [ ]

1973. (7") *<7793>* **NEW YORK CITY SONG. / RICHER THAN A RICH MAN** [–] [ ]

1974. (7") *<8234>* **HEY MY LOVE. / LOVER BOY SUPREME** [–] [ ]

1974. (7") *<8258>* **LOVER BOY SUPREME. / THE WAY YOU DO THE THINGS YOU DO** [–] [ ]

1974. (7") *<8293>* **QUEEN OF '59. / OH THE NIGHT** [–] [ ]

1975. (7") *<8406>* **YOUNG VIRGIN EYES (I'M ALL WRAPPED UP). / OH THE NIGHT** [–] [ ]

Phil Spector Int. — Phil Spector Int.

1975. (7") *<16063>* **BORN TO BE WITH YOU. / RUNNING CLOSE BEHIND YOU** [–] [ ]

Jun 75. (7") *<0403>* **MAKE THE WOMAN LOVE ME. / RUNNING CLOSE BEHIND YOU** [ ] [ ]

Oct 75. (lp) *(2307 002) <002>* **BORN TO BE WITH YOU** [ ] [ ]
– Born to be with you / ake the woman love me / Your own backyard / He's got the whole world in his hands / Only you know / New York City song / In and out of showers / Good vin' man.

Feb 76. (7") *(2010 012)* **BORN TO BE WITH YOU. / GOOD LOVIN' MAN** [ ] [–]

Aug 76. (7") *(2010 018)* **BABY LET'S STICK TOGETHER. / NEW YORK CITY SONG** [ ] [–]

Warners. — Warners

Aug 76. (lp) *(K 56279) <BS 2954>* **STREETHEART** [ ] [ ]
– Runaway man / Streetheart / Hey my love / On the night / Lover boy supreme / Queen of '59 / You showed me what love is / More to you / If I can just get through the night.

Aug 76. (7") *(K 16801)* **YOU SHOWED ME WHAT LOVE IS. / LOVER BOY SUPREME** [ ] [–]

not iss. — Lifesong

1978. (lp) *<35356>* **RETURN OF THE WANDERER** [–] [ ]
– Lookin' for the heart of Saturday night / Midtown American main street gang / You've awakened something in me / Guitar queen / The pattern of my lifeline / (I used to be a) Brooklyn Dodger / Streetheart theme / The power of love within / Spanish Harlem incident / Do you believe in magic. *(cd-iss. Jun90 on 'Ace')*

1978. (7") *<1765>* **LOOKING FOR THE HEART OF SATURDAY NIGHT. / YOU'VE AWAKENED SOMETHING IN ME** [–] [ ]

1978. (7") *<1770>* **GUITAR QUEEN. / MIDTOWN AMERICAN MAIN STREET GANG** [–] [ ]

1978. (7") *<1785>* **(I USED TO BE A) BROOKLYN DODGER. / STREETHEART THEME** [–] [ ]

Dayspring — Dayspring

1982. (lp/c) *<(DAY/TCDAY 4006)>* **INSIDE JOB** [ ] [ ]
– I believe / He's the one / Centre of my life / Truth will set you free / Gonna be ready / Old souvenirs / New Jersey wife / Man in the glass / Sweet Surrender.

Aura — Dayspring

Oct 83. (7") *(AUS 39)* **WE DON'T TALK ANYMORE. / MIDNIGHT LOVER** [ ] [–]

Aug 84. (7") *(AUS 42)* **THE WAY YOU DO THE THINGS YOU DO. / HEY MY LOVE** [ ] [–]

Dayspring — Dayspring

1984. (lp/c) *<(DAY/TCDAY 4016)>* **I PUT AWAY MY IDOLS** [ ] [ ]
– Here is my servant / Trust in my Lord / Day of the Lord / I put away my idols / Daddy / Very soon / He won't tell you / Healing / Give up and surrender / My prayer for you.

1985. (lp/c) *<(DAY/TCDAY 4032)>* **KINGDOM IN THE STREETS** [ ] [ ]

DION

— with **DAVE EDMUNDS** – guitar, bass / **JIM HORN** – sax / **PHIL CHEN** – bass / **CHUCK LEAVELL** – keyboards / **DAVE CHARLES** – percussion

		Arista	Arista
Jun 89.	(7") *(112 408)* <9797> **AND THE NIGHT STOOD STILL. / TOWER OF LOVE**		May89 75
	(12"+=/cd-s+=) *(612/662 408)* – The wanderer.		
Jun 89.	(lp/c/cd) *(209/409/259 766)* <8549> **YO FRANKIE**		May89
	– King of the New York streets / And the night stood still / Yo Frankie (she's all right with me) / I've got to get to you / Medley:- Written on the subway wall – Little star / Drive all night / Always in the rain / Loving you is killing me / Tower of love / Serenade.		
Jul 89.	(7") *(112 556)* **KING OF THE NEW YORK STREETS. / THE WANDERER**	74	
	(12"+=/cd-s+=) *(612/662 556)* – Serenade.		
Feb 90.	(7"ep/cd-ep) *(112/662 910)* **WRITTEN ON THE SUBWAY WALL – LITTLE STAR (medley) / KING OF THE NEW YORK STREETS. / AND THE NIGHT STOOD STILL / TOWER OF LOVE**		

– (selective) compilations, etc. –

Dec 62.	(lp) *Laurie; <2013>* **DION SINGS HIS GREATEST HITS**	–	29
Mar 63.	(7") *Stateside; (SS 161) / Laurie; <3153>* **SANDY. / FAITH**		Feb63 21
Jun 63.	(lp) *Laurie; <2017>* **DION SINGS TO SANDY (AND ALL HIS OTHER GIRLS)**	–	
Jul 63.	(7") *Stateside; (SS 209) / Laurie; <3171>* **COME GO WITH ME. / KING WITHOUT A QUEEN**		Jun63 48
Mar 73.	(lp) *Columbia; <31942>* **DION'S GREATEST HITS**	–	
	(re-iss. Apr74 & Dec81 on 'R.C.A.'-UK / 'Laurie'-US)		
Apr 76.	(7") *Philips; (6146 700)* **THE WANDERER. / LITTLE DIANE**	16	–
Mar 80.	(lp) *K-Tel; (NE 1057)* **DION AND THE BELMONTS' 20 GOLDEN GREATS**	31	–
Jun 90.	(cd) *Ace; (CDCHD 936)* **RETURN OF THE WANDERER / FIRE IN THE NIGHT**		–
Sep 90.	(cd) *Ace; (CDCH 945)* **WISH UPON A STAR / ALONE WITH DION**		–
Feb 91.	(cd) *Ace; (CDCHD 943)* **LOVERS WHO WANDER / SO WHY DIDN'T YOU DO THAT THE FIRST TIME**		–
Mar 91.	(cd) *Ace; (CDCHD 966)* **PRESENTING DION & THE BELMONTS / RUNAROUND SUE**		–
Sep 91.	(cd/c) *Ace; (CDFAB/FABC 002)* **THE FABULOUS DION & THE BELMONTS**		–
	– Where or when / A teenager in love / I wonder why / No one knows / Don't pity me / Every little thing I do / A lover's prayer / When you wish upon a star / In the still of the night / I can't go on (Rosalie) / That's my desire / Wonderful girl.		
Sep 91.	(cd/c) *Ace; (CDFAB/FABC 008)* **THE FABULOUS DION**		–
	– Runaround Sue / The wanderer / Lovers who wander / Little Diane / Love came to me / Lonely teenager / Little Miss Blue / The majestic / (I was) Born to cry / Sandy / Come go with me / Havin' fun.		
Aug 95.	(cd; by The BELMONTS) *Ace; (CDCHD 586)* **LAURIE, SABINA AND UNITED ARTISTS SIDES VOL.1**		
Dec 98.	(cd; by The BELMONTS) *Ace; (CDCHD 685)* **LAURIE, SABINA AND UNITED ARTISTS SIDES VOL.2**		
Apr 99.	(d-cd) *Collector's Choice; (WSCCM 0071-2)* **THE COMPLETE DION AND THE BELMONTS**		
Aug 00.	(cd) *Ace; (CDCHD 765)* **DEJA NU**		
Feb 01.	(cd) *See For Miles; (SEECD 723)* **THE EP COLLECTION**		
Feb 01.	(cd; as DION & THE BELMONTS) *EMI Plus; (5761540)* **THE STORY**		
Mar 01.	(cd) *Ace; (CDCHD 793)* **BORN TO BE WITH YOU / STREET HEART**		
Apr 01.	(cd) *Ace; (CDCHD 791)* **SIT DOWN OLD FRIEND / YOU'RE NOT ALONE**		
Sep 01.	(cd) *Ace; (CDCHD 792)* **SANCTUARY / SUITE FOR LATE SUMMER**		
Nov 01.	(cd; as DION & LITTLE KINGS) *Ace; (CDCHD 797)* **LIVE IN NEW YORK**		
Jun 03.	(cd) *Ace; (CDCHD 895)* **INSIDE JOB / ONLY JESUS**		
Aug 03.	(cd) *Ace; (CDCHD 898)* **I PUT AWAY MY IDOLS / KINGDOM IN THE STREET**		
Sep 03.	(cd) *E.M.I.; (513923-2)* **SUPER HITS**		

DIRE STRAITS

Formed: Deptford, London, England . . . mid-'77 by ex-teacher and journalist MARK KNOPFLER alongside brother DAVID, JOHN ILLSLEY and PICK WITHERS. After Radio 1 DJ, Charlie Gillett gave their demo an airing later the same year, they were signed to 'Vertigo' by A&R man, John Stainze, releasing a classic debut single, 'SULTANS OF SWING', in Spring '78. A driving but subtle slice of rootsy, bluesy R&B, the song was a wonderfully observed snapshot of the London pub rock scene where they'd initially plied their trade. Although it failed to chart, their eponymous debut album (released later that summer) made the UK Top 40 after rave live reviews and a major deal with 'Warners' in the States. Comparisons with BOB DYLAN's easier going material and the laidback (horizontal, even!) country-blues grooves of J.J. CALE were the favoured choice of salivating critics although KNOPFLER's dry wit and unmistakable guitar lines gave DIRE STRAITS the stamp of authenticity. In fact, DYLAN was so impressed he invited KNOPFLER to augment him on his 1979 set, 'SLOW TRAIN COMING'; by this point, both the debut single and album had amassed transatlantic Top 10 sales with the help of a sell-out US tour while a follow-up set, 'COMMUNIQUE' (1979), further developed KNOPFLER's narrative skills on the likes of the epic 'ONCE UPON A TIME IN THE WEST'. With HAL LINDES replacing the departing DAVID and ex-E STREET BAND man, ROY BITTAN drafted in on keyboards, 'MAKING MOVIES' (1980) took a harder-edged yet more melodic, accessible and expansive approach; vivid story-songs such as the bittersweet 'ROMEO AND JULIET' saw KNOPFLER compared to SPRINGSTEEN while the heady momentum of 'TUNNEL OF LOVE' effortlessly conjured up the giddy thrills and spills of a trip to the fairground. Opening with another compelling narrative in 'TELEGRAPH ROAD' and boasting the moody 'PRIVATE INVESTIGATIONS', 'LOVE OVER GOLD' (1982) became DIRE STRAITS' first UK No.1 album, the band flying in the face of fashion and selling millions. This was nothing, however, compared to the global phenomenon that was 'BROTHERS IN ARMS'; released in 1985 following the lengthy double live set, 'ALCHEMY' (1984), the record's glossy production and more focused pop-friendly approach saw it breaking UK sales records. Its biggest hit, 'MONEY FOR NOTHING', was an acerbic comment on US MTV domination, the accompanying video ironically caned by the channel in all its innovative, technology-enhanced glory. It was also the closest DIRE STRAITS ever veered towards heavy rock, the bulk of the material going in for coffee table, ear-massaging atmospherics and acoustic textures. The soft-focus minimalism of the title track is arguably DIRE STRAITS' finest moment and, despite the stigma surrounding the album, 'BROTHERS IN ARMS' remains an essential 80's release. Following the attendant mammoth touring commitments, DIRE STRAITS/KNOPFLER took an extended sabbatical with only a 1988 best of to keep fans happy. Having already scored soundtrack's for 'Local Hero' (1983) and 'Cal' (1984), KNOPFLER was commisioned for both 'The Princess Bride' (1987) and 'Last Exit To Brooklyn' (1989). He also got back to his pub-rock roots with The NOTTING HILLBILLIES, releasing an album, 'MISSING . . . PRESUMED HAVING A GOOD TIME', in 1990. Later that year, he hooked up with country picker, CHET ATKINS, for the 'NECK AND NECK' album. DIRE STRAITS eventually returned in 1991 with 'ON EVERY STREET', an album which couldn't hope to emulate 'BROTHERS . . .' and didn't even try. It made No.1 all the same and sold enough to keep their record company happy in the meantime. With KNOPFLER actually recording a solo set proper, 'GOLDEN HEART', in 1996, the chances of a further DIRE STRAITS release seemed slim although a split had yet to be confirmed. This was obvious to the record buying public when KNOPFLER delivered another chart-busting album, 'SAILING TO PHILADELPHIA' in 2000. If KNOPFLER fans must've wondered what was going on with another studio set so soon after the last, they wouldn't have been disappointed. 'THE RAGPICKER'S DREAM' (2002) inhabited that singular musical landscape sacred to KNOPFLER, where northern English tradition stalks the prairies and backwoods of rural America. It's a land far removed from DIRE STRAITS but one where the fleet-fingered singer moves with tranquil – if always strangely restless – ease, content to rein in his guitar prowess to the confines of acoustic roots music. • **Songwriters:** KNOPFLER compositions, except The NOTTING HILLBILLIES cover of FEEL LIKE GOING HOME (Charlie Rich). • **Trivia:** MARK penned 'PRIVATE DANCER' for TINA TURNER in 1983, and also produced to name but a few; 'Infidels' for BOB DYLAN and 'Knife' for AZTEC CAMERA.

Album rating: DIRE STRAITS (*8) / COMMUNIQUE (*5) / MAKING MOVIES (*6) / LOVE OVER GOLD (*6) / ALCHEMY – LIVE (*7) / BROTHERS IN ARMS (*8) / MONEY FOR NOTHING compilation (*8) / ON EVERY STREET (*5) / ON THE NIGHT (*5) / Mark Knopfler: LOCAL HERO (*5) / GOLDEN HEART (*4) / SAILING TO PHILADELPHIA (*6) / A SHOT IN THE DARK soundtrack (*5) / THE RAGPICKER'S DREAM (*6)

MARK KNOPFLER (b.12 Aug'49, Glasgow, Scotland) – vocals, lead guitar / **DAVID KNOPFLER** (b.1951, Glasgow) – guitar / **JOHN ILLSLEY** (b.24 Jun'49, Leicester, England) – bass / **PICK WITHERS** – drums

Vertigo Warners

May 78. (7") *(6059 206)* <8736> **SULTANS OF SWING. / EASTBOUND TRAIN** [ ] Jan79 [4]
(re-iss. Feb79; same) – (hit No.8)

Jun 78. (lp)(c) *(9102 021)(723 1015)* <3266> **DIRE STRAITS** [5] Oct78 [2]
– Down to the waterline / Water of love / Setting me up / Six blade knife / Southbound train / Sultans of swing / Wild west end / Lions / In the gallery. *(master edition Apr82; HS 9102 021) (cd-iss. 1987; 800 051-2) (cd re-iss. Jun96; same)*

Jul 79. (7") *(6059 230)* <49006> **LADY WRITER. / WHERE DO YOU THINK YOU'RE GOING** [ ] [45]

Aug 79. (lp)(c) *(9102 031)(723 1021)* <3330> **COMMUNIQUE** [5] Jun79 [11]
– Once upon a time in the west / News / Where do you think you're going / Communique / Lady writer / Angel of mercy / Portobello belle / Single-handed sailor / Follow me home. *(cd-iss. 1987; 800 052-2) (re-iss. Jun96; same)*

Oct 79. (7") <49082> **ONCE UPON A TIME IN THE WEST. / NEWS** [–] [ ]

—— **HAL LINDES** (b.30 Jun'53, Monterey, Calif.) – guitar repl. DAVID who later went solo, also added **ROY BITTAN** – keyboards / (ex-E-STREET BAND BRUCE SPRINGSTEEN)

Oct 80. (lp/c) *(6359/7150 034)* <3480> **MAKING MOVIES** [4] Nov80 [19]
– Tunnel of love / Romeo and Juliet / Skateaway / Expresso love / Hand in hand / Solid rock / Les boys. *(master edition Apr82; HS 6359 034) (cd-iss. 1987; 800 050-2) (cd re-iss. Jun96; same)*

Nov 80. (7") *(MOVIE 1)* <49688> **ROMEO AND JULIET / SOLID ROCK** [8] Mar81 [ ]

Dec 80. (7") <49632> **SKATEAWAY. / SOLID ROCK** [–] [58]

Mar 81. (7") *(MOVIE 2)* **SKATEAWAY. / EXPRESSO LOVE** [37] [–]

Sep 81. (7") *(MOVIE 3)* **TUNNEL OF LOVE. / TUNNEL OF LOVE (part 2)** [54] [–]

—— **ALAN CLARK** (b. 5 Mar'52, Durham, England) – keyboards repl ROY.

Aug 82. (7"/10") *(DSTR 1/+10)* **PRIVATE INVESTIGATIONS. / BADGES POSTERS STICKERS T-SHIRTS** [2] [–]

Sep 82. (lp/c) *(6359/7150 109)* <23728> **LOVE OVER GOLD** [1] [19]
– Telegraph road / Private investigations / Industrial disease / Love over gold / It never rains / If I had you / Twisting by the pool / Two young lovers / Badges, posters, stickers, T-shirts. *(cd-iss. 1984; 800 088-2) (cd re-iss. Jun96; same)*

Dec 82. (7") <29880> **INDUSTRIAL DISEASE. / BADGES POSTERS STICKERS T-SHIRT** [–] [75]

Jan 83. (7"/10"/12") *(DSTR 2/+10/12)* **TWISTING BY THE POOL. / TWO YOUNG LOVERS / IF I HAD YOU** [14] [–]

Mar 83. (m-lp) <29800> **TWISTING BY THE POOL** [–] [53]
– Twisting by the pool / Two young lovers / If I had you / Badges posters stickers T-shirts.

May 83. (7") <29706> **TWISTING BY THE POOL. / BADGES POSTERS STICKERS T-SHIRTS** [–] [ ]

—— **IOMAR HAKIM** – drums, percussion repl. PICK
above was replaced by **TERRY WILLIAMS** (b.11 Jan'48, Swansea, Wales) – drums (ex-MAN, ex-MOTORS, ex-ROCKPILE) / (both played on album below alongside **MARK, JOHN, HAL + ALAN**)

Feb 84. (7"/10"/12") *(DSRT 6/+10/12)* <> **LOVE OVER GOLD (live). / SOLID GOLD (live)** [50] [ ]

Mar 84. (d-lp/c)(cd) *(VERY/+C 11)(810243-2)* <25085> **ALCHEMY – LIVE (live)** [3] Apr84 [46]
– Once upon a time in the west / Romeo and Juliet / Expresso love / Private investigations / Sultans of swing / Two young lovers / Tunnel of love / Telegraph road / Solid rock / Going home (theme from 'Local Hero'). *(c+=/cd+=)* – Love over gold (live). *(cd re-iss. Jun96; same)*

—— added **GUY FLETCHER** – keyboards / also **JACK SONNI** – guitar (on tour)

Apr 85. (7"/10"/12") *(DSRT 9/+10/12)* **SO FAR AWAY. / WALK OF LIFE** [20] [–]

May 85. (lp/c)(cd) *(VERH/+C 25)(824499-2)* <25264> **BROTHERS IN ARMS** [1] [1]
– So far away / Money for nothing / Walk of life / Your latest trick / Why worry? / Ride across the river / The man's too strong / One world / Money for nothing / Brothers in arms. *(c+=/cd+=; extended versions)* – So far away / Money for nothing / Your latest trick / Why worry? *(cd re-iss. Jun96; ame)*

Jun 85. (7"/10"/12")(7"sha-pic-d) *(DSRT 10/+10/12)(DSPIC 10)* <28950> **MONEY FOR NOTHING. / LOVE OVER GOLD (live)** [4] [1]

Oct 85. (7") <28878> **WALK OF LIFE. / ONE WORLD** [–] [7]

Oct 85. (7"sha-pic-d)(10") *(DSPIC 11)(DSTR 11-10)* **BROTHERS IN ARMS. / GOING HOME – THEME FROM 'LOCAL HERO' (live)** [16] [ ]
(12"+=) *(DSTR 11-12)* – Why worry.
(d7"++=) *(DSTRD 11)* – Sultans of swing / Eastbound train.

Jan 86. (7") *(DSRT 12)* **WALK OF LIFE. / TWO YOUNG LOVERS (live)** [2] [–]
(12"+=) *(DSRT 12-12)* – Sultans of swing.
(d7"++=) *(DSTRD 12)* – Eastbound train (live).

Feb 86. (7") <28789> **SO FAR AWAY. / IF I HAD YOU** [–] [19]

Apr 86. (7") *(DSTR 13)* **YOUR LATEST TRICK. / IRISH BOY** [26] [ ]
(12"+=) *(DSTR 13-12)* – The long road.

Oct 88. (lp/c)(cd) *(VERH/+C 64)(836419-2)* <25794> **MONEY FOR NOTHING** (compilation) [1] Nov88 [62]
– Sultans of swing / Down to the waterline / Portobello belle (live) / Twisting by the pool / Tunnel of love / Romeo and Juliet / Where do you think you're going / Walk of life / Private investigations / Telegraph Road (live) / Money for nothing / Brothers in arms.

Nov 88. (7") *(DSTR 15)* **SULTANS OF SWING. / PORTOBELLO BELLE (live)** [62] [ ]
(12"+=)(cd-s+=) *(DSTR 15-12)(DSCD 15)* – Romeo and Juliet / Money for nothing.

Aug 91. (7"/c-s) *(DSTR/+C 16)* **CALLING ELVIS. / IRON HAND** [21] [ ]
(12"+=)(cd-s+=) *(DSTR 16-12)(DSCD 16)* – Millionaire blues.

Sep 91. (cd/c/lp) *(510160-2/-4/-1)* <26680> **ON EVERY STREET** [1] [12]
– Calling Elvis / On every street / When it comes to you / Fade to black / The bug / You and your friend / Heavy fuel / Iron hand / Ticket to Heaven / My parties / Planet of New Orleans / How long.

Oct 91. (7"/c-s) *(DSTR/+C 17)* <19094> **HEAVY FUEL. / PLANET OF NEW ORLEANS** [55] [ ]
(12"+=)(cd-s+=) *(DSTR 17-12)(DSCD 17)* – Kingdom come.

Feb 92. (7"/c-s) *(DSTR/+C 18)* **ON EVERY STREET. / ROMEO AND JULIET** [42] [–]
(cd-s+=) *(DSCD 18)* – Private investigations / Sultans of swing.

Jun 92. (7"/c-s) *(DSTR/+C 19)* **THE BUG. / TWISTING BY THE POOL** [67] [ ]
(cd-s+=) *(DSCD 19)* – ('A'version).

—— added touring band 91-93 **DANNY CUMMINGS** – percussion / **PHIL PALMER** – guitar / **PAUL FRANKLIN** – pedal steel / **CHRIS WHITE** – sax, flute / **CHRIS WHITTEN** – drums

May 93. (cd/c/lp) *(514766-2/-4/-1) <45259>* **ON THE NIGHT (live)** [4] [ ]
– Calling Elvis / Walk of life / Heavy fuel / Romeo & Juliet / Your latest trick / Private investigations / On every street / You and your friend / Money for nothing / Brothers in arms.

May 93. (c-ep/12"ep/cd-ep) *(DSTRC/DSTR12/DSCD 20)* **ENCORES LIVE EP (live)** [31] [ ]
– Your latest trick / The bug / Solid rock / Local hero (wild theme).

—— Oct'93; MARK was credited on HANK MARVIN's single 'Wonderful Land'.

—— DIRE STRAITS looked to have disbanded since its been five years since a recording.

– compilations, etc. –

Oct 88. (cd-video) *Vertigo; (080 128-2)* **SULTANS OF SWING / WILD WEST END / DOWN THE WATERLINE** [ ] [–]

Oct 88. (cd-video) *Vertigo; (080 130-2)* **MONEY FOR NOTHING (extended) / ONE WORLD / SO FAR AWAY** [ ] [–]

Oct 88. (cd-video) *Vertigo; (080 132-2)* **BROTHERS IN ARMS (extended) / YOUR LATEST TRICK / RIDE ACROSS THE RIVER** [ ] [–]

Oct 88. (cd-video) *Vertigo; (080 134-2)* **WALK OF LIFE / WHY WORRY / RIDE ACROSS THE RIVER** [ ] [–]

Oct 88. (cd-video) *Vertigo; (080 136-2)* **TWISTING BY THE POOL / TWO YOUNG LOVERS / IF I HAD YOU / TWISTING BY THE POOL** [ ] [–]

Jul 95. (cd/c/lp) *Windsong; (WIN CD/MC/LP 072)* **LIVE AT THE BBC (live)** [71] [–]

Oct 98. (cd/c) *Warners; (558658-2/-4) <47130>* **SULTANS OF SWING – THE VERY BEST OF DIRE STRAITS** [6] [ ]
– Sultans of swing / Lady writer / Romeo and Juliet / Tunnel of love / Private investigations / Twisting by the pool / Love over gold / So far away / Money for nothing / Brothers in arms / Walk of life / Calling Elvis / Heavy fuel / On every street / Your latest trick / Local hero – Wild theme. *(also d-cd; 538003-2)*

MARK KNOPFLER

(first with **CLARK, LINDES** plus **MIKE BRECKER** – sax)

Vertigo Warners

Feb 83. (7"/12") *(DSTR 4/+12) <29725>* **GOING HOME (THEME OF 'LOCAL HERO'). / SMOOCHING** [56] [ ]

Apr 83. (lp/c) *(VERL/+C 4) <23827>* **LOCAL HERO** [14] [ ]
– The rocks and the water / Wild theme / Freeway flyer / Boomtown / The way it always starts / The rocks and the thunder / The ceilidh and the northern lights / The mist covered mountains / The ceilidh: Louis' favourite Billy's tune / Whistle theme / Smooching / The rocks and the thunder / Going home (theme from 'Local Hero'). *(cd-iss. Jul84; 811 038-2)*

Jul 83. (7") *(DSTR 5)* **THEME FROM LOCAL HERO: WILD THEME. / GOING HOME** [ ] [–]

Jul 84. (12") *(DSTR 7-12)* **JOY (FROM 'COMFORT AND JOY'). / FISTFUL OF ICE CREAM** [ ] [–]

Sep 84. (7"/ext.12") *(DSTR 8/+12)* **THE LONG ROAD (THEME FROM CAL'). / IRISH BOY** [ ] [–]

Oct 84. (lp/c)(cd) *(VERH/+C 17)(<822 769-2>)* **CAL (MUSIC FROM THE FILM)** [65] [ ]
– Irish boy / The road / Waiting for her / Irish love / A secret place / Where will you go? / Father and son / Meeting under the trees / Potato picking / in a secret place / Fear and hatred / Love and guilt / The long road.

Oct 86. (7") *(DSTR 14)* **GOING HOME. / WILD THEME** [ ] [–]
(12"+=) *(DSTR 14-12)* – Smooching.
(cd-s+=) *(DSCD 14)* – Comfort (from 'Comfort And Joy').

Nov 87. (lp/c)(cd) *(VERH/+C 53)(832 864-2) <25610>* **MUSIC FROM THE FILM SOUNDTRACK 'THE PRINCESS BRIDE'** [ ] [ ]
– Once upon a time . . . storybook love / I will never love again / Florin dance / Morning ride / The friends' song / The cliffs of insanity / The sword fight / Guide my sword / The fireswamp and the rodents of unusual size / Revenge / A happy ending / Storybook love.

Mar 88. (7"/c-s; with WILLY DeVILLE) *(VER/+MC 37)* **THEME FROM 'THE PRINCESS BRIDE': STORYBOOK LOVE. / THE FRIENDS' SONG (with GUY FLETCHER)** [ ] [–]
(cd-s+=) *(VERCD 37)* – Once upon a time . . . storybook love.

Nov 89. (lp/c/cd) *(838725-1/-4/-2) <25986>* **LAST EXIT TO BROOKLYN (soundtrack)** [ ] [ ]
– Last exit to Brooklyn / Victims / Think fast / A love idea / Tralala / Riot / The reckoning / As low as it gets / Last exit to Brooklyn – finale.

NOTTING HILLBILLIES

MARK KNOPFLER – guitar, vocals, producer / **GUY FLETCHER** – guitar, vocals, producer / **BRENDAN CROKER** – guitar, vocals / **STEVE PHILLIPS** – guitar, vocals / with **PAUL FRANKLIN** – pedal steel guitar

Vertigo Warners

Feb 90. (7"/c-s) *(NHB/+MC 1)* **YOUR OWN SWEET WAY. / BEWILDERED** [ ] [–]
(12"+=)(cd-s+=) *(NHB 1-12)(NHBCD 1)* – That's where I belong.

Mar 90. (cd/c/lp) *(842 671-2/-4/-1) <26147>* **MISSING . . . PRESUMED HAVING A GOOD TIME** [2] [52]
– Railroad worksong / Bewildered / Your own sweet way / Run me down / One way gal / Blues stay away from me / Will you miss me / Please baby / Weapon of prayer / That's where I belong / Feel like going home.

Apr 90. (7"/c-s) *(NHB/+MC 2)* **FEEL LIKE GOING HOME. / LONESOME WIND BLUES** [ ] [–]
(12"+=)(cd-s+=) *(NHB 2-12)(NHBCD 2)* – One way gal.

Jun 90. (7"/c-s) *(NHB/+MC 3)* **WILL YOU MISS ME. / THAT'S WHERE I BELONG** [ ] [–]
(12"+=)(cd-s+=) *(NHB 3-12)(NHBCD 3)* – Lonesome wind blues.

CHET ATKINS & MARK KNOPFLER

C.B.S. Columbia

Oct 90. (7"/c-s) *(656 373-7/-4)* **POOR BOY BLUES. / SO SOFT YOUR GOODBYE** [ ] [ ]
(cd-s+=) *(656 373-2)* – There'll be some changes made.

Nov 90. (cd/c/lp) *(467435-2/-4/-1) <45307>* **NECK AND NECK** [41] Oct90 [ ]
– Poor boy blues / Sweet dreams / There'll be some changes made / Just one time / So soft / Your goodbye / Yakety axe / Tahitian skies / Tears / I'll see you in my dreams / The next time I'm in town.

MARK KNOPFLER

Vertigo Warners

Oct 93. (7"/c-s) *(VER/+MC 81)* **THEMES FROM LOCAL HERO: GOING HOME. / WILD THEME** [ ] [–]
(cd-s+=) *(VERCD 81)* – Comfort.
(above was obviously a re-issue. MARK also featured on HANK MARVIN's new version of 'Wonderful Land'; released Oct'93

Mar 96. (c-s/cd-s) *(VER MC/CD 88)* **DARLING PRETTY / GRAVY TRAIN** [33] [–]
(cd-s+=) *(VERDD 88)* – My claim to fame.

Apr 96. (cd/c) *(514732-2/-4) <46026>* **GOLDEN HEART** [9] [ ]
– Darling pretty / Imelda / Golden heart / No can do / Vic and Ray / Don't you get it / A night in summer long ago / Cannibals / I'm the fool / Je suis desole / Rudiger / Nobody's got the gun / Done with Bonaparte / Are we in trouble now.

May 96. (c-s/cd-s) *(VER MC/CD 89)* **CANNIBAL / TALL ORDER** [42] [–]
(cd-s+=) *(VERDD 89)* – What have I got to do.

—— In 1996, a collaboration cd with STEVE PHILIPS, 'JUST PICKIN' was issued by 'Buried Treasure' (TROV 2)

—— in 1998 + 1999, MARK released further soundtrack work, 'WAG THE DOG' and 'METROLAND', the first for 'Warners' <47006>, the second for 'Polygram' <536864>

Mercury Mercury

Sep 00. (c-s) *(562866-4)* **WHAT IT IS / LONG HIGHWAY** [ ] [–]
(cd-s+=) *(562866-2)* – Let's see you.

Sep 00. (cd/c) *(542981-2/-4) <47753>* **SAILING TO PHILADELPHIA** [4] Oct00 [60]
– What it is / Sailing to Philadelphia / Who's your baby now / Baloney again / The last laugh / Do America / Silvertown blues / El macho / Prairie wedding / Wanderlust / Speedway at Nazareth / Junkie doll / Sands of Nevada / One more matinee.

Warners Warners

Oct 01. (cd) *(548127-2) <48324>* **A SHOT AT GLORY** (soundtrack) [ ] Apr02 [ ]
– Sons of Scotland / Hard cases / He's the man / Training / The new laird / Say too much / Four in a row / All that I have in the world / Sons of Scotland – quiet theme / It's over / Wild mountain thyme.

Mercury Warners

Sep 02. (cd-s) *(63913-2)* **WHY AYE MAN / SMALL POTATOES / SO FAR AWAY (live at Shepherd's Bush Empire)** [ ] [–]

Sep 02. (cd/c/lp) *(63292-2/-4/-1)* <*48318*> **THE RAGPICKER'S DREAM** 7 Oct02 38
– Why aye man / Devil baby / Hill farmer's blues / A place where we used to live / Quality shoe / Fare thee well Northumberland / Marbletown / You don't know you're born / Coyote / The ragpicker's dream / Daddy's gone to Knoxville / Old Pigweed. *(ltd-cd+=; 63293-2)* – live:- Why aye man / Quality shoe / Sailing to Philadelphia / Brothers in arms / Why aye man (video).

– compilations, etc. –

Nov 93. (cd) *Warners;* <*45457-2/-4*> **SCREENPLAYING** (solo film work) –
Oct 00. (d-cd) *Universal; (E 546601-2)* **MISSING . . . PRESUMED HAVING A GOOD TIME (with the NOTTING HILLBILLIES) / SCREENPLAYING**

DIRTY VEGAS

Formed: London, England . . . 2000 by PAUL HARRIS, BEN HARRIS (no relation) and STEVE SMITH. Ranging from different backgrounds in dance and indie music, DIRTY VEGAS came together after the trio discovered that they all had the same philosophies and interests. PAUL was a regular dance DJ in London by the time he was 17, and contributed to nights at The Ministry of Sound and the legendary club The Milk Bar. BEN was an ex studio engineer who set up a seminal dance record shop with his brother SAM called 'Casa'. The two frequently made thumping house records under the BULLITT banner, and PAUL was a regular customer in his record shop. STEVE on the other hand was a seasoned live percussionist and vocalist, who had been doing the rounds in his indie/dance band HIGHER GROUND (they supported PAUL WELLER). When the group split, STEVE flitted to Ibiza and wrote a handful of songs; on his return he played a live set with PAUL HARRIS on the decks (who was now recording music with BEN under the moniker HYDROGEN ROCKERS). Thus, the trio were finally together. To mark their entry, SMITH played a track to PAUL and BEN entitled 'DAYS GO BY', which would eventually become their breakthrough hit, thanks to its inclusion on a Mitsubishi advert. Soulful melodies, breakbeat rhythms and SMITH's whimsical vocals made the single a hit both Stateside and Europe. A rushed released eponymous album, 'DIRTY VEGAS' hit the US Top 10 in 2002, a record that hovered somewhere between an edgier PAUL OAKENFOLD and a tamer RICHARD ASHCROFT.

Album rating: DIRTY VEGAS (*8)

PAUL HARRIS (b. 1975, Blackheath, South London) – keyboards, production / **BEN HARRIS** (b. 1974, Bromley, Kent) – guitars, production / **STEVE SMITH** (b. 1974, New Eltham, South London) – vocals, guitar, percussion (ex-HIGHER GROUND)

Credence Capitol

May 01. (c-s/cd-s) *(TC/CD CRED 011)* <*Y 77742*> **DAYS GO BY / DAYS GO BY (full vocal mix) / DAYS GO BY (acoustic)** 27 Apr02 14
(12") *(12CRED 011)* – ('A'version) / ('A'-Lucien Foort mix).
Jul 02. (12"/cd-s) *(12/CD CRED 028)* **GHOSTS. / GHOSTS (Joeski vocal/dub) / GHOSTS (Lexicon Avenue vocal)** 31 –
(12") *(12CREDX 028)* – ('A'-MAS collective vocal) / ('A'-Lexixon Avenue hard dub).
Aug 02. (cd/d-lp) *(<5 39985-2/-1>)* **DIRTY VEGAS** 40 Jun02 7
– I should know / Ghosts / Lost not found / Days go by / Throwing shapes / Candles / All or nothing / Alive / 7 am / The Brazilian / Simple things (pt.2). *(cd re-iss. Sep02 +=; 542999-2)* – Days go by (Steve Osborne mix).
Sep 02. (cd-s) *(CDCREDS 030)* **DAYS GO BY / DAYS GO BY (Steve Osborne acoustic mix) / 1979 (live) / ('A'-video)** 16 –
(12"/cd-s) *(12/CD CRED 030)* – ('A'side) / ('A'-Scumfrog vocal remix) / ('A'-Paul Oakenfold vocal remix).
Mar 03. (cd-s) *(CDCRED 032)* **SIMPLE THINGS / GHOSTS (live) / ALL OR NOTHING (XFM session) / ('A'-Jacknife Lee mix) / I SHOULD KNOW (Alex Neri club mix) / ('A'-video)** –
(12") *(12CRED 032)* – ('A'side) / I should know (flatline dub).

DISTILLERS

Formed: Detroit, Michigan, USA . . . 1998 by Aussie expat BRODY DALLE and KIM CHI, who subsequently recruited ROSE CASPAR and MATT. After inking a deal with 'Hellcat / Epitaph', the band laid bare their raw, unadulterated punk influences on 'THE DISTILLERS' (2000), as uncompromising a release as any amid the so-called punk revival of the late 90's. There was certainly nothing new or even particularly notable in their approach although DALLE's demented shrieking spoke of a deeper unrest than the usual rock star posturing, while a version of Patti Smith's 'ASK THE ANGELS' was more promising than the side-splitting pop covers of some nu-punk acts. Given the urgency of their sound, it was no surprise when follow-up 'SING SING DEATH HOUSE' was released later the same year, another discordant, discomfiting window on DALLE's troubled soul and even more troubled (at least judging by her lyrics) upbringing; she had also recently split from hubby TIM ARMSTRONG (of RANCID). By the time of the album's re-release in 2002 (to cash in on the interest in the feminist themed 'SENECA FALLS'), the line-up had been reduced to DALLE alongside new members RYAN SINN and ANDY OUTBREAK/GRANELLI, while TONY BRADLEY had stepped into the breach for the recording of 'CORAL FANG' (2003), The DISTILLERS' Gil Norton-produced major label debut (for 'Sire'). Appropriately perhaps, the album dispensed with the trashy quality of the earlier records, replacing it with a more composed, more intense and occasionally even a slightly theatrical dissection of shattered relationships and bruised emotions. Nevertheless, from the explicit cover art to the epic blitz of 'DEATH SEX', there was still enough subversion to please longtime fans (and 'Kerrang!') despite the corporate makeover.

Album rating: THE DISTILLERS (*6) / SING SING DEATH HOUSE (*7) / CORAL FANG (*6)

BRODY ARMSTRONG (b. BRODY DALLE) – vocals, guitar / **ROSE CASPER** – guitar / **KIM CHI** – bass / **MATT** – drums

Hellcat Hellcat

Jun 00. (cd/lp) <*(80422-2/-1)*> **THE DISTILLERS** Apr00
– Oh Serena / Idoless / The world comes tumblin' / L.A. girl / Distilla truant / Ask the angels / Old Scratch / Girlfixer / Open sky / Red carpet and rebellion / Colossus U.S.A. / Blackheart / Gypsy Rose Lee / The blackest years.

— **RYAN SINN** – bass; repl. KIM who joined ORIGINAL SINNERS

— **ANDY OUTBREAK** (b. GRANELLI) – drums; repl. MATT

Feb 02. (cd/lp) <*(80441-2/-1)*> **SING SING DEATH HOUSE**
– Sick of it all / I am revenant / Seneca falls / The young crazed peeling / Sing sing death house / Bullet and the bullseye / City of angels / Young girl / Hate me / Desperate / I understand / Lordy lordy.
Nov 02. (cd-s) *(1089-2)* **CITY OF ANGELS / SOLVENT / SING SING DEATH HOUSE** –

— **ARMSTRONG + SINN** brought in **TONY BRADLEY** – guitar, vocals

WEA Sire

Oct 03. (cd) *(9362 48586-2)* <*48420*> **CORAL FANG** 46 97
– Drain the blood / Dismantle me / Die on a rope / The gallow is God / Coral fang / The hunger / Hall of mirrors / Beat your heart out / Love is paranoid / For tonight you're only here to know / Death sex.
Nov 03. (cd-s) *(W 628CD)* **DRAIN THE BLOOD / DISMANTLE ME (acoustic version) / CINCINNATI** 51 –

DISTURBED

Formed: Chicago, Illinois, USA . . . early 90's by DAN DONEGAN, MIKE WENGREN and FUZZ. With the addition of severely angry young man DAVID DRAIMAN in 1997, the DISTURBED bandwagon began rolling with a vengeance as they built up a grassroots following from Chicago's mean streets. Subsequently signed to 'Giant' on the strength of a demo, the band joined the nu-metal melee in 2000 with debut album, 'THE SICKNESS'. Equal parts Big Rock chorus and itchy, rap-metal chops, naggingly addictive opening track 'VOICES' was as good a place as any to enter the unforgiving world of DISTURBED. The track was subsequently released as a single while the album itself made the US Top 75, a highlight being an updated 2000 version of Tear For Fears' 'SHOUT'. While few would've predicted a US No.1 placing for only their sophomore album, that's exactly what those DISTURBED boys enjoyed with 'BELIEVE' (2002). It might've been graced with a sleeve which wouldn't have looked out of place on a VENOM album back in the 80's, but its epic, much developed metal chops were tailor-made for a market that can't seem to get enough heavy music.

Album rating: THE SICKNESS (*5) / BELIEVE (*7)

DAVID DRAIMAN (b. Brooklyn, New York) – vocals / **DAN DONEGAN** (b. Oak Lawn, Illinois) – guitar / **FUZZ** (b. Covington, Kentucky) – bass / **MIKE WENGREN** – drums

R.C.A. | Giant – Warners

Jul 00. (cd) *(74321 70267-2)* <24738> **THE SICKNESS** [ ] | Mar00 [29]
– Voices / The game / Stupify / Down with the sickness / Violence fetish / Fear / Numb / Want / Conflict / Shout 2000 / Droppin' plates / Meaning of life. *(re-iss. Jul02 on 'Warners'+=; 9362 48315-2)* – God of the mind (Valentine soundtrack version) / Stupify (live) / The game (live) / Voices (live) / Down with the sickness (live).

Mar 01. (7"red) *(74321 84896-7)* <100410> **VOICES. / VOICES (live)** [52] | Nov00 [ ]
(cd-s) *(74321 84641-2)* – ('A'side) / Stupify (live) / The games (live).
(cd-s) *(74321 84896-2)* – ('A'side) / Down with the sickness (live) / ('A'-CD-ROM).

Warners | Warners

Sep 02. (7") *(W 591)* <93266> **PRAYER. / FEAR (live)** [31] | [58]
(cd-s+=) *(W 591CD1)* – Conflict (live).
(cd-s) *(W 591CD2)* – ('A'side) / Droppin' plates (live) / Shout 2000 (live).

Sep 02. (cd/lp/c) <*(9362 48320-2/-1/-4)*> **BELIEVE** [41] | [1]
– Prayer / Liberate / Awaken / Believe / Remember / Intoxication / Rise / Mistress / Breathe / Bound / Devour / Darkness.

Dec 02. (7"purple) *(W 596)* **REMEMBER. / REMEMBER (live)** [56] | [–]
(cd-s+=) *(W 596CD1)* – Rise (live).
(cd-s) *(W 596CD2)* – ('A'side) / Bound (live) / Mistress (live).

— (late 2003) FUZZ departed

DIVINE COMEDY

Formed: Londonderry, Northern Ireland . . . 1990 by bishop's son, NEIL HANNON, JOHN McCULLAGH and KEVIN TRAYNOR. Moving across the water to London, the three signed to maverick indie label, 'Setanta', releasing a SEAN O'NEILL (That Petrol Emotion)-produced debut, 'FANFARE FOR THE COMIC MUSE' (1990). A mini-set, it was followed by two further EP's, before the extroverted HANNON took over the reins as McCULLAGH and TRAYNOR bailed out. Free to pursue his own eccentric muse, HANNON steered The DIVINE COMEDY away from trad indie-rock towards a more self-consciously cultured approach which suggested the influence of everyone from SCOTT WALKER to JARVIS COCKER, in a cod-romantic ANDREW LLOYD-WEBBER-esque fashion of course! His first step towards educating the alternative pop scene came in the shape of 1993's 'LIBERATION' album, his debonair charisma in full effect on tracks such as 'EUROPOP', 'BERNICE BOBS HER HAIR' and 'I WAS BORN YESTERDAY'. His next set of songs, 'PROMENADE' (1994), was a loose concept affair and featured the Irish comedian, SEAN HUGHES, who provided verbal support on the track, 'THE BOOKLOVERS'. The name, DIVINE COMEDY, came to the attention of 'Father Ted' loving music fans after the instrumental, 'SONGS OF LOVE', was used as the theme tune to the popular Channel 4 programme. HANNON also co-wrote another ditty for the second series of the show; the downright silly 'My Beautiful Horse' was the singing priests' (Ted and Dougal) entry for the Eurovision Song Contest!!! In 1996, HANNON (together with his new DIVINE COMEDY recruits) released his most perfectly conceived pop masterpiece to date in 'CASANOVA', the Roger Moore of rock crooning his way through a dapper set of richly orchestrated diamonds. Duly encrusted into the Top 50, the album contained such memorably tongue-in-cheek hits as 'SOMETHING FOR THE WEEKEND', 'BECOMING MORE LIKE ALFIE' and 'THE FROG PRINCESS'. Now a firm critical fave, The DIVINE COMEDY (well, HANNON) had two more Top 20 successes with 'A SHORT ALBUM ABOUT LOVE' (a mini-set) and 'EVERYBODY KNOWS (EXCEPT YOU)' (a single). In August '98, "the Leslie Thomas" of indie-pop/rock, HANNON/DIVINE COMEDY had his first Top 10 album, 'FIN DE SIECLE', a record that boasted three further hits including 'GENERATION SEX' and 'NATIONAL EXPRESS'; a stop-gap UK Top 3 'best of' package, 'A SECRET HISTORY', was delivered the following year. The aptly titled 'REGENERATION' (2001) displayed a wholesale change of tack as HANNON and Co employed RADIOHEAD producer Nigel Godrich and ditched the arch theatricality of old for a more forthright, if not exactly earnest, musical and lyrical approach. A UK Top 20 success bolstered by the hit singles 'BAD AMBASSADOR' and 'LOVE WHAT YOU DO', the album suggested that the impish Irish chameleon was sufficiently savvy to carry the whole thing off. • **Covered:** THERE IS A LIGHT THAT NEVER GOES OUT (Smiths) / MIRANDA + LAST STAND IN METROLAND (Michael Nyman).

Album rating: FANFARE FOR THE COMIC MUSE mini (*4) / LIBERATION (*6) / PROMENADE (*7) / CASANOVA (*8) / A SHORT ALBUM ABOUT LOVE (*7) / FIN DE SIECLE (*7) / A SECRET HISTORY – THE BEST OF THE DIVINE COMEDY (*7) / REGENERATION (*6)

NEIL HANNON (b. 7 Nov'70) – vocals, guitar, bass, piano, etc. / **JOHN McCULLAGH** – bass, vocals / **KEVIN TRAYNOR** – drums

Setanta | Setanta

Aug 90. (m-cd/m-lp) *(SET CDM/LPM 002)* **FANFARE FOR THE COMIC MUSE** [ ] | [–]
– Ignorance is bliss / Indian rain / Bleak landscape / Tailspin / Rise and fall / Logic vs. emotion / Secret garden.

Nov 91. (12"ep) *(SET 008)* **TIMEWATCH. / JERUSALEM / THE RISE AND FALL** [ ] | [–]

Feb 92. (12"ep) *(SET 011)* **EUROPOP EP** [ ] | [–]
– New wave / Intifada / Monitor.
(cd-ep+=) *(SET 011CD)* – Timewatch / Jerusalem / The rise and fall.

— now **HANNON** solo after the other two departed

Jul 93. (7"ep) *(CAO 008)* **LUCY. / THE POP SINGER'S FEAR OF THE POLLEN COUNT / I WAS BORN YESTERDAY** [ ] | [–]

Aug 93. (cd/c/lp) *(SET CD/MC/LP 011)* **LIBERATION** [ ] | [–]
– Festive road / Death of a supernaturalist / Bernice bobs her hair / I was born yesterday / Your daddy's car / Europop / Timewatching / The singer's fear of the pollen count / Queen of the south / Victoria Falls / Three sisters / Europe by train / Lucy. *(re-iss. Aug96; same)*

Oct 93. (7"pic-d-ep) *(DC 001)* **INDULGENCE No.1** [ ] | [–]
– Untitled melody / Hate my way / Europe by train.

Mar 94. (cd/c/lp) *(SET CD/MC/LP 013)* **PROMENADE** □ [–]
– Bath / Going downhill / The booklovers / A seafood song / Geronimo / Don't look down / When the lights go out all over Europe / The summerhouse / Neptune's daughter / A drinking song / Ten seconds to midnight / Tonight we fly. *(re-iss. Aug96 & Aug97; same)*

Aug 94. (7"ep) *(DC 002)* **INDULGENCE No.2** □ [–]
– A drinking song / Tonight we fly (live) / When the lights go out all over Europe.

—— now one-man band **NEIL HANNON** and a large ensemble of musicians including main band; **STUART 'PINKIE' BATES** – hammond organ / **JOBY TALBOT** – piano, arranger / **IVOR TALBOT** – guitar / **BRYAN MILLS** – bass / **MIGUEL 'MIGGY' BARRADAS** – drums

Apr 96. (cd/c/lp) *(SET CD/MC/LP 025)* <36863> **CASANOVA** [48] □
– Something for the weekend / Becoming more like Alfie / Middle-class heroes / In & out of Paris & London / Charge / Songs of love / The frog princess / A woman of the world / Through a long & sleepless night / Theme from Casanova / The dogs & the horses.

—— <above issued on 'Tristar' in the US>

Jun 96. (c-s) *(SETMC 026)* **SOMETHING FOR THE WEEKEND / SONGS OF LOVE (theme from 'Father Ted')** [14] [–]
(cd-s+=) *(SETCD 026)* – Birds of Paradise farm / Love is lighter than air.

Aug 96. (7"/c-s) *(SET/+MC 027)* **BECOMING MORE LIKE ALFIE. / YOUR DADDY'S CAR (live)** [27] [–]
(cd-s+=) *(SETCD 027)* – Untitled melody (acoustic) / The dogs & the horses (acoustic).

Nov 96. (c-s) *(SETMC 032)* **THE FROG PRINCESS / MOTORWAY TO DAMASCUS** [15] [–]
(cd-s+=) *(SETCD 032)* – A woman of the world / Lucy (demo).
(cd-s) *(SETCDL 032)* – ('A'side) / Something before the weekend / Neptune's daughter / Tonight we fly.

Feb 97. (m-cd/m-c) *(<SET CD/MC 036>)* **A SHORT ALBUM ABOUT LOVE** [13] □
– In pursuit of happiness / Everybody knows (except you) / Someone / If . . . / If I were you (I'd be through with me) / Timewatching / I'm all you need.

Mar 97. (cd-ep) *(SETCDA 038)* **EVERYBODY KNOWS (EXCEPT YOU) / MAKE IT EASY ON YOURSELF (live) / A DRINKING SONG (live) / SOMETHING FOR THE WEEKEND (live)** [14] □
(cd-ep) *(SETCDB 038)* – ('A'side) / Johnny Mathis' feet (live) / Your daddy's car (live) / Europe by train (live).
(cd-ep) *(SETCDC 038)* – ('A'side) / Bath (live) / Tonight we fly (live) / Middle class heroes (live).

—— In April '98, The DIVINE COMEDY were part of a NOEL COWARD tribute album in which a single, 'I'VE BEEN TO A MARVELLOUS PARTY' was taken. It hit No.28 and was backed with a Shola Ama & Craig Armstrong track

—— added **ROB FARRER** – percussion

Setanta Imprint

Aug 98. (cd/c) *(SET CD/MC 057)* <111813> **FIN DE SIECLE** [9] Dec98 □
– Generation sex / Thrillseeker / Commuter love / Sweden / Eric the gardener / National express / Life on Earth / The certainty of chance / Here comes the flood / Sunrise. *(also ltd-cd; SETCDL 057)*

Sep 98. (7") *(SET 050)* **GENERATION SEX. / POSTCARD TO ROSIE** [19] Nov98 □
(cd-s) *(SETCDA 050)* <114195> – ('A'side) / London Irish / Time lapse.
(cd-s) *(SETCDB 050)* <114197> – ('A'side) / Chasing sheep is best left to shepherds / Little acts of kindness.

Setanta Tristar

Nov 98. (c-s) *(SETMC 067)* **THE CERTAINTY OF CHANCE / MARYLAND ELECTRIC RAINSTORM** [49] Mar99 □
(cd-s) *(<SETCDA 067>)* – ('A'side) / Last stand in Metroland / Miranda.
(cd-s) *(<SETCDB 067>)* – ('A'side) / Dead only quickly / Knowing the ropes.

Jan 99. (c-s) *(SETMC 069)* **NATIONAL EXPRESS / THE HEART OF ROCK AND ROLL** [8] [–]
(cd-s) *(SETCDA 069)* – ('A'side) / Going downhill fast / Radioactivity.
(cd-s) *(SETCDB 069)* – ('A'side) / Famous / Overstrand.

Aug 99. (c-s) *(SETMC 070)* **THE POP SINGER'S FEAR OF THE POLLEN COUNT / JACKIE** [17] [–]
(cd-s) *(SETCDA 070)* – ('A'side) / With whom to dance / Eric the gardener.
(cd-s) *(SETCDB 070)* – ('A'side) / This side of paradise / Vapour trail.

Aug 99. (cd/c) *(SET CD/MC 100)* <51080> **A SECRET HISTORY – THE BEST OF THE DIVINE COMEDY** (compilation) [3] Sep99 □
– National express / Something for the weekend / Everybody knows (except you) / Generation sex / Becoming more like Alfie / The summerhouse / Your daddy's car / The pop singer's fear of the pollen count / The frog princess / Gin soaked boy / Lucy / Songs of love / In pursuit of happiness / I've been to a marvellous city / The certainty of chance / Too young to die / Tonight we fly.

Nov 99. (c-s) *(SETMC 071)* **GIN SOAKED BOY / EUROPOP (live)** [38] [–]
(cd-s) *(SETCDA 071)* – ('A'side) / Songs of love / I am.
(cd-s) *(SETCDB 071)* – ('A'side) / Geronimo (livd) / My lovely horse.

Parlophone Nettwerk

Feb 01. (c-s) *(TCR 6554)* **LOVE WHAT YOU DO / SOUL TRADER / GET ME TO A MONASTERY** [26] [–]
(cd-s) *(CDRS 6554)* – (first 2 tracks) / You / ('A'-video).
(cd-s) *(CDR 6554)* – (first & third tracks) / ('A'-Deadly Avenger mix).

Mar 01. (cd/c) *(531761-2/-4)* <30237> **REGENERATION** [14] □
– Timestretched / Bad ambassador / Perfect lovesong / Note to self / Lost property / Eye of the needle / Love what you do / Dumb it down / Mastermind / Regeneration / The beauty regime.

May 01. (7") *(R 6558)* **BAD AMBASSADOR. / LIFE ON EARTH (live)** [34] [–]
(cd-s) *(CDRS 6558)* – ('A'side) / Edward the confessor / U.S.E. / ('A'video).
(cd-s) *(CDR 6558)* – ('A'live) / Sweden (live) / Pictures of matchstick men (live).

Oct 01. (cd-s) *(CDRS 6561)* **PERFECT LOVESONG / NO EXCUSES / LES JOURS TRISTES** [42] [–]
(cd-s) *(CDR 6561)* – ('A'side) / Thinking the unthinkable / Oh yeah.

Willie DIXON

Born: 1st July 1915, Vicksburg, Mississippi, USA. Interested in words and music from an early age and admiring the playing of LITTLE BROTHER MONTGOMERY, this 6 and a half foot, 250lb mountain of a man started singing with local gospel groups in his teens. After numerous scrapes with the law he decided to hitch-hike his way to Chicago, taking up boxing and winning the Golden Gloves Heavyweight title in 1936. DIXON became a professional musician on meeting BABY DOO CASTON in 1937 and together they formed the FIVE BREEZES, recording a blend of blues, jazz and vocal harmonies in the 40's. CASTON taught the young DIXON how to play bass and guitar although his progress was halted when he resisted the World War II draft and was imprisoned for 10 months. After the war he formed FOUR JUMPS OF JIVE before reuniting with CASTON in the BIG THREE TRIO, who went on to record for 'Columbia'. DIXON subsequently signed to 'Chess' as a recording artist but as he became more involved with the label his live performance work took a back seat and by 1951 he was a full time employee of the company with duties including producer, A&R man, session musician, talent scout and songwriter. He stayed with 'Chess', apart from an interlude with 'Cobra' (in a similar capacity, only reluctantly returning to 'Chess' when the label folded), until 1971 although his relationship with the label wasn't always a happy one and he once had to take them to court to regain copyright control of his songs. DIXON eventually left 'Chess' in 1957 because he felt that he was being underpaid and also because the label had rejected OTIS RUSH who DIXON thought was an exceptional talent. He subsequently set up 'Cobra' with ELI TOSCANO and signed OTIS RUSH, although TOSCANO gambled away the company's profits and DIXON returned to 'Chess', taking OTIS and BUDDY GUY with him. He was, on the whole, responsible for the sound of Chicago blues on both the aforementioned labels (furnishing MUDDY WATERS and HOWLIN' WOLF with most of their best known repertoire) with the black rock'n'roll of CHUCK BERRY and BO DIDDLEY also benefitting from his touch. DIXON teamed up with MEMPHIS SLIM in the early 60's to play folk festivals, also operating as a booking agent and manager, a role which proved crucial to the American Folk Blues Festival Tours of Europe. Many British R&B bands subsequently recorded his songs including The ROLLING STONES, JEFF BECK, CREAM and LED ZEPPELIN, all in their own inimitable style. On leaving 'Chess', DIXON went into independent production with his own labels, 'Yambo' and 'Spoonful', resuming his personal recording and performing career while also administering the Blues Heaven Foundation, a charity which promoted the awareness of the blues and offered support to old performers who had fallen on hard times. He once claimed "I am the blues", and although that may sound a bit arrogant, you can't take it away from the man that he was one of the major influences on the genre through his songwriting, production and performing. His songs, 'BACK DOOR MAN', 'MY BABE', 'HOOCHIE COOCHIE MAN', 'LITTLE RED ROOSTER', 'I JUST WANT TO MAKE LOVE TO YOU', 'I CAN'T QUIT YOU BABY', 'YOU NEED LOVE', 'YOU SHOOK ME', 'BRING IT ON HOME', 'I AIN'T SUPERSTITIOUS', 'SPOONFUL', 'WANG DANG DOODLE' and 'YOU CAN'T JUDGE A BOOK BY THE COVER' and hundreds more are a lasting legacy to his brilliance and may well make him the most recorded blues composer ever. His health suffered in the 70's and 80's, when he contracted diabetes and eventually had a leg amputated. He died of heart failure in California on the 29th of January 1992. • **Legacy:** Wrote for other blues artists MUDDY WATERS (I'm Ready / I Just Want To Make Love To You / Walking Blues / I'm Your Hoochie Coochie Man / Don't Go No Further / I Love The Life I Live, I Live The Life I Love / Close To You / My Captain / Same Thing / When The Eagle Flies); HOWLIN' WOLF (Spoonful / Wang Dang Doodle / Little Baby / The Red Rooster / Shake For Me / Built For Comfort / Do The Do / I Ain't Superstitious / Evil); LITTLE WALTER (My Babe); OTIS RUSH (I Can't Quit You Baby); LITTLE MILTON (I Can't Quit You Baby / Country Style / Too Late); BO DIDDLEY (You Can't Judge A Book By The Cover); KOKO TAYLOR (I Got What It Takes / Don't Mess With The Messer / Whatever I Am, You Made Me / Blue Heaven / (I Got) All You Need / Wang Dang Doodle / What Came First: The Egg Or The Hen? / Fire / Insane Asylum / I Don't Know Who Cares / Separate Or Integrate / Yes, It's Good For You); BUDDY GUY (co:-I Dig Your Wig / Crazy Love (Crazy Music) / Too Many Ways / Goin' Home / I Cry And Sing The Blues / Every Girl I See (DIXON-MURPHY); ETTA JAMES (Fire); EDDIE BOYD (Third Degree); JIMMY WITHERSPOON (Everything But You / Crazy Mixed Up World); ALBERT KING (Howlin' For My Darling / Down In The Bottom); SONNY BOY WILLIAMSON (co:- BUDDY GUY- I Dig Your Wig);

Best CD compilation: THE ORIGINAL WANG DANG DOODLE – THE CHESS RECORDINGS AND MORE (*8)

WILLIE DIXON & THE ALL-STARS

WILLIE DIXON – vocals, bass / **LAFAYETTE LEAKE** – piano / **FRED BELOW** – drums / **HAROLD ASHBY** – tenor sax

London | Checker

Aug 55. (7",78) *<822>* **WALKING THE BLUES. / IF YOU'RE MINE** [–] [ ]

Jan 56. (7",78) *<828>* **CRAZY FOR MY BABY. / I AM THE LOVER MAN** [–] [ ]

Jul 56. (7",78) *(HLU 8297)* **WALKING THE BLUES. / CRAZY FOR MY BABY** [ ] [–]
(re-iss. & flipped over Oct64 on 'Pye International'; 7N 25270)

Aug 57. (7",78) *<851>* **TWENTY NINE WAYS. / THE PAIN IN MY HEART** [–] [ ]

WILLIE DIXON

— now with **MEMPHIS SLIM** – piano / **WALLY RICHARDSON** – guitar / **HAROLD ASHBY** – tenor sax / **GUS JOHNSON** – drums

Bluesville | Prestige

Feb 60. (7") *<803>* **NERVOUS. / SITTIN' AND CRYIN' THE BLUES** [–] [ ]

1962. (lp) *(BV 1003)* *<1003>* **WILLIE'S BLUES** [ ] [ ]
– Nervous / Good understanding / That's my baby / Slim's thing / That's all I want baby / Don't you tell nobody / Youth to you / Sittin' and cryin' the blues / Built for comfort / I got a razor / Go easy / Move me. *<re-iss. Feb84 on 'O.B.C.'; OB 501> (cd-iss. Jun92 on 'Charly'; CDCHD 349)*

— now with – LUCKY THREE TRIO – (DIXON / **LEAKE** + **CLIFTON JAMES** – drums)

not iss. | Tuba

1962. (7") **BACK HOME IN INDIANA. / WRINKLES** [–] [ ]
WILLIE with drummer – **PHILIPPE COMBELLE**

Polydor | not iss.

1963. (lp) *(LPHM 46131)* **WILLIE DIXON & PHILIPPE COMBELLE** [ ] [–]
– African hunch with a boogie beat / Baby, baby, baby / Cold blooded / Do de do / Just you and I / New way to love / Shame, pretty girls / The way she loves a man.
now with The CHICAGO ALL-STARS: **WALTER HORTON** (aka SHAKY JAKE) – harmonica / **SUNNYLAND SLIM** – piano / **JOHNNY SHINES** – guitar / **CLIFTON JAMES** – drums

not iss. | Columbia

1969. (lp) <9987> **I AM THE BLUES** [–] [ ]
– Back door man / I can't quit you, baby / The seventh son / Spoonful / I ain't superstitious / You shook me / I'm your hoochie coochie man / The little red rooster / The same thing. *<cd-iss. 1986 on 'Mobile Fidelity'; MFCD 872>*

— now with **BUSTER BENTON** + **DENNIS MILLER** – guitar / **LAFAYETTE LEAKE** – piano / **FREDDIE DIXON** – bass / **CLIFTON JAMES** – drums / **CARRIE BELL HARRINGTON** – harmonica

Ovation | not iss.

1976. (lp; w-drawn) *(HA-O 8465)* **CATALYST** [–] [–]

1978. (lp) *(QD 1441)* **WHAT HAPPENED TO MY BLUES** [–] [ ]
– Moon cat / What happened to my blues / Pretty baby / Got to love you baby / Shakin' the shack / Hold me baby / It's so easy to love you / Oh Hugh baby / Put it all in there / Hey hey pretty mama.

not iss. | Spivey

1970's. (lp) **WILLIE DIXON AND THE CHICAGO BLUES BAND** [–] [ ]

1980's. (lp) **MIGHTY EARTHQUAKE AND HURRICANE** [–] [ ]

not iss. | Spoonful

1980's. (lp) **BACKSTAGE ACCESS (live)** [–] [ ]

Varese Sarabande Colosseum | Varese Sarabande Colosseum

Oct 89. (lp/c/cd) *<(VS/+C/CD 5234)>* **GINGER ALE AFTERNOON** (soundtrack) [ ] [ ]
– Miseries of memories / Wigglin' worm / I don't trust nobody / Earthquake and hurricane / The real thing / Move me baby / Save my child / I just want to make love to you / Sittin' and cryin' the blues / Save my child II / Shakin' the shake / That's my baby / Ginger ale blues / Save my child III / Good understanding.

Silvertone | Silvertone

Apr 91. (cd/c) *(ORE CD/C 515)* **HIDDEN CHARMS** (rec.1988) [ ] [ ]
– Blues you can't lose / I don't trust myself / Jungle swing / Don't mess with the messer / Study war no more / I love the life I live / I cry for you / Good advice / I do the job. *(re-iss. cd/c Mar94 & Apr95; same)*

— On 29th Jan'92, WILLIE died of heart failure at St.Thomas' Hospital, California.

– (selective) compilations, etc –

Jan 87. (lp/c) *Deja Vu; (DVLP/DVMC 2092)* **WILLIE DIXON: 20 BLUES GREATS** [ ] [–]
– Little red rooster / Built for comfort / Wang dang doodle / Ain't superstitious / Evil / Walking the blues / Fiery love / Alone / Mannish boy / All aboard / Rock me / I love the life I live / Sugar sweet / Thunderbird /

One more / Teenage beat / Snake dancer / Temperature / Rock bottom / Black angel blues.

Sep 90. (d-cd/d-c/t-lp; various artists) *Chess-MCA; (CHD 216500)* **THE CHESS BOX**
(d-cd re-iss. Apr97; MCD 16500)

Nov 92. (cd) *Chess; (CDRED 37)* **TRIBUTE TO WILLIE DIXON** –

Mar 93. (cd) *Blues Encore; (CD 52026)* **I'M THE BLUES** –

Mar 95. (cd; WILLIE DIXON & JOHNNY WINTER) *Thunderbolt; (CDTB 166)* **CRYING THE BLUES (LIVE AT LIBERTY HALL)** –

Jul 98. (cd) *Legacy; (489895-2)* **POET OF THE BLUES**

Sep 99. (cd) *Telarc Blues; (CD 83452)* **THE SONGS OG WILLIE DIXON**

Apr 01. (cd; with BIG THREE TRIO) *Catfish; (KATCD 189)* **BIG THREE BOOGIE**

May 01. (cd; with JIMMY REED) *Indigo; (IGOXCD 543)* **BIG BOSS MEN**

Mar 03. (cd) *Universal; (AACHD 9353)* **THE ORIGINAL WANG DOODLE**

DIZZEE RASCAL

Born: DYLAN MILLS, 1984, London, England. Blasting onto the UK rap/garage scene early 2003 with his much admired white-label release, 'I LUV U', DIZZEE RASCAL demanded as much attention as household names, such as MS. DYNAMITE and The STREETS. Like the former, his thick East London accent ensured rigorous airplay on pirate radio across the capital, whereas the crunching grind-core beats that accompanied his voice would surely mark him out amongst the left-field hip-hop crowd. Before becoming a Mercury Music Prize winner, the humble MILLS was raised on a council estate by his single mother in East London. Dodging school, stealing, and bumping cars, it wasn't until a music teacher encouraged DYLAN to focus all his energy on musical arrangement, backed by his radical whip-song lyrics and throbbing synchopated beats. At just eighteen he joined the in-demand ROLL DEEP CREW and issued the aforementioned 'I LUV U' which caught the attention of the eagle-eyed A&R men who stalked London's hip-hop scene looking to sign "the next big thing". They seemed to have found it in DIZZEE, as that year he signed a major deal with 'X.L.' records (home of The PRODIGY and more recently The WHITE STRIPES), releasing the album 'BOY IN DA CORNER' (2003), a record which was described by many journalists as "bling-bling hardcore". From the rhythmic industrial slam of lead single 'JUS A RASCAL' to the delicate flow of 'BRAND NEW DAY', the LP deservedly went on to be a massive success, with it topping many end-of-the-year polls and, of course, winning Britain's top music award. Oh, and the fact that DIZZEE was stabbed during a holiday in Ayia Napa, Cyprus didn't hurt promotion (no pun intended) of the album at the time. Taking off the cynical hat – here's to a fresh and brilliantly unique British talent!

Album rating: BOY IN DA CORNER (*8)

DIZZEE RASCAL – MC / with **GOD'S GIFT**

X.L. X.L.

May 03. (cd-s) *(XLS 165CD)* **I LUV U / (remix with WILEY & SHARKEY MAJOR) / (original)** 29 –
(12") *(XLT 165)* – ('A'-original) / ('A'radio) / Vexed.
(12") *(XLR 165)* – (first 2 mixes) / ('A'-instrumental).

Jul 03. (cd/lp) *(XLCD/XLLP 170)* <600> **BOY IN DA CORNER** 23 Jan04
– Sittin' here / Stop dat / I luv U / Brand new day / 2 far (with WILEY) / Fix up, look sharp / Cut 'em off / Hold ya mouf / Round we go / Jus a rascal / Wot U on / Jezebel / Seems 2 be / Live O / Do it / Vexed.

Aug 03. (cd-s) *(XLS 167CD)* **FIX UP, LOOK SHARP / STOP DAT / I LUV U (video)** 17 –
(12") *(XLT 167)* – ('A'-mixes).
(12") *(XLR 167)* – ('A'-mixes).

Nov 03. (12") *(XLT 175)* **JUS A RASCAL. / JUS A RASCAL (clean) / JUS A RASCAL (a cappella)** 30 –
(cd-s+=) *(XLS 175CD)* – Fix up, look sharp (video) / ('A'-video).

DJ SHADOW

Born: JOSH DAVIS, 1973, Hayward, San Francisco, California, USA. While hip hop continued to stagnate in a vicious circle of violence, recrimination and manicured beats, a handful of individuals are making leaps and bounds off the musical map. One such character is the aptly named DJ SHADOW, an elusive figure who entranced and beguiled the music world in 1996 with his groundbreaking debut album, 'ENDTRODUCING . . .' Eschewing rapping altogether, SHADOW took the form back to its roots in samples, scratching, beats, breaks and ingenious creativity, employing an obsessive knowledge of hip hop and vinyl culture to create something as funky and compulsive as it was cerebral, dark and complex. Working around a haunting central theme, the turntable guru moves in and out of musical focus, manipulating sounds and juxtaposing strings, creeping/rampaging beats, twilight zone organ and obscure samples with ever impressive cohesion. Located somewhere in the no-man's land between hip hop, trip-hop and avante-garde experimentalism, DJ SHADOW thankfully bypasses the head-nodding tendencies of much 'Mo-Wax' fodder while continuing to be feted by a wide cross section of both the dance and rock commumities. 1997's live 'Q-BERT MIX' was a scratch-athon taster of DJ SHADOW live in the flesh, an occurrence which remains, on UK shores at least, about as rare as . . . A few years earlier, DJ SHADOW had teamed up with label boss, JAMES LAVELLE on the UNKLE project, a mini-album, 'TIME HAS COME' (1996) surfaced, although it was 1998's 'PSYENCE FICTION', that broke them into the UK Top 10. 'RABBIT IN YOUR HEADLIGHTS' – co-written and sung by RADIOHEAD's THOM YORKE – was certainly the highlight, although amongst others, stars such as The Verve's RICHARD ASHCROFT and the Beastie Boys' MIKE D also contributed greatly to the classic. Shortly afterwards, DJ SHADOW returned to his daytime job. A long time coming, 'THE PRIVATE PRESS' (2002) confirmed that DJ SHADOW had lost nothing of his singular talent during his studio sabbatical. If anything, his sense of sonic possibility had been sharpened, probing the forgotten corners and blind alleys of popular music, synthesising cerebral masterpeices from the debris.

Album rating: ENTROPY (*6) / IN/FLUX mini (*7) / LOST AND FOUND (*6) / WHAT DOES YOUR SOUL LOOK LIKE (*7) / ENDTRODUCING . . . (*8) / THE PRIVATE PRESS (*8)

not iss. Sole Sides

1993. (cd) **ENTROPY** –

Mo'Wax Mo'Wax

Sep 94. (12"/cd-s) <*(MW 014/+CD)*> **IN FLUX. / HINDSIGHT** Dec93

Mar 95. (12"/cd-s) <*(MW 027/+CD)*> **WHAT DOES YOUR SOUL LOOK LIKE? / (3-'A'mixes)** 59
(cd-s) *(MW 027CDL)* – ('A'mixes).

May 95. (12"; DJ SHADOW & DJ KRUSH) <*(MW 024)*> **LOST AND FOUND. / DJ Krush: KEMURI** 1994

Sep 96. (12"/cd-s) <*(MW 057/+CD)*> **MIDNIGHT IN A PERFECT WORLD (mixes). / MUTUAL SLUMP** 54 –

Sep 96. (d-lp/c/cd) <*(MW 059/+MC/CD)*> **ENDTRODUCING** 17 Nov96
– Best foot forward / Building steam with a grain of salt / The number song / Changeling / (transmission #1) / What does your soul look like (part 4) / (untitled) / Stem – Long stem / (transmission #2) / Mutual slump / Organ donor / Why hip hop sucks in '96 / Midnight in a perfect world / Napalm brain – Scatter brain / What does your soul look like (part 1 – Blue sky revisit) / (transmission #3). *(d-lp re-iss. Jan98; same)*

Oct 96. (12"/cd-s) <*(MW 058/+CD)*> **STEM / RED BUS NEEDS TO LEAVE. / LONG STEM / SOUP** [74] [ ]

Jun 97. (12"; DJ SHADOW & XCEL) *(SS 005)* **HARDCORE HIP HOP. /** [ ] [–]
(above issued on 'Solesides')

Sep 97. (7"/c-s) <*(MW 063 S/MC)*> **HIGH NOON. / ORGAN DONOR (extended overhaul)** [22] [ ]
(12"+=/cd-s+=) <*(MW 063/+CD)*> – The Devil's advocate (Heaven and Hell bonus beats) / Hypnotize spoken word intro – outro.

Dec 97. (m-lp/m-cd) <*(MW 084/+CD)*> **"Q-BERT MIX-LIVE!!":- CAMEL BOBSLED RACE** (mixed by Q-BERT) [62] [ ]

Jan 98. (cd/c) <*540867*> **PREEMPTIVE STRIKE** [–] [ ]
– Strike one / In – Flux / Hindsight / Strike two / What does your soul look like (part 2) / What does your soul look like (part 3) / What does your soul look like (part 4) / What does your soul look like (part 1) / Strike three (and I'm out) / High noon / Organ donor (extended overhaul).

Jan 98. (12") <*(MW 087)*> **WHAT DOES YOUR SOUL LOOK LIKE (part 1). / (part 2)** [54] [ ]

Feb 98. (ltd-12") *(MW 086DJ)* **NUMBER SONG (Cut Chemist mix). / PAINKILLER (DJ Shadow Vs. Depeche Mode)** [ ] [–]

—— in Feb'99, he mixed the 'Funk Spectrum Vol.1' V/A double-set

Brainfreeze — Sixty 7

Oct 00. (cd/lp; by DJ SHADOW & CUT CHEMIST) *(SD 1001 CD/V)* **BRAINFREEZE** [ ] 1999 [ ]

—— in Nov'00, DJ SHADOW mixed the 'Bombay The Hard Way' V/A set

M.C.A. — M.C.A.

Feb 01. (7"/cd-s) *(155778-7/-2)* **DARK DAYS (main theme). / DARK DAYS (spoken for mix)** [ ] [–]

—— late in 2001, DJ SHADOW & CUT CHEMIST put together the very rare, 'PRODUCT PLACEMENT' LP for the 'One29 Recordings' imprint

Island — M.C.A.

May 02. (12"/cd-s) *(12IS/CID 797)* **YOU CAN'T GO HOME AGAIN! / DISAVOWED / TREACH BATTLE BEAT** [30] [–]

Jun 02. (cd/d-lp) *(CID/ILPSD 8118)* <*112937*> **THE PRIVATE PRESS** [8] [44]
– (Letter from home) / Fixed income / Un autre introduction / Walkie talkie / Giving up the ghost / Six days / Mongrel . . . / . . .Meets his maker / Right thing – GDMFSOB / Monosylabik / Mashin' on the motorway / Blood on the motorway / You can't go home again! / (Letter from home). *(ltd-d-cd+=)* – Giving up the ghost / Pushin' buttons (live w/ CUT CHEMIST & DJ NU-MARK).

Oct 02. (12"; as DJ SHADOW featuring MOS DEF) *(12IS 807)* **SIX DAYS. / SIX DAYS (original) / 100 METRE DASH** [28] [–]
(cd-s+=) *(CID 807)* – ('A'-instrumental) / ('A'-video).

DMX

Born: EARL SIMMONS, 18 Dec'70, Yonkers, New York, USA. As a troubled teen, with a chequered past, the apprehensive MC began his quest from the gutter and into rap stardom when he struck a deal with 'Columbia'; an unsigned talent show had panned the spotlight on the unknown 21-year-old. His debut, 'BORN LOSER' (1996), flopped unceremoniously when released in the States, most likely due to the fact that 2PAC and NOTORIOUS B.I.G. were stealing the show with their very own brand of humourless hardcore rap. It wasn't until 'Def Jam' were dumbfounded by a lost demo tape and the aforementioned rap martyrs were all dead that DMX and his RUFF RYDERS (a collection of friends and producers from his hood) could stand alone as the most outstanding artists of their generation. He cameo'd on songs by MA$E, LL COOL J and JAY-Z before issuing the haunting 'IT'S DARK AND HELL IS HOT' in 1998. Through subsequent months, the set began to slowly climb its way up the American Billboard charts before selling a whopping 3 million copies, gaining the talented gothic rapper the title "The Dawg". From its outset, the album was a bleak study into the underworld of hopelessness in the ghettos and the forgotten suburban neighbourhoods, where anything could and would happen. 'DAMIEN', the album's strongest moment, was a reflection from the point of view of a crazy murderer, commanded by his alter-ego to kill. The track began with a sinister orchestral riff accompanied by a beatbox before DMX began with the line: "Why is it that every move I make turns out to be a bad one, where's my guardian angel, need one, wish I had one . . ." which then segued into a biblical chorus: it was the most disturbing rap song since 2PAC's enraged 'HIT 'EM UP'. Other tracks induced DMX's disturbed imagery: in 'PRAYER', he pleads with God, questioning him about the decisions he could have helped the rapper make in his vexatious years; in 'X IS COMING' he fantasises about the rape and subsequent murder of a 15-year-old (and to think that he's MARIAH CAREY's favourite rapper!). SIMPSON surfaced again in the same year with the major label sophomore set, 'FLESH OF MY FLESH, BLOOD OF MY BLOOD' and it was much weaker than its heavyweight contender. DMX, "The Dawg", seemed to be barking phrases instead of rapping, loosening false pretentions with his overpowering ego. MARILYN MANSON and MARY J BLIGE were among the performers included on the album which had our anti-hero soaked in blood on the cover. His worst came in the form of ' . . .AND THEN THERE WAS X' (1999), a sloppy, inadequate fourth album, where The 'X droned on about his reign as the best rapper in the world. However, he was the most successful having had three US No.1 chartbusters. Things just began to get worse for the man when he issued his feeble shot at tough-love hip-hop with 'THE GREAT DEPRESSION' (2001). The album, which went number 1 in the US, drew on DMX's own personal conflicts within his life. But what personal conflicts did a millionaire rap artist have (apart from coming up with some original beats) and why did he have to share them with an entourage of producers like BINK, JUST BLAZE, BLACK KEY, KIDD KODD and SWIZZ BEATZ? 'WE RIGHT HERE' is a stonking, uptempo number that could have been a potential single, but the majority of the mood on ' . . . DEPRESSION' is dark with DMX's biblical good-versus-evil charade – that made his first two albums worth recommending in the first place – just repeated over and over. In the rap world it was already becoming clear that underground artists such as AESOP ROCK, CANNIBAL OX and The ANTI POP CONSORTIUM had a lot more to offer in terms of style, character, beats and rhythms. DMX was just becoming a tadpole swimming around in the stagnant pond of mainstream rap, when really he should have sprouted legs and leaped into the garden. The prolific DMX returned in 2003, with his overtly misogynistic 'GRAND CHAMP', a record which boasted the usual major label shout-outs, thug raps and cocaine party songs, with a few dark tunes to boot. Featuring a picture of a really mean looking dog (or should we say, "dawg") on the front cover, it was quite evident that DMX, with his polished production and slick beats was probably going to stay consistent with every album that he made. • **Note:** Not to be confused with the DMX CREW.

Album rating: IT'S DARK AND HELL IS NOT (*8) / FLESH OF MY FLESH BLOOD OF MY BLOOD (*7) / . . .AND THEN THERE WAS X (*6) / THE GREAT DEPRESSION (*5) / GRAND CHAMP (*6)

EARL SIMMONS – rapper, etc

not iss. — Sony

Jul 93. (c-s/12"/cd-s) <*74908*> **BORN LOSER (mixes)** [–] [ ]

not iss. — Metropolitan

Nov 94. (12"; by DMX & STEPHANIE MARANO) <*1034*> **SECRET GARDEN. / (version)** [–] [ ]

Def Jam Def Jam

Feb 98. (c-s/12"/cd-s; DMX featuring SHEEK of The LOX) *<568523>* **GET AT ME DOG (intro / street / instrumental / freestyle) / (interview) / STOP BEING GREEDY (street / instrumental)** [–] [39]

Jun 98. (cd/lp) *<(558227-2/-1)>* **IT'S DARK AND HELL IS NOT** [ ] May98 [1]
– Intro / Ruff Ryders' anthem / Fuckin' wit D / Storm / Look thru my eyes / Get at me dog / Let me fly / X-is coming / Damien / How's it goin' down / Mickey / Crime story / Stop being greedy / Ate / For my dogs / I can feel it / Prayer / Convo / Niggaz done started something.

—— DMX also featured on two V/A 12"ep's, 'SURVIVAL OF THE ILLEST' (Vols. 1 & 2) along with FAITH EVANS, ONYX and The DEF SQUAD

Aug 98. (cd-s) **STOP BEING GREEDY / (mixes)** [–] [79]

Oct 98. (12"/cd-s; by DMX featuring FAITH EVANS) *<566217>* **HOW'S IT GOIN' DOWN. / RUFF RYDERS' ANTHEM (radio)** [–] [70]

Jan 99. (cd/d-lp) *<(538640-2/-1)>* **FLESH OF MY FLESH BLOOD OF MY BLOOD** [ ] Dec98 [1]
– My niggas / Bring your whole crew / Pac man / Ain't no way / We don't give a fuck / Keep your shit the hardest / Coming from / It's all good / Omen / Slippin' / No love 4 me / Dogs for life / Blackout / Flesh of my flesh blood of my blood / Heat / Ready to meet him.

Feb 99. (c-s/cd-s) *<566217>* **RUFF RYDERS' ANTHEM (mixes)** [–] [94]

May 99. (12") *(563867-1) <870755>* **SLIPPIN'. / RUFF RYDERS' ANTHEM / STOP BEING GREEDY** [30] Apr99 [ ]
(cd-s) *(870755-2)* – (first 2 tracks) / How's it goin' down.
(cd-s) *(870753-2)* – ('A'side) / No love for me / Get at me dog (2 versions).

Nov 99. (12") *<562540>* **WHAT'S MY NAME (mixes)** [–] [67]

Dec 99. (cd/lp) *<(546933-2/-1)>* **. . .AND THEN THERE WAS X** [ ] [1]
– Kennel / One more road to cross / The professional / Fame / Alot to learn / Here we go again / Party up (up in here) / Make a move / What these bastards want / What's my name? / More 2 a song / Don't you ever / Shakedown / D-X-L / Comin' for ya / Prayer III / Angel / Good girls, bad guys.

Feb 00. (cd-s) *<562605>* **PARTY UP (UP IN HERE) / PARTY UP (instrumental) / SLIPPIN' / PARTY (video)** [–] [27]

Jun 00. (cd-s; by DMX featuring SISQO) *<562808>* **WHAT YOU WANT / WHAT THESE BASTARDS WANT (explicit) / RUFF RYDERS ANTHEM / (CD-Rom)** [–] [52]

Oct 01. (cd/d-lp) *<(586450-2/-1)>* **THE GREAT DEPRESSION** [20] [1]
– Sometimes / School street / Who we be / Trina Moe / We right here / Bloodline anthem / Shorty was da bomb / Damien III / When I'm nothing (with STEPHANIE MILLS) / I miss you (with FAITH EVANS) / Number 11 (with FAITH EVANS) / Pull up (skit) / I'm a bang / Pull out (skit) / You could be blind (with MaSHONDA) / The prayer IV / A minute for your son / Kennel (with JINX) / Loose / Big Stan / Problem child (with MYSONNE) / Drag-on / Shit's still real (with MIC GERONIMO) / Big Stan.

Dec 01. (12"/c-s) *(588851-1/-4) <572720>* **WHO WE BE. / WE RIGHT HERE** [34] Sep01 [60]
(cd-s+=) *(588851-2)* – ('A'-radio & video mixes).

Apr 03. (12") *(077904-1)* **X GON' GIVE IT TO YA. / (instrumental) / PARTY UP (UP IN HERE)** [6] [ ]
(cd-s) *(077904-2)* – ('A'side) / Get at me dog (with SHEEK) / Make a move.

Sep 03. (cd)(d-lp) *(9861021)<(633691)>* **GRAND CHAMP** [6] [1]
– Dog intro / My life (with CHINKY) / Where the hood at? / Dogs out / Get it on the floor (with SWIZZ BEATZ) / Come prepared / Shot down (with 50 CENT & STYLES P) / Bring the noize / Untouchable (with SHEEK, SYLEENA JOHNSON, INFA-RED & CROSS) / Fuck y'all / Ruff radio / We're back (with EVE & JADAKISS) / Ruff radio 2 / Rob all night (if I'm gonna rob) / We go hard (with CAM'RON) / We 'bout to blow (with BIG STAN) / The rain / Gotta go / Don't gotta go home (with MONICA) / A'yo kato (with MAGIC & VAL) / Thank you (with PATTI LaBELLE) / The prayer V. *(d-lp+=)* – On top (with BIG STAN).

Sep 03. (12") *(9811390)* **WHERE THE HOOD AT? / (Ruff Ryders anthem) / (instrumental)** [16] [–]
(cd-s) *(9811251)* – ('A'side) / Who we be / ('A'-video).

Fats DOMINO

Born: ANTOINE DOMINO, 26 Feb'28, New Orleans, Louisiana, USA. Growing up in a musical family, FATS began playing local honky tonk clubs before he even reached his teens. Nicknamed 'FATS' – for his 16 stone stature – by his bass player, BILLY DIAMOND, he was soon tinkling the ivories alongside Crescent City masters like PROFESSOR LONGHAIR and CHAMPION JACK DUPREE while digging the records of FATS WALLER and LOUIS JORDAN. DOMINO was barely over sixteen when he joined the band of trumpeter/producer/composer extrordinaire, Dave Bartholomew, although the pair would subsequently strike up a long and fruitful partnership. Also working as an A&R man for 'Imperial', Bartholomew helped the youngster sign to the label in 1949, the same year the pair co-penned what would become DOMINO's debut single, 'THE FAT MAN'. A rollicking piano groove oft cited as the first rock'n'roll record (alongside a host of others), the track was release by 'Imperial' in the Spring of 1950 and went on to sell a million copies over the ensuing three years. More importantly, it created a sizeable market for FATS' laid-back, free-rolling take on classic New Orleans R&B and with a crack band consisting of BARTHOLOMEW, RED TYLER and EARL PALMER, DOMINO cut a further succession of R&B hits over the next five years while touring almost constantly. It was only a matter of time before he crossed over to the mainstream pop charts and in summer 1955 FATS took his propulsive boogie-woogie to the masses with 'AIN'T THAT A SHAME', a US Top 10. Along with his appearance in two teen movies, 'Shake, Rattle & Roll' and 'The Girl Can't Help It', this success initiated almost a decade of regular chart action, his best-loved and most well known song, 'BLUEBERRY HILL', making the Top 10 on both sides of the pond in Autumn '56 (another classic 'IT'S KEEPS RAININ', has been cited as a precursor to Jamaican ska/reggae after import copies caused a musical storm – BITTY McLEAN took it to UK No.2 in 1993). This consolidated FATS as one of the most popular and respected performers of the rock'n'roll era, his unique encapsulation of his native city's multicultural musical heritage seeing him rack up more sales than any other American artist save ELVIS PRESLEY. Among the best and biggest of his hits were 'BLUE MONDAY' (sadly not an early version of NEW ORDER's electro classic), 'I'M WALKIN', 'WHOLE LOTTA LOVING' and 'WALKING TO NEW ORLEANS', all million-selling US Top 10's. By the time of FATS' move to 'ABC Paramount' in 1963, the hits were becoming thinner on the ground as the British Invasion heated up. Ironically, The BEATLES were big DOMINO fans and were no doubt both thrilled and amused when the Big Man covered 'LADY MADONNA' in 1968, one of his first singles for 'Reprise' and his last chart entry. Nevertheless, he continued to tour and record right up until the early 80's, when he finally retired from the music business. • **Covered:** WHEN THE SAINTS GO MARCHING IN (trad.) / JAMBALAYA + YOU WIN AGAIN (Hank Williams) / I HEAR YOU KNOCKIN' (Smiley Lewis) / DID YOU EVER SEE A DREAM WALKIN' (Eddy Duchin) / RED SAILS IN THE SUNSET (Platters) / I CAN'T STOP LOVING YOU (Ray Charles) / I LEFT MY HEART IN SAN FRANCISCO (Tony Bennett) / LOVELY RITA + EVERYBODY'S GOT SOMETHING TO HIDE EXCEPT ME AND THE MONKEY (Beatles) / etc. • **Trivia:** He married childhood sweetheart Rosemary in the late 40's, bringing up 8 children in homeland New Orleans.

Best CD compilation: MY BLUE HEAVEN: THE BEST OF FATS DOMINO (*7)

FATS DOMINO – vocals, piano with **DAVE BARTHOLOMEW** – trumpet / **RED TYLER** – bass / **EARL PALMER** – drums

not iss. Imperial

Apr 50. (78) *<5058>* **THE FAT MAN. / DETROIT CITY BLUES** [–] [ ]
May 50. (78) *<5065>* **BOOGIE WOOGIE BABY. / LITTLE BEE** [–] [ ]
Jul 50. (78) *<5077>* **SHE'S MY BABY. / HIDE AWAY BLUES** [–] [ ]
Sep 50. (78) *<5085>* **HEY LA BAS BOOGIE. / BRAND NEW BABY** [–] [ ]
Nov 50. (7",78) *<5099>* **KOREA BLUES. / EVERY NIGHT ABOUT THIS TIME** [–] [ ]

—— FATS now finds own musicians

Feb 51. (7",78) *<5114>* **TIRED OF CRYING. / WHAT'S THE MATTER BABY** [–] [ ]
May 51. (7",78) *<5123>* **DON'T LIE TO ME BABY. / SOMETIMES I WONDER** [–] [ ]
Aug 51. (7",78) *<5138>* **NO NO BABY. / RIGHT FROM WRONG** [–] [ ]
Nov 51. (7",78) *<5145>* **ROCKIN' CHAIR. / CARELESS LOVE** [–] [ ]
Jan 52. (7",78) *<5167>* **YOU KNOW I MISS YOU. / I'LL BE GONE** [–] [ ]
Mar 52. (7",78) *<5180>* **GOIN' HOME. / REELIN' AND ROCKIN'** [–] [ ]
Jun 52. (7",78) *<5197>* **POOR POOR ME. / TRUST IN ME** [–] [ ]
Sep 52. (7"red,78) *<5209>* **HOW LONG. / DREAMING** [–] [ ]
Jan 53. (7"red,78) *<5220>* **NOBODY LOVES ME. / CHEATIN'** [–] [ ]
May 53. (7"red,78) *<5231>* **GOING TO THE RIVER. / MARDI GRAS IN NEW ORLEANS** [–] [ ]
Jul 53. (7",78) *<5240>* **PLEASE DON'T LEAVE ME. / THE GIRL I LOVE** [–] [ ]

—— added **LEE ALLEN** – saxophone

London Imperial

Feb 54. (7",78) *(HL 8007) <5251>* **ROSE MARY. / YOU SAID YOU LOVED ME** [ ] Oct53 [ ]
Jul 54. (7",78) *(HL 8063) <5272>* **YOU DONE ME WRONG. / (HEY) LITTLE SCHOOL GIRL** [ ] Feb54 [ ]
Nov 54. (7",78) *(HL 8096) <5262>* **DON'T LEAVE ME THIS WAY. / SOMETHING'S WRONG** [ ] Dec53 [ ]
Jun 54. (7",78) *<5283>* **BABY PLEASE. / WHERE DID YOU STAY** [–] [ ]
Nov 54. (7",78) *<5301>* **YOU CAN PACK YOUR SUITCASE. / I LIVED MY LIFE** [–] [ ]
Feb 55. (7",78) *(HL 8124) <5313>* **LOVE ME. / DON'T YOU HEAR ME CALLIN' YOU** [ ] 1954 [ ]
Apr 55. (7",78) *(HL 8133) <5323>* **I KNOW. / THINKIN' OF YOU** [ ] Jan55 [ ]
Apr 55. (7",78) *<5340>* **DON'T YOU KNOW. / HELPING HAND** [–] [ ]

—— now with **WALTER NELSON** – guitar / **CORNELIUS COLEMAN** – drums.

Sep 55. (7",78) *(HLU 8173) <5348>* **AIN'T THAT A SHAME. / LA-LA-LA** [ ] Jun55 [10]
(above single hit UK chart No.23 in Jan57)
Nov 55. (lp) *<9004>* **CARRY ON ROCKIN'** [–] [ ]
– The fat man / Tired of crying / Goin' home / You said you love me / Going to the river / Please don't leave me / Rose Mary / All by myself / Ain't that a shame / Poor me / Bo Weevil / Don't blame it on me. *<re-iss. Mar57 as 'ROCK AND ROLLIN' WITH FATS DOMINO'; same> (UK-iss.Apr57; HA-P 2041)*
Sep 55. (7",78) *<5357>* **ALL BY MYSELF. / TROUBLES OF MY OWN** [–] [ ]
Nov 55. (7",78) *<5369>* **POOR ME. / I CAN'T GO ON (ROSALIE)** [–] [ ]
Mar 56. (7",78) *(HLU 8256) <5375>* **BO WEEVIL. / DON'T BLAME IT ON ME** [ ] Feb56 [35]
Jul 56. (7",78) *(HLU 8280) <5386>* **I'M IN LOVE AGAIN. / MY BLUE HEAVEN** [12] [3] [19]
Aug 56. (7",78) *(HLU 8309) <5396>* **WHEN MY DREAMBOAT COMES HOME. / SO-LONG** [ ] [14] Jul56 [44]
Sep 56. (7",78) *<5407>* **BLUEBERRY HILL. / HONEY CHILE** [–] [5]
Oct 56. (7",78) *(HLU 8330)* **BLUEBERRY HILL. / I CAN'T GO ON (ROSALIE)** [6] [–]
Oct 56. (lp) *(HA-U 2028) <9009>* **FATS DOMINO – ROCK AND ROLLIN'** [ ] [18]
– The fat man / Tired of crying / Goin' home / You said you love me / Going to the river / Please don't leave me / Rose Mary / All by myself / Ain't that a shame / Poor me / Bo Weevil / Don't blame it on me.
Jan 57. (7",78) *(HLU 8356)* **HONEY CHILE. / DON'T YOU KNOW** [29] [–]
Feb 57. (lp) *(HA-P 2073) <9028>* **THIS IS FATS DOMINO!** [ ] [19]
– Blueberry hill / Honey chile / What's the reason I'm not pleasing you / Blue Monday / So long / La la / Troubles of my own / You done me wrong / Reeling and rocking / The fat man's hop / Poor poor me / Trust in me.
Mar 57. (7",78) *(HLP 8377) <5417>* **BLUE MONDAY. / WHAT'S THE REASON I'M NOT PLEASING YOU** [23] [5] Dec56 [50]
Apr 57. (7",78) *(HLP 8407) <5428>* **I'M WALKIN'. / I'M IN THE MOOD FOR LOVE** [19] Feb57 [4]
Jul 57. (7",78) *(HLP 8449) <5442>* **VALLEY OF TEARS. / IT'S YOU I LOVE** [25] [8] May58 [6]
Aug 57. (7",78) *(HLP 8471) <5454>* **WHEN I SEE YOU. / WHAT WILL I TELL MY HEART** [ ] [29] [64]
Nov 57. (7",78) *(HLP 8519) <5467>* **WAIT AND SEE. / I STILL LOVE YOU** [ ] [23] Oct57 [79]

—— sessions incl. **ALLEN TOUSSAINT** – piano

Mar 58. (7",78) *(HLP 8575) <5477>* **THE BIG BEAT. / I WANT YOU TO KNOW** [20] [26] Dec57 [32]
Feb 58. (7",78) *<5492>* **YES, MY DARLING. / DON'T YOU KNOW I LOVE YOU** [–] [55]
May 58. (lp) *(HA-P 2052) <9038>* **HERE STANDS FATS DOMINO** [ ] [ ]
– Detroit City blues / Hide away blues / She's my baby / New baby / Little bee / Every night about this time / I'm walkin' / I'm in the mood for love / Cheatin' / You can pack your suitcase / Hey fat man / I'll be gone.
Jun 58. (7") *(HLP 8628) <5515>* **SICK AND TIRED. / NO, NO** [26] [22] Apr58 [55]
Jun 58. (lp) *(HA-P 2087) <9040>* **THIS IS FATS** [ ] [ ]
– The rooster song / My happiness / As time goes by / Hey la bas / ove me / Don't you hear me calling you / It's you I love / Valley of tears / Where did you stay / Baby please / Thinking of you / You know I miss you. *(re-iss. Apr79 on 'Flyover') (re-iss. US Jan83)*
Jul 58. (7",78) *(HLP 8663) <5526>* **LITTLE MARY. / PRISONER'S SONG** [ ] Jun58 [48]
Oct 58. (7",78) *(HLP 8727) <5537>* **YOUNG SCHOOL GIRL. / IT MUST BE LOVE** [ ] Sep58 [92]
Nov 58. (7",78) *(HLP 8759) <5553>* **WHOLE LOTTA LOVING. / COQUETTE** [ ] [6] [92]
Sep 58. (lp) *(HA-P 2135) <9055>* **THE FABULOUS "MR.D"** [ ] [ ]
– The big beat / I'll be glad when you're dead you rascal you / What will I tell my heart / Barrelhouse / Little Mary / Sick and tired / I want you to know / "44" / Mardi Gras in New Orleans / I can't go on / Long lonesome journey / Young school girl *(re-iss. US Jan83)*
Mar 59. (7",78) *(HLP 8822) <5569>* **WHEN THE SAINTS GO MARCHING IN. / TELLING LIES** [ ] Feb59 [50]
May 59. (7",78) *(HLP 8865) <5585>* **MARGIE. / I'M READY** [18] [51] [16]
(re-iss. Jul76 on 'United Artists')
Jun 59. (lp) *(HA-P 2223) <9065>* **LET'S PLAY FATS DOMINO** [ ] [ ]
– You left me / Ain't it good / Howdy podner / Stack & Billy / Would you / Margie / Hands across the table / When the saints go marching in / Ida Jane / Lil' Liza Jane / I'm gonna be a wheel some day / I want to walk you home.
Sep 59. (7",78) *(HLP 8942) <5606>* **I WANT TO WALK YOU HOME. / I'M GONNA BE A WHEEL SOMEDAY** [14] [8] Jul59 [17]
Dec 59. (7",78) *(HLP 9005) <5629>* **BE MY GUEST. / I'VE BEEN AROUND** [11] [8] Oct59 [33]
Dec 59. (lp) *<9062>* **FATS DOMINO SWINGS** [–] [ ]
– The fat man / Blue Monday / Blueberry Hill / I'm in love again / Going to the river / My blue Heaven / Bo Weevil / Goin' home / Please don't leave me / Ain't that a shame / I'm walkin' / Whole lotta lovin'. *(cd-iss. Nov99 on 'Magic'; 523017-2)*

Mar 60. (7",78) *(HLP 9073) <5645>* **COUNTRY BOY. / IF YOU NEED ME** [19] [25] Jan60 [98]

Jun 60. (7",78) *(HLP 9133) <5660>* **TELL ME THAT YOU LOVE ME. / BEFORE I GROW TOO OLD** [ ] [51] Apr60 [84]

Jul 60. (7",78) *(HLP 9163) <5675>* **WALKING TO NEW ORLEANS. / DON'T COME KNOCKIN'** [19] [6] Jun60 [21]

Oct 60. (7") *(HLP 9198) <5687>* **THREE NIGHTS A WEEK. / PUT YOUR ARMS AROUND ME HONEY** [45] [15] Aug60 [58]

Nov 60. (lp) *(HA-P 2312) <9127>* **A LOT OF DOMINOES** [ ] [ ]
– Put your arms around me honey / Three nights a week / Shu rah / Rising sun / My girl Josephine / The sheik of Araby / Walking to New Orleans / Don't come knockin' / Magic isles / You always hurt the one you love / It's the talk of the town / Natural born lover.

Dec 60. (7") *(HLP 9244) <5704>* **MY GIRL JOSEPHINE. / NATURAL BORN LOVER** [32] [14] Oct60 [38]

Mar 61. (7") *(HLP 9301) <5723>* **WHAT A PRICE. / AIN'T THAT JUST LIKE A WOMAN** [ ] [22] Jan61 [33]

Apr 61. (7") *(HLP 9327) <5734>* **SHU RAH. / FELL IN LOVE ON MONDAY** [ ] Mar61 [32]

Apr 61. (lp) *(HA-P 2364) <9138>* **I MISS YOU SO** [ ] [ ]
– I miss you so / It keeps rainin' / Ain't that just like a woman / Once in a while / I hear you knockin' / Isle of Capri / What a price / When I was young / Fell in love on Monday / My bleeding heart / Easter parade / I'll always be in love with you.

Jun 61. (7") *(HLP 9374) <5753>* **IT KEEPS RAININ'. / I JUST CRY** [49] May61 [23]

Sep 61. (7") *(HLP 9415) <5764>* **LET THE FOUR WINDS BLOW. / GOOD HEARTED MAN** [ ] Jul61 [15]

Sep 61. (lp) *(HA-P 2420) <9153>* **LET THE FOUR WINDS BLOW** [ ] [ ]
– Along the Navajo trail / You win again / One night / I'm alone because I love you / Won't you come on back / Trouble blues / I can't give you anything but love / Good hearted man / Your cheating heart / Let the four winds blow / In a shanty in Old Shanty Town / Am I blue.

Nov 61. (7") *(HLP 9456) <5779>* **WHAT A PARTY. / ROCKIN' BICYCLE** [ ] [22] Sep61 [83]

Nov 61. (lp) *(HA-P 2426) <9164>* **WHAT A PARTY** [ ] [ ]
– Did you ever see a dream / Walking rockin' bicycle / Before I grow too old ain't gonna do it / Bad luck and trouble / Hold hands / Trouble in mind / Coquette / What a party / I just cry / I've been calling / Tell me that you love me.

Nov 61. (7") *<5796>* **JAMBALAYA (ON THE BAYOU). / I HEAR YOU KNOCKIN'** [–] [30] [67]

Feb 62. (7") *<5816>* **YOU WIN AGAIN. / IDA JANE** [–] [22] [90]

Mar 62. (7") *(HLP 9520)* **JAMBALAYA. / YOU WIN AGAIN** [41] [–]

Apr 62. (lp) *(HA-P 2447) <9170>* **TWISTIN' THE STOMP** [ ] [ ]
– Twistin' the spots / The twist set me free / I know / Every night / Town talk / Wait and see / Twistin' the stomp / Don't deceive me / A long way from home / The girl I love / Do you know what it means to miss New Orleans / South of the border.

Jun 62. (7") *(HLP 9557) <5833>* **MY REAL NAME. / MY HEART IS BLEEDING** [ ] May62 [59]

Jul 62. (lp) *<9195>* **MILLION SELLERS BY FATS** (compilation) [–] [ ]
– You said you love me / I still love you / Be my guest / Country boy / If you need me / I want to walk you home / It's you I love / I've been around / I'm gonna be a wheel some day / I'm ready / Margie / I want you to know.

Aug 62. (7") *(HLP 9590) <5863>* **DANCE WITH MR.DOMINO. / NOTHING NEW (SAME OLD THING)** [ ] [98] Jun62 [77]

Oct 62. (7") *(HLP 9616) <5875>* **STOP THE CLOCK. / DID YOU EVER SEE A DREAM WALKING** [ ] Sep62 [79]

Dec 62. (7") *<5895>* **WON'T YOU COME ON BACK. / HANDS ACROSS THE TABLE** [–] [ ]

Jan 63. (7") *<5909>* **THOSE EYES. / HUM-DIDDY-DOO** [–] [ ]

H.M.V. ABC Paramount

May 63. (7") *(POP 1164) <10444>* **THERE GOES (MY HEART AGAIN). / CAN'T GO ON WITHOUT YOU** [ ] [59]

Jul 63. (7") *(POP 1917) <10475>* **WHEN I'M WALKING (LET ME WALK). / I'VE GOT A RIGHT TO CRY** [ ] [ ]

Sep 63. (7") *(POP 1219) <10484>* **RED SAILS IN THE SUNSET. / SONG FOR ROSEMARY** [34] [35]

Sep 63. (lp) *(CLP 1690) <455>* **HERE COMES . . . FATS DOMINO** [ ] [ ]
– When I'm walking / I got a right to cry / There goes (my heart again) / Just a lonely man / Red sails in the sunset / Bye baby, bye, bye / Forever, forever / I'm livin' right / Can't go on without you / Land of 1000 dances / Song for Rosemary / Tell me the truth, baby. *(cd-iss. Sep92 + Jul93 on 'Repertoire'; REP 4161)*

Jan 64. (7") *(POP 1265) <10512>* **WHO CARES. / JUST A LONELY MAN** [ ] Dec63 [63]

Feb 64. (lp) *(CLP 1740) <479>* **FATS ON FIRE** [ ] [ ]
– I don't want to set the world on fire / You know I miss you / Fats on fire / Land of make believe / Old man trouble / Love me / Mary, oh Mary / Gotta get a job / The fat man / Valley of tears / Fats shuffle / I'm a fool to care. *(cd-iss. Apr98 on 'Disky'; CDBB 9616)*

Mar 64. (7") *(POP 1281) <10531>* **LAZY LADY. / DON'T WANT TO SET THE WORLD ON FIRE** [ ] Feb64 [86]

May 64. (7") *(POP 1303) <10545>* **SOMETHING YOU GOT BABY. / IF YOU DON'T KNOW WHAT LOVE IS** [ ] Apr64 [ ]

Jul 64. (7") *(POP 1324) <10567>* **MARY OH MARY. / PACKIN' UP** [ ] Jun64 [ ]

Aug 64. (7") *<10584>* **SALLY WAS A GOOD OLD GIRL. / FOR YOU** [–] [99]

Nov 64. (7") *(POP 1370) <10596>* **HEARTBREAK HILL. / KANSAS CITY** [ ] Oct64 [99]

Apr 65. (7") *(POP 1421) <10631>* **WHY DON'T YOU DO RIGHT. / WIGS** [ ] [ ]

Jun 65. (lp) *(CLP 1821) <510>* **GETAWAY WITH FATS DOMINO** [ ] [ ]
– When the dreamboat comes home / Wigs / Trouble in mind / Man that's all / Kansas City / Reelin' and rockin' / On a slow boat to China / Monkey business / Heartbreak hill / Girl I'm gonna marry you / Why don't you do right / Ballin' the jack. *(re-iss. Dec83 on 'Ace-Charly'; CH 90)*

Jul 65. (7") *<10644>* **LET ME CALL YOU SWEETHEART. / GOODNIGHT SWEETHEART** [–] [ ]

Mercury Mercury

Sep 65. (7") *(MF 896) <72463>* **I LEFT MY HEART IN SAN FRANCISCO. / I DONE GOT FOR YOU** [ ] [ ]

Nov 65. (7") *(MF 873) <72485>* **WHAT'S THAT YOU GOT. / IT'S NEVER TOO LATE** [ ] [ ]

Dec 65. (lp; stereo/mono) *(S+/MCL 20070) <62039>* **DOMINO '65 (live)** [ ] [ ]
– (Introduction) / Blueberry hill / Please don't leave me / Domino twist / Let the four winds blow / I'm gonna be a wheel someday / I'm in the mood for love / Jambalaya (on the bayou) / Oh, what a price / Ain't that a shame / So long.

not iss. Broadmoor

Dec 67. (7") *<104>* **THE LADY IN BLACK. / WORK MY WAY UP STEADY** [–] [ ]

Feb 68. (7") *<105>* **BIG MOUTH. / WAIT TILL IT HAPPENS TO YOU** [–] [ ]

Reprise Reprise

Jun 68. (7"; UK w-drawn) *(RS 20696) <0696>* **ONE FOR THE HIGHWAY. / HONEST PAPAS LOVE THEIR MAMAS BETTER** [–] [ ]

Aug 68. (7") *(RS 20763) <0763>* **LADY MADONNA. / ONE FOR THE HIGHWAY** [ ] [100]

Sep 68. (lp) *(RSLP 107) <6304>* **FATS IS BACK** [ ] [ ]
– My old friends / I'm ready / So swell when you're well / Wait till it happens to you / I know / Lady Madonna / Honest papas love their mamas better / Make me belong to you / One for the highway / Lovely Rita / One more song for you. *(re-iss. Nov81 on 'Mercury' lp/c; 6463/7145 043) (cd-iss. Apr99 on 'Bullseye'; CDBB 9616)*

Nov 68. (7") *<0775>* **LOVEY RITA. / WAIT TILL IT HAPPENS TO YOU** [–] [ ]

1969. (7") *(RS 20810)* **EVERYBODY'S GOT SOMETHING TO HIDE EXCEPT ME AND THE DONKEY. / SO SWELL WHEN YOU'RE WELL** [–] [ ]

1970. (7") *<0891>* **MAKE ME BELONG TO YOU. / HAVE YOU SEEN MY BABY** [–] [ ]

1970. (lp) *<6439>* **FATS** [–] [ ]
– I'm going to cross that river / Big mouth / It's a sin to tell a lie / Wait till it happens to you / I'm going to help a friend / The lady in black / Another mule / When you're smiling (the whole world smiles with you) / These old shoes / Lawdy Miss Clawdy / Work my way up steady.

1970. (7") *<0944>* **NEW ORLEANS AIN'T THE SAME. / SWEET PATOOTIE** [–] [ ]

Atlantic — not iss.

Jun 74. (lp) *(K 50107)* **LIVE AT MONTREAUX – HELLO JOSEPHINE (live '73)** [ ] [–]
– Hello Josephine / I'm in love again / Blueberry hill / Jambalaya / Walking to New Orleans / I'm gonna be a wheel someday / Blue Monday / Mardi Gras in New Orleans / Stagger Lee / I want to walk you home / Let the four winds blow / I'm walking / When the saints go marching in / Sentimental journey.

Sonet — Polydor

May 79. (lp) *(SNTF 793) <PD 3215>* **SLEEPING ON THE JOB** [ ] [ ]
– Sleeping on the job / After hours / When I lost my baby / Something about you baby / Move with the groove / Any old time / Shame on you / I just can't get the girl I love / Love me.

Nov 78. (7") *(SON 2168)* **SLEEPING ON THE JOB. / AFTER HOURS** [ ] [–]

not iss. — Warners

Jan 81. (7") *<49610>* **WHISKEY HEAVEN. / BEERS TO YOU (by the Texas Opera Company)** [–] [ ]

—— FATS retired from music to spend time with his family, although he made a comeback album (see below)

Magnum Force — Toot Toot

1985. (7"; with DOUG KERSHAW) *<1>* **MY TOOT TOOT. / MY TOOT TOOT-THREE** [–] [ ]

Aug 85. (7"; with DOUG KERSHAW) *(MFS 4)* **MY TOOT TOOT. / DIGGY IGGY TO** [ ] [–]

—— he was now backed by many session men

not iss. — M.C.A.

1986. (lp) **HIS GREATEST HITS (live)** [–] [ ]
– My girl Josephine / The fat man / I'm gonna be a wheel someday / Blue Monday / Jambalaya (on the bayou) / Blueberry Hill / Going to the river / I'm ready / I want to walk you home / Whole lotta loving / Poor me / Ain't that a shame / I almost lost my mind / I'm in love again / I'm walkin' / Walking to New Orleans / Let the four winds blow / Shake, rattle and roll / My toot toot / I can't go on.

– (selective) compilations, etc. –

Apr 65. (lp) *Liberty; (LBY 3033)* **MILLION SELLERS BY FATS VOL.1** [ ] [–]
(re-iss. 1967; LBL 83023)

Jul 65. (lp) *Liberty; (LBY 3046)* **MILLION SELLERS BY FATS VOL.2** [ ] [–]
(re-iss. 1967; LBL 83024)

1968. (lp) *Liberty; (LBL 83101)* **MILLION SELLERS BY FATS VOL.3** [ ] [–]

Apr 70. (lp) *Liberty; (LBS 83331)* **THE VERY BEST OF FATS DOMINO: PLAY IT AGAIN FATS** [56] [–]

Feb 91. (cd/c) *E.M.I.; (CD/TC EMS 1381)* **MY BLUE HEAVEN: THE BEST OF FATS DOMINO** [ ] [–]
– My blue Heaven / The fat man / Please don't leave me / Ain't that a shame / I'm in love again / When my dreamboat comes home / Blueberry hill / Blue Monday / I'm walkin' / Valley of tears / Big beat / Yes my darling / Whole lotta loving / I'm ready / I'm gonna be a wheel someday / I want to walk you home / Be my guest / Walking to New Orleans (undubbed) / Let the four winds blow / What a party.

Jun 96. (cd) *Ace-Charly; (CDCHD 597)* **THE EARLY IMPERIAL SINGLES (1950-1952)** [ ] [–]

Apr 97. (cd) *Ace-Charly; (CDCHD 649)* **THE IMPERIAL SINGLES VOL.2 (1953-1956)** [ ] [–]

Jun 98. (cd) *Ace-Charly; (CDCHD 689)* **THE IMPERIAL SINGLES VOL.3: 1956-1958** [ ] [–]

May 00. (cd) *EMI Gold; (526777-2)* **THE FAT MAN SINGS** [ ] [ ]

Jul 00. (cd) *Members Edition; (UAE 31242)* **FATS DOMINO** [ ] [–]

Feb 01. (cd) *EMI Plus; (5760850)* **THE STORY** [ ] [ ]

Oct 01. (cd) *Catfish; (KATCD 213)* **REELING AND ROCKING** [ ] [ ]

Mar 02. (cd) *Classics; (5025)* **CLASSICS 1949-1951** [ ] [ ]

Mar 02. (4xcd-box) *537374-2)* **WALKING TO NEW ORLEANS** [ ] [ ]

Apr 02. (cd) *Indigo; (IGOCD 2513)* **THE FAT MAN: THE ESSENTIAL EARLY FATS DOMINO** [ ] [ ]

May 02. (cd) *E.M.I.; (537600-2)* **THE FATS DOMINO JUKEBOX – 20 GREATEST HITS** [ ] [ ]

Feb 03. (d-cd) *Proper Pairs; (PVCD 120)* **ROCKIN' ON RAMPART** [ ] [ ]

Feb 03. (8xcd-box+book) *Bear Family; (BCD 15541)* **OUT OF NEW ORLEANS** [ ] [ ]

Mar 03. (cd) *E.M.I.; (582212-2)* **THE ESSENTIAL FATS DOMINO** [ ] [ ]

Apr 03. (cd/c) *Castle Pulse; (PLS CD/MC 626)* **FABULOUS FATS DOMINO** [ ] [ ]

Jun 03. (cd) *Fabulous; (FABCD 159)* **ROCK AND ROLL LEGEND** [ ] [ ]

Jul 03. (d-cd) *Gemini; (220402303)* **ROCK RIGHT NOW WITH THE FAT MAN** [ ] [ ]

Jul 03. (cd) *Classics; (5060)* **CLASSICS 1951-1952** [ ] [ ]

Lonnie DONEGAN

Born: ANTHONY JAMES DONEGAN, 29 Apr'31, Glasgow, Scotland. The son of a classical violinist who played with the Scottish National Orchestra, DONEGAN began playing guitar in his teens. He was also an avid fan of folk, country, blues and jazz, immersing himself in the sounds of FRANK CRUMIT, JOSH WHITE, HANK WILLIAMS, LOUIS ARMSTRONG, LEADBELLY, WOODY GUTHRIE, etc. His musical ambitions eventually led him to London where he auditioned for CHRIS BARBER's band; the pair hit it off immediately and became lifelong friends. Following a stint of national service in Europe (where he was introduced to the musical delights of the American Forces Radio Network), DONEGAN returned to form The KEN COLYER JAZZMEN with BARBER and KEN COLYER. Between sets, DONEGAN took the spotlight and began developing the frantic hybrid of blues, jazz, folk and country that would come to be known as 'Skiffle'. Named – by COLYER's brother – after an old blues combo, the DAN BURLEY SKIFFLE GROUP, this unique sound kicked off a musical revolution almost as far reaching as ELVIS PRESLEY's lip-curling cross of rockabilly, gospel and jump-blues. When COLYER departed the group in 1954, BARBER took the helm and the band soon found themselves in the studio courtesy of 'Decca'. DONEGAN (who now took the stage name LONNIE after a compere confused him with guitarist LONNIE JOHNSON) persuaded the A&R man to let them cut a couple of tracks in his skiffle style, subsequently included on the 10" album, 'NEW ORLEANS JOY' (1955). One of them, 'ROCK ISLAND LINE' (a trad folk song cut by LEADBELLY amongst others), was released as a single – under the LONNIE DONEGAN SKIFFLE GROUP moniker – and proceeded to tear up the charts as well as the musical rule book; six months later it had sold an incredible three million copies, staying on the UK chart for 22 weeks and even making the US Top 10, a feat previously unheard of for a British act. Follow-up track, 'DIGGIN' MY POTATOES', was banned by the BBC for its suggestive title (hmmm . . .), giving old LONNIE (who duly signed to 'Pye') one of the first 'rebel' tags of the era. The ban only served to increase his popularity and over the next decade, an avalanche of hit singles buried the UK chart including No.1's 'CUMBERLAND GAP', 'PUTTING ON THE STYLE' (both 1957) and comic novelty track, 'MY OLD MAN'S A DUSTMAN' (1960). The latter track became the first ever single to go straight in at No.1, reflecting DONEGAN's 'King Of Skiffle' status. Imitators were ten a penny, utilising any DIY instruments they could lay their hands on i.e. washboards, soup spoons, etc.

In fact, a young PAUL McCARTNEY was one particularly mad keen fan, an early incarnation of The BEATLES playing at one of DONEGAN's folk appreciation society gigs in 1958. Ironically, though, the fab four's own adaptation of rock's roots steered the course of pop music in a different direction and skiffle mania was all but over by the early 60's. LONNIE's last Top 20 hit came in 1962 with 'PICK A BALE O' COTTON' and after 'THE FOLK ALBUM' (1965) failed to capture the imagination of the new folkies on the block, DONEGAN concentrated on production work for 'Pye'. 1970's flop 'LONNIEPOPS' album marked the end of his tenure with the label and he subsequently worked in Germany where there was a brief skiffle mini-revival. The man's curious brand of humour was showcased once more in 1976 with a one-off single, 'I'VE LOST MY LITTLE WILLIE'. Unfortunately he suffered a heart attack the same year and relocated to California to recuperate in the West Coast sun. 1978 saw the release of 'PUTTING ON THE STYLE', an all-star skiffle affair featuring the likes of RINGO STARR, RON WOOD and ELTON JOHN, all long time fans. The album actually made the UK Top 60 although the C&W follow-up, 'SUNDOWN' (1979) made little headway. 1981, meanwhile found him teaming up with Scots group, SHAKIN' PYRAMIDS for a one-off single although continuing heart problems curtailed him for much of the early-mid 80's. A further one-off single, 'DONEGAN'S DANCING SUNSHINE BAND', appeared in summer '87. In 1995, DONEGAN was presented with an Ivor Novello award, an occasion which saw him singing with longtime fan VAN MORRISON. The pair discussed cutting some tracks together, the results finally emerging in 1999 on 'MULESKINNER BLUES', an 'R.C.A.' set combining old and new material with contributions from the likes of ALBERT LEE, JACQUI McSHEE and even SAM BROWN. Standout tracks, though, were the two pairings with VAN the MAN, on the rabble-rousing title track and the brilliant remake of 'I'M ALABAMMY BOUND'. Clearly, DONEGAN (or VAN for that matter) hasn't reached the end of the rock island line just yet; he recently added Glastonbury to his already packed gig diary while his fans straddle both the generation gap and geographical boundaries (from Land's End to Falkirk, at least!). Basically DONEGAN IS SKIFFLE and we are not worthy.

Best CD collection: TALKING GUITAR BLUES – THE VERY BEST OF.. (*7)

LONNIE DONEGAN – vocals, guitar, banjo with his Skiffle Group: **DENNY WRIGHT** – lead guitar / **MICKY ASHMAN** – upright bass / **NICK NICHOLS** – drums

Decca London

Nov 55. (7"/78; as The LONNIE DONEGAN SKIFFLE GROUP) *(F/FJ 10647)* *<1650>* **ROCK ISLAND LINE. / JOHN HENRY** 8 Feb56 8

Feb 56. (7"/78; as The LONNIE DONEGAN SKIFFLE GROUP) *(F/FJ 10695)* **DIGGIN' MY POTATOES. / BURY MY BODY** – –

Pye Nixa Mercury

Apr 56. (7"/78) *(7N/N 15036)* *<70872>* **LOST JOHN. / STEWBALL** 2 May56 58

Jun 56. (7"ep) *(NJE 1017)* **SKIFFLE SESSION EP** 20 –
– Railroad Bill / Stackalee / Ballad of Jessie James / Ol' Riley.

Aug 56. (7"/78) *(7N/N 15071)* **BRING A LITTLE WATER, SYLVIE. / DEAD OR ALIVE** 7
(below lp hit the singles chart due to non-existence of UK lp chart)

Dec 56. (10"lp) *(NPT 19012)* **LONNIE DONEGAN SHOWCASE LP** 26 –
– Wabash cannonball / How long how long blues / Nobody's child / I shall not be moved / I'm Alabammy bound / I'm a rambling man / Wreck of the old '97 / Frankie and Johnny. *(re-iss. 1968 on 'Marble Arch'; MAL 797)*

Dec 56. (lp) *<M 920229>* **AN ENGLISHMAN SINGS AMERICAN FOLK SONGS** –

Jan 57. (7"/78) *(7N/N 15080)* **DON'T YOU ROCK ME, DADDY-O. / I'M ALABAMMY BOUND** 4

Mar 57. (7"/78) *(7N/N 15087)* **CUMBERLAND GAP. / LOVE IS STRANGE** 1

May 57. (7"/78) *(7N/N 15093)* **GAMBLIN' MAN. / PUTTING ON THE STYLE (live)** 1

Sep 57. (7"/78) *(7N/N 15108)* **MY DIXIE DARLING. / I'M JUST A ROLLING STONE** 10

Nov 57. (10"lp) *(NPT 19027)* **LONNIE** –
– Lonesome traveller / The sunshine of his love / Ain't no more cane on the Brazos / Ain't you glad you've got religion / Times are getting hard, boys / Lazy John / Light from the lighthouse / I've got my rocks in my bed / Long summer day. *(cd-iss. Feb00 on 'Sequel'+=; NEMCD 343)* – (extra tracks).

Dec 57. (7"/78) *(7N/N 15116)* **JACK O'DIAMONDS. / HAM 'N' EGGS** 14

Apr 58. (7"/78) *(7N/N 15129)* **THE GRAND COOLEE DAM. / NOBODY LOVES LIKE AN IRISHMAN** 6

Jun 58. (7"/78) *(7N/N 15148)* **SALLY, DON'T YOU GRIEVE. / BETTY, BETTY, BETTY** 11

Sep 58. (7"/78) *(7N/N 15158)* **LONESOME TRAVELLER. / TIMES ARE GETTING HARD BOYS** 28

Sep 58. (lp) *(NPL 18034)* **TOPS WITH LONNIE** –
– Don't you rock me, daddy-o / Putting on the style / Gamblin' man / My Dixie darling / Bring a little water, Sylvie / Cumberland gap / Grand Coulee Dam / Saly, don't you grieve / Nobody loves likes an Irishman / Lost John / Does your chewing gum lose it's flavour / Tom Dooley.

Nov 58. (7"/78) *(7N/N 15165)* **LONNIE'S SKIFFLE PARTY (medley part 1: LITTLE LIZA JANE – PUTTING ON THE STYLE – CAMPTOWN RACES – KNEES UP MOTHER BROWN. / (medley part 2: SO LONG – ON TOP OF OLD SMOKEY – DOWN IN THE VALLEY – SO LONG** 23 –

Nov 58. (7"/78) *(7N/N 15172)* **TOM DOOLEY. / ROCK O' MY SOUL** 3

Pye-Nixa Dot

Dec 58. (lp) *<DLP 3159>* **LONNIE DONEGAN** –

Jan 59. (7"/78) *(7N/N 15181)* *<15911>* **DOES YOUR CHEWING GUM LOSE ITS FLAVOUR. / AUNT RILEY** 3 Feb59
<US re-iss. Jul61; same> – hit No.5

Apr 59. (7"/78) *(7N/N 15198)* **FORT WORTH JAIL. / WHOA BUCK** 14

May 59. (lp) *(NPL 18043)* **LONNIE RIDES AGAIN**
– Fancy talking tinker / Miss Otis regrets / Jimmie Brown the newsboy / Mr. Froggy / Take this hammer / The gold rush is over / You pass me by / Talking guitar blues / John Hardy / House of the rising sun / San Miguel. *(re-iss. 1969 on 'Marble Arch'; MAL 1153) (cd-iss. Feb00 on 'Sequel'+=; NEMCD 344)* – (extra tracks).

Pye Atlantic

Jun 59. (7"/78) *(7N/N 15206)* **BATTLE OF NEW ORLEANS. / DARLING COREY** 2

Aug 59. (7"/78; Irish-only) *(7N/N 15219)* **KEVIN BARRY. / MY LAGAN LOVE** – –

Sep 59. (7"/78) *(7N/N 15223)* **SAL'S GOT A SUGAR LIP. / CHESAPEAKE BAY** 13

Nov 59. (7"/78) *(7N/N 15237)* **SAN MIGUEL. / TALKING GUITAR BLUES** 19

Dec 59. (lp) *<8038>* **SKIFFLE FOLK MUSIC** –

Mar 60. (7"/78) *(7N/N 15256)* **MY OLD MAN'S A DUSTMAN. / THE GOLDEN VANITY** 1

May 60. (7"/78) *(7N/N 15267)* **I WANNA GO HOME (THE WRECK THE THE JOHN). / JIMMY BROWN THE NEWSBOY** 5

Aug 60. (7"/78) *(7N/N 15275)* **LORELEI. / IN ALL MY WILDEST DREAMS** 10

Nov 60. (7") *(7N 15312)* **LIVELY. / BLACK CAT (CROSS MY PATH TODAY)** 13

Dec 60. (7") *(7N 15315)* **VIRGIN MARY. / BEYOND THE SUNSET** 27

Mar 61. (7") *(7N 15330)* **(BURY ME) BENEATH THE WILLOW. / LEAVE MY WOMAN ALONE**

Apr 61. (lp) *(NPL 18063)* **MORE! TOPS WITH LONNIE** –
– Battle of New Orleans / Lorelei / Lively! / Sal's got a sugar lip / I wanna go home / Leave my woman alone / My old man's a dustman / Fort Worth jail / Have a drink on me / (Bury me) Beneath the willow / Little Liza Jane / Puttin' on the style / Camptown races / Knees up, Mother Brown / On top of Old Smokey / Down in the valley / So long.

May 61. (7") *(7N 15354)* **HAVE A DRINK ON ME. / SEVEN DAFFODILS** [8] [ ]

Aug 61. (7") *(7N 15371)* **MICHAEL ROW THE BOAT. / LUMBERED** [6] [ ]

Jan 62. (7") *(7N 15410)* **THE COMMANCHEROS. / RAMBLIN' ROUND** [14] [ ]

Mar 62. (7") *(7N 15424)* **THE PARTY'S OVER. / OVER THE RAINBOW** [9] [ ]

Jun 62. (7") *(7N 15446)* **I'LL NEVER FALL IN LOVE AGAIN. / KEEP ON THE SUNNYSIDE** [ ] [–]

Aug 62. (7") *(7N 15455)* **PICK A BALE OF COTTON. / STEAL AWAY** [11] [ ]

Dec 62. (7") **THE MARKET SONG. / TIT-BITS (with MAX MILLER & The LONNIE DONEGAN GROUP)** [ ] [–]

Pye A.B.C.

Dec 62. (lp) *(NPL 18073)* **SING HALLELUJAH** [ ] [ ]
– Sing hallelujah / We shall walk through the valley / No hiding place / Good news, chariot's a-comin' / Noah found grace in the eyes of the Lord / Joshua fit the battle of Jericho / His eye is on the sparrow / Born in Bethlehem / This train / New burying ground / Steal away / Nobody knows the trouble I've seen. *(cd-iss. Feb00 on 'Sequel'+=; NEMCD 345)* – (extra tracks).

Apr 63. (7") *(7N 15514)* **LOSING BY A HAIR. / TRUMPET SOUNDS** [ ] [–]

Jun 63. (7") *(7N 15530)* **IT WAS A VERY GOOD YEAR. / RISE UP** [ ] [–]

Sep 63. (7") *(7N 15564)* **LEMON TREE. / I'VE GOTTA GIRL SO FINE** [ ] [–]

Nov 63. (7") *(7N 15579)* **500 MILES AWAY FROM HOME. / THIS TRAIN** [ ] [–]

Jul 64. (7") *(7N 15669)* **BEANS IN MY EARS. / IT'S A LONG ROAD TO TRAVEL** [ ] [–]

Sep 64. (7") *(7N 15679)* **FISHERMAN'S LUCK. / THERE'S A BIG WHEEL** [ ] [–]

Mar 65. (7") *(7N 15803)* **GET OUT OF MY LIFE. / WON'T YOU TELL ME** [ ] [–]

Jul 65. (7") *(7N 15893)* **LOUISIANA MAN. / BOUND FOR ZION** [ ] [–]

Aug 65. (lp) *(NPL 18126)* **THE LONNIE DONEGAN FOLK ALBUM** [ ] [–]
– I'm gonna be a bachelor / Interstate forty / After taxes / Where in the world are we going / Diamonds of dew / Bound for Zion / She was T-bone talking woman / Wedding bells / Reverend Mr. Black / The doctor's daughter / Blistered / Farewell. *(re-iss. 1967 on 'Golden Guinea'; GGL 0382) (cd-iss. Feb00 on 'Sequel'+=; NEMCD 346)* – (extra tracks).

Jan 66. (7") *(7N 15993)* **WORLD CUP WILLIE. / WHERE IN THIS WORLD ARE WE GOING** [ ] [–]

May 66. (7") *(7N 17109)* **I WANNA GO HOME. / BLACK CAT (CROSS MY PATH TODAY)** [ ] [–]

Jan 67. (7") *(7N 17232)* **AUNT MAGGIE'S REMEDY. / MY SWEET MARIE** [ ] [–]

Columbia not iss.

Mar 68. (7") *(DB 8371)* **TOYS. / RELAX YOUR MIND** [ ] [–]

Decca not iss.

Nov 69. (7") *(F 12984)* **MY LOVELY JUANITA. / WHO KNOWS WHERE THE TIME GOES** [ ] [–]

1970. (lp) *(SKL 5068)* **LONNIEPOPS – LONNIE DONEGAN TODAY** [ ] [–]
– Little green apples / Hey! hey! / First of May / Both sides now / If you go away / Love song to a princess / Who knows where the times goes / What the world needs now is love / My lovely Juanita / Windmills of your mind / Long haired lover from Liverpool / And you need me.

Pye not iss.

Nov 70. (7") *(7N 45009)* **BURNING BRIDGES. / I CAN'T TAKE IT ANY MORE** [ ] [–]

R.C.A. not iss.

Oct 71. (7") *(RCA 2128)* **COME TO AUSTRALIA. / DON'T BLAME THE CHILD** [ ] [–]

Pye not iss.

Oct 72. (7") *(7N 45184)* **SPEAK TO THE SKY. / GET OUT OF MY LIFE** [ ] [–]

Jun 73. (7"; by LONNIE DONEGAN & KENNY BALL) *(7N 45252)* **WHO'S GONNA PLAY THIS OLD PIANO. / SOUTH** [ ] [–]

Philips not iss.

1974. (lp) *(6305 227)* **LONNIE DONEGAN MEETS LEINEMANN** [–] German [–]
– Casey's last ride / Bottle of wine / Dixie darling / Frankie and Johnny / Tops at loving you / Gloryland / Leinemann's potatoes / Me and Bobby McGee / Does your chewing gum lose its flavour / Becky Deen / Jack o' diamonds.

1976. (lp) *(6305 288)* **COUNTRY ROADS** [–] German [–]
– Country roads / Rock island line / Keep on the sunny side / Dixie Lily / Louisiana man / Dead or alive / Midnight special / Muleskinner blues / Roll in my sweet baby's arms / Lost John / Have a drink on me / Dublin O'Shea.

Black Lion not iss.

Jul 76. (7") *(BSP 45105)* **LOST JOHN. / JENNY'S BALL** [ ] [–]

Decca not iss.

Aug 76. (7") *(FR 13669)* **I'VE LOST MY LITTLE WILLIE. / CENSORED** [ ] [–]

Chrysalis U.A.

Jan 78. (7") *(CHS 2205)* **ROCK ISLAND LINE. / HAM 'N' EGGS** [ ] [–]

Feb 78. (lp/c) *(CHR/ZCHR 1158)* *<UALA 827>* **PUTTIN' ON THE STYLE** [51] [ ]
– Rock Island line / Have a drink on me / Ham 'n' eggs / I wanna go home / Diggin' my potatoes / Nobody's child / Puttin' on the style / Frankie and Johnny / Drop down baby / Lost John.

Apr 78. (7") *(CHS 2211)* **PUTTIN' ON THE STYLE. / DROP DOWN BABY** [ ] [–]

May 79. (lp/c) *(CHR/ZCHR 1205)* **SUNDOWN** [ ] [–]
– I'm all out and down / Home / Streamline train / Sundown / Mama's got the know how / Morning light / Louisiana sun / The battle of New Orleans / Cajun / Dreaming my dreams with you.

Virgin not iss.

Nov 81. (7"ep; with the SHAKIN' PYRAMIDS) *(VS 460)* **CUMBERLAND GAP / WABASH CANNONBALL. / DON'T YOU ROCK ME DADDY-O / ONLY MY PILLOW / GRAB IT AND GROWL** [ ] [–]

—— next with guests MONTY SUNSHINE, CHRIS BARBER, KEN COLYER, etc

Dakota not iss.

Dec 81. (d-lp/d-c) *(ICSD/ZCICSD 2001)* **JUBILEE CONCERT (live Autumn 1981)** [ ] [–]
– Ace in the hole / Isle Of Capri / Going home / Shine / Jenny's ball / One sweet letter from you / Hush-a-bye / Bugle call march / Ice cream / John Henry / Take this hammer / Railroad Bill / Tom Dooley / New burying ground / Grand Coulee Dam / New York town / Miss Otis Regrets / Does your chewing gum lose its flavour on the bedpost overnight / One night of love / Rock island line / Gloryland / Corrina Corrina / Goodnight Irene.

Rosie's Records not iss.

Jul 87. (7"; with MONTY SUNSHINE) *(RR 015)* **DONEGAN'S DANCING SUNSHINE BAND. / LEAVING BLUES** [ ] [–]

—— In 1987 he turned actor, noteably in TV series 'Rockcliffe's Babies'

—— LONNIE returned with more stars as backing

Capo-RCA Capo-RCA

Jan 99. (cd) *(<CAPO 501>)* **MULESKINNER BLUES** [ ] [ ]
– Muleskinner blues (with VAN MORRISON) / Please don't call me in the morning / Rock island line / When I get off this feeling / Fancy talking tinker / I'm Alabammy bound (with VAN MORRISON) / Stewball / Skiffle / Welfare line / All together now / I don't wanna lose you / Poker club / Spanish nights / Always from the heart.

—— in Jan'2000, LONNIE hit the UK Top 20 (No.14) with VAN MORRISON and CHRIS BARBER on their album, 'THE SKIFFLE SESSIONS, LIVE IN BELFAST'

– (selective) compilations, etc. –

Aug 62. (lp) *Golden Guinea; (GGL 0135)* **A GOLDEN AGE OF DONEGAN** [3] [–]
(re-iss. 1966 on 'Marble Arch'; MAL 636)

Jan 63. (lp) *Golden Guinea; (GGL 0170)* **A GOLDEN AGE OF DONEGAN VOL.2** [15] [–]
(re-iss. 1967 on 'Marble Arch'; MAL 698)

Apr 92. (cd) *See For Miles; (SEECD 331)* **LONNIE DONEGAN – THE ORIGINALS** [ ] [–]

May 92. (cd/c) *See For Miles; (SEE CD/K 346)* **THE EP COLLECTION** [ ] [–]

Jul 92. (cd) *Kaz; (KAZCD 21)* **BEST OF LONNIE DONEGAN** [ ] [–]

Dec 92. (3xcd-box) *Sequel; (NXTCD 233)* **PUTTIN' ON THE STYLES** ☐ –

Oct 93. (cd) *See For Miles; (SEECD 382)* **THE EP COLLECTION VOL.2** ☐ –

Oct 93. (8xcd-box) *Bear Family; (BCD 15700)* **MORE THAN PIE IN THE SKY** ☐ ☐

Jun 99. (d-cd) *Jasmine; (JASCD 352/3)* **LONNIE DONEGAN MEETS LEINEMANN / COUNTRY ROADS** ☐ –

Aug 99. (cd) *Castle Pie; (PIESD 121)* **KING OF SKIFFLE** ☐ –

Sep 99. (d-cd) *Sequel; (NEECD 325)* **TALKING GUITAR BLUES – THE VERY BEST OF LONNIE DONEGAN** ☐ –

– Lost John / Stewball / Railroad Bill / Bring a little water, Sylvie / Dead or alive / Wabash cannonball / Nobody's child / Frankie and Johnny / Don't you rock me, daddy-o / Cumberland gap / Gamblin' man / Putting on the style / My Dixie darling / Jack O'Diamonds / On a Monday / Muleskinner blues / Grand Coulle Dam / Sally don't you grieve / Lonnie's skiffle (Little Liza Jane – Putting on the style – Camptown races – Little Liza Jane / Knees up mother Brown) / Tom Dooley / Does your chewing gum lose its flavour / Fort Worth jail / Battle of New Orleans / Sal's got a sugar lip / Take this hammer / You pass me by / San Miguel / Talking guitar blues / My old man's a dustman / I wanna go home / Lorelei / Sorry but I'm gonna have to pass / Lively / Virgin Mary / Have a drink on me / Michael row the boat ashore / Lumbered / The commancheros / The party's over / I'll never fall in love again / Pick a bale of cotton / This train / Noah found grace in the eyes of the Lord / Beans in my ears / She was T-bone talking woman / Farewell (fare thee well) / World Cup Willie.

Feb 00. (cd) *Sequel; (NEMCD 342)* **THE ORIGINAL ALBUMS REVISITED** ☐ –

Sep 00. (cd) *Delta; (47040)* **PUTTING ON THE STYLE** ☐ –

Sep 02. (3xcd-box) *Castle; (CMETD 580)* **ROCK ISLAND LINE: THE SINGLES ANTHOLOGY** ☐ ☐

Feb 03. (cd) *Sanctuary; (TYSAN 002)* **PUTTIN' ON THE STYLE – THE GREATEST HITS** 45 –

– Rock island line / Lost John / Bring a little water, Sylvie / Don't you rock me daddy-o / Cumberland gap / Gamblin' man / Puttin' on the style / My dixie darling / Jack o'Diamonds / The Grand Coolie dam / Sally don't you grieve / Tom Dooley / Does your chewing gum lose its flavour on the bedpost overnight / The battle of New Orleans / Sal's got a sugar lip / My old man's a dustman / I wanna go home / Lorelei / Lively! / Have a drink on me / Michael row the boat / Lumbered / The Comancheros / The party's over / Pick a bale o' cotton.

☐ Tanya DONELLY (see under ⇒ BELLY)

DONOVAN

Born: DONOVAN PHILIP LEITCH, 10 May'46, Maryhill, Glasgow, Scotland. At the age of 10, his family moved to Hatfield, England. In 1964, while playing small gigs in Southend, he was spotted by Geoff Stephens and Peter Eden, who became his managers. Later that year, after performing on the 'Ready Steady Go!' pop show over three consecutive weeks, the denim-clad beatnik signed to 'Pye'. His debut single, 'CATCH THE WIND' (issued the same time as DYLAN's 'The Times They Are A-Changin'), saw him break into the Top 5, later reaching Top 30 in America where he was enjoying the fruits of a burgeoning career. His follow-up, 'COLOURS', also made the Top 5 in the summer of '65, as did the debut album, 'WHAT'S BIN DID AND WHAT'S BIN HID'. Later in the year, the 'UNIVERSAL SOLDIER' EP saw DONOVAN begin to develop his uncompromising anti-war stance, a theme which he touched on with his second album, 'FAIRYTALE'. Initially heralded as Britain's answer to BOB DYLAN, he began to build on his folk/pop roots, progressing into flower-power with 'SUNSHINE SUPERMAN' in 1966. The album of the same name (issued only in the States) saw DONOVAN hit a creative high point and included the much revered, 'SEASON OF THE WITCH'. At the beginning of '67, the single 'MELLOW YELLOW' was riding high in the American hit parade, and 'EPISTLE TO DIPPY' soon followed suit. In the meantime, 'MELLOW YELLOW', was given a belated UK release (making Top 10), while its similarly titled parent album (again only issued in the US), hit No.14. 'SUNSHINE SUPERMAN', a UK compilation lp of both aforementioned albums, made the Top 30 in the middle of '67. His label, 'Pye', followed the same marketing strategy with his next UK album, the double 'A GIFT FROM A FLOWER TO A GARDEN', which was in actual fact, two US-only lp's in one. During this highly prolific period, which saw him inspired by the transcendental meditation of guru Maharishi Mahesh Yogi, he released two sublime pieces of acid-pop in 'THERE IS A MOUNTAIN' and 'JENNIFER JUNIPER'. The momentum continued with, 'HURDY GURDY MAN', another classic sojourn into psychedelia which hit Top 5 on both sides of the Atlantic. In 1969, he collaborated with The JEFF BECK GROUP on 'GOO GOO BARABAJAGAL', although this was his final 45 to make a major chart appearance. An album, 'OPEN ROAD' (1970), named after his new band, surprised many by cracking the US & UK charts. In 1971, he recorded a double album of children's songs 'H.M.S. DONOVAN', which led to a critical backlash from the music press. After a 3-year exile in Ireland for tax reasons, he set up home in California with his wife Linda Lawrence and daughters Astrella and Oriole. He has fathered two other children with his new American wife, Enid; DONOVAN LEITCH JNR. (star of the film 'Gas, Food, Lodging') and IONE SKYE, the latter said to be none too bothered about her famous father. DONOVAN enjoyed something of a renaissance in the early 90's when HAPPY MONDAYS' mainman SHAUN RYDER (now of BLACK GRAPE) sang his praises, leading to a comeback album, 'DONOVAN RISING'. He was still going strong in '96, releasing a well-received album, 'SUTRAS', for the RCA affiliated 'American' label. • **Songwriters:** Self-penned except, UNIVERSAL SOLDIER (Buffy Sainte-Marie) / LONDON TOWN (Tim Hardin) / REMEMBER THE ALAMO (Jane Bowes) / CAR CAR (Woody Guthrie) / GOLDWATCH BLUES (Mick Softley) / DONNA DONNA (Kevess-Secunda-Secanta-Schwartz-Zeitlin) / OH DEED I DO+ DO YOU HEAR ME NOW (Bert Jansch) / CIRCUS OF SOUR (Paul Bernath) / LITTLE TIN SOLDIER (Shawn Phillips / LORD OF THE DANCE (Sydney Carter) / ROCK'N'ROLL WITH ME (David Bowie-Warren Peace) / MY SONG IS TRUE (Darell Adams) / NO MAN'S LAND (Eric Bogle) / WIND IN THE WILLOWS (Eddie Hardin) / NEWEST BATH GUIDE + MOIRA McCAVENDISH (John Betjeman) / THE SENSITIVE KIND (J. J. Cale) / traditional:- KEEP ON TRUCKIN' + YOU'RE GONNA NEED SOMEBODY + CANDY MAN + THE STAR + COULTER'S CANDY + HENRY MARTIN + THE HEIGHTS OF ALMA + YOUNG BUT GROWING + STEALIN'. He also put music to words/poetry by; William Shakespeare (UNDER THE GREENWOOD TREE) / Gypsy Dave (A SUNNY DAY) / Lewis Carroll (WALRUS AND THE CARPENTER + JABBERWOCKY) / Thora Stowell (THE SELLER OF STARS + THE LITTLE WHITE ROAD) / Fifida Wolfe (LOST TIME) / Lucy Diamond (THE ROAD) / Agnes Herbertson (THINGS TO WEAR) / Edward Lear (THE OWL AND THE PUSSYCAT) / Eugene Field (WYNKEN, BLYNKEN AND NOD) / W. B. Yeats (THE SONG OF WANDERING AENGUS) / Natalie Joan (A FUNNY MAN) / Thomas Hood (QUEEN MAB) / Astella Leitch (MEE MEE I LOVE YOU) / Warwick Embury (ONE NIGHT IN TIME) / Note; HURLEY GURLEY MAN originally had a verse by GEORGE HARRISON but this was not recorded and he only added this for live appearances. • **Trivia:** DONOVAN sang co-lead on the title track from ALICE COOPER's 1973 lp 'Billion Dollar Babies'.

Album rating: WHAT'S BIN DID AND WHAT'S BIN HID (*7) / CATCH THE WIND (*6) / FAIRYTALE (*7) / SUNSHINE SUPERMAN (US version; *7) / MELLOW YELLOW (*6) / A GIFT FROM A FLOWER TO A GARDEN (*7; WEAR YOUR LOVE LIKE HEAVEN; *5 – FOR LITTLE ONES; *4) / DONOVAN IN CONCERT (*4) / HURDY GURDY MAN (*6) / DONOVAN'S GREATEST HITS compilation (*7) / BARABAJAGAL (*7) / OPEN ROAD (*5) / H.M.S. DONOVAN (*5) / COSMIC WHEELS (*5) / ESSENCE TO ESSENCE (*5) / 7-TEASE (*5) / SLOW DOWN WORLD (*4) / DONOVAN (*4) / NEUTRONICA (*4) / LADY OF THE STARS (*4) / GREATEST HITS AND MORE compilation (*8) / TROUBADOUR: THE DEFINITIVE COLLECTION compilation (*8) / SUTRAS (*5)

DONOVAN – vocals, acoustic guitar, harmonica with **BRIAN LOCKING** – bass / **SKIP ALLEN** – drums / **GYPSY DAVE** (b. DAVID MILLS) – kazoo, etc.

Pye Hickory

Mar 65. (7") *(7N 15801)* *<1309>* **CATCH THE WIND. / WHY DO YOU TREAT ME LIKE YOU DO** [4] Apr65 [23]

May 65. (7") *(7N 15866)* *<1324>* **COLOURS. / TO SING FOR YOU** [4] Jun65 [61]

May 65. (lp) *(NPL 18117)* *<123>* **WHAT'S BIN DID AND WHAT'S BIN HID** <US title 'CATCH THE WIND'> [3] [30]
– Josie / Catch the wind / Remember the Alamo / Cuttin' out / Car car * (riding in my car) / Keep on truckin' / Goldwatch blues / To sing for you / You're gonna need somebody on your bond / Tangerine puppet / Donna Donna * / Ramblin' boy *(re-iss. Jul68 on 'Marble Arch';)* – (omitted *)

Sep 65. (7") *<1338>* **UNIVERSAL SOLDIER. / DO YOU HEAR ME** [–] [53]

Sep 65. (7"ep) *(NEP 24219)* **THE UNIVERSAL SOLDIER EP** [13] [–]
– Universal soldier / The ballad of a crystal man / Do you hear me now* / The war drags on.

Oct 65. (lp) *(NPL 18128)* **FAIRYTALE** [20] Dec 65 [85]
– Colours * / To try for the sun / Sunny Goodge street / Oh deed I do / Circus of sour / The summer day reflection song / Candy man / Jersey Thursday / Belated forgiveness plea / Ballad of a crystal man / Little tin soldier * / Ballad of Geraldine. *(re-iss. Mar69 on 'Marble Arch';)* – (omitted *). *(re-iss. Feb91 on 'Castle' cd/c; CLA CD/MC 226)*

Nov 65. (7") *(7N 15984)* **TURQUOISE. / HEY GYP (DIG THE SLOWNESS)** [30] [–]

Nov 65. (7") *<1375>* **YOU'RE GONNA NEED SOMEBODY ON YOUR BOND. / THE LITTLE TIN SOLDIER** [–] [ ]

Jan 66. (7") *<1402>* **TO TRY FOR THE SUN. / TURQUOISE** [–] [ ]

Feb 66. (7") *(7N 17067)* **JOSIE. / LITTLE TIN SOLDIER** [ ] [–]

Apr 66. (7") *(7N 17088)* **REMEMBER THE ALAMO. / THE BALLAD OF A CRYSTAL MAN** [ ] [–]

—— **DONOVAN** plus **JOHN CAMERON** – piano, harpsicord / **HAROLD McNAIR** – flute

Pye Epic

Jul 66. (7") *(7N 17241)* *<10045>* **SUNSHINE SUPERMAN. / THE TRIP** [2] Jun66 [1]

Sep 66. (lp; mono><stereo) *<LN 24217><BN 26217>* **SUNSHINE SUPERMAN** [–] [11]
– Sunshine Superman / Legend of a girl child Linda / The observation / Guinevere / Celeste / Writer in the Sun / Season of the witch / Hampstead incident / Sand and foam / Young girl blues / Three kingfishers / Bert's blues. *(UK-iss.Feb91 on 'Beat Goes On' cd/c; BGO CD/MC 68) (cd re-iss. Oct96 on 'EMI Gold'; CDGOLD 1066)*

Nov 66. (7") *<10098>* **MELLOW YELLOW. / SUNNY SOUTH KENSINGTON** [–] [2]

Jan 67. (7") *<10127>* **EPISTLE TO DIPPY. / PREACHIN' LOVE** [–] [19]

Feb 67. (7") *(7N 17267)* **MELLOW YELLOW. / PREACHIN' LOVE** [8] [–]

Feb 67. (lp; mono><stereo) *<LN 24239><BN 26239>* **MELLOW YELLOW** [–] [14]
– Mellow yellow / Writer in the Sun / Sand and foam / The observation / Bleak city woman / House of Jansch / Young girl blues / Museum / Hampstead incident / Sunny South Kensington. *(cd-iss. Oct93 on 'Sony Europe';)*

Jun 67. (lp) *(NPL 18181)* **SUNSHINE SUPERMAN** [25] [–]
-(compilation of last 2 US albums)

Oct 67. (7") *(7N 17403)* *<10212>* **THERE IS A MOUNTAIN. / SAND AND FOAM** [8] Sep67 [11]

—— **DONOVAN** retained **HAROLD** and in came **TONY CARR** – percussion / **CANDY JOHN CARR** – bongos **CLIFF BARTON** – bass / **KEITH WEBB** – drums / **MIKE O'NEIL** – keyboards / **MIKE CARR** – vibraphone / **ERIC LEESE** – electric guitar

Dec 67. (7") *<10253>* **WEAR YOUR LOVE LIKE HEAVEN. / OH GOSH** [–] [23]

Dec 67. (lp; mono><stereo) *<LN 24349><BN 26349>* **WEAR YOUR LOVE LIKE HEAVEN** [–] [60]
– Wear your love like Heaven / Mad John's escape / Skip-a-long Sam / Sun / There was a time / Oh gosh / Little boy in corduroy / Under the greenwood tree / The land of doesn't have to be / Someone's singing / Song of the naturalist's wife / The enchanted gypsy.

—— **KEN BALDOCK** – bass repl. BARTON, LEESE, WEBB, O'NEIL + MIKE CARR

Dec 67. (lp; mono><stereo) *<LN 24350><BN 26350>* **FOR LITTLE ONES** [–] [ ]
– Voyage into the golden screen / Isle of Islay / The mandolin man and his secret / Lay of the last tinker / The tinker and the crab / Widow with shawl (a portrait) / The lullaby of spring / The magpie / Starfish-on-the-toast / Epistle to Derroll.

Feb 68. (7") *(7N 17457)* *<10300>* **JENNIFER JUNIPER. / POOR COW** [5] [26]

Apr 68. (d-lp-box; mono/stereo) *(NPL/NSPL 20000)* *<L2N6/B2N 171>* **A GIFT FROM A FLOWER TO A GARDEN** [13] [19]
– (contains 2 US Dec67 albums boxed) *(cd-iss. Jul93 & Jun97 on 'Beat Goes On'; BGOCD 194)*

May 68. (7") *(7N 17537)* *<10345>* **HURDY GURDY MAN. / TEEN ANGEL** [4] [5]

Sep 68. (lp; mono/stereo) *(NPL/NSPL 18237)* *<BN 26420>* **DONOVAN IN CONCERT (live)** [ ] Jul68 [18]
– Isle of Islay / Young girl blues / There is a mountain / Poor cow / Celeste / The fat angel / Guinevere / Widow with shawl (a portrait) / Preachin' love / The lullaby of Spring / Writer in the Sun / Rules and regulations / Pebble and the man / Mellow yellow. *(re-iss. May91 & Apr97 on 'Beat Goes On' cd/c/lp; BGO CD/MC/LP 90) (cd-iss. Nov94 on 'Start';) (re-iss. cd Jan96 on 'Happy Price'; HP 93432)*

Oct 68. (7") *<10393>* **LALENA. / AYE, MY LOVE** [–] [33]

Oct 68. (lp) *<BN 26420>* **HURDY GURDY MAN** [–] [20]
– Jennifer Juniper / Hurdy gurdy man / Hi, it's been a long time / Peregrine / The entertaining of a shy girl / Tangier / As I recall it / Get thy bearings / West Indian lady / Teas / The river song / The Sun is a very magic fellow / A sunny day.

Nov 68. (7") *(7N 17660)* **ATLANTIS. / I LOVE MY SHIRT** [23] [–]

Feb 69. (7") *<10434>* **ATLANTIS. / TO SUSAN ON THE WEST COAST WAITING** [–] [7] [35]

Mar 69. (lp) *(NPL/NSPL 18283)* *<BXN 26439>* **DONOVAN'S GREATEST HITS** (compilation) [ ] [4]
– Epistle to Dippy / Sunshine Superman / There is a mountain / Jennifer Juniper / Wear your love like Heaven / Season of the witch / Mellow yellow / Colours / Hurdy gurdy man / Catch the wind / Lalena. *<re-iss. 1972; PE 26439> <re-iss. 1973; BN 26836> (re-iss. Sep79 on 'CBS-Embassy' lp/c; CBS/40 31759) (cd-iss. Aug90 on 'Epic';)*

Jun 69. (7"; DONOVAN with The JEFF BECK GROUP) *(7N 17778)* **GOO GOO BARABAJAGAL (LOVE IS HOT). / BED WITH ME** [12] [–]

Sep 69. (7"; DONOVAN with The JEFF BECK GROUP) *<10510>* **GOO GOO BARABAJAGAL (LOVE IS HOT). / TRUDI** [–] [36]

Sep 69. (lp; DONOVAN with The JEFF BECK GROUP) *<BN 26481>* **BARABAJAGAL** [–] [ ]
– Barabajagal / Superlungs my supergirl / I love my shirt / The love song / To Susan on the West Coast waiting / Atlantis / Trudi / Pamela Jo / Happiness runs. *(cd-iss. Oct93 on 'Sony Europe';)*

—— with **JOHN CARR** – drums, vocals / **MIKE THOMPSON** – bass, vocals / **MIKE O'NEILL** – piano

Dawn Epic

Sep 70. (lp) *(DNLS 3009)* *<30125>* **OPEN ROAD** [30] Jul70 [16]
– Changes / Song for John / Curry land / Joe Bean's theme / People used to / Celtic rock / Riki tiki tavi / Clara clairvoyant / Roots of oak / Season of farewell / Poke at the Pope / New Year's resovolution. *(cd-iss. Sep00 on 'Repertoire'; REP 4880)*

Sep 70. (7"; DONOVAN with OPEN ROAD) *(DNS 1006)* *<10649>* **RIKI TIKI TAVI. / ROOTS OF OAK** [ ] [55]

—— (DANNY – double bass)

Dec 70. (7"; DONOVAN with DANNY THOMPSON) *(DNA 1007)* **CELIA OF THE SEALS. / MR.WIND** [ ] [–]

Feb 71. (7") *(10694>* **CELIA OF THE SEAS. / THE SONG OF THE WANDERING AENGUS** [–] [84]

Jul 71. (d-lp) *(DNLD 4001)* **H.M.S. DONOVAN** [–]
– The walrus and the carpenter / Jabberwocky / The seller of the stars / Lost time / The little white road / The star / Coulter's candy / The road / Things to wear / The owl and the pussycat / Homesickness / Fishes in love / Mr.Wind / Wynken, Bylnken and Nod / Celia of the seas / The pee song / The voyage to the Moon / The unicorn / Lord of dance / Little Ben / Can ye dance / In an old fashioned picture book / The song of the wandering Aengus / A funny man / Lord of the reedy river / Henry Martin / Queen Mab / La moor. *(cd-iss. Jan98 on 'Beat Goes On'; BGOCD 372)*

— with guests **CHRIS SPEDDING** – guitar / **JOHN 'RABBIT' BUNDRICK** – keyboards / **JIM HORN** – bass / **COZY POWELL** – drums

Epic Epic

Mar 73. (lp) *(SEPC 65450)* <32156> **COSMIC WHEELS** [15] [25]
– Cosmic wheels / Earth sign man / Sleep / Maria Magenta / Wild witch lady / Sleep / The music makers / The intergallactic laxative / I like you / Only the blues / Appearances. *(cd-iss. Sep94 on 'Epic-Rewind'; 477378-2)*

Apr 73. (7") *(EPC 1471)* <10983> **I LIKE YOU. / EARTH SIGN MAN** [66]

Jun 73. (7") *(EPC 1644)* <11023> **MARIA MAGENTA. / THE INTERGALLACTIC LAXATIVE**

— now with **STEVE MARRIOT, PETER FRAMPTON** and **NICKY HOPKINS**

Nov 73. (7") *(EPC 1960)* **SAILING HOMEWARD. / LAZY DAZE** [–]

Dec 73. (lp) *(SEPC 69050)* <32800> **ESSENCE TO ESSENCE**
– Operating manual for spaceship Earth / Lazy daze / Life goes on / There is an ocean / Dignity of man / Yellow star / Divine daze of deathless delight / Boy for every girl / Saint Valentine's angel / Life is a merry-go-round / Sailing homeward. *(cd-iss. Jan98; 489443-2)*

Jan 74. (7") <11108> **SAILING HOMEWARD. / YELLOW STAR** [–]

— Mainly used session musicians from now on.

Sep 74. (7") *(EPC 2661)* <50016> **ROCK'N'ROLL WITH ME. / THE DIVINE DAZE OF DEATHLESS DELIGHT** Nov74

Nov 74. (lp) *(SEPC 69104)* <33245> **7-TEASE**
– Rock and roll souljer / Your broken heart / Salvation stomp / The ordinary family / Ride-a-mile / Sadness / Moon rok / Love of my life / The voice of protest / How silly / The great song of the sky / The quest.

Jan 75. (7") <50077> **ROCK AND ROLL SOULJER. / HOW SILLY** [–]

Feb 75. (7") *(EPC 3037)* **ROCK AND ROLL SOULJER. / LOVE OF MY LIFE** [–]

Jun 76. (lp) *(SEPC 86011)* <33945> **SLOW DOWN WORLD**
– Dark-eyed blue jean angel / Cryin' shame / The mountain / Children of the world / My love is true (love song) / A well known has-been / Black widow / Slow down world / Liberation rag.

Jun 76. (7") <50237> **A WELL-KNOWN HAS-BEEN. / DARK EYED BLUE JEAN ANGEL** [–]

Rak Arista

Aug 77. (7") <0280> **DARE TO BE DIFFERENT. / THE INTERNATIONAL MAN** [–]

Oct 77. (lp) *(SRAK 528)* **DONOVAN** [–]
– Local boy chops wood / Astral angel / The light / Dare to be different / Brave new world / Lady of the stars / International man / Sing my song / Maya's dance / Kalifornia kids. *(cd-iss. Jun98 on 'Beat Goes On'; BGOCD 375)*

Nov 77. (7") *(RAK 265)* **THE LIGHT. / THE INTERNATIONAL MAN** [–]

Feb 78. (7") *(RAK 269)* **DARE TO BE DIFFERENT. / SING MY SONG** [–]

— (note:- on above US singles [Jan 73, Jan 75, Jun 76, Aug 77] the 'B' side was mono version on 'A').

Luggage-R.C.A. Allegiance

Aug 80. (lp) *(PL 28429)* **NEUTRONICA** [–]
– Shipwreck / Only to be expected / Comin' to you / No hunger / Neutron / Mee Mee I love you / The heights of Alma / No man's land / We are one / Madrigalinda / Harmony. *(cd-iss. May01 on 'Burning Airlines'+=; PILOT 089)* – (acoustic versions +).

— with **DANNY THOMPSON** – double bass / **JOHN STEPHENS** – drums / **TONY ROBERTS** – multi-wind instruments / and his 9 year-old daughter **ASTELLA** – dual vocals

Oct 81. (lp) *(PL 28472)* **LOVE IS ONLY FEELING** [–]
– Lady of the flowers / Lover o lover / The actor / Half Moon bay / The hills of Tuscany / Lay down Lassie / She / Johnny Tuff / Love is only feeling / Marjorie Margerine.

Oct 81. (7") *(7-LUG 03)* **LAY DOWN LASSIE. / LOVE IS ONLY FEELING** [–]

Jan 84. (lp) *(PL 70060)* <72857> **LADY OF THE STARS**
– Lady of the stars / I love you baby / Seasons of the witch / Bye bye girl / Every reason / Boy for every girl / Local boy chops wood / Sunshine superman / Til I see you again / Living for the lovelight.
After nearly 7 years in the wilderness, he returned on new label

Permanent Permanent

Nov 90. (cd/c/lp) *(PERM CD/MC/LP 2)* **DONOVAN RISING**
– Jennifer Juniper / Catch the wind / The hurdy gurdy man / Sunshine superman / Sadness / Universal soldier / Cosmic wheels / Atlantis / Wear your love like heaven / Colours / To Susan on the west coast waiting / Young girl blues / Young but growing / Stealing / Sailing homeward / Love will find a way / Lalena. *(d-cd-iss. Jul00 on 'Burning Airlines'; PILOT 059)*

— He had also credited on The SINGING CORNER's (Nov90) single version of his JENNIFER JUNIPER.

Silhouette not iss.

Apr 92. (cd-ep) *(MDCDKR 3)* **NEW BATH GUIDE / MOIRA McCAVENDISH / BROTHER SUN, SISTER MOON** [–]

American-RCA American

Oct 96. (cd) *(74321 39743-2)* **SUTRAS**
– Please don't bend / Give it all up / Sleep / Everlasting sea / High your love / The clear-browed one / The way / Deep peace / Nirvana / Eldorado / Be mine / Lady of the lamp / The evernow / Universe am I.

– (selective) compilations, etc. –

on 'Pye' UK / 'Hickory' (70's 'Epic') US unless otherwise mentioned

Sep 66. (lp) <135> **THE REAL DONOVAN** [–] [96]

Oct 67. (lp) *Marble Arch; (MAL 718)* **UNIVERSAL SOLDIER** [5] [–]
(re-iss. Feb83 on 'Spot'; SPR/SPC 8514)

Apr 68. (lp) <143> **LIKE IT IS, WAS AND EVERMORE SHALL BE** [–]

Jun 69. (lp) *United Artists; (UAS 29044)* **IF IT'S TUESDAY IT MUST BE BELGUIM** (soundtrack) [–]

Sep 89. (cd)(c/lp) *E.M.I.; (CZ 193)(TC+/EMS 1333)* **GREATEST HITS AND MORE** [–]
– Sunshine Superman / Wear your love like Heaven / Jennifer Juniper / Barabajagal (love is hot) / Hurdy gurdy man / Epistle to Dippy / To Susan on the West Coast waiting / Catch the wind / Mellow yellow / There is a mountain / Happiness runs / Season of the witch / Colours / Superlungs – My Supergirl / Lalena / Atlantis. *(cd+=)* – Preachin' love / Poor cow / Teen angel / Aye my love. *(lp re-iss. Dec99 on 'Simply Vinyl'; SVLP 155)*

Oct 90. (lp/c/cd) *See For Miles; (SEE/+K/CD 300)* **THE EP COLLECTION** [–]

Dec 90. (cd/c) *Castle; (CCS CD/MC 276)* **THE COLLECTION** [–]

Feb 91. (d-cd/d-c/d-lp) *E.M.I.; (CD/TC+/EM 1385)* **THE TRIP** (1964-1968 material)

Jul 98. (cd) *Epic; (480552-2)* **THE DEFINITE COLLECTION** [–]

Mar 00. (d-cd) *Essential; (ESDCD 861)* **ANTHOLOGY: SUMMER DAY REFLECTION SONGS**

Mar 99. (cd/c) *Platinum; (PLA TCD/C 435)* **THE TROUBADOUR**

Sep 02. (cd) *E.M.I.; (540777-2)* **SUNSHINE SUPERMAN: THE VERY BEST OF DONOVAN**

May 03. (d-cd) *Superior; (SU 2950-2)* **ATLANTIS: LIVE 1984-1986**

DOOBIE BROTHERS

Formed: San Jose, California, USA . . . 1970 by JOHN HARTMAN, TOM JOHNSTON (who had both played in an earlier incarnation of The DOOBIE BROTHERS, PUD, along with GREGG MURPHY) and DAVE SHOGREN. Starting out playing bar room boogie that was popular with local bikers, they signed to 'Warner Bros.'in 1971 and released an unsuccessful eponymous Ted Templeman produced album. Their second effort, 'TOULOUSE STREET', gave them their first gold disc and set the musical blueprint for the first half of their career. Coming on like an easy-listening ALLMANS, all crystal clear harmonies and laidback strumming, the band were quintessential Californian 70's rock. 'LISTEN TO THE MUSIC' was akin to an aural massage, while 'LONG TRAIN RUNNIN' from 'THE CAPTAIN AND ME' (1973) repeated the formula, its insidious chorus and foot shuffling groove taking it into the US Top 10. By now the DOOBIE's were selling millions, the country-rock of 'BLACK WATER', giving the band their No.1 in 1974. Its parent album, 'WHAT WERE ONCE VICES ARE NOW HABITS', and the follow-up, 'STAMPEDE' (1975) showed, however, that the sound was becoming tired. Thanks to JEFF BAXTER and MICHAEL McDONALD (both ex-STEELY DAN), the band underwent a timely, if subtle transformation from country boogie to polished, AOR funk. The former had joined before the band recorded 'STAMPEDE' while McDONALD arrived in late '75, initially to fill JOHNSTON's place on tour, the frontman giving up live commitments due to medical problems. McDONALD subsequently reworked the DOOBIE's back catalogue on stage, while writing most of the band's new material. Although many old fans were probably none too happy with the change, it certainly breathed new life into the band and while 'TAKIN' IT TO THE STREETS' (1976) was a marked improvement, the band were back at the top of the charts in 1978 with the multimillion selling 'MINUTE BY MINUTE'. The album also spawned a No.1 single in 'WHAT A FOOL BELIEVES', McDONALD's rich baritone now the essential ingredient in the DOOBIE BROTHERS sound (JOHNSTON having eventually left the previous year). The band then underwent a number of line-up changes before their final studio effort, 'ONE STEP CLOSER' (1980), although by this point McDONALD basically was the DOOBIE BROTHERS and it was inevitable he'd pack the band in for a solo career. The group officially split in March '82, recording a final farewell live album later that year. While McDONALD went on to a major solo success, The DOOBIE BROTHERS reformed in 1988 with a near-original line-up, JOHNSTON back in his role as frontman. The comeback album, 'CYCLES' (1989) went gold, spawning a Top 10 single with 'THE DOCTOR', although the follow-up set, 'BROTHERHOOD' (1991) was virtually ignored. Almost a decade on from that false re-start, the 'BROTHERS were back with the cheesily titled 'SIBLING RIVALRY' (2000). Again, the regrouped band attempted to relive that loose-hipped, harmony roots-rock of old and although they were never quite going to capture the heady atmosphere of those bearded, early 70's classics, they at least manage an enjoyably updated interpretation of it. • **Songwriters:** JOHNSTON or SIMMONS penned until MICHAEL McDONALD contributed on his 1975 arrival. JESUS IS JUST ALRIGHT (Byrds) / TAKE ME IN YOUR ARMS (Holland-Dozier-Holland) / LITTLE DARLIN' (I NEED YOU) (Marvin Gaye) / etc. WHAT A FOOL BELIEVES was co-written by McDONALD and KENNY LOGGINS. • **Trivia:** They took the name 'DOOBIE' from the slang for a joint.

Album rating: THE DOOBIE BROTHERS (*5) / TOULOUSE STREET (*6) / THE CAPTAIN AND ME (*7) / WHAT WERE ONCE VICES ARE NOW HABITS (*6) / STAMPEDE (*5) / TAKIN' IT TO THE STREETS (*7) / BEST OF THE DOOBIES compilation (*8) / LIVIN' ON THE FAULT LINE (*5) / MINUTE BY MINUTE (*7) / ONE STEP CLOSER (*4) / BEST OF THE DOOBIES, VOLUME II compilation (*6) / THE DOOBIE BROTHERS FAREWELL TOUR (*4) / CYCLES (*3) / BROTHERHOOD (*3) / LISTEN TO THE MUSIC – THE VERY BEST OF THE DOOBIES compilation (*7) / ROCKIN' DOWN THE HIGHWAY – THE WILDLIFE CONCERT (*4) / SIBLING RIVALRY (*4)

TOM JOHNSTON (b. Visalia, California) – vocals, guitar / **PAT SIMMONS** (b.23 Jan'50, Aberdeen, Washington) – guitar, vocals / **DAVE SHOGREN** (b. San Francisco, California) – bass / **JOHN HARTMAN** (b.18 Mar'50, Falls Church, Virginia) – drums

Warners Warners

Apr 71. (lp) *(K 46090) <1919>* **THE DOOBIE BROTHERS** [ ] [ ]
– Nobody / Slippery St. Paul / Greenwood creek / It won't be right / Travellin' man / Feelin' down farther / The master / rowin' a litle each day / Beehive state / Closer every day / Chicago. *(cd-iss. May95; 7599 26215-2)*

Apr 71. (7") *<7495>* **NOBODY. / SLIPPERY ST. PAUL** [–] [ ]

Jul 71. (7") *<7527>* **TRAVELIN' MAN. / FEELIN' DOWN FARTHER** [–] [ ]

Sep 71. (7") *<7544>* **BEEHIVE STATE. / CLOSER EVERY DAY** [–] [ ]

—— **TIRAN PORTER** (b. Los Angeles) – bass, vocals repl. SHOGREN.

added 2nd drummer **MICHAEL HOSSACK** (b.18 Sep'50, Paterson, New York, USA)

Jul 72. (lp) *(K 46183) <2634>* **TOULOUSE STREET** [ ] [21]
– Listen to the music / Don't start me talkin' / Mamaloi / Toulouse Street / Rockin' down the highway / Jesus is just alright / White sun / Cotton mouth / Disciple / Snake man. *(quad-lp 1976) (cd-iss. Jul88; K2 46183) (cd-iss. May93; 7599 27263-2)*

Aug 72. (7") *<7619>* **LISTEN TO THE MUSIC. / TOULOUSE STREET** [–] [11]
(UK-iss.Feb74; K 16208) – hit No.29

Dec 72. (7") *<7661>* **JESUS IS JUST ALRIGHT. / ROCKIN' DOWN THE HIGHWAY** [–] [35]

Mar 73. (lp) *(K 46217) <2694>* **THE CAPTAIN AND ME** [ ] [7]
– Natural thing / Long train runnin' / China Grove / Dark-eyed Cajun woman / Clear as the driven snow / Without you / South city midnight lady / Evil woman / Busted down around O'Connelly corners / Ukiah / The captain and me. *(cd-iss. Oct87 & Feb95; K2 46217)*

Apr 73. (7") *<7698>* **LONG TRAIN RUNNIN'. / WITHOUT YOU** [–] [8]
(UK-iss.Apr74; K 16267)

Aug 73. (7") *<7728>* **CHINA GROVE. / EVIL WOMAN** [–] [15]
(UK-iss.Aug74; K 16310)

—— **KEITH KNUDSON** (b.18 Oct'52, Ames, Iowa) – drums (ex-MANDELBAUM); repl. HOSSACK / added **BILL PAYNE** – keyboards (ex-LITTLE FEAT)

Feb 74. (lp/c) *(K/K4 56026) <2750>* **WHAT WERE ONCE VICES ARE NOW HABITS** [19] [4]
– Song to see you through / Spirit / Pursuit on 53rd street / Black water / Eyes of silver / Road angel / You just can't stop it / Tell me what you want / Down in the track / Another park, another Sunday / Flying cloud. *(quad-lp US 1976) (cd-iss. Jul88; K2 56026) (cd re-iss. May93; 7599 2780-2)*

Apr 74. (7") *<7795>* **ANOTHER PARK, ANOTHER SUNDAY. / BLACK WATER** [–] [32]

Aug 74. (7") *(K 16450) <7832>* **EYES OF SILVER. / YOU JUST CAN'T STOP IT** [ ] Jul74 [52]

Oct 74. (7") *<8041>* **NOBODY. / FLYING CLOUD** [–] [58]

Dec 74. (7") *<8062>* **BLACK WATER. / SONG TO SEE YOU THROUGH** [–] [1]

—— **JEFF BAXTER** (b.13 Dec'48, Washington, D.C.) – guitar (ex-STEELY DAN) repl. PAYNE who rejoined LITTLE FEAT

Apr 75. (lp/c) *(K/K4 56094) <2835>* **STAMPEDE** [14] [4]
– Sweet Maxine / Neal's fandango / Texas lullaby / Music man / Slat key sequel rag / Take me in your arms / I cheat the hangman / Precis / Rainy day crossroad blues / I've been workin' on you / Double dealin' four flusher. *(cd-iss. Jun89; 927289-2) (cd-iss. May93; 7599 27289-2)*

Apr 75. (7") *(K 16559) <8092>* **TAKE ME IN YOUR ARMS. / SLAT KEY SEQUEL RAG** [29] [ ]

Jul 75. (7") *(K 16601) <8126>* **SWEET MAXINE. / DOUBLE DEALIN' FOUR FLUSHER** [ ] [40]

Nov 75. (7") *<8161>* **I CHEAT THE HANGMAN. / MUSIC MAN** [–] [60]

—— **MICHAEL McDONALD** (b.12 Feb'52, St.Louis, Missouri) – keyboards, vocals (ex-STEELY DAN) repl. JOHNSTON who fell ill

Mar 76. (lp/c) *(K/K4 56196) <2899>* **TAKIN' IT TO THE STREETS** [42] [8]
– Wheels of fortune / Takin' it to the streets / 8th Avenue shuffle / Losin' end / Rio / For someone special / It keeps you runnin' / Turn it loose / Carry me away. *(cd-iss. Jun89 & Jul93; 927289-2)*

Mar 76. (7") *(K 16559) <8196>* **TAKIN' IT TO THE STREETS. / FOR SOMEONE SPECIAL** [ ] [13]

Aug 76. (7") *<8233>* **WHEELS OF FORTUNE. / SLAT KEY SEQUEL RAG** [–] [87]

Nov 76. (7") *<8282>* **IT KEEPS YOU RUNNIN'. / TURN IT LOOSE** [–] [37]

Nov 76. (lp/c) *(K/K4 56308) <2978>* **THE BEST OF THE DOOBIES** (compilation) [ ] [5]
– China Grove / Long train runnin' / Takin' it to the streets / Listen to the music / Black water / Rockin' down the highway / Jesus is just alright / It

keeps you runnin' / South city midnight lady / Take me in your arms (rock me a little while) / Without you. *(cd-iss. 1988; K2 56308)*

Jan 77. (7") *(K 16835)* **LISTEN TO THE MUSIC. / LONG TRAIN RUNNIN'** [ ] [–]

— **TOM JOHNSTON** returned but left again early '77 to go solo

Jul 77. (7") *(K 16989) <8408>* **LITTLE DARLING (I NEED YOU). / LOSING END** [ ] [48]

Aug 77. (lp/c) *(K/K4 56383) <3045>* **LIVIN' ON THE FAULT LINE** [25] [10]
– You're made that way / Echoes of love / Little darling (I need you) / You belong to me / Livin' on the fault line / Nothin' but a heartache / Chinatown / There's a light / Need a lady / Larry the logger two-step. *(cd-iss. Jun89; 927315-2)*

Sep 77. (7") *(K 17044) <8471>* **ECHOES OF LOVE. / THERE'S A LIGHT** [ ] [66]

Mar 78. (7") *<8500>* **LIVIN' ON THE FAULT LINE. / NOTHIN' BUT A HEARTACHE** [–] [ ]

Dec 78. (lp/c) *(K/K4 56486) <3193>* **MINUTE BY MINUTE** [ ] [1]
– Sweet feelin' / Open your eyes / Dependin' on you / Here to love you / Minute by minute / You never change / What a fool believes / Steamer lane breakdown / How do the fools survive? / Don't stop to watch the wheels. *(cd-iss. 1988; K2 56486)*

Feb 79. (7") *(K 17314) <8725>* **WHAT A FOOL BELIEVES. / DON'T STOP TO WATCH THE WHEELS** [31] Jan79 [1]

Apr 79. (12") *(K 17362)* **WHAT A FOOL BELIEVES. / DON'T STOP TO WATCH THE WHEELS / IT KEEPS YOU RUNNIN'** [72] [–]

Apr 79. (7") *<8828>* **MINUTE BY MINUTE. / SWEET FEELIN'** [–] [14]

Jul 79. (7") *(K 17411)* **MINUTE BY MINUTE. / HOW DO THE FOOLS SURVIVE?** [47] [–]

Jul 79. (7") *<49029>* **DEPENDIN' ON YOU. / HOW DO THE FOOLS SURVIVE?** [–] [25]

Aug 79. (7") *(K 17461)* **OPEN YOUR EYES. / STEAMER LANE BREAKDOWN** [ ] [–]

— **JOHN McFEE** (b.18 Nov'53, Santa Cruz, California) – guitar, vocals; repl. BAXTER / **CHET McCRACKEN** (b.17 Jul'52, Seattle, Washington) – drums, vibes (ex-session man) repl. HARTMAN / added **CORNELIUS BUMPUS** (b.13 Jan'52) – keyboards, sax (ex-MOBY GRAPE) / (now septet alongside **SIMMONS, McDONALD, PORTER + KNUDSEN**)

Aug 80. (7") *<49503>* **REAL LOVE. / THANK YOU LOVE** [–] [5]

Oct 80. (lp/c) *(K/K4 56824) <3452>* **ONE STEP CLOSER** [53] [3]
– Dedicate this heart / Real love / No stoppin' us now / Thank you love / One step closer / Keep this train a-rollin' / Just in time / South bay strut / One by one. *(cd re-iss. Jan96; 7599 26628-2)*

Nov 80. (7") *(K 17707) <49622>* **ONE STEP CLOSER. / SOUTH BAY STRUT** [ ] [24]

Jan 81. (7") *<49642>* **WYNKEN, BLYNKEN AND NOD. / IN HARMONY** [–] [76]
(above credited w/ KATE + SIMON TAYLOR)

Jan 81. (7") *<49642>* **KEEP THIS TRAIN A-ROLLIN'. / JUST IN TIME** [–] [62]

Nov 81. (lp/c) *(K/K4 56956) <3612>* **THE BEST OF THE DOOBIES VOLUME II** (compilation) [ ] [39]
– Little darlin' / Echoes of love / You belong to me / One step closer / What a fool believes / Dependin' on you / Here to love you / One by one / Real love / Minute by minute.

Jan 82. (7") *<50001>* **HERE TO LOVE YOU. / WYNKEN, BLYNKEN AND NOD** [–] [65]

— **WILLIE WEEKS** – bass repl. PORTER

— split Mar'82, recorded final concert album Sep'82

WEA WEA

Jun 83. (d-lp/d-c) *(923 772-1/-4) <23772>* **THE DOOBIE BROTHERS FAREWELL TOUR (live)** [ ] [79]
– Slippery St. Paul / Takin it to the streets / Jesus is just alright / Minute by minute / Can't let it get away / Listen to the music / Echoes of love / What a fool believes / Black water / You belong to me / Slat key sequel rag / Streamer lane breakdown / South city / Midnight lady / Olana / Don't start me to talking / Long train runnin' / China grove.

Jul 83. (7") *<29552>* **YOU BELONG TO ME (live). / SOUTH CITY MIDNIGHT LADY (live)** [–] [79]

— By this time MICHAEL McDONALD had gone solo, as did PATRICK SIMMONS. **DOOBIE BROTHERS** reformed mid'88. (JOHNSTON, HARTMAN, SIMMONS, PORTER) plus **MICHAEL HOSSACK** – drums / **BOBBY LaKIND** (b.1945) – percussion

Capitol Capitol

Jul 89. (7") *(CL 536) <44376>* **THE DOCTOR. / TOO HIGH A PRICE** [73] May89 [9]
(12"+=/cd-s+=) *(12/CD CL 536)* – Anything for love.

Jul 89. (cd/c/lp) *(CD/TC+/EST 2100) <90371>* **CYCLES** [ ] Jun89 [17]
– The doctor / One chain (don't make no prison) / Take me to the highway / South of the border / Time is here and gone / Need a little taste of love / I can read your mind / Wrong number / Tonight I'm coming through (the border) / Too high a price.

Sep 89. (7") *(CL 552) <44441>* **NEED A LITTLE TASTE OF LOVE. / I CAN READ YOUR MIND** [ ] Aug89 [45]
(12"+=/cd-s+=) *(12/CD CL 552)* – The doctor.

May 91. (cd/c/lp) *(CD/TC+/EST 2141) <94623>* **BROTHERHOOD** [ ] [82]
– Something you said / Is love enough / Dangerous / Our love / Divided highway / Under the spell / Excited / This train I'm on / Showdown / Rollin' on.

— On the 24th December '92, LaKIND died of cancer

— vocalists now **TOM JOHNSTON, MICHAEL McDONALD + PATRICK SIMMONS**

Columbia Sony

Aug 96. (d-cd) *(484452-2)* **ROCKIN' DOWN THE HIGHWAY – THE WILDLIFE CONCERT (live)** [ ] Jul96 [ ]
– China grove / What a fool believes / Dangerous / Jesus is just alright / Rockin' down the highway / Dependin' on you / Eyes of silver / Another park another Sunday / Slack key sequel rag (instrumental) / South city midnight lady / Clear as the driven snow / Black water / Wild ride / Slow burn / The doctor / Take me in your arms (rock me) / Long train runnin' / Without you / Excited / Dark eyed Cajun woman / Neal's fandango / Listen to the music / Minute by minute / Takin' it to the streets.

— **JOHNSTON + SIMMONS** with **KEITH KNUDSEN** – drums

Eagle Rhino

Oct 00. (cd) *(EAGCD 049) <8122 75809-2>* **SIBLING RIVALRY** [ ] [ ]
– People gotta love again / Leave my heartache behind / Ordinary man / Jericho / On every corner / Angels of madness / 45th floor / Can't stand to lose / Higher ground / Gates of Eden / Don't be afraid / Rocking horse / Five corners.

– compilations etc. –

on 'Warners' unless mentioned otherwise

Nov 84. (d-c) *(K4 66117)* **TAKIN' IT TO THE STREETS / LIVIN' ON THE FAULT LINE** [ ] [–]

Mar 86. (7") *Old Gold; (OG 9573)* **LISTEN TO THE MUSIC. / WHAT A FOOL BELIEVES** [ ] [–]

Jan 87. (7") *(W 8451)* **WHAT A FOOL BELIEVES. / MINUTE BY MINUTE** [57] [–]
(12"+=) *(W 8451T)* – Real love.

May 93. (cd) *F.N.A.C.; ()* **INTRODUCING . . .** [ ] [–]

May 93. (cd/c) *(9548 31094-2/-4)* **LISTEN TO THE MUSIC – THE VERY BEST OF THE DOOBIE BROTHERS** [ ] [ ]
(re-iss. May94 cd/c; 9548 32803-2/-4)

Nov 93. (7"/c-s) *(W 0217/+C)* **LONG TRAIN RUNNIN'. / ('A'mix)** [7] [–]
(12"+=/cd-s+=) *(W 0217 T/CD)* – ('A'mix).

Apr 94. (7"/c-s) *(W 0228/+C)* **LISTEN TO THE MUSIC ('94 remix). / ('A'mix)** [37] [–]
(12"+=/cd-s+=) *(W 0228 T/CD)* – ('A'remixes by MOTIV8 / RAMP . . . / DEVELOPMENT CORPORATION).

Feb 96. (cd) *B.A.M.; (KLMCD 055)* **THE EARLY YEARS** [ ] [–]

May 97. (cd) *Experience; (EXP 014)* **THE DOOBIE BROTHERS** [ ] [–]

— JOHN HARTMAN who was a reserve fireman /policeman was refused promotion by his home state court, due to his alleged drug-taking past

DOORS

Formed: Los Angeles, California, USA . . . July 1965 by RAY MANZAREK and JIM MORRISON. In 1966, after some personnel changes, they soon settled with JOHN DENSMORE and ROBBY KRIEGER and became The DOORS. They were released from a 'Columbia' recording contract, when ARTHUR LEE (of LOVE), recommended them to his 'Elektra' label boss Jac Holzman. Early in 1967, their eponymous debut album was issued, which soon climbed to US No.2 after an edited version of 'LIGHT MY FIRE' hit No.1 in July '67. The single and album showcased MORRISON's overtly sexual vocal theatrics against a backdrop of organ-dominated, avant-garde blues. The classic debut also contained two cover versions (see below), the lucid psychedelia of 'THE CRYSTAL SHIP', plus the extremely disturbing 11-minute epic, 'THE END' (which was later used on the soundtrack for the 1979 Francis Ford Coppola film, 'Apocalypse Now'). While other bands of the era were into peace and love, The DOORS found their salvation in a much darker vision, again in evidence on the follow-up (also in '67), 'STRANGE DAYS'. This was another classic, tracks like, 'LOVE ME TWO TIMES', 'YOU'RE LOST LITTLE GIRL' and 'PEOPLE ARE STRANGE' further enhancing the band's powerful mystique. As MORRISON's drink and drugs antics became increasingly problematic, he was arrested many times (on stage and off), mostly for lewd simulation of sexual acts and indecent exposure. Nevertheless, in the late summer of '68, they found themselves at the top of the US charts again with the 45, 'HELLO I LOVE YOU' and the album, 'WAITING FOR THE SUN'. A disappointing 4th album, 'THE SOFT PARADE' (1969), did, however, contain a classic US Top 3 hit, 'TOUCH ME'. More controversy was generated, when, in November '69, MORRISON was accused of interfering with an airline stewardess while a flight was in progress. He was later acquitted, but the following year, was given eights months hard labour after being found guilty of indecent exposure and profanity. He was freed on appeal and began work on 1970's, 'MORRISON HOTEL / HARD ROCK CAFE', a return to rawer, more basic rock'n'roll. After the recording of 'L.A. WOMAN', he relocated to Paris in the Spring of '71 with his girlfriend Pamela, amid rumours of an imminent split from the group. The aforementioned album was delivered in June, a masterpiece that carried on the re-evaluation of their blues roots. His over-indulgence in drugs and booze, had given his vocal chords a deeper resonance, showcased on such classics as, 'RIDERS ON THE STORM' (a Top 30 hit), 'LOVE HER MADLY', the JOHN LEE HOOKER cover 'CRAWLING KING SNAKE' and the freewheeling title track. Ironically, just as the band seemed to have found their feet again, JIM MORRISON was found dead in his bathtub on the 3rd of July 1971. Speculation was rife at the time, but it later became apparent he had died from a drugs/drink induced heart attack. He was also buried in Paris, his grave becoming a shrine to all but his parents, who disowned him in 1967. The others continued as a trio for the next two years, but sadly the public refused to acknowledge them as the real DOORS. The "god-like" cult of MORRISON has mushroomed to incredible proportions in the years following his death, rumours continuing, Elvis-like, to circulate that he was still alive. There have been many imitators over the last quarter of a century, although none have matched his/their dark majesty. MANZAREK and KRIEGER re-actified a new post-millennium version of the group in 2003 (The DOORS OF THE 21st CENTURY), choosing ex-CULT man IAN ASTBURY(!) to front them. • **Songwriters:** MORRISON – words/poetry (under the influence of explorative narcotics), Group/MANZAREK compositions. Covered; ALABAMA SONG (Brecht-Weill) / BACK DOOR MAN (Howlin' Wolf) / WHO DO YOU LOVE (Bo Diddley) / LITTLE RED ROOSTER (Willie Dixon) / BEEN DOWN SO LONG (J.B. Lenoir). • **Trivia:** In 1968, they featured on a UK TV documentary 'The Doors Are Open', which was later issued on video. In 1991, Oliver Stone released a feature film 'THE DOORS', with Val Kilmer playing the role of MORRISON.

Album rating: THE DOORS (*9) / STRANGE DAYS (*8) / WAITING FOR THE SUN (*6) / THE SOFT PARADE (*5) / MORRISON HOTEL – HARD ROCK CAFE (*8) / ABSOLUTELY LIVE (*6) / 13 compilation (*8) / L.A. WOMAN (*9) / OTHER VOICES (*4) / WEIRD SCENES INSIDE THE GOLDMINE compilation (*8) / FULL CIRCLE (*4) / AN AMERICAN PRAYER – JIM MORRISON exploitation (*4) / GREATEST HITS compilation (*8) / ALIVE, SHE CRIED exploitation (*4) / BEST OF THE DOORS compilation (*8) / LIVE AT THE HOLLYWOOD BOWL exploitation (*4) / THE DOORS soundtrack (*5) / IN CONCERT exploitation (*5) / GREATEST HITS compilation (*9) / THE COMPLETE STUDIO RECORDINGS boxed-set (*8)

JIM MORRISON (b. 8 Dec'43, Melbourne, Florida) – vocals / **RAY MANZAREK** (b.12 Feb'35, Chicago, Illinois) – keyboards, bass pedal / **ROBBY KRIEGER** (b. 8 Jan'46) – guitar / **JOHN DENSMORE** (b. 1 Dec'45) – drums / also guest **DOUG LUBAHN** – bass (of CLEAR LIGHT)

Date	Release	Elektra		Elektra
Feb 67.	(7") *(EKSN 45009)* <45611> **BREAK ON THROUGH (TO THE OTHER SIDE). / END OF THE NIGHT**		Jan67	
Mar 67.	(lp; mono/stereo) <*(EKL/EKS 74007)*> **THE DOORS** – Break on through (to the other side) / Soul kitchen / The crystal ship / Twentieth century fox / Alabama song (whiskey song) / Light my fire / Back door man / I looked at you / End of the night / Take it as it comes / The end. *(re-iss. Nov71 lp/c; K/K4 42012) (cd-iss. Jan84; K2 42012) (re-iss. cd Feb89; 974007-2) (re-hit UK No.43 in Apr91)*		Mar 67	1
Apr 67.	(7") *(EKSN 45012)* **ALABAMA SONG (WHISKEY BAR). / TAKE IT AS IT COMES**			–
Jul 67.	(7") *(EKSN 45014)* <45615> **LIGHT MY FIRE (edit). / THE CRYSTAL SHIP** *(re-iss. Jul71; same)*	49	Jun67	1
Sep 67.	(7") *(EKSN 45017)* <45621> **PEOPLE ARE STRANGE. / UNHAPPY GIRL**			12
Dec 67.	(lp; mono/stereo) <*(EKL/EKS 74014)*> **STRANGE DAYS** – Strange days / You're lost little girl / Love me two times / Unhappy girl / Horse latitudes / Moonlight drive / People are strange / My eyes have seen you / I can't see your face in my mind / When the music's over. *(re-iss. Nov71 lp/c; K/K4 42016) (cd-iss. Jan86; K2 42016) (cd re-iss. Feb89; 974014-2)*		Nov67	3
Dec 67.	(7") *(EKSN 45022)* <45624> **LOVE ME TWO TIMES. / MOONLIGHT DRIVE**			25
Apr 68.	(7") *(EKSN 45030)* <45628> **THE UNKNOWN SOLDIER. / WE COULD BE SO GOOD TOGETHER** *(re-iss. Jun71; K 12004)*		Mar68	39
Aug 68.	(7") *(EKSN 45037)* <45635> **HELLO, I LOVE YOU. / LOVE STREET**	15	Jul68	1

—— **LEROY VINEGAR** – acoustic bass repl. LABAHN

Date	Release	Elektra		Elektra
Sep 68.	(lp; mono/stereo) <*(EKL/EKS 74024)*> **WAITING FOR THE SUN** – Hello I love you / Love street / Not to touch the Earth / Summer's almost gone / Wintertime love / The unknown soldier / Spanish caravan / My wild love / We could be so good together / Yes, the river flows / Five to one. *(re-iss. Nov71 lp/c; K/K4 42041) (cd-iss. Jan86; K2 42041) (cd re-iss. Feb89; 974024-2)*	16	Aug68	1
Dec 68.	(7") *(EKSN 45050)* <45646> **TOUCH ME. / WILD CHILD**			3
May 69.	(7") *(EKSN 45059)* <45656> **WISHFUL SINFUL. / WHO SCARED YOU**		Mar69	44
Aug 69.	(7") *(EKSN 45065)* <45663> **TELL ALL THE PEOPLE. / EASY RIDE**		Jun69	57
Sep 69.	(lp) <*(EKS 75005)*> **THE SOFT PARADE** – Tell all the people / Touch me / Shaman's blues / Do it / Easy ride / Wild child / Runnin' blue / Wishful sinful / The soft parade. *(re-iss. Nov71 lp/c; K/K4 42079) (cd-iss. Feb89; 975005-2)*		Aug69	6
Sep 69.	(7") <*45675*> **RUNNIN' BLUE. / DO IT**	–		64

—— guest **LONNIE MACK** – bass repl. LUBAHN

Date	Release	Elektra		Elektra
Apr 70.	(7") <*45685*> **YOU MAKE ME REAL. / ROADHOUSE BLUES**	–		50
Apr 70.	(7") *(2101 004)* **YOU MAKE ME REAL. / THE SPY**			–
Apr 70.	(lp) <*(EKS 75007)*> **MORRISON HOTEL / HARD ROCK CAFE** – Land ho! / The spy / Queen of the highway / Indian summer / Maggie McGill / Roadhouse blues / Waiting for the sun / You make me real / Peace frog / Blue Sunday / Ship of fools. *(re-iss. Nov71 lp/c; K/K4 42080) (cd-iss. Apr86; K2 42080) (re-iss. cd.Feb89; 975007-2)*	12	Mar70	4
Jul 70.	(7") *(2101 008)* **ROADHOUSE BLUES. / BLUE SUNDAY**			–
Sep 70.	(d-lp) *(2665 002)* <*9002*> **ABSOLUTELY LIVE (live)** – Who do you love medley: Alabama song – Back door man – Love hides –	69	Aug70	8

Five to one / Build me a woman / When the music's over / Close to you / Universal mind / Break on through (to the other side) / The celebration of the lizard / Soul kitchen. *(re-iss. Nov71 d-lp; K 62005) (d-cd-iss. Mar87 w-drawn; 2665 002)*

Oct 70. (7") *<45708>* **UNIVERSAL MIND. / THE ICEWAGON FLEW** [–] [ ]

Mar 71. (lp/c) *(K/K4 42062) <74079>* **13** (compilation) [ ] Dec70 [25]
– Light my fire / People are strange / Back door man / Moonlight drive / The crystal ship / Roadhouse blues / Touch me / Love me two times / You're lost little girl / Hello, I love you / Land ho / Wild child / The unknown soldier.

—— guest **JERRY SCHEFF** – bass repl. MACK

May 71. (7") *<(EK 45726)>* **LOVE HER MADLY. / (YOU NEED MEAT) DON'T GO NO FURTHER** [ ] Apr71 [11]

Jun 71. (lp/c) *(K/K4 42090) <75011>* **L.A. WOMAN** [26] May71 [9]
– The changeling / Love her madly / Been down so long / Cars hiss by my window / L.A. woman / L'America / Hyacinth house / Crawling King Snake / The wasp (Texas radio and the big beat) / Riders on the storm. *(cd-iss. 1984; K2 42090) (cd re-iss. Feb89 & Apr91; 975011-2)*

Jul 71. (7") *(K 12021) <45738>* **RIDERS ON THE STORM (edit). / THE CHANGELING** [22] [14]

—— **RAY** – vocals, ROBBIE and JOHN carried on when JIM MORRISON died 3rd Jul'71 of a mysterious heart attack. The trio continued on

—— (MANZAREK now on vox). Used guest session bassmen **WILLIE RUFF, WOLFGANG MERTZ** and **JACK CONRAD**

Nov 71. (7") *(K 12036) <45757>* **TIGHTROPE RIDE. / VARIETY IS THE SPICE OF LIFE** [ ] [71]

Dec 71. (lp/c) *(K/K4 42104) <75017>* **OTHER VOICES** [ ] Nov71 [31]
– In the eye of the sun / Variety is the spice of life / Ships w.sails / Tightrope ride / Down on the farm / I'm horny, I'm stoned / Wandering musician / Hang on to your life

May 72. (7") *(K 12048) <45768>* **SHIP W. SAILS. / IN THE EYE OF THE SUN** [ ] [ ]

—— bass sessions **J. CONRAD, CHARLES LARKEY, LEE SKLAR and CHRIS ETHRIDGE.**

Aug 72. (7") *(K 12059) <45793>* **GET UP AND DANCE. / TREETRUNK** [ ] [ ]

Aug 72. (lp/c) *(K/K4 42116) <75038>* **FULL CIRCLE** [ ] [68]
– Get up and dance / Four billion souls / Verdilac / Hardwod floor / Good rockin' / The mosquito / The piano bird / It slipped my mind / The Peking king and the New York queen.

Sep 72. (7") *<45807>* **THE MOSQUITO. / IT SLIPPED MY MIND** [–] [85]

Dec 72. (7"w-drawn) **THE PIANO BIRD. / GOOD ROCKIN'** [–] [–]

—— They finally split 1973. MANZAREK went solo and KRIEGER & DENSMORE formed The BUTTS BAND. With JESS RODEN as lead singer / **PHILIP CHEN** – bass / **ROY DAVIS** – keyboards, they made 2 albums for 'Blue Thumb' records; 'THE BUTTS BAND' (1974) / 'HEAR AND NOW' (1975).

– compilations, etc. –

Note; All on 'Elektra' until mentioned otherwise

Mar 72. (d-lp/d-c) *(K/K4 62009) <6001>* **WEIRD SCENES INSIDE THE GOLD MINE** [50] Feb72 [55]
– Break on through (to the other side) / Strange days / Shaman's blues / Love street / Peace frog / Blue Sunday / The wasp (Texas radio and the big beat) / End of the night / Love her madly / Ship of fools / The spy / The end / Take it as it comes / Running blue / L.A. woman / Five to one / Who scared you? / Don't go no further / Riders on the storm / Maggie McGill / Horse latitudes / When the music's over.

Sep 74. (lp/c) *(K/K4 42143) <5035>* **THE BEST OF THE DOORS** [ ] [ ]

Feb 76. (7") *(K 12203)* **RIDERS ON THE STORM. / L.A. WOMAN** [33] [–]

Sep 76. (7") *(K 12227)* **LIGHT MY FIRE. / THE UNKNOWN SOLDIER** [ ] [–]

Sep 76. (7") *(K 12228)* **LOVE HER MADLY. / TOUCH ME** [ ] [–]

Nov 78. (lp/c; by JIM MORRISON) *(K/K4 52111) <502>* **AN AMERICAN PRAYER** (poetry recorded 8 Nov'70 with some DOORS tapes) [ ] [54]
– Awake / Ghost song / Dawn's highway / Newborn awakening / To come of age / Black polished chrome / Latino chrome / Angels and sailors / Stoned immaculate / The poet's dreams / The movie / Curses invocations / World on fire / American night / Roadhouse blues / Lament / The hitchhiker / An American prayer. *(re-iss. May95 cd/c/lp;)*

Jan 79. (7") *(K 12215)* **LOVE ME TWO TIMES. / HELLO I LOVE YOU** [ ] [–]
(w/ free 7"+=) *(SAM 94)* – GHOST SONG. / ROADHOUSE BLUES

Jan 79. (7") **ROADHOUSE BLUES. / AN AMERICAN PRAYER** [–] [ ]

Jan 80. (7")<12"> *(K 12400) <ELK 22032>* **THE END. / (b-side 'Delta' not by The DOORS)** [ ] [–]

Oct 80. (lp/c) *(K/K4 52254) <515>* **GREATEST HITS** [ ] [17]
– Hello, I love you / Light my fire / People are strange / Love me two times / Riders on the storm / Break on through / Roadhouse blues / Touch me / L.A. woman / Love her madly / The ghost song / The end. *(cd-iss. Oct95 cd/c; 7559 61860-2/-4)*

Oct 80. (7") **PEOPLE ARE STRANGE. / NOT TO TOUCH THE EARTH** [–] [ ]

Oct 82. (d-c) *(K4 62034)* **MORRISON HOTEL / L.A. WOMAN** [ ] [–]

Oct 83. (7") *<60269>* **GLORIA (live). / MOONLIGHT DRIVE (live)** [–] [71]

Oct 83. (12") *(E 9774T)* **GLORIA (live). / LOVE ME TWO TIMES (live)** [ ] [–]

Oct 83. (lp/c) *(960269-1/-4) <60269>* **ALIVE SHE CRIED (live)** [36] [23]
– Gloria / Light my fire / You make me real / The wasp (Texas radio and the big beat) / Love me two times / Little red rooster / Moonlight drive. *(cd-iss. Jul84; 960269-2)*

Aug 84. (d-c) *(K4 62040)* **THE SOFT PARADE / AN AMERICAN PRAYER** [ ] [ ]

Jun 85. (lp/c) *(EKT 9/+C) <60417>* **CLASSICS** [ ] [ ]

Sep 85. (7") *Old Gold; (OG 9520)* **RIDERS ON THE STORM. / LIGHT MY FIRE** [ ] [–]

Nov 85. (d-lp/c/cd) *(EKT 21/+C/CD) <60345>* **BEST OF THE DOORS** [ ] [ ]
– Break on through (to the other side) / Light my fire / The crystal ship / People are strange / Strange days / Love me two times / Five to one / Waiting for the Sun / Spanish caravan / When the music's over / Hello, I love you / Roadhouse blues / L.A. woman / Riders on the storm / Touch me / Love her madly / The unknown soldier / The end. (cd+=) – Alabama song (whiskey bar). *(re-iss. Apr91 hit UK No.17 & US No.32) (re-iss. Mar98, hit UK No.37)*

Jun 87. (m-lp/c)(cd) *(EKT 40/+C)(960741-2) <60741>* **LIVE AT THE HOLLYWOOD BOWL (live)** [ ] [ ]
– Wake up / Light my fire / The unknown soldier / A little game / The hill dwellers / Spanish caravan.

Mar 91. (lp/c)(cd) *(EKT 85/+C)(961047) <61047>* **THE DOORS: A FILM BY OLIVER STONE – MUSIC FROM THE ORIGINAL SOUNDTRACK** [11] [8]

Apr 91. (7") *(EKR 121)* **BREAK ON THROUGH. / LOVE STREET** [64] [ ]
(12"+=/cd-s+=) *(EKR 125 TW/CD)* – Hello I love you / Touch me.

May 91. (7") *(EKR 125)* **LIGHT MY FIRE. / PEOPLE ARE STRANGE** [7] [ ]
(ext; 12"+=/cd-s+=) *(EKR 125 TW/CD)* – Soul kitchen.

May 91. (t-lp/d-c)(d-cd) *(EKT 88/+C)(7559 61082) <61082>* **THE DOORS: IN CONCERT (live)** [24] [50]

Jul 91. (7") *(EKR 131)* **RIDERS ON THE STORM. / LOVE ME TWO TIMES (live)** [68] [ ]
(12"+=/cd-s+=) *(EKR 131 TW/CD)* – Roadhouse blues (live).

Jun 95. (c-s; by JIM MORRISON & THE DOORS) *(EKR 205C)* **THE GHOST SONG. / (interview)** [ ] [ ]
(cd-s+=) *(EKR 205CD)* – Love me two times (live) / Roadhouse blues (live).

Oct 97. (4xcd-box) *<(7559 62123-2)>* **THE DOORS BOX SET** [ ] [65]

Nov 99. (cd) *<(7559 62475-2)>* **STONED IMMACULATE** [ ] [ ]

Nov 99. (7xcd-box) *<(7559 62434-2)>* **THE COMPLETE STUDIO RECORDINGS** [ ] [ ]

Sep 00. (cd/c) *<(7559 62468-2/-4)>* **THE BEST OF THE DOORS** [9] [ ]
– Riders on the storm / Light my fire / Love me two times / Roadhouse blues (live) / Strange days / Break on through / Five to one / Moonlight drive / Alabama song / Love her madly / People are strange / Touch me / Backdoor man / The unknown soldier / L.A. woman / Hello I love you / The end. *<(d-cd+=; 7559 62569-2)>*

Sep 01. (cd) *<79376>* **THE VERY BEST OF THE DOORS** [–] [92]

Oct 01. (4xcd-box) *(7559 62716-2)* **THE DOORS BOX SET** [ ] [–]

DOVES

Formed: Manchester, England . . . 1998 out of dance/rave outfit, SUB SUB, by JIMI GOODWIN, along with brothers JEZ and ANDY WILLIAMS. After the hectic turbulence of the house scene in the late 80's/early 90's, SUB SUB protagonist GOODWIN rocketed straight into the number 5 spot with 'AIN'T NO USE (AIN'T NO LOVE)', which predictably ruined any future respect given to the man. A shambolic, rushed released debut album, 'FULL FATHOM FIVE' (1993), sent GOODWIN into hiding for four years (during which he cropped up on various material by TRICKY and BERNARD SUMNER). In 1998, a new direction forced out the 'CEDAR' EP, which The DOVES issued on their own 'Casino' label. Sounding similar to OASIS and heavy rivals SHACK, frontman GOODWIN did his best to capture the essence and mad-for-it-ness that he'd experienced during the early 1990's. However, the music lacked interest, and, although long drawn and enterprising at times, the tired trio sounded as magnificent as RADIOHEAD without any transmitter. With two further singles under their belt, 'Heavenly' records ('Astralwerks' in the US) gave The DOVES a lucrative signing-on deal, the single 'THE CEDAR ROOM' and its parent debut album, 'LOST SOULS', both making healthy chart positions in spring 2000. The feted DOVES were now darlings of Britain's emotional indie scene, ranking alongside major players such as COLDPLAY, STARSAILOR and troubadour DAVID GRAY. However, come the release of their sophomore album 'THE LAST BROADCAST' (2002), the bearded troupe of musing musicians had formally eclipsed any of the above in terms of musical and lyrical integrity. Taking its name from the 1998 "mocumentary", which was said to have inspired 'The Blair Witch Project', '. . .BROADCAST' generated emotional intensity from its dreamlike artwork to GOODWIN's vocals. The single, 'THERE GOES THE FEAR', used child-like guitar melodies and striking orchestral accompaniment courtesy of SEAN O'HAGAN (The HIGH LLAMAS), not to mention a tripped-out video to boot. Where most bands fall flat on their face come album Number deux, the DOVES had simply evolved into something splendid and sublime – well, like a pristine dove, walking amongst a flock of dirty pigeons that currently litter Britain's indie scene. • **Covers:** HIT THE GROUND RUNNING (Warren Zevon) / WILLOW'S SONG (trad.) / M62 SONG (King Crimson). • **Note:** Not to be confused with an early 90's DOVES who issued one album, 'Affinity', in 1991.

Album rating: Sub Sub: FULL FATHOM FIVE (*5) / Doves: LOST SOULS (*8) / THE LAST BROADCAST (*8) / LOST SIDES collection (*6)

SUB SUB

JIMI GOODWIN – vocals, guitar / **JEZ WILLIAMS** – vocals, guitar / **ANDY WILLIAMS** – vocals, drums

Rob's — not iss.

Jun 92. (12"ep) *(12ROB 7)* **COAST EP** □ –
– Coast / Inside of this / Inside out / Past.

Mar 93. (7"/c-s; as SUB SUB featuring MELANIE WILLIAMS) *(7/C ROB 9)* **AIN'T NO LOVE (AIN'T NO USE. / (parkside mix)** 3 –
(12"+=/cd-s+=) *(12/CD ROB 9)* – ('A'mixes; piano / on the house).

Feb 94. (7"/c-s) *(7/C ROB 19)* **RESPECT. / (original)** 49 –
(12"+=/cd-s+=) *(12/CD ROB 19)* – ('A'-DaSilva – McCreedy + acid) / ('A'-primetime).

Aug 94. (c-s) *(CROB 29)* **ANGEL / SOUTHERN TREES (instrumental)** □ –
(12"+=/cd-s+=) *(12/CD ROB 29)* – ('A'-Deep love + Primetime).
(12") *(12ROB 29X)* – ('A'mixes).

Sep 94. (cd/c/lp) *(CD/C/LP ROB 30)* **FULL FATHOM FIVE** □ □
– Coast / Angel / Valium jazz / Southern trees / Inside of this / Ain't no love (ain't no use) / Flute / Swamp / Respect / Past.

Jan 95. (12"/cd-s) *(12/CD ROB 39)* **SOUTHERN TREES (7" + 12" mixes). / JAGGERNATH / NORTHERN TREES** □ –

—— wisely decided to take some time out

DOVES

—— same line-up

Casino — not iss.

Nov 98. (10"ep) *(CHIP 001)* **CEDAR EP** □ –
– The cedar room / Rise / Zither.

—— the track, 'GUTTER GIRL', featured on the V/A Manchester compilation EP, 'Everyone Knows Everyone Else' alongside JANE WEAVER and ANDY VOTEL

May 99. (cd-ep) *(CHIP 002CD)* **SEA EP** □ –
– Sea song / Breakmegently (incidently) / Darker.

Aug 99. (10"/cd-s) *(CHIP 003/+CD)* **HERE IT COMES. / MEET ME AT THE PIER / ACOUSTIC NO.1** 73 –

Heavenly — Astralwerks

Mar 00. (10"/cd-s) *(HVN 95 10/CD)* **THE CEDAR ROOM. / ZITHER / KAREN** 33 –

Apr 00. (d-lp/cd) *(HVNLP 26/+CD)* *<ASW 50248 LP/CD>* **LOST SOULS** 16 Oct00 □
– Firesuite / Here it comes / Break me gently / Sea song / Rise / Lost souls / Melody calls / Catch the sun / The man who told everything / The cedar room / Reprise / A house.

May 00. (10"/cd-s) *(HVN 96 10/CDS)* **CATCH THE SUN. / VALLEY / DOWN TO SEA** 32 –
(cd-s) *(HVN 96CD)* – ('A'side) / Crunch / Lost in watts.

Oct 00. (7") *(HVN 98)* **THE MAN WHO TOLD EVERYTHING. / YOUR SHADOW LAY ACROSS MY LIFE** 32 –
(c-s+=/cd-s+=) *(HVN 98 CS/CD)* – Firesuite.
(cd-s) *(HVN 98CDS)* – ('A'side) / Rise (live) / Suitnoise.

Heavenly — Capitol

Apr 02. (10") *(HVN 111-10)* **THERE GOES THE FEAR. / HIT THE GROUND RUNNING** 3 –
(cd-s) *(HVN 111CD)* – ('A'side) / ('A'-video).

Apr 02. (d-lp/cd) *(HVNLP 35/+CD)* *<12232>* **THE LAST BROADCAST** 1 83
– Intro / Words / There goes the fear / M62 song / Where we're calling from / N.Y. / Satellites / Friday's dust / Pounding / The last broadcast / The sulphur man / Caught by the river.

Jul 02. (10") *(HVN 116-10)* **POUNDING. / SATELLITES (Soulsavers remix) / M62 SONG (Four Tet remix)** 21 –
(cd-s) *(HVN 116CD)* – ('A'side) / Far from grace / Northenden / ('A'-video).

Oct 02. (10") *(HVN 126-10)* **CAUGHT BY THE RIVER. / THE SULPHUR MAN (Rebelski remix) / WHERE WE'RE CALLING FROM (Hebden Bridge remix)** 29 –
(cd-s) *(HVN 126CD)* – ('A'side) / Hit the ground running / Willow's song / ('A'-video).

Sep 03. (cd) *(HVNLP 46CD)* **LOST SIDES** (collection) 50 –
– Break me gently (incidental) / Darker / Your shadow lay across my life / Meet me at the pier / Down to sea / Crunch / Zither / Valley / Northenden / Hit the ground running / Willow's song / Far from grace. *(ltd d-cd+=; HVNLP 46CDX)* – Words (Echoboy remix) / N.Y. (Chris Coco remix) / M62 song (Four Tet remix) / The sulphur man (Rebelski remix) / The last broadcast (Magnet remix) / Where we're calling from (Hebden Bridge remix) / Satellites (Soulsavers remix).

□ DOWN (see under ⇒ PANTERA)

Nick DRAKE

Born: 19 Jun'48, Burma. He moved to Britain in the mid 50's, first to Tamworth-in-Ardon then Stratford. Already a budding singer-songwriter by the time he reached Cambridge University, he was discovered playing a gig by ASHLEY HUTCHINGS of Fairport Convention, who, in turn, introduced him to Witchseason

Productions head JOE BOYD. Bowled over by his talent, BOYD helped him sign to 'Island', who released debut album 'FIVE LEAVES LEFT' in '69. The album highlighted his precocious talent and painful sensitivity, the music possessing a remarkable maturity not in keeping with DRAKE's young years. The melancholic resonance of DRAKE's voice and his crystalline guitar playing were complemented by delicate string arrangements, the effect one of understated intensity. After moving to London, DRAKE recorded the classic 'BRYTER LAYTER' in 1970 with BOYD again producing a cast of musicians that included RICHARD THOMPSON and JOHN CALE. The album boasted a jazzier flavour which saw DRAKE in a slightly more positive frame of mind. Ironically, like its predecessor, the album failed to sell in any great quantity. Due to his crippling shyness, DRAKE found live work too difficult, passing up the opportunity to promote his music. He fell into a deep depression, no doubt frustrated at his lack of success and inability to do something about it. After a spell in Europe he returned to record his tortured masterpiece, 'PINK MOON'. Recorded in just two nights, its spare, haunting songs were cloaked in regret and disillusionment. The bleak tone only let up occasionally as DRAKE attemted to exorcise his demons over a skeletal acoustic backing. Once again, the album was a commercial failure and DRAKE's mood blackened further, although he did begin work on a new album in 1973. He spent time in France with singer/friend FRANCOISE HARDY and his bouts of depression diminished when he decided to live there permanently. However, this didn't last long and he sadly overdosed on anti-depressants on 25th November 1974, a tragic end to a troubled but brilliant career. A questionable coroner's verdict was "Death By Suicide". The subsequent interest in DRAKE's work led to various compilations being released, including the excellent 'FRUIT TREE' boxed set. His music entrances more listeners with each passing year, a belated recognition that recently saw him grace the cover of 'Mojo' magazine. • **Trivia:** His sister Gabrielle was a TV actress in the 70's/80's 'Crossroads' soap.

Album rating: FIVE LEAVES LEFT (*8) / BRYTER LAYTER (*9) / PINK MOON (*9) / HEAVEN IN A WILD FLOWER posthumous (*7) / FRUIT TREE – THE COMPLETE RECORDED WORKS collection (*9) / TIME OF NO REPLY (*7) / WAY TO BLUE – AN INTRODUCTION TO NICK DRAKE compilation (*9)

NICK DRAKE – vocals, guitar, piano with **RICHARD THOMPSON** – guitar / **DANNY THOMPSON** – double bass / **PAUL HARRIS** – keyboards / **CLAIRE LOWTHER** and **ROCKY DZIDZORNU,** plus 15-piece orchestra.

Island Antilles

Sep 69. (lp) *(ILPS 9105) <AN 7010>* **FIVE LEAVES LEFT** [ ] [ ]
– Time has told me / River man / Three hours / Day is done / Way to blue / Cello song / The thoughts of Mary Jane / Man in a shed / Fruit tree / Saturday sun. *(cd-iss. Feb87; CID 9195) (re-iss. cd May89 & Jun00; IMCD 8) (lp re-iss. Jan00 on 'Simply Vinyl'; SVLP 163)*

— retained **RICHARD** bringing in other (FAIRPORT CONVENTION members: **DAVE PEGG** – drums / **DAVE MATTACKS** – bass. Also sessioned **PAUL HARRIS, RAY WARLEIGH, CHRIS McGREGOR.**

Nov 70. (lp) *(ILPS 9134) <7028>* **BRYTER LAYTER** [ ] [ ]
– Introduction / Hazey Jane II / At the chime of a city clock / One of these things first / Hazey Jane I / Bryter layter / Fly / Poor boy / Northern sky / Sunday. *(cd-iss. May87; CID 9134) (re-iss. cd Oct89 & Jun00; IMCD 71) (lp re-iss. Jun99 on 'Simply Vinyl'; SVLP 94)*

— **NICK DRAKE** – vocals, guitar (totally solo)

Feb 72. (lp) *(ILPS 9184)* **PINK MOON** [ ] [-]
– Pink moon / Place to be / Road / Which will / Horn / Things behind the sun / Know / Parasite / Ride / Harvest breed / From the morning / Voice from the mountain / Rider on the wheel / Black eyed dog / Hanging on a star. *(cd-iss. Apr90 & Jun00; IMCD 94) (lp re-iss. Feb00 on 'Simply Vinyl'; SVLP 172)*

— NICK had put down some tracks for new album, when on 25th Nov'74, he overdosed on medication/drugs.

– compilations, others, etc. –

1972. (lp) *Island; <9307>* **NICK DRAKE** (69-70 material) [-] [ ]

Apr 79. (3xlp-box) *Island; (NDSP 100)* **FRUIT TREE – THE COMPLETE RECORDED WORKS** [ ] [-]
– (contains all 3 albums)

May 85. (lp/c) *Island; (ILPS 9826)* **HEAVEN IN A WILD FLOWER** [ ] [ ]
– Fruit tree / Cello song / Thoughts of Mary Jane / Northern sky / River man / At the chime of the city clock / Introduction / Hazey Jane I / Hazey Jane II / Pink moon / Road / Which will / Things behind the sun / Time has told me. *(cd-iss. Apr90; IMCD 91)*

Aug 86. (4xlp-box) *Hannibal / Rykodisc; (HNBX 5302)* **FRUIT TREE** [ ] [ ]
– (all 3 lp's, plus 1987 album) *(4xcd-box-iss.Dec91; HNCD 5402)(+=)* – TIME OF NO REPLY / Fruit tree / Fly / Man in a shed / Thoughts of Mary Jane.

Mar 87. (lp/cd) *Hannibal / Rykodisc; (<HNBL/HNCD 1318>)* **TIME OF NO REPLY** [ ] [ ]
– Time of no reply / I was made to love magic / Joey / Clothes of sand / Man in a shed / Mayfair / Fly / The thoughts of Mary Jane / Been smoking too long / Strange meeting II / Rider on the wheel / Black eyed dog / Hanging on a star / Voice from the mountain.

Jun 94. (cd)(c/lp) *Island; (IMCD 196)(ICM/ILPM 2082) <1386>* **WAY TO BLUE – AN INTRODUCTION TO NICK DRAKE** [ ] [ ]
– Cello song / Hazey Jane I / Way to blue / Things behind the sun / River man / Poor boy / Time of no reply / From the morning / One of these things first / Northern sky / Which will / Hazey Jane II / Time has told me / Pink moon / Black eyed dog / Fruit tree. *(cd re-iss. May03; IMCD 299)*

Nov 99. (cd-ep) *Sonic Book; <SB 20>* **THE SWEET SUGGESTIONS OF THE PINK MOON** [ ] [-]
– When day is done / Saturday sun / Way to blue / Time has told me.

Jun 00. (lp) *Anthology; (ANT 1521)* **TAMWORTH IN ARDEN** [ ] [-]
(cd-iss. Jan02; ANT 1500)

Nov 02. (lp) *N.R.D.; (1)* **TIME HAS TOLD ME** [ ] [-]

☐ DR. DRE (see under ⇒ N.W.A.)

DREAM SYNDICATE

Formed: Los Angeles, California, USA . . . 1981 by STEVE WYNN and female bassist KENDRA SMITH. The former had previously cut his teeth with SID GRIFFIN in an embryonic LONG RYDERS. They soon completed the line-up with KARL PRECODA and DENNIS DUCK. After an untitled mini-lp back home, they caught the interest of UK indie, 'Rough Trade', in 1983, who released their debut full-length album 'THE DAYS OF WINE AND ROSES'. Cut from a distinctly rougher-hewn cloth than most of the band's 'Paisley Underground' contemporaries, the album's dark intensity caused enough of a stir to eventually get them snapped up by 'A&M'. By the release of their major label debut, 'MEDICINE SHOW' (1984), KENDRA SMITH had been replaced by DAVE PROVOST. Although more mainstream than its predecessor, the album still showed the ragged influence of NEIL YOUNG and THE VELVET UNDERGROUND and while it didn't accrue the success it was probably due, its critical acclaim paved the way for other majors to give them a shot at the big league. After a final album for 'A&M', the compilation of early live material, 'IT'S NOT THE NEW DREAM SYNDICATE ALBUM' (1985), the band released their next studio offering on 'Chrysalis', 1986's 'OUT OF THE GREY'. Despite the more commercial, straight ahead rock sound of the record, success continued to elude the band and they split in early 1989 after releasing a final well-received album for 'Enigma', 'GHOST STORIES'. With a vocal style more leaning towards NEIL YOUNG than LOU REED, STEVE WYNN embarked on a solo career at the turn of the decade. Albums such as 'KEROSENE MAN' (1990) and 'DAZZLING DISPLAY' (1991) set out his stall and further established the man as Paisley Underground's leader of the pack. From 1993 to 1995 he combined solo work alongside a new side project, GUTTERBALL (featuring BOB RUPE of The SILOS and ex-HOUSE OF FREAKS members), although this minor supergroup only delivered two sets, 'GUTTERBALL' and 'WEASEL'. In 2001, after a handful of unremarkable low-key sets ('PICK OF THE LITTER not even worthy of a British or American release), WYNN was back on song with 'HERE COME THE MIRACLES'. WYNN went on to a productive solo career, garnering plaudits for lean, hard-nosed albums such as 'MELTING IN THE DARK' (1996) and 'SWEETNESS AND LIGHT' (1997). Now well into middle age and still straining at the musical leash, WYNN reached a post-DREAM SYNDICATE career peak of sorts with 'STATIC TRANSMISSION' (2003), a record full of the kind of acerbic force of will which seems to have long deserted his peers. • **Songwriters:** Most written by WYNN, except covers CINNAMON GIRL (Neil Young) / BALLAD OF DWIGHT FRYE (Alice Cooper) / LET IT RAIN (Derek & The Dominoes) / SHAKE YOUR HIPS (Slim Harpo) / THE LONELY BULL (... Lake) / MR. SOUL (Buffalo Springfield). WYNN covered KOOL THING (Sonic Youth) / BONNIE & CLYDE (Serge Gainsbourg) / WATCHING THE RIVER FLOW (Bob Dylan) / VENUS (Shocking Blue) / TIGHTEN UP (Booker T & The MG's) / CRAZY FEELING (Lou Reed) / BOY IN THE BUBBLE (Paul Simon) / WHY DOES LOVE GOT TO BE SO SAD (Eric Clapton) / THE AIR THAT I BREATHE (Hollies) / GUTTERBALL mainly WYNN with HARVEY or McCARTHY. • **Trivia:** Early '85, STEVE WYNN was also in DANNY & DUSTY duo alongside old cohort DAN STUART (of GREEN ON RED).

Album rating: THE DAYS OF WINE AND ROSES (*7) / THE MEDICINE SHOW (*7) / THIS IS NOT THE NEW DREAM SYNDICATE ALBUM (*4) / OUT OF THE GREY (*6) / 50 IN A 25 ZONE (*4) / GHOST STORIES (*5) / LIVE AT RAJI'S (*7) / TELL ME WHEN IT'S OVER: THE BEST OF DREAM SYNDICATE compilation (*8) / Steve Wynn: KEROSENE MAN (*6) / DAZZLING DISPLAY (*6) / TAKE YOUR FLUNKY AND DANGLE collection (*5) / FLUORESCENT (*5) / GUTTERBALL by Gutterball (*5) / WEASEL by Gutterball (*5) / MELTING IN THE DARK (*6) / SWEETNESS & LIGHT (*5) / MY MIDNIGHT (*6) / THE SUITCASE SESSIONS collection (*4) / PICK OF THE LITTER (*6) / HERE COMES THE MIRACLES (*7) / STATIC TRANSMISSION (*6)

STEVE 'DUSTY' WYNN (b.21 Feb'60, Santa Monica, Calif.) – vocals / **KARL PRECODA** (b.1961) – guitar / **DENNIS DUCK** (b.25 Mar'53) – drums / **KENDRA SMITH** (b.14 Mar'60, San Diego, Calif.) – bass / guest on below; **TOM ZVONCHECK** – keyboards

not iss. | Down There

Dec 82. (m-lp) <*VEX 10*> **THE DREAM SYNDICATE** [–] [ ]
– Sure thing / Some kinda itch / That's what you always say / When you smile. *(UK-iss.Jun85 on 'Zippo'; ZANE 001) (cd-iss. Aug92; VEXCD 10)*

Rough Trade | Ruby

Nov 83. (lp) *(ROUGH 53)* **THE DAYS OF WINE AND ROSES** [ ] [ ]
– Tell me when it's over / Definitely clean / That's what you always say / Then she remembers / Halloween / When you smile / Until lately / Too little, too late / The days of wine and roses. *(re-iss. Jan87 on 'Slash'; 23844-1) (cd-iss. Jan95 & Aug99 on 'Normal'; NORMAL 176CD) <(cd re-mast.Jul01 on 'Rhino'+=; 8122 79937-2)>* – THE DREAM SYNDICATE ep tracks / (rehearsal/bonus tracks).

Dec 83. (12"ep) *(RTT 121)* **TELL ME WHEN IT'S OVER. / SOME KINDA ITCH (live) / MR. SOUL (live) / SURE THING (live)** [ ] [–]

— **DAVE PROVOST** – bass repl. KENDRA (she joined RAINY DAY then OPAL) (appeared on live album early '84) and later went solo

A&M | not iss.

Jun 84. (lp/c) *(AMLX/CXM 64990)* **MEDICINE SHOW** [ ] [–]
– Still holding on to you / Daddy's girl / Burn / Armed with an empty gun / Bullet with my name on it / The medicine show / John Coltrane stereo blues / Merrittville.

Feb 85. (lp) *(AMLH 12511)* **IT'S NOT THE NEW DREAM SYNDICATE ALBUM (live)** [ ] [–]
– Tell me when it's over / Bullet with my name on it / Armed with an empty gun / The medicine show / John Coltrane stereo blues.

— **PAUL B. CUTLER** (b. 5 Aug'54, Phoenix, Arizona) – lead guitar + **MARK WALTON** (b. 9 Aug'59, Fairfield, Calif.) – bass; repl. PRECODA + PROVOST

Chrysalis | Big Time

Jun 86. (lp/c) *(CHR/ZCHR 1539)* **OUT OF THE GREY** [ ] [ ]
– Out of the grey / Forest for the trees / 50 in a 25 zone / Boston / Slide away / Dying embers / Now I ride alone / Dancing blind / You can't forget. *(cd-iss. 1987; CCD 1539) (re-iss. Oct87 on 'Big Time' lp/c; ZL/ZK 71457X) <US cd-iss. 1997 on 'Atavistic'+=; 66> (cd re-iss. Aug99 on 'Normal'+=; NORMAL 184CD)* – Let it rain / Cinnamon girl / Ballad of Dwight Frye / Shake your hips / I won't forget / The lonely bull.

Sep 87. (12"ep) *(ZT 41420)* **50 IN A 25 ZONE. / DRINKING PROBLEM / BLOOD MONEY / THE LONELY BULL** [ ] [ ]

Enigma-Virgin | Enigma

Sep 88. (lp/c/cd) *(ENVLP/TCENV/CDENV 506) <73341-1/-4/-2>* **GHOST STORIES** [ ] [ ]
– The side I'll never show / My old haunts / Loving the sinner, hating the sin / Whatever you please / Weathered and torn / See that my grave is kept clean / I have faith / Some place better than this / Black / When the curtain calls. *(cd re-iss. Sep95 on 'Restless'; 72758-2)*

Nov 88. (7") *(ENV 6)* **I HAVE FAITH. / NOW I RIDE ALONE** [ ] [ ]
(12"+=) *(ENVT 6)* – I ain't living long like this.

— split early 1989, when WYNN decided to venture solo. He released a number of albums, the first two being 'KERSOSENE MAN' and 'DAZZLING DISPLAY'. He also formed GUTTERBALL with Long Ryder; STEPHEN McCARTHY. WALTON would subsequently form The CONTINENTAL DRIFTERS.

– compilations etc. –

Jun 89. (lp/cd) *Enigma-Virgin; (ENVLP/CDENV 531) / Restless; <72293-2>* **LIVE AT RAJI'S (live in Hollywood January '85)** [ ] [ ]
– Still holding on to you / Forest for the trees / Until lately / That's what you always say / Burn / Merritville / The days of wine and roses / The medicine show / Halloween / Boston / John Coltrane stereo blues. *(re-iss. Jun90 on 'Demon' lp/cd; DFIEND/FIENDCD 176)*

Sep 89. (lp) *Another Cowboy; (ANOTHER 1)* **IT'S TOO LATE TO STOP NOW** [ ] [–]

Apr 90. (d-lp/cd) *Demon; (FIEND/+CD 170)* **LIVE AT RAJI'S / GHOST STORIES** [ ] [ ]

Jun 92. (cd/c) *Rhino; <R2/R4 70373>* **TELL ME WHEN IT'S OVER: THE BEST OF DREAM SYNDICATE** [–] [ ]

Nov 93. (cd) *Normal; (NORMAL 156CD)* **THE LOST TAPES 1985-1988** [ ] [–]
(re-iss. Aug99; same)

STEVE WYNN

World Service | Rhino

May 90. (lp/c/cd) *(SERV 011/+MC/CD) <8122 70969-2>* **KEROSENE MAN** [ ] Apr90 [ ]
– Tears won't help / Carolyn / The blue drifter / Younger / Under the weather / Here on Earth as well / Something to remember me by / Killing time / Conspiracy of the heart / Kerosene man / Anthem. *(cd re-iss. Feb93 on 'Rhino'; same as US) <(cd re-iss. Nov98 on 'Prima'+=; SID 009)>* – demos:- Here on earth as well / Our little house / Under the weather / Killing time / Carolyn.

1991. (cd-ep) *<74427>* **KEROSENE MAN EP** [–] [ ]
– Kerosene man / Something to remember me by / Kool thing / Boy in the bubble / Conspiracy of the heart.

Rhino | Rhino

Dec 91. (cd-ep) *<PRO2 90114>* **DRAG EP** [–] [ ]
– Drag / Christine's tune / Younger (live) / How's my little girl.

Mar 93. (cd) *<(8122 02832-2)>* **DAZZLING DISPLAY** [ ] Nov91 [ ]
– Drag / Tuesday / When she comes around / A dazzling display / Halo / Dandy in disguise / Grace / As it should be / Bonnie and Clyde / 405 / Close your eyes / Light of hope. *<(cd re-iss. Mar00 on 'Prima'+=; SID 012)>* – Kool thing / Boy in the bubble / Conspiracy of the heart / Watching the river flow / Crazy feeling / The long goodbye.

— next with an array of backing musos including JOHN WESLEY HARDING

Brake Out | Mute

Nov 94. (cd) *(OUT 1162) <61652>* **FLUORESCENT** [ ] Mar94 [ ]
– Follow me / Collision course / Carelessly / Carry a torch / Open the door /

Older / Layer by layer / That's why I wear black / Wedding bells / The sun rises in the west / Look both ways / Never ending rain. *(re-mast.May02 on 'Blue Rose'+=; BLUDP 285)* <*US on 'Innerstate'; INNER 273*> – Animation / Gospel No.1 / Counting the days / Closer / The subject was roses / Dead roses / Gospel No.2 / Our little house.

— next with the group, COME

Brake Out / Zero Hour

Jul 96. (cd) *(OUT 1242)* <*ZEROCD 1160*> **MELTING IN THE DARK** ☐ ☐
– Why / Sheeley's blues / What we call love / Drizzle / Angels / Epilogue / Silence is our only friend / Stare it down / Smooth / For all I care / The way you punish me / Down / Melting in the dark.

Zero Hour / Zero Hour

Sep 97. (cd) <*(ZEROCD 2160)*> **SWEETNESS AND LIGHT** ☐ ☐
– Silver lining / Black magic / Sweetness and light / This strange effect / This deadly game / How's my little girl / Ghosts / Blood from a stone / In love with everyone / Great divide / That's the way love is / If my life was an open book.

— again with **CHRIS CACAVAS** – keyboards / **CHRIS BROKAW** – guitar / **LINDA PITMAN** – drums / **JOHN CONVERTINO + HOWE GELB**

Mar 99. (cd) <*(ZEROCD 3160)*> **MY MIDNIGHT** ☐ ☐
– Nothing but the shell / My favourite game / Cats and dogs / In your prime / Mandy breakdown / Lay of the land / Out of this world / My midnight / The mask of shame / We've been hanging on / 500 girl mornings. *(w/ bonus cd on 'Blue Rose'+=; BLUCD 0082)*

Glitterhouse / not iss.

Oct 99. (cd) **PICK OF THE LITTER** [–] German [–]
– My family / Invisible / James river incident / Ladies and gentlemen / Smoke from a distant flame / Halfway to the afterlife / Don't be afraid / The air that I breathe / The impossible / Smoke from a distant flame #2 / Why does love got to be so sad.

Blue Rose / Innerstate

Jun 01. (d-cd/d-lp) *(BLU DP/LP 237)* <*50063*> **HERE COME THE MIRACLES** ☐ ☐
– Here come the miracles / Shades of blue / Sustain / Blackout / Butterscotch / Southern California line / Morningside heights / Let's leave it like that / Crawling misanthropic blues / Drought / Death Valley rain / Strange new world / Sunset to the sea / Good and bad / Topanga Canyon freaks / Watch your step / Charity / Smash myself to bits / There will come a day.

Oct 01. (cd-ep) *(BLUS 10268)* **THERE WILL COME A DAY / live in Germany 2001:- DROUGHT / LET'S LEAVE IT LIKE THAT / DEATH VALLEY SUN / HALLOWEEN** ☐ [–]

Blue Rose / D.B.K.

Mar 03. (cd/d-lp; as STEVE WYNN & THE MIRACLE 3) *(BLU CD/LP 0300)* <*105*> **STATIC TRANSMISSION** ☐ Jun03 ☐
– What comes after / Candy machine / The ambassador of soul / Keep it clean / Amphetamine / California style / One less shining star / Maybe tomorrow / Hollywood / Charcoal sunset / A fond farewell / Riverside / Nothing like anything / Underneath the underground / Timing / Survival blues / Again / State trooper / Benediction.

– his compilations, etc. –

Nov 94. (cd) *Return To Sender;* <*(RTS 13)*> **TAKE YOUR FLUNKY AND DANGLE** (unissued material rec.1987-1993) ☐ Nov93 ☐
– Animation / Gospel #1 / How's my little girl / Counting the days / The subject was roses / Closer / Woodshed blues / Boxing song / AA / Gospel #2 / It only comes out at night. <*(re-iss. Oct99 on 'Innerstate'; INNER 7002)*> *(lp-iss.Mar00 on 'Fruit Tree'; FT 805)*

Aug 98. (cd) *Return To Sender; (RTS 28)* **THE SUITCASE SESSIONS** ☐ [–]
– Why / Waiting like Mary / This cdeadly game / The difference between right and wrong / Make it up to you / The way you punish me / The actress / Venus / Draggin' the line / Tighten up / The blue drifter / John Coltrane stereo blues.

GUTTERBALL

STEVE WYNN – vocals, guitar / **BRYAN HARVEY** – guitar, vocals (ex-HOUSE OF FREAKS) / **STEPHEN McCARTHY** – guitar, vocals (ex-LONG RYDERS) / **JOHNNY HOTT** – drums, vocals (ex-HOUSE OF FREAKS) / **BOB RUPE** – bass, vocals (ex-SILOS)

Brake Out / Mute

Jan 94. (cd) *(OUT 113-2)* <*61510*> **GUTTERBALL** ☐ Jun93 ☐
– Trial separation blues / Top of the hill / Lester Young / Motorcycle boy / One by one / When you make up your mind / Think it over / Falling from the sky / Please don't hold back / The preacher and the prostitute / Patent leather shoes / Blessing in disguise.

— **ARMISTEAD WELLFORD** – bass, vocals; repl. RUPE

Brake Out / Brake Out

Apr 95. (cd/lp) <*(OUT 119-2/-1)*> **WEASEL** ☐ ☐
– Transparency / Your best friend / Black and gold / Is there something I should know? / Hesitation / The firefly / Sugar fix / Maria / One-eyed dog / Tarzana, pt.2 / Angelene / California / Everything / Over 40 / Mickey's big mouth.

– compilations, etc. –

Aug 95. (cd) *Return To Sender;* <*(RTS 17)*> **TURNYOR HEDINKOV** ☐ ☐

DR. FEELGOOD

Formed: Canvey Island, Essex, England ... mid-'71 by LEE BRILLEAUX and WILKO JOHNSON alongside JOHN B. SPARKS and JOHN MARTIN aka The BIG FIGURE, taking their name from a 50's bluesman. After an initial period spent gigging in Southend-on-Sea, the group made a name for themselves in the capital, where their lean n' mean brand of revivalist R&B was going down a storm on the pub-rock circuit. While the band's mean faced assault was best sampled in the sweaty confines of a packed public house, DR. FEELGOOD secured a recording contract with 'United Artists' and proceeded to release an enjoyable series of albums beginning with 'DOWN BY THE JETTY' (1974). The band's JOHNNY KIDD & The PIRATES' influenced originals (stand out track being the piledriving 'KEEP IT OUT OF SIGHT') jostled for elbow room alongside covers material like 'BONY MORONIE' (Larry Williams) and 'TEQUILA' (The Champs). It was the follow-up set, 'MALPRACTICE' (1975), however, that saw the band make their break into the UK Top 20, the record's success a gauge of the changing musical climate; with their drainpipe suits, short hair (well, shorter than your average rock band of the day), stripped down sound and surly demeanour, DR. FEELGOOD were as influential as any band in the onset of punk. Their mushrooming popularity was confirmed when live set, 'STUPIDITY' (1976), topped the British charts. During the recording of subsequent set, 'SNEAKIN' SUSPICION' (1977), the band were dealt a potentially fatal blow with the departure of guitarist, co-writer and focal point, WILKO. Bearing up, they recruited JOHN 'GYPIE' MAYO as a replacement and, with NICK LOWE producing, introduced a slicker sound on 'BE SEEING YOU'. This was commercially rewarded when 1978's 'PRIVATE PRACTICE' spawned a Top 10 hit single (the only one of their career) in the classic 'MILK AND ALCOHOL'. Though their short period of chart grace was more or less over, the band remained a hot live ticket, releasing two concert sets in the space of three years, 'AS IT HAPPENS' (1979) and 'ON THE JOB' (1981). This marked the end of MAYO's tenure with the band, SPARKS and The BIG FIGURE departing around the same time and leaving BRILLEAUX as the sole constant in an ever changing line-up throughout the 80's. DR. FEELGOOD continued to record and perform to a loyal audience right up until BRILLEAUX's untimely death from throat cancer on 7th April '94, the band subsequently continuing with new singer PETE GAGE. • **Songwriters:** BRILLEAUX and JOHNSON, and later MAYO. Covered:- BONY MORONIE (Larry Williams) / TEQUILLA (Champs) / ROUTE 66 (Nelson Riddle) / DUST MY

BROOM (Elmore James) / MAD MAN BLUES + DIMPLES (John Lee Hooker) / ROCK ME BABY (B.B. King) / MY BABY (Willie Dixon) / SOMETHING YOU GET (Kenner) / CAN'T FIND THE LADY (Larry Wallis) / GOING DOWN (Don Nix) / NO TIME (JJ Cale) / STANDING AT THE CROSSROADS AGAIN (Mickey Jupp) / BEEN DOWN SO LONG (Doors) / DON'T WORRY BABY (Ritchie Valens) / YOU'VE GOT MY NUMBER (Undertones) / GET RHYTHM (Johnny Cash) / I'M A REAL MAN (John Hiatt) / AS LONG AS THE PRICE IS RIGHT (Larry Wallis) / GREAT BALLS OF FIRE (Jerry Lee Lewis) / etc. • **Trivia:** In 1977, NICK LOWE produced and co-wrote some material.

Album rating: DOWN BY THE JETTY (*7) / MALPRACTICE (*7) / STUPIDITY (*6) / SNEAKIN' SUSPICION (*6) / BE SEEING YOU (*6) / PRIVATE PRACTICE (*5) / AS IT HAPPENS (*5) / LET IT ROLL (*4) / A CASE OF THE SHAKES (*5) / ON THE JOB (*4) / CASEBOOK compilation (*6) / FAST WOMEN AND SLOW HORSES (*4) / DOCTOR'S ORDERS (*5) / MAD MAN BLUES (*6) / BRILLEAUX (*5) / CASE HISTORY – THE BEST OF DR. FEELGOOD compilation (*7) / SINGLES – THE UA YEARS compilation (*7) / LIVE IN LONDON (*4) / DOWN AT THE DOCTORS (*5) / ON THE ROAD AGAIN (*3) / CHESS MASTERS (*4)

LEE BRILLEAUX (b. LEE GREEN, 1953, Durban, S. Africa) – vocals, harmonica / **WILKO JOHNSON** (b. JOHN WILKINSON, 1947) – guitar (ex-ROAMERS) / **JOHN B.SPARKS** – bass / **THE BIG FIGURE** (aka. JOHN MARTIN, 1947) – drums (ex-ROAMERS)

U.A. Columbia

Nov 74. (7"; mono) *(UP 35760)* **ROXETTE. / (GET YOUR KICKS ON) ROUTE 66** [ ] [–]

Dec 74. (lp; mono) *(UAS 29727)* **DOWN BY THE JETTY** [ ] [–]
– She does it right / Boom boom / The more I give / Roxette / One weekend / That ain't the way to behave / I don't mind / Twenty yards behind / Keep it out of sight / All through the city / Cheque book / Oyeh / Bonie Moronie / Tequila. *(re-iss. May82 on 'Fame' lp/c; FA/TC-FA 3029) (re-iss. Oct85 on 'Edsel'; ED 160) (<re-iss. Jan90 on 'Grand' lp/cd; GRAND/+CD 05>)*

Mar 75. (7") *(UP 35815)* **SHE DOES IT RIGHT. / I DON'T MIND** [ ] [–]

Jul 75. (7") *(UP 35857)* **BACK IN THE NIGHT. / I'M A MAN** [ ] [–]

Oct 75. (lp) *(UAS 29880)* *<34098>* **MALPRACTICE** [17] [ ]
– I can tell / Going back home / Back in the night / Another man / Rolling and tumbling / Don't let your daddy know / Watch your step / Don't you just know it / Riot in cell block No.9 / Becaue you're mine / You shouldn't call the doctor (if you can't afford the bill). *(<re-iss. Aug90 on 'Grand' lp/cd; GRAND/+CD 09>)*

Sep 76. (lp) *(UAS 29990)* **STUPIDITY (live)** [1] [–]
– I'm talking about you / Twenty yards behind / Stupidity / All through the city / I'm a man / Walking the dog / She does it right / Going back home / I don't mind / Back in the night / I'm a hog for you baby / Checkin' up on my baby / Roxanne. *(free 7"-w.a.) (FEEL 1)* **RIOT IN CELL BLOCK NO.9. / JOHNNY B. GOODE** *(re-iss. Aug85 on 'Liberty'; lp/c; ED 260634-1/-4) (re-iss. Apr91 as 'STUPIDITY PLUS (LIVE 1976-1990)' on 'Liberty' d-lp)(d-cd; EM 1388)(CDP 795934-2)*

Sep 76. (7") *(UP 36171)* **ROXETTE (live). / KEEP IT OUT OF SIGHT (live)** [ ] [–]

May 77. (7") *(UP 36255)* **SNEAKIN' SUSPICION. / LIGHTS OUT** [47] [–]

May 77. (lp) *(UAS 30075)* **SNEAKIN' SUSPICION** [10] [–]
– Sneakin' suspicion / Paradise / Nothin' shakin' (but the leaves and trees) / Walking on the edge / Lights out / Lucky 7 / All my love / You'll be mine / Time and the Devil / Hey mama / Keep your big mouth shut. *(re-iss. May87 on 'Fame' lp/c; FA/TC-FA 3179) (<cd-iss. Jun91 on 'Grand' lp/cd; GRAND/+CD 13>)*

—— (Mar77) **JOHN 'GYPIE' MAYO** (b. JOHN CAWTHRA) – guitar; repl. HENRY McCULLOCH who had for 2 mths repl. WILKO JOHNSON (solo)

Sep 77. (7") *(UP 36304)* **SHE'S A WINDUP. / HI-RISE** [34] [–]
(12"+=) *(12UP 36304)* – Homework (live).

Sep 77. (lp) *(UAS 30123)* **BE SEEING YOU** [55] [–]
– Ninety-nine ana a half (won't do) / She's a windup / I thought I had it made / I don't wanna know / That's it, I quit / As long as the price is right / Hi-rise / My buddy buddy friends / Baby Jane / The blues had a baby, and they named it rock'n'roll / Looking back / 60 minutes of our love. *(re-iss. Oct87 on 'Edsel'; ED 238) (<cd-iss. Sep91 on 'Grand' lp/cd; GRAND/+CD 14>)*

Nov 77. (7") *(UP 36332)* **BABY JANE. / LOOKING BACK** [ ] [–]
(12"+=) *(12UP 36332)* – You upset me baby (live).

Sep 78. (7") *(UP 36444)* **DOWN AT THE DOCTORS. / TAKE A TIP** [48] [–]

Oct 78. (lp) *(UAG 30184)* **PRIVATE PRACTICE** [41] [–]
– Down at the doctors / Every kind of vice / Things get better / Milk and alcohol / Night time / Let's have a party / Take a tip / It wasn't me / Greaseball / Sugar shaker. *(<re-iss. Oct88 on 'Grand' lp/cd; GRAND/+CD 01>)*

Jan 79. (7",7"milky,7"beer-colrd) *(UP 36468)* **MILK AND ALCOHOL. / EVERY KIND OF VICE** [9] [–]

Apr 79. (7"blue/ 7"brown/ 7"purple/ 7") *(X/Y/Z+/UP 36506)* **AS LONG AS THE PRICE IS RIGHT (live). / DOWN AT THE DOCTORS (live)** [40] [–]

May 79. (lp) *(UAK 30239)* **AS IT HAPPENS (live)** [42] [–]
– Take a tip / Every kind of vice / Down at the doctors / Baby Jane / Sugar shaker / Things get better / She's a windup / Ninety-nine and a half (won't do) / My buddy buddy friends / Milk and alcohol / Matchbox / As long as the price is right / Night time. *(free live 7"ep)* **ENCORE EP** *(FEEL 2)* – Riot in cell block No.9 / Blues had a baby and they named it rock'n'roll / Lights out / Great balls of fire. *(<cd-iss. Dec92 on 'Grand' lp/cd+=; GRAND/+CD 15>)* – (EP tracks).

Aug 79. (7") *(BP 306)* **PUT HIM OUT OF YOUR MIND. / BEND YOUR EAR** [73] [–]

Sep 79. (lp/c) *(UAG/TCK 30269)* **LET IT ROLL** [ ] [–]
– Java blue / Feels good / Put him out of your mind / Bend your ear / Hong Kong money / Keeka smeeka / Shotgun blues / Pretty face / Riding on the L & N / Drop everything and run.

Jan 80. (7") *(BP 338)* **HONG KONG MONEY. / KEEKA SMEEKA** [ ] [–]

Aug 80. (7") *(BP 366)* **NO MO DO YAKAMO. / BEST IN THE WORLD** [ ] [–]

Sep 80. (lp/c) *(UAG/TC-UAG 30311)* **A CASE OF THE SHAKES** [ ] [–]
– Jumping from love to love / Going some place else / Best in the world / Punch drunk / King for a day / Violent love / No mo do Yakamo / Love hound / Coming to you / Who's winning / Drives me wild / A case of the shakes. *(re-iss. Aug86 on 'Edsel'; ED 189) (<re-iss. Oct90 on 'Grand' lp/cd; GRAND/+CD 10>)*

Nov 80. (7") *(BP 374)* **JUMPING FROM LOVE TO LOVE. / LOVE HOUND** [ ] [–]

Jan 81. (7") *(BP 386)* **VIOLENT LOVE. / A CASE OF THE SHAKES** [ ] [–]

Liberty not iss.

Aug 81. (lp) *(LBG 30328)* **ON THE JOB (live)** [ ] [–]
– Drives me wild / Java blue / Jumping from love to love / Pretty face / No mo do Yakomo / Love hound / Shotgun blues / Best in the world / Who's winning / Riding on the L' & 'N / Shotgun blues / Goodnight Vienna. *(<cd-iss. Dec92 on 'Grand' lp/cd; GRAND/+CD 16>)*

—— (early'81) **JOHNNY GUITAR** – guitar (ex-COUNT BISHOPS) repl. MAYO

Oct 81. (7") *(BP 404)* **WAITING FOR SATURDAY NIGHT. / EILEEN** [ ] [–]

—— **LEE & JOHNNY** recruited **PAT McMULLEN** – bass (ex-COUNT BISHOPS) repl. SPARKS / **BUZZ BARWELL** – drums (ex-LEW LEWIS BAND) repl. THE BIG FIGURE

Chiswick not iss.

Sep 82. (7") *(DICE 16)* **TRYING TO LIVE MY LIFE WITHOUT YOU. / MURDER IN THE FIRST DEGREE** [ ] [–]

Oct 82. (lp) *(TOSS 4)* **FAST WOMEN AND SLOW HORSES** [ ] [–]
– She's the one / Monkey / Sweet sweet lovin' (gone sour on me) / Trying to live my life without you / Rat race / Baby Jump / Crazy about girls / Sugar bowl / Educated fool / Bum's rush / Baby why do you treat me this way / Beautiful Delilah. *(<re-iss. May89 on 'Grand' lp/c/cd; GRAND/+C/CD 03>)*

Mar 83. (7") *(DICE 18)* **CRAZY ABOUT GIRLS. / SOMETHING OUT OF NOTHING** [ ] [–]

—— (1983) **GORDON RUSSELL** – guitar; repl. JOHNNY GUITAR

—— **PHIL MITCHELL** – bass repl. McMULLEN

—— (1984) **KEVIN MORRIS** – drums repl. BUZZ

Demon not iss.

Sep 84. (7") *(D 1030)* **DANGEROUS. / CAN'T FIND THE LADY** [ ] [–]

Oct 84. (lp) *(FIEND 29)* **DOCTOR'S ORDERS** [ ] [–]
– Close but no cigar / So long / You don't love me / My way / Neighbour, neighbour / Talk of the Devil / Hit git and split / I can't be satisfied /

Saturday night fish fry / Drivin' wheel / It ain't right / I don't worry about a thing / She's in the middle / Dangerous. *(<re-iss. Jan90 on 'Grand' lp/cd; GRAND/+CD 06>)*

Dec 84. (7") *(D 1032)* **MY WAY. / SHE'S IN THE MIDDLE**

I.D. not iss.

Oct 85. (lp) *(NOSE 5)* **MAD MAN BLUES**
– Dust my broom / Something you got / Dimples / Living on the highway / Tore down / Mad man blues / I've got news for you / My babe / Can't find the lady / Rock me baby. *(<re-iss. Oct88 on 'Grand' lp/cd; GRAND/+CD 02>)*

Stiff not iss.

Aug 86. (7") *(BUY 253)* **DON'T WAIT UP. / SOMETHING GOOD**
(w/free 7") *(FBUY 56)* – Back in the night / Milk and alcohol.
(12"+=) *(BUYIT 253)* – Rockin' with somebody new.

Aug 86. (lp/c) *(SEEZ/ZSEEZ 65)* **BRILLEAUX**
– I love you, so you're mine / You've got my number / Big enough / Don't wait up / Get rhythm / Here is the next one? / Play dirty / Grow too old / Rough ride / I'm a real man / Come over here / Take what you can get. *(<re-iss. May89 on 'Grand' lp/c/cd; GRAND/+C/CD 04>)*

Nov 86. (7") *(BUY 255)* **SEE YOU LATER ALLIGATOR. / I LOVE YOU SO YOU'RE MINE**
(12"+=) *(BUYIT 255)* – What do you think of that.

Jun 87. (7") *(BUY 259)* **HUNTING SHOOTING FISHING. / BIG ENOUGH**
(12"+=) *(BUYIT 259)* – Don't underestimate your enemy.
(c-s+=) *(CRASH 1)* – Crash Your Car Megamix.

Sep 87. (lp/c) *(SEEZ/ZSEEZ 67)* **CLASSIC**
– Hunting shooting fishing / Break these chains / Heartbeat / (I wanna) Make love to you / Hurricane / See you later alligator / Quit while you're behind / Nothing like it / Spy vs. spy / Highway 61 / Crack me up. *(<re-iss. Oct90 on 'Grand' lp+=/cd+=; GRAND/+CD 11>)*

E.M.I. not iss.

Apr 89. (7") *(EM 89)* **MILK AND ALCOHOL (new recipe). / SHE'S GOT HER EYES ON YOU**
(12"+=) *(12EM 89)* – Mad man blues.

— **BRILLEAUX + MITCHELL + MORRIS** recruited **STEVE WALWYN** – guitar (ex-STEVE MARRIOTT group)

Grand Grand

Apr 90. (lp/c/cd) *(<GRAND/+C/CD 08>)* **LIVE IN LONDON (live)**
– King for a day / You upset me baby / As long as the price is right / Mad man blues / She does it right / Baby Jane / Quit while you're behind / Back in the night / Milk and alcohol / See you later alligator / Down at the doctors / Route 66 / Going back home / Bony Moronie / Tequila.

Jun 91. (lp/cd) *(GRAND/+CD 12)* **PRIMO**
– Heart of the city / My sugar turns to alcohol / Going down / No time / World in a jug / If my baby quit me / Primo blues / Standing at the crossroads again / Been down so long / Don't worry baby / Down by the jetty blues / Two times nine.

— **DAVE BRONZE** – bass repl. MITCHELL

Jul 93. (lp/cd) *(<GRAND/+CD 17>)* **THE FEELGOOD FACTOR**
– The feelgood factor / Tranqueray / Tell me no lies / Styrofoam / I'm in the mood for you / Double crossed / Lying about the blues / She moves me / Wolfman calling / One step forward / One to ten / Fool for you.

— On the 7th Apr'94; LEE BRILLEAUX died of throat cancer

May 94. (lp/cd) *(<GRAND/+CD 18>)* **DOWN AT THE DOCTORS (live early '94)**
– If my baby quits me / Styrofoam / Tanqueray / Wolfman callin' / Roadrunner / One step forward / Got my mojo working / Milk and alcohol / Down at the doctors / Freddie's footsteps / Heart of the city.

— veteran **PETE GAGE** took over the role of singer and the group was reborn. Others in line-up **PHIL MITCHELL / DAVE BRONZE + STEVE WALWYN**

Aug 96. (cd) *(<GRAND 19>)* **ON THE ROAD AGAIN**
– Wine, women and whisky / Sweet Louise / The world keeps on turning / On the road again / Instinct to survive / Mellow down easy / Going out west / Cheap at half the price / Second opinion / What am I to believe / Repo man / You got me.

— **KEVIN MORRIS + WILL BIRCH** re-formed a new version of group

Liberty Grand

May 00. (cd) *(525844-2)* <GRAND 23> **CHESS MASTERS**
– Nadine / Date bait / You gotta help me / Talking about you / The walk / Twenty-nine ways to my baby's door / Who do you love / If walls could talk / Send for the doctor / Killing floor / Susie-Q / Don't start me talking / Gimme one more shot / (I'm your) Hoochie coochie man.

Grand Grand

May 03. (cd) *(<GRANDCD 27>)* **SPEEDING THRU EUROPE: DR. FEELGOOD LIVE IN CONCERT** (live 2002-2003)
– Nadine / Roxette / Don't start me talking / Going back home / Down by the jetty blues / Back in the night / Shake your moneymaker / Down at the doctors / Gimme one more shot / Mad man blues / Bony Moronie – Tequila.

– compilations, others, etc. –

Nov 81. (lp) *United Artists; (LBG 30341)* **CASEBOOK**

Apr 87. (cd) *E.M.I.; (CDP 746 711-2)* **CASE HISTORY – THE BEST OF DR.FEELGOOD**

May 89. (cd/c/d-lp) *Liberty; (CD/TC+/EM 1332)* **SINGLES (THE U.A. YEARS)**
– Roxette / She does it right / Back in the night / Going back home / Riot in cell block 9 / Sneakin' suspicion / She's a wind-up / Baby Jane / Down at the doctors / Milk and alcohol / As long as the price is right / Put him out of your mind / Hong Kong money / No modo Yakama / Jumping from love to love / Violent love / Waiting for Saturday night / Monkey / Trying to live my life without you / Crazy about girls / My way / Mad man blues / See you later alligator / Hunting shooting fishing. *(d-lp+=/c+=)* – Don't wait up / Milk and alcohol (new recipe).

Oct 95. (5xcd-box) *Liberty; (ACDFEEL 195)* **LOOKING BACK**

Apr 97. (d-cd) *Grand; (GRAND 20)* **TWENTY FIVE YEARS OF DR. FEELGOOD**

Oct 02. (cd) *Grand; (<GRANDCD 25>)* **FINELY TUNED – THE GUITAR ALBUM**

Oct 02. (cd) *Grand; (<GRANDCD 26>)* **DOWN AT THE BBC**

May 03. (cd) *Grand; (<GRANDCD 28>)* **WOLFMAN CALLING: THE BLUES OF LEE BRILLEAUX**

DR. JOHN

Born: MALCOLM REBENNACK, 20 Nov'42, New Orleans, Louisiana, USA. He became a noted session man in 1957 and soon branched out on his own the same year, taking up the piano after one of his fingers was shot off in a bar room brawl. Drawn to L.A. in the mid-60's, he continued his session work and began to assume his alter ego, DR. JOHN (CREAUX) THE NIGHT TRIPPER. Taking the name from a 19th Century New Orleans witchdoctor type, the character was a hybrid of psychedelic mysticism and deep South voodoo. 'GRIS GRIS' (1968) was the first DR. JOHN release on 'Atco', a sinister series of voodoo funk meditations that combined New Orleans R&B, creole soul and psychedelia. The next three releases, 'BABYLON' (1968), 'REMEDIES' (1970) and 'THE SUN, MOON AND HERBS' (1971) carried on in much the same vein without achieving quite the same foreboding effect. The JERRY WEXLER-produced 'GUMBO' (1972) saw DR. JOHN (by this time, he'd given up his nocturnal tripping) return to his bayou roots. A deeply satisfying journey through New Orleans' rich musical heritage, the record saw the good doctor belting out some spirited updates of standards like 'IKO IKO' and 'JUNKO PARTNER'. With impeccable credentials (produced by ALLEN TOUSSAINT, recorded with The METERS) 1973's 'IN THE RIGHT PLACE' concentrated on downhome funk. 'DESITIVELY BONNAROO' (1974) offered similar rhythmical remedies, spawning the rump shaking single '(EVERYBODY WANNA GET RICH) RITE AWAY'. Seemingly abandoning the New Orleans (black) magic, DR. JOHN made a misguided attempt at more rocking fare on the live 'HOLLYWOOD BE THY NAME' (1975). 'CITY LIGHTS' (1978) and 'TANGO PALACE' (1979) sounded confused and it was only with 1981's 'DR. JOHN PLAYS MAC REBENNACK' that he regained his focus. The album found him alone at his piano, effortlessly reeling off inspired tributes to New Orleans past masters.

'THE BRIGHTEST SMILE IN TOWN' (1983) proved that his return to form was no fluke although 'IN A SENTIMENTAL MOOD' (1989) sounded overwrought. DR. JOHN returned to his old stamping ground on funky 90's releases like 'GOIN' BACK TO NEW ORLEANS' (1992) and 'TELEVISION' (1994) while his far reaching influence was illustrated by his guesting on one of 1997's best albums, SPIRITUALIZED's 'LADIES AND GENTLEMEN WE ARE FLOATING IN SPACE BP'. Signing to 'Parlophone' records in the UK, DR. JOHN subsequently delivered two further sets of fine work, 'ANUTHA ZONE' (1998) and 'DUKE ELEGANT' (2000). After the creative diversions and belated critical rebirth of recent years, it was perhaps inevitable DR. JOHN was going to return to his roots with a vengeance and so he did on 2001's 'CREOLE MOON'. With FRED WESLEY presiding over the horn section, it was back to seriously funky New Orleans bizniz for the sexagenarian piano master, right down to the voodoo trappings of the cover art. • **Songwriters:** REBENNACK compositions except; IKO IKO (Dixie Cups) / THE WAY YOU DO THE THINGS YOU DO (Smokey Robinson) / YESTERDAY (Beatles) / IT'S ALL RIGHT WITH ME (Cole Porter) / BLUE SKIES (Irving Berlin) / etc. • **Trivia:** His organ playing featured heavily on ARETHA FRANKLIN's 1971 single 'Spanish Harlem'.

Album rating: GRIS GRIS (*7) / BABYLON (*6) / REMEDIES (*5) / SUN, MOON AND HERBS (*6) / DR. JOHN'S GUMBO (*7) / IN THE RIGHT PLACE (*6) / DESITIVELY BONAROO (*6) / HOLLYWOOD BE THY NAME (*4) / CUT ME WHILE I'M HOT (*5) / CITY LIGHTS (*6) / TANGO PALACE (*4) / DR. JOHN PLAYS MAC REBENNACK (*7) / THE BRIGHTEST SMILE IN TOWN (*6) / I BEEN HOODOOD compilation (*6) / IN THE NIGHT exploitation (*6) / SUCH A NIGHT – LIVE IN LONDON (*5) / IN A SENTIMENTAL MOOD (*5) / BLUESIANA TRIANGLE with Art Blakely & David 'Fathead' Newman (*4) / GOIN' BACK TO NEW ORLEANS (*5) / ANTHOLOGY compilation (*7) / TELEVISION (*4) / AFTERGLOW (*5) / THE VERY BEST OF DR. JOHN compilation (*7) / DUKE ELEGANT (*6) / CREOLE MOON (*6)

MAC REBENNACK

not iss. — Rex

1958. (lp) <2020> **DR. JOHN AND HIS NEW ORLEANS CONGREGATION** [–] [ ]

1959. (7") <1008> **STORM WARNING. / FOOLISH LITTLE GIRL** [–] [ ]

not iss. — A.F.O.

1962. (7") <309> **THE POINT. / ONE NAUGHTY FLAT** [–] [ ]

— He became a session man in the early 60's. He also formed numerous bands, including ZU ZU. Around 1963 he adopted the name of DR. JOHN THE NIGHT TRIPPER.

not iss. — Trip

1965. (lp) <9518> **ZU ZU MAN** (demos ?) [–] [ ]
– Cat and mouse game / She's just a square / Bald headed / In the night / Helpin' hand / Zu zu man / Mean cheatin' woman / Woman's the root of all evil / Trader John / Shoo-ra / Tipatina / One night late. *(cd-iss. Apr87 on 'Topline'; TOPCD 504) (re-iss. May89 on 'Thunderbolt' lp/cd; THBL/CDTB 069) (re-iss. Jul93 on 'Charly' cd/c; CDCD/CDCM 1090)*

DR. JOHN

– vocals, piano with various sessioners

Atlantic — Atco

1968. (7"; as DR. JOHN THE NIGHT TRIPPER) <6607> **I WALK ON GUILDED SPLINTERS. / (part 2)** [–] [ ]

1968. (lp; as DR. JOHN THE NIGHT TRIPPER) *(588 147)* <33234> **GRIS GRIS** [ ] [ ]
– Gris gris gumbo ya ya / Danse kalinda ba boom / Mama roux / Danse fambeaux / Croker court bullion / Jump steady / I walk on gilded splinters. *(re-iss. Aug87 on 'Sonet'; AL 3904) (cd-iss. Nov93; 7567 80437-2) (cd re-iss. Jun01 on 'Collector's Choice'; CCM 0131-2)*

Feb 69. (7"; as DR. JOHN THE NIGHT TRIPPER) <6635> **MAMA ROUX. / JUMP STEADY** [–] [ ]

Apr 69. (7") <6697> **PATRIOTIC FLAG WAVER. / ('A'-long version)** [–] [ ]

Apr 69. (lp) *(228 018)* <33-270> **BABYLON** [ ] [ ]
– Babylon / Glowin' / Black Widow spider / Barefoot lady / Twilight zone / The patriotic flag-waver / The lonesome guitar strangler. *(cd-iss. Nov93; 7567 80438-2)*

May 70. (7"; as DR.JOHN THE NIGHT TRIPPER) <6755> **WASH MAMA WASH. / LOUP GAROO** [–] [ ]

Jun 70. (7") *(2091 019)* **WASH MAMA WASH. / MAMA ROUX** [ ] [–]

Aug 70. (lp) *(2400 015)* <33-316> **REMEDIES** [ ] [ ]
– Loup garoo / What goes around comes around / Wash, mama, wash / Chippy, chippy / Mardi Gras day / Angola anthem. *(cd-iss. Nov93; 7567 80439-2)*

Nov 71. (lp; as DR. JOHN, THE NIGHT TRIPPER) *(2400 161)* <33-362> **SUN, MOON AND HERBS** [ ] Oct71 [ ]
– Black John the conqueror / Where ya at mule / Cranet crow / Familiar reality (opening) / Pots on fiyo / Zu Zu mama / Familiar reality (reprise). *(re-iss. 1971; K 40250) (cd-iss. Nov93; 7567 80440-2)*

Apr 72. (7") *(K 10158)* <6882> **IKO IKO. / HUEY SMITH MEDLEY** [ ] [71]

Jul 72. (lp) *(K 40384)* <7006> **DR. JOHN'S GUMBO** [ ] May71 [ ]
– Iko Iko / Blow wind blow / Big chief / The lock / Mess around / Let the good times roll / Junko partner / Stack-a-lee / Tipitina / Those lonely lonely nights / Huey Smith medley / High blood pressure / Don't you just know it / Well I'll be John Brown / Little Liza Jane. *(re-iss. Nov87 on 'Alligator'; AL 3901) (cd-iss. Feb95; 7567 80398-2)*

Jul 72. (7") *(K 10214)* **WANG DANG DOODLE. / BIG CHIEF** [ ] [–]

Nov 72. (7") <6900> **LET THE GOOD TIMES ROLL. / STACK-A-LEE** [–] [ ]

Mar 73. (7") *(K 10291)* <6914> **RIGHT PLACE, WRONG TIME. / I BEEN HOODOOED** [ ] [9]

Mar 73. (lp) *(K 50017)* <7018> **IN THE RIGHT PLACE** [ ] [24]
– Right place, wrong time / Same old same old / Just the same / Qualified / Travelling mood / Peace brother peace / Life / Such a nite / Shoo fly marches on / I been hoodooed / Cold cold cold. *(cd-iss. Jun93; 7567 80360-2)*

Jun 73. (7") *(K 10329)* **SUCH A NITE. / LIFE** [ ] [–]

Jun 73. (7") <6937> **SUCH A NITE. / COLD COLD COLD** [–] [42]

— In Aug'73 he was credited on album TRIUMVIRATE with JOHN HAMMOND and MIKE BLOOMFIELD.

Mar 74. (lp) *(K 50035)* <7043> **DESITIVELY BONNAROO** [ ] [ ]
– Quitters never win / Stealin' / What comes around / Me-You-Loneliness / Mos'scocious / Rite away / Let's make a better world / Ru four real / Sing along song / Can't git enuff / Go tell the people / Desitively Bonnaroo. *(cd-iss. Nov93; 7567 80441-2)*

Apr 74. (7") *(K 10445)* <6957> **(EVERYBODY WANNA GET RICH) RITE AWAY. / MOS'SCOCIOUS** [ ] [92]

Aug 74. (7") *(K 10501)* <6971> **LET'S MAKE A BETTER WORLD. / ME, YOU = LONELINESS** [ ] [ ]

D.J.M. — not iss.

Sep 75. (lp) *(22019)* **CUT ME WHILE I'M HOT (ANYTIME ANYPLACE)** [ ] [–]
– Woman is the root of all evil / Shoo ra / Tipatina / One night late / Cat and mouse game / She's just a square / Bald headed / In the night / Helpin' hand / Mean cheatin' woman. *(cd-iss. Feb95 on 'Thunderbolt'; CDTB 158)*

U.A. — U.A.

Dec 76. (lp) *(UAG 29902)* <UALA 552> **HOLLYWOOD BE THY NAME (live)** [ ] [ ]
– New island soiree / Reggae doctor / The way you do the things you do / Swanee river boogie / Yesterday / Babylon / Back by the river / Medley: It's all right with me – Blue skies – Will the circle be unbroken / Hollywood be thy name / I wanna rock. *(re-iss. Oct89 on 'Beat Goes On' lp/cd; BGO LP/CD 62) (cd re-iss. Aug98; same)*

— In 1977, he joined The R.C.O. ALL STARS with LEVON HELM and others.

— now with **STEVE GADD** – drums / **WILL LEE** – bass / **RICHARD TEE** – keyboards / **JOHN TROPEA** – guitar / **HUGH McCRACKEN** – guitar / **ARTHUR JENKINS** – percussion

not iss. — R.C.A.

1978. (7") <11285> **SWEET RIDER. / TAKE ME HIGHER** [–] [ ]

Horizon — A&M

Oct 78. (lp) *(AMLJ 732)* <SP 732> **CITY LIGHTS** [ ] [ ]
– Dance the night away with you / Street side / Wild honey / Rain II snake eyes / Fire of love / Senata – he's a hero / City lights.

1979. (lp) <SP 740> **TANGO PALACE** [–] [ ]
– Keep the music simple / Discotherapy / Renegade / Fonky side / Bon steps rouler / Something you got / I thought I heard New Orleans say / Tango palace / Louisiana lullabye.

— Early in 1981, DR. JOHN w/ LUBBY TITUS & AL JARREAU released 'Warner Bros' single, SAILOR AND THE MERMAID. / ONE GOOD TURN.

Demon Clean Cuts

Sep 82. (7") *(D 1015)* **THE NEARNESS OF YOU. / MAC'S BOOGIE** [ ] [ ]

Oct 82. (lp) *(FIEND 1) <705>* **DR. JOHN PLAYS MAC REBENNACK** [ ] [ ]
– Dorothy / Mac's boogie / Memories of Professor Longhair / The nearness of you / Delicado / Honeydripper / Big Mac / New island midnight / Saints / Pinetop. *(re-iss. Jan90 c/cd +=; FIEND CASS/CD 1)* – Silent night / Dance a la Negras / Wade in the water. *(cd re-iss. Sep02 on 'Acadia'; ACA 8034)*

Nov 83. (lp/c) *(FIEND/+CASS 9)* **THE BRIGHTEST SMILE IN TOWN** [ ] [–]
– Saddled the cow / Boxcar boogie / The brightest smile in town / Waiting for a train / Monkey puzzle / Average kind of guy / Pretty Libby / Marie Le Veau / Come rain or shine / Suite home New Orleans. *(cd-iss. 1992 +=;)* – Didn't he ramble / Touro infirmary / Closer walk with thee.

Beggars Banquet Streetwise

Mar 84. (7"/12") *(BEG/+T 107)* **JET SET. / ('A'dub)** [ ] [ ]

Spindrift not iss.

Jun 84. (lp) *(SPIN 107)* **SUCH A NIGHT – LIVE IN LONDON (live)** [ ] [–]

Topline not iss.

Jan 85. (lp/c) *(TOP/KTOP 118)* **IN THE NIGHT** [ ] [–]
– Bald head / Bring your love / Did she mention my name / Go ahead / Grass is greener / I pulled the cover off you two lovers / In the night / Just like America / Tipitina / Zuzu man / Mean cheatin' woman / New Orleans / Shoo-ra / The time has come / Noe night late / The ear is on strike.

Warners Warners

Apr 89. (lp/c/cd) *(925889-2/-4/-1) <25889>* **IN A SENTIMENTAL MOOD** [ ] [ ]
– Makin' whoopee / Candy / Ac-cent-tchu-ste the positive / My buddy / In a sentimental mood / Black night / Don't let the Sun catch you cryin' / Love for sale / More than you know.

Jun 89. (7") *(W 2976)* **MAKIN' WHOOPEE. / MORE THAN YOU KNOW** [ ] [ ]
(12"+=) *(W 2976T)* – In a sentimental mood.
(above 'A'side featured RICKIE LEE JONES)

Jul 92. (cd/c) *<(7599 26940-2/-4)>* **GOIN' BACK TO NEW ORLEANS** [ ] [ ]
– Litanie des saints / Careless love / My red Indian / Milneburg joys / I thought I heard Buddy Bolden say / Basin Street blues / Didn't he ramble / Do you call that a buddy? / How come my dog don't bark (when you come around) / Good night, Irene / Fess up / Since I fell for you / I'll be glad when you're dead, you rascal you / Cabbage head / Goin' home tomorrow / Blue Monday / Scald dog medley – I can't go on – Goin' back to New Orleans.

— next with **HUGH McCRACKEN** – guitar, harmonica / **GEORG WADENIUS** – guitar / **DAVID BARARD** – bass / **FREDDIE STAHLE** – drums

GRP-MCA GRP-MCA

Apr 94. (cd/c) *<(GRM 4025-2/-4)>* **TELEVISION** [ ] [ ]
– Television / Lissen / Limbo / Witchy red / Only the shadow knows / Shut d. fonk up / Thank you / Spaceship relationship / Hold it / Money / U lie too much / Same day service. *(cd re-iss. May98; same)*

Jul 95. (cd/c) *<(GRB 7000-2/-4)>* **AFTERGLOW** [ ] [ ]
– I know what I've got / Gee baby, ain't I good to you / I'm just a lucky so and so / Blue skies / So long / New York City blues / Tell me you'll wait for me / There must be a better world somewhere / I still think about you / I'm confessin' (that I love you).

Parlophone Virgin

Jun 98. (cd/c/lp) *(495490-2/-4/-1)* **ANUTHA ZONE** [33] [ ]
– Zonata / Ki ya gris gris / Voices in my head / Hello God / Party hellfire / I don't wanna know about evil / Anutha zone / I like ki yoka / Olive tree / Soulful warrior / The stroke / Sweet home New Orleans.

Parlophone Blue Note

Feb 00. (cd) *<(5 33220-2)>* **DUKE ELEGANT** [ ] [ ]
– On the wrong side of the railroad tracks / I'm gonna go fishin' / It don't mean a thing (if it ain't got that swing) / Perdido / Don't get around much anymore / Solitude / Satin doll / Mood indigo / Do nothin' till you hear from me / Things ain't what they used to be / Caravan / Flaming sword.

Oct 01. (cd) *<(5 34591-2)>* **CREOLE MOON** [ ] [ ]
– You swore / In the name of you / Food for thot / Holdin' pattern / Bruha bembe / Imitation of love / Now that you got me / Creole moon / Georgianna / Monkey and baboon / Take what I can get / Queen of cold / Litenin' / One 2 a.m. too many.

– compilations, others, etc. –

1975. (lp) *Rare Earth; <8014>* **NIGHT TRIPPER AT HIS BEST** [–] [ ]
(UK-iss.Jul88 on 'Bellaphon'; BID 8014)

Jan 77. (7") *Atlantic; (K 10877)* **RIGHT PLACE, WRONG TIME. / SUCH A NIGHT** [ ] [–]

1970's. (lp) *Trip; <TOP 16-1>* **16 GREATEST HITS** [–] [ ]

1970's. (lp) *Trip; <4018>* **DR. JOHN SUPERPAH** [–] [ ]

1982. (lp) *Fontana; (80023)* **LOSER FOR YOU BABY** (1960's material) [ ] [ ]
– The time had come / Loser for you baby / The ear is on strike / A little closer to my home / I pulled a cover off you two lovers / New Orleans / Go ahead on / Just like a mirror / Bring your love / Bald head. *(re-iss. Nov88 on 'Thunderbolt' lp/cd+=; THBL/CDTB 66)* – (2 extra tracks). *(cd-iss. Jun98 on 'MagMid'; MM 006)*

Jul 84. (lp) *Edsel; (ED 128)* **I BEEN HOODOOED** ('73 + '74) [ ] [ ]

Feb 86. (d-c) *Demon; (FIENDCASS 9)* **MAC REBENNACK / BRIGHTEST SMILE IN TOWN** [ ] [–]

Jun 88. (cd) *Warners; (WSP 2761-2)* **THE ULTIMATE DR. JOHN** [ ] [ ]

Feb 94. (d-cd) *Rhino; <(8122 71450-2)>* **MOS'SCOCIOUS – THE DR. JOHN ANTHOLOGY** [ ] [ ]
– Bad neighborhood (RONNIE & DELINQUENTS) / Morgus The Magnificent (MORGUS & THE 3 GHOULS) / Storm warning (MAC REBENNACK) / Sahara (MAC REBENNACK & HIS ORCHESTRA) / Down the road (ROLAND STONE) / Gris-gris gumbo ya ya / Mama Roux / Jump sturdy / I walk on guilded splinters / Black widow spider / Loop garoo / Wash, mama, wash / Mardi Gras day / Familiar reality – opening / Zu zu mamou / Mess around / Somebody changed the lock / / Iko iko / Junko partner / Tipitina / Huey Smith medley; a) High blood pressure, b) Don't you just know it, c) Well I'll be John Brown / Right place wrong time / Traveling mood / Life / Such a night / I been hoodood / Cold cold cold / Quitters never win / What comes around (goes around) / Mos'scocious / Let's make a better world / Back by the river / I wanna rock / Memories of Prof. Longhair / Honey dripper / Pretty Libby / Makin' whoopee! / Accentuate the positive / More than you know.

May 95. (cd) *Rhino; <(9548 33553-2)>* **THE VERY BEST OF DR.JOHN** [ ] [ ]

May 97. (cd) *Aim; (AIMA 4CD)* **CRAWFISH SAUCE** [ ] [–]

Mar 98. (cd) *Eagle; (EABCD 077)* **THE MASTERS** [ ] [–]

Apr 98. (cd/c) *Hallmark; (30598-2/-4)* **VOODOO BLUES** [ ] [–]

Apr 98. (d-cd) *Dressed To Kill; (AOP 64)* **DR. JOHN** [ ] [–]

Oct 98. (cd) *Laserlight; (12823)* **ZU ZU MAN** [ ] [–]

Oct 99. (cd) *MagMid; (MM 037)* **ZU ZU MAN** [ ] [–]

Nov 99. (cd) *Purple Pyramid; (CLP 713)* **NEXT HEX** [ ] [ ]

Jan 00. (cd) *Eagle; (EAGCD 003)* **TRIPPIN' LIVE** [ ] [ ]

Mar 00. (cd; with DONALD HARRISON BAND) *Metro; (METRCD 002)* **FUNKY NEW ORLEANS** [ ] [ ]

Jul 01. (cd) *Platinum; (PLATCD 666)* **ZU ZU MAN: THE NIGHT TRIPPER** [ ] [ ]

Feb 02. (d-cd) *Snapper; (SMDCD 365)* **EARLY PRESCRIPTIONS** [ ] [ ]

Apr 03. (cd) *Movieplay Gold; (MPG 74069)* **WOMAN IS THE ROOT OF ALL EVIL** [ ] [ ]

DROWNING POOL

Formed: Dallas, Texas, USA ... 1999 by DAVE WILLIAMS, C.J PIERCE, STEVIE BENTON and percussionist MIKE LUCE. After snatching their name from the Paul Newman movie, this band of prog-metallers smashed onto the scene in late 1999 when their demo tape was picked up by rockers SEVENDUST, who subsequently took the group on tour as a supporting act. With still no record contract, the quartet were signed after a song from their sophomore demo wound up in a local radio station's Top 10 rock chart. DROWNING POOL signed with the 'Wind Up' imprint (home to CREED, etc) and issued their debut album 'SINNER' (2001) to rave reviews. Produced by Nu-Metal honcho Jay Baumgardner, the record played out like a sports metal version of TOOL, with a hint of FEAR FACTORY thrown in for good measure. The effect was slightly better than the usual rock action, with WILLIAMS' vocals being a particular highlight. The ensemble went on to tour with acts such as KITTIE and old friends SEVENDUST, as well as having the honour of sharing OZZY OSBOURNE's stage at his annual 'Ozzfest' festival . . . poor buggers.

Album rating: SINNER (*6)

DAVE WILLIAMS – vocals / **C.J. PIERCE** – guitar / **STEVIE BENTON** – bass / **MIKE LUCE** – drums

		Wind-Up		Wind-Up
Feb 02.	(cd) *(504091-2)* <*13065*> **SINNER** – Sinner / Bodies / Tear away / All over me / Reminded / Pity / Mute / I am / Follow / Told you so / Sermon.	70	Jun01	14
Apr 02.	(7"blue) *(672317-7)* **BODIES. / BODIES (live)** (cd-s+=) *(672317-2)* – Sermon (session) / ('A'-uncensored video).	34		–
Jul 02.	(7") *(672983-7)* **TEAR AWAY. / BREAK YOU** (cd-s+=) *(672983-2)* – Game / ('A'video).	65		–

☐ D-12 (see under ⇒ EMINEM)

☐ DUKES OF STRATOSPHEAR (see under ⇒ XTC)

DURAN DURAN

Formed: Birmingham, England . . . 1978 by NICK RHODES, JOHN TAYLOR, STEPHEN DUFFY and clarinet player, SIMON COLLEY, taking their name from a character in cult space-kitsch movie, 'Barbarella'. The following year, ANDY WICKETT and ROGER TAYLOR replaced DUFFY (who went on to a briefly successful solo career as STEPHEN 'TIN TIN' DUFFY) and COLLEY respectively, while SIMON LE BON finally entered the fray as frontman in Spring '80. After a UK tour supporting HAZEL 'Breaking Glass' O'CONNOR, the band were snapped up by 'E.M.I.', initiating their manicured career in early '81 with 'PLANET EARTH'. The toast of the London cognoscenti, extravagantly coiffured (and even more outlandishly attired) poseurs ensured DURAN DURAN a near Top 10 hit as the scene that perpetrated one of the worst fashion crimes in history (i.e. legwarmers) was stepped up a gear. Later that summer, an eponymous debut album and a suitably po-faced follow-up single, 'GIRLS ON FILM', confirmed the band's synth-powered, post-ROXY MUSIC/BOWIE pretensions with lashings of attitude and mascara. Riding in on the floppy fringe of the New Romantic zeitgeist, the album made the UK Top 3 and, with help of heavy MTV rotation for the 'HUNGRY LIKE THE WOLF' video, eventually the US Top 10. The latter track was a transatlantic Top 5 and previewed the follow-up set, 'RIO' (1982). By this point the band's fanbase had grown from an arty clique to hordes of screaming girlies, ensuring massive success for the sub-panoramic warbling of 'SAVE A PRAYER', the streamlined aquatic rush of the title track and the whining 'IS THERE SOMETHING I SHOULD KNOW', youth centre dancefloor fillers the lot. Although the latter track wasn't included on the album, it did give the band their first UK No.1; with continuing support from MTV in the States, DURAN DURAN were also churning out ever more flamboyant videos to keep the Americans happy. A vague concept affair, 'SEVEN AND THE RAGGED TIGER' (1983) came in for a bit of a critical pasting, although the hits continued apace with the dodgy 'UNION OF THE SNAKE' and transatlantic No.1, 'THE REFLEX' (a quintessentially 80's effort complete with stuttering vocals, while the video was famous for five minutes with its water-coming-out-of-the-screen trickery, brilliant!). The zenith of DURAN DURAN's bombastic heyday came with 'THE WILD BOYS', a classic slice of white nouveau-funk with added rhythmic oomph courtesy of ex-CHIC man/producer in demand, NILE RODGERS, the accompanying video setting the boys in a storm-drenched, sub-Mad Max style netherworld. The single made No.2 in Britain and America, preceding the universally panned live effort, 'ARENA' (1984). A James Bond theme tune, 'VIEW TO A KILL' (another US No.1) nicely rounded off the first chapter in the band's career as the various members took time out to indulge themselves in solo projects. The less said about ARCADIA (LeBON, NICK RHODES and ROGER TAYLOR) the better, while the marginally more entertaining POWER STATION (ANDY/JOHN TAYLOR, ROBERT PALMER and ex-CHIC sticksman, TONY THOMPSON) released an eponymous album (1985) of sterile funk-rock, hitting the UK Top 10 with 'SOME LIKE IT HOT' and a cover of T.Rex's 'GET IT ON'. DURAN DURAN eventually returned in late '86 (minus ANDY and ROGER, the former setting out on a solo career while the latter quit the music business) with 'NOTORIOUS' (1986), the RODGERS-masterminded title track narrowly missing the top of the American charts. Gone were the hedonistic pop thrills of old, however, successive albums, 'BIG THING' (1988) and 'LIBERTY' (1990) indescribably bland. Nevertheless, ageing fans ensured continuing chart action, the latter album still making the UK Top 10, while 1993 saw them make something of a mini-comeback with 'ORDINARY WORLD', their best single for years and US Top 5 to boot. A second single, 'COME UNDONE', also made the grade, while the accompanying eponymous album gave a hint as to what was in store with an unlikely cover of The Velvet Underground's 'FEMME FATALE'. Even more unlikely was a cover of hip hop/electro landmark, 'WHITE LINES (DON'T DO IT)', just one of the many erm, "interpretations" on the 'THANK YOU' (1995) album. Incredibly, GRANDMASTER FLASH actually had a hand in this sacrilege, although what CHUCK D thought of the ridiculous rendition of '911 IS A JOKE' is anyone's guess. A well meant attempt at reinventing their heroes perhaps, but please, a cover of 'LAY LADY LAY'?! Of late, DURAN DURAN have plundered the past to regain some cred, a new (but old-sounding) American-only set, 'MEDAZZALAND' (1997) followed by a 'GREATEST HITS' package (again!) and worse still, a remix album in '99, entitled 'STRANGE BEHAVIOUR' (strange behaviour, indeed!). The millennial 'POP TRASH' (2000) proved that they couldn't even name an album title without resorting to cliche while the record's contents were hardly more adventurous. By this point, LE BON and RHODES were the only survivors from the classic line-up, WARREN CUCCURULLO (once again) completing the trio for a singularly uninspired set of overproduced, dinosaur pop. • **Songwriters:** LE BON – lyrics / RHODES – music. Covered; MAKE ME SMILE (Steve Harley & Cockney Rebel) / I WANNA TAKE YOU HIGHER (Sly & The Family Stone) / PERFECT DAY (Lou Reed) / WATCHING THE DETECTIVES (Elvis Costello) / SUCCESS (Iggy Pop) / CRYSTAL SHIP (Doors) / BALL OF CONFUSION (Temptations) / THANK YOU (Led Zeppelin). • **Trivia:** SIMON LE BON married top-model, Yasmin Parvanah, on the 27th of December '85, while a year previously, the other two, ROGER and NICK, had also married cosmopolitan models.

Album rating: DURAN DURAN (*7) / RIO (*7) / SEVEN AND THE RAGGED TIGER (*5) / ARENA (*4) / NOTORIOUS (*6) / BIG THING (*4) / DECADE compilation (*8) / LIBERTY (*2) / DURAN DURAN (THE WEDDING ALBUM) (*5) / THANK YOU (*4) / MEDAZZALAND (*3) / GREATEST compilation (*7) / STRANGE BEHAVIOUR (*2) / Power Station: THE POWER STATION (*5) / Arcadia: SO RED THE ROSE (*4)

SIMON LE BON (b.27 Oct'58, Bushley, Hertfordshire, England) – vocals / **ANDY TAYLOR** (b.16 Feb'61, Newcastle, England) – guitar / **NICK RHODES** (b. NICHOLAS BATES, 8 Jun'62) – keyboards / **JOHN TAYLOR** (b.20 Jul'60, Solihull, England) – bass / **ROGER TAYLOR** (b.26 Apr'60) – drums.

E.M.I. Harvest

Jan 81. (7") *(EMI 5137)* **PLANET EARTH. / LATE BAR** [12] [ ]
(12"+=) *(12EMI 5137)* – Planet earth (night version).
(re-iss. Aug83; same)

Apr 81. (7"/12") *(EMI/12EMI 5168)* **CARELESS MEMORIES. / KHANDA** [37] [ ]
(re-iss. Aug83, 7"+=/12"+=; same) – Fame.

Jun 81. (lp/c) *(EMC/TC-EMC 3372)* *<12158>* **DURAN DURAN** [3] [ ]
– Girls on film / Planet Earth / Anyone out there / To the shore / Careless memories / (Waiting for the) Night boat / Sound of thunder / Friends of mine / Tel Aviv. *<re-dist.Feb83, hit US No.10> (re-iss. Aug83; same) (cd-iss. Oct84; CZ) (re-iss. Sep87 on 'Fame' cd/c/lp; CD/TC+/FA 3185) (re-iss. Aug95 cd/c; CD/TC PRG 1003)*

Jul 81. (7") *(EMI 5206)* **GIRLS ON FILM. / FASTER THAN LIGHT** [5] [ ]
(12"+=) *(12EMI 5206)* – ('A'instrumental).
(re-iss. Aug83, 7"/12"; same)

Nov 81. (7") *(EMI 5254)* **MY OWN WAY. / LIKE AN ANGEL** [14] [ ]
(12"+=) *(12EMI 5254)* – ('A'night version).
(re-iss. Aug83, 7"/12"; same)

May 82. (7"/12") *(EMI/12EMI 5295)* *<5134>* **HUNGRY LIKE THE WOLF. / CARELESS MEMORIES (live)** [5] [ ]
(re-iss. Aug83, 7"/12"; same)
<re-iss. Dec82 with diff.B-side; 5195> – hit No.3.

E.M.I. Capitol

May 82. (lp/c) *(EMC/TC-EMC 3411)* *<12211>* **RIO** [2] Jan83 [6]
– Rio / My own way / Lonely in your nightmare / Hungry like the wolf / Hold back the rain / New religion / Last chance on the stairway / Save a prayer / The chauffeur. *(cd-iss. Aug83; CZ 291) (re-iss. Mar90 lp/c; ATAK/TC-ATAK 149) (re-iss. Sep93 cd/c; CD/TC PRG 1004)*

Aug 82. (7"/12") *(EMI/12EMI 5327)* **SAVE A PRAYER. / HOLD BACK THE RAIN (remix)** [2] [–]
(re-iss. Aug83, 7"/12"; same)

Sep 82. (m-lp) *Harvest; <15006>* **CARNIVAL** [–] [98]
– My own way / Hold back the rain / Girls on film / Hungry like the wolf.

Nov 82. (7") *(EMI 5346)* *<5175>* **RIO. / THE CHAUFFEUR (BLUE SILVER)** [9] [–]
(12") *(12EMI 5346)* – ('A'side) / Rio / (pt.2) / My own way. *(re-iss. Aug83, 7"/12"; same)*

Mar 83. (7") *<5215>* **RIO. / HOLD BACK THE RAIN** [–] [2]

Mar 83. (7"/12") *(EMI/12EMI 5371)* **IS THERE SOMETHING I SHOULD KNOW. / FAITH IN THIS COLOUR** [1] [–]
(re-iss. Aug83, 7"/12"; same)

May 83. (7") *<5233>* **IS THERE SOMETHING I SHOULD KNOW. / CARELESS MEMORIES** [–] [4]

Oct 83. (7") *(EMI 5429)* *<5290>* **UNION OF THE SNAKE. / SECRET OKTOBER** [3] [3]
(12"+=) *(12EMI 5429)* – ('A'-Monkey remix).

Nov 83. (lp/c) *(EMC/TC-EMC 1654)* *<12310>* **SEVEN AND THE RAGGED TIGER** [1] [8]
– The reflex / New Moon on Monday / (I'm looking for) Cracks in the pavement / I take the dice / Of crime and passion / Union of the snake / Shadows on your side / Tiger tiger / The seventh stranger. *(cd-iss. Mar84; CZ 36) (re-iss. Aug88 on 'Fame' cd/c/lp; CD/TC+/FA 3205) (re-iss. Sep93 cd/c; CD/TC PRG 1005)*

Jan 84. (7"/12") *(DURAN/12DURAN 1)* *<5309>* **NEW MOON ON MONDAY. / TIGER TIGER** [9] [10]

Apr 84. (7"/7"s) *(DURAN/+P 2)* **THE REFLEX. / MAKE ME SMILE (COME UP AND SEE ME) (live)** [1] [–]
(12"+=/12"pic-d+=) *(12DURAN/+P 2)* – ('A'dance mix).

Apr 84. (7") *<5345>* **THE REFLEX. / NEW RELIGION** [–] [1]

Oct 84. (7"/12") *(DURANC/12DURANC 3)* *<5417>* **THE WILD BOYS. / (I'M LOOKING FOR) CRACKS IN THE PAVEMENT** [2] [2]

Nov 84. (lp/c) *(DD/TC-DD 2)* *<12374>* **ARENA (live)** [6] [4]
– Is there something I should know / Hungry like the wolf / New religion / Save a prayer / The wild boys / The seventh stranger / The chauffeur / Union of the snake / Planet Earth / Careless memories. *(cd-iss. Dec84; CZ 79) (re-iss. Oct89 on 'Fame' cd/c/lp; CD/TC+/FA 3225)*

Jan 85. (7") *<5438>* **SAVE A PRAYER. / ('A'live version)** [–] [16]

Parlophone Capitol

May 85. (7"/7"white) *(DURAN/+G 007)* *<5475>* **A VIEW TO A KILL. / ('A'instrumental)** [2] [1]

—— took time off for own solo projects

The POWER STATION

(ANDY & JOHN TAYLOR) / **ROBERT PALMER** – vocals (solo artist see under own listing) / **TONY THOMPSON** – drums (ex-CHIC)

Parlophone Capitol

Mar 85. (7"/7"pic-d) *(R/+P 6091)* *<5444>* **SOME LIKE IT HOT. / THE HEAT IS ON** [14] [6]
(12"+=/12"pic-d+=) *(12R/+P 6091)* – ('A'extended).

Apr 85. (lp/c) *(POST/TC-POST 1)* *<12380>* **THE POWER STATION** [12] [6]
– Some like it hot / Murderess / Lonely tonight / Communication / Get it on (bang a gong) / Go to zero / Harvest for the world / Still in your heart. *(cd-iss. Jul85; CDP 746127-2) (re-iss. Sep88 on 'Fame' cd/c/lp; CD/TC+/FA 3206) (cd re-iss. Aug93; CDPRG 1011)*

May 85. (7")(12") *<5479>* **GET IT ON. / GO TO ZERO** [22] [9]

Nov 85. (7")(12") *<5511>* **COMMUNICATION. / MURDERESS** [75] [34]

—— **MICHAEL DES BARNES** – vocals; repl. PALMER on tour

ARCADIA

SIMON LE BON – vocals / **NICK RHODES** – keyboards / **ROGER TAYLOR** – drums / with session people

Oct 85. (7") *(NSR 1)* *<5501>* **ELECTION DAY. / SHE'S MOODY AND GREY SHE'S MEAN AND SHE'S RESTLESS** [7] [6]
(12"+=) *(12NSR 1)* – ('A'-Consensus mix).
(12") *(12NSRA 1)* – ('A'-Cryptic Cut No Voice mix) / ('A'mix) / ('A'-Consensus mix).

Dec 85. (lp/c) *(PCSD/TC-PCSD 101)* *<12428>* **SO RED THE ROSE** [30] [23]
– Election day / Keep me in the dark / Goodbye is forever / The flame / Missing / Rose Arcana / The promise / El Diablo / Lady Ice. *(re-iss. Aug93 cd/c; CD/TC PRG 1010)*

Dec 85. (7") *<5542>* **GOODBYE IS FOREVER. / MISSING** [–] [33]

Feb 86. (7") *(NSR 2)* **THE PROMISE. / ROSE ARCANE** [37] [ ]
(12"+=) *(12NSR 2)* – ('A'extended).

Jul 86. (7") *(NSR 3)* **THE FLAME. / FLAME AGAIN** [58] [ ]
(12") *(12NSR 3)* – ('A'extended) / ('B'-Homeboy mix) / Election day (Early Rough mix).

JOHN TAYLOR

Mar 86. (7") *(R 6125)* *<5551>* **I DO WHAT I DO . . . (theme from 9 1/2 weeks). / JAZZ (instrumental)** [42] [23]
(12"+=) *(12R 6125)* – ('A'-Film mix).

DURAN DURAN

—— ANDY went solo and subsequently released a handful of singles including a US Top 30 smash, 'TAKE IT EASY' (from the movie, 'American Anthem') and an album, 'THUNDER', a US Top 50 breaker in '87). (ROGER quit the music business)

—— now down to **SIMON, NICK + JOHN**

Oct 86. (7") *(DDN 45)* *<5648>* **NOTORIOUS. / WINTER MARCHES ON** [7] [2]
(c-s+=/12"+=) *(TC/12 DDNX 45)* – ('A'-Latin Rascals mix).

Nov 86. (lp/c)(cd) *(DDN/TCDDN 331)(CDP 746 415-2)* *<12540>* **NOTORIOUS** [16] [12]
– Notorious / American science / Skin trade / A matter of feeling / Hold me / Vertigo (do the demolition) / So misled / Meet el Presidente / Winter marches on / Proposition. *(re-iss. Sep93 cd/c; CD/TC PRG 1004)*

Feb 87. (7"/7"w-poster) *(TRADE/+X 1)* *<5670>* **SKIN TRADE. / WE NEED YOU** [22] [39]
(c-s+=) *(TCTRADE 1)* – ('A'-Stretch mix).

Apr 87. (7") *(TOUR 1)* **MEET EL PRESIDENTE. / VERTIGO (DO THE DEMOLITION)** [24] [70]
(ext.cd-s+=) *(CDTOUR 1)* – ('A'-Meet el Beat mix).

—— added **WARREN CUCCURULLO** – guitar (ex-FRANK ZAPPA, ex-MISSING PERSONS) / **STEVE FERRONE** – drums (ex-BRIAN AUGER, ex-AVERAGE WHITE BAND) (both on last lp

Sep 88. (7") *(YOUR 1)* *<44237>* **I DON'T WANT YOUR LOVE. / ('A'-lp version)** [14] [4]
(etched-12"+=/cd-s+=) *(12/CD YOURS 1)* – ('A'Big Mix version).

Oct 88. (cd/c/lp) *(CD/TC+/DDB 33)* *<90958>* **BIG THING** [15] [24]
– Big thing / I don't want your love / All she wants is / Too late Marlene / Drug (it's just a state of mind) / Do you believe in shame? / Palomino / Interlude one / Land / Flute interlude / The edge of America / Lake shore driving. *(re-iss. Mar90 on 'E.M.I.' lp/c; ATAK/TC-ATAK 148) (cd-iss. Mar90 on 'E.M.I'; CZ 290) (re-iss. Sep93 cd/c; CD/TC PRG 1007)*

Dec 88. (7") *(DD 11)* *<44287>* **ALL SHE WANTS IS. / I BELIEVE – ALL I NEED TO KNOW (medley)** [ ] [22]
(12"+=) *(12DDX 11)* *<44287>* – ('A'-US master mix).
(3"cd-s+=) *(CDDD 11)* – Skin trade (Parisian mix).

Apr 89. (7"/7"pic-d) *(DD/+PD 12)* *<44337>* **DO YOU BELIEVE IN SHAME? / ('A'-Krush Brothers LSD mix)** [30] Mar89 [72]
(10"+=) *(10DD 12)* – Notorious (live).
(3"cd-s++=) *(CDDD 12)* – God (London) / This is how a road gets made.
(3x7"box) *(DD A/B/C 12) – Do you believe in shame? / God (London) // Palomino (edit). / This is how a road gets made // Do you believe in shame? / Drugs – it's just a state of mind.*

Nov 89. (cd/c/lp) *(CD/TC+/DDX 10)* *<93178>* **DECADE** [5] [67]
– Planet Earth / Girls on film / Hungry like the wolf / Rio / Save a prayer / Is there something I should know / Union of the snake / The reflex / Wild boys / A view to a kill / Notorious / Skin trade / I don't want your love / All she wants is.

Dec 89. (c-s/7") *(TC+/DD 13)* **BURNING THE GROUND. / DECADENCE** [31] [–]
(12"+=/cd-s+=) *(12/CD DD 13)* – Decadence (extended).

—— **STERLING CAMPBELL** – drums repl. FERRONE

Jul 90. (c-s/7") *(TC+/DD 14)* **VIOLENCE OF SUMMER (LOVE'S TAKING OVER). / ('A'mix)** [20] [–]
(12"+=) *(12DD 14)* – ('A'extended).
(cd-s+=) *(CDDD 14)* – Throb.

Aug 90. (c-s) *<44608>* **VIOLENCE OF SUMMER (LOVE'S TAKING OVER) / YO BAD AZIZI** [–] [64]

Aug 90. (cd/c/lp) *(CD/TC+/PCSD 112)* *<94292>* **LIBERTY** [8] [46]
– Violence of summer (love's taking over) / Liberty / Hothead / Serious / All along the water / My Antartica / Read my lips / First impression / Can you deal with it / Venice drowning / Downtown. *(re-iss. Sep93 cd/c; CD/TC RG 1009)*

Nov 90. (c-s/7") *(TC+/DD 15)* **SERIOUS. / YO BAD AZIZI** [48] [–]
(12"+=/cd-s+=) *(12/CD DD 15)* – Water babies.

Jan 93. (c-s) *<44908>* **ORDINARY WORLD / ('A'acoustic) / SAVE A PRAYER (live)** [–] [3]

Jan 93. (c-s/7")(7"pic-d) *(TC+/DD 16)(DDP 16)* **ORDINARY WORLD. / MY ANTARTICA** [6] [–]
(cd-s+=) *(CDDDS 16)* – Save a prayer / Skin trade.
(cd-s) *(CDDDP 16)* – ('A'side) / The reflex / Hungry like the wolf / Girls on film.

Feb 93. (cd/c/lp) *(CD/TC+/DDB 34)* *<98876>* **DURAN DURAN** (THE WEDDING ALBUM) [4] [7]
– Too much information / Ordinary world / Love voodoo / Drowning man / Shotgun / Come undone / Breath after breath / UMF / Home of the above / Femme fatale / Shelter / To whom it may concern. *(cd-box Jan94; CDDDB 35)*

Mar 93. (c-s/7") *(TC+/DD 17)* **COME UNDONE. / ORDINARY WORLD (acoustic)** [13] [–]
(cd-s+=) *(CDDD 17)* – ('A'mixes).
(cd-s) *(CDDDS 17)* – ('A'side) / ('A'version) / Rio / Is there something I should know / A view to a kill.

Apr 93. (c-s) *<44918>* **COME UNDONE / ('A'-mix 2 master) / TIME FOR TEMPTATION** [–] [7]

Aug 93. (c-s/12") *(TC/12 DD 18)* **TOO MUCH INFORMATION. / COME UNDONE (live)** [35] [–]
(12"+=) *(12DD 18) – Come undone (12"mix Coming together) / Notorious (live).*
(cd-s) *(CDDD 18)* – ('A'side) / Drowning man.

Aug 93. (cd-s) *<44955>* **TOO MUCH INFORMATION / FIRST IMPRESSION / COME UNDONE (new mix)** [–] [45]
(with live free c-ep) **NO ORDINARY EP** – Hungry like the wolf / Notorious / Come undone.

Mar 95. (c-s/7") *(TC+/DD 20)* **PERFECT DAY. / FEMME FATALE (alt.mix)** [28] [ ]
(cd-s+=) *(CDDDS 20)* – Make me smile (come up and see me) / Perfect day (acoustic).
(cd-s) *(CDDDP 20)* – ('A'side) / Love voodoo / Needle and the damage done / 911 is a joke (alternative mix).

Mar 95. (cd/c) *(CD/TC DDB 36)* *<29419>* **THANK YOU** [12] [19]
– White lines / I wanna take you higher / Perfect day / Watching the detectives / Lay lady lay / 911 is a joke / Success / Crystal ship / Ball of confusion / Thank you / Drive by / I wanna take you higher again.
below actually featured GRANDMASTER FLASH

Jun 95. (c-s) *(TCDD 19)* **WHITE LINES (DON'T DO IT) / SAVE A PRAYER / NONE OF THE ABOVE (Drizabone mix)** [17] [ ]
(cd-s+=) *(CDDD 19)* – Ordinary world (acoustic).
(12") *(12DD 19)* – ('A'side) / ('A'-Junior Vasquez mix) / ('A'-Oakland fonk mix) / ('A'-70's club mix).

Virgin | Capitol

May 97. (7"/c-s/cd-s) *(VS LH/C/CDT 1639)* **OUT OF MY MIND / SILVA HALO** [21] [–]
(cd-s+=) *(VSCDX 1639)* – Sinner or saint / ('A'remix).

Sep 97. (c-s,cd-s) *<58674>* **ELECTRIC BARBARELLA /** [–] [52]

Oct 97. (cd,c) *<33876>* **MEDAZZALAND** [–] [58]
– Medazzaland / Big bang generation / Electric Barbarella / Out of my mind / Who do you think you are? / Silva halo / Be my icon / Buried in the sand / Michael you've got a lot to answer for / Midnight sun / So long suicide / Undergoing treatment.

E.M.I. | not iss.

Jan 99. (c-s) *(TCELEC 2000)* **ELECTRIC BARBARELLA / GIRLS ON FILM (Tin Tin Out mix)** [23] [–]
(cd-s+=) *(CDELEC 2000)* – ('A'-Tee's club mix).
(12"+=) *(12ELEC 2000)* – ('A'-Electric sex mix).

Hollywood | Hollywood

May 00. (c-s) *(0108845 HWR)* **SOMEONE ELSE NOT ME / (album version)** [53] [–]
(cd-s+=) *(0100849 HWR)* – Starting to remember.

Jun 00. (cd) *(0107512 HWR)* *<62266>* **POP TRASH** [53] [ ]
– Someone else not me / Lava lamp / Playing with uranium / Hallucinating Elvis / Starting to remember / Pop trash movie / Fragment / Mars meets Venus / Lady Xanax / The sun doesn't shine forever / Kiss goodbye / The last day on Earth. *<US+=>* – Someone else not me (en Espanol).

—— in 2002, NICK teamed up with STEPHEN DUFFY (again!) to form The DEVILS; one set 'DARK CIRCLES'.

– compilations, etc. –

Nov 98. (cd/c) *E.M.I.; (496239-2/-4) / Capitol; <96239>* **GREATEST** [15] Apr99 [ ]
– Is there something I should know? / The reflex / A view to a kill / Ordinary world / Save a prayer / Rio / Hungry like the wolf / Girls on film / Planet Earth / Union of the snake / New moon on Monday / Wild boys / Notorious / I don't want your love / All she wants is / Electric Barbarella / Serious / Skin trade / Come undone.

Mar 99. (d-cd) *E.M.I.; (493972-2)* **STRANGE BEHAVOIR** (remixes) [70] [ ]

POWER STATION

—— re-grouped (**PALMER / TAYLOR / TAYLOR / THOMPSON**)

Chrysalis | Chrysalis

Oct 96. (c-s) *(TCCHS 5039)* **SHE CAN ROCK IT / ('A'mix)** [63] [ ]
(cd-s+=) *(CDCHS 5039)* – Power trippin' / Charanga.

Oct 96. (cd/c) *(CD/TC CHR 6117)* **LIVING IN FEAR** [ ] [ ]
– Notoriety / Scarred / She can rock it / Let's get it on / Life forces / Fancy that / Living in fear / Shut up / Dope / Love conquers all / Taxman.

DURUTTI COLUMN

Formed: Manchester, England . . . early 1978 by VINI REILLY, CHRIS JOYCE and DAVE ROWBOTHAM. That year, they signed to TONY WILSON's indie label, 'Factory', although they dramatically split in mid-'79 leaving skinny VINI to pick up the pieces. Taking their name from the 1930's art-terrorists, Situationiste Internationale, and given free time by label boss, WILSON, under the wing of producer MARTIN HANNETT, the guitarist finally came up with DURUTTI's debut 'THE RETURN

OF . . .' (1980). This was a brilliant introduction to his minimalist yet picturesque guitar improvisations, although its gimmick sandpaper sleeve was not exactly the toast of the record retailers who had to protect the rest of their stock from its glassy debris. He subsequently supported on tour fellow Mancunian, JOHN COOPER CLARKE, PAULINE MURRAY and even JOHN MARTYN, while recording the follow-up, 'L.C.' (1981), another masterpiece that fused light jazz into barren but dreamy landscapes. However, not for the first time, ill-health was to dog VINI, and it took a few years to record 'ANOTHER SETTING' (1983). All the above albums featured eccentric percussionist BRUCE MITCHELL, he of former parody-rock outfit, ALBERTOS Y LOST TRIOS PARANOIAS, the man becoming a stalwart on all VINI/DURUTTI's further work. In 1986, VINI took a trip to California, where he invited punkette, DEBI DIAMOND, to sing on a version of JEFFERSON AIRPLANE's 'White Rabbit'. After the release of the 1987 album, 'GUITAR AND OTHER MACHINES', REILLY was invited by old fellow NOSEBLEEDS chum, MORRISSEY, to play guitar pieces on his 1988 solo debut, 'VIVA HATE'. In 1990, DURUTTI COLUMN returned in fine style with 'OBEY THE TIME', although this was the last for Factory, as the label went bankrupt in '92. Under the control of 'Polygram', the imprint was once again under way in 1994 as 'Factory Too', and a happier VINI unleashed another textured beauty, 'SEX AND DEATH'. REILLY resumed his intermittent recording schedule with low-key 'TIME WAS GIGANTIC . . . WHEN WE WERE KIDS' (1998), a set featuring ELEY RUDGE on vocals. For 'REBELLION' (2001), the ageing guitar wunderkind crafting a markedly more accessible long player with an unprecedented ceding of leeway to the basic tenets of song structure. Thus one of the record's standouts is an inspired rendition of Irish folk standard (and Celtic fans' anthem), 'THE FIELDS OF ATHENRY', while a willingness to augment his work with contemporary elements served to showcase the man's still burning talent. 2003's return, 'SOMEONE ELSE'S PARTY', was reflective and sombre due to death of VINI's mother, although it did reprise his classical guitar style of his early days. • **Songwriters:** All composed by REILLY, except cover; I GET ALONG WITHOUT YOU VERY WELL (Hoagy Carmichael). • **Note:** On the 8th of November '91, original member, DAVE ROWBOTHAM, was axed to death.

Album rating: THE RETURN OF THE DURUTTI COLUMN (*9) / L.C. (*7) / ANOTHER SETTING (*6) / WITHOUT MERCY (*6) / DOMO ARIGATO (*7) / CIRCUSES AND BREAD (*5) / VALUABLE PASSAGES compilation (*8) / THE GUITAR AND OTHER MACHINES (*6) / VINI REILLY (*7) / OBEY THE TIME (*5) / DRY (*5) / SEX AND DEATH (*7) / FIDELITY (*5) / TIME WAS GIGANTIC . . . WHEN WE WERE KIDS (*5) / REBELLION (*6) / SOMEONE ELSE'S PARTY (*7)

VINI REILLY (b. Aug'53) – guitar (ex-NOSEBLEEDS, ex-V2) / **DAVE ROWBOTHAM** – guitar / **CHRIS JOYCE** – drums / **BRUCE MITCHELL** – percussion / also **TONY BOWERS** – bass / **PHIL RAINFORD** – vocals (left Jul78)

— recorded for Various Artists EP – A FACTORY SAMPLER. Split mid'79, DAVE, CHRIS and TONY joined The MOTHMEN. **VINI REILLY** now brought in **MARTIN HANNETT** – switches, producer (ex-INVISIBLE GIRLS (JOHN COOPER CLARKE) with **PETER CROOKS** – bass / **TOBY** (b.PHILIP TOMANOV) – drums / **GAMMER** – melody

Factory not iss.

Feb 80. (lp) *(FACT 14)* **THE RETURN OF THE DURUTTI COLUMN** [ ] [–]
– Sketch for Summer / Requiem for a father / Katherine / Conduct / Beginning / Jazz / Sketch for winter / Collette / In "D". *(w/ free testcard flexi by MARTIN HANNETT)* **FIRST ASPECT OF THE SAME THING. / SECOND ASPECT OF THE SAME THING** *(re-iss. Jul80 lp/c; FACT 14/+C) (cd-iss. DEc96 on 'Factory Too'; 828829-2)*

— **VINI** on his own, featured **PHIL RAYNHAM** – vocals

Nov 80. (12") *Factory Benelux; (FACBN 2)* **LIPS THAT WOULD KISS (FORM PRAYERS TO BROKEN STONE). / MADELEINE** [–] Belgium [–]
(re-iss. Mar81; FACBN 2-005) (re-iss. cd-ep Mar91 & Nov96; FBN 2CD)

Mar 81. (7"ltd) *Sordide Sentimentale; (SS 45-005)* **ENIGMA. / DANNY** [–] Italy [–]

— now just a duo when **VINI** – guitars, now on extra vocals & keyboards / added **BRUCE MITCHELL** – percussion (ex-ALBERTOS Y LOST TRIOS PARANOIAS)

Sep 81. (lp/c) *(FACT 44/+C)* **LC** [ ] [–]
– Sketch for dawn 1 / Portrait for Frazier / Jacqueline / Messidor / Sketch for dawn 2 / Never known / The act committed / Detail for Paul / The missing boy / The sweet cheat gone. *(cd-iss. Dec96 on 'Factory Too'+=; 828827-2)* – For Mimi / Belgian friends / Self portrait / One Christmas for your thoughts / Danny / Enigma.

— VINI now completely solo

1982. (7"ltd) *Factory Benelux; (FBN 100)* **FOR PATTI. / WEARINESS AND FEVER** [–] Belgium [–]

Mar 82. (12"ep) *Factory Benelux; (FBN 10)* **DEUX TRIANGLES** [–] Belgium [–]
– Favourite painting / Zinni / Piece for out of tune grand piano.

— added guests **LINDSAY WILSON** – vocals / **MAUNAGH FLEMING** – cor anglais

Aug 82. (7") *(FAC 64)* **I GET ALONG WITHOUT YOU VERY WELL. / PRAYER** [ ] [–]

— **VINI** now augmented by **MERVYN FLETCHER** – saxophone / **TONY BOWERS** – bass / **CHRIS JOYCE** – drums / **TIM KELLETT** – trumpet (all ex-MOTHMEN)

Aug 83. (lp/c) *(FACT 74/+C)* **ANOTHER SETTING** [ ] [–]
– Prayer / Bordeaux / The beggar / The response / For a western / Francesca / Smile in the crowd / Dream of a child / Spent time / You've heard it before / Second family. *(cd-iss. Sep98 on 'Factory Once'+=; 556041-2)* – (Portuguese versions).

— **VINI** retained **MERVYN** and **TIM.** (TONY & CHRIS later joined SIMPLY RED with TIM). **BRUCE MITCHELL** rejoined (he had always been part of live set-up) / **MAUNAGH FLEMING** rejoined with new guests **CAROLINE LAVELLE** – cello / **RICHARD HENRY** – trombone / **BLAINE REININGER** – viola/violin (of TUXEDO MOON)

Dec 84. (lp/c) *(FACT 84/+C)* **WITHOUT MERCY** [ ] [–]
– Without mercy / Goodbye / Room / Little mercy / Silence / EE / Hellow / All that love and maths can do / Sea wall. *(cd-iss. Sep98 on 'Factory Once'; 556039-2)*

— now just basically **VINI** with **BRUCE** with old friends augmenting

Mar 85. (12"ep) *(FAC 114)* **SAY WHAT YOU MEAN, MEAN WHAT YOU SAY** [ ] [–]
– Goodbye / The room / E.E. / A little mercy / Silence / Hello.

Aug 85. (video-cd) *(FACD 144)* **DOMO ARIGATO (live Japan)** [ ] [–]
– Sketch for Summer / Mercy theme / Sketch for dawn / E.E. / Little mercy / Jacqueline / Dream of a child / Mercy dance / The room / Blind elevator girl / Tomorrow / Belgian friends / Missing boy / Self-portrait / (audience noise). *(cd-iss. Sep98 on 'Factory Once'+=; 556038-2)* – Our lady of the angels / White rabbit / Catos con guantos.

Mar 86. (7") *Factory Benelux; (FBN 51)* **TOMORROW. / TOMORROW (live)** [–] Belgium [–]
(12"+=) *(FBN 51)* – All that love and maths can do.

Mar 86. (lp)(cd) *(FBN 36)(FACD 154)* **CIRCUSES AND BREAD** [ ] [–]
– Pauline / Tomorrow / Dance 2 / For Hilary / Street fight / Royal infirmary / Black horses / Dance 1 / Blind elevator girl – Osaka. *(cd+=)* – (last 45). *(cd-iss. Nov93 on 'Crepescule'; TWI 9882)*

— **VINI** with **MITCHELL, KELLETT, JOHN METCALFE**

Oct 86. (12") *Materiali Sonori; (MASO 70003)* **GREETINGS THREE** [–] Italy [–]
– Florence sunset / All that love and maths can do / San Giovanni dawn / For friends in Italy.

Aug 87. (12"ep; w/ DEBI DIAMOND) *(FAC 184)* **THE CITY OF OUR LADY** [ ] [–]
– Our lady of the angels / White rabbit* / Catos con guantes.

Dec 87. (cd-ep) *(FACD 194)* **OUR LADY OF THE ANGELS / CATOS CON GUANTAS / WHEN THE WORLD (Newson mix)** [ ] [–]

— **VINI + BRUCE** were joined by guests **TIM KELLETT** (of SIMPLY RED) (1 track.) / **STANTON MIRANDA** – vocals (solo artist – 2 tracks.) **POL** – vocals (3 tracks.) / **STEPHEN STREET** – bass (1 track.) **JOHN METCALFE** – viola (1 track.) / **ROB GREY** – mouth organ

Factory Venture

Nov 87. (lp/cd)(c/dat) *(FAC T/D 204)(FACT 204 C/D) <90887-1/-4/-2>* **THE GUITAR AND OTHER MACHINES**
– When the world / Arpeggiator / What is it to me (woman) / U.S.P. / Red shoes / Jongleur grey / Bordeaux sequence / Miss Haynes / Don't think you're funny / English tradition landscape / Pol in 'B'. *(cd+=)* – Dream topping / You won't feel out of place / 28 Oldham Street. *(cd re-iss. Dec96 on 'Factory Too'+=; 828828-2)* – Otis / E.L.T. / Finding the sea / Bordeaux.

Dec 87. (7"flexi) *(FAC 214)* **THE GUITAR AND OTHER MARKETING DEVICES** –
– Jongleur grey / Bordeaux sequence / English landscape tradition / U.S.P.

—— added **ROBERT NEWTON** plus **DV8 PHYSICAL THEATRE**

Apr 88. (cd-s-video) *(FACDV 194)* **WHEN THE WORLD (soundtrack) / WHEN THE WORLD (lp) / FINAL CUT / WHEN THE WORLD (video)** –

Dec 88. (3"cd-ep) *(FACD 234)* **WOMAD LIVE (live)** –
– Otis / English landscape tradition / Finding the sea / Bordeaux.

Mar 89. (lp/cd)(dat) *(FAC T/CD 244)(FACT 244D)* **VINI REILLY** –
– Homage to Catalonea / Opera II / People's pleasure park / Pol in G / Love no more / Opera I / Finding the sea / Otis / They work every day / Requiem again / My country. *(lp w/ free 7" with MORRISSEY) (FAC 244+)* – I KNOW VERY WELL HOW I GOT MY NOTE WRONG *(cd w/ free 3"cd-ep) (FAC 244+)* – (above) / Red square / William B. *(cd re-iss. Nov99 on 'Factory Too'; 828826-2)*

—— Included sampled voices of OTIS REDDING, ANNIE LENNOX and TRACY CHAPMAN. **VINI** added **PAUL MILLER**

Dec 90. (cd/lp)(c/dat) *(FAC D/T 274)(FACT 274 C/D)* **OBEY THE TIME** –
– Vino della easa Bianco / Fridays / Home / Art and freight / Spanish reggae / Neon / The warmest rain / Contra-indications / Vino della casa rosso. *(cd re-iss. Sep98 on 'Factory Once'; 556040-2)*

Feb 91. (12"ep/cd-ep) *(FAC/+D 284)* **THE TOGETHER MIX. / CONTRA INDICATIONS (version) / FRIDAYS (up-person mix)** –

Jun 91. (cd)(lp) *Materiali Sonori; (CDMASO 90024)(33-065)* **DRY** – Italy –
– Dry / Paradise passage road / Rope around my neck / Short / Boat people / Boat people / Our lady / Grade 2 duet / Octaves / Out of the blue / Otis / English language tradition / Finding the sea / Bordeaux / Beggar. *(cd+=)* – WOMAD LIVE (tracks). *(UK cd-iss. Mar00; same)*

—— **VINI, BRUCE** w / guests **PETER HOOK** – bass (of NEW ORDER) + **MARTIN JACKSON** – keyboards (ex/of-SWING OUT SISTER)

Factory Too Factory Too

Nov 94. (cd) *(FACD 201) <697-124 043-2>* **SEX AND DEATH** Mar95
– Anthony / The rest of my life / For Colette / The next time / Beautiful lies / My irasable friend / Believe in me / Fermina / Where I should be / Fado / Madre mio / Blue period.

Crepescule not iss.

May 96. (cd) *(TWI 976-2)* **FIDELITY** May01
– Fidelity / For Suzanne / Future perfect / Abstract of expressio / G and T / Remember me / Sanko / Grace / Guitar for Steve / Storm for Steve.

—— next with **ELEY RUDGE** – vocals

Factory Once not iss.

Sep 98. (cd) *(558330-2)* **TIME WAS GIGANTIC . . . WHEN WE WERE KIDS** –
– Organ donor / Pigeon / I B yours / Twenty trees / Abuse / Drinking song / Sing to me / My last kiss / For Rachel / Highfield choir / Epilogue.

Artful Artful

Jun 01. (cd) *(<ARTFULCD 40>)* **REBELLION** Aug01
– 4 Sophia / Longsight romance / Ceh cak af en yam / The fields of Athenry / Overload (part 1) / Falling / Voluntary arrangement / Mello (part 1) / Mello (part 2) / Protest song / Meschugana.

Mar 03. (cd) *(<ARTFULCD 49>)* **SOMEONE ELSE'S PARTY**
– Love is a friend / Spanish lament / Somewhere / Somebody's party / Requiem for my mother / Remember / Vigil / Blue / No more hurt / Spasmic fairy / American view / Dribking time / Woman / Goodbye.

– compilations, etc. –

Jun 83. (lp) *V.U.; (VINI 1)* **LIVE AT THE VENUE (live VINI & BRUCE)** –
– Sketch for summer / Conduct / Never known / Jacqueline / Party / etc.

Dec 85. (lp) *Fundacao Atlantica; (1652071)* **AMIGOS EM PORTUGAL / DEDICATIONS FOR JACQUELINE** – Portu –
– Friends in Portugal / Small girl by a pool / Crumpled dress / Sara and Tristana / Nighttime Estoril / Lisbon / To end with / Wheels turning / Favourite descending intervals / Saudade / Games of rhythm / Lies of mercy.

Dec 86. (lp/cd)(d-c) *Factory; (FAC T/D 164)(FACT 164C) / Relativity; <88561 8123-1/-4/-2>* **VALUABLE PASSAGES** –
– Sketch for summer / Conduct / Sketch for winter / Lips that would kiss / Belgian friends / Danny / Piece for out-of-tune piano / Never know / Jacqueline / Missing boy / Prayer / Spent time / Without mercy stanzas 2-8 & 12-15 / Room / Blind elevator girl / Tomorrow / LFO MOD.

Nov 87. (c) *R.O.I.R.; (A-152)* **THE DURUTTI COLUMN LIVE AT THE BOTTOM LINE, NEW YORK (live)** –
– Prayer / Arpeggiator / Our lady of the angels / Pol in B / Miss Haymes / For mother / Requiem / Jaqueline / Elevator sequence / Missing boy / U.S.P. / Tomorrow. *(<re-iss. May93 & Feb95 cd/c; A-152 CD/C>) (<cd re-iss. Oct99 as 'A NIGHT IN NEW YORK' on 'R.O.I.R.'; RUSCD 8255>)*

Mar 88. (4xcd-box) *Factory; (FACD 224)* **THE DURUTTI COLUMN – THE FIRST FOUR ALBUMS** –

Dec 89. (ltd-cd) *Spore; (CD 1)* **THE SPORADIC RECORDINGS** –

Sep 94. (cd) *Materiali Sonori; (MASO 90037)* **RED SHOES** –

Jul 02. (cd) *Kooky; (KOOKYDISC 018)* **RETURN OF THE SPORADIC RECORDINGS / THE SPORADIC RECORDINGS** –

Ian DURY

Born: 12 May'42, Upminster, Essex, England. At age seven he became partially crippled from contracting polio. In 1970, he was employed as a teacher / lecturer at Canterbury College. The following year, he formed KILBURN & THE HIGH ROADS, who embarked on pub/college circuit in London. After 1 album in the mid-70's and many line-up changes, they disbanded, leaving DURY and manager DAVE ROBINSON to create solo deal for the singer. Signing to Jake Riviera's new indie label, 'Stiff', he soon raced up album charts in 1977 with the new wave favourite 'NEW BOOTS AND PANTIES!!!'. DURY's articulate patter and intelligent lyrics fused well with funky/jerky group backing which alternated between rock'n'roll and disco. He also developed many areas of Cockney rhyme-slang into rude but clever lyrics. The album made the UK Top 5, preceded by the brilliant 'SEX AND DRUGS AND ROCK AND ROLL', DURY's typically wry comment on the excesses of the music business. The following year, the singer's cast of sidemen became The BLOCKHEADS, the line-up of CHAZ JANKEL, NORMAN WATT-ROY, CHARLEY CHARLES, MICKEY GALLAGHER, JOHN TURNBULL and DAVY PAYNE playing on DURY's first hit single, 'WHAT A WASTE'. However, it was the follow-up, 'HIT ME WITH YOUR RHYTHM STICK' which really earned DURY a smutty place in the annals of pop history, its half-spoken narrative style breaking into a gloriously demented chorus. The track sat astride the UK singles chart for a few weeks, while the attendant album, 'DO IT YOURSELF' (1979) made No.2. The DURY/JANKEL writing partnership was to end soon after, however, the latter embarking on solo work and freeing up a position for ex-DR. FEELGOOD guitarist, WILKO JOHNSON. The resulting album, 'LAUGHTER' (1980), met with limited success, prompting a musical Spring clean from DURY; signing to 'Polydor', securing the esteemed services of SLY & ROBBIE and reuniting with JANKEL, the cheeky cockney released the acclaimed 'LORD UPMINSTER'. Commercial success continued to elude him, however, and DURY semi-retired in the mid-80's following the '4,000 WEEKS HOLIDAY' (1984) opus. He eventually resurfaced in 1989 with the 'APPLES' soundtrack, although he proved his inimitable sense of humour hadn't deserted him on 1992's 'THE BUS DRIVERS

PRAYER & OTHER STORIES'. Having been diagnosed with cancer of the colon in 1995 (it was soon to spread into his liver), IAN DURY wanted to bow out with a bang not a whimper. In the summer of '98, the man did just that (with the help from his ever faithful BLOCKHEADS). His comeback album, 'Mr LOVE PANTS', even returned him back into the charts, but sadly, this was IAN's last lyrical message – he died on the 27th March, 2000; they said he died with a smile on his face. A posthumous final recording, the LP 'TEN MORE TURNIPS FROM THE TIP' (2002), kept the man on a high note. • **Songwriters:** DURY – words / JANKEL – music, until his departure from The BLOCKHEADS. • **Trivia:** After he semi-retired in the mid-80's, he started an acting career in films:- NUMBER ONE (1985) / PIRATES (1986) / HEARTS OF FIRE (1987), and TV plays:- KING OF THE GHETTOS (1986) / TALK OF THE DEVIL (1986) / NIGHT MOVES (1987). His other work on TV was mainly for commercials, etc.

Album rating: NEW BOOTS AND PANTIES!! (*8) / DO IT YOURSELF (*7) / LAUGHTER (*6) / JUKEBOX DURY compilation (*6) / LORD UPMINSTER (*6) / 400 WEEKS HOLIDAY (*5) / SEX AND DRUGS AND ROCK AND ROLL compilation (*7) / APPLES (*5) / THE BUS DRIVER'S PRAYER AND OTHER STORIES (*6) / Mr LOVE PANTS (*6) / TEN MORE TURNIPS FROM THE TIP (*6)

KILBURN & THE HIGH ROADS

IAN DURY – vocals / **KEITH LUCAS** – guitar / **DAVEY PAYNE** – sax / **CHARLIE SINCLAIR** – bass repl. HUMPHREY OCEAN who had repl. CHARLIE HART / **LOUIS LAROSE** then **GEORGE BUTLER** – drums

— Early 1974, recorded lp for 'Raft', which was shelved after 'Warners' took over label. It was later issued by them in Oct'78 as 'WOTABUNCH', after DURY was top of the charts.

— (mid-74) **DAVID ROHOMAN** – drums repl. BUTLER / **ROD MELVIN** – piano repl. HARDY

Dawn — not iss.

Nov 74. (7") *(DNS 1090)* **ROUGH KIDS. / BILLY BENTLEY** [ ] [–]

Feb 75. (7") *(DNS 1102)* **CRIPPLED WITH NERVES. / HUFFETY PUFF** [ ] [–]

Jun 75. (lp) *(DNLS 3065)* **HANDSOME** [ ] [–]
– The roadette song / Pam's mood / Crippled with nerves / Broken skin / Upminster kid / Patience / Father / Thank you mum / Rough kids / The badger and the rabbit / The mumble rumble and the cocktail rock / The call up. *(re-iss. Nov85 on 'Flashback' lp/c; FBLP/ZCFBL 8094)*

— Disbanded mid-75, although IAN gigged at times with a new line-up as IAN DURY & THE KILBURNS. KEITH LUCAS was later to become NICK CASH and form 999. There were also other KILBURN material re-released after DURY's success.

1977. (lp) *Warners; (K 56513)* **WOTABUNCH** [ ] [–]

Sep 78. (7") *Warners; (K 17225)* **BENTLEY. / PAM'S MOODS** [ ] [–]

Jul 83. (lp/c) *P.R.T.; (DOW/ZCDOW 17)* **UPMINSTER KIDS** [ ] [–]

IAN DURY

— - vocals solo with **CHAZ JANKEL** – guitar, keyboards (ex-BYZANTIUM) plus session men that became The BLOCKHEADS (see below)

Stiff — Stiff

Aug 77. (7",7"orange) *(BUY 17)* **SEX AND DRUGS AND ROCK AND ROLL. / RAZZLE IN MY POCKET** [ ] [–]

Sep 77. (lp/gold-lp/c) *(SEEZ/SEEZG/ZSEEZ 4) <0002>* **NEW BOOTS AND PANTIES!!!** [5] Apr78 [ ]
– Sweet Gene Vincent / ake up and make love with me / I'm partial to your abracadabra / My old man / Billericay Dickie / Clevor Trever / If I was with a woman / Plainstow Patricia / Blockheads / Blackmail man. *(re-iss. Sep86 on 'Demon' lp/c/cd+=; FIEND/+CASS/CD 63)* – (interview). *(re-iss. cd May95 on 'Disky';) (cd re-iss. Aug98 & Apr00 on 'A Hit Label'; AHLCD 57) (cd re-iss. Jun00 on 'REpertoire'; REP 4546)*

Nov 77. (7") *(BUY 23)* **SWEET GENE VINCENT. / YOU'RE MORE THAN FAIR** [ ] [–]

IAN DURY AND THE BLOCKHEADS

— with **JANKEL** plus **NORMAN WATT-ROY** – bass (ex-LOVING AWARENESS, ex-GLENCOE) / **CHARLEY CHARLES** – drums (ex-LOVING AWARENESS, ex-GLENCOE) / **MICKEY GALLAGHER** – keyboards (ex-LOVING AWARENESS, ex-FRAMPTON'S CAMEL) / **JOHN TURNBULL** – guitar (ex-LOVING AWARENESS) / **DAVEY PAYNE** – saxophone (ex-WRECKLESS ERIC)

Apr 78. (7"/12") *(BUY 27/+12)* **WHAT A WASTE. / WAKE UP AND MAKE LOVE WITH ME** [11] [ ]

Nov 78. (7"; as IAN & THE BLOCKHEADS) *(BUY 38)* **HIT ME WITH YOUR RHYTHM STICK. / THERE AIN'T HALF BEEN SOME CLEVER BASTARDS** [1] [ ]

May 79. (lp/c) *(SEEZ/ZSEEZ 14) <36104>* **DO IT YOURSELF** [2] Jul79 [ ]
– Inbetweenies / Quiet / Don't ask me / Sink my boats / Waiting for your taxi / This is what we find / Uneasy sunny hotsy totsy / Mischief / Dance of the screamers / Lullaby for Francies. *(re-iss. Feb90 on 'Demon' lp/c/cd; FIEND/+CASS/CD 133) (re-iss. cd May95 on 'Disky';) (cd re-iss. Sep98 on 'Repertoire'; REP 4547) (cd re-iss. Apr00 on 'A Hit Label'; AHLCD 58)*

Jul 79. (7") *(BUY 50)* **REASONS TO CHEERFUL (pt.3). / COMMON AS MUCK** [3] [ ]

Aug 80. (7") *(BUY 90)* **I WANT TO BE STRAIGHT. / THAT'S NOT ALL HE WANTS** [22] [ ]

— **WILKO JOHNSON** – guitar (ex-DR. FEELGOOD, solo artist) repl. JANKEL who went solo

Oct 80. (7") *(BUY 100)* **SUEPERMAN'S BIG SISTER. / F***ING ADA** [51] [ ]
(12"+=) *(BUYIT 100)* – You'll see glimpses.

Nov 80. (lp/c) *(SEEZ/ZSEEZ 30) <36998>* **LAUGHTER** [48] Jan81 [ ]
– Sueperman's big sister / Pardon / Delusions of grandeur / Yes and no (Paula) / Dance of the crackpots / Over the points / (Take your elbow out of the soup you're sitting on the chicken) / Uncoolohol / Hey, hey, take me away / Manic depression / Oh, Mr. Peanut / F***ing Ada. *(cd-iss. May95 on 'Disky';) (cd re-iss. Aug98 & Apr00 on 'A Hit Label'; AHLCD 59)*

— IAN DURY now brought in the services of rhythm boys **SLY & ROBBIE** plus **JANKEL + TYRONE DOWNIE** – keyboards

Polydor — Polydor

Aug 81. (7"/12") *(POSP/+X 285)* **SPASTICUS AUSTICIOUS. / ('A'instrumental)** [ ] [ ]

Sep 81. (lp/c) *(POLD/+C 5042) <16337>* **LORD UPMINSTER** [53] [ ]
– Funky disco pops / Red letter / Girls watching / Wait for me / The body song / Lonely town / Trust is a must / Spasticus austicious. *(re-iss. Dec89 on 'Great Expectations' lp/cd; PIP LP/CD 005)*

IAN DURY & THE MUSIC STUDENTS

— with many musicians including **JANKEL, PAYNE + RAY COOPER**

Nov 83. (7"/12") *(POSP/+C 646)* **REALLY GLAD YOU CAME. / INSPIRATION** [ ] [ ]

Jan 84. (lp/c) *(POLD/+C 5112)* **4,000 WEEKS HOLIDAY** [54] [–]
– (You're my) Inspiration / Friends / Tell your daddy / Peter the painter / Ban the bomb / Percy the poet / Very personal / Take me to the cleaners / The man with no face / Really glad you came. *(re-iss. Dec89 on 'Great Expectations' lp/cd; PIP LP/CD 004)*

Feb 84. (7") *(POSP 673)* **VERY PERSONAL. / BAN THE BOMB** [ ] [ ]
(12"+=) *(POSPX 673)* – The sky's the limit.

IAN DURY

— solo, with **PAYNE, GALLAGHER, COOPER** plus **STEVE WHITE** – drums / **MICHAEL McEVOY** – bass, synth / **MERLIN RHYS-JONES** – guitar / **FRANCES RUFELLE** – vocals / etc.

E.M.I. — not iss.

Oct 89. (7"/7"pic-d) *(EMI/+P 5534)* **PROFOUNDLY IN LOVE WITH PANDORA. / EUGENIUS (YOU'RE A GENIUS)** [45] [–]
(above from the TV series, 'Adrian Mole')

WEA — not iss.

Oct 89. (7") *(YZ 437)* **APPLES. / BYLINE BROWN** [ ] [–]

Oct 89. (lp/c)(cd) *(WX 326/+C)(246355-2)* **APPLES** (soundtrack) [ ] [–]
– Apples / Love is all / Byline Browne / Bit of kit / Game on / Looking for Harry / England's glory / Bus driver's prayer / P.C. Honey / The right people / All those who say okay / Riding the outskirts of fantasy.

— In Sep'90 he reformed IAN DURY & THE BLOCKHEADS for two reunion gigs

IAN DURY

Demon / not iss.

Apr 91. (lp/cd) *(FIEND/+CD 777)* **WARTS 'N' AUDIENCE (live 22 December 1990)** [ ] [-]
– Wake up / Clever Trevor / If I was with a woman *[cd-only]* Billericay Dickie / Quiet / My old man / Spasticus autisticus / Plaistow Patricia / Clever bastards / Sweet Gene Vincent / What a waste / Hit me with your rhythm stick / Blockheads. *(cd re-iss. Sep00 on 'Diablo'+=; DIAB 8037)* – Inbetweenies / Reasons to be cheerful (part 3).

Nov 92. (cd/c) *(FIEND CD/CASS 702)* **THE BUS DRIVERS PRAYER & OTHER STORIES** [ ] [-]
– That's enough of that / Bill Haley's last words / Poor Joey / Quick quick slow / Fly in the ointment / O'Donegal / Poo-poo in the prawn / Ave a word / London talking / D'orine the cow / Your horoscope / No such thing as love / Two old dogs without a name / Bus driver's prayer.

IAN DURY & THE BLOCKHEADS

— with **CHAZ JANKEL, MICKEY GALLAGHER, DAVEY PAYNE, JOHN TURNBULL, NORMAN WATT-ROY, STEVEN MONTI** (drums) / **The BREEZEBLOCKS** – backing vocals

Ronnie Harris / Ronnie Harris

Jun 98. (cd) *(DUR 1) <61863>* **Mr LOVE PANTS** [57] [ ]
– Jack shit George / The passing show / You're my baby / Honeysuckle highway / Itinerant / Geraldine / Cacka boom / Bed 'o' roses No.9 / Heavy living / Mash it up Harry.

— sadly, IAN was to die on the 27th of March, 2000; his last recording was left for a few years . . .

Mar 02. (cd) *(DUR 002) <63145>* **TEN MORE TURNIPS FROM THE TIP** [60] Apr02 [ ]
– Dance little rude boy / I believe / It ain't cool / Cowboys / Ballad of the sulphate strangler / I could lie / One love / Happy hippy / Books and water / You're the why (with ROBBIE WILLIAMS).

May 02. (cd-s) *(DUR 004)* **ONE LOVE / JOCK'S POEM / BALLAD OF THE SULPHATE STRANGLER** [ ] [-]

– compilations etc. –

Nov 81. (lp/c) *Stiff; (SEEZ/ZSEEZ 41)* **JUKE BOX DURY** [ ] [-]
(re-iss. Sep82 as 'GREATEST HITS' on 'Fame' lp/c; FA/TC-FA 3031)

May 85. (7") *Stiff; (BUY 214)* **HIT ME WITH YOUR RHYTHM STICK (Paul Hardcastle mix). / SEX AND DRUGS AND ROCK AND ROLL** [55] [-]
(12"+=) *(BUYIT 214)* – Reasons to be cheerful / Wake up and make love to me (Paul Hardcastle mix).

Apr 87. (lp/c/cd) *Demon; (FIEND/+CASS/CD 69)* **SEX AND DRUGS AND ROCK AND ROLL** [ ] [-]
– Hit me with your rhythm stick / I want to be straight / There ain't half been some clever bastards / What a waste! / Common as muck / Reasons to be cheerful (pt.3) / Sex and drugs and rock and roll / Sueperman's big sister / Razzle in my pocket / You're more than fair / Inbetweenies / You'll see glimpses.

Jul 91. (7"/c-s) *Flying; (FLYR 1/+C)* **HIT ME WITH YOUR RHYTHM STICK '91 (The Flying Remix Version) / HIT ME WITH YOUR RHYTHM STICK** [73] [-]
(12"+=/cd-s+=) *(FLYR 1 T/CD)* – ('A'mix).

Aug 91. (3xcd-box) *Demon; (IAN 1)* **IAN DURY & THE BLOCKHEADS** [ ] [-]
– (NEW BOOTS AND PANTIES / DO IT YOURSELF / SEX AND DRUGS AND ROCK AND ROLL)

Aug 96. (cd) *Disky; (DC 88975-2)* **THE BEST OF IAN DURY** [ ] [-]

Sep 99. (cd) *E.M.I.; (522888-2)* **REASONS TO BE CHEERFUL – THE VERY BEST OF IAN DURY & THE BLOCKHEADS** [40] [-]
– Reasons to be cheerful / Wake up and make love with me / Hit me with your rhythm stick / Clevor Trever / What a waste / Sex and drugs and rock and roll / This is what we find / Itinerant child / Sweet Gene Vincent / I want to be straight / Blockheads / Mash it up Harry / There ain't half been some clever bastards / Billericay Dickie / Inbetweenies / Sparticus (autisticus) / My old man / Lullaby for Francis.

Apr 00. (d-cd) *Repertoire; (REP 4592)* **REASONS TO BE CHEERFUL** [ ] [-]

May 00. (cd) *Repertoire; (REP 4507)* **THE BEST OF IAN DURY** [ ] [-]

— The BLOCKHEADS also released their own singles and lp early 80's

□ DUST BROTHERS
(see under ⇒ CHEMICAL BROTHERS)

Bob DYLAN

Born: ROBERT ALLAN ZIMMERMAN, 24 May'41, Duluth, Minnesota, USA. In 1960 he left his local university, changing his name to BOB DYLAN. He also began a trek to New York where he played his first gig supporting JOHN LEE HOOKER on 11 April '61 at Gerde's Folk City. Soon after, he enjoyed harmonica session work for folk songstress Caroline Hester. Her employers 'Columbia' records, through John Hammond Snr., signed him in October '61. His eponymous debut album in 1962 gained sparse attention, although his live work created critical appraisal. In 1963 he unleashed 'THE FREEWHEELIN' BOB DYLAN', and after PETER, PAUL & MARY lifted a million seller from it, 'BLOWIN' IN THE WIND', the record gained enough respect to give him a US Top 30 album. The record also saw a pronounced development in DYLAN's songwriting dexterity on tracks like the cutting 'MASTERS OF WAR'. While his untrained, nasal vocals could be something of an acquired taste, they communicated the lyrics in a way that lent them greater depth and resonance. But DYLAN really hit his stride with 'THE TIMES THEY ARE A-CHANGIN' the following year, an album that represented his most pointed protest writing. On subsequent albums, DYLAN shied away from direct missives like 'WITH GOD ON OUR SIDE' and 'ONLY A PAWN IN THEIR GAME'. 'ANOTHER SIDE OF BOB DYLAN' (1964) was contrastingly personal in tone, 'I DON'T BELIEVE IN YOU' and 'IT AIN'T ME BABE' venting DYLAN's spleen on matters of the heart rather than the soapbox. The lyrics also began to assume an air of enigmatic suggestiveness, 'MY BACK PAGES' and 'CHIMES OF FREEDOM' boasting striking, lucid imagery which The BYRDS would later complement with their incandescent, chiming guitars and ringing harmonies. Influenced by the British R&B boom (especially The BEATLES), DYLAN stunned folk purists with the half electric/half acoustic 'BRINGING IT ALL BACK HOME' (1965). The newly plugged in DYLAN was a revelation and with the likes of the stream-of-consciousness 'SUBTERRANEAN HOMESICK BLUES', the album influenced in turn the bands DYLAN had taken his cue from. The acoustic tracks on the second side such as 'MR. TAMBOURINE MAN' and 'IT'S ALL OVER NOW BABY BLUE' rank among DYLAN's finest, the former giving The BYRDS their breakthrough hit. While the folk faithful dissed DYLAN at that summer's Newport Festival, he wowed the rock world with the masterful 'LIKE A ROLLING STONE' single and followed it up with the seminal 'HIGHWAY 61 REVISITED' (1965). A free flowing hybrid of blues, folk and R&B that used such esteemed musicians as AL KOOPER and PAUL BUTTERFIELD, rock music had never been graced with such complex, expansive lyrics. Backed by members of The HAWKS (who'd supported DYLAN on his recent tour and later become The BAND) and a posse of crack Nashville sessioneers, DYLAN recorded another rock milestone with 'BLONDE ON BLONDE' (1966). 'VISIONS OF JOHANNA' was DYLAN at his most lysergic, casting surreal lyrical spells with hypnotic ease. After a motorcycle accident that summer he sustained severe neck injuries and went into semi-retirement, looking after his family and holing up in Woodstock with The BAND. These sessions eventually saw the light of day in 1975 as 'THE BASEMENT TAPES', a classic double album of experimental roots rock. Upon his return to the music scene, DYLAN's vocals were slightly altered and his music had taken a distinct turn towards country-rock on 'JOHN WESLEY HARDING' (1968). The following year's 'NASHVILLE SKYLINE' was stone country, even featuring a bittersweet duet with JOHNNY CASH. After a lean spell, DYLAN returned with two harder-edged rock classics, 'BLOOD ON THE TRACKS' (1975) and 'DESIRE' (1975), providing him with a much needed boost in credibility both with the critics and the buying public. From 1979's 'SLOW TRAIN COMING' on through to his 80's work, he mellowed into more spiritual themes as a result of his new found Christianity; example 'SAVED' (1980), 'SHOT OF LOVE' (1981), 'INFIDELS' (1983), 'EMPIRE BURLESQUE' (1985), 'KNOCKED OUT LOADED' (1986) and 'DOWN IN THE GROOVE' (1988). Only the DANIEL LANOIS produced 'OH MERCY' (1989) came close to capturing the magic of old, the outtakes/rarities compilations 'BIOGRAPH' (1985) and 'THE BOOTLEG SERIES' (1991) of more interest to DYLAN fans than much of his new material. His first release of the new decade, the featherweight 'UNDER THE RED SKY' (1990) was roundly lambasted as his weakest effort since 'SELF PORTRAIT', while with 'GOOD AS I BEEN TO YOU' (1992), DYLAN again confounded fans and critics (and maybe even himself) by cutting a whole album of grizzled if endearing public domain folk songs. He then confounded fans and critics all over again with another volume, released almost a year to the day since the last one. 'WORLD GONE WRONG' (1993) was more than just a replay however, with a carefully chosen – if largely obscure – setlist interpreted with craft and obvious devotion. For fans of the man's rockier material, it seemed there was little respite as DYLAN released his own, inevitable chapter of 'MTV UNPLUGGED' (1995). There were few surprises, with most of the material drawn from his mid-60's golden period, although a few more 70's classics wouldn't have gone unwelcome. He finally emerged with a collection of original songs in 1997: 'TIME OUT OF MIND' (1997) marked the first chapter in one of his sporadic (in fact one of the most significant) periods of creative rebirth. Dark, disillusioned pre-millennial blues shot through with portentous, burbling hammond organ and a lingering sense of emotional impasse and encroaching old age, the record contained DYLAN's most naked songwriting in years; example the 16 min+ 'HIGHLANDS'. 'LOVE AND THEFT' (2001) was even more rapturously received although it was a completely different beast altogether. For the first time in decades – certainly since the 70's – rock's greatest living songwriter sounded liberated, inspired to stretch out and kick back in terms of both writing and performance. 'SUMMER DAYS' was possibly his most effervescent, carefree song since 'MOZAMBIQUE', while closer 'SUGAR BABY' was in the tradition of his finest album bookends. • **Songwriters:** 99% DYLAN compositions except; HOUSE OF THE RISING SUN + IN MY TIME OF DYIN' (trad.) / TAKE A MESSAGE TO MARY (Everly Brothers) / THE BOXER (Simon & Garfunkel) / EARLY MORNIN' RAIN (Gordon Lightfoot) / A FOOL SUCH AS I + CAN'T HELP FALLING IN LOVE (hits; Elvis Presley) / BIG YELLOW TAXI (Joni Mitchell) / MR.BOJANGLES (Jerry Jeff Walker) / LET'S STICK TOGETHER (Wilbert Harrison) / SPANISH IS THE LOVING TONGUE + SHENANDOAH (trad.) / ANGELS FLYING TOO CLOSE TO THE GROUND (Willie Nelson) / etc. **Writing credits/hits:** BLOWIN' IN THE WIND + DON'T THINK TWICE, IT'S ALRIGHT (Peter, Paul & Mary; 1963) / ALL I REALLY WANT TO DO (Cher; 1965) / IT AIN'T ME BABE (Turtles; 1965) / MR. TAMBOURINE MAN + ALL I REALLY WANT TO DO + MY BACK PAGES (Byrds; 1965-1967) / IT'S ALL OVER NOW, BABY BLUE + FAREWELL ANGELINA (Joan Baez; 1965) / IF YOU GOTTA GO, GO NOW + JUST LIKE A WOMAN + MIGHTY QUINN (Manfred Mann; 1965/66/68) / TOO MUCH OF NOTHING (Peter, Paul & Mary; 1967) / THIS WHEEL'S ON FIRE (Julie Driscoll, Brian Auger & The Trinity; 1968) / ALL ALONG THE WATCHTOWER (Jimi Hendrix; 1968) / IF NOT FOR YOU (Olivia Newton-John; 1971) / A HARD RAIN'S A-GONNA FALL (Bryan Ferry; 1973) / KNOCKIN' ON HEAVEN'S DOOR (Eric Clapton; 1975 / Guns n' Roses; 1992) / I'LL BE YOUR BABY TONIGHT (UB40 & Robert Palmer; 1990) / & some minor hits. **Filmography:** DON'T LOOK BACK (1965 documentary) / EAT THE DOCUMENTARY (1971 docu-film) / PAT GARRETT & BILLY THE KID (1973) / RENALDO AND CLARA (1978) / HEARTS OF FIRE (1987). • **Trivia:** On the 22 Nov'65, BOB married Sara Lowndes, but she divorced him in 1977. (Band members in discography are selective)

Album rating: BOB DYLAN (*7) / THE FREEWHEELIN' BOB DYLAN (*9) / THE TIMES THEY ARE A-CHANGIN' (*7) / ANOTHER SIDE OF BOB DYLAN (*8) / BRINGING IT ALL BACK HOME (*9) / HIGHWAY 61 REVISITED (*10) / BLONDE ON BLONDE (*10) / GREATEST HITS compilation (*10) / JOHN WESLEY HARDING (*6) / NASHVILLE SKYLINE (*6) / SELF PORTRAIT (*4) / NEW MORNING (*4) / MORE GREATEST HITS compilation (*7) / PAT GARRETT AND BILLY THE KID (*5) / PLANET WAVES (*6) / BEFORE THE FLOOD (*7) / BLOOD ON THE TRACKS (*10) / DESIRE (*10) / THE BASEMENT TAPES early recordings (*9) / HARD RAIN (*6) / SLOW TRAIN COMING (*5) / STREET LEGAL (*5) / AT BUDOKAN (*4) / SLOW TRAIN COMING (*5) / SAVED (*4) / SHOT OF LOVE (*4) / INFIDELS (*6) / REAL LIVE (*5) / EMPIRE BURLESQUE (*6) / BIOGRAPH boxed-set (*9) / KNOCKED OUT LOADED (*4) / DOWN IN THE GROOVE (*5) / DYLAN AND THE DEAD with Grateful Dead (*3) / OH MERCY (*6) / UNDER THE RED SKY (*5) / GOOD AS I BEEN TO YOU (*5) / WORLD GONE WRONG (*5) / 30th ANNIVERSARY CONCERT (*5) / GREATEST HITS, VOL.3 compilation (*6) / MTV UNPLUGGED (*5) / TIME OUT OF MIND (*7) / LOVE AND THEFT (*8) / BOB DYLAN LIVE 1975: THE ROLLING THUNDER REVUE exploitation (*7)

BOB DYLAN – vocals, guitar, harmonica

C.B.S. Columbia

Mar 62. (7") *<42656>* **MIXED UP CONFUSION. / CORRINA CORRINA** [–] [ ]

Jun 62. (lp; stereo/mono) *(S+/BPG 62022) <8579>* **BOB DYLAN** [ ] Mar62 [ ]
– She's no good / Talkin' New York / In my time of dyin' / Man of constant sorrow / Fixin' to die blues / Pretty Peggy-o / Highway 51 blues / Gospel plow / Baby, let me follow you down / House of the risin' sun / Freight train blues / Song to Woody / See that grave is kept clean. *(re-dist.May65, hit No.13) (re-iss. Mar81 lp/c; CBS/40 32001) (cd-iss. Nov89; CD 32001)*

— added musicians **HOWARD COLLINS** – guitar / **GEORGE BARNES** – bass / **HERB LOVELL** – drums / **LEONARD GASKIN** – bass / etc.

Nov 63. (lp; stereo/mono) *(S+/BPG 62193) <8786>* **THE FREEWHEELIN' BOB DYLAN** [16] May63 [22]
– Blowin' in the wind / Girl from the North Country / Masters of war / Down the highway / Bob Dylan's blues / A hard rains a-gonna fall / Don't think twice, it's all right / Bob Dylan's dream / Oxford Town / / Talking World War III blues / Corrina, Corrina / Honey, just allow me one more chance / I shall be free. *(re-dist.Apr65, hit No.1) (re-iss. Mar81 lp/c; CBS/40 62193) (cd-iss. Nov89; 32390)*

Jan 64. (7") *<42856>* **BLOWIN' IN THE WIND. / DON'T THINK TWICE IT'S ALRIGHT** [–] [ ]

Jun 64. (lp; stereo/mono) *(S+/BPG 62251) <8905>* **THE TIMES THEY ARE A-CHANGIN'** [20] Mar64 [20]
– The times they are a-changin' / Ballad of Hollis Brown / With God on our side / One too many mornings / North country blues / Only a pawn in their game / Boots of Spanish leather / When the ship comes in / The lonesome death of Hattie Carroll / Restless farewell. *(re-dist.Apr65, hit No.4) (re-iss. Mar81 lp/c; CBS/40 32021) (cd-iss. Nov89; CD 32021)*

Nov 64. (lp; stereo/mono) *(S+/BPG 62429) <8993>* **ANOTHER SIDE OF BOB DYLAN** [8] Sep64 [43]
– All I really want to do / Black crow blues / Spanish Harlem incident / Chimes of freedom / I shall be free No.10 / To Ramona / Motorpsycho nitemare / I don't believe you / Ballad in plain D / It ain't me babe. *(re-iss. Mar81 lp/c; CBS/40 32034) (cd-iss. Nov89; CD 32034)*

Mar 65. (7") *(201751)* **THE TIMES THEY ARE A-CHANGIN'. / HONEY, JUST ALLOW ME ONE MORE CHANCE** [9] [–]
(re-iss. May82; 1751)

—— with **BOBBY GREGG** – drums / **JOHN SEBASTIAN** – bass / **BRUCE LANGHORNE** – guitar

Apr 65. (7") *(201753) <43242>* **SUBTERRANEAN HOMESICK BLUES. / SHE BELONGS TO ME** 9 Mar65 39

May 65. (lp; stereo/mono) *(S+/BPG 62515) <9128>* **BRINGING IT ALL BACK HOME** 1 Apr65 6
– Subterranean homesick blues / She belongs to me / Maggie's farm / Love minus zero – No limit / Outlaw blues / On the road again / Bob Dylan's 115th dream / Mr. Tambourine man / Gates of Eden / It's alright, ma (I'm only bleeding) / It's all over now, baby blue. *(re-iss. Jul83 lp/c; CBS/40 32344) (cd-iss. Jul87; CD 62515) (cd re-iss. Jul89 as 'SUBTERRANEAN HOMESICK BLUES'; CD 32344)*

Jun 65. (7") *(201781)* **MAGGIE'S FARM. / ON THE ROAD AGAIN** 22 –

—— now with **AL KOOPER** – organ / **PAUL BUTTERFIELD** – guitar / **PAUL GRIFFIN** – keyboards / **CHARLIE McCOY** – guitar / **RUSS SAVAKUS** – bass

Aug 65. (7") *(201811) <43346>* **LIKE A ROLLING STONE. / GATES OF EDEN** 4 Jul65 2
(re-iss. May82; 1811)

Sep 65. (lp; stereo/mono) *(S+/BPG 62572) <9189>* **HIGHWAY 61 REVISITED** 4 3
– Like a rolling stone / Tombstone blues / It takes a lot to laugh, it takes a train to cry / From a Buick 6 / Ballad of a thin man / Queen Jane approximately / Highway 61 revisited / Just like Tom Thumb's blues / Desolation row. *(re-iss. Dec85 lp/c; CBS/40 62572) (cd-iss. Nov89; CD 62572)*

Oct 65. (7") *(201824) <43389>* **POSITIVELY 4th STREET. / FROM A BUICK 6** 8 Sep65 7

Jan 66. (7") *(201900) <43477>* **CAN YOU PLEASE CRAWL OUT YOUR WINDOW? / HIGHWAY 61 REVISITED** 17 Dec65 58

Apr 66. (7") *(202053) <43541>* **ONE OF US MUST KNOW (SOONER OR LATER). / QUEEN JANE APPROXIMATELY** 33 Feb66

—— Now augmented by members of The **BAND:- ROBBIE ROBERTSON** – guitar / **RICHARD MANUEL** – keyboards / **LEVON HELM** – drums / **RICK DANKO** – bass / **GARTH HUDSON** – keyboards plus also **KENNY BUTTREY** – drums

May 66. (7") *(202307) <43592>* **RAINY DAY WOMEN NOS.12 & 35. / PLEDGING MY TIME** 7 Apr66 2

Jul 66. (7") *(202258) <43683>* **I WANT YOU. / JUST LIKE TOM THUMB'S BLUES (live)** 16 Jun66 20

Aug 66. (d-lp; stereo/mono) *(S+/66012) <841>* **BLONDE ON BLONDE** 3 Jul66 9
– Rainy day women Nos.12 & 35 / Pledging my time / Visions of Johanna / One of us must know (sooner or later) / Most likely you go your way (and I'll go mine) / Temporary like Achilles / Absolutely sweet Marie / 4th time around / Obviously 5 believers / I want you / Stuck inside of Mobile with the Memphis blues again / Leopard-skin pill-box hat / Just like a woman / Sad eyed lady of the lowlands. *(re-iss. May82 d-lp/d-c; CBS/40 22130) (d-cd-iss. Jul87; CD 66012) (d-cd re-iss. Jun89; CD 22130) (d-cd re-iss. Feb95; CK 64411)*

Sep 66. (7") *<43792>* **JUST LIKE A WOMAN. / OBVIOUSLY 5 BELIEVERS** – 33

Jan 67. (lp; stereo/mono) *(S+/BPG 62847) <9463>* **BOB DYLAN'S GREATEST HITS** (compilation) <US diff.tracks> 6 Apr67 10
– Blowin' in the wind / It ain't me babe / The times they are a-changin' / Mr. Tambourine man / She belongs to me / It's all over now, baby blue / Subterranean homesick blues / One of us must know (sooner or later) / Like a rolling stone / Just like a woman / Rainy day women Nos. 12 & 35. *(re-iss. Mar88; 460907) (cd-iss. Nov89; 450882-2) (re-iss. Feb91 & Apr97 on 'Columbia'; 460907-2) (re-iss. cd Oct94 as 'BEST OF . . .';)*

May 67. (7") *(202700) <44069>* **LEOPARD-SKIN PILL-BOX HAT. / MOST LIKELY YOU GO YOUR WAY (AND I'LL GO MINE)** 81

—— now with **BUTTREY, McCOY** and **PETE DRAKE** – sitar, guitar

Feb 68. (lp; stereo/mono) *(S+/BPG 63252) <9604>* **JOHN WESLEY HARDING** 1 Jan68 2
– John Wesley Harding / As I went out one morning / I dreamed I saw St. Augustine / All along the watchtower / The ballad of Frankie Lee and Judas Priest / Drifter's escape / Dear landlord / I am a lonesome hobo / I pity the poor immigrant / The wicked messenger / Down along the cove / I'll be your baby tonight. *(re-iss. Nov89 lp/c/cd; 463359-1/-4/-2)*

—— next featured **CHARLIE DANIELS** – bass, guitar / etc.

May 69. (7") *(4219) <44826>* **I THREW IT ALL AWAY. / DRIFTER'S ESCAPE** 30 85

May 69. (lp) *(63601) <9825>* **NASHVILLE SKYLINE** 1 Apr69 3
– Girl from the North country (with JOHNNY CASH) / Nashville skyline rag / To be alone with you / I threw it all away / Pegy Day / Lady lady lay / One more night / Tell me that it isn't true / Country pie / Tonight I'll be staying here with you. *(re-iss. May87 lp/c; CBS/40 32675) (cd-iss. Jan86; CD 63601)*

Sep 69. (7") *(4434) <44926>* **LAY LADY LAY. / PEGGY DAY** 5 Jul69 7

Dec 69. (7") *(4611) <45004>* **TONIGHT I'LL BE STAYING HERE WITH YOU. / COUNTRY PIE** Oct69 50

Jul 70. (d-lp) *(66250) <30050>* **SELF PORTRAIT** 1 Jun70 4
– All the tired horses / Alberta #1 / I forgot more than you'll ever know / Days of 49 / Early mornin' rain / In search of little Sadie / Let it be me / Little Sadie / Woogie boogie / Belle isle / Living the blues / Like a rolling stone (version) / Copper kettle (the pale moonlight) / Gotta travel on / Blue Moon / The boxer / The mighty Quinn (Quinn, the eskimo) / Take me as I am / Take a message to Mary / It hurts me too / Minstrel boy / She belongs to me / Wigwam / Alberta #2. *(re-iss. Sep87 d-lp/c; 460112-1/-4) (re-iss. Feb91 on 'Columbia' cd/c; 460112-2/-4)*

Jul 70. (7") *(5122) <45199>* **WIGWAM. / COPPER KETTLE (THE PALE MOONLIGHT)** 41

Nov 70. (lp) *(69001) <30290>* **NEW MORNING** 1 7
– If not for you / Day of the locusts / Time passes slowly / Went to see the gypsy / Winterlude / If dogs ran free / New morning / Sign on the window / One more weekend / The man in me / Three angels / Father of the night. *(re-iss. Sep83 lp/c; CBS/40 32267) (re-iss. Feb91 & Feb94 on 'Columbia' cd/c; CD 32267)*

Mar 71. (7") *(7092)* **IF NOT FOR YOU. / NEW MORNING** –

Jun 71. (7") *(7329) <45409>* **WATCHING THE RIVER FLOW. / SPANISH IS THE LOVING TONGUE** 24 41

Dec 71. (7") *(7688) <45516>* **GEORGE JACKSON (acoustic). / GEORGE JACKSON (big band version)** Nov71 33

Dec 71. (d-lp/c) *(CBS/40 67239) <31120>* **MORE BOB DYLAN GREATEST HITS** <US-title 'BOB DYLAN'S GREATEST HITS, VOL.II'> (compilation) 12 14
– Watching the river flow / Don't think twice, it's alright / Lay lady lay / Stuck inside Mobile with the Memphis blues again / I'll be your baby tonight / All I really want to do / My back pages / Maggie's farm / Tonight I'll be staying here with you / Positively 4th Street / All along the watchtower / The mighty Quinn (Quinn, the eskimo) / Just like Tom Thumb's blues / A hard rain's a-gonna fall / If not for you / New morning / Tomorrow is a long time / When I paint my masterpiece / I shall be released / You ain't goin' nowhere / Down in the flood. *(cd-iss. Oct87; CD 67239) (cd re-iss. Aug92 on 'Columbia'; 467851-2) (re-iss. Mar93 on 'Columbia' cd/c; 471243-2/-4)*

Sep 73. (lp/c) *(CBS/40 69042) <32460>* **PAT GARRETT AND BILLY THE KID (Soundtrack)** 29 Jul73 16
– Main title theme / Cantina theme (working for the law) / Billy 1 / Bunkhouse theme / River theme / Turkey chase / Knockin' on Heaven's door / Final theme / Billy 4 / Billy 7. *(re-iss. Mar82 lp/c; CBS/40 32098) (re-iss. Feb91 on 'Columbia' cd/c;)*

Sep 73. (7") *(1762) <45913>* **KNOCKIN' ON HEAVEN'S DOOR. / TURKEY CHASE** 14 Aug73 12

Dec 73. (lp/c) *(CBS/40 69049) <32747>* **DYLAN** (rec.1970) 17
– Lily of the west / Can't help falling in love / Sarah Jane / The ballad of Ira Hayes / Mr. Bojangles / Mary Ann / Big yellow taxi / A fool such as I / Spanish is the loving tongue. *(re-iss. Mar83) (cd+c-iss.Feb91 on 'Columbia')*

Jan 74. (7") *(2006) <45982>* **A FOOL SUCH AS I. / LILY OF THE WEST** Dec73 55

Island Asylum

Feb 74. (lp/c) *(ILPS/ICT 9261) <1003>* **PLANET WAVES** 7 1
– On a night like this / Going going gone / Tough mama / Hazel / Something there is about you / Forever young / Dirge / You angel you / Never say goodbye / Wedding song. *(re-iss. Sep82 lp/c; CBS/40 32154) (cd-iss. Nov89 on 'C.B.S.'; CD 21154)*

Feb 74. (7") *<11033>* **ON A NIGHT LIKE THIS. / YOU ANGEL YOU** – 44

Feb 74. (7") *(WIP 6168)* **ON A NIGHT LIKE THIS. / FOREVER YOUNG** –

Apr 74. (7") **SOMETHING THERE IS ABOUT YOU. / GOING GOING GONE** –

Asylum Asylum

Jul 74. (d-lp/d-c; as BOB DYLAN & THE BAND) *(IBD 1)* *<201>* **BEFORE THE FLOOD** (tracks by The BAND) 8 3
– Most likely you go your way (and I'll go mine) / Lay lady lay / Rainy day

women Nos.12 & 35 / Knockin' on Heaven's door / It ain't me babe / The ballad of a thin man / Up on Cripple Creek * / I shall be released / Endless highway * / The night they drove old Dixie down * / Stage fright * / Don't think twice, it's all right / Just like a woman / It's alright ma (I'm only bleeding) / The shape I'm in * / When you awake * / The weight * / All along the watchtower / Highway 61 revisited / Like a rolling stone / Blowin' in the wind. *(re-iss. Sep82 on 'C.B.S.' d-lp/d-c; CBS/40 22137) (cd-iss. Jul87 + Nov89 + Jun96; CD 22137)*

—— The BAND had been his backing group from the mid '60's.

Aug 74. (7") *<11043>* **MOST LIKELY YOU GO YOUR WAY (AND I'LL GO MINE) (live). / STAGE FRIGHT (The BAND live)** [–] [66]

Nov 74. (7") **ALL ALONG THE WATCHTOWER (live). / IT AIN'T ME BABE (live)** [–] [ ]

C.B.S. Columbia

Feb 75. (lp/c) *(CBS/40 69097) <32235>* **BLOOD ON THE TRACKS** [4] [1]

– Tangled up in blue / Simple twist of fate / You're a big girl now / Idiot wind / You're gonna make me lonesome when you go / Meet me in the morning / Lily, Rosemary and the Jack of Hearts / If you see her, say hello / Shelter from the storm / Buckets of rain. *((cd-iss. Dec85; CD 69097) (re-iss. Sep93 on 'Columbia' cd/c; 467842-2/-4)*

Mar 75. (7") *(3160) <10106>* **TANGLED UP IN BLUE. / IF YOU SEE HER, SAY HELLO** [ ] [31]

Jul 75. (d-lp/c) *(CBS/40 88147) <33682>* **THE BASEMENT TAPES** (rec.1967) [8] [7]

– Odds and ends / Orange juice blues (blues for breakfast) / Million dollar bash / Yazoo street scandal / Goin' to Acapulco / Katie's been gone / Lo and behold / Bessie Smith / Clothes line saga / Apple suckling tree / Please Mrs. Henry / Tears of rage / Too much of nothing / Yea! heavy and a bottle of wine / Ain't no more Cane / Crash on the levee (down in the flood) / Ruben Remus / Tiny Montgomery / You ain't goin' nowhere / Don't ya tell Henry / Nothing was delivered / Open the doors, Homer / Long distance operator. *(cd-iss. Nov89; 466137-2)*

Oct 75. (7") *(3665)* **MILLION DOLLAR BASH. / TEARS OF RAGE** [ ] [ ]

—— next featured **EMMYLOU HARRIS** – vocals / **SCARLET RIVIERA** – violin / **RONNE BLAKELY** – vocals / **HOWIE WYTHE** – drums / **ROB STONER** – bass / **STEVEN SOLES** – guitar

Jan 76. (7") *(3879) <10245>* **HURRICANE (part 1). / HURRICANE (full version)** [43] Nov75 [33]

Jan 76. (lp/c) *(CBS/40 86003) <33893>* **DESIRE** [3] [1]

– Hurricane / Isis / Mozambique / One more cup of coffee / Oh, sister / Joey / Romance in Durango / Black diamond bay / Sara. *(re-iss. Apr85 lp/c; CBS/40 32570) (cd-iss. Jul87; 86003) (cd re-iss. Jun89; CD 32470)*

Apr 76. (7") *(4113) <10298>* **MOZAMBIQUE. / OH, SISTER** [ ] Mar76 [54]

—— His HARD RAIN tour added **MICK RONSON** – guitar / **DAVID MANSFIELD** – keyboards

Sep 76. (lp/c) *(CBS/40 86016) <34349>* **HARD RAIN (live)** [3] [17]

– Maggie's farm / One too many mornings / Stuck inside of Mobile with the Memphis blues again / Lay lady lay / Shelter from the storm / You're a big girl now / I threw it all away / Idiot wind. *(re-iss. Apr83 lp/c; CBS/40 32308) (cd-iss. Nov89; CD 32308)*

Feb 77. (7") *(4859) <10454>* **RITA MAY. / STUCK INSIDE OF MOBILE WITH THE MEMPHIS BLUES AGAIN (live)** [ ] [ ]

May 78. (7"/12") *(7/12 6499) <10805>* **BABY STOP CRYING. / NEW PONY** [13] [ ]

Jun 78. (lp/c) *(CBS/40 86067) <35453>* **STREET-LEGAL** [2] [11]

– Changing of the guards / New pony / No time to think / Baby stop crying / Is your love in vain / Senor (tales of Yankee power) / True love tends to forget / We better talk this over / Where are you tonight (journey through dark heat). *(cd-iss. Mar86; CD 86087) (re-iss. May95 cd/c; 403289)*

Oct 78. (7"/12") *(7/12 6718)* **IS YOUR LOVE IN VAIN. / WE BETTER TALK THIS OVER** [56] [–]

Dec 78. (7") *(6935) <10851>* **CHANGING OF THE GUARDS. / SENOR (TALES OF YANKEE POWER)** [ ] [ ]

1978. (7"ep) **4 SONGS FROM "RENALDO AND CLARA"** [–] [ ]

– People get ready / Never let me go / Isis / It ain't me babe.

May 79. (d-lp/d-c) *(CBS/40 96004) <36067>* **BOB DYLAN AT BUDOKAN (live)** [4] [13]

– Mr. Tambourine man / Shelter from the storm / Love minus zero – No limit / Ballad of a thin man / Don't think twice, it's all right / Maggie's farm / One more cup of coffee / Like a rolling stone / I shall be released / Oh sister / Is your love in vain? / Going going gone / Blowin' in the wind / Just like a woman / Simple twist of fate / All along the watchtower / I want you / All I really want to do / Knockin' on Heaven's door / It's alright ma (I'm only bleeding) / Forever young / The times they are a-changin'. *(cd-iss. Jul87; CD 96004)*

Jun 79. (7"m) *(7473)* **FOREVER YOUNG (live). / ALL ALONG THE WATCHTOWER (live) / I WANT YOU (live)** [ ] [–]

Aug 79. (7") *(7828)* **PRECIOUS ANGEL. / TROUBLE IN MIND** [ ] [–]

Sep 79. (lp/c) *(CBS/40 86095) <36120>* **SLOW TRAIN COMING** [2] [3]

– Gotta serve somebody / Precious angel / I believe in you / Slow train / Gonna change my way of thinking / Do right to me baby (do unto others) / When you gonna wake up / Man gave names to all the animals / When he returns. *(re-iss. Nov85 lp/c; CBS/40 32524) (cd-iss. Mar86; CD 86095) (cd re-iss. Apr89; CD 32524)*

Sep 79. (7") *<11072>* **GOTTA SERVE SOMEBODY. / TROUBLE IN MIND** [–] [24]

Oct 79. (7") *(7970)* **MAN GAVE NAMES TO ALL THE ANIMALS. / WHEN HE RETURNS** [ ] [–]

Jan 80. (7") *<11168>* **MAN GAVE NAMES TO THE ANIMALS. / WHEN YOU GONNA WAKE UP** [–] [ ]

Jan 80. (7") *(8134)* **GOTTA SERVE SOMEBODY. / GONNA CHANGE MY WAY OF THINKING** [ ] [–]

Mar 80. (7") *<11235>* **SLOW TRAIN. / DO RIGHT TO ME BABY (DO UNTO OTHERS)** [–] [ ]

May 80. (7") *<11318>* **SOLID ROCK. / COVENANT WOMAN** [–] [ ]

Jun 80. (lp/c) *(CBS/40 83113) <36553>* **SAVED** [3] [24]

– A satisfied mind / Saved / Covenant woman / What can I do for you? / Solid rock / Pressing on / In the garden / Saving Grace / Are you ready. *(reiss.Sep86 lp/c; CBS/40 32742) (re-iss. Feb91 & Mar93 on 'Columbia' cd/c; 403274-2/-4)*

Jun 80. (7") *(8743) <11370>* **SAVED. / ARE YOU READY** [ ] [ ]

Jun 81. (7") *<02510>* **HEART OF MINE. / THE GROOM'S STILL WAITING AT THE ALTAR** [–] [ ]

Jul 81. (7") *(A 1406)* **HEART OF MINE. / LET IT BE ME** [ ] [–]

Aug 81. (lp/c) *(CBS/40 85178) <37496>* **SHOT OF LOVE** [6] [33]

– Shot of love / Heart of mine / Property of Jesus / Lenny Bruce / Watered down love / Dead man, dead man / In the summertime / Trouble / Every grain of sand. *(re-iss. Feb91 on 'Columbia' cd+=/c+=; 467839-2/-4)* – The groom's still waiting at the altar. *(re-iss. cd Jun94 on 'Sony Europe'; 983338-2)*

Sep 81. (7") *(A 1460)* **LENNY BRUCE. / DEAD MAN, DEAD MAN** [ ] [–]

Oct 83. (7") *(A 3916)* **UNION SUNDOWN. / I AND I** [ ] [ ]

Nov 83. (lp/c) *(CBS/40 25539) <38819>* **INFIDELS** [9] [20]

– Jokerman / Sweetheart like you / Neighbourhood bully / License to kill / Man of peace / Union sundown / I and I / Don't fall apart on me tonight. *(cd-iss. Jul87; Cd 25539) (re-iss. Dec89 lp/c/cd; 460727-1/-4/-2)*

Dec 83. (7") *<04301>* **SWEETHEART LIKE YOU. / UNION SUNDOWN** [–] [55]

May 84. (7") *<04425>* **JOKERMAN. / ISIS** [–] [ ]

Jun 84. (7") *(A 4055)* **JOKERMAN. / LICENSE TO KILL** [ ] [–]

Dec 84. (lp/c/cd) *(CBS/40/CD 26334) <39944>* **REAL LIVE (live)** [54] [ ]

– Highway 61 revisited / Maggie's farm / I and I / License to kill / It ain't me babe / Tangled up in blue / Masters of war / Ballad of a thin man / Girl from the North country / Tombstone blues. *(re-iss. Feb91 on 'Columbia' cd/c; 467841-2/-4)*

Jan 85. (7"/7"g-f) *(A/GA 5020)* **HIGHWAY 61 REVISITED (live). / IT AIN'T ME BABE (live)** [ ] [ ]

Jun 85. (7") *(A 6303) <04933>* **TIGHT CONNECTION TO MY HEART. / WE'D BETTER TALK THIS OVER** [ ] [ ]

Jun 85. (lp/c/cd) *(CBS/40/CD 86313) <40110>* **EMPIRE BURLESQUE** [11] [33]

– Tight connection to my heart (has anybody seen my love) / Seeing the real you at last / I'll remember you / Clean cut kid / Never gonna be the same again / Trust yourself / Emotionally yours / When the night comes falling from the sky / Something's burning, baby / Dark eyes. *(re-iss. cd.1988; Cd 86313) (re-iss. Feb91 on 'Columbia' cd/c; 467840-2/-4)*

Aug 85. (7"/ext.12") *(A/TA 6469)* **WHEN THE NIGHT COMES FALLING FROM THE SKY. / DARK EYES** [ ] [–]

—— In Apr'86, he was credited next on the TOM PETTY ⇒ single 'BAND OF THE HAND'.

Oct 85. (7") *<05697>* **WHEN THE NIGHT COMES FALLING FROM THE SKY. / EMOTIONALLY YOURS** [–] [ ]

Jul 86. (lp/c/cd) *(CBS/40/CD 86326)* <40439> **KNOCKED OUT LOADED** [35] [53]
– You wanna ramble / They killed him / Driftin' too far from shore / Precious memories / Maybe someday / Brownsville girl / Got my mind made up / Under your spell. *(re-iss. Feb91 & Mar93 on 'Columbia' cd/c; 467040-2/-4)*

Oct 86. (7") *(651148-7)* **THE USUAL. / GOT MY MIND MADE UP** [ ] [ ]
(12"+=) *(651148-6)* – Precious memories / Driftin' too far from shore.

Jun 88. (lp/c/cd) *(460267-1/-4/-2)* <40957> **DOWN IN THE GROOVE** [32] [61]
– Let's stick together / When did you leave Heaven? / Sally Sue Brown / Death is not the end / Had a dream about you, baby / Ugliest girl in the world / Silvio / Ninety miles an hour (down a dead end street) / Shenandoah / Rank strangers to me.

Jul 88. (7") **SILVIO. / DRIFTIN' TOO FAR FROM SHORE** [–] [ ]

Jul 88. (7") *(651406-7)* **SILVIO. / WHEN DID YOU LEAVE HEAVEN?** [ ] [–]
(12"+=) *(651406-6)* – Driftin' too far from shore.

— Later in '88 & onwards, he was also part of supergroup TRAVELING WILBURYS

Feb 89. (lp/c/cd; BOB DYLAN & GRATEFUL DEAD) *(463381/-1/-4/-2)* <45056> **DYLAN & THE DEAD (live July'87)** [38] [37]
– Slow train / I want you / Gotta serve somebody / Queen Jane approximately / Joey / All along the watchtower / Knockin' on Heaven's door. *(re-iss. May94 on 'Columbia' cd/c; 463381-2/-4)*

Oct 89. (lp/c/cd) *(465800-1/-4/-2)* <45281> **OH MERCY** [6] [30]
– Political world / Where teardrops fall / Everything is broken / Ring them bells / Man in the long black coat / Most of the time / What good am I? / Disease of conceit / What was it you wanted / Shooting star.

Oct 89. (7") **EVERYTHING IS BROKEN. / DEAD MAN, DEAD MAN** [–] [ ]

Oct 89. (7") *(655358-7)* **EVERYTHING IS BROKEN. / DEATH IS NOT THE END** [ ] [–]
(12"/12"w-print) *(655358-6/-8)* – ('A'side) / Dead man, dead man / I want you (live).
(cd-s) *(655358-2)* – ('A'side) / Where the teardrops fall / Dead man, dead man (live) / Ugliest girl in the world (live).

Feb 90. (7") *(655643-7)* **POLITICAL WORLD. / RING THEM BELLS** [ ] [ ]
(12"+=/cd-s+=) *(655643-6/-2)* – Silvio / All along the watchtower (live).
(cd-s) *(655643-5)* – ('A'side) / Caribbean wind / You're a big girl now / It's all over now, baby blue.

Sep 90. (cd/c/lp) *(467188-2/-4/-1)* <46794> **UNDER THE RED SKY** [13] [38]
– Wiggle wiggle / Under the red sky / Unbelievable / Born in time / TV talkin' time / 10,000 men / 2x2 / God knows / Handy Dandy / Cat's in the well.

Sep 90. (7") *(656304-7)* **UNBELIEVABLE. / 10,000 MEN** [ ] [ ]
(cd-s+=) *(656304-2)* – In the summertime / Jokerman.

Feb 91. (7"/c-s) *(656707-7/-4)* **SERIES OF DREAMS. / SEVEN CURSES** [ ] [ ]
(cd-s+=) *(656707-5)* – Tangled up in blue / Like a rolling stone.

— totally solo DYLAN

Columbia Columbia

Nov 92. (cd/c/lp) *(472710-2/-4/-1)* <53200> **GOOD AS I BEEN TO YOU** [18] [51]
– Frankie & Albert / Jim Jones / Blackjack Davey / Canadee-i-o / Sittin' on top of the world / Little Maggie / Hard times / Step it up and go / Tomorrow night / Arthur McBride / You're gonna quit me / Diamond Joe / Froggie went a courtin'.

— In Aug93, a host of artists released a live tribute d-cd,d-c 'ANNIVERSARY CONCERT', which hit US No.30. Below all traditional tunes.

Nov 93. (cd/c) *(474857-2/-4)* <57590> **WORLD GONE WRONG** [35] [70]
– World gone wrong / Ragged and dirty / Love Henry / Blood in my eyes / Delia / Broke down engine / Two soldiers / Stack A Lee / Jack A Roe / Love pilgrim.

— with **TONY GARNIER** – bass / **JOHN JACKSON** – guitar / **BUCKY BAXTER** – pedal steel, dobro / **WINSTON WATSON** – drums / **BRENDAN O'BRIEN** – hammond organ

Apr 95. (cd/c/lp) *(478374-2/-4/-1)* <67000> **MTV UNPLUGGED** [10] May95 [23]
– Tombstone blues / Shooting star / All along the watchtower / The times they are a-changin' / John Brown / Desolation row / Rainy day women #12 & 35 / Love minus zero – No limit / Dignity / Knockin' on Heaven's door / Like a rolling stone / With God on our side.

May 95. (c-s) *(662076-4)* **DIGNITY / JOHN BROWN** [33] [ ]
(cd-s+=) *(662076-5)* – It ain't me babe (live).
(cd-s) *(662076-2)* – ('A'side) / A hard rain's a-gonna fall.

— To end '96, 'KNOCKIN' ON HEAVEN'S DOOR' hit UK No.1 for DUNBLANE; Scottish musicians and children of the town

Oct 97. (cd/c) *(486936-2/-4)* <68556> **TIME OUT OF MIND** [10] [10]
– Love sick / Dirt road blues / Standing in the doorway / Million miles / Tryin' to get to Heaven / 'Til I fell in love with you / Not dark yet / Cold irons bound / Make you feel my love / Can't wait / Highlands.

Jun 98. (cd-s) *(665997-2)* **LOVE SICK / COLD IRONS BOUND (live) / COCAINE (live) / BORN IN TIME (live)** [64] [–]
(cd-s) *(665997-5)* – ('A'side) / Can't wait (live) / Roving gambler (live) / Blind Willie McTell (live).

Oct 00. (cd-s) *(669379-2)* **THINGS HAVE CHANGED / TO MAKE YOU FEEL MY LOVE / HURRICANE / SONG TO WOODY** [58] [–]

Sep 01. (cd) *(504364-2)* <85975> **LOVE AND THEFT** [3] [5]
– Tweedle dee and tweedle dum / Mississippi / Summer days / Bye and bye / Lonesome day blues / Floater (too much to ask) / High water (for Charlie Patton) / Moonlight / Honest with me / Po' boy / Cry a while / Sugar baby. *(special cd+=; 504364-9)* – I was young when I left home / The times they are a-changin' (alternate version).

– (selective) compilations, etc. –

on 'CBS / Columbia' unless otherwise mentioned

Nov 85. (5xlp-box/3xc-box/3xcd-box) *(CBS/40/CD 66509)* <38830> **BIOGRAPH** [ ] [33]
– (above contains 16 unreleased tracks)

Apr 91. (3xcd/3xc/6xlp) *(468086-2/-4/-1)* <47382> **THE BOOTLEG SERIES VOLUMES 1-3 (RARE & UNRELEASED) 1961-1991** [32] [49]

Aug 92. (d-cd) *(466831-2)* **HIGHWAY 61 REVISITED / JOHN WESLEY HARDING** [ ] [–]

Oct 93. (3xcd-box) *(471621-2)* **BLONDE ON BLONDE / JOHN WESLEY HARDING / SELF PORTRAIT** [ ] [–]

Nov 94. (cd/c/d-lp) *(477805-2/-4/-1)* <66783> **GREATEST HITS VOLUME III** [ ] [ ]
– Tangled up in blue / Changing the guards / The groom's still waiting at the altar / Hurricane / Forever young / Jokerman / Dignity / Silvio / Ring them bells / Gotta serve somebody / Series of dream / Brownsville girl / Under the red sky / Knockin' on Heaven's door.

Jun 97. (d-cd/d-c) *Sony; (SONYTV 28 CD/MC)* **THE BEST OF BOB DYLAN** [8] [ ]
– Blowin' in the wind / The times they are a-changin' / Don't think twice, it's alright / Mr. Tambourine man / Like a rolling stone / Just like a woman / All along the watchtower / Lay lady lay / If not for you / Knockin' on Heaven's door / Forever young / Tangled up in blue / Shelter from the storm / I shall be released / Oh sister / Gotta serve somebody / Jokerman / Everything is broken.

Oct 98. (d-cd/d-c) *Legacy-Columbia; (491485-2/-4)* <65759> **LIVE AT THE ROYAL ALBERT HALL: THE BOOTLEG SERIES VOL.4** <US title 'BOB DYLAN LIVE 1966: THE 'ROYAL ALBERT HALL' CONCERT [19] [31]
– She belongs to me / Fourth time around / Visions of Johanna / It's all over now, baby blue / Desolation row / Just like a woman / Mr. Tambourine man / Tell me, momma / I don't believe you (she acts like we never met) / Baby, let me follow you down / Just like Tom Thumb's blues / Leopard-skin pillbox hat / One too many mornings / Ballad of a thin man / Like a rolling stone.

May 00. (cd/c) *(498361-2/-4)* **THE BEST OF BOB DYLAN VOL.2** [22] [–]
– Things have changed / A hard rain's a-gonna fall / It ain't me babe / Subterranean homesick blues / Positively 4th street / Highway 61 revisited / Rainy day women Nos.12 & 35 / I want you / I'll be your baby tonight / Quinn the eskimo / Simple twist of fate / Hurricane / Changing the guards / License to kill / Silvio / Dignity / Not yet dark / Blowin' in the wind (live) / Highlander (live).

May 01. (d-cd/d-c) *Sony TV; (STV CD/MC 116) / Columbia;* <85168> **THE ESSENTIAL BOB DYLAN** [9] Nov00 [67]
– Blowin' in the wind / Don't think twice, it's all right / The times they are a-changin' / It ain't me babe / Maggie's farm / It's all over now, baby blue / Mr. Tambourine man / Subterranean homesick blues / Like a rolling stone / Positively 4th Street / Just like a woman / Rainy day women #12 &

35 / All along the watchtower / The mighty Quinn (Quinn, the eskimo) / I'll be your baby tonight / Lay lady lay / If not for you / I shall be released / You ain't goin' nowhere / Knockin' on Heaven's door / Forever young / Tangled up in blue / Shelter from the storm / Hurricane / Gotta serve somebody / Jokerman / Silvio / Everything is broken / Not dark yet / Things have changed.

Sep 01. (3xcd-box) *(501621-2)* **Q 5 STAR REVIEWS VOL.1** ☐ ☐
– (THE FREEWHEELIN' . . . / BRINGING IT ALL BACK HOME / HIGHWAY 61 . . .)

Sep 01. (4xcd-box) *(501622-2)* **Q 5 STAR REVIEWS VOL.2** ☐ ☐
– (BLONDE ON BLONDE / BLOOD ON THE TRACKS / THE BASEMENT TAPES)

Sep 01. (3xcd-box) *(501623-2)* **Q 5 STAR REVIEWS VOL.3** ☐ ☐
– (DESIRE / OH MERCY / TIME OUT OF MIND)

Oct 02. (3xcd-box) *(509636-2)* **INFIDELS / OH MERCY / TIME OUT OF MIND** ☐ ☐

Oct 02. (3xcd-box) *(509637-2)* **BRINGING IT ALL BACK HOME / HIGHWAY 61 REVISITED / BLONDE ON BLONDE** ☐ ☐

Oct 02. (3xcd-box) *(509638-2)* **DESIRE / BLOOD ON THE TRACKS / STREET LEGAL** ☐ ☐

Oct 02. (3xcd-box) *(509639-2)* **ANOTHER SIDE OF BOB DYLAN / THE TIMES THEY ARE A-CHANGIN' / THE FREEWHEELIN' BOB DYLAN** ☐ ☐

Nov 02. (d-cd) *Columbia; (510140-2) / Sony; <87047>* **BOB DYLAN LIVE 1975 – THE ROLLING THUNDER REVUE (THE BOOTLEG SERIES VOL.5)** 69 56
– Tonight I'll be staying here with you / It ain't me babe / A hard rain's a-gonna fall / The lonesome death of Hattie Carroll / Romance in Durango / Isis / Mr. Tambourine man / Simple twist of fate / Blowin' in the wind (with JOAN BAEZ) / Mama, you been on my mind / I shall be released (with JOAN BAEZ) / It's all over now, baby blue / Love minus zero – No limit / Tangled up in blue / The water is wide / It takes a lot to laugh, it takes a train to cry / Oh, sister / Hurricane / One more cup of coffee / Sara / Just like a woman / Knockin' on Heaven's door (with ROGER McGUINN).

Dec 02. (d-cd) *(499858-2)* **BOB DYLAN / THE FREEWHEELIN' BOB DYLAN** ☐ ☐

Dec 02. (d-cd) *(499859-2)* **THE TIMES THEY ARE A-CHANGIN' / ANOTHER SIDE OF BOB DYLAN** ☐ ☐

EMINEM

EAGLES

Formed: Los Angeles, California, USA . . . 1971, by GLENN FREY and DON HENLEY who had previously been part of LINDA RONSTADT's backing band on her 'SILK PURSE' (1970) album. They duly recruited BERNIE LEADON and RANDY MEISNER (both seasoned hands; see discography) and gave birth to The EAGLES. The very name spelled out their musical ambitions; like The BYRDS they wanted to fly high with heavenly country harmonies although they wanted a tougher, more predatory sound. Signed to 'Asylum' records that year, they stormed the charts from the off with the FREY / JACKSON BROWNE-penned, open-road classic, 'TAKE IT EASY'. The eponymous debut album followed soon after, hitting the US Top 30. Not exactly groundbreaking, it contained more than a few duffers although 'PEACEFUL EASY FEELING' still sounds gorgeous. Considered by many to be the band's finest hour, 'DESPERADO' (1973) was a Wild West concept album. While the idea sounds too awful to contemplate on paper, they somehow managed to pull it off. Amid the twists and turns of the plot lay such goose-bump masterpieces as 'TEQUILA SUNRISE' and the elegiac title track, although no major hit singles were forthcoming. With the addition of guitarist DON FELDER and BILL SZYMCZYK on production duties, 'ON THE BORDER' (1974) introduced a more robust sound, spawning the US No.1, 'BEST OF MY LOVE'. The breakthrough came with 'ONE OF THESE NIGHTS' (1975), featuring three Top 5 hits in 'LYIN' EYES', 'TAKE IT TO THE LIMIT' and the hard-edged title track. LEADON was not a happy chappy however, his country boy sensibilities displeased at The EAGLES' increasing prediliction for "rawk". Maybe it was for the best, however, as he'd no doubt have been horrified by 'HOTEL CALIFORNIA' (1976), a decidedly harder affair with nary a hint of country to be found. In its place was a set of immaculately crafted, quintessentially Californian soft rock that was the stuff of radio programmer's dreams. Up there with 'Rumours' and 'Thriller' in terms of legendary and commercial status, its slow burning title track was an epic metaphor for that crazy, frozen-nosed Californian lifestyle that mere mortals could only dream of. Even punk champion JOHN PEEL was a fan (hipper-than-thou detractors take note!), playing the classic closing track, 'THE LAST RESORT', another song dealing with the jaded, faded City Of Angels. Guitarist JOE WALSH was partly responsible for the heavier sound, having replaced LEADON, while 1977 saw another line-up change with TIMOTHY B. SCHMIT taking the place of the departing MEISNER. The band's parting shot, 'THE LONG RUN' (1979) was another massive seller although it lacked the staying power of their previous efforts. After a live album in 1980, the band drifted apart with solo careers beckoning. HENLEY's career was set back somewhat in Nov'80, however, when a 16 year-old female was found naked and drugged in his Californian home (he was fined and ordered to attend a drug counselling scheme). The following year, he recorded his debut album, 'I CAN'T STAND STILL', with DANNY KORTCHMAR and GREG LADANYI, although this lay dormant until late 1982. In the meantime, he was credited on a US Top 10 single by STEVIE NICKS 'Leather And Lace'. Upon its release, his debut hit the US Top 30, helped by an appropriately titled Top 3 single, 'DIRTY LAUNDRY'. In '84, he moved to the 'Geffen' label, and secured a cross-Atlantic Top 20 single with the atmospheric 'THE BOYS OF SUMMER' and subsequent album, 'BUILDING THE PERFECT BEAST' (1985). Four years later, HENLEY garnered further critical acclaim with 'THE END OF THE INNOCENCE' album, his last solo work to date. FREY meanwhile, still contracted to 'Asylum' records, issued the US Top 40 album, 'NO FUN ALOUD', a easy-going set that found little sympathy with the British buying public. In 1984, his next Top 40 effort, 'THE ALLNIGHTER', prompted NBC TV to feature the sax-driven 'SMUGGLER'S BLUES' and FREY himself, on their 'Miami Vice' cop series. This gave him a cross-Atlantic Top 30 hit in 1985, and was followed by another hit song from the series, 'YOU BELONG TO THE CITY'. After a quiet two years, FREY returned to business with 1988's 'SOUL SEARCHIN' album. They had always insisted it would never happen, yet in 1994 a line-up of HENLEY, FREY, WALSH, FELDER and SCHMITT reformed for an MTV performance and tour. They even released an album, 'HELL FREEZES OVER', featuring material culled from the MTV show, together with four new cuts. Their Wembley Stadium show was eagerly anticipated although some of the new material was dodgy, 'ORDINARY AVERAGE GUY' springs to mind. The EAGLES have always been an easy and predictable target for the fashion police, yet their back catalogue contains some of the finest harmonies in rock history. With HENLEY unwilling to record any new material, 'Geffen' had to make do with a greatest hits set, 'ACTUAL MILES' (1995) and a re-released 'BOYS OF SUMMER' (a UK Top 20 hit in 1998) to see them through the final years of his contract. Eager for more creative control, HENLEY signed with 'Warners' and wasted no time in cutting his first album for over a decade, 'INSIDE JOB' (2000). Given how radically the music scene had changed since the late 80's, it was strangely heartening to hear the former EAGLE more or less taking up where he left off. So, no poorly judged trip hop experiments or Tom Jones covers, merely the pleasant sound of a singer/songwriter settling into middle age with only the occasional rant at society's downward spiral. To accompany yet another anthology (2003's double disc 'VERY BEST OF'), the EAGLES released their first new material in years in the shape of the 'HOLE IN THE WORLD' single. A stab of social conscience in the wake of 9/11, the single was typical harmony-rock fare with HENLEY in comfortably weathered vocal form. • **Songwriters:** All took turns writing and also covered; OL' 55 (Tom Waits) / OUTLAW MAN (David Blue) / PLEASE COME

HOME FOR CHRISTMAS (Charles Brown) / SEVEN BRIDGES ROAD (Steve Young). HENLEY covered EVERYBODY KNOWS (Leonard Cohen). • **Trivia:** In 1979, FREY, HENLEY and WALSH appeared on RANDY NEWMAN's 'Little Criminals'. In 1990, FREY was honoured by the Rock'n'charity foundation for his work to prevent against AIDS and cancer.

Album rating: EAGLES (*5) / DESPERADO (*8) / ON THE BORDER (*6) / ONE OF THESE NIGHTS (*8) / THEIR GREATEST HITS 1971-1975 compilation (*10) / HOTEL CALIFORNIA (*10) / THE LONG RUN (*6) / THE EAGLES LIVE (*4) / EAGLES GREATEST HITS, VOL.2 compilation (*6) / BEST OF THE EAGLES compilation (*7) / HELL FREEZES OVER (*5) / THE COMPLETE GREATEST HITS or THE VERY BEST OF . . . compilation (*8) / Glenn Frey: NO FUN ALOUD (*5) / THE ALLNIGHTER (*6) / SOUL SEARCHIN' (*5) / Don Henley: I CAN'T STAND STILL (*6) / BUILDING THE PERFECT BEAST (*7) / THE END OF THE INNOCENCE (*6) / ACTUAL MILES: HENLEY'S GREATEST HITS compilation (*6) / INSIDE JOB (*6) / ONE OF THESE NIGHTS (*6)

GLENN FREY (b. 6 Nov'48, Detroit, Mich.) – guitar, vocals (ex-LINDA RONSTADT Band, ex-LONGBRANCH PENWHISTLE) / **BERNIE LEADON** (b.19 Jul'47, Minneapolis, Minnesota) – guitar, vocals (ex-LINDA RONSTADT Band, ex-FLYING BURRITO BROTHERS) / **RANDY MEISNER** (b. 8 Mar'47, Scottsbluff, Nebraska) – bass, vocals (ex-LINDA RONSTADT Band, ex-POCO, ex-RICK NELSON) / **DON HENLEY** (b.22 Jul'47, Gilmer, Texas) – drums, vocals (ex-LINDA RONSTADT Band, ex-SHILOH)

Asylum Asylum

Jun 72. (7") *(AYM 505) <11005>* **TAKE IT EASY. / GET YOU IN THE MOOD** [ ] May72 [12]

Sep 72. (7") *(AYM 508) <11008>* **WITCHY WOMAN. / EARLY BIRD** [ ] [9]

Oct 72. (lp/c) *(SYLA/SYTC 101) <5054>* **EAGLES** [ ] Jun 72 [22]
– Take it easy / Witchy woman / Chug all night / Most of us are sad / Nightingale / Train leaves here this morning / Take the Devil / Early bird / Peaceful easy feeling / Tryin'. *(re-iss. Jun76 lp/c; K/K4 53009) (cd-iss. Feb87; K2 53009)*

Dec 72. (7") *<11013>* **PEACEFUL EASY FEELING. / TRYIN'** [-] [22]

Feb 73. (7") *(AYM 512)* **TRYIN'. / CHUG ALL NIGHT** [ ] [-]

Apr 73. (lp/c) *(SYLA/SYTC 9011) <5068>* **DESPERADO** [ ] [41]
– Doolin-Dalton / Twenty-one / Out of control / Tequila sunrise / Desperado / Certain kind of fool / Outlaw man / Saturday night / Bitter creek. *(re-iss. Aug75 lp/c; K/K4 53008)* – hit UK No.39 *(re-iss. Jun76; K/K4 53008) (cd-iss. 1989; K2 53008)*

Jul 73. (7") *<11017>* **TEQUILA SUNRISE. / TWENTY-ONE** [ ] Jun73 [64]

Oct 73. (7") *(AYM 523) <11025>* **OUTLAW MAN. / CERTAIN KIND OF FOOL** [ ] Sep73 [59]

— added **DON FELDER** (b.21 Sep'47, Gainsville, Florida) – guitar, vocals (ex-FLOW)

Apr 74. (lp/c) *(SYLA/SYTC 9016) <7E 1004>* **ON THE BORDER** [28] [17]
– Already gone / You never cry like a lover / Midnight flyer / My man / On the border / James Dean / Ol' 55 / Is it true / Good day in Hell / Best of my love. *(re-iss. Jun76 lp/c; K/K4 43005) (quad-lp 1977) (cd-iss. 1989; K2 43005)*

Apr 74. (7") *<11036>* **ALREADY GONE. / IS IT TRUE** [-] [32]

May 74. (7") *(AYM 527)* **JAMES DEAN. / IS IT TRUE** [ ] [-]

Jul 74. (7") *(AYM 530)* **ALREADY GONE. / OL' 55** [ ] [-]

Sep 74. (7") *<45202>* **JAMES DEAN. / GOOD DAY IN HELL** [-] [77]

Nov 74. (7") *<45218>* **BEST OF MY LOVE. / OL' 55** [-] [1]

Dec 74. (7") *(AYM 538)* **BEST OF MY LOVE. / MIDNIGHT FLYER** [ ] [-]

May 75. (7"m) *(AYM 542)* **MY MAN. / TAKE IT EASY / TEQUILA SUNRISE** [ ] [-]

Jun 75. (lp/c) *(SYLA/SYTC 8759) <1039>* **ONE OF THESE NIGHTS** [8] [1]
– One of these nights / Too many hands / Hollywood waltz / Journey of the sorceror / Lyin' eyes / Take it to the limit / Visions / After the thrill is gone / I wish you peace. *(re-iss. Jun76 lp/c; K/K4 53014) (quad-lp 1977) (cd-iss. 1989; K2 53014)*

Jun 75. (7") *(AYM 543) <45257>* **ONE OF THESE NIGHTS. / VISIONS** [23] May75 [1]

Oct 75. (7") *(AYM 548)* **LYIN' EYES. / JAMES DEAN** [23] [-]

Dec 75. (7") *(K 13025) <45279>* **LYIN' EYES. / TOO MANY HANDS** [ ] Sep75 [2]

Dec 75. (7") *<45293>* **TAKE IT TO THE LIMIT. / AFTER THE THRILL IS GONE** [-] [4]

Feb 76. (7") *(K 13029)* **TAKE IT TO THE LIMIT. / TOO MANY HANDS** [12] [-]

Feb 76. (lp/c) *(K/K4 53017) <1052>* **THEIR GREATEST HITS 1971-1975** (compilation) [2] [1]
– Take it easy / Witchy woman / Lyin' eyes / Already gone / Desperado / One of these nights / Tequila sunrise / Take it to the limit / Peaceful easy feeling / Best of my love. *(cd-iss. May87; 253 017-2)*

— **JOE WALSH** (b.20 Nov'47, Wichita, Kansas) – guitar, vocals (ex-Solo artist, ex-JAMES GANG),repl. LEADON who formed own duo band

Dec 76. (lp/c) *(K/K4 53051) <1084>* **HOTEL CALIFORNIA** [2] [1]
– Hotel California / New kid in town / Life in the fast lane / Wasted time / Wasted time (reprise) / Victim of love / Pretty maids all in a row / Try and love again / The last resort. *(cd-iss. May87; 253 051)*

Jan 77. (7") *(K 13069) <45373>* **NEW KID IN TOWN. / VICTIM OF LOVE** [20] Dec76 [1]

Apr 77. (7") *(K 13079) <45386>* **HOTEL CALIFORNIA. / PRETTY MAIDS ALL IN A ROW** [8] Feb77 [1]

Jun 77. (7") *(K 13085) <45403>* **LIFE IN THE FAST LANE. / THE LAST RESORT** [ ] May77 [11]

— **TIMOTHY B. SCHMIT** (b.30 Oct'47, Sacramento, Calif.) – bass, vocals (ex-POCO) repl. MEISNER who went solo.

— (SCHMIT now alongside FREY, HENLEY, WALSH and FELDER)

Dec 78. (7") *(K 13415) <45555>* **PLEASE COME HOME FOR CHRISTMAS. / FUNKY NEW YEAR** [30] [18]

— added p/t **JOE VITALE** – keyboards

Sep 79. (7") *(K 12394) <46545>* **HEARTACHE TONIGHT. / TEENAGE JAIL** [40] [1]

Sep 79. (lp/c) *(K/K4 52181) <508>* **THE LONG RUN** [4] [1]
– The long run / I can't tell you why / In the city / The disco strangler / King of Hollywood / Heartache tonight / Those shoes / Teenage jail / The Greeks don't want no freaks / The sad cafe. *(cd-iss. 1986; 252 181)*

Nov 79. (7") *(K 12404) <46569>* **THE LONG RUN. / THE DISCO STRANGLER** [66] [8]

Jan 80. (7") *(K 12418) <46608>* **I CAN'T TELL YOU WHY. / THE GREEKS DON'T WANT NO FREAKS** [ ] [8]

May 80. (7") *(K 12424)* **THE SAD CAFE. / THOSE SHOES** [ ] [-]

Jul 80. (7") *<47004>* **LYIN' EYES. / Johhny Lee: LOOKIN' FOR LOVE** [-] [ ]

Sep 80. (7") *<47073>* **LYIN' EYES. / Jimmy Buffet: HELLO TEXAS** [-] [ ]

Nov 80. (d-lp/d-c) *(K/K4 62032) <705>* **EAGLES LIVE (live)** [24] [6]
– Hotel California / Heartache tonight / I can't tell you why / The long run / New kid in town / Life's been good / Seven bridges road / Wasted time / Take it to the limit / Doolin-Dalton / Desperado / Saturday night / All night long / Life in the fast lane / Take it easy. *(d-cd-iss. Feb93; 7559 60591-2)*

Dec 80. (7") *<47100>* **SEVEN BRIDGES ROAD (live). / THE LONG RUN (live)** [-] [21]

Jan 81. (7") *(K 12504)* **TAKE IT TO THE LIMIT (live). / SEVEN BRIDGES ROAD (live) / TAKE IT EASY (live)** [ ] [-]

not iss. Full Moon

Mar 81. (7") *<49654>* **I CAN'T TELL YOU WHY. / Ambrosia: OUTSIDE** [-] [ ]

— By this time they had all mutually agreed to disband. All five went on to individual solo careers.

DON HENLEY

WEA Asylum

Sep 82. (7") *(K 13200) <69971>* **JOHNNY CAN'T READ. / LONG WAY HOME** [ ] Aug82 [42]

Elektra Asylum

Dec 82. (7") *(E 9849) <69894>* **DIRTY LAUNDRY. / LILAH** [59] Oct82 [3]
(12"+=) *(E 9849T)* – Them and us.
(re-iss. Jun85, 7"/12"; EKR 4/+T)

Jan 83. (7") *<69931>* **I CAN'T STAND STILL. / THEM AND US** [-] [48]

Asylum Asylum

Feb 83. (lp/c) *(K/K4 52365) <60048>* **I CAN'T STAND STILL** [ ] Aug82 [24]
– I can't stand still / You better hang up / Long way home / Nobody's business / Talking to the Moon / Dirty laundry / Johnny can't read / Them and us / La Eile / Lilah / The uncloudy day. *(cd-iss. Jun89; 960 048-2)*

May 83. (7") *(E 9876)* **THE UNCLOUDED DAY. / LONG WAY HOME** [ ] [-]
(12"+=) *(E 9876T)* – I can't stand still.

Jul 83. (7") *<69831>* **NOBODY'S BUSINESS. / LONG WAY HOME** [-] [ ]

Geffen Geffen

Dec 84. (7"/12") *(A/TA 4945)* <29141> **THE BOYS OF SUMMER. / A MONTH OF SUNDAYS** 12 Nov84 5

Feb 85. (lp/c) *(GEF/GEC 25939)* <24026> **BUILDING THE PERFECT BEAST** 14 Dec84 13
– The boys of summer / You can't make love / Man with a mission / You're not drinking enough / Not enough love in the world / Building the perfect beast / All she wants to do is dance / Sunset grill / Drivin' with your eyes closed / Land of the living. *(cd+=)* – A month of Sundays. *(re-iss. Sep86 lp/c; 924026-1/-4) (cd-iss. Feb87; 924026-2) (cd re-iss. 1988; CD 25939) (re-iss. Jan91 lp/c/cd; GEF/+C/D 24026) (cd re-iss. Mar95; GFLD 19267)*

Feb 85. (7") *<29065>* **ALL SHE WANTS TO DO IS DANCE. / BUILDING THE PERFECT BEAST** – 9

Apr 85. (7") *(A 6161)* **SUNSET GRILL. / BUILDING THE PERFECT BEAST** –

Jul 85. (7") *(A 6419)* <29012> **NOT ENOUGH LOVE IN THE WORLD. / MAN WITH A MISSION** May85 34

Aug 85. (7") *<28906>* **SUNSET GRILL. / MAN WITH A MISSION** – 22

— his basic back-up consisted of **DANNY KORTCHMAR** – guitar, keyboards / **STAN LYNCH** – drums / **PINO PALLADINO** – bass / **JAI WINDING** – keyboards / **MIKE CAMPBELL** – keyboards

Jun 89. (lp/c)(cd) *(WX 253/+C)(924217-2)* <24217> **THE END OF THE INNOCENCE** 17 8
– The end of the innocence / How bad do you want it? / I will not go quietly / The last worthless evening / New York minute / Shangri-la / Little tin god / Gimme what you got / If dirt were dollars / The heart of the matter. *(re-iss. Jan91 lp/c/cd; GEF/+C/D 24217) (cd re-iss. Oct95; GFLD 19285)*

Jul 89. (7"/c-s) *(GEF/+C 57)* <22925> **THE END OF THE INNOCENCE. / IF DIRT WERE DOLLARS** 48 Jun89 8
(12"+=/cd-s+=) *(GEF 57 T/CD)* – The boys of summer.

Oct 89. (7"/c-s) *(GEF 66)* **NEW YORK MINUTE. / GIMME WHAT YOU GOT** –
(10"+=/12"+=/cd-s+=) *(GEF 66 TE/T/CD)* – Sunset grill (live).

Oct 89. (7") *<22771>* **THE LAST WORTHLESS EVENING. / GIMME WHAT YOU GOT** – 21

Feb 90. (7"/c-s) *(GEF 71)* **THE LAST WORTHLESS EVENING. / ALL SHE WANTS TO DO IS DANCE** –
(12"+=) *(GEF 71T)* – You can't make love.
(cd-s++=) *(GEF 71CD)* – ('A'version).

Feb 90. (c-s) *<19898>* **THE HEART OF THE MATTER / LITTLE TIN GOD** – 21

Jun 90. (c-s) *<19699>* **HOW BAD DO YOU WANT IT? / NEW YORK MINUTE** – 48

Oct 90. (c-s) *<19660>* **NEW YORK MINUTE / THE HEART OF THE MATTER (acoustic)** – 48

— In Sep'92, HENLEY and PATTY SMYTH charted US No.2 / UK No.22 with 'SOMETIMES LOVE JUST AIN'T ENOUGH' on 'M.C.A.' <54403>

— In Mar'93, DON featured on TRISH YEARWOOD's single 'Walkaway Joe'.

Nov 95. (cd/c) *<(GED/GEC 24834)>* **ACTUAL MILES: HENLEY'S GREATEST HITS** (compilation + 2 new *) 48
– Dirty laundry / The boys of summer / All she wants to do is dance / Not enough love in the world / Sunset grill / The end of the innocence / The last worthless evening / New York minute / The heart of the matter / The garden of Allah * / You don't know me at all *. *(cd+=)* – I get the message.

Jul 98. (c-s/cd-s) *(GFS C/TD 22350)* **THE BOYS OF SUMMER / ALL SHE WANTS TO DO IS DANCE / SOMETIMES LOVE JUST AIN'T ENOUGH** 12 –

Warners Warners

May 00. (cd/c) *<(9362 47083-2/-4)>* **INSIDE JOB** 25 7
– Nobody else in the world but you / Taking you home / For my wedding / Everything is different now / Workin' it / Goodbye to a river / Inside job / They're not here, they're not coming / Damn it, Rose / Miss ghost / The genie / Annabel / My thanksgiving.

Jun 00. (-) *<radio cut>* **TAKING YOU HOME** – 58

– compilations, etc. –

Jul 02. (cd) *Traditional Line; <(TL 1350)>* **ONE OF THESE NIGHTS (live 1993 Labor Day benefit concert)**
– Hotel California / One of these nights / Desperado / End of innocence / Sunset grill / Boys of summer / Life in the fast lane / Volcano (with JIMMY BUFFET) / All she wants to do is dance / Margaritaville (with JIMMY BUFFET) / Dirty laundry / Well, well, well / The heart of the matter.

GLENN FREY

Asylum Asylum

Jun 82. (lp/c) *(K/K4 52395)* <60129> **NO FUN ALOUD** 32
– I found somebody / The one you love / Party town / I volunteer / I've been born again / Sea cruise / That girl / All those lies / She can't let go / Don't give up.

Jul 82. (7") *(K 13812)* <47466> **I FOUND SOMEBODY. / SHE CAN'T LET GO** Jun82 31

Oct 82. (7") *<69974>* **THE ONE YOU LOVE. / ALL THOSE LIES** – 15

Jan 83. (7") *<69857>* **ALL THOSE LIES. / THAT GIRL** – 41

M.C.A. M.C.A.

Jul 84. (lp/c) *(MCF/+C 3232)* <5501> **THE ALLNIGHTER** 37
– The allnighter / Sexy girl / I got love / Somebody else / Lover's moon / Smuggler's blues / Let's go home / Better in the U.S.A. / The heat is on / New love. *(re-act.Jun85, hit UK No.31) (cd-iss. Jul85; DMCF 3232) (cd re-iss. Aug89; DMCL 1893) (re-iss. Apr92 cd/c; MCL D/C 19009)*

Sep 84. (7") *(MCA 911)* <52413> **SEXY GIRL. / BETTER IN THE U.S.A.** Aug84 20

Oct 84. (7") *<52461>* **THE ALLNIGHTER. / SMUGGLER'S BLUES** – 54

Jan 85. (7"/12") *(MCA/+T 941)* <52513> **THE HEAT IS ON. / Harold Faltermeyer: SHOOT OUT** 12 Dec84 2
above was used for the film 'Beverly Hills Cop' starring Eddie Murphy

Mar 85. (7") *<52546>* **SMUGGLER'S BLUES. / NEW LOVE** – 12
below was issued on 'BBC' records in Britain only.

Jun 85. (7") *(RESL 170)* **SMUGGLER'S BLUES. / NEW LOVE** 22 –
(12"+=) *(12RSL 170)* – Living in darkness.

Jul 85. (7") *(MCA 965)* **SEXY GIRL. / BETTER IN THE U.S.A.** –
(12"+=) *(MCAT 965)* – The heat is on (dub) / New love.

Sep 85. (7") *<52651>* **YOU BELONG TO THE CITY. / SMUGGLER'S BLUES** – 2

Oct 85. (7") *(MCA 1008)* **YOU BELONG TO THE CITY. / I GOT LOVE** –
(12"+=) *(MCAT 1008)* – ('A'version).

Sep 88. (7") *(MCA 1284)* <53363> **TRUE LOVE. / WORKING MAN** Aug88 13
(12"+=/cd-s+=) *(MCAT/DMCA 1284)* – The heat is on.

Oct 88. (lp/c/cd) *(MCF/MCFC/DMCF 3429)* <6239> **SOUL SEARCHIN'** Aug88 36
– Soul searchin' / Livin' right / True love / I did it for your love / Working man / Two hearts / Some kind of blue / Can't put out this fire / Let's pretend we're still in love / It's your life.

Jan 89. (7") *(MCA 1294)* <53452> **SOUL SEARCHIN'. / IT'S COLD DOWN HERE**
(12"+=/cd-s+=) *(MCAT/DMCA 1294)* – True love.

Mar 89. (7") *<53497>* **LIVIN' RIGHT. / SOUL SEARCHIN'** – 90

May 89. (7") *<53684>* **TWO HEARTS. / SOME KIND OF BLUE** –

— now writes with keyboard player **JAY OLIVER** or **JACK TEMPCHIN**

Apr 91. (c-s) *<54060>* **PART OF ME, PART OF YOU** – 55
above taken from the film 'Thelma And Louise'

Jul 92. (c-s) *<54429>* **I'VE GOT MINE / A WALK IN THE DARK** – 91

Jul 92. (7"/c-s) **I'VE GOT MINE. / PART OF ME, PART OF YOU** –
(cd-s+=) – A walk in the dark.

Aug 92. (cd/c) *<(MCA D/C 10599)>* **STRANGE WEATHER** Jul92
– Silent spring / Long hot summer / Strange weather / Agua tranquillo / Love in the 21st century / He took advantage / River of dreams / Before the ship goes down / I've got mine / Rising sun / Brave new world / Delicious / A walk in the dark / Big life / Part of me, part of you.

Sep 92. (c-s) *<54461>* **RIVER OF DREAMS / HE TOOK ADVANTAGE** –

Mar 93. (c-s) *<54564>* **LOVE IN THE 21st CENTURY** –

May 93. (cd/c) *<(MCD/MCC 10826)>* **LIVE (live)** Jul93
– Peaceful easy feeling / New kid in town / The one you love / Wild mountain thyme / Strange weather / I've got mine / Lyin' eyes – Take it easy (medley) / River of dreams / True love / Love in the 21st century / Smuggler's blues / The heat is on / Heartache tonight / Desperado. *(cd re-iss. Mar03; AAMCAD 10826)*

Jul 93. (c-s) *<54699>* **STRANGE WEATHER (live)** –

– compilations, etc. –

Apr 95. (cd) *M.C.A.; <(MCD 11227)>* **SOLO CONNECTION**
– This way to happiness / Who's been sleeping in my bed / Common

ground / Call on me / The one you love / Sexy girl / Smuggler's blues / The heat is on / You belong to the city / True love / Soul searchin' / Part of me, part of you / I've got mine / River of dreams / Brave new world.

Jul 96. (d-cd) *M.C.A.; (MCD 33727)* **SOUL SEARCHIN' / STRANGE WEATHER** [ ] [ ]

Sep 00. (cd) *M.C.A.; <112359>* **THE BEST OF GLENN FREY – THE MILLENNIUM COLLECTION** [–] [ ]

Jul 01. (cd) *Universal; (E 112497-2)* **UNIVERSAL MASTERS COLLECTION** [ ] [–]

Jan 02. (cd) *Universal; <1073>* **THE BEST OF GLENN FREY** [–] [ ]

EAGLES

re-formed **HENLEY / FREY / WALSH / FELDER + SCHMIDT**

Geffen Geffen

Nov 94. (cd/c) *<(GED/GEC 24725)>* **HELL FREEZES OVER** [28] [1]
– Get over it / Love will keep us alive / The girl from yesterday / Learn to be still / Tequila sunrise / Hotel California / Wasted time / Pretty maids all in a row / I can't tell you why / New York minute / The last resort / Take it easy / In the city / Life in the fast lane / Desperado.

Nov 94. (c-s) *<19376>* **GET OVER IT / ('A'live version)** [–] [31]

Jul 96. (c-s) *(GFSC 21980)* **LOVE WILL KEEP US ALIVE / NEW YORK MINUTE** [52] [–]
(cd-s+=) *(GFSTD 21980)* – Help me through the night.

—— the EAGLES were back (**HENLEY, FREY, WALSH + SCHMIDT**)

Oct 03. (cd-s) *(8122 74547-2)* **HOLE IN THE WORLD / HOLE IN THE WORLD (live)** [69] [ ]

– compilations etc. –

Note; All releases on 'Asylum' unless mentioned otherwise

Sep 76. (7") *(K 13044)* **TAKE IT EASY. / WITCHY WOMAN** [ ] [–]

Sep 76. (7") *(K 13045)* **PEACEFUL EASY FEELING. / OL' 55** [ ] [–]

Sep 76. (7") *(K 13046)* **TEQUILA SUNRISE. / ON THE BORDER** [ ] [–]

Oct 82. (lp/c) *Elektra; (E 205-1/-4) / Asylum; <60205>* **EAGLES GREATEST HITS – VOLUME 2** [ ] [52]
– Hotel California / Heartache tonight / Life in the fast lane / Seven bridges road / The sad cafe / I can't tell you why / New kid in town / The long run / Victim of love / After the thrill is gone. *(cd-iss. Dec82; 960 205-2)*

Oct 83. (d-c) *(K4 62033)* **DESPERADO / ONE OF THESE NIGHTS** [ ] [–]

Nov 83. (d-c) *(960 275-4)* **HOTEL CALIFORNIA / THE LONG RUN** [ ] [–]

May 85. (lp/c) *Elektra; (EKT 5/+C)* **THE BEST OF THE EAGLES** [10] [–]
– Tequila sunrise / Lyin' eyes / Take it to the limit / Hotel California / Life in the fast lane / Heartache tonight / The long run / Take it easy / Peaceful easy feeling / Desperado / Best of my love / One of these nights / New kid in town. *(re-hit.Aug88 made UK No.8)*

Sep 85. (7") *Old Gold; (OG 9510)* **TAKE IT TO THE LIMIT. / BEST OF MY LOVE** [ ] [–]

Sep 85. (7") *Old Gold; (OG 9511)* **HOTEL CALIFORNIA. / DESPERADO** [ ] [–]

Oct 85. (7") *Old Gold; (OG 9526)* **LYIN' EYES. / ONE OF THESE NIGHTS** [ ] [–]

Jun 88. (7") *(EKR 10)* **HOTEL CALIFORNIA. / PRETTY MAIDS ALL IN A ROW** [ ] [–]
(12"+=) *(EKRT 10)* – The sad cafe.
(cd-s++=) *(EKRCD 10)* – Hotel California (live).

Jun 89. (cd-ep) **TAKE IT EASY / ONE OF THESE NIGHTS / DESPERADO / LYIN' EYES** [ ] [–]

Jul 94. (cd/c) *(9548 32375-2/-4)* **THE VERY BEST OF EAGLES** [5] [–]
– Take it easy / Witchy woman / Peaceful easy feeling / Doolin-Dalton / Desperado / Tequila sunrise / The best of my love / James Dean / I can't tell you why / Lyin' eyes / Take it to the limit / One of these nights / Hotel California / New kid in town / Life in the fast lane / Heartache tonight / The long run.

Nov 00. (4xcd-box) *<(7559 62575-2)>* **SELECTED WORKS: 1972-1999** [ ] [ ]

May 01. (cd/c) *Elektra; (7559 62680-2/-4)* **THE VERY BEST OF EAGLES** (diff. tracks) [3] [–]

Oct 03. (d-cd) *W.S.M.; (8122 73731-2) <73971>* **THE COMPLETE GREATEST HITS** <US title 'THE VERY BEST OF . . .'> [27] [3]
– Take it easy / Witchy woman / Peaceful easy feeling / Desperado / Tequila sunrise / Doolin-Dalton / Already gone / The best of my love / James Dean / Ol' 55 / Midnight flyer / On the border / Lyin' eyes / One of these nights / Take it to the limit / After the thrill is gone / Hotel California / Life in the fast lane / Wasted time / Victim of love / The last resort / New kid in town / Please come home for Christmas / Heartache tonight / The sad cafe / I can't tell you why / The long run / In the city / Those shoes / Seven bridges road (live) / Love will keep us alive / Get over it / Hole in the world.

Steve EARLE

Born: 17 Jan'55, Fort Monroe, Virginia, USA. The son of an air traffic controller, EARLE was raised in Schertz, Texas where his youth was spent immersed in guitar playing and rebelling against the authorities. At the age of 16, the long-haired would-be troubadour left home and eventually wound up in Houston where he befriended a coterie of songwriters that numbered the likes of TOWNES VAN ZANDT, JERRY JEFF WALKER and GUY CLARK. Subsequently relocating to Nashville, EARLE scraped by with a series of day jobs while playing in CLARK's backing band at night. A burgeoning talent for songwriting and a growing network of music biz contacts eventually saw him land a job as staff writer for a Nashville publishing company, his songs placed with PATTY LOVELESS and even ELVIS PRESLEY. Following a brief foray into acting (a bit part in Robert Altman's 'Nashville'), EARLE set about bringing together a backing band, The DUKES, who survived numerous incarnations over the first decade of EARLE's career. By this point (1980), he was already on his third wife, Carol, who temporarily helped put the brakes on his wilder instincts. EARLE took up a new job with publishers, 'DEA & CLARK', issuing a debut EP, 'PINK AND BLACK' on their small 'L.S.I.' label in 1982. A Nashville music journalist, John Lomax, was quick to spot EARLE's talent and offered his services as manager before helping net him a deal with 'Epic'. Unfortunately, the major label bods were at odds with EARLE over his musical direction, rejecting an album's worth of songs and demanding that he recut them in a more commercial style. A number of US-only tracks were eventually released in the space of a year or two including 'NOTHING BUT YOU', 'SQUEEZE ME IN' (featuring an early version of the scorching 'DEVIL'S RIGHT HAND'), 'WHAT'LL YOU DO ABOUT ME' and 'A LITTLE BIT IN LOVE'. None were successful, however, and after a mutual split, EARLE moved on to 'M.C.A.' with the help of producer Tony Brown. Finally, with the backing of a revamped DUKES (BUCKY BAXTER, RICHARD BENNETT, KEN MOORE, HARRY STINSON, EMORY GORDY JR., JOHN JARVIS, STEVE NATHAN and PAUL FRANKLIN), the self-styled Nashville renegade released a debut album, 'GUITAR TOWN' (1986). Walking the country line between threadbare folk, blues and rockabilly, the record found an audience with the 'new country' brigade looking for the next DWIGHT YOAKAM while commanding the respect of rock critics who praised his blue collar sentiments and gravel-throated troubadour approach. 'EXIT 0' (1987) continued in a similar, if slightly more countrified vein, featuring signature tune 'I AIN'T EVER SATISFIED' alongside the track he penned for Farm Aid, 'THE RAIN CAME DOWN'. Neither of these albums, however, hinted at the hard-bitten roots-rock of 'COPPERHEAD ROAD', EARLE's landmark 1988 effort that firmly established him within the mainstream rock community while simultaneously alienating many of his core country fans. From the epic grit of the title track to the frenetic POGUES collaboration, 'JOHNNY COME LATELY', EARLE never sounded so visceral. Neither had his lyrics been so vividly realised, bringing to life a motley cast of moonshiners, Vietnam vets and petty criminals. The record's success made EARLE a popular live attraction in Europe especially and he subsequently spent a large amount of time in London. His chaotic personal life was also catching up with him and besides coping with spiralling alcohol and drug dependency, he had to contend with an assault conviction (on a security guard at his own show) and the bankruptcy of 'Uni', the 'M.C.A.' subsidiary that'd handled his album. 'THE HARD WAY' (1990) then, was his dark night of the soul, a downbeat, introspective record that ironically furnished him with his highest UK chart placing (Top 30). Yet its relative commercial failure signalled the end of EARLE's tenure with his label and, burned out after a punishing few years of touring, he finally disbanded The DUKES. Things hardly improved for the beleaguered singer over the ensuing five years as he struggled with cocaine and heroin addiction, avoiding a one-year jail term by agreeing to enter a detox centre. Like the proverbial phoenix rising from the ashes, EARLE released what many critics considered his most accomplished record to date in 1995 with 'TRAIN A-COMIN''. Issued via the Nashville indie label, 'Winter Harvest' (the rejuvenated 'Transatlantic' in the UK), the album was an acoustic affair going back to EARLE's country roots and utilising such talents as EMMYLOU HARRIS. Critically, commercially and creatively reborn, EARLE subsequently signed a new contract with 'Warners' and released another winner in 1996's 'I FEEL ALRIGHT'. Older and wiser, EARLE has become one of the most respected elder statesmen in the country-roots field, going on to release the acclaimed 'EL CORAZON' (1997) and record and tour with the DEL McROURY BAND with whom he delivered his latest set, 'THE MOUNTAIN' (1999). While that was heavily steeped in bluegrass, the new millennium found EARLE taking a broader but no less worldy-wise sweep through the rugged country-rock which shaped his early career on 'TRANSCENDENTAL BLUES' (2000). As its title suggested, the singer was still seeking redemption through music, something that continued to lend his work a bruised authenticity missing in much modern country. The live 'TOGETHER AT THE BLUEBIRD CAFE' (2001) marked the belated release of a mid-90's benefit gig featuring EARLE and two of his musical/spiritual brethren, Texan singer-songwriters GUY CLARK and TOWNES VAN ZANDT. It was a tantalising bill which lent added poignancy given VAN ZANDT's subsequent demise. The concert's informal, back porch jam atmosphere only added to that feeling, with EARLE sounding as relaxed as he's ever done. 2002's 'JERUSALEM' was a quite different beast, EARLE's own personal meditation on the 9/11 tragedy and its aftermath and implications. Rather than trying to find blame, he sought explanations, even attempting to get inside the mind of the so-called "American Taliban" John Walker Lindh in 'JOHN WALKER'S BLUES'. Predictably, the singer came in from flack from the USA's right-wing, with the political fallout spilling over into 2003's excellent live set, 'JUST AN AMERICAN BOY' (2003). • **Covered:** THE CRUSH (John Hiatt) / THE DEVIL'S RIGHT HAND MAN (Waylon Jennings) / DEAD FLOWERS + BEFORE THEY MAKE ME RUN (Rolling Stones) / TECUMSEH VALLEY (Townes Van Zandt) / RIVERS OF BABYLON (Melodians) / BLUE YODEL NO.9 (Jimmie Rodgers) / WHAT'S YOUR NAME (Lynyrd Skynyrd) / JOHNNY TOO BAD (Slickers) / BREED (Nirvana) / TIME HAS COME TODAY (Chambers Brothers) / CREEPY JACKALOPE EYE (Supersuckers) / WILLIN' (Little Feat) / MY UNCLE (Flying Burrito Brothers) / MY BACK PAGES (Bob Dylan) / NEBRASKA (Bruce Springsteen) / SHE'S ABOUT A MOVER (Doug Sahm) / WHAT'S SO FUNNY 'BOUT PEACE, LOVE & UNDERSTANDING (Nick Lowe) / etc. MARIA McKEE (ex-LONE JUSTICE) co-wrote two songs on his 1990 album.

Album rating: GUITAR TOWN (*7) / EXIT 'O' (*6) / COPPERHEAD ROAD (*8) / THE HARD WAY (*6) / SHUT UP AND DIE LIKE AN AVIATOR (*7) / TRAIN A COMIN' (*7) / I FEEL ALRIGHT (*5) / EL CORAZON (*7) / THE MOUNTAIN with the Del Coury Band (*8) / EARLY TRACKS compilation (*5) / THE ESSENTIAL STEVE EARLE compilation (*7) / TRANSCENDENTAL BLUES (*7) / TOGETHER AT THE BLUEBIRD CAFE with Townes Van Zandt & Guy Clark (*6) / SIDE TRACKS collection (*6) / THE COLLECTION compilation (*5) / JERUSALEM (*5) / JUST AN AMERICAN BOY (*6)

STEVE EARLE – vocals, guitar + session players

		not iss.	L.S.I.
1982.	(7"ep) *<LSI 8209>* **PINK AND BLACK** – Nothin' but you / Continental trailway blues / Squeeze me in / My baby worships me.	-	

— **STEVE EARLE** – vocals, guitar (with The **DUKES**) **BUCKY BAXTER** – steel guitar, vocals / **RICHARD BENNETT** – guitars / **KEN MOORE** – organ, synthesizer, vocals / **HARRY STINSON** – drums, vocals / **EMORY GORDY JR.** – bass, mandolin / plus **JOHN JARVIS** – piano / **STEVE NATHAN** – synthesizer / **PAUL FRANKLIN** – pedal steel

		not iss.	Epic
Aug 83.	(7") *<04070>* **NOTHIN' BUT YOU. / CONTINENTAL TRAILWAY BLUES**	-	
Feb 84.	(7") *<04307>* **SQUEEZE ME IN. / DEVIL'S RIGHT HAND**	-	
Jun 84.	(7") *<04666>* **WHAT'LL YOU DO ABOUT ME. / CRY MYSELF TO SLEEP**	-	
Oct 84.	(7") *<04784>* **A LITTLE BIT IN LOVE. / THE CRUSH**	-	
		M.C.A.	M.C.A.
Aug 86.	(7") *(MCA 1083) <52920>* **SOMEDAY. / HILLBILLY HIGHWAY**		
Aug 86.	(lp/c) *(MCF/+C 3335) <5713>* **GUITAR TOWN** – Guitar town / Goodbye's all we've got left / Hillbilly highway / Good ol' boy (gettin' tough) / My old friend the blues / Someday / Think it over / Fearless heart / Little rock'n'roller / Down the road. *(cd-iss. Apr87; DMCF 3335) (cd re-iss. Jan90 +=; DMCL 1888)* – Good ol' boy (gettin' tough) (live).		89
Feb 87.	(7") *(MCA 1123)* **SOMEDAY. / GUITAR TOWN** (12"+=) *(MCAT 1123)* – Good ol' boy (gettin' tough) (live). (cd-s++=) *(MCACD 1123)* – Goodbye's all we've got left.		-
Feb 87.	(7") *<53011>* **GOODBYE'S ALL WE'VE GOT LEFT. / GOOD OL' BOY (GETTIN' TOUGH)**	-	

— credited on sleeve to "STEVE EARLE & THE DUKES" (EARLE, BAXTER, MOORE, STINSON plus **RENO KING** – bass / **MIKE McADAM** – guitars. Others included **BENNETT, GORDY JR. / JARVIS** and **K-MEAUX BOUDIN** – accordion

Apr 87.	(7") *(MCA 1141)* **FEARLESS HEART. / LITTLE ROCK'N'ROLLER** (12"+=) *(MCAT 1141)* – ('A'long version).		-
May 87.	(7"/12") *(MCA/+T 1162) <53103>* **I AIN'T EVER SATISFIED. / NOWHERE ROAD**		
Jun 87.	(lp/c/cd) *(MCF/MCFC/DMCF 3379) <5998>* **EXIT 'O'** – Nowhere road / Sweel little '66 / No.29 / Angry young man / San Antonio girl / The rain came down / I ain't ever satisfied / The week of living dangerously / I love you too much / It's all up to you. *(cd re-iss. Oct92; MCLD 19070)*	77	90
Sep 87.	(7") *<53182>* **SWEET LITTLE '66. / ANGRY YOUNG MAN**	-	
Nov 87.	(d7") *(MCA 1209)* **THE RAIN CAME DOWN. / GUITAR TOWN (live) // I LOVE YOU TOO MUCH (live). / No.29 (live)**		-
Feb 88.	(7") *<53249>* **THE WEEK OF LIVING DANGEROUSLY. / SIX DAYS ON THE ROAD**	-	
Jun 88.	(7") *(MCA 1249)* **I AIN'T EVER SATISFIED. / MY OLD FRIEND THE BLUES** (12"+=) *(MCAT 1249)* – I love you too much.		-
		M.C.A.	Uni
Sep 88.	(7") *(MCA 1280)* **COPPERHEAD ROAD. / LITTLE SISTER (live)** (12"+=) *(MCAT 1280)* – No.29. (cd-s+=) *(DMCA 1280)* – San Antonio girl / I ain't ever satisfied.	45	-
Oct 88.	(lp/c/cd) *(MCF/MCFC/DMCF 3426) <7>* **COPPERHEAD ROAD** – Copperhead road / Snake oil / Back to the wall / You belong to me / The Devil's right hand / Johnny come lately / Even when I'm blue / Waiting on you / Once you love / Nothing but a child. *(cd re-iss. Aug93; MCLD 19213)*	44	56

Dec 88. (7") *(MCA 1301)* **JOHNNY COME LATELY. / NOTHING BUT A CHILD** [75] [–]
(12"+=) *(MCAT 1301)* – Nebraska (live).
(3"cd-s++=) *(DMCA 1301)* – Copperhead Road (live).

Feb 89. (7") *(MCA 1319)* **BACK TO THE WALL. / SNAKE OIL** [ ] [–]
(12"+=/cd-s+=) *(MCAT/DMCA 1319)* – State trooper (live).

STEVE EARLE AND THE DUKES

— he retained **BAXTER, MOORE** and p/t **JARVIS** / newcomers = **ZIP GIBSON** – guitar, vocals / **KELLY LEONEY** – bass, vocals / **CRAIG WRIGHT** – drums / plus **PATRICK EARLE** – percussion and other guests

May 90. (7") *(MCA 1426)* **THE OTHER KIND. / WEST NASHVILLE BOOGIE** [ ] [–]
(12"+=/cd-s+=) *(MCAT/DMCA 1426)* – Guitar town (live) / Dead flowers (live).

Jun 90. (cd/c/lp) *(MCG/MCGC/DMCG 6095)* <6430> **THE HARD WAY** [22] Jul90 [100]
– The other kind / Promise you anything / Hopeless romantics / Esmeralda's Hollywood / This highway's mine (roadmaster) / Billy Austin / Justice in Ontario / Have mercy / Country girl / When the people find out / Regular guy / Close your eyes / West Nashville boogie. *(cd re-iss. Aug00; MCLD 19400)*

Sep 90. (7") *(MCA 1441)* **JUSTICE IN ONTARIO. / THIS HIGHWAY'S MINE (ROADMASTER)** [ ] [–]
(12"+=/cd-s+=) *(MCAT/DMCA 1441)* – Copperhead road (live) / I ain't ever satisfied (live).

— **STACEY EARLE-MIMS** – backing vocals, percussion; repl. JARVIS

Sep 91. (d-lp/c/cd) *<(MCA/+C/D 10315)>* **SHUT UP AND DIE LIKE AN AVIATOR (live)** [62] [ ]
– Good ol' boy (gettin' tough) / Devil's right hand / I ain't ever satisfied / Someday / West Nashville boogie / Snake oil / Blue yodel #9 / The other kind / Billy Austin / Copperhead road / Fearless heart / Guitar town / I love you too much / The rain came down / She's about a mover / Dead flowers. *(cd re-iss. Sep96; same)*

— now with PETER ROWAN / NORMAN BLAKE / ROY HUSKEY + EMMYLOU HARRIS

Transatla. Winter Harvest

Jul 95. (cd/c) *(TRA CD/MC 111)* <3302> **TRAIN A COMIN'** [ ] [ ]
– Mystery train part II / Hometown blues / Sometimes she forgets / you / Mercenary song / Goodbye / Tom Ames' prayer / Nothin' without you / Angel is the Devil / I'm looking through you / Northern winds / Ben McCulloch / Rivers of Babylon / Tecumseh Valley.

— now with The V-ROYS: **RICHARD BENNETT** – guitar, harmonium, percussion / **RAY KENNEDY** – guitar / **KELLEY LOONEY + GARRY TALLENT + ROY HUSKEY + RIC KIPP** – bass / **KEN MOORE** – organ / **CUSTER + GREG MORROW + RICK SCHELL** – drums / **DUB CORNETT** – percussion

Transatla. Warners

Mar 96. (cd/c) *(TRA CD/MC 227)* <46201> **I FEEL ALRIGHT** [44] [ ]
– Feel alright / Hard-core troubadour / More than I can do / Hurtin' me, hurtin' you / Now she's gone / Poor boy / Valentine's day / The unrepentant / CCKMP / Billy and Bonnie / South Nashville blues / You're still standin' there (with LUCINDA WILLIAMS).

Jun 96. (10"/12") *(TRA S/T 1026)* **JOHNNY TOO BAD (sunshine mix). / JOHNNY TOO BAD (Jamaican hillbilly mix) / STRAIGHT HIGHWAY** [ ] [–]
(cd-s+=) *(TRAX 1026)* – Ellis unit one.

Sub Pop Sub Pop

Jul 97. (cd-ep) *<(SPCD 388)>* **STEVE EARLE & THE SUPERSUCKERS** [ ] [ ]
– Creepy Jackalope eye / Angel is the Devil / Before they make me run / Creepy Jackalope eye (SUPERSUCKERS) / Angel is the Devil (STEVE EARLE). *(re-iss. Oct99; same)*

Warners Warners

Oct 97. (cd/c) *<(9362 46789-2/-4)>* **EL CORAZON** [59] [ ]
– Christmas in Washington / Taneytown / If you fall / I still carry you around / Telephone road / Someone out there / You know the rest / NYC / Poison lovers / The other side of town / Here I am / Fort Worth blues. *(cd re-iss. Jul00; same)*

STEVE EARLE and the DEL McCOURY BAND

Grapevine E-Squared

Feb 99. (cd) *(GRACD 252)* <1064> **THE MOUNTAIN** [51] [ ]
– Texas eagle / Your forever blue / Carrie Brown / I'm still in love with you / The graveyard shift / Harlan man / The mountain / Outlaw's honeymoon / Connemara breakdown / Leroy's dustbowl blues / Dixieland / Paddy on the beat / Long, lonesome highway blues / Pilgrim.

May 99. (cd-s) *(CDGPS 256)* **DIXIELAND / I'M STILL IN LOVE WITH YOU** [ ] [–]

Oct 99. (cd-s) *(CDGPS 270)* **THE MOUNTAIN / COPPERHEAD ROAD (live) / I AIN'T EVER SATISFIED (live)** [ ] [–]

STEVE EARLE

Artemis E-Squared

Jun 00. (cd) *(498074-2)* *<751033>* **TRANSCENDENTAL BLUES** [32] [66]
– Transcendental blues / Everyone's in love with you / Another town / I can wait / The boy who never cried / Steve's last ramble / The Galway girl / Lonelier than this / Wherever I go / When I fall / I don't want to lose you yet / Halo 'round the moon / Until the day I die / All of my life / Over yonder (Jonathan's song). *(cd w/cd+=; 498074-9)* – Copperhead road (live) / Galway girl (live) / Steve's last ramble (live) / I feel alright (live).

— STEVE also turned up with SHARON SHANNON on their version of the track/single, 'THE GALWAY GIRL'

Artemis Artemis

Sep 02. (cd) *(509480-2)* *<751147>* **JERUSALEM** [ ] [59]
– Ashes to ashes / Amerika v. 6.0 (the best we can do) / Conspiracy theory / John Walker's blues / The kind / What's a simple man to do? / The truth / Go Amanda / I remember you / Shadowland / Jerusalem.

Rykodisc Artemis

Sep 03. (d-cd) *(RCD 17002)* *<51256>* **JUST AN AMERICAN BOY: AN AUDIO DOCUMENTARY (live)** [ ] [ ]
– (audience intro) / Amerika v. 6.0 (the best we can do) / Ashes to ashes / Paranoia / Conspiracy theory / I remember you / Schertz, Texas / Hometown blues / The mountain / Pennsylvania miners / Harlan man / Copperhead road / Guitar town / I oppose the death penalty / Over yonder (Jonanthan's song) / Billy Austin // (audience intro 2) / South Nashville blues / Rex's blues – Ft. Worth blues / John Walker's blues / Jerusalem / The unrepentant / Christmas in Washington / Democracy / What's so funny 'bout peace, love & understanding / Time you waste.

– compilations etc. –

Jul 87. (lp/c) *Epic; (450873-1/-4)* **EARLY TRACKS** [ ] Oct86 [ ]
– Nothin' but you / If you need a fool / Continental trailway blues / Open up your door / Breakdown lane / Squeeze me in / Annie, is tonight the night / My baby worships me / Cadillac / Devil's right hand. *(cd-iss. Jul91 on 'Pickwick'; 982597) (cd re-iss. Feb98 on 'Koch'; 7903)*
(above was to have been released in '83 as 'CADILLAC')

Jun 92. (cd/c) *Windsong; (WIN CD/MC 020)* **BBC RADIO 1 IN CONCERT (live)** [ ] [–]

Oct 93. (cd/c) *Pickwick; (PWK S/MC 4178)* **THIS HIGHWAY'S MINE** [ ] [ ]

Aug 96. (cd) *Nectar; (NTMCD 532)* **ANGRY YOUNG MAN (THE VERY BEST OF STEVE EARLE)** [ ] [–]
(re-iss. Jun99 on 'Telstar Arena'; TAECD 4100)

Sep 96. (cd) *M.C.A.; (MCLD 19325)* **THE ESSENTIAL STEVE EARLE** [ ] [–]
– Guitar town / Hillbilly highway / The Devil's right hand / Goodbye's all we've got left / Six days on the road / Someday / Good ol' boy (gettin' tough) / Copperhead road / The rain came down / I ain't ever satisfied / Nowhere road / The week of living dangerously / Continental trailway blues.

Jul 00. (cd) *M.C.A.; <(MCLD 19399)>* **DEVIL'S RIGHT HAND – AN INTRODUCTION TO STEVE EARLE** [ ] [ ]

Nov 01. (cd; STEVE EARLE / TOWNES VAN ZANDT / GUY CLARK) *Catfish; <(KATCD 214) / American; <4006>* **TOGETHER AT THE BLUEBIRD CAFE (live)** [ ] Oct01 [ ]
– Baby took a limo to Memphis / My old friend the blues / Katie Belle – introduction / Katie Belle / The Cape / Valentine's day – introduction / Valentine's day / Ain't leavin' your love / Randall knife / Tom Ames' prayer / The interfaith dental clinic / A song for / Dublin blues / I ain't ever satisfied / Pancho and Lefty / Immigrant eyes / Sirocco's pizza / Mercenary song / Tecumseh valley / Copperhead road.

Apr 02. (cd) *Epic; (507837-2) / Artemis; <751128>* **SIDE TRACKS** [ ] [ ]
– Some dreams / Open your window / Me and the eagle / Johnny too bad / Dominick St. / Breed / Time has come today / Ellis unit one / Creepy jackalope eye / Willin' / Sara's angel / My uncle / My back pages.
May 02. (cd) *Spectrum; (544768-2)* **THE COLLECTION** [ ] [–]

EARTH, WIND & FIRE

Formed: Chicago, Illinois, USA . . . 1969 as The SALTY PEPPERS by ex-'Chess' session man, MAURICE WHITE, who gathered together a jazz/fusion/funk ensemble of VERDINE WHITE, WADE FLEMONS, DON WHITEHEAD, MICHAEL BEAL, SHERRY SCOTT, YACKOV BEN ISRAEL, CHET WASHINGTON and ALEX THOMAS. Changing their name to EARTH, WIND & FIRE the following year, the band signed to 'Warners' and released their eponymous debut set in Spring '71. A further set, 'THE NEED OF LOVE', appeared in early '72, prior to a major personnel upheaval (and a change of labels to 'Columbia') which saw the induction of the silky voiced PHILIP BAILEY as frontman; by the release of 1973's 'HEAD TO THE SKY', the line-up had stabilised around VERDINE, LARRY DUNN, RALPH JOHNSON, AL McKAY, ANDREW WOODFOLK, JESSICA CLEAVES and JOHNNY GRAHAM. While that album gave the group their first major US chart success, it was 'OPEN OUR EYES' (1974), which began to encompass WHITE's pseudo mystical concepts into a more commercially viable proposition. A laidback, creamy rich blend of soul/funk with a finely polished pop sensibiltiy, 'THAT'S THE WAY OF THE WORLD' (1975) and its flagship single, 'SHINING STAR' both topped the US charts, beginning an extended run of chart success. 'GRATITUDE' (1975), 'SPIRIT' (1976) and 'ALL 'N' ALL' (1978) made the American Top 3 while EARTH, WIND & FIRE got to grips with disco on the enduring glitter ball favourite, 'BOOGIE WONDERLAND'. Recorded with female backing group, The EMOTIONS, the track was one of their bigger British hits, culled from 1979 album, 'I AM' (1979). Though their success continued into the early 80's, the group's creative and commercial flame began to dampen and they split in '84. Three years later, a core of the WHITE brothers, BAILEY and WOODFOLK reformed the band and continued to release and record material into the 90's with mixed results. • **Songwriters:** WHITE penned with others, except covers MAKE IT WITH YOU (Bread) / WHERE HAVE ALL THE FLOWERS GONE (Pete Seeger) / GOT TO GET YOU INTO MY LIFE (Beatles) / AFTER THE LOVE HAS GONE (c.David Foster, Bill Champlin + Jay Graydon).

Album rating: EARTH, WIND & FIRE (*4) / THE NEED OF LOVE (*4) / LAST DAYS AND TIME (*4) / HEAD TO THE SKY (*6) / OPEN OUR EYES (*6) / THAT'S THE WAY OF THE WORLD (*7) / GRATITUDE (*6) / SPIRIT (*7) / ALL 'N ALL (*6) / THE BEST OF EARTH, WIND & FIRE, VOL.1 compilation (*8) / I AM (*6) / FACES (*6) / RAISE! (*5) / POWERLIGHT (*4) / ELECTRIC UNIVERSE (*4) / TOUCH THE WORLD (*5) / THE BEST OF EARTH, WIND & FIRE, VOL.II compilation (*6) / HERITAGE (*3) / MILLENNIUM (*4) / PLUGGED IN AND LIVE (*3) / IN THE NAME OF LOVE (*4)

MAURICE WHITE (b.19 Dec'41, Memphis, USA) – vocals, drums, percussion, etc (ex-RAMSEY LEWIS TRIO, also sessioned for IMPRESSIONS / JACKIE WILSON / etc.) / **VERDINE WHITE** (b.25 Jul'51) – bass / **WADE FLEMONS** – keyboards, vocals / **DON WHITEHEAD** – piano, vocals / **MICHAEL BEAL** – guitar, etc. / **SHERRY SCOTT** – vocals / **YACKOV BEN ISRAEL** – congas, etc. / **CHET WASHINGTON** – tenor sax / **ALEX THOMAS** – trombone

not iss. — Capitol

Feb 69. (7"; as the SALTY PEPPERS) *<2433>* **LA LA TIME. / (part II)** [–] [ ]
Sep 69. (7"; as the SALTY PEPPERS) *<2568>* **YOUR LOVE IS LIFE. / UH HUH YEAH** [–] [ ]

Warners — Warners

Jan 71. (7") *<7480>* **THIS WORLD TODAY. / FAN THE FIRE** [–] [ ]
Mar 71. (7") *<7492>* **LOVE IS LIFE. / THIS WORLD TODAY** [–] [93]
Mar 71. (lp) *<(WS 1905)>* **EARTH, WIND AND FIRE** [ ] [ ]
– Help somebody / Moment of truth / Love is life / Fan the fire / C'mon children / The world today / Bad tune. *(cd-iss. Jan96; 7599 26861-2)*
May 71. (7") *(WB 6125)* **HELP SOMEBODY. / LOVE IS LIFE** [ ] [–]
Nov 71. (7") *<7549>* **C'MON CHILDREN. / I THINK ABOUT LOVIN' YOU** [–] [ ]
Jan 72. (lp) *<WS 1958>* **THE NEED OF LOVE** [–] [89]
– Energy / Beauty / I can feel it in my bones / I think about lovin' you / Everything is everything. *(cd-iss. Jan96; 7599 26862-2)*

— **WHITE** retains only brother **VERDINE,** and recruited/**employed new line-up PHILIP BAILEY** (b. 8 May'51, Denver, Colorado) – vocals, percussion / **LARRY DUNN** (b.19 Jun'53, Colorado) – keyboards, clavinet /**RALPH JOHNSON** (b. 4 Jul'51, California) – drums, percussion / **ROLAND BAUTISTA** – guitar / **RONALD LAWS** – saxophone, flute / **JESSICA CLEAVES** (b.1943) – vocals

C.B.S. — Columbia

Oct 72. (lp/c) *(CBS/40 65208) <31702>* **LAST DAYS AND TIME** [ ] [87]
– Time is on your side / They don't see / Make it with you / Power / Remember the children / Where have all the flowers gone / I'd rather have you / Mom. *(re-iss. Oct79 lp/c; CBS/40 31761) (cd-iss. Feb92 on 'Columbia'; 982736-2)*

— **AL McKAY** (b. 2 Feb'48, Louisiana) – guitar repl. BAUTISTA / **ANDREW WOODFOLK** (b.11 Oct'50, Texas) – horns repl. LAWS who went solo / added **JOHNNY GRAHAM** (b. 3 Aug'51, Kentucky)

May 73. (lp/c) *(CBS/40 65604) <32194>* **HEAD TO THE SKY** [ ] [27]
– Evil / Keep your head to the sky / Build your nest / The world's masquerade / Clover / Zanzibar. *(quad-lp 1975; CBSQ 65604) (re-iss. Mar81 lp/c; CBS/40 32017) (cd-iss. Sep93 on 'Sony Collectors'; 982997-2)*
Oct 73. (7") *(CBS 1792) <45888>* **EVIL. / CLOVER** [ ] Jul73 [50]
Feb 74. (7") *(CBS 2033) <45953>* **KEEP YOUR HEAD TO THE SKY. / BUILD YOUR NEST** [ ] Nov73 [53]

— now w/out JESSICA

May 74. (7") *(CBS 2284) <46007>* **MIGHTY MIGHTY. / DRUM SONG** [ ] Mar74 [29]
Jun 74. (lp/c) *(CBS/40 65844) <32712>* **OPEN OUR EYES** [ ] Mar74 [15]
– Mighty mighty / Devotion / Fair but so uncool / Feelin' blue / Kalimba story / Drum song / Tee nine chee bit / Spasmodic mood / Caribou / Open our eyes. *(re-iss. Mar81; 32033)*
Sep 74. (7") *<10026>* **DEVOTION. / FAIR BUT SO UNCOOL** [–] [33]
Nov 74. (7") *(CBS 2782) <46070>* **KALIMBA STORY. / TEE NINE CHEE BIT** [ ] Jul74 [55]

— added other brother **FRED WHITE** (b.13 Jan'55, Chicago) – drums

— Early 1975, EARTH WIND & FIRE were credited on two US Top 50 singles by RAMSEY LEWIS; 'Hot Dawgit' <10056> and 'Sun Goddess' <10103>.

Apr 75. (lp/c) *(CBS/40 80575) <33280>* **THAT'S THE WAY OF THE WORLD** [ ] Mar75 [1]
– Shining star / That's the way of the world / Happy feelin' / All about love / Yearnin', learnin' / Reasons / Africano / See the light. *(re-iss. Nov81 on 'CBS-Embassy'; 32054) (cd-iss. May87; CD 80575) (cd re-iss. Feb97 on 'Columbia'; 484467-2)*
Apr 75. (7") *(CBS 3137) <10090>* **SHINING STAR. / YEARNIN', LEARNIN'** [ ] Feb75 [1]
Jul 75. (7") *(CBS 3519) <10172>* **THAT'S THE WAY OF THE WORLD. / AFRICANO** [ ] Jun75 [12]
Nov 75. (7") *(CBS 3847)* **SHININ' STAR (live). / HAPPY FEELIN'** [ ] [–]
Dec 75. (d-lp) *(CBS 88160) <33694>* **GRATITUDE (most live)** [ ] Nov75 [1]
– (introduction) / Sing a song / Gratitude / Celebrate / Can't hide love / Sunshine / Shining star / Sun Goddess / reasons / Sing a message to you / Devotion / Medley: Africano – Power / Yearnin', learnin'. *(re-iss. May82; CBS 22129) (cd-iss. 1987; CD 88160)*
Feb 76. (7") *(CBS 3859) <10251>* **SING A SONG (live). / (instrumental)** [ ] Nov75 [5]
Mar 76. (7") *<10309>* **CAN'T HIDE LOVE. / GRATITUDE** [–] [39]
May 76. (7") *(CBS 4240)* **REASONS (live). / GRATITUDE** [ ] [–]
Aug 76. (7") *(CBS 4532) <10373>* **GETAWAY. / (instrumental)** [ ] Jul76 [12]
Nov 76. (lp/c) *(CBS/40 81451) <34241>* **SPIRIT** [ ] Sep76 [2]
– Getaway / On your face / Imagination / Spirit / Saturday nite / Earth, wind and fire / Departure / Biyo / Burnin' bush. *(re-iss. Apr84 on 'Pickwick'; SHM 3133)*

Jan 77. (7") *(CBS 4835) <10439>* **SATURDAY NITE. / DEPARTURE** [17] Nov76 [21]
Apr 77. (7") *<10492>* **BIYO. / ON YOUR FACE** [–] [ ]
Jun 77. (7") *<10512>* **ON YOUR FACE. / SATURDAY NITE (live)** [–] [ ]
Dec 77. (7") *(CBS 5778) <10625>* **SERPENTINE FIRE. / (instrumental)** [ ] Oct77 [13]
Jan 78. (lp/c) *(CBS/40 86051) <34905>* **ALL 'N' ALL** [13] Nov77 [3]
– Serpentine fire / Fantasy / In the market place / Jupiter / Love's holiday / Brazillian rhyme / I'll write a song for you / Master mind / Runnin' / Be ever wonderful. *(re-iss. Mar83 lp/c; CBS/40 32266) (cd-iss. May87; CD 82238) (re-iss. Apr94 on 'Sony Collectors' cd/c; 982842-2/-4)*
Jan 78. (7") *<10688>* **FANTASY. / RUNNIN'** [–] [32]
Feb 78. (7") *(CBS 6056)* **FANTASY. / BOOGIE WONDERLAND** [14] [–]
Apr 78. (7") *(CBS 6267)* **JUPITER. / RUNNIN'** [41] [–]
Jul 78. (7") *(CBS 6490)* **MAGIC MIND. / LOVE'S HOLIDAY** [54] [–]
Sep 78. (7") *(CBS 6553) <10796>* **GOT TO GET YOU INTO MY LIFE. / I'LL WRITE A SONG FOR YOU** [33] Jul78 [9]
Oct 78. (7") *<10854>* **SEPTEMBER. / LOVE'S HOLIDAY** [–] [8]
Nov 78. (7") *(CBS 6922)* **SEPTEMBER. / CAN'T HAVE LOVE** [3] [–]
Dec 78. (lp/c) *(CBS/40 83284) <35647>* **THE BEST OF EARTH, WIND & FIRE, VOL.1** (compilation) [6] Nov78 [6]
– Got to get you into my life / Fantasy / Can't hide love / Saturday night / Love music / Getaway / That's the way of the world / September / Shining star / Reasons / Sing a song. *(re-iss. Nov84 lp/c; CBS/40 32536) (cd-iss. Jun89; CD 32536) (cd re-iss. Oct94 on 'Columbia'; 477508-2)*
May 79. (7"/12"; EARTH, WIND & FIRE WITH THE EMOTIONS) *(CBS 7292) <10956>* **BOOGIE WONDERLAND. / (instrumental)** [4] [6]
Jun 79. (lp/c) *(CBS/40 86084) <35730>* **I AM** [5] [3]
– In the stone / Can't let go / After the love has gone / Let your feelings show / Boogie wonderland / Star / Wait / Rock that / You and I. *(re-iss. Jun85 lp/c; CBS/40 32656) (cd-iss. May87; CD 86084)*
Jul 79. (7") *(CBS 7721) <11033>* **AFTER THE LOVE HAS GONE. / ROCK THAT** [4] [2]
Sep 79. (7") *(CBS 7902) <11165>* **STAR. / YOU AND I** [16] Dec79 [64]
Oct 79. (7") *<11093>* **IN THE STONE. / YOU AND I** [–] [58]
Dec 79. (7") *(CBS 8077)* **CAN'T LET GO. / LOVE MUSIC** [46] [–]
Feb 80. (7") *(CBS 8252)* **IN THE STONE. / AFRICAN BIYO** [53] [–]
Sep 80. (7") *(CBS 8982) <11366>* **LET ME TALK. / (instrumental)** [29] [44]
Oct 80. (d-lp/c) *(CBS/40 88498) <36795>* **FACES** [10] [10]
– Let me talk / Turn it into something good / Pride / You / Sparkle / Back on the road / Song in my heart / You went away / And love goes on / Sail away / Take it to the sky / Win or lose / Share your love / In time / Faces. *(cd-iss. Mar94 on 'Sony Collectors'; 983316-2) (cd-iss. Feb97 on 'Columbia'; 474679-2)*
Nov 80. (7") *<11407>* **YOU. / SHARE YOUR LOVE** [–] [ ]
Dec 80. (7") *(CBS 9377)* **BACK ON THE ROAD. / TAKE IT TO THE SKY** [63] [–]
Jan 80. (7") *<11434>* **AND LOVE GOES ON. / WIN OR LOSE** [–] [59]
Feb 81. (7") *(CBS 9521)* **AND LOVE GOES ON. / FACES** [ ] [–]
May 81. (7") *(A 1204)* **YOU. / PRIDE** [ ] [–]

— **ROLAND BAUTISTA** – guitar rejoined repl. McKAY who went into production.

Oct 81. (7") *(A 1679) <02536>* **LET'S GROOVE. / (instrumental)** [3] [3]
Nov 81. (lp/c) *(CBS/40 85272) <37548>* **RAISE!** [14] [5]
– Let's groove / Lady Sun / My love / Evolution orange / Kalimba tree / You are a winner / I've had enough / Wanna be with you / The changing times. *(cd-iss. Aug86; CD 85272)*
Jan 82. (7") *(A 1959)* **I'VE HAD ENOUGH. / KALIMBA TREE (instrumental)** [29] [–]
Jan 82. (7") *<02688>* **WANNA BE WITH YOU. / KALIMBA TREE (instrumental)** [–] [51]
Mar 82. (7") *(A 2074)* **WANNA BE WITH YOU. / MY LOVE** [ ] [–]
Jan 83. (7"/12") *(A/+12 2927) <03375>* **FALL IN LOVE WITH ME. / LADY SUN** [47] [17]
Feb 83. (lp/c) *(CBS/40 25120) <38367>* **POWERLIGHT** [22] [12]
– Fall in love with me / Spread your love / Side by side / Straight from the heart / The speed of love / Freedom of choice / Something special / Heart to heart / Miracles. *(cd-iss. 1988; CD 25120) (cd re-iss. Oct93 on 'Sony Europe')*
Mar 83. (7") *(A 3211)* **SPREAD YOUR LOVE. / HEART TO HEART** [ ] [–]
May 83. (7") *<03814>* **SIDE BY SIDE. / SOMETHING SPECIAL** [–] [76]
Jul 83. (7"/12") *<04002/04008>* **SPREAD YOUR LOVE. / FREEDOM OF CHOICE** [–] [ ]

— Still a member, PHIL BAILEY also takes on solo career.

Nov 83. (7"/12") *(A/TA 3887) <04210/04211>* **MAGNETIC. / SPEED OF LOVE** [ ] [57]
Dec 83. (lp/c) *(CBS/40 25775) <38980>* **ELECTRIC UNIVERSE** [ ] [40]
– Magnetic / Touch / Moonwalk / Could it be right / Spirit of a new world / Sweet sassy lady / We're living in our own time / Electic nation. *(cd-iss. 1988; CD 25772)*
Feb 84. (7") *(A 4164)* **TOUCH. / SEPTEMBER** [ ] [–]
(12"+=) *(TA 4164)* – After the love has gone / Boogie wonderland.
Feb 84. (7") *<04329>* **TOUCH. / SWEET SASSY LADY** [–] [ ]
May 84. (7") *<04427>* **MOONWALK. / WE'RE LIVING IN OUR OWN TIME** [–] [ ]

— disbanded March '84; both MAURICE and PHILIP continued solo

— they re-formed with (**MAURICE WHITE, VERDINE WHITE, PHILIP BAILEY, ANDREW WOODFOLK**)plus new man **SHELDON REYNOLDS** – guitar + loads of session people

Oct 87. (7") *(EWF 1) <07608>* **SYSTEM OF SURVIVAL. / WRITING ON THE WALL** [54] [60]
(12"+=) *(EWFT 1)* – ('A'acappella) / ('A'dub).
(12"+=/cd-s+=) *(EWFQT/CDEWF 1)* – ('A'-12"version).
Nov 87. (lp/c/cd) *(460409-1/-4/-2) <40596>* **TOUCH THE WORLD** [ ] [33]
– System of survival / Evil boy / Thinking of you / You and I / Musical interlude: new horizons / Money tight / Every now and then / Touch the world / Here today and gone tomorrow / Victim of the modern heart.
Dec 87. (7") *<07687>* **MUSICAL INTERLUDE: NEW HORIZONS. / YOU AND I** [–] [ ]
Feb 88. (7") *(EWF 2) <07695>* **THINKING OF YOU. / MONEY TIGHT** [ ] [67]
(12"+=) *(EWFT 2)* – ('A'version).
(12"+=/cd-s+=) *(EWFQT/CDEWF 2)* – ('A'-House mix).
Feb 88. (7") *<07687>* **EVIL BOY. / (part 2)** [–] [ ]
Nov 88. (7") *<08107>* **TURN ON (THE BEAT BOX). / (part 2)** [–] [ ]
Dec 88. (lp/c/cd) *<45013>* **THE BEST OF EARTH, WIND & FIRE, VOL.1** (compilation) [–] [ ]
– Turn on (the beat box) / Let's groove / After the love has gone / Fantasy / Devotion / Serpentine fire / Love's holiday / Boogie wonderland / Saturday nite / Mighty mighty. *(UK-iss.May91 on 'Columbia' cd/c; 463200-2/-4)*

— added **RALPH JOHNSON** – percussion / **SONNY EMORY** – drums / + **session people**

Feb 90. (7"/c-s) *(EWF/+M 3) <73205>* **HERITAGE. / GOTTA FIND OUT** [ ] [ ]
(12"+=) *(EWFT 3)* – ('A'acappella) / Let's groove (extended).
(cd-s+=) *(CDEWF 3)* – Fantasy / September / ('A'extended).
(12"+=) *(EWFQT 3)* – Brazillian rhyme (interlude) / Got to get you into my life / I've had enough.
Mar 90. (cd/c/lp) *(466242-2/-4/-1) <45268>* **HERITAGE** [ ] Feb90 [70]
– Soweto / Takin' chances / Heritage / Good time / Body wrap / Anything you want / Bird / Wanna be the man / Close to home / Daydreamin' / King of the groove / I'm in love / For the love of you / Gotta find out / Motor / Faith / Welcome / Soweto (reprise).
Apr 90. (c-s) *<73344>* **FOR THE LOVE OF YOU / MOTOR** [–] [ ]
Sep 90. (7"/c-s) *<73436>* **WANNA BE THE MAN. / WELCOME** [ ] [ ]
(ext.12"+=/cd-s+=) *<73396>* – ('A'dub version).

Reprise Reprise

Sep 93. (cd/c) *<(9362 45274-2/-4)>* **MILLENNIUM** [ ] [39]
– Even if you wonder / Sunday morning / Blood brothers / Kalimba interlude / Spend the night / Divine / Two hearts / Honor the magic / Love is the greatest story / The L word / Just another lonely night / Super hero / Wouldn't change a thing about you / Love across the wire / Chicago (Chitown) blues / Kalimba blues.
Oct 93. (7"/c-s) *(W 0205/+C) <18461>* **SUNDAY MORNING. / THE L WORD** [ ] Aug93 [53]
(cd-s+=) *(W 0205CD)* – Just another lonely heart.

Avex not iss.

Nov 95. (cd/c) *(AVEX CD/MC 20)* **PLUGGED IN AND LIVE (live)** [ ] [–]
– In the stone / September / Let your feelings show / Let's groove / Sun goddess / Can't hide love / Boogie wonderland / Fantasy / Reason / That's the way of the world / Africano / I'll write a song for you / Be ever wonderful / After the love is gone / Shining star / System of survival / Sing a song / Devotion.

		Eagle	Rhino
Jul 97.	(cd/c) *(EAG CD/MC 002) <R2/R4 72864>* **IN THE NAME OF LOVE**		

– Revolution / Rock it / In the name of love / Revolution / When loves goes wrong / Fill you up / The right time / Round and round / Keep it real / Cruising / Love is life / Avatar (interlude).

– compilations, others, etc. –

on 'C.B.S.' UK / 'Columbia' US unless mentioned otherwise

		Eagle	Rhino
Sep 74.	(d-lp) *Warners; <2798>* **ANOTHER TIME** (first 2 albums)	–	97
1975.	(7") *(13-33247)* **KEEP YOUR HEAD TO THE SKY. / EVIL**		–
Apr 77.	(7") *(CBS 5198)* **SING A SONG. / BIYO**		–
Oct 79.	(t-lp-box) *(CBS 66350)* **EARTH, WIND & FIRE** – (3 early albums)		–
Aug 80.	(7") *(CBS 8848)* **AFTER THE LOVE HAS GONE. / THAT'S THE WAY OF THE WORLD**		–
Aug 80.	(7") *(CBS 8876)* **FANTASY. / BOOGIE WONDERLAND**		–
Oct 80.	(lp) *Pickwick; (SSP 3078)* **EARTH, WIND & FIRE**		–
1982.	(c-ep) **SING A SONG / BIYO / SHINING STAR / THAT'S THE END OF THE WORLD**		–
Sep 85.	(7") *Old Gold; (OG 9556)* **FANTASY. / SEPTEMBER**		–
Sep 85.	(7") *Old Gold; (OG 9558)* **BOOGIE WONDERLAND. / LET'S GROOVE**		–
Feb 86.	(12"ep) *Old Gold; (OG 4008)* **STAR / SATURDAY NITE. / AFTER THE LOVE HAS GONE / I'VE HAD ENOUGH**		–
May 86.	(lp)(c)(cd) *K-Tel; (NE1/CD2/NCD3 322)* **THE COLLECTION**		–
Jun 86.	(7"/12") *(A/TA 7253)* **BOOGIE WONDERLAND. / LET'S GROOVE**		–
May 88.	(cd) *Arcade; (ADEHCD 821-0)* **THE VERY BEST OF . . . VOL.1**		–
May 88.	(cd) *Arcade; (ADEHCD 821-1)* **THE VERY BEST OF . . . VOL.2**		–
Dec 90.	(3xcd-box) *Columbia; (467388-2)* **I AM / ALL 'N' ALL / RAISE**		–
Jan 93.	(3xcd-box/3xc-box) *Columbia; (472614-2/-4)* **THE ETERNAL DANCE**		
Jul 94.	(3xcd-box) *Columbia; (468804-2)* **POWERLIGHT / ELECTRIC UNIVERSE / SPIRIT**		
Dec 95.	(cd/c) *Columbia; (467768-2/-4)* **THE LOVE SONGS**		
Sep 96.	(cd/c) *Telstar; (TCD/STAC 2879)* **BOOGIE WONDERLAND – THE BEST OF . . .**	35	–
Mar 97.	(cd/lp) *Stax; (CDSXE/SXD 103)* **SWEET SWEETBACK'S BAADASSS SONG** (original soundtrack)		
Jul 99.	(12"/c-s/cd-s) *Incredible; (INCR 24/+MC/CD)* **SEPTEMBER 99 (mixes)**	25	–
Jul 99.	(cd/c) *Sony TV; (SONYTV 66 CD/MC)* **THE ULTIMATE COLLECTION**	34	–

– Boogie wonderland / Shining star / That's the way of the world / September / Can't hide love / After the love has gone / Got to get you into my life / Sing a song / Gratitude / Serpentine fire / Fantasy / In the stone / Reasons / Saturday nite / Let's groove / Getaway / September '99 (Phats & Small remix) / Let's groove (Merchant Of Menace remix) / Boogie wonderland (Stretch & Vern remix).

□ EAZY-E (see under ⇒ N.W.A.)

ECHO & THE BUNNYMEN

Formed: Liverpool, England . . . Autumn 1978 by IAN McCULLOCH, WILL SERGEANT and LES PATTINSON. McCULLOCH had once been in The CRUCIAL THREE alongside future stars, JULIAN COPE and PETE WYLIE, the former two starting up another low key act, A SHALLOW MADNESS, together writing 'READ IT IN BOOKS' (the b-side of E&TB's debut single, 'PICTURES ON MY WALL'). The BUNNYMEN, complete with drum machine ECHO, released the aforementioned 45 as a one-off for the local 'Zoo' label, before signing to 'WEA/Warners' subsidiary, 'Korova', late in '79. By the following year, they'd had a Top 20 album, 'CROCODILES', and were soon breaking into the singles chart with 'RESCUE'. Overtly melancholy and DOORS-influenced, their material contained a fresher up-tempo feel which combined powerful melodrama and McCULLOCH's ego-fuelled attitude. From 1981-84, their albums 'HEAVEN UP HERE', 'PORCUPINE' and 'OCEAN RAIN', solidified a Merseyside revival that even crossed successfully over the Atlantic. They split after their last gig on the 26th April '88, and it surprised everyone, not least the solo bound McCULLOCH (he had issued a single in '84, Kurt Weill's 'SEPTEMBER SONG'), when The BUNNYMEN decided to carry on without him. However, in June '89, PETE DE FREITAS was tragically killed in a motorcycle accident. In the early 90's, The BUNNYMEN (SERGEANT, PATTINSON, plus NOEL BURKE – vocals, JACK BROCKMAN – keyboards and DAMON REECE – drums) struggled without their moody frontman. A disappointing album, 'REVERBERATION' (1990), did little to excite the public, the group forming their own 'Euphoric' label after 'Korova/WEA' dropped them. McCULLOCH meanwhile, had been continuing his search for glory, releasing two albums, the Top 20 'CANDLELAND' (1989) and the Top 50, 'MYSTERIO' (1992), the last of which was poorly received. Late in '94, McCULLOCH and SERGEANT were back with a new rock-driven tour de force, ELECTRAFIXION, their sole album, 'BURNED' (1995), was well received by the music press, went Top 40 and enjoyed moderate sales. There was considerably more media interest over the reformation of the original ECHO & THE BUNNYMEN line-up in 1997. A strong comeback single, 'NOTHING LASTS FOREVER', and album, 'EVERGREEN', both made the UK Top 10, while the band proved they could still cut it live with a tour and a series of summer festival appearances. McCULLOCH and SERGEANT returned in 1999 with the eagerly awaited 'WHAT ARE YOU GOING TO DO WITH YOUR LIFE?', a short but very, very sweet album (its running time is around thirty eight minutes). The set was very similar to other ECHO releases, but less jaded and cynical than the previous 'EVERGREEN', with songs 'HISTORY CHIMES' and 'GET IN THE CAR' all displaying McCULLOCH's tenderness towards songwriting. Meanwhile SERGEANT, who had been dabbling in psychedelic electronica since the late seventies (anyone remember the soundtrack album 'THEMES FOR GRIND' from 1983) had been completing a musical manifesto all on his ownsome. Named GLIDE, SERGEANT issued both live albums 'SPACE AGE FREAK OUT' ('97) and 'PERFORMANCE' along with a lost classic from 1978 called 'WEIRD AS FISH', both in 2000. All albums sounded similar to the Krautrock movement or BRIAN ENO in his better experimental stages. Lashings of psychedelia and weirdness was born from somebody who used to be a post-punk rocker, but that didn't diminish the originality of the albums. ECHO AND THE BUNNYMEN returned in 2001 with another accomplished set, 'FLOWERS'. Although considerably mellower than previous ECHO works, the album acted as a Part 2 to the fantastic 'WHAT ARE YOU GOING TO DO . . .?'. Mixing pop rock with classy melancholy, songs such as 'EVERYBODY KNOWS' and 'HIDE AND SEEK' had set the standards for future records by a band who were quite happy spending a third decade together. Now well into middle age, it was a more sure-footed and centered McCULLOCH that re-emerged in 2003 with 'SLIDELING', his first solo album in over a decade. Relying on acoustic-based arrangements with sympathetic string accompaniment, the singer put aside any residual attitude and artifice for a more candid and resolute portrayal of his artistic position in the post-millennial rock arena. • **Songwriters:** Mainly group compositions, except covers PEOPLE ARE STRANGE (Doors) / PAINT IT BLACK (Rolling Stones) / ALL YOU NEED IS LOVE + TICKET TO RIDE (Beatles) / FRICTION (Television) / RUN RUN RUN (Velvet Underground) / SHIP OF FOOLS (John Cale). McCULLOCH covered: RETURN TO SENDER (hit; Elvis Presley) / LOVER, LOVER, LOVER (Leonard Cohen) / THE PRETTIEST STAR (David Bowie) / JEALOUS GUY (John Lennon). • **Trivia:** DAVE BALFE (of DALEK I LOVE YOU) played keyboards on their first JOHN PEEL session in August 1979.

Album rating: CROCODILES (*9) / HEAVEN UP HERE (*9) / PORCUPINE (*7) / OCEAN RAIN (*7) / SONGS TO LEARN AND SING compilation (*9) / ECHO & THE BUNNYMEN (*5) / REVERBERATION (*3) / BALLYHOO: THE BEST OF ECHO & THE BUNNYMEN compilation (*8) / EVERGREEN (*7) / WHAT ARE YOU GOING TO DO WITH YOUR LIFE? (*8) / FLOWERS (*6) / LIVE IN LIVERPOOL (*5) / Ian McCulloch: CANDLELAND (*6) / MYSTERIO (*5) / SLIDELING (*6) / Electrafixion: BURNED (*6) / Will Sergeant: THEMES FOR GRIND (*3)

IAN McCULLOCH (b. 5 May'59) – vocals, guitar (ex-CRUCIAL THREE) **WILL SERGEANT** (b.12 Apr'58) – lead guitar / **LES PATTINSON** (b.18 Apr'58) – bass (& 'ECHO' a drum machine)

Zoo / not iss.

Mar 79. (7") *(CAGE 004)* **PICTURES ON MY WALL. / READ IT IN BOOKS** [ ] [–]
(re-iss. Mar91 on 'Document' 12"/cd-s; DC 3/+CD)

— **PETE DE FREITAS** (b. 2 Aug'61, Port Of Spain, Trinidad) – drums repl. 'ECHO'

Korova / Sire

Apr 80. (7") *(KOW 1)* **RESCUE. / SIMPLE STUFF** [62] [–]
(12"+=) *(KOW 1T)* – Pride.

Jul 80. (lp/c) *(KODE/CODE 1) <6096>* **CROCODILES** [17] [ ]
– Going up / Stars are stars / Pride / Monkeys / Crocodiles / Rescue / Villier's terrace / Pictures on my wall / All that jazz / Happy death men. *(re-iss. Nov80 w/ free 7"; SAM 128)* DO IT CLEAN. / READ IT IN BOOKS *(re-iss. 1989 on 'WEA' lp/c/cd; same/same/2423162)*

Sep 80. (7") *(KOW 11)* **THE PUPPET. / DO IT CLEAN** [ ] [ ]

Apr 81. (12"ep)(c-ep) *(ECHOZ 1)(ECHO 1M)* **SHINE SO HARD (live)** [37] [–]
– Crocodiles / Zimbo / Over the wall / All that jazz.

May 81. (lp/c) *(KODE/CODE 3) <3569>* **HEAVEN UP HERE** [10] [ ]
– Show of strength / With a hip / Over the wall / It was a pleasure / A promise / Heaven up here / The disease / All my colours / No dark things / Turquoise days / All I want. *(cd-iss. Jul88 on 'WEA'; 2432173)*

Jul 81. (7"/12") *(KOW 15/+T)* **A PROMISE. / BROKE MY NECK** [49] [–]

May 82. (7") *(KOW 24)* **THE BACK OF LOVE. / THE SUBJECT** [19] [–]
(12"+=) *(KOW 24T)* – Fuel.

Jan 83. (7") *(KOW 26)* **THE CUTTER. / WAY OUT AND UP WE GO** [8] [–]
(w/ free c-ep+=) *(KOW 26C)* – The cutter / Villier's terrace / Ashes to ashes (stars are stars) / Monkeys / Read it in books.
(12"+=) *(KOW 26T)* – Zimbo (live).

Jan 83. (lp/c) *(KODE/CODE 6) <23770>* **PORCUPINE** [2] [ ]
– The cutter / The back of love / My white devil / Clay / Porcupine / Heads will roll / Ripeness / Higher hell / Gods will be gods / In bluer skies. *(free ltd.c-ep w/ above lp)* – 'JOHN PEEL SESSIONS' *(re-iss. Jul88 on 'WEA' lp/c/cd; same/same/K 400 272)*

Feb 83. (7") **THE CUTTER. / GODS WILL BE GODS** [–] [ ]

Jul 83. (7") *(KOW 28)* **NEVER STOP. / HEADS WILL ROLL** [15] [–]
(12"+=) *(KOW 28T)* – ('A'-Discotheque) / ('B'-Summer version) / The original cutter (A drop in the ocean).

Jan 84. (7") *(KOW 32)* **THE KILLING MOON. / DO IT CLEAN** [9] [–]
(12"+=) *(KOW 32T)* – ('A'-All night version).

Jan 84. (m-lp) *<23987>* **ECHO AND THE BUNNYMEN** [–] [ ]
– Back of love / Never stop / Rescue / The cutter / Do it clean.

Apr 84. (lp/c)(cd) *(KODE/CODE 8)(K 240388-2) <25084>* **OCEAN RAIN** [4] Jun84 [87]
– Silver / Nocturnal me / Crystal days / The yo yo man / Thorn of crowns / The killing moon / Seven seas / My kingdom / Ocean rain.

Apr 84. (7") *(KOW 34)* **SILVER. / ANGELS AND DEVILS** [30] [–]
(12"+=) *(KOW 34T)* – Silver (Tidal wave).

Jun 84. (7") *(KOW 35)* **SEVEN SEAS. / ALL YOU NEED IS LOVE** [16] [–]
(12"+=/d7"+=) *(KOW 35 T/F)* – The killing Moon / Stars are stars (acoustic) / Villier's terrace (acoustic).

Oct 85. (7"/7"pic-d) *(KOW 43/+P)* **BRING ON THE DANCING HORSES. / OVER MY SHOULDER** [21] [–]
(ext.12"+=) *(KOW 43T)* – Beds, bugs and ballyhoo.
(d7"+=) *(KOW 43F)* – Villier's terrace / Monkeys.

Nov 85. (lp/c)(pic-lp)(cd) *(KODE/CODE 13)(KODE 13P)(240 767-2) <25360>* **SONGS TO LEARN AND SING** (compilation) [6] [ ]
– Rescue / The puppet / Do it clean / The promise / The back of love / The cutter / Never stop / The killing moon / Silver / Seven seas / Bring on the dancing horses. *(c+=/cd+=)* – Pride / Simple stuff / Read it in books / Angels and devils. *(free ltd.c-s w/ same extra tracks)*

— (Feb86) temp. **MARK FOX** – drums (ex-HAIRCUT 100) repl. DE FREITAS until return Sep'86.

WEA / Sire

Jun 87. (7") *(YZ 134)* **THE GAME. / SHIP OF FOOLS** [28] [–]
(12"+=/12"w poster+=) *(YZ 134T/+W)* – Lost and found.

Jul 87. (lp/c)(cd) *(WX 108/+C)(242 137-2) <25597>* **ECHO AND THE BUNNYMEN** [4] [51]
– The game / Over you / Bedbugs and ballyhoo / All in your mind / Bombers bay / Lips like sugar / Lost and found / New direction / Blue blue ocean / Satellite / All my life. *(re-iss. cd Nov94)*

Jul 87. (7"/7"gf/7"box) *(YZ 144/+V/B)* **LIPS LIKE SUGAR. / ROLLERCOASTER** [36] [–]
(12"+=) *(YZ 144T/+X)* – People are strange.

Feb 88. (7"/c-s) *(YZ 175/+C)* **PEOPLE ARE STRANGE. / RUN RUN RUN (live)** [29] [–]
(12"+=) *(YZ 175T)* – Paint it black / Friction. *(re-iss. Feb91 7"/c-s; YZ 567/+C /12"/cd-s; YZ 567 T/CD)* – hit UK No.34)

— They split some unofficial time in '88. Re-formed after McCULLOCH went solo. PETE DE FREITAS joined SEX GODS. He died in motorcycle accident 14 Jun '89.

— **SERGEANT** and **PATTINSON** reformed group early 1990, with newcomers **NOEL BURKE** (b.Belfast, N.Ireland) – vocals (ex-St.VITAS DANCE) / **JACK BROCKMAN** – keyboards / **DAMON REECE** – drums

Korova / Sire

Oct 90. (7"/c-s) *(9031 72796-7/-4)* **ENLIGHTEN ME. / LADY, DON'T FALL BACKWARDS** [ ] [ ]
(12"+=/cd-s+=) *(9031 72796-1/-2)* – ('A'extended).

Nov 90. (cd)(c/lp) *(9031 72553-2)(CODE/KODE 14) <26388>* **REVERBERATION** [ ] Dec90 [ ]
– Freaks dwell / Cut and dried / Revilement / Flaming red / Salvatore / Fine thing / Gone, gone, gone / Enlighten me / King of your castle / Senseless / Thick skinned world. *(cd+=)* – False goodbyes.

Euphoric / not iss.

Oct 91. (12"ep/cd-ep) *(E 001 T/CDS)* **PROVE ME WRONG. / FINE THING / REVERBERATION (live)** [ ] [–]

Mar 92. (12"/cd-s) *(K 002 T/CD)* **INSIDE ME, INSIDE YOU. / WIGGED OUT WORLD** [ ] [–]

— The BUNNYMEN disbanded soon after the above and LES joined TERRY HALL'S backing group.

WILL SERGEANT

WEA / not iss.

Jul 82. (7") *(K 19238)* **FAVOURITE BRANCHES. / (b-side by Ravi Shankar & Bill Lovelady)** [ ] [–]

92 Happy C. / not iss.

Mar 83. (lp) *(HAPLP 1)* **THEMES FOR "GRIND"** [ ] [–]
– Grind starts the generator / The wheel turns / The small screen flickers. *(cd-iss. Jan98 +=; HAPSCD 1)* – Theme / Favourite branches / Aquarius dub.

Ochre / not iss.

1995. (7"orange) *(OCH 003)* **COSMOS. / VENUS IN FLARES** [ ] [–]

— WILL went on to form project, GLIDE – (see Alt & Indie II book-only)

Ian McCULLOCH

IAN McCULLOCH – vocals while still a member of The BUNNYMEN

Korova / not iss.

Nov 84. (7"/10") *(KOW 40/+L)* **SEPTEMBER SONG. / COCKLES & MUSSELS** [51] [–]
(12"+=) *(KOW 40T)* – ('A'extended).

— Now solo his back-up came from **RAY SHULMAN** – keyboards, programmer, bass, producer / plus guests **MICHAEL JOBSON** – bass / **BORIS WILLIAMS** – drums / **OLLE REMO** – drum programmer / **LIZ FRASER** – vox (of COCTEAU TWINS)

WEA Sire

Aug 89. (7"/7"box/c-s) *(YZ 417/+B/C)* **PROUD TO FALL. / POTS OF GOLD** [51] [–]
(12") *(YZ 417T)* – ('A'extended) / ('A'side) / The dead end.
(cd-s) *(YZ 417CD)* – (above 3 tracks) / ('A'version).
(12") *(YZ 417TX)* – ('A'side / Everything is real / The circle game.

Sep 89. (lp/c)(cd) *(WX 303/+C)(2292 46225-2) <26012>* **CANDLELAND** [18] [ ]
– The flickering wall / The white hotel / Proud to fall / The cape / Candleland / Horse's head / Faith and healing / I know you well / In bloom / Start again.

Nov 89. (7"/c-s) *(YZ 436/+C)* **FAITH AND HEALING (remix). / TOAD** [ ] [–]
('A'mix-12"+=) *(YZ 436T)* – Fear of the known.
(cd-s++=) *(YZ 436CD)* – Rocket ship.
(12") *(YZ 436TX)* – ('A'side) / Fear of the known / Rocket ship.

Apr 90. (7"/c-s) *(YZ 436/+C)* **CANDLELAND (THE SECOND COMING). / THE WORLD IS FLAT** [75] [–]
(12"+=/12"gf+=/cd-s+=) *(YZ 452 T/TG/CD)* – Big days / Wassailing in the night.

— His backing band from late '89, were The PRODIGAL SONS; **MIKE MOONEY** – guitar / **JOHN McEVOY** – guitar, keyboards / **EDGAR SUMMERTIME** – bass / **STEVE HUMPHRIES** – drums

East West Warners

Feb 92. (7"/c-s) *(YZ 643/+C)* **LOVER, LOVER, LOVER. / WHITE HOTEL (acoustic) / THE GROUND BELOW** [47] [–]
('A'-Indian Dawn remix-12"+=/cd-s+=) *(YZ 643T)* – Vibor blue (acoustic).

Apr 92. (lp/c)(cd) *(WX 453/+C)(<9031 76264-2>)* **MYSTERIO** [46] [ ]
– Mayreal world / Close your eyes / Dug for love / Honeydrip / Damnation / Lover, lover, lover / Webbed / Pomegranate / Vibor blue / Heaven's gate / In my head.

Apr 92. (7"/c-s) *(YZ 660/+C)* **DUG FOR LOVE. / POMMEGRANITE (live)** [ ] [–]
(12"+=)(cd-s+=) *(YZ 660 T/CD)* – Do it clean (live) / In my head (live).

ELECTRAFIXION

— **IAN McCULLOCH** – vocals, guitar / **WILL SERGEANT** – guitar / **LEON DE SYLVA** – bass / **TONY McGUIGAN** – drums

WEA Warners

Nov 94. (c-ep/12"ep/cd-ep) *(YZ 865 C/T/CD)* **THE ZEPHYR EP** [47] [–]
– Zephyr / Burned / Mirrorball / Rain on me.

Sep 95. (7"red/c-s) *(YZ 977 X/C)* **LOWDOWN. / HOLY GRAIL** [54] [–]
(cd-s+=) *(YZ 977CD)* – Land of the dying sun / Razors edge.

Sep 95. (cd/c) *(0630 11248-2/-4) <61793>* **BURNED** [38] Oct95 [ ]
– Feel my pulse / Sister pain / Lowdown / Timebomb / Zephyr / Never / Too far gone / Mirrorball / Who's been sleeping in my head? / Hit by something / Bed of nails.

Oct 95. (c-s) *(WEA 022C)* **NEVER / NOT OF THIS WORLD** [58] [–]
(cd-s+=) *(WEA 022CD)* – Subway train / Lowdown (rest of the trash mix).
(cd-s) *(WEA 022CDX)* – ('A'side) / Lowdown / Work it on out / Never (Utah Saints blizzard on mix) / Sister pain.

Mar 96. (cd-ep) *(WEA 037CD1)* **SISTER PAIN / FEEL MY PULSE / ZEPHYR / LOWDOWN (live)** [27] [–]
(cd-ep) *(WEA 037CD2)* – ('A'side) / Burned / Loose (live) / Who's been sleeping in my head (acoustic).
(cd-ep) *(WEA 037CD3)* – ('A'live) / Holy grail (live) / Never (live) / Too far gone (live).

— the last set-up issued a very limited gold-7" in Sep'97, 'BASEBALL BILL' released on 'Phree' (PHREE 1)

ECHO & THE BUNNYMEN

— the original trio (**McCULLOCH, SEARGEANT + PATTINSON**) re-formed

London London

Jun 97. (7") *(LO 396)* **NOTHING LASTS FOREVER. / WATCHTOWER** [8] [–]
(cd-s+=) *(LONCD 396)* – Polly.
(cd-s) *(LONCDP 396)* – ('A'side) / Colour me in / Antelope.

Jul 97. (cd/c/lp) *(828905-2/-4/-1)* **EVERGREEN** [8] [–]
– Don't let it get you down / In my time / I want to be there (when you come) / Evergreen / I'll fly tonight / Nothing lasts forever / Baseball Bill / Altamont / Just a touch away / Empire state halo / Too young to kneel / Forgiven. *(d-cd-iss. Nov97; 828980-2) (cd re-iss. Sep99; 3984 29642-2)*

Aug 97. (cd-s) *(LOCD 399)* **I WANT TO BE THERE (WHEN YOU COME) / THE KILLING MOON (session) / NOTHING LASTS FOREVER (session)** [30] [–]
(cd-s) *(LOCDP 399)* – ('A'side) / Lips like sugar (live acoustic) / ('A'-live acoustic).

Oct 97. (cd-s) *(LOCD 406)* **DON'T LET IT GET YOU DOWN / BACK OF LOVE (live) / OVER THE WALL (live)** [50] [–]
(cd-s) *(LOCDP 406)* – ('A'side) / Rescue / Altamont.

— In Jun'98, McCULLOCH provided ENGLAND UNITED with their World Cup song, '(HOW DOES IT FEEL TO BE) ON TOP OF THE WORLD' which hit Top 10.

— a few months later, a joint single, 'GET IN THE CAR' with The FUN LOVIN' CRIMINALS, was withdrawn from release

Mar 99. (7") *(LO 424)* **RUST. / THE FISH HOOK GIRL** [22] [–]
(cd-s+=) *(LOCD 424)* – See the horizon.
(cd-s) *(LOCDP 424)* – ('A'side) / Sense of life / Beyond the green.

Apr 99. (cd/c) *(<556080-2/-4>)* **WHAT ARE YOU GOING TO DO WITH YOUR LIFE?** [21] Jun99 [ ]
– What are you going to do with your life? / Rust / Get in the car / Baby rain / History chimes / Lost on you / Morning sun / When it all blows over / Fools like us.

— **McCULLOCH + SERGEANT** brought in **CERI JAMES** – keyboards, synths

Cooking Vinyl Cooking Vinyl

Apr 01. (7") *(FRY 104)* **IT'S ALRIGHT. / SUPERMELLOW MAN (instrumental)** [41] [–]
(cd-s) *(FRYCD 104)* – ('A'side) / Marble towers / Rescue (Mindwinders remix).
(cd-s) *(FRYCD 104X)* – ('A'side) / Scratch the past / A promise (lo-fi lullaby #1) / ('A'-video).

May 01. (lp/cd) *(COOK/+CD 208) <608>* **FLOWERS** [56] [ ]
– King of kings / Supermellow man / Hide and seek / Make me shine / It's alright / Buried alive / Flowers / Everybody knows / Life goes on / An eternity turns / Burn for me.

Aug 01. (cd-s) *(FRYCD 112)* **MAKE ME SHINE / TICKET TO RIDE / NOTHING LASTS FOREVER (live)** [ ] [–]

— added **STEVE FLETT** – bass / **VINNY JAMIESON** – drums

Feb 02. (cd) *(COOKCD 223) <623>* **LIVE IN LIVERPOOL (live August 2001)** [ ] [ ]
– Rescue / Lips like sugar / King of kings / Never stop / Seven seas / Buried alive / Supermellow man / My kingdom / Zimbo / All the jazz / An eternity turns / The back of love / The killing moon / The cutter / Over the wall / Nothing lasts forever / Ocean rain.

– compilations, others, etc. –

Nov 88. (12"ep/cd-ep) *Strange Fruit; (SFPS/+CD 060)* **THE PEEL SESSIONS** (15.8.79) [ ] [–]
– Read it in books / Stars are stars / I bagsy yours / Villier's terrace. *(re-iss. cd-ep Dec94; same)*

Jul 90. (7") *Old Gold; (OG 9939)* **THE KILLING MOON. / SEVEN SEAS** [ ] [–]

Jul 90. (7") *Old Gold; (OG 9941)* **THE CUTTER. / THE BACK OF LOVE** [ ] [–]

Nov 91. (cd/lp) *Windsong; (WIN CD/LP 006)* **BBC RADIO 1 LIVE IN CONCERT (live)** [ ] [–]

Mar 93. (cd/c) *Pickwick-WEA; (4509-91886-2/-4)* **THE CUTTER** [ ] [–]
(re-iss. Sep95 on 'Warners'; same)

Jun 97. (cd/c) *W.E.A.; (0630 19103-2/-4)* **BALLYHOO – THE BEST OF ECHO & THE BUNNYMEN** [59] [–]
– Rescue / Do it clean / Villier's terrace / All that jazz / Over the wall / A promise / The disease / The back of love / The cutter / Never stop / The killing moon / Silver / Seven seas / Bring on the dancing horses / People are strange / The game / Lips like sugar / Bedbugs & ballyhoo.

Aug 01. (4xcd-box) *Rhino; (<8122 74263-2>)* **CRYSTAL DAYS 1979-1999** [ ] [ ]

IAN McCULLOCH

with session band, etc.

		Cooking Vinyl		SpinArt
Apr 03.	(cd-s) *(FRYCD 146)* **SLIDING / CRACKERJACK / BLUE SKIES UP AHEAD**	61		-
	(cd-s) *(FRYCD 146X)* – ('A'-acoustic) / Planet song / Jealous guy.			
Apr 03.	(cd) *(COOKCD 253)* *<SPIN 123>* **SLIDELING**		May03	
	– Love in veins / Playgrounds and city parks / Sliding / Baby hold on / Arthur / Seasons / Another train / High wires / She sings (all my life) / Kansas / Stake your claim.			
Jul 03.	(cd-s) *(FRYCD 158)* **LOVE IN VEINS / THE PRETTIEST STAR / ARTHUR (Prague)**			-

Duane EDDY

Born: 26 Apr'38, Corning, New York, USA. Moving with his family to Phoenix, Arizona, in his early teens, DUANE began getting seriously involved in the local music scene after dropping out of high school. Crucial to the development of his famous guitar twang was LEE HAZLEWOOD, a local DJ and all-round music biz hustler who signed EDDY's band, The REBELS (comprising AL CASEY, BUDDY WHEELER, DONNIE OWENS, CORKY CASEY, MIKE BERMANI and PIAS JOHNSON) to 'Jamie', a label he co-ran with 'American Bandstand' host, Dick Clark. Soon DUANE was touring with Clark's Caravan of Stars and following a one-off single for the small 'Ford' label, 'RAMROD' (released as The REBELS), the group released their debut single (now trading as DUANE EDDY & THE REBELS) for 'Jamie' in the shape of 'MOVIN 'N' GROOVIN''. EDDY's unique guitar sound was created by feeding the sound from the bass strings of his beloved Gretsch through a storage tank echo chamber in HAZLEWOOD's Ramco studio. The resulting grimy reverberation laid the basis for a string of transatlantic Top 40 hits beginning with 1958's definitive 'REBEL ROUSER', a single which narrowly missed the US Top 5 and established EDDY's instrumental guitar/honking sax sound at the forefront of the era's rapidly evolving pop/rock scene. The track was featured (alongside subsequent hits 'CANNONBALL', 'THE LONELY ONE' and a re-issued 'RAMROD') on his brilliantly titled debut album, 'HAVE TWANGY GUITAR WILL TRAVEL' (1959). That summer also saw EDDY score his biggest hit to date, narrowly missing the Top 5 in Britain with the classic Henry Mancini-penned 'PETER GUNN THEME'. While EDDY's sound was pivotal in the development of America's massive surf craze via his influence on the likes of The VENTURES and DICK DALE, he was also extremely influential and indeed more popular in the UK where The SHADOWS approximated their own take on instrumental twang; EDDY narrowly missed the UK No.1 spot with sophomore album, 'THE TWANG'S THE THANG' (1960) as well as singles, 'BECAUSE THEY'RE YOUNG' and 'PEPE'. In 1962 DUANE signed to 'R.C.A.' and embarked on a solo career, roaring back into the UK Top 10 after a lean spell with the 'TWISTIN' 'N' TWANGIN' album and glorious high noon cheesiness of 'THE BALLAD OF PALADIN'. He even hooked up with a gaggle of female backing singers (THE REBELETTES) for '(DANCE WITH THE) GUITAR MAN', another UK Top 5 smash later that year. Yet ironically it was to be the success of British Invasion acts like The BEATLES (whose GEORGE HARRISON was also clearly influenced by the twang) that would finally put paid to EDDY's five year chart run. His last Top 40 hit came in the shape of Spring 63's 'LONELY BOY, LONELY GUITAR', although the likes of the haunting DAVID GATES-penned 'BLOWIN' UP A STORM' (from the 1963 album, 'TWANGIN' UP A STORM') stands up against his best work. Thereafter a series of theme albums failed to cut the mustard ('DUANE GOES BOB DYLAN'?! c'mon!). A subsequent move to 'Reprise', more ridiculously titled albums and a final brace of independent singles later, EDDY took a sabbatical from the recording front, taking time out during which he produced PHIL EVERLY's 1973 solo album, 'Star Spangled Springer'. Back with The REBELETTES in 1975, he scored a one-off UK Top 10 hit for the 'G.T.O.' label with 'PLAY ME LIKE YOU PLAY YOUR GUITAR' although subsequent material for 'Elektra' and 'Capitol' failed to make any headway. More recently (1986), EDDY re-appeared on 'Top Of The Pops' alongside 80's electronic types, ART OF NOISE, who'd covered 'PETER GUNN' in suitably idiosyncratic style. This encouraged him to record an eponymous comeback album, released by 'Capitol' in 1987 and featuring the not inconsiderable production talents of PAUL McCARTNEY, JEFF LYNNE, GEORGE HARRISON and RY COODER. • **Trivia:** His photogenic appearance gained him acting experience in the 1960 film 'Because They're Young' (EDDY also cut the title track). A few years later he appeared in the films 'The Savage Seven' and 'Kona'.

Best CD compilation: TWANG THANG: ANTHOLOGY (*8)

The REBELS

featuring **DUANE EDDY** – guitar / **AL CASEY** – guitar, piano / **BUDDY WHEELER** – bass / **DONNIE OWENS** – guitar / **CORKY CASEY** – guitar / **MIKE BERMANI** – drums / **PIAS JOHNSON** – saxophone

		not iss.		Ford
Jan 58.	(7",78) *<500>* **RAMROD. / CARAVAN**	-		

DUANE EDDY & THE REBELS

		London		Jamie
Apr 58.	(7",78) *<1101>* **MOOVIN' N' GROOVIN'. / UP AND DOWN**	-		72
Aug 58.	(7",78) *(HL 8669)* *<1104>* **REBEL-ROUSER. / STALKIN'**	19	Jun58	6
Oct 58.	(7",78) *(HL 8723)* *<1109>* **RAMROD. / WALKER**		Aug58	27
Dec 58.	(7",78) *(HL 8764)* *<1111>* **CANNONBALL. / MASON-DIXON LINE**	22	Nov58	15
Mar 59.	(7",78) *(HLW 8821)* *<1117>* **THE LONELY ONE. / DETOUR**		Jan59	23
Apr 59.	(7",78) *(HLW 8879)* *<1122>* **YEP! / THREE-30 BLUES**	-		30
Jun 59.	(lp) *(HA-W 2160)* *<3000>* **HAVE "TWANGY" GUITAR – WILL TRAVEL**	6	Jan59	5
	– Lonesome road / I almost lost my mind / Rebel-rouser / Three-30-blues / Cannonball / The lonely one / Detour / Stalkin' / Ramrod / Anytime / Movin' n' Groovin' / Loving you. *(cd-iss. Feb90 on 'Motown'; WD 72688) (cd re-iss. Aug99 on 'Jamie'; JAMIE 4007-2)*			
Jun 59.	(7",78) *(HLW 8879)* **PETER GUNN THEME. / YEP!**	6		-
Aug 59.	(7",78) *(HLW 8929)* *<1126>* **FORTY MILES OF BAD ROAD. / THE QUIET THREE**	11		9
			Jun59	46
Oct 59.	(lp) *(HA-W 2191)* *<3006>* **ESPECIALLY FOR YOU**	6	Aug59	24
	– Peter Gunn / Only child / Lover / Fuzz / Yep! / Along the Navajo trail / Just because / Quiniela / Trouble in mind / Tuxedo Junction / Hard times / Along came Linda.			
Dec 59.	(7",78) *(HLW 9007)* **SOME KIND-A EARTHQUAKE. / FIRST LOVE, FIRST TEARS**	12		37
			Oct59	59
Dec 59.	(7",78) *<1144>* **BONNIE CAME BACK. / LOST ISLAND**	-		26
Feb 60.	(7",78) *(9050)* **BONNIE CAME BACK. / MOVIN' & GROOVIN'**	12		-
Apr 60.	(lp) *(HA-W 2236)* *<3009>* **THE "TWANGS" THE "THANG"**	2	Jan60	18
	– My blue Heaven / Tiger love and turnip greens / The last minute of innocence / Route No.1 / You are my sunshine / St.Louis blues / Night train to Memphis / The battle / Trombone / Blueberry hill / Rebel walk / Easy.			

— His touring REBELS were now **AL CASEY** – bass / **JIM HORN** – sax / **LARRY KNECHTEL** – piano / **JIMMY TROXEL** – drums

Apr 60. (7",78) *(HLW 9104) <1151>* **SHAZAM! / THE SECRET SEVEN** — 4 Mar60 45

Jul 60. (7",78) *(HLW 9162) <1156>* **BECAUSE THEY'RE YOUNG. / REBEL WALK** — 2 May60 4

Sep 60. (7") *<1158>* **(WHY MUST I DIE) THE GIRL ON DEATH ROW. / WORDS MEAN NOTHING** — – [ ]

Oct 60. (7") *(HLW 9225) <1163>* **KOMMOTION. / THEME FOR MOON CHILDREN** — 13 Aug60 78

Oct 60. (7") *<1168>* **PETER GUNN. / ALONG THE NAVAJO TRAIL** — – 27

Dec 60. (lp) *(HA-W 2285) <3011>* **SONGS OF OUR HERITAGE** — 13 [ ]
– Cripple Creek / Riddle song / John Henry / Streets of Laredo / Prisoner's song / In the pines / Ole Joe Clark / Wayfarin' stranger / Top of Old Smokey / Mule train / Scarlet ribbons.

Jan 61. (7") *(HLW 9257) <1175>* **PEPE. / LOST FRIEND** — 2 Dec60 18

Feb 61. (lp) *(HA-W 2325) <3021>* **A MILLION DOLLARS' WORTH OF TWANG** (compilation) — 5 Dec60 11
– Up and down / Lost island / The quiet three / Bonnie came back / Because they're young / Moon children / Shazam! / The secret seven / Forty miles of bad road / Some kinda earthquake / First love, first tears / Kommotion. *(cd-iss. Feb90 on 'Motown'; WD 72687)*

Apr 61. (7") *(HLW 9324)* **THEME FROM DIXIE. / THE BATTLE** — 7 –

Mar 61. (7") *<1183>* **THEME FROM DIXIE. / GIDGET GOES HAWAIIAN** — – 39

May 61. (7") *<1187>* **RING OF FIRE. / BOBBY** — – 84

Jun 61. (7") *(HLW 9370)* **RING OF FIRE. / GIDGET GOES HAWAIIAN** — 17 –

Aug 61. (7") *<1195>* **DRIVIN' HOME. / TAMMY** — – 87

Aug 61. (7") *(HLW 9406)* **DRIVIN' HOME. / MY BLUE HEAVEN** — 30 –

Aug 61 (7") *<1200>* **MY BLUE HEAVEN. / ALONG CAME LINDA** — – 50

Aug 61. (lp) *(HA-W 2373) <3019>* **GIRLS GIRLS GIRLS** — [ ] Jul61 93
– Brenda: I want to be wanted that's all you gotta do / I'm sorry / Sioux City Sue / Tommy / Big 'liza / Mary Ann / Annette / Tuesday / Sweet Cindy / Patricia / Mona Lisa / Connie / Carol.

DUANE EDDY

Parlophone — Gregmark

Sep 61. (7") *(R 4826) <5>* **CARAVAN. / (part 2)** — 42 [ ]

London — Jamie

Jan 62 (7") *(HLW 9477) <1206>* **THE AVENGER. / LONDONDERRY AIR** — [ ] [ ]

Feb 62 (7") *<1209>* **THE BATTLE. / TROMBONE** — – [ ]

Apr 62 (7") *<1224>* **RUNAWAY PONY. / JUST BECAUSE** — – [ ]

R.C.A. — R.C.A.

May 62. (7") *(RCA 1288) <7999>* **DEEP IN THE HEART OF TEXAS. / SAINTS AND SINNERS** — 19 Apr62 78

Aug 62. (lp) *(RD 27264) <LSP 2525>* **TWISTIN' N' TWANGIN'** — 8 May62 82
– The peppermint twist / Twistin' 'n' twangin' / Let's twist again / Miss Twist / Sugartime twist / Exactly like you / Walkin' 'n' twistin' (I'm walkin') / Dear lady twist / Moanin' 'n' twistin' / Country twist / The twist / Twisting off a cliff.

Aug 62. (7") *(RCA 1300) <8047>* **THE BALLAD OF PALADIN. / THE WILD WESTERNER** — 10 Jul62 33

DUANE EDDY & THE REBELETTES

(REBELETTES were female singers)

Oct 62. (7") *(RCA 1316) <8087>* **(DANCE WITH THE) GUITAR MAN. / STRETCHIN' OUT** — 4 12

Nov 62. (lp; mono/stereo) *(RD/SF 7510) <LSP 2576>* **TWANGY GUITAR – SILKY STRINGS** — 13 Oct62 72
– High noon / Born to be with you / Secret love / Unchained melody / When I fall in love / Mirriam / Moon river / Bali Ha'I / Hi-lili, hi-lo / Angel on my shoulder / Memories of Madrid / Love me tender. *(re-iss. 1970 on 'RCA-Camden'; CDS 1072)*

Jan 63. (lp; mono/stereo) *(RD/SF 7545) <LSP 2648>* **DANCE WITH THE GUITAR MAN** — [ ] 47
– Dance with the guitar man / Limbo rock / Wild Watusi / The scrape / New Hully Gully / Popeye (the hitchhiker) / Spanish twist / The climb / Loco-locomotion / Nashville stomp / Creamy mashed potatoes / Waltz of the wind. *(cd-iss. Apr93)*

Feb 63. (7") *(RCA 1329) <8131>* **BOSS GUITAR. / THE DESERT RAT** — 27 28

DUANE EDDY

May 63. (7") *(RCA 1344) <8180>* **LONELY BOY, LONELY GUITAR. / JOSHIN'** — 35 82

Aug 63. (7") *(RCA 1357) <8214>* **YOUR BABY'S GONE SURFIN'. / SHUCKIN'** — 49 93

Aug 63. (lp; mono/stereo) *(RD/SF 7560) <LSP 2681>* **TWANG A COUNTRY SONG** — [ ] [ ]
– Sugar foot rag / Weary blues / Fireball mail / Please help me I'm falling / Wildwood flower / Precious memories / Crazy arms / Have you ever been lonely / The window up above / A satisfied mind / Making believe / Peace in the valley.

Oct 63. (7") *(RCA 1369)* **MY BABY PLAYS THE SAME OLD SONG ON HIS GUITAR ALL NIGHT. / GUITAR'D AND FEATHERED** — [ ] –

Oct 63. (lp; mono/stereo) *(RD/SF 7568) <LSP 2700>* **TWANGIN' UP A STORM** — [ ] 93
– Guitar child / All you gave to me / Giddy goose / Walk right in / He's so fine / Beach bound / Mr.Guitar man / Blowin' up a storm / My baby plays the same old song on his guitar all night long / Guitar'd and feathered / Soldier boy / Soul twist.

Nov 63. (7") *(RCA 1389) <8276>* **THE SON OF REBEL ROUSER. / THE STORY OF THREE LOVERS** — [ ] 97

Dec 63 (7") *<8335>* **GUITAR CHILD. / JERKY JALOPY** — – [ ]

Apr 64. (lp; mono/stereo) *(RD/SF 7621) <LSP 2798>* **LONELY GUITAR** — [ ] [ ]
– I'm so lonesome I could cry / Long lonely days of winter / Along came Linda / Someday the rainbow / Gunsmoke / A home in the meadow / Danny boy / Shenandoah / Summer kiss / My destiny / Cryin' happy tears / Annie Laurie.

Jan 64 (7") *<8376>* **THEME FROM A SUMMER PLACE. / WATER SKIING** — – [ ]

Jul 64. (lp; mono/stereo) *(RD/SF 7656) <LSP 2918>* **WATER SKIING** — [ ] [ ]
– Water skiing / Slalom rooster tail / The backward swan / Whip off / Jitterboard / Deep-water start / The wake ballet / Toe-hold side slide / Banana peels / In gear / Jumping the wake.

Oct 64. (7") *(RCA 1425) <8442>* **GUITAR STAR. / THE IGUANA** — [ ] [ ]

Jan 65 (7") *<8507>* **MOONSHOT. / ROUGHNECK** — – [ ]

Colpix — Colpix

Aug 65. (7") *<(PX 779)>* **TRASH. / SOUTH PHOENIX** — [ ] [ ]

Oct 65. (lp) *<(PXL 490)>* **DUANE A-GO-GO-GO!** — [ ] [ ]
– Trash / Puddin' / Movin'n'groovin' / Choo choo a go go – toot toot! / Just to satisfy you / Around the block in 80 days (march in 'A') / Cottonmouth / If you've seen one, you've seen them all! / South Phoenix / Dream lover / Busted / I'm blue.

Dec 65. (7") *<(PX 788)>* **THE HOUSE OF THE RISING SUN. / DON'T THINK TWICE IT'S ALRIGHT** — [ ] [ ]

Mar 66. (lp) *<(PXL 494)>* **DUANE GOES BOB DYLAN** — [ ] [ ]
– Don't think twice / House of the rising sun / It ain't me babe / Not the loving kind / She belongs to me / All I really want to do / Houston / Love minus zero – no limit / Mr.Tambourine man / Blowin' in the wind / Swing low sweet chariot / Eve of destruction.

1966. (7") *<795>* **EL RANCHO GRANDE. / POPPA'S MOVIN' ON (I'M MOVIN' ON)** — – [ ]

Reprise — Reprise

1966. (7") *(RS 20504) <0504>* **DAYDREAM. / THIS GUITAR WAS MADE FOR TWANGIN'** — [ ] [ ]

1967. (7") *(RS 20557) <0557>* **MONSOON. / ROARIN'** — [ ] [ ]

1967. (7") *<0622>* **GUITAR ON MY MIND. / WICKED WOMAN FROM WICKENBURG** — – [ ]

1967. (lp; mono/stereo) *<(RLP/RSLP 6218)>* **THE BIGGEST TWANG OF THEM ALL** — [ ] [ ]
– This guitar was / Made for twangin' / Batman / Monday Monday / Strangers in the night / Night train / Ballad of the green berets / Daydream / What now my love / Younger girl / Where were you when I needed you / A groovy kind of love / Mame.

1967. (7") *<0662>* **THIS TOWN. / THERE IS A MOUNTAIN** — – [ ]

1967. (7") *(RS 20690) <0690>* **NIKI HOEKY. / VELVET NIGHTS** — [ ] [ ]

1967. (lp) *(RLP 6240) <6240>* **THE ROARING TWANGIES** — [ ] [ ]
– Bye bye blues / Roarin' / A happy girl / Goofus / American patrol / Out on the town / Undecided / Born free / St.Louis blues march / Hello, Dolly / A string of pearls / Wicked woman from Wickenburg.

C.B.S. / Columbia

1969. (7") *(CBS 3962)* **BREAK MY MIND. / LOVING BIRD** | | – |

not iss. / Uni

1970. (7") *<55237>* **THE FIVE-SEVENTEEN. / SOMETHING** | | |

not iss. / Big Tree

1970. (7") *<157>* **RENEGADE. / NIGHTLY NEWS** | | |

not iss. / Congress

1970. (7") *<6010>* **PUT A LITTLE LOVE IN YOUR HEART. / FREIGHT TRAIN** | – | |

DUANE EDDY & THE REBELETTES

G.T.O. / not iss.

Feb 75. (7") *GT 11)* **PLAY ME LIKE YOU PLAY YOUR GUITAR. / BLUE MONTANA SKY** | 9 | – |

Apr 75. (lp) *(GTLP 002)* **GUITAR MAN** | | – |
– Rock'n'roll guitar man / Night prowler / Son of a guitar man / Love theme from Romeo & Juliet / Play me like you play your guitar / Mark of Zorro / The man with the gold guitar / (Last night) I didn't get to sleep at all / Cannon ball rag / Blue Montana sky / Dance with the guitar man. *(re-iss. Apr78 on 'Hallmark'; SHM 947) (cd-iss. Nov02 on 'Planet Media'; PML 1015)*

Jun 75. (7") *(GT 25)* **THE MAN WITH THE GOLDEN GUITAR. / MARK OF ZORRO** | | – |

Target / Target

Oct 75. (7") *<(101)>* **LOVE CONFUSION. / LOVE IS A WARM EMOTION** | | |

Elektra / Elektra

Nov 78. (7") *<44018>* **SPIES. / ROCKABILLY HOLIDAY** | – | |

Mar 79. (7") *<45359>* **YOU ARE MY SUNSHINE. / 7 TO 8** | – | |

—— made his live comeback in 1983 and In May '86 he featured on the ART OF NOISE single version of 'PETER GUNN' (this hit UK No.8 / US No.50 enabling him to return to solo work)

Capitol / Capitol

Sep 87. (7") *(CL 463)* **ROCKESTRA THEME. / BLUE CITY** | | – |
(12"+=) *(12CL 463)* – ('A'version).

Sep 87. (lp/c/cd) *(EST/TCEST/CDEST 2034)* **DUANE EDDY** | | |
– Kickin' asphalt / Rockestra theme / Theme for something reading important / Spies / Blue city / The trembler / Los campaneros / Lost innocence / Rockabilly holiday / Last look back.

– (selective) compilations, etc. –

Jun 62. (lp) *(HA-W 2435) <3021>* **A MILLION DOLLARS' WORTH OF TWANG VOL.2** | 18 | |
– The walker / Pepe / Lost friend / Theme from Dixie / Gidget goes Hawaiian / Ring of fire / Bobbie / Drivin' home / Tammy / The avenger / Londonderry air / Liza Jane.

Jun 91. (cd)(c) *R.C.A.; (CZ 425)(TCEMS 1405)* **TWANGY PEAKS** | | – |
– (DUANE A GO-GO / DUANE GOES DYLAN)

Mar 93. (cd) *R.C.A.; (74321 12699-2)* **2GETHER ON ONE** | | – |

May 94. (cd) *Bear Family; (BCD 15702)* **THAT CLASSIC TWANG** | | |

May 94. (cd) *Bear Family; (BCD 15799)* **ESPECIALLY FOR YOU / GIRLS GIRLS GIRLS** | | |

May 94. (cd) *Bear Family; (BCD 15807)* **THE "TWANGS" THE "THANG" / SONGS OF OUR HERITAGE** | | |

Nov 94. (cd) *See For Miles; (SEECD 417)* **HIS TWANGY GUITAR AND THE REBELS** | | – |
(re-iss. Nov96 & Sep99; same)

Dec 94. (7xcd-box) *Bear Family; (BCD 15778)* **TWANGIN' FROM PHOENIX TO L.A. (THE JAMIE YEARS)** | | |

Jun 98. (cd) *One Way; (OW 34541)* **THE BEST OF DUANE EDDY / LONELY GUITAR** | | – |

Jun 98. (cd) *One Way; (OW 34542)* **DANCE WITH THE GUITAR MAN / TWISTIN' AND TWANGIN'** | | – |

Jun 98. (cd) *One Way; (OW 34543)* **TWANGIN' (THE GOLDEN HITS)** | | – |

Jun 98. (cd) *One Way; (OW 34545)* **TWANGY GUITAR / WATER SKIING** | | – |

Feb 99. (cd/c) *Pulse; (PLS CD/MC 309)* **MR. TWANGY GUITAR** | | – |
(re-iss. Mar02 on 'Disky'; SI 793142)

Oct 99. (6xcd-box) *Bear Family; (BCD 16271)* **DEEP IN THE HEART OF TWANGSVILLE** | | |

Nov 02. (d-cd; as DUANE EDDY & THE VENTURES) *Delta Blue; (63027)* **TWANGIN' GUITAR** | | |

Dec 02. (cd-ep) *Magic; (3930274)* **GUITAR MAN EP** | | – |

□ The EDGE (see under ⇒ U2)

Dave EDMUNDS

Born: 15 Apr'44, Cardiff, Wales. After being in two local bands: The 99'ers and The RAIDERS in the mid-60's, he joined The IMAGE in 1966, breaking away with their drummer the following year to form The HUMAN BEANS. In 1968, this bunch evolved into LOVE SCULPTURE and smashed into the UK Top 5 with 'SABRE DANCE'. Two years on and now solo, EDMUNDS topped the UK charts with his version of Smiley Lewis's 'I HEAR YOU KNOCKIN', which also broke the US Top 10. EDMUNDS scored a further couple of UK Top 10 hits in a similar vein with The Ronettes' 'BABY I LOVE YOU' and The Chordettes 'BORN TO BE WITH YOU'. As well as appearing in the 1974 film, 'Stardust' (alongside DAVID ESSEX and KEITH MOON), EDMUNDS also had his hands full with his Rockfield studio in Wales, a perenially popular operation where he first met NICK LOWE; then bass player for BRINSLEY SCHWARZ, LOWE would subsequently collaborate with EDMUNDS on a number of occasions, The BRINSLEY's initially helping out on 1975's 'SUBTLE AS A FLYING MALLET' set. Signing to LED ZEPPELIN's 'Swan Song' label shortly after, EDMUNDS formed a semi-permanent backing band, ROCKPILE, consisting of LOWE, guitarist BILLY BREMNER (no, not the wee Scottish footballer!) and drummer TERRY WILLIAMS, this formation making their debut on 'GET IT' (1977). With LOWE also co-writing, his knack for clever pop combined with EDMUNDS' instinctive rhythm and feel resulted in such enduring tracks as 'I KNEW THE BRIDE', a Top 30 hit in summer '77. Despite critical acclaim and the major success of the 'GIRLS TALK' (penned by ELVIS COSTELLO) and 'QUEEN OF HEARTS' singles in 1979, the accompanying album, 'REPEAT WHEN NECESSARY', only just scraped into the Top 40. Recorded under the ROCKPILE moniker, 1980's 'SECONDS OF PLEASURE' was EDMUNDS' first album under his new American contract with 'Columbia', the album achieving a healthy Top 30 US chart position on the back of an Stateside tour with BAD COMPANY. The singer fulfilled his obligations to 'Swan Song' with the following year's 'TWANGIN', his first without LOWE and Co. (LOWE continued to enjoy a relatively successful solo career, while WILLIAMS went on to join DIRE STRAITS). Recruiting a new band and signing to 'Arista' in the UK, EDMUNDS released the sturdy 'D.E. 7th' in 1982, before hooking up with ELO man, JEFF LYNNE for 'INFORMATION' (1983) and 'RIFF RAFF' (1984). He continued to produce an eclectic variety of acts throughout the 80's, the respect afforded him in this area a mark of the man's adaptability and musical intuition. The 90's meanwhile, saw EDMUNDS return with the star studded 'CLOSER TO THE FLAME' and his contribution to the MTV 'Unplugged' era, 'PLUGGED IN'. • **Covers:** The HUMAN BEANS covered MORNING DEW (Tim Rose). LOVE SCULPTURE covered WANG DANG DOODLE (Willie Dixon) / SABRE DANCE (Khachaturian) / ON THE ROAD AGAIN (Wilbert Harrison) / SUMMERTIME (Gershwin). EDMUNDS solo; BLUE MONDAY (Fats Domino) / GET OUT OF DENVER (Bob Seger) / HEY GOOD LOOKIN' (Hank Williams) / GIRLS TALK (Elvis Costello) / CRAWLING FROM THE WRECKAGE (Graham Parker) / SINGING THE BLUES (Guy Mitchell) / WRONG WAY

(Difford-Tilbrook of Squeeze) / ALMOST SATURDAY NIGHT (John Fogerty) / FROM SMALL THINGS BIG THINGS COME (Bruce Springsteen) / OUTLAW BLUES (Bob Dylan) / etc. • **Trivia:** EDMUNDS produced many artists, including SHAKIN' STEVENS & THE SUNSETS in 1970, BRINSLEY SCHWARZ (1974) / FLAMIN' GROOVIES (1976) / FABULOUS THUNDERBIRDS (1980-81) / EVERLY BROTHERS (1983-86) / k.d.LANG (1988) / NICK LOWE (1989) / DION (1989) / STRAY CATS (1980 + 1989).

Album rating: Love Sculpture: BLUES HELPING (*4) / FORMS AND FEELINGS (*4) / ROCKPILE (*5; as Dave Edmunds' Rockpile) / SUBTLE AS A FLYING MALLET (*5) / GET IT (*6) / TRACKS ON WAX (*6) / REPEAT WHEN NECESSARY (*7) / SECONDS OF PLEASURE (*7; as Rockpile) / THE BEST OF DAVE EDMUNDS compilation (*7) / TWANGIN' (*5) / D.E. 7th (*5) / INFORMATION (*4) / RIFF RAFF (*4) / I HEAR YOU ROCKIN' (*5; as Dave Edmunds Band) / CLOSER TO THE FLAME (*4) / THE ANTHOLOGY (1968-1990) compilation (*7) / PLUGGED IN (*5)

LOVE SCULPTURE

DAVE EDMUNDS – vocals, guitar / **TOMMY RILEY** – drums / **JOHN WILLIAMS** – bass

Columbia / not iss.

Jul 67. (7"; as HUMAN BEINGS) *(DB 8230)* **MORNING DEW. / IT'S A WONDER** [ ] [–]

Parlophone / Rare

Feb 68. (7") *(R 5664)* **RIVER TO ANOTHER DAY. / BRAND NEW WOMAN** [ ] [–]

— **BOB 'CONGO' JONES** – drums repl. RILEY

Sep 68. (7") *(R 5731)* **WANG-DANG-DOODLE. / THE STUMBLE** [ ] [–]

Nov 68. (7") *(R 5744)* **SABRE DANCE. / THINK OF LOVE** [5] [–]

Dec 68. (lp; mono/stereo) *(PMC/PCS 7059)* *<505>* **BLUES HELPING** [ ] [ ]
– The stumble / 3 o'clock blues / I believe to my soul / Blues helping / Summertime (from Porgy and Bess) / Don't answer the door / So unkind / On the road again / Wang-dang-doodle / Come back baby / Shake your hips.

Feb 69. (7") *(R 5807)* **FARENDOLE. / SEAGULL** [ ] [–]

Parlophone / Parrot

Jan 70. (lp) *<PCS 7090>* *<71035>* **FORMS AND FEELINGS** [ ] [ ]
– In the land of the few / Seagull / Nobody's talking / People people / Why (how now) / Sabre dance (from 'Gayaneh-Ballet') / You can't catch me / Farandole.

Feb 70. (7") *(R 5831)* **IN THE LAND OF THE FEW. / PEOPLE PEOPLE** [ ] [–]

— **TERRY WILLIAMS** (b.11 Jan'48, Swansea, Wales) – drums (ex-DREAM) repl. JONES who joined SASSAFRAS / added **MICKEY GEE** – guitar (ex-JOE COCKER'S GREASE BAND ex-TOM JONES)

— split soon after; GEE and WILLIAMS later joined MAN

DAVE EDMUNDS' ROCKPILE

EDMUNDS – multi-instrumentalist; retained **JOHN WILLIAMS**

M.A.M. / M.A.M.

Nov 70 (7") *(MAM 1)* *<3601>* **I HEAR YOU KNOCKING. / BLACK BILL** [1] [4]

Regal Zonophone / M.A.M.

Mar 71. (7") *(RZ 3032)* *<3608>* **I'M COMING HOME. / COUNTRY ROLL** [ ] [75]

Jul 71. (7") *(RZ 3037)* **BLUE MONDAY. / I'LL GET ALONG** [ ] [ ]

— guests included **TERRY WILLIAMS** – drums / **B.J. COLE** – pedal steel guitar / **ANDY FAIRWEATHER-LOW** – guitar (ex-AMEN CORNER)

Jun 72. (lp) *(SLRZ 1026)* *<MAM 3>* **ROCKPILE** [ ] [ ]
– Down down down / It ain't easy / I hear you knockin' / Hell of a pain / You can't catch me / Dance dance dance / Outlaw blues / Egg or the hen. *(cd-iss. Nov02 on 'Repertoire'; REP 4966)*

Jul 72. (7") *(RZ 3059)* **DOWN DOWN DOWN. / IT AIN'T EASY** [ ] [ ]

DAVE EDMUNDS

went solo playing nearly every instrument himself

Rockfield / R.C.A.

Dec 72. (7") *(ROC 1)* **BABY I LOVE YOU. / MAYBE** [8] [ ]

May 73. (7") *(ROC 2)* **BORN TO BE WITH YOU. / PICK AXE BLUES** [5] [ ]

Sep 74. (7") *(ROC 4)* **NEED A SHOT OF RHYTHM AND BLUES. / LET IT BE ME** [ ] [ ]

Feb 75. (7") *(ROC 6)* **I AIN'T NEVER. / SOME OTHER GUY** [ ] [ ]

— **EDMUNDS** added guests **BRINSLEY SCHWARTZ** – guitar and some of his band **NICK LOWE** – bass / **BOB ANDREWS** – keyboards / **IAN GOMM** – guitar / **PICK WITHERS, TERRY WILLIAMS and BILLY RANKIN** – drums

Apr 75. (lp) *(RRL 101)* *<APL-1 5003>* **SUBTLE AS A FLYING MALLET** [ ] [ ]
– Baby I love you / Leave my woman alone / Maybe / Let it rock / Let it be me / Da doo ron ron / No money down / I ain't never / Billy the kid / Shot of rhythm and blues / She's my baby / Born to be with you. *(re-iss. 1978 on 'R.C.A.' lp/c; RCA LP/K 5129) (re-iss. Oct81 on 'R.C.A.') (cd-iss. Jun98 on 'One Way'; OW 34504)*

Swan Song / Swan Song

Aug 76. (7") *(SSK 19408)* **HERE COMES THE WEEKEND. / AS LOVERS DO** [ ] [ ]

Oct 76. (7") *(SSK 19409)* **WHERE OR WHEN. / NEW YORK'S A LONELY TOWN** [ ] [ ]

— Now DAVE's band was **LOWE, T. WILLIAMS** and **BILLY BREMNER** – guitar plus session people as guests

Apr 77. (lp/c) *(SSK/SK4 59404)* *<8418>* **GET IT** [ ] [ ]
– Get out of Denver / Back to schooldays / Hey good lookin' / I knew the bride (when she used to rock'n'roll) / Get it / Here comes the weekend / Worn out suits and brand new pockets / Where or when / Ju ju man / Let's talk about us / What did I do last night? / My baby left me / Little darlin'.

Apr 77. (7") *(SSK 19410)* **JU JU MAN. / WHAT DID I DO LAST NIGHT?** [ ] [ ]

Jun 77. (7") *(SSK 19411)* **I KNEW THE BRIDE. / BACK TO SCHOOLDAYS** [26] [ ]

Aug 78. (7") *(SSK 19413)* **DEBORAH. / WHAT LOOKS BEST ON YOU** [ ] [ ]

Sep 78. (lp) *(SSK/SK4 59407)* *<8505>* **TRACKS ON WAX** [ ] [ ]
– Trouble boys / Never been in love / Not a woman, not a child / Television / What looks best on you / Readers wives / Deborah / Thread your needle / A.1 on the jukebox / It's my own business / Heart of the city.

Oct 78. (7") *(SSK 19414)* **TELEVISION. / NEVER BEEN IN LOVE** [ ] [ ]

Feb 79. (7") *(SSK 19417)* **A-1 ON THE JUKEBOX. / IT'S MY OWN BUSINESS** [ ] [ ]

Jun 79. (7"clear) *(SSK 19418)* **GIRLS TALK. / BAD IS BAD** [4] [–]

Jun 79. (lp/c) *(<SSK/SK4 8507>)* **REPEAT WHEN NECESSARY** [39] [54]
– Girls talk / Crawling from the wreckage / Sweet little Lisa / The creature from the black lagoon / Home in my hand / Take me for a little while / Queen of hearts / We were both wrong / Bad is bad / Dynamite / Goodbye Mr Good Guy. *(cd-iss. Jan93 on 'Warners'; 7567 90337-2)*

Aug 79. (7") *<71001>* **GIRLS TALK. / THE CREATURE FROM THE BLACK LAGOON** [–] [65]

Sep 79. (7") *(K 19419)* **QUEEN OF HEARTS. / CREATURE FROM THE BLACK LAGOON** [11] [ ]

Nov 79. (7") *(K 19420)* **CRAWLING FROM THE WRECKAGE. / AS LOVERS DO** [59] [ ]

Jan 80. (7") *(K 19422)* **SINGIN' THE BLUES. / BOYS TALK** [28] [ ]

— In Aug'80, EDMUNDS collaborated on a single, 'BABY RIDE EASY' with CARLENE CARTER (XX 8)

ROCKPILE

(EDMUNDS, LOWE, BREMNER and T. WILLIAMS)

F-Beat / Columbia

Sep 80. (7"/7"yellow) *(XX 9/+C)* **WRONG WAY. / NOW AND ALWAYS** [ ] [ ]

Oct 80. (lp/c) *(XX LP/C 7)* *<36886>* **SECONDS OF PLEASURE** [34] [27]
– Teacher teacher / If sugar was as sweet as you / Wrong way / Now and always / Knife and fork / When I write the book / Pet you and hold you / Oh what a thrill / Play that fast thing (one more time) / For too long / Heart / (You ain't nothing but) Fine fine fine. *(free 7"ep w/ above) (BEV 1)* **NICK LOWE & DAVE EDMUNDS SING THE EVERLY**

BROTHERS *(re-iss. Jun84 on 'Demon'; FIEND 28) (cd-iss. 1989 on 'Line'; LICD 0005)*

Nov 80. (7") *(XX 11) <11388>* **TEACHER TEACHER. / FOOL TOO LONG** [ ] [51]

Mar 81. (7") *<60503>* **TAKE A MESSAGE TO MARY. / ROCKPILE HEART** [–] [ ]

DAVE EDMUNDS

— solo again. NICK LOWE continued his solo career also WILLIAMS later joined DIRE STRAITS. **EDMUNDS** now used session people including past friends

Swan Song Swan Song

Mar 81. (7") *(SSK 19424) <72000>* **ALMOST SATURDAY NIGHT. / YOU'LL NEVER GET ME UP (IN ONE OF THOSE)** [58] [54]

Apr 81. (lp/c) *(SSK/SK4 59411) <16034>* **TWANGIN'** [37] [48]
– (I'm gonna start) Living again if it kills me / The race is on / Almost Saturday night / Singin' the blues / Something happens / It's been so long / Cheap talk, patter and jive / You'll never get me up (in one of those) / I'm only human / Baby let's play house.

Jun 81. (7"; DAVE EDMUNDS & THE STRAY CATS) *(SSK 19425)* **THE RACE IS ON. / (I'M GONNA START) LIVING AGAIN IF IT KILLS ME** [34] [ ]

— His touring band consisted of **MICKEY GEE** – guitar / **JOHN DAVID** – bass and **DAVID CHARLES** – drums. (They appear on album alongside sessioners)

Arista Columbia

Feb 82. (7") *(ARIST 439)* **WARMED OVER KISSES (LEFT OVER LOVE). / LOUISIANA MAN** [ ] [ ]

Mar 82. (lp/c) *(SPART/TC-SPART 1184) <37930>* **D.E. 7th** [60] [46]
– From small things big things come / Dear dad / Me and the boys / Bail you out / Generation number / Other guy's girls / Warmed over kisses (left over love) / Paula meet Jeanne / One more night / Deep in the heart of Texas / Louisiana man. *(free 7"ep w/a) (JUKE 1)* **LIVE AT THE VENUE (live)** *(re-iss. Mar84 on 'Fame' lp/c; FA41/TC-FA 41 3090-1/-4)*

Apr 82. (7") *(ARIST 471)* **ME AND THE BOYS. / QUEEN OF HEARTS (live)** [ ] [ ]

Jul 82. (7") *(ARIST 478)* **FROM SMALL THINGS BIG THINGS COME. / YOUR TRUE LOVE (live)** [ ] [–]

Jul 82. (7") **FROM SMALL THINGS BIG THINGS COME. / WARMED OVER KISSES (LEFT OVER LOVE)** [–] [ ]

— plus **JEFF LENNY** – bass, synthesizers and production

Mar 83. (7"/12") *(ARIST/+12 522) <03877>* **SLIPPING AWAY. / DON'T CALL ME TONIGHT** [60] [39]

Apr 83. (lp/c) *(205/405 348) <38651>* **INFORMATION** [92] [51]
– Slipping away / Don't you double / I want you bad / Wait / The watch on my wrist / The shape I'm in / Feels so right / What have I got to do to win / Have a heart / Information / Don't call me tonight.

May 83. (7"/12") *(ARIST/+12 532) <04080>* **INFORMATION. / WHAT HAVE I GOT TO DO TO WIN** [ ] [ ]

— **DAVE EDMUNDS** retained **JOHN DAVID** /**RICHARD TANDY** – keyboards (ex-ELECTRIC LIGHT ORCHESTRA) repl. GEE **TERRY WILLIAMS** – drums returned to repl. DAVID CHARLES

Jul 84. (7") *(ARIST 562) <04585>* **SOMETHING ABOUT YOU. / CAN'T GET ENOUGH** [ ] [ ]
(12"+=) *(ARIST12 562)* – Slipping away / Warmed over kisses (left over love) / From small things big things come.

Sep 84. (7") *<04700>* **BREAKING OUT. / HOW COULD I BE SO WRONG** [–] [ ]

Sep 84. (lp/c) *(206/406 396) <39273>* **RIFF RAFF** [ ] [ ]
– Something about you / Breaking out / Busted loose / S.O.S. / Far away / Rules of the game / Steel claw / Can't get enough / How could I be so wrong / Hang on.

Sep 84. (7") *(ARIST 583)* **STEEL CLAW. / HOW COULD I BE SO WRONG** [ ] [–]

Apr 85. (7") *<04923>* **DO YOU WANT TO DANCE. / DON'T CALL ME TONIGHT** [–] [ ]

Jul 85. (7") *(A 6277) <04762>* **HIGH SCHOOL NIGHTS. / PORKY'S REVENGE** [ ] Apr85 [91]

— (above from film 'Porky's Revenge', lp featured 3 more EDMUNDS tracks) 'RUN RUDOLPH RUN' appeared on 2 various comps. 'CHRISTMAS AT THE PATTI (live) and 'PARTY PARTY' soundtrack. They also appeared on 'STARDUST' soundtrack on 'CBS'/'Columbia'.

Jan 87. (lp/c/cd) *(208/408/258 228) <40603>* **I HEAR YOU ROCKIN' – LIVE: DAVE EDMUNDS BAND (live)** [ ] [ ]
– I hear you knocking / Down down down / Hell of a pain / I'll get along / It ain't easy / Country roll / Blue Monday / The promised land / Dance, dance, dance / Lover not a fighter / Egg or the hen / Sweet little rock and roller / Black bill / Outlaw blues / Sabre dance.

Apr 87. (7") *<06599>* **THE WANDERER (live). / INFORMATION (live)** [–] [ ]

— next featured **LEE ROCKER / BRIAN SETZER** (Stray Cats)

Capitol Capitol

Mar 90. (7") *(CL 568)* **KING OF LOVE. / STAY WITH ME TONIGHT** [68] [ ]
(12"+=/cd-s+=) *(12/CD CL 568)* – Everytime I see her.
(10"+=) *(10CL 568)* – King of love (at 78 rpm).

Apr 90. (cd/c/lp) *(CD/TC+/EST 2113) <90372>* **CLOSER TO THE FLAME** [ ] [ ]
– King of love / Don't talk to me / Everytime I see her / Test of love / Closer to the flame / Stockholm / Fallin' through a hole / Never take the place of you / I got your number / Sincerely.

Columbia Rhino

Aug 94. (cd/c/lp) *(477333-2/-4/-1) <71770>* **PLUGGED IN** [ ] Jul94 [ ]
– Chutes and ladders / New step back / I love music / Halfway down / Beach Boy blood (in my veins) / The claw / I got the will / Better word for love / Standing at the crossroads / It doesn't really matter / Sabre dance.

– compilations, etc. –

May 80. (7"ep) *R.C.A.; (PE 5243)* **BABY I LOVE YOU / DA DOO RON RON. / BORN TO BE WITH YOU / SHOT OF RHYTHM AND BLUES** [ ] [–]

Aug 80. (lp/c) *Harvest; (SHAM/TC-SHAM 2032)* **THE SINGLES A's & B's** [ ] [–]
(re-iss. 1989 on 'See For Miles' lp/cd; SEE/+CD 282)

Nov 81. (lp/c) *Swan Song; (SSK/SK4 59413) <8510>* **THE BEST OF DAVE EDMUNDS** [ ] [ ]
– Deborah / Girls talk / I knew the bride / A.1. on the jukebox / The race is on / I hear you knockin' / Almost Saturday night / Sabre dance / Queen of hearts / Crawling from the wreckage / Here comes the weekend / Trouble boys / Ju ju man / Singing the blues / Born to be with you. *(cd-iss. Mar97 on 'Warners'; 7567 90338-2)*

May 82. (7") *RCA Gold; (GOLD 548)* **BABY I LOVE YOU. / BORN TO BE WITH YOU** [ ] [–]

Oct 83. (7"; LOVE SCULPTURE) *Old Gold; (OG 9368)* **SABRE DANCE. / (track by other artist)** [ ] [–]

Aug 87. (lp/c) *E.M.I.; (EMS/TC-EMS 1126)* **THE ORIGINAL ROCKPILE VOL.II** [ ] [–]

Aug 87. (7") *Old Gold; (OG 9711)* **I HEAR YOU KNOCKIN'. / SHE'S ABOUT A MOVER / SABRE DANCE** [ ] [–]

Jul 91. (d-cd) *E.M.I.; (CDEM 1406)* **THE COMPLETE EARLY EDMUNDS** [ ] [–]

Sep 93. (cd) *Arista; (74321 12540-2)* **THE BEST OF DAVE EDMUNDS** [ ] [–]
– Something about you / I hear you knockin' (live) / Deep in the heart of Texas / Information / Breaking out / From small things big things come (live) / The shape I'm in / Some other guy / Bail you out / S.O.S. / Slipping away / Generation rumble / Your true love (live) / Steel claw / Queen of hearts / How could I be so wrong.

Dec 94. (cd) *Connoisseur; (VSOPCD 209)* **CHRONICLES** [ ] [–]

Feb 97. (cd) *RCA Camden; (74321 45192-2)* **ROCKIN' (THE BEST OF DAVE EDMUNDS)** [ ] [–]

Feb 97. (cd) *EMI Gold; (CDGOLD 1083)* **I HEAR YOU KNOCKING** [ ] [–]

Mar 97. (cd) *Disky; (DC 87862-2)* **THE COLLECTION** [ ] [–]

May 00. (cd) *Essential; (ESMCD 876) / Sanctuary; <81107>* **PILE OF ROCK – LIVE (live in Sweden 1997)** [ ] Sep01 [ ]

May 02. (cd) *Beat Goes On; (BGOCD 545)* **DE7TH / INFORMATION** [ ] [–]

May 02. (cd) *Disky; (SI 79418-2)* **C'MON EVERYBODY** [ ] [–]

Jul 02. (cd) *Beat Goes On; (BGOCD 559)* **RIFF RAFF / I HEAR YOU ROCKIN'** [ ] [–]

Nov 02. (cd) *Go-Disky; (<GO 90501-2>)* **SABRE DANCE** [ ] Feb03 [ ]

EELS

Formed: Los Angeles, California, USA ... 1995 by E (MARK EVERETT), who had previously released two solo albums under this rather minimalist moniker (only in America). Hooking up with fellow slippery characters TOMMY WALTER and BUTCH NORTON, they set free their electric debut album, 'BEAUTIFUL FREAK'. Lyrically grim, The EELS packaged their tales of dysfunctional Americana in deceptively effervescent indie melodies, the UK Top 10 singles 'NOVOCAINE FOR THE SOUL' and 'SUSAN'S HOUSE' being prime examples of post-NIRVANA lo-fi rock. 1998's 'ELECTRO-SHOCK BLUES' was a more private and personal exploration of life's darker side, E exorcising the demons of his sister's suicide and his mother's death from cancer (his father had died when MARK was 19). After the very morbid musings heard in 'ELECTRO ...', EELS frontman and mainman E decided to record an album that harked back to the softer, more upbeat version of the band – the kind of styles presented as an introduction on the 'BEAUTIFUL FREAK' LP. Entitled 'DAISIES OF THE GALAXY' (2000), it was a fantastic journey into the heart of EVERETT's, um, heart. Standout single 'BEAUTIFUL DAY' saw the man singing about something more positive, although however bleak his songs were the message still stood the same: life is a beautiful thing ... enjoy it! 'THE SOUND OF FEAR' displayed his brilliant backing band's use of instrumentation, with a creeping bass that sounded similar to NIRVANA's 'Lithium', before the jazzy snare kicked in. 'IT'S A MOTHERFUCKER' made an example of his songwriting talents in the way he could turn such a sour subject matter into such a sweet song. The amusing live set 'OH WHAT A BEAUTIFUL DAY' (2000), saw a collection of live recordings taken from everywhere including Glasgow, L.A., New York and London (by this point bassist TOMMY WALTER had fled, to be replaced by LISA GERMANO). The band threw in a few odd-ball covers along the way; EVERETT's staggering solo performances were awesome. The strange and disjointed 'SOULJACKER' album appeared in 2001 to tepid critical response. E, dressed as the notorious American terrorist the Unabomber, and taking the name from an equally notorious serial killer (who believed he stole his victim's souls when he killed them), the album was patchy at best. Full of strange, unfinished ideas, the set had an uneven quality reflecting the 'ELECTRO SHOCK ...' album almost to a tee. However, after the enigmatic and more mainstream 'DAISIES ...' album, it was nice to see a little diversity in the group's music. Mr EVERETT was back with more twisted humour and self-consciously bleak lyrical portraits on 'SHOOTENANNY!' (2003), sounding more and more like the contrary, wilfully wayward troubadour he's always threatened to become. There's a beguiling charm about E's determinedly downbeat outlook, a strength which he continued to play to with this release. • **Songwriters:** Most songs by E, some with JIM JACOBSEN, JIM WEATHERLY, MARK GOLDENBERG, JON BRION or JILL SOBULE.

Album rating: E: A MAN CALLED E (*7) / BROKEN TOY SHOP (*5) / Eels: BEAUTIFUL FREAK (*7) / ELECTRO-SHOCK BLUES (*6) / DAISIES OF THE GALAXY (*6) / OH WHAT A BEAUTIFUL MORNING (*5) / SOULJACKER (*6) / SHOOTENANNY! (*7)

(E)

E (b. MARK OLIVER EVERETT, 9 Apr'63, Virginia, USA) – vocals, piano, multi

not iss. Polydor

Dec 91. (cd-s) *<CDP 654>* **HELLO CRUEL WORLD** [–] [ ]

Feb 92. (cd/c) *<511570-2/-4>* **A MAN CALLED (E)** [–] [ ]

– Hello cruel world / Fitting in with the misfits / Are you and me gonna happen / Looking out the window with a blue / Nowheresville / Symphony for toy piano in G minor / Mockingbird Franklin / I've been kicked around / Pray / E's tune / You'll be the scarecrow.

Mar 92. (cd-s) **NOWHERESVILLE / STRAWBERRY BLONDE** [–] [ ]

— now with various personnel incl. **PARTHENON HUXLEY** + **SEAB COLEMAN**

Dec 93. (cd/c) *<519976-2/-4>* **BROKEN TOY SHOP** [–] [ ]

– Shine it all on / Standing at the gate / The only thing I care about / Manchester girl / L.A. river / Most unpleasant man / Mass / Tomorrow I'll be nine / The day I wrote you off / Someone to break the spell / She loves a puppet / My old raincoat / Permanent broken heart / Eight lives left.

Dec 93. (cd-ep) *<SACD 772>* **NOT FOR AIRPLAY** [–] [ ]

– Shine it all on / L.A. river / Tomorrow I'll be nine / Everything's gonna be cool this summer.

EELS

— E with **TOMMY WALTER** – bass, vocals / **BUTCH NORTON** (b. JONATHAN) – drums, vocals

Dreamworks Dreamworks

Aug 96. (cd-s; promo) **RAGS TO RICHES / ANIMAL** [–] [ ]

Feb 97. (cd/c) *<(DRD/DRC 50001)>* **BEAUTIFUL FREAK** [5] Aug96 [ ]

– Novocaine for the soul / Susan's house / Rags to rags / Beautiful freak / Not ready yet / My beloved monster / Flower / Guest list / Mental / Spunky / Your lucky day in Hell / Manchild. *(UK+=)* – BBC tracks:- Novocaine for the soul (live from Hell) / Manchester girl / My beloved mad monster party / Flower. *(re-iss. Feb00; same)*

Feb 97. (7"/c-s) *(DRM S/C 22174)* **NOVOCAINE FOR THE SOUL. / FUCKER** [10] [–]

(cd-s+=) *(DRMCD 22174)* – Guest list / My beloved monster (live).

May 97. (7"/c-s) *(DRM S/C 22238)* **SUSAN'S HOUSE. / STEPMOTHER** [9] [–]

(cd-s+=) *(DRMCD 22238)* – Manchester girl (BBC session).

Sep 97. (7"/c-s) *(DRM S/C 22277)* **YOUR LUCKY DAY IN HELL. / SUSAN'S APARTMENT** [35] [–]

(cd-s+=) *(DRMCD 22277)* – Altar boy.

Sep 98. (7"/c-s) *(DRM S/C 22346)* *<5112>* **LAST STOP: THIS TOWN. / FUNERAL PARLOUR** [23] [–]

(cd-s+=) *(DRMCD 22346)* – Novocaine for the soul (Moog Cookbook version).

Sep 98. (cd/c) *<(DRD/DRC 50052)>* **ELECTRO-SHOCK BLUES** [12] [ ]

– Elizabeth on the bathroom floor / Going to your funeral part 1 / Cancer for the cure / My descent into madness / 3 speed / Hospital food / Electro-shock blues / Efils' god / Going to your funeral part II / Last stop: this town / Baby genius / Climbing to the moon / Ant farm / Dead of winter / The medication is wearing off / P.S. you rock my world. *(re-iss. Feb00; same)*

Nov 98. (7"/c-s) *(DRM S/C 22373)* **CANCER FOR THE CURE. / EVERYTHING'S GONNA BE COOL THIS CHRISTMAS** [60] [–]

(cd-s+=) *(DRMCD 22373)* – Exodus part III.

— **ADAM SIEGAL** – bass; repl. TOMMY WALTER

Feb 00. (7"pic-d) *(450978-7)* **MR. E'S BEAUTIFUL BLUES. / BIRDGIRL ON A CELL PHONE** [15] [–]

(cd-s+=) *(450976-2)* – ('A'-CD-Rom).

(cd-s) *(450977-2)* – ('A'side) / Hospital food (live) / Cancer for the cure (video).

Feb 00. (cd) *<(450218-2)>* **DAISIES OF THE GALAXY** [8] Mar00 [ ]

– Grace Kelly blues / Packing blankets / The sound of fear / I like birds / Daisies of the galaxy / Flyswatter / It's a motherfucker / Estate sales / Tiger in my tank / A daisy through concrete / Jeannie's diary / Wooden nickels / Something is sacred / Selective memory / Mr. E's beautiful blues. *(lp-iss.Apr00 on 'Bongload'; BL 47)*

Jun 00. (7"pic-d/cd-s) *(45094 5-7/6-2)* **FLYSWATTER. / OPEN THE DOOR (BBC live) / FLYSWATTER (polka dot remix)** [55] [–]

(cd-s) *(450947-2)* – ('A'side) / Something is sacred / Vice President Fruitley.

— **LISA GERMANO** – bass (solo artist) repl. SIEGAL

Dec 00. (cd) *<net>* **OH WHAT A BEAUTIFUL MORNING (live)** [–] [–]

– Feeling good / Overture:- (a) Last stop: this town (b) Beautiful freak (c) Rags to riches (d) Your lucky day in Hell (e) My descent into madness (f) Novocaine for the soul (g) Flower / Oh what a beautiful morning / Abortion in the sky / It's a motherfucker / Fucker / Ant farm / Climbing to the Moon / Grace Kelly blues / Daisies of the galaxy / Flyswatter / Vice President Fruitley / Hot and cold / Mr. E's beautiful blues / Not ready yet / Susan's house / Something is sacred.

— **E + BUTCH** recruited **JOHN PARISH** – guitars, keyboards, co-writer, etc + **KOOOL G** – synthesizers / **ADAM** (still here!)

Sep 01. (7") *(450893-7)* **SOULJACKER (part 1). / I WRITE THE B-SIDES** [30] [–]
(cd-s+=) *(450893-2)* – Can't help falling in love / ('A'video).
(cd-s) *(450893-5)* – ('A'side) / Jennifer Eccles / My beloved monstrosity / Flyswatter (video).

Sep 01. (cd/lp) *(450335-2/-1)* <450346> **SOULJACKER** [12] [ ]
– Dog faced boy / That's not really funny / Fresh feeling / Woman driving, man sleeping / Souljacker, pt.I / Friendly ghost / Teenage witch / Bus stop boxer / Jungle telegraph / World of shit / Souljacker, pt.II / What is this note? *(d-cd+=; 450346-2)* – I write the B-sides / (hidden track) / Jehovah's witness / Rotten world blues.

Jun 03. (cd) *(4504588)* <03902> **HOOTENANNY!** [35] [ ]
– All in a day's work / Saturday morning / The good old days / Love of the loveless / Dirty girl / Agony / Rock hard times / Restraining order blues / Lone wolf / Wrong about Bobby / Numbered days / Fashion awards / Somebody loves you.

EIGHTIES MATCHBOX B-LINE DISASTER

Formed: Brighton, England . . . 1998 by GUY McKNIGHT, MARC NORRIS, ANDY HUXLEY, SYM GHARIAL and drummer TOM DIMANTEPOULO. A mish-mash of skull-busting sonics and frantic gothic rock'n'roll, The EIGHTIES MATCHBOX B-LINE DISASTER (an actual vintage 1940's hot-rod) would, probably, "fuck your mother" if they had the chance. They began playing riotous shows in their native Brighton, but since it wasn't a very rock'n'roll town these days, the group busted out and on to vinyl via the independent 'MORNING HAS BROKEN' single. They finally signed to 'M.C.A.' at the beginning of 2002. They issued the incestuous single 'CELEBRATE YOUR MOTHER' that September, a song so debased it actually sounded like The BIRTHDAY PARTY on crack (if that's possible); although singer McKNIGHT would deny it, his voice was an almost dead ringer of CAVE's. What followed? More debauchery; a twelve-track album entitled 'HORSE OF THE DOG' (2002) – that was under twenty-eight minutes long – evoked the same trashy scuzz-ball rockin' blues of The CRAMPS. A tour with The PARKINSONS followed which was said to have ended in happy chaos. Lock up your daughters because The EMB-LD want to "invent rock"!

Album rating: HORSE OF THE DOG (*8)

GUY McKNIGHT – vocals / **MARC NORRIS** – guitar / **ANDY HUXLEY** – guitar / **SYM GHARIAL** – bass / **TOM DIAMANTEPOULO** – drums

Radiate / not iss.

Mar 02. (cd-s/7") *(RDT/+S 5)* **MORNING HAS BROKEN. / ALEX** [ ] [–]

M.C.A. / not iss.

Sep 02. (7") *(MCS 40296)* **CELEBRATE YOUR MOTHER. / RETURN DECEMBER** [66] [–]
(cd-s+=) *(MCSTD 40296)* – Torrential abuse.

Sep 02. (cd/lp) *(MCD/MCA 60082)* **HORSE OF THE DOG** [ ] [–]
– Celebrate your mother / Chicken / Whack of shit / Psychosis safari / Giant bones / Fish fingers / Charge the guns / Morning has broken / Team meat / Presidential wave.

Jan 03. (7"pic-d) *(MCS 40308)* **PSYCHOSIS SAFARI. / CHARGE THE GUNS (demo) / WHACK OF SHIT (demo)** [26] [–]
(cd-s) *(MCSTD 40308)* – ('A'side) / Briefcases for girls (produced by CASEY CHAOS) / Presidential wave (live session) / ('A'-video).
(cd-s) *(MCSXD 40308)* – ('A'side) / Ho ha (live session) / Celebrate your mother (live session).

May 03. (7"pic-d) *(MCS 40317)* **CHICKEN. / TURKISH DELIGHTS OF THE DEVIL** [30] [–]
(cd-s+=) *(MCSTD 40317)* – Horse of the dog / ('A'-video).
(cd-s) *(MCSXD 40317)* – ('A'side) / Palomino's dream (The Boogs) / Sacred metal / Palomino's dream (The Boogs) (video).

808 STATE

Formed: Manchester, England . . . 1987 by MARTIN PRICE and GRAHAM MASSEY, along with programmer GERALD SIMPSON (aka A GUY CALLED GERALD). All met while working next to, and frequenting MARTIN PRICE's 'Eastern Bloc' record shop. After two albums on indie label, 'Creed', they signed to 'Island' off-shoot 'ZTT' in 1989. 808 STATE's first single, 'PACIFIC STATE' breeched the UK Top 10 and initially their onslaught around Europe. Techno-dance rave-rock using sampling and sparse anthemic vocals, they were once described as TANGERINE DREAM on speed. A further succession of early 90's Top 10 hits followed in 'THE ONLY RHYME THAT BITES' (a collaboration with Manc rapper, MC TUNES, who later formed The DUST JUNKYS), 'IN YER FACE' and the dancefloor shredding 'CUBIK'. Icelandic pop pixie, BJORK, guested on their Top 5 'EX:EL' (1991), a tougher set which also featured NEW ORDER's BERNARD SUMNER on the track, 'SPANISH HEART'. PRICE departed later that year, however, 808 STATE surfaced briefly in 1992 with an ill-advised UB40 collaboration, 'ONE IN TEN', before releasing the more textured 'GORGEOUS' album in early '93. Having already worked on QUINCY JONES and DAVID BOWIE material, the group remain increasingly dramatic and atmospheric, as evidenced on their 'DON SOLARIS' set in 1996. Save for a handful of singles on obscure labels, MASSEY and crew remained below the parapet until the release of 'OUTPOST TRANSMISSION' in late 2002. More oblique than their earlier efforts, with input from the likes of ALABAMA 3, ELBOW's GUY GARVEY and SIMIAN's SIMON LORD, the record was hardly in step with current trends but was probably all the better for it. • **Trivia:** In 1990, they omposed the theme tune for TV pop/chat programme 'The Word'.

Album rating: NEWBUILD (*7) / 808:90 (*6) / EX:EL (*7) / GORGEOUS (*6) / DON SOLARIS (*5) / 808:88:98 compilation (*7) / OUTPOST TRANSMISSION (*5)

GRAHAM MASSEY (b. 4 Aug'60) – programmer, engineer, keyboards (ex-BITING TONGUES) / **MARTIN PRICE** (b.26 Mar'55, Farnworth, England) – programmer, keyboards, engineer / **GERALD SIMPSON** (b.16 Feb'64) – programmer, engineer, keyboards

Creed / not iss.

Sep 88. (lp) *(STATE 002)* **NEWBUILD** [ ] [–]
– Sync – Swim / Flow coma / Dr Lowfruit (4am mix) / Headhunters / Narcossa / E talk / Compulsion. *(re-iss. Apr99 on 'Rephlex' cd/3x12"; CAT 080 CD/LP)*

Nov 88. (12") *(STATE 003)* **LET YOURSELF GO (303 mix). / LET YOURSELF GO (D50 mix) / DEEPVILLE** [ ] [–]

— **ANDREW BARKER** (b. 9 Mar'68) – DJ, drum programmer, keyboards + **DARREN PARTINGTON** (b. 1 Nov'69 – DJ, drum programmer repl. SIMPSON who became A GUY CALLED GERALD and had hit single 'Voodoo Ray'.

Jul 89. (m-lp) *(STATE 004)* **QUADRASTATE** [ ] [–]
– Pacific state / 106 / State ritual / Disco state / Fire cracker / State to state.

Z.T.T. / Tommy Boy

Oct 89. (7"/c-s) *(ZANG 1/+C)* <TB 949> **PACIFIC STATE. / PACIFIC B** [10] Mar90 [ ]
(12"/3"cd-s) *(ZANG 1 T/CD)* – Pacific 202 / Pacific state origin / Pacific 303 / Cobra bora shortcut. *<US 12"version; TB 949>*
(12") *(ZANG 1TX)* – Pacific 909 (mellow birds mega edit) / Bonus bird beats / Cobra bora.

Dec 89. (lp/c)(cd) *(ZTT 2/+C)(246 461-2) <TC/+C/CD 1033>*
808:90 [57] Jun90 [ ]
– Magical dream / Ancodia / Cobra bora / Pacific 202 / Donkey doctor / Sunrise / 808080808 / The fat shadow (pointy head mix). *<US-title 'UTD. STATE 90'; TB/+C/CD 1033> (cd re-iss. Jun98; ZTT 102CD)*

Mar 90. (12"ep) *(ZANG 2T)* **THE EXTENDED PLEASURE OF DANCE** [56] [–]
– Cobra bora (call the cops mix) / Ancodia (taters deep nit funky beat mix) / Cubik.

—— The below two singles and album were credited to "MC TUNES VERSUS 808 STATE". (MC TUNES = **NICHOLAS LOCKETT** – English rapper)

May 90. (7"/c-s/12") *(ZANG 3/+C/T)* **THE ONLY RHYME THAT BITES. / THE ONLY RHYME THAT BYTES** [10] [–]
(ext.cd-s+=) *(ZANG 3CD)* – (other version).

Sep 90. (7"/c-s) *(ZANG 6/+C)* **TUNES SPLIT THE ATOM (rap). / DANCE YOURSELF TO DEATH (bassless)** [18] [–]
('B'-Marley mix-12"+=) *(ZANG 6T)* – ('A'-Zero gravity mix).
(cd-s++=) *(ZANG 6CD)* – ('A'-original rap mix).
(12") *(ZANG 6TX)* – ('A'-Creamatomic mix) / ('A'-Creamatomic instrumental) / ('A'-Cool atom mix) / ('A'-Cool atom instrumental).

Oct 90. (lp/c/cd) *(ZTT 3/+C/CD)* **NORTH AT ITS HEIGHTS** [26] [–]
– The only rhyme that bites / This ain't no fantasy / Dance yourself to death / Own worst enemy / The north at it's heights / Tunes splits the atom / Mancunian blues / The sequel / Primary rhyming / Dub at it's heights.

—— MC TUNES also released own single (7"/c-s/12"/cd-s/s12") in November 'PRIMARY RHYMING'; *(ZANG 10/+C/T/CD/TW)*, with 808 STATE still in tow. It hit UK No.67.

Oct 90. (7"/c-s) *(ZANG 5/+C) <TB 959>* **CUBIK (original mix). / OLYMPIC (flutey mix)** [10] [ ]
(12"+=/cd-s+=) *(ZANG 5 T/CD)* – ('A'-Pan-Am mix) / Olympic (Euro-bass mix). *<US version 12"ep/cd-ep; TB 959>*
(12") *(ZANG 5TX)* – Cubik (tomix) / Olympic (August '90) / Lambrusco cowboy (mix).

Feb 91. (7"/c-s/12") *(ZANG 14/+C/T)* **IN YER FACE. / LEO LEO (featuring Raagman)** [9] [–]
(cd-s+=) *(ZANG 14CD)* – ('A'-In yer face mix).
(12") *(ZANG 14TX)* – ('A'-Facially yours remix) / ('B'-Poonchanting instrumental).

—— next featured **BJORK** (Sugarcubes) – vocals (*)

Mar 91. (cd)(lp/c) *(9031 73755-2)(ZTT 6/+C) <TB/+C/CD 1042>*
EX:EL [4] May91 [ ]
– San Francisco / Spanish heart / Leo Leo / Qwart * / Nephatiti / Lift / Ooops * / Empire / In yer face / Cubik / Lambrusco cowboy / Techno ball. *(cd+=)* – Olympic. *(cd re-iss. Jan97; same) (cd re-iss. Jun98; ZTT 103CD)*

Apr 91. (7"/c-s) *(ZANG 19/+C) <TB 986>* **OOOPS. / THE SKI FAMILY** [42] [ ]
(12"+=/cd-s+=) *(ZANG 19 T/CD)* – 808091 (live).
(12") *(ZANG 19TX)* – ('A'-Utsula mix) / ('A'-Mellow Birds mix). *<US version 12"ep/cd-ep; TB 986>*

Aug 91. (7"/c-s) *(ZANG 20/+C)* **LIFT. / OPEN YOUR MIND** [38] [ ]
(12"+=/cd-s+=) *(ZANG 20 T/CD)* – ('A'-heavy mix) / ('B'-sound galore mix). *<US version 12"ep/c-ep/cd-ep; TB 989>*

—— MARTIN PRICE departed Oct'91 and formed label 'Sun Text'.
In Feb'92, they collaborated with DAVID BOWIE on a version of 'SOUND AND VISION'. Below single as "808 STATE featuring BJORK".

Aug 92. (7"/c-s) *(ZANG 33/+C) <TB 540>* **TIME BOMB. / NIMBUS** [ ] [ ]
('Fon'mix-12"+=/cd-s+=) *(ZANG 33 T/CD)* – Reaper repo (short mix) / Reaper repo.

Nov 92. (7"/c-s) *(ZANG 39/+C) <TB 553>* **ONE IN TEN 808. / ONE IN TEN UB40 VOCAL** [17] [ ]
(cd-s+=) *(ZANG 39CD) <TB12 553>* – ('A'-808 original mix) / ('A'-Fast Fon mix) / ('A'instrumental) / ('A'-Forcable Labotomy mix).
(12") *(ZANG 39T) <TBCD 553>* – ('A'-original mix) / ('A'-Fast Fon mix) / ('A'side) / ('A'-Forcable Labotomy mix).
(12") *(ZANG 39TX)* – ('A'-UB 40 vocal) / ('A'-UB40 full instrumental).

Jan 93. (7"/c-s) *(ZANG 38/+C)* **PLAN 9. / OLYMPIC '93 (The Word mix)** [50] [–]
('A'-Choki Galaxy mix-12"+=) *(ZANG 38T)* – ('A'-Guitars on fire mix).
(cd-s++=) *(ZANG 38CD)* – Nbambi (the April showers mix).

Feb 93. (cd)(lp/c) *(4509 91100-2)(ZTT 12/+C) <TBCD 1067>*
GORGEOUS [17] [ ]
– Plan 9 / Moses / Contrique / 10 x 10 / Timebomb / One in ten / Europa / Orbit / Black morpheus / Southern cross / Nimbus / Colony. *(cd re-iss. Jan97; same) (cd re-iss. Jun98; ZTT 104CD)*

Jun 93. (c-s) *(ZANG 42C)* **10 x 10 (radio mix). / LA LUZ (chunky funky mix)** [67] [–]
(12"+=) *(ZANG 42T)* – ('A'-black eye mix) / ('A'-trance mix).
('A'-hit man's club-10"+=) *(ZANG 42X)* – ('A'instrumental).
(cd-s) *(ZANG 42CD)* – (3 'A'mixes above) / ('A'-Rockathon mix) / ('A'vox mix) / ('A'beats mix) / ('A'hit man's acapella mix).

Aug 94. (c-s/12"/cd-s) *(ZANG 54 C/T/CD) <TB 629>*
BOMBADIN. / MARATHON [67] [ ]

Z.T.T. Z.T.T.

Jun 96. (12") *(ZANG 80T)* **BOND. / CHISLER** [57] [–]
(c-s/cd-s) *(ZANG 80 C/CD)* – ('A'side) / Bonded.

Jun 96. (cd/c/lp) *(0630 14356-2/-4/-1) <14356>* **DON SOLARIS** [ ] [ ]
– Intro / Bond / Bird / Azura / Black Dartangnon / Joyrider / Lopez / Balboa / Kohoutek / Mooz / Jerusahat / Banacheq. *(re-iss. Feb97; same) <US version on 'Hypnotic'> (cd re-iss. Jun98; ZTT 105CD)*
below featured LOUISE (from LAMB) on vocals

Aug 96. (12"/cd-s) *(ZANG 84 T/CD2)* **AZURA. / JOYRIDER / GOA** [ ] [–]
(cd-s) *(ZANG 84CD1)* – ('A'-4 mixes).

Jan 97. (c-s; as 808 STATE featuring JAMES DEAN BRADFIELD) *(ZANG 87C)* **LOPEZ / ('A'mix)** [20] [–]
(cd-s) *(ZAND 87CD)* – ('A'mixes).
(12") *(ZANG 87T)* – ('A'mixes).

Z.T.T. ZTT-Universal

May 98. (12"/cd-s) *(ZTT 98 T/CD1)* **PACIFIC. / CUBIK** [21] [–]
(cd-s) *(ZTT 98CD2)* – ('A'mixes).

May 98. (cd/c) *(ZTT 100 CD/C) <53139>* **808:88:98 (compilation)** [40] Jun98 [ ]
– Pacific 707 / Cubik / In yer face / The only rhyme that bites / Olympic / Ooops / Lift / One in ten / Plan 9 / Bombadin / Bond / Azura / Lopez / Crash / Pacific 808:98 / Cubik:98.

Slut Smalls not iss.

Jan 99. (7") *(SMALL 002)* **QUINCY'S LUNCH. / Jega: MOVE U.R. BODY** [ ] [–]

All Saints not iss.

Oct 99. (cd-ep; as 808 STATE & JON HASSELL) *(ASCD 017)*
VOICEPRINT (mixes) / STREETFAXX [ ] [–]

Bellboy not iss.

Nov 99. (12") *(BL 043)* **INVADERS** [ ] [–]

Circus Shadow

Nov 02. (cd) *(FYL 012) <156>* **OUTPOST TRANSMISSION** [ ] Apr03 [ ]
– 606 / Chopsumwong / Wheatstraw / Lemonsoul / Suntower / Bent / Souflex / Crossword / Lungfoo / Quincy's lunch / Dissadis / Doctors and nurses / Brown sauce / Long orange. *(d-lp iss.Dec02 on 'S160'; 005)*

□ Mark EITZEL (see under ⇒ AMERICAN MUSIC CLUB)

ELASTICA

Formed: London, England ... October '92 by JUSTINE FRISCHMANN, who had been an embryonic member of SUEDE, with then boyfriend, BRETT ANDERSON. Signing for the new 'Deceptive' label in 1993, JUSTINE and Co (namely DONNA MATTHEWS, ANNIE HOLLAND and JUSTIN WELSH) collected critical acclaim from the music press for their debut 45, 'STUTTER'. Their (early '94) follow-up, 'LINE UP', gave them a UK Top 20 and made American labels take note. 'Geffen' soon took up the option for worldwide sales as all awaited 1995's tip for the top and their first album. New wave of the new wave featuring fuzzgun WIRE-like guitars, their blatant plagiarism didn't go without notice when they had to settle out of court with WIRE for the use of 'Three Girl Rhumba' riff on the 'CONNECTION' hit. Soon after this, The STRANGLERS were paid out of court for 'No More Heroes'-esque backing on another hit, 'WAKING UP' (however bassist, JEAN-JAQUES BURNEL, is said to be a great fan). Finally released in Spring '95, their eponymous debut album went straight into the UK charts at No.1, ELASTICA's spkiy, punk-inspired sound the toast of Brit-pop's golden year with FRISCHMANN as the scene's uncrowned ice queen. Although HOLLAND departed in summer '95, it was almost a year before replacements were found in SHEILA CHIPPERFIELD conspicuous by their absence from the recording front. FRISCHMANN subsequently refused any more press interviews following the media circus surrounding her relationship with BLUR frontman, DAMON ALBARN. The only action from the ELASTICA camp of late was the ME ME ME project (featuring STEPHEN DUFFY, Blur's ALEX JAMES and CHARLIE BLOOR) who scored a UK Top 20 hit in summer '96 with 'HANGING AROUND'. Early in '99 and despite rumours of their demise, ELASTICA were still around in one way or another. By that summer, JUSTINE, JUSTIN, 1996 acquisition DAVID BUSH, new players PAUL JONES and MEW (who took DONNA's place) plus the returning ANNIE (who replaced SHEILA CHIPPERFIELD) made up the 6-piece that were back in August '99. To coincide with a new EP/mini-set release (recorded between 1996-99) entitled, er, 'ELASTICA', the band were more than happy to return to the limelight playing the Leeds and Reading festivals. Of the six tracks (which were incidently not eligible for the charts!), probably the highlight was the number 'HOW WE WROTE ELASTICA MAN', a FALL song with MARK E. on guesting vocals. As the century came to a close, ELASTICA were in the studio polishing off a long-awaited sophomore set . . . That album did indeed arrive in 2000, 'THE MENACE' undergoing countless false starts and the attentions of numerous producers before finally seeing the light of day. Patient fans expecting another dose of addictive razor-pop hits were to be disappointed as JUSTINE and Co enmeshed themselves in the oblique, angular dissonance of their art-punk progenitors. Only a minor hit single, 'MAD DOG', was forthcoming and the band split in October 2001 after a swansong 45 for 'Wichita' records. • **Songwriters:** FRISCHMANN lyrics / group compositions. • **Trivia:** DAMON ALBARN (as DAN ABNORMAL – anagram) played keyboards on their debut album and featured with them on Top Of The Pops.

Album rating: ELASTICA (*8) / ELASTICA mini (*5) / THE MENACE (*6)

JUSTINE FRISCHMANN (b.1968, Twickenham) – vocals, rhythm guitar (ex-SUEDE) / **DONNA MATTHEWS** (b. Newport, Wales) – vocals, guitar / **ANNIE HOLLAND** (b. Brighton, England) – bass / **JUSTIN WELCH** (b. Nuneaton, England) – drums (ex-SUEDE)

Deceptive | Sub Pop

Oct 93. (7") *(BLUFF 003)* *<SB 275>* **STUTTER. / PUSSYCAT** [ ] Aug94 [ ]
Jan 94. (7") *(BLUFF 004)* **LINE UP. / VASELINE** [20] [ ]
(12"+=/cd-s+=) *(BLUFF 004 T/CD)* – Rockunroll / Annie (both John Peel sessions).

Deceptive | D.G.C.

Oct 94. (7"/c-s) *(BLUFF 010/+C)* **CONNECTION. / SEE THAT ANIMAL** [17] [–]
(12"+=/cd-s+=) *(BLUFF 010 T/CD)* – Blue (demo) / Spastica.
Feb 95. (7"/c-s) *(BLUFF 011/+C)* **WAKING UP. / GLORIA** [13] [ ]
(12"+=/cd-s+=) *(BLUFF 011 T/CD)* – Car wash / Brighton rock.
Mar 95. (cd/c/lp) *(BLUFF 014 CD/C/LP)* *<24728>* **ELASTICA** [1] [66]
– Line up / Annie / Connection / Car song / Smile / Hold me now / S.O.F.T. / Indian song / Blue / All-nighter / Waking up / 2:1 / Vaseline / Never here / Stutter.
Mar 95. (c-s) *<19385>* **CONNECTION / GLORIA** [–] [53]

— In Jul'95, they guested on 'Sub Pop' 4x7"box-set 'HELTER SHELTER'.

Jun 95. (10"gold-ep/cd-ep) *<DGC 10/CD 22001>* **STUTTER / ROCKUNROLL. / 2:1 (1 F.M. evening session) / ANNIE (John Peel session)** [–] [67]

— ANNIE departed in August '95, and was replaced nearly a year later by **SHEILA CHIPPERFIELD** – bass / **DAVID BUSH** – keyboards (ex-FALL).

— ELASTICA were back in '99; **JUSTINE, JUSTIN, DAVID** and the returning **ANNIE** recruited **PAUL JONES** – guitar (ex-LINOLEUM) who repl. DONNA + **MEW** – keyboards (ex-HEAVE)

Aug 99. (12"ep/cd-ep) *(BLUFF 071 T/CD)* **ELASTICA EP** [ ] [–]
– How we wrote Elastica man / Nothing stays the same / Miami nice / KB / Operator / Generator.
(above was ineligible for the singles chart)

Deceptive | Atlantic

Apr 00. (cd/lp) *(BLUFF 075 CD/LP)* *<83386>* **THE MENACE** [24] [ ]
– Mad dog / Generator / How he wrote Elastica man / Image change / Your arse my place / Human / Nothing stays the same / Miami nice / Love like ours / KB / My sex / The way I like it / Da da da.
Jun 00. (7") *(BLUFF 077)* **MAD DOG. / SUICIDE** [44] [–]
(cd-s+=) *(BLUFF 077CD1)* – Bush baby.
(cd-s) *(BLUFF 077CD2)* – ('A'mixes) / ('A'video).

Wichita | not iss.

Nov 01. (7") *(WEBB 0265)* **THE BITCH DON'T WORK. / NO GOOD** [ ] [–]

— ELASTICA split late in October 2001

– compilations, etc. –

Nov 01. (cd) *Strange Fruit; (SFRSCD 101) / Koch; <8624>* **THE RADIO ONE SESSIONS** [ ] [ ]

ME ME ME

JUSTIN WELCH + ALEX JAMES (Blur), STEPHEN DUFFY + CHARLIE BLOOR

Indolent | not iss.

Aug 96. (c-s/cd-s) *(DUFF 005 C/CD)* **HANGING AROUND / HOLLYWOOD WIVES / TABITHA'S ISLAND** [19] [–]

ELBOW

Formed: Bury, Manchester, England . . . 1994 by GUY GARVEY, RICHARD JUPP, CRAIG POTTER, his brother MARK POTTER and PETE TURNER. Shortlisted for the Mercury Music Prize, this bittersweet collective were living proof that the Manchester music scene didn't just comprise of arrogant guitar bands kissing the feet of major labels. That said, ELBOW have mostly been kicked in the face by the majors: 'Island' dropped them as did 'E.M.I.'. But thankfully, they came bounding back to astound us with their melancholic blend of (in their own words) "prog rock, without the solos". It began when all five members met at college and frequented local haunts before they attracted the watchful eye of 'Island'. This in turn led to their debut EP, 'THE NOISEBOX', its title track 'POWDER BLUE' gaining a spot in John Peel's Festive 50 late '98. Independent record label 'Uglyman' raised the money to fund the EP's 'THE NEWBORN' and 'ANY DAY NOW', two breezy, rousing tracks heir to TURIN BRAKES, KINGS OF CONVENIENCE and the spiralling New Acoustic Movement. The acclaim for the tracks was phenomenal, with music journos citing ELBOW as the millennium's answer to RADIOHEAD (if there was such a thing!). This led to the release of their debut set 'ASLEEP IN THE BACK' (2001), an album of inspired beauty and elegance. Tracks such as 'POWDER BLUE' and 'CAN'T STOP' made you wonder what the major labels were thinking when they gave them the proverbial elbow. The album, unsurprisingly, was nominated for a Mercury music prize while it also managed a few weeks in the Top 20. ELBOW would return in summer 2003 to issue the downbeat, but excellent 'CAST OF THOUSANDS', a record which saw the lads unrestrained and reaching new creative peaks via their complex melodies and lyrics of torn relationships. The poignancy of SPIRITUALIZED resonated somewhere in the background, especially when the large, full-on gospel choirs kicked in, but it never sounded cheesy or over-orchestrated. Predictably, the album was critically aclaimed on its release, also striking a chord with the introspective COLDPLAY crowd, as 'CAST OF THOUSANDS' deservedly entered the British Top 10.

Album rating: ASLEEP IN THE BACK (*8) / CAST OF THOUSANDS (*7)

GUY GARVEY – vocals / **CRAIG POTTER** – organ / **MARK POTTER** – guitar / **PETE TURNER** – bass / **RICHARD JUPP** – drums

Soft | not iss.

Jan 98. (ltd-cd-ep) **THE NOISEBOX EP** [ ] [–]
– Powder blue / Red / George lassoes the Moon / Theme from Munroe Kelly / Can't stop.

Uglyman | not iss.

Aug 00. (cd-ep) *(UGLY 20)* **THE NEWBORN EP** [ ] [–]
– Newborn / Kisses / Bitten by the tailfly / None one.

Jan 01. (cd-ep/10"ep) *(UGLY 25/+V)* **ANY DAY NOW EP** [ ] [–]
– Any day now / Wurzel / George lassoes the moon / Don't mix your drinks.
(cd-s) *(UGLY 25VID)* – ('A'-video).

V2 | V2

Apr 01. (7") *(VVR 501615-7)* **RED. / VUM GARDA** [36] [–]
(cd-s+=) *(VVR 501615-3)* – About time.
(cd-s) *(VVR 501615-8)* – ('A'side) / Crow (acoustic) / Newborn (acoustic).

May 01. (cd/d-lp) *(<VVR 101588-2/-1>)* **ASLEEP IN THE BACK** [14] Jun01 [ ]
– Any day now / Red / Little beast / Powder blue / Bitten by the tailfly / Newborn / Don't mix your drinks / Presuming Ed (rest easy) / Coming second / Can't stop / Scattered black and whites. *(cd re-iss. Feb02; VVR 101901-2)*

Jul 01. (cd-s) *(VVR 501616-3)* **POWDER BLUE / SUFFER / ABOUT TIME (acoustic)** [41] [–]
(cd-s) *(VVR 501616-8)* – ('A'side) / Red (session) / Powder blue (Andy Votel mix).

Oct 01. (12"/cd-s) *(VVR 501617-6/-3)* **NEWBORN. / LUCKY WITH DISEASE / PRESS YOUR LIPS (NEWBORN) – El Presidente remix** [42] [–]
(cd-s) *(VVR 501617-8)* – ('A'side) / One thing that was bothering me / None one.

Feb 02. (cd-s) *(VVR 501870-3)* **ASLEEP IN THE BACK / COMING SECOND / STUMBLE** [19] [–]
(cd-s) *(VVR 501870-8)* – ('A'side) / Coming second (Misery Lab mix) / Stumble.

Aug 03. (cd-s) *(VVR 502180-3)* **FALLEN ANGEL / LOSS / WHISPER GRASS** [19] [–]
(cd-s) *(VVR 502180-8)* – ('A'side) / Brave new shave / ('A'-remix).

Aug 03. (cd/lp) *(VVR 102181-2/-1)* *<27161>* **CAST OF THOUSANDS** [7] Jan04 [ ]
– Ribcage / Fallen angel / Fugitive motel / Snooks (progress report) / Switching off / Not a job / I've got a number / Buttons and zips / Crawling with idiot / Grace under pressure / Flying dream 143. *(cd re-iss. Nov03 +dvd; VVR 102181-0)*

Oct 03. (cd-s) *(VVR 502182-3)* **FUGITIVE MOTEL / SWITCHING OFF (acoustic) / RIBCAGE (Andy Cato mix)** [44] [–]
(cd-s) *(VVR 502182-8)* – ('A'-RJD2 mix) / Love blown down / Ribcage (Kinobe mix).

□ ELECTRAFIXION
(see under ⇒ ECHO & THE BUNNYMEN)

ELECTRIC FLAG

Formed: San Francisco, California, USA . . . April '67 by MIKE BLOOMFIELD, an ex-session man for the likes of BOB DYLAN, OTIS REDDING and WILSON PICKETT. With BUDDY MILES, NICK GRAVENITES, BARRY GOLDBERG, HARVEY BROOKS, MARCUS DOUBLEDAY, PETER STAZZA and HERBIE RICH completing the formidable line-up, they made their live debut at the seminal Monterey Pop Festival the same year. After laying down tracks (as The AMERICAN MUSIC BAND) for cult movie, 'The Trip' (directed by Jack Nicholson and starring Peter Fonda), they subsequently signed to 'Columbia'. The following year, the 'FLAG finally released their much-anticipated debut album, 'A LONG TIME COMIN'', the outfit's brassy blues excursions best sampled on 'GROOVIN' IS EASY' and 'SITTIN' IN CIRCLES'. Later in the year, BLOOMFIELD jumped ship to form the collaborative (and hugely popular) 'SUPER SESSIONS' project with AL KOOPER and STEVE STILLS. With BUDDY MILES now at the helm, The ELECTRIC FLAG limped on for a further six months, finally disbanding in '69 after the release of an eponymous follow-up. BLOOMFIELD released a few low-key solo albums (including a collaborative 1973 set, 'TRIUMVRATE', with DR. JOHN and JOHN HAMMOND) in the early 70's, before taking up the opportunity to reform the 'FLAG for a one-off 1974 set, 'THE BAND KEPT PLAYING'. In the mid 70's, BLOOMFIELD teamed up once more with GOLDBERG, forming the workmanlike KGB, before he delivered a string of trad blues sets later in the 70's. Tragically, the guitarist was to meet with an untimely death via a drug overdose on the 15th of February '81. • **Covered:** KILLING FLOOR (Howlin' Wolf) / YOU THREW YOUR LOVE ON ME TOO STRONG (Albert King) / IT TAKES A LOT TO LAUGH, IT TAKES A LOT TO CRY (Bob Dylan) / etc. KGB covered I'VE GOT A FEELING (Beatles).

Album rating: THE TRIP soundtrack (*4) / A LONG TIME COMIN' (*7) / THE ELECTRIC FLAG (*4) / THE BAND KEPT PLAYIN' (*3) / OLD GLORY: THE BEST OF ELECTRIC FLAG compilation (*7) / Michael Bloomfield: SUPER SESSION (*8; by Mike Bloomfield, Al Kooper & Steve Stills) / THE LIVE ADVENTURES OF MIKE BLOOMFIELD AND AL KOOPER (*4; with Al Kooper) / IT'S NOT KILLING ME (*4) / LIVE AT BILL GRAHAM'S FILLMORE EAST (*5) / TRIUMVIRATE (*6; with John Paul Hammond & Dr.John) / TRY IT BEFORE YOU BUY IT (*4) / KGB (*4; with KGB) / MOTION (*3; with KGB) / IF YOU LOVE THESE BLUES, PLAY 'EM AS YOU PLEASE (*5) / ANALINE (*4) / COUNT TALENT AND THE ORIGINALS (*4) / MICHAEL BLOOMFIELD (*4) / MICHAEL BLOOMFIELD & WOODY HARRIS (*4) / BETWEEN A HARD PLACE AND THE GROUND (*4) / CRUISIN' FOR A BRUISIN' (*4) / LIVIN' IN THE FAST LANE (*4) / BLOOMFIELD – A RETROSPECTIVE compilation (*6) / DON'T SAY THAT I AIN'T YOUR MAN compilation (*7)

MICHAEL BLOOMFIELD (b.28 Jul'44, Chicago, Illinois) – guitar, percussion (ex-PAUL BUTTERFIELD BLUES BAND) / **NICK GRAVENITES** (b. Chicago) – vocals, guitar / **BARRY GOLDBERG** – keyboards (ex-MITCH RYDER, ex-duo w/ STEVE MILLER) / **BUDDY MILES** (b. 5 Sep'46, Omaha, Nebraska) – drums, percussion / **HARVEY BROOKS** – bass, guitar / **MARCUS DOUBLEDAY** – trumpet, percussion / plus **PETER STRAZZA** – tenor sax / **HERBIE RICH** – guitar, saxophone

not iss. | Tower

Jun 67. (lp; The ELECTRIC FLAG, AN AMERICAN MUSIC BAND) *<ST 5908>* **THE TRIP (soundtrack)** [–] [ ]
– Peter's trip / Joint passing / Psyche soap / M-23 / Synethesia / A little head / Hobbit / Inner pocket / Fewghh / Green and gold / The other Ed Norton / Flash, bam pow / Home room / Peter gets off / Practice music / Fine jung thing / Senior citizen / Gettin' hard. *(UK-iss.Mar87 on 'Edsel'; ED 211) (cd-iss. Jun03 on 'Fabulous'; FABCD 142)*

Jul 67. (7") *<929>* **PETER'S TRIP. / GREEN AND GOLD** [–] [ ]

C.B.S. | Columbia

Jul 68. (lp) *(CBS 62394)* *<9597>* **A LONG TIME COMIN'** [ ] Apr68 [31]
– Killing floor / Groovin' is easy / Over-lovin' you / She should have just / Wine / Texas / Sittin' in circles / You don't realise / Another country / Easy rider. *(re-iss. Aug74 on 'Embassy-CBS'; 31061) <re-iss. Jul02; same>*

Jul 68. (7") *(CBS 3584)* *<44307>* **GROOVIN' IS EASY. / OVER-LOVIN' YOU** [ ] [ ]

—— BLOOMFIELD left to to go solo & collaborate with AL KOOPER, etc.

Jan 69. (lp) *(CBS 63462)* *<9714>* **THE ELECTRIC FLAG** [ ] [76]
– Soul searchin' / Sunny / With time there is change / Nothing to do / See to your neighbor / Qualified / Hey, little girl / Mystery / My woman that hangs around the house.

Mar 69. (7") *(CBS 4066)* *<44376>* **SUNNY. / SOUL SEARCHIN'** [ ] [ ]

—— Disband '69, GOLDBERG went solo and BROOKS joined FABULOUS RHINESTONES. BUDDY MILES formed his own EXPRESS and joined JIMI HENDRIX's BAND OF GYPSIES.

MIKE BLOOMFIELD, AL KOOPER & STEVE STILLS

(AL KOOPER ex-BLUES PROJECT) / (STEVE STILLS of-CROSBY, STILLS & NASH)

Sep 68. (lp) *(63396) <CS 9701>* **SUPER SESSION** Aug68 12
– Albert's shuffle / Stop / Man's temptation / His holy modal majesty / Really / It takes a lot to laugh, it takes a train to cry / Seasons of the witch / You don't love me / Harvey's tune. *(quad-lp 1973; Q 63396) (cd-iss. 1988; CD 63396) (re-iss. cd Aug91 on 'Essential'; ESSCD 951) <(cd re-iss. Apr03 on 'Sony'+=; 63406>* – Albert's shuffle (alt.) / Season of the witch (alt.) / Blues for nothing / Fat grey cloud (live).

Oct 68. (7") *(3770) <44657>* **SEASON OF THE WITCH. / ALBERT'S SHUFFLE**

MIKE BLOOMFIELD & AL KOOPER

— also featured **ELVIN BISHOP + CARLOS SANTANA**

Feb 69. (d-lp) *(66216) <PG 6>* **THE LIVE ADVENTURES OF MIKE BLOOMFIELD AND AL KOOPER (live)** Jan69 18
– The 59th Street Bridge song / I wonder who / Her holy modal highness / The weight – Mary Ann / Together 'til the end of time / That's all right – Green onions / Sonny Boy Williamson / No more lonely night / Dear Mr.Fantasy / You threw your love on me so strong / Finale – Refugee. *(re-iss. May88 on 'Edsel'; DED 261) (d-cd-iss. Jun94 & Mar97 on 'Legacy'; 485151-2)*

Feb 69. (7") *<44678>* **THE WEIGHT. / MAN'S TEMPTATION** –

Mar 69. (7") *(CBS 4094)* **THE WEIGHT. / THE 59th STREET BRIDGE SONG** –

— BLOOMFIELD then (Apr69) appeared on MUDDY WATERS live album 'Fathers And Sons'.

MICHAEL BLOOMFIELD

— solo **NICK GRAVENITES** – vocals / **JOHN KAHN** – bass / **MARK NAFTKAN** – keyboards / **IRA KAMIN** – keyboards / **BOB JONES** – drums

Nov 69. (lp) *(CBS 63652) <9883>* **IT'S NOT KILLING ME** Oct69
– If you see my baby / For anyone you meet / Good old guy / Far too many nights / It's not killing me / Next time you see me / Michael's lament / Why must my baby / The ones I loved are gone / Don't think about it, baby / Goofers.

Nov 70. (lp) *(CBS 63816) <9893>* **LIVE AT BILL GRAHAM'S FILLMORE EAST (live)**
– It takes time / Oh mama / Love got me / Blues on a westside / One more mile to go / It's about time / Carmelita skiffle.

— MIKE back into session work, until helping out NICK GRAVENITES on his soundtrack album 'Steelyard Blues' 1973. The same year he collaborated with **HAMMOND** – vocals / **DR. JOHN** – piano, vocals

Aug 73. (lp; by MIKE BLOOMFIELD, JOHN PAUL HAMMOND & DR. JOHN) *(CBS 65659) <32172>* **TRIUMVIRATE** Jun73
– Cha-dooky-doo / Last night / I yi yi / Just to be with you / Baby let me kiss you / Sho bout to drive me wild / It hurts me too / Rock me baby / Ground hog blues / Pretty thing. *(re-iss. May87 on 'Edsel'; ED 228) (cd-iss. Jun94 on 'Sony Europe')*

ELECTRIC FLAG

BLOOMFIELD with **GRAVENITES, GOLDBERG + MILES,** plus new man **ROGER 'Jellyroll' TROY** – bass, vocals

Atlantic Atlantic

Nov 74. (lp) *(K 50090) <18112>* **THE BAND KEPT PLAYING**
– Sweet soul music / Every now and then / Sudden change / Earthquake country / Doctor oh doctor / Lonely song / Make your love / Inside information / Talkin' won't get it / The band kept playing. *<(cd-iss. Apr02 on 'Wounded Bird'; WOU 8112)>*

Nov 74. (7") *<3222>* **SWEET SOUL MUSIC. / EVERY NOW AND THEN** –

Feb 75. (7") *<3237>* **THE BAND KEPT PLAYING. / DOCTOR OH DOCTOR** –

— Broke-up again in 1975

– compilations, etc. –

Nov 71. (lp) *C.B.S.; (64337) / Columbia; <10169>* **THE BEST OF THE ELECTRIC FLAG**

Nov 83. (lp) *Thunderbolt; (THBL 1.006)* **GROOVIN' IS EASY (live)** –
(cd-iss. Nov88; CDTB 1.006)

Jul 95. (cd) *Columbia; (CK 57629)* **OLD GLORY (THE BEST OF THE ELECTRIC FLAG)** –

KGB

BLOOMFIELD + GOLDBERG with **RAY KENNEDY** – vocals / **RICK GRECH** – bass / **CARMINE APPICE** – drums

M.C.A. M.C.A.

Jun 76. (lp) *(MCF 2749) <2166>* **KGB** Mar76
– Let me love you / Midnight traveler / I've got a feeling / High roller / Sail on sailor / Workin' for the children / You got the notion / Baby should I stay or go / It's gonna be a hard night / Magic in your touch.

Jun 76. (7") *<40544>* **MIDNIGHT TRAVELER. / MAGIC IN YOUR TOUCH** –

Sep 76. (7") *<40573>* **SAIL ON SAILOR. / WORKIN' FOR THE CHILDREN** –

— **GREG SUTTON** – bass repl. GRECH **BEN SCHULTZ** – guitar repl. BLOOMFIELD who went solo again (see further below)

Jan 77. (lp) *(MCF 2773) <2221>* **MOTION**
– Woman, stop watcha doin' / I only need a next time / My serene Coleene / Lookin' for a better way / Lay it all down / Treading water / Goin' through the motions / Je t'aime / Determination.

MICHAEL BLOOMFIELD

— with **NICK GRAVENITES** – guitar, vocals / **ROGER TROY + DOUG KILMER** – bass / **IRA KAMIN** – keyboards / **TOM DONLINGER + DAVE NEDITCH** – drums / **ERIC KRISS** – piano

Sonet Guitar Player

Aug 77. (lp) *(SNTF 726) <3002>* **IF YOU LOVE THESE BLUES, PLAY 'EM AS YOU PLEASE**
– If you love these blues / Hey foreman / India / Death cell rounder blues / City girl / Kansas City / Mama lion / Thrift shop rag / Death in the family / East Colorado blues / Blue ghost blues / The train is gone / The alter song.

— now w / **GRAVENITES / TROY + BOB JONES** – drums / **MARCIA ANN TAYLOR + ANNA RIZZO** – vocals

Sonet Takoma

Dec 77. (lp) *(SNTF 749) <1059>* **ANALINE**
– Peepin' an a moanin' / Mr. Johnson & Mr. Dunn / Frankie and Johnny / At the cross / Big 'C' blues / Hilo waltz / Effionna rag / Mood indingo / Analine.

1978. (lp) *(82516)* **COUNT TALENT AND THE ORIGINALS** –
– Love walk / You was wrong / Peach tree man / Sammy knows how to party / When I need you / I need your loving / Bad man / Saturday night / You're changin' / Let the people dance.
(above was issued on 'T.K.' in the UK)

— **DAVID SHOREY** – bass, vocals repl. TROY

Nov 78. (lp) *<1063>* **MICHAEL BLOOMFIELD** –
– Guitar king / Knockin' myself out / My children, my children / Women loving each other / Sloppy drunk / You took my money / See that my grave is kept clean / The gospel truth.

— **ROGER TROY** – bass returned to replace SHOREY

Nov 79. (lp) *<7070>* **BETWEEN THE HARD PLACE AND THE GROUND** –
– Lights out / Between the hard place and the ground / Big chief from New Orleans / Kid man blues / Orphans blues / Juke joint / Your friends. *(re-iss. Sep90 on 'Thunderbolt' cd/lp; CDTB/THBL 076) (cd re-iss. Dec99 on 'MagMid'; MM 041)*

— now w/ **HENRY ODEN** – bass / **TOM RIZZO** – drums / **JONATHAN CRAMER** – keyboards / **HART McNEE** – baritone sax / **KING PERKOFF + DERRICK WALKER** – tenor sax

Jun 81. (lp) *(SNTF 860) <7091>* **CRUISIN' FOR A BRUISIN'**
– Cruisin' for a bruisin' / Linda Lu / Papa mama rompah stompah / Jurker's blues / Midnight / It'll be me / Motorized blues / Mathilda / Winter bird / Snowblind.

— He brought back a near 1977 line-up.

Waterhouse not iss.

Apr 82. (lp) *(DAMP 100)* **LIVING IN THE FAST LANE** –
– Maudie / Shine on love / Roots / Let them talk / Watkin's rag / Andy's bad / When I get home / Used to it / Big "C" blues / The dizz rag. *(cd-iss. May91 on 'Line'; LICD 900395)*

— Above was his last album, recorded just before his death of a drug overdose on the 15th of February '81.

– (MIKE BLOOMFIELD) compilations –

Apr 80. (lp; MIKE BLOOMFIELD & WOODY HARRIS) *Kicking Mule; <(KM 164>)* **BLOOMFIELD & HARRIS – INITIAL SHOCK (live)**
– Eyesight to the blind / Woman lovin' each other / Linda Lu / Kansas City / Blues in B-flat / Medley: Darktown strutters ball – Mop top – Call me a dog / I'm glad I'm Jewish / Great gifts from Heaven / Lo, though I am thee / Jockey blues / Between the hard place and the ground / Don't lie to me / Cherry red / Uncle Bob's barrelhouse blues / Wee wee hours / Vamp in C / One of these days.

Jan 84. (d-lp/d-c) *C.B.S.; (CBS/40 22164)* **BLOOMFIELD – (A RETROSPECTIVE)** –
– I've got my mojo working / Born in Chicago / Texas / Groovin' is easy / Killing floor / You don't realise / Wine / Albert's shuffle / Stop / I wonder who / You're killing my love / Goofers / It hurts me too / Relaxin' blues / Blues for Jimmy Yancey / Sunnyland Slim and Otis Spann / Woodyard street / Midnight on my radio / Why Lord, oh why? / Easy rider.

Apr 84. (lp) *Thunderbolt; (THBL 1.009)* **AMERICAN HERO** –
(cd-iss. Mar88; CDTB 1.009)

Jun 87. (lp) *Demon; (FIEND 92)* **I'M WITH YOU ALWAYS** (rare) –
(cd-iss. Aug90; FIENDCD 92)

Nov 92. (cd) *Skyranch; (SR 652328)* **THE LOST WORKS** –

Mar 94. (cd/c) *Shanachie; (SHCD/SHMC 99007)* **BLUES, GOSPEL AND RAGTIME GUITAR INSTRUMENTALS** –

Jun 94. (cd/c) *Columbia; (476721-2/-4)* **DON'T SAY THAT I AIN'T YOU MAN (ESSENTIAL BLUES 1964-69)** –

Mar 96. (cd) *Prestige; (CDSGP 0216)* **KNOCKIN' MYSELF OUT** –

May 96. (cd) *Affinity; (840089-2)* **A TRUE SOUL BROTHER** –

Oct 96. (cd) *Thunderbolt; (CDTB 179)* **GOSPEL TRUTH** –

ELECTRIC LIGHT ORCHESTRA

Formed: Birmingham, England . . . 1968 by ROY WOOD, as an alternative to his other group The MOVE who were drifting into cabaret circuit decline. In 1969, he offered close friend JEFF LYNNE a place in The MOVE, although the singer he resisted and waited until ROY came up with ELO in 1971. Gathering in an array of outlandish but highly talented musicians (namely BEV BEVAN, RICHARD TANDY, BILL HUNT, WILF GIBSON, HUGH McDOWELL and ANDY CRAIG), the two outfits co-existed at this period, the eponymous ELECTRIC LIGHT ORCHESTRA debut, finally hitting the shops later that year. Much lawded by the critics, it didn't hit the UK Top 40 until the single, '10538 OVERTURE', made the Top 10 in August 1972. WOOD subsequently departed both ELO and The MOVE to form glam/flash rockers, WIZZARD, which left JEFF LYNNE as the group's main man. A creative BEATLES influenced rock/pop outfit who relied heavily on string-laden themes and a romanticised lyrical future, the new line-up (without WIZZARD bound HUNT and McDOWELL) rejuvenated a past Chuck Berry classic 'ROLL OVER BEETHOVEN' to the heights of the Top 10. The accompanying follow-up album, 'II' (1973), again made the British Top 40 and ELO enjoyed a further major chart hit with the infectious 'SHOWDOWN' single later that year. The track's more pop-friendly approach indicated the direction LYNNE would steer the band over the coming decade; both 'ON THE THIRD DAY' (1973) and 'EL DORADO . . .' (1974) saw him hone his songwriting skills, something which paid off when 'CAN'T GET IT OUT OF MY HEAD' became a surprise US Top 10 hit, boosting Statside sales of the latter album and taking it into the American Top 20. Subsequent album, 'FACE THE MUSIC' (1975), established the band as a major concert attraction across the Atlantic, where they spent much of their time touring. Though that album's 'EVIL WOMAN' had made the UK Top 10, they finally re-established themselves in their home country with 'A NEW WORLD RECORD' (1976). ELO reached a commercial peak towards the end of the decade when their finely crafted, harmony-laden songs represented everything the thriving punk scene set out to destroy; both 'OUT OF THE BLUE' (1977) and 'DISCOVERY' (1979) were massive transatlantic successes, while the band scored a formidable run of chart hits including 'MR. BLUE SKY', 'SWEET TALKIN' WOMAN', 'SHINE A LITTLE LOVE' and the classic 'DON'T BRING ME DOWN'. In summer 1980, a collaboration with OLIVIA NEWTON JOHN on the dreamy 'XANADU' provided the band with their only No.1 hit, the track taken from the soundtrack to the film of the same name. The hits continued to roll in with the inimitable cheesiness of 'TICKET TO THE MOON', 'HOLD ON TIGHT' and 'ROCK'N'ROLL IS KING', the latter track being their last Top 40 hit. As their chart success dried up in the mid-80's, LYNNE helped form The TRAVELING WILBURYS alongside BOB DYLAN, GEORGE HARRISON, ROY ORBISON and TOM PETTY. BEVAN eventually emerged in the early 90's with an ELO Mk.II, although their material inevitably lacked LYNNE's songwriting spark. The bearded one had produced DAVE EDMUNDS (1981-84), BRIAN WILSON (1988) and TOM PETTY (1989), to name just a few and released a solo album, 'ARMCHAIR THEATER' in 1990 which hit the UK Top 30. More than a decade later, LYNNE chose to resurrect the ELO moniker for 'ZOOM' (2001), a solo set in all but name but as close to the band's classic 70's sound as anything since, well, the 70's. Featuring JEFF's girlfriend (and former solo artiste), ROSIE VELA, the album touched all the bases that made ELO great way back when: a pristine pop sensibility, larger than life BEATLES-esque harmonies, retro bubblegum tendencies, lavish arrangements and flawless but sympathetic production. Unsurprisingly it failed to make much of a mark commercially, despite the fact that LYNNE knows more about so called "pop" music than most of the two-bit acts pimping their vacuous wares in the Top 20.

Album rating: ELECTRIC LIGHT ORCHESTRA (aka 'NO ANSWER' US) (*5) / ELECTRIC LIGHT ORCHESTRA II (*4) / ON THE THIRD DAY (*6) / THE NIGHT THE LIGHTS WENT ON IN LONG BEACH (*4) / ELDORADO (*7) / FACE THE MUSIC (*6) / OLE ELO compilation (*6) / A NEW WORLD RECORD (*6) / OUT OF THE BLUE (*8) / DISCOVERY (*5) / ELO'S GREATEST HITS compilation (*8) / XANADU with Olivia Newton-John (*4) / TIME (*4) / SECRET MESSAGES (*4) / BALANCE OF POWER (*4) / PART II (*2; as Electric Light Orchestra Part II) / MOMENT OF TRUTH (*3; as Electric Light Orchestra Part II) / STRANGE MUSIC: THE BEST OF ELECTRIC LIGHT ORCHESTRA compilation (*7) / ZOOM (*6)

ROY WOOD (b. 8 Nov'46) – cello, vocals, multi (ex-MOVE) / **JEFF LYNNE** (b.30 Dec'47) – vocals guitar (ex-MOVE, ex-IDLE RACE) / **BEV BEVAN** (b. BEVERLEY, 24 Nov'46) – drums, vocals (ex-MOVE) / **RICHARD TANDY** (b.26 Nov'48) – bass, keyboards, vocals (ex-BALLS, ex-UGLYS) / **BILL HUNT** – keyboards, French horn / **WILF GIBSON** – violin / **HUGH McDOWELL** (b.31 Jul'53, London, England) – cello / **ANDY CRAIG** – cello

Harvest U.A.

Dec 71. (lp) *(SHVL 797)* *<5573>* **THE ELECTRIC LIGHT ORCHESTRA** <US-title 'NO ANSWER'> 32
– 10538 overture / Look at me now / Nellie takes her bow / The battle of Marston Moor (July 2nd, 1644) / First movement (jumpin' biz) / Mr. Radio / Manhattan rumble (49th Street massacre) / Queen of the hours / Whisper in the night. *(re-iss. Nov83 on 'Fame' lp/c; FA/TCFA 4130841)*

Jul 72. (7") *(HAR 5053)* **10538 OVERTURE. / FIRST MOVEMENT (JUMPIN' BIZ)** 9 –

Sep 72. (7") *<50914>* **10538 OVERTURE. / THE BATTLE OF MARSTON MOOR (JULY 2ND, 1644)** –

— **MIKE EDWARDS** – cello repl. ROY WOOD who formed WIZZARD (also went solo) **MICHAEL DE ALBUQUERQUE** – bass repl. HUNT and McDOWELL who joined WIZZARD / **COLIN WALKER** – cello repl. ANDY CRAIG

Jan 73. (7") *(HAR 5063) <173>* **ROLL OVER BEETHOVEN. / QUEEN OF THE HOURS** [6] Apr73 [42]

Feb 73. (lp) *(SHVL 806) <040>* **ELECTRIC LIGHT ORCHESTRA II** [35] [62]
– In old England town (boogie #2) / Momma / Roll over Beethoven / From the sun to the world (boogie #1) / Kuiama. *(re-iss. May82 on 'Fame' lp/c; FA/TCFA 3003)*

Sep 73. (7") *(HAR 5077) <337>* **SHOWDOWN. / IN OLD ENGLAND TOWN** [12] Nov73 [53]

— **MIK KAMINSKI** (b. 2 Sep'51, Harrogate, England) – violin repl. GIBSON / **HUGH McDOWELL** – cello returned to repl. WALKER (above 2 in septet with **LYNNE, BEVAN, TANDY, WALKER ALBUQUERQUE** and **EDWARDS.**

Warners U.A.

Dec 73. (lp/c) *(K/K4 56021) <188>* **ON THE THIRD DAY** [ ] [52]
– Ocean breakup – King of the universe / Daybreaker / Bluebird is dead / Oh no, not Susan / New world rising / Ocean breakup (reprise) / Showdown / Daybreaker / Ma-Ma-Ma belle / Dreaming of 4000 / In the hall of the Mountain King. *(re-iss. 1977 on 'United Artists' lp/c; UAG/UAC 30091) (re-iss. Jun77 on 'Jet' clear-lp/c; JET LP/CA 202)*

Mar 74. (7") *(K 16349)* **MA-MA-MA BELLE. / CAN'T FIND THE TITLE** [22] [–]

Mar 74. (lp) *<UALA 318>* **THE NIGHT THE LIGHT WENT OUT IN LONG BEACH (live)** [–] [ ]
– Daybreaker / Showdown / Daytripper / 10538 overture / Mik's solo / Orange blossom special / Medley: In the hall of the mountain king – Great balls of fire / Roll over Beethoven. *(UK-iss.Nov85 on 'Epic' lp/c; EPC/40 32700)*

Apr 74. (7") *<405>* **DAYBREAKER (live). / MA-MA-MA BELLE (live)** [–] [87]

Jun 74. (7") *(K 16510) <573>* **CAN'T GET IT OUT OF MY HEAD. / ILLUSIONS IN G MAJOR** [ ] Dec74 [9]

Oct 74. (lp/c) *(K/K4 56090) <UALA 339>* **ELDORADO – A SYMPHONY BY THE ELECTRIC LIGHT ORCHESTRA** [ ] [16]
– Eldorado – overture / Can't get it out of my head / Boy blue / Larendo tornado / Poor boy (the greenwood) / Mister Kingdom / Nobody's child / Illusions in G major / Eldorado – finale. *(re-iss. 1977 on 'United Artists' lp/c; UAG/UAC 30092) (re-iss. Jun77 on 'Jet' yellow-lp/c; JET LP/CA 203) (re-iss. 1986; JETLP 32397)*

Nov 74. (7") **ELDORADO. / BOY BLUE** [–] [ ]

— **KELLY GROUCUTT** (b. 8 Sep'45, Coseley, England) – bass, vocals repl. ALBUQUERQUE / **MELVYN GALE** (b.15 Jan'52, London) – cello repl. EDWARDS

Jet Jet

Oct 75. (lp/c) *(JET LP/TC 11) <546>* **FACE THE MUSIC** [ ] [8]
– Fire on high / Waterfall / Evil woman / Night rider / Poker / Strange magic / Down home town / One summer dream. *(re-iss. Oct76 on 'Jet-United Artists' lp/c; UAG/UAC 30034) (re-iss. Mar77 green-lp/c; JET LP/CA 201) (re-iss. Jun85 on 'Epic'; lp/c; (EPC/40 32544) (cd-iss. Nov91 on 'Pickwick'; 9825962) (re-iss. cd Mar94 on 'Sony Collectors')*

Dec 75. (7") *(JET 764) <JET 729>* **EVIL WOMAN. / 10538 OVERTURE (live)** [10] Oct75 [10]

Mar 76. (7") *(JET 769)* **NIGHT RIDER. / DAYBREAKER** [ ] [–]

Mar 76. (7") *<JET 770>* **STRANGE MAGIC. / NEW WORLD RECORD** [–] [14]

Jun 76. (7") *(JET 779)* **STRANGE MAGIC. / SHOWDOWN (live)** [38] [–]

Jul 76. (7") *<JET 842>* **SHOWDOWN. / DAYBREAKER (live)** [–] [59]

U.A. Jet

Oct 76. (7",7"blue) *(UP 36184)* **LIVIN' THING. / FIRE ON HIGH** [4] [–]

Oct 76. (7") *<JET 888>* **LIVIN' THING. / MA-MA-MA BELLE** [–] [13]

Nov 76. (lp/c) *(UAG/UAC 30017) <679>* **A NEW WORLD RECORD** [6] Oct76 [5]
– Tightrope / Telephone line / Rockaria! / Mission (a new world record) / So fine / Livin' thing / Above the clouds / Do ya / Shangri-la. *(re-iss. Jun77 red-lp/c; JET LP/CA 200) (re-iss. 1985 on 'Epic' lp/c; JET LP/CA 32545) (cd-iss. Mar87; CDJET 200) (re-iss. cd Apr89; JETCD 32545) (re-iss. Sep89 on 'Pickwick' lp/c/cd; 902198-1/-4/-2)*

Jan 77. (7") *<JET 939>* **DO YA. / NIGHTRIDER** [–] [24]

Feb 77. (7") *(UP 36209)* **ROCKARIA!. / POKER** [9] [ ]
(re-iss. May78; SJET 100)

May 77. (7"m) *(UP 36254)* **TELEPHONE LINE. / POORBOY (THE GREENWOOD) / KING OF THE UNIVERSE** [8] [–]
(re-iss. May78; SJET 101)

May 77. (7") *<JET 1000>* **TELEPHONE LINE. / POORBOY (THE GREENWOOD)** [–] [7]

Oct 77. (7") *(UP 36313) <1099>* **TURN TO STONE. / MISTER KINGDOM** [18] Nov77 [13]
(re-iss. May78; SJET 103)

Nov 77. (d-lp/d-c) *(UAR/UAC 100) <823>* **OUT OF THE BLUE** [4] [4]
– Turn to stone / It's over / Sweet talkin' woman / Across the border / Night in the city / Starlight / Jungle / Believe me now / Steppin' out / Standing in the rain / Summer and lightning / Mr. Blue Sky / Sweet is the night / The whale / Wild west hero / Birmingham Blues. *(re-iss. 1978 on double-blue-lp; JETDP 400) (re-iss. May87 on 'Epic' d-lp/d-c/d-cd; 450885-1/-4/-2) (re-iss. cd Jun91 on 'Epic')*

Jan 78. (7") *(UP 36342) <5050>* **MR. BLUE SKY. / ONE SUMMER DREAM** [6] Jun78 [35]
(re-iss. May78 in 7"blue; SJET 104)

Jet Jet

Feb 78. (7") *<1145>* **SWEET TALKIN' WOMAN. / FIRE ON HIGH** [–] [17]

Jun 78. (7"/12"yellow) *(SJET/+12 109)* **WILD WEST HERO. / ELDORADO** [6] [–]

Oct 78. (7") *<5052>* **IT'S OVER. / THE WHALE** [–] [75]

Sep 78. (7",7"mauve/12"mauve) *(SJET/+12 121)* **SWEET TALKIN' WOMAN. / BLUEBIRD IS DEAD** [6] [–]

May 79. (7"/12",12"white) *(SJET/+12 144) <5057>* **SHINE A LITTLE LOVE. / JUNGLE** [6] [8]

Jun 79. (lp/c) *(JET LX/CX 500) <35769>* **DISCOVERY** [1] [5]
– Shine a little love / Confusion / Need her love / The diary of Horace Wimp / Last train to London / Midnight blue / On the run / Wishing / Don't bring me down. *(re-iss. Nov86 on 'Epic' lp/c; EPC/40 450083-1/-4) (cd-iss. Apr87; CDJET 500) (re-iss. cd Jun91 on 'Epic'; 450083-2)*

Jul 79. (7") *(JET 150)* **THE DIARY OF HORACE WIMP. / DOWN HOME TOWN** [6] [–]

Aug 79. (7"/12") *(JET/+12 153) <5060>* **DON'T BRING ME DOWN. / DREAMING OF 4000** [3] [4]

Oct 79. (7") *<5064>* **CONFUSION. / POKER** [–] [37]

Nov 79. (7") *(JET 166)* **CONFUSION. / LAST TRAIN TO LONDON** [8] [–]

Nov 79. Jet; (lp/c) *(JET LX/CX 525) <36310>* **ELO'S GREATEST HITS** (compilation) [7] [30]
– Telephone line / Evil woman / Livin' thing / Can't get it out of my head / Showdown / Turn to stone / Rockarai / Sweet talkin' woman / Ma-ma-ma belle / Strange magic / Mr. Blue sky. *(re-iss. Jan87 on 'Epic' lp/c; 450357-1/-4) (cd-iss. Dec86 on 'Epic; CDJET 525)*

Jan 80. (7") *<5067>* **LAST TRAIN TO LONDON. / DOWN HOME TOWN** [–] [39]

— Now trimmed basic quartet of **LYNNE, BEVAN, TANDY** and **GROUCUTT** (KAMINSKI formed VIOLINSKI) (McDOWELL and GALE also departed). For below album / singles they shared billing with OLIVIA NEWTON-JOHN

Jet M.C.A.

May 80. (7") *(JET 179) <41246>* **I'M ALIVE. / DRUM DREAMS** [2] [16]

Jun 80. (7"/10"pink; by OLIVIA NEWTON-JOHN and ELECTRIC LIGHT ORCHESTRA) *(JET/+10 185)* **XANADU. / FOOL COUNTRY** [1] [–]

Jun 80. (7") *<41285>* **XANADU. / (other track by GENE KELLY & OLIVIA NEWTON JOHN)** [–] [8]

Jul 80. (lp/c) *(JET LX/CX 526) <6100>* **XANADU** (film soundtrack) [2] [4]

Jul 80. (7"/10"blue) *(JET/+10 195)* **ALL OVER THE WORLD. / MIDNIGHT BLUE** [11] [–]

Jul 80. (7") *<41289>* **ALL OVER THE WORLD. / DRUM DREAMS** [–] [13]

Nov 80. (7") *(JET 7004)* **DON'T WALK AWAY. / ACROSS THE BORDER** [21] [–]

Jul 81. (7") *(JET 7011) <02408>* **HOLD ON TIGHT. / WHEN TIME STOOD STILL** [4] [10]

Aug 81. (lp/c) *(JET LP/CA 236) <37371>* **TIME** [1] [16]
– Prologue / Twilight / Yours truly, 2095 / Ticket to the Moon / The way life's meant to be / Another heart breaks / Rain is falling / From the end of the world / The lights go down / Here is the news / 21st century man / Hold on tight / Epilogue. *(re-iss. Feb88 on 'Epic'; 460212) (cd-iss. May88 on 'Jet'; ZK 37371) (re-iss. cd Jun91; 460212-2)*

Oct 81. (7") *(JET 7015) <02559>* **TWILIGHT. / JULIE DON'T LIVE HERE** [30] [33]

Dec 81. (7"/12"pic-d) *(JET/+P12 7018)* **TICKET TO THE MOON. / HERE IS THE NEWS** [24] [–]

Jan 82. (7") *<02693>* **RAIN IS FALLING. / ANOTHER HEART BREAKS** [–] [ ]

Mar 82. (7") *(JET 7021)* **THE WAY LIFE'S MEANT TO BE. / WISHING** [ ] [–]

Jet-Epic Jey-CBS

Jun 83. (7") *(JETA 3500) <03964>* **ROCK'N'ROLL IS KING. / AFTER ALL** [13] [19]
(12"+=) *(JETTA 3500)* – Time after time.

Jun 83. (lp/c) *(JET LX/CX 527) <38490>* **SECRET MESSAGES** [4] [36]
– Secret messages / Loser gone wild / Bluebird / Take me on and on / Four little diamonds / Stranger / Danger ahead / Letter from Spain / Train of gold / Rock'n'roll is king. *(cd-iss. May87; CDJET 527)* – Time after time. *(re-iss. Jun91 cd/c; 462487-2/-4) (re-iss. Mar93 cd/c)*

Aug 83. (7"/7"pic-d) *(JET A/WA 3720)* **SECRET MESSAGES. / BUILDINGS HAVE EYES** [48] [–]

Oct 83. (7") *(JETA 3869) <04130>* **FOUR LITTLE DIAMONDS. / LETTER FROM SPAIN** [ ] Sep83 [86]
(12"+=) *(JETTA 3869)* – The bouncer.

Jan 84. (7") *<04208>* **STRANGER. / TRAIN OF GOLD** [–] [ ]

— after a brief spell in BLACK SABBATH, **BEVAN** rejoined ELO with others **JEFF LYNNE** and the returning **MICK KAMINSKI**

Epic C.B.S.

Feb 86. (7") *(A 6844) <05766>* **CALLING AMERICA. / CAUGHT IN A TRAP** [28] Jan86 [18]
(12"+=) *(QTA 6844)* – Destination unknown.

Mar 86. (lp/c) *(EPC/40 26467) <40048>* **BALANCE OF POWER** [9] Feb86 [49]
– Heaven only knows / So serious / Getting to the point / Secret lives / Is it alright? / Sorrow about to fall / Without someone / Calling America / Endless lies / Send it. *(cd-iss. May87; CD 26467) (re-iss. Jun91 cd/c; 468576-2/-4) (re-iss. Mar93 cd/c)*

Apr 86. (7") *(A 7090)* **SO SERIOUS. / A MATTER OF FACT** [ ] [–]
(12"+=) *(TA 7090)* – ('A'-alternative mix).

May 86. (7") *<05892>* **SO SERIOUS. / ENDLESS LIES** [–] [ ]

Jul 86. (7") *(A 7317)* **GETTING TO THE POINT. / SECRET LIVES** [ ] [–]
(12"+=) *(TA 7317)* – Elo megamix.

— continued without LYNNE! who went solo and joined TRAVELING WILBURYS

— JEFF LYNNE had released two solo 45's while a ELO member. These were 'DOIN' THAT CRAZY THING'. / 'GOIN' DOWN TO RIO' in 1977. BEV BEVAN issued a single in 1976, 'LET THERE BE DRUMS'. / 'HEAVY HEAD'.

JEFF LYNNE

Virgin Virgin

Jul 84. (7"/12") *(VS 695/+12) <04570>* **VIDEO! / SOONER OR LATER** [ ] [85]

Reprise Reprise

Jun 90. (7") *(W 9799) <19799>* **EVERY LITTLE THING. / I'M GONE** [59] [ ]
(12"+=) *(W 9799T)* –

Jul 90. (cd)(lp/c) *(<7599 26134-2>)(WX 347/+C)* **ARMCHAIR THEATRE** [24] Jun90 [83]
– Every little thing / Don't let go / Lift me up / Nobody home / September song / Now you're gone / Don't say goodbye / What would it take / Stormy weather / Blown away / Save me now.

ELECTRIC LIGHT ORCHESTRA PART II

— now with **BEVAN, KAMINSKI, McDOWELL, GROUCUTT, LOUIS CLARK, PETE HAYCOCK** – vocals (ex-CLIMAX BLUES BAND) / session **NEIL LOCKWOOD, ERIC TROYER**

Telstar Scotti Bros

Apr 91. (7"/c-s) *(ELO 100/+C) <75248>* **HONEST MAN. / LOVE FOR SALE** [60] [ ]
(12"+=/cd-s+=) *(ELO 100 T/CD)* – ('A'extended).

May 91. (cd/c/lp) *(TCD/STAC/STAR 2503) <75222>* **PART II** [34] [ ]
– Hello / Honest man / Every night / Once upon a time / Heartbreaker / Thousand eyes / For the love of a woman / Kiss me red / Heart of hearts / Easy street.

Oct 91. (c-s) *<75292>* **FOR THE LOVE OF A WOMAN** [–] [ ]

— **ERIC TROYER + PHIL BATES** – guitar, vocals repl. HAYCOCK (now solo again)

Ultrapop Curb

Aug 94. (c-s/cd-s) *(9612-4/-5 ULT)* **POWER OF A MILLION LIGHTS** [ ] [–]

Oct 94. (cd/c) *(9610-2/-4 ULT) <77692>* **MOMENT OF TRUTH** [ ] [ ]
– Moment of truth (overture) / Breakin' down the walls / Power of a million lights / Interlude / One more tomorrow / Don't wanna / Voices / Interlude 2 / Vixen / The fox / Love or money / Blue violin / Whiskey girls / Interlude / Twist of the knife / So glad you said goodbye / Underture / The leaving.

Oct 94. (c-s/cd-s) **BREAKIN' DOWN THE WALLS / (album version) / DON'T WANNA** [ ] [–]

ELECTRIC LIGHT ORCHESTRA

— **JEFF LYNNE** + band **RICHARD TANDY** + guests ROSIE VELA, GEORGE HARRISON, RINGO STARR, etc

Epic Sony

Jun 01. (cd) *(502500-2) <85336>* **ZOOM** [34] [94]
– Alright / Moment in paradise / State of mind / Just for love / Stranger on a quiet street / In my own time / Easy money / It really doesn't matter / Ordinary dream / A long time gone / Melting in the sun / All she wanted / Lonesome lullaby.

Sep 01. (cd-s) *<671136>* **ALRIGHT** [–] [ ]

– compilations, etc. –

on 'Harvest' unless mentioned otherwise

Oct 74. (lp/c) *(SHSP/TC-SHSP 4037)* **SHOWDOWN** [ ] [–]

Apr 77. (lp/c) *(SHSM/TC-SHSM 2015)* **THE LIGHT SHINES ON** [ ] [–]

Dec 77. (7"/12") *(HAR/+12 5121)* **SHOWDOWN. / ROLL OVER BEETHOVEN** [ ] [–]

Jun 76. (lp) *Jet; (JETLP 19 w/drawn) <35528>* **OLE ELO** [–] [32]

Dec 78. (7"ep) *Jet; (ELO 1)* **E.L.O. EP** [34] [–]
– Can't get it out of my head / Strange magic / Evil woman / Ma-ma-ma-belle.

Dec 78. Jet; (3xlp-box) *(JETBX 1)* **THREE LIGHT YEARS** [38] [–]
– (ON THE THIRD DAY / ELDORADO / FACE THE MUSIC)

Mar 79. (lp/c) *(SHSM/TC-SHSM 2027)* **THE LIGHT SHINES ON (VOL.2)** [ ] [–]

Nov 80. (4xlp-box) *Jet; (JETBX 2)* **FOUR LIGHT YEARS** [ ] [–]
– (A NEW WORLD RECORD / OUT OF THE BLUE / DISCOVERY)

May 84. (7") *EMI Gold; (G45 22)* **ROLL OVER BEETHOVEN. / 10538 OVERTURE** [ ] [–]

Apr 86. (lp/c) *(EMS/EMC 1128)* **FIRST MOVEMENT** [ ] [–]
(cd-iss. Oct87; CZ 14)

1988. (cd) *Jet; (JETCD 24043)* **A PERFECT WORLD OF MUSIC** [ ] [–]

May 88. (cd) *Arcade; (01024661)* **ALL OVER THE WORLD** [ ] [–]

Dec 89. (lp/c/cd) *Telstar; (STAR/+T/CD 2370)* **THE VERY BEST OF ELO** [23] [–]
– Evil woman / Livin' thing / Can't get it out of my head / Showdown / Turn to stone / Rockaria! / Sweet talkin' woman / Telephone line / Ma ma ma belle / Strange magic / Mr blue sky *(re-iss. Oct90 as 'THE VERY BEST OF THE ELECTRIC LIGHT ORCHESTRA'; same)* – hit UK No.28

Aug 91. (cd/c/d-lp) *E.M.I.; (CD/TC/LP EM 1419)* **EARLY ELO** [ ] [ ]
– (first 2 albums, plus bonus tracks)

Sep 92. (cd/c) *Collection; (R 450357-2/-4)* **GREATEST HITS VOL.2** [ ] [–]

Oct 92. Epic; (3xcd-box) *(EPC 472267 123)* **BOXED SET** [ ] [–]
– (OUT OF THE BLUE / ELDORADO / A NEW WORLD RECORD)

Dec 92. (3xcd-box) *Epic; (472267-2)* **ELDORADO / A NEW WORLD RECORD / OUT OF THE BLUE** [ ] [–]

Jun 94. Dino; (cd/c) *(DIN CD/C 30)* **THE VERY BEST OF THE ELECTRIC LIGHT ORCHESTRA** [4] [–]

Jul 94. (3xcd-box) *Legacy-Epic; (CD 46090)* **AFTERGLOW** [ ] [–]

Oct 94. (3xcd-box) *Epic; (477526-2)* **TIME / SECRET MESSAGES / DISCOVERY** [ ] [–]

May 96. (cd/c) *EMI Gold; (CD/TC GOLD 1002)* **THE GOLD COLLECTION** [ ] [–]

Oct 97. (cd/c) *Epic; (3013-2/-4)* **ONE NIGHT IN AUSTRALIA LIVE VOL.1 (live)** [ ] [–]

Oct 97. (cd/c) *Epic; (3014-2/-4)* **ONE NIGHT IN AUSTRALIA LIVE VOL.2 (live)** [ ] [–]

Nov 97. (cd/c) *Epic; (489039-2/-4)* **LIGHT YEARS – THE VERY BEST OF** [60] [–]

Nov 97. (3xcd-box) *Epic; (485340-2)* **DISCOVERY / OUT OF THE BLUE / TIME** [ ] [-]
Oct 01. (d-cd) *Sony TV; (STVCD 126)* **THE ULTIMATE COLLECTION** [18] [ ]

ELECTRIC SIX

Formed: Detroit, Michigan, USA . . . 1996 as The WILDBUNCH by JACKSON POUNDER and MARTIN M. The pair released the warped garage single, 'I LOST CONTROL (OF MY ROCK'N'ROLL)', on the tiny 'Uchu Cult' label before recruiting MOJO FREZZATO, DISCO, THE ROCK-N-ROLL INDIAN and the brilliantly named DR. BLACKLIPS HOFFMAN for 1997's 'Flying Bomb' release, 'THE BALLADE OF MC SUCKA DJ'. More pseudonymous japery followed as DICK VALENTINE (i.e. JACKSON, accompanied by one FRANK LLOYD BONNAVENTURE and SURGE JOEBOT amongst others) took the mic for the calculated, demented stooge-rock of 'DANGER! HIGH VOLTAGE'. It was electrifying enough to come within sniffing distance of the UK No.1 spot and, newly signed to Britain's 'X.L.' label, ELECTRIC SIX released the long awaited 'FIRE' (2003). Mutant disco, swaggering, sardonic stadium rock and good old underground subversiveness were the key ingredients in the band's tongue-in-cheek armoury, proving that Detroit's font of alt-rock evangelism hasn't dried up quite yet. • **Covers:** ROCKSHOW (Peaches).

Album rating: FIRE (*7)

WILDBUNCH

JACKSON POUNDER (b. SPENCER) – vocals, guitar, bass, synthesizer / **MARTIN M.** (b. CORY MARTIN) – drums

not iss. Uchu Cult

1996. (7"ep) *<SC 001>* **I LOST CONTROL (OF MY ROCK & ROLL) / TINY LITTLE MEN. / GAY BAR / I KNOW KARATE** [-] [ ]
1996. (ltd;m-lp) *<none>* **AN EVENING WITH THE MANY MOODS OF THE WILDBUNCH'S GREATEST HITS . . . TONIGHT! 8 TRACK** [-] [ ]

—— added **THE ROCK-N-ROLL INDIAN** (b. ANTHONY SELPH) – guitar / **MOJO FREZZATO** – guitar / **DISCO** (b. STEVE NAWARA) – bass / plus **DR. BLACKLIPS HOFFMAN** – keyboards

not iss. Flying Bomb

1997. (7"m) *<FLB 105>* **THE BALLADE OF MC SUCKA DJ. / TAKE OFF YOUR CLOTHES / NUCLEAR WAR (ON THE DANCE FLOOR)** [-] [ ]

not iss. Off Woodward

1998. (cd) *<none>* **DON'T BE AFRAID OF THE ROBOT: LIVE AT THE GOLD DOLLAR (live)** [-] [ ]

—— **DICK VALENTINE** (was the new name for JACKSON)

—— **SURGE JOEBOT** – guitar; repl. MOJO

not iss. Flying Bomb

2001. (7"m) *<FLB 117>* **DANGER (HIGH VOLTAGE). / NEUROCAMERAMAN / SHE'S GUATEMALA** [-] [ ]

ELECTRIC SIX

VALENTINE, DISCO, SURGE + THE ROCK-N-ROLL INDIAN + M. with **TAIT NUCLEUS** – keyboards / **FRANK LLOYD BONNAVENTURE + DR. BLACKLIPS HOFFMAN + JEFF SIMMONS + TAIT NUCLEUS + JOHNNY VEGAS-HENTCH**

X.L. Beggars XL

Jan 03. (7") *(XLS 151) <BQTX 41157>* **DANGER! HIGH VOLTAGE. / I LOST CONTROL (OF MY ROCK'N'ROLL)** [2] Feb03 [ ]
(cd-s+=) *(XLS 151CD)* – Remote control (me).
('A'-Soulchild mix; 12"+=) *(XLT 151)* – ('A'-Thin White Duke remix).
(cd-s++=) *(XLS 151CD2)* – ('A'-kilogram mix).

—— now with **THE COLONEL + JOHNNY NAS$HINAL** repl. TAIT

Jun 03. (7") *(XLS 158)* **GAY BAR. / THE LIVING END** [5] [-]
(cd-s) *(XLS 158CD)* – ('A'side) / Don't be afraid of the robot / Take off your clothes.
Jun 03. (ltd-7") *(XLS 159)* **ROCKSHOW. / Peaches: ROCKSHOW** [ ] [-]
Jun 03. (cd/lp) *(XLCD/XLLP 169) <40169>* **FIRE** [7] May03 [ ]
– Dance commander / Electric demons in love / Naked pictures (of your mother) / Danger! high voltage / She's white / I invented the night / Improper dancing / Gay bar / Nuclear war (on the dance floor) / Getting into the jam / Vengeance and fashion / I'm the bomb / Synthesizer. *(w/ free video-cd)*
Oct 03. (cd-s) *(XLS 170CD)* **DANCE COMMANDER / I AM DETROIT / ('A'-Soulchild extended remix)** [40] [-]
(cd-s) *(XLS 170CD2)* – ('A'-Benny Benassi satisfaction remix) / ('A'-Fatboy Slim dub mix) / ('A'-video).
(12") *(XLT 170)* – ('A'-Soulchild mix) / ('A'-Benny . . . mix).

ELECTRIC SOFT PARADE

Formed: Brighton, England . . . 1998 by brothers TOM and ALEX WHITE, who then enlisted MATT THWAITES and STEVE LARGE. Originally called FIXED ASCENT and then The FELTRO MEDIA (the latter issued a few demos including 'NEON OF THE CITY' in August '99), the band subsequently settled on being called The SOFT PARADE. A promising debut single 'SILENT TO THE DARK' hit the shops in spring 2001, and a follow-up 'EMPTY AT THE END', broke the UK Top 75 later in the year. The lads then added "ELECTRIC" to the moniker after discovering there already existed a DOORS cover band of the same name. 'THERE'S A SILENCE' nearly cracked the Top 50 and paved the way for media interest for their debut album 'HOLES IN THE WALL' (2002). The Top 40 record was a more than competent homage to their musical influences whilst also managing to sound contemporary. Clearly influenced by 1960's psychedelia the band offered something different to the increasingly faceless Brit-pop movement. ELECTRIC SOFT PARADE and their 'Arista'-backed label 'DB' re-mixed and re-promoted both their first two SOFT PARADE 45's and they duly went Top 40. The group returned in 2003 with their highly ambitious second set entitled 'THE AMERICAN ADVENTURE'. Its lush orchestration was reminiscent of PHILIP GLASS on ice, a pastoral and cinematic affair that harked back to the days of The WALKER BROTHERS and BRIAN WILSON (circa 1966). Infusing instruments as diverse as harp, strings, creepy percussion, xylophones and pump organs, The ELECTRIC SOFT PARADE wove melodies in and out of each other to startling effect. Whilst perhaps not matching the emotional intensity of their debut LP, 'THE AMERICAN ADVENTURE' was all of the things that were great about lush records, invoking a meditative harmony in the listener's head whilst leaving them stunned and deeply moved simultaneously.

Album rating: HOLES IN THE WALL (*8) / THE AMERICAN ADVENTURE (*6)

ALEX WHITE (b. 1982) – vocals, guitar / **STEVE LARGE** – keyboards / **MATT THWAITS** – bass / **TOM WHITE** (b. 1985) – drums

DB – Arista not iss.

Apr 01. (7"/cd-s; as SOFT PARADE) *(DB 004 SP7/CD7)* **SILENT TO THE DARK. / SOMETHING'S GOT TO GIVE** [ ] [-]
Jul 01. (7"red/cd-s/cd-s; as SOFT PARADE) *(DB 006 SP7/CD7/CD7JC)* **EMPTY AT THE END. / SUMATRAN** [65] [-]
Oct 01. (7"silver) *(DB 007SP7)* **THERE'S A SILENCE. / ON THE WIRES** [52] [-]

(cd-s+=/cd-s+=) *(DB 007 CD7/CDJ7)* – Broadcast.

Feb 02. (cd/d-lp) *(DB 002 CD+/LP)* **HOLES IN THE WALL** [35] [–]
– Start again / Empty at the end / There's a silence / Something's got to give / It's wasting me away / Silent to the dark / Sleep alone / This given line / Why do you try so hard to hate me / Holes in the wall / Biting the soles of my feet / Red balloon for me. *(re-iss. Aug02 & Sep03; DB 002CDLPX)*

Mar 02. (7"blue) *(DB 008SP7)* **SILENT TO THE DARK II. / STAY WHERE YOU ARE** [23] [–]
(cd-s+=) *(DB 008CD7)* – ('A'-original video).
(cd-s) *(DB 008CDE7)* – ('A'side) / Hove park / Blitzed 6-4.

May 02. (7") *(DB 009SP7)* **EMPTY AT THE END (re-recording). / THIS GIVEN LINE** [39] [–]
(cd-s+=) *(DB 009CD7)* – The loop.
(cd-s+=) *(DB 009CDE7)* – Aerial roots.

Sep 02. (7") *(DB 013SP7)* **SAME WAY, EVERY DAY (BITING THE SOLES OF MY FEET). / POEMS** [ ] [–]
(cd-s+=) *(DB 013CD7JC)* – Zero return.
(cd-s) *(DB 013CD7)* – ('A'side) / Stop / Mood swing.

Arista — not iss.

Sep 03. (7"white) *(8287 65878-7)* **THINGS I'VE DONE BEFORE. / SUMMER'S SLOW MEANDER** [ ] [–]

Oct 03. (cd/lp) *(82876 56369-2/-1)* **THE AMERICAN ADVENTURE** [45] [–]
– Things I've done before / Bruxellisation / Lights out / The wrongest thing in town / Lose yr frown / The American adventure / Chaos / Headacheville / Existing.

Nov 03. (7") *(82876 56948-7)* **LOSE YR FROWN. / TAKE ME BACK / THIS IS WHERE I'M GONNA HIDE** [ ] [–]
(cd-s) *(82876 56948-2)* – ('A'side) / Empty at the end (live) / Blind cowboys' theme.

☐ ELECTRONIC (see under ⇒ NEW ORDER)

☐ Mama Cass ELLIOT
(see under ⇒ MAMAS AND THE PAPAS)

Missy ELLIOTT

Born: MELISSA ARNETTE ELLIOTT, 1 Jul'71, Portsmouth, Virginia, USA. Both a respected figure in the Hip-hop world and a self-proclaimed musical icon, MISSY ELLIOTT (along with DR DRE and super producer TIMBALAND) has contributed greatly to the rise of 'ghetto styl-ee' in modern music. MISSY began her musical legacy when DEVANTE SWING (of JODECI) signed her outfit SISTA to the 'Swing Mob' label. This is where she met TIMBALAND, a friend of SWING's and an inspiring Rap producer. JODECI's 'Diary Of A Mad Band' (1994) was to be the start of a long-term relationship with TIMBALAND, even if the 'Swing Mob' label eventually went bust. Abandoning SISTA, MISSY jumped at the chance to collaborate once again with her mentor on AALIYAH's 'One In A Million' album in '96, writing tracks 'Aaliyah' and the set's title track. After the astonishing success of the LP, MISSY was contracted to work with a number of rising stars by record execs, including writing, producing and rapping credits on songs from BOYZ II MEN, PAULA COLE and The RUFF RYDERS. She finally struck a solo deal with 'Elektra' in 1996 and issued the breakthrough album 'SUPA DUPA FLY' to critical and commercial acclaim, thanks to the stomping, adrenaline-fuelled single 'THE RAIN'. She continued producing tracks for WHITNEY HOUSTON, EVE and most notably DESTINY'S CHILD before the release of 1999's 'DA REAL WORLD' which spawned two massive singles 'SHE'S A BITCH' and 'HOT BOYZ' and boasted a collaboration with EMINEM. Between appearing in ads for Gap and Sprite, MISSY kept herself busy producing a rendition of 'LADY MARMALADE' featuring the girls from 'Moulin Rouge', aka PINK, CHRISTINA AGUILERA and LIL' KIM. The song was a Number One hit in both the States and the UK, paving the way for her third and best outing 'MISS E . . . SO ADDICTIVE' (2001), a record which featured the massive hit single 'GET UR FREAK ON', a tribal, operatic hip-hop track that sounded like no other. 'ONE MINUTE MAN' followed, and MISSY ELLIOTT was perhaps the most respected hip-hop artist/producer/rapper/songwriter in the industry. Southern rapper BUBBA SPARXXX asked to borrow elements from 'GET UR FREAK ON'. MISSY, of course obliged, but cheekily changed the lyrics to: "I'm Copywritten, so don't copy me . . .' However, many artists in the industry have, and with a talent this big, who could resist. The album 'UNDER CONSTRUCTION' was issued in 2002 to brilliant acclaim and featured possibly the most absurd and downright unusual single in the form of 'WORK IT'. Using spasmodic beats, industrial rhythms and elephant noises (!), it became a truly infectious bugged-out club hit. Elsewhere, MISSY ELLIOTT, brought in the cream of the R&B crop; from her right-hand man TIMBALAND (possibly the hardest working man in the Urban music game), JAY-Z and a duet with uber diva BEYONCE KNOWLES on 'NOTHING'S OUT THERE FOR ME'. It was a startling set of songs that put most R&B acts to shame with its use of warped time signatures, throbbing bass and colourful inventiveness. It would be hard to top the sheer size and scope of 'UNDER CONSTRUCTION', so it was no surprise that a year later and the release of 'THIS IS NOT A TEST!' failed to match up to the brilliance of its predecessor. However, the two albums were very similar, so much so, in fact, that they could have been issued as a double album. Single 'PASS THAT DUTCH', about dope-smoking among other things, was indeed 'WORK IT' only slightly watered down. The regulars were at the helm yet again, from TIMBALAND to JAY-Z, and a duet with Southern homeboy NELLY ('PUMP IT UP') being a particular highlight, although an R. KELLY collaboration 'IS THIS OUR LAST TIME' would have not been greatly missed.

Album rating: SUPA DUPA FLY (*6) / DA REAL WORLD (*7) / MISS E . . . SO ADDICTIVE (*8) / UNDER CONSTRUCTION (*7) / THIS IS NOT A TEST! (*5)

MISSY 'MISDEMEANOR' ELLIOTT

– vocals / with session people, etc

Elektra — Elektra

Jul 97. (cd/c) *<(7559 62062/-2/-4)>* **SUPA DUPA FLY** [ ] [3]
– Busta's intro / Hit 'em wit da hee / Sock it 2 me / The rain (supa dupa fly) / Beep me 911 / They don't wanna fuck wit me / Pass da blunt / Bite our style (interlude) / Friendly skies / Best friends / Don't be comin' (in my face) / Izzy izzy ahh / Why you hurt me / I'm talkin' (the biz) / Gettaway / Busta's outro / Missy's finale.

— In Jul'97, MISSY ELLIOTT was featured on the collaborative hit single 'Not Tonight' by LIL' KIM, DA BRAT, LEFT EYE and ANGIE MARTINEZ

Aug 97. (c-s) *(E 3919C)* **THE RAIN (SUPA DUPA FLY) / (instrumental)** [16] [ ]
(cd-s+=) *(E 3919CD)* – (acappella).

Nov 97. (c-s/cd-s) *(E 3890 C/CD)* **SOCK IT 2 ME / (Da Brat instrumental & acappella) / RELEASE THE TENSION** [33] Oct97 [12]
(cd-s) *(E 3890CDX)* – ('A'side) / The rain (supa dupa fly) / Release the tension.

Apr 98. (c-s) *(E 3859C)* **BEEP ME 911 / (instrumental)** [14] [ ]
(cd-s+=) *(E 3859CD)* – ('A'mix).

— in Jun'98, MISSY 'MISDEMEANOR' ELLIOTT (& MOCHA) featured on NICOLE's US Top 5 hit (UK No.22), 'Make It Hot' *(E 3821 C/T/CD)*
(below as MISSY 'MISDEMEANOR' ELLIOTT featuring LIL' KIM)

Aug 98. (12"/cd-s) *(E 3824 T/CD2)* **HIT 'EM WIT DA HEE. / BEEP ME 911** [25] [ ]
(12"/cd-s) *(E 3824 TX/CD1)* – ('A'mixes) / The rain.

— in Sep'98, MISSY featured on MELANIE B's UK No.1, 'I Want You Back'

— in Oct'98, she also guested for TOTAL on the US hit 'Trippin'

— in Nov'98, MISSY featured on LIL' MO's single, '5 Minutes'

—— in Mar'99, a three-way collaboration with TIMBALAND and MAGOO heralded another minor hit, 'Here We Come'

Jun 99. (cd/c/lp) *(7559 62436-2/-4/-1)* <62232> **DA REAL WORLD** [40] [10]
– Mysterious / Beat biter / Funky white boy / All 'n my grill / Smooth chick / Hot boyz / Mr DJ / You don't know / We did it / She's a bitch / Dangerous mouths / Sticking chickens / Checkin' for you / U can't resist / Crazy feelings / Religious / All 'n my grill.

Jul 99. (c-s) *(E 3745C)* <63751> **SHE'S A BITCH / (clean)** [ ] May99 [90]
(12"+=/cd-s+=) *(E 3745 T/CD)* – ('A'mixes).

Sep 99. (c-s) *(E 3742C)* <*radio cut*> **ALL 'N MY GRILL / (version)** [20] Jul99 [64]
(12"+=/cd-s+=) *(E 3742 T/CD)* – ('A'mixes).
(above as MISSY 'MISDEMEANOR' ELLIOTT featuring MC SOLAAR)
(below as MISSY 'MISDEMEANOR' ELLIOTT featuring NAS, EVE & Q-TIP)

Elektra — East West

Jan 00. (c-s) *(E 7002C)* <64029> **HOT BOYZ / (clean)** [18] Nov99 [5]
(12"+=/cd-s+=) *(E 7002 T/CD)* – (remix original).

—— in Jun'00, MISSY featured on TORREY CARTER's minior hit, 'Take That'

—— late 2000, she appeared on MEMPHIS BLEEK's hit, 'Is That Your Chick'

MISSY ELLIOTT

—— a slight change of moniker

Apr 01. (c-s) *(E 7206C)* <67190> **GET UR FREAK ON / (clean)** [4] Mar01 [7]
(12"+=/cd-s+=) *(E 7206 T/CD)* – (instrumental)

May 01. (cd/c) <*(7559 62639-2/-4)*> **MISS E . . . SO ADDICTIVE** [10] [2]
– So addictive (with CHARLENE 'TWEET' KAYE) / Dog n heat (with REDMAN & METHOD MAN) / One minute man (with LUDACRIA) / Old school joint / Get ur freak on / Lick shots / Take away (with GINUWINE) / 4 my people (with EVE) / Step off / Busta bus interlude (with BUSTA RHYMES) / Whatcha gon' do (with TIMBALAND) / Screen AKA itchin' / X tasy / Slap slap (with DA BRAT & JADE) / I've changed (with LIL' MO) / One minute man (with JAY-Z) / Higher ground. <*(clean version; 7559 62643-2/-4)*> *(new version cd-iss. Apr02 +=; 7559 62777-2)*

Aug 01. (c-s) *(E 7245C)* <*radio cut*> **ONE MINUTE MAN / (version)** [10] Jul01 [15]
(12"+=/cd-s+=) *(E 7245 T/CD)* – ('A'mixes).

Oct 01. (cd-s) **SUPERFREAKON (mixes)** [72] [–]

—— in Nov'01, MISSY featured on JANET JACKSON's hit, 'Son Of A Gun'

Dec 01. (c-s; by MISSY ELLIOTT featuring GINUWINE & TWEET) *(E 7263C)* **TAKE AWAY / (album version)** [ ] [50]
(cd-s+=) *(E 7263CD1)* – One minute man (original) / Get ur freak on (superchumba superfreakon remix + Cd-Rom).
(cd-s) *(E 7263CD2)* – ('A'mixes).

Jan 02. (cd-s) <6727-2> **TAKE AWAY** [–] [45]

Mar 02. (cd-s; by MISSY "MISDEMEANOR" ELLIOTT featuring EVE) *(E 7286CD1)* **4 MY PEOPLE / ('A'-Basement Jaxx mix) / TAKE AWAY** [5] [–]
(cd-s) *(E 7286CD2)* – ('A'side) / Get ur freak on (superchumbo's superfreakon remix) / Get ur freak on (video).

Nov 02. (c-s) *(E 7344C)* **WORK IT / (mix)** [6] Oct02 [2]
(12") *(E 7344T)* <*ELEK 67340*> – ('A'side) / P***ycat / My people.
(cd-s+=) *(E 7344CD)* – ('A'-video).

Nov 02. (cd/lp) <*(7559 62813-2/-4)*> **UNDER CONSTRUCTION** [23] [3]
– Intro – Go to the floor / Bring the pain (with METHOD MAN) / Gossip folks (with LUDACRIS) / Work it / Back in the day (with JAY-Z) / Funky fresh dressed (with MS. JADE) / P***ycat / Nothing out there for me (with BEYONCE KNOWLES) / Slide / Play that beat / Ain't that funny / Hot / Can you hear me (with TLC) / Work it (reprise with 50 CENT). *(cd re-iss. Mar03 +=; 7559 62875-2)* – Gossip folks (Fatboy Slim remix with LUDACRIS) / Gossip folks (Mousse T remix with LUDACRIS).

Mar 03. (12"/cd-s; by MISSY ELLIOTT & LUDACRIS) *(E 7380 T/CD)* <67356> **GOSSIP FOLKS (mixes by Fatboy Slim + video)** [9] [8]

—— late in 2003, MISSY ELLIOTT duetted with WYCLEF JEAN on the hit single, 'Party To Damascus'

Nov 03. (12"/cd-s) *(E 7509 T/CD)* **PASS THAT DUTCH / (version) / HURT SUMTHIN** [10] [27]

Nov 03. (cd/lp) <*(7559 62905-2/-1)*> **THIS IS NOT A TEST!** [49] [13]
– Baby girl intro (with MARY J. BLIGE) / Pass that Dutch / Wake up (with JAY-Z) / Keep it movin' (with ELEPHANT MAN) / Is this our last time (with FABOLOUS) / I'm really hot / Dats what I'm talkin about (with R. KELLY) / Don't be cruel / Toyz / Let it bump / Pump it up (with NELLY) / It's real / Let me fix my weave / Spelling bee / I'm not perfect (with CLARK SISTERS) / Outro (with MARY J. BLIGE).

☐ E.L.O. (see under ⇒ ELECTRIC LIGHT ORCHESTRA)

EMBRACE

Formed: Bradford/Huddersfield, England . . . 1993 by Irish-ancestry songwriting brothers, DANNY (lyrics) and RICHARD McNAMARA (the music), who enlisted the rhythm team of STEVE FIRTH and MIKE KEATON. After the stunning OASIS-esque grandeur of the early '97 debut, 'ALL YOU GOOD GOOD PEOPLE', for the 'Fierce Panda' set-up, they signed to Virgin offshoot, 'Hut'. The band made an immediate impact on the singles chart with the EP, 'FIREWORKS', increasing their chart exposure with the summer '97 follow-up, 'ONE BIG FAMILY'. However, the pop nation finally clutched them to their proverbial bosom with the re-issue of 'ALL YOU GOOD GOOD PEOPLE', which cracked the Top 10 in the Autumn. The following year, the much vaunted songwriting siblings scored a further two Top 10 hits, 'COME BACK TO WHAT YOU KNOW' and 'MY WEAKNESS IS NONE OF YOUR BUSINESS', both taken from their chart-topping debut album, 'THE GOOD WILL OUT'. Towards the end the decade and with part-timer MICKEY DALE now their official 5th member, EMBRACE previewed their forthcoming sophomore set via a Top 20 hit, 'HOOLIGAN'. When it finally arrived, 'DRAWN FROM MEMORY' (2000) revealed a more mature band, conscious of their more overblown tendencies and determined to pare their sound down somewhat. Thus the Britpop-inspired orchestration which characterised this album's predecessor wasn't quite so conspicuous, although the record's highlights were still centered around soul searching balladry such as the title track. In the event, 'DRAWN FROM MEMORY' (2000), in addition to making the UK Top 10 itself, spawned a further three hits in the shape of 'YOU'RE NOT ALONE', 'SAVE ME' and 'I WOULDN'T WANNA HAPPEN TO YOU'. Although the worst excesses of orchestration had been reined in, EMBRACE seemed to be working with the philosophy that if it ain't broke, don't fix it. If so, it was an ethos that ensured them a Top 10 placing for 'IF YOU'VE NEVER BEEN' (2001), along with two singles: the Top 20 'WONDER' and 'MAKE IT LAST'.

Album rating: THE GOOD WILL OUT (*8) / DRAWN FROM MEMORY (*6) / IF YOU'VE NEVER BEEN (*6) / FIREWORKS: SINGLES 1997-2002 compilation (*7)

DANNY McNAMARA – vocals / **RICHARD McNAMARA** – guitar, vocals / **STEVE FIRTH** – bass / **MIKE KEATON** – drums, vocals

Fierce Panda — not iss.

Feb 97. (ltd-7") *(NING 29)* **ALL YOU GOOD GOOD PEOPLE. / MY WEAKNESS IS NONE OF YOUR BUSINESS** [ ] [–]

Hut — Geffen

May 97. (c-ep/12"ep/cd-ep) *(HUT C/T/CD 84)* **FIREWORKS EP** [34] [–]
– The last gas / Now you're nobody / Blind / Fireworks. *(12"ep re-iss. Nov98; same)*

Jul 97. (c-ep/12"ep/cd-ep) *(HUT C/T/CD 86)* **ONE BIG FAMILY EP** [21] [–]
– One big family / Dry kids / You've only got to stop to get better / Butter wouldn't melt. *(12"ep re-iss. Nov98; same)*

Oct 97. (c-ep/12"ep/cd-ep) *(HUT C/T/DX 90)* **ALL YOU GOOD GOOD PEOPLE EP** [8] [–]
– All you good good people (extended) / You won't amount to anything – this time / The way I do / Free ride. *(12"ep re-iss. Nov98; same)*
(cd-ep) *(HUTCD 90)* – ('A'radio edit) / One big family (Perfecto mix) / ('A'-Fierce Panda version) / ('A'-orchestral mix).

May 98. (c-s) *(HUTC 93)* <*95132*> **COME BACK TO WHAT YOU KNOW / LOVE IS BACK** 6 Jul98
(12"+=/cd-s+=) *(HUT T/DX 93)* – If you feel like a sinner / Perfect way.
(cd-s) *(HUTCDX 93)* – ('A'side) / Butter wouldn't melt (live) / Dry kids (live) / ('A'orchestral).

Jun 98. (cd/c/d-lp) *(CDHUT/HUTMC/HUTDLP 46)* <*25165*> **THE GOOD WILL OUT** 1 Jul98
– Intro / All you good good people / My weakness is none of your business / Come back to what you know / One big family / Higher sights / Retread / I want the world / You've got to say yes / Fireworks / The last gas / That's all changed forever / Now you're nobody / The good will out.

Aug 98. (7") *(HUT 103)* **MY WEAKNESS IS NONE OF YOUR BUSINESS. / FEELINGS I THOUGHT YOU SHARED** 9 –
(c-s+=/cd-s+=) *(HUT C/CD 103)* – Don't turn your back on love.
(cd-s) *(HUTDX 103)* – ('A'live) / Higher sights (live) / Retread (live). *(12"ep re-iss. Nov98; HUTT 103)*

Nov 98. (12"ep) *(HUTT 107)* **THE GOOD WILL OUT. / BUTTER WOULDN'T MELT (live) / DRY KIDS (live) / BLIND** –

— added p/t (now f/t) 5th member **MICKEY DALE** – keyboards (ex-CUD)

Hut E.M.I.

Nov 99. (c-s/cd-s) *(HUT C/CD 123)* **HOOLIGAN / I'VE BEEN RUNNING / I CAN'T FEEL BAD ANYMORE** 18 –
(cd-s) *(HUTDX 123)* – ('A'side) / Like a believer / With the one who got me here.

Mar 00. (cd-s) *(HUTCD 126)* **YOU'RE NOT ALONE / BROTHERS AND SISTERS / HAPPY AND LOST** 14 –
(cd-s/12"+=) *(HUT DX/T 126)* – ('A'side) / Come on and smile / Tap on your shoulder.

Mar 00. (cd/c/lp) *(CDHUT/HUTMC/HUTLP 60)* <*849014*> **DRAWN FROM MEMORY** 8
– The love it takes / You're not alone / Save me / Drawn from memory / Bunker song / New Adam new Eve / Hooligan / Yeah you / Liars tears / I wouldn't wanna happen to you / I had a time.

May 00. (c-s/12"/cd-s) *(HUT C/X/CD 133)* **SAVE ME / GET ON BOARD / STILL SO YOUNG** 29 –
(cd-s) *(HUTDX 133)* – ('A'side) / ('A'mixes).

Aug 00. (7") *(HUT 137)* **I WOULDN'T WANNA HAPPEN TO YOU. / 3 IS A MAGIC NUMBER** 23 –
(cd-s+=) *(HUTCDX 133)* – Top of the heap.
(12"++=) *(HUTT 133)* – First cut / I know what's going on.
(cd-s) *(HUTCD 133)* – ('A'side) / First cut / I know what's going on.

Aug 01. (c-s/cd-s) *(HUT C/CD 142)* **WONDER / ANYWHERE YOU GO / EVERYDAY** 14 –
(cd-s) *(HUTDX 142)* – ('A'side) / Today / Caught in a rush.

Sep 01. (cd/c/lp) *(CDHUT/HUTMC/HUTLP 68)* <*810973*> **IF YOU'VE NEVER BEEN** 9 Oct01
– Over / I hope you're happy now / Wonder / Many will learn / It's gonna take time / Hey, what you trying to say / If you've never been in love with anything / Make it last / Happiness will get you in the end / Satellites.

Nov 01. (cd-s) *(HUTCD 144)* **MAKE IT LAST / FIGHT YER CORNER / IT'S YOU I MAKE FOR** 35 –
(cd-s) *(HUTDX 144)* – ('A'side) / ('A'-orchestral) / Giving forgiving and giving in / What you've never had you'll never have.

Mar 02. (cd) *(CDHUT 74)* <*812083*> **FIREWORKS: SINGLES 1997-2002** (compilation) 36
– All you good good people / You're not alone / Come back to what you know / Make it last / 3 is a magic number / One big family / My weakness is none of your business / I wouldn't wanna happen to you / Save me / Hooligan / The good will out / Wonder / Fireworks.

EMERSON, LAKE & PALMER

Formed: London, England ... mid-1970 by KEITH EMERSON, GREG LAKE and CARL PALMER, who had all cut their teeth in late 60's acts/combos (see below). After an aborted collaboration with HENDRIX (just prior to his death) and an appearance at the Isle Of Wight festival on the 29th August '70, they signed to 'Island'. Later in the year, they unleashed their eponymous debut, which immediately established the band as one of the leading purveyors of 70's prog-rock. In fact, they focused more on the classical side of things, proving that rock could be adapted for more high-brow tastes (EMERSON had previously explored this field while with The NICE). Next-up was 'TARKUS' (1971), a misguided concept piece which was based around a battle between a Manticore (a mythical beast) and a mechanised armadillo (!). Riding on the coat-tails of their debut success, it nevertheless reached No.1 (Top 10 in the States). Their third album was a live adaptation of Mussorgsky's 'PICTURES AT AN EXHIBITION', a fine effort which was let down by the closing track, a pointless cover of B.BUMBLE & THE STINGERS' early 60's hit 'NUTROCKER'. In 1972, they fulfilled their early potential with 'TRILOGY', an album that also made the Top 3, showcasing their most accomplished work to date on tracks such as 'THE ENDLESS ENIGMA', 'LIVING SIN' and 'ABADDON'S BOLERO'. The following year, ELP created the label 'Manticore', its first release being the 'BRAIN SALAD SURGERY' album which consolidated their position as one of the 70's leading bands, at least in commercial terms. Once again, former part-time KING CRIMSON member PETE SINFIELD was drafted in to collaborate on the lyrics. Tracks like the romantic 'STILL ... YOU TURN ME ON' and the grandiose epic, 'KARN EVIL 9' were skillfully placed side by side with an arresting re-working of the hymn 'JERUSALEM'. While the band took a 2-year hiatus, they released a stop-gap triple live set entitled, 'WELCOME BACK MY FRIENDS' that was a little too overblown, pricey and pretentious for many. In 1975, the fans cringed when a solo GREG LAKE returned with the festive 'I BELIEVE IN FATHER CHRISTMAS' which hit No.2. The multi-talented keyboard maestro, KEITH EMERSON, also had a solo outing, a surprisingly basic rock'n'roll cover of Meade Lux Lewis' 'HONKY TONK TRAIN BLUES'. In 1977, ELP eventually returned with the double album, 'WORKS 1', a patchy affair which nevertheless spawned an inspired cover of Aaron Copeland's 'FANFARE FOR THE COMMON MAN'. In its edited form, the track gave the band a near No.1 in the UK. This however, was to be their last work of any relevance. All went solo in the 80's, and when PALMER formed PM, ELP conviently found a replacement (P) in the guise of Cozy POWELL. This set-up was short-lived although the original EMERSON, LAKE & PALMER re-formed once more in 1991. They were found floundering on past glories with the mediocre 'BLACK MOON' album the following year. • **Trivia:** 'Manticore', the label they formed in 1973, also signed PETE SINFIELD, P.F.M. and LITTLE RICHARD!

Album rating: EMERSON, LAKE & PALMER (*6) / TARKUS (*5) / PICTURES AT AN EXHIBITION (*6) / TRILOGY (*8) / BRAIN SALAD SURGERY (*8) / WELCOME BACK MY FRIENDS TO THE SHOW THAT NEVER ENDS – LADIES AND GENTLEMEN ... EMERSON, LAKE & PALMER (*5) / WORKS 1 (*5) / WORKS 2 (*3) / LOVE BEACH (*3) / IN CONCERT (*4) / THE BEST OF EMERSON, LAKE & PALMER compilation (*5) / EMERSON, LAKE & POWELL (*4) / TO THE POWER OF THREE (er ... *3; by 3) / BLACK MOON (*4) / THE ATLANTIC YEARS compilation (*7) / LIVE AT THE ROYAL ALBERT HALL (*4) / IN THE HOT SEAT (*4)

KEITH EMERSON (b. 2 Nov'44. Todmorden, England) – keyboards (ex-NICE, ex-GARY FARR & THE T-BONES / **GREG LAKE** (b.10 Nov'48, Bournemouth, England) – vocals, guitar, bass (ex-KING CRIMSON) / **CARL PALMER** (b.20 Mar'47, Birmingham, England) – drums, percussion (ex-ATOMIC ROOSTER, ex-CRAZY WORLD OF ARTHUR BROWN)

Island Cotillion

Nov 70. (lp/c) *(ILPS/ILPC 9132)* <*9040*> **EMERSON, LAKE & PALMER** 4 18
– The barbarian / Take a pebble / Knife edge / The three fates:- Clotho – Lachesis – Acropus / Tank / Lucky man. *(re-iss. Dec73 on 'Manticore' lp/c; K/K4 43503) (cd-iss. 1988 on 'WEA'; 191202) (re-iss. cd Dec93 on 'Victory'; 828264-2) (cd re-iss. Mar96 on 'Essential'; ESMCD 340) (lp re-iss. Sep98 on 'Get Back'; GET 528) (cd re-iss. Mar01 on 'Castle'; CMRCD 165)*

Mar 71. (7") *<44106>* **LUCKY MAN. / KNIFE EDGE** [–] [48]
<US re-iss. Jan73 on 'Atlantic'; 13153> hit No.51>

Jun 71. (lp/c) *(ILPS/ILPC 9155) <9900>* **TARKUS** [1] [9]
– Tarkus:- Eruption – Stones of years – Iconoclast – The mass – Manticore – Battlefield – Aquatarkus – (conclusion) / Jeremy Bender / Bitches crystal / The only way / Infinite space / A time and a place / Are you ready Eddy?. *(re-iss. Dec73 on 'Manticore' lp/c; K/K4 43504) (cd-iss. Sep89 on 'WEA'; 781202) (re-iss. cd Dec93 on 'Victory'; 828465-2) (cd re-iss. Mar96 on 'Essential'; ESMCD 341)*

Sep 71. (7") *<44131>* **STONES OF YEARS. / A TIME AND A PLACE** [–] [ ]

Nov 71. (lp/c) *(HELP/HELC 1) <66666>* **PICTURES AT AN EXHIBITION** [3] Jan72 [10]
– Promenade: The gnome – Promenade – The sage – The old castle – Blues variation – Promenade / The hut of Baba Yaga – The curse of Baba Yaga – The hut of Baba Yaga – The great gates of Kiev – Nutrocker. *(re-iss. Dec73 on 'Manticore' lp/c; K/K4 33501) (cd-iss. 1988 on 'Cotillion'; 19122-2) (cd re-iss. Sep89 on 'WEA'; 781521-2) (re-iss. Dec93 on 'Victory'; 828466-2) (cd re-iss. Mar96 on 'Essential'; ESMCD 342) (cd re-iss. Mar01; CMRCD 167)*

Mar 72. (7") *<44151>* **NUTROCKER. / THE GREAT GATES OF KIEV** [–] [70]

Jul 72. (lp/c) *(ILPS/ILPC 9186) <9903>* **TRILOGY** [2] [5]
– The endless enigma (part 1) – Fugue – The endless enigma (part 2) / From the beginning / The sheriff / Hoedown / Trilogy / Living sin / Abaddon's bolero. *(re-iss. Dec73 on 'Manticore' lp/c; K/K4 43505) (cd-iss. Jun89 on 'Atlantic'; 781522-2) (re-iss. cd Dec93 on 'Victory'; 828467-2) (cd re-iss. Mar96 on 'Essential'; ESMCD 343)*

Aug 72. (7") *<44158>* **FROM THE BEGINNING. / LIVING SIN** [–] [39]

Manticore Manticore

Dec 73. (lp/c) *(K/K4 53501) <66669>* **BRAIN SALAD SURGERY** [2] [11]
– Jerusalem / Toccata / Still . . . you turn me on / Benny the bouncer / Karn evil 9. 1st impression – part 1 & 2 – 2nd impression – 3rd impression. *(cd-iss. Jun89 on 'WEA'; 781523-2) (re-iss. cd Dec93 on 'Victory'; 828468-2) (cd re-iss. Mar96 on 'Essential'; ESMCD 344) (<cd re-iss. May01 on 'Castle'+=; CMRCD 201)* – Brain salad surgery (single version) / When the apple blossoms bloom in the windmills of your mind / Excerpts from Brain Salad Surgery flexi.

Dec 73. (7") *(K 13503)* **JERUSALEM. / WHEN THE APPLE BLOSSOM BLOOMS IN THE WINDMILLS OF YOUR MIND, I'LL BE YOUR VALENTINE** [ ] [–]

Dec 73. (7") *<2003>* **BRAIN SALAD SURGERY. / STILL YOU TURN ME ON** [–] [ ]

Aug 74. (t-lp/d-c) *(K/K4 63500) <200>* **WELCOME BACK MY FRIENDS, TO THE SHOW THAT NEVER ENDS – LADIES AND GENTLEMEN . . . EMERSON, LAKE & PALMER (live)** [5] [4]
– Hoedown / Jerusalem / Toccata / Tarkus:- Eruption – Stones of years – Iconoclast – The mass – Manticore – Battlefield – Epitaph – Aquatarkus – (conclusion) / Take a pebble – Piano improvisations – Take a pebble (conclusion) / Jeremy Bender / The sheriff / Karn evil 9. 1st impression – 2nd impression – 3rd impression. *(re-iss. d-cd Dec93 on 'Victory'; 828474-2) (d-cd re-iss. Mar96 on 'Essential'; ESDCD 359)*

Nov 75. (7"; by GREG LAKE) *(K 13511) <3305>* **I BELIEVE IN FATHER CHRISTMAS. / HUMBUG** [2] [95]
(re-iss. Nov82, hit No.72 – Dec83 hit No.65) (re-iss. Nov92 on 'Atlantic'; A 7393)

Apr 76. (7"; by KEITH EMERSON) *(K 13513)* **HONKY TONK TRAIN BLUES. / BARREL HOUSE SHAKE DOWN** [21] [–]

Atlantic Atlantic

Mar 77. (d-lp/d-c) *(K/K4 80009) <7000>* **WORKS 1** [9] [12]
– Piano concerto No.1 – 1st movement: Allegro giojoso / 2nd movement: Andante molto cantabile / 3rd movement: Toccata con fuoco / Lend your love to me tonight / C'est la vie / Hallowed by thy name / Nobody loves you like I do / Closer to believing / The enemy God dances with the black spirits / L.A. nights / New Orleans / Bach: Two part invention in D minor / Food for your soul / Tank / Fanfare for the common man / Pirates. *(cd-iss. Jun89; 781372-2) (re-iss. d-cd Dec93 on 'Victory'; 828470-2)*

Jun 77. (7"/12") *(K 10946/+T) <3398>* **FANFARE FOR THE COMMON MAN (edit). / BRAIN SALAD SURGERY** [2] [ ]

Aug 77. (7"; A-side by GREG LAKE) *(K 10990) <3405>* **C'EST LA VIE. / JEREMY BENDER** [ ] [91]

Nov 77. (lp/c) *(K/K4 50422) <19147>* **WORKS 2** (compilation of rare and demo work) [20] [37]
– Tiger in a spotlight / When the apple blossoms bloom in the windmills of your mind, I'll be your valentine / Bullfrog / Brain salad surgery / Barrel house shake down / Watching over you / So far to fall / Maple leaf rag / I believe in Father Christmas / Close but not touching / Honky tonk train blues / Show me the way to go home. *(cd-iss. Jun89; 781538-2) (re-iss. cd Dec93 on 'Victory'; 828473-2)*

Jan 78. (7"; A-side by GREG LAKE) **WATCHING OVER YOU. / HALLOWED BE THY NAME** [ ] [ ]

Nov 78. (lp/c) *(K/K4 50552) <19211>* **LOVE BEACH** [48] [55]
– All I want is you / Love beach / Taste of my love / The gambler / For you / Canario / Memoirs of an officer and a gentleman – Prologue – The education of a gentleman / Love at first sight / Letters from the front / Honourable company. *(cd-iss. Jun89; K2 50552) (re-iss. cd Dec93 on 'Victory'; 828469-2)*

Nov 78. (7") *(K 11225)* **ALL I WANT IS YOU. / TIGER IN A SPOTLIGHT** [ ] [ ]

— disbanded December '78

Oct 79. (lp/c) *(K/K4 50652) <19255>* **EMERSON, LAKE & PALMER IN CONCERT (live 1978)** [ ] [73]
– (introductory fanfare) / Peter Gunn / Tiger in a spotlight / C'est la vie / The enemy god dances with the black spirits / Knife edge / Piano concerto No.1 / Pictures at an exhibition.

Dec 79. (7") *(K 11416)* **PETER GUNN (live). / KNIFE EDGE (live)** [ ] [ ]

KEITH EMERSON

Atlantic Atlantic

Sep 80. (7") *(K 11612)* **TAXI RIDE (ROME). / MATER TENEBRARUM** [ ] [ ]

Atlantic Cinevox

Dec 80. (lp) *(K 50753)* **INFERNO (Soundtrack)** [ ] [ ]
– Inferno / Rose's descent into a cellar / The taxi ride / The library / Sarah in the library vaults / Bookbinder's delight / Rose leaves the apartment / Rose gets it / Elisa's story / A cat attic attack / Kazanian's tarantella / Mark's discovery / Matter tenebarum / Inferno (finals) / Ices, cigarettes, etc. *(re-iss. Mar90 on 'Cinevox'; CIA 5022)*

— added **NEIL SYMONETTE** – drums / **TRISTAN FRY** – percussion / **GREG BOWEN** – trumpet / **JEROME RICHARDSON** – sax / **PAULETTE McWILLIAMS** – vocals

M.C.A. Backstreet

Apr 81. (7") *(MCA 697)* **I'M A MAN. / NIGHTHAWKS MAIN TITLE THEME** [ ] [ ]

Apr 81. (lp) *(MCF 3107)* **NIGHTHAWKS (Soundtrack)** [ ] [ ]
– Nighthawks – main title theme / Mean stalkin' / The bust / Nighthawking / The chase / I'm a man / The chopper / tramway / I'm comin' in / Face to face / The flight of the hawk. *(re-iss. Jan89; MCA 1521)*

Red Bus not iss.

Dec 83. (7") *(RBUS 85)* **UP THE ELEPHANT AND ROUND THE CASTLE. / ('A'instrumental)** [ ] [–]
(above featured comedian JIM DAVIDSON)

Chord not iss.

Apr 85. (lp) *(ESP 1)* **THE BEST OF KEITH EMERSON** (compilation) [ ] [–]

Apr 85. (lp/cd) *(CHORD/+CD 001)* **BEST REVENGE (Soundtrack with JOHN COLEMAN)** [ ] [–]
– Dream runner / The runner / Wha 'dya mean / Straight between the eyes / Orchestral suite to "Best Revenge" / Playing for keeps (main title theme). *(re-iss. Nov86)*

— **MOTT** – guitar / **DICK MORRISSEY + ANDREW BRENNAN + PETE KING** – saxophone

Apr 85. (lp/cd) *(CHORD/+CD 002)* **HONKY** [ ] [–]
– Hello sailor / Bach before the mast / Salt cay / Green ice / Intro-juicing / Big horn breakdown / Yancey special / Rum-a-thing / Jesus loves me. *(re-iss. May86)*

Apr 85. (lp) *(CHORD 003)* **HARMAGEDON / CHINA FREE FALL (Soundtracks; b-side by DEREK AUSTIN)** [ ] [–]
– Theme from Floi / Joe and Micheko / Children of the light / Funny's skate state / Zamedy stomp / Challenge of the psonic fighters. *(re-iss. Feb87)*

— Some with **DOREEN CHANTER** – vocals / **MIKE SEBBAGE** – vocals / **TOM NICOL + DEREK WILSON** – drums / **MICHAEL SHEPPARD** – bass, guitar, co-producer

May 86. (lp/cd) *(CHORD/+CD 004)* **MURDEROCK (soundtrack)** [ ] [–]
– Murderock / Tonight is your night / Streets to blame / Not so innocent / Prelude to Candice / Don't go in the shower / Coffee time / Candice / New York dash / Tonight is not your night / The spill one.

— next with The National Philharmonic Orchestra, plus **BRAD DELP, LEVON HELM.**

Dec 86. (cd) *(CDCOLL 1)* **THE EMERSON COLLECTION** (compilation) [ ] [–]

Priority — not iss.

Nov 88. (lp/c/cd) *(KEITH LP/MC/CD 1)* **EMERSON – THE CHRISTMAS ALBUM** [ ] [–]
(cd-iss. Jun93 & Dec95 on 'Amp'; AMPCD 018)

Emerson — not iss.

Dec 88. (7") *(KEITH 1)* **WE THREE KINGS OF ORIENT ARE. / CAPTAIN STARSHIP HOPKINS** [ ] [–]

Amp — not iss.

Apr 95. (cd) *(AMPCD 026)* **CHANGING STATES** [ ] [–]
Dec 95. (cd-s) **TROIKA (THE CHRISTMAS SINGLE). /** [ ] [–]

GREG LAKE BAND

GREG LAKE – vocals, guitar, bass with **TOMMY EYRE** – keyboards / **GARY MOORE** – guitar (ex-solo artist ex-THIN LIZZY ex-COLOSSEUM) / **TRISTRAM MARGETTS** – bass / **TED McKENNA** – drums (ex-SENSATIONAL ALEX HARVEY BAND)

Chrysalis — Chrysalis

Sep 81. (7") *(CHS 2553)* **LOVE YOU TOO MUCH. / SOMEONE** [ ] [–]
Oct 81. (lp/c) *(<CHR/ZCHR 1357>)* **GREG LAKE** [62] [62]
– Nuclear attack / Love you too much / It hurts / One before you go / Loving goodbye / Retribution drive / Black and blue / Let me love you once / The lies / For those who dare.
Dec 81. (7") *<2571>* **LET ME LOVE YOU ONCE. / RETRIBUTION DRIVE** [–] [48]
Feb 82. (7") *(CHS 2567)* **IT HURTS. / RETRIBUTION DRIVE** [ ] [ ]
Jul 83. (lp/c) *(<CHR/ZCHR 1392>)* **MANOEUVRES** [ ] [ ]
– Manoeuvres / Too young to love / Paralysed / A woman like you / I don't want to lose your love tonight / It's you, you've got to believe / Famous last words / Slave to love / Haunted / I don't know why I still love you.

— LAKE joined ASIA with PALMER

PM

CARL PALMER with **TODD COCHRAN** – keyboards / **BARRY FINNERTY** – guitar, vocals / **JOHN NITZINGER** – guitar, vocals / **ERIK SCOTT** – bass, vocals

Ariola — Ariola

May 80. (lp/c) *(ARL/ZCARL 5048)* **1 PM** [ ] [ ]
– Dynamite / You've got me rockin' / Green velvet splendour / Dreamers / Go on carry on / D'ya go all the way / Go for it / Madeleine / You're too much / Children of the air age.
Apr 80. (7") *(ARO 217)* **YOU GOT ME ROCKIN'. / GO FOR IT** [ ] [–]
Jul 80. (7") *(ARO 234)* **DYNAMITE. / D'YA GO ALL THE WAY** [ ] [–]

— (Jan81) PALMER joined ASIA

EMERSON, LAKE & POWELL

— are the new set up **COZY POWELL** (b.29 Dec'47, Cirencester, England) – drums, (ex-solo artist, ex-RAINBOW, etc.)

Polydor — Polydor

Jul 86. (lp/c)(cd) *(POLD/+C 5191)(<829 297-2>)* **EMERSON, LAKE & POWELL** [35] Jun86 [23]
– Mars, the bringer of war / The score / Learning to fly / Touch and go / Miracle / Love blind / Step aside / Lay down your guns.
Jul 86. (7") *(POSP 804)* *<885101>* **TOUCH AND GO. / LEARNING TO FLY** [ ] Jun86 [60]
(12"+=) *(POSPX 804)* – The locomotion.
Sep 86. (7") **LAY DOWN YOUR GUNS. /** [–] [ ]

— (1987 originals reformed but disbanded Oct87)

3

was the unit formed by **EMERSON, PALMER** and American **ROBERT BERRY** – vocals (ex-HUSH)

Geffen — Geffen

Feb 88. (lp/c/cd) *(924181-1/-4/-2)* *<24181>* **TO THE POWER OF THREE** [ ] [ ]
– Talkin' about / Lover to lover / Chains / Desde la vida / Eight miles high / Runaway / You do or you don't / On my way home.
Feb 88. (7") **TALKIN' ABOUT. / LA VISTA** [–] [ ]

EMERSON, LAKE & PALMER

— re-formed 1992

Victory-London — Victory

Apr 92. (cd/c/lp) *(828 318-2/-4/-2)* *<480003>* **BLACK MOON** [ ] Jun92 [78]
– Black Moon / Paper blood / Affairs of the heart / Romeo and Juliet / Farewell to arms / Changing states / Burning bridges / Close to home / Better days / Footprints in the snow. *(cd re-iss. Apr97 on 'Essential'; ESMCD 506)*

London — London

May 92. (7") *(LON 320)* **BLACK HOLE. / MILES IZ DEAD** [ ] [–]
(12"+=/cd-s+=) *(LON X/CD 320)* – A blade of grass.
Nov 92. (7"/c-s) *(LON/+C 327)* **AFFAIRS OF THE HEART. / BETTER DAYS** [ ] [–]
(cd-s+=) *(LONCD 327)* – A blade of grass / Black moon.
(cd-s) *(LOCDP 327)* – ('A'side) / Black moon (radio) / Fanfare for the common man / Jerusalem.
Feb 93. (cd/c) *(<828 933-2/-4>)* **LIVE AT THE ROYAL ALBERT HALL (live)** [ ] [ ]
– 1st impression part 2 / Tarkus: Eruption – Stones of years – Iconoclast / Knife edge / Paper blood / Romeo & Juliet / Creole dance / Still . . . you turn me on / Lucky man / Black moon / The pirates / Finale / Fanfare for the common man / America / Blue rondo A la Turk. *(cd re-iss. Apr97 on 'Essential'; ESMCD 504) (cd re-iss. Sep01; CMRCD 228)*
Nov 93. (4xcd-box) *(<828 459-2>)* **RETURN OF THE MANTICORE** (old & new material) [ ] [ ]
(re-iss. Nov96 on 'Essential'; ESFCD 421)
Dec 93. (cd) *(<828 477-2>)* **WORKS LIVE (live)** [ ] [ ]
Sep 94. (cd/c) *(<828 554-2/-4>)* **IN THE HOT SEAT** [ ] [ ]
– Hand of truth / Daddy / One by one / Heart on ice / Thin line / Man in the long black coat / Change / Give me a reason to stay / Gone too soon / Street war. *(cd+=)* – Pictures at an exhibition: a) Promenade – b) The gnome – c) Promenade – d) The sage – e) The hut of Baba Yaga – f) The great gates of Kiev.

Metal Minds — Metal Minds

Sep 99. (cd) *(PROGCD 006)* *<405613>* **LIVE IN POLAND (live 1997)** [ ] May01 [ ]
– Welcome back / Touch and go / From the beginning / Knife edge / Bitches crystal / Piano solo / Take a pebble / Lucky man / Medley: Tarkus – Pictures at an exhibition / Medley: Fanfare for the common man – Rondo. *(re-iss. Sep02 on 'Castle'; CMRCD 558)*

– compilations, others, etc. –

Nov 80. (lp/c) *Atlantic; (K/K4 50757)* *<19283>* **THE BEST OF EMERSON, LAKE & PALMER** [ ] [ ]
– Hoedown / Lucky man / Karn evil 9 / Trilogy / Fanfare for the common man / Still . . . you turn me on / Tiger in a spotlight / Jerusalem / Peter Gunn. *(cd-iss. 1983; K2 50757) (cd re-iss. Nov95 on 'Essential'; ESSCD 296)*
Jul 92. (cd/c/lp) *Atlantic; (<7567 82403-2/-4>)* **THE ATLANTIC YEARS** [ ] [ ]
Apr 97. (d-cd; GREG LAKE) *Essential; (ESDCD 522)* **FROM THE BEGINNING: THE GREG LAKE RETROSPECTIVE** [ ] [–]
Oct 98. (3xcd-box) *Essential; (ESMBX 303)* **EMERSON, LAKE & PALMER / TARKUS / PICTURES AT AN EXHIBITION** [ ] [ ]
Oct 98. (d-cd) *Eagle; (EDGCD 040)* **THEN & NOW (live 1974 & now)** [ ] [–]
Jan 01. (d-cd) *Castle; (CMEDD 110)* **FANFARE FOR THE COMMON MAN: THE ANTHOLOGY** [ ] [–]
Aug 01. (5xcd-box) *Castle; (<CMXBX 309>)* **THE ORIGINAL BOOTLEG SERIES FROM THE MANTICORE VAULTS VOL.1** [ ] [ ]

Aug 01. (8xcd-box) *Castle; (<CMXBX 330>)* **THE ORIGINAL BOOTLEG SERIES FROM THE MANTICORE VAULTS VOL.2** ☐ ☐
Oct 01. (d-cd) *Snapper; (SMDCD 370)* **THE SHOW THAT NEVER ENDS** ☐ –
Feb 02. (cd) *Castle; (CMRCD 458)* **LIVE AT THE ISLE OF WIGHT FESTIVAL 1970 (live)** ☐ –
May 02. (d-cd) *Castle; (<CMDDD 442>)* **BEST OF THE BOOTLEGS** ☐ ☐
Jul 02. (4xcd-box) *Castle; (<CMYBX 524>)* **THE ORIGINAL BOOTLEG SERIES FROM THE MANTICORE VAULTS VOL.3** ☐ ☐
Oct 02. (cd) *Delta; (CD 47098)* **FANFARE (THE 1997 WORLD TOUR)** ☐ –
Oct 02. (3xcd-box) *Burning Airlines; (<PILOT 145>)* **RE-WORKS** ☐ ☐
(lp-box-set-iss.Jul03 on 'Get Back'; GET 632)
Jan 03. (d-cd) *King Biscuit; (KBCCD 109)* **IN CONCERT (live)** ☐ –
May 03. (cd) *Music Club; (MCCD 520)* **FANFARE: THE BEST OF . . . LIVE** ☐ –
Aug 03. (cd) *Invisible Hands; (IHCD 23)* **RE-WORKS (BRAIN SALAD PERJURY)** ☐ –

EMF

Formed: Cinderford / Forest of Dean, Gloucestershire, England . . .late '89 by Oxford graduate IAN DENCH and JAMES ATKIN, DERRY BROWNSON, ZAC FOLEY, MARK DE CLOEDT and scratcher/DJ, MILF. After their 4th gig, they were spotted by ABBO (from former goth punks, UK DECAY) and his girlfriend, LINDA, who helped get them signed to 'E.M.I.' subsidiary, 'Parlophone' in March '90. Late that year, their debut single, 'UNBELIEVABLE', broke into the UK Top 3 and early the following year, they set about taking both sides of the Atlantic by storm. Similar in style, to say, JESUS JONES, or an uptempo DEPECHE MODE, EMF's brattish blend of indie dance and funky pop saw them hailed as the great white hopes of British music for as long as it took their teenybop fanbase to find someone new (i.e. not that long!). ATKIN's posh-accented whine was a bit much to take over the stretch of a whole album, although, spurred by the success of further singles, 'I BELIEVE' and 'CHILDREN', 'SCHUBERT DIP' (1991) was one of the year's biggest selling sets; it even did well in American where 'UNBELIEVABLE' had topped the charts. Touted as spearheading a second "British Invasion" along with JESUS JONES and Co., EMF's assault soon surrendered to the machinations of the music business as follow-up album, 'STIGMA' (1992) saw them making an ill-advised attempt at big boys' rock. Its heavier approach only succeeded in alienating their original fanbase, the band's apparent attempt to lighten up their image with a VIC REEVES and BOB MORTIMER collaboration (a Top 3 cover of The Monkees 'I'M A BELIEVER') not enough to prevent 'CHA CHA CHA' from virtually stiffing. Subsequently dropped by their label, EMF faced the inevitable and jacked it in. However, the story didn't quite finish there as DENCH resurfaced a few years later with his new trio, WHISTLER. Also comprising former disco singer, KERRY SHAW, and violin player JAMES TOPHAM, the group signed to the 'Wiiija' label and released a trio of singles (among them the music press fave, 'IF I GIVE YOU A SMILE') and an eponymous debut album in 1999. As starkly different to EMF as it was possible to get, the album's, pared-down folk-tinged indie-pop coalesced around SHAW's beguiling lullaby of a vocal. The band followed up with 'FAITH IN THE MORNING' (2000), another sweet treat that developed their easier-going approach. Sadly, on the 3rd of January 2002, IAN's old mucker, ZAC FOLEY, died. • **Covered:** LOW SPARK OF THE HIGH HEELED BOYS (Traffic) / SHADDAP YOU, FACE (Joe Dolce) / I'M A BELIEVER (Monkees) / STRANGE BREW (Cream). / WHISTLER:- AT SEVENTEEN (Janis Ian) / I JUST DON'T KNOW WHAT TO DO WITH MYSELF (hit; Dusty Springfield) / BLUE, RED AND GREY / ALL APOLOGIES (Nirvana). • **Trivia:** EMF was rumoured to stand for ECSTASY MOTHER FUCKERS, but later claimed to be EPSOM MAD FUNKERS.

Album rating: SCHUBERT DIP (*5) / STIGMA (*7) / CHA CHA CHA (*4) / EPSOM MAD FUNKERS: THE BEST OF EMF compilation (*6) / Whistler: WHISTLER (*6) / FAITH IN THE MORNING (*6)

JAMES ATKIN (b.28 Mar'67) – vocals / **IAN DENCH** (b. 7 Aug'64) – guitar, keyboards (ex-APPLE MOSAIC) / **DERRY BROWNSON** (b. DERRAN, 10 Nov'70) – samples, percussion (ex-LAC's) / **ZAC FOLEY** (b. ZACHARY, 9 Dec'70) – bass (ex-IUC's) / **MARK DE CLOEDT** (b.26 Jun'67) – drums (ex-ZU) / plus **MILF** – DJ scratcher

Parlophone E.M.I.

Oct 90. (c-s/7") *(TC+/R 6273)* **UNBELIEVABLE. / EMF (live)** 3 –
(12"+=/cd-s+=) *(12R/CDR 6273)* – ('A'-Cin City sex mix).
Jan 91. (c-s/7") *(TC+/R 6279)* **I BELIEVE. / WHEN YOU'RE MINE** 6 –
(12"+=/cd-s+=) *(12R/CDR 6279)* – Unbelievable (funk mix).
Mar 91. (c-s) *<50350>* **UNBELIEVABLE / ('A'-Cin City Sex mix)** – 1
Apr 91. (c-s/7") *(TC+/R 6288)* **CHILDREN. / STRANGE BREW (live remix)** 19 ☐
(12"+=) *(12R 6288)* – Children (mix).
(cd-s++=) *(CDR 6288)* – Children – Battle for the minds of North Amerika.
(7"ep+=) *(RX 6288)* – (live versions).
May 91. (cd/c/lp) *(CD/TC+/PCS 7353) <96238>* **SCHUBERT DIP** 3 12
– Children / Long summer days / When you're mine / Travelling not running / I believe / Unbelievable / Girl of an age / Admit it / Lies / Long time. *(re-iss. Mar94 cd/c; same) (cd re-iss. Oct00 on 'EMI Gold'; CDP 796238-2)*
Aug 91. (c-s/7") *(TC+/R 6295)* **LIES. / HEAD THE BALL** 28 –
(12"+=/cd-s+=) *(12R/CDR 6295)* – ('A'mix).
Sep 91. (c-s) *<50363>* **LIES / STRANGE BREW (live)** – 18
Apr 92. (7"ep) *(SGE 2026)* **UNEXPLAINED** 18 –
– Getting through / Far from me / The same.
(12"ep+=/cd-ep+=) *(12/CD SGE 2026)* – Search and destroy.
Sep 92. (c-s/7") *(TC+/R 6321)* **THEY'RE HERE. / PHANTASMAGORIC** 29 –
(12"+=) *(12R 6321)* – ('A'remix).
(cd-s+=) *(CDR 6321)* – Low spark of the high heeled boys.
Sep 92. (cd/c/lp) *(CD/TC+/PCSD 122) <80348>* **STIGMA** 19 ☐
– They're here / Arizona / It's you that leaves me dry / Never know / Blue highs / Inside / Getting through / She bleeds / Dog / The light that burns twice as bright . . .
Nov 92. (c-s/7") *(TC+/R 6327)* **IT'S YOU. / DOF (Foetus mix)** 23 –
(cd-s+=) *(CDR 6327)* – (2 other 'A'-Butch Vig mixes).
(cd-ep) *(CDRS 6327)* – It's you (Orbital mix) / The light that burns twice as bright . . . (mix) / They're here (mix).

Parlophone Parlophone

Feb 95. (c-s) *(TCR 6401)* **PERFECT DAY / ANGEL** 27 –
(cd-s+=) *(CDR 6401)* – I won't give into you / Kill for you (lo-fi mix).
(12"+=) *(12R 6401)* – ('A'-Temple of boom remix) / ('A'-Chris & James epic).
(cd-s) *(CDRS 6401)* – ('A'side) / ('A'-Chris & James mix) / ('A'-Black One mix) / ('A'-Toytown mix).
Mar 95. (cd/c) *(<CD/TC PCSD 165>)* **CHA CHA CHA** 30 ☐
– Perfect day / La plage / The day I was born / Secrets / Shining / Bring me down / Skin / Slouch / Bleeding you dry / Patterns / When will you come / West of the Cox / Ballad o' the bishop / Glass smash Jack.
Apr 95. (c-s) *(TCR 6407)* **BLEEDING YOU DRY / TOO MUCH / EASY / PERFECT DAY (acoustic)** ☐ –
(cd-s) *(CDRS 6407)* – (first 3 tracks) / Shining (acoustic).
(cd-s) *(CDR 6407)* – ('A'side) / I pushed the boat out so far it sank / Patterns (acoustic).
Jun 95. (c-s/7"; EMF and REEVES & MORTIMER) *(TC+/R 6412)* **I'M A BELIEVER. / AT LEAST WE'VE GOT OUR GUITARS** 3 –

(cd-s) *(CDR 6412)* – ('A'side) / At this stage I couldn't say / ('A'-Unbelievable mix) / La plage (mix).

Oct 95. (c-s) *(TCR 6416)* **AFRO KING / UNBELIEVABLE** [51] [–]
(cd-s+=) *(CDR 6416)* – Children / I believe.
(cd-s) *(CDRS 6416)* – ('A'side) / Too much / Easy / Bring me down.

— split not long after the relative failure of the above single. DENCH returned in 1998 with a new outfit, WHISTLER

– compilations, etc. –

1998. (cd,c; shared with JESUS JONES) *EMI Capitol special; <19641>* **BACK 2 BACK** [–] [ ]

Jun 01. (d-cd) *Parlophone; (533543-2)* **EPSOM MAD FUNKERS: THE BEST OF EMF** [ ] [–]

EMINEM

Born: MARSHALL MATHERS, 17 Oct'72, St. Joseph, Missouri, USA. Spending his childhood roaming from one State to the next, the gifted rapper and one time SOUL INTENT member began freestyling in his friend's basement at the age of fifteen. Five years (and, apparently, a lot of mushrooms and NWA albums) later, the white MC decided to try his luck in the increasing world of hip hop. He debuted with the poorly distributed album 'INFINITE' (1996) and failed blindly at attracting attention from any major labels. Legend DR DRE apparently discovered EMINEM (a word play on his initials) when he found a demo tape on Interscope's Jimmy Iovines' garage floor. To be fully convinced by the rapper, DRE travelled to watch him perform in the 1997 Rap Olympics before rushing over and signing him on the spot. His major label debut, 'THE SLIM SHADY LP', appeared in the Spring of '99, sales boosted after the rather offensive massive hit single, 'MY NAME IS'. The aforementioned platter rocketed to the top spot in America and sent parents into a fit of rage over the filth and obscenities our white chump was slobbering about on tape. The American media, senseless rock stars and a few bad words about his dear old momma were all mentioned in the single, that had such an infectious chorus it made listeners fall under the spell of EMINEM's crazy, high-speed, nasal-pinching slur. The sophomore album did not do so bad either, selling nearly a million copies in its first week and a further million in the months after its release. But the waging battle between him and the general public continued, when songs that depicted rape, murder, violence, excessive drug taking, child molesting and, erm, his poor old mother were all raised in frequent "morality" debates. The second single (and to some, his finest), 'GUILTY CONSCIENCE', featured DRE as his alter ego, who pops up to discuss EMINEM's relationship problems when he finds his wife in bed with another man. Not surprising to see then, that EMINEM returned the favour by contributing to DRE's '2001' LP on the brilliant and humourous track 'IT'S ALL ABOUT DRE'. The crown king of confrontation returned in 2001 with 'THE MARSHALL MATHERS LP', an even darker journey through his tortured psychscape, shot through with as much humour as ever but pinned back with (un)healthy doses of stark realism. The pairing of MATHERS and cooing pop songbird DIDO on 'STAN' was a true stroke of genius, one that resulted in a huge UK No.1 single. This was preceded by 'THE REAL SLIM SHADY', a shuffling, propulsive groove taking it to the top; he was now taking the alter-ego of the Texas Chainsaw Massacre on stage – a tough life indeed! 2001 saw the emergence of D-12, a project from the preceding decade initiated by BIZARRE and PROOF (aka RUFUS JOHNSON and DeSHAUN HOLTON). Joined by KON ARTIS, KUNIVA plus BUGZ (the latter was shot dead in 1998 and replaced by SWIFTY McVAY), the alter-ego outfit that was the DIRTY DOZEN soon got together with childhood buddy EMINEM. The Slim Shady MATHERS and his five cohorts soon put together some tracks, the first of which being the extremely controversial, '$#!* ON YOU'. A hit in the UK early 2001, it was pursued by their OTT set that was 'DEVIL'S NIGHT'. No.1 in America (No.2 in the UK) it showed EMINEM and his juvenile rap partners (aged between 23 and 25 at the time) full of expletives, explicit lyrics and explosive violence incorporating the usual drugs-talk; 'PURPLE PILLS' was a single hit on both sides of the Atlantic. The effable terrible of the rap scene returned in May 2002 with his ego firmly in place, delivering 'THE EMINEM SHOW'. The album consisted of the usual disgruntled outbursts at his critics and enemies, personal and international; if the 'MARSHAL MATHERS LP' was a concept album about his emotional strife, then this was centered upon the ever-looming media circle that surrounded him. Bad and good in equal measures, 'WHITE AMERICA', with its guitar riffs and bludgeoning beats was a poisoned reaction against the American government that recalled the recently defunct RAGE AGAINST . . . Elsewhere, 'WITHOUT ME' was typical jestering EMINEM, all jokey lyrics and poppy hooks. 'SQUARE DANCE' was also a particular highlight, with DRE at the helm once again, whereas 'SUPERMAN' was a sleazy as they come, demonstrating some warped synthesiser and a porn star endorsed video to boot. The weaker moments, the AEROSMITH sampled 'DREAM ON' and 'CLEANING OUT MY CLOSET' (Lennon's 'Jealous Guy', anyone?) were simply dripping in melted cheese. Not surprising then that both were massive hits, but, like they say, kids will do anything for the taste of Dairylee.

Album rating: INFINITE (*4) / THE SLIM SHADY LP (*9) / MARSHALL MATHERS LP (*9) / THE EMINEM SHOW (*7) / D-12: DEVIL'S NIGHT (*7)

EMINEM – vocals / with **MARKY + JEFF BASS**

not iss. Indep . . .

1996. (cd-s; as SOUL INTENT) *<none>* **FUCKING BACKSTABBER / BITERPHOBIA** [–] [ ]

1997. (d-lp) *<INF 01P>* **INFINITE** [–] [ ]
– Infinite / W.E.G.O. (interlude) / It's ok / 313 / Tonite / Maxine / Open mic / Never 2 far – Searchin' / Backstabber / Jealousy. *(UK-iss.Jan03; same as US)*

Interscope Interscope

Oct 98. (c-s,cd-s)(12") *<97044><95037>* **JUST DON'T GIVE A F***. / BRAIN DAMAGE** [–] [ ]

Mar 99. (c-s) *(INC 95638) <95040>* **MY NAME IS / (clean)** [2] Feb99 [36]
(cd-s) *(IND 95638)* – ('A'-instrumental).
(12") *(INT 95638)* – ('A'mixes).

Apr 99. (cd/c-d-lp)(clean;cd/c) *<(IND/INC/INT 90287)><(IND/INC 90321)>* **THE SLIM SHADY LP** [12] Feb99 [2]
– (Public service announcement) / My name is / Guilty conscience / Brain damage / Paul / If I had / 97' Bonnie & Clyde / Bitch / Role model / Lounge / My fault / Ken Kaniff / Cum on everybody / Rock bottom / Just don't give a fuck / Soap / As the world turns / I'm shady / Bad meets evil / Still don't give a fuck.

May 99. (12") *(RWK 193)* **ANY MAN. / ('A'mix)** [ ] [–]
(above issued on 'Rawkus')

Aug 99. (c-s; by EMINEM & DR.DRE) *(497129-4) <97097>* **GUILTY CONSCIENCE / ('A'mix with gunshots)** [5] Jun99 [25]
(cd-s) *(497128-2)* – ('A'side) / ('A'-acappella) / ('A'video).
(cd-s+=) *(497129-2)* – My name is (video).

May 00. (cd/c/d-lp) *<(490629-2/-4/-1)>* **THE MARSHALL MATHERS LP** [1] [1]
– (Public service announcement 2000) / Kill you / Stan / Paul (skit) / Who knew / Steve Berman / The way I am / The real Slim Shady / Remember me? / I'm back / Marshall Mathers / Kem Kaniff (skit) / Drug ballad / Amityville / Bitch please II / Kim / Under the influence / Criminal. *(censored version; 490632-2)*

— In Jun'00, EMINEM was also credited on DR DRE's UK Top single, 'Forget About Dre'

Jun 00. (c-s) *(497379-4)* *<497334>* **THE REAL SLIM SHADY / (instrumental)** 1 Apr00 4
(12"+=/cd-s+=) *(497379-1/-2)* – Bad influence / My fault (pizza mix).

Oct 00. (c-s) *(497425-4)* *<497399>* **THE WAY I AM / BAD INFLUENCE** 8 Aug00 58
(cd-s+=) *(497425-2)* – My fault (pizza mix) / ('A'-video).
(12") *(497425-1)* – ('A'side) / ('A'-instrumental).

Dec 00. (c-s; as EMINEM & DIDO) *(497470-4)* *<radio cut>* **STAN / MY NAME IS** 1 Nov00 51
(cd-s+=) *(497470-2)* – Get you mad / Stan (video).
(12") *(497470-1)* – ('A'side) / Get you mad / ('A'instrumental).

—— in Aug'01, EMINEM featured on BAD MEETS EVIL's hit, 'Scary Movies'

May 02. (c-s) *(497728-4)* *<497731>* **WITHOUT ME / (instrumental)** 1 2
(12"+=) *(497728-1)* – The way I am (w/ MARILYN MANSON).
(cd-s+=) *(497728-2)* – ('A'-acappella).

May 02. (cd/c/d-lp) *<(493290-2/-4/-1)>* **THE EMINEM SHOW** 1 1
– Curtains up / White America / Business / Cleanin' out my closet / Square dance / The kiss / Soldier / Say goodbye Hollywood / Drips (with OBIE TRICE) / Without me / (Paul Rosenberg – skit) / Sing for the moment / Superman (with DINA RAE) / Hailie's song / (Steve Berman – skit) / When the music stops (with D-12) / Say what you say (with DR. DRE) / 'Till I collapse (with NATE DOGG) / My dad's gone crazy (with HAILIE JADE) / Curtains close.

Sep 02. (c-s) *(497394-4)* *<radio>* **CLEANIN' OUT MY CLOSET / RENEGADE** 4 4
(cd-s+=) *(497394-2)* – ('A'-instrumental) / ('A'-video).
(12") *(497394-1)* – ('A'side) / ('A'-instrumental) / ('A'-acappella) / Stimulate.

Dec 02. (c-s) *(497828-4)* **LOSE YOURSELF / ('A'-instrumental)** 1 —
(cd-s+=) *(497828-2)* – Renegade / ('A'-video).
(12") *(497828-1)* *<INTR 7815>* – ('A'side & mixes).

Dec 02. (cd-s) **SUPERMAN (mixes)** – 15

Mar 03. (c-s/12") *(497871-4/-1)* **SING FOR THE MOMENT / SING FOR THE MOMENT (instrumental) / RABBIT RUN** 6 14
(cd-s+=) *(497871-2)* – ('A'video).

Jul 03. (12") *(980838-3)* **BUSINESS. / CONSPIRACY (freestyle – DJ Green Lantern version) / BUMP HEADS (DJ Green Lantern mix)** 6 –
(cd-s+=) *(980838-2)* – ('A'-live video).
(cd-s) *(980938-1)* – ('A'side) / Bump heads (DJ Green Lantern mix) / ('A'-live from Barcelona video).

D-12

EMINEM + **PETER S. BIZARRE** (b. RUFUS JOHNSON) – vocals (of OUTSIDAZ) / **PROOF** (b. DeSHAUN HOLTON) – vocals / **KUNIVA** (aka VON CARLISLE or HANNZ G) – vocals / **SWIFTY McVAY** (aka O. MOORE) – vocals; repl. BUGZ (who died 1998) + **KON ARTIS** (b. DENINE PORTER) – producer

Interscope Interscope

Mar 01. (c-s) *(497496-4)* *<497484>* **$#!* ON YOU / (version)** 10 Dec00 —
(12"+=) *(497496-1)* – Under the influence (explicit) / $#!* on you (instrumental).
(cd-s++=) *(497496-2)* – ('A'-CD-Rom).

Jun 01. (d-cd/c/d-lp) *(493079-2/-4/-1)* *<490897>* **DEVIL'S NIGHT** 2 1
– Another public announcement / Shit can happen / Pistol pistol / Bizarre (skit) / Nasty mind (with TRUTH HURTS) / Ain't nuthin' but music / American psycho / That's how (skit) / That's how . . . / Purple pills / Fight music / Instigator / Pimp like me (featuring DINA RAE) / Blow my buzz / Obie trice (skit by RONDELL BEENE & OBIE TRICE) / Devil's night / Steve Berman (by STEVE BERMAN & EMINEM) / Revelation / Girls / $#!* on you / Words are weapons / These drugs. *(clean version w/ less tracks Sep01; 490896-2)*

Jul 01. (c-s) *(497565-4)* *<497569>* **PURPLE PILLS / $#!* ON YOU (explicit)** 2 Jun01 19
(12"+=/cd-s+=) *(497587-1/-2)* – That's how . . . (explicit).
(cd-s) *(497569-2)* – ('A'-clean) / $#!* on you (clean) / That's how . . . (clean) / ('A'-CD-Rom).

Nov 01. (c-s/12") *(497652-4/-1)* *<497645>* **FIGHT MUSIC. / FREESTYLE / WORDS ARE WEAPONS** 11 —
(cd-s+=) *(497652-2)* – ('A'-CD-Rom).

ENIGMA

Formed: By the German-based duo of MICHAEL CRETU and wife SANDRA who almost immediately found themselves with an unusual worldwide hit in 'SADENESS', early in 1991. Born in Bucharest, Rumania (18th of May '57), CRETU had been trained as a classical pianist in Paris, although he subsequently moved to Frankfurt's Academy Of Music and to conducting. In the late 70's, he worked as a session musician and became a key figure for the European disco scene. Around the same period, CRETU released his debut album, 'MOON, LIGHT AND FLOWERS', for the German side of 'Polydor'. A few years later, his outfit, MOTI SPECIAL, hit the top of the German charts with a single, 'COLD DAYS HOT NIGHTS' (Carrere; 7"/12" CAR/+T 364) taken from the album 'MOTI VATION'. He subsequently left MOTI members, NILS TUXEN and DICKY TARRACH, when he discovered, then produced his wife's massive Euro hit, 'I'LL NEVER BE MARIA MAGDALENA'. The electronic wizard went onto produce several albums by SANDRA and went on to work with MIKE OLDFIELD, whom he had met at his Ibiza residence. With three albums, 'MCMXC a.D.' (1991), 'THE CROSS OF CHANGES' (1994) and 'LE ROI EST MORT, VIVE LE ROI!' (1996), now safely under their belt, ENIGMA have now sold nearly 20 million, their Gregorian chant musak (initially sampled from Munich's Kapelle Antiqua Choir) over a hip-hop dance beat, the toast of the coffee-table set. Back after an extended late 90's absence, CRETU took his ENIGMA project into the new millennium with 'THE SCREEN BEHIND THE MIRROR' (2000). The usual meditative ingredients – classical samples, religious choirs, experimental rhythms etc. – were all present and correct although this time around the German pastiche meister had decided to give his own vocals a bigger share of the spotlight. Having taken his medieval pot-pourri about as far as it could go, the Romanian changed tact on 'VOYAGEUR' (2003), freeing up his hermetic sound and embracing elements from contemporary electronica and dance. • **Sampled:** SONGS FROM THE VICTORIOUS CITY (Anne Dudley & Jaz Coleman) + THE CALLING (Mind Over Rhythm).

Album rating: MCMXC a.D. (*6) / THE CROSS OF CHANGES (*5) / LE ROI EST MORT, VIVE LE ROI! (*4) / THE SCREEN BEHIND THE MIRROR (*5) / LSD: LOVE SENSUALITY DEVOTION – THE GREATEST HITS compilation (*6) / VOYAGEUR (*5)

CURLY M.C. (MICHAEL CRETU) – electronics / **F. GREGORIAN** (b. SANDRA, France) – vocals / **DAVID-FAIRSTEIN** – etc.

Virgin Int Charisma

Nov 90. (7"/c-s) *(DINS/+C 101)* *<98864>* **SADENESS (part 1). / ('A'-Meditation mix)** 1 5
(12"+=/cd-s+=) *(DINS T/D 101)* – ('A'extended) / ('A'violent US mix).

Dec 90. (cd/c/lp) *(CD/MC+/VIR 11)* *<91642>* **MCMXC a.D.** 1 6
– The voice of Enigma / Principles of lust (a) Sadeness (b) Find love (c) Sadeness-(reprise) / Callas went away / Mea culpa / The voice & the snake / Knocking on-forbidden doors / Back to the rivers of belief (a) Way to eternity (b) Hallelujah (c) The rivers of belief. *(re-iss. Nov91)*

Mar 91. (7"/c-s) *(DINS/+C 104)* **MEA CULPA (part II). / ('A'-Catholic mix)** 55 –
(12"+=/cd-s+=) *(DINS T/D 104)* – ('A'-fading shades mix).

Sep 91. (7"/c-s) *(DINS 110)* **PRINCIPLES OF LUST. / SADENESS (pt.2 radio mix)** 59 –
(12"+=) *(DINST 110)* – ('A'extended) / ('A'-Owen mix).
(cd-s+=) *(DINSD 110)* – ('A'-jazz mix) / ('A'-Owen mix).

Jan 92. (7"/c-s) *(DINS/+C 112)* **THE RIVERS OF BELIEF. / KNOCKING ON FORBIDDEN-DOORS** 68 —
(12"/cd-s) *(DINS T/CD 112)* – ('A'mixes).

Jan 94. (7"/c-s) *(DINS/+C 123)* *<38423>* **RETURN TO INNOCENCE. / ('A'-380 midnight mix)** 3 4
(12"+=) *(DINST 123)* – ('A'extended mix).
(cd-s++=) *(DINSD 123)* – ('A'mix).

Feb 94. (cd/c/lp) *(CD/MC+/VIR 20)* <39236> **THE CROSS OF CHANGES** 1 9
– Second chapter / The eyes of truth / Return to innocence / Love you . . . I'll kill you / Silent warrior / The dream of the dolphin / Age of loneliness (Carly's song) / Out from the deep / The cross of changes. *(gold-cd-iss. Nov94; CDVIRX 20)*

May 94. (7"/c-s) *(DINS/+C 126)* **THE EYES OF TRUTH. / ('A'mix)** 21 -
(cd-s+=) *(DINSD 126)* – (2 other 'A'mixes).
(cd-s) *(DINSDX 126)* – ('A'side) / Sadeness (part I) / Mea culpa (part II) / Principles of lust.

Aug 94. (12"/c-s) *(DINS T/C 135)* **AGE OF LONELINESS. / ('A'-Jam & Spoon mix)** 21
(cd-s+=) *(DINSDX 135)* – Return to innocence (mix) / Sadeness part 1 (mix) / Principles of lust (everlasting lust).
(cd-s) *(DINSD 135)* – (5-'A'mixes).

Virgin Int Virgin

Nov 96. (cd/c) *(CD/MC VIR 60)* <42066> **LE ROI EST MORT, VIVE LE ROI!** 12 Dec96 25
– Le roi est mort, vive le roi / Morphing thru time / Third of its kind / Beyond the invisible / Why / Shadows in silence / Child in us / TNT for the brain / Almost full moon / Roundabout / Prism of life / Odyssey of the mind.

Jan 97. (c-s) *(DINSC 155)* <38572> **BEYOND THE INVISIBLE / ALMOST FULL MOON** 26 Nov96 81
(cd-s+=) *(DINSD 155)* – Light of your smile.

Apr 97. (c-s) *(DINSC 161)* **TNT FOR THE BRAIN / ('A'mix)** 60
(cd-s) *(DINSD 161)* – ('A'mixes).

Nov 99. (c-s/cd-s) *(DINS C/D 195)* **GRAVITY OF LOVE (mixes: radio / Judgement day club / Dark vocal)** -

Jan 00. (cd/c) *(CD/TC VIR 100)* <48616> **THE SCREEN BEHIND THE MIRROR** 7 33
– The gate / Push the limits / Gravity of love / Smell of desire / Modern crusaders / Traces (light and weight) / The screen behind the mirror / Endless quest / Camera obscura / Between mind & heart / Silence must be heard.

Jun 00. (12"/cd-s) *(DINS T/D 205)* **PUSH THE LIMITS (mixes; radio / ATB radio remix / remix)** -

Oct 01. (c-s) *(DINSC 225)* **TURN AROUND / GRAVITY OF LOVE (chilled club mix)** -
(cd-s+=) *(DINSD 225)* – ('A'-northern lights club mix).

Nov 01. (cd) *(CDVIR 150)* <11119> **LSD: LOVE SENSUALITY AND DEVOTION – THE GREATEST HITS** (compilation) 29 29
– The landing / Turn around / Gravity of love / TNT for the brain / Modern crusaders / Shadows in silence / Return to innocence / Love you . . . I'll kill you / Principles of lust / Sadness / Silence must be heard / Smell of desire / Mea culpa / Push the limits / Beyond the invisible / Age of loneliness / Morphing thru time / The cross of changes.

Nov 01. (cd) *(CDVIR 149)* **LSD: LOVE SENSUALITY AND DEVOTION – THE REMIX COLLECTION** -

Sep 03. (cd) *(CDVIRX 211)* <91929> **VOYAGEUR** 46 94
– From east to west / Voyageur / Incognito / Page of cups / Boum-boum / Total eclipse of the Moon / Look of today / In the shadow, in the light / Weightless / The piano / Following the sun.

– compilations, etc. –

Nov 98. (3xcd-box) *Virgin; (CDVRB 67)* **TRILOGY** -
– (first 3 albums)

Brian ENO

Born: BRIAN PETER GEORGE ST.JOHN LE BAPTISTE DE LA SALLE ENO, 15 May'48, Suffolk, England. After leaving art school, where he fronted heavy group MAXWELL DEMON, he joined ROXY MUSIC in 1971. Contributing greatly to their image and sound on the albums, 'ROXY MUSIC' & 'FOR YOUR PLEASURE', he left due to a dispute over their increasingly pop-rock orientated direction. His first post-ROXY venture was '(NO PUSSYFOOTING)' in 1973 with ROBERT FRIPP (of KING CRIMSON). This was nothing more than extreme experimentation of synth-electronics and treated guitar. However, it did provide art lovers with a photo-shot of ENO & FRIPP in a multi-mirrored room. His first solo work in early 1974, 'HERE COME THE WARM JETS', disappointed the critics, who gave it the thumbs down, bar one gem, 'BABY'S ON FIRE'. He released two more greatly improved efforts for 'Island' before he formed his own label in 1975, appropriately titled 'Obscure'. Preceding this, in a fit of depression, he joined The WINKIES for a short tour during Feb-Mar'74, but departed after being diagnosed with a collapsed lung. He recovered to find himself on an 'Island records' concert bill on '1st JUNE, 1974', alongside stablemates KEVIN AYERS, NICO and JOHN CALE. The following year, he was hit by a car, which caused slight but not lasting brain damage. 1975's 'ANOTHER GREEN WORLD' represented the fruition of ENO's aural experimentation, sculpting instrumental, insidiously melodic soundscapes while the title track was subsequently used as the theme tune for the BBC TV arts series, 'Arena'. 'BEFORE AND AFTER SCIENCE' (1977) was an equally brilliant, if colder sounding, tapestry of sonic delights. Around this time, ENO began working with DAVID BOWIE on a trilogy of lp's that included 'LOW' (1977) and 'HEROES' (1977), while the following year he hooked up with TALKING HEADS, producing three of their albums during the period 1978-'80. He also collaborated with DAVID BYRNE on the ethnic-flavoured 'MY LIFE IN THE BUSH OF GHOSTS' (1981). With 'AMBIENT 1: MUSIC FOR AIRPORTS' (1978), ENO created an innovative classic while 'APOLLO: ATMOSPHERS AND SOUNDTRACKS' (1983) was a beguiling fusion of country and ambient, the gorgeous 'DEEP BLUE DAY' belatedly cropping up on the 'TRAINSPOTTTING' (1996) soundtrack. After initially collaborating with Canadian producer/engineer DANIEL LANOIS for production duties on such early 80's projects as 'THE PEARL' (a HAROLD BUDD/ENO album), the two worked wonders on U2's seminal 'UNFORGETTABLE FIRE' (1984). ENO clocked up further U2 production credits on 'THE JOSHUA TREE' (1987) and 'ACHTUNG BABY' (1991), scooping a joint Grammy (with LANOIS) in 1992 for the latter. The same year saw the release of a long awaited ENO solo album, 'NERVE NET', which took its cue from the burgeoning ambient techno scene. Throughout the 90's, this electronic auteur has continued to work on a dizzying array of music and other multi media projects, even publishing a volume of diaries in 1996, 'A YEAR WITH SWOLLEN APPENDICES'. The balding genius once described himself as a non-musician who just turned dials and switches. Maybe, but he happens to turn the right dials and switches, and this technically brilliant ambient experimentalist's obscure new musak is possibly a direct link to what listeners will appreciate in the 21st century. Following on from his collaboration with JAH WOBBLE on 1995's 'SPINNER', 'DRAWN FROM LIFE' (2001) once again proved that ENO is probably most effective when he has someone to bounce ideas off. This time around it was J. PETER SCHWALM, a German DJ with whom he'd previously worked on a Japanese-only release. LAURIE ANDERSON also contributed her inimitable vocals although the bulk of the tracks were instrumental. • **Songwriters:** All composed by ENO. • **Trivia:** His 1977 song 'KING'S LEAD HAT' was in fact an anagram of TALKING HEADS. ENO has also done session and production work for JOHN CALE (1974-75), ROBERT WYATT (1975), ROBERT CALVERT (1975), DAVID BOWIE (1977) / DEVO (1978) / TALKING HEADS (1978-80) / U2 (1985-91 with Daniel Lanois) / etc.

Album rating: NO PUSSYFOOTIN' with Fripp (*2 at the time – *6 now!?) / HERE COME THE WARM JETS (*7) / TAKING TIGER MOUNTAIN (BY STRATEGY) (*7) / ANOTHER GREEN WORLD (*9) / DISCREET MUSIC (*6) /

EVENING STAR with Fripp (*2 at the time – *5 now!?) / BEFORE AND AFTER SCIENCE (*8) / CLUSTER AND ENO with Cluster (*6) / AFTER THE HEAT with Moebius & Roedelius (*6) / MUSIC FOR FILMS (*6) / AMBIENT 1: MUSIC FOR AIRPORTS (*7) / AMBIENT 2: THE PLATEAUX OF MIRROR with Harold Budd (*5) / FOURTH WORLD VOL.1: POSSIBLE MUSICS with Jon Hassell (*6) / MY LIFE IN THE BUSH OF GHOSTS with David Byrne (*8) / AMBIENT 4: ON LAND (*7) / APOLLO, ATMOSPHERES & SOUNDTRACKS with Daniel Lanois & Roger Eno (*8) / THE PEARL with Harold Budd & Daniel Lanois (*5) / THURSDAY AFTERNOON (*6) / HYBRID with Michael Brook & Daniel Lanois (*5) / VOICES with Roger Eno (*5) / MORE BLANK THAN FRANK compilation (*7) / DESERT ISLAND SELECTION compilation (*7) / MUSIC FOR FILMS 2 (*6) / WRONG WAY UP with JOHN CALE (*7) / NERVE NET (*6) / THE SHUTOV ASSEMBLY (*6) / :NEROLI: (*5) / SPINNER with Jah Wobble (*6) / THE DROP (*5) / DRAWN FROM LIFE with J. Peter Schwalm (*5)

FRIPP & ENO

ROBERT FRIPP – guitar of KING CRIMSON / **BRIAN ENO** – synthesizers, instruments

Island-Help Antilles

Nov 73. (lp) *(HELP 16) <7007>* **(NO PUSSYFOOTING)** ☐ ☐
– The heavenly music corporation / Swastika girls. *(re-iss. Oct77 on 'Polydor'; 2343 095) (re-iss. Jan87 on 'E.G.' lp/cd; EGED/EEGCD 2)*

ENO

now solo with guest session people, including ROXY MUSIC musicians and ROBERT FRIPP, CHRIS SPEDDING, PAUL RUDOLPH and others.

Island Island

Jan 74. (lp/c) *(ILPS/ICT <9268>)* **HERE COME THE WARM JETS** 26 ☐
– Needles in the camel's eye / The paw paw Negro blowtorch / Baby's on fire / Cindy tells me / Driving me backwards / On some faraway beach / Black rank / Dead finks don't talk / Some of them are old / Here come the warm jets. *(re-iss. Mar77 on 'Polydor'; 2302 063) (re-iss. Jan87 on 'E.G.' lp/c/cd; EG LP/MC/CD 11) (cd re-iss. Mar91; same)*

Mar 74. (7") *(WIP 6178)* **SEVEN DEADLY FINNS. / LATER ON** ☐ ☐

— guests incl. PORTSMOUTH SINFONIA ORCHESTRA, PHIL COLLINS – drums / etc.

Nov 74. (lp/c) *(ILPS/ICT <9309>)* **TAKING TIGER MOUNTAIN (BY STRATEGY)** ☐ ☐
– Burning airlines give you so much more / Back in Judy's jungle / The fat lady of Limbourg / Mother whale eyeless / The great pretender / Third uncle / Put a straw under baby / The truth wheel / China my China / Taking tiger mountain. *(re-iss. Mar77 on 'Polydor'; 2302 068) (re-iss. Jan87 on 'E.G.' lp/c/cd; EG LP/MC/CD 17) (cd re-iss. Mar91; same)*

Aug 75. (7") *(WIP 6233) <036>* **THE LION SLEEPS TONIGHT (WIMOWEH). / I'LL COME RUNNING** ☐ ☐

— now with **FRIPP** (3) / **COLLINS** (3) / **JOHN CALE** – viola (2) / **PAUL RUDOPLH** (3) / **PERCY JONES** – bass (3) / **ROD MELVIN** – piano (3) / **BRIAN TURRINGTON** – bass, piano (1)

Sep 75. (lp/c) *(ILPS/ICT <9351>)* **ANOTHER GREEN WORLD** ☐ ☐
– Sky saw / Over Fire Island / St. Elmo's fire / In dark trees / The big ship / I'll come running / Another green world / Sombre reptiles / Little fishes / Golden hours / Becalmed / Zawinul – Lava / Everything merges with the night. *(re-iss. Mar77 on 'Polydor'; 2302 069) (re-iss. Jan87 & Mar91 on 'E.G.' lp/c/cd; EG LP/MC/CD 21)*

Obscure Antilles

Nov 75. (lp) *(OBS 3) <7030>* **DISCREET MUSIC** ☐ ☐
– Discreet music 1 & 2 / Three Variations on canon in D major; a) Fullness of wind – b) French catalogues – c) Brutal ardour. *(re-iss. Jan87 on 'EG-Editions' lp/c/cd; EGED/EGEDC/EEGCD 23)*

FRIPP & ENO

collaborate again.

Help-Island Antilles

Dec 75. (lp) *(HELP 22) <7018>* **EVENING STAR** ☐ ☐
– Wind on water / Evening star / Evensong / Wind on wind / An index of metals. *(re-iss. Oct77 on 'Polydor'; 2343 094) (re-iss. Jan87 on 'E.G.' lp/cd; EGED/EEGCD 3)*

— For the next couple of years he worked with 801 (PHIL MANZANERA's band). He also produced his own 'Obscure' label, discovering people including PENGUIN CAFE ORCHESTRA, MICHAEL NYMAN, MAX EASTLEY & DAVID TOOP, HAROLD BUDD plus JAN STEELE / JOHN CAGE. More commercially he also played on and produced 1977 albums by DAVID BOWIE, TALKING HEADS, ULTRAVOX.

BRIAN ENO

Polydor Island

Dec 77. (lp) *(2302 071) <9478>* **BEFORE AND AFTER SCIENCE** ☐ May78 ☐
– No one receiving / Backwater / Kurt's rejoiner / Energy fools the magician / King's lead hat / Here he comes / Julie with . . . / By this river / Through hollow lands / Spider and I. *(re-iss. Jan87 on 'E.G.' lp/c/cd; EG LP/MC/CD 32) (cd re-iss. Mar91; same)*

Jan 78. (7") *(2001 762)* **KING'S LEAD HAT. / R.A.F. (by "ENO & SNATCH")** ☐ ☐

Polydor E.G.

Sep 78. (lp) *(2310 623) <EGS 105>* **MUSIC FOR FILMS** 55 ☐
– M386 / Aragon / From the same hill / Inland sea / Two rapid formations / Slow water / Sparrowfall 1 / Sparrowfall 2 / Sparrowfall 3 / Quartz / Events in dense fog / There is nobody / A measured room / Patrolling wire borders / Task force / Alternative 3 / Strange light / Final sunset. *(privately pressed 1976 on 'EG'; EGM 1) (re-iss. Jan87 on 'E.G.' lp/c/cd; EGED/EGEDC/EEGCD 5)*

Ambient P.V.C.

Mar 79. (lp/c) *(AMB/+C 001) <7908>* **AMBIENT 1: MUSIC FOR AIRPORTS** ☐ ☐
– 1'1 / 2'1 / 1'2 / 2'2. *(re-iss. Jan87 on 'E.G.' lp/c/cd; EGED/EGEDC/EEGCD 17)*

— Early in '79, ENO and MOEBIUS & ROEDILIUS (from CLUSTER) released album 'AFTER THE HEAT' *(Sky 021)*

— Late in 1979, ENO collaborated with trumpeter JON HASSELL on album 'FOURTH WORLD VOL.1: POSSIBLE MUSICS' on 'E.G.'; *EGED 007)*

— next with **HAROLD BUDD** – piano

E.G.-Ambient E.G.

Apr 80. (lp; ENO & BUDD) *(EGAMB 002) <EGS 107>* **AMBIENT 2: THE PLATEAUX OF MIRRORS** ☐ ☐
– First light / Steal away / The plateau of mirror / Above Chiangmai / An arc of doves / Not yet remembered / The chill air / Among fields of crystal / Wind in lonely fences / Failing light. *(re-iss. Jan87 on 'EG')*

— next with DAVID BYRNE, vocalist and instrumentalist w/ TALKING HEADS

E.G. Sire

Feb 81. (lp/c; BRIAN ENO & DAVID BYRNE) *(EG LP/MC 48) <6093>* **MY LIFE IN THE BUSH OF GHOSTS** 29 44
– America is waiting / Mea culpa / Regiment / Help me somebody / The Jezebel spirit / Qu'ran / Moonlight in glory / The carrier / A secret life / Come with us / Mountain of needles. *(re-iss. Jan87 on 'E.G.' lp/c/cd; EG LP/MC/CD 48)*

May 81. (7"; BRIAN ENO & DAVID BYRNE) *(EGO 1)* **THE JEZEBEL SPIRIT. / REGIMENT** ☐ ☐
(12"+=) *(EGOX 1)* – Very very hungry (Qu'ran).

Mar 82. (lp/c) *('EG-Editions'; EGED/+C 20)* **AMBIENT (4): ON LAND** 93 –
– Lizard point / The lost day / Tal coat / Shadow / Lantern marsh / Unfamiliar wind / A clearing / Dunwich Beach, Autumn 1960. *(cd-iss. Jan87 on 'E.G.'; EEGCD 20)*

Jul 83. (lp; BRIAN ENO with DANIEL LANOIS & ROGER ENO) *(EGLP 53)* **APOLLO: ATMOSPHERES & SOUNDTRACKS** ☐ –
– Under stars / The secret place / Matta / Signals / An ending (ascent) / Under stars II / Drift / Silver morning / Deep blue day / Weightless / Always returning / Stars. *(re-iss. Jan87 & Mar91 on 'E.G.' lp/c/cd; EG LP/MC/CD 53)*

EG-Editions not iss.

Aug 84. (lp; HAROLD BUDD & BRIAN ENO with DANIEL LANOIS) *(EGED 37)* **THE PEARL** ☐ –
– Late October / A stream with bright fish / The silver ball / Against the sky / Lost in the humming air / Dark-eyed sister / Their memories / The pearl / Foreshadowed / An echo of night / Still return. *(re-iss. Jan87 on 'E.G.' lp/c/cd; EG LP/MC/CD 37)*

— In 1984, he released 2 albums 'BEGEGNUNGEN I & II' with MOEBIUS, ROEDILUS & PLANK.

Aug 85. (lp/c; MICHAEL BROOK with BRIAN ENO & DANIEL LANOIS) *('EG-Editions'; EGED/+C 41)* **HYBRID** ☐ –
– Hybrid / Distant village / Mimosa / Pond life / Ocean motion / Midday /

Earth floor / Vacant. *(re-iss. Nov86 on 'E.G.' lp/c/cd; EG LP/MC/CD 41)*

Aug 85. (lp; ROGER ENO with BRIAN ENO) *('EG-Editions'; EGED 42)* **VOICES** [ ] [-]
– A place in the wilderness / The day after / At the water's edge / Grey promenade / A paler sky / Through the blue / Evening tango / Recalling winter / Voices / The old dance / Reflections on I.K.B. *(re-iss. Jan87 on 'E.G.' lp/c/cd; EG LP/MC/CD 42)*

Jan 87. (lp/cd) *(EG LP/CD 64)* **THURSDAY AFTERNOON** [ ] [-]
– Thursday afternoon. *(1 track only) (re-iss. cd Mar91; same)*

ENO / CALE

(collaboration **JOHN CALE** – vocals, multi-)with **ROBERT AHWAI** – rhythm guitar / **DARYL JOHNSON** – bass / **NEIL CATCHPOLE** – violin / **RONALD JONES** – drums, tabla / **DAVE YOUNG** – guitars, bass

Land | Opal-Warner

Oct 90. (lp/c/cd) *(AS/+C/CD 12) <7599 26421-1/-4/-2>* **WRONG WAY UP** [ ] [ ]
– Lay my love / One word / In the backroom / Empty frame / Cordoba / Spinning away / Footsteps / Been there done that / Crime in the desert / The river. *(re-iss. Jul92; same)*

Nov 90. (12"ep/cd-ep) *(LANDHO 4) <9 40001-1/-2>* **ONE WORD. / GRANDFATHER'S HOUSE / PALAQUIN** [ ] [-]

BRIAN ENO

Opal-WEA | Opal-Warner

Jul 92. (7") *(48496-7) <9 40539-2>* **FRACTIAL ZOOM. / ('A'-Moby mix)** [ ] [ ]
(12"+=) *(48496-1)* – (4 mixes).
(cd-s++=) *(48496-2)* – (another mix) / The roil, the choke.

Sep 92. (cd/c) *(<9362 45033-2/-4>)* **NERVE NET** [70] [ ]
– Fractial zoom / Wire shock / What actually happened? / Pierre in mist / My squelchy life / Decentre / Juju space jazz / The roil, the choke / Ali click / Distributing being / Web.

Oct 92. (7") *(40618-7) <9 40650-2>* **ALI CLICK (Beirut mix). / ('A'-Rural mix)** [ ] [ ]
(12"+=) *(40618-1)* – ('A'-Markus Draws + Grid mixes).
(cd-s) *(40618-2)* – ('A'side) / ('A'-Markus Draws + Grid mixes) / ('A'-trance long darkly mad mix) / ('A'-trance instrumental).

Nov 92. (cd/c) *(<9362 45010-2/-4>)* **THE SHUTOV ASSEMBLY** [ ] [ ]
– Triennale / Alhondiga / Markgraph / Lanzarote / Francisco / Riverside / Innocenti / Stedelijk / Ikebukero / Cavallino.
(above music inspired by Moscow painter Sergei Shutov)

— Around the same time as above, he lectured at Sadler's Wells, and is the brunt of NME jokes as Professor Eno.

All Saints | Caroline

Jun 93. (cd) *(ASCD 015) <6600-2>* **:NEROLI:** [ ] [ ]
– :Neroli:
above's long piece of music was used in hospitals for childbirth!

— Sep 94; he was credited on JAMES' ltd.album 'WAH WAH'.

All Saints | Gyroscope

Oct 95. (lp/c/cd; BRIAN ENO & JAH WOBBLE) *(AS/+C/CD 023) <8190 6614-2>* **SPINNER** [71] [ ]
– Where we lived / Like organza / Steam / Garden recalled / Marine radio / Unusual balance / Space diary 1 / Spinner / Transmitter and trumpet / Left where it fell.

All Saints | Thirsty Ear

Jun 97. (cd) *(ASCD 032) <6603-2>* **THE DROP** [ ] [ ]
– Slip dip / But if / Belgiam drop / Cornered / Black drop / Out-out / Swanky / Coasters / Blissed / M.C. Organ / Boomcubist / Hazard / Rayonism / Dutch blur / Back clack / Dear world / Iced world.

Venture | Astralwerks

May 01. (cd; as BRIAN ENO & J. PETER SCHWALM) *(CDVE 954) <10148>* **DRAWN FROM LIFE** [ ] [ ]
– From this moment / Persis / Like pictures (part 1) / Like pictures (part 2) / Night traffic / Rising dust / Intenser / More dust / Bloom / Two voices / Bloom (instrumental).

– his compilations, others, etc. –

on 'E.G.' unless mentioned otherwise

Apr 82. (d-c; FRIPP & ENO) *(EGDC 2)* **NO PUSSYFOOTIN' / EVENING STAR** [ ] [-]

Nov 83. (10xlp-box) *(EGBS 002)* **WORKING BACKWARDS 1983-1973** [ ] [-]
– (first 9 lp's, plus MUSIC FOR FILMS VOL.2 / + RARITIES m-lp:- Seven deadly finns / The lion sleeps tonight / Strong flashes of light / More volts / Mist rhythm)

Mar 86. (lp/c) *(EG LP/MC 65)* **MORE BLANK THAN FRANK** [ ] [-]
(cd-iss. Jun87 & Mar91; EGCD 65)

Jan 87. (cd) *(EGCD 65)* **DESERT ISLAND SELECTION** [ ] [-]
– Here he comes / Everything merges with the night / I'll come running (edit) / On some faraway beach (edit) / Spirits drifting / Back in Judy's jungle / St. Elmo's fire / No one receiving / Julie with . . . / Taking tiger mountain (edit) / 1'1.

Jan 87. (lp/c) *EG-Editions; (EGED/+C 35)* **MUSIC FOR FILMS 2** [ ] [-]
– The dove / Roman twilight / Matta / Dawn, marshland / Climate study / The secret place / An ending (ascent) / Always returning 1 / Signals / Under stars / Drift / Study / Approaching Taidu / Always returning 2.

Mar 89. (cd-s) *(CDT 41)* **ANOTHER GREEN WORLD / DOVER BEACH / DEEP BLUE DAY / 2'1** [ ] [-]

Dec 89. (3xc-box)(3xcd-box) *(EG BM/BC 7)* **ISLAND VARIOUS ARTISTS** [ ] [-]
– (ANOTHER GREEN WORLD / BEFORE AND AFTER SCIENCE / APOLLO)

Nov 93. (3xcd-box) *Virgin; (ENOBX 1)* **BRIAN ENO** (collaborations) [ ] [-]

Nov 93. (3xcd-box) *Virgin; (ENOBX 2)* **BRIAN ENO 2** (collaborations) [ ] [-]

Feb 94. (cd/c) *Venture; (CD/TC VE 920)* **THE ESSENTIAL FRIPP AND ENO** [ ] [-]

Oct 94. (3xcd-box) *Virgin; (TPAK 36)* **THE COMPACT COLLECTION** [ ] [-]

May 99. (cd) *Materiali Sonori; (129570110-2)* **SONORA PORTRAITS** [ ] [-]

— ENO contributed 2 tracks on live lp 'JUNE 1st, 1974' with KEVIN AYERS, NICO and JOHN CALE. He also with brother ROGER and DANIEL LANOIS provided one track to DUNE film (1984). For albums by CLUSTER & ENO; see CLUSTER.

□ JOHN ENTWISTLE (see under ⇒ WHO)

ENYA

Born: EITHNE NI BHRAONAIN, 17 May'61, Gweedore, County Donegal, Ireland. Classically trained as a pianist, she made her first inroads into the music business via contributions to her family's (CLANNAD) early 80's album, 'FUAIM', although her first solo project was a soundtrack for 'Island' records, 'The Frog Prince', in 1985. She had already been commissioned by the BBC to write the TV score to the cultural documentary, 'The Celts'. Built around new age synths, piano, wailing bagpipes and washes of ambient atmospherics, with ENYA singing in Irish, the record was different enough to attract interest from the mainstream music press and a subsequent Top 70 UK chart placing. Signed to 'Warners', ENYA began collaborating on the songwriting front with backing musicians, ROMA and NICKY RYAN, the latter also becoming her producer. Together they penned the acclaimed 'WATERMARK' (1988) opus, the hypnotic, aquatic orchestrations of 'ORINOCO FLOW' giving ENYA her first UK No.1 and bringing her worldwide recognition. The lavish arrangements and choral-like effects transported the singer's crystal pure vocals into an ethereal new dimension, the bulk of the album alternating between hymn-like grace and more expansively sublime sound collages. Spawning a further two singles in 'EVENING FALLS' and 'STORMS IN AFRICA', the record went on to become a multi-million seller, more of a landmark than a watermark. A subsequent follow-up, 'SHEPHERD MOONS' (1991), stuck more or less to the same formula if not quite capturing the otherworldly allure of its predecessor. Nevertheless, it became ENYA's first UK No.1 album, selling even more copies around the world and spending a staggering four years in the American charts. Though the demand was intense, the reclusive star once again chose not to tour, instead ensconcing herself in the studio once more to begin work on a third album, 'THE MEMORY OF TREES' (1995). The record deviated little from her previous output although if anything, it was more accessible, the positively jaunty 'ANYWHERE IS' coming as close to conventional pop music as ENYA had yet strayed. The single provided her with another Top 10 hit, while the album itself was another transatlantic success story. A compilation album, 'PAINT THE SKY WITH STARS – THE BEST OF ENYA' was released late in '97, filling in some time before her next effort. Predictably perhaps, 'A DAY WITHOUT RAIN' (2000) offered up little in the way of innovation or anything that might win over new fans. Longtime admirers, however, would've found little to fault in what amounted to another seamlessly crafted (if a little on the short side at just over the half hour mark) instalment of Celtic-tinged new age fluff/mood music (delete according to taste). Surprisingly, it again hit the US Top 20, and paved the way for her work via the first instalment of the mighty soundtrack for 'The Lord Of The Rings' trilogy. • **Trivia:** ENYA's father LED BRENNAN was a member of showband SLIEVE FOY BAND.

Album rating: ENYA (*4; + THE CELTS) / WATERMARK (*7) / SHEPHERD MOONS (*6) / MEMORY OF TREES (*6) / PAINT THE SKY WITH STARS – THE BEST OF ENYA compilation (*7) / A BOX OF DREAMS boxed set (*6) / A DAY WITHOUT RAIN (*7) / ONLY TIME – THE COLLECTION boxed set (*7)

ENYA – vocals, keyboards, percussion (ex-CLANNAD)

Island | not iss.

Oct 85. (lp/c) *(ISTA/ICT 10)* **THE FROG PRINCE** (soundtrack) [ ] [–]

B.B.C. | Atlantic

Feb 87. (lp/c/cd) *(REB/ZCF/BBCCD 605)* <81842> **ENYA** (rec.1980) [69] [ ]
– The Celts / Aldebaran / I want tomorrow / March of the Celts / Deireadh on tuath / The Sun in the stream / To go beyond (1) / Epona / Fairytale / Epona Triad: St. Patrick Cu Chulainn-oisin / Boadicea / Bard dance / Dan y dur / To go beyond (II). *(re-iss. Nov92 as 'THE CELTS' on 'WEA' hit UK No.10 – cd+=)(lp/c; 450991167-2)(WX 498/+C)* – Portrait (out of the blue).

Feb 87. (7") *(RESL 201)* **I WANT TOMORROW. / THE CELTS THEME** [ ] [–]
(12"+=/cd-s+=) *(RESL)* – To Go Beyond I + II. *(re-iss. Nov88; same)*

W.E.A. | Geffen

Sep 88. (lp/c)(cd) *(WX 199/+C)(246006-2)* <24233> **WATERMARK** [5] Jan89 [25]
– Watermark / Cursum perficio / On your shore / Storms in Africa / Exile / Miss Clare remembers / Orinoco flow / Evening falls / River / The longships / Na laetha geal m'oige / Storms in Africa (part II).

Oct 88. (7") *(YZ 312)* <27633> **ORINOCO FLOW. / OUT OF THE BLUE** [1] Jan89 [24]
(12"+=/cd-s+=) *(YZ 312 T/CD)* – Smaotin.

Dec 88. (7") *(YZ 356)* **EVENING FALLS. / OICHE CHIUN (SILENT NIGHT)** [20] [ ]
(12"+=/cd-s+=) *(YZ 356 T/CD)* – Morning glory.

Feb 89. (7"/c-s) *(YZ 368/+C)* **STORMS IN AFRICA (pt.II). / STORMS IN AFRICA** [41] [ ]
(12"+=/cd-s+=/3"cd-s+=) *(YZ 368 T/CD/CDX)* – The Celts / Aldebaran.

May 91. (7"/c-s) *(YX 580/+C)* **EXILE. / ON YOUR SHORE** [ ] [ ]
(12"+=/cd-s+=) *(YZ 580 T/CD)* – Watermark / River.

W.E.A. | Reprise

Oct 91. (7"/c-s) *(YZ 604/+C)* <19089> **CARIBBEAN BLUE. / ORINOCO FLOW** [13] Feb92 [79]
(cd-s+=) *(YZ 604CD)* – Angels.
(cd-s++=) *(YZ 604CDX)* – As baile / Oriel window.

— album guests **ROMA RYAN** – percussion / **STEVE SIDWELL** – cornet / **NICKY RYAN** and **ANDY DUNCAN** – perc. / **LIAM O'FLIONN** – vulcan pipes / **ROY JEWITT** – clarinet

Nov 91. (cd)(lp/c) *(903175572-2)(WX 431/+C)* <26775> **SHEPHERD MOONS** [1] [17]
– Shepherd moons / Caribbean blue / How can I keep from singing? / Ebudae / Angeles / No holly for Miss Quinn / Book of days / Evacuee / Lothlorien / Marble halls / Afer Ventus / Smaonte . . .

Dec 91. (7"/c-s) *(YZ 365/+C)* **HOW CAN I KEEP FROM SINGING? / ORCHE CHIUN (SILENT NIGHT)** [13] [ ]
(12"+=/cd-s+=) *(YZ 365 T/CD)* – 'S Fagain mo baile.

Jul 92. (7"/c-s) *(YZ 640/+C)* **BOOK OF DAYS. / AS BAILE** [10] [ ]
(cd-s) *(YZ 640CD)* – ('A'side) / Watermark / On your shoe / Exile.

Nov 92. (7"/c-s) *(YZ 705/+C)* **THE CELTS. / OFCHE CHIUN** [29] [ ]
(cd-s+=) *(YZ 705 T/CD)* – S'fagain mobhaile.

Nov 95. (c-s) *(WEA 023C)* **ANYWHERE IS / BOADICEA** [7] [ ]
(cd-s+=) *(WEA 023CD)* – Oriel window.
(cd-s) *(WEA 023CDX)* – ('A'side) / Book of days / Caribbean blue / Orinoco flow.

Nov 95. (cd/c) *(0630 12879-2/-4)* <46106> **THE MEMORY OF TREES** [5] [9]
– The memory of trees / Anywhere is / Pax deorum / Athair ar neamh / From where I am / China roses / Hope has a place / Tea-house moon / Once you had gold / La sonadora / On my way home.

Nov 96. (c-s) *(WEA 047C)* **ON MY WAY HOME / BOADICEA** [26] [–]
(cd-s+=) *(WEA 047CD)* – Eclipse / Storms in Africa (part 2).
(cd-s) *(WEA 047CDX)* – ('A'side) / Morning glory / I may not awaken.

Nov 97. (cd/c) *(3984 20895-2/-4)* <46835> **PAINT THE SKY WITH STARS – THE BEST OF ENYA** (compilation) [4] [30]
– Orinoco flow / Caribbean blue / Book of days / Anywhere is / Only if . . . / The Celts / China roses / Shepherd moons / Ebudae / Storms in Africa / Watermark / Paint the sky with stars / Marble halls / On my way home / Memory of trees / Boadicea.

Dec 97. (c-s/cd-s) *(WEA 143 C/CD)* **ONLY IF . . . / OICHE CHUIN (SILENT NIGHT Gaelic version)** [43] [–]
(cd-s+=) *(WEA 143CDX)* – Willows on the water.

Nov 00. (c-s) *(WEA 316C)* <radio cut> **ONLY TIME / THE FIRST OF AUTUMN** [32] Jun01 [10]
(cd-s+=) *(W 316CD)* – The promise.

Nov 00. (cd/c) *(8573 85986-2/-4)* <47426> **A DAY WITHOUT RAIN** [6] [2]
– A day without rain / Wild child / Only time / Tempus vernum / Deora ar mo chroi / Flora's secret / Fallen embers / Silver inches / Pilgrim / One by one / Lazy days.

Mar 01. (c-s) *(WEA 324C)* **WILD CHILD / MIDNIGHT BLUE** [72] [–]
(cd-s+=) *(WEA 324CD)* – Song of the sandman (lullaby).

Dec 01. (c-s) *(W 338C)* **ONLY TIME (remix) / OICHE CHIUN (SILENT NIGHT)** [ ] [–]
(cd-s+=) *(W 338CD)* <942420-2> – Willows on the water.

Jan 02. (c-s) *(W 578C)* **MAY IT BE / ISOBELLA** [50] [–]
(cd-s+=) *(W 578CD)* – The first of autumn.

– compilations, etc. –

Dec 97. (3xcd-box) *WEA; (<3984 21333-2>)* **A BOX OF DREAMS** [ ] [ ]

Dec 01. (cd) *WEA; <11006>* **THEMES FROM CALMI CUORI APPASSIONATI** [–] [ ]

Nov 02. (4xcd-box) *WEA; (<0927 49211-2>)* **ONLY TIME – THE COLLECTION** [ ] [ ]

ERASURE

Formed: London, England ... 1985 by VINCE CLARKE and one-time choirboy ANDY BELL, who answered a Melody Maker "vocalist wanted" ad. CLARKE's lucrative past had included spearheading other outfits; DEPECHE MODE ('81), YAZOO (82-83) and the one-off ASSEMBLY ('84) with FEARGAL SHARKEY and E.C.RADCLIFFE. In June 1985, he teamed up with PAUL QUINN (ex-Bourgie Bourgie) on another one-off, 'ONE DAY'. All were released on Daniel Miller's indie label 'Mute', as were his new outfit. ERASURE's debut single in September '85, 'WHO NEEDS LOVE LIKE THAT', only found a No.55 placing and things looked bleak when both of their follow-ups only managed to scrape into the

Top 100 (one of them, 'OH L'AMOUR', later became a Top 10 hit in late '87 for pop duo, DOLLAR). ERASURE finally broke through from the indie scene in October '86, when 'SOMETIMES' made UK No.2. BELL's vocal theatrics were almost as distinctive as his Liberace meets Sylvester stage persona, although the comparisons with ALISON MOYET were inevitable if a little unfair. The fact that CLARKE and BELL were successful in Europe before breaking in Britain speaks volumes. Basically, ERASURE was the shiny, happy, extrovert young pop kid to the sullen, rather aloof older brother of DEPECHE MODE and if you're looking for someone to blame for the 90's Euro-pop overload (SCATMAN, CULTURE BEAT, LA BOUCHE etc.), this dastardly duo are your men. Still, any group capable of such swoonful pop genius as 'BLUE SAVANNAH' and 'STAR', deserves leniency (and besides, 'Rhythm Of The Night' was a top tune!). Yet these were but two of ERASURE'S rather impressive run of 18 consecutive hits throughout the late 80's and early 90's, while 'THE INNOCENTS' (1988), 'WILD!' (1989) and 'CHORUS' (1991) were all No.1 albums. In the summer of '92, the band were again at the top of the charts, this time with the 'ABBA-ESQUE' EP; no prizes for guessing what this was all about. A fairly unoriginal, if charming tribute/parody to everybody's favourite Swedish popsters, it goes without saying that the boys did a brilliant ANNA/FRIDA for the video. A greatest hits collection, 'POP! THE FIRST 20 HITS' (1992), flew off the shelves that Christmas, with the group taking a well earned break. Returning to the scene in 1994, they found the going a little tougher; The PRODIGY were charting with much harder electronic sounds and the dance scene in general was becoming less pop-centric (and conversely, the pop scene was becoming more dance-centric). Perhaps bearing this in mind, then, the group duly drafted in the likes of ORBITAL and old hands KRAFTWERK to give 'ERASURE' (1995), more of an electro sheen. 1997's Top 10 'COWBOY' set went even further down the techno route, spawning the singles 'IN MY ARMS' and 'DON'T SAY YOUR LOVE IS KILLING ME'. CLARKE and BELL subsequently took an extended break from ERASURE duties, the former teaming up with HEAVEN 17's MARTIN WARE for 1999's THE CLARKE & WARE EXPERIMENT's 'PRETENTIOUS' – a second collaboration 'SPECTRUM PURSUIT VEHICLE' landed in 2001. If anything, 'LOVEBOAT' (2000) proved that the lay-off had done ERASURE no end of good, messrs BELL and CLARKE returning to their trademark melodicism with a vengeance. On the past evidence of the 'ABBA-ESQUE' EP, a full-blown covers set didn't seem like such a daunting prospect, especially bearing in mind BELL and CLARKE's ability to combine humour, irreverence and fondness for their material. In the event, 'OTHER PEOPLE'S SONGS' (2003) didn't quite come off, although it had its moments, chief among them an unlikely version of Steve Harley's 'MAKE ME SMILE (COME UP AND SEE ME)' and the Buggles' 'VIDEO KILLED THE RADIO STAR'. 'HITS! THE VERY BEST OF ERASURE' (2003), meanwhile, updated their earlier hits set without providing a competely satisfying best of. • **Songwriters:** CLARKE writes all material except covers; RIVER DEEP MOUNTAIN HIGH (Phil Spector) / GIMME GIMME GIMME + ABBA-ESQUE EP (Abba) / TOO DARN HOT (Cole Porter) / SOLISBURY HILL (Peter Gabriel) / EVERYBODY'S GOT TO LEARN SOMETIME (Korgis) / EVERYDAY + TRUE LOVE ALWAYS (Buddy Holly) / WHEN WILL I SEE YOU AGAIN (Three Degrees) / EBB TIDE + YOU'VE LOST THAT LOVIN' FEELIN' (Righteous Brothers) / WALKING IN THE RAIN (Shangri-la's) / GOODNIGHT (Eberhardt).

Album rating: WONDERLAND (*7) / THE CIRCUS (*6) / THE INNOCENTS (*7) / WILD! (*5) / CHORUS (*5) / POP! THE FIRST 20 HITS compilation (*8) / I SAY I SAY I SAY (*6) / COWBOY (*4) / LOVEBOAT (*5) / OTHER PEOPLE'S SONGS (*4) / HITS: THE VERY BEST OF ERASURE compilation (*6) / Vince Clarke & Martyn Ware: PRETENTIOUS (*5) / SPECTRUM PURSUIT VEHICLE (*6)

VINCE CLARKE (b. 3 Jul'60, South Woodford, England) – keyboards / **ANDY BELL** (b.25 Apr'64, Peterborough, England) – vocals (ex-The VOID)

Mute Sire

Sep 85. (7") *(MUTE 40)* **WHO NEEDS LOVE LIKE THAT. / PUSH ME SHOVE ME** [55] [ ]
(diff.mix-12"+=) *(12MUTE 40)* – ('A'instrumental work-out mix).
(12") *(L12MUTE 40)* – ('A'-Mexican mix) / ('B'-Tacos mix).
(re-iss. cd-s Sep93; CDMUTE 40)

Nov 85. (7") *(MUTE 42)* **HEAVENLY ACTION. / DON'T SAY NO** [100] [ ]
(12"+=) *(12MUTE 42)* – My heart . . . so blue (Incidental mix).
(d12"+=) *(D12MUTE 42)* – Who needs love like that (Mexican mix) / Push me shove me (Tacos mix).
(12") *(L12MUTE 42)* – ('A'-Yellow Brick mix) / ('B'-Ruby Red mix).
(re-iss. cd-s Sep93; CDMUTE 42)

Apr 86. (7") *(MUTE 45)* **OH L'AMOUR. / MARCH ON DOWN THE LINE** [85] [ ]
(12"+=) *(12MUTE 45)* – Gimme gimme gimme (a man after midnight).
('A'-Funky Sister mix-12"+=) *(L12MUTE 45)* – Gimme gimme gimme..
(re-iss. cd-s Sep93; CDMUTE 45)

Jun 86. (cd/c/lp) *(CD/C+/STUMM 25)* **WONDERLAND** [71] [ ]
– Who needs love like that / Reunion / Cry so easy / Push me shove me / Heavenly action / Say what / Love is a loser / My heart . . . so blue / Oh l'amour / Pistol. *(ltd-12"-w/lp)*– OH L'AMOUR / MARCH ON DOWN THE LINE / GIMME GIMME GIMME. *(cd+=)* – (remixes); Say what / Senseless / March on down the line.

Oct 86. (7") *(MUTE 51)* **SOMETIMES. / SEXUALITY** [2] [ ]
(ext-12"+=) *(12MUTE 51)* – Say what.
(diff.mix-12"+=) *(L12MUTE 51)* – Say what.
(d7"+=) *(DMUTE 51)* – Push me shove me / Who needs love like that.
(c-s+=) *(CMUTE 51)* – Who needs love like that / Heavenly action / Oh l'amour.
(re-iss. cd-s Sep93; CDMUTE 51)

Feb 87. (7") *(MUTE 56)* **IT DOESN'T HAVE TO BE. / IN THE HALL OF THE MOUNTAIN KING** [12] [ ]
('A'-diff.mix-12"+=) *(12MUTE 56)* – Who needs love like that.
('A'-diff.mix-12"+=) *(L12MUTE 56)* – Heavenly action.
(d7"+=) *(DMUTE 56)* – Sometimes / Sexuality.
(cd-s++=) *(CDMUTE 56)* – Sometimes / Oh l'amour / Heavenly action / Who needs love like that / Gimme gimme gimme.
(re-iss. cd-s Sep93; same)

Apr 87. (cd/c/lp) *(CD/C+/STUMM 35)* <25554> **THE CIRCUS** [6] [ ]
– It doesn't have to be / Hideaway / Don't dance / If I could / Sexuality / Victim of love / Leave me to bleed / Sometimes / The circus / Spiralling. *(ltd;d-c+=)* – WONDERLAND *(cd+=)* – Sometimes (remix) / It doesn't (mix) / In the hall of the mountain king.

May 87. (7"/7"pic-d) *(MUTE/+P 61)* **VICTIM OF LOVE (remix). / THE SOLDIER'S RETURN** [7] [ ]
('A'ext-12"+=/12"pic-d+=) *(12MUTE 61)* – ('A'dub).
(12"+=) *(L12MUTE 61)* – If I could help (Japanese mix).
(cd-s+=) *(CDMUTE 61)* – ('A' dub) / Safety in numbers (live) / Don't dance (live) / Leave me to bleed (live).

Sep 87. (7") *(1MUTE 66)* **THE CIRCUS (remix). / THE CIRCUS (version)** [6] [ ]
(12") *(1MUTE 66T)* – ('A'live) / Victim of love (live) / If I could (live) / Spiralling (live).
(12") *(2MUTE 66T)* – ('A'-Bareback Rider mix) / It doesn't have to be (live) / Who needs love like that (live) / Gimme gimme gimme (live).
(12") *(3MUTE 66T)* – ('A'-Gladiator mix) / Sometimes (live) / Say what (live) / Oh l'amour (live).
(re-iss. cd-s Sep93; CDMUTE 66)

Dec 87. (2x12"lp/cd) *(L/LCD STUMM 35)* <25667> **THE TWO RING CIRCUS** *(re-iss. last lp)* [ ] [ ]
(cd+=) – Victim of love / The Circus / Spiralling / Sometimes / Gimme gimme gimme / Oh l'amour / Who needs love like that.

Feb 88. (7") *(MUTE 74)* **SHIP OF FOOLS. / WHEN I NEEDED YOU** [6] [ ]
(diff.mix;12"+=/3"cd-s+=) *(12/CD MUTE 74)* – River deep mountain high (mix).
(diff.mix-12"+=) *(L12MUTE 74)* – River deep mountain high (dance).

Apr 88. (cd/c/lp) *(CD/C+/STUMM 55)* <25730> **THE INNOCENTS** [1] [49]
– A little respect / Ship of fools / Phantom bride / Chains of love / Sixty-five thousand / Heart of stone / Yahoo! / Imagination / Witch in the ditch /

Weight of the world. *(cd+=)* – River deep mountain high (mix) / When I needed you (mix).

May 88. (7") *(MUTE 83) <27844>* **CHAINS OF LOVE. / DON'T SUPPOSE** [11] Jul88 [12]
(diff.mixes;12"+=/cd-s+=) *(12/CD MUTE 83)* – The good, the bad and the ugly (mix).
(diff.mix-12"+=) *(L12MUTE 83)* – (extra track as above).

Sep 88. (s7"/7") *(P+/MUTE 85) <27738>* **A LITTLE RESPECT. / LIKE ZSA ZSA GABOR** [4] Dec88 [14]
(diff.mix;12"+=/cd-s+=) *(12/CD MUTE 85)* – Love is cooler than death.
(diff.mix;12"+=/cd-s+=) *(L12/LCD MUTE 85)* – (extra track as above).

Dec 88. (12"ep/cd-ep/7"ep) *(12/CD+/MUTE 93) <25904>* **CRACKERS INTERNATIONAL: EP** [3] Apr89 [73]
– Stop / Knocking on your door / She won't be home / The hardest part.
(d3"cd-ep+=/12"+=) *(L12/LCD MUTE 93)* – Stop (Mark Saunders remix) / Knocking on your door (Mark Saunders remix) / God rest ye merry gentlemen.

Jul 89. (c-s) *<22879>* **STOP! / SHIP OF FOOLS** [–] [97]

Sep 89. (c-s/7") *(C+/MUTE 89)* **DRAMA! / SWEET SWEET BABY** [4] [ ]
(diff.mixes;12"+=/3"cd-s+=) *(12/CD MUTE 89)* – Paradise (mix).

Oct 89. (cd/c/lp) *(CD/C+/STUMM 75) <26026>* **WILD!** [1] [57]
– You surround me / Drama! / How many times? / Crown of thorns / Piano song (instrumental) / Blue savannah / Star / La Gloria / Brother and sister / 2,000 miles / Piano song.

Dec 89. (c-s/7") *(C+/MUTE 99)* **YOU SURROUND ME. / 91 STEPS** [15] [ ]
(diff.mixes;12"+=/3"cd-s+=) *(12/CD MUTE 99)* – Supernature.
(diff.mixes;12"+=/cd-s+=) *(L12/LCD MUTE 99)* – Supernature (William Orbit mix).
(12") *(XL12MUTE 99)* – ('A'-Gareth Jones remix) / Supernature (Mark Saunders remix) / Supernature (Daniel Miller & Phil Legg dub mix).

Mar 90. (c-s/7") *(C+/MUTE 109)* **BLUE SAVANNAH. / NO G.D.M. (unfinished mix)** [3] [ ]
(12"+=/cd-s+=) *(12/CD MUTE 109)* – Runaround on the underground.
(extra-12") *(XL12MUTE 109)* – ('A'-Der Deutche mix 1 & 2).

May 90. (c-s/7") *(C+/MUTE 111)* **STAR. / ('A'soul mix)** [11] [ ]
(12"+=/cd-s+=) *(12/CD MUTE 111)* – ('A'-Dreamlike state 24 hour technicolour mix).

Jun 91. (c-s/7") *(C+/MUTE 125)* **CHORUS. / ('A'mix)** [3] [83]
(12"+=) *(12MUTE 125) <19202>* – (2-'A'mixes) / Snappy.
(cd-s+=) *(CDMUTE 125)* – Over the rainbow.

Sep 91. (c-s/7") *(C+/MUTE 131)* **LOVE TO HATE YOU. / VITAMIN C** [4] [ ]
(12"+=) *(12MUTE 131)* – La la la.
(cd-s++=) *(CDMUTE 131)* – ('A'version).

Oct 91. (cd/c/lp) *(CD/C+/STUMM 95) <26668>* **CHORUS** [1] [29]
– Chorus / Waiting for the day / Joan / Breath of life / Am I right? / Love to hate you / Turns the love to anger / Siren song / Perfect stranger / Home.

Nov 91. (cd-ep/12"ep/7"ep) *(CD/12+/MUTE 134)* **AM I RIGHT?** [15] [ ]
– Am I right? / Carry on clangers / Let it flow / Waiting for sex.

Jan 92. (7"ep-ltd.15,000) *(LMUTE 134)* **AM I RIGHT? (EP) (re-mix)** [22] [ ]
– Am I right? (The Grid remix) / Love to hate you (Mark Saunders remix) / Chorus (Moby remix).
(12"+=) *(12MUTE 134)* – B3.
(cd-s+=) *(CDMUTE 134)* – Perfect stranger.

Mar 92. (c-s/7") *(C+/MUTE 142)* **BREATH OF LIFE. / ('A'version)** [8] [ ]
(12"+=/cd-s+=) *(12/CD MUTE 142)* – (3 other 'A'versions).

Mute Elektra

Jun 92. (12"ep/c-ep/cd-ep/7"ep) *(12/C/CD+/MUTE 144) <61386>* **ABBA-ESQUE** [1] [85]
– Lay your love on me / S.O.S. / Take a chance on me / Voulez vous.

Oct 92. (12"/c-s/cd-s) *(12/C/CD MUTE 150)* **WHO NEEDS LOVE LIKE THAT (Hanbury mix). / SHIP OF FOOLS (Orb mix) / SOMETIMES (remix)** [10] [ ]
(cd-s) *(LCDMUTE 150)* – ('A'side) / Don't say no / Soldier's return / The circus (remix).

Nov 92. (cd/c/d-lp) *(CD/C+/MUTEL 2) <45153>* **POP! THE FIRST 20 HITS** (compilation) [1] [ ]
– Who needs love like that / Heavenly action / Oh l'amour / Sometimes / It doesn't have to be like that / Victim of love / The circus / Ship of fools / Chains of love / A little respect / Stop! / Drama! / You surround me / Blue Savannah / Star / Chorus / Love to hate you / Am I right? / Breathe of life / Take a chance on me. (c+=) – Who needs love like that (Hamburg mix).

Apr 94. (c-s/cd-s/7") *(C/CD+/MUTE 152)* **ALWAYS. / ('A'mix)** [4] [–]
(12"+=/cd-s+=) *(L12/LCD MUTE 152)* – (2 more 'A'mixes).

Apr 94. (c-s) *<64552>* **ALWAYS / TRAGIC** [–] [20]

May 94. (cd/c/lp) *(CD/C+/STUMM 115) <61633>* **I SAY I SAY I SAY** [1] [18]
– Take me back / I love Saturday / Man in the moon / So the story goes / Run to the sun / Always / All through the years / Blues away / Miracle / Because you're so sweet.

Jul 94. (c-s/7"yellow) *(C+/MUTE 153)* **RUN TO THE SUN. / TENDEREST MOMENT** [6] [ ]
(12"+=/cd-s+=) *(12/CD MUTE 153)* – ('A'-Beatmasters mix).
(cd-s++=) *(LCDMUTE 153)* – ('A'-Andy Bell remix).

Nov 94. (c-s) *(CMUTE 166)* **I LOVE SATURDAY / DODO / BECAUSE YOU'RE SO SWEET** [21] [ ]
(cd-s) *(EPCDMUTE 166)* – ('A'side) / Ghost / Truly, madly, deeply / Tragic (vocal version).
(cd-s) *(CDMUTE 166)* – ('A'side) / ('A'radio mix) / ('A'-JX mix) / ('A'-Beatmasters dub mix) / Dodo.
(cd-s) *(LCDMUTE 166)* – ('A'-Beatmasters club mix) / ('A'-Andy Bell mixes) / Always (x cut dub).

Sep 95. (c-s/cd-s) *(C/CD MUTE 174)* **STAY WITH ME / TRUE LOVE WARS** [15] [ ]
(12"+=/cd-s+=) *(12/LC MUTE 174)* – ('A'-Flow mix) / ('A'guitar mix) / ('A'-Castaway mix).

Oct 95. (cd/c/d-lp) *(CD/C+/STUMM 145) <61852>* **ERASURE** [14] [82]
– Guess I'm into feeling / Rescue me / Sono luminous / Fingers & thumbs (cold summer's day) / Rock me gently / Grace / Stay with me / Love the way you do so / Angel / I love you / A long goodbye.

Nov 95. (c-s/cd-s) *(C/CD MUTE 178)* **FINGERS & THUMBS (COLD SUMMER'S DAY) / HI NRG** [20] [ ]
(cd-s+=) *(LCDMUTE 178)* – ('A'-Tin Tin Out mix) / ('A'-Francois Kevorkian mix) / ('A'-Wire mix).

Mute Maverick

Jan 97. (c-s) *(CMUTE 190)* **IN MY ARMS / RAPTURE** [13] May97 [55]
(12"+=/cd-s+=) *(12/CD MUTE 190)* – ('A'mixes).
(cd-s) *(LCDMUTE 190)* – ('A'mixes).

Mar 97. (c-s) *(CMUTE 195)* **DON'T SAY YOUR LOVE IS KILLING ME / HEART OF GLASS (live)** [23] [ ]
(cd-s+=) *(CDMUTE 195)* – ('A'-Jon Pleased Wimmin flashback mix) / ('A'-Tall Pall mix).
(12"+=) *(12MUTE 195)* – Oh l'amour: Groove terminator.
(cd-s) *(LCDMUTE 195)* – ('A'-Jon Pleased Wimmin flashback mix) / Oh l'amour (Matt Darey mix) / Oh l'amour (Tin Tin Out mix).

Apr 97. (cd/c) *(CD/C STUMM 155) <46631>* **COWBOY** [10] [43]
– Rain / Worlds on fire / Reach out / In my arms / Don't say your love is killing me / Precious / Treasure / Boy / How can I say / Save me darling / Love affair.

Oct 00. (cd-s) *(CDMUTE 244)* **FREEDOM / BETTER / FREEDOM (acoustic)** [27] [–]
(cd-s) *(LCDMUTE 244)* – ('A'-Motiv8 mix) / ('A'-Jason Creasey mix) / ('A'-Mark Pichiotti mix).
(12") *(12MUTE 244)* – ('A'-Quake vocal mix) / ('A'-untidy dub) / ('A'-Mark Pichiotti dub).

Oct 00. (cd/c/lp) *(CD/C+/STUMM 175) <33298>* **LOVEBOAT** [45] [ ]
– Freedom / Where in the world / Crying in the rain / Perchance to dream / Alien / Mad as we are / Here in my heart / Love is the rage / Catch 22 / Moon and the sky / Surreal.

Jan 03. (cd-s) *(CDMUTE 275)* **SOLISBURY HILL / TELL IT TO ME / SEARCHING** [10] [ ]
(cd-s) *(LCDMUTE 275)* – ('A'-378 mix) / ('A'-Manhattan clique extended mix) / Ave Maria.

Jan 03. (cd/lp) *(CD+/STUMM 215) <9198>* **OTHER PEOPLE'S SONGS** [17] [ ]
– Solisbury hill / Everybody's got to learn sometime / Make me smile (come up and see me) / Everyday / When will I see you again / Walking in the rain / True love always / Ebb tide / Can't help falling in love / You've lost that lovin' feelin' / Goodnight / Video killed the radio star.

Apr 03. (cd-s) *(CDMUTE 292)* **MAKE ME SMILE (COME UP AND SEE ME) / OH L'AMOUR (acoustic) / WALKING IN THE RAIN (38B remix)** [14] [–]
(cd-s) *(LCDMUTE 292)* – ('A'-Dan Frampton radio mix) / ('A'-Manhattan clique extended) / When will I see you again (37B remix).

Oct 03. (cd-s) *(CDMUTE 312)* **OH L'AMOUR / LOVE ME ALL NIGHT LONG / NOTHING LASTS FOREVER** [13] [–]

(cd-s) *(LCDMUTE 312)* – ('A'-LMC extended mix) / ('A'-Shanghai surprise mix) / ('A'-Kenny Hayes mix).

Oct 03. (d-cd) *(CDMUTEL 10)* <73991> **HITS: THE VERY BEST OF ERASURE** (compilation) [15] [ ]
– Who needs love like that / Heavenly action / Oh l'amour / Sometimes / It doesn't have to be / Victim of love / Circus / Ship of fools / Chains of love / A little crespect / Stop! / Drama / You surround me / Blue Savannah / Star / Chorus / Love to hate you / Am I right / Breath of life / Lay all your love on me / S.O.S. / Take a chance on me / Voulez vous / Always / Run to the sun / I love Saturday / Stay with me / Fingers and thumbs / Rock me gently / In my arms / Don't say your love is killing me / Rain / Freedom / Solisbury hill / Make me smile (come up and see me). *(ltd-d-cd+=; LCDMUTEL 10)* – (Erasuremegamixes).

VINCE CLARKE + MARTYN WARE

MARTYN (of HEAVEN 17)

Mute Mute

Nov 99. (cd; as the CLARKE & WARE EXPERIMENT) *(CDSTUMM 181)* <9124> **PRETENTIOUS** [ ] Apr00 [ ]
– Music for multiple dimensions / Open your eyes / Too deep for tears / I think for tears / The east is falling / Wilderness – Turbulence / Disappearing breakthroughs / The light far away.

May 01. (cd) *(CDSTUMM 194)* <9155> **SPECTRUM PURSUIT VEHICLE** [ ] Jun01 [ ]
– White (you are in heaven) / Yellow (you are on a beach) / Red (you are in the womb) / Blue (you are underwater) / Green (you are in a forest) / White (you are in heaven again).

□ Roky ERICKSON
(see under ⇒ 13th FLOOR ELEVATORS)

Melissa ETHERIDGE

Born: 29 May'61, Leavenworth, Kansas, USA. A budding singer/songwriter by the time she'd reached her teens, ETHERIDGE went on to study at Boston's Berklee College Of Music. Relocating to California after graduating, she was spotted by 'Island' executive CHRIS BLACKWELL who signed her to a long term deal. Spring '88 saw the release of an eponymous debut album, her grainy blues-soaked vocals, angry, tough-talking lyrics and bar-band style attracting a loyal following which helped place the record in the US Top 30 and eventually saw it go gold. Subsequent albums, 'BRAVE AND CRAZY' (1989) and 'NEVER ENOUGH' (1992) attained similar chart positions although virtually all her singles failed to make a mark. This situation was rectified in 1993 when she scored a US Top 10 hit with 'I'M THE ONLY ONE', the track lifted from accompanying multi-platinum album, 'YES I AM'. ETHERIDGE had only recently "come out", appearing alongside other members of music's gay community at a concert organised to celebrate the election of Bill Clinton. By the release of 1995's 'YOUR LITTLE SECRET', her profile had been raised to the point that the album narrowly missed the Top 5 despite a mixed reaction from critics. ETHERIDGE's BONNIE TYLER-influenced vocals and rootsy, BRUCE SPRINGSTEEN-influenced songs continue to appeal to an adult, album oriented market, setting her apart somewhat from the new breed of young female singer/songwriters such as ALANIS MORISSETTE and JEWEL. Now signed to 'Mercury', ETHERIDGE saw out the decade with her long-awaited sixth album, 'BREAKDOWN' (1999), although it failed to build on her past successes. Informed by a break-up with her long term partner, 'SKIN' (2001) was perhaps the singer/songwriter's most painfully raw document to date. A Top 10 US success, the album ran the gamut of brokenhearted emotion, from self-accusation to outright anger, without resorting to self pity. • **Trivia:** After writing for the 'Weeds' film in 1988, she provided backing vox for DON HENLEY's 'New York Minute'. BONO of U2 guested on her second album 'BRAVE AND CRAZY'.

Album rating: MELISSA ETHERIDGE (*6) / BRAVE AND CRAZY (*5) / NEVER ENOUGH (*6) / YES I AM (*6) / YOUR LITTLE SECRET (*3) / BREAKDOWN (*4) / SKIN (*6)

MELISSA ETHERIDGE – vocals, guitar, piano / **KEVIN McCORMICK** – bass / **CRAIG KRAMPF** – drums, percussion / **WADDY WACHTEL** + **JOHNNY LEE SCHELL** – guitars / **SCOTT THURSTON** + **WALLY BADAROU** – keyboards

Island Island

Apr 88. (7") *(IS 356)* **SIMILAR FEATURES. / I WANT YOU** [ ] [ ]
(12"+=/cd-s+=) *(12IS/CID 356)* – Don't you need.

May 88. (lp/c/cd) *(ILPS/ICT/CID 9879)* <90875> **MELISSA ETHERIDGE** [ ] [22]
– Similar features / Chrome plated heart / Like the way I do / Precious pain / Don't you need / The late September dogs / Occasionally / Watching you / Bring me some water / I want you. <*(ltd-cd-iss. Sep03 +=; 9860688)*<104902> – (live tracks).

Jun 88. (7") *(IS 376)* **DON'T YOU NEED. / PRECIOUS PAIN** [ ] [ ]
(12"+=) *(12IS 376)* – ('A'live).
(cd-s++=) *(CID 376)* – Similar features.

Feb 89. (7") *(IS 393)* **BRING ME SOME WATER. / OCCASIONALLY** [ ] [ ]
(12"+=/cd-s+=) *(12IS/CID 393)* – I want you.

Mar 89. (7") <99251> **SIMILAR FEATURES. / BRING ME SOME WATER** [–] [94]

—— **MAURICIO FRITZ LEWAK** – drums + **BERNIE LARSEN** – guitar; repl. SCHELL + BADAROU

Jul 89. (7") *(IS 431)* <99176> **NO SOUVENIRS. / ('A'live)** [ ] [95]
(12"+=/cd-s+=) *(12IS/CID 431)* – Brave and crazy (live).

Sep 89. (lp/c/cd) *(ILPS/ICT/CID 9939)* <91285> **BRAVE AND CRAZY** [63] [22]
– No souvenirs / Brave and crazy / You used to love to dance / The angels / You can sleep while I drive / Testify / Let me go / My back door / Skin deep / Royal Station 4-16. *(cd re-iss. Mar97; IMCD 241)*

Nov 89. (7") *(IS 440)* **THE ANGELS. / ('A'live)** [ ] [ ]
(12"+=/cd-s+=) *(12IS/CID 440)* – Chrome plated heart (live) . *(re-iss. May90; same)*

Mar 90. (7") **YOU CAN SLEEP WHILE I DRIVE. / THE LATE SEPTEMBER DOGS (live)** [ ] [ ]
(12"+=) – ('A'live).

—— **STUART SMITH** + **MARK GOLDENBERG** – guitars; repl. LARSEN + WACHTEL

Feb 92. (c-s/7") **DANCE WITHOUT SLEEPING. / AIN'T IT HEAVY** [ ] [ ]
(12"+=/cd-s+=) – Similar features.

Apr 92. (cd/c/lp) *(CID/ICT/ILPS 9990)* <512120> **NEVER ENOUGH** [56] Mar92 [21]
– Ain't it heavy / 2001 / Dance without sleeping / Place your hand / Must be crazy for me / Meet me in the back / The boy feels strange / Keep it precious / The letting go / It's for you. *(cd re-iss. Mar96; IMCD 214)*

Apr 92. (7") **AIN'T IT HEAVY. / THE BOYS FEEL STRANGE** [ ] [ ]
(12"+=/cd-s+=) – Royal station 4-16 (live).

Jul 92. (c-s) *(866 893-4)* **2001. / ('A'remix)** [ ] [–]
(12"+=) *(866 893-1)* – Meet me in the back / Testify.
(cd-s+=) *(866 893-2)* – Meet me in the back / ('A'-12"remix).

Sep 93. (cd/c/lp) *(CID/ICT/ILPS 8010)* <848660> **YES I AM** [ ] [15]
– I'm the only one / If I wanted to / Come to my window / Silent legacy / I will never be the same / All American girl / Yes I am / Resist / Ruins / Talking to my angel. *(re-dist.Apr94)*

Nov 93. (c-s/7") *(C+/IS 579)* **I'M THE ONLY ONE. / ('A'version)** [ ] [–]
(cd-s) *(CID 579)* – ('A'side) / Bring me some water (live) / Yes I am (live).

Feb 94. (c-s) <858028> **COME TO MY WINDOW / AIN'T IT HEAVY (live)** [–] [25]

Jul 94. (c-s) <854068> **I'M THE ONLY ONE / MAGGIE MAY (live)** [–] [ ]

Oct 94. (c-s/cd-s) *(CIS/CID 604)* **COME TO MY WINDOW / AIN'T IT HEAVY (live) / THE LETTING GO (live) / I'M THE ONLY ONE (live)** [ ] [–]

Feb 95. (c-s) <854238> **IF I WANTED TO / LIKE THE WAY I DO** [–] [16] [42]

Oct 95. (c-s) *(CIS 608)* **YOUR LITTLE SECRET / ALL AMERICAN GIRL** [ ] [–]
(cd-s+=) *(CID 608)* – Bring me some water / Skin deep.

Nov 95. (cd/c) *(CID/ICT 8042)* <524154> **YOUR LITTLE SECRET** [ ] [6]
– Your little secret / I really like you / Nowhere to go / An unusual kiss / I want to come over / All the way to Heaven / I could have been you / Shriner's Park / Change / This war is over.

Feb 96. (c-s) *(CIS 627)* <854528> **I WANT TO COME OVER / YOUR LITTLE SECRET** [ ] [22]
(cd-s+=) *(CID 627)* – Must be crazy for me (live) / Let me go (live).

Jul 96. (c-s) *(CIS 642)* <854 664> **NOWHERE TO GO / BRING ME SOME WATER** [ ] Sep96 [40]
(cd-s+=) *(CID 642)* – Like the way I do.

Sep 99. (c-s/cd-s) <562 345> **ANGELS WOULD FALL / INTO THE DARK / BELOVED** [–] [51]

Oct 99. (cd/c) <(546 518-2/-4)> **BREAKDOWN** [ ] [12]
– Breakdown / Angels would fall / Stronger than me / Into the dark / Enough of me / Truth of the heart / Mama I'm strange / Scarecrow / How would I know / My lover / Sleep. *(some w/ extra cd+=; CDL 546608-2)* – Touch and go / Cherry avenue / Beloved.

Jul 01. (cd) <(548 661-2)> **SKIN** [ ] [9]
– Lover please / The prison / Walking on water / Down to one / Goodnight / It's only me / I want to be in love / Please forgive me / The different / Heal me.

EURYTHMICS

Formed: London, England ... 1976, by Aberdonian, ANNIE LENNOX and Sunderland-born, DAVE STEWART. They formed The CATCH in 1977 with PETE COOMBES, which, by 1979, had evolved into The TOURISTS. Signing to 'Logo' records, they scored with some Top 10 pop hits, namely'I ONLY WANT TO BE WITH YOU' and 'SO GOOD TO BE BACK HOME', before they broke with COOMBES late in 1980. The duo, now The EURYTHMICS, began recording their debut at Conny Plank's Cologne studio. Featuring contributions from the likes of CAN's HOLGER CZUKAY and JAKI LIEBEZEIT as well as MARCUS STOCHHAUSEN (son of KARLHEINZ), 'IN THE GARDEN' (1981) was a radical musical departure. Icy synth-pop with avant-garde tendencies, the band's closest musical compadres were the lipstick 'n' legwarmers 'New Romantic' crowd, although The EURYTHMICS vision was unique. So unique, in fact, that the record languished in relative obscurity, given scant support by 'R.C.A.'. Undeterred, the band recorded 'SWEET DREAMS (ARE MADE OF THIS)' (1983), the title track giving the band an international breakthrough. This time around, the sculpted synth soundscapes were fashioned with a studied pop nous, LENNOX's mournful vocals heavy with dark implications. Visually striking, the band's image was also highly marketable and ANNIE became the chameleon queen of the new video generation, leading to overnight success in the States. 'TOUCH' (1983) consolidated the EURYTHMICS position as pop frontrunners, the single 'HERE COMES THE RAIN AGAIN' going Top 10 on both sides of the Atlantic. While their next project, the soundtrack for the film '1984 – For The Love Of Big Brother' was a relative success in Britain, it stiffed big time in the US amid recriminations from both parties; the director, MICHAEL RADFORD and The EURYTHMICS themselves. 'BE YOURSELF TONIGHT' (1985) saw LENNOX in soul diva mode, belting out the likes of 'SISTERS ARE DOIN' IT FOR THEMSELVES' and putting in a breathtaking feat of vocal histrionics on the No.1 hit, 'THERE MUST BE AN ANGEL (PLAYING WITH MY HEART)'. Perhaps playing all those stadiums was beginning to affect the band, as 'REVENGE' saw the band veering towards big-rock, tracks like 'MISSIONARY MAN' sounding downright clumsy. By the release of 'WE TOO ARE ONE', (1989) the band were clearly on their last legs and it was obvious, on listening to the record, that the working relationship between LENNOX and STEWART had finally broken down. LENNOX went on to do charity work before releasing 'DIVA' in 1992, her multi-platinum selling solo debut. She also released a collection of covers, 'MEDUSA', in 1995. STEWART, meanwhile, recorded the soundtrack 'LILY WAS HERE' with sax-diva, CANDY DULFER, before going on to form his SPIRITUAL COWBOYS and generally receive a bit of a pasting from the critics. 1999 saw the return of The EURYTHMICS via the hit single, 'I SAVED THE WORLD TODAY' and Top 5 album, 'PEACE'. LENNOX and STEWART were briefly reunited musically for what will probably be their final set of melodic pop songs. ANNIE LENNOX returned in 2003 with one of her intermittent solo releases, 'BARE'. As its title intimated, it was the most unflinchingly personal and self-excoriating song cycle she's yet recorded. Completely self-penned and unrelentingly melancholy, yet blessed with sympathetic arrangements and alluring use of electronica, the record's naked emotional force was as hypnotic as it was unprecedented. • **Songwriters:** COOMBES penned songs in The TOURISTS, except I ONLY WANT TO BE WITH YOU (Dusty Springfield). DAVE and ANNIE wrote together in The EURYTHMICS. Now a solo writer, ANNIE LENNOX covered KEEP YOUNG AND BEAUTIFUL (Al Dubin-Harry Warren) / FEEL THE NEED (Detroit Emeralds) / RIVER DEEP MOUNTAIN HIGH (Phil Spector) / DON'T LET ME DOWN (Beatles) / NO MORE "I LOVE YOU'S" (The Lover Speaks) / TAKE ME TO THE RIVER (Al Green) / A WHITER SHADE OF PALE (Procol Harum) / DON'T LET IT BRING YOU DOWN (Neil Young) / TRAIN IN VAIN (Clash) / I CAN'T GET NEXT TO YOU (Strong-Whitfield) / DOWNTOWN LIGHTS (Blue Nile) / THE THIN BLUE LINE BETWEEN LOVE AND HATE (Pretenders; hit) / WAITING IN VAIN (Bob Marley) / SOMETHING SO RIGHT (Paul Simon) / LADIES OF THE CANYON (Joni Mitchell) / I'M ALWAYS TOUCHED BY YOUR PRESENCE DEAR (Blondie). DAVE STEWART's VEGAS covered SHE (Charles Aznavour). • **Trivia:** In March '84 ANNIE, now not involved intimately with DAVE, married German Hare Krishna RADHA RAMAR, although this only lasted six months. She married again in the early 90's and gave birth to her first child in the Spring pf '93. On the 1st of August '84, DAVE married SHAKESPEAR'S SISTER/ex-BANANARAMA singer, SIOBHAN FAHEY. The bearded one has also produced many artists including FEARGAL SHARKEY, MARIA McKEE, DARYL HALL, BOB GELDOF, BOB DYLAN, TOM PETTY, MICK JAGGER, BORIS GREBENSHIKOV (Russian rocker) and LONDONBEAT. Just a wee note to say, DAVE was not the DAVE STEWART that had a No.1 hit with BARBARA GASKIN.

Album rating: Tourists: THE TOURISTS (*4) / REALITY EFFECT (*4) / LUMINOUS BASEMENT (*5) / Eurythmics: IN THE GARDEN (*5) / SWEET DREAMS (ARE MADE OF THIS) (*8) / TOUCH (*7) / TOUCH DANCE mini remix (*3) / 1984 (FOR THE LOVE OF BIG BROTHER) (*4) / BE YOURSELF TONIGHT (*7) / REVENGE (*6) / SAVAGE (*5) / WE TOO ARE ONE (*6) / EURYTHMICS' GREATEST HITS compilation (*8) / EURYTHMICS LIVE 1983-1989 collection (*4) / Dave Stewart: LILY WAS HERE (*5) / DAVE STEWART & THE SPIRITUAL COWBOYS (*6) / HONEST (*5) / GREETINGS FROM THE GUTTER (*5) / Annie Lennox: ANNIE LENNOX – DIVA (*7) / MEDUSA (*5) / Eurythmics: PEACE (*5) / Annie Lennox: BARE (*6)

CATCH

ANNIE LENNOX (b.25 Dec'54, Aberdeen, Scotland) – vocals, keyboards, flute / **DAVE STEWART** (b. 9 Sep'52, Sunderland, England) – guitar, keyboards (ex-LONGDANCER) / **PETE COOMBES** – guitar, vocals

Logo — not iss.

Nov 77. (7") *(GO 103)* **BORDERLINE. / BLACK BLOOD** [ ] [–]

TOURISTS

added **EDDY CHIN** – bass / **JIM TOOMEY** – drums

Logo — Epic

May 79. (7") *(GO 350)* **BLIND AMONG THE FLOWERS. / HE WHO LAUGHS LAST LAUGHS LONGEST** [52] [ ]
(d7"+=) *(GOD 350)* – The golden lamp / Wrecked.

Jun 79. (lp) *(LOGO 1018)* **THE TOURISTS** [72] [ ]
– Blind among the flowers / Save me / Fool's paradise / Can't stop laughing / Don't get left behind / Another English day / Deadly kiss / Ain't no room / The loneliest man in the world / Useless duration of time / He who laughs last laughs longest / Just like you. *(re-iss. Jun81 on 'RCA Int.' lp/c; INT S/K 5096)*

Aug 79. (7"/7"pic-d) *(GO/+P 360)* **THE LONELIEST MAN IN THE WORLD. / DON'T GET LEFT BEHIND** [32] [ ]

Oct 79. (lp/c) *(LOGO/KLOGO 1019)* **REALITY EFFECT** [23] [ ]
– It doesn't have to be this way / I only want to be with you / In the morning / All life's tragedies / Everywhere you look / So good to be back home / Nothing to do / Circular fever / In my mind / Something in the air tonight / Summers night.

Oct 79. (7") *(GO 370)* <50850> **I ONLY WANT TO BE WITH YOU. / SUMMER NIGHT** [4] Apr80 [83]

Jan 80. (7") *(TOUR 1)* **SO GOOD TO BE BACK HOME. / CIRCULAR SAW** [6] [ ]

R.C.A. — R.C.A.

Sep 80. (7") *(TOUR 2)* **DON'T SAY I TOLD YOU SO. / STRANGE SKY** [40] [ ]

Oct 80. (lp/c) *(RCA LP/K 5001)* **LUMINOUS BASEMENT** [75] [ ]
– Walls and foundations / Don't say I told you so / Week days / So you want to go away now / One step nearer the edge / Angels and demons / Talk to me / Round round blues / Let's take a walk / Time drags so slow / I'm going to change my mind. *(free-7"yellow) (FREE 5001)* – FROM THE MIDDLE ROOM. / INTO THE FUTURE

— The TOURISTS split late '80.

EURYTHMICS

— were formed by **ANNIE LENNOX + DAVE STEWART** with guests **ROBERT GORL** and **GABI DELGADO** of D.A.F. / **JAKI LIEBEZEIT** – percussion and **HOLGER CZUKAY** – bass (both ex-CAN)

R.C.A. — R.C.A.

Jun 81. (7"/ext.12") *(RCA/+T 68)* **NEVER GONNA CRY AGAIN. / LE SINISTRE** [63] [ ]

Aug 81. (7") *(RCA 115)* **BELINDA. / HEARTBEAT, HEARTBEAT** [ ] [ ]

Oct 81. (lp/c) *(RCA LP/K 5061)* **IN THE GARDEN** [ ] [ ]
– English summer / Belinda / Take me to your heart / She's invisible now / Your time will come / Caveman head / Never gonna cry again / All the young (people of today) / Sing sing / Revenge. *(re-iss. Mar84 lp/c; PL/PK 70006) (cd-iss. Jan87; PD 70006) (re-iss. Sep91 cd/c/lp; ND/NK/NL 75036)*

— **ANNIE** and **DAVE** now augmented with synthesisers, also guests **CLEM BURKE** – drums (ex-BLONDIE, who later joined RAMONES in '87)

Mar 82. (7") *(RCA 199)* **THIS IS THE HOUSE. / HOME IS WHERE THE HEART IS** [ ] [ ]
(12") *(RCAT 199)* – ('A'side) / Your time will come (live) / 4-4 In leather (live) / Never gonna cry again (live) / Take me to your heart (live).

Jun 82. (7"m) *(RCA 230)* **THE WALK. / STEP ON THE BEAST / THE WALK (part 2)** [ ] [ ]
(12"+=) *(RCAT 230)* – Invisible hands / Dr. Trash.

Sep 82. (7"/7"pic-d) *(DA 1)* **LOVE IS A STRANGER. / MONKEY, MONKEY** [54] [ ]
(12"+=) *(DAT 1)* – Let's just close our eyes.
(re-iss. Apr83, hit No.6) <US re-iss. Sep83; 13618); hit No.23>

Jan 83. (7"/7"pic-d) *(DA/+P 2)* <13533> **SWEET DREAMS (ARE MADE OF THIS). / I COULD GIVE YOU (A MIRROR)** [2] Apr83 [1]
(12"+=) *(DAT 2)* – Baby's gone blue.

Feb 83. (lp/pic-lp/c) *(RCA LP/LPP/K 6063)* <4681> **SWEET DREAMS (ARE MADE OF THIS)** [3] May83 [15]
– Sweet dreams (are made of this) / Jennifer / This city never sleeps / This is the house / Somebody told me / The walk / I've got an angel / Love is a stranger / Wrap it up / I could give you (a mirror). *(re-iss. Aug84 lp/c; PL/PK 70014) (cd-iss. Jan84; RCD 25447) (re-iss. Oct87 lp/c/cd; NL/NK/ND 71471)*

Jul 83. (7"/7"pic-d) *(DA/+P 3)* **WHO'S THAT GIRL?. / YOU TAKE SOME LENTILS . . . AND YOU TAKE SOME RICE** [3] [–]
(12"+=) *(DAT 3)* – ABC (freeform).

Oct 83. (7"/7"pic-d) *(DA/+P 4)* <13695> **RIGHT BY YOUR SIDE. / ('A'party mix)** [10] Jul84 [29]
(7"w/ free-c-s) *(DA 4-EUC 001)* – Intro speech / Step on the beast / Invisible hands / Angel (dub) / Satellite of love.
(12"+=) *(DAT 4)* – Plus something else.

— **ANNIE** and **DAVE** were augmented on album by **CLEM** – drums plus **DICK CUTHELL** – brass MARTIN DOBSON – horns / **DEAN GARCIA** – bass(above 3 also went on tour adding) **VIC MARTIN** – synthesizers / **PETE PHIPPS** – drums / and backing singers **GILL O'DONOVAN, SUZIE O'LISZT and MAGGIE RYDER**

Nov 83. (lp/pic-lp/c) *(PL/PLP/PK 70109)* <4917> **TOUCH** [1] Jan84 [7]
– Here comes the rain again / Regrets / Right by your side / Cool blue / Who's that girl? / The first cut / Aqua / No fear, no hurt, no pain (no broken hearts) / Paint a rumour. *(cd-iss. Sep84; PD 70109) (re-iss. Sep89 lp/c/cd; NL/NK/ND 90369)*

Jan 84. (7"/7"pic-d) *(DA/+P 5)* <13725> **HERE COMES THE RAIN AGAIN. / PAINT A RUMOUR** [8] [4]
(ext.12"+=) *(DAT 5)* – This city never sleeps (live).

Apr 84. (7") <13800> **WHO'S THAT GIRL?. / AQUA** [–] [21]

Jun 84. (m-lp/c) *(PG/PH 70354)* <5086> **TOUCH DANCE** (remixes) [31] [ ]
– The first cut (instrumental) / Cool blue (instrumental) / Paint a rumour (instrumental) / The first cut / Cool blue / Paint a rumour / Regrets. *(cd-iss. Dec91; ND 75151)*

Oct 84. (7") *(VS 728)* <13956> **SEXCRIME (NINETEEN EIGHTY-FOUR). / I DID IT JUST THE SAME** [4] [81]
(12"/12"pic-d) *(VS 728-12)* – ('A'extended).

Nov 84. (lp/c) *(V/TCV 1984)* <5349> **1984 – FOR THE LOVE OF BIG BROTHER (soundtrack)** [23] [93]
– I did it just the same / Julia / Sexcrime (nineteen eighty-four) / Doubleplusgood / For the love of big brother / Ministry of love / Winston's diary / Room 101 / Greetings from a dead man. *(re-iss. Jan88 lp/c; OVED/+C 207) (cd-iss. Apr89; CDV 1984) (re-iss. cd.Dec95;)*

Jan 85. (7"/7"pic-d) *(VS 734)* **JULIA. / MINISTRY OF LOVE** [44] [ ]
(12"+=) *(VS 734-12)* – ('A'extended).
(above album & two singles were issued UK on 'Virgin')

Apr 85. (7",7"red,7"yellow,7"blue) *(PB 40101)* <14078> **WOULD I LIE TO YOU? / HERE COMES THAT SINKING FEELING** [11] [5]
(ext.remix; 12",12"red,12"yellow,12"blue;+=) *(PT 40102)* – ('A'-E.T.mix).

May 85. (lp/c/cd) *(PL/PK/PD 70711)* <5429> **BE YOURSELF TONIGHT** [3] [9]
– It's alright (baby's coming back) / Would I lie to you / There must be an angel (playing with my heart) / I love you like a ball and chain / Sisters are doin' it for themselves / Conditioned soul / Adrian / Here comes that sinking feeling / Better to have lost in love (than never to have loved at all). *(re-iss. May90 cd/c/lp; ND/NK/NL 74602)*

Jun 85. (7")(12"/dance mix-12") *(PB 40247)(PT 40248/+R)* <14160> **THERE MUST BE AN ANGEL (PLAYING WITH MY HEART). / GROWN UP GIRLS** [1] [22]

Oct 85. (7"; as EURYTHMICS & ARETHA FRANKLIN) *(PB 40339)* <14214> **SISTERS ARE DOIN' IT FOR THEMSELVES. / I LOVE YOU LIKE A BALL AND CHAIN** [9] [18]
(12"+=) *(PT 40340)* – ('A'-E.T. remix with ARETHA).

Jan 86. (7") *(PB 40375)* <14284> **IT'S ALRIGHT (BABY'S COMING BACK). / CONDITIONED SOUL** [12] [78]
(d7"+=/d12"+=) *(PB/PB 40375/40376; 2nd-free in yellow, blue or red)* – Would I lie to you? / Here comes that sinking feeling.
(12"+=) *(PT 40376)* – Tous les garcons et les filles.

Jun 86. (7") *(DA 7)* **WHEN TOMORROW COMES. / TAKE YOUR PAIN AWAY** [30] [ ]
(ext.12"+=) *(DAT 7)* – ('A'-orchestral).

Jul 86. (lp/c/cd) *(PL/PK/PD 71050)* <5847> **REVENGE** [3] [12]
– Let's go / Take your pain away / A little of you / Thorn in my side / In this town / I remember you / Missionary man / The last time / When tomorrow comes / The miracle of love. *(cd re-iss. Sep93; 74321 12529-2)*

Jul 86. (7"/12") <14414> **MISSIONARY MAN. / TAKE YOUR PAIN AWAY** [–] [14]

Aug 86. (7") *(DA 8)* <5058> **THORN IN MY SIDE. / IN THIS TOWN** [5] Oct86 [68]
(12"+=) *(DAT 8)* – ('A'extended or Houston mix).

Nov 86. (7"/7"sha-pic-d) *(DA/+P 9)* **THE MIRACLE OF LOVE. / WHEN TOMORROW COMES (live)** [23] [ ]
(12"+=) *(DAT 9)* – Who's that girl? (live).

Feb 87. (7"/ext.12") *(DA/+T 10)* **MISSIONARY MAN. / THE LAST TIME (live)** [31] [–]

Oct 87. (7"/7"w-poster) *(DA 11/+P)* **BEETHOVEN (I LOVE TO LISTEN TO). / HEAVEN** [25] [ ]
(ext.12"+=)(cd-s+=) *(DAT 11)(DA 11CD)* – ('A'dance mix).

Nov 87. (lp/c/cd) *(PL/PK/PD 71555)* <6794> **SAVAGE** [7] [41]
– Beethoven (I love to listen to) / I've got a lover (back in Japan) / Do you want to break up? / You have placed a chill in my heart / Shame / Savage / I need a man / Put the blame on me / Heaven / Wide eyed girl / I need you / Brand new day. *(re-iss. cd May93; 74321 13440-2)*

Dec 87. (7") *(DA 14)* **SHAME. / I'VE GOT A LOVER (BACK IN JAPAN)** [41] [ ]
(12"+=/12"s+=) *(DAT 14/+P)* – ('A'dance mix).
('A'dance mix-cd-s+=) *(DA 14CD)* – There must be an angel (playing with my heart).

Dec 87. (7") *<5361>* **I NEED A MAN. / HEAVEN** [–] [46]

Mar 88. (7") *(DA 15)* **I NEED A MAN. / I NEED YOU** [26] [–]
(12"+=) *(DAT 15)* – ('A'-macho mix).
(cd-s++=) *(DA 15CD)* – Missionary man (live).
(10"+=) *(DA 15X)* – There must be an angel (playing with my heart).
(7"m+=) *(DA 15R)* – I need a man (live).

May 88. (7") *(DA 16)* **YOU HAVE PLACED A CHILL IN MY HEART. / ('A'acoustic mix)** [16] [64]
(12"+=) *(DAT 16)* – ('A'dance).
(cd-s++=) *(DA 16CD)* – Do you want to break up / Here comes the rain again (live).

— In Oct'88, ANNIE was credited with AL GREEN on single 'PUT A LITTLE LOVE IN YOUR HEART' on 'A&M' 7"/12"; *(AM/+Y 484)*

R.C.A. Arista

Aug 89. (7"/c-s) *(DA/+K 17)* **REVIVAL. / PRECIOUS** [26] [ ]
(12"+=/cd-s+=) *(DAT/DACD 17)* – ('A'dance mix).
(12"+=/12"s+=) *(DAT 18/+P)* – ('A'-extended E.T. dance mix).

Sep 89. (lp/c/cd) *(PL/PK/PD 74251)* <8606> **WE TOO ARE ONE** [1] [34]
– We two are one / The King and Queen of America / (My my) Baby's gonna cry / Don't ask me why / Angel / Revival / You hurt me (and I hate you) / Sylvia / How long? / When the day goes down. *(re-iss. cd Jun94; 74321 20898-2)*

Oct 89. (7"/c-s) *(DA/+K 19)* <9880> **DON'T ASK ME WHY. / RICH GIRL** [25] Sep89 [40]
(12"+=/12"pic-d+=/cd-s+=) *(DA T/P/CD 19)* – Sylvia.
(12"+=/cd-s+=) *(DA T/CD 20)* – ('A'acoustic) / When the day goes down.

Jan 90. (7"/c-s) *(DA/+K 23)* **KING AND QUEEN OF AMERICA (remix). / SEE NO EVIL** [29] [–]
(cd-s+=) *(DACD 23)* – There must be an angel (playin' with my heart) (live) / I love you like a ball and chain (live) / ('A'dub).
(12") *(DAT 23)* – ('A'dance mix) / ('B'side) / ('A'dub mix).
(12"+=/cd-s+=) *(DA T/CD 24)* – (as extra above except 'A'dub).

Apr 90. (7"/c-s) *(DA/+K 21)* **ANGEL. / ANGEL (choir version)** [23] [–]
(12"+=/cd-s+=) *(DA T/CD 21)* – Missionary man (acoustic).
(12") *(DAT 25)* – ('A'remix) / Sweet dreams (are made of this) (Nightmare mix).

Apr 90. (c-s) *<9917>* **ANGEL / PRECIOUS** [–] [ ]

Jun 90. (c-s) *<9939>* **(MY MY) BABY'S GONNA CRY / ('A'acoustic)** [–] [ ]

— split after the above release

– compilations, others, etc. –

on 'RCA' UK / 'Arista' US unless otherwise stated

Nov 88. (3"cd-ep/5"cd-ep) *Virgin; (CDT/CDF 22)* **SEXCRIME (1984 extended mix) / JULIA (extended) / I DID IT JUST THE SAME** [ ] [–]

Mar 89. (3"cd-ep) *(PD 42651)* **SWEET DREAMS (ARE MADE OF THIS) / I COULD GIVE YOU (A MIRROR) / HERE COMES THE RAIN AGAIN / PAINT A RUMOUR** [ ] [–]

Mar 91. (cd/c/lp) *(PD/PK/PL 74856)* <8680> **EURYTHMICS' GREATEST HITS** [1] [72]
– Love is a stranger / Sweet dreams (are made of this) / Who's that girl? / Right by your side / Here comes the rain again / There must be an angel (playing with my heart) / Sisters are doin' it for themselves / It's alright (baby's coming back) / When tomorrow comes / You have placed a chill in my heart / Sexcrime (nineteen eighty-four) / Thorn in my side Don't ask me why. *(cd+=/c+=)* – Miracle of love / Angel / Would I lie to you? / Missionary man / I need a man.

Mar 91. (7"/c-s) *(PB/PK 44265)* **LOVE IS A STRANGER. / JULIA** [46] [–]
(12"+=/cd-s+=) *(PT/PD 44266)* – ('A'obsession mix) / There must be an angel (playin' with my heart).
(12") *(PT 44268)* – ('A'-JC meets the Obsessor mix) / ('A'instrumental) / ('A'-Coldcut mix).

Nov 91. (7"/c-s) *(PB/PK 45031)* <2243> **SWEET DREAMS (ARE MADE OF THIS) '91. / KING AND QUEEN OF AMERICA** [48] [ ]
(12") *(PT 45032)* – ('A'side) / ('A'-house mix) / ('A'-nightmare mix) / ('A'-hot remix).
(cd-s) *(PD 45032)* – ('A'side) / Beethoven (I love to listen to) / Shame / This city never sleeps.

Nov 93. (d-cd/d-c) *(74321 17145-2/-4)* **EURYTHMICS LIVE 1983-1989 (live)** [22] [–]
– Never gonna cry again / Love is a stranger / Sweet dreams (are made of this) / This city never sleeps / Somebody told me / Who's that girl? / Right by your side / Here comes the rain again / Sex crime / I love you like a ball and chain / There must be an angel (playing with my heart) / Thorn in my side / Let's go / Missionary man / The last time / Miracle of love / I need a man / We two are one / (My my) Baby's gonna cry / Don't ask me why / Angel. *(cd includes free 7 track EP) (re-iss. Oct95; same)*

Apr 95. (d-cd) *(74321 26442-2)* **BE YOURSELF TONIGHT / REVENGE** [ ] [–]

ANNIE LENNOX

in 1992 with **STEPHEN LIPSON** – guitars, prog., keyboards / **PETER-JOHN VITTESE** – keyboards, recorder / **MARIUS DE VRIES** – programming, keyboards/ also **LOUIS JARDIM** – percussion / **ED SHEARMUR** – piano / **KEITH LeBLANC** – drums / **DOUG WIMBUSH** – bass / **KENJI JAMMER** – guitar / **STEVE JANSON** – drum pro / **DAVE DeFRIES** – trumpet / **GAVON WRIGHT** – violin / **PAUL MOORE** – keyboards (co-writer on 1)

R.C.A. Arista

Mar 92. (7"/c-s) *(PB/PK 45317)* <12419> **WHY. / PRIMITIVE** [5] [34]
(12"+=) *(PT 45317)* – Keep young and beautiful.
(cd-s+=) *(PD 45317)* – ('A'instrumental).

Apr 92. (cd/c/lp) *(PL/PK/PD 75326)* <18704> **ANNIE LENNOX – DIVA** [1] [27]
– Why / Walking on broken glass / Precious / Legend in my living room / Cold / Money can't buy it / Little bird / Primitive / Stay by me / The gift. *(cd+=)* – Keep young and beautiful. *(re-iss. Feb96 cd/c; 74321 33102-2/-4)*

May 92. (7"/c-s) *(74321 10025-7/-4)* **PRECIOUS. / ('A'version)** [23] [ ]
(cd-s+=) *(74321 10025-2)* – Step by step / Why.

Aug 92. (7"/c-s/cd-s) *(74321 10722-7/-4/-2)* **WALKING ON BROKEN GLASS. / LEGEND IN MY OWN LIVING ROOM** [8] [–]
(12"+=/cd-s+=) *(74321 28483-1/-2)* – Don't let me down.

Aug 92. (c-s) *<12452>* **WALKING ON BROKEN GLASS / DON'T LET ME DOWN** [–] [14]

Oct 92. (7") *(74321 11688-7)* **COLD. / ('A'live)** [26] [ ]
(c-s) *(74321 11688-4)* – River deep mountain high / You have placed a chill in my heart / Why.
(cd-s) *(74321 11690-2)* – ('A'side) / River deep mountain high / Feel the need in me / Don't let me down.
(cd-s) *(74321 11689-2)* – ('A'side) / Why / The gift / Walking on broken glass.
(cd-s) *(74321 11688-2)* – ('A'side) / It's alright / Here comes the rain again / You have placed a chill in my heart.

Jan 93. (7"/c-s/12") *(74321 123383-7/-4/-1)* <12508> **LITTLE BIRD. / LOVE SONG FOR A VAMPIRE** [3] [49]
(cd-s+=) *(74321 12383-2)* – Feel the need (live).
(cd-s+=) *(74321 12383-5)* – River deep mountain high (live).
(cd-s+=) *(74321 12383-8)* – Don't let me down (live).

— with **STEPHEN LIPSON** – programmer, guitar, keyboards, bass

Feb 95. (7"/c-s) *(74321 25716-7/-4)* <12804> **NO MORE "I LOVE YOU'S". / LADIES OF THE CANYON** [2] [23]
(cd-s+=) *(74321 25551-2)* – Love song for a vampire.
(cd-s) *(74321 25716-2)* – ('A'side) / Why (acoustic) / Cold (acoustic) / Walking on broken glass (acoustic).

Mar 95. (cd/c/lp) *(<74321 25717-2/-4/-1>)* **MEDUSA** [1] [11]
– No more "I love you's" / Take me to the river / A whiter shade of pale / Don't let it bring you down / Train in vain / I can't get next to you /

Downtown lights / The thin line between love and hate / Waiting in vain / Something so right. *(re-iss. d-cd Dec95; 74321 33163-2)* – w/ free 'LIVE IN CENTRAL PARK')

May 95. (c-s) *(74321 28482-4)* **A WHITER SHADE OF PALE / HEAVEN** 16 [ ]
(cd-s+=) *(74321 26482-2)* – I'm always touched by your presence dear / Love song for a vampire.
(cd-s) *(74321 28483-2)* – ('A'side) / Don't let it bring you down / You have placed a chill in my heart / Here comes the rain again.

Sep 95. (c-s) *(74321 31612-4)* **WAITING IN VAIN. / NO MORE "I LOVE YOU'S"** 31 [ ]
(cd-s+=) *(74321 31613-2)* – (interview) / ('A'-Strong body mix).
(cd-s) *(74321 31612-2)* – ('A'side) / Train in vain (3 mixes).
(12") *(74321 31612-1)* – ('A'side) / ('A'-Strong body mix) / ('A'-Howie B mix).
(below featured PAUL SIMON)

Nov 95. (cd-s) *(74321 33238-2)* **SOMETHING SO RIGHT / SWEET DREAMS (ARE MADE OF THIS) (live)** 44 [ ]
(c-s+=) *(74321 33238-4)* – Who's that girl (live) / Waiting in vain (live).
(cd-s) *(74321 33239-2)* – ('A'side) / I love you like a ball and chain / Money can't buy it.

EURYTHMICS

—— re-formed in 1999 after a decade split

	Arista	Arista

Oct 99. (c-s/cd-s) *(74321 69563-4/-2)* **I SAVED THE WORLD TODAY / LIFTED** 11 [ ]
(cd-s) *(74321 69564-2)* – ('A'side) / You have placed a chill in my heart / There must be an angel playing with my heart.

Oct 99. (cd/c) *(74321 69582-2/-4)* *<14617>* **PEACE** 4 25
– 17 again / I saved the world today / Power to the meek / Beautiful child / Anything but strong / Peace is just a word / I've tried everything / I want it all / My true love / Forever / Lifted.

Jan 00. (c-s/cd-s) *(74321 72626-4/-2)* **17 AGAIN / GOSPEL MEDLEY:- BALL AND CHAIN – WOULD I LIE TO YOU – SISTERS ARE DOIN' IT FOR THEMSELVES** 27 [ ]
(cd-s) *(74321 72627-2)* – ('A'side) / Here comes the rain again / Why.

ANNIE LENNOX

	R.C.A.	J-Records

Jun 03. (cd) *(82876 52405-2)* *<52072>* **BARE** 3 4
– A thousand beautiful things / Pavement cracks / The hurting time / Honestly / Wonderful / Bitter pill / Loneliness / The saddest song I've got / Erased / Twisted / Oh God (prayer). *(ltd-cd w/ dvd+=; 82876 52247-2)* – A thousand beautiful things (live) / Wonderful (live) / (interview).

Oct 03. (12"/cd-s) *(82876 56920-1/-2)* **WONDERFUL / PAVEMENT CRACKS (Goldtrix full vocal mix) / A THOUSAND BEAUTIFUL THINGS (Gabriel & Dresden tech funk mix)** [ ] –
(cd-s) *(82876 56921-2)* – ('A'side) / Pavement cracks (Scumfrog mix) / A thousand beautiful things (Bimbo Jones stealth mix).

EVANESCENCE

Formed: Little Rock, Arkansas, USA ... 1998 by BEN MOODY and AMY LEE. Having first clocked the budding young singer/songwriter playing piano at a youth camp, MOODY quickly formed a musical partnership with her and the pair began crafting their gloomy, SARAH McLACHLAN goes nu-metal-lite, sub-goth, pro-Christian rock. A series of limited, self-financed EP's proved popular at live gigs and after expanding to a four piece – with the addition of ROCKY GRAY and JOHN LeCOMPT – they recorded the 'ORIGIN' demo. This in turn led to a major label deal with 'Sony' subsidiary 'Wind Up', who issued their debut album, 'FALLEN', in 2003. Spurred on by the chart success of the 'BRING ME TO LIFE' single (which had previously featured on the soundtrack to the awful movie, 'Daredevil'), the album made the US Top 3, showcasing LEE's admittedly powerful vocal chops against a piano-led backdrop swathed in the usual goth fallbacks of ominous keyboards, horror film strings and operatic choirs. • **Covered:** HEART-SHAPED BOX (Nirvana).

Album rating: FALLEN (*6)

AMY LEE – vocals, piano / **BEN MOODY** – guitar / **DAVID HODGES** – keyboards (left after debut EP)

	not iss.	own label

Dec 98. (cd-ep) *<none>* **EVANESCENCE** – [ ]

—— added **JOHN LeCOMPT** – guitar / **ROCKY GRAY** – drums

	Epic	Wind-Up

Apr 03. (cd) *(510879-2)* *<13063>* **FALLEN** 1 Mar03 3
– Going under / Bring me to life / Everybody's fool / My immortal / Haunted / Tourniquet / Imaginary / Taking over me / Hello / My last breath / Whisper.

Jun 03. (c-s) *(673976-4)* *<radio>* **BRING ME TO LIFE / FARTHER AWAY / BRING ME TO LIFE (bliss mix)** 1 5
(cd-s+=) *(673976-2)* – ('A'video).

Sep 03. (cd-s) *(674352-2)* **GOING UNDER / GOING UNDER (live acoustic) / HEART-SHAPED BOX (live acoustic) / GOING UNDER (video)** 8 –

EVE

Born: EVE JIHAN JEFFERS, 10 Nov'78, Philadelphia, Pennsylvania, USA. Having been raised by her mother and grandmother, the butch-like EVE went her own way at the tender age of 18 and initially paid her bills by stripping at the 'Golden Lady'. After performing (music, that is) in an all-girl R&B group for years on the Philadelphia music scene, EVE (or better known at that time as EVE OF DESTRUCTION) began rapping, hosting local talent shows, MC-ing to crowds as a support act and basically just honing her talents as a female rapper. A friend introduced her to legendary Hip-Hop producer DR. DRE, who was establishing his own 'Aftermath' records. He invited EVE to record tracks with him in his L.A. studio. One of the tracks 'EVE OF DESTRUCTION' featured on the 1996 soundtrack to Warren Beatty's ghetto-political satire 'Bullworth', however, due to management complications, DRE was unable to work with EVE. She found solace in DMX and his RUFF RYDER's crew (The LOX, DRAG-ON and SWIZZ BEATZ), contributing to their 'Ryde Or Die' album in '99. EVE's style was violent, sassy and nasty all in one. The new bad girl on the block was quickly becoming the female answer to DRE, before the overtly sexual LIL' KIM stole her crown. After a few more guest appearances (noteably for JANET JACKSON, BLACKstreet and JAY Z), EVE issued her debut album 'LET THERE BE EVE ... RUFF RYDER'S FIRST LADY' (1999), which somewhat surprised critics and rap afficionados everywhere. But it was her second album 'SCORPION' (2001) that really pulled in the crowds. A more serious and focused set, EVE demonstrated her talents at not only rapping but at musical production. The result was a fascinating insight into one of mainstream hip-hop's most underrated leading ladies – 'WHO'S THAT GIRL?', indeed. 'EVE-OLUTION' (2002) was a half decent attempt to partly diversify from hard ryhmin' into sensual R&B smooching although even the delicious tonsils of ALICIA KEYS couldn't lift 'GANGSTA LOVIN' much above the level of conveyor belt nu-soul.

Album rating: LET THERE BE ... EVE – RUFF RYDERS' FIRST LADY (*7) / SCORPION (*8) / EVE-OLUTION (*5)

EVE – vocals / with RUFF RYDERS crew on backing

	Ruff Ryders – Interscope	Ruff Ryders – Interscope

Jun 99. (-; by EVE & NOKIO) *<radio cut>* **WHAT Y'ALL WANT** – 29

Sep 99. (cd-s) *<97085>* **GOTTA MAN / (mixes)** [–] [26]

Sep 99. (cd/d-lp) *<(490453-2/-1)>* **LET THERE BE . . . EVE – RUFF RYDERS' FIRST LADY** [ ] [1]
– First lady (intro) / Let's talk about (featuring DRAG-ON) / Gotta man / Philly cheese steak (skit) / Philly, Philly (featuring BEANIE SIEGEL) / Stuck up (featuring CJ) / Ain't got no dough (featuring MISSY ELLIOTT) / Love is blind / Scenario 2000 (featuring DRAG-ON, The LOX & DMX) / Dog match (featuring DMX) / My bitches (skit) / We on that shit! (featuring P. KILLER TRACKS) / Chokie nikes (skit) / Maniac / My enemies (skit) / Heaven only knows. *(bonus+=)* – What y'all want (featuring NOKIO).

Dec 99. (-; EVE featuring FAITH EVANS) *<radio cut>* **LOVE IS BLIND** [–] [34]

— in Jan'00, EVE featured on MISSY ELLIOTT's hit single, 'Hot Boyz'

Mar 01. (cd/lp) *<(490845-2/-1)>* **SCORPION** [22] [4]
– Intro / Cowboy / Who's that girl? / Let me blow ya mind (with GWEN STEFANI) / 3 way (skit) / You had me, you lose me / Got what you need (with DRAG-ON) / Frontin' (skit) / Gangsta bitches (with DA BRAT & TRINA) / That's what it is (with STYLES) / Scream double R (with DMX) / Thug in the street (with The LOX & DRAG-ON) / No, no, no (with DAMIAN MARLEY & STEPHEN MARLEY) / You ain't gettin' none / Life is so hard (with TEENA MARIE) / Be me (with MASHONDA TIFRERE). *(bonus cd+=)* – Love is blind (with FAITH EVANS) / Got it all (with JADAKISS). *(clean version; 490848-2)*

May 01. (c-s) *(497557-4) <497488>* **WHO'S THAT GIRL? / (mix with NOKIO)** [6] Jan01 [47]
(12"+=) *(497557-1)* – ('A'-instrumental).
(cd-s+=) *(497557-2)* – ('A'-CLAS remix) / ('A'video).

Aug 01. (c-s; by EVE & GWEN STEFANI) *(497593-4) <497562>* **LET ME BLOW YA MIND / WHO'S THAT GIRL? (main pass)** [4] Apr01 [2]
(cd-s+=) *(497593-2)* – Gotta man / ('A'-video).
(12") *(497593-1)* – ('A'-instrumental) / ('A'-CLAS remix).
(cd-s) *(497605-2)* – ('A'-CLAS remix) / Ain't got no dough (with MISSY ELLIOTT) / ('A'video).

Aug 02. (cd)(d-lp) *<(493472-2)>(493381-1)* **EVE-OLUTION** [47] [6]
– Intro / What (with TRUTH HURTS) / Gangsta lovin' (with ALICIA KEYS) / Irresistible chick / Party in the rain (with MASHONDA) / Argument (skit with JAY "ICEPICK" JACKSON) / Let this go / Hey y'all (with SNOOP DOGG & NATE DOGG) / Figure you out / Stop hatin' (skit with EREX THE TRAVELER & TAKIA RIDEOUT) / Satisfaction / Neckbones / Double R what (with JADAKISS & STYLES OF THE LOX) / Ryde away / As I grow / Eve-olution. *(UK+=)* – Let me blow ya mind (with GWEN STEFANI) / U me and she.

Sep 02. (c-s/12"/cd-s; by EVE & ALICIA KEYS) *(497804-4/-1/-2) <INTR 7817>* **GANGSTA LOVIN'. / WHO'S THAT GIRL / ('A'-instrumental)** [6] Nov02 [2]

— in Mar'02, EVE and ALICIA KEYS featured on ANGIE STONE's hit single, 'Brotha Part II'

Mar 03. (12") *(497826-1)* **SATISFACTION. / DOUBLE R WHAT** [20] [27]
(cd-s+=) *(497826-2)* – ('A'-instrumental) / ('A'-video).

EVERCLEAR

Formed: Portland, Oregon, USA . . . 1991 by former teenage junkie, ART ALEXAKIS (he gave up alcohol, drugs and nicotine in June '84). Coming from a broken home, he was also dogged by the drug deaths of his girlfriend and older brother, George. At the turn of the decade, ART was involved in two bands, The EASY HOES (lp released 'Tragic Songs Of Life' on 'Shindig') and COLORFINGER (cd issued 'Deep In The Heart Of The Beast In The Sun' – a demo cassette was also issued with future EVERCLEAR tracks!). Another founder member, CRAIG MONTOYA (other two, STEVEN BIRCH and SCOTT CUTHBERT) helped produce their debut indie album, 'WORLD OF NOISE', in 1994 and after rave reviews they were whisked away by 'Capitol' A&R man PERRY WATTS-RUSSELL. It was alleged that they were released from the indie, only when the gun-totting ALEXAKIS convinced the boss to let them go. By Spring '96 (and now with GREG EKLUND who had replaced CUTHBERT and BIRCH), their second album, 'SPARKLE AND FADE', had climbed into the US Top 30. A stylish anti-drug affair, it was described as ELVIS COSTELLO fused with LED ZEPPELIN, HUSKER DU or NIRVANA! ALEXAKIS and Co. returned in 1998 with a third set proper (the previous year's 'WHITE TRASH HELL' consisted of outtakes), 'SO MUCH FOR THE AFTERGLOW', the US Top 40 album almost spawning another UK Top 40 single, 'EVERYTHING TO EVERYONE'. While many of the tail-end grunge acts imploded before the 90's were through, EVERCLEAR entered the new millennium with their most ambitious project to date, a two-volume concept set exploring ALEXAKIS' divorce. 'SONGS FROM AN AMERICAN MOVIE, VOL.1: LEARNING HOW TO SMILE' (2000) covered the dating years with a peppy soundtrack inspired by the A.M. pop/rock of the frontman's youth (including a cover of Van Morrison's timeless 'BROWN EYED GIRL'). 'SONGS FROM AN AMERICAN MOVIE, VOL.2: GOOD TIME FOR A BAD ATTITUDE' (2000), meanwhile, hit the shelves a few months later and documented the dream turning sour. Unsurprisingly, the music was harder and the subject matter heavier as ALEXAKIS exorcised the pain of lost love and broken friendship. The Portland songwriter returned in 2003 with 'SLOW MOTION DAYDREAM', a respectable effort but one which made it difficult to shake off the impression that the whole concept of EVERCLEAR and their approach to rock was perhaps a little dated. ALEXAKIS proved he can still cut to the quick on the likes of opener 'HOW TO WIN FRIENDS AND INFLUENCE PEOPLE', although the cliche-ridden 'VOLVO DRIVING SOCCER MUM', hinted at desperation rather than inspiration. • **Covered:** HOW SOON IS NOW (Smiths).

Album rating: WORLD OF NOISE (*6) / SPARKLE AND FADE (*9) / SO MUCH FOR THE AFTERGLOW (*7) / SONGS FROM AN AMERICAN MOVIE VOL.1: LEARNING HOW TO SMILE (*7) / SONGS FROM AN AMERICAN MOVIE VOL.2: GOOD TIME FOR A BAD ATTITUDE (*5) / SLOW MOTION DAYDREAM (*5)

ART ALEXAKIS (b.12 Apr'62) – vocals, guitar / **STEVEN BIRCH** – guitar / **CRAIG MONTOYA** (b.14 Sep'70) – bass, vocals / **SCOTT CUTHBERT** – drums, vocals

not iss. Tim/Kerr

Oct 93. (7",7"colrd) *<TK 937055>* **NERVOUS & WEIRD. / ELECTRA MADE ME BLIND** [–] [ ]
(cd-ep+=) *<TK 93CD57>* – Drunk again / Lame / Connection / Slow motion genius (instrumental).

Nov 93. (cd/lp) *(FIRE CD/LP 46) <TK 59>* **WORLD OF NOISE** [–] [ ]
– Your genius hands / Sick & tired / The laughing world / Fire maple song / Pennsylvania is . . . / Nervous and weird / Malevolent / Sparkle / Trust fund / Loser makes good / Invisible / Evergleam. *<US re-iss. Nov94 on 'Capitol' cd/c; 30562-2/-4> (UK-iss.Feb95 on 'Fire' cd/lp; FIRE CD/LP 46) (cd re-iss. Oct02; SFIRE 021CD)*

Fire Capitol

Nov 94. (cd-ep) *<58255>* **FIRE MAPLE SONG EP** [–] [ ]
– Fire maple song / Detroit / 1975 / Blondes / Pacific wonderland (instrumental) / Fire maple song (acoustic version).

Feb 95. (cd-ep) *(BLAZE 77CD)* **FIRE MAPLE SONG EP** [ ] [–]
– Fire maple song / Loser makes good / Lame / Connection.

— **GREG EKLUND** (b.18 Apr'70) – drums, vocals; repl. CUTHBERT + BIRCH

Nov 95. (7") *<23261-7>* **HEROIN GIRL. / AMERICAN GIRL** [–] [ ]
(cd-s+=) *<23261-2>* – Annabella's song / Nahalem (alt. mix).

Capitol Capitol

Mar 96. (cd/c/lp) *(CD/TC+/EST 2257) <30929>* **SPARKLE AND FADE** [ ] May95 [25]
– Electra made me blind / Heroin girl / You make me feel like a whore / Santa Monica / Summerland / Strawberry / Heartspark dollar / The twistinside / Her brand new skin / Nehalem / Queen of the air / Pale green stars / Chemical smile / My sexual life. *(d-cd re-iss. Jun98; CDESTX 2257)* – (extra tracks).

Apr 96. (cd-ep) *<58538>* **HEARTSPARK DOLLARSIGN / HEROIN GIRL (acoustic) / SIN CITY / HAPPY HOUR** [–] [85]

May 96. (7"clear) *(CL 773)* **HEARTSPARK DOLLARSIGN. / LOSER MAKES GOOD (live)** [48] [–]
(cd-s+=) *(CDCL 773)* – Sparkle (live).
(cd-s) *(CDCLS 773)* – ('A'side) / Pennsylvania is . . . (live) / Nervous & weird (live).

Aug 96. (7") *(CL 775)* **SANTA MONICA (WATCH THE WORLD DIE). / AMERICAN GIRL (KDGE version)** [40] [–]
(cd-s+=) *(CDCL 775)* – Strawberry (KDGE version) / Fire maple song (KDGE version).
(cd-s) *(CDCLS 775)* – ('A'side) / Heroin girl (KDGE version) / Summerland (KDGE version) / Sin city.

Sep 96. (cd-s) *<promo>* **YOU MAKE ME FEEL LIKE A WHORE / AMERICAN GIRL (live) / LIKE BRANDON DOES (by Klinger)** [–] [ ]

—— added **CHRIS BIRCH** – guitar

Mar 98. (cd/c) *<(36503-2/-4/-1)>* **SO MUCH FOR THE AFTERGLOW** [63] Oct97 [33]
– So much for the afterglow / Everything to everyone / Ataraxia / Normal like you / I will buy you a new life / Father of mine / One hit wonder / El distorto de melodica / Amphetamine / White men in black suits / Sunflower / Why don't I believe in God / Like a California king.

Apr 98. (7") *(CL 799)* **EVERYTHING TO EVERYONE. / OUR LIPS ARE SEALED** [41] [ ]
(cd-s+=) *(CDCL 799)* – What do I get / ('A'-CD-Rom video).
(cd-s) *(CDCLS 799)* – ('A'side) / Walk don't run / Search and destroy / Santa Monica heroin (CD-Rom video).

Jul 98. (cd-ep) *<85592>* **I WILL BUY YOU A NEW LIFE EP** [–] [ ]
– I will buy you a new life / So much for the afterglow (live) / Heroin girl (live) / Local god (live).

Nov 98. (cd-ep) *<86181>* **FATHER OF MINE EP** [–] [70]
– Father of mine / So much for the afterglow (live) / Heroin girl (live) / Local god (live).

Aug 00. (cd) *(527864-2) <97061>* **SONGS FROM AN AMERICAN MOVIE VOL.1 – LEARNING HOW TO SMILE** [51] Jul00 [9]
– Songs from an American movie (part 1) / Here we go again / AM radio / Brown eyed girl / Learning how to smile / The honeymoon song / Now that it's over / Thrift store chair / Otis Redding / Unemployed boyfriend / Wonderful / Annabella's song.

Oct 00. (c-s) *(TCCL 824) <58870>* **WONDERFUL / FATHER OF MINE (remix) / I'M ON YOUR TIME** [36] Aug00 [11]
(cd-s+=) *(CDCLS 824)* – ('A'-CD-ROM video)>

Mar 01. (cd-s) *(CDCL 827)* **AM RADIO / I'M ON YOUR TIME / SANTA MONICA (live from Woodstock)** [ ] [–]

Apr 01. (cd) *(530419-2) <95873>* **SONGS FROM AN AMERICAN MOVIE VOL.2 – GOOD TIME FOR A BAD ATTITUDE** [69] Nov00 [ ]
– When it all goes wrong again / Slide / Babytalk / Rock star / Short blonde hair / Misery whip / Out of my depth / The good witch of the north / Halloween Americana / All f**ked up / Overwhelming / Song from an American movie (part 2).

Mar 03. (cd) *<(5 38270-0)>* **SLOW MOTION DAYDREAM** [ ] [33]
– How to win friends and influence people / Blackjack / I want to die a beautiful death / Volvo driving soccer mom / Science fiction / New blue champion / TV show / Chrysanthemum / Sunshine (that acid summer) / A beautiful life / The New York Times. *<(bonus += untitled/dub)>*

– compilations, etc. –

Aug 95. (cd) *Imprint; <97633>* **LIVE FROM TORONTO (live)** [–] [ ]

Apr 97. (m-cd) *Fire; (MCD 45)* **WHITE TRASH HELL** [ ] [–]
– Heroin girl (demo) / Detroit / 1975 / Blondes / Pacific wonderland (instrumental) / For Pete's sake / Fire maple song (acoustic). *(re-iss. May02; SFIRE 009CD)*

☐ EVERLAST (see under ⇒ HOUSE OF PAIN)

EVERLY BROTHERS

Formed: Kentucky, USA . . . 1955 by brothers DON and PHIL EVERLY, the offspring of country singing parents, Ike and Margaret. No strangers to the music scene (the boys having appeared on numerous radio shows alongside their folks), they went to Nashville later that year hoping that hillbilly artists would buy their close harmony songs. The following year, they secured a deal with 'Columbia' records, the label releasing one country-style single, 'KEEP A LOVIN' ME', before opting out as the rock'n'roll era began to kick in. After a short struggle in an attempt to find another label, their father contacted old friend, star picker CHET ATKINS, who got them signed as writers for the legendary Roy Acuff/Wesley Rose songsmith team. ROSE subsequently became the siblings' manager, persuading Archie Bleyer of 'Cadence' records to take them on as recording artists in 1957. Adopting a new style combining their vocal harmonies with easy going pop'n'roll strumming, The EVERLY BROTHERS made an immediate impact with 'BYE BYE LOVE', a million selling single which peaked at No.2 that summer. Their profile heightened by a handful of TV appearances (i.e. the Ed Sullivan and Perry Como shows), the brothers' clean-cut apple-pie good looks and teen heartbreak appeal saw further singles, 'WAKE UP LITTLE SUSIE', 'ALL I HAVE TO DO IS DREAM' and 'BIRD DOG' fare equally well over the ensuing three years. In 1960, they signed to 'Warners', scoring a transatlantic chart topper with their label debut, 'CATHY'S CLOWN', a 45 that had to battle for chart supremacy against reissued 'Cadence' material. The lads were now also relying on their own material, having left the Felice & Boudleaux Bryant songwriting duo behind when they switched stables. A further clutch of major hits, 'SO SAD (TO WATCH GOOD LOVE GO BAD)', 'WALK RIGHT BACK', 'TEMPTATION', 'CRYIN' IN THE RAIN' etc, saw them dominate the pre-BEATLES pop charts in both America and Britain, although it would be the UK who stood by the duo when the onslaught of 1963-64 British Invasion took hold. In 1965, as their American profile was on the wane, they scored considerable critical and commercial success as the classic, 'THE PRICE OF LOVE' hit No.2 in Britain (criminally ignored in their homeland). Their records continued to sell moderately throughout the latter half of the 60's, although a dalliance with country rock in the early 70's brought little commercial reward; the increasingly estranged brothers finally parted company on less than amicable terms during a disastrous gig on the 14th of July '73. Over the next ten years, the brothers followed sporadically successful solo careers (PHIL, together with CLIFF RICHARD, had a 1983 UK Top 10 hit 'SHE MEANS NOTHING TO ME'), eventually coming together again for a reunion concert in '83; they were back on speaking terms after attending the funeral of their father. The resulting live album put The EVERLY BROTHERS back in the UK Top 50 as did the following year's eponymous (PAUL McCARTNEY-produced) comeback set, and although they maintained their working relationship they failed to keep up the momentum. • **Covered:** CLAUDETTE (Roy Orbison) / LET IT BE ME (Gilbert Becaud) / BE-BOP-A-LULA (Gene Vincent) / LUCILLE (Little Richard) / WALK RIGHT BACK (Sonny Curtis; of Crickets) / EBONY EYES + IT'S MY TIME (John D. Loudermilk) / TEMPTATION (Bing Crosby) / CRYING IN THE RAIN (Carole King & Howard Greenfield) / BOWLING GREEN (Terry Slater) / ABANDONED LOVE (Bob Dylan) / THE GIRL SANG THE BLUES + LOVE HER (Mann-Weill) / YVES (Scott McKenzie). After an inter-label rift between Wesley Rose was rectified, The BRYANTS returned on late 1964's 'GONE GONE GONE'. The album 'ROCK'N'SOUL' featured many classic rock'n'roll oldies. • **Trivia:** Many famous musicians have passed through their ranks, including FLOYD CHANCE – bass (1957) / JOEY PAGE – guitar (1962) / JIM GORDON and BILLY PRESTON. Other 60's sessioners stemmed from The BYRDS, The HOLLIES and LED ZEPPELIN!

Best CD compilation: THE DEFINITIVE EVERLY BROTHERS (*8)

DON EVERLY (b.ISAAC DONALD EVERLY, 1 Feb'37, Brownie, Kentucky, USA) – vocals, guitar / **PHIL EVERLY** (b.19 Jan'39, Chicago, Illinois, USA) – vocals, guitar

not iss. Columbia

Feb 56. (7") *<21496>* **KEEP A LOVIN' ME. / THE SUN KEEPS SHINING** –

London Cadence

Jun 57. (7",78) *(HLA 8440) <1315>* **BYE BYE LOVE. / I WONDER IF I CARE AS MUCH** 6 May57 2
(re-iss. Jul82 on 'Old Gold'; OG 9060)

Oct 57. (7",78) *(HLA 8498) <1337>* **WAKE UP LITTLE SUSIE. / MAYBE TOMORROW** 2 Sep57 1
(re-iss. Jul82 on 'Old Gold'; OG 9061)

Feb 58. (7",78) *(HLA 8554) <1342>* **THIS LITTLE GIRL OF MINE. / SHOULD WE TELL HIM** 26

Mar 58. (lp) *(HA-A 2081) <3003>* **THE EVERLY BROTHERS** Jan58 16
– This little girl of mine / Maybe tomorrow / Bye bye love / Brand new Heartache / Keep a knockin' / Be-bop-a-lula / Rip it up / I wonder if I care as much / Wake up little Susie / Leave my woman alone / Should we tell him / Hey doll baby.

May 58. (7",78) *(HLA 8554) <1348>* **ALL I HAVE TO DO IS DREAM. / CLAUDETTE** 1 1
Apr58 30
<re-iss. Jul61, A-side hit No.96> (re-iss. Jul82 on 'Old Gold'; OG 9062)

Sep 58. (7",78) *(HLA 8685)* **BIRD DOG. / DEVOTED TO YOU** 2 1
Jul58 10
(re-iss. Apr79 on 'Lightning; LIG 9018)

Nov 58. (lp) *(HA-A 2150) <3016>* **SONGS OUR DADDY TAUGHT US** Sep58
– Roving gambler / Down in the willow garden / Longtime gone / Lightning express / That silver haired daddy of mine / Who's gonna shoe your pretty little feet / Barbara Allen / Oh so many years / I'm here to get my baby out of jail / Rockin' alone (in an old rocking chair) / Kentucky / Put my little shoes away. *(re-iss. Aug83 on 'Charly' CH 75)*

Jan 59. (7",78) *(HLA 8781) <1355>* **PROBLEMS. / LOVE OF MY LIFE** 6 2
Nov58 40
(re-iss. Jul82 on 'Old Gold'; OG 9063)

May 59. (7",78) *(HLA 8863) <1364>* **POOR JENNY. / TAKE A MESSAGE TO MARY** 14 22
Apr59 16
(re-iss. Jul82 on 'Old Gold'; OG 9064)

Sep 59. (7",78) *(HLA 8934) <1364>* **TILL I KISSED YOU. / OH WHAT A FEELING** 2 Aug59 4
(re-iss. Jul82 on 'Old Gold'; OG 9065)

Feb 60. (7",78) *(HLA 9039) <1376>* **LET IT BE ME. / SINCE YOU BROKE MY HEART** 13 Jan60 7
(re-iss. Jul82 on 'Old Gold'; OG 9066)

Warners Warners

Apr 60. (7",78) *(WB 1) <5151>* **CATHY'S CLOWN. / ALWAYS IT'S YOU** 1 1
56

Jun 60. (lp) *(WM 4012) <1381>* **IT'S EVERLY TIME!** 2 May60 9
– So sad / Just in case / Memories are made of this / That's what you do to me / Sleepless nights / What kind of girl are you / Oh true love / Carol Jane / Some sweet day / Nashville blues / You thrill me / I want you to know. *(re-iss. May85 on 'Rollercoaster'; ROLI 313)*

Sep 60. (7",78) *(WB 19) <5163>* **LUCILLE. / SO SAD (TO WATCH GOOD LOVE GO BAD)** 4 21
Aug60 7

Jan 61. (7") *(WB 33) <5199>* **WALK RIGHT BACK. / EBONY EYES** 1 7
8

Feb 61. (lp) *(WM 4028) <1395>* **A DATE WITH THE EVERLY BROTHERS** 3 Nov60 9
– Made to love / That's just too much / Stick with me baby / Baby what you want me to do / Sigh cry almost die / Always it's you / Love hurts / Lucille / So how come / Donna Donna / A change of heart / Cathy's clown. *(re-iss. May85 on 'Rollercoaster'; ROLI 314)*

Jun 61. (7") *(WB 42) <5199>* **TEMPTATION. / STICK WITH ME BABY** 1 27
41

Sep 61. (7") *(WB 50) <5501>* **DON'T BLAME ME. / MUSKRAT** 20 20
82

1961. (lp) *(WM 4052) <1418>* **BOTH SIDES OF AN EVENING**
– My mamma / Muskrat / My gal Sal / My grandfather's clock / Bully of the town / Chloe / Mention my name in Sheboygan / Hi Lili hi lo / Wayward wind / Don't blame me / Now is the hour / Little old lady / When I grow too old to dream / Love is where you find it.

Jan 62. (7") *(WB 56) <5250>* **CRYIN' IN THE RAIN. / I'M NOT ANGRY** 6 6

May 62. (7") *(WB 67) <5273>* **HOW CAN I MEET HER. / THAT'S OLD FASHIONED (THAT'S THE WAY LOVE SHOULD BE)** 12 75
9

Jul 62. (lp) *(WM 4061) <1430>* **INSTANT PARTY** 20
– Jezebel / Oh my papa / Step it up and go / True love / Bye bye blackbird / Trouble in mind / Love makes the world go round / Long lost John / Autumn leaves / Party's over / Ground hawg / When it's night time in Italy. *(re-iss. Oct86 on 'Rollercoaster'; ROLI 321)*

Sep 62. (lp; mono/stereo) *(WM/WS 8108) <1471>* **THE GOLDEN HITS OF THE EVERLY BROTHERS** (compilation) 35
– That's old fashioned (that's the way love should be) / How can I meet her? / Crying in the rain / I'm not angry / Don't blame me / Ebony eyes / Cathy's clown / Walk right back / Lucille / So sad (to watch good love go bad) / Muskrat / Temptation. *(re-iss. Dec65 mono/stereo; W/WS 1471) (cd+c-iss 1991 on 'WEA')*

Oct 62. (7") *(WB 79) <5297>* **NO ONE CAN MAKE MY SUNSHINE SMILE. / DON'T ASK ME TO BE FRIENDS** 11 B-side 48

Dec 62. (lp; mono/stereo) *(WM/WS 8116) <1483>* **CHRISTMAS WITH THE EVERLY BROTHERS AND THE BOYS TOWN CHOIR** (trad Xmas songs)

Mar 63. (7") *(WB 94) <5346>* **SO IT WILL ALWAYS BE. / NANCY'S MINUET** 23

May 63. (lp; mono/stereo) *(WM/WS 8138) <1513>* **. . . SING GREAT COUNTRY HITS**
– Oh lonesome me / Born to lose / Just one time / Send me the pillow you dream on / Release me / Please help me I'm falling / I walk the line / Lonely street / Silver threads and golden needles / I'm so lonesome I could cry / Sweet dreams / This is the last song I'm ever going to sing. *(re-iss. Dec85 on 'Rollercoaster'; ROLI 329)*

Jun 63. (7") *(WB 99) <5362>* **IT'S BEEN NICE. / I'M AFRAID** 26

Oct 63. (7") *(WB 109) <5389>* **THE GIRL SANG THE BLUES. / LOVE HER** 25

Apr 64. (7") *(WB 129) <5422>* **AIN'T THAT LOVIN' YOU BABY. / HELLO AMY**

Jun 64. (7") *(WB 135) <5441>* **THE FERRIS WHEEL. / DON'T FORGET TO CRY** 22 72

Jan 65. (lp; mono/stereo) *(WM/WS 8163) <1554>* **THE VERY BEST OF THE EVERLY BROTHERS** (re-recorded hits) Jul64
– Bye bye love / (Til) I kissed you / Wake up little Susie / Crying in the rain / Walk right back / Cathy's clown / Bird dog / All I have to do is dream / Devoted to you / Lucille / So sad (to watch good love go bad) / Ebony eyes. *(re-iss. May74 lp/c; K/K4 46008)* – hit UK No.43

1964. (7") *<5466>* **RING AROUND MY ROSIE. / YOU'RE THE ONE I LOVE** –

Nov 64. (7") *(WB 146) <5478>* **GONE GONE GONE. / TORTURE** 36 31

Dec 64. (lp; mono/stereo) *(WM/WS 8169) <1585>* **GONE GONE GONE**
– Donna, Donna / Lonely island / The facts of life / Ain't that lovin' you baby / Love is all I need / Torture / The drop out / Radio and TV / Honolulu / It's been a long dry spell / The ferris wheel / Gone gone gone. *(re-iss. 1970 on 'Valient'; VS 109) (re-iss. May85 on 'Rollercoaster'; ROLI 316)*

Feb 65. (7") *(WB 154) <5600>* **YOU'RE MY GIRL. / DON'T LET THE WHOLE WORLD KNOW**

Apr 65. (7") *(WB 158) <5611>* **THAT'LL BE THE DAY. / GIVE ME A SWEETHEART** 30

May 65. (lp; mono/stereo) *(WM/WS 8171) <1578>* **ROCK'N'SOUL**
– That'll be the day / So fine / Maybelline / Dancing in the street / Kansas City / I got a woman / Love hurts / Slippin' and slidin' / Susie Q / Hound dog / I'm gonna move to the out-skirtsd of town / Lonely weekends. *(re-iss. May85 on 'Rollercoaster'; ROLI 317)*

May 65. (7") *(WB 161) <5628>* **THE PRICE OF LOVE. / IT ONLY COSTS A DIME** 2

Aug 65. (7") *(WB 5539) <5639)* **I'LL NEVER GET OVER YOU. / FOLLOW ME** 35

Sep 65. (lp) *<(WS 1605)>* **BEAT AND SOUL**
– Love is strange / Money / What am I living for / High heel sneakers / C.C.

rider / Lonely avenue / Man with money / People get ready / My babe / Walking the dog / I almost lost my mind / The girl can't help it. *(re-iss. Dec85 on 'Rollercoaster'; ROLI 319)*

Oct 65. (7") *<(WB 5649)>* **LOVE IS STRANGE. / MAN WITH MONEY** [11] [ ]

Mar 66. (7") *(WB 5743) <5808>* **THE POWER OF LOVE. / LEAVE MY GIRL ALONE** [ ] [ ]

Mar 66. (lp) *<(WS 1620)>* **IN OUR IMAGE** [ ] [ ]
– Leave my girl alone / Chained to a memory / I'll never get over you / The doll house is empty / Glitter and gold / The power of love / The price of love / It's all over / I used to love you / Lonely Kravezit / June is as cold as December / It only cost a dime. *(re-iss. May85 on 'Rollercoaster'; ROLI 318)*

Mar 66. (7") *<5682>* **I USED TO LOVE YOU. / IT'S ALL OVER** [–] [ ]

1966. (7") *<5698>* **THE DOLL HOUSE IS EMPTY. / LONELY KRAVEZIT** [–] [ ]

Jul 66. (lp) *<(WS 1646)>* **TWO YANKS IN ENGLAND** [ ] [ ]
– Somebody help me / So lonely / Kiss your man goodbye / Signs that will never change / Like everytime before / Pretty flamingo / I've been wrong before / Have you ever loved somebody / The collector / Don't run and hide / Fifi the flea / Hard, hard year. *(re-iss. Feb89 on 'Edsel'; ED 297)*

Aug 66. (7") *(WB 5754)* **I'VE BEEN WRONG BEFORE. / HARD, HARD YEAR** [ ] [–]

Sep 66. (7") *<5833>* **SOMEBODY HELP ME. / HARD, HARD YEAR** [–] [ ]

Dec 66. (7") *<5857>* **FIFI THE FLEA (by "DON"). / LIKE EVERYTIME BEFORE (by "PHIL")** [–] [ ]

Feb 67. (lp) *<(WS 1676)>* **THE HIT SOUND OF THE EVERLY BROTHERS** [ ] [ ]
– Blueberry Hill / Movin' on / Devil's child / Trains and boats and planes / Sea of heartbreak / Oh boy / (I'd be a) Legend in my time / Let's go get stoned / Sticks and stones / The house of the rising Sun / She never smiles anymore / Good golly Miss Molly.

Mar 67. (7") *<5901>* **THE DEVIL'S CHILD. / SHE NEVER SMILES ANYMORE** [–] [ ]

Mar 67. (7") *(WB 6074)* **OH BOY. / GOOD GOLLY MISS MOLLY** [ ] [–]

Jun 67. (7") *<(WB 7020)>* **BOWLING GREEN. / I DON'T WANT TO LOVE YOU** [ ] [40]

Sep 67. (7") *<(WB 7062)>* **MARY JANE. / TALKING TO THE FLOWERS** [ ] [ ]

Nov 67. (7") *<(WB 7088)>* **LOVE OF THE COMMON PEOPLE. / A VOICE WITHIN** [ ] [ ]

Apr 68. (7") *<(WB 7192)>* **IT'S MY TIME. / EMPTY BOXES** [39] [ ]

Aug 68. (7") *<(WB 7226)>* **MILK TRAIN. / LORD OF THE MANOR** [ ] [ ]

Nov 68. (lp) *<(WS 1752)>* **ROOTS** (new & re-old material) [ ] [ ]
– Introduction: The Everly family / Mama tried / Less of me / T for Texas / I wonder if I care as much / Ventura boulevard / Shady grove / Illinois / Living too close to the ground / You done me wrong / Turn around / Sing me back home / Montage : The Everly family-Shady grove-Kentucky. *(re-iss. 1971; K 46128) (re-iss. Sep86 on 'Rollercoaster'; ROLI 322) (re-iss. 1987 on 'Edsel'; ED 203) (cd-iss. May95)*

Apr 69. (7") *<7290>* **I'M ON MY WAY HOME AGAIN. / THE CUCKOO BIRD** [–] [ ]

1969. (7") *(7262>* **T – FOR TEARS. / I WONDER IF I CARE AS MUCH** [–] [ ]

1969. (7") *<7290>* **CAROLINA ON MY MIND. / MY LITTLE YELLOW BIRD** [–] [ ]

Feb 70. (d-lp) *<(WS 1858)>* **THE EVERLY BROTHERS SHOW (live at The Grand Hotel)** [ ] [ ]
– Mama tried / Kentucky / Bowling green / Till I kissed you / Wake up little Susie / Cathy's clown / Bird dog / Maybelline / Lord of the manor / I wonder if I care as much / Love is strange / Let it be me / Give peace a chance / Rock and roll music / The end / Aquarius / If I were a carpenter / The price of love / The thrill is gone / Games people play / Baby what you want me to do / All I have to do is dream / Walk right back / Susie Q / Hey Jude.

Oct 70. (7") *<(WB 7425)>* **YVES. / HUMAN RACE** [ ] Feb70 [ ]

RCA Victor RCA Victor

1972. (7") *(RCA 2232) <74-0717>* **RIDIN' HIGH. / STORIES WE COULD TELL** [ ] [ ]

Jun 72. (lp) *(SF 8270) <4620>* **STORIES WE COULD TELL** [ ] [ ]
– All we really want to do / Breakdown / Green river / Mandolin wind / Up in Mabel's room / Del Rio Dan / Ridin' high / Brand new Tennessee waltz / Stories we can tell / Christmas eve can kill you / I'm tired of singing my songs in Las Vegas.

1972. (7") *<74-0849>* **PARADISE. / LAY IT DOWN** [–] [ ]

1973. (7") *<74-0901>* **NOT FADE AWAY. / LADIES LOVE OUTLAWS** [–] [ ]

1973. (7") *(RCA 2286)* **NOT FADE AWAY. / LAY IT DOWN** [ ] [–]

Feb 73. (lp) *(SF 8332) <4781>* **PASS THE CHICKEN AND LISTEN** [ ] [ ]
– Lay it down / Husbands and wives / Woman don't you try to tie me down / Sweet memories / Ladies love outlaws / Not fade away / Watchin' it go / Paradise / Somebody nobody knows / Good-hearted woman / A nickel for the fiddler / Rocky top. *(re-iss. +cd.Jul91 on 'Edsel')*

— Announced their break-up at a 14 Jul'73 concert. PHIL went solo later.

DON EVERLY

with one lp under his belt, also continued with solo career.

A&M Ode

1971. (7") *<66009>* **TUMBLIN' TUMBLEWEEDS. / ONLY ME** [–] [ ]

1971. (lp) *(AMLS 2007) <77005>* **DON EVERLY** [ ] [ ]
– Don't drink the water / Eyes of Asia / February 15th / My baby / My friend / Omaha / Safari / Sweet dreams of you / Tumbling tumbleweed / Thinking it over / When I stop dreaming.

— His next album featured group HEADS, HANDS & FEET

Ode Ode

Aug 74. (7") *<(ODS 66046)>* **WARMIN' UP THE BAND. / EVELYN SWING** [ ] [ ]

Oct 74. (lp) *<(ODE 77023)>* **SUNSET TOWERS** [ ] [ ]
– Melody train / Jack Daniels Old No.7 / Warmin' up the band / Helpless when you're gone / Did it rain / Brand new rock and roll band / Takin' shots / The way you remain / Evelyn swing / Southern California.

D.J.M. Hickory

Jul 76. (7") *(DJS 10692) <368>* **YESTERDAY JUST PASSED MY WAY AGAIN. / NEVER LIKE THIS** [ ] [ ]

Mar 77. (7") *(DJS 10760)* **SO SAD TO WATCH GOOD LOVE GO BAD. / LOVE AT LAST SIGHT** [ ] [–]

1976. (7") *<54002>* **OH, I'D lIKE TO GO AWAY. / LOVE AT LAST SIGHT** [–] [ ]

1976. (7") *(54005)* **DEEP WATER. / SINCE YOU BROKE MY HEART** [–] [ ]

Mar 77. (lp) *(20501) <44003>* **BROTHER JUKE BOX** [ ] [ ]
– Brother juke box / Love at last sight / So sad to watch good love go bad / Lettin' go / Since you broke my heart / Never like this / Deep water / Yesterday just passed my way again / Oh I'd like to go away / Oh what a feeling / Turn the memories back again. *(re-iss. May88 on 'Sundown' lp/c; SDLP/SDC 002) (cd-iss. Aug94)*

Mar 78. (7") *(DJS 10842) <54012>* **BROTHER JUKE BOX. / OH, WHAT A FEELING** [ ] [ ]

Polydor Polydor

Aug 81. (7") *(POSP 315)* **LET'S PUT OUR HEARTS TOGETHER. / SO SAD TO WATCH GOOD LOVE GO BAD** [ ] [–]

Sundown Sundown

Nov 85. (7") *(SDS 1)* **BROTHER JUKE BOX. / NEVER LIKE THIS** [ ] [ ]

PHIL EVERLY

solo with **JAMES BURTON / WARREN ZEVON, JIM HORN and EARL PALMER**

R.C.A. R.C.A.

Sep 73. (7") *(RCA 2409)* **THE AIR THAT I BREATHE. / GOD BLESS OLD LADIES** [ ] [–]

Sep 73. (lp) *(SF 8370) <APL-1 0092>* **STAR SPANGLED SPRINGER** [ ] [ ]
– The air that I breathe / Sweet grass country / God bless older ladies (for they made rock and roll) / It pleases me to please you / Lady Anne / Red, white and blue / Our song / Poisonberry pie / La divorce / Snowflake bombadier.

Pye Pye

Mar 74. (7") *<71014>* **OLD KENTUCKY RIVER. / SUMMERSHINE** [–] [ ]

Jun 74. (7") *<71036>* **NEW OLD SONG. / BETTER THAN NOW** [–] [ ]

Aug 74. (7") *(7N 45398))* **INVISIBLE MAN. / IT'S TRUE** [ ] [–]

Nov 74. (7") *(7N 45415)* **SWEET MUSIC. / GOODBYE LINE** [ ] [–]

Jan 75. (lp) *(NSPL 18448) <12104>* **THERE'S NOTHING TOO GOOD FOR MY BABY** <US-title 'PHIL'S DINER'> [ ] [ ]
– Sweet music / Goodbye line / Feather bed / Summershine / Too blue / There's nothing too good for my baby / Invisible man / Caroline / We're running out / It's true / New old song. *(US title – 'PHIL'S DINER')*

Oct 75. (7") *(7N 45544)* **BETTER THAN NOW. / YOU AND I ARE A SONG** [ ] [ ]

Nov 75. (lp) *(NSPL 18473) <12121>* **MYSTIC LINE** [ ] [ ]
– Patiently / Lion and the lamb / Mystic line / Jammy butterfly / You and I are a song / Worlds in your eyes / Better than now / When will I be loved / Back when the bands played in ragtime / Friends.

1976. (7") *<71055>* **WORLDS IN YOUR EYES. / BACK WHEN THE BAND PLAYED IN RAGTIME** [–] [ ]

1976 (7") *(APBO 0064)* **GOD BLESS OLDER LADIES. / SWEET GRASS COUNTRY** [–] [ ]

not iss. Elektra

1979. (lp) *<6E 213>* **LIVING ALONE** [–] [ ]
– It was too late for the party / Ich bin dein (I am yours) / You broke it / Living alone / Buy me a beer / California gold / Love will pull us through / I just don't feel like dancing / Charleston guitar / The fall of '59.

— guested on SANDRA LOCKE single 'Don't Say You Don't Love Me No More'

1979 (7") *<46519>* **LIVING ALONE. / I JUST DON'T FEEL LIKE DANCING** [–] [ ]

1979. (7") *<46556>* **YOU BROKE IT. / BUY ME A BEER** [–] [ ]

Epic Curb

Mar 81. (7") *(EPCA 9575) <5401>* **DARE TO DREAM AGAIN. / LONELY DAYS LONELY NIGHTS** [ ] [ ]

1981. (7") *<ZS6 02116>* **SWEET SOUTHERN LOVE. / IN YOUR EYES** [–] [ ]

Capitol Capitol

Oct 82. (7") *(CL 266)* **LOUISE. / SWEET SUZANNE** [47] [–]

Jan 83. (7"; PHIL EVERLY & CLIFF RICHARD) *(CL 276)* **SHE MEANS NOTHING TO ME. / A WOMAN AND A MAN** [9] [–]

1983. (7") *<5197>* **WHO'S GONNA KEEP ME WARM. / ONE WAY LOVE ON A TWO WAY STREET)** [–] [ ]

Apr 83. (lp/c) *(EST/TC-EST 27670)* **PHIL EVERLY** [61] [ ]
– She means nothing to me / I'll mend your broken heart / God bless older ladies / Sweet pretender / Never gonna dream again / Better than now / A woman and a man / Louise / When I'm dead and gone / Sweet Suzanne / Oh baby oh (you're the star). *(re-iss. Aug87 as 'LOUISE' on 'Magnum Force' lp/c; MFLP/MFC 053) (cd-iss. Jan88; CDMF 053) (cd-iss. Oct93 & Feb95 on 'B.G.O.')*

Apr 83. (7") *(CL 285)* **SWEET PRETENDER. / BETTER THAN NOW** [ ] [–]

Jun 83. (7") *(CL 294)* **OH BABY OH (YOU'RE THE STAR). / GOD BLESS OLDER LADIES** [ ] [–]

EVERLY BROTHERS

re-united.

Impression Passport

Nov 83. (7"ep)(12"ep) *(IMS 1)* **DEVOTED TO YOU / EBONY EYES. / LOVE HURTS / THE PRICE OF LOVE (all live)** [ ] [–]

Dec 83. (lp/c) *(IMDP/IMDK 1) <11001>* **EVERLY BROTHERS' REUNION CONCERT** (Royal Albert Hall – Sep'83) [47] [ ]
– The price of love / Walk right back / Claudette / Crying in the rain / Love is strange / Live medley / Take a message to mary / Maybe tomorrow / I wonder if I care as much / When will I be loved / Bird dog / Live medley; Devoted to you – Ebony eyes – Love hurts / Barbara Allen / Lightning Express / Put my little shoes away / Long time gone / Down in the willow garden / Step it up and go / Cathy's clown / Gone, gone, gone / You send me / So sad (to watch good love go bad) / Blues (stay away from me) / Bye bye love / All I have to do is dream / Wake up little Susie / ('Til) I kissed you / Temptation / Be-bop-a-lula / Lucille / Let it be me / Good golly Miss Molly. *(cd-iss. May86 on 'Mercury') (re-iss. cd in 2 parts Jul95 on 'Charly'; CDCD 1226/7) (re-iss. cd/c Sep95 on 'Emporio'; EMPR CD/MC 587) (d-cd re-iss. May97 on 'Charly'; CPCD 8299-2) (d-cd re-iss. Nov99 on 'Snapper'; SMDCD 216) (d-cd re-iss. May00 on 'Castle Pie'; PIEDD 230) (d-cd re-iss. Jul01 on 'K-Box'; KBOX 226)*

Mercury Mercury

Aug 84. (7") *(MER 170) <880 213-7>* **ON THE WINGS OF A NIGHTINGALE. / ASLEEP** [41] [50]

Oct 84. (d-lp/c)(cd) *(MERH/+C 44)<822431-2)>* **THE EVERLY BROTHERS** <US-title 'EB 84'> [36] [38]
– Danger, danger / The first in line / On the wings of a nightingale / The story of me / I'm taking my time / Lay lady lay / Following the Sun / You make it seem so easy / More than I can handle / Asleep. *(re-iss. Jun87 lp/c; REICE/PRIMC 110) <(cd-iss. Nov98 as 'EB84' on 'Razor & Tie'; RE 2040)>*

Nov 84. (7") *(MER 180)* **THE STORY OF ME. / FOLLOWING THE SUN** [ ] [ ]

Nov 84. (7") *<880 423-7>* **THE STORY OF ME. / THE FIRST IN LINE** [–] [ ]

Oct 85. (7") *(MER 206)* **AMANDA RUTH. / BORN YESTERDAY** [ ] [ ]

Oct 85. (7") *<884 428-7>* **BORN YESTERDAY. / DON'T SAY GOODNIGHT** [–] [ ]

Nov 85. (lp/c)(cd) *(MERH/+C 80)<826142-2)>* **BORN YESTERDAY** [ ] [83]
– Amanda Ruth / I know love / Born yesterday / These shoes / Arms of Mary / That uncertain feeling / Thinkin' about you / Why worry / Abandoned love / Don't say goodnight / Always drive a Cadillac. (c-cd+=) – You send me.

Feb 86. (7') *<884 694-7>* **I KNOW LOVE. / THESE SHOES** [–] [ ]

Nov 88. (7"; EVERLY BROTHERS & The BEACH BOYS) *(MER 280)* **DON'T WORRY BABY. / BORN YESTERDAY** [ ] [–]
(cd-s+=) *(MERCD 280)* – On the wings of a nightingale.

Apr 89. (lp/c/cd) *<(832520-1/-4/-2)>* **SOME HEARTS** [ ] Nov88 [ ]
– Some hearts / Ride the wind / Can't get it over / Brown eyes / Julianne / Don't worry baby / Be my love again / Angel of the darkness / Three bands of steel / Any single – solitary heart.

Apr 89. (7") *<872 098-7>* **DON'T WORRY BABY. / RIDE THE WIND** [–] [ ]

– (selective) compilations, etc. –

Jul 60. (7") *(HLA 9157) <1380>* **WHEN WILL I BE LOVED. / BE-BOP-A-LULA** [4] [8] Jun60 [74]
(re-iss. Oct80 on 'Old Gold; OG 9067)

Oct 60. (lp) *London; (HA-A 2266) / <25040>* **THE FABULOUS STYLE OF THE EVERLY BROTHERS** [4] Aug60 [23]
<re-iss. Jan86 on 'Rhino'; RNLP 213> (cd-iss. Dec91 on 'Ace')

Nov 60. (7") *Cadence; <1388>* **LIKE STRANGERS. / BRAND NEW HEARTACHE** [–] [22]

Dec 60. (7") *London; (HLA 9250)* **LIKE STRANGERS. / LEAVE MY WOMAN ALONE** [11] [–]

Oct 62. (7") *Cadence; <1429>* **I'M HERE TO GET MY BABY OUT OF JAIL. / LIGHTNING EXPRESS** [–] [76]

Oct 75. (lp/c) *Warners; <(K/K4 56168)>* **WALK RIGHT BACK WITH THE EVERLYS** [10] [ ]

Mar 77. (lp) *Warwick; (WW 5027)* **LIVING LEGENDS** ('Cadence' hits) [12] [–]

Sep 77. (lp/c) *Warners; <(K/K4 56415)>* **THE NEW ALBUM** (from vaults) [ ] [ ]

Dec 82. (lp/c) *K-Tel; (NE1/CD2 197)* **LOVE HURTS** [31] [–]
(re-iss. Sep84; same)

Apr 90. (cd) *Ace; (CDCH 932)* **THE EVERLY BROTHERS (debut) / THE FABULOUS STYLE OF . . .** [ ] [–]

Apr 92. (3xcd-box) *Bear Family; (BCD 15618)* **CLASSIC EVERLY BROTHERS** [ ] [–]

Jun 93. (3xcd-box) *Sequel; (NXT 245)* **THE PERFECT HARMONY** [ ] [–]

May 93. (cd/c) *Warners; <(9548 31992-2/-4)>* **THE GOLDEN YEARS OF THE EVERLY BROTHERS – THEIR 24 GREATEST HITS** [26] [ ]

May 95. (cd/c) *Pickwick; (PWK S/MC 4259)* **THE BEST OF THE EVERLY BROTHERS – THE RARE SOLO CLASSICS** [ ] [–]
(re-iss. Apr99 on 'Curb'; CURCD 068)

Jul 95. (cd) *Music Club; (MC 209)* **THE BEST OF THE EVERLY BROTHERS** [ ] [–]

Jan 97. (cd) *Camden; (74321 43255-2)* **STORIES WE COULD TELL** [ ] [–]

Aug 97. (cd) *See For Miles; (SEECD 482)* **THE EP COLLECTION** [ ] [–]

Nov 97. (cd) *Eagle; (EABCD 002)* **THE MASTERS** [ ] [–]

Feb 98. (cd) *Disky; (TO 86552-2)* **THE ORIGINAL . . .** [ ] [–]

Feb 98. (d-cd) *Snapper; (SMDCD 179)* **BROTHERS IN RHYTHM** [ ] [ ]

Nov 98. (cd) *Laserlight; (21066)* **BEST OF THE EVERLY BROTHERS** [ ] [–]

Mar 99. (cd/c) *Platinum; (PLA TCD/C 459)* **20 ALL-TIME HITS** [ ] [–]

Apr 99. (cd) *Disky; <(LS 85616-2)>* **20 GREAT LOVE SONGS** Jan00
Jun 99. (cd) *Ronco; (CDSR 9012)* **BACK TOGETHER AGAIN** –
Oct 99. (cd) *Delta; (47021)* **20 ORIGINAL CLASSICS** –
Feb 00. (cd) *Connoisseur; (VSOPCD 237)* **EVERLY COUNTRY** –
Mar 00. (cd) *Varese Sarabande; <(VSD 6096)>* **DEVOTED TO YOU: THE LOVE SONGS**
May 00. (cd) *Music; (CD 6215)* **BYE BYE LOVE: RECORDED LIVE IN CONCERT** –
Feb 01. (cd) *EMI Plus; (5760210)* **THE STORY** –
May 01. (cd/c) *Castle Pulse; (PLS CD/MC 388)* **GREATEST HITS LIVE IN CONCERT (live)** –
Jul 01. (cd) *WEA; <(9362 47869-2)>* **IT'S EVERLY TIME / A DATE WITH THE EVERLY BROTHERS**
Jul 01. (cd) *WEA; <(9362 47870-2)>* **BOTH SIDES OF AN EVENING / INSTANT PARTY**
Apr 02. (cd) *Disky; <(GO 79388-2)>* **LET IT BE ME**
Apr 02. (d-cd) *Platinum; (PLATBX 2221)* **LOVE BALLADS / ROCK BALLADS** –
May 02. (d-cd) *W.S.M.; (0927 47304-2) <73049>* **THE DEFINITIVE EVERLY BROTHERS** 10 Oct02

– Bye bye love / I wonder if I care as much / Wake up little Susie / Maybe tomorrow / All I have to do is dream / Claudette / Bird dog / Devoted to you / Problems / Poor Jenny / Take a message to Mary / Till I kissed you / Let it be me / Since you broke my heart / Cathy's clown / When will I be loved / Love hurts / Lucille / So sad / Like strangers / Sleepless nights / Walk right back / Ebony eyes / Temptation / Muskrat / Don't blame me / Crying in the rain / How can I meet her / No one can my sunshine smile / So it was so it is so it always will be / It's been nice (goodnight) / The girl sang the blues / Love her / Ferris wheel / Gone gone gone / That'll be the day / The price of love / I'll never get over you / Love is strange / It's all over / Bowling queen / It's my time / Empty boxes / Lord of the manor / Milk train / Yves / The stories we could tell / Green river / Lay it down / On the wings of a nightingale.

Oct 02. (cd) *Metro; (METRCD 87)* **THE ESSENTIAL EVERLY BROTHERS** –
Jun 03. (d-cd) *Disky; (HR 905595)* **ORIGINAL GOLD** –

EVERYTHING BUT THE GIRL

Formed: Hull, England ... mid-1982 by ex-Hull university graduates TRACEY THORN (ex-MARINE GIRLS) and BEN WATT. They both had recorded solo efforts ('A DISTANT SHORE' and 'NORTH MARINE DRIVE' respectfully) for indie label 'Cherry Red', before venturing onto 'WEA' (in 1983) subsidiary 'Blanco Y Negro' (run by Geoff Travis & Mike Alway). They almost immediately struck gold, with 'EACH AND EVERY ONE' (1984), making the UK Top 30, while its parent album, 'EDEN', hit the Top 20. A publicly shy, melancholy duo, EBTG blended together light jazz, folk and agitpop, their influences ranging from COLE PORTER to the modern day JOHN MARTYN. The following year's 'LOVE NOT MONEY', however, was a more conventional indie affair which breached the UK Top 10, although the band went for an orchestrated country sound on 'BABY THE STARS SHINE BRIGHT' (1986), having been influenced by America's grassroots music scene while touring there. Thus far, EBTG's career had been grounded in album sales, their loyal student following ensuring a respectable placing for each successive release; no one really expected their tender cover of Danny Whitten's heartbreaking 'I DON'T WANT TO TALK ABOUT IT' to make the Top 3 in summer '88. The attendant album, 'IDLEWILD' (1988), considered by many to be their finest hour, made the Top 20, although no further singles were forthcoming. Employing yet another ensemble of classy musicians, the band cut the more overtly jazzy 'THE LANGUAGE OF LIFE' (1990) at the turn of the decade. The early 90's saw the pair scoring with covers of The Everly Brothers' 'LOVE IS STRANGE' and Simon & Garfunkel's 'THE ONLY LIVING BOY IN NEW YORK', although WATT was still recovering from a rare, life threatening illness (something he later documented in his book). THORN, meanwhile, found a perfect vehicle for her languorous vocal stylings with trip hop pioneers, MASSIVE ATTACK, the singer's contribution resulting in two of the best songs on their 1994 set, 'Protection' i.e. 'Better Things' and the title track. With contributions from such stalwarts as RICHARD THOMPSON, DAVE MATTACKS and the ubiquitous DANNY THOMPSON, 'AMPLIFIED HEART' (1994) was a return to form, showing the duo more willing to experiment with sound and atmosphere. One of the album's tracks, 'MISSING', was given an unlikely remix by house DJ, TODD TERRY; the result was a stunning combination of dancefloor dynamics and raw emotion which captured the imagination of record buyers around the world in late '95 (also a transatlantic Top 5). Suddenly, EBTG were big news, a hip name to drop in dance circles; the following year's 'WALKING WOUNDED' album took the logical next step and paired the duo's stripped down melancholy with cutting edge drum 'n' bass textures. Critically acclaimed by both dance critics and the mainstream rock media, the record became one of the biggest selling EBTG albums to date, spawning two Top 10 singles in 'WRONG' and the title track. BEN and TRACEY were cutting the rug once more with a fresh set of songs courtesy of 1999's 'TEMPERAMENTAL', this critically lambasted bedsit musak for the New Labour yuppie becoming a bit trite for the more discerning rock ear. • **Songwriters:** Most written by duo or individually, except the covers; NIGHT AND DAY (Cole Porter) / KID (Pretenders) / ALFIE (hit; Cilla Black) / DOWNTOWN TRAIN (Tom Waits) / I FALL TO PIECES (Patsy Cline) / TAKE ME (Womack And Womack) / ON MY MIND (?) / NO PLACE LIKE HOME (from 'Wizard Of Oz') / LOVE IS STRANGE (Everly Brothers) / TOUGHER THAN THE REST (Bruce Springsteen) / TIME AFTER TIME (Cyndi Lauper) / ALISON (Elvis Costello) / MY HEAD IS MY ONLY HOUSE UNLESS IT RAINS (Captain Beefheart) / THESE DAYS (Jackson Browne) / CORCOVADO (Antonio Carlos Jobim) / SINGLE contains a sample of Tim Buckley's (SONG TO THE SIREN). TRACEY THORN solo:- FEMME FATALE (Velvet Underground). • **Trivia:** EVERYTHING BUT THE GIRL was the name of a local second hand store in Hull.

Album rating: Tracey Thorn: A DISTANT SHORE mini (*6) / Ben Watt: NORTH MARINE DRIVE (*6) / Everything But The Girl: EDEN (*7) / LOVE NOT MONEY (*5) / BABY, THE STARS SHINE BRIGHT (*5) / IDLEWILD (*6) / THE LANGUAGE OF LIFE (*7) / WORLDWIDE (*5) / AMPLIFIED HEART (*6) / HOME MOVIES – THE BEST OF EVERYTHING BUT THE GIRL compilation (*8) / WALKING WOUNDED (*7) / TEMPERAMENTAL (*4) / LIKE THE DESERTS MISS THE RAIN compilation (*7)

TRACEY THORN

Cherry Red not iss.

Aug 82. (m-lp) *(MRED 35)* **A DISTANT SHORE** –

– Smalltown girl / Simply couldn't care / Seascape / Femme fatale / Dreamy / Plain sailing / New opened eyes / Too happy. *(cd-iss. Jun87 + Aug93; MRED 35CD)*

Dec 82. (7") *(CHERRY 53)* **PLAIN SAILING. / GOODBYE JOE** –

BEN WATT

Cherry Red not iss.

Jun 81. (7"m) *(CHERRY 25)* **CANT. / AUBADE / TOWER OF SILENCE** –
Apr 82. (12"ep; by BEN WATT & ROBERT WYATT) *(12CHERRY 36)* **SUMMER INTO WINTER** –

– Walter and John / Aquamarine / Slipping slowly / Another conversation with myself / A girl in winter.

Feb 83. (7") *(CHERRY 55)* **SOME THINGS DON'T MATTER. / ON BOX HILL** [ ] [–]

Feb 83. (lp) *(BRED 40)* **NORTH MARINE DRIVE** [ ] [–]
– On Box hill / Some things don't matter / Lucky one / Empty bottles / North Marine Drive / Waiting like mad / Thirst for knowledge / Long time no sea / You're gonna make me lonesome when you go. *(cd-iss. Jun87 + Jul93 w/ SUMMER INTO WINTER EP; BRED 40CD)*

EVERYTHING BUT THE GIRL

TRACEY THORN (b.26 Sep'62) – vocals, guitar / **BEN WATT** (b. 6 Dec'62, London, England) – vocals, guitar, piano

Jun 82. (7"m) *(CHERRY 37)* **NIGHT AND DAY. / FEELING DIZZY / ON MY MIND** [ ] [–]
(12"-iss.Dec85; 12CHERRY 37) (cd-s-iss.Mar89; CDCHERRY 37) (re-iss. Jul93)

— with **SIMON BOOTH** – guitar (of WORKING WEEK, ex-WEEKEND) / **CHUCHO MERCHAN** – double bass / **CHARLES HAYWARD** – drums / **BOSCO DE OLIVEIRA** – percussion / **PETER KING** – alto saxophone / **NIGEL NASH** – tenor saxophone / **DICK PEARCE** – flugel trumpet

Blanco Y Negro — Sire

Apr 84. (7") *(NEG 1)* **EACH AND EVERY ONE. / LAUGH YOU OUT THE HOUSE** [28] [–]
(12"+=) *(NEG 1T)* – Never could have been worse.

Jun 84. (lp/c)(cd) *(BYN/+C 2)(<240-395-2>)* **EDEN** [14] [ ]
– Each and every one / Bittersweet / Tender blue / Another bridge / The spice of life / The dustbowl / Crabwalk / Even so / Frost and fire / Fascination / I must confess / Soft touch. *(US-title 'EVERYTHING BUT THE GIRL'; 7599-25212-1>*

Jul 84. (7") *(NEG 3)* **MINE. / EASY AS SIN** [58] [–]
(12"+=) *(NEG 3T)* – Gun cupboard love.

Sep 84. (7") *(NEG 6)* **NATIVE LAND. / RIVERBED DRY** [73] [–]
(12"+=) *(NEG 6T)* – Don't you go.
(12"++=) *(NEG 6TX)* – Easy as sin / Gun cupboard love.

— now with **NEIL SCOTT** – guitars / **PHIL MOXHAM** – bass (ex-The GIST ex-YOUNG MARBLE GIANTS) / **JUNE MILES KINGSTON** – drums, vocals (ex-MODETTES, ex-FUN BOY THREE) and the wind section

Mar 85. (7") *(NEG 7)* **WHEN ALL'S WELL. / HEAVEN HELP ME** [ ] [–]
(12"+=) *(NEG 7T)* – Kid.

Apr 85. (lp/c)(cd) *(BYN 3/+C)(<240-657-2>)* **LOVE NOT MONEY** [10] [ ]
– When all's well / Ugly little dreams / Shoot me down / Are you trying to be funny / Sean / Ballad of the times / Anytown / This love (not for sale) / Trouble and strife / Angel. *(c+=)* – Heaven help me / Kid.

May 85. (7"m) *(NEG 15)* **ANGEL. / PIGEONS IN THE ATTIC ROOM / CHARMLESS, CALLOW WAYS** [ ] [–]
(12"+=) *(NEG 15T)* – Easy as sin.

— now **BEN + TRACEY** used new session people below plus an orchestra **CARA TIVEY** – keyboards / **MICKEY HARRIS** – bass / **PETER KING** – alto sax / **ROBERT PETERS** – drums (ex-DANGEROUS GIRLS)

Jul 86 (7") *(NEG 21)* **COME ON HOME. / DRAINING THE BAR** [44] [–]
(12"+=) *(NEG 21T)* – I fall to pieces.

Aug 86. (lp/c)(cd) *(BYN/+C 9)(<240-966-2>)* **BABY, THE STARS SHINE BRIGHT** [22] [ ]
– Come on home / Don't leave me behind / A country mile / Cross my heart / Don't let the teardrops rust your shining heart / Careless / Sugar Finney / Come hell or high water / Fighting talk / Little Hitler.

Sep 86. (7") *(NEG 23)* **DON'T LEAVE ME BEHIND. / ALFIE** [72] [–]
(12"+=) *(NEG 23T)* – Where's the playground, Susie?.
(d7"+=) *(NEG 23F)* – Come on home (acoustic) / Always on my mind (live).

Feb 87. (7") **DON'T LEAVE ME BEHIND. / DRAINING THE BAR** [–] [ ]

— **BEN and TRACEY** now with **PETER KING / IAN FRASER** – tenor saxophone / **STEVE PEARCE** – bass / **JAMES McMILLAN** – trumpet / **DAMON BUTCHER** – piano, synth.

Feb 88. (7") *(NEG 30)* **THESE EARLY DAYS. / DYED IN THE GRAIN** [75] [–]
(12"+=) *(NEG 30T)* – No place like home.
(12"ep+=/3"cd-ep+=) *(NEG 30TX)* – ('A'original demo) / Another day another dollar.

Mar 88. (lp/c)(cd) *(BYN/+C 14)(<242-288-2>)* **IDLEWILD** [13] [ ]
– Love is here where I live / These early days / I always was your girl / Oxford Street / The night I heard Caruso sing / Goodbye Sunday / Shadow on a harvest moon / Blue moon rose / Tears all over town / Lonesome for a place I know / Apron strings. *(re-iss. Jul88, hit UK No.21- lp/c/cd; BYN/+C 16)(243-840-2) (+=)* – I don't want to talk about it. *(re-iss. 2nd version cd Nov94)*

Mar 88. (7") *(NEG 33)* **I ALWAYS WAS YOUR GIRL. / HANG OUT THE FLAGS** [ ] [–]
(12"+=) *(NEG 33T)* – Home from home.
(3"cd-s++=) *(NEG 33CD)* – Almost blue.

Jun 88. (7") *(NEG 34)* **I DON'T WANT TO TALK ABOUT IT. / OXFORD STREET** [3] [ ]
(12"+=) *(NEG 34T)* – ('A'instrumental) / Shadow on a harvest moon.
(3"cd-s+=) *(NEG 34CD)* – ('A'instrumental) / Come on home.

Sep 88. (7") *(NEG 37)* **LOVE IS HERE WHERE I LIVE. / LIVING ON HONEYCOMB** [ ] [–]
(12"+=) *(NEG 37T)* – How about me?.
(3"cd-s++=) *(NEG 37CD)* – Each and every one.

Dec 88. (7") *(NEG 39)* **THESE EARLY DAYS (Dave Bascombe remix). / DYED IN THE GRAIN** [ ] [–]
(12"+=) *(NEG 39T)* – No place like home.
(3"cd-s++=) *(NEG 39CD)* – Another day another dollar.

— duo now with **OMAR HAKIM** – drums / **JOHN PATITUCCI** – bass / **LARRY WILLIAMS** – synth, piano / **LENNY CASTRO** – percussion / **MICHAEL LANDAU** – guitar / etc.

Blanco Y Negro — Atlantic

Jan 90. (7"/c-s) *(NEG 40/+C)* **DRIVING. / ME AND BOBBY D** [54] [–]
(12"+=/cd-s+=) *(NEG 40 T/CD)* – Downtown train / ('A'extended).
(ext.12"gf+=) *(NEG 40TG)* – Easy as sin / I don't want to talk about it.

Feb 90. (cd)(lp/c) *(246-260-2)(BYN/+C 21) <82057>* **THE LANGUAGE OF LIFE** [10] [77]
– Driving / Get back together / Meet me in the morning / Take me / Me and Bobby D / The language of life / Imagining America / My baby don't love me / Letting love go / The road. *(re-iss. cd Feb95)*

Mar 90. (7"/c-s) *(NEG 44/+C)* **TAKE ME. / DRIVING (acoustic)** [ ] [–]
(12"+=/cd-s+=) *(NEG 44 T/CD)* – ('A'-Hamblin remix).

— now with **GEOFF GISCOYNE and STEVE PEARCE** – bass / **DICK OATTS** – saxophone / **RALPH SALMINS** – drums, percussion

Aug 91. (7"/c-s) *(NEG 51/+C)* **OLD FRIENDS. / APRON STRINGS (live)** [ ] [–]
(12"+=) *(NEG 51T)* – Politics aside (instrumental).
(cd-s+=) *(NEG 51CD)* – Back to the old house (live).

Sep 91. (cd)(lp/c) *(9031-75308-2)(BYN/+C 25)* **WORLDWIDE** [29] [ ]
– Old friends / Understanding / You lift me up / Talk to me like the sea / British summertime / Twin cities / Frozen river / One place / Politics aside / Boxing and pop music / Feel alright. *(re-iss. cd Feb92 +=; 9031-76583-2)* – Love is strange.

Nov 91. (7"/c-s) *(NEG 53/+C)* **TWIN CITIES (Wildwood remix). / MEET ME IN THE MORNING (live)** [ ] [–]
(12"+=) *(NEG 53T)* – ('A'-The green plains a cappella mix). (cd-s++=) *(NEG 53CD)* – Mine.

Feb 92. (7"ep/c-ep/12"ep/cd-ep) *(NEG 54/+C/T/CD)* **COVERS EP** [13] [–]
– Love is strange / Tougher than the rest / Time after time / Alison. (above issued in the US as 'ACOUSTIC' w/ extra; *7567-82395-2>*

Apr 93. (7"ep/c-ep/12"ep/cd-ep) *(NEG 62/+C/T/CD)* **THE ONLY LIVING BOY IN NEW YORK EP** [42] [–]
– The only living boy in New York / Gabriel / Birds / Horses in the room.

May 93. (cd)(lp/c) *(4509-92319-2)(BYN/+C 29)* **HOME MOVIES – THE BEST OF EVERYTHING BUT THE GIRL** (compilation) [5] [ ]
– Each and every one / Another bridge / Fascination / Native land / Come on home / Cross my heart / Apron strings / I don't want to talk about it / The night I heard Caruso sing / Driving / Imagining America / Understanding / Twin cities / Love is strange / I didn't know I was looking for love / The only living boy in New York.

Jun 93. (7"ep/c-ep/cd-ep) *(NEG 64/+C/CD)* **I DIDN'T KNOW I WAS LOOKING FOR LOVE EP** [72] [–]
– I didn't know I was looking for love / My head is my only house unless it rains / Political science / A piece of my mind.

— with **DAVE MATTACKS** – drums / **DANNY THOMPSON** – double bass (both ex-FAIRPORT CONVENTION) / **MARTIN DITCHAM** – percussion / (guests) **RICHARD THOMPSON** – guitar / **PETER KING** – alto sax / **KATE ST.JOHN** – cor anglais

May 94. (7"ep/c-ep/cd-ep) *(NEG 69/+C/CD)* **THE ROLLERCOASTER EP** 65 –
– Rollercoaster / Straight back to you / Lights of Te Touan / I didn't know I was looking for love (demo).

Jun 94. (cd/c) *(4509-96482-2/-4)* *<82605>* **AMPLIFIED HEART** 20 46
– Rollercoaster / Troubled mind / I don't understand anything / Walking to you / Get me / Missing / Two star / We walk the same line / 25th December / Disenchanted. *(re-iss. Nov95 & Jul00; 0603-10453-2)*

Aug 94. (c-ep/cd-ep) *(NEG 71 C/CD1)* **MISSING – THE LIVE EP** 69 –
– Missing / Each and every one (live) / I don't want to talk about it (live) / These days (live).
(12"ep/cd-ep) *(NEG 71 T/CD2)* **THE (FULL) REMIX EP** – ('A'side) / ('A'-Chris & James remix) / ('A'-Little Joey remix) / ('A'-Ultramarine remix).

Oct 95. (c-s) *(NEG 84C)* *<87124>* **MISSING (Todd Terry club mix) / ('A'-Amplified Heart album mix)** 3 Jul95 2
(cd-s+=) *(NEG 84CD)* – ('A'-radio edit) / ('A'-Rockin' blue mix) / ('A'-Chris & James full on club mix) / ('A'-Todd Terry's piece).
(12") *(NEG 84T)* – (all above except 'B'side).

Virgin / Atlantic

Apr 96. (c-s/12"/cd-s) *(VS C/T/CDT 1577)* **WALKING WOUNDED (mixes; Spring Heel Jack / Omni Trio / Dave Wallace)** 6 –

May 96. (cd/c/lp) *(CD/TC+/V 2803)* *<82912>* **WALKING WOUNDED** 4 37
– Before today / Wrong / Single / The heart remains a child / Walking wounded / Flipside / Big deal / Mirrorball / Good cop bad cop / Wrong (Todd Terry remix) / Walking wounded (Omni Trio remix). *(lp re-iss. Apr01 on 'Simply Vinyl'; SVLP 321)*

Jun 96. (c-s/12"/cd-s) *(VS C/T/CDT 1589)* *<87059>* **WRONG (mixes; original / Todd Terry / Deep Dish / Mood II Swing)** 8 May96 68

Sep 96. (c-s) *(VSC 1600)* **SINGLE / CORCOVADO** 20 –
(cd-s+=) *(VSCDT 1600)* – ('A'-Photek remix) / ('A'-Brad Wood Memphis remix).
(12"+=) *(VST 1600)* – (above except 'Corcovado') / Wrong (Todd Terry remix).

Feb 97. (c-s/cd-s) *(VSC/+DT 1624)* **BEFORE TODAY (mixes; album / Adam F / Darren Emerson 1 & 2 / Dilinja / Chicane)** 25 –

—— in Sep'98, EBTG were credited on the DEEP DISH hit single, 'The Future Of The Future (Stay Gold)'.

Sep 99. (c-s/cd-s) *(VSC/+DT 1742)* **FIVE FATHOMS / FIREWALL** 27
(12"/cd-s) *(VST/VSCDX 1742)* – ('A'mixes).

Sep 99. (cd/c/lp) *(CD/TC+/V 2892)* *<83214>* **TEMPERAMENTAL** 16 65
– Five fathoms / Low tide of the night / Blame / Hatfield 1980 / Temperamental / Compression / Downhill racer / Lullaby of clubland / No difference / Future of the future (stay gold).

Dec 99. (12"/cd-s) *(VST/VSCDT 1752)* **BLAME (mixes; album / Grooverider Jeep dub / Fabio / J Majik VIP)** –

Feb 00. (c-s/12") *(VSC/+T 1761)* **TEMPERAMENTAL / (DJ Spen & Karizmo mix) / (Ralph Rosario mix)** 72 –
(cd-s+=) *(VSCT/+D 1761)* – ('A'-CD-Rom).
(cd-s) *(VSCDX 1761)* – ('A'side) / (Hex Hector mix) / (Amanda Project mix).

V.C. / not iss.

Jan 01. (c-s/cd-s; as EBTG vs. SOUL VISION) *(VCR C/D 78)* **TRACEY IN MY ROOM / (Lazy Dog bootleg mix)** 34 –
(12"+=) *(VCRT 78)* – ('A'-Lazy Dog bootleg vocal & dub).

– compilations, etc. –

Oct 96. (cd/c) *Blanco Y Negro; (0630 16637-2/-4)* **THE BEST OF EVERYTHING BUT THE GIRL** 23

Nov 96. (c-s) *Blanco Y Negro; (NEG 99C)* **DRIVING (remix) /** 36 –
(cd-s) *(NEG 99CD1)* – ('A'remixes).
(cd-s) *(NEG 99CD2)* – ('A'remixes).

Dec 01. (12") *Cosmic Flux; (EBTG 1)* **TEMPERAMENTAL** –

Nov 02. (cd/c) *Virgin; (CDV/TCV 2966) / E.M.I.; <542616>* **LIKE THE DESERTS MISS THE RAIN** 58
– My head is my only house unless it rains / Rollercoaster / Corcovado / Each and every one / Before today (Chicane remix) / Mine / Protection / Single / Tracey in my room (Lazy Dog bootleg vocal mix) / Missing (Todd Terry mix) / Almost blue / No difference / Cross my heart / Mirrorball / Piece of my mind / Walking wounded.

EVE6

Formed: Los Angeles, California, USA ... 1993 by 15 year-old bassist/singer MAX COLLINS and 13 year-old guitarist JON SIEBELS. They spent their High School years trying to develop their own brand of high velocity punk pop, although the end result gives more than just a nod to GREEN DAY and OFFSPRING. With drummer TONY FAGENSEN now on board, 'R.C.A.' signed them in '96, releasing the remarkably well received first album, 'EVE6' (1998), two years later. The preceding single, 'INSIDE OUT' was snapped up by a large portion of the US adolescent public hungry for a fresh anti-establishment sound. It topped the new Billboard rock chart and the album's release date was brought forward. Lyrically ambitious, 'EVE6' (which has now sold over half a million copies) showed the trio attempting an ELVIS COSTELLO-esque edge; on tracks such as 'INSIDE OUT' and 'LEECH' they showed that they were capable of playing with a rare gusto but more often than not found themselves held back by a severe naivety in the songwriting department. Standout track, 'JESUS NITELITE' relied more on talent than pace, giving a very brief insight into what this band could achieve should they choose this direction for the future. Sophomore set, 'HORRORSCOPE' (2000) seemed to be too predictable for their own good, although it still managed to reach the US Top 40 (Britain was not included in the band's release itinerary!). Packaged in yet another abysmal sleeve, the US Top 30(!) 'IT'S ALL IN YOUR HEAD' (2003) nevertheless showed the band to be at least slightly improved in the lyrical department, with decent attempts at broadening their sound.

Album rating: EVE6 (*6) / HORRORSCOPE (*6) / IT'S ALL IN YOUR HEAD (*5)

MAX COLLINS – vocals, bass / **JON SIEBELS** – guitar, vocals / **TONY FAGENSON** – drums

R.C.A. / R.C.A.

Sep 98. (ltd-7"red) *(74321 60569-7)* *<radio play>* **INSIDE OUT. / SATURDAY NIGHT** 28
(cd-s+=) *(74321 60569-2)* – Showerhead.

Oct 98. (cd) *<(07863 67617-2)>* **EVE6** Apr98 33
– How much longer / Inside out / Leech / Showerhead / Open road song / Jesus nitelite / Superhero girl / Tongue tied / Saturday night / There's a face / Small town trap.

Feb 99. (7") *(74321 63918-7)* **LEECH. / INSIDE OUT (acoustic)** –
(cd-s+=) *(74321 63918-2)* – Open road song (acoustic).

Jun 99. (7"/cd-s) *(74321 67985-7/-2)* **OPEN ROAD SONG** –

Jul 00. (cd,c) *<07863 67713-2>* **HORRORSCOPE** – 34
– Rescue / Promise / On the roof again / Sunset Strip bitch / Here's to the night / Amphetamines / Enemy / Nocturnal / Jet pack / Nightmare / Bang / Girl eyes.

May 01. (-) *<radio cut>* **HERE'S TO THE NIGHT** – 30

Jul 03. (cd) *<82876 52346-2>* **IT'S ALL IN YOUR HEAD** – 27
– Without you here / Think twice / At least we're dreaming / Still here waiting / Good lives / Hey Montana / Bring the night on / Friend of mine / Not gonna be alone tonight / Hokis / Arch drive goodbye.

☐ EXHAUST

(see under ⇒ GODSPEED YOU BLACK EMPEROR!)

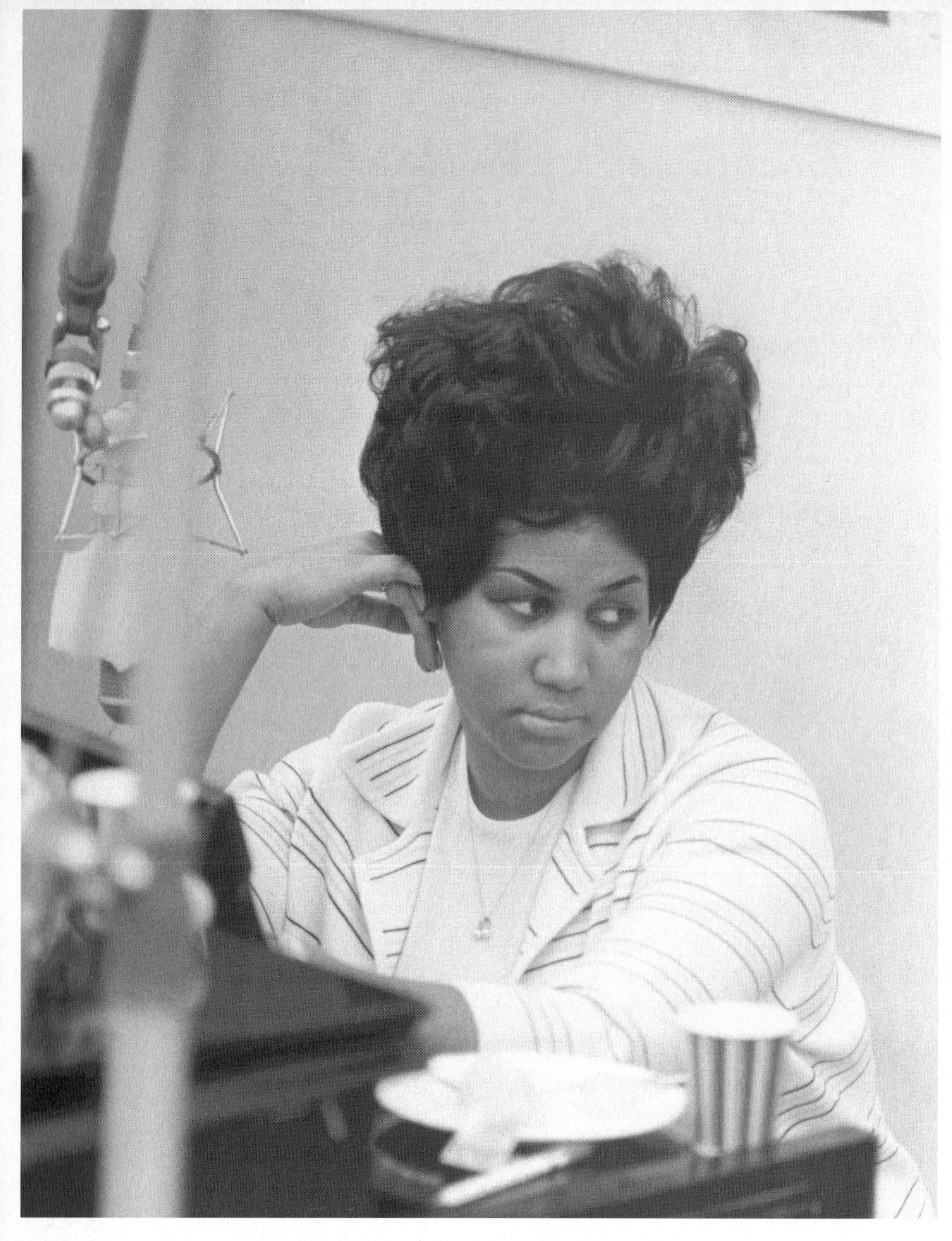

ARETHA FRANKLIN

☐ FACES (see under ⇒ SMALL FACES)

☐ Donald FAGEN (see under ⇒ STEELY DAN)

FAIRPORT CONVENTION

Formed: Muswell Hill, London, England ... mid-1967 by RICHARD THOMPSON, SIMON NICOL, ASHLEY HUTCHINGS, JUDY DYBLE and original drummer SHAUN FRATER. By the end of the year, FRATER was superseded by MARTIN LAMBLE, and after a debut 45 for 'Polydor', they added IAIN MATTHEWS. This new sextet with Joe Boyd on production, recorded their 1968 eponymous debut lp, although after its release, JUDY left and was replaced by SANDY DENNY. They signed to 'Island' around the same time and issued a second album, 'WHAT WE DID ON OUR HOLIDAYS' which was the last to feature MATTHEWS (a year later, he was at the UK No.1 spot with his SOUTHERN COMFORT version of 'Woodstock'). After the completion of their third set, 'UNHALFBRICKING', and while on tour, tragedy struck on the 14th of May '69, when MARTIN LAMBLE was killed as their van crashed. With the help of their Top 30 French version of a Dylan song ('IF YOU GOTTA GO, GO NOW'), 'SI TU DOIS PARTIR', the aforementioned album was the first of four consecutive UK Top 20 entries. At this stage, the band were Britain's answer to US West Coast folk-rock, although they increasingly adopted a more traditional folk sound in the 70's and subsequently influenced many other acts. After the classic, 'LIEGE AND LIEF' (1969), HUTCHINGS left for STEELEYE SPAN and DENNY formed FOTHERINGAY, both outfits enjoying their own bit of fame. Recruiting DAVE PEGG on bass, the band recorded another album, 'FULL HOUSE' (1970), before RICHARD THOMPSON departed for an acclaimed solo career which stretched a quarter of a century (plus). While 'ANGEL DELIGHT' (1971), hit the UK Top 10, the concept album 'BABBACOMBE LEE' (1971) stiffed and throughout the 70's, FAIRPORT underwent a dizzying series of personnel changes (DENNY eventually rejoining for 'LIVE CONVENTION' in '74). SANDY's stunning vocals made it one of the band's best releases of the 70's and she stayed for one further studio album, 'RISING FOR THE MOON' (1975), before going solo once more. Tragedy struck on the 21st of April 1978, when SANDY died from a brain haemorrhage after falling down a flight of stairs. Despite cutting a farewell live album in 1979, the band continued recording throughout the 80's and 90's amid constantly changing line-ups. In the early 80's, they limited their live appearances to an annual bash at Cropredy in Oxfordshire, an event which has now become something of a mini-festival attracting thousands of folk/roots fans each year. Various line-ups continued to record the occasional studio set through the 80's and 90's, with 1996's largely acoustic 'OLD NEW BORROWED BLUE' and 1997's 30th Anniversary set, 'WHO KNOWS WHERE THE TIME GOES', drawing favourable reviews. The latter featured a live version of SANDY DENNY's signature tune as well as an unlikely cover of Marvin Gaye's 'I HEARD IT THROUGH THE GRAPEVINE' and a reading of Jethro Tull's 'LIFE'S A LONG SONG'. 'TULL mainman ANDERSON, meanwhile, contributed his inimitable flute to 2002's 'XXXV', an album which took the veteran folk-rockers into the new millennium at the same time as it resurrected past classics. • **Songwriters:** Mainly group compositions, with numerous renditions of traditional English folk tunes. Other writers:- IF I HAD A RIBBON BOW (Maxine Sullivan) / NOTTAMUN TOWN + SHE MOVED THROUGH THE FAIR + loads more (trad.) / MILLION DOLLAR BASH (Bob Dylan) / GOLD (Peter Blegvad). The 1972 album as The BUNCH was full of covers. • **Trivia:** In 1970, their B-side, 'SIR B. McKENZIE'S DAUGHTER, ... ' entered The Guinness Book Of Records for having longest song title ever.

Album rating: FAIRPORT CONVENTION (*6) / WHAT WE DID ON OUR HOLIDAYS (*8) / UNHALFBRICKING (*8) / LIEGE AND LIEF (*8) / FULL HOUSE (*7) / ANGEL DELIGHT (*6) / BABBACOMBE LEE (*6) / THE HISTORY OF FAIRPORT CONVENTION compilation (*8) / ROSIE (*5) / FAIRPORT NINE (*5) / LIVE CONVENTION (*5) / RISING FOR THE MOON (*5) / GOTTLE O' GEER (*3) / BONNY BUNCH OF ROSES (*4) / TIPPLER'S TALES (*4) / FAREWELL, FAREWELL (*6) / MOAT ON THE LEDGE (*5) / GLADYS' LEAP (*6) / EXPLETIVE DELIGHTED (*5) / IN REAL TIME: LIVE '87 (*4) / RED AND GOLD (*4) / FIVE SEASONS (*5) / JEWEL IN THE CROWN (*5) / OLD NEW BORROWED BLUE (*7) / WHO KNOWS WHERE THE TIME GOES? (*7) / CROPREDY BOX (*5) / XXXV (*5)

RICHARD THOMPSON (b. 3 Apr'49) – guitar, vocals / **SIMON NICOL** (b.13 Oct'50) – guitar, banjo, dulcimer, bass, viola, vocals / **JUDY DYBLE** (b.1948) – vocals, autoharp / **ASHLEY HUTCHINGS** (b.Jan'45) – bass / **MARTIN LAMBLE** (b.Aug'49) – drums repl. SHAUN FRATER

Polydor | Cotillion

Nov 67. (7") *(604 020)* **IF I HAD A RIBBON BOW. / IF (STOMP)** ☐ ☐

— added **IAIN MATTHEWS** (b.IAN MATTHEW MacDONALD, 16 Jun'46, Scunthorpe, England) – vocals, guitar, percussion (ex-PYRAMIDS)

Jun 68. (lp) *(583 035) <SD 9024>* **FAIRPORT CONVENTION** ☐ ☐
– Time will show the wiser / I don't know where I stand / If (stomp) / Decameron / Jack O'Diamonds / Portfolio / Chelsea morning / Sun shade / The lobster / It's alright ma, it's only witchcraft / One sure thing / M1 breakdown. *(re-iss. Jul75; 238 4047) (re-iss. Aug90 cd/c; 835 230-2/-4) (<cd re-mast.Mar03 +=; 068291-2>)* – Suzanne / If I had a ribbon bow / Morning glory / Reno, Nevada.

— **SANDY DENNY** (b. 6 Jan'47) – vocals (ex-STRAWBS, etc) repl. JUDY who joined GILES, GILES and FRIPP

Island | A&M

Nov 68. (7") *(WIP 6047)* **MEET ON THE LEDGE. / THROWAWAY STREET PUZZLE** ☐ [–]

Jan 69. (lp) *(ILPS 9092)* **WHAT WE DID ON OUR HOLIDAYS** ☐ [–]
– Fotheringay / Mr. Lacey / Book song / The Lord is in his place / No man's land / I'll keep it with mine / Eastern rain / Nottamun town / Tale in hard time / She moves through the fair / Meet on the ledge / End of a holiday. *(re-iss. May89 on 'Carthage' lp/c; CG LP/C 4430) (cd-iss. Feb90; IMCD 97) (<cd re-mast.Mar03 +=; IMCD 294)<063597>* – Throwaway street puzzle / You're gonna need my help / Some sweet day.

1969. (7") <1108> **FOTHERINGAY. / I'LL KEEP IT WITH MINE** [–] [ ]

— Trimmed to a quintet when IAIN formed MATTHEW'S SOUTHERN COMFORT

Jul 69. (7") *(WIP 6064)* <1155> **SI TU DOIS PARTIR. / GENESIS HALL** [21] [ ]

Jul 69. (lp) *(ILPS 9102)* <4206> **UNHALFBRICKING** [12] [ ]
– Genesis Hall / Si tu dois partir / Autopsy / A sailor's life / Cajun woman / Who knows where the time goes? / Percy's song / Million dollar bash. *(cd-iss. Feb87; CID 9102) (re-iss. May89 on 'Carthage' lp/c; CG LP/C 4418) (cd-iss. Nov89; IMCD 61) (lp re-iss. Jan00 on 'Simply Vinyl'; SVLP 164) (<cd re-mast.Mar03 +=; IMCD 293)<63596>* – Dear landlord / The ballad of easy rider.

— **DAVE MATTACKS** (b.Mar'48, London) – drums; repl. MARTIN LAMBLE who died 14 May'69 in tour bus crash / also added **DAVE SWARBRICK** (b. 5 Apr'41, New Malden, Surrey, England) – fiddle, vocals

Dec 69. (lp) *(ILPS 9115)* <4257> **LIEGE & LIEF** [17] [ ]
– Come all ye / Reynardine / Matty Groves / Farewell, farewell / The deserter / The lark in the morning – Rakish Paddy – Foxhunter's jig – Toss the feathers / Tam Lin / Crazy man Michael. *(re-iss. Sep86 lp/c/cd; ILPM/ICM/CID 9115) (cd re-iss. Oct89; IMCD 60) (<cd re-mast.May02 +=; IMCD 291)<586929>* – Sir Patrick Spens (alt.) / Quiet joys of brotherhood.

— **DAVE PEGG** (b. 2 Nov'47, Birmingham, England) – bass, vocals (ex-UGLYS) repl HUTCHINGS who joined STEELEYE SPAN (**PEGG** now in quintet with **THOMPSON, NICOL, MATTACKS** and **SWARBRICK** because SANDY DENNY also departed to form FOTHERINGAY)

Jul 70. (lp) *(ILPS 9130)* <4265> **FULL HOUSE** [13] [ ]
– Walk awhile / Doctor of physick / Dirty linen / Sloth / Sir Patrick Spens / Flatback caper / Poor Will and the jolly hangman / Flowers of the forest. *(re-iss. Jul87 on 'Hannibal'; HNBL 4417) (c-iss.May89; HNBC 4417) (re-iss. Jan92 cd/c; HNCD/HNBC 4417) (<cd re-mast.Sep01 +=; IMCD 285)<586375>* – Now be thankful (mono) / Sir B. McKenzie's daughter's lament . . . / Bonny bunch of roses / Now be thankful (stereo).

Oct 70. (7") *(WIP 6089)* **NOW BE THANKFUL. / SIR B. McKENZIE'S DAUGHTER'S LAMENT FOR THE 77th MOUNTED LANCERS' RETREAT FROM THE STRAITS OF LOCH KOMBE IN THE YEAR OF OUR LORD 1727, ON THE LAIRD OF KINLEAKIE** [ ] [–]

Nov 70. (7") <1195> **WALK AWHILE. / SIR PATRICK SPENS** [–] [ ]

— Now a quartet when RICHARD THOMPSON left to go solo

Jun 71. (7") <1333> **THE JOURNEYMAN'S GRACE. / THE WORLD HAS SURELY LOST IT'S HEAD** [–] [ ]

Jun 71. (lp) *(ILPS 9162)* <4319> **ANGEL DELIGHT** [8] [ ]
– Lord Marlborough / Sir William Gower / Bridge over the River Ash / Wizard of the worldly game / The journeyman's grace / Angel delight / Banks of the sweet primroses / Instrumental medley:- Cuckoo's nest – Hardiman the fiddler – Papa stoor / The bonny black hare / Sickness and diseases. *(cd-iss. Mar93; IMCD 166)*

Sep 71. (7") *(WIP 6128)* <1348> **JOHN LEE. / THE TIME IS NEAR** [ ] [ ]

Nov 71. (lp) *(ILPS 9176)* <4333> **BABBACOMBE LEE** [ ] [ ]
– John Babbacombe Lee: (John's reflection of his boyhood / His struggle with his family / Then the happiest period of his life, the Navy / Returning reluctantly to his job after being invalided out of the service / And the senseless murder of his mistress and the three attempts to hang him – Hanging song). *(cd-iss. Aug92; IMCD 153)*

— **ROGER HILL** – guitar, vocals repl. NICOL who joined ALBION COUNTRY BAND / **TOM FARNAL** – drums repl. MATTACKS who joined ALBION COUNTRY BAND

— In Jun72, **DAVID REA** – guitar repl. ROGER HILL until Aug72 when **MATTACKS** returned to repl. FARNALL / **TREVOR LUCAS** (b.25 Dec'43, Bungaree, Australia) – guitar, vocals (ex-FOTHERINGAY) repl. REA / adding **JERRY DONAHUE** (b.24 Sep'46, New York City, N.Y.) – guitar, vocals (ex-FOTHERINGAY)

Mar 73. (7") *(WIP 6155)* **ROSIE. / KNIGHTS OF THE ROAD** [ ] [–]

Mar 73. (lp) *(ILPS 9208)* <4386> **ROSIE** [ ] [ ]
– Rosie / Matthew, Mark, Luke and John / Knights of the road / Peggy's pub / The plainsman / Hungarian rhapsodie / My girl / Me with you / The hen's march through the midden & the four-poster bed / Furs and feathers. *(cd-iss. Aug92; IMCD 152)*

Oct 73. (lp) *(ILPS 9246)* <4407> **FAIRPORT NINE** [ ] [ ]
– The Hexamshire lass / Polly on the shore / The brilliancy medley and Cherokee shuffle / To Althea from prison / Tokyo / Bring 'em down / Big William / Pleasure and pain / Possibly Parsons Green. *(cd-iss. Aug92; IMCD 154)*

— added the returning **SANDY DENNY** – vocals (from solo career)

Oct 74. (lp) *(ILPS 9285)* **LIVE CONVENTION (live)** [ ] [–]
– Matty Groves / Rosie / Fiddlestix / John the gun / Something you got / Sloth / Dirty linen / Down in the flood / Sir B. MacKenzie . . . *(cd-iss. Feb90; IMCD 95)*

— **PAUL WARREN** – drums repl. MATTACKS who rejoined ALBION DANCE BAND

— **BRUCE ROWLANDS** – drums (ex-RONNIE LANE, ex-JOE COCKER) repl. WARREN

Island Island

Jul 75. (7") *(WIP 6241)* **WHITE DRESS. / TEARS** [ ] [–]

Jul 75. (lp) *(ILPS <9313>)* **RISING FOR THE MOON** [52] [ ]
– Rising for the Moon / Restless / White dress / Let it go / Stranger to himself / What is true? / Iron lion / Dawn / After halloween / Night-time girl / One more chance. *(cd-iss. Aug92; IMCD 155)*

— FAIRPORT Basic trio **SWARBRICK, PEGG** and **ROWLANDS** recruited new folks **DAN AR BRAS** – guitar repl. SANDY DENNY who went solo again. (She later died of a brain haemorrage on 21 Apr78 after falling down her stairs) **BOB BRADY** – piano (ex-WIZZARD) repl. LUCAS who became producer. **ROGER BURRIDGE** – mandolin, fiddle repl. DONAHUE who became session man

Island not iss.

May 76. (lp; as FAIRPORT) *(ILPS 9389)* **GOTTLE O'GEER** [ ] [–]
– When first into this country / Our band / Lay me down easy / Cropedy capers / The frog up the pump / Don't be late / Sandy's song / Come and get it / Limey's lament. *(cd-iss. Aug99; IMCD 262)*

— **FAIRPORT CONVENTION** again because founder member **SIMON NICOL** – guitar returned to repl. BRADY, BRAS and BURRIDGE

Vertigo not iss.

Feb 77. (lp) *(9102 015)* **BONNY BUNCH OF ROSES** [ ] [–]
– James O'Donnell's jig / The Eynsham poacher / Adieu adieu / The bonny bunch of roses / The poor ditching boy / General Taylor / Run Johnny run / The last waltz / Royal Selection No.13. *(re-iss. Oct88 on 'Woodworm' lp/c/cd; WR/+C/CD 011)*

May 78. (lp) *(9102 022)* **TIPPLER'S TALES** [ ] [–]
– Ye mariner's all / Three drunken maidens / Jack O'rion / Reynard the fox / Lady of pleasure / Bankruptured / The widow of Westmorland / The hair of the dogma / As bitme / John Barleycorn. *(re-iss. 1989 on 'Beat Goes On' lp/c/cd; BGO LP/MC/CD 72)*

Simons not iss.

Oct 79. (7") *(PMW 1)* **RUBBER BAND. / BONNY BLACK HARE** [ ] [–]

Nov 79. (lp) *(GAMA 1)* **FAREWELL FAREWELL (live)** [ ] [–]
– Matty Groves / Orange blossom special / John Lee / Bridge over the River Ash / Sir Patrick Spens / Mr. Lacey / Walk awhile / Bonny black hare / Journeyman's grace / Meet on the ledge. *(re-iss. Apr80 on 'Woodworm'; BEAR 22) (cd-iss. May96 on 'Red Steel'; SIXCD 0002) (<cd re-mast.Sep97 as 'ENCORE ENCORE' on 'Folkprint'; FP 001CD)<4168> (cd re-iss. Jun99 as 'ENCORE ENCORE' on 'Eagle'; EMDCD 083)*

Woodworm Varrick

1982. (lp) *(WR 001)* **MOAT ON THE LEDGE – LIVE 1981 (live)** [ ] [–]
– Walk awhile / Country pie / Rosie / Matty Groves / Both sides now / Poor Will and the hangman / The brilliancy medley – Cherokee shuffle / Woman or man / High school confidential. *(c-iss.1985 on 'Stoney Plain'; SP5 1052) (cd-iss. Apr03 on 'Talking Elephant'; TECD 052)*

— **DAVE MATTACKS and DAVE PEGG** returned to repl. SWARBRICK and ROWLAND **NICOL** also recruited sessioners **MARTIN ALLCOCK** (b. 5 Jan'57, Manchester, England) – strings / **RIC SAUNDERS** – violin (ex-SOFT MACHINE)

Aug 85. (lp/c/cd) *(WR/+C/CD 007)* *<V/VRC/CDVR 023>* **GLADYS' LEAP** [ ] 1988 [ ]
– How many times / Bird from the mountain / Honour and praise / The hiring fair / Instrumental medley '85: The riverhead – Glady's leap – The wise maid / My feet are set for dancing / Wat Tyler / Head in a sack. *(cd-iss. Aug94 on 'Terrapin Truckin'; TRUCKCD 015) (cd re-iss. May96 on 'Red Steel'; SIVCD 0003) (cd re-mast.Sep01 on 'Talking Elephant'+=; TECD 034)* – Angel delight / Polly on the shore / Lucky old sun.

1986. (lp/c/cd) *(WR/+C/CD 009)* *<CDVR 029>* **EXPLETIVE DELIGHTED!** [ ] 1988 [ ]
– Medley; The Rutland reel – Sack the juggler / Medley; The cat on the mixer – Three left feet / Bankruptured / Portmeirion / James O'Donnell's jig / Expletive delighted / Sigh beg sigh mor / Innstuck / The gas almost works / Hanks for the memory; Shazam – Pipeline – Apache – Peter Gunn. *(re-iss. Aug94 on 'Terrapin Truckin' cd/c; TRUCK CD/MC 016) (cd re-iss. Jun96 on 'Red Steel'; SIVCD 0004)*

Island / not iss.

Nov 87. (lp/c/cd) *(ILPS/ICT/CID 9883)* **IN REAL TIME: LIVE '87 (live)** – –
– Reynard the fox / The widow of Westmorland's daughter / The hiring fair / Crazy man Michael / Close to the wind / Big three medley – the swirling pit: Matty groves – The Rutland reel – Sack the juggler / Meet on the ledge. *(cd re-iss. 1989; IMCD 10) (c re-iss. Jul93; ICM 2026)*

— now 7-piece of **ALLCOCK, SAUNDERS, PEGG, MATTACKS, NICOL, DONAHUE** and **RICHARD THOMPSON**

New Routes / Rough Trade

Jan 89. (lp/c/cd) *(RUE/+MC/CD 002)* <*ROUGH-US 63/+C/CD*> **RED AND GOLD** 74
– Set me up / The noise club / Red and gold / The beggars song / The battle / Dark eyed Molly / The rose hip / Summer before the war / Open the door Richard. *(cd re-iss. Dec95 on 'H.T.D.'; HTDCD 47) (<cd re-iss. Jun01 on 'Talking Elephant'+=; TECD 014>)* – Close to the wind.

Dec 90. (lp/c/cd) *(RUE/+MC/CD 005)* **THE FIVE SEASONS** –
– Cloudy beats: medley – Cup of tea! – A loaf of bread – Miss Monahan's / All your beauty / Sock in it / Gold / Ginnie / Mock Morris '90:- The green man – The cropedy badger – Molly on the jetty / Medley:- The card song – Shuffle the pack – The wounded whale. *(cd re-iss. Jan96 on 'H.T.D.'; HTDCD 48) (cd re-iss. Aug01 on 'Talking Elephant'+=; TECD 019) <cd re-iss. 2002 on 'Sanctuary'+=; 81217>* – Caught in a whisper.

— **NICOL, ALLCOCK, PEGG, MATTACKS + SAUNDERS**

Woodworm / Green Linnet

Jan 95. (c/cd) *(WRC/+D 023)* <*3103*> **JEWEL IN THE CROWN** Jun95
– Jewel in the crown / Slip jigs and reels / A surfeit of lampreys / Kind of fortune / Diamonds and gold / The naked highwayman / The islands / The youngest daughter / London Danny / Summer in December / Travelling by steam / (Travel by steam) / She's like the swallow / Red tide / Home is where the heart is / Closing time.

— In Jun'96, they featured on DAVE SWARBRICK's '50th Birthday Concert' on 'Cooking Vinyl'; *MASHCD 001)*

Jun 96. (cd) *(WRCD 024)* <*3114*> **OLD NEW BORROWED BLUE**
– Woodworm swing / Men / Aunt Sally shuffle / There once was love – Innstuck / Frozen man / Mr. Sands is in the building / Lalla rookh / Foolish you / Crazy man Michael / Widow of Westmorland's daughter / Genesis hall / The deserter / The swimming song / Struck it right / The hiring fair / Matty Groves – Dirty linen.

— FAIRPORT CONVENTION reunion of nearly all past members

Woodworm / Mooncrest

May 98. (3xcd-box) *(WR3CD 026)* <*6804*> **THE CROPREDY BOX: THIRTIETH ANNIVERSARY 3 CD SET (live August 1997)** 1999
– Rory McLeod to Joe Byrd (introduction) / Wings / Jack o' diamonds / Time will show the wiser / Mr. Lacey / Suzanne / Genesis hall / Million dollar bash / Come all ye / Reynardine / Matty Groves / Danny boy / Ashley (introduction) / Walk awhile / Now be thankful / Poor Will and the jolly hangman / Angel delight / Rain / Cut across Shorty / Sloth / Rosie / Solo / John Barleycorn / Wat Tyler / Red and gold / Jewel in the crown / Woodworm swing / John Gaudie / Fiddlestix / Dirty linen / Si tu dois partir / Meet on the ledge / Seventeen come Sunday / The April fool tape. *(re-iss. Sep99 on 'Mooncrest'; CRESTBCD 042)*

— **PEGG, MATTACKS, NICOL + MARTIN ALLCOCK + CHRIS LESLIE**

Woodworm / Green Linnet

Aug 97. (cd/c) *(WRCD/WRC 025)* <*3122*> **WHO KNOWS WHERE THE TIME GOES?**
– John Gaudie / Sailing boat / Here's to Tom Paine / The bowman's retreat / Spanish main / The golden glove / Slipology / The wishfulness waltz / Life's a long song / Dangerous / Heard it through the grapevine (with RICHARD THOMPSON & ROY WOOD) / Who knows where the time goes? (live). *<US cd-iss. Mar00 as 'WISHFULNESS WALTZ' on 'Mooncrest'++; CRESTCD 48>* – Poor Will and the jolly hangman / Rosie / Jack o' diamonds / Come all ye.

Woodworm / Compass

Jan 02. (cd) *(WRCD 038)* <*4332*> **XXXV – 1967-2002: THE 35th ANNIVERSARY ALBUM** Feb02
– Madeleine / My love is in America / The happy man / Portmeiron / The crowd / Banks of the sweet primroses / The deserter / The light of day / I wandered by a brookside / Niel Gow's apprentice / Everything but the skirl / Talking about my love / Now be thankful / The crowd revosited.

Talking Elephant / not iss.

Jun 03. (d-cd) *(TECD 054)* **CROPREDY FESTIVAL 2002 (live)** –
(re-iss. Nov03 on 'Castle'; CMETD 815)

– compilations etc. –

on 'Island' unless mentioned otherwise

Jul 70. (7") *Polydor; (2058 014)* **IF (STOMP). / CHELSEA MORNING**

Nov 72. (d-lp) *(ICD 4)* **THE HISTORY OF FAIRPORT CONVENTION**
– Meet on the ledge / Fotheringay / Mr.Lacey / Book song / Sailor's life / Si tu dois partir / Who knows where the time goes / Matty Groves / Crazy man Michael / Now be thankful (medley) / Walk awhile / Sloth / The bonny black hare / Angel delight / Bridge over the river Ash / John Lee / Breakfast in Mayfair / Hanging song / The hen's march through the midden / The four-poster bed. *(cd-iss. Apr88; CIDD 4)* – (omits 2 tracks). *(re-iss. Jul91 cd)(c; IMCD 128)(ICM 2073)*

1976. (lp) *A&M; <3530>* **FAIRPORT CHRONICLES** –

Dec 76. (lp) *Help-Island; (HELP 28)* **LIVE AT THE L.A. TROUBADOUR 1970 (live)** –
(re-iss. Jan87 as 'HOUSE FULL' on 'Hannibal' lp/c; HN BL/BC 1319) (re-iss. Jan92 cd/c; HNCD/HNBC 1319) (cd re-mast.Oct01 on 'Island'+=; IMCD 289) – (bonus tracks).

1982. (c) *Woodworm; (none)* **THE AIRING CUPBOARD TAPES** –
(cd-iss. Nov02 on 'Talking Elephant'; TECD 046)

Sep 84. (c) *Woodworm; (WRC 1)* **AT 2 (THE AIRING CUPBOARD TAPES)** –

1985. (d-c) *Woodworm; (none)* **THE BOOT** –

1987. (d-c) *Woodworm; (none)* **THE OTHER BOOT** –

May 87. (7") *(IS 324)* **MEET ON THE LEDGE (re-recorded). / SIGH BHEG SIGH MHOR (live)** –
(12"+=) *(12IS 324)* – John Barleycorn (live).

Sep 87. (lp/c/cd) *Hannibal; (HN BL/BC/CD 1329)* **HEYDAY (BBC sessions '68-'69)** –
(<cd re-iss. Mar02 on 'Island'; IMCD 290>)

Apr 88. (cd) *(CIDD 4)* **THE BEST OF FAIRPORT CONVENTION** –

Aug 89. (d-c) *Woodworm; (none)* **THE THIRD LEG** –

Jan 92. (cd/c) *Woodworm; (WR CD/C 015)* **THE WOODWORM YEARS** –
(cd re-iss. Feb98 on 'Folkprint'; FP 003CD)

Aug 92. (4xcd-box) *(FCBX 1)* **25th ANNIVERSARY PACK** –
– (ROSIE / JOHN BABBACOMBE LEE / NINE / RISING FOR THE MOON)

Feb 98. (d-cd) *Folkprint; (FP 002CD)* **GLADYS' LEAP / EXPLETIVE DELIGHTED** –

Apr 98. (cd) *Mooncrest; (CRESTCD 035)* **CLOSE TO THE WIND** –

Nov 98. (cd) *Raven; (<RVCD 47>)* **FIDDLESTIX: THE BEST OF FAIRPORT CONVENTION 1972-1984**

Apr 99. (d-cd) *(<564687-2>)* **MEET ON THE LEDGE: THE CLASSIC YEARS**

Sep 99. (cd) *Delta; (4700-2)* **RHYTHM OF THE TIME** –

Feb 00. (d-cd) *Snapper; (SMDCD 214)* **KING FORTUNE** –

Mar 01. (cd) *Rialto; (RMCD 2312)* **THE FAIRPORT CONVENTION ARCHIVE** –

Nov 01. (d-cd) *Castle; (CMDDD 367)* **ANTHOLOGY**

Feb 02. (cd) *Metro; (METRCD 076)* **THEN AND NOW: 1982-1996 – THE BEST OF FAIRPORT CONVENTION**

May 02. (4xcd-box) *(FRQCD 35)* **FAIRPORT UNCONVENTIONAL**

May 02. (cd) *Talking Elephant; (TECD 042)* **FROM CROPREDY TO PORTMEIRON (live)** –

Jun 02. (d-cd) *Burning Airlines; (<PILOT 133>)* **BEFORE THE MOON (live in Denver, 1974)**

Mar 03. (cd) *Disky; (<SI 905323>)* **HERITAGE**

Aug 03. (3xcd-box) *Eureka; (<EURBX 1>)* **SHINES LIKE GOLD**

Oct 03. (d-cd) *Snapper; (SMDCD 484)* **ACROSS THE DECADES** –

Marianne FAITHFULL

Born: 29 Dec'46, Hampstead, London, England, daughter of a university lecturer and an Austrian baroness, who sent her to St. Joseph's convent school in Reading, Berkshire. At the age of 17, while attending a party with her artist boyfriend, JOHN DUNBAR, she was spotted by ANDREW LOOG OLDHAM (the ROLLING STONES' manager), who signed her to 'Decca' records. MARIANNE's debut 45, 'AS TEARS GO BY' (from the pen of JAGGER and RICHARDS), soon careered into the UK Top 10 and the US Top 30, however, her follow-up, Dylan's 'BLOWIN' IN THE WIND', flopped. Early in '65, 'COME AND STAY WITH ME' gave MARIANNE her biggest hit to date (and subsequently ever) and this was followed by two simultaneously issued folk/pop albums, 'COME MY WAY' and the eponymous, 'MARIANNE FAITHFULL' (both of which hit the Top 20). Later the same year, she gave birth to a son, Nicholas, although she was soon to separate from DUNBAR. The sultry blonde bombshell then began a much-publicised affair with MICK JAGGER after allegedly bedding the other three! (not WATTS). Busted for drugs with JAGGER and Co. on many occasions, the couple visiting the Maharishi Yogi in '68, although her career in the flower-power years had taken a sharp nosedive. Around the same time, she also began acting and starred in 'The Three Sisters' (a Chekhov play) and in the film, 'Girl On A Motorcycle', with Alain Delon. Later in '68, she miscarried with JAGGER's baby and six months later, both were arrested in their London home for possession of marijuana. A single, 'SISTER MORPHINE' (written with JAGGER and RICHARDS), was withdrawn and it looked like her music career was about to end. In the summer of '69, while on the set of the movie, 'Ned Kelly', alongside JAGGER, she was found in a coma after overdosing on barbituates (100+ Tuinal). MARIANNE was sadly dropped from the film and subsequently went into hospital to try and cure her heroin addiction and depression. A year later, after a season playing Ophelia in 'Hamlet' (alongside Nicol Williamson), much was made out of her suspected suicide bids which were reported by the press; her divorce from DUNBAR and split with JAGGER, also in the dailys. After five years in the proverbial wilderness, MARIANNE returned with a new contract on 'Nems', the single, 'DREAMING MY DREAMS' a pleasant if not brilliant comeback. Two albums appeared for the label, 'DREAMIN' MY DREAMS' (1977) and 'FAITHLESS' (1978), before she signed to 'Island', returning to the UK Top 50 in 1979 with her rendition of Shel Silverstein's, 'THE BALLAD OF LUCY JORDAN' (once a hit by DR. HOOK). On the 23rd of November '79, she married BEN BRIERLY (of punk rock band, The VIBRATORS), although her future seemed always to be dogged by her drug intake. Her last album's unfruitful attempt at C&W was soon forgotten when she unleashed what was to become her greatest achievement, the 'BROKEN ENGLISH' album. Released nearing the end of, what was for her, a torturous 70's, it marked a pinnacle in her up and down career and was helped in the writing department by her long-time guitarist, BARRY REYNOLDS. Highlighted by her explicit, 'WHY D'YA DO IT' track, the leather-clad mistress was in full swing using sex as her vocal weapon backed by "the in-thing" electro/new wave; her cover of John Lennon's 'WORKING CLASS HERO' also a must-hear. Two albums followed in relatively quick succession, 'DANGEROUS ACQUAINTANCE' (1981) and 'A CHILD'S ADVENTURE' (1983), showing too desperately for some, that she wanted to retain her new "rock" street cred. In 1987, still surprisingly contracted to 'Island' and now living in Cambridge, Massachusetts with new husband and writer, Giorgio Della, she issued a comeback album of sorts, 'STRANGE WEATHER'. It delivered some powerful and poignant messages, showing her once croaky voice to shining effect; EDITH PIAF would have been proud of her. However, the following year, MARIANNE was deported from the States, the singer subsequently choosing to settle in Ireland to finish off her autobiography, simply titled 'Faithfull'. In the mid-90's, she released a handful of albums (including 1995's 'A SECRET LIFE' and 1996's '20th CENTURY BLUES'), she even took time out to appear with the likes of The CHIEFTAINS. A few years onwards, MARIANNE chose to sing a full set of Kurt Weill songs under the banner of 'THE SEVEN DEADLY SINS' (1998) – very ambitious with a full orchestra as backing. Like a 'BROKEN ENGLISH' part II, in the sense that it was just as lyrically intriguing, 'VAGABOND WAYS' (1999) delivered her back into the critical limelight. Tracks such as 'ELECTRA' (accounting all the infamous women of history), 'INCARCERATION OF A FLOWER CHILD' (a late 60's number written by ROGER WATERS about SYD BARRETT) and a cover of Leonard Cohen's 'TOWER OF SONG' were excellent by today's high standards – FAITHFULL was indeed the saving grace amongst her contemporary divas. With 'KISSIN' TIME' (2002), the seemingly indomitable singer surpassed herself yet again, roping in a raft of cutting edge artists from the rock world to create one of her most intriguing and challenging works to date. The presence of BECK, DAMON ALBARN, JARVIS COCKER and BILLY CORGAN might at best, have threatened to overshadow FAITHFULL's singular talent, at worst, have become a muddled celebrity knees-up. In the event, she managed to meld the various link-ups into a seamless whole without compromising either her own artistic vision or that of her guests, each of whom succeeded in teasing out different facets of FAITHFULL's musical character. • **Songwriters:** Penned some herself, although she initially covered others; I'LL BE YOUR BABY TONIGHT (Bob Dylan) / GREENSLEEVES + HOUSE OF THE RISING SUN + SCARBOROUGH FAIR (trad.) / COME AND STAY WITH ME (Jackie DeShannon) / GREEN ARE YOUR EYES (Bert Jansch) / THE LAST THING ON MY MIND (Tom Paxton) / THE FIRST TIME EVER I SAW YOUR FACE (Ewan MacColl) / SALLY FREE AND EASY (... Tannery) / COCKLESHELLS (... Taylor) / THIS LITTLE BIRD (John D.Loudermilk) / SUNNY GOODGE STREET + THE MOST OF WHAT IS LEAST (Donovan) / YESTERDAY (Beatles) / SOMETHING BETTER (Goffin-King) / IS THIS WHAT I GET FOR LOVING YOU (Ronettes) / DREAMING MY DREAMS (Waylon Jennings) / STRANGE WEATHER (Tom Waits) / MADAME GEORGE (Van Morrison) / GHOST DANCE (Patti Smith), etc. • **Trivia:** In 1967, she appeared and supplied backing vocals for The BEATLES on their 'All You Need Is Love', single & TV video.

Album rating: COME MY WAY (*4) / MARIANNE FAITHFULL (*6) / GO AWAY FROM MY WORLD (*5) / NORTH COUNTRY MAID (*4) / FAITHFULL FOREVER (*4) / LOVE IN A MIST (*4) / DREAMING MY DREAMS (*3) / FAITHLESS (*4) / BROKEN ENGLISH (*8) / DANGEROUS ACQUAINTANCES (*6) / A CHILD'S ADVENTURE (*5) / THE VERY BEST OF MARIANNE FAITHFULL compilation (*7) / STRANGE WEATHER (*7) / BLAZING AWAY (*6) / FAITHFULL: A COLLECTION OF HER BEST RECORDINGS compilation (*6) / A SECRET LIFE (*5) / 20th CENTURY BLUES (*4) / THE SEVEN DEADLY SINS (*6) / VAGABOND WAYS (*7) / KISSIN' TIME (*6)

MARIANNE FAITHFULL – vocals (with session people)

		Decca		London
Jul 64.	(7") *(F 11923)* *<9697>* **AS TEARS GO BY. / GREENSLEEVES**	9	Oct64	22
Oct 64.	(7") *(F 12007)* **BLOWIN' IN THE WIND. / THE HOUSE OF THE RISING SUN**			

Feb 65. (7") *(F 12075) <9731>* **COME AND STAY WITH ME. / WHAT HAVE I DONE WRONG** [4] [26]

Apr 65. (7") *(F 12162) <9759>* **THIS LITTLE BIRD. / MORNING SUN** [6] May65 [32]

May 65. (lp) *(LK 4688)* **COME MY WAY** [12] [-]
– Come my way / Jabberwock / Portland town / The house of the rising sun / Spanish is a loving tongue / Fare thee well / Lonesome traveller / Down in the Salley garden / Mary Ann / Full fathom five / Four strong winds / Black girl / Once I had a sweetheart / Bells of freedom. *(re-iss. Sep91 on 'Deram' lp/cd+=; 820 629-2)* – Blowin' in the wind / Et maintenant (what now my love) / That's right baby / Sister Morphine.

May 65. (lp) *(LK 4689) <3423>* **MARIANNE FAITHFULL** [15] [12]
– Come and stay with me / They will never leave you *(UK-only)* / / What have they done to the rain / In my time of sorrow / What have I done wrong / I'm a loser / As tears go by / If I never get to love you / Time takes time / He'll come back to me / Paris bells / Plasir d'amour. *(re-iss. Aug84; DOA 3) (cd-iss. Jun89 on 'London'+=; 820 630-2)* – Can't you hear my heartbeat? / Downtown.

Jul 65. (7") *(F 12193) <9780>* **SUMMER NIGHTS. / THE SHA LA LA SONG** [10] Aug65 [24]

Oct 65. (7") *(F 12268)* **YESTERDAY. / OH LOOK AROUND YOU** [36] [ ]

Nov 66. (7") *<9802>* **GO AWAY FROM MY WORLD. / OH, LOOK AROUND YOU** [-] [89]

Dec 65. (lp) *<3452>* **GO AWAY FROM MY WORLD** [-] [81]
– Go away from my world / Yesterday / Come my way / Last thing on my mind / How should true love / Wild mountain time / Summer nights / Mary Ann / Scarborough Fair / Lullabye / North country maid / Sally free and easy.

Apr 66. (lp) *(LK 4778)* **NORTH COUNTRY MAID** [ ] [-]
– Green are your eyes / Scarborough fair / Cockleshells / The last thing on my mind / The first time ever I saw your face / Sally free and easy / Sunny Goodge Street / How should your true love know / She moved through the fair / North country maid / Lullaby / Wild mountain thyme. *(cd-iss. Aug90+=; 820 631-2)* – The most of what is least / Come my way / Mary Ann.

May 66. (7") *(F 12408)* **TOMORROW'S CALLING. / THAT'S RIGHT BABY** [ ] [ ]

Jul 66. (7") *(F 12443)* **COUNTING. / I'D LIKE TO DIAL YOUR NUMBER** [ ] [ ]

Nov 66. (lp) *<3482>* **FAITHFULL FOREVER** [-] [ ]
– Counting / Tomorrow's calling / The first time / With you in mind / In the night time / Ne me quitte pas (love theme from Umbrellas of Cherbourg) / Monday Monday / Some other Spring / That's right baby / Lucky girl / I'm the sky / I have a love.

Feb 67. (7") *(F 22524)* **IS THIS WHAT I GET FOR LOVING YOU?. / TOMORROW'S CALLING** [43] [ ]

Feb 67. (lp; mono/stereo) *(LK/SKL 4854)* **LOVEINAMIST** [ ] [-]
– Yesterday / You can't go where the roses go / Our love has gone / Don't make promises / In the night time / This little bird / Ne me quite pas / Counting / Reason to believe / Conquillage / With you in mind / Young girl blues / Good guy / I love a love. *(cd-iss. Oct88+=; 820 632-2)* – Rosie, Rosie.

Feb 69. (7"; w-drawn) *(F 12889)* **SOMETHING BETTER. / SISTER MORPHINE** [ ] [ ]

—— She retired from music business for around half a decade

NEMS — not iss.

Nov 75. (7") *(NES 004)* **DREAMIN' MY DREAMS. / LADY MADELAINE** [ ] [-]

Sep 76. (7") *(NES 013)* **ALL I WANNA DO IN LIFE. / WRONG ROAD AGAIN** [ ] [-]

Jan 77. (lp)(c) *(NEL 6007)* **DREAMIN' MY DREAMS** [ ] [-]
– Fairy tale hero / This time / I'm not Lisa / he way you want me to be / Wrong road again / All I wanna do in life / I'm looking for blue eyes / Somebody loves you / Vanilla O'lay / Dreamin' my dreams / Lady Madelaine / Sweet little sixteen.

Jan 77. (7") *(NES 014)* **WRONG ROAD AGAIN. / THE WAY YOU WANT ME TO BE** [ ] [-]

—— she was now backed by **The GREASE BAND**

Mar 78. (lp) *(NEL 6012)* **FAITHLESS** [ ] [-]
– Dreamin' my dreams / Vanilla O'Lay / Wait for me down by the river / I'll be your baby tonight / Lady Madelaine / All I wanna do in life / The way you want me to be / Wrong road again / This was the day (Nashville) / This time / I'm not Lisa / Honky tonk angels. *(re-iss. Apr89 on 'Castle' lp/c/cd; CLA LP/MC/CD 148) (cd re-iss. Apr99 on 'Essential'; ESSCD 713)*

Mar 78. (7") *(NES 117)* **THE WAY YOU WANT ME TO BE. / THAT WAS THE DAY (NASHVILLE)** [ ] [-]

—— now with **BARRY REYNOLDS** – guitar, co-producer / **STEVE YORK** – bass / **TERRY STANNARD** – drums / **JOE HAVETY** – keys / etc.

Island — Island

Oct 79. (7") *(WIP 6491)* **THE BALLAD OF LUCY JORDAN. / BRAIN DRAIN** [48] [ ]

Oct 79. (lp) *(M 1) <ILPS 9570>* **BROKEN ENGLISH** [57] [82]
– Broken English / Witches song / Brain drain / Guilt / The ballad of Lucy Jordan / What's the hurry / Working class hero / Why d'ya do it? *(c-iss.May81; ICT 9570) (re-iss. Sep86 lp/c; ILPM/ICM 9570) (cd-iss. May89; IMCD 11) (re-iss. May94; ILPS 9570)*

Jan 80. (7") *<49121>* **BROKEN ENGLISH. / BRAIN DRAIN** [-] [ ]

Jan 80. (7") *(WIP 6542)* **BROKEN ENGLISH. / WHAT'S THE HURRY** [ ] [-]
(12") *(12WIP 6542)* – ('A'side) / Why d'ya do it?.

Oct 81. (7") *(WIP 6737)* **INTRIGUE. / FOR BEAUTY'S SAKE** [ ] [ ]

Oct 81. (lp/c) *(ILPS/ICT 9648)* **DANGEROUS ACQUAINTANCE** [45] [ ]
– Sweetheart / Intrigue / Easy in the city / Strange one / Tenderness / For beautie's sake / So sad / Eye communication / Truth bitter truth. *(cd-iss. May95; IMCD 205)*

Nov 81. (7") *(WIP 6752)* **SWEETHEART. / OVER HERE** [ ] [-]

Jan 82. (7") **SWEETHEART. / FOR BEAUTIE'S SAKE** [-] [ ]

May 82. (7") *(MF 100)* **BROKEN ENGLISH. / SISTER MORPHINE** [ ] [ ]

—— **BEN BRIERLEY + MIKEY CHUNG** – guitar repl. MAVETY **FERNANDO SAUNDERS** – bass + **WALLY BADAROU** – keyboards repl. YORK

Feb 83. (lp) *(ILPS 9734) <90066>* **A CHILD'S ADVENTURE** [99] [ ]
– Times Square / The blue millionaire / Falling from grace / Morning come / Ashes in my hand / Running for our lives / Ireland / She's got a problem. *(re-iss. Apr87 lp/c; ILPM/ICM 9734) (cd-iss. May95; IMCD 206)*

Mar 83. (7") *(IS 105)* **RUNNING FOR OUR LIVES. / SHE'S GOT A PROBLEM** [ ] [ ]

—— now w/ **many on session, incl. SAUNDERS**

Jun 87. (7") *(IS 323)* **AS TEARS GO BY. / TROUBLE IN MIND (THE RETURN)** [ ] [-]
(12"+=) *(12IS 323)* – This hawk el Galvion.

Jul 87. (lp/c/cd) *(ILPS/ICT/CID 9874) <842593>* **STRANGE WEATHER** [78] [ ]
– Stranger intro / Boulevard of broken dreams / I ain't goin' down to the well no more / Yesterdays / Sign of judgement / Strange weather / Love, life and money / I'll keep it with mine / Hello stranger / Penthouse serenade / As tears go by / A stranger on Earth. *(cd re-iss. May89; IMCD 12)*

—— now with **BARRY REYNOLDS** – guitar / **MARC RIBOT / LEW SOLOFF / GARTH HUDSON**

May 90. (cd/c/lp) *(CID/ICT/ILPS 9957) <842794>* **BLAZING AWAY (live + 1 studio)** [ ] [ ]
– Les prisons du roi / Guilt / Sister morphine / Why d'ya do it? / The ballad of Lucy Jordan / Blazing away / Broken English / Strange weather / Working class hero / As tears go by / When I find my life / Times Square / She moved through the fair. *(re-iss. cd May95; IMCD 207) (c re-iss. May95; same)*

Sep 94. (cd/c) *(DID/ICT 8023) <524004>* **FAITHFULL – A COLLECTION OF HER BEST RECORDINGS** (compilation) [ ] [ ]
– Broken English / Ballad of Lucy Jordan / Working class hero / Guilt / Why d'ya do it? / Ghost dance / Trouble in mind (the return) / Times Square (live) / Strange weather / She / As tears go by.
below from a VAN MORRISON tribute album on 'Exile-Polydor' / 'M.C.A.'

Sep 94. (c-s) **MADAME GEORGE. / ('b'side by Brian Kennedy)** [ ] [ ]
(cd-s+=) – (other by Brian Kennedy + Shana Morrison).
below with composer ANGELO BADALEMENTI

Apr 95. (cd/c) *(CID/ICT 8038) <524096>* **A SECRET LIFE** [ ] [ ]
– Prologue / Sleep / Love in the afternoon / Flaming September / She / Bored by dreams / Losing / The wedding / The stars line up / Epilogue. *(cd re-iss. Jul02 on 'Spectrum'; 524096-2)*

RCA Victor — RCA Victor

Sep 96. (cd) *(<74321 38656-2>)* **20th CENTURY BLUES** [ ] Jan97 [ ]
– Alabama song / Want to buy some illusions / Pirate Jenny / Salomon song / Boulevard of broken dreams / Complainte de la Seine / The ballad of the soldier's wife / Intro / Mon ami (my friend) / Falling in love again / Mack the knife / 20th century blues / Don't forget me / Surabaya Johnny / Outro: street singers farewell.

Aug 97. (cd-ep) *(CDDISC 10)* **HANG IT ON YOUR HEART / (TV theme version) / (instrumental)** [ ] [-]
(above issued on 'EMI Disc')

— next with the Vienna Radio Orchestra conducted – Dennis Russell Davis

Sep 98. (cd) *(<74321 60119-2>)* **THE SEVEN DEADLY SINS** ☐ ☐
– Prologue / Sloth / Pride / Anger / Gluttony / Lust / Covetousness / Envy / Epilogue / Alabama song / The ballad of sexual dependency / Bilbao song / Pirate Jenny.

I.T.R. I.T.R.

Jun 99. (cd) *(ITRCD 1) <47759>* **VAGABOND WAYS** ☐ ☐
– Vagabond ways / Incarceration of a flower child / File it under fun from the past / Electra / Wilder shores of love / Marathon kiss / For wanting you / Great expectations / Tower of song / After the ceasefire.

Nov 99. (cd-s) *(896309)* **ELECTRA** – Europe –

Hut E.M.I.

Mar 02. (cd) *(CDHUT 71) <12009>* **KISSIN' TIME** ☐ ☐
– Sex with strangers / The pleasure song / Like being born / I'm on fire / Wherever I go / Song for Nico / Sliding through life on charm / Love and money / Nobody's fault / Kissin' time / Something good.

– compilations, etc. –

on 'Decca' unless mentioned otherwise

May 65. (7"ep) *(DFE 8624)* **MARIANNE FAITHFULL** ☐ –
– Go away from my world / The most of what is least / El main tenant (what now my love) / The sha la la song.

Feb 69. (lp) *(SPA 17)* **THE WORLD OF MARIANNE FAITHFULL** ☐ –

Apr 69. (lp) *London; <3547>* **MARIANNE FAITHFULL'S GREATEST HITS** (same tracks as above) – ☐

Jul 80. (7"ep) *(F 13890)* **AS TEARS GO BY / COME AND STAY WITH ME. / THIS LITTLE BIRD / SUMMER NIGHTS** ☐ –

Feb 81. (lp) *(TAB 13)* **AS TEARS GO BY** ☐ –

Apr 83. (7") *Old Gold; (OG 9335)* **AS TEARS GO BY. / COME AND STAY WITH ME** ☐ –

Mar 84. (lp) *(TAB 78)* **SUMMER NIGHTS** ☐ –

Nov 85. (d-lp/c/cd) *Castle; (CCS LP/MC/CD 107)* **RICH KID BLUES** ☐ –
(cd re-iss. Jul98 on 'Diablo'; DIAB 861) (cd re-iss. Jun02 on 'Diablo'; DIAB 8043)

Mar 87. (cd) *London; (820 482-2)* **THE VERY BEST OF MARIANNE FAITHFULL** ☐ –
– As tears go by / Come and stay with me / Scarborough Fair / Monday, Monday / Yesterday / The last thing on my mind / What have they done to the rain / This little bird / Something better / In my time of sorrow / Is this what I get for loving you? / Tomorrow's calling / Reason to believe / Sister Morphine / Go away from my world / Summer nights *(re-iss. Sep87 lp/c; 820 482-1/-4)*

Nov 92. (d-cd) *Island; (IRSCD 10)* **BROKEN ENGLISH / STRANGE WEATHER** ☐ –

Oct 93. (cd/c) *Spectrum; (550 097-2/-4)* **THIS LITTLE BIRD** ☐ –

Nov 98. (d-cd) *Island; (<524579-2>)* **PERFECT STRANGER: THE ISLAND ANTHOLOGY** ☐ ☐

Nov 99. (cd) *Spectrum; (544 180-2)* **THE BEST OF MARIANNE FAITHFULL** ☐ –

Jan 00. (cd) *Repertoire; (REP 4799)* **IT'S ALL OVER NOW, BABY BLUE** ☐ –

Oct 00. (d-cd) *Universal; (E 542853-2)* **BROKEN ENGLISH / FAITHFULL** ☐ –

Sep 01. (cd) *Mercury; (585152-2)* **STRANGER ON EARTH: AN INTRODUCTION TO MARIANNE FAITHFULL** ☐ –

FAITHLESS

Formed: London, England . . . early '96 by veterans of the hip-hop dance scene MAXI JAZZ and ROLLO. The former had founded "The Soul Food Cafe Sound System" in 1984, later spending time at the 'Acid Jazz' label before forming his own imprint in '92; 'Namu'. He released three solo outings under various guises and toured the world supporting SOUL II SOUL and JAMIROQUAI. The man also worked with JAH WOBBLE on his 'INVADERS OF THE HEART', just prior to meeting ROLLO in the studio. ROLLO (a member of Mensa), worked on FELIX's massive seller 'DON'T YOU WANT ME', before remixing the likes of SIMPLY RED, GABRIELLE, LIVIN' JOY, M-PEOPLE and The PET SHOP BOYS. One of the top producers/mixers in the world, he also worked on GLOWORM's 'Lift My Cup' among others on his own 'Cheeky' records. JAMIE CATTO was a singer/songwriter, who became frontman for BIG TRUTH BAND, while SISTER BLISS had outings as a solo singer. FAITHLESS revived 'Cheeky' records and had a Top 10 hit with the house dramatics of 'INSOMNIA' at the end of '96, pushing their album into the big league. ROLLO's ascendance from the narrow confines of the dance scene to muso acceptance was confirmed with FAITHLESS' appearance on Jools Holland's 'Later With . . .' show. 1998's 'SUNDAY 8PM' was a well-anticipated follow-up, but although it contained a handful of major UK hits ('GOD IS A DJ', 'TAKE THE LONG WAY HOME' and 'BRING MY FAMILY BACK'), it failed to match its predecessor, at least with the critics. Three years in the making, 'OUTROSPECTIVE', hit the shops in 2001. A Top 5 hit only in Britain, it nevertheless yielded another massive smash for ROLLO and BLISS in the shape of 'WE COME 1'. • **Songwriters:** Permutation of quartet, some with ROLLO's younger sister, DIDO. • **Trivia:** ROLLO had four hits:- 'Get Off Your High Horse' by ROLLO GOES CAMPING, which hit the UK Top 50 twice in 1994, while 'Love Love Love – Here I Come' by ROLLO GOES MYSTIC hit No.32 in the summer of '95. His final effort, 'Let This Be A Prayer' hit No.26 around a year later and was as ROLLO GOES SPIRITUAL WITH PAULINE TAYLOR.

Album rating: REVERENCE (*7) / SUNDAY 8PM (*6) / OUTROSPECTIVE (*7)

MAXI JAZZ (b. MAXWELL FRASER) – vocals / **JAMIE CATTO** – vocals / **SISTER BLISS** (b. AYALAH BEN-TOVIM) – keyboards, vocals / **ROLLO** (b. ROLAND ARMSTRONG) – programming / with others **DIDO** (ARMSTRONG) – vocals / **PAULINE TAYLOR** – vocals / + more musicians

Cheeky Arista

Jul 95. (c-s) *(CHEKK 008)* **SALVA MEA (SAVE ME) / ('A'-Epic mix)** 30 –
(12"+=/cd-s+=) *(CHEK 12/CD 008)* – ('A'mixes; Tuff / Sister Bliss).

Nov 95. (c-s) *(CHEKK 010)* **INSOMNIA / ('A'-monster mix)** 27 –
(12"+=/cd-s+=) *(CHEK 12/CD 010)* – ('A'-moody mix).

Mar 96. (c-s) *(CHEKK 012)* **DON'T LEAVE / ('A'-deep mix)** 34 –
(12"+=/cd-s+=) *(CHEK 12/CD 012)* – ('A'mixes; Nellee Hooper / simple).

Apr 96. (cd/c/d-lp) *(CHEK CD/K/LP 500) <18966>* **REVERENCE** 63 Nov96 ☐
– Reverence / Don't leave / Salva Mea / If lovin' you is wrong / Angeline / Insomnia / Dirty ol' man / Flowerstand man / Baseball cap / Drifting away. *(re-dist.Nov96 hit UK No.26; same)* (free cd w/cd) *(CHEKXCD 500)* **IRREVERENCE** – Flowerstand man (Matty's remix) / Angeline (The Innocents mix) / Reverence (Tamsin's re-fix) / Soundcheck jam / Salva Mea (Way Out West remix) / Don't leave (Floating remix) / Drifting away (Paradiso mix) / Insomnia (Moody mix) / Baseball dub (Cheeky All Stars remix). *(re-iss. Jun01 on 'Arista'; 74321 85859-1) <US-iss.May01 on 'Mushroom'; 54150>*

Jun 96. (12") *(VENMX 07ST)* **SALVA MEA (mixes)** ☐ –
(above issued on 'Vendetta')

Oct 96. (c-s) *(CHEKK 017) <13333>* **INSOMNIA / ('A'mix)** 3 Mar97 62
(12"+=/cd-s+=) *(CHEK 12/CD 017)* – ('A'mixes; CEC / monster).
(cd-s+=) *(CHEKXCD 017)* – ('A'mixes; moody / tuff).

Dec 96. (c-s) *(CHEKK 018)* **SALVA MEA / ('A'-C.E.C. mix) / ('A'-Epic mix)** 9 ☐
(12"+=/cd-s+=) *(CHEK 12/CD 018)* – ('A'mixes; '96 / Way Out West / Tuff).
(cd-s+=) *(CHEKXCD 018)* – ('A'mixes; Sister Bliss / DJ Quicksilver).

Apr 97. (c-s) *(CHEKK 019)* **REVERENCE / INSOMNIA** 10 ☐
(12"/cd-s) *(CHEK 12/CD 019)* – ('A'mixes; Matty's / monster).
(cd-s) *(CHEKXCD 019)* – ('A'mixes; Epic / Tamsin's drum & bass).

Nov 97. (c-s) *(CHEKK 024)* **DON'T LEAVE / ('A'-floating mix)** 21 ☐
(cd-s+=) *(CHEKCD 024)* – ('A'-big mixes, etc).
(cd-s+=) *(CHEKXCD 024)* – ('A'-euphoric mixes, etc).

— **DAVE RANDALL** – guitar; repl. ROLLO (still producer, etc)

Aug 98. (c-s) *(CHEKK 028)* **GOD IS A DJ / ('A'-monster mix)** 6 ☐
(12"+=/cd-s+=) *(CHEK 12/CD 028)* – ('A'mixes; serious danger / sharp, etc).

Sep 98. (cd/c/d-lp) *(CHEK CD/K/LP 503)* *<19029>* **SUNDAY 8PM** 10
– The garden / Bring my family back / Hour of need / Postcards / Take the long way home / Why go? / She's my baby / God is a DJ / Hem of his garment / Sunday 8 pm / Killer's lullaby.

Nov 98. (c-s) *(CHEKK 031)* *<INT 886486-6>* **TAKE THE LONG WAY HOME / ('A'-Rollin' mix)** 15 Dec98
(cd-s+=) *(CHEKCD 031)* – ('A'-Epic mix) / ('A'-16c+ mix) / ('A'-Grant Nelson / Driver's powerpack / Timewriter's where the heart is.
(12") *(CHEK12 031)* – ('A'mixes).

Apr 99. (12") *(CHEK12 035)* **BRING MY FAMILY BACK (mixes; Boombastic / Robbie Rivera's Phat Funked up mix)** 14
(cd-s) *(CHEKCD 035)* – ('A'side) / ('A'-Paul Van Dyk mix) / ('A'-Jan Driver boombastic mix) / ('A'-Rollo & Sister Bliss monster mix).
(cd-s) *(CHEKXCD 035)* – ('A'side) / God is a DJ (first ever mix) / Insomnia (Armand's unreleased mix).

Oct 99. (d-cd) *(CHEKXCD 503)* **SATURDAY 3AM** (remixes)

Nov 99. (12"/cd-s; by FAITHLESS & BOY GEORGE) *(CHEK 12/CD 038)* **WHY GO? (mixes; Ferry Corsten)**
(cd-s) *(CHEKXCD 038)* – ('A'mixes; Lange / Fused why).

Arista Arista

Jun 01. (cd-s) *(74321 85084-2)* **WE COME 1 / WE COME 1 (Rollo & Sister Bliss remix) / WE COME 1 (Dave Clarke remix)** 3
(cd-s) *(74321 85835-2)* – ('A'side) / ('A'-Wookie remix) / ('A'-Rocket vs Jeno remix).
(12") *(74321 85084-1)* – ('A'-Rollo & Sister Bliss remix) / ('A'-Elliott J remix).

Jun 01. (cd/d-lp) *(74321 85083-2/-1)* *<14713>* **OUTROSPECTIVE** 4
– Donny X / Not enuff love / We come 1 / Crazy English summer / Muhammad Ali / Machines R us / One step too far / Tarantula / Giving myself away / Code / Evergreen / Lion tamer. *(cd+=)* – We come 1 (video).

Sep 01. (cd-s) *(74321 88544-2)* **MUHAMMAD ALI / (mixes: full intention club / Rollo & Sister Bliss sweet love)** 29
(12") *(74321 88544-1)* – ('A'side & mixes, etc.)
(cd-s) *(74321 88645-2)* – ('A'side) / ('A'-Architech's remix) / ('A'-Inland Knight's alley mix).

Dec 01. (12"/cd-s) *(74321 90359-1/-2)* **TARANTULA (mixes; radio / Rollo & Sister Bliss funky as fuck / Tiesto)** 29 –
(cd-s) *(74321 90360-2)* – ('A'mixes; Rollo & Sister Bliss / Hiver & Hammer).

Apr 02. (12"/cd-s; by FAITHLESS & DIDO) *(74321 92641-1/-2)* **ONE STEP TOO FAR (mixes; radio / Rollo & Sister Bliss / Alex Neri club rah / Alex Neri club vocal)** 6

Aug 02. (d-cd/d-lp) *(74321 95346-2/-1)* **REPERSPECTIVE** (remixes) 64 –

– compilations, etc. –

on 'Arista' unless mentioned otherwise

Nov 00. (d-cd) *(74321 81165-2)* **SUNDAY 8PM / SATURDAY 3AM** –

Nov 00. (d-cd) *(74321 81169-2)* **REVERENCE / IRREVERENCE** –

Feb 01. (cd) *Ultra; <1080>* **BACK TO MINE** (compiled and mixed by ROLLO & SISTER BLISS) –

FAITH NO MORE

Formed: Los Angeles & San Francisco, California, USA . . . 1980 by BILL GOULD and MIKE BORDIN, although they only started gigging in 1982. With CHUCK MOSELEY and JIM MARTIN completing the line-up, the band began to carve out their innovative fusion of funk, rap, hardcore and metal. In 1985, they issued their eponymous debut album on local indie label, 'Mordam', the single, 'WE CARE A LOT' drawing the attention of 'Slash' records, who unleashed 'INTRODUCE YOURSELF' the same year. In 1988, due to musical differences and off-beat stage humour, MOSELEY was discharged from the band. His replacement was magnetic, Kyle Mclachlan-like, MIKE PATTON who immediately became a focal point, his impressive vocal theatrics and commanding stage presence transforming FAITH NO MORE into a formidable live act. PATTON also penned the bizarre, enigmatic lyrics for the band's breakthrough record, 'THE REAL THING' (1989). Arguably the best metal album of the decade, if you could call it metal, it veered from the stuttering rap-rock of 'EPIC' to the sublimely aquatic 'UNDERWATER LOVE' and on to a searing cover of BLACK SABBATH's 'WAR PIGS'. The record went on to sell over a million copies, gave a tired heavy metal scene a much needed boot up the arse and more importantly, gave FAITH NO MORE the convenience of a bigger budget for their next album. 'ANGEL DUST' (1992) wreaked aural havoc, a mish-mash of styles even more diverse than its predecessor. By turns defiantly inaccessible ('MALPRACTICE') and pop-friendly ('MIDLIFE CRISIS'), the record was characterised by a fractured, schizophrenic sound that seemed to tally with PATTON's increasingly outrageous antics. Following on from their live TECHNOTRONIC/NEW KIDS ON THE BLOCK (ironic? Americans? nah) medley, the band released their rather uninspired cover of The COMMODORES' 'I'M EASY'. It became their biggest selling UK single to date, while the album also sold by the truckload following a world tour with GUNS N' ROSES. By the release of 'KING FOR A DAY . . . FOOL FOR A LIFETIME' (1995), MARTIN had been replaced with TREY SPRUANCE, who played alongside PATTON in his part-time side project, MR. BUNGLE. The record was as uncompromising as ever, venom-spewing hardcore rage sitting side by side with wilful weirdness. A blistering headlining set at that year's Phoenix festival (almost topping PUBLIC ENEMY's poignant farewell slot earlier that day) proved once more that live, FAITH NO MORE have few peers and even less scruples. While the group maintain they're simply a rock band and nothing more, they remain one of the genre's quintessential outsiders, image-unfriendly and maverick to the last, as evidenced on their last studio set, 'ALBUM OF THE YEAR' (1997). If not quite living up to the rather presumptious title, the record illustrated that FAITH NO MORE still have their collective finger in more than one pie, 'LAST CUP OF SORROW' being their most affecting single for years. Unfortunately, it would also be their epitaph as the band split up the following April. • **Covered:** THE RIGHT STUFF (Edwin Starr) / MIDNIGHT COWBOY (John Barry) / MALPRACTICE (sampled: Kronos Quartet No.8) / LET'S LYNCH THE LANDLORD (Dead Kennedys) / I'M EASY (Commodores) / I STARTED A JOKE (Bee Gees) / GREENFIELDS (Gilykson-Dehr-Miller) / SPANISH EYES (hit; Al Martino) / THIS GUY'S IN LOVE WITH YOU (Burt Bacharach) / HIGHWAY STAR (Deep Purple). IMPERIAL TEEN covered SHAYLA (Blondie).

Album rating: FAITH NO MORE (*5) / INTRODUCE YOURSELF (*8) / THE REAL THING (*8) / LIVE AT BRIXTON ACADEMY (*6) / ANGEL DUST (*8) / KING FOR A DAY – FOOL FOR A LIFETIME (*7) / ALBUM OF THE YEAR (*6) / WHO CARES A LOT? compilation (*9) / Mr. Bungle: MR. BUNGLE (*4) / DISCO VOLANTE (*4) / CALIFORNIA (*6) / Imperial Teen: SEASICK (*4) / WHAT IS NOT TO LOVE (*5)

CHUCK MOSELEY – vocals / **BILLY GOULD** (b.24 Apr'63, L.A.) – bass / **RODDY BOTTUM** (b. 1 Jul'63, L.A.) – keyboards / **JIM MARTIN** (b.JAMES, 21 Jul'61, Oakland, Calif.) – guitar / **MIKE BORDIN** (b.27 Nov'62) – drums

not iss. Mordan

1985. (lp) *<MDR 1>* **FAITH NO MORE** –
– We care a lot / The jungle / Mark Bowen / Jim / Why do you bother / Greed / Pills for breakfast / As the worm turns / Arabian disco / New beginnings. *(imported into UK.Feb88 as 'WE CARE A LOT'; same)*

Slash Slash

Oct 87. (lp/c)(cd) *(SLAP/SMAC 21)<(828051-2)>* **INTRODUCE YOURSELF**
– Faster disco / Anne's song / Introduce yourself / Chinese arithmetic / Death march / We care a lot / R'n'r / Crab song / Blood / Spirit.

Jan 88. (7") *(LASH 17)* <28287> **WE CARE A LOT. / SPIRIT** [53] [ ]
(12"+=) *(LASHX 17)* – Chinese Arithmetic (radio mix).

Apr 88. (7"/7"pic-d/12") *(LASH/+P/X 18)* **ANNE'S SONG (remix). / GREED** [ ] [ ]

— **MIKE PATTON** (b.27 Jan'68, Eureka, Calif.) – vocals (of-MR. BUNGLE) repl. CHUCK who later (1991) joined BAD BRAINS

Jul 89. (lp/c/cd) *(828154-1/-4/-2)* <25878> **THE REAL THING** [30] [11]
– From out of nowhere / Epic / Falling to pieces / Surprise, you're dead / Zombie eaters / The real thing / Underwater love / The morning after / Woodpecker from Mars. *(cd+=)* – Edge of the world / War pigs. *(actually hit charts early 1990) (re-iss. Sep92 cd/c; same)*

Oct 89. (7") *(LASH 19)* **FROM OUT OF NOWHERE. / COWBOY SONG** [ ] [ ]
(12"+=) *(LASHX 19)* – The grave.

Jan 90. (7"/7"sha-pic-d) *(LASH/LASPD 21)* **EPIC. / WAR PIGS (live)** [37] [–]
(7"m+=) *(LASHG 21)* – Surprise you're dead (live).
(12"++=/cd-s++=) *(LASHX/LASCD 21)* – Chinese arithmetic.

Apr 90. (c-s) *(LASCS 24)* **FROM OUT OF NOWHERE. / WOODPECKER FROM MARS (live)** [23] [ ]
(7"m+=) *(LASHG 24)* – Epic (live).
(12"++=/12"pic-d++=/cd-s++=) *(LASHX/LASPX/LASCD 24)* – The real thing (live).

Jun 90. (c-s) *<19813>* **EPIC / EDGE OF THE WORLD** [–] [9]

Jul 90. (7") *(LASHP 25)* **FALLING TO PIECES. / WE CARE A LOT (live)** [41] [–]
(7"m+=)(c-s+=) *(LASHG/LASCS 25)* – Underwater love (live).
(12"++=/12"w-poster++=/cd-s++=) *(LASHX/LASPX/LASCD 25)* – From out of nowhere (live).

Sep 90. (7"sha-pic-d) *(LASPD 26)* **EPIC. / FALLING TO PIECES (live)** [25] [–]
(7"m+=/c-s+=) *(LASH/LASCS 26)* – Epic (live).
(12"++=/cd-s++=) *(LASHX/LASCD 26)* – As the worm turns.

Oct 90. (c-s) *<19563>* **FALLING TO PIECES / ZOMBIE EATERS** [–] [92]

Feb 91. (cd/c/lp) *(828238-2/-4/-1)* **LIVE AT BRIXTON ACADEMY (live)** [20] [–]
– Falling to pieces / The real thing / Pump up the jam / Epic / War pigs / From out of nowhere / We care a lot / The right stuff / Zombie eaters / Edge of the world. *(cd+=/c+=)* – The grade / Cowboy song.

May 92. (7"/7"colrd/c-s) *(LASH//LASCS 37)* **MIDLIFE CRISIS. / JIZZLOBER / CRACK HITLER** [10] [ ]
(12"pic-d+=/pic-cd-s+=) *(LASHX/LASCD 37)* – Midnight cowboy.

Jun 92. (cd/c/lp) *(828321-2/-4/-1)* <26785> **ANGEL DUST** [2] [10]
– Land of sunshine / Caffeine / Midlife crisis / RV / Smaller and smaller / Everything's ruined / Malpractise / Kindergarten / Be aggressive / A small victory / Crack Hitler / Jizzlober / Midnight cowboy. *(lp w/ free-12"ep)* – MIDLIFE CRISIS (remix) / (2). *(re-iss. Feb93) (+=)* – I'm easy.

Aug 92. (7"/c-s) *(LASH/LASCS 39)* **A SMALL VICTORY. / LET'S LYNCH THE LANDLORD** [29] [ ]
(12"+=)(12"pic-d+=) *(LASHX 39)* – Malpractise.
(cd-s++=) *(LASCD 39)* – ('A'extended).

Sep 92. (12"ep/cd-ep) *(LASHX/LASCD 40)* **A SMALL VICTORY (Youth remix) / R-EVOLUTION 23 (Full Moon mix) / SUNDOWN (mix) / SUNDOWN (instrumental)** [55] [–]

Nov 92. (7"/c-s) *(LASH/LASCS 43)* **EVERYTHING'S RUINED. / MIDLIFE CRISIS (live)** [28] [ ]
(cd-s+=) *(LASCD 43)* – Land of sunshine (live).
(cd-s) *(LASHCD 43)* – ('A'side) / Edge of the world (live) / RV (live).

Jan 93. (7"/c-s/12"/cd-s) *(LASH/LASCS/LASHX/LACDP 44)* **I'M EASY. / BE AGGRESSIVE** [3] [–]

Mar 93. (c-s) *<18569>* **EASY / DAS SCHUTENFEST** [–] [58]

Oct 93. (12"ep/c-ep/cd-ep; by FAITH NO MORE & BOO-YAA TRIBE) *(659794-6/-4/-2)* **ANOTHER BODY MURDERED. / Just Another Victim (by "HELMET / HOUSE OF PAIN")** [26] [ ]

— (above from the film 'Judgement Day', released on 'Epic')

— **DEAN MENTA** – guitar; repl. JIM MARTIN (TREY SPRUANCE played on below album) – JIM MARTIN released a solo album, 'MILK AND BLOOD' for 'S.P.V.' in 1997

Mar 95. (7"/c-s) *(LASH/LASCS 51)* **DIGGING THE GRAVE. / UGLY IN THE MORNING** [16] [ ]
(12"blue+=) *(LASHX 51)* – Absolute zero / Get out.
(cd-s+=) *(LASCD 51)* – Absolute zero / Cuckoo for Caca.
(cd-s) *(LASHCD 51)* – ('A'side) / I started a joke / Greenfields.

Mar 95. (cd/c/lp) *(828 560-2/-4/-1)* <45723> **KING FOR A DAY – FOOL FOR A LIFETIME** [5] [31]
– Get out / Ricochet / Evidence / The great art of making enemies / Star A.D. / Cuckoo for Caca / Caralho Voador / Ugly in the morning / Digging the grave / Take this bottle / King for a day / What a day / The last to know / Just a man. *(7"box-set)* – (interviews). *(re-iss. Sep97 cd/c; same)*

May 95. (c-s) *(LASCS 53)* **RICOCHET / SPANISH EYES** [27] [ ]
(cd-s+=) *(LASCD 53)* – I wanna f**k myself.
(cd-s) *(LACDP 53)* – ('A'side) / Midlife crisis (live) / Epic (live) / We care a lot (live).

Jul 95. (c-s) *(LASCS 54)* **EVIDENCE / EASY (live)** [32] [ ]
(cd-s+=) *(LASCD 54)* – Digging the grave (live) / From out of nowhere (live).
(cd-s) *(LACDP 54)* – ('A'side) / Das schutzenfest / (interview).

— **JON HUDSON** – guitar; repl. MENTA

May 97. (cd-ep) *(LASCD 61)* <5915> **ASHES TO ASHES / LIGHT UP AND LET GO / COLLISION / ASHES TO ASHES (DJ Icey & Mystero mix)** [15] [ ]
(cd-ep) *(LASCDP 61)* <5909> – ('A'side) / The big Kahuna / Mouth to mouth / ('A'-Hard Knox alternative mix).
(12"ep) *(LASX 61)* – ('A'side) / ('A'-Hard Knox alternative mix) / ('A'-DJ Icey & Mystero mix) / ('A';-DJ & Mystero dub mix).

Jun 97. (cd/c/lp) *(828 901-2/-4/-1)* <46629> **ALBUM OF THE YEAR** [7] [41]
– Collision / Strip search / Last cup of sorrow / Naked in front of the computer / Helpless / Mouth to mouth / Ashes to ashes / She loves me not / Got that feeling / Paths of glory / Home sick home / Pristina. *(cd with free cd Jan98; 828902-2)*

Jul 97. (cd-ep) *(LASCD 62)* **LAST CUP OF SORROW / LAST CUP OF SORROW (Bonehead mix) / SHE LOVES ME NOT (Spinna main mix) / SHE LOVES ME NOT (Spinna crazy dub)** [ ] [–]
(cd-ep) *(LASDP 62)* – ('A'side) / Pristina (Billy Gould mix) / Last cup of sorrow (Roli Mosimann mix) / Ashes to ashes (Dillinja remix).

— In Nov'97, they teamed up with 70's popsters SPARKS on a combined version of 'THIS TOWN AIN'T BIG ENOUGH FOR BOTH OF US'.

Jan 98. (cd-s) *(LASCD 63)* **ASHES TO ASHES / LAST CUP OF SORROW (Rammstein mix) / LAST CUP OF SORROW (Sharam Vs FNM club mix)** [29] [–]
(cd-s) *(LASCX 63)* – ('A'side) / ('A'-Dillinja remix) / The gentle art of making enemies / ('A'live).
(12") *(LASHX 63)* – ('A'-Dillinja mix) / ('A'-Hardknox mix).

— the band had already split in April '98

Oct 98. (cd-s) *(LONCD 65)* <570331> **I STARTED A JOKE / THE WORLD IS YOURS / THEME FROM MIDNIGHT COWBOY** [49] Nov98 [ ]
(cd-s) *(LASCX 65)* <570333> – ('A'side) / This guy's in love with you / We care a lot (CD-rom).

Nov 98. (d-cd/d-c) *(556 057-2/-4)* <47149> **WHO CARES A LOT? – THE GREATEST HITS** (compilation) [37] [ ]
– We care a lot (original) / Introduce yourself / From out of nowhere / Epic / Falling to pieces / Midlife crisis / A small victory / Easy / Digging the grave / The gentle art of making enemies / Evidence / I started a joke / Last cup of sorrow / Ashes to ashes / Stripsearch // The world is yours / Hippie jam song / Instrumental / I won't forget you / Introduce yourself (4-track demos) / Highway star / Theme from Midnight Cowboy / This guy's in love with you.

FALL

Formed: Salford, Manchester, England ... late '76 by vocalist MARK E. SMITH, guitarist MARTIN BRAMAH and bassist TONY FRIEL. Completing the line-up with UNA BAINES (electric piano) and KARL BURNS (drums), the unusual punk band completed a 1977 session for Radio One's John Peel show, before signing to indie outlet, 'Step Forward'. In summer of the following year, The FALL released their debut, the 'BINGO-MASTERS BREAK-OUT! EP'. Sharp-witted right from the outset, the shrieking MARK E traversed the minefield of punk sterotypes, the last track, 'REPETITION' a slow teaser to the other quickfire numbers, 'PSYCHO MAFIA' and

'BINGO-MASTER'. The first of many personnel changes was to occur soon after, MARC RILEY and YVONNE PAWLETT coming in for the departing FRIEL (to The PASSAGE) and BAINES (to The BLUE ORCHIDS) respectively. A weird, disappointing follow-up, 'IT'S THE NEW THING' was thankfully not on their glorious Bob Sergeant-produced debut album, 'LIVE AT THE WITCH TRIALS'. Unleashed to an ever-changing alternative rock audience (who were probably now holding down office jobs while daydreaming of their pogoing dancefloor days of yore!?), the studio set (recorded in two days) packed a lyrical angst not heard since the days of The VELVET UNDERGROUND (one of MARK E's inspirators). Quirky punk tracks such as 'FUTURES AND PASTS' and 'REBELLIOUS JUKEBOX' fitted in nicely with longer excursions into experimentation, 'FRIGHTENED' and 'MUSIC SCENE', making this a classic debut worthy of more listeners. MARK E was now in full control after the remaining founding members, BRAMAH and BURNS bailed out (also joining BLUE ORCHIDS and The PASSAGE) to be subsequently replaced by STEVE HANLEY and MIKE LEIGH respectively. What came next was a piece of punk rock genius, the single 'ROWCHE RUMBLE' ditching conventional rhythms in mindblowing style. PAWLETT left the band soon after and was replaced by guitarist, CRAIG SCANLON, just in time for yet another masterful set that year, 'DRAGNET' (1979). A darker, even more experimental affair, MARK E's twisted tales of life's stranger characters were summed up best on tracks such as 'MUZOREWI'S DAUGHTER', 'A FIGURE WALKS', 'SPECTRE VS. RECTOR' and the "rockabilly" 'PSYKICK DANCEHALL'. The FALL kickstarted the 80's in fine fashion with another punkabilly classic, 'FIERY JACK', an ever better version appearing on 'THE FALL LIVE – TOTALE'S TURNS', their first for 'Rough Trade' a couple of months later. With PAUL HANLEY taking over the vacant drum stool, Mark and Co. delivered two more classic 45's, 'HOW I WROTE ELASTIC MAN' and 'TOTALLY WIRED', their third studio set, 'GROTESQUE (AFTER THE GRAMME)', being released later in 1980. An impressive if not brilliant album, it featured such acidic, "Manc-abilly" screechers, 'THE CONTAINER DRIVERS', 'PAY YOUR RATES' and 'NEW FACE IN HELL', the kazoo backing provided by the group's manager and MARK E's girlfriend, KAY CARROLL. Next up was another unusual concept, the 10" mini-set that was 'SLATES' (1981), a patchy affair that nevertheless contained another gem, 'AN OLDER LOVER ETC'. With founder member KARL BURNS (the second drummer! and extra keyboard player) now back in tow, The FALL signed to 'Kamera', releasing another diamond of a single, 'LIE DREAM OF A CASINO SOUL' (backed by 'FANTASTIC LIFE' on the B-side; like all 45's at this time, not from the accompanying album). They finally found some degree of commercial success when 1982's 'HEX ENDUCTION HOUR' broke silently into the Top 75. Recorded in Iceland, it was sixty minutes of lyrical abandon, excellent songs, however confusing, came in the shape of 'THE CLASSICAL', 'WHO MAKES THE NAZIS?', 'HIP PRIEST' and their most commercial tune to date, 'JAW-BONE AND THE AIR-RIFLE'. Later that year, the most prolific band on earth issued yet another long-player, 'ROOM TO LIVE', a more self-indulgent delivery that disappointed their growing college/uni fanbase. In 1983, they lost the talents of MARC RILEY, who formed his own outfit, The CREEPERS (another great band!), KAY also leaving after she split (not for the first time!) with the grumpy one. Returning to 'Rough Trade', The FALL excelled once more with two splendid singles, 'THE MAN WHOSE HEAD EXPANDED' and 'KICKER CONSPIRACY', before MARK E's new Californian girlfriend, BRIX, came into the fold. She immediately made her mark, augmenting on vocals, playing guitar and co-writing a few numbers on The FALL's late 1983 album, 'PERVERTED BY LANGUAGE'. This set was another to whet the appetite of the faithful (and another illustrious indie chart topper), MARK's mental execution of tracks like 'EAT Y'SELF FITTER' and 'TEMPO HOUSE' the pick of a bizarre bunch. Advancing to 'Beggars Banquet', MARK E, BRIX E and Co. delivered a couple of odd pop singles in the shape of 'OH BROTHER' and 'C.R.E.E.P.', the records not featuring on their forthcoming eighth set, 'THE WONDERFUL AND FRIGHTENING WORLD OF . . .' (1984). Their buoyant rockabilly was back in full flow on two numbers, 'LAY OF THE LAND' and '2 x 4', while GAVIN FRIDAY of The VIRGIN PRUNES guested on a couple of tracks. A month later, a 12"ep, 'CALL FOR ESCAPE ROUTE', saw The FALL experimenting once more, although this was their last with PAUL HANLEY, who was superseded by the numerous talents of SIMON ROGERS (he had been a member of panpipes afficionados, INCANTATION!). With STEVE HANLEY on summer vacation in 1985, the band released the disappointing 'COULDN'T GET AHEAD' single, its flipside containing their first cover, Gene Vincent's 'ROLLIN DANY'. STEVE was back in time to record their most accessible recording to date, 'THIS NATION'S SAVING GRACE' (1985). Regarded as their best work since their debut, the UK Top 60 album housed the excellent 'PAINTWORK', 'MY NEW HOUSE' and 'I AM DAMO SUZUKI', the latter track MARK E's tribute (sort of!) to the CAN singer. BURNS jumped ship after the obligatory set of singles, SIMON WOOLSTENCROFT taking his place for The FALL's first hit (well, No.75), a cover version of The Other Half's 'MR. PHARMACIST'. This seemed to pay off commercially, especially when the accompanying (for once) 'BEND SINISTER' album reached the dizzy heights of the Top 40 in 1986. Another minor hit 45, 'HEY! LUCIANI' (Top 60 this time), preceded the following year's Top 30 embarrassment coming in the shape of R. Dean Taylor's 'THERE'S A GHOST IN MY HOUSE'. Some time later in 1987, BRIX brought in her old friend, MARSHA SCHOFIELD (both were in BANDA DRATSING together), the keyboard player and vocalist arriving in time for two more hits, 'HIT THE NORTH' and 'VICTORIA' (the latter from the pen of Ray Davies). Now without SIMON, who stayed on as their producer, MARK E and Co. hit the charts (Top 20!) with 'THE FRENZ EXPERIMENT' (1988), a confused set that nevertheless contained one standout song, 'CARRY BAG MAN'. Having also been a friend of ballet dancer, MICHAEL CLARK (who used FALL tapes as his backing soundtrack), MARK E and The FALL collaborated with the bare-arsed performer on the band's next ambitious concept, 'I AM KURIOUS ORANJ' (1988). It was indeed, curious, although the Top 60 album did have its moments, especially in 'CAB IT UP!' and a tongue-in-cheek rendition of William Blake's 'JERUSALEM' (segued with the 'DOG IS LIFE' poem). A concert set, 'SEMINAL LIVE' (1989) filled in time during which MARK and BRIX split up, the blonde (who had initiated her own band, ADULT NET, some time ago) eventually becoming the girlfriend of posh/cockney (you choose) classical violinist, NIGEL KENNEDY; he had previously guested on an earlier FALL album (she stunned many after appearing on 'This Is Your Life', which looked back over NIGEL's short career). BRAMAH was now back in the fold, enrolling in time for their umpteenth long-player, 'EXTRICATE' (1990), their first album jointly controlled by the group's new imprint, 'Cog Sinister' and major 'Fontana' label. Premiered by a hit version of Cold Cut's 'TELEPHONE THING', the cynical but accessible set featured other acidic attacks, 'SING! HARPY', 'THE LITTLEST REBEL' and two more obscure covers, 'POPCORN DOUBLE FEATURE' (Searchers) and 'BLACK MONK THEME' (Monks). MARK then trimmed the band down to a quartet, retaining only CRAIG, STEVE and JOHN to record an excellent SID VICIOUS-esque version of Big Bopper's 'WHITE LIGHTNING'. This minor hit was followed by an uncharacteristic flop, 'HIGH TENSION LINE', although both tracks appeared on the follow-up album, 'SHIFT-WORK' (1991), which added a fifth member, violinist KENNY BRADY. Split into two, titled sides, the UK Top 20 record was highlighted by two more excellent pieces of wordplay, 'EDINBURGH MAN' (still makes me sad) and their umpteenth rockabilly delivery, 'A LOT OF WIND' (as in, you talk . . .). BRADY was let go soon after, DAVID BUSH coming in as a more permanent fixture on their next set, 'CODE: SELFISH' (1992). The album disappointed many of the faithful, although some FALL diehards regard it as one of the best (I'm in the former I'm afraid), its re-working of Hank Williams' 'JUST WAITING' not the MARK E of old, although the hit single, 'FREE RANGE' gets back to grips. Moving to 'Permanent' records (not the most appropriate label title for them), MARK and the lads released their biggest seller to date, 'THE INFOTAINMENT SCAN', which went Top 10 in 1993. Short of a classic MARK E song, it collected together another bunch of covers, this time in the shape of Sister Sledge's 'LOST IN MUSIC', S. Bent's (who?!) 'I'M GOING TO SPAIN' and Lee Perry's 'WHY ARE PEOPLE GRUDGEFUL?' (a Top 50 hit). For many, The FALL "lost it" from then on, their formula of sticking several good (not brilliant) songs together with a few obscure covers saw their fanbase dwindle dramatically. Early in '94, a collaboration between MARK and The INSPIRAL CARPETS on the brilliant 'I WANT YOU' single gave him another hit, the mainman subsequently being invited to do similar things for other acts (notably, COLD CUT and DOSE). The return of KARL BURNS for the disappointing 'MIDDLE CLASS REVOLT' (Top 50, 1994) and BRIX for the bittersweet 'CEREBRAL CAUSTIC' (Top 75, 1995), did little to rectify this change in commercial climate. Now signed to 'Jet' records (once home to ELO!), they added JULIA NAGLE and a few guest members to the fold for their next effort, 'THE LIGHT USER SYNDROME' (1996), gaining some critical respect once again, as well as brief chart action. Returning early '98 on 'Artful' records with 'LEVITATE', MARK E and his crew seemed a tad "lost in music", the album being under par for once. Evidently, there had been friction between him and his "employees", three of them (STEVE HANLEY, KARL BURNS and guitarist TOMMY CROOKS) subsequently bailing out after the frontman became "impossible" to work with. Unperturbed, MARK E talked about a spoken-word album, 'THE POST NEARLY MAN', while the DOSE track, 'INCH' (a No.7 in John Peel's 1997 Festive 50), finally hit the shops early in '99. The FALL (Mk.1998/99) were back soon after, NAGLE standing by her man while newcomers NEVILLE WILDING, TOM HEAD and ADAM HALAL (the former two both session men on the last set – ADAM replaced KAREN LATHAM) were beginning to "fall" into place. That spring, album number thirty odd, 'THE MARSHALL SUITE', was dispatched to the shops and although it was a slight improvement the record found no new fans in the way of sales. Never far from the music biz tabloids, MARK E appeared (as a janitor!) in the low-budget movie, 'Glow Boys', while he collaborated with the CLINT BOON EXPERIENCE (ex-INSPIRAL CARPETS man) on the track, 'I Wanna Be Your Dog'. The millennium finally kicked off for The FALL in November 2000 via studio set, 'THE UNUTTERABLE'. Synth-riddled, sharp-lyrically and positively beaming with chaotic rhythms, the set shone out in all the right places, the obscure cover this time being 'HANDS UP BILLY'. A year on and returning to their own 'Cog Sinister' imprint (having escaped for the previous shot on elephant's graveyard label 'Eagle' – once home to STATUS QUO and GARY NUMAN), MARK E and his "classmates" drove out album #f---knows, 'ARE YOU ARE MISSING WINNER' (2001). A winner it was certainly not, from the obscure nine and a half minutes of 'IBIS-AFRO MAN' trailing after a decent cover of R Dean Taylor's 'GOTTA SEE JANE', it failed to register among even the loyal fanbase. Get back to basics was the call. MARK E and his cohorts issued a rather disappointing album of studio outtakes and nine new live tracks (mostly culled from the band's 2001 US tour) in the form of '2G+2' (2002). Suffering from bad quality and even worse musicianship, the album didn't highlight the full live potential of the group, whilst the studio tracks seemed like the same regurgitated garage riffs over SMITH's stammering/strained vocals. A typical FALL release, nonetheless, but just not their best effort. Towards the end of 2003, The FALL (MARK E., JIM WATTS, BEN PRITCHARD, DAVE MILNER and ELINI POULOU) delivered their umpteenth studio set, 'THE REAL NEW FALL LP', a confusing title that was to have been called 'COUNTRY ON THE CLICK'. With producer Grant Showbiz at the controls, the band even managed a love song of sorts, 'GREEN EYED LOCO-MAN'. • **Other covers:** A DAY IN THE LIFE (Beatles) / LEGEND OF XANADU (Dave Dee, Beaky, Mick and Tich) / SHUT UP! (Monks) / JUNK MAN (McFree) / WAR (Slapp Happy) / I'M NOT SATISFIED (Frank Zappa) / JUST WAITING (Hank Williams) / ROADHOUSE (John Barry) / STAY AWAY (OLD WHITE TRAIN) (Johnny Paycheck) / LAST CHANCE TO TURN AROUND (hit; Gene Pitney) / JUNGLE ROCK (Hank Mizell) / THIS PERFECT DAY (Saints) / F-'OLDIN' MONEY (Tommy Blake) / LOOP41 'HOUSTON (Lee Hazlewood). • **Trivia:** MARK E. featured on TACKHEAD b-side of 'Dangerous Sex' in mid 1990, alongside ADRIAN SHERWOOD and GARY CLAIL. Just previous to this, he had a solo track 'ERROR-ORROR I' for the Various Artists compilation 'HOME'.

Album rating: LIVE AT THE WITCH TRIALS (*9) / DRAGNET (*8) / THE FALL LIVE – TOTALE'S TURNS (IT'S NOW OR NEVER) (*6) / GROTESQUE (AFTER THE GRAMME) (*7) / SLATES (*6) / EARLY YEARS 77-79 compilation (*7) / HEX ENDUCTION HOUR (*7) / ROOM TO LIVE (*6) / PERVERTED BY LANGUAGE (*7) / THE WONDERFUL AND FRIGHTENING WORLD OF . . . (*7) / HIP PRIESTS & KAMERADS compilation (*6) / THIS NATION'S SAVING GRACE (*8) / BEND SINISTER (*7) / IN PALACE OF SWORDS REVERSED collection (*6) / THE FRENZ EXPERIMENT (*6) / I AM KURIOUS, ORANJ (*7) / SEMINAL LIVE (*4) / 458489 A-SIDES compilation (*8) / 458489 B-SIDES compilation (*7) / EXTRICATE (*8) / SHIFT-WORK (*8) / CODE: SELFISH (*7) / THE INFOTAINMENT SCAN (*7) / MIDDLE CLASS REVOLT (*6) / CELEBRAL CAUSTIC (*6) / THE TWENTY-SEVEN POINTS (*5) / THE LIGHT USER SYNDROME (*7) / LEVITATE (*6) / THE MARSHALL SUITE (*7) / THE UNUTTERABLE (*7) / ARE YOU ARE MISSING WINNER (*5) / 2G + 2 (*4) / THE REAL NEW FALL LP: FORMERLY 'COUNTRY ON THE CLICK' (*7)

MARK E. SMITH (b. MARK EDWARD SMITH, 5 Mar'57) – vocals / **TONY FRIEL** – bass / **MARTIN BRAMAH** – guitar / **UNA BAINES** – electric piano / **KARL BURNS** – drums

Step Forward I.R.S.

Jun 78. (7"ep) *(SF 7)* **BINGO-MASTERS BREAK-OUT!** [ ] [–]
– Psycho Mafia / Bingo-Master / Repitition.

—— **MARC RILEY** – bass; repl. ERIC and JOHNNIE BROWN who had repl. FRIEL (he formed The PASSAGE) / **YVONNE PAWLETT** – keyboards; repl. BAINES who formed BLUE ORCHIDS

Nov 78. (7") *(SF 9)* **IT'S THE NEW THING. / VARIOUS TIMES** [ ] [–]

Jan 79. (lp) *(SFLP 1) <SP 003>* **LIVE AT THE WITCH TRIALS** [ ] [ ]
– Frightened / Crap rap 2 – Like to blow / Rebellious jukebox / No Xmas for John Quays / Mother-sister! / Industrial estate / Underground medecin / Two steps back / Live at the witch trials / Futures and pasts / Music scene. *(cd-iss. Jun97 & Nov01 on 'Cog Sinister'; COGVP 103CD) <US cd-iss. 1997 on 'Resurgent'; 4107> (lp re-iss. Aug02 on 'Turning Point'; TPM 02208) (cd re-iss. Nov01 on 'Cog Sinister'; COGVP 103CD) <(US+cd re-iss. Nov02 on 'Cog Sinister'+=; COGVP 138CD>)* – Bingo master / Psycho mafia / Repetition.

— **MARK E.** (now sole founder), **RILEY** (now guitar) and **PAWLETT** recruited **STEVE HANLEY** (b.20 May'59, Dublin, Ireland) – bass repl. BRAMAH who also joined BLUE ORCHIDS / **MIKE LEIGH** – drums repl. BURNS who also joined The PASSAGE and P.I.L.

Jul 79. (7") *(SF 11)* **ROWCHE RUMBLE. / IN MY AREA** –

— **CRAIG SCANLON** (b. 7 Dec'60) – guitar (RILEY now guitar, keyboards) repl. PAWLETT

Oct 79. (lp) *(SFLP 4)* **DRAGNET** –
– Psykick dancehall / A figure walks / Printhead / Dice man / Before the Moon falls / Your heart out / Muzorewi's daughter / Flat of angles / Choc-stock / Spectre vs. rector / Put away. *(re-iss. Dec90 lp/cd; SFAL/SPLPCD 4) (cd re-iss. Nov01 on 'Cog Sinister'; COGVP 113CD) (lp re-iss. Aug02 on 'Turning Point'; TPM 02209) (<US+cd re-iss. Nov02 on 'Cog Sinister'+=; COGVP 140>)* – Rowche rumble / In my area / Fiery Jack / 2nd dark age / Psykick dancehall No.2.

Jan 80. (7") *(SF 13)* **FIERY JACK. / SECOND DARK AGE / PSYKICK DANCEHALL II** –

Rough Trade not iss.

May 80. (lp) *(ROUGH 10)* **THE FALL LIVE – TOTALE'S TURNS (IT'S NOW OR NEVER) (live)** –
– (intro) – Fiery Jack / Rowche rumble / Muzorewi's daughter / In my area / Choc-stock / Spectre vs. rector 2 / Cary Grant's wedding / That man / New puritan / No Xmas for John Quays. *(cd-iss. Nov92 on 'Dojo'; DOJOCD 83)*

— **PAUL HANLEY** – drums repl. LEIGH

Jun 80. (7") *(RT 048)* **HOW I WROTE ELASTIC MAN. / CITY HOBGOBLINS** –

Sep 80. (7") *(RT 056)* **TOTALLY WIRED. / PUTTA BLOCK** –

— **KAY CARROLL** their manager augmented p/t on backing vocals, kazoo

Nov 80. (lp) *(ROUGH 18)* **GROTESQUE (AFTER THE GRAMME)**
– Pay your rates / English scheme / New face in Hell / C'n'c Smithering / The container drivers / Impression of J. Temperance / In the park / W.M.C. – Blob 59 / Gramme Friday / The N.W.R.A. *(<cd-iss. Sep93 on 'Castle'; CLACD 391>) (cd re-iss. Jun98 on 'Essential'; ESMCD 640) (lp re-iss. Oct02 on 'Turning Point'; TPM 02210)*

Apr 81. (10"m-lp) *(RT 071)* **SLATES** –
– Middle mass / An older lover etc. / Prole art threat / Fit and working again / Slates, slags, etc. / Leave the capitol.

— **KARL BURNS** – drums returned now alongside **SMITH, RILEY, SCANLON, S and P HANLEY**

Kamera not iss.

Nov 81. (7") *(ERA 001)* **LIE DREAM OF A CASINO SOUL. / FANTASTIC LIFE** –

Mar 82. (lp) *(KAM 005)* **HEX ENDUCTION HOUR** 71 –
– The classical / Jaw-bone and the air-rifle / Hip priest / Fortress – Deer park / Mere psued mag. ed / Winter / Winter 2 / Just step s'ways / Who makes the Nazis? / Iceland / And this day. *(re-iss. 1987 on 'Line'; LILP 400126) (<cd-iss. Sep89 & Mar98; LICD 900126>) <US cd-iss. 1999 on 'Resurgent'; 4486> (<cd re-iss. Nov02 on 'Cog Sinister'; COGVP 141CD>)*

Apr 82. (7") *(ERA 004)* **LOOK KNOW. / I'M INTO C.B.** –

Nov 82. (lp) *(KAM 011)* **ROOM TO LIVE** –
– Joker hysterical face / Marquee cha-cha / Hard life in the country / Room to live / Detective instinct / Solicitor in studio / Papal visit. *(re-iss. Oct87 on 'Line'; LILP 400109) (cd-iss. Apr98 & Nov01 on 'Cog Sinister'; COGVP 105CD) <US cd-iss. 1998 on 'Resurgent'; 4257> (cd re-iss. Apr02 on 'Cog Sinister'; COGVP 119CD) (<US+cd-iss. Nov02 on 'Cog Sinister'; COGVP 139CD>)*

— reverted to quintet when RILEY left to form MARC RILEY & THE CREEPERS (note that their manager and p/t member KAY CARROLL also departed)

Rough Trade not iss.

Jun 83. (7") *(RT 133)* **THE MAN WHOSE HEAD EXPANDED. / LUDD GANG** –

Oct 83. (d7") *(RT 143)* **KICKER CONSPIRACY. // WINGS / CONTAINER DRIVERS (live) / NEW PURITANS (live)** –

— added **LAURA-ELISE** (now BRIX E. SMITH) (b. California, USA) – guitar, vocals (ex-BANDA DRATSING) P. HANLEY added keyboards and BURNS added lead bass to their repertoire

Dec 83. (lp/c) *(ROUGH/+C 62)* **PERVERTED BY LANGUAGE** –
– Eat y'self fitter / Neighbourhood of infinity / Garden / Hotel Bloedel / I feel voxish / Tempo house / Hexen definitive / Strife knot. *(re-iss. Oct87 on 'Line'; LILP 400116) (cd-iss. Sep89+=; LICD 900116)* – Oh! brother / God-box / C.R.E.E.P. / Pat-trip dispenser. *(<cd re-iss. Sep93 on 'Castle'; CLACD 392>) (cd re-iss. Feb98 on 'Cog Sinister – Voiceprint'; COGVP 104CD) (cd re-iss. Jun98 on 'Essential'; ESMCD 639)*

Beggars Banquet Beggars Banquet

Jun 84. (7") *(BEG 110)* **OH BROTHER. / GOD-BOX** –
(12"+=) *(BEG 110T)* – ('A'instrumental).

Aug 84. (7") *(BEG 116)* **C.R.E.E.P. / PAT-TRIP DISPENSER** –
(12"green+=/12"s) *(BEG 116T/+P)* – ('A'extended).

— added **GAVIN FRIDAY** – some vocals (of VIRGIN PRUNES) (on next 2 releases)

Sep 84. (lp/c) *(<BEGA/+C 58>)* **THE WONDERFUL AND FRIGHTENING WORLD OF . . .** 62
– Lay of the land / 2 x 4 / Copped it / Elves / Slang king / Bug day / Stephen song / Craigness / Disney's dream debased. *(re-iss. Jul88 on 'Beggars Banquet' lp/c)(cd+=; BBL/+C 58)(BBL 58CD)* – Oh! brother / Draygo's guilt / God-box / Clear off! / C.R.E.E.P. / Pat-trip dispenser / No bulbs.

Oct 84. (12"ep) *(BEG 120E)* **CALL FOR ESCAPE ROUTE** –
– Draygo's Guilt / No bulbs / Clear Off!.
(with free-7") **NO BULBS 3. / SLANG KING**

— **SIMON ROGERS** – bass, keyboards repl. P. HANLEY (he cont. with KISS THE BLADE) (GAVIN returned to VIRGIN PRUNES and S. HANLEY took a holiday)

Jul 85. (7") *(BEG 134)* **COULDN'T GET AHEAD. / ROLLIN' DANY**
(12"+=) *(BEG 134T)* – Petty (thief) lout.

— **STEVE HANLEY** returned to join **MARK E., BRIX, CRAIG, KARL and SIMON**

Sep 85. (lp/c)(cd) *(<BEGA/BEGC 47)(BEGA 67CD>)* **THIS NATION'S SAVING GRACE** 54
– Mansion / Bombast / Barmy / What you need / Spoilt Victorian child / L.A. / Out of the quantifier / My new house / Paintwork / I am Damo Suzuki / To nkroachment: yarbles. *(re-iss. Feb90 lp/c)(cd+=; BBL/+C 67)(BBL 67CD)* – Vixen / Couldn't get ahead / Pretty (thief) lout / Rollin' Dany / Cruiser's creek.

Oct 85. (7") *(BEG 150)* **CRUISER'S CREEK. / L.A.** –
(12"+=) *(BEG 150T)* – Vixen.

Jul 86. (7") *(BEG 165)* **LIVING TOO LATE. / HOT AFTER-SHAVE BOP** –
(12"+=) *(BEG 165T)* – Living too long.

— **JOHN SIMON WOOLSTENCROFT** (b.19 Jan'63, Altringham, England) – drums (ex-WEEDS) repl. BURNS who formed THIRST

Sep 86. (7") *(BEG 168)* **MR. PHARMICIST. / LUCIFER OVER LANCASHIRE** 75
(12"+=) *(BEG 168T)* – Auto-tech pilot.

Oct 86. (lp/c) *(BEGA/BEGC 75)* **BEND SINISTER** 36
– R.O.D. / Dktr. Faustus / Shoulder pads #1 / Mr. Pharmicist / Gross chapel – British grenadiers / U.S. 80's-90's / Terry Waite sez / Bournemouth runner / Riddler / Shoulder pads #2. *(cd-iss. Jan88+=; BEGA 75CD)* – Living too late / Auto-tech pilot.

Nov 86. (7") *(BEGA 176)* **HEY! LUCIANI. / ENTITLED** 59
(12"+=) *(BEG 176T)* – Shoulder pads.

Apr 87. (7") *(BEG 187)* **THERE'S A GHOST IN MY HOUSE. / HAF FOUND, BORMAN** 30
(12"+=/c-s+=) *(BEG 187 T/C)* – Sleepdebt / Snatches / Mark'll sink us.

— added **MARSHA SCHOFIELD** (b.1963, Brooklyn, N.Y.) – keyboards, vocals of ADULT NET, (ex-BANDA DRATSING)

Oct 87. (7"/7"pic-d) *(BEG 200/+P)* **HIT THE NORTH. / (part 2)** 57
(12"+=) *(BEG 200T)* – Australians in Europe.
(cd-s+=) *BEG 200C)* – Northerns in Europe / (Hit the north versions).

— reverted back to sextet of **MARK E., BRIX, CRAIG, JOHN S., STEVE** and **MARSHA** when **SIMON** became their producer & studio guitarist only

Jan 88. (7") *(BEG 206)* **VICTORIA. / TUFF LIFE BOOGIE** 35
(12"+=) *(BEG 206T)* – Guest informant / Twister.

Mar 88. (lp/c)(cd) *(BEGA/BEGC 91)(BEGA 91CD) <6987>* **THE FRENZ EXPERIMENT** 19
– Frenz / Carry bag man / Get a hotel / Victoria / Athlete cured / In these times / The steak place / Bremen nacht / Guest informant (excerpt) / Oswald defence lawyer. *(c/cd+=)* – Tuff life boogie / Guest informant / Twister / There's a ghost in my house / Hit the north (part 1).

Oct 88. (lp/c)(cd) *(BEGA/BEGC 96)(BEGA 96CD) <9582>* **I AM KURIOUS, ORANJ** 54
– New big prinz / Overture from 'I Am Curious, Orange' / Dog is life – Jerusalem / Wrong place, right time / Guide me soft * / C.D. win fall 2088

ad / Yes, o yes / Van plague? / Bad news girl / Cab it up! / Last nacht * / Big new priest *. *(c+=/cd+= *)*

Nov 88. (d7"ep/d3"cd-ep) *(FALL 2 B/CD)* **JERUSALEM / ACID PRIEST 2088. / BIG NEW PRINZ / WRONG PLACE, RIGHT TIME** 59 –

Jun 89. (7") *(BEG 226)* **CAB IT UP. / DEAD BEAT DESCENDENT (out take from ballet** –
(12"+=) *(BEG 226T)* – Kurious oranj (live) / Hit the north (live).

Beggars Banquet – Lowdown | not iss.

Jun 89. (lp/c)(cd) *(BBL/+C 102)(BBL 102CD) <9807>* **SEMINAL LIVE (some studio)** 40 –
– Dead beat descendant / Pinball machine / H.O.W. / Squid law / Mollusc in Tyrol / 2 x 4 / Elf prefix – L.A. / Victoria / Pay your rates / Cruiser's creek. *(c+=/cd+=)* – Kurious oranj / Hit the north / In these times / Frenz.

— **MARTIN BRAMAH** – guitar returned to repl. BRIX E. who continued with ADULT NET.

Cog Sinister-Fontana | Fontana

Jan 90. (7"/c-s) *(SIN/+MC 4)* **TELEPHONE THING. / BRITISH PEOPLE IN HOT WEATHER** 58 –
(12"+=)(cd-s+=) *(SIN 4-12)(SINCD 4)* – Telephone (dub).

Feb 90. (cd/c/lp) *(<842204-2/-4/-1>)* **EXTRICATE** 31
– Sing! Harpy / I'm Frank / Bill is dead / Black monk theme part 1 / Popcorn double feature / Telephone thing / Hilary / Chicago, now! / The littlest rebel / British people in hot weather / And therein. (c+cd+=) – Arms control poseur / Black monk theme part II / Extricate. *(cd re-iss. Nov01 on 'Cog Sinister'; COGVP 122CD)*

Mar 90. (7"/c-s) *(SIN/+MC 5)* **POPCORN DOUBLE FEATURE. / BUTTERFLIES 4 BRAINS** –
(12"+=) *(SIN 5-12)* – Arms control poseur.
(cd-s+=) *(SINCD 5)* – Zandra / Black monk theme part II.

— trimmed to basic quartet of **MARK E, CRAIG, STEVE and JOHN.**

Aug 90. (7") *(SIN 6)* **WHITE LIGHTNING. / BLOOD OUTTA STONE** 56 –
(12"+=) *(SINR 6-12)* – Zagreb.
(12"ep+=)(cd-ep+=) **THE DREDGER EP** *(SIN 6-12)(SINCD 6)* – Life just bounces.

Dec 90. (7") *(SIN 7)* **HIGH TENSION LINE. / XMAS WITH SIMON** –
(12"+=)(cd-s+=) *(SIN 7-12)(SINCD 7)* – Don't take the pizza.

— added guest **KENNY BRADY** – violin

Apr 91. (cd/c/lp) *(<848594-2/-4/-1>)* **SHIFT-WORK** 17
– EARTH'S IMPOSSIBLE DAY :-So what about it? / Idiot joy showland / Edinburgh man / Pittsville direkt / The book of lies / High tension line / The war against intelligence/ / NOTEBOOKS OUT PLAGIARISTS :-Shift-work / You haven't found it yet / The mixer / White lightning / A lot of wind / Rose / Sinister waltz. *(<US+cd re-iss. Sep02 on 'Cog Sinister'+=; COGVP 134CD>)* – Blood outta stone / Xmas with Simon.

— **DAVID BUSH** (b. 4 Jun'59, Taplow, England) – keyboards, machines repl. BRADY

Mar 92. (7") *(SINS 8)* **FREE RANGE. / EVERYTHING HURTZ** 40 –
(12"+=)(pic-cd-s+=) *(SIN 8-12)(SINCD 8)* – Dangerous / Return.

Mar 92. (cd/c/lp) *(<512162-2/-4/-1>)* **CODE: SELFISH** 21
– The Birmingham school of business school / Free range / Return / Time enough at last / Everything hurtz / Immorality / Two-face! / Just waiting / So-called dangerous / Gentlemen's agreement / Married, 2 kids / Crew filth. *(cd re-iss. Aug93; same) (<US+cd re-iss. Sep02 on 'Cog Sinister'+=; COGVP 133CD>)* – Ed's babe / Free ranger.

Jun 92. (12"ep)(cd-ep) *(SIN 9-12)(SINCD 9)* **ED'S BABE / PUMPKIN HEAD XSCAPES / THE KNIGHT, THE DEVIL AND DEATH / ARID'S AL'S DREAM / FREE RANGER** –

Permanent | Matador

Apr 93. (7") *(SPERM 9) <OLE 053>* **WHY ARE PEOPLE GRUDGEFUL? / GLAM-RACKET** 43
(12"+=/cd-s+=) *(12/CD SPERM 9) <OLE 054>* – The re-mixer / Lost in music.

Apr 93. (cd/c/lp) *(PERM CD/MC/LP 12) <OLE 055>* **THE INFOTAINMENT SCAN** 9 May93
– Ladybird (green grass) / Lost in music / Glam-racket / I'm going to Spain / It's a curse / Paranoia man in cheap sh*t room / Service / The league of bald-headed men / A past gone mad / Light fireworks / League Moon monkey mix. *(cd+=)* – Why are people grudgeful? *(cd re-iss. Jul99 on 'Artful'; ARTFULCD 22)*

— added the returning **KARL BURNS** – percussion(now 6-piece yet again)

Dec 93. (d-cd-ep/d12"ep) *(CD/12 SPERM 13)* **BEHIND THE COUNTER EP** 75 –
– Behind the counter / War / M5 / Happy holiday / Cab driver / (1).

— Feb94; MARK guested for INSPIRAL CARPETS on their single 'I Want You'

Apr 94. (10"clear-ep/12"ep/cd-ep) *(10/12/CD SPERM 14) <OLE 094>* **15 WAYS. / HEY! STUDENT / THE $500 BOTTLE OF WINE** 65 May94

May 94. (cd/c/lp) *(PERM CD/MC/LP 18) <OLE 095>* **MIDDLE CLASS REVOLT (aka THE VAPOURISATION OF REALITY** 48 Jul94
– 15 ways / The reckoning / Behind the counter / M5#1 / Surmount all obstacles / Middle class revolt! / You're not up to much / Symbol of Mordgan / Hey! student / Junk man / The $500 bottle of wine / City dweller / War / Shut up!. *(cd re-iss. Jul99 on 'Artful'; ARTFULCD 23)*

— added on tour the returning **BRIX SMITH**– guitar, vocals

Permanent | Permanent

Feb 95. (cd/c/lp) *(<PERM CD/MC/LP 30>)* **CEREBRAL CAUSTIC** 67 May95
– The joke / Don't call me darling / Rainmaster / Feeling numb / Pearl city / Life just bounces / I'm not satisfied / The aphid / Bonkers in Phoenix / One day / North west fashion show / Pine leaves. *(cd re-iss. Jul99 on 'Artful'; ARTFULCD 24)*

Aug 95. (d-cd/d-c/d-lp) *(<PERM CD/MC/LP 36>)* **THE TWENTY-SEVEN POINTS (live)** Sep95
– Mollusc in Tyrol / Return / Lady bird (green grass) / Idiot – Walk-out / Ten points / Idiot – Walk-out / Big new prinz / Intro: Roadhouse / The joke / ME's jokes – The British people in hot weather / Free range / Hi-tension line / The league of the bald headed men / Glam racket: Star / Lost in music / Mr. Pharmacist / Cloud of black / Paranoia man in cheap shit room / Bounces / Outro / Passable / Glasgow advice / Middle class revolt: Simon, Dave and John / Bill is dead / Strychnine / War! / Noel's chemical effluence / Three points – Up too much.

— added **JULIA NAGLE** – keyboards, guitar / + 7th & 8th members **LUCY RIMMER** – vocals / **MIKE BENNETT** – vocals, co-producer (to MARK E., BRIX, SIMON, STEPHEN + KARL)

Jet | Jet

Feb 96. (12"ep/c-ep/cd-ep) *(JET/+MC/SCD 500)* **THE CHISELERS / CHILINIST. / INTERLUDE / CHILINISM** 60 –

— MARK E. worked with DOSE on their single 'PLUG MYSELF IN', released on Pete Waterman's new label 'Coliseum'!

Jun 96. (cd/c/lp) *(<JET CD/MC/LP 1012>)* **THE LIGHT USER SYNDROME** 54
– D.I.Y. meat / Das vulture ans ein nutter-wain / He Pep! / Hostile / Stay away (old white train) / Spinetrak / Interlude – Chilinism / Powder keg / Oleano / Cheetham Hill / The Coliseum / Last chance to turn around / The ballard of J. Drummer / Oxymoron / Secession man. *(cd re-iss. Feb99 on 'Receiver'; RRCD 264) (cd re-iss. Sep02 on 'Castle'; CMRCD 570)*

Artful | Artful

Feb 98. (10"ep/cd-ep) *(10/CD ARTFUL 1)* **MASQUERADE / CALENDAR. / SCAREBALL / OL' GANG (live)** 69 –
(cd-ep) *(CXARTFUL 001)* – ('A'side) / Ivanhoes two pence / Spencer must die / Ten houses of Eve.

Feb 98. (cd/c/lp) *(<ARTFUL CD/MC/LP 9>)* **LEVITATE**
– Ten houses of Eve / Masquerade / Hurricane Edward / I'm a mummy / Quartet of Doc Shanley / Jap kid / 4 1/2 inch / Spencer must die / Jungle rock / Ol' gang / Tragic days / I come and stand at your door / Levitate / Everybody but myself. *(cd re-iss. May99; ARTFULCDX 9)*

— **SMITH** retained **NAGLE** and recruited **NEVILLE WILDING** – guitar + **TOM HEAD** – drums

— **ADAM HALAL** – bass; repl. temp. KAREN LATHAM

Mar 99. (12"/cd-s) *(12/CD ARTFUL 2)* **TOUCH SENSITIVE. / ANTIDOTE / TOUCH SENSITIVE (dance mix)** –

Apr 99. (cd/c/lp) *(<ARTFUL CD/MC/LP 17>)* **THE MARSHALL SUITE** Oct99
– Touch sensitive / F-'oldin' money / Snake-off / Bound / This perfect day / (Jung Nev's) Antidotes / Inevitable / Anecdotes + anecdotes in B# / Early life of crying Marshal / Birthday song / Mad. men-eng, dog / On my own.

Aug 99. (cd-s) *(CDARTFUL 3)* **F-'OLDIN' MONEY / THIS PERFECT DAY (remix) / BIRTHDAY SONG (remix)** –
(cd-s) *(CDXARTFUL 3)* – ('A'side) / The early life of the crying marshall (remix) / Tom Raggazzi (remix).

Eagle | Mister E

Nov 00. (cd) *(EAGCD 164) <3>* **THE UNUTTERABLE**
– Cyber insekt / Two Librans / W.B. / Sons of temperance / Dr. Buck's

letter / Hot runes Way round / Octo realm – Ketamine sun / Serum / The unutterable / Pumpkin soup and mashed potatoes / Hands up Billy / Midwatch 1953 / Devolute / Das katerer.

—— **SMITH + NAGLE** with **BERNARD FANNING** – guitar, vocals / **JIM WATTS** – bass, guitar

Cog Sinister Cog Sinister

Nov 01. (cd) *(<COGVP 131CD>)* **ARE YOU ARE MISSING WINNER** Dec01
– Jim's the fall / Bourgeois town / Crop dust / My ex-classmate's kids / Kick the can / Gotta see Jane / Ibis afro man / Acute / Hollow mind / Reprise (Jane – Prof Mick – Ey bastardo). *(pic-lp iss.Feb02; COGVP 131LP)*

Action Telegraph

Jun 02. (cd) *(TAKE 018CD) <1099-2>* **2G + 2 (live)** Aug02
– The joke / New formation sermon / My ex-classmates' kids / Enigrammatic dream / I wake up in the city / Kick the can / F-'oldin' money / Bourgeois town / Distilled mug art / Ibis Afro-man / Mr. Pharmacist / I am Damo Suzuki.

Nov 02. (7"ep/cd-ep) *(TAKE 020/+CD)* **FALL VS. 2003** 64 –
– Susan vs. nightclub / Janet vs. Johnny.

—— **SMITH + WATTS** plus **BEN PRITCHARD** – lead guitar / **DAVE MILNER** – drums, keyboards / **ELINI POULOU** – keyboards

Oct 03. (lp/cd) *(TAKE 021/+CD)* **THE REAL NEW FALL LP: FORMERLY 'COUNTRY ON THE CLICK'** –
– Green eyed loco-man / Mountain energei / Theme from Sparta F.C. / Contraflow / Last commands of xyralothep via M.E.S. / Open the boxoctosis #2 / Janet, Johnny + James / The past #2 / Loop41 'Houston / Mike's love xexagon / Proteinprotection / Recovery kit.

Dec 03. (d7"ep/cd-ep) *(TAKE 022/+CD)* **(WE WISH YOU) A PROTEIN CHRISTMAS** –
– (We wish you) A protein Christmas / (We are) Mod mock goth / (Birtwistle's) Girl in shop / Recovery kit 2#.

– compilations, etc. –

Sep 81. (lp) *Step Forward; (ROUGH 18)* **77-EARLY YEARS-79** –
– Repetition / Bingo-masters breakout / Psycho mafia / Various times / It's the new thing / Rowche rumble / In my area / Dice man / Psykick dancehall / Second dark age / Fiery Jack / Stepping out / Last orders. *<US cd-iss. 2000 on 'Resurgent'; 4540> (cd-iss. Nov01 on 'Cog Sinister'; COGVP 123CD) (cd re-iss. Dec02 as 'THE EARLY SINGLES 1978-1982' on 'Cog Sinister'; COGVP 136CD)*

Mar 82. (c) *Chaos; (LIVE 006)* **LIVE AT ACKLAM HALL, LONDON 1980** –
(cd-iss. Jan96 as 'THE LEGENDARY CHAOS TAPES'; SAR 1005) (cd re-iss. Jul97 & Nov01 on 'Cog Sinister – Voiceprint'; COGVP 101CD)

Nov 82. (lp) *Cottage; <none>* **A PART OF AMERICA THEREIN** –

Nov 83. (7") *Kamera; (KAM 014)* **MARQUEE CHA-CHA. / ROOM TO LIVE / / (PAPAL VISIT original b-side)** –

Mar 85. (lp/c) *Situation 2; (SIT U/C 13)* **HIP PRIESTS AND KAMERADS** (81-82 material) –
(c+=) – (has 4 extra tracks) *(cd-iss. Mar88+= same 4; SITU 13CD) (re-iss. 1988 on 'Situation 2-Lowdown' lp/c)(cd+=; SITL/+C 13)(SITU 13CD) (cd re-iss. Sep95 on 'Beggars Banquet')*

May 87. (12"ep/c-ep) *Strange Fruit; (<SFPF/SFPSC 028>)* **THE PEEL SESSIONS** (28.11.78) 1991
– Put away / No Xmas for John Quay / Like to blow / Mess of my.

Nov 87. (cd/c/lp) *Cog Sinister; (CD/C+/COG 1)* **IN PALACE OF SWORDS REVERSED (80-83)** –
(cd re-iss. Nov01; COGVP 107CD)

Sep 90. (cd)(lp/c) *Beggars Banquet; (BEGA 111CD)(BEGA/+C 111) <2430>* **458489** ('A'sides; 1984-89) 47
– Oh! brother / C.R.E.E.P. / No bulbs 3 / Rollin' Dany / Couldn't get ahead / Cruiser's creek / L.A. / Living too late / Hit the north (part 1) / Mr. Pharmacist / Hey! Luciani / There's a ghost in my house / Victoria / Big new prinz / Wrong place, right time No.2 / Jerusalem / Dead beat descendant. // God-box / Pat-trip dispenser / Slang king 2 / Draygo's guilt / Clear off! / No bulbs / Petty thief lout / Vixen / Hot aftershave bop / Living too long / Lucifer over Lancashire / Auto tech pilot / Entitled / Shoulder pads #1 / Sleep debt snatches / Mark'll sink us / Haf found Bormann / Australians in Europe / Northerns in Europe / Hit the north (part 2) / Guest informant / Tuff life boogie / Twister / Acid priest 2088 / Cab it up. *<US cd re-iss. 1994 on 'Atlantic'; 92380>*

Dec 90. (cd)(d-lp/c) *Beggars Banquet; (BEGA 116CD)(BEGA/+C 116) <2430>* **458489** (B'sides; 1984-89)
– God-box / Pat-trip dispenser / Slang king 2 / Draygo's guilt / Clear off! / No bulbs / Petty thief lout / Vixen / Hot aftershave bop / Living too long / Lucifer over Lancashire / Auto tech pilot / Entitled / Shoulder pads £1 / Sleep debt snatches / Mark'll sink us / Haf found Bormann / Australians in Europe / Northerns in Europe / Hit the north (part 2) / Guest informant / Tuff life boogie / Twister / Acid priest 2088 / Cab it up. *(cd+=)* – Bremen nache run out / Mark'll sink us (live) / Kurious oranj. *<US cd re-iss. 1994 on 'Atlantic'; 92474>*

Mar 93. (7"ep/cd-ep) *Strange Fruit; (SFPS/SFPCD 087) / Dutch East India; <8355>* **KIMBLE**
– Kimble / C'n'c hassle schmuk / Spoilt Victorian child / Words of expectation.

Apr 93. (cd) *Castle; (CCSCD 365)* **THE COLLECTION** –

Aug 93. (m-cd) *Windsong; (WINCD 038) / Griffin; <404>* **BBC RADIO 1 LIVE IN CONCERT** –

Feb 94. (cd) *Loma; (LOMACD 10)* **SLATES / PART OF AMERICA IN THERIN 1981** –

Aug 94. (cd) *Matador; <OLE 62>* **THE LEAGUE OF BALD HEADED MEN** –

Feb 96. (cd) *Receiver; (<RRCD 209>)* **SINISTER WALTZ**

Apr 96. (cd) *Receiver; (<RRCD 211>)* **FIEND WITH A VIOLIN**

Apr 96. (cd/lp) *Receiver; (<RRCD/RRLP 213>)* **OSWALD DEFENCE LAWYER**

Oct 96. (3xcd-box) *Receiver; (<RRXCD 506>)* **THE OTHER SIDE OF THE FALL** (above 3 albums)

Apr 97. (d-cd) *Cog Sinister – Voiceprint; (COGVP 102CD)* **FALL IN A HOLE** –
(was originally a New Zealand release on 'Flying Nun') (re-iss. Nov97 on 'Resurgence'; RSG 4016) (re-iss. Nov01 on 'Cog Sinister'; COGVP 102CD) (re-iss. Dec02 on 'Cog Sinister'; COGVP 137CD)

Jun 97. (d-cd) *Snapper; (<SMDCD 132>)* **THE LESS YOU LOOK THE MORE YOU FIND**

Aug 97. (cd) *Receiver; (RRCD 239)* **15 WAYS TO LEAVE YOUR MAN (live)** –

Nov 97. (cd) *Receiver; (<RRCD 246>)* **OXYMORON**

Nov 97. (cd) *Rialto; (<RMCD 214>)* **THE FALL ARCHIVES**

Dec 97. (cd) *Receiver; (<RRCD 247>)* **CHEETHAM HILL**

Mar 98. (cd) *Strange Fruit; (SFRSCD 048)* **THE PEEL SESSIONS** –

Mar 98. (cd) *Castle; (CCSCD 823)* **SMILE . . . IT'S THE BEST OF THE FALL** –

Apr 98. (cd) *Cog Sinister – Voiceprint; (COGVP 108CD)* **LIVE ON AIR IN MELBOURNE 1982 (live)** –
(re-iss. Nov01; same)

Jun 98. (cd) *M.C.I.; (MCCD 350)* **NORTHERN ATTITUDE** –

Jun 98. (cd) *Artful; (ARTFULCD 3)* **IN THE CITY (live in Manchester 1995)**

Aug 98. (cd) *Cog Sinister – Voiceprint; (COGVP 111CD)* **LIVE VARIOUS YEARS (live)** –
(re-iss. Nov01; same)

Jan 99. (3xcd-box) *Receiver; (RRXCD 508)* **THE FALL BOX SET** –

Jan 99. (cd) *Strange Fruit; (SFRSCD 048)* **THE PEEL SESSIONS** –

Feb 00. (cd/d-lp) *Artful; (ARTFUL CD/LP 30)* **A PAST GONE MAD (THE BEST OF 1990-2000)** –

Aug 00. (3xcd-box) *Eagle; (EEECD 010)* **PSYKICK DANCEHALL – THE MASTERS** –

Feb 01. (d-cd) *Artful; (ARTFULCD 35)* **A WORLD BEWITCHED – THE BEST OF THE FALL 1990-2000** –

Feb 01. (cd) *Cog Sinister; (COGVP 115CD)* **LIVE IN CAMBRIDGE 1988 (live)** –

Jun 01. (cd) *Cog Sinister; (COGVP 109CD)* **LIVE IN ZAGREB (live)** –

Nov 01. (cd) *Cog Sinister; (COGVP 125CD)* **LIVE IN REYKJAVIK (May 6th 1983)** –

Nov 01. (cd) *Cog Sinister; (COGVP 127CD)* **BACKDROP** –

Nov 01. (cd) *Cog Sinister; (COGVP 110CD)* **LIVE IN NOTTINGHAM (live)** –

Dec 01. (cd) *Cog Sinister; (COGVP 115CD)* **LIVE IN CAMBRIDGE 1988 (live)** –

Dec 01. (cd) *Cog Sinister; (COGVP 118CD)* **LIVERPOOL '78 – LIVE AT MR. PICKWICK'S LIVERPOOL 1978** –

Apr 02. (cd) *Cog Sinister; (COGVP 114CD)* **LIVE 1977** –

Jun 02. (cd) *Cog Sinister; (COGVP 112CD)* **LIVE AT THE DERBY HALL, BURY 1982 (live)** –

Jul 02. (d-cd) *Castle; (CMDDD 461) / Sanctuary; <81205>* **TOTALLY WIRED: THE ROUGH TRADE ANTHOLOGY** Aug02

Jul 02. (4xcd-box) *Castle; (CMEBX 526)* **THE ROUGH TRADE SINGLES BOX** –

Sep 02. (d-cd) *Snapper; (SMDCD 443) / Recall; <443>* **HIGH TENSION LINE** Oct02

Nov 02. (cd) *Cog Sinister; (COGVP 132CD)* **LISTENING IN: LOST SINGLES TRACKS 1990-92** [ ] [-]
Feb 03. (cd) *Cog Sinister; (COGVP 143CD)* **LIVE IN AMERICA (live)** [ ] [-]
Mar 03. (cd) *Castle; (CMQCD 697) / Sanctuary; <81303>* **IT'S THE NEW THING! – THE STEP FORWARD YEARS** [ ] Jun03 [ ]
Apr 03. (3xcd-box) *Castle; (CMETD 706) / Sanctuary; <81304>* **TIME ENOUGH AT LAST** (out-takes & live) [ ] [ ]
– OXYMORON / CHEETHAM HILL / 15 WAYS TO LEAVE YOUR MAN)
Jun 03. (d-cd) *Burning Airlines; (<PILOT 173>)* **THE IDIOT JOY SHOW** (rare live) [ ] Sep03 [ ]
Jul 03. (5xcd-box) *Castle; (CMYBX 752) / Sanctuary; <81315>* **TOUCH SENSITIVE . . .BOOTLEG BOX SET (live)** [ ] Sep03 [ ]
Aug 03. (cd) *Strange Fruit; (SFRSCD 120)* **LIVE AT THE PHOENIX FESTIVAL (live)** [ ] [-]
Sep 03. (d-cd) *Voiceprint; (VO 241 004CD)* **LIVE IN CAMBRIDGE / LIVE VARIOUS YEARS** [ ] [-]
Sep 03. (d-cd) *Voiceprint; (VP 241 019CD)* **IN A HOLE / LIVERPOOL 1978 (live)** [ ] [-]
Oct 03. (cd) *Fontana; (077000-2)* **THE WAR AGAINST INTELLIGENCE: THE FONTANA YEARS** [ ] [-]

FAMILY

Formed: Leicester, England . . . 1967 by CHARLIE WHITNEY, ROGER CHAPMAN, JIM KING and RIC GRECH. They had stemmed from The FARINAS, a band who existed for 5 years and who issued one single in 1964 for 'Fontana'; YOU'D BETTER STOP / I LIKE IT LIKE THAT. After moving to London, the band made their debut at The Royal Albert Hall in July '67 supporting TIM HARDIN. Signing to 'Reprise' in 1968, following a one-off 7" for 'Liberty', TRAFFIC's DAVE MASON & JIMMY MILLER produced the debut album, 'MUSIC FROM A DOLL'S HOUSE', which made the UK Top 40. CHAPMAN's unmistakable, frog-in throat vocal style, complemented by WHITNEY's distinctive guitar and GRECH's violin, created an enduring classic and soon marked the band out as cult favourites. The follow-up, 'ENTERTAINMENT', included 'WEAVER'S ANSWER', a song which went on to become a staple of the band's infamous live show. Soon after the album's release, GRECH departed for BLIND FAITH, being replaced by JOHN WEIDER. The band also recruited POLI PALMER on keyboards in place of saxophonist KING before releasing two Top 10 albums within a year, 'A SONG FOR ME' & 'ANYWAY'. Unusually for a prog-rock outfit, FAMILY were no strangers to hit singles, the classic 'IN MY OWN TIME' (from 'ANYWAY') reaching No.4, following on from the memorable successes 'NO MULES FOOL' and 'STRANGE BAND'. During the next three years the band went through yet more personnel shifts, perhaps accounting for the inconsistency of their last two albums. While 'FEARLESS' was quite impressive, 'BANDSTAND' was patchy, although it did spawn one of their last hits, 'BURLESQUE'. FAMILY then moved to the 'Raft' label where they recorded their final, slightly disappointing effort, 'IT'S ONLY A MOVIE', in 1973. The album was a complete flop and the band broke up, CHAPMAN and WHITNEY going on to form the more basic STREETWALKERS. CHAPMAN has released numerous solo albums, beginning with 'CHAPPO' in '79. Included on these albums were a number of covers:- LET'S SPEND THE NIGHT TOGETHER (Rolling Stones) / I'M YOUR HOOCHIE COOCHIE MAN + THAT SAME THING (Willie Dixon) / KEEP A KNOCKIN' (Little Richard) / I'M A KING BEE (Sam Moore) / STONE FREE (Jimi Hendrix) / LOVE LETTERS IN THE SAND (Pat Boone?) / SLOW DOWN (Hank Williams) / BUSTED LOOSE (Paul Brady) / KEEP FORGETTING (Leiber-Stoller) / TALKING ABOUT YOU (Chuck Berry).

Album rating: MUSIC IN A DOLL'S HOUSE (*8) / ENTERTAINMENT (*7) / A SONG FOR ME (*6) / ANYWAY (*6) / OLD SONGS NEW SONGS remixes (*7) / FEARLESS (*7) / BANDSTAND (*6) / IT'S ONLY A MOVIE (*4) / THE BEST OF FAMILY compilation (*9) / Streetwalkers: STREETWALKERS (*4) / DOWNTOWN FLYERS (*4) / RED CARD (*5) / VICIOUS BUT FAIR (*4) / LIVE (*4) / THE BEST OF STREETWALKERS compilation (*5) / Roger CHAPMAN: CHAPPO (*5) / LIVE IN HAMBURG (*5) / MAIL ORDER MAGIC (*4) / HYENAS ONLY LAUGH FOR FUN (*4) / HE WAS SHE WAS YOU WAS WE WAS (*4) / MANGO CRAZY (*4) / THE SHADOW KNOWS (*5) / ZIPPER (*4) / TECHNO-PRISONERS (*4) / WALKING THE CAT (*5) / HYBRID AND LOWDOWN (*5) / UNDER NO OBLIGATION (*4) / KICK IT BACK compilation (*6) / KISS MY SOUL (*4)

ROGER CHAPMAN (b. 8 Apr'44) – vocals / **CHARLIE WHITNEY** (b. 4 Jun'44) – guitar, vocals / **JIM KING** (b.1945) – saxophone, flute / **RICK GRECH** (b. 1 Nov'46, Bordeaux, France) – bass / **HARRY OVENALL** – drums

Liberty — not iss.

Sep 67. (7") *(LBF 15031)* **SCENE THRU THE EYE OF A LENS. / GYPSY WOMAN** [ ] [-]

— **ROB TOWNSEND** (b. 7 Jul'47) – drums repl. HARRY

Reprise — Reprise

Jun 68. (7") *(RS 23270)* **ME AND MY FRIEND. / HEY MR. POLICEMAN** [ ] [ ]
Jul 68. (7") *<0786>* **OLD SONGS NEW SONGS. / HEY MR. POLICEMAN** [-] [ ]
Jul 68. (lp; mono/stereo) *(<RLP/RSLP 6312>)* **MUSIC IN A DOLL'S HOUSE** [35] [ ]
– The chase / Mellowing grey / Never like this / Me and my friend / Variation on a theme of Hey Mr. Policeman / Winter / Old songs new songs / Variation on a theme of the breeze / Hey Mr. Policeman / See through windows / Variation on a theme of me and my friend / Peace of mind / Voyage / The breeze / 3 x time. *(re-iss. Sep87 on 'See For Miles' lp/c/cd; SEE/+K/CD 100) (<cd re-mast.Jun03 on 'Pucka'; PUC 701>)*
Nov 68. (7") *(RS 23315) <0809>* **SECOND GENERATION WOMAN. / HOME TOWN** [ ] [ ]
Mar 69. (lp; mono/stereo) *(<RLP/RSLP 6340>)* **FAMILY ENTERTAINMENT** [6] [ ]
– The weaver's answer / Observations from a hill / Hung up down / Summer '67 / How-hi-the-li / Second generation woman / From past archives / Dim / Processions / Face in the crowd / Emotions. *(re-iss. Sep87 on 'See For Miles' lp/c/cd; SEE/+K/CD 200) (<cd re-mast.Jun03 on 'Pucka'; PUC 702>)*

— **JOHN WEIDER** (b.21 Apr'47) – bass, violin (ex-ERIC BURDON & ANIMALS) repl. GRECH who joined BLIND FAITH

Oct 69. (7") *(RS 27001) <0881>* **NO MULE'S FOOL. / GOOD FRIEND OF MINE** [29] [ ]

— **POLI PALMER** (b. JOHN, 25 May'43) – keyboards, vibes (ex-ECLECTION) repl. KING who joined RING OF TRUTH

Jan 70. (lp) *(RSLP 9001) <6384>* **A SONG FOR ME** [4] [ ]
– Drowned in wine / Some poor soul / Love is a sleeper / Stop for the traffic (through the heart of me) / Wheels / Song for sinking lovers / Hey let it rock / The cat and the rat / 93's ok J. / A song for me. *(re-iss. Nov88 on 'See For Miles' lp/cd; SEE/+CD 240) (cd re-iss. Nov93 on 'Castle'; CLACD 376) (cd re-iss. Mar98 on 'Essential'; ESMCD 616)*
Apr 70. (7") *(RS 27005)* **TODAY. / SONG FOR SINKING LOVERS** [ ] [ ]
Aug 70. (7"m) *(RS 27009)* **STRANGE BAND. / THE WEAVER'S ANSWER / HUNG UP DOWN** [11] [ ]

Reprise — U.A.

Nov 70. (lp) *(RSX 9005) <5527>* **ANYWAY . . .** (half live) [7] [ ]
– Good news bad news / Holding the compass / Strange band / Willow tree / Part of the load / Anyway / Normans / Lives and ladies. *(re-iss. Nov88 on 'See For Miles' lp/cd; SEE/+CD 245) (re-iss. cd May94 on 'Castle'; CLACD 375) (cd re-iss. Mar98 on 'Essential'; ESMCD 615) (cd re-mast.Sep03 on 'Mystic'+=; MYSCD 171)* – Strange band (alt.) / Part of the load (live) / Lives and ladies (live).
Mar 71. (lp) *(RMP 9007) <6413>* **OLD SONGS NEW SONGS** (compilation remixed) [ ] [ ]
– Hung up down / Today / Observations from a hill / Good friend of mine / Drowned in wine / Peace of mind / Home town / The cat and the rat / No mule's fool / See through windows / The weaver's answer. *(cd-iss. Mar92 on 'See For Miles'; SEECD 334)*

Jun 71. (7") *(K 14090) <50832>* **IN MY OWN TIME. / SEASONS** [4] [ ]

—— **JOHN WETTON** (b.12 Jul'49, Derby, England) – bass, vocals (ex-MOGUL THRASH) repl. WEIDER who joined STUD

Oct 71. (lp) *(K 54003) <5562>* **FEARLESS** [14] [ ]
– Between blue and me / Sat'd'y barfly / Larf and sing / Spanish tide / Save some for thee / Take your partners / Children / Crinkly grin / Blind / Burning bridges. *(re-iss. cd Feb93 on 'Castle'; CLACD 324) (cd re-iss. Aug97 on 'Essential'; ESMCD 567) (cd re-mast.Sep03 on 'Mystic'+=; MYSCD 172)* – In my own time / SEasons / Between blue and me (live) / Sing 'em the way I feel (live).

Nov 71. (7") *<50882>* **BETWEEN BLUE AND ME. / LARF & SING** [–] [ ]

Sep 72. (7") *(K 14196) <50951>* **BURLESQUE. / THE ROCKIN' R'S** [13] [ ]

Sep 72. (lp) *(K 54006) <5644>* **BANDSTAND** [15] [ ]
– Burlesque / Bolero babe / Coronation / Dark eyes / Broken nose / My friend the sun / Glove / Ready to go / Top of the hill. *(re-iss. Nov88 on 'See For Miles' lp/cd; SEE/+CD 241) (cd re-iss. Mar94 on 'Castle'; CLACD 322) (cd re-iss. Aug97 on 'Essential'; ESMCD 565) (cd re-mast.Sep03 on 'Mystic'+=; MYSCD 173)* – The rockin' R's / No mule's fool (live) / Good news bad news (live) / The weaver's answer (live).

Jan 73. (7") *(K 14218) <171>* **MY FRIEND THE SUN. / GLOVE** [ ] [ ]

—— CHAPMAN, WHITNEY and TOWNSEND were joined by **JIM CREGAN** – bass, guitar (ex-STUD) repl. WETTON who joined KING CRIMSON / **TONY ASHTON** (b. 1 Mar'46, Blackburn, England) – keyboards (ex-ASHTON, GARDNER and DYKE) repl. PALMER

Raft U.A.

Apr 73. (7") *(RA 18501)* **BOOM BANG. / STOP THIS CAR** [ ] [ ]

Sep 73. (7") *(RA 18503)* **SWEET DESIREE. / DRINK TO YOU** [ ] [ ]

Sep 73. (lp) *(RA 58501) <UALA 181>* **IT'S ONLY A MOVIE** [30] [ ]
– It's only a movie / Leroy / Buffet tea for two / Boom bang / Boots 'n' roots / Banger / Sweet Desiree / Suspicion / Check out. *(cd-iss. Aug97 on 'Essential'; ESMCD 566) (cd re-mast.Sep03 on 'Mystic'+=; MYSCD 174)* – Hometown / Hold the compass (live) / Weaver's answer (live) / Dim (live) / Procession / No mules fool (live).

Oct 73. (7") *<416>* **IT'S ONLY A MOVIE. / SUSPICION** [–] [ ]

—— They split late '73 with TOWNSEND joining MEDICINE HEAD and CREGAN went to COCKNEY REBEL, ASHTON went into production. ROGER and CHARLIE formed CHAPMAN / WHITNEY STREETWALKERS, who released a number of albums before ROGER went solo in 1979 (see GREAT ROCK DISCOGRAPHY)

– compilations, etc. –

on 'Reprise' UK, or 'United Artists' in the States

Sep 74. (lp) *Reprise; (K 54023)* **THE BEST OF FAMILY** [ ] [–]
– Burlesque / My friend the Sun / The chase / Old songs, new songs / Part of the load / In my own time / It's only a movie / Sweet desiree / Sat'd'y barfly / Children / No mule's fool / The weaver's answer. *(re-iss. Nov91 on 'See For Miles' lp/cd+=; SEE/+CD 330) (cd re-iss. Jul94 on 'Line'; CRCD 901238)*

Nov 74. (7") *(K 14378)* **MY FRIEND THE SUN. / BURLESQUE** [ ] [–]

May 78. (7"ep) *(K 14487)* **BURLESQUE. / IN MY OWN TIME / THE WEAVER'S ANSWER** [ ] [–]

Oct 81. (lp) *Rebecca; (BEC 777)* **RISE . . . VERY BEST OF FAMILY** [ ] [–]

Jan 82. (7") *Rebecca; (BECS 77)* **BURLESQUE. / MY FRIEND THE SUN** [ ] [–]

Nov 88. (12"ep/cd-ep) *Strange Fruit; (SFPS/+CD 061)* **THE PEEL SESSIONS** (8.5.73) [ ] [–]

Aug 89. (d-lp/d-c/d-cd) *That's Original; (TFO LP/MC/CD 22)* **IT'S ONLY A MOVIE / FEARLESS** [ ] [–]

Oct 91. (cd) *Windsong; (WINCD 001)* **BBC RADIO 1 LIVE IN CONCERT** [ ] [–]

Nov 92. (cd) *Castle; (CCSCD 354)* **THE COLLECTION – THE SINGLES A's & B's** [ ] [–]

Mar 93. (cd/c) *Castle; (CCS CD/MC 374)* **THE BEST OF FAMILY** [ ] [–]

Mar 93. (cd) *Dutch East India; (DEI 8333-2)* **THE PEEL SESSIONS** [ ] [–]

Feb 00. (d-cd) *Essential; (ESDCD 839)* **ANTHOLOGY** [ ] [–]

Apr 00. (d-lp) *Get Back; (TPM 204)* **BBC RADIO SHOW 1973 (live)** [ ] [–]

Sep 03. (cd) *Mystic; (MYSCD 176)* **LIVE (live)** [ ] [–]

Oct 03. (d-cd) *Pucka; (PUC 1968)* **MUSIC IN A DOLL'S HOUSE / FAMILY ENTERTAINMENT** [ ] [–]

STREETWALKERS

ROGER CHAPMAN – vocals / **CHARLIE WHITNEY** – guitar / **BOBBY TENCH** – guitar, vocals (ex-JEFF BECK) / **PHILIP CHEN** – bass / **TIM HINKLEY** – keyboards / **MEL COLLINS** – saxophone, flute / **IAN WALLACE** – drums (both ex-KING CRIMSON)

Reprise Mercury

May 74. (lp) *(K 54017) <SRMI 1060>* **STREETWALKERS** [ ] [ ]
– Parisienne high heels / Roxianna / Systematic stealth / Call ya / Creature feature / Sue and Betty Jean / Showbiz Joe / Just four men / Tokyo rose / Hangman.

Jun 74. (7") *(K 14357)* **ROXIANNA. / CRACK** [ ] [–]

—— **JON PLOTEL** – bass (ex-CASABLANCA) repl. CHEN & HINKLEY (to sessions) / **NICKO McBAIN** – drums repl. WALLACE & COLLINS (to ALVIN LEE ⇒ TEN YEARS AFTER)

Vertigo Mercury

Oct 75. (lp) *(6360 123)* **DOWNTOWN FLYERS** [ ] [–]
– Downtown flyers / Toenail draggin' / Raingame / Miller / Crawfish / Walking on waters / Gypsy moon / Burn it down / Ace o' spades. *(cd-iss. Apr02 on 'Beat Goes On'; BGOCD 542)*

Oct 75. (7") *(6059 130)* **RAINGAME. / MILLER** [ ] [–]

May 76. (red-lp) *(9102 010) <SRMI 1083>* **RED CARD** [16] [ ]
– Run for cover / Me an' me horse an' me rum / Crazy charade / Daddy rolling stone / Roll up, roll up / Between us / Shotgun messiah / Decadence code. *(cd-iss. Aug91 on 'Repertoire'; REP 4147WP)*

Jun 76. (7") *(6059 144)* **DADDY ROLLING STONE. / HOLE IN YOUR POCKET** [ ] [–]

—— **CHAPMAN, WHITNEY + TENCH** were joined by **MICKY FEAT** – bass / **DAVID DOWLE** – drums / **BRIAN JOHNSON** – keyboards (**McBAIN** joined **PAT TRAVERS** and later **IRON MAIDEN**)

Jan 77. (lp) *(9102 012) <SRMI 1135>* **VICIOUS BUT FAIR** [ ] [ ]
– Mama was mad / Chili con carne / Dice man / But you're beautiful / Can't come in / Belle star / Sam (maybe he can come to some arrangement) / Cross time woman. *(cd-iss. Aug92 on 'See For Miles'+=; SEECD 352)* – Downtown flyers / Gypsy Moon / Crawfish / Raingame / Crazy charade / Shotgun Messiah / Decadence code / Daddy rolling stone.

Dec 77. (d-lp) *(6641 703)* **LIVE (live)** [ ] [–]
– Chilli con carne / Crazy charade / Walking on waters / Dice man / My friend the Sun / Toenail draggin' / Mama was mad / Me an' me horse an' me rum / Run for cover / Burlesque / Can't come in.

—— Had already split, TENCH and FEAT joined VAN MORRISON. JOHNSON and DOWLE joined DAVID COVERDALE'S WHITESNAKE.

– compilations, etc. –

Dec 90. (cd/c/lp) *Vertigo; (846661-2/-4/-1)* **THE BEST OF STREETWALKERS** [ ] [–]

Jun 94. (cd) *Windsong;* **BBC RADIO 1 LIVE IN CONCERT** [ ] [–]

ROGER CHAPMAN

went solo, augmented by MICKEY JUPP

Arista Arista

Mar 79. (lp/c) *(SPART/TC-SPART 1083)* **CHAPPO** [ ] [ ]
– Midnite child / Moth to a flame / Keep forgettin' / Shape of things / Face of stone / Who pulled the nite down / Always gotta pay in the end / Hang on to a dream / Pills / Don't give up. *(re-iss. 1988 on 'Maze' lp/cd; 604629/764630) (cd-iss. Jul92 on 'Castle' cd/c; CLACD/CLAMC 299) (cd re-iss. Mar99 on 'Essential'; ESMCD 678)*

Mar 79. (7") *(ARIST 244)* **MIDNITE CHILD. / MOTH TO A FLAME** [ ] [–]

Acrobat not iss.

May 79. (7") *(BAT 5)* **WHO PULLED THE NIGHT DOWN. / SHORTLIST** [ ] [–]

Jul 79. (7") *(BAT 9)* **LET'S SPEND THE NIGHT TOGETHER. / SHAPE OF THINGS** [ ] [–]

Dec 79. (lp/c) *(ACT/TC-ACT 6)* **LIVE IN HAMBURG (live w/ The SHORTLIST)** [ ] [–]
– Moth to a flame / Keep forgettin' / Midnite child / Who pulled the nite down / Talking about you / Shortlist / Can't get in / Keep a knockin' / I'm your hoochie coochie man / Let's spend the night together. *(re-iss. 1988 on 'Maze' lp/cd; 604627/764635) (cd re-iss. Nov92 on 'Castle'; CLACD 320) (cd re-iss. Mar99 on 'Essential'; ESMCD 692)*

B.B.C. not iss.

Oct 80. (7") *(RESL 85)* **SPEAK FOR YOURSELF. / SWEET VANILLA** [ ] [–]

— with **PALMER / HINKLEY / WHITEHORN**

Kamera not iss.

Sep 81. (lp) *(KAM 001)* **MAIL ORDER MAGIC** ☐ –
– Unknown soldier (can't get to Heaven) / He was, she was / Barman / Right to go / Duelling man / Making the same mistake / Another little hurt / Mail order magic / Higher ground / Ground floor. *(re-iss. 1988 on 'Maze' lp/cd; 604627/764636) (re-iss. Dec92 on 'Castle' cd/c; CLA CD/MC 301) (cd re-iss. Mar99 on 'Essential'; ESMCD 564) (cd re-mast.Jul03 on 'Mystic'; MYSCD 167)*

Teldec not iss.

Dec 81. (lp) *(AS6/HCT4 24850)* **HYENAS ONLY LAUGH FOR FUN** – German –
– Prisoner / Hyenas only laugh for fun / Killing time / Want's nothing chained / The long goodbye / Blood and sand / Common touch / Goodbye (reprise) / Hearts on the floor / Step up – Take a bow / Jukebox mama. *(UK-iss.1988 on 'Maze' lp/cd; 604625/764626) (cd re-iss. Jun92 on 'Castle'; CLACD 305)*

Polydor not iss.

Oct 82. (d-lp) *(2646 106)* **HE WAS SHE WAS YOU WAS WE WAS (live)** – German –
– Higher ground / Ducking down / Making the same mistake / Blood and sand / Medley:- I'm a king bee – That same thing – Face of stone / Hyeanas only laugh for fun / Prisoner / Medley:- Slow down – Common touch / Jukebox mama No.3 / He was, she was / Stone free / Bitches brew / Unknown soldier. *(UK-iss.1988 on 'Maze' lp/cd; 084 624/854633) (cd re-iss. Apr94 on 'Castle'; CLACD 373)*

Mar 83. (lp) *(on 'Instant'; 28532)* **MANGO CRAZY** – German –
– Mango crazy / Toys: Do you? / I read your file / Los dos Bailadores / Blues breaker / Turn it up loud / Let me down / Hunt the man / Rivers run dry / I really can't go straight / Room service / Hegoshegoyougoamigo. *(re-iss. 1988 on 'Maze' lp/cd; 604623/764634) (cd-iss. Jun92 on 'Castle'; CLACD 304)*

— (CHAPMAN provided vocals for MIKE OLDFIELD on single 'Shadow On The Wall')

Apr 84. (7") *(POSP 683)* **HOW HOW HOW. / HOLD THAT TIDE BACK** ☐ –

R.C.A. not iss.

May 85. (lp/c) *(ZL/ZK 70482)* **THE SHADOW KNOWS** ☐ –
– Busted loose / Leader of men / Ready to roll / I think of you now / The shadow knows / How how how / Only love is in the red / Sweet vanilla / I'm a good boy now. *(cd-iss. 1988; ZD 70482) (re-iss. cd Mar94 on 'Castle'; CLACD 370)*

1986. (lp/c/cd) *(PL/PK/PD 70989)* **ZIPPER** – German –
– Zipper / Running with the flame / On do die day / Never love a rolling stone / Let the beat get heavy / It's never too late to do-ron-ron / Woman of destiny / Hoodoo me up.

1987. (lp/cd) *(PL/PD 71516)* **TECHNO-PRISONERS** – German –
– The drum / Wild again / Techno-prisoner / Black forest / We will touch again / Run for your love / Slap bang in the middle / Who's been sleeping in my bed / Ball of confusion. *(re-iss. cd Mar94 on 'Castle'; CLACD 371) (cd re-mast.Jul03 on 'Mystic'; MYSCD 168)*

Maze not iss.

1989. (cd) *(854632)* **WALKING THE CAT** – German –
– Kick it back / Son of Red moon / Stranger than strange / Just a step away (let's go) / The fool / Walking the cat / J & D / Come the dark night / Hands off / Jivin' / Saturday night kick back. *(UK cd-iss. Nov93 on 'Castle'; CLACD 372)*

Nov 89. (m-lp) *(604639)* **LIVE IN BERLIN (live)** ☐ –
– Shadow on the wall / Let me down / How how how / Mango crazy. *(cd-iss. Dec92 on 'Castle'; CLACD 313)*

Polydor not iss.

1990. (lp) *(847117-1)* **HYBRID AND LOWDOWN** – German –
– Hot night to rhumba / Holding on / Breaking away / Beautifully indecent / Susie roll / Someone else's clothes / Chicken fingers / House behind the sun / Sushi rock / Is there anybody out there? / Cops in shades / Bye bye love. *(cd-iss. Feb00 on 'Essential'; ESMCD 731)*

Essential not iss.

1992. (cd/c) *(ESM CD/MC 175)* **KICK IT BACK** (compilation) ☐ –
– Walking the cat / Cops in shades / House behind the sun / Chicken fingers / Kick it back / Son of red Moon / Someone else's clothes / Hideaway / Toys: Do you? / Hot night to rhumba / Stranger than strange / Just a step away (let's go) / Jesus and the Devil. *(re-iss. Aug96; same)*

May 96. (cd) *(ESSCD 382)* **KISS MY SOUL** ☐ –
– Into the bright / Habits of a lifetime / A cat called Komono / Pne more whisky / Kiss my soul / Outside looking in / Beautiful dreamers / It's all over now baby blue / Mistreated / Song of desire / Two pieces of silver / Really started something. *(re-iss. Mar01 on 'Castle'; CMRCD 182)*

– compilations, etc. –

Oct 98. (d-cd) *Essential; (ESDCD 665)* **THE BEST OF ROGER CHAPMAN** ☐ –
Feb 00. (cd) *Line; (901357)* **THE LEGENDARY FUNNY CIDER SESSIONS 1081/83** ☐ –
Dec 00. (cd) *Thunderbolt; (CDTB 217)* **MOTH TO A FLAME** ☐ –
May 01. (d-cd) *Thunderbolt; (CDTBD 017)* **BEFORE YOUR VERY EYES / RIFF BURGLAR** ☐ –
May 01. (cd) *Thunderbolt; (CSA 110)* **SELECTA: THE BEST OF 1979-1981** ☐ –
Feb 02. (cd) *S.P.V.; (2301895-2)* **A TURN UNSTONED** ☐ –
Feb 03. (cd) *Mystic; (MYSCD 146)* **ROLLIN' AND TUMBLIN'** ☐ –
Mar 03. (4xcd-box) *Mystic; (MYSCD 161)* **FAMILY AND FRIENDS** ☐ –
Mar 03. (3xcd-box) *Trilogie; (205975)* **IN MY OWN TIME** ☐ –
Jul 03. (d-cd) *Gemini; (220454303)* **ROGER CHAPMAN** ☐ –

☐ FANATICS (see under ⇒ OCEAN COLOUR SCENE)

☐ Jay FARRAR (see under ⇒ SON VOLT)

☐ Perry FARRELL (see under ⇒ JANE'S ADDICTION)

☐ FATBOY SLIM (see under ⇒ COOK, Norman)

FAUST

Formed: Hamburg, Germany ... 1970 by producer UWE NETTELBECK, who was given money to assemble a collective of musicians in his Wumme studios. These numbered RUDOLF SOSNA, HANS-JOACHIM IRMLER, JEAN-HERVE PERON, GUNTER WUSTHOFF and ARNULF MEIFERT; the latter being replaced by WERNER DIERMEYER in 1971. Following in the footsteps of CAN, TANGERINE DREAM and AMON DUUL II, they became an integral part of the burgeoning underground "krautrock" scene. Early recordings for 'Polydor', although strikingly innovative, failed to gain any widespread commercial appeal outside Germany. However, 'THE FAUST TAPES' (a 'Virgin' sampler of unreleased tunes) introduced them to the UK and sold a respectable quantity due to its 49p price-tag. This unfortunately disqualified it from chart returns. Inspired by a myriad of influences that took in everything from KARL-HEINZ STOCKHAUSEN to The BEATLES to The MOTHERS OF INVENTION, they left conventional song structures at the starting gate. Instead they opted for a continuous collage of musical set pieces which nevertheless had the potential to be great 3-minute songs. Alternately delighting and disgusting audiences, they were prone to playing pinball machines and wielding pneumatic drills on stage. They toured this bizarre spectacle around Europe after Richard Branson's 'Virgin' issued 'FAUST IV' while in 1974, they recorded an album with American minimalist TONY CONRAD (he had earlier been in The DREAM SYNDICATE; part of JOHN CALE's pre-VELVET days). Eventually FAUST faded away into obscurity but were re-called for a one-off gig at London's Marquee on the 25th of October '92. Their comeback albums, 'RIEN' and 'YOU KNOW FAUST', were issued between 1996-1997 and they were lined up for another rare live appearance at the Edinburgh Festival. • **Trivia:** UWE also produced for SLAPP HAPPY. Were and still are one of JULIAN COPE's (ex-TEARDROP EXPLODES) fave bands.

Album rating: FAUST (*7) / FAUST SO FAR (*8) / THE FAUST TAPES (*5 at the time – *8 now!?) / FAUST IV (*5) / MUNICH & ELSEWHERE collection (*5) / 71 MINUTES OF FAUST compilation (*7) / RIEN (*4) / YOU KNOW FAUST (*6) / LIVE IN EDINBURGH – AUGUST 1997 (*6) / FAUST WAKES NOSFERATU (*5) / RAVVIVANDO (*7)

RUDOLF SOSNA – guitar, keyboards / **HANS-JOACHIM IRMLER** – organ / **WERNER DIERMEIER** – drums; repl. ARNULF MEIFERT who contributed to recordings in 1971 / **JEAN-HERVE PERON** – bass / **GUNTER WUSTHOFF** – saxophone, synthesizer

Polydor not iss.

Jan 72. (clear-lp) *(2310 142)* **FAUST**
– Why don't you eat carrots / Meadow meal / Miss Fortune. *(re-iss. Oct79 as 'FAUST ONE' on 'Recommended'; RRA 1) (cd-iss. Nov96 on 'Klangbad'; KLANG 01) (cd re-iss. Jul01 on 'ReR'; RERF 6)*

Jul 72. (lp) *(2310 196)* **FAUST SO FAR**
– It's a rainy day, sunshine girl / On the way to Abamae / No harm / So far / Mamie is blue / I've got my car and my T.V. / Picnic on a frozen river / Me back space . . . / . . . In the spirit. *(re-iss. Oct79 on 'Recommended'; R.R.TWO) (cd-iss. Jul01 on 'ReR'; RERF 7)*

Aug 72. (7") *(2001 299)* **IT'S A BIT OF A PAIN. / SO FAR**
(re-iss. 1979 on 'Recommended'; RR 2)

Caroline not iss.

1972. (lp; by TONY CONRAD & FAUST) *(C 1501)*
OUTSIDE THE DREAM SYNDICATE
– From the side of man and womankind / From the side of the machine / From the side of woman and mankind. *(cd-iss. Feb94 on 'Southern'; LITHIUM 2) <(cd re-iss. Apr98 on 'Table Of Elements'; LITHIUM 6)> (d-cd-iss. Nov02 on 'Table Of The Elements'+=; SWCCD 3)* – (bonus CD).

Virgin not iss.

1973. (lp) *(V 2004)* **FAUST IV**
– Krautrock / The sad skinhead / Jennifer / Just a second (starts like that!) / Picnic on a frozen river, deuxieme tableux / Giggy smile / Lauft . . . heisst das es lauft oder es kommt bald . . . lauft / It's a bit of a pain. *(cd-iss. Oct92 & Jul97; CDV 2004) <US cd-iss. Oct92 on 'Caroline'; CAROL 1885-2>*

1973. (lp) *(VC 501)* **THE FAUST TAPES** (rec. 1971-73; tracks were originally untitled)
– Flash-back Caruso / J'ai mal aux dents (I have a toothache) / Humphrey Bogart / Doctor Schwitters / 7/5/4 / Los Hideros / Finnish Autumn / Stretch out / Der baum (the tree) / Ma chambre (my room). *(re-iss. 1980 on 'Recommended'; RRA 6) (cd-iss. Apr91 as 'THE LAST ALBUM'; RERF 2CD) (cd re-iss. Feb94 & Jun96 & Dec01 on 'ReR'; RERF 2CD)*

— added **PETER BLEGVAD** – guitar, clarinet, vocals

— disbanded in 1973 and PETER BLEGVAD went solo. However, they (**IRMLER, DEIRMEIER + PERON**) did re-form in 1990 for a Prinzenbar, Hamburg concert and London Marquee gig on 25th October '92

Recommended Recommended

Jan 97. (cd) *(<RERF 3CD>)* **YOU KNOW FAUST** Feb97
– Hurricane / Tenne laufen / C pluus / Pause / Irons / Cendre / Sixty sixty / Winds / Liebeswehen / Elektron 2 / Ella / Pause / Men from the Moon / Der pfad / Noizes from Pythagoras / Na sowas / L'oiseau / Huttenfreak / Teutonentango. *(lp-iss.Feb98 on 'Klangbad'; KLANGBAD 1) (re-iss. Oct98 on 'Recommended'; F 4CD)*

— the trio added **KEIJI HAINO + MICHAEL MORLEY + STEVEN WRAY LOBDELL** – guitars / **JIM O'ROURKE** – tapes

Table Of Elements Table Of Elements

Jun 97. (cd) *(<CHROMIUM 24>)* **RIEN** (rec. 1995) 1996
– Rien / untitled / Long distance calls in the desert / Eroberung der stille, teil II / untitled / Eroberung der stille, teil I / Fin.

— Table Of The Elements also split a 45 with SLAPP HAPPY, 'SORT OF'

— **DIERMEIER, IRMLER + LOBDELL** recruited **MICHAEL STOLL** – bass / **LARS PAUKSTAT** – percussion

Klangbad EFA

Nov 97. (cd) *(FAUSTLIVECD 1) <KLANGF 2>* **LIVE IN EDINBURGH – AUGUST 1997 (live)**
– (untitled tracks). *(re-iss. Dec97 on 'Think Progressive'; EFA 03560-2) (re-iss. Mar99; C 8326)*

Mar 98. (cd)(lp) *(C 8173)(FL 15) <3558>* **FAUST WAKES NOSFERATU**
– Ausbruch nach Rumanien / Verwirrung / Telepathia / Kampf der machte / Das unheil breitet sich aus / Die entscheidung.

— added **ULRIKE HELMHOLZ**

Apr 99. (cd) *(EFA 36000-2)* **RAVVIVANDO**
– Ein neuer tag / Carousel II / Wir brauchen dich #6 / Four plus seven means eleven / Take care / Spiel / Dr' hansl / Apokalypse / D.I.G. / Du weist schon / Livin' Tokyo / T-electronique.

Nov 01. (cd-s) *(efa 06283-2)* **WIR BRAUCHEN DICH 6 (Dave Ball & Ingo Vauk remixes)**

Mar 02. (cd/lp) *(efa 06289-2/-1)* **FREISPIEL** (remixes)

– compilations, others, etc. –

on 'Recommended' unless mentioned otherwise

Mar 80. (7"ep) *(RRI 15)* **EXTRACTS FROM FAUST PARTY 3**

1980. (lp; with SLAPP HAPPY) *(RR 5)* **CASABLANCA MOON** (or ACNALBASAC NOOM)

Sep 86. (lp) *(RR 25)* **MUNICH AND ELSEWHERE (live)**

Nov 92. (cd) *(RERF 1CD)* **71 MINUTES OF FAUST** (out-takes 1971-1975)
– Munic A / Baby / Meer / Munic B / Don't take roots / Faust party 3 / Party 2 / Party 8 / Spalter / Party 5 / Party 1 / Party 3 / Party 6 / Party 4. *(re-iss. Feb94 & Jun96 & Dec01; same)*

Oct 96. (cd) *(RERHCD 2)* **KIRK**

Jun 97. (cd) *(RER 25)* **RETURN OF A LEGEND**

Dec 97. (cd) *Table of Elements; (CHROMIUM 26)* **FAUST CONCERTS VOL.1 (live at Prinzenbar, Hamburg 1990)**
– As tu ton ticket? / Legendare gleichgultigkeit / The sad head / Haarscharf / Schempal buddha / 13/8 / Rainy day / Volitaire / Rien.

Dec 97. (cd) *Table Of Elements; (CHROMIUM 27)* **FAUST CONCERTS VOL.2 (live at the Marquee, London 1992)**
– Opening of the Marquee / Abamae / Das (s)tier part 1: as tu ton tickets? / Das (s)tier part 2: (Du rouge du bleu / Dying pigs / Viel obst / Stadtluft / Axel goes straight / Pentatonische kinderlied / Promotion / Ex..cess.

Jun 98. (lp) *(RERFV 3)* **THE BBC SESSIONS**
(cd-iss. Jul01; RERF 5)

Nov 00. (5xcd-box) *ReR; (<RERFB 1>)* **THE WUMME YEARS 1970-73**

Nov 02. (cd/lp) *Staubgold; (37/+L)* **PATCHWORK 1971-2002**

FEAR FACTORY

Formed: Los Angeles, California, USA . . . 1991 by BURTON C. BELL, the very-large DINO CAZARES and RAYMOND HERRERA. The group completed two BILL GOULD (Faith No More)-produced tracks for compilation album, 'L.A. Death Metal' before being snapped up by 'Roadrunner'. Instrumental in ushering in the current era of fertile cross-breeding between extreme metal and extreme techno, FEAR FACTORY debuted with the COLIN RICHARDSON-produced album, 'SOUL OF A NEW MACHINE' (1992), the record indicating expansive new possibilities for a flagging death-metal scene. Following US live work with BIOHAZARD and SICK OF IT ALL, they teamed up with veteran Canadian industrialists, FRONT LINE ASSEMBLY, who remixed their debut as 'FEAR IS THE MINDKILLER', NIN style. 1995 saw them grow into frontrunners of the new electronic-industrial death-metal brigade with the groundbreaking 'DEMANUFACTURE' set, a brutally uncompromising album which continued their obsession with technology and the darker side of the human psyche. The record broke the UK Top 30, while another follow-up remix project, 'REMANUFACTURE (CLONING TECHNOLOGY)' (1997), made an even bigger dent in the UK charts. Featuring rhythmic (ranging from the funky to the synapse-shattering) reworkings from the likes of JUNKIE XL and DJ DANO, the album further blurred the fine line between organic and electronic music. CAZARES, with the help of BELL and FAITH NO MORE's BILL GOULD, were the mysterious members (although they denied this) behind BRUJERIA, a mock death-metal (pseudo-Mexican) septet, who released two albums, 'MATANDO GUEROS' (1993) and 'RAZA ODLADA' (1995). In 1998, FEAR FACTORY released another set, 'OBSOLETE', while the following year they took on Gary Numan's 'CARS' and released it as a single. The Angeleno doom-mongers were back on the production line in 2001 with 'DIGIMORTAL', a reliably menacing album concerning itself with portents of computer-aided oblivion and man's electronic heart of darkness. As ever, digitally-enhanced jackhammer rhythms, relentless riffing and grim soundscapes drove the message home as the FEAR FACTORY team took their militant industrial action to new extremes. • **Songwriters:** BELL / CAZARES / HERRERA, except DOG DAY SUNRISE (Head Of David).

Album rating: SOUL OF A NEW MACHINE (*6) / FEAR IS THE MINDKILLER mini (*5) / DEMANUFACTURE (*6) / REMANUFACTURE (CLONING TECHNOLOGY) (*8) / OBSOLETE (*7) / DIGIMORTAL (*6) / CONCRETE (*6)

BURTON C. BELL – vocals / **DINO CAZARES** – guitar (also of BRUJERIA) / **ANDREW SHIVES** – bass / **RAYMOND HERRERA** – drums

Roadrunner Roadrunner

Sep 92. (cd) *<(RR 9160-2)>* **SOUL OF A NEW MACHINE** [ ] [ ]
– Martyr / Leechmaster / Scapegoat / Crisis / Crash test / Flesh hold / Lifeblind / Scumgrief / Natividad / Big god – Raped souls / Arise above oppression / Self immolation / Suffer age / W.O.E. / Desecrate / Escape confusion / Manipulation. *(re-iss. Feb01; same)*

Apr 93. (m-cd) *<(RR 9082-2)>* **FEAR IS THE MINDKILLER** [ ] [ ]
– Martyr (suffer bastard mix) / Self immolation (vein tap mix) / Scapegoat (pigf*** mix) / Scumgrief (deep dub trauma mix) / Self immolation (liquid sky mix) / Self immolation (album version).

— **CHRISTIAN OLDE WOLBERS** – bass; repl. SHIVES

Jun 95. (cd/c/lp) *<(RR 8956-2/-4/-1)>* **DEMANUFACTURE** [27] [ ]
– Demanufacture / Self bias resistor / Zero signal / Replica / New breed / Dog day sunrise / Body hammer / H-K (Hunter-Killer) / A therapy for pain / Flashpoint / Pisschrist. *(d-lp+=)* – Resistancial! / New breed (revolutionary designed mix).

Nov 95. (12"ep/cd-ep) *(RR 2330-6/-3)* **DOG DAY SUNRISE / ('A'version) / CONCRETO / REPLICA (electric sheep mix)** [ ] [–]
(12"/cd-s) *(NRR 2330-6/-3)* – ('A'remixes).

Jun 97. (cd/c/lp) *<(RR 8834-2/-4)>* **REMANUFACTURE (CLONING TECHNOLOGY)** [22] [ ]
– Remanufacture / National panel beating / Genetic blueprint / Faithless / Bionic chronic / Cloning technology / Burn / T-1000 / Machines of hate / 21st century Jesus / Bound for forgiveness / Refinery / Remanufacture (edit).

Jul 97. (12"ep) **THE BABBER MIXES** [ ] [–]
– New breed (Steel gun mix) / Flashpoint (Chosen few mix) / T-1000 (DJ Dano mix) / Manic cure.

Oct 97. (cd-ep) *(RR 2271-3)* **BURN / CYBERDYNE / TRANSGENIC / REFUELLED** [ ] [–]

Jul 98. (cd/c) *<(RR 8752-2/-4)>* **OBSOLETE** [20] [77]
– Shock / Edgecrusher / Smasher – Devourer / Securiton / (Police state 2000) Descent / Hi-tech hate / Freedom or fire / Obsolete / Resurrection / Timelessness.

Dec 98. (cd-ep) *(RR 2232-5)* **RESURRECTION / 0-0 (WHERE EVIL DWELLS) / SOULWOUND** [ ] [–]

Sep 99. (cd-s) *(RR 2189-3)* **CARS / DESCENT (Falling Deeper mix) / EDGECRUSHER (Urban Assault mix)** [ ] [–]

Apr 01. (cd) *<(RR 8561-2)>* **DIGIMORTAL** [24] [32]
– What will become? / Damaged / Digimortal / No one / Linchpin / Invisible wounds (dark bodies) / Acres of skin / Back the f*** up / Byte block / Hurt conveyor / (Memory imprints) Never end. *(other cd+=; RR 8561-5)* – Dead man walking / Strain vs resistance / Repentance / Full metal contact.

Jul 02. (cd) *<(RR 84392-2)>* **CONCRETE** [ ] [ ]
– Big god / Raped souls / Arise above oppression / Concrete / Crisis / Escape confusion / Sangre de ninos / Soulwomb / Echoes of innocence / Dragged down by the weight of existence / Deception / Desecate / Sufferage / Anxiety / Self immolation / Piss Christ / Ulceration.

– compilations, etc. –

Apr 03. (cd) *<(RR 8398-2)>* **HATEFILES** (rare mixes) [ ] [ ]

FEEDER

Formed: London, England . . . 1993 by Newport-born frontman GRANT NICHOLAS, fellow Welshman JON HENRY LEE on bass and through many auditions, Japanese bassist TAKA HIROSE, the group now set out to become the British answer to The SMASHING PUMPKINS. After slogging around the toilet circuit, the band signed to 'Echo' (home of JULIAN COPE and BABYBIRD), releasing their debut single 'TWO COLOURS' at the end of '95. The mini-album, 'SWIM' (mid '96), consolidated their pop-metal/grunge credentials, while an appearance at the CMJ music business conference in New York, led them to sign for 'Elektra'. Following on from the glistening dynamics and sonic confetti of their well-received debut album, 'POLYTHENE' (1997), they scored a number of minor UK chart successes culminating in the Top 30 single 'HIGH'. Never far from the pages of Kerrang! or the NME, FEEDER continued to scale the charts via two equally enterprising hard rock-meets-indie sets, 'YESTERDAY WENT TOO SOON' (1999) and 'ECHO PARK' (2001). The band were subsequently dealt the cruellest of blows with the suicide of JON LEE in early 2002. After deciding to carry on at the behest of LEE's family, they recruited former SKUNK ANANSIE drummer MARK RICHARDSON and set about recording 'COMFORT IN SOUND' (2002). As its title inferred, this was an attempt to both come to terms with, and find some kind of meaning in tragedy. Often uncomfortably intimate, the record nevertheless achieved its own natural catharsis over the course of its song cycle and reached the UK Top 10. • **Covered:** CAN'T STAND LOSING YOU (Police) / THE POWER OF LOVE (Frankie Goes To Hollywood).

Album rating: POLYTHENE (*6) / YESTERDAY WENT TOO SOON (*6) / ECHO PARK (*6) / COMFORT IN SOUND (*7)

GRANT NICHOLAS (b. 1967, Newport, Wales) – vocals, guitar / **TAKA HIROSE** (b. Tokyo) – bass / **JON HENRY LEE** (b. Wales)- drums

Echo Elektra

Oct 95. (7"/cd-s) *(ecs/+cd 13)* **TWO COLOURS** [ ] [–]
– Chicken on a bone / Pictures of pain.

May 96. (m-cd/m-c/m-lp) *(ech cd/mc/lp 9)* **SWIM** [ ] [–]
– Sweet 16 / Stereo world / W.I.T. / Descend / World asleep / Swim. *(m-cd re-iss. Oct98; same) (re-iss. Jul01 as 'SWIM (resurfaced)'+=; echcd 38)* – Shade / Elegy / Chicken on a bone / Spill / Forgiven / Crash (video) / Cement (video).

Oct 96. (7") *(ecs 27)* **STEREO WORLD. / MY PERFECT DAY** [ ] [–]
(cd-s+=) *(ecscd 27)* – World asleep / Change.

Feb 97. (7") *(ecs 32)* **TANGERINE. / RHUBARB** [60] [–]
(cd-s+=) *(ecscd 32)* – Rain.
(cd-s+=) *(ecscx 32)* – ('A'side) / TV me / Elegy.

Apr 97. (7") *(ecs 36)* **CEMENT. / PICTURES OF PAIN** [53] [–]
(cd-s+=) *(ecscd 36)* – Undivided.
(cd-s) *(ecscx 36)* – ('A'live) / Tangerine (live) / Shade (live) / Stereo world (live).

May 97. (cd/c/lp) *(ech cd/mc/lp 15)* *<62085>* **POLYTHENE** [65] [ ]
– Polythene girl / My perfect day / Cement / Crash / Radiation / Suffocate / Descend / Stereo world / Tangerine / Waterfall / Forgive / Twentieth century trip. *(re-iss. Oct97 & Oct99 cd/c; ech cd/mc 19)*

Aug 97. (7") *(ecs 42)* **CRASH. / HERE IN THE BUBBLE** [48] [–]
(cd-s+=) *(ecscd 42)* – Forgive (acoustic) / Stereo world (video).
(cd-s) *(ecscx 42)* – ('A'side) / Undivided / Swim (version) / Tangerine (video).

Oct 97. (7"colrd) *(ecs 44)* **HIGH. / WHEN THE MORNING COMES** [24] [–]
(cd-s+=) *(ecscd 44)* – Women in towels / Cement (video cd-rom).
(cd-s) *(ecscx 44)* – ('A'side) / ('A'acoustic) / Sweet 16 / Crash (video cd-rom).

Feb 98. (7"purple) *(ecs 52)* **SUFFOCATE. / ECLIPSE** [37] [–]
(cd-s+=) *(ecscd 52)* – Cockroach / High (video – live).
(cd-s) *(ecscx 52)* – ('A'side) / Dry (acoustic) / Teddy bear / Descend (live).

Mar 99. (7") *(ecs 75)* **DAY IN DAY OUT. / CAN'T DANCE TO DISCO / HONEYFUZZ** [31] [–]
(cd-s) *(ecscd 75)* – ('A'side) / I need a buzz / Fly.
(cd-s) *(ecscx 75)* – ('A'side) / Can't dance to disco / Don't bring me down.
May 99. (c-s/cd-s) *(ecs mc/cd 77)* **INSOMNIA / SPACE AGE HERO / LIVING IN PARANOID** [22] [–]
(cd-s) *(ecscx 77)* – ('A'side) / Divebomb / Fly.
Aug 99. (c-s) *(ecsmc 79)* **YESTERDAY WENT TOO SOON / OXIDISE / TOMORROW SHINE** [20] [–]
(cd-s) *(ecscd 79)* – ('A'side) / Getting to know you well / Tomorrow shine.
(cd-s) *(ecscx 79)* – ('A'side) / Rubberband / Slide.
Aug 99. (cd/c/lp) *(ech cd/mc/lp 28)* *<62400>* **YESTERDAY WENT TOO SOON** [8] Oct99 [ ]
– Anaesthetic / Insomnia / Picture of perfect youth / Yesterday went too soon / Waiting for changes / Radioman / Day in day out / Tinsel town / You're my evergreen / Dry / Hole in my head / So well / Paperfaces. *(d-cd; echcx 28)* – Bubble head.
Nov 99. (c-s) *(ecsmc 85)* **PAPERFACES / WHOOEY / WAITING FOR CHANGES (session)** [41] [–]
(cd-s) *(ecscd 85)* – (first two tracks) / Tinsel town (session).
(cd-s) *(ecscx 85)* – ('A'side) / Crash mat / You're my evergreen (session).

Echo / Pony Canyon

Jan 01. (7"orange) *(ecs 106)* **BUCK ROGERS. / SEX TYPE DRUG** [5] [–]
(cd-s) *(ecscd106)* – ('A'side) / Purple / Heads.
(cd-s) *(ecscx 106)* – ('A'side) / We the electronic / 21st Century meltdown / ('A'-CD-Rom).
Apr 01. (7") *(ecs 107)* **SEVEN DAYS IN THE SUN. / JUST A DAY** [14] [–]
(c-s+=/cd-s+=) *(esc mc/cd 107)* – Home for the summer.
(cd-s) *(ecscx 107)* – ('A'side) / Reminders / Forever glow / ('A'-CD-Rom).
Apr 01. (cd/c/lp) *(ech cd/mc/lp 34)* **ECHO PARK** [5] [–]
– Standing on the edge / Buck Rogers / Piece by piece / Seven days in the sun / We can't rewind / Turn / Choka / Oxygen / Tell all your friends / Under the weather / Satellite news / Bug / Just a day.
Jul 01. (7"/cd-s) *(ech/+cd 116)* **TURN. / COMING BACK AROUND / BRING IT HOME** [27] [–]
(c-s) *(echcs 116)* – (first & third tracks) / San Diego.
(cd-s) *(echcx 116)* – ('A'side) / Bad hair day / ('A'-CD-Rom) / (the making of Echo Park).
Sep 01. (cd) *<1521>* **SEVEN DAYS IN THE SUN** [–] [ ]
– Seven days in the sun / Satellite news / Home for summer / Reminders / Forever glow / We the electronic / W.I.T. / High acoustic / Sry acoustic.
Dec 01. (7"orange) *(ecs/+mc 121)* **JUST A DAY. / EARLY** [12] [–]
(cd-s+=) *(ecscd 121)* – Slowburn.
(cd-s) *(ecscx 121)* – ('A'side) / Can't stand losing you / Piece by piece (video).

—— JON LEE committed suicide in January 2002; **MARK RICHARDSON** – drums (ex-SKUNK ANANSIE) joined other two

Echo / Universal

Sep 02. (cd-s) *(ecscd 130)* **COME BACK AROUND / FEEL IT AGAIN / BULLET** [14] [–]
(cd-s) *(ecscx 130)* – ('A'side) / Opaque / ('A'-acoustic).
Oct 02. (cd/c/lp) *(ech cd/mc/lp 43)* *<01180-2>* **COMFORT IN SOUND** [6] May03 [ ]
– Just the way I'm feeling / Come back around / Helium / Child in you / Comfort in sound / Forget about tomorrow / Summers gone / Godzilla / Quick fade / Find the colour / Love pollution / Moonshine. *(cd re-iss. Sep03 w/dvd+=; echdv 43)*
Jan 03. (cd-s) *(ecscd 133)* **JUST THE WAY I'M FEELING / BROKEN / THE POWER OF LOVE** [10] [–]
(cd-s) *(ecscx 133)* – ('A'-radio) / Redemption / Child in you (acoustic living room session) / ('A'-video).
May 03. (cd-s) *(ecscd 135)* **FORGET ABOUT TOMORROW / LOSE THE FEAR / TINSELTOWN (acoustic) / ('A'-video)** [12] [–]
(cd-s) *(ecscx 135)* – ('A'side) / Bring it together / Helium (acoustic) / ('A'-live video from Brixton Academy).
Sep 03. (7"white) *(ecs 145)* **FIND THE COLOUR. / REMEMBER THE SILENCE** [24] [–]
(cd-s+=) *(ecscd 145)* – Circles / ('A'-video).

☐ Bryan FERRY (see under ⇒ ROXY MUSIC)

☐ FFWD (see under ⇒ ORB)

50 CENT

Born: CURTIS JACKSON, 6 Jul'76, Queens, New York, USA. One of the most highly anticipated and hyped MCs in recent years, the much lauded 50 CENT, it seems, spent years on the street, and on the shelf, before breaking through to the mainstream with his DR.DRE/EMINEM-endorsed set, 'GET RICH OR DIE TRYIN', in 2003. Raised by his drug-dealing mother (who died when he was eight), and then subsequently his grandmother in the impoverished area of Southside Jamaica, 50 CENT himself took to hustling crack-cocaine in his late teens, seeing a stint of prison sentences which eventually turned his attention towards hip-hop. Somehow, he managed to acquaint himself with the late JAM MASTER JAY (of RUN-D.M.C.), who signed him to his 'J.M.J.' imprint, although nothing much arose from the deal. However, through this young JACKSON made friends with the producing duo TRACKMASTERS (POKE and TONE, respectively) whose work with JAY-Z and NAS was notorious on the East Coast scene. They signed him to their 'Columbia' subsidiary, and recorded a batch of singles, the best of the bunch being 'THUG LOVE' (featuring, of all people, DESTINY'S CHILD) and the minor hit 'HOW TO ROB'. Tradegy would strike, when, after being stabbed three months earlier, 50 CENT was shot several times outside a studio in Queens as he was sitting in the passenger seat of a friend's car. 'Columbia' balked and his 'POWER OF THE DOLLAR' album was shelved indefinitely, turning a wounded and disappointed 50 CENT back on the streets, broke and disgruntled. Refusing to quit the music industry, he formed the underground trio G-UNIT with LLOYD BANKS and TONY YAYO and started touting himself on the underground "mix-tape" circuit, his bootlegged songs all appearing on 2002's 'GUESS WHO'S BACK?' outtakes compilation. After EMINEM openly cited 50 CENT as an inspiration on a live radio broadcast, the bidding wars for this notorious enigmatic MC began to escalate, with – guess who – EMINEM finally winning over, signing 50 CENT to his and DRE's 'Shady/Aftermath' imprint; EMINEM even included the underground hit 'WANKSTA' on his '8-MILE' movie soundtrack. Which would bring us to the crossover hit of 2003, and perhaps the most massive hip-hop single of the year, 'IN DA CLUB'. Beginning with the now famous lines "Hey Shorty, it's your birthday, we're gonna party like it's your birthday . . .", the single with its DRE produced beats and catchy hooks proved to be a massive hit in clubs and saw the once rebuked hip-hop artist win massive acclaim with sales and music awards et al. Around the same time, he issued his debut album proper 'GET RICH OR DIE TRYIN', which was critically acclaimed during the hype. 2003 also saw him strike chart gold with a special DVD/CD, 'THE NEW BREED' and two further singles, '21 QUESTIONS' and 'P.I.M.P.'.

Album rating: GUESS WHO'S BACK? (*5) / GET RICH OR DIE TRYIN' (*7) / THE NEW BREED multimedia (*5)

50 CENT – vocals

not iss. / Sony

Aug 99. (cd-s) *<79252>* **HOW TO ROB** [–] [ ]
Sep 99. (cd-s; as 50 CENT & DESTINY'S CHILD) *<79271>* **THUG LOVE (mixes; extra clean / instrumental / clean)** [–] [ ]
Oct 99. (12") *<79296>* **YOUR LIFE'S ON THE LINE** [–] [ ]
Feb 00. (12"; by 50 CENT & DESTINY'S CHILD) *<79297>* **THUG LOVE (mixes; explicit / clean / instrumental / explicit acappella)** [–] [ ]
Aug 00. (12"; with DESTINY'S CHILD, NOREAGA & The MADD RAPPER) *<79479>* **THUG LOVE. / I'M A HUSTLER** [–] [ ]

		Full Clip	Full Clip
Aug 02.	(cd) <*(FCR 2003)*> **GUESS WHO'S BACK?** – Killa tape intro / Rotten apple / Drop (skit) / That's what's up (with G UNIT) / U not like me / 50 bars / Life's on the line / Get out the club / Be a gentleman / Fuck you / Too hot (with NAS & NATURE) / Who U rep with (with NAS & BRAVEHEARTS) / Corner bodega / Ghetto qua ran / As the world turns (with U.G.K.) / Whoo kid (freestyle) / Stretch Armstrong (freestyle) / Doo wop (freestyle). <*(d-lp-iss.Nov02; FCR 2003DLP)*>		Apr02 28
Nov 02.	(12") <*7816*> **WANKSTA**	–	13
Nov 02.	(12") <*(FCR 4001)*> **ROTTEN APPLE**		Jan03
		Polydor	Interscope
Feb 03.	(cd) *(493564-2)* <*493544*> **GET RICH OR DIE TRYIN'** – Intro / What up gangsta / Patiently waiting (with EMINEM) / Many men (wish death) / In da club / High all the time / Heat / If I can't / Blood hound (with YOUNG BUCK) / Back down / P.I.M.P. / Like my style (with TONY YAYO) / Poor lil rich / 21 questions (with NATE DOGG) / Don't push me (with LLOYD BANKS & EMINEM) / Gotta make it to Heaven / Wanksta / U not like me / Life's on the line. *(ltd-d-cd+=; 493564-2)* – In da club (acappella) / Wanksta (video).	2	1
Mar 03.	(c-s) *(497874-4)* <*497856*> **IN DA CLUB / IN DA CLUB (explicit)** (12"+=/cd-s+=) *(497874-1/-2)* – Wanksta.	4	1
May 03.	(dvd+cd) *(493678-0)* <*10800DVD*> **THE NEW BREED** – (the documentary) / (the interview) / Wanksta / Wanksta (video) / In da club / In da club (video) / Not like me (live) / Wanksta (live) / Patiently waiting (live) / Love me (live) / Rap game (live) / In da club (live) / The Detroit show: behind the scenes / Wanksta (AOL sessions) / In da club (AOL sessions) / Round here (AOL sessions) / 8 Mile (DVD trailer) / True loyalty / 8 Mile road / In da hood.		Apr03 2
May 03.	(12"; as 50 CENT & NATE DOGG) <*INT 063511*> **21 QUESTIONS / 21 QUESTIONS (instrumental). / MANY MEN (WISH DEATH) / MANY MEN (WISH DEATH) (instrumental)**	–	1
Jun 03.	(c-s; as 50 CENT & NATE DOGG) *(980877-4)* **21 QUESTIONS / SOLDIER (with G UNIT)** (12"+=) *(9808773)* – ('A'-live in NY) / ('A'-instrumental). (cd-s++=) *(9807195)* – ('A'-video).	6	–
Oct 03.	(c-s) *(9812336)* **P.I.M.P. / 8 MORE MILES (freestyle with G UNIT)** (12"+=) *(9812334)* <*INT 088811*> – ('A'-version). (cd-s++=) *(9812333)* – ('A'-video).	5	Jul03 3

FILTER

Formed: Cleveland, Ohio, USA . . . 1995 by RICHARD PATRICK and BRIAN LIESEGANG (once both of NINE INCH NAILS). With the addition of GENO LENARDO, FRANK CAVANAGH and MATT WALKER, the group scraped into the lower regions of the US chart with their debut album, 'SHORT BUS' (1995). A basement industrial outfit utilising dense Euro-rock sounds, the group eventually secured some widespread exposure when they hit the UK Top 40 via a collaboration with The CRYSTAL METHOD, '(CAN'T YOU) TRIP LIKE I DO', featured on the soundtrack to 'The Spawn'. Mixing a cocktail of metal and goth once again (the kids just loved it, didn't they!), FILTER resurfaced with that difficult second album. Entitled confusingly enough, 'TITLE OF RECORD' (1999), the set made it all the way into the US Top 30 (UK Top 75), 'WELCOME TO THE FOLD' and 'TAKE A PICTURE' were worthy specimens. 'THE AMALGAMUT' (2002) found PATRICK attempting to make sense of his country's various ills, not least the 9/11 tragedy, in unprecedented lyrical outpourings. It was a risky strategy although the man's sincerity gave it some weight, while the relatively safe musical backing also shored it up. • **Note:** Don't let yourself buy the different house/club act, FILTER, who released a single, 'RUNNING AWAY', in '97.

Album rating: SHORT BUS (*8) / TITLE OF RECORD (*6) / THE AMALGAMUT (*7)

RICHARD PATRICK (b.1967) – vocals, guitar, bass / **BRIAN LIESEGANG** (b.1970) – keyboards, drums / with **KEVIN HANLEY** – guitars / **SCOTT KERN** + **MIKE PEFFER** – drums

		Warners	Reprise
May 95.	(cd/c) <*(9362 45864-2/-4)*> **SHORT BUS** – Hey man, nice shot / Dose / Under / Spent / Take another / Stuck in here / It's over / Gerbil / White like that / Consider this / So cool.		59

— basic duo now with **GENO LENARDO** – guitar / **FRANK CAVANAGH** – bass / **MATT WALKER** – drums

Aug 95.	(12"/cd-s) *(W 0299 T/CD1)* <*43531*> **HEY MAN NICE SHOT (sober mix) / ('A'-1/2oz mix) / ('A'-1/4lb mix) / ('A'-Big Mac mix)** (cd-s) *(W 0299 CD2)* <*43531*> – ('A'-Bud gets the lead out mix) / ('A'-Sawed off edit) / ('A'-Nickel bag mix) / White like that. *(re-iss. May96; same)*		Jul95 76

— WALKER joined the SMASHING PUMPKINS in '96

— In Sep'97, FILTER & The CRYSTAL METHOD hit UK Top 40 with '(CAN'T YOU) TRIP LIKE I DO' from the film 'The Spawn'.

Aug 99.	(cd/c) *(9362 47519-2/-4)* <*47388*> **TITLE OF RECORD** – Sand / Welcome to the fold / Captain Bleigh / It's gonna kill me / The best things / Take a picture / Skinny / I will lead you / Cancer / I'm not the only one / Miss Blue.	75	30
Sep 99.	(cd-s) *(W 502CD)* <*44738*> **WELCOME TO THE FOLD / ONE (IS THE LONELIEST NUMBER) / (CAN'T YOU) TRIP LIKE I DO** (cd-s) *(W 502CDX)* – ('A'-Freaq Nasty remix) / ('A'-Militant Moving Fusion remix) / ('A'-video).		
Mar 00.	(c-s) *(W 515C)* <*44788*> **TAKE A PICTURE (Letterman edit) / TAKE A PICTURE (live)** (cd-s) *(W 515CD)* – ('A'side) / ('A'-Hybrid mix) / ('A'-Rennie Pilgrem mix). (cd-s) *(W 515CDX)* – ('A'side) / Welcome to the fold (live) / Hey man, nice shot (live).	25	Nov99 12
Jul 02.	(cd) <*(9362 47963-2)*> **THE AMALGAMUT** – You walk away / American cliche / Where do we go from here / Columind / The missing / The only way (is the wrong way) / My long walk to jail / So I quit / God damn me / It can never be the same / World today / The 4th.	68	32
Sep 02.	(cd-s) *(W 587CD1)* <*42444*> **WHERE DO WE GO FROM HERE / IT'S GONNA KILL ME (live) / CAN'T YOU TRIP LIKE I DO / ('A'-video)** (cd-s) *(W 587CD2)* – ('A'side) / ('A'mixes; Richard Morel's pink noise vocal / X-Ecutioner's / DJ Hyper).		Jul02 94

☐ Neil / Tim FINN (see under ⇒ CROWDED HOUSE)

☐ FIRM (see under ⇒ LED ZEPPELIN)

FISH

Born: DEREK WILLIAM DICK, 25 Apr'58, Dalkeith, Midlothian. After leaving top progsters, MARILLION, in less than agreeable circumstances in September '88, he finally released a debut single, 'STATE OF MIND', a year later. This hit the UK Top 40, as did his early 1990 follow-up, 'BIG WEDGE'. A Top 5 album, 'VIGIL IN A WILDERNESS OF MIRRORS' was soon in the charts, FISH solo following a more commercial yet ambitiously diverse guitar-based sound while retaining the PETER GABRIEL-esque vocal theatrics. Through an ever changing cast of backing musicians, FISH recorded another two major label albums for 'Polydor', 'INTERNAL EXILE' (1991) and a covers set, 'SONGS FROM THE MIRROR' (1993), the latter of which stalled outside the Top 40. Moving back to Scotland after living in London, the singer then set up his own label, 'Dick Bros.', proceeding to maintain a prolific recording schedule over the ensuing four years as well as producing and releasing other low-key Scottish-based projects. Much of the material consisted of concert recordings, FISH retaining a loyal live following, especially in Europe. Studio wise, he released the 'SUITS' set in 1994, another Top 20 hit despite criticisms from the usual quarters. The Caledonian maverick even recorded a duet with forgotten 80's starlet SAM BROWN although predictably it failed to make the chart. 1995 saw the release of two complementary best of/live affairs, 'YIN' and 'YANG', while the singer returned in 1997 with 'SUNSETS ON EMPIRE'. The aquatic one subsequently became an unusual signing for 'Roadrunner' after a series of legal hassles with previous labels. The resulting Elliot Ness-produced 'RAINGODS WITH ZIPPOS' (1999) was hailed by many critics and fans as his most complete effort since splitting from MARILLION more than a decade previously. The new 'Roadrunner' deal also resulted in a veritable avalanche of live sets and oddity collections in late '98, among them 'KETTLE OF FISH 88-98', 'UNCLE FISH AND THE CRYPT CREEPERS' and 'TALES FROM THE BIG BUS'. • **Songwriters:** FISH co-wrote most of material with MICKEY SIMMONDS. He covered; THE FAITH HEALER (Sensational Alex Harvey Band). In early 1993, he released full covers album with tracks: QUESTION (Moody Blues) / BOSTON TEA PARTY (Sensational Alex Harvey Band) / FEARLESS (Pink Floyd) / APEMAN (Kinks) / HOLD YOUR HEAD UP (Argent) / SOLD (Sandy Denny) / I KNOW WHAT I LIKE (Genesis) / JEEPSTER (T.Rex) / FIVE YEARS (David Bowie) / ROADHOUSE BLUES (Doors). • **Trivia:** October '86, FISH was credited on TONY BANKS (Genesis) single 'Short Cut To Nowhere'.

Album rating: VIGIL IN A WILDERNESS OF MIRRORS (*6) / INTERNAL EXILE (*5) / SONGS FROM THE MIRROR (*3) / SUSHI (*5) / ACOUSTIC SESSION (*5) / SUITS (*4) / YIN collection (*6) / YANG collection (*6) / SUNSETS ON EMPIRE (*6) / RAINGODS WITH ZIPPOS (*4)

FISH – vocals (ex-MARILLION) with guest musicians on debut album **FRANK USHER** – guitar / **HAL LINDES** – guitar / **MICKEY SIMMONDS** – keyboards / **JOHN GIBLIN** – bass / **MARK BRZEZICKI** – drums / **CAROL KENYON** – backing vocals / plus **LUIS JARDIM** – percussion / **JANICK GERS** – guitar

E.M.I. E.M.I.

Oct 89. (c-s/7") *(TC+/EM 109)* **STATE OF MIND. / THE VOYEUR (I LIKE TO WATCH)** [32] [–]
(12"+=/cd-s+=) *(12/CD EM 109)* – ('A'-Presidential mix).

Dec 89. (7"/7"s)(c-s) *(EM/+S 125)(TC 125)* **BIG WEDGE. / JACK AND JILL** [25] [–]
(12"+=/12"pic-d)(cd-s+=) *(12EM/+PD 125)(CDEM 125)* – Faith healer (live).

Feb 90. (lp/c/cd)(pic-lp) *(CD/C+/EMD 1015)(EMPD 1015)* *<2202>* **VIGIL IN A WILDERNESS OF MIRRORS** [5] [ ]
– Vigil / Big wedge / State of mind / The company / A gentleman's excuse me / The voyeur (I like to watch) / Family business / View from the hill / Cliche. *(cd re-iss. Nov98 on 'Roadrunner'+=; RR 8687-2)* – Jack and Jill / Internal exile / A gentleman's excuse me / Whiplash. *(cd re-iss. Sep02 on 'Chocolate Frog – Voiceprint'; CFVP 009CD)*

Mar 90. (7"/7"red/7"sha-pic-d)(c-s) *(EM/+S/PD 135)(TCEM 135)* **A GENTLEMAN'S EXCUSE ME. / WHIPLASH** [30] [–]
(12"+=/12"pic-d+=)(cd-s+=) *(12EM/+PD 135)(CDEM 135)* – ('A'demo version).

—— retained SIMMONDS and USHER, and brought in **ROBIN BOULT** – lead guitar, vocals / **DAVID PATON** – bass / **ETHAN JOHNS** – drums, percussion / guest drummer **TED McKENNA**

Polydor Polydor

Sep 91. (7") *(FISH Y/C 1)* **INTERNAL EXILE. / CARNIVAL MAN** [37] [–]
(12"+=) *(FISHS 1)* – ('A'-Karaoke mix).
(cd-s++=) *(FISCD 1)* – ('A'remix).

Oct 91. (cd/c/lp) *(511049-2/-4/-1)* *<513765>* **INTERNAL EXILE** [21] [ ]
– Shadowplay / Credo / Just good friends (close) / Favourite stranger / Lucky / Dear friend / Tongues / Internal exile. *(re-iss. cd Apr95; same) (cd re-iss. Nov98 on 'Roadrunner'+=; RR 8683-2)* – Poet's moon / Something in the air / Carnival man. *(cd re-iss. Sep02 on 'Chocolate Frog – Voiceprint'; CFVP 010CD)*

Dec 91. (7"/c-s) *(FISH Y/C 2)* **CREDO. / POET'S MOON** [38] [–]
(12"box+=/cd-s+=) *(FISHS/FISCD 2)* – ('A'mix).
(12"+=) *(FISHX 2)* – (the 2 'A'versions) / Tongues (demo).

Jun 92. (7"/c-s) *(FISH Y/C 3)* **SOMETHING IN THE AIR. / DEAR FRIEND** [51] [–]
(12"+=) *(FISHX 3)* – ('A'-Teddy bear mix).
(cd-s++=) *(FISHP 3)* – ('A'radio mix).
(cd-s) *(FISHL 3)* – ('A'side) ('A'-Christopher Robin mix) / Credo / Shadowplay.

—— **FOSTER PATTERSON** – keyboards, vocals; repl. SIMMONS / **KEVIN WILKINSON** – drums, percussion; repl. JOHNS.

Jan 93. (cd/c/lp) *(517499-2/-4/-1)* **SONGS FROM THE MIRROR** [46] [–]
– Question / Boston tea party / Fearless / Apeman / Hold your head up / Solo / I know what I like (in your wardrobe) / Jeepster / Five years. *(re-iss. cd Apr95; same) (cd re-iss. Nov98 on 'Roadrunner'; RR 8682-2) (cd re-iss. Feb03 on 'Chocolate Frog'; CFVP 015CD)*

Dick Bros Griffin

Mar 94. (d-cd) *(DDICK 002CD)* *<158>* **SUSHI (live)** [ ] [ ]
– Fearless / Big wedge / Boston tea party / Credo / Family business / View from a hill / He knows you know / She chameleon / Kayleigh / White Russian / The company / / Just good friends / Jeepster / Hold your head up / Lucky / Internal exile / Cliche / Last straw / Poet's Moon / Five years. *(re-iss. Sep96 on 'Blueprint'; DDICK 2CD) (re-iss. Nov98 on 'Roadrunner'; RR 8680-2)*

Apr 94. (c-s/ext-12"pic-d/cd-s) *(DDICK 3 CAS/PIC/CD1)* **LADY LET IT LIE / OUT OF MY LIFE. / BLACK CANAL** [46] [–]
(cd-s) *(DDICK 3CD2)* – ('A'extended) / ('B'live) / Emperors song (live) / Just good friends.

May 94. (cd/c/lp/pic-lp) *(DDICK 004 CD/MC/LP/PIC)* **SUITS** [18] [–]
– 1470 / Lady let it lie / Emperor's song / Fortunes of war / Somebody special / No dummy / Pipeline / Jumpsuit city / Bandwagon / Raw meat. *(cd re-iss. Sep96 on 'Blueprint'; DDICK 4CD) (cd re-iss. Nov98 on 'Roadrunner'; RR 8686-2) (cd re-iss. Sep02 on 'Chocolate Frog – Voiceprint'; CFVP 01CD)*

Sep 94. (cd-ep) *(DDICK 008CD1)* **FORTUNES OF WAR (edit) / SOMEBODY SPECIAL (live) / STATE OF MIND (live) / LUCKY (live)** [67] [–]
(cd-ep) *(DDICK 008CD2)* – ('A'live) / Warm wet circles / Jumpsuit city / The company (all live).
(cd-ep) *(DDICK 008CD3)* – ('A'acoustic) / Kayleigh (live) / Internal exile (live) / Just good friends (acoustic).
(cd-ep) *(DDICK 008CD4)* – ('A'acoustic) / Sugar mice (live) / Dear friend (live) / Lady let it lie (acoustic).

—— Above 4-cd single (nearly 90 mins.) / can be fitted in together as 1 package.

Aug 95. (c-s; FISH featuring SAM BROWN) *(DDICK 014MC)* **JUST GOOD FRIENDS / SOMEBODY SPECIAL** [63] [–]
(cd-s+=) *(DDICK 014CD1)* – State of mind.
(cd-s) *(DDICK 014CD2)* – ('A'side) / Raw meat (live) / Roadhouse blues (live).

Sep 95. (cd/c) *(DDICK 011 CD/MC)* **YIN** (THE BEST OF FISH & '95 remixes) [58] [–]
– Incommunicado / Family business / Just good friends / Pipeline / Institution waltz / Tongues / Favourite stranger / Boston tea party / Raw meat / Time & a word / Company / Incubus / Solo. *(cd re-iss. Sep96 on 'Blueprint'; DDICK 11CD) (cd re-iss. Sep00 & May02 on 'Chocolate Frog – Voiceprint'; CFVP 004CD)*

Sep 95. (cd/c) *(DDICK 012 CD/MC)* **YANG** (THE BEST OF FISH & '95 remixes) [52] [–]
– Lucky / Big wedge / Lady let it lie / Lavender / Credo / A gentleman's excuse me / Kayleigh / State of mind / Somebody special / Sugar mice / Punch & Judy / Internal exile / Fortunes of war. *(cd re-iss. Sep96 on 'Blueprint'; DDICK 12CD) (cd re-iss. Sep00 & May02 on 'Chocolate Frog – Voiceprint'; CFVP 005CD)*

Dick Bros. Lightyear

May 97. (cd-s) *(DDICK 24CD1)* **BROTHER 52 / BROTHER 52 (Stateline mix) / DO NOT WALK OUTSIDE THIS AREA / BROTHER 52 (album version)** [ ] [–]
(cd-s) *(DDICK 24CD2)* – (first 2 tracks) / ('A'-4 am dub mix).

May 97. (cd) *(DDICK 25CD)* *<54197>* **SUNSETS ON EMPIRE** [42] Jun97 [ ]
– Perception of Johnny punter / Goldfish and clowns / Change of heart / What colour is God / Tara / Jungle ride / Worm in a bottle / Brother 52 / Sunsets on empire / Say it with flowers / Do not walk outside this area. *(special-cd; DDICK 26CD) (re-iss. Nov98 on 'Roadrunner'; RR 8679-2) (<cd re-iss. Dec02 on 'Chocolate Frog'+=; CFVP 012CD)* – (bonus track).

Aug 97. (cd-s) *(DDICK 27CD)* **CHANGE OF HEART / GOLDFISH AND CLOWNS / THE PERCEPTION OF JOHNNY PUNTER** [ ] [–]

Roadrunner Roadrunner

Apr 99. (7"pic-d/cd-s; as FISH with ELIZABETH ANTWI) *(RR 2185-7/-3)* **INCOMPLETE. / MAKE IT HAPPEN (acoustic mix) / INCOMPLETE (castle demo)** [ ] [–]

Apr 99. (cd) *(<RR 8677-2>)* **RAINGODS WITH ZIPPOS** [57] [ ]
– Tumbledown / Mission statement / Incomplete / Tilted cross / Faith healer / Rites of passage / Plague of ghosts – (i) Old haunts, (ii) Digging deep, (iii) Chocolate frogs, (iv) Waving at stars, (v) Raingods dancing, (vi) Wake-up call (make it happen). *(re-iss. Dec02 on 'Chocolate Frog'; CFVP 013CD)*

Chocolate Frog Chocolate Frog

Aug 01. (cd) *(<CFVP 007CD>)* **FELLINI DAYS** [ ] Sep02 [ ]
– 3d / So Fellini / Tiki 4 / Our smile / Long cold day / Dancing in fog / Obligatory ballad / The pilgrim's address / Clock moves sideways. *(cd bonus+=)* – Hold your head up / I know what I like / Jeepster / Five years.

Dec 02. (cd) *(CFVP 014CD)* **FELLINI NIGHTS (live)** [ ] [–]
– 3D / So Fellini / Brother 52 / Tumbledown / Long cold day / Tki 4 / Our smile / Perception of Johnny Punter / Pilgrim's address / Medley:- Lucky – Credo – Vigil in a wilderness of mirrors / Clock moves sideways / The company / Flower of Scotland.

– compilations, others, etc. –

Sep 94. (cd) *Blueprint; (DDICK 6CD)* **ACOUSTIC SESSIONS (live)** [ ] [–]
– Lucky / Internal exile / Kayleigh / Fortunes of war / Dear friend / Sugar mice / Somebody special / Jumpsuit city / Lady let it lie. *(re-iss. d-cd Jan01 & May02 on 'Chocolate Frog – Voiceprint'+=; CFVP 006CD)* – KRAKOW

Sep 96. (d-cd) *Blueprint; (DDICK 16CD)* **PIGPENS BIRTHDAY** [ ] [–]
(re-iss. Nov98 on 'Roadrunner'; RR 8684-2)

Nov 98. (cd) *Roadrunner; (<RR 8678-2>)* **KETTLE OF FISH 88-98** [ ] [ ]
– Big wedge / Just good friends (with SAM BROWN) / Brother 52 / Chasing Miss Pretty / Credo / A gentleman's excuse me / Goldfish and clowns / Lady let it lie / Lucky / State of mind / Mr Buttons / Fortunes of war / Internal exile. *(also w/ CD-ROM; RR 8678-8)*

Nov 98. (d-cd) *Roadrunner; (RR 8681-2)* **KRAKOW (live acoustic 1995)** [ ] [–]
– Somebody special / Jumpsuit city / Lady let it lie / Out of my life / State of mind / Kayleigh / Solo / Company / Giz a bun / Lavender.

Nov 98. (d-cd) *Roadrunner; (RR 8685-2)* **UNCLE FISH AND THE CRYPT CREEPERS** [ ] [ ]

Nov 98. (d-cd) *Roadrunner; (RR 8688-2)* **TALES FROM THE BIG BUS (live)** [ ] [–]

Nov 98. (cd) *Roadrunner; (RR 8689-2)* **FORTUNES OF WAR** [ ] [ ]

May 99. (d-cd) *Blueprint; (BP 297CD)* **THE COMPLETE BBC SESSIONS** [ ] [–]

Jan 01. (d-cd) *Chocolate Frog – Voiceprint; (CFVP 001CD)* **TOILING IN THE REEPERBAHN** [ ] [–]
(re-iss. May02; same)

Mar 01. (d-cd) *Chocolate Frog – Voiceprint; (CFVP 002CD)* **FOR WHOM THE BELL TOLLS** [ ] [–]
(re-iss. May02; same)

Mar 01. (d-cd) *Chocolate Frog – Voiceprint; (CFVP 003CD)* **DEREK DICK AND HIS AMAZING BEAR** [ ] [–]
(re-iss. May02; same)

Dec 02. (d-cd) *(CFVP 008CD)* **SASHAMI** [ ] [–]

FLAMIN' GROOVIES

Formed: Bay Area, San Francisco, California, USA … 1965 originally as The CHOSEN FEW and then The LOST AND FOUND, by CYRIL JORDAN, ROY LONEY, GEORGE ALEXANDER and TIM LYNCH. In 1967, they issued a self-financed debut lp, the 10" 'SNEAKERS', which resulted in a deal with 'Epic'. After one poorly promoted lp, 'SUPERSNAZZ', they left to join the roster of the 'Kama Sutra' label, aided by producer Richard Robinson in 1970. There, they issued two well-received albums, 'FLAMINGO' and 'TEENAGE HEAD', before again moving stables to 'United Artists' in '72. Critically acclaimed, the albums highlighted The 'GROOVIES' characteristic high-energy rock'n'roll, updating 50's material into 60's-style garage punk. The following years resulted in many personnel changes, and after touring Europe in 1976, they finally released the DAVE EDMUNDS-produced 'Sire' comeback, 'SHAKE SOME ACTION' (he had previously worked on their 1972 album, 'SLOW DEATH'). Although the band were associated with the embryonic new wave/punk movement, the album's power-pop harmonies found little credibility with this scene. The band released a further two albums in the same vein before splitting then re-forming for the live comeback lp, 'ONE NIGHT STAND' (1987). • **Songwriters:** JORDAN-LONEY, until the latter's departure in '71. Recorded many covers including; SOMETHIN' ELSE (Eddie Cochran) / PISTOL PACKIN' MAMA (Gene Vincent) / SHAKIN' ALL OVER (Johnny Kidd) / THAT'LL BE THE DAY (Buddy Holly) / KEEP A KNOCKIN' (Little Richard) / MOVE IT (Cliff Richard) / FEEL A WHOLE LOT BETTER (Byrds) / PAINT IT BLACK + JUMPIN' JACK FLASH + 19th NERVOUS BREAKDOWN (Rolling Stones) / MARRIED WOMAN (Frankie Lee Sims) / TEENAGE CONFIDENTIAL (Jerry Lee Lewis) / WEREWOLVES OF LONDON (Warren Zevon) / ABSOLUTELY SWEET MARIE (Bob Dylan) / TALLAHASSEE LASSIE (Freddy Cannon) / KICKS (Mann-Weill) / CALL ME LIGHTNING (Who) / MONEY (Barrett Strong) / PLEASE PLEASE ME + MISERY + THERE'S A PLACE (Beatles) / etc. • **Trivia:** Long-time fan GREG SHAW, issued 1975 single 'YOU TORE ME DOWN', for his own 'Bomp' magazine label.

Album rating: SNEAKERS (*5) / SUPERSNAZZ (*6) / FLAMINGO (*7) / TEENAGE HEAD (*8) / SHAKE SOME ACTION (*8) / FLAMIN' GROOVIES NOW! (*7) / JUMPIN' IN THE NIGHT (*6) / ONE NIGHT STAND (*4) / GROOVIES GREATEST GROOVES compilation (*8)

ROB LONEY (b.13 Apr'46) – vocals / **CYRIL JORDAN** (b. 1948) – lead guitar / **TIM LYNCH** (b.18 Jul'46) – rhythm guitar / **GEORGE ALEXANDER** (b.18 May'46, San Mateo, Calif.) – bass / **DANNY MIHM** – drums (ex-WHISTLING SHRIMP) repl. RON GRECO

not iss. Snazz

1967. (10"m-lp) *<2371>* **SNEAKERS** [–] [ ]
– The slide / I'm drowning / Babes in the sky / Love time / My yada / Golden clouds / Prelude in A flat to afternoon of a plad. *<US re-iss. 1975 on 'Skydog'; FGG 803>*

not iss. Epic

1968. (7") *<10501>* **ROCKIN' PNEUMONIA AND THE BOOGIE WOOGIE FLU. / THE FIRST ONE'S FREE** [–] [ ]

1968. (7") *<10564>* **SOMETHIN' ELSE. / LAURIE DID IT** [–] [ ]

1970. (lp) *<26487>* **SUPERSNAZZ** [–] [ ]
– Love have mercy / The girl can't help it / Laurie did it / Apart from that / Rockin' pneumonia and the boogie woogie flu / The first one's free / Pagan Rachel / a) Somethin' else, b) Pistol packin' mama / Brushfire / Bam balam / Around the corner. *(UK-rel.Feb86 on 'Edsel'; ED 173) (cd-iss. Aug93 on 'Columbia'; 467073-2)*

Kama Sutra Kama Sutra

1971. (lp) *<KSBS 2021>* **FLAMINGO** [–] [ ]
– Roadhouse / Headin' for the Texas border / Gonna rock tonite / Comin' after you / Sweet roll me on down / Keep a knockin' / Second cousin / Childhood's end / Jailbait. *(UK cd-iss. Jan90 on 'Big Beat'+=; CDWIK 925)* – Walkin' the dog / Somethin' else / My girl Josephine / Louie Louie / Rockin' pneumonia and the boogie woogie flu / Going out theme (version 2).

1971. (d-lp) *<KSBS 2031>* **TEENAGE HEAD** [–] [ ]
– Teenage head / Whiskey women / Yesterday's numbers 32:20 / High flyin' baby / City lights / Have you seen my baby / Evil-hearted Ada / Doctor Boogie / Rumble / Shakin' all over / That'll be the day / Round and round / Going out theme. *('FLAMINGO' + 'TEENAGE HEAD' iss.UK as 'FLAMIN' GROOVIES' on 'Kama Sutra' d-lp; 2683 003) (UK re-iss. 1989 on 'Dojo' lp/cd; DOJO LP/CD 58) (cd re-iss. Jan90 on 'Big Beat'; CDWIK 926)*

Aug 71. (7") *(2013 031)* **TEENAGE HEAD. / EVIL-HEARTED ADA** [ ] [ ]

Mar 72. (7"ep) *(2013 042)* **GONNA ROCK TONITE / KEEP A-KNOCKIN'. / (3 others by 'Sha Na Na')** [ ] [ ]

— **CHRIS WILSON** (b.10 Sep'52, Waltham, Massachusetts, USA) – vocals (ex-LOOSE GRAVEL) repl. LONEY / **JAMES FARRELL** – guitar (ex-LOOSE GRAVEL) repl. LYNCH who formed HOT KNIVES

— changed to The DOGS for a short while, before returning to same

U.A. U.A.

Jun 72. (7") *(UP 35392)* **SLOW DEATH. / TALAHASSIE LASSIE**

Jun 72. (lp) *<7521>* **SLOW DEATH** –
– Sweet little rock'n'roller / Doctor Boogie / Walking the dog / Roadhouse / Teenage head / Slow death / Shakin' all over / Louie Louie / Have you seen my baby / Can't explain.

Jan 73. (7") *(UP 35464)* **MARRIED WOMAN. / GET A SHOT OF RHYTHM & BLUES**

— **JORDAN, WILSON, FARRELL and ALEXANDER** recruited new member **DAVID WRIGHT** – drums; repl. TERRY RAE who had repl. MIHM (to HOT KNIVES)

Skydog not iss.

1974. (7") **JUMPIN' JACK FLASH. / BLUES FROM PHILLYS** – France –
(re-iss. '77 on 12";)

1974. (7"ep) *<66001>* **GREASE** – France –
– Let me rock / Dog meat / Sweet little rock'n'roller.

Philips not iss.

1975. (7") **LET THE BOY ROCK'N'ROLL. / YES IT'S TRUE** – France –

not iss. Bomp

1975. (7") *<101>* **YOU TORE ME DOWN. / HIM OR ME** –

Sire Sire

Jun 76. (lp) *(9103 251)* **SHAKE SOME ACTION**
– Shake some action / Sometimes / Yes it's true / St. Louis blues / You tore me down / Please please girl / Let the boy rock'n'roll / Don't you lie to me / She said yeah / I'll cry alone / Misery / I saw her / Teenage confidential / I can't hide. *(re-iss. Sep78; SRK 6021) (cd-iss. Sep93 on 'Aim'; AIMCD 1017)*

Jul 76. (7"m) *(6198 086)* **DON'T YOU LIE TO ME. / SHE SAID YEAH / SHAKE SOME ACTION**

Nov 76. (7") *(6078 602)* **SHAKE SOME ACTION. / TEENAGE CONFIDENTIAL**

Nov 76. (7") *<731>* **TEENAGE CONFIDENTIAL. / I CAN'T HIDE** –

— **MIKE WILHELM** – guitar; repl. FARRELL who joined PHANTOM MOVERS

Apr 78. (lp) *(9103 333)* **THE FLAMIN' GROOVIES NOW!**
– Feel a whole lot better / Bewteen the lines / Ups and downs / There's a place / Take me back / Reminiscing / Good laugh man / Yeah my baby / House of blue lights / All I wanted / Blue turns to grey / When I heard your name / Move it / Don't put me on. *(re-iss. Sep78; SRK 7059)*

Apr 78. (7"m,12"m) *(6078 619)* **FEEL A WHOLE LOT BETTER. / PAINT IT BLACK / SHAKE SOME ACTION**

Aug 78. (7") *(SIR 4002)* **MOVE IT. / WHEN I HEARD YOUR NAME**

Jun 79. (lp) *(SRK 6067)* **JUMPING IN THE NIGHT**
– Please please girl / Next one crying / Down down down / Tell me again / Absolutely sweet Marie / (You're my) Wonderful one / Jumpin' in the night / 19th nervous breakdown / Boys / 5D / First plane home / Lady friend / In the U.S.A. *<US-different tracks>*

1979. (7"m) *(SIR 4018)* **ABSOLUTELY SWEET MARIE. / WEREWOLVES OF LONDON / NEXT ONE CRYING**

— **DANNY MIHM** – drums (ex-PHANTOM MOVERS) re-repl. WRIGHT before split CHRIS WILSON joined BARRACUDAS in '82, **CYRIL JORDAN** re-formed **FLAMIN' GROOVIES** in 1986

— **JACK JOHNSON** – guitar + **PAUL ZAHL** – drums; repl. WILSON, WRIGHT + WILHELM

A.B.C. not iss.

Jul 87. (7") *(ABCS 015)* **SHAKE SOME ACTION (live). / ?** –

Jul 87. (lp) *(ABCLP 10)* **ONE NIGHT STAND (live)** –
– Kicks / Bittersweet / I can't hide / Money / Call me Lightning / Shake some action / Slow death / Teenage head / Slow down / Tallahassee lassie. *(cd-iss. Apr89; ABCD 10) (re-iss. Sep93 on 'Aim' cd/c; AIM CD/C 1008)*

– compilations etc. –

Jun 76. (7") *Kama Sutra; (KSS 707)* **TEENAGE HEAD. / HEADIN' FOR TEXAS BORDER** –

Nov 76. (7"ep) *United Artists; (REM 406)* **SLOW DEATH EP** –
– Slow death / Talahassie lassie / Married woman / Get a shot of rhythm & blues.

May 84. (lp) *Skydog; (SK 12226)* **SUPERGREASE** – France –

1980's. (7") *Skydog;* **I CAN'T EXPLAIN. / LITTLE QUEENIE** – France –

Nov 84. (lp) *Eva; (12044)* **'68 (live)** – France –

Nov 84. (lp) *Eva; (12045)* **'70 (live)** – France –

Jul 85. (lp/c) *Buddah; (252262-1/-4)* **STILL SHAKIN'** –

May 86. (lp/c) *Edsel; (ED/CED 183)* **ROADHOUSE** –
– (compilation of 'FLAMINGO' + 'TEENAGE HEAD').

Aug 88. (lp) *Voxx; (200009)* **BUCKET OF BRAINS** –
(UK cd-iss. Apr95 on 'E.M.I.'; CZ 542)

Aug 89. (lp/c/cd) *Sire; (K 925948-1/-4/-2)* **GROOVIES GREATEST GROOVES**
– Shake some action / Teenage head / Slow death / Tallahassie lassie / Yeah my baby / Yes it's true / First plane home / In the U.S.A. / Between the lines / Don't you lie to me / Down down down / I'll cry alone / You tore me down / Please please girl / Yes I am / Teenage confidential / I can't hide / Absolutely sweet Marie / Don't put me on / I saw her / All I wanted / Jumpin' in the night / There's a place / River deep, mountain high. *(cd re-iss. Jan96 on 'Warners'; 7599 25948-2)*

Nov 89. (lp) *Aim; (COLLECT 2)* **ROCKFIELD SESSIONS** –

Apr 93. (cd/lp) *Marilyn;* **RARE DEMOS & LIVE RECORDINGS** –

Sep 93. (cd/c) *Ain; (AIM CD/C 1030)* **STEP UP** –

Oct 93. (cd) *Aim; (COLLECT 1-2)* **SNEAKERS / ROCKFIELD SESSIONS** –

Nov 93. (cd) *Mystery;* **ROCKIN' AT THE ROUNDHOUSE – LIVE IN LONDON 1976/78 (live)** –

May 94. (cd) *Eva; (842070)* **LIVE 68/70 (live)** –

Nov 94. (10"lp) *Bomp;* **EP** –

Apr 95. (cd) *Aim; (AIM 1051CD)* **LIVE AT THE FESTIVAL OF THE SUN BARCELONA (live)** –

Apr 97. (cd) *Aim; (AIM 2001CD)* **OLDIES BUT GOLDIES: BEST OF** –

Jan 98. (cd) *Camden; (74321 55843-2)* **YESTERDAY'S NUMBERS** –

Jan 00. (cd) *Ranch Life; (CRANCH 17)* **BACKTRACKS** –

Nov 02. (cd) *Norton; <(CED 243)>* **CALIFORNIA BORN AND BRED**

FLAMING LIPS

Formed: Oklahoma City, Oklahoma, USA . . . 1983 by the COYNE brothers WAYNE and MARK, who reputedly stole instruments from a church hall to get their act off the ground. After a rare and weird EP in 1985, MARK left brother WAYNE to recruit new members for the 'Enigma' album, 'HEAR IT IS'. Their next, 'OH MY GAWD!!!', in '87, saw them strike with many poetic assaults, including the near 10-minute track 'ONE MILLION BILLIONTH OF A MILLISECOND ON A SUNDAY MORNING'. Their reputation grew, with wild, climactic live appearances, highlighting albums 'TELEPATHIC SURGERY' and 'IN A PRIEST-DRIVEN AMBULANCE (WITH SILVER SUNSHINE STARES)'. Phew!!!. Signed to 'Warners' in 1992, and between appearing at the Reading Festival, they released 'HIT TO DEATH IN THE MAJOR HEAD' and the US No.108 (!) album 'TRANSMISSIONS FROM THE SATELLITE HEART'. By the mid-90's, they had secured weirdo posterity, after giving birth to the drug-orientated, narrative track, 'WATERBUG'. Their avant-garde psychedelic (BARRETT / FLOYD) approach was now well behind them, their barrage of sound, once described as The JESUS & MARY CHAIN meeting BLACK FLAG or The DEAD KENNEDYS, took a sharp detour and ended up in DAVE FRIDMANN's (of MERCURY REV) up state New York studio, where the LIPS (now consisting of only three; WAYNE COYNE, STEVE DROZD and MICHAEL IVINS) recorded the spooky but highly commercial 'THE SOFT BULLETIN' (1999) for 'Warners'. The album spawned two hit singles, 'RACE FOR THE PRIZE' and the echo fronted 'WAITIN' FOR A SUPERMAN', which was their most pop orientated work since the 1995 release 'BAD DAYS'. 'THE SOFT BULLETIN' marked the work of a band who had matured in age and in sound. Adding the FRIDMANN formula, the album sounded similar to MERCURY REV's 'Deserter's Songs', although relying largely on its YES-type chord changes/structures and BEACH BOYS harmonies with COYNE attempting to sing in tune (possibly for the very first time). The group returned three years later with an album just as stunning and as beautiful as 'THE SOFT BULLETIN', influenced by Japanese counter-culture named 'YOSHIMI BATTLES THE PINK ROBOTS' (it's a concept album, kind of). From the lush title track, with its swirling analogue synth to the emotionally sweeping 'DO YOU REALIZE', 'YOSHIMI . . .' could be categorized easily alongside GRANDADDY's 'The Sophtware Slump' and RADIOHEAD's 'Kid A', although it seems that The FLAMING LIPS had a lot more fun. 'FIGHT TEST' was issued on the back of 'YOSHIMI . . .' in 2003, an EP of B-sides, remixes and obscure covers that extended the band's diversity even further. In amongst the oddities was the truly hilarious and rather downbeat cover of Kylie's monster hit 'CAN'T GET YOU OUT OF MY HEAD', beginning in a dramatic orchestral sweep, the listener couldn't help but think that the 'LIPS were extracting the urine a little, while making a notable improvement on the original. More obvious was their choices of covering Radiohead's 'KNIVES OUT' and touring partner Beck's 'GOLDEN AGE'. Both songs were given that added weirdness and would probably sit well with their original authors. As for the remix side, there was the overlong but joyous Scott Hardkiss redux of 'YOSHIMI . . .'s 'DO YOU REALIZE', clocking in at almost nine-and-a-half minutes it's always interesting to hear another musicians take on what was already a brilliant song. • **Songwriters:** Group except; SUMMERTIME BLUES (Eddie Cochran) / WHAT'S SO FUNNY 'BOUT PEACE, LOVE & UNDERSTANDING (Brinsley Schwarz) / THANK YOU + COMMUNICATION BREAKDOWN (Led Zeppelin) / DEATH VALLEY '69 (Sonic Youth & Lydia Lunch) / STRYCHNINE (Sonics) / AFTER THE GOLD RUSH (Neil Young) / ALL THAT JAZZ + HAPPY DEATH MEN (Echo & The Bunnymen) / LIFE ON MARS (David Bowie) / WHAT A WONDERFUL WORLD (Nat King Cole) / ICE DRUMMER (Suicide) / CHOSEN ONE + LITTLE DRUMMER BOY (Smog).

Album rating: HEAR IT IS (*5) / OH MY GAWD!!! . . . THE FLAMING LIPS (*7) / TELEPATHIC SURGERY (*5) / IN A PRIEST-DRIVEN AMBULANCE (*6) / HIT TO DEATH IN THE FUTURE HEAD (*6) / TRANSMISSIONS FROM THE SATELLITE HEART (*8) / CLOUDS TASTE METALLIC (*7) / ZAIREEKA (*7) / THE SOFT BULLETIN (*9) / YOSHIMI BATTLES THE PINK ROBOTS (*8)

MARK COYNE – vocals / **WAYNE COYNE** – guitar / **MICHAEL IVINS** – bass / **RICHARD ENGLISH** – drums

not iss. — Lovely Sorts Of Death

1985. (7"green-ep) *<L-19679>* **THE FLAMING LIPS E.P.** [ ] [ ]
– Bag full of thoughts / Out for a walk / Garden of eyes – Forever is a long time / Scratching the door / My own planet. *(re-iss. 1986 red-ep; same)* *(re-iss. 1987 on 'Pink Dust' 7"ep/c-ep; 731881-1/-4)*

— **WAYNE** now on vox, when MARK departed

Enigma — Restless

Nov 86. (white-lp,lp/c/cd) *<72173-1/-4/-2>* **HEAR IT IS** [–] [ ]
– With you / Unplugged / Trains, brains and rain / Jesus shootin' heroin / Just like before / She is death / Charles Manson blues / Man from Pakistan / Godzilla flick / Staring at sound – With you. *(cd+=)* – Bag full of thoughts / Out for a walk / Garden of eyes – Forever is a long time / Scratching the door / My own planet / Summertime blues. *(cd re-iss. Jul99; same)*

Nov 87. (clear-lp,lp/c/cd) *<72207-1/-4/-2>* **OH MY GAWD!!! . . . THE FLAMING LIPS** [–] [ ]
– Can't exist / Can't stop the spring / Ceiling is bending / Everything's explodin' / Love yer brain / Maximum dream for Evil Knievel / Ode to CC / One million billionth / Prescription: Overkill / Thank.

Feb 89. (lp/c/cd) *(ENVLP/TCENV/CDENV 523) <72350-1/-4/-2>* **TELEPATHIC SURGERY** [ ] [ ]
– Drug machine / Michael time to wake up / Miracle on 42nd Street / UFO story / Shaved gorilla / Begs and achin' / Right now / Hare Krishna stomp wagon / Chrome plated suicide / Redneck school of technology / Spontaneous combustion of John / The last drop of morning dew. *(cd re-iss. Jul99 on 'Restless'; same as US)*

— **JONATHAN PONEMANN** – guitar + **JOHN DONAHUE** – guitar

City Slang — Sub Pop

Jun 89. (7"m) *(EFA 40153) <SP-28>* **DRUG MACHINE / STRYCHNINE. / (WHAT'S SO FUNNY ABOUT) PEACE, LOVE AND UNDERSTANDING** [ ] Jan89 [ ]

— **NATHAN ROBERTS** – drums repl. ENGLISH

City Slang — Atavistic

Jan 91. (12"ep) *(EFA 04063-05)* **UNCONSCIOUSLY SCREAMIN' EP** [ ] [ ]
– Unconsciously screamin' / Lucifer rising / Ma, I didn't notice / Let me be it.

City Slang — Restless

Feb 91. (pink-lp,lp/c/cd) *(SLANG 005/+C/CD) <72359>* **IN A PRIEST-DRIVEN AMBULANCE (WITH SILVER SUNSHINE STARES)** [ ] Sep90 [ ]
– Shine on sweet Jesus – Jesus song No.5 / Unconsciously screamin' / Rainin' babies / Take me ta Mars / Five stop Mother Superior rain / Stand in line / God walks among us now / Jesus song No.6 / There you are / Jesus song No.7 / Mountain song / What a wonderful world. *(cd re-iss. Sep96 on 'Restless'; 72359-2)*

Warners — Warners

Jul 92. (cd-ep) *<40244>* **. . .WASTIN' PIGS IS STILL RADICAL** [–] [ ]
– Talkin' 'bout the smiling deathporn immorality blues (everyone wants to live forever) / All that jazz – Happy death men / Jets (Cupid's kiss vs. the psyche of death).

Aug 92. (cd/c/lp) *<(7599 26838-2/-4/-1)>* **HIT TO DEATH IN THE MAJOR HEAD** [ ] [ ]
– Talkin' about the smiling deathporn immorality blues (everyone wants to live forever) / Hit me like you did the first time / The Sun / Felt good to burn / Gingerale afternoon (the astrology of a Saturday) / Halloween on the Barbary Coast / The magician vs. the headache / You have to be joking (autopsy of the Devil's brain) / Frogs / Hold your head. *(re-iss. Apr95; same)*

— **RONALD JONES** – guitar repl. JOHN who joined MERCURY REV

— **STEVEN DROZD** – drums repl. NATHAN

Jun 93. (cd/c/lp) *<(9362 45334-2/-4/-1)>* **TRANSMISSIONS FROM THE SATELLITE HEART** [ ] [ ]
– Turn it on / Pilot can at the queer of God / Oh my pregnant head (labia in the sunlight) / She don't use jelly / Chewin' the apple of your eye / Superhumans / Be my head / Moth in the incubator / Plastic Jesus / When yer twenty-two / Slow nerve action.

Aug 94. (7"/c-s) *(W 0246/+C) <9362 18131-2>* **SHE DON'T USE JELLY. / TURN IT ON (bluegrass version)** [ ] Nov94 [55]
(cd-s+=) *(WO 246CD)* – Translucent egg.
(cd-s) *(WO 246CDX)* – ('A'side) / The process / Moth in the incubator.

Apr 95. (cd-s) *<9362 43509-2>* **TURN IT ON / PUT THE WATERBUG IN THE POLICEMAN'S EAR / SHE DON'T USE JELLY (demo)** [–] [ ]

Jul 95. (m-cd) *<9362 45748-2>* **PROVIDING NEEDLES FOR YOUR BALLOONS** [–] [ ]
– Bad days / Jets part 2 (my two days as an ambulance driver) / Ice drummer / Put the waterbug in the policeman's ear / Chewin the apple of yer ear / Chosen one / Little drummerboy / Slow nerve action.

Sep 95. (cd/c) *<(9362 45911-2/-4)>* **CLOUDS TASTE METALLIC** [ ] [ ]
– The abandoned hospital ship / Psychiatric explorations of the fetus with needles / Placebo headwood / This here giraffe / Brainville / Guy who lost a headache and accidentally saves the world / When you smile / Kim's watermelon gun / They punctured my yolk / Lightning strikes the postman / Christmas at the zoo / Evil will prevail / Bad days (aurally excited version).

Dec 95. (c-s) *(W 0322C)* **BAD DAYS / GIRL WITH HAIR LIKE AN EXPLOSION** [ ] [–]
(cd-s+=) *(W 0322CD)* – She don't use jelly / Giraffe (demo).
(cd-s) *(W 0322CDX)* – ('A'side) / Ice drummer / When you smiled I lost my only idea / Put the water bug in the policeman's ear.

Mar 96. (cd-s) *(W 0335CD)* **THIS HERE GIRAFFE / JETS pt.2 (MY TWO DAYS AS AN AMBULANCE DRIVER) / LIFE ON MARS** 72 –
(c-s/cd-s) *(W 0335 C/CDX)* – ('A'side) / The sun / Hit me like you did the first time.
above was the first ever shaped cd single.

Aug 96. (3D-cd-s) *(W 0370CD)* **BRAINVILLE / EVIL WILL PREVAIL (live) / WATERBUG (live)** –
(c-s/cd-s) *(W 0370 C/CDX)* – ('A'side) / Brainville (live) / Raindrops keep falling on my head.

Oct 97. (4xcd-box) <*(9362 46804)*> **ZAIREEKA**
– Okay I'll admit that I really don't care / Riding to work in the year 2025 (your invisible now) / Thirty-five thousand feet of despair / Machine in India / The train runs over the camel but is . . . / How will we know? (futuristic crashendos) / March of the rotten vegetables / Big ol' bug is the new baby now.
(above was an unusual concept in that you needed 4 separate CD players to hear the simultaneous recordings at its full potential)

— now down to a trio of **WAYNE COYNE, STEVEN DROZD + MICHAEL IVINS**

May 99. (cd/c) <*(9362 47393-2/-4)*> **THE SOFT BULLETIN** 39
– Race for the prize / A spoonful weighs a ton / The spark that bled / Slow motion / What is the light? / The observer / Waitin' for a superman / Suddenly everything has changed / The gash / Feeling yourself disintigrate / Sleeping on the roof / Race for the prize (remix) / Waitin' for a superman (remix) / Buggin' (remix). *<(lp-iss.Aug02 on 'PIAS USA'; PIASA 09LP)>*

Jun 99. (cd-s) *(W 494CD1)* **RACE FOR THE PRIZE / RIDING TO WORK IN THE YEAR 2025 (YOUR INVISIBLE NOW) (from 'Zaireeka' disc 1 / THIRTY THOUSAND FEET OF DESPAIR (from 'Zaireeka' disc 1)** 39 –
(cd-s) *(W 494CD2)* – ('A'side) / (same B's except from 'Zaireeka' disc 2).

Nov 99. (c-s/cd-s) *(W 505 C/CD2)* <*44793*> **WAITIN' FOR A SUPERMAN / RIDING TO WORK IN THE YEAR 2025 / YOU'RE INVISIBLE / 35,000 FEET OF DESPAIR** Feb00
(cd-s) *(W 505CD1)* – ('A'mixes).

Jul 02. (cd) <*(9362 48141-2)*> **YOSHIMI BATTLES THE PINK ROBOTS** 13 50
– Fight test / One more robot – 3000-21 / Yoshimi battles the pink robots pt.1 / Yoshimi battles the pink robots pt.2 / In the morning of the magicians / Ego tripping at the gates of Hell / Are you a hypnotist? / It's summertime / Do you realize? / All we have is now / Approaching pavonis mons by balloon (utopia planitia). *<(lp-iss.Aug02 on 'PIAS USA'; PIASA 101LP)>*

Aug 02. (cd-s) *(W 586CD1)* **DO YOU REALIZE? / IF I GO MAD – FUNERAL IN MY HEAD / SYRTIS MAJOR** 32 –
(cd-s) *(W 586CD2)* – ('A'side) / Up above the daily hum / Zanthe terra.

Aug 02. (7"pic-d) <*RE-1*> **DO YOU REALIZE? / UP ABOVE THE DAILY HUM** –

Jan 03. (cd-s) *(W 597CD1)* **YOSHIMI BATTLES THE PINK ROBOTS PT.1 / CAN'T GET YOU OUT OF MY HEAD (KEXP version) / YOSHIMI BATTLES THE PINK ROBOTS PT.1 (AOL sessions version)** 18 –
(cd-s) *(W 597CD2)* – ('A'side) / Do you realize?? (Scott Hardkiss floating in space vocal mix) / ('A'-Japanese version).

Feb 03. (7"pic-d) <*FL 1*> **YOSHIMI BATTLES THE PINK ROBOTS PT.1 / YOSHIMI BATTLES THE PINK ROBOTS PT.1 (AOL sessions live in L.A.)** –

Apr 03. (m-cd) <*48433*> **FIGHT TEST** – 93
– Fight test / Strange design of conscience / Thank you Jack White (for the fiber-optic Jesus that you gave me) / Do you realize (Scott Hardkiss mix) / Can't get you out of my head / The golden age / Knives out.

Jun 03. (cd-s) *(W 611CD1)* **FIGHT TEST / THANK YOU JACK WHITE (FOR THE FIBER-OPTIC JESUS THAT YOU GAVE ME) / DETEORATION OF THE FIGHT OR FLIGHT RESPONSE** 28 –
(cd-s) *(W 611CD2)* – ('A'side) / Strange design of conscience / ('A'-helium voice demo).

Jul 03. (7"pic-d) <*16659*> **FIGHT TEST. / THANK YOU JACK WHITE (FOR THE FIBER-OPTIC JESUS THAT YOU GAVE ME)** –

Nov 03. (m-cd) <*48514*> **EGO TRIPPING AT THE GATES OF HELL** –
– Assassination of the sun / I'm a fly in a sunbeam (following the funeral procession of a stranger) / Sunshine balloons / Do you realize?? / Ego tripping (ego in acceceration) / Ego tripping / A change at Christmas (say it isn't so).

– compilations, etc. –

Oct 98. (cd) *Restless;* <*(RST 72963)*> **A COLLECTION OF SONGS REPRESENTING AN ENTHUSIASM FOR RECORDING . . . BY AMATEURS** (1984-1990) Sep98
– Bag full of thoughts / Jesus shootin' heroin / One million billionth / Chrome plated suicide / Michael time to wake up / Hell's angels cracker factory / Unconsciously screamin' / God walks among us now / Stychnini – Peace, love and understanding / Death valley '69 / Thank you / Ma, I didn't notice / After the gold rush / I want to kill my brother: The cymbal.

Sep 02. (3xcd-box) *Restless;* <*(REST 73764)*> **FINALLY, THE PUNK ROCKERS ARE TAKING ACID**
– (THE FLAMING LIPS ep / HEAR IT IS / OH MY GAWD!!! / TELEPATHIC SURGERY / others).

Sep 02. (2xcd-box) *Restless;* <*(REST 73765)*> **THE DAY WE SHOT A HOLE IN THE JESUS EGG**
– (IN A PRIEST DRIVEN AMBULANCE / DRUG MACHINE / UNCONSCIOUSLY SCREAMIN' / etc.)

FLEETWOOD MAC

Formed: London, England . . . July 1967, by MICK FLEETWOOD, PETER GREEN and BOB BRUNNING. They quickly inducted JEREMY SPENCER and made their live debut at the prestigious Windsor Jazz & Blues Festival on the 12th of August '67. Replacing BRUNNING with another ex-BLUESBREAKERS member, JOHN McVIE, they signed to 'Blue Horizon'. Initially billed as PETER GREEN'S FLEETWOOD MAC, the group made little impact in late '67 with their first 45, 'I BELIEVE MY TIME AIN'T LONG'. Around the same time, they became the in-house band for blues artists like OTIS SPANN and DUSTER BENNETT. Early in '68, the debut album, 'PETER GREEN'S FLEETWOOD MAC' hit the Top 5, a fairly derivative set of white-boy blues which nevertheless introduced GREEN's incredibly instinctive feeling for the music, both in his guitar playing and his bruised, soulful vocals. The promise was fully realised with 'BLACK MAGIC WOMAN', a classic slice of brooding voodoo blues with a lean, blistering GREEN solo. Another single, 'NEED YOUR LOVE SO BAD', followed into the lower regions of the chart soon after, while the follow-up album, 'MR. WONDERFUL', again made the Top 10 album charts. But the real breakthrough came with the billowy wistfulness of the GREEN instrumental, 'ALBATROSS', which made No.1 and saw the band melding their blues fixation into something more original. Listening to 'MAN OF THE WORLD', arguably GREEN's most affecting composition (presumably included for those who found the single too sensitive, was the charmingly titled B-side, 'SOMEBODY'S GONNA GET THEIR HEAD KICKED IN TONIGHT'!) , it was clear that all was not well with the band's frontman, and indeed he abruptly left the band the following year. Taking LSD had seriously affected GREEN and he began giving all his money away in line with his newly acquired religious beliefs, his last recording with the band, 'GREEN MANALISHI (WITH THE TWO PRONGED CROWN)', giving light to his demons in chilling style. Truly one of the most tragic cases in the history of rock, GREEN never really recovered from his mental problems and at one particularly low ebb in the 80's, was even sleeping rough around Richmond, Surrey. Despite his difficulties, GREEN did record a number of solo albums in the 70's and more recently, the man undertook a 1997 comeback tour under the moniker PETER GREEN & THE SPLINTER GROUP. Rarely has a white man played the blues with such feeling (legendary bluesman B.B. KING was one of his biggest fans) and it was inevitable that with his departure, FLEETWOOD MAC would be a radically different proposition. The remaining quartet of FLEETWOOD, McVIE, SPENCER and (DANNY) KIRWAN (who had joined a couple of years previous) cut a further album, 'KILN HOUSE' (1970), before recruiting CHRISTINE PERFECT (ex-CHICKEN SHACK) on keyboards/vocals. The next casualty to depart from FLEETWOOD MAC in bizarre circumstances was JEREMY SPENCER, who, in an infamous incident, went AWOL while the band were on tour in Los Angeles. When they eventually tracked him down, he was living with a religious cult, the Children Of God, and informed the band he was staying put. Surprisingly, GREEN returned briefly to fill in on the remainder of the tour although SPENCER was eventually replaced with session pro BOB WELCH. The addition of WELCH saw the band move ever further into the melodic rock vein in which PERFECT and KIRWAN had been steering the band since GREEN's departure. KIRWAN was next to leave, however, DAVE WALKER (ex-SAVOY BROWN) and BOB WESTON (ex-LONG JOHN BALDRY) briefly joining up. When the band cancelled a US tour, manager CLIFFORD DAVIS formed a 'new' FLEETWOOD MAC around WALKER and WESTON, the real FLEETWOOD MAC not unreasonably slapping an injunction on the imposters. Amid much legal wrangling, the band severed themselves from DAVIS and moved to California in 1974, only FLEETWOOD and JOHN and CHRISTINE McVIE (the pair had since been hitched) remaining. And so began the second chapter in the marathon MAC saga, as the band hooked up with studio maestro LINDSEY BUCKINGHAM and the sexiest woman to ever walk the planet, STEVIE NICKS. This girlfriend/boyfriend team had previously released an album on 'Polydor', 'BUCKINGHAM-NICKS', and FLEETWOOD was suitably impressed. For once, the band line-up gelled and by the following year, in an incredible reversal of fortunes, FLEETWOOD MAC were sitting pretty at the top of the US charts with the eponymous 'FLEETWOOD MAC' album. Highly melodic, airbrushed pop/rock was the order of the day while in NICKS, the band had a singer of a distinctiveness to match the likes of EMMYLOU HARRIS. The classic 'RHIANNON' found NICKS at her most alluring, fuelling the fantasies of clean cut American boys the country over with her breathy purr. While creatively the band were reaching for the stars, personally they were hitting the depths; JOHN and CHRISTINE divorced the following year, while BUCKINGHAM and NICKS had split acrimoniously. To top it all, FLEETWOOD was in the process of divorcing his wife, JENNY. Instead of imploding, the band channelled the emotional turmoil into writing songs, creating one of the most phenomenally successful records ever released. 'RUMOURS' (1977) remains the quintessential break-up record, every track, from 'GO YOUR OWN WAY' to 'GOLD DUST WOMAN' giving a different perspective on the situation. The songwriting was impeccable, not a duffer in sight, and in terms of AOR the record has yet to meet its match. 'TUSK' (1979), meanwhile, was a completely different kettle of fish; expensive, often experimental and bloody long. A double album, it was hard going in places yet there were moments of genius, notably NICKS' 'SARA', a beautifully melancholic ballad which arguably stands as the highlight of her career. Come 1980, various members began work on solo projects, FLEETWOOD recording 'THE VISITOR' (1981) with African musicians while NICKS started out on a successful solo career with 'BELLADONNA' (1981). The next MAC project was 'MIRAGE' (1982), a pleasant but ultimately unsatisfying attempt to recreate their winning 70's formula. It was relatively successful nevertheless, reaching No.1 in the States, although it would be the last band effort for five years. In the interim, BUCKINGHAM released his well-received 'GO INSANE' (1984) album (he'd made his solo debut three years earlier with 'LAW AND ORDER') while CHRISTINE McVIE released a self-titled album in 1984. Eventually regrouping in 1985, the band began working on what would become 'TANGO IN THE NIGHT' (1987). Basically the MAC sound translated into modern musical currency, the record surprisingly made more of an impact in Britain than the States. Like 'RUMOURS', the record was characterised by varying moods and textures, from BUCKINGHAM's clever, insistent 'BIG LOVE' to the cascading 'LITTLE LIES', and spawned a number of major chart hits. This marked the end of the classic line-up, however, as BUCKINGHAM departed the following summer after escalating tension with NICKS. RICK VITO and BILLY BURNETT were drafted in as replacements but on the showing of 'BEHIND THE MASK' (1990), BUCKINGHAM's midas touch was sorely missed. While the record made No.1 in the States, it failed to produce any singles, more calamity befalling the band later that year as NICKS bailed out following allegations in MICK FLEETWOOD's recently published autobiography. While BUCKINGHAM and NICKS played with the band at Bill Clinton's inauguration in 1993, there was no question of them rejoining, and ex-TRAFFIC man, DAVE MASON was hired along with BEKKA BRAMLETT (daughter of the legendary DELANEY & BONNIE). The resultant album, 'TIME' (1995), was released to general indifference although it was competent enough. Maybe the album should've been titled 'TIME, GENTLEMEN' as the band seemed something of an irrelevance in the 1990's. Then again, given their chequered history, anything is possible, an album of drum 'n' bass remixes, anyone? Anything is usually possible with the 'MAC and in 'SAY YOU WILL' (2003), they indeed pulled off the seemingly impossible: getting the original mid-70's band back together to record a fully fledged album – a double set no less – of new material. Admittedly, CHRISTINE McVIE was only a bit-part player but it was as close to a fully fledged reunion as longtime fans could have wished. The end result wasn't exactly spectacular, however, coming in at just under the hour and a half mark. With NICKS and BUCKINGHAM dominating the songwriting, there was an uneveness to proceedings, someting only exacerbated by the wildly indulgent running time. • **Songwriters:** GREEN compositions, except early covers; NEED YOUR LOVE SO BAD (Little Willie John) / NO PLACE TO GO (Howlin' Wolf) / DUST MY BROOM (Robert Johnson) / LOVE MINUS ZERO – NO LIMIT (Bob Dylan) / etc. • **Trivia:** Late 1973, their manager Clifford Davis, put together a bogus FLEETWOOD MAC, which resulted in a legal court battle, in which they won. The bogus group became STRETCH, and had a late '75 UK Top 20 hit with 'Why Did You Do It'.

Album rating: PETER GREEN'S FLEETWOOD MAC (*7) / MR. WONDERFUL (*6) / ENGLISH ROSE (*7) / PIOUS BIRD OF GOOD OMEN compilation (*7) / THEN PLAY ON (*7) / KILN HOUSE (*6) / FLEETWOOD MAC IN CHICAGO exploitation (*5) / FUTURE GAMES (*6) / GREATEST HITS compilation on 'CBS' (*9) / BARE TREES (*5) / PENGUIN (*4) / MYSTERY TO ME (*5) / HEROES ARE HARD TO FIND (*6) / FLEETWOOD MAC (*8) / RUMOURS (*10) / TUSK (*7) / FLEETWOOD MAC LIVE (*5) / MIRAGE (*6) / TANGO IN THE NIGHT (*6) / GREATEST HITS compilation on 'Warners' (*8) / BEHIND THE MASK (*5) / TIME (*3) / THE DANCE (*4) / THE VERY BEST OF FLEETWOOD MAC double compilation (*8) / SAY YOU WILL (*5) / Mick Fleetwood: THE VISITOR (*4) / I'M NOT ME with Zoo (*3) / SHAKIN' THE CAGE with Zoo (*3) / Lindsey Buckingham: LAW AND ORDER (*6) / GO INSANE (*5)

JEREMY SPENCER (b. 4 Jul'48, Hartlepool, England) – guitar, vocals / **PETER GREEN** (b. PETER GREENBAUM, 29 Oct'49) – guitar, vocals (ex-JOHN MAYALL'S BLUESBREAKERS, ex-SHOTGUN EXPRESS) / **MICK FLEETWOOD** (b.24 Jun'42, Redruth, England) – drums (ex-JOHN MAYALL'S BLUESBREAKERS) / **JOHN McVIE** (b.26 Nov'45) – bass (ex-JOHN MAYALL'S

BLUESBREAKERS) repl. BOB BRUNNING who formed SUNFLOWER BLUES BAND after recording B-side)

Blue Horizon Epic

Nov 67. (7"; as PETER GREEN'S FLEETWOOD MAC) *(57-3051)* **I BELIEVE MY TIME AIN'T LONG. / RAMBLING PONY** [ ] [–]
(re-iss. 1969 on 'C.B.S.'; 3051)

Feb 68. (lp; stereo/mono) *(S+/7-63200)* *<26402>* **PETER GREEN'S FLEETWOOD MAC** <US-title 'FLEETWOOD MAC'> [4] Aug68 [ ]
– My heart beat like a hammer / Merry go round / Long grey mare / Shake your moneymaker / Looking for somebody / No place to go / My baby's good to me / I love another woman / Cold black night / The world keep on turning / Got to move. *(re-iss. Oct73 on 'CBS-Embasssy'; EMB 31036) (re-iss. Jul77 on 'CBS' lp/c; CBS/40 31494) (cd-iss. Aug94 as 'FLEETWOOD MAC' on 'Columbia Rewind'; 477 358-2)*

Mar 68. (7") *(57-3138)* **BLACK MAGIC WOMAN. / THE SUN IS SHINING** [37] [–]

Apr 68. (7") *<10351>* **BLACK MAGIC WOMAN. / LONG GREY MARE** [–] [ ]

Jul 68. (7") *(57-3139) <10386>* **NEED YOUR LOVE SO BAD. / STOP MESSIN' ROUND** [31] [ ]

Aug 68. (lp) *(7-63025)* **MR. WONDERFUL** [10] [–]
– Stop messin' round / Coming home / Rollin' man / Dust my broom / Love that burns / Doctor Brown / Need your love tonight / If you be my baby / Evenin' boogie / Lazy poker blues / I've lost my baby / Trying so hard to forget. *(re-iss. Nov89 on 'Essential' lp/c/cd; ESS LP/MC/CD 010) (re-iss. cd on 'Castle'; CCSCD 368)*

—— added **DANNY KIRWAN** (b.13 Mar'50) – guitar, vocals (ex-BOILERHOUSE)

Nov 68. (7") *(57-3145) <10436>* **ALBATROSS. / JIGSAW PUZZLE BLUES** [1] [ ]
(re-iss. Nov71 on 'C.B.S.'; CBS 3145)

Feb 69. (lp) *<BN 26446>* **ENGLISH ROSE** [–] [ ]
– Stop messin' round / Jigsaw puzzle blues / Doctor Brown / Something inside of me / Evenin' boogie / Love that burns / Black magic woman / I've lost my baby / One sunny day / Without you / Coming home / Albatross.

Immediate not iss.

Apr 69. (7"; b-side by EARL VINCE & THE VALIENTS) *(IM 080)* **MAN OF THE WORLD. / SOMEBODY'S GONNA GET THEIR HEAD KICKED IN TONIGHT** [2] [–]
(re-iss. Feb83; same)

Reprise Reprise

Sep 69. (7") *<0860>* **RATTLESNAKE SHAKE. / COMING YOUR WAY** [–] [ ]

Sep 69. (7") *(RS 27000) <0883>* **OH WELL (part 1). / OH WELL (part 2)** [2] Jan70 [55]

—— (note that SPENCER, for some reason did not play on the below album)

Sep 69. (lp) *(RSLP 9000) <6368>* **THEN PLAY ON** [6] [ ]
– Coming your way / Closing my eyes / Showbiz blues / Underway / Oh well / Although the sun is shining / Rattlesnake shake / Searching for Madge / Fighting for Madge / Closing my eyes / When you say / One sunny day / Although the sun is shining / Like crying / Before the beginning. *(re-iss. Jul71 lp/c; K/K4 44103) ;re-iss. Apr77) (cd-iss. Jun88 with extra tracks; 927 448-2)*

May 70. (7") *(RS 27007) <0925>* **THE GREEN MANALISHI (WITH THE TWO-PRONG CROWN). / WORLD IN HARMONY** [10] [ ]

—— Now a quartet of **FLEETWOOD, McVIE, SPENCER and KIRWAN** when GREEN went solo

Sep 70. (lp) *(RSLP 9004) <6408>* **KILN HOUSE** [39] [69]
– This is the rock / Station man / Blood on the floor / Hi ho silver / Jewel eyed Judy / Buddy's song / Earl Grey / One together / Tell me all the things you do / Mission bell. *(re-iss. Jul71 lp/c; K/K4 54001) (cd-iss. Feb93 on 'Warners'; 7599 27453-2)*

Jan 71. (7") *<0984>* **JEWEL EYED JUDY. / STATION MAN** [–] [ ]

—— added **CHRISTINE** (PERFECT) **McVIE** (b.12 Jul'43, Birmingham, England) – keyboards, vocals (ex-CHICKEN SHACK) (she had already guested on 'MR. WONDERFUL' album)

Mar 71. (7") *(RS 27010)* **DRAGONFLY. / PURPLE DANCER** [ ] [–]

—— **BOB WELCH** (b.31 Jul'46, Los Angeles, Calif.) – guitar, vocals (ex-HEAD WEST) repl. SPENCER who formed CHILDREN OF GOD

Sep 71. (lp/c) *(K/K4 44153) <6465>* **FUTURE GAMES** [ ] [91]
– Women of 1000 years / Morning rain / What a shame / Future games / Sands of time / Sometimes / Lay it all down / Show me a smile. *(re-iss. Apr77; same) (cd-iss. Feb93 on 'Warners'; 7599 27458-2)*

Sep 71. (7") *<1057>* **SANDS OF TIME. / LAY IT ALL DOWN** [–] [ ]

Apr 72. (lp/c) *(K/K4 44181) <2080>* **BARE TREES** [ ] [70]
– Child of mine / The ghost / Homeward bound / Sunny side of Heaven / Bare trees / Sentimental lady / Danny's chant / Spare me a little of your love / Dust / Thoughts on a grey day. *(re-iss. Apr77; same) (cd-iss. Feb93 on 'Warners'; 7599 27240-2)*

Aug 72. (7") *<1093>* **SENTIMENTAL LADY. / SUNNY SIDE OF HEAVEN** [–] [ ]

Aug 72. (7") *(K 14194)* **SPARE ME A LITTLE OF YOUR LOVE. / SUNNY SIDE OF HEAVEN** [ ] [–]

—— **DAVE WALKER** – vocals (ex-SAVOY BROWN) repl. KIRWAN who went solo / added **BOB WESTON** – guitar, vocals (ex-LONG JOHN BALDRY) (above two now with FLEETWOOD, J. McVIE, C. McVIE and WELCH)

May 73. (7") *<1157>* **REMEMBER ME. / DISSATISFIED** [–] [ ]

May 73. (lp/c) *(K/K4 44235) <2138>* **PENGUIN** [ ] Apr73 [49]
– Remember me / Bright fire / Dissatisfied / (I'm a) Road runner / The derelict / Revelation / Did you ever love me / Night watch / Caught in the rain. *(re-iss. Apr77; same) (cd-iss. Feb93 on 'Warners'; 7599 26178-2)*

Jun 73. (7") *<1172>* **DID YOU EVER LOVE ME. / REVELATION** [–] [ ]

Jun 73. (7") *(K 14280)* **DID YOU EVER LOVE ME. / THE DERELICT** [ ] [–]

—— Reverted to a quintet when WALKER departed forming HUNGRY FIGHTER

Jan 74. (lp/c) *(K/K4 44248) <2158>* **MYSTERY TO ME** [ ] Nov73 [67]
– Emerald eyes / Believe me / Just crazy love / Hypnotized / Forever / Keep on going / The city / Miles away / Somebody / The way I feel / Good things come to those who wait / Why / For your love. *(re-iss. Apr77; same) (cd-iss. Feb93 on 'Warners'; 7599 25982-2)*

Mar 74. (7") *(K 14315) <1188>* **FOR YOUR LOVE. / HYPNOTIZED** [ ] [ ]

—— Trimmed to quartet when WESTON also left

Sep 74. (lp/c) *(K/K4 54026) <2196>* **HEROES ARE HARD TO FIND** [ ] [34]
– Heroes are hard to find / Coming home / Angel / The Bermuda Triangle / Come a little bit closer / She's changing me / Bad loser / Silver heels / Prove your love / Born enchanter / Safe harbour. *(cd-iss. Feb93 on 'Warners'; 7599 27216-2)*

Feb 75. (7") *(K 14388) <1317>* **HEROES ARE HARD TO FIND. / BORN ENCHANTER** [ ] [ ]

—— **LINDSEY BUCKINGHAM** (b. 3 Oct'47. Palo Alto, Calif.) – guitar, vocals (as below; ex-BUCKINGHAM-NICKS) repl. WELCH / added **STEVIE NICKS** (b. STEPHANIE NICKS, 26 May'48, Phoenix, Arizona) – vocals

Aug 75. (lp,white-lp/c) *(K/K4 54043) <2225>* **FLEETWOOD MAC** [ ] [1]
– Monday morning / Warm ways / Blue letter / Rhiannon / Over my head / Crystal / Say you love me / Landslide / World turning / Sugar daddy / I'm so afraid. *(Nov76 hit UK No.23) (cd-iss. 1983; 2281-2) (cd-iss. Dec85 on 'Warners'; K2 54043) (re-iss. Feb93 cd/c/lp; 7599 27241-2/-4/-1)*

Oct 75. (7") *(K 14403)* **WARM WAYS. / BLUE LETTER** [ ] [–]

Feb 76. (7") *(K 14413) <1339>* **OVER MY HEAD. / I'M SO AFRAID** [ ] Nov75 [20]

Apr 76. (7") *(K 14430) <1345>* **RHIANNON. / SUGAR DADDY** [ ] Feb76 [11]
(re-iss. Feb78 reached UK-No.46)

Sep 76. (7") *(K 14447) <1356>* **SAY YOU LOVE ME. / MONDAY MORNING** [40] Jun76 [11]

Warners Warners

Jan 77. (7") *(K 16872) <8304>* **GO YOUR OWN WAY. / SILVER SPRINGS** [38] [10]

Feb 77. (lp,white-lp/c) *(K/K4 56344) <3010>* **RUMOURS** [1] [1]
– Second hand news / Dreams / Never going back again / Don't stop / Go your own way / Songbird / The chain / You make loving fun / I don't want to know / Oh daddy / Gold dust woman. *(cd-iss. Dec83; K2 56344) (re-iss. Jun88 lp/c; K/K4 56344) (re-iss. Feb93 cd/c/lp; 7599 27313-2/-4/-1) (re-hit No.18 UK in Sep'97)*

Apr 77. (7") *(K 16930) <8413>* **DON'T STOP. / GOLD DUST WOMAN** [32] Jul77 [3]

Jun 77. (7") *(K 16969) <8371>* **DREAMS. / SONGBIRD** [24] Apr77 [1]

Sep 77. (7") *(K 17013)* **YOU MAKE LOVING FUN. / NEVER GOING BACK AGAIN** [45] [–]

Oct 77. (7") *<8483>* **YOU MAKE LOVING FUN. / GOLD DUST WOMAN** [–] [9]

Sep 79. (7") *(K 17468) <49077>* **TUSK. / NEVER MAKE ME CRY** [6] [8]

Oct 79. (d-lp/c) *(K/K4 66088)* <3350> **TUSK** [1] [4]
– Over & over / The ledge / Think about me / Save me a place / Sara / What makes you think you're the one / That's all for everyone / Not that funny / Sisters of the Moon / Angel / That's enough for me / Brown eyes / Never make me cry / I know I'm not wrong / Honey hi / Beautiful child / Walk a thin line / Tusk / Never forget. *(cd-iss. Mar87; K2 66088) (re-iss. Feb93 cd/c/d-lp; 7599 27395-2/-4/-1)*

Dec 79. (7") *(K 17533)* <49150> **SARA. / THAT'S ENOUGH FOR ME** [37] [7]

Feb 80. (7") *(K 17577)* **NOT THAT FUNNY. / SAVE ME A PLACE** [ ] [–]

Mar 80. (7") <49196> **THINK ABOUT ME. / SAVE ME A PLACE** [–] [20]

Mar 80. (7") *(K 17614)* **THINK ABOUT ME. / HONEY HI** [ ] [–]

Jun 80. (7") <49500> **SISTERS OF THE MOON. / WALK A THIN LINE** [–] [86]

Nov 80. (d-lp/c) *(K/K4 66097)* <3500> **FLEETWOOD MAC LIVE (live)** [31] [14]
– Monday morning / Say you love me / Dreams / Oh well / Over & over / Sara / Not that funny / Never going back again / Landslide / Fireflies / Over my head / Rhiannon / Don't let me down again / One more night / Go your own way / Don't stop / I'm so afraid / The farmer's daughter.

Jan 81. (7") <49660> **FIREFLIES. / OVER MY HEAD** [–] [60]

Feb 81. (7") *(K 17746)* **THE FARMER'S DAUGHTER (live). / DREAMS (live)** [ ] [–]

Mar 81. (7") <49700> **THE FARMER'S DAUGHTER (live). / MONDAY MORNING (live)** [–] [ ]

Jul 82. (7") *(K 17965)* <29966> **HOLD ME. / EYES OF THE WORLD** [ ] Jun82 [4]

Jul 82. (lp/c) *(K/K4 56952)* <23607> **MIRAGE** [5] [1]
– Love in store / Can't go back / That's alright / Book of love / Gypsy / Only over you / Empire state / Straight back / Hold me / Oh Diane / Eyes of the world / Wish you were here. *(cd-iss. Dec83; K2 56952) (re-iss. Feb93 cd/c/lp; 7599 23607-2/-4/-1)*

Sep 82. (7") *(K 17997)* <29918> **GYPSY. / COOL WATER** [46] Aug82 [12]

Nov 82. (7") <29848> **LOVE IN STORE. / CAN'T GO BACK** [–] [22]

Dec 82. (7"/7"pic-d) *(FLEET 1/+P)* **OH DIANE. / ONLY OVER YOU** [9] [–]
(12"+=) *(FLEET 1T)* – The chain.

Feb 83. (7") <29698> **OH DIANE. / THAT'S ALRIGHT** [–] [ ]

Apr 83. (7") *(W 9848)* **CAN'T GO BACK. / THAT'S ALRIGHT** [ ] [–]
(12") *(W 9848T)* – ('A'side) / Rhiannon / Tusk / Over and over.

Mar 87. (7"/ext.12"/ext.12"pic-d) *(W 8398/+T/TP)* <28398> **BIG LOVE. / YOU AND I, PART 1** [9] [5]
(d7"+=) *(W 8398F)* – The chain / Go your own way.

Apr 87. (lp/c)(cd) *(WX 65/+C)(925 471-2)* <25471> **TANGO IN THE NIGHT** [1] [7]
– Big love / Seven wonders / Everywhere / Caroline / Tango in the night / Mystified / Little lies / Family man / Welcome to the room . . . Sara / Isn't it midnight / When I see you again / You and I, part II.

Jun 87. (7") *(W 8317)* <28317> **SEVEN WONDERS. / BOOK OF MIRACLES (instrumental)** [56] [19]
(ext-remix.12"+=/ext-remix.12"pic-d+=) *(W 8317T/+P)* – ('A'dub).

Aug 87. (7") *(W 8291)* <28291> **LITTLE LIES. / RICKY** [5] [4]
(ext.c-s+=/ext.12"+=/ext.12"pic-d+=) *(W 8291/+C/T/TP)* – ('A'dub).

Nov 87. (7") *(W 8114)* <28114> **FAMILY MAN. / DOWN ENDLESS STREET** [54] Mar88 [90]
(7"box/12") *(W 8114 B/T)* – ('A'extended vocal remix) / Family party bonus beats / You and I, part II.

Feb 88. (7") *(W 8143)* <28143> **EVERYWHERE. / WHEN I SEE YOU AGAIN** [4] Nov 87 [14]
(12"+=) *(W 8143T)* – ('A'extended) / ('A'dub version).
(3"cd-s+=) *(W 8143CD)* – Rhiannon / Say you love me.

Jun 88. (7") *(W 7860)* **ISN'T IT MIDNIGHT. / MYSTIFIED** [60] [–]
(12"+=/3"cd-s+=) *(W 7860 T/CD)* – Say you love me / Gypsy.

Nov 88. (7") *(W 7644)* <27644> **AS LONG AS YOU FOLLOW. / OH WELL (live)** [66] [43]
(12"+=/3"cd-s+=) *(W 7644 T/CD)* – Gold dust woman.

Nov 88. (lp/c)(cd) *(WX 221/+C)(925 838-2)* <25801> **FLEETWOOD MAC'S GREATEST HITS** (compilation) [3] [14]
– As long as you follow / No questions asked / Rhiannon / Don't stop / Go your own way / Hold me / Everywhere / Gypsy / Say you love me / Dreams / Little lies / Sara / Tusk. *(c+=/cd+=)* – Oh Diane / Big love / You making loving fun / Seven wonders.

Feb 89. (7") *(W 7528)* **HOLD ME. / NO QUESTIONS ASKED** [ ] [–]
(12"+=/3"cd-s+=) *(W 7528 T/CD)* – I loved another woman (live).

—— (Jul'88) when BUCKINGHAM departed, he was repl. by **RICK VITO** (b.13 Oct'49, Darby, Pennsylvania) – guitar / **BILLY BURNETT** (b. 8 May'53, Memphis, Tenn.) – guitar (ex-MICK FLEETWOOD'S ZOO)

Apr 90. (7"/c-s) *(W 9866/+C)* <19866> **SAVE ME. / ANOTHER WOMAN (live)** [53] [33]
(12"+=/cd-s+=/s-cd-s+=) *(W 9866 T/CD/CDX)* – Everywhere (live).

Apr 90. (cd)(lp/c) *(<7599 26111-2>)(WX 335/+C)* **BEHIND THE MASK** [1] [18]
– The skies the limit / In the back of my mind / Do you know / Save me / Affairs of the heart / When the Sun goes down / Behind the mask / Stand on the rock / Hard feelings / Freedom / When it comes to love / The second time. *(also cd-box; 7599 26206) (cd re-iss. Feb95; same)*

Aug 90. (7"/c-s) *(W 9739/+C)* **IN THE BACK OF MY MIND. / LIZARD PEOPLE** [58] [–]
(12"/cd-s) *(W 9739 T/CD)* – ('A'side) / Little lies (live) / The chain (live).
(s-cd-s+=) *(W 9739CDX)* – Lizard people.

Nov 90. (7"/c-s) *(W 9740/+C)* **THE SKIES THE LIMIT. / LIZARD PEOPLE** [ ] [–]
(12"/cd-s) *(W 9740 T/CD)* – ('A'side) / Little lies (live) / The chain (live).

Feb 91. (7") **SKIES THE LIMIT. / THE SECOND TIME** [–] [ ]

—— (late 1990) STEVIE NICKS left to go solo, and CHRISTINE departed due to MICK's new book allegations.

Jan 93. (7"/c-s) *(W 0145/+C)* **LOVE SHINES. / THE CHAIN (alt.mix)** [ ] [ ]
(cd-s+=) *(W 0145CD)* – The chain (Not That Funny live version) / Isn't it midnight (alt.version).

—— **MICK FLEETWOOD, JOHN McVIE, CHRISTINE McVIE** (latter departed in '94, but on below) + **BILLY BURNETTE** added **DAVE MASON** (b.10 May'46, Worcester, England) – vocals, guitars (ex-TRAFFIC, ex-solo artist)/ **BEKKA BRAMLETT** (b.19 Apr'68, Westwood, Calif.) – vocals (daughter of DELANEY & BONNIE)

Oct 95. (cd/c) *(<9362 45920-2/-4>)* **TIME** [47] [ ]
– Talkin' to my heart / Hollywood (some other kind of town) / Blow by blow / Winds of change / I do / Nothing without you / Dreamin' the dream / Sooner or later / I wonder why / Nights in Estoril / I got it in for you / All over again / These strange times.

—— the famous mid-late 70's line-up reformed for one-off MTV performance below (complete with orchestra/band!)

Aug 97. (cd/c) *(<9362 46702/-2/-4>)* **THE DANCE** [15] [1]
– The chain / Dreams / Everywhere / Rhiannon / I'm so afraid / Temporary one / Bleed to love her / Big love / Landslide / Say you love me / My little demon / Silver springs / You make loving fun / Sweet girl / Go your own way / Tusk / Don't stop.

Jul 98. (12"ep/cd-ep) *<9362 44540-1/-2>* **LANDSLIDE (mixes; live album version / remix / string / analog)** [–] [51]

—— line-up **MICK FLEETWOOD + JOHN McVIE** brought back **STEVIE NICKS + LINDSEY BUCKINGHAM** (CHRISTINE McVIE was a guest player)

Apr 03. (cd) *(9362 48479-2)* *<49467>* **SAY YOU WILL** [6] [3]
– What's the world coming to / Murrow turning over in his grave / Illume / Thrown down / Miranda / Red rover / Say you will / Peacekeeper / Come / Smile at you / Running through the garden / Silver girl / Steal your heart away / Bleed to love her / Everybody finds out / Destiny rules / Say goodbye / Goodbye baby. *(ltd d-cd+=; 9362 48467-2)* – Love minus zero – No limit / Not make believe / Peacekeeper (live) / Say you will (live).

Nov 03. (cd-s) *(W 632CD)* *<radio>* **PEACEKEEPER (Tin Tin Out radio edit) / PEACEKEEPER / SMILE AT YOU** [ ] [80]

– (with PETER GREEN) compilations, others, etc. –

Note all 'Blue Horizon' releases were on 'Epic' US.

Jul 69. (7") *Blue Horizon; (57-3157)* **NEED YOUR LOVE SO BAD. / NO PLACE TO GO** [32] [–]

Aug 69. (lp) *Blue Horizon; (7-63215)* **PIOUS BIRD OF GOOD OMEN** [18] [–]
– Need your love so bad / Coming home / Rambling pony / The big boat / I believe my time ain't long / The sun is shining / Albatross / Black magic woman / Just the blues / Jigsaw puzzle blues / Looking for somebody / Stop messin' around. *(re-iss. Jun81 on 'C.B.S.'; CBS 32050) (cd-iss. Jun95 on 'Columbia-Rewind'; 480 524-2)*
Note all CBS releases were on 'Epic' US.

May 71. (lp) *C.B.S.; (63875)* **THE ORIGINAL FLEETWOOD MAC BEFORE THE SPLIT** [ ] [ ]
(re-iss. +c/cd.Jun90 on 'Castle')

Jun 71. (d-lp) *Blue Horizon; <3801>* **FLEETWOOD MAC IN CHICAGO** [–] [ ]
<US-iss.Nov75 on 'Sire'; SASH 37152> <re-iss. 1977; 2XS 6009>

Oct 71. (d-lp) *Epic; <KE 30632>* **BLACK MAGIC WOMAN** [-] [ ]
– (US lp's; 'FLEETWOOD MAC' (1968) & 'ENGLISH ROSE')

Nov 71. (lp/c) *C.B.S.; (CBS/40 69011)* **GREATEST HITS** [36] [ ]
– The green Manalishi (with the two-pronged crown) / Oh well (part 1 & 2) / Shake your moneymaker / Need your love so bad / Rattlesnake shake / Dragonfly / Black magic woman / Albatross / Man of the world / Stop messin' around / Love that burns. *(re-iss. Feb88 lp/c; CBS 460 704-1/4) (cd-iss. Apr89; 460 704-2) (re-iss. cd Dec94 on 'Columbia-Rewind'; 477 512-2)*

May 72. (7") *Reprise; (K 14174)* **THE GREEN MANALISHI (WITH THE TWO-PRONG CROWN). / OH WELL (Pt.1)** [ ] [ ]
(re-iss. Mar73 & Nov76; same)

May 73. (7") *C.B.S.; (CBS 8306)* **ALBATROSS. / NEED YOUR LOVE SO BAD** [2] [ ]
(re-iss. Feb78; CBS 5957) (re-iss. Nov90 on 'Old Gold'; OG 9955)

Aug 73. (7") *C.B.S.; (CBS 1722)* **BLACK MAGIC WOMAN. / STOP MESSIN' ROUND** [ ] [ ]

Jun 75. (d-lp) *C.B.S.; (CBS 22025)* **THE ORIGINAL FLEETWOOD MAC / ENGLISH ROSE** [ ] [ ]
(re-iss. Jun76; 81308-9) (re-iss. Jun90 on 'Essential' cd/c/lp; ESS CD/MC/LP 026) (re-iss. cd May94 on 'Castle'; CLACD 344)

Oct 75. (7"; b-side by DANNY KIRWAN) *D.J.M.; (DJS 10620)* **MAN OF THE WORLD. / SECOND CHAPTER** [ ] [-]
(re-iss. Feb76 & Jun78 on 'Epic'; EPC 6466)

Mar 77. (d-lp/c) *C.B.S. / Sire; (CBS/40 88227) <3706>* **VINTAGE YEARS** [ ] [ ]
(re-iss. May82 as 'THE VINTAGE YEARS: HISTORY OF FLEETWOOD MAC'; CBS 22122)

Aug 77. (lp) *Embassy; (EMB 31569)* **ALBATROSS** (1 side by 'CHRISTINE PERFECT') [ ] [-]
(cd-iss. Feb91 on 'Columbia'; CD 31569)

Sep 78. (lp/c) *C.B.S.; (CBS/40 83110)* **MAN OF THE WORLD** [ ] [-]

Feb 80. (lp) *C.B.S.; (CBS 31798)* **BLACK MAGIC WOMAN** [ ] [-]

Aug 83. (c) *C.B.S.; (40-22163)* **FLEETWOOD MAC / THE PIOUS BIRD OF GOOD OMEN** [ ] [-]

Jul 84. (7") *C.B.S.; (A 4578)* **ALBATROSS. / MAN OF THE WORLD** [ ] [-]

Jan 85. (lp) *Shanghai; (HAI 107)* **LIVE IN BOSTON (live)** [ ] [-]
(re-iss. May88 on 'Line'; IMLP 400129) (cd-iss. Oct85 on 'Shanghai'; HAI 400) (cd-iss. Oct89 on 'Castle')

Aug 85. (d-lp/c) *Shanghai; (HAI/HAC 300)* **CERULEAN (LIVE IN BOSTON Part II)** [ ] [-]

Sep 85. (7") *Old Gold; (OG 9529)* **MAN OF THE WORLD. / ('Natural Born boogie' by Humble Pie)** [ ] [-]

Oct 85. (lp) *Platinum; (24076)* **RATTLESNAKE SHAKE** [ ] [-]

Oct 85. (lp) *Platinum;(24077)* **MADISON BLUES** [ ] [-]

Dec 85. (lp) *Platinum; (24082)* **OH WELL** [ ] [-]

Apr 86. (lp) *Commander; (LP 39006)* **RATTLESNAKE SHAKE LIVE** [ ] [-]

Apr 86. (lp) *Commander; (LP 39007)* **OH WELL LIVE** [ ] [-]

Apr 86. (lp) *Commander; (LP 39008)* **GREEN MANALISHI LIVE** [ ] [-]

Nov 86. (cd) *Commander; (CD 99011)* **FLEETWOOD MAC LIVE (live 1968)** [ ] [-]
(re-iss. May88; same) (re-iss. May94//Nov94 on 'Arc'; MEC 949020//MO 3016) (re-iss. Aug95 on 'Abracadabra'; AB 3017)

Nov 86. (lp/c/cd) *Thunderbolt; (THBL/THBC/CDTB 1.038)* **LONDON LIVE '68 (live)** [ ] [-]

Jul 87. (d-lp/c/cd) *Castle; (CCS LP/MC/CD 157)* **THE COLLECTION** [ ] [-]
(re-iss. cd Jan94)

Sep 87. (lp) *Commander; (224 821-7)* **GREATEST HITS LIVE** [ ] [-]
(re-iss. Dec89 lp/c/cd; 264 821-7/-4/-2) (re-iss. cd Apr93 on 'Zillion'; 261 0992)

1988. (lp) *Varrick; <VR 020>* **JUMPING AT SHADOWS** [-] [ ]
– (same as above)

Feb 89. (7") *C.B.S.; (654 613-7)* **ALBATROSS. / MAN OF THE WORLD** [ ] [-]
(12"+=/cd-s+=) *(654 613-6/-2)* – Black magic woman / Love that burns.

Apr 89. (lp/c/cd) *Castle; (CCS LP/MC/CD 216)* **THE BLUES COLLECTION** [ ] [-]

1989. (3"cd-ep) *C.B.S.; (655 171-3)* **ALBATROSS / BLACK MAGIC WOMAN / NEED YOUR LOVE SO BAD / I'D RATHER GO BLIND** [ ] [-]

Oct 89. (lp/c/cd) *Castle; (CLA LP/MC/CD 152)* **BOSTON LIVE** [ ] [-]

Nov 89. (lp/c/cd) *Mainline; (264 824-1/-4/-2)* **OH WELL** [ ] [-]

Nov 89. (lp/c) *Hallmark; (SHM/HSC 3268)* **LOOKING BACK ON FLEETWOOD MAC** [ ] [-]
(cd-iss. May90 on 'Pickwick'; PWKS 533)

Jul 90. (cd) *Marble Ach; (CMACD 125)* **FLEETWOOD MAC LIVE (live)** [ ] [-]

Feb 91. (3xcd/5xlp) *Essential; (ESB CD/LP 138)* **THE BLUES YEARS** [ ] [ ]

Jun 91. (cd/c) *Elite; (ELITE 008 MC/CD)* **LIKE IT THIS WAY** [ ] [-]
(re-iss. Sep93; same)

Mar 92. (cd/lp; as PETER GREEN'S FLEETWOOD MAC) *Receiver; (RR CD/LP 157)* **LIVE AT THE MARQUEE (live)** [ ] [-]
(re-iss. cd Jun92 on 'Sunflower'; SF-CD 104)

Sep 92. (cd; as PETER GREEN'S FLEETWOOD MAC) *Dojo Early Years; (EARLD 5)* **THE EARLY YEARS** [ ] [-]

Feb 93. (cd) *Castle; (SSLCD 207)* **LIVE** [ ] [-]

Jun 93. (cd) *Point; (261 0202)* **21 GREATEST HITS LIVE** [ ] [-]

Mar 94. (cd) *Castle; (MACCD 187)* **MADISON BLUES LIVE** [ ] [-]

May 94. (cd) *Castle; (MATCD 266)* **THE BLUES YEARS** [ ] [-]

Jul 94. (cd/c) *Success;* **LIVE (live)** [ ] [-]

Jun 95. (cd) *Renaissance; (551 776-2)* **FLEETWOOD MAC** [ ] [-]

Sep 95. (d-cd/d-c; as PETER GREEN'S FLEETWOOD MAC) *Fleetwood; (EDF CD/MC 297)* **LIVE AT THE BBC** [48] [-]

– (GREEN on some) compilations, others, etc –

on 'Warners' unless mentioned otherwise

1978. (lp/c) *Reprise; (K/K4 44138)* **THE BEST OF FLEETWOOD MAC** [ ] [-]

Oct 82. (c) *(K4 66103)* **RUMOURS / FLEETWOOD MAC** [ ] [ ]

Nov 92. (4xcd-box/4xc-box) *(<9362 45129-2/-4>)* **25 YEARS – THE CHAIN** [ ] [ ]

Feb 93. (d-cd) *(<9362 45188-2>)* **25 YEARS – SELECTIONS FROM THE CHAIN** [ ] [-]

Oct 02. (cd) *W.S.M.; (8122 73635-2)* **THE VERY BEST OF FLEETWOOD MAC** [7] [-]
– Go your own way / Don't stop / Dreams / Little lies / Everywhere / Albatross / You make loving fun / Rhiannon / Black magic woman / Tusk / Say you love me / Man of the world / Seven wonders / Family man / Sara / Monday morning / Gypsy / Over my head / Landslide / The chain / Big love (live 1997).

Oct 02. (d-cd) *Reprise; <73775>* **THE VERY BEST OF FLEETWOOD MAC** [-] [12]
– Monday morning / Dreams / You make loving fun / Go your own way / Rhiannon / Say you love me / I'm so afraid / Silver springs / Over my head / Never going back again / Sara / Love in store / Tusk / Landslide / Songbird / Big love / Storms / The chain / Don't stop / What makes you think you're the one / Gypsy / Second hand news / Little lies / Think about me / Go insane / Gold dust woman / Hold me / Seven wonders / World turning / Everywhere / Sisters of the Moon / Family man / As long as you follow / No questions asked / Skies the limit / Paper doll.

FLYING BURRITO BROTHERS

Formed: Los Angeles, California, USA ... late 1968 by ex-BYRDS members GRAM PARSONS and CHRIS HILLMAN. While PARSONS had left The BYRDS on the eve of their South African tour, HILLMAN departed upon their return, the pair duly hooking up to realise GRAM's long held vision of a 'Cosmic American Music'. Recruiting pedal steel maestro, SNEAKY PETE KLEINOW, bassist CHRIS ETHRIDGE and drummer JON CORNEAL (who'd played with GRAM previously in The INTERNATIONAL SUBMARINE BAND), this troupe of musical outlaws recorded one of the all-time great country records and one of the first country-rock records in 'THE GILDED PALACE OF SIN' (1969). Equal parts country soul/rock/R&B, alongside the poignant 'HOT BURRITO No.1' (GRAM's fragile voice eternally on the point of cracking) and 'JUANITA', the album featured sublime versions of standards 'DO RIGHT WOMAN' and 'DARK END OF THE STREET' (both written by the legendary DAN PENN). On more uptempo numbers like 'CHRISTINE'S TUNE', the BURRITO's cut a swaggering country rug like no-one else. Onstage and image-wise, the band were just as vivid, custom made Nudie suits and foxy hippy chicks the order of the day. Clearly, playing the Grand Ole Opry as The BYRDS had done before them, was out of the question, PARSONS no doubt past caring about the head-in-the-sand opinion of the country establishment. Yet the rock establishment was equally blinkered in its outlook, the band making little impact outside their native L.A., despite a slot at The ROLLING STONES' ill-fated Altamont gig. MICK JAGGER and KEITH RICHARDS were big fans of the band, RICHARDS especially, building up a close friendship with GRAM. As the pair spent more and more time together, however, GRAM's interest in The BURRITO's began to dwindle. By the release of the follow-up, 'BURRITO DELUXE' (1970), MICHAEL CLARKE and BERNIE LEADON had been drafted in to replace the departed ETHERIDGE and CORNEAL. The album was more upbeat than the debut, but despite such enduring PARSONS/HILLMAN material as 'CODY, CODY', the record lacked the focus and sense of purpose of its predecessor. In spirit, GRAM was only half there, his mind on thoughts of solo stardom, and he left soon after the album's release. In effect, the FLYING BURRITO BROTHERS was GRAM's baby, the band failing to grow, creatively or otherwise after its founding father's departure. They made a further eponymous album with RICK ROBERTS taking PARSONS' place, but by late '71, HILLMAN had split (he joined STEPHEN STILLS in MANASSAS, later going on to C&W success with the DESERT ROSE BAND) and the band were verging on a parody of their former selves. While LEADON went on to success with The EAGLES and ROBERTS (to a lesser degree) with FIREFALL, through various line-ups and label changes, The FLYING BURRITO BROTHERS continued as a kind of clearing house for ageing country-rockers, still releasing albums way into the 90's. SNEAKY PETE KLEINOW returned to the fold for 1999's 'SONS OF THE OLD WEST', written primarily by new member JOHN BELAND. One of the better latter day 'BURRITO records, it featured a slew of new and old country stars ranging from bluegrass diva ALISON KRAUSS to the late MERLE HAGGARD, an indication of the esteem in which the band are still held. • **Songwriters:** PARSONS wrote most, until his premature departure after the second LP. The rest of group took over writing credits from then on. Covered; WILD HORSES (Rolling Stones) / IF YOU GOTTA GO, GO NOW (Bob Dylan) / etc. • **Trivia:** DAVID CROSBY guested his harmonies on their 1969 track 'DO RIGHT WOMAN'.

Album rating: THE GILDED PALACE OF SIN (*9) / BURRITO DELUXE (*7) / THE FLYING BURRITO BROTHERS (*6) / THE LAST OF THE RED HOT BURRITOS (*6) / CLOSE UP THE HONKY TONKS compilation (*8) / FLYING AGAIN (*4) / SLEEPLESS NIGHTS some by Gram Parsons solo (*5) / AIRBORNE (*4) / LIVE IN TOKYO (*4) / DIM LIGHTS, THICK SMOKE AND LOUD MUSIC collection (*6) / FARTHER ALONG: BEST OF compilation (*8) / BACK TO THE SWEETHEARTS OF THE RODEO (*5) / SOUTHERN TRACKS (*5) / ENCORE – LIVE IN EUROPE (*4) / EYE OF THE HURRICANE (*4) / CALIFORNIA JUKEBOX (*4) / SONS OF THE GOLDEN WEST (*4) / HOT BURRITOS! compilation (*8) / SIN CITY: THE VERY BEST OF . . . compilation (*7)

GRAM PARSONS (b. INGRAM CECIL CONNOR, 5 Nov'46, Winter Haven, Florida) – vocals, guitar (ex-BYRDS) / **CHRIS HILLMAN** (b. 4 Dec'42) – guitar, vocals (ex-BYRDS) / **SNEAKY PETE KLEINOW** (b.1935, South Bend, Indiana) – pedal steel guitar (ex-BYRDS part-time) / **CHRIS ETHERIDGE** – bass / **JON CORNEAL** – drums (half) / other guest drummers **POPEYE PHILLIPS / EDDIE HOH + SAM GOLDSTEIN**

A&M A&M

Apr 69. (lp) *(AMLS 931)* *<4175>* **THE GILDED PALACE OF SIN** Mar69
– Christine's tune / Sin city / Do right woman / Dark end of the street / My uncle / Wheels / Juanita / Hot burrito #1 / Hot burrito #2 / Do you know how it feels / Hippie boy. *(re-iss. Jul86 on 'Edsel' lp/c; ED/CED 191) (cd-iss. 1988; EDCD 191)*

Jun 69. (7") *(AMS 756)* *<1067>* **THE TRAIN SONG. / HOT BURRITO #1**

— **BERNIE LEADON** (b.19 Jul'47, Minneapolis, Minnesota) – guitar, vocals (ex-DILLARD & CLARK) repl. ETHERIDGE / **MICHAEL CLARKE** (b. 3 Jun'44, New York City) – drums (ex-DILLARD & CLARK) repl. CORNEAL (exchanged to D&C) (HILLMAN now switched to bass, vocals)

Apr 70. (7") *<1166>* **IF YOU GOTTA GO, GO NOW. / CODY, CODY** –

May 70. (lp) *(AMLS 983)* *<4258>* **BURRITO DELUXE**
– Lazy day / Image of me / High fashion queen / If you gotta go, go now / Man in the fog / Further along / Older guys / Cody, Cody / God's own singer / Down in the churchyard / Wild horses. *(re-iss. Jul86 on 'Edsel'; ED 194) (cd-iss. Jun90; EDCD 194)*

Jul 70. (7") *(AMS 794)* *<1189>* **OLDER GUYS. / DOWN IN THE CHURCHYARD**

— **RICK ROBERTS** (b.1950, Florida) – guitar, vocals repl. PARSONS (went solo, died 19 Sep'73)

Dec 70. (7") *(AMS 816)* **TRIED SO HARD. / LAZY DAY** –

Jun 71. (lp) *(AMLS 64295)* *<SP 4295>* **THE FLYING BURRITO BROTHERS**
– White line fever / Colorado / Hand to mouth / Tried so hard / Just can't be / To Romana / Four days of rain / Can't you hear me calling / All alone / Why are you crying.

Jul 71. (7") *<1277>* **COLORADO. / WHITE LINE FEVER** –

— **HILLMAN, ROBERTS, CLARKE** bring in new members **AL PERKINS** – pedal steel (ex-SHILOH) repl. SNEAKY PETE who went into sessions / **KENNY WERTZ** – guitar, vocals (ex-DILLARD & CLARK) repl. LEADON (later EAGLES) / added **ROGER BUSH** – bass / **BYRON BERLINE** – drums (both ex-COUNTRY GAZETTE)

Jul 72. (lp) *(AMLS 74343)* *<SP 4343>* **LAST OF THE RED HOT BURRITOS (live)** Feb72
– Devil in disguise / Six days on the road / My uncle / Dixie breakdown / Don't let your deal go down / Orange blossom special / Ain't that a lot of love / High fashion queen / Don't fight it / Hot burrito #2 / Losing game. *(cd-iss. Apr89; CDA 4343)*

— Had already split late '71. HILLMAN and PERKINS joined STEPHEN STILLS band. **ROBERTS** Enlisted **BUSH, BERLINE, WERTZ, DON BECK, ALAN MUNDE + ERIC DALTON.** They tour Europe and the Netherlands release 2 live albums for 'Ariola'; 'LIVE IN AMSTERDAM' (d-lp; Feb73) & 'BLUEGRASS SPECIAL' (1974). **KLEINOW** returned but they made no recordings.

— **SNEAKY PETE + ETHERIDGE** re-formed band with **FLOYD 'GIB' GUILBEAU** – fiddle / **GENE PARSONS** – drums (ex-BYRDS) / **JOEL SCOTT HILL** – bass (ex-CANNED HEAT) ROBERTS & CLARKE later formed FIREFALL

C.B.S. Columbia

Nov 75. (7") *(CBS 3724)* *<10229>* **BUILDING FIRES. / HOT BURRITO #3**

Dec 75. (lp) *(CBS 61984)* *<33817>* **FLYING AGAIN** Oct75
– Easy to get on / Wind and rain / Why baby why / Dim lights, thick smoke (and loud, loud music) / You left the water running / Building fires / Desert childhood / Bon soir blues / River road / Hot burrito #3.

Feb 76. (7") *<10287>* **BON SOIR BLUES. / HOT BURRITO #3** –

— **SKIP BATTIN** – bass (ex-BYRDS, ex-NEW RIDERS OF THE PURPLE SAGE) repl. ETHERIDGE

Jul 76. (lp) *(CBS 81433)* *<34222>* **AIRBORNE** Jun76
– Waitin' for love to begin / Out of control / Big bayou / Toe tappin' music / Linda Lu / Walk on the water / Northbound bus / Jesus broke the wild horse / She's a sailor / Quiet man / Border town.

Aug 76. (7") *<10389>* **BIG BAYOU. / WAITIN' FOR LOVE TO BEGIN** –

— disbanded when BATTIN re-joined NEW RIDERS . . . / His replacement ED PONDERS also departed as did PARSONS.

SIERRA

— were formed by **GUILBEAU, KLEINOW + HILL** plus **THAD MAXWELL** – bass / **MICKEY McGEE** – drums / **BOBBY COCHRAN**

not iss. Mercury

1977. (lp) *<SRM-1 1179>* **SIERRA** –
– Gina / Farmer's daughter / Honey dew / I found love / Strange here in the night / I'd rather be with you / If I could only get to you / She's the tall one / Don't plant roses / You give me lovin' / Let me live.

1977. (7") <73966> **GINA. / STRANGE HERE IN THE NIGHT** [-] [ ]

FLYING BURRITO BROTHERS

were once again with **GUILBEAU, KLEINOW + GREG HARRIS** – guitar / **ED PONDER + SKIP BATTIN**

Sundown Regency

Jun 79. (lp) *<79001>* **LIVE IN TOKYO (live)** [-] [ ]
– Big bayou / White line fever / Dim lights, thick smoke / There'll be no teardrops tonight / Roll in my sweet baby's arms / Hot burrito #2 / Colorado / Rocky top / Six days on the road / Truck drivin' man. *(UK-iss.Jan86 on 'Sundown' lp/cd; SDLP/CDSD 025)*

Dec 79. (7") *<45001>* **WHITE LINE FEVER (live). / BIG BAYOU (live)** [-] [ ]

The BURRITO BROTHERS

— **JOHN BELAND** – vocals, guitar (ex-SWAMPWATER) repl. HARRIS + PONDER

not iss. Curb

Dec 80. (7") *<5402>* **SHE'S A FRIEND OF A FRIEND. /** [-] [ ]

Jan 81. (lp) *<JZ 37004>* **HEARTS ON THE LINE** [-] [ ]
– That's the way you know it's over / She's a friend of a friend / Isn't that just like love / She belongs to everyone but me / Why must the ending be so sad / Family tree / Damned if I'll be lonely tonight / Does she wish she was single again / Too much honky tonkin' / Oh lonesome me.

Apr 81. (7") *<01011>* **DOES SHE WISH SHE WAS SINGLE AGAIN. / OH LONESOME ME** [-] [ ]

Jul 81. (7") *<02243>* **SHE BELONGS TO EVERYONE BUT ME. / WHY MUST THE ENDING ALWAYS BE SO SAD** [-] [ ]

— Trimmed to a duo of **BELAND + GUILBEAU**

Dec 81. (7") *<02641>* **IF SOMETHING SHOULD COME BETWEEN US (LET IT BE LOVE). / DAMNED IF I'LL BE LONELY TONIGHT** [-] [ ]

Jan 82. (lp) *<FZ 37705>* **SUNSET SUNDOWN** [-] [ ]
– If something should come between us / Louisiana / I'm drinkin' Canada dry / When you're giving yourself to a stranger / What's one more time / Run to the night / How'd we ever get this way / Coast to coast / Closer to you / Save the wild life.

Apr 82. (7") *<02835>* **CLOSER TO YOU. / COAST TO COAST** [-] [ ]

Jul 82. (7") *<03023>* **I'M DRINKIN' CANADA DRY. / HOW'D WE EVER GET THAT WAY** [-] [ ]

Nov 82. (7") *<03314>* **BLUE AND BROKEN HEARTED ME. / OUR ROOTS ARE COUNTRY MUSIC** [-] [ ]

M.C.A. Curb

1983. (7";with EARL SCRUGGS) **COULD YOU LOVE ME ONE MORE TIME. / ROLLER COASTER** [-] [ ]

— The duo cut another lp for 'Curb' but this was shelved.

Jan 84. (7") *(MCA 868) <52329>* **ALMOST SATURDAY NIGHT. / JUKEBOX KIND OF NIGHT** [ ] [ ]

May 84. (7") *<52379>* **MY KIND OF LADY. / DREAM CHASER** [-] [ ]

— Signed to LEON RUSSELL's 'Paradise', but album was shelved until '95.

The FLYING BROTHERS

— with **SNEAKY PETE, SKIP BATTIN, GREG HARRIS + JIM GOODALL**

not iss. Relix

Oct 85. (lp) *<RRLP 2008>* **CABIN FEVER (live)** [-] [ ]
– Wheels / Hot burrito #2 / Hickory wind / Do right woman / Uncle Penn / Louisiana man / She belongs to me / Six days on the road / Mr. Spaceman / Bugles.

Sep 86. (lp) *<RRLP 2022>* **LIVE FROM EUROPE (live)** [-] [ ]
– Streets of Baltimore / Cash on the barrelhead / Help is on it's way / Roll on brother / Come a little closer / Star of the show / Spitting image / Sin city / Christin's tune / Foggy mountain breakdown / Steam-powered airplane / Mystery train.

The FLYING BURRITO BROTHERS

reformed by **GUILBEAU + BELAND**

Disky Disky

Dec 87. (d-lp/c/cd) *<(DLP2/DC4/DCD5 025)>* **BACK TO THE SWEETHEARTS OF THE RODEO** [ ] [ ]
– Back to the sweethearts of the rodeo / Burning embers / Red shoes / Shoot for the Moon / Moonlight raider / Gold guitar / True true love / I'm impressed / Let's do something crazy / Like a shadow / I don't believe you met my baby / My heart stops a beat / Take a message to Mary / Last call / You're running wild / This could be the night / My shoes keep walking back to you / You should know my name by now / I've got a new heartache / Roadmaster. *(re-iss. d-cd Jul95 as The BURRITO BROTHERS on 'Appalosa'+=; AP 05455-2)* – Carry me / Baby won't you let me be the one / You're a fool to love / Mean streets / Burn the midnight oil / Should we tell him / One man woman / Do you know Mary Lou. *(cd re-iss. Feb96 on 'Sundown'; SDCD 502) <(VOL.1-iss.Feb00 on 'Sundown'; CDSD 085)*

— **KLEINOW, GUILBEAU & BELAND** added **GEORGE GRANTHAM** – bass (ex-POCO)

Voodoo not iss.

1990. (cd) *(VD 103)* **SOUTHERN TRACKS** [-] France [-]
– Crazy horses / Born for honky tonkin' / Armed and dangerous / Shelly's little girl / Thunder road / Matchbox / She's your lover now / Love minus zero / They want to hang a bad boy / My believing heart / Christine's tune (live) / My bucket's got a hole in it (live). *(UK-iss.Oct93; same)*

— **LARRY PATTON + RICK LANOW** – bass + drums repl.GRANTHAM

Sundown not iss.

May 91. (cd) *(CDSD 069)* **ENCORE – LIVE IN EUROPE (live)** [ ] [-]
– Dim lights, thick smoke / You ain't goin' nowhere / Hickory wind / White line fever / Sweet little Colette / Big bayou / Sweet Suzanna / Wild horses / Silverwings / Help wanted / Cannonball rag / When it all comes down to love / Wheels.

— **CHRIS ETHERIDGE / BRIAN CADD** (b. Australia) – keyboards / **RONNIE TUTT** – drums; repl. PATTON + LANOW

Oct 93. (cd) *(CDSD 075)* **EYE OF THE HURRICANE** [ ] [-]
– Wheel of love / Like a thief in the night / Bayou blues / Angry words / Rosetta knows / Heart highway / I sent your saddle home / Jukebox Saturday night / Arizona moon / Wild wild west / Eye of a hurricane / Sunset boulevard / Smile. *(re-iss. Jul94 on 'One Way'; OW 30330)*

— **KLEINOW + BELAND** plus numerous

not iss. Arista

May 99. (cd) *<14065>* **SONS OF THE GOLDEN WEST** [-] [ ]
– Sons of the golden west / Honky tonkin' / Area 51 / Hungry eyes / Pioneer zephyr train / When I was a cowboy / Down at the Palomino / Genuine healer / Pull this / Anyone else but you / Honky tonk blues / Up on Sycamore / Locked away / Ode to Gram.

– compilations, etc. –

1972. (lp; shared with DILLARD & CLARK) *Mayfair; (AMLB 51038)* **GRASS ROOTS** [ ] [-]

1973. (lp) *Bumble; (GEXD 301)* **SIX DAYS ON THE ROAD – LIVE IN AMSTERDAM** [ ] [-]

Jul 74. (d-lp) *A&M; (AMLH 63631) <SD 3631>* **CLOSE UP THE HONKY TONKS** (out-takes) [ ] [ ]

Mar 87. (lp/cd) *Edsel; (ED/+CD 197)* **DIM LIGHTS, THICK SMOKE AND LOUD, LOUD MUSIC** [ ] [-]
– Train song / Close up the honky tonks / Sing me back home / Tonight the bottle let me down / Your angel steps out of Heaven / Crazy arms / Together again / Honky tonk women / Green, green grass of home / Dim lights / Bony Moronie / To love somebody / Break my mind / Dim lights, thick smoke and loud music.

Dec 88. (cd/c) *A&M; <75021 5216-2/-4>* **FARTHER ALONG: THE BEST OF THE FLYING BURRITO BROTHERS** [-] [ ]

May 90. (cd/lp) *Sundown; (CDSD/CDSD 067)* **HOLLYWOOD NIGHTS** (demos 1979-81) [ ] [-]

May 91. (cd) *Sundown; (CDSD 072)* **FROM ANOTHER TIME** (live 1975) [ ] [-]

1992. (cd) *Relix; <RRCD 2052>* **SIN CITY (live 1976)** [-] [ ]

Mar 93. (cd) *Castle; (CCSCD 366)* **THE COLLECTION** [ ] [-]

Nov 94. (cd) *Start; (HP 9342-2)* **IN CONCERT** [ ] [-]

Dec 95. (cd) *Sundown; (CDSD 079)* **DOUBLE BARREL** (rec.1984) [ ] [ ]
– She's single again / New shade of blue / Price of love / Ain't love just like the rain / One more time / Sailor / No easy way out / Tonight / Hearts in my eyes / Ain't worth the powder / Late in the night / I'm confessing / Let your heart do the talking.

Apr 96. (d-cd) *A&M; (540408-2)* **OUT OF THE BLUE** [ ] [-]

May 96. (cd) *Country Stars; (CTS 55439)* **TOO MUCH HONKY TONIK'** [ ] [-]

Mar 97. (cd) *A&M; (540704-2)* **GUILDED PALACE OF SIN / BURRITO DELUXE** [ ] [-]

Sep 99. (cd) *Relix; <(RRCD 2098)>* **BICENTENNIAL BURRITOS** [ ] Apr99 [ ]

Jul 00. (d-cd) *Universal; <(69 490610)>* **HOT BURRITOS! – THE FLYING BURRITOS ANTHOLOGY 1969-1972** [ ] Apr00 [ ]
– (the first 3 sets + rarities)

Jul 02. (cd) *Universal; <(493264-2)>* **SIN CITY: THE VERY BEST OF THE FLYING BURRITO BROTHERS** [ ] [ ]

Aug 03. (cd) *Corazong; (255057)* **THE RED ALBUM: LIVE STUDIO PARTY IN HOLLYWOOD 1976** [ ] [ ]

□ FLY PAN AM

(see under ⇒ GODSPEED YOU BLACK EMPEROR!)

FOCUS

Formed: Amsterdam, Netherlands . . . late 1969 by THIJS VAN LEER, HANS CLEUVER and MARTIN DRESDEN, who became backing band for the Dutch version of the musical 'HAIR'. In 1970, they enlisted virtuso guitarist JAN AKKERMAN, who had previously departed from BRAINBOX. Signing to the 'Bovema' label in Holland, their first lp, 'IN AND OUT OF FOCUS', hit the shelves. Following the European success of the 'HOUSE OF THE KING' track, 'Blue Horizon' picked it up for release in the UK and it subsequently provided the theme tune for many a British TV documentary. Their 2nd album, 'MOVING WAVES', was a more progressively innovative set, containing the extended version of 'HOCUS POCUS', furnishing them with a surprise UK Top 20 hit for new label 'Polydor'. It was described by some as a novelty single due to LEER's strangulated yodel intermittently punctuating AKKERMAN's blistering guitar-work. Fairly unrepresentative of the FOCUS sound, the majority of the band's material was characterised by more pronounced neo-classical and jazz-rock leanings. They consolidated this early chart success with 'SYLVIA', a less frantic, more melodic piece, which fared even better than its predecessor. The single was gleaned from the 1972 double-set, 'FOCUS 3', another album which surprised many by also hitting the charts Stateside. However, after a stop-gap live album recorded at The Rainbow, the band disappointed critics and fans alike with the more conventional 'HAMBURGER CONCERTO' in 1974. From then on the band chose jazz-fusion as their raison d'etre, leading to a sharp commercial decline and inevitable split. AKKERMAN and VAN LEER had already moonlighted with solo outings, going full-time after FOCUS's demise. Come the new millennium, VAN LEER was back – alongside new faces JAN DUMEE, BOBBY JACOBS and BERT SMAAK – with 'FOCUS 8' (2002), two decades after his band first hit the UK Top 20 with 'HOCUS POCUS'. Proving if nothing else, that the man's flute chops could still cut it, the record found the familiar FOCUS formula little varied from its heyday. • **Songwriters:** AKKERMAN & VAN LEER, except TOMMY (Tom Barlage). • **Trivia:** On Apr'90, FOCUS of late'72 re-formed for Dutch TV special.

Album rating: IN AND OUT OF FOCUS (*5) / MOVING WAVES (*7) / FOCUS III (*6) / LIVE AT THE RAINBOW (*4) / HAMBURGER CONCERTO (*4) / MOTHER FOCUS (*3) / SHIP OF MEMORIES exploitation (*4) / FOCUS CON PROBY with P.J. Proby (*4) / HOCUS POCUS – THE BEST OF FOCUS compilation (*7) / FOCUS 8 (*4)

BRAINBOX

JAN AKKERMAN – guitar, organ / **KAZIMIRZ LUX** – vocals, percussion / **ANDRE REYNEN** – bass / **PIERRE VAN DER LINDEN** -drums

Parlophone Elektra

Jun 69. (7") *(R 5775) <45673>* **WOMAN'S GONE. / DOWN MAN** [ ] [ ]

Parlophone Capitol

1969. (lp) *(PCS 7094) <ST 596>* **BRAINBOX** [ ] 1970 [ ]
– Dark rose / Reason to believe / Baby, what you want me to do / Scarborough Fair / Summertime / Sinner's prayer / Sea of delight. *(cd-iss. Jun97 by BRAINBOX & JAN AKKERMAN on 'Oseudonym'; CDP 1033DD)*

May 70. (7") *(R 5842)* **TO YOU. / SO HELPLESS** [ ] [–]

FOCUS

THIJS VAN LEER (b.31 Mar'48) – organ, flute, some vocals / **JAN AKKERMAN** (b.24 Dec'46) – lead guitar, lute (ex-HUNTERS) / **MARTIN DRESDEN** – guitar / **HANS CLEUVER** – drums

Polydor Sire

Jan 71. (lp) *(2344 003) <97027>* **IN AND OUT OF FOCUS** [ ] [ ]
– Focus (instrumental) / Why dream / Happy nightmare (mescaline) / Anonymous / Black beauty / Sugar Island / House of the king / Focus (vocal). *<US re-iss. Jun73; 7404> (re-iss. Dec73; same as above) (<cd-iss. Jan02 on 'Red Bullet'; RB 66187>)*

Jan 71. (7") *(2001 134) <352>* **HOUSE OF THE KING. / BLACK BEAUTY** [ ] [ ]

— **PIERRE VAN DER LINDEN** (b.19 Feb'46) – drums (ex-BRAINBOX, ex-HUNTERS) repl. CLEUVER / **CYRIL HAVERMANS** – bass, vocals repl. DRESDEN

Blue Horizon Sire

Oct 71. (lp) *(2931 002) <7401>* **MOVING WAVES** [ ] [ ]
– Hocus pocus / Le clochard ("bread") / Janus / Moving waves / Focus II / Eruption: Orpheus – Pupilla – Tommy – Pupilla – Answer – The bridge – Euridice – Dayglow – Endless road – Answer – Orfeus – Euridice. *(re-dist.Nov72 by 'Polydor' lp/c; same); hit No.2) <US re-dist.Nov72; same> (cd-iss. Jun96 on 'Premier-EMI'; PRMCD 9) (<cd re-iss. Jan02 on 'Red Bullet'; RB 66198>)*

Oct 71. (7") *(2094 006)* **HOCUS POCUS. / JANIS** [ ] [–]

Jan 72. (7") *(2094 008)* **TOMMY. / FOCUS II** [ ] [–]

Polydor Sire

Oct 72. (7") *(2001 211)* **HOCUS POCUS. / JANIS** [20] [ ]

— **BERT RUITER** (b.26 Nov'46) – bass, vocals repl. CYRIL who went solo

Nov 72. (d-lp/c) *(2659/ 016) <3901>* **FOCUS III** [6] Mar73 [35]
– Round goes the gossip / Love remembered / Sylvia / Carnival fugue / Focus III / Answers? questions! questions? answers! / Anonymous II (part 1) / Elspeth of Nottingham / House of the king. *(<cd-iss. Jan02 on 'Red Bullet'; RB 66189>)*

Dec 72. (7") *(2001 422)* **SYLVIA. / HOUSE OF THE KING** [4] [–]

Feb 73. (7") *<704>* **HOCUS POCUS (pt.1). / HOCUS POCUS (pt.2)** [–] [9]

Jul 73. (7") *<708>* **SYLVIA. / LOVE REMEMBERED** [–] [89]

Oct 73. (lp/c) *(2443/ 118) <7408>* **FOCUS AT THE RAINBOW (live)** [23] [ ]
– Focus III / Answers? questions! questions? answers! / Focus II / Eruption: Orfeus – Answer – Pupilla – Tommy – Pupilla / Hocus pocus / Sylvia / Hocus pocus (reprise). *(cd-iss. Apr97 on 'E.M.I.'; REPLAYCD 40) (<cd re-iss. Jan02 on 'Red Bullet'; RB 66190>)*

— (Oct73) **COLIN ALLEN** – drums (ex-STONE THE CROWS, ex-JOHN MAYALL) repl. LINDEN (He later briefly returned)

Polydor Atco

Apr 74. (7") *(2058 466)* **HAREM SCAREM. / EARLY BIRTH** [ ] [ ]

May 74. (lp/c) *(2442/ 124) <36-100>* **HAMBURGER CONCERTO** [20] [66]
– Delitiae musicae / Harem scarem / La cathedrale de Strasbourg / Birth / Hamburger concerto:- Starter – Rare – Medium I – Medium II – Well done – One for the road. *(<cd-iss. Jan02 on 'Red Bullet'; RB 66191>)*

Jul 75. (lp) *(2384 070)* **FOCUS** (compilation) [23] [–]

— (mid'75) **DAVID KEMPER** (b.USA) – drums repl. ALLEN

Oct 75. (lp/c) *(2302/ 036) <36-117>* **MOTHER FOCUS** [ ] [ ]
– Mother Focus / I need a bathroom / Bennie Helder / Soft vanilla / Hard vanilla / Tropic bird / Focus IV – Someone's crying . . .what! / All together . . .oh that! / No hang ups / My sweetheart / Father Bach. *(cd-iss. Apr97 on 'E.M.I.'; REPLAYCD 41) (<cd re-iss. Jan02 on 'Red Bullet'; RB 66192>)*

Mar 76. (7") *(2001 640)* **HOUSE OF THE KING. / O AVENDROOD** [ ] [–]

— (Mar76) **PHILIP CATHERINE** (b.27 Oct'42, London) – guitar (ex-JEAN LUC PONTY, ex-JOHN McLAUGHLIN) repl. JAN AKKERMAN who went solo / **STEVE SMITH** – drums (ex-JEAN LUC PONTY) repl. VAN DER LINDEN / added **EEF ALBERS** – guitar

Harvest Sire

Sep 77. (lp) *(SHSP 4068) <7531>* **SHIP OF MEMORIES** (rare 1973) □ □
– P's march / Can't believe my eyes / Focus V / Out of Vesuvius / Glider / Red sky at night / Spoke the Lord Creator / Crackers / Ship of memories. *(<cd-iss. Jan02 on 'Red Bullet'; RB 66193>)*

Jan 78. (lp) *(SHSP 11721)* **FOCUS CON PROBY** □ [-]
– Wingless / Orion / Night flight / Eddy / Sneezing bull / Brother / Tokyo Rose / Maximum / How long.

— They split around the same time but managed to leave a collaboration with 60's pop star **P.J.PROBY** above

— **RICHARD JAMES** – drums repl. SMITH who joined JOURNEY. THIJS VAN LEER continued his solo career, further below.

— **AKKERMAN + VAN LEER** re-formed for Dutch gigs and album (with **TATO GOMEZ + RUUS JACOBS** – bass / **ED STARING** – synthesizers / **SERGIO CASTILLO** – drums / **USTAD ZAMIR AHMED KHAN** – tabla

Vertigo not iss.

Aug 85. (lp/cd) *(824 524-1/-2)* **FOCUS** □ [-]
– Russian roulette / King Kong / Le tango / Indian summer / Beethoven's revenge / Ole Judy / Who's calling.

— In April 1990, the 1972/73 line-up were back again

— post-millennium line-up **THIJS VAN LEER** plus **BOBBY JACOBS + JAN DUMEE + BERT SMAAK**

Musea not iss.

Jan 03. (cd) *(FGBG 4472)* **FOCUS 8** □ [-]
– Rock & Rio / Tamara's move / Fretless love / Hurkey Turkey / De ti O de mi / Focus 8 / Sto ces raditi ostatac zivota? / Neurotica / Brother / Blizu tebe / Flower shower.

– compilations, others, etc. –

Feb 75. (lp) *Sire; <7505>* **DUTCH MASTERS – A SELECTION OF THEIR FINEST RECORDINGS 1969-1973** [-] □

Sep 84. (lp/c) *Fame; (FA 41 3112-1/-4)* **GREATEST HITS OF FOCUS** □ [-]
– Focus / Moving waves / Focus II / Tommy / Hocus pocus / House of the king / Sylvia / Janis.

Feb 85. (7") *Golden 45's; (G 4539)* **SYLVIA. / HOCUS POCUS** □ [-]

Apr 87. (7") *Old Gold; (OG 9696)* **SYLVIA. / HOCUS POCUS** □ [-]

May 94. (cd) *E.M.I.; (CDP 828162-2)* **HOCUS POCUS – THE BEST OF FOCUS** □ [-]
(<re-iss. Jan02 on 'Red Bullet'; RB 66194>)

Jul 03. (cd) *Classic Rock Legends; (CRP 1090)* **LIVE IN THE USA (live)** □ [-]

Aug 03. (cd) *Classic Rock Legends; (CRP 1112)* **MASTERS FROM THE VAULTS** □ [-]

□ John FOGERTY
(see under ⇒ CREEDENCE CLEARWATER REVIVAL)

FOO FIGHTERS

Formed: Seattle, Washington, USA ... April/May '94, after the death of KURT COBAIN (Nirvana), by drummer turned singer/guitarist DAVE GROHL. He subsequently brought in COBAIN stand-in, PAT SMEAR, along with NATE MANDEL and WILLIAM GOLDSMITH, taking the group name from the mysterious lights reported by pilots during World War II. Continuing the UFO concept, the group founded their own 'Roswell' label, (funded by 'Capitol') and debuted in the summer of '95 with UK Top 5 single, 'THIS IS A CALL'. More harmonic and positively life-affirming than NIRVANA (comparisons were inevitable), The FOO FIGHTERS' offered up one of the most exciting debuts of the year; while the lyrics may have been somewhat cryptic, the obvious grunge influences were tempered with an infectious, pop-hardcore rush that was impossible to resist. The album sold well on both sides of the Atlantic, with GROHL & Co heading out on a successful series of festival dates. Work on the Gil Norton-produced follow-up, 'THE COLOUR AND THE SHAPE', got off to a difficult start with initial sessions in Seattle being scrapped. Further problems arose with the departure of sticksman GOLDSMITH halfway through recording, although GROHL subsequently completed the drum parts and the record was finally released in Spring '97 to rave reviews. Outpacing even the debut, The FOO FIGHTERS had come on leaps and bounds in the songwriting department, their rich post-grunge tapestry markedly more diverse. With good old romantic love as the driving theme of the record, the likes of the heart-rending (UK Top 20) 'EVERLONG' took starry-eyed, melodic distortion-pop to new (neck) hair-raising limits (complete with 'Evil Dead'-style video for that true-love atmosphere!), while more mellow musings like 'WALKING AFTER YOU' (used on the movie 'X-Files: Fight The Future') and 'DOLL' suggested GROHL was gaining enough confidence in his writing to chill out and reflect rather than continually going for the jugular. The group's growing self-belief was confirmed by some storming festival sets, while the album later came out top in rock 'bible', 'Kerrang!'s yearly critic's poll. After GROHL's brief expedition into film score work (with soundtrack 'TOUCH' being issued mid-'98), the band inked a deal with 'R.C.A.' and were ready to unleash a third album. 'THERE IS NOTHING LEFT TO LOSE' (1999), which disappointed no one with its melodic, HUSKER DU/PIXIES-inspired rock tunes, especially the hit 'LEARN TO FLY' (although I hear RUSH's 'Finding My Way' every time). GROHL and the mighty FOO FIGHTERS went straight to No.1 in October 2002, courtesy of album, 'ONE BY ONE', a clean, polished-up rock album that seemed to be lacking any kind of sparkle or charisma or just plain damn rawness. Top 10 hit, 'ALL MY LIFE' was very remiscent of the thrash-attack of QUEENS OF THE STONE AGE (well, GROHL had joined as drummer!), while elsewhere on the album, ballads were stuck clumsily alongside clean-cut out-and-out rock songs, and with no attempt made at rekindling the punk spirit. In short, papa GROHL's gonna have to get a brand new bag. Whenever! • **Covers:** OZONE (Kiss) / GAS CHAMBER (Angry Samoans) / DRIVE ME WILD (Vanity 6) / BAKER STREET (Gerry Rafferty) / DANNY SAYS (Ramones) / IRON & STONE (Obsessed) / REQUIEM (Killing Joke) / DOWN IN THE PARK (Tubeway Army) / SISTER EUROPE (Psychedelic Furs) / HAVE A CIGAR (Pink Floyd) / NEVER TALKING TO YOU AGAIN (Husker Du) / DARLING NIKKI (Prince). • **Trivia:** GREG DULLI (Afghan Whigs) played guitar on 'X-static'.

Album rating: FOO FIGHTERS (*8) / THE COLOUR AND THE SHAPE (*9) / TOUCH soundtrack by Dave Grohl (*6) / THERE IS NOTHING LEFT TO LOSE (*8) / ONE BY ONE (*6)

DAVE GROHL (b.14 Jan'69, Warren, Ohio) – vocals, guitar / **PAT SMEAR** – guitar (ex-GERMS) / **NATE MANDEL** – bass / **WILLIAM GOLDSMITH** – drums (both of SUNNY DAY REAL ESTATE)

Roswell Roswell

Jun 95. (7",7"red) *(CL 753)* **THIS IS A CALL. / WINNEBAGO** [5] [-]
(12"luminous+=/cd-s+=) *(12/CD CL 753)* – Podunk.

Jun 95. (cd/c/lp) *(CD/TC+/EST 2266) <34027>* **FOO FIGHTERS** [3] [23]
– This is a call / I'll stick around / Big me / Alone + easy target / Good grief / Floaty / Weenie beenie / Oh, George / For all the cows / X-static / Wattershed / Exhausted.

Sep 95. (c-s/7"red) *(TC+/CL 757)* **I'LL STICK AROUND. / HOW I MISS YOU** [18] [-]
(12"+=/cd-s+=) *(12/CD CL 757)* – Ozone.

Nov 95. (c-s/7"blue) *(TC+/CL 762)* **FOR ALL THE COWS. / WATTERSHED (live at Reading)** [28] [–]
(cd-s+=) *(CDCL 762)* – ('A'-live at Reading).

Mar 96. (c-s/7"white) *(TC+CL 768)* **BIG ME. / FLOATY (BBC session) / GAS CHAMBER (BBC session)** [19] [–]
(cd-s+=) *(CDCL 768)* – Alone + easy target (BBC session).

— **TAYLOR HAWKINS** – drums (of-ALANIS MORISSETTE) repl. GOLDSMITH

Apr 97. (7") *(CL 788)* **MONKEY WRENCH. / THE COLOUR AND THE SHAPE** [12] [–]
(cd-s+=) *(CDCLS 788)* – Up in arms (slow version).
(cd-s) *(CDCL 788)* – ('A'side) / Down in the park / See you (acoustic).

May 97. (cd/c/lp) *(CD/TC+/EST 2295)* *<58530>* **THE COLOUR AND THE SHAPE** [3] [10]
– Doll / Monkey wrench / Hey Johnny Park / My poor brain / Wind up / Up in arms / My hero / See you / Enough space / February stars / Everlong / Walking after you / New way home.

Aug 97. (7"blue) *(CL 792)* **EVERLONG. / DRIVE ME WILD** [18] [–]
(cd-s+=) *(CDCL 792)* – See you (live).
(cd-s) *(CDCLS 792)* – ('A'side) / Requiem / I'll stick around (live).

— now without SMEAR who was repl. by **FRANZ STAHL** (ex-SCREAM)

Jan 98. (7"red) *(CL 796)* **MY HERO. / DEAR LOVER** [21] [–]
(cd-s+=) *(CDCL 796)* – Baker Street (BBC session). *(with enhanced cd+=)* – Everlong (video) / Monkey wrench (video).

Jun 98. (cd; by DAVE GROHL) *<(7243 855632-25)>* **TOUCH** (music from the motion picture) [ ] [ ]
– Bill Hill theme / August Murray theme / How do you do / Richie Baker's miracle / Making popcorn / Outrage / Saints in love / Spinning newspapers / Remission my ass / Scene 6 / This loving thing / Final miracle / Touch.
above featured guests LOUISE POST + JOHN DOE plus BARRETT JONES keyboards + ERIC RICHARDS slide guitar

Aug 98. (7"/c-s/cd-s) *(E 4100/+C/CD)* **WALKING AFTER YOU (remix). / (Ween: Beacon Light)** [20] [–]
(above from the movie, 'X-Files: Fight The Future' on 'Elektra')

— now trio of **GROHL, MENDEL + HAWKINS**/ added on tour **CHRIS SHIFLETT** – guitar (ex-NO USE FOR A NAME)

R.C.A. R.C.A.

Oct 99. (c-s) *(74321 71308-4)* *<album cut>* **LEARN TO FLY / HAVE A CIGAR** [21] [19]
(cd-s+=) *(74321 71308-2)* – Iron & stone.
(cd-s+=) *(74321 71310-2)* – Make a bet.

Nov 99. (cd/c/lp) *<(07863 67892-2/-4/-1)>* **THERE IS NOTHING LEFT TO LOSE** [10] [10]
– Stacked actors / Breakout / Learn to fly / Gimme stitches / Generator / Aurora / Live-in skin / Next year / Headwires / Ain't it the life / M.I.A.

Mar 00. (cd-ep) *(74321 74958-2)* **GENERATOR EP** [ ] [–]
– Generator / Ain't it the life (two meter Dutch session) / Floaty (two meter Dutch session) / Fraternity / Breakout (live).
(cd-ep) *<74321 74617-2>* – ('A'side) / Learn to fly (live in Australia) / Stacked actors (live in Australia) / Breakout (live).

Sep 00. (7") *(74321 79012-7)* **BREAKOUT. / STACKED ACTORS (live)** [29] [–]
(cd-s+=) *(74321 79011-2)* – Monkey wrench.
(cd-s) *(74321 79010-2)* – ('A'side) / Iron and stone / Learn to fly (live).

Dec 00. (7"/c-s) *(74321 80926-7/-4)* **NEXT YEAR. / BIG ME (live/session)** [42] [–]
(cd-s+=) *(74321 80926-2)* – Next year (live/session).
(cd-s) *(74321 80927-2)* – ('A'side) / Baker street (live/session) / ('A'-CD-ROM).

Oct 02. (7") *(74321 97315-7)* **ALL MY LIFE. / SISTER EUROPE** [5] [–]
(cd-s+=) *(74321 97314-2)* – Win or lose / ('A'-video).
(cd-s) *(74321 97315-2)* – ('A'side) / Danny says / One.

Oct 02. (cd/lp) *(74321 97348-2/-1)* *<68008>* **ONE BY ONE** [1] [3]
– All my life / Low / Have it all / Times like these / Disenchanted lullaby / Tired of you / Halo / Lonely as you / Overdrive / Burn away / Come back.

Jan 03. (7") *(74321 98955-7)* **TIMES LIKE THESE. / LIFE OF ILLUSION** [12] [–]
(cd-s+=) *(74321 98955-2)* – Planet Claire / ('A'-video).
(cd-s) *(74321 98956-2)* – ('A'side) / Normal / Learn to fly (live) / (video footage).

Jun 03. (7") *(82876 52256-7)* **LOW. / NEVER TALKING TO YOU AGAIN (live)** [21] [–]
(cd-s+=) *(82876 52256-2)* – ('A'-video).
(cd-s) *(82876 52257-2)* – ('A'side) / Enough space (live) / ('A'video).

Sep 03. (7") *(82876 56370-7)* **HAVE IT ALL. / DARLING NIKKI** [37] [–]
(cd-s+=) *(82876 56370-2)* – Times like these (session).

☐ FOR CARNATION (see under ⇒ SLINT)

FOREIGNER

Formed: New York, USA . . . early 1976 by English expatriot MICK JONES, who was already the owner of a rather chequered music biz CV. After beginning his career in England with 60's outfit NERO & THE GLADIATORS, he later worked with French singer JOHNNY HALLIDAY as well as undergoing a stint in SPOOKY TOOTH before moving to New York and securing a job as an A&R man. Eventually hooking up with Englishmen, IAN McDONALD and DENNIS ELLIOTT alongside New Yorkers, LOU GRAMM, AL GREENWOOD and ED GAGLIARI, JONES formed FOREIGNER. After a year in the studio, the group unleashed an eponymous debut album for 'Atlantic'. Although the record failed to chart in the UK, it hit Top 5 in the States, becoming a multi-million seller and staying in the chart for a year. Its success boosted by two hit singles, 'FEELS LIKE THE FIRST TIME' and 'COLD AS ICE', FOREIGNER rapidly became established as prime staples for American FM radio. Though their material was harder-edged than the likes of REO SPEEDWAGON etc., FOREIGNER captured the middle ground perfectly, their AOR/hard rock-straddling sound gaining them massive sales for subsequent releases such as 'DOUBLE VISION' (1978) and 'HEAD GAMES' (1979), the former's title track narrowly missing the US top spot. Despite the group headlining the 1978 Reading Festival, the latter album (which saw another seasoned player, RICK WILLS, replacing GREENWOOD) failed to chart in the UK. FOREIGNER would have to wait until the release of the huge, Mutt Lange-produced '4' (1981) album, before they enjoyed transatlantic success. This was secured on the back of the UK/US Top 10, 'WAITING FOR A GIRL LIKE YOU'. It would be another histrionic AOR ballad, 'I WANT TO KNOW WHAT LOVE IS' (featuring the gospel talents of the New Jersey Mass Choir), that would become the group's best known song, its success even furnishing the band with a UK No.1 album. Released after a lengthy sabbatical, 'AGENT PROVOCATEUR' (1984), gave FOREIGNER yet another multi-million selling set, the success of the single making the band a household name. While LOU GRAMM cut a successful solo set in 1987, 'READY OR NOT', MICK JONES flopped with an eponymous set in '89, GRAMM eventually leaving the band for a time at the beginning of the 90's. While FOREIGNER had enjoyed reasonable success with the 1987 set, 'INSIDE INFORMATION', their first GRAMM-less set (with JOHNNY EDWARDS on vocals) was a relative commercial failure. GRAMM finally returned in 1994 although it was clear FOREIGNER's glory days were over. • **Songwriters:** JONES penned some with GRAMM, until his 1987 departure.

Album rating: FOREIGNER (*5) / DOUBLE VISION (*6) / HEAD GAMES (*6) / 4 (*7) / RECORDS compilation (*8) / AGENT PROVOCATEUR (*6) / INSIDE INFORMATION (*5) / UNUSUAL HEAT (*5) / THE VERY BEST OF FOREIGNER or THE VERY BEST . . . AND BEYOND compilations (*7) / MR. MOONLIGHT (*4) / JUKEBOX HEROES: THE FOREIGNER ANTHOLOGY compilation (*7) / THE DEFINITIVE compilation (*8)

LOU GRAMM (b. 2 May'50, Rochester, New York) – vocals (ex-BLACK SHEEP) / **MICK JONES** (b.27 Dec'47, London, England) – guitar (ex-SPOOKY TOOTH) / **IAN McDONALD** (b.25 Jun'46, London) – guitar, keyboards (ex-KING CRIMSON) / **AL GREENWOOD** (b. New York) – keyboards / **ED GAGLIARI**

(b.13 Feb'52, New York) – bass (ex-STORM) / **DENNIS ELLIOTT** (b.18 Aug'50, London) – drums (ex-IAN HUNTER BAND)

Atlantic Atlantic

Apr 77. (7") *(K 10917) <3394>* **FEELS LIKE THE FIRST TIME. / WOMAN OH WOMAN** [ ] Mar77 [4]

Apr 77. (lp/c) *(K/K4 50356) <18215>* **FOREIGNER** [ ] Mar77 [4]
– Feels like the first time / Cold as ice / Starrider / Headknocker / The damage is done / Long, long way from home / Woman oh woman / At war with the world / Fool for you anyway / I need you. *(cd-iss. Apr85; 250356) (re-iss. cd Oct95; same) <(cd re-mast.May02 on 'Rhino'+=; 8122 74270-2)>* – Feels like the first time (demo) / Woman oh woman (demo) / At war with the world (demo) / Take me to your leader (demo).

Jul 77. (7",7"clear) *(K 10986) <3410>* **COLD AS ICE. / I NEED YOU** [ ] [6]
(hit UK No.24 in Jul'78)

Dec 77. (7") *<3439>* **LONG, LONG WAY FROM HOME. / THE DAMAGE IS DONE** [–] [20]

Apr 78. (7"m) *(K 11086)* **FEELS LIKE THE FIRST TIME. / LONG, LONG WAY FROM HOME / COLD AS ICE** [39] [–]

Aug 78. (lp/c) *(K/K4 50476) <19999>* **DOUBLE VISION** [32] Jul78 [3]
– Hot blooded / Blue morning, blue day / You're all I am / Back where you belong / Love has taken its toll / Double vision / Tramontaine / I have waited so long / Lonely children / Spellbinder. *(cd-iss. 1988 & Oct95; K2 50476) <(cd re-mast.Aug02 on 'Rhino'+=; 8122 78187-2)>* – Hot blooded (live) / Love maker (live).

Oct 78. (7",7"red) *(K 11167) <3488>* **HOT BLOODED. / TRAMONTANE** [42] Jun78 [3]

Dec 78. (7") *(K 11199) <3514>* **DOUBLE VISION. / LONELY CHILDREN** [ ] Sep78 [2]

Feb 79. (7",7"pic-d) *(K 11236) <3543>* **BLUE MORNING, BLUE DAY. / I HAVE WAITED SO LONG** [45] Dec78 [15]

— **RICK WILLS** – bass (ex-ROXY MUSIC, ex-SMALL FACES) repl. AL (he joined The SPYS)

Sep 79. (7") *(K 11373) <3618>* **DIRTY WHITE BOY. / REV ON THE RED LINE** [ ] [12]

Sep 79. (lp/c) *(K/K4 50651) <29999>* **HEAD GAMES** [ ] [5]
– Dirty white boy / Love on the telephone / Women / I'll get even with you / Seventeen / Head games / The modern day / Blinded by science / Do what you like / Rev on the red line. *(cd-iss. Feb93 on 'Atco'; 7567 81598-2) (re-iss. cd Nov95; 250651) <(cd re-mast.Aug02 on 'Rhino'+=; 8122 78198-2)>* – Zalia.

Feb 80. (7") *(K 11417) <3633>* **HEAD GAMES. / DO WHAT YOU LIKE** [ ] Nov79 [14]

Apr 80. (7") *(K 11456) <3651>* **WOMEN. / THE MODERN DAY** [ ] Feb80 [41]

Sep 80. (7") *(K 11602)* **I'LL GET EVEN WITH YOU. / BLINDED BY SCIENCE** [ ] [–]

— Trimmed to quartet, when GAGLIARI and McDONALD left

Jul 81. (7") *(K 11665) <3831>* **URGENT. / GIRL ON THE MOON** [54] Jun81 [4]

Jul 81. (lp/c) *(K/K4 50796) <16999>* **4** [5] [1]
– Night life / Juke box hero / Break it up / Waiting for a girl like you / Luanne / Urgent / I'm gonna win / Woman in black / Urgent / Girl on the Moon / Don't let go. *(cd-iss. Aug85; 250796) (re-iss. cd Feb91; 7567 82795-2) <(cd re-mast.May02 on 'Rhino'+=; 8122 78275-2)>* – Juke box hero (nearly unplugged) / Waiting for a girl like you (nearly unplugged).

Sep 81. (7") *(K 11678) <4017>* **JUKE BOX HERO. / I'M GONNA WIN** [48] Feb82 [26]

Oct 81. (7") *<3868>* **WAITING FOR A GIRL LIKE YOU. / I'M GONNA WIN** [–] [2]

Nov 81. (7"m) *(K 11696)* **WAITING FOR A GIRL LIKE YOU. / FEELS LIKE THE FIRST TIME / COLD AS ICE** [8] [–]

Mar 82. (7") *(K 11718)* **DON'T LET GO. / FOOL FOR YOU ANYWAY** [ ] [–]

Apr 82. (7") *<4044>* **BREAK IT UP. / LUANNE** [–] [26]

Apr 82. (7") *(K 11728)* **URGENT. / HEAD GAMES (live)** [45] [–]
(12") *(K 11728T)* – ('A'side) / Hot blooded (live).

Jul 82. (7") *<4072>* **LUANNE. / FOOL FOR YOU ANYWAY** [–] [75]

Dec 82. (lp/c)(cd) *(A 0999/+4)(780 999-2) <80999>* **RECORDS (THE BEST OF . . .)** (compilation) [58] [10]
– Cold as ice / Double vision / Head games / Waiting for a girl like you / Feels like the first time / Urgent / Dirty white boy / Jukebox hero / Long, long way from home / Hot blooded. *<(re-iss. cd Oct95; 7567 82800-2)>*

Nov 84. (7",7"sha-pic-d) *(A 9596) <89596>* **I WANT TO KNOW WHAT LOVE IS. / STREET THUNDER** [1] [1]
(12"+=) *(A 9596T)* – Urgent.

Dec 84. (lp/c/cd) *(781999-1/-4/-2) <81999>* **AGENT PROVOCATEUR** [1] Nov84 [4]
– Tooth and nail / That was yesterday / I want to know what love is / Growing up the hard way / Reaction to action / Stranger in my own house / A love in vain / Down on love / Two different worlds / She's too tough. *(re-iss. cd Oct95; same)*

Mar 85. (7") *(A 9571) <89571>* **THAT WAS YESTERDAY (remix). / TWO DIFFERENT WORLDS** [28] [12]
(12"+=) *(A 9571T)* – ('A'-orchestral version).

May 85. (7") *<89542>* **REACTION TO ACTION. / SHE'S TOO TOUGH** [–] [54]

Jun 85. (7") *(A 9539)* **COLD AS ICE (remix). / REACTION TO ACTION** [64] [–]
(12"+=) *(A 9539T)* – Head games (live).
(d7"++=) *(A 9539/SAM 247)* – Hot blooded (live).

Aug 85. (7") *<89493>* **DOWN ON LOVE. / GROWING UP THE HARD WAY** [–] [54]

— LOU GRAMM left to go solo

Jul 87. (7") *(A 9169) <89169>* **SAY YOU WILL. / A NIGHT TO REMEMBER** [71] Nov87 [6]
(7"box+=/12"+=/cd-s+=) *(A 9169 B/T/CD)* – Hot blooded (live).

Dec 87. (lp/c)(cd) *(WX 143/+C)(781808-2) <81808>* **INSIDE INFORMATION** [64] [15]
– Heart turns to stone / Can't wait / Say you will / I don't want to live without you / Counting every minute / Inside information / The beat of my heart / Face to face / Out of the blue / A night to remember.

May 88. (7") *(A 9101) <89101>* **I DON'T WANT TO LIVE WITHOUT YOU. / FACE TO FACE** [ ] Mar88 [5]
(12"+=/cd-s+=) *(A 9101 T/CD)* – Urgent.

Jul 88. (7") *<89046>* **HEART TURNS TO STONE. / COUNTING EVERY MINUTE** [–] [56]

— (1990) added **JOHNNY EDWARDS** – vocals to join **JONES + THOMAS**

Jun 91. (7"/c-s) *(A 7666/+C)* **LOWDOWN AND DIRTY. / FLESH WOUND** [ ] [ ]
(12"+=/cd-s+=) *(A 7666 T/CD)* – No hiding place.

Jul 91. (cd)(lp/c) *<(7567 82299-2)>(WX 424/+C)* **UNUSUAL HEAT** [56] [ ]
– Only Heaven knows / Lowdown and dirty / I'll fight for you / Moment of truth / Mountain of love / Ready for the rain / When the night comes down / Safe in my heart / No hiding place / Flesh wound / Unusual heat. *(cd-iss. Nov93; same)*

Aug 91. (7"/c-s) *(A 7608/+MC)* **I'LL FIGHT FOR YOU / MOMENT OF TRUTH** [ ] [ ]
(12"+=/cd-s+=) *(A 7608 T/CD)* – Dirty white boy (live).

Apr 92. (cd)(lp/c) *(7597 80511-2)(WX 469/+C) <89999>* **THE VERY BEST OF FOREIGNER** (compilation) [19] [ ]
– Feels like the first time / Cold as ice / Starrider / Hot blooded / Blue morning, blue day / Double vision / Dirty white boy / Women / Head games / Juke Box hero / Waiting for a girl like you / Urgent / That was yesterday / I want to know what love is / Say you will / I don't want to live without you. *(re-iss. Dec92 as 'THE VERY BEST . . . AND BEYOND' cd; 7567 89999-2)(+=)* – (3 extra tracks).

Apr 92. (7"/c-s) *(7567 85696-7/-4)* **WAITING FOR A GIRL LIKE YOU (live). / COLD AS ICE (live)** [ ] [–]
(cd-s+=) *(7567 85696-2)* – That was yesterday (live) / Feels like the first time (live).

Dec 93. (cd/c) *<(7567 82525-2/-4)>* **CLASSIC HITS LIVE (live)** [ ] [ ]
– Double vision / Cold as ice / Damage is done / Women / Dirty white boy / Fool for you anyway / Head games / Not fade away – Mona / Waiting for a girl like you / Juke box hero / Urgent / Love maker / I want to know what love is / Feels like the first time.

— **JONES + GRAMM** recruited **MARK SCHULMAN** – drums / **JEFF JACOBS** – keyboards / **BRUCE TURGON** – bass

B.M.G. Rhythm Safari

Oct 94. (7"/c-s) *(74321 23286-7/-4)* **WHITE LIE. / UNDER THE GUN** [58] [ ]
(cd-s+=) *(74321 23286-2)* – ('A'-alternate version).

Nov 94. (cd/c) *<(74321 23285-2/-4)>* **MR. MOONLIGHT** [59] [ ]
– Under the gun / Rain / Until the end of time / White lie / Big dog / Real world / All I need to know / Hole in my soul / I keep hoping / Running the risk / Hand on my heart.

Mar 95. (c-s) *<53183>* **UNTIL THE END OF TIME / UNDER THE GUN** [–] [42]

Mar 95. (c-s) *(74321 25457-4)* **UNTIL THE END OF TIME / HAND ON MY HEART** [ ] [–]
(cd-s+=) *(74321 25457-2)* – ('A'mix).

– compilations, etc. –

Oct 00. (d-cd) *Rhino; <(8122 79884-2)>* **JUKEBOX HEROES – THE FOREIGNER ANTHOLOGY** ☐ Aug00 ☐
– Feels like the first time / Long, long way from home / Cold as ice / Headknocker / Starrider / At war with the world / Double vision / Blue morning, blue day / Hot blooded / I have waited so long / Dirty white boy / Head games / Women / Rev on the red line / Break it up / Juke box hero / Luanne / Urgent / Waiting for a girl like you / All sewn up (SPOOKY TOOTH) / The hoofer (SPOOKY TOOTH) / I want to know what love is / Down on love / Street thunder / Reaction to action / That was yesterday / Ready or not / Midnight blue / Heart turns to stone / I don't want to live without you / Say you will / Can't wait / Just wanna hold (MICK JONES) / Everything that comes around (MICK JONES) / Just between you and me (LOU GRAMM) / Lowdown and dirty / Soul doctor / Until the end of time / Under the gun.

Sep 02. (cd) *Rhino; <(8122 73596-2)>* **THE DEFINITIVE FOREIGNER** ☐ ☐
– Cold as ice / Waiting for a girl like you / I want to know what love is / That was yesterday / Urgent / Say you will / Double vision / Blue morning, blue day / Heart turns to stone / Feels like the first time / Long, long way from home / I don't want to live without you / Starrider / White lie / Break it up / Hot blooded / Dirty white boy / Down on love / Juke box hero / Urgent (live).

☐ FORMINX (see under ⇒ VANGELIS)

☐ Robert FORSTER (see under ⇒ GO-BETWEENS)

☐ FOTHERINGAY (see under ⇒ DENNY, Sandy)

☐ FOUR TET (see under ⇒ FRIDGE)

FOUR TOPS

Formed: Detroit, Michigan, USA . . . 1953 as vocal quartet, The FOUR AIMS by LEVI STUBBS, RENALDO 'OBIE' BENSON, LAWRENCE PAYTON and ABDUL 'DUKE' FAKIR. In order to avoid confusion with the AMES BROTHERS, the group subsequently changed their name to The FOUR TOPS and cut a one-off single, 'KISS ME BABY', for the 'Chess' label in 1956. 'AIN'T THAT LOVE' and 'WHERE ARE YOU' followed on 'Columbia' and 'Riverside' respectively in the early 60's before the boys were picked up by long-time acquaintance, Berry Gordy, for his new 'Tamla Motown' operation. As astute as ever, Gordy paired them up with his crack writing team of Holland/Dozier/Holland, the resultant 'BABY I NEED YOUR LOVING' (reputedly the inspiration for the Mann/Weil-penned RIGHTEOUS BROTHERS classic, 'You've Lost That Lovin' Feelin'') narrowly missing the Top 10 in 1964. This served notice that 'Motown' had yet another ace up their sleeve in their bid for total domination of the pop/soul scene as the 60's began to swing. It also unveiled the emotionally fired-up tour de force that was STUBBS in full vocal flight, singing his pain against the towering harmonies of messrs BENSON, PAYTON and FAKIR. Summer '65 found them at No.1 with 'I CAN'T HELP MYSELF' while follow-up, 'IT'S THE SAME OLD SONG', made the Top 5 a few months later. The FOUR TOPS reached their dramatic peak in 1966 with transatlantic No.1, 'REACH OUT I'LL BE THERE', a soul symphony of epic proportions that remains their signature tune. The formula was repeated early the following year with 'STANDING IN THE SHADOWS OF LOVE', again achieving similar sales on both sides of the pond (Top 10). The hits kept coming – 'BERNADETTE', '7 ROOMS OF GLOOM', 'YOU KEEP RUNNING AWAY' – but towards the end of the year, Holland/Dozier/Holland departed 'Motown' to form their own label. Divorced from their songwriting/production team, The FOUR TOPS fell back on covers, making the US Top 20 (UK Top 10) with such seemingly incongruous material as The Left Banke's 'WALK AWAY RENEE' and Tim Hardin's 'IF I WERE A CARPENTER'. Although they continued to hit the UK Top 20 with the likes of 'WHAT IS A MAN?', 'DO WHAT YOU GOTTA DO' and 'I CAN'T HELP MYSELF', it'd be 1970 before they were back in the US Top 40 with 'IT'S ALL IN THE GAME' (Top 5 in the UK). 'STILL WATER (LOVE)' finally put them back in the American Top 20 while a duet with The SUPREMES on the Phil Spector classic, 'RIVER DEEP MOUNTAIN HIGH' was a similar sized hit in 1971. That year's album, 'CHANGING TIMES', couldn't have been more aptly named with The FOUR TOPS struggling to find their place amid a radically altered 'Motown' set-up (the label had relocated its main operation to L.A.) wherein the likes of STEVIE WONDER and MARVIN GAYE (although OBIE actually co-wrote GAYE's seminal 'What's Goin' On') were making massive steps as "serious" artists in their own right and 60's stalwarts (GLADYS KNIGHT, The ISLEY BROTHERS etc.) were defecting in droves. STUBBS and Co themselves parted company with Gordy in 1972, signing with 'Dunhill' ('Probe' in the UK) and initially enjoying something of a mini revival with major hits like 'KEEPER OF THE CASTLE', 'AIN'T NO WOMAN (LIKE THE ONE I'VE GOT)' and 'ARE YOU MAN ENOUGH?', the latter The FOUR TOPS' token contribution to blaxploitation mania with the film in question being 'Shaft In Africa'. From that point on the hits dried up with R&B Top 10 'CATFISH' being their last (very minor i.e. Top 75) pop hit of the decade in 1976. Veterans of the supper club circuit, The FOUR TOPS continued to sell out both nightclubs and major tour venues despite their lack of commercial recording success. The inevitable comeback came at the dawn of the 80's courtesy of a new deal with 'Casablanca', the group scoring a UK Top 3 (US Top 20) hit with 'WHEN SHE WAS MY GIRL' and again hitting the Top 20 in Britain with 'DON'T WALK AWAY'. A brief mid-80's reunion with 'Motown' failed to provide any hits although a double header tour with The TEMPTATIONS packed the crowds in and The FOUR TOPS enjoyed another one-off hit (UK Top 10) in 1988 with 'LOCO IN ACAPULCO' after signing to 'Arista'. While their enduring popularity ensures they're always a hot live ticket. • **Covered:** DO WHAT YOU GOTTA DO + MacARTHUR PARK (Jimmy Webb) / IT'S ALL IN THE GAME (Tommy Edwards) / A SIMPLE GAME + SO DEEP WITHIN YOU (Moody Blues) / WONDERFUL BABY (Smokey Robinson) / LAST TRAIN TO CLARKSVILLE (Boyce-Hart) / I'M A BELIEVER (Neil Diamond) / etc. • **Trivia:** BILLY BRAGG made one Four Top famous again, after singing about LEVI STUBBS' TEARS on a 1986 single. That year LEVI also provided the voice for the man-eating plant in the film musical 'Little Shop Of Horrors'.

Best CD compilation: THE SINGLES COLLECTION (*8)

LEVI STUBBS (b. LEVI STUBBLES) – lead vocals (ex-ROYALS) / **RENALDO 'OBIE' BENSON** – vocals / **LAWRENCE PAYTON** – vocals / **ABDUL 'DUKE' FAKIR** (b.26 Dec'35) – vocals

		not iss.	Chess
Jul 56.	(7") *<1623>* **KISS ME BABY. / COULD IT BE YOU**	–	
		not iss.	Columbia
Oct 60.	(7") *<41755>* **AIN'T THAT LOVE. / LONELY SUMMER** *<re-iss. Jul65; 43356>* – hit No.93	–	
		not iss.	Riverside
1962.	(7") *<4534>* **WHERE ARE YOU? / PENNIES FROM HEAVEN**	–	

Stateside Motown

Sep 64. (7") *(SS 336)* <1062> **BABY I NEED YOUR LOVING. / CALL ON ME** [ ] Jul64 [11]

Jan 65. (7") *(SS 371)* <1069> **WITHOUT THE ONE YOU LOVE (LIFE'S NOT WORTH WHILE). / LOVE HAS GONE** [ ] Nov64 [43]

Tamla Motown Motown

Mar 65. (7") *(TMG 507)* <1073> **ASK THE LONELY. / WHERE DID YOU GO?** [ ] Jan65 [24]

Jun 65. (7") *(TMG 515)* <1076> **I CAN'T HELP MYSELF (SUGAR PIE, HONEY BUNCH). / SAD SOUVENIRS** [23] May65 [1]

Jun 65. (lp) *(TML 11010)* <622> **FOUR TOPS** [ ] Feb65 [63]
– Baby I need your loving / Without the one you love / Where did you go / Ask the lonely / Your love is amazing / Sad souvenirs / Don't turn away / Tea house in Chinatown / Left with a broken heart / Love has gone / Call on me. *(re-iss. Mar77 & Feb82)*

Aug 65. (7") *(TMG 528)* <1081> **IT'S THE SAME OLD SONG. / YOUR LOVE IS AMAZING** [34] Jul65 [5]

Nov 65. (7") *(TMG 542)* <1084> **SOMETHING ABOUT YOU. / DARLING I HUM OUR SONG** [ ] [19]

Mar 66. (lp; mono/stereo) *(TML/STML 11021)* <647> **FOUR TOPS SECOND ALBUM** [ ] Nov65 [20]
– Baby I need your loving / Without the one you love / Where did you go / Ask the lonely / Your love is amazing / Sad souvenirs / Tea house in China / Left with a broken heart / Love has gone / Call on me / I can't help myself / Love feels like fire / Is there anything that I can do / Something about you / It's the same old song. *(re-iss. Jan80 + Oct82)*

Mar 66. (7") *(TMG 553)* <1090> **SHAKE ME, WAKE ME (WHEN IT'S OVER). / JUST AS LONG AS YOU NEED ME** [ ] Feb66 [18]

Jul 66. (7") *(TMG 568)* <1096> **LOVING YOU IS SWEETER THAN EVER. / I LIKE EVERYTHING ABOUT YOU** [21] May66 [45]

Oct 66. (7") *(TMG 5790)* <1098> **REACH OUT I'LL BE THERE. / UNTIL YOU LOVE SOMEONE** [1] Aug66 [1]

Nov 66. (lp; mono/stereo) *(TML/STML 11037)* <634> **4 TOPS ON TOP** [9] Aug66 [32]
– I got a feeling / Brenda / Loving you is sweeter tha ever / Shake me, wake me (when it's over) / Until you love someone / There's no one left / Matchmaker / Michelle / In the still of the night / Bluesette / Quiet nights of quiet stars / Then.

Jan 67. (7") *(TMG 589)* <1102> **STANDING IN THE SHADOWS OF LOVE. / SINCE YOU'VE BEEN GONE** [6] Dec66 [6]

Feb 67. (lp; mono/stereo) *(TML/STML 11041)* <654> **FOUR TOPS LIVE! (live)** [4] Dec66 [17]
– (Introduction) / It's the same old song / It's not unusual / Baby I need your loving / Reach out I'll be there / I'll turn to stone / I left my heart in San Francisco / You can't hurry love / Ask the lonely / Climb ev'ry mountain / The girl from Ipanema / If I had a hammer / I can't help myself / I like everything about you. *(re-iss. Apr85)*

Mar 67. (7") *(TMG 601)* <1104> **BERNADETTE. / I GOT A FEELING** [8] [4]

Apr 67. (lp; mono/stereo) *(TML/STML 11046)* <657> **4 TOPS ON BROADWAY** [ ] [79]

Jun 67. (7") *(TMG 612)* <1110> **7 ROOMS OF GLOOM. / I'LL TURN TO STONE** [12] [14]
May66 [76]

Oct 67. (lp; mono/stereo) *(TML/STML 11056)* <660> **FOUR TOPS REACH OUT** [4] Aug67 [11]
– What else is there to do (but think about you?) / If I were a carpenter / Reach out, I'll be there / Walk away Renee / 7 nights of gloom / Last train to Clarksville / I'll turn to stone / I'm a believer / Standing in the shadows of love / Bernadette / Cherish / Wonderful baby. *(cd-iss. Sep95)*

Oct 67. (7") *(TMG 623)* <1113> **YOU KEEP RUNNING AWAY. / IF YOU DON'T WANT MY LOVE** [26] Sep67 [19]

Dec 67. (7") *(TMG 634)* **WALK AWAY RENEE. / MAME** [3] [–]

Jan 68. (lp; mono/stereo) *(TML/STML 11061)* <662> **THE FOUR TOPS GREATEST HITS** (compilation) [1] Sep67 [4]
– Baby i need your loving / It's the same old song / Reach out i'll be there / Ask the lonely / Standing in the shadows of love / Loving you is sweeter than ever / I can't help myself / Without the one you love (life's not worthwhile) / 7 rooms of gloom / Something about you / Bernadette / Shake me, wake me (when it's over).

Jan 68. (7") <1119> **WALK AWAY RENEE. / YOUR LOVE IS WONDERFUL** [–] [14]

Mar 68. (7") *(TMG 647)* **IF I WERE A CARPENTER. / YOUR LOVE IS WONDERFUL** [7] [–]

Apr 68. (7") *(TMG 647)* <1124> **IF I WERE A CARPENTER. / WONDERFUL BABY** [–] [20]

Aug 68. (7") *(TMG 665)* <1127> **YESTERDAY'S DREAMS. / FOR ONCE IN MY LIFE** [23] Jul68 [49]

Nov 68. (7") *(TMG 675)* <1132> **I'M IN A DIFFERENT WORLD. / REMEMBER WHEN** [27] Sep68 [51]

Jan 69. (lp; mono/stereo) *(TML/STML 11087)* <669> **YESTERDAY'S DREAMS** [37] Sep68 [91]
– Yesterday's dreams / Can't seem to get you out of my mind / I'm in a different world / We've got a strong love (on our side) / By the time I get to Phoenix / Remember when / Sunny / Never my love / Daydream believer / Once upon a time / The sweetheart tree / A place in the sun.

May 69. (7") *(TMG 698)* <1147> **WHAT IS A MAN. / DON'T BRING BACK MEMORIES** [16] [53]

Sep 69. (lp; mono/stereo) *(TML/STML 11113)* <675> **FOUR TOPS NOW!** [ ] Jun69 [74]
– The key / What is a man / My past just crossed my future / Don't let him take your love from me / Eleanor Rigby / Little green apples / Do what you gotta do / MacArthur Park / Don't bring back memories / Wish I don't love you so / Opportunity knock (for me) / The fool on the hill.

Sep 69. (7") *(TMG 710)* **DO WHAT YOU GOTTA DO. / CAN'T SEEM TO GET YOU OUT OF MY MIND** [11] [–]

Sep 69. (7") <1159> **DON'T LET HIM TAKE YOUR LOVE FROM ME. / THE KEY** [–] [45]

Feb 70. (lp; mono/stereo) *(TML/STML 11138)* <695> **SOUL SPIN** [ ] Dec69 [ ]
– Look out your window / Barbara's boy / Lost in a pool of red / Got to get you into my life / Stop the world / Nothing / This guy's in love with you / Light my fire / Honey / The look of love / California dreamin'.

Mar 70. (7") *(TMG 732)* **I CAN'T HELP MYSELF. / BABY I NEED YOUR LOVING** [10] [–]

May 70. (7") *(TMG 736)* <1164> **IT'S ALL IN THE GAME. / LOVE IS THE ANSWER** [5] Apr70 [24]

Jun 70. (lp)(c) *(STML 11149)* <704> **STILL WATERS RUN DEEP** [29] Apr70 [21]
– Still water (love and peace) / Reflections / It's all in the game / Everybody's talkin' / Love is the answer / I wish I were your mirror / Elusive butterfly / Ring me together / L.A. (my town) / I'm a believer / Standing in the shadows of love / Cherish / Bernadette / Wonderful baby. *(re-iss. Jun82) (re-iss. Mar91)*

Sep 70. (7") *(TMG 752)* <1170> **STILL WATER (LOVE). / STILL WATER (PEACE)** [10] Aug70 [11]

—— (with The SUPREMES ⇒, they release (Nov'70) album THE MAGNIFICENT 7, this was issued UK May71 hit No.6. At same time 7" – RIVER DEEP MOUNTAIN HIGH hit US No.14, and UK No.11 in Jun71.

Jan 71. (lp) *(STML 11173)* <721> **CHANGING TIMES** [ ] Oct70 [ ]
– In these changing times / Just seven numbers / Raindrops keep fallin' on my head / Right before my eyes / I almost had her / Try to remember / Something's tearing at the edges of time / Sing a song of yesterday / The long and winding road.

May 71. (7") *(TMG 770)* <1175> **JUST SEVEN NUMBERS (CAN STRAIGHTEN OUT MY LIFE). / I WISH I WERE YOUR MIRROR** [36] Jan71 [40]

Jun 71. (7") <1185> **IN THESE CHANGING TIMES. / RIGHT BEFORE MY EYES** [–] [70]

—— again with The SUPREMES, they issued (Jun71) album RETURN OF THE MAGNIFICENT 7 and single YOU GOTTA HAVE LOVE IN YOUR HEART

Sep 71. (7") <1189> **MACARTHUR PARK (part II). / (part 1)** [–] [38]

Sep 71. (7") *(TMG 785)* **A SIMPLE GAME. / YOU STOLE MY LOVE** [3] [–]

Nov 71. (lp) *(STML 11195)* <740> **FOUR TOPS GREATEST HITS VOL.2** (compilation) [25] Sep71 [ ]
– In these changing times / Still water (love) / Still water (peace) / Don't let him take your love from me / It's all in the game / I'm in a different world / If I were a carpenter / What is a man / Walk away Renee / You keep running away / Yesterday's dreams / Just seven numbers.

Jan 72. (7") <1196> **A SIMPLE GAME. / L.A. (MY TOWN)** [–] [90]

Feb 72. (7"m) *(TMG 803)* **BERNADETTE. / I GOT A FEELING / IT'S THE SAME OLD SONG** [23] [–]

—— final collaborations with The SUPREMES, came out (US Jan72 / UK Apr72) with DYNAMITE lp. Singles WITHOUT THE ONE YOU LOVE + REACH OUT AND TOUCH (SOMEBODY'S HAND) were issued May72 + Nov72 respectively.

May 72. (7") <1198> **I CAN'T QUIT YOUR LOVE. / HAPPY (IS A BUMPY ROAD)** [–] [ ]

Jun 72. (lp) *(STML 11206)* <748> **NATURE PLANNED IT** [ ] May72 [50]
– I am your man / (It's the way) Nature planned it / I'll never change /

She's an understanding woman / I can't quit your love / Walk with me, talk with me, darling / Medley: Hey man – We got to get you a woman / You got to forget him darling / If you let me / Happy (is a bumpy road) / How will I forget you.

Jul 72. (7") *(TMG 823)* **WALK WITH ME, TALK WITH ME DARLING. / L.A. (MY TOWN)** [32] [–]

Sep 72. (7") *<1210>* **(IT'S THE WAY) NATURE PLANNED IT. / I'LL NEVER CHANGE** [–] [53]

Sep 72. (7") *(TMG 829)* **I'LL TURN TO STONE. / LOVE FEELS LIKE FIRE** [ ] [–]

Probe Dunhill

Nov 72. (7") *(PRO 575) <4330>* **KEEPER OF THE CASTLE. / JUBILEE WITH SOUL** [18] [10]

Nov 72. (lp) *(SPB 1064) <50129>* **KEEPER OF THE CASTLE** [ ] [33]
– Keeper of the castle / Ain't no woman / Put a little love away / Turn on the light of your love / When tonight meets tomorrow / Love music / Remember what I told you to forget / Love makes you human / Dreaming / The good Lord knows / Jubilee with soul / Keeper of the castle (reprise). *(re-iss. Oct74 on 'A.B.C.'; ABCL 5023)*

Jan 73. (7") *<4339>* **AIN'T NO WOMAN (LIKE THE ONE I'VE GOT). / THE GOOD LORD KNOWS** [–] [4]

Jul 73. (7") *(PRO 596) <4354>* **ARE YOU MAN ENOUGH?. / PEACE OF MIND** [ ] Jun73 [15]
(above from the soundtrack 'Shaft In Africa' issued on 'Probe-ABC')

Oct 73. (7") *(PRO 604) <4366>* **SWEET UNDERSTANDING LOVE. / MAIN STREET PEOPLE** [ ] [33]

Dec 73. (lp)(c) *(SPBA 6277) <50144>* **MAIN STREET PEOPLE** [ ] Sep73 [66]
– Main street people intro / I just can't get you out of my mind / It won't be the first time / Sweet understanding love / Am I my brother's keeper / Are you man enough? / Whenever's there's blue / Too little, too late / Peace of mind / One woman man / Main street people. *(re-iss. Oct74 on 'A.B.C.') (cd-iss. Jun86 on 'Charly'; CRB 1129)*

Feb 74. (7") *(PRO 612) <4377>* **I JUST CAN'T GET YOU OUT OF MY MIND. / AM I MY BROTHER'S KEEPER** [ ] Jan74 [62]

Apr 74. (7") *<4386>* **ONE CHAIN DON'T MAKE A PRISON. / TURN ON THE LIGHT OF YOUR LOVE** [–] [41]

Jul 74. (lp) *(SPBA 6283) <50166>* **MEETING OF THE MINDS** [ ] Apr74 [ ]
– One chain don't make no prison / Midnight flower / The well is dry / Love ain't easy to come by / No sad songs / Right on, brother / Tell me you love me / All my love / I found the spirit / Meeting of the minds. *(re-iss. Oct74 on 'A.B.C.')*

Aug 74. (7") *<15005>* **MIDNIGHT FLOWER. / ALL MY LOVE** [–] [55]

A.B.C. A.B.C.

Oct 74. (7") *(ABC 4013)* **THE WELL IS DRY. / MIDNIGHT FLOWER** [ ] [–]

Oct 74. (lp) *(ABCL 5062) <50188>* **LIVE & IN CONCERT (live)** [ ] [92]
– Intro and countdown / Are you man enough / Love ain't easy to come by / Medley / Love music / Reach out I'll be there / Standing in the shadow of love / Midnight flower / Baby I need your loving / Keeper of the castle / I am your man / Ain't no woman (like the one I've got) / One chain don't make no prison / I can't help myself (sugar pie honey bunch). *(cd-iss. Aug89 on 'M.C.A.'; DMCL 1890)*

Jun 75. (7") *(ABC 4057) <120960>* **SEVEN LONELY NIGHTS. / I CAN'T HOLD ON MUCH LONGER** [ ] May75 [71]

Jul 75. (lp) *(ABCL 5132) <862>* **NIGHT LIGHTS HARMONY** [ ] Jun75 [ ]
– Seven lonely nights / Is this the price / We all gotta stick together / I've got what you need / I can't hold on much longer / Drive me out of my mind / I'm glad you walked into my life / Let me know the truth.

Dec 75. (7") *<12123>* **WE ALL GOTTA STICK TOGETHER. / (IT WOULD ALMOST) DRIVE ME OUT OF MY MIND** [–] [97]

Sep 76. (7") *(ABC 4143) <12214>* **CATFISH. / LOOK AT ME BABY** [ ] [71]

Nov 76. (lp) *(ABCL 5197) <968>* **CATFISH** [ ] [ ]
– Catfish / Feel free / You can't hold back on love / I know you like it / Strung out for your love / Love don't come easy / Disco daddy / Look at me baby.

Nov 76. (7") *<12236>* **FEEL FREE. / I KNOW YOU LIKE IT** [–] [ ]

Feb 77. (7") *<12267>* **STRUNG OUT FOR YOUR LOVE. / YOU CAN'T HOLD BACK ON LOVE** [–] [ ]

Jan 78. (7") *(ABC 4199)* **FOR YOUR LOVE. / YOU'LL NEVER A BETTER MAN** [ ] [–]

Nov 77. (lp) *(ABCL 5223) <1014>* **THE SHOW MUST GO ON** [ ] [ ]
– The show must go on / I can't live without you / Save it for a rainy day / Runnin' from your love / See the real me / Love is a joy / You'll never find a better man / Candy.

Jan 78. (7") *<12315>* **THE SHOW MUST GO ON. / RUNNIN' FROM YOUR LOVE** [–] [ ]

Oct 78. (7") *<12427>* **H.E.L.P. / INSIDE A BROKEN HEARTED MAN** [–] [ ]

Oct 78. (7") *(ABC 4235)* **PUT IT ON THE NEWS. / WINGS** [ ] [–]

Jan 79. (lp) *(ABCL 5262)* **AT THE TOP** [ ] Nov78 [ ]
– H.E.L.P. / Bits and pieces / Seclusion / Put it on the news / This house / Just in time / Inside a broken hearted man / When your dreams take wings and fly.

Jan 79. (7") *<12457>* **JUST IN TIME. / THIS HOUSE** [–] [ ]

not iss. Reliant

1980. (7") *<1691>* **I'M HERE AGAIN. / ('A'instrumental)** [–] [ ]

Casablanca Casablanca

Sep 81. (7"/12") *(CAN/+X 1005) <2338>* **WHEN SHE WAS MY GIRL. / SOMETHING TO REMEMBER** [3] Aug81 [11]

Nov 81. (lp/c) *(6480/7190 058) <7258>* **TONIGHT!** [ ] Sep81 [37]
– When she was my girl / Don't walk away / Tonight / I'm gonna love you / Who's right, who's wrong / Let me set you free / Something to remember / From a distance / All I do / I'll never leave again. *(cd-iss. Feb89; 836967-2)*

Nov 81. (7") *<2344>* **LET ME SET YOU FREE. / FROM A DISTANCE** [–] [ ]

Dec 81. (7"/12") *(CAN/+X 1006)* **DON'T WALK AWAY. / I'LL NEVER EVER LEAVE AGAIN** [16] [–]

Jan 82. (7") *<2345>* **TONIGHT I'M GONNA LOVE YOU ALL OVER. / I'LL NEVER EVER LEAVE AGAIN** [–] [–]

Feb 82. (7"/12") *(CAN/+X 1008)* **TONIGHT I'M GONNA LOVE YOU ALL OVER. / FROM A DISTANCE** [43] [–]

May 82. (7") *(RSO 89) <1069>* **BACK TO SCHOOL AGAIN. / (B-side by the 'Grease' cast)** [62] [71]
(above from the film 'Grease' and issued on 'R.S.O.')

Jul 82. (7"/12") *(CAN/+X 1012) <2353>* **SAD HEARTS. / I BELIEVE IN YOU AND ME** [ ] Aug82 [84]

Aug 82. (lp/c) *(CANS/+C 3)* **ONE MORE MOUNTAIN** [ ] [ ]
– Sad hearts / One more mountain to climb / Givin' it up / I believe in you and me / I'm the one / Keep on lightin' my fire / Nobody's gonna love you like I do / Dream on / Whatever it is.

Motown Motown

Oct 83. (7"/12") *(TMG/+T 1321) <1706>* **I JUST CAN'T WALK AWAY. / HANG** [ ] [71]

Nov 83. (lp/c) *(STML/CSTML 12197)* **BACK WHERE I BELONG** [ ] [ ]
– Make yourself right at home / I just can't walk away / Sail on / Back where I belong / What have we got to lose / The masquerade is over / Body and soul / Hang.

Jan 84. (7") *<1718>* **MAKE YOURSELF RIGHT AT HOME. / SING A SONG OF YESTERDAY** [–] [ ]

Jun 85. (7") *<1790>* **SEXY WAYS. / BODY AND SOUL** [–] [ ]

Jul 85. (lp/c) *)ZL/ZK 72301) <6130>* **MAGIC** [ ] Jun85 [ ]
– I can feel the magic / Don't tell me that it's over / Sexy ways / Easier said than done / Don't turn away / I'm ready for love / Again / Maybe tomorrow / Remember me.

Oct 85. (7") *<1811>* **I'M READY FOR LOVE. / DON'T TELL ME THAT IT'S OVER** [–] [ ]

Sep 86. (7") *<1854>* **HOT NIGHTS. / AGAIN** [–] [ ]

Oct 86. (lp/cd) *(ZL/ZD 72480)* **HOT NIGHTS** [ ] [ ]
– Hot nights / Red hot love / I believe in you and me / Let's jam / We got bus'ness / This is love / 80 up for you / Livin' it up too much / The four of us.

Arista Arista

Aug 88. (7") *(111 717) <9706>* **INDESTRUCTIBLE. / ARE YOU WITH ME** [55] [35]
(12"+=/cd-s+=) *(611/661 717)* – ('A'version).

Sep 88. (lp/c/cd) *(208/408/258 840) <8492>* **INDESTRUCTIBLE** [ ] [ ]
– Indestructible / Change of heart / If ever a love there was / The Sun ain't gonna shine / Next time / Loco in Acapulco / Are you with me / I'm only wounded / When you dance / Let's jam. *(re-iss. Jun91 cd/c/lp; 261/411/211 567)*

Oct 88. (7") *<9801>* **LOVE IN ACAPULCO. / CHANGE OF HEART** [–] [ ]

Nov 88. (7") *(111 850)* **LOCO IN ACAPULCO. / THE FOUR OF US** [9] [–]
(12"+=/cd-s+=) *(611/661 850)* – ('A'-Body mix).

Feb 89. (7"; by FOUR TOPS featuring ARETHA FRANKLIN) *<9850>* **IF EVER A LOVE THERE WAS. / LET'S JAM** [–] [ ]

Feb 89. (7"; by FOUR TOPS featuring SMOKEY ROBINSON) *(112 074)* **INDESTRUCTIBLE. / ARE YOU WITH ME** [30] [-]
(12"+=/cd-s+=) *(612/662 074)* – ('A'versions).
(7"pic-d) *(112 151)* – ('A'side) / Next time.

Jul 89. (7") *(112 252)* **THE SUN AIN'T GONNA SHINE (The Ben Liebrand Remix) / LOCO IN ACAPULCO** [-]
(12"+=/cd-s+=) *(612/662 252)* – ('A'versions).

— retired to the cabaret circuit for the rest of the 90's

– (selective) compilations, etc. –

on 'Motown' unless mentioned otherwise

Oct 73. (d-lp) *(TMSP 11241-2) <764>* **THE FOUR TOPS STORY 1964-72** <US-title 'THE BEST OF THE FOUR TOPS'> [35]

Jun 80. (lp/c) *EMI-TV; (EMTV/CMTV 26)* **20 GOLDEN GREATS** [-]

Feb 82. (lp/c) *K-Tel; (NE1/CE2 160)* **THE BEST OF THE FOUR TOPS** [13] [-]

Sep 82. (d-lp/d-c) *(TMSP/CTMSP 6013)* **ANTHOLOGY** [-]
(cd-iss. Apr89; WD 72528)

May 88. (7") *(ZB 41943)* **REACH OUT I'LL BE THERE. / STANDING IN THE SHADOWS OF LOVE** [11] [-]
(12"+=/cd-s+=) *(ZT/ZD 41944)* – ('A'instrumental).

Jan 91. (cd/c/lp) *Telstar; (TCD/STAC/STAR 2437)* **THEIR GREATEST HITS** [47] [-]

Sep 92. (cd/c/lp) *Polygram; (515710-2/-4/-1)* **THE SINGLES COLLECTION** [11]
– Reach out I'll be there / Standing in the shadows of love / Bernadette / Walk away Renee / If i were a carpenter / Simple game / 7 Rooms of gloom / Loving you is sweeter than ever / You keep running away / Yesterday's dreams / I'm in a different world / What is a man / Loco in Acapulco / Indestructible / When she was my girl / It's all in the game / Still water (love) / I can't help myself / Do what you gotta do / Keeper of the castle / Don't walk away.

Aug 98. (cd) *(530825-2)* **THE ULTIMATE COLLECTION** [-]

Jul 00. (cd) *(15365-2)* **MOTOWN LOST AND FOUND: BREAKING THROUGH 1963-1964**

Dec 00. (cd) *(AA314 560824-2)* **ULTIMATE COLLECTION**

Jan 01. (d-cd) *Bianco; (BIA 2002)* **KEEPER OF THE CASTLE**

Jan 01. (cd) *Bianco; (BIA 4071)* **REACH OUT**

Jul 01. (cd) *Universal; (E 157523-2)* **UNIVERSAL MASTERS COLLECTION**

Nov 01. (cd) *(013359-2)* **THE FOUR TOPS / SECOND ALBUM**

Nov 01. (cd) *(013360-2)* **FOUR TOPS ON TOP / REACH OUT**

Nov 01. (cd) *(013361-2)* **YESTERDAY'S DREAMS / SOUL SPIN**

Nov 01. (cd) *(013362-2)* **STILL WATERS RUN DEEP / CHANGING TIMES**

Jan 02. (cd) *Exclusive; (4123)* **REACH OUT**

Jan 02. (d-cd) *BR Music; (BS 8121-2)* **THE SINGLES PLUS** [-]

Feb 02. (cd) *M.C.A.; (MCAD 11647)* **KEEPERS OF THE CASTLE: THE BEST OF THE FOUR TOPS 1972-1978**

Feb 02. (d-cd) *Delta Blue; (63017)* **LOCO IN ACAPULCO**

Jun 02. (4xcd-box) *(5562252-2)* **FOUREVER**

Jun 02. (d-cd; shared with the TEMPTATIONS) *Mercury; (583014-2)* **AT THEIR VERY BEST**

Aug 03. (3xcd-box) *Spectrum; (9808966)* **KEEPER OF THE CASTLE / REACH OUT / EARLY CLASSICS**

☐ Roddy FRAME (see under ⇒ AZTEC CAMERA)

Peter FRAMPTON

Born: 22 Apr'50, Beckenham, Kent, England. After leaving HUMBLE PIE late in '71, FRAMPTON signed a solo deal with 'A&M', a debut album, 'WINDS OF CHANGE', was subsequently supported by a US tour with headliners The J. GEILS BAND. In 1973, his next album, 'FRAMPTON'S CAMEL' (as FRAMPTON'S CAMEL), failed to make any substantial commercial impact and it was decided to drop the CAMEL part of the name to avoid confusion with the British band of same name. A year later, FRAMPTON gained his first US Top 40 entry with his third set, 'SOMETHIN'S HAPPENING' and followed it the next year with another hit album, 'FRAMPTON'. In 1976, his live double-lp, 'FRAMPTON COMES ALIVE' (recorded live at Winterland, California), soon topped the US chart, becoming a multi-million seller in the process. Its sales were boosted by three smash hits, 'SHOW ME THE WAY', 'BABY, I LOVE YOUR WAY' and 'DO YOU FEEL LIKE WE DO', the former seeing the singer/guitarist trademarking his new "Voxbox" guitar sound. His 1977 studio follow-up, 'I'M IN YOU', became an even greater success (Top 3 US and Top 20 UK), its title track hit US Top 3, while his version of Stevie Wonder's 'SIGNED, SEALED, DELIVERED (I'M YOURS) made the Top 20. A 1979 effort, 'WHERE I SHOULD BE', proved to be his last major success as he all but faded commercially in the 80's. A very talented guitarist, FRAMPTON established himself as the "Golden boy of US mainstream AOR". His curly locks and youthful face were still all the rage in the 70's having been idolized as a kid with 60's outfit, The HERD. The English boy made good kept up a fairly rigourous recording schedule through the 80's and 90's, including an inevitable – but not quite so million selling – 'FRAMPTON COMES ALIVE II' (1995) and a stint with DAVID BOWIE. He also began the new millennium with a concert set, 'LIVE IN DETROIT' (2000), original keys man BOB MAYO still on board and even co-writing one tune. A belated studio album, 'NOW', also appeared in 2003, showing the ageing axemeister to be ticking along nicely if not exactly at the top of his game, covering George Harrison's 'WHILE MY GUITAR GENTLY WEEPS' in tribute to the late Beatle. • **Songwriters:** Self-penned numbers, except; JUMPING JACK FLASH (Rolling Stones) / (I'M A) ROADRUNNER (Junior Walker) / FRIDAY ON MY MIND (Easybeats) / etc. • **Trivia:** Late in 1988, the group, WILL TO POWER, hit US No.1 with a segue of his 'BABY I LOVE YOUR WAY' and LYNYRD SKYNYRD's 'Freebird'.

Album rating: WIND OF CHANGE (*5) / FRAMPTON'S CAMEL (*6) / SOMETHIN'S HAPPENING (*4) / FRAMPTON (*5) / FRAMPTON COMES ALIVE! (*8) / I'M IN YOU (*5) / WHERE I SHOULD BE (*4) / BREAKING ALL THE RULES (*4) / THE ART OF CONTROL (*3) / PREMONITION (*2) / WHEN ALL THE PIECES FIT (*3) / SHINE ON – A COLLECTION compilation (*5) / PETER FRAMPTON (*5) / FRAMPTON COMES ALIVE II (er . . . *II) / LIVE IN DETROIT (*4) / NOW (*4)

PETER FRAMPTON – vocals, guitar (ex-HUMBLE PIE, ex-HERD) with **MIKE KELLIE** – drums (ex-SPOOKY TOOTH) / **RICK WILLS** – bass (ex-COCHISE) / & guests **BILLY PRESTON** – keyboards (solo artist) / **RINGO STARR** – drums, vox (solo artist) /**ANDY BOWN** – keyboards (ex-HERD) / **KLAUS VOORMAN** – keyboards (ex-MANFRED MANN)

A&M A&M

May 72. (7") *<1379>* **JUMPING JACK FLASH. / OH FOR ANOTHER DAY** [-]

May 72. (lp) *(AMLH 68099) <4348>* **WIND OF CHANGE**
– Fig tree bay / Wind of change / Lady lie right / Jumping Jack Flash / It's a plain shame / Oh for another day / All I want to be (is by your side) / The lodger / Hard / Alright. *<(cd-iss. Mar03; 490728-2)>*

Sep 72. (7") *(AMS 7025)* **IT'S A PLAIN SHAME. / OH FOR ANOTHER DAY** [-]

— FRAMPTON retained only WILLS and brought in **MICKEY GALLAGHER** – keyboards (ex-BELL & ARC) / **JOHN SIOMES** (b. USA) – drums (ex-MITCH RYDER)

May 73. (lp) *(AMLH 68150) <4389>* **FRAMPTON'S CAMEL**
– I got my eyes on you / All night long / Lines on my face / Which way the wind blows / I believe (when I fall in love with you it will be forever) / White sugar / Don't fade away / Just the time of year / Do you feel like we do. *<(cd-iss. Sep00; 490715-2)>*
(above lps & below 45s, credited to "FRAMPTON'S CAMEL")

May 73. (7") *(AMS 7069) <1456>* **ALL NIGHT LONG. / DON'T FADE AWAY**

Jul 73. (7") *<1470>* **WHICH WAY THE WIND BLOWS. / I BELIEVE (WHEN I FALL IN LOVE IT WILL BE FOREVER)** [–] [ ]

—— disbanded, bringing in session people

May 74. (lp) *(AMLH 63619) 3619>* **SOMETHIN'S HAPPENING** [ ] Mar74 [25]
– Doobie wah / Golden goose / Underhand / I wanna go to the sun / Baby (somethin's happening) / Waterfall / Magic Moon / Sail away. *<(cd-iss. Sep00; 490730-2>*

May 74. (7") *<1506>* **BABY (SOMETHIN'S HAPPENING). / I WANNA GO TO THE SUN** [–] [ ]

—— **ANDY BOWN** – keyboards, bass returned to repl. GALLAGHER (to GLENCOE) and WILLS (to ROXY MUSIC)

Mar 75. (lp) *(AMLH 64512) <4512>* **FRAMPTON** [ ] [32]
– Day's dawning / Show me the way / One more time / The crying clown / Fanfare / Nowhere's too far (for my baby) / Nassau / Baby, I love your way / Apple of your eye / Penny for your thoughts / (I'll give you) Money. *<(cd-iss. Aug00; 490729-2)>*

Jun 75. (7") *(AMS 7174) <1693>* **SHOW ME THE WAY. / THE CRYING CLOWN** [ ] [ ]

Aug 75. (7") *<1738>* **BABY, I LOVE YOUR WAY. / (I'LL GIVE YOU MONEY)** [–] [ ]

Oct 75. (7") *<1763>* **(I'LL GIVE YOU) MONEY. / NOWHERE'S TOO FAR (FOR MY BABY)** [–] [ ]

—— still with SIOMOS, also now w/ **STANLEY SHELDON** – bass / **BOB MAYO** – keyboards

Apr 76. (d-lp/d-c) *(AMLH/CLM 63703) <3703>* **FRAMPTON COMES ALIVE! (live)** [6] Jan76 [1]
– Somethin's happening / Doobie wah / Show me the way / It's a plain shame / All I want to be (is by your side) / Wind of change / Baby, I love your way / I wanna go to the sun / Penny for your thoughts / (I'll give you) Money / Shine on / Jumping Jack Flash / Lines on my face / Do you feel like we do. *<US pic-lp 1978> (re-iss. Feb85 as 'THE BEST OF FRAMPTON COMES ALIVE' on 'Hallmark' lp/c; SHM/HSC 3165) (cd-iss. 1988; CDA 6505) (re-iss. Jun91 cd/c; CD/C MID 164) <(cd re-mast.Oct98; 540930-2)>*

Apr 76. (7") *(AMS 7218) <1795>* **SHOW ME THE WAY (live). / SHINE ON (live)** [10] Feb76 [6]

Jun 76. (7") *<1832>* **BABY, I LOVE YOUR WAY (live). / IT'S A PLAIN SHAME (live)** [–] [12]

Aug 76. (7") *(AMS 7246)* **BABY, I LOVE YOUR WAY (live). / (I'LL GIVE YOU) MONEY (live)** [43] [–]

Oct 76. (7") *(AMS 7260) <1867>* **DO YOU FEEL LIKE WE DO (live). / PENNY FOR YOUR THOUGHTS (live)** [39] Sep76 [10]

Jun 77. (lp/c) *(AMLK/CAM 64039) <4704>* **I'M IN YOU** [19] [2]
– I'm in you / (Putting my) Heart on the line / St.Thomas (don't you know how I feel) / Won't you be my friend / You don't have to worry / Tried to love / Rocky's hot club / (I'm a) Roadrunner / Signed, sealed, delivered (I'm yours). *<(cd-iss. Aug00; 490714-2)>*

Jul 77. (7") *(AMS 7298) <1941>* **I'M IN YOU. / ST. THOMAS (DON'T YOU KNOW HOW I FEEL)** [41] May77 [2]

Sep 77. (7") *(AMS 7312) <1972>* **SIGNED, SEALED, DELIVERED (I'M YOURS). / ROCKY'S HOT CLUB** [ ] Aug77 [18]

Dec 77. (7") *<1988>* **TRIED TO LOVE. / YOU DON'T HAVE TO WORRY** [–] [41]

May 79. (7") *<2148>* **I CAN'T STAND IT NO MORE. / WHERE SHOULD I BE** [–] [14]

Jun 79. (7") *(AMS 7449)* **I CAN'T STAND IT NO MORE. / MAY I BABY** [ ] [–]

Jun 79. (lp/c) *(AMLK/CAM 63701) <3710>* **WHERE I SHOULD BE** [ ] [19]
– I can't stand it no more / Got my feet back on the ground / Where I should be / Everything I need / May I baby / You don't know like I know / She don't reply / We've just begun / Take me by the hand / It's a sad affair.

Aug 79. (7") *<2174>* **SHE DON'T REPLY. / ST. THOMAS (DON'T YOU KNOW HOW I FEEL)** [–] [ ]

Jun 81. (lp/c) *(AMLK/CAM 63722) <3722>* **BREAKING ALL THE RULES** [ ] [43]
– Dig what I say / I don't wanna let you go / Rise up / Wasting the night away / Going to L.A. / You kill me / Friday on my mind / Lost a part of you / Breaking all the rules.

Aug 81. (7") *(AMS 8154) <2350>* **BREAKING ALL THE RULES. / NIGHT TOWN** [ ] [ ]

Nov 81. (7") *<2362>* **WASTING THE NIGHT AWAY. / YOU KILL ME** [–] [ ]

Aug 82. (7") *<2442>* **SLEEPWALK. / THEME FROM NIVRAM** [–] [ ]

Sep 82. (lp/c) *(AMLH/CAM 64905) <4905>* **THE ART OF CONTROL** [ ] Aug82 [ ]
– I read the news / Sleepwalk / Save me / Back to Eden / An eye for an eye / Don't think about me / Heart in the fire / Here comes Caroline / Barbara's vacation.

—— PETER now used guitar & synthesizers, etc. plus band **TONY LEVIN** – guitar / **STEVE FERRONE + OMAR HAKIM** – drums / **PETE SOLLEY** – piano / **RICHARD COTTLE** – keys / **RICHIE PUENTE** – percussion

Virgin Atlantic

Nov 85. (7") *<89463>* **LYING. / INTO VIEW** [–] [74]

Dec 85. (7"pic-d/12") *(VS 827/+12)* **LYING. / YOU KNOW SO WELL** [ ] [–]

Jan 86. (lp/c/cd) *(C/TCV/CDV 2365) <81290>* **PREMONITION** [ ] [80]
– Stop / Hiding from a heartache / You know so well / Premonition / Lying / Moving a mountain / All eyes on you / Into view / Call of the wild. *(re-iss. Jul87 lp/c; OVED/+C 220)*

Feb 86. (7") *<89426>* **ALL EYES ON YOU. / SO FAR AWAY** [–] [ ]

Apr 86. (7"/12") *(VS 847/+12)* **ALL EYES ON YOU. / INTO VIEW** [ ] [–]

May 86. (7") *<89395>* **HIDING FROM A HEARTACHE. / INTO VIEW** [–] [ ]

—— He became guitarist for DAVID BOWIE in 1987. The following year he sessioned for KARLA BONOFF and returned to solo work in 1989.

Atlantic Atlantic

Sep 89. (7") *<88820>* **HOLDING ON TO YOU. / GIVE ME A LITTLE LOVE THAT'S REAL** [–] [ ]

Oct 89. (lp,c,cd) *<82030>* **WHEN ALL THE PIECES FIT** [–] [ ]
– More ways than one / Holding on to you / My heart goes out to you / Hold tight / People all over the world / Back to the start / Mind over matter / Now and again / Hard earned love / This time around.

—— His new back-up band now featured **DAVE MENIKETTI** – guitar (ex-Y&T) after signing to 'Geffen' (no releases)

Relativity Relativity

Apr 94. (cd/c/lp) *<(475876-2/04/-1)>* **PETER FRAMPTON** [ ] [ ]
– Day in the Sun / You can be sure / It all comes down to you / You can't take that away / Young island / Off the hook / Waiting for your love / So hard to believe / Out of the blue / Shelter through the night / Changing all the time.

I.R.S. I.R.S.

Oct 95. (cd/c) *(EIRS CD/TC 1074)* **FRAMPTON COMES ALIVE II (live)** [ ] [ ]
– (intro) / Day in the sun / Lying / For now / Most of all / You / Waiting for your love / I'm in you / Talk to me / Hang on to a dream / Can't take that away / More ways than one / Almost said goodbye / Off the hook. *(cd with free live cd; EIRSCDX 1074)* – Show me the way / Baby, I love your way / Lines on my face / Do you feel like we do.

In-Akustik not iss.

Oct 96. (cd) *(INAK 11004)* **MOON'S TRAIN** [–] German [–]

S.P.V. S.P.V.

Jul 00. (cd) *<(SPV 089 3000-2)>* **LIVE IN DETROIT (live 1999)** [ ] May00 [ ]
– (introduction) / Lying / Lines on my face / Show me the way / All I wanna be (is by your side) / If you say goodbye / Oh for another day / Nassau / Baby, I love your way / Can't take that away / Do you feel like we do / Off the hook / You had to be there / I don't need no doctor.

not iss. 33rd Street

Aug 03. (cd) *<3321>* **NOW** [–] [ ]
– Verge of a thing / Flying without wings / Love stands alone / Not forgotten / Hour of need / Mia rose / I'm back / I need ground / While my guitar gently weeps / Greens / Above it all.

– compilations, others –

Jun 79. (lp) *Flyover;* **THE SUPER DISC OF PETER FRAMPTON** [ ] [–]

Oct 83. (7") *Old Gold; (OG 9363)* **SHOW ME THE WAY. / BABY I LOVE YOUR WAY** [ ] [–]

Jun 84. (7"ep/c-ep) *Scoop; (7SR/7SC 5039)* **6 TRACK HITS** [ ] [–]
– Show me the way / Baby, I love your way / Penny for your thoughts / I'm in you / Wind of change / Signed, sealed, delivered (I'm yours).

Dec 92. (d-cd) *A&M; (CDMID 174)* **SHINE ON – A COLLECTION** [ ] [ ]
– Wind of change / It's a plain shame / Jumping Jack Flash / All I want to be (is by your side) / The lodger / I got my eyes on you / All night long / Lines on my face / Don't fade away / I wanna go to the sun / Baby (somethin's happening) / Nowhere's too far (for my baby) / Nassau – Baby I love your

way / The crying clown / Penny for your thoughts / (I'll give you) Money / Show me the way / Shine on / Do you feel like we do / I'm in you / (Putting my) Heart on the line / Signed sealed delivered (I'm yours) / I can't stand it no more / Breaking all the rules / Theme from Nivram / Lying / More ways than one / Holding on to you / The bigger they come / I won't let you down.

Mar 94. (cd/c) *Spectrum; (550 103-2/-4)* **PETER FRAMPTON SHOWS THE WAY** –

Dec 95. (cd; PETER FRAMPTON & FRIENDS) *Javelin; (HADCD 199)* **LOVE TAKER** –

Feb 96. (cd) *Prestige; (CDSGP 0243)* **PACIFIC FREIGHT** –

FRANKIE GOES TO HOLLYWOOD

Formed: Liverpool, England ... August '80 (initially as HOLLYCAUST) by HOLLY JOHNSON, who had issued two solo singles, 'YANKEE ROSE' and 'HOBO JOE', after once being part of punk experimentalists, BIG IN JAPAN. Taking their name from a news headline concerning singer, FRANKIE VAUGHAN going into the movies, FGTH enjoyed some on TV exposure in late 1982. After a session on David Jensen's Radio One show, they were invited onto Channel 4's 'The Tube', where they sang an embryonic, 'RELAX'. This led to 'Z.T.T.' (Zang Tumb Tumm) label, run by PAUL MORLEY and TREVOR HORN (ex-BUGGLES) signing them in Autumn 1983. With HORN's clever production, the song 'RELAX' soon climbed to the top in the UK, aided by another Radio One DJ, Mike Read, who helped it get banned from airplay due to its risqué lyrics. In June '84, with 'RELAX' still in the chart, the follow-up, 'TWO TRIBES', went straight in at No.1, and gave a new lease of life to the debut (it resurged back up to No.2, while 'TWO TRIBES' was at No.1!). This well-produced, power-disco/rock outfit were always at the front end of controversy (so to speak!), their gay/S&M sex themes (provided by leather clad HOLLY and boyfriend/dancer, PAUL RUTHERFORD) were the toast of the burgeoning mid-80's dance scene. Their debut (a double!) album in October '84, 'WELCOME TO THE PLEASURE DOME', also hit peak position, as did their third consecutive No.1 single, 'THE POWER OF LOVE' (a feat only previously achieved by another Mersey group, GERRY & THE PACEMAKERS). In March '85, their fourth single, the title track from the album, spoiled the run when it stalled at No.2. The group returned in late summer '86 after over a year off, their fifth single, 'RAGE HARD', only just scraping into the UK Top 5. Poor reviews of their follow-up album, 'LIVERPOOL', saw the group fading into a sharp commercial decline with each subsequent single release. HOLLY JOHNSON was back early in 1989. Having signed a contract with 'M.C.A.', the singer subsequently charted high with the singles, 'LOVE TRAIN' and 'AMERICANOS', which previewed his No.1 album, 'BLAST'. In mid-1990, HOLLY was asked by friend RICHARD O'BRIEN, to act as FRANK 'N' FURTER in the 'Rocky Horror Picture Show'. HOLLY's second solo album, 'DREAMS THAT MONEY CAN'T BUY' (1991), failed miserably, its sales so poor that the set didn't achieve a Top 75 placing. Sadly, HOLLY was subsequently diagnosed with the AIDS virus and was HIV postive as he wrote his autobiography, entitled 'A Bone In My Flute' (1994). Prior to delivering his third solo set, 'SOULSTREAM' (1999) – on his own 'Pleasuredome' imprint', JOHNSON exhibited his artwork at a London gallery. • **Songwriters:** All group compositions except; FERRY ACROSS THE MERSEY (Gerry & The Pacemakers) / BORN TO RUN (Bruce Springsteen) / WAR (Edwin Starr) / SUFFRAGETTE CITY (David Bowie) / GET IT ON (T.Rex) / SAN JOSE (Bacharach-David). HOLLY solo covered; LOVE ME TENDER (Elvis Presley). The track 'ACROSS THE UNIVERSE' was not The BEATLES original. • **Trivia:** The 'TWO TRIBES' video (directed by GODLEY & CREME) featured Ronald Reagan & Chernenko lookalikes fighting in a wrestling ring.

Album rating: WELCOME TO THE PLEASURE DOME (*7) / LIVERPOOL (*5) / Holly Johnson: BLAST (*5) / DREAMS THAT MONEY CAN'T BUY (*3) / SOULSTREAM (*3)

HOLLY JOHNSON (b. WILLIAM JOHNSON, 9 Feb'60, Khartoum, Sudan) – vocals (ex-solo artist, ex-BIG IN JAPAN) / **PAUL RUTHERFORD** (b. 8 Dec'59) – vocals (ex-SPITFIRE BOYS) / **BRIAN NASH** (b.20 Mar'63) – guitar repl. GED O'TOOLE / **MARK O'TOOLE** (b. 6 Jan'64) – bass / **PETER GILL** (b. 8 Mar'64) – drums

ZTT-Island Island

Oct 83. (7"pic-d/7") *(P+/ZTAS 1) <99805>* **RELAX. / ONE SEPTEMBER MORNING** 1 Mar84 67
(12"/12"pic-d) *(12/+P ZTAS 1)* – ('A'version) / Ferry across the Mersey.
(c-ep) *(CTIS 102)* – "Relax's Greatest Bits" – (various mixes).

Jun 84. (7"pic-d/7") *(P+/ZTAS 3) <99695>* **TWO TRIBES. / ONE FEBRUARY MORNING** 1 Oct84 43
(12"/12"pic-d) *(12/+P ZTAS 3)* – ('A'version) / War (hide yourself).
(12"pic-d) *(XZTAS 3)* – (all 3 tracks above)
(c-ep) *(CTIS 103)* – "Two Tribes (Keep The Peace)" – (various mixes).

Nov 84. (d-lp/c/cd) *(ZTTIQ/ZCIQ/CDIQ 1) <90232>* **WELCOME TO THE PLEASURE DOME** 1 33
– Well . . . / The world is my oyster / Snatch of fury / Welcome to the pleasure dome / Relax / War / Two tribes / Ferry / Born to run / San Jose / Wish the lads were here (inc. 'Ballad of 32') / Black night white light / The only star in Heaven / The power of love / Bang . . . *(also d-pic-lp; NEAT 1) (re-iss. May94 & Feb95 cd/c; same) (re-hit No.16 in Jun99) (cd re-iss. Jul00 on 'Repertoire'; RR 4896) (cd re-iss. Aug00 on 'ZTT'; ZTT 157CD)*

Nov 84. (7"pic-d/7") *(P+/ZTAS 5)* **THE POWER OF LOVE. / THE WORLD IS MY OYSTER** 1
(12"+=) *(12XZTAS 5)* – ('A'-Pleasurefix mix) / ('A'-Starfix mix).
(12"pic-d)(c-s) *(12PZTAS 5)(CTIS 105)* – ('A'side) / Trapped and scrapped / Holier than thou.

Mar 85. (7"sha-pic-d/7") *(P+/ZTAS 7) <99653>* **WELCOME TO THE PLEASURE DOME. / HAPPY HI / GET IT ON** 2 48
(12"+=) *(XTAS 7)* – Born to run (live).
(c-s+=) *(CTIS 107)* – How to remake the world.

Aug 86. (7") *(ZTAX 22)* **RAGE HARD. / (DON'T LOSE WHAT'S LEFT) OF YOUR LITTLE MIND** 4
(12"+=) *(12ZTAQ 22)* – Suffragette City.
(12"+=/12"box+=) *(12ZTAX/+B 22)* – Roadhouse blues.
(cd-s+=) *(ZCID 22)* – Suffragette city / Roadhouse blues.

Sep 86. (lp/c/cd) *(ZTT/ZC/ZCD IQ 8) <90546>* **LIVERPOOL** 5 88
– Warriors of the wasteland / Rage hard / Kill the pain / Maximum joy / Watching the wildlife / Lunar bay / For Heaven's sake / Is anybody out there?. *(re-iss. 1989 on 'Island'; IMCD 13) (re-iss. May94 & Nov98 cd/c; ZTT 107CD) (cd re-iss. Jul00 on 'Repertoire'; RR 4897)*

Nov 86. (7") *(ZTAS 25)* **WARRIORS OF THE WASTELAND. / WARRIORS (instrumental)** 19
(12"+=/c-s+=/cd-s+=) *(12ZTAS/CTIS/ZCID 25)* – Warriors (lots of different mixes).

Feb 87. (7") *(ZTAS 26)* **WATCHING THE WILDLIFE. / THE WAVES** 28
(12"+=) *(12ZTAX 26)* – Wildlife (Bit 3 & 4).
(c-s+=/cd-s+=) *(CTIS/ZCID 26)* – (various mixes, etc).

—— they split after legal contractual problems; RUTHERFORD went solo

—— In the spring of '93, HOLLY revealed he was HIV positive (AIDS)

– compilations, etc. –

releases on 'ZTT'

Sep 93. (7"/c-s) *(FGTH 1/+C)* **RELAX. / RELAX MCMXCIII** 5
(12"+=/cd-s+=) *(FGTH 1 T/CD)* – ('A'mixes; Jam & Spoon, etc).

Oct 93. (cd/c/lp) *(4509 93912-2/-4/-1)* **BANG! . . . THE GREATEST HITS OF . . .** 4
– Relax / Two tribes / War / Ferry / Warriors of the wasteland / For Heaven's sake / The world is my oyster / Welcome to the Pleasure dome / Watching the wildlife / Born to run / Rage hard / The power of love / Bang . . . *(re-iss. Jun94 cd/c; same) (cd re-iss. Jul00 on 'Repertoire'; RR 4898) (cd re-iss. Aug00; ZTT 159CD)*

Nov 93. (7"/c-s) *(FGTH 2/+C)* **WELCOME TO THE PLEASURE DOME. / ('A'-Elevatorman's non-stop top floor mix)** [18] [ ]
(12"+=/cd-s+=) *(FGTH 2 T/CD)* – ('A'mixes; Brothers In Rhythm, etc).
Dec 93. (7"/c-s) *(FGTH 3/+C)* **THE POWER OF LOVE. / ('A'mix)** [10] [ ]
(cd-s+=) *(FGTH 3CD)* – Rage hard (original DJ mix) / Holier than thou.
Feb 94. (7"/c-s) *(FGTH 4/+C)* **TWO TRIBES (Fluke's minimix). / ('A'mix)** [16] [ ]
(12"+=/cd-s+=) *(FGTH 4 T/CD)* – ('A'mixes).
May 94. (cd/c/lp) *(4509 95292-2/-4/-1)* **RELOAD – THE WHOLE 12 INCHES** [ ] [–]
(cd re-iss. Jul00 on 'Repertoire'; RR 4899) (cd re-iss. Aug00; ZTT 160CD)
Jun 00. (c-s/12"/cd-s) *(ZTT 150 C/T/CD)* **THE POWER OF LOVE (mixes)** [6] [–]
Jul 00. (cd-s) *Repertoire; (RR 8024)* **THE POWER OF LOVE (remix)** [ ] [–]
Aug 00. (c-s/12"/cd-s) *(ZTT 154 C/T/CD)* **TWO TRIBES (mixes)** [17] [–]
Sep 00. (cd/c) *(ZZT 160 CD/C)* **MAXIMUM JOY** [54] [–]
Nov 00. (c-s/12"/cd-s) *(ZTT 166 C/T/CD)* **WELCOME TO THE PLEASURE DOME** [45] [–]

HOLLY JOHNSON

had earlier returned to a solo career

M.C.A. Uni

Jan 89. (7") *(MCA 1306)* **LOVE TRAIN. / MURDER IN PARADISE** [4] [ ]
(12"+=/cd-s+=) *(MCAT/DMCA 1306)* – ('A'mix).
Mar 89. (7"/c-s) *(MCA/+C 1323)* **AMERICANOS. / ('A'dub version)** [4] [ ]
(cd-s+=/12"+=) *(D+/MCAT 1323)* – ('A'-Liberty mix).
(12") *(MCAX 1323)* – ('A'remixes).
Apr 89. (lp/c/cd) *(DMCG/MCGC/MCG 6042)* <603> **BLAST** [1] [ ]
– Atomic city / Heaven's here / Americanos / Deep in love / S.U.C.C.E.S.S. / Love train / Got it made / Love will come / Perfume / Feel good.
Jun 89. (12"/c-s) *(MCA T/C 1342)* **ATOMIC CITY. / BEAT THE SYSTEM** [18] [–]
(12"+=/cd-s+=) *(MCAX/DMCAT 1342)* – ('A'extended).
Sep 89. (7"/7"pic-d/c-s) *(MCA/+P/C 1365)* **HEAVEN'S HERE. / HALLELUJAH** [62] [–]
(cd-s+=/12"+=) *(D+/MCAT 1365)* – ('A'version).
Jul 90. (cd/c/lp) *(DMCL/MCLC/MCL 1902)* **HALLELUJAH, THE REMIX ALBUM** (BLAST remixed) [ ] [–]
Nov 90. (7"/c-s) *(MCA/+C 1460)* **WHERE HAS LOVE GONE. / PERFUME** [73] [–]
(cd-s+=/12"+=) *(D+/MCAT 1460)* – ('A'version).
Mar 91. (7"/c-s) **ACROSS THE UNIVERSE. / FUNKY PARADISE** [ ] [–]
(cd-s+=/12"+=) – ('A'-Space a-go-go mix).
May 91. (lp/c/cd) *(MCA/+C/D 10278)* **DREAMS THAT MONEY CAN'T BUY** [ ] [–]
– Across the universe / When the party's over / The people want to dance / I need your love / Boyfriend '65 / Where has love gone? / Penny arcade / Do it for love / You're a hit / The great love story.
Aug 91. (7"/c-s) **PEOPLE WANT TO DANCE. / ('A'-Apollo 440 mix)** [ ] [ ]
(12"+=/cd-s+=) – Love train (anxious big beat version).

Club Tool not iss.

Sep 94. (12"ep/cd-ep) **LEGENDARY CHILDREN (ALL OF THEM QUEER). / (4-'A'mixes)** [ ] [–]

Pleasuredome not iss.

Aug 99. (12"/cd-s) *(PLD/+CD1 004)* **DISCO HEAVEN (mixes; Sicario club radio / Daz & Andy's Heavenly / Sicario club)** [ ] [–]
Oct 99. (cd/c) *(PLD CD/MC 001)* **SOULSTREAM** [ ] [–]
– Lady luck / Soulstream / Disco heaven / Don't give up / Hope / The best invention / Hallelujah! / All U need is love / Legendary children (2000) / The power of love / Urban jungle – In the house of the rising sun.
Dec 99. (c-s/cd-s) *(PLD MC/CD1 005)* **THE POWER OF LOVE (mix) / IN THE HOUSE OF THE RISING SUN (mixes; 12" & Doggs House)** [56] [–]
(cd-s) *(PLCD 2005)* – ('A'-Millennium mix) / In the house of the rising sun (DNA instrumental) / All U need is love (demo).

HOLLY

early solo

Eric's not iss.

Dec 79. (7"m) *(ERIC'S 003)* **YANKEE ROSE. / TREASURE ISLAND / DESPERATE DAN** [ ] [–]
Jun 80. (7") *(ERIC'S 007)* **HOBO JOE. / STARS OF THE BARS** [ ] [–]

Aretha FRANKLIN

Born: 25 Mar'42, Memphis, Tennessee, USA. She was one of six children (future recording artists ERMA and CAROLYN among them) raised by her well-to-do preacher father, Rev. C.L. Franklin (a much revered figure, who himself had released a catalogue of recordings of his famous sermons) after they moved to Detroit, Michigan. In the early 50's, ARETHA was given singing lessons by family friends, MAHALIA JACKSON and CLARA WARD, who influenced her early career. ARETHA's initial recordings (included in the recently re-released 'Chess Masters' CD series) were primarily gospel releases, the celebratory, acappella black religious singing style that had developed from the old time spirituals and which went on to form a cornerstone of popular music. Inspired by the secular success of SAM COOKE, ARETHA subsequently moved to New York where she found manager, Joe King. There, she was spotted by music biz legend, JOHN HAMMOND, and in 1960 she signed to 'Columbia', releasing her debut single, 'TODAY I SING THE BLUES' In the autumn. After a minor hit, 'WON'T BE LONG', the gospel diva scored her first US Top 40 entry in 1961 with the standard, 'ROCK-A-BYE YOUR BABY WITH A DIXIE MELODY'. She continued to break the Hot 100 many times but FRANKLIN's wild creative spirit was essentially stifled by record company attempts to market her as a mainstream blues torch singer. Things really took off when she signed to 'Atlantic' in late '66, veteran producer Jerry Wexler relocating FRANKLIN to the legendary 'Muscle Shoals' studio in Alabama, the combination of WEXLER's experience and the "down home" style of the resident musicians, allowing FRANKLIN's formidable talents to flower in a manner that previous producer, Mitch Miller, hadn't touched on. With a team of WEXLER, engineer TOM DOWD and arranger ARIF MARDIN behind her, ARETHA was unstoppable and in the ensuing two years notched up a staggering run of hit singles, every one a timeless classic. 'I NEVER LOVED A MAN (THE WAY I LOVE YOU)' heralded her creative rebirth, FRANKLIN marking her territory with a seductive, primal femininity. The flip side was a sensitive cover of the DAN PENN/SPOONER OLDHAM classic, 'DO RIGHT WOMAN, DO RIGHT MAN', a potential hit in its own right. The same could be said of the follow-up, a blistering interpretation of Otis Redding's 'RESPECT', released with FRANKLIN's slow burning 'DR. FEELGOOD' in America and backed with the equally impressive 'SAVE ME' in Britain. The single was a US chart topper, the album 'I NEVER LOVED A MAN (THE WAY I LOVE YOU)' (1967) arguably her magnum opus and certainly a landmark soul release. More hits followed in the shape of the GOFFIN/KING-penned, '(YOU MAKE ME FEEL LIKE) A NATURAL WOMAN' (No.8 US), a cover of Don Covay's 'CHAIN OF FOOLS' (No.2 US) and 'SINCE YOU'VE BEEN GONE (SWEET SWEET BABY)'. All were included on 'LADY SOUL' (1968), another essential album which could've conceivably been titled 'FIRST LADY OF SOUL', ARETHA consolidating her position as the most talented female soul vocalist in the world as well as a highly accomplished piano player. 'THINK' was next up, a sexy soul juggernaut of a record and arguably the most uplifting call to feminist arms in the history of recorded music, while 'I SAY A LITTLE PRAYER', a beautifully sweet cover of the BACHARACH & DAVID number, was another million selling single, backed with the insidiously funky 'HOUSE THAT JACK BUILT' on the American release. As the decade drew to a close however, FRANKLIN began to lose her focus, splitting with her husband and sometime songwriting partner, TED WHITE. Nevertheless, 1970 saw a masterful gospel set, 'SPIRIT IN THE DARK', which contained the brilliant 'DON'T PLAY THAT SONG'. 'LIVE AT FILLMORE WEST' (1971) was a smoking concert set, while 'YOUNG GIFTED AND BLACK' (1972) featured the gritty funk of FRANKLIN's 'ROCK STEADY', proving that the 'Queen Of Soul' could compete with the Godfather, JAMES BROWN. 1972 also saw the release of 'AMAZING GRACE', Aretha's spellbinding double gospel set recorded with JAMES CLEVELAND & THE SOUTHERN CALIFORNIA COMMUNITY CHOIR. 'UNTIL YOU COME BACK TO ME (THAT'S WHAT I'M GONNA DO)', partly composed by STEVIE WONDER, was FRANKLIN's last major hit of the 70's and despite a reunion in 1974 with WEXLER and MARDIN, she couldn't match the depth and power of her late 60's heyday. Following a move to 'Arista' at the turn of the decade, FRANKLIN teamed up with LUTHER VANDROSS, releasing a string of slicker and poppier, if equally bland albums, the best of which, 'WHO'S ZOOMIN' WHO' (1985), providing her with her last Top 10 hit to date in the title track (excluding her smash hit duets with ANNIE LENNOX snd GEORGE MICHAEL). More interesting was the 1987 gospel album, 'ONE LORD, ONE FAITH, ONE BAPTISM', her voice still a revelation on a set which included contributions from the likes of MAVIS STAPLES and JESSE JACKSON. More's the pity then, that ARETHA seems to be lost without some kind of guiding hand, her wonderful voice wasted on uninspired projects. All her records from the golden period of '67-'72 are worth shelling out for, as is the Grammy Award-winning 4CD Box Set, covering the cream of the 'Atlantic' years. While the hip-hop smarts of 1998's 'A ROSE IS STILL A ROSE' had endeared her to a younger audience and regained her a place in the Top 40, FRANKLIN undertook a bonafide return to the roots with 2003's 'SO DAMN HAPPY'. If the hip-hop inlfuence remained courtesy of two – admittedly rather wonderful – MARY J. BLIGE collaborations, ARETHA soared once more on the wholesome, retro soul likes of 'WONDERFUL'.

• **Songwriters:** Although ARETHA wrote many songs herself, her greatest success came with 'Atlantic' covers: SEE SAW (Don Covay) / YOU SEND ME (Sam Cooke) / SATISFACTION (Rolling Stones) / THE WEIGHT (Band) / TRACKS OF MY TEARS (Miracles) / GENTLE ON MY MIND (John Hartford) / ELEANOR RIGBY + LET IT BE (Beatles) / SON OF A PREACHER MAN (Dusty Springfield) / BRIDGE OVER TROUBLED WATER (Simon & Garfunkel) / DON'T PLAY THAT SONG + SPANISH HARLEM (Ben E. King) / WHOLY HOLY (Marvin Gaye) / YOU'RE ALL I NEED TO GET BY + AIN'T NOTHING LIKE THE REAL THING (Marvin Gaye & Tammi Terrell) / ANGEL (Jimi Hendrix) / WHEN YOU GET RIGHT DOWN TO IT (Ronnie Dyson) / WHAT A FOOL BELIEVES (Doobie Brothers) / EVERYDAY PEOPLE (Staple Singles) / etc. • **Trivia:** On her 1969 recordings, DUANE ALLMAN played slide guitar. She had been produced by many greats including QUINCY JONES (1973) / CURTIS MAYFIELD (1976) / LAMONT-DOZIER (1977) / ARIF MARDIN (1980) / LUTHER VANDROSS (1982-83) / NARADA MICHAEL WALDEN (1985-87). In 1980, she appeared as a waitress in the film, 'The Blues Brothers'.

Album rating: ARETHA (*4) / THE ELECTRIFYING ARETHA FRANKLIN (*4) / THE TENDER, THE MOVING, THE SWINGING (*5) / LAUGHING (ON THE OUTSIDE) (*4) / UNFORGETTABLE: A TRIBUTE TO DINAH WASHINGTON (*4) / SONGS OF FAITH gospel (*4) / RUNNIN' OUT OF FOOLS (*5) / YEAH!!! (*4) / SOUL SISTER (*4) / I NEVER LOVED A MAN (THE WAY I LOVE YOU) (*9) / ARETHA FRANKLIN'S GREATEST HITS exploitation compilation (*6) / ARETHA ARRIVES (*7) / ARETHA: LADY SOUL (*9) / ARETHA NOW (*8) / ARETHA IN PARIS (*6) / ARETHA FRANKLIN: SOUL '69 (*7) / ARETHA'S GOLD compilation (*8) / THIS GIRL'S IN LOVE WITH YOU (*6) / SPIRIT IN THE DARK (*6) / ARETHA LIVE AT FILLMORE WEST (*6) / ARETHA'S GREATEST HITS compilation (*7) / YOUNG, GIFTED & BLACK (*5) / AMAZING GRACE (*7) / HEY NOW HEY (THE OTHER SIDE OF THE SKY) (*6) / LET ME IN YOUR LIFE (*6) / WITH EVERYTHING I FEEL IN ME (*5) / YOU (*4) / SPARKLE (*5) / SWEET PASSION (*4) / ALMIGHTY FIRE (*4) / LA DIVA (*3) / ARETHA (*5) / LOVE ALL THE HURT WAY (*4) / JUMP TO IT (*5) / GET IT RIGHT (*5) / WHO'S ZOOMIN' WHO (*6) / ARETHA [1986] (*5) / ONE LORD, ONE FAITH, ONE BAPTISM (*4) / THROUGH THE STORM (*5) / WHAT YOU SEE IS WHAT YOU SWEAT (*4) / QUEEN OF SOUL – THE VERY BEST OF ARETHA FRANKLIN compilation (*8) / RESPECT – THE VERY BEST OF ARETHA FRANKLIN compilation (*9) / SO DAMN HAPPY (*6)

ARETHA FRANKLIN – vocals (with session people)

		not iss.	Checker
1960.	(7") *<861>* **NEVER GROW OLD. / YOU GROW CLOSER**	–	
1960.	(7") *<941>* **PRECIOUS LORD. / (part 2)**	–	
		Fontana	**Columbia**
Jan 61.	(7") *(H 271) <41793>* **LOVE IS THE ONLY THING. / TODAY I SING THE BLUES** *<re-iss. 1970>*		Oct60
Feb 61.	(7") *<41923>* **WON'T BE LONG. / RIGHT NOW**	–	76
Jul 61.	(7") *<41985>* **MAYBE I'M A FOOL. / ARE YOU SURE**	–	
Oct 61.	(7") *(H 343) <42157>* **ROCK-A-BYE YOUR BABY WITH A DIXIE MELODY. / OPERATION HEARTBREAK**		37
Jan 62.	(lp) *(TFL 5173) <8412>* **ARETHA** – Won't be long / Over the rainbow / Love is the only thing / Sweet lover / All night long / Who needs you? / Right now / Are you sure / Maybe I'm a fool / It ain't necessarily so / Blue by myself / Today I sing the blues. *(re-iss. Jan84 on 'Cameo-CBS')*		Oct61
		C.B.S.	**Columbia**
Jan 62.	(7") *<42266>* **I SURRENDER, DEAR. / ROUGH RIDER**	–	87 / 94
Apr 62.	(lp) *<8561>* **THE ELECTRIFYING ARETHA FRANKLIN** – You made me love you / I told you so / Rockabye your baby with a Dixie melody / Nobody like you / Exactly like you / It's so heartbreakin' / Rough lover / Blue holiday / Just for you / That lucky old sun / I surrender, dear / Ac-cent-tchu-ate the positive.	–	
Jun 62.	(7") *<42456>* **DON'T CRY BABY. / WITHOUT THE ONE YOU LOVE**	–	92
Sep 62.	(7") *<42520>* **TRY A LITTLE TENDERNESS. / JUST FOR A THRILL**	–	100
Nov 62.	(lp) *<8676>* **THE TENDER, THE MOVING, THE SWINGING ARETHA FRANKLIN** – Don't cry baby / Try a little tenderness / I apologize / Without the one you love / Look for the silver lining / I'm sitting on top of the world / Just for a thrill / God bless the child / I'm wandering / How deep is the ocean / I don't know you anymore / Lover come back to me.	–	69
Dec 62.	(7") *<42625>* **TROUBLE IN MIND. / GOD BLESS THE CHILD**	–	86
Jan 63.	(lp) *<8897>* **LAUGHING (ON THE OUTSIDE)** – Skylark / For all we know / Make someone happy / I wonder / Solitude / Laughing on the outside / Say it isn't so / Until the real thing comes along / If ever I would leave you / Where are you / Mr.Ugly / I wanna be around.	–	
1963.	(7") *<42796>* **SAY IT ISN'T SO. / HERE'S WHERE I CAME IN**	–	
1963.	(7") *<42874>* **SKYLARK. / YOU'VE GOT HER**	–	
1963.	(7") *<42933>* **JOHNNY. / KISSIN' BY THE MISTLETOE**	–	
1964.	(7") *<43009>* **SOULVILLE. / EVIL GAL BLUES**	–	
Sep 64.	(7") *<43113>* **RUNNIN' OUT OF FOOLS. / IT'S JUST A MATTER OF TIME**	–	57
Oct 64.	(lp) *<8963>* **UNFORGETTABLE: A TRIBUTE TO DINAH WASHINGTON** – Unforgettable / Cold cold heart / What a difference a day made / Drinking again / Evil gal blues / Nobody knows the way I feel this morning / Don't say you're sorry again / This bitter Earth / If I should lose you / Soulville. *(cd-iss. Jun95)*	–	

Nov 64. (7") *<43177>* **WINTER WONDERLAND. / THE CHRISTMAS SONG** –

Dec 64. (lp) *<9081>* **RUNNIN' OUT OF FOOLS** – 84
– Mockingbird / How glad I am / Walk on by / My guy / Every little bit hurts / Shoop shoop song / You'll lose a good thing / I can't wait until I see my baby's face / It's just a matter of time / Runnin' out of fools / Two sides of love / One room Paradise.

Mar 65. (7") *<43203>* **CAN'T YOU JUST SEE ME. / LITTLE MISS RAGGEDY ANNE** Jan65 96

May 65. (7") *<43241>* **I CAN'T WAIT UNTIL I SEE MY BABY'S FACE. / ONE STEP AHEAD** –

Nov 65. (lp; stereo/mono) *(S+/BPG 62566) <9151>* **YEAH!!! – IN PERSON** Jul65
– This could be the start of something / Once in a lifetime / Misty / More / There is no greater love / Muddy water / If I had a hammer / Impossible / Today I love everybody / Without the one you love / Trouble in mind / Love for sale.

Jul 66. (7") *<4333>* **SWEET BITTER LOVE. / I'M LOSING YOU** –

Aug 66. (lp; stereo/mono) *(S+/BPG 62744) <9321>* **SOUL SISTER**
– Until you were gone / You made me love you / Follow your heart / Ol' man river / Sweet bitter love / Mother's love / Swanee / I'm losing you / Take a look / Can't you just see me / Cry like a baby.

1966. (7") *<43442>* **THERE IS NO GREATER LOVE. / YOU MADE ME LOVE YOU** –

1966. (7") *<43515>* **HANDS OFF. / TIGHTEN UP YOUR TIE, BUTTON UP YOUR JACKET** –

1967. (7") *<43637>* **UNTIL YOU WERE GONE. / SWANEE** –

Atlantic Atlantic

Apr 67. (7") *(584 084) <2386>* **I NEVER LOVED A MAN (THE WAY I LOVE YOU). / DO RIGHT WOMAN, DO RIGHT MAN** Mar67 9

Apr 67. (7") *<2403>* **RESPECT. / DR. FEELGOOD** – 1

May 67. (7") *(584 115)* **RESPECT. / SAVE ME** 10 –

Jul 67. (lp; mono/stereo) *(587/588 066) <8139>* **I NEVER LOVED A MAN (THE WAY I LOVE YOU)** 36 Apr67 2
– Respect / Drown in my own tears / I never loved a man (the way I loved you) / Soul serenade / Don't let me lose this dream / Baby, baby, baby / Dr. Feelgood / Good times / Do right woman – do right man / Save me / A change is gonna come. *(re-iss. 1972) (cd-iss. Jun93)*

Aug 67. (7") *(584 127) <2427>* **BABY I LOVE YOU. / GOING DOWN SLOW** 39 Jul67 4

Sep 67. (7") *<2441>* **A NATURAL WOMAN (YOU MAKE ME FEEL LIKE). / BABY BABY BABY** – 8

Oct 67. (lp; mono/stereo) *(587/588 085) <8150>* **ARETHA ARRIVES** Aug67 5
– Satisfaction / You are my sunshine / Never let me go / 96 tears / Prove it / Night life / That's life / I wonder / Ain't nobody (gonna turn me around) / Going down slow / Baby, I love you. *(re-iss. 1972) (cd-iss. Aug93 on 'Rhino')*

Oct 67. (7") *(584 141)* **(YOU MAKE ME FEEL LIKE A) NATURAL WOMAN. / NEVER LET ME GO** –

Nov 67. (7") *<2464>* **CHAIN OF FOOLS. / PROVE IT** – 2

Dec 67. (7") *(584 157>* **CHAIN OF FOOLS. / SATISFACTION** 37 –

Mar 68. (7") *(584 172) <2486>* **(SWEET SWEET BABY) SINCE YOU'VE BEEN GONE. / AIN'T NO WAY** 47 5
Feb68 16

Mar 68. (lp; mono/stereo) *(587/588 099) <8176>* **ARETHA: LADY SOUL** 25 Feb68 2
– Chain of fools / Money won't change You / People get ready / Niki Hoeky / (You make me feel like) A natural woman / Since you've been gone (sweet sweet baby) / Good to me as I am to you / Come back baby / Groovin' / Ain't no way. *(re-iss. Jun88, cd-iss. Sep89) (cd-iss. Jun93)*

May 68. (7") *(584 186) <2518>* **THINK. / YOU SEND ME** 26 7
56

Jul 68. (7") *(584 206)* **I SAY A LITTLE PRAYER. / SEE-SAW** 4 –

Aug 68. (7") *<2546>* **THE HOUSE THAT JACK BUILT. / I SAY A LITTLE PRAYER** – 6
10

Sep 68. (7") *(584 239)* **THE HOUSE THAT JACK BUILT. / DON'T LET ME LOSE THIS DREAM** –

Sep 68. (lp; mono/stereo) *(587/588 114) <8186>* **ARETHA NOW** 6 Jul68 3
– Think / I say a little prayer / See saw / Night time is the right time / You send me / You're a sweet sweet man / I take what I want / Hello sunshine / A change / I can't see myself leaving you *(cd-iss. Aug93 on 'Rhino')*

Nov 68. (7") *<2574>* **SEE SAW. / MY SONG** – 14
31

Dec 68. (lp; mono/stereo) *(587/588 149) <8207>* **ARETHA IN PARIS – LIVE AT THE OLYMPIA (live)** Nov68 13
– (I can't get no) Satisfaction / Don't let me lose this dream / Soul serenade / Night life / Baby I love you / Groovin' / Natural woman / Come back baby / Dr. Feelgood / Since you've been gone / I never loved a man (the way I love you) / Chain of fools / Respect. *(re-iss. cd Dec94 on 'Rhino-Atlantic')*

Mar 69. (7") *(584 252) <2603>* **THE WEIGHT. / THE TRACKS OF MY TEARS** 19
Feb69 71

Mar 69. (lp) *(588 169) <8212>* **SOUL '69** Feb69 15
– Ramblin' / Today I sing the blues / River's invitation / Pitiful / Crazy he calls me / Bring it on home to me / Tracks of my tears / If you gotta make a fool of somebody / Gentle on my mind / So long / I'll never be free / Elusive butterfly *(cd-iss. Feb94 on 'Rhino-Atlantic')*

Apr 69. (7") *<2619>* **I CAN'T SEE MYSELF LEAVING YOU. / GENTLE ON MY MIND** – 28
76

Aug 69. (7") *(584 285) <2650>* **SHARE YOUR LOVE WITH ME. / PLEDGING MY LOVE / THE CLOCK** Jul69 13

Nov 69. (7") *(584 306) <2683>* **ELEANOR RIGBY. / IT AIN'T FAIR** Oct69 17

Mar 70. (7") *(584 322) <2706>* **CALL ME. / SON OF A PREACHER MAN** Feb70 13

Apr 70. (lp) *(2400 004) <8248>* **THIS GIRL'S IN LOVE WITH YOU** Feb70 17
– Son of a preacher man / Share your love with me / The dark end of the street / Let it be / Eleanor Rigby / This girl's in love with you / It ain't fair / The weight / Call me / Sit down and cry *(cd-iss. Feb94 on 'Rhino-Atlantic')*

May 70. (7") *(2091 008)* **LET IT BE. / MY SONG** –

May 70. (7") *<2731>* **SPIRIT IN THE DARK. / THE THRILL IS GONE** – 23

— Her new band comprised **KING CURTIS** – saxophone / **CORNELL DUPREE** – guitar / **RICHARD TEE** – piano / **JERRY JEMMOTT** – bass / **BERNARD PURDIE** – drums

Jul 70. (7") *<2751>* **DON'T PLAY THAT SONG. / LET IT BE** – 11

Aug 70. (7") *(2091 027)* **DON'T PLAY THAT SONG. / THE THRILL IS GONE** 13 –

Sep 70. (lp) *(2400 021) <8265>* **DON'T PLAY THAT SONG** <US-title 'SPIRIT IN THE DARK'> 25
– Don't play that song / The thrill is gone / Pullin' / You and me / Honest I do / Spirit in the dark / When the battle is over / One way ticket / Try Matty's / That's all I want from you / Oh no, not my baby / When I sing the blues. *(cd-iss. Feb94 on 'Rhino-Atlantic')*

Dec 70. (7") *(2091 044)* **OH NO NOT MY BABY. / YOU AND ME** –

Dec 70. (7") *<2772)* **BORDER SONG (HOLY MOSES). / YOU AND ME** – 37

Feb 71. (7") *<2787>* **YOU'RE ALL I NEED TO GET BY. / PULLIN'** – 19

Mar 71. (7") *(2091 063)* **YOU'RE ALL I NEED TO GET BY. / BORDER SONG** –

May 71. (7") *(2091 090) <2796>* **BRIDGE OVER TROUBLED WATER. / A BRAND NEW ME** Apr71 6

Jul 71. (lp) *(2400 136) <7205>* **LIVE AT FILLMORE WEST (live)** May71 7
– Respect / Love the one you're with / Bridge over troubled water / Eleanor Rigby / Make it with you / Don't play that song / Dr. Feelgood / Spirit in the dark / Spirit in the dark (reprise with RAY CHARLES) / Reach out and touch (somebody's hand). *(cd-iss. Feb94 on 'Rhino-Atlantic')*

Jul 71. (7"m) *(2091 111)* **I SAY A LITTLE PRAYER (live). / (I CAN'T GET NO) SATISFACTION (live)** –

Aug 71. (7") *(2091 127)* **A BRAND NEW ME. / SPIRIT IN THE DARK** –

— On the 13th August '71, her legendary sax player and soloist, KING CURTIS, was stabbed to death on the street. She and her father sang and gave sermon at funeral. She attended another funeral 6 months later of her friend/mentor Mahalia Jackson.

Sep 71. (7") *(2091 138) <2817>* **SPANISH HARLEM. / LEAN ON ME** 14 Jul71 2

Oct 71. (7") *<2838>* **ROCK STEADY. / OH ME OH MY (I'M A FOOL FOR YOU BABY)** – 9
73

Mar 72. (7") *(K 10154) <2866>* **DAYDREAMING. / I'VE BEEN LOVING TOU TOO LONG** 5

Mar 72. (lp) *(K 40323)* *<7213>* **YOUNG, GIFTED AND BLACK** Feb72 11
– Oh me oh my (I'm a fool for you baby) / Daydreaming / Rock steady / Young, gifted and black / All the king's horses / A brand new me / April fools / I've been loving you too long / First snow in Kokomo / The long and winding road / Didn't I (blow your mind this time) / Border song. *(cd-iss. Feb94 on 'Rhino-Atlantic')*

May 72. (7") *<2883>* **ALL THE KING'S HORSES. / APRIL FOOLS** – 26

Aug 72. (7") *<2901>* **WHOLY HOLY. / GIVE YOURSELF TO JESUS** – 81

Sep 72. (7") *(K 10224)* **ALL THE KING'S HORSES. / ROCK STEADY** –

Sep 72. (d-lp) *(K 60023)* *<906>* **AMAZING GRACE (live)** Jun72 7
– Mary don't you weep / Medley / Precious Lord, Take my hand / You've got a friend / Old landmark / Give yourself to Jesus / How I got over / What a friend we have in Jesus / Amazing grace – Precious memories / Climbing higher mountains / Remarks by Reverend C L Franklin / God will take care of you / Wholy holy / You'll never walk alone / Never grow old. *(re-iss. Nov87)(cd-iss. Aug93)*

Mar 73. (7") *(K 10288)* *<2941>* **MASTER OF EYES (THE DEEPNESS OF YOUR EYES). / MOODY'S MOOD FOR LOVE** Feb73 33

Aug 73. (7") *(K 10346)* *<2969>* **ANGEL. / SISTER FROM TEXAS** 37 Jul73 20

Aug 73. (lp/c) *(K/K4 40504)* *<7265>* **HEY NOW HEY (THE OTHER SIDE OF THE SKY)** Jul73 30
– Hey now hey / Somewhere / So well when you're well / Angel / Sister from Texas / Mister Spain / That's the way I feel about cha / Moody's mood / Just right tonight. *(re-iss. cd Dec94 on 'Rhino-Atlantic')*

Jan 74. (7") *(K 10399)* *<2995>* **UNTIL YOU COME BACK TO ME (THAT'S WHAT I'M GONNA DO). / IF YOU DON'T THINK** 26 Nov73 3

Apr 74. (lp/c) *(K/K4 50031)* *<7292>* **LET ME IN YOUR LIFE** Mar74 14
– Let me in your life / Every natural thing / Ain't nothing like the real thing / I'm in love / Until you come back to me (that's what I'm gonna do) / The masquerade is over / With pen in hand / Oh baby / Eight days on the road / If you don't think / A song for you. *(re-iss. cd Dec94 on 'Rhino-Atlantic')*

Jun 74. (7") *(K 10447)* *<2999>* **I'M IN LOVE. / OH BABY** Apr74 19

Aug 74. (7") *<3200>* **AIN'T NOTHING LIKE THE REAL THING. / EIGHT DAYS A WEEK** – 47

Jan 75. (7") *(K 10543)* *<3224>* **WITHOUT LOVE. / DON'T GO BREAKING MY HEART** Nov74 45

Feb 75. (lp/c) *(K/K4 50093)* *<18116>* **WITH EVERYTHING I FEEL IN ME** Jan75 57
– Without love / Don't go breaking my heart / When you get right down to it / You'll never get to Heaven / With everything I feel in me / I love every little thing about you / Sing it again – say it again / All of these things / You move me.

Mar 75. (7") *(K 10577)* **WHEN YOU GET RIGHT DOWN TO IT. / SING IT AGAIN – SAY IT AGAIN** –

Apr 75. (7") *<3249>* **SING IT AGAIN – SAY IT AGAIN. / WITH EVERYTHING I FEEL IN ME** –

Oct 75. (7") *(K 10669)* *<3289>* **MR. D.J. (5 FOR THE D.J.). / AS LONG AS YOU ARE THERE** Sep75 53

Dec 75. (7") *<3311>* **YOU. / WITHOUT LOVE** –

Dec 75. (lp/c) *(K/K4 50159)* *<18151>* **YOU** Nov75 83
– Mr D.J. / It only happens / I'm not strong enough to love you again / Walk softly / You make my life / Without you / The sha-la bandit / You / You got all the aces / As long as you are there.

Jun 76. (7") *(K 16765)* *<3326>* **SOMETHING HE CAN FEEL. / LOVING YOU BABY** 28

Jun 76. (lp/c) *(K/K4 56248)* *<18176>* **SPARKLE (Soundtrack)** 18
– Sparkle / Giving him something he can feel / Hooked on your love / Look into your heart / I get high / Jump / Loving you baby / Rock with me.

Sep 76. (7") *<3358>* **JUMP. / HOOKED ON YOUR LOVE** – 72

Jan 77. (7") *<3373>* **LOOK INTO YOUR HEART. / ROCK WITH ME** – 82

May 77. (7") *(K 10938)* *<3393>* **BREAK IT TO ME GENTLY. / MEADOWS OF SPRINGTIME** 85

Jun 77. (lp/c) *(K/K4 50368)* *<19102>* **SWEET PASSION** 49
– Break it to me gently / When I think about you / What I did for love / No one could ever love you more / Tender touch / Touch me up / Sunshine will never be the same / Meadows of Springtime / Mumbles / I've got the music in me / Passion.

Sep 77. (7") *(K 11007)* *<3418>* **WHEN I THINK ABOUT YOU. / TOUCH ME**

Jun 78. (lp/c) *(K/K4 50445)* *<19161>* **ALMIGHTY FIRE** May78 63
– Almighty fire (woman of the future) / Lady day / More than just a joy / Keep on loving you / I needed you baby / Close to you / No matter who you love / This you can believe / I'm your speed.

Jun 78. (7") *<3468>* **ALMIGHTY FIRE. / I'M YOUR SPEED** –

Nov 78. (7") *<3495>* **THIS YOU CAN BELIEVE. / MORE THAN JUST A JOY** –

Oct 79. (7") *(K 11390)* *<3605>* **LADIES ONLY. / WHAT IF I SHOULD EVER NEED YOU**

Oct 79. (lp/c) *(K/K4 50637)* *<19248>* **LA DIVA**
– Ladies only / It's gonna get a bit better / What if I should ever need you / Honey I need your love / I was made for you / Only star / Reasons why / You brought me back to life / Half a love / The feeling.

Jan 80. (7") *<3632>* **HALF A LOVE. / ONLY STAR** –

Arista Arista

Oct 80. (7"/12") *(ARIST/+12 377)* **WHAT A FOOL BELIEVES. / SCHOOLDAYS** 46 –

Oct 80. (lp/c) *(SPART/TCART 1147)* *<9538>* **ARETHA** 47
– Come to me / I can't turn you loose / United together / Take me with you / Whatever it is / What a fool believes / Together / Love me forever / Schooldays. *(re-iss. May88 lp/c/cd; 208/408/258 883)*

Mar 81. (7") *(ARIST 395)* *<0569>* **UNITED TOGETHER. / I CAN'T TURN YOU LOOSE** Dec80 56

May 81. (7") *<0600>* **COME TO ME. / SCHOOL DAYS** – 84

Aug 81. (7"/12"; ARETHA FRANKLIN & GEORGE BENSON) *(ARIST/+12 428)* *<0624>* **LOVE ALL THE HURT AWAY. / HOLD ON I'M COMING** 49 46

Sep 81. (lp/c) *(SPART/TCART 1170)* *<9552>* **LOVE ALL THE HURT AWAY** 36
– Hold on I'm coming / You can't always get what you want / It's my turn / Living in the streets / Love all the hurt away / There's a star for everyone / Truth and honesty / Search on / Whole lot of me / Kind of man *(cd-iss. 1988; 253 913)*

Jan 82. (7") *<0646>* **IT'S MY TURN. / KIND OF MAN** –

Feb 82. (7"/12") *(ARIST/+12 442)* **HOLD ON I'M COMING. / KIND OF MAN** –

Apr 82. (7") *<0665>* **LIVIN' IN THE STREETS. / THERE'S A STAR FOR EVERYONE** –

Aug 82. (7"/12") *(ARIST/+12 479)* *<0699>* **JUMP TO IT. / JUST MY DAYDREAM** 42 24

Aug 82. (lp/c) *(204/404 742)* *<9602>* **JUMP TO IT** 23
– Love me right / 16 she don't want your love / This is for real / (It's just) Your love / I wanna make it up to you / It's your thing / Just my day dream. *(re-iss. May88 lp/c/cd; 209/409/259 060)*

Jan 83. (7"/12") *(ARIST/+12 500)* *<1023>* **LOVE ME RIGHT. / (IT'S JUST) YOUR LOVE**

Mar 83. (7") *<1043>* **THIS IS FOR REAL. / I WANT TO MAKE IT UP TO YOU** –

Jul 83. (7"/12") *(ARIST/+12 537)* **GET IT RIGHT. / JUMP TO IT** 74 –

Jul 83. (7") *<9034>* **GET IT RIGHT. / GIVING IN** – 61

Jul 83. (lp/c) *(205/405 544)* *<8019>* **GET IT RIGHT** 36
– Get it right / Pretender / Every girl (wants my guy) / When you love me like that / I wish it would rain / Better friends than lovers / I got your love / Giving in.

Oct 83. (7") *<9095>* **EVERY GIRL (WANTS MY GIRL). / I GOT YOUR LOVE** –

—— In Jul'85, while attending a civil rights campaign, her father C.L. is shot and went into a coma. He never recovered fully and died in Jul'87.

Jul 85. (7") *(ARIST 624)* *<9354>* **FREEWAY OF LOVE. / UNTIL YOU SAY YOU LOVE ME** 68 Jun85 3
(12"+=) *(ARIST12 624)* – Jump to it.
(d7"++=) *(ARIST22 624)* – Zoomin' to the freeway.
(7"/12" – re-dist.Apr86, hit UK No.51)

—— (Oct85) She duets with EURYTHMICS on her 'SISTERS ARE DOIN' IT FOR THEMSELVES'. It hit UK No.9 + US No.18.

Nov 85. (lp/c/cd) *(207/407 202)* *<8286>* **WHO'S ZOOMIN' WHO?** 49 Jul85 13
– Who's zoomin' who / Freeway of love / Another night / Sweet bitter love / Sisters are doin' it for themselves / Until you say love me / Push / Ain't nobody ever loved you / Integrity. *(re-iss. Jul88 lp/c/cd; 259/409/259 053)*

Nov 85. (7") *(ARIST 633)* *<9410>* **WHO'S ZOOMIN' WHO. / SWEET BITTER LOVE** 11 Sep85 7
(12"+=) *(ARIST12 633)* – ('A'dub version) / ('A'acappella mix).

Feb 86. (7")(12") *(ARIST 657)* *<9453>* **ANOTHER NIGHT. / KIND OF MAN** 54 22
(12"+=) *(ARIST12 657)* – School days / Together again.
(d7"++=) *(ARIST22 657)* – ('A'-Nightlife mix).

Aug 86. (7") *(ARIST 667)* *<9474>* **AIN'T NOBODY EVER LOVED YOU. / INTEGRITY**
(12"+=) *(ARIST12 667)* – ('A'dub mix) / ('A-Percappella mix).

Oct 86. (lp/c/cd) *(208/408/258 020)* *<8442>* **ARETHA** [51] [32]
– Jimmy Lee / I knew you were waiting (for me) / Do you still remember / Jumpin' Jack Flash / Rock-a-lott / An angel cries / He'll come along / If you need my love tonight / Look to the rainbow. *(cd re-iss. Nov93 on 'Entertainers')*

Oct 86. (7") *(ARIST 678)* *<9528>* **JUMPIN' JACK FLASH. / INTEGRITY** [58] Sep86 [21]
(12"+=) *(ARIST12 678)* – Who's zoomin' who / Sweet bitter love.

Nov 86. (7") *<9546>* **JIMMY LEE. / IF YOU NEED MY LOVE TONIGHT** [–] [28]

—— She hit No.1 UK/US with GEORGE MICHAEL duet 'I KNEW YOU WERE WAITING (FOR ME)', This was released 'Epic' UK / 'Arista' US.

Feb 87. (7") *(RIS 6)* *<9557>* **JIMMY LEE. / AN ANGEL CRIES** Apr87
(12"+=/cd-s+=) *(RIST/RICD 6)* – ('A'dub version) / Aretha megamix.

Jun 87. (7") *(RIS 20)* *<9574>* **ROCK-A-LOTT. / LOOK TO THE RAINBOW** [82]
(12") *(RIST 20)* – ('A'side) / ('A'dub) / ('A'cappella mix).

Oct 87. (7") *<9623>* **IF YOU NEED MY LOVE TONIGHT. / HE'LL COME ALONG** [–]

Nov 87. (lp/c/cd) *(208/408/258 715)* *<8497>* **ONE LORD, ONE FAITH, ONE BAPTISM**
– Walking in the light / Prayer invitation by Cecil Franklin / Introduction by Rev. Jesse Jackson / Jesus hears every prayer / Surely God is able / The Lord's prayer / Oh happy day / We need prayer / Speech by Rev. Jesse Jackson / Ave Maria / Introduction by Rev. Jasper Williams / Higher ground / Prayer by Rev. Donald Person / I've been in the storm too long / Waking up ready to go.

Feb 88. (7"/12") *(109780/610978)* *<9672>* **OH HAPPY DAY. / THE LORD'S PRAYER**
(above featured MAVIS STAPLES)

Apr 89. (7"/c-s/7"pic-d; ARETHA FRANKLIN & ELTON JOHN) *(112 185/409957/112377)* *<9809>* **THROUGH THE STORM. / COME TO ME** [41]
(12"+=/cd-s+=) *(612/162 185)* – Oh happy day.

May 89. (lp/c/cd) *(209/409/259 842)* *<8572>* **THROUGH THE STORM** [46] [55]
– Through the storm / Gimme your love / He's the boy / It ain't never gonna be / Think / Mercy / It isn't, it wasn't, it ain't never gonna be / If ever a love there was.

Jun 89, (7"; ARETHA FRANKLIN & WHITNEY HOUSTON) *<9850>* **IT ISN'T, IT WASN'T, IT AIN'T NEVER GONNA BE. / IF EVER A LOVE THERE WAS** [–] [41]

Sep 89. (7"/c-s; ARETHA FRANKLIN & WHITNEY HOUSTON) *(112545/410093)* **IT ISN'T, IT WASN'T, IT AIN'T NEVER GONNA BE. / THINK '89** [29] [–]
(12"+=) *(612545)* – ('A'extended remix).
(cd-s++=) *(662545)* – ('A'-Hip hop remix).

Nov 89. (7") *(112728)* *<9884>* **GIMME YOUR LOVE. / HE'S THE BOY**
(12"+=/cd-s+=) *(612/662 727)* – ('A'parts 1 & 2 versions).

Jul 91. (7") *(114420)* *<2239>* **EVERYDAY PEOPLE. / YOU CAN'T TAKE ME FOR GRANTED** [69]
(12") *(114420)* *<2340>* – ('A'side) / ('A'people remix) / ('A'people dub).
(cd-s+=) *(114420)* – ('A'remixed).

Aug 91. (cd/c/lp) *(261/411/211 724)* *<8628>* **WHAT YOU SEE IS WHAT YOU SWEAT**
– Everyday people / Everchanging times (with MICHAEL McDONALD / What you see is what you sweat / Mary goes round / I dreamed a dream / Someone' else's eyes / Doctor's orders / You can't take me for granted / What did you give / Everyday people (remix). *(cd re-iss. Feb94; same)*

Sep 91. (c-s) *<2350>* **SOMEONE ELSE'S EYES / WHAT DID YOU GIVE** [–]

Nov 91. (c-s) *<2380>* **WHAT YOU SEE IS WHAT YOU SWEAT /** [–]

Feb 92. (c-s) *<2394>* **YOU CAN'T TAKE ME FOR GRANTED / EVERCHANGING TIMES** [–]

Jan 94. (c-s) *(74321 18702-4)* *<12657>* **A DEEPER LOVE. / ('A'-Tribesman mix)** [5] [63]
(12"+=/cd-s+=) *(74321 18702-1/-2)* – (2 other mixes).

Mar 94. (cd/c) *(74321 16202-2/-4)* *<18722>* **GREATEST HITS 1980-1994** (compilation) [27] [85]
– Freeway of love / I knew you were waiting (for me) (w/ GEORGE MICHAEL) / Jump to it / Willing to forgive / Doctor's orders / United together / Who's zoomin' who / A deeper love / Honey / Get it right / Another night / Ever changing times / Jimmy Lee / (You make me fee like) A natural woman / I dreamed a dream / Jumpin' Jack Flash.

Jun 94. (c-s) *(74321 21334-4)* *<12680>* **WILLING TO FORGIVE / JUMP TO IT** [17] [26]
(12"+=/cd-s+=) *(74321 21334-1/-2)* – ('A'mix).

Apr 98. (c-s/cd-s) *(74321 56974-4/-2)* *<13465>* **A ROSE IS STILL A ROSE / ('A'mix)** [22] Mar98 [26]
(cd-s) *(74321 58035-2)* – ('A'mixes).

May 98. (cd/c) *<(0782 2 18987-2/-4)>* **A ROSE IS STILL A ROSE** Apr98 [30]
– A rose is still a rose / Never leave you again / In case you forgot / Here we go again / Every little bit hurts / In the morning / I'll dip / How many times / Watch my back / Love pang / Woman.

Sep 98. (c-s/cd-s) *(74321 61274-4/-2)* *<13502>* **HERE WE GO AGAIN / IN THE MORNING / NESSUN DORMA (live)** [68] Jul98 [76]
(cd-s) *(74321 61275-2)* – ('A'side) / Who's zoomin' who / Everyday people.

Sep 03. (12") *<56474>* **THE ONLY THING MISSIN. / (mix)** [–]

Sep 03. (cd) *(82876 55279-2)* *<50174>* **SO DAMN HAPPY** [33]
– The only thing missin' / Wonderful / Holdin' on / No matter what / Everybody's somebody's fool / So damn happy / You are my joy / Falling out of love / Ain't no way / Good news / You are my joy (reprise).

– (selective) compilations, etc. –

on 'CBS' / 'Columbia' unless mentioned otherwise

Jun 67. (lp) *(CBS 64536)* *<9473>* **GREATEST HITS: ARETHA FRANKLIN 1960-65** [94]
(re-iss. Apr87 lp/c;)

Aug 67. (7") *<44270>* **TAKE A LOOK. / FOLLOW YOUR HEART** [–] [56]

Dec 67. (7") *<44381>* **MOCKINGBIRD. / A MOTHER'S LOVE** [–] [94]

Jan 68. (lp) *(CBS 63269)* *<9554>* **TAKE A LOOK** Oct67

Feb 68. (7") *<44441>* **SOULVILLE. / EVIL GAL BLUES** [–] [83]

on 'Atlantic' unless mentioned otherwise

Jul 69. (lp) *(588 182)* *<8227>* **ARETHA'S GOLD** [18]
(re-iss. 1972) (cd-iss. Aug93)

1970. (lp) *(2464 007)* **I SAY A LITTLE PRAYER** [–]

Sep 71. (lp) *(K 40279)* *<8295>* **ARETHA'S GREATEST HITS** [19]
(re-iss. 1982) (cd-iss. Aug93)

May 86. (d-lp/d-c) *Stylus; (SMR/SMC 8506)* **THE FIRST LADY OF SOUL** [89] [–]

Mar 90. (7") *East West; (A 7951)* **THINK. / (b-side by Blues Brothers)** [31] [–]
(12"+=/cd-s+=) (TA/CDA 7951) – ('A'mixes).

May 93. (cd) *<(7567 81230)>* **ARETHA'S JAZZ**

Jun 93. (d-cd) *<(7567 81668-2)>* **30 GREATEST HITS**

Oct 94. (cd/c) *<(7567 80606-2/-4)>* **QUEEN OF SOUL – THE VERY BEST OF . . .** [23]

Apr 97. (cd) *Chess-MCA; <(MCD 91521)>* **ARETHA GOSPEL**

May 97. (cd) *Rhino; <(8122 72576-2)>* **LOVE SONGS**

May 98. (cd) *Sony Jazz; (CK 65050)* **THIS IS JAZZ**

May 98. (cd) *Rhino; <(8122 72942-2)>* **DELTA MEETS DETROIT: ARETHA'S BLUES**

Aug 98. (cd) *C.B.S.; (491454-2)* **SOUL SISTER (THE BEST OF ARETHA FRANKLIN)**

Nov 98. (d-cd/d-c) *Global TV; (RAD CD/MC 110)* **GREATEST HITS** [38]

Jul 99. (d-cd) *<(8122 75627-2)>* **AMAZING GRACE: THE COMPLETE GOSPEL RECORDINGS**

Sep 00. (cd) *Universal; (AAMCAD 11850)* **YOU GROW CLOSER: THE PEACOCK GOSPEL CLASSICS**

Feb 01. (cd) *Columbia; (501495-2)* **LOVE SONGS** [–]

Apr 01. (cd) *Camden; (74321 84088-2)* **LOVE SONGS** [–]

Jun 02. (d-cd) *Warners; (0927 47054-2)* **RESPECT – THE VERY BEST OF ARETHA FRANKLIN** [15] [–]
– Respect / Think / Spanish Harlem / You make me feel like a natural woman / I say a little prayer / Son of a preacher man / I never loved a man / Chain of fools / Don't play that song / Angel / Border song (holy Moses) / Rock steady / See saw / The house that Jack built / Oh no not my baby / Until you come back to me / Good times / Since you've been gone / You're all I need to get by / Ain't nothing like the real thing / Do right woman do right man / Share your love with me / Something he can feel / Ain't no way / Sisters are doin' it for themselves (with ANNIE LENNOX) / I knew you were waiting (for me) (with GEORGE MICHAEL) / Through the storm (with ELTON JOHN) / Love all the hurt away / Willing to forgive /

Let it be / Never let me go / The night time is the right time / Call me / Drown in my tears / People get ready / My song / The dark end of the street / Today I sing the blues / A rose is still a rose / Who's zoomin' who / Freeway of love / Daydreaming / Bridge over troubled water.

Oct 02. (d-cd) *Sony Music; (508621-2)* **THE QUEEN IN WAITING**

Jan 03. (cd) *Columbia; (509619-2)* **COLUMBIA JAZZ: 1960-1965**

Jun 03. (cd) *Paradiso; (PA 7902)* **THE BEST OF ARETHA FRANKLIN**

□ FRANTIC ELEVATORS (see under ⇒ SIMPLY RED)

□ FREAK POWER (see under ⇒ COOK, Norman)

FREE

Formed: London, England ... Spring 1968 by PAUL RODGERS (vocals), PAUL KOSSOFF (guitar) and SIMON KIRKE (drums). The latter two had been members of blues combo BLACK CAT BONES before poaching RODGERS from another blues outfit, BROWN SUGAR. With the addition of young ex-BLUESBREAKER, ANDY FRASER, on bass, this precocious line-up was complete, adopting the name FREE at the suggestion of blues grandaddy ALEXIS KORNER. KORNER also tipped off 'Island' supremo CHRIS BLACKWELL, and after resisting an extremely misguided BLACKWELL attempt to rename them The HEAVY METAL KIDS, FREE duly signed to his label and began work on their debut album, TONS OF SOBS (1968). Emerging from the shadow of CREAM, the album was an impressive set of heavy, organic blues, KOSSOFF stealing the show with his emotionally charged, liquid gold guitar style, in full effect on BOOKER T's 'THE HUNTER'. By the release of 'FREE' (1969), RODGERS soulful voice was developing into one of the best in rock, while FRASER had taken on joint songwriting duties with RODGERS. The band also had a blistering live reputation and had already built up a sizeable following by the time 'ALL RIGHT NOW' was a massive worldwide hit. It's gritty R&B stomp paved the way for FREE's magnum opus, 'FIRE AND WATER' (1970), a No.3 UK album that boasted such enduring fare as the introspective ballads, 'OH I WEPT' and 'HEAVY LOAD' while RODGERS' wonderfully evocative vocals lent 'REMEMBER' a mellow resonance. That summer, cresting the wave of their popularity, the band played to over half a million people at the Isle Of Wight festival. With pressure to come up with a successful follow-up to 'ALL RIGHT NOW', FREE were confident that the 'THE STEALER' would do the business. When it stiffed completely things started to go seriously awry, the 'HIGHWAY' (1970) album receiving a similarly lukewarm reception. This relative commercial failure increased tensions in what was already a perilously fraught intra-band relationship, the group deciding to call it a day after fulfilling touring commitments in Japan and Australia. The split eventually came in May '71, ironically almost coinciding with their biggest hit since 'ALL RIGHT NOW', a FACES-style romp entitled 'MY BROTHER JAKE'. Solo projects by RODGERS (PEACE) and FRASER (TOBY) came to little, although KOSSOFF and KIRKE's eponymous collaboration with Texan keyboard player, JOHN 'RABBIT' BUNDRICK, and Japanese bassist TETSU YAMAUCHI, was released to relative critical and commercial success, KOSSOFF relishing the opportunity to realise his ideas outwith the confines of FREE. The band subsequently regrouped in early 1972 and recorded the 'FREE AT LAST' album, a reasonable effort which spawned a Top 20 hit with the 'LITTLE BIT OF LOVE' single, a highly melodic slice of rock, the sort of thing RODGERS would go on to perfect with BAD COMPANY. While the album made the Top 10, KOSSOFF was spiralling into serious drug dependence, and following a disastrous American tour, the band's stability received a further blow when FRASER departed for the group SHARKS (he subsequently released a few melodic rock albums in the mid 70's). With TETSU and RABBIT filling in, FREE undertook a Japanese tour prior to recording a final album, 'HEARTBREAKER' (1973). Although KOSSOFF was too ill to make much of a contribution, the album stands among FREE's best, boasting RODGER's desperate plea to KOSSOFF, 'WISHING WELL', and the superb, BEATLES-esque 'COME TOGETHER IN THE MORNING'. Following a final tour of America with TRAFFIC, FREE finally split in summer '73, RODGERS and KIRKE going on to form BAD COMPANY. KOSSOFF, meanwhile, had already begun his ill-fated solo career, forming BACK STREET CRAWLER. After a handful of relatively well-received albums, KOSSOFF finally succumbed to heroin addiction, dying in his sleep on the 19th March '76. It was a tragic end for a guitarist who was once destined to be remembered in the same breath as the likes of ERIC CLAPTON and JIMI HENDRIX.

Album rating: TONS OF SOBS (*7) / FREE (*6) / FIRE AND WATER (*8) / HIGHWAY (*5) / FREE LIVE (*6) / FREE AT LAST (*5) / HEARTBREAKER (*6) / THE FREE STORY compilation (*8) / COMPLETELY FREE compilation (*7) / THE BEST OF FREE – ALL RIGHT NOW compilation (*8) / MOLTEN GOLD: THE ANTHOLOGY compilation (*8) / KOSSOFF, KIRKE, TETSU & RABBIT (*4) / Back Street Crawler: BACK STREET CRAWLER (*6) / AND THE BAND PLAYS ON (*5) / posthumous:- KOSS (*6) / THE COLLECTION (*6) / STONE FREE (*6)

PAUL RODGERS (b.12 Dec'49, Middlesbrough, England) – vocals (ex-BROWN SUGAR) / **PAUL KOSSOFF** (b.14 Sep'50, Hampstead, London, England) – guitar (ex-BLACK CAT BONES) / **SIMON KIRKE** (b.28 Jul'49, Shrewsbury, England) – drums (ex-BLACK CAT BONES) / **ANDY FRASER** (b. 7 Aug'52, Shropshire, England) – bass (ex-JOHN MAYALL'S BLUESBREAKERS)

Island A&M

Nov 68. (lp) *(ILPS 9089) <4198>* **TONS OF SOBS** Aug69
– Over the green hills (part 1) / Worry / Walk in my shadow / Wild Indian woman / Goin' down slow / I'm a mover / The hunter / Moonshine / Sweet tooth / Over the green hills (part 2). *(cd-iss. Jun88; CID 9089) (cd re-iss. 1989; IMCD 62) (<cd re-mast.Oct01 on 'Island-Universal'+=; IMCD 289><586149>* – I'm a mover (BBC session) / Waitin' on you (BBC session) / Guy Stevens blues (blues jam) / Moonshine (alt.) / Sweet tooth (alt.) / Visions of Hell (mix) / Woman by the sea (alt.) / Over the green hills (BBC session).

Mar 69. (7") *<1099>* **I'M A MOVER. / WORRY** –

Mar 69. (7") *(WIP 6054)* **BROAD DAYLIGHT. / THE WORM** –

Jul 69. (7") *(WIP 6062)* **I'LL BE CREEPIN'. / SUGAR FOR MR. MORRISON** –

Aug 69. (7") *<1172>* **I'LL BE CREEPIN'. / MOUTHFUL OF GRASS** –

Oct 69. (lp) *(ILPS 9104) <4204>* **FREE** 22
– I'll be creepin' / Songs of yesterday / Lying in the sunshine / Trouble on double time / Mouthful of grass / Woman / Free me / Broad daylight / Mourning sad morning. *(cd-iss. Jun88; CID 9104) (lp re-iss. Jan00 on 'Simply Vinyl'; SVLP 165) (cd re-mast.Oct01 on 'Island-Universal'+=; IMCD 282)* – Broad daylight (mono) / Worm (mono) / I'll be creepin' (mono) / Sugar for me Mr. Morrison (mono) / Broad daylight (BBC session) / Songs of yesterday (BBC session) / Mouthful of grass (solo acoustic) / Woman (alt.) / Trouble on double time (Songs of yesterday version) / Mourning sad morning (alt.).

May 70. (7") *(WIP 6082) <1206>* **ALL RIGHT NOW. / MOUTHFUL OF GRASS** 2 Jul70 4
(re-iss. Jul73 hit UK No.15)

Jun 70. (lp) *(ILPS 9120) <4268>* **FIRE AND WATER** 2 Aug70 17
– Fire and water / Oh I wept / Remember / Heavy load / Mr. Big / Don't say you love me / All right now. *(re-iss. Sep86 lp/c/cd; ILPM/ICM/CID 9120) (cd-iss. Apr90; IMCD 80) (re-iss. lp Jan94 + May94; ILPS 9120) (lp re-iss. Jul99 on 'Simply Vinyl'; SVLP 97) (<cd re-mast.Oct01 on 'Island-Universal'+=; IMCD 284><586227>* – Oh I wept (alt.) / Fire and water (new stereo) / Fire and water (BBC session) / All right now (BBC session) / All right now (single version) / All right now (Songs of yesterday version).

Nov 70. (7") *(WIP 6093)* **THE STEALER. / LYING IN THE SUNSHINE** [ ] [–]
Nov 70. (7") *<1230>* **THE STEALER. / BROAD DAYLIGHT** [–] [49]
Dec 70. (lp) *(ILPS 9138) <4287>* **HIGHWAY** [41] Feb71 [ ]
– The highway song / The stealer / On my way / Be my friend / Sunny day / Ride on pony / Love you so / Bodie / Soon I will be gone. *(cd-iss. Jun88; CID 9138) (cd re-iss. 1989; (IMCD 63) (<cd re-mast.Feb02 on 'Island-Universal'+=; IMCD 283)<586226>* – My brother Jake / Only my soul / Ride on a pony (BBC session) / Be my friend (BBC session) / Rain (alt.) / The stealer (single version).
Jan 71. (7") *<1248>* **THE HIGHWAY SONG. / LOVE YOU SO** [–] [ ]
Mar 71. (7") *<1266>* **I'LL BE CREEPIN'. / MR. BIG** [–] [ ]
Apr 71. (7") *(WIP 6100) <1276>* **MY BROTHER JAKE. / ONLY MY SOUL** [4] [ ]
Jun 71. (lp) *(ILPS 9160) <4306>* **FREE LIVE! (live)** [4] Aug71 [89]
– All right now / I'm a mover / Be my friend / Fire and water / Ride on pony / Mr. Big / The hunter / Get where I belong (studio). *(cd-iss. Jun88; CID 9160) (cd re-iss. 1989; IMCD 73) (<cd re-mast.Feb02 on 'Island-Universal'+=; IMCD 286)<586228>* – Woman / Walk in my shadow / Moonshine / Trouble on double time / Mr. Big / All right now / Get where I belong (alt.).

—— they had already split May'71. FRASER formed TOBY, while RODGERS formed the short-lived PEACE.

KOSSOFF, KIRKE, TETSU & RABBIT

were formed by the other two plus **TETSU YAMAUCHI** (b.21 Oct'47, Fukuoka, Japan) – bass / **JOHN 'RABBIT' BUNDRICK** – keyboards, vocals / and guest **B.J. COLE** – steel guitar

Nov 71. (lp) *(<ILPS 9188>)* **KOSSOFF, KIRKE, TETSU & RABBIT** [ ] [ ]
– Blue grass / Sammy's alright / Just for the box / Colours / Hold on / Yellow house / Dying fire / Fool's life / Anna / I'm on the run. *(re-iss. Aug91 cd)(c; IMCD 139)(ICM 9188)*

FREE

—— re-formed originals Feb'72 (**RODGERS, KOSSOFF, FRASER + KIRKE**)

May 72. (7") *(WIP 6129) <1352>***LITTLE BIT OF LOVE. / SAIL ON** [13] [ ]
Jun 72. (lp/c) *(ILPS/ICT 9192) <4349>* **FREE AT LAST** [9] [69]
– Catch a train / Soldier boy / Magic ship / Sail on / Travelling man / Little bit of love / Guardian of the universe / Child / Goodbye. *(cd-iss. Jun88; CID 9192) (cd re-iss. Feb90; IMCD 82) (<cd re-mast.Feb02 on 'Island-Universal'+=; IMCD 287)<586229>* – Burnin' (molten gold) (alt.) / Honky tonk women / Magic ship / Little bit of love / Guardian of the universe (Paul Rodgers solo) / Child (early version).

—— **TETSU YAMAUCHI** – bass (see above); repl. FRASER who joined SHARKS / added **JOHN 'RABBIT' BUNDRICK** – keyboards (see above) / **RODGERS** – also added guitar

Dec 72. (7") *(WIP 6146)* **WISHING WELL. / LET ME SHOW YOU** [7] [–]
Jan 73. (lp/c) *(ILPS 9217) <9324>* **HEARTBREAKER** [9] [47]
– Wishing well / Come together in the morning / Travellin' in style / Heartbreaker / Muddy water / Common mortal man / Easy on my soul / Seven angels. *(cd-iss. Jun88; CID 9217) (cd re-iss. Feb90; IMCD 81) (<cd re-mast.Feb02 on 'Island-Universal'+=; IMCD 288)<586230>* – Wishing well (US mix) / Let me show you / Muddy water (alt.) / Hand me down – Turn me around / Heartbreaker (rehearsal) / Easy on my soul (rehearsal).
Mar 73. (7") *(WIP 6160)* **TRAVELLIN' IN STYLE. / EASY ON MY SOUL** [ ] [–]
(re-iss. Mar74; WIP 6223)

—— **WENDELL RICHARDSON** – guitar of OSIBISA, on UK & US tour early '73) repl. KOSSOFF who formed BACK STREET CRAWLER. He died in his sleep 19 Mar'76 after years of drug abuse. FREE split early '73. RABBIT went solo before joining (KOSSOFF's) CRAWLER. TETSU joined The FACES. RODGERS and KIRKE formed BAD COMPANY.

– compilations, etc. –

on 'Island' UK / 'A&M' US unless mentioned otherwise

Mar 74. (d-lp) *(ISL D4)* **THE FREE STORY** [2] [ ]
– I'm a mover / I'll be creepin' / Mourning sad morning / All right now / Heavy load / Fire and water / Be my friend / The stealer / Soon I will be gone / Mr. Big / The hunter / Get where I belong / Travelling man / Just for the box / Lady / My brother Jake / Little bit of love / Sail on / Come together in the morning. *(re-iss. Oct89 lp/c/cd; ILPS/ICT/CID 9945) (cd re-iss. Sep96; IMCD 226)*
1974. (7") *<1629>* **LITTLE BIT OF LOVE. / THE STEALER** [–] [ ]
1974. (7") *<1720>* **ALL RIGHT NOW. / THE STEALER** [–] [ ]
Apr 75. (lp) *<3663>* **THE BEST OF FREE** [–] [ ]
Nov 76. (lp) *(ILPS 9453)* **FREE AND EASY, ROUGH AND READY** [ ] [–]
Nov 76. (7") *(WIP 6351)* **THE HUNTER. / WORRY** [ ] [–]
Feb 78. (7"ep) *(IEP 6)* **THE FREE EP** [11] [–]
– All right now / My brother Jake / Wishing well. *(re-iss. Oct82 as 12"pic-d; PIEP 6)* – hit UK No.57.
Oct 82. (lp/c) *(ILPS/ICT 9719)* **COMPLETELY FREE** [ ] [–]
May 85. (7") *(IS 221)* **WISHING WELL. / WOMAN** [ ] [–]
(12"+=) *(12IS 221)* – Walk in my shadow.
Feb 91. (c-s/7") *(C+/IS 486)* **ALL RIGHT NOW. / I'M A MOVER** [8] [ ]
(12"+=/cd-s+=) *(12IS/CID 486)* – Get where I belong.
Feb 91. (cd/c/lp) *(CID/IC/ILP TV 2)* **ALL RIGHT NOW – THE BEST OF FREE** [9] [ ]
– Wishing well / All right now / Little bit of love / Come together in the morning / The stealer / Sail on / Mr. Big / My brother Jake / The hunter / Be my friend / Travellin' in style / Fire and water / Travelling man / Don't say you love me.
Apr 91. (c-s/7") *(C+/IS 495)* **MY BROTHER JAKE (remix). / WISHING WELL (remix)** [ ] [ ]
(12"+=/cd-s+=) *(12IS/CID 495)* – The stealer (extended) / Only my soul (extended).
Nov 92. (d-cd) *(ITSCD 3)* **FIRE AND WATER / HEARTBREAKER** [ ] [–]
May 94. (d-cd) *(CRNCD 2) <518456>* **MOLTEN GOLD: THE ANTHOLOGY** [ ] [–]
Nov 98. (cd) *(IMCD 255)* **WALK IN MY SHADOW – AN INTRODUCTION TO FREE** [ ] [–]
Oct 99. (cd) *Spectrum; (544167-2)* **ALL RIGHT NOW** [ ] [–]
May 00. (5xcd-box) *(IBXCD 3)* **SONGS OF YESTERDAY** [ ] [–]
Oct 01. (cd) *Universal; (<E 586315>)* **THE UNIVERSAL MASTERS COLLECTION** [ ] [ ]

☐ FREEHEAT (see under ⇒ JESUS & MARY CHAIN)

☐ FREUR (see under ⇒ UNDERWORLD)

☐ Glenn FREY (see under ⇒ EAGLES)

FRIDGE

Formed: Putney, London, England . . . 1995 by former classmates, KIERAN HEBDEN, ADEM ILHAN and SAM JEFFERS. Lucky enough to sign a deal almost immediately with Trevor Jackson's 'Output', FRIDGE dished out their first vinyl helping in the shape of 7", 'LOJEN', followed closely by debut album (a double!), 'CEEFAX' (1997). Obviously turned on by the ever expanding list of outfits experimenting in the post-rock grey area of indie electronica, FRIDGE clearly liked to chill out to ambient noodling in the vein of TORTOISE and ROME. A busy year for the cool teenagers, they would go on to deliver another two singles, the radio-friendly 'ANGLEPOISED' and a shared effort with ADD N TO (X). Precociously prolific, the FRIDGE boys passed their critical exams with early 1998's 'SEMAPHORE', a brooding, intoxicating series of undulating anti-rock frequencies that endeared them to more discerning indie fans. A neat overview of the band's career trajectory was presented later that year with the 'SEVENS AND TWELVES' singles compilation. Member KIERAN HEBDEN, meanwhile concentrated on his own FOUR TET project, right about the time when other members of FRIDGE were attending college. A strange mix between folk, electronica and post-rock, FOUR TET's debut release was the 35-minute long 'THIRTYSIXTWENTYFOUR' (1998), a fascinating slide of musical genres, mostly hip-hop and electronica based, with breakbeats, voice samples/loops, sirens and sound effects et al. HEBDEN's first album proper was the eclectic and mellow 'DIALOGUE' issued in 1999. Acoustic guitars, thumb pianos and a whole host of weird instruments collided with the scathing electronic drum samples, all to startling effect. FRIDGE, meanwhile, continued pushing out their own hybrid of electro-indie sounds, 'EPH' (1999) highlighted by the opener 'ARK'. FOUR TET issued the double A-side 'CALAMINE' / 'GLASSHEAD' (the latter being one of his greatest achievements in music, a transcending, hallucinogenic 11-minute adventure in stereo) and a collaboration with elecro-wizard POLE before returning with the excellent sophomore album 'PAUSE' (2001). Possibly one of the best albums of the year, 'PAUSE' carried on in the same vein as 'DIALOGUE', but with HEBDEN more focused on the hazy, dreamy, folk aspect of his music. With 'UNTANGLE' and 'TWENTY THREE', the listener could just imagine driving along a coast-line on a warm clear afternoon, gazing at the sea; whereas the heavy dud-electronic of standout track 'NO MORE MOSQUITOES' reminded people that FOUR TET's music, although 70% organic, was still deeply rooted in experimental electronica. In the same year, FRIDGE regrouped to record 'HAPPINESS' (2001), the follow-up to 1999's 'EPH'. A humble and minimalistic album from the outset, FRIDGE managed to escape the 'post-rock' tag by using less jazzy instrumentations and a more un-plugged theme. The tracks did what it said on the tin; 'MELODICA AND TROMBONE' was just that, while 'CUT UP PIANO AND XYLOPHONE' was a short poignant piece of music played for the saddest of hearts. Taking a break from FRIDGE's quiet minimilism, HEBDEN returned with a fuller, more focused album, 2003's 'ROUNDS'. Not to say that 'PAUSE' was none of the above, it was just more dreamlike in its conviction, whereas HEBDEN's latest was a thoroughly composed piece of electronica with a touch of folk here and there. Still, a marvellous effort from one of the world's leading laptop folktronicists.

Album rating: CEEFAX (*5) / SEMAPHORE (*7) / SEVENS AND TWELVES double compilation (*7) / EPH (*6) / HAPPINESS (*8) / Four Tet: DIALOGUE (*8) / PAUSE (*9) / ROUNDS (*8)

KIERAN HEBDEN – guitar, samples / **ADEM ILHAN** – bass, keyboards / **SAM JEFFERS** – drums, trombone

Output — not iss.

Jan 97. (7") *(OPR 5)* **LOJEN. / MORE EDH4800 (PHASE SHIFTER)**

Mar 97. (d-lp/cd) *(OPR 6/+CD)* **CEEFAX**
– EDM / Helicopter / Tricity / More EH4-800 / FDM / Robots in disguise / EDM 2 / Oracle / EDM 3 / Zed ex ay-ti-wan. *(cd re-iss. Jul98 & Nov99 & Dec01; same)*

Sep 97. (12"ep) *(OPR 9)* **ANGLEPOISED**
– Anglepoised / Astrozero / Simple harmonic motion / Concert in your house / Config.

Nov 97. (one-sided-12") *(OPR 10)* **ASTHMA**

Nov 97. (ltd-12") *(Piao! 10)* **ASTHMA. / (other track by Add N To (X)**
(above issued on 'Piao!' records)

Feb 98. (7"ep) *(OPR 11)* **LIGN EP**
– Lign / For force / Must be magic.
(12"ep) *(OPR 11T)* – ('A'extended) / Sequioia / The traps / Fisa.

Feb 98. (d-lp/cd) *(OPR 12/+CD)* **SEMAPHORE**
– Cassette / Furniture boy / A slow / Motorbus / Teletexed / Chroma / Low fat diet / Swerve and spin / Curdle / Lign / Stamper / There is no try / Michael Knight. *(cd re-iss. Dec01; same)*

May 98. (12"; w/7") *(OPR 15D)* **ORKO. / DISTANCE // IT'S ALL ON / JESSICA**

Aug 98. (one-sided-7"; as FRIDGE + D) *(SOUL 22)* **INDEGUISE**
(above issued on 'Soul Static')

Oct 98. (d-cd) *(OPRCD 19)* **SEVENS AND TWELVES** (compilation)
– Anglepoised / For force / Astrozero / Jessica / Single harmonic motion / Lign (extended) / It's all on / EH4-800 (phase shifter) / Sequoia // Orko / The traps / Concert in your house / Must be magic / Asthma / Fisa / Config / Lojen / Distance. *(re-iss. Dec01; same)*

Earworm — not iss.

Oct 98. (7") *(WORM 37)* **DEADLY CUBE. / (track by Portal)**

Go! Beat — not iss.

May 99. (12"/cd-s) *(GOB X/CD 15)* **KINOSHITA. / TERASAKA**

Jun 99. (cd/lp) *(GOB 16 CD/LP)* **EPH**
– Ark / Meum / Transience / Of / Tuum / Bad Ischl / Yttium / Aphelion. *<US cd-iss. Apr02 on 'Temporary Residence – Brainwashed'+=; 48>* – Kinoshita / Terasaka / Of (version) / Of (remix) / Of (edit) / Of (dub) / Ark (Herberts fully flooded mix) / Bad Ischl (Patrick Pulsinger mix).

Jul 99. (12"ep/cd-ep) *(GOB X/CD 17)* **OF EP**
– Of (version / remix / edit / dub).

not iss. — Box Theory

Nov 99. (cd-s) **PLUXUSVSFRIDGEVSPLUXUS**
– Take or leave it.

Text — Temporary Residence

Sep 01. (cd/d-lp) *(TEXT 002 CD/LP)* <43> **HAPPINESS**
– Melodica and trombone / Drum machines and glockenspiels / Cut up piano and xylophone / Tone guitar and drum noise / Five four child voice / Sample and clicks / Drum bass sonics and edit / Harmonics / Long singing.

FOUR TET

KIERAN HEBDEN – instruments, etc.

Output — not iss.

Jul 97. (7"; as 4T RECORDINGS) *(OPR 7)* **DOUBLE DENSITY. / LIKE SIAMESE FIGHTING FISH**

Aug 98. (d12"ep/cd-ep) *(OPR 14)* **THIRTYSIXTWENTYFIVE**
– (part one) / (part two).

Jan 99. (12"ep) *(OPR 20)* **MISNOMER EP**
– Misnomer (long version) / Aying / Fume / Charm.

Feb 99. (lp/cd) *(OPR 21/+CD)* **DIALOGUE**
– Space of two weeks / Chiron / Alambradas / 3.3 degrees from the pole / Misnomer / Liquefaction / She scanned / Calamine / The butterfly effect. *(cd+=)* – Aying / Fume / Charm. *(re-iss. May01 & Jun03; same)*

May 99. (12") *(LOEP 09)* **RIVERS BECOME OCEANS. / Rothko: RIVERS BECOME OCEANS (COLOUR DEFINES THE CITYSCAPE)**
(above issued on 'Lo Recordings')

Jul 99. (12"/cd-s) *(OPR/+CD 24)* **GLASSHEAD. / CALAMINE (radio mix)**

Leaf — not iss.

Jun 00. (12"ep) *(DOCK 20)* **POLE v FOUR TET ep**
– Heim (by POLE remixed by FOUR TET) / Cload (by FOUR TET) / Cload (by FOUR TET remixed by POLE) / Heim (by POLE).

Domino — Domino

May 01. (cd/lp) *(<WIG 94 CD/LP>)* **PAUSE**
– Glue of the world / Twenty three / Harmony one / Parks / Leila came round and we watched a video / Untangle / Everything is alright / No more mosquitoes / Tangle / You could ruin my day / Hilarious movie of the 90's. *(d-cd-iss. Jan02 +=; WIGCD 94X)* – PAWS

Jun 01. (12"ep/cd-ep) *(RUG 126 T/CD)* **NO MORE MOSQUITOES. / FLON / LOOK AFTER YOUR MERMAIDS / WARMER PLACES**

Dec 01. (12"ep) *(RUG 130T)* **PAWS**
– Glue of the other world (remix) / Hilarious movie of the 90's (Koushik funny flick remix) / Hilarious movie of the 90's (Manitoba remix) / No more mosquitos (boom bip remix).

May 02. (7") *(RUG 139)* **I'M ON FIRE (pt.1). / I'M ON FIRE (pt.2)**

Mar 03. (12") *(RUG 155T)* **SHE MOVES SHE. / CRADLE**

May 03. (cd/d-lp) *(WIG CD/LP 126)* <14> **ROUNDS** — 60
– Hands / She moves she / First thing / My angel rocks back and forth / Spirit fingers / Unspoken / Chia / As serious as your life / And they all look broken hearted / Slow jam.

Oct 03. (12") *(RUG 167T)* <23> **AS SERIOUS AS YOUR LIFE. / (Jay Dee remix 1) / (live)**

☐ Robert FRIPP (see under ⇒ KING CRIMSON)

☐ Edgar FROESE (see under ⇒ TANGERINE DREAM)

FUGAZI

Formed: Arlington, Virginia, USA ... 1987 by IAN MacKAYE (now of Washington DC), who had the previous year featured on an album by EMBRACE (not the more recent outfit!). MacKAYE and drummer JEFF NELSON subsequently founded the 'Dischord' label, a bedrock of the Washington DC hardcore scene and an outlet for the pair's new band, MINOR THREAT. Completing the line-up with LYLE PRESLAR and BRIAN BAKER, this highly influential outfit released two singles in 1981, before they added STEVE HANSEN to boost their minimalist sound on the album, 'OUT OF STEP' (1983). A further album, the eponymous 'MINOR THREAT', contained the track 'STRAIGHT EDGE', a term which would be adopted by a generation of fans who followed MacKAYE and Co.'s example of abstinence and individual responsibility. Following their split, mainman MacKAYE formed FUGAZI, sharing vocal and songwriting duties with GUY PICCOTTO (ex-leader of RITES OF SPRING and INSURRECTION – the latter outfit having released a self-titled effort for 'Peaceville'). With the FUGAZI line-up crystallising around BRENDAN CANTY and JOE LALLY, they released two HENRY ROLLINS-produced mini-sets, the eponymous 'FUGAZI' and 'MARGIN WALKER' (1989), before fully realising their aggressively economical sound on the acclaimed 'REPEATER' (1990) album. Bringing to mind the once wilfully obscure vocals of DAVID THOMAS (PERE UBU) backed by the hardcore of NO MEANS NO, FUGAZI delivered a fourth set, 'STEADY DIET OF NOTHING' (1991), their perseverance paying off with a minor placing in the UK charts. Two years later, 'IN ON THE KILLTAKER' scored a deserved UK Top 30 and dominated the indie charts for months; despite persistent major label interest, FUGAZI have admirably refused to play the corporate game (how many bands can you say that about?). The mid 90's saw the release of 'RED MEDICINE', the album taking the staunchly independent hardcore crusaders into previously uncharted territory, i.e. the UK Top 20 (appropriately enough, the commercial behemoth that is the American music industry has so far prohibited the band's domestic success). MacKAYE, PICCIOTTO and crew were back in '98, although 'END HITS' (not a compilation) suffered a little commercially due to their long absence. Unperturbed, FUGAZI worked on a soundtrack album. Jem Cohen's docu-film, 'INSTRUMENT', was delivered the following Spring, the music (with sparse vocals!) a return of sorts to their abrasive best. Now with the addition of second sticksman, JERRY BUSHER, FUGAZI returned via the 2001 set, 'THE ARGUMENT', a record that even boasted a minor UK hit single, 'FURNITURE' and the classic 'CASHOUT'. • **Covered:** 12XU (Wire). • **Trivia:** MacKAYE produced the early '89 BEEFEATER single, 'House Burning Down'.

Album rating: 13 SONGS compilation (*8) / REPEATER (*8) / STEADY DIET OF NOTHING (*7) / IN ON THE KILLTAKER (*7) / RED MEDICINE (*6) / END HITS (*6) / INSTRUMENT soundtrack (*7) / THE ARGUMENT (*&) / Minor Threat: COMPLETE DISCOGRAPHY compilation (*8)

MINOR THREAT

IAN MacKAYE (b.1963) – vocals, guitar / **LYLE PRESLAR** – guitar / **BRIAN BAKER** – bass (ex-GOVERNMENT ISSUE) / **JEFF NELSON** – drums

Dischord Dischord

Jun 81. (7"ep) *<Dischord 3>* **MINOR THREAT EP** [–] [ ]
– Out of step (with the world) / Guilty of being white / Steppin' stone.

Dec 81. (7",7"red) *<Dischord 5-Limp 41>* **IN MY EYES. / STAND UP / 12XU** [–] [ ]

—— added **STEVE HANSEN** – bass (BAKER now on second guitar)

1983. (lp/c) *<(DISCHORD 10/+C)>* **OUT OF STEP** [ ] [ ]
– Betray / It follows / Think again / Look back and laugh / Sob story / No reason / Little friend / Out of step.

Jun 84. (lp/c) *<(DISCHORD 12/+C)>* **MINOR THREAT** [ ] [ ]
– Filler / I don't wanna hear it / Seeing red / Straight edge / Small man, big mouth / Screaming at a wall / Bottled violence / Minor threat.

Aug 85. (7"ep) *<(DISCHORD 15)>* **SALAD DAYS / GOOD GUYS (DON'T WEAR WHITE). / STUMPED / CASHING IN** [ ] [ ]

Mar 90. (cd) *<(DISCHORD 40)>* **COMPLETE DISCOGRAPHY** (compilation) [ ] [ ]

FUGAZI

IAN MacKAYE – vocals, guitar (ex-MINOR THREAT, ex-TEEN IDES, ex-EMBRACE) / **GUY PICCIOTTO** (b.1966) – vocals (ex-INSURRECTION, ex-RITES OF SPRING, ex-ONE LAST WISH) / **JOE LALLY** (b.1964, Rockville, Maryland) – bass / **BRENDAN CANTY** (b.1967) – drums

Dischord Dischord

Dec 88. (m-lp/m-c) *<(DISCHORD 30/+C)>* **FUGAZI** [ ] [ ]
– Waiting room / Bulldog front / Bad mouth / Burning / Give me the cure / Suggestion / Glue man. *(re-iss. Apr98; same)*

Jul 89. (m-lp/m-c) *<(DISCHORD 35/+C)>* **MARGIN WALKER** [ ] [ ]
– Margin walker / And the same / Burning too / Provisional / Lockdown / Promises. *(cd-iss. Oct89 as '13 SONGS'+=; DIS 36)* – FUGAZI *(re-iss. Apr98; same)*

Feb 90. (7",7"green) *<(DISCHORD 43)>* **JOE #1. / BREAK IN / SONG #1** [ ] [ ]

Mar 90. (lp/c/cd) *<(DISCHORD 44/+C/CD)>* **REPEATER** [ ] [ ]
– Turnover / Repeater / Brendan /1 / Merchandise / Blueprint / Sieve-fisted grind / Greed / Two beats off / Styrofoam / Reprovisional / Shut the door. *(cd+=)* – Song #1 / Joe /1 / Break in. *(re-iss. Apr98; same)*

Aug 91. (lp/c/cd) *<(DISCHORD 60/+C/CD)>* **STEADY DIET OF NOTHING** [63] [ ]
– Exit only / Reclamation / Nice new outfits / Stacks / Latin roots / Steady diet / Long division / Runaway return / Polish / Dear justice letter / K.Y.E.O. *(re-iss. Apr98; same)*

Jun 93. (m-lp/m-c/m-cd) *<(DIS 70/+C/D)>* **IN ON THE KILLTAKER** [24] [ ]
– Facet squared / Public witness program / Returning the screw / Smallpox champion / Rend it / 23 beats off / Sweet and low / Cassavetes / Great cop / Walken's syndrome / Instrument / Last chance for a slow dance. *(re-iss. Apr98; same)*

May 95. (lp/cd) *(DIS 90/+CD) <EFA 17990-2>* **RED MEDICINE** [18] [ ]
– Do you like me / Bed for the scraping / Latest disgrace / Birthday pony / Forensic scene / Combination lock / Fell, destroyed / By you / Version / Target / Back to base / Downed city / Long distance runner. *(re-iss. Apr98; same)*

—— FUGAZI were put in backburner until their return below

Apr 98. (cd/c/lp) *<(DIS 110 CD/C/V)>* **END HITS** [47] [ ]
– Break / Place position / Recap modotti / No surprise / Five corporations / Caustic acrostic / Closed captioned / Floating boy / Foreman's dog / Arpeggiation / Guilford fall / Pink frosty / F/D.

Apr 99. (cd/c/lp) *<(DIS 120 CD/C/V)>* **INSTRUMENT** (soundtrack) [ ] [ ]
– Pink frosty (demo) / Lusty scripps / Arpeggiator (demo) / Afterthought / Trio's / Turkish disco / Me and Thumbelina / Floating boy (demo) / Link track / Little Debbie / H.B. / I'm so tired / Rend it (demo) / Closed caption (demo) / Guildford fall (demo) / Swingset / Shaken all over / Slo crostic.

—— now with second drummer **JERRY BUSHER**

Oct 01. (7"/cd-s) *<(DIS 129/+CD)>* **FURNITURE. / NUMBER / HELLO MORNING** [61] [ ]

Oct 01. (cd/lp) *<(DIS 130 CD/V)>* **THE ARGUMENT** [63] [ ]
– Untitled / Cashout / Full disclosure / Epic problem / Life and limb / The kill / Strangelight / Oh / Ex-spectator / Nightshop / Argument.

FUGEES

Formed: East Orange, New Jersey, USA . . . early 90's by expatriate Haitian (hence the name FUGEES, as in refugees) cousins, PRAKAZREL 'PRAS' MICHEL and WYCLEF JEAN, who recruited sweet-voiced vocalist, LAURYN HILL; she had previously scored a bit part in US comedy, 'Sister Act II', and had just completed a degree at Columbia university. Signed to 'Ruffhouse' (part of 'Columbia'), The FUGEES' debut set, 'BLUNTED ON REALITY' (1994), reflected their more intelligent, socially conscious approach to hip hop while musically they were also more enlightened, fusing reggae and African folk-style acoustic guitar parts over their laidback rapping. Although the debut garnered critical acclaim, the group would have to wait a further two years for any real commerical rewards. Fuelled by the massive success (UK No.1) of their intuitive, innovative cover of Lori Lieberman's 'KILLING ME SOFTLY', Bob Marley's 'NO WOMAN, NO CRY' and the tough but soulful 'READY OR NOT', 'THE SCORE' (1996) became a multi- million worldwide seller, The FUGEES possibly one of the most commercially successful hip hop acts to make it in recent years. After the excitement of 1996, JEAN released a solo project under the moniker, WYCLEF JEAN & THE REFUGEE ALLSTARS the following year as well as a charming collaborative single with HILL, 'THE SWEETEST THING'. While PRAS worked on his solo set, entitled 'GHETTO SUPASTAR' (featuring the massive hit of the same name) and released in November '98, LAURYN HILL was conjuring up some magic of her own. 'THE MISEDUCATION OF . . .' (1998), pushed all the right buttons and was a massive success all over the world, especially America where it won a plethora of Grammy's the following year. Its everso cool songs – segued with a "back-in-time" LAURYN in the classroom – grooved high and mighty above any of today's soul and hip hop, tracks such as 'DOO WOP (THAT THING)' (also a chart-topper), 'EX-FACTOR' and 'EVERYTHING IS EVERYTHING', giving her top marks all round. WYCLEF JEAN was the first FUGEE to release an album in the new millennium, 'ECLEFTIC: 2 SIDES II A BOOK' (2000). His samples were as wide ranging as ever, even stretching to country crooner KENNY ROGERS . . . If that was a bit much to take for some fans, then at least he kept up his street savvy with a raft of biting social commentaries including four top hits, 'IT DOESN'T MATTER', '911', 'PERFECT GENTLEMAN' and 'WISH YOU WERE HERE'. You can only imagine the reaction of LAURYN HILL's record company when she delivered the uncompromisingly stripped-down 'MTV UNPLUGGED' (2002) as her sophomore solo set. Gone were the sassy rhymes and killer hooks. In their place was a rambling double live set of acoustic song sketches, often seemingly half finished and about as raw and intimate as any album in the Unplugged series. Reference points might be TERRY CALLIER or BOB MARLEY's 'Redemption Song', perhaps even JOAN ARMATRADING. While pop fans may have baulked, HILL proved that she doesn't need production gloss to polish her phenomenal talent. And while the segued songs were often way too long – and occasionally too worthy – many of the tracks blazed with the zeal of the newly converted. 'MYSTERY OF INIQUITY' was a tour de force of hip-hop/folk-soul, HILL living every line of her conscious, rapid-fire lyrics, while the traditional 'CONQUERING LION' summed up her newfound faith. Less focused was the album from her erstwhile colleague, WYCLEF JEAN. 'MASQUERADE' (2002) was perhaps an unfortunate choice of title for an album which found the ambitious rapper being just a little too ambitious for his own good. The record was too long for a start and while the straight-up hip-hop and reggae-flavoured tracks hit home, ill-advised forays into lounge/easy listening territory were downright embarrassing. A new year and a new deal (with 'J' Records) seemed to rejuvenate the unpredictable Haitian, while a raft of guest stars on 'THE PREACHER'S SON' (2003), together with some conciliatory lyrics, confirmed JEAN as a much needed positive force in hip hop. • **Trivia:** FUGEE is a slang American term for a Haitian refugee, thus the suffix of REFUGEE CAMP on 'THE SCORE' after their group name.

Album rating: BLUNTED ON REALITY (*5) / THE SCORE (*8) / THE SCORE – BOOTLEG VERSIONS (*5) / Wyclef Jean: THE CARNIVAL (*6) / THE ECLEFTIC: TWO SIDES II A BOOK (*7) / MASQUERADE (*5) / GREATEST HITS compilation (*7) / THE PREACHER'S SON (*6) / Pras: GHETTO SUPASTAR (*6) / Lauryn Hill: THE MISEDUCATION OF LAURYN HILL (*9) / MTV UNPLUGGED 2.0 (*7)

LAURYN HILL (b.19 Oct'75, East Orange, New Jersey, USA) – vocals, guitar / **PRAS MICHEL** (b. SAMUEL PRAKAZREL MICHEL, 19 Oct'72, Haiti) – vocals / **WYCLEF JEAN** (b. JEANNEL WYCLEF JEAN, 17 Oct'72, Haiti) – vocals

Ruffhouse – Columbia | Ruffhouse – Columbia

Mar 94. (cd/c) *(474713-2/-4)* <57462> **BLUNTED ON REALITY** [ ] [ ]
– (Introduction) / Nappy heads / (Blunted interlude) / Recharge / (Freestyle interlude) / Vocab / (Special news bulletin interlude) / Boof baf / Temple / How hard is it? / (Harlem chit chat interlude) / Some seek stardom / Giggles / (Da kid from Haiti interlude) / Refugees on the mic / Living like there ain't no tomorrow / Shouts out from the block. *(cd+=)* – Nappy heads (remix). *(re-iss. Oct96; same)*

May 94. (c-s) *(660421-4)* <77149> **BOOF BAF / NAPPY HEADS** [ ] Oct93 [ ]
(12"s+=/cd-s+=) *(660421-6/-2)* – ('A'mixes).

Jun 94. (c-s; as FUGEES – Tranzlator Crew) <77431> **NAPPY HEADS / ('A'instrumental)** [–] [49]
(cd-s+=) *<77432>* – (4-'A'versions) / Some seek stardom.
(cd-s) *<CSK 6427>* – ('A'side) / ('A'-remix) / Vocab (instrumental).

Oct 94. (c-s; as FUGEES – Tranzlator Crew) <77634> **VOCAB / (mixes)** [–] [ ]
(cd-s+=) *<77633>* – ('A'mixes; Refugees hip hop / Refugees acoustic) / Refugees on the mic / ('A'mixes; instrumental / Salaam's acoustic / Vibey) / Nappy heads (Mad Spider mix).

Jan 95. (c-s) **TEMPLE / (mixes)** [–] [ ]

Mar 96. (cd/c) *(483549-2/-4)* *<67147>* **THE SCORE** [2] Feb96 [1]
– Red intro / How many mics / Ready or not / Zealots / The beast / Fu-gee-la / Family business / Killing me softly / The score / The mask / Cowboys / No woman, no cry / Manifest – outro / Fu-gee-la (Refugee Camp remix) / Fu-gee-la (Refugee Camp global remix) / Mista mista. *(cd+=)* – Fu-gee-la (Refugee Camp global remix).

Mar 96. (c-s) *(663066-4)* *<78195>* **FU-GEE-LA / HOW MANY MICS** [21] [29]
(cd-s+=) *(663066-2)* – ('A'mixes; instrumental / Refugee Camp / Refugee Camp instrumental).
(12") *(663066-6)* – ('A'mixes; North Side / Sly & Robbie).

Jun 96. (c-s) *(663343-4)* **KILLING ME SOFTLY / ('A'instrumental)** [1] [–]
(cd-s+=) *(663343-2)* – Cowboys (version) / Nappy heads (remix).
(cd-s) *(663343-5)* – ('A'side) / Cowboys / Nappy heads (remix) / Vocab (Refugees hip hop mix).

Sep 96. (c-s) *(663721-4)* **READY OR NOT / THE SCORE** [1] [–]
(cd-s) *(663721-2)* – ('A'side) / ('A'-Salaam's ready for the show mix) / ('A'-Handel's yard vibe mix).
(12") *(663721-6)* – ('A'side) / Killing me softly / Cowboys.

Nov 96. (c-s) *(6639224-4)* **NO WOMAN, NO CRY / ('A'remix)** [2] [–]
(cd-s+=) *(6639224-2)* – ('A'mixes; radio / instrumental) / Killing me softly (live).
(cd-s) *(6639224-5)* – ('A'side) / Don't cry, dry your eyes / Don't cry, dry your eyes (instrumental) / A change is gonna come.

Nov 96. (cd/c) *(486824-2/-4)* **THE SCORE . . . BOOTLEG VERSIONS** [55] [–]
– Ready or not / Nappy heads / Don't cry, dry your eyes / Vocab / Killing me softly / No woman no cry.

—— In Mar'97, FUGEES featured on BOUNTY KILLER's US hit, 'Hip-Hopera'.

Mar 97. (c-s) *(574069-4)* **RUMBLE IN THE JUNGLE / ('A'extended)** [3] [ ]
(cd-s+=) *(574069-2)* – I'm so mean I made medicine sick (snippet) / ('A'-acappella mix).
(above featured A TRIBE CALLED QUEST & BUSTA RHYMES and was issued on 'Mercury' records)

WYCLEF JEAN

Jun 97. (c-s/cd-s; WYCLEF JEAN & THE REFUGEE ALL STARS) *(664681-4/-2)* **WE TRYING TO STAY ALIVE / FLAVOR FROM THE CARNIVAL** [13] [46]
(cd-s+=) *(664681-5)* – Anything can happen / Imagio.

Jun 97. (cd/c; WYCLEF JEAN featuring the REFUGEE ALL STARS) *(487442-2/-4/-1)* *<67974>* **THE CARNIVAL** [40] [16]
– Intro-Court-Clef-Intro / Apocalypse / Guantanamera / Pablo Diablo /

Bubblegoose / Prelude to all the girls / Down to ho / Anything can happen / Gone till November / Words of wisdom / Year of the dragon / Sang Fezi / Fresh interlude / Mona Lisa / Street jeopardy / Killer MC / We trying to stay alive / Gunpowder / Closing arguments / Enter the carnival / Jaspora / Yele / The carnival. *(re-iss. May98 & Apr00; same)*

Aug 97. (c-s; REFUGEE ALL STARS & LAURYN HILL) *(664978-4)* **THE SWEETEST THING / ('A'mix)** [18] [ ]
(cd-s+=) *(664978-2)* – ('A'mixes).

Sep 97. (c-s,12"/cd-s; REFUGEE CAMP ALL STARS featuring PRAS – with KY-MANI) *<13411>* **AVENUES / ('A'mix)** [–] [35]
(above from the film, 'Money Talks'; issued on 'Arista' records)

Sep 97. (c-s) *(665085-4)* **GUANTANAMERA / ROXANNE ROXANNE** [25] [ ]
(cd-s+=) *(665085-2)* – Trying to stay alive.
(cd-s) *(665085-5)* – ('A'side) / Bubble goose bakin' cake / No airplay men in blue.

— LAURYN HILL featured on the PAID & LIVE single 'All The Time', which hit UK Top 60 in Dec'97.

May 98. (12"/c-s) *(665871-6/-4) <78752>* **GONE TILL NOVEMBER (The Makin' Runs remixes; original / instrumental / acappella) / NO AIRPLAY / NO AIRPLAY (instrumental)** [3] Jan98 [9]
(cd-s+=) *(665871-5)* – ('A'mixes) / Bubblegoose / Guantanamera.

Jul 98. (c-s,12",cd-s) *<78993>* **CHICKENHEAD / WHAT'S CLEF / CHEATED (R&B mix) / CHEATED (rock remix) / TO ALL THE GIRLS** [–] [61]
(above featured SPRAGGA BENZ)

Oct 99. (c-s/cd-s; WYCLEF JEAN featuring BONO) *(668212-4/-2)* **NEW DAY / NEW DAY (clean mix)** [23] Sep99 [ ]
(cd-s) *(668212-5)* – ('A'mix) / Gone till November / We trying to stay alive.

Aug 00. (cd/c/lp) *(497979-2/-4/-1) <62180>* **THE ECLEFTIC: 2 SIDES II A BOOK** [34] Jul00 [9]
– Columbia records / Where Fugees at? / Kenny Rogers (Pharoahe Monch dub plate) / Thug angels / It doesn't matter (with The ROCK & MELKY SEDECK) / 911 (with MARY J. BLIGE) / Pullin' me in / Da cypha / Runaway (with EARTH, WIND & FIRE) / Product G&B / Red light district / Perfect gentleman / Low income / Whitney Houston dub plate / However you want it / Hollyhood to Hollywood / Diallo (with YOUSSOU N'DOUR) / MB2 / Something about Mary / Bus search / Wish you were here / Younger days. *(re-iss. Jul01 cd+=/c/lp; same)* – (video remixes). hit UK No.5

Sep 00. (c-s; by WYCLEF JEAN featuring the ROCK & MELKY SEDECK) *(669778-4)* **IT DOESN'T MATTER / (mix)** [3] [–]
(cd-s+=) *(669778-2)* – Thug angels.
(cd-s) *(669778-5)* – ('A'side) / We trying to stay alive / Younger days.

Dec 00. (c-s; by WYCLEF JEAN featuring MARY J. BLIGE) *(670612-4) <79460>* **911 / 911 (ghetto love mix)** [9] Sep00 [38]
(cd-s+=) *(670612-2)* – 911 (emergency mix).
(cd-s) *(670612-5)* – ('A'side) / Gone till November / It doesn't matter (Wyclef mix).

Jul 01. (c-s) *(671052-4)* **PERFECT GENTLEMAN / PERFECT GENTLEMAN (Xzibit remix)** [4] [–]
(12"+=) *(671052-6)* – ('A'-Kelly G remix).
(cd-s++=) *(671052-2)* – ('A'-video).

Nov 01. (c-s) *(672156-4)* **WISH YOU WERE HERE / Wyclef Jean & Xzibit / King Yellowman: PERFECT GENTLEMAN** [28] [–]
(cd-s+=) *(672156-2)* – No woman no cry (FUGEES) / 911 (with MARY J. BLIGE) / ('A'video).

Jun 02. (cd-s; by WYCLEF JEAN featuring CLAUDETTE ORTIZ) *(672890-2) <672575>* **TWO WRONGS / AFRICA / PJ'S / ('A'-video)** [14] May02 [28]

Jul 02. (cd) *(507854-2) <86542>* **MASQUERADE** [30] Jun02 [6]
– Message to the streets / Peace God / PJ's (with GOVERNOR & PROLIFIC) / 800 bars / Masquerade (with M.O.P., BUMPY KNUCKLES & MIRI) / (1-800-henchmen) / You say keep it gangsta (with BUTCH CASSIDY & SHARISSA) / Party like I party / Oh what a night / (Hot 93.1) / Pussycat (with TOM JONES) / (Midnight lovers) / Two wrongs / (Instant request) / Thus like me / Daddy / Knockin' on Heaven's door / The eulogy / War no more / The mix show / MVP Kompa (with MELKY) / Ghetto racine (with JA RAH RAH).

Nov 02. (cd-s) *(673377-2)* **PUSSYCAT (mixes)** [ ] [–]

Nov 03. (cd) *(513533-2) <90726>* **GREATEST HITS** [ ] Oct03 [ ]
– Ghetto religion (with R. KELLY) / Hey girl (with AYESHA & PAPA DON) / We trying to stay alive (with JOHN FORTE & PRAS) / It doesn't matter (with ROCK & MELKY SEDECK) / Anything can happen / 911 (with MARY J. BLIGE) / Two wrongs (with CLAUDETTE ORTIZ) / Gone till November (with CANIBUS) / Knockin' on Heaven's door / Diallo (with YOUSSOU N'DOUR & MB2) / Something about Mary / Wish you were here / Gone till November (the makin' runs remix with CANIBUS). *(d-cd+=; 513533-9)* – (bonus tracks).

J-Records J-Records

Oct 03. (cd) *(82876 56543-2) <55425>* **THE PREACHER'S SON** [ ] Oct03 [22]
– Intro / Industry / Party to Damascus (with MISSY ELLIOTT) / Celebrate (with PATTI LaBELLE & CASSIDY) / Baby daddy (with REDMAN) / Three nights in Rio (with CARLOS SANTANA) / Class reunion (with MONICA) / Baby / I am your doctor (with WAYNE WONDER & ELEPHANT MAN) / Linda (with CARL RESTIVO) / Take me as I am (with SHARISSA) / Grateful / Next generation (with SCARFACE & RAH DIGGA) / Rebel music (with The PRODIGY) / Who gave the order (with BUJU BANTON) / Party by the sea (with BUTU BANTON & T-VICE) / Party to Damascus (remix with MISSY ELLIOTT).

Jan 04. (12"/cd-s; by WYCLEF JEAN & MISSY ELLIOTT) *(82876 57951-1/-2) <54960>* **PARTY TO DAMASCUS (mixes)** [–] Sep03 [65]

PRAS

Interscope Interscope

Jun 98. (c-s/12"/cd-s; PRAS MICHEL featuring OL' DIRTY BASTARD & introducing MYA) *(INC/INT/IND 95593) <95021>* **GHETTO SUPASTAR (THAT IS WHAT YOU ARE) / ('A'instrumental) / DON'T BE AFRAID** [2] [15]

Columbia Columbia

Oct 98. (c-s/cd-s) *(666621-4/-2)* **BLUE ANGELS (mixes; radio / instrumental / acappella) / 1ST PHONE (instrumental)** [6] [ ]
(cd-s) *(666621-5)* – ('A'side) / Ghetto supastar / M.Y.A. / Murder death.

Nov 98. (cd/c) *(491489-2/-4) <69516>* **GHETTO SUPASTAR** [44] [55]
– Hallelujah / Ghetto supastar (that is what you are) / 1st phone interlude / What'cha' wanna do / For the love of this / Blue angels / Can't stop the shinning (RIP rock part 2) / Get your groove on / Frowsey (part 2) / Dirty cash / For the love of this / Wha'wha'wha'what / 2nd phone interlude / Lowriders / Yeah 'eh yeah 'eh / Murder dem / 3rd phone interlude / Final interlude / Amazing Grace / Avenues / Another one bites the dust.

— In Nov'98, QUEEN and WYCLEF JEAN (featuring PRAS & FREE) hit UK No.5 with a re-working of, 'ANOTHER ONE BITES THE DUST' (from the movie, 'Small Soldiers')

— in Jul'01, PRAS featured on DANTE THOMAS' hit 'Miss California'

LAURYN HILL

Columbia Columbia

Sep 98. (c-s/cd-s) *(666515-4/-2) <78868>* **DOO WOP (THAT THING) / (Gordon's mix) / (instrumental)** [3] Nov98 [1]
(cd-s) *(666515-5)* – ('A'side) / Lost ones / Forgive them father.

Sep 98. (cd/c) *(489843-2/-4) <69035>* **THE MISEDUCATION OF LAURYN HILL** [2] [1]
– Intro / Lost ones / Ex-factor / To Zion / Doo wop (that thing) / Superstar / Final hour / When it hurts so bad / I used to love him / Forgive them father / Every ghetto, every city / Nothing even matters / Everything is everything / The miseducation of Lauryn Hill. *(cd hidden+=)* – Can't take my eyes off you / Tell him.

Feb 99. (c-s/cd-s) *(666945-4/-2) <radio cut>* **EX-FACTOR / ('A'-part II) / ('A'-simple mix)** [4] Jan99 [21]
(cd-s) *(666945-5)* – ('A'side) / ('A'-A simple breakdown mix) / Lost ones.

Jun 99. (c-s/cd-s) *(667574-4/-2) <79206>* **EVERYTHING IS EVERYTHING / EX-FACTOR (a simple mix)** [19] [35]
(cd-s+=) *(667574-5)* – ('A'radio & instrumental) / Ex-fator (a simple breakdown).

May 02. (cd) *(508003-2) <86580>* **MTV UNPLUGGED 2.0 (live)** [40] [3]
– (intro) / Mr. Intentional / Adam lives in theory / (interlude 1) / Oh Jerusalem / (interlude 2) / Freedom time / (interlude 3) / I find it hard to say (rebel) / Just like water / (interlude 4) / Just want you around / I gotta find peace of mind / (interlude 5) / Mystery of iniquity / (interlude 6) / I get out / (interlude 7) / I remember / So much things to say / The conquering lion / (outro).

FUNERAL FOR A FRIEND

Formed: Wales . . . 2001 by singer MATT 'THE RAT' DAVIES, KRIS ROBERTS, DARREN SMITH, drummer RANDY RICHARDS and bassist GARETH DAVIES. Issuing a plethora of singles and EP's during 2002 and receiving considerable interest from the UK music press, FUNERAL FOR A FRIEND took their emo-infused prog-metal to 'Warners' and began work on their 2003 debut 'CASUALLY DRESSED AND IN DEEP CONVERSATION'; a set which was to later reach the Top 20. Melding AT THE DRIVE-IN's synthetic funk with TOOL's dark metal offerings, FFAF out-sold their subsequent tour and were regularly featured during music slots on MTV2. They had recently delivered a compilation of the best material from their earlier EPs, acting as an introduction for US distribution only, entitled 'SEVEN WAYS TO SCREAM YOUR NAME' (2003).

Album rating: CASUALLY DRESSED & DEEP IN CONVERSATION (*6)

MATT "THE RAT" DAVIES – vocals / **KRIS ROBERTS** – guitar / **DARREN SMITH** – guitar / **GARETH DAVIES** – bass / **RANDY RICHARDS** – drums

Mighty Atom — not iss.

Sep 02. (cd-ep) *(MTY 338CD)* **BETWEEN ORDER AND MODEL** [ ] [–]
– 10:45 Amsterdam conversations / Juno / Red is the new black / The art of American football. *(re-iss. Nov03; same)*

Infectious — not iss.

Apr 03. (7"ep/cd-ep) *(INFEC 126 S/CDS)* **FOUR WAYS TO SCREAM YOUR NAME** [ ] [–]
– This year's most open heartbreak / She drove me to daytime television / Kiss and makeup (all bets are off) / Escapes artists never die.

East West — Ferret

Jul 03. (7"white) *(EW 269)* **JUNEAU. / THE GETAWAY PLAN** [19] [–]
(cd-s+=) *(EW 269CD1)* – Kiss and makeup.
(cd-s) *(EW 269CD2)* – ('A'side) / The art of American football (BBC Wales session) / This year's most open heartbreak (Radio 1 session) / ('A'-video).

Oct 03. (m-cd) *<41>* **SEVEN WAYS TO SCREAM YOUR NAME** [–] [ ]
– 10:45 Amsterdam conversations / Red is the new black / The art of American football / The getaway plan / This year's most open heartbreak / Kiss and makeup / Escape artists never die.

Oct 03. (7") *(EW 274)* **SHE DROVE ME TO DAYTIME TELEVISION. / BULLET THEORY** [20] [–]
(cd-s+=) *(EW 274CD1)* – The system (session).
(cd-s+=) *(EW 274CD2)* – Juno (session).

Oct 03. (cd/lp) *(82564 60947-2/-1)* **CASUALLY DRESSED AND DEEP IN CONVERSATION** [12] [–]
– Rookie of the year / Bullet theory / Juneau / Bend your arms to look like wings / Escape artists never die / Storytelling / Moments forever faded / She drove me to daytime television / Red is the new black / Your revolution is a joke / Waking up / Novella.

☐ FUNHOUSE (see under ⇒ WATERBOYS)

☐ FUNKADELIC (see under ⇒ CLINTON, George)

FUN LOVIN' CRIMINALS

Formed: Manhattan, New York, USA . . . 1993 by former marine HUEY MORGAN (of Puerto-Rican/Irish decent), FAST and STEVE. This hard-bitten NY hip hop-rock posse, took on the mantle of early BEASTIE BOYS, fusing it together with "acid"-ic jazz and the mandatory drug references. The slow-rollin' CHEECH & CHONG-esque 'SCOOBY SNACKS' and 'SMOKE 'EM', were highlights from their much touted debut album, 'COME FIND YOURSELF'. Initially unleashed in '96, it was virtually ignored in the States, although it created quite a stir in Britain almost a year on, when 'SCOOBY SNACKS' (sampling 'Movement Of Fear' by TONES ON TAILS), 'THE FUN LOVIN' CRIMINAL' and 'THE KING OF NEW YORK' all had Top 30 success. In the summer of '97, they played major festivals including Scotland's 'T In The Park', while HUEY (was it him or FAST who was seeing SAFFRON of REPUBLICA?) chilled out on the Various Artists/LOU REED No.1 smash 'Perfect Day'. The following year, FLC were back in fine suggestive form with their sophomore long-player, '100% COLOMBIAN' (1998), a UK Top 3 entry. Premiered by the "Barry White saved my life" single/tribute, 'LOVE UNLIMITED', the record was indeed laid back, laid back enough to bury yourselves between the sheets for a marathon session and hope rigor mortis or viagra take hold. Certifying that there was always an easy listening element to their scuzz-hop, FLC went the whole hog with 'MIMOSA (The LOUNGE ALBUM)' (1999) wherein HUEY and co dished the laidback dirt on a hodge-podge of covers (from 10cc's 'I'M NOT IN LOVE' to Ozzy's 'CRAZY TRAIN') and reworked originals. Criminal indeed (in places) but an interesting diversion that reached the UK Top 40. Normal service was resumed in early 2001 with the 'LOCO' album, a Top 5 UK success that featured a great saucy video for the title track. After the obligatory compilation, 'BAG OF HITS' (2002), everyones favourite wise guys were back in studio business with 'WELCOME TO POPPY'S' (2003). The record worked best when it was taking liberties with their own city's cosmopolitan musical heritage – everything from DAS EFX to LOU REED – roughing it up just enough to make it talk but not so badly as to bleed all over their threads. • **Songwriters:** Group, except WE HAVE ALL THE TIME IN THE WORLD (Hal David & John Barry) / I'M NOT IN LOVE (10cc). Sampled LYNYRD SKYNYRD's 'Freebird' on 'BOMBIN' THE L' and the soundtracks from QUENTIN TARANTINO's 'Reservoir Dogs' & 'Pulp Fiction' on 'SCOOBY SNACKS'. 'KING OF NEW YORK' used pieces of 'Insensatez' (Ray Brown Trio) & 'Also Sprach Zarathestra' (Deodato).

Album rating: COME FIND YOURSELF (*8) / 100% COLOMBIAN (*7) / MIMOSA (THE LOUNGE ALBUM) (*5) / LOCO (*6) / BAG OF HITS – 15 INTERGLOBAL CHARTSTOPPERS compilation (*7) / WELCOME TO POPPY'S (*6)

HUEY MORGAN – vocals, guitar / **FAST** – bass, keyboards, trumpet / **STEVE** – drums

not iss. — Silver Spotlight

Nov 95. (cd-ep) <36515> **ORIGINAL SOUNDTRACK FOR HI-FI LIVING** [–] [ ]
– Passive – Aggressive / Blues for suckers / I can't get with that / Coney Island girl.

Chrysalis — Capitol

Jun 96. (7") *(CHS 5031)* **THE GRAVE AND THE CONSTANT. / BOMBIN' THE L / BLUES FOR SUCKERS** [72] [–]
(12"+=/cd-s+=) *(12/CD CHS 5031)* – King of New York.

Jul 96. (cd/c/lp) *(CD/TC+/CHR 6113)* <35703> **COME FIND YOURSELF** [7] Feb96 [ ]
– The fun lovin' criminal / Passive – Aggressive / The grave and the constant / Scooby snacks / Smoke 'em / Bombin' the L / I can't get with that / King of New York / We have all the time in the world / Bear hug / Come find yourself / Crime and punishment / Methadonia / I can't get with that (schmoove version) / Coney Island girl.

Aug 96. (7") *(CHS 5034)* **SCOOBY SNACKS. / I'LL BE SEEING YOU** [22] [–]
(cd-s) *(CDCHS 5034)* – ('A'side) / Smoke 'em (live) / Come find yourself (live) / I can't get with that (live).
(cd-s) *(CDCHSS 5034)* – ('A'mixes).

Nov 96. (7"pic-d) *(CHSPD 5040)* <58581> **THE FUN LOVIN' CRIMINAL. / COME FIND YOURSELF (live BBC session)** [26] Feb97 [ ]
(cd-s+=) *(CDCHSS 5040)* – ('A'-Hee Haw version) / The grave and the constant (Stephen Lironi 12"mix).

(cd-s) *(CDCHS 5040)* – ('A'side) / The grave and the constant (live) / Coney Island girl (live) / Scooby snacks.

Mar 97. (7"colrd) *(CHS 5049)* **KING OF NEW YORK. / SCOOBY SNACKS (Schmoove version)** 28 –
(cd-s+=) *(CDCHS 5049)* – ('A'-Jack Dangers complex mix).
(cd-s) *(CDCHSS 5049)* – ('A'side) / ('A'-Jack Dangers complex mix) / Blues for suckers / ('A'instrumental).

Jun 97. (7"m) *(CHS 5060)* **SCOOBY SNACKS. / I'M NOT IN LOVE / CONEY ISLAND GIRL (Schmoove version)** 12 –
(cd-ep) *(CDCHS 5060)* – (first 2 tracks) / Scooby snacks (live) / I can't get with that (live).
(cd-ep) *(CDCHSS 5060)* – (2nd & 3rd tracks) / Scooby snacks (Schmoove version) / Bombin the L (Schmoove version).

Chrysalis Virgin

Aug 98. (c-s/cd-s) *(TC/CD CHS 5096)* **LOVE UNLIMITED / SHINING STAR / 10th STREET** 18 –
(cd-s) *(CDCHSS 5096)* – ('A'side) / ('A'mix) / ('A'instrumental).

Aug 98. (cd-ep) *<97463>* **MUSIC FROM 100% COLOMBIAN** – ☐
– Love unlimited / Back on the block / Up on the hill / The view belongs to everyone / Sugar / Big night out.

Aug 98. (cd/c/lp) *(497056-2/-4/-1) <23140>* **100% COLOMBIAN** 3 ☐
– Up on the hill / Love unlimited / The view belongs to everyone / Korean bodega / Back on the block / 10th street / Sugar / South side / We are all very worried about you / All for self / All my time is gone / Big night out / Mini bar blues.

Oct 98. (c-s/cd-s) *(TC/CD CHS 5101)* **BIG NIGHT OUT / SUMMER WIND (with IAN McCULLOCH) / LOVE UNLIMITED** 29 –
(cd-s) *(CDCHSS 5101)* – ('A'side) / We are all very worried about you / My D (slight return).

Apr 99. (c-s) *(TCCHS 5108)* **KOREAN BODEGA / KOREAN BODEGA (Aero Mexicana mix)** 15 ☐
(cd-s) *(CDCHS 5108)* – ('A'side) / The ballad of Larry Davis / Sleepyhead.
(cd-s) *(CDCHSS 5108)* – ('A'side) / The fun lovin' criminal / Big night out (full length video).

Chrysalis Chrysalis

Nov 99. (cd) *<(523459-2)>* **MIMOSA (THE LOUNGE ALBUM)** 37 ☐
– Couldn't get it right / Scooby snacks (schmoove version) / Shining star / Bombin' the L (circa 1956 version) / I'm not in love / The summer wind / Crazy train / I can't get with that (schmoove version) / We have all the time in the world (Copa Capana version) / Coney Island girl (schmoove version) / I'll be seeing you.

Jan 01. (c-s) *(TCCHS 5121)* **LOCO / EVERYTHING UNDER THE STARS / SPECIAL DEDICATION (from Maui homocide 2001)** 5 –
(cd-s+=) *(CDCHS 5121)* – ('A'-video).
(cd-s) *(CDCHSS 5121)* – ('A'side) / ('A'-Latin quarter instrumental) / Kill the bad guy (from Maui homocide 2001).

Feb 01. (cd) *<(531471-2)>* **LOCO** 5 ☐
– Where the bums go / Loco / The biz / Run daddy run / Half a block / Swashbucklin' in Brooklyn / Bump / Microphone fiend / My sin / Underground / She's my friend / There was a time / Dickholder / Little song.

Aug 01. (c-s) *(TCCHS 5128)* **BUMP / RUN DADDY RUN / BUMP (live in Dubai)** 50 –
(cd-s+=) *(CDCHS 5128)* – Maui homocide 2001 (medley).
(cd-s) *(CDCHSS 5128)* – ('A'side) / ('A'-Mark Berkley's remix) / Run daddy run (remix).

Jul 02. (cd) *<(539954-2)>* **BAG OF HITS: 15 INTERGLOBAL CHARTSTOPPERS** (compilation) 11 ☐
– The fun lovin' ciminal / Up on the hill / Loco / Korean bodega / King of New York / Run daddy run / The grave and the constant / Swashbucklin' in Brooklyn / Love unlimited / Bump / Scooby snacks / Smoke 'em / Couldn't get it right / Big night out / We have all the time in the world. *(d-cd edition +=; 539953-2)* – (remixes).

—— now down to **HUEY + FAST**

Sanctuary Sanctuary

Sep 03. (cd-s) *(SANXD 205)* **TOO HOT / TOO HOT (dub) / SAVE THE BABIES** 61 –
(cd-s) *(SANXD 205X)* – ('A'side) / ('A'-drum'n'bass) / ('A'-straight up).

Sep 03. (cd) *(SANCD 187) <84616>* **WELCOME TO POPPY'S** 20 ☐
– Too hot / Stray bullit / Living on the streets / Lost it all / Friday night / You got a problem / Running for cover / Take me back / What had happened? / Got our love / This sick world / Steak knife / Beautiful / Baby / You just can't have it all.

– compilations, etc. –

Jul 03. (cd) *EMI Gold; (590206-2)* **SCOOBY SNACKS – THE COLLECTION** ☐ –

Nelly FURTADO

Born: 2 Dec'78, Victoria, British Columbia, Canada. Born into Portuguese parentage, NELLY's up bringing was dominated by her strict working-class family who had always encouraged her to work hard in whatever field she'd follow. Little did they know that the one-time chambermaid would grow up to be a best-selling, Grammy nominated singer/songwriter. During her time as a housekeeper (under her mother's wing), FURTADO began experimenting with music, creating a hobby out of guitar and ukelele playing. She enjoyed the songs of R&B acts such as TLC and SALT 'N' PEPA, but her versatile inspiration came from the discovery of "real" bands like The BEATLES, The VERVE and RADIOHEAD. Hip-hop also became a driving force in her relentless pursuit of music, as did the Brazilian tinged works of AMALIA RODRIGUES. After she graduated from high school, FURTADO took off to Toronto where she picked up a job as an alarm salesperson. The move to a big city enabled her to fully appreciate the joys of the local music scene, and, not before long, she had joined a Hip-Hop duo named, NELSTAR. During this period she began writing her own free-style melodies, listening to the influential records of DE LA SOUL for reference. It wasn't until she began performing at open-mic nights in the bohemian quarters of Toronto that she drew the attention of BRIAN WEST and GERALD EATON, two inspiring producers who moonlighted in the funk band The PHILOSOPHER KINGS. They offered to produce a demo tape, which would land her a recording contract with 'DreamWorks'. By 2000, NELLY FURTADO had issued the single 'I'M LIKE A BIRD', a swirling pop anthem for romantics everywhere. The song featured a heavy hip-hop bass beat, lush strings and sweet, sweet vocals, which enabled the world to see just how talented Miss FURTADO had become. The single was a hit, reaching the Top Ten in both Canada and the UK and paved the way for the equally catchy 'TURN OFF THE LIGHT' and her sublime debut album 'WHOA, NELLY!' (2000). The NELLY which returned in 2003 with 'FOLKLORE' was – as the cover art suggested – a more mature proposition, undoubtedly sacrificing some of the youthful sweetness and naivety of old for the weight of adult concerns. Sadly missing was the sparky wit and knowing drollery of the debut, although this ambitious song cycle admittedly showed potential if self-analysing songwriting is really the direction she intends to head in.

Album rating: WHOA, NELLY! (*7) / FOLKLORE (*5)

NELLY FURTADO – vocals / with session people

DreamWorks DreamWorks

Feb 01. (c-s) *(450919-4) <radio cut>* **I'M LIKE A BIRD / PARTY (reprise)** 5 9
(cd-s+=) *(450919-2)* – My love grows deeper / ('A'-video).

Mar 01. (cd/c) *(450285-2/-4) <450217>* **WHOA, NELLY!** 2 Oct00 24
– Hey, man! / Shit on the radio (remember the days) / Baby girl / Legend / I'm like a bird / Turn off the light / Trynna finda way / Party / Well, well / My love grows deeper (pt.1) / I will make U cry / Scared of you / Oude estes. *(re-iss. May01; 450329-2)* – I feel you (with ESTHERO) / My love grows deeper / I'm like a bird (video).

Aug 01. (c-s) *(450891-4) <459093>* **TURN OFF THE LIGHT / I'M LIKE A BIRD (acoustic)** 4 5
(cd-s+=) *('A'-version with Ms JADE & TIMBALAND).*
(12") *(450891-1)* – ('A'side) / ('A'-So Solid Crew remix) / ('A'-sunshine reggae mix).

Jan 02. (c-s) *(450856-4)* **. . . ON THE RADIO (REMEMBER THE DAYS) / (semi clean version)** 18 ☐
(cd-s+=) *(450856-2)* – ('A'-Carl H vocal mix) / I'm like a bird (Nelly vs Asha remix) / ('A'video).

Nov 03. (cd) *(450505-2)* *<00010071-2>* **FOLKLORE** 62 38
– One-trick pony (with the KRONOS QUARTET) / Powerless (say what you want) / Explode / Try / Fresh off the boat / Forca / The grass is green / Picture perfect / Saturdays (with JARVIS CHURCH) / Build you up / Island of wonder (with CAETANO VELOSO) / Childhood of dreams.

Dec 03. (cd-s) *(450464-2)* **POWERLESS (SAY WHAT YOU WANT) / ('A'-Josh's desl mix) / ('A'-alt. acoustic mix)** 13 ☐

☐ FUSE (see under ⇒ CHEAP TRICK)

GUNS N' ROSES

Peter GABRIEL

Born: 13 May'50, Cobham, Surrey, England. After 8 years as leader of GENESIS, he left in May '75 to pursue a solo career, releasing the first of his four self-titled studio albums in 1977. Produced by BOB EZRIN (more often found working with heavy-rock acts), the album's overwrought feel found GABRIEL struggling for a musical identity despite including such enduring songs as the classic 'SOLISBURY HILL', a Top 20 hit single, and its creepy flipside, 'MORIBUND THE BURGERMEISTER'. 1978's follow-up boasted ROBERT FRIPP at the production helm, and a somewhat pared-down sound, GABRIEL illustrating his admiration for the punk ethos on 'D.I.Y.' and rocking out on the raging 'ON THE AIR'. His third, in 1980, moved towards a radically different style of songwriting, based around rhythm rather than chord sequences. With the use of a pioneering sampler, the Fairlight CMI, GABRIEL was able to construct tracks around the rhythm, adding instrumentation to enhance the sound. With STEVE LILLYWHITE producing and a cast of collaborators including FRIPP, KATE BUSH and PHIL COLLINS, he created a compelling set of minimalistic songs, the hypnotic anti-war single 'GAMES WITHOUT FRONTIERS', taking GABRIEL into the Top 5. The album also included his inspired tribute to murdered black South African activist (STEVE) 'BIKO'. This introduced GABRIEL's growing interest in world music, an area he would explore further on his fourth album (released in the States as 'SECURITY'). Incorporating ethnic sounds and rhythms into his distinctive songwriting technique, GABRIEL discovered a new found artistic freedom, creating one of his most accomplished and inventive albums in the process. Highlights included the single, 'SHOCK THE MONKEY', the African tribal drumming of 'RHYTHM OF THE HEAT', and the exotic 'THE FAMILY AND THE FISHING NET'. His increasing immersion in all things ethnic saw him become involved with the newly conceived WOMAD festival in 1982, highlighting music from the furthest flung corners of the globe. After a shaky start, the festival has now become an annual event with an affiliated world music label, 'Real World'. The 80's also saw GABRIEL record two soundtrack albums, Alan Parker's 'BIRDY' (1985) and Martin Scorsese's 'THE LAST TEMPTATION OF CHRIST' (1989). The former was made-up largely of revamped tracks from his earlier work, the original songs transformed into atmospheric mood pieces to impressive effect, while the latter was an eerily affecting collage of folksy, world music stylings. Sandwiched between these two, was the album which finally marked his arrival as a major league rock star. 'SO', released in 1986, saw GABRIEL incorporating his ethnic experimentation into the pop format with remarkable dexterity. The track, 'SLEDGEHAMMER', with its polished funk and famous, award winning video, shot into the upper regions of the charts, propelling the album to No.1 in the UK (No.2 in America). The record was a free ranging world trip, showcasing strong melodies ('DON'T GIVE UP' with KATE BUSH) against exotic backdrops, the culmination of his work to date. The long awaited "proper" follow-up, 'US' was eventually released in 1992, just held off the top spot on both sides of the Atlantic. The album was a markedly more downbeat, introspective affair, the single 'DIGGING IN THE DIRT', highlighting GABRIEL's return to more personal songwriting. It was also inspired by his mid-80's divorce from childhood sweetheart JILL MOORE and the split with his girlfriend, actress ROSANNA ARQUETTE. GABRIEL continued to devote much of his time to the 'Real World' label, although he did find some time for a tour and a live album, 'SECRET WORLD' in 1994. Not strictly a solo album as such, 'OVO: MILLENNIUM SHOW' (2000) was the ambitious soundtrack to an installation commissioned for London's Millennium Dome. A healthy list of collaborators as varied as The BLACK DYKE MILLS BAND, NENEH CHERRY and The AFRO-CELT SOUND SYSTEM ensured that the record encomapassed everything from hip hop to folk and ethnic percussion. Released a full decade since his last album, 'UP' (2002) was even more hermetic and insular, an often impenetrably personal work destined to appeal to dedicated fans with the patience and perseyerence to coax out its secrets. • **Covered;** STRAWBERRY FIELDS FOREVER (Beatles) / SUZANNE (Leonard Cohen). • **Trivia:** In 1982, he co-wrote & produced 'Animals Have More Fun' for JIMMY PURSEY (ex-SHAM 69). He has also guested for ROBBIE ROBERTSON (his 1987 album) & JONI MITCHELL (her 1991 album).

Album rating: PETER GABRIEL [1] (*7) / PETER GABRIEL [2] (*6) / PETER GABRIEL [3] (*7) / PETER GABRIEL (SECURITY) (*6) / PETER GABRIEL – PLAYS LIVE (*5) / BIRDY soundtrack (*5) / SO (*8) / PASSION: MUSIC FOR THE LAST TEMPTATION OF CHRIST (*6) / SHAKIN' THE TREE: SIXTEEN GOLDEN GREATS compilation (*8) / US (*6) / SECRET WORLD LIVE (*5) / OVO (*4) / UP (*5) / HIT – THE DEFINITIVE COLLECTION compilation (*8)

PETER GABRIEL – vocals, keyboards (ex-GENESIS, ex-GARDEN WALL) with **TONY LEVIN** – bass / **STEVE HUNTER** – guitar / **LARRY FAST** – keyboards / **JIMMY MAELEN** – percussion / **ALAN SCHWARTZBERG** – drums / **ROBERT FRIPP** – guitar

Charisma | Atco

Feb 77. (lp/c) *(CDS/+MC 4006) <36-147>* **PETER GABRIEL** | 7 | 38
– Moribund the burgermeister / Solisbury Hill / Modern love / Excuse me / Humdrum / Slowburn / Waiting for the big one / Down the Dolce Vita / Here comes the flood. *(cd-iss. May83; CDSCD 4006) (re-iss. Aug88 lp/c; CHC/+MC 38) (cd re-iss. May87; PGCD 1)*

Mar 77. (7") *(CB 301) <7079>* **SOLISBURY HILL. / MORIBUND THE BURGERMEISTER** | 13 | 68

Jun 77. (7") *(CB 302)* **MODERN LOVE. / SLOWBURN** | | –

—— now with **FRIPP,** plus **JERRY MAROTTA** – drums / **ROY BITTAN** – piano / **SID McGINNIS** – guitar / **BAYETE** – keyboards

May 78. (7") *(CB 311)* **D.I.Y. / PERSPECTIVE (long)** | | –

Charisma | Atlantic

Jun 78. (lp/c) *(CAS/+MC 4013) <19181>* **PETER GABRIEL** | 10 | 45
– On the air / D.I.Y. / Mother of violence / A wonderful day in a one-way

world / White shadow / Indigo / Animal magic / Exposure / Flotsam and jetsam / Perspective / Home sweet home. *(re-iss. Mar84 lp/c; CHC/+MC 24) (cd-iss. May87; PGCD 2)*

Jun 78. (7") *(CB 319)* **D.I.Y. (remix). / MOTHER OF VIOLENCE / TEDDY BEAR** [ ] [–]

Charisma Mercury

Feb 80. (7"m) *(CB 354)* **GAMES WITHOUT FRONTIERS. / THE START / I DON'T REMEMBER** [4] [–]

May 80. (7") *(CB 360)* **NO SELF CONTROL. / LEAD A NORMAL LIFE** [33] [–]

Jul 80. (7") *<76086>* **GAMES WITHOUT FRONTIERS. / LEAD A NORMAL LIFE** [–] [48]

Sep 80. (7") *<76086>* **I DON'T REMEMBER. /** [–] [ ]

— now with **FRIPP, LEVIN + MAROTTA** plus guests **PHIL COLLINS** – drums / **KATE BUSH** – vocals + **PAUL WELLER** – guitar

May 80. (lp/c) *(CAS/+Mc 4019) <3848>* **PETER GABRIEL** [1] [22]
– Intruder / No self control / Start / I don't remember / Family snapshot / And through the wire / Not one of us / Lead a normal life / Biko. *(re-iss. Sep83 lp/c; CDS/+MC 4019) (cd-iss. May87; PGCD 3) (cd's re-iss. Jul02; PGCDX/PGCDR 1)*

Aug 80. (7"/12") *(CB 370/+12)* **BIKO. / SHOSHOLOZA / JETZT KOMMT DIE FLUT** [38] [ ]

— guests on next incl. **DAVID LORD** – synthesizers, co-producer / **JOHN ELLIS** – guitar / + some of last line-up

Charisma Geffen

Sep 82. (lp/c) *(PG/+MC 4) <2011>* **PETER GABRIEL** <US-title 'SECURITY'> [6] [28]
– The rhythm of the heat / San Jacinto / I have the touch / The family and the fishing net / Shock the monkey / Lay your hands on me / Wallflower / Kiss of life. *(re-iss. Sep83 lp/c; same) (cd-iss. 1986; PGCD 4)*

Sep 82. (7"/7"pic-d/12") *(SHOCK 1/+22/12) <29883>* **SHOCK THE MONKEY. / SOFT DOG (instrumental)** [58] [29]
(7"/12") *(SHOCK 1/350)* – ('A'side) / ('B'-instrumental).

Dec 82. (7") *(CB 405)* **I HAVE THE TOUCH. / ACROSS THE RIVER** [ ] [–]

Jun 83. (d-lp/c) *(PGD L/MC 1) <4012>* **PETER GABRIEL PLAYS LIVE (live)** [8] [44]
– The rhythm of the heat / I have the touch / Not one of us / Family snapshot / D.I.Y. / The family and the fishing net / Intruder / I go swimming / San Jacinto / Solisbury Hill / No self control / I don't remember / Shock the monkey / Humdrum / On the air / Biko. *(cd-iss. Jun85; PGDLD 1) (cd re-iss. 1988; CDPGD 100)* – (omits 4 tracks).

Jun 83. (7") *(GAB 1)* **I DON'T REMEMBER (live). / SOLISBURY HILL (live)** [62] [–]
(12"+=) *(GAB 12)* – Kiss of life (live).
(free-12"w- 12") *(GAB 122)* – GAMES WITHOUT FRONTIERS (live). / SCHNAPPSCHUSS (EIN FAMILIENFOTO)

Virgin Geffen

Nov 83. (7") *<29542>* **SOLISBURY HILL (live). / I GO SWIMMING (live)** [–] [84]

May 84. (7") *(VS 689)* **WALK THROUGH THE FIRE. / THE RACE (by Larry Carlton)** [69] [ ]
(12"+=) *(VS 689-12)* – I have the touch (remix).

Mar 85. (lp/c/cd) *(CAS/+MC/CD 1167) <24070>* **BIRDY – MUSIC FROM THE FILM (soundtrack)** [51] [ ]
– At night / Floating dogs / Quiet and alone / Close up / Slow water / Dressing the wound / Birdy's flight / Slow marimbas / The heat / Sketchpad with trumpet and voice / Under lock and key / Powerhouse at the foot of the mountain. *(re-iss. Apr90 on 'Virgin' lp/c; OVED/+C 283)*

— with **MAROTTA, LEVIN** plus **DANIEL LANOIS** – guitar, co-producer / **MANU KATCHE** – percussion / **YOUSSOU N'DOUR + KATE BUSH** – guest vocals / **STEWART COPELAND** – drums / etc.

Apr 86. (7") *(PGS 1) <28718>* **SLEDGEHAMMER. / DON'T BREAK THIS RHYTHM** [4] May86 [1]
(12"+=) *(PGS 112)* – ('A'dance mix).
('A'dance-12"+=) *(PGS 113)* – Biko (extended) / I have the touch ('85 remix).

May 86. (lp/c/cd) *(PG/+MC/CD 5) <24088>* **SO** [1] [2]
– Red rain / Sledgehammer / Don't give up / That voice again / In your eyes / Mercy street / Big time / We do what we're told. *(pic-cd.Dec88+=; PGCDP 5)* – This is the picture (excellent birds). *(re-iss. Feb97 on 'E.M.I.'; LPCENT 16)*

Sep 86. (7") *<28622>* **IN YOUR EYES. / ('A'-Special mix)** [–] [26]

Oct 86. (7"; PETER GABRIEL & KATE BUSH) *(PGS/+P 2)* **DON'T GIVE UP. / IN YOUR EYES (special mix)** [9] [–]
(12"+=) *(PGS 2-12)* – This is the picture (excellent birds).

Jan 87. (7") *<28503>* **BIG TIME. / WE DO WHAT WE'RE TOLD** [–] [8]

Mar 87. (7") *(PGS 3)* **BIG TIME. / CURTAINS** [13] [–]
(12"+=) *(PGS 312)* – ('A'extended).
('A'ext-c-s) *(PGT 312)* – Across the river / No self control (live). *(re-iss. 3"cd-s.1989; GAIL 312)*

Mar 87. (7"; PETER GABRIEL & KATE BUSH) *<28463>* **DON'T GIVE UP / CURTAINS** [–] [72]

Jun 87. (7") *(PGS 4)* **RED RAIN. / GA GA (I GO SWIMMING instrumental)** [46] [–]
(12"+=/c-s+=) *(PGS/+C 412)* – Walk through the fire.

Jan 88. (7"/c-s) *(PGS/+C 6)* **BIKO (live). / NO MORE APARTEID** [49] [–]
(12"+=/cd-s+=) *(PGS/CDPGS 6-12)* – I have the touch ('85 remix).

— In May 89, PETER ws credited with YOUSSOU N'DOUR on minor hit single 'SHAKING THE TREE' *(VS/+T/CD 1167)*

Real World Geffen

Jun 89. (d-lp/c/cd) *(RW LP/MC/CD 1) <24206>* **PASSION (music for The Last Temptation Of Christ)** [29] [60]
– The feeling begins / Gethsemane / Of these, hope / Lazarus raised / Of these, hope – reprise / In doubt / A different drum / Zaar / Troubled / Open* / Before night falls / With this love / Sandstorm / Stigmata** / Passion / With this love – choir / Wall of breath / The promise of shadows / Disturbed / It is accomplished / Bread and wine. *(*= with SHANKAR) (**= with MAHMOUD TABRIZI ZADEH)*

Nov 90. (lp/c/cd) *(PGTV/+C/D 6) <24326>* **SHAKING THE TREE – SIXTEEN GOLDEN GREATS** (compilation) [11] [48]
– Solisbury Hill / I don't remember / Sledgehammer / Family snapshot / Mercy Street / Shaking the tree / Don't give up / Here comes the flood / Games without frontiers / Shock the monkey / Big time / Biko. *(cd+=/c+=)* – San Juanito / Red rain / I have the touch / Zaar. *(cd re-iss. Feb02; PGTVDR 6)* – (hit No.61)

Dec 90. (7"/c-s) *(VS/+C 1322)* **SOLISBURY HILL. / SHAKING THE TREE** (w/ YOUSSOU N'DOUR) [57] [–]
(12"+=/cd-s+=) *(VS T/CD 1322)* – Games without frontiers.

Sep 92. (7"/c-s) *(PGS/+C 7) <19136>* **DIGGING IN THE DIRT. / QUIET STEAM** [24] [52]
(cd-s+=) *(PGSDG 7)* – ('A'instrumental).
(cd-s++=) *(PGSCD 7)* – Bashi-bazouk.

Oct 92. (lp/c/cd) *(PG/+MC/CD 7) <24473>* **US** [2] [2]
– Come talk to me / Love to be loved / Blood of Eden / Steam / Digging in the dirt / Fourteen black paintings / Kiss that frog / Secret world.

Dec 92. (c-s) *<19145>* **STEAM / GAMES WITHOUT FRONTIERS (live)** [–] [32]

Jan 93. (7"/c-s) *(PGS/+C 8)* **STEAM. / ('A'-Carter mix)** [10] [–]
(cd-s) *(PGSDG 8 / PGSDX 8)* – ('A' mix) / Games without frontiers (mix) / (2 'A' extended + dub mix or Games (other mix)

Mar 93. (7"/c-s) *(PGS/+C 9)* **BLOOD OF EDEN. / MERCY STREET** [43] [ ]
(cd-s+=) *(PGSDG 9)* – ('A'-special mix)
(cd-s+=) *(PGCDX 9)* – Sledgehammer.

Sep 93. (7"/c-s) *(PGS/+C 10)* **KISS THAT FROG. / ('A'-mindblender mix)** [46] [ ]
(cd-s+=) *(PGSDG 10)* – Digging in the dirt.
(cd-s+=) *(PGSDX 10)* – Across the river / Shaking the tree (Bottrill remix).

— Below single, another from 'Philadelphia' film on 'Epic' records.

Jun 94. (7"/c-s) *(660480-7/-4)* **LOVE TOWN. / LOVE TO BE LOVED** [49] [ ]
(cd-s+=) *(660480-2)* – Different drum.

— live with **TONY LEVIN** – bass, vocals / **DAVID RHODES** – guitar, vocals / **MANU KATCHE** – drums / **PAULA COLE** – vocals / **JEAN CLAUDE NAIMRO** – keyboards, vocals / **RAVI SHANKAR** – violin, vocals / **LEVON MINASSIAN** – doudouk

Aug 94. (c-s) *(PGSC 11)* **SECRET WORLD (live). / COME TALK TO ME** [39] [ ]
(cd-ep) *(PGSCD 11)* – ('A'live) / Red rain (live) / San Jacinto (live) / Mercy Street (live).

Sep 94. (d-cd/d-c) *(PG DCD/MC 8) <24722>* **SECRET WORLD LIVE (live)** [10] [23]
– Come talk to me / Steam / Across the river / Slow marimbas / Shaking the tree / Red rain / Blood of Eden / Kiss that frog / Washing of the water / Solisbury Hill / Digging in the dirt / Sledgehammer / Secret world / Don't give up / In your eyes.

Real World E.M.I.

Jun 00. (cd) *(PGCD 9) <849540>* **OVO (live millennium show)** [24] Aug00 [ ]
– The story of Ovo / Low light / The time of the turning / The man who

loved the earth – The hand that sold shadows / The time of the turning (reprise) / Father, son / The tower that ate people / Revenge / White ashes / Downside up / The nest that sailed the sky / Make tomorrow.

Sep 02. (cd-s) *(PGSCD 13)* **THE BARRY WILLIAMS SHOW / (unadulterated) / MY HEAD SOUNDS LIKE THAT (Royksopp remix) / CLOUDLESS (radio edit)** [ ] [–]

Sep 02. (cd/c/d-lp) *(PG CD/MC/DLP 11) <493536>* **UP** [11] [9]
– Darkness / Growing up / Sky blue / No way out / I grieve / The Barry Williams show / My head sounds like that / More than this / Signal to noise / The drop.

Dec 02. (cd-s) *(PGSCD 14)* **MORE THAN THIS / MORE THAN THIS (Polyphonic Spree remix) / MORE THAN THIS (Elbow mix)** [47] [–]
(12") *(PGST 14)* – ('A'side) / My head sounds like this (Royksopp mix).

Nov 03. (d-cd) *(595237-2) <14860-2>* **HIT – THE DEFINITIVE COLLECTION** (compilation) [29] [100]
– Solisbury hill / Shock the monkey / Sledgehammer / Don't give up (with KATE BUSH) / Games without frontiers / Big time / Burn you up, burn you down / Growing up (Tom Lord – Alge mix) / Digging in the dirt / Blood of Eden / More than this / Biko / Steam / Red rain / Here comes the flood / San Jacinto / No self control *[UK-only]* / I don't remember *[US-only]* / Cloudless / The rhythm of the heat / I have the touch *[UK-only]* / Loved to be loved *[US-only]* / I grieve / D.I.Y. *[UK-only]* / Family snapshot *[US-only]* / Different drum *[UK-only]* / In your eyes *[US-only]* / The drop / The tower that ate people (Steve Osborne mix) / Lovetown / Father, son / Signal to noise / Downside up (live) / Washing of the water *[UK-only]*.

Nov 03. (cd-s) *(GABRIEL 003)* **BURN YOU UP, BURN YOU DOWN / DARKNESS (Engelspost remix)** [ ] [–]

– compilations, others, etc. –

on 'Virgin' UK / 'Geffen' US, unless mentioned otherwise

Jan 83. (7") *Old Gold; (OG 9265)* **SOLISBURY HILL. / GAMES WITHOUT FRONTIERS** [ ] [–]

Mar 83. (d-c) *Charisma; (CASMC 102)* **PETER GABRIEL 1 / PETER GABRIEL 2** [ ] [–]

1988. (3"cd-ep) *(CDT 33)* **SOLISBURY HILL / MORIBUND THE BURGERMEISTER / SOLISBURY HILL (live)** [ ] [–]
(re-iss. Apr90; VVCS 8)

Jun 88. (cd) *XCDSD 4018)* **PETER GABRIEL 3 (German version)** [ ] [–]

May 89. (7") *W.T.G.; <68936>* **IN YOUR EYES. / (track by Fishbone)** [–] [41]
(above from the movie, 'Say Anything')

Oct 90. (3xcd-box) *(TPAK 9)* **PETER GABRIEL 1 / 2 / 3** [ ] [ ]

☐ GADGETS (see under ⇒ THE THE)

☐ Dave GAHAN (see under ⇒ DEPECHE MODE)

Serge GAINSBOURG

Born: LUCIEN GINZBERG, 2 Apr'28, Paris, France. The son of Russian Jewish immigrants, GAINSBOURG attended art college and initially tried to scrape a living as a painter. To supplement his income, he worked nights as a bar pianist before being snapped up for an unwilling singing role in the musical 'Milord L'Arsoille'. Reluctant to take to the stage himself (partly due to his less than conventionally handsome appearance), GAINSBOURG felt more comfortable as a songwriter, composing for major-league French stars such as SACHA DISTEL and JOHNNY HALLIDAY. Nevertheless, he ventured into the studio himself in the late 50's for debut album, 'DU CHANTE A LA UNE!' (1958), following it up with 'NO.2' (1959), 'L'ETONNANT SERGE GAINSBOURG' (1961), 'NO.4' (1962), 'GAINSBOURG CONFIDENTIEL' (1964) and 'GAINSBOURG PERCUSSIONS' (1964). Although these weren't great successes (outside France) in their own right, his material was exposed to English audiences via the likes of DIONNE WARWICK and PETULA CLARK. A close association with French actress/sex symbol BRIGITTE BARDOT inspired some of GAINSBOURG's finest work, the pair cutting a series of celebrated duets including 'BONNIE & CLYDE' and 'HARLEY DAVIDSON'. Even the infamous 'JE T'AIME . . . MOI NON PLUS' was penned for BARDOT who subsequently declined to perform it. Instead, the increasingly wayward Frenchman duetted on the track with another actress-cum-sex-kitten, JANE BIRKIN. Released as a single on 'Fontana' in July 1969, this breathy ode to sweaty love was banned by the BBC although it crowned the UK chart all the same (in October '69 the 'Major Minor' re-issue was No.1 while its identical counterpart was still in the charts having made No.2!); it even made the Top 60 in the USA. 1971's 'HISTOIRE DE MELODY NELSON' album found GAINSBOURG preoccupied with life's darker side (MELODY was a 14-year old girl with whom the writer – as narrator – was having an affair!), a trait which would become more pronounced as his reputation grew ever more lecherous and provocative. His concept-type sets in the the mid-70's were weird to say the least. From 1973's 'VU DE L'EXTERIEUR' – with its fart joke song ('DES VENTS DES PETS DES POUM') – to 75's Adolf Hitler concept! 'ROCK AROUND THE BUNKER' and 'L'HOMME A TETE DE CHOU' ('THE MAN WITH A CABBAGE HEAD'), all were extremely shocking and OTT; LOU REED meeting 50's rock'n'roll was how one could describe it. 1979's cod-reggae 'AUX ARMES ET CETERA' (his only UK release) was also diverse, SLY & ROBBIE giving it their Jamaican dub treatment. SERGE even recorded a concept album about male prostitutes, 'LOVE ON THE BEAT' (1984), which updated 'HARLEY . . .' as 'HARLEY DAVID SON OF A BITCH'. Also guaranteed to shock was a duet with his daughter (actress Charlotte Gainsbourg), 'LEMON INCEST'; the Gallic Jew going a little astray even by his standards. Controversy was SERGE's middle name, while appearances on French chat shows were often accompanied by outrageous comments and remarks; actor Oliver Reed must have been watching. A pillar of the French anti-establishment, GAINSBOURG's hard-drinking lifestyle eventually caught up with him on 2nd March 1991 when he died of heart complications.

Album rating: DU CHANT A LA UNE! (*5) / NO.2 (*5) / L'ETONNANT SERGE GAINSBOURG (*5) / NO.4 (*5) / GAINSBOURG CONFIDENTIEL (*5) / GAINSBOURG PERCUSSIONS (*5) / ANNA soundtrack (*6) / INITIALES B.B. (*7) / BONNIE AND CLYDE with Brigitte Bardot (*6) / JANE BIRKIN & SERGE GAINSBOURG – JE T'AIME (*6) / HISTOIRE DE MELODY NELSON (*7) / VU DE L'EXTERIEUR (*6) / ROCK AROUND THE BUNKER (*7) / L'HOMME A TETE DE CHOU (*6) / AUX ARMES ET CAETERA (*4) / MAUVAISES NOUVELLES DES ETOILES (*4) / LOVE ON THE BEAT (*3) / YOU'RE UNDER ARREST (*3) / LE ZENITH DE GAINSBOURG (*3) / COMIC STRIP compilation (*7) / INITIALS S.G. compilation (*9)

Best CD compilation: DE GAINSBOURG A GAINSBARRE boxed-set (*9)

SERGE GAINSBOURG – vocals, piano, guitar / (with sessioners)

Philips not iss.

1958. (7") *(432307BE)* **LA POINCONNEUR DES LILAS** [–] French [–]

1958. (10"lp) *(76447R)* **DU CHANT A LA UNE!** [–] French [–]
– Le poinconneur de lilas / Recette de l'amour fou / Douze belles dans la peau / Ce mortel ennui / Ronsard / Femmes des uns sous le corps des autres / L'alcool / Du jazz dans le ravin / Charleston des demenageurs de piano / Jambe de bios "Friedland" / Claquer de doigts. *(cd-iss. Feb01 on 'Mercury' France; 548421-2) (cd/10"lp re-iss. Nov02 on 'Mercury' France; 548606-2/-1)*

1958. (7") *(432325BE)* **LA JAMBE DE BOIS "FRIEDLAND"** [–] French [–]

1959. (lp) *(76473R)* **NO.2** [–] French [–]
– Nuit d'Octobre / Adieu creature / L'anthracite / Mambo miam miam / Indifferente / Jeunes femmes et vieux messieurs / L'amour a la papa / Cha cha cha du loup / Sois belle et tais toi / Laissez-moi tranquille / Judith / L'eau a la bouche. *(cd-iss. Feb01 on 'Mercury' France'; 548422-2)*

1959. (7") *(432397BE)* **INDIFFERENTE** [–] French [–]

1959. (7") *(432398BE)* **JEUNES FEMMES ET VIEUX MESSIEURS** – French –
1960. (7") **B.O. DU FILM L'EAU A LA BOUCHE** – French –
1960. (7") **B.O. DU FILM LES LOUPS DANS LA BERGERIE** – French –
1961. (lp) *(76516R)* **L'ETONNANT SERGE GAINSBOURG** – French –
– Chanson de prevert / En relisant ta lettre / Rock de nerval / Oubliettes / Chanson de Maglia / Viva villa / Amours perdues / Femmes c'est du chinois / Personne / Sonnet d'Arvers. *(cd-iss. Feb01; 548423-2)*
1961. (7") *(432533BE)* **LA CHANSON DE PREVERT** – French –
1961. (7") *(432564BE)* **LES OUBLIETTES** – French –
1962. (lp) *(76553R)* **NO.4** – French –
– Goemons / Black trombone / Baudelaire / Intoxicated man / Quand tu t'y mets / Cigarillos / Requiem pour un twister / Ce grand mechant vous / L'appareil a sous. *(cd-iss. Feb01 on 'Mercury' France; 548424-2)*
1962. (7") *(432771BE)* **LES GOEMONS** – French –
1962. (7") **REQUIEM POUR UN TWISTER** – French –
1963. (7"ep) *(432862BE)* **VILAINES FILLES ET VIEUX GARCONS** – French –
– Vilaines filles et vieux garcons / Violin, un jambon / La Javanaise.
1963. (7") **B.O. DU FILM STRIP-TEASE** – French –
1963. (7") *(434888BE)* **CHEZ LES YE YE** – French –
1964. (lp) *(76553R)* **GAINSBOURG CONFIDENTIEL** – French –
– Chez le ye-ye / Sait-on jamais ou va une femme quand elle …. / Le talkie-walkie / Fille au rasoir / Saison des pluies / Alaeudania teiteia / Scenic railway / Tempes de yoyos / Amour sans amour / No no thanks no / Maxim's / Negative blues. *(cd-iss. Feb01 on 'Mercury' France; 548425-2)*
1964. (7") **B.O. DU FILM COMMENT TROUVEZ-VOUS MA SOEUR?** – French –
1964. (lp) *(77842L)* **GAINSBOURG PERCUSSIONS** – French –
– Joanna / La-bas c'est naturel / Pauvre Lola / Quand mon 6.35 me fait les yeux doux / Machins choses / Sambassadeurs / New York City U.S.A. / Couleur cafe / Marabout / Ces petits riens / Tatoue Jeremie / Coco and Co / Comment trouvez vous ma soeur? *(cd-iss. Feb01 on 'Mercury' France; 548426-2)*
1964. (7") *(434994BE)* **COULEUR CAFE** – French –
1964. (7") **MACHINS CHOSES** – French –
1966. (7") *(437167BE)* **QUI EST IN QUI EST OUT** – French –
1967. (lp; V/A soundtrack) **BANDE ORIGINALE DE LA COMEDIE MUSICALE ANNA** – French –
– Soul le soleil exactement / Sous le soleil exactement II / C'est la cristallisation comme dit / Pas mal'pas mal du tout / J'etais fait pour le sympathies / Photographes et religieuses / Rien rien j'disais ca comme ca / Jour comme un autre / Boomerang / Poison violent, c'est ca l'amour / De plus en plus, de moins en moins / Roller girl / Ne dis risen / Pistolet Jo / G.I. Jo / Je n'avais qu'un seul mot a lui dire. *(UK cd-iss. Oct98 on 'Mercury'+=; 558 837-2)* – JE T'AIME MOI NON PLUS "BALLADE DE JOHNNY-JANE" soundtrack + others.
1967. (7") *(437355BE)* **COMIC STRIP** – French –
1967. (7"ep) **EXTRAIT DE LA B.O. DE LA COMEDIE MUSICALE ANNA** – French –
1967. (7"ep) **B.O. DU FILM TOUTES FOLLES DE LUI** – French –
(above issued on 'Barclay')
1967. (7"ep) **B.O. DU FEUILLETON TELEVISE VIDOCQ** – French –
1967. (7"ep) **B.O. DU FILM L'HORIZON** – French –

BRIGITTE BARDOT & SERGE GAINSBOURG

1968. (lp) *(GU 885529)* **BRIGITTE BARDOT ET SERGE GAINSBOURG** – French –
– Bonnie and Clyde / Bubble gum / Comic strip / Un jour comme un autre / Pauvre Lola / L'eau a la bouche / La Javanaise / Madrague / Intoxicated man / Everybody loves my baby / Baudelaire / Docteur Jekyll et Monsieur Hyde.
(above issued on 'Fontana')
1968. (7") *(460247HE)* **BONNIE AND CLYDE** – French –
1968. (lp) *(LP 844784B4)* **INITIALS B.B.** – French –
– Chanson du forcat / Chanson du forcat II / Manon / Requiem pour un con / L herbe tendre / Initials B.B. / Comic strip / Bloody Jack / Docteur Jeckyll et Monsieur Hyde / Torrey canyon / Shu ba du ba loo ba / Ford Mustang. *(cd-iss. Jun00 on 'Mercury' France; 546534-2) (cd re-mast.Feb01 on 'Mercury' France; 548612-2)*
1968. (7") *(437431BE)* **INITIALS B.B.** – French –

SERGE GAINSBOURG

1968. (7"ep) **B.O. DU FILM CE SACRE GRAND-PERE** – French –
1968. (7") **B.O. DU FILM MANON 70** – French –
1968. (7") **B.O. DU FILM LE PACHA** – French –
1969. (7") **B.O. DU FILM SLOGAN** – French –
Barclay not iss.
1969. (lp) **B.O. DU FILM MISTER FREEDOM** – French –

JANE BIRKIN & SERGE GAINSBOURG

Fontana Fontana
1969. (lp) *(885545)* **JANE BIRKIN & SERGE GAINSBOURG** – French –
– Chanson de slogan / L'anamour / Orang outan / Souse le soleil exactement / 18-39 / 69 Annee erotique / Jane B / Elisa / Canari est sur la balc / Manon. *(UK-iss.Jun88 as 'JE T'AIME . . . MOI NON PLUS' on 'Bam Caruso'; DN 2002) (cd-iss. Oct98 as 'JE T'AIME . . . MOI NON PLUS' on 'Mercury'; 558 774-2)*
Jul 69. (7") *(TF 1042)* **JE T'AIME . . . MOI NON PLUS. / Jane Birkin: JANE B** 2 Nov69 58
(re-iss. Sep69 on 'Major Minor'; MM 645) – hit UK No.1 *(re-iss. Nov74 on 'Atlantic'; K 11511)* – hit No.31
1969. (7") **69 ANNEE EROTIQUE** – French –

SERGE GAINSBOURG

Philips not iss.
1969. (7") **ELISA** – French –
1970. (lp) **B.O. DU FILM CANNABIS** – French –
1970. (7") **EXTRAIT DE LA B.O. DU FILM CANNABIS** – French –
Mar 71. (lp) *(6325 071)* **HISTOIRE DE MELODY NELSON** – French –
– Melody (extrait de Melody Nelson) / Ballade de Melody Nelson / Valse de Melody / Ah! Melody / L'hotel particulieur (extrait de bof Melody) / En Melody / Cargo culte. *(UK cd-iss. 1988; 812826-2) (<cd re-iss. Oct98 on 'Mercury'; 532 073-2>)*
1971. (7"; by JANE BIRKIN & SERGE GAINSBOURG) *(6118 014)* **BALLADE DU MELODY NELSON** – French –
Fontana not iss.
1971. (7") *(6010 054)* **LA DECADANSE** – French –
1972. (7") **B.O. DU FILM SEX SHOP** – French –
1972. (7") **B.O. DU FILM TROP JOLIES POUR ETRE HONNETES** – French –
Philips not iss.
1973. (lp) *(6499 731)* **VU DE L'EXTERIEUR** – French –
– Je suis venu te dire que je m'en vais / Vu de l'exterieur / Panpan cucul / Par hasard et pas rase / Des vents des pets des poums / Titicaca / Pamela popo / Poupee qui fait / L'hippopodame / Sensuelle et sans suite. *<US cd-iss. Oct98 on 'Mercury'; 532 075-2>*
1973. (7") *(6009 459)* **JE SUIS VENU TE DIRE QUE M'EN VAIS** – French –
1975. (lp) *(6325 195)* **ROCK AROUND THE BUNKER** – French –
– Nazi rock / Tata teutonne / J'entends des voix off / Eva / Smoke gets in your eyes / Zig zag avec toi / Est-ce est-ce si bon / Yellow star / Rock around the bunker / S.S. in Uruguay. *<US cd-iss. Oct98 on 'Mercury'; 532 074-2>*
1975. (7") *(6009 630)* **ROCK AROUND THE BUNKER** – French –
1975. (7") *(6009 678)* **L'AMI CAOUETTE** – French –
1976. (lp; soundtrack) **JE T'AIME MOI NON PLUS "BALLADE DE JOHNNY-JANE"** – French –
– Ballade de Johnny-Jane / Camion Jane / Banjo au bord du Styx / Rock'n'roll autor de Johnny / L'abominable strip-tease / Joe Banjo / Je t'aime moi non plus / Je t'aime moi non plus au lac vert / Je t'aime moi non plus au motel / Ballade de Johnny-Jane (finale).
1976. (7") **EXTRAIT DE LA B.O. DU FILM JE T'AIME . . . MOI NON PLUS** – French –
1976. (lp) *(9101 097)* **L'HOMME A TETE DE CHOU** – French –
– L'homme a tete de chou / Chez max coiffeur pour hommes / Marilou reggae / Transit a Marilou / Flash-forward / Aeroplanes / Premiers symptomes / Ma Lou Marilou / Variations sur Marilou / Meurtre a l'extincteur / Marilou sous la neige / Lunatic asylum. *(UK cd-iss. 1988; 812825-2) <US cd-iss. Oct98 on 'Mercury'; 532 076-2>*
1976. (7") *(6042 272)* **MARILOU SOUS LA NIEGE** – French –
1977. (lp; soundtrack) **MADAME CLAUDE** – French –
– Diapositivisme / Discophoteque / Mi corasong / Ketchup in the night / Fish-eye blues / Teleobjectivisme / Putain que ma joie demeure / Burnt island / Yesterday yes a day / Dusty lane / First class ticket / Long focal rock / Arabysance / Passage a tobacco / Yesterday on Fender.
1977. (7") **EXTRAIT DE LA B.O. DU FILM MADAME CLAUDE** – French –
1977. (7") **EXTRAIT DE LA B.O. DU FILM GOOD-BYE EMMANUELLE** – French –
1977. (7") *(6042 272)* **MY LADY HEROINE** – French –

1977. (7") **EXTRAIT DE LA B.O. DU FILM VOUS N'AUREZ PAS L'ALSACE ET LA LORRAINE** French
1978. (12") *(6172 147)* **B.O. DU FILM LES BRONZES** French
Jan 79. (12") *(6042 412)* **SEA, SEX & SUN. / MISTER ICEBERG**
1979. (7"; by SERGRE GAINSBOURG & BIJOU) **B.O. DU FILM TAPAGE NOCTURNE** French

—— next with **SLY & ROBBIE** – rhythm, etc / **ANSEL COLLINS** – organ / **I-THREES** :- MARCIA GRIFFITHS, RITA MARLEY + JUDY MOWATT

Island Polydor

Aug 79. (7") *(WIP 6518)* **AUX ARMES ET CAETERA. / DAISY TEMPLE**
Aug 79. (lp) *(ILPS 9581)* **AUX ARMES ET CAETERA**
– La Javanaise remake / Aux armes et caetera / Les cocataires / Des laids des laids / Brigade des stups / Vielle canaille / Lola rastaquourere / Relax baby be cool / Daisy temple / Eau et gaz a tous le etages / Pas long feu / Marilou reggae dub. *US cd-iss. Oct98 on 'Mercury'; 532 077-2>*

Philips Mercury

1979. (7") *(6172 287)* **VIELLE CANAILLE** French
1979. (7") *(6172 250)* **DES LAIDS DES LAIDS** French
1980. (d-lp) *(6681 013)* **ENREGISTREMENT PUBLIC AU THEATRE LE PALACE** French
1980. (7") *(6172 316)* **HARLEY DAVIDSON** French
1980. (lp) **B.O. DU FILM JE VOIS AIME** French
1980. (7") **EXTRAIT DE LA B.O. DU FILM JE VOUS AIME** French
1981. (7") **B.O. DU COURT-METRAGE PHYSIQUE ET LE FIGURE** French
1981. (lp) *(6313 270)* **MAUVAISES NOUVELLES DES ETOILES** French
– Overseas telegram / Ecce homo / Mickey Maosse / Juif et dieu / Shush shush Charlotte / Toi mourir / Nostalgie camarade / Bana basadi balalo / Eugenie Sokolov / Negusa nagast / Strike / Bad news from the stars. *(UK cd-iss. 1988; 812823-2)* *<US cd-iss. Oct98 on 'Mercury'; 532 078-2>*
1981. (7") *(6010 448)* **ECCE HOMO** French
1981. (7") *(6010 557)* **BANA BASADI BALALO** French
1984. (lp/c) *(822 849-1/-4)* **LOVE ON THE BEAT** French
– Love on the beat / Sorry angel / Hmm hmm hmm / Kiss me Hardy / No comment / I'm the boy / Harley David son of a bitch / Lemon incest.
1984. (7"/12") *(880 538-7/-1)* **LOVE ON THE BEAT** French
1985. (7"/12") *(880 620-7/-1)* **NO COMMENT** French
1985. (12"; by CHARLOTTE GAINSBOURG & SERGE GAINSBOURG) *(880 620-1)* **LEMON INCEST** French
1986. (d-lp) *(826 721-1)* **SERGE GAINSBOURG LIVE (live)** French
1986. (7") **SORRY ANGEL** French
1986. (7") **MY LADY HEROINE** French
1986. (lp) **B.O. DU FILM TENUE DE SOIREE** French
(above issued on 'Apache-WEA')
1987. (lp/cd) *(834 034-1/-2)* **YOU'RE UNDER ARREST** French
– You're under arrest / Five easy pisseuses / Baille baille Samantha / Suck baby suck / Gloomy Sunday / Aux enfants de la chance / Shotgun / Glass securit / Dispatch box / Mon legionnaire.
1987. (7"/12") **YOU'RE UNDER ARREST** French
1988. (7"/12") **AUX ENFANTS DE LA CHANCE** French
1988. (7"/12") **MON LEGIONNAIRE** French
1989. (d-lp/cd) *(838 162-1/-2)* **LE ZENITH DE GAINSBOURG (live 1988)** French
– You're under arrest / Qui est "in" qui est "out" / Five easy pisseuses / Hey man amen / L'homme ae tate de chou / Manon / Valse de melody / Dispatch box / Harley David son of a bitch / You you you but not you / Seigneur et saigneur / Bonnie & Clyde / Gloomy Sunday / Couleur cae / Aux armes etcaetera / Aux enfants de la chance / Les dessouos chics / Mon Legionnaire.
1989. (7") **HEY MAN AMEN** French
1989. (7") **COULEUR CAFE** French
1990. (7") **B.O. DU FILM STAN THE FLASHER** French
1991. (7") **REQUIEM POUR UN CON (remix 91)** French

—— sadly, SERGE was to die (2nd March, 1991) of heart complications

– compilations, etc. –

1988. (cd) *Philips; (812 877-2)* **1958 – 25 ANS – 1983**
Oct 96. (cd) *Philips; (<522 629-2>)* **DU JAZZ DANS LE RAVIN**
– Angoisse / Du jazz dans le ravin / Requiem pour un twisteur / Chez les ye-ye / Black march / Black trombone / Ce mortel ennui / Generique / Coco and Co / Intoxicated man / Elaeudania tetia / Le talkie-walkie / Some small chance / Quend tu t'y mets / La fille au rasor / Quand mon 6.35 me fait les yeux doux / Fugue / Machins choses / Negative blues / Wake me at five.
Oct 96. (cd) *Philips; (<528 949-2>)* **COULEUR CAFE** (the 1964 albums) Feb97
Feb 97. (cd) *Philips; <528 951-2>* **COMIC STRIP** (1966-1969)
Apr 98. (10xcd-box) *Polygram; <532 130-2>* **DE GAINSBOURG A GAINSBARRE**
– (LE POINCONNEUR DES LILAS; collection of first 2 albums / LA JAVANAISE; collection of second 2 albums / COULEUR CAFE; collection of 1964 albums / ANNA; collection of 1967 lp and BALLADE DE JOHNNY-JANE soundtrack / INITIALES B.B.; collection of 1968 album and BRIGITTE BARDOT duets / JE T'AIME MOI NON PLUS; collection of the JANE BIRKIN duets / JE SUIS VENU TE DIRE QUE JE M'EN VAIS; collection of 2 singles, the albums VU DE L'EXTERIEUR and ROCK AROUND THE BUNKER / L'HOMME A TETE DE CHOU; collection of the album and a 70's singles compilation / AUX ARMES ET CAETERA; collection of the album and MAUVAISES NOUVELLES DES ETOILES / LOVE ON THE BEAT; collection of the album and YOU'RE UNDER ARREST).
Dec 01. (cd) *Universal; (<E 522242-2>)* **DE GAINSBOURG A GAINSBARRE – THE BEST OF . . .**
– Le poinconneur des lilas / Le sucettes / La javanaise / Chez les ye-ye / Couleur cafe / New York U.S.A. / Je t'aime . . . moi non plus / Elisa / Ballade de Melody Nelson / Je suis venu te dire que je m'en vais / L'ami caouette / Sea, sex and sun / Sorry angel / Aux enfants de la chance.
Apr 98. (cd) *Polygram; <830 599-2>* **LE PALACE 80 (live)**
Aug 98. (cd) *Mercury; <558 842-2>* **CLASSE X**
– Je t'aime . . . moi non plus / Sucettes / Sex shop / Decadanse / Raccrochez c'est une horreur / Sea, sex and sun / Je pense queue / Good bye Emmanuelle / Vu de l'exterieur / Chez max coiffeur pour hommes / Panpan cucul / Des vents des pets des poums / Variations sur Marilou / Lola rastaquouere / Eau et gaz a tous le etages / Mickey Maousse / Eugenie Sokolov / Love on the beat / No comment / Suck baby suck.
Jan 03. (cd) *Universal; (514065-2)* **MASTER SERIES 2003**
Feb 03. (cd/d-lp) *Mercury; (<063230-2/-1>)* **INITIALS S.G.**
– Le poinconneur des lilas / Intoxicated man / La javanaise / Chez les ye-ye / Couleur cafe / Qui est in qui est out / Docteur Jekyll et Monssieur Hyde / Bonnie and Clyde (with BRIGITTE BARDOT) / Ford Mustang / Initials BB / Requiem pour un c . . . / Je t'aime moi non plus (with JANE BIRKIN) / L'anamour / 69 Annee erotique (with JANE BIRKIN) / Sous le soleil exactement / Ballade de melody Nelson / La decadanse (with JANE BIRKIN) / Je suis venu te dire que je m'en vais / L'homme a tete de chou / Marilou sous la neige / Sea sex and sun / Aux armes et caetera / Dieu fumeur de Havanes (with CATHERINE DENEUVE).

Rory GALLAGHER

Born: 2 Mar'49, Ballyshannon, Donegal, Ireland. After playing in various school bands in Cork, RORY formed The FONTANA SHOWBAND, who subsequently became The IMPACT. By 1965, they'd secured residencies in Hamburg, mostly playing CHUCK BERRY songs to post-BEATLES audiences. A year later, just as the British blues revival was gathering steam, he formed TASTE with NORMAN DAMERY and ERIC KITTERINGHAM, although the latter two were eventually replaced by CHARLIE McCRACKEN and JOHN WILSON. After an eponymous debut album failed to break through, TASTE hit the UK Top 20 in 1970 with the follow-up set, 'ON THE BOARDS'. The album established GALLAGHER as Ireland's ambassador of the blues guitar, setting the stage for his forthcoming solo career. A self-titled debut appeared in 1971, the record selling enough initial copies to give it a Top 40 placing. Worshipping at the altar of blues KING-s; B.B., FREDDIE and ALBERT that is, GALLAGHER was revered by loyal fans for his musical integrity and down-to-earth approach (described as the working man's guitarist, due to his unconformist attire – i.e. lumberjack shirt, jeans and ruffled hair – GALLAGHER could also drink many a rock star under the table, eventually into the grave). After another blistering studio set in 1971, 'DEUCE', he scored a massive UK Top 10 with the concert album, 'LIVE IN EUROPE' (1972). Recorded at the peak of GALLAGHER's powers,

'BLUEPRINT' (1972) and 'TATTOO' (1973) stand among the Irishman's most overlooked albums, although the former nearly hit the UK Top 10. To coincide with the projected release of an in-concert rockumentary, GALLAGHER released yet another live set, the electrifying double set, 'IRISH TOUR '74'. Moving to 'Chrysalis' records soon after, GALLAGHER's form slumped slightly just as the new, leaner breed of guitar acts were up and coming, his commercial appeal subsiding under this pressure with each successive release. Nevertheless he continued to record some worthwhile material and perform live for a hardcore following, persevering with the rock industry well into the 90's. Death was the only thing that could prise GALLAGHER away from his guitar, the Irishman passing away on the 14th June '95 after suffering complications with a liver transplant. • **Covers:** SUGAR MAMA + DON'T START ME TALKING (Sonny Boy Williamson) / I'M MOVING ON (Hank Snow) / I TAKE WHAT I WANT (Hayes-Porter-Hedges) / ALL AROUND MAN (Davenport) / OUT ON THE WESTERN PLAINS (Leadbelly) / RIDE ON RED, RIDE ON (Levy-Glover-Reid) / I WONDER WHO (. . . Boyle) / AS THE CROW FLIES (Josh White) / JUST A LITTLE BIT (Dexter Gordon) / MESSING WITH THE KID (Julie London) / PISTOL SLAPPER BLUES (. . . Allen) / etc. • **Trivia:** VINCENT CRANE of ATOMIC ROOSTER guested on RORY's debut lp in '71. GALLAGHER also sessioned on albums by MUDDY WATERS (London Sessions) / JERRY LEE LEWIS (London Sessions) / LONNIE DONEGAN (Putting On The Style) / etc.

Album rating: Taste: TASTE (*6) / ON THE BOARDS (*7) / LIVE TASTE (*4) / LIVE AT THE ISLE OF WIGHT exploitation (*4) / Rory Gallagher: RORY GALLAGHER (*6) / DEUCE (*5) / LIVE IN EUROPE (*6) / BLUEPRINT (*7) / TATTOO (*7) / IRISH TOUR '74 (*8) / SINNER . . . AND SAINT early stuff (*5) / AGAINST THE GRAIN (*5) / THE STORY SO FAR compilation (*6) / CALLING CARD (*7) / PHOTO FINISH (*5) / TOP PRIORITY (*5) / STAGE STRUCK (*5) / JINX (*5) / DEFENDER (*4) / THE BEST OF RORY GALLAGHER & TASTE compilation (*6) / EDGED IN BLUE (*7)

TASTE

RORY GALLAGHER – vocals, guitar / **CHARLIE McCRACKEN** (b.26 Jun'48) – bass repl. ERIC KITTERINGHAM / **JOHN WILSON** (b. 3 Dec'47) – drums (ex-THEM) repl. NORMAN DAMERY

Major Minor not iss.

Apr 68. (7") *(MM 560)* **BLISTER ON THE MOON. / BORN ON THE WRONG SIDE OF TIME** [ ] [–]
(re-iss. Jul70; MM 718)

Polydor Atco

Mar 69. (7") *(56313)* **BORN ON THE WRONG SIDE OF TIME. / SAME OLD STORY** [ ] [–]

Apr 69. (lp) *(583 042)* **TASTE** [ ] [ ]
– Blister on the moon / Leaving blues / Sugar mama / Hail / Born on the wrong side of time / Dual carriageway pain / Same old story / Catfish / I'm moving on. *(re-iss. 1977; 2384 076) (cd-iss. Aug92; 841 600-2)*

Jan 70. (lp) *(583 083)* **ON THE BOARDS** [18] [ ]
– What's going on / Railway and gun / It's happened before, it'll happen again / If the day was any longer / Morning sun / Eat my words / On the boards / If I don't sing I'll cry / See here / I'll remember. *(cd-iss. Apr94; 841 599-2)*

Feb 71. (lp) *(2310 082)* **LIVE TASTE (live)** [ ] [–]
– Sugar mama / Gamblin' blues / Feel so good (part 1) / Feel so good (part 2) / Catfish / Same old story.

— GALLAGHER went solo. The other two formed STUD. McCRACKEN also joined SPENCER DAVIS GROUP

RORY GALLAGHER

solo – vocals, guitar with **GERRY MacAVOY** – bass (ex-DEEP JOY) / **WILGAR CAMPBELL** – drums (ex-METHOD)

Polydor Atlantic

May 71. (lp) *(2383 044) <33368>* **RORY GALLAGHER** [32] [ ]
– Laundromat / Just the smile / I fall apart / Wave myself goodbye / Hands up / Sinner boy / For the last time / It's you / I'm not surprised / Can't believe it's true. *(re-iss. 1979 on 'Chrysalis' lp/c; CHR/ZCHR 1258) (cd-iss. Sep98 on 'Capo'; CAPO 101)*

Jun 71. (7"m) *(2814 004)* **IT'S YOU. / JUST THE SMILE / SINNER BOY** [ ] [ ]

Nov 71. (lp) *(2383 076) <7004>* **DEUCE** [39] [ ]
– Used to be / I'm not awake yet / Don't know where I'm going / Maybe I will / Whole lot of people / In your town / Should've learn't my lesson / There's a light / Out of my mind / Crest of a wave. *(re-iss. 1979 on 'Chrysalis' lp/c; CHR/ZCHR 1254) (cd-iss. Sep98 on 'Capo'; CAPO 102)*

Polydor Polydor

May 72. (lp) *(2383 112) <5513>* **LIVE! IN EUROPE (live)** [9] [ ]
– Messin' with the kid / Laundromat / I could've had religion / Pistol slapper blues / Going to my home town / In your town / Bullfrog blues. *(re-iss. 1979 on 'Chrysalis' lp/c; CHR/ZCHR 1257) (cd-iss. Mar95 on 'Castle'; CLACD 406) (cd re-iss. Feb99 on 'Capo'; CAPO 103)*

— **ROD DE'ATH** – drums (ex-KILLING FLOOR) repl. CAMPBELL / added **LOU MARTIN** – keyboards, mandolin (ex-KILLING FLOOR)

Feb 73. (lp) *(2383 189) <5522>* **BLUEPRINT** [12] [ ]
– Walk on hot coals / Daughter of the Everglades / Banker's blues / Hands off / Race the breeze / The seventh son of a seventh son / Unmilitary two-step / If I had a reason. *(re-iss. 1979 on 'Chrysalis' lp/c; CHR/ZCHR 1253) (cd-iss. Feb94 on 'Castle; CLACD 316) (cd re-iss. Feb00 on 'Capo'; CAPO 104)*

Aug 73. (lp) *(2383 230) <5539>* **TATTOO** [32] [ ]
– Tattoo'd lady / Cradle rock / 20:20 vision / They don't make them like you anymore / Livin' like a trucker / Sleep on a clothes-line / Who's that coming / A million miles away / Admit it. *(re-iss. 1979 on 'Chrysalis' lp/c; CHR/ZCHR 1259) (cd-iss. Jan94 on 'Castle'; CLACD 315) (cd re-iss. Feb00 on 'Capo'; CAPO 105)*

Jul 74. (d-lp) *(2659 031) <9501>* **IRISH TOUR '74 (live)** [36] [ ]
– Cradle rock / I wonder who (who's gonna be your sweet man) / Tattoo'd lady / Too much alcohol / As the crow flies / A million miles away / Walk on hot coals / Who's that coming / Back on my (stompin' ground) / Just a little bit. *(re-iss. 1979 on 'Chrysalis' lp/c; CTY/ZCTY 1256) (re-iss. May88 on 'Demon' d-lp)(d-c/d-cd; DFIEND 120)(FIEND CASS/CD 120) (cd re-iss. Sep98 on 'Capo'; CAPO 106)*

Chrysalis Chrysalis

Oct 75. (lp/c) *(<CHR/ZCHR 1098>)* **AGAINST THE GRAIN** [ ] [ ]
– Let me in / Cross me off your list / Ain't too good / Souped-up Ford / Bought and sold / I take what I want / Lost at sea / All around man / Out on the western plain / At the bottom. *(re-iss. May91 on 'Castle' cd/c/lp; CLA CD/MC/LP 223) (cd re-iss. Feb99 on 'Capo'; CAPO 107)*

Nov 75. (7") *(CDV 102)* **SOUPED-UP FORD. / I TAKE WHAT I WANT** [ ] [–]

Oct 76. (lp/c) *(<CHR/ZCHR 1124>)* **CALLING CARD** [32] [ ]
– Do you read me / Country mile / Moonchild / Calling card / I'll admit you're gone / Secret agent / Jack-knife beat / Edged in blue / Barley and grape rag. *(re-iss. Apr91 on 'Essential' cd/c/lp; ESS CD/MC/LP 143) (re-iss. cd Mar94 on 'Castle'; CLACD 352) (cd re-iss. Sep98 on 'Capo'; CAPO 108)*

— **TED McKENNA** – drums (ex-SENSATIONAL ALEX HARVEY BAND) repl.DE'ATH and MARTIN (to RAMROD)

Oct 76. (lp/c) *(<CHR/ZCHR 1170>)* **PHOTO FINISH** [ ] [ ]
– Shin kicker / Brute force and ignorance / Cruise on out / Cloak and dagger / Overnight bag / Shadow play / The Mississippi sheiks / The last of the indepenents / Fuel to the fire. *(cd-iss. Sep98 on 'Capo'; CAPO 109)*

Jan 79. (7"m) *(CHS 2281)* **SHADOW PLAY. / SOUPED UP FORD / BRUTE FORCE AND IGNORANCE** [ ] [–]
(10"+=) *(CXP 2281)* – Moonchild

Aug 79. (7",7"colrd) *(CHS 2364)* **PHILBY. / HELLCAT / COUNTRY MILE** [ ] [ ]

Sep 79. (lp/c) *(<CHR/ZCHR 1235>)* **TOP PRIORITY** [56] [ ]
– Follow me / Philby / Wayward child / Keychain / At the depot / Bad penny / Just hit town / Off the handle / Public enemy No.1. *(re-iss. May88 on 'Demon' lp/c/cd; FIEND/+CASS/CD 123) (cd re-iss. Feb99 on 'Capo'; CAPO 110)*

Aug 80. (7",7"colrd) *(CHS 2453)* **WAYWARD CHILD (live). / KEYCHAIN** [ ] [–]

Sep 80. (lp/c) *(<CHR/ZCHR 1280>)* **STAGE STRUCK (live)** [40] [ ]
– Shin kicker / Wayward child / Brute force and ignorance / Moonchild / Follow me / Bought and sold / The last of the independents / Shadow play. *(cd-iss. Mar95 on 'Castle'; CLACD 407) (cd re-iss. Feb00 on 'Capo'; CAPO 111)*

Dec 80. (7") *(CHS 2466)* **HELLCAT. / NOTHIN' BUT THE DEVIL** [ ] [ ]

— (May'81) **GALLAGHER** with **McAVOY** brought in **BRENDAN O'NEILL** – drums; repl. McKENNA who joined GREG LAKE BAND then MSG

Chrysalis / Mercury

Apr 82. (lp/c) *(CHR/ZCHR 1359)* <SRMI 4051> **JINX** [68] [ ]
– Signals / The Devil made me do it / Double vision / Easy come, easy go / Big guns / Jinxed / Bourbon / Ride on Red, ride on / Loose talk. *(re-iss. May88 on 'Demon' lp/c/cd; FIEND/+CASS/CD 126) (cd re-iss. Feb00 on 'Capo'; CAPO 112)*

Jun 82. (7") *(CHS 2612)* **BIG GUNS. / THE DEVIL MADE ME DO IT** [ ] [ ]

1983. (10"ep) *(CXP 2281)* **SHADOW PLAY / BRUTE FORCE AND IGNORANCE. / MOONCHILD / SOUPED UP FORD** [ ] [–]

Capo-Demon / Intercord

Jul 87. (lp)(c/cd) *(XFIEND 98)(FIEND CASS/CD 98)* **DEFENDER** [ ] [–]
– Kickback city / Loanshark blues / Continental op / I ain't no saint / Failsafe day / Road to Hell / Doing time / Smear campaign / Don't start me talkin' / Seven days. *(c+=/cd+=) (free-7")* – SEEMS TO ME. / NO PEACE FOR THE WICKED *(cd-iss. Feb99 on 'Capo'+=; CAPO 113)* – Seems to me / No peace for the wicked.

— guests **MARK FELTHAM** – harmonica / **LOU MARTIN** – piano / **JOHN EARL** – saxophones / **GERAINT WATKINS** – accordion / **JOHN COOKE** – keyboards / **RAY BEAVIS** – tenor sax / **DICK HANSON** – trumpet

Capo / Intercord

Jun 90. (cd/c/lp) *(CAPO CD/MC/LP 14)* **FRESH EVIDENCE** [ ] [ ]
– 'Kid' gloves / The king of Zydeco (to: Clifton Chenier) / Middle name / Alexis / Empire state express / Ghost blues / Heaven's gate / The loop / Walkin' wounded / Slumming angel. *(re-iss. cd Oct92 on 'Essential'; ESSCD 155) (cd re-iss. Sep98 on 'Capo'; CAPO 114)*

— on the 14th June 1995, RORY died after complications from a liver transplant operation

– compilations etc. –

1974. (c) *Emerald-Gem; (GES 1110) / Springboard; <SPB 4056>* **IN THE BEGINNING (VOCAL AND GUITAR)** (rec.'67) <US-title 'TAKE IT EASY BABY'> [ ] 1976 [ ]

Aug 72. (lp; by TASTE) *Polydor; (2383 120)* **TASTE – LIVE AT THE ISLE OF WIGHT (live)** [41] [–]
(cd-iss. Apr94; 841 601-2)

Feb 75. (lp) *Polydor; (2383 315) <6510>* **SINNER . . . AND SAINT** (1971 material) [ ] [ ]

Oct 82. (7"ep/12"ep) *Polydor; (POSP/+X 609)* **BLISTER ON THE MOON / SUGAR MAMA. / CATFISH / ON THE BOARDS** [ ] [–]

Feb 76. (lp) *Polydor; (2383 376) <6519>* **THE STORY SO FAR** [ ] [ ]

1977. (lp) *Polydor: (2384 079)* **LIVE** [ ] [–]

May 80. (lp) *Hallmark; (HSC 3041)* **RORY GALLAGHER** [ ] [–]

Feb 88. (cd) *Razor; (MACH 10D)* **THE BEST OF RORY GALLAGHER & TASTE** [ ] [–]
– Blister on the moon / Hail / Born on the wrong side of time / Dual carriageway pain / Same old story / On the boards / See here / I'll remember / Sugar mama (live) / Sinner boy (live) / I feel so good (live) / Catfish / I'm movin' on / What's going on / Ralway and gun / Morning Sun / Eat my words.

May 89. (d-lp/d-c/d-cd) *That's Original; (TFO LP/MC/CD 20)* **LIVE! IN EUROPE / STAGE STRUCK** [ ] [–]

Jul 89. (d-lp/d-c/d-cd) *That's Original; (TFO LP/MC/CD 21)* **TATTOO / BLUEPRINT** [ ] [–]

May 91. (4xcd-box) *Demon; (RORY G1)* **RORY GALLAGHER** [ ] [–]
– (IRISH TOUR '74 / DEFENDER / TOP PRIORITY / JINX)

Jun 92. (lp/c/cd) *Demon; (FIEND/+C/CD 719)* **EDGED IN BLUE** [ ] [–]

Nov 92. (3xcd-box) *Essential; (ESBCD 187)* **G-MEN: BOOTLEG SERIES VOLUME ONE** [ ] [–]

Nov 98. (cd) *I.R.S.; (35783)* **A BLUE DAY FOR THE BLUES** [ ] [–]

Nov 98. (cd) *Camden; (74321 62797-2)* **ETCHED IN BLUE** [ ] [–]

Aug 99. (d-cd) *Capo; (CAPO 701)* **THE BBC SESSIONS** [ ] [ ]

Oct 01. (4xcd-box) *Capo; (CAPO 702)* **LET'S GO TO WORK** [ ] [–]

Mar 03. (cd) *Capo; (82876 50387-2) / Buddha; <99787>* **WHEELS WITHIN WHEELS** [ ] [ ]

GANG OF FOUR

Formed: Leeds, England . . . 1977 by journalist ANDY GILL, JON KING, DAVE ALLEN and HUGO BURNHAM. After releasing a debut EP, 'DAMAGED GOODS' for Bob Last's 'Fast' label, they signed to 'E.M.I.' in late '78. Their debut 45 for the label, 'AT HOME HE'S A TOURIST', hit the Top 60 and should have reached a lot higher but for a BBC ban due to the use of the word 'Rubbers' (i.e. contraceptives) in the lyrics. In Autumn '79, their debut album 'ENTERTAINMENT' hit the Top 50, a startling showcase for the band's adrenaline fuelled post-punk sound, GILL's rifling staccato guitar slicing through the twisted funk rhythms. Lyrically, they were also pretty incendiary, although their radical political agenda rarely descended into heavy handed preaching or took precedence over the music. It would be another couple of years before they released a follow-up, 'SOLID GOLD' (1981) mixing down GILL's patented feedback assault and coming in for some critical stick. Although he played on the landmark 'TO HELL WITH POVERTY' single (released in summer '81), ALLEN subsequently left the band to form his own outfit, SHRIEKBACK, his replacement being SARA LEE. Thereafter, the band favoured a more conventional approach, 'SONGS OF THE FREE' (1982) notable for its barbed comments on the Falklands war, 'CALL ME UP' and 'I LOVE A MAN IN UNIFORM (another single blacklisted by Radio 1). Following the departure of BURNHAM, they moved further towards a slick funk/Philly sound with 'HARD' (1983), employing a cast of studio professionals and female backing singers. With diminishing artistic and commercial returns, the band finally split in mid-'84 following the release of live set, 'AT THE PALACE' (1984). While GILL subsequently relocated to America and concentrated on production work, renewed interest in the band towards the end of the decade saw a GANG OF FOUR reformation, although GILL and KING were the only original members involved in the project. The result was a one-off album for 'Polydor', 'MALL' (1991), the label soon losing interest after it failed to sell; there was more grief for them the following year when, despite their best efforts in supplying the soundtrack for the Labour Party's 1992 campaign, the Tories romped home yet again. The duo initiated yet another reincarnation of the band in 1995 for the 'SHRINKWRAPPED' set, although sales were again disappointing. • **Songwriters:** Penned by KING / ALLEN / GILL, until ALLEN departed. Covered SOUL REBEL (Bob Marley).

Album rating: ENTERTAINMENT (*7) / SOLID GOLD (*6) / SONGS OF THE FREE (*6) / HARD (*5) / AT THE PALACE (*3) / A BRIEF HISTORY OF THE 20TH CENTURY compilation (*8) / MALL (*4) / SHRINKWRAPPED (*5)

JON KING (b. 8 Jun'55, London) – vocals, melodica / **ANDY GILL** (b. 1 Jan'56, Manchester) – guitar / **DAVE ALLEN** (b.23 Dec'55, Cumbria) – bass / **HUGO BURNHAM** (b.25 Mar'56, London) – drums

Fast / not iss.

Oct 78. (7"m) *(FAST 5)* **DAMAGED GOODS. / LOVE LIKE ANTHRAX / ARMALITE RIFLE** [ ] [–]

E.M.I. / Warners

Mar 79. (7") *(EMI 2956)* **AT HOME HE'S A TOURIST. / IT'S HER FACTORY** [58] [–]

Sep 79. (lp/c) *(EMC/TC-EMC 3313)* <BSK 3446> **ENTERTAINMENT** [45] [ ]
– Ether / Natural's not in it / Not great men / Damaged goods / Return the gift / Guns before butter / I found that essence rare / Glass / Contract / At home he's a tourist / 5-45 / Anthrax. *(re-iss. 1985 lp/c; ATAK/TC-ATAK 41) (cd-iss. Feb95; CZ 541) <cd-iss. 1995 on 'Infinite Zero'+=; 14502-2>* – YELLOW EP

Regal Zono. / not iss.

Apr 80. (7") *(Z 1)* **OUTSIDE THE TRAINS DON'T RUN ON TIME. / HE'D SEND IN THE ARMY** [ ] [–]

Regal Zonophone — Warners

Oct 80. (12"ep) *<MINI 3494>* **OUTSIDE THE TRAINS DON'T RUN ON TIME / HE'D SEND IN THE ARMY. / IT'S HER FACTORY / ARMALITE RIFLE** [–] [ ]
Mar 81. (7"/12") *(EMI/12EMI 5146)* **WHAT WE ALL WANT. / HISTORY'S BUNK** [ ] [–]
Mar 81. (lp/c) *(EMC/TC-EMC 3364) <BSK 3565>* **SOLID GOLD** [52] [ ]
– Paralysed / What we all want / If I could keep it for myself / Outside the trains don't run on time / Why theory? / Cheeseburger / The republic / In the ditch / A hole in the wallet / He'd send in the army.
May 81. (7") *(EMI 5177)* **CHEESEBURGER. / PARALYSED** [ ] [–]

—— (tour) **BUSTA CHERRY JONES** – bass (ex-SHARKS) repl. ALLEN (to SHRIEKBACK)

Jul 81. (7"/12") *(EMI/12EMI 5193)* **TO HELL WITH POVERTY. / CAPITAL (IT FAILS US NOW)** [ ] [–]
Feb 82. (m-lp) *<MINI 3646>* **ANOTHER DAY / ANOTHER DOLLAR** [–] [ ]
– To hell with poverty / What we all want / Cheeseburger / Capital (it fails us now) / History's bunk!

—— **SARA LEE** – bass, vocals (ex-JANE AIRE, ex-ROBERT FRIPP) repl. BUSTA

Apr 82. (7"/12") *(EMI/12EMI 5299)* **I LOVE A MAN IN A UNIFORM. / WORLD AT FAULT** [65] [–]
May 82. (lp/c) *(EMC/TCEMC 3412) <23683>* **SONGS OF THE FREE** [61] [ ]
– Call me up / I love a man in a uniform / Muscle for brains / It is not enough / Life, it's a shame / I will be a good boy / History of the world / We live as we dream, alone / Of the instant.
Jun 82. (7") *<29921>* **I LOVE A MAN IN A UNIFORM. / I WILL A GOOD BOY** [–] [ ]
(12"+=) *<29907>* – ('A'extended).
Jul 82. (7") *(EMI 5320)* **CALL ME UP. / I WILL BE A GOOD BOY** [ ] [–]

—— (**KING, GILL + BURNHAM** were joined by) **JON ASTROP / CHUCK KIRKPATRICK + JOHN SOMBATERO** – bass repl. SARA / added backing singers **ALFA ANDERSON** and **BRENDA WHITE**

Aug 83. (7"/12") *(EMI/12EMI 5418)* **IS IT LOVE. / MAN WITH A GOOD CAR** [ ] [–]
Sep 83. (lp/c) *(EMC 165219-1/-4) <23936>* **HARD** [ ] [ ]
– Is it love / I fled / Silver lining / Woman town / A man with a good car / It don't matter / Arabic / A piece of my heart / Independence.
Sep 83. (7") *<29449>* **IS IT LOVE. / ARABIC** [–] [ ]
Nov 83. (7") *(EMI 5440)* **SILVER LINING. / INDEPENDENCE** [ ] [–]

—— **STEVE GOULDING** – drums (ex-RUMOUR) repl. BURNHAM who joined ILLUSTRATED MAN

Mercury — not iss.

Oct 84. (12"m) *(GANG 12)* **I WILL BE A GOOD BOY (live). / IS IT LOVE (live) / CALL ME UP (live)** [ ] [–]
Nov 84. (lp/c) *(MERL/+C 51)* **AT THE PALACE (live)** [ ] [–]
– We live as we dream, alone / History is not made by great men / Silver lining / The history of the world / I love a man in uniform / Paralysed / Is it love / Damaged goods / At home he's a tourist / To hell with poverty. *(c+=)* – I will be a good boy / Call me up.

—— (split mid-84) **JON** later formed KING BUTCHER

ANDY GILL

—— finally went solo

Survival — not iss.

Aug 87. (12") *(SUR12 039)* **DISPOSSESSION. / GENUINE** [ ] [–]

GANG OF FOUR

—— re-formed 1990 w/ **JON KING + ALAN GILL** added **HIROMI + STAN LOUBIERES**

Scarlett — not iss.

Jun 90. (7") *(SCART 4)* **MONEY TALKS (The Money mix). / USE THE COLOUR FROM THE TUBE** [ ] [–]
(12") *(SCART 4T)* – ('A'side) / ('A'dub version).
(cd-s) *(SCART 4CD)* – ('A'extended) / (above 3 tracks).

Polydor — Polydor

May 91. (cd/c/lp) *<849 124-2/-4/-1>* **MALL** [–] [ ]
– Cadillac / Motel / Satellite / F.M.U.S.A. / Don't fix what ain't broke / Impossible / Money talks / Soul rebel / Hiromi & Stan talk / Colour from the tube / Hey yeah / Everybody wants to come / World falls apart.
Aug 91. (12") *(P2 152DJ)* **CADILLAC. / MOTEL / FAVOURITES** [ ] [–]

—— disbanded again when their record label dropped them. GILL then supplied the soundtrack in 1992 for the Labour Party's unsuccessful general election campaign. Re-formed again in 1994.

—— **GILL + KING + STEVE MONTI** (ex-CURVE) + **PHIL BUTCHER** (ex-IGGY POP)

When! — not iss.

Aug 95. (7"/c-s) *(WEN 7/M 1002)* **TATTOO. / BANNED WORDS / COP GOES HOME** [ ] [–]
(cd-s+=) *(WENX 1002)* – ('A'-Quiet guy mix).
Sep 95. (cd/c) *(WEN CD/MC 003)* **SHRINKWRAPPED** [ ] [–]
– Tattoo / Sleepwalker / I parade myself / Unburden / Better him than me / Something 99 / Showtime, valentine / Unburden, unbound / The dark side / I absolve you / Shrinkwrapped. *(cd re-iss. Apr01 on 'Castle'; CMRCD 197)*

– compilations etc. –

Oct 86. (12"ep) *Strange Fruit; (SFPS 008)* **THE PEEL SESSIONS** (16.1.89) [ ] [–]
– I found that essence rare / Return the gift / 5-45 / At home he's a tourist. *(c-ep.iss.Jun87; SFPSC 008)*
May 90. (lp/c/cd) *Strange Fruit; (SFR LP/C/CD 107) / Dutch East India; <8101>* **THE PEEL SESSIONS (COMPLETE SESSIONS 1979-81)** [ ] [ ]
Mar 90. (cd)(c/lp) *Greenlight – Capitol; (CDP 795051-2)(TC+/GO 2028)* **YOU CATCH UP WITH HISTORY (1978-1983)** [ ] [–]
Nov 90. (cd/c/lp) *E.M.I.; (CD/TC+/EMC 3583) / Warners: <26448>* **A BRIEF HISTORY OF THE 20th CENTURY** [ ] Dec90 [ ]
– At home he's a tourist / Damaged goods / Natural's not in it / Not great men / Anthrax / Return the gift / It's her factory / What we all want (live) / Paralysed / A hole in the wallet / Cheeseburger / To hell with poverty / Capital (it fails us now) / Call me up / I will be a good boy / History of the world / I love a man in a uniform / Is it love / Woman town / We live as we dream, alone. (c+cd.+=) – (4 tracks)
Jan 91. (7"ep/c-ep/12"ep/cd-ep) *E.M.I.; (EMS/TCEM/12EM/CDEM 172)* **TO HELL WITH POVERTY (the loaded edit) / ('A'-original version). / CHEESEBURGER (live) / CALL ME UP** [ ] [–]
Oct 95. (cd) *Warners; <43035>* **SOLID GOLD / ANOTHER DAY – ANOTHER DOLLAR** [–] [ ]
Nov 98. (d-cd) *Rhino; <RCD 75479>* **100 FLOWERS BLOOM** (rare tracks) [–] [ ]
Jan 03. (cd) *Wounded Bird; (WOU 3936)* **HARD / SOLID GOLD** [ ] [–]

GANG STARR

Formed: Brooklyn, New York, USA . . . 1988. One part organic turntable negotiator DJ PREMIER aka CHRIS MARTIN, one part worthy wordsmith GURU (Gifted Unlimited Rhymes Universal) aka KEITH ELAM, GANG STARR shake up a potent cocktail of Afro-centric hip hop and jazz far removed from the gangsta rap cliches their name might suggest. Although ELAM had initiated the GANG STARR project some years before in his hometown of Boston, the blue juice only really started flowing after the rapper hooked up with PREMIER having earlier heard his demo tape. Signed to local label 'Wild Pitch', the duo's debut album, 'NO MORE MR. NICE GUY' appeared in 1989, film director Spike Lee sufficiently impressed to offer GANG STARR the opportunity of recording with saxophonist BRANFORD MARSALIS. The result was 'JAZZ THING', a funky, free flowing history lesson on the finer points of the genre used in LEE's seminal 'Mo' Better Blues'. Ensuing interest helped secure a major label deal (with 'Chrysalis' off-shoot, 'Cooltempo') and 'STEP IN THE ARENA' (1991) announced the arrival of a vibrant figurehead in the emerging rap/jazz fusion movement. One of the few acts to favour vinyl and live mixing on stage, GANG STARR's experimental sound – personified by the moog-sampling 'JUST TO GET A REP' – gripped the imagination of the hip hop community and DJ PREMIER soon became a producer in demand, going on to work with the likes of JERU THE DAMAJA and NAS. GURU, in turn, was developing into one of the most articulate and socially aware commentators on the scene, initiating the acclaimed 'JAZZMATAZZ' project after GANG STARR's third album, 'DAILY OPERATION' (1992). Having already collaborated with The BRAND NEW HEAVIES, GURU rounded up an impressive posse of respected musicians/vocalists including MARSALIS, DONALD BYRD, COURTNEY PINE, SHARA NELSON and DC LEE, an achievement in itself. Conceived with GURU's pro-positive vision of black music, 'JAZZMATAZZ VOLUME 1' (1993) proved to be much more than just another superstar jam session, more a stylish, sophisticated marriage of street and studio and a perfect companion piece to US 3's 'Blue Note' homage, 'Hand On The Torch'. Blessed with the inimitable guitar groove of RONNY JORDAN, 'NO TIME TO PLAY' was a definite highlight and one of summer 93's best singles. Back on GANG STARR duty, GURU and PREMIER came up with their most focused album to date, 'HARD TO EARN' (1994), both obviously having honed their respective disciplines in the interim. While a second instalment of 'JAZZMATAZZ VOLUME 2: THE NEW REALITY' (1995) didn't meet with the same dizzy heights as its predecessor, GURU remains something of an erm . . . guru for the hip hop scene, a willing spokesman on the ever controversial issues affecting the genre. It was to be another four years before the return of GANG STARR proper, 1998's hugely successful 'MOMENT OF TRUTH' breaking the duo big time in the States. The new decade found GURU instigating the third instalment of his JAZZMATAZZ project with 'STREETSOUL' (2000). As its title suggested, the record was more centered around nu-soul than jazz-rap, reflecting the mood of the times with a guest list that featured the likes of ERYKAH BADU, KELIS and MACY GRAY. Hardly surprising then that it didn't possess that exciting, innovative spark of the earlier records, especially bearing in mind the fact that hip hop and soul have been cross-pollinated to death already. 'BALDHEAD SLICK & DA CLICK' arrived the following year, GURU's album was disappointing to say the least, America, even, giving it the bums' rush. Consisting of much of the same repertoire as his previous outings, ELAM replaced his usual finely tuned patter with egotistical nonsense. 2003 saw the release of 'THE OWNERZ', a refreshing antidote to much of the insipid "bling-bling" horseshit clogging up the airwaves. Robust, no nonsense rhyming and well aimed lyrical potshots at deserving targets, complete with DJ PREMIER's much missed turntable maneouvres, made this one of the year's more palatable hip hop albums.

Album rating: STEP IN THE ARENA (*6) / DAILY OPERATION (*6) / HARD TO EARN (*6) / MOMENT OF TRUTH (*6) / FULL CLIP: A DECADE OF GANG STARR compilation (*7) / THE OWNERZ (*7) / Guru: JAZZMATAZZ VOLUME 1 (*7) / JAZZMATAZZ VOLUME 2: THE NEW REALITY (*6) / JAZZMATAZZ STREETSOUL (*5) / BALDHEAD SLICK & DA CLICK (*3)

GURU (b. KEITH ELAM, 18 Jul'66, Boston, Mass.) – rapper / **DJ PREMIER** (b. CHRISTOPHER MARTIN) – turntables, etc

S.B.K. — Wild Pitch

Nov 89. (12"ep) *<(SBK 004)>* **THE MANIFEST EP** [ ] [ ]

Dec 89. (lp/cd) *<98709>* **NO MORE MR NICE GUY** [–] [ ]
– Premier & the Guru / Jazz music / Gotch U / Manifest / Gusto / DJ Premier in deep concentration / Postivity / Manifest / Conscience be free / Cause and effect / 2 steps ahead / No more Mr. Nice guy / Knowledge / Postivity. *(re-iss. Jul99 on 'Wild Pitch'; WPL 2001-2/-1)*

C.B.S. — Columbia

Sep 90. (7") *(356377-7)* **JAZZ THING. / (mix)** [66] [ ]
(12"+=/cd-s+=) *(356377-6/-2)* – (mixes).
(above from the Spike Lee movie, 'Mo Better Blues')

Cooltempo — Chrysalis

Jan 91. (cd)(c/lp) *(CCD 1798)(Z+/CTLP 21)* <21798> **STEP IN THE ARENA** [36] [ ]
– Game plan / Take a rest / What you want this time? / Street ministry / Just to get a rep / Say your prayers / As I read my S-A / Precisely the right rhymes / The meaning of the name / Name tag (Premier & the Guru) / Step in the arena / Form of intellect / Execution of a chump (no more Mr. Nice Guy pt.2) / Who's gonna take the weight? / Beyond comprehension / Check the technique / Lovesick / Here today, gone tomorrow.

Feb 91. (7") *(COOL 230)* **TAKE A REST (remix). / (mix)** [63] [ ]
(12"+=/cd-s+=) *(12/CD COOL 230)* – Just to get a rep / Who's gonna take the weight.

May 91. (7") *(COOL 234)* **LOVESICK. / (mix)** [50] [ ]
(12"+=/cd-s+=) *(12/CD COOL 234)* – (mix).

Apr 92. (7") **TAKE IT PERSONAL. / (mix)** [ ] [ ]
(12"+=/cd-s+=) – (mix).

May 92. (cd)(c/lp) *(CCD 1910)(Z+/CTLP 27)* <21910> **DAILY OPERATION** [ ] [65]
– Intro / The place where we dwell / Flip the script / Ex girl to next girl / Soliloquy of chaos / I'm the man / 92 interlude / Take it personal / 2 deep / 24-7/365 / No shame in my game / Conspiracy / The illest brother / Hardcore composer / B.Y.S. / Much too much (mack a mil) / Take two and pass / Stay tuned (interlude).

Jun 92. (7") *(COOL 256)* **2 DEEP. / TAKE IT PERSONAL** [67] [ ]
(12"+=/cd-s+=) – ('A'mixes).

Cooltempo — Chrysalis

Feb 94. (cd-s) *<58111>* **MASS APPEAL / (versions)** [–] [67]

Feb 94. (cd/c/lp) *(CT CD/TC/LP 38)* <28435> **HARD TO EARN** [29] [25]
– Intro – The first steps / ALONGWAYTOGO / Code of the streets / Brainstorm / Tonz 'O' gunz / The planet / Aiiight chill / Speak ya clout / DWYCK / Words from the nutcracker / Mass appeal / Blowin' up the spot / Suckas need bodyguards / Now you're mine / Mostly the voice / F.A.L.A. / Comin' for the datazz.

Oct 94. (12") *(Y 58265)* **SUCKAS NEED BODYGUARDS. / (mixes)** [ ] [ ]

— during the mid 90's, GURU and PREMIER concentrated more on their own label 'Illkid' and production work noteably for a part-time GANG STARR collaborator, JERU THE DAMAJA on his US Top 40 set, 'The Sun Rises In The East'.

Nov 97. (ltd-12"/cd-s) *(12COOL 330)* <38624> **YOU KNOW MY STEEZ (versions) / SO WASSUP?! (versions)** [ ] [76]

Apr 98. (cd/c/lp) *<(8 45585-2/-4/-1)>* **MOMENT OF TRUTH** [43] [6]
– You know my steez / Robbin hood theory / Work / Royalty / Above the clouds / JFK 2 Lax / Itz a set up / Moment of truth / B.I. vs. friendship / The militia / The rep grows bigga / What I'm here for / She knowz what she wantz / New York strait talk / My advice 2 you / Make 'em pay / The mall / Betrayal / Next time / In memory of . . .

Jul 98. (12"/cd-s) *(12/CD COOL 337)* **YOU KNOW MY STEEZ. / (mixes)** [ ] [–]

Virgin — Virgin

Nov 02. (12") *<VIR 038849>* **SKILLS (mixes) / NATURAL (mixes)** [–] [ ]

Jun 03. (cd/t-lp) *(CDVUS/VUSLP 235)* <80247> **THE OWNERZ** [74] [18]
– Intro (HQ, Goo, Panch) / Put up or shut up (with KRUMBSNATCHA) / Werdz from the ghetto child (with SMILEY) / Sabotage / Rite where U stand (with JADAKISS) / Skills / Deadly habitz / Nice girl, wrong place (with BOY BIG) / Peace of mine / Who got gunz (with FAT JOE & M.O.P.) / Capture (militia, pt.3) (with BIG SHUG & FREDDIE FOXXX) / Playtawin / Riot akt / (hiney) / Same team, no games (with NYG'z & H. STAX) / In this life . . . (with SNOOP DOGG & UNCLE REO) / The ownerz / Zonin' / Eulogy.

Jun 03. (12"/cd-s) *(VUS T/CD 267)* <VIR 38860> **NICE GIRL, WRONG PLACE (mixes) / RIGHT WHERE U STAND (with Jadakiss)** [ ] Apr03 [ ]

– compilations, etc. –

Mar 99. (12") *Wild Pitch; (DRI 2004)* **DWYCK. / (mixes)** [ ] [ ]

Jul 99. (d-cd/q-lp) *Cooltempo; (521189-2/-1) / Noo Trybe;* <47279> **FULL CLIP: A DECADE OF GANG STARR** [47] [33]
– Intro / Full clip / Discipline / Words (manifest mix) / Ex girl to the next girl / I'm the man / Lil dap / Mass appeal / Jazz think / Militia / Freddie

Foxxx / Tonz o' gunz / Royalty / Who's gonna take the weight / You know my steez / Allbove the clouds / Just to get a rep / DWYCK / All 4 the ca$h / Step in the arena / Work / Sililoquy of chaos / Take it personal / Speak ya clout / Lil dap / Gotta get over (taking loot) / 1/2 and 1/2 / The question remains / Code of the streets / So wassup / Now you're mine / Betrayal / BYS / Credit is due / Militia II / You know my steez (mix).

GURU

with **DONALD BYRD, ROY AYERS, LONNIE LISON SMITH, CARLEEN ANDERSON, N'DEA DAVENPORT, RONNY JORDAN, DC LEE, COURTNEY PINE + MC SOLAAR**

Cooltempo Chrysalis

Nov 92. (12") *<24830>* **BIEN ET AL MAL** [–] [ ]
Apr 93. (12") *<24837>* **LOUNGIN'** [–] [ ]
May 93. (cd/c/lp) *(CT CD/TC/LP 34) <21998>* **JAZZMATAZZ VOLUME 1** [ ] [94]
– Introduction / Loungin' / When you're near / Transit ride / No time to play / Down the backstreets / Respectful dedications / Take a look (at yourself) / Trust me / Slicker than most / Le bien, le mal / Sights in the city.
Jul 93. (c-s) *<24849>* **TRUST ME** [–] [ ]
Nov 93. (12",c-s) *<58081>* **NO TIME TO PLAY** [–] [ ]

— now with **CHAKA KHAN, ME'SHELL NDEGEOCELLO, PATRA, DONALD BYRD, MICA PARIS, SHARA NELSON, RAMSEY LEWIS, JAMIROQUAI, RONNY JORDAN, FREDDIE HUBBARD, COURTNEY PINE, DC LEE, IN KAMOZE** etc.

Jul 95. (cd/c/lp) *(CT CD/TC/LP 47) <34290>* **JAZZMATAZZ VOLUME II: THE NEW REALITY** [ ] [71]
– Intro / Lifesaver / Living in this world / Looking through darkness / Watch what you say / Defining purpose / For you / Medicine / Lost souls / Nobody knows / Hip hop as a way of life / Respect the architect / Feel the music / Young ladies / The traveller / Count your blessings / Maintaining focus / Choice of weapons / Something in the past / Revelation.
Jul 95. (12"/cd-s; GURU featuring CHAKA KHAN) *<58438>* **WATCH WHAT YOU SAY** [–] [ ]

Virgin Virgin

Oct 00. (cd/c/d-lp) *(CDVUS/VUSC/VUSLP 178) <50189>* **JAZZMATAZZ STREETSOUL** [74] [32]
– Intro / Keep your worries (street version with ANGIE STONE) / Hustlin' daze (with DONELL JONES) / All I said (with MACY GRAY) / Certified (with BILAL) / Plenty (with ERYKAH BADU) / Lift your fist (with ROOTS) / Guidance (with AMEL LARRIEUX) / Interlude (Brooklyn skit) / Supalove (with KELIS) / No more (with CRAIG DAVID) / Where's my ladies? (with BIG SHUG) / Night vision (with ISAAC HAYES) / Who's there? (with LES NUBIANS) / Mashin' up da world (with JUNIOR REID) / Prodigal son / Timeless (with HERBIE HANCOCK).
Dec 00. (c-s; by GURU & ANGIE STONE) *(VUSC 177)* *<38732>* **KEEP YOUR WORRIES / I WONDER WHY (featuring Bobbi Humphrey & Melodie Davies) / LOUNGIN'** [57] Sep00 [ ]
(cd-s) *(VUSCD 177)* – (first 2 tracks) / ('A'-Sweet P remix).
(12") *(VUST 177)* – ('A'side) / ('A'-Sweet P remix) / ('A'-instrumental) / ('A'-Sweet P instrumental).
Apr 01. (12") *<97509>* **SUPALOVE** [–] [ ]
May 01. (12"/cd-s; by GURU & BILAL / SKAT D / MAC) *(VUS T/CD 201)* **CERTIFIED / CERTIFIED (Mr. Shabz remix). / TRUST ME** [ ] [–]

Landspeed Landspeed

Sep 01. (cd/d-lp) *<(LSR CD/LP 9205)>* **BALDHEAD SLICK & DA CLICK** [ ] [ ]
– Where's our money?! / Back 2 back / Rollin' dolo / No surviving / Underground connections / Niggaz know / In here / The come up / Cry / O.G. talk / Pimp shit / Never ending saga / War tactics / Collectin' props / Revolutionist / No grease / How you gonna be a killa? / Stay outta my face / The anthem.

– compilations, etc. –

Jul 96. (d-cd) *Cooltempo; (CTCD 54)* **JAZZMATAZZ VOLUMES ONE & TWO** [ ] [–]

GARBAGE

Formed: Madison, Wisconsin, USA ... 1994 by BUTCH VIG, DUKE ERIKSON and STEVE MARKER, out of the ashes of FIRE TOWN and SPOONER. BUTCH's latter ham-pop/rock act, had been on the go since early 1978 and released their debut ep 'CRUEL SCHOOL' a year later <Boat; SP 4001>. Another soon followed, 'WHERE YOU GONNA RUN?' <Boat; SP 3001>, before an album, 'EVERY CORNER DANCE' surfaced in '82; <Mountain Railroad; HR 8005>. BUTCH then set up his own studio and produced KILLDOZER, before giving SPOONER another outing with the album 'WILDEST DREAMS' <Boat; SP 1004>. In 1986, their final flop 45, 'MEAN OLD WORLD' <Boat; SP 1018>, made BUTCH form FIRE TOWN, with old buddy STEVE MARKER and co-songwriter DOUG ERIKSON. A few singles, 'CARRY THE TORCH' <7-89242> and 'RAIN ON YOU' <7-89204>, appeared from the 'Atlantic' stable alongside albums 'IN THE HEART OF THE HEART COUNTRY' <Boat; 1013 / re-iss. Atlantic; 81754> & 'THE GOOD LIFE' cd/lp; <781945-2/-1>. In 1989/90, BUTCH re-formed with the original line-up of SPOONER, DUKE ERIKSON, DAVE BENTON, JEFF WALKER and JOEL TAPPERO, to release one-off comeback cd 'THE FUGITIVE DANCE' <Dali-Chameleon; 89026>. He was then to find fame in production work for greats like NIRVANA, SONIC YOUTH, SMASHING PUMPKINS, NINE INCH NAILS and U2, before coming across Edinburgh-born vixen SHIRLEY MANSON fronting the band ANGELFISH on MTV. The new-look GARBAGE contributed the electro-goth of 'VOW' to a 'Volume' various artists compilation and this ended up as their limited edition debut 45 in 1995. By that year's summer, they had signed to Geffen's 'Almo Sounds' (UK 'Mushroom') records, which helped them break into the UK Top 50 with 'SUBHUMAN'. Success finally came with the 'ONLY HAPPY WHEN IT RAINS' single, a grungey, more tuneful affair that retained the goth overtones, MANSON weaving her deep throat vocals around the melody like a spider's web. She was an obvious focal point for the group; on their Top Of The Pops debut the singer made like a brooding, 90's incarnation of CHRISSIE HYNDE while the rest of the band remained comfortably anonymous in uniform black. The eponymous debut album, released later that year, was a mixed bag of styles that worked fairly effectively. Subsequent single, 'QUEER', kind of summed up the GARBAGE ethos, a deceptively poppy number featuring a MANSON vocal positively dripping with loathing, self or otherwise. GARBAGE continued their rise to the top of the pile with a UK chart-topping second set, 'VERSION 2.0', masterfully treading the finest of lines between alternative credibility and outright mainstream success; the hits kept on coming with 'PUSH IT', 'I THINK I'M PARANOID' and 'SPECIAL' all making the UK Top 20. After the phenomenal success of their previous albums, the group re-united in the studio to record their third album proper, the strange and often confused 'BEAUTIFUL GARBAGE' (2001). A slice of every popular genre imaginable, the set offered the listener a wide range of uncommercial tracks, shot through with MANSON's sexual imagery and VIG's scorching production techniques. The sassy 'SILENCE IS GOLDEN' saw MANSON taking some hints from feminine hero PJ HARVEY, while 'SHUT YOUR MOUTH' and hit single 'ANDROGYNY' were classic GARBAGE and would have fitted anywhere on the group's debut album. 'CHERRY LIPS (GO BABY GO!)' was the surprise track out of them all; a funky, sexy take-on of new wave, which just proves that GARBAGE may have a few tricks up their sleeves yet. • **Covered:**

KISS MY ASS (Vic Chesnutt) / WILD HORSES (Rolling Stones) / sampled the CLASH's 'Train In Vain' on 'STUPID GIRL'.

Album rating: GARBAGE (*8) / VERSION 2.0 (*7) / BEAUTIFUL GARBAGE (*6)

SHIRLEY MANSON (b. 3 Aug'66, Edinburgh, Scotland) – vocals, guitar (ex-GOODBYE MR MACKENZIE) / **STEVE MARKER** – guitar, samples, loops / **DUKE ERIKSON** (b. DOUG) – guitar, keyboards, bass / **BUTCH VIG** (b. BRYAN VIG, Viroqua, Wisconsin) – drums, loops, efx

Discordant AlmoSounds

Mar 95. (7") *(CORD 001)* <89000> **VOW. / VOW (Torn Apart version)** [ ] Jul95 [97]

Mushroom AlmoSounds

Aug 95. (s7"/7") *(SX/S 1138)* <89001> **SUBHUMAN. / £1 CRUSH** [50] [ ]
(cd-s+=) *(D 1138)* – Vow.

Sep 95. (7"/c-s/cd-s) *(SX/C/D 1199)* <89002> **ONLY HAPPY WHEN IT RAINS. / GIRL DON'T COME / SLEEP** [29] Feb96 [55]

Oct 95. (cd/c/2x45rpm-lp/6x7"box) *(D/C/L/LX 31450)* <80004> **GARBAGE** [6] Aug95 [20]
– Supervixen / Queer / Only happy when it rains / As Heaven is wide / Not my idea / A stroke of luck / Vow / Stupid girl / Dog new tricks / My lover's box / Fix me now / Milk. *(d-lp re-iss. Sep99 on 'Simply Vinyl'+=; SVLP 123)* – Dumb (live) / Stupid girl (live) / Temptation waits (live) / Vow (live).

— on above **MIKE KASHAN** – bass / **PAULI RYAN** – percussion

Nov 95. (7") *(SX 1237)* <89003> **QUEER. / QUEER (Adrian Sherwood remix)** [13] Mar96 [ ]
(silver-cd-s) *(D 1237)* – ('A'side) / Trip my wire / ('A'-The very queer dub-bin mix) / ('A'-The most beautiful girl in town mix).
(gold-cd-s) *(DX 1237)* – ('A'side) / Butterfly collector / ('A'-Rabbit in the Moon remix) / ('A'-Danny Saber remix).

Mar 96. (7") *(SX 1271)* **STUPID GIRL. / DOG NEW TRICKS (pal mix)** [4] [–]
(red-cd-s+=) *(D 1271)* – Driving lesson / ('A'-Red Snapper mix).
(blue-cd-s) *(DX 1271)* – ('A'side) / Alien sex fiend / ('A'-Dreadzone dub) / ('A'-Dreadzone vox).

Jul 96. (c-s) <89004> **STUPID GIRL / DRIVING LESSON** [–] [24]

Nov 96. (7") *(SX 1494)* <89007> **MILK (The wicked mix). / MILK (the Tricky remix)** [10] [ ]
(cd-s) *(D 1494)* – Milk (the wicked mix featuring TRICKY) / ('A'-Goldie's completely trashed remix) / ('A'-original version) / Stupid girl (Tees radio mix by TODD TERRY).
(cd-s) *(DX 1494)* – Milk (the wicked mix featuring TRICKY) / ('A'-Massive Attack classic remix) / ('A'-Rabbit in the moon udder remix) / Stupid girl (the Danny Saber remix).

May 98. (c-s) *(MUSH 28MCS)* <89014> **PUSH IT / LICK THE PAVEMENT** [9] [52]
(cd-s+=) *(MUSH 28CDS)* – ('A'-Boom Boom Satellites remix).
(3"cd-s) *(MUSH 28CDSX)* – ('A'side) / Thirteen.

May 98. (cd/c/lp) *(74321 55410-2/-4/-1)* <80018> **VERSION 2.0** [1] [13]
– Temptation waits / I think I'm paranoid / When I grow up / Medication / Special / Hammering in my head / Push it / The trick is to keep breathing / Dumb / Sleep together / Wicked ways / You look so fine. *(d-cd-iss. Jun99; MUSH 29CDX)*

Jul 98. (c-s) *(MUSH 35MCS)* <40035> **I THINK I'M PARANOID / DEADWOOD** [9] [ ]
(cd-s+=) *(MUSH 35CDS)* – Afterglow.
(cd-s) *(MUSH 35CDX)* – ('A'side) / ('A'extended) / ('A'-Purity mix).
(3"cd-ep+=) *(MUSH 35CDXXX)* – (all of the above).

Oct 98. (c-s) *(MUSH 39MCS)* <827> **SPECIAL / THIRTEEN X FOREVER** [15] Nov98 [52]
(cd-s+=) *(MUSH 39CDS)* – ('A'-Brothers In Rhythm mix).
(cd-s) *(MUSH 39CDSX)* – ('A'side) / Medication (acoustic) / Push it (Victor Calderone remix).
(3"cd-s) *(MUSH 39CDSXXX)* – (all 5 above).

Jan 99. (c-s) *(MUSH 43MCS)* **WHEN I GROW UP / CAN'T SEEM TO MAKE YOU MINE** [9] [ ]
(cd-s+=) *(MUSH 43CDS)* – ('A'-Danny Tenaglia club mix).
(cd-s+=) *(MUSH 43CDSXXX)* – Tornado / ('A'-Danny Tenaglia club).
(cd-s) *(MUSH 43CDSX)* – ('A'side) / Tornado / Special (Rickidy raw mix).

May 99. (c-s) *(MUSH 49MCS)* **YOU LOOK SO FINE / SOLDIER THROUGH THIS** [19] [ ]
(cd-s+=) *(MUSH 49CDS)* – ('A'-Fine Young Cannibals remix).
(cd-s) *(MUSH 49CDSX)* – ('A'side) / Get busy with the fizzy / ('A'-Eric Kupper mix).
(3"cd-s) *(MUSH 49CDSXXX)* – ('A'side) / ('A'-Fine Young Cannibals mix) / ('A'-Eric Kupper mix) / ('A'-Plaid mix).

Nov 99. (c-s/cd-s) *(RAX C/TD 40)* **THE WORLD IS NOT ENOUGH (mixes; original / UNKLE / Ice Bandits)** [11] [ ]
(above from Bond movie of the same name – issued on 'Radioactive')

Sep 01. (cd-s) *(MUSH 94CDS)* **ANDROGYNY / BEGGING BONE / ANDROGYNY (Felix Da Housecat 'thee glitz remix')** [24] [–]
(cd-s) *(MUSH 94CDX)* – ('A'side) / ('A'-Neptunes remix) / ('A'-Architechs remix).

Oct 01. (cd/c/lp) *(MUSH 95 CD/MC/LP)* <493115> **BEAUTIFUL GARBAGE** [6] [13]
– Shut your mouth / Androgyny / Can't cry these tears / Till the day I die / Cup of coffee / Silence is golden / Cherry lips (go baby go!) / Breaking up the girl / Drive you home / Parade / Nobody loves you / Untouchable / So like a rose.

Jan 02. (cd-s) *(MUSH 98CDSE)* **CHERRY LIPS / CHERRY LIPS (Roger Sanchez tha S man's release mix)** [22] [–]
(cd-s+=) *(MUSH 98CDSX)* – Enough is never enough.
(cd-s) *(MUSH 98CDS)* – ('A'side) / Use me / ('A'-Howie B remix) / ('A'-video).
(12") *(MUSH 98T)* – ('A'-Roger Sanchez tha S man's release mix) / ('A'-mauve dark vocal mix with accapella mix).

Apr 02. (cd-s) *(MUSH 101CDS)* **BREAKING UP THE GIRL / CANDY SAYS / BREAKING UP THE GIRL (Brothers In Rhythm remix) / BREAKING UP THE GIRL (video)** [27] [–]
(cd-s) *(MUSH 101CDSX)* – ('A'version) / Happiness (p.2) / ('A'-Tino Maas remix).
(cd-s) *(MUSH 101CDSXXX)* – ('A'-acoustic version) / Confidence / Cherry lips (go go jam; Eli Janey remix).

Sep 02. (cd-s) *(MUSH 106CDS)* **SHUT YOUR MOUTH / SEX NEVER GOES OUT OF FASHION / SHUT YOUR MOUTH (jolly scary music mix) / SHUT YOUR MOUTH (video)** [20] [–]
(cd-s) *(MUSH 106CDSX)* – ('A'side) / April tenth / ('A'-Jags Kooner full vocal mix).
(cd-s) *(MUSH 106CDSXXX)* – ('A'side) / I'm really into techno / Wild horses (live).

□ Jerry GARCIA (see under ⇒ GRATEFUL DEAD)

□ Art GARFUNKEL (see under ⇒ SIMON & GARFUNKEL)

□ David GATES (see under ⇒ BREAD)

Marvin GAYE

Born: MARVIN PENTZ GAY JR., 2 Apr'39, Washington, D.C., USA, son of an apostolic minister. In 1957, after being discharged from the army, MARVIN joined doo-wop outfit The MARQUEES, releasing two singles (HEY LITTLE SCHOOL GIRL; produced by Bo Diddley, + BABY YOU'RE THE ONLY ONE) for the 'Okeh' label. The following year, HARVEY FUQUA invited them to become his new MOONGLOWS, and after moving to 'Chess' land, Chicago, they recorded the 'ALMOST GROWN' and 'MAMA LOOCIE' singles. In 1960, FUQUA, who accompanied GAY to the motor city of Detroit with the intention of becoming a solo artist, helped arrange for GAY to play session drums on 45's by The MIRACLES. In 1961, after more session work for 'Motown' artists such as The MARVELETTES, he signed as a solo artist to 'Tamla Motown' as well as marrying boss BERRY GORDY's younger sister, ANNA. Suffixing his surname with an E, MARVIN initially had his heart set on becoming a jazz balladeer, although an album, 'THE SOULFUL MOODS OF MARVIN GAYE' (1961), flopped and he was eventually cajoled into recording R&B/soul. The result was the rawer, 'STUBBORN KIND OF FELLOW' single, an immediate success which provided MARVIN with his first R&B Top 10 hit in 1962. 'HITCH HIKE', 'PRIDE AND JOY' and CAN I GET A

WITNESS followed in quick succession, all charting in the US Top 50 and establishing GAYE as one of Motown's foremost talents. Like most artists on the label, GAYE was assigned material by various writers (mainly the in-house team of HOLLAND-DOZIER-HOLLAND) although even in those early days, many of his songs were self-penned, including the classic 'WHEREVER I LAY MY HAT (THAT'S MY HOME)' (later made famous again by PAUL YOUNG). In 1964, although still mainly a credible solo artist, Berry Gordy teamed him up with MARY WELLS, and later KIM WESTON with whom he recorded the Top 20 soul-pop brilliance of 'IT TAKES TWO' as well as recording a whole album of duets under a similar title. The mid-60's also saw him developing the super smooth vocal prowess that would become his trademark on such hits as 'HOW SWEET IT IS (TO BE LOVED BY YOU)' and 'ONE MORE HEARTACHE'. The WESTON alliance was dissolved in mid-67 when GAYE found Philadelphia born singer, TAMMI TERRELL, their charmed partnership yielding a three-year run of hits on both sides of the Atlantic and producing some of the most sublime duets in the history of soul ('AIN'T NO MOUNTAIN HIGH ENOUGH', 'YOU'RE ALL I NEED TO GET BY', 'AIN'T NOTHING LIKE THE REAL THING' etc.). Tragically, to the obvious dismay of MARVIN, TAMMI died of a brain tumour in March 1970, aged only 24. The previous year, MARVIN had scored his biggest hit to date when 'I HEARD IT THROUGH THE GRAPEVINE' hit No.1 in America and Britain, a brooding, experimental epic that became Motown's biggest selling record in the label's history. But TERRELL's death hit MARVIN hard and his subsequent work was to take on a considerably more introspective bent. Although MARVIN didn't write it, the melancholy 'ABRAHAM, MARTIN AND JOHN' single (released in Spring '70) was an indicator of the direction GAYE was headed. Taking his cue from STEVIE WONDER, MARVIN decided to take complete control of his career, from the writing to the recording, making his first major artistic statement with 'WHAT'S GOING ON' (1971). A radical departure, the album (along with WONDER's early 70's material) changed the way soul music was made and challenged people's perceptions of the genre. Like a black 'Astral Weeks' (in feeling if not lyrically), the album was a lush, orchestral stream of consciousness collage, GAYE gazing into the ether and pleading for some kind of redemption for mankind. Addressing such pertinent issues as war, environmental disaster and God, 'Motown' were extremely reluctant to release the album, only relenting when GAYE threatened to leave the label. The singer was vindicated when the record became his biggest seller to date, as well as being recognised as one of the greatest albums in recording history. GAYE solved the problem of following up such a milestone by recording the soundtrack to blaxploitation flick, 'TROUBLE MAN'. Largely instrumental, the album was an enjoyable collection of jazz-funk grooves, a stop gap rather than a step forward. A bona fide successor came with 1973's steamy 'LET'S GET IT ON', the title track providing GAYE with the second No.1 of his career. The album itself reached No.2, becoming the most commercially successful release of his career. Like all truly transcendent artists, GAYE embraced both the profane and the sacred, his best work both overtly sexual and deeply spiritual; for GAYE, spiritual healing was sexual healing. Yet, ironically, GAYE's marriage to ANNA GORDY foundered in 1975, MARVIN detailing the break-up in his underrated double album, 'HERE MY DEAR' (1979), its title a sarcastic reference to the fact that GORDY was to receive all royalties from the disc as part of the divorce settlement. Despite having scored a third No.1 single two years previously with the disco epic, 'GOT TO GIVE IT UP', GAYE's personal life was a mess. As well as a second failed marriage, GAYE was constantly hounded by the taxman and fell into heavy cocaine use. Escaping to Europe, GAYE worked on another concept album, 'IN OUR LIFETIME'. Following its release in 1981, GAYE accused Motown of tampering with both the sound of the album and the artwork prior to release. This marked the bitter end to his long standing relationship with the label, and he subsequently signed with 'Columbia'. 'MIDNIGHT LOVE' (1982) was a resounding return to form, the seminal 'SEXUAL HEALING' going Top 5 in Britain and America. Lyrically, the album explored familiar GAYE themes on the nature of God and love, but while the singer was still actively following some kind of spiritual path, he was also sinking deeper into drug dependence and depression. Retreating to his parents' home in L.A., MARVIN's depression and mood swings brought him into continual conflict with his father and after one particularly violent argument on the 1st of April 1984, MARVIN GAYE SNR. shot his son dead. It was a tragic end to the life of one of the most pivotal figures soul music has produced. • **Covered:** ... GRAPEVINE (Whitfield-Strong) / ABRAHAM, MARTIN AND JOHN (c.Dick Holler). MARVIN's songs have been recorded by many international stars including ROBERT PALMER (Mercy Mercy Me) / CYNDI LAUPER (What's Going On).

Album rating: THE SOULFUL MOODS OF MARVIN GAYE (*5) / THAT STUBBORN KINDA FELLA (*6) / RECORDED LIVE ON STAGE (*4) / WHEN I'M ALONE I CRY (*4) / TOGETHER with Mary Wells (*6) / MARVIN GAYE GREATEST HITS compilation (*7) / HOW SWEET IT IS TO BE LOVED BY YOU (*5) / HELLO BROADWAY THIS IS MARVIN (*5) / A TRIBUTE TO THE GREAT NAT KING COLE (*4) / MOODS OF MARVIN GAYE (*5) / TAKE TWO with Kim Weston (*5) / MARVIN GAYE GREATEST HITS, VOL.2 compilation (*6) / UNITED with Tammi Terrell (*6) / YOU'RE ALL I NEED (*6) / IN THE GROOVE (*6) / M.P.G. (*6) / MARVIN GAYE AND HIS GIRLS collection (*6) / EASY with Tammi Terrell (*6) / THAT'S THE WAY LOVE IS (*5) / MARVIN GAYE & TAMMI TERRELL GREATEST HITS compilation (*6) / MARVIN GAYE SUPER HITS exploitation (*6) / WHAT'S GOING ON (*10) / TROUBLE MAN soundtrack (*5) / LET'S GET IT ON (*9) / ANTHOLOGY compilation (*8) / MARVIN GAYE LIVE! (*4) / I WANT YOU (*6) / MARVIN GAYE'S GREATEST HITS compilation (*7) / MARVIN GAYE LIVE AT THE LONDON PALLADIUM (*5) / HERE, MY DEAR (*7) / IN OUR LIFETIME (*6) / MIDNIGHT LOVE (*7) / DREAM OF A LIFETIME posthumous (*5)

MARVIN GAYE – vocals, drums, etc. (ex-MOONGLOWS, etc.) with Motown session people

not iss. | Tamla Motown

May 61. (lp) *<221>* **THE SOULFUL MOODS OF MARVIN GAYE** | – |
– The masquerade is over / Love for sale / My funny valentine / Let your conscience be your guide / etc.

May 61. (7") *<54041>* **LET YOUR CONSCIENCE BE YOUR GUIDE. / NEVER LET YOU GO (SHA LA BOP)** | – |

1962. (7") *<54055>* **I'M YOURS, YOU'RE MINE. / SANDMAN** | – |

1962. (7") *<54063>* **TAKING MY TIME. / SOLDIER'S PLEA** | – |

Nov 62. (lp) *<239>* **THAT STUBBORN KINDA FELLA** | – |
– That stubborn kinda fella / Pride and joy / Hitch hike / Get my hands on some lovin' / Soldier's plea / I'm yours, you're mine / Wherever I lay my hat (that's my home) / Taking my time / It hurt me too / Hello there angel.

Dec 62. (7") *<54075>* **HITCH HIKE. / HELLO THERE ANGEL** | – | 30

Oriole | Tamla

Feb 63. (7") *(CBA 1803) <54068>* **STUBBORN KIND OF FELLOW. / IT HURT ME TOO** | | Jul62 46

Jul 63. (7") *(CBA 1846) <54079>* **PRIDE AND JOY. / ONE OF THESE DAYS** | | Apr63 10

Jul 63. (lp) *<242>* **RECORDED LIVE ON STAGE (live)** | – |
– That stubborn kinda fella / Hitch hike / One of these days / Days of wine and roses / You are my sunshine / etc.

Stateside | Tamla

Nov 63. (7") *(SS 243) <54087>* **CAN I GET A WITNESS. / I'M CRAZY 'BOUT MY BABY** | | 22 Oct63 77

1964. (lp) *<251>* **WHEN I'M ALONE I CRY** | – |
– You've changed / I was telling her about you / I wonder / I'll be around / Because of you / I don't know why / I've grown accustomed to her face / When your lover has gone / When I'm alone I cry / If my heart could sing.

Apr 64. (7") *(SS 284) <54093>* **YOU'RE A WONDERFUL ONE. / WHEN I'M ALONE I CRY** [ ] Feb64 [15]

—— Apr64, saw MARVIN duet with MARY WELLS on hit single ONCE UPON A TIME and album TOGETHER. (See further below and for collaborations/duets with **KIM WESTON and TAMMI TERRELL**)

Aug 64. (7") *<54095>* **TRY IT BABY. / IF MY HEART COULD SING** [ ] May64 [15]

Sep 64. (7") *<54101>* **BABY DON'T YOU DO IT. / WALK ON THE WILD SIDE** [–] [27]

Nov 64. (lp) *(SL 10100)* **MARVIN GAYE** (compilation from '63 & '64 lp's) [ ] [–]
– You're a wonderful one / Get my hands on some lovin' / Taking my time / Soldier's plea / Hello there, angel / I'm crazy 'bout my baby / Try it, baby / I'm yours, you're mine / Sandman / Hitch hike / Wherever I lay my hat / Can I get a witness.

Nov 64. (7") *(SS 360) <54107>* **HOW SWEET IT IS TO BE LOVED BY YOU. / FOREVER** [49] [6]
Tamla Motown — Tamla

Apr 65. (lp) *(STML 11004) <258>* **HOW SWEET IT IS TO BE LOVED BY YOU** [ ] Feb65 [ ]
– How sweet it is to be loved by you / Try it baby / Baby don't you do it / You're a wonderful one / Now that you've won me / Me and my lonely room / Stepping closer to your heart / No good without you / One of these days / Need your lovin' (want you back) / Forever. *<US-tracks slightly different> (cd-iss. Mar91; WD 72732)*

Apr 65. (7") *(TMG 510) <54112>* **I'LL BE DOGGONE. / YOU'VE BEEN A LONG TIME COMING** [ ] Feb65 [8]

Aug 65. (7") *(TMG 524) <54117>* **PRETTY LITTLE BABY. / NOW THAT YOU'VE WON ME** [ ] Jun65 [25]

Sep 65. (lp) *(STML 11015) <259>* **HELLO BROADWAY THIS IS MARVIN** [ ] [ ]
– Walk on the wild side / What kind of fool am I / Party's over / Days of wine and roses / People / My way / On the street where you live / Hello Dolly / Hello Broadway / My kind of town / This is the life.

Nov 65. (7") *(TMG 539) <54122>* **AIN'T THAT PECULIAR. / SHE'S GOT TO BE REAL** [ ] Sep65 [8]

Feb 66. (lp) *(STML 11022) <261>* **A TRIBUTE TO GREAT NAT KING COLE** [ ] [ ]
– Nature boy / Ramblin' Rose / Too young / Pretend / Straighten up and fly right / Mona Lisa / Unforgettable / To the ends of the Earth / Sweet Lorraine / It's only a paper Moon / Send for me / Calypso blues. *(re-iss. Jul82 lp/c; WL/WK 72210) (cd-iss. Jul92; 530054-2)*

Mar 66. (7") *(TMG 552) <54129>* **ONE MORE HEARTACHE. / WHEN I HAD YOUR LOVE** [ ] Feb66 [29]

Jun 66. (7") *(TMG 563) <54132>* **TAKE THIS HEART OF MINE. / NEED YOUR LOVIN' (WANT YOU BACK)** [ ] May66 [44]

Sep 66. (7") *(TMG 574) <54138>* **LITTLE DARLING (I NEED YOU). / HEY DIDDLE DIDDLE** [50] Aug66 [47]

Aug 67. (7") *(TMG 618) <54153>* **YOUR UNCHANGING LOVE. / I'LL TAKE CARE OF YOU** [ ] Jul67 [33]

Jan 68. (7") *(TMG 640) <54160>* **YOU. / CHANGE WHAT YOU CAN** [ ] [34]

Nov 68. (7") *(TMG 676) <54170>* **CHAINED. / AT LAST (I FOUND A LOVE)** [ ] [32]

Nov 68. (7") *<54176>* **I HEARD IT THROUGH THE GRAPEVINE. / YOU'RE WHAT'S HAPPENING (IN THE WORLD TODAY)** [–] [1]

Jan 69. (lp) *(STML 11091) <285>* **IN THE GROOVE** [ ] Oct68 [63]
– You / Tear it on down / Chained / I heard it through the grapevine / At last (I found a love) / Some kind of wonderful / Loving you is sweeter than ever / Change what you can / It's love I need / Every now and then / You're what's happening (in the world today) / There goes my baby. *(re-iss. Apr85 as 'I HEARD IT THROUGH THE GRAPEVINE' lp/c; WL/WK 72374) (cd-iss. Jun89; WD 72374)*

Feb 69. (7") *(TMG 686)* **I HEARD IT THROUGH THE GRAPEVINE. / NEED SOMEBODY** [1] [–]

Jul 69. (7") *(TMG 705) <54181>* **TOO BUSY THINKING ABOUT MY BABY. / WHEREVER I LAY MY HAT** [5] Apr69 [4]
(re-iss. Oct81 on 'Motown'; same)

Nov 69. (lp) *(STML 11119) <292>* **M.P.G.** [ ] Jun69 [33]
– Too busy thinking about my baby / This magic moment / I got to get to California / That's the way love is / The end of our road / Seek and you shall find / It's a bitter pill to swallow / Only a lonely man would know / Try my true love / Memories / More than a heart can stand / It don't take too much to keep me. *(re-iss. Jul82 lp/c; STMS/CSTMS 5064) (cd-iss. Aug93; 530210-2)*

Nov 69. (7") *(TMG 718) <54185>* **THAT'S THE WAY LOVE IS. / GONNA KEEP TRYIN' TILL I WIN YOUR LOVE** [ ] Aug 69 [7]

Jan 70. (7") *<54190>* **HOW CAN I FORGET. / GONNA GIVE HER ALL THE LOVE I'VE GOT** [–] [41] [67]

Apr 70. (lp) *(STML 11136) <299>* **THAT'S THE WAY LOVE IS** [ ] Oct69 [ ]
– Gonna give her all the love i've got / Yesterday / Groovin' / I wish it would rain / That's the way love is / How can I forget / Abraham, Martin and John / Gonna keep on tryin' till I win your love / No time for tears / Cloud nine / Don't you miss me a little bit baby / So long. *(cd-iss. Apr91; WD 72736) (cd re-iss. Aug93; 530214-2)*

Apr 70. (7") *(TMG 734)* **ABRAHAM, MARTIN AND JOHN. / HOW CAN I FORGET** [9] [–]

Jun 70. (7") *<54195>* **THE END OF OUR ROAD. / ME AND MY LONELY ROOM** [–] [40]

Jun 71. (7") *(TMG 775) <54201>* **WHAT'S GOING ON. / GOD IS LOVE** [ ] Feb71 [2]
(re-iss. Mar83 on 'Motown')

Oct 71. (lp) *(STML 11190) <310>* **WHAT'S GOING ON** [ ] Jun71 [6]
– What's going on / What's happening brother / Flyin' high (in the friendly sky) / Save the children / God is love / Mercy mercy me (the ecology) / Right on / Wholy holy / Inner city blues (make me wanna holler). *(re-iss. Apr88 lp/c/cd; WL/WK/WD 72611) (re-iss. Jul94; 530022-2/-4) (deluxe d-cd-iss. Mar01 +=; 013404-2)* – (alt. mixes). *<(cd re-mast.Jan03 +=; 064022-2)>* – God is love (version) / Sad tomorrows (aka Flyin' high – in the friendly sky).

Nov 71. (7") *(TMG 796)* **SAVE THE CHILDREN. / LITTLE DARLING** [41] [ ]

Feb 72. (7") *(TMG 802)* **MERCY MERCY ME. / SAD TOMORROWS** [ ] Jul71 [4]

May 72. (7") *(TMG 817) <54209>* **INNER CITY BLUES (MAKE ME WANNA HOLLER). / WHOLY HOLY** [ ] Oct71 [9]

May 72. (7") *<54221>* **YOU'RE THE MAN. / (part 2)** [–] [50]

Feb 73. (lp) *(STML 11225) <322>* **TROUBLE MAN** [ ] Dec72 [14]
– Main theme from "Trouble Man" / "T" plays it cool / Poor Abbey Walsh / The break-in (police shoot big) / Cleo's apartment / Trouble man / Theme from "Trouble Man" / "T" stands for trouble / Life is a gamble / Deep in it / Don't mess with Mister "T" / There goes Mister "T". *(re-iss. Jul82 lp/c; STMS/CSTMS 5065) (re-iss. 1986 lp/c; WL/WK 72215) (cd-iss. Sep91; WD 72215) (cd re-iss. Apr93; 530097-2)*

Mar 73. (7") *(TMG 846) <54228>* **TROUBLE MAN. / DON'T MESS WITH MISTER "T"** [ ] Dec72 [7]

Aug 73. (7") *(TMG 868) <54234>* **LET'S GET IT ON. / I WISH IT WOULD RAIN** [31] Jul73 [1]

Nov 73. (lp) *(STMA 8013) <329>* **LET'S GET IT ON** [39] Sep73 [2]
– Let's get it on / Please don't stay (once you go away) / If I should die tonight / Keep gettin' it on / Come get to this / Distant lover / You sure love to ball / Just to keep you satisfied. *(re-iss. Mar82 lp/c; STMS/XSTMS 5034) (re-iss. Apr84 on 'Motown' lp/c; WL/WK 72085) (cd-iss. Apr88; WD 72085) (cd-iss. Jul92; 530055-2) (deluxe d-cd-iss. Oct01 +=; 014757-2)* – (alt. versions). *(cd re-mast.Jan03 +=; 064021-2)* – Let's get it on (single version) / You sure love to ball (version).

—— Around this time MARVIN teams up with DIANA ROSS, on album DIANA AND MARVIN. Many hits were lifted from it including YOU ARE EVERYTHING.

Jan 74. (7") *(TMG 882) <54241>* **COME GET TO THIS. / DISTANT LOVER** [ ] Nov73 [21]

Jan 74. (7") *<54244>* **YOU SURE LOVE TO BALL. / JUST TO KEEP YOU SATISFIED** [–] [50]

Sep 74. (lp) *(STMA 8018) <333>* **MARVIN GAYE LIVE! (live)** [ ] Jul74 [8]
– (the beginning: introduction & overture) / Trouble man – Inner city blues – Distant lover / Jan / Fossil medley: I'll be doggone – Try it baby – Can I get a witness – Subborn kind of fellow – How sweet it is to be loved by you / Now: Let's get it on – What's going on. *(re-iss. Mar82; same) (cd-iss. Feb88) (cd-iss. Sep93 on 'Stardust'; STAMCD 536)*

Sep 74. (7") *<54253>* **DISTANT LOVER. / TROUBLE MAN** [–] [28]

Apr 76. (7") *(TMG 1026) <54264>* **I WANT YOU. / I WANT YOU (instrumental)** [ ] [15]

May 76. (lp) *(STML 12025) <342>* **I WANT YOU** [22] Mar76 [4]
– I want you / Come live with me angel / After the dance (instrumental) / Feel all my love inside / I wanna be where you are / I want you / All the way around / Since I had you / Soon I'll be loving you again / I want you (intro jam) / After the dance. *(re-iss. Oct81; same) (re-iss. 1986 on 'Motown'; WL 72027) (cd-iss. Mar90; WD 72027) (cd re-iss. Jul94 & Sep98; 530887-2) (deluxe d-cd-iss. Aug03 +=; 038656-2)* – (alt. versions).

Aug 76. (7") *(TMG 1035) <54273>* **AFTER THE DANCE. / FEEL ALL MY LOVE INSIDE** [ ] [74]

Motown Motown

Apr 77. (7") *(TMG 1069) <54280>* **GOT TO GIVE IT UP (part 1). / GOT TO GIVE IT UP (part 2)** [7] [1]

— next d-lp, * – duets with FLORENCE LYLES

May 77. (d-lp) *(TMSP 6006) <352>* **LIVE AT THE LONDON PALLADIUM (live)** [ ] Mar77 [3]
– (intro theme) / All the way around / Since I had you / Come get to this / Let's get it on / Trouble man / Ain't peculiar / You're a wonderful one / Stubborn kind of fellow / Pride and joy / Little darling (I need you) / I heard it through the grapevine / Hitch hike / You / Too busy thinking about my baby / How sweet it is to be loved by you / Inner city blues (make me wanna holler) / God is love / What's going on / Save the children / You're all I need to get by * / Ain't nothing like the real thing * / Your precious love * / It takes two * / Ain't no mountain high enough * / Distant lover / (closing theme) / Got to give it up. *(re-iss. Aug86 lp/c; WL/WK 72213) (cd-iss. Mar87; ZD 72213) (cd re-iss. May89; WD 72213) (cd re-iss. Sep98; 530886-2)*

Jan 79. (d-lp) *(TMSP 6008) <364>* **HERE, MY DEAR** [ ] [26]
– Here, my dear / I met a little girl / When did you stop loving me, when did I stop loving you / Anger / Is that enough / Everybody needs love / Time to get it together / Sparrow / Anna's song / When did you stop loving me, when did I stop loving you (instrumental) / A funky space reincarnation / You can leave, but it's going to cost you / Falling in love again / When did you stop loving me, when did I stop loving you (reprise). *(re-iss. Oct81 lp/c; TMSP/CTMSP 6008) (cd-iss. Nov93; 530253-2)*

Feb 79. (7") *(TMG 1138) <54298>* **A FUNKY SPACE REINCARNATION (part 1). / (part 2)** [ ] [ ]
(12"+=) *(TMGT 1138)* – ('A'disco).

— Around this a collaboration with SMOKEY ROBINSON, DIANA ROSS and STEVE WONDER gave them a minor hit single 'POPS WE LOVE YOU'.

Nov 79. (7") *(TMG 1168) <54305>* **EGO TRIPPING OUT. / ('A' instrumental)** [ ] [ ]
(12") *(TMGT 1168)* – ('A'side) / What's going on / What's happening brother.

Feb 81. (lp) *(STML 12149) <374>* **IN OUR LIFETIME** [48] [ ]
– Praise / Life is for learning / Love party / Funk me / Far cry / Love me now or love me later / Heavy love affair / In our lifetime. *(cd-iss. Oct94; 530274-2)*

Feb 81. (7") *(TMG 1225) <54322>* **PRAISE. / FUNK ME** [ ] [ ]

Oct 81. (7") *(TMG 1232) <54326>* **HEAVY LOVE AFFAIR. / FAR CRY** [ ] [ ]

— MARVIN now played all instruments (or most of anyway)

C.B.S. Columbia

Oct 82. (lp/c) *(CBS/40 85977) <38197>* **MIDNIGHT LOVE** [10] [7]
– Midnight lady / Sexual healing / Rockin' after midnight / 'Til tomorrow / Turn on some music / Third world girl / Joy / My love is waiting. *(re-iss. Apr86 lp/c; CBS/40 32776) (cd-iss. Jul94; CD 85977) (cd re-iss. Aug00; 498169-2)*

Oct 82. (7"/12") *(A/TA 2855) <03302>* **SEXUAL HEALING. / ('A'instrumental)** [4] [3]

Nov 82. (7") *<03589>* **ROCKIN' AFTER MIDNIGHT. / 'TIL TOMORROW** [–] [ ]

Jan 83. (7"/12") *(A/TA 3048)* **MY LOVE IS WAITING. / ROCKIN' AFTER MIDNIGHT** [34] [–]

Jan 83. (7") *<03860>* **JOY. / ('A' instrumental)** [–] [ ]

Feb 83. (7") *<03870>* **STAR SPANGLED BANNER. / TURN ON SOME MUSIC** [–] [ ]

Mar 83. (7") *(A 3242) <03935>* **JOY. / TURN ON SOME MUSIC** [ ] [ ]

— On the 1st April 1984, MARVIN was shot dead by his father.

May 85. (7"/12") *(A/TA 4894) (04861>* **SANCTIFIED LADY. / ('A'instrumental)** [51] [ ]
(d7"+=) *(DA 4894)* – Sexual healing / Rockin' after midnight.

Jun 85. (lp/c) *(CBS/40 26239) <39916>* **DREAM OF A LIFETIME** (2 new & recordings from the 70's) [46] [41]
– Sanctified lady / Savage in the sack / Masochistic beauty / It's madness / Ain't it funny (how things turn around) / Symphony / Life's opera / Dream of a lifetime. *(cd-iss. Jun91 on 'Pickwick'; 982591-2)*

Jul 85. (7") *(A 6462) <05542>* **IT'S MADNESS. / AIN'T IT FUNNY (HOW THINGS TURN AROUND)** [ ] [ ]
(12"+=) *(TA 6462)* – Joy.

Dec 85. (lp/c) *(CBS/40 26744) <40208>* **ROMANTICALLY YOURS** [ ] [ ]
– More / Why did I choose you? / Maria / The shadow of your smile / Fly me to the Moon (in other words) / I won't cry anymore / Just like / Walkin' in the rain / I live for you / Stranger in my life / Happy go lucky. *(cd-iss. Jul89 on 'Pickwick' 902121-2) (re-iss. Jun94 on 'Sony Collectors' cd/c; 463158-2/-4)*

Jan 86. (7") *<05791>* **JUST LIKE. / MORE** [–] [ ]

Jun 86. (7") *(ZB 40758)* **THE WORLD IS RATED X. / LONELY LOVER** [ ] [–]
(12"+=) *(ZT 40758)* – ('A'instrumental).

Jun 86. (7") *<1836>* **THE WORLD IS RATED X. / NO GREATER LOVE** [–] [ ]

– (selective) compilations, etc. –

note all below on 'Tamla Motown' unless mentioned otherwise

Mar 64. (lp) *<252>* **GREATEST HITS** [–] [72]

Feb 68. (lp) *(STML 11065)* **MARVIN GAYE'S GREATEST HITS** [40] [–]

Jun 74. (d-lp) *(TMSP 1128)* **ANTHOLOGY** [ ] [61]
(d-cd-iss. Oct86) (d-cd re-iss. Apr93)

Nov 76. (lp) *(STML 12042) <348>* **THE BEST OF MARVIN GAYE** [56] [ ]
(re-iss. Oct81)

Oct 83. (lp) *<6058>* **EVERY GREAT MOTOWN HIT OF MARVIN GAYE** [–] [80]
(cd-iss. Jul00; AA314 549517-2)

Nov 83. (lp/c) *Telstar; (STAR/STAC 2234)* **GREATEST HITS** [13] [–]
– I heard it through the grapevine / Let's get it on / Too busy thinking about my baby / How sweet it is to be loved by you / You're all I need to get by / Got to give it up / You are everything / Midnight lady / Sexual healing / What's going on / Abraham, Martin & John / It takes two / Stop, look, listen (to your heart) / My love is waiting / The onion song / Wherever I lay my hat.

Apr 85. (lp/c) *(WK/WL 72374)* **I HEARD IT THROUGH THE GRAPEVINE** [ ] [–]
(cd-iss. Nov86; ZD 72457) (cd re-iss. Jun89; WD 72374) (cd re-iss. Aug99 on 'Spectrum'; 530793-2)

Mar 86. (cd) *(ZD 72422)* **COMPACT COMMAND PERFORMANCES VOL.1** [ ] [–]

Apr 86. (7") *(ZB 40701)* **I HEARD IT THROUGH THE GRAPEVINE. / CAN I GET A WITNESS** [8] [–]
(ext; 12"/c-s) *(ZT/ZV 40702)* – ('A'side) / That's the way love is / You're a wonderful one.

Jun 86. (lp/c) *(ZL/ZK 72463) <6172>* **MOTOWN REMEMBERS MARVIN GAYE** [ ] Apr86 [ ]

Jul 86. (cd) *(TCD 2234)* **THE VERY BEST OF MARVIN GAYE** [ ] [–]

Nov 86. (d-cd) *(ZD 72456)* **WHAT'S GOING ON / LET'S GET IT ON** [ ] [ ]

Feb 87. (d-cd) *(ZD 72500)* **TROUBLE MAN / M.P.G.** [ ] [–]

Mar 87. (cd) *(ZD 72508)* **COMPACT COMMAND PERFORMANCES – VOL.2** [ ] [–]

Jul 87. (d-cd) *(ZD 72562)* **THAT STUBBORN KINDA FELLA / HOW SWEET IT IS** [ ] [–]

Nov 88. (lp/c/cd; shared with SMOKEY ROBINSON) *Telstar; (STAR/STAC/TCD 2331)* **LOVE SONGS** [69] [–]

Oct 90. (cd/c/lp) *Telstar; (TCD/STAC/STAR 2427)* **LOVE SONGS** [39] [–]

Oct 92. (cd) *Columbia; (461017-2)* **MIDNIGHT LOVE / DREAM OF A LIFETIME** [ ] [–]

Mar 94. (cd/c) *(530292-2/-4)* **THE VERY BEST OF MARVIN GAYE** [3] [–]

May 94. (7"/c-s) *(TMG/+C 1426)* **LUCKY LUCKY ME. / ('A'extended)** [67] [ ]
(12"+=/cd-s+=) *(TMG T/CD 1426)* – ('A'instrumental mix) / ('A'jazz mix) / ('A'ragga vibe mix).

Oct 94. (3xcd-box) *Columbia; (477525-2)* **DREAM OF A LIFETIME / ROMANTICALLY YOURS / MIDNIGHT LOVE** [ ] [–]

Nov 95. (3xcd-box) **HOW SWEET IT IS / TRIBUTE TO NAT KING COLE / M.P.G.** [ ] [–]

Jul 96. (cd) *Spectrum; (552118-2)* **MOTOWN EARLY CLASSICS** [ ] [ ]

Nov 96. (cd) *Summit; (SUMCD 4043)* **THE MIDNIGHT LOVER: LIVE IN CONCERT (live)** [ ] [–]

May 97. (cd) *A-Play; (10030-2)* **IN CONCERT (live)** [ ] [–]

Sep 97. (d-cd) *Alpha; (ALPCD 102)* **THE LEGENDARY MARVIN GAYE** [ ] [ ]

Nov 98. (cd) *Creole; (CP 1008)* **THE LEGEND** [ ] [ ]
Nov 98. (cd) *Columbia; (491572-2)* **MIDNIGHT LOVE / THE SEXUAL HEALING SESSIONS** [ ] [ ]
Dec 99. (cd) *Castle Pie; (PIESD 180)* **LIVE** [ ] [–]
Feb 00. (cd/c) *Universal TV; (545470-2/-4)* **THE LOVE SONGS** [8] [–]
May 00. (4xcd-box) *(530492-2)* **THE MASTER 1961-1984** [ ] [ ]
Jul 00. (cd) *(153868-2)* **MOTOWN LOST AND FOUND: LOVE STARVED HEART** [ ] [ ]
Jul 00. (cd) *157609-2)* **AIN'T NOTHING LIKE THE REAL THING: AN INTRODUCTION TO MARVIN GAYE** [ ] [ ]
Oct 00. (d-cd) *(E 530831-2)* **WHAT'S GOING ON / IN OUR LIFETIME** [ ] [ ]
Oct 00. (cd) *(153426-2)* **I HEARD IT THROUGH THE GRAPEVINE / WHAT'S GOING ON** [ ] [ ]
Oct 00. (3xcd-box) *(E 530910-2)* **WHAT'S GOING ON / LET'S GET IT ON / TROUBLE MAN** [ ] [ ]
Oct 00. (d-cd) *(E 530832-2)* **LET'S GET IT ON / HERE, MY DEAR** [ ] [ ]
Feb 01. (cd) *(013184-2)* **THAT STUBBORN KINDA FELLOW / HOW SWEET IT IS TO BE LOVED BY YOU** [ ] [ ]
Feb 01. (cd) *(013185-2)* **MOODS OF MARVIN GAYE / IN THE GROOVE** [ ] [ ]
Feb 01. (cd) *(013187-2)* **M.P.G. / THAT'S THE WAY LOVE IS** [ ] [ ]
Feb 01. (cd) *(013216-2)* **HERE, MY DEAR / IN OUR LIFETIME** [ ] [ ]
Feb 01. (cd) *Burning Airlings; (PILOT 005)* **THE REAL THING** [ ] [ ]
(re-iss. Aug03 on 'Snapper'; SNAP 157CD)
Aug 01. (d-cd) *Universal TV; (014367-2)* **THE VERY BEST OF MARVIN GAYE** [15] [ ]
Feb 02. (cd) *016815-2)* **LOVE SONGS: BEDROOM BALLADS** [ ] [ ]
Aug 02. (d-cd) *Proper Pairs; (PVCD 110)* **MARVIN GAYE LIVE** [ ] [ ]
Sep 02. (cd) *Cleopatra; (CLP 1204CD)* **PERFORMANCE** [ ] [ ]
Oct 02. (cd) *Armoury; (ARMCD 069)* **BEST OF LIVE** [ ] [–]
Oct 02. (d-cd) *Delta Blues; (63060)* **GOT TO GIVE IT UP (live)** [ ] [–]
Nov 02. (cd) *Planet Media; (PML 1090)* **FINAL CONCERT (live)** [ ] [ ]
Jan 03. (cd) *Universe; (UV 061)* **NORTH AMERICAN TOUR** [ ] [ ]
Mar 03. (cd) *Universal; (AA121 53363-2)* **20th CENTURY MASTERS VOL.1** [ ] [ ]
Mar 03. (cd) *Universal; (AA121 53732-2)* **20th CENTURY MASTERS VOL.2** [ ] [ ]
May 03. (d-cd) *Eagle; (EDGCD 234)* **LIVE IN MONTREUX 1980 (live)** [ ] [–]
Aug 03. (3xcd-box) *Spectrum; (9808968)* **I HEARD IT THROUGH THE GRAPEVINE / MARVIN GAYE AND FRIENDS / EARLY CLASSICS** [ ] [ ]

– duets –

MARVIN GAYE & MARY WELLS

Stateside Tamla

Jul 64. (7") *(SS 316) <1057>* **ONCE UPON A TIME. / WHAT'S THE MATTER WITH YOU BABY** [50] [19]
Apr64 [17]
Oct 64. (lp) *(SL 10097) <613>* **TOGETHER** [ ] May64 [42]
– Once upon a time / What's the matter with you baby / Deed I do / Until I met you / After the lights go down low / Together / Squeeze me / For sentimental reasons / You came a long way from St. Louis / Late late show.

MARVIN GAYE & KIM WESTON

Dec 64. (7") *(SS 363) <54104>* **WHAT GOOD AM I WITHOUT YOU. / I WANT YOU AROUND** [ ] Oct64 [61]

Tamla Motown Tamla

Jan 67. (7") *(TMG 590) <54141>* **IT TAKES TWO. / IT'S GOT TO BE A MIRACLE** [16] [14]
May 67. (lp) *(STML 11049) <270>* **TAKE TWO** [ ] [ ]
– It takes two / I love you, yes I do / Baby I need your loving / It's got to be a miracle / Baby say yes / What good am I without you / Till there was you / Love fell on me / Secret love / I want you 'round / Heaven sent you I know / When.

MARVIN GAYE & TAMMI TERRELL

Jun 67. (7") *(TMG 611) <54149>* **AIN'T NO MOUNTAIN HIGH ENOUGH. / GIVE A LITTLE LOVE** [ ] May67 [19]
Sep 67. (7") *(TMG 625) <54156>* **YOUR PRECIOUS LOVE. / HOLD ME OH MY DARLING** [ ] [5]
Dec 67. (7") *(TMG 635) <54161>* **IF I COULD BUILD MY WHOLE WORLD AROUND YOU. / IF THIS WORLD WERE MINE** [41] [10] [68]
Jan 68. (lp) *(STML 11062) <277>* **UNITED** [ ] Oct67 [69]
– Ain't no mountain high enough / Hold me oh my darling / You got wht it takes / If I could build my whole world around you / Somethin' stupid / Your precious love / Two can have a party / Little ole boy, little ole girl / Give a little love / If this world were mine / Sad wedding / Oh how I'd miss you. *(re-iss. Mar82 on 'Motown' lp/c; STMS/CSTMS 5036) (re-iss. Feb88 lp/c/cd; WL/WK/WD 72211)*
Apr 68. (7") *(TMG 655) <54163>* **AIN'T NOTHING LIKE THE REAL THING. / LITTLE OLE BOY LITTLE OLE GIRL** [34] [8]
Jul 68. (7") *(TMG 668) <54169>* **YOU'RE ALL I NEED TO GET BY. / TWO CAN HAVE A PARTY** [19] [7]
Oct 68. (7") *<54173>* **KEEP ON LOVING ME HONEY. / YOU AIN'T LIVIN' TIL YOU'RE LOVIN'** [–] [28]
Nov 68. (lp) *(STML 11084) <284>* **YOU'RE ALL I NEED** [ ] Sep68 [60]
– Ain't nothing like the real thing / Keep on loving me honey / You're all I need to get by / Baby don'tcha worry / Give in you can't win / You ain't livin' till you're lovin' / That's how it is (since you've been gone) / I'll never stop loving you / When love comes knockin' at my heart / Memory chest / I can't help but love you. *(re-iss. Oct81 lp/c; STMS/CSTMS 5005) (re-iss. May91 cd/c; WD/WK 72208) (cd-iss. Sep93; 530216-2)*
Jan 69. (7") *(TMG 681)* **YOU AIN'T LIVIN' TILL YOU'RE LOVIN'. / OH HOW I MISS YOU** [21] [–]
May 69. (7") *(TMG 697) <54173>* **GOOD LOVIN' AIN'T EASY TO COME BY. / SATISFIED FEELIN'** [26] Jan69 [30]
Nov 69. (7") *(TMG 715)* **THE ONION SONG. / I CAN'T BELIEVE YOU LOVE ME** [9] [–]
Nov 69. (7") *<54187>* **WHAT YOU GAVE ME. / HOW YOU GONNA KEEP IT (AFTER YOU GET IT)** [–] [49]
Feb 70. (lp) *(STML 11132) <294>* **EASY** [ ] Oct69 [ ]
– Good lovin' ain't easy to come by / California soul / Love wake me up this morning / This poor heart of mine / I'm your puppet / Onion song / What you gave me / Baby I need your loving / I can't believe you love me / How you gonna keep it / More, more, more / Satisfied feeling. *(re-iss. Sep86 lp/c; WL/WK 72507)*
Apr 70. (7") *<54192>* **THE ONION SONG. / CALIFORNIA SOUL** [–] [50]

—— Aged 23, TAMMI from a brain tumor after collapsing in the Autumn of '69. A few exploitation releases were forthcoming.

Aug 70. (lp) *(STML 11153) <302>* **MARVIN GAYE & TAMMI TERRELL'S GREATEST HITS** [ ] [ ]
(re-iss. Jul82 lp/c; STMS/CSTMS 5066) (re-iss. Sep86 lp/c/cd; WL/WK/WD 72103)
Apr 85. (7"/12") *(TMG/+T 993)* **THE ONION SONG. / YOU AIN'T LIVIN' TIL YOU'RE LOVIN'** [ ] [–]
Mar 74. (lp) *Music For Pleasure;* **THE ONION SONG** [ ] [–]

– duet compilations –

Nov 69. (lp) *(STML 11123) <293>* **MARVIN GAYE & HIS GIRLS** [ ] [ ]
(re-iss. Feb83 on 'Motown' lp/c; STMS/CSTMS 5088) cd-iss. Oct87; WD 72115)
Jan 86. (cd) *(WD 72397)* **MARVIN GAYE & HIS WOMEN** [ ] [–]
Sep 98. (cd; with TAMMI TERRELL) *(064987-2)* **GREATEST DUETS** [ ] [ ]
Feb 01. (cd) *(013217-2)* **UNITED / YOU'RE ALL I NEED** [ ] [ ]
Feb 01. (cd) *(013309-2)* **TOGETHER / TAKE TWO** [ ] [ ]
Mar 01. (cd) *Spectrum; (544520-2)* **MARVIN GAYE AND FRIENDS** [ ] [ ]
Dec 01. (d-cd) *(016402-2)* **THE COMPLETE DUETS** [ ] [ ]
Jan 03. (cd) *(064987-2)* **GREATEST DUETS** [ ] [ ]
Mar 03. (cd; with TAMMI TERRELL) *Universal; (AA121 57600-2)* **20th CENTURY MASTERS** [ ] [ ]

□ Bob GELDOF (see under ⇒ BOOMTOWN RATS)

□ GENERATION X (see under ⇒ IDOL, Billy)

GENESIS

Formed: Godalming, Surrey, England ... early 1967 by Charterhouse public school boys PETER GABRIEL and TONY BANKS (both ex-The GARDEN WALL). They teamed up with former members of The ANON; MICHAEL RUTHERFORD, ANTHONY PHILLIPS and CHRIS STEWART. Still at school, they signed to 'Decca', having sent demos to solo artist and producer JONATHAN KING. Their first 2 singles flopped, as did their 1969 MOODY BLUES-styled album, 'FROM GENESIS TO REVELATION', which only sold around 500 copies. Early in 1970, they were seen live by TONY STRATTON-SMITH, who became their manager after signing them to his 'Charisma' label. Their second album, 'TRESPASS', failed to break through, although it contained the live favourite and edited 45, 'THE KNIFE'. After its release, they found new members PHIL COLLINS and STEVE HACKETT, who replaced recent additions JOHN MAYHEW and ANTHONY PHILLIPS. Late in '71, they issued their set, 'NURSERY CRYME', which featured another two gems, 'THE MUSICAL BOX' and 'THE RETURN OF THE GIANT HOGWEED'. By this point the band transformed into one of the leading purveyors of progressive rock, bizarre extrovert GABRIEL proving a compelling, theatrical focus for the critically-lauded group. It was also the brief debut on lead vox for COLLINS, who sang on the track, 'FOR ABSENT FRIENDS'. A year later, with many gigs behind them, they had their first taste of chart success when 'FOXTROT' hit the UK Top 20. This contained the excellent concept piece, 'SUPPER'S READY', which lasted all of 23 minutes. In 1973, a live album of their best work so far, hit the Top 10, as did their studio follow-up, 'SELLING ENGLAND BY THE POUND'. This boasted another epic track, 'THE BATTLE OF EPPING FOREST', plus another COLLINS lead vocal in 'MORE FOOL ME'. Lifted from it, was a near Top 20 single, 'I KNOW WHAT I LIKE (IN YOUR WARDROBE)'. Late in 1974, they again made Top 10, with the concept double album, 'THE LAMB LIES DOWN ON BROADWAY', which was their first US Top 50 placing, the band performing the album in its entirety as part of a worldwide live show. Shortly after a last concert in May '75, GABRIEL left for a solo career, COLLINS taking over the vocal duties. Surprisingly, this did not harm the commercial appeal of the group when they returned in 1976 with the Top 3 album, 'A TRICK OF THE TAIL'. His drum-stool was filled for live gigs by the seasoned BILL BRUFORD, then CHESTER THOMPSON, who appeared on the 1977 live double album, 'SECONDS OUT'. This was also the last album to feature STEVE HACKETT, who also left for a lucrative solo career. In 1978, their next album, appropriately titled ' ... AND THEN THERE WERE THREE' (COLLINS, BANKS & RUTHERFORD), hit No.3 and also climbed into the US Top 20. The 80's were even more fruitful for the band, as they hit the top spot in the UK with each successive album, also amassing a number of hit singles over the same period. During this era, PHIL COLLINS (who had moonlighted in his own BRAND X) scored a number of easier-listening hit singles and albums. Although they remain one of the stadium rock circuit's largest grossing bands, the band have lost all trace of their pioneering 70's sound. With PHIL COLLINS now out of the picture, BANKS and RUTHERFORD took on the relatively younger Scotsman, RAY WILSON, who had previously fronted chart-toppers, STILTSKIN. TONY BANKS also released some solo work, as did MIKE RUTHERFORD, who made coffee-table pop/rock with his outfit, MIKE + THE MECHANICS. • **Songwriters:** GABRIEL lyrics and group compositions. From 1978, the trio collaborated on all work.

Album rating: FROM GENESIS TO REVELATION (*5) / TRESPASS (*6) / NURSERY CRYME (*8) / FOXTROT (*9) / GENESIS LIVE (*7) / SELLING ENGLAND BY THE POUND (*10) / THE LAMB LIES DOWN ON BROADWAY (*9) / A TRICK OF THE TAIL (*7) / WIND & WUTHERING (*6) / ... AND THEN THERE WERE THREE (*6) / DUKE (*6) / ABACAB (*6) / THREE SIDES LIVE (*6) / GENESIS (*5) / INVISIBLE TOUCH (*6) / WE CAN'T DANCE (*5) / THE WAY WE WALK VOLUME 1: THE SHORTS (*5) / LIVE – THE WAY WE WALK VOLUME 2: THE LONGS (*6) / CALLING ALL STATIONS (*4) / TURN IT ON AGAIN – THE HITS compilation (*8) / Tony Banks: A CURIOUS FEELING (*5) / THE FUGITIVE (*4) / SOUNDTRACKS (*5) / BANKSTATEMENT (*5; by Bankstatement) / STILL (*4) / Mike Rutherford: SMALLCREEP'S DAY (*5) / ACTING VERY STRANGE (*5) / Mike + The Mechanics: MIKE + THE MECHANICS (*4) / THE LIVING YEARS (*5) / WORD OF MOUTH (*5) / BEGGAR ON A BEACH OF GOLD (*4) / HITS compilation (*6)

PETER GABRIEL (b.13 May'50, London, England) – vocals / **TONY BANKS** (b.27 Mar'51, East Heathly, Sussex, England) – keyboards, vocals / **ANTHONY PHILLIPS** (b.Dec'51, Putney, England) – guitar, vocals / **MICHAEL RUTHERFORD** (b. 2 Oct'50, Guildford, Surrey, England) – bass, guitar / **CHRIS STEWART** – drums

Decca — Parrot

Feb 68. (7") *(F 12735) <3018>* **THE SILENT SUN. / THAT'S ME**

May 68. (7") *(F 12775)* **A WINTER'S TALE. / ONE-EYED HOUND** — [ ] [-]

—— **JOHN SILVER** – drums repl. CHRIS

Mar 69. (lp; mono/stereo) *(LK/SKL 4990)* **FROM GENESIS TO REVELATION**
– Where the sour turns to sweet / In the beginning / Fireside song / The serpent / Am I very wrong? / In the wilderness / The conqueror / In hiding / One day / Window / In limbo / The silent sun / A place to call my own. *(re-iss. 1974 as 'IN THE BEGINNING'; same) (re-iss. Oct93 on 'Music Club' cd/c;)*

Jun 69. (7") *(F 12949)* **WHERE THE SOUR TURNS TO SWEET. / IN HIDING** — [ ] [-]

—— (Jul69) **JOHN MAYHEW** – drums repl. JOHN SILVER

Charisma — Impulse

Oct 70. (7"w-drawn) *(GS 1)* **LOOKING FOR SOMEONE. / VISIONS OF ANGELS** — [-] [-]

Oct 70. (lp) *(CAS 1020) <9295>* **TRESPASS**
– Looking for someone / White mountain / Visions of angels / Stagnation / Dusk / The knife. *<US re-iss. 1974 on 'ABC'; 816> (re-iss. Mar83; CHC/+MC 12)(hit 98; Apr84) (cd-iss. Jun88; CASCD 1020) (cd re-iss. Aug94; CASCDX 1020)*

Jun 71. (7") *(CB 152)* **THE KNIFE (part 1). / THE KNIFE (part 2)** — [ ] [-]

—— (Dec70) **GABRIEL, BANKS + RUTHERFORD** recruited new members **PHIL COLLINS** (b.31 Jan'51, Chiswick, London, England) – drums, vocals (ex-FLAMING YOUTH) repl. MAYHEW / **STEVE HACKETT** (b.12 Feb'50, London) – guitar (ex-QUIET WORLD) repl. ANTHONY PHILLIPS who went solo

Charisma — Charisma

Nov 71. (lp)(c) *(<CAS 1052>)(7208 552)* **NURSERY CRYME**
– The musical box / For absent friends / The fountain of Salmacis / Seven stones / Harold the barrel / Harlequin / The return of the giant hogweed. *(hit UK No.39 May74) (re-iss. Feb84 lp/c; CHC/+MC 22); hit 68) (cd-iss. Sep85; CASCD 1052) (cd re-iss. Aug94; CASCDX 1052)*

May 72. (7") *(CB 181)* **HAPPY THE MAN. / SEVEN STONES**

Oct 72. (lp)(c) *(<CAS 1058>)(7208 553)* **FOXTROT** — [12] [ ]
– Get 'em out by Friday / Time-table / Watcher of the skies / Can-utility and the coastliners / Horizon / Supper's ready; (i) Lover's leap, (ii) The guaranteed eternal sanctuary man, (iii) Ikhaton and Itsacon and their band of merry men, (iv) How dare I be so beautiful, (v) Willow farm, (vi) Apocalypse in 9/8 co-starring the delicious talents of Gabble Ratchet, (vii) As sure as eggs is eggs (aching men's feets). *(re-iss. Sep83 lp/c; CHC/+MC 38) (cd-iss. Jul86; CASCD 1058) (cd re-iss. Aug94; CASCDX 1058)*

Feb 73. (7") *<103>* **WATCHER OF THE SKIES. / WILLOW FARM** — [-] [ ]

Jul 73. (lp)(c) *(CLASS 1)(7299 288) <1066>* **GENESIS LIVE (live)** — [9] May74 [ ]
– Watcher of the skies / Get 'em out by Friday / The return of the giant hogweed / The musical box / The knife. *(re-iss. Feb86 lp/c; CHC/+MC 23) (cd-iss. Jul87; CLACD 1) (cd re-iss. Aug94; CLACDX 1)*

Oct 73. (lp)(c) *(CAS 1074)(7208 554)* <6060> **SELLING ENGLAND BY THE POUND** [3] [70]
– Dancing with the moonlit knight / I know what I like (in your wardrobe) / Firth of fifth / More fool me / The battle of Epping Forest / After the ordeal / The cinema show / Aisle of plenty. *(re-iss. Oct86 lp/c; CHC/+MC 46) (cd-iss. Feb86; CASCD 1074) (cd re-iss. Aug94; CLACDX 1074) (re-iss. Feb97 on 'E.M.I.'; LPCENT 17)*

Mar 74. (7") *(CB 224)* <26002> **I KNOW WHAT I LIKE (IN YOUR WARDROBE). / TWILIGHT ALEHOUSE** [21] [ ]

Charisma Atco

Nov 74. (d-lp)(d-c) *(CGS 101)(7599 121)* <401> **THE LAMB LIES DOWN ON BROADWAY** [10] [41]
– The lamb lies down on Broadway / Fly on a windshield / Broadway melody of 1974 / Cuckoo cocoon / In the cage / The grand parade of lifeless packaging / Back in N.Y.C. / Hairless heart / Counting out time / Carpet crawlers / The chamber of 32 doors // Lilywhite Lilith / The waiting room / Anyway / Here comes the supernatural anaesthetist / The lamia / Silent sorrow in empty boats / The colony of Slippermen (The arrival – A visit to the doktor – Raven) / Ravine / The light dies down on Broadway / Riding the scree / It. *(re-iss. Sep83 d-lp/c; CGS/+MC 101) (d-cd-iss. Feb86; CGSCD 1) (cd re-iss. Aug94; CGSCDX 1)*

Nov 74. (7") *(CB 238)* **COUNTING OUT TIME. / RIDING THE SCREE** [ ] [–]

Dec 74. (7") <7013> **COUNTING OUT TIME. / THE LAMB LIES DOWN ON BROADWAY** [–] [ ]

Apr 75. (7") *(CB 251)* **CARPET CRAWLERS. / THE WAITING ROOM (evil jam) (live)** [ ] [–]

—— Now just a quartet when PETER GABRIEL left to go solo.

Feb 76. (lp)(c) *(CDS 4001)* <129> **A TRICK OF THE TAIL** [3] [31]
– Dance on a volcano / Entangled / Squonk / Mad mad Moon / Robbery, assault and battery / Ripples / A trick of the tail / Los endos. *(re-iss. Sep83 lp/c; CDS/+MC 4001) (cd-iss. Apr86; CDSCD 4001) (re-iss. Apr90 on 'Virgin' lp/c; OVED/+C 306) (cd re-iss. Oct94; CDSCDX 4001)*

Mar 76. (7") *(CB 277)* **A TRICK OF THE TAIL. / RIPPLES** [ ] [–]

Mar 76. (7") <7050> **RIPPLES. / ENTANGLED** [–] [ ]

Jan 77. (lp)(c) *(CDS 4005)(7208 611)* <144> **WIND AND WUTHERING** [7] [26]
– Eleventh Earl of Mar / One for the vine / Your own special way / Wot gorilla? / All in a mouse's night / Blood on the rooftops / Unquiet slumbers for the sleepers . . .In that quiet Earth / Afterglow. *(re-iss. Sep83 lp/c; CDS/+MC 4005) (cd-iss. Apr86; CDSCD 4005) (re-iss. Apr90 on 'Virgin' lp/c; OVED/+C 332) (cd re-iss. Oct94; CDSCDX 4005)*

Feb 77. (7") *(CB 300)* **YOUR OWN SPECIAL WAY. / IT'S YOURSELF** [43] [–]

Feb 77. (7") <7076> **YOUR OWN SPECIAL WAY. / . . .IN THAT QUIET EARTH** [–] [62]

May 77. (7"ep) *(GEN 001)* **SPOT THE PIGEON** [14] [–]
– Match of the day / Inside and out / Pigeons. *(cd-ep-iss.1988 on 'Virgin'; CDT 40)*

—— added **BILL BRUFORD** – drums (ex-YES, ex-KING CRIMSON) **CHESTER THOMPSON** – drums (ex-FRANK ZAPPA) they were both used on live album below, with CHESTER augmenting on tours.

Oct 77. (d-lp)(d-c) *(GE 2001)(7649 067)* <9002> **SECONDS OUT (live)** [4] [47]
– Sqounk / Carpet crawlers / Robbery, assault and battery / Afterglow / Firth of fifth / I know what I like (in your wardrobe) / The lamb lies down on Broadway / The musical box / Supper's ready / The cinema show / Dance on a volcano / Los endos. *(re-iss. Sep83 d-lp/d-c; GE/+MC 2001) (d-cd-iss. Nov85; GECD 2001) (d-cd re-iss. Oct94; GECDX 2001)*

—— (Jun77) Now a trio of **COLLINS, BANKS & RUTHERFORD** when STEVE HACKETT continued solo career.

Charisma Atlantic

Mar 78. (7") *(CB 309)* **FOLLOW YOU FOLLOW ME. / BALLAD OF BIG** [7] [–]

Mar 78. (7") <3474> **FOLLOW YOU FOLLOW ME. / INSIDE AND OUT** [–] [23]

Apr 78. (lp)(c) *(CDS 4010)(7208 619)* <19173> **. . .AND THEN THERE WERE THREE** [3] [14]
– Down and out / Undertow / Ballad of big / Snowbound / Burning rope / Deep in the motherlode / Many too many / Scene from a night's dream / Say it's alright Joe / The lady lies / Follow you follow me. *(re-iss. Sep83 lp/c; CDS/+MC 4010) (cd-iss. May83; 800 059-2) (re-iss. Aug91 on 'Virgin' lp/c; OVED/+C 368) (cd re-iss. Oct94; CDSCDX 4010)*

Jun 78. (7") *(CB 315)* **MANY TOO MANY. / THE DAY THE LIGHT WENT OUT IN VANCOUVER** [43] [–]

Jul 78. (7") <3511> **SCENE FROM A NIGHT'S DREAM. / DEEP IN THE MOTHERLODE** [–] [ ]

Mar 80. (7") *(CB 356)* **TURN IT ON AGAIN. / BEHIND THE LINES (part 2)** [8] [–]

Mar 80. (lp/c) *(CBR/+C 101)* <16014> **DUKE** [1] [11]
– Behind the lines / Duchess / Guide vocal / Man of our time / Misunderstanding / Heathaze / Turn it on again / Alone tonight / Cul-de-sac / Please don't ask / Duke's end / Duke's travels. *(re-iss. Sep83 lp/c; CBR/+C 101) (cd-iss. Apr85; CBRCD 101) (re-iss. Mar91 on 'Virgin' lp/c; OVED/+C 345) (cd re-iss. Oct94; CBRCDX 101)*

May 80. (7") *(CB 363)* **DUCHESS. / OPEN DOOR** [46] [–]

May 80. (7") <3662> **MISUNDERSTANDING. / BEHIND THE LINES** [–] [14]

Sep 80. (7") *(CB 369)* **MISUNDERSTANDING. / EVIDENCE OF AUTUMN** [42] [–]

Sep 80. (7") <3751> **TURN IT ON AGAIN. / EVIDENCE OF AUTUMN** [–] [58]

Aug 81. (7") *(CB 388)* **ABACAB. / ANOTHER RECORD** [9] [–]

Sep 81. (lp/c) *(CBR/+C 102)* <19313> **ABACAB** [1] [7]
– Abacab / No reply at all / Me and Sarah Jane / Keep it dark / Dodo / Lurker / Who dunnit? / Man on the corner / Like it or not / Another record. *(cd-iss. May83; 800 044-2) (re-iss. Mar91 on 'Virgin' lp/c; OVED/+C 344) (cd re-iss. Oct94; CBRCDX 102) (lp re-iss. Jan01 on 'Simply Vinyl'; SVLP 278)*

Oct 81. (7") *(CB 391)* **KEEP IT DARK. / NAMINANU** [33] [–]
(12"+=) *(CB 391-12)* – Abacab (long version).

Oct 81. (7") <3858> **NO REPLY AT ALL. / HEAVEN LOVE MY LIFE** [–] [29]

Jan 82. (7") <3891> **ABACAB. / WHO DUNNIT?** [–] [26]

Feb 82. (7") *(CB 393)* <4025> **MAN IN THE CORNER. / SUBMARINE** [41] Mar82 [40]

May 82. (7") <4053> **PAPERLATE. / YOU MIGHT RECALL** [–] [32]

May 82. (7"ep) *(GEN 1)* **3 X 3 E.P.** [10] [–]
– Paperlate / You might recall / Me and Virgil.

Jun 82. (d-lp/d-c) *(GE/+MC 2002)* <2000> **THREE SIDES LIVE (live except ***)** [2] [10]
– Turn it on again / Dodo / Abacab / Behind the lines / Duchess / Me and Sarah Jane / Follow you follow me / Misunderstanding / In the cage / Afterglow / One for the vine * / Fountain of Salmacis * / Watcher of the skies * / It * / Paperlate *** / You might recall *** / Me and Virgil *** / Evidence of Autumn *** / Open door *** / You might recall II ***. *(cd-iss. Apr85; GECD 2002) <US-cd.repl.* w/ The cinema show + The colony of Slippermen> (re-iss. Apr92 d-lp/c; DOVD/+C 2) (cd re-iss. Oct94; GECDX 2002)*

Virgin Atco

Aug 83. (7"/ext.12") *(MAMA 1/+12)* <89770> **MAMA. / IT'S GONNA GET BETTER** [4] [73]
(cd-ep.iss.Jun88; CDT 5)

Oct 83. (lp/c/cd) *(GEN LP/MC/CD 1)* <80116> **GENESIS** [1] [9]
– Mama / That's all / Home by the sea / Second home by the sea / Illegal alien / Taking it all too hard / Just a job to do / Silver rainbow / It's gonna get better. *(re-iss. Jul87; same)*

Nov 83. (7") *(TATA 1)* **THAT'S ALL. / TAKING IT ALL TOO HARD** [16] [–]
(12"+=) *(TATAY 1)* – Firth of fifth (live).

Nov 83. (7") <89724> **THAT'S ALL. / SECOND HOME BY THE SEA** [–] [6]

Feb 84. (7"/7"sha-pic-d) *(AL/+S 1)* <89698> **ILLEGAL ALIEN. / TURN IT ON AGAIN (live)** [46] [44]
(12"+=) *(AL 1-12)* – ('A'extended).

Jun 84. (7") <89656> **TAKING IT ALL TOO HARD. / SILVER RAINBOW** [–] [50]

May 86. (7",7"clear) *(GENS 1)* **INVISIBLE TOUCH. / THE LAST DOMINO** [15] [1]
(12"+=) *(GENS 1-12)* – ('A'extended).

Jun 86. (lp/c/cd) *(GEN LP/MC/CD 2)* <81641> **INVISIBLE TOUCH** [1] [3]
– Invisible touch / Tonight, tonight, tonight / Land of confusion / In too deep / Anything she does / Domino:- In the glow of the night – The last domino / Throwing it all away / The Brazilian. *(pic-cd.Dec88; GENCDP 2)*

Aug 86. (7"/12") *(GENS 2/+12)* **IN TOO DEEP. / DO THE NEUROTIC** [19] [–]

Aug 86. (7") <89372> **THROWING IT ALL AWAY. / DO THE NEUROTIC** [–] [4]

Nov 86. (7") *(GENS 3)* <89336> **LAND OF CONFUSION. / FEEDING THE FIRE** [14] Oct86 [4]
(12"+=) *(GENS 3-12)* – Dance the neurotic.
(cd-s++=) *(SNEG 3-12)* – ('A'extended).

Mar 87. (7"/12") *(GENS 4/+12)* **TONIGHT, TONIGHT, TONIGHT. / IN THE GLOW OF THE NIGHT (part 1)** [18] Feb87 [3]
(12"+=/cd-s+=) *(GENS/DRAW 4-12)* – Paperlate / ('A'ext.remix).
(cd-s+=) *(CDEP 1)* – Invisible touch (extended) / ('A'-John Potoker remix).
Apr 87. (7") *<89316>* **IN TOO DEEP. / I'D RATHER BE WITH YOU** [–] [3]
Jun 87. (7") *(GENS 5)* **THROWING IT ALL AWAY. / I'D RATHER BE WITH YOU** [22] [–]
(12"+=/c-s+=) *(GENS/+C 5-12)* – Invisible touch (live).
Oct 91. (7"/c-s) *(GENS/+C 6) <87571>* **NO SON OF MINE. / LIVING FOREVER** [6] [13]
(12"+=/cd-s+=) *(GENS/GENCD 6)* – Invisible touch (live).
Nov 91. (cd/c/d-lp) *(GEN CD/MC/LP 3) <82344>* **WE CAN'T DANCE** [1] [4]
– No son of mine / Jesus he knows me / Driving the last spike / I can't dance / Never a time / Dreaming while you sleep / Tell me why / Living forever / Hold on my heart / Way of the world / Since I lost you / Fading lights.
Jan 92. (7"/c-s) *(GENS/+C 7) <87532>* **I CAN'T DANCE. / ON THE SHORELINE** [7] [7]
(cd-s+=) *(GENDG 7)* – In too deep (live) / That's all (live).
(cd-s+=) *(GENDX 7)* – ('A'-sex mix).
Apr 92. (7"/c-s) *(GENS/+C 8) <87481>* **HOLD ON MY HEART. / WAY OF THE WORLD** [16] [12]
(cd-s+=) *(GENDG 8)* – Your own special way (live).
(cd-s+=) *(GENDX 8)* – Home by the sea.
Jul 92. (7"/c-s) *(GENS/+C 9) <87454>* **JESUS HE KNOWS ME. / HEARTS OF FIRE** [20] [23]
(cd-s+=) *(GENDG 9)* – I can't dance (mix).
(cd-s+=) *(GENDX 9)* – Land of confusion (rehearsal version).
Nov 92. (cd/c/d-lp) *(GEN CD/MC/LP 4) <82452>* **THE WAY WE WALK VOLUME 1: THE SHORTS (live)** [3] [35]
– Land of confusion / No son of mine / Jesus he knows me / Throwing it all away / I can't dance / Mama / Hold on my heart / That's all / In too deep / Tonight, tonight, tonight / Invisible touch.
Nov 92. (7"/c-s) *(GENS/+C 10)* **INVISIBLE TOUCH (live). / ABACAB (live)** [7] [–]
(cd-s+=) *(GENDG 10)* – The Brazilian.
Nov 92. (c-s) *<87411>* **NEVER A TIME / TONIGHT, TONIGHT, TONIGHT (live) / INVISIBLE TOUCH (live)** [–] [21]
Jan 93. (cd/c/lp) *(GEN CD/MC/LP 5) <82461>* **LIVE / THE WAY WE WALK VOLUME 2: THE LONGS (live)** [1] Feb93 [20]
– Old medley: Dance on a volcano – Lamb lies down on Broadway – The musical box – Firth of fifth – I know what I like . . . / Driving the fast spike / Domino: part I – In the glow of the night, part II – The last domino / Home by the sea – Second home by the sea / Drum duet.
Feb 93. (7"/c-s) *(GENS/+C 11)* **TELL ME WHY. / DREAMING WHILE YOU SLEEP** [40] [–]
(cd-s+=) *(GENDG 11)* – Tonight, tonight, tonight.
— **RAY WILSON** – vocals (ex-STILTSKIN) repl. COLLINS who continued his solo career (see own entry ⇒)
Sep 97. (cd/c/lp) *(GEN CD/MC/LP 6) <83037>* **CALLING ALL STATIONS** [2] [54]
– Calling all stations / Congo / Shipwrecked / Alien afternoon / Not about us / If that's what you need / The dividing line / Uncertain weather / Small talk / There must be some other way / One man's fool.
Sep 97. (c-s/cd-s) *(GENS C/D 12)* **CONGO / PAPA HE SAID / BANJO MAN** [29] [–]
Nov 97. (c-s/cd-s) *<84063>* **NOT ABOUT US / TURN IT ON AGAIN (live acoustic)** [–] [ ]
(cd-s+=) *(GENSDX 12)* – Second by the sea.
Dec 97. (c-s/cd-s) *(GENS C/D 14)* **SHIPWRECKED / NO SON OF MINE / LOVERS LEAP / TURN IT ON AGAIN** [54] [–]
(cd-s) *(GENSDX 14)* – ('A'side) / Phret / 7-8.
Feb 98. (c-s/cd-s) *(GENS C/D 15)* **NOT ABOUT US / (extended)** [66] [–]
(cd-s+=) *(GENSDX 15)* – Dancing with the moonlit knight / Follow you, follow me.
Oct 99. (cd) *(GENMD 8) <83244>* **TURN IT ON AGAIN – THE HITS** (compilation) [4] [65]
– Turn it on again / Invisible touch / Mama / Land of confusion / I can't dance / Follow you, follow me / Hold on my heart / Abacab / I know what I like (in your wardrobe) / No son of mine / Tonight, tonight, tonight / In too deep / Congo / Jesus he knows me / That's all / Misunderstanding / Throwing it all away / The carpet crawlers (1999).

– compilations etc. –

on 'Charisma' unless mentioned otherwise
May 74. (d-lp-box) *(CGS 102)* **GENESIS COLLECTION VOLUME ONE** [ ] [–]
– (TRESPASS / NURSERY CRYME)
May 74. (d-lp-box) *(CGS 103)* **GENESIS COLLECTION VOLUME TWO** [ ] [–]
– (FOXTROT / SELLING ENGLAND BY THE POUND)
May 76. (lp/c) *Decca; (ROOTS/KRTC 1)* **ROCK ROOTS: GENESIS** [ ] [–]
– (debut lp + early 45's)
Mar 83. (d-c) *(CASMC 112)* **FOXTROT / SELLING ENGLAND BY THE POUND** [ ] [–]
Apr 86. (lp/pic-lp) *Metal Masters; (MACHM/+P 4)* **WHEN THE SOUR TURNS TO SWEET** [ ] [–]
(cd-iss. Oct87; MACD 4) (re-iss. Jul91;)
Mar 87. (cd) *London; (820496-2)* **AND THE WORLD WAS** (early) [ ] [–]
Jun 88. (7") *Old Gold; (OG 9263)* **I KNOW WHAT I LIKE (IN YOUR WARDROBE). / COUNTING OUT TIME** [ ] [–]
Jun 88. (7") *Old Gold; (OG 9264)* **FOLLOW YOU FOLLOW ME. / A TRICK OF THE TAIL** [ ] [–]
Nov 90. (pic-cd-box) *Virgin; (TPAK 1)* **GENESIS CD COLLECTORS EDITION** [ ] [ ]
– (TRESPASS / NURSERY CRYME / FOXTROT)
Jun 98. (4xcd-box) *(CDBOX 6)* **ARCHIVE 1967-1975** [35] [ ]
Nov 00. (d-cd) *(MILBOX 41)* **GENESIS / ABACAB** [ ] [–]
Nov 00. (3xcd-box) *(CDBOX 7)* **ARCHIVE VOL.2 1976-1992** [ ] [ ]

TONY BANKS

Charisma Charisma

Oct 79. (7") *(CB 344)* **FOR A WHILE. / FROM THE UNDERTOW** [ ] [–]
Oct 79. (lp/c) *(CAS/+MC 1148) <2207>* **A CURIOUS FEELING** [21] [ ]
– From the undertow / Lucky me / The lie / After the lie / A curious feeling / Forever morning / You / Somebody else's dream / The waters of Lethe / For a while / In the dark. *(re-iss. Oct86 lp/c; CHC/+MC 42) (cd-iss. 1988; CASCD 1148)*
Jul 80. (7") *(CB 365)* **A CURIOUS FEELING. / FOR A WHILE** [ ] [–]
Apr 83. (7"/12") *(BANKS 1/+12)* **THIS IS LOVE. / CHARM** [ ] [–]
May 83. (7") *(A 9825)* **THE WICKED LADY. / (part 2)** [ ] [–]
(above from the film soundtrack 'THE WICKED LADY; on 'WEA')
Jun 83. (lp/c) *(TB/+MC 1)* **THE FUGITIVE** [50] [ ]
– This is love / Man of spells / And the wheels keep turning / Say you'll never leave me / Thirty three's / By you / At the edge of night / Charm / Moving under. *(re-iss. Oct86 lp/c; CHC/+MC 43) (cd-iss. 1988; TBCD 1)*
Aug 83. (7") *(BANKS 2)* **AND THE WHEELS KEEP TURNING. / MAN OF SPELLS** [ ] [–]
(12"+=) *(BANKS 2/+12)* – Sometime never.
(below with JIM DIAMOND and TOYAH on vocals)
Sep 85. (7"ep) *(CBEP 415)* **TONY BANKS** [ ] [–]
– Red wing (instrumental) / You call this victory / Line of symmetry.
Oct 86. (7"; by FISH & TONY BANKS) *(CB 426)* **SHORT CUT TO NOWHERE. / SMILIN JACK CASEY** [ ] [–]
(12"+=) *(CB 426-12)* – K.2.
Jul 87. (cd) *(CASCD 1173)* **SOUNDTRACKS** ('Quicksilver' // 'Lorca And The Outlaws') [ ] [ ]
– Short cut to nowhere / Smilin' Jack Casey / Quicksilver suite: Rebirth – Gypsy – Final chase // You call this victory / Lion of symmetry / Redwing suite: Redwing – Lorca – Kid and Detective Droid – Lift off – Death of Abby. *(re-iss. Nov89 lp/c; CHC/+MC 82)*

BANKSTATEMENT

TONY BANKS with friends, etc.

Virgin Atlantic

Jul 89. (7") *(VS 1200)* **THROWBACK. / THURSDAY THE 12th** [ ] [–]
(12"+=/cd-s+=) *(VS T/CD 1200)* – This is love.
Aug 89. (lp/c/cd) *(V/TCV/CDV 2600)* **BANKSTATEMENT** [ ] [ ]
– Throwback / I'll be waiting / Queen of darkness / That night / Raincloud / he border / Big man / A house needs a roof / The more I hide it. *(cd+=)* – Diamonds aren't so bad / Thursday the 12th.
Oct 89. (7") *(VS 1208)* **I'LL BE WAITING. / DIAMONDS AREN'T SO BAD** [ ] [–]
(12"+=/cd-s+=) *(VS T/CD 1208)* – And the wheels keep turning.

TONY BANKS

solo, with guest vocals **ANDY TAYLOR, FISH, JAYNEY KLIMEK**

May 91. (7"/c-s) **I WANNA CHANGE THE SCORE. / HERO FOR AN HOUR** [ ] [–]
(12"+=) – Big man (BANKSTATEMENT).
(cd-s++=) – The waters of Lethe.

Jun 91. (cd/c/lp) *(CD/TC+/V 2658)* **STILL** [ ] [ ]
– Red day on blue street / Angel face / The gift / Still it takes me by surprise / Hero for an hour / I wanna change the score / Water out of wine / Another murder of a day / Back to back / The final curtain.

MIKE RUTHERFORD

Charisma Passport

Jan 80. (7") *(CB 353)* **WORKING IN LINE. / COMPRESSION** [ ] [–]

Feb 80. (lp) *(CAS 1149) <9843>* **SMALLCREEP'S DAY** [13] [ ]
– Smallcreep's day: Between the tick and the tock – Working in line – After hours – Cats and rats in the neighbourhood – Smallcreep alone – Out into the daylight – At the end of the day / Moonshine / Time and time again / Romani / Every road / Overnight job. *(re-iss. Oct86 lp/c; CHC/+MC 53) (cd-iss. Jun89; CASCD 1149)*

Mar 80. (7") **WORKING IN LINE. / MOONSHINE** [–] [ ]

Jul 80. (7") *(CB 364)* **TIME AND TIME AGAIN. / AT THE END OF THE DAY** [ ] [–]

W.E.A. Atlantic

Aug 82. (7") *(K 79331) <89976>* **HALFWAY THERE. / A DAY TO REMEMBER** [ ] Nov82 [ ]

Aug 82. (7") *<89981>* **A DAY TO REMEMBER. / MAXINE** [–] [ ]

Sep 82. (lp/c) *(K/K4 99249) <80015>* **ACTING VERY STRANGE** [23] [ ]
– Acting very strange / A day to remember / Maxine / Halfway there / Who's fooling who / Couldn't get arrested / I don't wanna know / Hideaway.

Oct 82. (7"/12") *(RUTH 1/+T)* **ACTING VERY STRANGE. / COULDN'T GET ARRESTED** [ ] [–]

Jan 83. (7") *(U 9967)* **HIDEAWAY. / CALYPSO** [ ] [–]

—— MIKE then formed the pop outfit MIKE + THE MECHANICS

MIKE + THE MECHANICS

RUTHERFORD with **PAUL CARRACK** (b.22 Apr'51, Sheffield, England) – vocals, keyboards (ex-ACE, ex-SQUEEZE, ex-Solo artist) / **PAUL YOUNG** (b.17 Jun'47, Manchester, England) – vocals (ex-SAD CAFE) / **PETER VAN HOOKE** (b. 4 Jun'50, London) – drums / **ADRIAN LEE** (b. 9 Sep'47) – keyboards

WEA Atlantic

Oct 85. (lp/c) *(WX 49/+C) <81287>* **MIKE + THE MECHANICS** [78] [26]
– Silent running (on dangerous ground) / All I need is a miracle / Par Avion / Hanging by a thread / I get the feeling / Take the reins / You are the one / A call to arms / Taken in. *(cd-iss. Jul86; 252496-2)*

Nov 85. (7") *<89488>* **SILENT RUNNING (ON DANGEROUS GROUND). / PAR AVION** [–] [6]

Feb 86. (7") *(U 8908)* **SILENT RUNNING (ON DANGEROUS GROUND). / I GET THE FEELING** [21] [–]
(12"+=) *(U 8908T)* – Too far gone.

May 86. (7") *(U 8765) <89450>* **ALL I NEED IS A MIRACLE. / YOU ARE THE ONE** [53] Mar86 [5]
(12"+=) *(U 8908T)* – A call to arms.

Jun 86. (7") *<89404>* **TAKEN IN. / A CALL TO ARMS** [–] [32]

—— added **TIM RENWICK** – guitar (ex-SUTHERLAND BROTHERS & QUIVER)

Nov 88. (7") *(U 7789) <88990>* **NOBODY'S PERFECT. / NOBODY KNOWS** [ ] Oct88 [63]
(12"+=/3"cd-s+=) *(U 7789 T/CD)* – All I need is a miracle.

Nov 88. (lp/c)(cd) *(WX 203/+C)(256004-2) <81923>* **THE LIVING YEARS** [2] [13]
– Nobody's perfect / The living years / Seeing is believing / Nobody knows / Poor boy down / Blame / Don't / Black and blue / Beautiful day / Why me?.

Feb 89. (7") *(U 7717) <88964>* **THE LIVING YEARS. / TOO MANY FRIENDS** [2] Dec88 [1]
(12"+=/cd-s+=) *(U 7717 T/CD)* – I get the feeling (live).

Apr 89. (7") *(U 7602)* **NOBODY KNOWS. / WHY ME?** [ ] [ ]
(c-s+=/12"+=/cd-s+=) *(U 7602 C/T/CD)* – The living years / ('A'edit).

Apr 89. (c-s) *<88921>* **SEEING IS BELIEVING / DON'T** [–] [62]

Virgin Atlantic

Mar 91. (7"/c-s/12"/cd-s) *(VS/+C/T/CD 1345) <87714>* **WORD OF MOUTH. / LET'S PRETEND IT DIDN'T HAPPEN** [13] [78]
(cd-s+=) *(VSCDG 1345)* – Taken in (live).

Apr 91. (cd/c/lp) *(CD/TC+/V 2662) <82233>* **WORD OF MOUTH** [11] [ ]
– Get up / Word of mouth / A time and place / Yesterday, today, tomorrow / The way you look at me / Everybody gets a second chance / Stop baby / My crime of passion / Let's pretend it didn't happen / Before (the next heartache falls).

May 91. (7"/c-s) *(VS/+C 1351)* **A TIME AND A PLACE. / GET UP** [58] [ ]
(12"+=/cd-s+=) *(VS T/CD 1351)* – I think I've got the message.
(cd-s) *(VSCDG 1351)* – ('A'side) / I think I've got the message / My crime of passion (acoustic).

Sep 91. (7"/c-s) **STOP BABY. / GET UP** [ ] [ ]
(cd-s+=) – Before the heartache falls.

Feb 92. (7"/c-s) *(VS/+C 1396)* **EVERYBODY GETS A SECOND CHANCE. / THE WAY YOU LOOK AT ME** [56] [ ]
(cd-s+=) *(VSCD 1396)* – At the end of the day (MIKE RUTHERFORD).

—— now without RENWICK, who was repl. by guests **B.A. ROBERTSON / GARY WALLIS / WIX + CLEM CLEMPSON**

Feb 95. (7"/c-s) *(VS/+C 1526)* **OVER MY SHOULDER. / SOMETHING TO BELIEVE IN** [12] [ ]
(cd-s+=) *(VSCDG 1526)* – Always the last to know.
(cd-s+=) *(VSCDX 1526)* – Word of mouth / ('A'version).

Mar 95. (cd/c) *(CD/TC V 2772) <82738>* **BEGGAR ON A BEACH OF GOLD** [9] [ ]
– A beggar on a beach of gold / Another cup of coffee / You've really got a hold on me / Mea culpa / Over my shoulder / Someone always hates someone / The ghost of sex and you / Web of lies / Plain & simple / Something to believe in / A house of many rooms / I believe (when I fall in love it will be forever) / Going going . . .home.

Jun 95. (c-s/cd-s) *(VSC/+DT 1535)* **BEGGAR ON A BEACH OF GOLD / HELP ME / NOBODY TOLD ME** [33] [ ]
(cd-s) *(VSCDX 1535)* – ('A'side) / Boys at the front / Little boy / ('A'acoustic).

Aug 95. (c-s) *(VSC 1554)* **ANOTHER CUP OF COFFEE / YOU NEVER CHANGE** [65] [ ]
(cd-s+=) *(VSCDG 1554)* – You don't know what love is.
(cd-s) *(VSCDX 1554)* – ('A'side) / Everyday hurts / How long.

Feb 96. (c-s) *(VSC 1576)* **ALL I NEED IS A MIRACLE '96 (remix) / THE WAY YOU LOOK AT ME** [27] [–]
(cd-s) *(VSCDG 1576)* – Don't / Over my shoulder (live).

Mar 96. (cd/c) *(CD/TC V2797)* **HITS** (compilation) [3] [–]
– All I need is a miracle '96 / Over my shoulder / Word of mouth / The living years / Another cup of coffee / Nobody's perfect / Silent running / Nobody knows / Get up / A time and place / Taken in / Everybody gets a second chance / A beggar on a beach of gold.

May 96. (c-s) *(VSC 1585)* **SILENT RUNNING / PLAIN & SIMPLE** [ ] [–]
(cd-s+=) *(VSCDT 1585)* – Stop baby.

May 99. (c-s) *(VSC 1732)* **NOW THAT YOU'VE GONE / WORD OF MOUTH (live) / BEGGAR ON A BEACH OF GOLD (live)** [35] [–]
(cd-s) *(VSCDT 1732)* – (first & third tracks) / Silent running (live).
(cd-s) *(VSCDX 1732)* – (first two tracks) / I believe when I fall in love it will be forever.

May 99. (cd/c) *(CDV/TCV 2885)* **MIKE & THE MECHANICS** [14] [–]
– Whenever I stop / Now that you've gone / Ordinary girl / All the light I need / What will you do / My little island / Open up / When I get over you / If only / Asking for the last time / Did you see me coming / Look across at dreamland.

Aug 99. (c-s/cd-s) *(TCV/CDV 1743)* **WHENEVER I STOP / NOW THAT YOU'VE GONE (live)** [73] [–]
(cd-s) *(VSCDX 1743)* – ('A'side) / Ordinary girl (unplugged) / My little island (live).

□ GENIUS / GZA (see under ⇒ WU-TANG CLAN)

GENTLE GIANT

Formed: Portsmouth, England ... 1966 as SIMON DUPREE & THE BIG SOUND, by SHULMAN brothers DEREK, RAY and PHIL. Early in '67, they had a UK Top 50 hit with 'I SEE THE LIGHT'. By the end of the year, 'KITES', gave them a Top 10 smash, although they soon opted out of the psychedelic pop market in favour of the burgeoning prog-rock scene. Late in 1969, the three brothers, with three new recruits (KERRY MINEAR, GARY GREEN and MARTIN SMITH), re-launched themselves as the more experimental GENTLE GIANT. A year later, they appeared on the pivotal 'Vertigo' label, their eponymous debut album regaining support from stalwart Radio One DJ, ALAN 'Fluff' FREEMAN. Their fourth album, 'OCTOPUS' (1972), although not a major success in Britain, hit the Top 200 in north America. They might have built upon this Stateside interest, but for Columbia's decision not to release their next project, 'IN A GLASS HOUSE'. However, in 1974, they finally cracked the Top 100 with their much-improved, 'THE POWER AND GLORY'. Signing a new deal in Britain with 'Chrysalis' records, their seventh album, 'FREE HAND', again only found a paying audience across the water. However, it did contain more impressive vocal gymnastics, much in evidence on the opening two tracks, 'JUST THE SAME' and 'ON REFLECTION'. The band was subsequently crushed under the jack-booted heels of punk rock, although they did soldier on under 1980. DEREK moved to New York, becoming an A&R executive and going on to sign hard-rock acts, CINDERELLA and KINGDOM COME. • **Songwriters:** MINNEAR and the SHULMANS collaborated on most recordings. SIMON DUPREE covered; DAY TIME, NIGHT TIME (Mike Hugg of Manfred Mann). • **Trivia:** MINNEAR had graduated from the Royal Academy Of Music in the late 60's.

Album rating: Simon Dupree & The Big Sound: WITHOUT RESERVATIONS (*5) / Gentle Giant: GENTLE GIANT (*6) / ACQUIRING THE TASTE (*6) / THREE FRIENDS (*6) / OCTOPUS (*5) / IN A GLASS HOUSE (*5) / THE POWER AND THE GLORY (*5) / FREE HAND (*6) / GIANT STEPS ... THE FIRST FIVE YEARS compilation (*7) / INTERVIEW (*5) / THE OFFICIAL "LIVE" GENTLE GIANT – PLAYING THE FOOL (*6) / THE MISSING PIECE (*4) / GIANT FOR A DAY (*4) / CIVILIAN (*4)

SIMON DUPREE & THE BIG SOUND

DEREK SHULMAN (b. 2 Feb'47, Glasgow, Scotland) – vocals / **RAY SCHULMAN** (b. 8 Dec'49, Portsmouth, England) – lead guitar / **PHIL SCHULMAN** (b.27 Aug'37, Glasgow) – saxophone, trumpet / **ERIC HINE** – keyboards / **PETE O'FLAHERTY** – bass / **TONY RANSLEY** – drums

Parlophone Tower

Dec 66. (7") *(R 5542)* **I SEE THE LIGHT. / IT IS FINISHED** [45] [–]

Feb 67. (7") *(R 5574) <347>* **RESERVATIONS. / YOU NEED A MAN** [ ] [ ]

May 67. (7") *(R 5594) <427>* **DAY TIME, NIGHT TIME. / I'VE SEEN IT ALL BEFORE** [ ] [ ]

Aug 67. (lp; mono/stereo) *(PCM/PCS 7029) <T 5097>* **WITHOUT RESERVATIONS** [39] [ ]
– Medley: Sixty minutes of your love – A lot of love / Love / Get off my Bach / There's a little playhouse / Day time, night time / I see the light / What is soul / Teacher, teacher / Amen / Who cares / Reservations. *(re-dist.1969; same)*

Oct 67. (7") *(R 5646)* **KITES. / LIKE THE SUN LIKE THE FIRE** [9] [ ]

Mar 68. (7") *(R 5670)* **FOR WHOM THE BELL TOLLS. / SLEEP** [43] [ ]

May 68. (7") *(R 5697)* **PART OF MY PAST. / THIS STORY NEVER ENDS** [ ] [ ]

Sep 68. (7") *(R 5727)* **THINKING ABOUT MY LIFE. / VELVET AND LACE** [ ] [ ]

Nov 68. (7"; as The MOLES) *(R 5743)* **WE ARE THE MOLES (part 2) / (part 2)** [ ] [–]

Feb 69. (7") *(R 5757)* **BROKEN HEARTED PIRATES. / SHE GAVE ME THE SUN** [ ] [–]

— **GERRY KENWORTHY** – keyboards repl. HINE

Nov 69. (7") *(R 5816)* **THE EAGLE FLIES TONIGHT. / GIVE IT ALL BACK** [ ] [–]

— Split late '69. The SHULMAN's formed GENTLE GIANT while the others left the business.

– compilations etc. –

Nov 78. (7"ep) *E.M.I.; (EMI 2893)* **SIMON DUPREE & THE BIG SOUND** [ ] [–]
– Kites / For whom the bells toll / Reservations / I see the light.

Mar 82. (lp/c) *See For Miles; (CM/+K 109)* **AMEN** [ ] [–]
– Kites / Like the sun like the fire / Sleep / For whom the bells toll / Broken hearted pirates / 60 Minutes of your love / A lot of love / Love / Get off my Bach / There's a little picture playhouse / Day time, night time / I see the light / What is soul / Amen / Who cares / She gave me the sun / Thinking about my life / It is finished / I've seen it all before / You need a man / Reservations. *(re-iss. Dec86 as 'KITES'; same) (cd-iss. May93 & May97 as 'KITES' on 'See For Miles'; SEECD 368)*

Mar 87. (7") *Old Gold; (OG 9655)* **KITES. / (b-side by other artist)** [ ] [–]

GENTLE GIANT

DEREK SHULMAN – vocals, bass, saxophone / **RAY SHULMAN** – guitar, bass, violin, keyboards, drums / **PHIL SHULMAN** – saxophone, trumpet / **KERRY MINNEAR** (b.2 Apr'48, Salisbury, England) – keyboards, vocals (ex-RUST) / **GARY GREEN** (b.20 Nov'50, Stroud Green, England) – guitar, vocals / **MARTIN SMITH** – drums (ex-MOJOS)

Vertigo Vertigo

Nov 70. (lp) *(6360 020)* **GENTLE GIANT** [ ] [–]
– Giant / Funny ways / Alucard / Isn't it quiet and cold / Nothing at all / Why not? / The Queen. *(cd-iss. Aug89 on 'Line'; LICD 900722) (cd re-iss. Nov94 on 'Repertoire';) (cd re-iss. Feb97 on 'Mercury'; 842624-2)*

Aug 71. (lp) *(6360 041) <1005>* **ACQUIRING THE TASTE** [ ] [ ]
– Pantagruel's nativity / Edge of twilight / The house, the street, the room / Acquiring the taste / Wreck / The Moon is down / Black cat / Plain truth. *(cd-iss. Oct89 on 'Line'; LICD 900726) (cd re-iss. Aug90; 842917-2) (cd re-iss. Feb97 on 'Mercury'; 842917-2)*

— **MALCOLM MORTIMER** – drums repl. MARTIN

Vertigo Columbia

Jul 72. (lp) *(6360 070) <31649>* **THREE FRIENDS** [ ] [ ]
– (prologue) / Schooldays / Working all day / Peel the paint / Mister Class and quality? / Three friends. *(cd-iss. Oct89 on 'Line'; LICD 900730)*

— **JOHN WEATHERS** (b.Wales) – drums (ex-GRAHAM BOND, ex-EYES OF BLUE, ex-ANCIENT GREASE, ex-PETE BROWN, etc.) repl. MALCOLM

Dec 72. (lp) *(6360 080) <32022>* **OCTOPUS** [ ] [ ]
– The advent of Panurge / Raconteur troubadour / A cry for everyone / Knots / The boys in the band / Dog's life / Knots / Think of me with kindness / River. *(cd-iss. Oct89 on 'Line'; LICD 900736) (cd re-iss. Nov94 on 'Repertoire';) (cd re-iss. Feb97 on 'Mercury'; 842694-2)*

— now quintet of **DEREK, RAY, KERRY, GARY + JOHN** when PHIL left.

W.W.A. Capitol

Dec 73. (lp) *(WWA 002)* **IN A GLASS HOUSE** [ ] [–]
– The runaway / An inmate's lullaby / Way of life / A reunion / Experience / In a glass house / Index. *(cd-iss. Dec92 on 'Road Goes On Forever'; RGFCD 1001) (cd re-iss. Jul94 on 'Terrapin Truckin'; TRUCKCD 1)*

Jan 74. (7") *(WWP 1001)* **IN A GLASS HOUSE. / AN INMATE'S LULLABY** [ ] [–]

Oct 74. (lp) *(WWA 010) <11337>* **THE POWER AND THE GLORY** [ ] [78]
– Proclamation / So sincere / Aspirations / Playing the game / Cogs in cogs / No god's a man / The face / Valedictory. *(cd-iss. Dec92 on 'Road Goes On Forever'; RGFCD 1002)*

Nov 74. (7") *(WWS 017)* **THE POWER AND THE GLORY. / PLAYING THE GAME** [ ] [–]

Chrysalis Capitol

Aug 75. (lp/c) *(CHR/ZCHR 1093) <11428>* **FREE HAND** [ ] [48]
– Just the same / On reflection / Free hand / Time to kill / His last voyage / Talybont / Mobile. *(cd-iss. Aug93 on 'Road Goes On Forever'; RGFCD 1004) (cd-iss. Jul94 on 'Terrapin Truckin'; TRUCKCD 4)*

Apr 76. (lp/c) *(CHR/ZCHR 1115) <11532>* **INTERVIEW** [ ] [ ]
– Interview / Give it back / Design / Another show / Empty city / Timing / I lost my head. *(cd-iss. Mar93 on 'Road Goes On Forever'; RGFCD 1005)*

(cd-iss. Jul94 on 'Terrapin Truckin'; TRUCKCD 5) (cd re-iss. Oct95 on 'One Way';)

Jan 77. (d-lp/d-c) *(CTY/ZCTY 1133) <11592>* **PLAYING THE FOOL – LIVE (live)** [ ] [89]
– Just the same / Proclamation / On reflection / Excerpts from Octopus (Boys in the band, etc) / Funny ways / In a glass house / So sincere / Free hand / Sweet Georgia Brown (breakdown in Brussels) / Peel the paint / I lost my head. *(re-iss. May89 on 'Essential' d-lp/cd; ESS LP/CD 006) (cd re-iss. Dec94 on 'Terrapin Truckin'; TRUCKCD 9)*

Aug 77. (lp/c) *(CHR/ZCHR 1152) <11696>* **THE MISSING PIECE** [ ] [81]
– Two weeks in Spain / I'm turning around / Betcha thought we couldn't do it / Who do you think you are? / Mountain time / As old as you're young / Memories of old days / Winning / For nobody. *(cd re-iss. Aug93 on 'Road Goes On Forever'; RGFCD 1006) (cd-iss. Jul94 on 'Terrapin Truckin'; TRUCKCD 6) (cd re-iss. Oct99 on 'One Way'; S 211846-2)*

Aug 77. (7") *(CHS 2160)* **I'M TURNING AROUND. / JUST THE SAME (live)** [ ] [–]

Sep 77. (7") *<4484>* **I'M TURNING AROUND. / COGS IN COGS** [–] [ ]

Oct 77. (7") *(CHS 2181)* **TWO WEEKS IN SPAIN. / FREE HAND** [ ] [–]

Sep 78. (7") *(CHS 2245)* **THANK YOU. / SPOOKY BOOGIE** [ ] [–]

Sep 78. (lp/c) *(CHR/ZCHR 1186) <11813>* **GIANT FOR A DAY** [ ] [ ]
– Word from the wise / Thank you / Giant for a day / Spooky boogie / Take me / Little brown bag / Friends / No stranger / It's only goodbye / Rock climber. *(cd-iss. Aug93 on 'Road Goes On Forever'; RGFCD 7) (cd-iss. Jul94 on 'Terrapin Truckin'; TRUCKCD 7) (cd re-iss. Oct99 on 'One Way'; S 2118470)*

Jan 79. (7") *(CHS 2270)* **WORD FROM THE WISE. / NO STRANGER** [ ] [–]

Jan 79. (7") *<4652>* **WORD FROM THE WISE. / SPOOKY BOOGIE** [–] [ ]

Chrysalis Columbia

Aug 80. (lp/c) *(CHR/ZCHR 1285) <36341>* **CIVILIAN** [ ] [ ]
– Convenience / All through the night / Shadows on the street / Number one / Underground / I'm a camera / Inside out / It's not imagination. *(cd-iss. Jul94 on 'Terrapin Truckin'; TRUCKCD 8)*

—— split 1980. RAY SHULMAN went into production; WEATHERS joined MAN.

– compilations, others, etc. –

on 'Vertigo' unless otherwise mentioned

Nov 75. (d-lp) *(6641 334)* **GIANT STEPS . . . (THE FIRST FIVE YEARS) 1970-75** [ ] [–]
– Giant / Alucard / Nothing at all / Plain truth / Prologue / A cry for everyone / Why not / Peel the paint / Mister Class and quality? / River / The face / The runaway / Power and the glory / Playing the game / In a glass house.

Oct 77. (d-lp) *(6641 629)* **PRETENTIOUS (FOR THE SAKE OF IT)** [ ] [–]

Aug 81. (lp/c) *(6381/7215 045)* **GREATEST HITS** [–] Dutch [–]

Apr 94. (cd) *Terrapin Truckin'; (TRUCKCD 1010)* **THE LAST TIME (LIVE 1980)** [ ] [–]

Dec 94. (cd) *Windsong; (WINCD 066)* **IN CONCERT (live)** [ ] [–]

Jul 96. (cd) *Strange Fruit; (BOJCD 018)* **LIVE IN CONCERT (live)** [ ] [–]

Sep 96. (cd) *Red Steel; (RMCCD 0205)* **LAST STEPS (live 1980)** [ ] [–]

Aug 97. (cd) *Strange Fruit; (SFRSCD 023)* **LIVE AT THE BBC** [ ] [–]

1997. (d-cd) *Vertigo; <534101>* **EDGE OF TWILIGHT** [–] [ ]

Apr 98. (cd) *King Biscuit; (<KBFHCD 004>)* **KING BISCUIT PRESENTS . . .** [ ] [ ]

Sep 98. (d-cd) *Hux; (<HUX 008>)* **OUT OF THE FIRE: LIVE ON THE BBC 1973 & 1978 (live)** [ ] [ ]

Oct 98. (cd) *Beat Goes On; (<BGOCD 421>)* **FREE HAND / INTERVIEW** [ ] [ ]

Jan 99. (cd) *Beat Goes On; (<BGOCD 435>)* **PLAYING THE FOOL / CIVILIAN** [ ] [ ]

Mar 99. (cd) *Beat Goes On; (<BGOCD 431>)* **THE MISSING PIECE / GIANT FOR A DAY** [ ] [ ]

Mar 00. (d-cd) *Hux; (<HUX 018>)* **TOTALLY OUT OF THE WOODS** [ ] [ ]

Sep 00. (cd) *La Cooka Ratcha; (LCVP 101CD) / Blueprint; <4720>* **LIVE ROME 1974** [ ] [–]
(re-iss. May02 on 'Glasshouse'; GLASS 101CD)

Dec 01. (cd) *Disky; (SI 64040-2)* **EXPERIENCE** [ ] [–]

May 02. (cd) *Glasshouse; (<GLASS 102CD>)* **IN A PALESPORT HOUSE (live)** [ ] [ ]

Jul 02. (cd) *Glasshouse; (<GLASS 103CD>)* **INTERVIEW (IN CONCERT) (live)** [ ] [ ]

Jan 03. (d-cd) *Glasshouse; (<GLASS 108CD>)* **ENDLESS LIFE (live)** [ ] [ ]

Feb 03. (cd) *Glasshouse; (<GLASS 105CD>)* **THE MISSING FACE (live)** [ ] [ ]

Mar 03. (cd) *Glasshouse; (<GLASS 104CD>)* **ARTISTICALLY CRYME (live)** [ ] [ ]

Mar 03. (cd) *Glasshouse; (<GLASS 106CD>)* **PLAYING THE CLEVELAND (live)** [ ] [ ]

Mar 03. (cd) *Glasshouse; (<GLASS 107CD>)* **PROLOGUE (live)** [ ] [ ]

May 03. (d-cd) *Snapper; (SMDCD 455)* **WAY OF LIFE** [ ] [–]

May 03. (cd) *King Biscuit; (<KBBCD 138>)* **IN CONCERT** [ ] [ ]

☐ Lowell GEORGE (see under ⇒ LITTLE FEAT)

☐ Lisa GERRARD (see under ⇒ DEAD CAN DANCE)

GERRY & THE PACEMAKERS

Formed: Liverpool, England ... 1959 as The MARS BARS by GERRY MARSDEN, his brother FREDDIE, LES CHADWICK and ARTHUR MACK. Following objections from the confectionary manufacturers, GERRY and Co rather sensibly renamed themselves as they began building up a fanbase at famous Merseyside haunts like The Cavern. MACK was replaced by LES MAGUIRE prior to a stint in Hamburg; there they were spotted by BEATLES manager, Brian Epstein who in turn, secured them a contract with 'Columbia'. Incredibly, perhaps, the quartet were initially more successful than Epstein's other Merseybeat proteges, The BEATLES (with whom they also shared producer George Martin), scoring three UK No.1 hits in a row with their first three single releases. 'HOW DO YOU DO IT?' kicked off their career in Spring '63, a Mitch Murray-penned tune originally intended for The BEATLES. Murray also penned 'I LIKE IT', another moronically cheery ditty that scaled the chart a few months later. Best of the three was 'YOU'LL NEVER WALK ALONE', a cover of the Rogers & Hammerstein standard that at least had some substance to it (the track was later adopted as a terrace anthem by Liverpool football fans). By the close of 1963, GERRY & THE PACEMAKERS had set an unlikely chart record that stood for 21 years before it was equalled by another – decidedly more risqué – Merseyside outfit, FRANKIE GOES TO HOLLYWOOD (HOLLY JOHNSON's mob actually cut 'FERRY CROSS THE MERSEY' as a B-side to the infamous 'Relax'). MARSDEN took over on the songwriting front with early 64's 'I'M THE ONE' (No.2) while the group joined The BEATLES, The ROLLING STONES, The ANIMALS, etc., in the frontline of the British Invasion when 'DON'T LET THE SUN CATCH YOU CRYING' hit the US Top 5 a few months later. The end of that vintage year saw the release of GERRY & THE PACEMAKERS' most enduring song, 'FERRY CROSS THE MERSEY', also the title of 'A Hard Day's Night'-style film and soundtrack aired in early '65. While the band's string of UK singles became American hits all over again, their sound was becoming outmoded in the rapidly evolving British music scene. A final UK hit, 'WALK HAND IN HAND' made the Top 30 in late '65 and they carried on for a further year before disbanding in October '66. MARSDEN cut a number of low-key solo singles over the next decade although he was more well known for his work in children's TV. He re-formed the 'PACEMAKERS in the mid-70's for a USA revival tour, the group reuniting sporadically thereafter for dates on the golden oldie circuit. 1985 saw GERRY back at the top of the UK singles chart when he sang on a charity re-make of 'YOU'LL NEVER WALK ALONE', the track credited to The CROWD with proceeds going towards the Bradford FC Disaster Fund (after a tragic fire). Another 'PACEMAKERS nugget, 'FERRY CROSS THE MERSEY', was dusted down for No.1 reinterpretation in 1989 courtesy of STOCK, AITKEN & WATERMAN together with The CHRISTIANS, PAUL McCARTNEY, GERRY himself, etc.

Best CD compilation: THE ESSENTIAL GERRY & THE PACEMAKERS (*7)

GERRY MARSDEN (b.24 Sep'42) – vocals, lead guitar / **LES CHADWICK** (b.JOHN LESLIE CHADWICK, 11 May'43) – bass / **FREDDIE MARSDEN** (b.23 Oct'40) – drums / **LES MAGUIRE** (b.27 Dec'41, Wallasey, England) – piano, saxophone (ex-UNDERTAKERS) repl. ARTHUR MACK

		Columbia	Laurie
Mar 63.	(7") *(DB 4987) <3162>* **HOW DO YOU DO IT? / AWAY FROM YOU**	1 Apr63	
May 63.	(7") *(DB 7041) <3196>* **I LIKE IT. / IT'S HAPPENED TO ME**	1 Sep63	
Oct 63.	(7") *(DB 7126) <3218>* **YOU'LL NEVER WALK ALONE. / IT'S ALRIGHT**	1 Dec63	
Oct 63.	(lp) *(33SX 1546)* **HOW DO YOU LIKE IT?** – A shot of rhythm and blues / Jambalaya / Where have you been / Here's hoping / Pretend / Maybellene / You'll never walk alone / The wrong yo yo / You're the reason / Chills / You can't fool me / Don't you ever / Summertime / Slow down. *(re-iss. 1967 as 'YOU'LL NEVER WALK ALONE' on 'Music For Pleasure'; MPF 1153) (re-iss. Sep89 on 'Beat Goes On'; BGOLP 57) (cd-iss. Aug94 on 'Repertoire'; REP 4422)*	2	–
Jan 64.	(7") *(DB 7189) <3233>* **I'M THE ONE. / YOU'VE GOT WHAT I LIKE**	2 Feb64	82
Apr 64.	(7") *(DB 7268)* **DON'T LET THE SUN CATCH YOU CRYING. / SHOW ME THAT YOU CARE**	6	–
May 64.	(7") *<3251>* **DON'T LET THE SUN CATCH YOU CRYING. / AWAY FROM YOU**	–	4
Jul 64.	(lp) *<2024>* **DON'T LET THE SUN CATCH YOU CRYING** – Don't let the sun catch you crying / I'm the one / Away from you / Jambalaya / Maybellene / You'll never walk alone / How do you do it / You're the reason / Don't you ever / Summertime / Slow down / Show me that you care.	–	29
Jul 64.	(7") *<3261>* **HOW DO YOU DO IT? / YOU'LL NEVER WALK ALONE**	–	9
Aug 64.	(7") *(DB 7353)* **IT'S GONNA BE ALRIGHT. / IT'S JUST BECAUSE**	24	–
Oct 64.	(7") *<3271>* **I LIKE IT. / JAMBALAYA**	–	17
Nov 64.	(lp) *<2027>* **GERRY & THE PACEMAKERS' SECOND ALBUM** – I like it / A shot of rhythm and blues / Where have you been / Here's hoping / Pretend / The wrong yo-yo / Chills / You can't fool me / It happened to me / It's all right / Slow down / Jambalaya.	–	
Dec 64.	(7") *(DB 7437)* **FERRY CROSS THE MERSEY. / YOU YOU YOU**	8	–
Dec 64.	(7") *<3279>* **I'LL BE THERE. / YOU YOU YOU**	–	14
Jan 65.	(lp) *(33SX 1693) <6387>* **FERRY CROSS THE MERSEY (live Film Soundtrack on 'United Artists' US)** – It's gonna be alright / Why oh why / Fall in love / Think about love / I love you too (FOURMOST) / All is quiet on the Mersey front (GEORGE MARTIN AND ORCHESTRA) / This thing called love / Baby you're so good to me / I'll wait for you / She's the only girl for me / Is it love (CILLA BLACK) / Ferry cross the Mersey. *(re-iss. Mar88 on 'Beat Goes On'; BGOLP 10) (cd-iss. Aug94 on 'Repertoire'+=; REP 4423)* – (14 tracks). *(cd re-iss. Jul97 +=; DORIG 114)*	19 Feb65	13
Jan 65.	(7") *<3284>* **FERRY CROSS THE MERSEY. / PRETEND**	–	6
Feb 65.	(lp) *<2030>* **I'LL BE THERE!** – I'll be there / What'd I say / Rip it up / You win again / You you you / Now I'm alone / My babe / Reelin' and rockin' / I count the tears / Whole lotta shakin' goin' on / It'll be me / Skinny Minnie.	–	
Mar 65.	(7") *(DB 7504)* **I'LL BE THERE. / BABY YOU'RE SO GOOD TO ME**	15	–
Apr 65.	(7") *<3293>* **IT'S GONNA BE ALRIGHT. / SKINNY MINNIE**	–	23
May 65.	(lp) *<2031>* **GERRY AND THE PACEMAKERS' GREATEST HITS** (compilation)	–	44
Aug 65.	(7") *<3313>* **GIVE ALL YOUR LOVE TO ME. / YOU'RE THE REASON**	–	68
Nov 65.	(7") *(DB 7738)* **WALK HAND IN HAND. / DREAMS**	29	
Feb 66.	(7") *(DB 7835) <3337>* **LA LA LA. / WITHOUT YOU**		90
May 66.	(7") *<3370>* **LOOKING FOR MY LIFE. / BRIGHT GREEN PLEASURE MACHINE**	–	
Sep 66.	(7") *(DB 8044) <3354>* **GIRL ON A SWING. / FOOL TO MYSELF**		28

—— Disbanded Oct'66. MARSDEN went solo in 1967 (see GREAT ROCK DISCOG.)

GERRY MARSDEN

		C.B.S.	Columbia
Jun 67.	(7") *(2784)* **PLEASE LET THEM BE. / I'M NOT BLUE**		
1967.	(7") *(2946)* **GILBERT GREEN. / WHAT MAKES ME LOVE YOU**		

—— In 1968, GERRY landed leading role in stage play 'Charlie Girl'.

Jun 68.	(7"; by GERRY MARSDEN & DEREK NIMMO) *(3575)* **LIVERPOOL. / CHARLIE GIRL**		–
		NEMS	not iss.
1968.	(7") *(56-3831)* **IN THE YEAR OF APRIL. / EVERY DAY**		–
May 69.	(7") *(56-4229)* **EVERY LITTLE MINUTE. / IN DAYS OF OLD**		–
		Decca	not iss.
May 71.	(7") *(F 13172)* **I'VE GOT MY UKELELE. / WHAT A DAY**		–
		Phoenix	not iss.
1972.	(7") *(SNIX 129)* **AMOCREDO. / ('A'version)**		–

GERRY MARSDEN & THE PACEMAKERS

(with new line-up)

Apr 74.	(7") *D.J.M.; (DJS 298)* **REMEMBER (THE DAYS OF ROCK AND ROLL). / THERE'S STILL TIME**		–

GERRY MARSDEN

went solo again.

		D.J.M.	not iss.
Aug 74.	(7") *(DJS 10314)* **THEY DON'T MAKE DAYS LIKE THAT. / CAN'T YOU HEAR THE SONG**		–
Apr 75.	(7") *(DJS 10362)* **YOUR SONG. / DAYS I SPENT WITH YOU**		–
Sep 76.	(7") *(DJS 10708)* **MY HOMETOWN. / LOVELY LADY**		–

—— GERRY semi-retired from biz, until his vocal contribution May '85 on Disaster Fund (Bradford F.C. fire) No.1 re-indition of YOU'LL NEVER WALK ALONE by 'The CROWD'. The band are still regulars on the cabaret circuit.

– (selective) compilations, etc. –

on 'Columbia' unless stated otherwise

Jun 63.	(7"ep) *(SEG 8257)* **HOW DO YOU DO IT?**	34	–
Oct 77.	(lp/c) *E.M.I.; (NUT/TC-NUT 10)* **THE BEST OF GERRY & THE PACEMAKERS**		–
Jun 92.	(cd/c) *E.M.I.; (CD/TC EMS 1443)* **THE BEST OF THE EMI YEARS** – How do you do it / Maybellene / I like it / Chills / Pretend / Jambalaya / You're the reason / Hello little girl / You'll never walk alone / A shot of rhythm and blues / Slow down / It's all right / I'm the one / Don't let the sun catch you crying / You've got what I like / It's just because / You you you / It's gonna be all right / Ferry cross the Mersey / I'll wait for you / Hallelujah I love her so / Reelin' & rockin' / Why oh why / Baby you're so good to me / Walk hand in hand / Dreams / Give all your love to me / I'll be there / La la la / Fool to myself / Girl on a swing.		–
Oct 97.	(cd) *E.M.I.; (CDABBEY 102)* **AT ABBEY ROAD 1063-1966**		
Jun 99.	(cd/c) *Castle Pulse; (PLS CD/MC 129)* **FERRY 'CROSS THE MERSEY: THE BEST OF GERRY & THE PACEMAKERS**		
Apr 00.	(cd) *Disky; (SI 25073-2)* **THE BEST OF THE 60'S**		

Feb 01. (cd) *EMI Plus; (5760320)* **THE STORY**

Apr 02. (cd) *E.M.I.; (538847-2)* **HOW DO YOU LIKE IT / FERRY 'CROSS THE MERSEY**

Mar 03. (cd) *E.M.I.; (582098-2)* **THE ESSENTIAL GERRY & THE PACEMAKERS**

GETO BOYS

Formed: Houston, Texas, USA . . . mid-80's as The GHETTO BOYS by 'Rap-A-Lot' boss, James 'Li'l J' Smith, who brought together rapper / multi instrumentalist, SCARFACE, DJ READY RED and rappers WILLIE D and the Jamaican born, BUSHWICK BILL. Making NWA look like choirboys, these Deep South gangsta rappers traded in possibly the most stomach churningly explicit lyrics ever laid down on vinyl, the first two albums, 'MAKING TROUBLE' (1988) and 'GRIP IT! ON THAT OTHER LEVEL' (1990) setting out the splatter-core blueprint of rape, dismemberment and general criminal insanity. Signed to Rick Rubin's 'Def American' label in 1990, the group found themselves at the centre of a national US debate on censorship following 'Geffen's' refusal to distribute their third album, 'THE GETO BOYS' (1990), basically a repackaged 'GRIP IT . . .' with a few extra tracks. Though the controversy was fairly minor in comparison to the subsequent ICE-T/'Cop Killer' storm, it nevertheless saw heated debate on the validity of such violent gangsta lyrics, the majority of critics of the opinion that any valuable insights into ghetto life were largely buried under a hail of expletives and sensationalism. Musically, The GETO BOYS were no great shakes, though with the compelling 'MIND PLAYING TRICKS ON ME', the group scored a US Top 30 hit in 1992. The track was a highlight of 'WE CAN'T BE STOPPED' (1992), the group's first Top 30 album, BUSHWICK BILL (who had lost an eye the previous year after he persuaded his girlfriend to shoot him!) and Co. by this point having returned to 'Rap-A-Lot'. The internal tensions within the group were well documented and it came as no surprise when WILLIE D left at the end of '92, having already released a number of solo efforts. With MIKE BARNETT (aka BIG MIKE) as a replacement, The GETO BOYS almost broke into the US Top 10 with 'TILL DEATH US DO PART' (1993), the album making No.1 on the R&B chart. SCARFACE had also been enjoying a fairly successful simultaneous solo career alongside The GETO BOYS, scoring his biggest success in 1994 with 'The DIARY' album, the title track one of the most penetrating and revealing in the gangsta canon. The record narrowly missed the US top spot, paving the way for a Top 10 GETO BOYS' comeback album in 1996, 'THE RESURRECTION', and another Top 3 solo effort from SCARFACE the following year, 'THE UNTOUCHABLE', the latter featuring collaborations with DR DRE, ICE CUBE and the late 2PAC SHAKUR. Not even issued in the UK (Top 10 in the States), 'THE LAST OF A DYING BREED' (2000) was a relatively revelatory effort from the veteran gangsta rapper, taking a more thoughtful but no less nihilistic look at the brutality of ghetto life. Another US Top 5 album entry, 'THE FIX' (2002), saw SCARFACE collaborate with more rap faces – i.e. JAY-Z, BEANIE SIGEL, FAITH EVANS, NAS and KELLY PRICE – that was really necessary, all held together by 'Def Jam' head A&R honcho, Brad Jordan. The following years' cut-n-paste set, 'BALLS AND MY WORD' (2003), attempted to stick together all his unavailable 'Rap-A-Lot' material. In one word, "ball-ocks".

Album rating: GRIP IT! ON THAT OTHER LEVEL (*5; as Ghetto Boys) / THE GETO BOYS (*6) / WE CAN'T BE STOPPED (*7) / BEST UNCUT DOPE compilation (*7) / TILL DEATH US DO PART (*6) / THE RESURRECTION (*7) / DA GOOD DA BAD AND DA UGLY (*5) / Scarface: MR. SCARFACE IS BACK (*6) / THE WORLD IS YOURS (*7) / THE DIARY (7) / THE UNTOUCHABLE (*6) / MY HOMIES (*4) / THE LAST OF A DYING BREED (*5) / THE FIX (*5) / BALLS AND MY WORD outtakes (*3)

SCARFACE (b. BRAD JORDAN, 9 Nov'69) – vocals, multi-instrumentalist / **WILLIE D** (b. WILLIE DENNIS, 1 Nov'66) – vocals / **BUSHWICK BILL** (b. RICHARD SHAW, 8 Dec'66, Kingston, Jamaica) – vocals / **READY RED** (b. COLLINS LYASETH) – DJ

not iss. Rap-A-Lot

1988. (cd; as GHETTO BOYS) **MAKING TROUBLE** –

Mar 90. (cd; as GHETTO BOYS) *<103>* **GRIP IT! ON THAT OTHER LEVEL** –
– Gangster of love / Scarface / Size ain't shit / Talkin' loud ain't saying nothin' / Seek and destroy / No sell out / Read these nikes / Do it like a G.O. / Let a ho be a ho. / Mind of a lunatic / Life in the fast lane.

Def American Def American

Oct 90. (cd/c) *<(DEF 24306-2/-4)>* **THE GETO BOYS**
– F#@* 'em / Size ain't shit / Mind of a lunatic / Gangster of love / Trigga happy nigga / Life in the fast lane / Assassins / Do it like a G.O. / Read these Nikes / Talkin' loud ain't sayin' nothin' / Scarface / Let a ho be a ho / City under siege.

Z.Y.X. Rap-A-Lot

Sep 91. (c-s) *<7241>* **MIND PLAYING TRICKS ON ME / ('A'version)** – 23

Jan 92. (cd) *(20214-2) <57161>* **WE CAN'T BE STOPPED** Jul91 24
– Rebel rap family / We can't be stopped / Homie don't play that / Another nigger in the morgue / Chuckie / Mind playing tricks on me / I'm not a gentleman / Gota let your nuts hang / F___a war / Ain't with being broke / Quickie / Punk-B game / The other level / Trophy.

—— **BIG MIKE** (b. MIKE BARNETT, 27 Sep'71, New Orleans, Louisiana) – vocals; repl. WILLIE D who went solo. He made four albums from late 1989 onwards; 'CONTROVERSY', 'I'M GOIN' OUT LIKE SOLDIER' (Sep'92; US No.88) 'TROUBLE MAN' (1993; with SHO) and 'PLAY WICHA MAMA' (1994).

Nov 92. (cd) *<57183>* **BEST UNCUT DOPE** (part compilation) –
– Action speaks louder than words / Mind playing tricks on me / The unseen / Scarface / Damn it feels good to be a gangsta / Chuckie / Assassins / And my word / Do it like a G.O. / Mind of a lunatic / Gota let your nuts hang / Size ain't shit.

Mar 93. (cd) *<57191>* **TILL DEATH US DO PART** – 11
– Crooked officer / Bring it on / Cereal killer / No nuts no glory / Murder after midnight / G.E.T.O. / This's for you / Raise up / Six feet deep / Straight gangstaism / Street life / Murderavenue / It ain't.

Apr 93. (c-s) *<53823>* **SIX FEET DEEP / ('A'instrumental)** – 40

—— BUSHWICK BILL also released a solo album, 'LITTLE BIG MAN' in 1992 for 'Rap-A-Lot'.

Virgin America Rap-A-Lot

Apr 96. (cd/c/lp) *(CDVUS/VUSMC/VUSLP 103) <41555>* **THE RESURRECTION** 6
– Ghetto prisoner / Still / The world is a ghetto (with FLAJ) / Open minded / Killer for scratch / Hold it down / Blind leading the blind / First light of day / Time taker / Geto boys and girls / Geto fantasy / I just wanna die / Niggas and flies / Visit with Larry Hoover / Point of no return.

Apr 96. (c-s; GETO BOYS featuring FLAJ) *(VUSMC 104) <38544>* **THE WORLD IS A GHETTO / STILL (2 versions)** 49 82
(12"+=/cd-s+=) *(VUS T/CD 104)* – ('A'versions).

Dec 98. (cd/lp) *(CDVUS/VUSLP 152) <46780>* **DA GOOD DA BAD AND DA UGLY** Nov98 26
– Intro / Dawn 2 dust (featuring DMG – CAINE – YUKMOUTH) / Livin' 4 the moment (featuring DMG) / Niggas ain't doin' shit / Eye 4 an eye / Bitches & hoes (featuring TELA) / Why U playin' (featuring DORACELL) / Like some hoes (featuring DEVIN) / I don't fubk with you (featuring OUTLAWZ – DMG / GOTTI) / Do yo time (featuring GHETTO TWIINZ) / Free / Thugg niggaz (featuring DMG – DORACELL) / They bitches / Big faces (featuring YUKMOUTH – The GORILLA CLICK) / Gangsta (put me down) / Retaliation (featuring 007 – K.B. – MADD DOGG) / Gun in your mouth (featuring OUTLAWZ).

SCARFACE

not iss. Rap-A-Lot

Oct 91. (cd) *<57167>* **MR. SCARFACE IS BACK** – 51
– Mr. Scarface / Body snatchers / I'm dead / Minute to prey and a second

to die / Murder by reason of insanity / PD roll 'em / Your ass got took / Born killer / Diary of a madman / Money and the power.

Jul 93. (c-s) *<53831>* **LET ME ROLL / ('A'instrumental)** – 87

Aug 93. (cd) *<53861>* **THE WORLD IS YOURS** – 7
– Mr. Scarface: part III the final chapter / Comin' agg / Good girl gone bad / I'm black / Now I feel ya / Still that aggin' / One time / Strictly for the funk lovers / The wall / You don't hear me doc / Dying with your boots on / Funky lil aggin' / He'd dead / Lettin 'em know.

Virgin America — Rap-A-Lot

Oct 94. (cd/c/lp) *(CDVUS/VUSMC/VUSLP 81) <39946>* **THE DIARY** 2
– (intro) / The white sheet / No tears / Jesse James / G's / I seen a man die (I never seen a man cry) / One / Goin' down / One time / Hand of the dead body (aka People don't believe) / Mind playin' tricks '94 / The diary / (outro).

Feb 95. (c-s; SCARFACE featuring ICE CUBE) *(VUSC 88)* *<38469>* **PEOPLE DON'T BELIEVE (aka HAND OF THE DEAD BODY) / MIND PLAYIN' TRICKS** 41 74
(12"+=/cd-s+=) *(VUS T/CD 88)* – (3-'A'mixes).

Jul 95. (c-s) *(VUSC 94) <38461>* **I NEVER SEEN A MAN CRY / ('A'instrumental))** 55 Nov94 37
(12"+=/cd-s+=) *(VUS T/CD 94)* – G's (2 versions).

Mar 97. (cd/c/lp) *(CDVUS/VUDMC/VUSLP 125) <42799>* **THE UNTOUCHABLE** 1
– (intro) / The untouchable / No warning / Southside / Sunshine (with LISA CRAWFORD) / Money makes the world go around (with DAZ) / For real / Ya money or ya life / Mary Jane / Smile (with 2PAC & JOHNNY P) / Smartz / Faith / Game over (with DR DRE & ICE CUBE) / Too short / (outro).

Jun 97. (cd-s; SCARFACE featuring 2PAC & JOHNNY P) *<38581>* **SMILE / ('A'mixes)** – 12

Jun 97. (c-s/12"/cd-s) *(VUS C/T/CD 121)* **GAME OVER. / FOR REAL** 34

Mar 98. (d-c/d-cd) *<45471>* **MY HOMIES** – 4
– Ma homiez / Hustler / Do what you do / Southside: Houston, Texas / Don't testify / Homies & thugs / The geto / Fuck faces / What's goin' on / 2 real / Rules 4 real niggas / Win, lose or draw / Overnight / Small time / Krunch time / City under siege / Do what you want / Dog these ho's / Boo boo'n / You owe me / In my blood / Sleepin in my Nikes / Greed / Who run this / Cocaine / All night long / Use them ho's / Menace niggas never die / Homies & thugs.

Oct 00. (cd,c) *<49867>* **THE LAST OF A DYING BREED** – 7
– 11-09-70 / The last of a dying breed / Look me in the eyes / It ain't (part 2) / They down with us / Sorry for what? / O.G. to me / The gangsta shit / Conspiracy theory / Watch ya step / Get out / In and out / And yo / In my time / 11-09-2000.

Mercury — Def Jam

Apr 02. (12") *<582865>* **GUESS WHO'S BACK. / ON MY BLOCK** – 79

Aug 02. (cd) *(063239-2) <586909>* **THE FIX** 4
– The fix / Safe / In cold blood / Guess who's back (with JAY-Z & BEANIE SIGEL) / On my block / Keep me down / What can I do? (with KELLY PRICE) / In between us (with NAS) / Someday (with FAITH EVANS) / Sellout / Heaven / I ain't the one (with W.C.) / Fixed.

Apr 03. (12") *<039911>* **SOMEDAY / IN COLD BLOOD** –

– compilations, etc. –

Mar 03. (cd) *Rap-A-Lot; <42024>* **BALLS AND MY WORD** – 20
– Balls and my word / Recognize / On my grind (with Z-RO) / Bitch nigga (with Z-RO, DIRT BOMB & BUN B) / Stuck at a standstill / Strapped / Only your mother (with DEVIN THE DUDE & TELA) / Make your peace / Spend the night (with ARIES) / Mary II / Dirty money (with TANYA HERRON) / F*ck'n with face / Invincible / Real nigga blues (with LIL' PAPA ROACH).

☐ G-FORCE (see under ⇒ MOORE, Gary)

☐ GHOSTFACE KILLAH (see under ⇒ WU-TANG CLAN)

☐ Beth GIBBONS & RUSTIN MAN (see under ⇒ PORTISHEAD)

☐ GILES, GILES & FRIPP (see under ⇒ KING CRIMSON)

☐ Andy GILL (see under ⇒ GANG OF FOUR)

☐ David GILMOUR (see under ⇒ PINK FLOYD)

☐ GLASS ONION (see under ⇒ TRAVIS)

☐ GLOVE (see under ⇒ SIOUXSIE AND THE BANSHEES)

GO-BETWEENS

Formed: Brisbane, Australia ... 1978 by ROBERT FORSTER (guitar, vocals) and GRANT McLENNAN (vocals, lead guitar, bass) with DENNIS CANTWELL on drums. After a debut Australian-only 7" single, 'LEE REMICK', CANTWELL was replaced with TIM MUSTAFA while organist MALCOLM KELLY was brought in briefly for the early classic, 'PEOPLE SAY', the band's second and final domestic release (were also on the books of 'Beserkley' UK for a few months). Finally settling with LINDY MORRISON on drums, The GO-BETWEENS recorded two singles for seminal Scottish indie label, 'Postcard', before settling in London and signing with 'Rough Trade'. Their debut, 'SEND ME A LULLABY' (1982), drew comparisons with The TALKING HEADS, although their root influences remained the classic songwriting of BOB DYLAN and The VELVET UNDERGROUND. Following the addition of ROBERT VICKERS on bass, allowing McLENNAN to switch to guitar, 'BEFORE HOLLYWOOD' (1983) was a marked improvement. The twin songwriting and singing strength of McLENNAN and FORSTER was developing apace, the former's 'CATTLE AND CANE' a yearning, melancholy highlight. Rave reviews abounded and the band were soon signed to the Warner Brothers-affiliated 'Sire' label. 'SPRING HILL FAIR' (1984) marked the GO-BETWEENS major label debut, their swooning melodies enhanced by a superior production on classics like 'BACHELOR KISSES'. Again the band were heralded by the press and adored by a cult following yet a commercial breakthrough proved elusive. The group switched labels yet again (moving to 'Beggar's Banquet') for 'LIBERTY BELLE AND THE BLACK DIAMOND EXPRESS' (1986), the band's most accessible, and probably finest effort of their career; it remains a mystery why the lush guitar-pop of 'SPRING RAIN' failed to breach the charts. With the addition of AMANDA BROWN (guitar, violin, oboe, keyboards), the band cut the more ambitious 'TALLULAH' (1987) and despite a couple of strong singles, were still confined to the indie margins. Understandably, the group were miffed at their lack of any real success and '16 LOVERS LANE' (1988), another sterling set of consummate, painstakingly crafted songs, proved to be their final effort. The record reached a lowly No.81 on the UK chart, The GO-BETWEENS finally going their own way with McLENNAN and FORSTER both embarking on solo careers. FORSTER's 1991 debut, 'DANGER IN THE PAST' was a fine effort, its sound not much of a departure from the later GO-BETWEENS albums. 'CALLING FROM A COUNTRY PHONE' (1993) was rootsier, employing such traditional instrumentation as banjo and mandolin. McLENNAN initially worked on the more avant-garde project, JACK FROST, with STEVE KILBEY of The CHURCH, before releasing 'WATERSHED' in 1991 as G.W. McLENNAN. Another two fine albums followed with 'FIREBOY' (1993) and 'HORSEBREAKER STAR' (1994), FORSTER releasing an album of covers the same year, 'I HAD A NEW YORK GIRLFRIEND'. 'BELLAVISTA TERRACE: THE BEST OF THE GO-BETWEENS' was issued as a sort of updated version of the lost and very rare '1978-1990', containing some of the group's best tracks that never made it into the charts (FORSTER's bitter linear notes are a tad tiresome). Yes, they was all there in their full glory: 'PART COMPANY', 'HEAD FULL OF STEAM' and the truly fantastic 'BYE BYE PRIDE' were some of the best singles that nobody heard for a long time. In a strange twist to the band's legacy, FORSTER and McLENNAN re-joined to split the songwriting credits on a brand new GO-BETWEENS album entitled 'FRIENDS OF RACHEL WORTH' (2000). Enlisting the help of SLEATER-KINNEY (the other members of the GO-B's refused to take part), the album sounded like it was recorded by LOU REED's mountain dwelling brother, with tracks such as 'GOING BLIND' and 'GERMAN FARMHOUSE' both returing back to the folksy, rock/pop sound that made the band so attractive in the beginning. 'BRIGHT YELLOW BRIGHT ORANGE' (2003) basically picked up where that album left off with FORSTER and McLENNAN cementing their renewed partnership. Bolstered this time around by the rhythm section of ADELE PICKVANCE and GLENN THOMPSON, the pair eased into their performances with the kind of confident intimacy and almost telepathic anticipation that only comes with such long-term collaboration. Largely acoustic, satisfyingly literate and unadorned, with harmony vocals from PICKVANCE, the songs basked in the rosy glow of bittersweet, middle-aged contentment.

• **Songwriters:** All compositions by FORSTER and McLENNAN, with LINDY MORRISON contributing some. McLENNAN covered BALLAD OF EASY RIDER (Byrds). FORSTER covered; NATURE'S WAY (Spirit) / BROKEN HEARTED PEOPLE (Guy Clark) / ECHO BEACH (Martha & The Muffins) / TELL ME THAT IT ISN'T TRUE (Bob Dylan) / 2541 (Bob Mould) / ANYTIME (. . . Nelson) / LOCKED AWAY (Richards-Jordan) / LOOK OUT HERE COMES TOMORROW (Neil Diamond) / ALONE (I-Ten) / BIRD (. . .Hansoms) / FRISCO DEPOT (Mickey Newbury) / 3 A.M. (Anderson-Todd) / TOWER OF SONG (Leonard Cohen).

• **Trivia:** In 1991, FORSTER and McLENNAN did support slot to LLOYD COLE on a Toronto gig, which prompted GO-BETWEENS reformation rumours.

Album rating: SEND ME A LULLABY (*7) / BEFORE HOLLYWOOD (*8) / SPRING HILL FAIR (*7) / LIBERTY BELLE AND THE BLACK DIAMOND EXPRESS (*7) / TALULAH (*7) / 16 LOVERS LANE (*8) / THE GO-BETWEENS 1979-1990 compilation (*9) / Robert Forster: DANGER IN THE PAST (*6) / CALLING FROM A COUNTRY PHONE (*6) / I HAD A NEW YORK GIRLFRIEND (*5) / WARM NIGHTS (*5) / G.W. McLennan: WATERSHED (*7) / FIREBOY (*6) / HORSEBREAKER STAR (*7) / IN YOUR BRIGHT RAY (*6) / Go-Betweens: BELLAVISTA TERRACE compilation (*8) / THE FRIENDS OF RACHEL WORTH (*7) / BRIGHT YELLOW BRIGHT ORANGE (*7)

GRANT McLENNAN (b.12 Feb'58, Rock Hampton, Australia) – vocals, lead guitar, bass / **ROB FORSTER** (b.29 Jun'57) – guitar, vocals / **DENNIS CANTWELL** – drums

Abel | not iss.

Oct 78. (7") *(AB 001)* **LEE REMICK. / KAREN** [–] Austra [–]

— added **TIM MUSTAFA** – drums + **MALCOLM KELLY** – organ to repl. CANTWELL

Oct 79. (7") *(AB 004)* **PEOPLE SAY. / DON'T LET HIM COME BACK** [–] Austra [–]
(above released UK Nov86 as 12"ep on 'Situation 2'; *SIT 44T)*

— **LINDY MORRISON** (b. 2 Nov'51) – drums (ex-ZERO) repl. TIM + MALCOLM

Postcard | not iss.

Nov 80. (7") *(80-4)* **I NEED TWO HEADS. / STOP BEFORE YOU SAY IT** [–]

Jul 81. (7") *(81-9)* **YOUR TURN, MY TURN. / WORLD WEARY** [–]
(possibly not issued in UK, released on their Australian label, 'Missing Link'; MISS 29)

Rough Trade | not iss.

Jun 82. (lp) *(ROUGH 45)* **SEND ME A LULLABY** [–]
– Your turn, my turn / One thing can hold us / People know / The girls have moved / Midnight to neon / Eight pictures / Careless / All about strength / Ride / Hold your horses / Arrow in a bow / It could be anyone. *<US cd-iss. 1990 on 'Beggars Banquet'; 92702> (cd re-mast.Jun02 on 'Circus'+=; FYL 009)* – Sunday night / One word / I need two heads / Clowns are in town / Serenade sound / Hope / Stop before you say it / World weary / Distant hands / Undo what you did / Cracked wheat / After the fireworks / Your turn my turn (video).

Jul 82. (7") *(RT 108)* **HAMMER THE HAMMER. / BY CHANCE** [–]

— added **ROBERT VICKERS** (b.25 Nov'59) – bass

Feb 83. (7") *(RT 124)* **CATTLE AND CANE. / HEAVEN SAYS** [–]

Sep 83. (lp) *(ROUGH 54)* **BEFORE HOLLYWOOD** [–]
– A bad debt follows you / Two steps step out / Before Hollywood / Dusty in here / Ask / Cattle and cane / By chance / As long as that / On my block / That way. *(cd-iss. Jun90; LCD 54) <US cd-iss. 1990 on 'Beggars Banquet'; 92703> (cd re-mast.Jun02 on 'Circus'+=; FYL 010)* – Hammer the hammer / Heaven says / Just a king in mirrors / Peaceful wreck / Man o' sand to girl o' sea / Near the chimney / This girl black girl / Exception of deception / Cattle and cane (video).

Oct 83. (7") *(RT 114)* **MAN O' SAND TO GIRL O' SEA. / THIS GIRL BLACK GIRL** [–]

Sire | not iss.

Jul 84. (7") *(W 9211)* **PART COMPANY. / JUST A KING IN MIRRORS** [–]
(12"+=) *(W 9211T)* – Newton told me.

Sep 84. (lp) *(925 179-1)* **SPRING HILL FAIR** [–]
– Bachelor kisses / Five words / The old way out / You've never lived / Part company / Slow slow music / Draining the pool for you / River of money / Unkind and unwise / Man o' sand girl o' sea. *<US cd-iss. 1990 on 'Beggars Banquet'; 82003> (cd re-mast.Jun02 on 'Circus'+=; FYL 011)* – Emperor's courtesan / Rare breed / Newton told me / Just right for him / Attraction / The power that I now have / Second hand furniture / Marco Polo Jr. / Sweet tasting hours / Unkind and unwise (instrumental) / Bachelor kisses (video).

Sep 84. (7") *(W 9156)* **BACHELOR KISSES. / RARE BREED** [–]
(12"+=) *(W 9156T)* – Unkind and unwise (instrumental).

Beggars Banquet | Big Time

Feb 86. (7") *(BEG 155)* **SPRING RAIN. / LIFE AT HAND** [–]
(12"+=) *(BEG 155T)* – Little Joe.

Mar 86. (lp/c) *(BEGA/BEGC 72)* *<6010>* **LIBERTY BELLE AND THE BLACK DIAMOND EXPRESS**
– Spring rain / The ghost and the black hat / The wrong road / To reach me / Twin layers of lightning / In the core of the flame / Head full of steam / Palm Sunday (on board the S.S.Within) / Apology accepted. *(re-iss. Feb89 on 'Beggars Banquet-Lowdown' lp/c)(cd; BBL/+C 72)(BBL 72CD)*

May 86. (7") *(BEG 159)* **HEAD FULL OF STEAM. / DON'T LET HIM COME BACK** [–]
(12"+=) *(BEG 159T)* – The wrong road.

— added **AMANDA BROWN** (b.17 Nov'65) – keyboards, violin, guitar, oboe

Feb 87. (7") *(BEG 183)* **RIGHT HERE. / WHEN PEOPLE ARE DEAD** [–]
(12"+=) *(BEG 183T)* – Don't call me gone.
(d7"++=) *(BEG 183D)* – A little romance (live).

May 87. (7") *(BEG 190)* **CUT IT OUT. / TIME IN DESERT** [–]
(12"+=) *(BEG 190T)* – Doo wop in "A".

Jun 87. (lp/c)(cd) *(BEGA/BEGC 81)(BEGA 81CD) <6042>* **TALLULAH** [91]
– Right here / You tell me / Someone else's wife / I just get caught out / Cut it out / The house that Jack Kerouac built / Bye bye pride / Spirit of a vampyre / The Clarke sisters / Hope then strife. *(re-iss. Feb90 on 'Beggars Banquet-Lowdown' cd)(c/lp; BEGA 81CD)(BEGC/BEGA 81)*

Aug 87. (7"/12") *(BEG 194/+T)* **BYE BYE PRIDE. / THE HOUSE THAT JACK KEROUAC BUILT** [–]

— **JOHN WILSTEED** (b.13 Feb'57) – bass; repl. VICKERS

Beggars Banquet | Capitol

Jul 88. (7") *(BEG 218) <4BX 44262>* **STREETS OF YOUR TOWN. / WAIT UNTIL JUNE**
(12"+=) *(BEG 218T)* – Casanova's last words.
(cd-s++=) *(BEG 218CD)* – Spring rain / Right here.

Aug 88. (lp/c)(cd) *(BEGA/BEGC 95)(BEGA 95CD) <91230>* **16 LOVERS LANE** [81]
– Love goes on / Quiet heart / Love is a sign / You can't say no forever / The

Devil's eye / Streets of your town / Clouds / Was there anything I could do? / I'm alright / Dive for your memory.

Oct 88. (7") *(BEG 219)* **WAS THERE ANYTHING I COULD DO. / ROCK'N'ROLL FRIEND** ☐ -
(12"+=) *(BEG 219T)* – Mexican postcard.
(cd-s++=) *(BEG 219CD)* – Bye bye pride.

— split on the day we moved into the 90's. FORSTER and McLENNAN went solo. The latter also being part of JACK FROST with STEVE KILBEY of The CHURCH. AMANDA formed CLEOPATRA WONG.

ROBERT FORSTER

— (solo, with MICK HARVEY – producer)

Beggars Banquet | Beggars Banquet

Sep 90. (7") *(BEG 245)* **BABY STONES. / THE LAND THAT TIME FORGOT** ☐ -

Oct 90. (cd)(c/lp) *(BEGA 113CD)(BEGA/BEGC 113) <3028>* **DANGER IN THE PAST** ☐ ☐
– Baby stones / The river people / Leave here satisfied / Heart out to tender / Is this what you call change / Dear black dream / Danger in the past / I've been looking for somebody / Justice.

Apr 93. (cd/c) *(BBQ CD/MC 127)* **CALLING FROM A COUNTRY PHONE** ☐ -
– Atlanta lie low / 121 / The circle / Falling star / I want to be quiet / Cats life / Girl to a world / Drop / Beyond theit law / Forever & time. *(cd re-iss. Sep95 on 'Beggars Banquet-Lowdown'; BBL 127CD)*

— with **JOHN KEANE** – guitars, banjos, keyboards, bass, etc / **JOEL MORRIS** – drums / **STEVE VENZ** – bass / **ANDY CARLSON** – guitars, mandolin / **TIM WHITE & BILL HOLMES** – porga & piano / **DWIGHT MANNING** – oboe / **SYD STRAW** – backing vocals

Beggars Banquet | Atlantic

Jul 94. (cd-ep) *(BBQ 38CD)* **2541 / 3 a.m. / FREDDIE FENDER / DANGER IN THE PAST (live)** ☐ -

Aug 94. (cd/c) *(BBQ CD/MC 161) <92482>* **I HAD A NEW YORK GIRLFRIEND** ☐ ☐
– Nature's way / Broken hearted people / Echo beach / Tell me that it isn't true / 2541 / Anytime / Locked away / Look out loves comes tomorrow / Alone / Bird / Frisco depot / 3 a.m.

Beggars Banquet | Beggars Banquet

Jul 96. (cd-ep) *(BEG 300CD)* **CRYIN' LOVE / HALF THE WAY HOME / HYPNOTIZED** ☐ -

Aug 96. (cd)(lp) *(BEGL 185CD)(BEGA 185) <80185>* **WARM NIGHTS** ☐ Sep96 ☐
– I can do / Warn nights / Cryin' love / Snake skin lady / Loneliness / Jug of wine / Fortress / Rock-n-roll friend / On a street corner / I'll jump.

G.W. McLENNAN

Beggars Banquet | Beggars Banquet

Mar 91. (12"ep/cd-ep) *(BEG 247 T/CD)* **WHEN WORD GETS AROUND / BLACK MULE / SHE'S SO STRANGE / THE MAN WHO DIED IN RAPTURE** ☐ -

May 91. (12"ep/cd-ep) *(BEG 254 T/CD)* **EASY COME EASY GO. / MAKING IT RIGHT FOR HER / STONES FOR YOU (trumpet version)** ☐ -

Jun 91. (cd)(c/lp) *(BEGACD 118)(BEG/BEGC 118)* **WATERSHED** ☐ -
– When word gets around / Haven't I been a fool / Haunted house / Stones for you / Easy come easy go / Black mule / Rory the weeks back on / You can't have everything / Sally's revolution / Broadway bride / Just get that straight / Dream about tomorrow.

Beggars Banquet | Atlantic

Jan 93. (cd-ep) *(BBQ 2CD)* **FINGERS / WHOSE SIDE ARE YOU ON? / WHAT WENT WRONG (original)** ☐ -

Feb 93. (cd-ep) *(BBQ 11CD)* **LIGHTING FIRES / DARK SIDE OF TOWN / IF I SHOULD FALL BEHIND** ☐ -

Mar 93. (cd/c) *(BBQ CD/MC 127) <92387>* **FIREBOY** ☐ Jun94 ☐
– Lighting fires / Surround me / One million miles from here / The dark side of town / Things will change / The pawnbroker / Whose side are you on? / Fingers / Signs of life / The day my eyes Came back / Bathe (in the water) / When I close my eyes / Riddle in the rain.

Nov 94. (d-cd/c) *(BBQ CD/MC 162)* **HORSEBREAKER STAR** ☐ -
– Simone & Perry / Ice in Heaven / What went wrong / Race day rag / Don't you cry for me no more / Put you down / Late afternoon in early August / Coming up for air / Ballad of Easy Rider / Open invitation / Open my eyes / From my lips / / Dropping you / Hot water / Keep my word / Do your own thing / That's that / If I was a girl / Head over heels / Girl in a beret / All her songs / No peace in the palace / I'll call you wild / Horsebreaker star. *(re-iss. d-cd Sep95 on 'Beggars Banquet-Lowdown'; BEGA 162CD)*

Jun 95. (cd-ep) *(BBQ 57CD)* **SIMONE & PERRY / DON'T YOU CRY FOR ME NO MORE / BALLAD OF EASY RIDER / WHAT WENT WRONG (original)** ☐ -

Jul 97. (cd) *(BBQCD 192)* **IN YOUR BRIGHT RAY** ☐ -
– In your bright ray / Cave in / One plus one / Sea breeze / Malibu '69 / Who said love was dead / Room for skin / All them pretty angels / Comet scar / Down here / Lamp by lamp / Do you see the lights / Parade of shadows.

GO-BETWEENS

— re-formed with **FORSTER + McLENNAN** plus SLEATER-KINNEY:- **CORIN TUCKER, CARRIE BROWNSTEIN + JANET WEISS**

Circus | Jetset

Sep 00. (cd) *(CIRCUSCD 004) <TWA 31>* **THE FRIENDS OF RACHEL WORTH** ☐ ☐
– Magic in here / Spirit / The clock / German farmhouse / He lives my life / Heart and home / Surfing magazines / Orpheus beach / Going blind / When she sang about angels. *(lp-iss.on 'Clear Spot'; 054251) (re-mast.JUn02; FYL 003)*

Oct 00. (cd-s) *(CIRCUSCDS 002) <TWA 32>* **GOING BLIND / WOMAN ACROSS THE WAY / THE LOCUST GIRLS** ☐ ☐

— **FORSTER + McLENNAN** added **ADELE PICKVANCE** – vocals, bass / **GLENN THOMPSON** – drums

Feb 03. (cd) *(CIRCUSCD 016) <TWA 58>* **BRIGHT YELLOW BRIGHT ORANGE** ☐ ☐
– Caroline and I / Poison in the walls / Mrs. Morgan / In her diary / Too much of one thing / Crooked lines / Old Mexico / Make her day / Something for myself / Unfinished business. *(lp-iss.Mar03 on 'Clearspot'; efa 60211-1)*

– compilations, others, etc. –

1982. (lp) *Man Made;* **VERY QUICK ON THE EYE – BRISBANE 1981 (demo)** ☐ -

1985. (lp) *P.V.C.; <PVC 8942>* **METAL AND SHELLS** - ☐

Oct 89. (12"ep/cd-ep) *Strange Fruit; (SFPS/+CD 074) / Dutch East India; <8339>* **THE PEEL SESSIONS** ☐ 1991 ☐
– The power that I have now / Second hand furniture / Fire woods / Rare breed.

Mar 90. (cd)(c/d-lp) *Beggars Banquet; (BEGA 104CD)(BEGC/BEGA 104) / Capitol; <94681>* **THE GO-BETWEENS 1979-1990** ☐ ☐
– Hammer the hammer / I need two heads / Cattle and cane / When people are dead / Man o' sand to girl o' sea / Bachelor kisses / People say / Draining the pool for you / World weary / Spring rain / Rock and roll friend / Dusty in here / The Clarke sisters / Right here / Second-hand furniture / Bye bye pride / This girl, black girl / The house that Jack Kerouac built / Don't call me gone / Streets of our own town / Love is a sign / You won't find it again. *(c+=/d-lp+=)* – Karen / 8 pictures / The sound of rain / The wrong road / Mexican postcard.

Apr 99. (cd) *Tag; (TAGCD 002) / Jetset; <TWA 019>* **THE LOST ALBUM 1978-1979** ☐ ☐

May 99. (d-cd) *Beggars Banquet; (BBL2 020CD) <82020>* **BELLAVISTA TERRACE: THE BEST OF THE GO-BETWEENS** ☐ ☐
– Was there anything I could do? / Head full of steam / That way / Part company / Cattle and cane / Draining the pool for you / The wrong road / Bye bye pride / Man o' sand to girl o' sea / The house that Jack Kerouac built / Bachelor kisses / Streets of your town / Spring rain / Dive for your memory.

☐ GODLEY & CREME (see under ⇒ 10cc)

GODSMACK

Formed: Boston, Massachusetts, USA ... 1996 by frontman SALLY ERNA and his musical mates, TONY ROMBOLO, ROBBIE MERRILL and TOMMY STEWART, who named themselves after an ALICE IN CHAINS track. If you were to put the aforementioned ALICE IN CHAINS, METALLICA and the rest of the Grunge crew together – and without getting too sarcy – you would probably come up with GODSMACK. This dour 4-piece got their break from noneother than PAUL GEARY (former sticksman with EXTREME), who sorted out a contract with 'Universal' in 1998. By the following year, their self-titled debut album was high in the US Top 30, with an invite to Woodstock and Ozzfest to boot. Heralded by young trendy Americans into "that sort of thing", the band also had a surprise alternative rock hit with probably their finest five minutes, 'WHATEVER'. By late 2000, the lads thought we'd enjoy a second set. 'AWAKE' was not an appropriate title. 'FACELESS' (2003) was much more appropriate given their utterly derivative take on what rock music has descended into over the last five years or so. That GODSMACK and their ilk continued to make not the slightest impression on the UK Top 40 was less surprising than ever.

Album rating: GODSMACK (*3) / AWAKE (*4) / FACELESS (*4)

SULLY ERNA – vocals / **TONY ROMBOLO** – guitar / **ROBBIE MERRILL** – bass / **TOMMY STEWART** – drums; repl. JOE D'ARCO (although he did return)

Universal Universal

Aug 99. (cd) *(UND 53190) <153190>* **GODSMACK** [ ] Aug98 [22]
– Moon baby / Whatever / Keep away / Time bomb / Bad religion / Immune / Someone in London / Get up, get out! / Now or never / Stress / Situation / Voodoo. *<clean version as 'ALL WOUND UP'; UND 53183>*

Oct 00. (cd) *<(159688-2)>* **AWAKE** [ ] [5]
– Sick of life / Awake / Greed / Bad magick / Goin' down / Mistakes / Trippin' / Forgive me / Vampires / The journey / Spiral. *(re-iss. Apr01; same)*

— **SHANNON LARKIN** – drums (ex-AMEN) repl. D'ARCO

Apr 03. (cd) *(19900-2) <067854>* **FACELESS** [ ] [1]
– Straight out of line / Faceless / Changes / Make me believe / I stand alone / Re-align / I fucking hate you / Releasing the demons / Dead and broken / I am / The awakening / Serenity. *(UK+=)* – Keep away (live) / Awake (live).

Nov 03. (cd-s) *<19866>* **STRAIGHT OUT OF LINE** [–] [73]
(above was actually a Canadian import!)

GODSPEED YOU BLACK EMPEROR!

Formed: Mile End district, Montreal, Canada ... 1994 by EFRIM and MAURO (the original pair issuing a very limited 33 copy cassette, 'ALL LIGHTS FUCKED ON THE HAIRY AMP DROOLING'). Enlarging the outfit to a 9-piece collective and enlisting DAVE, AIDAN GIRT, BRUCE, THIERRY, NORSOLA and SOPHIE with STEPH, SYLVIA, COLIN, CRISTOPHE, JESSE, DAN C, SHANEABERG, PETER and AMANDA making up contributors at various times. Revolting against the "pay to play" system that many of the local establishments employed, the ensemble took to playing empty warehouses and other such venues, enabling them to gain popularity among the more alternative centred individuals in their town. In 1996, GYBE! retreated to Hotel2Tango (a mythological apartment which certain members of the band were said to occupy), putting down material with the assistance of Chemical Daryl at his Chemical Sound studio. Broke again, they obtained free reel to reel tape from a friend and remixed their old material, adding two tracks and sequencing their efforts at Mile End studio. The result was the devastatingly bleak 'F#A#oo' album, issued in limited numbers in the summer of '98 for 'Constellation', harbouring the attention of Chicago-based cult experimental imprint, 'Kranky' for UK and US release. From its post-apocalyptic opener 'THE DEAD FLAG BLUES' (with the memorable spoken dialogue of 'The Car's On Fire And There's No Driver At The Wheel And The Sewers Are All Muddied With A Thousand Lonely Suicides And A Dark Wind Blows ...') segued together with the eerie rumbling effects on the self-explanatory 'SLOW MOVING TRAINS' cruising into the epic tour de force of 'THE COWBOY' (a landscape of spiralling David Lynch-esque peaks that quite literally tickle the ears into orgasmic proportions on headphone experience!) and uplifted by the bright and folky denouement of its 'OUTRO'. The album's second piece, 'EAST HASTINGS', fades into the broken ramblings of a distressed street anarchist (see below) complaining "NOTHING'S ALRITE IN OUR LIFE" lamented by distant bagpipes and overlapped with soft vibrato acoustics and paranoid MOGWAI meets TANGERINE DREAM (their cinematic period!) slow burning crescendo culminating with ear-bashing orchestral avant-metal. Section two of this lengthy piece, 'THE SAD MAFIESE', navigated the psyche into further headbusting headphone gymnastics with its plucking harmonics swaying continuously like a rocking chair uneasy in a derelict porch. The track's third instalment, 'DRUGS IN TOKYO – BLACK HELICOPTER', was arguably the most disturbing piece of the set, its Oriental chimes festooned between sounds of bees trapped in a generator. Song(!) number three, 'PROVIDENCE', begins with a doubtful riddle lecturing about the current state of America linking that with the end of time, waking up to a sunrise owned by (BRIAN) ENO. Each of its four pieces were like a homage to late 60's/early 70's experimental rock (i.e. PINK FLOYD) battling on a stranger plateau of military percussion and space-age guitars. The following Spring, the group (now with new guitarist ROGER TELLIER-CRAIG) returned with 'SLOW RIOT FOR NEW ZER0 KANADA E.P.' an unusual two-track mini-set that again stunned audiences and critics alike. Soft violins, rattling guitars, orchestrated crescendoes and bizarre vox-pops were all the standard on opening track, 'MOYA', while the deeply negative 'BBF3' (named eponymously after the aforementioned street/soapbox anarchist, Mister Blaise Bailey Finnegan the third!) attacked world society and all its corruptive forces. Arguably this band were the most promising act to hit the year 2000, ironically it's everything that they rebel against. During all the hype and journo commotion, ROGER'S side-project, FLY PAN AM, took off on their campaign of climax-enduced minimalist (s)Lo-Fi, the result being a well-received eponymous album in October '99. GODSPEED ... had now secured such a reputation on the leftfield scene that tours were being sold-out all over Europe and America, with film director Oliver Stone requesting to use the band's old music in a film, they politely declined. EFRIM, SOPHIE and NORSOLA established A SILVER MT. ZION, just one of the many militant groups which were springing up around Canada from the GODSPEED camp. They issued their debut album 'HE HAS LEFT US ALONE ... BUT SHAFTS OF LIGHT STILL GRACE THE CORNERS OF OUR ROOM' (2000), a beautiful lament for what the band called "a falling/fallen world". The music was slow burning with the first few tracks backed by post-apocalyptic religious rantings, thundering piano and dashing strings. Later EFRIM sang (accompanied only by his fragile piano) about the collapse of capitalism. The set was a truly dazzling affair, with the eerie loop and drone of '13 ANGELS CIRCLING AROUND MY BED' being a particular treasure. MOLACES, 1-SPEED BIKE, EXHAUST and FLY PAN AM all issued equally brilliant albums in the time it took GODSPEED to complete the recording of their eagerly awaited sophomore set, 'LIFT YR. SKINNY FISTS LIKE ANTENNAS TO HEAVEN' (2000), a roaring 2-CD set that astounded and bewildered fans and critics alike. The set boasted some of the most poignant and musically mature tracks in the history of rock, outing any Prog-rock band with semi-classical pieces evoking sadness, hope and worry. It was a wonder GODSPEED had even made a record this non-conformist, this loud, this brash and still get away with releasing it in such a mafia-like music industry. So triumphant was their glory that when the words 'freedom can be achieved' flashed at the end of their shows, it was almost as if GODSPEED had been sent from the heavens themselves to save mankind from dull, unimaginative music. 'MONHEIM', their most powerful track evoked the same crescending substance as 'BBF111' on the 'SLOW RIOT . . .' EP. 'SHE DREAMT SHE WAS A BULLDOZER, SHE DREAMT SHE WAS ALONE IN AN EMPTY FIELD' began with sweeping violins, distorted guitar before crashing unannounced into a full on rock-out, before fading into a beautiful middle section reminiscent of "empty wet streets at dawn". Perhaps the most effective piece was 'THE BUILDINGS THEY ARE SLEEPING NOW', just a drone of feedback that sounded like Chinese symbols being played with violin bows, to create a stark and haunting sound. The members of GODSPEED excelled themselves once again by issuing the remarkable 'BORN INTO TROUBLE AS THE SPARKS FLY UPWARD' (2001), a joint collaboration between A SILVER MT. ZION (now renamed THE SILVER MT. ZION MEMORIAL ORCHESTRA) and The TRA-TRA-LA-LA-LA BAND. On one particular track EFRIM sings "Musicians are cowards . . .", providing the whole basis for GODSPEED as not just a collective from Montreal but as a philosophy; be brave, be free, help one another, don't let the greediness of man ruin our communities. Other musicians may be cowards, but GODSPEED suggested that they were all the above and no sell-out – a true democratic group of musicians. Anybody who was lucky enough to live in their time should be grateful, and for those who weren't, there's always the future. In 2002, along with fractions of FLY PAN AM and HANGED UP, GODSPEED collaborated on 'SINGS REIGN REBUILDER', under the collective nom de plum of SET FIRE TO FLAMES. The LP (with gorgeous packaging as standard) was mostly a collection of fragmented field recordings, taped around Vancouver and Montreal, respectively. Using brass, reed and a whole host of eerie guitar effects and strange percussion instruments, SET FIRE TO FLAMES had delivered the most sonically poetic album of the year. Like GODSPEED's 'SKINNY FISTS . . .' offering, instrumentals collided with broken down noises and bizarre, but always welcoming, voices which faded in and drifted out of the recording. Meanwhile, in Chicago, the band themselves were perfecting five long pieces with legendary producer STEVE ALBINI, which would eventually end up as 'YANQUI U.X.O.' (2002), meaning un-coordinated cluster bombs, dropped by American planes in the Gulf War. The set, from its quietly building opener, to the scary swirling percussion orientated ending was a sight to behold. ALBINI, as usual had just left the microphones on to tell it like it was: pure live orchestrations for a "falling/fallen world". But this time the BLACK EMPERORs weren't messing about. Firstly, they knew a war was imminent, and from the military-funded major label berating on the back cover to the blitzing beauty and sadness of 'ROCKETS FALL ON ROCKET FALLS' (with added clarinets, reeds and stand up bass to brilliant effect), 'YANQUI U.X.O.' was a deliberate warning to us of the brutality that was about to ensue. Years ago, GODSPEED YOU BLACK EMPEROR! were deemed by music critics as just a "cinematic orchestra for a post apocalyptic generation". Their music and what they stood for has never been more relevant. EFRIM and ROGER returned in 2002 with the latter issuing a new FLY PAN AM album and the former riding the faders. 'CEUX QUI INVENTENT N'ONT JAMAIS VECU' followed the ensemble's strict template of barraging sounds backed by delicate post-rock melodies and static hiss. Much the same as EXHAUST, whose 'ENREGISTREUR' (also 2002) was another foray into experimental doodling and cut'n'paste fuzz. Perhaps more melodic was EFRIM and Co's SILVER MT. ZION project 'THIS IS OUR PUNK ROCK, THEE RUSTED SATELLITES GATHER + SING' which was issued in 2003 under the once again lengthier moniker. Another achievement for the ZION crew, the album with its soaring coral arrangements (courtesy of The CHOIR) and ambient orchestrations were possibly the ensemble's most accessible work to date, with even EFRIM doing a decent NEIL YOUNG impersonation/homage on finale 'GOODBYE DESOLATE RAILYARD'. Meanwhile, SET FIRE TO FLAMES, another excellent GODSPEED! offshoot delivered their sophomore set 'TELEGRAPHS IN NEGATIVE . . .' (2003), a lonely and drifting record that took a lot of patience to appreciate at first, but subtly defined the spaces and textures in their music, much akin to their debut 'SINGS REIGN REBUILDER'.

Album rating: ALL LIGHTS FUCKED ON THE HAIRY AMP DROOLING (*5) / F#A#oo (*9) / SLOW RIOT FOR NEW ZER0 KANADA mini (*8) / LIFT YR. SKINNY FISTS LIKE ANTENNAS TO HEAVEN! (*7) / YANQUI U.X.O. (*7) / Exhaust: 230596 (*5) / EXHAUST (*6) / ENREGISTREUR (*7) / Fly Pan Am: FLY PAN AM (*7) / CEUX QUI INVENTENT N'ONT JAMAIS VECU (*6) / Silver Mt. Zion: HE HAS LEFT US ALONE . . . (*7) / BORN INTO TROUBLE AS THE SPARKS FLY UPWARD (*7) / THIS IS OUR PUNK ROCK, THEE RUSTED SATELLITES GATHER + SING (*6) / 1-Speed Bike: DROOPY BUTT BEGONE! (*4) / Set Fire To Flames: SINGS REIGN REBUILDER (*6) / TELEGRAPHS IN NEGATIVE, MOUTHS TRAPPED IN STATIC (*6)

EFRIM – guitar, tape loops / **MAURO** – bass

not iss. not listed

Dec 94. (ltd-c) *<none>* **ALL LIGHTS FUCKED ON THE HAIRY AMP DROOLING** [–] Canada [–]
– Drifting intro open / Shot thru tubes / Three three three / When all the furnaces exploded / Beep / Hush / Son of a diplomat, daughter of a politician / Glencairn 14 / $13.13 / Loose the idiot dogs / Diminishing shine / Random luvly moncton blue(s) / Dadmomdaddy / Frames per second / Revisionist alternatif wounds to the hair-cut hit head / Ditty for Moya / Buried ton / And the hair guts shine / Hoarding / Deterior 23 / All angels gone / Deterior 17 / Deterior three / Devil's in the church / No job / Dress like shit / Perfumed pink corpses from the lips of Ms. Celine Dion.

— added **DAVE** – guitar, tape loops / **AIDAN GIRT** – percussion, drums (also of EXHAUST) / **BRUCE** – percussion, glockenspiel / **THIERRY** – bass / **NORSOLA** – cello / **SOPHIE TRUDEAU** – violin

Kranky Kranky

Jun 98. (cd)<lp> *<(KRANKY 27CD)><cst 003>* **F#A#oo** [ ] Aug97 [ ]
– The dead flag blues: 1. The dead flag blues, 2. Slow moving trains, 3. The cowboy, 4. (; Outro) / East Hastings: 1. "Nothing's alrite in our life" – Dead flag blues (reprise), 2. The sad Mafiese, 3. Drugs in Tokyo – Black helicopter / Providence: 1. Divorce and fever, 2. Dead mothery, 3. Kicking horse on broken hill, 4. String loop manufacturer during downpour.

— added **ROGER TELLIER-CRAIG** – guitar

Apr 99. (m-lp/m-cd) *<(KRANKY 34/+CD)><cst 006>* **SLOW RIOT FOR NEW ZER0 KANADA E.P.** [ ] Mar99 [ ]
– Moya / BBF3 (voice by Mister Blaise Bailey Finnegan the third).

— <above releases also on 'Constellation' in Canada>

Sep 99. (7",7"white) *<MAZE 01>* **SUNSHINE & GASOLINE. / Fly Pan Am: L'ESPACE AU SOL EST REDESSINE PAR DES IMMENSES PANNEAUX BLEUS** [–] [ ]

— <above issued for 'aMAZEzine!' fanzine>

Oct 00. (d-cd)(d-lp) *<(KRK 43D)>* *<cst 012>* **LIFT YR. SKINNY FISTS LIKE ANTENNAS TO HEAVEN!** [66] [ ]
– Lift yr. skinny fists like antennas to heaven / Gathering storm / Il pleut amourir (+ clatters like worry) / Welcome to Barco AM/PM . . . / Cancer towers on Holy road hi-way / Terrible canyons of state / Atomic

clock / World police and friendly fire / (. . .+ the buildings they are sleeping now) / Murray Ostril: they don't sleep anymore on the beach / Monheim / Broken windows, locks of love pt.III / Moya sings "baby-o" / Edgyswingsetacid / Glockenspiel duet recorded on a campsite in Rhineback, N.Y. / Attention . . . mon ami . . . fa-lala-lala-la-la (55-St.Laurent) / She dreamt she was a bulldozer, she dreamt she was alone in an empty field / Deathkamp drone / (Antennas to heaven . . .).

Nov 02. (cd/d-lp) *<(cst 024-2/-1)>* **YANQUI U.X.O.**
– 09-15-00 / 09-15-00 / Rockets fall on Rocket Falls / Motherfucker = redeemer / Motherfucker = redeemer.

EXHAUST

AIDAN GIRT – drums, etc / **GORDON KRIEGER** – bass, clarinet, (some) guitar / **MIKE ZABITSKY** – tape loops

Constellation Constellation

Oct 96. (c) *<none>* **230596** –
– Cat face / Hork pitou / Wool fever dub / That cost you $116 / High Aidan diminished by fists / The bass and the trouble / Free shuttle from Bifteck / Bubbles will harm Nick / Tripolar depression.

Aug 98. (lp) *<(cst 004)>* **EXHAUST**
– A history of guerilla warfare / Metro Mile End / Homemade maggot beer / We support Iran in their bid to win the 1998 World Cup / Two years on welfare / This is our (borrowed) equipment Wool fever / A medley of late night buffet commercials / Winterlude / The black horns of H2T. *<(cd-iss. Aug00; cst 004cd)>*

— AIDAN had now left GODSPEED

Sep 02. (cd/lp) *<(cst 21-2/-1)>* **ENREGISTREUR**
– Gauss / Behind the water tower / Voiceboxed / Ice storm / Dither / Behind the paint factory / My country is winter / Silence sur le plateau / Degauss.

FLY PAN AM

ROGER TELLIER-CRAIG – guitar / **J.S.** – bass (ex-WISIGOTH) / **JONATHAN PARANT** – guitar / **FELIX MOREL** – drums

Constellation Constellation

Oct 99. (3-sided-lp/cd) *<(cst 008/+cd)>* **FLY PAN AM**
– L'espace au sol est redesine par d'immeses panneaux bleus / Et aussi L'eclairge de plastique au centre de tout ces compartiments lateraux / Dans ses cheveux soixante circuits / Bibi a nice, 1921 / Nice est en feu!

Oct 00. (12"ep/cd-ep) *<(cst 011 v/cd)>* **SEDATIFS EN FREQUENCIES ET SILLONS**
– De cercle en cercle . . . / Efferant – Afferant / Stereo stupefiant – (micro sillons).

Apr 02. (cd/lp) *<(cst 019 cd/lp)>* **CEUX QUI INVENTENT N'ONT JAMAIS VECU**
– Jeunesse sonique, tu dors (en cage) / Rompre l'indifference de l'inexitable avant que l'on vienne / Partially sabotaged distraction partiellement sabotee / Univoque – Equivoque / Arcades-Pamelor / Sound-support surface noises reaching out to you / Erreur, errance; interdits de par leurs nouvelles possibilities / La vie se doit d'etre vecue ou commencons a vivre.

a SILVER MT. ZION

EFRIM, THIERRY + SOPHIE with guests **AIDAN, GORDON KRIEGER, SAM SHALABI** (of The Shalabi Effect) – guitar

Mar 00. (lp/cd) *<(cst 009/+cd)>* **HE HAS LEFT US ALONE BUT SHAFTS OF LIGHT SOMETIMES GRACE THE CORNERS OF OUR ROOMS . . .**
– Broken chords can sing a little / Sit in the middle of three galloping dogs / Stumble and then rise on some awkward morning / Movie (never made) / 13 angels standing guard 'round the side of your bed / Long march rocket or doomed airliner / Blown out joy from Heaven's mercied hole.

SILVER MT. ZION MEMORIAL ORCHESTRA & TRA-LA-LA BAND

— the trio plus **BECKIE, IAN ILAVSKY** (of SACKVILLE, of SOFA, of RE:) + **JESSICA**, etc.

Oct 01. (10"d-lp/cd) *<(cst 018/+cd)>* **BORN INTO TROUBLE AS THE SPARKS FLY UPWARD**
– Sisters! brothers! small boats of fire are falling from the sky! / This gentle hearts like shot bird's fallen / Built then burnt (hurrah! hurrah!) / Take these hands and throw them in the river / Could've moved mountains / Tho you are gone I still often walk w/ you / C'mon come on (loose an endless longing) / The triumph of our tired eyes.

Aug 03. (cd/d-lp) *<(cst 027-2/-1)>* **THIS IS OUR PUNK-ROCK, THEE RUSTED SATELLITES GATHER + SING** Sep03
– So someone lonesome corner so many flowers bloom / Babylon was built on fire – Starnostars / American motor over smoldered field / Goodbye desolate railyard.

1-SPEED BIKE

AIDAN GIRT solo

Oct 00. (cd/lp) *<(cst 014 cd/v)>* **DROOPY BUTT BEGONE!**
– The day that Mauro ran over Elwy Yost / Seattle – Washington – Prague 00-68 – Chicago – Nixon – Reagan circle-fighting ma / Yuppie restaurant-goers beware because this song is for the dishwasher / Just another jive-assed white colonial theft / Why are all the doges dying of cancer? / My kitchen is Tianamen Square / Any movement that forgets about class is a bowel movement / (untitled).

SET FIRE TO FLAMES

AIDAN + SOPHIE

13071 13071

Oct 01. (cd/d-lp) *<(CD/LP 13 01)>* **SINGS REIGN REBUILDER**
– I will be true – Reign rebuilder (head) / Vienna arcweld – Fucked gameplan – Rigid tracking / Steal compass – Drive north – Disappear / Wild dogs of the thunderbolt – They cannot lock me up . . . / Ohama / There is no dance in frequency and balance / Cote d'Abrahams room tone – What's going on / Love song for 15 Ontario / In jur gutted two track / When I first get to Phoenix / Shit heap Gloria of the new town planning / Jesus – Pop / Esquimalt harbour / Two tears in a bucket / Fading lights are fading – Reign rebuilder (tail out).

Jun 03. (d-cd/d-lp) *<(CD/LP 13 03)>* **TELEGRAPHS IN NEGATIVE / MOUTHS TRAPPED IN STATIC**
– Deja, comme des trous de vent, comme reproduit / Small steps against inertia – Echo of a dead end / Measure de mesure / Holy throat hiss tracts to the sedative-hypnotic / When sorrow shoots her darts / Kill fatigue frequencies / In prelight isolate / Tehran in seizure / Telegraphs in negative // Your guts are like mine / Fukt perkusiv – Something about bad drugs, schizophrenics and grain silos . . . / Sleep maps / Something about Eva Mattes in the halo of exploding street lamps . . . / Buzz of barn flies like faulty electronics / And the birds are about to bust their guts with singing / Rites of spring reverb / Mouths trapped in static / This thing between us is a rickety bridge of impossible crossing – Bonfires for nobody . . .

GO-GO'S

Formed: Hollywood, California, USA . . . May '78 as all-girl band The MISFITS by BELINDA CARLISLE, CHARLOTTE CAFFEY, JANE WIEDLIN, MARGOT OLAVERRA and ELISA BELLO (subsequently replaced by GINA SHOCK). An integral part of the punk/new wave scene centered on Hollywood's 'Masque' club and nearby 'Canterbury Arms' apartment building, the group subsequently adopted the GO-GO'S moniker. Although they'd later project a more wholesome image, the earliest incarnation of the band lived the drug-taking punk lifestyle to the full, one of their shows even ending in an infamous 1979 riot. Yet their sound gradually lost its early rawness and mutated into a more commerical power-pop style at the turn of the decade; British ska revival nutters MADNESS were sufficiently impressed to offer the girls a support slot on their 1980 UK tour. The resultant exposure led to interest from premier UK indie label, 'Stiff', who released the ladettes' debut single, 'WE GOT THE BEAT', in Spring of the same year. Back in the States, POLICE manager Miles Copeland signed the group to his burgeoning 'I.R.S.' roster and helped put them in the US Top 20 with summer 81's pink vinyl classic 'OUR LIPS ARE SEALED' (co-written by SPECIALS man, TERRY HALL). Debut album, 'BEAUTY AND THE BEAT' (1981) followed hot on its heels, a frothy, surf-influenced set which couched occasionally hard-bitten lyrics in a buoyant, typically Californian veneer. The record topped the charts and suddenly The GO-GO'S were hot property. A more overtly commercial, polished follow-up, 'VACATION' (1982), made the Top 10 and spawned a similarly placed, cheesy summer single in its title track. Yet the band's fast-living ethos had taken its toll and after a third album, 'TALK SHOW' (1984) and final Top 20 single, 'HEAD OVER HEELS', the various members split to do their own thing. While WIEDLIN would go on to have a couple of 80's hits (the biggest and best being 'RUSH HOUR'), it was the cutesy CARLISLE (incredibly a brief member of legendary L.A. punks, The GERMS) who'd emerge as a typically airbrushed 80's pop/rock clone with big hair and even bigger songs. Following on from the Stateside success of her 1986 eponymous debut album and its Top 3 hit, 'MAD ABOUT YOU', she scored a massive transatlantic No.1 towards the end of '87 with the anthemic schlock of 'HEAVEN IS A PLACE ON EARTH'. Now signed to 'Virgin' in the UK, she became one of Britain's biggest late 80's female pop stars, churning out Top 5 doe-eyed dross like 'CIRCLE IN THE SAND' and 'LEAVE A LIGHT ON'. Although she began the new decade on a commercial high with the huge 1990 hit, '(WE WANT) THE SAME THING', her singles increasingly only scraped the Top 30. Nevertheless, the strength of her British following was illustrated by the No.1 success of a 1992 greatest hits set (which didn't even chart in America) while the following year's 'REAL' album made the Top 10. Having already reunited in 1990 to promote a retrospective set (during which time they played a naked but discreet anti-fur campaign benefit), The GO-GO'S got back together again in late '94. This time around they cut a handful of fresh tracks for an anthology of earlier material, 'RETURN TO THE VALLEY OF THE GO-GO'S' (1995), incredibly scoring their first ever UK Top 30 hit with 'THE WHOLE WORLD LOST ITS HEAD'. Presumably prompted by a bad case of millennial fever, The GO-GO's unveiled their first set of new material in over 15 years with 'GOD BLESS THE GO-GO'S' (2001). You might be forgiven for thinking BELINDA CARLISLE's solo career had never happened, what with a BILLIE JOE ARMSTRONG (GREEN DAY) collaboration (on the single 'UNFORGIVEN') and a healthy dose of alt-rock riffing. Still, the fact that it only scraped the US Top 60 might indicate that some of their old fans have got more sensible things to spend their money on these days. • **Songwriters:** WIEDLIN or CARLISLE; when the latter went solo, her songs were largely written by producer RICK NOWELS and ELLEN SHIPLEY. In 1992, she collaborated on some with new producer RICHARD FELDMAN. Others writers; I GET WEAK + WORLD WITHOUT YOU (Dianne Warren) / SUMMER RAIN (Seidman-Vidal) / I FEEL FREE (Cream) / THE AIR YOU BREATHE (Weiss-White) / JEALOUS GUY (John Lennon) / ALWAYS BREAKING MY HEART (Per Gessle; Roxette).

Album rating: BEAUTY AND THE BEAT (*6) / VACATION (*5) / TALK SHOW (*4) / GREATEST compilation (*6) / RETURN TO THE VALLEY OF THE GO-GO'S compilation (*5) / Belinda Carlisle: BELINDA (*5) / HEAVEN ON EARTH (*6) / RUNAWAY HORSES (*5) / LIVE YOUR LIFE BE FREE (*4) / THE BEST OF BELINDA CARLISLE compilation (*6) / REAL (*4) / A WOMAN AND A MAN (*3) / . . .A PLACE ON EARTH – THE GREATEST HITS compilation (*5) / Go-Go's: GOD BLESS THE GO-GO'S (*5)

BELINDA CARLISLE (b.17 Aug'58) – vocals (ex-GERMS) / **CHARLOTTE CAFFEY** (b.21 Oct'53, Santa Monica, Calif.) – lead guitar, vocals / **JANE WIEDLIN** (b.20 May'58, Oconomowoc, Wisconsin) – rhythm guitar, vocals / **MARGOT OLAVERRA** – bass / **GINA SHOCK** (b.31 Aug'57, Baltimore, Maryland) – drums (ex-EDDIE MASSEY & HER EGGS) repl. ELISA BELLO

Stiff — not iss.

May 80. (7") *(BUY 78)* **WE GOT THE BEAT. / HOW MUCH MORE** [ ] [–]

— **KATHY VALENTINE** (b. 7 Jan'59, Austin, Texas) – bass (ex-TEXTONES) repl. MARGOT.

I.R.S. — I.R.S.

Jul 81. (7"pink) *(PFP 1007)* <9901> **OUR LIPS ARE SEALED. / SURFING AND SPYING** [ ] [20]

Aug 81. (lp/c) <*(SP/CS 70021)*> **BEAUTY AND THE BEAT** [ ] Jul 81 [1]
– Our lips are sealed / This town / How much more / Fading fast / We got the beat / Tonite / Skidmarks on my heart / Lust to love / Automatic / You can't walk in your sleep (if you can't sleep) / Can't stop the world. *(cd-iss. 1988; CD 70021)*

Nov 81. (7",7"pic-d) *(PFP 1010)* **WE GOT THE BEAT. / SKIDMARKS ON MY HEART** [ ] [–]

Jan 82. (7") <9903> **WE GOT THE BEAT. / CAN'T STOP THE WORLD** [–] [2]

Feb 82. (7",7"pic-d) *(GON 101)* **AUTOMATIC. / TONITE** [ ] [–]

Apr 82. (7") *(GON 102)* **OUR LIPS ARE SEALED. / WE GOT THE BEAT** [47] [–]

Aug 82. (7") *(GON 103)* <9907> **VACATION. / BEATNIK BEACH** [ ] Jul82 [8]

Aug 82. (lp/c) <*(SP/CS 70031)*> **VACATION** [75] [8]
– Vacation / This old feeling / He's so strange / Girl of 100 lists / It's everything but partytime / Get up and go / Beatnik beach / I think it's me / The way you dance / We don't get along / Worlds away / Cool jerk.

Sep 82. (7") <9910> **GET UP AND GO. / SPEEDING** [–] [50]

Nov 82. (7") *(GON 104)* **GIRL OF 100 LISTS. / I THINK IT'S ME** [ ] [–]

Dec 82. (7") **IT'S EVERYTHING BUT PARTYTIME. / THIS OLD FEELING** [–] [ ]

Nov 83. (7") **BELONG TO ME. / DON'T YOU LOVE ME** [–] [ ]

Apr 84. (7") *(104)* <9926> **HEAD OVER HEELS. / GOOD FOR GONE** [ ] Mar84 [11]

May 84. (lp/c) <*(IRS A/C 70041)*> **TALK SHOW** [ ] Apr84 [18]
– Turn to you / You thought / Capture the light / I'm the only one / Mercenary / I'm with you / Yes or no / Head over heels / Forget that day / Beneath the blue sky. *(cd-iss. 1988; CD 70041)*

Jun 84. (7") <9928> **TURN TO YOU. / I'M WITH YOU** [–] [32]

Sep 84. (7") <9933> **YES OR NO. / MERCENARY** [–] [84]

— **PAULA JEAN BROWN** – rhythm guitar repl. JANE WIEDLIN who went solo. They disbanded May 1985 when CAFFEY and CARLISLE left.

BELINDA CARLISLE

— went solo initially taking with her; **CHARLOTTE CAFFEY**

I.R.S. — I.R.S.

Jun 86. (7") *(IRM 118)* <52815> **MAD ABOUT YOU. / I NEVER WANTED A RICH MAN** [ ] May86 [3]
(12"+=) *(IRMT 118)* – ('A'extended). *(re-iss. Jan88; same)* – hit UK No.67 *(re-iss. Jul88; DIRM 118)*

Jul 86. (lp/c) *(MIRF/+C 1012)* <5741> **BELINDA** [ ] [13]
– Mad about you / I need a disguise / Since you've gone / I feel the magic / I never wanted a rich man / Band of gold / Gotta get to you / From the heart / Shot in the dark / Stuff and nonsense. *(cd-iss. 1988; DMIRF 1012) (cd re-iss. Jan90 & Apr92 cd/c; IRLD/IRLC 19002)*

Sep 86. (7") <52889> **I FEEL THE MAGIC. / FROM THE HEART** [–] [82]

Virgin — M.C.A.

Nov 87. (7") *(VS 1036)* <53181> **HEAVEN IS A PLACE ON EARTH. / WE CAN CHANGE** [1] Sep87 [1]
(12"+=) *(VST 1036)* – ('A'-heavenly version).
(cd-s++=) *(VSCD 1036)* – ('A'-acappella version).

Dec 87. (cd/c/lp) *(CD/TC+/V 2496)* <42080> **HEAVEN ON EARTH** [4] Oct87 [13]
– Heaven is a place on Earth / Circle in the sand / I feel free / Should I let you in? / World without you / I get weak / We can change / Fool for love / Nobody owns me / Love never dies . . . *(pic-cd-iss. Nov88; CDVP 2496) (re-iss. Jan91; OVED/+C 330); hit No.46)*

Feb 88. (7") *(VS 1046)* <53242> **I GET WEAK. / SHOULD I LET YOU IN** [10] Jan88 [2]
(12"+=/c-s+=/pic-cd-s+=) *(VS T/TC/CD 1046)* – ('A'extended).

Apr 88. (7") <53308> **CIRCLE IN THE SAND. / WE CAN CHANGE** [–] [7]

Apr 88. (7") *(VS 1074)* **CIRCLE IN THE SAND. / ('A'-seaside mmod groove mix)** [4] [–]
(12"+=/12"pic-d+=) *(VST/+Y 1074)* – ('A'-beach party mix).
(c-s+=/cd-s+=) *(VS TC/CD 1074)* – ('A'-sandblast multi-mix).

Jul 88. (c-s) *<53308>* **I FEEL FREE. / SHOULD I LET YOU IN** [–] [88]

Aug 88. (7") *(VS 1114)* **WORLD WITHOUT YOU (remix). / NOBODY OWES ME** [34] [ ]
(12"+=) *(VST 1114)* – ('A'extended worldwide mix).
(cd-s) *(VSCD 1114)* – ('A'extended worldwide mix) / ('A'side) / ('A'-panavision mix).

Nov 88. (7") *(VS 1150)* **LOVE NEVER DIES. / I FEEL FREE (live)** [54] [ ]
(12"+=) *(VST 1150)* – Heaven is a place on Earth (live).
(cd-s++=) *(VSCD 1150)* – Circle in the sand (live).

Sep 89. (7"/c-s) *(VS/+C 1210)* *<53706>* **LEAVE A LIGHT ON. / SHADES OF MICAELANGELO** [4] [11]
(12"+=) *(VST 1210)* – ('A'extended).
(cd-s++=) *(VSCD 1210)* – ('A'-acappella).

Oct 89. (cd/c/lp) *(CD/TC+/V 2599)* *<6339>* **RUNAWAY HORSES** [4] [37]
– Leave a light on / Runaway horses / Vision of you / Summer rain / La Luna / (We want) The same thing / Deep deep ocean / Valentine / Whatever it takes / Shades of Michaelangelo. *(re-iss. Jan91 hit No.6).*

Nov 89. (7"/7"g-f/c-s) *(VS/+X/C 1230)* **LA LUNA. / WHATEVER IT TAKES** [38] [ ]
(12"/12"g-f/3"cd-s) *(VS T/TP/CD 1230)* – ('A'side) / ('A'extended dance mix) / ('A'extended dub).

Dec 89. (7") *<53783>* **SUMMER RAIN. / SHADES OF MICHAELANGELO** [–] [30]

Mar 90. (7"/c-s) *(VS/+C 1244)* **RUNAWAY HORSES. / HEAVEN IS A PLACE ON EARTH (live)** [40] [ ]
(12"+=/3"cd-s+=/cd-s+=) *(VS T/TD/CD 1244)* – Circle in the sand (beach party mix).

May 90. (7"/c-s) *(VS/+C 1264)* **VISION OF YOU. / LEAVE A LIGHT ON (kamikaze mix)** [41] [ ]
(12"+=/cd-s+=) *(VS T/CD 1264)* – I feel free (extended).
(re-iss. Apr91; same); hit UK No.71)

Oct 90. (7"/c-s) *(VS 1291)* **(WE WANT) THE SAME THING (summer remix). / SHADES OF MICHAELANGELO** [6] [ ]
(12"+=) *(VSTA 1291)* – Heaven is a place on Earth / I get weak.
(pic-cd+=) *(VSCDP 1291)* – Circle in the sand (sandblast multi).

Dec 90. (7"/c-s) *(VS/+C 1323)* **SUMMER RAIN. / LEAVE A LIGHT ON (mix)** [23] [–]
(12"+=/cd-s+=) *(VS T/CDX 1323)* – ('A'-Justin Strauss mix).

Sep 91. (7"/c-s) *(VS/+C 1370)* **LIVE YOUR LIFE BE FREE. / LONELINESS GAME** [12] [ ]
(12"pic-d+=/cd-s+=) *(VS T/CD 1370)* – ('A'club version).

Oct 91. (cd/c/lp) *(CD/TC+/V 2680)* *<10446>* **LIVE YOUR LIFE BE FREE** [7] [ ]
– Live your life be free / Do you feel like I feel? / Half the world / You came out of nowhere / You're nothing without me / I plead insanity / Emotional highway / Little black book / Love revolution / World of love / Loneliness game.

Nov 91. (7"/7"pic-d) *(VS/+P 1383)* *<54183>* **DO YOU FEEL LIKE I FEEL. / WORLD OF LOVE** [29] [73]
(12"+=) *(VST 1383)* – ('A'dance version).
(cd-s++=) *(VSCD 1383)* – Live your life be free (dance instrumental).

Jan 92. (7"/c-s) *(VS/+C 1388)* **HALF THE WORLD. / ONLY A DREAM** [35] [ ]
(cd-s+=) *(VSCDT 1388)* – Live your life be free (original).
(cd-s) *(VSCDX 1388)* – ('A'side) / Vision of you ('91 remix) / Circle in the sand / Love never dies.

Aug 92. (7"/c-s) *(VS/+C 1428)* **LITTLE BLACK BOOK. / ONLY A DREAM** [28] [–]
(cd-s+=) *(VSCDT 1428)* – The air you breathe.
(cd-s+=) *(VSCDG 1428)* – ('A'mix) / ('A'house mix).

Sep 92. (cd/c/lp) *(BEL CD/MC/TV 1)* *<10606>* **THE BEST OF BELINDA CARLISLE VOLUME 1** (compilation) [1] [ ]
– Heaven is a place on Earth / (We want) The same thing / Circle in the sand / Leave a light on / Little black book / Summer rain / Vision of you / Live your life be free / I get weak / La Luna / I plead insanity / World without you / Do you feel like I feel? / Half the world / Runaway horses.

— <US title 'HER GREATEST HITS' w/ diff. order tracks>

— with writers **CAFFEY** + brothers **THOMAS** + **RICHARD**, plus **JEFFREY McDONALD & STEVEN McDONALD** / and a host of musicians

Sep 93. (7"/c-s) *(VS/+C 1472)* **BIG SCARY ANIMAL. / WINDOWS OF THE WORLD** [12] [–]
(cd-s+=) *(VSCDT 1472)* – Change (demo) / Too much water (demo).

Oct 93. (cd/c/lp) *(CD/TC+/V 2725)* *<39102>* **REAL** [9] [ ]
– Goodbye day / Big scary animal / Too much water / Lay down your arms / Where love hides / One with you / Wrap my arms / Tell me / Windows of the world / Here comes my baby.

Nov 93. (7"/c-s) *(VS/+C 1476)* **LAY DOWN YOUR ARMS. / TELL ME** [27] [–]
(cd-s+=) *(VSCDX 1476)* – Wrap my arms (demo).
(cd-s++=) *(VSCDG 1476)* – Here comes my baby (demo).

Chrysalis Ark 21

Jul 96. (7"pic-d/c-s) *(CHSPD/TCCHS 5033)* **IN TOO DEEP. / (WE WANT) THE SAME THING** [6] [–]
(cd-s+=) *(CDCHS 5033)* – I see no ships / Jealous guy.

Sep 96. (c-s) *(TCCHS 5037)* **ALWAYS BREAKING MY HEART / HEAVEN IS A PLACE ON EARTH** [8] [–]
(cd-s+=) *(CDCHS 5037)* – Circle in the sand / I get weak.
(cd-s) *(CDCHSS 5037)* – ('A'side) / Love walks in / The ballad of Lucy Jordan.

Sep 96. (cd/c) *(CD/TC CHR 6115)* *<10010>* **A WOMAN AND A MAN** [12] [ ]
– In too deep / California / A woman and a man / Remember September / Listen to love / Always breaking my heart / Love doesn't live here anymore / He goes on / Kneel at your feet / Love in the key of C / My heart goes out to you.

Nov 96. (c-s) *(TCCHS 5044)* **LOVE IN THE KEY OF C / HEAVEN IS A PLACE ON EARTH / CIRCLE IN THE SAND** [20] [–]
(cd-s) *(CDCHS 5044)* – ('A'side) / Don't cry (demo) / Watcha doin' to me (demo) / Too much water (demo).
(cd-s) *(CDCHSS 5044)* – ('A'side) / Kneel at your feet / In too deep (acoustic) / Circle in the sand (acoustic).

Feb 97. (c-s) *(TCCHS 5047)* **CALIFORNIA / LEAVE A LIGHT ON (live)** [31] [–]
(cd-s+=) *(CDCHSS 5047)* – Live your life be free (live) / Heaven is a place on earth (live).
(cd-s) *(CDCHS 5047)* – ('A'side) / Big scary animal (live) / In too deep (live) / I get weak (live).

Virgin E.M.I.

Nov 99. (cd/c) *(CDVX/TCV 2901)* *<848470>* **. . . A PLACE ON EARTH – THE GREATEST HITS** (compilation) [15] [ ]
– Heaven is a place on Earth / I get weak / Circle in the sand / Leave a light on / La Luna / We want the same thing / Summer rain / Live your life be free / Do you feel like I feel / Little black book / Big scary animal / In too deep / California / Always breaking my heart / Love in the key of C / Feels like I've known you forever / Prayer for everyone / All God's children. *<US w/ extra CD of mixes>*

Nov 99. (c-s/cd-s) *(VSC/+DT 1756)* **ALL GOD'S CHILDREN / RUNAWAY HORSES / ONLY A DREAM** [66] [–]

GO-GO'S

— had briefly re-united in 1990 and late in '94

A&M A&M

Jan 91. (12") *(AM 712)* **COOL JERK. / WE GOT THE BEAT** [60] [ ]

Feb 91. (cd/c/lp) *(395333-2/-4/-1)* *<447797>* **GO-GO'S GREATEST** (compilation) [ ] Nov90 [ ]
– Our lips are sealed / Cool jerk / We got the beat / Head over heels / Get up and go / Vacation / Beatnik beach / You thought / I'm the only one / This town / Lust to love / Mercenary / How much more / Turn to you. *(re-iss. cd Mar93 on 'A&M'; CDMID 184)*

I.R.S. I.R.S.

Feb 95. (7"/c-s) *(EIRS/+C 190)* **THE WHOLE WORLD LOST ITS HEAD. / OUR LIPS ARE SEALED** [29] [ ]
(cd-s+=) *(CDEIRS 190)* – Automatic / Lust to love.

Mar 95. (cd/c) *(EIRS CD/MC 1071)* **RETURN TO THE VALLEY OF THE GO-GO'S** (compilation) [52] [ ]
– Living at the Canterbury – Party pose / Fashion seekers (live) / He's so strange / London boys (live) / Beatnik beach (live) / Cool jerk / We got the beat / Our lips are sealed / Surfing and spying / Vacation / Speeding / Good for gone / Head over heels / Can't stop the world (live) / Mercenary (acoustic) / Good girl / Beautiful / The whole world lost its head.

— re-formed yet again

not iss. Beyond

May 01. (cd,c) *<5 78182>* **GOD BLESS THE GO-GO'S** [–] [57]
– La la land / Unforgiven / Apology / Stuck in my car / Vision of nowness / Here you are / Automatic rainy day / Kissing asphalt / Insincere / Superslide / Throw me a curve / Talking myself down / Daisy chain.

GOLDFRAPP

Formed: Bath, England . . . 1998 by vocalist/keyboardist ALISON GOLDFRAPP and composer WILL GREGORY. Before bringing GOLDFRAPP together, ALISON was a regular contributor to the independent music scene in Britain. She began experimenting with music as part of her fine-art degree studies at Middlesex University, and while still majoring, managed to appear on TRICKY's debut album 'Maxinquaye' in 1995. Throughout the decade she seemed rather busy, appearing on both ORBITAL's 'Snivilization' in '96 and ADD N TO (X)'s undisputed masterpiece 'Avant Garde' in '98. Cameo appearances on alternative records such as these helped ALISON establish a reputation in both the independent and mainstream circles. By 1999, ALISON had completed a tape of demo material that would ultimately find its way onto the startling debut album proper, 'FELT MOUNTAIN' (2000), a set which was co-written with composer and fellow group member, WILL GREGORY. It took the music press by surprise, with many critics placing the set high on their top Albums Of The Year list. 'FELT MOUNTAIN' displayed such beauty and inspiration that peers PORTISHEAD and BROADCAST paled in comparison. The lush strings on 'HORSE TEARS' or ALISON's wilting vocals on 'PILOTS' set the standards for anybody who dared to be as good as them. But 'LOVELY HEAD', with its strange creeping JOHN BARRY-meets-STREISAND esque orchestra, reminiscent of MERCURY REV's darker period, and nostalgic whistling (very MORRICONE, indeed!), was perhaps the stand-out track on the entire album. Unfortunately, it was spoiled by an appearance in an Altman-esque mobile phone ad starring a very creepy Gary Oldman in cameo role. That said, everybody went about the next day asking everybody else: "Who sings that tune in that Gary Oldman advert?" Of course, it was GOLDFRAPP, and by the following year, both the album and singles ('UTOPIA' and 'LOVELY HEAD') were hitting the lower rungs of the UK charts. 2003's 'BLACK CHERRY' (featuring hits 'TRAIN', 'STRICT MACHINE' and 'TWIST') served up more glacially intoxicating, strangely familiar and deceptively futuristic pop, less traditionalist and more experimental than the debut but still operating broadly within that record's parameters.

Album rating: FELT MOUNTAIN (*8) / BLACK CHERRY (*7)

ALISON GOLDFRAPP – vocals, keyboards / **WILL GREGORY** – keyboards / with session people + guests

Mute Mute

May 00. (12"/cd-s) *(12/CD MUTE 247)* **LOVELY HEAD. / ('A'-star mix) / ('A'-Miss World mix)** [ ] [–]

Sep 00. (cd/lp) *(CD+/STUMM 188) <9135>* **FELT MOUNTAIN** [ ] [ ]
– Lovely head / Paper bag / Human / Pilots / Deer stop / Felt mountain / Oompa radar / Utopia / Horse tears. *(d-cd iss.Oct01+=; LCDSTUMM 188)* – Pilots (on a star) / UK girls (physical) / Lovely head (Miss World mix) / Utopia (new ears mix) / Human (Calexico vocal) / Human (Massey's cro-magnon mix) / Utopia (Tom Middleton cosmos vocal). *(re-dist.Aug01)* – hit No.57

Oct 00. (12"/cd-s) *(12/CD MUTE 253)* **UTOPIA. / UTOPIA (new ears mix) / UTOPIA (sunroof mix)** [ ] [–]

Feb 01. (12") *(12MUTE 259)* **HUMAN. / HUMAN (Calexico vocal mix) / HUMAN (Calexico instrumental) / HUMAN (Massey's neanderthal mix)** [ ] [–]
(cd-s) *(CDMUTE 259)* – ('A'side) / ('A'-Massey's cro-magnon).

Jun 01. (cd-s) *(CDMUTE 264)* **UTOPIA / UK GIRLS (physical) / HUMAN (live)** [62] [–]
(12"/cd-s) *(12/CDS MUTE 264)* – ('A'side) / ('A'-Jori Hulkonnen mix) / ('A'-Tom Middleton cosmos vocal) / ('A'-Tim Wright mix).

Nov 01. (cd-s) *(CDMUTE 267)* **LOVELY HEAD / PILOTS (ON A STAR) / HORSE TEARS (live)** [68] [–]
(cd-s) *(LCDMUTE 267)* – ('A'side) / ('A'-stare mesto mix) / Utopia (Tom Middleton cosmos acid dub) / Pilots (on a star) (video).

Apr 03. (cd-s) *(CDMUTE 291)* **TRAIN / TRAIN (village hall mix) / BIG BLACK CLOUD LITTLE WHITE LIE / TRAIN (video)** [23] [–]
(12") *(12MUTE 291)* – ('A'side) / El train (T Raumschmiere remix) / ('A'-Ewan Pearson 4/4 instrumental).
(cd-s) *(LCDMUTE 291)* – El train (T Raumschmiere remix) / ('A'-Ewan Pearson 6/8 vocal mix) / ('A'-Ewan Pearson 4/4 instrumental).

Apr 03. (cd/lp) *(CD+/STUMM 196) <9206>* **BLACK CHERRY** [19] May03 [ ]
– Crystalline green / Train / Black cherry / Tiptoe / Deep honey / Hairy trees / Twist / Strict machine / Forever / Slippage.

Jul 03. (cd-s) *(CDMUTE 295)* **STRICT MACHINE / WHITE SOFT ROPE (featuring the Midwich Children Choir) / HAIRY TREES (live)** [25] [–]
(cd-s) *(LCDMUTE 295)* – ('A'-Ewan Pearson instrumental remix) / ('A'-Rowan's remix) / Train (Ewan Pearson dub).

Nov 03. (cd-s) *(CDMUTE 311)* **TWIST / YES SIR / DEER STOP (live)** [31] [–]
(cd-s) *(LCDMUTE 311)* – ('A'-Jacques Le Cont's conversation perversion mix) / Forever (Mountaineers remix) / ('A'-Dimitri Tokovol remix).

GOLDIE

Born: CLIFFORD PRICE, 1965, Wolverhampton, England. After a rough'n'ready childhood spent in foster homes, GOLDIE was a streetwise dude with a penchant for electro, hip hop and graffiti art. After a spell in Miami with his father, he returned to Britain and met up with DJ duo KEMISTRY and STORM, who took him to the hardcore rave club "Rage" in London's Charing Cross. Worked with Mancunian (A GUY CALLED) GERALD ('Voodoo Ray' man) on his 'ENERGY' single. GOLDIE was hooked and soon became one of the prime movers at 'Reinforced', a small hardcore label which had grown out of the embryonic rave scene and flourished under the entrepreneurial spirit of the time. In the early 90's, GOLDIE (named so, due to his gold-plated molars) released his first recorded music under the RUFIGE KRU moniker. Along with other cutting edge releases of the day, the records heralded a move away from the smiley sounds of rave culture, replacing the uplifting piano breaks with disturbing sound effects, razor-sharp breakbeats and way-deep sub-basslines. Then, in 1993, under the alias METALHEADZ, a name he'd later use for his own label, GOLDIE recorded the pivotal 'TERMINATOR'. With its deconstructed fluid beats and futuristic samples, the record saw jungle coming of age. The follow-up 'ANGEL' took the blueprint and pushed the parameters ever further. Haunting female vocals and 'Tomorrow Never Knows'-like squawls melted into amphetamine-rush snares, creating music of exquisite beauty and dark grace. After signing to 'Ffrr', GOLDIE released the lush 'INNER CITY LIFE' towards the end of '94. Already a godfather-like figure within the tight-knit breakbeat community, GOLDIE was a charismatic character with a talent for the off-the-cuff soundbites and duly adopted by the music press as the drum'n'bass spokesman. His high media profile helped propel his landmark opus, 'TIMELESS' to the upper reaches of the album charts. Beloved of the inky press as well as the dance mags, the album went on to sell more than 100,000 copies, inspiring a slew of ambient-jungle imitators and even galvanising Radio One into covering the burgeoning breakbeat movement. In addition to live work, at home and abroad, GOLDIE has continued to release pioneering material on his 'Metalheadz' label, anticipating the move towards more jazz-infected rhythms evident in the work of contemporaries like RONI SIZE. The Metalheadz club night in London also continues to pack in the crowds, all of which will ensure that, for the time being at least, GOLDIE will remain as the larger than life spokesperson for one of the most innovative musical developments of the last decade. Along with LTJ BUKEM's 'Logical Progression' collection, GOLDIE's epochal 'TIMELESS' album is one of the few jungle releases you'd be likely to see on the well-heeled CD buyer's coffee table. His love life too, became more fodder for the gossip columns, when he became the beau of Icelandic pixie BJORK around 1996. GOLDIE's 'SATURNZRETURN' in early '98 was a little disappointing to say the least. A double-disc taking up two and a half hours, the ambitious, schizophrenic and excessive record comprised mainly long-drawn pieces ranging from drum'n'bass symphonies to inconsistent collaborations with the likes of KRS-ONE and NOEL GALLAGHER; cut to one-disc it might well have worked. Pity. Of late, GOLDIE has set himself new tasks of bringing through new talent on his GOLDIE.CO.UK various artists project.

Album rating: TIMELESS (*8) / SATURNZRETURN (*6)

METALHEADZ

GOLDIE – vocals / with

		Reinforced	not iss.
1992.	(12"ep) **KILLERMUFFIN EP**		–
		Synthetic	not iss.
Nov 92.	(12"ep/c-ep/cd-ep) *(SYNTH/+K/CD 003)* **TERMINATOR EP**		–
	– Terminator / Kemistry / Knowledge / Sinister. *(re-iss. Oct93; SYNTH 3 /+C/CD)*		
Aug 93.	(12"ep) *(SYNTH 7)* **ANGEL EP**		–
	(12") *(SYNTH 7R)* – Angel (remixes).		
1994.	(12"ep) **ENFORCERS EP**		–

GOLDIE

		Ffrr-London	London
Nov 94.	(12"/c-s/cd-s; as GOLDIE PRESENTS METALHEADZ) *(FX/FCS/FCD 251)* **INNER CITY LIFE / ('A'mixes)**	49	
	(12") *(FXX 251)* – ('A'mixes; Roni Size / Nookie remix).		
Mar 95.	(c-s/cd-s) **TIMELESS / INNER CITY LIFE**		
Jul 95.	(d-cd/d-c/d-lp) *(<828 646-2/-4/-1>)* **TIMELESS**	7	
	– Timeless / Saint Angel / State of mind / This is a bad / Sea of tears / Jah the seventh / State of rage (sensual V.I.P. mix) / Still life / Angel / Adrift / Kemistry / You & me. *(d-lp+=)* – (2 other mixes). *(cd re-iss. Feb98; 828614-2)*		
Aug 95.	(12"/c-s) *(FX/FCS 266)* **ANGEL. / SAINT ANGEL / YOU AND ME (THE BEAUTY – THE BEAST)**	41	
	(cd-s+=) *(FCD 266)* – Angel (Peshay back from Narm mix).		
	(above vocals by D. CHARLEMAGNE)		
Nov 95.	(c-s) *(FCS 267)* **INNER CITY LIFE / ('A'-Peshay mix)**	39	
	(cd-s+=) *(FCD 267)* – Kemistry (Doc Scott mix).		
	(12") *(FX 267)* – ('A'radio mix) / ('A'extended) / ('A'-4 Hero part 1 mix) / ('A'-Roni Size instrumental).		
——	following album featured an orchestra arranged by GAVYN WRIGHT		
Oct 97.	(12"/cd-s; GOLDIE feat KRS ONE) *(FX/FCD 316)* **DIGITAL / ('A'-original mix) / ('A'-V.I.P. mix)**	13	
	(cd-s) *(FXX/FCDP 316)* – ('A'remixes).		
Jan 98.	(12"/cd-s) *(FX/FCD 325)* **TEMPERTEMPER – (short temper). / TEMPERTEMPER / TEMPERTEMPER – (vipmix)**	13	
	(cd-s) *(FCDP 325)* –		
Feb 98.	(d-cd/c/t-lp) *(828990-2/-4/-1)* *<828983>* **SATURNZRETURN**	15	
	– MOTHER: Mother / Truth // SATURN: Tempertemper / Digital / I'll be there for you / Believe / Dragonfly / Chico-death of a rockstar / Letter of fate / Fury – the origin / Crystal clear / Demonz.		
Mar 98.	(12"/cd-s) *(FX/FCD 332)* **BELIEVE. / (MJ Cole remix)**	36	–
	(cd-s) *(FCDP 332)* – ('A'mixes).		
	(12" re-iss. Oct01 on 'Swing City Renegade'; REN 1003)		
——	late in 2001, GOLDIE put together a mix album, 'GOLDIE.CO.UK' of people he'd been working with since the millennium		

☐ GOLLIWOGS (see under ⇒ CREEDENCE CLEARWATER REVIVAL)

GOMEZ

Formed: Southport, England . . . 1997 originally as GOMEZ, KILL, KILL THE VORTEX by college lads BEN OTTERWELL, TOM GRAY, IAN BALL, PAUL BLACKBURN and OLLY PEACOCK. A home-recorded tape of the band found its way into the hands of record shop worker and former COMSAT ANGELS member, STEVE FELLOWS, who almost immediately became their manager. He in turn set up time in a Sheffield rehearsal studio in which he invited a plethora of A&R men to witness the unique talent of the band. After a fortnight, over thirty record labels were showing signs of interest, although FELLOWS and his protegees opted for Virgin offshoot, 'Hut'. Their early 70's to early 90's sound – like a hybrid of LOWELL GEORGE, GRATEFUL DEAD and BECK – was much in debt to the bluesy whisky-throated chords of lead singer, BEN, whose boyish, bespectacled look stunned an unsuspecting but appreciative audience on their debut single, '78 STONE WOBBLE'. It was their first UK Top 50 entry and was pursued a month later – in April '98 – by their classic debut album, 'BRING IT ON'. A critical and soon-to-be commercial success, its highlights were the tracks, 'GET MILES' (gruffly reminiscent of The BEATLES' 'Come Together'), 'WHIPPIN' PICCADILLY' and 'GET MYSELF ARRESTED', all of which helped it win the much lauded Mercury prize early in '99. Later that year, two brand-new GOMEZ tracks 'BRING IT ON' (surprisingly not a part of the debut!) and 'RHYTHM & BLUES ALIBI' hovered around the Top 20, while parent follow-up set, 'LIQUID SKIN' (1999) smashed in at No.2. On reflection, the band might've been better to wait a little longer. Good on GOMEZ though, as it says a lot for a band who release a fresh set of songs every year – here's hoping America could be their next prize. Prior to that difficult third album, GOMEZ stopped the proverbial gap with 'ABANDONED SHOPPING TROLLEY HOTLINE' (2000). Ostensibly a collection of the usual B-sides, live material and outtakes, this record merely served to underline GOMEZ's talent by transcending the implied second division quality of such material. Indeed, this could almost have been a third album proper in its own right save for the fact there are no obvious singles. 'IN OUR GUN' (2002) was a welcome return from GOMEZ. Still not surpassing the initial brilliance of their debut, the boys had a good shot at recreating that timid, stoned and gruff sound. Even more stoned here, with a lot of dub influences thrown in for good measure, these romantic-orientated ballads didn't seem too out of place (i.e. the title track). However, the production was as smooth as a polished stone, and the songs could get a little too Americana for their own good. Despite these small gripes, GOMEZ delivered one of the most enjoyable and entertaining records of the year.

Album rating: BRING IT ON (*9) / LIQUID SKIN (*7) / ABANDONED SHOPPING TROLLEY HOTLINE collection (*6) / IN OUR GUN (*6)

BEN OTTERWELL – vocals / **IAN BALL** – guitar, vocals, harmonica (ex-SEV) / **TOM GRAY** – keyboards, vocals, guitar, multi / **PAUL BLACKBURN** – bass / **OLLY PEACOCK** – percussion

		Hut	Virgin
Mar 98.	(cd-s) *(HUTCD 95)* **78 STONE WOBBLE / WHO'S GONNA GO TO THE BAR / STEVE McCROSKI**	44	–
	(12"+=/c-s+=) *(HUT T/C 95)* – Wham bam.		
Apr 98.	(cd-c/d-lp) *(CDHUT/HUTMC/HUTDLP 49)* *<45592>* **BRING IT ON**	11	May98
	– Get miles / Whippin' Piccadilly / Make no sound / 78 stone wobble / Tijuana lady / Here comes the breeze / Love is better than a warm trombone / Get myself arrested / Free to run / Bubble gum years / Rie's wagon / The comeback.		

Jun 98. (c-s) *(HUTC 97)* **GET MYSELF ARRESTED / THE COWBOY SONG** [45] [–]
(12"+=/cd-s+=) *(HUT T/CD 97)* – Flavours / Old school shirt.

Aug 98. (c-s) *(HUTC 105) <95293>* **WHIPPIN' PICCADILLY / PUSSYFOOTIN'** [35] Nov98 [ ]
(12"+=/cd-s+=) *(HUT T/CD 105)* – Pick up the pieces.

Jun 99. (c-s/cd-s) *(HUT C/CD 112)* **BRING IT ON / DIRE TRIBE / M57** [21] [–]
(cd-s) *(HUTDX 112)* – ('A'side) / Chicken bones / Step inside.
(12"+=) *(HUTT 112)* – (all 5 tracks above).

Aug 99. (c-s/cd-s) *(HUT C/CD 114)* **RHYTHM & BLUES ALIBI / THE BEST IN THE TOWN / SO** [18] [–]
(cd-s) *(HUTDX 114)* – ('A'-Pre-mellotron version) / ZYX / Tijuanalaska (Tijuana lady – live version).
(12"+=) *(HUUT 114)* – (all 6 tracks above).

Sep 99. (cd/c/d-lp) *(CDHUT/HUTMC/HUTDLP 54) <48218>* **LIQUID SKIN** [2] [ ]
– Hangover / Revolutionary kind / Bring it on / Blue moon rising / Las Vegas dealer / We haven't turned around / Fill my cup / Rhythm & blues alibi / Rosalita / California / Devil will ride.

Nov 99. (c-s/cd-s) *(HUT C/CD 117)* **WE HAVEN'T TURNED AROUND / FLIGHT / ROSEMARY** [38] [–]
(cd-s/12") *(HUT DX/T 117)* – ('A'mix) / Gomez in a bucket (a seaside town made of ice cream slowly melting) / Emergency surgery.

Sep 00. (cd/c/lp) *(CDHUTX/HUTMCX/HUTLP 64) <50260>* **ABANDONED SHOPPING TROLLEY HOTLINE** (collection) [10] Oct00 [ ]
– Shitbag 9 / Bringin' your lovin' back here / Emergency surgery (remix) / Hit on the head / Flavors / 78 stone shuffle (BBC live session) / We haven't turned around (x-ray version) / Buena vista / Shitbag / Steve McCroski (BBC live session) / Wharf me / High on liquid skin / Rosemary (BBC live session) / Cowboy song / Getting better.

Mar 02. (7") *(HUT 149)* **SHOT SHOT. / SILHOUETTES** [28] [–]
(cd-s+=) *(HUTCD 149)* – Coltrane.
(cd-s) *(HUTDX 149)* – Shot shot (folk shot) / Air hostess song / Pop juice.

Mar 02. (cd/d-lp) *(CDHUT/HUTDLP 72) <811950>* **IN OUR GUN** [8] [ ]
– Shot shot / Rex Kramer / Detroit swing 66 / In our gun / Even song / Ruff stuff / Sound of sounds / Army dub / Miles end / Ping one down / 1000 times / Drench / Ballad of nice and easy.

Jun 02. (7") *(HUT 154)* **SOUND OF SOUNDS. / PING ONE DOWN** [48] [–]
(cd-s+=) *(HUTCD 154)* – Where are your friends / ('A'video).
(cd-s) *(HUTDX 154)* – ('B'side) / ('A'instrumental) / Click click / ('B'video).

– compilations, etc. –

Oct 02. (d-cd) *Hut; (543175-2)* **IN OUR GUN / ABANDONED SHOPPING TROLLEY HOTLINE** [ ] [–]

Oct 02. (d-cd) *Hut; (543416-2)* **LIQUID SKIN / BRING IT ON** [ ] [–]

GONG

Formed: Paris, France . . . c.1970 by Australian DAEVID ALLEN, who had been part of the embryonic Canterbury beatnik scene in England since the mid-60's. Previous to this, he had hung-out with the likes of WILLIAM BURROUGHS and ALLEN GINSBERG at the famous Beat Hotel in Paris, cultivating his bohemian leanings and free-form poetry skills. He hitched back to England and soon met a young ROBERT WYATT while lodging at his parents' house. Through WYATT, he was introduced to MIKE RATLEDGE and HUGH HOPPER, with whom he subsequently formed the jazz-influenced WILDE FLOWERS. A prototype SOFT MACHINE, they also numbered another youngster; KEVIN AYERS. ALLEN remained for a one-off 45, 'Love Makes Sweet Music', in 1967, while he was subsequently refused re-entry into Britain after a gig in St. Tropez. This effectively ended his tenure with the group, providing the impetus to set up his own commune of hippies who later evolved into GONG. A flexible outfit at this stage, they provided the backing for two albums, 'MAGICK BROTHER, MYSTIC SISTER' and 'BANANA MOON', the latter being credited to ALLEN. Theirs was an enchanting blend of whimsical, unconventional psychedelia that combined spaced-out rock and weird experimentation. 1971 produced the excellent 'CAMEMBERT ELECTRIQUE', which crystalised their innovative sound, the album finally being issued in the UK when Richard Branson's newly formed 'Virgin' label virtually gave it away for 49p (new money!). Titles like 'SQUEEZING SPONGES OVER POLICEMEN'S HEADS', 'WET CHEESE DELIRIUM' and the not-so ridiculously named 'TRIED SO HARD', were perfect examples of GONG's acid-fried humour. They had been part of the Glastonbury scene following a slot at the 1971 festival, although ALLEN broke up the band soon after. A year later, they reformed with a slightly altered line-up; GILLI SMYTH, DIDIER MALHERBE, LAURIE ALLEN, CHRISTIAN TRITSCH and FRANCIS MOZE, along with new space-cadets STEVE HILLAGE and TIM BLAKE. Now on 'Virgin', the band began work on a trilogy of albums entitled 'RADIO GNOME INVISIBLE', beginning with 'THE FLYING TEAPOT'. The second and third of these; 'ANGEL'S EGG' and 'YOU', came out the following year, ALLEN later decamping to Majorca. With their leading light gone, the band went through a dizzying series of personnel changes; HILLAGE went solo, while MOERLEN left a couple of times before he finally took control of the reins in 1976. This resulted in the creatively poor NICK MASON-produced set, 'SHAMAL'. Another, 'GAZEUSE!', was just as bad, the group taking some time to recover from the stagnant jazz-rock they peddled during the MOERLEN period. Meanwhile, ALLEN was carving out his own solo career; the punk-rock number, 'OPIUM FOR THE PEOPLE', in 1978 introducing a harder edge, while PLANET GONG and MOTHER GONG (GILLI's outfit) was as zany as anything the original GONG had ever produced. By the late 80's, GONG (and occasionally GONG MAISON) was again under the control of ALLEN, who had (predictably!) set up home in Glastonbury.

Album rating (selective): MAGICK BROTHER, MYSTIC SISTER (*5) / CONTINENTAL CIRCUS (*6) / BANANA MOON (*5; by Daevid Allen) / CAMEMBERT ELECTRIQUE (*8) / THE FLYING TEAPOT (*7) / ANGEL'S EGG (*6) / YOU (*6) / SHAMAL (*4) / GOOD MORNING! (*4; by Daevid Allen & Euterpe) / NOW IS THE HAPPIEST TIME OF YOUR LIFE (*5; by Daevid Allen) / LIVE FLOATING ANARCHY 77 (*7; as Planet Gong) / GAZEUSE! (*4) / LIVE, ETC (*4) / EXPRESSO II (*4) / DOWNWIND (*3) / TIME IS THE KEY (*3) / PIERRE MOERLEN'S GONG (*3) / LEAVE IT OPEN (*3) / BREAKTHROUGH (*3) / SECOND WIND (*2) / SHAPESHIFTER (*6) / THE BEST OF GONG compilation (*8) / 25th BIRTHDAY PARTY (*6)

DAEVID ALLEN (b.Australia) – guitar, vocals (ex-SOFT MACHINE) / **GILLI SMYTH** (b.France) – whispered vocals / **DIDIER MALHERBE** – sax, flute / **RACHID HOUARI** – drums, tabla / **DIETER GEWISSLER** – contrabass / **CARL FREEMAN** – contrabass / **BARE PHILLIPS** – contrabass / **BURTON GREEN** – piano, piano harp / **TASMIN SMYTH** (Gilli's daughter) – vocals

Byg Actuel not iss.

Feb 70. (lp) *(5-529 029)* **MAGICK BROTHER, MYSTIC SISTER** [–] France [–]
– Mystick sister, Magick brother / Glad to say to say / Rational anthem / Chainstore chant – Pretty Miss Titty / Fable of a Fredfish – Hope you feel o.k.? / Ego / Gong song / Princess dreaming / 5 & 20 schoolgirls / Cos you got green hair. *(UK-iss.Nov77 on 'Charly'; CRL 5052) (cd-iss. Nov86 on 'Decal'; CDLIK 31)*

1970. (7") *(129021)* **EST-CE-QUE JE SUIS. / HIP HIPNOTIZE YOU** [–] France [–]

—— now with Englishmen **PIP PYLE, CHRISTIAN TRITSCH + ROBERT WYATT**

1971. (lp; by DAEVID ALLEN) *(45 529 345)* **BANANA MOON** [–] France [–]
– Time of our life / Memories / All I want is out of here / Fred the fish / White rock blues and cabin code / Stoned innocent / Frankenstein, and his adventures in the land of Flip / I am a bowl. *(UK-iss.Jul75 on 'Caroline'; C*

1512) (re-iss. May79 on 'Charly'; CR 30165) (cd-iss. May90 on 'Decal'; CDLIK 63) (lp re-iss. Aug99 on 'Get Back'; GET 557)

— **CHRISTIAN TRITSCH** – bass / **GERRY FIELDS** – violin / **DANIEL LALOU** – multi horns, percussion repl. **FREEMAN, GREEN, PHILLIPS** and **T. SMYTH**

1971. (lp) *(45 529 533)* **CAMEMBERT ELECTRIQUE** [–] France [–]
– Radio gnome / You can't kill me / I've bin stone before / Mister long shanks: O mother – I am your fantasy / Dynamite: I am your animal / Wet cheese delirium / Squeezing sponges over policemen's heads / Fohat digs holes in space / Tried so hard / Tropical fish: Selene / Gnome the second. *(UK-iss.Jun74 on 'Caroline'; VC 502) (re-iss. 1982 on 'Charly'; CRM 2003) (cd-iss. Mar86 on 'Decal'; CDLIK 11) (re-iss. cd 1988 on 'Caroline'; C 1520) (re-iss. cd Mar90 on 'Decal'; CDLIK 64) (cd-iss. Nov94 on 'Gas'; AGASCD 001) (re-iss. Sep95 on 'Spalax';)*

Jan 71. (lp; Philips UK) *(6332 033)* **CONTINENTAL CIRCUS (Soundtrack)** [ ] [–]
– Blues for Findlay / Continental circus world / What do you want / Blues for Findlay (instrumental). *(cd-iss. May96 on 'Mantra'; 642089)*

— **LAURIE ALLEN** (b.England) – drums repl. PYLE who joined HATFIELD + THE NORTH / added **FRANCIS MOZE** – bass (ex-MAGMA)

— Disbanded early '72 after Glastonbury Fayre, but re-formed by end of year. Added **STEVE HILLAGE** (b. 2 Aug'51, England) – guitar (ex-KEVIN AYERS, ex-KHAN, ex-URIEL) / **TIM BLAKE** (b.England) – synthesizers

Virgin Virgin

May 73. (lp) *(V 2002)* **FLYING TEAPOT (RADIO GNOME INVISIBLE PART 1)** [ ] [–]
– Radio gnome invisible / Flying teapot / The pot head pixies / The octave doctors and the crystal machine / Zero to hero and the witch's spell / Witch's song / I am your pussy. *(re-iss. Jan82 on 'Charly'; CR 30202) (re-iss. Mar84; OVED 14) (cd-iss. May91 on 'Decal'; CDLIK 67) (re-iss. cd Sep95 on 'Spalax';)*

— Although DAEVID and GILLI moved to Majorca, Spain, they returned mid 1973. / **PIERRE MOERLEN** (b.Colmar, France) – drums repl. LAURIE / **MIKE HOWLETT** (b.Fiji) – bass, vocals repl. MOZE

Dec 73. (lp) *(V 2007)* **ANGEL'S EGG (RADIO GNOME INVISIBLE PART 2)** [ ] [–]
– Other side of the sky / Sold to the highest Buddha / Castles in the clouds / Prostitute poem / Givin' my luv to you / Selene / Flute salad / Oily way / Outer temple – Inner temple / Percolations / Love is how you make it / I never glid before / Eat that phonebook coda. *(re-iss. Aug82 on 'Charly'; CR 30219) (re-iss. Mar84; OVED 15) (cd-iss. 1989; CDV 2007) (re-iss. cd Apr91 on 'Decal'+=; CDLIK 75)* – Ooby-Stooby doomsday or The D-Day DJs got the DDT blues.

— **MIQUETTE GIRAUDY** – keyboards repl. GILLI

Oct 74. (lp) *(V 2019)* **YOU** [ ] [ ]
– Thoughts for nought / A.P.H.P.'s advice / Magick mother invocation / Master builder / A sprinkling of clouds / Perfect mystery / The isle of everywhere / You never blow your trip forever. *(re-iss. Aug82 on 'Charly'; CR 30220) (re-iss. Mar84; OVED 16) (cd-iss. 1989; CDV 2019) (re-iss. cd Aug91 on 'Decal'; CDLIK 76)*

— Virtually break-up, when DAEVID and GILLI move to Spain again. In May'76, DAEVID continued solo career and re-formed GONG in the late 80's. Meanwhile back in 1975, after he recorded solo FISH RISING album, STEVE HILLAGE also became solo artist using most of GONG!.

GONG

re-formed with only one original **DIDIER MALHERBE.** He recruited **JORGE PINCHEVSKY** – violin / **MIQUETTE GIRAUDY** – keyboards / **MIKE HOWLETT** – drums / **MIREILLE BAUER** – percussion, xylophone, etc. / **PATRICE LEMOINE** – keyboards

— (HOWLETT went on to become producer of A FLOCK OF SEAGULLS, etc)

Feb 76. (lp) *(V 2046)* **SHAMAL** [ ] [ ]
– Wingful of eyes / Chandra / Bambooji / Cat in Clark's shoes / Mandrake / Shamal. *(re-iss. Mar84; OVED 17) (cd-iss. 1989; CDV 2046)*

— **PIERRE MOERLEN** returned to repl. BRIAN DAVISON (ex-REFUGEE) who had toured with them in 1976 after BILL BRUFORD left to join GENESIS, etc. / **ALLAN HOLDSWORTH** – guitar (ex-SOFT MACHINE, etc) / **FRANCIS MOZE** – bass returned / **BENOIT MOERLEN** – keyboards / **MINO CINELOU** – percussion / **DIDIER & MIREILLE** also

Feb 77. (lp) *(V 2074)* **GAZEUSE!** (US title 'EXPRESSO') [ ] [ ]
– Expresso / Night illusion / Percolations part 1 & 2 / Shadows of Mireille. *(re-iss. Mar84; OVED 18) (cd-iss. Jun90; CDV 2074)*

— Disbanded again Spring 1977 (aargghh!!!). Left behind retrospective below (all line-ups).

Aug 77. (d-lp) *(VGD 3501)* **LIVE! ETC. (live)** [ ] [–]
– You can't kill me / Zero the hero and the witches spell / Flying teapot / Dynamite: I am your animal / 6/8 (coit) / Est ce que je suis / Ooby Scooby doomsday or the D-day DJ's got the DDT blues / Radio gnome invisible / Oily way / Outer temple – Inner temple / Where have all the flowers gone / Isle of everywhere / Get it inner / Master builder / Flying teapot. *(cd-iss. Jun90; CDVM 3501)*

— **PIERRE MOERLEN** retained group name with **HOLDSWORTH, BENOIT MOERLEN, BAUER** (on next lp only), plus **DARYL WAY** – violin (ex-CURVED AIR) / **HANNY ROWE** – bass / **FRANCOISE CHAUSSE** – percussion / **BON LOZANGA** – percussion

Feb 78. (lp) *(V 2099)* **EXPRESSO II** [ ] [–]
– Heavy tune / Golden dilemma / Sleepy / Soli / Burning / Three blind mice. *(re-iss. 1986; OVED 65) (cd-iss. Jun90; CDV 2099)*

PIERRE MOERLEN'S GONG

Arista Arista

Feb 79. (lp) *(SPART 1080)* **DOWNWIND** [ ] [ ]
– Aeroplane / Crooscurrents / Downwind / Jin go la ba / What you know / Emotions / Xtasea. *(re-iss. Jul91 on 'Great Expectations' cd/lp; PIP CD/LP 025)*

Oct 79. (lp) *(SPART 1105)* **TIME IS THE KEY** [ ] [ ]
– And na greine / Earthrise / Supermarket / Faerie steps / An American in England / The organ grinder / Sugar street / The bender / Arabesque intro / Esnuria two / Time is the key. *(re-iss. Nov90 on 'Great Expectations' cd/lp; PIP CD/LP 018)*

Jul 80. (lp) *(SPART 1130)* **PIERRE MOERLEN'S GONG LIVE (live)** [ ] [–]
– Downwind / Mandrake / Golden dilemma / Soli / Drum solo / Esnurio / Crosscurrents. *(re-iss. Nov90 on 'Great Expectations' cd/lp; PIP CD/LP 019)*

— (featured **MIKE OLDFIELD** – guitar)

— **BRIAN HOLLOWAY** – guitar repl. HOLDSWORTH (to various groups)

1981. (lp) *(202955)* **LEAVE IT OPEN** [–] Dutch [–]
– Leave it open / How much better it has become / I woke up this morning felt like playing the guitar / It's about time / Stok stok stok sto-gak / Adrien.

Eulenspiegel not iss.

1986. (lp/c/cd) *(EU LP/MC/CD 1053)* **BREAKTHROUGH** [–] Dutch [–]
– Breakthrough / Spaceship disco / Rock in seven / Six 8 / Poitou / Children's dreams / Portrait / The road out / Romantic punk / Far east.

Line not iss.

1988. (lp) *(LIDLP 5.0003)* **SECOND WIND** [ ] [–]
– Second wind / Time and space / Say no more / Deep end / Crystal funk / Exotic / Beton / Alan Key / Crash and co. *(cd-iss. Nov92 on 'Line'+=; LICD 900698)* – Crash and co. (# 2 & 3).

– compilations, others –

Jan 87. (cd) *Virgin; (COMCD 1)* **A WINGFUL OF EYES** [ ] [–]
(re-iss. Jan96; CDOVD 462)

Apr 89. (lp) *Demi-Monde; (DMLP 018)* **THE MYSTERY AND THE HISTORY OF THE PLANET GONG** (rarities 1971-72) [ ] [–]
(cd-iss. 1989 & 1993 on 'Thunderbolt'; CDTL 010 & CDTB 116) (cd-iss. Jun97 on 'Spalax'; 14518)

Nov 95. (cd) *Nectar; (NTMCD 517)* **THE BEST OF GONG** [ ] [–]

Dec 95. (3xcd-box) *Spalax;* **THE RADIO GNOME TRILOGY** [ ] [–]

Dec 95. (cd) *Strange Fruit; (SFRCD 137)* **PRE MODERNIST WIRELESS ON RADIO** [ ] [–]

May 96. (cd) *Mantra; (890025)* **LIVE AU BATACLAN 1973 (live)** [ ] [–]

May 96. (cd) *Mantra; (890042)* **LIVE AT SHEFFIELD 1974 (live)** [ ] [–]

Jun 96. (cd; as GONG MAISON) *Gas; (AGASCD 004)* **GLASTONBURY 1989 (live)** [ ] [–]

Jun 96. (cd) *Summit; (SUMCD 4117)* **THE VERY BEST OF GONG** [ ] [–]

Mar 97. (cd) *Gas; (AGASCD 001)* **CAMEMBERT ELECTRIQUE (Not What You Think . . . Unreleased studio tracks)** [ ] [–]

May 97. (cd) *Sound & Media; (SUMCD 4117)* **THE VERY BEST OF GONG** [ ] [–]

DAEVID ALLEN

DAEVID + PEPSI MILAN – guitar, mandolin / **ANA CAMPS** – vocals / **TONI PASCUAL** – synths, keyboards / **TONI ARES** – bass / **TONI FREE FERNANDEZ** – guitar / with GONG guests; **MIKE HOWLETT** – bass / **PIERRE MOERLEN** – percussion

Virgin not iss.

May 76. (lp; by DAEVID ALLEN & EUTERPE) *(V 2054)* **GOOD MORNING!** ☐ [–]
– Children of the new world / Good morning! / Spirit / Song of satisfaction / Have you seen my friend / French garden / Wise man in your heart / She doesn't she. *(cd-iss. Jun90; CDV 2054) (+=)* – Euterpe gratitude piece.

DAEVID + PEPSI + JUAN BIBLIONI – guitar / **SAM GOPAL** - percussion, synthesizers / **VICTOR PERAINO** – synth, keyboards / **MARIANNE OBERASCHER** – harp

Affinity not iss.

Nov 77. (lp) *(AFF 3)* **NOW IS THE HAPPIEST TIME OF YOUR LIFE** ☐ [–]
– Flamenco zero / Why do we treat ourselves like we do / Tally & Orlando / Meet the cockpit pixie / See you on the moontower / Poet for sale / Crocodile nonsense poem / Only make love if you want to / I am / Deya goddess. *(cd-iss. Nov90 on 'Decal'; CDLIK 69) (re-iss. cd Dec95 on 'Spalax'; 542825)*

PLANET GONG

DAEVID ALLEN + HERE AND NOW (London musicians); **GILLIE SMYTH** – vocals / **PROF. S.SHARPSTRINGS** -guitar, vocals / **KEITH MISSILE** – bass / **KIF KIF LE BATTEUR** – drums / **GAVIN DA BLITZ** – synthesizers / **SUZA DA BLOOZ + ANNI WOMBAT** – vocals

Feb 78. (7") *(AF 5101)* **OPIUM FOR THE PEOPLE. / POET FOR SALE** ☐ [–]

Charly not iss.

Apr 78. (10") *(CYX 202)* **OPIUM FOR THE PEOPLE. / STONED INNOCENT FRANKENSTEIN** ☐ [–]
Apr 78. (lp) *(CRM 2000)* **LIVE FLOATING ANARCHY 77 (live)** ☐ [–]
– Psychological overture / Floating anarchy / Stoned innocent Frankenstein / New age transformation / Try no more sages / Opium for the people / Allez Ali Baba blacksheep have you any bullshit – Mama mya mantram. *(cd-iss. Oct90 on 'Decal'; CDLIK 68) (re-iss. cd Dec95 on 'Spalax';)*

— with **PEPSI + CHRIS CUTLER** – percussion / **GEORGE BISHOP** – sax, clarinet / **ANGEL ADUANO** – banjo / **BRIAN DAMAGE** – drums / **RONALD WALTHERN** – pipes

May 79. (lp; by DAEVID ALLEN) *(CRL 5015)* **N'EXISTE PAS!** ☐ [–]
– Professor Sharpstrings says / The freedom of the city in a suitable box / The say the say / Something tells me / H's a fine air for fliss / But it's really not real / Because barroom philoshers / 333 / No other than the mother is my song / Theme from hashish to ashes / The turkeybirds breakfast / Rajneesh with thanks / No God will not go on or the wrong way to be right / O man you.

NEW YORK GONG

DAEVID ALLEN + MATERIAL; BILL LASWELL – bass / **MICHAEL BEINHORN** – synthesizers / **DON DAVIS** – alto sax / **FRED MAHER** – drums / **CLIFF CULTRERI** – guitar / + **BILL BACON** – drums / **MARK KRAMER** – organ / **GARY WINDO** – tenor sax

Jan 80. (7") *(CY 51056)* **MUCH TOO OLD. / I AM A FREUD** ☐ [–]
Apr 80. (lp) *(CRL 5021)* **ABOUT TIME** ☐ [–]
– Preface / Much too old / Black September / Materialism / Strong woman / I am a freud / O my photograph / Jungle windo(w) / Hours gone. *(cd-iss. Dec90 on 'Decal'; CDLIK 73)*
1980. (10"ep) *(CYX 203)* **JUNGLE WINDO(W). / MUCH TOO OLD / MATERIALISM** ☐ [–]

DAEVID ALLEN

HARRY WILLIAMSON – bass, sax (repl.DAVIS, WINDO + KRAMER)

1981. (lp) *(CR 30218)* **DIVIDED ALIEN PLAYBAX '80** ☐ [–]
– When / Well / Bell / Boon / Dab / Gray / Rude / Disguise / Pearls / Bodygas / Froghello / Fastfather / Smile. *(cd-iss. Dec95 on 'Spalax'; 14837)*
May 83. (12"ep) *(CY 2101)* **ALIEN IN NEW YORK** ☐ [–]
– Bananareggae / Are you ready / Oo lala / Side windo.

— with **MARK KRAMER** – piano / **ELIZABETH MIDDLETON** – piano, vocals / **W.S. BURROUGHS**

Shanghai not iss.

Nov 82. (m-lp) *(HAI 201)* **THE DEATH OF ROCK AND OTHER ENTRANCES** ☐ [–]
– Death of rock / Poet for sale / Tally's birthday song / You never existed at all / Afraid. *(cd-iss. Jan93 on 'Voiceprint'+=; VP 114CD)* – Radio Gnome concert intro loop / the switch doctor / Gong ORFT invasion 1971. *(cd re-iss. Aug96 on 'Blueprint'; BP 114CD)*

— He returned to Australia and teamed up with DAVID TOLLEY

Aug 86. (m-lp; as The EX) *(HAI 202)* **DON'T STOP** ☐ [–]
– Do / Eat / Work / Dinosaur / What they say.

Invisible not iss.

1987. (7"; as INVISIBLE OPERA COMPANY OF TIBET) *(INV 001)* **TRIAL BY HEADLINE. / TRIAL BY HEADLINE** [–] Aust. [–]

Demi Monde not iss.

Oct 89. (lp/cd) *(DM LP/CD 1019; one-side by MOTHER GONG)* **THE OWL AND THE TREE** ☐ [–]
– The owly song / I am my own lover / I am a tree / Lament for the future of the forest / Hands / Unseen alley / La dee Madri.

GONG

DAEVID + GRAHAM CLARKE – violin / **DIDIER MALHERBE / KEITH MISSILE** – bass

Dec 89. (cd/lp; as GONG MAISON) *(DM CD/LP 1022)* **GONG MAISON** [–]
– Flying teacup / 1989 / Titti-caca / Tatlas Logorythique / Negotiate / We circle around. *(cd+=)* – (1 track).

— In 1991, their touring line-up of GONG MAISON was **DAEVID ALLEN, DIDIER MALHERBE, GRAHAM CLARKE** – violin / **SHYAMAL MAITRA + KEITH MISSILE**

Celluloid not iss.

Oct 92. (cd) *(66914-2)* **SHAPESHIFTER** [–] France [–]
– Flying teacup / 1989 / Titti-caca / Tatlas Logorythique / Negotiate / We circle around. *(re-iss. Jan97 on 'Viceroy'; VIC 80392)*

Code 90 not iss.

Mar 93. (cd) *(NINETY 2)* **LIVE ON TV 1990 (live)** ☐ [–]
– Planetary introduction / You can't kill me / I've bin stoned before – Long Shanks – Omotha / Radio gnome invisible / Pot-head pixies / Voix lactee / Outer vision / Inner vision / Gorbachev cocktail – I am your animal / Flying teacup / I am you.
Sep 95. (d-cd) *(VPGAS 101CD)* **25th BIRTHDAY PARTY – OCTOBER 8-9, 1994, THE FORUM (live)** ☐ [–]
– Thom intro / Floating into a birthday gig / You can't kill me / adio gnome 25 / I am your pussy / ot head pixies / Never glid before / Eat that phonebook / Gnomic address / Flute salad / Oily way. *(re-iss. Mar97; same)*
Sep 95. (m-cd; as GONG GLOBAL FAMILY) *(VPGASCD 102)* **HOW TO NUKE THE EIFFEL TOWER** ☐ [–]
– Away away (South Pacific version) / Away away (twelve selves version) / Nuclear megawaste / Chernobyl rain.

Gliss not iss.

Aug 97. (12") *(GLISS12 001)* **A SPRINKLING OF CLOUDS** ☐ [–]

DAEVID ALLEN

Demi Monde not iss.

Feb 90. (cd/lp) *(DM CD/LP 1025)* **AUSTRALIA AQUARIA / SHE** ☐ [–]
– Gaia / Peaceful warrior / Australia aquaria / She / Isis is calling / Slave queen / Voice of Om / Voice of Om dub. *(re-iss. cd Feb91 as 'THE AUSTRALIAN YEARS' on 'Voiceprint'+=; VP 101)* – Don't stop. *(cd re-iss. Oct97 on 'Demi-Monde'; DMCD 1025)*

Amp not iss.

1990. (cd; by DAEVID ALLEN, HARRY WILLIAMSON & GILLI SMYTH) *(CD 011)* **STROKING THE TAIL OF THE BIRD** ☐ [–]
– Stroking the tail of the bird (part 1 & 2) / Moonpeople gliss / Deep sea / Rainbow meditation. *(re-iss. Nov99 on 'Voiceprint'; VP 207CD)*

Voiceprint not iss.

Feb 91. (cd) *(VPCD 102)* **THE SEVEN DRONES** ☐ [–]
– C drone (muladhara) / D drone (swadhishthana) / E drone (manipura) / F drone (anahata) / G drone (visuddha) / A drone (njna) / B drone (sahaiara) / Hello me.

1991. (cd; as INVISIBLE OPERA COMPANY OF TIBET) *(VP 106CD)* **JEWEL IN THE LOTUS** | | – |
(re-iss. Apr96 on 'Gas'; AGASCD 006)

— Next with; **GRAHAM CLARK + MARK ROBSON**

1992. (cd; by DAEVID ALLEN & THE MAGICK BROTHERS) *(VP 107CD)* **LIVE AT THE WITCHWOOD 1991 (live)** | | – |
– Zero theme / Why do we treat ourselves like we do? / I am my own roadie / Herbacious border / Have you seen my friend / Wayland Smithy / Trial by headline / Isle of glass / Children of the new world / Wise man in your heart / Magick brother.

Shimmy Disc | Shimmy Disc

Nov 92. (lp/cd; by DAEVID ALLEN & KRAMER) *(SHIMMY 060/+CD)* **WHO'S AFRAID** | | |
(above was augmented by label boss & BONGWATER man MARK KRAMER)

Voiceprint | not iss.

Nov 93. (cd) *(VP 111CD)* **TWELVE SELVES** | | – |
– Introdrone / Mystico fanatico / Away away away / Colage – Bellyphone of telephone / She – Isis is calling / Colage patafisico – Divided alien manifesto / I love sex but / Wargasm / Children of the new world / O Wichito / Sexual blueprint / Gaia / My heart's song.

Mar 97. (cd; as INVISIBLE OPERA COMPANY OF TIBET) *(VP 147CD)* **GLISSANDO SPIRIT** | | – |
– Landing / Uluwatu / Electric bird / Baliman energy / Cosmic dancer / Inner voice / High mountains dance / Dreaming / Moon in the sky / Mirage / Distant shore / Stars can frighten you / 7 keys / Wizard's garden / Eastside.

G.A.S. | not iss.

May 96. (cd) *(AGASCD 007)* **DREAMING A DREAM** | | – |
– Dear friends / High points / Brothers / Big daddy / Wotsa use / Garden song / Came to find you / Rapist / Sittin' in a teashop / Fire becomes her / No one's slave / For song / Dear friends. *(re-iss. Oct97 on 'Cleopatra'; CLP 0106)*

Jan 99. (cd) *(cd) (AGASCD 016)* **EAT ME BABY, I'M A JELLY BEAN** | | – |
– So what / Gold top / I can't get started / Slow boat / It ain't necessarily so / My funny valentine / Au privave / St. Petersburg cafe / Salt peanuts.

Gliss | not iss.

May 99. (cd; by DAEVID ALLEN & HARRY WILLIAMSON) *(GLISSCD 005)* **22 MEANINGS** | | – |

Innerstate | not iss.

Sep 99. (cd; as DAEVID ALLEN & THE UNIVERSITY OF ERRORS) *(INNER 7707)* **MONEY DOESN'T MAKE IT** | | – |
– Money doesn't make it / Prince of sidewalk scooter / False teacher / Involve me / Mullumbimby mother / Submarine of salt / Professor Improbable's preamble / Cunning style construct / Talkwind upswerve / Wedding music / Burn your money (remix) / Can't buy me sex.

Voiceprint | not iss.

Dec 99. (cd; by DAEVID ALLEN & RUSSELL HIBBS) *(VP 206CD)* **NECTAN'S GLEN** | | – |
– Ring the bells / Turn / Leshy / We came down / Nectan's glen / Spring song / Watching / Brother / Envirolament / Spirit / Man in the green / Avalon / Queen of hearts / She and I / Bees / Sonic tonic.

– his compilations, etc. –

Feb 94. (m-cd) *Voiceprint; (VPR 012CD)* **VOICEPRINT RADIO SESSION** | | – |

Mar 94. (cd; DAEVID ALLEN TRIO) *Voiceprint; (VP 122CD)* **LIVE 1963 (live)** | | – |

Mar 95. (cd) *Legend; (KZLM 1505-1)* **BANANA MOON GONG** (late 60's material) | | – |

Oct 97. (cd) *Blueprint; (BP 269CD)* **DIVIDED ALIEN CLOCKWORK BAND – LIVE AT SQUAT THEATRE NEW YORK AUGUST 1980 (live)** | | – |
(re-iss. Nov97 on 'Gas'; AGASCD 005)

GOOD CHARLOTTE

Formed: Waldorf, Maryland, USA . . . 1996 by twins JOEL and BENJI MADDEN, together with schoolfriends PAUL and BILLY. Famously inspired to pick up a guitar by a show on the BEASTIE BOYS' 'Ill Communication' tour of the mid-90's, the lads unfortunately failed to absorb much of the BEASTIES' style, wit, charisma and originality, never mind their awkward, endearing funkiness or encyclopaedic knowledge of black music. Instead, they took the usual route of local gigging then demo straight to major label amid the continuing corporate rush to sign anything with a faint whiff of adolescent angst or spiky hair. The fact that the MADDEN twins were moonlighting as MTV presenters didn't exactly do the band much harm either. Settling for a deal with 'Epic/Sony', GOOD CHARLOTTE released their eponymous debut album in 2000, sounding as assembly line-manufactured as they looked. Which was great if you were a fan of BLINK-182, GREEN DAY and their ilk, but not so great if you'd heard those chugging guitar chords and whining lyrics just once too often. 'THE YOUNG AND THE HOPELESS' (2002) was as tired as its title suggested, with more heavy handed hormonal musings and join-the-dots "punk" – example major hit singles, 'LIFESTYLES OF THE RICH AND FAMOUS', 'GIRLS AND BOYS' and 'THE ANTHEM'.

Album rating: GOOD CHARLOTTE (*5) / THE YOUNG AND THE HOPELESS (*6)

JOEL MADDEN – vocals / **BENJI MADDEN** – guitar, vocals / **BILLY** – guitar / **PAUL** – bass / **AARON** – drums

Epic | Sony

Sep 00. (cd) <61452> **GOOD CHARLOTTE** | – | |
– Little things / Waldorfworldwide / Motivation proclamation / East Coast anthem / Festival song / Complicated / Seasons / I don't wanna stop / I heard you / Walk by / Let me go / Screamer / Change. *(UK-iss.Feb03 on 'Epic'+=; 510974-2)* – Thank you mom.

Mar 01. (cd-s) <670738> **LITTLE THINGS / CLICK / THANK YOU MOM** | – | |

Aug 01. (cd-s) <671309> **MOTIVATION PROCLAMATION / YEP / YEP (version)** | – | |

Jan 03. (cd) *(509488-9)* <86486> **THE YOUNG AND THE HOPELESS** | 15 | Sep02 | 7 |
– A new beginning / The anthem / Lifestyles of the rich and famous / Wondering / The story of my old man / Girls and boys / My bloody valentine / Hold on / Riot girl / Say anything / The day that I die / The young and the hopeless / Emotionless / Movin' on.

Feb 03. (cd-s) *(673556-2)* **LIFESTYLES OF THE RICH AND FAMOUS / THE ANTHEM (demo) / LIFESTYLES OF THE RICH AND FAMOUS (live acoustic) / CEMETERY (live acoustic)** | 8 | 20 |
(cd-s) *(673556-5)* – ('A'side) / Little things / ('A'-live acoustic).

May 03. (c-s) *(673877-4)* **GIRLS AND BOYS / LIFESTYLES OF THE RICH AND FAMOUS (instrumental)** | 6 | 48 |
(cd-s) *(673877-2)* – ('A'side) / Riot girl (acoustic) / ('A'video).
(cd-s) *(673877-5)* – ('A'side) / Lifestyles of the rich and famous (live acoustic) / The young and the hopeless (live acoustic).

Aug 03. (c-s) *(674255-4)* <79932> **THE ANTHEM / THE ANTHEM (instrumental)** | 10 | Jul03 | 43 |
(cd-s) *(674255-2)* – ('A'side) / If you leave / Motivation proclamation (live acoustic) / ('A'-video).
(cd-s) *(674255-5)* – ('A'side) / Acquiesce (live on BBC3) / Complicated (version).

Dec 03. (7") *(674543-7)* **THE YOUNG AND THE HOPELESS. / LIFESTYLES OF THE RICH AND FAMOUS** | 34 | |
(cd-s) *(674543-5)* – ('A'side) / Girls and boys (Abbey Road session) / Hold on (video).
(cd-s) *(674543-2)* – Hold on / The story of my old man (Abbey Road session) / ('A'video).

GOO GOO DOLLS

Formed: Buffalo, New York, USA . . . 1985 by ROBBY TAKAC (a former DJ), JOHNNY RZEZNIK and GEORGE TUTUSKA. Like a grunge-punk fusion of CHEAP TRICK, The LEMONHEADS and The DESCENDENTS, they debuted the following year with a low-rent eponymous debut album thankfully not given a release in Britain. A follow-up, 'JED' (1989), was also sprinkled with the odd cover version, a reading of Creedence Clearwater Revival's 'DOWN ON THE CORNER' presided over by guest crooner, LANCE DIAMOND. In the early 90's, 'Metal Blade' took over the reins, their powerful metal-punk winning new audiences after the release of their third set, 'HOLD ME UP' (1990). Three years on, the GOO GOO DOLLS returned with 'SUPERSTAR CARWASH', a transitional set preceding their break for the big time. GEORGE had now been replaced by MIKE MALININ, the sticksman coming in for the band's LOU GIORDANO-produced set, 'A BOY NAMED GOO' (1995), a US Top 30 success that featured Top 5 smash, 'NAME'. However, unlike many of their peers (GREEN DAY, OFFSPRING, etc), the 'DOLLS didn't really translate to the saturated British market despite having another two radio airplay hits in the States, both taken from 1998 album, 'DIZZY UP THE GIRL'. Now irrevocably part of the major league despite their unassuming aesthetic, the band recorded 'GUTTERFLOWER' (2002) as an unashamedly major league album with a suitably pristine production to match. That said, the spirit – if not the sound – of their more ragged earlier releases was still intact, indicating a potential longevity which might yet outlast many of their formative influences. • **Covered:** I WANNA DESTROY YOU (Soft Boys) / DON'T FEAR THE REAPER (Blue Oyster Cult) / SUNSHINE OF YOUR LOVE (Cream) / I COULD NEVER TAKE THE PLACE OF YOUR MAN (Prince) / GIMME SHELTER (Rolling Stones) / I DON'T WANNA KNOW (Fleetwood Mac) / etc.

Album rating: GOO GOO DOLLS (*4) / JED (*4) / HOLD ME UP (*5) / SUPERSTAR CARWASH (*5) / A BOY NAMED GOO (*7) / DIZZY UP THE GIRL (*5) / EGO, OPINION, ART & COMMERCE compilation (*7) / GUTTERFLOWER (*6)

JOHNNY RZEZNIK (b. 5 Dec'65) – vocals, guitar / **ROBBY TAKAC** (b.30 Sep'64) – bass, vocals / **GEORGE TUTUSKA** – drums

Celluloid / Mercenary

1987. (lp) *(2211)* *<97292-2>* **GOO GOO DOLLS** [–] French [ ]
– Torn apart / Messed up / Livin' in a hut / I'm addicted / Sunshine of your love / Hardsores / Hammering eggs (the metal song) / (Don't fear) The reaper / Beat me / Scream / Slaughterhouse / Different light / Come on / Don't beat my ass (with a baseball bat). *(re-iss. Nov95 on 'Metal Blade'; 14079-2)*

Roadracer / Death-Enigma

Apr 89. (lp/cd) *(RO 9477-1/-2)* *<847859>* **JED** [ ] [ ]
– Out of sight / Up yours / No way out / 7th of last month / Love dolls / Sex maggot / Down on the corner / Had enough / Road to Salinas / Em Elbmuh / Misfortune / Artie / Gimme shelter / James Dean. *(cd re-iss. Feb94 on 'Metal Blade'; CDZORRO 70)*

Fun After All / Metal Blade

Nov 90. (lp/cd) *(AFTER 8/+CD)* *<26259-1/-2>* **HOLD ME UP** [ ] [ ]
– Laughing / Just the way you are / So outta line / There you are / You know what I man / Out of the red / I could never take the place of your man / Hey / On your side / 22 seconds / Kevin's song / Know my name / Million miles away / Two days in February. *(cd re-iss. May96 on 'Metal Blade'; 3984 17018CD)*

Warners / Warners

1993. (cd/c) *<9362 45206-2/-4>* **SUPERSTAR CARWASH** [–] [ ]
– Fallin' down / Lucky star / Cuz you're gone / Don't worry / Girl right next to me / Domino / We are the normal / String of lies / Another second time around / Stop the world / Already there / On the lie / Close your eyes / So far away. *(UK-iss.Aug99 on 'Edel'; 0102702HWR)*

— **MIKE MALININ** (b.10 Oct'67, Washington, DC) – drums, vocals; repl. GEORGE

Apr 95. (cd/c) *<9362 45750-2/-4>* **A BOY NAMED GOO** [ ] [27]
– Long way down / Burnin' up / Naked / Flat top / Impersonality / Name / Only one / Somethin' bad / Ain't that unusual / So long / Eyes wide open / Disconnected / Slave girl. *(cd re-iss. Aug99 on 'Edel'; 0103122HWR)*

May 95. (c-s) *(W 0293C)* **ONLY ONE / IMPERSONALITY** [ ] [ ]
(cd-s+=) *(W 0293CD)* – Hit or miss.

Sep 95. (c-s) *<17758>* **NAME / BURNIN' UP / HIT OR MISS** [–] [5]

Feb 96. (c-s) *(W 0333C)* **NAME / NOTHING CAN CHANGE YOU** [ ] [–]
(cd-s+=) *(W 0333CD)* – I wanna destroy you.

Jul 96. (c-s) *(W 0362C)* **LONG WAY DOWN / NAME (live)** [ ] [–]
(cd-s+=) *(W 0362CD)* – Don't change (live).

Jul 98. (c-s) *(W 0449C)* *<44525>* **IRIS / LAZY EYE** [50] Sep98 [9]
(cd-s+=) *(W 0449CD)* – I don't want to know.

Hollywood / Imprint-Warners

Mar 99. (c-s) *(010239HWR)* *<1763>* **SLIDE / ACOUSTIC #3** [43] Nov98 [8]
(cd-s+=) *(010205HWR)* – Nothing can change you.

Jul 99. (c-s/cd-s) *(01024 89/42 HWR)* **IRIS / IRIS (acoustic)** [26] [–]

Jul 99. (cd/c) *(0102042HWR)* *<47058-2/-4>* **DIZZY UP THE GIRL** [47] Sep98 [15]
– Dizzy / Slide / Broadway / January friend / Black balloon / Bullet proof / Amigone / All eyes on me / Full forever / Acoustic #3 / Iris / Extra pale / Hate this place.

Nov 99. (c-s/cd-s) *(010535 9/5 HWR)* **DIZZY / SLIDE (acoustic)** [ ] [–]

Feb 00. (c-s/cd-s) *(010311 9/5 HWR)* *<16946>* **BLACK BALLOON / BLACK BALLOON (album version) / NAKED** [ ] Jul99 [16]

Apr 00. (cd-s) **BROADWAY / NAKED (live) / BLACK BALLOON (live)** [–] [24]

Jul 01. (cd) *(0127112HWR)* *<47945>* **EGO, OPINION, ART & COMMERCE** (compilation) [ ] May01 [ ]
– Bulletproof / All eyes on me / Amigone / Acoustic #3 / Naked / Ain't that unusual / Burning up / Flat top / Eyes wide open / Fallin' down / Another second time around / Cuz you're gone / We are the normal / Girl right next to me / Lucky star / On the lie / Just the way you are / Two days in February / Laughing / There you are / Up yours / I'm addicted.

Warners / Warners

Apr 02. (cd) *(9362 48311-2)* *<48206>* **GUTTERFLOWER** [56] [4]
– Big machine / Think about me / Here is gone / You never know / What a scene / Up, up, up / It's over / Sympathy / What do you need? / Smash / Tucked away / Truth is a whisper.

Jul 02. (c-s) *(W 583C)* *<radio>* **HERE IS GONE / WE ARE THE NORMAL** [ ] [18]
(cd-s+=) *(W 583CD1)* – Burnin' up / Two days in February.
(cd-s+=) *(W 583CD2)* – Burnin' up.

Sep 02. (cd-s) *<42475>* **BIG MACHINE / BLACK BALLOON / BROADWAY** [–] [64]

□ Martin L. GORE (see under ⇒ DEPECHE MODE)

□ GORILLAZ (see under ⇒ BLUR)

GORKY'S ZYGOTIC MYNCI

Formed: Carmarthen, South Wales . . . early 1991 by EUROS CHILD, RICHARD JAMES and JOHN LAWRENCE. Naming themselves after the Russian writer MAXIM GORKY, they were signed to the Bangor-based 'Ankst' label by owner ALUN LLWYD and issued their 1992 debut 45, 'PATIO'. Two years later, their first album 'TATAY', found favour in the indie circuit, while they toured supporting The FALL (The GORKY's were banned in some Welsh clubs for combining the Welsh and English language!). A youthful Welsh-language psychedelic/folk/pop-rock outfit, they were largely influenced by the likes of The INCREDIBLE STRING BAND, early

SOFT MACHINE, or the even medieval, GRYPHON. Two brilliant singles were released in 1995; 'MISS TRUDY' (from 'LLANFROG' EP) and the classic 'IF FINGERS WERE XYLOPHONES', while they progressed with their second album proper, 'BWYD TIME', in 1995 (another in 1994; 'PATIO' was demos, etc from '91-93). Early in '96, they inked a deal with the major 'Fontana' label, through A&R man Steve Greenberg. Their first single for the label, the excellent 'PATIO SONG', was their initial breakthrough into the UK Top 50. In April '97, this song and 15 others, were featured on their best offering to date, the trippy 'BARAFUNDLE' which included the excellently folky 'SOMETIMES THE FATHER IS THE SON'. The following year, with cult glory seemingly at their feet, the GORKY'S released their fifth proper album, 'GORKY 5', a comparatively disappointing effort which, with mediocre reviews, only managed one week in the Top 75. After being dropped by Mercury in '99, they hooked up with Beggars Banquet subsidiary 'Mantra', only for JOHN LAWRENCE to become disillusioned just days before signing. However, a new-line (with RHODRY PUGH in tow) promoted the much-improved 'SPANISH DANCE TROUPE' (1999), the Catalonian-inspired title track scraping into the Top 50. By the time GORKY'S had issued the brilliant and timeless mini-set, 'THE BLUE TREES' (2001), their sound had mellowed so much it was hardly recognisable. The set included eight songs, all produced by GORWELL OWEN (his poignant diary entry about 'Bambi', written when he was nine years-old is worth the album alone), were written by CHILDS with the occasional track by JAMES. But what remained standard on the album was the acoustic reverberation of mandolins, violins, pianos, strummed guitars and songs about summer. So folksy and introverted was the title track that once the piano trills began you had forgotten that you were listening to the champions of Welsh Indie, and instead convinced yourself that you had put on something by NICK DRAKE. 'THE SUMMER'S BEEN GOOD FROM THE START' saw CHILDS reminiscing over blue skies and green fields while a country-blues fiddle quietly wailed over the acoustic guitar. If GORKY'S had been invited to play on MTV's 'Unplugged', this is what it would've sounded like. The sunny theme was denoted even further when the group issued the album 'HOW I LONG TO FEEL THAT SUMMER IN MY HEART' (2001), a more back-to-basics for the MYNCI's. However, this wasn't a bad thing as tracks such as 'CAN MEGAN' and 'HOW I LONG' (which ends up turning into a kind of homage to the seventies, with its brass-led outro) still evoked the calm heard on 'BLUE TREES'. If 'SPANISH DANCE TROUPE' amazed music listeners with its complex structure and blinding ambiguity, then with 'HOW I LONG . . .' and the beyond-sublime 'BLUE TREES', GORKY'S ZYGOTIC MYNCI had re-invented their own wheel. The hushed 'SLEEP / HOLIDAY' (2003) continued the Welsh dreamers' addictive preoccupation with impossible nostalgia and pastoral paradise lost, while never quite foregoing their trademark unpredictability. • **Songwriters:** Mostly EUROS CHILDS, some by or with JOHN LAWRENCE (until his departure) and RICHARD JAMES, and a few by MEGAN. Covered; A DAY IN THE LIFE (Beatles) / WHY ARE WE SLEEPING? (Soft Machine) / O CAROLINE (Matching Mole).

Album rating: TATAY (*6) / PATIO (*5) / BWYD TIME (*6) / INTRODUCING . . . compilation US (*6) / BARAFUNDLE (*9) / GORKY 5 (*6) / SPANISH DANCE TROUPE (*7) / THE BLUE TREES mini (*7) / HOW I LONG TO FEEL THAT SUMMER IN MY HEART (*8) / 20 (SINGLES & EP'S '94-'96) compilation (*6) / SLEEP – HOLIDAY (*7)

EUROS CHILDS – vocals, keyboards, synthesizer / **RICHARD JAMES** – guitars, bass / **JOHN LAWRENCE** – bass, guitars, keyboards / **SION LANE** – keyboards / **STEFFAN** – violin

Mynci | not iss.

1991. (c) *(001)* **ALLUMETTE** [ ] [–]

—— **OSIAN EVANS** – drums; repl. SION + STEFFAN

G.Z.M. | not iss.

1992. (c) *(none)* **PEIRIANT PLESER** [ ] [–]

—— added **MEGAN CHILDS** – violin

Ankst | not iss.

Oct 93. (10"lp;ltd) *(ANKST 40)* **PATIO** [ ] [–]
– Peanut dispenser / Lladd eich gwraig / Dafad yn sirad / Mr Groovy / Ti! Moses / Barbed wire / Miriam o Farbel / Oren, mefus a chadno / Gwallt rhegi Pegi / Sally Webster / Diamonds o Monte Carlo / Siwt nofio. *(re-iss. Jan95 & Apr97 cd+=/c+=; ANKST 055 cd/c)* – Blessed are the meek / Reverend Oscar Marzaroli / Oren, mefus a chadno / Dean ser / Siwmper heb grys / Llenni ar gloi / Anna apera / Siwf nofio / Hi ar gan.

Mar 94. (cd/c) *(ANKST 047 cd/c)* **TATAY** [ ] [–]
– Thema o cartref (Theme from home) / Beth sy'n digwydd i'r fuwch (What happens to the cow?) / Tatay / Y ffordd oren (Orange way) / Gwres prynhawn (Afternoon heat) / Amsermaemaiyndod (When May comes) – Cinema / O, Caroline / Naw.e.pimp (Nine for a pimp) / Kevin Ayers / When you hear the captain sing / O, Caroline II / Tatay (moog mix) / Anna apera:- a. Anna apera – b. Gegin nos (Night kitchen) – c. Silff ffenest (Window sill) – d. Backward dog. *(re-iss. Apr97; same)*

Jun 94. (7") *(ANKST 048)* **MERCHED YN GWALLT EI GILYDD. / BOCS ANGELICA / WHEN YOU LAUGH AT YOUR OWN GARDEN IN A BLAZER** [ ] [–]
(cd-s+=) *(ANKST 048cd)* – Mewn. *(re-iss. Apr97; same)*

Nov 94. (7") *(ANKST 053)* **THE GAME OF EYES. / PENTREF WRTH Y MOR** [ ] [–]
(cd-s+=) *(ANKST 053cd)* – Cwpwrdd sadwrn. *(re-iss. Apr97; same)*

—— **EUROS ROWLANDS** – percussion, drums; repl. EVANS

Mar 95. (10"ep/cd-ep) *(ANKST 056/+cd)* **LLANFWROG EP** [ ] [–]
– Miss Trudy / Eira / Methu aros tan haf / Why are we sleeping? *(re-iss. Apr97; same)*

Jun 95. (7"w-drawn) *(ANKST 058)* **GEWN NI GORFFEN. / 12 IMPRESSIONISTIC SOUNDSCAPES** [ ] [–]

Jul 95. (lp/c/cd) *(ANKST 059/+c/cd)* **BWYD TIME** [ ] [–]
– Bwyd time / Miss Trudy / Paid cheto ar Pam (Don't cheat on Pam) / Oraphis yndelphie / Eating salt is easy / Gewn ni gorffen (Let's finish) / Iechyd da (Good health) / Ymwelwyr a gwrachod (Visitors and witches) / The telescope and the bonfire / The man with salt hair / The game of eyes / Blood chant / Ffarm-wr. *(re-iss. Apr97; same)*

Nov 95. (7") *(ANKST 064)* **IF FINGERS WERE XYLOPHONES. / MOON BEATS YELLOW** [ ] [–]
(cd-s+=) *(ANKST 064cd)* – Pethau. *(re-iss. Apr97; same)*

Jul 96. (10"ep/cd-ep) *(ANKST 068/+cd)* **AMBLER GAMBLER EP** [ ] [–]
– Lucy's hamper / Heart of Kentucky / Sdim yr adar yn canu / 20. *(re-iss. Apr97; same)*

Fontana | Polygram

Aug 96. (cd) *<532818-2>* **INTRODUCING . . .** (compilation) [–] [ ]
– Merched ya neod gwalt eu gilydd / If fingers were xylophones / PenTree WRTH Y mor / Games of eyes / Kevin Ayers / Miss Trudy / Why are we sleeping? / Y ffordd oren / Meth aros tan haf / Era / Iechyd da / The moon beats yellow.

Oct 96. (7") *(GZMX 1)* **PATIO SONG. / NO ONE LOOKED AROUND** [41] [–]
(cd-s+=) *(GZMCD 1)* – Morwyr o hyd yn lladd eu hun ar y tir.

Mar 97. (7"/c-s/cd-s) *(GZM/+MC/CD 2)* **DIAMOND DEW. / QUEEN OF GEORGIA / TEARS IN DISGUISE** [42] [–]

Apr 97. (cd/c) *(534 769-2/-4) <536122>* **BARAFUNDLE** [46] [ ]
– Diamond dew / The barafundle bumbler / Starmoonsun / Patio song / Better rooms . . . / Heywood lane / Pen gwag glas / Bola bola / Cursed, coined and crucified / Sometimes the father is the son / Meirion Wylit / The wizard and the lizard / Miniature kingdoms / Dark night / Hwyl fawr i pawb / Wordless song.

Jun 97. (7"/c-s) *(GZM/+MC 3)* **YOUNG GIRLS & HAPPY ENDINGS. / DARK KNIGHT** [49] [–]
(cd-s) *(GZMCD 3)* – Marching ants.

May 98. (7") *(GZM 4)* **SWEET JOHNNY. / UN HOGYN UN HOGAN DRIST** [60] [–]
(cd-s+=) *(GZMCD 4)* – Mifi Mihafan.

Aug 98. (7") *(GZM 5)* **LET'S GET TOGETHER (IN OUR MINDS). / TONIGHT** [43] [–]
(cd-s) *(GZMCD 5)* – ('A'side) / Billy and the sugarloaf mountain / Hwiangerdd mair.

Aug 98. (cd/c/lp) *(558 822-2/-4/-1)* **GORKY 5** [67] [–]
– The tidal wave / Dyle fi / Let's get together (in our minds) / Tsunami / Not yet / Only the sea makes sense / Softly / Frozen smile / Sweet Johnny / Theme from Gorky 5 (Russian song) / Hush the warmth / Catrin.

Mantra — Beggars Banquet

Sep 99. (7") *(MNT 047)* **SPANISH DANCE TROUPE. / (DO THE) CHICKEN IN THE JUNGLE** [47] [–]
(cd-s+=) *(MNT 047CD)* – The Johnny Cash lawsuit song.

Oct 99. (cd/c/lp) *(MNT CD/MC/LP 1015)* <81015> **SPANISH DANCE TROUPE** [ ] [ ]
– Hallway / Poodle rockin' / She lives on a mountain / Drws / Over and out / Don't you worry / Faraway eyes / The fool / Hair like monkey teeth like dog / Spanish dance troupe / Desolation blues / Murder ballad / Freckles / Christmas eve / The humming song.

— (Jun'99) now without JOHN who formed the INFINITY CHIMPS (after partly recording with GZM on above) **RHODRY PUGH** (took his place)

Feb 00. (7") *(MNT 052)* **POODLE ROCKIN'. / FLU MUSIC** [51] [–]
(cd-s+=) *(MNT 052CD)* – Girl I've always known.

Oct 00. (m-cd/m-lp) *(MNT CDM/LP 1023)* <81023> **THE BLUE TREES** [ ] Feb01 [ ]
– The blue trees / This summer's been good from the start / Lady fair / Foot and mouth '68 / Wrong turnings / Fresher than the sweetness in water / Face like summer / Sbia ar y seren.

— **EUROS & MEGAN CHILDS + EUROS ROWLANDS** recruited **RICHARD JAMES** – guitar, vocals / **GORWEL OWEN** – piano / **PETER RICHARDSON** – bass / **RHODRI PHU** – drums / plus **ASHLEY COOKE, ANDY FUNG, NORMAN BLAKE + JASPER**

Sep 01. (7") *(MNT 64)* **STOOD ON GOLD. / MY HONEY** [65] [–]
(cd-s+=) *(MNT 64CD)* – Out on the side.

Sep 01. (cd/lp) *(MNT CD/LP 1025)* <81025> **HOW I LONG TO FEEL THAT SUMMER IN MY HEART** [ ] Oct01 [ ]
– Where does yer go now? / Honeymoon with you / Stood on gold / Dead-aid / Can Megan / Christina / Easy love / Let those blue skies / These winds are in my heart / How I long / Her hair hangs long / Hodgeston's hallelujah.

Sanctuary — Sanctuary

Aug 03. (cd) *(SANCD 183)* <84635> **SLEEP / HOLIDAY** [ ] Oct03 [ ]
– Waking for winter / Happiness / Mow the lawn / Single to Fairwater / Shore light / Country / Eyes of green, green, green / The south of France / Leave my dreaming / Only takes a night / Pretty as a bee / Red rocks.

Oct 03. (7") *(SANSE 226)* **MOW THE LAWN. / HOT SURFACE (part 2)** [ ] [–]
(cd-s+=) *(SANXD 226)* – Old Fanny Mahoney.

– compilations, etc. –

Feb 03. (cd) *Castle; (CMFCD 663) / Sanctuary; <81283>* **20 (SINGLES & EP'S '94-'96)** [ ] Mar03 [ ]

☐ GRADUATE (see under ⇒ TEARS FOR FEARS)

GRANDADDY

Formed: Modesto, California, USA . . . 1992 by ex-skater, JASON LYTLE, who, with the help of HOWE GELB (of GIANT SAND), found a sympathetic ear at 'Big Cat' records. The line-up around this time also included JIM FAIRCHILD, TIM DRYDEN, KEVIN GARCIA and AARON BURTCH, although it took time aplenty to finally emerge with debut release, the mini-set, 'A PRETTY MESS BY THIS ONE BAND'. 'UNDER THE WESTERN FREEWAY' followed in '98, another based on classic West Coast Americana, their BRIAN WILSON/MERCURY REV-esque sound marked them out as the Sunday drivers of the alt-country brigade. JASON LYTLE and his band of beardy brothers returned one year after the release of the 'BROKEN DOWN COMFORTER COLLECTION' with perhaps the best album of the year, 'THE SOPHTWARE SLUMP' (2000). As prog and as concept as you can get, 'THE SOPHTWARE SLUMP' began with what could only be described as an American Lo-Fi version of 'Paranoid Android' entitled 'HE'S SIMPLE, HE'S DUMB, HE'S THE PILOT'. On it LYTLE sang "How's it going 2000 man, I heard all of your controls were jammed . . .", and continued the theme of man against machine through the entirety of the set. Backed by FAIRCHILD's psychedelic, effect-laden guitar and DRYDEN's electric piano, that doubled up as a space-age synth, LYTLE wandered like a lost child in a daunting sc-fi mountain landscape singing eleven sad songs about drunken robots, smashed up computers, lost love and ultimately, hope, all in his unsure NEIL YOUNG/DANIEL JOHNSON-esque croon. Tracks 'HEWLETT'S DAUGHTER' and 'THE CRYSTAL LAKE' must've been two of the best psychedelic pop songs ever written, whereas on 'CHARSANDGRAFS', the band cranked up all of their instruments for what sounded like progressive grunge. In turn, a humble band who were thought to only make sad, sun-blasted Lo-Fi had created one of the strongest concept albums since 'Ok Computer'. Even if it was pitched somewhere between the aforementioned set, THE FLAMING LIPS' 'The Soft Bulletin' and MERCURY REV's 'Deserters Songs', the biggest compliment the listener could've paid GRANDADDY was by saying that it sounded mostly like them. After all of the acclaim, GRANDADDY issued the somewhat disappointing third set proper, 'SUMDAY', in 2003. Not that the album was bad, it was just many fans had expected something a bit more extravagant or even adventerous. What they got instead seemed like a watered-down version of their first two albums, with LYTLE's production moving towards a more polished, mainstream direction. Single 'NOW IT'S ON' was far too simple for a band that had given us the mindbending prog of 'HE'S DUMB . . .', and their slamming synth sounds, fuzzy guitars and looped beats were becoming a tad tiresome. But, it still seemed like an average album by GRANDADDY was still twice as good as other bands' outputs.

Album rating: A PRETTY MESS BY THIS ONE BAND mini (*6) / UNDER THE WESTERN FREEWAY (*8) / THE BROKEN DOWN COMFORTER COLLECTION compilation (*8) / THE SOPHTWARE SLUMP (*9) / CONCRETE DUNES collection (*5) / SUMDAY (*6)

JASON LYTLE – vocals / **JIM FAIRCHILD** – guitar / **TIM DRYDEN** – keyboards / **KEVIN GARCIA** – bass / **AARON BURTCH** – drums

not iss. — Big Jesus

Apr 94. (c) <*none*> **COMPLEX PARTY COME-ALONG THEORIES** [–] [ ]

1994. (7") <*none*> **COULD THIS BE LOVE. / KIM, YOU BORE ME TO DEATH** [–] [ ]

1994. (7") <*none*> **TASTER. / NEBRASKA** [–] [ ]

1995. (c) <*w-drawn*> **DON'T SOCK THIS TRYER** [–] [–]

Big Cat — Will

Apr 96. (m-cd) <*041*> **A PRETTY MESS BY THIS ONE BAND** [–] [ ]
– Away birdies with special sounds / Taster / Peeano / Kim you bore me to death / Pre Merced / Gentle spike resort / Egg hit and Jack too.

1997. (7"ep) <*none*> **MACHINES ARE NOT SHE E.P.** [–] mail-o [ ]
– Levitz / For the dishwasher / Lava kiss / Wretched songs / Sikh in a Baja VW bug / Fentry. *<re-iss. 1998 on 'Big Cat'; ABB 128P>*

Feb 98. (7") *(ABB 157S)* **EVERYTHING BEAUTIFUL IS FAR AWAY. / FOR THE DISHWASHER** [ ] [–]
(cd-s+=) *(ABB 157SCD)* – Glass dusty.

Mar 98. (7"/cd-s) *(ABB 161S/+CD)* **LAUGHING STOCK. / G.P.C. / 12-PAK 599** [ ] [–]

Apr 98. (lp/cd) *(ABB 152/+CD)* <33646> **UNDER THE WESTERN FREEWAY** [ ] Oct97 [ ]
– Nonphenomenal lineage / A.M. 180 / Collective dreamwish of upper class / Summer here kids / Laughing stock / Under the western freeway / Everything beautiful is far away / Poisoned at Hartsy Thai food / Go progress chrome / Why took your advice / Lawn and so on. *(cd re-iss. Aug00; ABB 100248-2)*

May 98. (7"/cd-s) *(ABB 162S/+CD)* **SUMMER HERE KIDS. / LEVITZ (BIRDLESS) / MY SMALL LOVE** [ ] [–]

Oct 98. (7") *(ABB 500 350-7)* **A.M. 180. / HERE** [ ] [–]
(cd-s) *(ABB 164SCD)* – ('A'side) / For the dishwasher.

V2 — V2

Sep 99. (7"ep) <27612> **SIGNAL TO SNOW** [–] [ ]
– Hand crank transmitter / Jeddy's 3's poem / MGM grand / Protected from the rain.

May 00. (cd) *(VVR 101225-2)* *<27068>* **THE SOPHTWARE SLUMP** [36] [ ]
– He's simple, he's dumb, he's the pilot / Hewlett's daughter / Jed the humanoid / The crystal lake / Chartsengrafs / Underneath the weeping willow / Broken household appliance national forest / Jed's other poem (beautiful ground) / E. Knievel interlude (the perils of keeping it real) / Miner at the dial-a-view / So you'll aim toward the sky. *(re-iss. Aug00 +=; VVR 101225-8)* – THE CRYSTAL LAKE tracks *(d-cd iss.Nov00 +=; VVR 101389-8)* – OUR DYING BRAIN tracks *(d-cd iss.Feb01 +=; VVR 101613-2)* – SIGNAL TO SNOW tracks

May 00. (7") *(VVR 501301-7)* **THE CRYSTAL LAKE. / OUR DYING BRAIN** [ ] [–]
(cd-s+=) *(VVR 501301-3)* – First movement / Message send: ID#5646766.

Aug 00. (7") *(VVR 501433-7)* **HEWLETT'S DAUGHTER. / LFO** [71] [–]
(cd-s) *(VVR 501433-3)* – ('A'side) / XD-data-II / Street bunny.
(cd-s++=) *(VVR 501465-3)* – Wonder why in L.A. / ('A'mix).
(cd-s) *(VVR 501433-8)* – ('A'side) / Wonder why in L.A. / Chartsengrafs.

Nov 00. (12"/cd-s) *(VVR 501493-6/-3)* **HE'S SIMPLE, HE'S DUMB, HE'S THE PILOT. / WIVES OF FARMERS / N. BLENDER** [ ] [–]

Jan 01. (7") *(VVR 501515-7)* **THE CRYSTAL LAKE. / RODE MY BIKE TO MY STEPSISTER'S WEDDING** [38] [–]
(cd-s) *(VVR 501515-3)* – ('A'side) / Moe Bandy mountaineers / She-deleter.
(cd-s) *(VVR 501515-8)* – ('A'-chilly mix) / What can't be erased / I don't want to record anymore.

Jun 03. (7") *(VVR 502224-7)* **NOW IT'S ON. / TROUBLE WITH A CAPITAL T** [23] [–]
(cd-s+=) *(VVR 502224-3)* – Hey cowboy, the phone's for you.
(cd-s) *(VVR 502224-8)* – ('A'side) / Getting jipped.

Jun 03. (cd/lp) *(VVR 102223-2/-1)* *<27155>* **SUMDAY** [22] May03 [84]
– Now it's on / I'm on standby / The go in the go-for-it / The group who couldn't say / Lost on yer merry way / El caminos in the west / "Yeah" is what we had / Saddest vacant lot in all the world / Stray dog and the chocolate shake / O.K. with my decay / The warming sun / The final push to the sum. *(ltd-d-cd-iss. Nov03 +=; VVR 102223-0)* – Crystal lake (live) / For the dishwasher / "Yeah" is what we had / A.M. 180 / Our dying brains / Laughing stock / The go in go-for-it (Radio Frances Black session) / Saddest vacant lot in all the world / He's simple, he's dumb, he's the pilot.

Aug 03. (cd-s) *(VVR 502366-3)* **EL CAMINOS IN THE WEST / BEAUTIFUL GROUND (live XM satellite radio) / MY LITTLE SKATEBOARDING PROBLEM** [48] [–]
(cd-s) *(VVR 502366-8)* – ('A'side) / Now it's on (Colin Murray Radio 1 session) / Derek Spears.

– compilations, etc. –

1996. (cd) *none;* *<none>* **THE WINDFALL VARIETAL** [–] [ ]

Jun 99. (cd) *Big Cat; (ABB 100569-2)* **THE BROKEN DOWN COMFORTER COLLECTION** [ ] [–]
– (A PRETTY MESS BY THIS ONE BAND / MACHINES ARE NOT SHE).

Oct 02. (cd) *Lakeshore;* *<(LAK 33690CD)>* **CONCRETE DUNES** [ ] Feb02 [ ]
– Why should I want to die / My small love / 12-pak-599 / Wretched songs / Levitz / For the dishwasher / Sikh in a baja VW bug / Lava kiss / Fentry / Gentle spike resort / Away birdies with spacial sounds / Kim you bore me to death / Pre merced / Taster / Egg hit and Jack too.

GRAND FUNK RAILROAD

Formed: Flint, Michigan, USA ... 1964 as TERRY KNIGHT & THE PACK, by RICHARD KNAPP, MARK FARNER and DON BREWER. A few years into their career, the soulful rock trio scored a US Top 50 hit with 'I (WHO HAVE NOTHING)'. KNIGHT subsequently became their manager in 1969, FARNER (now on vocals and guitar) and BREWER (drums) recruiting bass player MEL SCHACHER, the revamped threesome adopting the GRAND FUNK RAILROAD moniker. Along with STEPPENWOLF, MOUNTAIN, etc, they formulated their own brand of populist proto-heavy metal/rock with an emphasis on extreme volume. Having signed to 'Capitol' around the same time as their Atlanta Pop Festival appearance (mid '69), they immediately hit the US Top 50 with the single, 'TIME MACHINE', a track from their debut Top 30 album, 'ON TIME'. From that point on, the group proceeded to enjoy increasing and extremely profitable popularity with each successive release despite regular critical derision. Highly prolific, GFR delivered an album approximately every six months, the American public seemingly never tiring of their formulaic approach (in June '71, they broke The BEATLES' box-office record, selling out New York's Shea Stadium). By Spring '72, the group had split from the management of TERRY KNIGHT, hiring John Eastman (brother-in-law of PAUL McCARTNEY) to control their finances. The following year, with their moniker clipped to GRAND FUNK, the group enjoyed their finest three minutes with the US chart-topping, 'WE'RE AN AMERICAN BAND'. The similarly-titled, TODD RUNDGREN-produced parent album also shifted millions of copies, although British rock fans were more interested in prog rock or glam. In 1974, they fleshed out their sound with the brief addition of keyboard player, CRAIG FROST, who graced their second US No.1, a rock version of Little Eva's 'LOCOMOTION'. The group proceeded to churn out the inevitable hard rockin' pop hits and patchy albums, culminating in FRANK ZAPPA's disastrous 1976 attempt to redefine the band's sound with 'GOOD SINGIN', GOOD PLAYIN''. This release finally saw GRAND FUNK RAILROAD hitting the buffers at the end of the commercial line. MARK FARNER subsequently took off on a solo sojourn, returning in 1981 with some more below par GRAND FUNK material. • **Covers:** WE'VE GOTTA GET OUT OF THIS PLACE (Animals) / GIMME SHELTER (Rolling Stones) / etc.

Album rating: ON TIME (*6) / GRAND FUNK (*6) / CLOSER TO HOME (*6) / LIVE ALBUM (*6) / SURVIVAL (*6) / E PLURIBUS FUNK (*5) / PHOENIX (*5) / WE'RE AN AMERICAN BAND (*6) / SHININ' (*5) / ALL THE GIRLS IN THE WORLD BEWARE!!! (*5) / CAUGHT IN THE ACT (*4) / BORN TO DIE (*4) / GOOD SINGIN' GOOD PLAYIN' (*6) / GRAND FUNK HITS compilation (86) / GRAND FUNK LIVES (*3) / WHAT'S FUNK? (*3) / CAPITOL COLLECTORS SERIES compilation (*7) / MORE OF THE BEST compilation (*6)

TERRY KNIGHT & THE PACK

TERRY KNIGHT (b. RICHARD KNAPP) – vocals / **MARK FARNER** (b. 29 Sep'48) – vocals, bass (guitar from 1969) / **DONALD BREWER** (b. 3 Sep'48) – drums (ex-JAZZ MASTERS)

not iss. / A&M

1965. (7") *<769>* **YOU LIE. / THE KIDS WILL BE THE SAME** [–] [ ]

Cameo Parkway / Lucky 11

1966. (7") *<225>* **I'VE BEEN TOLD. / HOW MUCH MORE?** [–] [ ]
1966. (7") *<226>* **BETTER MAN THAN I. / I GOT LOVE** [–] [ ]
1966. (7") *<228>* **LOVIN' KIND. / LADY JANE** [–] [ ]
1966. (7") *<229>* **WHAT'S ON YOUR MIND? / A CHANGE ON THE WAY** [–] [ ]

Nov 66. (lp) *<S-8000>* **TERRY KNIGHT & THE PACK** [–] [ ]
– Numbers / What's on your mind / Where do you go / Better man than I / Lovin' kind / The shut-in / Got love / A change on the way / Lady Jane / Sleep talkin' / I've been told / I (who have nothing).

Jan 67. (7") *(C 102)* *<230>* **I (WHO HAVE NOTHING). / NUMBERS** [ ] [46]

Apr 67. (7") *<235>* **THIS PRECIOUS TIME. / LOVE, LOVE, LOVE, LOVE, LOVE** [–] [ ]

Jul 67. (7") *<236>* **ONE MONKEY DON'T STOP NO SHOW. / THE TRAIN** [–] [ ]

1968. (7"; as MARK FARNER & DON BREWER) **WE GOTTA HAVE LOVE. / DOES IT MATTER TO YOU GIRL** [–] [ ]

GRAND FUNK RAILROAD

KNIGHT became their manager. Added **MEL SCHACHER** (b. 3 Apr'51, Owosso, Michigan) – bass (ex-? AND THE MYSTERIANS)

Capitol / Capitol

Sep 69. (7") *<2567>* **TIME MACHINE. / HIGH ON A HORSE** [–] [48]

Sep 69. (lp) *<(E-ST 307)>* **ON TIME** [ ] [27]
– Are you ready / Anybody's answer / Time machine / High on a horse / T.N.U.C. / Into the sun / Heartbreaker / Call yourself a man / Can't be too long / Ups and down. *<cd-iss. Aug02 +=; 39502>* – High on a horse (original) / Heartbreaker (original).

Nov 69. (7") *<2691>* **MR. LIMOUSINE DRIVER. / HIGH FALOOTIN' WOMAN** [–] [97]

Jan 70. (lp) *<(E-ST 406)>* **GRAND FUNK** [ ] [11]
– Got this thing on the move / Please don't worry / High falootin' woman / Mr. Limousine driver / In need / Winter and my soul / Paranoid / Inside looking out. *<cd-iss. Aug02 +=; 39381>* – Nothing is the same (demo) / Mr. Limousine driver (alt.).

Mar 70. (7") *(CL 15632) <2732>* **HEARTBREAKER. / PLEASE DON'T WORRY** [ ] Jan70 [72]

Jun 70. (7") *<2816>* **NOTHING IS THE SAME. / SIN'S A GOOD MAN'S BROTHER** [–] [ ]

Jul 70. (lp) *<(E-ST 471)>* **CLOSER TO HOME** [ ] [6]
– Sin's a good man's brother / Aimless lady / Nothing is the same / Mean mistreater / Get it together / I don't have to sing the blues / Hooked on love / I'm your captain. *<cd-iss. Aug02 +=; 39380>* – Mean mistreater (alt.) / In need (live) / Heartbreaker (live) / Mean mistreater (live).

Oct 70. (7") *(CL 15661) <2877>* **CLOSER TO HOME. / AIMLESS LADY** [ ] Aug70 [22]

Dec 70. (7") *<2996>* **MEAN MISTREATER. / MARK SAYS ALRIGHT** [–] [47]

Jan 71. (d-lp) *(E-STDW 1-2) <633>* **LIVE ALBUM (live)** [ ] Nov70 [5]
– (introduction) / Are you ready / Paranoid / In need / Heartbreaker / Inside looking out / Words of wisdom / Meam mistreater / Mark says alright / T.N.U.C. / Into the sun. *<cd-iss. Aug02; 39326>*

Jan 71. (7";33rpm) *(CL 15668)* **INSIDE LOOKING OUT. / PARANOID** [40] [–]

Apr 71. (7") *(CL 15683) <3095>* **FEELIN' ALRIGHT. / I WANT FREEDOM** [ ] [54]

Apr 71. (lp) *<(E-SW 764)>* **SURVIVAL** [ ] [6]
– Country road / All you've got is money / Comfort me / Feelin' alright / I want freedom / I can feel him in the morning / Gimme shelter. *<(cd-iss. Nov02 +=; CAP 41725)>* – I can't get along with society / Jam (footstompin' music) / Country road (extended) / All you've got is money (extended) / Feelin' alright (extended).

Jul 71. (7"m;B-33rpm) *(CL 15689)* **I CAN FEEL HIM IN THE MORNING. / ARE YOU READY / MEAN MISTREATER** [ ] [–]

Aug 71. (7") *<3160>* **GIMME SHELTER. / I CAN FEEL HIM IN THE MORNING** [–] [61]

Sep 71. (7") *(CL 15694)* **GIMME SHELTER. / COUNTRY ROAD** [ ] [–]

Dec 71. (7") *(CL 15705)* **PEOPLE, LET'S STOP THE WAR. / SAVE THE LAND** [ ] [ ]

Jan 72. (lp) *(EA-SW 853) <E-AS 853>* **E PLURIBUS FUNK** [ ] Nov71 [5]
– Footstompin' music / People, let's stop the war / Upsetter / I come tumblin' / Save the land / No lies / Loneliness. *(UK cd-iss. Feb01 on 'EMI Plus'; 576223-2) <(cd-iss. Nov02 +=; CAP 41724)>* – Medley:- I'm your captain – Closer to home (live) / Hooked on love (live) / Get it together (live) / Mark says it's alright (live).

Mar 72. (7") *(CL 15709) <3255>* **FOOTSTOMPIN' MUSIC. / I COME TUMBLIN'** [ ] Dec71 [29]

May 72. (7") *(CL 15720) <3316>* **UPSETTER. / NO LIES** [ ] Apr72 [73]

Nov 72. (7") *(CL 15738) <3363>* **ROCK'N'ROLL SOUL. / FLIGHT OF THE PHOENIX** [ ] Sep72 [29]

Jan 73. (lp) *<(E-AST 11099)>* **PHOENIX** [ ] Oct72 [7]
– Flight of the Phoenix / Trying to get away / Someone / She got to move me / Rain keeps fallin' / I just gotta know / So you won't have to die / Freedom is for children / Gotta find me a better day / Rock 'n roll soul. *<(cd-iss. Nov02 +=; CAP 41723)>* – Flight of the phoenix.

GRAND FUNK

Aug 73. (7")<7"US-pic-d> *(CL 15760) <3660>* **WE'RE AN AMERICAN BAND. / CREEPIN'** [ ] Jul73 [1]

Aug 73. (lp) *<(E-AST 11027)>* **WE'RE AN AMERICAN BAND** [ ] [2]
– We're an American band / Stop lookin' back / Creepin' / Black licorice / The railroad / Ain't got nobody / Walk like a man / Loneliest rider. *<(cd-iss. Nov02 +=; CAP 41726)>* – Hooray / The end / Stop lookin' back (acoustic) / We're an American band (remix).

Nov 73. (7") *(CL 15771) <3760>* **WALK LIKE A MAN. / RAILROAD** [ ] [19]

— added **CRAIG FROST** (b.20 Apr'48) – keyboards

May 74. (7") *(CL 15780) <3840>* **THE LOCO-MOTION. / DESTITUTE & LOSIN'** [ ] Mar74 [1]

Jun 74. (lp) *<(SWAE 11278)>* **SHININ' ON** [ ] Mar74 [5]
– Shinin' on / To get back in / The loco-motion / Carry me through / Please me / Mr. Pretty boy / Gettin' over you / Little Johnny Hooker. *(UK cd-iss. Mar03 on 'EMI Plus'; 76383-2) <(cd re-iss. Jun03 +=; CAP 80531)>* – Destitute and losin' / Shinin' on (alt.).

Jul 74. (7") *(CL 15789) <3917>* **SHININ' ON. / MR. PRETTY BOY** [ ] [11]

— reverted back to trio.

Dec 74. (lp) *(E-ST 11356) <SO 11356>* **ALL THE GIRLS IN THE WORLD BEWARE!!!** [ ] [10]
– Responsibility / Runnin' / Life / Look at granny run run / Memories / All the girls in the world beware / Wild / Good & evil / Bad time / Some kind of wonderful. *<(cd-iss. Jun03; CAP 80532)>*

Feb 75. (7") *(CL 15805) <4002>* **SOME KIND OF WONDERFUL. / WILD** [ ] Dec74 [3]

Apr 75. (7") *(CL 15816) <4046>* **BAD TIME. / GOOD AND EVIL** [ ] Mar75 [4]

GRAND FUNK RAILROAD

Dec 75. (d-lp) *(E-STSP 15) <11445>* **CAUGHT IN THE ACT (live)** [ ] Sep75 [21]
– Footstompin' music / Rock'n'roll soul / Closer to home / Some kind of wonderful / Heartbreaker / Shinin' on / The loco-motion / Black licorice / The railroad / We're an American band / T.N.U.C. / Inside looking out / Gimme shelter. *<(cd-iss. Jun03; CAP 80592)>*

Dec 75. (7") *<4199>* **TAKE ME. / GENEVIEVE** [–] [53]

Mar 76. (7") *<4235>* **SALLY. / LOVE IS DYIN'** [–] [69]

Apr 76. (lp) *<(E-ST 11482)>* **BORN TO DIE** [ ] Jan76 [47]
– Born to die / Duss / Sally / I fell for your love / Talk to the people / Take me / Genevieve / Love is dying / Politician / Good things. *<(cd-iss. Jun03 +=; CAP 80498)>* – Bare naked woman / Genevieve.

EMI Inter. M.C.A.

Aug 76. (7") *(INT 523) <40590>* **CAN YOU DO IT. / 1976** [ ] [45]

Aug 76. (lp) *(EMC 1503) <2216>* **GOOD SINGIN' GOOD PLAYIN'** [ ] [52]
– Just couldn't wait / Can you do it / Pass it around / Don't let 'em take your gun / Miss my baby / Big buns / Out to get you / Crossfire / 1976 / Release your love / Goin' for the pastor. *<(cd-iss. Jan99 & Mar03 on 'Hip-O'+=; HIPCD 40144)>* – Rubberneck.

Jan 77. (7") *(INT 528)* **PASS IT AROUND. / DON'T LET 'EM TAKE YOUR GUN** [ ] [–]

Jan 77. (7") *<40641>* **JUST COULDN'T WAIT. / OUT TO GET YOU** [–] [ ]

— disbanded when the rest formed FLINT; FARNER went solo for a while

GRAND FUNK

re-formed with **FARNER, BREWER + DENNIS BELLINGER** – bass, vocals / (FROST had joined BOB SEGER)

Full Moon Full Moon

Nov 81. (7") *<49823>* **Y-O-U. / TESTIFY** [–] [ ]

Jan 82. (lp) *(K 99251) <3625>* **GRAND FUNK LIVES** [ ] Oct81 [ ]
– Good times / Queen bee / Testify / Can't be with you tonight / No reason why / We gotta get out of this place / Y.O.U. / Stuck in the middle / Greed of man / Wait for me. *<cd-iss. 2001 on 'Lissmark'; 6346>*

Feb 82. (7") *<49866>* **STUCK IN THE MIDDLE. / NO REASON WHY** [–] [ ]

Jan 83. (lp) *(K 99251) <923750-1>* **WHAT'S FUNK?** [–] German [ ]
– Rock & roll American style / Nowhere to run / Innocent / Still waitin' / Borderline / El Salvador / It's a man's world / I'm so true / Don't lie to me / Life in outer space. *<cd-iss. 2001 on 'Lissmark'; 6347>*

— disbanded again after appearing on 'Heavy Metal' soundtrack. BREWER joined BOB SEGER'S SILVER BULLET BAND. FARNER went solo again in 1988, releasing an album 'JUST ANOTHER INJUSTICE' for 'Frontline'.

– compilations, others, etc. –

on 'Capitol' unless mentioned otherwise

May 72. (d-lp) *(E-STSP 10) <11042>* **MARK, DON & MEL 1969-1971** [ ] [17]

		UK	US
Oct 72.	(d-lp) *Abkco; <4217>* **MARK, DON AND TERRY 1966-67**	–	
Nov 76.	(lp) *<11579>* **GRAND FUNK HITS**	–	
May 89.	(c-s) *<44394>* **WE'RE AN AMERICAN BAND. / THE LOCO-MOTION**	–	
Mar 91.	(cd) *(CDP 790608-2)* **CAPITOL COLLECTORS**		–
	– Time machine / Heartbreaker / Inside looking out / Medley / Closer to home / I'm your captain / Mean mistreater / Feelin' alright / Gimme shelter / Footstompin' music / Rock & roll soul / We're an American band / Walk like a man / The Loco-motion / Shinin' on / Some kind of wonderful / Bad time.		
Sep 91.	(cd/c) *Rhino; <R2/R4 70530>* **MORE OF THE BEST**	–	
May 92.	(cd/c) *Castle; (CCS CD/MC 332)* **THE COLLECTION**		–
	– The loco-motion / Gimme shelter / Inside looking out / Closer to home / I'm your captain / We're an American band / Into the Sun / Loneliness / Paranoid / Walk like a man / Shinin' on / Creepin' / Sally.		
Jun 99.	(3xcd-box) *<CAP 99523>* **THIRTY YEARS OF FUNK: 1969-1999** (w/ new recordings)	–	
	(UK-iss.Jul03; same as US)		
Dec 99.	(cd) *<50119>* **SUPER BEST**	–	
Jul 02.	(cd) *<(CAP 39501)>* **LIVE: THE 1971 TOUR (live)**	Jun02	
	(re-iss. of 'LIVE ALBUM' Feb01 on 'EMI Plus'; 576239-2)		
Nov 02.	(4xcd-box) *<(CAP 41422)>* **TRUNK OF FUNK**	Aug02	
Mar 03.	(cd) *EMI Plus; (76380-2)* **ROCK CHAMPIONS**		–
May 03.	(cd) *<(5 39857-2)>* **CLASSIC MASTERS**	Jul02	

GRANDMASTER FLASH

Born: 1 Jan'58, Barbados, West Indies as JOSEPH SADDLER, although he moved to the Bronx district of New York at an early age. Taking his cue from pioneering DJ's like KOOL HERC, a teenage SADDLER began spinning records at local block parties, eventually developing the complex technique of "cutting" between records on two separate turntables, creating a continuous flow of beats punctuated by repetitive rhythmic "breaks". While these tricks later proved to be one of the most revolutionary and money-spinning developments in the evolution of popular music, for the time being SADDLER aka DJ GRANDMASTER FLASH (so called for his lightning speed turntable techniques) was content to demonstrate his considerable skills at local hip hop events. Enlisting a cast of rappers to complement his spinning, FLASH created The FURIOUS FIVE, originally consisting of GRANDMASTER MELLE MEL (born MELVIN GLOVER), brother KID CREOLE (born NATHANIEL GLOVER and no, not THAT KID CREOLE!), COWBOY (born KEITH WIGGINS), DUKE BOOTEE (born EDWARD FLETCHER) and KURTIS BLOW. The latter was subsequently replaced by RAHIEM (born GUY TODD WILLIAMS), the crew creating a buzz around New York and finally making their vinyl debut in 1979 for 'Enjoy' records with the track 'SUPERRAPPIN'. Like its follow-up, 'WE RAP MORE MELLOW', the track was a massive underground hit, although the band failed to grab the attention of the wider music community. It was only after signing to Sylvia and Joe Robinson's 'Sugar Hill' records that FLASH and his FURIOUS FIVE began to make major waves. With the addition of SCORPIO (born ED MORRIS), the group released the 'FREEDOM' single which hit the American R&B Top 20, closely followed by 'BIRTHDAY PARTY', but it was 'THE ADVENTURES OF GRANDMASTER FLASH ON THE WHEELS OF STEEL' (1981) that really set the hip hop world alight. A revolutionary cut'n'paste of sampling, scratching, breaks and boisterous rapping, the record used Chic's 'GOOD TIMES' and Queen's 'ANOTHER ONE BITES THE DUST' as its base material. Another precedent was set almost a year later with the SYLVIA ROBINSON/DUKE BOOTEE-penned 'THE MESSAGE', as powerful a record as has ever emerged from hip hop. With its hard hitting account of inner city life, the record pre-empted Gangsta-rap with half the bluster and twice the effectiveness, topping the charts on both sides of the Atlantic in 1982. Financial and personal squabbling led to a split in the ranks the following year during the recording of 'WHITE LINES (DON'T DO IT)', FLASH heading off with RAHEIM and KID CREOLE, eventually securing a contract with 'Elektra'. The latter track, released under the moniker GRANDMASTER FLASH & MELLE MEL was another revelatory piece of old skool electro-hip hop, all reverberating bass and apocalyptic vocals warning of the dangers of drug addiction. It was a warning that FLASH would've done well to heed, now a freebase cocaine addict himself, and although he eventually won a court battle with MELLE MEL over the use of the group name, his major label records made little impact, FLASH fading into obscurity as the 80's wore on, while young bucks like ERIC B and PUBLIC ENEMY took over. MELLE MEL, meanwhile, who had remained with COWBOY and SCORPIO, continued to record for 'Sugarhill' although he too, was afforded about as much interest with his later work as his estranged colleague. FLASH, MELLE MEL and THE FURIOUS FIVE eventually re-united in 1987 for a New York charity concert organised by PAUL SIMON. Tragically, it was the last time the original line-up would be on the same stage together as COWBOY died on the 8th of September '89 as a result of crack addiction. More recently, FLASH played at the 1997 Essential Music Festival in Brighton, England, while MELLE MEL released a solo album the same year. • **Songwriters:** All written by FLASH and MELLE (VAUGHAN), except loads of sampling and covers, including WHO'S THAT LADY (Isley Brothers).

Album rating: THE MESSAGE (*7) / GREATEST MESSAGES compilation (*6) / THEY SAID IT COULDN'T BE DONE (*4) / THE SOURCE (*5) / BA-DOP-BOOM-BANG (*4) / ON THE STRENGTH (*3) / THE GREATEST HITS compilation (*7)

GRANDMASTER FLASH & THE FURIOUS FIVE

GRANDMASTER FLASH (b. JOSEPH SADDLER, 1 Jan '58, Barbados) – turntables / **MELLE MEL** (b. MELVIN GLOVER) – vocals / **COWBOY** (b. KEITH WIGGINS, 20 Sep'60) – vocals / **KID CREOLE** (b. NATHANIEL GLOVER) – vocals / added **MR. NESS** (b. EDDIE MORRIS) – rapper / and **RAHEIM** (b. GUY WILLIAMS) – vocals repl. KURTIS BLOW who went solo

		not iss.	Enjoy
1979.	(7") **SUPERRAPPIN'. / ('A'instrumental)**	–	
		not iss.	Brass
1979.	(7"; as The YOUNGER GENERATION) **WE RAP MORE MELLOW. / ('A' instrumental)**	–	
——	added **SCORPIO** – electronics		
		Sugar Hill	Sugar Hill
Apr 81.	(7") *(SH 555) <759>* **BIRTHDAY PARTY. / ('A'instrumental)**		
Jul 81.	(7") **FREEDOM. / ('A'instrumental)**	–	
Dec 81.	(12") *(SHL 557)* **THE ADVENTURES OF GRANDMASTER FLASH ON THE WHEELS OF STEEL. / THE BIRTHDAY PARTY**	Oct81	
Dec 81.	(7") **FLASH TO THE BEAT. / ('A'instrumental)**	–	
	(originally issued 1979 on 'Bozo Meko')		
Mar 82	(7"/12") *(SH/+L 111)* **IT'S NASTY (GENIUS OF LOVE). / BIRTHDAY PARTY**		–
May 82.	(7"/12") *(SH/+L 117) <584>* **THE MESSAGE. / THE MESSAGE (part 2)**	8 Sep82	62
Oct 82.	(lp/c) *(SHLP/ZCSH 1007) <268>* **THE MESSAGE**	77	53
	– She's fresh / It's nasty (genius of love) / Scorpio / It's a shame / Dreamin' / You are / The message / Adventures of Grandmaster Flash on the wheels of steel.		
Dec 82.	(7"/12") *(SH/+L 118) <790>* **SCORPIO. / IT'S A SHAME**		
Jan 83.	(7"/12"; by MELLE MEL & DUKE BOOTEE) *(SH/+L 119) <792>* **MESSAGE II (SURVIVAL). / ('A'instrumental)**	74	

May 83. (7"/12"; by The FURIOUS FIVE) *(SH/+L 125)* **NEW YORK, NEW YORK. / ('A'instrumental)** [ ] [–]

GRANDMASTER FLASH & MELLE MEL

Sugarhill Sugarhill

Nov 83. (7"/12") *(SH/+L 130)* *<465>* **WHITE LINES (DON'T DO IT). / ('A'version)** [7] [ ]
(Jul84; 12"pic-d+=) *(SHLX 130)* – White lines (New York remix) / ('A'original) / ('A'-US mix). *(re-iss. Oct84 as 'CONTINUOUS WHITE LINES'; SHLM 130) (re-iss. Jun87 on 'Blatant' 7"/12"; BLAT 7/12 1)*

— GRANDMASTER FLASH, MELLE MEL & THE FURIOUS FIVE split Nov83. FLASH and MEL split two ways, and went to court to use full group name. MEL adopted

GRANDMASTER MELLE MEL & THE FURIOUS FIVE

— taking with him **SCORPIO** and **COWBOY**. He recruited new members **LEWIS GLOVER** (MEL's brother) / **TOMMY GUN CHEV / LES DE LA CRUZ**

Sugar Hill Sugar Hill

1984. (7"/12") *(SH/+L 133)* **JESSE. / ('A' instrumental)** [ ] [–]

— (below from the film 'Beat Street' on 'Atlantic')

Jun 84. (7") *(A 9659)* *<89659>* **BEAT STREET BREAKDOWN. / (part II)** [42] [86]
(12"+=) *(TA 9659)* – Internationally known.

Jun 84. (lp/c) *(SHLP/ZCSH 5552)* **GREATEST MESSAGES** (compilation) [41] [–]
– The message / Survival (The message II) / Freedom / Flash to the beat / Jesse / White lines (don't do it) / New York New York / Internationally known / Birthday party / Adventures on the wheels of steel / Scorpio / It's nasty (genius of love).

Sep 84. (7"/12") *(SH/+L 136)* *<92011>* **WE DON'T WORK FOR FREE. / ('A'instrumental)** [45] [ ]

Oct 84. (lp/c) *(SHLP/ZCSH 5553)* **WORK PARTY** [45] [ ]
– Rustler's convention / Yesterday / At the party / The truth / White lines (new UK master mix) / We don't work for free / World war III / Can't keep running away / The new adventures of Grandmaster.

Nov 84. (7") *(SH 139)* **STEP OFF (part 1). / STEP OFF (part 2)** [8] [ ]
(12"+=) *(SHL 139)* – The message.
(12"+=) *(SHLX 139)* – Continuous white lines.

Mar 85. (7") *(SH 141)* **PUMP ME UP. / ('A' instrumental)** [45] [–]
(12"+=/12"pic-d+=) *(SHL/+X 141)* – ('A'version).

May 85. (lp/c) *(SHLP/ZCSH 5555)* **STEPPING OFF** (compilation) [ ] [–]
– Pump me up / Step off / The message / We don't work for free / White lines (don't do it) / Jesse / Survival (the message II) / The megaMelle mix.

Jul 85. (7") *(SH 143)* **WORLD WAR III. / THE TRUTH** [ ] [–]
(12"+=) *(SHL 143)* – Step off / The message (version).

Nov 85. (7") *(SH 146)* *<92015>* **VICE (from 'Miami Vice' TV). / KING OF THE STREET** [ ] [ ]

GRANDMASTER FLASH

— went solo, taking **RAHEIM** and **KID CREOLE** plus new people **LEVON, BROADWAY** and **LARRY LOVE**

Elektra Elektra

Feb 85. (7") *(E 9677)* *<69677>* **SIGN OF THE TIMES. / LARRY'S DANCE THEME** [72] [ ]
(12"+=) *(E 9677T)* – ('A'instrumental).

Feb 85. (lp/c) *(960389-1/-4)* *<60389>* **THEY SAID IT COULDN'T BE DONE** [95] [ ]
– Girls love the way he spins / The joint is jumpin' / Rock the house / Jailbait / Sign of the times / Larry's dance theme / Who's that lady / Alternative groove / Paradise.

May 85. (7") *<69643>* **GIRLS LOVE THE WAY HE SPINS. / LARRY'S DANCE THEME** [–] [ ]

Jul 85. (7") *<69617>* **WHO'S THAT LADY. / ALTERNATIVE GROOVE** [–] [ ]

Apr 86. (lp/c) *(960476-1/-4)* *<60476>* **THE SOURCE** [ ] [ ]
– Street scene / Style (Peter Gunn theme) / Ms. Thang / P.L.U. (Peace, Love and Unity) / Throwin' down / Behind closed doors / Larry's dance theme (part 2) / Lies / Fastest man alive / Freelance.

May 86. (7") *(EKR 39)* *<69552>* **STYLE (PETER GUNN THEME). / ('A'instrumental)** [ ] [ ]
(12"+=) *(EKR 39T)* – ('A'remix).

Jul 86. (7") *<69530>* **LIES. / BEHIND CLOSED DOORS** [–] [ ]

Mar 87. (7"/12") *(EKR 54/+T)* *<69490>* **U KNOW WHAT TIME IT IS? / BUS DIS (WOO)** [ ] [ ]

Mar 87. (lp/c/cd) *(960723-1/-4/-2)* *<60723>* **BA-DOP-BOOM-BANG** [ ] [ ]
– Ain't we funkin' now / U know what time it is? / Underarms / Kid named Flash / Get yours / Then jeans / We will rock you / All wrapped up / Tear the roof off / Big black caddy / House that rocked / Bus dis / I am somebody / Ain't we funkin' now (reprise).

May 87. (7") *<69459>* **ALL WRAPPED UP. / KID NAMED FLASH** [–] [ ]

GRANDMASTER FLASH & THE FURIOUS FIVE

(originals re-formed for 'Elektra')

Feb 88. (7") *(EKR 70)* *<69416>* **GOLD. / BACK IN THE OLD DAYS OF HIP HOP** [ ] [ ]
(12"+=) *(EKR 70T)* – ('A'acappella) / ('A'acappella dub).

Mar 88. (lp/c/cd) *(960769-1/-4/-2)* *<60769>* **ON THE STRENGTH** [ ] [ ]
– Gold / Cold in effect / Yo baby / On the strength / The king / Fly girl / Magic carpet ride / Leave here / This is where you got it from / The boy is dope. *(cd+=)* – Back in the old days of hip-hop. *(cd re-iss. Jan97; 7559 60769-2)*

May 88. (7") *<69400>* **COLD IN EFFECT. / FLY GIRL** [–] [ ]

Jul 88. (7") *<69380>* **ON THE STRENGTH. / MAGIC CARPET RIDE** [–] [ ]

GRANDMASTER MELLE MEL

Edel unknown

Jul 97. (12") *(0098470 RAP)* **MR. BIG STUFF. / CHINA WHITE** [ ] [–]

– compilations, etc. –

1988. (3"cd-ep) *Special Edition; (CD3-1)* **WHITE LINES (DON'T DO IT). / JESSE / THE MESSAGE II** [ ] [–]

1988. (3"cd-ep) *Special Edition; (CD3-2)* **THE ADVENTURES OF GRANDMASTER FLASH ON THE WHEELS OF STEEL. / THE MESSAGE / IT'S NASTY (GENIUS OF LOVE)** [ ] [–]

Mar 89. (d-c) *Sugar Hill; (IED 33)* **THE BEST OF GRANDMASTER FLASH & THE FURIOUS FIVE** [ ] [–]

Nov 89. (12") *Old Gold; (OG 4152)* **THE MESSAGE. / THE ADVENTURES ON THE WHEELS OF STEEL** [ ] [–]

Jul 90. (7") *Castle;* **WHITE LINES (DON'T DON'T DO IT) (freestyle Ben Legrand mix). / (Part 2)** [ ] [–]

Jul 91. (cd/c) *Kwest; (KWEST 5/4 193)* **WHITE LINES & OTHER MESSAGES – THE SILVER COLLECTION** [ ] [–]

May 92. (cd) *Sequel; (NEMCD 622)* **THE GREATEST HITS** [ ] [–]
– White lines (don't do it) / Step off / Pump me up / Jesse / Beat Street / Vice / Freedom / Birthday party / Flash to the beat / It's nasty (genius of love) / The message / Scorpio / Survival (Message II) / New York, New York.

Dec 93. (12"/cd-s) *W.G.A.F.; (WGAF/+CD 103)* **WHITE LINES (DON'T DO IT) (D&S 7" Remix) / HEY HEY (D&S 7" Remix)** [59] [–]

Mar 94. (12"/cd-s) *W.G.A.F.; (WGAF/+CD 104)* **THE MESSAGE. / ('A'remixes)** [ ] [–]

Aug 95. (cd-s) *Old Gold; (OG 6314)* **WHITE LINES (DON'T DO IT) / PUMP ME UP** [ ] [–]

Sep 95. (cd-s) *Old Gold; (12623 6300-2)* **THE MESSAGE / SURVIVAL (MESSAGE II)** [ ] [–]

Nov 96. (cd/lp) *Deep Beats; (DEEP M/X 004)* **MORE HITS** [ ] [–]

Jul 97. (12"/cd-s) *Deep Cuts; (DEEP 12/CD 001)* **THE MESSAGE (mixes)** [ ] [–]

Jul 97. (d-cd; shared with SUGARHILL GANG) *Snapper; (SMDCD 164)* **GRANDMASTER FLASH VS THE SUGARHILL GANG** [ ] [–]

Mar 99. (12") *Sugarhill-Sequel; (NEET 1003)* **THE MESSAGE. / THE ADVENTURES OF GRANDMASTER FLASH ON THE WHEELS OF STEEL** [ ] [–]

Mar 99. (12") *Sugarhill-Sequel; (NEET 1007)* **WHITE LINES (DON'T DO IT). / SCORPIO** [ ] [–]

Mar 99. (3xcd-box) *Sequel; (NXTCD 305)* **BACK TO THE OLD SCHOOL** ☐ -
Oct 99. (12") *Hot Classics; (HCL 2261)* **THE MESSAGE. / IT'S NASTY** ☐ -
Oct 99. (12") *Hot Classics; (HCL 2262)* **WHITE LINES. / THE MESSAGE II** ☐ -
May 02. (cd; & MELLE MEL) *Sequel; (NEMCD 622)* **GREATEST HITS** ☐ -
Sep 02. (cd) *Camden; (74321 96051-2)* **GRANDMASTER FLASH & THE SUGARHILL GANG** ☐ ☐

☐ GRANDPABOY (see under ⇒ REPLACEMENTS)

☐ GRASSHOPPER & THE GOLDEN CRICKETS (see under ⇒ MERCURY REV)

GRATEFUL DEAD

Formed: San Francisco, California, USA ... 1965 by JERRY GARCIA, who had spent nine months of 1959 in the army before finding lyricist extrordinaire ROBERT HUNTER and forming folk outfit The THUNDER MOUNTAIN TUB THUMPERS. Along the way, this loose collective of musicians included soon-to-be GRATEFUL DEAD members BOB WEIR and RON McKERNAN (aka PIGPEN), JERRY going on to make demos in 1963 as duo JERRY & SARAH GARCIA. It wasn't until 1965 that the earliest incarnation of The GRATEFUL DEAD, The WARLOCKS, set out on their "golden road to unlimited gigging", when they took centre stage as house band for KEN KESEY's (author of 'One Flew Over The Cuckoo's Nest') legendary acid tests. Created by KESEY and his band of merry pranksters, the main objective of these psychedelic shindigs was to bombard the tripping hordes with as much sensory overload as posible; flashing lights, pre-recorded chants, hidden speakers hissing subversive messages and of course, the ear splitting racket of The WARLOCKS. With crowd and band liberally dosed with LSD courtesy of acidmeister AUGUSTUS STANLEY III, the events were clearly a formative part of their career. By this time, the band had gone electric, inspired by the raucous rock'n'roll of The BEATLES, bolstering the sound with drummer BILL KREUTZMANN and bassist PHIL LESH. Changing their name to the equally hoary sounding GRATEFUL DEAD (picked at random from a dictionary), the band toured California alongside JEFFERSON AIRPLANE. In 1966, they issued a one-off 45, 'DON'T EASE ME IN' for 'Fantasy' off-shoot label 'Scorpio', which led to 'Warners' signing them up in 1967. Recorded in three amphetamine-fuelled days, 'THE GRATEFUL DEAD' was released to the expectant hippy faithful in December of the same year, an admirable but untimately doomed attempt to recreate their fabled live sound in the studio. After an impromptu guest spot at one of their early shows, drummer MICKEY HART augmented the band's rhythm section, creating a more subtly complex rather than powerful sound. The group also recruited keyboardist TOM CONSTANTEN, whose avant-garde influences included JOHN CAGE and STOCKHAUSEN. Adding to the DEAD's psychedelic stew, these two further inspired the band's live improvisation, partly captured on 'ANTHEM OF THE SUN' in 1968. An ambitious collage of live and studio pieces, the album was another flawed attempt to seize the essence of the elusive beast that was the band's live show. It did however, contain bizarrely experimental sections with wonderful cod-hippy titles like, 'CRYPTICAL ENVELOPMENT' and 'THE FASTER WE GO, THE ROUNDER WE GET', these worth the admission price alone. The experimentation continued with 'AOXOMOXOA' in 1969, GARCIA's old mate ROBERT HUNTER marking his first collaboration with the band and helping to contain the explorations inside defined song structures. Highlights included 'MOUNTAINS OF THE MOON', with its celestial harpsicord and 'ST STEPHEN', a song that would go on to become a staple of the band's live set. With the release of 'LIVE DEAD' in 1970, The GRATEFUL DEAD finally did itself justice on vinyl, silencing the critics of their previous output who couldn't understand why the band were held in such high esteem by their fiercely loyal San Franciscan fanbase. On the track 'DARK STAR', the band crystallised their free-flowing improvisation in breathtaking style, while the celebratory 'TURN ON YOUR LOVE LIGHT', was also a standard of the band's now legendary live shows. Attracting multitudes of tye-dyed freaks, affectionately nicknamed "Deadheads", the band's gigs became communal gatherings, where both the crowd and band could lose themselves in the spaced-out jams which would often stretch songs over an hour or more. Forget 15 minutes of fame (as ANDY WARHOL once gave us all), the DEAD needed 15 minutes just for the intro! Ironically the band's next two studio albums marked a radical new direction with pared-down sets of harmony laden country-folk. With CONSTANTEN out of the picture by early 1970 and mounting debts, the group went for a simpler sound, clearly influenced by CROSBY, STILLS and NASH and GARCIA's part-time dabblings with The NEW RIDERS OF THE PURPLE SAGE. 'WORKINGMAN'S DEAD' was symptomatic of the times as bands began to move away from the psychedelic claustrophobia of the late 60's (note 'NEW SPEEDWAY BOOGIE' about the end of the hippy dream; the Altamont Festival at which a ROLLING STONES fan was killed by a drug-crazed Hell's Angel). 'AMERICAN BEAUTY' carried on where the previous album left off, 'SUGAR MAGNOLIA' and 'RIPPLE' being the highlights of this highly regarded piece of roots rock. By 1971, HART had departed and the band were reduced to five core members. Two live albums followed, the double 'GRATEFUL DEAD' and 'EUROPE 72', the latter stretching to three slabs of vinyl. 1972 also saw the release of WEIR's solo album, 'ACE', actually a GRATEFUL DEAD album in all but name. It included the glorious tongue-in-cheek romp, 'MEXICALI BLUES' and also saw WEIR begin writing with JOHN PERRY BARLOW, a partnership that would see HUNTER's input diminish over the following years. Years of alcohol abuse led to PIGPEN dying on 8th May '73 and he was replaced by KEITH GODCHAUX, who had toured with them the previous year. His wife DONNA also joined, taking up vocal duties. Around this time the band set up their own label, imaginatively titled 'Grateful Dead Records', releasing 'WAKE OF THE FLOOD' in July '73. The album was their most successful to date, containing the melancholy 'STELLA BLUE', although ironically, profits were lost to bootleggers. 'BLUES FOR ALLAH', from 1975, signalled a jazzier, fuller sound, though by this juncture the band were in financial deep water and signed with 'United Artists'. The source of much of their money problems was a concert movie which ate up most of their resources. 'STEAL YOUR FACE' was next in line and was intended for the movie, although it remained in the can due to the album's relative critical failure. Signing to 'Arista' and drafting in KEITH OLSEN on production duties they released 'TERRAPIN STATION' in 1977, an album which showcased a lusher, fuller sound. For '78's 'SHAKEDOWN STREET', the band collaborated with LOWELL GEORGE, and what could have been an interesting pairing, came out sounding limp and uninspiring; a pale reflection of what the DEAD were capable of. Despite the inconsistent quality of their studio work, the DEAD were always a safe live bet and they played the gig to surely top all gigs with their series of dates at the Pyramids in Egypt. Still carrying a hippy torch (even through the punk days), they filled large venues wherever they played and became a multi-million dollar industry in their own right. However, as they concentrated on live work, their studio outings suffered, their 1980 album 'GO TO HEAVEN' being particularly disappointing although it spawned their first success in the US singles chart with 'ALABAMA GETAWAY'. Another two live sets followed in 1981, 'DEAD SET' and 'RECKONING'. The latter was an acoustic album featuring classics like 'RIPPLE' and 'CASSIDY'. Soon after their release, GARCIA became a full blown heroin addict, narrowly escaping death when he fell into a diabetic coma in in 1986. Once he rehabilitated, the DEAD came back to life with 'IN THE DARK', a spirited set that reached the Top 10 in the US chart, even resulting in top selling 45, 'TOUCH OF GREY'. Their tribute to growing old with pride, it was a first when the band agreed to make a video for MTV. The awful 'DYLAN & THE DEAD' (yes with Mr. Zimmerman) was muted and dull, as was the studio 1989 offering, 'BUILT TO LAST'. Tragedy hit the band yet again, when keyboardist BRENT MYDLAND (who himself had replaced KEITH GODCHAUX in '79) was killed by a hard drugs cocktail. BRUCE HORNSBY (yes that solo geezer) was drafted in temporarily for touring commitments, while VINCE WELNICK joined full-time. The band released yet another live album the same year, the hardly dangerous 'WITHOUT A NET' and also started issuing the DICK'S PICKS series of archive recordings from great days of yore. On 9th August, 1995, the ailing JERRY GARCIA died of heart failure in a rehab unit after his arteries clogged up. It seemed inevitable that the long strange trip of The GRATEFUL DEAD had come to an end, GARCIA's guiding light relocating to find his "Dark Star" once again. The DEAD left behind a rich musical legacy, including numerous solo outings and off-shoot projects, but will always be remembered, by the Deadheads at least, for their transcendental live performances. WEIR, HART and LESH formed a new 'Dead' outfit, The OTHER ONES (along with BRUCE HORNSBY, DAVE ELLIS, MARK KARAN, JOHN MOLO and STEVE KIMOCK, etc), delivering a surprise oddity set, 'ONLY THE STRANGE REMAIN' (1999). • **Songwriters:** Most by HUNTER-GARCIA or WEIR, LESH and some by others, including JOHN BARLOW. Covered; GOOD MORNING LITTLE SCHOOLGIRL (Don & Bob) / NEW MINGLEWOOD BLUES + SAMSON AND DELILAH (trad.) / JOHNNY B. GOODE (Chuck Berry) / NOT FADE AWAY (Buddy Holly) / ME AND BOBBY McGEE (Kris Kristofferson) / BIG BOSS MAN (Bo Diddley) / DANCING IN THE STREET (hit; Martha & The Vandellas) / STAGGER LEE (Lloyd Price) / LITTLE RED ROOSTER (Willie Dixon) / DEAR MR. FANTASY (Traffic) / WALKIN' BLUES (Robert Johnson) / NEXT TIME YOU SEE ME (Junior Parker) / etc. GARCIA covered; IT TAKES A LOT TO LAUGH + POSITIVELY 4TH STREET + KNOCKIN' ON HEAVEN'S DOOR (Bob Dylan) / LET'S SPEND THE NIGHT TOGETHER + WILD HORSES (Rolling Stones) / HE AIN'T GIVE YOU NONE (Van Morrison) / THAT'S ALL RIGHT MAMA (Arthur Crudup) / MY FUNNY VALENTINE / WHEN THE HUNTER GETS CAPTURED BY THE GAME (Smokey Robinson) / LET IT ROCK (Chuck Berry) / RUSSIAN LULLABY (Irving Berlin) / MIDNIGHT TOWN (Kahn-Hunter) / I SAW HER STANDING THERE (Beatles) / etc. • **Trivia:** An edited 'DARK STAR', was used as theme in the US 70's series of 'Twilight Zone'.

Album rating: THE GRATEFUL DEAD (*5) / ANTHEM OF THE SUN (*7) / AOXOMOXOA (*8) / LIVE/DEAD (*7) / WORKINGMAN'S DEAD (*8) / AMERICAN BEAUTY (*10) / GRATEFUL DEAD live double (*6) / EUROPE '72 (*6) / HISTORY OF THE GRATEFUL DEAD, VOL.1 (BEAR'S CHOICE) (*5) / WAKE OF THE FLOOD (*5) / SKELETON'S FROM THE CLOSET: THE BEST OF . . . compilation (*5) / GRATEFUL DEAD FROM THE MARS HOTEL (*5) / BLUES FOR ALLAH (*5) / STEAL YOUR FACE (*4) / TERRAPIN STATION (*6) / WHAT A LONG STRANGE TRIP IT'S BEEN compilation (*8) / SHAKEDOWN STREET (*4) / GO TO HEAVEN (*1) / RECKONING (*5) / DEAD SET (*5) / IN THE DARK (*7) / BUILT TO LAST (*4) / WITHOUT A NET (*4) / ONE FROM THE VAULT early concert (*5) / INFRARED ROSES concert (*4) / TWO FROM THE VAULT early concert (*5) / DICK'S PICK, VOL.1 early concert (*5) / DICK'S PICK, VOL.2 early concert (*5) / HUNDRED YEAR HALL early concert (*5) / DICK'S PICK, VOL.3 early concert (*6) / DICK'S PICK, VOL.4 early concert (*8) / THE VERY BEST OF THE GRATEFUL DEAD compilation (*8) / Jerry Garcia: HOOTEROLL (*5) / GARCIA (*7) / LIVE AT THE KEYSTONE (*4) / GARCIA on 'Round' (*6) / OLD & IN THE WAY (*4) / REFLECTIONS (*5) / CATS UNDER THE STARS (*6) / RUN FOR THE ROSES (*6) / ALMOST ACOUSTIC (*6) / JERRY GARCIA BAND (*6) / JERRY GARCIA & DAVID GRISMAN (*6) / NOT FOR KIDS ONLY with David Grisman (*5) / HOW SWEET IT IS early gig (*5) / Other Ones: ONLY THE STRANGE REMAIN (*5)

JERRY GARCIA (b. JEROME JOHN GARCIA, 1 Aug'42) – vocals, lead guitar / **BOB WEIR** (b. ROBERT HALL, 6 Oct'47) – rhythm guitar / **RON 'PIGPEN' McKERNAN** (b. 8 Sep'45, San Bruno, Calif.) – keyboards, vocals, mouth harp / **PHIL LESH** (b. PHILIP CHAPMAN, 15 Mar'40, Berkeley, Calif.) – bass / **BILL KREUTZMANN** (b. 7 Apr'46, Palo Alto, Calif.) – drums (DAN MORGAN left before recording)

not iss. Scorpio

Jun 66. (7") *<003-201>* **DON'T EASE ME IN. / STEALIN'** [–] [ ]

Warners Warners

Feb 67. (7") *<7016>* **THE GOLDEN ROAD (TO UNLIMITED DEVOTION). / CREAM PUFF WAR** [–] [ ]

Dec 67. (lp; mono/stereo) *(<W/+S 1689>)* **THE GRATEFUL DEAD** [ ] Feb67 [73]
– The golden road (to unlimited devotion) / Cold rain and snow / Good morning little schoolgirl / Beat it on down / Sitting on top of the world / Cream puff war / Morning dew / New, new Minglewood blues / Viola Lee blues. *(re-iss. Mar87 on 'Edsel'; ED 221) <US cd-iss. 1987; 2-1689> (cd-iss. Jul88 on 'Atlantic'; K 259302) <(cd-iss. Feb94; 7599 27167-2)> <(cd re-mast.Mar03 on 'Rhino'+=; 8122 74398-2)>* – Alice D. millionaire / Overseas stomp (the Lindy) / Tastebud / Death don't have no mercy / Viola Lee blues (edit) / Viola Lee blues (live).

—— added **TOM CONSTANTEN** – keyboards / **MICKEY HART** (b.1950, Long Island, N.Y.) – percussion and returning lyricist **ROBERT HUNTER**

Oct 68. (7") *(WB <7186>)* **BORN CROSS-EYED. / DARK STAR** [ ] [ ]

Nov 68. (lp) *(<WS 1749>)* **ANTHEM OF THE SUN** [ ] Aug 68 [87]
– That's it for other one:- Cryptical envelopment – Quadlibet for tender feet – The faster we go, the rounder we get – We leave the castle / New potato caboose / Born cross-eyed / Alligator / Caution (do not stop on the tracks). *(re-iss. Jul71; K 46021) <US cd-iss. 1987; 2-1749> (re-iss. Jul88 on 'WEA' lp/cd; K2 4602-1/2) <(re-iss. cd Feb94; 7599 27173-2)> <(cd re-mast.Mar03 on 'Rhino'+=; 8122 74393-2)>* – Alligator (live) / Caution (do not stop on the tracks) (live) / Feedback (live) / (untitled).

Oct 69. (lp) *(<WS 1790>)* **AOXOMOXOA** [ ] Jun 69 [73]
– St. Stephen / Dupree's diamond blues / Rosemary / Doin' the rag / Mountains of the Moon / China cat sunflower / What's become of the baby / Cosmic Charlie. *(re-iss. Jul71; K 46027) ;re-iss. Jan77) <US cd-iss. 1987; 2-1790> (re-iss. Jun89 on 'WEA' c/cd; K4 46027/ K927128-2) <(cd re-iss. Feb94; 7599 27178-2)> <(cd re-mast.Mar03 on 'Rhino'+=; 8122 74394-2)>* – Clementine jam / Nobody's spoonful jam / The eleven jam / Cosmic Charlie (live).

Oct 69. (7") *<7324>* **DUPREE'S DIAMOND BLUES. / COSMIC CHARLIE** [–] [ ]

Feb 70. (d-lp) *<2(WS 1830)>* **LIVE/DEAD (live in the studio)** [ ] Dec 69 [64]
– Dark star / St. Stephen / The eleven / Turn on your love light / Death don't have no mercy / Feedback / And we bid you goodnight. *(re-iss. Jul71; K 66002) <US cd-iss. 1987; 2-1830> (cd-iss. Jun89 on 'WEA'; K927 181-2) <(cd re-mast.Mar03 on 'Rhino'; 8122 74395-2)>*

—— **DAVID NELSON** – acoustic guitar; repl. CONSTANTEN / added guest **JOHN DAWSON** – guitar, vocals (on some)
above pairing also formed off-shoot band The NEW RIDERS OF THE PURPLE SAGE, who initially toured as support to DEAD, with GARCIA in their ranks.

Sep 70. (lp) *(<WS 1869>)* **WORKINGMAN'S DEAD** [ ] Jun 70 [27]
– Uncle John's band / High time / Dire wolf / New speedway boogie / Cumberland blues / Black Peter / Easy wind / Casey Jones. *(re-iss. Jul71; K 46049) <US cd-iss. 1987; 2-1889> (re-iss. 1988 lp/c) (cd-iss. Jun89 on 'WEA'; K2 46049) <(cd re-mast.Mar03 on 'Rhino'+=; 8122 74396-2)>* – New speedway boogie (alt.) / Dire wolf (live) / Black Peter (live) / Easy wind

(live) / Cumberland blues (live) / Mason's children (live) / Uncle John's band (live).

Aug 70. (7") *(WB <7410>)* **UNCLE JOHN'S BAND. / NEW SPEEDWAY BOOGIE** [ ] [69]

—— added guest **DAVID TORBERT** – bass (1)

Dec 70. (lp) *(<WS 1893>)* **AMERICAN BEAUTY** [ ] [30]
– Box of rain / Friend of the Devil / Sugar magnolia / Operator / Candyman / Ripple / Brokedown palace / Till the morning comes / Attics of my life / Truckin'. *(re-iss. Jul71; K 46074) ;re-iss. Jan77) <US cd-iss. 1987; 2-1893> (re-iss. Jun89 on 'WEA' c/cd; K2/K4 46074) <(cd re-mast.Mar03 on 'Rhino'+=; 8122 74397-2)>* – Truckin' (single version) / Friend of the DEvil (live) / Candyman (live) / Till the morning comes (live) / Attics of my life (live) / Truckin' (live).

Jan 71. (7") *<7464>* **TRUCKIN. / RIPPLE** [–] [64]

—— Now **GARCIA, WEIR, LESH, KREUTZMANN** and **'PIGPEN'** with new members **MERL SAUNDERS** – keyboards (repl. PIGPEN for a while when he was ill) all guests had departed, incl. HART and NELSON.

Oct 71. (d-lp) *(K 66009) <2WS 1935>* **GRATEFUL DEAD** (SKULL & ROSES) (live) [ ] [25]
– Bertha / Mama tried / Big railroad blues / Playing in the band / The other one / Me & my uncle / Big boss man / Me & Bobby McGhee / Johnny B. Goode / Wharf rat / Not fade away / Goin' down road feeling bad. *<US cd-iss. 1987; 2-1935> (cd-iss. 1988; 927 192-2) <(cd re-iss. Feb03; 7599 27192-2)> <(cd re-mast.Mar03 on 'Rhino'+=; 8122 74392-2)>* – Oh, boy! / I'm a hog for you.

Jan 72. (7") **JOHNNY B. GOODE. / SO FINE (by 'Elvin Bishop')** [–] [ ]

—— added on tour **KEITH GODCHAUX** (b.14 Jul'48) – keyboards (ex-DAVE MASON band) and **DONNA GODCHAUX** (b.22 Aug'47) – vocals (They both repl. SAUNDERS)

Dec 72. (t-lp) *(K 66019) <3WS 2668>* **EUROPE '72 (live)** [ ] Nov 72 [24]
– Cumberland blues / He's gone / One more Saturday night / Jack Straw / You win again / China cat sunflower / I know you rider / Brown-eyed woman / Hurts me too / Ramble on Rose / Sugar magnolia / Mr. Charlie / Tennessee Jed / The stranger (two souls in communion) *[re-mast.only]* / Truckin' / Epilogue / Prelude / Morning dew. *<(cd-iss. Nov94; 7599 27265-2)> <(cd re-mast.Mar03 on 'Rhino'+=; 8122 74399-2)>* – Looks like rain / Good lovin' / Caution (do not stop on the tracks) / Who do you love? / Caution (do not stop on the tracks) (alt.) / Good lovin' (alt.).

Dec 72. (7") *<7667>* **SUGAR MAGNOLIA (live). / MR. CHARLIE (live)** [–] [91]

—— Now just basic 4 of **GARCIA, WEIR, LESH, KREUTZMANN** and both **GODCHAUX'S.** ('PIGPEN' sadly died 8 May'73 after a long and threatening bout of illness) note that ROBERT HUNTER was still writing their lyrics, next 2 albums also included ten or more session people.

Warners / Grateful Dead

Jul 73. (lp/c) *(K/K4 49301) <GD 01>* **WAKE OF THE FLOOD** [ ] Oct 73 [18]
– Mississippi half-step uptown toodeloo / Let me sing your blues away / Row Jimmy / Stella blue / Here comes sunshine / Eyes of the world / Weather Report suite (part 1; Prelude – part 2; Let it grow). *(re-iss. Jan76 on 'United Artists'; UAS 29903) (<re-iss. Apr89 on 'Grateful Dead' lp/c/cd; GDV/GDTCGDCD 4002>) (pic-cd Feb90; GDPD 4002) <(cd re-iss. Oct03 on 'Falcon'; UN 3862)>*

Nov 73. (7") *(K 19301) <01>* **LET ME SING YOUR BLUES AWAY. / HERE COMES SUNSHINE** [ ] [ ]

Jan 74. (7") *<02>* **EYES OF THE WORLD. / WEATHER REPORT SUITE (part 1; PRELUDE)** [–] [ ]

Jul 74. (lp/c) *(K/K4 59302) <GD 102>* **FROM THE MARS HOTEL** [47] [16]
– Scarlet begonias / Ship of fools / Pride of Cucamonga / Loose Lucy / U.S. blues / Unbroken chain / China doll / Money money. *(re-iss. Jan76 on 'United Artists'; UAS 29904) <US cd-iss. Dec85 on 'Mobile Fidelity'; MFCD 830> (re-iss. Mar89 on 'Grateful Dead' lp/c/cd; GDV/GDTCGDCD 4007) (pic-cd Feb90; GDPD 4007)*

Aug 74. (7") *(UP 36030) <03>* **U.S. BLUES. / LOOSE LUCY** [ ] [ ]

—— added the returning **MICKEY HART** – percussion

U.A. / Grateful Dead

Oct 75. (lp) *(UAS 29895) <LA 494>* **BLUES FOR ALLAH** [45] Sep75 [12]
– Help on the way / Slipknot / Franklin's tower / King Solomon's marbles / Stronger than dirt or milkin' the turkey / The music never stopped / Crazy fingers / Sage & spirit / Blues for Allah / Sand castles & glass camels / Unusual occurances in the desert. *(<re-iss. Mar89 on 'Grateful Dead' lp/c/cd; GDV/GDTCGDCD 4001>) (pic-cd Feb90; GDPD 4001)*

Oct 75. (7") *<718>* **THE MUSIC NEVER STOPPED. / HELP IS ON THE WAY** [–] [81]

Jun 76. (d-lp) *(UAD 60131-2) <LA 620>* **STEAL YOUR FACE (live)** [42] [56]
– The promised land / Cold rain and snow / Around and around / Stella blue / Mississippi half-step uptown toodeloo / Ship of fools / Beat it down the line / Big river / Black-throated wind / U.S. blues / El Paso / Sugaree / It must have been the roses / Casey Jones. *(re-iss. Mar89 on 'Grateful Dead' lp/c/cd; GDV2/GDTCGDCD2 4006) (pic-cd Feb90; GDPD2 4006)*

1976. (7") *<762>* **FRANKLIN'S TOWER. / HELP IS ON THE WAY** [–] [ ]

Arista / Arista

Aug 77. (lp/c) *(SPART/TC-ARTY 1016) <AL 7001>* **TERRAPIN STATION** [ ] [28]
– Estimated prophet / Samson and Delilah / Passenger / Dancing in the street / Sunrise / Terrapin station. *(re-iss. 1983; SPARTY 1016) (re-iss. Jan87 lp/c; 201/401 190) <US cd-iss. 1986; ARCD 8065> (cd-iss. Nov90; 260175)*

Oct 77. (12")<7"> *(DEAD 1) <0276>* **DANCING IN THE STREETS. / TERRAPIN STATION** [ ] [ ]

Feb 78. (7") *<0291>* **PASSENGER. / TERRAPIN STATION** [–] [ ]

Dec 78. (lp/c) *(ARTY/TC-ART 159) <AB 4198>* **SHAKEDOWN STREET** [ ] [41]
– Good lovin' / France / Shakedown street / Serangetti / Fire on the mountain / I need a miracle / From the heart of me / Stagger Lee / New, new Minglewood blues / If I had the world to give. *<US cd-iss. 1986; ARCD 4198> (cd-iss. Jun91; 251 133)*

Dec 78. (7") *(ARIST 236) <0383>* **GOOD LOVIN'. / STAGGER LEE** [ ] [ ]

Mar 79. (7") *<0410>* **SHAKEDOWN STREET. / FRANCE** [–] [ ]

—— **BRENT MYDLAND** (b.1953, Munich, Germany) – keyboards repl. both GODCHAUX'S (KEITH was killed in car crash 23 Jul'80)

May 80. (lp/c) *(SPART/TCART 1115) <AL 9508>* **GO TO HEAVEN** [ ] [23]
– Far from home / Althea / Feel like a stranger / Alabama getaway / Don't ease me in / Easy to love you / Lost sailor / Saint of circumstance. *<US cd-iss. 1986; ARCD 9508>*

Jun 80. (7") *<0519>* **ALABAMA GETAWAY. / FAR FROM ME** [–] [68]

Jan 81. (7") *<0546>* **DON'T EASE ME IN. / FAR FROM ME** [–] [ ]

Apr 81. (d-lp) *(DARTY 9) <A2L 8604>* **RECKONING (live)** (all line-ups) [ ] [43]
– Dire wolf / The race is on / Oh babe it ain't no lie / It must have been the roses / Dark hollow / China doll / Been all around the world / Monkey and the engineer / Jack-a-roe / Deep Elam blues / Cassidy / To lay me down / Rosalie McFall / On the road again / Bird song / Ripple.

1981. (7") *<116>* **ALABAMA GETAWAY. / SHAKEDOWN STREET** [–] [ ]

Sep 81. (d-lp) *(DARTY 11) <A2L 8606>* **DEAD SET (live)** [ ] [29]
– Samson and Delilah / Friend of the Devil / New, new Minglewood blues / Deal / Candyman / Little red rooster / Loser / Passenger / Feel like a stranger / Franklin's tower / Fire on the mountain / Rhythm devils / Greatest story ever told / Brokedown palace. *<US cd-iss. 1986; ARCD 8112>*

Sep 87. (7"/12") <cd-s/7",7"grey> *(RIS/+T 35) <ASCD+/9606>* **TOUCH OF GREY. / MY BROTHER ESAU** [ ] Jul87 [9]

Oct 87. (lp/c/cd) *(208/408/258 564) <AL/AC/ARCD 8452>* **IN THE DARK** [57] Jul87 [6]
– Touch of grey / Hell in a bucket / When push comes to shove / West L.A. fadeaway / Tons of steel / Throwing stones / Black muddy river. *(re-iss. Nov90 cd/lp; 261/211 145)*

Nov 87. (cd-s/7") *<ASCD+/9643>* **THROWING STONES. / WHEN PUSH COMES TO SHOVE** [–] [ ]

—— Late '87, they recorded live album 'DYLAN AND THE DEAD' with BOB DYLAN, which was released early 1989, and hit US No.37.

Nov 89. (lp/c/cd) *(210/410/260 326) <AL/AC/ARCD 875>* **BUILT TO LAST** [ ] [27]
– Foolish heart / Just a little light / Built to last / Blow away / Standing on the Moon / Victim or the crime / We can run / Picasso moon / I will take you home.

Nov 89. (cd-s/7") *<ASCD+/9899>* **FOOLISH HEART. / WE CAN RUN** [–] [ ]

Oct 90. (d-cd/t-lp) *(303/353 935) <ACD2 8634>* **WITHOUT A NET (live)** [ ] [43]
– Feel like a stranger / Mississippi half-step uptown toodeloo / Walkin' blues / Althea / Cassidy / Let it grow / China cat sunflower – I know you rider / Looks like rain / Eyes of the world / Victim or the crime / Help on the way – Slipknot! – Franklin's tower / Bird song / One more Saturday night / Dear Mr. Fantasy.

— BRETT MYDLAND died 26 Jul'90 of a drug overdose. Replaced by **VINCE WELNICK** (b.22 Feb'52, Phoenix, Arizona) – keyboards (ex-TUBES, ex-TODD RUNDGREN)

– compilations etc. –

on 'Grateful Dead' records unless mentioned otherwise

Apr 72. (lp) *Polydor; (2310 171) / Sunflower; <SNF 5004>* **HISTORIC DEAD** (rare '66) [ ] Jun71 [ ]

Apr 72. (lp) *Polydor; (2310 172) / Sunflower; <SUN 5001>* **VINTAGE DEAD (live '66)** [ ] Oct70 [ ]

1972. (lp) *Pride; <PRD 0016>* **THE HISTORY OF GRATEFUL DEAD** [–] [ ]

Sep 73. (lp) *Warners; (K 46246) <BS 2721>* **HISTORY OF THE DEAD – BEAR'S CHOICE (live rarities)** [ ] Jul73 [60]
– Katie Mae / Dark hollow / I've been all around the world / Wake up little Susie / Black Peter / Smokestack lightnin' / Hard to handle. *<US cd-iss. 1988; 2721-2> <(cd re-iss. Jun00; 7599 27274-2)> <(cd re-mast.Mar03 on 'Rhino'+=; 8122 74400-2)>* – Good lovin' / Big boss man / Smokestack lightnin' (version 2) / Sitting on top of the world.

Mar 74. (lp) *Warners; (K 56024) <BS 2674>* **SKELETONS FROM THE CLOSET** [ ] [75]
(re-iss. Oct86 on 'Thunderbolt' lp/c/cd; THBL/THBCCDTB 018) <US cd-iss. 1988; 2764-2>

Apr 74. (7") *Warners; <WB 21988>* **SUGAR MAGNOLIA. / MR. CHARLIE** [–] [ ]

— All below on 'Grateful Dead' US records, unless otherwise mentioned.

Feb 77. (d-lp) *United Artists; (UDM 103-4)* **WAKE OF THE FLOOD / FROM MARS HOTEL** [ ] [ ]

Feb 78. (d-lp) *Warners; (K 66073)* **WHAT A LONG STRANGE TRIP IT'S BEEN: THE BEST OF GRATEFUL DEAD** [ ] Nov 77 [ ]
– New, new Minglewood blues / Cosmic Charlie / Truckin' / Black Peter / Born cross-eyed / Ripple / Doin' that rag / Dark star / High time / New speedway boogie / St. Stephen / Jack Straw / Me & my uncle / Tennessee Jed / Cumberland blues / Playing in the band / Brown-eyed woman / Ramble on Rose. *<US cd-iss. 1989; 3091-2>*

1987. (6xcd-box) *Arista; <ACD6 8530>* **DEAD ZONE: THE GRATEFUL DEAD CD COLLECTION 1977-1987** [–] [ ]
– (Arista albums from 77-87)

1987. (cd) *Pair; <ARP2 1053>* **FOR THE FAITHFUL** [–] [ ]

Jun 91. (d-cd/d-c/t-lp) *<(GDCD2/GDTC2/GDV2 4015)>* **ONE FROM THE VAULT** (live 13 Aug'75, Great American Music Hall, San Francisco) [ ] May91 [ ]
– (introduction) / Help on the way / Franklin's tower / Music never stopped / It must have been the roses / Eyes of the world – drums / King Solomon's marbles / Around and around / Sugaree / Big river / Crazy fingers – drums / The other one / Sage and spirit / Goin' down the road feeling bad / U.S. blues / Blues for Allah.

Jan 92. (cd) *<(GDCD 4016)>* **INFRARED ROSES (live)** [ ] [ ]
– Crowd sculpture / Parallelogram / Little Nemo in Lightland / Riverside rhapsody / Post-modern highrise table top stomp / Infrared roses / Silver apples of the Moon / Speaking in swords / Magnesium night light / Sparrow hawk row / River of nine sorrows / Apollo at the Ritz.

Aug 92. (d-cd/d-lp) *<(GDCD2/GDV2 4018)>* **TWO FROM THE VAULT** (live 23/24 Aug'68, Shrine Auditorium, L.A.) [ ] May92 [ ]
– Good morning little schoolgirl / Dark star / St. Stephen / The eleven / Death don't have no mercy / The other one / New potato caboose / Turn on your lovelight / Morning dew.

Dec 93. (d-cd) *<(GDCD 4019)>* **DICK'S PICK: VOLUME ONE (live Tampa, Florida 12/19/73)** [ ] [ ]
– Here comes sunshine / Big river / Mississippi half-step uptown toodeloo / Weather report suite (Prelude – part 1, Let it grow – part 2) / Big railroad blues / Playing in the band / He's gone / Truckin' / Nobody's fault but mine / Jam / The other one / Jam / Stella blue / Around and around.

Jan 94. (cd/c) *Dare International; (DIL CD/C 1001)* **RISEN FROM THE VAULTS** [ ] [ ]

Jun 95. (cd) *<(GDCD 4020)>* **DICK'S PICKS: VOLUME TWO** (live Columbus, Ohio 10/3/71) [ ] [ ]
– Dark star / Jam / Sugar magnolia / St. Stephen / Not fade away / Going down the road feeling bad / Not fade away.

Oct 95. (d-cd/d-c) *<(GD CD/MC 4021)>* **HUNDRED YEAR HALL** (live 26th April 1972, Jahrhundert Halle, Frankfurt) [ ] [26]
– Bertha / Me & my uncle / The next time you see me / China cat sunflower / I know you rider / Jack Straw / Big railroad blues / Playing in the band / Turn on your love light / Going down the road feeling bad / One more Saturday night / Truckin' / Cryptical envelopment / Comes a time / Sugar magnolia.

Nov 95. (d-cd) *<(GDCD2 4022)>* **DICK'S PICKS: VOLUME THREE** (live Pembroke Pines, Florida, 5/22/77) [ ] [ ]

Oct 96. (d-cd/d-c) *Arista; <(07822 18934-2/-4)>* **THE ARISTA YEARS 1977-95** [ ] [95]

Dec 96. (t-cd) *<(GRCD3 4023)>* **DICK'S PICK: VOLUME FOUR** (live February 13-14 1970) [ ] [ ]

Jan 97. (t-cd) *<(GDCD3 4024)>* **DOZIN' AT THE KNICK** [ ] Nov96 [74]

Dec 96. (t-cd) *<(GDCD3 4025)>* **DICK'S PICKS: VOLUME FIVE** (live Oakland Auditorium Arena 12/26/79) [ ] [ ]

Jan 97. (t-cd) *<(GDCD3 4026)>* **DICK'S PICKS: VOLUME SIX** (live Hartford Civic Center 10/04/83) [ ] [ ]

Apr 97. (t-cd) *<(GDCD3 4027)>* **DICK'S PICKS: VOLUME SEVEN** (live Alexandra Palace 9-11 Sep'74) [ ] [ ]

May 97. (cd) *Metro; (OTR 1100024)* **NIGHT OF THE GRATEFUL DEAD** [ ] [–]

Jun 97. (d-cd) *<(GDCD2 4052)>* **FALLOUT FROM THE PHIL ZONE** [ ] [83]

Jun 97. (d-cd; with JOHN OSWALD) *Swell Artifact; (SA 1969)* **GRAYFOLDED** [ ] [ ]
(re-iss. Aug99 on 'Snapper'; SMDCD 215)

Jun 97. (cd; MICKEY & THE HEARTBEATS) *Anthology; (ANT 2912)* **HARTBITS VOL.2** [ ] [ ]

Jul 97. (t-cd) *<GDCD3 4028>* **DICK'S PICK: VOLUME EIGHT** (live Harpur College 5/02/70) [–] [ ]

Oct 97. (t-cd) *<GDCD3 4029>* **DICK'S PICKS: VOLUME NINE** (live Madison Square Garden September 16, 1990) [ ] [ ]

Nov 97. (d-cd) *<GDCD2 4054>* **FILLMORE EAST 2-11-69 (live)** [–] [77]

Jun 98. (t-cd) *<ARI1 4031>* **DICK'S PICKS: VOLUME ELEVEN** (live August 27, 1972 Oregon & Jersey City) [–] [ ]

Mar 99. (t-cd) *<ARI1 4033>* **DICK'S PICKS: VOLUME THIRTEEN** (live 6/5/81 Nassau Coliseum, Long Island, NY) [–] [ ]
(UK-iss.May02; same as US)

Jun 99. (q-cd) *<ARI1 4034>* **DICK'S PICKS: VOLUME FOURTEEN** (live Boston Music Hall 11/30/73 & 12/2/73) [–] [ ]
(UK-iss.May02; same as US)

Aug 99. (t-cd) *<ARI1 4035>* **DICK'S PICKS: VOLUME FIFTEEN** (live English Town New Jersey 9/3/77) [–] [ ]
(UK-iss.May02; same as US)

Nov 99. (5xcd-box) *<14066>* **SO MANY ROADS (1965-1995) (live)** [–] [ ]

Dec 99. (pic-lp) *Ugo; (UGO 2)* **THE DEAD LIVE IN CONCERT (live)** [ ] [–]

Mar 00. (t-cd) *<ARI1 4036>* **DICK'S PICKS: VOLUME SIXTEEN** (live Fillmore Auditorium 11/8/69) [–] [ ]
(UK-iss.May02; same as US)

May 00. (t-cd) *<ARI1 4037>* **DICK'S PICKS: VOLUME SEVENTEEN** (live Boston Garden 9/25/91) [–] [ ]
(UK-iss.May02; same as US)

Jun 00. (t-cd) *<ARI1 4038>* **DICK'S PICKS: VOLUME EIGHTEEN** (live Dane County Coliseum 3/2/78 + University of North Iowa 5/2/78) [–] [ ]
(UK-iss.May02; same as US)

Jul 00. (t-cd) *<ARI1 4030>* **DICK'S PICKS: VOLUME TEN** (live 1977 San Francisco) [–] [ ]

Jul 00. (t-cd) *<ARI1 4032>* **DICK'S PICKS: VOLUME TWELVE** (live 1974 Providence & Boston) [–] [ ]

Oct 00. (t-cd) *<ARI1 4039>* **DICK'S PICKS: VOLUME NINETEEN** (live Fairgrounds Arena, Oklahoma City 10/19/73) [–] [ ]

Oct 00. (4xcd-box) *<14075>* **LADIES AND GENTLEMEN . . . FILLMORE EAST: NEW YORK CITY: APRIL 1971** [–] [ ]

Jan 01. (4xcd) *<ARI1 4040>* **DICK'S PICKS: VOLUME TWENTY** (live September 1976) [–] [ ]

Feb 01. (t-cd) *<ARI1 4041>* **DICK'S PICKS: VOLUME TWENTY-ONE** (live Richmond Coliseum 11/1/85 & 9/2/80 Community War Memorial, Rochester, NY) [–] [ ]

Jul 01. (d-cd) *<ARI1 4042>* **DICK'S PICKS: VOLUME TWENTY-TWO** (live 23/24 February 1968, Kings Beach, Lake Tahoe) [–] [ ]

Sep 01. (d-cd) *ARI1 4081>* **NIGHTFALL OF DIAMONDS** (live October 10, 1989) [–] [ ]

Oct 01. (t-cd) *<ARI1 4043>* **DICK'S PICKS: VOLUME TWENTY-THREE** (live September 17, 1972, Baltimore Civic Center) –

Oct 01. (12xcd-box) *Rhino; <(8122 74401-2)>* **THE GOLDEN ROAD (1965-1973)**

Feb 02. (d-cd) *<ARI1 4044>* **DICK'S PICKS: VOLUME TWENTY-FOUR** (live Bay Area 1974) –

Mar 02. (cd) *<ARI1 4069>* **POSTCARDS OF THE HANGING: . . .PERFORM THE SONGS OF BOB DYLAN** –

Jul 02. (t-cd) *<ARI1 4045>* **DICK'S PICKS 25** (live 1978 New Haven, CT, May 10 – Springfield, MA, May 11) –

Jul 02. (4xcd) *<(ARI1 4084)>* **STEPPIN' OUT WITH THE GRATEFUL DEAD (live)**

Oct 02. (t-cd) *<ARI1 4046>* **DICK'S PICKS: TWENTY-SIX** (live Electric Theater, Chicago, IL, April 26, 1969 & Labor Temple, Minneapolis, MN, April 27, 1969) –

Nov 02. (d-cd) *<(ARI1 4085)>* **GO TO NASSAU (live May 15-16, 1980)** Oct02

Jan 03. (t-cd) *<ARI1 4047>* **DICK'S PICKS: VOLUME TWENTY-SEVEN** (live December 16, 1992, Oakland Coliseum Arena) –

Mar 03. (d-cd) *Rhino; <(8122 74391-2)>* **BIRTH OF THE DEAD**

Apr 03. (t-cd) *<ARI1 4048>* **DICK'S PICKS 28** (live Salt Palace, Salt Lake City, UT, February 28, 1973 & Lincoln, NE, February 28, 1973) –

Jul 03. (6xcd-box) *<ARI1 4049>* **DICK'S PICKS 29** (live spring & summer 1977) –

Sep 03. (cd) *Rhino; <(8122 73899-2)>* **THE VERY BEST OF THE GRATEFUL DEAD** 69
– Truckin' / Touch of grey / Sugar magnolia / Casey Jones / Uncle John's band / Friend of the Devil / Franklin's tower / Estimated prophet / Eyes of the world / Box of rain / U.S. blues / The golden road (to unlimited devotion) / One more Saturday night (live) / Fire on the mountain / The music never stopped / Hell in a bucket / Ripple.

Oct 03. (t-cd) *<ARI1 4050>* **DICK'S PICKS 30** (live Academy Of Music, New York City, March 25 & 26, 1972) –

JERRY GARCIA

solo – used session men from the DEAD plus others

C.B.S. Douglas

Jul 71. (lp; by HOWARD WALES & JERRY GARCIA) *(69013)* *<KZ 30859>* **HOOTEROLL?**
– South side strut / A trip to what next / Up from the desert / DC-502 / One a.m. approach / Uncle Martin's / Da bird song. *(cd-iss. Oct87 & Jul92 on 'Rykodisc'; <RCD 10052>) <US cd+=>* – Morning in Marin / Evening in Marin.

Jan 72. (7"; by HOWARD WALES & JERRY GARCIA) *<7-6501>* **SOUTH SIDE STRUT. / UNCLE MARTIN'S** –

Warners Warners

Jan 72. (lp) *(K 46139)* *<BS 2582>* **GARCIA** (aka 'The Wheel') 35
– Deal / Bird song / Sugaree / Loser / Late for supper / Spiderdawg / Eep hour / To lay me down / An odd little place / The wheel. *(<re-iss. Feb89 as 'THE WHEEL' on 'Grateful Dead' lp/c/cd; GDV/GDTC/<GDCD 4003>)*

1973. (7") *<7551>* **THE WHEEL. / DEAL** –

1973. (7") *<7569>* **SUGAREE. / EEP HOUR** –

not iss. Fantasy

Dec 73. (d-lp) *<F 79002>* **LIVE AT THE KEYSTONE (live with MERLE SAUNDERS)** –
– Let's spend the night together / It takes a lot to laugh, it takes a train to cry / The harder they come / That's all right mama / He ain't give you none / Positively 4th street / My funny valentine / etc.

Round Round

Jun 74. (lp) *(RX 59301)* *<RX 102>* **GARCIA** (aka 'Compliments Of Garcia') 49
– Let it rock / When the hunter gets captured by the game / That's what love will make us do / Russian lullabye / Turn on the bright lights / He ain't give you none / What goes around / Let's spend the night together / Mississippi moon / Midnight town. *(<re-iss. Apr89 as 'COMPLIMENTS OF GARCIA' on 'Grateful Dead' lp/c/cd; GDV/GDC/<GDCD 4011>)*

Jul 74. (7") *<4504>* **LET IT ROCK. / MIDNIGHT TOWN** –

—— **GARCIA, DAVID GRISMAN, PETER ROWAN, JOHN KAHN, VASSAR CLEMENTS**

Mar 75. (lp; by OLD & IN THE WAY) *<RX 103>* **OLD AND IN THE WAY** –
– Pig in a pen / Midnight moonlight / Old and in the way / Knockin' on your door / The hobo song / Panama red / Wild horses / Kissimmee kid / White dove / Land of the Navajo. *(UK-iss.Feb85 on 'Sugarhill' lp/cd; SH/+CD 3746) <US cd-iss. 1987 on 'Rykodisc'; RCD 1009> (re-iss. cd 1990 on 'Grateful Dead'; GDCD 4014)*

U.A. Round

Feb 76. (lp) *(UAG 29921)* *<RX 107>* **REFLECTIONS** 42
– Might as well / Mission in the rain / They love each other / I'll take a melody / It must have been the roses / Tore up over you / Catfish John / Comes a time. *(re-iss. Feb89 on 'Grateful Dead' lp/cd; GDV/GDTC/GDCD 4008)*

Arista Arista

Apr 78. (lp; by JERRY GARCIA BAND) *(SPART 1053)* *<AB 4160>* **CATS UNDER THE STARS**
– Rubin and Cherise / Love in the afternoon / Palm Sunday / Cats under the stars / Rhapsody in red / Rain / Down home / Gomorrah. *<US cd-iss. 1988; ARCD 8535>*

Nov 82. (lp) *(1204973)* *<AL 9603>* **RUN FOR THE ROSES**
– Run for the roses / I saw her standing there / Without love / Midnight getaway / Leave the little girl alone / Valerie / Knockin' on Heaven's door. *<US cd-iss. 1986; ARCD 8557>*

not iss. Fantasy

1988. (lp) *<MPF 4533>* **KEYSTONE ENCORES VOLUME 1** –

1988. (cd) *<FCD 7701-2>* **LIVE AT KEYSTONE VOLUME 1** –

1988. (lp) *<MPF 4534>* **KEYSTONE ENCORES VOLUME 2** –

1988. (cd) *<FCD 7702-2>* **LIVE AT KEYSTONE VOLUME 2** –

1988. (cd) *<FCD 7703-2>* **KEYSTONE ENCORES** (compilation of above) –
(above credited with MERLE SAUNDERS; lp/cd's with diff.titles)

Grateful Dead Grateful Dead

Mar 89. (lp/c/cd; as JERRY GARCIA ACOUSTIC BAND) *(GDV/GDC/GDCD 4005)* **ALMOST ACOUSTIC**
– Swing low, sweet chariot / Deep Elam blues / Blue yodel £9 (standing on the corner) / Spike driver blues / I've been all around this world / I'm here to get my baby out of jail / I'm troubled / Oh, the wind and the rain / The girl at the Crossroads bar / Oh babe it ain't no lie / Casey Jones / Diamond Joe / Gone home / Ripple.

—— with **JOHN KAHN** – bass / **DAVID KEMPER** – drums / **MARVIN SEALS** – keyboards / and backing vocalists **JACKIE LA BRANCH** and **GLORIA JONES**

Arista Arista

Sep 91. (d-cd) *(354284)* *<18690-2>* **JERRY GARCIA BAND (live)** 97
– The way you do the things you do / Waiting for a miracle / Simple twist of fate / Get out of my life / My sister and brothers / I shall be released / Dear Prudence / Deal / Stop that train / Senor (tales of Yankee power) / Evangeline / The night they drove old Dixie down / Don't let go / That lucky old Sun / Tangled up in blue.

not iss. Acoustic Disc

1993. (cd; by DAVID GRISMAN / JERRY GARCIA) *<ACD-9>* **NOT FOR KIDS ONLY** –

Apr 97. (cd; JERRY GARCIA & DAVID GRISMAN) *<(ACD-21)>* **SHADY GROVE**

Grateful Dead Grateful Dead

May 97. (cd; JERRY GARCIA BAND) *(GDCD 4051)* **HOW SWEET IT IS** Apr97 81

OTHER ONES

—— (see biog for line-up)

not iss. Grateful Dead

Feb 99. (d-cd) *<14062>* **ONLY THE STRANGE REMAIN** –
– St. Stephen – The eleven / Jack Straw / Sugaree / Corrina / Only the strange remain / White-wheeled limosine / Estimated prophet / Playing in the band / The other one / Banyan tree / Rainbow's cadillac / Mountains of the moon / Friend of the Devil / Baba jingo / China cat sunflower – I know you rider.

David GRAY

Born: 13 Jun'70, Manchester, England. As a young boy of nine, GRAY moved to Solva (in Wales) with his family where he found the joys of guitar playing while taking in the local punk and folk scene. In 1992 (through manager/A&R man Rob Holden), he signed to Virgin offshoot, 'Hut' and issued his debut set 'A CENTURY ENDS' (1993), which brilliantly displayed his tender and sparse songwriting skills. 'FLESH' (1994) appeared one year later, by now, GRAY had made a promising name for himself, attracting a huge cult following around Britain and Europe. The aforementioned album was not bad for somebody who was still learning his trade, comparisons to DYLAN, EDDIE VEDDER and MIKE SCOTT were bandied about like confetti at a wedding. The acoustic guitars, bouncing pedal steel and occasional piano made stand out tracks 'WHAT ARE YOU NOW', 'FALLING FREE' and 'NEW HORIZONS' levitate above some recent attempts at melancholic music, proving GRAY to be one of Britain's best kept secrets and filing him along with assets THOM YORKE and RICHARD ASHCROFT. 'SELL, SELL, SELL' (1996) was perhaps too proverbial for its own good and thus it didn't gain enough exposure to hit the shops in the UK. Nevertheless, it still received some airplay from Radio One's Steve Lamaque and went on to sustain GRAY's reputation in the alt-music world. It was 1999's 'WHITE LADDER' (on new imprint 'iht' through 'eastwest') which caught the attention of music critics and audiences alike. A fine album in every sense, GRAY took us into the underworld of his soul . . . and deeper, with tracks 'SAIL AWAY' and Soft Cell's 'SAY HELLO WAVE GOODBYE' bringing something delicate and strangely human to the work. Easily the highlight from the set was 'BABYLON', a chart flop first time around although album opener 'PLEASE FORGIVE ME' slightly compensated for this, clocking in at No.72. Aaah! what a difference a year can make. Now signed to 'east west', the single 'BABYLON' was re-issued to a wider audience and after massive playlisting it finally peaked at No.5. A resurrected 'WHITE LADDER' also climbed the charts post-millennium, rising to No.1 a whole year later. A newcomer of sorts (tell that to the struggling 30-something troubadour!), GRAY proceeded to have three further hits during 2001, 'PLEASE FORGIVE ME', 'THIS YEARS LOVE' and 'SAIL AWAY'. The tender singer/songwriter returned in 2002 to issue 'A NEW DAY AT MIDNIGHT', an altogether more thoughtful and intimate set than 'WHITE LADDER'. It included the soaring piano lament 'SEE YOU ON THE OTHER SIDE', a deep but nevertheless uplifting feel through GRAY's psyche. Another surefire hit with fans was the song 'BE MINE', a slight hark back to GRAY's earlier days. But it was the bitterly bitter-sweet sound of his piano on the frosty ballad 'DECEMBER' which set him apart from many copyists.

Album rating: A CENTURY ENDS (*6) / FLESH (*6) / SELL, SELL, SELL (*6) / WHITE LADDER (*9) / LOST SONGS 95-98 collection (*6) / THE EP'S 1992-1994 ALBUM collection (*5) / A NEW DAY AT MIDNIGHT (*7)

DAVID GRAY – vocals, guitar, keyboards / with **NEILL MacCOLL** – guitar, mandolin, vocals / **ROBIN MILLAR** – guitar / **"FAMOUS DAVE" ANDERSON** – keyboards / **STEVE SIDELNYK** – programming

Hut — Caroline

Nov 92. (12"/cd-s) *(HUT/+CD 23)* **BIRDS WITHOUT WINGS. / L'S SONG / THE LIGHT** [ ] [–]

Mar 93. (12"/cd-s) *(HUT/+CD 27)* **SHINE. / BRICK WALLS / THE RICE** [ ] [–]

Apr 93. (cd/c/lp) *(CDHUT/HUTMC/HUTLP 9)* <CAROL 1739> **A CENTURY ENDS** [ ] Nov93 [ ]
– Shine / A century ends / Debauchery / Let the truth sting / Gathering dust / Wisdom / Lead me upstairs / Living room / Birds without wings / It's all over. *(cd re-iss. Jul01; CDHUTX 9)*

Jul 93. (12"/cd-s) *(HUT/+CD 32)* **WISDOM. / LOVERS / 4AM** [ ] [–]

— with **MacCOLL** plus **ANDY METCALFE** – hammond organ / **SIMON EDWARDS + DAVID NOLTE** – bass / **ROY DODS** – drums / **CLUNE** – drums, vocals, keyboards, bass, co-writer

Hut — not iss.

Sep 94. (cd/c) *(CDHUT/HUTMC 17)* **FLESH** [ ] [–]
– What are you? / The light / Coming down / Falling free / Mystery of love / Lullaby / New horizons / Loves old song / Flesh. *<US cd-iss. Jul00 on 'Vernon Yard'; 39770> (cd re-iss. Jul01; CDHUTX 17)*

— now with different session people incl. **CLUNE + TIM BRADSHAW**

E.M.I. — not iss.

Apr 96. (cd) *(7243 8 37357)* **SELL, SELL, SELL** [–] Europe [–]
– Faster, sooner, now / Late night radio / Sell, sell, sell / Hold on to nothing / Everytime / Magdalena / Smile / Only the lonely / What am I doing wrong? / Gutters full of rain / Forever is tomorrow is today / Folk song. *(UK-iss.Jul00; CDEMC 3755) <US-iss.Sep00 on 'Nettwerk'; >*

— GRAY with **(Mc)CLUNE** + 3rd p/t co-writer/producer, **POLSON**

Iht — A.T.O.

Mar 99. (cd) *(ihtcd 001) <21539>* **WHITE LADDER** [ ] Jan00 [ ]
– Please forgive me / Babylon / My oh my / We're not right / Nightblindness / Silver lining / White ladder / This years love / Sail away / Say hello wave goodbye. *(re-iss. Apr00 on 'eastwest'; 8573 82983-2)* – hit No.2 – No.1 a year later! *<US re-iss. Aug00 on 'R.C.A.'; 69351>* – hit No.35

Mar 99. (cd-s) *(ihtcds 001)* **THIS YEARS LOVE / NIGHTBLINDNESS / OVER MY HEAD** [ ] [–]

Jul 99. (cd-s) *(ihtcds 002)* **BABYLON / LEAD ME UPSTAIRS (live) / NEW HORIZONS (live)** [ ] [–]

Nov 99. (12")(cd-s) *(ihtv 001)(ihtcds 003)* **PLEASE FORGIVE ME. / PLEASE FORGIVE ME (Paul Hartnoll remix)** [72] [–]

eastwest — R.C.A.

Jun 00. (c-s/cd-s) *(EW 215 C/CD1) <radio cut>* **BABYLON / TELL ME MORE LIES / OVER MY HEAD** [5] Nov00 [57]
(cd-s+=) *(EW 215CD2)* – ('A'-video).

Oct 00. (c-s) *(EW 219C)* **PLEASE FORGIVE ME / (Paul Hartnoll remix)** [18] [–]
(cd-s+=) *(EW 219CD)* – Babylon (live at the Point) (video).

Mar 01. (c-s/cd-s) *(EW 228 C/CD1)* **THIS YEARS LOVE (strings remix) / FLAME TURNS BLUE / THE LIGHTS OF LONDON** [20] [–]
(cd-s) *(EW 228CD2)* – ('A'live) / Roots of love / Tired of me.

Jul 01. (c-s) *(EW 234C)* **SAIL AWAY / (club mix)** [26] [–]
(cd-s+=) *(EW 234CD)* – ('A'-Rae & Christian remix).

Dec 01. (cd-s) *(EW 244CD)* **SAY HELLO WAVE GOODBYE (mixes)** [26] [–]

Oct 02. (cd) *(5046 61658-2) <68154>* **A NEW DAY AT MIDNIGHT** [1] Nov02 [17]
– Dead in the water / Caroline / Long distance call / Freedom / Kangaroo / Last boat to America / Real love / Knowhere / December / Be mine / Easy way to cry / The other side.

Dec 02. (cd-s) *(EW 259CD)* **THE OTHER SIDE / LORELEI / DECIPHER** [35] [–]

Apr 03. (cd-s) *(EW 264CD)* **BE MINE / LOVERBOY / FALLING DOWN FROM THE MOUNTAINSIDE (live 2002)** [23] [–]

– compilations, etc. –

Jul 00. (cd) *iht; (IHTCD 002) / A.T.O.; <69375>* **LOST SONGS 95-98** [ ] Apr01 [ ]
– Flame turns blue / Twilight / Hold on / As I'm leaving / If your love is real / Tidal wave / Falling down the mountainside / January rain / Red moon / A clean pair of eyes / Wurlitzer. *(re-iss. Feb01 on 'eastwest' cd/c; 8573 86953-2/-4)* – hit No.7

Jul 01. (cd) *Hut; (CDHUT 67)* **THE EP'S 1992-1994 ALBUM** [68] [ ]

Oct 02. (d-cd) *Hut; (543413-0)* **FLESH / A CENTURY ENDS** [ ] [–]

Oct 02. (d-cd) *Hut; (543414-0)* **SELL, SELL, SELL / THE EP'S 1992-1994 ALBUM** [ ] [–]

Macy GRAY

Born: NATALIE McINTYRE, 9 Sep'70, Canton, Ohio, USA. An exceptionally accomplished pianist, MACY began to sing one afternoon (her voice had been established after a bout of bronchitis!) when a former vocalist had failed to show at a band practice she had organised in the University of Southern California. While studying screenwriting in L.A., MACY soon became involved with a local jazz group and made extra money singing as a session musician. She signed to 'Epic' records in 1998 and issued her first release, 'DO SOMETHING', a hit song subsequently lifted from her debut Top 3 album, 'ON HOW LIFE IS', the following summer. The CD soared through a collection of influences such as hip-hop, R&B and soul, all backed with MACY's uniquely chocolate-coated, croaky style (BILLIE HOLIDAY and JANIS JOPLIN come to mind). A Top 10 hit single, 'I TRY', was a classy 'Motown'-esque breakup song set to modern times and cleverly produced by Andrew Slater, of FIONA APPLE fame. The self-styled black sheep of nu-soul, GRAY let it all hang out on 'The ID' (2001), an ambitious update of the kind of kaleidoscopic soul extravaganza beloved of Motown artists keen to assert their creative independence back in the 70's. Not as endearing or as unique as her debut then, although it had its moments, chief among them a duet with ERYKAH BADU entitled 'SWEET BABY'. 'THE TROUBLE WITH BEING MYSELF' (2003) lost yet more creative ground with a meandering set of songs lacking much of any focus save GRAY's black coffee-stained vocal chops. Dressed up in R&B artifice when they should've been graced with arrangements as unwieldy and engaging as that singular voice itself, her vocals may yet be her saviour although it was difficult to avoid the impression of them having been at least partly squandered this time around.

Album rating: ON HOW LIFE IS (*7) / THE ID (*6) / THE TROUBLE WITH BEING MYSELF (*5)

MACY GRAY – vocals / with session people incl. co-writers **JEREMY RUZUMNA** – keyboards / **MILES OM TACKETT** – guitar / **KILU BECKWITH** – programming

Epic Sony

Jun 99. (c-s) *(667593-4)* *<79209>* **DO SOMETHING / RATHER HAZY** [51] Jul99 [ ]
(cd-s+=) *(667593-2)* *<79241>* – ('A'-Organized Noize mix featuring Cee Lo).
(cd-s) *(667593-5)* – ('A'mixes; album / Jay's subliminal funk / King Britt).

Jul 99. (cd/c) *(494423-2/-4)* *<69490>* **ON HOW LIFE IS** [3] [4]
– Why didn't you call me / Do something / Caligula / I try / Sex-o-matic Venus freak / I can't wait to meetchu / Still / I've committed murder / Moment to myself / Letter.

Sep 99. (c-s) *(668193-4)* *<radio cut>* **I TRY / I TRY (full crew mix)** [6] Jan00 [5]
(cd-s+=) *(668193-2)* – Don't come around.
(cd-s) *(668193-5)* – ('A'side) / ('A'mixes; Jay Dee / Bob Power).

Mar 00. (c-s/cd-s) *(668982-4/-2)* **STILL / STILL (Attica blues mix) / I TRY (grand style mix)** [18] [–]
(cd-s) *(668982-5)* – ('A'side) / ('A'-X-executioners remix) / I try (Jo Whiley radio session) / ('A'video).

Jul 00. (c-s) *(669668-4)* **WHY DIDN'T YOU CALL ME / I'VE COMMITTED MURDER (Gang Starr mix) / ('A'live)** [38] [ ]
(cd-s) *(669668-2)* – (first 2 tracks) / ('A'-88 Keys mix).
(cd-s) *(669668-5)* – ('A'side) / I can't wait to meetchu / ('A'-Black Eyed Peas mix) / ('A'video).

— in Jan'01, MACY featured on FATBOY SLIM's UK Top 20 hit, 'Demons'

— in Mar'01, MACY featured on BLACK EYED PEAS' hit, 'Request Line'

— in Apr'01, she also featured on COMMON's hit, 'Geto Heaven'

Sep 01. (c-s; by MACY GRAY & ERYKAH BADU) *(671882-4)* **SWEET BABY / BETTER WHERE YOU ARE / SWEET BABY (8-jam mix)** [23] [ ]
(cd-s+=) *(67188-2-2)* – ('A'-video).
(12") *(671882-6)* – Hey young world II (with SLICK RICK).

Sep 01. (cd/c/lp) *(504089-2/-4/-1)* *<85200>* **THE ID** [1] [11]
– Relating to a psychopath / Boo / Sexual revolution / Hey young world II (with SLICK RICK) / Sweet baby (with ERYKAH BADU) / Harry / Gimme all your lovin' or I will kill you / Don't come around (with SUNSHINE ANDERSON) / My nutmeg phantasy (with ANGIE STONE & MOS DEF) / Freak like me / Oblivion / Forgiveness / Blowin' up your speakers. *(special cd+=; 504089-9)* – Shed.

Nov 01. (12"/cd-s) *(672146-6/-2)* **SEXUAL REVOLUTION (mixes; Miguel Mags petalpusher vocal 12"/ album = CD / Norman Cook 128bpm / blaze main shelter)** [45] [–]
(cd-s) *(672146-5)* – ('A'mixes; radio / Miguel Migs / video) / Winter wonderland.

Apr 03. (cd-s)<12"> *(673840-2)* *<4979869>* **WHEN I SEE YOU / WHEN I SEE YOU (bugz in the attic remix) / I TRY (grand style mix)** [26] [ ]
(cd-s) *(6738405)* – ('A'side) / Lie to me / It's love.

Apr 03. (cd) *(510810-2)* *<86535>* **THE TROUBLE WITH BEING MYSELF** [17] [44]
– When I see you / It ain't the money (with PHAROAHE MONCH & BECK) / She ain't right for you / Things that made me change / Come together / She don't write songs about you / Jesus for a day / My fondest childhood memories / Happiness / Speechless / Screamin' / Every now and then.

Al GREEN

Born: AL GREENE, 13 Apr'46, Forrest City, Arkansas, USA. AL got off to an early start when, at the age of nine, he formed his first group, The GREEN BROTHERS, a gospel outfit which included siblings ROBERT, WALTER and WILLIAM. After touring throughout the South, AL was dropped from the group after his Dad caught him listening to the sweet sounds of JACKIE WILSON, and in doing so instilled an instant love for soul music. By the time AL was sixteen, he had formed his own outfit, AL GREEN & THE CREATIONS, who performed R&B tracks before drifting more into soul. Two members of the group, meanwhile, had formed their own label, 'Hot Line Music Journal', recording the newly-renamed AL GREENE & THE SOUL MATES. Their one and only hit, 'BACK UP TRAIN', was the sole measure of success until 1969 when AL met WILLIE MITCHELL, then bandleader and vice-president of 'Hi' Records. After hearing GREEN sing, MITCHELL immediately signed him to the label, where the soul brother recorded his most soulful and funky tracks. The debut album, 'GREEN IS BLUES', released in early '70, proved MITCHELL had made the right move. GREEN's incredible falsetto voice blended with the MITCHELL-arranged horn and strings punctuated a sexy groove that led to the trademark "love man" persona in the early 70's. Although no hits were forthcoming, his second set, 'AL GREEN GETS NEXT TO YOU', proved more accessible, spawning the classic 'TIRED OF BEING ALONE'; this benchmark was to precede four further hits in the next two years. Lifted from his next album, 'LET'S STAY TOGETHER', the title track became the first No.1 of GREEN's glorious career, his alluring voice subsequently gracing the heart-stopping 'I'M STILL IN LOVE WITH YOU' and the spicy 'HERE I AM (COME AND TAKE ME)'. By this point in his career, GREEN was widely recognised as a commercial and critical success, an artist at the pinnacle of his singing career who scored with six consecutive Top 10 singles between '72-'73. His life and career took a dramatic change of course when, on the 25th of October '74, his former girlfriend inflicted second degree burns on his back by pouring boiling grits over him before killing herself with the singer's gun. This led GREEN to follow a life in the Church, believing that the assault was a sign from God; by 1976 he had become pastor of the Full Gospel Tabernacle in Memphis. Though still making albums with MITCHELL, his sound had become too formulaic and he began to record solely self-produced religious music through his own studio ('American Music') to mixed critical acclaim and significantly smaller sales. The '80s saw GREEN releasing Gospel sets on the 'Myrrh' label, as well as the curious duet with ANNIE LENNOX, 'PUT A LITTLE LOVE IN YOUR HEART'. Now primarily a Gospel artist, the 90's have seen GREEN recording the occasional R&B number, the best of the bunch being 1995's 'YOUR HEART IN GOOD HANDS'. Over the years, his songs have been interpreted by many top artists; TAKE ME TO THE RIVER (Talking Heads), L.O.V.E. (Orange Juice), LET'S STAY TOGETHER (Tina Turner), HERE I AM (UB 40), to name but a few. All the more reason for celebration among classic soul fans then, when news leaked out that GREEN was back in the Hi studio with WILLIE MITCHELL at the controls and original sessioneers backing him up. The end result was 'I CAN'T STOP' (2003), an album which allayed fears of a limp retread with the soul don sounding like he'd never hung up his funk chops in the first place. Highlights included the joyous title track, as revelatory a slice of retro-soul as has been aired this decade. • **Covered:** I WANT TO HOLD YOUR HAND + GET BACK (Beatles) / MEMPHIS, TENNESSEE (Chuck Berry) / CAN'T GET NEXT TO YOU (Temptations) / etc. • **Trivia:** On the 13th of February '78, L.A. declared this the 'Al Green Day'.

Album rating: BACK UP TRAIN (*5) / GREEN IS BLUES (*6) / AL GREEN GETS NEXT TO YOU (*7) / LET'S STAY TOGETHER (*8) / I'M STILL IN LOVE WITH YOU (*8) / CALL ME (*8) / LIVIN' FOR YOU (*8) / AL GREEN EXPLORES YOUR MIND (*7) / AL GREEN'S GREATEST HITS compilation (*9) / AL GREEN IS LOVE (*6) / FULL OF FIRE (*5) / HAVE A GOOD TIME (*5) / AL GREEN'S GREATEST HITS, VOLUME II compilation (*7) / THE BELLE ALBUM (*7) / TRUTH 'N' TIME (*6) / THE LORD WILL MAKE A WAY (*6) / HIGHER PLANE (86) / TOKYO LIVE (*7) / TRUST IN GOD (*5) / HE IS THE LIGHT (*6) / GOING AWAY (*5) / SOUL SURVIVOR (*5) / I GET JOY (*6) / LOVE IS REALITY (*5) / THE SUPREME AL GREEN: THE GREATEST HITS compilation (*8) / YOUR HEART'S IN GOOD HANDS (*4) / HI AND MIGHTY: THE STORY OF AL GREEN 1969-78 compilation (*8) / TESTIFY: THE BEST OF THE A&M YEARS compilation (*7) / I CAN'T STOP (*7) / LOVE – THE ESSENTIAL AL GREEN compilation (*8)

AL GREEN – vocals with **CURTIS ROGERS + PALMER JONES**

Stateside — Bell

Jan 68. (7"; by AL GREEN & The SOUL MATES) *(SS 2079)* *<1188>* **BACK UP TRAIN. / DON'T LEAVE ME** [ ] Oct67 [41]

Action — Hot Line

Feb 69. (7"; as AL GREENE) *(ACT 4540)* **DON'T HURT ME NO MORE. / GET YOURSELF TOGETHER** [ ] [–]

Mar 69. (lp) *(ACLP 6008)* *<1500>* **BACK UP TRAIN** [ ] [ ]
– Back up train / Hot wire / Stop and check myself / Let me help you / I'm reaching out / Don't hurt me no more / Lovers hideaway / Don't leave me / What's it all about / I'll be good to you / Guilty / That's all it takes (lady) / Get yourself together. *<(cd-iss. Mar02 on 'Camden'; 74321 92482-2)>*

— now using 'Hi' records house band **THE MEMPHIS HORNS** who were **WAYNE JACKSON** – trumpet / **JAMES MITCHELL** – baritone sax. / **ANDREW LOVE** – tenor sax. / **JACK HALE** – trombone / **ED LOGAN** – tenor sax. / plus **LEROY HODGES** – bass / **MABON HODGES** – guitar. / **CHARLES HUGHES** – organ and **HOWARD GRIMES** – drums who repl. AL JACKSON who joined BOOKER T.

London — Hi

1969. (7") *<2159>* **I WANT TO HOLD YOUR HAND. / WHAT AM I TO DO WITH MYSELF** [–] [ ]

1969. (7") *<2164>* **ONE WOMAN. / TOMORROW'S DREAM** [–] [ ]

1969. (lp) *<32055>* **GREEN IS BLUES** [–] [ ]
– One woman / Talk to me / My girl / I stand accused / Gotta find a new world / What am I gonna do with myself / Tomorrow's dream / What am I gonna do with myself / Get back baby / Get back / Summertime. *<re-iss. Jan73, hit No.19> (UK-iss.Apr86 on 'Hi'; HIUKLP 401) <(cd-iss. Jan99; HILO 150)> <cd re-mast.Feb03 on 'Capitol'+=; CAP 42474>* – I want to hold your hand / Nothing impossible with love / Baby, what's wrong with you? / Memphis, Tennessee.

Feb 70. (7") *(HLU 10300)* *<2172>* **YOU SAY IT. / GOTTA FIND A NEW WORLD** [ ] [ ]

Apr 70. (7") *<2177>* **RIGHT NOW RIGHT NOW. / ALL BECAUSE I'M A FOOLISH ONE** [–] [ ]

Jan 71. (7") *(HLU 10324)* *<2182>* **I CAN'T GET NEXT TO YOU. / RIDE SALLY RIDE** [ ] Nov70 [60]

Apr 71. (7") *<2188>* **DRIVIN' WHEEL. / TRUE LOVE** [–] [ ]

Jul 71. (7") *<2194>* **TIRED OF BEING ALONE. / GET BACK BABY** [–] [11]

Aug 71. (7") *(HLU 10337)* **TIRED OF BEING ALONE. / RIGHT NOW RIGHT NOW** [4] [–]

Nov 71. (lp) *(SHU 8424)* *<32062>* **AL GREEN GETS NEXT TO YOU** [ ] Aug71 [58]
– I can't get next to you / Are you lonely for me baby / God is standing by / Tired of being alone / I'm a ram / Drivin' wheel / Light my fire / You say it / Right now right now / All because. *(re-iss. Apr86 on 'Hi' lp/cd; HIUK LP/CD 403) <(cd-iss. Jan99; HILO 151)> <cd re-mast.Feb03 on 'Capitol'+=; CAP 42679>* – Ride Sally ride / True love / I'll be standing by.

Dec 71. (7") *(HLU 10348)* *<2202>* **LET'S STAY TOGETHER. / TOMORROW'S DREAM** [7] Nov71 [1]

Mar 72. (lp) *(SHU 8430)* *<32070>* **LET'S STAY TOGETHER** [ ] Feb72 [8]
– Let's stay together / La-la for you / So you're leaving / What is this feeling / Old time lovin' / I've never found a girl / How can you mend a broken heart / Judy / It ain't no fun to me. *(re-iss. Jul86 on 'Hi' lp/cd; HIUK LP/CD 405) <(cd-iss. Nov98; HILO 152)> <cd re-mast.Feb03 on 'Capitol'+=; CAP 42678>* – Eli's game / Listen.

Mar 72. (7") *<2211>* **LOOK WHAT YOU DONE FOR ME. / LA-LA FOR YOU** [–] [4]

May 72. (7") *(HLU 10369)* **LOOK WHAT YOU DONE FOR ME. / I'VE NEVER FOUND A GIRL** [44] [–]

Jul 72. (7") *(HLU 10382)* *<2216>* **I'M STILL IN LOVE WITH YOU. / OLD TIME LOVIN'** [35] Jun72 [3]

Oct 72. (7") *(HLU 10393)* *<2227>* **YOU OUGHT TO BE WITH ME. / WHAT IS THIS FEELING** [ ] [3]

Dec 72. (lp) *(SHU 8443)* *<32074>* **I'M STILL IN LOVE WITH YOU** [ ] Oct72 [4]
– I'm still in love with you / I'm glad you're mine / Love and happiness / What a wonderful thing love is / Simply beautiful / Oh, pretty woman / For the good times / Look what you done for me / One of these good old days. *(re-iss. Jul86 on 'Hi'; HIUKLP 407) <(cd-iss. Nov98; HILO 153)> <cd re-mast.Feb03 on 'Capitol'+=; CAP 42677>* – I think it's for the feeling / Up above my head.

Feb 73. (7") *(HLU 10406)* *<2235>* **CALL ME (COME BACK HOME). / WHAT A WONDERFUL THING LOVE IS** [ ] [10]

Apr 73. (7") *(HLU 10419)* **LOVE AND HAPPINESS. / SO YOU'RE LEAVING** [ ] [–]

Jul 73. (7") *(HLU 10426)* *<2247>* **HERE I AM (COME AND TAKE ME). / I'M GLAD YOU'RE MINE** [ ] Jun73 [10]

Nov 73. (lp) *(SHU 8457)* *<32077>* **CALL ME** [ ] May73 [10]
– Call me (come back home) / Have you been making out o.k. / Stand up / I'm so lonesome I could cry / Your love is like the morning sun / Here I am (come and take me) / You ought to be with me / Jesus is waiting. *(re-iss. Jul86 on 'Hi'; HIUKLP 409) <(cd-iss. Nov98; HILO 154)>*

Jan 74. (7") *(HLU 10443)* *<2257>* **LIVIN' FOR YOU. / IT AIN'T NO FUN TO ME** [ ] Dec73 [19]

Apr 74. (lp) *(SHU 8464)* *<32082>* **LIVIN' FOR YOU** [ ] Dec73 [24]
– Livin' for you / Home again / Free at last / Let's get married / So good to be here / My sweet sixteen / Unchained melody / My God is real / Beware. *(re-iss. Jul86 on 'Hi'; HIUKLP 411) <(cd-iss. Mar99; HILO 155)>*

Apr 74. (7") *(HLU 10452)* *<2262>* **LET'S GET MARRIED. / SO GOOD TO BE HERE** [ ] Mar74 [32]

Oct 74. (7") *(HLU 10470)* *<2274>* **SHA-LA-LA (MAKE ME HAPPY). / SCHOOL DAYS** [20] Sep74 [7]

Dec 74. (lp) *(SHU 8479)* *<32087>* **AL GREEN EXPLORES YOUR MIND** [ ] Nov74 [15]
– Sha-la-la (make me happy) / Take me to the river / God blessed our love / The city / One nite stand / Stay with me forever / Hangin' on / School days. *(re-iss. Sep86 on 'Hi' lp/cd; HIUK LP/CD 413) <(cd-iss. Mar99; HILO 156)>*

Feb 75. (7") *(HLU 10482)* *<2282>* **L-O-V-E. (LOVE). / I WISH YOU WERE HERE WITH ME** [24] [13]

Jul 75. (7") *(HLU 10493)* *<2288>* **OH ME, OH MY (DREAMS IN MY ARMS). / STRONG AS DEATH (SWEET AS LIFE)** [ ] [48]

Oct 75. (lp) *(SHU 8488)* *<32092>* **AL GREEN IS LOVE** [ ] Sep75 [28]
– L.O.V.E. (love) / Rhymes / The love sermon / There is love / Could I be the one / Love ritual / I didn't know / Oh me, oh my (dreams in my heart) / I wish you were here. *(re-iss. Jul86 on Hi'; HIUKLP 415) <(cd-iss. Jun99; HILO 157)>*

Nov 75. (7") *(HLU 10511)* <2300> **FULL OF FIRE. / COULD I BE THE ONE** [ ] [28]
Mar 76. (lp) *(SHU 8493)* <32097> **FULL OF FIRE** [ ] [59]
– Glory glory / That's the way it is / Always / There's no way / I'd fly away / Full of fire / Together again / Soon as I get home / Let it shine. *(re-iss. Sep86 on 'Hi'; HIUKLP 417) <(cd-iss. Jun99; HILO 158)>*
May 76. (7") *(HLU 10527)* <2306> **LET IT SHINE. / THERE'S NO WAY** [ ] [ ]
Oct 76. (7") *(HLU 10542)* <2319> **KEEP ME CRYIN'. / THERE IS LOVE** [ ] [37]
Dec 76. (lp) *(SHU 8505)* <32103> **HAVE A GOOD TIME** [ ] Nov76 [93]
– Keep on cryin' / Smile a little bit more / I tried to tell myself / Something / The truth marches on / Have a good time / Nothing takes the place of you / Happy / Hold on forever. *(re-iss. Jul86 on 'Hi'; HIUKLP 419)*
Apr 77. (7") <2322> **I TRIED TO TELL MYSELF. / SOMETHING** [–] [ ]
May 77. (7"ep) **I TRIED TO TELL MYSELF / SOMETHING. / WHAT AM I GONNA DO WITH MYSELF / SUMMERTIME** [ ] [–]
Nov 77. (7") <2324> **LOVE AND HAPPINESS. / GLORY GLORY** [–] [ ]
Jan 78. (lp) <6009> **TRUTH 'N' TIME** [–] [ ]
– Blow me down / Lo and behold / Wait here / To sir with love / Truth 'n' time / King of all / Say a little prayer / Happy days. *<(cd-iss. Nov99; HILO 161)>*

— AL GREEN completely changed his backing musicians recruiting **JAMES BASS** – guitar / **RUEBEN FAIRFAX** – bass / **JOHNNY TONEY** – drums / **FRED JORDAN** – trumpet / **BUDDY JARRETT** – alto sax. / **RON ECHOLS** – baritone sax

Hi-Cream | Hi

Jan 78. (7") <77505> **BELLE. / CHARIOTS OF FIRE** [–] [83]
Aug 78. (7") <78511> **FEELS LIKE SUMMER. / I FEEL GOOD** [–] [ ]
Nov 78. (7") <78522> **TO SIR WITH LOVE. / WAIT HERE** [–] [ ]
Aug 79. (7") *(HCS 101)* **BELLE. / TO SIR WITH LOVE** [ ] [–]
Sep 79. (lp) <(6004)> **THE BELLE ALBUM** [ ] Dec77 [ ]
– Belle / Loving you / Feels like summer / Georgia boy / I feel good / Chariots of fire / All in all / Dream. *(re-iss. Nov86 on 'Hi'; HIUKLP 421) <(cd-iss. Nov99; HILO 160)>*
Jul 81. (d-lp/d-c) *(HCD/ZHCD 5001)* <6005> **TOKYO LIVE (live)** [ ] [ ]
– L.O.V.E. (love) / Tired of being alone / Let's stay together / How can you mend a broken heart / All n all / Belle / Sha-la-la (make me happy) / Let's get married / God blessed our love / You ought to be with me / For the good times / Dream / I feel good / Love and happiness. *(re-iss. Aug87; 8302 ML2) (cd-iss. Mar90; HIUKCD 104) <(cd re-iss. Nov99; HILO 162)>*

— The Rev. now used mainly session people and gospel backing singers.

Hi | Hi

Feb 82. (lp/c) *<(HLP/ZCHLP 6006)>* **HIGHER PLANE** [ ] [ ]
– Where love rules / Amazing Grace / His name is Jesus / Battle hymn of the republic / Higher plane / People get ready / By my side / Amazing grace / The spirit might come – on and on. *(re-iss. Nov86; HIUKLP 431)*
Nov 82. (lp) *<(HLP 6007)>* **PRECIOUS LORD** [ ] [ ]
– Glory to his name / Rock of ages / In the garden / Hallelujah (I just want to praise the Lord) / Precious Lord / What a friend we have in Jesus / The old rugged cross / Morningstar / How great thou art. *(re-iss. Nov86; HIUKLP 429)*
Feb 85. (lp) *(HIUKLP 423)* **TRUST IN GOD** [ ] [ ]
– Don't it make you wanna go home / Trust in God / Holy Spirit / Up the ladder to the roof / Ain't no mountain high enough / No not one / Lean on me / Never met anybody like you / Trust in God (reprise) / All we need is a little more love. *(cd-iss. Jul86; HIUKCD 423)*
Feb 85. (7") *(UK45 7003)* **NEVER MET NOBODY LIKE YOU. / HIGHER PLANE** [ ] [–]

A&M | A&M

Nov 85. (7") <2786> **GOING AWAY. / BUILDING UP** [–] [ ]
Nov 85. (lp/c) *<(AMA/AMC 5120)>* **GOING AWAY** [ ] [ ]
– Going away / True love / He is the light / I feel like going on / Be with me Jesus / You brought the sunshine / Power / Building up / Nearer my God to thee.
Jan 86. (7") *(AM 302)* **TRUE LOVE. / YOU BROUGHT THE SUNSHINE** [ ] [–]
(12"+=) *(AMY 302)* – Going away.
Jan 86. (7") <2807> **TRUE LOVE. / HE IS THE LIGHT** [–] [ ]
Feb 87. (7") <2919> **EVERYTHING'S GONNA BE ALRIGHT. / SO REAL TO ME** [–] [ ]
Apr 87. (lp/c) *<(AMA/AMC 5150)>* **SOUL SURVIVOR** [ ] [ ]
– Everything's gonna be alright / Jesus will fix it / You know and I know / Yield not to temptation / So real to me / Soul survivor / You've got a friend / He ain't heavy / 23rd psalm.
Jun 87. (7") <2952> **YOU KNOW AND I KNOW. / TRUE LOVE** [–] [ ]
Sep 87. (7") <2962> **SOUL SURVIVOR. / JESUS WILL FIX IT** [–] [ ]
Nov 88. (7"; ANNIE LENNOX & AL GREEN) *(AM 484)* <1255> **PUT A LITTLE LOVE IN YOUR HEART. / Spheres Of Celestial Influence: A GREAT BIG PIECE OF LOVE** [28] [9]
(12"+=/cd-s+=) *(AMY/CDEE 484)* – (2-'A'versions).

Breakout-A&M | Brreakout-A&M

Jun 89. (7") *(USA 654)* **AS LONG AS WE'RE TOGETHER. / BLESSED** [ ] [ ]
(12"+=) *(USAT 654)* – ('A'other mix).
Jun 89. (lp/c/cd) *(395228-1/-4/-2)* **I GET JOY** [ ] [ ]
– You're everything to me / All my praise / The end is near / Mighty clouds of joy / I get joy / As long as we're together / Praise him / Blessed / Tryin' to do the best I can / Tryin' to get over you.

— He provided the vocals on ARTHUR BAKER + BACKSTREET DISCIPLES Oct89 single THE MESSAGE IS LOVE.

— Co-writes w / **DAVID STEELE** (ex-BEAT). **ANDY COX** also appears and is co-producer. The song 'DON'T LOOK BACK' was written by SMOKEY ROBINSON, and featured CURTIS STIGERS. JOE ROBERTS + A.GLASS wrote 'Fountain of Love'. LOVE IN MOTION was a cover, as was his single below, which was penned by S.SWIRSKY.

Word | Word

Apr 92. (cd/c) *(7019271 60X/502)* **LOVE IS REALITY** [ ] [ ]
– Just can't let you go / I can feel it / Love is reality / Positive attitude / Again / Sure feels good / I like it / You don't know me / A long time / A lone time / Why (with DON BYAS).

Arista | R.C.A.

Sep 93. (7"/c-s) *(74321 16269-7/-4)* **LOVE IS A BEAUTIFUL THING. / ('A'mix)** [56] [ ]
(12"+=/cd-s+=) *(74321 16269-6/-2)* – ('A'mixes).
Sep 93. (cd/c/lp) *(74321 16310-2/-4/-1)* **DON'T LOOK BACK** [ ] [ ]
– Best love / Love is a beautiful thing / Waiting on you / What does it take / Keep on pushing love / You are my everything / One love / People in the world (keep on lovin' you) / Give it everything / Your love (is more than I ever hoped for) / Fountain of love / Don't look back / Love in motion. *(cd re-iss. Feb97; same)*
Mar 94. (7"/c-s) *(74321 19694-7/-4)* **KEEP ON PUSHING LOVE. / ('A'mix)** [ ] [ ]
(12"+=/cd-s+=) *(74321 19694-1/-2)* – ('A'mix).

— In May 94, AL did duet 'Funny How Time Slips Away' with LYLE LOVETT on 'Geffen' c-s/cd-s; (MCS C/TD 1974). Originally a 1962 hit for JIMMY ELLEDGE.

Jul 94. (c-s) *(74321 19349-4)* **WAITING ON YOU. / ('A'mix)** [ ] [ ]
(12"+=/cd-s+=) *(74321 19349-1/-2)* – (2-'A'mixes).

not iss. | M.C.A.

Nov 95. (cd) <AAMCAD 11350> **YOUR HEART'S IN GOOD HANDS** [–] [ ]
– Your heart's in good hands / Keep on pushing love / Could this be love / Love is a beautiful thing / On love / Don't look back / The best love / Your love (is more than I ever hoped for) / What does it take / People in the world (keep on lovin' you). *(UK-iss.Mar03; same as US)*

Blue Note | Blue Note

Nov 03. (cd/d-lp) <(5 93556-2/-1)> **I CAN'T STOP** [ ] [53]
– I can't stop / Play to win / Rainin' in my heart / I've been waitin' on you / You / Not tonight / Million to one / My problem is you / I'd still choose you / I've been thinkin' 'bout you / I'd write a letter / Too many.

– compilations, etc. –

on 'Hi' unless mentioned otherwise

Sep 72. (lp) *Bell;* <6076> **AL GREEN** (early recordings) [–] [ ]
Sep 72. (7") *Bell;* <45258> **GUILTY. / LET ME HELP YOU** [–] [69]
Jan 73. (7") *Bell;* <45305> **HOT WIRE. / DON'T LEAVE ME** [–] [71]
Mar 75. (lp) *London; (SHU 8481) / Hi;* <32089> **AL GREEN'S GREATEST HITS** [18] Mar75 [17]
– Let's stay together / I can't get next to you / You ought to be with me / Look what you done to me / Let's get married / Tired of being alone / Call me / I'm still in love with you / Here I am (come and take me) / How can you mend a broken heart. *(re-iss. Jul86 on 'Hi' lp/c/cd; HIUK LP/CASS/CD 425)*

Jul 77. (lp) *<32105>* **GREATEST HITS VOL.2** –
(UK-iss.Oct87 as 'TAKE ME TO THE RIVER – GREATEST HITS VOL.2' on 'Hi' lp/c/cd; HIUK LP/CASS/CD 438)

Jan 80. (lp/c) *Cream; (HLPC/ZCHLP 101)* **THE CREAM OF AL GREEN** –

Jan 80. (7"/12") *Cream; (HCS/12HCS 102)* **TIRED OF BEING ALONE. / HOW CAN YOU MEND A BROKEN HEART** –

May 81. (lp) *Myrrh; (MYR 1109)* **THE LORD WILL MAKE A WAY**
– Highway to heaven / Pass me not / The Lord will make a way / Too close / None but the righteous / I have a friend above all others / Saved / In the holy name of Jesus. *(re-iss. Jul86 on 'Hi'; HIUKLP 433)*

Oct 81. (d-lp/d-c) *P.R.T.; (SPOT/ZCSPT 1016)* **SPOTLIGHT ON AL GREEN** –

1984. (7") *Cream; (HCS 107)* **TIRED OF BEING ALONE. / LET'S STAY TOGETHER**
(12"+=) *(12HCS 107)* – How can you mend a broken heart.

Sep 85. (7") *(HIUK45 7001)* **LET'S STAY TOGETHER. / I'M STILL IN LOVE WITH YOU** –
(12"+=) *(HIUK45T 7001)* – You ought to be with me.

Jul 86. (lp) *(HIUKLP 425)* **THE BEST OF AL GREEN**

Jul 86. (lp) *(XHIUKLP 437)* **WHITE CHRISTMAS**
(cd-iss. Nov95 +=; HILOCD 21) – (extra tracks).

Sep 88. (lp/c/cd) *K-Tel; (NE1/CD2/NCD3 420)* **HI LIFE – THE BEST OF AL GREEN** 34 –

Mar 89. (lp/c/cd) *(HIUK LP/CASS/CD 443)* **LOVE RITUAL – RARE AND PREVIOUSLY UNRELEASED (1968-76)**

Jun 90. (lp) *(HIUK 444)* **YOU SAY IT!** –

1990. (cd) *Word;* **ONE IN A MILLION** – –

Apr 91. (cd/c) *(HIUK CD/CASS 107* **COVER ME GREEN** –

May 91. (cd) *(HIUKCD 113)* **LIVIN' FOR YOU / AL GREEN EXPLORES YOUR MIND** –

May 91. (cd) *(HIUKCD 114)* **AL GREEN IS LOVE / FULL OF FIRE** –

Sep 91. (cd) *(HIUKCD 119)* **HAVE A GOOD TIME / THE BELLE ALBUM** –

Apr 92. (cd/c) *(HIUK CD/CASS 130)* **THE SUPREME AL GREEN: THE GREATEST HITS** –
– Tired of being alone / I can't get next to you / Let's stay together / How can you mend a broken heart / Love & happiness / I'm still in love with you / Simply beautiful / What a wonderful thing love is / Call me (come back home) / My God is real / Let's get married / Sha-la-la (make me happy) / Take me to the river / Love ritual / L-O-V-E / I didn't know / Full of fire / Belle.

Oct 92. (cd; AL GREEN & ACE CANNON) *(HIUKCD 126)* **CHRISTMAS CHEERS**

Nov 92. (cd/c/lp) *Beechwood; (AGREE CD/MC/LP 1)* **AL** 41 –

Jul 93. (cd) *(HIUKCD 141)* **THE FLIP SIDE OF AL GREEN**

May 95. (cd) *Universal; (E 540255-2)* **. . .AND THE MESSAGE IS LOVE** –

Feb 97. (3xcd-box) *(HIBOOK 12)* **A DEEP SHADE OF GREEN**

Aug 98. (cd) *<(HEX 35)>* **THE HI MASTERS**

Sep 98. (cd/lp) *D.C.C.; (CDZ/LPZ 2058)* **GREATEST HITS** –

Oct 98. (d-cd) *<(HEXD 41)>* **HI AND MIGHTY – THE STORY OF AL GREEN (1969-78)**

Mar 99. (cd) *Music Club; (MCCD 378)* **TRUE LOVE (A COLLECTION)** –

Jul 00. (d-cd) *<(HEXD 52)>* **THE HI SINGLES A'S AND B'S**

Sep 00. (cd) *(HIUKCD 251)* **LISTEN – THE RARITIES** –

Apr 01. (cd) *Spectrum; (544294-2)* **THE GOSPEL COLLECTION** –

Aug 01. (3xcd-box+book) *(FBOOK 26)* **LOVE AND HAPPINESS** –

Aug 01. (cd) *Capitol; <33603>* **FEELS LIKE CHRISTMAS** –

Sep 01. (cd) *A&M; <(493122-2)>* **TESTIFY: THE BEST OF THE A&M YEARS**
– Put a little love in your heart (with ANNIE LENNOX) / Going away / True love / I feel like going on / You brought the sunshine / Power / Building up / Everything's gonna be alright / You know and I know / You've got a friend / He ain't heavy (he's my brother) / Soul survivor / You're everything to me / Mighty clouds of joy / As long as we're together / Tryin' to do the best I can / I get joy / So real to me.

Oct 01. (cd) *Music Club; (MCCD 476)* **THE VERY BEST OF AL GREEN** –

Jun 02. (cd) *<(HILO 189)>* **THE LORD WILL MAKE A WAY / HIGHER PLANE**

Aug 02. (cd) *<(HILO 190)>* **PRECIOUS LORD / I'LL RISE AGAIN**

Sep 02. (cd) *(HIUKCD 252)* **UNCHAINED MELODIES** –

Oct 02. (cd) *<(HILO 191)>* **TRUST IN GOD / WHITE CHRISTMAS**

Feb 02. (d-cd) *<(ALTV 2002)>* **LOVE: THE ESSENTIAL AL GREEN** 18 Feb04
– I can't get next to you / Tired of being alone / Look what you done for me / Let's stay together / What am I gonna do with myself / Light my fire / I've never found a girl / I'm still in love with you / How can you mend a broken heart / What a wonderful thing love is / You ought to be with me / Call me (come back home) / Judy / Here I am (come and take me) / I wish you were here / Lean on me / I'm hooked on you / Simply beautiful / L.O.V.E. / Livin' for you / Love and happiness / My girl / Take me to the river / Sha la la (makes me happy) / Let's get married / Oh me oh my (dreams in my arms) / Full of fire / Have a good time / Let it shine / Could I be the one / Keep me cryin' / I tried to tell myself / Belle / Love is a beautiful thing / The message is love (with ARTHUR BAKER).

Peter GREEN

Born: 29 Oct'46, Bethnal Green, London, England. Early in 1966, he joined PETER B'S LOONERS (aka with PETER BARDENS; future CAMEL), who cut one 'Columbia' 45, 'IF YOU WANNA BE HAPPY' / 'JODRELL BLUES', before evolving into SHOTGUN EXPRESS (who boasted a young ROD STEWART on vocals) in May '66. GREEN's tenure only lasted a few months, however, the guitarist subsequently replacing ERIC CLAPTON in JOHN MAYALL's BLUESBREAKERS. GREEN appeared on the album, 'A Hard Road', but by summer 1967 he was on the move again, forming FLEETWOOD MAC along with MICK FLEETWOOD. Initially going under the moniker PETER GREEN'S FLEETWOOD MAC, the group gained considerable credibility in both the blues field and the charts with a string of Top 10 albums and Top 3 singles. GREEN was the chief songwriter and his early 'MAC compositions remain among the most enduring of that band's long and pockmarked career. Songs like 'BLACK MAGIC WOMAN', 'ALBATROSS', 'OH WELL' and 'MAN OF THE WORLD'. The guitarist's spare, incredibly intuitive interpretation of the blues was almost unique for a skinny white kid and the latter track was all the more poignant for its portrayal of GREEN's precarious emotional state. Like many great artists before him, it seemed that GREEN's genius traversed a parallel borderline with mental fragmentation and following a final howl at his demons (real or imagined) with the spine-chilling 'GREEN MANALISHI', the guitarist left FLEETWOOD MAC in early 1970 (and, in line with his new religious beliefs, stated his intention to give away all royalties to charity). While many rockstars have been flippantly written off as "acid casualties", the devastating effect of LSD on GREEN was all too real and has been well documented over the years, one of the most tragic tales in rock that ultimately saw PETER alternating between the street and a mental home. Following his departure from FLEETWOOD MAC, he deliberately distanced himself from the machinations of the music industry, refusing press interviews etc., although he did release a lacklustre solo debut effort, 'END OF THE GAME', later that year. This stodgy collection of blues jams gained little support from the critics or buying public and following a brief reunion with FLEETWOOD MAC on an American tour, GREEN went to ground. Details of the subsequent six years are hazy to say the least, with rumours abounding as to GREEN's activities and whereabouts. It seems he gave away his guitar as well as growing his fingernails and beard, working on a kibbutz in Israel for a while, before taking up various menial jobs in England (i.e. grave-digger, hospital porter, etc.), but little was heard of his low-key activities until . . . early in 1977, he was tragically committed to a mental hospital after returning an unwanted royalty cheque with rifle in hand, to his accountant. (No doubt subtlely wanting to re-form SHOTGUN EXPRESS). This signalled the beginning of GREEN's intermittent periods of hospital treatment for his mental problems although he enjoyed a brief flurry of recording activity at the turn of the decade; in 1978, he signed a new solo contract with 'P.V.K.', surprisingly hitting the UK Top 40 with albums 'IN THE SKIES' (1979) and 'LITTLE DREAMER' (1980). After a final effort in 1983, 'KOLORS', little was heard from GREEN bar the odd insensitive tabloid feature centering on his haggard, unkempt appearance, the guitarist seemingly having hit rock bottom (with rumours that he was sleeping rough in Richmond). More positively, GREEN has made something of a comeback with his SPLINTER BAND, apparently the first time he's picked up a guitar in years, having to relearn many parts from scratch. He even toured with the outfit in 1996, playing to fans who'd literally waited decades to see him. One of those fans was veteran bluesman B.B. KING with whom GREEN subsequently enjoyed an onstage jam. Two volumes of ROBERT JOHNSON songs, 'THE ROBERT JOHNSON SONGBOOK' (1998) and 'HOT FOOT POWDER' (2000), found GREEN teaming up with longtime collaborator NIGEL WATSON and paying charmingly indolent if heartfelt homage to one of his idols, while studio sets such as 'TIME TRADERS' (2001) and 'REACHING THE COLD 100' (2003) were further testament to the man's untapped reservoir of talent.

Album rating: THE END OF THE GAME (*4) / IN THE SKIES (*5) / LITTLE DREAMER (*5) / WHATCHA GONNA DO (*4) / BLUE GUITAR (*4) / WHITE SKY (*4) / KOLORS (*4) / LEGEND (*4) / PETER GREEN 'Backtrackin'' compilation (*6) / Peter Green Splinter Group: SPLINTER GROUP (*6) / THE ROBERT JOHNSON SONGBOOK with Nigel Watson (*5) / SOHO SESSION (*5) / DESTINY ROAD (*5) / HOT FOOT POWDER with Nigel Watson Splinter Group (*4) / TIME TRADERS (*5) / REACHING THE COLD 100 (*4)

PETER GREEN – guitar, vocals / with **ZOOT MONEY** – piano / **NICK BUCK** – keyboards / **ALEX DMOCHOWSKI** – bass / **GODFREY MacLEAN** – drums

Reprise | Reprise

Nov 70. (lp) *(RSLP 9006)* **THE END OF THE GAME**
– Bottoms up / Timeless time / Descending scales / Burnt foot / Hidden depths / The end of the game. *(re-iss. 1972; K 44106) (<cd-iss. Jan96; 7599 26758-2>)*

Jun 71. (7") *(RS 27012)* **HEAVY HEART. / NO WAY OUT**
(re-iss. Nov71; K 14092)

Jan 72. (7"; by PETER GREEN & NIGEL WATSON) *(K 14141)* **BEASTS OF BURDEN./ UGANDA WOMAN**

— Between 1971-78 PETER concentrated on religious activities, and after a time recovering in a mental hospital in 1977, he was gladly making a comeback with **SNOWY WHITE** – guitar / **PETER BARDENS** – keyboards / **KUMA HARADA** – bass and **REG ISADORE** – drums (all mainly on following album) (first 45 below quickly withdrawn)

P.V.K. | Sail

Jun 78. (7"w-drawn) *(PV 16)* **THE APOSTLE. / TRIBAL DANCE** | | –

May 79. (lp,green-lp) *(PVLS 101)* **IN THE SKIES** | 32 | –
– In the skies / Slaybo day / A fool no more / Tribal dance / Seven stars / Funky chunk / Just for you / Proud Pinto / The apostle. *(cd-iss. 1988 on 'Creole'; 823793) (<cd re-iss. Jun96 on 'Rhino'; RNCD 1001>) (cd re-iss. Feb01 on 'EMI Plus'; 576028-2)*

Jun 79. (7") *(PV 24)* **IN THE SKIES. / PROUD PINTO**

— Continued to work with noted session people, too numerous to mention

Apr 80. (lp) *(PVLS 102)* <0112> **LITTLE DREAMER** | 34 | Oct80
– Loser two times / Momma don'tcha cry / Born under a bad sign / I could not ask for more / Baby when the sun goes down / Walkin' the road / One woman love / Cryin' won't bring you back / Little dreamer. *(cd-iss. Jun96 on 'Rhino'; RNCD 1002)*

Apr 80. (7") *(PV 36)* **WALKIN' THE ROAD. / WOMAN DON'T** | | –

Jun 80. (7"w-drawn) *(PV 41)* **LOSER TWO TIMES. / MOMMA DONTCHA CRY** | – | –

Mar 81. (lp) *(PET 1)* **WHATCHA GONNA DO** | | –
– Gotta see her tonight / Promised land / Bullet in the sky / Give me back my freedom / Last train to San Antone / To break your heart / Bizzy Lizzy / Lost my love / Like a hot tomato / Head against the wall. *(cd-iss. Feb93 on 'Rhino';)*

Mar 81. (7") *(PV 103)* **GIVE ME BACK MY FREEDOM. / LOST MY LOVE**

Jul 81. (7") *(PV 112)* **PROMISED LAND. / BIZZY LIZZY** | | –

Headline | not iss.

Jun 82. (lp/c) *(HED/+C 1)* **WHITE SKY** | | –
– Time for me to go / Shining star / The clown / White sky (love that evil woman) / It's gotta be me / Born on the wild side / Fallin' apart / Indian lover / Just another guy. *(cd-iss. Nov92 & Jun96 on 'Rhino'; RNCD 1004)*

Jun 82. (7") *(LIN 2)* **THE CLOWN. / TIME FOR ME TO GO** | | –

Nov 83. (lp/c) *(HED/+C 2)* **KOLORS** | | –
– What am I doing here / Bad bad feelings / Big boy now / Black woman / Bandit / Same old blues / Liquor and you / Gotta do it with me / Funky jam. *(cd-iss. Nov92 on 'Rhino'; RNCD 1005)*

Creole | not iss.

1984. (7") *(614035)* **BIG BOY. / BANDIT** | | –

— Virtually retired from the biz in '86 after a recording session with MICK GREEN (ex-PIRATES)

PETER GREEN SPLINTER GROUP

— **PETER GREEN** – guitar, vocals; with **NIGEL WATSON** – guitars, vocals / **ROGER COTTON** – keyboards, vocal / **NEIL MURRAY** – bass / **LARRY TOLFREE** – drums

Snapper | Artisan

May 97. (d-cd/d-c) *(SAR CD/MC 101)* **SPLINTER GROUP** | 71 | –
– Hitch hiking woman / Travelling riverside blues / Look on yonder wall / Homework / Stumble / Help me / Watch your stepm / From 4 till late / Steady rolling man / It takes time / Dark end of the street / Going down. *(d-cd re-iss. Feb00; SMMCD 590) <US-iss.2000 on 'Original'; 15590>*

May 98. (cd; with NIGEL WATSON) *(SARCD 002)* <10002-2> **THE ROBERT JOHNSON SONGBOOK** | 57 |
– When you got a good friend / 32-20 blues / Phonograph blues / Last fair deal gone down / Stop breakin' down blues / Terraplane blues / Walkin' blues / Love in vain blues / Ramblin' on my mind / Stones in my passway / Me and the Devil blues / Honeymoon blues / Kind hearted woman blues / I believe I'll dust my broom / If I had possession over judgement day / Sweet home Chicago. *(re-iss. Sep03; SDPCD 141)*

Mar 99. (d-cd) *(SDDCD 816)* **SOHO SESSION (live)** | | –
– It takes time / Homework / Black magic woman / Indians / Hey mama keep your big mouth shut / The supernatural / Rattlesnake shake / Shake your hips / Albatross // Travelling Riverside blues / Steady rollin' man / Terraplane blues / Honeymoon blues / Last fair deal gone down / If I had possession over judgement day / Green manalishi / Goin' down / Help me / Look over yonder wall. *(re-iss. Sep01; SMDCD 327)*

Jun 99. (cd) *(SMACD 817)* <12817> **DESTINY ROAD** | | Jul99
– A big change is gonna come / Say that you want to / Heart of stone / Tribal dance / Burglar / Turn your love away / Madison blues / I can't help myself / Indians / Hiding in shadows / There's a river / You'll be sorry someday. (

Apr 00. (cd; as PETER GREEN with NIGEL WATSON SPLINTER GROUP) *(SMACD 828)* **HOT FOOT POWDER** | | –
– I'm a steady rollin' man / From four until late / Dead shrimp blues / Little queen of spades / They're red hot / Preachin' blues / Hellhound on my trail / Travelling riverside blues / Malted cow / Milkcow's calf blues / Drunken hearted man / Cross road blues / Come on in my kitchen.

Eagle | Spitfire

Sep 01. (cd) *(EAGCD 193)* <3006> **TIME TRADERS** | | Oct01
– Until the well runs dry / Real world / Running after you / Shadow on my door / Lies / (Down the road of) Temptation / Downsize blues (repossess my body) / Feeling good / Time keeps slipping away / Wild dogs / Home / Underway / Uganda woman.

Feb 03. (cd) *(EAGCD 224)* <20004> **REACHING THE COLD 1000**
– Ain't nothin' gonna change it / Look out for yourself / Cool down / Dangerous man / Needs must the Devil drives / Must be a fool / Don't walk away / Can you tell me why (aka Legal fee) / Spiritual thief / I'm ready for you / Smile / Nice girl like you / When somebody cares. *(cd bonus+=)* – Black magic woman / It takes time / Green manalishi / Albatross.

– compilations, etc. –

Nov 81. (lp/c) *Creole; (CRX/+C 5)* **BLUE GUITAR** [ ] [-]
– Gotta see her tonight / Last train to San Antone / Woman don't / Whatcha gonna do / Walking in the road / The apostle / A fool no more / Loser two times / Slaybo day / Cryin' won't bring you back. *(cd-iss. Jun96 on 'Rhino'; RNCD 1003)*

Feb 86. (lp) *Homestead; <HMS 031>* **COME ON DOWN** [-] [ ]

Aug 87. (lp/cd) *Nightflite; (NTFL 2001)* **A CASE FOR THE BLUES** [ ] [-]
(cd-iss. Sep87 on 'Compact Company'; 74001) (cd re-iss. Jun99 on 'Saraja'; SARCD 007)

Jan 88. (lp/c/cd) *Creole; (CRX/+C/CD 12)* **LEGEND** [ ] [-]
– Touch my spirit / Six string guitar / Proud Pinto / The clown / You won't see me anymore / Long way from home / In the skies / Rubbing my eyes / What am I doing here? / Corner of my mind / Carry my love / Bandit / White skies. *(cd+=)* – Little dreamer. *(re-iss. cd Feb93 on 'Rhino'; RNCD 1009)*

Jan 90. (cd/c/d-lp) *Backtrackin'; (TRK CD/MC/LP 101)* **PETER GREEN** [ ] [-]
– In the skies / A fool no more / Tribal dance / Just for you / Born on the wild side / Proud Pinto / Shining star / Slaybo day / Indian lover / Carry my love / Corner of my mind / Cryin' won't bring you back / Little dreamer / Momma dontcha cry / Baby when the sun goes down / Born under a bad sign / Walkin' the road / Loser two times / What am I doing here / Big boy now / Time for me to go now / It's gonna be me / You won't see me anymore / Bad bad feeling.

Apr 91. (cd; by MICK GREEN with PETER GREEN & THE ENEMY WITHIN) *Red Lightnin'; (RLCD 0087)* **TWO GREENS MAKE A BLUES** [ ] [-]
(re-iss. Mar97 on 'Castle'; CLACD 426)

Jun 92. (cd/c/lp) *Creole; (FG 2/4/1 802)* **LAST TRAIN** [ ] [-]

Feb 93. (cd) *Disky; (PACD/PAMC 7013)* **ONE WOMAN LOVE** [ ] [-]

Jun 96. (cd/c) *Music Club; (MC CD/TC 244)* **GREEN AND GUITAR (BEST OF PETER GREEN)** [ ] [-]

Apr 97. (cd) *Milan; (74321 47464-2)* **BANDIT** [ ] [-]

May 97. (cd/c) *A-Play; (10064-2/-4)* **KATMANDU** [ ] [-]
(cd re-iss. May03 on 'Falcon'; UN 388-2)

Jun 97. (cd) *Appaloosa; (APCD 052)* **RARITIES** [ ] [-]

Feb 98. (cd) *Disky; (WB 88600-2)* **THE VERY BEST OF PETER GREEN** [ ] [-]

Jul 98. (cd/c) *K-Tel; (ECD2/EMC3 356)* **BORN ON THE WILD SIDE** [ ] [-]

Nov 98. (cd) *Laserlight; (CD 21064)* **IN THE SKIES / LITTLE DREAMER** [ ] [-]

Apr 01. (3xcd-box) *Snapper; (SMBCD 844)* **ME AND THE DEVIL** [ ] [-]

Jun 01. (cd) *Armoury; (ARMCD 047)* **A FOOL NO MORE** [ ] [-]

Jul 02. (d-cd) *Snapper; (SMADD 849)* **THE BEST OF PETER GREEN SPLINTER GROUP** [ ] [-]

May 03. (d-cd) *Snapper; (SMDCD 457)* **THE ROBERT JOHNSON SONGBOOK / HOT FOOT POWDER** [ ] [-]

GREEN DAY

Formed: Rodeo, nr. Berkeley, California, USA . . . early 90's out of The SWEET CHILDREN by BILLY JOE ARMSTRONG and MIKE DIRNT. When TRE COOL replaced BILLY JOE's sister ANA on drums, they became GREEN DAY, this line-up releasing their debut LP, '39 / SMOOTH', which was recorded in under 24 hours. Their third album, 'DOOKIE' (their first for 'Reprise'), was a surprise US smash in 1994 due to its college/MTV favourite, 'BASKET CASE'. Retro punk-rock for young Americans (and now older Brits) who missed out on BUZZCOCKS, DICKIES, RAMONES (and even earlier 60's pop outfit, the MONKEES), GREEN DAY became a phenomenon in the States; like the SEX PISTOLS' revolution all over again, without the danger, unpredictability and raw excitement. Instead we got formulaic, annoyingly and yes, inanely catchy punk retreads that took you way back to '77. Still, the multi-millions who bought the record ensured that GREEN DAY were indeed radio-friendly unit shifters. A follow-up set, 'INSOMNIAC' (1995), was another massive seller, although it had to compete with the hordes of equally faceless acts clogging up the charts with similar material. A fifth set, 'NIMROD' (1997), made sure they were still in touch with their fanbase, the tried and tested formula again getting them into the Top 10. The album also spawned a surprise hit single in the shape of a rare ballad, 'TIME OF YOUR LIFE (GOOD RIDDANCE)', geeing the band on to er, express their more feminine side, or at least their less frantic side. With 'WARNING' (2000), GREEN DAY went ahead and exorcised those pop demons which had clearly been haunting them since way back when. By investing their punk-pop formula with a measure of melodic sparkle and a hint of vintage 60's flavour, the 3-chord thumpers had come up with their most consistently listenable album to date. • **Songwriters:** Lyrics; BILLIE JOE, group songs except TIRED OF WAITING FOR YOU (Kinks). • **Trivia:** DIRNT guested on The SCREAMING WEASEL album, 'How to Make Enemies And Irritate People'. BILLIE JOE was also a member of PINHEAD GUNPOWDER, who released an album, 'Jump Salty', plus a few EP's (also for 'Lookout').

Album rating: 39/SMOOTHED OUT SLAPPY HOUR compilation (*5) / KERPLUNK! (*5) / DOOKIE (*7) / INSOMNIAC (*6) / NIMROD (*6) / WARNING (*6) / INTERNATIONAL SUPERHITS compilation (*7) / SHENANIGANS compilation (*6)

BILLIE JOE ARMSTRONG (b.17 Feb'72, San Pablo, Calif.) – vocals, guitar / **MIKE DIRNT** (b. PRITCHARD, 4 May'72) – bass, vocals / **TRE COOL** (b. FRANK EDWIN WRIGHT III, 9 Dec'72, Germany) – drums (ex-LOOKOUTS) repl. JOHN KIFTMEYER who had repl. AL SOBRANTE

not iss. Lookout

Apr 89. (7"ep) *<LK 17>* **1000 HOURS EP** [-] [ ]
– 1000 hours / Dry ice / Only of you / The one I want. *(UK-iss.Dec94; as above)*

Apr 90. (lp/c/cd) *<LO 22/+CS/CD>* **39 / SMOOTH** [-] [ ]
– At the library / Don't leave me / I was there / Disappearing boy / Green day / Going to Pasalacgua / 16 / Road to exceptance / Rest / The judge's daughter / Paper lanterns / Why do you want him? / 409 in your coffeemaker / Knowledge / 1000 hours / Dry ice / Only of you / The one I want / I want to be alone. *<re-iss. Nov91 lp/cd; LOOKOUT 22/+CD> (UK-iss.Sep94 as '1,039 / SMOOTHED OUT SLAPPY HOURS'; as above) (cd re-iss. Aug97 on 'Epitaph'; 6522-2)*

Mar 90. (7"ep) *<LK 35>* **SLAPPY EP** [-] [ ]
– Paper lanterns / Why do you want him? / 409 in your coffeemaker / Knowledge. *(UK-iss.Sep94; as above)*

Dec 91. (lp) *<LOOKOUT 46>* **KERPLUNK!** [-] [ ]
– 2000 light years away / One for the razorbacks / Welcome to Paradise / Christie Road / Private ale / Dominated love slave / One of my lies / 80 / Android / No one knows / Who wrote Holden Caulfield? / Words I might have ate. *(UK-iss.Sep94 on 'Lookout' lp/cd+=; LOOKOUT 46/+CD)* – Sweet children / Best thing in town / Strangeland / My generation. *(by SWEET CHILDREN and released US 1990 on 'Skene') (cd re-iss. Aug97 on 'Epitaph'; 6517-2)*

Reprise Reprise

Feb 94. (cd/c) *<(9362 45529-2/-4)>* **DOOKIE** [ ] [2]
– Burnout / Having a blast / Chump / Longview / Welcome to Paradise / Pulling teeth / Basket case / She / Sassafras roots / When I come around / Coming clean / Emenius sleepus / In the end / F.O.D. *(cd+=)* – (hidden track). *(re-dist.Oct94 on green-lp soon hit UK No.13; 9362 45795-2/-4)*

Jun 94. (7") *(W 0247)* **LONGVIEW. / ON THE WAGON** [ ] [-]
(10"/cd-s) *(W 0247 T/CD)* – ('A'side) / Going to Pasalacqua (infatuation) / F.O.D. (live) / Christy Road (live).

Aug 94. (7"green/c-s) *(W 0257/+C)* **BASKET CASE. / TIRED OF WAITING FOR YOU** [55] [-]
(cd-s+=) *(W 0257CD2)* – On the wagon / 409 in your coffeemaker.
(cd-s) *(W 0257CD)* – ('A'side) / Longview (live) / Burnout (live) / 2000 light years away (live).

Oct 94. (c-s) *(W 0269C)* **WELCOME TO PARADISE. / CHUMP (live)** [20] [-]
(12"green+=/cd-s+=/cd-s+=) *(W 0269 T/CD/CDX)* – Emenius sleepus.

Jan 95. (7"green/c-s) *(W 0279/+C)* **BASKET CASE. / 2,000 LIGHT YEARS AWAY (live)** [7] [-]
(cd-s+=) *(W 0279CD)* – Burnout (live) / Longview (live).

Mar 95. (7"/c-s) *(W 0278/+C)* **LONGVIEW. / WELCOME TO PARADISE (live)** | 30 | – |
(cd-s+=) *(W 0278CD)* – One of my lies (live).

May 95. (7"pic-d/c-s) *(W 0294/+C)* **WHEN I COME AROUND. / SHE (live)** | 27 | – |
(cd-s+=) *(W 0294CD)* – Coming clean (live).

Sep 95. (7"red/c-s) *(W 0320/+C)* **GEEK STINK BREATH. / I WANT TO BE ON T.V.** | 16 | – |
(cd-s+=) *(W 0320CD)* – Don't want to fall in love.

Oct 95. (cd/c/lp) *<(9362 46046-2/-4/-1)>* **INSOMNIAC** | 8 | 2 |
– Armatage Shanks / Brat / Stuck with me / Geek stink breath / No pride / Bab's Uvula who? / 86 / Panic song / Stuart and the Ave. / Brain stew / Jaded / Westbound sign / Tight wad hill / Walking contradiction.

Dec 95. (7") *(W 0327X)* **STUCK WITH ME. / WHEN I COME AROUND (live)** | 24 | – |
(c-s+=) *(W 0327C)* – Jaded (live).
(cd-s) *(W 0327CD)* – ('A'side) / Dominated love slave (live) / Chump (live).

Jun 96. (c-s) *(W 0339C)* **BRAIN STEW / JADED / TIME OF YOUR LIFE (GOOD RIDDANCE)** | 28 | – |
(cd-s+=) *(W 0339CD)* – Do da da.
(brain-shaped cd-s++=) *(W 0339CDX)* – Brain stew (radio).

Sep 97. (c-s) *(W 0424C)* *<43945>* **HITCHIN' A RIDE / SICK** | 25 | Jun98 | |
(cd-s+=) *(W 0424CD)* – Espionage.

Oct 97. (cd/c) *<(9362 46794-2/-4)>* **NIMROD** | 11 | 10 |
– Nice guys finish last / Hitchin' a ride / The grouch / Reduntant / Scattered / Worry rock / Desensitized / All the time / Platypus (I hate you) / Last ride in / Jinx / Haushinka / Walking alone / Suffocate / Uptight / Take back / King for a day / Good riddance / Prosthetic head.

Jan 98. (c-s) *(W 0430C)* *<43974>* **TIME OF YOUR LIFE (GOOD RIDDANCE) / DESENSITIZED** | 11 | Jun98 | |
(cd-s+=) *(W 0430CD1)* – Rotting.
(cd-s) *(W 0430CD2)* – ('A'side) / Suffocate / You lied.

Apr 98. (7") *(W 0438)* **REDUNDANT. / THE GROUCH (live)** | 27 | – |
(cd-s+=) *(W 0438CD1)* – Paper lanterns (live).
(cd-s) *(W 0438CD2)* – ('A'side) / Reject all American (live) / She (live).

Sep 00. (c-s) *(W 532C)* **MINORITY / BRAT (live)** | 18 | – |
(cd-s+=) *(W 532CD)* – 86 (live).
(7"ep iss.Nov00 on 'Adeline'+=; ADELINE 013) – Jackass.

Oct 00. (cd/c) *<(9362 48030-2/-4)>* **WARNING** | 4 | 4 |
– Warning / Blood, sex and booze / Church on Sunday / Fashion victim / Castaway / Misery / Deadbeat holiday / Hold on / Jackass / Waiting / Minority / Macy's day parade. *<US version+=; 47857>* – Brat (live) / 86 (live). *<(lp; 9362 47613-1)> <US lp-iss.Oct00 on 'Adeline'; ADELINE 012>*

Dec 00. (7"orange) *(W 548)* **WARNING. / SUFFOCATE** | 27 | – |
(c-s+=/cd-s+=) *(W 548 C/CD2)* – Outsider. *(7"iss.Feb01 on 'Adeline'; ADELINE 014)*
(cd-s) *(W 548CD1)* – ('A'side) / Scumbag / I don't want to know if you are lonely.

Oct 01. (cd-s) *(W 570CD)* **WAITING / MACY'S DAY PARADE / BASKET CASE** | 34 | – |
(cd-s) *(W 570CDX)* – ('A'side) / She / F.O.D.

Nov 01. (cd/c) *<(9362 48145-2/-4)>* **INTERNATIONAL SUPERHITS** (compilation) | 15 | 40 |
– Maria / Poprocks and coke / Longview / Welcome to paradise / Basket case / When I come around / She / J.A.R. (Jason Andrew Relva) / Geek stink breath / Brain stew / Jaded / Walking contradiction / Stuck with me / Hitchin' a ride / Good riddance (time of your life) / Reduntant / Nice guys finish last / Macy's day parade.

Jul 02. (cd/c) *<(9362 48208-2/-4)>* **SHENANIGANS** (B-sides, etc, compilation) | 32 | 27 |
– Suffocate / Desensitized / You lied / Outsider / Don't wanna fall in love / Espionage / I want to be on T.V. / Scumbag / Tired of waiting for you / Sick of me / Rotting / Do da da / On the wagon / Ha ha you're dead.

GREEN ON RED

Formed: Tucson, Arizona, USA ... 1979 by DAN STUART, CHRIS CACAVAS, JACK WATERSON and VAN CRISTIAN. The latter was replaced by ALEX MacNICOL prior to the release of their eponymous mini-lp for STEVE WYNN's 'Down There' label. Their debut album, 'GRAVITY TALKS' (1984), drew comparisons with NEIL YOUNG's more rocky outings, moving away from the ramshackle garage of their earlier releases. This influence was even more evident on their 1985 offering 'GAS FOOD LODGING', which featured the distinctive guitar style of the newly recruited CHUCK PROPHET. Signing to 'Mercury' the same year, they released the disappointing 'NO FREE LUNCH', an album that saw the band attempting a BYRDS-like country sound, and even included a WILLIE NELSON cover 'AIN'T IT FUNNY NOW'. After the similarly poor 'THE KILLER INSIDE ME' in 1987, the group disbanded although DAN and CHUCK re-formed, using session players to flesh out the sound. Always on the verge of a commercial breakthrough, they were dogged by label failures and by the time of 1989's 'HERE COME THE SNAKES', the band had signed to 'China' in the UK although the record, which showcased a bolshier, heavy guitar sound, was previously to have been issued in August '88 by the soon-to-be bust 'Red Rhino' records. Undaunted, the band played a blinding live set in London, documented on 'LIVE AT THE TOWN AND COUNTRY' (1989). The band issued another three albums (including AL KOOPER-produced 'SCAPEGOATS') to no commercial success and after the ironically titled 'TOO MUCH FUN' (1992), PROPHET and STUART went on to release well-received solo albums. • **More covers:** KNOCKIN' ON HEAVEN'S DOOR (Bob Dylan) / SMOKESTACK LIGHTNIN' (Howlin' Wolf) / RAINY DAYS AND MONDAYS (Carpenters).

Album rating: GREEN ON RED mini (*6) / GRAVITY TALKS (*7) / GAS FOOD LODGING (*8) / NO FREE LUNCH mini (*4) / THE KILLER INSIDE ME (*5) / HERE COME THE SNAKES (*7) / LIVE AT THE TOWN AND COUNTRY (*4) / THIS TIME AROUND (*6) / SCAPEGOATS (*5) / ROCK'N'ROLL DISEASE – THE BEST OF GREEN ON RED compilation (*7) / TOO MUCH FUN (*4) / Danny & Dusty: THE LOST WEEKEND (*5) / Dan Stuart: RETRONEUVO with Al Perry (*5) / CANO'WORMS (*5)

DAN STUART – vocals, guitar / **CHRIS CACAVAS** – keyboards, vocals / **JACK WATERSON** – bass / **ALEX MacNICOL** – drums; repl. VAN CRISTIAN who joined GIANT SAND

not iss. | Private

Jul 81. (ltd-12"red-ep) *<R-714>* **TWO BIBLES** | – | |
– Two bibles / La vida muerta / New world / Not today / A tragedy.

not iss. | Down There

Jul 82. (m-lp) *<71026>* **GREEN ON RED (UNTITLED)** | – | |
– Death and angels / Hair and skin / Black night / Illustrated crawling / Aspirin / Lost world / Apartment 6. *(UK-iss.Jun85 on 'Zippo'; ZANE 002)*

Slash | Slash

Aug 84. (lp) *(SR 207)* *<23964-1>* **GRAVITY TALKS** | | 1983 | |
– Gravity talks / Old chief / 5 easy pieces / Deliverance / Over my head / Snake bite / Blue parade / That's what you're here for / Brave generation / Abigail's ghost / Cheap wine / Narcolepsy. *(re-iss. Jan87 lp/c; SLM P/C 16) <(cd-iss. Jan03 on 'Wounded Bird'+=; WOU 3964)>* – Alice.

— added **CHUCK W. PROPHET** – steel guitar, vocals

Zippo | Enigma

May 85. (lp/c) *(ZONG/+CASS 005)* *<ST/4XT 73249>* **GAS FOOD LODGING** | | 1986 | |
– That's what dreams / Black river / Hair of the dog / This I know / Fading away / Easy way out / Sixteen ways / The drifter / Sea of Cortez / We shall overcome. *(cd-iss. 1990 on 'Enigma'; D2-73249)*

— **KEITH MITCHELL** – percussion repl. ALEX

Mercury | Mercury

Oct 85. (m-lp/m-c) *(MERM/+C 78)* *<82646-1>* **NO FREE LUNCH** | 99 | |
– Time ain't nothing / Honest man / Ballad of Guy Fawkes / No free lunch / Funny how time slips away / Jimmy boy / Keep on moving. *(c+=)* – Smokestack lightning.

Nov 85. (7") *(MER 202)* **TIME AIN'T NOTHING. / NO FREE LUNCH** | | – |

Feb 87. (7") *(GOR 1)* **CLARKSVILLE. / NO DRINKIN'** | | – |
(12"+=) *(GOR 1-12)* – Broken.

Mar 87. (lp/c)(cd) *(GOR LP/MC 1)(839122-2)* *<830912-2>* **THE KILLER INSIDE ME** | | |
– Clarksville / Mighty gun / Jamie / Whispering wind / Ghost hand / Sorry Naomi / No man's land / Track you down (his master's voice) / Born to fight / We ain't feee / The killer inside me. *(cd+=)* – NO FREE LUNCH (m-lp)

Jun 87. (7") *(GOR 2)* **BORN TO FIGHT. / DON'T SHINE YOUR LIGHT ON ME** ☐ -
(ext.12"+=) *(GOR 2-12)* – While the widow weeps.

— Disbanded late 1987, DAN and CHUCK reformed and brought in new sessioners. WATERSON released an album 'WHOSE DOG' in 1988, while CHRIS CACAVAS & THE JUNKYARD LOVE released self-titled one in 1989.

China Restless

Apr 89. (7") *(CHINA 16)* **KEITH CAN'T READ. / THAT'S THE WAY THE WORLD GOES ROUND / VAYA CON DIOS** ☐ -
(12") *(CHINX 16)* – (1st & 3rd tracks) / Tenderloin.

Apr 89. (lp/c/cd) *(839294-1/-4/-2) <72351-1>* **HERE COME THE SNAKES** ☐ ☐
– Keith can't read / Rock and roll disease / Morning blue / Zombie for love / Broken radio / Change / Tenderloin / Way back home / We had it all / D.T. blues.

Aug 89. (ltd; 10"lp/c) *(841013-0/-4)* **LIVE AT THE TOWN & COUNTRY CLUB (live)** ☐ -
– 16 ways / Change / DT blues / Fading away / Morning blue / Are you sure Hank done it this way / Zombie for love / Hair of the dog. *(c+=)* – Rock and roll disease / We had it all.

— duo now with **RENE COMAN** – upright bass, bass / **MIKE FINNEGAN** – keyboards / **DAVID KEMPER** – drums, percussion / plus **BERNIE LEADON** – mandolin, acoustic guitar (4) / **PAT DONALDSON** – bass (4) / **SPOONER OLDHAM** – piano (3)

China Catalina

Oct 89. (7") *(CHINA 21)* **THIS TIME AROUND. / FADING AWAY (live)** ☐ -
(12"+=/cd-s+=) *(CHINX/CHICD 21)* – 16 ways (live).

Nov 89. (lp/c/cd) *(841720-1/-4/-2) <841519-2>* **THIS TIME AROUND** ☐ -
– This time around / Cool million / Rev. Luther / Good patient woman / You couldn't get arrested / The quarter / Foot / Hold the line / Pills and booze / We're all waiting. *(free-7"w.a.)* – MORNING BLUE / ROCK AND ROLL DISEASE. / (interview) *(re-iss. Jul91 cd/c; WOL CD/MC 1019)*

Dec 89. (7") *(CHINA 22)* **YOU COULDN'T GET ARRESTED. / BROKEN RADIO** ☐ -
(ext.12"/ext.cd-s) *(CHINX/CHICD 22)* – Hair of the dog.

— DAN and CHUCK recruit **MICHAEL RHODES** – bass / **DAREN HESS** – drums

China China

Mar 91. (7") *(WOK 2001)* **LITTLE THINGS IN LIFE. / CHERRY KIND** ☐ -
(12"+=/cd-s+=) *(WOK 2001 T/CD)* – Sun goes down / Waiting for love.

Mar 91. (cd/c/lp) *<(WOL CD/MC/LP 1001)>* **SCAPEGOATS** ☐ ☐
– A guy like me / Little things in life / Two lovers (waitin' to die) / Gold in the graveyard / Hector's out / Shed a tear (for the lonesome) / Blowfly / Sun goes down / Where the rooster crows / Baby loves her gun.

Jun 91. (7") *(WOK 2002)* **TWO LOVERS (WAITIN' TO DIE). / KEITH CAN'T READ** ☐ -

Sep 91. (cd/c/lp) *(WOL/+MC/CD 1021)* **THE BEST OF GREEN ON RED** (compilation) ☐ -
– Time ain't nothing / Born to fight / Hair of the dog / Keith can't read / Morning blue / This time around / Little things in life / You couldn't get arrested / That's what dreams / Zombie for love / Baby loves her gun.

— added **J.D. FOSTER**

Oct 92. (cd-ep) *(WOKCD 2029)* **SHE'S ALL MINE / TWO LOVERS (live) / BABY LOVES HER GUN (live) / LITTLE THINGS IN LIFE (live)** ☐ -

Oct 92. (lp/c/cd) *<(WOL/+MC/CD 1029)>* **TOO MUCH FUN** ☐ ☐
– She's all mine / Frozen in my headlights / Love is insane / Too much fun / The getaway / I owe you one / Man needs woman / Sweetest thing / Thing or two / Hands and knees / Wait and see / Rainy days and Mondays.

– compilations, others, etc. –

Sep 91. (cd/c) *Music Club; <(MC CD/TC 037)>* **THE LITTLE THINGS IN LIVE (live)** ☐ ☐

May 92. (cd) *Mau Mau; <(MAUCD 612)>* **GAS FOOD LODGING / GREEN ON RED** ☐ Jan96 ☐
<(re-iss. Aug03 on 'Restless'+=; REST 72999)> – (bonus 2).

Jun 94. (cd) *China; <(WOLCD 1047)>* **ROCK'N'ROLL DISEASE – THE BEST OF . . .** ☐ 1995 ☐
– Rock'n'roll disease / This time around / 16 ways (live) / Fading away (live) / Hair of the dog / Keith can't read / Morning blue / Zombie for love / Change / Tenderloin / You couldn't get arrested / Little things in life / Two lovers (waitin' to die) / Hector's out / Baby loves her gun / The quarter / She's all mine / Frozen in my headlights / Too much fun. *(re-iss. Jul99; 4509 96106-2)*

Dec 97. (cd/lp) *Corduroy; (CORD 026/+LP)* **ARCHIVES VOL.1: WHAT WERE WE THINKING** ☐ -
(cd re-iss. Aug99 on 'Normal'; NORMAL 194CD)

Dec 98. (cd) *Edsel; (EDCD 591)* **THIS TIME AROUND / TOO MUCH FUN** ☐ -

☐ GREEN RIVER (see under ⇒ PEARL JAM)

☐ Sid GRIFFIN (see under ⇒ LONG RYDERS)

Nanci GRIFFITH

Born: 6 Jul'53, Seguin, Texas, USA. This self-styled 'Folkabilly' poet/singer began performing from an early age, initially with her parents in the region's honky tonks and later on the Texas folk circuit, her pure, girly cute voice and girl-next-door appeal gaining her a sizeable following. After completing a degree in education at the University of Texas, GRIFFITH focused wholly on music, making her recording debut a year later in 1978 with 'THERE'S A LIGHT BEYOND THESE WOODS'. Released on the small independent label, 'B.F. Deal', the album was largely self-penned, introducing her talent for vivid storytelling and snapshot vignettes. It was another four years before she recorded a follow-up, 1982's 'POET IN MY WINDOW', released on another small label, 'Featherbed'. However, it wasn't until GRIFFITH signed with folk/country label, 'Philo', that her highly original singing/songwriting style began to develop significantly. Backed by established musicians like Irish (electric) lead guitarist PHIL DONNELLY and acoustic maestros such as LLOYD GREEN, ROY HUSKEY JR. and BELA FLECK, GRIFFITH cut her acclaimed 'ONCE IN A VERY BLUE MOON' (1985). Again the album consisted mainly of her own compositions, although there were a few fine covers including LYLE LOVETT's 'IF I WAS THE WOMAN YOU WANTED' and the exceptional PAT ALGER-penned title track after which NANCI would subsequently name the backing band she formed the following year, The BLUE MOON ORCHESTRA. 1986 also saw the release of the Grammy Award winning (Best Folk Album) 'LAST OF THE TRUE BELIEVERS', KATHY MATTEA subsequently scoring a US country smash with one its tracks, the GRIFFITH-penned 'LOVE AT THE FIVE AND DIME'. The album was the first to be released in the UK through the independently distributed 'Demon' and the same year, 'Philo' re-released GRIFFITH's first two albums, her star firmly in the ascendant as she inked a new deal with M.C.A. The singer made her major label debut with 'LONE STAR STATE OF MIND' (1987), the most successful release of her career thus far and an album featuring two of her most famous tracks, the bittersweet reminiscence of the PAT ALGER/GENE LEVINE/FRED KOLLER-penned title track (a minor hit) and the crystal clear, definitive reading of JULIE GOLD's 'FROM A DISTANCE'. Other highlights numbered the re-recorded 'THERE'S A LIGHT BEYOND THESES WOODS (MARY MARGARET)' from the debut and ROBERT EARL KEEN JNR.'s 'SING ONE FOR SISTER'. 'LITTLE LOVE AFFAIRS' (1988) marked a new songwriting maturity, GRIFFITH creating a thematic continuity on the subject of love in various contexts, over the course of the album. After the live 'ONE FAIR SUMMER EVENING' (1988), GRIFFITH moved into moved into more AOR-esque territory with 'STORMS' (1989), recorded in

L.A. and produced by GLYN JOHNS, a man who's had a hand in some of the best albums in rock history. His midas touch gave NANCI her commercial breakthrough, in the UK at least, where the record made the Top 40. 'LATE NIGHT GRANDE HOTEL' (1991), continued in a similar vein, employing PETER VAN HOOKE and ROD ARGENT on production duties and adding strings to her primarily acoustic-based sound. Already a major star in Ireland (she's also contributed to a number of CHIEFTAINS releases) where she regularly has sell-out tours, GRIFFITH finally made the UK Top 20 in 1993 with 'OTHER VOICES, OTHER ROOMS', an album that saw a return to her folk/country roots. A tribute to her favourite songwriters, among the album's many highlights was a plaintive reading of JOHN PRINE's 'SPEED OF THE SOUND OF LONELINESS' as well as a sensitive cover of the late TOWNE VAN ZANDT's 'TECUMSHEH' valley, the record seeing GRIFFITH renewing her partnership with her early producer JIM ROONEY. More recently, 'THE FLYER' (1994) and 'BLUE ROSES FROM THE MOONS' (1997) have seen GRIFFITH consolidate her position as one of the most respected artists in the singer/songwriter/interpretor genre, alongside EMMYLOU HARRIS. Following on from 1998's cover set 'OTHER VOICES, TOO (A TRIP TO THE BOUNTIFUL)', GRIFFITH released the ambitious and not entirely successful 'DUST BOWL SYMPHONY' (1999). A brace of past favourites underscored by the London Symphony Orchestra, the record was a rather uncomfortable meeting of classical and country, formal and informal. 'CLOCK WITHOUT HANDS' (2001) found her back on more familiar, if not exactly inspiring, ground, her first set of wholly original material in almost five years. The live 'WINTER MARQUEE' (2002) was much more heartening, a back-to-the roots concert set with NANCI in fine voice, accompanied by EMMYLOU HARRIS and TOM RUSSELL, and covering the likes of Bob Dylan's 'BOOTS OF SPANISH LEATHER', Phil Och's 'WHAT'S THAT I HEAR' and Townes Van Zandt's 'WHITE FREIGHT LINER', as well as her trademark version of 'SPEED OF THE SOUND OF LONELINESS'. • **Covered:** DEADWOOD, SOUTH DAKOTA (Eric Taylor) / ROSEVILLE FAIR (Bill Staines) / HEAVEN (Julie Gold) / NEVER MIND (Harlan Howard) / BALLAD OF ROBIN WINTERSMITH (Richard Dobson) / LET IT SHINE ON ME (P.Kennerly) / NICKEL DREAMS (M.McAnally-D.Lowery) / THE SUN, MOON, AND STARS (Vince Bell) / SAN DIEGO SERENADE (Tom Waits). OTHER VOICES, OTHER ROOMS covers album; ACROSS THE GREAT DIVIDE (Kate Wolf) / WOMAN OF THE PHOENIX (Vince Bell) / TECUMSEH VALLEY (Townes Van Zandt) / THREE FLIGHTS UP (Frank Christian) / BOOTS OF SPANISH LEATHER (Bob Dylan) / FROM CLARE TO HERE (Ralph McTell) / CAN'T HELP BUT WONDER WHERE I'M BOUND (Tom Paxton) / DO RE MI (Woody Guthrie) / THIS OLD TOWN (Janis Ian) / COMIN' DOWN IN THE RAIN (Buddy Mondlock) / TEN DEGREES AND GETTING OLD (Gordon Lightfoot) / MORNING SONG FOR SALLY (Jerry Jeff Walker) / NIGHT RIDER'S LAMENT (Michael Burton) / ARE YOU TIRED OF ME DARLING (G.P.Cook & Ralph Roland) / TURN AROUND (Harry Belafonte) / WIMOWEH (c.Paul Campbell) / GRAVITY OF THE SITUATION with Hootie & The Blowfish (Vic Chesnutt) / etc.

Album rating: THERE'S A LIGHT BEYOND THESE WOODS (*4) / POET IN MY WINDOW (*4) / ONCE IN A VERY BLUE MOON (*6) / LAST OF THE TRUE BELIEVERS (*7) / LONE STAR STATE OF MIND (*7) / LITTLE LOVE AFFAIRS (*7) / ONE FAIR SUMMER EVENING (*7) / STORMS (*8) / LATE NIGHT GRANDE HOTEL (*7) / OTHER VOICES, OTHER ROOMS (*7) / THE BEST OF NANCI GRIFFITH compilation (*8) / FLYER (*7) / BLUE ROSES FROM THE MOON (*6) / OTHER VOICES, TOO (*6) / THE DUST BOWL SYMPHONY (*6) / WINGS TO FLY AND A PLACE TO BE – AN INTRODUCTION TO . . . collection (*7) / CLOCK WITHOUT HANDS (*6) / WINTER MARQUEE (*5)

NANCI GRIFFITH – vocals, acoustic guitar

not iss. B.F. Deal

Feb 78. (lp) <6> **THERE'S A LIGHT BEYOND THESE WOODS** [–] [ ]
– I remember Joe / Alabama soft spoken blues / Michael's song / Song for remembered heroes / West Texas sun / There's a light beyond these woods / Dollar matinee / Montana backroads / John Philipp Griffith. *<re-iss. 1982 on 'Featherbed'; FB 903> <re-iss. Aug87 on 'Philo' lp/c/cd; PH 1097/+C/CD> (UK-iss.Jul89 on 'M.C.A.'; MCG/MCGC/DMCG 6052)*

not iss. Featherbed

May 82. (lp) *<FB 902>* **POET IN MY WINDOW** [–] [ ]
– Marilyn Monroe – Neon and waltzes / Heart of a miner / Julie Ann / You can't go home again / October reasons / Wheels / Workin' in corners / Trouble with roses / Tonight I think I'm gonna go downtown / Poet in my window. *<re-iss. Aug87 on 'Philo' lp/c/cd; PH 1098/+C/CD> (UK-iss.Jul89 on 'M.C.A.' lp/c/cd; MCG/MCGC/DMCG 6053) (re-iss. Oct91 cd/c; DMCL/MCLC 1911) <(cd re-mast.Jan02 on 'Philo'+=; CDPH 1235)>* – Can't love wrong.

not iss. Philo

Jul 85. (7") **ONCE IN A VERY BLUE MOON. /** [–] [ ]
Dec 85. (lp) *<PH 1096>* **ONCE IN A VERY BLUE MOON** [–] [ ]
– Ghost in the music / Love is a hard waltz / Mary & Omie / Roseville fair / Friend out in the madness / Time alone / I'm not drivin' these wheels / Spin on a red brick floor / Ballad of Richard Wintersmith / If I were a woman you wanted. *(UK-iss.Jul89 on 'M.C.A.' lp/c/cd; MCG/MCGC/DMCG 6054)*
Dec 86. (cd/c/lp) *<CD/C+/PH 1109>* **LAST OF TRUE BELIEVERS** [–] [ ]
– Last of the true believers / Love at the Five & Dime / St. Olav's gate / More than a whisper / Banks of the Pontchatrain / Looking for the time / Goin' gone / One of these days / Love's found a shoulder / Fly by night / The wing and the wheel. *(UK-iss.Jun88 on 'Rounder' lp/c/cd; REU/+C/CD 1013) (cd re-iss. Nov96; same as US)*

M.C.A. M.C.A.

Apr 87. (7") *<53008>* **LONE STAR STATE OF MIND. / THERE'S A LIGHT BEOND THE WOODS (MARY MARGARET)** [–] [ ]
Apr 87. (lp/c) *(MCF/+C 3364) <5927>* **LONE STAR STATE OF MIND** [ ] [ ]
– Lone star state of mind / Cold hearts – closed minds / From a distance / Beacon Street / Nickel dreams / Sing one for sister / Ford Econoline / Trouble in the fields / Love in a memory / Let it shine on me / There's a light beyond these woods (Mary Margaret). *(cd-iss. Jul87; MCAD 5927) (cd re-iss. Oct98; MCLD 19176)*
Jun 87. (7") *<53082>* **LOVE IN A MEMORY. / TROUBLE IN THE FIELDS** [–] [ ]
Jul 87. (7") *(MCA 1169)* **FROM A DISTANCE. / SING ONE FOR SISTER** [ ] [–]
(cd-s) *(DMCA 1169)* – ('A'side) / De Lejos / Gulf Coast highway.
Nov 87. (7"ep) *(MCA 1221) <53147>* **COLD HEARTS** [ ] [ ]
– Cold hearts, closed minds / Ford Econoline / Lone star state of mind.
Jan 88. (7") *<53184>* **FROM A DISTANCE. / NEVER MIND** [–] [ ]
Feb 88. (7") *(MCA 1230)* **OUTBOUND PLANE. / SO LONG AGO** [ ] [–]
(12"+=) *(MCAT 1230)* – Trouble in the fields.
Mar 88. (lp/c/cd) *(MCF/MCFC/DMCF 3413) <42102>* **LITTLE LOVE AFFAIRS** [78] [ ]
– Anyone can be somebody's fool / I knew love / Never mind / Love wore a halo (back before the war) / So long ago / Gulf Coast highway / Little love affairs / I wish it would rain / Outbound plane / I would change my life / Sweet dreams will come. *(cd re-iss. Oct98; MCLD 19211)*
Mar 88. (7") *<53306>* **I KNEW LOVE. / SO LONG AGO** [–] [ ]
Apr 88. (7") *(MCA 1240)* **I KNEW LOVE. / NEVER MIND** [ ] [–]
(12"+=) *(MCAT 1240)* – Lone star state of mind.
Sep 88. (7") *<53374>* **ANYONE CAN BE SOMEBODY'S FOOL. / LOVE WORE A HALO (BACK BEFORE THE WAR)** [–] [ ]
Sep 88. (7") *(MCA 1282)* **FROM A DISTANCE. / LOVE WORE A HALO (BACK BEFORE THE WAR)** [ ] [–]
(cd-s+=) *(DMCA 1282)* – There's a light beyond these woods (Mary Margaret).

—— with musicians **JAMES HOOKER** – keyboards / **DENNY BIXBY** – bass

Nov 88. (lp/c/cd) *(MCF/MCFC/DMCF 3435) <42255>* **ONE FAIR SUMMER EVENING (live)** [ ] [ ]
– Once in a very blue moon / Looking for the time (workin' girl) / Deadwood, South Dakota / More than a whisper / I would bring you Ireland / Roseville fair / Workin' in corners / Trouble in the fields / The wing and the wheel / From a distance / Love at the Five & Dime / Spin on a red brick floor. *(cd re-iss. Oct98; MCLD 19388)*

Jun 89. (7") *<53700>* **IT'S A HARD LIFE WHEREVER YOU GO. / FROM A DISTANCE** [–] [ ]

Jul 89. (7") *(MCA 1358)* **IT'S A HARD LIFE WHEREVER YOU GO. / GULF COAST HIGHWAY** [ ] [–]

(cd-s+=/12"+=) *(D+/MCAT 1358)* – If wishes were changes.

Sep 89. (lp/c/cd) *(MCG/MCGC/DMCG 6066) <6319>* **STORMS** [38] [99]

– I don't wanna talk about love / Drive-in movies and dashboard lights / You made this love a teardrop / Brave companion of the road / Storms / It's a hard life wherever you go / If wishes were changes / Listen to the radio / Leaving the harbor / Radio Fragile. *(cd re-iss. Oct98; MCLD 19389) (lp re-iss. Dec98 on 'Alto'; AA 004)*

Sep 89. (7") *<53761>* **I DON'T WANT TO TALK ABOUT LOVE. / DRIVE-IN MOVIES AND DASHBOARD LIGHTS** [–] [ ]

Sep 89. (7") **I DON'T WANT TO TALK ABOUT LOVE. / SPIN ON A RED BRICK FLOOR** [ ] [–]

Nov 89. (7") *(MCA 1379)* **YOU MADE THIS LOVE A TEARDROP. / MORE THAN A WHISPER** [ ] [ ]

(cd-s+=/12"+=) *(D+/MCAT 1379)* – Little love affairs.

Sep 91. (7"/c-s) **LATE NIGHT GRANDE HOTEL. / IT'S JUST ANOTHER MORNING HERE** [ ] [ ]

(12"+=) – Wooden heart.

(cd-s++=) – From a distance.

Sep 91. (lp/c/cd) *<(MCA/+C/D 10306)>* **LATE NIGHT GRANDE HOTEL** [40] [ ]

– It's just another morning here / Late night Grande Hotel / It's too late / Fields of summer / Heaven / The power lines / Hometown streets / Down'n'outer / One blade shy of a sharp edge / The Sun, Moon, and stars / San Diego serenade. *(re-iss. cd Oct95; MCLD 10304)*

Nov 91. (7"/c-s) **HEAVEN. / DOWN 'N' OUTER** [ ] [ ]

(12"+=) – Tumble and fall.

(cd-s+=) – Love at the Five And Dime (live).

Feb 93. (c-s) *(MCSC 1743)* **SPEED OF THE SOUND OF LONELINESS / FROM CLARE TO HERE** [ ] [ ]

(cd-s+=) *(MCSTD 1743)* – Boots of Spanish leather.

Feb 93. (cd/c) *(MCD/MCC 10796) <61464>* **OTHER VOICES, OTHER ROOMS** [18] [54]

– Across the great divide / Woman of the Phoenix / Tecumseh Valley / Three flights up / Boots of Spanish leather / Speed of the sound of loneliness / From Clare to here / Can't help but wonder where I'm bound / Do re mi / This old town / Comin' down in the rain / Ten degrees and getting colder / Morning song to Sally / Night rider's lament / Are you tired of me darling / Turn around / Wimoweh.

May 93. (c-s) *(MCSC 1771)* **FROM CLARE TO HERE / CRADLE OF THE INTERSTATE** [ ] [ ]

(cd-s+=) *(MCSTD 1771)* – De Lejos (From a distance) (Spanish version) / ('A'extended).

Nov 93. (cd/c) *(MCD/MCC 10966)* **THE BEST OF NANCI GRIFFITH** (compilation) [27] [–]

– Trouble in the fields / From a distance / Speed of the sound of loneliness / Love at the five and dime / Listen to the radio / Gulf Coast highway / I wish it would rain / Ford Econoline / If wishes were changes / The wing and the wheel / Late night Grande hotel / From Clare to here / It's just another morning here / Trouble and fall / There's a light beyond these woods (Mary Margaret) / Outbound plane / Lone star state of mind / It's a hard life wherever you go / The road to Aberdeen.

M.C.A. Elektra

Sep 94. (cd/c) *(MCD/MCC 11155) <61681>* **FLYER** [20] [48]

– The flyer / Nobody's angel / Say it isn't so / Southbound train / These days in an open book / Time of inconvenience / Don't forget about me / Always will / Going back to Georgia / Talk to me while I'm listening / Fragile / On Grafton Street / Anything you need but me / Goodnight to a mother's dream / This heart.

Sep 94. (c-s) **ON GRAFTON STREET / THIS HEART** [ ] [ ]

(cd-s+=) – These days in an open book.

Warners Warners

Mar 97. (cd/c) *<(7559 62015-2/-4)>* **BLUE ROSES FROM THE MOONS** [64] [ ]

– Everything's coming up roses / Two for the road / Wouldn't that be fine / Battlefield / Saint Teresa of Avila / Gulf Coast highway / I fought the law / Not my way home / Is this all there is / Maybe tomorrow / Waiting for love / I'll move along / Morning train / She ain't goin' nowhere.

Elektra Elektra

Sep 98. (cd/c) *<(7559 62235-2/-4)>* **OTHER VOICES, TOO (A TRIP TO THE BOUNTIFUL)** [ ] Jul98 [85]

– Wall of death / Who knows where the time goes? / You were on my mind / Walk right by / Canadian whiskey / Desperadoes waiting on a train / Wings of a dove / Dress of laces / Summer wages / He was a friend of mine / Hard times come again no more / Wasn't that a mighty storm / Deportee (plane wreck at Los Gatos) / Yarrington town / I still miss someone / Try the love / The streets of Baltimore / Darcy, Farrow / If I had a hammer.

Sep 99. (cd/c) *<(7559 62418-2/-4)>* **THE DUST BOWL SYMPHONY** [ ] [ ]

– Trouble in the fields / The wing and the wheel / These days in an open book / Love at the five and dime / It's a hard life wherever you go / Late night grande hotel / Tell me how / Not my way home / 1937 pre-war kimball / Waiting for love / Nobody's angel / Always will / Drops from the faucet / Dust bowl reprise.

above also credited The LONDON SYMPHONY ORCHESTRA

Jul 01. (cd) *<(7559 62660-2)>* **CLOCK WITHOUT HANDS** [61] [ ]

– Clock without hands / Travelling through this part of you / Where would I be / Midnight in Missoula / Lost him in the sun / The ghost inside of me / Truly something fine / Cotton / Pearl's eye view (the life of Dickey Chapelle) / Roses on the 4th of July / Shaking out the snow / Armstrong / Last song for mother / In the wee small hours.

Rounder Rounder

Sep 02. (cd) *<(ROUCD 3220)>* **WINTER MARQUEE (live)** [ ] [ ]

– Speed of sound of loneliness / I wish it would rain / Boots of Spanish leather / Two for the road / Listen to the radio / There's a light beyond these woods / Gulf Coast highway / The flyer / Good night, New York / Traveling through this part of you / Last train home / I'm not drivin' these wheels / What's that I hear / White fright liner.

– compilations, etc. –

Mar 00. (cd) *M.C.A.; <(MCLD 19395)>* **WINGS TO FLY AND A PLACE TO BE – AN INTRODUCTION TO NANCI GRIFFITH** [ ] [ ]

☐ GRIN (see under ⇒ LOFGREN, Nils)

GROUNDHOGS

Formed: New Cross, London, England . . . 1963 by TONY McPHEE, who named them after a JOHN LEE HOOKER track. In 1964, they signed with Mickie Most's Anglo-American agency, soon having their debut 45, 'SHAKE IT', issued on 'Interphon'. Around the same time, they recorded an lp, 'LIVE AT THE AU-GO CLUB, NEW YORK', with their hero, HOOKER. They returned to England in 1965 and subsequently went through a series of false starts before finally stablising their line-up in 1968. Just prior to this, McPHEE had teamed up with The JOHN DUMMER BLUES BAND, who released two singles for 'Mercury'. However, with advice from Andrew Lauder of 'United Artists', the new GROUNDHOGS took-off with (their) debut, 'SCRATCHING THE SURFACE'. In 1969, the single 'BDD' (Blind Deaf Dumb) flopped in the UK, although it bizarrely hit the top spot in Lebanon! In the early 70's, they scored with two UK Top 10 lp's, 'THANK CHRIST FOR THE BOMB' (which caused controversy with its sarcastic praise of the nuclear deterrent) and 'SPLIT' (which they always seemed to do, from then on). One of the tracks from the latter, 'CHERRY RED', featured on Top Of The Pops (22nd of April '71). Although they had lost none of their white-boy Chicago blues elements, the aforementioned couple of albums moved towards a more mellotron-based prog-rock sound. Two albums in 1972, 'WHO WILL SAVE THE WORLD?' and 'HOGWASH', revisited their blues roots. 1974's 'SOLID' album, meanwhile, saw a return to the charts, a feat TONY McPHEE & his GROUNDHOGS couldn't emulate with further releases. They were still going strong well into the 90's, releasing albums for the discerning blues connoisseur. • **Songwriters:** McPHEE penned except; EARLY IN THE MORNING (Sonny Boy Williamson) / STILL A FOOL (Muddy Waters) / MISTREATED (Tommy Johnson) / etc. • **Trivia:** TONY McPHEE appeared on JOHN DUMMER BAND releases between 1968-69. Around the same time he guested on BIG JOE WILLIAMS recordings.

Album rating: SCRATCHING THE SURFACE (*5) / BLUES OBITUARY (*6) / THANK CHRIST FOR THE BOMB (*8) / SPLIT (*7) / WHO WILL SAVE THE WORLD? THE MIGHTY GROUNDHOGS? (*6) / HOGWASH (*5) / SOLID (*4) / CROSSCUT SAW (*4) / BLACK DIAMOND (*4) / RAZOR'S EDGE (*4) / BACK AGAINST THE WALL (*4) / HOGS ON THE ROAD (*4) / NO SURRENDER (*4) / FOOLISH PRIDE (*4) / DOCUMENT SERIES PRESENTS . . . THE GROUNDHOGS (*8)

TONY McPHEE (b.22 Mar'44, Lincolnshire, England) – guitar, vocals, keyboards / **JOHN CRUIKSHANK** – vocals, mouth harp / **PETE CRUIKSHANK** (b. 2 Jul'45) – bass / **DAVID BOORMAN** – drums / on session **TOM PARKER** – piano repl. BOB HALL

not iss. — Interphon

Jan 65. (7") *<7715>* **SHAKE IT. / ROCK ME** –

JOHN LEE'S GROUNDHOGS

HOOKER – solo blues guitarist **TERRY SLADE** – drums repl. BOORMAN + added 3-piece brass section

Planet — Planet

Jan 66. (7") *(<PLF 104>)* **I'LL NEVER FALL IN LOVE AGAIN. / OVER YOU BABY**

—— TONY McPHEE joined The TRUTH for a short stint before sessioning for CHAMPION JACK DUPREE on his '66 single 'Get Your Head Happy'

T.S. McPHEE

– solo with **PETE CRUICKSHANK / BOB HALL** / and **VAUGHN REES** – drums / **NEIL SLAVEN** – guitar

Purdah — not iss.

Aug 66. (7") *(45-3501)* **SOMEONE TO LOVE ME. / AIN'T GONNA CRY NO MO'** –

—— This band also backed JO-ANN KELLY. In summer McPHEE formed HERBAL MIXTURE around the same time he joined JOHN DUMMER BLUES BAND on two 1966 singles.

GROUNDHOGS

re-formed (**TONY McPHEE** and **PETE CRUICKSHANK**) recruited **STEVE RYE** – vocals, mouth harp / **KEN PUSTELNIK** – drums

Liberty — World Pacific

Nov 68. (lp; mono/stereo) *(LBL/LBS 83199E) <21892>* **SCRATCHING THE SURFACE (live in the studio)**
– Man trouble / Married men / Early in the morning / Come back baby / You don't love me / Rocking chair / Walkin' blues / No more daggin' / Still a fool. *(re-iss. Sep88 & Apr97 on 'Beat Goes On' lp/cd+=; BGO LP/CD 15)* – Oh death / Gasoline / Rock me / Don't pass the hat around. *(cd-iss. Jan99 on 'Akarma'; AKCD 038CD)*

Dec 68. (7") *(LBF 15174)* **YOU DON'T LOVE ME. / STILL A FOOL**

—— trimmed to a trio when RYE left due to illness

Liberty — Imperial

Jul 69. (lp) *(LBS 83253) <12452>* **BLUES OBITUARY**
– B.D.D. / Daze of the weak / Times / Mistreated / Express man / Natchez burning / Light was the day. *(re-iss. Jan89 on 'Beat Goes On' lp/cd; BGO LP/CD 6) (cd re-iss. Jan99 on 'Akarma'; AK 039CD)*

Aug 69. (7") *(LBF 15263)* **BDD. / Tony McPhee: GASOLINE**

Liberty — Liberty

May 70. (lp) *(LBS 83295) <7644>* **THANK CHRIST FOR THE BOMB** 9
– Strange town / Darkness is no friend / Soldier / Thank Christ for the bomb / Ship on the ocean / Garden / Status people / Rich man, poor man / Eccentric man. *(re-iss. 1975 on 'Sunset'; 50376) (re-iss. May86 on 'Fame' lp/c; FA41/TCFA 3152) (re-iss. Dec89 on 'Beat Goes On' lp/cd; BGO LP/CD 67) (cd re-iss. Jan99 on 'Akarma'; AK 040CD)*

1970. (7") *(LBF 15346)* **ECCENTRIC MAN. / STATUS PEOPLE** –

1970. (7") *<56205>* **SHIP ON THE OCEAN. / SOLDIER** –

Liberty — U.A.

Mar 71. (lp) *(LBS 83401) <UA 5513>* **SPLIT** 5
– Split (parts 1-4) / Cherry red / A year in the life / Junkman / Groundhog. *(re-iss. Aug80; LBR 1017) (re-iss. Mar86 on 'E.M.I.' lp/c; ATAK/TC-ATAK 73) (re-iss. Dec89 on 'Beat Goes On'; BGO LP/CD 76) (cd re-iss. Jan99 on 'Akarma'; AK 041CD)*

U.A. — U.A.

Mar 72. (lp) *(UAG 29237) <UA 5570>* **WHO WILL SAVE THE WORLD? THE MIGHTY GROUNDHOGS**
– Earth is not room enough / Wages of peace / Body in mind / Music is the food of thought / Bog roll blues / Death of the sun / Amazing Grace / The grey maze. *(re-iss. Dec89 & Apr91 on 'Beat Goes On' lp/cd; BGO LP/CD 77)*

—— **CLIVE BROOKS** – drums (ex-EGG) repl. PUSTELNIK

Oct 72. (lp) *(UAG 29419) <UA 008>* **HOGWASH**
– I love Miss Ogyny / You had a lesson / The ringmaster / 3744 James Road / Sad is the hunter / S'one song / Earth shanty / Mr. Hooker, Sir John. *(re-iss. Apr89 on 'Beat Goes On' lp/cd; BGO LP/CD 44) (cd re-iss. May91;)*

W.W.A. — W.W.A.

Oct 73. (lp; T.S. McPHEE; solo) *(WWA 1)* **THE TWO SIDES OF TONY (T.S.) McPHEE** –
– Three times seven / All my money, alimoney / Morning's eyes / Dog me, bitch / Take it out / The hunt. *(cd-iss. Dec92 on 'Castle';)*

Nov 73. (7") *(WWS 006)* **SAD GO ROUND. / OVER BLUE**

Jun 74. (lp) *(WWA 004)* **SOLID** 31
– Light my light / Free from all alarm / Sins of the father / Sad go round / Corn cob / Plea sing plea song / Snowstorm / Jokers grave. *(cd-iss. Oct91 on 'Castle'; CLACD 266)*

Aug 74. (7") *(WWS 012)* **PLEA SING – PLEA SONG. / Tony McPhee: DOG ME BITCH**

—— **McPHEE** brought back **PETE CRUIKSHANK** – rhythm guitar, / plus new members **DAVE WELLBELOVE** – guitar / **MARTIN KENT** – bass / **MICK COOK** – drums

U.A. — U.A.

Feb 76. (lp) *(UAG 29917) <LA 603>* **CROSSCUT SAW**
– Crosscut saw / Promiscuity / Boogie withus / Fulfilment / Live a little lady / Three way split / Mean mistreater / Eleventh hour.

Mar 76. (7") *(UP 36095)* **LIVE A LITTLE LADY. / BOOGIE WITHUS**

—— **RICK ADAMS** – rhythm guitar repl. PETE

Oct 76. (lp) *(UAG 29994) <LA 680>* **BLACK DIAMOND**
– Body talk / Fantasy partner / Live right / Country blues / Your love keeps me alive / Friendzy / Pastoral future / Black diamond.

Oct 76. (7"; as TONY McPHEE & GROUNDHOGS) *(UP 36177)* **PASTORAL FUTURE. / LIVE RIGHT**

—— split '77. **McPHEE** formed **TERRAPLANE,** with **ALAN FISH** – bass / **WILGUR CAMPBELL** – drums. They appeared on album CHECKIN' IT OUT by 'BILLY BOY ARNOLD'. (1979 split) **TONY** formed TURBO ('79-'83) with **CLIVE BROOKS** – drums / **PAUL RAVEN**

TONY McPHEE BAND

with **MICK MIRTON** – drums / **STEVE TOWNER** – bass

T.S. — not iss.

May 83. (7"; sold at gigs) *(TS 001)* **TIME OF ACTION. / BORN TO BE WITH YOU** –

GROUNDHOGS

McPHEE with **ALAN FISH** – bass / **MICK MIRTON** – drums

Conquest — not iss.

May 85. (lp) *(QUEST 1)* **RAZOR'S EDGE** –
– Razor's edge / I confess / Born to be with you / One more chance / The protector / Superseded / Moving fast, standing still / I want you to love me. *(re-iss. Nov89 on 'Landslide'; BUTLP 005) (cd-iss. Oct92; BUTCD 005) (cd re-iss. Nov97 on 'Blueprint'; BP 270CD)*

—— (Early'86) **DAVE THOMPSON** – bass repl. FISH who joined DUMPY'S RUSTY NUTS / **KEN PUSTELNIK** – drums returned to repl. MIRTON who joined DUMPY'S RUSTY NUTS. They gigged several times and appeared on Radio 2's 'Rhythm and Blues'.

—— **DAVE ANDERSON** – bass (ex-AMON DUUL II, ex-HAWKWIND) repl. THOMPSON / **MIKE JONES** – drums repl. PUSTELNIK

Demi-Monde — not iss.

May 87. (lp) *(DMLP 1014)* **BACK AGAINST THE WALL** –
– Back against the wall / No to submission / Blue boar blues / Waiting in shadows / Ain't no slaver / Stick to your guns / In the meantime / 54156. *(cd-iss. Jul87 on 'The CD Label'; CDTL 005)*

— ANDERSON re-formed AMON DUUL II, taking with him McPHEE as guest

TONY McPHEE and the GROUNDHOGS

recorded album below

Apr 88. (d-lp) *(DMLP 1016)* **HOGS ON THE ROAD (live)** ☐ ☐
– Express man / Strange town / Eccentric man / 3744 James Road / I want you to love me / Split IV / Soldier / Back against the wall / Garden / Split I / Waiting in shadows / Light my light / Me and the Devil / Mistreated / Groundhogs blues / Split II / Cherry red. *(cd-iss. Aug88 on 'The CD Label'; CDTL 008) (cd re-iss. Mar94 on 'Thunderbolt'; CDTB 114)*

H.T.D. Gopaco

Aug 89. (lp/cd) *(HTD LP/CD 2)* **NO SURRENDER** ☐ ☐
– Razor's edge / 3744 James Road / Superseeded / Light my light / One more chance / Garden. *(cd+=)* – Split (pt.2) / Eccentric man / Strange town / Cherry red. *(re-iss. Dec90 cd/lp; same) <US cd-iss. Oct95 on 'Magnum'; 8> (cd re-iss. Feb00 on 'Transatlantic'; TRACD 328)*

Feb 93. (cd; TONY McPHEE) *(HTDCD 10)* **FOOLISH PRIDE** ☐ ☐
– Foolish pride / Every minute / Devil you know / Masqueradin' / Time after time / On the run / Took me by surprise / Whatever it takes / Been there done that / I'm gonna win. *(re-iss. Sep96; same)*

Jul 93. (d-cd) *(HTDCD 12) <169>* **GROUNDHOG NIGHT – GROUNDHOGS LIVE (live)** ☐ 1994 ☐
– Shake for me / No more doggin' / Eccentric man / 3744 James Road / I want you to love me / Garden / Split pt.1 / Split pt.2 / Still a fool / I love you Miss Ogyny / Thank Christ for the bomb / Soldier / Mistreated / Me and the Devil blues / Cherry red / Groundhog blues / Been there, done that / Down in the bottom. *(re-iss. Feb00; same)*

Dec 94. (cd; as TONY (T.S.) McPHEE) *(HTDCD 26)* **SLIDE T.S. SLIDE** ☐ ☐
– Reformed man / Mean dispostion / Slide to slide / From a pawn to a king / Tell me baby / Hooker & the hogs / Someday, baby / Driving duck / No place to go / Me & the Devil / Death letter / Can't be satisfied / Still a fool / Write me a few short lines / Down in the bottom. *(re-iss. Sep96; same)*

Apr 97. (cd) *(HTDCD 72)* **BLEACHING THE BLUES** ☐ ☐
– When you're down / All your women / There's a light / Went in like a lamb / When your man has gone / Many times / All last night / When you're walking down the street / Meeting of the minds / Bleaching the blues / If I had possession / Love in vain / Floatin' bridge / Terraplane blues / Little red rooster.

H.T.D. Transatla.

Jan 98. (cd) *(HTDCD 81) <314>* **HOGS IN WOLF'S CLOTHING** ☐ Apr99 ☐
– Smokestack lightnimg / Baby how long / Commit a crime / Forty-four / No place to go / I ain't superstitious / Evil / So glad / My life / Sittin' on top of the world / Shake for me / Wang dang doodle / How many more years / Nature / Down in the bottom.

– compilations, etc. –

Sep 74. (d-lp) *United Artists; (UDF 31) <60063-4>* **GROUNDHOGS' BEST 1969-1972** ☐ ☐
– Groundhog / Strange town / Bog roll blues / You had a lesson / Express man / Eccentric man / Earth is not room enough / BDD / Split part 1 / Cherry red / Mistreated / 3744 James Road / Soldier / Sad is the hunter / Garden / Split part 4 / Amazing grace. *(re-iss. Mar88 on 'Beat Goes On' d-lp/cd; BGO DLP/MC 1) (cd-iss. Mar90 on 'E.M.I.'; CDP 7-90434-2)*

Apr 84. (d-lp) *Psycho; (PSYCHO 24)* **HOGGIN' THE STAGE** ☐ ☐
(with free 7") (cd-iss. Nov95 on 'Receiver'; RRCD 207)

May 86. (d-lp/c) *Raw Power; (RAW LP/TC 021)* **MOVING FAST, STANDING STILL** ☐ ☐
– RAZOR'S EDGE' & 'THE TWO SIDES OF T.S. McPHEE', incl. 4 extra 'Immediate' 45's)

Jun 92. (cd) *Beat Goes On; (BGOCD 131)* **CROSSCUT SAW / BLACK DIAMOND** ☐ ☐

Dec 92. (cd/c) *Connoisseur; (CSAP CD/MC 112)* **DOCUMENT SERIES PRESENTS (CLASSIC ALBUM CUTS 1968-1976)** ☐ ☐
– Still a fool / Walking blues / Mistreated / Express man / Eccentric man / Status people / Cherry red / Split (part IV) / Wages of peace / Amazing Grace / Love you Miss Ogyny / Earth shanty / Live a little lady / Boogie with us / Pastoral future / Live right.

Sep 94. (cd) *Windsong; (WINCD 064)* **BBC RADIO 1 LIVE IN CONCERT** ☐ ☐

Feb 96. (4xcd-box) *E.M.I.; (CDHOGS 1)* **FOUR GROUNDHOGS ORIGINALS** ☐ ☐
– (SCRATCHING THE SURFACE / BLUES OBITUARY / THANK CHRIST FOR THE BOMB / SPLIT)

Oct 96. (cd; as TONY McPHEE'S GROUNDHOGS) *Indigo; (IGOCD 2058)* **WHO SAID CHERRY RED?** ☐ ☐

Feb 97. (cd) *EMI Gold; (CDGOLD 1074)* **THE BEST OF** ☐ ☐

Jun 97. (cd; with HERBAL MIXTURE) *Distortions; (D 1012)* **PLEASE LEAVE MY MIND** ☐ ☐

Feb 98. (cd) *Strange Fruit; (SFRSCD 053)* **ON AIR 1970-72** ☐ ☐

Aug 98. (lp) *Akarma; (AK 010)* **LIVE AT LEEDS** ☐ ☐

Mar 98. (cd) *Eagle; (EABCD 087)* **THE MASTERS** ☐ ☐
(re-iss. Sep98 on 'Cleopatra'; CLEO 370)

Sep 98. (cd) *H.T.D.; (HTDCD 68)* **NO SURRENDER / RAZOR'S EDGE TOUR** ☐ ☐

Apr 99. (cd) *H.T.D.; (HTDCD 91) / Castle; <548>* **MUDDY WATERS SONGBOOK** ☐ ☐

May 99. (cd) *Music; (CD 6189)* **GROUNDHOG BLUES** ☐ ☐

Sep 99. (lp/cd) *Akarma; (AK/+CD 073)* **US TOUR** ☐ ☐

Aug 00. (cd) *Mooncrest; (CRESTCD 049Z)* **BOOGIE WITH US** ☐ ☐

Mar 01. (d-cd) *Burning Airlines; (PILOT 084)* **BACK AGAINST THE WALL** ☐ ☐

Jul 01. (d-cd) *Castle; (CMDDD 277)* **THE HTD ANTHOLOGY** ☐ ☐

Oct 01. (cd) *Talking Elephant; (TECD 026)* **LIVE AT THE ASTORIA (live)** ☐ ☐

Jul 02. (cd) *Strange Fruit; (SFRSCD 106)* **THE RADIO 1 SESSIONS** ☐ ☐

Nov 02. (cd) *Strange Fruit; (SFRSCD 112)* **BBC LIVE IN CONCERT** ☐ ☐

Mar 03. (cd) *Blue Flame; (BFBL 004)* **THE LOST TAPES VOL.1** ☐ ☐

Mar 03. (cd) *Blue Flame; (BFBL 005)* **THE LOST TAPES VOL.2** ☐ ☐

TONY McPHEE

also released other solo work.

1968. (lp) *Liberty; (LBS 83190)* **ME AND THE DEVIL** ☐ ☐
(contributed some tracks to below compilation)

1969. (lp) *Liberty; (LBS 83252)* **I ASKED FOR WATER, SHE GAVE ME GASOLINE** ☐ ☐

— Next credited with **JO-ANN KELLY**

1971. (lp) *Sunset; (SLS 50209)* **SAME THING ON THEIR MINDS** ☐ ☐

Apr 98. (cd) *Beat Goes On; (BGOCD 332)* **ME AND THE DEVIL / I ASKED FOR WATER SHE GAVE ME GASOLINE** ☐ ☐

☐ GULLIVER (see under ⇒ HALL, Daryl)

GUNS N' ROSES

Formed: Los Angeles, California, USA ... early 1985 by AXL ROSE, IZZY STRADLIN and moonlighting L.A. GUNS member TRACII GUNS, who was soon to return to said outfit. With the addition of SLASH, DUFF McKAGAN and STEVEN ADLER, the seminal G N' R line-up was complete, the ramshackle collection of fun loving musical vagabonds subsequently embarking on the 'hell' tour of the US. Although this outing was a disaster, the band created a major buzz with their residency at L.A.'s Troubadour club and in the summer of '86 unleashed their debut recording, a 7"ep entitled 'LIVE ?!*' LIKE A SUICIDE'. A short, sharp shock of visceral rock'n'raunch, the record struck a major chord with critics and fans alike, quickly selling out of its limited 10,000 pressing. Snapped up by 'Geffen', the band released their debut album, 'APPETITE FOR DESTRUCTION', the following year. A head-on collision of AC/DC, AEROSMITH and The SEX PISTOLS, what the record lacked in originality, it made up for with sheer impact.

The opening unholy trinity ('WELCOME TO THE JUNGLE', 'IT'S SO EASY', 'NIGHTRAIN') alone laid the rest of the L.A. hairspray pack to waste, while with 'PARADISE CITY' and 'SWEET CHILD O' MINE', the band staked their claim to chart domination and stadium stardom. In spite of its controversial cover art featuring a robot raping a woman (later withdrawn), the record went on to sell a staggering 20 million copies worldwide and remains one of metal's defining moments. It also remains one of the most vivid portrayals of the claustrophobic seediness of the L.A. metal scene in much the same way as N.W.A. captured the fuck-you nihilism of the city's black ghetto with 'Straight Outta Compton'. Live, GUNS N' ROSES were caustic and volatile, as likely to produce tabloid headlines as blistering performances. Image wise, they had SLASH as an unmistakable focal point; his trademark top hat perched on a nest of thick curls that all but obscured his face, fag constantly hanging from his lips a la KEITH RICHARDS. Controversy turned into tragedy the following summer, however, when two fans were crushed to death during a G N' R set at the 1988 Castle Donington Monsters Of Rock festival. Later that year, the band released 'G N' R LIES', a half live/ half studio affair that combined their earlier EP with four new acoustic numbers. On the lovely 'PATIENCE', ROSE was transformed from sneering vocal acrobat to mellow songsmith, although by 'ONE IN A MILLION', he was back to his old ways with a vengeance. While the song was performed with undeniable passion, it was all the more worrying given the subjects he was railing against. The track was basically an unforgivable tirade of abuse aimed at 'niggers', 'faggots' and 'immigrants', hmmm.. ironic? Yeah, right. Still, the good citizens of America snapped up the record and it peaked at No.2. in the US, No.22 in Britain. Come 1990, the band were supporting The ROLLING STONES on a world tour, their star status rapidly assuming the same magnitude as their drug habits. ADLER's heroin problems eventually saw him kicked out later that summer, CULT drummer MATT SORUM taking his place on the drum stool. The band also recruited a keyboard player, DIZZY REED, a sure sign they were beginning to lose the plot. A terminally dull cover of DYLAN's 'KNOCKIN' ON HEAVEN'S DOOR' (included on the 'Days Of Thunder' soundtrack) seemed to confirm this although 'CIVIL WAR', their contribution to Romanian orphan project, 'Nobody's Child', was more encouraging. When it eventually surfaced, the band's next studio project, 'USE YOUR ILLUSION' (1991), was a resounding disappointment. The very fact they released the disc in 2 volumes showed a severe lack of objectivity and needless to say, the quality control was non-existent. A sprawling, unfocused jumble, the collection nevertheless included a few inspired moments (notably the classic 'NOVEMBER RAIN') and both albums reached No.1 and 2 respectively in both Britain and America. During the subsequent world tour, STRADLIN walked out, finally leaving the band soon after for a solo career (his replacement was GILBY CLARKE). Among the dates on the record-breaking 28 month world tour was a performance at AIDS benefit concert, The Freddie Mercury Tribute, rather ironic in light of ROSE's lyrical homophobic tendencies. The bandana'ed one courted further outrage when the group included a CHARLES MANSON song on their 1993 covers album, 'THE SPAGHETTI INCIDENT', a record that also saw the band rework their faves from NAZARETH to The UK SUBS. They also massacred 'SYMPATHY FOR THE DEVIL' for the 'Interview With The Vampire' soundtrack, their last outing to date. CLARKE has subsequently left the band following a solo release, 'PAWNSHOP GUITARS', while SLASH also released a side project, 'IT'S FIVE O'CLOCK SOMEWHERE', in 1995 under the moniker SLASH'S SNAKEPIT. • **Songwriters:** All written by AXL except; MAMA KIN (Aerosmith) / NICE BOYS DON'T PLAY ROCK'N'ROLL (Rose Tattoo) / WHOLE LOTTA ROSIE (Ac-Dc) / LIVE AND LET DIE (Paul McCartney & Wings). Punk covers album; SINCE I DON'T HAVE YOU (Skyliners) / NEW ROSE (Damned) / DOWN ON THE FARM (UK Subs) / HUMAN BEING (New York Dolls) / RAW POWER (Iggy & The Stooges) / AIN'T IT FUN (Dead Boys) / BUICK MAKANE (T.Rex) / HAIR OF THE DOG (Nazareth) / ATTITUDE (Misfits) / BLACK LEATHER (Sex Pistols) / YOU CAN'T PUT YOUR ARMS AROUND A MEMORY (Johnny Thunders) / I DON'T CARE ABOUT YOU (Fear) / WHAT'S YOUR GAME! (Charles Manson). McKAGAN covered CRACKED ACTOR (David Bowie) • **Trivia:** On 28 Apr'90, AXL was married to ERIN, daughter of DON EVERLY (Brothers), but a couple of months later, they counterfiled for divorce. BAILEY was AXL's step-father's surname, and he found out real surname ROSE in the 80's.

Album rating: APPETITE FOR DESTRUCTION (*9) / G N' R LIES (*7) / USE YOUR ILLUSION I (*7) / USE YOUR ILLUSION II (*6) / THE SPAGHETTI INCIDENT (*5) / LIVE ERA '87-'93 exploitation (*6)

W. AXL ROSE (b. WILLIAM BAILEY, 6 Feb'62, Lafayette, Indiana, USA) – vocals / **SLASH** (b. SAUL HUDSON, 23 Jul'65, Stoke-On-Trent, England) – lead guitar / **IZZY STRADLIN** (b.JEFFREY ISBELL, 8 Apr'62, Lafayette) – guitar / **DUFF McKAGAN** (b. MICHAEL, 5 Feb'64, Seattle, Wash.) – bass (ex-10 MINUTE WARNING, ex-FASTBACKS) / **STEVE ADLER** (b.22 Jan'65, Ohio) – drums repl. ROB to L.A. GUNS again.

not iss. — Uzi Suicide

Aug 86. (7"ep) *<USR 001>* **LIVE ?!*' LIKE A SUICIDE** [–] [ ]
– Mama kin / Reckless life / Move to the city / Nice boys (don't play rock'n'roll). *<re-iss. Jan87 on 'Geffen'; >*

Geffen — Geffen

Jun 87. (7") *(GEF 22)* **IT'S SO EASY. / MR. BROWNSTONE** [ ] [ ]
(12"+=/12"pic-d+=) *(GEF 22T/+P)* – Shadow of your love / Move to the city.

Aug 87. (lp/c)(cd) *(WX 125/+C)(924148-2) <24148>* **APPETITE FOR DESTRUCTION** [5] [1]
– Welcome to the jungle / It's so easy / Nightrain / Out ta get me / Mr. Brownstone / Paradise city / My Michelle / Think about you / Sweet child o' mine / You're crazy / Anything goes / Rocket queen. *(peaked UK-No.5 in 1989) (re-iss. Nov90 lp/c/cd; GEF/+C/D 24148) (re-iss. Oct95 cd/c;)*

Sep 87. (7") *(GEF 30)* **WELCOME TO THE JUNGLE. / WHOLE LOTTA ROSIE (live)** [67] [ ]
(12"+=/12"w-poster/12"pic-d+=) *(GEF 30 T/TW/P)* – It's so easy (live) / Knockin' on Heaven's door (live).

Aug 88. (7") *(GEF 43) <27963>* **SWEET CHILD O' MINE. / OUT TA GET ME** [24] Jun88 [1]
(12"+=/12"s+=/10"+=) *(GEF 43T/+V/E)* – Rocket queen.

Oct 88. (7") *(GEF 47) <27759>* **WELCOME TO THE JUNGLE. / NIGHTRAIN** [24] [7]
(12"+=/12"w-poster+=/12"w-patch+=/12"pic-d+=/cd-s+=) *(GEF 47 T/TW/TV/TP/CD)* – You're crazy.

Dec 88. (lp/c)(cd) *(WX 218/+C)(924198-2) <24198>* **G N' R LIES (live)** [22] [2]
– Reckless life / Nice boys (don't play rock'n'roll) / Move to the city / Mama kin / Patience / I used to love her / You're crazy / One in a million. *(re-iss. Nov90 lp/c/cd; GEF/+C/D 24198) (re-iss. Oct95 cd/c;)*

Mar 89. (7"/7"sha-clear/7"white-pic-d) *(GEF 50/+P/X) <27570>* **PARADISE CITY. / I USED TO LOVE HER** [6] Jan89 [5]
(c-s+=)(12"+=) *(9275 704)(GEF 50T)* – Anything goes.
(cd-s++=) *(GEF 50CD)* – Sweet child o' mine.

May 89. (7"/7"s/c-s) *(GEF 55/+W/C)* **SWEET CHILD O' MINE (remix). / OUT TA GET ME** [6] [–]
(7"sha-pic-d+=) *(GEF 55P)* – Rocket queen.
(12"/3"cd-s) *(GEF 55 T/CD)* – ('A'side) / Move to the city / Whole lotta Rosie (live) / It's so easy (live).

Jun 89. (7"/c-s) *(GEF 56/+C) <22996>* **PATIENCE. / ROCKET QUEEN** [10] Apr89 [4]
(12"+=/3"cd-s+=) *(GEF 56 T/CD)* – (W. Axl Rose interview).

Aug 89. (7"/7"sha-pic-d/c-s) *(GEF 60/+P/C) <22869>* **NIGHTRAIN. / RECKLESS LIFE** [17] Jul89 [93]
(12"+=/3"cd-s+=) *(GEF 60 T/CD)* – Knockin' on Heaven's door (live '87).

— (Aug90) **MATT SORUM** (b.19 Nov'60, Long Beach, Calif.) – drums (ex-CULT) repl. ADAM MARPLES (ex-SEA HAGS) who repl. ADLER due to bouts of drunkenness / added **DIZZY REED** (b. DARREN REED, 18 Jun'63, Hinsdale, Illinois) – keyboards

Jul 91. (7"/c-s/12"clear-pic-d/cd-s) *(GFS/+C/TP/TD 6)* *<19039>* **YOU COULD BE MINE. / CIVIL WAR** 3 29

Sep 91. (d-lp/c/cd) *<(GEF/+C/D 24415)>* **USE YOUR ILLUSION I** 2 2
– Right next door to Hell / Dust n' bones / Live and let die / Don't cry (original) / Perfect crime / You ain't the first / Bad obsession / Back off bitch / Double talkin' jive / November rain / The garden / Garden of Eden / Don't damn me / Bad apples / Dead horse / Coma.

Sep 91. (d-lp/c/cd) *<(GEF/+C/D 24420)>* **USE YOUR ILLUSION II** 1 1
– Civil war / 14 years / Yesterdays / Knockin' on Heaven's door / Get in the ring / Shotgun blues / Breakdown / Pretty tied up / Locomotive / So fine / Estranged / You could be mine / Don't cry (alt.lyrics) / My world.

Sep 91. (7"/c-s) *(GFS/+C 9)* *<19027>* **DON'T CRY (original). / DON'T CRY (alternate lyrics)** 8 10
(12"+=/cd-s+=) *(GFST/+D 9)* – ('A'demo).

Dec 91. (7"/c-s/12") *(GFS/+C/X 17)* *<19114>* **LIVE AND LET DIE. / ('A'live)** 5 33
(cd-s+=) *(GFSTD 17)* – Shadow of your love.

— (Sep'91) **DAVID NAVARRO** – guitar (of JANE'S ADDICTION) repl. IZZY who walked out on tour. **GILBY CLARKE** (b.17 Aug'62, Cleveland, Ohio) – guitar finally repl. IZZY who formed IZZY STRADLIN & THE JU JU HOUNDS

Feb 92. (7"/c-s) *(GFS/+C 18)* *<19067>* **NOVEMBER RAIN. / SWEET CHILD O' MINE (live)** 4 Jun92 3
(12"+=/pic-cd-s+=) *(GFST/+D 18)* – Patience.

May 92. (7"/c-s/12"/cd-s) *(GFS/+C/T/TD 21)* **KNOCKIN' ON HEAVEN'S DOOR (live '92 at Freddie Mercury tribute). / ('A'studio)** 2 –

Oct 92. (7"/c-s) *(GFS/+C 27)* **YESTERDAYS. / NOVEMBER RAIN** 8 –
(12"pic-d+=/cd-s+=) *(GFST/+D 27)* – ('A'live) / Knockin' on Heaven's door (live '87).

Nov 92. (c-s) *<19142>* **YESTERDAYS / ('A'live)** – 72

May 93. (cd-ep) *(GFSTD 43)* **CIVIL WAR EP** 11 –
– Civil war / Garden of Eden / Dead horse / (interview with Slash).

Nov 93. (c-s) *(GFSC 62)* **AIN'T IT FUN. / DOWN ON THE FARM** 9 –
(cd-s+=) *(GFSTD 62)* – Attitude.

Nov 93. (cd/c/lp) *<(GED/GEC/GEF 24617)>* **THE SPAGHETTI INCIDENT** 2 4
– Since I don't have you / New rose / Down on the farm / Human being / Raw power / Ain't it fun / Buick Makane / Hair of the dog / Attitude / Black leather / You can't put your arms around a memory / I don't care about you / What's your game!.

May 94. (7"colrd/c-s) *(GFS/+C 70)* *<19266>* **SINCE I DON'T HAVE YOU. / YOU CAN'T PUT YOUR ARMS AROUND A MEMORY** 10 Feb94 69
(cd-s+=) *(GFSTD 70)* – Human being.
(cd-s) *(GFSXD 70)* – ('A'side) / Sweet child o' mine / Estranged.

— **PAUL HUGE** – guitar; repl. the sacked and solo bound GILBY
(below from the movie 'Interview With A Vampire')

Jan 95. (c-s) *(GFSC 86)* **SYMPATHY FOR THE DEVIL / LIVE AND LET DIE** 9 Dec94 55
(cd-s) *(GFSTD 86)* *<19381>* – ('A'side) / (track by Elliot Goldenthal).

— DUFF and MATT teamed up with STEVE JONES (Sex Pistols) and JOHN TAYLOR (Duran Duran) to form mid '96 supergroup, The NEUROTIC OUTSIDERS; released an eponymous album and single, 'JERK', for 'Maverick' records. In early November, SLASH quit, citing ill feeling between him and AXL.

– compilations, etc. –

Nov 99. (d-cd/d-c) *Geffen; <(490514-2/-4)>* **LIVE ERA '87-'93 (live)** 45 45
– Nightrain / Mr. Brownstone / It's so easy / Welcome to the jungle / Dust n' bones / My Michelle / You're crazy / Used to love her / Patience / It's alright / November rain / Out to get me / Pretty tied up (the perils of rock'n'roll) / Yesterdays / Move to the city / You could be mine / Rocket queen / Sweet child o' mine / Knockin' on Heaven's door / Don't cry / Estranged / Paradise city.

□ GURU (see under ⇒ GANG STARR)

Woody GUTHRIE

Born: WOODROW WILSON GUTHRIE, 14 July 1912, Okemah, Oklahoma, USA. The son of a professional boxer, GUTHRIE first began performing in public in his teens before landing a job as a DJ in Los Angeles. By the time musicologist Alan Lomax made his first field recordings of GUTHRIE in 1940, the self-confessed ramblin' man had amassed a staggering catalogue of songs, many based on his experiences as a travelling hobo living on his wits, talent and staunch political beliefs. While he was refused membership of the US communist party after refusing to give up his religious beliefs, socialist ideals permeated much of his work nevertheless; with the now famous message 'This machine kills fascists' (imitated countless times since) emblazoned across his battered acoustic guitar, few were left in doubt as to where his heart lay. 'THIS LAND IS YOUR LAND', perhaps his best known track, remains a populist anthem and an unofficial alternative to 'The Star Spangled Banner' although this message of equality somehow rings hollow in the corporate miasma of modern day America. GUTHRIE's views had been shaped by years of struggling on the breadline and huddling in boxcars, watching his people leaving their homes to escape the 'dustbowl' of Oklahoma, only to arrive in sunny California and be turned back, beaten up or worse. Songs like 'I AIN'T GOT NO HOME', 'TALKIN' DUST BOWL BLUES' and 'HARD TRAVELIN', sung by GUTHRIE in his weatherbeaten, heavily accented husk of a voice evoke the trials of the migrants just as vividly as Steinbeck's 'Grapes Of Wrath'. Lomax's Library Of Congress recordings were subsequently issued commercially by 'R.C.A.' although GUTHRIE's work wasn't afforded any significant recognition in his own lifetime. Suffering from alcohol problems, he was consigned to a mental institution before being diagnosed with the genetic degenerative disease, Huntington's Chorea. Confined to a hospital bed for the latter stages of his life, the illness finally claimed him on October 3rd, 1967. By this time, a young BOB DYLAN had already been crowned America's king of cool, his inspiration (particularly his earlier work and indeed the whole Greenwich Village folk revival) taken largely from GUTHRIE; during the ailing troubadour's final years, DYLAN had been a regular visitor at his bedside, including tribute 'SONG TO WOODY' on his 1962 debut set. Aside from the obvious influence of his work on artists like DYLAN, PETE SEEGER and his own son ARLO, everyone from U2 to BRUCE SPRINGSTEEN paid tribute to the man on 1988's 'Folkways: A Vision Shared'. Round about the same time, 'Folkways' the label released a split album of GUTHRIE and LEADBELLY material. More recently, GUTHRIE's wife unearthed and submitted some of his unfinished 'work in progress' to the combined talents of US roots rockers WILCO & English protest bard, BILLY BRAGG. The results were issued in 1998 in the shape of the critically acclaimed 'Mermaid Avenue', a highly entertaining and often moving collection of songs interpreted with surprising sensitivity and intuition. It also sounded utterly relevant, some thirty years after the man's death. A veritable cornerstone of popular music, both GUTHRIE's fame and the continuing influence of his music grow with each passing year.

Album rating (selective): MORE SONGS BY GUTHRIE (*8) / BOUND FOR GLORY (*8) / DUST BOWL BALLADS (*9) / LIBRARY OF CONGRESS RECORDINGS (*8) / THIS IS YOUR LAND (*8) / STRUGGLE (*7) / BALLADS OF SACO & VANZETTI (*5) / SONGS TO GROW ON FOR MOTHER AND CHILD (*6)

WOODY GUTHRIE – vocals, acoustic guitar

Melodisc not iss.

1951. (78) *(1141)* **RAMBLIN' BLUES. / TALKIN' COLUMBIA BLUES** –

1955. (7"ep) *(EPM7 84)* **RANGER'S COMMAND** –
– Ranger's command / Hard, ain't it hard / Ain't gonna be treated this way / Buffalo skinners.

1955. (7"ep) *(EPM7 85)* **WORRIED MAN BLUES** –
– Worried man blues / Poor boy / Gypsy Davie / More pretty girls than one.

1955. (7"ep) *(EPM7 91)* **HEY LOLLY LOLLY** –

1955. (lp) *(MLP12 106)* **MORE SONGS BY GUTHRIE** –
– Columbus Georgia stockade / Johnny hard / Foggy mountain top / Bury me beneath the willow / Skip to meet Lou / Ezekiel saw the wheel / Take a whiff on me / Bad Lee Brown / The golden vanity / Cumberland gap / Sourwood mountain / Old time religion.

Topic Folkways

1958. (lp) *(12T 31)* **BOUND FOR GLORY**
– Stagolee / Little stack of sugar / Ship in the sky / Swim swim swimmy / Pastures of plenty / Grand Coulee Dam / This land is your land / Talking fish blues / The sinking of the Reuben James / Jesus Christ / There's a better world.

1960. (lp) *<5485>* **BALLADS OF SACCO & VANZETTI** –
– The flood and the storm / Two good men / I just want to sing your name / Red wine / Suassos lane / You souls of Boston / Old Judge Thayer / Vanzetti's rock / Vanzetti's letter / Root hog and die / We welcome to Heaven / Sacco's letter to his son. *<(cd/c-iss.Apr96 on 'Smithsonian Folkways'; SFW CD/MC 40060)>*

— WOODY died in hospital on the 3rd of October, 1967, having been ill and inactive for over a decade

– compilations, etc. –

1964. (lp) *R.C.A.; (RD 7642) / Folkways; <FH 5212>* **DUST BOWL BALLADS** (rec.1940)
– The great dust storm / I ain't got no home / Talkin' dust bowl blues / Vigilante man / Dust can't kill me / Pretty boy Floyd / Dust pneumonia blues / Blowin' down this road / Tom Joad / Dust bowl refugee / Do re mi / Dust bowl blues / Dusty old dust. *(re-iss. Jul78 as 'A LEGENDARY PERFORMER' lp/c; PL/PK 12099) <(re-iss. 1988 on 'Rounder' lp/c/cd; ROUNDER 1040/+C/CD)> <(cd-iss. Feb96 as 'A LEGENDARY PERFORMER'; 74321 31774-2)>*

— next also featured **SONNY TERRY, CISCO HOUSTON & LEADBELLY**

1965. (lp) *Xtra; (XTRA 1012) / Everest;* **WOODY GUTHRIE** 1964
– Lindburgh / Hard travellin' / Jiggy jiggy bum bum / Hey little water boy / Chisholm trail / Rubber dolly / I ain't got nobody / Philadelphia lawyer / Springfield mountain / Put my little shoes / Ida red / Yeller gal. *(re-iss. 1966; XTRA 1064)*

1966. (t-lp) *Elektra; <(EKL 27 1/2/3)>* **LIBRARY OF CONGRESS RECORDINGS** (rec.1940)
– Lost train blues / Railroad blues / Rye whiskey / Old Joe Clark / Beaumont rag / Greenback dollar / The boll weevil song / So long, it's been so good to know you / Talking dustbowl blues / Do re mi / Hard times / Pretty boy Floyd / They laid Jesus Christ in his grave / Jolly banker / I ain't got no home / Dirty overalls / Chain around my leg / Worried man blues / Lonesome valley / Walking down that railroad line / Goin' down the road feelin' bad / Dust storm disaster / Foggy mountain top / Dust pneumonia blues / California blues / Dust bowl refugees / Will Rogers' highway / Los Angeles New Year's flood. *<(t-cd-box-iss.1988 on 'Rounder'; CD 1041/2/3)> (iss.separately 1988 as VOL.1 & VOL.2 & VOL.3; ROUNDER 1041/+C/CD & ROUNDER 1042/+C/CD & ROUNDER 1043/+C/CD)>*

1966. (lp) *Xtra; (XTRA 1065)* **POOR BOY** –
– Baltimore to Washington / Little black train / Who's going to shoe your little feet / Slip knot / Poor boy / Mean talking blues / Stepstone / Bed on the floor / Little darling / Miner's song / Train blues / Danville girl No.2 / Ride old paint. *(re-iss. Oct81 on 'Transatlantic'; TRS 113)*

1967. (lp) *Xtra; (XTRA 1067)* **SONGS TO GROW ON VOL.1** –

1967. (lp) *Folkways; <FTS 31001>* **THIS LAND IS YOUR LAND** –
– Talking Columbia blues / Pastures of plenty / New found land / Oregon trail / End of my line / Miner's song / This land is your land / Grand Coulee Dam / Ramblin' round / Goin' down the road / Little black train / Slip knot.

1968. (lp) *Ember; (CW 129)* **WOODY GUTHRIE – IN MEMORIAM** –
– Gypsy Dave / More perty galz / Pretty boy Floyd / Poor boy / Hey lolly lolly / Lonesome day – John Henry / Ranger's command / Ain't gonna be treated this way / Buffalo skinners / Hard, ain't it hard / Worried man blues.

1968. (lp) *Ember; (CW 135)* **CISCO HOUSTON AND WOODY GUTHRIE** –

1968. (lp) *Ember; (CW 136)* **BLIND SONNY TERRY & WOODY GUTHRIE** –

1976. (lp) *Folkways; <FA 2485>* **STRUGGLE** –
– Struggle blues / Dollar down / Get along little doggies / Hang knot / Waiting at the gate / The dying miner / Union burying ground / Lost John / Buffalo skinners / Pretty boy Floyd / Ludlow massacre / 1913 massacre. *<(re-iss. Aug90 on 'Special Delivery' lp/c/cd; SPD/+C/CD 1034)>*

Jun 77. (lp) *Warners; <(K 56335)>* **SONGS FROM 'BOUND FOR GLORY'** (original recordings 1940-1946)
– Gypsy Dave / Jesus Christ / Pastures of plenty / Columbus Georgia stockade / So long (it's been good to know ya) / Howdido / Pretty boy Floyd / Hard travellin' / Better world / This land is your land.

Jan 88. (lp/cd) *Topic; (12T/TSCD 448) / Rounder; <ROUNDER 1036/+CD>* **COLUMBIA RIVER COLLECTION** Aug88

1988. (lp/c) *Joker; (lp/c) <SM/MC 3960>* **VOLUME 1** –

1988. (lp) *Folkways; <FA 2483>* **WOODY GUTHRIE SINGS FOLKSONGS OF LEADBELLY** –

1988. (lp) *Folkways; <FA 2484>* **WOODY GUTHRIE SINGS FOLKSONGS OF LEADBELLY VOL.2** –
(above also featured CISCO HOUSTON & SONNY TERRY)

1988. (cd; by Various Artists) *Vanguard; <VMD 73105>* **THE GREATEST SONGS OF WOODY GUTHRIE** –
<(re-iss. Jan96; same)>

Jun 88. (lp/c) *Deja Vu; (DVLP/DVMC 2128)* **THE WOODY GUTHRIE COLLECTION: 20 GOLDEN GREATS** –

Jun 92. (cd/c) *Music Club; (MCCD/MCTC 067)* **THE VERY BEST OF WOODY GUTHRIE** –

Jun 94. (cd/c) *Smithsonian Folkways; <(SFW CD/MC 40046)>* **LONG WAYS TO TRAVEL: UNRELEASED FOLKWAYS MASTERS 1944-1949**

Dec 94. (cd/c) *Smithsonian Folkways; <(SFW CD/MC 45036)>* **NURSERY DAYS – GROW BIG SONGS VOL.1** 1993

Mar 95. (cd/c) *Smithsonian Folkways; <(SFW CD/MC 45035)>* **SONGS TO GROW ON FOR MOTHER AND CHILD** 1993

May 96. (cd) *Tradition; <(TCD 1017)>* **EARLY MASTERS**

May 97. (cd) *Smithsonian Folkways; <(SFWCD 40100)>* **THIS LAND IS YOUR LAND – THE ASCH RECORDINGS VOL.1**

Aug 97. (cd) *Collectables; <(COLCD 5095)>* **GOLDEN CLASSICS VOL.1 – WORRIED MAN BLUES**

Aug 97. (cd) *Collectables; <(COLCD 5098)>* **GOLDEN CLASSICS VOL.2 – THE IMMORTAL**

Aug 97. (cd) *Collectables; <(COLCD 5605)>* **WOODY GUTHRIE & CISCO HOUSTON VOL.1** 1995

Nov 97. (cd) *Smithsonian Folkways; <(SFWCD 40101)>* **MULESKINNER BLUES – THE ASCH RECORDINGS VOL.2**

Jun 98. (cd) *Smithsonian Folkways; <(SFWCD 40102)>* **HARD TRAVELLIN' – THE ASCH RECORDINGS VOL.3**

Jan 99. (cd) *Prism; <427>* **PASTURES OF PLENTY** –

Feb 99. (cd) *United Audio . . .; (UAE 30242)* **WOODY GUTHRIE – MEMBERS EDITION** –

May 99. (cd) *Smithsonian Folkways; <(SFW 40103)>* **BUFFALO SKINNERS – THE ASCH RECORDINGS VOL.4**

Jun 99. (cd) *Hallmark; (31172-2)* **THIS IS YOUR LAND – THE BEST OF WOODY GUTHRIE** –

Aug 99. (4xcd-box) *Smithsonian Folkways; <(SFW CD/MC 40112)>* **THE ASCH RECORDINGS VOLS.1-4**

Nov 99. (4xcd-box) *Chrome Dreams; (ABCD 016)* **THE WOODY GUTHRIE STORY** –

Jun 01. (cd) *Catfish; (KATCD 199)* **HARD LUCK BLUES**

Aug 03. (cd/c) *Castle Pulse; (PLS CD/MC 652)* **COUNTRY AND FOLK ROOTS**

Arlo GUTHRIE

Born: 10 Jul'47, Coney Island, New York, USA, son of legendary folk singer, WOODY GUTHRIE, who bought him his first electric guitar. ARLO went to school in Stockbridge, Massachusetts, where he sang his fathers' songs (his father was the inspiration behind DYLAN). In the mid-60's, ARLO met school librarian, ALICE, and they opened a restaurant named as his debut album, 'ALICE'S RESTAURANT', late 1967. This renovated old church became a meeting place for mainly middle-class hippies, who were radically opposed to the US involvement in Vietnam; he had earlier been refused induction into the army due to a petty criminal charge. With help from his father's agent and friend, Harold Leventhal, he gained tour work (i.e, Newport Festival), which helped his finely crafted debut reach the US Top 20. Sadly, prior to its success, his father passed away on the 3rd of October '67, the victim of a long-lasting Huntingdon's chorea disease. In 1970, an Arthur Penn movie 'ALICE'S RESTAURANT', was made, ARLO playing himself alongside some intentionally amateurish actors. A year previous, after playing Woodstock (August 1969), he bought a 250-acre farm where he settled with wife-to-be, Jackie Hyde. Political but satirical folk-singer, in the mould of early BOB DYLAN, ARLO never quite emerged from the towering shadow of his father, although he did release a series of fine albums including 'RUNNING DOWN THE ROAD' (1969), 'WASHINGTON COUNTY' (1969), 'HOBO'S LULLABY' (1972) and the eclectic 'LAST OF THE BROOKLYN COWBOYS' (1973). His only singles chart success came with a version of Steve Goodman's 'THE CITY OF NEW ORLEANS' in 1972 and as the decade wore on, ARLO became more of a cult artist. In 1974, he wrote an attack on President Nixon, 'PRESIDENTIAL RAG', which understandably didn't sell in great heaps. 1976's 'AMIGO' brought further critical acclaim but no chart success, while 'ONE NIGHT' (1978), was the first in a series of albums recorded with folk/country act, SHENANDOAH. In the interim, he became a Catholic and appeared on 'The Muppet Show', as well as touring alongside JOE COCKER and JOHN SEBASTIAN on a 'Woodstock' reunion European tour. GUTHRIE remained a staunch social activist throughout, playing all manner of benefit gigs, while in the late 80's, he set up his own label, 'Rising Son'. From 1989 onwards, ARLO has released a handful of albums from 'SOMEDAY' to 'ALICE'S RESTAURANT VOL.2' (1997). • **Covered:** DON'T THINK TWICE, IT'S ALRIGHT + PERCY'S SONG + WHEN THE SHIP COMES IN (Bob Dylan) / 1913 MASSACRE (Woody Guthrie) / LIGHTNIN' BAR BLUES + SOMEBODY TURNED ON THE LIGHT (Hoyt Axton) / WHEN I GET TO THE BORDER (Richard Thompson) / etc.

Album rating: ALICE'S RESTAURANT (*8) / ARLO (*4) / ALICE'S RESTAURANT soundtrack with Various Artists (*5) / RUNNING DOWN THE ROAD (*6) / WASHINGTON COUNTY (*6) / HOBO'S LULLABY (*7) / THE LAST OF THE BROOKLYN COWBOYS (*5) / ARLO GUTHRIE (*4) / TOGETHER IN CONCERT (*6; with Pete Seeger) / AMIGO (*7) / THE BEST OF ARLO GUTHRIE compilation (*7) / ONE NIGHT (*4; with Shenandoah) / OUTLASTING THE BLUES (*5; with Shenandoah) / POWER OF LOVE (*5) / PRECIOUS FRIEND (*5; with Pete Seeger) / SOMEDAY (*5) / ALL OVER THE WORLD (*5) / SON OF THE WIND (*5) / MORE TOGETHER AGAIN (*4; with Pete Seeger) / MYSTIC JOURNEY (*6) / ALICE'S RESTAURANT VOL.2: THE MASSACRE REVISITED (*4)

ARLO GUTHRIE – vocals, guitar (with various session people)

Reprise Reprise

Dec 67. (lp) <*(RLP 6267)*> **ALICE'S RESTAURANT** Nov67 17
– Alice's restaurant massacre / Chilling of the evening / Ring-a-round-rosy rag / Now and then / I'm going home / Motorcycle song / Highway in the wind. *(re-iss. 1972; K 44045) <cd-iss. Jul88; K2 44045>*

Mar 68. (7") *(RS 20644)* **MOTORCYCLE SONG. / NOW AND THEN** –

Sep 68. (7") <*0793*> **MOTORCYCLE SONG. / (part 2)** –

Oct 68. (lp) <*(RSLP 6269)*> **ARLO (live)** 100
– Motorcycle song / Wouldn't you believe it / Try me one more time / John looked down / Meditation / Standing at the threshold / The pause of Mr. Claus. *(re-iss. 1972; K 44052)*

Oct 69. (lp) <*(RSLP 6346)*> **RUNNING DOWN THE ROAD** 54
– Running down the road / Oklahoma hills / Every hand in the land / Living in the country / Wheel of fortune / Creole belle / Coming in to Los Angeles / Oh, in the morning / Stealin' / My front pages. *(re-iss. 1972; K 44071)*

Dec 69. (lp) <*(RSLP 6411)*> **WASHINGTON COUNTY** 33
– (introduction) / Fence post blues / Gabriel's mother's hiway ballad #16 blues / Washington County / Valley to pray / Lay down little doggies / I could be singing / If you would just drop by / Percy's song / I want to be around. *(re-iss. 1972; K 44049)*

Jan 70. (7") *(RS 20877)* <*0877*> **ALICE'S ROCK'N'ROLL RESTAURANT. / COMING IN TO LOS ANGELES** Nov69 97

May 70. (7") <*0951*> **GABRIEL'S MOTHER'S HIWAY BALLAD #16 BLUES. / VALLEY TO PRAY** –

May 71. (7") *(RS 20994)* <*0994*> **THE BALLAD OF TRICKY FRED. / SHACKLES AND CHAINS**

Jul 72. (7") *(K 14188)* **UKELELE LADY. / WHEN THE SHIP COMES IN** –

Jun 72. (lp) *(K 44169)* <*2060*> **HOBO'S LULLABY** 52
– Anytime / The city of New Orleans / Lightning bar blues / Shackles and chains / 1913 massacre / Somebody turned on the light / Ukelele lady / When the ship comes in / Mapleview (20%) rag / Days are short / Hobo's lullabye.

Sep 72. (7") *(K 14202)* <*1103*> **THE CITY OF NEW ORLEANS. / DAYS ARE SHORT** Jul72 18

Nov 72. (7") <*1137*> **UKELELE LADY. / COOPER'S LAMENT** –

Feb 73. (7") *(K 14257)* **LOVESICK BLUES. / FARREL O'GALA** –

Apr 73. (7") <*1158*> **GYPSY DAVE. / WEEK ON THE RAG** –

Apr 73. (lp) *(K 44236)* <*2142*> **LAST OF THE BROOKLYN COWBOYS** 87
– Farrell O'Gara / Gypsy Davy / This troubled mind of mine / Week of the rag / Miss the Mississippi and you / Lovesick blues / Uncle Jeff / Gates of Eden / Last train / Cowboy's song / Sailor's bonnett / Cooper's lament / Ramblin' round. *(re-iss. Aug77 +quad)*

Aug 74. (7") *(K 14365)* <*1211*> **PRESIDENTIAL RAG. / NOSTALGIA RAG**

Jul 74. (lp) *(K 54019)* <*2183*> **ARLO GUTHRIE** Jun74
– Won't be long / Presidential rag / Deportee (plane wreck at Los Gatos) / Children of Abraham / Nostalgia rag / When the cactus is in bloom / Me and my goose / Bling blang / Go down Moses / Hard times / Last to leave.

May 75. (d-lp; with PETE SEEGER) *(K 64023)* <*2214*> **TOGETHER IN CONCERT (live)**
– Way out there / Yodelling / Roving gambler / Declaration of independence / Don't think twice, it's alright / Get up and go / City of New Orleans / Estradio Chile / Guantanamera / On a Monday / Presidential rag / Walkin' down the line / Well may the world go / Henry my son / Mother, the queen of my heart / Deportee (plane wreck at Los Gatos) / Joe Hill / May there always be sunshine / Three rules of discipline and the eight rules of attention / Stealin' / Golden vanity / Lonesome valley / Quite early morning / Sweet Rosyanne.

Sep 76. (lp) *(K 54077)* <*2239*> **AMIGO**
– Guabi, Guabi / Darkest hour / Massachusetts / Victor Jara / Patriot's dream / Grocery blues / Walking song / My love / Manzanillo Bay / Ocean crossing / Connection.

Sep 76. (7") <*1363*> **PATRIOT'S DREAM. / OCEAN CROSSING** –

Nov 76. (7") <*1376*> **GUABI, GUABI. / GROCERY BLUES** –

Mar 77. (7") <*1388*> **MASSACHUSETTS. / MY LOVE** –

Feb 78. (lp) *(K 56431)* <*3117*> **THE BEST OF ARLO GUTHRIE** (compilation)
– Alice's restaurant massacre / Gabriel's mother's hiway ballad £16 blues / Cooper's lament / The motorcycle song / Coming in to Los Angeles / Last train / City of New Orleans / Darkest hour / Last to leave. *(re-iss. 1984 lp/c; K/K4 56431) (cd-iss. Feb93; 7599 27340-2)*

Warners Warners

1978. (lp; with SHENANDOAH) <*3232*> **ONE NIGHT** –
– One nite / I've just seen a face / Tennessee stud / Anytime / Little beggar man / Buffalo skinners / St.Louis tickle / The story of Reuben Clamzo and his strange daughter / In the hey of A / Strangest dream.

Jul 79. (lp; with SHENANDOAH) *(K 56658)* *<3336>* **OUTLASTING THE BLUES** [ ] [ ]
– Weddding song / Epilogue / Sailing down this golden river / Evangelina / Prologue / Which side / World away from me / Telephone / Carry me over / Drowning man / Underground.

Nov 79. (7"; with SHENANDOAH) *<49037>* **WEDDING SONG. / PROLOGUE** [–] [ ]

Jul 81. (lp) *(K 56910)* *<3558>* **POWER OF LOVE** [ ] Jun81 [ ]
– Power of love / Oklahoma nights / If I could only touch your life / Waimanalo blues / Living like a legend / Give it all you got / When I get to the border / Jamaica farewell / Slow boat / Garden song.

Aug 81. (7") *<49796>* **IF I COULD ONLY TOUCH YOUR LIFE. / SLOW BOAT** [–] [ ]

Feb 82. (7") *<49889>* **POWER OF LOVE. / OKLAHOMA NIGHTS** [–] [ ]

1982. (d-lp; with SHENANDOAH & PETE SEEGER) *<3644>* **PRECIOUS FRIEND** [–] [ ]
– Wabash cannonball / Circles / Hills of Glenshee / Ocean crossing / Celery-time / Run, come see Jerusalem / Sailin' up, sailin' down / How can I keep from singing / Old time religion / Pretty Boy Floyd / Ladies auxiliary / Please don't talk about me / When I'm gone / Precious friend you will be there / Do re mi / Tarantella / The neutron bomb / I'm changing my name to Chrysler / St.Louis tickle / Wimoweh / Will the circle be unbroken? / Garden song / Kisses sweeter than wine / Raggedy raggedy / In dead earnest / If I had a hammer / Amazing Grace.

Rising Sun Rising Sun

1989. (cd) *<RSR 0001>* **SOMEDAY** [–] [ ]
– All over the world / Russian girls / Here we are – way out in the country / Someday / Satellite / Oh mom / Unemployment line / Eli / Major blues / You and me.

1991. (cd) *<RSR 0002>* **ALL OVER THE WORLD** [–] [ ]
– All over the world / Oklahoma nights / Massachusetts / Ukelele lady / Manzanillo Bay / Miss the Mississippi and you / When I get to the border / City of New Orleans / Russian girls / Guabi, Guabi / Waimanalo blues / Evangelina / (Last night I had the) Strangest dream.

1992. (cd) *<RSR 0003>* **SON OF THE WIND** [–] [ ]
– Buffalo gals / Dead or alive / Streets of Laredo / Ridin' down the canyon / South coast / Shenandoah / Gal I left behind / When the cactus is in bloom / Woody's rag (hard work) / I ride an old paint / Utah Carroll / Red river valley.

Oct 94. (d-cd; by ARLO GUTHRIE & PETE SEEGER) *<(RSR 0007-8)>* **MORE TOGETHER AGAIN IN CONCERT (live)** [ ] [ ]
– Midnight special / Abiyoyo / Where have all the flowers gone? / Mooses come walking / When the ship comes in / Guantanamera / Ross Perot guide to answering embarrassing / Sailing down this golden river / If I had a hammer (the hammer song) / When a soldier makes it home / Can't help falling in love // De Colores / Solo le pido a dios / Wake up dead / Gabriel's mother highway ballad No.16 / Hills of Glenshee / Little a this 'n that / City of New Orleans / Jacob's ladder / Wimoweh (Mbube) / Amazing grace / This land is your land.

Feb 96. (cd) *<RSR 0009>* **MYSTIC JOURNEY** [–] [ ]
– Moon song / Face of time / Mystic journey / Under cover of night / You are the song / Doors to Heaven / Wake up dead / When a soldier makes it home / Stairs / All this stuff takes time / I'll be with you tonight.

Dec 97. (cd) *<RSR 0010>* **ALICE'S RESTAURANT VOL.2: THE MASSACRE REVISITED** [–] [ ]

– compilations, others, etc. –

Mar 70. (lp) *United Artists; (UAS 29061)* *<5195>* **ALICE'S RESTAURANT (Soundtrack)** **[44]** Oct69 **[63]**
– Travelin' music / Alice's restaurant massacre – 1 / The let down / Songs to aging children (by TIGGER OUTLAW) / Amazing Grace (by The GARRY SHERMAN CHORUS) / Trip to the city / Alice's restaurant massacre – 2 / Crash pad improvs / You're a fink (by AL SCHACKMAN) / Harps and marriage.

Sep 00. (cd) *Koch; <7956>* **OUTLASTING THE BLUES / POWER OF LOVE** [–] [ ]

—— also contributed to various albums including 'Woodstock'.

☐ Robin GUTHRIE (see under ⇒ COCTEAU TWINS)

☐ GUTTERBALL (see under ⇒ DREAM SYNDICATE)

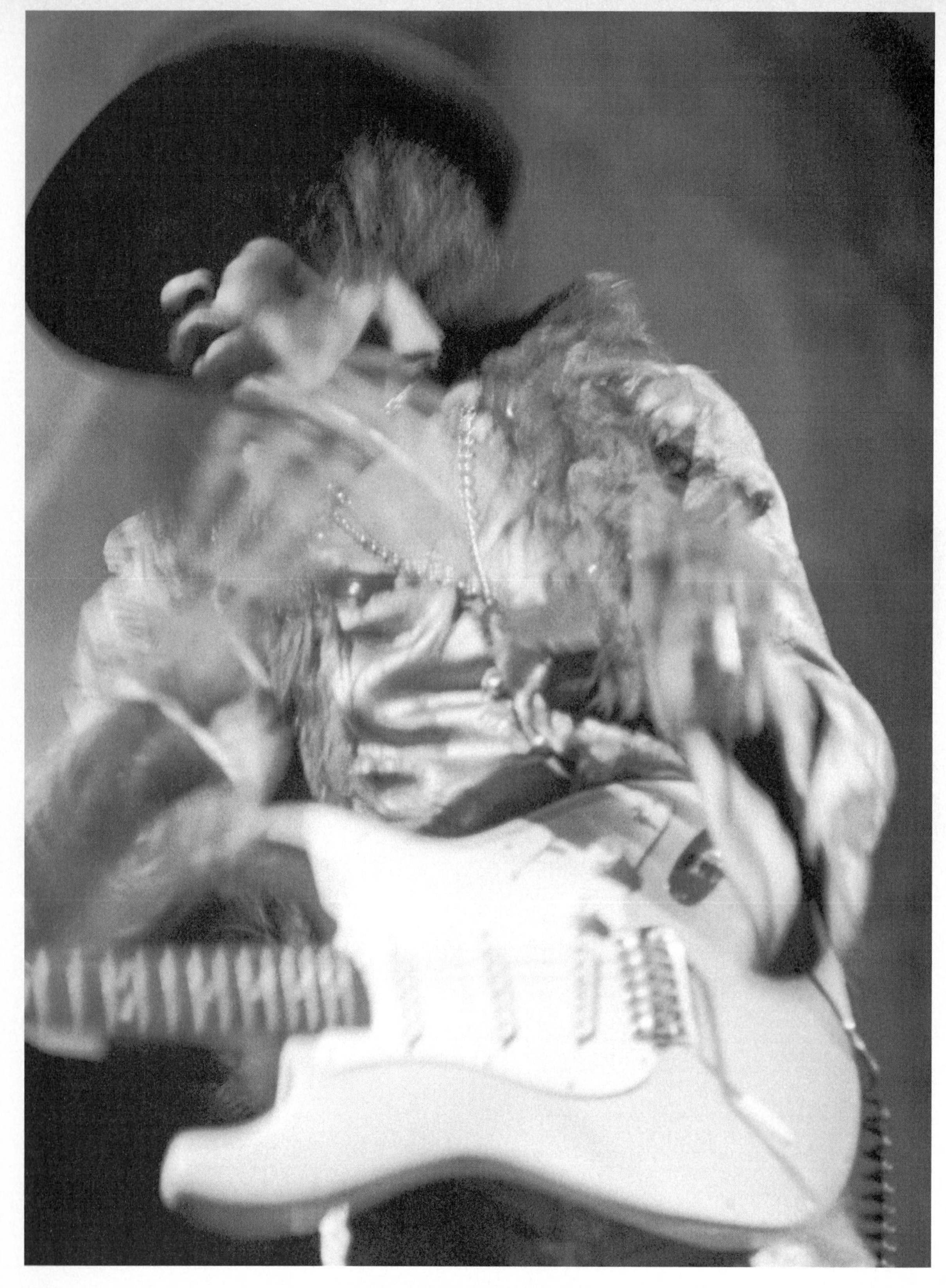

JIMI HENDRIX

Sammy HAGAR

Born: 13 Oct'47, Monterey, California, USA. Honing his inimitably hoary vocal style in a number of local bands, including FABULOUS CASTILLAS and The JUSTICE BROTHERS, HAGAR subsequently joined MONTROSE in 1973. A prototype 80's hair-metal band, MONTROSE recorded two lauded albums with HAGAR as frontman, 'MONTROSE' (1973) and 'PAPER MONEY' (1974). These sets featured a clutch of classy HAGAR numbers, namely 'SPACE STATION No.5', 'ROCK THE NATION' and 'BAD MOTOR SCOOTER', the singer resurrecting these tracks as the core of his feted stage show. After parting company with MONTROSE, he formed a few short-lived outfits (i.e. DUST COWBOYS and SAMMY WILD), before inking a deal with 'Capitol' records and releasing a solo debut album, 'NINE ON A TEN SCALE' in 1976. Initially he struggled to break through commercially, that is, until 1979's triumphant 'STREET MACHINE', an album that hit the UK! Top 40. Crossover success followed with the more overtly commercial (but hard-rockin' nonetheless) 'DANGER ZONE' (1980) set, although HAGAR only really came into his own in the live arena. Signing to 'Geffen', he delivered a further handful of workmanlike albums, before stunning the rock community by joining VAN HALEN in 1985. Faced with the nigh-on impossible task of replacing the charismatic DAVE LEE ROTH, HAGAR nonetheless won over the fans with his solid and dependable style on such massive 80's albums as '5150' (1986) and 'OU812' (1988). He fulfilled his contractual obligations to 'Geffen', by delivering an eponymous set in 1987 – later re-promoted for MTV as 'I NEVER SAID GOODBYE'. HAGAR continued to enjoy worldwide stardom with VAN HALEN right up until the mid 90's, when he left to resume his solo career. In 1997 and 1999, the man returned to the US Top 30 with two further sets, 'MARCHING TO MARS' and 'RED VOODOO', the latter credited with his new backing band, The WABORITAS. The party monster kept rocking into the new millennium with 'TEN 13' (2000), the title alluding to HAGAR's birthday (itself reportedly an excuse for a bit of annual ball down at the singer's bar in Mexico). Again beefed up by the WABORITAS, the record was another instalment of rowdy, thunderous party-rock softened slightly by the heat of the tropics. 'NOT 4 SALE' (2002) continued in similar style while 'LIVE – HALLELUJAH' (2003) proved that birthdays apparently have no effect on the ageing process of hardcore hard rockers like HAGAR. • **Covers:** THE DOCK OF A BAY (Otis Redding) / A WHITER SHADE OF PALE (Procol Harum). • **Trivia:** BETTE MIDLER covered his 'KEEP ON ROCKIN'', in the film 'The Rose'.

Album rating: NINE ON A TEN SCALE (*5) / SAMMY HAGAR (*5) / MUSICAL CHAIRS (*5) / ALL NIGHT LONG (aka LOUD AND CLEAR) (*7) / STREET MACHINE (*5) / DANGER ZONE (*6) / STANDING HAMPTON (*6) / THREE LOCK BOX (*6) / REMATCH compilation (*6) / THROUGH THE FIRE (*5; by HAGAR, SCHON, AARONSON, SHRIEVE) / VOA (*6) / SAMMY HAGAR – I NEVER SAID GOODBYE (*5) / THE BEST OF SAMMY HAGAR compilation (*6) / MARCHING TO MARS (*5) / RED VOODOO (*5) / TEN 13 (*5) / NOT 4 SALE (*4) / LIVE HALLELUJAH (*4)

SAMMY HAGAR – vocals (ex-MONTROSE) / with **GARY PHIL** – guitar / **BILL CHURCH** – bass (ex-MONTROSE) / **ALAN FITZGERALD** – keyboards / plus session drummers, etc.

Capitol — Capitol

May 76. (lp) <*(E-ST 11489)*> **NINE ON A TEN SCALE**
– Keep on rockin' / Urban guerilla / Flamingos fly / China / Silver lights / All American / Confession / Please come back / Young girl blues / Rock'n'roll Romeo. *(re-iss. Jun81 on 'Greenlight'; GO 2017) (re-iss. May83 on 'Fame' lp/c; FA/TC-FA 3068) (cd-iss. May93 on 'Beat Goes On'; BGOCD 182) <(cd re-iss. Mar01 on 'Repertoire'; REP 4889)*

Jun 76. (7") *(CL 15872)* **FLAMINGOS FLY. / URBAN GUERILLA**

— **SCOTT MATTHEWS** – drums (repl. session people)

Mar 77. (red-lp) <*(E-ST 11599)*> **SAMMY HAGAR** — Feb77
– Red / Catch the wind / Cruisin' and boozin' / Free money / Rock'n'roll weekend / Fillmore shuffle / Hungry / The pits / Love has found me / Little star – Eclipse. *(re-iss. May81 on 'Greenlight'; GO 2007) (cd-iss. May93 as 'RED' on 'Beat Goes On'; BGOCD 181)*

Mar 77. (7") <*4388*> **CATCH THE WIND. / RED** — –

Mar 77. (7") *(CL 15913)* **CATCH THE WIND. / ROCK'N'ROLL WEEKEND** — –

Jun 77. (7") <*4411*> **CRUISIN' AND BOOZIN'. / LOVE HAS FOUND ME** — –

— **DENNY CARMASSI** – drums repl. SCOTT / added **DAVID LEWARK** – guitar

Jan 78. (7") *(CL 15960)* <*4502*> **YOU MAKE ME CRAZY. / RECKLESS** — Nov77 62

Jan 78. (lp) <*(E-ST 11706)*> **MUSICAL CHAIRS** — 100
– Turn up the music / It's gonna be alright / You make me crazy / Reckless / Try (try to fall in love) / Don't stop me now / Straight from the hip kid / Hey boys / Someone out there / Crack in the world. *(re-iss. Jul81 on 'Greenlight'; GO 2021) (cd-iss. May94 on 'Beat Goes On'; BGOCD 201)*

Apr 78. (7") <*4550*> **TURN UP THE MUSIC. / HEY BOYS** — –

May 78. (7") *(CL 15983)* **TURN UP THE MUSIC. / STRAIGHT FROM THE HIP KID** — –

May 78. (7") <*4596*> **SOMEONE OUT THERE. / I'VE DONE EVERYTHING FOR YOU** — –

— **GARY PIHL** – guitar repl. LEWARK

Aug 78. (lp) <*E-ST 11812*> **ALL NIGHT LONG (live)** — – 89
– Red / Rock'n'roll weekend / Make it last – Reckless / Turn up the music / I've done everything for you / Young girl blues / Bad motor scooter. *(UK-iss.Mar80 as 'LOUD & CLEAR' red-lp +=; E-ST 25330)* – Space station No.5. *(hit No.12) (cd-iss. Aug92 as 'LOUD & CLEAR' on 'Beat Goes On'; BGOCD 149)*

Sep 78. (7") *(CL 160010)* **I'VE DONE EVERYTHING FOR YOU (live). / BAD MOTOR SCOOTER (live)** — –

Jun 79. (7") *(CL 16083)* <*4699*> **(SITTIN' ON) THE DOCK OF THE BAY. / I'VE DONE EVERYTHING FOR YOU** — Mar79 65

— **CHUCK RUFF** – drums repl. DENNY / **NEAL SCHON** – guitar (of JOURNEY) repl. FITZGERALD

Sep 79. (7") *(CL 16101)* <*4757*> **PLAIN JANE. / WOUNDED IN LOVE** — 77

Sep 79. (lp) <*(E-ST 11983)*> **STREET MACHINE** — 38 71
– Growing pains / Child to man / Trans am (highway wonderland) / Feels like love / Plain Jane / Never say die / This planet's on fire (burn to hell) /

Wounded in love / Falling in love / Straight to the top. *(re-iss. Jun86 on 'Revolver'; REVLP 72) (cd-iss. Dec92 on 'Beat Goes On'; BGOCD 150)*

Nov 79. (7") *<4825>* **GROWING PAINS. / STRAIGHT TO THE TOP** [-] [ ]

Nov 79. (7") *(CL 16114)* **THIS PLANET'S ON FIRE (BURN IN HELL). / SPACE STATION No.5 (live)** [52] [-]

Jan 80. (7") *(CL 16120)* **I'VE DONE EVERYTHING FOR YOU. / RED** [36] [-]

— added **GEOFF WORKMAN** – keyboards

May 80. (lp) *<(E-ST 12069)>* **DANGER ZONE** [25] [85]
– Love or money / 20th century man / Miles from boredom / Mommy says, daddy says / In the night (entering the danger zone) / The iceman / Bad reputation / Heartbeat / Run for your life / Danger zone. *(cd-iss. Jul95 on 'Beat Goes On'; BGOCD 261)*

May 80. (7") *(RED 1)* **HEARTBEAT. / LOVE OR MONEY** [67] [-]

May 80. (7") *<4893>* **HEARTBEAT. / MILES FROM BOREDOM** [-] [ ]

— **DAVID LAUSER** – drums repl. CHUCK

Epic Epic

Sep 81. (7"/12") *(EPCA/+13 1600)* **HEAVY METAL. / SATISFIED** [ ] [ ]
(above from film 'Heavy Metal')

Geffen Geffen

Dec 81. (7"/7"pic-d) *(GEFA/+11 1884)* **PIECE OF MY HEART. / BABY'S ON FIRE** [67] [-]

Dec 81. (7") *<49881>* **I'LL FALL IN LOVE AGAIN. / SATISFIED (by Journey)** [-] [43]
(also issued on 'B'side of CRAZY FOR YOU by 'Madonna' Jun85 hit)

Jan 82. (lp) *(GEF 85456) <GHS 2006>* **STANDING HAMPTON** [84] [28]
– There's only one way to rock / Baby's on fire / Can't get loose / I'll fall in love again / Heavy metal / Baby it's you / Surrender / Inside looking in / Sweet hitchhiker / Piece of my heart. *(re-iss. Sep86 lp/c; 902006-1/-4)*

May 82. (7") *<50059>* **PIECE OF MY HEART. / SWEET HITCHHIKER** [-] [73]

Jan 83. (lp)(c) *(GEF 25454)(402425-4) <GHS 2021>* **THREE LOCK BOX** [ ] Dec82 [17]
– Three lock box / Remote love / Remember the heroes / Your love is driving me crazy / In the room / Rise of the animal / I wouldn't change a thing / Growing up / Never give up / I don't need love. *(re-iss. Sep96 lp/c; 902021-1/-4) <(cd re-iss. Nov00 on 'Universal'; AA 22021)>*

Jan 83. (7") *(GEF 3043) <29816>* **YOUR LOVE IS DRIVING ME CRAZY. / I DON'T NEED LOVE** [ ] Dec82 [13]

Mar 83. (7") *<29718>* **NEVER GIVE UP. / FAST TIMES AT RIDGEMONT HIGH** [-] [46]

— **SCHON** – guitar / **AARONSON** – bass / **SHRIEVE** – drums

May 84. (lp/c; by HAGAR, SCHON, AARONSON, SHRIEVE) *(GEF/GEC 25893) <4023>* **THROUGH THE FIRE** [92] Mar84 [42]
– Top of the rock / Missing you / Animation / Valley of the kings / Giza / Whiter shade of pale / Hot and dirty / He will understand / My home town. *(cd-iss. Jan96 on 'Retroactive'; RETRO 50059CD) (<cd re-iss. Mar03 on 'Universal'; AAGEFD 4023)>*

May 84. (7"; by HAGAR, SCHON, AARONSON, SHRIEVE) *<29280>* **A WHITER SHADE OF PALE. / HOT AND DIRTY** [-] [94]

— added to 1982 line-up **JESSE HARMS** – keyboards, vocals

Aug 84. (7") *(GEF 4696) <29246>* **TWO SIDES OF LOVE. / BURNING DOWN THE CITY** [ ] Jul84 [38]

Sep 84. (7") *<29173>* **I CAN'T DRIVE 55. / PICK IN THE DIRT** [-] [26]

Sep 84. (lp/c) *(GEF/GEC 26054) <24043>* **VOA** (Voice Of America) [ ] Aug84 [32]
– I can't drive 55 / Swept away / Rock is in my blood / Two sides of love / Dick in the dirt / VOA / Don't make me wait / Burnin' down the city. *(re-iss. Sep86 lp/c/cd; GEF/GEC/GED 924043-1/-4/-2)*

— It was around this time he replaced DAVE LEE ROTH in VAN HALEN

Apr 87. (7") *(650407-7) / Columbia; <06647>* **WINNER TAKES ALL. / THE FIGHT (by Giorgio Moroder)** [ ] Feb87 [54]
(above from the 'Columbia' movie, 'Over The Top')

— **EDDIE VAN HALEN** – bass, vocals repl. CHURCH + PIHL

Jul 87. (lp/c)(cd) *(WX 114/+C)(924144-2) <24144>* **SAMMY HAGAR** <re-promoted as 'I NEVER SAID GOODBYE'> [86] [14]
– When the hammer falls / Hands and knees / Give to live / Boy's night out / Returning home / Standin' at the same old crossroads / Privacy / Back into you / Eagles fly / What they gonna say now. *(some w/ free conversation disc) <(cd re-iss. Mar03 as 'I NEVER SAID GOODBYE'; AAGEFD 24144)>*

Aug 87. (7") *(GEF 23) <28314>* **GIVE TO LIVE. / WHEN THE HAMMER FALLS** [ ] Jun87 [23]
(12"+=) *(GEF 23T)* – Standing at the same old crossroads.

Oct 87. (7") *<28185>* **EAGLES FLY. / HANDS AND KNEES** [-] [82]

Mar 94. (cd/c) *<(GED/GEC 24702)>* **UNBOXED** (compilation) [ ] [51]
– High hopes / Buying my way into Heaven / I'll fall in love again / There's only one way to rock / Heavy metal / Eagles fly / Baby's on fire / Three lock box / Two sides of love / I can't drive / Give to live / I don't need to love. *<(cd re-iss. Mar03 on 'Universal'; AAGEFD 24702)>*

Track Factory Track Factory

May 97. (cd) *<(AATKRD 11627)>* **MARCHING TO MARS** [ ] [18]
– Little white lie / Salvation on Sand Hill / Who has the right / Would you do it for free / Leaving the warmth of the womb / Kama / On the other hand / Both sides now / Yogi's so high (I'm stoned) / Amnesty is granted / Marching to Mars. *(re-iss. Mar03 on 'Universal'; AATRKD 1627)*

Mar 99. (cd/c; as SAMMY HAGAR AND THE WABORITAS) *<AATKRD 11872>* **RED VOODOO** [-] [22]
– Mas tequila / Shag / Sympathy for the human / Red voodoo / Lay your hand on me / High and dry again? / Revival / Don't fight it (feel it) / Love / Right on right / Returning of the wish. *(UK-iss.Mar03; same as US)*

not iss. Beyond

Sep 00. (cd-ep) *<78160>* **SERIOUS JUJU / 3 IN THE MIDDLE** [-] [ ]

Oct 00. (cd) *<78110>* **TEN 13** [-] [52]
– Shaka doobie (the limit) / Let Sally drive / Serious juju / The message / Deeper kind of love / A little bit more / Ten 13 / Protection / 3 in the middle / The real deal / Tropic of Capricorn.

not iss. 33rd Street

Oct 02. (cd; as SAMMY HAGAR AND THE WABORITAS) *<3315>* **NOT 4 SALE** [-] [ ]
– Stand up / Hallelujah / Halfway to Memphis / Things've changed / Whole lotta Zep / The big nail / Make it alright / Not 4 sale / The big square inch / Karma wheel.

Metal-Is Sanctuary

May 03. (cd; as SAMMY AND THE WABO'S) *(MISCD 26) <84619>* **LIVE HALLELUJAH (live)** [ ] [ ]
– Shaka doobie (the limit) / Three lock box / There's only one way to rock / Give to live / Top of the world / Deeper kinda love / Why can't this be love / Eagles fly / Little white lies / Rock candy / I can't drive 55 / Mas tequila / Heavy metal / When it's love / Right now / Dreams / Hallelujah.

– compilations, etc. –

1979. (7"m) *Capitol; (SPSR 441)* **TURN UP THE MUSIC. / RED / BAD MOTOR SCOOTER** [ ] [-]

Oct 82. (lp/c) *Capitol; (EST/TC-EST 26882)* **RED ALERT – DIAL NINE (THE VERY BEST OF SAMMY HAGAR)** [ ] [ ]

Jan 83. (lp) *Capitol; <12238>* **REMATCH (some live)** [-] [ ]
– Trans am (highway wonderland) / Love or money / Plain Jane / 20th century man / This planet's on fire (burn in Hell) / In the night / Danger zone / Space Station No.5.

Jan 87. (lp/c) *Geffen; (924127-1/-4)* **LOOKING BACK** [ ] [-]

Aug 89. (lp/c)(cd) *Warners; (WX 291/+C)<(K 924255-2)>* **THE BEST OF SAMMY HAGAR** [ ] [ ]
– Red / (Sittin' on) The dock of the bay / I've done everything for you / Rock'n'roll weekend / Cruisin' and boozin' / Turn up the music / Reckless / Trans am (highway wonderland) / Love or money / This planet's on fire (burn in Hell) / Plain Jane / Bad reputation / Bad motor scooter / You make me crazy.

Nov 94. (cd) *Connoisseur; (VSOPCD 207)* **THE ANTHOLOGY** [ ] [-]

Jun 97. (cd) *EMI Gold; (CPD 780262-2)* **THE BEST OF SAMMY HAGAR** [ ] [-]

Aug 01. (cd) *E.M.I.; (534694-2)* **MASTERS OF ROCK: THE VERY BEST OF SAMMY HAGAR** [ ] [-]

Oct 02. (cd) *Capitol; <41798>* **CLASSIC MASTERS** [-] [ ]

Oct 03. (cd) *EMI-Capitol; <36820>* **GREATEST HITS LIVE!** [-] [ ]

□ Luke HAINES (see under ⇒ AUTEURS)

Bill HALEY

Born: WILLIAM HALEY, 6 Jul'25, Highland Park, Detroit, USA. After leaving school in Pennsylvania, BILL became a travelling musician and yodeller for country bands, The DOWN HOMERS and The RANGE DRIFTERS. In 1948, he was hired as a DJ for the local W-PWA station in Chester, taking up the opportunity to air recordings of his new outfit, The FOUR ACES. He subsequently abandoned them in the early 50's, recruiting new backers, The SADDLEMEN, whose reputation was beginning to spread around the hillbilly community. In 1952, HALEY signed to 'Essex' and issued the 78, 'ICY HEART' / 'ROCK THE JOINT', although this was only a minor seller. Renaming the outfit BILL HALEY & HIS COMETS, they hit upon a winning combination of rockabilly fused with their own interpretation of black R&B, scoring their first US Top 20 hit with 'CRAZY MAN CRAZY'. In 1954, the group shifted stables to 'Decca', where they cut 'THIRTEEN WOMEN' as a single, although this was to initially flop. The record's flip side, 'ROCK AROUND THE CLOCK', began to garner airplay from some of the more non-conformist radio stations and their next single, 'SHAKE, RATTLE AND ROLL' became a Top 20 hit (on both! sides of the Atlantic). Due to unprecedented public demand, 'ROCK AROUND THE CLOCK' was reissued, this landmark track eventually becoming a transatlantic chart topper. It was undeniably the birth of popular rock'n'roll, the youth culture transforming virtually overnight (parents hated its rebellious overtones, their offspring bopping uninhibitedly around the nation's dancehalls). HALEY was now giving legendary performances up and down the States, although his clean-cut and well-dressed appearance disappointed his newfound British following who were looking for a thinner, unmarried figurehead to portray this hip new sound. The formula was repeated on subsequent 45's/78's throughout the mid-late 50's, songs such as 'ROCK-A-BEATIN' BOOGIE', 'SEE YOU LATER, ALLIGATOR', 'THE SAINTS ROCK'N'ROLL' and 'ROCKIN' THROUGH THE RYE' dominating the charts prior to the advent of rock'n'roll as an image industry for fresh faced youngsters (i.e. ELVIS, EDDIE, and even CLIFF). The 60's were virtually a non-starter for HALEY, although his revival concerts of the following decade saw obligatory reissues of 'ROCK AROUND THE CLOCK' hit the UK Top 20. Sadly, after a year spent in and out of hospital with a brain tumor, he died of a heart attack at his home in Harlingen, Texas on the 9th of February, 1981. • **Songwriters:** HALEY adapted songs from obscure originals, writing many himself. Covered ROCK THE JOINT (Jimmy Preston) / ROCKET 88 (hit. Jackie Brenston) / RIP IT UP (Little Richard) / WHEN THE SAINTS GO MARCHING IN (trad.) / ROCKIN' THROUGH THE RYE (Scot. trad) / etc.

Best CD compilation: THE VERY BEST OF BILL HALEY & HIS COMETS (*7)

BILL HALEY and the 4 ACES OF WESTERN SWING

BILL HALEY – vocals, guitar; and unknown backers

not iss. | Cowboy

1948. (78) *<1201>* **TOO MANY PARTIES, TOO MANY PALS. / FOUR LEAF CLOVER BLUES** [–] [ ]

1948. (78) *<1202>* **CANDY KISSES. / TENNESSEE BORDER** [–] [ ]

JOHNNY CLIFTON & HIS STRING BAND

not iss. | Center

1949. (78) *<102>* **STAND UP AND BE COUNTED. / LOVELESS BLUES** [–] [ ]

— In 1950, BILL HALEY's vocals were credited on RENO BROWNE and her BUCKAROOS single, 'MY SWEET LITTLE GIRL FROM NEVADA' <1701>

BILL HALEY and his SADDLEMEN

— with **JOHNNY GRANDE** – piano / **BILLY WILLIAMSON** – steel guitar

not iss. | Keystone

1950. (78) *<5101>* **DEAL ME A HAND (I PLAY THE GAME ANYWAY). / TEN GALLON STETSON (WITH A HOLE IN THE CROWN)** [–] [ ]

1950. (78) *<5102>* **SUSAN VAN DUREN. / I'M NOT TO BLAME** [–] [ ]

(below was backing for **LOU GRAHAM**

not iss. | Atlantic

1950. (78) *<727>* **WHY DO I CRY OVER YOU. / I'M GONNA DRY EVERY TEAR WITH A KISS** [–] [ ]

not iss. | Holiday

1951. (78) *<105> (TU 103)* **ROCKET 88. / TEARSTAINS ON MY HEART** [–] [ ]

(UK-iss.Feb81 on 'Thumbs Up')

1951. (78) *<108>* **GREEN TREE BOOGIE. / DOWN DEEP IN MY HEART** [–] [ ]

1951. (78) *<110>* **I'M CRYING. / PRETTY BABY** [–] [ ]

1951. (78) *<111>* **A YEAR AGO THIS CHRISTMAS. / I DON'T WANT TO ALONE THIS CHRISTMAS** [–] [ ]

1952. (78) *<113>* **JUKEBOX CANNONBALL. / SUNDOWN BOOGIE** [–] [ ]

not iss. | Essex

1952. (78) *<303>* **ICY HEART. / ROCK THE JOINT** [–] [ ]

1952. (78) *<305>* **ROCKING CHAIR ON THE MOON. / DANCE WITH THE DOLLY (WITH A HOLE IN HER STOCKING)** [–] [ ]

BILL HALEY and his COMETS

— with **GRANDE + WILLIAMSON** plus **DANNY SEDRONE** – lead guitar / **MARSHALL PINGATORE** – up.bass / **DICK RICHARDS** – drums / **JOEY D'AMBROSIA** – tenor sax.

London | Essex

1952. (78) *<310>* **STOP BEATIN' ROUND THE MULBURRY BUSH. / REAL ROCK DRIVE** [–] [ ]

Aug 53. (78) *(L 1190) <321>* **CRAZY MAN, CRAZY. / WHATCHA GONNA DO** [ ] Feb53 [ ]

Nov 53. (78) *(L 1216) <327>* **PAT-A-CAKE. / FRACTURED** [ ] Apr53 [ ]

1953. (78) *<332>* **LIVE IT UP. / FAREWELL, SO LONG, GOODBYE** [–] [ ]

1953. (78) *<340>* **I'LL BE TRUE. / TEN LITTLE INDIANS** [–] [ ]

1953. (78) *<348>* **STRAIGHT JACKET. / CHATTANOOGA CHOO-CHOO** [–] [ ]

1954. (78) *<374>* **SUNDOWN BOOGIE. / JUKEBOX CANNONBALL** [–] [ ]

1954. (78) *<381>* **ROCKET 88. / GREEN TREE BOOGIE** [–] [ ]

1954. (lp) *<LP 202>* **ROCK WITH BILL HALEY & THE COMETS** [–] [ ]

(re-iss. 1954 on 'Trans World'; same)

— **BILLY GUSACK** – session drums (only 1)

Brunswick | Decca

Sep 54. (7",78) *(05317) <29124>* **ROCK AROUND THE CLOCK. / THIRTEEN WOMEN** [ ] May54 [ ]

(re-dist.UK Dec54 hit No.17, Oct55 hit No.1, Sep56 hit No.5, stayed Top 30 until early next year) (re-dist.US Apr55, after 'Blackboard Jungle' film appearance, hit No.1, stayed in Top 50 for 1/2 a year)

— **FRANNY BEECHER** – lead guitar repl. CEDRONE who died of heart attack / **RUDY POMPILLI** – saxophone / **AL POMPILLI** – bass / **RALPH JONES** – drums repl. others

Nov 54. (7",78) *(05338) <29204>* **SHAKE, RATTLE AND ROLL. / ABC BOOGIE** [4] Jul54 [12]

Jan 55. (7",78) *(05373) <29317>* **DIM, DIM THE LIGHTS (I WANT SOME ATMOSPHERE). / HAPPY BABY** [ ] Nov54 [11]

Mar 55. (7",78) *(05405) <29418>* **MAMBO ROCK. / BIRTH OF THE BOOGIE** 14 18
Feb55 17

Jul 55. (7",78) *(05405) <29552>* **RAZZLE-DAZZLE. / TWO HOUND DOGS** 15
(UK re-dist.Sep56; hit No.13)

Sep 55. (10"lp) *<DL 5560>* **SHAKE RATTLE AND ROLL** –

Nov 55. (7",78) *(05509) <29713>* **ROCK-A-BEATIN' BOOGIE. / BURN THAT CANDLE** 4 9
23

Feb 56. (7",78) *(05530) <29791>* **SEE YOU LATER, ALLIGATOR. / THE PAPER BOY** 7 Jan56 6
(re-dist.UK Sep56; hit No.12)

May 56. (7",78) *(05565) <29870>* **THE SAINTS ROCK'N'ROLL. / R-O-C-K** 5 Mar56 18
16

Jun 56. (lp) *(LAT 8117) <DL 8225>* **ROCK AROUND THE CLOCK** Jan56 12
– (virtually a compilation, didn't make it in UK due to no lp chart until Nov'58)
– Rock around the clock / Shake rattle and roll / ABC boogie / (You hit the wrong note) Billy goat / Thirteen women (and only one man in town) / Tonight's the night / Razzle dazzle / Two hound dogs / Dim dim the lights / Happy baby / Birth of the boogie / Rockin' rollin' Rover / Mambo rock / Hide and seek / Burn that candle / Rock-a-beatin' boogie. *(re-iss. 1961 on 'Ace Of Hearts', re-iss. May68, hit UK No.34) (re-iss. Jan71 on 'Coral') (re-iss. Sep81 on 'M.C.A.')*

Aug 56. (7",78) *(05582) <29948>* **ROCKIN' THROUGH THE RYE. / HOT DOG BUDDY BUDDY** 3 78
60

Nov 56. (7",78) *(05615) <30028>* **RIP IT UP. / TEENAGER'S MOTHER (ARE YOU RIGHT?)** 4 25
Aug56 68

Nov 56. (lp) *(LAT 8139> <DL 8345>* **ROCK'N'ROLL STAGE SHOW** (hit singles chart=) 30 Sep56 18
– Calling all comets / Rockin' through the rye / A rocking little tune / Hide and seek / Hey then there now / Goofin' around / Hook line and sinker / Rudy's rock / Choo choo ch'boogie / Blue comet blues / Hot dog buddy buddy / Tonight's the night. *(re-iss. Aug83 on 'Charly')*

Nov 56. (7",78) *(05615) <30085>* **RUDY'S ROCK. / BLUE COMET BLUES** 26 34

Dec 56. (7") *<30148>* **DON'T KNOCK THE ROCK. / CHOO CHOO CH'BOOGIE** – 45

Feb 57. (7",78) *(05640)* **DON'T KNOCK THE ROCK. / CALLING ALL COMETS** 7 –

Feb 57. (7",78) *(05641)* **HOOK, LINE AND SINKER. / GOOFIN' AROUND** –

Mar 57. (7") *<30214>* **FORTY CUPS OF COFFEE. / HOOK, LINE AND SINKER** – 70

Apr 57. (7",78) *(05658)* **FORTY CUPS OF COFFEE. / CHOO CHOO CH'BOOGIE** –

—— **FRANKIE SCOTT** – saxophone repl. RUDY (He was to die 5 Feb'76)

Jul 57. (7",78) *(05688) <30314>* **(YOU HIT THE WRONG NOTE) BILLY GOAT. / ROCKIN' ROLLIN' ROVER**

Oct 57. (7",78) *(05719) <30394>* **MISS YOU. / THE DIPSY DOODLE**

Dec 57. (lp) *(LAT 8219) <DL 8569>* **ROCKIN' THE OLDIES**
– The dipsy doodle / You can't stop me from dreamin' / (I'll be with you) In apple blossom time / Moon over Miami / Is it true what they say about Dixie / Carolina in the morning / Miss you / Please don't talk about me when I'm gone / Ain't misbehavin' (I'm savin' my love for you) / One sweet letter from you / I'm gonna sit right down and write myself a letter / Somebody else is taking my place. *(re-iss. Oct62 on 'Ace Of Hearts')*

Feb 58. (7",78) *(05735) <30530>* **MARY, MARY LOU. / IT'S A SIN**

Apr 58. (7",78) *(05742) <30592>* **SKINNY MINNIE. / HOW MANY** 22

Aug 58. (7",78) *(05753) <30681>* **LEAN JEAN. / DON'T NOBODY MOVE** 67

Nov 58. (lp) *(LAT 8268) <DL 8775>* **ROCKIN' THE JOINT**
– Rock the joint / Rockin' chair on the Moon / Farewell – So long – Goodbye / Real rock drive / Fractured / Stop beatin' around the mulberry bush / Crazy man, crazy / Pat-a-cake / Live it up / Watcha gonna do / I'll be true to you / Dance with a dolly (with a hole in her stockin').

Nov 58. (7",78) *(05766) <30741>* **WHOA MABEL! / CHIQUITA LINDA**

Jan 59. (7",78) *<30781>* **CORRINE, CORRINA. / B-B-BETTY** –

Mar 59. (7",78) *(05788) <30844>* **I GOT A WOMAN. / CHARMAINE**

Jun 59. (lp) *(LAT 8295) <DL 8821>* **BILL HALEY'S CHICKS**
– Whoa Mabel! / Ida, sweet as apple cider / Eloise / Dinah / Skinny Minnie / Mary, Mary Lou / Sweet Sue – Just you / B-B-Betty / Charmaine / Corrine Corrina / Marie / Lean Jean. *(re-iss. 1960 stereo; STA 3011) (re-iss. Jan64 on 'Ace Of Hearts'; AH 66)*

Jun 59. (7") *<30873>* **WHERE DID YOU GO LAST NIGHT? / (NOW AND THEN THERE'S) A FOOL SUCH AS I** –

Aug 59. (7",78) *(05805) <30926>* **SHAKY. / CALEDONIA**

Jan 60. (7",78) *(05810) <30956>* **JOEY'S SONG. / LOOK-A-THERE, AIN'T SHE PRETTY** Sep59 46

Feb 60. (7") *(05818) <31030>* **SKOKIAAN. / PUERTO RICAN JUGGLER** Dec59 70

Apr 60. (7") *<31080>* **MUSIC! MUSIC! MUSIC!. / STRICTLY INSTRUMENTAL** –

Apr 60. (lp) *(LAT 8326) <DL 8964>* **STRICTLY INSTRUMENTAL**
– Joey's song / (Put another nickel in) Music, music, music / Mack the knife / In a little Spanish town ('twas on a night like this) / Two shadows / Shaky / Strictly instrumental / Skokiaan (South African song) / Puerto Rican peddlar / Drowsy waters / Chiquita Linda (un poquito de tu amor) / The catwalk.

Warners Warners

May 60. (7") *(WB 6)* **CANDY KISSES. / TAMIAMI** –

1960. (7") *<5154>* **CHUCK SAFARI. / HAWK** –

1960. (7") *<5171>* **SO RIGHT TONIGHT. / LET THE GOOD TIMES ROLL, CREOLE** –

Nov 60. (lp) *(W 1391)* **HALEY'S JUKE BOX**
– Sing the blues / Candy kisses / No letter today / This is the thanks I get / Bouquet of roses / There's a new Moon over my shoulder / Cold, cold heart / Wild side of life / Any time / Afraid / I don't hurt anymore.

1960. (7") *<5228>* **FLIP, FLOP AND FLY. / HONKY TONK** –

London Gone

Dec 61. (7") *(HLU 9471) <5111>* **SPANISH TWIST. / MY KIND OF WOMAN**

1962. (7") *<5116>* **RIVIERA. / WAR PAINT** –

not iss. Orfeon

1962. (7") **FLORIDA TWIST. / NEGRA CONSENTIDA** – Mexico –

1962. (7") **PURE DE PAPAS. / ANOCHE** – Mexico –

not iss. Logo

1962. (7") *<7005>* **YAKETY SAX. / BOOTS RANDOLPH – BOOTS BLUES** –

Columbia Columbia

Oct 62. (lp) *(33SX 1460)* **TWISTIN' KNIGHTS AT THE ROUNDTABLE (LIVE!)**
– Lullaby of Birdland twist / Twist Marie / One two three twist / Down by the riverside twist / Queen of the twisters / Caravan twist / I want a little girl / Whistlin' and walkin' twist / Florida twist / Eight more miles to Louisville. *(re-iss. May81 on 'P.R.T.')*

Stateside Newtown

Jun 63. (7") *(SS 196) <5013>* **TENOR MAN. / UP GOES MY LOVE**

1963. (7") *<5014>* **MIDNIGHT IN WASHINGTON. / WHITE PARAKEET** –

1963. (7") *<5024>* **DANCE AROUND THE CLOCK. / WHAT CAN I SAY AFTER I SAY I'M SORRY** –

1963. (7") *<5025>* **TANDY. / YOU CALL EVERYBODY DARLING** –

Brunswick Decca

Aug 64. (7") *(05910)* **HAPPY BABY. / BIRTH OF THE BOOGIE** –

Oct 64. (7") *(05917) <31650>* **GREEN DOOR. / (YEAH!) SHE'S EVIL**

not iss. Apt

1965. (7") *<25051>* **BIG DADDY. / ST. LOUIS** –

1965. (7") *<25081>* **BURN THAT CANDLE. / STOP, LOOK AND LISTEN** –

1965. (7") *<25087>* **HALEY A GO-GO. / TONGUE TIED TONY** –

not iss. U.A.

1969. (7") *<50483>* **THAT'S HOW I GOT TO MEMPHIS. / AIN'T LOVE FUNNY, HA! HA! HA!** –

not iss. Kama Sutra

1970. (7") *<508>* **ROCK AROUND THE CLOCK. / FRAMED** [–] [ ]

Sonet GNP Cres

1971. (lp) *(SNTF 623) <2097>* **ROCK AROUND THE COUNTRY** [ ] [–]
– Dance around the clock / Games people play / A little piece at a time / I wouldn't have missed it for the world / Bony Moronie / There's a new Moon over my shoulder / Me and Bobby McGee / How many / Who'll stop the rain / Pink eyed pussycat / Travelin' band / No letter today. *(re-iss. Jun74 on 'Hallmark')*

1972. (7") *<162>* **A LITTLE PIECE AT A TIME. / TRAVELIN' BAND** [–] [ ]

May 73. (7") *(SON 2016)* **ME AND BOBBY McGEE. / I WOULDN'T HAVE MISSED IT FOR THE WORLD** [ ] [–]

1973. (lp) *(SNTF 645)* **JUST ROCK AND ROLL MUSIC** [ ] [ ]
– I'm walkin' / High-heel sneakers / Blue suede shoes / Tossin' and turnin' / Flip, flop and fly / Whole lotta shakin' goin' on / CC rider / Lawdy Miss Clawdy / Bring it on home to me / Personality / Crazy man crazy / Rock'n'roll music.

1974. (lp) **LIVE IN SWEDEN (live)** [–] [ ]

Jun 74. (7") *(SON 2043)* **CRAZY MAN CRAZY (live). / LAWDY MISS CLAWDY (live)** [ ] [–]

Atlantic Atlantic

Jun 74. (lp) *(K 51501)* **LIVE IN LONDON '74 (live)** [ ] [ ]
– Shake, rattle & roll / Rudy's rock / Rip it up / Spanish eyes / Razzle dazzle / Rock-a-beatin' boogie / Caravan / See you later alligator / Saints rock and roll / Rock around the clock / Rock the joint.

—— HALEY became ill, leading him into retirement. Although in England, he had given final appearance at Royal Variety Show, Nov79. In 1980, now at age 55, he was diagnosed with brain tumor. On 9 Feb'81 he died of a heart attack.

– (selective) compilations, etc. –

Feb 57. (7") *London; (HLF 8371)* **ROCK THE JOINT. / YES INDEED** [20] [–]

Mar 68. (7") *M.C.A.; (MU 1013)* **ROCK AROUND THE CLOCK. / SHAKE RATTLE AND ROLL** [20] [ ]

May 68. (lp) *M.C.A.; (MUP 318)* **RIP IT UP** [ ] [ ]

Mar 74. (7") *M.C.A.; (MCA 128)* **ROCK AROUND THE CLOCK. / RIP IT UP** [12] [–]

Mar 74. (7") *M.C.A.; <60025>* **(WE'RE GONNA) ROCK AROUND THE CLOCK. / THIRTEEN WOMEN (AND ONLY ONE MAN IN TOWN)** [–] [39]

Apr 81. (7") *M.C.A.; (MCA 694)* **HALEY'S GOLDEN MEDLEY. / ABC BOOGIE** [50] [ ]

Sep 82. (5xlp-box) *Bear Family; <BFX 15068-5>* **ROCKIN' ROLLIN' HALEY** [–] [ ]
(UK-iss.Sep84 on 'Rollercoaster'; same) <(5xcd-box iss.Oct90; BCD 15506)>

Dec 89. (cd/c) *Accord; (30137-2/-4)* **SEE YOU LATER ALLIGATOR** [ ] [–]

Jul 92. (cd/c) *Music Club; (MC CD/TC 068)* **THE VERY BEST OF BILL HALEY & HIS COMETS** [ ] [–]
– Rock around the clock / Shake, rattle and roll / See you later alligator / The saints rock and roll / Rock-a beatin' boogie / Rockin' thru the rye / Rip it up / Don't knock the rock / Mambo rock / Rudy's rock / Razzle dazzle / Skinny Minnie / R.O.C.K. / Thirteen women / ABC boogie / Birth of the boogie / Forty cups of coffee / Two hound dogs / Burn that candle / Calling all Comets.

Oct 94. (cd) *Timeless Treasures; (CD 114)* **BILL HALEY & THE COMETS** [ ] [–]

Feb 95. (cd/c) *More Music; (MOCD/MOMC 3015)* **ROCK AROUND THE CLOCK** [ ] [–]

Aug 96. (cd) *Marble Arch; (MACCD 231)* **BEST OF BILL HALEY** [ ] [–]

May 97. (cd) *A-Play; (10059-2)* **THE HITS COLLECTION** [ ] [ ]

Jan 98. (cd) *Members Edition; (UAE 3001-2)* **BILL HALEY** [ ] [–]

Mar 98. (cd) *Eagle; (EABCD 083)* **THE MASTERS** [ ] [–]

May 99. (6xcd-box) *Bear Family; <(BCD 16157)>* **THE WARNER BROTHERS YEARS AND MORE** [ ] [ ]

Jun 99. (cd) *Half Moon; (HMNCD 043)* **THE VERY BEST OF BILL HALEY & THE COMETS** [ ] [ ]

Aug 99. (cd) *Ultimate; (ULT 4019-2)* **ULTIMATE LEGENDS** [ ] [ ]

Oct 99. (cd) *Nervous; (RSRCD 013)* **THE HOUSE IS ROCKIN'** [ ] [ ]

Jan 00. (cd) *Members Edition; (UAE 30886-2)* **BILL HALEY & HIS COMETS** [ ] [–]

Jan 00. (cd) *Universal; (E 112174-2)* **THE UNIVERSAL MASTERS COLLECTION** [ ] [ ]

Jan 00. (cd) *Hydra; (BCK 27100)* **WE'RE GONNA PARTY** [ ] [–]

Jan 00. (cd) *Hydra; (BCL 27103)* **YOU'RE NEVER TOO OLD TO ROCK** [ ] [–]

Jul 00. (d-cd) *Duoline; (99011)* **ROCK AROUND THE CLOCK** [ ] [–]

Jan 01. (d-cd) *Ember; (EMCDCD 004)* **MR. ROCK 'N' ROLL / FRIENDS FROM THE BEGINNING (Little Richard & Jimi Hendrix)** [ ] [–]

Jul 01. (cd) *Platinum; (PLATCD 664)* **ROCK'N'ROLL LEGEND** [ ] [–]

Jul 01. (cd) *Hydra; (BCK 2711-2)* **ON THE AIR** [ ] [ ]

Sep 01. (cd) *Ember; (EMBCD 3401)* **MR. ROCK 'N' ROLL** [ ] [ ]

Feb 02. (cd/c) *Castle Pulse; (PLS CD/MC 566)* **THE BEST OF BILL HALEY** [ ] [ ]

Nov 02. (cd) *Planet Media; (PML 1051)* **ROCK AROUND THE CLOCK** [ ] [ ]

Dec 02. (cd) *Jerden; (JRCD 7023)* **THE BILL HALEY TAPES** [ ] [–]

Mar 03. (cd) *Universal; (AAMCAD 11957)* **20th CENTURY MASTERS** [ ] [ ]

Mar 03. (cd) *Universal; (E 320161-2)* **GREATEST HITS** [ ] [ ]

Jul 03. (cd) *Rock'n'roll Heroes; (RR 005)* **ROCK'N'ROLL HERO** [ ] [–]

☐ HALF NELSON (see under ⇒ SPARKS)

Daryl HALL & John OATES

Formed: Philadelphia, Pennsylvania, USA . . . 1972 by the duo, who signed to 'Atlantic', following their work with the band, GULLIVER. They had originally met in 1967, while attending local Temple University; HALL had undergone classical training as a boy, and progressed to doo-wop groups while also featuring on a single recorded by future producer KENNY GAMBLE & THE ROMEOS. He then sessioned for many including THE TEMPTONES and SMOKEY ROBINSON, before forming GULLIVER with TIM MOORE, TOM SELLERS and JIM HELMER. They released one self-titled lp in 1969 for 'Elektra', before being joined by OATES, although they broke up before OATES could cut any songs with them. The duo's debut album, 'WHOLE OATS', was produced by Arif Mardin, and was followed in 1974 by 'ABANDONED LUNCHEONETTE', the latter set containing the first of HALL & OATES' chartbound torch ballads in 'SHE'S GONE'. Though not a hit upon its original release, the single made the US Top 10 two years later. The latter track featured on 'WAR BABIES' (1974), a heavier, more experimental set (produced by TODD RUNDGREN) whose commercial failure marked the end of their ill-fated tenure with 'Atlantic'. Moving to 'R.C.A.', the group concentrated on developing their white soul-rock/R&B, scoring almost immediately when their eponymous 1975 set climbed into the US Top 20 following the massive success of the infectious 'SARA SMILE' (co-written by HALL's sometime collaborator and girlfriend, Sara Allen). A follow-up set, 'BIGGER THAN BOTH OF US' (1976) was even more successful, spawning the duo's first No.1 hit, 'RICH GIRL'. Though their profile took a bit of a battering towards the end of the decade, HALL & OATES emerged with a gleaming new synth/pop-soul sound on 'VOICES' (1980), making the Top 20 with a cover of The Righteous Brothers' 'YOU'VE LOST THAT LOVIN' FEELIN' and scoring a belated second No.1 with 'KISS ON MY LIST' (it also included the original version of 'EVERY TIME YOU GO AWAY', later a hit for PAUL YOUNG). Vaguely akin to a two-headed American version of PHIL COLLINS (granted, a disturbing thought), HALL & OATES cleaned up in both the singles and albums market with a string of MOR hits including 'PRIVATE EYES', 'I

CAN'T GO FOR THAT' (NO CAN DO)', 'MANEATER' and 'SAY IT ISN'T SO'; 'PRIVATE EYES' (1981) and 'H2O' (1982) remain among their best selling albums. The mid-80's concert set, 'LIVE AT THE APOLLO', saw them hooking up with TEMPTATIONS heroes, DAVID RUFFIN and EDDIE KENDRICKS, after which they took time out to work on side projects. Returning in 1988, they scored with the Top 5 hit, 'EVERYTHING YOUR HEART DESIRES', although subsequent albums, 'OOH YEAH!' (1988) and 'CHANGE OF SEASON' (1990) failed to scale the commercial heights of yesteryear. While 1997's 'MARIGOLD SKY' garnered few column inches, 2003's 'DO IT FOR LOVE' (2003) enjoyed a more hospitable reception from both the press and longtime fans. While hardly breaking any new ground, the record was a more than passable attempt at resurrecting the slick, blue-eyed soul vibe of their best work while both DARYL and JOHN were in fine voice throughout, if a little burnished by the intervening years. • **Songwriters:** HALL-OATES except; THE WAY YOU DO THE THINGS YOU DO – MY GIRL (Temptations) / CAN'T HELP FALLING IN LOVE (Elvis Presley) / LOVE TRAIN (O'Jays) / etc. HALL covered; WRITTEN IN STONE (J.Allen-S.Dubin-K.Savigar) / ME AND MRS. JONES (Billy Paul). • **Trivia:** ROBERT FRIPP (of KING CRIMSON) produced HALL's solo outing 'SACRED SONGS'.

Album rating: WHOLE OATS (*5) / ABANDONED LUNCHEONETTE (*7) / WAR BABIES (*4) / DARYL HALL & JOHN OATES (*6) / BIGGER THAN BOTH OF US (*5) / NO GOODBYES copilation (*4) / BEAUTY ON A BACK STREET (*6) / LIVETIME (*4) / ALONG THE RED LEDGE (*6) / X-STATIC (*4) / SACRED SONGS (*4; by Daryl Hall) / VOICES (*6) / PRIVATE EYES (*7) / H20 (*7) / ROCK'N'SOUL PART 1 compilation (*8) / BIG BAM BOOM (*6) / LIVE AT THE APOLLO with David Ruffin & Eddie Kendrick (*5) / THREE HEARTS IN A HAPPY ENDING MACHINE (*4; by Daryl Hall) / OOH YEAH! (*4) / CHANGE OF SEASON (*4) / THE BEST OF HALL & OATES – LOOKING BACK compilation (*8) / SOUL ALONE (*4; by Daryl Hall) / MARIGOLD SKY (*3)

DARYL HALL (b.DARYL HOHL, 11 Oct'48, Pottstown, Philadelphia) – vocals, keyboards (ex-TEMPTONES, ex-solo artist, ex-CELLAR DOOR, ex-EXECUTIVE SUITE, ex-GULLIVER) / **JOHN OATES** (b. 7 Apr'49, New York, USA) – vocals, guitar (ex-MASTERS) with various personnel session players.

Atlantic Atlantic

Sep 72. (7"; as WHOLE OATS) *<2922>* **GOODNIGHT AND GOOD MORNING. / ALL OUR LOVE** [–] [ ]

Nov 72. (lp) *<7242>* **WHOLE OATS** [–] [ ]
– I'm sorry / All our love / Georgie / Fall in Philadelphia / Water wheel / Lazy man / Good night & good morning / They needed each other / Southeast city window / Thank you for . . . / Lily (are you happy). *(UK-iss.Sep76; K 50306) (cd-iss. Feb93; 7567 81423)*

Nov 72. (7") *<2939>* **I'M SORRY. / LILY (ARE YOU HAPPY)** [–] [ ]

Jan 74. (lp) *(K 40534) <7269>* **ABANDONED LUNCHEONETTE** [ ] [ ]
– I'm just a kid (don't make me feel like a man) / Laughing boy / She's gone / Las Vegas turnaround / Had I known you better then / Lady rain / When the morning comes / Abandoned luncheonette / Everytime I look at you. *<US re-iss. Oct76 hit No.33> (cd-iss. Jun93; 7567 81537-2)*

Jan 74. (7") *(K 19422)* **LAS VEGAS TURNAROUND. / I'M JUST A KID** [ ] [–]

Feb 74. (7") *<2993>* **SHE'S GONE. / I'M JUST A KID (DON'T MAKE ME FEEL LIKE A MAN)** [–] [60]

Jul 74. (7") *(K 10459) <3026>* **WHEN THE MORNING COMES. / LADY RAIN** [ ] [ ]

Sep 74. (7") *(K 10502)* **SHE'S GONE. / ABANDONED LUNCHEONETTE** [ ] [–]

Nov 74. (lp) *(K 50086) <18109>* **WAR BABIES** [ ] Oct74 [86]
– Can't stop the music (he played it much too long) / Is it a star / Beanie G and the rose tattoo / You're much too soon / 70's scenario / War baby son of Zorro / I'm watching you (a mutant romance) / Better watch your back / Screaming through December / Johnny Gone and the "C" eaters. *(cd-iss. Jul96; 7567 81489-2)*

Nov 74. (7") *<3239>* **CAN'T STOP THE MUSIC (HE PLAYED IT MUCH TOO LONG). / 70'S SCENARIO** [–] [ ]

R.C.A. R.C.A.

Sep 75. (lp) *<(APL-1 1144)>* **DARYL HALL & JOHN OATES** [56] [17]
– Camelia / Sara smile / Alone too long / Out of me, out of you / Nothing at all / Gino (the manager) / (You know) It doesn't matter anymore / Ennui on the mountain / Grounds for separation / Soldering. *(re-iss. Apr80; INTS 5010)*

Sep 75. (7") *(2614) <10373>* **CAMELIA. / ENNUI ON THE MOUNTAIN** [ ] [ ]

Nov 75. (7") *<10436>* **ALONE TOO LONG. / NOTHING AT ALL** [–] [ ]

Jan 76. (7") *(2656) <10530>* **SARA SMILE. / SOLDERING** [ ] [4]

May 76. (7") *(2684)* **GINO (THE MANAGER). / SOLDERING** [ ] [–]

Sep 76. (lp) *<(APL-1 1467)>* **BIGGER THAN BOTH OF US** [25] Aug76 [13]
– Back together again / Rich girl / Crazy eyes / Do what you want, be what you are / Kerry / London luck and love / Room to breathe / You'll never learn / Falling.

Oct 76. (7") *<10808>* **DO WHAT YOU WANT, BE WHAT YOU ARE. / YOU'LL NEVER LEARN** [–] [39]

—— late in '76 DARYL duetted with RUTH COPELAND on single 'Heaven'.

Jan 77. (7") *<10860>* **RICH GIRL. / LONDON LUCK & LOVE** [–] [1]

Jan 77. (7") *(2757)* **RICH GIRL. / YOU'LL NEVER LEARN** [ ] [–]

May 77. (7") *<10970>* **BACK TOGETHER AGAIN. / ROOM TO BREATHE** [–] [28]

May 77. (7") *(PB 9053)* **BACK TOGETHER AGAIN. / ENNUI ON THE MOUNTAIN** [ ] [–]

Oct 77. (lp/c) *(PL/PK 12300) <2300>* **BEAUTY ON A BACK STREET** [40] Sep77 [30]
– Don't change / Why do lovers (break each other's heart?) / You must be good for something / The emptyness / Love hurts (love heals) / Bigger than both of us / Bad habits and infections / Winged bull / The girl who used to be. *(re-iss. Jul84; NL 82300)*

Oct 77. (7") *(PB 1132) <11132>* **WHY DO LOVERS (BREAK EACH OTHER'S HEART?). / THE GIRL WHO USED TO BE** [ ] [73]

Jan 78. (7") *<11181>* **DON'T CHANGE. / THE EMPTYNESS** [–] [ ]

—— **CHARLES DE CHANT** – saxophone, keyboards, perc. repl. TOM SCOTT / **KENNY PASSARELLI** – bass repl. LEE SKLAR & SCOTT EDWARDS / **ROGER POPE** – drums repl. JEFF PORCARO / **CALEB QUAYE** – lead guitar / **DAVID KENT** – keyboards repl. other sessioners.

Jun 78. (lp/c) *(PL/PK 12802) <2802>* **LIVE TIME (live)** [ ] May78 [42]
– Rich girl / The emptyness / Do what you want, be what you are / I'm just a kid / Sara smile / Abandoned luncheonette / Room to breathe. *(re-iss. Jun83; INTS 5252)*

Aug 78. (7") *<111371>* **IT'S A LAUGH. / SERIOUS MATTER** [–] [20]

Sep 78. (7") *(PB 9324)* **THE LAST TIME. / SERIOUS MATTER** [ ] [–]

Sep 78. (lp/c) *(PL/PK 12804) <2894>* **ALONG THE RED LEDGE** [ ] [27]
– It's a laugh / Melody for a memory / The last time / I don't wanna lose you / Have I been away too long / Alley katz / Don't blame it on love / Serious matter / Pleasure beach / August day. *(re-iss. Jun83; INTS 5258) (re-iss. 1987 lp/c; NL/NK 84231)*

Jan 79. (7") *(PB 1424) <11424>* **I DON'T WANNA LOSE YOU. / AUGUST DAY** [ ] Dec78 [42]

—— They retained **DECHANT, PASSARELLI** (on next only), and brought in **TOM 'T-Bone' WOLK** – bass, synthe / **G.E. SMITH** – guitar / **MICKEY CURRY** – drums

Nov 79. (7") *(PB 9466)* **PORTABLE RADIO. / NUMBER ONE** [ ] [–]

Nov 79. (lp/c) *<(AFL-1 3494)>* **X-STATIC** [ ] Oct79 [33]
– The woman comes and goes / Wait for me / Portable radio / All you want is Heaven / Who said the world was fair / Running from Paradise / Number one / Bebop – Drop / Hallofon / Intravino.

May 80. (7") *(PB 1747) <11747>* **WAIT FOR ME. / NO BRAIN NO PAIN** [ ] Oct79 [18]

May 80. (7") *<11920>* **WHO SAID THE WORLD WAS FAIR. / ALL YOU WANT IS HEAVEN** [–] [ ]

Jun 80. (7") *(RUN 1)* **RUNNING FROM PARADISE. / BEBOP – DROP** [41] [–]

Jul 80. (7") *<12048>* **HOW DOES IT FEEL TO BE BACK. / UNITED STATE** [–] [30]

Aug 80. (lp/c) *(PL/PK 13646) <AQL-1 3646>* **VOICES** [ ] [17]
– How does it feel to be back / Big kids / United state / Hard to be in love with you / Kiss on my list / Gotta lotta nerve (perfect perfect) / You've lost that lovin' feelin' / You make my dreams / Everytime you go away / Africa / Diddy doo wop (I hear the voices). *(re-iss. Sep81; RCALP 3044) (re-iss. Oct87 lp/c/cd; NL/NK/ND 90078)*

Sep 80. (7") *<12103>* **YOU'VE LOST THAT LOVIN' FEELIN' / DIDDY DOO WOP (I HEAR THE VOICES)** [–] [12]

Sep 80. (7") *(RCA 1)* **YOU'VE LOST THAT LOVIN' FEELIN'. / UNITED STATE** [55] [–]

Nov 80. (7") *(RCA 15)* <12142> **KISS ON MY LIST. / AFRICA** 33 Jan81 1

Jun 81. (7") *(RCA 86)* <12217> **YOU MAKE MY DREAMS. / GOTTA LOTTA NERVE (PERFECT PERFECT)** Apr81 5

Sep 81. (7"/12") *(RCA/+T 134)* <12296> **PRIVATE EYES. / TELL ME WHAT YOU WANT** Aug81 1
(re-promoted.Mar82; hit UK No.32)

Sep 81. (lp/c) *(RCA LP/K 6001)* <AFL-1 4028> **PRIVATE EYES** 8 5
– Private eyes / Loking for a good gun / I can't go for that (no can do) / Mama a mano / Did it in a minute / Head above water / Tell me what you want / Friday let me down / Ungaurded minute / Your imagination / Some men. *(cd-iss. Dec84; PD 84028) (re-iss. Oct87 lp/c/cd; NL/NK/ND 90079)*

Jan 82. (7"/12") *(RCA/+T 172)* <12361> **I CAN'T GO FOR THAT (NO CAN DO). / UNGUARDED MINUTE** 8 Nov81 1

Mar 82. (7") <13065> **DID IT IN A MINUTE. / HEAD ABOVE WATER** – 9

Jun 82. (7"/12") *(RCA/+T 239)* <13252> **YOUR IMAGINATION. / SARA SMILE** 33

Oct 82. (7"/12") *(RCA/+T 290)* <13354> **MANEATER. / DELAYED REACTION** 6 1

Oct 82. (lp/c) *(RCA LP/K 6056)* <4383> **H2O** 24 3
– Maneater / Crime pays / One on one / Art of heartbreak / Open all night / Family man / Italian girls / Guessing games / Delayed reaction / At tension / Go solo. *(cd-iss. 1985; PD 84383)*

Jan 83. (7"/12") *(RCA/+T 305)* <13421> **ONE ON ONE. / ART OF HEARTBREAK** 63 7
(US 12") <13421> – ('A'club) / I can't go for that (no can do) (extended).

Apr 83. (7") <13507> **FAMILY MAN. / OPEN ALL NIGHT** – 6

Apr 83. (7") *(RCA 323)* **FAMILY MAN. / CRIME PAYS** 15 –
(12") *(RCAT 323)* – Open All Night.

Sep 83. (7") <13654> **SAY IT ISN'T SO. / KISS ON MY LIST** – 2

Oct 83. (7"/12") *(RCA/+T 375)* **SAY IT ISN'T SO. / DID IT IN A MINUTE** 69 –

Oct 83. (lp/c) *(PL/PK 84858)* <4858> **ROCK'N SOUL, PART 1** (compilation) 16 7
– Sara smile / She's gone / Rich girl / Kiss on my list / You make my dreams / Private eyes / I can't go for that (no can do) / Maneater / One on one / Wait for me (live) / Adult education / Say it isn't so. *(cd-iss. Oct84; PD 84858)*

Feb 84. (7") <13714> **ADULT EDUCATION. / MANEATER** – 8

Feb 84. (7") *(RCA 396)* **ADULT EDUCATION. / SAY IT ISN'T SO** 63 –
(12"+=) *(RCAT 396)* – I can't go for that (no can do).

Oct 84. (7"/12") *(RCA/+T 449)* <13916> **OUT OF TOUCH. / COLD DARK AND YESTERDAY** 48 Sep84 1

Oct 84. (lp/c/cd) *(PL/PK/PD 85309)* <5309> **BIG BAM BOOM** 28 5
– Going thru the motions / Cold dark and yesterday / All American girl / Possession obsession / Dance on your knees / Out of touch / Method of modern love / Bank on your love / Some things are better left unsaid.

Jan 85. (7"/12") *(RCA/+T 472)* <13960> **METHOD OF MODERN LOVE. / BANK ON YOUR LOVE** 21 Dec84 5
(d7"+=) *(RCAD 472)* – I can't go for that (live) / Maneater (live).

Mar 85. (7") <14035> **SOME THINGS ARE BETTER LEFT UNSAID. / ALL AMERICAN GIRL** – 18

May 85. (7") *(PB 49967)* **OUT OF TOUCH (remix). / DANCE ON YOUR KNEES** 62 –
(12"+=) *(PT 49968)* – Every time you go away.

May 85. (7") <14098> **POSSESSION OBSESSION. / DANCE ON YOUR KNEES** – 30

Aug 85. (7") <14178> **A NITE AT THE APOLLO! (live medley:- THE WAY YOU DO THE THINGS YOU DO – MY GIRL). / EVERY TIME YOU GO AWAY** – 20

Sep 85. (7")(12") *(PB 49935)(PT 49936)* **A NITE AT THE APOLLO LIVE! (live medley: – THE WAY YOU DO THE THINGS YOU DO – MY GIRL). / ADULT EDUCATION** 58 –
(above & below credited eith DAVID RUFFIN & EDDIE KENDRICKS; ex-Temptations)

Sep 85. (lp/c/cd) *(PL/PK/PD 87035)* <7035> **LIVE AT THE APOLLO (WITH DAVID RUFFIN & EDDIE KENDRICKS)** 32 21
– Get ready – Ain't too proud to beg – The way you do the things you do – My girl / When something is wrong with my baby / Everytime you go away / I can't go for that (no can do) / One by one / Possession obsession / Adult education. *(cd-iss. Sep93; 74321 16003-2)*

—— In 1986, they split for a while, HALL made solo album

Arista Arista

Apr 88. (7"/12") *(109/609 869)* <9684> **EVERYTHING YOUR HEART DESIRES. / REALOVE** 3

Jun 88. (lp/c/cd) *(208/408/258 895)* <8539> **OOH YEAH!** 52 May88 24
– Downtown life / Everything your heart desires / I'm in pieces / Missed opportunity / Talking all night / Rockability / Rocket to God / Soul love / ReaLove / Keep on pushin' love.

Jul 88. (7") <9727> **MISSED OPPORTUNITY. / SOUL LOVE** – 29

Sep 88. (7") <9753> **DOWNTOWN LIFE. / ('A'-Urban mix)** – 31

Sep 90. (7") <2085> **SO CLOSE. / SO CLOSE (unplugged version)** – 11

Sep 90. (7")(c-s) *(113600)(411050)* **SO CLOSE. / CAN'T HELP FALLING IN LOVE** 69 –
(12"+=)(cd-s+=) *(613600)(663600)* – She's gone (live).

Nov 90. (cd/c/lp) *(210/410/260 548)* <8614> **CHANGE OF SEASON** 44 Oct90 61
– So close / Starting all over again / Sometimes a mind changes / Change of season / I ain't gonna take it this time / Everywhere I look / Give it up (old habits) / Don't hold back your love / Halfway there / Only love / Heavy rain / So close – unplugged.

Dec 90. (c-s) <2157> **DON'T HOLD BACK YOUR LOVE / CHANGE OF SEASON** – 41

Jan 91. (7")(c-s) *(113980)411329)* **EVERYWHERE I LOOK. / SOMETIMES A MIND CHANGES** 74 –
(12"+=)(cd-s+=) *(613980)(663980)* – I can't go for that (Ben Liebrand mix).

Oct 91. (cd/c) *(PD/PK 90388)* **LOOKING BACK – THE BEST OF DARYL HALL & JOHN OATES** (compilation) 9
– She's gone / Sara smile / Rich girl / You've lost that lovin' feelin' / Kiss on my list / Every time you go away / Private eyes / I can't go for that (no can do) / Maneater / One on one / Family man / Adult education / Out of touch / Method of modern love / Starting all over again. *(cd+/c+=)* – Back together again / So close / Everything your heart desires.

DARYL HALL

not iss. Parallex

1968. (7") *(404>* **A LONELY GIRL / VICKY, VICKY** –

not iss. Amy

1968. (7") <11049> **THE PRINCESS & THE SOLDIER. / (part 2)** –

R.C.A. R.C.A.

Apr 80. (lp/c) *(PL/PK 13573)* <3573> **SACRED SONGS** (rec.1977) 58
– Sacred songs / Something in 4/4 time / Babs and Babs / Urban landscape / NYNCY / The farther away (I am) / Why was it so easy / Don't leave me alone with her / Survive / Without tears. *(re-iss. Jul84; NL 83573)*

Apr 80. (7") <12001> **SACRED SONGS. / SOMETHING IN 4-4 TIME** –

Jul 86. (7"/12") *(HALL/+T 1)* <14387> **DREAMTIME. / LET IT OUT** 28 5

Aug 86. (lp/c/cd) *(PL/PK/PD 87196)* <7196> **THREE HEARTS IN THE HAPPY ENDING MACHINE** 26 29
– Dreamtime / Only a vision / I wasn't born yesterday / Someone like you / Next stop / For you / Foolish pride / Right as rain / Let it out / What's going to happen to us. *(re-iss. May88)*

Oct 86. (7") <5038-7> **FOOLISH PRIDE. / WHAT'S GOING TO HAPPEN TO US** – 33

Nov 86. (7") *(HALL 2)* **I WASN'T BORN YESTERDAY. / WHAT'S GONNA HAPPEN TO US** –
(12"+=) *(HALLT 2)* – Dreamtime.

Jan 87. (7") <5105-7> **SOMEONE LIKE YOU. / ('A'sax solo version)** – 57

—— writes with **PETER LORD MORELAND** – keyboards / **V. JEFFREY SMITH** – synth.bass / **ALAN GORRIE** – bass / other musicians **TOMMY EYRE** – keyboards / **MEL WESSON** – programming / **TREVOR MURRELL** – drums / **BOB BITSAND** – bass / **MYLES BOULD** – percussion

Epic Epic

Sep 93. (7"/c-s) *(659 555-7/-4)* <77139> **I'M IN A PHILLY MOOD (Edit) / MONEY CHANGES EVERYTHING** 59 82
(cd-s+=) *(659 555-2)* – I've finally seen the light.
(cd-s) *(659 555-5)* – ('A'side) / Love T.K.O. (live) / Me and Mrs. Jones (live).
(re-iss. Mar94, hit UK 52)

Oct 93. (cd/c/lp) *(473921-2/-4/-1)* <53937> **SOUL ALONE** 57
– Power of seduction / This time / Love revelation / I'm in a Philly mood / Borderline / Stop loving me, stop loving you / Help me find a way to your

heart / Send me / Wildfire / Money changes everything / Written in stone. *(re-dist.Jan94)*

Jan 94. (c-s) *(659 998-4)* **STOP LOVING ME, STOP LOVING YOU. / MONEY CHANGES EVERYTHING** [30] [ ]
(12"+=/cd-s+=) *(659 998-6/-2)* – (4 more 'A'mixes).

May 94. (7"/c-s) *(660 410-7/-4)* **HELP ME FIND A WAY TO YOUR HEART. / POWER OF SEDUCTION** [70] [ ]
(cd-s+=) *(660 410-2)* – Stop loving me, stop loving you (live) / I'm in a Philly mood (live).

— Below on 'Mercury' & the theme from USA soccer World Cup Finals.

Jun 94. (7"pic-d/c-s/cd-s; DARYL HALL & SOUNDS OF BLACKNESS) *(662 059-7/-4/-2)* **GLORYLAND. / ('A'mixes)** [36] [ ]

Aug 94. (c-s) *(660 719-4)* **WILDFIRE / THIS TIME** [ ] [–]
(cd-s+=) *(660 719-2)* – ('A'extended).

— DARYL surfaced again when credited in May95 on DUSTY SPRINGFIELD's UK Top 50 hit single 'WHEREVER WOULD I BE'.

C.N.R. Liquid 8

Jul 03. (cd) *(2299957-2) <12109>* **CAN'T STOP DREAMING** (issued Japan 1999) [ ] [ ]
– Cab driver / Let me be the one / Can't stop dreaming / Never let me go / Holding out for love / Justify / What's in your world / Hold on to me / She's gone / All by myself / Fools rush in.

DARYL HALL & JOHN OATES

— reformed in 1997

Eagle Push

Nov 97. (cd/c) *(EAG CD/MC 011) <90200>* **MARIGOLD SKY** [ ] Oct97 [95]
– Romeo is bleeding / Marigold sky / The sky is falling / Out of the blue / Want to / Love out loud / Throw the roses away / I don't think so / Promise ain't enough / Time won't pass me by / Hold on to yourself / War of words / Hold on to yourself (remix).

Feb 98. (c-s) *(EAGCS 011)* **THE SKY IS FALLING / SHE'S GONE (live)** [ ] [ ]
(cd-s+=) *(EAGXA 011)* – Sara smile (live) / Out of touch (live).

Sanctuary U-Watch

Mar 03. (cd) *(SANCD 166) <480100>* **DO IT FOR LOVE** [37] Feb03 [ ]
– Man on a mission / Do it for love / Someday we'll know / Forever for you / Life's too short / Getaway car / Make you stay / Miss DJ / "She" got me bad / Breath of your life / Intuition / Heartbreak time / Something about you / Love in a dangerous time.

Jun 03. (cd-s) *(SANXD 199)* **MAN ON A MISSION / KISS ON MY LIST (live) / OUT OF TOUCH (live)** [ ] [–]

– compilations, etc. –

on 'Atlantic' unless mentioned otherwise

Jul 76. (7") *<3332>* **SHE'S GONE. / I'M JUST A KID (DON'T MAKE ME FEEL LIKE A MAN)** [–] [ ]

Sep 76. (7"ep) *(K 10828)* **SHE'S GONE / WAR BABY SON OF ZORRO / LAZY MAN** [42] [–]

Jan 77. (7") *(K 10887)* **LAS VEGAS TURNAROUND. / HAD I KNOWN YOU BETTER THEN** [ ] [–]

Mar 77. (lp) *(K 50347) <18213>* **NO GOODBYES** [ ] [92]
(cd-iss. Jul96; 7567 80430-2)

Apr 77. (7") *(K 10915)* **IT'S UNCANNY. / BEANIE G. & THE ROSE TATTOO** [ ] [–]

Apr 77. (lp) *Chelsea; (CHL 547)* **PAST TIMES BEHIND** (71-72) [ ] [ ]

May 77. (7") *Chelsea; <3063>* **THE REASON WHY (Daryl Hall & GULLIVER). / IF THAT'S WHAT MAKES YOU HAPPY (Hall & Oates)** [ ] [–]

Jun 77. (7") *<3397>* **IT'S UNCANNY. / LILY (ARE YOU HAPPY)** [–] [80]

Jul 81. (7") *(K 11597)* **SHE'S GONE. / WHEN THE MORNING COMES** [ ] [–]

May 82. (7") *RCA Gold; (GOLD 547)* **KISS ON MY LIST. / RUNNING FROM PARADISE** [ ] [–]

May 83. (c-ep) *R.C.A.; (RCXK 007)* **CASSETTE EP** [ ] [–]
– I can't go for that (no can do) / Maneater / Private eyes / Kiss on my list.

Jun 84. (lp) *Magnum Force; (THBM 003)* **THE PROVIDER** [ ] [–]

Oct 85. (lp) *Thunderbolt; (THBL 035)* **REALLY SMOKIN'** [ ] [–]
(cd-iss. Jul93; CDTB 122)

Apr 86. (lp/c) *Showcase; (SHLP/SHTC 134)* **THE EARLY YEARS** [ ] [–]

Nov 86. (7") *Old Gold; (OG9658)* **MANEATER. / I CAN'T GO FOR THAT (NO CAN DO)** [ ] [–]

Nov 86. (lp/c/cd) *Meteor; (SMT/SMTC/CDSM 006)* **20 CLASSIC TRACKS** [ ] [–]

Nov 88. (lp/c/cd) *Big Time; (221/211/241 5012)* **FIRST SESSIONS** [ ] [–]

Oct 92. (cd-ep) *Old Gold; (OG 6184)* **I CAN'T GO FOR THAT (NO CAN DO) / PRIVATE EYES / KISS IS ON MY LIST** [ ] [–]

Oct 92. (cd-ep) *Old Gold; (OG 6188)* **MANEATER / FAMILY MAN / METHOD OF MODERN LOVE** [ ] [–]

Feb 94. (cd/c) *Javelin; (HAD CD/MC 107)* **SPOTLIGHT ON HALL & OATES** [ ] [–]

Sep 94. (cd) *Wisepack; (LECD 084)* **LEGENDS IN MUSIC** [ ] [–]

Sep 94. (cd) *Prestige; (CDSGP 0128)* **A LOT OF CHANGES COMIN'** [ ] [–]

Feb 95. (cd) *B.A.M.;* **PEARLS OF THE PAST** [ ] [–]

Oct 95. (cd) *R.C.A.; (74321 28983-2)* **ROCK'N'SOUL PART 2 (GREATEST HITS)** [ ] [–]

Jul 96. (cd) *(812272205-2)* **ATLANTIC COLLECTION – THE BEST OF HALL & OATES** [ ] [–]

Feb 98. (cd) *R.C.A.; (74321 43662-2)* **WITH LOVE FROM HALL & OATES (THE BEST OF THE BALLADS)** [ ] [ ]

Sep 01. (cd/c) *(74321 88697-2/-4)* **THE ESSENTIAL COLLECTION** [26] [ ]
– Sara smile / She's gone / Rich girl / Wait for me / Kiss on my list / I can't go for that (no can do) / Private eyes / Maneater / One on one / Family man / Say it isn't so / Adult education / Out of touch / Method of modern love / Everything your heart desires / So close / Starting it all over again / I can't go for that (no can do) (Hoax remix).

Oct 01. (c-s) *(74321 89092-4)* **I CAN'T GO FOR THAT (NO CAN DO) (remix) / ('A'mix)** [ ] [–]
(12"+=/cd-s+=) *(74321 89092-1/-2)* – ('A'mixes).

GULLIVER

with **DARYL HALL**

Elektra Elektra

1969. (7") *<45689>* **EVERY DAY'S A LOVELY DAY / ANGELINA** [–] [ ]

1970. (lp) *(2410 006) <EKS 74070>* **GULLIVER** [ ] 1969 [ ]
– Every day's a lovely day / I'm really smokin' / Christine / Rose come home / Enough – Over the mountain / Angelina / Flogene / Lemon road / Seventy / Truly good song. *<(cd-iss. Sep02 on 'Collectors Choice'; CCM 0310-2)>*

1970. (7") *<45698>* **A TRULY GOOD SONG. / EVERY DAY'S A LOVELY DAY** [–] [ ]

☐ Pete HAM (see under ⇒ BADFINGER)

☐ Peter HAMMILL
(see under ⇒ VAN DER GRAAF GENERATOR)

Herbie HANCOCK

Born: 12 Apr'40, Chicago, Illinois, USA. While at Iowa college in the late 50's, HANCOCK formed a 17-piece band/ensemble to play local gigs. At the turn of the 60's, he was invited to play piano in DONALD BYRD's combo, the trumpeter inspiring HANCOCK to issue his 1962 debut solo lp, 'TAKIN' OFF'; an interpretation of 'WATERMELON MAN' by MONGO SANTAMARIA became a surprise Top 10 hit the following year. HANCOCK's classically-trained, confident delivery was noted by legendary trumpeter, MILES DAVIS, who swiftly poached him for his own quintet. The pianist remained an integral part of MILES' pioneering jazz outfit, HANCOCK taking the group's fusion experiments in his own direction following his departure in 1968. Although he had made several albums for 'Blue Note' during the mid 60's (as well as scoring the soundtrack for MGM's cult classic, 'BLOW-UP'), HANCOCK moved on to 'Warner Bros', releasing the highly acclaimed set, 'MWANDISHI' (1971). After relocating to L.A., he signed to 'Columbia' and assembled The HEADHUNTERS (who scored a massive mid-70's dancefloor hit in their own right with the classic 'GOD MADE ME FUNKY') backing group, achieving Top 20 crossover success early in 1974 with an album of the same name. A seminal release, the record found HANCOCK flirting with funk and initiating the most critical and commercial period of his career to date. Subsequent HANCOCK albums such as 'THRUST' (1974), 'MAN-CHILD' (1975), 'SECRETS' (1976), 'SUNLIGHT' (1978) and 'FEETS DON'T FAIL ME NOW' (1979), all made the mainstream US charts, while the man had two UK Top 20 hits (from the latter two sets), 'I THOUGHT IT WAS YOU' and 'YOU BET YOUR LOVE'. Two live collaborations in 1979 with CHICK COREA kept his jazz roots intact, while he also got back to basics with 'V.S.O.P.' (1977), an acoustic formation featuring TONY WILLIAMS, RON CARTER, FREDDIE HUBBARD and WAYNE SHORTER. In 1980, HANCOCK delivered his umpteenth set, 'MONSTER', which, like its studio predecessor, utilized his new toy, an electronic vocoder (voice-box). Just as he'd anticipated the jazz-funk scene of the mid-70's, HANCOCK was in at the frontline of the electro/hip-hop explosion with his groundbreaking, BILL LASWELL-produced 'ROCKIT' single in 1983. Lifted from his best selling album, 'FUTURE SHOCK', the track became a Top 10 hit in Britain (only Top 75 in the States), and although HANCOCK dabbled in further experimentation, it was to be his only major crossover success of the decade. During the latter half of the 80's, he became more noted for his soundtrack work (he had previously worked on 'DEATH WISH' in '75), scoring for such box-office smashes as 'Colors' and 'Round Midnight'. Recorded at the height of the jazz-rap crossover scene in the early 90's 'DIS IS DA DRUM' (1995) found HANCOCK again pursuing the cross-fertilisation integral to his best work. Backed up by the likes of BERNIE MAUPIN, HUBERT LAWS and BILL SUMMERS, and roping in a slew of hip-hop faces, HANCOCK served up another tasty set of up-to-the-minute fusion, embracing hip-hop recording techniques and updating past glories like 1974's 'BUTTERFLY'. 'NEW STANDARD' (1995), meanwhile, translated songs as diverse as Don Henley's 'NEW YORK MINUTE', Stevie Wonder's 'YOU'VE GOT IT BAD GIRL' and Nirvana's 'ALL APOLOGIES' into the acoustic jazz idiom with surprisingly effective results. On the acclaimed 'GERSHWIN'S WORLD' (1998) – recorded and released to mark the 100th anniversary of GERSHWIN's birth – it was the turn of the legendary songwriter to undergo the HANCOCK treatment, although the not inconsiderable contributions of guests such as JONI MITCHELL, STEVIE WONDER and the ORPHEUS CHAMBER ORCHESTRA deserve mention in their own right. Almost two decades on from 'ROCKIT', HERBIE teamed up with BILL LASWELL once more for another stab at futureshock electronica in the shape of 'FUTURE 2 FUTURE' (2001).

Album rating: TAKIN' OFF (*8) / MY POINT OF VIEW (*7) / INVENTIONS AND DIMENSIONS (*6) / EMPYREAN ISLES (*8) / MAIDEN VOYAGE (*9) / BLOW-UP soundtrack (*6) / SPEAK LIKE A CHILD (*6) / THE PRISONER (*5) / FAT ALBERT ROTUNDA (*5) / MWANDISHI (*7) / CROSSINGS (*7) / SEXTANT (*5) / HEADHUNTERS (*7) / THRUST (*5) / DEATH WISH soundtrack (*4) / FLOOD (*6) / MAN-CHILD (*6) / SECRETS (*5) / V.S.O.P. – THE QUINTET (*7) / SUNLIGHT (*5) / FEETS DON'T FAIL ME NOW (*5) / AN EVENING WITH HERBIE HANCOCK & CHICK COREA (*6) / MONSTER (*4) / MR. HANDS (*5) / MAGIC WINDOWS (*5) / LITE ME UP (*4) / FUTURE SHOCK (*7) / SOUND SYSTEM (*5) / VILLAGE LIFE (*7) / PERFECT MACHINE (*5) / DIS IS DA DRUM (*4) / THE COLLECTION compilation (*7) / THE NEW STANDARD (*5) / GERSHWIN'S WORLD (*7) / FUTURE 2 FUTURE (*6)

HERBIE HANCOCK – keyboards, etc. (ex-DONALD BYRD Band) with **DEXTER GORDON** – tenor sax / **FREDDIE HUBBARD** – trumpet / **BUTCH WARREN** – bass / **BILLY HIGGINS** – drums

Blue Note Blue Note

May 62. (lp) *<(BLP 4109)>* **TAKIN' OFF** ☐ ☐
– Watermelon man / Three bags full / Empty pockets / The maze / Driftin' / Alone and I. *(re-iss. Sep84; BST 84109) (cd-iss. May86; CDP 746506-2) (cd re-iss. Jun96; CDP 837643-2)*

Jun 62. (7") *<45-1862>* **WATERMELON MAN. / THREE BAGS FULL** – ☐

Aug 62. (7") *<45-1863>* **DRIFTIN'. / ALONE AND I** – ☐

— In 1963, he joined MILES DAVIS until 1968. Carried on solo career).

— Now a septet w/ **DONALD BYRD** – trumpet / **GRACKEN MONCUR** – trombone / **HANK MOBLEY** – tenor sax / **GRANT GREEN** – guitar / **CHUCK ISRAELS** – bass / **ANTHONY WILLIAMS** – drums

Mar 63. (lp) *<(BLP 4126)>* **MY POINT OF VIEW** ☐ 1963 ☐
– Blind man, blind man / A tribute to someone / King Cobra / The pleasure is mine / And what if I don't. *(re-iss. Oct84; same) (cd-iss. Apr88; BNZ 44)*

Apr 63. (7") *<(45-1887)>* **BLIND MAN, BLIND MAN. / (part 2)** ☐ ☐

— with **PAUL CHAMBER** – bass / **WILLIE BOBO** – percussion / **OSVALDO MARTINEZ** – percussion

1964. (lp) *<(BLP 4147)>* **INVENTIONS AND DIMENSIONS** ☐ Aug63 ☐
– Sucotash / Triangle / Jack rabbit / Mimoson / Jump ahead. *(cd-iss. Apr89 on 'Blue Note'; CDP 784147-2)*

— now with **FREDDIE HUBBARD** / **RON CARTER** – bass / **TONY WILLIAMS** – drums

1965. (lp) *<(BLP 4175)>* **EMPYREAN ISLES** ☐ Jul64 ☐
– One finer snap / Oliloqui valley / Cantaloupe Island / The egg. *(re-iss. Oct85; BST 84175) (cd-iss. Aug89; CDP 784175-2)*

— added **GEORGE COLEMAN** – tenor sax

1966. (lp) *<(BLP 4195)>* **MAIDEN VOYAGE** ☐ Mar65 ☐
– Maiden voyage / The eye of the hurricane / The little one / Survival of the fittest / Dolphin dance. *(re-iss. May85; BST 84195) (cd-iss. Jul87; CDP 746339-2) (cd re-iss. Mar95)*

May 67. (lp; mono/stereo) *(MGM-C/+S 8039) <E/SE 4447>* **BLOW-UP** (soundtrack on 'M.G.M.') ☐ ☐
– Main title "Blow Up" / Verushka part I / Verushka part II / The naked camera / Bring down the birds / Jane's theme / Stroll on (YARDBIRDS) / The thief / The kiss / Curiosity / Thomas studies photos / The bed / End title "Blow Up". *(cd-iss. Jan97 on 'EMI Soundtracks'+=; CDODEON 15)* – (tracks by TOMORROW). *<cd-iss. 1992 on 'Sony'; > (cd re-iss. Dec99 on 'Vintage Classics'+=; VCS 005)* – (extra sessions).

— with **RON CARTER** – bass / **MICKEY ROKER** – drums / **THAD JONES** – flugelhorn / **JERRY DODGION** – flute / **PETER PHILLIPS** – trombone

Mar 68. (lp) *<(BST 84279)>* **SPEAK LIKE A CHILD** ☐ ☐
– Riot / Speak like a child / First trip / Toys / Goodbye to childhood / The sorcerer. *(cd-iss. Jul87; CDP 746136-2)*

Apr 69. (lp) *<(BST 84321)>* **THE PRISONER** ☐ ☐
– I have a dream / The prisoner / Firewater / He who lives in fear / Promise of the Sun. *(cd-iss. Sep87; CDP 746845-2)*

— Set up new sextet **BERNIE MAUPIN** – reeds / **BUSTER WILLIAMS** – bass, percussion / **BILLY HART** – drums, percussion / **LEON NDUGU CHANCLER** – drums / **JULIAN PRIESTER** – trombone / **EDDIE HENDERSON** – trumpet

Warners Warners

1971. (lp) *(WS 1834) <56293>* **FAT ALBERT ROTUNDA** ☐ ☐
– Wiggle-waggle / Fat mama / Tell me a bedtime story / Oh! oh! here he comes / Jessica / Fat Albert Rotunda / Lil' brother. *(re-iss. 1974; K 46039)*

1971. (7") *<(WB 7358)>* **FAT MAMA. / WIGGLE-WAGGLE** ☐ ☐

1971. (lp) *(K 46077) <1898>* **MWANDISHI** ☐ ☐
– Ostinato (suite for Angela) / You'll know when you get there / Wondering spirit song.

Feb 72. (lp) *(K 46164) <2617>* **CROSSINGS** ☐ ☐
– Sleeping giant (part 1-5) / Quasar / Water torture / Crossings.

Mar 72. (7") *<WB 7598>* **WATER TORTURE. / CROSSINGS** – ☐

C.B.S. Columbia

May 73. (lp/c) *(CBS/40 65582) <32212>* **SEXTANT** ☐ ☐
– Rain dance / Hidden shadows / Hornets.

Jan 74. (lp/c) *(CBS/40 65928) <32731>* **HEAD HUNTERS** ☐ 13
– Chameleon / Watermelon man / Sly / Vein melter. *(re-iss. Mar84; 32008) (cd-iss. Jul84; CD 65928)*

Jan 74. (7") *<46073>* **WATERMELON MAN (edit). / SLY (edit)** – ☐

Apr 74. (7") *(CBS 2329) <46002>* **CHAMELEON (edit). / VEIN METER (edit)** ☐ Mar74 42

Oct 74. (lp/c) *(CBS/40 80193)* <32965> **THRUST** [ ] Sep74 [13]
– Spank-a-lee / Butterfly / Actual proof / Palm grease.

Feb 75. (7") *(CBS 3059)* <10050> **PALM GREASE. / BUTTERFLY** [ ] Nov74 [ ]

Feb 75. (7") <10094> **SPANK-A-LEE. / ACTUAL PROOF** [–] [ ]

1975. (lp) *(CBS 80546)* <33199> **DEATH WISH (Soundtrack)** [ ] [ ]
– Death wish / Joanna's theme / Do a thing / Paint her mouth / Rich country / Suite revenge: (a) Striking back – (b) Riverside Park – (c) The alley – (d) Last stop – (e) 8th Avenue Station – Ochoa knose – Party people – Fill your hand.

1975. (d-lp) *(98-99)* **FLOOD (live in Japan)** [–] Japan [–]
– Introduction – Maiden voyage / Actual proof / Spank-a-Lee / Watermelon man / Butterfly / Chameleon / Hang up your hang ups.

Oct 75. (lp) *(CBS 69185)* <33812> **MAN-CHILD** [ ] [21]
– Hang up your hang ups / Sun touch / The traitor / Bubbles / Steppin' in it / Heartbeat.

Oct 75. (7") <10239> **HANG UP YOUR HANG UPS. / SUNTOUCH** [–] [ ]

Sep 76. (lp/c) *(CBS/40 81591)* <34280> **SECRETS** [ ] [ ]
– Doin' it / People music / Cantalope Island / Spider / Gentle thoughts / Swamp rat / Sansho Shima.

Sep 76. (7") <10408> **DOIN' IT. / PEOPLE MUSIC** [–] [ ]

—— His quintet:- **WAYNE SHORTER, RON CARTER, TONY WILLIAMS, FRED HUBBARD**

May 77. (lp/c) *(CBS/40 88235)* <34976> **V.S.O.P. (live Newport)** [ ] [79]
– (piano introduction) / Maiden voyage / Nefertiti / (introduction of players) / The eye of the hurricane / Toys / (introductions) / You'll know when you get there / Hang up your hang ups / Spider.

Jun 77. (7") <10563> **SPIDER. / MAIDEN VOYAGE** [–] [ ]

—— HANCOCK now introduced his voice, incorporated into music.

Jul 78. (lp/c) *(CBS/40 82240)* <34907> **SUNLIGHT** [27] [58]
– I thought it was you / Come running to me / Sunlight / No means yes / Good question.

Aug 78. (7") *(CBS 6530)* <10781> **I THOUGHT IT WAS YOU. / NO MEANS YES** [15] [ ]

Oct 78. (7") <10835> **SUNLIGHT. / COME RUNNING TO ME** [–] [ ]

Jan 79. (7") *(CBS 7010)* <10894> **YOU BET YOUR LOVE. / KNEE DEEP** [18] [ ]

Feb 79. (lp/c) *(CBS/40 83491)* <35764> **FEETS DON'T FAIL ME NOW** [28] [38]
– You bet your love / Trust me / Ready or not / Tell everybody / Honey from the jar / Knee deep. *(cd-iss. Sep85; CD 83491) (cd re-iss. Oct93 on 'Sony Collectors'; 983311-2)*

Apr 79. (7") <10936> **READY OR NOT. / TRUST ME** [–] [ ]

Apr 79. (7") *(CBS/+12 7229)* **TELL EVERYBODY. / TRUST ME** [ ] [–]

Jun 79. (7") <11019> **TELL EVERYBODY. / HONEY FROM THE JAR** [–] [ ]

Jun 79. (d-lp) *(CBS 88329)* <35663> **AN EVENING WITH HERBIE HANCOCK & CHICK COREA IN CONCERT (live)** [ ] Mar 79 [100]
– Someday my Prince will come / Liza / Button up / February moment / Maiden voyage / La fiesta. *(d-cd-iss. Nov94 on 'Columbia'; 477296-2)*

Dec 79. (7") <11122> **DOIN' IT. / HONEY FROM THE JAR** [–] [ ]

Apr 80. (7") <11227> **GO FOR IT. / TRUST ME** [–] [ ]

Apr 80. (7") *(CBS 8529)* **GO FOR IT. / MAKING LOVE** [ ] [–]

May 80. (lp/c) *(CBS/40 84237)* <36415> **MONSTER** [ ] Apr80 [94]
– Saturday night / Stars in your eyes / Go for it / Don't hold it in / Making love / It all comes round.

Sep 80. (7") <11310> **GO FOR IT. / STARS IN YOUR EYES** [–] [ ]

Nov 80. (7") <11323> **MAKING LOVE. / IT ALL COMES ROUND** [–] [ ]

Nov 80. (lp/c) *(CBS/40 84638)* <36578> **MR. HANDS** [ ] [ ]
– Spiralling prism / Calypso / Just around the corner / 4 a.m. / Shiftless shuffle / Textures.

—— on next with **RAY PARKER JNR.** – guitar, drums / **GEORGE JOHNSON** – rhythm guitar / **ADRIAN BELEW** – lead guitar / **FREDDIE WASHINGTON & LOUIS JOHNSON** – bass / **JOHN ROBINSON & ALPHONSE MOUZON** – drums / guest vocalists **SYLVESTER / VICKI RANDLE / GAVIN CHRISTOPHER**

Oct 81. (lp/c) *(CBS/40 85144)* <37387> **MAGIC WINDOWS** [ ] [ ]
– Magic number / Tonight's the night / Everybody's broke / Help yourself / Satisfied with love / The twilight clone.

Oct 81. (7") <02404> **EVERYBODY'S BROKE. / HELP YOURSELF** [–] [ ]
(12") <02461> – ('A'side) / Magic number.

Jan 82. (7") <02615> **MAGIC NUMBER. / HELP YOURSELF** [–] [ ]

Apr 82. (7") *(A 2222)* <02824> **LITE ME UP. / SATISFIED WITH LOVE** [ ] [ ]

May 82. (lp/c) *(CBS/40 32474)* <37928> **LITE ME UP** [ ] [ ]
– Lite me up / The bomb / Gettin' to the good part / Paradise / Can't hide your love / The fun tracks / Motor mouth / Give it all your heart.

Jul 82. (7") *(A 2563)* **THE FUN TRACKS. / GIVE IT ALL YOUR HEART** [ ] [–]

Jul 82. (7") <03004> **THE FUN TRACKS. / GETTIN' TO THE GOOD PART** [–] [ ]

Jan 83. (7") <03318> **PARADISE. / THE FUN TRACKS** [–] [ ]

—— with **RON CARTER** – bass / **TONY WILLIAMS** – drums / **WYNSTON MARSALIS** – trumpet

Jan 83. (d-lp) *(CBS 22219)* **HERBIE HANCOCK QUARTET (live)** [ ] [ ]
– Well you needn't / 'Round midnight / Clearways / A quick sketch / The eye of the hurricane / Parade / The sorcerer / Pee Wee / I fall in love too easily. *(cd-iss. Dec93 on 'Columbia'; 465626-2)*

Jul 83. (7")(12") <03978><04200> **ROCKIT. / (part 2)** [–] [71]

Jul 83. (7"/12") *(A/TA 3577)* **ROCKIT. / ROUGH** [8] [–]

Aug 83. (lp/c) *(CBS/40 25540)* <38814> **FUTURE SHOCK** [27] [ ]
– Rockit / Future shock / TFS / Earthbeat / Autodrive / Rough. *(re-iss. Apr87 lp/c; 450625-1/-4) (cd-iss. CD 25540)*

Sep 83. (7") <04268> **AUTODRIVE. / CHAMELEON** [–] [ ]

Sep 83. (7") *(A 3802)* **AUTODRIVE. / THE BOMB** [33] [–]
(12"+=) *(TA 3802)* – Chameleon.

Jan 84. (7") *(A 4075)* <04473> **FUTURE SHOCK. / EARTHBEAT** [54] [ ]
(12"+=) *(TA 4075)* – Herbie Hancock megamix; Rockit – Autodrive – Future shock – TFS – Rough – Chameleon.

—— with **WAYNE SHORTER** – lyricon / **HENRY KAISER + NICKY SKOPELITIS** – guitar / **BILL CASWELL** – bass, synth. / **WILL ALEXANDER + BOB STEVENS** – electronics / **JOHNNY ST CYR** – turntables / **ANTON FIER** – drums, percussion / **HAMID DRAKE + DANIEL PONCE + AIYB DIENE** – percussion / **JALI FODAY MUSA SUSO** – balafon / **BERNARD FOWLER + TOSHINORI KONDO** – vocals

Jul 84. (7") <04565> **HARDROCK. / ('A'version)** [–] [ ]

Jul 84. (7") *(A 4616)* **HARDROCK. / TFS** [65] [–]
(12"+=) *(TA 4616)* – ('A'-US megamix).

Aug 84. (lp/c) *(CBS/40 26062)* <39478> **SOUND-SYSTEM** [ ] [71]
– Hardrock / Metal beat / Karabali / Junkie / People are changing / Sound-system. *(c+=)* – (extra mixes).

Sep 84. (7")(ext-12") <04633><04637> **METAL BEAT. / KARABALI** [–] [ ]
(below w / FODAY MUSA SUSO)

May 85. (lp/c) *(CBS/40 23697)* <39870> **VILLAGE LIFE** [ ] [ ]
– Moon – Light / Ndan Ndan Nyaria / Early warning / Kanatente.

1986. (lp) <40464> **ROUND MIDNIGHT (Soundtrack)** [–] [ ]
– Round midnight / Body and soul / Berangeres nightmare / Fair weather / Una noche con Francis / The peacocks / How long has this been going on / Rhythm-a-ning / Still time / Minuit aux champs – Elysees / Chan's song (never said).

May 88. (7"/12") *(651432-7/-8)* **VIBE ALIVE. / MAIDEN VOYAGE** [ ] [ ]
(cd-s+=) *(651432-9)* – ('A'extended) / ('A'bonus beats).

Jun 88. (lp/c/cd) *(460679-1/-4/-2)* <40025> **PERFECT MACHINE** [ ] [ ]
– Perfect machine / Obsession / Vibe alive / Beat wise / Maiden voyage – P bop / Chemical residue.

Sep 88. (7") <07987> **BEAT WISE. / CHEMICAL RESIDUE** [–] [ ]

—— HERBIE featured on 'Yanarete' cd with MILTON NASCIMENTO early 1992.

Mercury Mercury

Jun 95. (cd/c) <(528185-2/-4)> **DIS IS DA DRUM** [ ] [ ]
– Call it '94 / Dis is da drum / Shooz / The melody (on the deuce by 44) / Mojuba / Butterfly / Juju / Hump / Come and see me / Rubber soul / Bo ba be ba.

Verve Verve

Mar 96. (cd) *(527715-2)* <529584> **THE NEW STANDARD** [ ] [ ]
– New York minute / Mercy street / Norwegian wood (this bird has flown) / When can I see you / / You've got it bad girl / Love is stronger than pride / Scarborough fair / Thieves in the temple / All apologies / Manhattan (island of lights and love).

—— in 1997, HERBIE collaborated with jazz giant WAYNE SHORTER on the album, '1 + 1'

Oct 98. (cd) <(557797-2)> **GERSHWIN'S WORLD** [ ] [ ]
– Overture (fascinating rhythm) / It ain't neccessarily so / The man I love /

Here come da honey man / St. Louis blues / Lullaby / Blueberry rhyme / It ain't neccessarily so (interlude) / Cotton tail / Summertime / My man's gone now / Prelude in C sharp minor / Concerto for piano and orchestra in G (2nd movement) / Embraceable you.

Transparent Transparent

Oct 01. (cd)(lp) *<(50012)>(HERBIELP 1)* **FUTURE 2 FUTURE** ☐ Sep01 ☐
– Kebero (part 1) / Wisdom / The essence / This is Rob Swift / Black gravity / Tony Williams / Be still / Ionosphere / Kebero (part 2) / Alphabeta / Virtual hornets.

— in 2002, HERBIE, MICHAEL BRECKER and ROY HARGROVE collaborated 'DIRECTIONS IN MUSIC – LIVE AT MASSEY HALL', a set attributed to the 75th birthdays of both MILES DAVIS and JOHN COLTRANE

– compilations, etc. –

1970. (lp) *Blue Note; (33199) / <80546>* **THE BEST OF HERBIE HANCOCK** ☐ ☐
Oct 74. (d-lp) *Warners; <2-2807>* **TREASURE CHEST** (rare 69-70) – ☐
1975. (lp) *Blue Note; <LA 152>* **SUCOTASH** – ☐
1975. (lp) *Blue Note; <LA 399>* **HANCOCK** – ☐
Apr 81. (lp; HERBIE HANCOCK & ALPHONSE MOUZON) *MPS Jazz; (MPS 68266)* **BY ALL MEANS** ☐ –
(cd-iss. Apr84 on 'Verve'; 817485-2)
Nov 84. (lp) *C.B.S.; (CBS/40 32526)* **THE BEST OF HERBIE HANCOCK** ☐ –
Nov 84. (lp/c) *Premier; (CBR/KCBR 1030) / Chase; <SJAZC 4>* **HOT AND HEAVY** ☐ ☐
<re-iss. Apr86 on 'Star Jazz' lp/c; SJAZZ/+C 4)
Sep 85. (7") *Old Gold; (OG 9561)* **YOU BET YOUR LOVE / I THOUGHT IT WAS YOU** ☐ –
Feb 91. (cd/c) *Castle; (CCS CD/MC 283)* **THE COLLECTION** ☐ –
– Chameleon / Watermelon man / Maiden voyage / I thought it was you / No means yes / You bet your love / Tell everybody / Lite me up / Rockit / Auto drive / Hardrock / Round midnight.
Jul 91. (cd) *Jazz Collection; (ORO 153)* **HOT PIANO** ☐ –
Jul 94. (cd) *Blue Note; (CDP 829331-2)* **CANTALOUPE ISLAND** ☐ ☐
Nov 94. (cd) *Jazz Door; (JD 1274)* **LIVE IN NEW YORK (TRIO live)** ☐ –
Nov 94. (d-cd) *Warners; (9362 45732-2)* **MWANDISHI – THE COMPLETE WARNER BROS. RECORDINGS** ☐ ☐
Jul 95. (cd) *Jazz Collection; (CK 64665)* **SINGLES COLLECTION** ☐ –
Nov 95. (3xcd-box) *Blue Note; (CDOMB 009)* **TAKIN' OFF / INVENTIONS & DIMENSIONS / EMPRYEAN ISLES** ☐ –
Nov 98. (6xcd-box) *Blue Note; (495569-2)* **THE COMPLETE BLUE NOTE SIXTIES SESSIONS** ☐ ☐
Oct 99. (cd) *Sony Jazz; (CK 65963)* **THE BEST OF HERBIE HANCOCK: THE HITS** ☐ ☐
Nov 00. (3xcd-box) *Sony Jazz; (492739-2)* **THRUST / SECRETS / MR. HANDS** ☐ ☐
Feb 01. (cd) *Sony Jazz; (501036-2)* **THE DEFINITIVE . . .** ☐ ☐
Sep 01. (3xcd-box) *Sony Jazz; (489346-2)* **HEADHUNTERS / FUTURE SHOCK / MAN-CHILD** ☐ ☐
Oct 02. (4xcd-box) *Sony Jazz; (508072-2)* **THE COLUMBIA YEARS 1972-1986** ☐ ☐
Dec 02. (d-cd) *Sony Jazz; (508934-2)* **HEADHUNTERS / THRUST** ☐ ☐
Mar 03. (cd) *E.M.I.; (583488-2)* **THE ESSENTIAL HERBIE HANCOCK** ☐ ☐

HANDSOME FAMILY

Formed: Chicago, Illinois, USA . . . 1993 by songwriter BRETT SPARKS, his wife and co-conspirator RENNIE SPARKS plus third bespectacled member, drummer MIKE WERNER. The husband and wife team were the Gomez and Morticia of alt-country (or even a distorted, updated version of TIMBUK 3!) to the GEORGE JONES and TAMMY WYNETTE of classic Nashville, although BRETT and RENNIE's sound was, well . . . er . . . miles apart. Born of acute personal difficulties, The HANDSOME FAMILY's music set against a background of strife; BRETT suffered a mental breakdown attempting to write his own bible!, while RENNIE was the "school freak" who immersed herself in literature (Greek classic, 'The Iliad', is apparently her favourite). From the onset, the trio toured extensively promoting their early releases, 'ODESSA' (1995), 'MILK AND SCISSORS' (1996) and foreign mini-set 'INVISIBLE HANDS' (1997), dark country tales and lifesize plastic animals unsettling audiences in both America and Europe. Initially aided by co-producer DAVE TRUMFIO, the band of renegade "true country" folk were augmented on the aforesaid releases by studio helpers, et all. Recorded on collaborator JEFF TWEEDY's (WILCO/UNCLE TUPELO) mobile studio, 1998's pioneering (in every sense of the word!) 'THROUGH THE TREES' kicked-off with the delightfully disturbing 'WEIGHTLESS AGAIN'. These peerless lyrics describe their 'Dead Man' emotions; "This is why people O.D. on pills, And jump . . . from the Golden Gate Bridge, Anything to feel weightless again". Cloaked in the gothic GORDON LIGHTFOOT/BILLY BRAGG-esque vocals of BRETT, The HANDSOME FAMILY's mournful tales of tragic 19th century Wild West folklore conjure up cinematic images of barren canyons and Red Indian ghosts dancing on General Custer's grave. The gothic husband and wife team returned in 2001, with the deliciously bleak, but achingly tender 'TWILIGHT', which was their first album not to be recorded in a studio (it was made in their house on a computer, apparently). However, despite a usual turn of brilliance, there were faults within the set; sometimes the lyrics seemed too complex for the simplistics of BRETT's music . . . such as the opener 'SNOW WHITE DINER' which tried to tell a rather moving story, only to be ruined by the singer's off-kilter voice and lyrics that didn't really fit around the guitar part. But these were minor qualms and the LP delivered the standard backwoods humour, with 'ALL THE TV'S IN TOWN' being a particular highlight. In 2002 they issued 'LIVE AT SCHUBA'S TAVERN', a rather good live album, that was initially intended for diehard fans, although all of the classics turned up in one way or another and the banter was not bad either! The 'FAMILY made a welcome comeback in 2003, via their most established work since 'THROUGH THE TREES', comprising of eleven songs entitled 'THE SINGING BONES'. Richer in songwriting structure and lyrical composition, the set display some of the duo's best work to date; the eerie '24 HOUR STORE', the Nick Cave-esque 'BOTTOMLESS HOLE' and the a cappella's 'IF THE WORLD SHOULD END IN FIRE' and ' . . .END IN ICE', which, for some reason sounded like Auld Lang Syne being sung by a troupe of Norweigan opera singers(!). • **Covers:** BARBARA ALLEN (Merle Travis) / SUNDAY MORNING COMING DOWN (Kris Kristofferson) / I HEAR A SWEET VOICE CALLING (Bill Monroe) / TRAIL OF TIME (Delmore Brothers) / FARAWAY EYES (Rolling Stones) / KNOXVILLE GIRL + BANKS OF THE OHIO (trad.) / etc.

Album rating: ODESSA (*5) / MILK AND SCISSORS (*5) / INVISIBLE HANDS mini (*5) / THROUGH THE TREES (*8) / DOWN IN THE VALLEY compilation (*8) / IN THE AIR (*6) / TWILIGHT (*6) / LIVE AT SCHUBA'S TAVERN (*5) / SMOTHERED AND COVERED collection (*5) / SINGING BONES (*7)

BRETT SPARKS – vocals, guitar, keyboards / **RENNIE SPARKS** – bass, vocals / **MIKE WERNER** – drums / with additional musicians DAVE TRUMFIO – acoustic guitar, keyboards, co-producer / MICHAEL HAGLER – guitar / STEVE THOMAS – pedal steel

not iss. Carrot Top

Jan 95. (cd) *<SAKI 005CD>* **ODESSA** – ☐
– Here's hopin' / Arlene / Pony / One way up / Water into wine / Giant ant / Everything that rises must converge / Gorilla / The last / Claire said / Moving furniture around / Big bad wolf / She awoke with a jerk / Happy harvest. *(German-iss.Jan96 on 'Scout'; SR 1004) (UK-iss.Oct99 & Oct01; same as US)*

— the trio's guests included MICHAEL, DAVE, HARRY TRUMFIO, DARRELL SPARKS and MARK STRUZYNSKI

Feb 96. (cd) *<SAKI 011CD>* **MILK AND SCISSORS** [–] [ ]
– Lake Geneva / Winnebago skeletons / Drunk by noon / The house carpenter / The Dutch boy / The king who wouldn't smile / Emily Shore 1819-1839 / 3-legged dog / #1 country song / Amelia Earhart vs. the dancing bear / Tin foil / Puddin' fingers. *(German-iss.Sep96 on 'Scout'; SR 1011) (UK-iss.Oct99 & Oct01; same as US)*

— now without WERNER who retired from music

Scout — not iss.

Sep 97. (m-lp) *(SR 1012)* **INVISIBLE HANDS** [–] German [–]
– Tin foil / Cathedrals / Grandmother waits for you / Bury me here / Barbara Allen / Birds you cannot see. *<(re-iss. Oct99 & Oct01 on 'Carrot Top'; SAKI 016CD)>*

— the husband and wife duo added guests DAVE, JEFF TWEEDY, JESSICA BILLEY, DAVE SMITH and DAVE WINER

Loose — Carrot Top

Apr 98. (cd) *(VJCD 105)* *<SAKI 20CD>* **THROUGH THE TREES** [ ] Jan98 [ ]
– Weightless again / My sister's tiny hands / Stalled / Where the birch trees lean / Cathedrals / Down in the ground / The giant of Illinois / Down in the valley of hollow logs / I fell / The woman downstairs / Last night I went out walking / Bury me here / My ghost.

Aug 99. (7") *(MAG 025)* **MY BEAUTIFUL BRIDE. / (other by Sackville)** [–] Canada [–]
(above issued on 'Magwheel')

Vinyl Junkie — Carrot Top

Oct 99. (cd) *(VJCD 110)* **DOWN IN THE VALLEY** (compilation) [ ] [–]
– Tin foil / My sister's tiny hands / Lake Geneva / Weightless again / No.1 country song / Giant of Illinois / Drunk by noon / Don't be scared / House carpenter / Arlene / Woman downstairs / Cathedrals / Moving furniture around / Dutchboy.

Feb 00. (cd) *(VJCD 112)* *<SAKI 23CD>* **IN THE AIR** [ ] [ ]
– Don't be scared / The sad milkman / In the air / A beautiful thing / So much wine / Up falling Rock Hill / Poor, poor Lenore / When that helicopter comes / Grandmother waits for you / Lie down / My beautiful bride.

Oct 01. (cd) *(VJCD 126)* *<SAKI 27CD>* **TWILIGHT** [ ] [ ]
– The snow white diner / Passenger pigeons / A dark eye / There is a sound / All the TV's in town / Gravity / Cold, cold, cold / No one fell asleep alone / I know you are there / Birds you cannot see / The white dog / So long / Peace in the vallet once again.

Sep 03. (cd) *(VJCD 144)* *<SAKI 36CD>* **SINGING BONES** [ ] Oct03 [ ]
– The forgotten lake / Gail with the golden hair / 24-hour store / The bottomless hole / Far from any road / If the world should end in fire / A shadow underneath / Dry bones / Fallen peaches / Whitehaven / Sleepy / The song of a hundred toads / If the world should end in ice.

– compilations, others, etc. –

Jul 02. (cd) *D.C.N.; <(DCN 1005CD)>* **LIVE AT SCHUBA'S TAVERN** (live in Chicago, December 2000) [ ] [ ]
– Amelia Earhart vs. the dancing bear / The good toothpicks / So much wine / The Czar bar / Tin foil / A beautiful thing / Vienna sausage hotline / The giant of Illinois / My sister's tiny hands / Names for all his shirts / Cathedrals / Weightless again / Bony bread / Winnebago skeletons / Drunk by noon / Magic balls (introduction) / The sad milkman / Magic balls (conclusion) / I know you are there / Down in the ground / Arlene / Moving furniture around / Freebird / My ghost / The woman downstairs.

Aug 02. (cd) *Handsome Family; <(HF 001CD)>* **SMOTHERED AND COVERED** [ ] Apr02 [ ]
– There's a city / Sunday morning coming down / Prepared piano #1 / I hear a sweet voice calling / Down in the ground (demo) / Cello #1 / Trail of time / Faraway eyes / Knoxville girl / Prepared piano #2 / The last (demo) / Banks of the Ohio / Cello #2 / Natalie Wood / #1 country song (demo) / Prepared piano #3 / Stupid bells / The weinermobile.

HAPPY MONDAYS

Formed: Salford, Manchester, England . . . 1984 by brothers SHAUN and PAUL RYDER. In 1985, with the help of A&R man and producer Mike Pickering, they signed a contract with Tony Wilson's 'Factory' records, issuing a debut 12", 'FORTY-FIVE'. With the addition of MARK BERRY aka BEZ on 'percussion', the band released the 'FREAKY DANCIN' single, as good a description as any for BEZ's onstage contortions. A JOHN CALE-produced debut album followed in 1987, the acclaimed mutant indie funk of 'SQUIRREL AND G-MAN . . .' winning the band many converts in the music press and the beginnings of a cult following. The early live shoes have been elevated to almost mythical status, SHAUN & Co. allegedly giving away drugs on the door to their own fans in true scally style. Despite sounding like it'd been recorded in a shed, the Martin Hannett-produced 'BUMMED' (1988) was a classic, a freewheeling groovy noise, punctuated intermittently by RYDER's stoned Mancunian slur. 'MAD CYRIL', 'LAZYITIS' and 'WROTE FOR LUCK' were all brilliant singles, the latter given a dance remix treatment by VINCE CLARKE (Erasure). 'Factory' supremo WILSON decided to take this a step further and set the band to work with the DJ/production team of PAUL OAKENFOLD and STEVE OSBORNE. The result was the pivotal 'MADCHESTER RAVE ON EP', a druggy mash-up of dance, indie, pop and funk that acted as a catylyst for the "Baggy" scene alongside The STONE ROSES' 'FOOL'S GOLD' single (spookily released exactly the same month), inspiring a whole string of bands in Manchester and beyond, some good, some not so good (just don't mention The FARM). Early the following year, The 'MONDAYS hit the Top 5 with their anthemic remake of JOHN KONGOS' 'He's Gonna Step On You Again', retitled 'STEP ON' and injected with typically laissez faire funk. 'KINKY AFRO' also made the Top 5, preceding the band's biggest success of their career, the 'PILLS 'N' THRILLS AND BELLYACHES' (1990) album. This time around there was a cleaner production and a melodic accessibility coating the trademark melange of dirty 'STONES'-style guitar, raggedy-assed funk and cheesy disco. In addition to the singles, the album's highlights included a tribute to 60's folk-popster DONOVAN, a leering piece of porn-funk, 'BOB'S YER UNCLE' and the classic 'GOD'S COP' (featuring the timeless RYDER line "God laid his E's all on me"). While much of the band's music sounded continuously on the point of collapse and live, The HAPPY MONDAYS often seemed as if they'd arrived onstage purely by accident, RYDER was no space cadet, his inimitable lyrical couplets sussed, sharp and dryly witty. Almost inevitably though, the backlash began in earnest with an NME interview painting RYDER and BEZ as dim witted homophobes. Whatever RYDER actually said, it's likely that his tongue was planted firmly in cheek, and besides, to expect The HAPPY MONDAYS to stand up as right-on, PC role models for student NME readers displays a naivety that beggars belief. Retreating to the Bahamas with Talking Heads' CHRIS FRANTZ and TINA WEYMOUTH at the production helm, the band struggled through sessions for the ' . . .YES PLEASE!' album, amid tales of general strife, severe drug abuse and obligatory debauchery. The album, an expensive disaster (critically and commercially) that reputedly bankrupted 'Factory', eventually emerged in late '92. Generally ignored and panned by the press, the album nevertheless contained some stellar 'MONDAYS moments, not least the low-key brilliance of 'STINKIN' THINKIN' and the darkly hypnotic 'ANGEL', both tracks using female backing vocals to impressive effect. After a washout of a tour, The HAPPY MONDAYS drifted apart, a messy end for a band that were capable of true musical genius against all the odds. The loose limbed spirit of The 'MONDAYS lived on, though, in BLACK GRAPE, the band RYDER formed along with rapper KERMIT and JED from the RUTHLESS RAP ASSASSINS and a host of extras. SHAUN's brilliant return from oblivion was complete by summer 1995 when the storming 'REVEREND BLACK GRAPE' launched him back into the Top 10. The mouthiest, grooviest low-slung Manc rave-up to grace the charts since the 'MONDAYS peak, the record pointed squarely in the direction where the party was really happening, bypassing completely the tedious Brit-pop posturing. As ever, RYDER and entourage were never far from controversy, both the song and video subsequently banned from TV as the Catholic church alleged the lyrics condoned Venezuelan terrorist, Carlos The Jackal (which also angered the New York based ADL – Anti-Defamation League). Another classic single, 'IN THE NAME OF THE FATHER', followed into the Top 10, funk rhythms and a sitar tinged intro previewing the eclecticism of the accompanying No.1 album, 'IT'S GREAT WHEN YOU'RE STRAIGHT . . . YEAH!'. Its title a reference to RYDER's clean living new ways (his inimitable cut 'n' paste lyrics apparently fuelled solely by Guinness!?), the record was compared favourably against The HAPPY MONDAYS' best work, and the second coming-style fuss over RYDER's critical rebirth seemed at least partly justified. Loping through a dayglo musical smarty pack of hip-hop, rock, indie-dance, soul and indeed, anything close to hand, RYDER proved his subversive genius was well intact, while KERMIT's hyperactive rapping assaults were a perfect foil for his stoned immaculate drawl. During this time, they were one of the successes at Hamilton Park's 'T In The Park' 2-day festival (near Glasgow), even though KERMIT broke his leg and had to sit out most of the gig on a speaker! During an eventful 1996 of regular touring and high profile press coverage, BEZ and RYDER finally parted ways, while KERMIT embarked on a side project, MAN MADE, the following year. A follow-up album, 'STUPID, STUPID, STUPID' finally emerged at the end of '97 amid furious interband disputes, claims and counter claims. The feuding saw the band cancel their New Year's Eve show at London's Alexandra Palace. SHAUN resurrected The HAPPY MONDAYS and in the meantime, BEZ was up to all sorts, including a TV spot on the Lee & Herring Sunday brunch show (dedicated to strange scientific happenings, mad for it, man). He also began writing an autobiography, no really man! The HAPPY MONDAYS (i.e. SHAUN, his brother PAUL, GAZ, 'WAGS', 'NUTS', ROWETTA and of course a reluctant BEZ!) were "smokin" once again when a new single, 'THE BOYS ARE BACK IN TOWN' (described as only inspired by the THIN LIZZY number!) hit the Top 30. However, after all the hype, the promise and the fuss, only an accompanying 'GREATEST HITS' package was supplied as a stop-gap to feed their fans; PAUL RYDER left on the 11th of August after the Eclipse '99 festival in Cornwall. By which time, SHAUN had paid off the taxman (and child maintenance) from his royalties, but really what did the 'MONDAYS give us during this spell apart from another chance to see the bleary-eyed singer trying to read a cue card on a stage monitor; you're answers please on the back of a postage stamp. In the month of July 2000, the most embarrassing sham on TV since the days of Oliver Reed and George Best when a sober-looking SHAUN was a guest on the Jim Davidson Friday show, er . . . singing 'BARCELONA' (yes, that one!) side by side with opera singer RUSSELL WATSON. With ongoing legal wrangles stalling RYDER from recording under his old banners, the man took off to his cousin Pete's house in Perth, Australia. There, SHAUN talked about retiring and, with the help of 'MONDAY's sleeve designer Pete, he set about putting his memoirs to music. In the summer of 2003, his fun tales of drugs, fights, prison and er . . . drugs, were duly delivered as 'CLOWNS AND PET SOUNDS' under the AMATEUR NIGHT IN THE BIG TOP banner. Opener 'THE STORY' and the single, 'SCOOTER GIRL' (the latter produced by CABARET VOLTAIRE man STEPHEN MALLINDER), were both experimental and techno showcasing his dark wit and cheeky Mancunian humour to the fore. • **Songwriters:** Group compositions except; DESMOND (Ob-la-di Ob-la-da; Beatles) / LAZYITIS (Ticket To Ride; Beatles) / TOKOLOSHE MAN (John Kongos). For BLACK GRAPE, SHAUN & KERMIT wrote alongside DANNY SABER, although in October '95, INTASTELLA members MARTIN WRIGHT and MARTIN MITTLER served a writ, claiming they co-wrote with SHAUN on early demos before they departed.

Album rating: SQUIRREL AND G-MAN TWENTY FOUR HOUR PARTY . . . (*8) / BUMMED (*8) / PILLS N' THRILLS AND BELLYACHES (*9) / LIVE (BABY BIG HEAD Bootleg album) (*4) / . . .YES PLEASE (*6) / LOADS – THE BEST OF . . . compilation (*8) / Black Grape: IT'S GREAT WHEN YOU'RE STRAIGHT . . . YEAH! (*9) / STUPID, STUPID, STUPID (*7) / Happy Mondays: THE GREATEST HITS compilation (*8) / Amateur Night In The Big Top: CLOWNS AND PET SOUNDS (*7)

SHAUN RYDER (b.23 Aug'62) – vocals / **PAUL RYDER** (b.24 Apr'64) – bass / **MARK DAY** (b.29 Dec'61) – guitar / **PAUL DAVIS** (b. 7 Mar'66) – keyboards / **GARY 'GAZ' WHELAN** (b.12 Feb'66) – drums

		Factory	Rough Trade
Sep 85.	(12"ep) *(FAC 129)* **FORTY-FIVE EP** – Delightful / This feeling / Oasis.		–
——	added **BEZ** (b. MARK BERRY, 18 Apr'64) – percussion, dancer		
Jun 86.	(7") *(FAC 142)* **FREAKY DANCIN'. / THE EGG** (ext.12"+=) *(FAC 142)* – ('A'live).		–
Mar 87.	(12") *(FAC 176)* **TART TART. / LITTLE MATCHSTICK OWEN'S RAP**		–
Apr 87.	(lp) *(FACT 170)* **SQUIRREL & G-MAN TWENTY-FOUR HOUR PARTY PEOPLE PLASTIC FACE CARNT SMILE (WHITE OUT)** – Kuff dam / Tart tart / 'Enery / Russell / Olive oil / Weekends / Little matchstick Owen / Oasis / Desmond * / Cob 20. *(re-iss. Nov88; same)(track * repl. by)* – Twenty four hour party people. *(cd-iss. Mar90 +=; FACD 170)* – Little matchstick Owen's rap. *(cd re-iss. May99 on 'London'; 520012-2) (cd re-iss. Jan00 on 'Factory Too'; 3984 28252-2)*		–
Oct 87.	(12") *(FAC 192)* **TWENTY FOUR HOUR PARTY PEOPLE. / YAHOO / WAH WAH (THINK TANK)**		–
Nov 88.	(7") *(FAC 212-7)* **WROTE FOR LUCK. / BOOM** (12"+=/cd-s+=) *(FAC/+D 212)* – ('A'dance mix) / ('A'club mix).		–
Nov 88.	(lp/cd)(d/dat) *(FACT/FACD 220)(FACT 220 C/D)* **BUMMED** – Country song / Moving in with / Mad Cyril / Fat lady wrestlers / Performance / Brain dead / Wrote for luck / Bring a friend / Do it better / Lazyitis. *(hit UK 59 UK Jan90) (cd re-iss. May99 on 'London'; 520013-2) (cd re-iss. Jan00 on 'Factory Too'; 3984 28250-2)*		–
May 89.	(12"/7"/c-s; as HAPPY MONDAYS & KARL DENVER) *(FAC 222/+7/C)* **LAZYITIS – ONE ARMED BOXER. / MAD CYRIL – HELLO GIRLS** *(re-iss. May90; same); hit No.46)*	85	–
Sep 89.	(12"/7") *(FAC 232/+7)* **WFL (Vince Clarke mix). / WFL – THINK ABOUT THE FUTURE (the Paul Oakenfold mix)** (cd-s+=) *(FACD 232)* – Lazyitis – one armed boxer.	68	–
Nov 89.	(7"clear/12"clear) **MAD CYRIL – HELLO GIRLS. / DO IT BETTER**	–	
Nov 89.	(12"ep/cd-ep)(7"ep/c-ep) *(FAC/+D 242)(FAC 242-7/-C)* **MADCHESTER RAVE ON EP** – Hallelujah / Holy ghost / Clap your hands / Rave on. (7") *(FAC 242R-7)* – Hallelujah (the MacColl mix). / Hallelujah (in out mix). (c-s)(12"/cd-s) *(FAC 242RC)(FAC/+D 242R)* – ('A'club mix) / Rave on (club mix).	19	–
——	added guest **ROWETA** – backing vocals to repl. other guest KIRSTY MacCOLL		

Factory Elektra

Mar 90. (12"/7") *(FAC 272/+7) <64899>* **STEP ON (stuff it in mix). / ('A'-One louder mix)** [5] Feb91 [57]
(c-s+=)(cd-s+=) *(FAC 272C)(FACD 272)* – ('A'-Twistin' my melons mix).

Oct 90. (12"/7"/c-s) *(FAC 302/+7/C)* **KINKY AFRO. / KINKY AFRO (live)** [5] [–]
(cd-s+=) *(FACD 302)* – ('A'radio edit).

Nov 90. (cd/lp)(c) *(FACD/FACT 320)(FAC 320C) <60986>* **PILLS 'N THRILLS AND BELLYACHES** [4] [89]
– Kinky Afro / God's cop / Donovan / Grandbag's funeral / Loose fit / Dennis & Lois / Bob's your uncle / Step on / Holiday / Harmony. *(cd re-iss. May99 on 'London'; 828223-2) (re-hit.Jul02 at No.47) (cd re-iss. Sep99 on 'Factory Too'; 3984 28251-2)*

Feb 91. (12"/7"/c-s) *(FAC 312/+7/C)* **LOOSE FIT. / BOB'S YOUR UNCLE** [17] [–]
(cd-s+=) *(FACD 312)* – Kinky Afro (Euro mix).

Sep 91. (cd/d-lp)(c) *(FACD/FACT 322)(FAC 322C)* **LIVE** (live BABY BIG HEAD Bootleg album) [21] [–]
– Hallelujah / Donovan / Kinky Afro / Clap your hands / Loose fit / Holiday / Rave on / E / Tokoloshe man / Dennis and Lois / God's cop / Step on / W.F.L. *(d-lp+=)(c+=)* – Bob's your uncle.

Nov 91. (12"/7"/c-s) *(FAC 332/+7/C)* **JUDGE FUDGE. / TOKOLOSHE MAN** [24] [–]
(cd-s+=) *(FACD 332)* – ('A'version).

Sep 92. (7"/c-s) *(FAC 362 7/C)* **STINKIN' THINKIN'. / ('A'-Boys Own mix)** [31] [–]
(12"+=/cd-s+=) *(FAC/+D 362)* – ('A'-Terry Farley mix) / Baby bighead.

Oct 92. (cd/lp)(c) *(FACD/FACT 420)(FAC 420C) <61391>* **. . . YES PLEASE!** [14] [ ]
– Stinkin' thinkin' / Monkey in the family / Sunshine & love / Dustman / Angel / Cut 'em loose Bruce / Theme from Netto / Love child / Total Ringo / Cowboy Dave. *(cd re-iss. May99 on 'London'; 520026-2) (cd re-iss. Jan00 on 'Factory Too'; 3984 28253-2)*

Nov 92. (7"/c-s) *(FAC 372 7/C)* **SUNSHINE & LOVE. / STAYING ALIVE (mix) / TWENTY FOUR HOUR PARTY PEOPLE (remix)** [62] [–]
(12"+=/cd-s+=) *(FAC/+D 372)* – ('A'dance mix).

—— they disbanded early '93, with SHAUN and other two briefly forming The MONDAYS which evolved into BLACK GRAPE

BLACK GRAPE

SHAUN RYDER + **BEZ** with **KERMIT** (b.PAUL LEVEREDGE) – rapper (ex-RUTHLESS RAP ASSASINS) / **JED BIRTWHISTLE** – rapper (ex-RUTHLESS RAP ASSASSINS) / **WAGS** – guitar (ex-PARIS ANGELS) / **CRAIG GANNON** – guitar (ex-SMITHS) who replaced INTASTELLA guitarists **MARTIN WRIGHT** + **MARTIN MITTLER**

Radioactive Radioactive

May 95. (c-s) *(RAXC 16)* **REVEREND BLACK GRAPE / STRAIGHT OUT OF TRUMPTON (BASEMENT TAPES)** [9] [ ]
(cd-s+=) *(RAXTD 16)* – ('A'-dark side mix).
(12") *(RAXT 16)* – ('A'side) / ('A'-dub collar mix) / ('A'-dark side mix).

Jul 95. (c-s) *(RAXC 19)* **IN THE NAME OF THE FATHER / LAND OF A THOUSAND KAMA SUTRA BABIES** [8] [ ]
(cd-s+=) *(RAXTD 19)* – ('A'-chopper's mix) / ('A'-chopper's instrumental).
(12") *(RAXT 19)* – ('A'side) / (above 2).

Aug 95. (cd/c/lp) *(<RAD/RAC/RAR 11224>)* **IT'S GREAT WHEN YOU'RE STRAIGHT . . . YEAH** [1] [ ]
– Reverend Black Grape / In the name of the father / Tramazi party / Kelly's heroes / Yeah yeah brother / Big day in the north / Shake well before opening / Shake your money / Little Bob.

Nov 95. (c-s) *(RAXC 22)* **KELLY'S HEROES / ('A'-The Milky Bar Kid mix)** [17] [ ]
(cd-s+=) *(RAXTD 22)* – ('A'-The Archibald mix) / Little Bob (live).
(cd-s) *(RAXXD 22)* – ('A'live) / In the name of the father (live) / Fat neck.

—— BEZ quit due to argument with SHAUN over his role in the group.

—— On Channel 4's TFI Friday, SHAUN caused more controversy by adding loads of live f words on their version on SEX PISTOLS 'Pretty Vacant'.

May 96. (c-s) *(RAXC 24)* **FAT NECK / PRETTY VACANT (live)** [10] [ ]
(cd-s+=) *(RAXTD 24)* – Yeah yeah brother (Outlaw Josey Wales mix).
(12") *(RAXT 24)* – ('A'-GOLDIE Beat the f*** down mix) / Yeah yeah brother (Clockwork Orange mix) / Yeah yeah brother (Dog day afternoon mix).

Jun 96. (c-s) *(RAXC 25)* **ENGLAND'S IRIE / (Pass the Durazac mix)** [6] [ ]
(12"+=/cd-s+=) *(RAXT/+D 25)* – ('A'-Suedehead dub) / ('A'-Mel's L.A. Irie mix).
above featured JOE STRUMMER and KEITH ALLEN

—— In Oct'96, SHAUN moonlighted with The HEADS (ex-TALKING HEADS) on minor hit single 'Don't Take My Kindness For Weakness'.

Oct 97. (c-s/cd-s) *(RAX C/TD 32)* **GET HIGHER / ('A'mixes)** [24] [–]
(cd-s) *(RAXXD 32)* – ('A'mixes).

Nov 97. (lp/c/cd) *(RAR/+C/D 11716)* **STUPID STUPID STUPID** [11] [–]
– Get higher / Squeaky / Marbles / Dadi was a badi / Rubber band / Spotlight / Tell me something / Money back guarenteed / Lonely / Words.

Feb 98. (cd-s) *(RAXTD 33)* **MARBLES (remixes by R.I.P. and FABIO PARAS) / MARBLES (demo)** [46] [–]
(12"+=) *(RAXT 33)* – ('A'-Tricky remix).
(cd-s) *(RAXXD 33)* – ('A'-Tricky remix) / Harry the dog / Get higher (uncensored video on CD-ROM).

HAPPY MONDAYS

—— re-formed **SHAUN + PAUL RYDER , GAZ WHELAN, PAUL 'WAGS' WAGSTAFF, 'NUTS', BEZ + ROWETTA**

London not iss.

May 99. (12") *(LONX 432)* **THE BOYS ARE BACK IN TOWN. / ('A'-Dirty mix)** [24] [–]
(cd-s) *(LONCD 432)* – ('A'side) / Kinky Afro / ('A'extended).
(cd-s) *(LOCDP 432)* – ('A'-Dirty mix) / Loose fit (Perfecto mix) / Bob's yer uncle (Perfecto mix).

May 99. (cd/c) *(556105-2/-4)* **GREATEST HITS** (compilation) [11] [–]
– Step on / WFL (Vince Clarke mix) / The boys are back in town / Kinky Afro (Perfecto mix) / Hallelujah (club mix) / Mad Cyril / Lazyitis (One Armed Boxer mix) / Loose fit (Perfecto mix) / Bob's yer uncle / Judge fudge / Stinkin' thinkin' / 24 hour party people / WFL (Think About The Future mix) / Stayin' alive / Step on (Twisting My Melon mix).

—— in Jul'00, SHAUN RYDER er, collaborated on a version of 'BARCELONA' with opera singer RUSSELL WATSON (it hit UK No.68)

– compilations, etc. –

May 90. (12"ep/c-ep/cd-ep) *Strange Fruit; (SFPS/+C/CD 077) / Dutch East India; <8306>* **THE PEEL SESSION** [ ] [ ]
– Tart tart / Mad Cyril / Do it better. *(cd-ep re-iss. Feb92; same)*

Nov 91. (cd-ep) *Strange Fruit;* **THE PEEL SESSION (1986)** [ ] [–]
– Freaky dancin' / Kuff dam / Olive Oil / Cob 20.

Sep 93. (cd,c) *Elektra; <61543>* **DOUBLE EASY: THE US SINGLES** [–] [ ]

Oct 95. (cd/c) *London; (520036-2/-4)* **LOADS** [41] [–]
– Step on / W.F.L. / Kinky Afro / Hallelujah – MacColl mix / Mad Cyril / Lazyitis / Tokoloshe man / Loose fit / Bob's yer uncle / Judge fudge / Stinkin' thinkin' / Sunshine & love / Angel / Tart tart / Kuff dam / Twenty four hour party people. *(some cd's w/ free cd+=)* **LOADS MORE** – Lazyitis – one armed boxer mix / W.F.L. (Perfecto mix) / Bob's yer uncle (Perfecto mix) / Loose fit (Perfecto mix) / Hallelujah (Deadstock mix) / Freaky dancing / Delightful.

May 02. (12") *Londpn; (LONX 466)* **24 HOUR PARTY PEOPLE (mixes)** [ ] [–]

AMATEUR NIGHT IN THE BIG TOP

SHAUN RYDER – vocals / + cohorts on electronics, etc.

Offworld not iss.

Jun 03. (12"/cd-s) *(LOWS/COWS 1)* **SCOOTER GIRL. / CLOWNS (Gripper remix) / SCOOTER GIRL (Soundlab remix)** [ ] [–]

Jul 03. (cd) *(POWS 1)* **CLOWNS AND PET SOUNDS** [ ] [–]
– The story / Long legs (parts 1-3) / Scooter girl / Clowns / Murder / Northern soul brother (shapeshifter) / Monster / In 1987.

Ed HARCOURT

Born: EDWARD HARCOURT-SMITH, 14 Aug'77, Lewes, East Sussex, England. Known for his youthfulness and eager talent, this musing troubadour erupted into the pages of critics come his first release 'MAPLEWOOD' (2000). An edgy and sometimes frustrating mini-album, HARCOURT ambitiously recorded the whole thing on a 4-track, and appeared to be running through a cornfield on the cover sleeve. There were certain elements that suggested he was in love with the romanticism of TOM WAITS' lush Americana; tracks such as the gruff hobo dirge 'BECOME MISGUIDED', with its plinky-plonky banjo and obsure drifting lyrics et al, gave HARCOURT the confusing tag of "new country", when clearly it was the old one he was really obsessed with. Jazzy, late-nighter 'ATTABOY, GO SPIN A YARN' showcased his tender vocal muscles, while 'WHISTLE OF A DISTANT TRAIN' harked back to DONOVAN's 'Summer Day Reflections' period. After supporting SPARKLEHORSE on a brief tour, HARCOURT recorded his sophomore release, 'HERE BE MONSTERS' (2001) for 'Heavenly' records. More technically improved, the album went on to receive rave reviews, and earned HARCOURT a 'Mercury Music Prize' nomination. It was also a pleasant surprise to hear muted trumpets, soft strings and whispering piano all included on the set. HARCOURT followed up his acclaimed debut with 'FROM EVERY SPHERE' (2003), an album just as delicate in arrangement and structure as his first. Taking the troubadour mantle head-on, the young crooner displayed his knack for songwriting once again with the timid 'ALL OF YOUR DAYS WILL BE BLESSED', while flirting with the more jazzy aspects of his musicianship with the swagger of standout track 'GHOSTWRITER'. While he's still only in his mid-twenties, the future can only be bright for young ED.

Album rating: MAPLEWOOD mini (*5) / HERE BE MONSTERS (*7) / FROM EVERY SPHERE (*8)

ED HARCOURT – vocals, keyboards, guitars, multi / with **HADRIAN GARRARD** – multi

Heavenly | Capitol

Nov 00. (lp/cd) *(HVNLP 27/+CD)* **MAPLEWOOD** [ ] [ ]
– Hanging with the wrong crowd / I've become misguided / Apple of my eye / Attaboy go spin a yarn / He's a building a swamp / Whistle of a distant train.

—— added **LEO ABRAHAMS** – guitars / + strings

Jun 01. (7") *(HVN 101)* **SOMETHING IN MY EYE. / HERE BE MONSTERS** [ ] [–]
(cd-s+=) *(HVN 101CD)* – T-bone tombstone.

Jun 01. (lp/cd) *(HVNLP 31/+CD)* <37688> **HERE BE MONSTERS** [ ] Jul01 [ ]
– Something in my eye / God protect your soul / She fell into my arms / Those crimson tears / Hanging with the wrong crowd / Apple of my eye / Beneath the heart of darkness / Wind through the trees / Birds fly backwards / Shanghai / Like only lovers can.

Sep 01. (7") *(HVN 104)* **SHE FELL INTO MY ARMS. / I'VE BECOME MISGUIDED** [ ] [–]
(cd-s+=) *(HVN 104CD)* – When Americans come to London.

Jan 02. (7") *(HVN 107)* **APPLE OF MY EYE. / WEARY AND BLEARY EYED** [61] [–]
(c-s/cd-s) *(HVN 107 CS/CD)* – ('A'side) / The last of the troubadours / Little silver bullet.

Heavenly | Astralwerks

Nov 02. (cd-s) *(HVN 121CD)* **STILL I DREAM OF IT / GHOSTS PARADE** [ ] [–]

Feb 03. (cd-s) *(HVN 127CD)* **ALL OF YOUR DAYS WILL BE BLESSED / COAL BLACK HEART / BLACKWOODS BACK HOME / ('A'-video)** [35] [–]

Feb 03. (lp/cd) *(HVNLP 39/+CD)* <40505> **FROM EVERY SPHERE** [39] May03 [ ]
– Bittersweetheart / All your days will be blessed / Ghost writer / The birds will sing for us / Sister Renee / Undertaker strut / Bleed a river deep / Jetsetter / Watching the sun come up / Fireflies take flight / Metaphorically yours / From every sphere. *<US+=>* – The hammer and the nail.

May 03. (cd-s) *(HVN 130CD)* **WATCHING THE SUN COME UP / SUGARBOMB / PAID TO GET DRUNK / ('A'-video)** [ ] [–]

Tim HARDIN

Born: EUGENE HARDIN, 23 Dec'41, Oregon, U.S.A. After a short-lived and miserable spell in the marines, HARDIN moved to Greenwich village in the early 60's with little financial means and a heroin habit. He briefly attended the American Academy of Dramatic Art before dropping out and heading for the Boston folk scene, his earliest forays into the music world. There, TIM received a call from manager/producer ERIK JACOBSEN asking him back up to New York to record some demos for 'Columbia'. The company were less than impressed with the results; at this point HARDIN had yet to develop his subtle, jazz-inflected folk-style, instead peddling a rather forgettable strain of awkward, white-boy blues. Some of the material from this period later ended up on 'TIM HARDIN IV' (1969), passed off as new work and subsequently enraging HARDIN, not the first time he'd clash with those trying to guide his career. Nevertheless, HARDIN was already possessed of a unique vocal style, the jazz influence apparent in his phrasing and the way he manipulated notes. JACOBSEN, however, showed faith in the singer and eventually HARDIN was signed to the new 'Verve-Forecast' label with the help of producers CHARLES KOPPELMAN and DON RUBIN. 'TIM HARDIN 1' (1966) showcased a marked improvement in TIM's playing, singing and songwriting, the blues pretensions substituted for a meditative, painfully intimate folk-confessional style, exemplified by the likes of 'MISTY ROSES' and 'HOW CAN WE HANG ON TO A DREAM'. The album was also overdubbed with strings, apparently without HARDIN's consent and much to his disgust although ironically, they added an austere beauty to many of the tracks. The debut also featured 'REASON TO BELIEVE', like many of HARDIN's songs, much covered and made famous by other artists (in this case ROD STEWART) while TIM lingered in obscurity. One cover version that really incensed HARDIN was BOBBY DARIN's reading of 'IF I WERE A CARPENTER', TIM allegedly claiming that DARIN had the original playing on headphones so he could replicate his phrasing. The song was just one of the many classics on 'TIM HARDIN 2' (1967), the singer's most affecting and realised album. Written immediately prior to the birth of his son, DAMION, 'BLACK SHEEP BOY' (later, appropriately enough, covered by SCOTT WALKER) was heart-rending, 'RED BALLOON' bleakly moving, while HARDIN's hesitant, fragile 'TRIBUTE TO HANK WILLIAMS' saw the singer detail his ambiguous feelings about live performance. 'Who watched the pain in his heart and then they sat and then they clapped their hands'; for HARDIN, performing (when he deigned to turn up) was more about internal catharsis than pleasing the crowd. Heralded by BOB DYLAN as the greatest songwriter of the decade, the singer is said to have inspired DYLAN's 'John Wesley Harding' (HARDIN often boasted that he was a descendant of the famed outlaw, JOHN WESLEY HARDIN). Yet despite the brilliance of these two albums, his muse increasingly deserted him as he fell deeper into heroine abuse. 'TIM HARDIN 3' (1968) was a jazzy live set that featured reworkings of songs from the first two albums as well as a smattering of new tracks. Shortly after the record's release, it was announced that HARDIN was suffering fom the respiratory disease, pleurisy, making his live appearances even more erratic. After an English tour with Family ended in disaster at the Royal Albert Hall (Hardin fell asleep on stage), the singer made a concerted effort to wean himself off heroine. When this failed he retreated to Woodstock, writing the brutally naked confessional of 'SUITE FOR SUSAN MOORE AND DAMION' (1969), the first fruits of his new deal with 'Columbia'. The SUSAN MOORE of the title was his wife, who eventually left him soon after the record's release, HARDIN subsequently spiralling into despair. He moved to England, registering as an addict in order to procure drugs on the NHS, releasing a further couple of patchy albums, 'BIRD ON A WIRE' (1971) and 'PAINTED HEAD' (1973), the latter a set of covers. Neither sold well and a film role as WOODY GUTHRIE in a proposed biopic, 'Bound For Glory', came to nothing. He recorded a final album, 'TIM HARDIN 9' (1974) before moving back to L.A. where he finally overdosed on the 29th December '80, aged only 39. • **Covers:** HOUSE OF THE RISING SUN (trad) / BO DIDDLEY (Bo Diddley).

Album rating: TIM HARDIN 1 (*6) / TIM HARDIN 2 (*8) / THIS IS TIM HARDIN early stuff (*5) / TIM HARDIN 3 – LIVE IN CONCERT (*6) / TIM HARDIN 4 (*5) / SUITE FOR SUSAN MOORE AND DAMION-WE ARE-ONE, ONE, ALL IN ONE (*5) / THE BEST OF TIM HARDIN compilation (*6) / BIRD ON A WIRE (*4) / PAINTED HEAD (*5) / NINE (*5) / THE SHOCK OF GRACE posthumous (*5) / HANG ON TO A DREAM (THE BEST OF TIM HARDIN) (*8) / SIMPLE SONGS OF FREEDOM – THE TIM HARDIN COLLECTION compilation (*7)

TIM HARDIN – vocals, guitar, piano

Verve Folkways — Verve Folkways

Oct 66. (7") *<5008>* **HANG ON TO A DREAM. / IT'LL NEVER HAPPEN AGAIN** –

Dec 66. (lp) *(5018) <3004>* **TIM HARDIN 1**
– Don't make promises / Green rocky road / Smugglin' man / How long / While you're on your way / It'll never happen again / Reason to believe / Never too far / Part of the wind / Ain't gonna do without / Misty roses / How can we hang on to a dream. *(cd-iss. Sep92 on 'Line'; LMCD 951113)*

Dec 66. (7") *(VS 1504)* **HANG ON TO A DREAM. / REASON TO BELIEVE** 50 –

Feb 67. (7") *<5017>* **DON'T MAKE PROMISES. / MISTY ROSES** –

May 67. (7") *<5031>* **HANG ON TO A DREAM. / MISTY ROSES** –

Sep 67. (lp) *(6002) <3022>* **TIM HARDIN 2** May67
– If I were a carpenter / Red balloon / Black sheep boy / Lady came from Baltimore / Baby close its eyes / You upset the grace of living when you lie / Speak like a child / See where you are and get out / It's hard to believe in love for long / Tribute to Hank Williams. *(cd-iss. Sep92 on 'Line'; LMCD 951069)*

Sep 67. (7") *<5042>* **NEVER TOO FAR. / GREEN ROCKY ROAD** –

Nov 67. (7") *<5048>* **BLACK SHEEP BOY. / MISTY ROSES** –

Nov 67. (7") *(VS 1511)* **LADY CAME FROM BALTIMORE. / BLACK SHEEP BOY** –

Jun 68. (7") *<5059>* **TRIBUTE TO HANK WILLIAMS. / YOU UPSET THE GRACE OF LIVING** –

Jun 68. (lp) *(6010) <3049>* **TIM HARDIN 3 – LIVE IN CONCERT (live)**
– Lady came from Baltimore / Reason to believe / You upset the grace of living when you lie / Misty roses / Black sheep boy / Lenny's tune / Don't make promises / Danville dame / If I were a carpenter / Red balloon / Tribute to Hank Williams / Smugglin' man. *(cd-iss. Sep92 on 'Line'; LMCD 951073)*

Jul 68. (7") *(VS 1516)* **DON'T MAKE PROMISES. / SMUGGLIN' MAN** –

Apr 69. (7") *<5097>* **SMUGGLIN' MAN. / REASON TO BELIEVE** –
<re-iss. 1970; 5116>

May 69. (lp) *(6016) <3064>* **TIM HARDIN IV**
– Airmobile / Whiskey whiskey / Seventh son / How long / Danville dame / Ain't gonna do without (part 1 & 2) / House of the rising son / Bo Diddley / I can't slow down / Hello baby. *(cd-iss. Sep92 on 'Line'; LMCD 951091)*

C.B.S. — Columbia

May 69. (lp) *(63571) <9787>* **SUITE FOR SUSAN MOORE AND DAMION . . . WE ARE . . . ONE, ONE, ALL IN ONE** Apr69
– First love song / Everything good become more true / Question of birth / Once-touched by flame / Last sweet moments / Magician / Loneliness she knows / The country I'm living in / One, one, the perfect sum / Susan.

May 69. (7") *<44920>* **ONE-TOUCHED BY FLAME. / QUESTION OF BIRTH** –

Aug 69. (7") *(4441) <44920>* **SIMPLE SONG OF FREEDOM. / QUESTION OF BIRTH** Jul69 50

Aug 71. (lp) *(64335) <30551>* **BIRD ON A WIRE** Jul71
– Bird on the wire / Moonshiner / Southern butterfly / A satisfied mind / Soft summer breeze / Hoboin' / Georgia on my mind / Andre Johray / If I knew / Love hymn.

Aug 71. (7") *<45426>* **BIRD ON THE WIRE. / SOFT SUMMER BREEZE** –

Jan 73. (lp) *(65209) <31764>* **PAINTED HEAD**
– You can't judge a book by the cover / Midnight caller / Yankee lady / Lonesome valley / Sweet lady / Do the do / Perfection / Till we meet again / I'll be home / Nobody knows you when you're down and out.

Jan 73. (7") *(1016) <45695>* **DO THE DO. / SWEET LADY**

G.M. — Antilles

Jan 74. (lp) *(1004) <7023>* **NINE**
– Shiloh town / Never too far / Rags & old iron / Look our love over / Person to person / Darling girl / Blues on my ceiling / Is there no rest for the weary / Fire and rain / While you're on your way / Judge and jury. *(re-iss. Dec90 on 'Marquee' cd/c/lp; MQC CD/MC/LP 003) (cd-iss. Apr92 & Feb97 on 'See For Miles'; SEECD 335)*

Feb 74. (7") *(GMS 14)* **DARLING GIRL. / PERSON TO PERSON** –

—— Resided in the UK from 1974. He died in L.A. of drug abuse in 1980.

– compilations, etc. –

Apr 68. (lp) *Atlantic; (588 082) / Atco; <33210>* **THIS IS TIM HARDIN** (rec.1962) Sep67
– I can't slow down / Blues on the ceilin' / I'm your hoochie coochie man / Stagger Lee / I've been working on the railroad / House of the rising Sun / Fast freight / Cocaine Bill / You got to have more than one woman / Danville dame. *(re-iss. Jul89 on 'Edsel'; ED 309) <(cd-iss. Jun00; 7567 80780-2)>*

1970. (lp) *Verve; (2317 003) <3078>* **THE BEST OF TIM HARDIN**

1971. (7") *Verve; (2009 006)* **IF I WERE A CARPENTER. / HANG ON TO A DREAM** –

1973. (lp) *M.G.M.; <4952>* **ARCHETYPES** – –

1974. (d-lp) *Verve; (2683 048)* **TIM HARDIN I & II** – –

1981. (lp) *Columbia; <37164>* **THE STATE OF GRACE** –

Feb 82. (lp) *Polydor; (PD 16333)* **TIM HARDIN MEMORIAL ALBUM**

May 82. (lp) *Kamera; (KAM 004)* **HOMECOMING CONCERT** –
(cd-iss. 1989 & Aug94 on 'Line'; LICD 90040)

May 88. (cd) *Polydor; (835706-2)* **REASON TO BELIEVE – THE BEST OF TIM HARDIN** –

Jan 93. (d-cd) *Polydor; (521583-2)* **HANG ON TO A DREAM (THE VERVE RECORDINGS)** –
(re-iss. Feb97; same)

Nov 99. (cd) *Beat Goes On; (BGOCD 470)* **SUITE FOR SUSAN MOORE AND DAMION . . . WE ARE ONE, ONE, ALL IN ONE / BIRD ON A WIRE** –

Aug 00. (cd) *Raven; (RVCD 104)* **ESSENTIAL CLASSIC HARDIN 1963-1980 – PERSON TO PERSON** –

☐ HARDLINE (see under ⇒ JOURNEY)

☐ Morten HARKET (see under ⇒ A-HA)

Steve HARLEY

Born: STEVEN NICE, 27 Feb'51, London, England. After an initial stint as a music journalist, HARLEY formed COCKNEY REBEL, recruiting the interestingly named, MILTON REAME-JAMES, JEAN-PAUL CROCKER, PAUL AVON JEFFREYS and STUART ELLIOT. Signed to 'E.M.I.', the group's debut album, 'THE HUMAN MENAGERIE' (1973) sank without trace, although their avant-glam stylings were attracting a growing following in the capital and, in Spring '74, they scored a Top 5 hit with 'JUDY TEEN'. HARLEY's affected enunciation backed by the group's quirky pop creations amounted to a distant 70's cousin of prime KINKS, although the frontman lacked the prolific songwriting prowess of RAY DAVIES. A second album, 'THE PSYCHOMODO' (1974), followed into the Top 10 later that summer, while the 'MR. SOFT' single gave them further chart success. Despite these advances, HARLEY's war of words with the music press continued to escalate, eventually prompting the singer to disband the outfit and re-invent his whole approach. Retaining only ELLIOT from this first incarnation, HARLEY recruited a new line-up of JIM CREGAN, DUNCAN MACKAY and GEORGE FORD (now under the slightly revised moniker of STEVE HARLEY & COCKNEY REBEL), almost immediately hitting the UK No.1 spot with the gorgeous 'MAKE ME SMILE (COME UP AND SEE ME)'. Yet despite its lush melody and harmonies, the track was actually a sarcastic rebuff to his sworn critical enemies in the media. The accompanying album, 'THE BEST YEARS OF OUR LIVES' (1975), reached the Top 5 and became the most successful set of HARLEY's career; the DAVIES/IAN HUNTER-esque lyrical flourishes were still in evidence, just wrapped in more conventional tunes. Subsequent albums, 'TIMELESS FLIGHT' (1976) and 'LOVE'S A PRIMA DONNA' (1976), weren't quite so successful although HARLEY scored a surprise Top 10 in summer '76 with an unlikely cover of The Beatles' 'HERE COMES THE SUN'. The latter set was HARLEY's first full solo attempt, the singer relocating to America where he continued to record low-key albums through till the end of the decade. In the mid-80's, HARLEY came to prominence once more when he duetted with SARAH BRIGHTMAN on the Top 10 excerpt from 'PHANTOM OF THE OPERA', although he was surprised when MICHAEL CRAWFORD was chosen for the lead role in the stage version of the musical. A series of singles followed on Mickie Most's 'R.A.K.' label as well as a collaborative effort with JON ANDERSON, and although HARLEY has sporadically reformed COCKNEY REBEL over the years, mainstream success has proved elusive. • **Also:** An ex-original member JEFFREYS died in the Lockerbie plane crash on the 21st December '88.

Album rating: Cockney Rebel: THE HUMAN MENAGERIE (*5) / THE PSYCHOMODO (*6) / Steve Harley & Cockney Rebel: THE BEST YEARS OF OUR LIVES (*5) / Steve Harley: LOVE'S A PRIMA DONNA (*4) / FACE TO FACE – A LIVE RECORDING (*3) / HOBO WITH A GRIN (*4) / MAKE ME SMILE – THE BEST OF STEVE HARLEY & COCKNEY REBEL compilation (*7) / YES YOU CAN (*4) / LIVE IN THE UK (*4) / POETIC JUSTICE (*4) / STRIPPED TO THE BARE BONES (*4)

COCKNEY REBEL

STEVE HARLEY – vocals, guitar / **MILTON REAME-JAMES** – keyboards / **JEAN-PAUL** (b. JOHN) **CROCKER** – violin / **PAUL AVRON JEFFERIES** – bass / **STUART ELLIOT** – drums

E.M.I. E.M.I.

Aug 73. (7") *(EMI 2051)* *<3846>* **SEBASTIAN. / ROCK AND ROLL PARADE** [ ] [ ]

Nov 73. (lp/c) *(EMA/TC-EMA 759)* *<11294>* **THE HUMAN MENAGERIE** [ ] [ ]
– Hideaway / What Ruthy said / Loretta's tale / Crazy raver / Sebastian / Mirror freak / My only vice / Muriel the actor / Chameleon / Death trip. *(cd-iss. Jul90+=; CDP 794756-2)* – Rock and roll parade / Judy Teen / Spaced out.

Mar 74. (7") *(EMI 2128)* **JUDY TEEN. / SPACED OUT** [5] [–]

Jun 74. (lp/c) *(EMC/TC-EMC 3033)* *<11330>* **THE PSYCHOMODO** [8] [ ]
– Sweet dreams / Psychomodo / Mr. Soft / Singular band / Ritz / Cavaliers / Bed in the corner / Sling it / Tumbling down. *(re-iss. 1983 on 'Fame' lp/c; FA41 3135-1/-4) (cd-iss. Jul90+=; CDP 794755-2)* – Big big deal / Such a dream. *(<cd re-iss. Jun01 on 'Beat Goes On'+=; BGOCD 529>)*

Jul 74. (7") *(EMI 2191)* **MR. SOFT. / SUCH A DREAM** [8] [–]

Nov 74. (7"; by STEVE HARLEY) *(EMI 2233)* **BIG BIG DEAL. / BED IN THE CORNER** [ ] [–]

Nov 74. (7") *<4023>* **SINGULAR BAND. / TUMBLING DOWN** [–] [ ]

STEVE HARLEY & COCKNEY REBEL

—— retained only **ELLIOT** with **JIM CREGAN** – guitar (ex-FAMILY)repl. CROCKER / **DUNCAN MACKAY** – keyboards repl. REAME-JAMES / **GEORGE FORD** – bass repl. JEFFERIES (he died early '89 in the Lockerbie disaster).

Feb 75. (7") *(EMI 2263)* *<4070>* **MAKE ME SMILE (COME UP AND SEE ME). / ANOTHER JOURNEY** [1] [ ]

Mar 75. (lp/c) *(EMC/TC-EMC 3068)* *<11394>* **THE BEST YEARS OF OUR LIVES** [4] [ ]
– introducing "the best years" / Mad mad moonlight / Mr. Raffles (man it was mean) / It wasn't me / Panorama / Make me smile (come up and see me) / Back to the farm / 49th parallel / The best years of our lives. *(re-iss. Mar91 cd/lp; CDP 795926-2/-1) (<cd re-iss. Apr01 on 'Beat Goes On'+=; BGOCD 525>)* – Another journey / Sebastian (live).

May 75. (7") *(EMI 2299)* **MR. RAFFLES (MAN IT WAS MEAN). / SEBASTIAN (live)** [13] [–]

—— now a quartet when JIM CREGAN left to join ROD STEWART's band

Nov 75. (7") *(EMI 2369)* **BLACK OR WHITE. / MAD MAD MOONLIGHT (live)** [ ] [–]

Feb 76. (7") *<4201>* **MAKE ME SMILE (COME UP AND SEE ME). / ANOTHER JOURNEY** [–] [96]

Feb 76. (7") *(EMI 2409)* **WHITE WHITE DOVE. / THROW YOUR SOUL DOWN HERE** [ ] [–]

Feb 76. (lp/c) *(EMA/TC-EMA 775)* *<11500>* **TIMELESS FLIGHT** [18] [ ]
– Red is a mean, mean colour / White, white dove / Understand / All men are hungry / Black or white (and step on it) / Everything changes / Nothing is sacred / Don't go, don't cry. *(cd-iss. Mar91; CZ 386) (<cd re-iss. Dec02 on 'Beat Goes On'+=; BGOCD 574>)* – Throw your soul down here / Mad, mad moonlight (live).

Jul 76. (7") *(EMI 2505)* **HERE COMES THE SUN. / LAY ME DOWN** [10] [–]

Aug 76. (7") *<4335>* **HERE COMES THE SUN. / ALL MEN ARE HUNGRY** [–] [ ]

Oct 76. (7") *(EMI 2539)* **(I BELIEVE) LOVE'S A PRIMA DONNA. / SIDETRACK ONE** [41] [–]

Oct 76. (lp/c) *(EMC/TC-EMC 3156)* *<11596>* **LOVE'S A PRIMA DONNA** [28] [ ]
– Seeking a love / G.I. valentine / Finally a card game / Too much tenderness / Love compared with you / (I believe) Love's a prima donna / Seeking a love (pt.2) / (If this is love) Give me more / Carry me again / Here comes the sun / Innocence and guilt / Is it true what they say.

Dec 76. (7") *<4397>* **LOVE COMPARED WITH YOU. / TOO MUCH TENDERNESS** [–] [ ]

Jun 77. (lp/c) *(EMSP/TC-EMSP 320)* *<11661>* **FACE TO FACE – A LIVE RECORDING (live)** [40] [ ]
– Here comes the sun / (I believe) Love's a prima donna / Mad, mad moonlight / Red is a mean, mean colour / Sweet dreams / Finally a card game / Psychomodo / (If this is love) Give me more) / The best years of our lives / Love compared with you / Mr. Soft / Sebastian. *(<cd-iss. Aug00 on 'Beat Goes On'+=; BGOCD 501>)* – Seeking a love / Tumbling down / Make me smile (come up and see me).

Aug 77. (7"/12") *(EMI/12EMI 2673)* **THE BEST YEARS OF OUR LIVES (live). / TUMBLING DOWN (live)** [ ] [ ]

STEVE HARLEY

Jul 78. (7") *(EMI 2830) <4622>* **ROLL THE DICE. / WAITING**
Jul 78. (lp/c) *(EMC/TC-EMC 3254) <11770>* **HOBO WITH A GRIN**
– Roll the dice / America the brave / Living in a rhapsody / I wish it would rain / Riding the waves (with Virginia Woolf) / Someone's coming / Hot youth / (I don't believe) God is an anarchist / Faith, hope and charity. *<US cd-iss. 2000 on 'Blueprint'+=; 4646>* – Spaced out (original) / That's my life in your hands (live). *(cd-iss. Apr00 on 'Comeuppance'+=; CMUP 101CD)*
Sep 79. (7") *(EMI 2994)* **FREEDOM'S PRISONER. / ONE MORE TIME** 58
Sep 79. (lp/c) *(EMC/TC-EMC 3311)* **THE CANDIDATE** –
– Audience with the man / Woodchopper / Freedom's prisoner / Love on the rocks / Who's afraid? / One more time / How good it feels / From here to eternity / Young hearts (the candidate). *<US cd-iss. 2000 on 'Blueprint'+=; 4647>* – I can't even touch you / Psychomodo (live). *(cd-iss. Apr00 on 'Comeuppance'; CMUP 102CD)*

Chrysalis not iss.

Mar 82. (7") *(CHS 2594)* **I CAN'T EVEN TOUCH YOU. / I CAN'T BE ANYONE** –
(above featured MIDGE URE of ULTRAVOX)

Stiletto-RCA not iss.

Jul 83. (7") *(STIL 14)* **BALLERINA (PRIMA DONNA). / FACE TO FACE** 51 –
(12") *(STLT 14)* – ('A'extended) / Sebastian (new version).

Polydor not iss.

Dec 85. (7"/ext.12"; by SARAH BRIGHTMAN & STEVE HARLEY) *(POSP/+X 800)* **PHANTOM OF THE OPERA. / OVERTURE (From the Musical)** 7 –

— now solo with a backing band.

R.A.K. not iss.

Jun 85. (7") *(RAK 383)* **IRRESISTABLE. / SUCH IS LIFE** –
(12") *(RAK 383-12)* – ('A'extended) / Sebastian (original).
Apr 86. (7"/ext.12") *(RAK 387/+12)* **HEARTBEAT LIKE THUNDER. / WARM MY COLD HEART** –
Jun 86. (7"/ext.12") *(RAK 389/+12)* **IRRESISTABLE. / LUCKY MAN** –

— Late in '88, HARLEY teamed up with JON ANDERSON (of YES) and MIKE BATT for single 'WHATEVER YOU BELIEVE' on 'Epic'; *PEEPS/+12P 1)*

Vital Vinyl not iss.

Jun 89. (7") *(VIT 3)* **WHEN I'M WITH YOU. / THEME FROM BABBACOMBE LEE** –

— In Apr'90, STEVE HARLEY and several ex-COCKNEY REBEL members re-formed as RAFFLES UNITED, and played 4 consecutive Sunday nights live in a Sudbury pub.

Food For Thought not iss.

May 93. (cd/c) *(CD/T GRUB 28)* **YES YOU CAN** –
– Irresistable / Victim of love / Rain in Venice / Star for a week (Dino) / Promises / Fire in the night / The alibi / New-fashioned way / The lighthouse / Dancing on the telephone. *(re-iss. Dec95 on 'CTE'; 0843180-2/-4) <US cd-iss. Aug00 on 'Blueprint'; 4648> (cd re-iss. Apr00 on 'Comeuppance'; CMUP 103CD)*

Realisation not iss.

Nov 93. (cd/c) *(RLBT C/M 005)* **LIVE IN THE UK (live)** –
– Mr. Soft / Mr. Raffles (man it was mean) / When I'm with you / Star for a week / Riding the waves (for Vigínia Woolf) / The lighthouse / The best years of our lives / Sweet dreams / The psychomodo / Sling it! / Sebastian / Make me smile (come up and see me) / Love's a prima donna.

Transatla. not iss.

Aug 96. (cd) *(TRACD 242)* **POETIC JUSTICE** –
– That's my life in your hands / What becomes of the broken-hearted? / Two dam'd lies / Loveless / Strange communications / All in a life's work / Love minus zero – No limit / Safe / The last time I saw you / Crazy love / Riding the waves (for Virginia Woolf). *(re-iss. Oct02; same)*

Burning Airlines Burning Airlines

Aug 99. (cd) *(<PILOT 043>)* **STRIPPED TO THE BARE BONES (live and acoustic from the Jazz Cafe London 1998)**
– My only vice / Star for a week (Dino) / The best years of our lives / Judy teen / The last time I saw you / Mr. Soft / (Love) Compared to you / Tumbling down / Only you / Bed in the corner / Sling it! / Riding the waves (for Virgina Woolf) / Sebastian / Make me smile (come up and see me).

– (COCKNEY REBEL) compilations, etc. –

releases on 'EMI' unless otherwise mentioned
Apr 76. (lp) *Capitol; <ST 11456>* **A CLOSER LOOK** –
Sep 80. (lp/c) *(EMI/TC-EMI 13345)* **THE BEST OF STEVE HARLEY AND COCKNEY REBEL** –
(re-iss. May82 on 'Fame' lp/c; FA/TC-FA 3007)
Oct 80. (7") *(EMI 5112)* **MAKE ME SMILE (COME UP AND SEE ME). / SEBASTIAN** –
Sep 83. (d-lp) *(EDP 1546-773)* **THE HUMAN MENAGERIE / THE PSYCHOMODO** –
Oct 83. (7") *Old Gold; (OG 9375)* **MAKE ME SMILE (COME UP AND SEE ME). / JUDY TEEN** –
Feb 88. (7") *(EM 50)* **MR. SOFT. / MAD MAD MOONLIGHT**
May 88. (lp/c)(cd) *(EM/TC-EM 1291)(CDP 746 714-2)* **GREATEST HITS: STEVE HARLEY AND COCKNEY REBEL** –
(cd+=) – (3 extra).
1988. (lp) *Connoisseur; (VSOP 124)* **MR. SOFT** –
1988. (lp/c) *Castle; (CCS LP/MC 197)* **THE COLLECTION** –
Apr 92. (c-s/7") *(TC+/EM 5)* **MAKE ME SMILE (COME UP AND SEE ME). / MR. SOFT** 46 –
(cd-s+=) *(EMCT 5)* – Spaced out / (Love) Compared with you.
May 92. (cd) *(CDGO 2036)* **MAKE ME SMILE – THE BEST OF STEVE HARLEY & COCKNEY REBEL** –
– Mr. Soft / Riding the waves (for Virginia Woolf) / Irresistable (remix) / Mr. Raffles / Freedoms prisoner / Hideaway / Judy Teen / Best years of our lives (live) / Make me smile (come up and see me) / If this is love (give me more) (live) / Here comes the sun / Sebastian / Roll the dice / Understand / I believe (love's a prima donna) / Tumbling down.
May 94. (cd) *Magnum; (MCD 5)* **MAKE ME SMILE** –
Jul 95. (cd) *Windsong; (WINCD 073)* **LIVE AT THE BBC (live)** –
Nov 95. (cd-s) *Old Gold; (12623 6337-2)* **MAKE ME SMILE (COME UP AND SEE ME) / JUDY TEEN** –
Dec 95. (c-s/7") *Premier; (TC+/HARLEY 1)* **MAKE ME SMILE (COME UP AND SEE ME). / JUDY TEEN** 33 –
(cd-s+=) *(CDHARLEY 1)* – Another journey / (I believe) Love's a prima donna.
May 97. (cd) *Experience; (EXP 017)* **STEVE HARLEY & COCKNEY REBEL** –
Aug 97. (cd) *BR Music; (RM 1511)* **GREATEST HITS LIVE** –
Mar 98. (cd) *E.M.I.; (493764-2)* **MORE THAN SOMEWHAT: THE VERY BEST OF STEVE HARLEY** –
Mar 99. (cd) *EMI Gold; (<499419-2>)* **THE CREAM OF STEVE HARLEY & COCKNEY REBEL** Apr01
Apr 00. (cd) *Disky; (SI 99032-2)* **THE BEST OF THE 70'S** –
Feb 01. (cd) *Music Deluxe; (MDCD 005)* **MAKE ME SMILE (live 1989)** –
May 01. (cd) *Beat Goes On; (<BGOCD 527>)* **A CLOSER LOOK / LOVE'S A PRIMA DONNA**
Jul 01. (cd) *Burning Airlines; (<PILOT 053>)* **IN PURSUIT OF ILLUSION** (live Bremen, Germany 1976)

□ HARMONY ROCKETS (see under ⇒ MERCURY REV)

Ben HARPER

Born: 28 Oct'69, Pomona, California, USA. Born to music loving parents, HARPER was hooked by the blues as a child, subsequently taking up the guitar and graduating from a hands-on apprenticeship that found him playing on the same stage as such respected veterans as TAJ MAHAL. It was MAHAL who "discovered" HARPER, drawing attention to the distinctive sound the young musician would ring from his vintage Weissenborn lap steel guitar and before long, the lad was added to the roster of 'Virgin America'. Prior to this, the man had made his recording debut, 'PLEASURE AND PAIN' (1992), with fellow troubadour TOM FREUND. Steeped in the essence of the blues but written in a thoroughly modern context, HARPER's songs addressed current events while reflecting age old themes. Racism for one; released as his debut single, 'LIKE

A KING' was a barbed comment on the Rodney King affair. Cloaked in the sparsest of arrangements, HARPER's more personal material on 'WELCOME TO THE CRUEL WORLD' (1994) was equally forthright, succinct and resonant. While many cited him as the new HENDRIX (how many times have we heard that?), more sympathetic comparisons would be GIL SCOTT-HERON (who he subsequently played and toured with) and, if only for the purity and soulfulness of his slide playing, the late LOWELL GEORGE (of LITTLE FEAT). Yet while his influences were manifold, HARPER was singing the blues in his own style, accumulating gushing critical praise for his cathartic live performances. 1995's follow-up set, 'FIGHT FOR YOUR MIND', saw the addition of a drummer, OLIVER CHARLES, and a bassist, JUAN NELSON, although the songs were as sparingly radical as ever, if even more intense and imbued with a sense of human truth. Incredibly, perhaps, HARPER maintains that he has only written a handful of "blues" songs in his life, with only one ('HOMELESS CHILD') making it into the recording studio. What can't be disputed is that HARPER's music is about as far from the conception of blues as crusty old pub-rock as it is possible to get, a fact borne out by the continuing support of a wide cross-section of the music press, from the dance and style mags to the inkies. While major chart success continues to elude him, HARPER's third full-length release, 'THE WILL TO LIVE' (1997), suggested that, like his mate TAJ MAHAL, the best is yet to come. Now credited as BEN HARPER AND THE INNOCENT CRIMINALS, the man and his 3-piece backing combo had a well-deserved US Top 75 entry with fourth set, 'BURN TO SHINE' (1999). 2001's concert double set, 'LIVE FROM MARS', was an enjoyable, occasionally visceral insight into HARPER's hard-touring ethos. It only takes a couple of spins to realise that the guitarist lives and breathes this music, never more so than when he's onstage and inspired by the live dynamic. Two whole discs in one sitting may be a bit much for the average listener but even the covers (Marvin Gaye's 'SEXUAL HEALING' and Led Zep's 'WHOLE LOTTA LOVE') are soaked in HARPER's 100% proof soul power. The cleverly titled 'DIAMONDS ON THE INSIDE' (2003), his first new studio material in four years, was almost certainly worth the wait. As the likes of 'TOUCH FROM YOUR LUST', 'TEMPORARY REMEDY' and 'BRING THE FUNK' demonstrated, HARPER was perhaps more in tune with the spirit of raw funk than he's ever been, while guest vocals by LADYSMITH BLACK MAMBAZO lent the record an even deeper, African-rooted appeal. • **Covers:** STRAWBERRY FIELDS FOREVER (Beatles).

Album rating: WELCOME TO THE CRUEL WORLD (*6) / FIGHT FOR YOUR MIND (*7) / THE WILL TO LIVE (*6) / BURN TO SHINE (*6) / LIVE FROM MARS (*6) / DIAMONDS ON THE INSIDE (*7)

BEN HARPER – vocals, acoustic guitar / **TOM FREUND** – guitar

not iss. Cardas

Mar 92. (lp; as BEN HARPER & TOM FREUND) *<none>*
PLEASURE AND PAIN – ltd –
– Whipping boy / Jesus on the main line / Pay the man / Quarter of a man / Mama's got a girlfriend now / Angel from Montgomery / Click'yo heels / You should have come to me / Dust my broom / Sweet home Chicago / Pleasure and pain.
(above album was half covers w/ BEN + TOM writing 2 each separately)

—— now with **JOHN McKNIGHT** – bass + **ROCK DEADRICK** – drums

Virgin Virgin

Jul 94. (cd/c) *(CDVUS/VUSMC 69) <V2/V4 39320>*
WELCOME TO THE CRUEL WORLD Feb94
– The three of us / Whipping boy / Breakin' down / Don't take that attitude to your grave / Waiting on an angel / Mama's got a girlfriend now / Forever / Like a king / Pleasure and pain / Walk away / How many miles must we march / Welcome to the cruel world / I'll rise.

Nov 94. (12"/cd-s) *(VUS T/DG 86)* **LIKE A KING / (remix). / WHIPPING BOY / (remix)** –

—— now with **JUAN NELSON** – bass / **OLIVER CHARLES** – drums

Jul 95. (cd/c/d-lp) *(CDVUS/VUSMC/VUSDLP 93) <40620>*
FIGHT FOR YOUR MIND
– Oppression / Ground on down / Another lonely day / Please me like you want to / Gold to me / Burn one down / Excuse me Mr. / People lead / Fight for your mind / Give a man a home / By my side / Power of the gospel / God fearing man / One road to freedom.

Mar 96. (c-ep/cd-ep) *(VUS C/CD 99)* **GROUND ON DOWN EP** –
– Ground on down / Not fire not ice / Wicked man / If I could only hear my mother pray again.

May 97. (cd/c/lp) *(CDVUS/VUSMC/VUSLP 128) <44178>* **THE WILL TO LIVE** 89
– Faded / Homeless child / Number three / Roses from my friends / Jah work / I want to be ready / The will to live / Ashes / Widow of a living man / Glory and consequence / Mama's trippin' / I shall not walk alone. *(cd re-iss. Apr98; CDVUSX 128)*

Oct 97. (c-s) *(VUSC 120)* **FADED / VOODOO CHILE** –
(cd-s+=) *(VUSCD 120)* – Gold to me (live) / Fight for your mind.

Mar 98. (cd-s) *(VUSCD 134)* **FADED / REMEMBER – SUPERSTITION (live) / LIKE A KING (remix)** 54 –
(cd-s) *(VUSCDX 134)* – ('A'side) / Fight for your mind (live) / Faded:- Heroes Dollis Hill groove (instrumental).

Jul 98. (cd-s) *<95139>* **MAMA'S TRIPPIN' / MAMA'S TRIPPIN' (the Freedom mix) / EXCUSE ME MUSTER – BURNIN' & LOOTIN' (live)** –

Feb 99. (cd-s) *<893726>* **EXCUSE ME MISTER / NOBODY'S FAULT BUT MINE / SEXUAL HEALING (live)** –

BEN HARPER & THE INNOCENT CRIMINALS

Sep 99. (cd/d-lp) *(CDVUS/VUSLP 160) <48151>* **BURN TO SHINE** 67
– Alone / The woman in you / Less / Two hands of a prayer / Please bleed / Suzie blue / Steal my kisses / Burn to shine / Show me a little shame / Forgiven / Beloved one / In the Lord's arms.

Nov 99. (cd-s) **JAH WORK / MAMA'S TRIPPIN' (live) / POWER OF THE GOSPEL (live) / EXCUSE ME MR – BURNIN' & LOOTIN' (live)** –

Jan 00. (cd-s) *<896471>* **PLEASE BLEED** –

2000. (cd-s) **STEAL MY KISSES / NUMBER THREE (live) / BY MY SIDE (live) / STEAL MY KISSES (Neptune beat box)** –

May 01. (d-cd) *(CDVUSDX 187) <10079>* **LIVE FROM MARS (live)** Mar01 70
– Glory & consequence / Excuse me Mr. / Alone / Sexual healing / Woman in you / Ground on down / Steal my kisses / Burn one down / Mama's got a girlfriend / Welcome to the cruel world / Forgiven / Faded – Whole lotta love / Waiting on an angel / Roses from my friends / Power of the gospel / Pleasure and pain / Please bleed / The drugs don't work / In the Lord's arms / Not fire not ice / Beloved one / Number three / Walk away / Another lonely day / Like a king – I'll rise.

Mar 03. (cd; as BEN HARPER) *(CDVUS 234) <83003>*
DIAMONDS ON THE INSIDE 19
– With my own two hands / When it's good / Diamonds on the inside / Touch from your lust / When she believes / Brown eyed blues / Bring the funk / Everything / Amen omen / Temporary remedy / So high so low / Blessed to be a witness / Picture of Jesus / She's only happy in the sun.

Jun 03. (cd-s) *(VUSCD 266)* **DIAMONDS ON THE INSIDE / AMEN OMEN (solo acoustic version) / STRAWBERRY FIELDS FOREVER** –

– compilations, etc. –

Oct 02. (3xcd-box) *Virgin; (812906-2)* **BURN TO SHINE / WELCOME TO THE CRUEL WORLD / FIGHT FOR YOUR MIND**

Roy HARPER

Born: 12 Jun'41, Manchester, England. He was raised by his father, following his mother's death during childbirth. His step-mother was a Jehovah's Witness, leading to him becoming anti-religious. As a young teenager, he played in a skiffle group with his brother DAVID, but at 15, after leaving school, he joined the R.A.F. Not finding it to his liking, he feigned madness to escape further service. Roy then underwent ECT treatment at a mental hospital, later being institutionalised in Lancaster Moor. He then spent a year in jail at Walton Prison, Liverpool. In 1964, after busking around Europe, he moved to London and gained a solo residency at LES COUSINS' folk club in Soho. In 1966, he was signed to Peter Richards's 'Strike' records, who issued his debut lp, 'THE SOPHISTICATED BEGGAR'. The record encompassed his best pieces of poetry, only using a simple revox machine as backing. The following year, he signed to 'C.B.S.', issuing a second flop 45, which preceded the album, 'COME OUT FIGHTING, GENGHIS SMITH'. This featured an 11-minute track, 'CIRCLE' another of his highly personal folk/blues confessionals. In the summer of '68, he played free concerts at London's Hyde Park, which brought him a new underground audience. In 1969, he released the album, 'FOLKJOKEOPUS', which also featured a similarily lengthy track, the 15-minute 'McGOOGHAN'S BLUES'. Signing to 'Harvest' early in 1970, he released his fourth album in as many years, 'FLAT BAROQUE AND BERSERK' (it featured an uncredited guest spot from The NICE on the track, 'HELL'S ANGEL'). ROY then embarked on a US tour, but after arriving there drunk and jet-lagged he was arrested for abusive behaviour. He slept on West Coast beaches, while playing many gigs. In 1971, he released the highly regarded 'STORMCOCK' set, which hosted DAVID BEDFORD on orchestration and friend JIMMY PAGE (of LED ZEPPELIN) on the first of many guitar sessions for him. PAGE had already written an ode, 'Hats Off To Harper' for their LED ZEPPELIN III album. In 1972, he made his acting debut in the low-budget British film, 'Made', alongside Carol White. Most of the music from the film appeared in his next project, 'LIFEMASK', which was written as his last will and testament, following a near fatal, recurring blood disorder. On the 14th of February '74, he released the appropriately titled, 'VALENTINE', which gave him his first entry into the UK album chart. It was premiered at a concert on Valentine's Day at London's Rainbow theatre, with backing from PAGE, BEDFORD, KEITH MOON and JOHN BONHAM. Later in 1974, he formed the band TRIGGER (with BILL BRUFORD – drums / CHRIS SPEDDING – guitar & DAVE COCHRAN – bass), and supported PINK FLOYD at Knebworth. In 1975, he sang lead vox on PINK FLOYD's 'Have A Cigar', featured on the album, 'Wish You Were Here'. FLOYD had already guested on his next album, 'HQ', which, like its 1977 follow-up, 'BULLINAMINGVASE', hit the UK Top 40. In between the aforementioned projects, he had briefly resided in the States. In 1982 with MARK THOMPSON, he set up his own 'Public' records, who issued ROY's return to form with the 'WORK OF HEART' album. Early in 1985, he scored his last UK Top 50 album, the JIMMY PAGE collaboration, 'WHATEVER HAPPENED TO JUGULA'. He continued to take an active part in the music scene, the album, 'DEATH OR GLORY' being his last effort for some time in 1992. HARPER's son NICK proved he was a chip off the old block when he contributed some fine acoustic guitar to the opening track ('SONGS OF LOVE') on ROY's 1998 album, 'The DREAM SOCIETY'. Other guests included former JETHRO TULL man, IAN ANDERSON, who obliged with his trademark flute on the ambitious 'THESE FIFTY YEARS'. 'THE GREEN MAN' (2000), on the other hand, was a back to basics acoustic set recorded by HARPER alone with lyrics which were as reliably oblique as ever.
• **Trivia:** PAUL and LINDA McCARTNEY guested on his 'ONE OF THOSE DAYS IN ENGLAND' album. Meanwhile, KATE BUSH guested on ROY's 'THE UNKNOWN SOLDIER' album, returning the compliment by appearing on her hit 45, 'Breathing'.

Album rating: THE SOPHISTICATED BEGGAR (*8) / COME OUT FIGHTING GENGHIS SMITH (*6) / FOLKJOKEOPUS (*5) / FLAT BAROQUE AND BERSERK (*6) / STORMCOCK (*8) / LIFEMASK (*7) / VALENTINE (*6) / FLASHES FROM THE ARCHIVES OF OBLIVION (*6) / HQ (*7) / BULLINAMINGVASE (*7) / ROY HARPER 1970-75 compilation (*6) / THE UNKNOWN SOLDIER (*4) / WORK OF HEART (*6) / BORN IN CAPTIVY (*5) / WHATEVER HAPPENED TO JUGULA with Jimmy Page (*5) / IN BETWEEN EVERY LINE (*4) / DESCENDENTS OF SMITH (*6) / LOONY ON THE BUS early/rare (*4) / ONCE (*5) / BURN THE WORLD (*5) / DEATH OR GLORY (*6) / AN INTRODUCTION TO ROY HARPER collection (*6) / THE DREAM SOCIETY (*6) / THE GREEN MAN (*5)

ROY HARPER – vocals, guitar (with session people)

Strike — not iss.

Mar 66. (7") *(JH 304)* **TAKE ME IN YOUR EYES. / PRETTY BABY** [ ] [–]

Dec 66. (lp) *(JHL 105)* **THE SOPHISTICATED BEGGAR** [ ] [–]
– China girl / Goldfish / Sophisticated beggar / My friend / Big fat silver aeroplane / Blackpool / Legend / Girlie / October the twelfth / Black clouds / Mr. Station master / Forever / Committed. *(re-iss. Aug70 & 1972 as 'RETURN OF THE SOPHISTICATED BEGGAR' on 'Youngblood' and 'Birth' respectively; SSYB 7 & RAB 3) (re-iss. 1977 on 'Big Ben'; BBX 502) (re-iss. Jan89 on 'Sundown' lp/cd; SDLP/CDSM 051) (cd re-iss. Oct94 on 'J.H.D.'; JHDCD 064) (cd re-iss. Oct96 on 'Science Friction'; HUCD 007)*

C.B.S. — not iss.

Oct 67. (7") *(CBS 203001)* **MIDSPRING DITHERING. / ZENGEM** [ ] [–]

Jan 68. (lp) *(CBS 63184)* **COME OUT FIGHTING GHENGIS SMITH** [ ] [–]
– Freak street / You don't need money / Ageing raver / In a beautiful rambling mess / All you need is / What you have / Circle / Highgate Cemetary / Come out fighting Ghengis Smith / Zaney Janey / Ballad of songwriter / Midspring dithering / Zenjem / It's tomorrow and today is yesterday / Francesca / She's the one / Nobody's got any money in the summer. *(re-iss. Jun77 as 'THE EARLY YEARS' on 'CBS-Embassy'; EMB 31544) (re-iss. Sep91 on 'Awareness' lp/cd;) (cd re-iss. Nov94 & Oct96 on 'Science Friction'; HUCD 006)*

Apr 68. (7") *(CBS 3371)* **LIFE GOES BY. / NOBODY'S GOT ANY MONEY IN THE SUMMER** [ ] [–]

Liberty — World Pacific

Apr 69. (lp; mono/stereo) *(LBL/LBS 83231)* *<21888>* **FOLKJOKEOPUS** [ ] [ ]
– Sergeant Sunshine / She's the one / In the time of water / Composer of life / One for all / Exercising some control / McGoohan's blues / Manana. *(re-iss. Sep77 on 'Sunset'; SLS 50373) <US re-iss. 1978 on 'Chrysalis'; 1160> (re-iss. Aug86 & Nov88 on 'Awareness' lp/c; AWL/AWT 1003) (cd-iss. Oct89; AWCD 1003) (cd re-iss. Oct94 & Oct96 on 'Science Friction'; HUCD 009)*

Harvest — Harvest

Jun 70. (lp) *(SHVL 766)* <418> **FLAT BAROQUE AND BERSERK** [ ] [ ]
– Don't you grieve / I hate the white man / Feeling all the Saturday / How does it feel / Goodbye / Another day / Davey / East of the sun / Tom Tiddler's ground / Francesca / Song of the ages / Hell's angels. *(re-iss. Jul85 lp/c; 260585-1/-4) (cd-iss. 1992 & Jun94 on 'Hard Up' respectively; HUCD 003 & HUP 3LTDCD)*

May 71. (lp) *(SHVL 789)* **STORMCOCK** [ ] [–]
– Hors d'oeuvres / The same old rock / One man rock and roll band / Me and my woman. *<US-iss.1978 on 'Chrysalis'; 1161> (re-iss. Apr87 on 'Awareness' lp/c; AWL/AWT 2001) (cd re-iss. Oct94 & Oct96 on 'Science Friction'; HUCD 004)*

Oct 72. (7") *(HAR 5059)* **BANK OF THE DEAD (VALERIE'S SONG). / LITTLE LADY** [ ] [–]

Feb 73. (lp) *(SHVL 808)* **LIFEMASK** (music from film soundtrack 'MADE') [ ] [–]
– Highway blues / All Ireland / Little lady / Bank of the dead (Valerie's song) / South Africa / The Lord's prayer: Poem – Modal song (part 1-4) –

Front song – Middle song – End song – Front song (reprise). *<US-iss.1978 on 'Chrysalis'; 1162> (re-iss. Apr87 on 'Awareness' lp/c; AWL/AWT 1007) (cd-iss. Sep94 & Oct96 & Sep02 on 'Science Friction'+=; HUCD 005)* – Ballad of songwriter / Zaney Janey / Midspring dithering / Zenjam.

Feb 74. (7") *(HAR 5080)* **(DON'T YOU THINK WE'RE) FOREVER. / MALE CHAUVINIST PIG BLUES** –

Feb 74. (lp) *(SHSP 4027)* **VALENTINE** 27 –
– Forbidden fruit / Male chauvinist pig blues / I'll see you again / Twelve hours of sunset / Acapulco gold / Commune / Magic woman / Che / North country / (Don't you think we're) Forever. *<US-iss.1978 on 'Chrysalis'; 1163> (re-iss. Apr89 on 'Awareness' lp/c/cd; AWL/AWT/AWCD 1015)* – Home (studio) / Too many movies / Home (live). *(cd re-iss. Nov94 & Oct96 & Sep02 on 'Science Friction'+=; HUCD 015)*

Oct 74. (7") *(HAR 5089)* **HOME (live). / HOME (studio)** –

Nov 74. (d-lp) *(SHDW 405)* **FLASHES FROM THE ARCHIVES OF OBLIVION (live)** –
– Home / Commune / Don't you grieve / Twelve hours of sunset / Kangaroo blues / All Ireland / Me and my woman / South Africa / Interference / Highway blues / One man rock and roll band / Another day / M.C.P. blues / Too many movies / Home (studio version) *<US-iss.1978 on 'Chrysalis'; 1164> (re-iss. Apr89 on 'Awareness' d-lp/c/cd; AW CD/TD/LD 1012) (cd re-iss. Sep94 & Oct96 on 'Science Friction'; HUCD 010)*

Harvest Chrysalis

May 75. (lp) *(SHSP 4046)* *<1105>* **HQ** <US-title 'WHEN AN OLD CRICKETER LEAVES THE CREASE'> 31 Feb 76
– The game (part I-V) / The spirit lives / Grown-ups are just silly children / Referendum / Forget-me-not / Hallucinating light / When an old cricketer leaves the crease / Referendum. *(re-iss. Mar86 on 'E.M.I.' lp/c; ATAK/TCATAK 68) (cd-iss. Aug95 & Oct96 on 'Science Friction'; HUCD 019)*

May 75. (7") *(HAR 5096)* **WHEN AN OLD CRICKETER LEAVES THE CREASE. / HALLUCINATING LIGHT (acoustic)**

Oct 75. (7") *(HAR 5102)* **GROWN-UPS ARE JUST SILLY CHILDREN. / REFERENDUM (LEGEND)** –

Feb 77. (lp) *(SHSP 4060)* **BULLINAMINGVASE** 25 –
– One of those days in England / These last days / Cherishing the lonesome / Naked flame / Watford Gap * / One of those days in England (parts 2-10). *(free 7"w/a) (PSR 407)* REFERENDUM / ANOTHER DAY (live). / TOM TIDDLER'S GROUND (live) *(lp re-iss. Mar77, track * repl. by;* – Breakfast in bed. *(re-iss. Apr87 on 'E.M.I.' lp/c; EMS/TCEMS 1259)*

Mar 77. (7") *(HAR 5120)* **ONE OF THOSE DAYS IN ENGLAND. / WATFORD GAP** –

Nov 77. (7"; as ROY HARPER'S BLACK SHEEP) *(HAR 5140)* **SAIL AWAY. / CHERISHING THE LONESOME** –

Mar 80. (7") *(HAR 5203)* **PLAYING GAMES. / FIRST THING IN THE MORNING** –

Jun 80. (lp) *(SHVL 820)* **THE UNKNOWN SOLDIER** –
– Playing games / I'm in love with you / The flycatcher / You / Old faces / Short and sweet / First thing in the morning / The unknown soldier / Ten years ago / True story.

Jun 80. (7"m) *(HAR 5207)* **SHORT AND SWEET. / WATER SPORTS (live) / UNKNOWN SOLDIER (live)** –

Public not iss.

Oct 82. (7") *(PUBS 1001)* **NO ONE EVER GETS OUT ALIVE. / CASUALITY (live)** –

Nov 82. (lp/c) *(PUBLP/TCPUBLP 5001)* **WORK OF HEART** –
– Drawn to the flames / Jack of hearts / I am a child / Woman / I still care / Work of heart; (i) No one ever gets out alive – (ii) Two lovers in the Moon – (iii) We are the people – (iv) All us children (so sadly far apart) – (v) We are the people (reprise) – (vi) No one ever gets out alive (finale). *(re-iss. Nov86 on 'Awareness' lp,c; AWL 1002) (lp w/free 7"x2; PUBS 1001/1002; 2nd very ltd) (cd-iss. Oct89; AWCD 1002)*

Mar 83. (7") *(PUBS 1002)* **I STILL CARE. / GOODBYE LADYBIRD** –

Hardup not iss.

1984. (lp; ltd) *(PUB 5002)* **BORN IN CAPTIVITY** (demos) –
– Stan / Drawn to the flames / Come to bed eyes / No woman is safe / I am a child / Elizabeth / Work of heart; (i) No one ever gets out alive – (ii) Two lovers on the Moon – (iii) We are the people – (iv) All us children (so sadly far apart) – (v) We are the people (reprise) – (vi) No one ever gets out alive (finale). *(re-iss. Jul85 & Nov88 on 'Awareness' lp/c; AWL/AWT 1001) (cd-iss. Apr89; AWCD 1001) (cd re-iss. Oct96 on 'Blueprint'; HUCD 008)*

ROY HARPER and JIMMY PAGE

with **JIMMY PAGE** – guitar (ex-LED ZEPPELIN)

Beggars Banquet P.V.C.

Feb 85. (lp/c) *(BEGA/BEGC 60)* *<8937>* **WHATEVER HAPPENED TO JUGULA** 44
– Nineteen forty-eightish / Hangman / Elizabeth / Advertisement / Bad speech / Hope / Twentieth century man. *(re-iss. Aug88 & Jul91 on 'Lowdown – Beggars Banquet' lp/c/cd; BBL/+C 60/+CD)*

Mar 85. (7") *(BEG 131)* **ELIZABETH. / ADVERTISEMENT** –
(12"+=) *(BEG 131T)* – (I hate the) White man (live).

ROY HARPER

E.M.I. not iss.

Jun 86. (d-lp/c) *(EM/TCEM 5004)* **IN BETWEEN EVERY LINE (live)** –
– One of those days in England / Short and sweet / True story / Referendum / Highway blues / One man rock and roll band / The game / Hangman. *(cd-iss. Nov94 & Oct96 on 'Science Friction'; HUCD 018)*

Mar 88. (7") *(EM 46)* **LAUGHING INSIDE. / LAUGHING INSIDE (acoustic)** –
(above single was also released as 3 promos in the disguise of palindromes; RORY PHARE / HARRY ROPE / PER YARROH; *(Regal Zonophone; RP 1 / HP 1 / PY 1)*

Mar 88. (cd/c/lp) *(CD/TC+/EMC 3524)* **DESCENDANTS OF SMITH** –
– Laughing inside / Garden of uranium / Still life / Pinches of salt / Desert island / Government surplus / Surplus liquorice / Liquorice alltime / Maile lei / Same shoes / Descendants of Smith. *(cd+=)* – Laughing inside (rough and ready version). *(cd-iss. Sep94 & Oct96 as 'GARDEN OF URANIUM' on 'Science Friction' respectively; HUCD 014)*

below featured DAVE GILMOUR, KATE BUSH & STEVE BROUGHTON

Awareness I.R.S.

May 90. (cd/c/lp) *(AW CD/T/L 1018)* *<13078>* **ONCE**
– Once / Once in the middle of nowhere / Nowhere to run to / Black cloud of Islam / If / Winds of change / Berliners / Sleeping at the wheel / For longer than it takes / Ghost dance. *(cd re-iss. Oct94 on 'Line'; LICD 900892) (cd re-iss. Oct96 on 'Science Friction'; HUCD 011)*

Nov 90. (cd/c/lp) *(AW CD/T/L 1019)* **BURN THE WORLD** –
– Burn the world (studio) / Burn the world (live). *(cd re-iss. Oct94 & Oct96 on 'Science Friction'; HUCD 013)*

Nov 92. (cd/c/lp) *(AW CD/T/L 1037)* **DEATH OR GLORY** –
– Death or glory / War came home / Tonight duty / Waiting for Godot / Part zed next to me / Man kind / Tallest tree / Miles remains / Fourth world / Why / Cardboard city / One more tomorrow / Plough / On summer day / If I can. *(cd re-iss. Dec94 & Oct96 & Sep99 on 'Science Friction'; HUCD 012)*

Resurgent not iss.

Jun 98. (cd) *(4305)* **THE DREAM SOCIETY** –
– Songs of love / Songs of love (part 2) / Dancing all the night / Psychopath / I want to be in love / Drugs for everybody / Come the revolution / Angel of the night / The dream society / Broken wing / These fifty years. *(re-iss. Sep99 on 'Science Friction'; HUCD 030)*

Science Friction Science Friction

Apr 01. (cd) *(<HUCD 033>)* **THE GREEN MAN** May01
– The green man / Wishing well / Sexy woman / The apology / Midnight sun / Glasto / The monster / New England / Solar wind sculptures / Rushing Camelot / All in all.

– compilations etc. –

May 78. (7") *Harvest; (HAR 5160)* **WHEN AN OLD CRICKETER LEAVES THE CREASE. / HOME (studio)**

May 78. (lp) *Harvest; (SHSM 2025)* **ROY HARPER 1970-75** –
– Don't you grieve / (I hate the) White man / Tom Tiddler's ground / Me and my woman / Little lady / South Africa / Forbidden fruit / I'll see you again / Commune / Another day / When an old cricketer leaves the crease / Home.

Dec 88. (lp/c/cd) *Awareness; (AWL/AWT/AWCD 1011)* **LOONY ON THE BUS** (rare) –
– No change (ten years ago) / Sail away / / Playing prison / I wanna be part of the news / Burn the world / Casuality / Cora / Loony on the bus / Come up and see me / The flycatcher / Square boxes.

1992. (c) *Hard Up; (HU 2)* **BORN IN CAPTIVITY II (live)** –

Nov 94. (cd) *Awareness;* **BORN IN CAPTIVITY / WORK OF HEART** –
(re-iss. cd Nov94 on 'Science Friction'; HUCD 008)

Dec 94. (cd) *Awareness;* **COMMERCIAL BREAKS** (unreleased from 1977 on 'Harvest'; *SHSP 4077)*
– My little girl / I'm in love with you / Ten years ago / Sail away / I wanna be part of the news / Cora / Come up and see me / The flycatcher / Too many movies / Square boxes / Burn the world (part 1) / Playing prisons. *(re-iss. Feb95 & Oct96 on 'Science Friction'; HUCD 016)*

Dec 94. (cd) *Awareness; (234)* **AN INTRODUCTION TO ROY HARPER**
– Legend / She's the one / Tom Tiddler's ground / Highway blues / Che / Hallucinating light / One of those days in England / You / Nineteen forty-eightish / Pinches of salt / Ghost dance / The tallest tree / Miles remains. *(re-iss. Feb95 & Oct96 on 'Science Friction'; HUCD 017)*

Aug 95. (cd) *Griffin; (132-2)* **UNHINGED**
– Descendants of Smith / Legend / North country / When an old cricketer leaves the crease / Three hundred words / Hope / Naked flame / Commune / South Africa / Back to the stones / Frozen moment / Highway blues / The same old rock. *(re-iss. Oct96 on 'Blueprint'; HUCD 020)*

May 96. (cd) *Blueprint; (BP 220CD)* **LIVE AT LES COUSINS (live)**

Apr 97. (cd) *Science Friction; (HUCD 022)* **LIVE AT THE BBC VOL.1**

Apr 97. (cd) *Science Friction; (HUCD 023)* **LIVE AT THE BBC VOL.2**

Jun 97. (cd) *Science Friction; (HUCD 024)* **LIVE AT THE BBC VOL.3**

Jun 97. (cd) *Science Friction; (HUCD 025)* **LIVE AT THE BBC VOL.4**

Jun 97. (cd) *Science Friction; (HUCD 026)* **LIVE AT THE BBC VOL.5**

Jun 97. (cd) *Science Friction; (HUCD 027)* **LIVE AT THE BBC VOL.6**

Jun 01. (cd) *Capitol; <27640>* **HATS OFF**

Emmylou HARRIS

Born: 2 Apr'47, Birmingham, Alabama, USA. She later moved to Washington, playing sax in a high school band before going to the University of North Carolina where she made her first forays into the world of folk music, playing as part of a duo. From here it was but a short step to the folk clubs of Greenwich Village in New York where she released her debut 1969 album, 'GLIDING BIRD' for the 'Jubilee' label. The record was hardly a resounding success and after a spell in Nashville in the early 70's, she drifted back with baby Hallie to Washington following the failure of her first marriage. By a twist of fate, this apparent setback proved to be the beginning of her career proper after she was spotted in a local club by the The FLYING BURRITO BROTHERS. The band informed ex-member and founding father of Cosmic American Music (country-rock, basically), GRAM PARSONS, who was after a partner for his forthcoming solo project. The two hit it off immediately, GRAM schooling her in the ways of classic country. Over the course of two albums, 'G.P.' (1972) and 'GRIEVOUS ANGEL' (1973), the pair recorded some of the most sublime duets in the history of recorded music ('WE'LL SWEEP OUT THE ASHES IN THE MORNING', 'LOVE HURTS' etc.), HARRIS' mournful soprano combining with PARSON's cracked chords to create music of a fragile beauty. PARSONS was on a crash course in self-destruction, however, and after he O.D.'d in 1973, HARRIS's career was once again in limbo. Down but not out, she eventually formed a new backing outfit from the ashes of GRAM's FALLEN ANGELS, retaining JAMES BURTON (guitar, previously of ELVIS PRESLEY's band) and GLENN D.HARDIN (piano), bringing in EMORY GORDY (bass), RODNEY CROWELL (rhythm guitar, vocals), HANK DE VITO (pedal steel) and JOHN WARE (drums). Remaining with PARSON's label, 'Reprise', HARRIS released 'PIECES OF THE SKY' in 1975, a masterful set which included one of her finest compositions, 'BOULDER TO BIRMINGHAM', a lilting eulogy to GRAM, alongside the beautiful 'SLEEPLESS NIGHTS' and a rousing cover of the LOUVIN BROTHERS 'IF I COULD ONLY WIN YOUR LOVE' which became an American country No.1. HARRIS possessed one of the most haunting and alongside STEVIE NICKS, one of the most distinctive, white female voices in the business. Over a string of excellent albums and consummate choice of cover material, she built up a reputation as one of country's leading ladies as well as winning over rock and pop fans. Her tonsils much in demand, she even appeared in The BAND's 'Last Waltz', performing ROBBIE ROBERTSON's 'EVANGELINE', and during the 70's provided backing vocals on a number of classic albums, including LITTLE FEAT's 'Dixie Chicken' and BOB DYLAN's 'Desire'. Following her marriage to producer BRIAN AHERN, HARRIS released her second Top 30 album, 'LUXURY LINER' (1977), arguably her strongest set of the decade wherein she performed a spine-tingling run through of the late, great Townes Van Zandt's 'PANCHO AND LEFTY' while covering The Carter Family's 'HELLO STRANGER' in fine style. With 'QUARTER MOON IN A TEN CENT TOWN' (1978), the singer moved towards straight country, scoring a Top 3 country hit with her touching cover of Dolly Parton's 'TO DADDY'. 'BLUE KENTUCKY GIRL' (1979) and 'ROSES IN THE SNOW' (1980) were rootsier, the latter stripped down to bare acoustic guitar. 'EVANGELINE' (1981) once more saw HARRIS at her best covering classic material, GRAM's 'HOT BURRITO No.2' and CREEDENCE CLEARWATER REVIVAL's 'BAD MOON RISING' both given a thorough going over. Heading back to Nashville in the mid-80's, HARRIS even recorded a country concept album (!), 'THE BALLAD OF SALLY ROSE' (1985). As the decade wore on, HARRIS and her HOT BAND were met with an increasingly cold reception, commercially at least, and she eventually replaced said backing crew with The NASH RAMBLERS, a rootsier acoustic group. The 90's saw HARRIS re-appraising her sound, hip producer DANIEL LANOIS working on her acclaimed 1995 album, 'WRECKING BALL', a set that also saw the likes of a similarly revamped STEVE EARLE guesting. If anyone can keep the spirit of roots country alive and relevant in an increasingly hi-tech musical world, then it's EMMYLOU, whose dedication to the genre through the ever changing dictats of fashion is admirable. Three whole decades and nearly thirty albums under her belt, HARRIS finally tapped her latent songwriting talent on the acclaimed 'RED DIRT GIRL' (2000). She may still dress like a cowgirl but you'd be hard pushed to find anything to tempt the Nashville mainstream on this record. Instead, EMMYLOU – with the help of producer Malcolm Burn and an extensive cast of friends that included BRUCE SPRINGSTEEN, GUY CLARK, KATE McGARRIGLE and DAVE MATTHEWS – put in some of the best performances of her career against a backdrop that encompassed elements of starry-eyed pop, atmospheric rock, ethnic textures and driving percussion. 2003's 'STUMBLE INTO GRACE', meanwhile, found the singer growing – if not exactly stumbling – older with as much elegance as the title suggested. Although she's arguably been working towards a state of musical grace since the earliest days of her career, in recent years she seems to have intensified that quest and the mistitled 'STUMBLE..' was another step in the right direction. Again laying its arrangements open to elements outwith her previous remit, the record found HARRIS flirting with haunting fragments of folk, pop and world music to often mesmerising effect. • **Songwriters:** Writes some herself, collaborates with others, except covers I'LL BE YOUR BABY TONIGHT (Bob Dylan) / THE PRICE YOU PAY + MY FATHER'S HOUSE + BORN TO RUN +

TOUGHER THAN THE REST (Bruce Springsteen) / YOU NEVER CAN TELL (Chuck Berry) / THE BOXER (Simon & Garfunkel) / MISTER SANDMAN (Chordettes) / TO DADDY (Dolly Parton) / BURN THAT CANDLE (Bill Haley) / TWO MORE BOTTLES OF WINE (Delbert McClinton) / PLEDGING MY LOVE (Johnny Ace) / DIAMONDS ARE A GIRL'S BEST FRIEND (Jule Styne) / WILD MONTANA SKIES (duet w / JOHN DENVER) / HERE, THERE AND EVERYWHERE + FOR NO ONE (Beatles) / NO REGRETS (Tom Rush) / ICY BLUE HEART (John Hiatt) / LOVE IS (Kate McGarrigle) / WHEELS OF LOVE (Marjy Plant) / SAVE THE LAST DANCE FOR ME (Drifters) / JAMBALAYA (Hank Williams) / BAD MOON RISING + LODI (Creedence Clearwater Revival) / ROSE OF CIMARRON (Poco) / HOT BURRITO + SLEEPLESS NIGHTS (Gram Parsons) / BRAND NEW DANCE (Paul Kennerley) / SWEET DREAMS OF YOU (Kennerley-David) / BETTER OFF WITHOUT YOU (Chapman-Walker-Brown) / NEVER BE ANYONE ELSE BUT YOU (Baker Knight) / RED RED ROSE (David Mallett) / GUITAR TOWN (Steve Earle) / ROLLIN' AND RAMBLIN' (Williams-Williams-Clark) / EASY FOR YOU TO SAY (Routh-Sharp) / IN HIS WORLD (Kostas-Reynolds) / ABRAHAM, MARTIN & JOHN (hit; Marvin Gaye) / SCOTLAND (. . . Monroe) / CATTLE CALL (Buck Owens) / THANKS TO YOU (Jesse Winchester) / BALLAD OF A RUNNING HORSE (Leonard Cohen) / etc. • **Trivia:** In 1980, she won a Grammy for her country lp 'BLUE KENTUCKY GIRL'.

Album rating: GLIDING BIRD (*4) / PIECES OF THE SKY (*7) / ELITE HOTEL (*8) / LUXURY LINER (*8) / QUARTER MOON IN A TEN CENT TOWN (*7) / PROFILE – BEST OF . . . compilation (*7) / BLUE KENTUCKY GIRL (*6) / ROSES IN THE SNOW (*7) / LIGHT OF THE STABLE (*6) / EVANGELINE (*7) / CIMARRON (*6) / LAST DATE (*6) / WHITE SHOES (*6) / PROFILE II – BEST OF . . . compilation (*6) / THE BALLAD OF SALLY ROSE (*5) / THIRTEEN (*5) / TRIO with Dolly Parton & Linda Ronstadt (*5) / ANGEL BAND (*5) / BLUEBIRD (*5) / DUETS (*5) / BRAND NEW DANCE (*5) / AT THE RYMAN (*7) / NASHVILLE COUNTRY DUETS with Carl Jackson (*5) / COWGIRL'S PRAYER (*6) / SONGS OF THE WEST (*6) / WRECKING BALL (*8) / NASHVILLE (*5) / RED DIRT GIRL (*8) / STUMBLE INTO GRACE (*7)

EMMYLOU HARRIS – vocals, acoustic guitar; with session people

not iss. Jubilee

1969. (lp) *<JGS 0031>* **GLIDING BIRD** [–] [ ]
– I'll be your baby tonight / Fugue for the fox / I saw the light / Clocks / Black gypsy / Gliding bird / Everybody's talkin' / Bobbie's gone / I'll never fall in love again / Waltz of the magic man. *(UK-iss.Apr79 as 'THE LEGENDARY GLIDING BIRD ALBUM' on 'Pye Special'; PKL 5577)*

1969. (7") *<5679>* **I'LL BE YOUR BABY TONIGHT. / I'LL NEVER FALL IN LOVE AGAIN** [–] [ ]

1969. (7") *<5697>* **FUGUE FOR THE FOX. / PADDY** [–] [ ]

— he then went solo, augmented soon by The HOT BAND:- **JAMES BURTON** – guitar / **GLEN D.HARDIN** – piano / **EMORY GORDY** – bass / **RODNEY CROMWELL** – rhythm guitar, vocals / **HANK DE VITO** – pedal steel guitar / **JOHN WARE** – drums

Reprise Reprise

Apr 75. (lp/c) *(L/K4 54037) <2213>* **PIECES OF THE SKY** [ ] Mar75 [45]
– Bluebird wine / Too far gone / If I could only win your love / Boulder to Birmingham / Before believing / Bottle let me down / Sleepless nights / Coat of many colours / For no one / Queen of the silver dollar. *(cd-iss. Feb89; 7599 27244-2)*

May 75. (7") *<1326>* **BOULDER TO BIRMINGHAM. / TOO FAR GONE** [–] [ ]

Jun 75. (7") *(K 14396)* **BOULDER TO BIRMINGHAM. / QUEEN OF THE SILVER DOLLAR** [ ] [–]

Nov 75. (7") *(K 14404) <1332>* **IF I COULD ONLY WIN YOUR LOVE. / QUEEN OF THE SILVER DOLLAR** [ ] Aug75 [58]

Jan 76. (7") *(K 14410) <1341>* **LIGHT OF THE STABLE. / BLUEBIRD WINE** [ ] [ ]

Jan 76. (lp/c) *(K/K4 54060) <2213>* **ELITE HOTEL** [17] [25]
– Amarillo / Together again / Feelin' single – seeing double / Sin city / One of these days / Till I gain control again / Here, there and everywhere / Ooh Las Vegas / Sweet dreams / Jambalaya / Satan's jewel crown / Wheels. *(re-iss. May89 on 'Edsel'; ED 306)*

Feb 76. (7") *(K 14415)* **HERE, THERE AND EVERYWHERE. / AMARILLO** [30] [–]

Mar 76. (7") *<1346>* **HERE, THERE AND EVERYWHERE. / TOGETHER AGAIN** [–] [65]

May 76. (7") *(K 14439)* **TOGETHER AGAIN. / WHEELS** [ ] [–]

Jul 76. (7") *<1353>* **ONE OF THESE DAYS. / TILL I GAIN CONTROL AGAIN** [–] [ ]

Sep 76. (7") *<1371>* **AMARILLO. / SWEET DREAMS** [–] [ ]

Nov 76. (7") *<1379>* **LIGHT OF THE STABLE. / BOULDER TO BIRMINGHAM** [–] [ ]

— **ALBERT LEE** – guitar (ex-Solo artist) repl. BURTON (returned to ELVIS)

Warners Warners

Jan 77. (lp/c) *(K/K4 56334) <3115>* **LUXURY LINER** [17] [21]
– Luxury liner / Pancho & Lefty / Making believe / You're supposed to be feeling good / I'll be your San Antone rose / (You never can tell) C'est la vie / When I stop dreaming / Hello stranger / She / Tulsa queen. *(cd-iss. Jun89; 927338-2)*

Feb 77. (7") *(K 16888)* **(YOU NEVER CAN TELL) C'EST LA VIE. / HELLO STRANGER** [ ] [–]

Feb 77. (7") *<8329>* **(YOU NEVER CAN TELL) C'EST LA VIE. / YOU'RE SUPPOSED TO BE FEELING GOOD** [–] [ ]

May 77. (7") *<8388>* **MAKING BELIEVE. / I'LL BE YOUR SAN ANTONE ROSE** [–] [ ]

Jan 78. (lp/c) *(K/K4 56443) <3141>* **QUARTER MOON IN A TEN CENT TOWN** [40] [29]
– Easy from now on / Two more bottles of wine / To daddy / My songbird / Leavin' Louisiana in the broad daylight / Defying gravity / I ain't livin' long like this / One paper kid / Green rolling hills / Burn that candle. *(cd-iss. 1989; 927345-2)*

Feb 78. (7") *(K 17095) <8498>* **TO DADDY. / TULSA QUEEN** [ ] [ ]

Apr 78. (7") *<8553>* **I AIN'T LIVIN' LONG LIKE THIS. / TWO MORE BOTTLES OF WINE** [–] [ ]

Apr 78. (7") *(K 17133)* **I AIN'T LIVIN' LONG LIKE THIS. / ONE PAPER KID** [ ] [–]

Jun 78. (7") *<8623>* **EVEN FROM NOW ON. / YOU'RE SUPPOSED TO BE FEELING GOOD** [–] [ ]

May 79. (7") *<8815>* **SAVE THE LAST DANCE FOR ME. / EVEN COWGIRLS GET THE BLUES** [–] [ ]

Jun 79. (lp/c) *(K/K4 56627) <3318>* **BLUE KENTUCKY GIRL** [ ] May79 [43]
– Sister's coming home / Beneath still waters / Rough and rocky / Hickory wind / Save the last dance for me / Sorrow in the wind / They'll never take his love from me / Everytime you leave / Blue Kentucky girl / Even cowgirls get the blues. *<(cd-iss. Jan93; 7599 29392-2)>*

Jul 79. (7") *<49056>* **BLUE KENTUCKY GIRL. / LEAVIN' LOUISIANA IN THE BROAD DAYLIGHT** [–] [ ]

Oct 79. (7") *<49164>* **BENEATH STILL WATERS. / TILL I GAIN CONTROL AGAIN** [–] [ ]

Nov 79. (lp/c) *(K/K4 56757) <3484>* **LIGHT OF THE STABLE (THE CHRISTMAS ALBUM)** (festive) [ ] Nov80 [ ]

Nov 79. (7") *(K 17528)* **THE FIRST NOEL. / SILENT NIGHT** [ ] [–]

May 80. (7") *<49239>* **GREEN PASTURES. / WAYFARING STRANGERS** [–] [ ]

May 80. (lp/c) *(K/K4 56796) <3422>* **ROSES IN THE SNOW** [ ] [26]
– Roses in the snow / Wayfaring stranger / Green pastures / The boxer / Darkest hour just before dawn / I'll go stepping too / You're learning / Jordan / Miss the Mississippi / Gold watch and chain. *<(cd-iss. Feb90; 7599 23422-2)> <(cd re-mast.Jul02 on 'W.S.M.'+=; 8122 78140-2)>* – You're gonna change / Root like a rose.

Jul 80. (7") *(K 17649) <49262>* **THAT LOVIN' YOU FEELIN' AGAIN. / (b-side by Craig Hindley)** [ ] Jun80 [55]
(above from the film 'Roadie' and credited with ROY ORBISON)

Jul 80. (7") *<49551>* **THE BOXER. / PRECIOUS LOVE** [–] [ ]

Nov 80. (7") *<49633>* **BEAUTIFUL STAR OF BETHLEHEM. / LITTLE DRUMMER BOY** [–] [ ]

Dec 80. (7") *<49645>* **LIGHT OF THE STABLE. / LITTLE DRUMMER BOY** [–] [ ]

Feb 81. (7") *<49684>* **MISTER SANDMAN. / FOOLS THIN AIR** [–] [37]

Feb 81. (7") *(K 17758)* **MISTER SANDMAN. / ASHES BY NOW** [ ] [–]

Feb 81. (lp/c) *(K/K4 56880) <3508>* **EVANGELINE** [53] [22]
– I don't have to crawl / How high the Moon / Spanish Johnny / Bad Moon rising / Evangeline / Hot burrito £2 / Millworker / Oh Atlanta / Mister Sandman / Ashes by now.

May 81. (7") *<49739>* **COLORS OF YOUR HEART. / I DON'T HAVE TO CRAWL** [–] [ ]

May 81. (7") *(K 17804)* **BAD MOON RISING. / I DON'T HAVE TO CRAWL** [ ] [–]
Nov 81. (7") *<49892>* **MAMA HELP. / TENNESSEE ROSE** [–] [ ]
Nov 81. (lp/c) *(K/K4 56955) <3603>* **CIMARRON** [ ] [46]
– Rose of cimarron / Spanish is a loving tongue / If I needed you / Another lonesome morning / The last cheater's waltz / Born to run / The price you pay / Son of a rotten gambler / Tennessee waltz / Tennessee rose.
Feb 82. (7") *<29993>* **BORN TO RUN. / COLORS OF YOUR HEART** [–] [ ]
Feb 82. (7") *(K 17896)* **BORN TO RUN. / ASHES BY NOW** [ ] [–]
Nov 82. (lp/c) *(923740-1/-4) <23740>* **LAST DATE (live)** [ ] [65]
– I'm moving on / It's not love (but it's not bad) / So sad (to watch good love so bad) / Grevious angel / Restless / Racing in the streets / Long may you run / Well sweep out the ashes (in the morning) / Juanita / Devil in disguise / (Lost his love) On our last date / Buckaroo / Love's gonna live here.
Nov 82. (7") *<29898>* **(LOST HIS LOVE) ON OUR LAST DATE. / ANOTHER POT O' TEA** [–] [ ]
Feb 83. (7") *<29729>* **I'M MOVIN' ON (live). / MAYBE TONIGHT** [–] [ ]
Apr 83. (7") *<29583>* **SO SAD (TO WATCH GOOD LOVE GO BAD) (live). / AMARILLO (live)** [–] [ ]
Oct 83. (7") *<29443>* **DRIVIN' WHEEL. / GOOD NEWS** [–] [ ]
Oct 83. (lp/c) *(923961-1/-4) <23961>* **WHITE SHOES** [ ] [ ]
– Drivin' wheel / Pledging my love / In my dreams / White shoes / On the radio / It's only rock'n'roll / Diamonds are a girl's best friend / Good news / Baby, better start turnin' 'em down / Like an old fashoined waltz. *(cd-iss. Jan84; 923961-2) (cd re-iss. Jan96; 7599 23961-2)*
Jan 84. (7") *<29329>* **LIKE AN OLD FASHIONED WALTZ. / IN MY DREAMS** [–] [ ]
May 84. (7") *<29218>* **PLEDGING MY LOVE. / BABY, BETTER START TURNIN' 'EM DOWN** [–] [ ]
May 84. (7") *(W 9364)* **ON THE RADIO. / GOOD NEWS** [ ] [–]
Nov 84. (7") *<29138>* **SOMEONE LIKE YOU. / LIGHT OF THE STABLE** [–] [ ]
Feb 85. (7") *<29041>* **WHITE LINE. / LONG TALL SALLY ROSE** [–] [ ]
Feb 85. (lp/c/cd) *(925205-1/-4/-2) <25205>* **THE BALLAD OF SALLY ROSE** [ ] [ ]
– The ballad of Sally Rose / Rhythm guitar / I think I love him – (instrumental; You are my flower) – Heart to heart / Woman walk the line / Bad news / Timberline / Long tall Sally Rose / White line / Diamond in my crown / The sweetheart of the rodeo / K-S-O-S (instrumental medley; Ring of fire – Wildwood flower – Six days on the road) – Sweet chariot. *(cd re-iss. Jan96; 7599 25205-2)*
May 85. (7") *<28952>* **DIAMOND IN MY CROWN. / RHYTHM GUITAR** [–] [ ]
Aug 85. (7") *<28852>* **TIMBERLINE. / SWEET CHARIOT** [–] [ ]
Mar 87. (7") *<28770>* **I HAD MY HEART SET ON YOU. / YOUR LONG JOURNEY** [–] [ ]
Apr 87. (lp/c/cd) *(925352-1/-4/-2) <25352>* **THIRTEEN** [ ] Mar87 [ ]
– Mystery train / You're free to go / Sweetheart of the pines / Just someone in the know / My father's house / Lacassine special / Today I started loving you again / When I was yours / I had my heart set on you / Your long journey.
Jun 87. (7") *<28770>* **TODAY I STARTED LOVING YOU AGAIN. / WHEN I WAS YOURS** [–] [ ]
Jul 87. (lp/c/cd) *<25585-1/-4/-2>* **ANGEL BAND** [–] [ ]
– Where could I go to the Lord / Angel band / If I be lifted up / Precious memories / Bright morning stars / When he calls / We shall rise / Drifting too far / Who will sing for me / Someday my ship will sail / The other side of your life / When they ring those golden bells.
Aug 87. (7") *<28302>* **SOMEDAY MY SHIP WILL SAIL. / WHEN HE CALLS** [–] [ ]
Feb 89. (7") *<27635>* **HEARTBREAK HILL. / ICY BLUE HEART** [–] [ ]
Feb 89. (lp/c/cd) *(925776-1/-4/-2) <25776>* **BLUEBIRD** [ ] [ ]
– Heaven only knows / You've been on my mind / Icy blue heart / Love is / No regrets / Lonely street / Heartbreak hill / I still miss someone / A river for him / If you were a bluebird.

Reprise | Reprise

May 89. (7") *<22999>* **HEAVEN ONLY KNOWS. / A RIVER FOR HIM** [–] [ ]
Aug 89. (7") *<22850>* **I STILL MISS SOMEONE. / NO REGRETS** [–] [ ]
Jul 90. (cd/c/lp) *Reprise; <(7599 25791-2/-4/-1)>* **DUETS** [ ] [ ]
Nov 90. (lp/c/cd) *(WX 396/+C/CD)* **BRAND NEW DANCE** [ ] [ ]
– Wheels of love / Tougher than the rest / In his world / Sweet dreams of you / Easy for you to say / Rollin' and ramblin' (the death of Hank Williams) / Better off without you / Never be anyone else but you / Brand new dance / Red red rose. *(cd re-iss. Feb95; same)*
Jan 91. (7") *<19870>* **GULF COAST HIGHWAY (w/ WILLIE NELSON). / EVANGELINE** [–] [ ]
Apr 91. (7") *<19707>* **RED RED ROSE. / NEVER BE ANYONE ELSE BUT YOU** [–] [ ]
Jan 92. (cd/c/d-lp; EMMYLOU HARRIS & The NASH RAMBLERS) *<(7599 26664-2/-4/-1)>* **AT THE RYMAN (live)** [ ] [ ]
– Guitar town / Halk as much / Cattle call / Guess things happen that way / Hard times / Mansion on the hill / Scotland / Montana cowboy / Like strangers / Lodi / Calling my children home / If I could be there / Walls of time / Get up John / Medley:- It's a hard life wherever you go / Smoke along the track. *(cd re-iss. Feb95; same)*

Grapevine | Asylum

Apr 94. (cd-s) *(CDGPS 101)* **HIGH POWERED LOVE. / BALLAD OF A RUNAWAY HORSE** [ ] [–]
May 94. (cd/c/lp) *(GRA 101 CD/C) <61541>* **COWGIRL'S PRAYER** [ ] [ ]
– A ways to go / The night / High powered love / You don't know me / Prayer in open D / Cresent city / Lovin' you again / Jerusalem tomorrow / Thanks to you / I hear a call / Ballad of a runaway horse.
Sep 94. (c-s/cd-s) *(CS/CD GPS 102)* **YOU DON'T KNOW ME. / A WAYS TO GO** [ ] [–]
Oct 95. (cd/c/lp) *(GRA CD/MC/LP 102) <61854>* **WRECKING BALL** [46] [94]
– Where will I be / Goodbye / All my tears / Wrecking ball / Goin' back to Harlan / A deeper well / Every grain of sand / Sweet old world / May this be love / Orphan girl / Blackhawk / Waltz across Texas tonight.
Aug 98. (cd/c) *(GRA CD/MC 241) <25001>* **SPYBOY (live)** [57] [ ]
– My songbird / Where will I be / I ain't living long like this / Love hurts / Green pastures / A deeper well / Prayer in open D / Calling my children home / Tulsa queen / Wheels / Born to run / Boulder to Birmingham / All my tears / Maker.

—— In Sep'99, she and LINDA RONSTADT released the 'WESTERN WALL – THE TUCSON SESSIONS' set, which scraped into the US Top 75

Grapevine | Nonesuch

Sep 00. (cd) *(GRACD 103) <79616>* **RED DIRT GIRL** [45] [54]
– The pearl / Michelangelo / I don't wanna talk about it now / Tragedy / Red dirt girl / My baby needs a shepherd / Bang the drum slowly / J'ai fait tout / One big love / Hour of gold / My Antonia / Boy from Tupelo.
Sep 03. (cd) *<(7559 79805-2)>* **STUMBLE INTO GRACE** [52] [58]
– Here I am / I will dream / Little bird / Time in Babylon / Can you hear me now / Strong hand (just one miracle) / Jupiter rising / O Evangeline / Plaisir d'Amour / Lost unto this world / Cup of kindness.

– compilations, etc. –

on 'Warners' unless mentioned otherwise

Nov 78. (lp/c) *(K/K4 56570)* **PROFILE – THE BEST OF EMMYLOU HARRIS** [ ] [81]
– One of these days / Sweet dreams / To daddy / You never can tell (C'est la vie) / Making believe / Easy from now on / Together again / If I could only win your love / Too far gone / Two more bottles of wine / From Boulder to Birmingham / Hello stranger. *(cd-iss. Jul84; 256570)*
Nov 78. (7") *<8732>* **TOO FAR GONE. / TULSA QUEEN** [–] [ ]
Mar 80. (7") *(K 17580)* **(YOU NEVER CAN TELL) C'EST LA VIE. / BOULDER TO BIRMIMGHAM** [ ] [–]
Mar 80. (lp) *K-Tel; (NE 1058)* **HER BEST SONGS** [36] [–]
Oct 82. (d-c) **ELITE HOTEL / LUXURY LINER** [ ] [–]

—— In Nov '83, 'Magnum Force' released lp 'LIVE' with GRAM PARSONS

Oct 84. (lp/c) *<25161>* **PROFILE II – THE BEST OF EMMYLOU HARRIS** [–] [ ]
(UK-iss.Feb94; 7599 25161-2)

—— In July '93, 'Magnum Force' released a cd 'NASHVILLE COUNTRY DUETS' with CARL JACKSON

Nov 94. (cd/c) *<(9362 45725-2/-4)>* **SONGS OF THE WEST** [ ] [ ]
Dec 96. (3xcd-box) *(9362 45308-2)* **PORTRAIT** [ ] [ ]
Jul 02. (cd) *Catfish; (KATCD 226)* **NOBODY'S DARLING BUT MINE** [ ] [–]

DOLLY PARTON, LINDA RONSTADT, EMMYLOU HARRIS

Warners Warners

Mar 87. (lp/c/cd) *(925491-1/-4/-1)* <25491> **TRIO** 60 6
– The pain of lovin' you / Making plans / To know him is to love him / Hobo's meditation / Wildflowers / Telling me lies / My dear companion / These memories of you / I've had enough / Rosewood casket. *(cd+=/c+=)* – Farther along. *(cd re-iss. Feb95; same)*

Apr 87. (7") *(W 8492)* **TO KNOW HIM IS TO LOVE HIM. / FARTHER ALONG**

Jun 87. (7") *<28371>* **TELLING ME LIES. / ROSEWOOD CASKET** –

Sep 87. (7") *<28248>* **THOSE MEMORIES OF YOU. / MY DEAR COMPANION** –

Nov 87. (7") *<27970>* **WILDFLOWERS. / HOBO'S MEDITATION** –

Asylum Asylum

Feb 99. (cd/c) *<62275>* **TRIO II** – 62
– Lover's return / High Sierra / Do I ever cross your mind / After the gold rush / The blue train / I feel the blues movin' in / You'll never see the sun / He rode all the way to Texas / Feels like home / When you're gone, long gone.

George HARRISON

Born: 25 Feb'43, Wavertree, Liverpool, England. Released in late 1968, HARRISON's 'WONDERWALL' was the first solo release by a BEATLE, although it flopped in the UK. He followed it up with a classic piece of late 60's self-indulgence, the awful 'ELECTRONIC SOUNDS' (released on his own 'Zapple' label). While HARRISON's pioneering sitar work was praise-worthy, the same experimental spirit applied to a Moog synthesizer, (strung out over a whole album), was downright dull. Despite being overshadowed by the writing partnership of LENNON and McCARTNEY, HARRISON's songs rank among the BEATLES' best, not least 'SOMETHING' and 'HERE COMES THE SUN'. When the BEATLES officially split in 1969, it was perhaps an opportunity for GEORGE to really go for it and prove his writing skills over a whole album. Not content with two sides of vinyl, he went for six, releasing the triple-set 'ALL THINGS MUST PASS' in 1970. The Herculean task of keeping a consistently high standard over three albums was beyond even the mercurial talent of HARRISON, although the peaks definitely outweigh the troughs. PHIL SPECTOR's legendary production skills enhance the gorgeous melodies of 'MY SWEET LORD' and DYLAN's 'IF NOT FOR YOU', while HARRISON's well-documented spirituality is given a voice in the title track and 'THE ART OF DYING'. The aforementioned 'MY SWEET LORD' was released as a single in early '71 topping the charts on both sides of the Atlantic. Success was bittersweet though, as BRIGHT TUNES (owners of songwriter RONNIE MACK's estate) claimed the song plagiarised their CHIFFONS song, 'HE'S SO FINE'. Five years later, the court gave 6-figure royalties to the plaintiff. HARRISON helped to organise a huge famine relief benefit gig in New York, playing alongside a cast of musicians that included his old mucker RINGO STARR as well as BOB DYLAN. The gig was released on another triple-set in 1972 as 'CONCERT FOR BANGLADESH'. May '73 saw yet another No.1 US single, 'GIVE ME LOVE (GIVE ME PEACE ON EARTH)' taken from the similarly successful album, 'LIVING IN THE MATERIAL WORLD'. If HARRISON was riding the crest of a wave, then he was soon to be dallying listlessly in a stagnant creative pond. In 1974, he set up his own 'Dark Horse' label, releasing the clueless album of the same name as well as signing up artists like RAVI SHANKAR and SPLINTER. He and his wife PATTI were divorced in June '77, after her much publicised affair with ERIC CLAPTON. In 1979, he founded his own 'Homemade' film productions, which released the 80's movies: 'Life Of Brian', 'The Long Good Friday', 'Time Bandits', 'The Missionary', 'Mona Lisa', 'A Private Function', 'Water', and 'Shanghai Surprise'. Mediocre albums were his forte at the turn of the decade, and even the tribute to LENNON, 'ALL THOSE YEARS AGO', (from 1981's 'SOMEWHERE IN ENGLAND'), seemed uninspired. HARRISON teamed up with ELO's JEFF LYNNE for 1987's 'CLOUD NINE'; his production, along with the hit, 'GOT MY MIND SET ON YOU', helping to make the record HARRISON's most successful of the 80's (and 90's for that matter). In the decade since, HARRISON has been involved in the relatively brief TRAVELING WILBURYS project (with LYNNE, DYLAN, PETTY & ROY ORBISON under various brotherly guises) as well as releasing 'LIVE IN JAPAN' in 1992, culled from a series of Japanese concerts with CLAPTON. In the mid-90's, he was involved in the archive project which saw the release of a BEATLES documentary, rarities/outtakes albums and even a "new" single, 'FREE AS A BIRD'. As ever though, the man remained an enigma, the quintessential rock star hermit content to do his own thing with a minimum of fuss. In December 1999, just when things looked settled and peaceful for the quiet man of rock, HARRISON and his wife Olivia were subjected to a break-in from a so-called fan at their mansion home in Henley-on-Thames. Both received injuries and, for a time, HARRISON's stab wounds looked serious enough for the media to speculate on his survival. It was also around this time that GEORGE found out he had cancer of the throat (later spreading to lung and brain cancer). By the 29th of November, 2001, tributes were overwhelming when GEORGE finally lost his battle for life. At the subsequent tribute concert at London's Royal Albert Hall, JEFF LYNNE featured prominently, as did HARRISON's son Dhani. In fact, the pair were to finish off GEORGE's final work, 'BRAINWASHED' (2002), roundly hailed as among the best of the former Beatle's career. Surprisingly light of touch in view of the pain of his final years, the album was the sound of a man content in himself and in his music. • **Covered:** I'D HAVE YOU ANYTIME + I DON'T WANT TO DO IT (Bob Dylan) / BYE BYE LOVE (Everly Brothers) / GOT MY MIND SET ON YOU (James Ray) / ROLL OVER BEETHOVEN (Chuck Berry).

Album rating: WONDERWALL MUSIC (*4) / ELECTRONIC SOUND (*3) / ALL THINGS MUST PASS (*9) / THE CONCERT FOR BANGLA DESH with Various Artists (*6) / LIVING IN THE MATERIAL WORLD (*6) / DARK HORSE (*3) / EXTRA TEXTURE (READ ALL ABOUT IT) (*4) / THE BEST OF GEORGE HARRISON compilation (*6) / THIRTY-THREE & 1/3 (*6) / GEORGE HARRISON (*5) / SOMEWHERE IN ENGLAND (*4) / GONE TROPPO (*3) / CLOUD NINE (*7) / THE BEST OF DARK HORSE 1976-89 compilation (*7) / LIVE IN JAPAN (*4) / BRAINWASHED (*7)

GEORGE HARRISON – instruments (no vocals)

Apple Apple

Nov 68. (lp; stereo/mono) *(S+/APCOR 1)* <3350> **WONDERWALL MUSIC (Soundtrack)** Jan69 49
– Microbes / Red lady too / Tabla and Pavajak / In the park / Drilling a hole / Guru Vandana / Greasy legs / Ski-ing / Gat Kirwani / Dream scene / Party Seacombe / Love scene / Crying / Cowboy music / Fantasy sequins / On the bed / Glass box / Wonderwall to be here / Singing om. *(cd-iss. Jun92; CDSAPCOR 1)*

—— **GEORGE** – moog synthesizer (no vocals)

Zapple Zapple

May 69. (lp) *(02)* <3358> **ELECTRONIC SOUND**
– Under the Mersey wall / No time or space.

—— He became in-house 'Apple' producer, before gigging with DELANEY & BONNIE late 1969. The BEATLES broke-up and he went solo again. Now with vocals, etc + augmented by **DEREK & THE DOMINOES** (Eric Clapton and his band) / **BADFINGER** / **BILLY PRESTON** – keyboards / **RINGO STARR, GINGER BAKER** – drums / etc.

Apple Apple

Nov 70. (t-box-lp) *(<STCH 639>)* **ALL THINGS MUST PASS** [4] [1]
– I'd have you anytime / My sweet Lord / Wah-wah / Isn't it a pity / What is life / If not for you / Behind that locked door / Let it down / Run of the mill / Beware of darkness / Apple scruffs / Ballad of Frankie Crisp (let it roll) / Awaiting on you all / All things must pass / I dig love / Art of dying / Isn't it a pity / Hear me Lord / Out of the blue / It's Johnny's birthday / Plug me in / I remember Jeep / Thanks for the pepperoni. *(d-cd.iss.May87 on 'E.M.I.'; CDS 746688-2) (d-cd/t-lp re-iss. Jan01; 530474-2/-1)* – hit No.68

Nov 70. (7") *<2995>* **MY SWEET LORD. / ISN'T IT A PITY** [–] [1]

Jan 71. (7") *(R 5884)* **MY SWEET LORD. / WHAT IS LIFE** [1] [–]
(re-iss. Nov76; same)

Feb 71. (7") *<1828>* **WHAT IS LIFE. / APPLE SCRUFFS** [–] [10]

Jul 71. (7") *(R 5912) <1836>* **BANGLA-DESH. / DEEP BLUE** [10] [23]

—— In Jan72, he with other artists released live triple album 'CONCERT FOR BANGLADESH'; *(<STCX 3385>)*. It hit UK No.1 & US No.2. *(re-iss. Aug91 d-cd/d-c; 468835-2/-4)*

—— **GEORGE** now with various session people

May 73. (7") *(R 5988) <1862>* **GIVE ME LOVE (GIVE ME PEACE ON EARTH). / MISS O'DELL** [8] [1]

Jun 73. (lp/c) *(PAS 10006) <3410>* **LIVING IN THE MATERIAL WORLD** [2] [1]
– Give me love (give me peace on earth) / Sue me, sue you blues / The light that has lighted the world / Don't let me wait too long / Who can see it / Living in the material world / The Lord loves the one (that loves the Lord) / Be here now / Try some buy some / The day the world gets 'round / That is all. *(cd-iss. Jan92 on 'E.M.I.'; CDPAS 10006)*

Dec 74. (7") *(R 6002) <1879>* **DING DONG; DING DONG. / I DON'T CARE ANYMORE** [38] Jan75 [36]

Dec 74. (lp/c) *(PAS 10008) <3418>* **DARK HORSE** [ ] [4]
– Hari's on tour (express) / Simply shady / So sad / Bye bye love / Maya love / Ding dong; ding dong / Dark horse / Far East man / Is it he (Jai Sri Krishna). *(re-iss. Dec80 on 'Music For Pleasure'; MFP 50510) (cd-iss. Jan92 on 'E.M.I.'; CDPAS 10008)*

Feb 75. (7") *(R 6001) <1877>* **DARK HORSE. / HARI'S ON TOUR (EXPRESS)** [ ] Nov74 [15]

Sep 75. (7") *(R 6007) <1884>* **YOU. / WORLD OF STONE** [38] [20]

Oct 75. (lp/c) *(PAS 10009) <3420>* **EXTRA TEXTURE (READ ALL ABOUT IT)** [16] [8]
– The answer's at the end / This guitar (can't keep from crying) / You / Ooh baby (you know that I love you) / World of stone / A bit more of you / Can't stop thinking about you / Tired of midnight blue / Grey cloudy lies / His name is legs (ladies & gentlemen). *(cd-iss. Jan92 on 'E.M.I.'; CDPAS 10009)*

Feb 76. (7") *(R 6012) <1885>* **THIS GUITAR (CAN'T KEEP FROM CRYING). / MAYA LOVE** [ ] [ ]

Apple Capitol

Oct 76. (lp/c) *(PAS 10011) <11578>* **THE BEST OF GEORGE HARRISON** (compilation) [ ] [31]
– Something (BEATLES) / If I needed someone (BEATLES) / Here comes the sun (BEATLES) / Taxman (BEATLES) / Think for yourself (BEATLES) / While my guitar gently weeps (BEATLES) / For you blue (BEATLES) / My sweet Lord / Give me love (give me peace on Earth) / You / Bangla-Desh / Dark horse / What is life. *(re-iss. Oct81 on 'Music For Pleasure' lp/c; MFP 50523) (cd-iss. May87 on 'Parlophone'; CDP 746682-2)*

Dark Horse Dark Horse

Nov 76. (7") *(K 16856) <8294>* **THIS SONG. / LEARNING HOW TO LOVE YOU** [ ] [25]

Nov 76. (lp/c) *(K/K4 56319) <3005>* **THIRTY-THREE AND A THIRD** [35] [11]
– Woman don't you cry for me / Dear one / Beautiful girl / This song / See yourself / It's what you value / True love / Pure Smokey / Crackerbox palace / Learning how to love you.

Jan 77. (7") *<8313>* **CRACKERBOX PALACE. / LEARNING HOW TO LOVE YOU** [–] [19]

Feb 77. (7") *(K 16896)* **TRUE LOVE. / PURE SMOKEY** [ ] [–]

Jun 77. (7") *(K 16967)* **IT'S WHAT YOU VALUE. / WOMAN DON'T YOU CRY FOR ME** [ ] [–]

Feb 79. (7") *<8763>* **BLOW AWAY. / SOFT-HEARTED HANA** [–] [16]

Feb 79. (7") *(K 17327)* **BLOW AWAY. / SOFT TOUCH** [51] [–]

Feb 79. (lp/c) *(K/K4 56562) <3255>* **GEORGE HARRISON** [39] [14]
– Love comes to everyone / Not guilty / Here comes the moon / Soft-hearted Hana / Blow away / Faster / Your love is forever / Dark sweet lady / Soft touch / If you believe.

Apr 79. (7") *(K 17284)* **LOVE COMES TO EVERYONE. / SOFT-HEARTED HANA** [ ] [–]

Apr 79. (7") *<8844>* **LOVE COMES TO EVERYONE. / SOFT TOUCH** [–] [ ]

Jul 79. (7"/7"pic-d) *(K 17423/+P)* **FASTER. / YOUR LOVE IS FOREVER** [ ] [–]

May 81. (7") *(K 17807) <49725>* **ALL THOSE YEARS AGO. / WRITING'S ON THE WALL** [13] [2]

Jun 81. (lp/c) *(K/K4 56870) <3492>* **SOMEWHERE IN ENGLAND** [13] [11]
– Blood from a clone / Unconsciousness rules / Life itself / All those years ago / Baltimore oriole / Teardrops / That which I have lost / Writing's on the wall / Hong Kong blues / Save the world.

Jul 81. (7") *(K 17837) <49785>* **TEARDROPS. / SAVE THE WORLD** [ ] [ ]

Oct 82. (7") *(929864-2) <29864>* **WAKE UP MY LOVE. / GREECE** [ ] [53]

Nov 82. (lp/c) *(K 923734-1/-4) <23734>* **GONE TROPPO** [ ] [ ]
– Wake up my love / That's the way it goes / I really love you / Greece / Gone troppo / Mystical one / Unknown delight / Baby don't run away / Dream away / Circles.

Jan 83. (7") *<29744>* **I REALLY LOVE YOU. / CIRCLES** [–] [ ]

—— Took long time off from solo career to establish his film production work. Returned after nearly five years with new session people.

Sep 87. (lp/c)(cd) *(WX 123/+C)(925643-2) <25643>* **CLOUD NINE** [10] Nov87 [8]
– Cloud 9 / That's what it takes / Fish on the sand / Just for today / This is love / When we was fab / Devil's radio / Someplace else / Wreck of the Hesperus / Breath away from Heaven / Got my mind set on you.

Oct 87. (7") *(W 8178) <28178>* **GOT MY MIND SET ON YOU. / LAY HIS HEAD** [2] [1]
(12"+=/12"pic-d+=) *(W 8178T/+P)* – ('A'extended).

Feb 88. (7") *(W 8131) <28131>* **WHEN WE WAS FAB. / ZIGZAG** [25] [23]
(12"+=/12"pic-d+=/3"cd-s+=) *(W 8131 T/TX/CD)* – That's the way it goes (remix) / ('A'mix).

Jun 88. (7") *(W 7913) <27913>* **THIS IS LOVE. / BREATH AWAY FROM HEAVEN** [55] [ ]
(12"+=) *(W 7913T)* – All those wasted years ago.
(3"cd-s++=) *(W 7913CD)* – Hong Kong blues.

—— Later in 1988, HARRISON teamed up with BOB DYLAN, ROY ORBISON, JEFF LYNNE and TOM PETTY in The TRAVELLING WILBURYS. He also continued solo work below.

Oct 89. (lp/c)(cd) *(WX 312/+C)(K 925643-2) <25726>* **THE BEST OF DARK HORSE (1976-1989)** (compilation) [ ] [ ]
– Poor little girl / Blow away / That's the way it goes / Cockamamie business / Wake up my love / Life itself / Got my mind set on you / Here comes the Moon / Gone troppo / When we was fab / Love comes to everyone / All those years ago / Cheer down. *(c+=/cd+=)* – Crackerbox Palace.

Nov 89. (7") *(W 2696)* **CHEER DOWN. / POOR LITTLE GIRL** [ ] [–]
(12"+=/cd-s+=) *(W 2696 T/CD)* – Crackerbox palace.

Jul 92. (cd/c) *(<7599 26964-2/-4>)* **LIVE IN JAPAN (with ERIC CLAPTON AND BAND)** [ ] [ ]
– I want to tell you / Old brown shoe / Taxman / Give me love (give me peace on Earth) / If I needed someone / Something / What is life / Dark horse / Piggies / Got my mind set on you / Cloud nine / Here comes the Sun / My sweet Lord / All those years ago / Cheer down / Devil's radio / Isn't it a pity / While my guitar gently weeps / Roll over Beethoven.

—— GEORGE died of cancer on the 29th November, 2001

Parlophone Capitol

Jan 02. (cd-s) *(CDR 6571) <50438>* **MY SWEET LORD / LET IT DOWN / MY SWEET LORD (2000)** [1] [94]

E.M.I. Capitol

Nov 02. (cd)(lp/c) *(543246-2)(541969-1/-4) <41969>* **BRAINWASHED** [52] [18]
– Any road / P2 Vatican blues (last Saturday night) / Pisces fish / Looking for my life / Rising sun / Marwa blues / Stuck inside a cloud / Run so far / Never get over you / Between the Devil and the deep blue sea / Rocking chair in Hawaii / Brainwashed. *(cd-iss. w/ dvd+=; 580345-0)* – (extra tracks).

May 03. (7") *(R 6601)* **ANY ROAD. / MARWA BLUES** [37] [ ]
(cd-s+=) *(CDRS 6601)* – ('A'-video).

– compilations etc. –

Oct 82. (d-cd) *Dark Horse; (K 466101)* **THIRTY-THREE AND A THIRD / GEORGE HARRISON** ☐ [-]

☐ Jerry HARRISON (see under ⇒ TALKING HEADS)

☐ Deborah / Debbie HARRY (see under ⇒ BLONDIE)

Alex HARVEY

Born: 5 Feb'35, "the Gorbals" area, Glasgow, Scotland. ALEX grew up in a politically aware, well-read family, taking his stance as a conscientious objector from his father. Following loads of jobs (36 to be exact, including a stint lion-taming!) he played in various skiffle groups and after winning a local talent contest in 1956, he was dubbed "The TOMMY STEELE Of Scotland". In 1959, his BIG SOUL BAND backed touring American stars, EDDIE COCHRAN and GENE VINCENT, the former subsequently being killed in a car crash a few months later. By 1964, ALEX HARVEY AND HIS SOUL BAND were taking the well-trodden path to Hamburg, Germany, while back home LULU was capitalising on a hit version of 'Shout!', an ISLEY BROTHERS track which featured prominently in HARVEY's repertoire. During this heady mid-60's period, HARVEY himself released two LP's, the second of which 'THE BLUES' (1965) featured the precocious guitar playing of his younger brother LES. Travelling between London and Glasgow, ALEX subsequently struggled on with his ever evolving musical vision, psychedelic GIANT MOTH backing him up during the flower-power era of '67. After a run of flop singles, HARVEY joined the crew of the 'Hair' musical in London's West End, earning his crust by night (mainly as the guitarist but also contributing the occasional vocal) and continuing to write his own material by day. Towards the end of the decade, HARVEY released his first bonafide solo album, 'ROMAN WALL BLUES' (1969), backed up by his brother LES and some of the crew from the ROCK WORKSHOP ensemble in which ALEX was briefly involved. Through a third party, ALEX was introduced to Glasgow band TEAR GAS (ZAL CLEMINSON, HUGH McKENNA, CHRIS GLEN and TED McKENNA), with whom he was so impressed he moved back to Scotland and secured them as his backing outfit. Early in 1972 they became The SENSATIONAL ALEX HARVEY BAND, and, after nationwide tours and a signature for 'Vertigo', released their debut album 'FRAMED'. 1972 was set to be an eventful, often traumatic year for ALEX, what with the tragic death of his brother LES (electrocuted while on stage with STONE THE CROWS) and a challenging support slot to Brummie chart-toppers SLADE. ALEX had his own way of approaching such a challenge, frequently goading audiences (especially if they happened to be from south of the border!) into a reaction, negative or otherwise – JOHNNY ROTTEN obviously took note. Visually, HARVEY was a larger than life JOHNNY KIDD-esque pirate figure with more than a hint of hidden menace. With his buccaneer attitude and dishevelled look, he was nothing less than a musical visionary, only matched by his clown-faced guitarist, ZAL CLEMINSON. Late in '73, SAHB issued the excellent 'NEXT . . .', promoting the album with an extensive tour which included of all places, Falkirk Town Hall. The unadulterated combination of European style seediness, OTT theatrics and futuristic comic book imagery came together in such classics as 'THE FAITH HEALER' (a 7 minute+ masterpiece), the self-explanatory 'GANG BANG' and Jacques Brel's 'NEXT'. HARVEY was also a rather unlikely advocate of cleaning up the nation's streets, inventing the "Vambo" comic book character to push home his anti-vandal message. The track 'VAMBO MARBLE EYE', was the first and also the most memorable in a series of "Vambo" songs, urging fans "don't pish in your own water supply". A year later, SAHB secured their first UK Top 20 album spot with 'THE IMPOSSIBLE DREAM' (1974), a more accessible effort which sacrificed some of its predecessor's grubby intensity although 'THE TOMAHAWK KID' and 'ANTHEM' kept the fans on HARVEY's alternative yellow brick road. The pinnacle of HARVEY and SAHB's colourful career came in 1975, a year that saw both a UK Top 10 album 'TOMORROW BELONGS TO ME' and a Top 10 rendition of Tom Jones' 'DELILAH' (from the 'LIVE' set), culminating in a series of three sold out Xmas shows at Glasgow's Apollo theatre. Gallus as ever, HARVEY entered the stage to the strains of Irving Berlin's 'CHEEK TO CHEEK', joined by a troupe of dancing girls who eventually turned their backs to the crowd and revealed their cheeky bare-ass attire; ALEX was so impressed he kissed each bum in turn before blessing each one with a rose . . . The aforementioned 'CHEEK . . .' featured on SAHB's next offering 'THE PENTHOUSE TAPES' (1976), a slightly disappointing covers set that led to the band signing a fresh deal with 'Mountain' records (also home to NAZARETH). Shortly afterwards, ALEX and the boys scored their second major UK hit, 'BOSTON TEA PARTY', although again the accompanying album 'SAHB STORIES' (1976), left most fans let down. While ALEX took off to Northern Scotland for a bizarre documentary album, ' . . .PRESENTS THE LOCH NESS MONSTER', SAHB WITHOUT ALEX (as they were briefly billed!) released their own set, 'FOURPLAY' (1977). Even though ALEX had in some respects anticipated the advent of Punk Rock, SAHB were ill-equipped to compete in the brave new (wave) world. The 'ROCK DRILL' (1978) album was a final disappointing nail in the coffin while the death of HARVEY's mentor/manager BILL dealt him an emotional hammer blow. The band effectively came to an end when ALEX refused to board a plane for Stockholm, claiming that he'd seen a purple light and therefore couldn't cross water. Although his drinking and eccentric behaviour became more pronounced, he did subsequently form the not so sensational ALEX HARVEY BAND, returning to the recording studio with a new line-up for 1979's cult fave 'THE MAFIA STOLE MY GUITAR'. Years of hard living finally took its toll on ALEX as he succumbed to a heart attack on the 4th of February 1982, bizarrely enough just prior to boarding a return ferry from Belgium; he left behind wife Trudy and two sons. • **Songwriters:** Most by himself and HUGH McKENNA, with additions from either ZAL or producer DAVE BATCHELOR. Covered; FRAMED (Leiber-Stoller) / I JUST WANT TO MAKE LOVE TO YOU (Willie Dixon) / GIDDY-UP-A-DING-DONG (Freddie Bell & The Bellboys) / THE IMPOSSIBLE DREAM (Leigh-Darion) / MONEY HONEY (. . . Stone) / RIVER OF LOVE / TOMORROW BELONGS TO ME (Ebb-Kander) / DELILAH (hit; Tom Jones) / GAMBLIN' BAR ROOM BLUES (Alley-Rodgers) / CHEEK TO CHEEK (Irving Berlin) / LOVE STORY (Jethro Tull) / CRAZY HORSES (Osmonds) / SCHOOL'S OUT (Alice Cooper) / RUNAWAY (Del Shannon) / GOODNIGHT IRENE (Leadbelly) / SHAKIN' ALL OVER (Johnny Kidd) / SNOWSHOES THOMPSON (Buddy Ebson). • **Trivia:** HARVEY's 'LOCH NESS' lp, released unusually on 'K-Tel', featured only interviews from sightings of the monster.

Album rating: ALEX HARVEY & HIS SOUL BAND (*5) / THE BLUES (*5) / ROMAN WALL BLUES (*4) / Sensational Alex Harvey Band: FRAMED (*6) / NEXT . . . (*9) / THE IMPOSSIBLE DREAM (*7) / TOMORROW BELONGS TO ME (*7) / THE SENSATIONAL ALEX HARVEY BAND "LIVE" (*7) /

PENTHOUSE TAPES (*5) / SAHB STORIES (*5) / FOURPLAY without Alex (*4) / ROCK DRILL (*5) / THE MAFIA STOLE MY GUITAR (*5) / THE SOLDIER ON THE WALL (*5) / THE BEST OF THE SENSATIONAL ALEX HARVEY BAND compilation (*8)

ALEX HARVEY & HIS SOUL BAND

ALEX HARVEY – vocals / **RICKY BARNES** – saxophone, vocals / **ISOBEL BOND** – vocals / **GIBSON KEMP** – drums / **IAN HINDS** – organ / **BILL PATRICK** – guitar

Polydor not iss.

Jan 64. (7"; as ALEX HARVEY) *(NH 52264)* **I JUST WANNA MAKE LOVE TO YOU. / LET THE GOOD TIMES ROLL** [ ] [–]

Mar 64. (lp) *(LPHM 46424)* **ALEX HARVEY AND HIS SOUL BAND (live)** [ ] [–]
– Framed / I ain't worrying baby / Backwater blues / Let the good times roll / Going home / I've got my mojo working / Teensville U.S.A. / New Orleans / Bo Diddley is a gunslinger / When I grow too old to rock / Evil hearted man / I just wanna make love to you / The blind man / Reeling and rocking. *(Germany re-iss. Oct87 lp/c; 831887-1/-4)*

Jun 64. (7") *(NH 52907)* **GOT MY MOJO WORKING. / I AIN'T WORRIED BABY** [ ] [–]

—— ALEX HARVEY brought in new soul band, (his brother **LES HARVEY** – guitar / **BOBBY THOMPSON** – bass / **GILSON KEMP** – drums)

Jul 65. (7") *(BM 56017)* **AIN'T THAT JUST TOO BAD. / MY KIND OF LOVE** [ ] [–]

Nov 65. (lp) *(LPHM 46441)* **THE BLUES** [ ] [–]
– Trouble in mind / Honey bee / I learned about woman / Danger zone / The riddle song / Waltzing Matilda / The blues / The big rock candy mountain / The Michegan massacre / No peace / Nobody knows you when you're down and out / St. James infirmary / Strange fruit / Kisses sweeter than wine / Good God almighty.

ALEX HARVEY

solo with session musicians.

Fontana not iss.

Sep 65. (7") *(TF 610)* **AGENT OO SOUL. / GO AWAY BABY** [ ] [–]

Nov 66. (7") *(TF 764)* **WORK SONG. / I CAN'T DO WITHOUT YOUR LOVE** [ ] [–]

—— HARVEY now backed by **GIANT MOTH:- JIM CONDRON** – guitar, bass / **MOX** – flute / **GEORGE BUTLER** – drums

Decca not iss.

Jul 67. (7") *(F 12640)* **THE SUNDAY SONG. / HORIZON'S** [ ] [–]

Sep 67. (7") *(F 12660)* **MAYBE SOME DAY. / CURTAINS FOR MY BABY** [ ] [–]

—— next with backing from ROCK WORKSHOP which incl. brother LES and loads of others. In 1970/71 for 'CBS', they released two lp's 'ROCK WORKSHOP' *(64075) & not with ALEX, a double 'THE VERY LAST TIME' (64394).* Taken from first lp was 45; 'YOU TO LOSE'.

Fontana not iss.

Oct 69. (lp; stereo/mono) *(S+/TL 5534)* **ROMAN WALL BLUES** [ ] [–]
– Midnight Moses / Hello L.A., bye bye Birmingham / Broken hearted fairytale / Donna / Roman wall blues / Jumping Jack Flash / Hammer song / Let my bluebird sing / Maxine / Down at Bart's place / Candy. *(cd-iss. May02 on 'Red Bus'; RF 609)*

Nov 69. (7") *(TF 1063)* **MIDNIGHT MOSES. / ROMAN WALL BLUES** [ ] [–]

—— ALEX then formed his trio (**IAN ELLIS** – bass, ex-CLOUDS, **DAVE DUFORT** – drums) This was broken up after the death, by stage electrocution, of his brother LES, who had been part of STONE THE CROWS since '69 (Aug72) **ALEX** recruited a whole band

—— **TEAR GAS** who had already made two albums – Nov70 'PIGGY GO BETTER' on 'Famous', without the McKENNA brothers. Aug71. 'TEAR GAS' on 'Regal Zonophone', with all the members of below . . .

SENSATIONAL ALEX HARVEY BAND

ALEX – vocals, guitar / **ZAL CLEMINSON** (b. 4 May'49) – guitar, vocals / **CHRIS GLEN** (b. 6 Nov'50) – bass / **HUGH McKENNA** (b.28 Nov'49) – keyboards / **TED McKENNA** (b.10 Mar'50) – drums

Vertigo Vertigo

Dec 72. (7") *(6059 070)* **THERE'S NO LIGHTS ON THE CHRISTMAS TREE, MOTHER, THEY'RE BURNING BIG LOUIE TONIGHT. / HARP** [ ] [–]

Jan 73. (lp) *(6360 081)* **FRAMED** [ ] [–]
– Framed / Hammer song / Midnight Moses / Isobel Goudie (part 1 – My lady of the night, part 2 – Coitus interruptus, part 3 – The virgin and the hunter) / Buff's bar blues / I just want to make love to you / Hole in her stocking / There's no lights on the Christmas tree, mother, they're burning big Louie tonight / St. Anthony. *(re-iss. Mar79 on 'Mountain';) (re-iss. Jul86 on 'Sahara' lp/c; (SAH 119/+TC) (cd-iss. 1986 on 'Samurai'+=; SAMRCD 00119)* – Smouldering / Chase it into the night.

Mar 73. (7") *(6059 075)* **JUNGLE JENNY. / BUFF'S BAR BLUES** [ ] [–]

Nov 73. (lp) *(6360 103)* <1017> **NEXT . . .** [ ] [ ]
– Swampsnake / Gang bang / The faith healer / Giddy up a ding dong / Next / Vambo marble eye / The last of the teenage idols (part I-III). *(re-iss. Mar79 on 'Mountain';) (re-iss. Nov84 on 'Sahara'; SAH 114) (pic-lp May86; SAH 114CD) (cd-iss. 1986 on 'Samurai'; SAMRCD 00114) (re-iss. Mar87 on 'Fame' lp/c; FA/TC-FA 3169)*

Feb 74. (7") *(6059 098)* **THE FAITH HEALER (edit). / ST. ANTHONY** [ ] [–]

Feb 74. (7") <113> **SWAMPSNAKE. / GANG BANG** [–] [ ]

Aug 74. (7") *(6059 106)* **SERGEANT FURY. / GANG BANG** [ ] [–]

Sep 74. (7") <200> **SERGEANT FURY. / TOMAHAWK KID** [–] [ ]

Sep 74. (lp)(c) *(6360 112)* <2000> **THE IMPOSSIBLE DREAM** [16] [ ]
– The hot city symphony; (part 1 – Vambo, part 2 – Man in the Jar) / River of love / Long hair music / Sergeant Fury / Weights made of lead / Money honey – The impossible dream / Tomahawk kid / Anthem. *(re-iss. Mar79 on 'Mountain';) (re-iss. Jul86 on 'Samurai' lp/c; SAH 116/+TC)*

Nov 74. (7") *(6059 112)* **ANTHEM. / ANTHEM (version)** [ ] [–]

Apr 75. (lp)(c) *(6360 120)* <2004> **TOMORROW BELONGS TO ME** [9] [ ]
– Action strasse / Snake bite / Soul in chains / The tale of the giant stoneater / Ribs and balls / Give my compliments to the chef / Sharks teeth / Ribs and balls / Shake that thing / Tomorrow belongs to me / To be continued . . . *(re-iss. Nov84 on 'Sahara'; SAH 111) (cd-iss. Jul86 on 'Samurai'+=; SAMRCD 00111)* – Big boy / Pick it up and kick it.

Vertigo Atlantic

Jul 75. (7") *(ALEX 001)* <3293> **DELILAH (live). / SOUL IN CHAINS (live)** [7] [ ]

Sep 75. (lp)(c) *(9102 007)* <18184> **THE SENSATIONAL ALEX HARVEY BAND "LIVE" (live)** [14] [100]
– Fanfare (justly, skillfully, magnanimously) / The faith healer / Tomahawk kid / Vambo / Give my compliments to the chef / Delilah / Framed. *(re-iss. Jul86 on 'Sahara' c/lp/pic-lp; TC+/SAH 117/+PD) (re-iss. Oct86 on 'Fame' lp/c; FA/TC-FA 3161) (cd-iss. 1986 on 'Samurai'; SAMRCD 00117)* – I wanna have you back / Jungle Jenny / Runaway / Love story / School's Out.

Nov 75. (7") *(ALEX 002)* **GAMBLIN' BAR ROOM BLUES. / SHAKE THAT THING** [38] [–]

Mar 76. (7") *(ALEX 003)* **RUNAWAY. / SNAKE BITE** [ ] [–]

Mar 76. (lp)(c) *(9102 007)* **PENTHOUSE TAPES** (old covers) [14] [–]
– I wanna have you back / Jungle Jenny / Runaway / Love story / School's out / Goodnight Irene / Say you're mine / Gamblin' bar room blues / Crazy horses / Cheek to cheek. *(re-iss. Mar79 on 'Mountain';) (re-iss. Nov84 on 'Sahara'; SAH 112) (cd-iss. Jul86 on 'Samurai'; SAMRCD 00112)*

Mountain not iss.

May 76. (7") *(TOP 12)* **BOSTON TEA PARTY. / SULTAN'S CHOICE** [13] [–]

Jul 76. (lp)(c) *(TOPS 112)* **SAHB STORIES** [11] [–]
– Boston Tea Party / Sultan's choice / $25 for a massage / Dogs of war / Dance to your daddy / Amos Moses / Jungle rub out / Sirocco. *(re-iss. Nov84 on 'Sahara'; SAH 115)*

Aug 76. (7") *(TOP 19)* **AMOS MOSES. / SATCHEL AND THE SCALP HUNTER** [ ] [–]

—— now all 4 members without ALEX HARVEY. (HUGH on vocals)

Jan 77. (lp; SAHB WITHOUT ALEX) *(TOPC 5006)* **FOURPLAY** [ ] [–]
– Smouldering / Chase it into the night / Shake your way to Heaven / Outer boogie / Big boy / Pick it up and kick it / Love you for a lifetime / Too much American pie. *(re-iss. Nov84 on 'Sahara'; SAH 113)*

Jan 77. (7"; SAHB WITHOUT ALEX) **PICK IT UP AND KICK IT. / SMOULDERING** [ ] [–]

—— In Apr'77, **ALEX HARVEY** released but withdrew, solo narrative lp 'PRESENTS THE LOCH NESS MONSTER' on 'K-Tel'; *NE 984)*

— re-formed **HARVEY, CLEMINSON, TED McKENNA and GLEN** recruited **TOMMY EYRE** – keyboards who repl. HUGH McKENNA

Aug 77. (7") *(TOP 32)* **MRS. BLACKHOUSE. / ENGINE ROOM BOOGIE** [ ] [–]

Mar 78. (lp)(c) *(TOPS 114)* **ROCK DRILL** [ ] [–]
– The rock drill suite: Rock drill – The dolphins – Rock and roll – King Kong / Booids / Who murdered sex / Nightmare city / Water beastie / Mrs. Blackhouse. *(re-iss. Nov84 on 'Sahara'; SAH 118)*

— (had already split late '77) CHRIS and TED joined ZAL in his own named band. ZAL later joined NAZARETH. TED later joined RORY GALLAGHER and then GREG LAKE BAND. TED and CHRIS later moved on to the MICHAEL SCHENKER GROUP.

ALEX HARVEY BAND

with **TOMMY EYRE** – keyboards / **MATTHEW CANG** – guitar / **GORDON SELLAR** – bass (ex-BEGGARS OPERA) / **SIMON CHATTERTON** – drums

R.C.A. not iss.

Oct 79. (7") *(PB 5199)* **SHAKIN' ALL OVER. / WAKE UP DAVIS** [ ] [–]

Nov 79. (lp/c) *(PL/PK 25257)* **THE MAFIA STOLE MY GUITAR** [ ] [–]
– Don's delight / Back in the depot / Wait for me mama / The Mafia stole my guitar / Shakin' all over / The whalers (thar she blows) / Oh Sparticus / Just a gigolo / I ain't got nobody. *(cd-iss. Sep91 on 'Mau Mau'; MAUCD 608) (cd re-iss. May98 on 'Edsel'; EDCD 562)*

May 80. (7") *(PB 5252)* **BIG TREE SMALL AXE. / THE WHALERS (THAR SHE BLOWS)** [ ] [–]

— ALEX HARVEY died of a heart attack on the 4th of February 1982 while on a ferry from Belgium; he recorded last set late in 1981

Power Supply not iss.

Nov 83. (7") *(OHM 3)* **THE POET AND I. /** [ ] [–]

Nov 83. (c/lp) *(C+/AMP 2)* **SOLDIER ON THE WALL** (rec.late 1981) [ ] [–]
– Mitzi / Billy Bolero / Snowshoes Thompson / Roman wall blues / The poet and I / Nervous / Carry the water / Flowers Mr. Florist / The poet and I (reprise). *(<cd-iss. Aug03 on 'Diablo'; DIAB 8047>)*

SENSATIONAL ALEX HARVEY BAND

— actually re-formed for live gigs without ALEX!

Meantime not iss.

Apr 94. (cd/c) *(JIMBO/JIMMC 001)* **LIVE IN GLASGOW 1993 (live)** [ ] [–]
– The faith healer / St. Anthony / Framed / Gang bang / Amos Moses / Boston tea party / Midnight Moses / Vambo / Armed and dangerous / Delilah.

– SAHB compilations, etc. –

May 77. (lp) *Vertigo; (6360 147)* **BIG HITS AND CLOSE SHAVES** [ ] [–]
(re-iss. Apr79 on 'Mountain')

Jun 77. (7") *Vertigo; (6059 173)* **CHEEK TO CHEEK. / JUNGLE JENNY** [ ] [–]

Jul 80. (c/lp) *Mountain; (T+/TOPS 129)* **COLLECTOR'S ITEMS** [ ] [–]

Jul 80. (7"m) *Mountain; (HOT 2)* **DELILAH (live). / BOSTON TEA PARTY / THE FAITH HEALER** [ ] [–]

Aug 82. (d-lp/d-c) *R.C.A.; (RCA LP/K 9003)* **THE BEST OF THE SENSATIONAL ALEX HARVEY BAND** [ ] [–]
– Next / Framed / The faith healer / Tomahawk kid / The hot city symphony; part 1 – Vambo, part 2 – Man in the jar / Sergeant Fury / The tale of the giant stoneater / Action strasse / Delilah / Weights made of lead / Boston Tea Party / Anthem / Runaway / Crazy horses / Big tree small axe / The Mafia stole my guitar / Gang bang / Tomorrow belongs to me. *(re-iss. May84 d-lp/d-c; PL/PK 70276)*

Nov 85. (lp/c) *Sahara; (SAH/+TC 041)* **LEGEND** [ ] [–]
(cd-iss. 1986 on 'Samurai'; SAMR 041CD)

Jan 86. (c) *Sahara; (SAH 041TC)* **ANTHOLOGY** [ ] [–]

Apr 86. (c) *Aura;* **DOCUMENT** [ ] [–]

Sep 86. (d-lp/c/cd) *Castle; (CCS LP/MC/CD 149)* **THE COLLECTION** [ ] [–]
– $25 for a massage / The tale of the giant stoneater / Action strasse / Gang bang / Next / Give my compliments to the chef / Framed / Tomorrow belongs to me / Dance to your daddy / Sgt.Fury / Sultan's choice / Delilah (live) / Soul in chains / The faith healer / Boston tea party / Vambo (part 1) / Dogs of war / There's no lights on the Christmas tree mother, they're burning big Louie tonight / Giddy up a ding dong.

Jul 87. (lp/c)(cd) *K-Tel; (NE1/CE2 368)(NCD 5139)* **THE BEST OF THE SENSATIONAL ALEX HARVEY BAND** [ ] [–]
– Delilah / The faith healer / Framed / Sergeant Fury / Jungle rub out / Love story / School's out / Boston Tea Party / Gamblin' bar room blues / Next / The man in the jar / Snake bite / Give my compliments to the chef / Cheek to cheek.

Sep 87. (lp/c/cd) *Start; (STF L/C/CD 1)* **PORTRAIT** [ ] [–]
(re-iss. Jan91 lp/c/cd; same)

Feb 91. (cd/c) *Music Club; (MC CD/TC 001)* **THE BEST OF THE SENSATIONAL ALEX HARVEY BAND** [ ] [–]
(re-iss. Jul94 on 'Success';)

Oct 91. (lp) *Windsong; (WINCD 002)* **BBC RADIO 1 LIVE IN CONCERT (live)** [ ] [–]

Jun 92. (cd/c) *Vertigo; (512 201-2/-4)* **ALL SENSATIONS** [ ] [–]

Nov 94. (cd) *Windsong; (WHISCD 004)* **LIVE ON THE TEST** [ ] [–]

Sep 94. (cd/c) *Spectrum; (550 663-2/-4)* **DELILAH** [ ] [–]

Feb 99. (lp) *Get Back; (GET 536)* **THE RISE AND FALL OF THE SENSATIONAL ALEX HARVEY BAND** [ ] [–]

May 99. (cd) *Bear Family; (<BCD 1630-2>)* **ALEX HARVEY AND HIS SOUL BAND** (not original LP) [ ] [ ]

Feb 02. (cd) *Mercury; (<586392-2>)* **FAITH HEALER – AN INTRODUCTION TO THE SENSATIONAL ALEX HARVEY BAND** [ ] [ ]

Apr 02. (d-cd) *Mercury; (<586696-2>)* **FRAMED / NEXT . . .** [ ] May02 [ ]

Apr 02. (d-cd) *Mercury; (<586697-2>)* **THE IMPOSSIBLE DREAM / TOMORROW BELONGS TO ME** [ ] May02 [ ]

Apr 02. (d-cd) *Mercury; (<586698-2>)* **THE PENTHOUSE TAPES / LIVE** [ ] May02 [ ]

Apr 02. (d-cd) *Mercury; (<586699-2>)* **ROCK DRILL / SAHB STORIES** [ ] May02 [ ]

Mar 03. (d-cd) *Mercury; (<065005-2>)* **CONSIDERING THE SITUATION: THE ANTHOLOGY** [ ] [ ]

May 03. (cd) *Neon; (NE 34559)* **ICE COLD** [ ] [–]

Jun 03. (cd) *Burning Airlines; (<PILOT 159>)* **TEENAGE A GO GO**

PJ HARVEY

Born: POLLY JEAN HARVEY, 9 Oct'69, Corscombe, nr.Yeovil, England. Born to music-loving hippie parents, HARVEY was acquainted with music and musicians from an early age. Her first songwriting experience was with rootsy outfit The POLEKATS, HARVEY later joining Somerset-based group AUTOMATIC DLAMINI, who had been around for some five years. Numbered in their ranks were ROBERT ELLIS on drums, JOHN PARISH (ex-THIEVES LIKE US) on guitar and vocals (both ex-HEADLESS HORSEMEN; alongside bassist DAVE DALLIMORE). With bassist JAMIE ANDERSON, they finally released a well-received debut EP, 'THE CRAZY SUPPER', in June '86 on the 'D For Drum' label (DLAM 1). PARISH also went into production work for The CHESTERFIELDS and BRILLIANT CORNERS. Early members of AUTOMATIC DLAMINI included ex-CLEANERS FROM VENUS keyboard man and future rock critic GILES SMITH, and IAN OLLIVER. 1987 was their busiest year, releasing a single, 'I DON'T KNOW YOU BUT . . .' / 'I'VE NEVER BEEN THAT COLOUR ANYWHERE BEFORE' (DLAM 2) / 7"+12" 'ME AND MY CONSCIENCE' for 'Idea' (IDEA+T 009), and album, 'THE D IS FOR DRUM' (on 'Idea' IDEALP 001). ELLIS departed soon after and POLLY finally convinced PARISH to let her play guitar, sax and contribute backing vocals. Unfortunately, recordings (i.e. 12" 'WATER', an album, 'HERE CATCH SHOUTED HIS FATHER') didn't quite reach the retail stage. In August 1992, the group released 'FROM A DIVA TO A DIVER' (BOT/+CD 04), after which PARISH took time out to produce WALL OF VOODOO and play with ENSENADA JOYRIDE, whose 'Hey Lady' POLLY has always wanted to cover. She then turned up on GRAPE's single 'BABY IN A PLASTIC BAG' and two tracks by The FAMILY CAT; 'COLOUR ME GREY' and 'RIVER OF DIAMONDS'. With ELLIS and OLLIVER, she had already formed PJ HARVEY in 1991, and they signed for 'Too Pure'. With POLLY on vocals, their first release, 'DRESS', immediately caught the attention of JOHN PEEL and achieved the dubious honour of a Melody Maker single of the week. A driving, primal howl of a record, it introduced HARVEY's lyrical preoccupation with the darker corners of female sexuality, a theme continued with 'SHEELA-NA-GIG' (without OLLIVER who was subsequently replaced by STEPHEN VAUGHAN) in early '92. The single hit the UK Top 75 and and there was enough of a buzz around the band for the debut album, 'DRY', to reach the fringes of the Top 10. HARVEY's impact had been immediate, her raw, defiantly individual interpretation of feminism sparking much debate in the music press, especially after an NME cover shot in which she appeared topless, back to the camera. Signing to 'Island', PJ HARVEY began work on the Steve Albini (ex-BIG BLACK)-produced follow-up, 'RID OF ME', which went Top 3 upon its release in the Spring of'93. As one might expect from the man who gave us 'Songs About Fucking', Albini's production didn't exactly make for an easy listen, HARVEY turning in her most ferocious performance to date. With the likes of 'LEGS', 'MAN SIZE' and 'RUB TILL IT BLEEDS', the singer continued to explore the contradictory and unsavoury aspects of sexuality/relationships with unparallelled feminine fury. Following the departure of ROB ELLIS, HARVEY assembled a backing band that includuded JOHN PARRISH (guitar, ex-AUTOMATIC DLAMINI), NICK BAGNALL (keyboards/bass), JOE GORE (guitar) and ERIC FELDMAN (keyboards) and JEAN-MARC BUTTY (drums). In 1995, with FLOOD and BAD SEED, MICK HARVEY on production duties, she/they unleashed HARVEY's finest work to date, 'TO BRING YOU MY LOVE', which also hit the US Top 40 and was nominated for a UK "Mercury" award. A more balanced affair, HARVEY's dark rage chose to simmer below the surface this time around, creating the feeling of creeping unease that runs through much of NICK CAVE's work (her new acquaintance!?). In 1996, she gave JOHN PARISH a full credit on their dual album 'DANCE HALL AT LOUSE POINT', which sold relatively poorly. As well as featuring on TRICKY's 'Broken Homes' single, 1998 saw the release of 'IS THIS DESIRE', the singer's most introspective, inscrutable work to date. Recorded amid a period of retreat from the vagaries and distractions of the rock world, the album's relatively restrained textures suggested an artist in transition. This was confirmed with the release of the widely acclaimed 'STORIES FROM THE CITY, STORIES FROM THE SEA' (2000), an album – a Mercury prize contender – with the energy of New York (where it was partly written) and the visceral thrill of self discovery coursing through its glamorous veins. Many commentators mentioned PATTI SMITH, a reference that HARVEY would be unlikely to dispute given the cathartic power she wielded throughout. • **Songwriters:** POLLY, and covers; HIGHWAY 61 (Bob Dylan) / DADDY (Willie Dixon) / BALLAD OF THE SOLDIER'S WIFE (Kurt Weill).

Album rating: DRY (*9) / RID OF ME (*8) / TO BRING YOU MY LOVE (*9) / DANCE HALL AT LOUSE POINT with John Parish (*5) / IS THIS DESIRE (*6) / STORIES FROM THE CITY, STORIES FROM THE SEA (*9)

POLLY HARVEY – vocals, guitar, cello, violin, organ / **IAN OLLIVER** – bass / **ROBERT ELLIS** (b.13 Feb'62, Bristol, England) – drums, vocals

Too Pure Indigo

Oct 91. (12"ep) *(PURE 5)* **DRESS. / WATER (demo) / DRY (demo)** [ ] [–]
(cd-iss. Mar92; PURECD 5)

— **STEPHEN VAUGHAN** (b.22 Jun'62, Wolverhampton, England) – bass repl. OLLIVER who returned to brief reformation of AUTOMATIC DLAMINI

Feb 92. (7"ltd.) *(PURE S8)* **SHEELA-NA-GIG. / JOE (demo)** [69] [–]
(12"+=/cd-s+=) *(PURE 8/+CD)* – Hair (demo).

Mar 92. (lp/cd/s-lp) *(PURE 10/+CD/D)* <ING 5001> **DRY** [11] Jun92 [ ]
– Oh my lover / O Stella / Dress / Victory / Happy and bleeding / Sheela-na-gig / Hair / Joe / Plants and rags / Fountain water. *(s-lp w/ free 'Demonstration' lp; PURED 10)*

Island Island

Apr 93. (7"/c-s) *(IS/CIS 538)* **50FT QUEENIE. / REELING / MAN-SIZE (demo)** [27] [–]
(12"+=/cd-s+=) *(12IS/CID 538)* – Hook (demo).

Apr 93. (cd/c/lp) *(CID/ICT/ILPS 8002)* <514696> **RID OF ME** [3] May93 [ ]
– Rid of me / Missed / Legs / Rub 'til it bleeds / Hook / Man-size sextet / Highway '61 revisited / 50ft Queenie / Yuri-G / Man-size / Dry / Me-Jane / Snake / Ecstasy.

Jul 93. (12"ep/cd-ep) *(12IS/CID 569)* **MAN-SIZE. / WANG DANG DOODLE / DADDY** [42] [–]

— drummer ELLIS departed after above.

Oct 93. (cd/c/lp) *(IMCD/ICT/ILPM 2079)* <518450> **4-TRACK DEMOS** (demos) [19] Nov93 [ ]
– Rid of me / Legs / Reeling / Snake / Hook / 50ft Queenie / Driving / Ecstasy / Hardly wait / Rub 'til it bleeds / Easy / M-bike / Yuri-G / Goodnight.

— POLLY now with **JOHN PARISH** – drums, guitar / **JOE GORE** (b. San Francisco) – guitar (ex-TOM WAITS) / **NICK BAGNALL** – keyboards, bass / **ERIC FELDMAN** (b. San Francisco) – keyboards (ex-CAPTAIN BEEFEART) / **JEAN-MARC BUTTY** (b. France) – drums

Feb 95. (7"ep/12"ep/cd-ep) *(IS/12IS/CID 607)* **DOWN BY THE WATER. / LYING IN THE SUN / SOMEBODY'S DOWN, SOMEBODY'S NAME** [38] [–]

Feb 95. (cd/c/lp) *(CID/ICT/ILPS 8035)* <524085> **TO BRING YOU MY LOVE** [12] [40]
– To bring you my love / Meet ze monsta / Working for the man / C'mon Billy / Teclo / Long snake moan / Down by the water / I think I'm a mother / Send his love to me / The dancer. *(re-iss. d-cd Dec95 w/ extra B-sides; CIDZ 8035)*

Jul 95. (12"/cd-s) *(12IS/CID 614)* **C'MON BILLY. / DARLING BE THERE / MANIAC** [29] [–]
(cd-s+=) *(CIDX 614)* – One time too many.

Oct 95. (7"pic-d) *(IS 610)* **SEND HIS LOVE TO ME. / LONG TIME COMING (session)** [34] [–]
(cd-s+=) *(CID 610)* – Harder.
(cd-s) *(CIDX 610)* – ('A'side) / Hook (live) / Water (live).

— Enjoyed more chart success on duet with NICK CAVE; 'Henry Lee' single released early '96.

JOHN PARISH & POLLY JEAN HARVEY

— with **JEREMY HOGG** – guitar / **ERIC DREW FELDMAN** – bass, keyboards (ex-CAPTAIN BEEFHEART) / **ROB ELLIS** – drums

Island Island

Sep 96. (cd/c/lp) *(CID/ICT/ILPS 8051)* <524278> **DANCE HALL AT LOUSE POINT** [46] [ ]
– Girl / Rope bridge crossing / City of no sun / That was my veil / Urn with dead flowers in a drained pool / Civil war correspondent / Taut / Un cercle autour du soleil / Heela / Is that all there is / Dance hall at Louse Point / Lost fun zone.

Nov 96. (7") *(IS 648)* **THAT WAS MY VEIL. / LOSING GROUND** [75] [–]
(12"+=/cd-s+=) *(12IS/CID 648)* – Who will love me now? / Civil war correspondent (Global Communications mix).

— ELLIS joined 'Too Pure' outfit, LAIKA

PJ HARVEY

— In 1998, she featured with TRICKY on his 'Broken Homes' single.

Island Polygram

Sep 98. (7") *(IS 718)* <572408> **A PERFECT DAY ELISE. / SWEETER THAN ANYTHING / INSTRUMENTAL #3** [25] Oct98 [ ]
(cd-s) *(CID 718)* – (first & third tracks) / The Northwood.
(cd-s) *(CIDX 718)* – (first two tracks) / The bay.

Sep 98. (cd/c/lp) *(CID/ICT/ILPS 8076)* <524563> **IS THIS DESIRE?** [17] [54]
– Angelene / Sky lit up / Wind / My beautiful Leah / A perfect day Elise /

Catherine / Electric light / Garden / Joy / River / No girl so sweet / Is this desire?

Jan 99. (7") *(IS 730)* **THE WIND. / NINA IN ECSTASY 2** [29] [ ]
(cd-s+=) *(CID 730)* – The faster I breathe, the further I go.
(cd-s) *(CIDX 730)* – ('A'side) / Rebecca / Instrumental No.2.

Oct 00. (cd/c/lp) *(CID/ICT/ILPS 8099)* *<548144>* **STORIES FROM THE CITY, STORIES FROM THE SEA** [23] Nov00 [42]
– Big exit / Good fortune / A place called home / One line / Beautiful feeling / The whores hustle and the hustlers whore / This mess we're in / You said something / Kamikaze / This is love / Horses in my dreams / We float. *(cd+=)* – This wicked tongue.

Nov 00. (7") *(IS 769)* **GOOD FORTUNE. / 66 PROMISES** [41] [–]
(cd-s+=) *(CID 769)* – Memphis.
(cd-s) *(CIDX 769)* – ('A'side) / Memphis / 30.

Feb 01. (7") *(IS 771)* **A PLACE CALLED HOME. / KICK TO THE GROUND (demo)** [43] [–]
(cd-s) *(CID 771)* – ('A'side) / As close as this / My own private revolution.

Oct 01. (7") *(IS 785)* **THIS IS LOVE. / ANGELINE (live)** [41] [–]
(cd-s) *(CID 785)* – ('A'side) / You said something / Place called home (live).

Richie HAVENS

Born: 21 Jan'41, Brooklyn, New York, USA and raised as the oldest of nine children in the New York ghetto area of Bedford-Stuyvesant. After inclinations of following in his pianist father's footsteps had lost their attraction due to lack of money, he began to busk the street-corners as a young teenager. He also formed The McCREA GOSPEL SINGERS, before he relocated to Greenwich Village, painting portraits of tourists to earn a living. It was now the early 60's and the folk revival was taking hold in the area to the extent that everybody (now even RICHIE) was picking up their guitar again. His unorthodox technique (tuning with an E-chord) helped him quickly adapt and characterise his own style. In 1965 having gained notoriety around the underground 'Village' scene, he was picked up by 'Douglas' records, who quickly shifted out copies of his debut lp, 'THE RICHIE HAVENS ALBUM'. It was followed by another, before 'Verve' took over and set free his 'MIXED BAG' album, which contained a remarkable cover of 'ELEANOR RIGBY'. In 1968, he played a benefit gig for dust-bowl folk hero idol, WOODY GUTHRIE, who had died the year previous. In August of 1969 he opened for the Woodstock Festival, which (overnight) made him into a star. One song, 'FREEDOM', became not only his anthem but the American people's anthem, delivered from the ashes of hippy psychedelia, to a hopeful early 70's generation that never quite disappeared. This showed itself to be the case in the Spring of 1971, when he resurrected (into the US Top 20), a GEORGE HARRISON written BEATLES song, 'HERE COMES THE SUN'. The accompanying album, 'ALARM CLOCK' made it into the Top 30 as a result. Now on the 'Stormy Forest' label, HAVENS continued in his inimitably earnest style throughout the 70's with albums such as 'THE GREAT BLIND DEGREE' (1972) and 'MIXED BAG II' (1975). He also continued to build up his bulging repertoire of BEATLES and BOB DYLAN covers (see below) and develop his knack for covering the most unlikely artists, material which no black artist would ordinarily go near. Although HAVENS' output diminished in the 80's, fans could console themselves (or not) with his TV advertising voiceovers (!). In 1994, he sued 'Time-Warner' for using his opening Woodstock footage for a new version of the film soundtrack. 'WISHING WELL' (2002), HAVENS' first new material in almost a decade, was cast in the kind of warm, wise, verging on transcendental mould which has brought TERRY CALLIER such respect and acclaim since his re-emergence in the mid-90's. A sage veteran of the original hippy era who grew old gracefully rather than burning himself out, HAVENS sounded like a man at peace with both his maker and his past on this record, remodelling Pink Floyd's 'ON THE TURNING AWAY' with fascinating results. • **Songwriters:** Self-penned except; CHAIN GANG (Sam Cooke) / OXFORD TOWN + BOOTS OF SPANISH LEATHER + JUST LIKE A WOMAN + SAD EYED LADY + IF NOT FOR YOU + LAY LADY LAY + ALL ALONG THE WATCHTOWER + THE TIMES THEY ARE-A CHANGIN' + IT'S ALL OVER NOW, BABY BLUE + LICENSE TO KILL (Bob Dylan) / C.C. RIDER (hit; Chuck Willis) / ELEANOR RIGBY + STRAWBERRY FIELDS FOREVER + LADY MADONNA + SHE'S LEAVING HOME + WITH A LITTLE HELP FROM MY FRIENDS + ROCKY RACCOON + IN MY LIFE + THE LONG AND WINDING ROAD + LET IT BE (Beatles) / WEAR YOUR LOVE LIKE HEAVEN (Donovan) / FIRE AND RAIN (James Taylor) / TOMMY (Who) / TEACH YOUR CHILDREN (Crosby, Stills, Nash & Young) / GOD BLESS THE CHILD (Billie Holiday) / TUPELO HONEY (Van Morrison) / WHERE HAVE ALL THE FLOWERS GONE (hit; Kingston Trio) / THE LONER (Neil Young) / BAND ON THE RUN (Paul McCartney) / IMAGINE + WORKING CLASS HERO (John Lennon) / MY SWEET LORD (George Harrison) / DO IT AGAIN (Steely Dan) / LONG TRAIN RUNNING (Doobie Brothers) / I'M NOT IN LOVE (10 cc) / OL' 55 (Tom Waits) / WE'VE GOT TONIGHT (Bob Seger) / LIVES IN THE BALANCE (Jackson Browne) / THEY DANCE ALONE (Sting) / THE HAWK (Kris Kristofferson) / HOW THE NIGHTS CAN FLY (Bob Lind) / MY FATHER'S SHOES (Eberhardt) / COMING BACK TO ME (Marty Balin) / etc. • **Miscellaneous:** In 1972, he also took part in the stage production of The Who's 'Tommy'.

Album rating: A RICHIE HAVENS RECORD (*4) / ELECTRIC HAVENS (*4) / MIXED BAG (*8) / SOMETHING ELSE AGAIN (*6) / RICHARD P. HAVENS (*7) / STONEHENGE (*4) / ALARM CLOCK (*5) / THE GREAT BLIND DEGREE (*4) / RICHIE HAVENS ON STAGE (*6) / PORTFOLIO (*5) / MIXED BAG II (*4) / THE END OF THE BEGINNING (*4) / MIRAGE (*4) / CONNECTIONS (*4) / COMMON GROUND (*4) / SIMPLE THINGS (*3) / SINGS BEATLES AND DYLAN (*6) / LIVE AT THE CELLAR DOOR (*3) / NOW (*4) / RESUME – BEST OF . . . compilation (*7) / CUTS TO THE CHASE (*5) / WISHING WELL (*6)

RICHIE HAVENS – vocals, guitar

not iss. Douglas

1965. (lp) *<779>* **A RICHIE HAVENS RECORD** [–] [ ]
– I'm gonna make you glad / It hurts me / Chain gang / Drown in my own tears / I'm on my way / Baby, I'm leavin' / Nora's dove / Daddy roll 'em / The bag I'm in. *(UK-iss.1969 on 'Transatlantic'; TRA 199)*

1966. (lp) *<780>* **ELECTRIC HAVENS** [–] [ ]
– Oxford Town / 900 miles from home / I'm a stranger here / My own way / Boots of Spanish leather / C.C. rider / 3:10 to Yuma / Shadow town. *<re-dist.Nov68> (UK-iss.1969 on 'Transatlantic'; TRA 187)*

— added **PAUL HARRIS** – piano, organ / **PAUL WILLIAMS** + **HOWARD COLLINS** – guitar / **HARVEY BROOKS** – bass / **BILL LA VORGNA** – drums / **JOE PRICE** – tabla

Verve Verve Folkways

Feb 67. (lp) *<3006>* **MIXED BAG** [–] [ ]
– High flyin' bird / I can't make it anymore / Morning morning / Adam / Follow / Three day eternity / Sandy / Handsome Johnny / San Francisco Bay blues / Just like a woman / Eleanor Rigby. *<re-dist.Jul68> (UK-iss.1968; SVLP 6008) <re-iss. Nov70 on 'M.G.M.'; 4698> (cd-iss. May88 & Jul94 & Jul02; 835210-2)*

Mar 67. (7") *<5022>* **I CAN'T MAKE IT ANYMORE. / MORNING MORNING** [–] [ ]

Jun 67. (7") *<5039>* **I'VE GOTTA GO. / MORNING MORNING** [–] [ ]

— **DANIEL BEN ZEBULON** + **DON McDONALD** + **SKIP PROKOP** – drums / **WARREN BERNHARDT** – keyboards / **JEREMY STEIG** – flute / **ADRIAN GULLEY** – guitar / **EDDIE GOMEZ** + **DON PAYNE** – bass / **JOHN BLAIR** – violin; repl. everyone except WILLIAMS

Feb 68. (lp) *(SVLP 6005)* *<3034>* **SOMETHING ELSE AGAIN** [ ] [ ]
– No opportunity necessary, no experience needed / Inside of him / The klan / Don't listen to me / Sugarplums / From the prison / New city / Run, shaker life / Maggie's farm / Something else again.

Jan 69. (7") *(VS 1512)* <*5068*> **NO OPPORTUNITY NECESSARY, NO EXPERIENCE NEEDED. / THREE DAY ETERNITY**

— **ERIC OXENDINE** – bass repl. GOMEZ + PAYNE / (added others on session)

May 69. (d-lp) *(SVLP 6014/5)* <*3047*> **RICHIE P. HAVENS, 1983** (some live) Jan69 80
– Stop pulling and pushing me / For Haven's sake / Strawberry fields forever / What more can I say John? / I pity the poor immigrant / Lady Madonna / Priests / Indian rope man / Cautiously / Just above my hobby horse's head / She's leaving home / Putting out the vibration, and hoping it comes home / The parable of Ramon / With a little help from my friends / Wear your love like Heaven / Run shaker life / Do you feel good?.

May 69. (7") <*5092*> **INDIAN ROPE MAN. / JUST ABOVE MY HOBBY HORSES HEAD** –

May 69. (7") *(VS 1519)* **LADY MADONNA. / INDIAN ROPE MAN** –

Verve / Stormy Forest

Jul 69. (7") *(VS 1521)* <*650*> **ROCKY RACCOON. / STOP PULLING AND PUSHING ME**

Sep 69. (7") *(VS 1523)* <*651*> **THERE'S A HOLE IN THE FUTURE. / MINSTREL FROM GAULT**

Oct 69. (7") *(VS 1524)* <*652*> **HANDSOME JOHNNY. / SANDIE**

Polydor / Stormy Forest

Jan 70. (lp) *(SVLP 6021)* <*6001*> **STONEHENGE**
– Open our eyes / Minstrel from Gault / It could be the first day / Ring around the Moon / Baby blue / There's a hole in the future / I started a joke / Prayer / Tiny little blues / Shouldn't all the world be dancing. <*(cd-iss. Jul02 on 'Evangeline'; GEL 4054)*>

Nov 70. (7") <*653*> **TO GIVE ALL MY LOVE AWAY. / NOBODY KNOWS** –

Jan 71. (lp) *(2310 080)* <*6005*> **ALARM CLOCK** 29
– Here comes the Sun / To give all your love away / Younger men grow older / Girls don't run away / End of the seasons / Some will wait / Patient lady / Missing train / Alarm clock.

Apr 71. (7") <*656*> **HERE COMES THE SUN. / YOUNGER MEN GET OLDER** – 16

Apr 71. (7") *(2001 162)* **HERE COMES THE SUN. / SOME WILL WAIT** –

Jul 71. (7") <*658*> **MISSING TRAIN. / I'VE GOT TO GET TO KNOW MYSELF** –

Jan 72. (lp) *(2480 049)* <*6010*> **THE GREAT BLIND DEGREE** Nov71
– What about me / Fire and rain / Tommy / In these flames / Think about the children / Fathers & sons / Teach your children / What have we done.

Feb 72. (7") <*660*> **THINK ABOUT THE CHILDREN. / FIRE AND RAIN** –

Mar 72. (7") *(2121 098)* **WHAT ABOUT ME. / FIRE AND RAIN** –

HAVENS still with **WILLIAMS** + **ZEBULON** live BBC, London, 19 Oct'71.

Sep 72. (d-lp) *(2659 015)* <*6012*> **RICHIE HAVENS ON STAGE (live)** 55
– From the prison / Younger men grow older / God bless the child / High flying bird / Tupelo honey / Just like a woman / Handsome Johnny / Where have all the flowers gone / Rocky raccoon / Teach the children / Minstrel from Gault / Freedom.

Oct 72. (7") <*664*> **I'VE GOT TO GET TO KNOW MYSELF (live). / WHERE YOU GONNA RUN TO (live)** –

Feb 73. (7") <*666*> **FREEDOM. / HANDSOME JOHNNY**

— added **OXENDINE** / **JERRY FRIEDMAN** – guitar / **ERIC WEISBERG** – steel guitar / etc.

Jul 73. (lp) *(2480 166)* <*6013*> **PORTFOLIO** Jun73
– It was a very good year / Dreaming my life away / 23 days in September / I know I won't be there / I don't need nobody / Woman / What's goin' on / Tightrope / Mama loves you. <*(cd-iss. Apr03 on 'Evangeline'; GEL 4063)*>

Aug 73. (7") <*671*> **IT WAS A VERY GOOD YEAR. / I KNOW I WON'T BE THERE** –

Oct 73. (7") <*672*> **TIGHTROPE. / WOMAN** –

Nov 73. (7") *(2121 181)* **TIGHTROPE. / IT WAS A VERY GOOD YEAR** –

Jan 75. (lp) *(2310 356)* <*6201*> **MIXED BAG II** Oct74
– Ooh child / Headkeeper / Wandering Angus / Sad eyed lady (of the lowlands) / Someone suite / Band on the run / The loner / The makings of you / The Indian prayer.

— now with numerous session including **HERMAN ERNST** – drums / **DARRYL JOHNSON** – guitar / + (on first) **BOOKER T. & THE MG's**

A&M / A&M

Sep 76. (7") <*1869*> **WE CAN'T HIDE IT ANYMORE. / DREAMING AS ONE** –

Nov 76. (lp) *(AMLH 64598)* <*4598*> **THE END OF THE BEGINNING** Sep76
– I'm not in love / We can't hide it anymore / Dreaming as one / You can close your eyes / I was educated by myself / Daughter of the night / If not for you / Do it again / Wild night / Long train running.

Nov 76. (7") *(AMS 7266)* <*1882*> **I'M NOT IN LOVE. / DREAMING AS ONE**

Mar 77. (7") <*1901*> **YOU CAN CLOSE YOUR EYES. / WE CAN'T HIDE IT ANYMORE** –

Oct 77. (lp) *(AMLH 64641)* <*4641*> **MIRAGE** Apr77
– Live it up (one time) / Shadows of the past / I don't complain / Touch the sky / Billy John / We all wanna boogie / Avalon / Aviation man / Nobody left to crown / The end.

Jan 78. (7") <*1984*> **WE ALL WANNA BOOGIE. / NOBODY LEFT TO CROWN** –

— Around mid-78, RICHIE guested on STEVE HACKETT's single 'How Can I.' Later that year, he wrote and apeared in film 'Greased Lightning'. He now employed totally new session men incl. on next **JEFF BAXTER** + **RICHARD TEE**

Elektra / Elektra

Nov 79. (7") <*46619*> **EVERY NIGHT. / HERE'S A SONG** –

Mar 80. (lp) *(K 52186)* <*242*> **CONNECTIONS** Nov79
– Mama we're gonna dance / Every night / You send me / We've got tonight / Ol' 55 / Going back to my roots / Dreams / She touched my heart / Fire down below / Here's a song. <*(cd-iss. Apr02 on 'Wounded Bird'; WOU 242)*>

Mar 80. (7") <*46657*> **THE GIRL, THE GOLD WATCH AND EVERYTHING. / TWO HEARTS IN PERFECT TIME** –

Bagaria / not iss.

Jun 83. (lp) *(165155-1)* **COMMON GROUND** – Italian –
– Death at an early age / Gay cavalier / Lay ye down boys / This is the hour / Stand up / Dear John / Leave well enough alone / Moonlight rain / Things must change.

Connexion / not iss.

Jun 83. (7") *(CX 5381)* **DEATH AT AN EARLY AGE. / MOONLIGHT RAIN**

R.B.I. / R.B.I.

Sep 87. (lp/c/cd) <*(RB L/C/D 400)*> **SIMPLE THINGS**
– Drivin' / Simple things / Songwriter / Passin' by / Wake up and dream / I don't wanna know / Shouldn't we all be having a good time / Arrow through me / Runner in the night.

not iss. / Five Star

1990. (cd) <*1001*> **LIVE AT THE CELLAR DOOR** –
– Can't make it anymore / All along the watchtower / Helplessly hoping / God bless the child / The night they drove old Dixie down / No more, no more / Preparation / Here comes the sun / Fire and rain / Superman / The dolphins / Nobody knows the trouble I've seen – My sweet Lord.

not iss. / Solar-Epic

1991. (cd) <*75325*> **NOW** –
– Angel / You are the one / That's the way I see you / After all these years / Love sometimes says goodbye / Message from the doctor / Time after time / You're my tomorrow / Let the walls fall down / It ain't over til it's over.

Rykodisc / Rykodisc

May 92. (cd) <*(RCD 20035)*> **SINGS BEATLES AND DYLAN** (rec.1987) 1990
– Here comes the sun / If not for you / Lay lady lay / In my life / Strawberry fields forver / All along the watchtower / Imagine / My sweet Lord / It's all over now, baby blue / Eleanor Rigby / Just like a woman / The long and winding road / Let it be / License to kill / The times they are a-changin' / Working class hero / Rocky raccoon / With a little help from my friends.

— In Jul'93, HAVENS and FRANCESCO BRUNO (jazz artist) released the single 'THE WORLD IS SO SMALL' from the 'Prestige' album 'EL LUGAR (THE PLACE)'.

Essential / Garden

Jun 94. (cd/c) *(ESS CD/MC 212)* <*71735*> **CUTS TO THE CHASE**
– Lives in the balance / They dance alone / My father's shoes / Darkness, darkness / The hawk / Young boy / The times they are a-changin' / Fade to blue medley: Intro – Old love / How the nights can fly / Comin' back to me / Don't pass it up / At a glance.

		Evangeline	Stormy Forest
Apr 02.	(cd) *(GEL 4040)* <SFS 2021> **WISHING WELL**		
	– The well / Handouts in the rain / Love is alive / You'll never know / Slow down / On the road to Calvary / Stardust & passion / Paradise / Alone together / On the turning away.		

– compilations, etc. –

Apr 69.	(7") *Big T; (BIG 119)* **OXFORD TOWN. / MY OWN WAY**		–
Jul 71.	(lp) *Polydor; (2304 050)* **A STATE OF MIND**		–
Mar 76.	(lp) *Polydor; (2482 273)* **RICHIE HAVENS**		–
Nov 87.	(cd) *Rykodisc;* <RCD 20036> **COLLECTION**	–	
Apr 93.	(cd) *Rhino;* <71187> **RESUME: THE BEST OF RICHIE HAVENS**	–	
	– High flyin' bird / Drown in my own tears / Morning, morning / Just like a woman / The dolphins / Here comes the sun / God bless the child / The klan / Handsome Johnny / Follow / Younger men grow older / Medley: Run shake life – Do you feel good / What about me / The monstrel from Gaul / Rocky raccoon / San Francisco Bay blues / Freedom.		
Sep 95.	(cd) *Rebound;* <520291> **THE CLASSICS**	–	
1999.	(cd) *Silver Lining;* <DJA 1114> **TIME**	–	
Mar 03.	(cd) *Universal;* <(AA314 547900-2)> **THE BEST OF RICHIE HAVENS: THE MILLENNIUM COLLECTION**		Feb00

☐ HAWKETTS (see under ⇒ NEVILLE BROTHERS)

Screamin' Jay HAWKINS

Born: JALACY HAWKINS, 18 Jul'29, Cleveland, Ohio, USA. He decided upon a musical career after being orphaned and fostered as a young boy. Unfortunately he was not suited to the operatic style of performing (he chose at the time) and began his lifelong ambitions in 1951; he was pianist on several tracks by TINY GRIMES. However, a year later, the tables were turned when his solo career was aided with the help of GRIMES AND HIS ROCKING HIGHLANDERS. HAWKINS' delivered his finest 3-minutes in 1956 with the single, 'I PUT A SPELL ON YOU', a meisterwork in its time that has since achieved great things although never a hit for the man. The infamous grunting sections were reputedly recorded while HAWKINS was in a state of severe intoxication. The single, with its tongue very firmly placed in its cheek, fused swinging R&B instrumentation and backing vocals with a then new care-less attitude to the lead vocals, the drum-lines and guitar licks were provided by his motley crew of friends. It could be said that the man achieved little else in his lifetime, although he tried time and time again to breach the unsympathetic charts. HAWKINS was more famous for his onstage antics, shaped around shock-horror voodoo R'n'R, something not practised before but has since been associated with ARTHUR BROWN and ALICE COOPER. His antics included appearing from a coffin and also carrying HENRY, a macabre flaming skull companion, while shouting his words like a demented preacher man. This eccentric flair saw him being rebuked in the early 60's, with angry parents and God-fearing Americans having a field day due to its banning on radio. It also translated well onto the cinema screen when HAWKINS had minor memorable roles in a share of films: 'Two Moon Junction', 'Dance With The Devil' and cult director Jim Jarmush's masterpiece 'Mystery Train'. More recently, albums from HAWKINS included 'BLACK MUSIC FOR WHITE PEOPLE' (1991), 'STONE CRAZY' (1993) and 'SOMETHIN' FUNNY GOIN' ON' (1994), although all were nothing short of incoherent ramblings. However, the man did achieve his first hit single (albeit minor) when his version of Tom Waits' 'HEART ATTACK AND VINE' made it into the UK Top 50 in Spring '93; WAITS would subsequently sue the accompanying TV advert. HAWKINS died in Paris, France on the 12th February 2000 after an operation to his brain (aneurysm) failed. His legacy was quickly established when, on a Channel 4 TV documentary, it was revealed he had over 50 children in his lifetime – and a lot of them (and their mothers) were interviewed on this chin-dropping programme!

Best CD compilation: PORTRAIT OF A MAN – A HISTORY OF ... (*6)

SCREAMIN' JAY HAWKINS – vocals, piano, saxophone

		not iss.	Timely
1954.	(78) <1004> **BAPTIZE ME IN WINE. / NOT ANYMORE**	–	
1954.	(78) <1005> **PLEASE TRY TO UNDERSTAND. / I FOUND MY WAY TO WINE**	–	
		not iss.	Mercury
1955.	(78; as JAY HAWKINS) <70549> **SHE PUT THE WHAMMY ON ME. / THIS IS ALL**	–	
		not iss.	Wing
1955.	(78; as JAY HAWKINS) <90005> **YOU'RE ALL OF MY LIFE TO ME. / WELL I TRIED**	–	
1956.	(78; as JAY HAWKINS) <90055> **EVEN THOUGH. / TALK ABOUT ME**	–	
		not iss.	Grand
1956.	(78) <135> **TAKE ME BACK. / I IS**	–	
		not iss.	Okeh
1956.	(78) <7072> **I PUT A SPELL ON YOU. / LITTLE DEMON**	–	
	(UK-iss.Jan58 on 'Fontana'; H 107) (7"-iss.1969 on 'Direction'; 58-4097) (re-iss. 1975 on 'Epic'; 15-2209)		
1956.	(78) <7084> **YOU MADE ME LOVE YOU. / DARLING, PLEASE FORGIVE ME**	–	
1956.	(78) <7087> **FRENZY. / PERSON TO PERSON**	–	
1957.	(78) <7101> **ALLIGATOR WINE. / THERE'S SOMETHING WRONG WITH YOU**	–	
		not iss.	Epic
1957.	(lp) <LN 3448> **AT HOME WITH SCREAMIN' JAY HAWKINS**	–	
		not iss.	Apollo
1957.	(78) <506> **PLEASE TRY TO UNDERSTAND. / NOT ANYMORE**	–	
1958.	(78) <528> **BAPTIZE ME IN WINE. / NOT ANYMORE**	–	
		not iss.	Enrica
1962.	(7") <1010> **I HEAR VOICES. / JUST DON'T CARE (with the Chicken Hawks)**	–	
	(UK-iss.Jun65 on 'Sue'; WI 379)		
		not iss.	Chancellor
1962.	(7") <1117> **ASHES. / NITTY GRITTY (with PAT NEWBORN)**	–	
		Columbia	Roulette
Jan 65.	(7") *(DB 7460)* <4579> **THE WHAMMY. / STRANGE**		
		not iss.	Providence
Feb 65.	(7") <411> **PO' FOLKS. / MY KIND OF LOVE**	–	
		Planet	not iss.
1966.	(lp) *(PLL 1001)* **THE NIGHT AND DAY OF SCREAMIN' JAY HAWKINS**		–
		not iss.	Decca
1967.	(7") <32019> **I'M NOT MADE OF CLAY. / ALL NIGHT**	–	
1967.	(7") <32100> **I PUT A SPELL ON YOU. / YOU'RE AN EXCEPTION TO THE RULE**	–	
		Direction	Epic
1969.	(lp; stereo/mono) *(S+/8-63481)* <26457> **I PUT A SPELL ON YOU** (compilation)		
	– You made me love you / I put a spell on you / Alligator wine / Little demon / There's something wrong with you / Orange-coloured sky / Yellow coat / Give me back my boots and saddle / Hong Kong / Person to person / Frenzy / I love Paris.		

—— now with a back-up session band

		Mercury	Philips
1969.	(7") <40606> **I'M LONELY. / STONE CRAZY**	–	
1969.	(7") <40645> **DO YOU REALLY LOVE ME. / CONSTIPATION BLUES**	–	

1969. (7") *<40668>* **MOANIN'. / CONSTIPATION BLUES**

1969. (lp) *(SMCL 20178) <PHS 600-319>* **WHAT THAT IS!**
– What that is / Feast of the Mau Mau / Do you really love me / Stone crazy / I love you / Constipation blues / I'm lonely / Thing called woman / Dig / I'm your man / Ask him / Reprise. *(cd-iss. Aug95 on 'Verve'+=; 527490-2)*

1970. (lp) *<PHS 600-336>* **SCREAMIN' JAY HAWKINS**

1970. (7") *<40674>* **OUR LOVE IS NOT FOR THREE. / TAKE ME BACK**

not iss. Sound Of Hawaii

1970. (lp) *<5013>* **A NIGHT AT THE FORBIDDEN CITY (live)** Hawaii

1970. (7") **TOO MANY TEARDROPS. / MAKAHA WAVES** Hawaii

not iss. Queen Bee

1971. (7") **MONKBERRY MOON DELIGHT. / SWEET GINNY**

not iss. Hot Line

1972. (lp) *<10024>* **PORTRAIT OF A MAN AND HIS WOMAN** (part compilation)

not iss. London

1973. (7") **AFRICA GONE FUNKY. / (part 2)**

not iss. R.C.A.

1974. (7") **VOODOO. / YOU PUT THE SPELL ON ME**

not iss. Versatile

1977. (7") **I PUT A SPELL ON YOU. / AFRICA GONE FUNKY**

Polydor not iss.

Sep 80. (7") *(POSP 183)* **I PUT A SPELL ON YOU. / ARMPIT #6 (with KEITH RICHARDS)**

—— recorded next set with French musicians

Paris not iss.

1983. (lp) *(C 3358)* **REAL LIFE** French
– Deep in love / Your kind of love / Get down France / All night / Serving time / Feast of the Mau Mau / I feel alright / Poor folks / Mountain jive / Constipation blues. *(UK-iss.Feb89 on 'Charly' lp)(cd; CRB 1205)(CDCHARLY 163) (cd re-iss. Feb93 on 'Blues Collection'; 15755-2) (cd re-iss. Jul03 on 'Snapper'; SNAP 127CD)*

Midnight not iss.

Mar 86. (m-lp; with The FUZZTONES) *(MIRLP 114)* **LIVE (live 1985)**
– Alligator wine / I put a spell on you / It's that time again / Constipation blues.

Demon Rhino

Mar 91. (cd/c) *(FIEND CD/CASS 211) <R2/R4 70556>* **BLACK MUSIC FOR WHITE PEOPLE**
– Is you is or is you ain't my baby? / I feel alright / I put a spell on you (dance version) / I hear you knockin' / Heart attack and vine / Ignant and shit / Swamp gas / Voodoo priestess / Ice cream man / I want your body / Ol' man river / Strokin'. *(cd re-iss. Mar98 on 'Manifesto'; BP 40102CD)*

Mar 93. (7"/c-s/cd-s) *(659109-7/-4/-2)* **HEART ATTACK AND VINE. / I PUT A SPELL ON YOU / ON THE JOB** 42
(above issued on 'Columbia')

Apr 93. (cd) *(FIENDCD 728) <R2 71184>* **STONE CRAZY**
– Strange / I don't know / Who's been talkin' / I believe / Stone crazy / Last Saturday night / Call the plumber / I wanna know / Sherilyn Fenn / Late night Hawkins / On the job / I am the queen.

—— next featured **BUDDY BLUE** – guitar (ex-BEAT FARMERS)

Demon Bizarre – Straight

Feb 94. (cd) *(FIENDCD 750) <40105>* **SOMETHIN' FUNNY GOIN' ON** Apr95
– Somethin' funny goin' on / I am the cool / Whistling past the graveyard / Rock the house / Scream the blues / Brujo / You make me sick / Give it a break / When you walked out the door / Fourteen wives.

Last Call Valley

Feb 98. (cd) *(302742-2) <15008>* **AT LAST**
– Listen / Because of you / Coulda', woulda', shoulda' / Pot luck / You took me / Deceived / I'll be there / I played the fool / Shut your mouth when you sneeze / Life goes on / You want love / Make me happy / I shot the sheriff.

Last Call Last Call

Dec 99. (d-cd) *<(305256-2)>* **LIVE – OLYMPIA, PARIS 1998 (live)**
– I feel alright / Don't love you no more / Pretty girls everywhere / I'm lonely / Deceived / I don't know / I want to know / I'll be there / Stand by me / Bite it / Constipation blues / What'd I say / Alligator wine / I put a spell on you / Itty bitty pretty one / Shout / You took me / Please don't leave me / Goodnight sweetheart / Frankly speaking. *(lp-iss.Dec01 on 'Munster'; MR 197)*

—— sadly, HAWKINS was to die the following February

– compilations, etc. –

Sep 79. (lp) *Red Lightnin'; (RL 0025)* **SCREAMIN' THE BLUES** (material from 1953-1970)
(cd-iss. Aug89; RLCD 75) (cd re-iss. Aug02 on 'Blue Boar'; CDBB 1002)

Oct 82. (lp) *Edsel; (ED 104)* **FRENZY** (the 'Okeh' recordings)
(re-iss. Mar86 cd/c/lp; CD/C+/ED 104)

Mar 88. (d-lp) *Edsel; (DED 252)* **FEAST OF THE MAU MAU**
(re-iss. Mar91 cd/c; ED/C ED 252)

Jun 89. (lp)(cd) *Charly; (CRB 1211)(CDCHARLY 181)* **I PUT A SPELL ON YOU** (not the original)
(cd re-iss. Apr93 on 'Instant'; CDINS 5078) (cd re-iss. Jun96; CPCD 8221) (cd re-iss. Mar01 on 'Snapper'; SNAP 006CD)

Feb 90. (cd/c) *Rhino; <R2/R4 70947>* **VOODOO JIVE: THE BEST OF SCREAMIN' JAY HAWKINS**

Dec 90. (d-cd) *Bear Family; <(BCD 15530-BH)>* **SPELLBOUND! 1955-1974**

Oct 91. (cd) *(SJHCD 71829)* **SCREAMIN' JAY HAWKINS 1952-1955 – THE COMPLETE GOTHAM & GRAND RECORDINGS**

Jan 92. (cd) *Evidence; <(ECD 26003-2)>* **LIVE & CRAZY (live)**

Mar 92. (cd/c) *Legacy; (471270-2/-4) / Epic; <EK/ET 47933>* **COW FINGERS AND MOSQUITO PIE**
(cd re-iss. Apr00 on 'Columbia'; 498088-2)

Sep 93. (cd/c) *Aim; (AIM CD/C 1031)* **I SHAKE MY STICK AT YOU**

Jan 95. (cd) *Edsel; (EDCD 414)* **PORTRAIT OF A MAN – A HISTORY OF SCREAMIN' JAY HAWKINS**
– Little demon / I put a spell on you / Baptize me in wine / Not anymore / I hear voices / Just don't care / Ashes / There's something wrong with you / Strange / The whammy / All night / Poor folks / Your kind of love / Mountain jive / Voodoo / You put the spell on me / Portrait of a man / Ol' man river / Heart attack and vine / I don't know / Don't deceive me / Whistling past the graveyard / Armpit #6 / I put a spell on you (1979 version) / Scream the blues.

Nov 97. (cd) *Prestige; (CDSGP 358)* **DON'T FOOL WITH ME**

Nov 97. (cd) *Music Club; (MCCD 322)* **THE BEST OF ALLIGATOR WINE**

Sep 98. (cd) *M.I.L.; <6121>* **SHE PUT THE WAMMEE ON ME**

Jun 00. (cd) *Snapper; (SMDCD 294)* **SPELLS AND POTIONS**

HAWKWIND

Formed: London, England ... mid-69 as GROUP X, by ex-FAMOUS CURE members DAVE BROCK and MICK SLATTERY, who were joined by NIK TURNER, TERRY OLLIS, DIK MIK and JOHN HARRISON. They subsequently became HAWKWIND ZOO, although SLATTERY opted out for a gypsy lifestyle in Ireland after they signed to 'United Artists' in late '69. Now as HAWKWIND and many free concerts later (mostly at open-air festivals), they released their eponymous debut in late summer 1970. While this album was a melange of bluesy, heavy psychedelic rock, the band added more personnel for the follow-up, 'IN SEARCH OF SPACE' (1971), including synth player DEL DETTMAR and vocalist/poet ROBERT CALVERT. His sci-fi musings featured heavily on the album, while the scattered electronic stabs and saxophone honking merged with the driving rhythm section to create their own tripped-out take on space rock. The record saw HAWKWIND break into the Top 20, while the following summer they smashed into the Top 3 with the classic 'SILVER MACHINE' (1972) single, LEMMY KILMISTER's pile driving bass fuelling the beast with a turbo-charged power. The track previously featured on the live various artists 'GREASY TRUCKERS' PARTY' album, as well as appearing on the similar 'GLASTONBURY FAYRE' compilation. The success of the single secured the band Top 20 placings on all four of their future albums for 'United Artists', although come 1975, after the semi-classic 'WARRIOR ON THE EDGE OF TIME' album, LEMMY had departed to form MOTORHEAD, while CALVERT had been replaced by sci-fi writer, MICHAEL MOORCOCK. HAWKWIND signed to 'Charisma' and despite continuing moderate success, were dogged by legal battles over their moniker (HAWKLORDS was used for one album, 1978's '25 YEARS ON'). With a substantially altered line-up, HAWKWIND continued to release albums on their own 'Flicknife' label throughout the 80's. Tragedy struck when CALVERT died from a heart attack on 14 August '88, although yet another line-up saw HAWKWIND into the 90's with the 'SPACE BANDITS' (1990) album. The band continue to attract a loyal following of die-hard hippies and the emergence of the psychedelic/crusty techno scene has done them no harm, many young stoners citing HAWKWIND as a prominent influence. • **Songwriters:** Mostly by BROCK or CALVERT until the latter's departure, ALAN DAVEY eventually replacing him. Other various personnel over the years also took part in writing.

Album rating: HAWKWIND (*6) / IN SEARCH OF SPACE (*8) / DOREMI FASOL LATIDO (*5) / SPACE RITUAL ALIVE (*8) / HALL OF THE MOUNTAIN KING (*6) / WARRIOR ON THE EDGE OF TIME (*7) / ROADHAWKS live collection (*6) / ASTOUNDING SOUNDS AND AMAZING MUSIC (*5) / QUARK, STRANGENESS AND CHARM (*4) / 25 YEARS ON (*4) / PRX 5 (*5) / LIVE 1979 (*4) / LEVITATION (*5) / SONIC ATTACK (*6) / CHURCH OF HAWKWIND (*6) / CHOOSE YOUR MASQUES (*6) / ZONES (*5) / THIS IS HAWKWIND, DO NOT PANIC (*4) / CHRONICLE OF THE BLACK SWORD (*6) / THE XENON CODEX (*6) / STASIS – THE U.A. YEARS 1971-1975 compilation (*8) / SPACE BANDITS (*6) / ELECTRIC TEEPEE (*6) / IT'S THE BUSINESS OF THE FUTURE TO BE DANGEROUS (*6) / THE BUSINESS TRIP (*4) / ALIEN 4 (*5) / LOVE IN SPACE (*5)

DAVE BROCK (b. 20 Aug'41, Isleworth, England) – vocals, guitar / **NIK TURNER** (b. 26 Aug'40, Oxford, England) – vocals, saxophone / **HUW-LLOYD LANGTON** – guitar repl. MICK SLATTERY (Oct69, when as HAWKWIND ZOO) **JOHN HARRISON** – bass / **TERRY OLLIS** – drums / **DIK MIK** (b. S. McMANUS, Richmond, England) – electronics engineer, synthesizers

Liberty U.A.

Jul 70. (7") *(LBF 15382)* **HURRY ON SUNDOWN. / MIRROR OF ILLUSION**

Aug 70. (lp) *(LBS 83348) <5519>* **HAWKWIND**
– Hurry on sundown / The reason is? / Be yourself / Paranoia (part 1) / Paranoia (part 2) / Seeing it as you really are / Mirror of illusion. *(re-iss. Sep75 on 'Sunset'; SLS 50374) (re-iss. Feb80 as 'ROCKFILE' on 'United Artists'; LBR 1012) (re-iss. Feb84 on 'E.M.I.' lp/pic-lp; SLS/+P 1972921) (hit UK 75) (cd-iss. Feb94 & Nov02 on 'Repertoire'; REP 4403) (cd re-mast.Aug01 on 'E.M.I.'+=; 530028-2)* – Bring it on home / Hurry on sundown (alt.) / Kiss of the velvet whip / Cymbaline.

— (Sep'70) **THOMAS CRIMBLE** – bass repl. JOHN HARRISON / **DEL DETTMAR** – synthesizer repl. LANGTON (partway through next album)

— (May'71) **DAVE ANDERSON** – bass (ex-AMON DUUL II) repl. CRIMBLE On stage they also added on vocals **ROBERT CALVERT** (b. 9 Mar'45, Pretoria, South Africa) – poet, vocals, **MICHAEL MOORCOCK** – sci-fi writer and **STACIA** – exotic dancer

U.A. U.A.

Oct 71. (lp) *(UAG 29202) <5567>* **IN SEARCH OF SPACE** [18]
– You shouldn't do that / You know you're only dreaming / Master of the universe / We took the wrong step years ago / Adjust me / Children of the sun. *(re-iss. Jan81 on 'Liberty'; LBG 29202) (re-iss. Jun85 on 'Liberty-EMI' lp/c; ATAK/TCATAK 9) (re-iss. Oct87 on 'Fame' lp/c; FA/TCFA 3192) (cd-iss. May89 & Dec95 on 'Fame'; CDFA 3192) (cd re-mast.Aug01 on 'E.M.I.'+=; 530030-2)* – Silver machine / Seven by seven / Born to go (live).

— (Sep'71) **LEMMY** (b. IAN KILMISTER, 24 Dec'45, Stoke-On-Trent, England) – bass, vocals repl. ANDERSON

— (Jan'72) **SIMON KING** – drums (ex-OPAL BUTTERFLY) repl. OLLIS (group now **KING, LEMMY, BROCK, TURNER, DIK MIK, DETTMAR, CALVERT, STACIA** and p/t **MOORCOCK**)

Jun 72. (7") *(UP 35381) <50949>* **SILVER MACHINE. / SEVEN BY SEVEN** [3]
(re-iss. '76) (re-iss. Oct78, hit UK 34) (re-hit 67 when re-iss. Dec82 7"/7"pic-d/12"; UP/UPP/12UP 35381)

Nov 72. (lp) *(UAG 29364) <LA 001>* **DOREMI FASOL LATIDO** [14]
– Brainstorm / Space is deep / One change / Lord of light / Down through the night / Time we left this world today / The watcher. *(re-iss. 1979) (re-iss. Jun85 on 'Liberty-EMI') (US cd-iss. Jul91 on 'One Way') (cd re-iss. Mar96 on 'E.M.I.'+=; HAWKS 3)* – Urban guerilla / Brainbox pullution / Lord of light / Ejection. *(cd re-mast.Aug01 on 'E.M.I.'+=; 530031-2)*

May 73. (d-lp) *(UAD 60037-8) <LA 120>* **SPACE RITUAL – RECORDED LIVE IN LIVERPOOL AND LONDON (live)** [9]
– Earth calling / Born to go / Down through the night / The awakening / Lord of light / The black corridor / Space is deep / Electronic No.1 / Orgone accumulator / Upside down / 10 seconds of forever / Brainstorm / 7 by 7 / Sonic attack / Time we left this world today / Master of the universe / Welcome to the future. *(re-iss. 1979;) (cd re-mast.Aug01 on 'E.M.I.'+=; 530032-2)* – You shouldn't do that / Masters of the universe / Born to go.

Aug 73. (7") *(UP 25566) <314>* **URBAN GUERILLA. / BRAINBOX POLLUTION** [39]

— Now a trim sex/septet when DIK MIK and CALVERT departed. The latter going solo. (Apr74) **SIMON HOUSE** – keyboards, synthesizers, violin (ex-THIRD EAR BAND, ex-HIGH TIDE) repl. DETTMAR who emigrated to Canada

Aug 74. (7") *(UP 35715)* **PSYCHEDELIC WARLORDS (DISAPPEAR IN SMOKE). / IT'S SO EASY**

Sep 74. (lp/c) *(UAG/UAC 29672) <LA 328>* **HALL OF THE MOUNTAIN GRILL** [16]
– The psychedelic warlords (disappear in smoke) / Wind of change / D-rider / Web weaver / You'd better believe it / Hall of the Mountain Grill / Lost Johnnie / Goat willow / Paradox. *(re-iss. Jan81 on 'Liberty'; LBG 29672) (re-iss. Jun85 on 'Liberty-EMI';) (re-iss. Sep85 on 'Fame'; FA41 3133-1) (cd-iss. May89 & Dec95; CD-FA 3133) (cd re-mast.Aug01 on 'E.M.I.'+=; 530030-2)* – You'd better believe it (single version) / Psychedelic warlords (disappear in smoke) (single version) / Paradox / It's so easy.

— added **ALAN POWELL** – 2nd drums (ex-STACKRIDGE, ex-CHICKEN SHACK, etc)

Charisma Atco

Mar 75. (7") *(UP 35808)* **KINGS OF SPEED. / MOTORHEAD**

May 75. (lp/c) *(UAG/UAC 29766) <35115>* **WARRIOR ON THE EDGE OF TIME** [13]
– Assault and battery – part one / The golden void – part two / The wizard blew his horn / Opa-Loka / The demented man / Magnu / Standing at the edge / Spiral galaxy 28948 / Warriors / Dying seas / Kings of speed. *(re-iss. 1979; same) (re-iss. Jan81 + Jun85 on 'Liberty-EMI'; TCK 29766) (re-iss. Feb94 on 'Dojo'; DOJOCD 84) (cd re-iss. Aug03 on 'Hawkwind'; HAWKVP 6CD)*

— **PAUL RUDOLPH** – bass (ex-PINK FAIRIES) repl. LEMMY who formed MOTORHEAD **BOB CALVERT** – vocals returned, STACIA the dancer left to get married. **CALVERT** and **RUDOLPH** now with **BROCK, TURNER, KING, HOUSE** and **POWELL**. note also that MOORCOCK left to form his DEEP FIX

Charisma Sire

Jul 76. (7") *(CB 289)* **KERB CRAWLER. / HONKY DORKY** [–]

Aug 76. (lp/c) *(CDS 4004)* **ASTOUNDING SOUNDS, AMAZING MUSIC EMPORIUM** [33] [–]
– Reefer madness / Steppenwolf / City of lagoons / The aubergine that ate Rangoon / Kerb crawler / Kadu flyer / Chronoglide skyway. *(re-iss. Mar83; CHC 14) (cd-iss. Apr89 on 'Virgin'; CDSCD 4004) (cd re-iss. Aug03 on 'Hawkwind'; HAWKVP 28CD)*

Jan 77. (7") *(CB 299)* **BACK ON THE STREETS. / THE DREAM OF ISIS**

— **ADRIAN SHAW** – bass TURNER who formed SPHINX then INNER CITY BLUES

Jun 77. (lp/c) *(CDS/CDC 4008) <6047>* **QUARK, STRANGENESS AND CHARM** [30]
– Spirit of the age / Damnation alley / Fable of a failed race / Quark, strangeness and charm / Hassan I Sahba / The forge of Vulcan / Days of the underground / Iron dream. *(re-iss. Oct86 lp/c; CHC/MC 50) (cd-iss. Apr89 on 'Virgin'; CDSCD 4008) (cd re-iss. Aug03 on 'Hawkwind'; HAWKVP 26CD)*

Jul 77. (7") *(CB 305)* **QUARK, STRANGENESS AND CHARM. / THE FORGE OF VULCAN** [–]

— **PAUL HAYLES** – keyboards repl. HOUSE who joined DAVID BOWIE on tour

HAWKLORDS

BROCK and **CALVERT** recruiting new members **STEVE SWINDELLS** – keyboards (ex-STRING DRIVEN THING, ex-PILOT) / **HARVEY BAINBRIDGE** – bass / **MARTIN GRIFFIN** – drums

Charisma Charisma

Oct 78. (lp/c) *(CDS/CDC 4014)* *<2203>* **25 YEARS ON** [48] [ ]
– PSI power / Free fall / Automoton / 25 years / Flying doctor / The only ones / (only) The dead dreams of the cold war kid / The age of the micro man. *(re-iss. Aug82; CHC 10) (cd-iss. Apr89 on 'Virgin'; CDS4014)*

Oct 78. (7") *(CB 323)* **PSI POWER. / DEATH TRAP** [ ] [–]

Dec 78. (7") *<CAS 701>* **PSI POWER. / ('A'extended)** [–] [ ]

Mar 79. (7") *(CB 332)* **25 YEARS. / (ONLY) THE DEAD DREAMS OF THE COLD WAR KID** [ ] [ ]
(12"grey+=) *(CB 332-12)* – P.X.R. 5.

HAWKWIND

recorded '78 by **BROCK, TURNER, SHAW, KING / + HAYLES**

May 79. (lp/c) *(CDS 4016)* **P.X.R. 5** [59] [–]
– Death trap / Jack of shadows / Uncle Sam's on Mars / Infinity / Life form / Robot / High rise / P.X.R. 5. *(re-iss. Mar84; CHC 25) (cd-iss. Apr89 on 'Virgin'; CDSCD 4016)*

— **HAWKWIND** in 1979 were **SIMON KING** – drums returned from QUASAR, to repl. GRIFFITHS in Dec78 (CALVERT left to go solo). **TIM BLAKE** – keyboards (ex-GONG) repl. SWINDELLS who went solo

— added **HUW-LLOYD LANGTON** – guitar who returned from QUASAR

— now:- **BROCK, LANGTON, BAINBRIDGE, KING + BLAKE**

Bronze not iss.

Jul 80. (lp/c) *(BRON/TCBRON 527)* **LIVE 1979 (live)** [15] [–]
– Shot down in the night / Motorway city / Spirit of the age / Brainstorm / Lighthouse / Master of the universe / Silver machine (requiem). *(cd-iss. Feb92 on 'Castle'; CLACD 243) (cd re-iss. Jul99 on 'Essential'; ESMCD 735)*

Jul 80. (7") *(BRO 98)* **SHOT DOWN IN THE NIGHT (live). / URBAN GUERILLA (live)** [59] [–]

— **GINGER BAKER** – drums (ex-CREAM, ex-BLIND FAITH, ex-AIRFORCE etc) repl. KING who teamed up with SWINDELLS

Nov 80. (7") *(BRO 109)* **WHO'S GONNA WIN THE WAR. / NUCLEAR TOYS** [ ] [ ]

Nov 80. (blue-lp/c) *(BRON/TCBRON 530)* **LEVITATION** [21] [–]
– Levitation / Motorway city / Psychosis / World of tiers / Prelude / Who's gonna win the war / Space chase / The 5th second forever / Dust of time. *(re-iss. Jul87 on 'Castle' lp/cd; CLA/+CD 129) (cd-iss. Jul99 on 'Essential'; ESMCD 736)*

— **MARTIN GRIFFIN** – drums returned to repl. BAKER / **KEITH HALE** – keyboards repl. BLAKE

RCA Active not iss.

Oct 81. (7") *(RCA 137)* **ANGELS OF DEATH. / TRANS-DIMENSIONAL** [ ] [–]

Oct 81. (lp/c) *(RCA LP/K 6004)* **SONIC ATTACK** [19] [–]
– Sonic attack / Rocky paths / Psychosonia / Virgin of the world / Angels of death / Living on a knife edge / Coded languages / Disintigration / Streets of fear / Lost chances. *(cd-iss. Nov97 on 'Emergency Broadcast'; EBSCD 123)*

May 82. (lp/c) *(RCA LP/K 9004)* **CHURCH OF HAWKWIND** [26] [–]
– Angel voices / Nuclear drive / Star cannibal / The phenomena of luminosity / Fall of Earth city / The church / The joker at the gate / Some people never die / Light specific data / Experiment with destiny / The last Messiah / Looking in the future. *(cd-iss. Jun94 on 'Dojo')*

— **NIK TURNER** – vocals, saxophone returned to repl. HALE

Aug 82. (7"/7"pic-d) *(RCA/+P 267)* **SILVER MACHINE (remix). / PSYCHEDELIC WARLORDS (remix)** [ ] [–]

Oct 82. (lp/c) *(RCA LP/K 6055)* **CHOOSE YOUR MASQUES** [29] [–]
– Choose your masques / Dream worker / Arrival in Utopia / Utopia / Silver machine / Void city / Solitary mind games / Fahrenheit 451 / The scan / Waiting for tomorrow. *(cd-iss. Nov97 on 'Emergency Broadcast'; EBSCD 124)*

Flicknife not iss.

Oct 83. (lp) *(SHARP 014)* **ZONES** (live, with other 80's line-ups) [57] [–]
– Zones / Dangerous vision / Running through the back brain / The island / Motorway city / Utopia 84 / Society alliance / Sonic attack / Dream worker / Brainstorm. *(re-iss. Mar84 on pic-lp; PSHARP 014)*

Oct 83. (7") *(FLS 025)* **MOTORWAY CITY (live). / MASTER OF THE UNIVERSE (live)** [ ] [–]

Jan 84. (7") *(7FLEP 104)* **NIGHT OF THE HAWKS. / GREEN FINNED DEMON** [ ] [–]
(12"ep+=) *(FLEP 104)* - **THE EARTH RITUAL PREVIEW** – Dream dancers / Dragons + fables.

Nov 84. (lp) *(SHARP 022)* **STONEHENGE: THIS IS HAWKWIND, DO NOT PANIC** [ ] [–]
– Psy power / Levitation / Circles / Space chase / Death trap / Angels of death / Shot down in the night / Stonehenge decoded / Watching the grass grow. *(cd-iss. May92 on 'Anagram'; CDM GRAM 54)*

— **ALAN DAVEY** – bass, vocals repl. BAINBRIDGE and TURNER / **CLIVE DEAMER** – drums repl. GRIFFIN

Nov 85. (lp/c/cd) *(SHARP 033/+C/CD)* **CHRONICLE OF THE BLACK SWORD** [65] [–]
– Song of the swords / Shade gate / The sea king / The pulsing cavern / Elric the enchanter / Needle gun / Zarozinia / The demise / Sleep of a thousand tears / Chaos army / Horn of destiny. *(cd-iss. w / 3 extra tracks) (re-iss. cd Aug92 on 'Dojo'; DPJPCD 72)*

Nov 85. (7") *(FLS 032)* **NEEDLE GUN. / ARIOCH** [ ] [–]
(12"+=) *(FLST 032)* – Song of the swords.

Mar 86. (7") *(FLS 033)* **ZAROZINIA. / ASSAULT AND BATTERY** [ ] [–]
(12"+=) *(FLST 033)* – Sleep of a 1000 tears.

— **HAWKWIND** are now **BROCK**, as DR. HASBEEN – vocals, guitar, keyboards, synthesizers, **LANGTON, DAVEY, BAINBRIDGE** now vocals, keyboards, synthesizer and **DANNY THOMPSON** – drums, percussion, vocals

G.W.R. Roadrunner

May 88. (lp/c/cd) *(GW/+C/CD 26)* **THE XENON CODEX** [79] 1989 [ ]
– The war I survived / Wastelands of sleep / Neon skyline / Lost chronicles / Tides / Heads / Mutation zone / E.M.C. / Sword of the east / Good evening. *<US-iss. on pic-d> (cd re-iss. Jul99 on 'Essential'; ESMCD 737)*

— **BROCK, BAINBRIDGE, DAVEY** plus **SIMON HOUSE, RICHARD CHADWICK & BRIDGETT WISHART**

Oct 90. (lp/c/cd) *(GW/+C/CD 103)* **SPACE BANDITS** [70] [–]
– Images / Black elk speaks / Wings / Out of the shadows / Realms / Ship of dreams / TV suicide. *(re-iss. cd Feb92 on 'Castle'; CLACD 282) (cd re-iss. Jul99 on 'Essential'; ESMCD 738)*

Essential not iss.

May 92. (cd/c/d-lp) *(ESSCD/ESSMC/ESSD 181)* **ELECTRIC TEPEE** [53] [–]
– LSD / Blue shift / Death of war / The secret agent / Garden pests / Space dust / Snake dance / Mask of the morning / Rites of Netherworld / Don't understand / Sadness runs deep / Right to decide / Going to Hawaii / Electric teepee. *(re-iss. Jul95 on 'Dojo'; DOJOCD 244) (cd re-iss. May00; ESMCD 885)*

Oct 93. (cd/c/lp) *(ESD CD/MC/LP 196)* **IT IS THE BUSINESS OF THE FUTURE TO BE DANGEROUS** [75] [ ]
– It's the business of the future to be dangerous / Space is their (Palestine) / Tibet is not China (pt.1 & 2) / Let barking dogs lie / Wave upon wave / Letting in the past / The camera that could lie / 3 or 4 erections during the course of the night / Technotropic zone exists / Give me shelter / Avante. *(cd re-iss. Jul99; ESMCD 740)*

4 Real not iss.

Jun 93. (12"ep/c-ep/cd-ep) *(4R 1 T/CS/D)* **SPIRIT OF THE AGE (The Solstice remixes)** [ ] [–]
– (Full Vocal / Hard Trance / Cyber Trance / Flesh To Phantasy)

Nov 93. (12"ep/cd-ep) *(4R 2 T/D)* **DECIDE YOUR FUTURE EP** [ ] [–]
– Right to decide / The camera that could lie / Right to decide (radio edit mix) / Assassin (Magick Carpet mix).

Emergency not iss.

Sep 94. (12"ep/cd-ep) *(EBT/+D 110)* **QUARK, STRANGENESS AND CHARM** [ ] [–]
– Uncle Sam's on Mars (Red Planet radio mix) / Quark, strangeness and charm / Black sun / Uncle Sam's on Mars (Martian Conquest mix).

Sep 94. (cd/c/d-lp) *(EBS CD/MC/LP 111)* **THE BUSINESS TRIP (live)** [ ] [–]
– Altair / Quark, strangeness and charm / LSD / The camera that would lie / Green finned demon / Do that / The day a wall came down / Berlin axis / Void of golden light / Right stuff / Wastelands / The dream goes on / Right to decide / The dream has ended / The future / Terra mystica.

Sep 95. (12"ep/cd-ep) *(EB T/CD 107)* **AREA S.4.** [ ] [–]
– Alien / Sputnik Stan / Medley: Death trap – Wastelands of sleep – Dream has . . ..

Oct 95. (cd/lp) *(EB SCD/LP 118)* **ALIEN 4** [ ] [–]
– Abducted / Alien (I am) / Reject your human touch / Blue skin / Beam me up / Vega / Xenomorph / Journey / Sputnik Stan / Kapal /

Festivals / Deah trap / Wastelands / Are you losing your mind? / Space sex.

May 96. (cd/lp) *(EBS CD/LP 120)* **LOVE IN SPACE (live October 1995)** –
– Abducted / Death trap / Wastelands / Are you losing your mind? / Photo encounter / Blue skin / Robot / Alien I am / Sputnik Stan / Xenomorph / Vega / Love in space / Kapal / Elfin / Silver machine / Welcome.

– compilations, etc. –

1973. (d7") *United Artists;* **HURRY ON SUNDOWN. / MASTER OF THE UNIVERSE/ / SILVER MACHINE. / ORGONE ACCUMULATOR** –

Apr 76. (lp) *United Artists; (UAK 29919)* **ROADHAWKS** 34
– Hurry on sundown / Paranoia (excerpt) / You shouldn't do that (live) / Silver machine (live) / Urban guerilla / Space is deep / Wind of change / The golden void. *(re-iss. Apr84 on 'Fame' lp/c; FA 413096-1/-4)*

Feb 77. (lp) *United Artists; (UAG 30025)* **MASTERS OF THE UNIVERSE** –
– Master of the universe / Brainstorm / Sonic attack / Orgone accumulator / It's so easy / Lost Johnnie. *(re-iss. May82 on 'Fame' lp/c; FA/C 3008) (re-iss. Jun87 & Dec95 on 'Liberty' lp/c; EMS/TCEMS 1258) (re-iss. May89 on 'Fame' lp/c/cd; FA/TCFA/CDFA 3220) (re-iss. Jul90 on 'Marble Arch' c/cd; CMA/+CD 129) (re-iss. Jul94 on 'Success' cd/c;) (cd-iss. Apr97 on 'Spalax'; 14972)*

Sep 80. (lp/c) *Charisma; (BG/+C 2)* **REPEAT PERFORMANCE** –
– Kerb crawler / Back on the streets / Quark strangeness and charm / Spirit of the age / Steppenwolf / 25 years / PSI power / The only ones / High rise / Uncle Sam's on Mars.

May 81. (12"ep; as HAWKWIND ZOO) *Flicknife; (FLEP 100)* **HURRY ON SUNDOWN. / SWEET MISTRESS OF PAIN / KINGS OF SPEED (live)** –
(re-iss. Dec83)

Jul 81. (7"/12") *Flicknife; (FLS/+EP 205)* **MOTORHEAD. / VALIUM TEN** –
(re-iss. 12" Oct82)

Nov 81. (12"ep; as SONIC ASSASSINS) *Flicknife; (FLEP 101)* **OVER THE TOP. / FREEFALL / DEATH TRAP** –

Mar 82. (lp) *Flicknife; (SHARP 001)* **FRIENDS & RELATIONS** –
(1/2 live '77-78, 1/2 studio '82)
(re-iss. Nov83) (re-iss. Nov94 on 'Emporio' cd/c)

Jun 82. (7"; as HAWKLORDS) *Flicknife; (FLS 209)* **WHO'S GONNA WIN THE WAR. / TIME OFF** –

Feb 83. (7") *Flicknife; (FLS 14)* **HURRY ON SUNDOWN. / LORD OF THE HORNETS / DODGEM DUKE** –

Mar 83. (d-c) *Charisma; (CASMC 110)* **QUARK, STRANGENESS & CHARM / PXR 5** –
(re-iss. '88)

1983. (lp) *Flicknife; (SHARP 107)* **TWICE UPON A TIME: HAWKWIND FRIENDS AND RELATIONS VOL.2** –

Jul 83. (d-lp) *Illuminated; (JAMS 29)* **TEXT OF FESTIVAL (live '70-72)** –
(1-lp re-iss. Jul85 as 'IN THE BEGINNING' on 'Demi Monde'; DM 005) (re-iss. cd Mar94 on 'Charly') (re-iss. Dec88 on 'Thunderbolt'; THBL 2.068) (cd-iss. first 3 sides) (cd re-iss. Mar97; CDTB 068)

Jun 84. (10"m-lp) *Flicknife; (SHARP 109)* **INDEPENDENTS DAY** –

Nov 84. (d-lp/d-c) *A.P.K.; (APK/+C 8)* **SPACE RITUAL 2 (live)** –
(cd-iss. 1987 on 'The CD Label'; CDTL 003)

Feb 85. (lp) *Demi-Monde; (DM 002)* **BRING ME THE HEAD OF YURI GAGARIN** (live '73 Empire Pool) –
(cd-iss. Nov86 on 'Charly'; CDCHARLY 40) (cd-iss. Nov92 on 'Thunderbolt'; CDTB 101) (cd re-iss. Apr97 on 'Spalax'; 14846)

Feb 85. (lp) *Flicknife; (SHARP 024)* **HAWKWIND, FRIENDS AND RELATIONS VOL.3** –
(c-iss.Apr84 with VOL.1 on reverse; *SHARP C1024) (other c-iss.Apr84 with VOL.2 on reverse; SHARP C2024)*

Jul 85. (lp) *Dojo; (DOJOLP 11)* **LIVE 70-73 (live)** –

May 85. (lp) *Mausoleum; (SKULL 8333369)* **UTOPIA 1984** –

Nov 85. (lp) *Mausoleum; (SKULL 83103)* **WELCOME TO THE FUTURE** –

Nov 85. (lp) *Obsession; (OBLP 1)* **RIDICULE** –
(re-iss. of disc 2 of 'SPACE RITUAL') (re-iss. 1990 cd/lp; OBSESS CD/LP 1)

Nov 85. (lp/pic-lp)(cd) *Samurai; (SAMR 038/+PD)(SAMRCD 038)* **ANTHOLOGY – HAWKWIND VOL.1** –
(cd+=) – Silver machine. *(re-iss. pic-lp.Nov86 as 'APPROVED HISTORY OF HAWKWIND'; SAMR 046) (re-iss. Apr90 as 'ACID DAZE 1' on 'Receiver'; RR 125)*

Mar 86. (lp/cd)(c) *Samurai; (SAMR/+CD 039)(TCSAMR 039)* **ANTHOLOGY – HAWKWIND VOL. 2** –
(cd-iss. 1986 extra 4 tracks) (re-iss. Apr90 as 'ACID DAZE 2' on 'Receiver'; RR 126)

May 86. (7"/7"sha-pic-d) *Samurai; (HW 7001/001)* **SILVER MACHINE. / MAGNU** –
(12"+=) *(HW12-001)* – Angels of death.

Jul 86. (7") *Flicknife; (FLS 034-A)* **MOTORHEAD. / HURRY ON SUNDOWN** –

Jul 86. (lp/c) *Samurai; (SAMR 040/+TC)* **ANTHOLOGY – HAWKWIND VOL.3** –
(re-iss. Apr90 as 'ACID DAZE 3' on 'Receiver'; RR 127)

Jul 86. (lp) *Hawkfan; (HWFB 2)* **HAWKFAN 12** –

Sep 86. (d-lp/d-c/cd) *Castle; (CCS LP/MC/CD 148)* **THE HAWKWIND COLLECTION (Pts. 1 & 2)** –
(cd-iss. Dec86 omits some tracks)

Nov 86. (lp/c) *Flicknife; (SHARP 036/+C)* **INDEPENDENTS DAY VOL.2** –

Jan 87. (lp/c) *R.C.A.; (NL/NK 71150)* **ANGELS OF DEATH** –

Apr 87. (lp/c/cd) *Flicknife; (SHARP 040/+C/CD)* **OUT AND INTAKE** –
(cd+=) – (2 extra tracks).

Sep 87. (lp/c/cd) *Start; (STF L/C/CD 2)* **BRITISH TRIBAL MUSIC** –

Oct 87. (3xbox-pic-lp) *Flicknife; (HWBOX 1)* **OFFICIAL PICTURE LOGBOOK** –
– ('STONEHENGE' / 'BLACK SWORD' / 'OUT & INTAKE' / '(interview)' lp *(cd-iss. Nov94 on 'Dojo';)*

Dec 87. (lp/c) *Thunderbolt; (THBL/THBC 044)* **EARLY DAZE (THE BEST OF HAWKWIND)** –
(cd-iss. Jun88; CDTB CDTB 044)

Sep 88. (cd) *Virgin; (COMCD 8)* **SPIRIT OF THE AGE** –
(re-iss. Oct91 on 'Elite'; ELITE 021CD) (re-iss. Sep 93)

Nov 88. (cd) *Flicknife; (SHARP 1422CD)* **ZONES / STONEHENGE** –

Nov 88. (cd) *Flicknife; (SHARP 1724CD)* **BEST OF HAWKWIND, FRIENDS & RELATIONS** –

Dec 88. (d-lp/cd) *Flicknife; (SHARP 2045/+CD)* **THE TRAVELLERS AID TRUST** –

Dec 88. (d-lp/d-cd) *That's Original; (TFO 17/+CD)* **LEVITATION / HAWKWIND LIVE** –

Mar 89. (cd) *Avanti; (ISTCD 004)* **IRONSTRIKE** –

May 89. (lp) *Legacy; (GWSP 1)* **LIVE CHRONICLES** –
(re-iss. Feb92 cd/c on 'Castle; CCS CD/MC 123) (cd re-iss. Sep00 on 'Essential'; CMDDD 013)

May 89. (lp/c/cd) *Powerhouse; (POW/+C/CD 5502)* **NIGHT OF THE HAWK** –
(cd-iss. has 3 extra tracks)

1990. (cd/c) *Action Replay; (ARLC/CDAR 1018)* **BEST AND THE REST OF HAWKWIND** –

Mar 90. (2xcd-box)(3xlp-box) *Receiver; (RRDCD 1X)(RRBX 1)* **ACID DAZE (re-issue)** –
(3 VOLUMES re-iss. cd Jul93)

May 90. (cd)(c/lp) *E.M.I.; (CDP 746694-2)(TC+/NTS 300)* **STASIS, THE U.A. YEARS 1971-1975** –
– Urban guerilla / Psychedelic warlords (disappear in smoke) / Brainbox pollution / 7 by 7 / Paradox / Silver machine / You'd better believe it / Lord of light / The black corridor (live) / Space is deep (live) / You shouldn't do that (live). *(re-iss. cd Dec95 on 'Fame')*

Dec 90. (12"blue-ep) *Receiver; (REPLAY 3014)* **THE EARLY YEARS LIVE** –
– Silver machine / Spirit of the age / Urban guerilla / Born to go.

1990. (c) *Capitol; <4XLL 57286>* **METAL CLASSICS 2: BEST OF HAWKWIND** –

1990. (cd/c) *Knight; (KN CD/MC 10017)* **NIGHT RIDING** –

Jun 91. (lp/c/cd) *G.W.R.; (GW/+MC/CD 104)* **PALACE SPRINGS** –
– (remixed tracks from 'WARRIORS . . . ' & 'XENON . . .) *(re-iss. cd Jul92 on 'Castle'; CLACD 303) (cd re-iss. Jul99 on 'Essential'; ESMCD 739)*

Oct 91. (cd/c) *Windsong; (WIN CD/MC 007)* **BBC RADIO 1 LIVE IN CONCERT (live)** –

Feb 92. (3xcd-box) *Castle; (CLABX 911)* **3 ORIGINALS** –

Feb 92. (cd) *Raw Fruit; (FRSCD 005)* **THE FRIDAY ROCK SHOW SESSIONS (live '86)** –

Jun 92. (cd) *Anagram; (GRAM 53)* **MIGHTY HAWKWIND CLASSICS 1980-1985** –

Aug 92. (cd) *Dojo; (DOJOCD 71)* **HAWKLORDS LIVE** –

Apr 94. (cd) *Cleopatra; (CLEO 57732)* **LORD OF LIGHT** –

Apr 94. (cd) *Cleopatra; (CLEO 57412)* **PSYCHEDELIC WARLORDS** ☐ ⊟
Dec 94. (cd) *Cyclops; (CYCL 021)* **CALIFORNIA BRAINSTORM** ☐ ⊟
Feb 95. (cd) *Emergency Broadcast; (EMBSCD 114)* **UNDISCLOSED FILES – ADDENDUM** ☐ ⊟
Mar 95. (cd) *Anagram; (CDMGRAM 91)* **THE RARITIES . . .** ☐ ⊟
May 95. (cd) *Spectrum; (550764-2)* **SILVER MACHINE** ☐ ⊟
Oct 95. (cd) *Anagram; (CDGRAM 94)* **INDEPENDENTS DAY VOLUMES 1 & 2** ☐ ⊟
Mar 97. (cd) *Emporio; (EMPRCD 710)* **ONWARD FLIES THE BIRD – LIVE AND RARE** ☐ ⊟
Jul 97. (cd-ep) *E.B.S.; (EBCD 106)* **LOVE IN SPACE / LORD OF LIGHT / SONIC ATTACK** ☐ ⊟
Sep 97. (d-cd) *Snapper; (SMDCD 121)* **AMBIENT ANARCHISTS** ☐ ⊟
Nov 97. (cd/lp) *Emergency Broadcast; (EBS CD/LP 117)* **RITUAL OF THE SOLSTICE** ☐ ⊟
Nov 97. (cd) *Emergency Broadcast; (EBSCD 139)* **DISTANT HORIZONS** ☐ ⊟
Nov 97. (d-cd) *E.M.I.; (HAWKS 6)* **1999 PARTY** ☐ ⊟
Mar 98. (cd) *Eagle; (EABCD 084)* **THE MASTERS** ☐ ⊟
Apr 98. (cd) *Cleopatra; <(CLEO 2202)>* **WELCOME TO THE FUTURE** ☐ ⊟
Sep 98. (cd) *Repertoire; (REP 4676)* **SONIC BOOM KILLERS** ☐ ⊟
Sep 98. (d-cd) *Essential; (<ESDCD 664>)* **ANTHOLOGY** ☐ ☐
Feb 99. (cd) *Cleopatra; <(CLP 0471-2)>* **GOLDEN VOID 1969-1979** ☐ ☐
Mar 99. (lp) *Black Widow; (BWR/+CD 026)* **THE ELF AND THE HAWK** ☐ ⊟
Apr 99. (cd) *Blueprint; (BP 309CD)* **THE DAWN OF HAWKWIND** ☐ ⊟
May 99. (cd) *Anagram; (CDMGRAM 61)* **THE BEST OF FRIENDS AND RELATIONS** ☐ ⊟
May 99. (4xcd-box) *Dressed To Kill; (REDTK 98)* **ENTIRE AND INFINITE** ☐ ⊟
– (MASTERS OF THE UNIVERSE / BRING ME THE HEAD OF URI GAGARIN / SPACE RITUAL / TEXT OF FESTIVAL)
Jun 99. (cd) *Thunderbolt; (CDTB 099)* **SPACE RITUAL VOL.2** ☐ ⊟
Aug 99. (cd) *EMI; (521747-2)* **EPOCH – ECLIPSE (THE ULTIMATE BEST OF HAWKWIND)** ☐ ⊟
Aug 99. (3xcd-box) *EMI; (521751-2)* **EPOCH – ECLIPSE 30 YEAR ANTHOLOGY** ☐ ⊟
Nov 99. (cd) *Hawkwind; (HAWKVP 1CD)* **LIVE AT THE GLASTONBURY FESTIVAL 1990** ☐ ⊟
Nov 99. (cd) *Hawkwind; (HAWKVP 2CD)* **GREASY TRUCKERS (live at the Roundhouse 1972)** ☐ ⊟
Nov 99. (d-cd) *Hawkwind; (HAWKVP 3CD)* **COLLECTORS SERIES VOL.1** ☐ ⊟
Dec 99. (d-cd) *Hawkwind; (HAWKCD 4CD)* **COLLECTORS SERIES VOL.2** ☐ ⊟
Apr 00. (cd) *Hawkwind; (HAWKVP 5CD)* **ATOM HENGE** ☐ ⊟
Apr 00. (d-cd) *Hawkwind; (HAWKVP 13CD)* **LIVE IN NOTTINGHAM 1990** ☐ ⊟
Apr 00. (cd) *Hawkwind; (HAWKVP 17CD)* **IN YOUR AREA** ☐ ⊟
Jul 00. (d-cd) *Burning Airlines; (PILOT 033)* **YEAR 2000 – CODENAME HAWKWIND VOL.1 (live)** ☐ ⊟
Jul 00. (cd) *Burning Airlines; (PILOT 064)* **LIVE FROM THE DARKSIDE** ☐ ⊟
Jul 00. (d-cd) *Cleopatra; <(CLP 850)>* **THE STONEHENGE COLLECTION** ☐ ☐

Isaac HAYES

Born: 20 Aug'38, Covington, Tennessee, USA. As a teenager he moved to Memphis, where he learned to play sax and piano. He was soon invited to session for the 'Stax' label in the mid-60's, eventually forming a writing partnership with DAVID PORTER. The pair were highly successful, going on to pen for 'Stax' artists such as OTIS REDDING, SAM & DAVE, EDDIE FLOYD and CARLA THOMAS. After a rambling, jazz-based debut album in 1968, the follow-up, 'HOT BUTTERED SOUL' (1969), gave him a US Top 10 placing and gained widespread respect from critics for its highly original interpretations of standards like JIMMY WEBB's 'BY THE TIME I GET TO PHOENIX'. Establishing himself as the original medallion man, self-styled love-God HAYES created sophisticated mood pieces; stretching songs over seemingly unfeasible, elaborately orchestrated lengths, the singer patented a breathy, often spoken, vocal style, his black velvet tones proving a hit with fans of easy listening, jazz, R&B, pop and rock. Subsequent efforts like 'TO BE CONTINUED' (1970) and 'BLACK MOSES' (1972) followed the same formula although in late '71, his score for blaxploitation movie, 'SHAFT' provided him with an international smash hit in the wah wah-funk of the main theme. Both the single and the soundtrack album itself toppped the American charts, the latter winning an academy award. Its success spawned a glut of similar films such as BLACK CAESAR (scored by JAMES BROWN) and SUPERFLY (scored by CURTIS MAYFIELD), HAYES himself issuing two further soundtracks on 'Stax', 'TOUGH GUYS' (1974) and TRUCK TURNER (1974) as well as releasing a theme from US cop TV series 'The Men' in 1972. The singer left 'Enterprise-Stax' in 1975 following a disagreement over non-payment of royalties, signing to 'A.B.C.' the same year. As he experimented with disco (a genre he'd laid the foundations for), however, his work lost its impact and amid mediocre album sales and bankruptcy in '77, he shifted to 'Polydor'. The move failed to resurrect his flagging career and in the 80's, after serving a brief jail term for drug offences, he became more interested in film acting. HAYES had previously acted in the likes of 'TRUCK TURNER' as well as appearing in 'The Rockford Files' in 1977 with DIONNE WARWICK (with whom he also recorded an album of duets the same year). 1981 saw him playing a baddie (what else!) in the film 'Escape From New York' while the mid-80's were marked by cameo appearances in TV series' 'The A-Team' and 'Hunter'. The HAYES' legend was given a bit of a dusting down in the late 80's when numerous hip hop and house tunes sampled 'THEME FROM SHAFT'. Similarly, in the 90's, trip hop artists like MASSIVE ATTACK, TRICKY and PORTISHEAD borrowed from the singer's back catalogue, coinciding with HAYES' best album since his early 70's heyday, 'BRANDED' (1995). With the singer back on smoking form, he puts in typically elaborate readings of STING's 'FRAGILE' and THE LOVIN' SPOONFUL's 'SUMMER IN THE CITY' (not as ridiculous as it appears on paper) as well as updating classics like 'SOULSVILLE' and 'HYPERBOLICSYLLABICSESQUEDALYMYSTIC'. The latter features a guest spot by PUBLIC ENEMY's CHUCK D, things coming full circle and illustrating the pivotal influence of HAYES on the development of rap. Of recent times, HAYES has contributed his deep-throated larynx as CHEF to adult(!?) animation, 'South Park'. He was even even back in the charts with the team's 'Chocolate Salty Balls'; who killed ISAAC? • **Covers:** WALK ON BY + THE LOOK OF LOVE (Bacharach-David) / I STAND ACCUSED (Jerry Butler) / NEVER CAN SAY GOODBYE (Jackson 5) / YOU'VE LOST THAT LOVIN' FEELIN' (Righteous Brothers) / LET'S STAY TOGETHER (Al Green) / HEY GIRL (Freddie Scott) / LET'S GO OUT TONIGHT (Blue Nile) / etc.

Album rating: PRESENTING ISAAC HAYES (*5) / HOT BUTTERED SOUL (*9) / THE ISAAC HAYES MOVEMENT (*8) / TO BE CONTINUED (*6) / SHAFT soundtrack (*7) / BLACK MOSES (*5) / LIVE AT THE SAHARA TAHOE (*4) / JOY (*5) / TOUGH GUYS (*4) / TRUCK TURNER (*4) / CHOCOLATE CHIP (*6) / THE BEST OF ISAAC HAYES compilation (*6) / DISCO CONNECTION (*4) / GROOVE-A-THON (*3) / JUICY FRUIT (DISCO FREAK) (*3) / A MAN AND A WOMAN with Dionne Warwick (*3) / NEW HORIZON (*3) / FOR THE SAKE OF LOVE (*3) / DON'T LET GO (*4) / ROYAL RAPPIN'S with Millie Jackson (*4) / AND ONCE AGAIN (*4) / LIFETIME THING (*4) / U-TURN (*4) / LOVE ATTACK (*4) / ISAAC'S MOODS – THE BEST OF ISAAC HAYES compilation (*8) / BRANDED (*6) / THE MAN! – THE ULTIMATE ISAAC HAYES 1969-1977 compilation (*8)

ISAAC HAYES – vocals, keyboards, etc. with Stax session men **DUCK DUNN + AL JACKSON**

Stax | Enterprise

1968. (lp) <*13100*> **PRESENTING ISAAC HAYES** [–] [ ]
– Precious, precious / When I fall in love / I just want to make love to me / Rock me baby / Going to Chicago blues / Misty / You don't know like I know. *<re-iss. Mar72 as 'IN THE BEGINNING' on 'Atlantic'; 1599>*

1968. (7") <*ENA 002*> **GOING TO CHICAGO BLUES. / PRECIOUS PRECIOUS** [–] [ ]

Oct 69. (lp) *(SXATS 1028)* <*1001*> **HOT BUTTERED SOUL** [ ] Jul69 [8]
– Walk on by / Hyperbollesyllacisce squelalymistc / One woman / By the time I get to Phoenix. *(re-iss. Aug71; 2325 011) (re-iss. Aug81 lp/c; STAXL/STAXK 5002) (re-iss. Nov87; SXE 005) (cd-iss. Jun91 on 'Stax-Ace')*

Sep 69. (7") *(STAX 133)* <*ENA 9003*> **BY THE TIME I GET TO PHOENIX. / WALK ON BY** [ ] Aug69 [37] [30]

Nov 69. (7") <*ENA 9006*> **THE MISTLETOE AND ME. / WINTER SNOW** [–] Xmas [ ]

May 70. (lp) *(SXATS 1032)* <*1010*> **THE ISAAC HAYES MOVEMENT** [ ] Apr70 [8]
– I stand accused / One big unhappy family / I just don't know what to do with myself / Something. *(re-iss. Aug71; 2325 014) (re-iss. Feb90 cd/lp; CD+/SXE 025)*

Aug 70. (7") *(STAX 154)* <*ENA 9017*> **I STAND ACCUSED. / I JUST DON'T KNOW WHAT TO DO WITH MYSELF** [ ] Jul70 [42]
<re-iss. US 1975>
<other 45's from early to mid'70's were also re-issued>

Dec 70. (lp) *(2325 026)* <*1014*> **TO BE CONTINUED** [ ] Nov70 [11]
– (monologue) / Ike's rap 1 / Our day will come / The look of love / Ike's mood – You've lost that lovin' feelin' / Runnin' out of fools. *(re-iss. Oct81 lp/c; STAX L/K 5008) (cd-iss. Feb91 on 'Stax-Ace')*

Feb 71. (7") <*ENA 9028*> **THE LOOK OF LOVE. / IKE'S MOOD** [–] [79]

May 71. (7") *(2025 020)* **YOU'VE LOST THAT LOVIN' FEELIN'. / OUR DAY WILL COME** [ ] [–]

Sep 71. (7") *(2025 029)* <*ENA 9031*> **NEVER CAN SAY GOODBYE. / I CAN'T HELP IT IF I'M STILL IN LOVE** [ ] May71 [22]

Nov 71. (7") *(2025 069)* <*ENA 9038*> **THEME FROM "SHAFT". / CAFE REGIO'S** [4] Oct71 [1]

Dec 71. (d-lp) *(2659 007)* <*5002*> **SHAFT (Soundtrack)** [17] Aug71 [1]
– Theme from Shaft * / Bumpy's lament / Walk from Regio's / Ellie's love theme / Shaft's cab ride / Cafe Regio's / Early Sunday morning / Be yourself / A friend's place / Soulsville * / No name bar / Bumpy's blues / Shaft strikes again / Do your thing * / (the end theme). *(tracks *= have vocals)*
(above has background vocals by **HOT BUTTERED + SOUL**)

Feb 72. (d-lp) *(2628 004)* <*5003*> **BLACK MOSES** [38] Dec71 [10]
– Never can say goodbye / (They long to be) Close to you / Nothing takes the place of you / Man's temptation / Part time love / Ike's rap – A brand new me / Going in circles / Gonna give you up / Ike's rap 2 – Help me love / Need to belong / Good love / Ike's rap 3 – Your love is so doggone good / For the good times / I'll never fall in love again. *(re-iss. +cd.Sep90 on 'Stax-Ace')*

Feb 72. (7") <*ENA 9042*> **DO YOUR THING. / ELLIE'S LOVE THEME** [–] [30]

Apr 72. (7") **LET'S STAY TOGETHER. / AIN'T THAT LOVING YOU (FOR MORE REASONS THAN ONE)** [ ] [–]

Apr 72. (7") <*ENA 9045*> **LET'S STAY TOGETHER. / SOULSVILLE** [–] [48]

May 72. (7"; by ISAAC HAYES & DAVID PORTER) <*ENA 9049*> **AIN'T THAT LOVING YOU (FOR MORE REASONS THAN ONE). / BABY I'M A WANT YOU** [–] [ ]

Nov 72. (7") *(2025 146)* <*ENA 9058*> **THEME FROM THE MEN. / TYPE THANG** [ ] Oct72 [38]
(above was from US TV cop series, 'The Men')

Jun 73. (d-lp) *(2659 026)* <*5005*> **LIVE AT SAHARA TAHOE (live)** [ ] May73 [14]
– Theme from "Shaft" / The come on / Light my fire / Ike's rap / Never can say goodbye / Windows of the world / The look of love / Ellie's love theme / Use me / Do your thing / Theme from The Men / It's too late / Rock me baby / Stormy Monday blues / Type thang / The first time ever I saw your face / Ike's rap VI / Ain't no sunshine / Feelin' alright. *(re-iss. Nov86 lp/c; MPS/+5 88004) (cd-iss. Oct92)*

Nov 73. (lp) *(2325 111)* <*5007*> **JOY** [ ] Oct73 [16]
– Joy / I love you that's all / A man will be a man / The feeling keeps on coming / I'm gonna make it (without you). *(cd-iss. Jun92)*

Nov 73. (7") *(2025 177)* <*ENA 9065*> **(IF LOVING YOU IS WRONG) I DON'T WANT TO BE RIGHT. / ROLLING DOWN A MOUNTAINSIDE** [ ] [ ]

Dec 73. (7") *(202 5220)* <*ENA 9085*> **JOY (part 1). / JOY (part 2)** [ ] [30]

May 74. (7") <*ENA 9095*> **WONDERFUL. / SOMEONE MADE YOU FOR ME** [–] [71]

Jun 74. (lp) *(STXH 5001)* <*7504*> **TOUGH GUYS (Soundtrack)** [ ] [ ]
– (title theme) / Randolph & Dearborn / The red rooster / Joe Bell / Hung up on my baby / Kidnapped / Run Fay run / Buns o'plenty / (the end theme).

Aug 74. (7") *(STXS 2004)* <*ENA 9104*> **TITLE THEM ('TRUCK TURNER'). / HUNG UP ON MY BABY** [ ] [ ]

Aug 74. (d-lp) *(STXD 4001-2)* <*7507*> **TRUCK TURNER (Soundtrack)** [ ] Jul74 [ ]
– Truck Turner / House of beauty / Blue's crib / Driving in the Sun / You're in my arms again / Give it to me / Drinking / Insurance company / Breakthrough / Now we're one / The duke / Dorinda's party / Pursuit of the pimpmobile / We need each other girl / A house full of girls / Hospital shootout / (end theme).

A.B.C. | A.B.C.

Jun 75. (lp) *(ABCL 5129)* <*874*> **CHOCOLATE CHIP** [ ] [18]
– That loving feeling / Body language / Chocolate chip / Chocolate chip (instrumental) / I want to make love to you so bad / Come live with me / I can't turn around.

Jul 75. (7") *(ABC 4076)* <*12118*> **CHOCOLATE CHIP. / ('A'instrumental)** [ ] [92]

Dec 75. (lp; as ISAAC HAYES MOVEMENT) <*923*> **DISCO CONNECTION** [–] [85]
– The first day of forever / St. Thomas Square / Vykkii / Disco connection / Disco shuffle / Choppers / After five / Aruba.

Feb 76. (7") *(ABC 4100)* <*12171*> **DISCO CONNECTION. / ST. THOMAS SQUARE** [10] [ ]

Feb 76. (lp) *(ABCL 5155)* <*925*> **GROOVE A THON** [ ] [45]
– Groove-a-thon / Your loving is much too strong / Rock me easy baby / We've got a whole lot of love / Wish you were here / Make a little love to me.

Jun 76. (7") *(ABC 4111)* <*12176*> **ROCK ME EASY BABY. / (part 2)** [ ] [ ]

Jul 76. (lp) <*953*> **JUICY FRUIT (DISCO FREAK)** [–] [ ]
– Juicy fruit (disco freak) / Let's don't ever blow our thing / The storm is over / Music to make love by / Thank you love / Lady of the night / Love me or lose me.

Aug 76. (7") *(ABC 4136)* <*12206*> **JUICY FRUIT (DISCO FREAK). / (part 2)** [ ] [ ]

Mar 77. (d-lp; by ISAAC HAYES & DIONNE WARWICK) *(ABCD 613)* <*996*> **A MAN AND A WOMAN** [ ] Feb77 [49]
– Unity / Just don't know what to do with myself / Walk on by / My love / The way I want to touch you – Have you never been mellow – Love will keep us together – I love music – This will be (an everlasting love) – That's the way I like it – Get down tonight / By the time I get to Phoenix / I say a little prayer / Then came you / Feelings / My eyes adored you / Body language / Can't hide love / Come love with me / Once you hit the road / Chocolate chip.

Aug 77. (12") *(ABE12 007)* **DISCO CONNECTION. / CHOCOLATE CHIP** [ ] [–]

not iss. | Stax

Nov 77. (7") <*3209*> **FEEL LIKE MAKIN' LOVE. / (part 2)** [–] [ ]

Polydor | Polydor

Dec 77. (lp) <*6120*> **NEW HORIZON** [–] [78]
– Stranger in Paradise / Moonlight lovin' / Don't take your love away / Out of the ghetto / It's heaven to me.

Jan 78. (7") <*14446*> **OUT OF THE GHETTO. / IT'S HEAVEN TO ME** [–] [ ]

May 78. (7") *(2066 904)* <*14464*> **MOONLIGHT LOVIN'. / IT'S HEAVEN TO ME** [ ] [ ]

Dec 78. (lp) *(2480 475)* <*6164*> **FOR THE SAKE OF LOVE** [ ] Nov78 [75]
– Just the way you are / Believe in me / If we ever needed peace / Shaft II / Zeke the freak / Don't let me be lonely tonight.

Jan 79. (7"/12") *(POSP/+X 23)* **ZEKE THE FREAK. / IF WE EVER NEEDED PEACE** [ ] [ ]

Mar 79. (7") <*14534*> **JUST THE WAY YOU ARE. / (part 2)** [–] [ ]

— (Later '79, he was credited with MILLIE JACKSON on 'Royal Rappin's' album <6229> which hit US No.80)

— Also issued 2 US singles with her on 'Polydor'; DO YOU WANNA MAKE LOVE / I CHANGED MY MIND <2036> and YOU NEVER CROSS MY MIND / FEELS LIKE THE FIRST TIME <2063>

Nov 79. (lp) *(2480 510)* <6224> **DON'T LET GO** ☐ Sep79 39
– Don't let go / What does it take / Few more kisses to go / Fever / Someone who will take the place of you.

Dec 79. (7"/12") *(STEP/+X 4)* <2011> **DON'T LET GO. / YOU CAN'T HOLD YOUR WOMAN** ☐ Oct79 18

Feb 80. (7") *<2068>* **FEW MORE KISSES TO GO. / WHAT DOES IT TAKE** – ☐

May 80. (lp) *(2480 538)* <6269> **AND ONCE AGAIN** ☐ 59
– It's all in the game / Ike's rap VII – This time I'll be sweeter / I ain't ever / Wherever you are / Love has been good to us.

Jun 80. (7") *(2001 965)* <2090> **I AIN'T EVER. / LOVE HAS BEEN GOOD TO US** ☐ ☐

Sep 80. (7") *<2102>* **IT'S ALL IN THE GAME. / WHEREVER YOU ARE** – ☐

Sep 81. (7") *<2182>* **I'M GONNA MAKE ME LOVE YOU. / I'M SO PROUD** – ☐

Sep 81. (lp) *(2311 074)* **LIFETIME THING** ☐ –
– I'm gonna make you love me / Three times a lady / Fugitive / Summer / I'm so proud / Lifetime thing.

Nov 81. (7") *<2192>* **LIFETIME THING. / FUGITIVE** – ☐

— Took time out to concentrate on spiraling acting career. He had previously acted in own soundtrack films, 'Truck Turner', etc. He also appeared in 'The Rockford Files' with DIONNE WARWICK in 1977. In 1981, he plays a baddie (what else!) in the film 'Escape From New York'. In 85-86, he cameod in TV for series 'The A-Team' + 'Hunter'.

(Returned in '86, plays everything)

C.B.S. Columbia

Dec 86. (7") *(650236-7)* <06363> **HEY GIRL. / IKE'S RAP VIII** ☐ ☐
(12"+=) *(650236-6)* – Hey Fred (you need a sunbed).

Dec 86. (lp) *(450 155-1)* <40316> **U-TURN** ☐ ☐
– If you want my lovin' (do me right) / Flash backs / You turn me on / Ike's rap VIII – Hey girl / Doesn't rain in London / Can't take my eyes off you / Thing for you / Thank God for love.

Mar 87. (7") *<06655>* **THING FOR YOU. / THANK GOD FOR LOVE** – ☐

Jun 87. (7") *<07104>* **IF YOU WANT MY LOVIN' (DO ME RIGHT). / (part 2)** – ☐

Jul 88. (7") *<07978>* **SHOWDOWN. / (part 2)** – ☐

Nov 88. (lp/c) *(462515-1/-4/-2)* <FC 40941> **LOVE ATTACK** ☐ Oct88 ☐
– Love attack / Let me be your everything / Showdown / Eye of the storm / Accused rap / I stand accused '88 / She's got a way / Foreplay rap / Love won't let me wait.

Dec 88. (7") *<08116>* **LET ME BE YOUR EVERYTHING. / CURIOUS** – ☐

— He once again appeared in films (i.e. 'Counter Force' + 'The Sofia Conspiracy').

PointBlank Pointblank

May 95. (cd/c/lp) *(VPB CD/TC/LP 24)* **BRANDED** ☐ ☐
– Ike's plea / Life's mood / Fragile / Life's mood II / Summer in the city / Let me love you / I'll do anything (to turn you on) / Thanks to the fool / Branded / Soulsville / Hyperbolicsyllabicsesquedalymistic.

Jun 95. (c-s/12") *(POB C/T 12)* **FRAGILE. / FRAGILE / BIRTH OF SHAFT** ☐ ☐
(cd-s+=) *(POBD 12)* – Let's go out tonight.

Jul 95. (cd/c/lp) *(VPB CD/MC/LP 25)* **RAW AND REFINED** ☐ ☐
– Birth of Shaft / Urban nights / Funkalicious / Tahoe Spring / The night before / Memphis trax / Soul fiddle / Funky junky / You make me live / Making love at the ocean / Southern breeze / Didn't know love was so good / 405.

— ISAAC (as CHEF) hit UK No.1 with the single, 'CHOCOLATE SALTY BALLS (P.S. I LOVE YOU)'

LaFace-Arista LaFace-Arista

Sep 00. (c-s) *(74321 79258-4)* **THEME FROM SHAFT 2000 / (radio mix)** 53 ☐
(12"/cd-s) *(74321 79258-1/-2)* – ('A'side) / ('A'-Karmadelic sex machine mix) / ('A'-Razor'n'Guido Shaft 2000).

– compilations, others, etc. –

on 'Stax' UK / 'Enterprise' US unless mentioned otherwise

Sep 75. (lp) **THE BEST OF ISAAC HAYES** ☐ ☐

Oct 75. (7") *(STX 2035)* **GOOD LOVE 6-9969. / I'M GONNA HAVE TO TELL HER** ☐ –

Nov 75. (lp) **USE ME** ☐ ☐

Mar 76. (lp/c) *Golden Hour; (GH 844)* **THE GOLDEN HOUR OF . . .** ☐ –

1977. (lp) **MEMPHIS MOVEMENT** ☐ ☐

1977. (7") *(STAX 2002)* **THEME FROM SHAFT. / DO YOUR THING** ☐ –

Nov 77. (7") *(STAX 1009)* **THEME FROM SHAFT. / I DON'T WANT TO BE RIGHT** ☐ ☐

1978. (lp) *<4102>* **HOT BED** (rarities) – ☐
(cd-iss. Aug94)

Apr 78. (lp) *(STM 7003)* **THE ISAAC HAYES CHRONICLES** ☐ ☐

Jan 80. (lp) *(STM 7008)* **LIGHT MY FIRE** ☐ –

Nov 80. (d-lp)(c) *(STX 88003)* **HIS GREATEST HITS** ☐ ☐

Oct 81. (lp/c) *(STAX L/K 5012)* **THE BEST OF SHAFT** ☐ ☐
(re-iss. Jun86; 1052504)

Sep 85. (7") *Old Gold; (OG 9528)* **THEME FROM SHAFT. / NEVER CAN SAY GOODBYE** ☐ –

Apr 88. (lp/c/cd) *(SX/SXC/CDSX 011)* **ISAAC'S MOODS – THE BEST OF ISAAC HAYES** ☐ ☐
– Ike's mood / Soulsville / Joy (part 1) / If loving you is wrong I don't want to be right / Never can say goodbye / The theme from Shaft / Ike's rap VI / A brand new me / Do your thing / Walk on by / I stand accused. *(cd+=)* – Ike's rap I / Hyperbolic-syllabic-sesquedaly-mystic / Ike's rap III / Ike's rap II.

May 89. (7") *Southbound; (SEWS 701))* **THEME FROM SHAFT. / THEME FROM THE MEN** ☐ –
(12"+=) *(SEWT 701)* – Theme from The Men / Type thang.
(cd-s++=) *(CDSEW 701)* – Walk on by.

Aug 93. (d-cd) **TOUGH GUYS / TRUCK TURNER** ☐ ☐

Mar 95. (cd) *Connoisseur; (VSOPCD 210)* **THE COLLECTION** ☐ –

Sep 98. (cd) *Polydor; (529487-2)* **THE BEST OF THE POLYDOR YEARS** ☐ ☐

Oct 98. (cd) *Stax; (CDSXK 124)* **THE BEST OF ISAAC HAYES** ☐ ☐

Aug 00. (cd) *Universal; <(544318-2)>* **OUT OF THE GHETTO: THE POLYDOR YEARS** ☐ ☐

Apr 01. (d-cd) *Stax; (CDSXE 2133)* **THE MAN! THE ULTIMATE ISAAC HAYES 1969-1977** ☐ –
– Ike's mood 1 / Walk on by / Never can say goodbye / Feel like making love / Do your thing / Joy / I can't turn around / Disco connection / Chocolate chip / Storm is over / I stand accused / Ike's rap 2 / Theme from Shaft / The from The Men / Good love / Wonderful / Rolling down a mountainside / Black Moses (radio ad) / Part time love / By the time I get to Phoenix / The look of love.

Apr 01. (cd) *Stax; (SCD 248515)* **GREATEST HIT SINGLES** ☐ –

☐ Michael HEAD (see under ⇒ SHACK)

☐ HEADS (see under ⇒ TALKING HEADS)

HEART

Formed: Vancouver, Canada . . . 1975 by sisters ANN and NANCY WILSON, who had graduated from Seattle groups The ARMY and WHITE HEART. In these line-ups were brothers ROGER and MIKE FISHER, the respective boyfriends of ANN and NANCY. The latter had arrived from the solo-folk scene to replace MIKE, who became their sound engineer, the group moving to Vancouver to avoid his draft papers. With bassist STEVE FOSSEN completing the line-up, the group named themselves HEART and were duly signed to the local 'Mushroom' label by owner Shelley Siegal, issuing their well-received debut album, 'DREAMBOAT ANNIE', in 1976. With the help of two US Top 40 singles, 'MAGIC MAN' and 'CRAZY ON YOU', the album made the American Top 10, its JEFFERSON STARSHIP meets LED ZEPPELIN folky pop/rock sound sitting well with FM radio. Following the record's success, HEART returned to Seattle in late '76 and inked a new deal with 'CBS-Portrait', Mushroom promptly sueing them for breach of contract. Despite the legal hassles, the group ploughed on, adding keyboardist HOWARD LEESE and permanent drummer

MICHAEL DEROSIER for the 'LITTLE QUEEN' (1977) album. A heavier affair, the record was another critical and commercial success, spawning the hard rocking single, 'BARRACUDA'. While punk precluded any real UK success, the band were consistently popular in the States, the rock babe glamour of the WILSON sisters and impressive vocal acrobatics of younger sibling ANNE marking them out from the AOR pack. In 1978, a Seattle judge gave Mushroom the rights to issue their out-takes album, 'MAGAZINE', but ruled that the group could re-record it. Inevitably, the record was a patchy affair, although it surprised many, even the band themselves, by making the Top 20. Later that year, their fourth album, 'DOG AND BUTTERFLY' was another Top 20 success, their last for 'Portrait' as the band underwent personal upheavals and signed a new deal with 'Epic'. The FLEETWOOD MAC-style inter-band relationship problems resulted in ROGER FISHER departing, and though 'BEBE LE STRANGE' (1980) wasn't quite 'Rumours', it was an improvement on their previous effort. The line-up remained unsettled, however, as the band went through a kind of mid-period slump, MARK ANDES and DENNY CARMASI having replaced FOSSEN and DEROSIER respectively by the release of 'PASSIONWORKS' (1983). This album signalled the end of their tenure with 'Epic', although HEART's fortunes were given a bit of a boost when ANN WILSON duetted with LOVERBOY's MIKE RENO on the Top 10 hit single, 'ALMOST PARADISE' (used in the film 'FOOTLOOSE'). Signing a new deal with 'Capitol', the band rose phoenix-like to top the American charts with the eponymous 'HEART' in 1985. Full of gleaming, MTV-friendly power ballads (i.e.'THESE DREAMS', 'WHAT ABOUT LOVE'), the band had practically re-invented themselves and had the leather'n'lace-style soft-rock market well and truly cornered. 'BAD ANIMALS' was more of the same, ANNE flexing maximum vocal muscle on the 'ALONE' single and duly breaking the band in Britain where the song went Top 3. 'BRIGADE' (1990) was almost as successful though not quite as convincing, the WILSONs taking time out for solo projects after touring the record. HEART returned with an almost original line-up for 1993's 'DESIRE WALKS ON', while 'THE ROAD HOME' showcased a stripped down acoustic sound. • **Songwriters:** ANN WILSON or the group wrote most except; TELL IT LIKE IT IS (Aaron Neville) / I'M DOWN (Beatles) / LONG TALL SALLY (Little Richard) / UNCHAINED MELODY (hit; Righteous Brothers) / I'VE GOT THE MUSIC IN ME (Kiki Dee) / THESE DREAMS (Martin Page & Bernie Taupin) / ALONE (Billy Steinberg & Tom Kelly) / ALL I WANNA DO IS MAKE LOVE TO YOU (Mutt Lange) / THE BATTLE OF EVERMORE + BLACK DOG (Led Zeppelin) / etc. • **Trivia:** In 1967, ANN WILSON AND THE DAYBREAKS issued a couple of singles on 'Topaz'; STANDIN' WATCHIN' YOU. / WONDER HOW I MANAGED and THROUGH EYES AND GLASS. / I'M GONNA DRINK MY HURT AWAY.

Album rating: DREAMBOAT ANNIE (*8) / LITTLE QUEEN (*5) / MAGAZINE (*5) / DOG AND BUTTERFLY (*7) / BEBE LE STRANGE (*5) / GREATEST HITS / LIVE live compilation (*5) / PRIVATE AUDITION (*6) / PASSION WORKS (*6) / HEART (*7) / BAD ANIMALS (*7) / BRIGADE (*5) / ROCK THE HOUSE LIVE (*5) / THESE DREAMS – GREATEST HITS compilation (*8) / THE ESSENTIAL HEART compilation (*8) / ALIVE IN SEATTLE (*5)

ANN WILSON (b.19 Jun'51, San Diego, Calif.) – vocals, guitar, flute / **NANCY WILSON** (b.16 Mar'54, San Francisco, Calif.) – guitar, vocals / **ROGER FISHER** (b.1950) – guitar / **STEVE FOSSEN** – bass with session keyboard player and drummer

Arista | Mushroom

Apr 76. (7") *<7021>* **CRAZY ON YOU. / DREAMBOAT ANNIE** [–] [35]
<re-hit US No.62 early 1978>

Oct 76. (7") *(ARISTA 71) <7011>* **MAGIC MAN. / HOW DEEP IT GOES** [ ] Feb76 [ ]
<finally climbed to No.9 by mid-'76>

Oct 76. (lp/c)<US-pic-lp> *(ARTY/TC-ARTY 139) <5005>* **DREAMBOAT ANNIE** [36] Mar76 [7]
– Magic man / Dreamboat Annie (fantasy child) / Crazy on you / Soul of the sea / Dreamboat Annie / White lightning and wine (love me like music) / I'll be your song / Sing child / How deep it goes / Dreamboat Annie (reprise). *(re-iss. Oct87 on 'Capitol' cd/c/lp; CD/TC+/EMS 1277) (<cd re-iss. Jul97 on 'Disky'; DC 88124-2>)*

Feb 77. (7") *(ARISTA 86)* **CRAZY ON YOU. / SOUL OF THE SEA** [ ] [–]

Apr 77. (7") *(ARISTA 104) <7023>* **DREAMBOAT ANNIE. / SING CHILD** [ ] Dec76 [42]

—— added **HOWARD LEESE** (b.13 Jun'51) – keyboards, synthesizer, guitar (appeared as guest on debut album) / **MICHAEL DEROSIER** – drums

Portrait | Portrait

Jul 77. (lp/c) *(PRT 82075) <34799>* **LITTLE QUEEN** [34] May77 [9]
– Barracuda / Love alive / Sylvan song / Dream of the archer / Kick it out / Little queen / Treat me well / Say hello / Cry to me / Go on cry. *(re-iss. Aug86; same) (cd-iss. May87; CDPRT 82075) (cd re-iss. Sep93 on 'Sony Collectors';) (cd re-is.Feb97 on 'Columbia'; 474678-2)*

Aug 77. (7") *(PRT 5402) <70004>* **BARRACUDA. / CRY TO ME** [ ] May77 [11]

Oct 77. (7") *(PRT 5570)* **LOVE ALIVE. / KICK IT OUT** [ ] [–]

Nov 77. (7") *(PRT 5751) <70008>* **LITTLE QUEEN. / TREAT ME WELL** [ ] Sep77 [62]

Nov 77. (7") *<70010>* **KICK IT OUT. / GO ON CRY** [–] [79]
(The following few releases on 'Arista' UK & 'Mushroom' US were contractual)

Arista | Mushroom

Sep 77. (7"w-drawn) *(ARISTA 140)* **HEARTLESS. / HERE SONG** [–] [–]

Mar 78. (7") *<7031>* **HEARTLESS. / JUST THE WINE** [–] [24]

Apr 78. (lp)<US-pic-lp> *(SPART 1024) <5008>* **MAGAZINE** [–] [17]
– Heartless / Devil delight / Just the wine / Without you / Magazine / Here song / Mother Earth blues / I've got the music in me (live). *(UK-iss.Oct87 on 'Capitol' cd/c/lp; CD/TC+/EMS 1278)*

May 78. (7") *(ARIST 187)* **HEARTLESS (version II). / HERE SONG** [ ] [–]

May 78. (7") *<7035>* **WITHOUT YOU. / HERE SONG** [–] [ ]

Jul 78. (7") *<7043>* **MAGAZINE. / DEVIL DELIGHT** [–] [ ]

Aug 78. (7") *(ARIST 206)* **MAGAZINE. / JUST THE WINE** [ ] [–]

Portrait | Portrait

Oct 78. (7") *(PRT 6704) <70020>* **STRAIGHT ON. / LIGHTER TOUCH** [ ] Sep78 [15]

Dec 78. (lp/c) *(PRT 83080) <35555>* **DOG & BUTTERFLY** [ ] Oct78 [17]
– Cook with fire / High time / Hijinx / Straight on / Lighter touch / Dog & butterfly / Nada one / Mistral wind. *(re-iss. Aug86; PRT 32803) (cd-iss. May87; CDPRT 32803)*

Jan 79. (7") *<70025>* **DOG & BUTTERFLY. / MISTRAL WIND** [–] [34]

—— Now a quartet when Nancy's boyfriend ROGER FISHER left the band

Epic | Epic

Mar 80. (7") *(EPC 8270)* **EVEN IT UP. / PILOT** [ ] Feb 80 [34]

Mar 80. (lp/c) *(EPC/40 84135) <36371>* **BEBE LE STRANGE** [ ] [5]
– Bebe le strange / Down on me / Silver wheels / Break / Rockin' heaven down / Even it up / Strange night / Raised on you / Pilot / Sweet darlin'. *(cd-iss. 1988; CDEPC 84135) (cd re-iss. May93 on 'Sony Collectors' cd/c;)*

May 80. (7") *<50874>* **DOWN ON ME. / RAISED ON YOU** [–] [ ]

Jul 80. (7") *<50892>* **BEBE LE STRANGE. / SILVER WHEELS** [–] [ ]

Nov 80. (7") *<50950>* **TELL IT LIKE IT IS. / STRANGE EUPHORIA** [–] [8]

Jan 81. (7") *(EPC 9436)* **TELL IT LIKE IT IS. / BARRACUDA (live)** [ ] [–]

Mar 81. (lp/c)<US-d-lp> *(EPC/40 84829) <36888>* **GREATEST HITS / LIVE** (half comp / half live) [ ] Nov80 [13]
– Tell it like it is / Barracuda / Straight on / Dog & butterfly / Even it up / Bebe le strange / Sweet darlin' / I'm down – Long tall Sally – Unchained melody / Rock and roll. *(re-iss. +cd Dec88)*

Mar 81. (7") *<51010>* **UNCHAINED MELODY (live). / MISTRAL WIND** [–] [83]

Jun 82. (7") *(EPCA 2436) <02925>* **THIS MAN IS MINE. / AMERICA** [ ] May82 [33]

Jun 82. (lp/c) *(EPC/40 85792) <38049>* **PRIVATE AUDITION** [77] [25]
– City's burning / Bright light girl / Perfect stranger / Private audition /

Angels / This man is mine / The situation / Hey darlin' darlin' / One word / Fast times / America. *(re-iss. Feb88 on 'C.B.S.' lp/c; 460174-1/-4) (cd-iss. 1988; CDEPC 85792) (re-iss. cd May94)*

Sep 82. (7") *<03071>* **PRIVATE AUDITION. / BRIGHT LIGHT GIRL** [–] [ ]

—— **MARK ANDES** (b.19 Feb'48, Philadelphia, Pennsylvania) – bass (ex-SPIRIT, ex-JO JO GUNNE, ex-FIREFALL) repl. FOSSEN / **DENNY CARMASSI** – drums (ex-MONTROSE, ex-SAMMY HAGAR, ex-GAMMA) repl. DEROSIER who formed ORION THE HUNTER

Aug 83. (7") *<04047>* **HOW CAN I REFUSE. / JOHNNY MOON** [–] [ ]

Sep 83. (lp/c) *(EPC/40 25491) <38800>* **PASSIONWORKS** [ ] [39]
– How can I refuse / Blue guitar / Johnny Moon / Sleep alone / Together now / Allies / (Beat by) Jealousy / Heavy heart / Love mistake / Language of love / Ambush. *(cd-iss. Feb88; CDEPC 25391)*

Sep 83. (12"m) *(TA 3695)* **HOW CAN I REFUSE. / BARRACUDA / LITTLE QUEEN** [ ] [–]

Oct 83. (7") *<04184>* **ALLIES. / TOGETHER NOW** [–] [83]

—— While HEART looked for new contract ANN WILSON teamed up in '84 with MIKE RENO of LOVERBOY on 7" 'ALMOST PARADISE' from the film 'Footloose'.

Capitol Capitol

Jul 85. (7") *(CL 361) <5481>* **WHAT ABOUT LOVE?. / HEART OF DARKNESS** [ ] May85 [10]

Oct 85. (lp/c) *(EJ 0372-1/-4) <12410>* **HEART** [50] Jul85 [1]
– If looks could kill / What about love? / Never / These dreams / The wolf / All eyes / Nobody home / Nothin' at all / What he don't know / Shell shock. *(cd-iss. Feb86; CDP 746157-2) (re-iss. cd Sep94;)*

Oct 85. (7") *(CL 380) <5512>* **NEVER (remix). / SHELL SHOCK** [ ] Sep85 [4]
(12"+=) *(12CL 380)* – ('A'extended remix).

Jan 86. (7") *<5541>* **THESE DREAMS. / SHELL SHOCK** [–] [1]

Mar 86. (7") *(CL 394)* **THESE DREAMS. / IF LOOKS COULD KILL (live)** [62] [–]
(12"+=) *(12CL 394)* – Shell shock.
(d7"+=) *(CLD 394)* – What about love? / Heart of darkness.

May 86. (7"/7"sha-pic-d) *(CL/+P 406) <5572>* **NOTHIN' AT ALL (remix). / THE WOLF** [ ] Apr86 [1]
(12"+=) *(12CL 406)* – ('A'extended remix).

Jul 86. (7") *<5605>* **IF LOOKS COULD KILL. / WHAT HE DON'T KNOW** [–] [54]

Dec 86. (7") *<5654>* **THE BEST MAN IN THE WORLD. /** [–] [61]
(above from the film 'The Golden Child' starring Eddie Murphy)

May 87. (7") *(CL 448) <44002>* **ALONE. / BARRACUDA (live)** [3] [1]
(c-s+=/12"+=) *(CCL/12CL 448)* – Magic man (live).

May 87. (cd/c/lp) *(CD/TC+/ESTU 2032) <12546>* **BAD ANIMALS** [7] [5]
– Who will you run to / Alone / There's the girl / I want you so bad / Wait for the answer / Bad animals / You ain't so tough / Strangers of the heart / Easy target / RSVP. *(re-iss. cd Jul94;)*

Aug 87. (7") *<44040>* **WHO WILL YOU RUN TO. / MAGIC MAN** [–] [ ]

Sep 87. (7"/7"pic-d) *(CL/+P 457)* **WHO WILL YOU RUN TO. / NOBODY HOME** [30] [–]
('A'-Rock mix-12"+=) *(12CL 457)* – These dreams.
(cd-s++=) *(CDCL 457)* – ('A'-Rock mix).

Nov 87. (7") *(CL 473) <44089>* **THERE'S THE GIRL (remix). / BAD ANIMALS** [34] [12]
(12"+=) *(12CL 473)* – ('A'extended remix).
(c-s++=/cd-s++=) *(TC/CD CL 473)* – Alone.

Jan 88. (7"/7"g-f/7"pic-d) *(CL/+G/P 482)* **NEVER. / THESE DREAMS** [8] [–]
(12"+=) *(12CL 482)* – ('A'extended remix) / These dreams (version).
(etched-12") *(12CLE 482)* – These dreams (remixes & instrumental) / ('A'extended remix).
(ext-remix.cd-s+=) *(CDCL 482)* – Heart of darkness / If looks could kill (live).

Feb 88. (7") *<44116>* **I WANT YOU SO BAD. / EASY TARGET** [–] [49]

May 88. (7"/7"pic-d) *(CL/+P 487)* **WHAT ABOUT LOVE. / SHELL SHOCK** [14] [–]
(12"+=/12"g-f+=) *(12CL/+G 487)* – ('A'extended remix).
(cd-s+=) *(CDCL 487)* – Crazy on you / Dreamboat Annie.

Oct 88. (7") *(CL 507)* **NOTHIN' AT ALL (remix). / I'VE GOT THE MUSIC IN ME (live)** [38] [–]
(12"+=/12"pic-d+=) *(12CL/+P 507)* – I want you so bad (extended remix).
(cd-s++=) *(CDCL 507)* – ('A'extended).

(below with ZANDER (CHEAP TRICK) and from the film 'Tequila Sunrise')

Feb 89. (7"; ANN WILSON & ROBIN ZANDER) *(CL 525) <44288>* **SURRENDER TO ME. / (B-side by Dave Grusin featuring Lee Ritenour)** [ ] [6]
(12"+=/cd-s+=) *(12/CD CL 525)* – (by Diamond & Cerney).

Dec 89. (7") *<44488>* **HERE IS CHRISTMAS. /** [–] [ ]

Mar 90. (c-s/7") *(TC+/CL 569) <44507>* **ALL I WANNA DO IS MAKE LOVE TO YOU. / CALL OF THE WILD** [8] [2]
(12"+=/12"pic-d+=/12"clear+=/cd-s+=) *(12CL/12CLPD/12CLE/CDCL 569)* – Cruel tears.

Apr 90. (cd/c/lp) *(CD/TC+/ESTU 121) <91820>* **BRIGADE** [2] [3]
– Wild child / All I wanna do is make love to you / Secret / Tall, dark handsome stranger / I didn't want to need you / The night / Fallen from grace / Under the sky / Cruel nights / Stranded / Call of the wild / I want your world to turn / I love you. *(re-iss. Mar94 cd/c; CD/TC ESTU 2121)*

Jul 90. (7") *(CL 580) <44553>* **I DIDN'T WANT TO NEED YOU. / THE NIGHT** [47] Jun90 [23]
(c-s+=/12"+=/12"pic-d+=/cd-s+=) *(TCCL/12CL/12CLPD/CDCL 580)* – The will to love.

Nov 90. (c-s/7") *(TC+/CL 595) <44621>* **STRANDED. / UNDER THE SKY** [60] Sep90 [13]
(12"+=/12"pic-d+=/cd-s+=) *(12CL/12CLP/CDCL 595)* – I'll never stop loving you.

Feb 91. (c-s/7") *(TC+/CL 603) <44614>* **SECRET. / I LOVE YOU** [ ] Jan91 [64]
(12"+=/cd-s+=) *(12/CD CL 603)* – How can I refuse (live).

Sep 91. (cd/c/lp) *(CD/TC+/ESTU 2154) <95797>* **ROCK THE HOUSE (live)** [45] [ ]
– Wild child / Fallen from grace / Call of the wild / How can I refuse / Shell shock / Love alive / Under the sky / The night / Tall, dark, handsome stranger / If looks could kill / Who will you run to / You're the voice / The way back machine / Barracuda.

Sep 91. (c-s/7") *(TC+/CL 624)* **YOU'RE THE VOICE (live). / CALL OF THE WILD (live)** [56] [ ]
(10"colrd+=/cd-s+=) *(10/CD CL 624)* – Barracuda (live).

—— In 1992, the WILSONS were in splinter group LOVEMONGERS. The latter (which also included SUE ENNIS + FRANK COX) released a self-titled cd-ep on 'Capitol' w/tracks – Battle of evermore / Love of the common man / Papa was a rollin' stone / Crazy on you.

—— **FERNANDO SAUNDERS** (b.17 Jan'54, Detroit, Mich.) – bass repl. ANDES / **DENNY FONGHEISER** (b.21 Apr'59, Almeda, Calif.) – drums repl. CARMASSI

Nov 93. (7"pic-d/c-s) *(CLPD/TCCL 700)* **WILL YOU BE THERE (IN THE MORNING). / THESE DREAMS (live)** [19] [–]
(cd-s) *(CDCLS 700)* – ('A'side) / What about love? / Risin' suspicion / Who will you run to.

Nov 93. (cd/c) *(CD/TC EST 2216) <99627>* **DESIRE WALKS ON** [32] [48]
– Desire / Black on black II / Back to Avalon / The woman in me / Rage / In walks the night / My crazy head / Ring them bells / Will you be there (in the morning) / Voodoo doll / Anything is possible / Avalon (reprise) / Desire walks on *[UK+=]* / La mujer que hay en mi / Te quedaras (en la manana).

Dec 93. (c-s) *<58041>* **WILL YOU BE THERE (IN THE MORNING) / RISIN' SUSPICION** [–] [39]

Mar 94. (cd-s) **BACK TO AVALON / WILL YOU BE THERE (IN THE MORNING) / ALL I WANNA DO IS MAKE LOVE TO YOU** [ ] [ ]

Aug 95. (cd/c) *(CD/TC EST 2258) <30489>* **THE ROAD HOME (live)** [ ] [87]
– Dreamboat Annie (fantasy child) / Dog and butterfly / (Up on) Cherry blossom road / Back to Avalon / Alone / These dreams / Love hurts / Straight on / All I wanna do is make love to you / Crazy on you / Seasons / The river / Barracuda / Dream of the archer. *(re-iss. Sep97; same)*

not iss. Beyond

Nov 01. (cd) *<57822-2>* **LOVEMONGERS' CHRISTMAS** (festive) [–] [ ]

not iss. Epic

Jun 03. (cd) *<90287>* **ALIVE IN SEATTLE (live)** [–] [ ]
– Crazy on you / Sister wild rose / The witch / Straight on / These dreams / Mistral wind / Alone / Dog and butterfly / Mona Lisas and mad hatters / The battle of Evermore / Heaven / Magic man / Two faces of Eve / Love alive / Break the rock / Barracuda / Wild child / Black dog / Dreamboat Annie (reprise). *(UK-iss.dvd)*

– compilations etc. –

Sep 87. (d-lp/c) *Epic; (460174-1/-4)* **HEART (THE BEST OF . . .)** –
Nov 88. (d-lp-box/d-c-box/d-cd-box) *Capitol; (CD/TC+/LOVE 2)* **WITH LOVE FROM HEART** (HEART / BAD ANIMALS) –
Nov 90. (t-cd-box)(t-lp-box) *Capitol; (795247-2)(HGIFT 1)* **HEART BOX SET** (HEART / BAD ANIMALS / BRIGADE) –
Nov 91. (d-cd) *Epic; (465222-2)* **DOG & BUTTERFLY / LITTLE QUEEN** –
May 94. (cd/c) *Columbia; (460174-2/-4)* **GREATEST HITS**
Apr 97. (cd) *Capitol; (7243 8 53376 2 8)* **THESE DREAMS – HEART'S GREATEST HITS** 35
– Crazy on you / All I wanna do is make love to you / If looks could kill / Never / Alone / Who will you run to / Straight on (acoustic) / Magic man / What about love / Dreamboat Annie / Dog and butterfly (acoustic) / Nothin' at all / Heartless / Stranded / Will you be there (in the morning) / These dreams / Barracuda (live).
Jul 98. (cd) *Epic; (480561-2)* **THE DEFINITIVE COLLECTION** –
Jul 00. (cd) *Liberty; (527128-2)* **GREATEST HITS** –
Feb 03. (d-cd) *Sony; <(510519-2)>* **THE ESSENTIAL HEART**

□ HEARTBREAKERS (see under ⇒ THUNDERS, Johnny)

□ HEATMISER (see under ⇒ SMITH, Elliott)

□ Paul HEATON (see under ⇒ BEAUTIFUL SOUTH)

Richard HELL

Born: RICHARD MYERS, 2 Oct'49, Lexington, Kentucky, USA. Raised in Wilmington, Delaware, he later moved to New York in his late teens, where he wrote poetry and experimented with drugs. Along with his sidekick, TOM MILLER and BILLY FICCA, he formed The NEON BOYS in 1971. By '73, they'd metamorphosed into TELEVISION, MYERS adopting his RICHARD HELL moniker (while MILLER became TOM VERLAINE) and helping to initiate the city's new wave/punk scene. As legend has it, a sharp eyed MALCOLM McLAREN was rather taken by HELL's dragged-through-a-hedge-backwards attire and mop of spiked hair, initially attempting to secure his services for his new baby, The SEX PISTOLS; when this failed, well, at least he could go back to England with a few ideas . . . HELL subsequently split with VERLAINE and co., briefly joining JOHNNY THUNDERS in The HEARTBREAKERS, where he co-penned (along with a RAMONE!) the seminal 'CHINESE ROCKS'; like THUNDERS, HELL was well acquainted with the pleasures of heroin, which no doubt accounted for his haphazard career. HELL subsequently formed his own outfit, RICHARD HELL & THE VOIDOIDS along with future LOU REED guitarist ROBERT QUINE, IVAN JULIAN and MARC BELL. They hastily recorded an independently released debut EP before signing to 'Sire'; with the resulting 'BLANK GENERATION' (1977) album, HELL had finally succeeded in capturing his brutally nihilistic poetical/musical vision, if only fleetingly. With his drug problems reaching critical levels, HELL's only release over the next five years was 'THE KID WITH THE REPLACEABLE HEAD', a 1978 NICK LOWE-produced single. A belated follow-up album, 'DESTINY STREET' (1982), eventually appeared in Spring '82, although the momentum had long since dissipated. HELL was absent from the music scene for the next ten years (although he did star in the film, 'Smithereens' as well as scoring a cameo role as MADONNA's boyfriend in 'Desperately Seeking Susan'), finally re-emerging with art-noise veterans, THURSTON MOORE and DON FLEMING for a solo EP, before adding STEVE SHELLEY and recording an album under the DIM STARS moniker. • **Songwriters:** HELL penned all, co-writing 'LOVE COMES IN SPURTS' with VERLAINE. He also covered CRUEL WAY TO GO DOWN (Allen Toussaint) / I'M FREE + VENTILATOR BLUES (Rolling Stones) / CROSSTOWN TRAFFIC (Jimi Hendrix) / WALKING ON THE WATER (Creedence Clearwater Revival) / I WANNA BE YOUR DOG (Stooges); DIM STARS covered RIP OFF (Marc Bolan) / NATCHEZ BURNING (Johnny Burnette). • **Trivia:** He also wrote a column for East Village Eye in the 80's. His biography 'Artifact: Notebooks from Hell' was issued by Hanuman in 1990.

Album rating: BLANK GENERATION (*8) / DESTINY STREET (*5) / R.I.P. – THE ROIR SESSIONS collection (*5) / FUNHUNT live collection (*5) / ANOTHER WORLD collection (*4) / TIME double compilation (*7) / Dim Stars: DIM STARS (*6)

RICHARD HELL & THE VOID-OIDS

RICHARD HELL – vocals, bass / **ROBERT QUINE** (b.30 Dec'42, Akron, Ohio) – guitar, vocals / **IVAN JULIAN** (b.26 Jun'55, Washington, D.C.) – guitar, vocals / **MARC BELL** (b.15 Jul'56, New York City) – drums (ex-WAYNE COUNTY & THE ELECTRIC CHAIRS)

Stiff Ork

Nov 76. (7"ep) *(BUY 7) <81976>* **(I COULD LIVE WITH YOU IN) ANOTHER WORLD. / YOU GOTTA LOSE / (I BELONG TO THE) BLANK GENERATION**
(re-iss. Jun94 on 'Overground' 7"ep/cd-ep; OVER 36/+CD)

Sire Sire

Sep 77. (7") *(6078 608) <SRE 1003>* **BLANK GENERATION. / LOVE COMES IN SPURTS**
(12") *(6078 608)* – ('A'side) / Liars beware / Who says.
Sep 77. (lp) *(SR 6037) <6037>* **BLANK GENERATION**
– Love comes in spurts / Liars beware / New pleasure / Betrayal takes two / Down at the rock and roll club / Who says / Blank generation / Walking on the water / The plan / Another world. *<(cd-iss. Jun90; 7599 26137-2)>*

— **FRED MAURO** – drums repl. BELL who joined RAMONES

— added **JERRY ANTONIUS** – keyboards, vocals

Radar not iss.

Nov 78. (7") *(ADA 30)* **THE KID WITH THE REPLACEABLE HEAD. / I'M YOUR MAN** –

— **HELL** and **JULIAN** recruited **FRED MAHER** – drums repl. MAURO / **NAUX** (b.29 Jul'51, San Jose, Calif.) – guitar repl. QUINE to LYDIA LUNCH

I.D. Red Star

May 82. (lp) *(NOSE 2)* **DESTINY STREET**
– The kid with the replaceable head / You gotta move / Going going gone / Lowest common dominator / Downtown at dawn / Time / I can only give you everything / Ignore that door / Staring in her eyes / Destiny street. *<US cd-iss. 1991 on 'Relativity'; 5036> (cd-iss. Sep93 & Mar95 on 'Danceteria'; DAN 9306CD) (cd re-iss. Jul97 on 'Essential'; ESMCD 574) (lp re-iss. Dec00 on 'Munster'; MR 192)*

— Split 1982, RICHARD HELL starred in the film 'Smithereens'. MAHER joined SCRITTI POLITTI. In 1986, he made brief cameo in the film 'Desperately Seeking Susan' as Madonna's boyfriend.

RICHARD HELL

— (solo) with **THURSTON MOORE** + **DON FLEMING** – guitar (of GUMBALL)

Overground not iss.

Feb 92. (7"ep/cd-ep) *(OVER 24/+CD)* **3 NEW SONGS EP** –
– The night is coming on / Baby Huey (Baby do you wanna dance?) / Frank Sinatra.

Codex Tim Kerr

Apr 95. (cd-ep/10"ep) *(CODE 3/+X) <TK 9410 080 CD>* **GO NOW** (spoken word) Oct96

– compilations etc. –

Feb 80. (7"ep; The NEON BOYS) *Shake; <SHK 101>* **DON'T DIE / TIME. / LOVE COMES IN SPURTS ('73) / THAT'S ALL I KNOW (RIGHT NOW)** [–] [ ]
(UK-iss.Feb90 as 'TIME EP' on 'Overground' 7"purple; OVER 11)

Dec 84. (c) *R.O.I.R.; <A-134>* **R.I.P. (live)** [–] [ ]
– Love comes in spurts / Can't keep my eyes on you / Hurt me / I'm your man / Betrayal takes two / Crack of dawn / Ignore that door / I live my life / Going, going, gone / I can only give you everything (live) / I been sleepin' on it / Cruel way to go down / The hunter was drowned / Hey sweetheart. *(UK cd-iss. Jun90 on 'Danceteria'; DANCD 040) (lp-iss.Sep92; DANLP 040)*

Apr 90. (c) *R.O.I.R.; <A-172>* **FUNHUNT (live at the CBGB's & Max's 1978 & 1979)** [–] [ ]
– Love comes in spurts / I'm free / Funhunt / Lowest common dominator / Staring in her eyes / You gotta lose / Crosstown traffic / Liars beware / Don't die / Ignore that door / Walking on the water / Ventilator blues / Blank generation / I wanna be your dog / Hell has left the building – All the way. *(cd/lp-iss.Jul92 on 'Danceteria'; DAN CD/LP 088)*

Apr 91. (12"clear/cd-ep; A-side as The NEON BOYS) *Overground; (OVER 19/+CD)* **THAT'S ALL I KNOW (RIGHT NOW) / LOVE COMES IN SPURTS / HIGH HEELED WHEELS. / DON'T DIE / TIME** [ ] [–]

Jan 98. (cd) *Overground; <(OVER 36)>* **ANOTHER WORLD** [ ] [ ]

Mar 02. (d-cd) *Matador; <(OLE 530-2)>* **TIME** [ ] [ ]
– (R.I.P. + other sessions/live).

DIM STARS

RICHARD HELL + DON FLEMING with **THURSTON MOORE + STEVE SHELLEY** (both of SONIC YOUTH)

Paperhouse / Caroline

Apr 92. (12"ep/cd-ep) *(PAPER 015 T/CD) <CAROL 1468>* **THE PLUG / DIM STAR THEME. / CHRISTIAN RAP ATTACK / YOU GOTTA LOSE** [ ] [ ]

Jun 92. (cd/lp) *(PAP CD/LP 014) <CAROL 1724>* **DIM STARS** [ ] [ ]
– She wants to die / All my witches come true / Memo to Marty / Monkey / Natchez burning / Stop breakin' down / Baby Huey (do you wanna dance?) / The night is coming on / Downtown at dawn / Try this / Stray cat generation / Rip off.

HELL IS FOR HEROES

Formed: London, England … October 2000 by former SYMPOSIUM men WILL McGONAGLE and JOE BIRCH along with TOM O'DONOHUE and JAMES 'FIN' FINDLAY. Completed by the addition of singer JUSTIN SCHLOSBERG, the band (incidentally named after a classic Steve McQueen movie) garnered effusive plaudits from the likes of NME, Kerrang! and Xfm for debut single 'SICK / HAPPY', released on the 'Superior Quality' label. A second single, 'YOU DROVE ME TO IT', surfaced on indie label 'Wishakismo' in early 2002, while their intense, heroic, jittery brand of nu-rock was fully showcased on the Andy Gill-produced, 'E.M.I.'-released UK Top 20 debut album, 'NEON HANDSHAKE' (2002).

Album rating: NEON HANDSHAKE (*7)

JUSTIN SCHLOSBERG – vocals / **TOM O'DONAHUE** – guitar / **WILL McGONAGLE** – guitar (ex-SYMPOSIUM) / **JAMES 'FIN' FINDLAY** – bass / **JOE BIRCH** – drums (ex-SYMPOSIUM)

Superior Quality / not iss.

Jun 01. (cd-s) *(HERO 001CD)* **SICK – HAPPY / CUT DOWN** [ ] [–]

Wishakismo / not iss.

Jan 02. (7") *(7WISH 003)* **YOU DROVE ME TO IT. / THINGS FALL APART** [63] [–]
(cd-s+=) *(CDWISH 003)* – Kill the silence.

Chrysalis / not iss.

Aug 02. (7") *(CHS 5143)* **I CAN CLIMB MOUNTAINS. / I GET LOW** [41] [–]
(cd-s+=) *(CDCHS 5143)* – You and me and a whole lot of funk 45's / ('A'-video).

Oct 02. (7") *(CHS 5147)* **NIGHT VISION. / CAN'T YOU HEAR IT** [38] [–]
(cd-s+=) *(CDCHSS 5147)* – Folded paper figures.
(cd-s) *(CDCHS 5147)* – ('A'side) / This is why / Leave me gently / ('A'-video).

Jan 03. (7") *(CHS 5149)* **YOU DROVE ME TO IT. / INSIDE** [28] [–]
(cd-s+=) *(CDCHSS 5149)* – Gravity / ('A'video).
(cd-s) *(CDCHS 5149)* – ('A'live session) / Night vision (live session) / Sick – Happy (live session).

Feb 03. (cd/lp) *(540923-2/-1)* **NEON HANDSHAKE** [16] [–]
– Five kids go / Out of sight / Night vision / Cut down / Few against many / Three of clubs / I can climb mountains / Disconnector / You drove me to it / Slow song / Sick – Happy / Retreat.

E.M.I. / not iss.

May 03. (7") *(EM 619)* **RETREAT. / WE'RE MAKING IT UP** [39] [–]
(cd-s+=) *(CDEMS 619)* – ('A'-video).
(cd-s) *(CDEM 619)* – ('A'side) / Slow song (live session) / Changes / Boys don't cry.

Jimi HENDRIX

Born: JOHNNY ALLEN HENDRIX, 27 Nov'42, Seattle, Washington, USA. He was raised by a part Cherokee Indian mother and black father, who, at age 3, changed his forenames to JAMES MARSHALL and bought him his first guitar. Being left-handed, he turned it upside down and reversed the strings, teaching himself by listening to blues and rock'n'roll artists such as ROBERT JOHNSON, MUDDY WATERS, B.B. KING and CHUCK BERRY. In the early 60's, he enlisted in the paratroopers, thus avoiding the draft into the US army. He was subsequently discharged for medical reasons in 1962, after injuring himself during a jump. Two years later, the young HENDRIX moved to New York and backed acts LITTLE RICHARD, The ISLEY BROTHERS and IKE & TINA TURNER. He soon struck up a partnership with soul singer CURTIS KNIGHT, also obtaining a contract with Ed Chalpin (KNIGHT is said to have written 'The Ballad Of Jimi' in 1965, after JIMI prophesied his own death circa 1970!). Early the following year, HENDRIX's first real band, JIMMY JAMES & THE BLUE FLAMES, were born. With JIMI's reputation now spreading, he was seen by ex-ANIMALS bassman CHAS CHANDLER, who invited him to London. After auditions, they found a rhythm section of NOEL REDDING and MITCH MITCHELL, smashing their way into the UK Top 10 in early '67 with the 'Polydor' one-off 45, 'HEY JOE'. CHANDLER then set up a deal with Kit Lambert's new 'Track' label, and The JIMI HENDRIX EXPERIENCE exploded onto the scene. Their first Hendrix-penned 45, the thundering acid-fever of 'PURPLE HAZE', made the UK Top 3, as did the scintillating debut album, 'ARE YOU EXPERIENCED?'. This was released hot on the heels of their third Top 10 single, 'THE WIND CRIES MARY'. Hendrix was a revelation, a black super-freak whose mastery of the guitar was above and beyond anything previously heard. In fact, he virtually re-invented the instrument, duly illustrating various methods of on-stage abuse (i.e. biting it, playing it with his teeth, shagging it and even setting fire to it!). He was duly booked on the Monterey International Pop Festival bill, where he proceeded to play an orgasmic version of 'WILD THING'. From the sublime to the ridiculous, the following month saw a wholly inappropriate US support tour with The MONKEES, leaving both him and teenybop audiences baffled, but no doubt entertained for seven nights. After another classic UK hit, 'THE BURNING OF THE MIDNIGHT LAMP', he released his second LP, 'AXIS: BOLD AS LOVE', which made the Top 5 early in '68, and was the first to chart and hit the Top 3 in his native America. In the Autumn of '68, JIMI revived and transformed BOB DYLAN's 'ALL ALONG THE WATCHTOWER', a song that broke into the US Top 20 and UK Top 5. It was trailed by a superb British Top 10 (US No.1) double-LP, 'ELECTRIC LADYLAND', the record featuring the now infamous naked women sleeve (much to JIMI's displeasure), which some shops sold in a brown cover! The beginning of the end came in 1969, when he was busted for drugs, leading to his band disintegrating; the trio played together for the last time on the 29th June at the Denver Pop Festival. REDDING had already formed FAT MATTRESS, MITCHELL returning with other musicians BILLY COX and LARRY LEE to make the group a quartet. The new "Experience" played the Woodstock Festival on the 17-18 August '69, performing an excellent version of 'STAR SPANGLED BANNER' that went down in the folklore of rock music. To end the year, JIMI was found not guilty of an earlier charge of heroin and marijuana possession and at the same time, he formed all-black outfit, BAND OF GYPSYS, along with COX and drummer BUDDY MILES. They released the self-titled live set in May '70 (recorded at FILLMORE EAST, New Year's Eve/Day 1969/70). This hit the Top 5 in the States, and, following a court order, he paid ex-manager Ed Chalpin $1m in compensation and a percentage of royalties. Tragically, after a few more open-air festival concerts and some bad drugs trips, he died in London on the 18th of September '70. He was said to have left a phoned message to Chandler saying "I need help bad, man". The official cause of death was an inhalation of vomit, due to barbiturate intoxication, leading to a coroner's decision of an open verdict. To many rock music buffs, he remains the greatest axegrinder of all-time and who knows what he might have become had he survived the heady sixties. • **Songwriters:** HENDRIX except other covers; HEY JOE (William Roberts) / JOHNNY B.GOODE (Chuck Berry) / GLORIA (Them) / SGT. PEPPER (Beatles) / HANG ON SLOOPY (McCoys) / TUTTI FRUTTI + LUCILLE (Little Richard) / BO DIDDLEY (Bo Diddley) / PETER GUNN (Henry Mancini) / HOOCHIE COOCHIE MAN (Muddy Waters) / BLUE SUEDE SHOES (Carl Perkins) / etc. • **Trivia:** In Jan'69, he and band play live tribute of CREAM's 'Sunshine Of Your Love' on The LULU Show, much to annoyance of TV controllers.

Album rating (selective): ARE YOU EXPERIENCED? (*10) / AXIS: BOLD AS LOVE (*9) / SMASH HITS compilation (*8) / ELECTRIC LADYLAND (*10) / BAND OF GYPSYS (*8) / posthumous:- THE CRY OF LOVE (*7) / EXPERIENCE (*3) / AT THE ISLE OF WIGHT (*4) / RAINBOW BRIDGE (*4) / HENDRIX IN THE WEST (*5) / WAR HEROES (*4) / SOUNDTRACK RECORDINGS FROM THE FILM 'JIMI HENDRIX' (*5) / CRASH LANDING (*4) / MIDNIGHT LIGHTNING (*4) / THE JIMI HENDRIX CONCERTS (*5) / THE SINGLES ALBUM (*7) / LIVE AT WINTERLAND (*7) / RADIO ONE (*7) / CORNERSTONES 1967-1970 (*8) / THE ULTIMATE EXPERIENCE (*10) / BLUES (*6) JIMI HENDRIX: WOODSTOCK (*6) / VOODOO SOUP (*5) / FIRST RAYS OF THE NEW RISING SUN (*6) / VOODOO CHILD – THE JIMI HENDRIX COLLECTION (*8)

JIMI HENDRIX EXPERIENCE

JIMI HENDRIX – vocals, lead guitar (ex-CURTIS KNIGHT) with **NOEL REDDING** (b.DAVID REDDING, 25 Dec'45, Folkstone, Kent, England) – bass / **MITCH MITCHELL** (b.JOHN MITCHELL, 9 Jun'47, Ealing, London, England) – drums

Polydor / Reprise

Dec 66. (7"; as JIMI HENDRIX) *(56139)* **HEY JOE. / STONE FREE** [6] [–]
(re-iss. Jul84 on 'Old Gold')

Track / Reprise

Mar 67. (7") *(604 001)* **PURPLE HAZE. / 51ST ANNIVERSARY** [3] [–]
Mar 67. (7") *<0572>* **HEY JOE. / 51st ANNIVERSARY** [–] [ ]
May 67. (7") *(604 004)* **THE WIND CRIES MARY. / HIGHWAY CHILE** [6] [–]
May 67. (lp; mono/stereo) *(612/613 001) <6261>* **ARE YOU EXPERIENCED?** [2] Aug67 [5]
– Foxy lady / Manic depression / Red house / Can you see me / Love or confusion / I don't live today / May this be love / Fire / Third stone from the sun / Remember / Are you experienced? *(re-iss. Nov70; 2407 010) (re-iss. Nov81; 612 001) (re-iss. Sep85 on 'Polydor' lp/c; SPE LP/MC 97) (cd-iss. Jun91 & Oct93 cd/c; 521036-2/-4) (re-iss. Apr97 on 'MCA' cd/c; MCD/MCC 11608)*
Aug 67. (7") *<0597>* **PURPLE HAZE. / THE WIND CRIES MARY** [–] [65]
Aug 67. (7") *(604 007)* **THE BURNING OF THE MIDNIGHT LAMP. / THE STARS THAT PLAY WITH LAUGHING SAM'S DICE** [18] [–]
Dec 67. (7"; by JIMI HENDRIX) *<0641>* **FOXY LADY. / HEY JOE** [–] [67]
Dec 67. (lp; mono/stereo) *(612/613 003) <6281>* **AXIS: BOLD AS LOVE** [5] Feb68 [3]
– Experience / Up from the skies / Spanish castle magic / Wait until tomorrow / Ain't no telling / Little wing / If six was nine / You've got me floating / Castles made of sand / She's so fine / One rainy wish / Little Miss Lover / Bold as love. *(re-iss. Nov70;) (re-iss. Aug83 on 'Polydor' lp/c; (SPE LP/MC 71) (cd-iss. 1987 on 'Polydor'; 813 572-2) (re-iss. Jul91 & Oct93 on 'Polydor' lp/c/cd; 847243-1/-4/-2) (re-iss. Apr97 on 'MCA' cd/c; MCD/MCC 11601)*
Feb 68. (7") *<0665>* **UP FROM THE SKIES. / ONE RAINY WISH** [–] [82]
Apr 68. (lp; mono/stereo) *(612/613 004) <2025>* **SMASH HITS** (compilation) [4] Jul69 [6]
– Purple haze / Fire / The wind cries Mary / Can you see me / 51st anniversary / Hey Joe / Stone free / The stars that play with laughing Sam's dice / Manic depression / Highway chile / The burning of the midnight lamp / Foxy lady. *(re-iss. Jun73 on 'Polydor'; 2310 268) (re-iss. Aug83 on 'Polydor' lp/c; SPE LP/MC 3) (cd-iss. Feb85; 813 572-2)*
May 68. (7") *<0728>* **FOXY LADY. / PURPLE HAZE** [–] [ ]
Jul 68. (7") *<0742>* **ALL ALONG THE WATCHTOWER. / CROSSTOWN TRAFFIC** [–] [ ]

—— JIMI now brought in old session campaigners **AL KOOPER** and **STEVE WINWOOD** – keyboards plus **JACK CASADY** – bass / **BUDDY MILES** – drums / (to repl. MITCHELL and REDDING)

Sep 68. (7") *<0767>* **ALL ALONG THE WATCHTOWER. / BURNING OF THE MIDNIGHT LAMP** [–] [20]
Oct 68. (7") *(604 025)* **ALL ALONG THE WATCHTOWER. / LONG HOT SUMMER NIGHT** [5] [–]
Nov 68. (d-lp) *(613 008-9) <6307>* **ELECTRIC LADYLAND** [6] Oct68 [1]
– And the gods made love / (Have you ever been to) Electric Ladyland / Crosstown traffic / Voodoo chile / Rainy day, dream away / 1983 (a merman I should turn to be) / Moon, turn the tide . . . gently gently away / Little Miss Strange / Long hot summer night / Come on / Gypsy eyes / The burning of the midnight lamp / Still raining still dreaming / House burning down / All along the watchtower / Voodoo chile (slight return). *(also iss.lp/lp; 613 010/017) (re-iss. Jun73 on 'Polydor'; 2657 012) (re-iss. Jan84 on 'Polydor'; 350011-2) (re-iss. Jul91 & Oct93 on 'Polydor' lp/c/cd; 847233-1/-4/-2) (re-iss. Apr97 on 'MCA' cd/c; MCD/MCC 11600) (hit UK No.47 in Aug97)*
Apr 69. (7") *(604 029) <0798>* **CROSSTOWN TRAFFIC. / GYPSY EYES** [37] Nov68 [52]
Oct 69. (7") *(604 033)* **(LET ME LIGHT YOUR) FIRE. / THE BURNING OF THE MIDNIGHT LAMP** [ ] [ ]
Feb 70. (7") *<0853>* **STONE FREE. / IF 6 WAS 9** [–] [ ]
Apr 70. (7") *<0905>* **STEPPING STONE. / IZABELLA** [–] [ ]

JIMI HENDRIX

retained **BUDDY MILES** + recruited **BILLY COX** – bass

Track / Capitol

Jun 70. (lp) *(2406 002) <472>* **BAND OF GYPSYS (live)** [6] Apr70 [5]
– Who knows / Machine gun / Changes / Power of soul / Message to love / We gotta live together. *(re-iss. Aug83 on 'Polydor'; SPELP 16) (cd-iss. May88; 821 933-2) (re-iss. Dec89 & Jul91 on 'Polydor' lp/c/cd; 847 237-1/-4/-2) (re-iss. Apr97 on 'MCA' cd/c; MCD/MCC 11607)*

—— on the 18th September 1970 HENDRIX died of a drug overdose

– (selective) compilations, etc. –

on 'Polydor' unless mentioned otherwise / 'Reprise' US

Feb 68. (lp; with CURTIS KNIGHT) *London; (HA 8349) / Capitol; <2856>* **GET THAT FEELING (live 1964)** [39] [75]
Oct 70. (7"; JIMI HENDRIX with CURTIS KNIGHT) *London; (HLZ 10321)* **BALLAD OF JIMI. / GLOOMY MONDAY** [ ] [ ]

Sep 70. (lp) *Reprise; <2029>* **MONTEREY INTERNATIONAL POP FESTIVAL (live soundtrack)** [–] [16]

Oct 70. (7"m) *Track; (2095 001)* **VOODOO CHILE (SLIGHT RETURN). / HEY JOE / ALL ALONG THE WATCHTOWER** [1] [–]

Mar 71. (lp) *Track; (2408 101) <2034>* **THE CRY OF LOVE** [2] [3]
– Freedom / Drifting / Ezy rider / Night bird flying / My friend / Straight ahead / Astro man / Angel / In from the storm / Belly button window. *(re-iss. Jun73 on 'Polydor' lp)(c; 2302 023)(3194 025) (re-iss. Sep85 on 'Polydor' lp/c; SPE LP/MC 98) (cd-iss. Mar89; 829 926-2) (re-iss. Jul91 & Mar93 on 'Polydor' cd/c/lp; 847242-2/-4/-1)*

Mar 71. (7") *Reprise; <1000>* **FREEDOM. / ANGEL** [–] [59]

Aug 71. (lp) *Ember; (NR 5057)* **EXPERIENCE (live)** [9] [–]
– The sunshine of your love / Room full of mirrors / Bleeding heart / Smashing of amps. *(re-iss. Sep79 on 'Bulldog'; BDL 4002) (cd-iss. Jan87 & Nov91; BDCD 40023) (cd-iss. Mar95 on 'Nectar';)*

Oct 71. (7") *Reprise; <1044>* **DOLLY DAGGER. / STAR SPANGLED BANNER** [–] [74]

Oct 71. (7"ep) *Track; (2094 010)* **GYPSY EYES. / REMEMBER / PURPLE HAZE / STONE FREE** [35] [ ]

Nov 71. (lp) *Reprise; (K 44159) <2040>* **RAINBOW BRIDGE (live soundtrack)** [16] Oct71 [15]
– Dolly dagger / Earth blues / Pali gap / Room full of mirrors / Star spangled banner / Look over yonder / Hear my train a comin' / Hey baby. *(cd-iss. Mar87; K2 44159) (cd re-iss. Apr89; 831 312-2)*

Nov 71. (lp) *(2302 016)* **JIMI HENDRIX AT THE ISLE OF WIGHT (live)** [17] [–]
– Midnight lightning / Foxy lady / Lover man / Freedom / All along the watchtower / In from the storm. *(re-iss. Apr84 lp/c; SPE LP/MC 71) (cd-iss. Mar89; 831 813-2) (re-iss. Jul91 & Mar93 cd/c/lp; 847 236-2/-4/-1)*

Jan 72. (lp) *(2302 018) <2049>* **HENDRIX IN THE WEST (live)** [7] [12]
– Johnny B. Goode / Lover man / Blue suede shoes / Voodoo chile (slight return) / The queen / Sergeant Pepper's lonely hearts club band / Little wing / Red house.

Feb 72. (7") *(2001 277)* **JOHNNY B. GOODE. / LITTLE WING** [35] [–]

Nov 72. (lp) *(2302 020) <2103>* **WAR HEROES** [23] [48]
– Bleeding heart / Highway chile / Tax free / Peter Gunn / Catastrophe / Stepping stone / Midnight / 3 little bears / Beginning / Izabella. *(re-iss. Aug83 on 'Polydor' lp/c; SPE LP/MC 4) (cd-iss. Mar89; 813 573-2) (re-iss. Jul91 cd/c/lp;) (re-iss. cd+c Mar93)*

Jul 73. (d-lp) *Reprise; (K 64017)* **SOUNDTRACK RECORDINGS FROM THE FILM 'JIMI HENDRIX'** [37] [ ]

Mar 75. (lp) *(2343 080)* **JIMI HENDRIX** [35] [–]

Sep 75. (lp) *(2310 398) <2204>* **CRASH LANDING** [35] Mar75 [5]
– Message to love / Somewhere over the rainbow / Crash landing / Coming down hard on me / Peace in Mississippi / With the power / Stone free again / Captain Coconut. *(re-iss. Mar83 lp/c; SPE LP/MC 94) (cd-iss. Mar89;) (cd-iss. Jun91 & Mar93 cd/c/lp; 847263-2/-4/-1)*

Nov 75. (lp) *(2310 415) <2229>* **MIDNIGHT LIGHTNING** [46] [43]
– Trashman / Midnight lightning / Hear my train a coming / Hey baby (new rising sun) / Blue suede shoes / Machine gun / Once I had a woman / Beginnings. *(re-iss. Mar89 lp/c/cd; 825 166-1/-4/-2)*

Aug 82. (d-lp) *C.B.S.; (88592) / Reprise; <22306>* **THE JIMI HENDRIX CONCERTS (live)** [16] [79]
– Fire / I don't live today / Red house / Stone free / Are you experienced? / Little wing / Voodoo chile (slight return) / Bleeding heart / Hey Joe / Wild thing / Hear my train a-comin'. *(re-iss. Aug89 on 'Media Motion' lp/c/cd; MEDIA/+C/CD 1) (re-iss. Feb90 on 'Castle' lp+=/c+=/cd+=; CCS LP/MC/CD 235)* – Foxy lady.

Feb 83. (lp/c) *(PODV/+C 6)* **SINGLES ALBUM** [77] [–]

Nov 88. (12"ep/cd-ep) *Strange Fruit; (SFPS/+CD 065)* **THE PEEL SESSIONS** [ ] [–]
– Radio One theme / Day tripper / Wait until tomorrow / Hear my train a'comin' / Spanish castle magic. *(cd re-iss. Apr96; same)*

Feb 89. (d-lp/c/cd) *Castle; (CCS LP/MC/CD 212) / Rykodisc; <RALP 00782>* **THE RADIO ONE SESSIONS** [30] [ ]
– Stone free / Radio one theme / Day tripper / Killing floor / Love or confusion / Catfish blues / Drivin' south / Wait until tomorrow / Hear my train a-comin' / Hound dog / Fire / Hoochie coochie man / Purple haze / Spanish castle magic / Hey Joe / Foxy lady / The burning of the midnight lamp.

Nov 89. (5xlp/3xc/3xcd-box) *Castle; (HB LP/MC/CD 100)* **LIVE AND UNRELEASED – THE RADIO SHOWS (live)** [ ] [ ]

Mar 90. (7"/c-s) *(PO/+CS 71)* **CROSSTOWN TRAFFIC. / PURPLE HAZE** [61] [ ]
(12"+=) *(PZ 71)* – All along the watchtower.
(cd-s++=) *(PZCD 71)* – Have you ever been (to Electric Ladyland).

Oct 90. (cd/c/lp) *(847 231-2/-4/-1)* **CORNERSTONES (1967-1970, FOUR YEARS THAT CHANGED THE MUSIC) (live)** [5] [ ]
– Hey Joe / Foxy lady / Purple haze / The wind cries Mary / Have you ever been to (Electric Ladyland) / Crosstown traffic / All along the watchtower / Voodoo chile (slight return) / Star spangled banner / Stepping stone / Room full of mirrors / Ezy rider / Freedom / Drifting / In from the storm / Angel. *(cd+=/c+=)* – Fire (live) / Stone free (live).

Oct 90. (7"ep) *(PO 100)* **ALL ALONG THE WATCHTOWER. / VOODOO CHILE / HEY JOE** [52] [ ]
(12"+=/c-s+=) *(POCS/PZCD 100)* – Crosstown traffic.

Nov 90. (4xcd-box) *<9-26435-2>* **LIFELINES: THE JIMI HENDRIX STORY (live)** [–] [ ]

Feb 91. (4xcd-box) *(847232-2)* **SESSIONS BOX – ARE YOU EXPERIENCED? / AXIS: BOLD AS LOVE / ELECTRIC LADYLAND / CRY OF LOVE** [ ] [ ]

Mar 91. (4xcd-box) *(847 235-2)* **FOOTLIGHTS (live)** [ ] [ ]
– JIMI PLAYS MONTEREY / ISLE OF WIGHT / BAND OF GYPSIES / LIVE AT WINTERLAND

Feb 92. (4xcd-box) *(511 763-2)* **STAGES (live)** [ ] [ ]
– (Stockholm 5 Sep'67 / Paris 29 Jan'68 / San Diego 24 May'69 / Atlanta 4 Jul'70)

Nov 92. (cd/c) *Polygram TV; (517235-2/-4) / M.C.A.; <10829>* **THE ULTIMATE EXPERIENCE** [25] Jul93 [72]
– All along the watchtower / Purple haze / Hey Joe / The wind cries Mary / Angel / Voodoo chile (slight return) / Foxy lady / Burning of the midnight lamp / Highway chile / Crosstown traffic / Castles made of sand / Long hot summer night / Red house / Manic depression / Gypsy eyes / Little wing / Fire / Wait until tomorrow / Star spangled banner (live) / Wild thing (live). *(re-iss. Sep95; same)*

Feb 94. (cd) *I.T.M.; (ITM 960004)* **PURPLE HAZE IN WOODSTOCK (live)** [ ] [ ]

Apr 94. (3xcd-box) *Pulsar; (PULSE 301)* **GREATEST HITS** [ ] [–]
'Polydor' (the ones not mentioned), were issued on 'M.C.A.' in US.

Apr 94. (cd/c) *(521037-2/-4) <11060>* **BLUES** [10] [45]

Aug 94. (cd/c) *(523384-2/-4) <11063>* **AT WOODSTOCK (live)** [32] [37]

Apr 95. (cd/c) *(527 520-2/-4) <11236>* **VOODOO SOUP** [ ] [66]
– The new rising sun / Belly button window / Stepping stone / Freedom / Angel / Room full of mirrors / Midnight / Night bird flying / Drifting / Ezy rider / Pali gap / Message to love / Peace in Mississippi / In from the storm.

May 97. (cd/c/d-lp) *M.C.A.; (MCD/MCC/MCA2 11599)* **FIRST RAYS OF THE NEW RISING SUN** [37] [49]

Sep 97. (cd/c) *Telstar; (TTV CD/MC 2930)* **EXPERIENCE HENDRIX – THE BEST OF** [21] [ ]
– Purple haze / Fire / The wind cries Mary / Hey Joe / All along the watchtower / Stone free / Crosstown traffic / Manic depression / Little wing / If six was nine / Foxy lady / Bold as love / Castles made of sand / Red house / Voodoo chile (slight return) / Freedom / Night bird flying / Angel / Dolly dagger / Star spangled banner.

Oct 97. (cd/c/d-lp) *M.C.A.; (MCD/MCC/MCA 11684)* **SOUTH SATURN DELTA** [ ] [51]

Jun 98. (d-cd/d-c/t-lp) *M.C.A.; <(MCD/MCC/MCA 11742)>* **THE BBC SESSIONS** [42] [50]

Feb 99. (d-cd/d-c/t-lp) *M.C.A.; <(MCD/MCC/MCA 11931)>* **LIVE AT FILLMORE EAST** [ ] [65]

Jul 99. (d-cd/d-c) *M.C.A.; <(MCD 11987)>* **JIMI HENDRIX LIVE AT WOODSTOCK (live)** [ ] [90]

Jul 99. (10x7"box) *M.C.A.; (MCA 55578)* **THE CLASSIC SINGLES COLLECTION** [ ] [ ]

Apr 00. (cd) *Stony Plain; (7253 20068-2)* **WOKE UP THIS MORNING AND FOUND MYSELF DEAD** [ ] [ ]

Sep 00. (4xcd-box/8xlp-box) *Universal TV; <(112316-2/-1)>* **EXPERIENCE HENDRIX: THE BEST OF JIMI HENDRIX** [10] [78]

Apr 01. (d-cd) *Dressed To Kill; (TOPAK 952)* **THE LEGENDS COLLECTION** [ ] [–]

May 01. (3xcd-box) *K-Box; (KBOX 3270)* **THE BEST OF JIMI HENDRIX** [ ] [–]

Jul 02. (d-cd) *M.C.A.; (170322-2) / Universal; <112603-2>* **VOODOO CHILD – THE JIMI HENDRIX COLLECTION** [10] May01 [ ]
– Purple haze / Hey Joe / The wind cries Mary / Fire / Highway chile / Are you experienced? / Burning of the midnight lamp / Little wing / All along the watchtower / Crosstown traffic / Voodoo child (slight return) / Spanish castle magic / Stone free / Izabella / Band of gypsys / Stepping stone / Angel / Dolly dagger / Hey baby (new rising sun) / Fire (live) / Hey Joe (live) / I don't live today (live) / Hear my train a comin' (live) /

Foxy lady (live) / Machine gun (live) / Johnny B. Goode (live) / Red house (live) / Freedom (live) / Purple haze (live) / Star spangled banner (live) / Wild thing (live).

Oct 02. (3xcd-box) *Snapper; (SNAJ 720CD)* **THE LAST EXPERIENCE** □ □

Mar 03. (3xcd-box) *Trilogie; (205998)* **VOODOO GUITAR** □ □

□ Don HENLEY (see under ⇒ EAGLES)

□ Kristin HERSH (see under ⇒ THROWING MUSES)

John HIATT

Born: 20 Aug'52, Indianapolis, Indiana, USA. In his late teens, HIATT became a staff songwriter for a Nashville publishing house ('Tree'), where he had songs covered by THREE DOG NIGHT and CONWAY TWITTY (the latter took 'HEAVY TEARS' to the top of the country charts). A deal with 'Epic' presented him with the opportunity to record two creatively diverse but commercially unsuccessful albums with producer Norbert Putnam, 'HANGIN' AROUND THE OBSERVATORY' and 'OVERCOATS', seeing the light of day in the mid-70's. In 1978, HIATT was given another chance by 'M.C.A.', who groomed the singer-songwriter as an American answer to ELVIS COSTELLO with the toughened-up and critically acclaimed 'SLUG LINE' and 'TWO BIT MONSTERS' at the turn of the decade. With his songs now being performed by the likes of RICK NELSON, DAVE EDMUNDS, MARIA MULDAUR, etc, etc, HIATT's professional reputation led him to movie soundtrack work ('American Gigolo' and 'Cruising'). This golden early 80's period also saw him strike up a friendship with RY COODER, the roots scholar inviting HIATT to sing and play on two albums 'Borderline' and 'The Slide Area'. In 1982, JOHN switched to 'Geffen', where he released the Tony Visconti-produced set, 'ALL OF A SUDDEN', following it up with the NICK LOWE-produced 'RIDING WITH THE KING' (1983). LOWE in fact, became a close friend of HIATT and the pair would regularly work together over the coming decade. When 'Geffen' dropped HIATT after 1985's soul-tinged 'WARMING UP TO THE ICE-AGE', he subsequently signed to 'A&M' ('Demon'-only in the UK) and formed a backing band comprising LOWE, COODER and session veteran JIM KELTNER. Having finally won a long battle against alcoholism (and the tragedy of his wife's suicide), a rejuvenated HIATT came up with his sharpest set of songs to date in the Glyn Johns-produced 'BRING THE FAMILY' (1987). His commercial and critical rehabilitation continued with 'SLOW TURNING' (1988) and 'STOLEN MOMENTS' (1990), the former featuring BERNIE LEADON (ex-EAGLES) and DENNIS LOCORRIERE (of DR. HOOK). In 1992, HIATT and backing band became a bonafide group, LITTLE VILLAGE. Although these 'Reprise'-signed super-troubadours made the UK Top 30 (Top 75 in the States) with their eponymous debut album, the generally critical consensus deemed the record and accompanying tour slightly disappointing. However, a solo HIATT was back in town for 1993's 'PERFECTLY GOOD GUITAR', its title reflecting the rockier grooves contained within (supplied in part by CRACKER and SCHOOL OF FISH). A sardonically titled stop-gap concert set, 'HIATT COMES ALIVE AT BUDOKAN?' (1994), found the singer backed by The GUILTY DOGS. Signing to 'Capitol' for his next set, 'WALK ON' (1995), the man again made the US Top 50, although it failed to provide the chart longevity of previous efforts. While 1997's 'LITTLE HEAD' also performed poorly saleswise, HIATT retains a cult following and his songs have been covered by everyone from IGGY POP to BONNIE RAITT. The new millennium found the ageing troubadour undergoing a creative rebirth of sorts, going back to his roots on the stripped down 'CROSSING MUDDY WATERS' (2000). Released on the legendary 'Vanguard' label, the record was perhaps a primer for the more full-on electric action of 'The TIKI BAR IS OPEN' (2001) wherein HIATT once again hooked up with backing outfit The GONERS (who originally accompanied him on 1988's 'SLOW TURNING'. Like that album, 'The TIKI BAR . . .' scraped into the US Top 100, demonstrating that the man's fanbase remains as reliable as his muse. 'BENEATH THIS GRUFF EXTERIOR' (2003), meanwhile, found HIATT letting it all hang out loose and free, more so than he had in many a year. The results were as raggedly charming as might have been expected with the GONERS – and particularly guitarist SONNY LANDRETH – whipping up a storm. • **Trivia:** 1986's 'WARMING UP TO THE ICE-AGE' featured a duet with ELVIS COSTELLO: the Detroit Spinners cover 'LIVING A LITTLE, LAUGHING A LITTLE'.

Album rating: HANGIN' AROUND THE OBSERVATORY (*5) / OVERCOATS (*4) / SLUG LINE (*5) / TWO BIT MONSTERS (*5) / ALL OF A SUDDEN (*5) / RIDING WITH THE KING (*7) / WARMING UP TO THE ICE-AGE (*7) / BRING THE FAMILY (*8) / SLOW TURNING (*7) / Y'ALL CAUGHT compilation (*6) / STOLEN MOMENTS (*7) / PERFECTLY GOOD GUITAR (*6) / HIATT COMES ALIVE AT BUDOKAN (*5) / WALK ON (*5) / LITTLE HEAD (*4) / THE BEST OF JOHN HIATT compilation (*7) / CROSSING MUDDY WATERS (*5) / THE TIKI BAR IS OPEN (*6) / BENEATH THIS GRUFF EXTERIOR (*6)

JOHN HIATT – vocals, guitar / with many on session incl. **SHANE KEISTER** – keyboards

not iss. Epic

1973. (7") *<10990>* **BOULEVARD AIN'T SO BAD. / WE MAKE SPIRIT** [-] □

1974. (lp) *<EK 32688>* **HANGIN' ROUND THE OBSERVATORY** [-] □

– Maybe baby, say you do / Whistles in my ears / Sure as I'm sittin' here / Rose / Hangin' around the observatory / Full Moon / Wild-eyed gypsies / It's alright with me / Little blue song for you / Ocean. *(cd-iss. Jun94 on 'Sony Europe')*

1974. (7") *<11095>* **SURE AS I'M SITTIN' HERE. / OCEAN** [-] □

1974. (7") *<50022>* **FULL MOON. / HANGIN' ROUND THE OBSERVATORY** [-] □

1975. (7") *<50115>* **MOTORBOAT TO HEAVEN. / DOWN HOME (KEEP ON FALLIN')** [-] □

1975. (lp) *<EK 33190>* **OVERCOATS** [-] □

– One more time / Smiling in the rain / I'm tired of your stuff / Distance / Down home / Overcoats / I want your love inside of me / I killed an ant with my guitar / Motorboat to Heaven / The lady of the night. *(cd-iss. Jun94 on 'Sony Europe')*

M.C.A. M.C.A.

Jul 79. (7") *(MCA 502) <41019>* **SHARON'S GOT A DRUGSTORE. / RADIO GIRL** □ Jun79 □

Aug 79. (lp/c) *(MCF/+C 3005) <3088>* **SLUG LINE** □ □

– You used to kiss the girls / The negroes were dancing / Slug line / Madonna road / (No more) Dancin' in the street / Long night / The night that Kenny died / Radio girl / You're my love interest / Take off your uniform / Sharon's got a drugstore / Washable ink.

Oct 79. (7") *(MCA 528) <41132>* **SLUG LINE. / MADONNA ROAD** □ Aug79 □

—— now w / **SHANE KEISTER** – keyboards / **HOWARD EPSTEIN** – bass / **DARYL VERDUSCO** – drums

May 80. (7") **I SPY (FOR THE F.B.I.). / IT HASN'T HAPPENED YET** [-] □

Jul 80. (7") *(MCA 625)* **I SPY (FOR THE F.B.I.). / GOOD GIRL, BAD WORLD** □ [-]

Oct 80. (lp) *(MCF 3078) <5123>* **TWO BIT MONSTERS** □ □

– Back to normal / Down in front / I spy (for the F.B.I.) / Pink bedroom / Good girl, bad world / Face the nation / Cop party / Back to the war / It hasn't happened yet / String pull job / New numbers.

Oct 80. (7") *(MCA 649)* **BACK TO THE WAR. / PINK BEDROOM** □ [-]

Feb 81. (7") *(MCA 664)* **BACK TO NORMAL. / STRING PULL JOB** □ [-]

— **JESSE HARMS** – keyboards + **JAMES ROLLESTON** – bass; repl. KEISTER + EPSTEIN

Apr 82. (7") **LOOK FOR LOVE. / TAKE TIME TO KNOW HER** [–] [ ]

Geffen Geffen

Apr 82. (lp/c) *(GEF/40 85580)* <2009> **ALL OF A SUDDEN** [ ] [ ]
– I look for love / The secret life / Overnight story / Forever yours / Some fun now / The walking dead / I could use an angel / Getting excited / Doll hospital / Something happens / Marianne / My edge of the razor.

— now w / **MARTIN BELMONT** – guitar / **PAUL CARRACK** – keyboards / **NICK LOWE** – bass, vocals / **SCOTT MATTHEWS** – drums, bass, sax, guitar / **BOBBY IRWIN** – drums

Feb 84. (7") *(A 4086)* **SHE LOVES THE JERK. / LOVE LIKE BLOOD** [ ] [–]

Apr 84. (lp/c) <*(GEF/GEC 25593)*> **RIDING WITH THE KING** [ ] [ ]
– I don't even try / Death by misadventure / Girl on a string / Lovers will / She loves the jerk / Say it with flowers / Riding with the king / You may already be a winner / Love like blood / Love that harms / Book lovers / Falling up. *(re-iss. May91 cd/c; GEF D/C 04017) (re-iss. Apr92 cd/c; GFL D/C 19056) (cd re-iss. Feb99 on 'Mobile Fidelity'; UDCD 740)*

— now w / **RANDY McCORMICK** – keyboards / **JESSE BOYCE** – bass / **LARRIE LONDON** – drums

Jan 85. (7"m) *(A 5033)* **SHE SAID THE SAME THINGS TO ME. / SHE LOVES THE JERK / SOMETHING HAPPENS** [ ] [–]

May 85. (7") *(A 6121)* **LIVING A LITTLE, LAUGHING A LITTLE. / I'M A REAL MAN** [ ] [–]
(12"+=) *(X 6121)* – When we ran / Everybody's girl.

Apr 86. (7") *(A 9461)* **THIS IS YOUR DAY. / SNAKE CHARMER** [ ] [–]
(above was issued on 'Atlantic')

Sep 86. (lp/c) <*(K9 24055-1/-4)*> **WARMING UP TO THE ICE AGE** [ ] [ ]
– The usual / Crush / When we ran / She said the same things to me / Living a little, laughing a little / Zero house / Warming up to the ice age / I'm a real man / Number one honest game / I got a gun. *(re-iss. May91 cd/c; GEF D/C 24055) (re-iss. Apr92 cd/c; GFL D/C 19057) <(cd re-iss. Sep03 on 'Lemon'; CDLEM 8)>*

— now w / **RY COODER** – guitar, vocals / **NICK LOWE** – bass, vocals / **JIM KELTNER** – drums

Demon A&M

May 87. (7") *(D 1050)* **THANK YOU GIRL. / MY GIRL** [ ] [–]

May 87. (lp/c/cd) *(FIEND/+CASS/CD 100)* <5158> **BRING THE FAMILY** [ ] [ ]
– Memphis in the meantime / Alone in the dark / A thing called love / Lipstick sunset / Have a little faith in me / Thank you girl / Tip of my tongue / Your dad did / Stood up / Learning how to love you.

Jul 87. (7") <2950> **THANK YOU GIRL. / LIPSTICK SUNSET** [–] [ ]

Oct 87. (7") <2970> **HAVE A LITTLE FAITH IN ME. / THANK YOU GIRL** [–] [ ]

— now w / **BERNIE LEADON** – guitar, mandolin, banjo / **DAVID RANSON** – bass / **SONNY LANDRETH** – steel guitar / **KEN BLEVINS** – drums / **JAMES HOOKER** – organ

A&M A&M

Aug 88. (7") <1245> **SLOW TURNING. / YOUR DAD DID (live)** [–] [ ]

Aug 88. (lp/c/cd) <*(AMA/AMC/CDA 5206)*> **SLOW TURNING** [ ] [98]
– Drive south / Trudy and Dave / Tennessee plates / Icy blue heart / Sometime other than now / Georgia Rae / Ride along / Slow turning / It'll come to you / Is anybody there? / Paper thin / Feels like rain. *(cd re-iss. Feb99 on 'Mobile Fidelity'; UDCD 741)*

Oct 88. (7") *(AM 478)* **SLOW TURNING. / IS ANYBODY THERE?** [ ] [–]
(12"+=) *(AMY 478)* – Already love.

Feb 89. (7") *(AM 499)* **TENNESSEE PLATES. / GEORGIA RAE (live)** [ ] [–]
(12"+=) *(AMY 499)* – Thank you girl (live).

Jun 90. (cd/c/lp) <*(395310-2/-4/-1)*> **STOLEN MOMENTS** [72] [61]
– A real fine love / Seven little Indians / Child of the wild blue yonder / Back of my mind / Stolen moments / Bring back your love to me / The rest of the dream / Thirty years of tears / Rock back Billy / Listening to old voices / Through your hands / One kiss. *(cd re-iss. May95; same)*

Jul 90. (7") **A REAL FINE LOVE. / JUST ENOUGH ASLAND CITY** [ ] [ ]
(12"+=/cd-s+=) – Feels like rain.

— In 1992, he joined LITTLE VILLAGE with NICK LOWE, JIM KELTNER + RY COODER.

— solo (vocals, guitar, piano, organ) again w/ **MATT WALLACE** – guitar / **MICHAEL WARD** – lead guitar / **JOHN PIERCE** – bass / **BRIAN MacLEOD** – drums, percussion / **RAVI OLI** – electric sitar

Sep 93. (cd/c) <*(540135-2/-4)*> **PERFECTLY GOOD GUITAR** [67] [47]
– Something wild / Straight outta time / Perfectly good guitar / Buffalo River home / Angel / Blue telescope / Cross my fingers / Old habits / The wreck of the Barbie Ferrari / When you hold me tight / Permanent hurt / Loving a hurricane / I'll never get over you.

Oct 93. (7"/c-s) *(580426-7/-4)* **ANGEL. / LITTLE GOODNIGHT** [ ] [ ]
(cd-s+=) *(580427-2)* – Drive south / I'll never get over you.

Nov 94. (cd/c) <*(540284-2/-4)*> **HIATT COMES ALIVE AT BUDOKAN (live)** [ ] [ ]
– Through your hands / Real fine love / Memphis in the meantime / Icy blue heart / Paper thin / Angel eyes / You dad did / Have a little faith in me / Drive south / A thing called love / Perfectly good guitar / Feels like rain / Tennessee plates / Lipstick sunset / Slow turning.

Capitol Capitol

Oct 95. (c-s) *(TCCL 759)* **CRY LOVE / THE OTHER SIDE / TWENTY ONE** [ ] [ ]
(cd-s+=) *(CDCL 759)* – Your love is my rent.

Nov 95. (cd/c) <*(CD/C 33416)*> **WALK ON** [74] [48]
– Cry love / You must go / Walk on / Good as she could be / The river knows your name / Native son / Dust down a country road / Ethylene / I can't wait / Shedding the document / Wrote it down and burned it / Your love is my rest / Friend of mine / Mile high.

Parlophone Capitol

Jun 97. (cd/c) <*(CD/TC EST 2296)*> **LITTLE HEAD** [ ] [ ]
– Little head / Pirate radio / My sweet girl / Feelin' again / Graduated / Sure Pinocchio / Runaway / Woman sawwed in half / Far as we go / After all this time.

Sanctuary Vanguard

Oct 00. (cd) *(SANCD 003)* <79576> **CROSSING MUDDY WATERS** [ ] [ ]
– Lincoln town / Crossing muddy waters / What do we do now / Only the song survives / Lift up every stone / Take it down / Gone / Take it back / Mr. Stanley / God's golden eyes / Before I go.

Sep 01. (cd) *(SANCD 006)* <79593> **THE TIKI BAR IS OPEN** [ ] [89]
– Everybody went low / Hangin' round here / All the lilacs in Ohio / My old friend / I know a place / Something broken / Rock of your love / I'll never get over you / The tiki bar is open / Come home to you / Farther stars.

— next with **SONNY LANDRETH** – guitar / **DAVID RANSON** – bass / **KENNETH BLEVINS** – drums

Sanctuary New West

May 03. (cd; as JOHN HIATT & THE GONERS) *(SANCD 181)* <6045> **BENEATH THIS GRUFF EXTERIOR** [ ] [73]
– Uncommon connection / How bad's the coffee / The nagging dark / My baby blue / My dog and me / Almost fed up with the blues / Circle back / Window on the world / Missing pieces / Fly back home / The last time / The most unoriginal sin.

– compilations, etc. –

Sep 89. (lp/c/cd) *Geffen;* <*(K9 24247-1/-4/-2)*> **Y'ALL CAUGHT?** [ ] [ ]
– The crush / She said the same things to me / Love like blood / Slug line / She loves the jerk / My edge of the razor / Pink bedroom / It hasn't happened yet / Radio girl / I look for love / Washable ink / Riding with the King / When we ran.

Jul 93. (cd) *Beat Goes On; (BGOCD 176)* **SLUG LINE / TWO BIT MONSTERS** [ ] [–]

Aug 98. (cd) *Capitol; (859179-2)* **THE BEST OF JOHN HIATT** [ ] [ ]
– Have a little faith / A thing called love / Riding with the king / Cry love / Slow turning / The way we make a broken heart / Memphis in the meantime / Child of the wild blue yonder / Drive south / Angel eyes / Buffalo river home / Feels like rain / Love in flames / Perfectly good guitar / Tennessee plates / Take off your uniform / Don't know much.

Jan 00. (cd) *Universal;* <*(E 540929-2)*> **GREATEST HITS (THE A&M YEARS 1987-1994)** [ ] Oct98 [ ]

Aug 01. (d-cd) *Hip-O;* <556134> **ANTHOLOGY** [–] [ ]

Sep 03. (cd) *Universal;* <(90202)> **THE BEST OF JOHN HIATT – THE MILLENNIUM COLLECTION** [ ] [ ]

☐ HIGHWAYMEN (see under ⇒ CASH, Johnny)

☐ Lauryn HILL (see under ⇒ FUGEES)

☐ HINDU LOVE GODS (see under ⇒ R.E.M.)

Robyn HITCHCOCK

Born: 3 Mar'53, East Grinstead, London, England. Aged 21, he set out for Cambridge to locate the home of his idol, SYD BARRETT but ended up busking instead. 1976 found him forming a string of bands including The WORST FEARS, The BEETLES, MAUREEN & THE MEATPACKERS and, finally by the end of the year, DENNIS AND THE EXPERTS, who were the embryonic SOFT BOYS; alongside ROBYN were ALAN DAVIES, ANDY METCALFE and MORRIS WINDSOR. In March '77, they were offered a deal with indie label, 'Raw', who soon issued their debut release, 'GIVE IT TO THE SOFT BOYS EP'. The record included three trash-punk songs, notably 'WADING THROUGH A VENTILATOR'. KIMBERLEY REW replaced DAVIES before the band embarked on a UK tour supporting ELVIS COSTELLO and The DAMNED. This, in turn, led to a contract with 'Radar', although after only one 45 and many disagreements, they parted company. Taking matters into their own hands, the SOFT BOYS set up their own label, 'Two Crabs', and issued a debut album, 'A CAN OF BEES' (1979). The record was a resounding failure although it has since been the subject of many re-issues in different versions. In 1980 – by which time MATTHEW SELIGMAN had replaced METCALFE – they eventually established themselves, critically at least, with the much loved follow-up, 'UNDERWATER MOONLIGHT'. HITCHCOCK and Co. had finally managed to translate their quirky post-punk psychedelia to vinyl, pointing the way towards the direction of the frontman's erratic solo career. By the following year The SOFT BOYS had split, playing their final shows to more appreciative US audiences. HITCHCOCK subsequently completed a solo album, 'BLACK SNAKE DIAMOND ROLE' (1981), featuring the cult classics, 'BRENDA'S IRON SLEDGE' and the single, 'THE MAN WHO INVENTED HIMSELF'. Clearly the man had lost none of his BARRETT-esque lyrical daftness in the interim, his tongue-in-cheek, surreal humour occasionally even outstripping CAPTAIN BEEFHEART. After the disastrous STEVE HILLAGE-produced 'GROOVY DECAY' (1982), however, ROBYN decided enough was enough. Until 1984, that is, when he returned with an affecting acoustic album, 'I OFTEN DREAM OF TRAINS', the record seeing him reinstate the SOFT BOYS rhythm section (MORRIS WINDSOR and ANDY METCALFE) under the guise of ROBYN HITCHCOCK & THE EGYPTIANS. In 1985, their first product, 'FEGMANIA!', hit the shops, songs like 'THE MAN WITH THE LIGHTBULB HEAD' and 'EGYPTIAN CREAM', resurrecting the man's public profile. After a few more albums in the mid-80's, he and his band were signed to 'A&M', the resulting album, 'GLOBE OF FROGS' (1988), worthy of anything he'd previously recorded. It brought recommendations from R.E.M., who were longtime fans of HITCHCOCK. His band became firm faves on the US college circuit, especially when indie idols, MICHAEL STIPE and PETER BUCK guested on the two mediocre either-side-of-the-decade albums, 'QUEEN ELVIS' and 'PERSPEX ISLAND'. In 1993, he returned to the eccentric brilliance of old with the highly regarded, John Leckie-produced 'RESPECT', a creative renaissance of sorts which even inspired him to re-unite The SOFT BOYS early in 1994 for some Bosnia benefit concerts. A further couple of solo sets appeared in the mid-90's, 'YOU AND OBLIVION' (1995) and 'MOSS ELIXIR' (1996), the latter with a quintessentially HITCHCOCK, engagingly fantastical life-after-death yarn printed on the inner sleeve. Back to the zaniness of his old self, the man was to bow out of the 90's with a low-key effort, 'JEWELS FOR SOPHIA' (1999). Towards the end of 2002, ROBYN delivered a whole set of Dylan tunes under the guise of 'ROBYN SINGS', while he also found time to re-form The SOFT BOYS for a one-off album 'NEXTDOORLAND' (2002); HITCHCOCK, REW, SELIGMAN and WINDSOR had performed live the previous year. Had it really been over 21 years since their last? Back in 2003 with 'LUXOR', HITCHCOCK was still plying the kind of kooky quasi-folk which moves some to label him as a wayward genius. With lyrics as engagingly impenetrable as ever, and acoustic guitar playing as wildly impressive as ever, the record was another minor classic for the man's diehard fanbase.

Album rating: A CAN OF BEES (*7) / UNDERWATER MOONLIGHT (*8) / INVISIBLE HITS compilation (*7) / THE SOFT BOYS 1976-81 compilation (*8) / Robyn Hitchcock: BLACK SNAKE DIAMOND ROLE (*6) / GROOVY DECAY (*4) / I OFTEN DREAM OF TRAINS (*7) / FEGMANIA! (*8) / GOTTA LET THIS HEN OUT (*8) / ELEMENT OF LIGHT (*7) / INVISIBLE HITCHCOCK collection (*5) / GLOBE OF FROGS (*7) / QUEEN ELVIS (*7) / EYE (*7) / PERSPEX ISLAND (*4) / RESPECT (*5) / YOU & OBLIVION (*4) / MOSS ELIXIR (*6) / GREATEST HITS compilation (*8) / JEWELS FOR SOPHIA (*5) / ROBYN SINGS (*5) / LUXOR (*6) / Soft Boys: NEXTDOORLAND (*7)

SOFT BOYS

ROBYN HITCHCOCK – vocals, guitar, bass / **ALAN DAVIS** – guitar / **ANDY METCALFE** – bass / **MORRIS WINDSOR** (aka OTIS FAGG) – drums

Raw — not iss.

Jul 77. (7"ep) *(RAW 5)* **GIVE IT TO THE SOFT BOYS** — –
– Wading through a ventilator / The face of death / Hear my brane. *(re-iss. Oct79; RAW 37)*

— **KIMBERLEY REW** – guitar, harmonica, vocals repl. DAVIS

Radar — not iss.

May 78. (7") *(ADA 8)* **(I WANT TO BE AN) ANGELPOISE LAMP. / FAT MAN'S SON** — –

Two Crabs — not iss.

Feb 79. (lp) *(CLAW 1001)* **A CAN OF BEES** — –
– Give it to the soft boys / The pigworker / Human music / Leppo and the jooves / The rat's prayer / Do the chisel / Sandra's having her brain out / The return of the sacred crab / Cold turkey / Skool dinner blues / Wading through a ventilator. *(re-iss. Feb80 on 'Aura'; AUL 709) (re-iss. Jun84 on 'Two Crabs'; same) (cd-iss. Feb95 on 'Rhino'+=; RCD 20231)* – Leppo and the jooves / Sandra's having her brain out / Skool dinner blues / Fatman's son / (I want to be an) Angelpoise lamp / Ugly Nora. *(<cd re-iss. Nov92 & May96 on 'Rykodisc'; RCD 20231>)*

— In Oct'79, 'Raw' quickly withdrew release of 45 'WHERE ARE THE PRAWNS'; *RAW 41)*

— **MATTHEW SELIGMAN** – bass, keyboards (ex-SW9) repl. ANDY to FISH TURNED HUMAN

Armageddon — Armageddon

Jun 80. (7"ep) *(AEP 002)* **NEAR THE SOFT BOYS** — –
– Kingdom of love / Vegetable man / Strange.

Jul 80. (lp) *(ARM 1)* **UNDERWATER MOONLIGHT** — –
– I wanna destroy you / Kingdom of love / Positive vibrations / I got the job / Insanely jealous / Tonight / You'll have to go sideways / Old pervert / The queen of eyes / Underwater moonlight. *(cd-iss. Feb95 on 'Rhino'+=;)* – Vegetable man / Strange / Only the stones remain / Where are the prawns / Dreams / Black snake diamond role / There's nobody like you / Song No.4. *(<cd re-iss. Nov92 & May96 on 'Rykodisc'; RCD 20232>) (<re-iss. Mar01 on 'Matador' as t-lp+7"/d-cd+=; OLE 500-1/-2>)* – (extra tracks).

Aug 80. (7") *(AS 005)* **I WANNA DESTROY YOU. / (I'M AN) OLD PERVERT (DISCO)** — –

Oct 81. (7") *(AS 029)* **ONLY THE STONES REMAIN. / THE ASKING TREE**

Mar 82. (lp) *(BYE 1)* **TWO HALVES FOR THE PRICE OF ONE** (half live) — Oct81
– Only the stones remain / Where are the prawns / The bells of Rhymney /

There's nobody like you / Innocent box / Black snake diamond role / Underwater moonlight / Astronomy domine / Outlaw blues / Mystery train. *<US-title; ONLY THE STONES REMAIN>*

— disbanded in 1982, SELIGMAN who joined The THOMPSON TWINS

ROBYN HITCHCOCK

was already solo, using session people, including most ex-SOFT BOYS

Armageddon not iss.

Apr 81. (7") *(AS 008)* **THE MAN WHO INVENTED HIMSELF. / DANCING ON GOD'S THUMB** –
(free 7"flexi w-above) (4SPURT 1) IT'S A MYSTIC TRIP. / GROOVING ON AN INNER PLANE

May 81. (lp) *(ARM 4)* **BLACK SNAKE DIAMOND ROLE** –
– The man who invented himself / Brenda's iron sledge / Do policemen sing? / The lizard / Meat / Acid bird / I watch the cars / Out of the picture / City of shame / Love. *(re-iss. May86 on 'Aftermath'; AFT 1) (cd-iss. 1988; AFTCD 1) (cd re-iss. Feb95 on 'Rhino-Sequel'+=; RSACD 819)* – Dancing on God's thumb / Happy the golden prince / I watch the cars / It was the night / Grooving on an inner plane.

— now w / **SARA LEE** – bass / **ANTHONY THISTLETWAITE** – sax / **ROD JOHNSON** – drums repl. SELIGMAN to THOMAS DOLBY (and REW who re-joined The WAVES, who added Czech KATRINA; now KATRINA & THE WAVES)

Albion not iss.

Mar 82. (7") *(ION 103)* **AMERICA. / IT WAS THE NIGHT / HOW DO YOU WORK THIS THING?** –

Mar 82. (lp) *(ALB 110)* **GROOVY DECAY** –
– Night ride to Trinidad / Fifty-two stations / Young people scream / The rain / America / The cars she used to drive / Grooving on an inner plane / St. Petersburg / When I was a kid / Midnight fish. *(some with free various 'Albion' artists; RH track '52 STATIONS') (re-iss. Dec85 on 'Midnight Music'; CHIME 00.15) (cd-iss. Nov89 & Oct94 on 'Line'; ALCD 9.000008) (cd-iss. Feb95 as 'GRAVY DECO (THE COMPLETE GROOVY DECAY / DECOY SESSIONS)' on 'Rhino-Sequel'+=; RSACD 820)* – (extra mixes)

Midnight Music Slash

Nov 82. (7"m) *(DING 2)* **EATEN BY HER OWN DINNER. / LISTENING TO THE HIGSONS / DR. STICKY** –
(12"ep; Oct86) *(DONG 2)* – ('A'side) / Grooving on an inner plane / Messages of the dark / The abandoned brain / Happy the golden prince.

— now w / **WINDSOR + METCALFE / + ROGER JACKSON** – keyboards

Aug 84. (lp) *(CHIME 00.05S)* **I OFTEN DREAM OF TRAINS** –
– Nocturne / Uncorrected personality traits / Sounds great when you're dead / Flavour of night / This could be the day / Trams of old London / Furry green atom bowl / Heart full of leaves / Autumn is your last chance / I often dream of trains. *(cd-iss. Oct86; CHIME 00.05CD) (cd re-iss. Feb95 on 'Rhino-Sequel'+=; RSACD 821)* – Ye sleeping knights of Jesus / Sometimes I wish I was a pretty girl / Cathedral / Mellow together / Winter love / The bones in the ground / My favourite buildings / I used to say I love you.

Nov 84. (12"m) *(DONG 8)* **THE BELLS OF RHYMNEY / FALLING LEAVES. / WINTER LOVE / THE BONES IN THE GROUND** –

ROBIN HITCHCOCK & THE EGYPTIANS

— same as solo line-up

Mar 85. (lp) *(CHIME 00.08) <25316>* **FEGMANIA!**
– Egyptian cream / Another bubble / I'm only you / My wife and my dead wife / Goodnight I say / The man with the lightbulb head / Insect mother / Strawberry mind / Glass / The fly / Heaven. *(cd-iss. 1986 +=; CHIME 00.08CD)* – The bells of rhymney / Dwarfbeat / Some body. *(re-iss. Mar95 on 'Rhino-Sequel'+=; RSACD 822)* – Egyptian cream (demo) / Heaven (live) / Insect mother (demo) / Egyptian cream (live) / The pit of souls: I) The plateau – II) The descent – III) The spinal dance – IV) Flight of the iron lung.

May 85. (12"m) *(DONG 12)* **HEAVEN. / DWARFBEAT / SOME BODY** –

Midnight Relativity

Oct 85. (lp/c) *(CHIME 00.15 S/C)* **GOTTA LET THIS HEN OUT (live)** –
– Sometimes I wish I was a pretty girl / Kingdom of love / Acid bird / The cars she used to drive / My wife and my dead wife / Brenda's iron sledge / The fly * / Only the stones remain * / Egyptian cream * / Leppo & the Jooves / America / Heaven / Listening to The Higsons / Face of death. *(cd-iss. Oct86 += *; CHIME 00.15CD) (re-iss. cd Mar95 on 'Rhino-Sequel'; RSACD 823)*

Feb 86. (12"ep) *(DONG 17)* **BRENDA'S IRON SLEDGE (live). / ONLY THE STONES REMAIN (live) / THE PIT OF SOULS (part I-IV)** –

Mar 86. (pic-lp)(c) *(BM 80)(BMC 80-4) <EMC 8074>* **EXPLODING IN SILENCE**

Glass Fish Combat

Jun 86. (lp) *(MOIST 2)* **INVISIBLE HITCHCOCK** (compilation)
– All I wanna do is fall in love / Give me a spanner, Ralph / A skull, a suitcase, and a long red bottle of wine / It's a mystic trip / My favourite buildings / Falling leaves / Eaten by her own dinner / Pits of souls / Trash / Mr. Deadly / Star of hairs / Messages of dark / Vegetable friend / I got a message for you / Abandoned brain / Point it at gran / Let there be more darkness / Blues in A. *(re-iss. cd Mar95 on 'Rhino-Sequel'+=; RSACD 825)* – Listening to the higsons / Dr. Sticky.

Sep 86. (lp/cd) *(MOIST 3/+CD) <885618130>* **ELEMENT OF LIGHT**
– If you were a priest / Winchester / Somewhere apart / Ted, Woody and Junior / The president / Raymond Chandler evening / Bass / Airscape / Never stop bleeding / Lady Waters & the hooded one / The black crow knows / The crawling / The leopard / Tell me about your drugs. *(re-iss. cd Mar95 on 'Rhino-Sequel'+=; RSACD 824)* – The can opener / Raymond Chandler evening (demo) / President (demo) / If you were a priest (demo) / Airscape (live) / The leopard (demo).

Jan 87. (7") *(OOZE 1)* **IF YOU WERE A PRIEST. / THE CRAWLING** –
(12"+=) *(OOZE 1T)* – Tell me about your drugs / The can opener.

A&M A&M

Feb 88. (lp/c/cd) *<(AMA/AMC/CDA 5182)>* **GLOBE OF FROGS**
– Trapped flesh Mandela / Vibrating / Balloon man / Luminous rose / Sleeping with your devil mask on / Unsettled / Flesh number one / Chinese bones / A globe of frogs / Beatle Dennis / The shapes between us / Turn to animals.

Apr 88. (7") **GLOBE OF FROGS. / BALLOON MAN** –

— still with **METCALFE + WINDSOR** + guest **PETER BUCK** – guitar (of R.E.M.)

Mar 89. (lp/c/cd) *<395241-1/-4/-2>* **QUEEN ELVIS** –
– Madonna of the wasps / The Devils coachman / Wax doll / Knife / Swirling / One long pair of eyes / Veins of the Queen / Freeze / Autumn sea / Superman. *(cd+=)* – Veins of the Queen (royal mix) / Freeze (shatter mix).

Jul 89. (7") **MADONNA OF THE WASPS. / RULING CLASS** –
(12"+=/cd-s+=) – Veins of the queen (royal mix) / Freeze (shatter mix).

ROBIN HITCHCOCK

Glass Fish Twin/Tone

Nov 90. (lp/cd) *(MOIST 8/CD) <89175>* **EYE**
– Cynthia mask / Certainly clickot / Queen Elvis / Flesh cartoons / Chinese water python / Executioner / Linctus House / Sweet ghosts of light / College of ice / Transparent lover / Beautiful girl / Raining twilight coast / Clean Steve / Agony of pleasure / Glass hotel / Satellite / Aquarium / Queen Elvis II. *(UK cd-iss. Mar95 on 'Rhino-Sequel'+=; RSACD 826)* – Raining twilight coast (demo) / Agony of pleasure (demo) / Queen Elvis III (demo).

Go! Discs A&M

Oct 91. (cd/c) *(828 292-2/-4) <75021 5368-2>* **PERSPEX ISLAND** Aug91
– Oceanside / So you think you're in love / Birds in perspex / Ultra unbelievable love / Vegetations and dines / Lysander / Child of the universe / She doesn't exist / Ride / If you go away / Earthly Paradise.

Jan 92. (7") *(GOD 65)* **SO YOU THINK YOU'RE IN LOVE. / WATCH YOUR INTELLIGENCE**
(12"+=/cd-s+=) *(GOD X/CD 65)* – Dark green energy.
(above featured STIPE + BUCK of R.E.M.)

Jun 93. (cd/c; with ARCHIE ROACH) *(RHE CD/MC 1) <540064>* **RESPECT** Feb93
– The yip song / The arms of love / The moon inside / Railway shoes / When I was dead / The wreck of Arthur Lee / Driving aloud (radio storm) / erpnt at the gates of wisdom / Then you're dust / Wafflehead. *(cd re-iss. Oct96; same)*

Rhino-Sequel Rhino-Sequel

Mar 95. (cd) *(<RSACD 827>)* **YOU & OBLIVION**
– You've got / Don't you / Birdshead / She reached for a light / Victorian squid / Captain Dry / Mr. Rock I / August hair / Take your knife out of

my back / Surgery / The dust / Polly on the shore / Aether / Fiend before the shrine / Nothing / Into it / Stranded in the future / Keeping still / September clones / Ghost ship / You & me / If I could look.

Feb 95. (cd-ep) *(CDSEQ 2)* **MY WIFE AND MY DEAD WIFE / I SOMETHING YOU / ZIPPER IN MY SPINE / MAN WITH A WOMAN'S SHADOW** ☐ –

— now with **DENI BONET** – violin / **NITSHUKS BONGA** – sax / **TIM KEEGAN** – guitar / **JAKE KYLE** – bass / **PATCH HANNAN** – drums / **MORRIS WINDSOR** – vocals, percussion / etc

Warners Warners

Aug 96. (cd/c) *(<9362 46302-2/-4>)* **MOSS ELIXIR** ☐ ☐
– Sinister but she was happy / The Devil's radio / Heliotrope / Alright, yeah / Filthy bird / The speed of things / Beautiful queen / Man with a woman's shadow / I am not me / De Chirico Street / You and oblivion / This is how it feels.

Sep 99. (cd) *(<9362 47433-2>)* **JEWELS FOR SOPHIA** ☐ Jul99 ☐
– Mexican God / Cheese alarm / Viva! sea-tac / I feel beautiful / You've got a sweet mouth on you, baby / NASA clapping / Sally was a legend / Antwoman / Elizabeth Jade / No, I don't remember Guildford / Dark princess / Jewels for Sophia.

Editions PAF Editions PAF

Jul 02. (d-cd) *(<PAF 002CD>)* **ROBYN SINGS: A TRIBUTE TO BOB DYLAN** ☐ Nov02 ☐
– Visions of Johanna / Tangled up in blue / Not dark yet / 4th time around / Desolation row / It's all over now, baby blue / Dignity / Visions of Johanna // live:- Tell me mama / I don't believe you / Baby let me follow you down / Just like Tom Thumb's blues / Leopard-skin pillbox hat / One too many mornings / Ballad of a thin man / Like a rolling stone.

Apr 03. (cd) *(<PAF 004>)* **LUXOR** ☐ ☐
– The sound of sound / One L / Penelope's angles / The idea of you / You remind me of you / Luxor / Keep finding me / Maria Lyn / Round song / Ant corridor / Idonia / The wolf house / Solpadeine.

– compilations, etc. –

May 83. (12"ep) *Albion; (12ION 1036)* **NIGHT RIDE TO TRINIDAD (long version). / KINGDOM OF LOVE / MIDNIGHT FISH** ☐ –

1984. (7"flexi; w-mag) *Bucketful Of Brains; (BOB 8)* **HAPPY THE GOLDEN PRINCE** – –

Jun 94. (cd) *Strange Roots; (ROOTCD 001)* **KERSHAW SESSIONS** ☐ –
(re-iss. Jul98 on 'Strange Fruit'; SFRSCD 075)

Sep 96. (cd) *A&M; (540 570-2)* **GREATEST HITS** ☐ –

Jan 98. (cd) *Rhino-Sequel; (<RSACD 957>)* **THE COLLECTION: UNCORRECTED PERSONALITY TRAITS** ☐ ☐

Oct 98. (cd) *Strange Fruit; (CAFECD 004)* **LIVE AT THE CAMBRIDGE FOLK FESTIVAL (live)** ☐ –
(re-iss. Jul00 on 'Varese Sarabande'; 0302061070-2)

Nov 98. (cd) *Warners; (<9362 46846-2)>* **STOREFRONT HITCHCOCK: MUSIC FROM DEMME PICTURE (live)** ☐ Oct97 ☐
– 1974 / Let's go thundering / I'm only you / Glass hotel / I something you / Yip! song / Freeze / Alright, yeah / Where do you go when you die? / The wind cries Mary / No, I don't remember Guildford / Beautiful queen.

2000. (cd) *Editions PAF; <PAF 001CD>* **A SONG FOR BRAM** – ☐
(UK-iss.Sep03; same as US)

SOFT BOYS

ROBYN HITCHCOCK with **KIMBERLEY REW, MATTHEW SELIGMAN** + **MORRIS WINDSOR**

Matador Matador

Sep 02. (cd/lp) *(<OLE 553-2/-1>)* **NEXTDOORLAND** ☐ ☐
– I love Lucy / Pulse of my heart / Mr. Kennedy / Unprotected love / My mind is connected to your dreams / Sudden town / Strings / Japanese captain / La cherite / Lions and tigers.

– compilations, others, etc –

1982. (7"w/mag) *Bucketful Of Brains; (BOB 1)* **LOVE POISONING. / WHEN I WAS A KID** – –

Nov 83. (7") *Midnight Music; (DING 4)* **HE'S A REPTILE. / SONG NO.4** ☐ –

Nov 83. (7") *Midnight Music; (CHIME 0002)* **INVISIBLE HITS** ☐ –
– Wey-wey-hep-uh-hole * / Have a heart Betty (I'm not fireproof) * / The asking tree / Muriel's hoof / The rout of the clones / Let me put it next to you / When I was a kid * / Rock & roll toilet * / Love poisoning * / Empty girl / Blues in the dark / He's a reptile. *(cd-iss. Feb95 on 'Rhino" +=;)* – (alt.takes of *). *(cd re-iss. May96 on 'Rykodisc'; RCD 20233)*

Aug 85. (lp/pic-lp) *De Laurean; (SOFT 1/+P)* **WADING THROUGH A VENTILATOR** ☐ –

1987. (7"flexi; w-mag) *Bucketful Of Brains; (BOB 17)* **DECK OF CARDS. / Robyn Hitchcock & Peter Buck: FLESH NO.1** – –

Dec 87. (lp) *Midnight Music; (MOIST 4)* **LIVE AT THE PORTLAND ARMS (live)** ☐ –

1989. (7"yellow,7"white; ltd) *Overground; (OVER 4)* **THE FACE OF DEATH. / THE YODELLING HOOVER** ☐ –

Sep 93. (d-cd) *Rykodisc; (RCD 10234-35)* **THE SOFT BOYS 1976-1981** ☐ –
– (mostly all of their material).

HIVES

Formed: Fagersta, Sweden . . . 1993 by NICHOLAUS ARSON, his brother HOWLIN' PETE ALMQVIST – later, CHRIS DANGEROUS, DR. MATT DESTRUCTION AND VIGILANTE CARLSTROEM were added to the line-up. Owing as much style and zeitgeist to The STOOGES, The KINKS and The ROLLING STONES as The STROKES did, this punky, mod-looking collective were banging out quasi-garage rock tunes before The STROKES had even left private school. In hindsight, possibly the only reason The HIVES became so popular after four years of industry/consumer ignorance was because of the Garage rock explosion during the summer of 2001, but, unlike the dull-ish LOU REED drone of The STROKES, The HIVES partied like it was 1969 . . . and boy did they rock some! Clad in Al Capone gangster uniform (black suit, white tie, naturally), The HIVES originally began playing rock'n'roll to annoy the commercial punk pundits who sifted around their hometown of Fagersta. After an inaugural EP in '96 ('OH LORD! WHEN? HOW?'), the quintet issued their debut album 'BARELY LEGAL' in September 1997 and practically became local heroes, selling-out clubs and venues and rocking up a storm with the Swedish music press. Soon the word spread like wildfire around Scandinavia and The HIVES issued 'aka I-D-I-O-T' as a mini-set at the beginning of '98. A thrash blend of rawk'n'roll and punk, the release was to be the band's last for almost two years as they began to experience management problems. However, this break turned out to be a blessing in disguise as they re-emerged in 2000 with a killer album and a re-invented, semi-fictional history involving a mysterious MONKEES-esque manufacturing. 'VENI VIDI VICIOUS' smacked the European music press in the face with its screeeeeching guitars, fuzz-bass and hollering, but nobody seemed to be paying any attention – for now. The British music buying public missed the soaring KINKS driven anthems that were 'HATE TO SAY I TOLD YOU SO' and 'MAIN OFFENDER' the first time around when they were issued as singles in 2000 and 2001, but thanks to a Garage-rock revival, a few TV promos and ALAN McGEE (now boss at the newly-formed 'Poptones' imprint), The HIVES legacy was finally realised with the premiere of their "Best Of. . ." compilation 'YOUR NEW FAVOURITE BAND' (2001, and a title taking a subtle dig at the histrionic coverage that The STROKES received in the NME). The two aforementioned singles were re-released the following year to – hurrah! – critical acclaim, which just shows that sometimes you can't just lead a horse to the water, you have to make it drink the damn thing as well. • **Trivia:** Their mysterious 6th member/writer, FITZSIMMONS was actually mainman PETE who seemingly took the name of his old school teacher.

Album rating: BARELY LEGAL (*7) / a.k.a. I-D-I-O-T mini (*5) / VENI VIDI VICIOUS (*8) / YOUR NEW FAVOURITE BAND (*8)

HOWLIN' PETE ALMQVIST – vocals / **NICHOLAUS ARSON** (b. ALMQVIST) – guitar / **VIGILANTE CARLSTROEM** – guitar / **DR MATT DESTRUCTION** – bass / **CHRIS DANGEROUS** – drums

		Burning Heart	Gearhead
Jun 96.	(cd-ep) *(JABSCD 001)* **OH LORD! WHEN? HOW?** – You think you're so darn special / Cellblock / Some people / How will I cope with that? / Bearded lady / Let me go.		-
Sep 97.	(cd) *(BHR 068CD)* **BARELY LEGAL** – Well, well, well / a.k.a. I-D-I-O-T / Here we go again / I'm a wicked one / Automatic schmuck / King of asskissing / Hail hail spit n' drool / Black Jack / What's that spell? . . . go to hell! / Theme from . . . / Uptempo venomous poison / Oh Lord! when? how? / The stomp / Closed for the season. *<(US+re-iss. cd/lp-iss.Mar01/Jan02 on 'Gearhead'; RPM 030 CD/LP)>*		-
Mar 98.	(m-cd,m-lp) *(BHR 072) <RPM 023>* **a.k.a. I-D-I-O-T** – a.k.a. I-D-I-O-T / Outsmarted / Untutored youth / Fever / Mad man / Numbers. *(re-iss. Mar01 on 'Gearhead' m-lp/m-cd; same as US)*		
Apr 00.	(cd/lp) *(BHR 107-2/-1) <82005-2>* **VENI VIDI VICIOUS** – The Hives – declare guerre nucleaire / Die, all right! / A get together to tear it apart / Main offender / Outsmarted / Hate to say I told you so / The Hives – introduce the metric system in time / Find another girl / Statecontrol / Inspection wise 1999 / Knock knock / Supply and demand. *(lp re-iss. Jul02 on 'Gearhead'; RPM 040LP)(hit US No.63)*		Sep00
Dec 00.	(7"/cd-s) *(BHR 122-2) <RPM 024/+CD>* **HATE TO SAY I TOLD YOU SO. / DIE, ALL RIGHT! / THE HIVES ARE LAW, YOU ARE CRIME** *(re-iss. Jan02 on 'Gearhead'; same as US)*		
Sep 01.	(cd-s) *(BHR 134-2)* **MAIN OFFENDER / LOST AND FOUND / HOWLIN' PELLE TALKS TO THE KIDS**		-
		Poptones	Poptones
Sep 01.	(7") *(MC 50555)* **SUPPLY AND DEMAND. / THE STOMP**		-
Oct 01.	(cd) *(<MC 5055CD>)* **YOUR NEW FAVOURITE BAND** (compilation) – Hate to say I told you so / Main offender / Supply and demand / Die, all right! / Untutored youth / Outsmarted / Mad man / Here we go again / a.k.a. I-D-I-O-T / Automatic schmuck / Hail hail spit n' drool / Hives are law you are crime. *(cd bonus+=)* – Main offender (video) / Hate to say I told you so (video) / a.k.a. I-D-I-O-T (video) / Die, all right! (video). *(lp-iss.Mar02; MC 5055LP)*	7	Apr02
Nov 01.	(7") *(7SN 006)* **MAIN OFFENDER. / LOST AND FOUND / HOWLIN' PELLE TALKS TO THE KIDS** *(above issued on 'Sweet Nothing') (re-iss. Dec01 on 'Big Wheel' 7"/cd-s; BWR 0248/+CD)*		-
Feb 02.	(7") *(BHR 1058-7)* **HATE TO SAY I TOLD YOU SO. / UPTEMPO VENOMOUS POISON** (cd-s+=) *(BHR 1057-2)* – Gninrom ytic kcorknup. (cd-s) *(BHR 1059-2)* – ('A'side) / Fever / Barely homosapien. (above issued on 'Burning Heart') (below on 'Hard On' records)	23	86
Mar 02.	(7"ep; split w/ PRICKS) *(HARDON 2)* **3:30 PUNK ROCK CITY MORNING / GNINROM YTIC KCOR KNUP 3:30 / NUMBERS. / (other side by The Pricks)**		-
May 02.	(7") *(MC 5076S)* **MAIN OFFENDER. / LOST AND FOUND** (cd-s+=) *(MC 5076SCD)* – Hate to say I told you so (live on Top Of The Pops + video).	24	-
Oct 02.	(cd-s) *(MC 5078SCD)* **DIE, ALL RIGHT! / SUPPLY AND DEMAND**		-

HOLE

Formed: Los Angeles, California, USA . . . late 1989 by COURTNEY LOVE (bizarrely enough, a two-piece indie band of the same moniker – see under LOIS – surfaced with a few 45's a year later!) and six foot plus guitarist and Capitol records employee, ERIC ERLANDSON. LOVE, who had previously worked as an exotic dancer and an actress (she appeared in the 1986 punk movie, 'Sid & Nancy') and played alongside JENNIFER FINCH (L7) and KAT BJELLAND (Babes In Toyland) in a band called SUGAR BABY DOLL, was also involved in an early incarnation of FAITH NO MORE. Taking the name HOLE from a line in Euripides' Medea, they placed an ad in a local paper, 'Flipside', finding a bassist and drummer, namely JILL EMERY and CAROLINE RUE. In the Spring of 1990, HOLE released the 'RAT BASTARD' EP, subsequently relocating to the burgeoning Seattle area. Early the following year, 'Sub Pop' issued the 'DICKNAIL' EP, the band duly signing to 'Caroline' records for their debut album, 'PRETTY ON THE INSIDE'. Produced by KIM GORDON and DON FLEMING, it hit the lower regions of the US charts, the record being voted album of the year by New York's Village Voice magazine. A harrowing primal howl of a record, LOVE's demons were confronted mercilessly on such psyche-trawling dirges as 'TEENAGE WHORE' and 'GARBAGE MAN'. Around the same time, LOVE's relationship with NIRVANA's KURT COBAIN, was the talk of the alternative rock world, the singer subsequently marrying him in February '92, giving birth to his daughter, Frances Bean, later that summer. The following year, with newcomers PATTY SCHEMEL (drums) and KRISTEN PFAFF (bass), the group secured a deal with the David Geffen Company ('D.G.C.'), much to the dismay of MADONNA who wanted HOLE for her newly formed 'Maverick' label. In Spring 1994, LOVE finally celebrated a UK Top 20 album, 'LIVE THROUGH THIS', although its success was overshadowed by the shocking suicide of KURT on the 8th of April. She subsequently held a memorial two days later, hailing everyone there to call him an asshole. More press coverage followed later that summer, when PFAFF was found dead in her bath on the 16th June (it was believed to be another tragic drug related death). Despite the press circus surrounding LOVE, the band played a rather disappointing Reading Festival stint in August that year, her at times lethargic vox letting some of the more discerning fans down (EVAN DANDO of The LEMONHEADS was rumoured to be her new boyfriend, although a number of lucky people – including DANDO – were privy to her womanly charms – both of them – when she "flashed" at the side of the stage). With a new bassist, MELISSA AUF DER MAUR, the group released two UK hits, 'DOLL PARTS' and 'VIOLET', LOVE certainly back on top form with her incendiary Top Of The Pops performances (LYDIA LUNCH eat your heart out!?). Back in the news again, she was fined for assaulting BIKINI KILL's KATHLEEN HANNA, LOVE and SCHEMEL conversely taking three security guards to court following an alleged assault incident while signing autographs stagefront at a GREEN DAY concert in Lakefront Arena (yet more column inches were devoted to the controversial singer in August '96, when LOVE was acquitted of a stage assault nine months previous on two teenage fans in Florida). More recently, LOVE has played down her wild child character, exchanging the Seattle grunge mantle for a more respectable Hollywood career. This was largely down to her acclaimed roles in the movies, 'Feeling Minnesota' and more so with the controversial, 'The People Vs. Larry Flint'. On the recording front, only a lone version of FLEETWOOD MAC's 'GOLD DUST WOMAN' has surfaced (this was included on the film soundtrack from 'The Crow II: City Of Angels'). In '98, COURTNEY (and HOLE) was once again writing new material, this time with BILLY CORGAN of the SMASHING PUMPKINS, although a dispute over who actually wrote what the public thought were collaborations was subsequent tabloid news. The album in question, 'CELEBRITY SKIN' (1998), was worthy of its Top 10 placing although a little commercialised for some. The following year (in November), MELISSA bailed out of the band and more shocking still was that she joined COURTNEY's old pal CORGAN in The SMASHING PUMPKINS. After a Golden Globe performance in the movie 'The People Vs. Larry Flynt' in '99, LOVE subsequently entered a legal wrangle over her dead husband's legacy once again. She tried to hault CHRIS NOVOSELIC and DAVE GROHL as they prepared to mix two new NIRVANA tracks and issue a 'Best Of . . .' compendium. Opening the situation up to the press as well as the television media, LOVE sought even more attention by publicly warring with the ex-NIRVANA casualties. However, it was all in vein as a settlement was agreed by both camps, leaving our favourite female rock'n'roll attention-seeker to direct her anger towards her own record company (whom she sued), before getting arrested over numerous drug-related offences during 2002-03. • **Covers:** STAR BELLY sampled DREAMS (Fleetwood Mac) + INTO THE BLACK (Neil Young) / DO IT CLEAN (Echo & The Bunnymen) / CREDIT IN THE STRAIGHT WORLD (Young Marble Giants) / HUNGRY LIKE THE WOLF (Duran Duran) / SEASON OF THE WITCH (Donovan) / HE HIT ME (IT FELT LIKE A KISS) (Goffin-King) / IT'S ALL OVER NOW, BABY BLUE (Bob Dylan). 'I THINK THAT I WOULD DIE' was co-written w / KAT BJELLAND (Babes In Toyland). • **Note:** Not to be confused with band who released in the late 80's; OTHER TONGUES, OTHER FLESH (LP) and DYSKINSIA (12") both on 'Eyes Media'.

Album rating: PRETTY ON THE INSIDE (*7) / LIVE THROUGH THIS (*9) / MY BODY, THE HAND GRENADE collection (*6) / CELEBRITY SKIN (*7)

COURTNEY LOVE (b. MICHELLE HARRISON, 9 Jul'64, San Francisco, Calif.) – vocals, guitars / **ERIC ERLANDSON** (b. 9 Jan'63) – guitars / **JILL EMERY** – bass, vocals / **CAROLINE RUE** – drums

not iss. — Sympathy F

Jul 90. (7"white-ep) *<SFTRI 53>* **RETARD GIRL. / PHONEBILL SONG / JOHNNIES IN THE BATHROOM** [–] [ ]
(UK-iss.cd-ep Sep97 +=; SFTRI 53CD) – Turpentine.

not iss. — Sub Pop

Apr 91. (7"colrd-various) *(SP 93)* **DICKNAIL. / BURNBLACK** [–] [ ]

City Slang — Caroline

Aug 91. (7"colrd-various) *(EFA 04070-45)* **TEENAGE WHORE. / DROWN SODA** [ ] [ ]
(12"+=/cd-s+=) *(EFA 04070-02/-03)* – Burnblack.

Oct 91. (cd/c/lp-some red) *(EFA 0407-2/-C/-1)* *<SLANG 012>* **PRETTY ON THE INSIDE** [59] Jul91 [ ]
– Teenage whore / Babydoll / Garbage man / Sassy / Goodsister – bad sister / Mrs. Jones / Berry / Loaded / Star belly / Pretty on the inside / Clouds. *(re-iss. Sep95; same)*

— **LESLEY** – bass repl. JILL / **PATTY SCHEMEL** (b.24 Apr'67, Seattle Washington) – drums repl. CAROLINE

City Slang — D.G.C.

Apr 93. (7") *(EFA 04916-45)* **BEAUTIFUL SON. / OLD AGE** [54] [–]
(12"+=/cd-s+=) *(EFA 04916-02/-03)* – 20 years in the Dakota.

— **KRISTEN PFAFF** – bass, piano, vocals repl. LESLEY

Mar 94. (7"some pink) *(EFA 04936-7)* **MISS WORLD. / ROCK STAR (alternate mix)** [64] [ ]
(cd-s+=) *(EFA 04936-2)* – Do it clean (live).

Apr 94. (cd/c/lp;some white) *(EFA 04935-2/-4/-1)* *<24631>* **LIVE THROUGH THIS** [13] [52]
– Violet / Miss World / Plump / Asking for it / Jennifer's body / Doll parts / Credit in the straight world / Softer, softest / She walks on me / I think that I would die / Gutless / Rock star. *(re-iss. cd/lp Mar95 on 'Geffen'; GED/GEF 24631)*

— KRISTEN was found dead in her bath 16th June 1994. COURTNEY, ERIC + PATTI continued and later recruited **MELISSA AUF DER MAUR** (b.17 Mar'72, Montreal, Canada) – bass. As HOLEZ (HOLE + PAT SMEAR of GERMS) they released tribute GERMS cover 'CIRCLE 1' on 'Dutch East India' Mar95.

Geffen — D.G.C.

Nov 94. (c-s) *<19379>* **DOLL PARTS / PLUMP (live)** [–] [58]

Apr 95. (7") *(GFS 91)* **DOLL PARTS. / THE VOID** [16] [–]
(cd-s+=) *(GFSTD 91)* – Hungry like the wolf (live).
(cd-s) *(GFSXD 91)* – ('A'side) / Plump (live) / I think that I would die (live) / Credit in the straight world (live).

Jul 95. (7") *(GFS 94)* **VIOLET. / OLD AGE** [17] [ ]
(7"colrd) *(GFSP 94)* – ('A'side) / He hit me (it felt like a kiss).
(cd-s++=) *(GFSCD 94)* – Who's porno you burn (black).

Nov 96. (etched-d7") *(573164-7)* **GOLD DUST WOMAN. / (NY LOOSE: Spit)** [ ] [ ]
(above 45 was a limited edition on 'Polydor' UK, 'Hollywood' US)

Sep 98. (7"/c-s) *(GFS/+C 22345)* *<radio play>* **CELEBRITY SKIN. / BEST SUNDAY DRESS** [19] [85]
(cd-s+=) *(GFSTD 22345)* – Dying (original demo).

Sep 98. (cd/c/lp) *<(GED/GEC/GEF 25164)>* **CELEBRITY SKIN** [11] [9]
– Celebrity skin / Awful / Hit so hard / Malibu / Reasons to be beautiful / Dying / Use once & destroy / Northern star / Boys on the radio / Heaven tonight / Playing your song / Petals. *(special cd w/tour cd Jun99 +=; IND 90385)* – Pretty on the inside / Heaven tonight / Northern star / Awful / Paradise city / Celebrity skin.

Jan 99. (7") *(GFS 22369)* *<radio cut>* **MALIBU. / DRAG** [22] [81]
(cd-s+=) *(GFSTD 22369)* – It's all over now, baby blue.
(cd-s) *(GFSCX 22369)* – ('A'side) / Celebrity skin (live) / Reasons to be beautiful (live).

Interscope — Interscope

Jun 99. (7") *(INTS7 97098)* **AWFUL. / VIOLET (live)** [42] [ ]
(cd-s) *(INTDE 97099)* – ('A'side) / Miss World (live) / Celebrity skin (CD-Rom video).
(cd-s) *(INTDE 97098)* – ('A'side) / She walks on me (live) / Malibu (CD-Rom video).

– compilations, etc. –

Oct 95. (m-cd) *Caroline; <1470>* **ASK FOR IT** (radio session) [–] [ ]

Sep 97. (cd/c/lp) *City Slang; <(EFA 04995-2/-4/-1)>* **MY BODY, THE HAND GRENADE** [ ] Oct97 [ ]
– Turpentine / Phonebill song / Retard girl / Burn black / Dicknail / Beautiful son / 20 years in Dakota / Miss World / Old age / Softer softest / He hit me (it felt like a kiss) / Season of the witch / Drown soda / Asking for it.

HOLLIES

Formed: Manchester, England . . . 1961 by ALLAN CLARKE and GRAHAM NASH, who quickly found DON RATHBONE and ERIC HAYCOCK. In 1963, they signed to EMI's 'Parlophone' label, adding a 5th member, TONY HICKS. Their debut 45, '(AIN'T THAT) JUST LIKE ME', made the UK Top 30, being followed by 'SEARCHIN'', their first of 21 consecutive Top 20 hits until 1971's 'HEY WILLY' (later a hit for the SWEET as 'Little Willy') failed to register. During the early part of their career, The HOLLIES were basically a pop industry beat group, jumping on the psychedelic bandwagon in 1968 with the mythical pretentiousness of 'KING MIDAS IN REVERSE'. However, following the departure of NASH, they increasingly moved into the cabaret scene. They regained a bit of credibility in late 1969, however, with the much-loved ballad, 'HE AIN'T HEAVY'. In December '71, CLARKE left for the first time, returning in mid-73 after his Swedish replacement MICHAEL RICKFORS failed to impress the buying public. They immediately reinstated themselves when a Top 30 hit was followed by near No.1 smash, 'THE AIR THAT I BREATHE'. Although future hits were few and far between, they ploughed on throughout the 70's & 80's. • **Songwriters:** CLARKE-HICKS-NASH, until latter's departure to CROSBY, STILLS & NASH. HOLLIES covered; (AIN'T THAT) JUST LIKE ME + SEARCHIN' (Coasters) / STAY (Maurice Williams & The Zodiacs) / JUST ONE LOOK (Doris Troy) / YES I WILL (Goffin-Titelman) / I'M ALIVE (Clint Ballard Jr.) / LOOK THROUGH ANY WINDOW + BUS STOP (Graham Gouldman) / IF I NEEDED SOMEONE (George Harrison; Beatles) / I CAN'T LET GO + THE BABY (Chip Taylor) / SORRY SUZANNE (T.MacAuley & G.Stephens) / GASOLINE ALLEY BRED (T.MacAuley-R.Cook-R.Greenaway) / WHEN THE SHIP COMES IN (Bob Dylan) / JESUS WAS A CROSSMAKER (Judee Sill) / SANDY (Bruce Springsteen) / STOP IN THE NAME OF LOVE (Supremes) / SOLDIER'S SONG (Mike Batt) / CARRIE (John Miles) / STAND BY ME (Ben

E.King) / SHINE SILENTLY (Nils Lofgren) / etc. Also cover albums 'HOLLIES SING (Bob) DYLAN' and 'BUDDY HOLLY'. KENNY LYNCH collaborated on several with HICKS on 1971's 'DISTANT LIGHT'. • **Trivia:** In 1988 after exposure on Miller lite UK TV ad, the 1969 hit 'HE AIN'T HEAVY, HE'S MY BROTHER' re-charted, hitting No.1.

Best CD compilation: GREATEST HITS (*8)

ALLAN CLARKE (b. 5 Apr'42, Salford, Manchester, England) – vocals / **TONY HICKS** (b.16 Dec'43, Nelson, Lancashire, England) – lead guitar / **GRAHAM NASH** (b. 2 Feb'42, Blackpool, England) – guitar / **ERIC HAYDOCK** (b. 3 Feb'43) – bass / **DON RATHBONE** – drums

Parlophone Liberty

May 63. (7") *(R 5030)* **(AIN'T THAT) JUST LIKE ME. / HEY WHAT'S WRONG WITH ME** 25 –

Aug 63. (7") *(R 5052)* **SEARCHIN'. / WHOLE WORLD OVER** 12 –

— **BOBBY ELLIOTT** (b. 8 Dec'42, Burnley, England) – drums (ex-SHANE FENTON & THE FENTONES) repl. RATHBONE (still on next single b-side and album track – *)

Nov 63. (7") *(R 5077)* <55674> **STAY. / NOW'S THE TIME** 8 Mar64

Jan 64. (lp) *(PMC 1220)* **STAY WITH THE HOLLIES** 2 –
– I'm talkin' 'bout you / Mr. Moonlight / You better move on / Lucille / Baby don't cry / Memphis / Stay / Rockin' Robin / What'cha gonna do about it? / Do you love me / It's only make believe / What kind of girl are you / Little lover / Candy man. *(re-iss. Oct87 on 'Beat Goes On'; BGOLP 4) (cd-iss. Oct88; BGOCD 4) (cd re-iss. Dec99 on 'Magic'; 524412-2)*

Parlophone Imperial

Feb 64. (7") *(R 5104)* <66026> **JUST ONE LOOK. / KEEP OFF THAT FRIEND OF MINE** 2 Apr64 98

May 64. (7") *(R 5137)* **HERE I GO AGAIN. / BABY THAT'S ALL** 4 –

Jul 64. (7") <66044> **HERE I GO AGAIN. / LUCILLE** –

Sep 64. (7") *(R 5178)* <66070> **WE'RE THROUGH. / COME ON BACK** 7 Oct64

Nov 64. (lp) *(PMC 1235)* **IN THE HOLLIES STYLE** –
– Nitty gritty – Something's got a hold on me / Don't you know / To you my love / It's in her kiss / Time for love / What kind of boy / Too much monkey business / I thought of you last night / Please don't feel too bad / Come on home / Set me free. *(re-iss. Mar88 & Apr97 on 'Beat Goes On' lp/cd; BGO LP/CD 8) (cd re-iss. Oct00 on 'Magic'; 525127-2)*

Jan 65. (7") *(R 5232)* **YES I WILL. / NOBODY** 9 –

May 65. (7") *(R 5287)* **I'M ALIVE. / YOU KNOW HE DID** 1 –

Aug 65. (7") *(R 5322)* <66134> **LOOK THROUGH ANY WINDOW. / SO LONELY** 4 Nov65 32

Sep 65. (lp) *(PMC 1261)* <12312> **THE HOLLIES** 8 Jun66
– Put yourself in my place / When I come home to you / That's my desire / Mickey's monkey / Very last day / Down the line / Lawdy Miss Clawdy / You must believe me / Too many people / Fortune teller / I've been wrong. *(re-iss. Nov69 as 'REFLECTION' on 'Regal Starline'; SRS 5008) (re-iss. Jul88 on 'Beat Goes On'; BGOLP 25) (cd-iss. Apr91; BGOCD 25)*

Dec 65. (7") *(R 5392)* **IF I NEEDED SOMEONE. / I'VE GOT A WAY OF MY OWN** 20 –

Jan 66. (lp) <12299> **HEAR! HERE!** –
– I'm alive / Very last day / You must believe me / Put yourself in my place / Down the line / That's my desire / Look through any window / Lawdy Miss Clawdy / When I come home to you / Lonely / I've been wrong / Too many people.

Feb 66. (7") *(R 5409)* <66158> **I CAN'T LET GO. / I'VE GOT A WAY OF MY OWN** 2 Mar66 42

Jun 66. (lp; mono/stereo) *(PMC/PCS 7008)* <12330> **WOULD YOU BELIEVE?** <US-title 'BUS STOP'> 16 Oct66 75
– I take what I want / Hard hard year / That's how strong my love is / Sweet little sixteen / Oriental sadness (I'll never trust in anybody no more) / I am a rock / Take your time / Don't you even care (what's gonna happen) / Fifi the flea / Stewball / I've got a way of my own / I can't let go. *(re-iss. Oct88 on 'Beat Goes On'; BGOLP 24) (cd-iss. Apr91; BGOCD 24)*

— **BERNIE CALVERT** (b.16 Sep'43, Burnley) – bass repl. HAYDOCK who formed HAYDOCK'S ROADHOUSE **JOHN PAUL JONES** – bass sessioned on the next b-side. (Later to LED ZEPPELIN)

Jun 66. (7") *(R 5469)* <66186> **BUS STOP. / DON'T RUN AND HIDE** 5 Jul66 5

— in Aug'66, they teamed up with actor/comedian PETER SELLERS on single 'AFTER THE FOX', from the film on 'United Artists'

Oct 66. (7") *(R 5508)* <66214> **STOP! STOP! STOP!. / IT'S YOU** 2 7

Oct 66. (lp; mono/stereo) *(PMC/PCS 7011)* <12339> **FOR CERTAIN BECAUSE . . .** <US-title 'STOP! STOP! STOP!'> 23 Feb67 91
– What's wrong with the way I live / Pay you back with interest / Tell me to my face / Clown / Suspicious look in your eyes / It's you / High classed / Peculiar situation / What went wrong / Crusader / Don't even think about changing / Stop! stop! stop! *(re-iss. Dec71 as 'STOP! STOP! STOP!' on 'Regal Starline'; SRS 5088) (re-iss. Apr88 on 'Beat Goes On' lp/c; BGO MC/CD 9) (cd-iss. Dec89; BGOCD 9) (cd re-iss. Jan99 on 'E.M.I.'; 528241-2)*

Feb 67. (7") *(R 5562)* <66231> **ON A CAROUSEL. / ALL THE WORLD IS LOVE** 4 Mar67 11

May 67. (7") <66240> **PAY YOU BACK WITH INTEREST. / WHAT'CHA GONNA DO ABOUT IT** – 28

— between Feb'67 and Mar'67 they used session drummer **DOUGIE WRIGHT** to repl. ill ELLIOTT (CLEM CATTINI + MITCH MITCHELL also guested)

Parlophone Epic

May 67. (7") *(R 5602)* <10180> **CARRIE-ANNE. / SIGNS THAT WILL NEVER CHANGE** 3 Jun67 9

Jun 67. (lp; mono/stereo) *(PMC/PCS 7022)* <26315> **EVOLUTION** 13 Jul67 43
– Then the heartaches begin / Stop right there / Water on the brain / Lullaby to Tim / Have you ever loved somebody / You need love / Rain on the window / Heading for a fall / Ye olde toffee shoppe *[UK-only]* / When your lights turned on / Leave me *[UK-only]* / The games we play. <US+=> – Carrie-Anne / Jennifer Eccles / Signs that will never change / Open up your eyes. *(re-iss. Feb72 as 'HOLLIES' on 'Music For Pleasure'; MFP 5252) (re-iss. 1989 on 'Beat Goes On'; BGOLP 80) (cd-iss. Jun93; BGOCD 80) (cd re-iss. Feb99 on 'E.M.I.'; 528247-2) <(cd re-iss. Jun99 on 'Sundazed'++=; SC 6122)> (cd re-iss. Oct00 on 'Magic'; 497579-2)*

Sep 67. (7") *(R 5637)* **KING MIDAS IN REVERSE. / EVERYTHING IS SUNSHINE** 18 –

Sep 67. (7") <10234> **KING MIDAS IN REVERSE. / WATER ON THE BRAIN** – 51

Oct 67. (lp; mono/stereo) *(PMC/PCS 7039)* <26344> **BUTTERFLY** <US-title 'DEAR ELOISE / KING MIDAS IN REVERSE'> Jan68
– Dear Eloise / Away away away / Maker / Pegasus the flying horse / Would you believe / Wish you a wish / Postcard / Charlie and Fred / Try it / Elevated observations / Step inside / Butterfly. <US+=> – King Midas in reverse / Leave me / Do the best you can. *(re-iss. 1989 on 'Beat Goes On' lp/cd; BGO LP/CD 79) <(cd re-iss. Dec97 as US title on 'Sundazed'+=; SC 6123)> (cd re-iss. Mar99 on 'E.M.I.'; 528243-2)*

Nov 67. (7") <10251> **DEAR ELOISE. / WHEN YOUR LIGHTS TURNED ON** – 50

Mar 68. (7") *(R 5680)* **JENNIFER ECCLES. / OPEN UP YOUR EYES** 11 –

Mar 68. (7") <10298> **JENNIFER ECCLES. / TRY IT** – 40

Jun 68. (7") <10361> **DO THE BEST YOU CAN. / ELEVATED OBSERVATIONS** – 93

Sep 68. (7") *(R 5733)* **LISTEN TO ME. / DO THE BEST YOU CAN** 11 –

Sep 68. (7") <10400> **LISTEN TO ME. / EVERYTHING IS SUNSHINE** –

— **TERRY SYLVESTER** (b. 8 Jan'45, Liverpool, England) – vocals, guitar (ex-SWINGING BLUE JEANS) repl. NASH who joined CROSBY, STILLS & NASH. (**ELLIOT** also returned)

Feb 69. (7") *(R 5765)* <10454> **SORRY SUZANNE. / NOT THAT WAY AT ALL** 3 56

May 69. (lp; mono/stereo) *(PMC/PCS 7078)* <26447> **HOLLIES SING DYLAN** 3
– When the ship comes in / I'll be your baby tonight / I want you / This wheel's on fire / I shall be released/ / Blowin' in the wind / Quit your low down ways / Just like a woman / The times they are a-changin' / All I really want to do / My back pages / The mighty Quinn (Quinn, the eskimo). *(re-iss. Oct87 on 'Music For Pleasure' lp/c; MFP/TC-MFP 5811) (cd-iss. Jun93 on 'E.M.I.'; CZ 520) (cd re-iss. Apr99 on 'E.M.I.'; 528246-2)*

Sep 69. (7") *(R 5806)* <10532> **HE AIN'T HEAVY, HE'S MY BROTHER. / 'COS YOU LIKE TO LOVE ME** 3 Dec69 7

Nov 69. (lp) *(PCS 7092)* <26538> **HOLLIES SING HOLLIES** <US-title 'HE AIN'T HEAVY, HE'S MY BROTHER'> 32
– Do you believe in love / Please sign your letters / Please let me please / Goodbye tomorrow / My life is over with you / Soldier's dilemma / Marigold; Gloria swansong / You love 'cos you like it / Why didn't you believe / Look at life / Don't give up easily / Reflections of a time gone

past. *<US version replaced; 'Marigold – Gloria Swansong' with>* – He ain't heavy, he's my brother. *(cd-iss. Apr99 on 'Magic'; 497757-2)*

Apr 70. (7") *(R 5837) <10613>* **I CAN'T TELL THE BOTTOM FROM THE TOP. / MAD PROFESSOR BLYTH** [7] May70 [82]

Sep 70. (7") *(R 5862) <10677>* **GASOLINE ALLEY BRED. / DANDELION WINE** [14] [ ]

Nov 70. (lp) *(PCS 7116) <30255>* **CONFESSIONS OF THE MIND** <US-title 'MOVING FINGER'> [30] [ ]
– Survival of the fittest / Man without a heart / Little girl / Isn't it nice? / Perfect lady housewife / Confessions of a mind / Lady please / Frightened lady / Too young to be married / Separated / I wanna shout. <US+=> – Marigold – Gloria Swansong / Gasoline alley bred / Dandelion wine / Mad Professor Blyth. *(re-iss. 1989 on 'Beat Goes On'; BGOLP 96) (cd-iss. Apr91; BGOCD 96) <(cd re-iss. Nov97 as US title on 'Sundazed'+=; SC 6126)> (cd re-iss. May99 on 'E.M.I.'; 528243-2)*

Jan 71. (7") *<10716>* **SURVIVAL OF THE FITTEST. / MAN WITHOUT A HEART** [–] [ ]

May 71. (7") *(R 5905)* **HEY WILLY. / ROW THE BOAT TOGETHER** [ ] [ ]

Jun 71. (lp) *(PAS 10005) <30958>* **DISTANT LIGHT** [ ] Jul71 [21]
– What a life I've led / Look what we've got / Hold on / Pull down the blind / To do with love / Promised land / Long cool woman (in a black dress) / You know the score / Cable car / A little thing like love / Long dark road. *(re-iss. Jul91 on 'Beat Goes On'; BGO LP/CD 97) (cd re-iss. May99 on 'E.M.I.'; 528242-2)*

Jun 72. (7") *<10871>* **LONG COOL WOMAN (IN A BLACK DRESS). / LOOK WHAT WE'VE GOT** [–] [2]

Aug 72. (7") *(R 5939)* **LONG COOL WOMAN (IN A BLACK DRESS). / CABLE CAR** [32] [–]

Nov 72. (7") *<10920>* **LONG DARK ROAD. / INDIAN GIRL** [–] [26]

—— (Aug71) **MICHAEL RICKFORS** – vocals (ex-BAMBOO) repl. CLARKE who went solo

Polydor Epic

Feb 72. (7") *(2058 199) <10842>* **THE BABY. / OH! GRANNY** [26] [ ]

Nov 72. (7") *(2058 289)* **MAGIC WOMAN TOUCH. / INDIAN GIRL** [ ] [–]

Nov 72. (lp) *(2383 144) <31992>* **ROMANY** [ ] [84]
– Won't we feel good that morning / Touch / Words don't come easy / Magic woman touch / Lizzy and the rainman / Down river / Slow down – Go down / Delaware Taggett and the outlaw boys / Jesus was a crossmaker / Romany / Blue in the morning / Courage of your convictions. *(cd-iss. Oct00 on 'Magic'+=; 497578-2)* – The baby / Oh! granny / Indian girl / I had a dream / Don't leave the child alone / If it wasn't for the reason / A better place / The last wind.

Jan 73. (7") *<10951>* **MAGIC WOMAN TOUCH. / BLUE IN THE MORNING** [–] [60]

Mar 73. (7") *<10989>* **JESUS WAS A CROSSMAKER. / I HAD A DREAM** [–] [ ]

May 73. (7") *<11025>* **SLOW DOWN. / WON'T WE FEEL GOOD** [–] [ ]

not iss. Polydor

May 73. (lp) **OUT ON THE ROAD (studio)** [–] German [–]
– Out on the road / A better place / They don't realize I'm down / The last wind / Mr. Heartbreaker / I was born a man / Slow down – Go down / Don't leave the child alone / Nearer to you / Pick up the pieces again / Transatlantic west bound jet.

—— (Jul73) **ALLAN CLARKE** – vocals returned to repl. RICKFORS (CLARKE now joining others HICKS, SYLVESTER, CALVERT and ELLIOTT)

Oct 73. (7") *(2058 403) <11051>* **THE DAY THAT CURLY BILLY SHOT CRAZY SAM McGEE. / BORN A MAN** [24] [ ]

Jan 74. (7") *(2058 435) <11100>* **THE AIR THAT I BREATHE. / NO MORE RIDERS** [2] Apr74 [6]

Mar 74. (lp) *(2383 262) <32574>* **THE HOLLIES** [38] May74 [28]
– Falling calling / It's a shame, it's a game / Don't let me down / Out on the road / The air that I breathe / Rubber Lucy / Transatlantic west bound jet / Pick up the pieces again / Down on the run / Love makes the world go round / The day that Curly Billy shot down crazy Sam McGee. *(cd-iss. Dec99 on 'Magic'; 497577-2)*

May 74. (7") *(2058 476)* **SON OF A ROTTEN GAMBLER. / LAYIN' TO THE MUSIC** [ ] [–]

May 74. (7") *<50029>* **DON'T LET ME DOWN. / LAY INTO THE MUSIC** [–] [ ]

Nov 74. (7") *(2058 533)* **I'M DOWN. / HELLO LADY GOODBYE** [ ] [–]

Feb 75. (lp) *(2441 128) <33387>* **ANOTHER NIGHT** [ ] [ ]
– Another night / 4th of July, Asbury Park (Sandy) / Lonely hobo lullaby / Secondhand hang-ups / Time machine jive / I'm down / Look out Johnny (there's a monkey on your back) / Give me time / You gave me life (with that look in your eyes) / Lucy. *(cd-iss. Dec99 on 'Magic'; 524408-2)*

May 75. (7") *(2058 595) <50086>* **4TH OF JULY, ASBURY PARK (SANDY). / SECONDHAND HANG-UPS** [ ] Mar75 [85]
<US re-iss. Apr76; 50359>

Jun 75. (7") *<50110>* **ANOTHER NIGHT. / TIME MACHINE JIVE** [–] [71]

Aug 75. (7") *<50144>* **I'M DOWN. / LOOK OUT JOHNNY (THERE'S A MONKEY ON YOUR BACK)** [–] [ ]

—— **ROD ARGENT** – moog, piano (on next opening track)

Jan 76. (lp) *(2442 141)* **WRITE ON** [ ] [–]
– Star / Write on / Sweet country calling / Love is the thing / I won't move over / Narida / Stranger / Crocodile woman (she bites) / My island / There's always goodbye. *(cd-iss. Dec99 on 'Magic'+=; 524414-2)* – Boulder to Birmingham / Samuel / Star (live) / My island (live) / Born to run.

Feb 76. (7") *<50204>* **WRITE ON. / CROCODILE WOMAN (SHE BITES)** [–] [ ]

Feb 76. (7") *(2058 694)* **BOULDER TO BIRMINGHAM. / CROCODILE WOMAN (SHE BITES)** [ ] [–]

Apr 76. (7") *(2058 719)* **STAR. / LOVE IS THE THING** [ ] [–]

Aug 76. (7") *(2058 779)* **DADDY DON'T MIND. / C'MON** [ ] [–]

Oct 76. (7") *(2058 799)* **WIGGLE THAT WOTSIT. / CORRINE** [ ] [–]

Dec 76. (lp) *(2382 421)* **RUSSIAN ROULETTE** [ ] [–]
– Wiggle that wotsit / Forty-eight hour patrol / Thanks for the memories / My love / Lady of the night / Russian roulette / Draggin' my heels / Louise / Be with you / Daddy don't mind.

Dec 76. (7") *<50422>* **DRAGGIN' MY HEELS. / I WON'T MOVE OVER** [–] [ ]

Mar 77. (lp) *(2383 428)* **HOLLIES LIVE HITS** (live in New Zealand) [4] [–]
– I can't let go / Just one look / I can't tell the bottom from the top / Another night / Bus stop / 4th of July, Asbury Park (Sandy) / Star / My island / I'm down / Stop, stop, stop / Long cool woman (in a black dress) / Carrie-Anne / The air that I breathe / Too young to be married / He ain't heavy, he's my brother.

May 77. (7") *(2058 880)* **HELLO TO ROMANCE. / 48 HOUR PAROLE** [ ] [–]

Jul 77. (7") *(2058 906)* **AMNESTY. / CROSSFIRE** [ ] [–]

Mar 78. (lp) *(2383 474) <3534>* **A CRAZY STEAL** [ ] [ ]
– Writing on the wall / What am I gonna do? / Let it pour / Burn out / Hello to romance / Amnesty / Caracas / Boulder to Birmingham / Clown service / Feet on the ground.

Apr 78. (7") *<50522>* **BURN OUT. / WRITING ON THE WALL** [–] [ ]

Mar 79. (7") *(POSP 35)* **SOMETHING TO LIVE FOR. / SONG OF THE SUN** [ ] [–]
(12"+=) *(POSPX 35)* – The air that I breathe.

Mar 79. (lp) *(2442 160)* **FIVE THREE ONE – DOUBLE SEVEN O FOUR** [ ] [–]
– Say it ain't so, Joe / Maybe it's dawn / Song of the sun / Harlequin / When I'm yours / Something to live for / Stormy waters / Boys in the band / Satellite three / It's in every one of us.

Mar 80. (7") *(2059 246)* **SOLDIER'S SONG. / DRAGGIN' MY HEELS** [58] [–]

Sep 80. (7") *(POSP 175)* **HEARTBEAT. / TAKE YOUR TIME** [ ] [–]

Oct 80. (lp/c) *(POLTV/+M 12)* **BUDDY HOLLY** [ ] [–]
– Take your time / Wishing / Peggy Sue / Heartbeat / Love's made a fool of you / That'll be the day / Think it over / Tell me how / Maybe baby / I'm gonna love you too / What to do / It doesn't matter / Peggy Sue got married / Midnight shift / Everyday.

—— trimmed to a trio of CLARKE, HICKS and ELLIOTT when CALVERT and SYLVESTER left. Latter teamed with JAMES GRIFFIN (ex-BREAD) (next single b-side with **ALAN JONES** – bass)

Nov 81. (7") *(POSP 379)* **TAKE MY LOVE AND RUN. / DRIVER** [ ] [–]

—— added returning **GRAHAM NASH** – vocals, guitar

WEA Atlantic

Jul 83. (7") *(U 9888) <89819>* **STOP! IN THE NAME OF LOVE. / MUSICAL PICTURES** [ ] May83 [29]

Jul 83. (lp/c) *(250139-1/-4) <80076>* **WHAT GOES AROUND** [ ] [90]
– Casualty / Take my love and run / Say you'll be mine / Something ain't right / If the lights go out / Stop! In the name of love / I got what you want / Just one look / Someone else's eyes / Having a good

time. <(cd-iss. Jan02 on 'Wounded Bird'+=; WOU 8076)> – Musical pictures.

Aug 83. (7") *<89784>* **SOMEONE ELSE'S EYES. / IF THE LIGHTS GO OUT** – ☐

Oct 83. (7") *<89768>* **CASUALTY. / IF THE LIGHTS GO OUT** – ☐

—— basic trio of **CLARKE, HICKS** and **ELLIOTT** plus **ALAN COATES** – harmonies / **STEVE STROUD** – bass / **DENNIS HAYNES** – keyboards

Columbia / not iss.

May 85. (7") *(DB 9110)* **TOO MANY HEARTS GET BROKEN. / YOU'RE ALL WOMAN** ☐ –
(12"+=) *(12DB 9110)* – Laughter turns to tears.

Jan 87. (7") *(DB 9146)* **THIS IS IT. / YOU GAVE ME STRENGTH** ☐ –
(12"+=) *(12DB 9146)* – You're all woman.

Mar 87. (7") *(DB 9151)* **REUNION OF THE HEART. / TOO MANY HEARTS GET BROKEN** ☐ –
(12"+=) *(12DB 9151)* – Hollidaze (medley).

—— **RAY STILES** – bass (ex-MUD) repl. STROUD

Coconut / not iss.

Jan 88. (7") **STAND BY ME. / FOR WHAT IT'S WORTH** – German –

Jun 88. (7") **SHINE SILENTLY. / YOUR EYES** – German –

E.M.I. / not iss.

Feb 89. (7") *(EM 86)* **FIND ME A FAMILY. / NO RULES** ☐ –

Mar 93. (c-s/7") *(TC+/EM 264)* **THE WOMAN I LOVE. / PURPLE RAIN (live)** 42 –
(cd-s+=) *(CDEM 264)* – The air that I breathe / (Ain't) That just like me.

Mar 93. (cd/c/lp) *(CD/TC+/EMTV 74)* **THE AIR THAT I BREATHE (THE BEST OF THE HOLLIES)** (compilation) 15 –
– The air that I breathe / Bus stop / Just one look / Yes I will / Look through any window / He ain't heavy, he's my brother / I can't let go / We're through / Searchin' / Stay / I'm alive / If I needed someone / Here I go again / Stop stop stop / On a carousel / Carrie Ann / King Midas in reverse / Jennifer Eccles / Listen to me / Sorry Suzanne / I can't tell the bottom from the top / Gasoline alley bred / Hey Willy / The day that curly Billy shot down crazy Sam McGee / The woman I love.

– (selective) compilations, etc. –

on 'Parlophone' unless mentiond otherwise

Sep 67. (7") *Imperial; <66258>* **JUST ONE LOOK. / RUNNING THROUGH THE NIGHT** – 44

Aug 68. (lp) *(7057) <12350>* **HOLLIES' GREATEST HITS** 1 11
(US version different)

Jul 78. (lp/c) *E.M.I.; (EMTV/TC-EMTV 11)* **20 GOLDEN GREATS** 2 –
– The air that I breathe / Carrie Anne / Bus stop / Listen to me / Look through any window / I can't let go / Long cool woman in a black dress / Here I go again / I can't tell the bottom from the top / I'm alive / Yes I will / Stay / Sorry Suzanne / Gasoline alley bred / We're through / Jennifer Eccles / Stop! stop! stop! / On a carousel / Just one look / He ain't heavy, he's my brother. *(cd-iss. Mar87 & Jan89; CDP 238-2)*

Aug 81. (7") *E.M.I.; (EMI 5229)* **HOLLIEDAZE (MEDLEY). / HOLLIEPOPS** 28 –

Aug 88. (7") *E.M.I.; (EM 74)* **HE AIN'T HEAVY, HE'S MY BROTHER. / CARRIE** 1 ☐
(12"+=/cd-s+=) *(12/CD EM 74)* – The air that I breathe.

Sep 88. (d-lp/d-c)(d-cd) *E.M.I.; (EM/TCEM 1301)(CDS 790 850-2)* **ALL THE HITS AND MORE – THE DEFINITIVE COLLECTION** 51 –

Nov 88. (7") *E.M.I.; (EM 80)* **THE AIR THAT I BREATHE. / WE'RE THROUGH** 60 ☐
(12"+=) *(12EM 80)* – King Midas in reverse / Just one look.
(cd-s+=) *(CDEM 80)* – He ain't heavy, he's my brother.

Feb 95. (4xcd-box) *E.M.I.; (HOLLIES 1)* **FOUR HOLLIES ORIGINALS** ☐ –
– (ANOTHER NIGHT / RUSSIAN ROULETTE / 5317704 / BUDDY HOLLY)

Mar 95. (cd) *See For Miles; (SEECD 94)* **THE EP COLLECTION** ☐ ☐

Feb 96. (4xcd-box) *Premier-EMI; (CDHOLLIES 2)* **FOUR MORE HOLLIES ORIGINALS** ☐ –
– (ROMANY / WRITE ON / THE HOLLIES / A CRAZY STEAL)

Feb 97. (cd) *E.M.I.; (CTMCD 311)* **THE BEST OF THE HOLLIES: CENTENARY COLLECTION** ☐ ☐

Sep 97. (cd) *Connoisseur; (NSPCD 518)* **ARCHIVE ALIVE: LIVE AT KING'S ISLAND, CINCINNATI, OHIO)** ☐ ☐

Oct 97. (cd) *E.M.I.; (CDABBEY 103)* **AT ABBEY ROAD 1963-1966** ☐ ☐

Nov 97. (d-cd) *BR Music; (BS 81032)* **THE AIR THAT I BREATHE** ☐ –

Feb 98. (cd) *E.M.I.; (493450-2)* **AT ABBEY ROAD 1966-1970** ☐ ☐

Feb 98. (cd) *Disky; (LS 86521-2)* **20 GREAT LOVE SONGS** ☐ ☐

Apr 00. (cd) *Disky; (SI 99075-2)* **THE BEST OF THE 60'S** ☐ ☐

Jul 00. (cd) *Disky; (SI 99028-2)* **THE BEST OF THE 70'S** ☐ ☐

Aug 00. (cd) *E.M.I.; (CDP 746238-2)* **20 GOLDEN GREATS** ☐ ☐

Apr 02. (cd) *Disky; (GO 79349-2)* **HERE I GO AGAIN** ☐ ☐

Jul 02. (cd) *Capitol; <CAP 36266>* **CAPITOL MASTERS** – ☐

Mar 03. (d-cd) *E.M.I.; (<5 82012-2>)* **GREATEST HITS** 21 ☐
– I'm alive / Sorry Suzanne / Here I go again / On a carousel / King Midas in reverse / Look through any window / Blowin' in the wind / The air that I breathe / Pay you back with interest / I've got a way of my own / Stay / The very last day / We're through / Carrie Anne / Magic woman touch / I'm down / Gasoline alley bred / I can't let go / 4th of July, Asbury Park (Sandy) / Long cool woman (in a black dress) / Stop, stop, stop / If I needed someone / Dear Eloise / Long dark road / I can't tell the bottom from the top / He ain't heavy, he's my brother / Bus stop / Jennifer Eccles / The day that Curly Billy shot down Crazy Sam McGee / Too young to be married / Listen to me / Just one look / Searchin' / Ain't that just like me / Yes I will (I'll be true to you) / What's wrong with the way I live / Lonely hobo lullaby / Daddy don't mind / The baby / Hey Willy / Son of a rotten gambler / Write on / Star / Boulder to Birmingham / Soldier's song / The woman I love / How do I survive.

☐ Mark HOLLIS (see under ⇒ TALK TALK)

Buddy HOLLY

Born: CHARLES HARDIN HOLLEY, 7 Sep'36, Lubbock, Texas, USA. In the late 40's, the young HOLLY formed a C&W duo with schoolmate, BOB MONTGOMERY. As BUDDY & BOB, they became regulars on a Saturday afternoon TV show (around 1953/54), the pair subsequently putting together a number of demos, later issued as 'HOLLY IN THE HILLS'. With the addition of bassman, LARRY WELBORN and drummer JERRY ALLISON in 1955, the revamped unit began to make a name for themselves locally. After a gig supporting BILL HALEY & HIS COMETS, and through agent Eddie Crandall, BUDDY HOLLY was signed up by 'Decca' early the following year. Rejecting MONTGOMERY (who went on to become a successful producer, etc), the bespectacled HOLLY formed backing band, The THREE TUNES, retaining JERRY and recruiting SONNY CURTIS on guitar, DON GUESS on bass. Following two flop singles, BUDDY and JERRY left the label, travelling to New Mexico in search of producer, NORMAN PETTY, who was soon to become their manager. Early in 1957, the pair were joined by NIKI SULLIVAN (rhythm guitar) and JOE B. MAUDLIN (bass), becoming The CRICKETS. Their debut single, 'THAT'LL BE THE DAY', hit the top of the charts on both sides of the Atlantic, selling a million in the process. As a solo artist (with CRICKETS backing), BUDDY set up a deal with 'Coral', who released 'PEGGY SUE', another transatlantic Top 10 smash. The single also introduced HOLLY's idiosyncratic vocal mannerisms, his exaggerated hiccuping framed by simple but effective arrangements and infectious hooks which influenced many of the biggest 60's rock/pop stars, including DYLAN, The BEATLES and The 'STONES. Over the course of the following year, he balanced a series of CRICKETS hits ('OH BOY', 'MAYBE BABY' and 'THINK IT OVER') with his own solo classics ('LISTEN TO ME', 'RAVE ON' and 'EARLY IN THE MORNING').

His partnership with The CRICKETS was eventually severed in August '58, BUDDY marrying Maria Elena Santiago and moving to New York. His first CRICKETS-less single, 'HEARTBEAT', was surprisingly disappointing in terms of native chart success (i.e. No.82), although it managed to scrape into the UK Top 30. This was certainly a transitional period, things looking promising early the following year when the singer set out as headliner on a winter-long package tour of the States. Tragically, on the morning of the 3rd of February 1959, HOLLY, along with fellow pop stars, RICHIE VALENS and the BIG BOPPER were killed when their chartered plane crashed just after take-off from Mason City airport in Iowa. A posthumous release (written by PAUL ANKA), 'IT DOESN'T MATTER ANYMORE' – backed by 'RAINING IN MY HEART' – became one of his biggest UK hits, while climbing the US Top 20. With a bulging vault of HOLLY material at his disposal, NORMAN PETTY proceeded to keep the legend's name alive via a series of hit releases during the early 60's. Although fans might have disagreed on what direction HOLLY's career might have taken, there was no disputing the fact that the 22 year-old surely still had a wealth of music inside of him. • **Songwriters:** HOLLY wrote most himself, except EARLY IN THE MORNING + NOW WE'RE ONE (Bobby Darin) / BABY I DON'T CARE (Elvis Presley) / etc. His songs were later covered by Rolling Stones (NOT FADE AWAY) / Mud (OH BOY) / Showaddywaddy (HEARTBEAT) / Leo Sayer (RAINING IN MY HEART). • **Trivia:** In Sep'58, HOLLY produces his new bass player's (WAYLON JENNINGS) debut single 'JOLE BLON'.

Best CD compilation: THE BUDDY HOLLY COLLECTION (*9)

BUDDY HOLLY – vocals, guitar (backed by The **CRICKETS**

Brunswick Decca

Jul 56. (7",78) *(05581) <29854>* **BLUE DAYS BLACK NIGHTS. / LOVE ME** [ ] Apr56 [ ]

Dec 56. (7",78) *<30166>* **MODERN DON JUAN. / YOU ARE MY ONE DESIRE** [–] [ ]

(with The CRICKETS ⇒ , he hit No.1 (May57-US / Sep57-UK) with the single **THAT'LL BE THE DAY. / I'M LOOKING FOR SOMEONE TO LOVE**

Coral Coral

Jun 57. (7",78) *<61852>* **WORDS OF LOVE. / MAILMAN BRING ME NO MORE BLUES** [–] [ ]

Nov 57. (7",78) *(Q 72293) <61885>* **PEGGY SUE. / EVERYDAY** [6] Sep57 [3]

(re-iss. Jul82 on 'Old Gold')

— (with The CRICKETS ⇒ again, he hit US No.10 (Nov57) / UK No.3 (Dec57) with single **OH BOY. / NOT FADE AWAY.**

— An album **THE CHIRPING CRICKETS** was issued Nov57-US / Mar58-UK. Another single **MAYBE BABY. / TELL ME HOW** hit US No.17 (Feb58) / UK No.4 (Mar58).

Mar 58. (7",78) *(Q 72288) <61947>* **LISTEN TO ME. / I'M GONNA LOVE YOU TOO** [16] [ ]

Jun 58. (7",78) *(Q 72325) <61985>* **RAVE ON. / TAKE YOUR TIME** [5] Apr58 [37]

Jul 58. (lp) *(LVA 9085) <57210>* **BUDDY HOLLY** [ ] Mar58 [ ]

– I'm gonna love you too / Peggy Sue / Look at me / Listen to me / Valley of tears / Ready Teddy / Everyday / Mailman, bring me no more blues / Words of love / Baby I don't care / Rave on / Little baby. *(re-iss. Jul75) (re-iss. Mar83 + Nov86 on 'M.C.A.', cd-iss. Nov92 on 'Sequel') (re-iss. Jul68 as 'LISTEN TO ME' on 'MCA', re-iss. Feb74; all UK)*

(with The CRICKETS ⇒ again, he hit US No.27 (Jun58) / UK No.11 (Jul58) with single **THINK IT OVER. / FOOL'S PARADISE**

Aug 58. (7",78) *(Q 72333) <62006>* **EARLY IN THE MORNING. / NOW WE'RE ONE** [ ] Jul58 [32]

— (with The CRICKETS ⇒ again, he was heard on their last single collaboration **IT'S SO EASY. / LONESOME TEARS** (which didn't chart US-Sep58 / UK-Oct58)

He had now left The CRICKETS to hop away on their own Oct'58.

Nov 58. (7",78) *(Q 72346) <62051>* **HEARTBEAT. / WELL ALL RIGHT** [30] [82]

Feb 59. (7",78) *(Q 72360) <62074>* **IT DOESN'T MATTER ANYMORE. / RAINING IN MY HEART** [1] [13] Jan59 [88]

(re-iss. Apr83 on 'Old Gold')

— On the 3rd of Feb'59, BUDDY was killed in a plane crash alongside other pop stars RICHIE VALENS and BIG BOPPER.

– (selective) compilations, etc. –

Jul 59. (7",78) *Brunswick; (05800)* **MIDNIGHT SHIFT. / ROCK AROUND WITH OLLIE VEE** [26] [–]

(some below featured CRICKETS' songs)

Apr 59. (lp) *Coral; (LVA 9105)* **THE BUDDY HOLLY STORY** [2] Mar 59 [11]

(UK re-iss. Jul68 as 'RAVE ON' on 'M.C.A.', re-iss. Feb74, also iss.Aug75 on 'M.F.P.') (cd-iss. Oct01 on 'Spectrum'; 544670-2)

Aug 59. (7",78) *Coral; (Q 72376) <62134>* **PEGGY SUE GOT MARRIED. / CRYING, WAITING, HOPING** [13] Jul59 [ ]

Mar 60. (7",78) *Coral; (Q 72392)* **HEARTBEAT. / EVERYDAY** [30] [–]

May 60. (7") *Coral; (Q 72397)* **TRUE LOVE WAYS. / MOONDREAMS** [25] [–]

Jun 60. (7") *Coral; <62210>* **TRUE LOVE WAYS. / THAT MAKES IT TOUGH** [–] [ ]

Oct 60. (7") *Coral; (Q 72411)* **LEARNING THE GAME. / THAT MAKES IT TOUGH** [36] [–]

Oct 60. (lp) *Coral; (LVA 9127)* **THE BUDDY HOLLY STORY VOL.2** [7] Mar60 [ ]

(UK re-iss. Jul68 as 'TRUE LOVE WAYS' on 'M.C.A.', re-iss. Feb74)

Jan 61. (7") *Coral; (Q 72419)* **WHAT TO DO. / THAT'S WHAT THEY SAY** [34] [–]

Jun 61. (7") *Coral; (Q 72432) <62283>* **BABY I DON'T CARE. / VALLEY OF TEARS** [12] [ ]

Feb 62. (7") *Coral; (Q 724490)* **LISTEN TO ME. / WORDS OF LOVE** [48] [–]

Sep 62. (7") *Coral; (Q 72455) <62329>* **REMINISCING. / WAIT TILL THE SUN SHINES NELLIE** [17] Aug62 [ ]

Mar 63. (7") *Coral; (Q 72459)* **BROWN-EYED HANDSOME MAN. / SLIPPIN' & SLIDIN'** [3] [–]

(below album was dubbed in 1962 with musicians The FIREBALLS)

Apr 63. (lp) *Coral; (LVA 9212) <57246>* **REMINISCING** [2] Feb63 [40]

– Reminiscing / Slippin' and slidin' / Bo Diddley / Wait till the Sun shines, Nellie / Baby, won't you come out tonight / Brown-eyed handsome man / Because I love you / It's not my fault / I'm gonna set my foot down / Changing all those changes / Rock-a-bye-rock. *(UK re-iss. Nov86 on 'M.C.A.') (UK re-iss. Jul68 as 'BROWN-EYED HANDSOME MAN' on 'M.C.A.', re-iss. Feb74) (re-iss. Feb89; MCL/+C/CD 1826) (cd-iss. Nov92 on 'Castle'; CLACD 308) (cd re-iss. Feb03 on 'Spectrum'; 112099-2)*

May 63. (7") *Coral; (Q 72463)* **BO DIDDLEY. / IT'S NOT MY FAULT** [4] [–]

Aug 63. (7") *Coral; (Q 72466)* **WISHING. / BECAUSE I LOVE YOU** [10] [–]

Dec 63. (7") *Coral; (Q 72469)***WHAT TO DO. / UMM OH YEAH (DEAREST)** [27] [–]

Apr 64. (7"; BUDDY HOLLY & THE CRICKETS) *Coral; (Q 72472)* **YOU'VE GOT LOVE. / AN EMPTY CUP** [40] [–]

Jun 64. (lp) *Coral; (LVA 9222) <57450>* **SHOWCASE** [3] May64 [ ]

(UK re-iss. Nov86 & Feb89 on 'M.C.A.') (UK re-iss. Jul68 as 'HE'S THE ONE' on 'M.C.A.') (cd-iss Apr 93 on 'Castle')

Sep 64. (7") *Coral; (Q 724750)* **LOVE'S MADE A FOOL OF YOU. / YOU'RE THE ONE** [39] [–]

Jun 65. (lp) *Coral; (LVA 9227) <57463>* **HOLLY IN THE HILLS** (1954 demos) [13] Jan65 [ ]

(some lp's have track 'Reminiscing' instead of 'Wishing') (UK re-iss. Jul86 as 'WISHING' on 'M.C.A.')

Jun 67. (lp) *Ace Of Hearts; (AH 148)* **BUDDY HOLLY'S GREATEST HITS** [9] [–]

(UK re-iss. Nov69, re-iss. Aug71; hit No.32, on 'Coral')

Mar 68. (7") *M.C.A.; (MU 1012)* **PEGGY SUE. / RAVE ON** [32] [–]

Mar 69. (lp) *M.C.A.; (MUPS 371)* **GIANT** [13] Jan69 [ ]

(re-iss. Feb74 + Nov86)

Mar 78. (lp/c) *M.C.A.; (MCTV/+C 1)* **20 GOLDEN GREATS** [1] [55]

– That'll be the day / Peggy Sue / Words of love / Everyday / Not fade away / Oh! boy / Maybe baby / Listen to me / Heartbeat / Think it over / It doesn't matter anymore / It's so easy / Well all right / Rave on / Raining in my heart / True love ways / Peggy Sue got married / Bo Diddley / Brown-eyed handsome man / Wishing. *(re-iss. Jun79; same) (cd-iss. Feb89 & Aug93; DMCTV 1)*

Feb 89.	(lp/c/cd) *Telstar; (STAR/STAC/TCD 2339)* **TRUE LOVE WAYS**	8	–
May 94.	(cd/c) *M.C.A.; (MCLD 19242)* **THAT'LL BE THE DAY / BUDDY HOLLY**		
Oct 94.	(cd/c) *Music Club; (MCCD 177)* **COVER TO COVER (20 SONGS THAT INFLUENCED THE WORLD OF POPULAR MUSIC)**		
Dec 94.	(3xcd-box) *Pickwick; (BOXD 26T)* **A SPECIAL COLLECTION**		–
Mar 96.	(cd; BUDDY HOLLY & THE PICKS) *Magnum Force; (CDMF 088)* **THE ORIGINAL VOICES OF THE CRICKETS**		
Nov 96.	(cd/c) *Dino; (DIN CD/MC 133)* **THE VERY BEST OF BUDDY HOLLY**	24	–
May 98.	(d-cd) *Charly; (CPCD 83372)* **BUDDY HOLLY & THE PICKS**		
Mar 99.	(cd) *M.C.A.; (MCLD 19186)* **FROM THE ORIGINAL MASTER TAPES**		
Aug 99.	(cd/c) *Universal TV; (112048-2/-4)* **THE VERY BEST OF BUDDY HOLLY**	25	–
Sep 99.	(cd) *Platinum; (PLATCD 518)* **THE VERY BEST OF BUDDY HOLLY & THE PICKS**		
Sep 99.	(cd) *Platinum; (PLATCD 521)* **THE RARITIES COLLECTION 1957-1959**		–
Oct 99.	(cd) *Rockstar; (RSRCD 002)* **RAVIN' ON – FROM CALIFORNIA TO CLOVIS**		–
Jan 00.	(cd) *Universal; (E 112176-2)* **UNIVERSAL MASTERS COLLECTION**		
Jun 00.	(d-cd) *Snapper; (SMDCD 293)* **FOREVER 22**		
Jan 01.	(cd) *Beat Goes On; (BGOCD 517)* **CHIRPING CRICKETS / BUDDY HOLLY**		
Feb 01.	(cd) *M.C.A.; (MCBD 19522)* **LOVE SONGS**		
Mar 01.	(cd; BUDDY HOLLY & THE PICKS) *K-Tel; (ECD 3634)* **ONLY THE LOVE SONGS**		–
Jul 01.	(d-cd) *Platinum; (PLATBX 2201)* **39 GOLDEN GREATS: THE RARITIES COLLECTION / THE VERY BEST OF**		
Sep 01.	(d-cd) *See For Miles; (SFM 1970)* **THE EP COLLECTION**		
Jan 02.	(cd) *BR Music; (BS 81262)* **THE SINGLES PLUS**		–
Aug 02.	(cd) *Beat Goes On; (BGOCD 563)* **HOLLY IN THE HILLS / GIANT**		
Sep 02.	(cd) *Beat Goes On; (BGOCD 564)* **THAT'LL BE THE DAY / REMEMBER**		
Sep 02.	(cd) *M.C.A.; (MCBD 19506)* **THE BEST OF BUDDY HOLLY**		
Oct 02.	(cd) *Jerden; (JRCD 7013)* **THE BUDDY HOLLY TAPES**		
Nov 02.	(cd) *Planet Media; (PML 1105)* **RAINING IN MY HEART**		–
Mar 03.	(cd) *Universal; (AAMCAD 11956)* **20th CENTURY MASTERS**		

☐ HOLY BARBARIANS (see under ⇒ CULT)

☐ HONEYDRIPPERS (see under ⇒ LED ZEPPELIN)

HOOBASTANK

Formed: Agoura Hills, California, USA . . . 1994 by DOUG ROBB and DAN ESTRIN, together with MARKKU LAPPALAINEN and CHRIS HESSE. The self-financed, self-consciously titled 'THEY SURE DON'T MAKE BASKETBALL SHORTS LIKE THEY USED TO' marked their long-playing debut in 1998, while a millennial deal with 'Island' saw them secure tour spots with the likes of ALIEN ANT FARM. The heavily rotated likes of 'CRAWLING IN THE DARK' pushed up sales of the band's 2001-released eponymous major label debut, itself a fairly rote collection high on energy and low on inspiration. It nevertheless went platinum, while 2003's 'THE REASON' offered yet more meat and potatoes angst-rock lovingly sculpted for the restrictive confines of US radio play.

Album rating: HOOBASTANK (*4) / THE REASON (*6)

DOUG ROBB – vocals / **DAN ESTRIN** – guitar / **MARKKU LAPPALAINEN** – bass / **CHRIS HESSE** – drums

		not iss.	own label
1998.	(cd) **THEY SURE DON'T MAKE BASKETBALL SHORTS LIKE THEY USED TO**	–	
		Mercury	Island
Jan 02.	(cd) *<(586435-2)>* **HOOBASTANK**		Nov01 25
	– Crawling in the dark / Remember me / Running away / Pieces / Let you know / Better / Ready for you / Up and gone / Too little too late / Hello again / To be with you / Give it back. *(ltd cd-iss. Jul02 +=; 586873-2)* – Critic.		
Apr 02.	(c-s) *(582862-4) <radio>* **CRAWLING IN THE DARK / PIECES**	47	68
	(cd-s+=) *(582862-2)* – Losing my grip / ('A'-video).		
Jul 02.	(c-s) *(582969-4) <radio>* **RUNNING AWAY / CRAWLING IN THE DARK (acoustic)**		44
	(cd-s+=) *(582969-2)* – Up and gone (acoustic) / ('A'-video).		
Dec 03.	(cd) *(9860881) <14880-2>* **THE REASON**		38
	– Same direction / Out of control / What happened to us? / Escape / Just one / Lucky / From the heart / The reason / Let it out / Unaffected / Never there / Disappear.		

John Lee HOOKER

Born: 22 Aug'20, Clarksdale, Mississippi, USA. The last of the original bluesmen who travelled north from the Delta, VAN MORRISON once said that HOOKER was "a window into another age". Doubts remain about his actual birth date although HOOKER recently admitted that he lied about his age as a teenager to get into the army. Taught to play guitar by his stepfather (his birth father disapproved of the blues), a popular local blues guitarist by the name of WILL MOORE, HOOKER drifted north during his teens to Memphis, Cincinatti and finally, to Detroit, where he settled in 1943. The budding bluesman was given his first guitar by the legendary T-BONE WALKER in 1947, sitting in on early sessions with Robert Nighthawk. He worked as a janitor in a car factory by day and performed in clubs around Hastings Street (a notorious area known as 'Black Bottom' from which the dance was named) at night, slowly gaining a reputation which paralleled such Chicago masters as MUDDY WATERS, SONNY BOY WILLIAMSON and HOWLIN' WOLF. HOOKER always maintained that he didn't like Chicago because there were too many other blues guitarists there, his relocation to Detroit paying off when he was introduced to local distributor, record store owner and kingpin of the 'Sensation' record label, Bernie Bessman, in 1948. In November that year he undertook his debut recording session (just himself and his guitar, with his distinctive tapping sounds coming from Coca-Cola bottle tops attached to the soles of his shoes), his first single from the set, 'BOOGIE CHILLUN' topping the "race" chart, as it was then known. After Bessman leased the master to 'Modern', it eventually sold more than a million copies (when it broke, HOOKER was still working as a janitor in the Chrysler car factory). As well as a demon guitarist, he was also a wicked womaniser, almost copping it in 1950 when an aggrieved husband poisoned his whisky (12 years after ROBERT JOHNSON had fatally suffered in a similar manner). HOOKER subsequently signed to 'Modern' in 1951, staying with the label for five years; as with other blues artists of the time, he recorded for anyone who was willing to pay him and got round his contractual obligations by recording 70 singles on 21 different labels under 10 pseudonyms, TEXAS SLIM ('BLACK MAN BLUES' for 'KING' Records), BIRMINGHAM SAM ('Savoy' Records), JOHN LEE BOOKER ('Chess' Records), JOHN LEE COOKER

('King' Records), DELTA JOHN ('Regent' Records), JOHNNY LEE ('Deluxe' Records), JOHNNY WILLIAMS ('Gotham' Records), LITTLE PORK CHOPS, THE BOOGIE MAN ('Acorn' Records) and JOHN L'HOOKER. During this period, 'I'M IN THE MOOD' became his second major R&B hit and matched the one million sales of 'BOOGIE CHILLUN', while the following year he made his debut as a DJ on a local radio station. Although B.B. KING outshone him in the 50's, HOOKER signed to 'Vee-Jay', who recognised his wider appeal and crafted him into a tighter performer, backing him with seasoned session players including guitarist, EDDIE TAYLOR and drummer, TOM WHITEHEAD. During a subsequent 1959 session, HOOKER cut new versions of his most successful songs including 'I'M IN THE MOOD', 'BOOGIE CHILLUN', 'HOBO BLUES' and 'CRAWLIN' KINGSNAKE' (all with his distinctive guttural singing). The following year, he was one of only a few (traditional) blues artists to perform at the 2nd Newport Folk Festival (his set was recorded and later released as 'CONCERT AT NEWPORT'), while the following year, BOB DYLAN made his New York debut opening for HOOKER at Gerde's Folk City venue. 1964 saw the British R&B explosion in full flow with 'BOOM BOOM' becoming a US hit for The ANIMALS (they also covered three HOOKER compositions on their debut album) and HOOKER himself entering the UK chart at 23 with 'DIMPLES'. This success led to numerous UK tours backed by the likes of The SPENCER DAVIS GROUP and The GROUNDHOGS (who took their name from HOOKER's, 'GROUNDHOG BLUES'); many other British bands of the time including The YARDBIRDS, The WHO, The SMALL FACES and, in particular, The ROLLING STONES, were inspired by, and recorded many of HOOKER's songs. In America, meanwhile, he influenced many bands from ZZ TOP (whose 'LA GRANGE' is pure HOOKER) to BRUCE SPRINGSTEEN, the latter including 'BOOM BOOM' as part of his set on the 'Tunnel Of Love' tour in 1988. In 1966, the veteran bluesman signed to 'ABC' Records and, over the next eight years, recorded albums for their subsidiaries, 'Impulse' and 'Bluesway', as well as 'ABC' themselves. HOOKER left Detroit in 1970 after a nasty divorce, settling in San Francisco where he met CANNED HEAT; together they recorded the double album, 'HOOKER 'N' HEAT' (1971), which became the guitarists first US chart success, reaching the Top 75. Unfortunately, CANNED HEAT's ALAN 'Blind Owl' WILSON died before the album was mixed, the sleeve depicting everyone in sombre mood with a black framed picture of WILSON hanging in the background. HOOKER's ABC contract ended in 1974 and, on the verge of quitting to open a motel, he signed a deal with 'Atlantic' Records. He recorded two albums for the major, 'DETROIT SPECIAL' and 'DON'T TURN ME FROM YOUR DOOR', although by 1978's, 'THE CREAM', he had downshifted to 'Tomato' Records. In 1980, he had a cameo role in 'The Blues Brothers' alongside RAY CHARLES, JAMES BROWN and ARETHA FRANKLIN, while his music also featured in another movie, 'The Color Purple'. Later in the 80's, HOOKER starred in the title role of PETE TOWNSHEND's musical, 'THE IRON MAN' (singing 'I EAT HEAVY METAL' – far removed from his normal style but performed with typical HOOKER panache nonetheless) and at the turn of the decade he paired up with MILES DAVIS for the soundtrack to the Dennis Hopper movie, 'The Hot Spot' (which featured HOOKER's, 'I'M IN THE MOOD'). He's become more popular with age, 'THE HEALER' (1989) attracting a whole new army of fans and breaking him into the mainstream rock world. The project came about because the contributing artists were all fans of "THE HOOK" (they all lived locally), including CARLOS SANTANA on the title track, BONNIE RAITT on 'I'M IN THE MOOD' (a Grammy winner), ROBERT CRAY on 'CUTTIN' OUT' and LOS LOBOS on 'THINK TWICE BEFORE YOU GO', while most of the songs were completed in one or two takes (a hallmark of HOOKER's career). His next album was the stunning 'Charisma' debut, 'MR. LUCKY', which, in reaching number 3 in Britain (only made number 101 in the US!), became the highest charting "real" blues album ever, and at the age of 71, it made HOOKER the oldest artist to reach the UK Top 5. This album was another collection of duets, including the collaborations 'CRAWLIN KINGSNAKE' with KEITH RICHARDS, 'MR. LUCKY' with the ROBERT CRAY BAND, 'SUZIE' with JOHNNY WINTER and 'I COVER THE WATERFRONT' with his No.1 fan, VAN MORRISON, although the stand-outs were 'THIS IS HIP' with RY COODER, 'STRIPPED ME NAKED' (on which HOOKER sounds like a man possessed and CARLOS SANTANA is at his wailing best) and the top of the lot, 'I WANT TO HUG YOU' with CHUCK BERRY's former pianist, JOHNNIE JOHNSON. 1992 saw a rare appearance on Top Of The Pops as 'BOOM BOOM' reached the UK Top 20, further singles, 'BOOGIE AT RUSSIAN HILL' and 'GLORIA' (recorded with VAN MORRISON) also reaching the charts. Although clocking in at a remarkable three quarters of a century, HOOKER retained his humour, ability and style, as witnessed on the 1995 and 1997 releases, 'CHILL OUT' and 'DON'T LOOK BACK'. Sadly, HOOKER was to die of natural causes on the 21st June, 2001, aged 80.

Album rating (selective): THE FOLK BLUES OF JOHN LEE HOOKER (*8) / I'M JOHN LEE HOOKER (*8) / TRAVELLIN' (*7) / SINGS THE BLUES (*7) / THAT'S MY STORY (*8) / THE FOLKLORE OF JOHN LEE HOOKER (*8) / THE BEST OF JOHN LEE HOOKER compilation (*7) / JOHN LEE HOOKER AT NEWPORT (*7) / REAL FOLK BLUES (*7) / THE HEALER (*10) / MR. LUCKY (*7) / BOOM BOOM (*6) / CHILL OUT (*7) / DON'T LOOK BACK (*6) / THE BEST OF FRIENDS (*5) / THE ULTIMATE COLLECTION compilation (*8)

JOHN LEE HOOKER – vocals, guitars

not iss. / Modern

Jan 49. (78) *<20-627>* **BOOGIE CHILLEN (BOOGIE CHILDREN). / SALLY MAE (THERE'S A DAY COMIN' BABY)** [–] [ ]

— now with **JAMES WATKINS** – piano / **CURTIS FOSTER** – drums

not iss. / King

Mar 49. (78; as TEXAS SLIM) *<4283>* **BLACK MAN BLUES. / STOMP BOOGIE (FLUB)** [–] [ ]

— now w/ **ANDREW DUNHAM** – guitar / **EDDIE BURNS** – harmonica

— released many US 78's over the next several years (some with pseudonyms)

not iss. / Regent

1949. (78; as DELTA JOHN) *<1001>* **HELPLESS BLUES. / GOIN' MAD BLUES** [–] [ ]

not iss. / Savoy

1949. (78; as BIRMINGHAM SAM & HIS MAGIC GUITAR) *<5558>* **LOW DOWN MIDNITE BOOGIE. / LANDING BLUES** [–] [ ]

not iss. / Modern

1949. (78) *<20-663>* **HOBO BLUES. / HOOGIE BOOGIE** [–] [ ]

1949. (78) *<20-688>* **WEEPING WILLOW (BOOGIE). / WHISTLIN' AND MOANIN' BLUES (HUMMIN' THE BLUES)** [–] [ ]

1949. (78) *<20-714>* **CRAWLING KING SNAKE. / DRIFTING FROM DOOR TO DOOR** [–] [ ]

not iss. / Prize

1949. (78; as JOHNNY WILLIAMS) *<704>* **MISS ROSIE MAE. / HIGHWAY BLUES** [–] [ ]

not iss. / Sensation

Mar 50. (78) *<21>* **MISS SADIE MAE. / BURNIN' HELL** [–] [ ]

Apr 50. (78) *<26>* **CANAL STREET BLUES. / HUCKLE UP BABY** [–] [ ]

May 50. (78) *<30>* **GOIN' ON HIGHWAY 51 (GOIN' DOWN HIGHWAY 51). / LET YOUR DADDY RIDE (SLOW DOWN YOUR CHATTER BABY)** [–] [ ]

Jun 50. (78) <33> **MY BABY'S GOT SOMETHIN'. / DECORATION DAY BLUES (LORD TAKETH MY BABY AWAY)**

Jul 50. (78) <34> **BOOGIE CHILLEN 2 (I GOTTA BE COMIN' BACK). / MISS ELOISE (MISS ELOISE, MISS ELOISE)**

Aug 50. (78; as JOHN LEE COOKER) <4504> **MOANING BLUES. / STOMP BOOGIE (FLUB)**

not iss. Acorn

1949. (78; as THE BOOGIE MAN) <308> **DO THE BOOGIE. / MORNING BLUES**

not iss. Chance

1949. (78; as JOHN LEE BOOKER) <1108> **MISS LORRAINE. / TALKIN' BOOGIE**

1949. (78; as JOHN LEE BOOKER) <1110> **GRAVEYARD BLUES. / I LOVE TO BOOGIE**

1949. (78; as JOHN L. BOOKER) <1122> **609 BOOGIE. / ROAD TROUBLE**

not iss. King

1950. (78; as TEXAS SLIM) <4315> **THE NUMBERS. / DEVIL'S JUMP**

1950. (78; as TEXAS SLIM) <4323> **I'M GONNA KILL THAT WOMAN. / NIGHTMARE BLUES**

1950. (78; as TEXAS SLIM) <4329> **HEART TROUBLE BLUES. / SLIM'S STOMP (instrumental)**

1950. (78; as TEXAS SLIM) <4334> **DON'T GO BABY. / WANDERING BLUES**

Oct 50. (78; as TEXAS SLIM) <4366> **LATE LAST NIGHT. / DON'T YOU REMEMBER ME**

Nov 50. (78; as TEXAS SLIM) <4377> **MOANING BLUES. / THINKING BLUES**

not iss. Modern

Apr 50. (78) <20-730> **PLAYIN' THE RACES (DREAM A NUMBER). / WELL I GOT TO LEAVE**

May 50. (78) <20-746> **NO FRIEND AROUND (T.B.'S KILLIN' ME). / WEDNESDAY EVENING (SHE LEFT ME – ON MY BENDED KNEE)**

Jun 50. (78) <20-767> **GIMME YOUR PHONE NUMBER (IT'S A CRIME AND A SHAME). / ROCK'N'ROLL (I CRIED THE WHOLE NIGHT LONG)**

Jul 50. (78) <20-790> **ONE MORE TIME (LET'S TALK IT OVER). / LET YOUR DADDY RIDE**

not iss. Regal

1950. (78) <3304> **NEVER SATISFIED (JUST LIKE A WOMAN). / NOTORIETY WOMAN (NO PLACE TO STAY)**

not iss. Gone

1950. (78; as JOHN LEE BOOKER) **MAD MAN BLUES. / BOOGIE NOW (HEY BOOGIE)**

not iss. Modern

1950. (78) <814> **QUEEN BEE. / JOHN L'S HOUSE RENT BOOGIE (OUT THE DOOR I WENT)**

not iss. Staff

1950. (78; as JOHNNY WILLIAMS) <710> **HOUSE RENT BOOGIE. / WANDERING BLUES**

1950. (78; as JOHNNY WILLIAMS) <718> **PRISON BOUND. / BUMBLE BEE BLUES**

not iss. Gotham

1951. (78; as JOHNNY WILLIAMS) <509> **REAL GONE GAL. / QUESTIONNAIRE BLUES**

1951. (78; as JOHNNY WILLIAMS) <513> **LITTLE BOY BLUE. / MY DADDY WAS A JOCKEY**

1951. (78' as JOHN LEE) <515> **CATFISH. / MEAN OLD TRAIN**

not iss. Chess

Jun 51. (78; as JOHN LEE BOOKER) <1467> **LEAVE MY WIFE ALONE. / RAMBLIN' BY MYSELF**

Jul 51. (78; as JOHN LEE BOOKER) <1482> **GROUND HOG BLUES. / LOUISE**

<above also iss.Jan52 as JOHN L. HOOKER on 'Modern'; 852>

Aug 51. (78) <1505> **HIGH PRICED WOMAN. / UNION STATION BLUES**

Jul 52. (78) <1513> **WALKIN' THE BOOGIE. / SUGAR MAMA**

not iss. Modern

Sep 51. (78) <829> **(FOUR) WOMEN IN MY LIFE. / TEASE ME BABY (TEASE YOUR DADDY)**

Nov 51. (78) <835> **I'M IN THE MOOD. / HOW CAN YOU DO IT**

Dec 51. (78; as JOHN L. HOOKER) <847> **TURN OVER A NEW LEAF. / ANYBODY SEEN MY BABY (JOHNNY SAYS COME BACK)**

Feb 52. (78) <862> **ROCK ME MAMA (GOOD ROCKIN' MAMA). / COLD CHILLS (ALL OVER ME)**

Vogue Modern

1952. (78) *(V 2102)* **HOOGIE BOOGIE. / WHISTLIN' AND MOANIN' BLUES**

Sep 52. (78; as JOHN LEE HOOKER & "LITTLE" EDDIE KIRKLAND) <876> **IT HURTS ME SO. / I GOT EYES FOR YOU**

Nov 52. (78) <886> **KEY TO THE HIGHWAY. / BLUEBIRD BLUES**

Feb 53. (78) <897> **IT'S BEEN A LONG TIME BABY. / ROCK HOUSE BOOGIE**

Apr 53. (78) <901> **RIDE 'TIL I DIE. / IT'S STORMIN' AND RAININ'**

Jun 53. (78) <1562> **IT'S MY OWN FAULT (BABY, I PROVE MY LOVE TO YOU). / WOMEN AND MONEY**

1953. (78; as JOHNNY LEE HOOKER) <30> **BOOGIE RAMBLER. / NO MORE DOGGIN'**

<above issued on 'J.V.B.'>

Jul 53. (78; as JOHNNY LEE HOOKER) <908> **PLEASE TAKE ME BACK. / LOVE MONEY CAN'T BUY**

Aug 53. (78; as JOHNNY LEE HOOKER) <916> **NEED SOMEBODY. / TOO MUCH BOOGIE**

(UK-iss.1954 on 'London'; HL 8037)

Sep 53. (78; as JOHNNY LEE HOOKER) <931> **I WONDER (LITTLE DARLING). / JUMP ME (ONE MORE TIME)**

not iss. DeLuxe

Sep 53. (78; as JOHN LEE BOOKER) <6004> **BLUE MONDAY (I AIN'T GOT NOBODY). / LOVIN' GUITAR MAN**

Oct 53. (78; as JOHNNY LEE) <6009> **I'M A BOOGIE MAN. / I CAME TO SEE MY BABY**

Dec 53. (78; as JOHN LEE BOOKER) <6046> **MY BABY DON'T LOVE ME. / REAL REAL GONE**

not iss. Rockin'

Oct 53. (78; as JOHN LEE BOOKER) <524> **BLUE MONDAY (I AIN'T GOT NOBODY). / LOVIN' GUITAR MAN**

Nov 53. (78; as JOHN LEE BOOKER) <525> **STUTTERIN' BLUES. / POURING DOWN RAIN (WOBBLIN' BABY)**

not iss. Chart

1954. (78) <609> **GOIN' SOUTH. / WOBBLIN' BABY**

1954. (78) <614> **BLUE MONDAY (I AIN'T GOT NOBODY). / MISBELIEVING BABY (MY BABY PUT YOU DOWN)**

not iss. Modern

1954. (78) <923> **DOWN CHILD. / GOTTA BOOGIE (GONNA BOOGIE)**

1954. (78) <935> **LET'S TALK IT OVER. / I TRIED HARD**

1954. (78) <942> **BAD BOY. / COOL LITTLE CAR**

1954. (78) <948> **SHAKE, HOLLER AND RUN. / HALF A STRANGER**

1955. (78) <958> **TAXI DRIVER. / YOU RECEIVE ME**

1955. (78) <966> **HUG AND SQUEEZE (YOU). / THE SYNDICATOR (SYNDICATE)**

1955. (78) <978> **LOOKIN' FOR A WOMAN. / I'M READY**

not iss. Vee Jay

Dec 55. (7") <164> **MAMBO CHILLUN. / TIME IS MARCHING**

Apr 56. (7") <188> **TROUBLE BLUES. / EVERY NIGHT**

Jun 56. (7") <205> **DIMPLES. / BABY LEE**

Sep 56. (7") <233> **I'M SO WORRIED BABY. / THE ROAD IS SO ROUGH**

Apr 57. (7") <245> **I'M SO EXCITED. / I SEE YOU WHEN YOU'RE WEAK**

Aug 57. (7") <255> **LITTLE WHEEL. / ROSIE MAE**

Sep 57. (7") <265> **YOU CAN LEAD ME BABY. / UNFRIENDLY WOMAN**

Jul 58. (7") <293> **I LOVE YOU HONEY. / YOU'VE TAKEN MY WOMAN**

Feb 59. (7") <308> **I'M IN THE MOOD. / MAUDIE**

Apr 59. (7") *<319>* **BOOGIE CHILLUN. / TENNESSEE BLUES** [–] [ ]

Jun 59. (7") *<331>* **CRAWLIN' KINGSNAKE. / HOBO BLUES** [–] [ ]

Riverside Riverside

1960. (lp) *<321>* **THAT'S MY STORY** [–] [ ]
– I need some money / I'm wanderin' / Democrat man / I want to talk about you / Gonna use my rod / Wednesday evening blues / No more doggin' / One of these days, I'll believe I'll go back home / You're leavin' me baby / That's my story / Black snake / How long blues / Wobblin' baby / She's long, she's tall, she weeps like . . . / Peavine special / Tupelo blues / I rowed a little boat / Water boy / Church bell tone / Bundle up and go. *(UK-iss.Nov88 on 'Ace')*

1962. (lp) *(RLP 12-838) <838>* **THE FOLK BLUES OF JOHN LEE HOOKER** [ ] 1959 [ ]
– Black snake / How long blues / Wobblin' baby / She's long, she's tall, she weeps like a willow tree / Pea-vine special / Tupelo blues / I'm prison bound / I rowed a little boat / Water boy / Church bell tone / Bundle up and go / Good mornin' lil' school girl / Behind the plow.
– singles on other labels at the time

not iss. Elmor

1959. (7") *<303>* **609 BOOGIE. / (MISS SADIE MAE) CURL MY BABY'S HAIR** [–] [ ]

not iss. Fortune

1960. (7") *<853>* **CRY BABY. / LOVE YOU BABY** [–] [ ]

1960. (7") *<855>* **CRAZY ABOUT THAT WALK. / WE'RE ALL GOD'S CHILLUN** [–] [ ]

not iss. Hi-Q

1959. (7") *<5018>* **BIG FINE WOMAN. / BLUES FOR CHRISTMAS** [–] [ ]

not iss. Lauren

1960. (7") *<361>* **BALLAD TO ABRAHAM LINCOLN (HE GOT ASSASSINATED). / MOJO HAND (RISIN' SUN)** [–] [ ]

1960. (7") *<362>* **I LOST MY JOB (TELL YOU A STORY). / DEEP DOWN IN MY HEART (HOW LONG CAN THIS GO ON)** [–] [ ]

not iss. Galaxy

1960. (7") *<716>* **SHAKE IT UP (JOHNNY LEE & THE THING). / (I) LOST MY JOB (TELL YOU A STORY)** [–] [ ]

Stateside Vee Jay

Apr 60. (7") *<349>* **SOLID SENDER. / NO SHOES** [–] [ ]

Jul 60. (7") *<366>* **TUPELO (BACKWATER BLUES). / DUSTY ROAD** [–] [ ]

Feb 61. (7") *<379>* **I'M MAD AGAIN. / I'M GOING UPSTAIRS** [–] [ ]

Apr 61. (7") *<397>* **WANT AD BLUES. / TAKE ME AS I AM** [–] [ ]

Feb 62. (7") *<438>* **BOOM BOOM. / DRUG STORE WOMAN** [–] [60]

Apr 62. (7") *<453>* **SHE'S MINE (KEEP YOUR HANDS TO YOURSELF). / A NEW LEAF** [–] [ ]

1962. (lp) *(SL 10014)* **THE FOLK LORE OF JOHN LEE HOOKER** [ ] [–]
– Tupelo / I'm mad again / I'm going upstairs / Wanted blues / Five years long / I like to see you walk / The hobo / Hard headed woman / Wednesday evening blues / Take me as I am / My first wife left me / You're looking good tonight. *(re-iss. 1974 on 'Joy')*

Nov 62. (7") *<493>* **FRISCO BLUES. / TAKE A LOOK AT YOURSELF** [–] [ ]

1963. (7") *<538>* **I'M LEAVING. / BIRMINGHAM BLUES** [–] [ ]

1963. (7") *<575>* **DON'T LOOK BACK. / SEND ME YOUR PILLOW** [–] [ ]

1964. (lp) *(SL 10053)* **THE BIG SOUL OF JOHN LEE HOOKER** [ ] [–]
– Frisco blues / Take a look at yourself / Send me your pillow / She shot me down / I love her / Old time shimmy / You know I love you / Big soul / Good rocking mama / Onions / No one told me. *(re-iss. 1969 + 1974 on 'Joy')*

Jul 63. (7") *(SS 203)* **BOOM BOOM. / FRISCO BLUES** [ ] [–]

May 64. (7") *(SS 297)* **DIMPLES. / I'M LEAVING** [23] [–]

Sep 64. (7") *(SS 341)* **I LOVE YOU HONEY. / SEND ME YOUR PILLOW** [ ] [–]

1964. (lp) *(SL 10074)* **I WANT TO SHOUT THE BLUES** [ ] [–]
– I'm leaving / Love is a burning thing / Birmingham blues / I want to shout / Don't look back / I want to hug you / Poor me / I want to ramble / Half a stranger / My grinding mill / Bottle up and go / One way ticket.

1964. (7") *<670>* **YOUR BABE AIN'T SWEET LIKE MINE. / BIG LEGS, TIGHT SHIRT** [–] [ ]

1964. (7") *<708>* **IT SERVES ME RIGHT (TO SUFFER). / FLOWERS ON THE HOUR** [–] [ ]

Polydor not iss.

1964. (7") *(NH 52930)* **SHAKE IT BABY. / LET'S MAKE IT BABY** [ ] [–]

Pye Int. Chess

Aug 64. (7") *(7N 25255)* **HIGH PRICED WOMAN. / SUGAR MAMA** [ ] [ ]

Nov 64. (7"ep) *(NEP 44034)* **LOVE BLUES** [ ] [–]

Sue not iss.

Jun 65. (7") *(WI 361)* **I'M IN THE MOOD. / BOOGIE CHILLUN'** [ ] [–]

Fontana not iss.

Nov 65. (lp) *(FJL 119)* **BLUE** (rec.1960) [ ] [–]

not iss. Impulse

Jan 66. (7") *<242>* **BOTTLE UP AND GO. / MONEY** [–] [ ]

Planet Planet

Feb 66. (7"; as JOHN LEE'S GROUNDHOGS) **I'LL NEVER FALL IN LOVE AGAIN. / OVER YOU BABY** [–] [ ]

May 66. (7") *<(PLF 114)>* **MAI LEE. / DON'T BE MESSING WITH MY BREAD** [ ] [ ]

Chess Chess

Aug 66. (7") *(CRS 8039) <1965>* **LET'S GO OUT TONIGHT. / I'M IN THE MOOD** [ ] [ ]

Jan 67. (7") *(CRL 4527)* **REAL FOLK BLUES** [ ] [ ]
– Let's go out tonight / Please lovin' man / Stella Mae / I put my trust in you / I'm in the mood / You know, I know / I'll never trust your love again / One bourbon, one Scotch, one beer / The waterfront. *(cd-iss. Feb90 on 'M.C.A.';)*

H.M.V. Impulse

1968. (lp) *(CLP 5032) <9103>* **IT SERVES YOU RIGHT TO SUFFER** [ ] Feb66 [ ]
– Sugar mama / Declaration day / Money (that's what I want) / It serves you right to suffer / Shake it baby / Country boy / Bottle up and go / You're wrong. *(re-iss. 1977 on 'Impulse') (re-iss,Feb84 on 'Jasmine')*

H.M.V. Bluesway

1968. (lp) *(CLP 3612) <BLS 6002>* **LIVE AT THE CAFE AU GO-GO (live)** [ ] Jul66 [ ]
– I'm bad like Jesse James / She's long, she's tall / When my first wife left me / Heartaches and misery / One bourbon, on scotch and one beer / I don't want no trouble / I'll never get out of these blues alive / Seven days. *(re-iss. 1973 on 'Bluesway') (re-iss. +c+cd.Oct88 on 'B.G.O.')*

Jan 68. (7") *<61010>* **WANT AD BLUES. / THE MOTOR CITY IS BURNING** [–] [ ]

Mar 68. (7") *<61014>* **CRY BEFORE I GO. / MR. LUCKY** [–] [ ]

Stateside Bluesway

1968. (lp) *(SSL 10246) <BLS 6012>* **URBAN BLUES** [ ] [ ]
– Cry before I go / Boom boom / Backbiters & syndicaters / Mr.Lucky / I can't stand to leave you / My own blues / Think twice before you go / I'm standing in line / Hot water springs (pt.1 & 2) / Wand ad blues *(re-iss. Oct91 on 'B.G.O.')*

Jun 68. (7") *<61017>* **THINK TWICE BEFORE YOU GO. / BACKBITERS AND SYNDICATER** [–] [ ]

1969. (lp) *(SSL 10208)* **SIMPLY THE TRUTH** [ ] [–]
– I don't wanna go to Vietnam / I wanna boogaloo / Tantalizing with the blues / I'm just a drifter / Mini skirts / Mean mean woman / One room country shack. *(re-iss. +cd.Feb89 on 'B.G.O.')*

Probe Bluesway

1969. (lp) *(SPB 1016) <BLS 6038>* **IF YOU MISS 'IM . . . I GET 'IM** [ ] [ ]
– Hookers (if you miss 'im . . .I got 'im) / Baby I love you / Lonesome mood / Bang bang bang / If you take care of me, I'll take care of you / Baby, be strong / I wanna be your puppy / I don't care when you go / Have mercy on my soul.

—— next with **PRETTY PURDIE** – drums / **ERNIE HAYES** – mouth harp

Feb 69. (7") *<61023>* **MEAN MEAN WOMAN. / I DON'T WANNA GO TO VIETNAM** [–] [ ]
– below set are exploitation releases

1968. (lp) *(RLP 008)* **BURNIN'** [ ] [–]
– Boom boom / Process / Lost a good girl / A new leaf / Blues before sunrise / Let's make it / I got a letter / Thelma / Drug store woman / Keep you hands to yourself / What do you say. *(re-iss. 1974 on 'Joy'; JOYS 124) (re-iss. +c.May87 on 'Topline')*

Joy Vee-Jay

1968. (lp) *(JOYS 101)* **I'M JOHN LEE HOOKER** [ ] [ ]

1969. (lp) *(JOYS 129)* **TRAVELIN'** [ ] [ ]
– No shoes / I wanna walk / Canal Street blues / Keep on / I'm a stranger /

Whiskey and wimmen / Solid sender / Sunny land / Goin' to California / I can't believe / I'll know tonight / Dusty road. *(re-iss. 1974)*

1969. (lp) *(JOYS 142)* *<VJS 1078>* **CONCERT AT NEWPORT (live 24 Jun'60)** [ ] [ ]
– I can't quit you now blues / Stop baby don't hold me that way / Tupelo / Bus station blues / Freight train be my friend / Boom boom boom Talk that talk baby / Sometime baby you make me feel so bad / You've got to walk by yourself / Let's make it / The mighty fire.

1969. (lp) *(JOYS 152)* **IN PERSON** [ ] [–]
– I'm leaving Love is a burning thing / Birmingham blues / I want to shout / Don't look back / I want to hug youu / Poor me / I want to ramble / Half a stranger / My grinding mill / Bottle up and go / One way ticket.

— In 1970, he recorded dual live album 'HOOKER'N'HEAT' with CANNED HEAT

Probe A.B.C.

May 71. (7") **KICK HIT 4 HIT KIX U. / DOIN' THE SHOUT** [–] [ ]

May 71. (d-lp) *(SPB 1034)* *<ABCX 720>* **ENDLESS BOOGIE** [ ] Mar71 [ ]
– (I got) A good 'un / Pots on, gas on high / Kick hit 4 hit kix u / I don't need no stream heart / We might as well call it through . . . / Sittin' in my dark room / Endless boogie parts 27 & 28.

— next with **ROBERT HOOKER** – organ / **LUTHER TUCKER** – guitar / **ELVIN BISHOP + DON 'Sugarcane' HARRIS** – piano / **CHARLIE MUSSELWHITE** – harmonica / **VAN MORRISON**

Apr 72. (lp) *(SPB 1057)* *<ABCX 736>* **NEVER GET OUT OF THESE BLUES ALIVE** [ ] Mar72 [ ]
– Bumblebee bumblebee / Hit the road / Country boy / Boogee with the Hook / If you take care of me (I'll take care of you) / I've got a go / T.B. sheets / Letter to my baby / Never get out of these blues alive / Baby I love you / Lonesome road. *(cd-iss. Feb90 & Jan91 on 'See For Miles', 4 extra tracks)*

Apr 72. (7") **BOOGIE WITH THE HOOK. / NEVER GET OUT OF THESE BLUES ALIVE** [–] [ ]

Dec 72. (lp) *<ABCX 761>* **LIVE AT SOLEDAD PRISON (live)** [–] [ ]
– Super lover / I'm your crosscut saw / What's the matter baby Lucille / Boogie everywhere I go / Serve me right to suffer / Bang bang bang bang.

1973. (lp) *<ABCX 768>* **BORN IN MISSISSIPPI, RAISED UP IN TENNESSEE** [–] [ ]
– Born in Mississippi, raised up in Tennessee / How many more years you gonna dog me 'round / Going down ./ Younger stud / King of the world / Tell me you love me.

A.B.C. A.B.C.

Nov 74. (lp) *(ABCL 5059)* **FREE BEER & CHICKEN** [ ] [ ]
– Make it funky / Five long years / 713 blues / 714 blues / One bourbon one Scotch one beer / Homework / Bluebird / Sittin' on top of the world / (You'll never amount to anything if you don't go to) College (a fortuitous concatenation of events (a) I know how to rock, (b) Nothin' but the best, (c) The scratch. *(re-iss. +cd.Oct91 on 'B.G.O.')*

not iss. Tomato

1977. (d-lp) *<2-7009>* **THE CREAM (live)** [–] [ ]
– Hey hey / Rock steady / Tupelo / You know it ain't right / She's gone / T.B. sheets / Sugar mama / One room country shack / Drug store woman / I want you to roll me / Bar room drinking / Little girl / Louise / When my first wife left me* / Boogie on*. *(UK-iss.+c+cd.Jan88 on 'Charly', cd-omits*)(re-iss. cd Jun93)*

— In 1980, he cameos with loads of other stars in the film, 'BLUES BROTHERS'.

Silvertone Chameleon

Oct 89. (lp/c/cd) *(ORE LP/C/CD 508)* *<74808>* **THE HEALER** [63] [62]
– The healer / I'm in the mood / Baby Lee / Cuttin' out / Think twice before you go / Sally Mae / That's alright / Rockin' chair / My dream / No substitute.

Dec 89. (7"/12"; JOHN LEE HOOKER & CARLOS SANTANA) *(ORE/+T 10)* **THE HEALER. / ROCKIN' CHAIR** [ ] [ ]
(cd-s+=) *(ORECD 10)* – ('A'mix) / No substitute.

May 90. (7"; JOHN LEE HOOKER & BONNIE RAITT) *(ORE 18)* **I'M IN THE MOOD. / MY DREAM** [ ] [ ]
(cd-s+=) *(ORECD 18)* – ('A'version) / That's alright.

Oct 90. (7"/c-s; JOHN LEE HOOKER & ROBERT CRAY) **BABY LEE. / CUTTIN' OUT** [ ] [–]
(cd-s+=) – ('A'mix).
(re-iss. Apr96; ORECD 81) – hit UK No.65

— with **STEVE EHERMAN** – bass / **SCOTT MATTHEWS** – drums + loads on sessions **CARLOS SANTANA / ALBERT COLLINS / VAN MORRISON / KEITH RICHARDS / BOOKER T. / RY COODER / etc.**

Silvertone Charisma

Aug 91. (cd/c/lp) *(ORE CD/C/LP 519)* *<91724>* **MR. LUCKY** [3] [ ]
– I want to hug you / Mr. Lucky / Backstabbers / This is hip / I cover the waterfront / Highway 13 / Stripped me naked / Susie / Crawlin' Kingsnake / Father was a jockey.

Aug 91. (7") *(ORE 29)* **MR. LUCKY. / THIS IS HIP** [ ] [–]
(12"+=/cd-s+=) *(ORE T/CD 29)* – ('A'-mix).

Pointblank Pointblank

Oct 92. (7"/c-s) *(POB/+C 3)* **BOOM BOOM. / HOMEWORK** [16] [ ]
(cd-s+=) *(POBCD 3)* – The blues will never die / Thought I heard.
(cd-s) *(POBDX 3)* – ('A'version) / Thought I heard.

Nov 92. (cd/c/lp) *(VPB CD/TC/LP 12)* **BOOM BOOM** (new rec.old tunes) [15] [–]
– Boom boom / I'm bad like Jesse James / Same old blues again / Sugar mama / Trick bag (shoppin' for my tombstone) / Boogie at Russian Hill / Hittin' the bottle again / Bottle up and go / Thought I heard / I ain't gonna suffer no more. *(re-iss. Oct93)*

Jan 93. (7"/c-s) *(POB/+C 4)* **BOOGIE AT RUSSIAN HILL. / THE BLUES WILL NEVER DIE** [53] [ ]
(cd-s+=) *(POBDX 4)* – I'm bad like Jesse James / Driftin' blues (w/ JOHN HAMMOND).

— In May'93, he teamed up with VAN MORRISON on UK No.31 hit 'GLORIA'.

— with **ROY ROGERS** – slide guitar / **CHARLES BROWN** – piano / **DANNY CARON** – guitar / **RUTH DAVIS + JIM GYETT** – bass / **GAYLORD BIRCH + BOWEN BROWN** – drums / guests **CARLOS SANTANA + CHESTER THOMPSON** (track 1) / **VAN MORRISON + BOOKER T** (track 4)

Feb 95. (7"/c-s) *(POB/+C 10)* **CHILL OUT (THINGS GONNA CHANGE). / TUPELO** [45] [ ]
(cd-s+=) *(POBDG 10)* – Boom boom.
(cd-s+=) *(POBD 10)* – Up and down / Thought I heard.

Feb 95. (cd/c/lp) *(VPB CD/TC/LP 22)* *<40107>* **CHILL OUT** [23] [ ]
– Chill out (things gonna change) / Deep blue sea / Kiddio / Medley: Serves me right to suffer – Syndicator / One bourbon, one scotch, one beer / Tupelo / Woman on my mind / Annie Mae / Too young / Talkin' the blues / If you've never been in love / We'll meet again.

Mar 97. (cd/c) *(VPB CD/TC 39)* *<42771>* **DON'T LOOK BACK** [63] [ ]
– Dimples / Healing game / Ain't no gig thing / Don't look back / Blues before sunrise / Spellbound / Travellin' blues / I love you honey / Frisco blues / Red house / Rainy day.

— next feat. duets with VAN MORRISON, ERIC CLAPTON, ROBERT CRAY, BONNIE RAITT, CARLOS SANTANA, RY COODER, etc.

Oct 98. (cd) *(VPBCD 49)* *<46424>* **THE BEST OF FRIENDS** [ ] [ ]
– Boogie chillen / This is hip / The healer / I cover the waterfront / Boom boom / I'm in the mood / Burning hell / Tupelo / Baby Lee / Dimples / Chill out (things gonna change) / Big legs, tight skirt / Don't look back.

— JOHN LEE HOOKER died in Los Altos, Ca., on the 21st of June 2001

– (selective) compilations, etc. –

Jul 64. (lp) *Pye Int./ US= Chess; (NPL 28042)* **HOUSE OF THE BLUES** (50's recordings) [ ] 1960 [ ]
(UK re-iss. Jan67 on 'Marble Arch'; MAL 663) – hit No.34 *(re-iss. Oct87 on 'Chess') (cd-iss. Dec86 on 'Vogue')*

1971. (lp) *United Artists; (UAS 29235)* **COAST TO COAST** [ ] [–]
(cd-iss. Sep97 on 'Beat Goes On'; BGOCD 363)

Feb 77. (d-lp) *D.J.M.; (DJD 28026)* **DIMPLES** [ ] [–]

Apr 82. (lp) *Chess; (CXMD 4005)* **CHESS MASTERS** [–] [ ]

Feb 87. (cd) *Charly; (CDCHARLY 62)* **HOUSE RENT BOOGIE** [ ] [–]
(re-iss. Mar01 on 'Ace'; CDCHD 799)

May 91. (cd) *Music Club; (MCCD 020)* **THE BEST OF JOHN LEE HOOKER** [ ] [–]
– Boom boom / Shake it baby (original) / The right time / Dimples / Boogie chillun / Mambo chillun / Wheel and deal / I'm so excited / Trouble blues / Everybody's rockin' / Unfriendly woman / Time is marchin' / I see you when you're weak / I'm in the mood / Will the circle be unbroken / This is hip / Hobo blues / Solid sender.

Sep 92. (cd) *Ace; (CDCHD 421)* **GRAVEYARD BLUES** [ ] [–]

May 93. (cd) *Ace; (CDCHD 315)* **THE LEGENDARY MODERN RECORDINGS 1948-1954** [ ] [–]

Jul 93. (cd) *Ace; (CDCHD 474)* **EVERYBODY'S BLUES** [ ] [–]
Nov 93. (cd) *Ace; (CDCHD 405)* **BLUES BROTHER** [ ] [ ]
Mar 94. (cd) *Ace; (CDCHM 530)* **ORIGINAL FOLK BLUES OF JOHN LEE HOOKER** [ ] [–]
Jul 94. (cd) *See For Miles; (SEECD 402)* **THE EP COLLECTION** [ ] [–]
Feb 95. (cd) *Castle; (CCSCD 410)* **THE COLLECTION: 20 BLUES GREATS** [ ] [–]
Apr 95. (4xcd-box+book) *Charly; (CDDIG 5)* **THE BOOGIE MAN** [ ] [–]
Jul 95. (3xcd-box) *Charly; (VBCD 301)* **THE VERY BEST OF JOHN LEE HOOKER** [ ] [–]
Aug 95. (cd) *Imp; (IMP 301)* **WHISKEY & WIMMEN** [ ] [–]
Oct 96. (d-cd) *Charly; (CPCD 8242-2)* **THE VERY BEST OF JOHN LEE HOOKER** [ ] [ ]
Jun 99. (d-cd) *Snapper; (SMDCD 187)* **THIS IS HIP: THE BEST OF JOHN LEE HOOKER** [ ] [ ]
Sep 99. (cd/c) *Platinum; (PLATCD 535)* **THE BEST OF JOHN LEE HOOKER** [ ] [–]
Oct 99. (cd) *Castle Pie; (PIESD 148)* **BOOM BOOM** [ ] [ ]
Mar 00. (cd) *Krazy Kat; (KKCD 05)* **BOOGIE AWHILE 1948-1953** [ ] [ ]
Feb 01. (cd) *M.C.A.; (MCBD 19507)* **THE BEST OF JOHN LEE HOOKER** [ ] [ ]
Jun 01. (cd) *Indigo; (IGOCD 2122)* **BOOGIE CHILLEN: THE ESSENTIAL RECORDINGS OF JOHN LEE HOOKER 1948-1949** [ ] [ ]
Sep 01. (cd) *R.P.M.; (RPMSH 208)* **THE COMPLETE 1964 RECORDINGS** [ ] [ ]
Sep 01. (3xcd-box) *Snapper; (SNAJ 705CD)* **TESTAMENT** [ ] [ ]
Sep 01. (3xcd-box) *E.M.I.; (833912-2)* **ALTERNATIVE BOOGIE: EARLY STUDIO RECORDINGS 1948-1952** [ ] [ ]
Oct 01. (d-cd) *Pointblank; (810908-2)* **BOOM BOOM / THE HEALER** [ ] [ ]
Jun 02. (cd) *Delta Blue; (63049)* **BLUES IS MY MIDDLE NAME** [ ] [ ]
Mar 03. (d-cd) *E.M.I.; (581727-2)* **BOOM BOOM / CHILL OUT** [ ] [ ]
Mar 03. (cd) *Corazong; (255018)* **ALONE – THE 1ST CONCERT (live)** [ ] [ ]
Mar 03. (cd) *Corazong; (255028)* **ALONE – THE 2ND CONCERT (live)** [ ] [ ]

HOOTIE & THE BLOWFISH

Formed: Columbia, South Carolina, USA ... 1993 by DARIUS RUCKER, MARK BRYAN, DEAN FELBER and JIM 'SONI' SONEFELD. Their debut single 'HOLD MY HAND' (helped by backing vox from DAVID CROSBY) stormed America, as did multi-million selling No.1 album 'CRACKED REAR VIEW'. In Britain, they were lauded by the likes of TV/radio presenter, Danny Baker, which (I suppose) helped gain growing reputation on Virgin FM safe rock music station. Corporate and melodic, MTV adult-orientated rock, with similar vox references of African-American DARIUS, to BRAD ROBERTS (Crash Test Dummies) or EDDIE VEDDER (Pearl Jam), HOOTIE & THE BLOWFISH struck gold again with their second set, 'FAIRWEATHER JOHNSON' (1996). Another massive No.1 hit in the States, the album even cracked the UK Top 10; their appeal wasn't that universal, though, one MAX CAVALERA (ex-SEPULTURA) making his thoughts pretty explicit on the track 'No!' from the SOULFLY debut. Regardless of whether 'HOOTIE & THE BLOWFISH' (2003) was so named due to a statement of intent or just plain laziness, the results were entirely in keeping with their reputation for earnest pop/rock workmanship. • **Covered:** DRIVER 8 (R.E.M.) / I GO BLIND (54:40) / GRAVITY OF THE SITUATION with Nanci Griffith (Vic Chesnutt) / HEY HEY WHAT CAN I DO (Led Zeppelin) / I HOPE THAT I DON'T FALL IN LOVE WITH YOU (Tom Waits) / USE ME (Bill Withers) / PLEASE, PLEASE, PLEASE LET ME GET WHAT I WANT (Smiths) / RENAISSANCE EYES (Willie Dixon) / etc.

Album rating: CRACKED REAR VIEW (*7) / FAIRWEATHER JOHNSON (*6) / MUSICAL CHAIRS (*5) / SCATTERED, SMOTHERED & COVERED collection (*5) / HOOTIE & THE BLOWFISH (*5)

DARIUS RUCKER – vocals, acoustic guitar, percussion / **MARK BRYAN** – guitars, vocals, etc / **DEAN FELBER** – bass, clavinet, vocals / **JIM 'SONI' SONEFELD** – drums, vocals, piano, etc.

Atlantic Atlantic

Feb 95. (c-s) *(A 7230C) <87230>* **HOLD MY HAND / I GO BLIND** [50] Sep94 [10]
(cd-s+=) *(A 7230CD)* – Running from an angel.
Mar 95. (cd/c) *<(7567 82613-2/-4)>* **CRACKED REAR VIEW** [12] Jul94 [1]
– Hannah Jane / Hold my hand / Let her cry / Only wanna be with you / Running from an angel / I'm goin' home / Drowning / Time / Look away / Not even the trees / Goodbye.
Mar 95. (c-s) *<87231>* **LET HER CRY / ('A'version)** [–] [9]
May 95. (c-s) *(A 7188C)* **LET HER CRY / FINE LINE** [75] [–]
(cd-s+=) *(A 7188CD)* – Hannah Jane (live) / Where were you.
(cd-s) *(A 7188CDX)* – ('A'side) / Goodbye (live) / The ballad of John and Yoko (live) / Hold my hand (live).
Jul 95. (c-s) *<87132>* **ONLY WANNA BE WITH YOU / WHERE WERE YOU** [–] [6]
Aug 95. (c-s) *(A 7138C)* **ONLY WANNA BE WITH YOU / USE ME (live)** [ ] [–]
(cd-s+=) *(A 7138CD)* – ('A'live).
Nov 95. (c-s) *<87095>* **TIME / GOODBYE (live)** [–] [14]
Apr 96. (c-s) *(A 5513C) <87074>* **OLD MAN & ME (WHEN I GET TO HEAVEN) / BEFORE THE HEARTACHE ROLLS IN** [57] [13]
(cd-s+=) *(A 5513CD)* – Time (live) / Only wanna be with you (live).
Apr 96. (cd/c) *<(7567 82886-2/-4)>* **FAIRWEATHER JOHNSON** [9] [1]
– Be the one / Sad caper / Tucker's town / She crawls away / So strange / Old man & me / Earth stopped cold at dawn / Fairweather Johnson / Honeyscrew / Let it breathe / Silly little pop song / Fool / Tootie / When I'm lonely.
Jul 96. (c-s) *<87051>* **TUCKER'S TOWN / ARABY** [–] [38]
Jul 96. (c-s) *(A 5498C)* **TUCKER'S TOWN / NOT EVEN THE TREES** [ ] [–]
(cd-s) *(A 5498CD)* – ('A'side) / Araby.
Jan 97. (cd-s) *<87054>* **SAD CAPER** [–] [ ]
Sep 98. (cd/c) *<(7567 83136-2/-4)>* **MUSICAL CHAIRS** [15] [4]
– I will wait / Wishing / Las Vegas nights / Only lonely / Answer man / Michelle post / Bluesy revolution / Home again / One by one / Desert mountain showdown / What's going on here / What do you want from me now.
Oct 98. (c-s/cd-s) *(AT 0048 C/CD)* **I WILL WAIT / DRIVER 8 / I WILL WAIT (acoustic)** [57] [ ]
May 99. (c-s/cd-s) *(AT 0059 C/CD)* **ONLY LONELY / MICHELLE POST / FRANCES** [ ] [ ]
Nov 00. (cd/c) *<(7567 83048-2/-4)>* **SCATTERED, SMOTHERED & COVERED** (B-sides, etc.) [ ] [71]
– Fine line / I go blind / Almost home / Hey hey what can I do / Renaissance eyes / Before the heartache rolls in / Araby / I'm over you / Gravity of the situation / I hope that I don't fall in love with you / Dream baby / Driver 8 / Let me be your man / Please, please, please let me get what I want / Use me.
Mar 03. (cd) *<(7567 83564-2)>* **HOOTIE & THE BLOWFISH** [ ] [46]
– Deeper side / Little brother / Innocence / Space / I'll come runnin' / Tears fall down / The rain song / Show me your heart / When she's gone / Little darlin' / Woody / Go and tell him (soup song) – Alright.

HOT HOT HEAT

Formed: Victoria, British Columbia, Canada ... 1999 by MATT MARNIK, STEVE BAYS, PAUL HAWLEY and DUSTIN HAWTHORNE. The band began as guitar-less new wave/punk revival rock outfit, using disturbing synthesizer sound and pounding bass to create a lively and vital piece of alt rock while carving their space out amongst their more garage rock obsessed peers. This early sound was probably best witnessed on subsequent compilation, 'SCENES ONE THROUGH TO THIRTEEN' (2002), which collected material from the period from about 2000 through to 2001. The following year saw the departure of frontman MARNIK, who was replaced by guitarist DANTE DECARO. This led the band's sound down a punkier road as evidenced on the EP, 'KNOCK KNOCK KNOCK', released on the influential 'Sub Pop' indie imprint. A packed year of touring ensued to support this record and their subsequent debut album, 'MAKE UP THE BREAKDOWN' (2002) which, with its non-stop synth-punk attack, led to a major deal with 'Warners' by the year end. An album laden with catchy hooks and screaming keyboards, HOT HOT HEAT were certainly disproving their critics who had written them off as bandwagon jumping retroists hitching a ride on The STROKES' cart. Nevertheless, they joined the growing number of no-wave bands popping out of the underground scene; from YEAH YEAH YEAHS to The RAPTURE, something seemed different about HHH's spasmo-techno punk/funk assault. First of all they were great songwriters, as evident on 'NO, NOT NOW' and the infectious 'BANDAGES'. Second, they were just great young musicians, very tight, focused and well-oiled both in the studio and live. 'MAKE UP THE BREAKDOWN' sold a truck-load of albums and sent the band on a whirlwind tour in 2003.

Album rating: SCENES ONE THROUGH THIRTEEN compilation (*6) / MAKE UP THE BREAKDOWN (*7)

MATT MARNIK – vocals, guitar / **STEVE BAYS** – keyboards / **DUSTIN HAWTHORNE** – bass, vocals / **PATRICK HAWLEY** – drums

Apr 00. (7"red-ep) <*ACHE 001*> **HOT HOT HEAT** [-] [ ]
– Fashion fight pause / Tourist in your town / Matador at the door / Spelling live backwards. *(UK-iss.Sep02; same)*

Nov 00. (lp) <*ACHE 002*> **HOT HOT HEAT / THE RED LIGHT STING** [-] [ ]
– Case that they gave me / Haircut economics / Circus maximus / Tokyo vogue / I blew a fuse in my personality / (others by RED LIGHT STING). *(UK cd-iss. Aug03; ACHE 002CD)*

not iss. — Monoton Studios

Jun 01. (7"ep) **HOT HOT HEAT** [-] [ ]
– Keep my name out of your mouth / Word to water / Paco Pena.

Ohev — Ohev

Feb 02. (cd) <*(OHEV 009CD)*> **SCENES ONE THROUGH THIRTEEN** (compilation) [ ] [ ]
– Keep my name out of your mouth / Word to water / Haircut economics / The case that they gave me / Paco Pena / Circus maximus / I blew a fuse in my personality / Tokyo vogue / Fashion fight pause / Spelling live backwards / Matador at the door / Tourist in your own town / You're ruining it for everyone.

— **DANTE DECARO** – vocals, guitar; repl. MATT

Sub Pop — Sub Pop

Jul 02. (cd-ep) <*(SPCD 594)*> **KNOCK KNOCK KNOCK** [ ] Apr02 [ ]
– Le le low / 5 times out of 100 / Have a good sleep / Touch you touch you / More for show. <*(12"ep iss.Oct02; SP 594)*> *(re-iss. Sep03; same)*

B-Unique — Sub Pop

Mar 03. (7") *(BUN 045-7)* **BANDAGES. / APT. 101** [25] [-]
(cd-s+=) *(BUN 045CDS)* – Move on.

Mar 03. (lp/cd) *(5046 64225-2)* <*SP/+CD 599*> **MAKE UP THE BREAKDOWN** [35] Oct02 [ ]
– Naked in the city again / No, not now / Get in or get out / Bandages / Oh, godamnit / Aveda / This town / Talk to me, dance with me / Save us S.O.S. / In Cairo.

Warners — not iss.

Jul 03. (7") *(W 615)* **NO NOT NOW. / 5 TIMES OUT OF A 100 (thoughts out of a 100 remix)** [38] [-]
(cd-s+=) *(W 615CD)* – This town (live).

Nov 03. (cd-s) *(W 626CD)* **TALK TO ME, DANCE WITH ME / OH GODDAMMIT** [ ] [-]

□ HOTLEGS (see under ⇒ 10cc)

□ HOURGLASS
(see under ⇒ ALLMAN BROTHERS BAND)

HOUSEMARTINS

Formed: Hull, England . . . late 1983 by PAUL HEATON and STAN CULLIMORE, CHRIS LANG and TED KEY soon completing the line-up. After local gigs, many of them for political causes (i.e. the miners & CND), they signed to Andy McDonald's new 'Go! Discs' label. With HUGH WHITAKER replacing LANG, they released their debut single, 'FLAG DAY', a record that left you in no doubt where the band's political loyalties lay. Although the single failed to chart, with the follow-up, 'SHEEP' (prior to which, NORMAN COOK replaced TED KEY) faring little better, The HOUSEMARTINS imprinted themselves on mid-80's consciousness with 'HAPPY HOUR'. An outrageously catchy single, this was Brit-pop before Brit-pop was even invented; shiny, happy melodies, chiming guitars and nifty footwork, as always with an underlying right-on message. The record reached No.3 in the UK charts, the debut album, 'LONDON 0 HULL 4' (1986) attaining the same position later that summer. An endearing collection of witty, finely crafted songs which, above all, had a big heart and a deep soul, attributes which were at a premium in those dark 80's days with the twin spectres of Thatcher and Stock, Aitken & Waterman never far away. That Christmas, the band became a household name when they scaled the charts with a lovely a cappella cover of ISLEY JASPER ISLEY's 'CARAVAN OF LOVE'. The following Spring, WHITAKER was replaced by DAVE HEMMINGWAY, the band releasing their follow-up album later that year, 'THE PEOPLE WHO GRINNED THEMSELVES TO DEATH'. Even more politically pointed than the debut, the record nevertheless delivered its barbs in unerringly melodic packages, its highlight being the gorgeous gospel-pop of penultimate single, 'BUILD'. Yet the band had almost reached the end of their woefully short lifespan, HEATON and CULLIMORE agreeing from the start that it shouldn't exceed three years. Bowing out with a cover of Burt Bacharach's 'THERE'S ALWAYS SOMETHING THERE TO REMIND ME', The HOUSEMARTINS officially split in early '88. While HEATON went on to even greater success with The BEAUTIFUL SOUTH, the pseudo-Christian, Socialist sentiments he propounded in his earlier career seem a little hollow in light of his alleged penchant for soccer hooliganism. Working Class to the bone, eh mate? WHITAKER's subsequent conduct was little better, the man being sentenced to six years in prison in 1993 for assault and arson offences. NORMAN COOK, on the other hand, became a major player on the dance scene under various aliases, including BEATS INTERNATIONAL, PIZZAMAN and more recently the storming FATBOY SLIM. • **Songwriters:** Penned by HEATON-CULLIMORE except covers; HE AIN'T HEAVY, HE'S MY BROTHER (Hollies) / CARAVAN OF LOVE (Isley Jasper Isley). • **Trivia:** LONDON 0 HULL 4, stemmed from group's promotional hometown pride. They often described themselves as Hull's 4th best group. Who were better? RED GUITARS, EVERYTHING BUT THE GIRL and GARGOYLES?

Album rating: LONDON 0 HULL 4 (*8) / THE PEOPLE WHO GRINNED THEMSELVES TO DEATH (*7) / NOW THAT'S WHAT I CALL QUITE GOOD compilation (*8)

PAUL HEATON (b. 9 May'62, Bromborough, England) – vocals / **STAN CULLIMORE** (b.IAN, 6 Apr'62) – guitar, vocals / **TED KEY** – bass / **HUGH WHITAKER** – drums; repl. CHRIS LANG

		Go! Discs	Elektra
Oct 85.	(7") *(GOD 7)* **FLAG DAY. / STAND AT EASE**		-
	(12"+=) *(GODX 7)* – Coal train to Hatfield Main.		

— **NORMAN COOK** (b. QUENTIN COOK, 31 Jul'63, Brighton, England) – bass repl. TED KEY who formed GARGOYLES

Mar 86.	(7"/7"pic-d) *(GOD/+P 9)* **SHEEP. / DROP DOWN DEAD**	54	-
	(d7"+=) *(GOD 9/+7)* – Flag day / Stand at ease.		
	(12"+=) *(GODX 9)* – I'll be your shelter / Anxious / People get ready.		
May 86.	(7"/7"sha-pic-d) *(GOD/+P 11)* *<69515>* **HAPPY HOUR. / THE MIGHTY SHIP**	3	Sep86
	(12"+=) *(GODX 11)* – Sitting on a fence / He ain't heavy.		
Jun 86.	(lp/c)(cd) *(A/Z GOLP 7)(CCD 1537)* *<60501>* **LONDON 0 HULL 4**	3	Feb87
	– Happy hour / Get up off our knees / Flag day / Anxious / Reverends revenge / Sitting on a fence / Sheep / Over there / Think for a minute / We're not deep / Lean on me / Freedom. *(c+=)* – I'll be your shelter. *(cd++=)* – People get ready / The mighty ship / He ain't heavy. *(re-iss. Oct92 cd/c; same)*		
Sep 86.	(7"/7"sha-pic-d) *(GOD/+P 13)* **THINK FOR A MINUTE. / WHO NEEDS THE LIMELIGHT**	18	
	(12"+=) *(GODX 13)* – I smell winter / Joy joy joy / Rap around the clock.		
Nov 86.	(7"/7"sha-pic-d) *(GOD/+P 16)* **CARAVAN OF LOVE. / WHEN I FIRST MET JESUS**	1	-
	(12"+=) *(GODX 16)* – We shall not be moved / So much in love / Heaven help us all.		
	(7"box-set+=) *(GODB 16)* **THE HOUSEMARTINS CHRISTMAS BOX SET** – (all 4 singles +=; *GOD 9)* – I'll be your shelter. – hit No.84		
Feb 87.	(7") *<69491>* **FLAG DAY. / THE MIGHTY SHIP**	-	

— **DAVE HEMMINGWAY** (b.20 Sep'60) – drums; repl. WHITAKER who joined GARGOYLES full-time

May 87.	(7") *(GOD 18)* **FIVE GET OVER EXCITED. / REBEL WITHOUT THE AIRPLAY**	11	-
	(c-s+=/12"+=) *(XGOD/GODX 18)* – So glad / Hopelessly devoted to them.		
Aug 87.	(7") *(GOD 19)* **ME AND THE FARMER. / I BIT MY LIP**	15	-
	(c-s+=/12"+=) *(XGOD/GODX 19)* – He will find you out / Step outside.		
Sep 87.	(lp/c) *(A/Z GOLP 9)* *<60761>* **THE PEOPLE WHO GRINNED THEMSELVES TO DEATH**	9	Jan88
	– The people who grinned themselves to death / I can't put my finger on it / The light is always green / The world's on fire / Pirate aggro / We're not coming back / Me and the farmer / Five get over excited / Johannesburg / Bow down / You better be doubtful / Build. *(re-iss. Oct92 cd/c; same)*		
Nov 87.	(7") *(GOD 21)* **BUILD. / PARIS IN FLARES**	15	-
	(c-s+=)(10"+=/12"+=/cd-s+=) *(ZGOD 21)(GOD X/T/CD 21)* – Forwards and backwards / The light is always green (cheaper version).		
Apr 88.	(7") *(GOD 22)* **THERE IS ALWAYS SOMETHING THERE TO REMIND ME. / GET UP OFF YOUR KNEES (live)**	35	-
	(12"+=/cd-s+=) *(GOD X/CD 22)* – Five get over excited (live) / Johannesburg (live).		
Apr 88.	(d-lp/d-c/cd) *(AGOLP/ZGOLP/AGOCD 11)* **NOW THAT'S WHAT I CALL QUITE GOOD** (compilation)	8	-
	– I smell winter / Bow down / Think for a minute / There is always something there to remind me / The mighty ship / Sheep / I'll be your shelter / Five get over excited / Everybody's the same / Build / Step outside / Flag day / Happy hour / You've got a friend / He ain't heavy / Freedom / The people who grinned themselves to death / Caravan of love / The light is always green / We're not deep / Me and the farmer / Lean on me.		

— They had already decided to split up late '87. NORMAN COOK developed several solo projects including the unashamedly commercial BEATS INTERNATIONAL. HEATON and HEMINGWAY formed The BEAUTIFUL SOUTH. The HOUSEMARTINS briefly returned to the UK charts via a (collab/vs.) single, 'Change The World'

HOUSE OF PAIN

Formed: Woodland Hills, Los Angeles, California, USA . . . 1990 by solo artist/rapper EVERLAST (whose 1990 eponymous 'Warners' debut featured rap don, ICE T), fellow wordsmith DANNY BOY and DJ LETHAL. Signing to 'Tommy Boy', the band hit the American Top 3 with their debut single, 'JUMP AROUND', a hip hop juggernaut of a record that employed thuggish vocal rhyming, a big 'n' bouncy bassline and screeching PUBLIC ENEMY-style noise to create one of the year's most memorable rap tunes. The self-titled debut was released soon after, hitting the US Top 20 although a follow-up single, 'SHAMROCKS AND SHENANIGANS (BOOM SHALOCK LOCK BOOM)' flopped. Once you got past the gimmicky Irish-American facade there really wasn't much substance to this lot (we thought) apart from cliched macho lyrics and gangsta posturing (degrading women, a speciality). But while their success petered out in America, 'JUMP AROUND' was re-released in the UK the following Spring, making the Top 10. This coincided with EVERLAST being arrested at New York's JFK airport, charged with illegal possession of a firearm, the rapper eventually being sentenced to four months house arrest the following year. Controversy continued to dog the group when, in a particularly nasty incident, a HOUSE OF PAIN road crew member was involved in a fight with the security crew at a gig in Manchester. Such publicity obviously did the band's hard-man image and public profile no harm, 1994's follow-up album, 'SAME AS IT EVER WAS' going Top 10 in the UK, Top 20 in America. A marked improvement on the debut, the album was more impassioned with EVERLAST railing against his perceived role as media fall guy. A third set, 'TRUTH CRUSHED TO EARTH SHALL RISE AGAIN' (1996), did little to resurrect the HOUSE OF PAIN of old and it was inevitable that the group would split; meanwhile, Murphy's beer were screeching out 'JUMP AROUND' for a TV commercial. In 1998, the reformed EVERLAST (he's now a Muslim) re-invented himself as a hip-hop minstrel and turned out his best work in years (if not ever!) with the US Top 10 set, 'WHITEY FORD SINGS THE BLUES'. The record contained at least two classic numbers, the US Top 20 hit, 'WHAT IT'S LIKE' and the man's cautionary tale of greed, 'ENDS'. Follow-up set, 'EAT AT WHITEY'S' (2000) continued in a similar vein of charismatic, bohemian folk-hop, the rap survivor getting by just fine – and getting into the US Top 20 – with a little help from his friends. No bad thing when they happen to be as famous and as talented as SANTANA although EVERLAST sounded most convincing performing on his proverbial tod. • **Songwriters:** Group penned, and partly produced by DJ MUGGS (Cypress Hill). Sampled HARLEM SHUFFLE (Bob Earl) / I COME TO YOU BABY (John Lee Hooker). • **Trivia:** DANNY BOY's preoccupation with his Irish ancestry made him mark his body with a 'Sinn Fein' tattoo, although he admitted to being more influenced by actor Mickey Rourke than the Irish political party.

Album rating: HOUSE OF PAIN (*8) / SAME AS IT EVER WAS (*7) / TRUTH CRUSHED TO EARTH SHALL RISE AGAIN (*4) / Everlast: FOREVER EVERLAST (*5) / WHITEY FORD SINGS THE BLUES (*8) / TODAY (WATCH ME SHINE) mini (*6) / EAT AT WHITEY'S (*7)

EVERLAST

w/ **ICE-T** – vocals / **BILAL BASHIR** – keyboards / **CLARENCE METHENY** – synthesizer / **JOHN BREYER** – guitar / **MIKE GREG** – sax

		Warners	Warners
Sep 88.	(7") *<27771>* **SYNDICATION. / BUSTIN' LOOSE**	-	
Feb 90.	(cd/c/lp) *<(7599 26097-2/-4/-1)>* **FOREVER EVERLAST**		
	– Syndicate soldier / Speak no evil / Syndication (remix) / What is this? /		

The rhythm / I got the knack / On the edge / Fuck everyone / Goodbye / Pass it on / Never missin' a beat. *(cd re-iss. Jun99 on 'Rhino'; 8122 75786-2)*

Mar 90. (7") *<22739>* **SYNDICATE SOLDIER. / NEVER MISSIN' A BEAT** –

Jun 90. (12") *<19973>* **PAY THE PRICE / I GOT THE KNACK** –

HOUSE OF PAIN

EVERLAST (b. ERIC SCHRODY, 18 Aug'69, Valley Stream, N.Y.) – vocals / **DANNY BOY** (b. DANIEL O'CONNOR, 12 Dec'68) – vocals / **DJ LETHAL** (b. LEOR DiMANT, 18 Dec'72, Latvia) – turntable

X.L. Tommy Boy

Sep 92. (7"/c-s/12") *(XLS/XLC/XLT 32) <526>* **JUMP AROUND / HOUSE OF PAIN ANTHEM** 32 Jun92 3
(cd-s+=) *(XLS 32CD)* – ('A'mixes).

Nov 92. (cd/c) *(XL CD/TC 111) <1056>* **HOUSE OF PAIN** 73 Jul92 14
– Salutations / Jump around / Put your head out / Top o' the morning to ya / House and the rising sun / Shamrocks and shenanigans (boom shalock lock boom) / House of pain anthem / Danny boy, Danny boy / Guess who's back / Put on your shit kickers / Come and get some of this / Life goes on / One for the road / Feel it / All my love.

Nov 92. (7"/c-s/12") *(XLS/XLC/XLT 38) <543>* **SHAMROCKS AND SHENANIGANS (BOOM SHALOCK LOCK BOOM). / PUT YOUR HEAD OUT** 65
(cd-s+=) *(XLS 38CD)* – (3-'A'versions).

May 93. (c-s) *<556>* **WHO'S THE MAN? / ('A'instrumental) / PUT ON YOUR SHIT KICKERS (2 versions)** – 96

May 93. (12"/c-s) *(XLC/XLT 43)* **JUMP AROUND (remix). / TOP O' THE MORNING TO YA (remix)** 8 –
(cd-s+=) *(XLS 43CD)* – ('A'mixes).

Oct 93. (12"/c-s) *(XLC/XLT 46)* **SHAMROCKS & SHENANIGANS. / WHO'S THE MAN** 23 –
(cd-s+=) *(XLS 46CD)* – ('A'mixes).

—— early in '94, EVERLAST was sentenced to 3 months – served at home (tagged), for earlier carrying a weapon. 'IT AIN'T A CRIME' sampled UNDER THE BRIDGE (Red Hot Chili Peppers).

Jul 94. (c-s) *(XSC 52) <623>* **ON POINT (The Beatminerz mix). / ('A'-DJ Lethal mix)** 19 85
(12"+=)(cd-s+=) *(XST 52)(XLS 52CD)* – Word is bond.

Jul 94. (cd/c/d-lp) *(XL CD/MC/LP 115) <1089>* **SAME AS IT EVER WAS** 8 Jun94 12
– Back from the dead / I'm a swing it / All that / On point / Runnin' up on ya / Over the shit / Word is bond / Keep it comin' / Interlude / Same as it ever was / It ain't a crime / Where I'm from / Still got a lotta love / Who's the man? / On point (lethal dose remix).

Oct 94. (12"/c-s) *(XLT/XLC 55)* **IT AIN'T A CRIME (madhouse remix). / LEGEND** 37
(cd-s) *(XLS 55CD)* – ('A'side) / Word is bond (Diamond D + Darkman remixes).

Jun 95. (12"/c-s) *(XLT/XLC 61)* **OVER THERE (I DON'T CARE). / JUMP AROUND (mastermix)** 20
(cd-s+=) *(XLS 61CD1)* – Shamrocks and shenanigans / Top o' the morning to ya.
(cd-s) *(XLS 61CD2)* – ('A'side) / Runnin' up on ya (versions incl. House of Pain vs. Kerbdog).

Tommy Boy Tommy Boy

Sep 96. (c-s) *(TBC 7744)* **FED UP / ('A'mix)** 68
(cd-s) *(TBCD 7744)* – ('A'mix).
(12") *(12TC 7744)* – ('A'mix).

Oct 96. (cd/c/lp) *<(TB CD/C/V 1161)>* **TRUTH CRUSHED TO EARTH SHALL RISE AGAIN** 47
– Have nots / Fed up / What's that smell / Heart full of sorrow / Earthquake / Shut the door / Pass the Jinn / No doubt / Choose your poison / X-files / Fed up / Killa rhyme klik / While I'm here.

—— when HOUSE OF PAIN broke-up, DJ LETHAL joined metallers, LIMP BIZKIT

EVERLAST

—— solo once more

Tommy Boy Tommy Boy

Feb 99. (c-s/cd-s) *(TBC/+D7 470) <radio play>* **WHAT IT'S LIKE / WHAT IT'S LIKE (clean) / WHAT IT'S LIKE (original)** 34 Dec98 13

Mar 99. (cd/c/d-lp) *<(TB CD/C/V 1236)>* **WHITEY FORD SINGS THE BLUES** 65 Sep98 9
– The white boy is back / Money (dollar bill) feat. SADAT X / Ends / What it's like / Get down / Sen Dog / Tired / Hot to death / Painkillers / Prince Paul / Praise the Lord / Today (watch me shine) feat. BRONX STYLE BOB / Guru / Death comes callin' / Funky beat feat. CASUAL and SADAT X / The letter / 7 years. *(cd+=)* – Next man.

Jun 99. (7") *(TB7 346)* **ENDS / ('A'live)** 47
(12"/cd-s) *(12TB/TBCD 346)* – ('A'side) / What it's like (live) / Hot to death.

Nov 99. (m-cd) *(<TBCD 2045>)* **TODAY (WATCH ME SHINE)**
– Today (watch me shine) / Put your lights on (with SANTANA) / Only love can break your heart / What it's like (live) / Jump around (live) / Some nights are better than others / Hot to death (live).

Oct 00. (cd-s) *(TBCD 2150)* **BLACK JESUS (mixes)** –

Oct 00. (cd/d-lp) *<(TB CD/V 1411)>* **EAT AT WHITEY'S** 20
– Whitey / Black Jesus / I can't move / Black coffee / Babylon feeling / Deadly assassins / Children's story / Love for real / One and the same / We're all gonna die / Mercy on my soul / One, two / Graves to die / Put your lights on: EVERLAST & SANTANA.

Jan 01. (12") *(TBV 2180)* **BLACK JESUS. / CHILDREN'S STORY: Everlast & Rahzel / GRAVES TO DIG** 37 –
(cd-s) *(TBCD 2180A)* – ('A'side) / ('A'versions).
(cd-s) *(TBCD 2180B)* – (first 2 tracks) / What's it like (video).

Mar 01. (12"/cd-s) *(TB V/CD 2113)* **DEADLY ASSASSINS. / ONE, TWO (featuring KURUPT) / DEADLY ASSASSINS (instrumental)** –

May 01. (promo-cd-s) *(BCD 2214)* **I CAN'T MOVE / CALL OUT HOOK** – –

☐ Steve HOWE (see under ⇒ YES)

HOWLIN' WOLF

Born: CHESTER ARTHUR BURNETT, 10 June 1910, West Point, Mississippi, USA. One of the most important of the Southern expatriates who created the 'Chicago Sound' of the 50's, his earliest musical experience, as with many other blues artists, was singing in the local Baptist church choir. Inspired by CHARLEY PATTON (who taught him how to play guitar) and TOMMY JOHNSON, he gleaned much of his showmanship from them, although his powerful voice and "howlin'" were very much his own (further influences were to be ROBERT JOHNSON and SON HOUSE). BURNETT was a farmer to trade until his late 30's when he was introduced by IKE TURNER to SAM PHILLIPS of Sun Records. PHILLIPS, in turn, made deals with 'Modern' Records in California, 'Chess' Records in Chicago issuing WOLF's other recordings. His first single, 'MOANING AT MIDNIGHT', was released by both companies concurrently, although 'Chess' avoided split sales by promoting the b-side, 'HOW MANY MORE YEARS'. This track was by far the heaviest blues song (in rock terms) released in America to date, both versions of the song reaching the R&B Top 20. After much wrangling between the two record companies, he decided to sign exclusively for 'Chess' in 1952, subsequently moving to Chicago and leaving his band behind in the process. The records never sold well after his initial success, although 'Chess' were making plenty of money through CHUCK BERRY and BO DIDDLEY and could afford to keep the WOLF in business to maintain their core ghetto audience. He eventually went back "down home" to pick up some Delta musicians, including a teenage guitarist going by the name of HUBERT SUMLIN. Despite initial conflict, including one incident in which they punched out each other's front teeth, SUMLIN virtually became WOLF's adopted son, remaining by his side for the rest of his career. During the next 10 years, he recorded most of his classic repertoire, including his own compositions

'SMOKESTACK LIGHTNING', 'NO PLACE TO GO', 'SITTING ON TOP OF THE WORLD', 'EVIL', 'KILLING FLOOR', 'I AIN'T SUPERSTITIOUS' and 'WHO'S BEEN TALKING', plus the WILLIE DIXON songs, 'SPOONFUL','DOWN IN THE BOTTOM', 'BACK DOOR MAN', 'THE RED ROOSTER' and 'WANG DANG DOODLE'. HOWLIN' WOLF came to Britain in 1961, 'Pye' releasing 'LITTLE BABY' as his first single, although it failed to chart. In 1963, he was recorded live with OTIS SPANN, BUDDY GUY and MUDDY WATERS, the performance being released the following year on the album, 'FOLK FESTIVAL OF THE BLUES'. WOLF was allegedly not easy to work with, being described by some of his associates as "bone stupid", illiterate and slow witted. He was also chronically suspicious that everyone was out to cheat him and convinced that MUDDY WATERS was his most deadly enemy, even though MUDDY had helped him get work when he first came to Chicago. WILLIE DIXON, who wrote and arranged much of WOLF's 'Chess' material, claimed that the only way he could get the WOLF to record a song was to tell him that MUDDY wanted it! His fans in Britain included The ROLLING STONES and The YARDBIRDS, these groups publicising his work both in Europe and in white America, leading to his music becoming a significant influence on the emerging rock music of the day. Many of his songs were covered by a number of diverse artists, although only CAPTAIN BEEFHEART came close to the raucous aggressiveness of the originals. His only pop hit, the magnificent 'SMOKESTACK LIGHTNING', arrived in June 1964, eight years after its original US release. In 1967 he recorded the album, 'SUPER SUPER BLUES BAND' with BO DIDDLEY and MUDDY WATERS, although disappointingly, it only contained reworkings of familiar songs rather than new material. 1969 was a year of dramatic contrasts for him; 'Chess' and WOLF were impressed by the success of MUDDY WATERS' 'ELECTRIC MUD' album and they decided to release the similarly conceived psychedelic opus, 'THE HOWLIN' WOLF ALBUM'. The record was an unmitigated disaster, WOLF himself even commenting that it was "dog-shit". He was back on familiar ground with 'THE LONDON SESSIONS' album, recorded with, among others, ERIC CLAPTON, STEVE WINWOOD, BILL WYMAN and CHARLIE WATTS. During the recording of the album he attempted to teach the correct beat of 'RED ROOSTER' to the musicians (The STONES already having had a worldwide success with the track) by playing bottleneck guitar. He later suffered a heart attack and then a kidney ailment which left him permanently dependent on dialysis. As a result, WOLF did little between 1969 and 1976, although he did have one final bellow at the world with the extraordinary, 'COON ON THE MOON' from the 1971 album, 'MESSAGE TO THE YOUNG'. The album remains unavailable while the song is yet to make it onto any compilation (probably down to our politically correct times). HOWLIN' WOLF died on the 10th of January 1976 in Hines, Illinois, USA and although he was not the first bluesman to call himself HOWLIN' WOLF (that distinction belongs to J.T. SMITH) he will be the only HOWLIN' WOLF to everyone involved with blues music. Delta bluesman or Chicago titan – who knows?, but whatever you think, there's not been anything like him. The blues can boast better guitarists, better composers, better harmonica players and yes, better singers, but no one has produced a better recorded voice or a more compelling human presence. • **Rock/pop artists to cover his material:** SPOONFUL (Cream) / I AIN'T SUPERSTITIOUS (Savoy Brown) + (Jeff Beck) / BACK DOOR MAN (Doors) / HOW MANY MORE YEARS? (Little Feat) / KILLIN' FLOOR (Electric Flag) / etc.

Album rating (selective): MOANIN' IN THE MOONLIGHT (*8) / HOWLIN' WOLF aka THE ROCKING CHAIR (*7) / THE REAL FOLK BLUES (*8) / EVIL (*6) / MORE REAL FOLK BLUES (*7) / THE BACK DOOR WOLF (*7) / THE GENUINE ARTICLE – THE BEST OF.. compilation (*8)

HOWLIN' WOLF – vocals, guitar with **HUBERT SUMLIN** + **WILLIE JOHNSON** – guitar / **WILLIE STEZZ** – drums / **IKE TURNER** – piano

		not iss.	R.P.M.
Oct 51.	(78) *<333>* **MOANIN' AT MIDNIGHT. / RIDIN' IN THE MOONLIGHT**	–	
Nov 51.	(78; as HOWLING WOLF) *<340>* **CRYING AT DAYBREAK. / PASSING BY BLUES**	–	
Dec 51.	(78; as THE HOWLING WOLF) *<347>* **MY BABY STOLE OFF. / I WANT YOUR PICTURE**	–	

		London	Chess
Dec 51.	(78) *<1479>* **MOANIN' AT MIDNIGHT. / HOW MANY MORE YEARS**	–	
Feb 52.	(78; as THE HOWLING WOLF) *<1497>* **THE WOLF IS AT YOUR DOOR (HOWLIN' FOR MY BABY). / HOWLIN' WOLF BOOGIE**	–	
Mar 52.	(78; as THE HOWLING WOLF) *<1510>* **GETTING OLD AND GREY. / MR. HIGHWAY MAN**	–	
Jun 52.	(78; THE HOWLING WOLF) *<1515>* **SADDLE MY PONY. / WORRIED ALL THE TIME**	–	
Nov 52.	(78) *<1528>* **OH! RED. / MY LAST AFFAIR**	–	
Feb 53.	(78) **ALL NIGHT BOOGIE (ALL NIGHT LONG). / I LOVE MY BABY**	–	

—— now w / **WILLIE DIXON** – bass / **OTIS SPANN** – piano / **LEE COOPER** – guitar / **FRED BELOW** – drums

		London	Chess
May 54.	(78) *<1566>* **ROCKING DADDY. / NO PLACE TO GO (YOU GONNA WRECK MY LIFE)**	–	
Jul 54.	(78) *<1575>* **BABY HOW LONG. / EVIL IS GOING ON**	–	
Dec 54.	(78) *<1584>* **I'LL BE AROUND. / FORTY FOUR**	–	
May 55.	(78; THE HOWLING WOLF) *<1593>* **WHO WILL BE NEXT. / I HAVE A LITTLE GIRL**	–	
Jul 55.	(78) *<1607>* **COME TO ME BABY. / DON'T MESS WITH MY BABY**	–	

—— now w / **HOSEA LEE KENNARD** – piano / **HUBERT SUMLIN** + **WILLIE JOHNSON** – guitar / **EARL PHILLIPS** – drums

		London	Chess
Mar 56.	(78) *<1618>* **SMOKESTACK LIGHTNIN'. / YOU CAN'T BE BEAT**	–	
Sep 56.	(78) *<1632>* **I ASKED FOR WATER (SHE GAVE ME GASOLINE). / SO GLAD**	–	
Dec 56.	(7"ep) *(REU 1072)* **RHYTHM & BLUES WITH HOWLIN' WOLF** – Smokestack lightnin' / You can't be beat / Don't mess with me baby / Come to me baby.		–
Mar 57.	(78) *<1648>* **GOING BACK HOME. / MY LIFE**	–	
Jul 57.	(78) *<1668>* **NATURE. / SOMEBODY IN MY HOME**	–	
Feb 58.	(78) *<1679>* **SITTIN' ON TOP OF THE WORLD. / POOR BOY**	–	
May 58.	(78) *<1695>* **MOANIN' FOR MY BABY (MIDNIGHT BLUES). / I DIDN'T KNOW**	–	
Oct 58.	(78) *<1712>* **I'M LEAVING YOU. / CHANGE MY WAY**	–	
Nov 58.	(78) *<1726>* **I BETTER GO NOW. / HOWLIN' BLUES**	–	

—— added **WILLIE DIXON** – bass / **OTIS SPANN** – piano / **EARL PHILLIPS** – drums

—— now used various personnel

		London	Chess
Aug 59.	(7") *<1735>* **MR. AIRPLANE MAN. / I'VE BEEN ABUSED**	–	
Nov 59.	(7") *<1744>* **THE NATCHEZ BURNING. / YOU GONNA WRECK MY LIFE**	–	
Mar 60.	(7") *<1750>* **WHO'S BEEN TALKING. / TELL ME**	–	
Jul 60.	(7") *<1762>* **HOWLIN' FOR MY BABY. / SPOONFUL**	–	
Nov 60.	(7") *<1777>* **WANG-DANG-DOODLE. / BACK DOOR MAN**	–	

		Pye Int.	Chess
Sep 61.	(7") *(7N 25101)* *<1793>* **LITTLE BABY. / DOWN IN THE BOTTOM**		
Nov 61.	(7") *<1804>* **THE RED ROOSTER. / SHAKE FOR ME**	–	
Feb 62.	(7") *<1813>* **GOING DOWN SLOW. / YOU'LL BE MINE**	–	
Nov 62.	(7") *<1844>* **MAMA'S BABY. / DO THE DO**	–	

Sep 63. (7") *<1870>* **THREE HUNDRED POUNDS OF JOY. / BUILT FOR COMFORT** [–]

Apr 63. (7") *(7N 25192) <1823>* **JUST LIKE I TREAT YOU. / I AIN'T SUPERSTITIOUS** Apr62

Nov 63. (7"ep) *(NEP 44015)* **SMOKESTACK LIGHTNIN'** [–]
– Smokestack lightnin' / Howling for my baby / Going down slow / You'll be mine.

May 64. (7") *(7N 25244)* **SMOKESTACK LIGHTNIN'. / GOING DOWN SLOW** [42] [–]
(re-iss. Jul85 on 'Chess'; CHESS 4008)

Oct 64. (7"ep) *(NEP 44032)* **TELL ME** [–]
– Tell me / Who's been talking / Shake for me / Back door man.

Oct 64. (7") *(7N 25269)* **LITTLE BABY. / TAIL DRAGGER** [–]

Dec 64. (7") *(7N 25283) <1911>* **LOVE ME DARLING. / MY COUNTRY SUGAR MAMA**

Chess Chess

Feb 65. (lp) *(CRL 4006) <1434>* **MOANIN' IN THE MOONLIGHT** (compilation 50's)
– Moanin' in the moonlight / How many more years / Smokestack lightnin' / Baby how long / No place to go / Evil / I'm leading you / Moanin' for my baby / I ask for water / Forty-four / Somebody in my home. *(re-iss. Jan67 on 'Marble Arch'; MAL 665) (re-iss. Apr87 on 'Charly')*

Apr 65. (7") *(CRS 8010) <1923>* **KILLING FLOOR. / LOUISE**

JUn 65. (lp) *(CRL 4508)* **POOR BOY** [–]
– Cause of it all / The killing floor / Little red rooster / Built for comfort / Commit a crime / Do the do / Highway 49 / Worried about you / Poor boy / Wang dang doodle.

Jun 65. (7") *(CRS 8016) <1928>* **OOH BABY. / TELL ME WHAT I'VE DONE**

Aug 65. (7") *<1945>* **I WALKED FROM DALLAS / DON'T LAUGH AT ME** [–]

1966. (lp) *<1502>* **REAL FOLK BLUES** [–]
– Killing floor / Lousie / Poor boy / Sittin' on top of the world / Nature / My country / Sugar mama / Tail draggerr / 300 lb. of joy / Natchez burning / Built for comfort / Ooh baby, hold me / Tell me what I've done. *(UK cd-iss. Feb90 on 'M.C.A.')*

Jun 66. (7") *<1968>* **NEW CRAWLIN' KING SNAKE. / MY MIND IS RAMBLIN'** [–]

1966. (7"ep) *(CRE 6017)* **REAL FOLK BLUES** [–]
– Three hundred pounds of joy / My country sugar mama / Oh baby hold me / Louise.

1967. (lp) *<1512>* **MORE REAL FOLK BLUES** (compilation 1952-56) [–]

Aug 67. (7") *<2009>* **I HAD A DREAM. / POP IT TO ME** [–]

May 68. (lp; HOWLIN' WOLF, MUDDY WATERS & BO DIDDLEY) *(CRL 4537) <4537>* **SUPER SUPER BLUES BAND**
– Long distance call / Goin' down slow / You don't love me / I'm a man / Who do you love / The red rooster / Diddley daddy / I just want to make love to you.

Chess Cadet

Feb 69. (7") *(CRS 8097) <7013>* **EVIL. / TAIL DRAGGER**

Apr 69. (lp) *(CRLS 4543)* **THE NEW ALBUM** [–]
– Spoonful / Tail dragger / Smokestack lightning / Moanin' at midnight / Built for comfort / The red rooster / Evil / Down in the bottom / Three hundred pounds of joy / Back door man.

Chess Chess

Aug 69. (7") *<2081>* **MARY SUE. / HARD LUCK** [–]

Syndicate Syndicate

May 70. (lp) **GOING BACK HOME** (compilation 1948-58)
– Saddle my pony / Worried all the time / Howlin' Wolf boogie / The Wolf is at your door / On red / My last affair / Mr. Highway man / Gettin' old and grey / Come to me baby / Don't mess with me baby / So glad / My life / Going back home / I don't know / Howlin' blues / I better go now. *(re-iss. Sep82)*

—— In June '70, he and LITTLE WALTER collaborated with MUDDY WATERS on the album, 'WE THREE KINGS' (Syndicate Chapter; SC 005)

Nov 70. (7") *<2108>* **IF I WERE A BIRD. / JUST AS LONG** [–]

Feb 71. (7") *<2118>* **DO THE DO. / THE RED ROOSTER** [–]

1971. (lp) *(6310 108)* **MESSAGE TO THE YOUNG**
– If I were a bird / I smell a rat / Miss James / Message to the young / She's looking good / Just as long / Romance without finance / Turn me on.

—— (Below lp, featured **BILL WYMAN & CHARLIE WATTS** (of The ROLLING STONES) / **ERIC CLAPTON** – guitar / **STEVE WINWOOD** – keyboards / **RINGO STARR** – drums

Rolling Stones Chess

Sep 71. (lp) *(COC 49101) <60008>* **THE LONDON SESSIONS** Aug71 [79]
– I ain't superstitious / Poor boy / The red rooster / Worried about my baby / Do the do / Built for comfort / Sittin' on top of the world / Highway 49 / What a woman / Who's been talkin' / Rockin' daddy / Wang dang doodle. *(re-iss. Apr82) (re-iss. Dec85 on 'Charly', cd-iss. Jan91)*

1972. (lp) *<50015>* **LIVE & COOKIN' AT ALICES REVISITED (live)** [–]
– When I laid down I was troubled / I don't know / Mean mistreater / I had a dream / Call me The Wolf / Don't laugh at me / Just passing by / Sitting on top of the world.

1973. (7") *<2145>* **BACK DOOR WOLF. / COME ON THE MOON** [–]

1973. (lp) *<50045>* **THE BACK DOOR WOLF** [–]
– Movin' / Coon on the Moon / Speak now woman / Trying to fight you / Stop using me / Leave here walking / The back door wolf / You turn slick on me / Watergate blues / Can't stay here. *(UK-iss.+c.1989)*

1972. (d-lp) *<60016>* **AKA CHESTER BURNETT** (compilation 1951-65) [–]

1974. (lp) *<60026>* **LONDON REVISITED** [–]
(re-iss. Jul93 on 'Charly')

—— earlier in the 70's, he suffered two heart attacks and subsequently a car crash in which he acrued kidney damage. After a concert at Chicago Amphitheater Nov'75 with B.B. KING, BOBBY BLAND and LITTLE MILTON, he was re-hospitalized and died there on the 10th January '76 following brain surgery.

– (selective) compilations, etc. –

1977. (lp) *Chess; (2ACBM 201)* **BLUES MASTERS** [–]

Jun 81. (d-lp) *Chess; (CXMD 4004)* **CHESS MASTERS**

Apr 82. (d-lp) *Chess; (CXMD 4007)* **CHESS MASTERS VOL.2**

May 83. (d-lp) *Chess; (CXMD 4014)* **CHESS MASTERS VOL.3**

Nov 85. (lp/c) *Deja Vu; (DV LP/MC 2032)* **COLLECTION: 20 BLUES GREATS** [–]
– Little red rooster / My baby walked off / Killing floor / My country sugar mama / My life / Going back home / Louise / Highway 49 / Hold on to your money / Built for comfort / Ain't superstitious / My last affair / Dorothy Mae / Commit a crime / Moanin' at midnight / Wang dang doodle / Ridin' in the moonlight / Everybody's in the mood / The wolf is at your door / I better go now. *(cd-iss. Aug87)*

Dec 88. (lp/c) *Chess; (CHX L/T 102)* **CHESS MASTERS VOL.4 – MOANIN' AND HOWLIN'**

Apr 89. (cd) *Bear Family; (BCD 15460)* **MEMPHIS DAYS (THE DEFINITIVE COLLECTION, VOL.1)** [–]

Jan 91. (cd) *Bear Family; (BCD 15500)* **MEMPHIS DAYS (THE DEFINITIVE COLLECTION, VOL.2)** [–]

May 94. (cd) *Charly; (CDRB 2)* **SPOONFUL** [–]

Apr 95. (cd) *Deja Vu; (DVBC 9022)* **COLLECTOR'S EDITION** [–]

Feb 97. (cd) *Last Call; (422329)* **LIVE IN CAMBRIDGE, MASS. 1966**

Apr 97. (cd) *Chess-MCA; (MCD 11073)* **THE GENUINE ARTICLE: THE BEST OF HOWLIN' WOLF**

Mar 98. (cd) *Eagle; (EABCD 080)* **THE MASTERS**

Sep 00. (cd) *Spectrum; (112047-2)* **THE COLLECTION**

Mar 01. (cd) *MagMid; (MM 074)* **KINGS OF THE BLUES**

Jul 02. (cd/c) *Castle Pulse; (PLS CD/MC 595)* **KING OF THE BLUES**

Mar 03. (3xcd-box) *Chess; (AACHD 3933-2)* **THE CHESS BOX**

Mar 03. (d-cd) *M.C.A.; (112985-2)* **THE LONDON HOWLIN' WOLF SESSIONS**

Apr 03. (cd) *Classics; (5056)* **CLASSICS 1951-52**

Jun 03. (cd) *Universal; (0003580-2)* **THE MILLENNIUM COLLECTION**

Jun 03. (cd) *Snapper; (SNAP 123CD)* **HOWLIN' AT THE SUN**

Aug 03. (cd) *Tomato; (TOM 2103)* **CHICAGO BLUE**

☐ Alan HULL (see under ⇒ LINDISFARNE)

HUMAN LEAGUE

Formed: Sheffield, England . . . Autumn 1977 by computer operators MARTYN WARE and IAN CRAIG-MARSH. As The FUTURE, with vocalist ADI NEWTON, they recruited former hospital porter PHIL OAKEY, who soon replaced ADI (later to CLOCKDVA). Now as HUMAN LEAGUE, the trio recorded demo, which was accepted by Edinburgh-based indie 'Fast', run by Bob Last. Their debut 45 'BEING BOILED', became NME single of the week in mid-78. They added ADRIAN WRIGHT on visuals and synths, and after a dire instrumental EP 'THE DIGNITY OF LABOUR', they signed to 'Virgin' in Apr'79. Their first 45 for the label, 'I DON'T DEPEND ON YOU', was credited to The MEN, but their credibility was restored later that year when 'EMPIRE STATE HUMAN', nearly gave them a hit. This was duly followed by a debut album, 'REPRODUCTION', which failed to build on their early promise. In Spring 1980, they went into UK Top 60 with double-7" EP, 'HOLIDAY '80', and Top 20 with album, 'TRAVELOGUE'. In October '80, OAKEY and WRIGHT brought in teenage girls JOANNE and SUZANNE to replace WARE and CRAIG-MARSH who left to form HEAVEN 17. Twelve months later, with new additions IAN BURDEN and JO CALLIS, they were at No.1 with both the 'DARE' album, and 'DON'T YOU WANT ME' single, which also peaked at the top in the States. By now, the experimental industrial leanings of their early work had given way to a chart dominating new romantic/pop synth sound which made 'DARE' one of the definitive albums of the era. They were also responsible, or at least OAKEY was, for perhaps the worst 80's haircut of them all (yes, even worse than the mullet), the accident-with-a-pair-of-garden-shears number that featured one side long and erm . . . one side short! Barnet's aside, the hits were consistent ('KEEP FEELING FASCINATION', 'MIRROR MAN', 'THE LEBANON'), if not exactly prolific and, like many similar 80's acts, by the time they got around to releasing a follow-up set, the fuss had died down. Nevertheless, 'HYSTERIA' (1984) made the UK Top 3, while OAKEY teamed up with disco veteran, GIORGIO MORODER, for the soppy but brilliant 'TOGETHER IN ELECTRIC DREAMS', another massive Top 5 hit in Autumn '84 (the pair subsequently recorded a full length album together, 'CHROME'). Produced by the soul/R&B team of Jimmy Jam and Terry Lewis, 'CRASH' (1986) didn't do the band any favours, although it did spawn the melancholy 'HUMAN', a surprise US No.1 and their biggest hit single since the early 80's heyday. Though a 1988 greatest hits album kept the band's profile high, poor sales of 'ROMANTIC' (1990) saw the end of their tenure with 'Virgin', and it looked like permanent relegation was imminent. A new deal with 'East West' and a 1994 Top 10 album, 'OCTOPUS', suggested otherwise, things coming full circle when a remixed version of 'DON'T YOU WANT ME' made the Top 20 in late '95. Conspicuous only by his absence, PHIL OAKEY has since provided some vocals (alongside 60's crooner, TONY CHRISTIE) on the ALL SEEING I album in '99. With 'SECRETS' (2001), The HUMAN LEAGUE entered their fourth decade of recording although you wouldn't have guessed it by OAKEY's ever youthful looks. A fair attempt at reconciling current trends in electronic music with their classic sound, this largely instrumental effort scraped into the UK Top 50. • **Songwriters:** WARE and CRAIG-MARSH before their departure, and OAKEY and WRIGHT on all since early 80's. The 90's, featured OAKEY composing alongside new member NEIL SUTTON. Covered:- YOU'VE LOST THAT LOVIN' FEELIN' (Righteous Brothers) / ROCK'N'ROLL (Gary Glitter) / NIGHTCLUBBIN' (Iggy Pop) / ONLY AFTER DARK (Mick Ronson).

Album rating: REPRODUCTION (*5) / TRAVELOGUE (*5) / DARE (*8) / LOVE AND DANCING mixes set (*4) / HYSTERIA (*5) / CRASH (*5) / GREATEST HITS compilation (*8) / ROMANTIC? (*4) / OCTOPUS (*6) / SECRETS (*4) / THE VERY BEST OF . . . compilation (*7) / Phil Oakey & Giorgio Moroder: CHROME (*4)

PHIL OAKEY (b. 2 Oct'55) – vocals / **IAN CRAIG-MARSH** (b.19 Nov'56) – synthesizers / **MARTYN WARE** (b.19 May'56) – synthesizers

Fast | not iss.

Jun 78. (7") *(FAST 4)* **BEING BOILED. / CIRCUS OF DEATH** [ ] [–]
(re-iss. Jan82 reached No.6 UK; same)

—— added **ADRIAN WRIGHT** (b.30 Dec'56) – synthesizers, visuals

Apr 79. (12"ep) *(FAST 10)* **THE DIGNITY OF LABOUR** [ ] [–]
– (part 1 / part 2 / part 3 / part 4) *(contains free spoken word flexi; VF 1)*

Virgin | A&M

Jul 79. (7"/12"; as The MEN) *(VS 269/+12)* **I DON'T DEPEND ON YOU. / CRUEL (instrumental)** [ ] [–]

Sep 79. (7") *(VS 294)* **EMPIRE STATE HUMAN. / INTRODUCING** [ ] [–]

Oct 79. (lp/c) *(V/TCV 2133)* **REPRODUCTION** [ ] [–]
– Almost medieval / Circus of death / The path of least resistance / Blind youth / The word before last / Empire state human / Morale / You've lost that lovin' feelin' / Austerity / Girl one / Zero as a limit. *(re-pro.Aug81, hit UK No.49) (re-iss. Jun88 lp/c; OVED/+C 114) (cd-iss. Dec88; CDV 2133)*

Apr 80. (d7"ep) *(SV 105)* **HOLIDAY '80** [56] [–]
– Rock'n'roll / Being boiled / Nightclubbing / Dancevision. *(re-iss. Nov81 as 12"ep+=)* – Marianne. *(hit UK No.46)*

May 80. (lp/c) *(T/TCV 2160)* **TRAVELOGUE** [16] [–]
– The black hit of space / Only after dark / Life kills / Dreams of leaving / Toyota city / Crow and a baby / The touchables / Gordon's Gin / Being boiled / WXJL tonight. *(re-iss. Jun88 lp/c; OVED/+C 115)*

Jun 80. (7") *(VS 351)* **ONLY AFTER DARK. / TOYOTA CITY** [62] [–]
(free 7" w/) – EMPIRE STATE HUMAN. / INTRODUCING

—— **JO CATHERALL** (b.18 Sep'62) **& SUSANNE SULLEY** (b.22 Mar'63) – b.vocals repl. WARE and MARSH who formed HEAVEN 17. also added **IAN BURDEN** (b.24 Dec'57) – bass, synthesizers

Feb 81. (7") *(VS 395)* **BOYS AND GIRLS. / TOM BAKER** [48] [–]

Apr 81. (7"/ext.12"; as HUMAN LEAGUE RED) *(VS 416/+12)* **THE SOUND OF THE CROWD. / ('A'instrumental)** [12] [–]

—— added **JO CALLIS** (b. 2 May'55, Glasgow, Scotland) – guitar (ex-REZILLOS, ex-BOOTS FOR DANCING, ex-SHAKE)

Jul 81. (7"; as HUMAN LEAGUE RED) *(VS 435)* **LOVE ACTION (I BELIEVE IN LOVE). / HARD TIMES** [3] Apr82 [ ]
(12"+=) *(VS 435-12)* – ('A'&'B'instrumental).
(cd-ep.iss.Jun88; – the four 12"tracks)

Oct 81. (7"; as HUMAN LEAGUE BLUE) *(VS 453)* **OPEN YOUR HEART. / NON-STOP** [6] [–]
(12"+=) *(VS 453-12)* – ('A'instrumental) / ('B'instrumental).

Oct 81. (lp/pic-lp/c) *(T/TP/TCV 2192)* *<4892>* **DARE** [1] Feb82 [3]
– Things that dreams are made of / Open your heart / The sound of the crowd / Darkness / Do or die / Get Carter / I am the law / Seconds / Love action (I believe in love) / Don't you want me. *(cd-iss. 1983; OVED 177) (re-iss. Sep90 lp/c; OVED/+C 333) (cd-iss. Nov01; SACDV 2192)*

Nov 81. (7"; as HUMAN LEAGUE 100) *(VS 466)* *<2397>* **DON'T YOU WANT ME. / SECONDS** [1] Feb82 [1]
(2"+=) *(VS 466-12)* – ('A'extended).

Jul 82. (lp/c; as LEAGUE UNLIMITED ORCHESTRA) *(OVED/OVEC 6)* *<3209>* **LOVE AND DANCING** [6] Sep92 [ ]
– (instrumental versions of "DARE" except;) / Get Carter / Darkness. *(cd-iss. Jan86; CDOVED 6)*

Aug 82. (7") **THINGS THAT DREAMS ARE MADE OF. / ('A' instrumental)** [–] [ ]

Oct 82. (7"; as LEAGUE UNLIMITED ORCHESTRA) **DON'T YOU WANT ME. / (part 2)** [–] [ ]

Nov 82. (7"/7"pic-d) *(VS/+Y 522)* **MIRROR MAN. / (YOU REMIND ME OF) GOLD** [2] [–]
(ext.12"+=) *(VS 522-12)* – Gold (instrumental).

Apr 83. (7"; as HUMAN LEAGUE RED) *(VS 569)* *<2547>* **(KEEP FEELING) FASCINATION. / TOTAL PANIC** [2] May83 [8]
(ext.12"+=) *(VS 569-12)* – ('A'improvisation).

Jul 83. (m-lp) *<12501>* **FASCINATION** (import, recent hits) [–] [22]

Sep 83. (7") *<2587>* **MIRROR MAN. / NON-STOP** [–] [30]

Apr 84. (7") *(VS 672)* *<2641>* **THE LEBANON. / THIRTEEN** [11] Jul84 [64]
(ext.12"+=) *(VS 672-12)* – ('A'instrumental).

May 84. (lp/c/cd) *(T/TCV/CDV 2315) <4923>* **HYSTERIA** [3] [62]
– I'm coming back / I love you too much / Rock me again and again and again and again and again and again / Louise / The Lebanon / Betrayed / The sign / So hurt / Life on your own / Don't you know I want you. *(re-iss. Feb88 lp/c; OVED/+C 177)*

Jun 84. (7") *(VS 688)* **LIFE ON YOUR OWN. / THE WORLD TONIGHT** [16] [–]
(12"+=) *(VS 688-12)* – ('A'extended).

Aug 84. (7") **DON'T YOU KNOW I WANT TO. / THIRTEEN** [–] [ ]

Oct 84. (7"/7"pic-d)(12") *(VS/+Y 723)(VS 723-12)* **LOUISE. / THE SIGN** [13] [–]

Oct 84. (7") **LOUISE. / THE WORLD TONIGHT** [–] [ ]

— Trimmed down to main trio of **PHIL, SUSANNE, JOANNE** plus **ADRIAN / JIM RUSSELL** – synthesizer repl. BURDEN and CALLIS

Aug 86. (7") *(VS 880) <2861>* **HUMAN. / ('A'instrumental)** [8] [1]
(ext.12"+=) *(VS 880-12)* – ('A'acappella).

Sep 86. (lp/c/cd) *(V/TCV/CDV 2391) <5129>* **CRASH** [7] [24]
– Money / Swang / Human / Jam / Are you ever coming back? / I need your loving / Party / Love on the run / The real thing / Love is all that matters.

Nov 86. (7") *(VS 900)* **I NEED YOUR LOVING. / ('A'instrumental)** [72] [–]
(ext.12"+=) *(VS 900-12)* – ('A'dub).

Nov 86. (7") *<2893>* **I NEED YOUR LOVING. / ARE YOU EVER COMING BACK** [–] [44]

Jan 87. (7") **LOVE IS ALL THAT MATTERS. / ('A'instrumental)** [–] [ ]

Apr 87. (7") **ARE YOU EVER COMING BACK. / JAM** [–] [ ]

Oct 88. (7") *(VS 1025)* **LOVE IS ALL THAT MATTERS. / I LOVE YOU TOO MUCH** [41] [ ]
('B'dub.12"+=/'B'dub.cd-s+=) *(VS T/CD 1025)* – ('A'extended).

Nov 88. (lp/c/cd/pic-cd) *(HL TV/MC/CD/CDP 1) <75021 5227-1/-4/-2>* **GREATEST HITS** (compilation) [3] [ ]
– Mirror man / (Keep feeling) Fascination / The sound of the crowd / The Lebanon / Human / Together in electric dreams (PHIL OAKEY & GIORGIO MORODER) / Don't you want me? / Being boiled (re-boiled) / Love action (I believe in love) / Louise / Open your heart / Love is all that matters / Life on your own. *(re-iss. Nov95 cd/c;)*

— The basic trio, added **RUSSELL BENNETT** – guitar / **NEIL SUTTON** – keyboards

Aug 90. (7"/c-s) *(VS/+C 1262) <1520>* **HEART LIKE A WHEEL. / REBOUND** [29] Sep90 [32]
(12"+=) *(VST 1262)* – ('A'extended).
(cd-s++=) *(VSCDT 1262)* – ('A'remix).
(cd-s++=) *(VSCDX 1262)* – A doorway (dub mix).

Sep 90. (cd/c/lp) *(V/TCV/CDV 2624) <75021 5316-2/-4/-1>* **ROMANTIC?** [24] [ ]
– Kiss the future / A doorway / Heart like a wheel / Men are dreamers / Mister Moon and Mister Sun / Soundtrack to a generation / Rebound / The stars are going out / Let's get together again / Get it right this time.

Nov 90. (7"/c-s) *(VS/+C 1303)* **SOUNDTRACK TO A GENERATION. / ('A'instrumental)** [ ] [–]
(12"+=) *(VST 1303)* – ('A'-Orbit mix).
(cd-s++=) *(VSCDT 1303)* – ('A'-Pan Belgian mix).
(cd-s) *(VSCDX 1303)* – ('A'-Pan Belgian dub) / ('A'-808 instrumental mix) / ('A'-Dave Dodd's mix) / ('A'-acappella).

East West — East West

Dec 94. (c-s) *(YZ 882C) <64443>* **TELL ME WHEN. / ('A'mix 1)** [6] Mar95 [31]
(cd-s+=) *(YZ 882CD1)* – Kimi ni mune kyun / The bus to Crookes.
(12"/cd-s) *(YZ 882 T/CD2)* – ('A'side) / ('A'-Overworld mix) / ('A'-Red Jerry mix) / ('A'-Strictly blind dub mix).

Jan 95. (cd/c/lp) *(4509 98750-2/-4/-1) <61788>* **OCTOPUS** [6] [ ]
– Tell me when / These are the days / One man in my heart / Words / Filling up with Heaven / House full of nothing / John Cleese; is he funny? / Never again / Cruel young lover.

Mar 95. (c-s/cd-s) *(YZ 904 C/CD1)* **ONE MAN IN MY HEART / THESE ARE THE DAYS (Ba ba mix)** [13] [–]
(cd-s+=) *(YZ 904CD2)* – These are the days (sonic radiation) / ('A'version).
(12") *(YZ 904T)* – ('B'side) / ('B'-Symphone Ba Ba mix) / ('B'instrumental) / ('A'-T.O.E.C. unplugged).

Jun 95. (c-s/cd-s) *(YZ 944 C/CD1)* **FILLING UP WITH HEAVEN / JOHN CLEESE, IS HE FUNNY?** [36] [–]
(cd-s) *(YZ 944CD2)* – ('A'side) / ('A'-Hardfloor mix) / ('A'-Neil McLellen mix).

Jan 96. (c-s) *(EW 020C)* **STAY WITH ME TONIGHT / ('A'mix)** [40] [–]
(cd-s) *(EW 020CD)* – ('A'mixes).

Papillion — Ark 21

Jul 01. (cd-s) *(BTFLYS 0012) <1220>* **ALL I EVER WANTED / TRANQUILITY / ALL I EVER WANTED (vanity case mix)** [47] [ ]
(cd-s) *(BTFLYX 0012)* – ('A'-original) / ('A'-Oliver Lieb mix).

Aug 01. (cd) *(BTFLYCD 0019) <810075>* **SECRETS** [44] [ ]
– All I ever wanted / Nervous / Love me madly? / Shameless / 122.3 bpm / Never give your heart / Ran / The snake / Ringinglow / Liar / Lament / Reflections / Brute / Sin city / Release / You'll be sorry.

— in Apr'03, PHILIP OAKEY featured on ALEX GOLD's single, 'LA Today'

– compilations, etc. –

Oct 90. (3xcd-box) *Virgin; (TPAK 3)* **DARE / HYSTERIA / CRASH** [ ] [–]

Oct 95. (c-s) *Virgin; (VSC 1557)* **DON'T YOU WANT ME (remix) / ('A'-Snap remix) / (2-'A'-Red Jerry mix)** [16] [ ]
(12") *(VST 1557)* – ('A'-Snap remix extended) / ('A'-Red Jerry remix extended).
(cd-s) *(VSCDT 1557)* – (all 6-'A'versions).

Oct 96. (cd) *Disky; (VI 87530-2)* **SOUNDTRACK TO A GENERATION** [ ] [ ]

Apr 02. (12") *Klang; (KLANG 62)* **ALL I EVER WANTED (mixes)** [ ] [–]

Sep 03. (d-cd) *Virgin; (HLCDX 2) / E.M.I.; <592391>* **THE VERY BEST OF THE HUMAN LEAGUE** [24] [ ]
– Don't you want me / Love action (I believe in love) / Open your heart / The sound of the crowd / Mirror man / (Keep feeling) Fascination / The Lebanon / Life on your own / Together in electric dreams / Louise / Human / Heart like a wheel / Tell me when / One man in my heart / All I ever wanted / Being boiled (Fast version) / Empire State human // Don't you want me (Majik J original booty vocal mix) / Open your heart (Laid remix) / The sound of the crowd (Trisco's popclash mix) / Love action (Brooks red line vocal mix) / (Keep feeling) Fascination ((groove collision TMC mix) / Empire State human (Chamber's reproduced mix) / The things that dreams are made of (Jimmy 19 the A509 PWC remix) / The sound of the crowd (Freaksblamredo) / Open your heart (Strand remix) / The sound of the crowd (Rilton re-dub) / Love action (Fluke's dub action remix).

PHIL OAKEY & GIORGIO MORODER

– synthesizers

Virgin — A&M

Sep 84. (7"/7"pic-d/ext.12") *(VS/+Y 713/+12)* **TOGETHER IN ELECTRIC DREAMS. / ('A'instrumental)** [3] [ ]

Jun 85. (7") *(VS 772)* **GOODBYE BAD TIMES. / ('A'instrumental)** [44] [ ]

Jul 85. (lp/c/cd) *(V/TCV/CDV 2351)* **CHROME** [52] [ ]
– Goodbye bad times / Together in electric dreams / Valerie / Why must the show go on / Be me lover now / Shake it up / Brand new lover / In transit / Now. *(re-iss. Oct87; OVED 187)*

Aug 85. (7"/12") *(VS 800/+12)* **BE MY LOVER NOW. / ('A' instrumental)** [ ] [ ]

Nov 88. (7") *Old Gold; (OG 9825)* **TOGETHER IN ELECTRIC DREAMS. / GOODBYE BAD TIMES** [ ] [–]

HUMBLE PIE

Formed: Essex, England . . . Spring 1969 as a mini-supergroup by STEVE MARRIOT (ex-SMALL FACES, vocals, guitar) and PETER FRAMPTON (ex-HERD, vocals, guitar). Recruiting GREG RIDLEY (bass, ex-SPOOKY TOOTH) and JERRY SHIRLEY (drums, ex-LITTLE WOMEN), the band signed to Andrew Loog Oldham's 'Immediate' label and released their debut album, 'AS SAFE AS YESTERDAY', in the summer of '69. A solid collection of rootsy rock, the record spawned a Top 5 UK single with 'NATURAL BORN BUGIE', MARRIOT ditching the chirpy cockney popster persona he'd developed with the SMALL FACES in favour of an 'authentic' R&B rasp. The more acoustic-based follow-up, 'TOWN AND COUNTRY' (1969) flopped, and HUMBLE PIE returned from an American tour in late '69 to discover that their record label had gone under. Severe financial problems ensued until help came in the form of US lawyer, Dee Anthony, who helped secure the band a new deal with A&M. The eponymous 'HUMBLE PIE' (1970) failed to resurrect their fortunes, as did the harder-edged 'ROCK ON' (1971), Anthony subsequently packing the band off to America on another tour from whence came the US gold-selling live album, 'PERFORMANCE-ROCKIN' THE FILLMORE' (1971). Despite his diminutive size, MARRIOT had a towering stage presence, the singer blazing his way through a fiery set of boogie-based blues-rock, both HUMBLE PIE originals and frenetic covers including Muddy Waters' 'ROLLIN' STONE' and Dr. John's 'I WALK ON GILDED SPLINTERS'. FRAMPTON departed for a solo career later that year, ex-COLOSSEUM man, DAVE CLEMPSON taking his place. While FRAMPTON had proved a melodic acoustic-rock foil to MARRIOT's hard rockin' excess, the new-look 'PIE continued to move in a heavier direction with 'SMOKIN' (1972), the highest charting album in the band's career, reaching No.6 in the States. Augmented by all-girl backing trio, The BLACKBERRIES (CLYDIE KING, BILLIE BARNUM & VANETTA FIELDS), the band attempted a hard rock/soul fusion with the half live/half studio double set, 'EAT IT' (1973). The album was another American Top 20 hit but HUMBLE PIE's popularity was on the wane, a further two efforts, 'THUNDERBOX' (1974) and 'STREET RATS' (1975) barely making the charts and receiving a scathing critical reaction. The group finally split shortly after the release of the latter album, SHIRLEY forming NATURAL GAS with ex-BADFINGER guitarist JOEY MOLLAND while MARRIOT put together the short lived STEVE MARRIOTT ALL-STARS with MICKEY FINN (guitar, ex-T.REX), IAN WALLACE (drums, ex-KING CRIMSON) and DAMON BUTCHER (keyboards). CLEMPSON, meanwhile, joined GREENSLADE. After a brief SMALL FACES reunion in the late 70's, MARIOTT reformed HUMBLE PIE along with SHIRLEY and new members BOBBY TENCH (guitar, ex-STREETWALKERS, ex-JEFF BECK GROUP) and ANTHONY JONES (bass). Signed to 'Atco', the band released two generally ignored albums, 'ON TO VICTORY' (1980) and 'GO FOR THE THROAT' (1981) before disbanding finally in 1981. MARRIOT continued to tour, releasing a low key solo album, 'PACKET OF THREE', in 1986. Hopes of a musical reunion between MARIOTT and FRAMPTON were finally dashed on 20th April '91 when MARIOTT was tragically killed in a fire at his Essex cottage. • **Songwriters:** All took a shot at writing, with MARRIOTT the main contributor. Covers:- C'MON EVERYBODY + HALLELUJAH I LOVE HER SO (Eddie Cochran) / ROADRUNNER (Junior Walker) / HONKY TONK WOMAN (Rolling Stones) / ROCK'N'ROLL MUSIC (Chuck Berry) / ALL SHOOK UP (Elvis Presley) / etc.

Album rating: AS SAFE AS YESTERDAY (*6) / TOWN AND COUNTRY (*5) / HUMBLE PIE (*5) / ROCK ON (*6) / PERFORMANCE – ROCKIN' THE FILLMORE (*7) / SMOKIN' (*5) / EAT IT (*5) / THUNDERBOX (*4) / STREET RATS (*3) / ON TO VICTORY (*3) / GO FOR THE THROAT (*2) / HOT N' NASTY – THE ANTHOLOGY compilation (*7) / Steve Marriott: MARRIOTT (*4) / PACKET OF THREE (what else ... *3) / 30 SECONDS TO MIDNIGHT exploitation (*4)

STEVE MARRIOTT (b.30 Jan'47, London, England) – vocals, guitar, keyboards (ex-SMALL FACES) / **PETER FRAMPTON** (b.22 Apr'50, Beckenham, England) – vocals, guitar (ex-HERD) / **GREG RIDLEY** (b.23 Oct'47, Carlisle, England) – bass (ex-SPOOKY TOOTH) / **JERRY SHIRLEY** (b. 4 Feb'52) – drums (ex-LITTLE WOMEN)

Immediate Immediate

Jul 69. (lp) *(IMSP 025)* <101> **AS SAFE AS YESTERDAY** [32] [ ]
– Desperation / Stick shift / Buttermilk boy / Growing closer / As safe as yesterday / Bang? / Alabama '69 / I'll go alone / A nifty little number like you / What you will. *(cd-iss. Nov89 on 'Line'; LICD 900296) (cd re-iss. Dec92 on 'Repertoire'+=;)* – Natural born bugie / Wrist job. *(lp re-iss. Dec99 on 'Get Back'; GET 549)*

Sep 69. (7") *(IM 082)* **NATURAL BORN BUGIE. / WRIST JOB** [4] [ ]
(re-iss. Feb83; same)

Oct 69. (7") <101> **NATURAL BORN BUGIE. / I'LL GO ALONE** [–] [ ]

Dec 69. (lp) *(IMSP 027)* **TOWN AND COUNTRY** [ ] [–]
– Take me back / The sad bag of shaky Jake / The light of love / Cold lady / Down home again / Ollie Ollie / Every mother's son / Heartbeat / Only you can say / Silver tongue / Home and away. *(re-iss. 1978 on 'Charly'; CR 300016) (cd-iss. Nov93; CDIMM 020) (cd-iss. Dec92 on 'Repertoire'+=;)* – Greg's song / 79th Street blues. *(cd re-iss. Feb95 on 'Charly'; CDIMM 020)*

A&M A&M

Jul 70. (lp) *(AMLS 986)* <4270> **HUMBLE PIE** [ ] [ ]
– Live with me / Only a roach / One eyed trouser-snake rumba / Earth and water song / I'm ready / Theme from Skint (see you later liquidator) / Red light mamma / Red hot / Sucking on the sweet vine.

Mar 71. (lp) *(AMLS 203)* <4301> **ROCK ON** [ ] [ ]
– Shine on / Sour grain / 79th and sunset / Stone cold fever / Rollin' stone / A song for Jenny / The light / Big George / Strange days / Red neck jump. *(cd-iss. 1988 on 'Mobile Fidelity'; MFCD 847)*

Sep 71. (7") <1282> **I DON'T NEED NO DOCTOR (live). / SONG FOR JENNY** [–] [73]

Nov 71. (d-lp/d-c) *(AMLH/CDM 63506)* <3506> **PERFORMANCE – ROCKIN' THE FILLMORE (live)** [32] [21]
– Four day creep / I'm ready / Stone cold fever / I walk on guilded splinters / Rollin' stone / Hallelujah (I love her so) / I don't need no doctor. *(re-iss. 1974;)*

— **DAVE CLEMPSON** (b. 5 Sep'45) – guitar (ex-COLOSSEUM) repl. FRAMPTON who went solo

Mar 72. (lp) *(AMLS 64342)* <4342> **SMOKIN'** [28] [6]
– Hot 'n' nasty / The fixer / You're so good to me / C'mon everybody / Old time feelin' / 30 days in the hole / (I'm a) Road runner / Roadrunner "G" jam / I wonder who / Sweet peace and time.

Apr 72. (7") <1349> **HOT 'N' NASTY. / YOU"RE SO GOOD FOR ME** [–] [52]

Sep 72. (7") <1366> **30 DAYS IN THE HOLE. / SWEET PEACE AND TIME** [–] [ ]

— now augmented by all-girl backing trio The BLACKBERRIES (**CLYDIE KING / BILLIE BARNUM + VANETTA FIELDS**)

Jan 73. (7") *(AMS 7052)* <1406> **BLACK COFFEE. / SAY NO MORE** [ ] [ ]

Apr 73. (d-lp) *(AMLD 6004)* <3701> **EAT IT** (1-side live) [34] Mar73 [13]
– Get down to it / Good booze and bad women / Is it for love / Drugstore cowboy / Black coffee / I believe to my soul / Shut up and don't interrupt me / That's how strong my love is / Say no more / Oh, Bella (all that's hers) / Summer song / Beckton dumps / Up our sleeve / Honky tonk woman / (I'm a) Road runner.

Jun 73. (7") *(AMS 7070)* <1440> **GET DOWN TO IT. / HONKY TONK WOMAN (live)** [ ] [ ]

Oct 73. (7") *(AMS 7090)* **OH LA DE DA. / THE OUTCROWD** [ ] [–]

Feb 74. (lp) *(AMLH 63611)* <3611> **THUNDERBOX** [ ] [52]
– Thunderbox / Groovin' with Jesus / I can't stand the rain / Anna / No way / Rally with Ali / Don't worry, be happy / Ninety-nine pounds / Every single day / No money down / Drift away / Oh la de da.

May 74. (7") <1530> **NINETY-NINE POUNDS. / RALLY WITH ALI** [–] [ ]

Feb 75. (lp) *(AMLS 68282)* <4514> **STREET RATS** [ ] [100]
– Street rat / Rock'n'roll music / We can work it out / Scored out / Road hog / Rain / Funky to the bone / Let me be your lovemaker / Countryman / Stomp / Drive my car / Queens and nuns.

Mar 75. (7") *(AMS 7185)* **ROCK'N'ROLL MUSIC. / SCORED OUT** [ ] [–]

Jul 75. (7") <1711> **ROCK'N'ROLL MUSIC. / ROAD HOG** [–] [ ]

— Disbanded Spring 1975. JERRY SHIRLEY formed NATURAL GAS, and the others joined

STEVE MARRIOTT ALL-STARS

also included **DAMON BUTCHER** – keyboards / **IAN WALLACE** – drums (ex-KING CRIMSON) / **MICKEY FINN** – guitar (ex-T.REX)

A&M A&M

May 76. (lp) *(AMLH 64572)* <4572> **MARRIOTT** [ ] [ ]
– Star in my life / Are you lonely for me baby / You don't know me / Late night lady / Early evening light / East side struttin' / Lookin' for love /

Help me through the day / Midnight rock'n'rollin' / Wam bam thank you ma'am.

Jun 76. (7") *(AMS 7230)* **STAR IN MY LIFE. / MIDNIGHT ROCK'N'ROLLIN'** [ ] [–]

Jun 76. (7") *<1825>* **STAR IN MY LIFE. / EAST SIDE STRUTTIN'** [–] [ ]

— CLEMPSON and BUTCHER joined ROUGH DIAMOND. WALLACE toured with BOB DYLAN. MICKEY FINN joined PHIL MAY'S FALLEN ANGELS. MARRIOTT re-formed The SMALL FACES

HUMBLE PIE

also re-formed in 1979, with **STEVE MARRIOTT** – vocals, guitar / **JERRY SHIRLEY** – drums / **BOBBY TENCH** – guitar (ex-STREETWALKERS, ex-JEFF BECK) / **ANTHONY JONES** – bass

Jet | Atco

Apr 80. (7") *(JET 180) <7216>* **FOOL FOR A PRETTY FACE. / YOU SOPPY PRATT** [ ] [52]

Apr 80. (lp) *(JET LP/CA 231) <38122>* **ON TO VICTORY** [ ] [60]
– Fool for a pretty face / You soppy pratt / Get it in the end / Infatuation / Further down the road / My lover's prayer / Take it from here / Baby don't do it.

Jun 81. (lp) *(38131) <131>* **GO FOR THE THROAT** [ ] May81 [ ]
– All shook up / Chip away / Driver / Go for the throat / Keep it on the island / Lottie and the charcoal queen / Restless blood / Teenage anxiety / Tin soldier.

— Finally called it a day in '81

– compilations, others –

Sep 72. (d-lp) *A&M; <3513>* **LOST AND FOUND** (1st-2 lp's) [–] [37]

Jul 76. (lp) *Immediate; (IML 1005)* **BACK HOME AGAIN** [ ] [–]

Jan 78. (lp) *Immediate; (IML 2005)* **HUMBLE PIE'S GREATEST HITS** [ ] [–]

Sep 85. (7") *Old Gold; (OG 9529)* **NATURAL BORN BUGIE. / (other artist)** [ ] [–]

Nov 85. (d-lp/c/cd) *Castle; (CCS LP/MC/CD 104)* **THE COLLECTION** [ ] [–]
– Bang? / Natural born bugie / I'll go alone / Buttermilk boy / Desperation / Nifty little number like you / Wrist job / Stick shift / Growing closer / As safe as yesterday / Heartbeat / Down home again / Take me back / Only you can see / Silver tongue / Every mother's son / The sad bag of Shaky Jake / Cold lady / Home and away / Light of love. *(cd-iss. Apr94;)*

1988. (cd) *A&M; (393 208-2)* **THE BEST OF HUMBLE PIE** [ ] [ ]

Nov 92. (cd) *Dojo; (EARLD 4)* **THE EARLY YEARS** [ ] [–]

Feb 95. (cd) *Band Of Joy; (BOJCD 101)* **NATURAL BORN BOOGIE** [ ] [–]

May 95. (cd) *A&M; (540 179-2)* **A PIECE OF THE PIE** [ ] [ ]

Nov 95. (d-cd) *Charly; (CDIMMBOX 3)* **THE IMMEDIATE YEARS** [ ] [–]

Jul 98. (cd) *Strange Fruit; (SFRSCD 066)* **NATURAL BORN BOOGIE** [ ] [–]

Aug 98. (cd) *King Biscuit; (<KBFHCD 017>)* **KING BISCUIT PRESENTS . . .** [ ] [ ]

Nov 99. (cd) *Eagle; (EAGCD 114)* **THE SCRUBBERS SESSIONS** [ ] [–]

Jul 00. (cd) *Burning Airlines; (<PILOT 048>)* **RUNNING WITH THE PACK** [ ] [ ]

STEVE MARRIOTT

solo again

Aura | not iss.

Jan 85 (7") *(AUS 145)* **WHAT'CHA GONNA DO ABOUT IT. / ALL SHOOK UP** [ ] [–]

Aura | not iss.

Apr 86. (lp/c; STEVE MARRIOTT'S PACKET OF THREE) *(AUL/AUC 729)* **PACKET OF THREE** [ ] [–]
– What'cha gonna do about it / Bad moon rising / All shook up / The fixer / All or nothing / Five long years / I don't need no doctor.

— STEVE MARRIOT died 20 Apr'91, after accidentally setting his Essex cottage on fire with a lighted cigarette.

– his compilations, others –

Sep 89. (lp/c/cd) *Trax; (MOD EM/EMC/CD 1037)* **30 SECONDS TO MIDNIGHT** [ ] [–]
(re-iss. Apr93 on 'Castle' cd/c; CLA CD/MC 386)

Nov 91. (cd) *Mau Mau; (MAUCD 609)* **DINGWALLS 6.7.84 (live)** [ ] [–]

Feb 92. (cd) *Maste – Elastic Cat;* **SCRUBBERS** (rec.1974, **STEVE MARRIOTT / TIM HINKLEY / GREG RIDLEY)** [ ] [–]

May 97. (cd) *Metro; (OTR 1100020)* **LIVE AT THE PALACE (with A PACKET OF THREE)** [ ] [–]

May 97. (d-cd) *Metro; (OTR 1100021)* **THE MARRIOTT ANTHOLOGY** [ ] [–]

May 97. (cd) *Metro; (OTR 1100023)* **INTEREPRETATIONS** [ ] [–]

HUNDRED REASONS

Formed: based – Surrey, England . . . early 2000 from the remnants of JETPAK and FLOOR by COLIN DORAN, LARY HIBBIT, PAUL TOWNSEND, ANDY GILMOUR and ANDY BEWS. Plucked from relative obscurity by Kerrang! Magazine to support Canadian band KITTIE, the lads were subsequently picked up by Simon Williams and his 'Fierce Panda' label. A debut EP, 'ONE', a session on Steve Lamacq's Radio 1 show and a wholly unexpected Kerrang!-sponsored Best New British Band award got 2000 off to a flyer. After more hard touring and general acclaim, the group finished off the year with yet another Kerrang! Award, this time for Best Unsigned Band as voted for by readers. They didn't remain unsigned for long with 'Columbia' scooping their signatures and eventually releasing a second EP and a debut UK Top 10 album, 'IDEAS ABOVE OUR STATION' (2002). While their various awards might have been hard earned, the one dimensional, pedestrian if passionately executed fare served up on the album was just another disappointing chapter in the annals of corporate rock as grunge continued to exact its revenge.

Album rating: IDEAS ABOVE OUR STATION (*6)

COLIN DORAN – vocals / **LARRY HIBBIT** – guitar, vocals / **PAUL TOWNSEND** – guitar, vocals / **ANDY GILMOUR** – bass / **ANDY BEWS** – drums

Fierce Panda | not iss.

Jul 00. (7"clear) *(NING 099)* **CEREBRA. / CLEAR (FLAWED)** [ ] [–]
(cd-s+=) *(NING 099CD)* – Slow learner. *(re-iss. Jun02)*

Columbia | Sony

Aug 01. (7") *(671392-7)* **REMMUS. / SOAP BOX RALLY** [47] [–]
(cd-ep+=) **EPTWO** *(671392-2)* – Shine / ('A'-video).

Aug 01. (cd-s) *(SIM 014-2)* **HUNDRED REASONS / GARRISON** [ ] [–]
– Counting the days / Lefthanded throwback / (2 by GARRISON).
(above issued on 'Simba' records)

Dec 01. (7") *(672078-7)* **I'LL FIND YOU. / SUNNY** [37] [–]
(cd-ep+=) **EPTHREE** *(672078-2)* – Slow motion / ('A'-video).

Mar 02. (7") *(672440-7)* **IF I COULD. / NO.5** [19] [–]
(cd-s+=) *(762440-2)* – One moment / ('A'-video).
(cd-s) *(762440-5)* – ('A'side) / Formula 1 / Out the window / ('A'-director's cut video).

May 02. (7") *(672664-7)* **SILVER. / RUSH-IN** [15] [–]
(cd-s+=) *(672664-2)* – Aerodrome / ('A'-video).
(cd-s) *(672664-5)* – ('A'side) / Seems to register zero / Punctual if nothing else.

May 02. (cd/lp) *(<508148-2/-1>)* **IDEAS ABOVE OUR STATION** [6] Jun02 [ ]
– I'll find you / Answers / Dissolve / What thought did / If I could / Falter / Shine / Drowning / Oratorio / Silver / Gone too far / Avalanche.

Sep 02. (7") *(673145-7)* **FALTER. / SAFE DISTANCE** [38] [–]
(cd-s+=) *(673145-2)* – Introduction to pop / ('A'-video).
(cd-s) *(673145-5)* – ('A'side) / Little toys / Your day / ('A'-video).

Nov 03. (7") *(674370-6)* **THE GREAT TEST. / CHANGE OF SEASON** [29] [–]
(cd-s+=) *(674376-2)* – ('A'-video).
(cd-s) *(674376-5)* – ('A'side) / Anyone else's conclusion / Seven years / Anyone else's conclusion (video).

☐ Miles HUNT (CLUB) (see under ⇒ WONDER STUFF)

Ian HUNTER

Born: IAN HUNTER PATTERSON, 3 Jun'46, Shrewsbury, England. After years spent playing clubs in Hamburg, Germany, he joined AT LAST THE 1958 ROCK & ROLL SHOW, who released a one-off 45 for 'CBS' in 1967, 'I CAN'T DRIVE' / 'WORKIN' ON THE RAILROAD'. The following year, he wrote a few songs for the CHARLIE WOLFE demos, which remained unissued until 'Nems' released them in mid-70's ('STAY STAY STAY' / 'HOME'). After answering an ad in the music press, HUNTER successfully auditioned in June '69 for lead singer in MOTT THE HOOPLE. For the next five years, they became one of Britain's best rock acts, until HUNTER decided to opt for solo career in 1975. His debut 45, 'ONCE BITTEN TWICE SHY', took up where 'THE HOOPLE left off, making the UK Top 20 in the process. With help from stalwart supporter and guitarist MICK RONSON, he continued to surface either in England or New York, with credible material, having already toured supporting each other's solo projects, as the HUNTER-RONSON BAND. Following the Top 30 success of the 'ALL AMERICAN ALIEN BOY' (1976) set, the shady (as in dark spectacled) rock'n'roll hero/icon formed touring band, The OVERNIGHT ANGELS featuring EARL SLICK amongst others (RONSON had joined DYLAN's 'Rolling Thunder' tour in mid-'76), the group backing up HUNTER on a one-off eponymous album which the curly locked frontman was allegedly none too happy with. Signing to 'Chrysalis' at the end of the decade, HUNTER teamed up with RONSON once more on 'YOU'RE NEVER ALONE WITH A SCHIZOPHRENIC' (1979), while 1981's 'SHORT BACK 'N' SIDES' featured such esteemed guests as TODD RUNDGREN, MICK JONES and TOPPER HEADON (the latter two both members of The CLASH; HUNTER also proved his punk credentials by producing GENERATION X's 'VALLEY OF THE DOLLS' album the same year). He subsequently went to ground following 1983's 'ALL THE GOOD ONES ARE TAKEN', eventually re-emerging in 1990 with another RONSON collaboration, 'Y U I ORTA', released on 'Mercury' (his old pal was to die of cancer in '94). Though HUNTER has never quite risen above second division status in his post-HOOPLE career, he remains, especially among his peers, one of the most respected figures in the rock world. The aptly titled 'RANT' (2001) found HUNTER in as feisty and as passionate a mood as he's been in since his 70's glory years, spewing bile at various, usually deserving targets and backing it all up with confident, consummate forays into surprisingly diverse rock textures.

Album rating: IAN HUNTER (*7) / ALL AMERICAN ALIEN BOY (*5) / OVERNIGHT ANGELS (*4) / YOU'RE NEVER ALONE WITH A SCHIZOPHRENIC (*7) / SHADES OF IAN HUNTER compilation (*7) / WELCOME TO THE CLUB (*6) / SHORT BACK AND SIDES (*7) / ALL THE GOOD ONES ARE TAKEN (*6) / YUI ORTA (*6; as Hunter-Ronson) / THE VERY BEST OF IAN HUNTER compilation (*6) / IAN HUNTER'S DIRTY LAUNDRY (*4) / THE ARTFUL DODGER (*4) / RANT (*6)

IAN HUNTER – vocals, guitar (ex-MOTT THE HOOPLE, ex-AT LAST THE 1958 . . .) with **MICK RONSON** – guitar, vocals (ex-MOTT THE HOOPLE, ex-DAVID BOWIE, Solo artist) / **PETE ARNESEN** – keyboards / **JEFF APPLEBY** – bass / **DENNIS ELLIOTT** – drums

C.B.S. Columbia

Mar 75. (7") *(CBS 3194) <10161>* **ONCE BITTEN TWICE SHY. / 3,000 MILES FROM HERE** [14] [ ]

Apr 75. (lp/c) *(CBS/40 80710) <33480>* **IAN HUNTER** [21] [50]
– Once bitten twice shy / Who do you love / Lounge lizard / Boy / 3,000 miles from here / The truth, the whole truth, nuthin' but the truth / It ain't easy when you fall / Shades off / I get so excited. *<US cd-iss. Jul90; CK 33480> (re-iss. cd Sep94 on 'Sony Rewind'; COL 477359-2)*

Jul 75. (7") *(CBS 3486)* **WHO DO YOU LOVE. / BOY** [ ] [–]

— HUNTER with RONSON, brought in mainly session people including **AYNSLEY DUNBAR** – drums / **CORNELL DUPREEE** – guitar / **JACO PASTORUS** – bass / **CHRIS STAINTON** – keyboards / guests **BRIAN MAY + FREDDIE MERCURY** – vocals (QUEEN) All replaced PETE and JEFF who went into sessions + DENNIS who joined FOREIGNER

May 76. (7") *(CBS 4268)* **ALL AMERICAN ALIEN BOY. / RAPE** [ ] [–]

May 76. (lp/c) *(CBS/40 81310) <34142>* **ALL AMERICAN ALIEN BOY** [29] [ ]
– Letter to Brittania from the Union Jack / All American alien boy / Irene Wilde / Restless youth / Rape / You nearly did me in / Apathy 83 / God (take 1). *<US cd-iss. Jan90; CK 34142> (cd-iss. Aug98 on 'Columbia'; 491695-2)*

Aug 76. (7") *(CBS 4479)* **YOU NEARLY DID ME IN. / LETTER TO BRITANNIA FROM THE UNION JACK** [ ] [–]

— HUNTER formed tour band OVERNIGHT ANGELS:- **EARL SLICK** – guitar (ex-BOWIE) / **PETER OXENDALE** – keyboards / **BOB RAWLINSON** – bass / **CURLY SMITH** – drums (MICK RONSON joined BOB DYLAN's Rolling Thunder Tour mid-76)

May 77. (7"; as IAN HUNTER'S OVERNIGHT ANGELS) *(CBS 5229)* **JUSTICE OF THE PEACE. / THE BALLAD OF LITTLE STAR** [ ] [ ]

May 77. (lp/c) *(CBS/40 81993) <34721>* **OVERNIGHT ANGELS** [ ] [ ]
– Golden opportunity / Shallow crystals / Overnight angels / Broadway / Justice of the peace / Silver dime / Wild'n'free / The ballad of little star / To love a woman. *(re-iss. cd Jun94 on 'Sony Europe'; 474 780-2) (cd re-iss. Jan02 on 'Sony'+=; 50603-2)* – England rocks.

Jul 78. (7"; as IAN HUNTER'S OVERNIGHT ANGELS) *(CBS 5497)* **ENGLAND ROCKS. / WILD'N'FREE** [ ] [–]

— now with **RONSON** plus **ROY BITTAN** – keyboards / **MAX WEINBERG** – drums / **GEORGE YOUNG + LEW DELGATTO** – sax / **GARY TALLENT** – bass / **ELLEN FOLEY** – vocals

Chrysalis Chrysalis

Apr 79. (7"white) *(CHS 2324)* **WHEN THE DAYLIGHT COMES. / LIFE AFTER DEATH** [ ] [–]

Apr 79. (lp/c) *(<CHR/ZCHR 1214>)* **YOU'RE NEVER ALONE WITH A SCHIZOPHRENIC** [49] [35]
– Just another night / Wild east / Cleveland rocks / When the daylight comes / Ships / Life after death / Standin' in my light / Bastard / The outsider. *<cd-iss. Jun94 on 'Razor & Tie'; RE 2011> (re-iss. cd Mar94; CD 25CR 03) (cd re-iss. Aug99 on 'E.M.I.'; 521853-2)*

Jul 79. (7") *(CHS 2346)* **SHIPS. / WILD EAST** [ ] [–]

Aug 79. (7") *<2352>* **JUST ANOTHER NIGHT. / CLEVELAND ROCKS** [–] [68]

Oct 79. (7") *(CHS 2390)* **CLEVELAND ROCKS. / BASTARD** [ ] [–]

— **MARTIN BRILEY** – bass repl. TALLENT / **ERIC PARKER** – drums repl. WEINBERG / **GEORGE MEYER + TOM MANDEL** – keyboards repl. BITTAN also to BRUCE SPRINGSTEEN / **TOMMY MORRONGIELLO** – guitar, bass repl. YOUNG + DELGATTO

Apr 80. (d-lp/c) *(CJT/ZCJT 6) <1269>* **WELCOME TO THE CLUB (live)** [61] [69]
– F.B.I. / Once bitten twice shy / Angelline / Laugh at me / All the way from Memphis / I wish I was your mother / Irene Wilde / Just another night / Cleveland rocks / Standin' in my light / Bastard / Walkin' with a mountain / Rock'n'roll queen / All the young dudes / Slaughter on Tenth Avenue / We gotta get out of here / Silver needles / Man o' war / Sons and daughters. *(re-iss. d-cd May94; CDCHR 6075)*

Jun 80. (d7") *(2434)* **WE GOTTA GET OUT OF HERE (live). / MEDLEY: PNCE BITTEN TWICE SHY – BASTARD – CLEVELAND ROCKS (live) // SONS AND DAUGHTERS (live). / ONE OF THE BOYS (live)** [ ] [–]

— virtualy same band except featured guests **TODD RUNDGREN** – vocals, bass / **MICK JONES** – guitar / **TOPPER HEADON** – drums (both of CLASH) / **TYMON DOGG** – violin

Aug 81. (7"clear) *(CHS 2542)* **LISA LIKES ROCK'N'ROLL. / NOISES** [ ] [–]

Aug 81. (lp/c) *(<CHR/ZCHR 1326>)* **SHORT BACK 'N' SIDES** [79] [62]
– Central Park'n'West / Lisa likes rock'n'roll / I need your love / Old records never die / Noises / Rain / Gun control / Theatre of the absurd / Leave me alone / Keep on burning. *(re-iss. d-cd.May94+=; CDCHR 6074)* – LONG ODDS AND OUT TAKES *(cd re-iss. Feb00 on 'Liberty'; 524625-2)*

— now with **RONSON + ROBBIE ALTER + JIMMY RIP** – guitar / **MARK CLARKE + DAN HARTMAN** – bass / **MANDAL / JEFF BOVA + BOB MAYO** – keyboards / **CLARENCE CLEMONS + LOU CORTLEZZI** – sax / **HILLY MICHAELS** – drums

C.B.S. Columbia

Jul 83. (7") *(A 3855)* **ALL THE GOOD ONES ARE TAKEN. / DEATH 'N' GLORY BOYS** [ ] [–]
(12"+=) *(TA 3855)* – Traitor.

Aug 83. (lp/c) *(CBS/40 25379) <38628>* **ALL THE GOOD ONES ARE TAKEN** [ ] [ ]
– All the good ones are taken / Every step of the way / Fun / Speechless / Death 'n' glory boys / Somethin's goin' on / That girl is rock'n'roll / Captain Void 'n' the video jets / Seeing double / All the good ones are taken (reprise). *(re-iss. cd Jun94 on 'Sony Europe'; 474780-2)*

Oct 83. (7") *(A 3541)* **SOMETHIN'S GOIN' ON. / ALL THE GOOD ONES ARE TAKEN** [ ] [–]

Oct 83. (7") *<04166>* **SEEING DOUBLE. / THAT GIRL IS ROCK'N'ROLL** [–] [ ]

— HUNTER retired from public eye until late '89 . . .

HUNTER-RONSON

— IAN HUNTER + MICK RONSON's band, with **PAT KILBRIDE** – bass / **MICKEY CURRY** – drums / **TOMMY MANDEL** – keyboards

Mercury Mercury

Jan 90. (cd/c/lp) *(<838 973-2/-4/-1>)* **Y U I ORTA** [ ] Oct89 [ ]
– American music / The loner / Women's intuition / Tell it like it is / Livin' in a heart / Big time / Cool / Beg a little love / Following in your footsteps * / Sons 'n' lovers / Pain * / How much more can I take * / Sweet dreamer. *(c+=/cd+= *) (<cd re-iss. Apr03 on 'Burning Airlines'; PILOT 154>) (<cd re-iss. Sep03 on 'Lemon'; CDLEM 6>)*

Feb 90. (7"/c-s) *(MER/+MC 315)* **AMERICAN MUSIC. / TELL IT LIKE IT IS** [ ] [ ]
(12"+=/cd-s+=) *(MER X/CD 315)* – Sweet dreamer.

Norsk Plateproduksjon not iss.

Feb 95. (cd-s; as IAN HUNTER'S DIRTY LAUNDRY) *(IDS 44)* **MY REVOLUTION / DANCING ON THE MOON** [–] Norway [–]

Mar 95. (cd; as IAN HUNTER'S DIRTY LAUNDRY) *(IDCD 44)* **IAN HUNTER'S DIRTY LAUNDRY** [–] Norway [–]

Polydor not iss.

Sep 96. (cd) *(531 794-2)* **THE ARTFUL DODGER** [ ] [–]
– Too much / Now is the time / Something to believe in / Resurrection Mary / Walk on water / 23a Swan Hill / Michael Picasso / Open my eyes / Artful dodger / Skeletons in your closet / Still the same. *(UK-iss.Sep97 on 'Citadel' pic-cd; CID 1-CD)*

Citadel not iss.

Apr 97. (cd-s) *(CIT 101)* **THE ARTFUL DODGER / NOW IS THE TIME / FUCK IT UP** [ ] [–]

Papillon Varese

May 01. (cd) *(BTFLYCD 0016) <061116>* **RANT** [ ] Apr01 [ ]
– Still love rock and roll / Wash us away / Death of a nation / Morons / Purgatory / American spy / Dead man walkin' / Good samaritan / Soap 'n' water / Ripoff / Knees of my heart / No one.

– compilations, etc. –

Feb 80. (lp/c) *Columbia; (CBS/40 88476)* **SHADES OF IAN HUNTER – THE BALLAD OF IAN HUNTER & MOTT THE HOOPLE** [ ] [ ]
<US cd-iss. Nov88; VK 41670>

Apr 91. (cd/c/lp) *C.B.S.; (467508-2/-4/-1)* **THE VERY BEST OF IAN HUNTER** [ ] [ ]

Jul 91. (cd/c) *Castle; (CCS CD/MC 290)* **THE COLLECTION** [ ] [–]
(Includes tracks by MOTT THE HOOPLE)

Oct 95. (cd) *Windsong; (WINCD 078)* **THE HUNTER-HONSON BAND BBC LIVE IN CONCERT** [ ] [–]

Jul 99. (cd) *Citadel; (CIT 1BOX)* **THE ARTFUL DODGER / THE DIARY OF A ROCK'N'ROLL STAR** [ ] [–]

May 00. (d-cd) *Columbia; (496284-2) <61406>* **ONCE BITTEN TWICE SHY** [ ] Aug00 [ ]

Jul 00. (cd; as IAN HUNTER BAND) *Burning Airlines; (<PILOT 052>)* **MISSING IN ACTION** [ ] [ ]

HUSKER DU

Formed: St. Paul, Minnesota, USA . . . 1978 by MOULD, HART and NORTON. In 1980-82, they issued a few 45's and a live LP 'LAND SPEED RECORD', on their own label, 'New Alliance'. The record typified the band's early uncompromising hardcore which was often tediously workmanlike in its adherence to the steadfast confines of the genre. 'EVERYTHING FALLS APART' (1983) was also unflinching in its intensity and it was all the more surprising when the band showed glimmers of noise-pop greatness on their 1983 debut for 'SST', 'METAL CIRCUS'. They consolidated this by cross-fertilising the previously polarised worlds of psychedelia and hardcore punk on an electrifying cover of The BYRDS' 'EIGHT MILES HIGH' (1984). The follow-up double set, 'ZEN ARCADE' (1984) was a further giant step for hardcore-kind. A concept album no less, the twin songwriting attack of MOULD and HART was becoming sharper and even the sprawling, unfocused feel of the whole affair wasn't enough to blunt the edges of songs like 'WHATEVER' and 'TURN ON THE NEWS'. The songwriting on 'NEW DAY RISING' (1985) was even more trenchant, the band's adrenaline fuelled pop-core hybrid developing at breakneck speed. 'FLIP YOUR WIG' (1985), the band's last indie release, marked a stepping stone to their major label debut for 'Warners', 'CANDY APPLE GREY' (1986). While HART perfected HUSKER DU's melodic dischord on tracks like 'DEAD SET ON DESTRUCTION', MOULD showcased darkly introspective, acoustic elegies 'TOO FAR DOWN' and 'HARDLY GETTING OVER IT'. The more musically-challenged among HUSKER DU's following were none too taken with this new fangled unplugged business although the album was released to unanimous critical acclaim. The band's swansong, 'WAREHOUSE: SONGS AND STORIES' (1987) was the culmination of a decade's experimentation and possessed an unprecedented depth, clarity and consistency. By the time of its release, though, tension in the band was reaching breaking point and HUSKER DU was disbanded in 1987. While GRANT HART and BOB MOULD went on to solo careers, as well as respectively forming NOVA MOB and SUGAR, they were always better together and the magic of HUSKER DU is inestimable in its influence on a generation of alternative guitar bands. The new millennium saw HART return with a new set, 'GOOD NEWS FOR THE MODERN MAN' (1999). • **Songwriters:** MOULD-HART compositions except; SUNSHINE SUPERMAN (Donovan) / TICKET TO RIDE + SHE'S A WOMAN + HELTER SKELTER (Beatles) / EIGHT MILES HIGH (Byrds). NOVA MOB covered I JUST WANT TO MAKE LOVE TO YOU (Willie Dixon) / SHEENA IS A PUNK ROCKER (Ramones). Solo GRANT HART covered SIGNED D.C. (Love). • **Trivia:** HUSKER DU means DO YOU REMEMBER in Swedish.

Album rating: LAND SPEED RECORD mini (*6) / EVERYTHING FALLS APART (*5) / ZEN ARCADE (*9) / NEW DAY RISING (*9) / FLIP YOUR WIG (*9) / CANDY APPLE GREY (*7) / WAREHOUSE: SONGS & STORIES (*9) / THE LIVING END live compilation (*6) / Grant Hart: INTOLERANCE (*6) / Nova Mob: THE DAYS DAYS OF POMPEII (*6) / NOVA MOB (*6) / ECCE HOMO (*5) / Grant Hart: GOOD NEWS FOR THE MODERN MAN (*7)

BOB MOULD (b.12 Oct'61, Malone, New York) – vocals, guitar, keyboards, percussion / **GRANT HART** (b. GRANTZBERG VERNON HART, 18 Mar'61) – drums, keyboards, percussion, vocals / **GREG NORTON** (b.13 Mar'59, Rock Island, Illinois) – bass

not iss. Reflex

Jan 81. (7") *<38285>* **STATUES. / AMUSEMENT (live)** [–] [ ]

Alternative Tentacles / New Alliance

Jan 82. (m-lp) *(VIRUS 25)* <*NAR 007*> **LAND SPEED RECORD (live)**
– All tensed up / Don't try to call / I'm not interested / Big sky / Guns at my school / Push the button / Gilligan's Island / MTC / Don't have a life / Bricklayer / Tired of doing things / You're naive / Strange week / Do the bee / Ultracore / Let's go die / Data control. *(re-iss. Nov88 on 'S.S.T.'; SST 195) (re-iss. cd/c/lp Oct95)*

May 82. (7"m) <*NAR 010*> **IN A FREE LAND. / WHAT DO I WANT? / M.I.C.** — –

not iss. / Reflex

Jan 83. (lp; @45rpm) <*D*> **EVERYTHING FALLS APART** — –
– From the gut / Blah, blah, blah / Punch drunk / Bricklayer / Afraid of being wrong / Sunshine Superman / Signals from above / Everything falls apart / Wheels / Obnoxious / Gravity. *(cd-iss. May93 on 'WEA'+=; 8122 71163-2)* – In a free land / What do I want / M.I.C. / Statues / Let's go die / Amusement (live) / Do you remember?

S.S.T. / S.S.T.

Dec 83. (m-lp) <*(SST 020)*> **METAL CIRCUS** — Oct83
– Real world / Deadly skies / It's not funny anymore / Diane / First of the last calls / Lifeline / Out on a limb.

Apr 84. (7"colrd) <*(SST 025)*> **EIGHT MILES HIGH. / MASOCHISM WORLD**
(3"cd-s iss.Dec88; SST 025CD)

Sep 84. (d-lp) <*(SST 027)*> **ZEN ARCADE** — Jul84
– Something I learned today / Broken home, broken heart / Never talking to you again / Chartered trips / Dreams reoccurring / Indecision time / Hare Krishna / Beyond the threshold / Pride / I'll never forget you / The biggest lie / What's going on / Masochism world / Standing by the sea / Somewhere / One step at a time / Pink turns to blue / Newest industry / Monday will never be the same / Whatever / The tooth fairy and the princess / Turn on the news / Reoccurring dreams. *(cd-iss. Oct87; SST 027CD) (re-iss. cd/c/d-lp Oct95 & Jun97; same)*

Feb 85. (lp) <*(SST 031)*> **NEW DAY RISING** — Jan85
– New day rising / Girl who lives on Heaven Hill / I apologize / Folklore / If I told you / Celebrated summer / Perfect example / Terms of psychic warfare / 59 times the pain / Powerline / Books about UFO's / I don't know what you're talking about / How to skin a cat / Watcha drinkin' / Plans I make. *(cd-iss. Oct87; SST 031CD) (re-iss. cd/c/lp Oct95; same)*

Aug 85. (7") <*(SST 051)*> **MAKE NO SENSE AT ALL. / LOVE IS ALL AROUND (MARY'S THEME)**

Oct 85. (lp) <*(SST 055)*> **FLIP YOUR WIG** — Sep85
– Flip your wig / Every everything / Makes no sense at all / Hate paper doll / Green eyes / Divide and conquer / Games / Find me / The baby song / Flexible flyer / Private plane / Keep hanging on / The wit and the wisdom / Don't know yet. *(cd-iss. Oct87; SST 055CD) (re-iss. cd/c/lp Oct95; same)*

Warners / Warners

Feb 86. (7") *(W 8746)* **DON'T WANT TO KNOW IF YOU ARE LONELY. / ALL WORK NO PLAY**
(12"+=) *(W 8746T)* <*20446-0*> – Helter skelter (live).

Mar 86. (lp/c) *(WX 40/+C)* <*25385*> **CANDY APPLE GREY**
– Crystal / Don't want to know if you are lonely / I don't know for sure / Sorry somehow / Too far down / Hardly getting over it / Dead set on destruction / Eiffel Tower high / No promises have I made / All this I've done for you. *(cd-iss. Nov92; 7599 25385-2)*

Sep 86. (7") *(W 8612)* **SORRY SOMEHOW. / ALL THIS I'VE DONE FOR YOU** — –
(d7+=/12"+=) *(W 8612 F/T)* – Flexible flyer / Celebrated summer.

Jan 87. (7") *(W 8456)* **COULD YOU BE THE ONE. / EVERYTIME** — –
(12"+=) *(W 8456T)* – Charity, chastity, prudence, hope.

Jan 87. (d-lp/d-c) *(925544-1/-4)* <*25544*> **WAREHOUSE: SONGS & STORIES** — 72
– These important years / Charity, chastity, prudence and hope / Standing in the rain / Back from somewhere / Ice cold ice / You're a soldier / Could you be the one? / Too much spice / Friend, you've got to fall / Visionary / She floated away / Bed of nails / Tell you why tomorrow / It's not peculiar / Actual condition / No reservations / Turn it around / She's a woman (and now he is a man) / Up in the air / You can live at home. *(cd-iss. Oct92; 7599 25544-2)*

Jun 87. (7") *(W 8276)* **ICE COLD ICE. / GOTTA LETTA** — –
(12"+=) *(W 8276T)* – Medley.

—— disbanded in '87 after manager DAVID SAVOY Jr. committed suicide. GRANT HART went solo as did BOB MOULD; in 1992 the latter formed SUGAR

– compilations, etc. –

May 94. (cd/c) *Warners;* <*(9362 45582-2/-4)*> **THE LIVING END (live)** — Apr94
– New day rising / Heaven Hill / Standing in the rain / Back from somewhere / Ice cold ice / Everytime / Friend you're gonna fall / She floated away / From the gut / Target / It's not funny anymore / Hardly getting over it / Terms of psychic warfare / Powertime / Books about UFO's / Divide and conquer / Keep hangin' on / Celebrated summer / Now that you know me / Ain't no water in the well / What's goin' on / Data control / In a free land / Sheena is a punk rocker.

☐ Michael HUTCHENCE (see under ⇒ INXS)

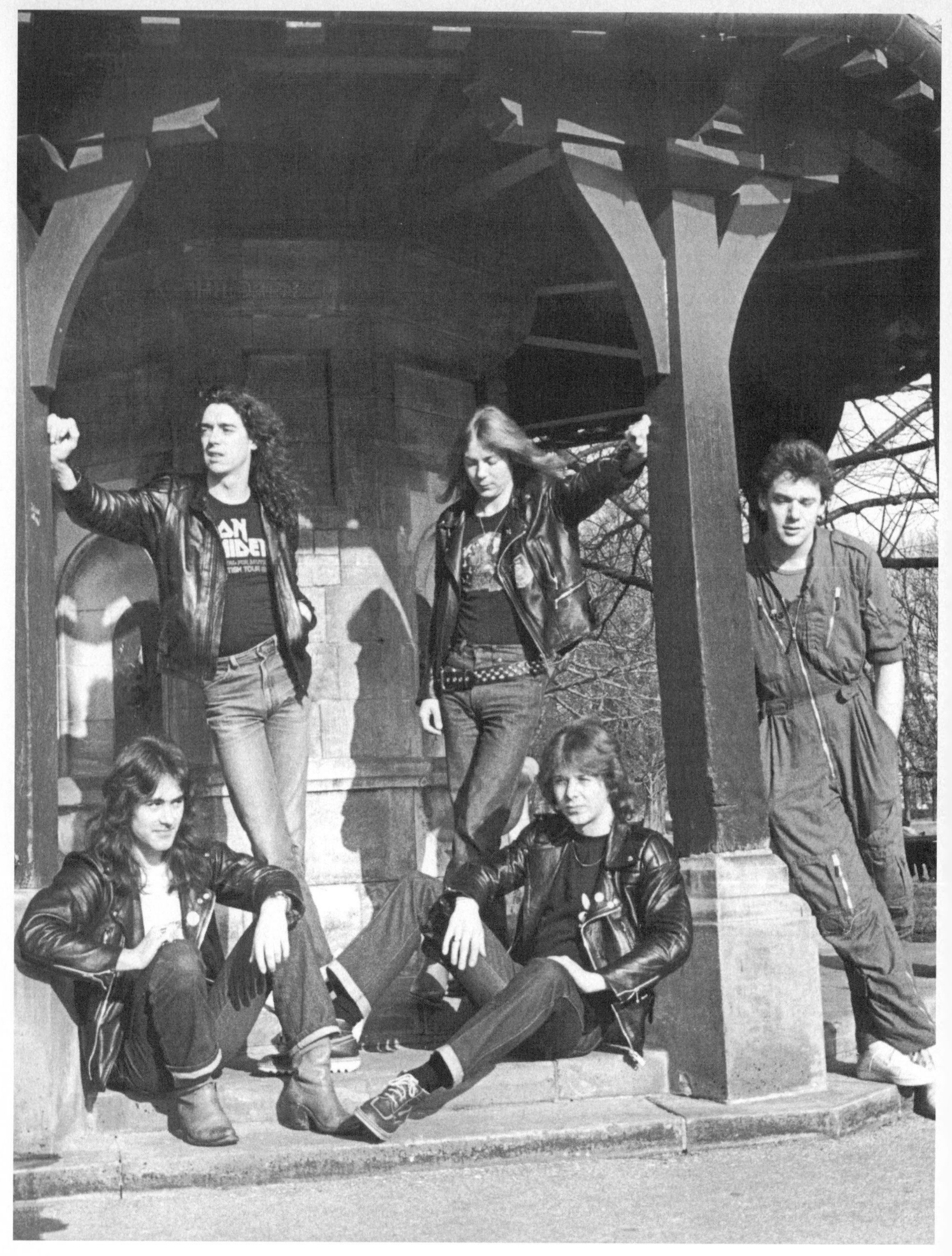

IRON MAIDEN

Janis IAN

Born: JANIS EDDY FINK, 7 May'51, New York City, New York, USA. While attending Manhattan High School of Music & Art, she had her first song 'HAIR OF SPUN GOLD' published by Broadside magazine. In 1965, while singing at The Village Gate, she signed as a songwriter to 'Elektra' records, but was soon dropped when she wanted to sing herself!. Early in 1966, after her family moved from New Jersey to New York, she secured another contract, this time with 'M.G.M.'. Her debut single, 'SOCIETY'S CHILD', released while she was still aged 15, broke into the US chart, and finally reached the Top 20 in 1967. At the same time, her eponymous debut album also made Top 30, but although failed to establish herself and subsequently moved to Philadelphia. In 1971, she uprooted again, this time to California (after she married), 'Capitol' records issuing her fifth set, 'PRESENT COMPANY'. In 1974, she resurfaced on 'Columbia' and hit critically with 'STARS', both the album's title track and 'JESSE' enjoying a series of interpretations by leading artists, the latter track covered in heart-renderingly beautiful style by ROBERTA FLACK on her 'Killing Me Softly' album. By now, IAN's angst-ridden folk-rock outpourings had given way to a more contemporary, jazzy and lyrical style, 'BETWEEN THE LINES' (1975) landing her a No.1 US slot amid the singer/songwriter boom (even if its massive hit single, 'AT SEVENTEEN', was about high school trauma). Although the following year's 'AFTERTONES' made the Top 20, her subsequent albums failed to make any commercial impact and IAN retured from studio work in late '81. Though she continued to undertake live work and release dance set, 'UNCLE WONDERFUL' in Australia in '84, it would be nearly a decade before she recorded another album, 'BREAKING SILENCE' eventually surfacing in 1993. Though it failed to chart, BETTE MIDLER had a hit with one track, 'SOME PEOPLE'S LIVES'. Two further JANIS IAN albums, 'REVENGE' (1995) and 'HUNGER' (1997) were slightly a slight let down although her fanbase in America might disagree. A great title and a decent album into the bargain, 'GOD & THE FBI' (2000) found JANIS running her inimitable commentary on everything from state security to cultural decadence, with her instrumental weave more adventurous than usual. 'LIVE: WORKING WITHOUT A NET' (2003), meanwhile, was a double disc concert set spanning the length and breadth of her career and creating a intimate atmosphere with a clutch of spoken word intros.

Album rating: JANIS IAN (*6) / FOR ALL THE SEASONS OF YOUR MIND (*5) / THE SECRET LIFE OF J. EDDY FINK (*4) / WHO REALLY CARES (*3) / PRESENT COMPANY (*4) / STARS (*6) / BETWEEN THE LINES (*8) / AFTERTONES (*6) / MIRACLE ROW (*5) / JANIS IAN on 'Columbia' (*4) / NIGHT RAINS (*4) / THE BEST OF JANIS IAN compilation (*6) / RESTLESS EYES (*4) / UNCLE WONDERFUL (*5) / BREAKING SILENCE (*6) / REVENGE (*6) / SOCIETY'S CHILD: THE VERVE RECORDINGS compilation (*7) / HUNGER (*4) / GOD & THE FBI (*5) / LIVE: WORKING WITHOUT A NET (*5)

JANIS IAN – vocals, acoustic guitar, piano (w/ session people)

Verve Folkways / Verve Folkways

Oct 66. (7") *(VS 1503)* <5027> **SOCIETY'S CHILD (BABY I'VE BEEN THINKING). / LETTER TO JOHN**
(re-iss. May67; VS 1506) <re-iss. May67, hit US No.14>

Jun 67. (lp; stereo/mono) *(S+VLP 6001)* <3017> **JANIS IAN** — 29
– Society's child (baby I've been thinking) / Too old to go 'way little girl / Hair of spun gold / Then tangles of my mind / I'll give you a stone if you throw it (changing tymes) / Pro-girl / Younger generation blues / New Christ cardiac hero / Lover be kindly / Mrs. McKenzie / Janey's blues. *(re-iss. Jun82 on 'Polydor'; PD 6058)*

Oct 67. (7") *<5041>* **YOUNGER GENERATION BLUES. / I'LL GIVE YOU A STONE IF YOU THROW IT (CHANGING TYMES)** — -

Jan 68. (lp) *(SVLP 6003)* *<FTS 3024>* **FOR ALL THE SEASONS OF YOUR MIND** — Dec67
– A song for all the seasons of your mind / And I did ma / Honey d'ya think? / Bahimsa / Queen Merka & me / There are times / Lonely one / Sunflakes fall, snowrays call / Evening star / Shady acres / Insanity comes quietly to the structured mind.

Nov 68. (7") *(VS 1513)* *<5072>* **SUNFLAKES FALL, SNOWRAYS CALL. / INSANITY COMES QUIETLY TO THE STRUCTURED MIND**

Jan 69. (7") *<5079>* **A SONG FOR ALL THE SEASONS OF YOUR MIND. / LONELY ONE** — -

Feb 69. (lp) *(SVLP 6009)* *<FTS 3048>* **THE SECRET LIFE OF J. EDDY FINK**
– Everybody knows / Mistaken identity / Friends again / 42nd St. psycho blues / She's made of porcelain / Sweet misery / When I was a child / What do you think of the dead / Look to the rain / Son of love / Baby's blue.

Mar 69. (7") *<5090>* **FRIENDS AGAIN. / LADIES OF THE NIGHT** — -

Jul 69. (7") *<5099>* **EVERYBODY KNOWS. / JANEY'S BLUES** — -

Nov 69. (7") *<5113>* **CALLING YOUR NAME. / MONTH OF MAY** — -

Nov 69. (lp) *(SVLP 6023)* *<FTS 3063>* **WHO REALLY CARES**
– Time on my hands / Snowbird / Love you more than yesterday / Orphan of the wind / Sea and sand / Galveston / Do you remember / Month of May / Calling your name.

Capitol / Capitol

Feb 71. (7") *<3107>* **HE'S A RAINBOW. / HERE IN SPAIN** — -

May 71. (7") *(CL 15685)* **HE'S A RAINBOW. / SEE MY GRAMMY RIDE** — -

Jun 71. (lp) *(VMP 1014)* *<SM 683>* **PRESENT COMPANY** — Feb71
– The seaside / Present company / See my Grammy ride / Here in Spain / On the train / He's a rainbow / Weary lady / Nature's at peace / See the river / Let it run free / Alabama / Liberty / My land / Hello Jerry / Can you reach me / The sunlight. *(cd-iss. Nov92 on 'Beat Goes On'; BGOCD 165)*

C.B.S. / Columbia

May 74. (7") *<46034>* **JESSE. / THE MAN YOU ARE IN ME** — -

Jun 74. (lp/c) *(CBS/40 80224)* *<32857>* **STARS** — May74 83
– Stars / The man you are in me / Sweet sympathy / Page nine / Thankyous / Dance with me / Without you / Jesse / You've got me on a string / Applause. *(re-iss. Jun81; CBS 32049) (re-iss. Aug95 on 'Grapevine' cd/c; GRA CD/MC 302) (cd re-iss. Oct03 on 'Cooking Vinyl'+=; COOKCD 279)* – Jesse (live).

Jul 74. (7") *(CBS 2501)* **WITHOUT YOU. / YOU'VE GOT ME ON A STRING** [ ] [–]

May 75. (7") *<10119>* **WHEN THE PARTY'S OVER. / BRIGHT LIGHTS AND PROMISES** [–] [ ]

Aug 75. (7") *(CBS 3498) <10154>* **AT SEVENTEEN. / STARS** [ ] Jun75 [3]

Aug 75. (lp/c) *(CBS/40 80635) <33394>* **BETWEEN THE LINES** [ ] Mar75 [1]
– When the party's over / At seventeen / From me to you / Brights lights and promises / In the winter / Water colors / Between the lines / The come on / Light a light / Tea or symphony / Lover's lullaby. *(re-iss. Aug95 on 'Grapevine' cd/c; GRA CD/MC 303) (cd re-iss. Oct03 on 'Cooking Vinyl'+=; COOKCD 271)* – Between the lines (live).

Oct 75. (7") *<10228>* **IN THE WINTER. / THANKYOUSE** [–] [ ]

Nov 75. (7") *(CBS 4798)* **IN THE WINTER. / WHEN THE PARTY'S OVER** [ ] [–]

Feb 76. (lp/c) *(CBS/40 69220) <33919>* **AFTERTONES** [ ] Jan76 [12]
– Aftertones / I would like to dance / Love is blind / Roses / Belle of the blues / Goodbye to morning / Boy I really tied one on / This must be wrong / Don't cry, old man / Hymn. *(re-iss. Mar81; CBS 32018) (re-iss. Aug95 on 'Grapevine' cd/c; GRA CD/MC 304) (cd re-iss. Oct03 on 'Cooking Vinyl'+=; COOKCD 270)* – Love is blind (live).

Mar 76. (7") *(CBS 4100) <10297>* **BOY I REALLY TIED ONE ON. / AFTERTONES** [ ] [ ]

May 76. (7") *<10331>* **I WOULD LIKE TO DANCE. / GOODBYE TO MORNING** [–] [ ]

Sep 76. (7") *<10391>* **LOVE IS BLIND. / ROSES** [–] [ ]

Jan 77. (7") *<10484>* **MIRACLE ROW. / TAKE IT TO THE SKY** [–] [ ]

Mar 77. (lp/c) *(CBS/40 81879) <34440>* **MIRACLE ROW** [ ] Jan77 [45]
– Party lights / I want to make you love me / Sunset of your life / Take to the sky / Candlelight / Let me be lonely / Slow dance romance / Will you dance? / I'll cry tonight / Miracle row – Maria. *(re-iss. Aug95 on 'Grapevine' cd/c; GRA CD/MC 305) (cd re-iss. Oct03 on 'Cooking Vinyl'+=; COOKCD 275)* – Will you dance? (live).

May 77. (7") *<10526>* **CANDLELIGHT. / I WANT TO MAKE YOU LOVE ME** [–] [ ]

Sep 78. (7") *<10813>* **THAT GRAND ILLUSION. / HOPPER PAINTING** [–] [ ]

Sep 78. (lp/c) *(CBS/40 82700) <35325>* **JANIS IAN** [ ] [ ]
– That grand illusion / Some people / Tonight will last forever / Hotels & one-night stands / Do you wanna dance? / Silly habits / The bridge / My mama's house / Streetlife serenaders / I need to live alone again / Hopper painting. *(re-iss. Aug95 on 'Grapevine' cd/c; GRA CD/MC 306) (cd re-iss. Oct03 as 'JANIS IAN II' on 'Cooking Vinyl'+=; COOKCD 274)* – Silly habits (live).

Dec 78. (7") *<10864>* **DO YOU WANNA DANCE?. / THE BRIDGE** [–] [ ]

Apr 79. (7") *<10979>* **TONIGHT WILL LAST FOREVER. / HERE COMES THE NIGHT** [–] [ ]

Oct 79. (7") *(CBS 7936) <11111>* **FLY TOO HIGH. / NIGHT RAINS** [44] [ ]

Oct 79. (lp/c) *(CBS/40 83802) <36139>* **NIGHT RAINS** [ ] [ ]
– The other side of the sun / Fly too high / Memories / Night rains / Here comes the night / Day by day / Have mercy love / Lay low / Photographs / Jenny (Iowa sunrise). *(re-iss. Mar83; CBS 32298) (re-iss. Aug95 on 'Grapevine' cd/c; GRA CD/MC 307) (cd re-iss. Oct03 on 'Cooking Vinyl'+=; COOKCD 276)* – Fly too high (live).

Jan 80. (7") *(CBS 8136)* **HAVE MERCY LOVE. / JENNY (IOWA SUNRISE)** [ ] [–]

May 80. (7") *(CBS 8611)* **THE OTHER SIDE OF THE SUN. / PHOTOGRAPHS** [44] [–]

Jul 80. (7") *<11327>* **THE OTHER SIDE OF THE SUN. / MEMORIES** [–] [ ]

Nov 80. (7") *(CBS 9324)* **HERE COMES THE NIGHT. / MEMORIES** [ ] [–]

Mar 81. (7") *<02176>* **UNDER THE COVERS. / SUGAR MOUNTAIN** [–] [71]

Jun 81. (7") *(A 1324)* **UNDER THE COVERS. / PASSION PLAY** [ ] [–]

Jul 81. (lp/c) *(CBS/40 85040) <37360>* **RESTLESS EYES** [ ] [ ]
– Under the covers / I remember yesterday / I believe I'm myself again / Restless eyes / Get ready to roll / Passion play / Down and away / Bigger than real / Dear Billy / Sugar mountain. *(re-iss. Aug95 on 'Grapevine' cd/c; GRA CD/MC 308) (cd re-iss. Oct03 on 'Cooking Vinyl'; COOKCD 277)*

Oct 81. (7") *(A 1603) <02546>* **I REMEMBER YESTERDAY. / RESTLESS EYES** [ ] [ ]

— she retired from studio work 1981; although guested on a MEL TORME album in 1982 and continued to appear live throughout the 80's.

unknown — not iss.

1984. (lp) **UNCLE WONDERFUL** (rec.1981-1983) [–] Austra [–]
– Just a girl / Uncle Wonderful / Why can't you and I / Trigger happy love / Heart skip too many beats / Body slave / Hit you with guilt / Sniper of the heart / This night / Mechanical telephone. *(UK-iss.Jan96 on 'Grapevine' cd/c; GRA CD/MC 309) (cd re-iss. Oct03 on 'Cooking Vinyl'; COOKCD 280)*

Sony — Morgan Creek

Jun 93. (cd) *(519614-2) <2959 20023-2>* **BREAKING SILENCE** [ ] [ ]
– All roads to the river / Ride me like a wave / Tattoo / Guess you had to be there / What about the love? / His hands / Walking on sacred ground / This train still runs / Through the years / This house / Some people's lives / Breaking silence. *<(re-iss. Jun99 on 'Analogue'; CAPPG/AAPP 027)> (re-iss. Oct03 on 'Cooking Vinyl'+=; COOKCD 272)* – Ride me like a wave (wet mix) / This train still runs (live).

Grapevine — Beacon

May 95. (cd/c/lp) *(GRA CD/MC/LP 301) <51559>* **REVENGE** [ ] [ ]
– Ready for the war / Take no prisoners / Tenderness / No one else like you / Davy / When the silence falls / Take me walking in the rain / Berlin / Stolen fire / Ruby / The mission / When angels cry. *(cd re-iss. Oct03 on 'Cooking Vinyl'+=; COOKCD 278)* – Take me walking in the rain (live).

Jul 95. (c-s/cd-s) *(CDGPS 301)* **TENDERNESS / TAKE NO PRISONERS / WHEN ANGELS CRY** [ ] [–]

Oct 97. (cd/c) *(GRA CD/MC 233) <11274>* **HUNGER** [ ] Sep97 [ ]
– Black and white / On the dark side of town / Might as well be Monday / Getting over you / Searching for America / Hunger / Welcome to Acousticville / Honor them all / Empty / House without a heart / Shadow / Getting over you (with strings). *(cd re-iss. Nov03 on 'Cooking Vinyl'; COOKCD 273)*

Windham Hill — Windham Hill

Apr 00. (cd) *<(01934 11498-2)>* **GOD & THE FBI** [ ] Mar00 [ ]
– God & the FBI / On the other side / Memphis / Jolene / When you love someone / Play like a girl / Days like these / Boots like Emmy Lou's / She must be beautiful / The last comeback / Murdering Stravinsky.

Cooking Vinyl — Rude Girl

Oct 03. (d-cd) *(COOKCD 268) <26>* **LIVE: WORKING WITHOUT A NET (live)** [ ] [ ]
– This train still runs / Fly too high / (intro: "We love you") / Take me walking in the rain / Jesse / Paris in your eyes / Ride me like a wave / Love is blind / (intro: "Vote for me") / Boots like Emmy Lou's / Days like these / Society's child / (intro: "My pal Tiffany") / Between the lines / (intro: "How lucky am I?") / Take no prisoners / (intro: "Has-been at 19") / Stars / Will you dance? / Honor them all / (intro: "Moving back home") / At seventeen / Cosmopolitan girl / Tattoo / Watercolors / Breaking silence / Berlin / Silly habits / In the winter / (intro: "Kumbaya") / These boots were made for walking.

– compilations, others, etc. –

1975. (7") *Polydor; <14299>* **SOCIETY'S CHILD (BABY I'VE BEEN THINKING). / I'LL GIVE YOU A STONE IF YOU THROW IT (CHANGING TYMES)** [–] [ ]

Dec 80. (lp/c) *C.B.S.; (CBS/40 84711)* **THE BEST OF JANIS IAN** [ ] [ ]
– At seventeen / Have mercy love / Aftertones / When the party's over / In the winter / Stars / Fly too high / The other side of the sun / Without you / Here comes the night / Jesse (Iowa sunrise) / The bridge / Between the lines / Miracle row / Maria.

Aug 83. (d-c) *C.B.S.; (40 22158)* **STARS / NIGHT RAINS** [ ] [ ]

Jan 94. (d-cd) *Polydor; (527591-2) <7591>* **SOCIETY'S CHILD – THE VERVE RECORDINGS** [ ] Aug95 [ ]

Jun 95. (cd) *Whistle Test; (WHISCD 008)* **LIVE ON THE TEST (live)** [ ] [–]

May 99. (cd) *Bottom Line; <(63440 47402-2)>* **THE BOTTOM LINE ENCORE COLLECTION (live 1980)** [ ] Feb99 [ ]

Jul 02. (cd) *Festival; <36453>* **BEST OF JANIS IAN** [–] [ ]

ICE CUBE

Born: O'SHEA JACKSON, 15 Jun'69, Crenshaw, Los Angeles, California, USA. After starting out as a founding member of seminal rap terrorists N.W.A., CUBE took a sabbatical from the band following the release of the first album, going to study architecture at the Phoenix Institute of Technology. Returning in 1988, he worked on the pivotal 'STRAIGHT OUTTA COMPTON' (1989). After touring the record, the rapper had a dispute with manager JERRY HELLER over royalties, eventually settling in court in 1990. Following the incident, CUBE went solo with his backing crew DA LENCH MOB, releasing his debut, 'AMERIKKKA'S MOST WANTED' the same year. Produced by PUBLIC ENEMY's BOMB SQUAD, the album was as uncompromising, both lyrically and musically, as his best work for N.W.A., following the same gangsta rap blueprint and never budging from his old adage that "Life ain't nothing but bitches and money". Consistently controversial and contradictory, ICE CUBE puts down women at every opportunity yet offers female rapper YO YO a chance to have her say on 'IT'S A MAN'S WORLD', and say it she does, in fine style. 'DEATH CERTIFICATE' (1991) was an even more vicious verbal attack, CUBE railing against the usual targets like the police and the media, although the track's 'NO VASELINE' and 'BLACK KOREA' brought the most criticism. The former was an anti-Semitic outburst against his former boss, the jewish JERRY HELLER, while the latter advocated setting fire to Korean-owned grocery stores. He didn't stop there though, going on to include white "devils", middle class blacks and gay men in his litany of hate. Inevitably, the album brought widespread condemnation, the only thanks the rapper received for his troubles was from the Ku Klux Klan. On 'THE PREDATOR' (1992) CUBE's anger was more focused, the record debuting at No.1 in America and becoming a million seller within a month. It also spawned CUBE's biggest UK hit to date in the deceptively mellow 'IT WAS A GOOD DAY'. The rapper's P-Funk preoccupation continued with 'LETHAL INJECTION' (1993), wherein he spars with GEORGE CLINTON on the 'One Nation Under A Groove'-sampling 'BOP GUN (ONE NATION)', a single that almost made the Top 20 in both Britain and America. The remainder of the 90's was characterised by the rapper's absence from the scene save for a couple of compilations (1994's 'BOOTLEGS & B-SIDES' and '97's 'FEATURING . . .'), a one-off flop single ('WORLD IS MINE') and a collaborative effort with KRS-ONE, B-REAL and SHAQUE O'NEILL ('Men Of Steel'). He finally emerged with a new album's worth of material in 1998's 'WAR & PEACE VOL.1 (THE WAR DISC)', the first instalment in a double whammy partnered by 'VOL.2 THE PEACE DISC' (2000). • **Songwriters:** Co-writes with SADLER or JINX. Sample The ISLEYS, JAMES BROWN, STEELY DAN and MICHAEL JACKSON, OHIO PLAYERS, PUBLIC ENEMY, DAS EFX, MOMENTS + GRANDMASTER FLASH. • **Trivia:** ICE-T starred and contributed to soundtracks for the films 'Boyz 'n' The Hood' and 'Trespass' (circa early 90's). In 1991, he co-wrote with JAMES BROWN and produced female hardcore rapper YO-YO on their 'East-West' debut US hit single 'You can't Play With My World'.

Album rating: AMERIKKKA'S MOST WANTED (*8) / DEATH CERTIFICATE (*8) / THE PREDATOR (*6) / LETHAL INJECTION (*5) / BOOTLEGS & B-SIDES collection (*5) / WAR & PEACE VOL.1 (THE WAR DISC) (*5) / WAR & PEACE VOL.2 (THE PEACE DISC) (*5) / GREATEST HITS compilation (*8)

ICE CUBE – vocals (with backing from DA LENCH MOB)

Ruthless Priority

May 90. (12") *(VL 7220)* **AMERIKKKA'S MOST WANTED. / ONCE UPON A TIME IN THE PROJECTS**

4th & Broad Priority

Jun 90. (cd/c/lp) *(CR CD/CA/LP 551)* <57120> **AMERIKKKA'S MOST WANTED** 48 May90 19
– Better off dead / The nigga ya love to hate / Amerikkka's most wanted / What they hittin' foe? / You can't fade me / JD's gaffilin' / Once upon a time in the projects / Turn off the radio / Endangered species (tales from the darkside) / A gangsta's fairytale / I'm only out for one thing / Get off my Dick and tell yo bitch to come here / The drive-by / Rollin' with the Lench Mob / Who's the Mack? / It's a man's world / The bomb. *(cd re-iss. Sep96 on 'Island'; IMCD 230) <(cd re-mast.Mar03 on 'Priority'+=; 5 37601)>* – KILL AT WILL

Mar 91. (m-cd/m-c/m-lp) *(BRECD/BRCM/BRLM 572) <7230>* **KILL AT WILL** (above remixes) 66 Dec90 34
– Endangered species (tales from the darkside) / Jackin' for beats / Get off my Dick and tell yo bitch to come here / The product / Dead Homiez / JD's gaffilin (part 2) / I gotta say what up!!!.

Nov 91. (cd/c/lp) *(BR CD/CA/LP 581) <57155>* **DEATH CERTIFICATE** 2
– The funeral / The wrong nigga to fuck wit / My summer vacation / Steady mobbin' / Robin Lench / Givin' up the nappy dug out / Look who's burnin' / A bird in the hand / Man's best friend / Alive on arrival / Death / The birth / I wanna kill Sam / Horny lil' devil / True to the game / Color blind / Doing dumb shit / Us. *(cd+=)* – No Vaseline / Black Korea. *(cd re-iss. Sep96 on 'Island'; IMCD 232) <(cd re-mast.Mar03 on 'Priority'+=; 5 543341-2)>*– How to survive in South Central.

Dec 91. (7") *<7247>* **STEADY MOBBIN' / US**
(12"+=/cd-s+=) – Dead Homrez / Endangered species (tales from the dark side) (remix).

Nov 92. (cd-s) *<53813>* **WICKED (2 versions) / U AIN'T GONNA TAKE MY LIFE (2 versions)** – 55

Nov 92. (7"/c-s) *(BRW/BRCA 282)* **WICKED. / WE HAD TO TEAR THIS MOTHAFUCKA UP** –
(12"+=/cd-s+=) *(12BRW/BRCD 282)* – ('A'instrumental) / The wrong nigga to fuck wit. *(re-iss. Aug93, hit UK 62; same)*

Nov 92. (cd/c/lp) *(BR CD/CA/LP 592) <57185>* **THE PREDATOR** 73 1
– (the first day of school intro) / When will they shoot? / (I'm scared) / Wicked / Now I gotta wet 'cha / The predator / It was a good day / We had to tear this mothafucka up / **** 'em / Dirty Mack / Don't trust 'em / Gangsta's fairytale 2 / Check yo self / Who's got the camera? / Integration / Say hi to the bad guy. *(cd re-iss. Sep96 on 'Island'; IMCD 328) <(cd re-mast.Mar03 on 'Priority'+=; 5 43339-2)>* – Check yo self (the message remix) / It was a good day (remix) / 24 with an L / U ain't gonna take my life.

Feb 93. (c-s) *<53813>* **IT WAS A GOOD DAY / ('A'instrumental)** – 15

Mar 93. (c-s) *(BRCA 270) <53817>* **IT WAS A GOOD DAY. / AIN'T GONNA TAKE MY LIFE** 27 –
(12"+=/cd-s+=) *(12BRW/BRCD 270)* – ('A'&'B'instrumentals).

Jul 93. (c-s; as ICE CUBE featuring DAS EFX) *(BRCA 283) <53830>* **CHECK YO SELF / IT WAS A GOOD DAY (radio mix)** 36 20
(12"+=/cd-s+=) *(12BRW/BRCD 283)* – 24 with an L / ('A'version).
(cd-s+=) *(BRCDX 283)* – It was a good day (instrumental) / Who got the camera.

Dec 93. (cd/c/lp) *(BR CD/CA/LP 609) <53876>* **LETHAL INJECTION** 52 5
– The shot / Really doe / Ghetto bird / You know how we do it / Cave bitch / Bop gun (one nation) / What can I do? / Lil ass gee / Make it ruff, make it smooth / Down for whatever / Enemy / When I get to Heaven. *(cd re-iss. Sep96 on 'Island'; IMCD 229) <(cd re-mast.Mar03 on 'Priority'+=; 5 37602-2)>* – What can I do? (westside remix) / What can I do? (eastside remix) / You know how we do it (part 2) / Lil ass gee (eerie gumbo remix).

Dec 93. (12") *(12BRW 302) <53843>* **REALLY DOE. / MY SKIN IS MY SKIN** 66 54
(cd-s+=) *(BRCD 302)* – ('A'&'B'mixes).

Mar 94. (7"/c-s) *(BRW/BRCA 303) <53847>* **YOU KNOW HOW WE DO IT. / 2 N THE MORNING** 41 30
(12"+=/cd-s+=) *(12BRW/BRCD 303)* – ('A'instrumental). *(re-entered UK No.46 Dec94)*
(cd-s+=) *(BRCDX 303)* – D-voidofpopniggafiedmegamix.

Aug 94. (7"/c-s; by ICE CUBE featuring GEORGE CLINTON) *(BR W/CA 308) <53155>* **BOP GUN (ONE NATION). / DOWN FOR WHATEVER** 22 Jul94 23
(12"+=) *(12BRW 308)* – ('A'-MYR mix) / Ghetto jam.
(cd-s+=) *(BRCD 308)* – Ghetto bird (Dr. Jam's mix).

— snippets from the FUNKADELIC song 'One Nation Under A Groove'.

Dec 94. (cd/c/d-lp) *(BR CD/CA/LP 616) <53921>* **BOOTLEGS AND B-SIDES** (compilation) 19
– Robin Hood (cause it ain't all good) / What can I do (remix) / 24 with an L / You know how we do it (remix) / 2 n the morning / Check yo self (remix) / You don't want to fuck with these (unreleased '93 shit) / Lil piss gee (eerie gumbo mix) / My skin is my sin / It was a good day (remix) / D'voidofpopniggafied – megamix. *(cd re-iss. Sep96 on 'Island'; IMCD 231)*

— In 1995, ICE CUBE featured on minor hits by SCARFACE ('People Don't Believe') and WC AND THE MAAD CIRCLE 'West Up!'.

Priority Priority

Mar 97. (cd-s) *(894176-2)* **WORLD IS MINE / ('A'mixes)** 60 [ ]

— In Aug'97, ICE CUBE collaborated with KRS-ONE, B-REAL and SHAQUE O'NEILL on minor US hit single, 'Men Of Steel'.

Dec 97. (cd) *<51037>* **FEATURING . . . ICE CUBE** (compilation) – [ ]
– Bend a corner with me / Natural born killaz / Bow down / Bop gun (one nation) / Check yo self / Endangered species (tales from the . . . .) / Trespass / It's a man's world / West up! / Game over / Wicked ways / Two to the head.

Oct 98. (c-s,12",cd-s; ICE CUBE featuring MR. SHORT KHOP) *<5345>* **PUSHIN' WEIGHT / (mixes)** – 26

Nov 98. (cd/lp) *(CDPTY/PTYLP 1616) <50700>* **WAR & PEACE VOL.1 (THE WAR DISC)** [ ] 7
– Ask about me / Pushin weight / Dr. Frankenstein / Fuck dying / War & peace / Ghetto vet / Greed / MP / Cash over ass / Curse of money / Peckin' order / Limos, demos & bimbos / Once upon a time in the projects 2 / If I was fuckin you / X-bitches / Extradition / 3 strikes you in / Penitentiary.

Mar 00. (cd/d-lp) *(CDPTY/PTYLP 183) <50015>* **WAR & PEACE VOL.2 (THE PEACE DISC)** 56 Feb00 3
– Hello / (pimp homeo) / You ain't gonna lie (ta kick it) / The guitar shit / Supreme hustle / (mental warfare) / 24 mo' hours / Until we rich / You can do it / (mackin' and drivin') / Gotta be insanity / Roll all day / Can you bounce? / (dinner with the CEO) *[d-lp-only]* / Record company pimpin' *[d-lp-only]* / Waitin' ta hate / Nigga of the century / You can do it (instrumental).

May 00. (12"/cd-s; as ICE CUBE featuring MACK 10 & MS. TOI) *(PTY ST/CD 125) <53562>* **YOU CAN DO IT. / UNTIL WE RICH** [ ] Nov99 35

Dec 01. (cd) *(CDPTY 221) <29091>* **GREATEST HITS** (compilation) [ ] 54
– Pushin' weight / Check yo' self / We be clubbin' / $100 bill y'all / Once upon a time in the projects / Bow down (WESTSIDE CONNECTION) / Hello / You can do it / You know how we do it / It was a good day / Bop gun (one nation) / What can I do? (remix) / My summer vacation / Steady mobbin' / Jackin' for beats / The nigga ya love to hate / Late night hour.

ICE-T

Born: TRACY MORROW, 16 Feb'58, Newark, New Jersey, USA. With a ghetto background that reportedly involved copious amounts of unlawful activity, a name derived from superpimp, ICEBERG SLIM, and a mean line in caustic wit, ICE-T set himself up as the original 'gangsta' rapper. The fact of the matter is he wasn't actually the first gangsta rapper, although he did invent the particularly potent West Coast strain. With backing from AFRIKA ISLAM and DJ ALADDIN, his debut for 'Warners', 'RHYME PAYS' (1987), set out the ICE-T agenda of unashamed criminal glorification over tough, made-to-measure beats. 'POWER' (1988) thankfully laid off the "I'm mental, me" sentiments to a certain degree, allowing room for more objectively intelligent lyrics, although that obviously couldn't be applied to 'GIRLS L.G.B.N.A.F.' (LET'S GET BUTT NAKED AND FUCK, dummy). Hardly the most offensive or potentially damaging lyrics in the ICE-T canon, the song nevertheless upset those nice people at the PMRC (an American institutionalised neighbourhood watch scheme for bad pop stars), not the first time he'd upset the powers that be (or would be). This storm in a teacup informed much of 1989's 'THE ICEBERG: FREEDOM OF SPEECH . . . JUST WATCH WHAT YOU SAY', a more rock-based, anti-censorship rant that laid the ground-work for his subsequent BODY COUNT project. The record that really took ICE-T's dubious message to the masses was the landmark 'O.G. ORIGINAL GANGSTER' (1991), a UK Top 5 album that saw ICE powering his way through a hardcore rap set of unrelenting intensity. As ever, the lyrics were sharp, witty and artfully articulate but ultimately offensive. While ICE-T argues that he tells it like it is, his lame attempts to justify his continual objectification of women are rarely satisfactory. It's one of hip hop's great tragedies that a rapper as charismatic, intelligent and creative as ICE-T continues to reinforce prejudice and stereotyping; for every inch that CHUCK D advances the black cause, ICE-T drags it back two. The next logical step for ICE was a foray into the world of heavy metal, another genre not exactly noted for its tolerance. Recruiting ERNIE-C (guitar), D-ROC (guitar), MOOSEMAN (bass) and BEATMASTER V (drums), ICE-T debuted his hardcore/speed metal band, BODY COUNT, on the 1991 Lollapalooza tour prior to the release of their eponymous debut the following year. While the record addressed racism on the likes of 'MOMMA'S GOTTA DIE TONIGHT', the rapper's trademark misogyny was ever present, notably on 'KKK BITCH'. However, the track that really hit the fan squarely with the shit was 'COP KILLER', a nasty little ditty about "taking out" some lawmen. While the LAPD were hardly in a postion to come over all moral, they perhaps understandibly took offence to such sentiments. As did President George Bush and good ol' Ollie North, ICE-T subsequently being given the honour of the biggest threat to American security since McCARTHY flushed out "those damn commies" in the 50's. The final straw for 'Warners' was when record company personnel started receiving death threats, the label finally giving in and removing the offending song from subsequent pressings. While it's arguably one of the functions of art to question the "norm", to go about it in such a club-footed manner ultimately benefits no-one. ICE-T was as defiant as ever, though, moving to 'Virgin' for 'BORN DEAD' (1994), another accomplished collection that wasn't quite so inflammatory. The rapper's solo career continued, meanwhile, with 'HOME INVASION' (1993) upon which, gasp!, the rapper actually admitted to feelings for his fellow man in 'GOTTA LOTTA LOVE' while remaining as unrepentant about his lifestyle as ever, ('THAT'S HOW I'M LIVIN'). It was to be another three years before the next album and in the interim, ICE-T used his not inconsiderable talent to host a Channel 4 documentary on Blaxploitation movies as well as presenting 'Baadaasss TV', a semi-successful attempt at catering for black culture. He also published a book of his forthright opinions which only served to furnish his opponents with yet more ammunition. ICE-T resumed his recording career in typically bigoted fashion with, 'VI: RETURN OF THE REAL' (1996), a cliched gangsta affair that added anti-semitic sentiment to his litany of hate. After a third BODY COUNT effort, 'VIOLENT DEMISE (THE LAST DAYS)' in '97, ICE-T was out on his own once more courtesy of the David Fincher 'Seven'-inspired 'THE SEVENTH DEADLY SIN' (1999). Featuring the 2PAC and BIGGIE tribute track, 'VALUABLE GAME', the album failed to generate much media or chart interest. Had ICE-T finally lost out to his younger rivals.

Album rating: RHYME PAYS (*5) / POWER (*5) / THE ICEBERG: FREEDOM OF SPEECH . . . JUST WATCH WHAT YOU SAY (*7) / O.G. ORIGINAL GANGSTER (*8) / BODY COUNT (*8; with Body Count) / HOME INVASION (*6) / BORN DEAD (*5; with Body Count) / IV: RETURN OF THE REAL (*5) / VIOLENT DEMISE (THE LAST DAYS (*4; with Body Count) / THE SEVENTH DEADLY SIN (*5) / GREATEST HITS: THE EVIDENCE compilation (*7)

ICE-T – vocals / w/**AFRIKA ISLAM** – synthesizers

Sire Sire

Jul 87. (12") *(YZ 145)* **MAKE IT FUNKY. / SEX** [ ] [ ]

Jul 87. (lp/c/cd) *(925602-1/-4/-2) <25602>* **RHYME PAYS** [ ] 93
– (intro) / Rhyme pays / 6 'n the mornin' / Make it funky / Somebody gotta do it (pimpin' ain't easy) / 409 / I love ladies / Sex / Pain / Squeeze the trigger. *(cd-iss. Jan93 on 'Warners'; 7599 25602-2)*

Nov 87. (12") *<020805>* **SOMEBODY GOT DO IT (PIMPIN' AIN'T EASY). / OUR MOST REQUESTED RECORD** [ ] [ ]

Jun 88. (12") *<27902>* **COLORS. / SQUEEZE THE TRIGGER** – 10

Sep 88. (lp/c/cd) *(925765-1/-4/-2)* **POWER** [ ] [35]
– (intro) / Power / Drama / Heartbeat / The syndicate / Radio suckers / I'm your pusher / Personal / High rollers / Girls L.G.B.N.A.F. / Grand larceny / Soul on ice / (outro).

Nov 88. (7") <27768> **I'M YOUR PUSHER. / GIRLS L.G.B.N.A.F.** [–] [ ]
(12"+=) – ('A'instrumental) / ('A'acappella) / ('B'instrumental) / ('B'acappella).

Warners Sire

Mar 89. (7") *(W 7574)* <27574> **HIGH ROLLERS. / THE HUNTED CHILD** [63] [ ]
(12"+=/12"s+=) *(W 7574T/+W)* – Power.

Sep 89. (7") *(W 2802)* <11810> **LETHAL WEAPON. / HEARTBEAT (remix)** [ ] [ ]
(12"+=/cd-s+=) *(W 2802 T/CD)* – ('A'instrumental).

Oct 89. (lp/c)(cd) *(WX 316/+C)*<(926028-2)> **THE ICEBERG: FREEDOM OF SPEECH . . . JUST WATCH WHAT YOU SAY** [42] [37]
– (intro) / Shut up, be happy / The iceberg / Lethal weapon / You played yourself / Peel their caps back / The girl tried to kill me / Black'n'decker / Hit the deck / This one's for me / The hunted child / What ya wanna do? / Freedom of speech / My word is bond. *(cd re-iss. Feb95)*

— guested on CURTIS MAYFIELD's re-make of classic 'Superfly'.

Feb 90. (c-s) <19994> **YOU PLAYED TOURSELF / FREEDOM OF SPEECH** [–] [ ]

Feb 90. (7") *(W 9994)* **YOU PLAYED YOURSELF. / MY WORD IS BOND** [64] [–]
(12"+=) *(W 9994T)* – Freedom of speech (with HENDRIX sample)

Apr 90. (c-s) **WHAT DO YOU WANNA DO? / THE GIRL TRIED TO KILL ME** [–] [ ]

Apr 91. (c-s) <19442> **NEW JACK HUSTLER (NINO'S THEME) / ('A'instrumental)** [ ] [67]

— <above from the film of the same name on US label 'Giant-Sire'>

May 91. (7") **O.G. ORIGINAL GANGSTER. / BITCHES 2** [ ] [ ]
(12"+=/cd-s+=) – Mind over matter / Midnight.

May 91. (cd)(lp/c) <*(7599 26492-2)*>*(WX 412/+C)* **O.G. ORIGINAL GANGSTER** [38] [5]
– Home of the bodybag / First impression / Ziplock / Mic contract / Mind over matter / New Jack hustler / Ed / Bitches 2 (incl. sample:- Dr. Funkenstein) / Straight up nigga / O.G. Original Gangster / The house / Evil E – what about sex? / Fly by / Midnight / Fried chicken / M.V.P.'s / Lifestyles of the rich and infamous / Body count / Prepared to die / Escape from the killing fields / Street killer / Pulse of the rhyme / The tower / Ya should killed me last year. *(cd re-iss. Feb95; same)*

Rhyme Syndicate Rhyme Syndicate

Mar 93. (d-lp/d-c/d-cd) *(RSYN/+C/D 1)* <53858> **HOME INVASION** [15] [14]
– Warning / It's on / Ice MFT / Home invasion / G style / Addicted to danger / Question and answer / Watch the ice break / Race war / That's how I'm livin' / I ain't new ta this / Pimp behind the wheels (DJ Evil E the great) / Gotta lotta love / Hit the fan / Depths of Hell (featuring DADDY NITRO) / 99 problems (featuring BROTHER MARQUIS) / Funky gripsta / Message to the soldier / Ain't a damn thing changed.

Apr 93. (12"ep/c-ep/cd-ep) *(SYND D/C/R 1)* **I AIN'T NEW TA THIS. / MIXED UP / MIXED UP (instrumental)** [62] [ ]

Dec 93. (12"ep/c-ep/cd-ep) *(SYND T/C/D 2)* **THAT'S HOW I'M LIVIN'. / COLOURS – RICOCHET – NEW JACK HUSTLER (film excerpts)** [21] [ ]

Mar 94. (c-s/12"/cd-s) *(SYND C/T/D 3)* **GOTTA LOTTA LOVE. / (2-'A'mixes) / excerpt from book 'The Ice Opinion (who gives a f***)'** [24] [ ]
(cd-s) *(SYNDD 3)* – ('A'mix) / Addicted to danger / G style / Racewar (remixes).

— In Dec 94, ICE-T was credited with WHITFIELD CRANE (Ugly Kid Joe) on MOTORHEAD single 'Born To Raise Hell', hit UK No.47

May 96. (12"/cd-s) *(SYND T/D 5)* **I MUST STAND. / ('A'mixes)** [41] [ ]

May 96. (d-lp/c/cd) *(RSYN/+C/D 3)* <53933> **VI – THE RETURN OF THE REAL** [26] [89]
– Pimp anthem / Where the shit goes down / Bouncin' down the strezeet / Return of the real / I must stand / (Alotta niggas) / Rap games hijacked / How does it feel / The lane / (Rap is fake) / Make the loot loop / Syndicate 4 ever / The 5th / (It's goin' down) / They want me back in / Inside of a gangsta / Forced to do dirt / (Haters) / Cramp your style / (Real).

Nov 96. (12"ep/cd-ep) *(SYND T/D 6)* **THE LANE / ('A'mixes). / BOUNCIN' DOWN THE STREZEET / GET MY CASH ON** [18] [ ]

Roadrunner Coroner

Oct 99. (cd/d-lp) *(RR 8614-2/-1)* <3> **THE SEVENTH DEADLY SIN** [ ] [ ]
– (intro) / Don't hate the playa / Check your game / Get your moneyman / 7th / NY NY / Valuable game / Eye of the storm / Always wanted to be a ho / Brother Marguis (interlude) / Fuck it / CJ Mac (interlude) / Retaliation / Threat / Check your heart / Sondoobiest (interlude) / Hardcore / In common sense / Numbskull (interlude) / God forgive me / Exodus.

Nov 99. (cd-s) *(RR 2137-3)* **VALUABLE GAME / VALUABLE GAME (instrumental) / ICE'S EXODUS (clean version)** [ ] [ ]

– compilations, etc. –

May 93. (cd/c) *Warners; (8122 71170-2/-4)* **THE CLASSIC COLLECTION** [ ] [ ]

Oct 00. (cd/c/lp) *Street Knowledge; (9362 46500-2/-4/-1) / Atomic Pop;* <11> **GREATEST HITS: THE EVIDENCE** [ ] Aug00 [ ]
– 6 'n the mornin' / I'm your pusher / High rollers / You played yourself / Peel their caps back / O.G. Original Gangster / Colors / New jack hustler / Power / I ain't new ta this / That's how I'm livin' / I must stand / Squeeze the trigger / The tower / The lane / Money, power, women.

BODY COUNT

ICE-T with **ERNIE C** – lead guitar / **D-ROC** – rhythm guitar / **MOOSEMAN** – bass / **BEATMASTER 'V'** – drums

Sire Sire

Jan 92. (12"/cd-s; w-drawn) **COP KILLER. / (withdrawn)** [–] [ ]

Mar 92. (cd/c) *(9362 45139-2/-4)* <26876> **BODY COUNT** [ ] [26]
– Smoked pork / Body Count's in the house / New sports / Body count / A statistic / Bowels of the Devil / The real problem / KKK bitch / C note / Voodoo / The winner loses / There goes the neighborhood / Oprah / Evil Dick / Body Count anthem / Momma's gotta die tonight / Freedom of speech.

Jun 92. (12") **THERE GOES THE NEIGHBORHOOD. / KKK BITCH** [ ] [ ]

Rhyme Syndicate Virgin

Sep 94. (red-lp/c/cd) *(RSYN/+C/D 2)* <39802> **BORN DEAD** [15] [74]
– Body M-F Count / Masters of revenge / Killin' floor / Necessary evil / Drive by / Last breath / Hey Joe / Shallow graves / Surviving the game / Who are you / Sweet lobotomy / Born dead.

Sep 94. (c-s) *(SYNDC 4)* **BORN DEAD / BODY COUNT'S IN THE HOUSE (live)** [28] [ ]
(12"pic-d+=) *(SYNDTP 4)* – ('A'live).
(cd-s+=) *(SYNDD 4)* – Body M-F Count (live) / On with the Body Count (live).

Virgin Virgin

Dec 94. (etched-10"pic-d) *(VSA 1529)* **NECESSARY EVIL / NECESSARY EVIL (live) / BOWELS OF THE DEVIL (live)** [45] [ ]
(cd-s) *(VSCDX 1529)* – ('A'side) / Body Count anthem (live) / Drive by (live) / There goes the neighborhood (live).

— **GRIZ** – bass + **O.T.** – drums; repl. MOOSEMAN + BEATMASTER V

Mar 97. (cd/c/lp) *(CD/TC+/V 2813)* <41915> **VIOLENT DEMISE (THE LAST DAYS)** [ ] [ ]
– (interview) / My way (BODY COUNT & RAW BREED) / Strippers intro / Strippers / Truth or death / Violent demise / Bring it to pain / Music business / I used to love her / Root of all evil / Dead man walking / (interview end) / You're fuckin' with BC / Ernie's intro / Dr. K / Last days.

☐ ICICLE WORKS (see under ⇒ McNABB, Ian)

IDLEWILD

Formed: Edinburgh, Scotland . . . late '95 by RODDY WOOMBLE, ROD JONES and COLIN NEWTON, each having a penchant for noise veterans, SONIC YOUTH and FUGAZI. Having met at a party, the erstwhile students whittled away their revision time with ramshackle rehearsals, eventually channelling their frustrations into a debut single, 'QUEEN OF THE TROUBLED TEENS'. Famously financed by a student loan (and issued on their own 'Human Condition' imprint), the track was championed by Radio One DJ Steve Lamacq, duly rescuing the band from eternal toilet gig hell and setting in motion the mechanics of A&R overload. A follow-up single, 'CHANDELIER', appeared on 'Fierce Panda' while an acclaimed mini-album on 'Deceptive', 'CAPTAIN', kickstarted '98 and became their final fully fledged indie release prior to a deal with 'Food'. Somewhere along the way the band also picked up bassist BOB FAIRFOULL and began to coax some melancholic tunefulness from the blizzard of sound and fury that characterised their youthful approach. 'A FILM FOR THE FUTURE' announced their major label arrival in fittingly convulsive style, the first of many minor hits which have cemented the band's reputation as one of Scotland's most talked about and possibly most dedicated sonic abusers. Their highly anticipated first album proper, 'HOPE IS IMPORTANT' (late '98), made the UK Top 60 and the band's steady rise proves that noisy guitars never go out of fashion. '100 BROKEN WINDOWS' (2000) might've been the casualties of noise, perhaps. But surprisingly enough, the four-piece turned the screeching guitars down for this commercially-orientated release. The single, 'THESE WOODEN IDEAS' unveiled another side to the band that used to literally knee-cap themselves on stage. Still, with its edge intact 'LITTLE DISCOURAGE' found IDLEWILD adopting an REM-esque style (circa 1995), and 'THERE'S A GLORY IN YOUR STORY' saw them unplugging their guitars altogether. Still, this set could make ears bleed if played at the correct volume. They toned it down, however, for their next release, the bleakly entitled 'THE REMOTE PART' (2002), an album which flirted with a lot of influences; from the Top 20, AZTEC CAMERA-inspired single 'YOU HELD THE WORLD IN YOUR ARMS' to the punky R.E.M. 'Murmur'-era led 'AMERICAN ENGLISH'. The same formula (seen on the latter LP) remained with 'I NEVER WANTED', a soft, heartfelt acoustic number and even a bit of spoken-word on 'THE REMOTE PART'. The album also crashed into the UK charts at No.3, providing one of Scotland's premier rock bands with the recognition they've been striving for since their musical birth.

Album rating: HOPE IS IMPORTANT (*7) / 100 BROKEN WINDOWS (*7) / THE REMOTE PART (*8)

RODDY WOOMBLE (b.13 Aug'76) – vocals / **ROD JONES** (b. 3 Dec'76) – guitar / **COLIN NEWTON** (b.18 Apr'77) – drums / **PAUL TIPLER** (helped out on) bass

Human Condition — not iss.

Mar 97. (7") *(HC 0017)* **QUEEN OF THE TROUBLED TEENS. / FASTER / SELF HEALER** [ ] [–]
(re-iss. Jan98; same)

—— **BOB FAIRFOULL** (b. 6 Aug'76) – bass; repl. PAUL

Fierce Panda — not iss.

Dec 97. (ltd-7") *(NING 42)* **CHANDELIER. / I WANT TO BE A WRITER** [ ] [–]

Deceptive — not iss.

Jan 98. (m-cd) *(BLUFF 058CD)* **CAPTAIN** [ ] [–]
– Self healer / Annihilate now / Captain / Last night I missed all the fireworks / Satan polaroid / You just have to be who you are.

Feb 98. (7") *(BLUFF 057)* **SATAN POLAROID. / HOUSE ALONE** [ ] [–]

Food — Odeon-EMI

Apr 98. (7") *(FOOD 111)* **A FILM FOR THE FUTURE. / MINCE SHOWERCAP (part I)** [53] [–]
(cd-s+=) *(CDFOOD 111)* – What am I going to do?

Jul 98. (7") *(FOOD 113)* **EVERYONE SAYS YOU'RE SO FRAGILE. / MINCE SHOWERCAP (part II)** [47] [–]
(cd-s+=) *(CDFOOD 113)* – Theory of achievement.

Oct 98. (7") *(FOOD 114)* **I'M A MESSAGE. / MINCE SHOWERCAP (part III)** [41] [–]
(cd-s+=) *(CDFOOD 114)* – This is worse.
(cd-s) **THE SESSIONS EP** *(CDFOODS 114)* – ('A'live) / Satan polaroid (live) / You've lost your way (live).

Oct 98. (cd/c/lp) *(497132-2/-4/-1)* <9504> **HOPE IS IMPORTANT** [53] [ ]
– You've lost your way / A film for the future / Paint nothing / When I argue I see shapes / 4 people do good / I'm happy to be here tonight / Everyone says you're so fragile / I'm a message / You don't have the heart / Close the door / Safe and sound / Low light.

Feb 99. (7") *(FOOD 116)* **WHEN I ARGUE I SEE SHAPES. / (1903-70) / CHANDELIER (10.15 version)** [19] [–]
(cd-s) *(CDFOOD 116)* – (first 2 tracks) / Last night I missed all the fireworks (live).
(cd-s) *(CDFOODS 116)* – (first & third tracks) / Palace flophouse.

Sep 99. (7") *(FOOD 124)* **LITTLE DISCOURAGE. / BROKEN WINDOWS** [24] [–]
(cd-s+=) *(CDFOOD 124)* – A-Tone.
(cd-s) *(CDFOODS 124)* – ('A'side) / You don't have the heart (live) / 1990 – night-time.

Mar 00. (7") *(FOOD 127)* **ACTUALLY IT'S DARKNESS. / MEET ME AT THE HARBOUR** [23] [–]
(cd-s+=) *(CDFOODS 127)* – West Haven.
(cd-s) *(CDFOOD 127)* – ('A'side) / Forgot to follow / It'll take a long time.

Apr 00. (cd/c/lp) *(FOOD CD/TC/LP 32)* <65397> **100 BROKEN WINDOWS** [15] May00 [ ]
– Little discourage / I don't have the map / These wooden ideas / Roseability / Idea track / Let me sleep (next to the mirror) / Listen to what you've got / Actually it's darkness / Rusty / Mistake pageant / Quiet crown / The bronze medal.

Jun 00. (7") *(FOOD 132)* **THESE WOODEN IDEAS. / THERE'S GLORY IN YOUR STORY** [32] [–]
(c-s) *(TCFOOD 132)* – ('A'side) / When the ship comes in.
(cd-s+=) *(CDFOODS 132)* – (three tracks above).
(cd-s) *(CDFOOD 132)* – ('A'side) / Actually it's darkness (acoustic) / Rescue.

Oct 00. (7") *(FOOD 134)* **ROSEABILITY. / RUSTY (the poop soldier mix)** [38] [–]
(cd-s+=) *(CDFOOD 134)* – A thousand.
(cd-s) *(CDFOODS 134)* – ('A'side) / I've only just begun / Self healer (live acoustic version) / ('A'-CD-Rom).

Parlophone — E.M.I.

Apr 02. (7") *(R 6575)* <55078-2> **YOU HELD THE WORLD IN YOUR ARMS. / A DISTANT HISTORY** [9] May02 [ ]
(cd-s+=) *(CDR 6575)* – I was made to think it.
(cd-s) *(CDRS 6575)* – ('A'side) / All this information / No generation.

Jul 02. (7") *(R 6582)* **AMERICAN ENGLISH. / POOR THING** [15] [–]
(cd-s+=) *(CDRS 6582)* – These are just years / ('A'-CD-video).
(cd-s) *(CDR 6582)* – ('A'side) / The nothing I know / We always have to impress.

Jul 02. (cd/lp) *(540243-2/-1)* **THE REMOTE PART** [3] [–]
– You held the world in your arms / A modern way of letting go / American English / I never wanted / (I am) What I am not / Live in a hiding place / Out of routine / Century after century / Tell me ten words / Stay the same / In remote part – Scottish fiction.

Oct 02. (7") *(R 6587)* **LIVE IN A HIDING PLACE. / GREAT TIMES WASTED** [26] [–]
(cd-s+=) *(CDR 6587)* – Everything flows / ('A'-video).
(cd-s) *(CDRS 6587)* – ('A'side) / Found that essence rare / I'm happy to be here tonight (live).

—— FAIRFOUL had already departed September 2002

Feb 03. (7") *(R 6598)* **A MODERN WAY OF LETTING GO. / IN REMOTE PART** [28] [–]
(cd-s+=) *(CDR 6598)* – Scottish fiction (live) / ('A'-live).

– compilations, etc. –

Oct 02. (d-cd) *Parlophone; (543148-2)* **100 BROKEN WINDOWS / HOPE IS IMPORTANT** [ ] [–]

Billy IDOL

Born: WILLIAM BROAD, 30 Nov'55, Stanmore, Middlesex, England. In 1976, this aspring punk formed GENERATION X alongside BOB ANDREWS and ex-CHELSEA members, TONY JAMES and JOHN TOWE (the latter was soon replaced by former SUBWAY SECT man, MARK LAFF). Though they attracted a loyal fanbase, GENERATION X were never considered a dyed-in-the-wool punk band per se, their more commercial, hooky power pop at odds with the genre's inherent nihilism. Signed to 'Chrysalis', the band hit the Top 40 with their first single, 'YOUR GENERATION', following it up with 'WILD YOUTH' and 'READY STEADY GO', the latter track a decidedly un-punk 60's tribute. An eponymous debut album hit the Top 30 in Spring '78, while the band's sound grew increasingly commercial on successive albums, 'VALLEY OF THE DOLLS' (1979; produced by IAN HUNTER) and 'KISS ME DEADLY' (1981; released under the slightly clipped moniker of GEN X). Following their split in '81, JAMES later formed SIGUE SIGUE SPUTNIK, while the bleached-blond IDOL was free to pursue his barely concealed desire for pop stardom. Relocating to New York, he met manager, Bill Aucoin and producer, Keith Forsey, recruiting guitarist STEVE STEVENS and cutting a cover of Tommy James & The Shondells' 'MONY MONY' (along with a few other tracks – including the GENERATION X song, 'DANCING WITH MYSELF' – it formed part of a US-only mini-set, 'DON'T STOP'). A full length eponymous debut album followed in summer '82, the record including many songs which wouldn't hit the UK charts for another five years. The loping 'HOT IN THE CITY', for example, which became IDOL's first major US success; with the not inconsiderable, IDOL transformed himself into a leather-clad, lip-sneering hard rocker, his anthemic, dancefloor-friendly tunes lapped up by American teeny boppers and older fans alike. 'REBEL YELL' (1984) and the attendant 'EYES WITHOUT A FACE' single gave him further Stateside success, while a re-released 'WHITE WEDDING' gave IDOL a belated UK Top 10 hit in summer '85. A remix compilation, 'VITAL IDOL', was rush released the following month to build on the breakthrough, precipitating a rash of re-issued singles; while sales of his 'WHIPLASH SMILE' (1986) opus certainly benefitted, these re-issues were all bigger hits than his new material, not exactly a good sign. Just prior to the release of 'CHARMED LIFE' (1990), IDOL, ironically enough, suffered a near fatal motorbike crash, the climax to a troubled late 80's period which had seen the singer living out the rock'n'roll lifestyle to the full in sunny L.A. Bluesy and confessional, the album's only hit was 'CRADLE OF LOVE', while the less said about IDOL's cover of The Doors' 'L.A. WOMAN', the better. An ill-advised concept album, 'CYBERPUNK' (1993), was even less well received, fallen IDOL indeed. • **Songwriters:** GENERATION X:- IDOL – JAMES, except GIMME SOME TRUTH (John Lennon) / SHAKIN' ALL OVER (hit; Johnny Kidd & The Pirates). Solo, IDOL & STEVENS collaborated until 1990 when IDOL wrote with WERNER. Solo Covers; HEROIN (Lou Reed) / MOTHER DAWN (McBrook – Youth).

Album rating: Generation X: GENERATION X (*6) / VALLEY OF THE DOLLS (*5) / KISS ME DEADLY (*5) / PERFECT HITS compilation (*7) / Billy Idol: BILLY IDOL (*6) / REBEL YELL (*7) / WHIPLASH SMILE (*5) / VITAL IDOL remixes (*5) / CHARMED LIFE (*6) / CYBERPUNK (*3) / IDOL SONGS – 11 OF THE BEST compilation (*7) / GREATEST HITS compilation (*7)

GENERATION X

BILLY IDOL – vocals (ex-CHELSEA, ex-INFANTS) / **BOB 'Derwood' ANDREWS** – guitar / **TONY JAMES** – bass, vocals (ex-CHELSEA, ex-INFANTS) / **MARK LAFF** – drums (ex-SUBWAY SECT) repl. JOHN TOWE (ex-CHELSEA, ex-INFANTS) who joined ALTERNATIVE TV then ADVERTS, etc

		Chrysalis	Chrysalis
Sep 77.	(7") *(CHS 2165)* **YOUR GENERATION. / DAY BY DAY**	36	
Dec 77.	(7") *(CHS 2189)* **WILD YOUTH. / WILD DUB**		
	(some copies were mispressed with b-side 'NO NO NO')		
Mar 78.	(7") *(CHS 2207)* **READY STEADY GO. / NO NO NO**	47	
Mar 78.	(lp/c) *(CHR/ZCHR 1169)* **GENERATION X**	29	
	– From the heart / One hundred punks / Listen / Ready steady go / Kleenex / Promises promises / Day by day / The invisible man / Kiss me deadly / Too personal / Youth, youth, youth. *(cd-iss. Jan86; CCD 1169) (re-iss. cd Mar94; CD25CR 14) (cd re-iss. Jul96 on 'EMI Gold'; CDGOLD 1039)*		
Jan 79.	(7",7"red,7"pink,7"orange,7"yellow) *(CHS 2261)* **KING ROCKER. / GIMME SOME TRUTH**	11	
Jan 79.	(lp/c) *(CHR/ZCHR 1193)* **VALLEY OF THE DOLLS**	51	
	– Running with the boss sound / Night of the Cadillacs / Paradise west / Friday's angels / King rocker / Valley of the dolls / English dream / Love like fire / Paradise west / The prime of Kenny Silvers. *(cd-iss. Jan86; CCD 1193)*		
Mar 79.	(7",7"brown) *(CHS 2310)* **VALLEY OF THE DOLLS. / SHAKIN' ALL OVER**	23	
Jun 79.	(7",7"pink) *(CHS 2330)* **FRIDAY'S ANGELS. / TRYING FOR KICKS / THIS HEAT**	62	

— **TERRY CHIMES** – drums (ex-CLASH, ex-COWBOYS INTERNATIONAL) repl. LAFF / **JAMES STEPHENSON** – guitar (ex-CHELSEA) repl. 'DERWOOD' (later to WESTWORLD)

GEN X

Sep 80.	(7") *(CHS 2444)* **DANCING WITH MYSELF. / UGLY RASH**	62	
	(12"+=) *(CHS12 2444)* – Loopy dub / What do you want		
Jan 81.	(lp/c) *(CHR/ZCHR 1327)* **KISS ME DEADLY**		
	– Dancing with myself / Untouchables / Happy people / Heaven's inside / Triumph / Revenge / Stars look down / What do you want / Oh mother. *(cd-iss. Jan86; CCD 1327)*		
Jan 81.	(7"ep,7"clear-ep/12"ep) *(CHS/+12 2488)* **DANCING WITH MYSELF / UNTOUCHABLES. / KING ROCKER / ROCK ON**	60	

— split early '81, when BILLY went solo. CHIMES rejoined The CLASH, TONY JAMES later formed SIGUE SIGUE SPUTNIK. STEPHENSON later joined GENE LOVES JEZEBEL, then The CULT.

– compilations, etc. –

on 'Chrysalis' unless otherwise mentioned

Nov 85.	(lp/c) *(CHM/ZCHM 1521)* **THE BEST OF GENERATION X**		
Feb 87.	(7") *Old Gold; (OG 9693)* **KING ROCKER. / VALLEY OF THE DOLLS**		-
Jun 87.	(lp) *M.B.C.; (JOCKLP 9)* **THE ORIGINAL GENERATION X**		-
Jun 88.	(lp) *M.B.C.; (JOCKLP 11)* **GENERATION X LIVE (live)**		-
Oct 91.	(cd/c/lp) *(CCD/ZCHR/CHR 1854)* **PERFECT HITS (1975-81)**		
	– Dancing with myself / Your generation / Ready steady go / The untouchables / Day by day / Wild youth / Wild dub / One hundred punks / King rocker / Kiss me deadly / Gimme some truth / New order / English dream / Triumph / Youth, youth, youth.		

BILLY IDOL

— with **STEVE STEVENS** – guitar / **PHIL FEIT** – bass / **STEVE MISSAL** – drums (same label)

Sep 81.	(7") *(CHS 2543)* **MONY MONY. / BABY TALK**		
	(12"+=) *(CHS12 2543)* – Untouchables / Dancing with myself (extended). *<US-title 'DON'T STOP' m-lp; 4000>; hit No.71.*		
Jul 82.	(lp/c) *(CHR/ZCHR 1377) <41377>* **BILLY IDOL**		45
	– Come on, come on / White wedding (part 1 & 2) / Hot in the city / Dead on arrival / Nobody's business / Love calling / Hole in the wall / Shooting stars / It's so cruel / Congo man. *(cd-iss. Jan86; CCD 1377) (re-iss. Jul94 cd/c;) (cd re-iss. Jan02 ++; 532860-2)* – Dancing with myself.		
Aug 82.	(7"/7"pic-d/ext.12") *(CHS/+P/12 2625) <2605>* **HOT IN THE CITY. / DEAD ON ARRIVAL**	58 Jun82	23
Oct 82.	(7"/ext.12") *(CHS/+12 2656) <42697>* **WHITE WEDDING. / HOLE IN THE WALL**		36
Sep 83.	(7",7"clear) *(IDOL 1)* **WHITE WEDDING. / HOT IN THE CITY**		-
	(12"+=) *(IDOLX 1)* – Love calling / Dancing with myself.		
Jan 84.	(lp/c) *(CHR/ZCHR 1450) <41450>* **REBEL YELL**	Nov83	6
	– Rebel yell / Daytime drama / Eyes without a face / Blue highway / Flesh for fantasy / Catch my fall / Crank call / (Do not) Stand in the shadows / The dead next door. *(hit UK No.36 Sep85) (cd-iss. Jan86; CCD 1450) (re-iss. cd Mar94;)*		

Feb 84. (7"/7"square-pic-d) *(IDOL/+P 2) <42762>* **REBEL YELL. / CRANK CALL** [62] Jan84 [46]
(12"+=) *(IDOLX 2)* – White wedding.
(d7"++=) *(IDOLD 2)* – Hot in the city.

Jun 84. (7") *(IDOL 3) <42786>* **EYES WITHOUT A FACE. / THE DEAD NEXT DOOR** [18] Apr84 [4]
(d7"+=/12"+=/12"pic-d+=) *(IDOL D/X/P 3)* – Dancing with myself / Rebel yell.

Sep 84. (7") *(IDOL 4) <42809>* **FLESH FOR FANTASY. / BLUE HIGHWAY** [54] Aug84 [29]
(12"+=/12"pic-d+=) *(IDOL X/P 4)* – ('A'extended).

Oct 84. (7") *<42840>* **CATCH MY FALL. / DAYTIME DRAMA** [–] [50]

Jun 85. (7",7"white) *(IDOL 5)* **WHITE WEDDING. / FLESH FOR FANTASY** [6] [–]
(7"clear/12",12"white/12"pic-d) *(IDOL/+X/P 5)* – ('A'-Shotgun mix pts.1 & 2) / Mega-Idol-mix.

Jul 85. (lp/c) *(CUX/ZCUX 1502) <41620>* **VITAL IDOL** (remix compilation) [7] Oct87 [10]
– White wedding (part 1 & 2) / Mony mony (downtown mix) / Hopt in the city / Dancing with myself (uptown mix) / Flesh for fantasy (below the belt mix) / To be a lover (mother of mercy mix) / Love calling (rub a dub dub mix) / Catch my fall (remix). *(cd-iss. Jan86; CCD 1502) (cd re-iss. Jan02; 532859-2)*

Sep 85. (7"/7"pic-d) *(IDOL/+P 6)* **REBEL YELL. / (DO NOT) STAND IN THE SHADOWS (live)** [6] [ ]
(12"+=/12"pic-d+=) *(IDOL X/P 6)* – Blue highway.

Sep 86. (7",7"colrd) *(IDOL 8) <43024>* **TO BE A LOVER. / ALL SUMMER SINGLE** [22] [6]
(12"+=/12"pic-d+=) *(IDOL X/P 8)* – ('A'-Mercy mix).
(d12"++=) *(IDOLD 8)* – White wedding.

Oct 86. (lp/c/cd) *(CDL/ZCDL/CCD 1514) <41514>* **WHIPLASH SMILE** [8] [6]
– Worlds forgotten boy / To be a lover / Soul standing by / Sweet sixteen / Man for all seasons / Don't need a gun / Beyond belief / Fatal charm / All summer single / One night, one chance. *(re-iss. Mar93 cd/c;)*

Feb 87. (7",7"colrd) *(IDOL 9) <43087>* **DON'T NEED A GUN. / FATAL CHARM** [26] Jan87 [37]
(12"+=/12"pic-d+=) *(IDOL X/P 9)* – ('A'version).
(d7"+=) *(IDOLD 9)* – (free single).

May 87. (7") *(IDOL 10) <43114>* **SWEET 16. / BEYOND BELIEF** [17] Apr87 [20]
(12"+=/12"pic-d+=) *(IDOL X/P 10)* – Rebel yell.

Sep 87. (7") *(IDOL 11) <43161>* **MONY MONY (live). / SHAKIN' ALL OVER (live)** [7] Aug87 [1]
(12"+=) *(IDOLX 11)* – ('A'-Hung like a pony mix).

Jan 88. (7") *(IDOL 12) <43203>* **HOT IN THE CITY (remix). / CATCH MY FALL (remix)** [13] Dec87 [48]
(12"+=) *(IDOLX 12)* – Soul standing by.
('A'-Exterminator mix-cd-s++=) *(IDOLCD 12)* – Mony Mony (live).

Jun 88. (lp/c/cd) *(BILTV/ZBILTV/BILCD 1)* **IDOL SONGS – 11 OF THE BEST** (compilation) [2] [–]
– Rebel yell / Hot in the city / White wedding / Eyes without a face / Catch my fall / Mony mony / To be a lover / Sweet sixteen / Flesh for fantasy / Don't need a gun / Dancing with myself.

Aug 88. (7"/12"/cd-s) *(IDOL/+X/CD 13)* **CATCH MY FALL (the remix fix). / ALL SUMMER SINGLE (remix)** [63] [–]

—— now with **MARK YOUNGER-SMITH** – guitar, bass / **KEITH FORSEY** – drums, producer **VITO** and **PHIL SOUSSAN** – bass / **ARTHUR BARROW** – keyboards / **MIKE BAIRD** – drums

Apr 90. (7"/c-s) *(IDOL/+C 14) <23509>* **CRADLE OF LOVE. / 311 MAN** [34] [2]
(12") *(IDOLX 14)* – ('A'extended) / Rob the cradle of love.
(cd-s) *(IDOLCD 14)* – (all 3 tracks above).

Apr 90. (cd/c/lp) *(CD/Z+/CHR 1735) <21735>* **CHARMED LIFE** [15] [11]
– The loveless / Pumping on steel / Prodigal blues / L.A. woman / Trouble with the sweet stuff / Cradle of love / Mark of Caine / Endless sleep / Love unchained / The right way / License to thrill.

Jul 90. (7"/c-s) *(IDOL/+C 15) <23571>* **L.A. WOMAN. / LICENSE TO THRILL** [70] [52]
(12"+=/cd-s+=) *(IDOL X/CD 15)* – Love child.

Dec 90. (7"/c-s) *(IDOL/+C 16)* **PRODIGAL BLUES. / MARK OF CAINE** [47] [ ]
(12"+=/cd-s+=) *(IDOL X/CD 16)* – Flesh for fantasy.

—— retained co-writer **YOUNGER-SMITH** + recruited **ROBIN HANCOCK** – keyboards, producer / **DOUG WIMBUSH** – bass / **JAMIE MAMOBERAC** – organ / **TAL BERGHAN** – drums

Jun 93. (7"/12") *(CHS/+12 3994)* **SHOCK TO THE SYSTEM. / HEROIN (overloads mix) / HEROIN (durge trance dub)** [30] [ ]
(cd-s) *(CHSCD1 3994)* – ('A'side) / Heroin (original) / Rebel yell.
(cd-s) *(CHSCD2 3994)* – ('A'side) / Heroin (smack attack) / White wedding.

Jun 93. (cd/c/lp) *(CD/Z+/CHR 6000) <26000>* **CYBERPUNK** [20] [48]
– Wasteland / Shock to the system / Tomorrow people / Adam in chains / Neuromancer / Power junkie / Love labours on / Heroin / Shangrila / Concrete kingdom / Venus / Then the night comes / Mother Dawn.

Sep 93. (c-s/7") *(TC+/CHS 5002)* **ADAM IN CHAINS. / SHOCK TO THE SYSTEM / VENUS** [ ] [–]
(cd-s) *(CSCHSS 5002)* – (first 2) / Eyes without a face.
(cd-s) *(CDCHS 5002)* – ('A'side) / Tomorrow people / Mony Mony.

Fox-Arista Fox-Arista

Sep 94. (7"/c-s/cd-s) *(74321 22347-7/-4/-2)* **SPEED. / REBEL YELL (acoustic)** [47] [ ]
(above from the film of the same name)

—— BILLY was to give up the music biz after above

– compilations, etc. –

on 'Chrysalis' unless mentioned otherwise

Mar 01. (cd) *(<5 28812-2>)* **GREATEST HITS** [ ] [74]
– Dancing with myself / Mony Mony (studio) / Hot in the city / White wedding / Rebel yell / Eyes without a face / Flesh for fantasy / Catch my fall / To be a lover / Don't need a gun / Sweet sixteen / Cradle of love / L.A. woman / Shock to the system / Rebel yell (live acoustic) / Don't you forget about me.

Feb 02. (cd) *(<536919-2>)* **VH-1 STORYTELLERS (live)** [ ] [ ]

Mar 03. (cd) *E.M.I.; (58221-2)* **THE ESSENTIAL BILLY IDOL** [ ] [–]

Mar 03. (d-cd) *(581768-2)* **VITAL IDOL / CHARMED LIFE** [ ] [–]

☐ James IHA (see under ⇒ SMASHING PUMPKINS)

Natalie IMBRUGLIA

Born: 4 Feb'75, Sydney, Australia. Before becoming one of Europe's biggest selling pop/rock artists in 1998, IMBRUGLIA was just one of the many soap actresses groomed to become a singer/performer. The childlike brunette was born in a small beach community and grew up with her three sisters who had all been a major influence in her ambitions to become an actress. IMBRUGLIA's lucky break came when Australian soap 'Neighbours' offered her a leading part. The role subsequently led her to widespread popularity amongst pre-pubescent teenagers, who heralded her as their new pin-up. After becoming tired of her acting life, she flitted to London in 1996 in the hope of becoming a pop star, hooking up with former CURE guitarist PHIL THORNALLY and signing an album contract with 'R.C.A.'. Her debut single, 'TORN' was launched in October 1997, a track that had previously been a local hit in 1994 for L.A. outfit, EDNASWAP. NATALIE's version became one of the most heavily rotated songs on UK radio, narrowly missing No.1 and spending an amazing 14 weeks in the charts. Few had predicted the runaway success of the single, many critics writing-off IMBRUGLIA as a lightweight ALANIS MORISSETTE impersonator. A month later, her debut set 'LEFT OF THE MIDDLE' (1997) was released in Australia and Britain (the following Spring in the USA) and included follow-up hits 'BIG MISTAKE' and 'WISHING I WAS THERE', the latter displaying more ALANIS traits through its use of heavy distortion and angry, but radio-friendly vocals. Another highlight was 'SMOKE', a soft ballad in the mould of FIONA APPLE or perhaps LISA LOEB. NATALIE returned in 1999 to sing on a Various Superstar charity re-vamp of the Rolling Stones' 'IT'S ONLY ROCK'N'ROLL', while also guesting on TOM JONES' star-studded cover album 'RELOAD' (the track in question being the

INXS song, 'Never Tear Us Apart'). After such a long hiatus from the music industry, IMBRUGLIA returned in 2001 with 'WHITE LILIES ISLAND', a more accomplished album than her debut 'LEFT OF THE MIDDLE'. The themes were pretty much the same; betrayal, lost love, but this time all shot through with a 'songwriter' sensibility. The single, 'THAT DAY', where IMBRUGLIA was doing her best SHERYL CROW impression (and trying to fit in as many words into one line as humanly possible), entered the charts at No.11, a far cry from her Top 3 'TORN'. Meanwhile the album itself didn't even manage to reach the Top 10.

Album rating: LEFT OF THE MIDDLE (*6) / WHITE LILIES ISLAND (*5)

NATALIE IMBRUGLIA – vocals / with various session people

R.C.A. R.C.A.

Oct 97. (c-s) *(74321 52798-4)* *<radio play>* **TORN / SOMETIMES** [2] 1998 [42]
(cd-s+=) *(74321 52798-2)* – Frightened child.
(cd-s) *(74321 52799-2)* – ('A'side) / Contradictions / Diving in at the deep end.

Nov 97. (cd/c) *(74321 54441-21/-45)* <67634> **LEFT OF THE MIDDLE** [5] Mar98 [10]
– Torn / One more addiction / Big mistake / Leave me alone / Intuition / Smoke / Pigeons and crumbs / Don't you think? / Impressed / Wishing I was there / City / Left of the middle.

Mar 98. (c-s) *(74321 56678-4)* **BIG MISTAKE / SOMETHING BETTER** [2] [–]
(cd-s+=) *(74321 56678-2)* – Torn (MTV unplugged) / ('A'-video).
(cd-s) *(74321 56679-2)* – ('A'side) / I've been watching you / Tomorrow morning.

May 98. (c-s) *(74321 58506-4)* **WISHING I WAS THERE / WHY** [19] [–]
(cd-s+=) *(74321 58506-2)* – Big mistake (live for MTV).
(cd-s) *(74321 58515-2)* – ('A'side) / ('A'-transistor remix) / Impressed (Tim Bran remix).

Oct 98. (c-s) *(74321 62194-4)* **SMOKE / CITY (live in Manhattan)** [5] [–]
(cd-s+=) *(74321 62194-2)* – ('A'-Martyn Phillips & Marc Fox mix) / ('A;-video).
(cd-s) *(74321 62149-5)* – ('A'side) / ('A'remixes; Ganja Kru / Way Out West / Beloved hypnoxic).

Oct 01. (c-s) *(74321 89357-4)* **THAT DAY / SHIKALYA** [11] [–]
(cd-s+=) *(74321 89357-2)* – Just another day / ('A'video).
(cd-s) *(74321 89679-2)* – ('A'mixes).

Nov 01. (cd/c/lp) *(74321 89120-2/-4/-1)* <68082> **WHITE LILIES ISLAND** [15] Jan02 [35]
– That day / Beauty on the fire / Satellite / Do you love? / Wrong impression / Goodbye / Everything goes / Hurricane / Sunlight / Talk in tongues / Butterflies / Come September.

Mar 02. (c-s) *(74321 92835-4)* *<radio>* **WRONG IMPRESSION / ALWAYS NEVER** [10] [64]
(cd-s+=) *(74321 92835-2)* – Hide behind the sun / ('A'-video).

Jul 02. (c-s) *(74321 94702-4)* **BEAUTY ON THE FIRE / (mix)** [26] [–]
(cd-s+=) *(74321 94702-2)* – Broken thread / ('A'-video).
(cd-s) *(74321 95036-2)* – ('A'side) / Cold air / Standing there.

□ IN-BE-TWEENS (see under ⇒ SLADE)

INCREDIBLE STRING BAND

Formed: Glasgow, Scotland ... early 1966 by ROBIN WILLIAMSON, London-born CLIVE PALMER and MIKE HERON. From the early 60's, WILLIAMSON had played London gigs alongside BERT JANSCH (future PENTANGLE), before he returned to Glasgow. In April 1961, he formed a duo with Englishman PALMER, although they found it difficult to establish themselves, that is, until 1965 when PALMER set up the 'Incredible' folk club in Sauchiehall Street. That same year, the pair performed at the Edinburgh Folk Festival, catching the eye of Nathan Joseph of 'Transatlantic' records who recorded them for the concert's Various Artists compilation. After their folk club was shut down by the police, they became a trio, adding MIKE HERON to become The INCREDIBLE STRING BAND. After months tracking them down, American producer JOE BOYD finally found them and duly signed them to 'Elektra'. He subsequently took them to London, where they recorded their eponymous debut album (summer '66). With this well-received record under their belt, PALMER departed for Afghanistan. When he returned he declined to re-join the act, who were now broke but under the management of BOYD. Upon ROBIN's return from Morocco, the duo (augmented by some friends), played an 'Elektra' records package alongside TOM PAXTON and JUDY COLLINS, at The Royal Albert Hall. It helped promote their second album, 'THE 5000 SPIRITS OR THE LAYERS OF THE ONION', which made the UK Top 30 in 1967. Their underground blend of psychedelic folk was crystallised on such charming tracks as, 'CHINESE WHITE', 'FIRST GIRL I LOVED' and 'PAINTING BOX'. In Spring '68, they surprisingly crashed into the UK Top 5 with their third set, 'THE HANGMAN'S BEAUTIFUL DAUGHTER'. The album's witty lyrics (alternately penned by HERON or WILLIAMSON) and ethnic multi-instrumentation was embellished with the vocals of the duo's girlfriends, LICORICE and ROSE. The highlights of this album, arguably the group's finest hour, were 'A VERY CELLULAR SONG', 'THE MINOTAUR'S SONG' and 'KOEEOADDI THERE'. Late that year, they issued 2 single lp's as a double-set, 'WEE TAM' & 'THE BIG HUGE'. However, this brilliant but confused package failed to sell. Over the next two years, they released three UK Top 40 albums ('I LOOKED UP', a collection of baroque eclecticism – 'U' verging on pantomine), but after a move to 'Island' in 1971, they soon faded from the commercial limelight. Nevertheless, the second 'Island' album, 'LIQUID ACROBAT AS REGARDS THE AIR', hit the Top 50, boasting the spine-tingling melancholy of the 11-minute 'DARLING BELLE'. HERON and WILLIAMSON went their separate ways in the mid-70's, the former writing 'DON'T KILL IT CAROL' (later a hit for MANFRED MANN'S EARTH BAND), the latter becoming something of a self-styled cosmic folk storyteller (complete with harp). WILLIAMSON recorded a plethora of albums and poetry between 1977 to the present day and even established his own imprint, 'Pig's Whisker'. Although HERON hasn't been quite as visible since the ISB's split, he has surfaced with the occasional solo set, harking back to an ISB-style sound on 1996's 'WHERE THE MYSTICS SWIM'. Another old ISB face cropped up in 1999 as ROBIN recorded 'AT THE PURE FOUNTAIN' with CLIVE PALMER, the pair completing a second set, 'JUST LIKE THE IVY', the following year. The big news, however, was a full INCREDIBLE STRING BAND reunion at the 2001 Celtic Connections Festival in Glasgow, messrs WILLIAMSON, HERON, PALMER plus newcomers LAWSON DANDO and BINA WILLIAMSON (ROBIN's wife) putting in an acclaimed performance which more than justified the hype and boded well for the future.

Album rating: THE INCREDIBLE STRING BAND (*6) / THE 5000 SPIRITS OR THE LAYERS OF THE ONION (*9) / THE HANGMAN'S BEAUTIFUL DAUGHTER (*9) / WEE TAM (*8) / THE BIG HUGE (*7) / CHANGING HORSES (*5) / I LOOKED UP (*4) / "U" (*4) / RELICS OF . . . compilation (*7) / BE GLAD FOR THE SONG HAS NO ENDING (*4) / LIQUID ACROBAT AS REGARDS THE AIR (*5) / EARTHSPAN (*4) / NO RUINOUS FEUD (*5) / HARD ROPE AND SILKEN TWINE (*4) / SEASONS THEY CHANGE – THE BEST OF THE INCREDIBLE STRING BAND compilation (*8)

ROBIN WILLIAMSON (b.24 Nov'43, Edinburgh, Scotland) – vocals, guitars, etc. / **CLIVE PALMER** (b. 1943, Edmonton, London, England) – guitar, banjo, vocals / **MIKE HERON** (b.12 Dec'42, Glasgow, Scotland) – vocals, rhythm guitar, sitar, etc.

Elektra Elektra

Jun 66. (lp) *(EUK 254)* *<EKS 7322>* **THE INCREDIBLE STRING BAND**
– Maybe someday / October song / When the music starts to play / Schaeffer's jig / Womankind / The tree / Whistle tune / Dandelion blues / How happy am I / Empty pocket blues / Smoke shovelling song / Can't keep me here / Good as gone / Footsteps of the heron / Niggertown / Everything's fine right now. *(re-iss. Jul68; EKL 254); hit No.34) (cd-iss. Jul93; 7559 61547-2) (cd re-iss. Jun94 on 'Hannibal'; HNCD 4437)*

— now a duo when PALMER went to abroad; he later formed FAMOUS JUG BAND — added **CHRISTINA 'LICORICE' McKECHNIE** – some vocals, organ (a guest on below) plus guests **DANNY THOMPSON** – double bass (of PENTANGLE) / **JOHN HOPKINS** – piano

Jul 67. (lp; mono/stereo) *(EUK/+S7 257)* *<EKS 74010>* **THE 5000 SPIRITS OR THE LAYERS OF THE ONION** 26
– Chinese white / No sleep blues / Painting box / The Mad Hatter's song / Little cloud / The eyes of fate / Blues for the muse / The hedgehog's song / First girl I loved / You know that you could be / My name is death / Gently tender / Way back in the 1960s. *(re-iss. 1968; EKS 7257) (re-iss. Jan73 + 1976; K 42001) (cd-iss. Mar92; 7559 60913-2) (cd re-iss. Jun94 on 'Hannibal'; HNCD 4438)*

Mar 68. (7") *(EKSN 45028)* **PAINTING BOX. / NO SLEEP BLUES** –

Mar 68. (lp; mono/stereo) *(EUK/+S7 258)* *<EKS 74021>* **THE HANGMAN'S BEAUTIFUL DAUGHTER** 5 Jun68
– Koeeoaddi there / The minotaur's song / Witches hat / A very cellular song / Mercy I cry city / Waltz of the new Moon / The water song / Three is a green crown / Swift as the wind / Nightfall. *(re-iss. Jan73 + 1976; K 42002) (cd-iss. Mar92; 7559 60835-2) (cd re-iss. Jun94 on 'Hannibal'; HNCD 4437)*

— **MIKE, ROBIN** and his girlfriend **LICORICE** introduced MIKE'S girlfriend **ROSE SIMPSON** – some vocals, bass, percussion, violin

Oct 68. (d-lp; mono/stereo) *(EKL/EKS7 4036-7)* **WEE TAM / THE BIG HUGE** –
(d-cd-iss. Nov94 on 'Hannibal'; HNCD 4802) (d-cd re-iss. Jul02 on 'Collector's Choice'; CCM 0290-2)

Oct 68. (lp; mono/stereo) *(EKL/<EKS7 4036>)* **WEE TAM** Mar69
– Job's tears / Puppies / Beyond the see / The yellow snake / Log cabin home in the sky / You get brighter / The half-remarkable question / Air / Ducks on a pond. *(re-iss. Jan73 + 1976; K 42021) (cd-iss. Feb92 & Sep99; 7559 60914-2) (<cd re-iss. Nov94 on 'Hannibal'; HNCD 4802>)*

Oct 68. (lp; mono/stereo) *(EKL/<EKS7 4037>)* **THE BIG HUGE** Mar69
– Maya / Greatest friend / The son of Noah's brother / Lordly nightshade / The mountain of God / Cousin caterpillar / The iron stone / Douglas Traherne Harding / The circle is unbroken. *(re-iss. Jan73 + 1976; K 42022) (cd-iss. Jul93; 7559 61548-2)*

— LICORICE was now a full-time member

Oct 69. (7") *(EKSN 45074)* **BIG TED. / ALL WRIT DOWN** –

Nov 69. (lp) *(<EKS 74057>)* **CHANGING HORSES** 30
– Big Ted / White bird / Dust be diamonds / Sleepers, awake! / Mr. & Mrs. / Creation. *(cd-iss. Jul93 & May01; 7559 61549-2) (cd-iss. Dec94 on 'Hannibal'; HNCD 4439)*

— added guest **DAVE MATTACKS** – drums of FAIRPORT CONVENTION

Apr 70. (lp) *(<EKS 7401>)* **I LOOKED UP** 30 Jul70
– Black Jack Davey / Letter / Pictures in a mirror / This moment / When you find out who you are / Fair as you. *(re-prom.1970; 2469 002) (cd-iss. Dec94 on 'Hannibal'; HNCD 4440) (cd re-iss. Jul02; 7559 62760-2)*

Apr 70. (7") *(2101 003)* **THIS MOMENT. / BLACK JACK DAVEY** –

May 70. (7") *<45696>* **THIS MOMENT. / BIG TED** –

— augmented by **JANET SHANKMAN** – b.vocals (ROBIN married her Dec70) **PETE GRANT** – banjo / **GREG HART** – sitar (of STONE MONKEY) plus guest **MALCOLM LE MAISTRE** – keyboards, bass (of EXPLODING GALAXY)

Oct 70. (d-lp) *(2665 001)* *<7E 2002>* **"U"** 34 Jan71
– El wool suite / The juggler's song / Time / Bad Sadie Lee / Queen of love / Partial belated overture / Light in the time of darkness – Glad to see you / Walking along with you / Hirem pawnitof – Fairies' hornpipe // Bridge theme / Bridge song / Astral plane theme / Invocation / Robot blues / Puppet song / Cutting the strings / I know you / Rainbow. *(re-iss. Jan73; K 62002) (d-cd iss.Jul02 on 'Collector's Choice'; CCM 0288-2) (d-cd re-iss. Aug02; 7559 62761-2)*

— Back to basic duo of **ROBIN + MIKE** plus **LICORICE + ROSE**

Island Elektra

Apr 71. (lp) *(ILPS 9140)* **BE GLAD FOR THE SONG HAS NO ENDING** –
– Come with me / All writ down / Vishangro / See all the people / Waiting for you / (Be glad for) The song has no ending. *(cd-iss. Jun98 on 'Edsel'; EDCD 564)*

— **MALCOLM LE MAISTRE** – keyboards, bass, vocals returned to repl. ROSE

Oct 71. (lp) *(ILPS 9172)* *<74112>* **LIQUID ACROBAT AS REGARDS THE AIR** 46 Feb72
– Talking of the end / Dear old battlefield / Cosmic boy / Worlds they rise and fall / Evloution rag / Painted chariot / Adam and Eve / Red hair / Here till here is there / Tree / Jigs: Eyes like leaves – Sunday is my wedding day – Drops of whiskey – Grumbling old men / Darling Belle. *(re-iss. Aug91 cd)(c; IMCD 130)(ICM 9172)*

— added **GERARD DOTT** – clarinet, saxophone (he played on HERON's 1972 solo album) and guest on one **STUART GORDON** – viola

Oct 72. (lp) *(ILPS 9211)* **EARTH SPAN** –
– My father was a lighthouse keeper / Antoine / Restless night / Sunday song / Black Jack David / Banks of sweet Italy / The actor / Moon hang low / The sailor and the dancer / Seagull. *(cd-iss. Dec92 on 'Edsel'; EDCD 360)*

Nov 72. (7") *(WIP 6145)* **BLACK JACK DAVID. / MOON HANG LOW** –

— **STAN LEE** – bass repl. LICORICE who joined WOODY WOODMANSEY Band **JACK INGRAM** – drums (added to ROBIN, MIKE, MALCOLM, GERARD and STAN)

Island Reprise

Feb 73. (7") *(WIP 6158)* **AT THE LIGHTHOUSE DANCE. / JIGS** –

Feb 73. (lp) *(ILPS 9229)* *<2139>* **NO RUINOUS FEUD**
– Explorer / Down before Cathy / Saturday maybe / Jigs / Old Buccaneer / At the lighthouse dance / Second fiddle / Circus girl / Turquoise blue / My blue tears / Weather the storm / Little girl. *(cd-iss. Nov92 on 'Edsel'; EDCD 367)*

— **GRAHAM FORBES** – electric guitar (ex-POWERHOUSE) repl. GERARD / **JOHN GILSTON** – drums repl. INGRAM

Mar 74. (lp) *(ILPS 9270)* *<2198>* **HARD ROPE & SILKEN TWINE**
– Maker of islands / Cold February / Glancing love / Dreams of no return / Dumb Kate / Ithkos. *(cd-iss. Feb93 on 'Edsel'; EDCD 368)*

— WILLIAMSON + HERON went onto solo careers; the pair re-formed late 1999 with PALMER, LAWSON DANDO + BINA WILLIAMSON

Pig's Whisker Pig's Whisker

Aug 01. (cd) *(<PWMD 5024>)* **BLOOMSBURY 2000 (live)** Nov01
– Maker of islands / Ducks on a pond / Air / The storm is on the ocean / Big city blues / Waltz of the new moon / Goodbye / You know what you could be / October song.

– compilations etc. –

Mar 71. (lp) *Elektra; (EKS 74065) / Reprise; <7E 2004>* **RELICS OF THE INCREDIBLE STRING BAND**

Nov 76. (d-lp) *Island; (ISLD 9)* **SEASONS THEY CHANGE – BEST OF THE INCREDIBLE STRING BAND** –
– Black Jack Davey / Blues for the muse / Nightfall / Puppies / Cold days of February / Worlds they rise and fall / Chinese white / Empty pocket blues / When the music starts to play / Saturday maybe / Red hair / The circle is unbroken / First girl I loved / Cosmic boy / Darling Belle / My father was a lighthouse keeper / Queen Juanita and her fisherman lover.

Oct 91. (cd/lp) *Band Of Joy; (BOJ CD/LP 004)* **ON AIR (live)** –

Nov 92. (cd) *Windsong; (WINCD 029)* **BBC RADIO 1 LIVE IN CONCERT** –

Jun 97. (cd) *Blueprint; (PWMD 5003)* **CHELSEA SESSIONS 1967** –
(<re-iss. Mar98 on 'Pig's Whisker'; PWCD 5003)> (re-iss. Jul00; PWCD 5023)

Aug 98. (cd) *Mooncrest; (<CRESTCD 002>)* **FIRST GIRL I LOVED (live)**
– Cousin caterpillar / I know that man / The circle is unbroken / Wild cat blues / The first girl I loved / Everything's fine right now / Old buccaneer / Catwalk rag / Giles crocodile / Turquoise blue / My father was a lighthouse keeper / Black Jack Davey / Ithkos.

May 01. (cd) *Island; (IMCD 280)* **HERE TILL THERE IS HERE (AN INTRODUCTION TO THE INCREDIBLE STRING BAND)** –

Jul 01. (cd) *Warner ESP; (9548 39803-2)* **THE BEST OF THE INCREDIBLE STRING BAND 1966-1970** –

Jul 02. (d-cd) *Collector's Choice; (CCM 0289-2)* **5000 SPIRITS OR THE LAYERS OF THE ONION / THE HANGMAN'S BEAUTIFUL DAUGHTER** [ ] [–]

Jul 02. (d-cd) *Collector's Choice; (CCM 0291-2)* **CHANGING HORSES / I LOOKED UP** [ ] [–]

Mar 03. (cd) *Disky; (<SI 90532-2>)* **HERITAGE** [ ] [ ]

— HERON and WILLIAMSON also released solo albums before their split. HERON = 'SMILING MEN WITH BAD REPUTATIONS' and WILLIAMSON = 'MYRRH'. Plus they went onto solo careers in 1975.

INCUBUS

Formed: Calabasas, California, USA . . . 1991 by BRANDON BOYD, MIKE EINZIGER, ALEX KATUNICH, GAVIN POPPEL and JOSE ANTONIO PASILLAS II. Taking their moniker from an evil spirit purported to indulge in sexual activities with sleeping women, the band were nevertheless an uptempo funk/metal combo rather than a ghoulish death-metal act. One of the better acts to stay faithful to the spirit of classic RED HOT CHILI PEPPERS and FAITH NO MORE, updating the jack-in-the-box slap bass of the former and the resounding vocal depth of the latter, the group signed to Epic subsidiary 'Immortal' for their debut album, 'ENJOY INCUBUS' (1996) – actually they had self-financed a "real" debut album in '94. Well received in the metal press, 'ENJOY . . .' transcended the barriers of the genre to successfully embrace everything from reggae to laid-back jazz, and still sounded funkin' great! Equally challenging and inventive, their next set, 'S.C.I.E.N.C.E.', was another mish-mash of styles even incorporating BOYD's didgeridoo, although don't let that put you off! In 1999, INCUBUS were back with a second full-set, 'MAKE YOURSELF', an album that finally gave them a US Top 50 success. • **Note:** Not the same group who released records on 'Nuclear Blast'.

Album rating: ENJOY INCUBUS mini (*6) / S.C.I.E.N.C.E. (*6) / MAKE YOURSELF (*7) / WHEN INCUBUS ATTACKS VOL.1 mini (*5) / FUNGUS AMONGUS collection (*5) / MORNING VIEW (*6)

BRANDON OF THE JUNGLE (b. BRANDON BOYD) – vocals, percussion / **DYNAMIKE** (b. MIKE EINZIGER) – guitar / **DIRK LANCE** (b. ALEX KATUNICH) – bass / **KID LYFE** (b. GAVIN POPPEL) – scratches / **JOSE ANTONIO PASILLAS II** – drums

Immortal-Epic Immortal-Epic

Feb 97. (m-cd/m-c) *<(487102-2/-4)>* **ENJOY INCUBUS** [ ] Nov96 [ ]
– You will be a hot dancer / Shaft / Trouble in 421 / Take me to your leader / Medium / Speak free / The answer / Psychopsilocybin / Sink beneath the line / Hilikus. *<US re-iss. Nov00 as 'FUNGUS AMONGUS'; 61497>*

Oct 97. (cd) *<(4882616)>* **S.C.I.E.N.C.E.** [ ] [ ]
– Redefine / New skin / Idiot box / Glass / Magic medicine / Certain shade of green / Favourite things / Anti-gravity love song / Nebula / Deep inside / Calgon. *(re-iss. Jan01 & Jan02; same)*

Oct 99. (cd/c) *(495040-2/-4) <63652>* **MAKE YOURSELF** [ ] [47]
– Privilege / Nowhere fast / Consequence / Warmth / When it comes / Stellar / Make yourself / Drive / Clean / Battle star / I miss you / Pardon me / Out from under. *(cd re-iss. May01 w/ extra cd; 495040-9)* – Pardon me (acoustic) / Stellar (acoustic) / Make yourself (acoustic) / Drive (live orchestral).

May 00. (7"red) *(669346-7)* **PARDON ME. / PARDON ME (acoustic)** [61] [–]
(cd-s) *(669346-2)* – ('A'side) / I miss you / Crowded elevator / ('A'-CD-Rom).

Aug 00. (m-cd) *<61395>* **WHEN INCUBUS ATTACKS VOL.1** [–] [41]
– Pardon me (acoustic) / Stellar (acoustic) / Make yourself (acoustic) / Crowded elevator / Favorite things (live) / Pardon me (live).

Jun 01. (cd-s) *(671378-2) <radio play>* **DRIVE / DRIVE (acoustic) / CLEAN (live)** [40] Feb01 [9]
(7"m) *(671378-7)* – ('A'live) / Favourite things (live) / Pardon me (live).

Jan 02. (cd-s) *(672255-2) <671976>* **WISH YOU WERE HERE / NEW SKIN / DRIVE (orchestra) / ('A'video)** [27] Sep01 [60]
(cd-s) *(672255-5)* – ('A'side) / ('A'live) / Warmth (live) / Mexico (live).

Oct 01. (cd) *(504061-2) <85272>* **MORNING VIEW** [15] [2]
– Nice to know you / Circles / Wish you were here / Just a phase / 11 a.m. / Blood on the ground / Mexico / Warning / Echo / Have you ever / Are you in? / Under my umbrella / Aqueous transmission. *(special cd+=; 504061-9)*– (the making of Morning View).

Sep 02. (cd-s) *(672848-2) <67283-2>* **ARE YOU IN? / ARE YOU IN? (Paul Oakenfold remix) / STELLAR (acoustic) / ARE YOU IN? (video)** [34] Jun02 [ ]
(cd-s) *(672848-5)* – ('A'side) / Wish you were here (live) / Pardon me (live video).

— **BEN KENNEY** – bass (of TIME-LAPSE CONSORTIUM) repl. DIRK

INDIGO GIRLS

Formed: Decatur, Georgia, USA ... 1980 by AMY RAY and EMILY SALIERS, who had written and performed together since childhood. The duo made their vinyl debut in summer '85 with an independently released single, 'CRAZY GAME', following up with an eponymous EP and a self-financed debut album, 'STRANGE FIRE' (1987). With the success of such female nu-folk artists as SUZANNE VEGA and TRACY CHAPMAN, The INDIGO GIRLS' folksy, apple-pie college strumming became hot property and the group were signed up by 'Epic'. Featuring contributions from the likes of R.E.M. and HOTHOUSE FLOWERS, 'INDIGO GIRLS' (1989) was a strong major label debut which had no problem crossing over from their loyal grassroots following to the pop market. Similar to British outfits such as EVERYTHING BUT THE GIRL and FAIRGROUND ATTRACTION, if a bit deeper and (socially/environmentally) lyrically aware, The INDIGO GIRLS' harmony-laden folk pop/rock found particular favour with the burgeoning US feminist movement. Again featuring an array of respected names including MARY CHAPIN CARPENTER and JIM KELTNER, 'NOMADS – INDIANS – SAINTS' (1990) wasn't quite so successful although the more adventurous 'RITES OF PASSAGE' (1992) almost made the US Top 20 and was nominated for a Grammy. The latter's more expansive approach was further developed on 'SWAMP OPHELIA' (1994), which employed the violin of LISA GERMANO to similarly impressive results alongside the acoustic bass playing of the ubiquitous DANNY THOMPSON. The record finally took the pair into the American Top 10 and while that achievement was repeated with 'SHAMING OF THE SUN' (1997), their success in Britain remains minimal. With its cast of guests – including SHERYL CROW, NATACHA ATLAS, JOAN OSBORNE and ME'SHELL NDEGEOCELLO – and thrillingly diverse approach, 'COME ON NOW SOCIAL' (1999) was as likely as any of their past records to change that situation. While the album dabbled in heads-down rock and even straight-up country, the soulful single, 'PEACE TONIGHT' showcased the 'GIRLS at the height of their art. 'BECOME YOU' (2002), in contrast, was a pared back affair, shorn of any production or guest star excess, and concentrating on the kind of obliquely personal songwriting with which the group originally made their name. • **Covered:** ALL ALONG THE WATCHTOWER + TANGLED UP IN BLUE (Bob Dylan) / FREE OF HOPE (Vic Chesnutt) / LAND OF CANAAN (Joni Mitchell) / DOWN BY THE RIVER (Neil Young) / MIDNIGHT TRAIN TO GEORGIA (Gladys Knight & The Pips) / etc.

Album rating: STRANGE FIRE (*4) / INDIGO GIRLS (*8) / NOMADS – INDIANS – SAINTS (*7) / LIVE: BACK ON THE BUS Y'ALL (*4) / RITES OF PASSAGE (*6) / SWAMP OPHELIA (*6) / 4.5 THE BEST OF compilation (*6) / 1200 CURFEWS (*7) / SHAMING OF THE SUN (*6) / COME ON NOW SOCIAL (*6) / RETROSPECTIVE compilation (*7) / BECOME YOU (*6)

AMY RAY (b.12 Apr'64) – vocals, guitars / **EMILY SALIERS** (b.22 Jul'63, New Haven, Connecticut) – vocals, acoustic guitar

not iss. / J Ellis

Jun 85. (7") *<A 1264>* **CRAZY GAME. / EVERYBODY'S WAITING (FOR SOMEONE TO COME HOME)** [–] [ ]

not iss. / DragonPath

Nov 86. (12"ep) *<LMM I>* **INDIGO GIRLS** [–] [ ]

not iss. / Indigo Music

Oct 87. (lp) *<LMM II>* **STRANGE FIRE** [–] [ ]
– Strange fire / Crazy game / Left me a fool / I don't wanna know / Hey Jesus / Get together / Walk away / Make it easier / You left it up to me / Land of Canaan. *<US re-iss. Nov89 on 'Epic'; EK 45427> (cd re-iss. Oct00 on 'Epic'; 500750-2)*

— now with **JAY DEE DAUGHERTY** – drums (ex-HOTHOUSE FLOWERS, ex-WATERBOYS, etc.) / **JOHN KEANE** – guitar, bass / **JOHN VAN TONGEREN** – keyboards / **KASIM SULTAN + DEDE VOGT** – bass / **PAULINHO DA COSTA** – percussion / **JAI WINDING** – piano

Epic / Epic

Jun 89. (7") *<68912>* **CLOSER TO FINE. / COLD AS ICE** [–] [52]

Jun 89. (7") *(654907-7)* **CLOSER TO FINE. / HISTORY OF US** [ ] [–]
(12"+=/cd-s+=) *(654907-5/-2)* – Center stage.

Jul 89. (lp/c/cd) *(463491-1/-4/-2) <45044>* **INDIGO GIRLS** [ ] Apr89 [22]
– Closer to fine / Secure yourself / Kid fears / Prince of darkness / Blood and fire / Tried to be true / Love's recovery / Land of Canaan / Center stage / History of us. *(cd re-iss. Oct00; 500751-2)*

Sep 89. (7") *<73003>* **LAND OF CANAAN. / NEVER STOP** [–] [ ]

Nov 89. (12"ep/cd-ep) *(655135-8/-2)* **CLOSER TO FINE / CLOSER TO FINE (live). / MONA LISAS AND MAD HATTERS (live) / AMERICAN TUNE (live)** [ ] [–]

Feb 90. (7") *<73255>* **GET TOGETHER. / FINLANDIA** [–] [ ]

— now w / **DAUGHERTY / PETER BUCK** (of R.E.M.) / **SARA LEE** – bass (ex-GANG OF FOUR) / **MARY CHAPIN CARPENTER / KENNY ARONOFF / BENMONT TENCH / JIM KELTNER / PETER HOLSAPPLE / JOHN JENNINGS / DA COSTA / CHRIS McGUIRE / CRAIG EDWARDS** / etc.

Oct 90. (c-s) *<73607>* **HAMMER AND NAIL / WELCOME (live)** [–] [ ]

Nov 90. (cd/c/lp) *(467308-2/-4/-1) <46820>* **NOMADS – INDIANS – SAINTS** [ ] Sep90 [43]
– Hammer and nail / Welcome me / World falls / Southland in the springtime / 1,2,3 / Keeper of my heart / Watershed / Hand me downs / You and me of the 10,000 wars / Pushing the needle too far / The girl with the weight of the world in her hands. *(cd re-iss. Oct00; 500752-2)*

Jun 91. (m-cd) *(468415-2) <EK 047508>* **BACK ON THE BUS Y'ALL (live)** [ ] [ ]
– 1 2 3 / Tried to be true / You and me of the 10,000 wars / Prince of darkness / Kid fears / Left me a fool / All along the watchtower / 1 2 3 (studio version).

— now w / **SARA LEE** – bass / **BUDGIE** – drums (of SIOUXSIE & THE BANSHEES) / **LISA GERMANO** – fiddle / **JERRY MAROTTA** – drums / **MARTIN McCARRICK** – cello / **DONAL LUNNY** – bouziki, bodhran / **JENNINGS** – guitar / **KAI WINDING** – piano

Jun 92. (cd/c/lp) *(471363-2/-4/-1) <EK 048865>* **RITES OF PASSAGE** [ ] May92 [21]
– Three hits / Galileo / Ghost / Joking / Jonas & Ezekial / Love will come to you / Romeo & Juliet / Virginia Woolf / Chicken man / Airplane / Nashville / Let it be me / Cedar tree. *(cd re-iss. Oct00; 500753-2)*

Aug 92. (cd-s) *<74326>* **GALILEO / GHOST / JOKING / LOVE WILL COME TO YOU / JONAS & EZEKIAL** [–] [89]

Oct 92. (7"/c-s) *(658768-7/-4)* **GALILEO. / KID FEARS** [ ] [–]
(cd-s) *(658768-2)* – ('A'side) / Closer to fine / Tried to be true / Hammer and a nail.

— Augmented by **SARA LEE** – bass (ex-GANG OF FOUR, etc.) / **JERRY MAROTTA** – drums / **JAMES HALL** – trumpet / **DANNY THOMPSON** – acoustic bass / **LISA GERMANO** – violin / **JOHN PAINTER** – flugel horn / **JANE SCARPANTONI** – cello / **MICHAEL LORANT** – drums, b.vocals

May 94. (cd-ep) *(660340-2)* **LEAST COMPLICATED / DEAD MAN'S HILL (acoustic) / MYSTERY (acoustic) / KID FEARS** [ ] [–]

May 94. (cd/c/lp) *(475931-2/-4/-1) <EK 057621>* **SWAMP OPHELIA** [66] [9]
– Fugitive / Least complicated / Language or the kiss / Reunion / Power of two / Touch me fall / The wood song / Mystery / Dead man's hill / Fare thee well / This train revised.

Jun 95. (c-s) *(662166-4)* **CLOSER TO FINE / ROCKIN' IN THE FREE WORLD** [ ] [–]
(cd-s+=) *(662166-2)* – Dead man's hill (acoustic) / Mystery (acoustic).
(cd-s) *(662166-5)* – ('A'side) / Kid fears / All along the watchtower (live) / Let me a fool (live).

Jul 95. (cd/c) *(480439-2/-4)* **4.5 (THE BEST OF THE INDIGO GIRLS)** (compilation) [43] [–]
– Joking / Hammer and nail / Kid fears / Galileo / Tried to be true / Power of love / Pushing the needle too far / Reunion / Closer to fine / Three hits / Least complicated / Touch me fall / Love's recovery / Land of Canaan / Ghost.

Oct 95. (d-cd) *<EK 067229>* **1200 CURFEWS (live)** [–] [40]
– Joking / Least complicated / Thin line / River / Strange fire / Power of two / Pushing the needle too far / Virginia Woolf / Jonas and Ezekial / Tangled up in blue / World falls / Bury my heart at Wounded Knee / Ghost / Dead man's hill // I don't wanna know / Galileo / Down by the river / Love's recovery / Land of Canaan / Mystery / This train revised / Back together again / Language or the kiss / Chickenman / Midnight train to Georgia / Closer to fine / Bury my heart at Wounded Knee / Go go go. (above featured a number of cover versions)

May 97. (cd/c) *(486982-2/-4) <EK 067891>* **SHAMING OF THE SUN** [ ] Apr97 [7]
– Shame on you / Get out the map / Shed your skin / It's alright / Caramia / Don't give that girl a gun / Leeds / Scooter boys / Everything in its own time / Cut it out / Burn all the letters / Hey kind friend.

— **RAY + SALIERS** recruited band:- **CAROL ISAACS** – keyboards / **CLAIRE KENNY** – bass / **BRADY BLADE** – drums

Oct 99. (cd/c) *(495091-2/-4) <EK 069914>* **COME ON NOW SOCIAL** [ ] [34]
– Go / Soon to be nothing / Gone again / Trouble / Sister / Peace tonight / Ozilline / We are together / Cold beer and remote control / Compromise / Andy / Faye Tucker.

Oct 00. (cd/c) *(500988-2/-4) <EK 61602>* **RETROSPECTIVE** (compilation + 2 new) [ ] [ ]
– Strange fire / Closer to fine / Kid fears / Watershed / Three hits / Galileo / Ghost / Reunion / Power of two / Least complicated / Shame on you / Get out the map / Go / Trouble / Devotion / Leaving.

May 02. (cd) *(507575-2) <86401>* **BECOME YOU** [ ] Mar02 [30]
– Moment of forgiveness / Deconstruction / Become you / You've got to show / Yield / Collecting you / Hope alone / Bitterroot / Our deliverance / Starkville / She's saving me / Nuevas senoritas.

INME

Formed: Essex, England ... 2001 by songwriter/bassist JOE MORGAN, along with DAVE McPHERSON and SIMON TAYLOR. Influenced by the wave of early '90's pre-grunge acts such as MUDHONEY, SOUNDGARDEN and NIRVANA, INME wielded a screeching flash of distorted rock at the beginning of 2003 when they issued the Top 75 single 'UNDERDOSE'. 'FIREFLY' followed later on in the year and crashed the Top 50 before the floppy-haired McPHERSON and Co delivered the group's UK Top 20 debut album 'OVERGROWN EDEN' and embarked on a UK tour at the end of the year. Mixing thick and fast hardcore grunge with wayward ballads (think SOUNDGARDEN's 'Black Hole Sun' and you get the idea), the album was no revelation in the music world, but displayed enough verve and musical proliferation to keep the ears suitably pricked.

Album rating: OVERGROWN EDEN (*5)

DAVE McPHERSON – vocals, guitar / **JOE MORGAN** – bass / **SIMON TAYLOR** – drums

Music For Nations / not iss.

Jul 02. (cd) *(CDKUT 195)* **UNDERDOSE / GLEOSEA / RUINS** [66] [–]

Sep 02. (cd-s) *(CDKUT 197)* **FIREFLY / WEB / MIRACLE** [43] [–]
(cd-s+=) *(CDXKUT 197)* – ('A'side) / Miracle / Underdose (video).

Jan 03. (cd-s) *(CDKUT 200)* **CRUSHED LIKE FRUIT / SPUR OF MOMENT / GENTLY HURTING** [25] [–]
(cd-s) *(CDXKUT 200)* – ('A'side) / Deep regret / May (as well kiss me).

Jan 03. (cd) *(CDMFN 275)* **OVERGROWN EDEN** [15] [–]
– Underdose / Firefly / Wounds / Lava twilight / Natural / Her mask /

Energy / Crushed like fruit / Ice warm / Trenches / Neptune / Mosaic. *(special cd+=; CDMFNX 275)*

Apr 03. (cd-s) *(CDKUT 201)* **NEPTUNE / RECEIPT OF LIFE / LOW AS YOU ARE** [46] [–]
(cd-s) *(CDXKUT 201)* – ('A'-live) / Natural (live) / Gently hurting (live).

INSANE CLOWN POSSE

Formed: Detroit, Michigan, USA . . . 1989 as The INNER CITY POSSE, by SHAGGY 2 DOPE and VIOLENT J, two face-painted rappers with er . . . a wicked sense of fun. They changed their moniker in 1992, releasing their debut album 'CARNIVAL OF CARNAGE' the same year. Championed by the metal press, INSANE CLOWN POSSE are basically nevertheless a dyed-in-the-wool rap duo, albeit an extremely offensive one with a bizarre line in twisted circus trappings. Following a little contretemps with the Walt Disney corporation (and a short-lived spell with 'Jive' records), the gruesome jokers delivered their breakthrough release, 'THE GREAT MILENKO' in 1997, although this initially ran into difficulties with the all-powerful moral majority (the old record company recalling all copies due to its offensive content). Predictably, sales of the album (released by 'Island') soared, culminating in a US Top 75 placing. Just in time for Yuletide festivities, the 'POSSE laid their Christmas gift 45, 'SANTA'S A FAT BITCH' under the tree of hypocritical middle class America. 1998 saw a further couple of minor UK hit singles while 'THE AMAZING JECKEL BROTHERS' (1999) amazingly made the US Top 5. Yet the posse's most ambitious moment was still to come: in the year 2000, the jokers released 'BIZZAR' – accompanied by the US-only 'BIZAAR'. Confused? You might well be, especially by the former's choice of cover material, a reading of the 80's Sly Fox hit, 'LET'S GO ALL THE WAY'. With the release of 'THE WRAITH: SHANGRI-LA' (2002), the INSANE ones revealed that there was actually some kind of metaphysical form to their dastardly lyrical deeds, and that us listeners had all been taken along for the grotesque, carnivalesque ride. If you could get past these underwhelming revelations, there was the usual fix of degenerate, sniggering trash-rap barely made more palatable by their newfound bonhomie.

Album rating: CARNIVAL OF CHANGE (*4) / THE RING MASTER (*4) / RIDDLE BOX (*6) / THE GREAT MILENKO (*5) / THE AMAZING JECKEL BROTHERS (*4) / BIZAAR (*4) / BIZZAR (*4) / THE WRAITH (SHANGRI-LA) (*4)

SHAGGY 2 DOPE (b. MIKE CLARK) – rapper / **VIOLENT J** (b. BROWN) – rapper; with guests **SLASH + STEVE JONES** – guitars

not iss. Psychopathic

1992. (cd) <*PSY 1004*> **CARNIVAL OF CARNAGE** [–] [ ]
– Intro / Carnival of carnage / The juggla / First day out / Red neck hoe / Wizard of the hood / Is that you? / Psychopathic / Guts on the ceiling / Never had made it / Your rebel flag / Ghetto freak show / Taste. *(UK-iss.Jun98 on 'Island'; 524514-2)*

1993. (m-lp) <*PSY 1005*> **BEVERLY HILLS 50187** [–] [ ]
– Beverly Hills 50187 / 17 dead / The stalker / In the haughhh! / Chop! chop! with Esham / Joke your mind.

Mar 94. (cd) <*PSY 1006*> **THE RING MASTER** [–] [ ]
– Wax museum / Murder go round / Chicken huntin' / Mr. Johnson's head / Southwest song / Get off me, dog! / Who asked you / The dead one / My funhouse / For the maggots / Wagon wagon / The loons / Ghetto funk show / Bugz on my nugzs / House of mirrors / Ringmaster's word. *(UK-iss.Jun98 on 'Island'; 524515-2)*

Aug 94. (m-lp) <*PSY 1007*> **THE TERROR WHEEL** [–] [ ]
– The dead body man / Skitsofrantic / The smog / Out / I stuck her with my wang / Amys in the attic.

Dec 94. (cd-ep) <*PSY 1009*> **A CARNIVAL XMAS** [–] [ ]
– Santa's a fat bitch / Red Christmas / Santa killas / It's coming.

not iss. Jive

Aug 95. (c-s) <*46505*> **CHICKEN HUNTIN' (slaughterhouse street) / CHICKEN HUNTIN' (slaughterhouse mixtramental)** [–] [ ]
(cd-s+=) <*46504*> – I didn't mean to kill him / Fabulous / Riddle box sampler / Chicken huntin' (original recipe).

not iss. Battery

Oct 95. (cd) <*02141-46001-2*> **RIDDLE BOX** [–] [ ]
– Riddle box / The show must go on / Chicken huntin' / Toy box / Cemetery girl / 3 rings / Headless boogie / Joker's wild / Dead body man / Lil' somethin' somethin' / Ol' evil eye / 12 / Killing fields / I'm coming home.

not iss. Psychopathic

Nov 96. (m-cd) <*PSY 1015*> **TUNNEL OF LOVE** [–] [ ]
– Intro / Cotton candy / Super balls / Ninja / Stomp / Prom queen / My kind of bitch / When I get out / (untitled). *(UK-iss.Feb98; same as US)*

Apr 97. (cd) <*PSY 1016*> **MUTILATION MIX** [–] [ ]
– Request #1 / Cemetary girl / Clown luv / Wagon wagon / Request #2 / Psychopathic / Southwest strangla / Never had it made / Chicken huntin' (slaughterhouse mix) / I stuck her with my wang / The neck cutta / Red neck hoe / Request #3 / I'm comin' home / Super balls / The stalker / Wizard of the hood / Skitsofrantic / 3 rings / Request #4 / Murder go 'round / Request #5 / Southwest song / Fxck off! / The dead body man / Cotton candy / 17 dead / Request #6 / The Neden game / House of wonders + Mike Clark.

Island Hollywood

Oct 97. (cd/c) *(CID/ICT 8061)* <*524442-2*> **THE GREAT MILENKO** [ ] Jul97 [63]
– Intro / The great Milenko / Hokus pokus / Piggy pie / How many times? / Southwest voodoo / Halls of illusion / Under the moon / What is a juggalo? / House of horrors / Boogie woogie wu / Neden game / Hellalujah / Down with the clown / Just like that / Pass me by.

Dec 97. (cd-s) <*57219-2*> **SANTA'S A FAT BITCH / RED CHRISTMAS** [–] [67]

Jan 98. (7") *(IS 685)* **HALLS OF ILLUSION. / SMOG** [56] [–]
(cd-s+=) *(CID 685)* – Southwest voodoo / Cotton candy.

May 98. (7"pic-d) *(ISP 705)* **HOKUS POKUS. / PROM QUEEN** [53] [ ]
('A'-Headhunta'z mix; cd-s+=) *(CID 705)* – My kind of bitch / Skitzofrantic.
(cd-s) *(CIDX 705)* – ('A'-Headhunta'z mix) / ('A'-radio mix) / ('A'-lp version) / ('A'-Headhunta'z instrumental).

May 99. (cd) <*(524661-2)*> **THE AMAZING JECKEL BROTHERS** [ ] [4]
– Intro / Jake Jeckel / Bring it on / I want my shit / Bitches! / Terrible / I stab people / Another love song / Everyone rize / Play with me / Jack Jeckel / Fuck the world / The Shaggy show / Mad professor / Assassins / Echo side / Nothing left.

Nov 00. (cd) <*548174-2*> **BIZAAR** [–] [20]
– Intro / Take me away / Fearless / Rainbows and stuff / What / Still stabbin' / Tilt-a-whirl / We gives no fuck / Please don't hate me / Behind the paint / My homie baby mama / The pendulum's promise.

Nov 00. (cd) <*(548175-2)*> **BIZZAR** [ ] [21]
– Intro / Bizzar / Cherry pie (I need a freak) / Questions / Mr. Happy / Radio stars / My axe / If / Let's go all the way / Let a killa / Juggalo paradise / Crystal ball.

Riviera Riviera

Nov 02. (cd) <*(RIV 9912-2)*> **THE WRAITH (SHANGRI-LA)** [ ] [15]
– Walk into the light / Welcome to the show / Get ya wicked on / Murder rap / Birthday bitches / Blaaam!!! / It rains diamonds / The staleness / Hell's forecast / Juggalo homies / Ain't yo bidness / We belong / Cotton candy & popsicles / Crossing the bridge / The raven's mirror / The wraith / The unveiling.

– compilations, etc.

Aug 98. (d-cd,d-c) *Island;* <*524552*> **FORGOTTEN FRESHNESS VOL.1 & 2** (B-sides, outtakes, remixes) [–] [46]

Dec 01. (cd) *Psychopathic;* <*3000*> **FORGOTTEN FRESHNESS VOL.3** [–] [ ]
(UK-iss.Mar03 on 'Universal'; AA314 524552-2)

☐ INSPECTAH DECK (see under ⇒ WU-TANG CLAN)

INSPIRAL CARPETS

Formed: Manchester, England . . . 1980 initially as The FURS, by schoolboy GRAHAM LAMBERT. He was joined in the mid-80's by STEPHEN HOLT, TONY WELSH and CHRIS GOODWIN. In 1986, as The INSPIRAL CARPETS, they replaced GOODWIN and WELSH with CRAIG GILL, DAVE SWIFT and CLINT BOON. Early in '87, they recorded a version of 'GARAGE' for a 7" flexi-disc given free with 'Debris' magazine. After gigs supporting the WEDDING PRESENT, JAMES, STONES ROSES and The SHAMEN, they issued their official debut, the 'PLANE CRASH EP' in mid-'88 for indie, 'Playtime' records. Early in 1989, they set up their own 'Cow' label, after their distributers, 'Red Rhino', went bust. At the same time, HOLT and SWIFT left to form The RAINKINGS, and were replaced by HINGLEY and WALSH. After a late 1988 recording, 'TRAIN SURFING EP', was issued, they recorded the 808 STATE-produced 'JOE' single/EP. A year later, they had their first UK Top 50 entry with 'MOVE', which led to Daniel Miller of 'Mute' records taking on both band and label. In April 1990, they broke into UK Top 20 with the poignant single, 'THIS IS HOW IT FEELS', pushing their debut album, 'LIFE', to No. 3. A heavy, organ-orientated psychedelic-pop group, their music lay somewhere between The DOORS and The FALL. The INSPIRAL CARPETS continued with a run of hit singles that included, 'SHE COMES IN THE FALL', 'CARAVAN' and 'DRAGGING ME DOWN', the latter two featured on the Top 5 album, 'THE BEAST INSIDE' (1991). The following year, with a further clutch of hit singles under their belt, they scraped into the Top 20 with 'REVENGE OF THE GOLDFISH', a weaker effort. A year of reflection in 1993 preceded a return to form with a MARK E. SMITH (The Fall) collaboration 45, 'I WANT YOU' (and featured on a certain TV ad). This helped the album, 'DEVIL HOPPING', reach the Top 10 but when their next single, 'UNIFORM', failed to even dent the Top 50, they were unceremoniously dropped by their label, 'Mute'. The band split soon after, leaving behind the customary cash-in compilation. The man behind their trademark keyboard sound eventually struck out on his own with The CLINT BOON EXPERIENCE, accompanied by RICHARD STUBBS aka STUBBSY, KATHRYN STUBBS aka SISTA STUBBS, PAPA T aka TONY THOMPSON, MATT HAYDEN and MOOSE. After a trio of singles on 'Rabid Badger' (namely 'ONE WAY I CAN GO', 'WHITE NO SUGAR' and 'COMET THEME #1'), the outfit signed to 'Artful' for a further single, 'CAN'T KEEP A GOOD MAN DOWN' (featuring Manchester's very own MARK E) and debut album, '(THE COMPACT GUIDE TO) POP MUSIC AND SPACE TRAVEL' (1999). Poking fun at various easy targets, the album was a more easy-going listening experience after the intensity of The INSPIRALS, BOON and co delivering a millennial follow-up in the shape of 'LIFE IN TRANSITION' (2000). The heady memory of The INSPIRALS was resurrected once again in 2003 with a reunion tour and a more comprehensive anthology encompassing another singles package, 'COOL AS' (featuring shelved track, 'COME BACK TOMORROW'), a disc of lesser known tracks, 'RARE AS' and a DVD of live clips and promos, 'SPOOL AS'. • **Songwriters:** Group penned except; 96 TEARS (? & The Mysterians) / GIMME SHELTER (Rolling Stones) / TAINTED LOVE (Soft Cell) / PARANOID (Black Sabbath). • **Trivia:** To promote debut album, they employed the services of the Milk Marketing Board who ran a TV ad on their bottles. Early 1990, they penned 'THE 8.15 FROM MANCHESTER' (theme) from children's Saturday morning TV show.

Album rating: LIFE (*8) / THE BEAST INSIDE (*7) / REVENGE OF THE GOLDFISH (*6) / DEVIL HOPPING (*5) / THE SINGLES compilation (*8) / COOL AS compilation (*7) / Clint Boon Experience!: (THE COMPACT GUIDE TO) POP MUSIC & SPACE TRAVEL (*7) / LIFE IN TRANSITION (*6)

GRAHAM LAMBERT (b.10 Jul'64, Oldham, England) – guitar / **STEPHEN HOLT** – vocals / **DAVE SWIFT** – bass repl. TONY WELSH / **CRAIG GILL** (b. 5 Dec'71) – drums repl. CHRIS GOODWIN who joined ASIA FIELDS (later BUZZCOCKS F.O.C. and The HIGH) / added **CLINT BOON** (b.28 Jun'59, Oldham) – organ, vocals (ex-INCA BABIES)

Playtime / not iss.

Jul 88. (7"ltd.) *(AMUSE 2)* **KEEP THE CIRCLE AROUND. / THEME FROM COW** [ ] [-]
(12"ep+=) **PLANE CRASH EP** *(AMUSE 2T)* – Seeds of doubt / Garage full of flowers / 96 tears.

Cow / not iss.

Mar 89. (12"ep) *(MOO 2)* **TRAIN SURFING** [ ] [-]
– Butterfly / Causeway / You can't take the truth / Greek wedding song.

—— **TOM HINGLEY** (b. 9 Jul'65, Oxford, England) – vocals (ex-TOO MUCH TEXAS) repl. HOLT who formed RAINKINGS **MARTIN WALSH** (b. 3 Jul'68) – bass (ex-NEXT STEP) repl. SWIFT who formed RAINKINGS

May 89. (12"ep) *(MOO 3)* **JOE. / COMMERCIAL MIX / DIRECTING TRAFFIK / COMMERCIAL RAIN** [ ] [-]

May 89. (c;ltd) *(DUNG 4)* **DEMO CASSETTE** (rec.Dec'87) [ ] [-]
– Keep the circle around / Seeds of doubt / Joe / Causeway / 26 / Inside my head / Sun don't shine / Theme from Cow / 96 tears / Butterfly / Garage full of flowers.

Aug 89. (7") *(DUNG 5)* **FIND OUT WHY. / SO FAR** [ ] [-]
(12"+=/cd-s+=) *(DUNG 5 T/CD)* – Plane crash (live).

Oct 89. (7"/s7") *(DUNG 6/+X)* **MOVE. / OUT OF TIME** [49] [-]
(12"+=/cd-s+=) *(DUNG 6 T/CD)* – Move in.

Cow-Mute / Elektra

Mar 90. (7") *(DUNG 7)* <66581> **THIS IS HOW IT FEELS. / TUNE FOR A FAMILY** [14] [ ]
(12"+=/cd-s+=) *(DUNG 7 T/CD)* – ('A'extended) / Seeds of doubt.
(c-s+=) *(DUNG 7MC)* – ('A'extended) / Whiskey.
(12") *(DUNG 7R)* – ('A'-Robbery mix) / ('B'drum mix).

Apr 90. (lp/c/cd) *(DUNG 8/+C/CD)* <60987> **LIFE** [2] Oct90 [ ]
– Real thing / Song for a family / This is how it feels / Directing traffik / Besides me / Many happy returns / Memories of you / She comes in the fall / Monkey on my back / Sun don't shine / Inside my head / Move * / Sackville. *(cd+= *)* *<US++=>* – Commercial rain / Weakness / Biggest mountain / I'll keep it in mind.

Jun 90. (7") *(DUNG 10)* **SHE COMES IN THE FALL. / SACKVILLE** [27] [-]
(12"+=/cd-s+=) *(DUNG 10 T/CD)* – Continental reign (version).
(12"+=) *(DUNG 10R)* – ('A'acappella version).

Nov 90. (7"ep/12"ep) *(DUNG 11/+T)* **ISLAND HEAD** [21] [ ]
– Biggest mountain / I'll keep it in mind / Weakness / Gold to . . .
(cd-ep+=) *(DUNG 11CD)* – Mountain sequence.

Mar 91. (7") *(DUNG 13)* <66543> **CARAVAN. / SKIDOO** [30] Apr91 [ ]
(7"/12") *(DUNG 13 R/T)* – ('A'side) / ('B'-Possession mix).
(cd-s) *(DUNG 13CD)* – ('A'-What noise rethink mix) / ('B'side).

Apr 91. (lp/c/cd) *(DUNG 14/+C/CD)* <61089> **THE BEAST INSIDE** [5] May91 [ ]
– Caravan / Please be cruel / Born yesterday / Sleep well tonight / Grip / Beast inside / Niagara / Mermaid / Further away / Dreams are all we have.

Jun 91. (7"/c-s) *(DUNG/+C 15)* **PLEASE BE CRUEL. / THE WIND IS CALLING YOUR NAME** [50] [-]
(12"+=/cd-s+=) *(DUNG 15 T/CD)* – St.Kilda (version).

Feb 92. (7") *(DUNG 16)* **DRAGGING ME DOWN. / I KNOW I'M LOSING YOU** [12] [-]
(12"+=/cd-s+=) *(DUNG 16 T/CD)* – (2 other 'A'mixes).

May 92. (7") *(DUNG 17)* **TWO WORLDS COLLIDE. / BOOMERANG** [32] [-]
(12"+=/cd-s+=) *(DUNG 17 T/CD)* – ('A'-Mike Pickering remix).

Sep 92. (7") *(DUNG 18)* **GENERATIONS. / ('A'remix)** [28] [-]
(c-s) *(DUNG 18C)* – Lost in space again.
(12"/cd-s) *(DUNG 18 T/CD)* – ('A'side) / She comes in the fall (live) / Move (live) / Directing traffik (live).
(cd-s) *(DUNG 18CDR)* – ('A'side) / Joe (live) / Commercial rain (live) / Butterfly (live).

Oct 92. (lp/c/cd) *(DUNG 19/+C/CD)* <61397> **REVENGE OF THE GOLDFISH** [17] [ ]
– Generations / Saviour / Bitches brew / Smoking her clothes / Fire / Here comes the flood / Dragging me down / A little disappeared / Two worlds collide / Mystery / Rain song / Irresistable force.

Nov 92. (c-ep/12"ep) *(DUNG 20 C/T)* **BITCHES BREW / TAINTED LOVE. / BITCHES BREW (Fortran 5 remix) / IRRESISTABLE FORCE (Fortran 5 mix)** 36 –
(cd-ep+=) *(DUNG 20CD)* – Mermaid (live) / Born yesterday (live) / Sleep well tonight (live).
(cd-ep+=) *(DUNG 20CDR)* – Dragging me down (live) / Smoking her clothes (live) / Fire (live).

— parted company with 'Cow' co-founder/manager Anthony Boggiano.

May 93. (7"/c-s) *(DUNG 22/+C)* **HOW IT SHOULD BE. / IT'S ONLY A PAPER MOON** 49 –
(12"+=/cd-s+=) *(DUNG 22 T/CD)* – I'm alive.

Jan 94. (7"/c-s) *(DUNG 23/+C)* **SATURN 5. / PARTY IN THE SKY** 20 –
(cd-s+=/12"+=) *(DUNG 23 T/CD)* – ('A'mixes).
(cd-s) *(DUNG 23CDR)* – ('A'side) / Well of seven heads / Two cows / Going down.

Feb 94. (7"/c-s; by INSPIRAL CARPETS featuring MARK E. SMITH) *(DUNG 24/+C)* **I WANT YOU. / I WANT YOU (version)** 18 –
(cd-s+=) *(DUNG 24CD)* – We can do everything / Inside of you.
(cd-s) *(DUNG 24CDR)* – ('A'side) / Dragging me down / Party in the sky / Plutoman.

Mar 94. (lp/c/cd) *(DUNG 25/+C/CD)* *<61632>* **DEVIL HOPPING** 10
– I want you / Party in the sky / Plutoman / Uniform / Lovegrove / Just Wednesday / Saturn 5 / All of this and more / The way the light falls / Half way there / Cobra / I don't want to go blind. *(w / free ltd-cd of 'BBC SESSIONS' or free ltd.red-10"lp)*

Apr 94. (7"/c-s/cd-s) *(DUNG 26/+C/CD)* **UNIFORM. / PARANOID** 51 –
(cd-s) *(DUNG 26 CDR)* – ('A'side) / Paranoid (Collapsed Lung mix).

Aug 95. (7"m) *(DUNG 27L)* **JOE (acoustic). / SEEDS OF DOUBT / WHISKEY** 37 –
(7"m) *(DUNG 27R)* – Joe (live) / Sackville (live) / Saviour (live).
(cd-s) *(DUNG 25CD)* – ('A'side) / I want you / I'll keep it in mind / Tainted love.

Sep 95. (cd/c/d-lp) *(CD/C+/MOOTEL 3)* *<9010>* **THE SINGLES** (compilation) 17
– Joe / Find out why / Move / This is how it feels / (extended) / She comes in the fall / Commercial reign / Sackville / Biggest mountain / Weakness / Caravan / Please be cruel / Dragging me down / Two worlds collide / Generations / Bitches brew / How it should be / Saturn 5 / I want you / Uniform.

— had already been dropped from the 'Mute' roster late in 1994

– compilations, etc. –

Jul 89. (12"ep/cd-ep) *Strange Fruit; (SFPS/+CD 072) / Dutch East India; <8305>* **THE PEEL SESSIONS**
– Out of time / Directing traffic / Keep the circle around / Gimme shelter.

Aug 92. (cd/10"lp) *Strange Fruit; (SFRSCD 082) / Dutch East India; <8502>* **THE PEEL SESSIONS**

— also released import 7"colrd/12"colrd/pic-cd-s 'GIMME SHELTER'.

May 03. (d-cd+dvd) *Mute; (DUNG 30CD)* *<1008>* **COOL AS** 65
– Keep the circle around / Butterfly / Joe / Find out why / Move / This is how it feels / She comes in the fall / Biggest mountain / Weakness / Caravan / Please be cruel / Dragging me down / Two worlds collide / Generations / Bitches brew / How it should be / Saturn 5 / I want you (with MARK E. SMITH) / Uniform / Come back tomorrow / Theme from cow / Seeds of doubt / Garage full of flowers / 96 tears / You can't take the truth / Greek wedding song / Causeway / Directing traffic / Sackville / Commercial reign / Skidoo / Tainted love / Paper moon / I don't want to go blind (with BASIL CLARKE) / Paranoid (with COLLAPSED LUNG) / Iron / You've got what it takes. *(dvd+=)* – (videos).

Jul 03. (7") *Mute; (DUNG 31)* **COME BACK TOMORROW. / THIS IS HOW IT FEELS (live from G-Mex)** 43 –
(cd-s) *(DUNG 31CD)* – ('A'side) / Misbeliever / Breath to sorrow / ('A'-video).

☐ INTERNATIONAL SUBMARINE BAND
(see under ⇒ PARSONS, Gram)

INTERPOL

Formed: New York City, New York, USA . . . 1998 by students DANIEL KESSLER, CARLOS DENGLER, and an old acquaintance PAUL BANKS. After some early gigging in the millennium the band settled on the inclusion of drummer SAM FOGARINO, they were then set for a busy 2001. In that year, in true indie fashion, the band delivered on their own an EP, as well as another EP on the Scottish imprint 'Chemikal Underground' on the 'fukd i.d.' run. The group could also be found on several compilations not least the British indie label Fierce Panda's 'Clooney Tunes'. INTERPOL were garnering interest in the music press both in their stateside homeland and in the UK; they toured Britain in April, and took the well-trodden track of alternative acts by appearing on the, need it be said, legendary John Peel slot on Radio 1. Comparisons were being bandied around by the music hacks, not least of which was their likeness to celebrated Mancunian post-New Wavers The CHAMELEONS. The darker tones of the band's material did echo back to MARK BURGESS' et al's melancholy output, but it would have been wrong to have taken this analogy too far, as INTERPOL also ran in the tradition of many of the great American East-coast alternative acts. These New Yorkers were brought to the attention of 'Matador', who signed them up in 2002, and released a triple-track single in the early summer of that year. Hot on its heels came the release of their debut album 'TURN ON THE BRIGHT LIGHTS' (2002). Fairly despondent stuff was showcased here but, in mood, rather than quality, which on the whole was promising. Thus more rave reviews followed, not least by NME, who had them play in their UK touring NME awards show at the beginning of 2003.

Album rating: TURN ON THE BRIGHT LIGHTS (*8)

DANIEL KESSLER – vocals, guitar / **PAUL BANKS** – guitar, vocals / **CARLOS DENGLER** – bass, keyboards / **SAM FOGARINO** – drums; repl. GREG

Chemikal U/ground — Chemikal U/ground

Dec 00. (12"ep/cd-ep) *(<CHEM 047/+CD>)* **fukd i.d. #3: PDA**
– PDA / Precipitate / Roland / 5.

Matador — Matador

Jul 02. (7"ep/cd-ep) *<(OLE 546-7/-2)>* **THE INTERPOL EP** Jun02
– PDA / NYC / Specialist.

Aug 02. (cd/lp) *<(OLE 545-2/-1)>* **TURN ON THE BRIGHT LIGHTS**
– Untitled / Obstacle 1 / NYC / PDA / Say hello to the angels / Hands away / Obstacle 2 / Stella was a diver and she was always down / Roland / The new / Leif Erikson.

Nov 02. (7") *(OLE 570-7)* **OBSTACLE 1. / OBSTACLE 2 (Peel session)** 72 –
(cd-s) *(OLE 570-2)* – ('A'side) / PDA (KCRW session) / Hands away (Peel session).

Apr 03. (7") *(OLE 582-7)* **SAY HELLO TO THE ANGELS. / N.Y.C. (demo)** 65 –
(cd-s+=) *(OLE 582-2)* – N.Y.C.

Sep 03. (7") *(OLE 594-7)* **OBSTACLE 1 (remix). / OBSTACLE 1 (live black session)** 41 –
(cd-s) *(OLE 594-2)* – ('A'-Arthur Baker remixes).

INXS

Formed: Sydney, Australia . . . 1977 as The FARRISS BROTHERS by TIM, ANDREW and JON, plus MICHAEL HUTCHENCE, KIRK PENGILLY and GARRY BEERS. After briefly moving to Perth in 1978, they returned the following year as INXS, gigging extensively and eventually landing a deal with 'Deluxe' through 'RCA'. Their second single, 'JUST KEEP WALKING' was a domestic hit in 1980 and after a couple of straightahead rock efforts, 'INXS' (1980) and 'UNDERNEATH THE COLOURS' (1981), the band were eventually picked up by the American-based, 'Atlantic'-affiliated 'Atco' label. Their major label debut, 'SHABOOH SHOOBAH' (1982) eventually reached the lower fringes of the US Top 40 on the strength of single, 'THE ONE THING', which MTV had latched onto, the band's new groove-rock sound and HUTCHENCE's classic rock-god looks making them hot property in the emerging video generation. They caught the eye of top producer and ex-CHIC maestro NILE RODGERS who worked on the 'ORIGINAL SIN' single, a propulsive slice of funk rock that was the highlight of 'THE SWING', the band's 1984 album that once again almost breached the US Top 40. The break eventually came with the 'LISTEN LIKE THIEVES' opus, a Top 20 album in Britain with the single 'WHAT YOU NEED' reaching the UK Top 5. The band also gained valuable exposure by playing the Australian Live Aid that year, rather ironic bearing in mind HUTCHENCE's future relationship with BOB GELDOF. With 'KICK' (1987), the band moved into the mega stardom league, the album a multi-million worldwide success, spawning four international hit singles. 'NEW SENSATION' and 'NEED YOU TONIGHT' (UK No.1) typified the INXS sound; glossy, supple, danceable rock with chunky basslines and HUTCHENCE's breathy vocals magnifying the raunch factor. 'NEVER TEAR US APART', meanwhile, was a rare ballad, uncharacteristically poignant with atmospheric strings. 1987 also saw the frontman's acting debut in Richard Lowenstein's cult movie, 'Dogs In Space'. The following year, after a gruelling world tour, HUTCHENCE recorded an album with IAN OLSEN under the title of MAX Q (named after his dog!), before re-emerging in 1990 with a new INXS album, 'X'. The record trod the same territory as 'KICK' without achieving quite the same effect, only 'SUICIDE BLONDE' and 'DISAPPEAR' making any impact on the singles charts. After packing out London's Wembley Stadium in 1991, an admirable feat for any band, INXS attempted to cast off the stadium rock tag by recording a more ambitious and experimental record, 'WELCOME TO WHEREVER YOU ARE' (1992). As well as a couple of US hits, the album contained the lovely 'BEAUTIFUL GIRL' single, as good as anything the band have recorded to date. With 'FULL MOON, DIRTY HEARTS' (1993), INXS aimed for a rocking return to their earliest recordings, featuring contributions from RAY CHARLES and CHRISSIE HYNDE. The result was only partly successful, the record stiffing completely in the UK. HUTCHENCE had always played the part of the decadent rock star to the max (Q), dating supermodels and allegedly indulging in copious drug use. Although HUTCHENCE had apparently found some sort of stability through a very public romance with PAULA YATES (the final nail in the coffin of her doomed marriage to BOB GELDOF), friends and colleagues were apparently worried about his increasing drug use in recent years. However, no one could have predicted that HUTCHENCE would take his own life, the apparent cause of death after the singer was tragically found hanging from his hotel room door in Sydney, Australia on November 22, 1997. With tabloids speculating that HUTCHENCE was a casualty of a bizarre sex act gone wrong, and PAULA YATES (also now deceased) laying the blame firmly at GELDOF's feet (hysterically calling him "the devil"). Whatever the outcome, the sad fact is that the music world has lost a talented and well loved star, the future of INXS looking decidedly shakey. 'V2' delivered MICHAEL's final solo recordings as his eponymous debut album in October '99, although what critics might have said – had he been still alive – about this basic self-written set (featuring guests BONO and JOE STRUMMER), we'll never know.

• **Songwriters:** Most by ANDREW FARRISS and HUTCHENCE, except some B-sides by TIM. Covered; THE LOVED ONE (The Loved One).

Album rating: INXS (*4) / UNDERNEATH THE COLOURS (*5) / SHABOOH SHOOBAH (*5) / THE SWING (*6) / LISTEN LIKE THIEVES (*7) / KICK (*7) / X (*5) / LIVE BABY LIVE (*3) / WELCOME TO WHEREVER YOU ARE (*6) / FULL MOON, DIRTY HEARTS (*5) / INXS – THE GREATEST HITS compilation (*8) / ELEGANTLY WASTED (*5) / DEFINITIVE INXS compilation (*8) / Max Q: MAX Q (*5) / Michael Hutchence: MICHAEL HUTCHENCE (*4)

MICHAEL HUTCHENCE (b.12 Jan'60, Lain Cove, Sydney, Australia) – vocals / **ANDREW FARRISS** (b.27 Mar'59, Perth, Australia) – keyboards, guitar / **TIM FARRISS** (b.16 Aug'57, Perth) – guitar / **KIRK PENGILLY** (b. 4 Jul'58) – saxophone, guitar, vocals / **GARRY GARY BEERS** (b.22 Jun'57) – bass, vocals / **JON FARRISS** (b.18 Aug'61, Perth) – drums

Deluxe | not iss.

May 80. (7") *(103586)* **SIMPLE SIMON. / WE ARE ALL VEGETABLES** – Austra –

Oct 80. (lp) *(790184-1)* **INXS** – Austra –
– On a bus / Doctor / Just keep walking / Learn to smile / Jumping in vain / Roller skating / Body language / Newsreel babies / Wishy washy. *<US-iss.Aug84 on 'Atco' lp/c; 7.90184-1/-4> (UK-iss.Jul89 on 'Vertigo' lp/c/cd; 838776-1/-4/-2) (re-iss. May90 on 'Vertigo' cd/c/lp; 838925-2/-4/-1)*

Feb 81. (7") *(103741)* **THE LOVED ONE. / THE UNLOVED ONE** – Austra –

Sep 81. (7") *(103884)* **STAY YOUNG. / LACA VOCAL** – Austra –

Jan 82. (7") *(103734)* **NIGHT OF REBELLION. / PREHISTORIA** – Austra –

R.C.A. | not iss.

Sep 81. (7") *(RCA 89)* **JUST KEEP WALKING. / SCRATCH** –

Mar 82. (lp) *(RCALP 3058)* **UNDERNEATH THE COLOURS** –
– Stay young / Horizons / Big go-go / Underneath the colours / Fair weather ahead / Night of rebellion / What would you do / Follow / Barbarian / Just to learn again. *(re-iss. Jul89 on 'Vertigo' lp/c/cd; 838777-1/-4/-2)*

Mercury | Atco

Oct 82. (lp) *<90072>* **SHABOOH SHOOBAH** – 46
– The one thing / To look at you / Spy of love / Soul mistake / Here comes / Black and white / Golden playpen / Jan's song / Old world new world / Don't change. *(UK-iss.Jun87 lp/c; PRICE/PRIMC 94) (cd-iss. May90; 812084-2)*

Oct 82. (7") *(100232)* **DON'T CHANGE. / GO WEST** – Austra –

Mar 83. (7") *<99905>* **THE ONE THING. / PHANTOM OF THE OPERA** – 30

Jun 83. (7") *<99874>* **DON'T CHANGE. / LONG IN TOOTH** – 80

Jun 83. (7") *(INXS 1)* **DON'T CHANGE. / YOU NEVER USED TO CRY** –
(12"+=) *(INXS 12-1)* – Golden playpen.

Sep 83. (7") *(INXS 2)* **THE ONE THING. / THE SAX THING** –
(12") *(INXS 2-12)* – ('A'extended) / Black and white.
(12") *(INXS 2-22)* – ('A'side) / Black and white / Here comes II.

Sep 83. (m-lp) *<7.90115>* **DEKADANCE** (remixes) –
– Black and white / Here comes / The one thing / To look at you.

Feb 84. (7") *(INXS 3)* **ORIGINAL SIN. / JAN'S SONG (live) / TO LOOK AT YOU (live)** –
(12"+=) *(INXS 3-12)* – ('A'extended).

Apr 84. (7") *<99766>* **ORIGINAL SIN. / STAY YOUNG** – 58

May 84. (lp/c) *(MERL/+C 39) <90160>* **THE SWING** 52
– Original sin / Melting in the sun / I send a message / Dancing on the jetty / The swing / Johnson's aeroplane / Love is (what I say) / Face the change / Burn for you / All the voices. *(cd-iss. Jul86; 818 553-2)*

Philips | Atco

May 84. (7") *(PH 2) <99731>* **I SEND A MESSAGE. / MECHANICAL** Jul84 77
(12"+=) *(PH 2-12)* – ('A'-long distance version).

Oct 84. (7") *<99703>* **BURN FOR YOU. / JOHNSON'S AEROPLANE** –

Mercury | Atlantic

Oct 85. (lp/c)(cd) *(MERH/+C 82)(824 957-2) <81277>* **LISTEN LIKE THIEVES** 48 11
– What you need / Listen like thieves / Kiss the dirt (falling down the mountain) / Shine like it does / Good and bad times / Biting bullets / This time / Three sisters / Same direction / One x one / Red red sun. *(initial copies cont. 'THE SWING') (re-iss. Apr95 cd/c;)*

Feb 86. (7") *(INXS 4) <89497>* **THIS TIME. / ORIGINAL SIN (long)** Nov85 81
(12"+=/d7"+=) *(INXS 4-12/D4)* – Burn for you / Dancing on the jetty.

Apr 86. (7") *(INXS 5) <89460>* **WHAT YOU NEED. / SWEET AS SIN** 51 Jan86 5
(w/ free c-s+=) *(INXSC 5)* – This time / What you need (live) / I'm over you / (lp excerpts).
(remix-12"+=) *(INXS 5-12)* – ('A'live) / The one thing.
(remix-d12"++=) *(INXSD 5-12)* – Don't change / Johnsons aeroplane.

Jun 86. (7"/7"sha-pic-d) *(INXS/+P 6) <89429>* **LISTEN LIKE THIEVES. / BEGOTTEN** 46 May86 54
(ext.12"+=) *(INXS 6-12)* – ('A'instrumental remix) / ('A'live).
(d7"+=) *(INXSSD 6)* – One x one / Xs verbiage (band interview).

Aug 86. (7") *(INXS 7)* **KISS THE DIRT. / 6 KNOTS / THE ONE THING (live)** 54 –
(12"+=) *(INXS 7-12)* – Spy of love.
(d7"+=) *(INXSD 7)* – This time / Original sin.

— In Jun'87, INXS were credited with JIMMY BARNES (ex-COLD CHISEL singer), on US single 'GOOD TIMES' <Atlantic; *89237*>, which hit No.47 and was lifted from the film 'The Lost Boys'. Early in 1991, it was finally a UK No.18 hit (Atlantic; *A 7751).*

Oct 87. (7") *(INXS 8) <89188>* **NEED YOU TONIGHT. / I'M COMING (HOME)** 58 1
(12"+=/cd-s+=) *(INXS 8-12/CD8)* – Mediate.

Nov 87. (lp/c)(cd) *(MERH/+C 114)(832 721-2) <81796>* **KICK** 9 3
– Guns in the sky / New sensation / Devil inside / Need you tonight / Mediate / The loved one / Wild life / Never tear us apart / Mystify / Kick / Calling all nations / Tiny daggers. *(pic-lp.Nov88; MERHP 114)*

Dec 87. (7"/7"pic-d) *(INXS/+R 9)* **NEW SENSATION. / DO WOT YOU DO** 25 –
(ext.12"+=) *(INXSR 9-12)* – Love is (what I say).
(12"++=/12"w-poster++=)(c-s++=/cd-s++=) *(INXS/+P 9-12)(INSM/INXSCD 9)* – Same direction.

Feb 88. (7"/7"s) *(INXS/+P 10) <89144>* **DEVIL INSIDE. / ON THE ROCKS** 47 2
(12"+=) *(INXS 10-12)* – ('A'extended).
(cd-s++=) *(INXSCD 10)* – What you need.
(10"+=) *(INXS 10-10)* – Dancing on the jetty / Shine like it does (live).

May 88. (7") *<89080>* **NEW SENSATION. / GUNS IN THE SKY (kookaburra mix)** – 3

Jun 88. (7"/7"w-poster)(7"pic-d/ext.12") *(INXS/+P 11)(INXS 11/+12/00)* **NEVER TEAR US APART. / GUNS IN THE SKY (Kickass remix)** 24 –
(12"+=) *(INXSG 11-12)* – Burn for you / One world new world.
(ext.cd-s+=) *(INXSCD 11)* – Different world / This time.
(10"white+=) *(INXS 11-10)* – Need you tonight / Listen like thieves.

Aug 88. (7") *<89038>* **NEVER TEAR US APART. / DIFFERENT WORLD** – 7

Oct 88. (7"/7"s) *(INXS/+G 12)* **NEED YOU TONIGHT. / MOVE ON** 2 –
('A'-Mendolsohn mix-cd-s+=) *(INXSCD 12)* – Original sin / Don't change.
(12"+=) *(INXS 12-12)* – Kiss the dirt / ('A'-Mendelsohn mix).
('A'-Ben Liebrand mix-12"+=) *(INXSR 12-12)* – New sensation.

Mar 89. (7"/7"g-f) *(INXS/+G 13)* **MYSTIFY. / DEVIL INSIDE (extended)** 14 –
(cd-s+=) *(INXSCD 13)* – What you need (extended) / Listen like thieves.
(12"+=) *(INXS 13-12)* – Never tear us apart (live) / Shine like it does (live).
(12") *(INXS 13-22)* – ('A'side) / Biting bullets / Shine like it does (live) / Never tear us apart (live).

Sep 90. (7") *(INXS 14) <87860>* **SUICIDE BLONDE. / EVERYBODY WANTS U TONIGHT** 11 9
(12"+=)(cd-s+=) *(INXS 14-12)(INXSCD 14)* – ('A'-milk mix).

Sep 90. (cd/c/lp) *(846668-2/-4/-1) <82140>* **X** 2 5
– Suicide blonde / Disappear / The stairs / Faith in each other / By my side / Lately / Who pays the price / Know the difference / Bitter tears / On my way / Hear that sound. *(re-iss. cd/c Apr95)*

Nov 90. (7") *(INXS 15) <87784>* **DISAPPEAR. / MIDDLE BEAST** 21 8
(12"+=)(cd-s+=) *(INXS 15-12)(INXSCD 15)* – What you need (Cold Cut force mix).
(12") *(INXS 15-22)* – ('A'side) / Need you tonight (mix) / New sensation.

Mar 91. (7"/c-s) *(INX S/MC 16)* **BY MY SIDE. / THE OTHER SIDE** 42 –
(12"+=) *(INXS 16-12)* – Faith in each other (live).
(cd-s++=) *(INXSCD 16)* – Disappear (mix).

Mar 91. (c-s) *<87760>* **BITTER TEARS / THE OTHER SIDE** – 46

Jul 91. (7") *(INXS 17)* **BITTER TEARS. / SOOTHE ME** 30 –
(12"+=) *(INXS 17-12)* – Disappear (mix) / ('A'tears are bitter mix) / ('A'other mix).
(cd-s+=) *(INXSCD 17)* – Original sin / Listen like thieves (extended remix).

Oct 91. (7"ep/12"ep/cd-ep) *(INXS/+12/CD 18)* **SHINING STAR** 27
– Shining star / Send a message (live) / Faith in each other (live) / Bitter tears (live).

Nov 91. (cd/c/lp) *(510580-2/-4/-1) <82294>* **LIVE BABY LIVE (live)** 8 72
– New sensation / Mystify / Never tear us apart / Need you tonight / Suicide blonde / By my side / Mediate / Hear that sound / The stairs / What you need / Shining star (studio).

Jul 92. (7"/7"pic-d/c-s/12"/cd-s) *(INX S/P/T/D 19)* **HEAVEN SENT. / IT AIN'T EASY** 31 –

Aug 92. (c-s) *<87437>* **NOT ENOUGH TIME / DEEPEST RED** – 28

Aug 92. (cd/c/lp) *(512507-2/-4/-1) <82394>* **WELCOME TO WHEREVER YOU ARE** 1 16
– Questions / Heaven sent / Communication / Taste it / Not enough time / All around / Baby don't cry / Beautiful girl / Wishing well / Back on line / Strange desire / Men and women. *(re-iss. cd/c Apr95)*

Sep 92. (7"/c-s) *(INX S/MC 20)* **BABY DON'T CRY. / (part 2)** 20
(cd-s+=) *(INXSCD 20)* – Ptar speaks / Question 8 (instrumental) / ('A'acappella mix).

Nov 92. (7"/c-s) *(INX S/MC 23)* **TASTE IT. / LIGHT THE PLANET** 21
(cd-s+=) *(INXCD 23)* – Youth / Not enough time (mix).

Feb 93. (7"/c-s) *(INX S/MC 24)* **BEAUTIFUL GIRL. / IN MY LIVING ROOM / ASHTAR SPEAKS** 23 –
(cd-s) *(INXCD 24)* – ('A'side) / Strange desire.
(cd-s) *(INXCT 24)* – ('A'side) / Underneath my colours / Wishing well.

Feb 93. (c-s) *<87383>* **BEAUTIFUL GIRL / STRANGE DESIRE** – 46

Oct 93. (7"/c-s) *(INX S/MC 25)* **THE GIFT. / ('A'mix)** 11
(cd-s+=) *(INXCD 25)* – Born to be wild.
(cd-s+=) *(INXCT 25)* – Heaven sent (live).

Nov 93. (cd/c/lp) *(518637-2/-4/-1) <82541>* **FULL MOON, DIRTY HEARTS** 3 53
– Days of rust / The gift / Make your peace / Time / I'm only looking / Please (you got that . . .) / Full moon, dirty hearts / Freedom deep / Kill the pain / Cut your roses down / The messenger / Viking juice.
(below single featured RAY CHARLES)

Dec 93. (12"/c-s) *(INX S/MC 26)* **PLEASE (YOU GOT THAT . . .). / TASTE IT (live)** 50
(cd-s) *(INXCD 26)* – ('A'side) / ('A'edit) / Freedom deep (extended 12"mix) / Communication (live).

Oct 94. (7"red/c-s) *(INX S/MC 27)* **THE STRANGEST PARTY (THESE ARE THE TIMES). / WISHING WELL** 15
(cd-s+=) *(INXCD 27)* – ('A'mix) / Sing something.
(cd-s) *(INXCT 27)* – ('A'side) / Need you tonight (remix) / I'm only looking (remix).

Nov 94. (cd/c/lp) *(526230-2/-4/-1) <82622>* **INXS – THE GREATEST HITS** (compilation) 3
– Mystify / Suicide blonde / Taste it / The strangest party (these are the times) / Need you tonight / Original sin / Heaven sent / Disappear / Never tear us apart / The gift / Devil inside / Beautiful girl / Deliver me / New sensation / What you need / Listen like thieves / Bitter tears / Baby don't cry.

— From mid-90's, HUTCHENCE and BOB GELDOF's estranged missus PAULA YATES starting living together. In 1996, complete with breast implants, she had HUTCHENCE's baby (another with a long silly Christian name)

Mar 97. (c-s/cd-s) *(INX MC/CD 28)* **ELEGANTLY WASTED / I'M ONLY LOOKING** 20
(cd-s+=) *(INXDD 28)* – Need you tonight / Original sin (mix).

Apr 97. (cd/c) *(<534 613-2/-4>)* **ELEGANTLY WASTED** 16 41
– Show me (cherry baby) / Elegantly wasted / Everything / Don't lose your head / Searching / I'm just a man / Girl on fire / We are thrown together / Shake the tree / She is rising / Building bridges / Shine.

May 97. (c-s) *(INXMC 29)* **EVERYTHING / BELIEVE** 71 –
(cd-s+=) *(INXCD 29)* – Suicide blonde.
(cd-s) *(INXDD 29)* – ('A'side) / Never tear you apart / What you need.

Sep 97. (promo;cd-s) *(INXCD 30)* **SEARCHING (mixes; leadstation / album / Alex Reece drum n' bass / Linslee Campbell R'n'B)** –

— On the 22nd November '97, HUTCHENCE committed suicide after a party in his hotel room. Obviously, the band look like calling it a day

– compilations, etc. –

on 'Mercury' unless mentioned otherwise

Oct 02. (d-cd) *Raven; (RVCD 145)* **STAY YOUNG 1979-1982: THE COMPLETE DELUXE YEARS** ☐ ☐

Oct 02. (cd-s) *(63885-2)* **TIGHT (mixes; Randy Nicklaus / Thick Dick vocal / Dino Lenny)** ☐ –
(cd-s) *(63884-2)* – ('A'side) / ('A'-Automator mix).

Oct 02. (cd/c) *(<63356-2/-4>)* **DEFINITIVE INXS** 15 Dec02 ☐
– Need you tonight / What you need / Disappear / Baby don't cry / Elegantly wasted / Mystify / Just keep walking / Suicide blonde / Never tear us apart / Shining star / Beautiful girl / Listen like thieves / New sensation / Bitter tears / Original sin / The Devil inside / Gift / By my side / Born to be wild / Salvation Jane / Tight (Randy Nicklaus mix). *(<ltd d-cd+=; 63355-2>)* – Mystify (live) / Suicide blonde (live) / New sensation (live) / Tight (automator mix) / Precious heart / I'm so crazy / Suicide blonde / Need you tonight / Mystify.

– some other AUSTRALIA only releases –

on 'WEA' unless mentioned otherwise

Oct 83. (7") *(259727-7)* **ORIGINAL SIN. / IN VAIN / JUST KEEP WALKING (live)** – –

1984. (12") *(259443-1)* **BURN FOR YOU. / JOHNSON'S AEROPLANE** – –

1984. (7"/12") *(259198)* **DANCING ON THE JETTY. / THE HARBOUR** – –

MICHAEL HUTCHENCE also released below single

1987. (7") **ROOMS FOR THE MEMORY. / GOLFCOURSE** – –

MAX Q

(HUTCHENCE with **IAN 'OLLIE' OLSEN** duo named after his dog!)

Mercury Atlantic

Sep 89. (7") *(MXQ 1) <88844>* **WAY OF THE WORLD. / ZERO 2-0** ☐ ☐
(c-s+=/cd-s+=)(12"+=) *(MXQ MC/CD 1)(MXQ 1-12)* – Ghost of the year (Todd Terry mix).

Oct 89. (lp/c/cd) *(838942-1/-4/-2) <82014>* **MAX Q** 69 ☐
– Sometimes / Way of the world / Ghost of the year / Everything / Zero 2-0 / Soul engine / Buckethead / Monday night by satellite / Tight / Ot-ven-rot.

Feb 90. (7"/7"w-poster/c-s) *(MXQ/+P/MC 2)* **SOMETIMES. / LOVE MAN** 53 –
(12"+=) *(MXQ 22-12)* – ('A'instrumental).
(12"+=/cd-s+=) *(MXQ 2-12/CD2)* – ('A'-land of Oz mix) / ('A'-rock house mix).

Feb 90. (7") *<88754>* **SOMETIMES. / GHOST OF THE YEAR** – ☐

MICHAEL HUTCHENCE

V2 Sony

Oct 99. (c-s/cd-s) *(VVR 501079-5/-3)* **A STRAIGHT LINE / STANDING ON THE ROOFTOP / THE PASSENGER** ☐ –

Oct 99. (cd) *(VVR 100788-2) <707888>* **MICHAEL HUTCHENCE** ☐ Dec99 ☐
– Let me show you / Possibilties / Get on the inside / Fear / All I'm saying / A straight line / Baby it's alright / Don't save me from myself / She flirts for England / Flesh and blood / Put the pieces back together / Breathe / Slide away.

☐ Tony IOMMI (see under ⇒ BLACK SABBATH)

IRON BUTTERFLY

Formed: San Diego, California, USA . . . 1966 by DOUG INGLE, RON BUSHY, DANNY WEIS, JERRY PENROD and DARRYL DeLOACH. They soon moved to Los Angeles and after being spotted at the Whiskey A-Go-Go, they signed to Atlantic subsidiary label, 'Atco'. Early in 1968, they issued the 'HEAVY' album, which bulldozed its way into the lower regions of the US Top 100. Later that summer, WEIS and PENROD departed, superseded by LEE DORMAN and ERIK BRAUN. This line-up subsequently recorded the organ-driven, progressive proto-metal of 'IN-A-GADDA-DA-VIDA' (aka 'The Garden of Life'), a classic album which hit the US Top 5, going on to sell over three million copies. The edited title track (trimmed from 17-minute LP version) gave them additional success in the singles chart. With the aforementioned album still riding high in the charts, their 1969 'BALL' album bounced into the Top 3. In 1970, IRON BUTTERFLY introduced the twin-guitar assault of MIKE PIERA and LARRY REINHARDT, who featured on their Top 20 set, 'METAMORPHOSIS'. They split soon after, only to surface again in 1975 with two poor efforts, 'SCORCHING BEAUTY' and 'SUN AND STEEL'. • **Songwriters:** INGLE and BUSHY were main contributors until the addition/departure of BRAUN and DORMAN. • **Trivia:** In 1968, two tracks, 'POSSESSION' and 'UNCONSCIOUS POWER' were used on the film soundtrack of 'The Savage Seven'.

Album rating: HEAVY (*6) / IN-A-GADDA-DA-VIDA (*9) / BALL (*6) / IRON BUTTERFLY LIVE (*3) / METAMORPHOSIS (*5) / THE BEST OF IRON BUTTERFLY – EVOLUTION compilation (*6) / SCORCHING BEAUTY (*4) / SUN AND STEEL (*3) / LIGHT AND HEAVY – THE BEST OF IRON BUTTERFLY compilation (*7)

DOUG INGLE (b. 9 Sep'46, Omaha, Nebraska) – keyboards, vocals /**JERRY PENROD** – guitar / **DANNY WEIS** – guitar (both ex-DAVID ACKLES band) / **RON BUSHY** (b.23 Sep'45, Washington, D.C.) – drums, vocals / **DARRYL DeLOACH** – bass, vocals

Atco Atco

Feb 68. (lp) *(2465 015) <33227>* **HEAVY** ☐ 78
– Possession / Unconscious power / Get out of my life, woman / Gentle as it may seem / You can't win / So-lo / Look for the sun / Fields of sun / Stamped ideas / Iron butterfly theme. *(cd-iss. 1992 on 'Repertoire'+=;)* – I can't help but deceive you little girl / To be alone.

Atlantic Atco

Jun 68. (7") *(584 188) <6573>* **POSSESSION. / UNCONSCIOUS POWER** ☐ May68 ☐

— **ERIK BRAUN** (b.11 Aug'50, Boston, Mass.) – lead guitar, vocals repl. WEIS and PENROD who formed RHINOCEROS / **LEE DORMAN** (b.19 Sep'45, St.Louis, Missouri) – bass, multi repl. DeLOACH

Jul 68. (lp; mono/stereo) *(587/588 116) <33250>* **IN-A-GADDA-DA-VIDA** ☐ 4
– Most anything you want / Flowers and beads / My mirage / Termination / Are you happy / In-a-gadda-da-vida. *(re-iss. Jan73; K 40022) (cd-iss. Jul87 & Jun93; K2 40022) <(special cd-iss. Nov95 on 'Rhino'; 8122 72196-2)> (lp re-iss. Oct97 on 'Simply Vinyl'; SVLP 15)*

Aug 68. (7") *<6606>* **IN-A-GADDA-DA-VIDA (edit). / IRON BUTTERFLY THEME** – 30

Feb 69. (lp) *(228 011) <33280>* **BALL** ☐ 3
– In the time of our lives / Soul experience / Lonely boy / Real fright / In the crowds / It must be love / Her favourite style / Filled with fear / Belda-beast. *<(cd-iss. May00 on 'Collector's Choice'; CCM 0088-2)>*

Mar 69. (7") *(584 254) <6647>* **SOUL EXPERIENCE. / IN THE CROWDS** ☐ Feb69 75

Jul 69. (7") *<6676>* **IN THE TIME OF OUR LIVES. / IT MUST BE LOVE** – 96

Nov 69. (7") *<6712>* **I CAN'T HELP BUT DECEIVE YOU LITTLE GIRL. / TO BE ALONE** – ☐

Apr 70. (lp) *(2400 014) <33318>* **IRON BUTTERFLY LIVE (live)** ☐ 20
– In the time of our lives / Filled with fear / Soul experience / You can't win / Are you happy / In-a-gadda-da-vida. *(re-iss. 1972; K 40086) (re-iss. 1981; K 40088)*

Jul 70. (7") *(2091 024)* **IN-A-GADDA-DA-VIDA (edit). / TERMINATION** ☐ –

— **INGLE, BUSHY and DORMAN** recruited new members **MIKE PINERA** (b.29 Sep'48, Tampa, Florida) – guitar, vocals (ex-BLUES IMAGE) repl. BRAUN who later formed FLINTWHISTLE / added **LARRY REINHARDT** (b. 7 Jul'48, Florida) – guitar

Oct 70. (7") *<6782>* **EASY RIDER (LET THE WIND PAY THE WAY). / SOLDIER IN OUR TOWN** – 66

Feb 71. (7") *<6818>* **SILLY SALLY. / STONE BELIEVER** – ☐

Apr 71. (lp) *(2401 003)* <33339> **METAMORPHOSIS** ☐ Aug70 16
– Free flight / New day / Shady lady / Best years of our lives / Slower than guns / Stone believer / Soldier in our town / Easy rider (let the wind pay the way) / Butterfly bleu. *(re-iss. 1971; K 40294) (cd-iss. Jun92 on 'Repertoire'; RR 4262)*

— Disbanded Spring '71, with DORMAN and REINHARDT forming CAPTAIN BEYOND. PINERA formed RAMATAM before later joining ALICE COOPER (1981-82). Re-formed 1974, as 4-piece with **BUSHY, BRAUN** and newcomers **HOWARD REITZES** (b.22 Mar'51, Southgate, Calif.) – keyboards, vocals / **PHIL KRAMER** (b.12 Jul'52, Youngstown, Ohio) – bass, vocals

M.C.A. M.C.A.

Feb 75. (lp) *(MCF 2694)* <465> **SCORCHING BEAUTY** ☐ ☐
– 1975 overture / Hard miseree / High on a mountain top / Am I down / People of the world / Searchin' circles / Pearly Gates / Lonely hearts / Before you go. *(cd-iss. Jun95 & Nov02 on 'Repertoire'; RR 4558)*

Feb 75. (7") <40379> **SEARCHIN' CIRCLES. / PEARLY GATES** – ☐

— **BILL DeMARTINES** – keyboards repl. REITZES

Dec 75. (lp) *(MCF 2738)* <2164> **SUN AND STEEL** ☐ ☐
– Sun and steel / Lightnin' / Beyond the Milky Way / Free / Scion / Get it out / I'm right, I'm wrong / Watch the world goin' by / Scorching beauty. *(cd-iss. Mar95 on 'Edsel'; EDCD 408)*

Jan 76. (7") *(MCA 221)* <40494> **BEYOND THE MILKY WAY. / GET IT OUT** ☐ ☐

— Broke up again in 1976, BUSHY formed JUICY GROOVE.

— In May'89, IRON BUTTERFLY reformed w/**DORMAN, BRAUN, REINHARDT** and new men **STEVE FELDMANN** – vocals / **DEREK HILLARD** – keyboards / **KENNY SUAREZ** – drums

– compilations, others, etc. –

on 'Atlantic' UK & 'Atco' US unless mentioned otherwise

Jan 72. (lp) *(K 40298)* <33369> **EVOLUTION – THE BEST OF IRON BUTTERFLY** ☐ Dec71 ☐
– Iron Butterfly theme / Possession / Unconscious power / Flowers and beads / Termination / In-a-gadda-da-vida / Soul experience / Stone believer / Belda-beast / Easy rider (let the wind pay the way) / Slower than guns.

1973. (lp) *(30038)* **STAR COLLECTION** ☐ –

Oct 75. (d-lp) *(K 80003)* **TWO ORIGINALS OF . . .** ☐ –
– (BALL / METAMORPHISIS)

Feb 93. (cd) *Rhino; (8122 71166-2)* **LIGHT AND HEAVY: THE BEST OF IRON BUTTERFLY** ☐ ☐

☐ IRONHORSE

(see under ⇒ BACHMAN-TURNER OVERDRIVE)

IRON MAIDEN

Formed: Leytonstone, East London, England . . . mid 1976 by STEVE HARRIS, DAVE MURRAY, PAUL DiANNO and DOUG SAMPSON, who played their earliest gigs around mid '77 – an embryonic late '75 IRON MAIDEN included HARRIS, PAUL DAY (vocals), DAVE SULLIVAN (guitar), TERRY RANCE (guitar) and RON MATTHEWS (drums). The band's amphetamine-fuelled trad-metal soon procured them a rabid following around the capital and the following year they released a self-financed debut EP, 'THE SOUNDHOUSE TAPES'. The cassette came to the attention of Rock DJ, Neal Kay, who sent them on a 'Heavy Metal Crusade' tour at London's Music Machine, the resultant publicity and increasing interest in the band leading to a deal with 'E.M.I.' in 1979 (this coincided with personnel changes, CLIVE BURR replacing SAMPSON, while DENNIS STRATTON replaced brief member TONY PARSONS. Their debut single, the 100 horsepower outlaw fantasy, 'RUNNING FREE', hit the shops and UK Top 40 early in 1980, soon followed by a self-titled debut album which made the Top 5. IRON MAIDEN were the leading lights of the New Wave Of British Heavy Metal; carrying on where BLACK SABBATH and URIAH HEEP left off, they helped to create and embody the cartoon caricature that the genre would become. Despite production problems, the debut album remains one the most enduring of their career, the material raw and hungry where later efforts have tended towards flabbiness. Masters of the power chord, tracks like 'IRON MAIDEN' and 'CHARLOTTE THE HARLOT' (Politically Correct this band were not, although the phrase could be interpreted in a different way with regards to the 'KILLERS' album sleeve, a depiction of Thatcher meeting an untimely end) were prime headbanging material, DI'ANNO's vocals more guttural punk than metal warbling. Yet the band were no musical novices, the stop-start exhilaration of 'PHANTOM OF THE OPERA' sounding considered and spontaneous at the same time. A hasty follow-up, the aforementioned 'KILLERS' (1981), lacked the focus of the debut, something which didn't deter metal fans from buying it in droves. By the release of 'THE NUMBER OF THE BEAST' (1982), DI'ANNO had been replaced by BRUCE DICKINSON, more of a vocal acrobat in the traditional metal sense. More accessible and melodic, if not as exciting, the record was a massive success (No.1 in Britain), packed with songs that would go on to form the backbone of the 'MAIDEN live set. 'RUN TO THE HILLS' was a particular favourite, giving the band their first Top 10 placing in the pop singles chart. 'PIECE OF MIND' (1983) and 'POWERSLAVE' (1984) carried on in much the same anthemic vein, the band capitalising on their staggering worldwide popularity with a mammoth touring schedule. With their trademark ghoulish mascot, 'EDDIE', horror fantasy artwork and readily identifiable sound, the band were arguably the very essence of 'Heavy Metal', a phenomenon which traversed all language boundaries in much the same way as dance music in the 90's. 'SOMEWHERE IN TIME' (1986) marked something of a departure, a more ambitious and musically diverse collection both in terms of songwriting and playing. This avenue was further explored on 'SEVENTH SON OF A SEVENTH SON' (1988), a concept affair that piled on the synth and sharpened the harmonies, resulting in four consecutive Top 10 singles. The steadfast reliability of the band's fanbase was amply illustrated when a series of EP's repackaging the band's singles went Top 10 almost without exception. But there was tension in the ranks with HARRIS favouring a return to their chest beating roots while guitarist ADRIAN SMITH was less than pleased with the prospect. In the event, SMITH was replaced with JANICK GERS and the band released the no-frills 'NO PRAYER FOR THE DYING' (1990), a back to basics effort which spawned IRON MAIDEN's first No.1 single, the side-splittingly titled 'BRING YOUR DAUGHTER . . . TO THE SLAUGHTER'. 'FEAR OF THE DARK' (1992) gave the band yet another No.1 album, the last to feature the tonsils of DICKINSON, who soon departed for a solo career. DICKINSON's eventual replacement was BLAZE BAILEY (ex-WOLFSBANE) who made his debut on 'THE X-FACTOR' (1995), a record that achieved their lowest chart placing since 'KILLERS'. 1998's 'VIRTUAL XI' was another relative disappointment although the MAIDEN hordes took heart when BRUCE DICKINSON returned to the fray in early '99. The resulting tour was a blockbuster and paved the way for a new studio album featuring the classic line-up of DICKINSON, HARRIS, MURRAY, McBRAIN and SMITH alongside JANICK GERS who was retained as a third guitarist. 'BRAVE NEW WORLD' was released in spring 2000 amid much fanfare and expectation, the album's return to MAIDEN's halcyon mid-80's period – in terms of both gothic fantasy songwriting and crunching powerchord assault – pleasing longtime fans no end and seemingly securing the band's place in the post-metal wilderness. If the rather pointless 'ROCK IN RIO' (2002) live set perhaps showed up – however unintentionally – the gap in ambition between classic 'MAIDEN and their stodgier latter day fare, the back to basics 'DANCE OF DEATH' (2003) succeeded in harnessing at least some of that kinetic energy of old as they fast approached their 30th year in business. • **Songwriters:** All mostly HARRIS and group. In the 90's, HARRIS or DICKINSON + GERS. Covered; COMMUNICATION BREAKDOWN (Led Zeppelin) / KILL ME, CE SOIR (Golden Earring) / SPACE STATION No.5 (Montrose). DICKINSON solo re-hashed; ALL THE YOUNG DUDES (hit; Mott The Hoople). • **Trivia:** Derek Riggs became the group's artistic designer and created 'EDDIE', an evil skeleton comic-strip character, who appeared on album sleeves, poster bills & theatrical stage shows. Banned in Chile for being interpreted as 'devils and satanists'. First band to play 'live' on Top Of The Pops since The Who.

Album rating: IRON MAIDEN (*9) / KILLERS (*6) / THE NUMBER OF THE BEAST (*7) / PIECE OF MIND (*6) / POWERSLAVE (*6) / LIVE AFTER DEATH (*8) / SOMEWHERE IN TIME (*6) / SEVENTH SON OF A SEVENTH SON (*7) / NO PRAYER FOR THE DYING (*7) / FEAR OF THE DARK (*7) / A REAL LIVE ONE (*5) / A REAL DEAD ONE (*5) / LIVE AT DONINGTON 1992 (*5) / THE X FACTOR (*6) / THE BEST OF THE BEAST compilation (*9) / VIRTUAL XI (*5) / BRAVE NEW WORLD (*7) / BACK IN RIO (*4) / EDWARD THE GREAT: THE GREATEST HITS compilation (*8) / DANCE OF DEATH (*6)

PAUL DI'ANNO (b.17 May'59, Chingford, Essex, England) – vocals / **DAVE MURRAY** (b.23 Dec'58) – guitar / **STEVE HARRIS** (b.12 Mar'57) – bass, vocals / **DOUG SAMPSON** – drums

Rock Hard — not iss.

Jan 79. (7"ep) *(ROK 1)* **THE SOUNDHOUSE TAPES** [ ] [–]
– Invasion / Iron Maiden / Prowler.

—— (Nov79) **CLIVE BURR** (b. 8 Mar'57) – drums repl. SAMPSON / **DENNIS STRATTON** (b. 9 Nov'54) – guitar repl. TONY PARSONS (brief stay)

E.M.I. — Harvest

Feb 80. (7") *(EMI 5032)* **RUNNING FREE. / BURNING AMBITION** [34] [–]

Apr 80. (lp/c) *(EMC/TCEMC 3330)* **IRON MAIDEN** [4] [ ]
– Prowler / Remember tomorrow / Running free / Phantom of the opera / Transylvania / Strange world / Charlotte the harlot / Iron maiden. *(re-iss. May85 on 'Fame' lp/c; FA/TCFA 41-3121-1)* – hit 71 *(cd-iss. Oct87 on 'Fame'; CDFA 3121) (re-iss. cd Jul94; CDEMS 1538) (re-iss. cd Dec95; CDEM 1570) (cd re-iss. Sep98; 496916-0)*

May 80. (7"m) *(EMI 5065)* **SANCTUARY. / DRIFTER / I'VE GOT THE FIRE (live)** [29] [–]

Oct 80. (7") *(EMI 5105)* **WOMEN IN UNIFORM. / INVASION** [35] [–]
(12"+=) *(12EMI 5105)* – Phantom of the opera (live).

—— **ADRIAN SMITH** (b.27 Feb'57) – guitar (ex-URCHIN) repl. STRATTON who formed LIONHEART

Feb 81. (lp/c) *(EMC/TCEMC 3357)* <12141> **KILLERS** [12] [78]
– The ides of march / Wrathchild / Murders in the Rue Morgue / Another life / Ghenghis Khan / Innocent exile / KIllers / Prodigal son / Purgatory / Drifter. *(re-iss. May85 on 'Fame' lp/c; FA/TCFA 41-3122-1) (cd-iss. Oct87 on 'Fame'; CDFA 3122) (re-iss. cd Jul94; CDEMS 1539) (re-iss. cd Dec95; CDEM 1571) (cd re-iss. Sep98; 496917-0)*

Mar 81. (7",7"clear,7"red,c-s) *(EMI 5145)* **TWILIGHT ZONE. / WRATH CHILD** [31] [–]

Jun 81. (7") *(EMI 5184)* **PURGATORY. / GHENGIS KHAN** [52] [–]

Sep 81. (12"ep)<m-lp> *(12EMI 5219)* <15000> **MAIDEN JAPAN** [43] [89]
– Remember tomorrow / Killers / Running free / Innocent exile.

—— **BRUCE DICKINSON** (b. PAUL BRUCE DICKINSON, 7 Aug'58, Sheffield, England) – vocals (ex-SAMSON) repl. DI'ANNO who formed LONE WOLF

Feb 82. (7"/7"pic-d) *(EMI/+P 5263)* **RUN TO THE HILLS. / TOTAL ECLIPSE** [7] [–]

Mar 82. (lp/pic-lp)(c) *(EMC/EMCP/TCEMC 3400)* <12202> **THE NUMBER OF THE BEAST** [1] [33]
– Invaders / Children of the damned / The prisoner / 22, Acacia Avenue / The number of the beast / Run to the hills / Gangland / Hallowed be thy name. *(re-iss. May87 on 'Fame'; FA/TCFA 3178) (cd-iss. Apr88 on 'Fame'; CDFA 3178) (re-iss. cd Jul94; CDEMS 1533) (re-iss. Dec95 on d-cd w/bonus tracks; CDEM 1572) (cd re-iss. Sep98; 496918-0)*

Apr 82. (7"/7"red) *(EMI 5287)* **THE NUMBER OF THE BEAST. / REMEMBER TOMORROW** [18] [–]

—— now **HARRIS, MURRAY, DICKINSON** and **SMITH** were joined by **NICKO McBRAIN** (b. MICHAEL, 5 Jun'54) – drums (ex-PAT TRAVERS, ex-TRUST, ex-STREETWALKERS) repl. BURR who joined STRATUS

E.M.I. — Capitol

Apr 83. (7"/12"pic-d)(c-s) *(EMI/12EMIP 5378)(TC IM4)* <5248> **FLIGHT OF ICARUS. / I'VE GOT THE FIRE** [11] [ ]

May 83. (lp/c) *(EMA/TCEMA 800)* <12274> **PIECE OF MIND** [3] [14]
– Where eagles dare / Revelations / Flight of Icarus / Die with your boots on / The trooper / Still life / Quest for fire / Sun and steel / To tame a land. *(cd-iss. Dec86; CZ 82) (re-iss. 1989 lp/c; ATAK/CDATAK 139) (re-iss. cd Jun91 on 'Fame'; CDFA 3245) (re-iss. cd Jul94; CDEMS 1540) (re-iss. Dec95 on d-cd w/bonus tracks; CDEM 1573) (cd re-iss. Sep98; 496919-0)*

Jun 83. (7",7"sha-pic-d) *(EMI 5397)* **THE TROOPER. / CROSS-EYED MARY** [12] [–]

Aug 84. (7") *(EMI 5489)* **2 MINUTES TO MIDNIGHT. / RAINBOW'S GOLD** [11] [–]
(12"pic-d+=) *(12EMI 5489)* – Mission from 'Arry.

Sep 84. (lp/pic-lp)(c)(cd) *(POWER/+P 1)(TCPOWER 1)(746045-2)* <12321> **POWERSLAVE** [2] [21]
– Aces high / 2 minutes to midnight / Losfer words (big 'orra) / Flash of the blade / The duellists / Back in the village / Powerslave / Rime of the ancient mariner. *(re-iss. 1989 lp/c; ATAK/TCATAK 140) (re-iss. Jun91 on 'Fame'; FA 3244) (re-iss. cd Jul94; CDEMS 1539) (re-iss. Dec95 d-cd w/bonus tracks; CDEM 1574) (cd re-iss. Sep98; 496920-0)*

Oct 84. (7") *(EMI 5502)* **ACES HIGH. / KING OF TWILIGHT** [20] [–]
(12"+=/12"pic-d+=) *(12EMI/+P 5502)* – The number of the beast (live).

Sep 85. (7") *(EMI 5532)* **RUNNING FREE (live). / SANCTUARY (live)** [19] [–]
(12"+=/12"pic-d+=) *(12EMI/+P 5532)* – Murders in the Rue Morgue (live).

Oct 85. (d-lp/c)(cd) *(RIP/TCRIP 1)(746186-2)* <12441> **LIVE AFTER DEATH (live)** [2] [19]
– Aces high / 2 minutes to midnight / The trooper / Revelations / Flight of Icarus / The rime of the ancient mariner / Powerslave / The number of the beast / Hallowed be thy name / Iron maiden / Run to the hills / Running free. *(d-lp+=/c+=)* – Wrathchild / 22 Acacia Avenue / Children of the damned / Die with your boots on / Phantom of the opera. *(re-iss. 1989 lp/c; ATAK/TCATAK 141) (re-iss. Jun91 on 'Fame' w/ less tracks; CDFA 3248) (re-iss. cd Jul94 w/ fewer tracks; CDEMS 1535) (re-iss. Dec95 d-cd w/ bonus tracks; CDEM 1575) (d-cd re-iss. Sep98; 496921-0)*

Nov 85. (7") *(EMI 5542)* **RUN TO THE HILLS (live). / PHANTOM OF THE OPERA (live)** [26] [–]
(12"+=/12"pic-d+=) *(12EMI/+P 5542)* – Losfer words (The big 'orra) (live).

Aug 86. (7"/7"sha-pic-d) *(EMI/+P 5583)* **WASTED YEARS. / REACH OUT** [18] [–]
(12"+=) *(12EMI 5583)* – The sheriff of Huddersfield.

Sep 86. (lp/c)(cd) *(EMC/TCEMC 3512)(746341-2)* <12524> **SOMEWHERE IN TIME** [3] [11]
– Caught somewhere in time / Wasted years / Sea of madness / Heaven can wait / The loneliness of the long distance runner / Stranger in a strange land / Deja-vu / Alexander the Great. *(re-iss. 1989 lp/c; ATAK/TCATAK 142) (re-iss. Jun91 on 'Fame'; CDFA 3246) (re-iss. cd Jul94; CDEMS 1537) (re-iss. Dec95 d-cd w/bonus tracks; CDEM 1576) (cd re-iss. Sep98; 496924-0)*

Nov 86. (7") *(EMI 5589)* **STRANGER IN A STRANGE LAND. / THAT GIRL** [22] [–]
(12"+=/12"pic-d+=) *(12EMI/+P 5589)* – Juanita.

Mar 88. (7"/7"w sticker & transfer/7"sha-pic-d) *(EM/+S/P 49)* <44154> **CAN I PLAY WITH MADNESS. / BLACK BART BLUES** [3] [ ]
(12"+=/cd-s+=) *(12EM/CDEM 49)* – Massacre.

Apr 88. (cd/c/lp)(pic-lp) *(TC/CD+/EMD 1006)(EMDP 1006)* <90258> **SEVENTH SON OF A SEVENTH SON** [1] [12]
– Moonchild / Infinite dreams / Can I play with madness / The evil that men do / Seventh son of a seventh son / The prophecy / The clairvoyant / Only the good die young. *(re-iss. 1989 lp/c; ATAK/TCATAK 143) (re-iss. Jun91 on 'Fame'; CDFA 3247) (re-iss. cd Jul94; CDEMS 1534) (re-iss. Dec95 d-cd w/bonus tracks; CDEM 1577) (cd re-iss. Sep98; 496864-0)*

Aug 88. (7"/7"g-f/7"sha-pic-d) *(EM/+G/P 64)* **THE EVIL THAT MEN DO. / PROWLER '88** [5] [ ]
(12"+=/12"poster)(cd-s+=) *(12EM/+S 64)(CDEM 64)* – Charlotte the harlot '88.

Nov 88. (7"/7"clear/7"sha-pic-d) *(EM/+S/P 79)* **THE CLAIRVOYANT (live). / THE PRISONER (live)** [6] [ ]
(12"+=/12"pic-d+=)(cd-s+=) *(12EM/+P 79)(CDEM 79)* – Heaven can wait (live).

Nov 89. (7"/7"sha-pic-d)(c-s) *(EM/+PD 117)(TCEM 117)* **INFINITE DREAMS (live). / KILLERS (live)** [6] [ ]
(12"+=/cd-s+=)(12"etched+=) *(12/CD EM 117)* – Still life (live).

— (Feb'90) **JANICK GERS** – guitar (ex-GILLAN, ex-WHITE SPIRIT, etc.) repl. SMITH who formed A.S.A.P.

E.M.I. Epic

Sep 90. (7"/c-s) *(EM/TCEM 158)* **HOLY SMOKE. / ALL IN YOUR MIND** [3] [ ]
(12"+=/12"pic-d+=)(cd-s+=) *(12EM/+P 158)(CDEM 158)* – Kill me ce soir.

Oct 90. (cd/c/lp)(pic-lp)<red-lp> *(CD/TC+/EMD 1017)(EMPD 1017) <E 46905>* **NO PRAYER FOR THE DYING** [2] [17]
– Tailgunner / Holy smoke / No prayer for the dying / Public enema number one / Fates warning / The assassin / Run silent run deep / Hooks in you / Bring your daughter . . . to the slaughter / Mother Russia. *(re-iss. cd Jul94; CDEMS 1541) (re-iss. Dec95 d-cd w/bonus tracks; CDEM 1578) (cd re-iss. Sep98; 496865-4)*

Dec 90. (7"/7"pic-d)(c-s) *(EM/+PD 171)(TCEM 171)* **BRING YOUR DAUGHTER . . . TO THE SLAUGHTER. / I'M A MOVER** [1] [ ]
(12"+=/12"pic-d+=)(cd-s+=) *(12EM/+P 171)(CDEM 171)* – Communication breakdown.

— In Summer 1991, HARRIS and McBAIN back up tennis stars McENROE & CASH on their version of LED ZEPPELIN'S 'Rock And Roll'. In Mar'92, BRUCE DICKINSON was to feature on single with Rowan Atkinson's comic character 'MR.BEAN & SMEAR CAMPAIGN' on a version of an Alice Cooper song '(I Want To Be) Elected'.

Apr 92. (7") *(EM 229)* **BE QUICK OR BE DEAD. / NODDING DONKEY BLUES** [2] [ ]
(12"+=/12"pic-d+=)(cd-s+=) *(12EM/+P 229)(CDEM 229)* – Space station No.5.

May 92. (cd/c/d-lp) *(CD/TC+/EMD 1032) <48993>* **FEAR OF THE DARK** [1] [12]
– Be quick or be dead / From here to eternity / Afraid to shoot strangers / Fear is the key / Childhood's end / Wasting love / The fugitive / Chains of misery / The apparition / Judas be my guide / Weekend warrior / Fear of the dark. *(re-iss. cd Jul94; CDEM 1542) (re-iss. Dec95 d-cd w/bonus tracks +=; CDEM 1579)* – Nodding donkey blues / Space station No.5 / I can't see my feeling / No prayer for the dying (live) / Public enema No.1 (live) / Hook in you (live). *(cd re-iss. Sep98; 496925-0)*

Jul 92. (7"etched) *(EM 240)* **FROM HERE TO ETERNITY. / ROLL OVER VIC VELLA** [21] [ ]
(12"+=/cd-s+=) *(12/CD EM 240)* – Public enema number one / No prayer for the dying.
(7"sha-pic-d) *(EMPD 240)* – ('A'side) / I can't see my feeling.

E.M.I. Capitol

Mar 93. (7"/7"sha-pic-d) *(EMP/+D 263)* **FEAR OF THE DARK (live). / TAILGUNNER (live)** [8] [ ]
(cd-s+=) *(CDEM 263)* – Hooks in you (live) *(on some 7"sha-pic-d)* / Bring your daughter . . .to the slaughter (live).

Mar 93. (cd/c/lp) *(CD/TC+/EMD 1042) <81456>* **A REAL LIVE ONE (live)** [3] [ ]
– Be quick or be dead / From here to eternity / Can I play with madness / Wasting love / Tailgunner / The evil that men do / Afraid to shoot strangers / Bring your daughter . . .to the slaughter / Heaven can wait / The clairvoyant / Fear of the dark.

— DICKINSON had already announced he had departed to go solo in '94

Oct 93. (7"red) *(EM 288)* **HALLOWED BE THY NAME (live). / WRATHCHILD (live)** [9] [ ]
(12"pic-d+=/cd-s+=) *(12EMP/CDEM 288)* – The trooper (live) / Wasted years (live).

Oct 93. (cd/c/lp) *(CD/TC+/EMD 1048) <89248>* **A REAL DEAD ONE (live)** [12] [ ]
– The number of the beast / The trooper / Prowler / Transylvania / Remember tomorrow / Where eagles dare / Sanctuary / Running free / Run to the hills / 2 minutes to midnight / Iron Maiden / Hallowed be thy name. *(this & last "live" set, re-iss. Sep98; 496926-0)*

Nov 93. (d-cd/d-c/t-lp) *(CD/MC+/DON 1)* **LIVE AT DONINGTON 1992 (live)** [23] [–]
– Be quick or be dead / The number of the beast / Wrathchild / From here to eternity / Can I play with madness / Wasting love / Tailgunner / The evil that men do / Afraid to shoot strangers / Fear of the dark / Bring your daughter . . . to the slaughter / The clairvoyant / Heaven can wait / Run to the hills / 2 minutes to midnight / Iron maiden / Hallowed be thy name / The trooper / Sanctuary / Running free. *(re-iss. Sep98; 496929-0)*

— **BLAZE BAILEY** – vocals (ex-WOLFSBANE) now his replacement

E.M.I. CMC Int.

Sep 95. (c-s) *(TCEM 398)* **MAN ON THE EDGE / THE EDGE OF DARKNESS** [10] [ ]
(12"pic-d+=) *(12EM 398)* – I live my way.
(cd-s+=) *(CDEMS 398)* – Judgement day / (Blaze Bailey interview part 1).
(cd-s+=) *(CDEM 398)* – Justice of the peace / (Blaze Bailey interview part 2).

Oct 95. (cd/c/clear-d-lp) *(+CD/TC EMD 1087) <8003>* **THE X FACTOR** [9] [ ]
– Sign of the cross / Lord of the flies / Man on the edge / Fortunes of war / Look for the truth / The aftermath / Judgement of Heaven / Blood on the world's hands / The edge of darkness / 2 a.m. / The unbeliever.

Sep 96. (12") *(12EM 443)* **VIRUS. / PROWLER (the Soundhouse tapes) / INVASION (the Soundhouse tapes)** [16] [ ]
(cd-s) *(CDEM 443)* – ('A'side) / My generation / Doctor, doctor.
(cd-s) *(CDEMS 443)* – ('A'side) / Sanctuary (metal for muthas) / Wrathchild (metal for muthas).

Sep 96. (d-cd/q-lp) *(CDEMDS 1097)* **BEST OF THE BEAST** (compilation with all line-ups) [16] [ ]
– Virus / Sign of the cross / Afraid to shoot strangers (live) / Man on the edge / Be quick or be dead / Fear of the dark (live) / Holy smoke / Bring your daughter . . . to the slaughter / Seventh son of a seventh son / Can I play with madness / The evil that men do / The clairvoyant / Heaven can wait / Wasted years / / 2 minutes to midnight / Running free (live) / Rime of the ancient mariner (live) / Aces high / Where eagles dare / The trooper * / The number of the beast / Revelations * / The prisoner * / Run to the hills / Hallowed be thy name / Wrathchild / Killers * / Remember tomorrow * / Phantom of the opera / Sanctuary / Prowler * / Invasion * / Strange world / Iron maiden. *(q-lp+= *)*

Mar 98. (7"pic-d) *(EM 507)* **THE ANGEL AND THE GAMBLER. / BLOOD ON THE WORLD'S HANDS (live) / THE AFTERMATH (live)** [18] [ ]
(cd-s) *(CDEMS 507)* – (first 2 tracks) / Afraid to shoot strangers (CD-Rom video).
(cd-s) *(CDEM 507)* – (first & third tracks) / The aftermath (live) / Man on the edge (CD-Rom video).

Mar 98. (cd/c/d-lp) *(493915-2/-4/-1) <86240>* **VIRTUAL XI** [16] [ ]
– Futureal / The angel and the gambler / Lightning strikes twice / Clansman / When two worlds collide / Educated fool / Don't look to the eyes of a stranger / Como estais amigos.

Sep 98. (7"pic-d) *(EM 525)* **FUTUREAL. / THE EVIL THAT MEN DO (live) / MAN ON THE EDGE (live)** [–] [–]
(cd-s) *(CDEM 525)* – (first 2) / Futureal (CD-rom).
(cd-s) *(CDEMS 525)* – (first & third) / The angel and the gambler (CD-rom).
(above only available through the internet shopping channel)

— early in '99, BRUCE DICKINSON was now back at the helm (as was **ADRIAN SMITH** – guitar (now a six-piece)

May 00. (12"pic-d) *(12EM 568)* **THE WICKER MAN. / POWERSLAVE (live) / Killers (live)** [9] [ ]
(cd-s) *(CDEMS 568)* – (first two tracks) / Man on the edge (live) / ('A'-CD-Rom).
(cd-s) *(CDEM 568)* – (first & third tracks) / Futureal (live) / Futureal (CD-Rom).

May 00. (cd/c/d-lp) *(526605-2/-4/-1) <62208>* **BRAVE NEW WORLD** [7] [39]
– The wicker man / Ghost of the navigator / Brave new world / Blood brothers / The mercenary / Dream of mirrors / The fallen angel / The nomad / Out of the silent planet / The thin line between love and hate.

Oct 00. (7"red) *(EM 576)* **OUT OF THE SILENT PLANET. / ACES HIGH (live)** [20] [–]
(12"pic-d+=) *(12EM 576)* – Wasted years (live).
(cd-s+=) *(CDEM 576)* – ('A'-CD-ROM video).

Mar 02. (7"red) *(EM 612)* **RUN TO THE HILLS (live in Rio 2001). / RUN TO THE HILLS (original) / TOTAL ECLIPSE (live 1982)** [9] [–]
(cd-s+=) *(CDEM 612)* – Children of the damned (live 1982) / ('A'-video live in Rio 2001).
(cd-s) *(CDEMS 612)* – ('A'side) / 22 Acacia Avenue (live 1982) / Prisoner (live 1982) / ('A'-video Camp Chaos version of 1982 promo).

Mar 02. (d-cd/d-c/t-lp) *(538643-0/-4/-1) <54269>* **ROCK IN RIO (live)** [15] [ ]
– Intro / The wicker man / Ghost of the navigator / Brave new world / Wrathchild / 2 minutes to midnight / Blood brothers / Sign of the cross / The mercenary / The trooper / Brave new world (enhanced video) // Dream of mirrors / The clansman / The evil that men do / Fear of the

dark / Iron maiden / The number of the beast / Hallowed be thy name / Sanctuary / Run to the hills / A day in the life (enhanced video).

E.M.I. Columbia

Sep 03. (7"green) *(EM 627)* **WILDEST DREAMS. / PASS THE JAM** 6 –
(cd-s+=) *(CDEM 627)* – Blood brothers (orchestral mix).

Sep 03. (cd/d-lp) *(592340-2/-1)* <89061> **DANCE OF DEATH** 2 18
– Wildest dreams / Rainmaker / No more lies / Montsegur / Dance of death / Gates of tomorrow / New frontier / Paschendale / Face in the sand / Age of innocence / Journeyman.

Nov 03. (7"blue) *(EM 633)* **RAINMAKER. / DANCE OF DEATH (orchestral version 2)** 13 –
(cd-s+=) *(CDEM 633)* – More tea vicar.

– compilations, etc. –

on 'E.M.I.' unless otherwise stated

Feb 90. (cd-ep/d12") *(CD+/IRN 1)* **RUNNING FREE / BURNING AMBITION / SANCTUARY / DRIFTER (live) / I'VE GOT THE FIRE (live) / Listen with Nicko (part 1)** 10

Feb 90. (cd-ep/d12") *(CD+/IRN 2)* **WOMEN IN UNIFORM / INVASION / PHANTOM OF THE OPERA / TWILIGHT ZONE / WRATHCHILD / Listen with Nicko (part 2)** 10

Feb 90. (cd-ep/d12") *(CD+/IRN 3)* **PURGATORY / GENGHIS KHAN / RUNNING FREE / REMEMBER TOMORROW / KILLERS / INNOCENT EXILE / Listen with Nicko (part 3)** 5

Mar 90. (cd-ep/d12") *(CD+/IRN 4)* **RUN TO THE HILLS / TOTAL ECLIPSE / THE NUMBER OF THE BEAST / REMEMBER TOMORROW (live) / Listen with Nicko (part 4)** 3

Mar 90. (cd-ep/d12") *(CD+/IRN 5)* **FLIGHT OF ICARUS / I'VE GOT THE FIRE / THE TROOPER / CROSS-EYED MARY / Listen with Nicko (part 5)** 7

Mar 90. (cd-ep/d12") *(CD+/IRN 6)* **2 MINUTES TO MIDNIGHT / RAINBOW'S GOLD / MISSION FROM 'ARRY / ACES HIGH / KING OF TWILIGHT / THE NUMBER OF THE BEAST (live) / Listen with Nicko (part 6)** 11

Apr 90. (cd-ep/d12") *(CD+/IRN 7)* **RUNNING FREE / SANCTUARY / MURDERS IN THE RUE MORGUE / RUN TO THE HILLS / PHANTOM OF THE OPERA / LOSFER WORDS (THE BIG 'ORRA) / Listen with Nicko (part 7)** 9

Apr 90. (cd-ep/d12") *(CD+/IRN 8)* **WASTED YEARS / REACH OUT / THE SHERIFF OF HUDDERSFIELD / STRANGER IN A STRANGE LAND / THAT GIRL / JUANITA / Listen with Nicko (part 8)** 9

Apr 90. (cd-ep/d12") *(CD+/IRN 9)* **CAN I PLAY WITH MADNESS / BLACK BART BLUES / MASSACRE / THE EVIL THAT MEN DO / PROWLER '88 / CHARLOTTE THE HARLOT '88 / Listen with Nicko (part 9)** 10

Apr 90. (cd-ep/d12") *(CD+/IRN 10)* **THE CLAIRVOYANT (live) / THE PRISONER (live) / HEAVEN CAN WAIT (live) / INFINITE DREAMS (live) / KILLERS (live) / STILL LIFE (live) / Listen with Nicko (part 10)** 11

—— (all 10 singles above, basically hit peak number before crashing out)

Aug 94. (cd,cd-vid) *(SAV 4913103)* **MAIDEN ENGLAND (live)** –
– Moonchild / The evil that men do / Prisoner / Still life / Die with your boots on / Infinite dreams / Killers / Heaven can wait / Wasted years / The clairvoyant / Seventh son of a seventh son / The number of the best / Iron maiden.

Dec 98. (16xcd-box) *(4979990)* **EDDIE'S HEAD**

May 99. (3xcd-ROM) *(5205200)* **ED HUNTER** –

Nov 02. (cd/c/d-lp) *(543103-2/-4/-1) / Sony;* <86969> **EDWARD THE GREAT: THE GREATEST HITS** 57
– Run to the hills / The number of the beast / Flight of Icarus / The trooper / 2 minutes to midnight / Wasted years / Can I play with madness / The evil that men do / The clairvoyant / Infinite dreams / Holy smoke / Bring your daughter . . . to the slaughter / Man on the edge / Futureal / The wicker man / Fear of the dark.

Nov 02. (6xcd-box) *(541277-2)* **EDDIE'S ARCHIVE**

Chris ISAAK

Born: 6 Jun'56, Stockton, California, USA. In 1984, after graduating with a degree in English & Communications, he formed his own rockabilly backing outfit, SILVERTONE, who comprised JAMES CALVIN WILSEY (lead guitar), ROWLAND SALLEY (bass, vocals), and KENNEY DALE JOHNSON (drums, vocals). They were soon spotted by Erik Jacobsen, who became their manager, helping them secure a deal with 'Warners' and subsequently producing the debut album, 'SILVERTONE', in 1985. A moody cross between heroes ELVIS PRESLEY and ROY ORBISON, ISAAK crooned his way through tales of lost love that functioned best as emotive mood pieces. The 1987 eponymous follow-up and 1989's 'HEART SHAPED WORLD' didn't exactly break any new ground although they perfected the ISAAK formula, the understated tragedy of 'WICKED GAME' becoming a trans-Atlantic Top 10 hit in 1990 after featuring on the soundtrack to the David Lynch movie, 'Wild At Heart'. Signing a new contract with 'Reprise', the success of 'WICKED GAME' resurrected sales of 'HEART SHAPED WORLD', propelling the album back into the US Top 10. The singer had already scored a big hit in France with 'BLUE HOTEL' (from 'CHRIS ISAAK'), the song finally making the UK Top 20 when it was re-released in early 1991. ISAAK re-emerged in 1993 with 'SAN FRANCISCO DAYS', a relatively more uptempo collection which nevertheless included a brooding cover of Neil Diamond's 'SOLITARY MAN'. Another highlight was the country-tinged melancholy of 'EXCEPT THE NEW GIRL'. 'FOREVER BLUE' (1995) saw the prince of heartache reverting back to his rockabilly roots with a new band. 1998's 'SPEAK OF THE DEVIL', meanwhile, found ISAAK adding at least a few modern brush strokes to his retro-pop canvas although highlights such as 'THIS TIME' confirmed that he sounded more convincing on familiar ground. 2002's 'ALWAYS GOT TONIGHT' also made some reluctant nods towards contemporary musical fashion, again only serving to highlight the fact that ISAAK is a classicist first and foremost. • **Songwriters:** BAJA SESSIONS included covers SOUTH OF THE BORDER (DOWN MEXICO WAY) (Meleon – Roy Orbison) / I WONDER (hit; Brenda Lee) / TWO HEARTS (hit; Pat Boone) / RETURN TO ME (hit; Dean Martin) / LEILANI (Harry – Dyens). • **Trivia:** CHRIS has also played bit parts in movies, 'Married To The Mob' & 'The Silence Of The Lambs'. In 1987, he appeared for the first time on Channel 4 TV's 'The Last Resort' which was hosted by fan, Jonathan R/W oss (delete as appropriate).

Album rating: SILVERTONE (*5) / CHRIS ISAAK (*5) / HEART SHAPED WORLD (*6) / WICKED GAME (*7) / SAN FRANCISCO DAYS (*6) / FOREVER BLUE (*5) / BAJA SESSIONS (*4) / SPEAK OF THE DEVIL (*4) / ALWAYS GOT TONIGHT (*5)

CHRIS ISAAK – vocals, guitar with back-up from **SILVERTONE** who feature **JAMES CALVIN WILSEY** – lead guitar / **ROWLAND SALLEY** – bass, vocals / **KENNEY DALE JOHNSON** – drums, vocals

Warners Warners

Mar 85. (lp) *(925156-1)* <25156> **SILVERTONE**
– Dancin' / Talk to me / Livin' for your lover / Back on your side / Voodoo / Funeral in the rain / The lonely one / Unhappiness / Tears / Goin' ridin' / Pretty girls don't cry / Western stars. *(cd-iss. Dec87; 925156-2)*

Apr 85. (7") <29073> **DANCIN'. / HAPPINESS** –

Jul 85. (7") <28971> **TALK TO ME. / LIVIN' FOR YOUR LOVER** –

Oct 85. (7") <28907> **GONE RIDIN' (theme from 'American Flyer'). / TEARS** –

Mar 87. (lp/c)(cd) *(WX 138/+C)(925536-2)* <25536> **CHRIS ISAAK**
– You owe me some kind of love / Heart full of soul / Blue

hotel / Lie to me / Fade away / Wild love / This love will last / You took my heart / Cryin' / Lovers game / Waiting for the rain to fall.

Apr 87. (7"/12") *(W 8467/+T)* **YOU OWE ME SOME KIND OF LOVE. / WAITING FOR THE RAIN TO FALL** [ ] [–]

Jul 87. (7") *(W 8374)* **BLUE HOTEL. / WAITING FOR THE RAIN TO FALL** [ ] [–]
(12"+=/12"pic-d+=) *(W 8374T)* – Wild love.

Jun 89. (lp/c)(cd) *(WX 264/+C)(925837-2)* *<25837>* **HEART SHAPED WORLD** [ ] [ ]
– Heart shaped world / I'm not waiting / Don't make me dream about you / Kings of the highway / Wicked game / Blue Spanish sky / Wrong to love you / Forever young / Nothing's changed / In the heart of the jungle / Diddley daddy. *<re-dist.Jan91, hit No.7>*

Nov 90. (c-s) *<19704>* **WICKED GAME / ('A'instrumental)** [–] [6]

Nov 90. (7"/c-s) *(LON/+CS 279)* **WICKED GAME. / COOL CAT WALK** [10] [–]
(12"+=/cd-s+=) *(LON X/CD 279)* – Dark Spanish symphony / Blue Hawaiian music.
(above from the movie, 'Wild At Heart' on 'London' records)

Reprise Reprise

Jan 91. (cd)(lp/c) *(7599 26513-2)(WX 406/+C)* **WICKED GAME** (compilation) [3] [–]
– Wicked game / You owe me some kind of love / Blue Spanish sky / Heart shaped world / Funeral in the rain / Blue hotel / Dancin' / Nothing's changed / Voodoo / Lie to me / Wicked game (instrumental).

Jan 91. (7"/c-s) *(W 0005/+C)* **BLUE HOTEL. / WICKED GAME** [17] [–]
(12"+=/cd-s+=) *(W 0005 T/CD)* – Wrong to love you.

Mar 91. (7"/c-s) **DANCIN'. / NOTHING'S CHANGED** [ ] [–]
(12"+=/cd-s+=) – Wild love.

Sep 91. (7"/c-s) *<19133>* **BLUE SPANISH SKY. / WICKED GAME (instrumental)** [ ] [ ]
(12"/cd-s) – ('A'side) / Don't make me dream about you / The lovely ones / Lovers game.

Mar 93. (7"/c-s) *(W 0161/+C)* **CAN'T DO A THING (TO STOP ME). / BLUE HOTEL** [36] [–]
(cd-s) *(W 0161CD1)* – ('A'side) / Tears / Blue Spanish sky / Lonely with a broken heart.
(cd-s) *(W 0161CD2)* – ('A'side) / Talk to me / Gone ridin' / Waiting for the rain to fall.

Apr 93. (cd/c/lp) *<(9362 45116-2/-4)>* **SAN FRANCISCO DAYS** [12] [35]
– San Francisco days / Beautiful homes / Round 'n' round / Two hearts / Can't do a thing (to stop me) / Except the new girl / Waiting / Move along / I want your love / 5:15 / Lonely with a broken heart / A solitary man.

Jul 93. (7"/c-s) *(W 0182/+C)* **SAN FRANCISCO DAYS. / 5:15** [62] [–]
(cd-s+=) *(W 0182CD1)* – Shake little sister.
(cd-s) *(W 0182CD2)* – ('A'side) / Western stars / Suspicion of love.

Sep 93. (7"/c-s) *(W 0202/+C)* **A SOLITARY MAN. / WICKED GAME** [ ] [–]
(cd-s+=) *(W 0202CD)* – Lie to me / Lovers game.

—— SILVERTONE band; **MARK GOLDENBERG / GREGG ARREGUIN / FRANK MARTIN / JASON MORGAN / JEFF WATSON / STEPHEN BISHOP / DAVID GRISMAN / DAVID GRISSOM / BRUCE KAPHAN**

May 95. (c-s) *(W 0295C)* *<17872>* **SOMEBODY'S CRYING / CHANGED YOUR MIND** [ ] [45]
(cd-s+=) *(W 0295CD)* – Little white cloud that lied.
(re-iss. Oct95; same)

May 95. (cd/c) *<(9362 45845-2/-4)>* **FOREVER BLUE** [27] [31]
– Baby did a bad bad thing / Somebody's crying / Graduation day / Go walking down there / Don't leave me on my own / Things go wrong / Forever blue / There she goes / Goin' nohere / Changed your mind / Shadows in a mirror / I believe / The end of everything.

Sep 95. (c-s) *<17781>* **GO WALKING DOWN THERE** [–] [ ]

Oct 96. (cd/c) *<(9362-46325-2/-4)>* **BAJA SESSIONS** [ ] [33]
– Pretty girls don't cry / Back on your side / Only the lonely / South of the border (down Mexico way) / I wonder / Wrong to love you / Waiting for my lucky day / Yellow bird / Two hearts / Return to me / Dancin' / Sweet Leilani / Think of tomorrow.

Sep 98. (c-s/cd-s) *(W 0454 C/CD)* **PLEASE / EVERYONE GETS DOWN** [ ] [–]

Oct 98. (cd/c) *<(9362 46849-2/-4)>* **SPEAK OF THE DEVIL** [ ] Sep98 [41]
– Please / Flying / Walk slow / Breakin' apart / This time / Speak of the devil / Like the way she moves / Wanderin' / Don't get so down on yourself / Black flowers / I'm not sleepy / Lonely nights / Talkin' 'bout a home / Super magic 2000.

Sep 99. (cd-s) *(W 0503C)* **BABY DID A BAD BAD THING / WICKED GAME** [44] [–]
(cd-s+=) *(W 0503CD)* – I wonder.
(cd-s) *(W 0503CDX)* – ('A'side) / ('A'remix) / ('A'acoustic).

Apr 02. (cd-s) *<42439>* **LET ME DOWN EASY / BEST I EVER HAD / IT WOULDN'T BE THE SAME WITHOUT YOU** [–] [ ]

May 02. (cd) *<(9362 48016-2)>* **ALWAYS GOT TONIGHT** [ ] Feb02 [24]
– One day / Let me down easy / Worked it out wrong / Courthouse / Life will go on / Always got tonight / Cool love / Notice the ring / I see you everywhere / American boy / Somebody to love / Nothing to say.

ISLEY BROTHERS

Formed: Cincinatti, Ohio, USA ... early 50's by RONALD, RUDOLPH, O'KELLY and VERNON ISLEY, all experienced gospel singers. The subsequent death of VERNON led to the remaining brothers moving from Cincinnati to New York in '56, where they began their recording career. After achieving some early success with 'SHOUT' in '59, the siblings recorded the enduring 'TWIST AND SHOUT' a couple of years later, a song The BEATLES would later cover to significantly greater commercial success. Eager for more creative control, The ISLEY BROTHERS took the unprecedented step of setting up their own label, 'T-Neck' (named after their new location, Teaneck in New Jersey). Their first homegrown recording, 'TESTIFY', was largely ignored although the featured lead guitarist would go on to influence the playing of generations, the axe-man in question one JIMI HENDRIX. In an effort to achieve a higher profile, the group signed to 'Motown' in '65. Unfortunately, the label insisted on moulding the band to their formulaic 'hit-factory' approach, stifling their creative input and producing only one hit, 1966's 'THIS OLD HEART OF MINE'. The brothers' finest recordings came after they split with Berry Gordy and Co. in '68, relaunching 'T-Neck' the following year. With creative control firmly back in the hands of the outfit, they let rip with funky grooves and even funkier outfits, their evolution complete with the addition of three more members of the ISLEY clan, brothers ERNIE and MARVIN and cousin CHRIS JASPER. The latter contributed the classic single, 'IT'S YOUR THING', a record which became an instant hit and earned the band a Grammy. Touring frequently in the late 60's and early 70's, a distribution deal with 'C.B.S.' in '73 led to the release of '3 + 3', an album which showcased the roots of the "Isley Sound"; ERNIE's Hendrix-influenced guitar work was a vital component in the trademark blend of dance rhythms and funk laden grooves best sampled on the sexy 'THAT LADY'. Through '73 to '83, the band scored nine consecutive gold or platinum albums, their sound switching back and forth between RONALD's soulfully smooth ballads and the hard and funky stuff. The two styles combined especially well on the 1975 offering, 'THE HEAT IS ON', alternating the furious vocals of 'FIGHT THE POWER' with a song addressing the need for social awareness and global peace in 'HARVEST FOR THE WORLD'. Towards the early 80's the family released a series of songs with a highly erotic content, a sure-fire winner in terms of sales, which produced the hits 'BETWEEN THE SHEETS' and 'CHOOSY LOVER'. There was a certain amount of compromise to their output, however, and in '84, the band split; the original members signed to 'Warner Bros.' while the "youngsters" went on to form the short-lived ISLEY-JASPER-ISLEY unit. The latter outfit penned the hymnal 'CARAVAN OF LOVE' in '85, later a UK No.1 hit for The HOUSEMARTINS. ERNIE ISLEY subsequently recorded a blistering solo album on 'Elektra', while RONALD, together with his future wife ANGELA WINBUSH, topped the R&B

charts with 'SPEND THE NIGHT'. Influencing legions of recording artists throughout their four decades, The ISLEY BROTHERS were inducted into the Rock & Roll Hall Of Fame in '92. While a mid-90's effort on 'Island', 'MISSION TO PLEASE' (1996) made the US Top 40, The ISLEY BROTHERS became one of the few old skool soul acts to roll with the punches on the new R&B block come the new millennium. Deservedly, the acclaimed 'ETERNAL' (2001) made the US Top 3 alongside the Top 20 hit, 'CONTAGIOUS'. While the record featured a roll call of R&B scenesters such as R KELLY and JILL SCOTT, the real star of the show was RONALD's falsetto vocal, still as fresh as that 70's summer breeze after all these years. KELLY was to play a much bigger role in 2003's huge 'BODY KISS', producing and writing the bulk of the album. A No.1 hit in the States, the record fulfilled the potential hinted at in its predecessor, freeing up the full, stratospheric power of RONALD's vocals with a collection of contemporary R&B love songs. • **Songwriters:** Producers LEIBER & STOLLER provided them with their 'Atlantic' material in '61, while the following year, producer BERT BERNS wrote 'RIGHT NOW' and produced their hit Medley-Russell-penned 'TWIST AND SHOUT'. In 1966, with 'Tamla Motown', HOLLAND-DOZIER-HOLLAND provided them with some hits. In 1969, their formation of 'T-Neck' saw them writing their own material. During this time they also covered LOVE THE ONE YOU'RE WITH (Stephen Stills) / LAY LADY LAY (Bob Dylan) / SPILL THE WINE (War) / COLD BOLOGNA (Bill Withers) / FIRE AND RAIN (James Taylor) / MACHINE GUN (Jimi Hendrix) / OHIO (Neil Young) / SUMMER BREEZE (Seals & Croft) / IT'S TOO LATE + BROTHER, BROTHER, BROTHER (Carole King) / etc.

Album rating: SHOUT! (*5) / TWIST & SHOUT! (*6) / THE FABULOUS ISLEY BROTHERS TWISTING AND SHOUTING (*4) / THIS OLD HEART OF MINE (*5) / SOUL ON THE ROCKS (*4) / IT'S OUR THING (*7) / THE BROTHERS: ISLEY (*4) / GIVIN' IT BACK (*5) / BROTHER, BROTHER, BROTHER (*6) / THE ISLEYS LIVE (*5) / 3 + 3 (*8) / LIVE IT UP (*6) / THE HEAT IS ON (*7) / HARVEST FOR THE WORLD (*6) / GO FOR YOUR GUNS (*6) / FOREVER GOLD compilation (*7) / SHOWDOWN (*6) / WINNER TAKES ALL (*6) / GO ALL THE WAY (*6) / GRAND SLAM (*6) / INSIDE YOU (*5) / THE REAL DEAL (*5) / BETWEEN THE SHEETS (*6) / MASTERPIECE (*5) / SMOOTH SAILIN' (*5) / Isley Brothers featuring Ronald Isley: SPEND THE NIGHT (*4) / TRACKS OF LIFE (*4) / MISSION TO PLEASE (*6) / ISLEY BROTHERS STORY VOL.1 (THE ROCK'N'ROLL YEARS 1959-68) compilation (*8) / ISLEY BROTHERS STORY VOL.2 (THE T-NECK YEARS 1969-1985) compilation (*8) / ETERNAL (*5) / BODY KISS (*6)

RONALD ISLEY (b.21 May'41) – lead vocals / **RUDOLPH ISLEY** (b. 1 Apr'39) – vocal / **O'KELLY ISLEY** (b.25 Dec'37) – vocals

not iss. / Teenage

1957. (7") *<1004>* **THE COW JUMPED OVER THE MOON. / ANGELS CRIED** –

not iss. / Mark-X

1957. (7") *<7003>* **ROCKIN' McDONALD. / DON'T BE JEALOUS** –

not iss. / Gone

1958. (7") *<5022>* **EVERYBODY'S GONNA ROCK'N'ROLL. / I WANNA KNOW** –

1958. (7") *<5048>* **THE DRAG. / THE LOVE** –

not iss. / Cindy

1958. (7") *<3009>* **THIS IS THE END. / DON'T BE JEALOUS** –

R.C.A. / R.C.A.

1959. (7") *<7537>* **TURN TO ME. / I'M GONNA KNOCK ON YOUR DOOR** –

Oct 59. (7") *(RCA 1149) <7588>* **SHOUT. / SHOUT (Pt.2)** Sep59 47
(re-iss. US Mar 62, hit No.94)

Jun 60. (lp) *(RD 27165) <LSP 2156>* **SHOUT!** Oct59
– Shout! (part 1 & 2) / Tell me who / How deep is the ocean (part 1 & 2) / Respectable (parts 1 & 2) / Say you love me / Open up your heart / He's got the whole world in his hands / Without a song / Yes indeed / Ring a ling a ling / That lucky old sun / When the saints go marching in / Gypsy love song / St. Louis blues / Rock around the clock / Turn to me / Not one minute more / I'm gonna knock on your door. *(re-iss. Nov70; INTS 1098) (cd-iss. DEc88 on 'Bear Family'; BCD 15425)* – (extra tracks).

Feb 60. (7") *<7657>* **RESPECTABLE. / WITHOUT A SONG** –

Feb 60. (7") *(RCA 1172)* **RESPECTABLE. / I'M GONNA KNOCK ON YOUR DOOR** –

May 60. (7") *(RCA 1190) <7718>* **HE'S GOT THE WHOLE WORLD IN HIS HANDS. / HOW DEEP IS THE OCEAN**

Aug 60. (7") *<7746>* **GYPSY LOVE SONG. / OPEN UP YOUR HEART** –

Nov 60. (7") *(RCA 1213) <7787>* **TELL ME WHO. / SAY YOU LOVE ME TOO**

not iss. / Atlantic

1961. (7") *<2092>* **TELL ME HOW TO SHIMMY. / JEEPERS CREEPERS** –

1961. (7") *<2100>* **SHINE ON HARVEST MOON. / STANDING ON THE DANCE FLOOR** –

1961. (7") *<2110>* **WRITE TO ME. / YOUR OLD LADY** –

1961. (7") *<2122>* **A FOOL FOR YOU. / JUST ONE MORE TIME** –

Stateside / Wand

Feb 62. (7") *<118>* **RIGHT NOW. / THE SNAKE** –

Jun 62. (7") *(SS 112) <124>* **TWIST AND SHOUT. / I.B. Special: SPANISH TWIST** May62 17
(re-act.Jul63 reached UK No.42)

Oct 62. (7") *(SS 132) <127>* **TWISTING WITH LINDA. / YOU BETTER COME HOME** Sep62 54

Oct 62. (lp) *<653>* **TWIST AND SHOUT** – 61
– Twist and shout / Don't you feel / Hold on baby / Time after time / Twisting with Linda / I say love / Right now / Spanish twist / The drag / Don't be jealous / This is the end / Rockin' McDonald. *(UK-iss.Feb76 on 'D.J.M.'; 2628) (c-iss.Oct82 on 'Orchid'; ORC 009) (cd-iss. 1988 on 'K-Tel'; NCD 5162)*

Aug 63. (7") *(SS 128) <127>* **NOBODY BUT ME. / I'M LAUGHING TO KEEP FROM CRYING**

Oct 63. (7") *<137>* **HOLD ON BABY. / I SAY LOVE** –

U.A. / U.A.

Oct 63. (7") *(UP 1034) <605>* **TANGO. / SHE'S GONE**

Dec 63. (7") *<638>* **SURF AND SHOUT. / WHAT'CHA GONNA DO** –

Feb 64. (7") *<659>* **YOU'LL NEVER LEAVE HIM. / PLEASE, PLEASE, PLEASE** –

Apr 64. (7") *<714>* **WHO'S THAT LADY. / MY LITTLE GIRL** –

Apr 64. (7") *(UP 1050)* **SHAKE IT WITH ME BABY. / STAGGER LEE** –

May 64. (lp) *(ULP 1064) <6313>* **THE FABULOUS ISLEY BROTHERS – TWISTING AND SHOUTING**
– Surf and shout / Please please please / Do the twist / She's the one / Tango / What'cha gonna do / Stagger Lee / You'll never leave him / Let's go, let's go, let's go / Shake it with me baby / She's gone / Long tall Sally.

Atlantic / T-Neck

May 64. (7") *<501>***TESTIFY. / (part 2)** –

Atlantic / Atlantic

Oct 64. (7") *(AT 4010) <2263>* **THE LAST GIRL. / LOOKING FOR A LOVE**

1965. (7") *<2277>* **SIMON SAYS. / WILD AS A TIGER** –

1965. (7") *<2303>* **MOVE OVER AND LET ME DANCE. / HAVE YOU EVER BEEN DISAPPOINTED** –

Tamla Motown / Tamla

Mar 66. (7") *(TMG 555) <54128>* **THIS OLD HEART OF MINE (IS WEAK FOR YOU). / THERE'S NO LOVE LEFT** 47 Jan66 12
(re-act.Oct68 reached UK No.3)

Oct 66. (lp) *(TML 11034) <269>* **THIS OLD HEART OF MINE (IS WEAK FOR YOU)** Jun66
– Nowhere to run / Stop in the name of love / This old heart of mine (is weak for you) / Take some time out for love / I guess I'll always love you / Baby don't you do it / Who could ever doubt my love / Put yourself in my place / Just ain't enough love / I hear a symphony / There's no love left / Seek and you shall find. *(re-act.Dec68 hit UK No.23) (re-iss. Jul81 lp/c; STMS/CSTMS 5026)*

Jun 66. (7") *(TMG 556) <54133>* **TAKE SOME TIME OUT FOR LOVE. / WHO COULD EVER DOUBT MY LOVE** May66 66
(re-iss. Nov69; TMG 719)

Aug 66. (7") *(TMG 572) <54135>* **I GUESS I'LL ALWAYS LOVE YOU. / I HEAR A SYMPHONY** 45 Jul66 61

1967. (lp) *<37080>* **TAMLA MOTOWN PRESENTS . . . THE ISLEY BROTHERS** [–] [ ]
(UK-iss.Mar73 on 'Music For Pleasure';)

May 67. (7") *(TMG 606) <54146>* **GOT TO HAVE YOU BACK. / JUST AIN'T ENOUGH LOVE** [ ] [93]

Jan 68. (7") *<54154>* **ONE TOO MANY HEARTACHES. / THAT'S THE WAY LOVE IS** [–] [ ]

Feb 68. (lp) *(STML 11066) <275>* **SOUL ON THE ROCKS** [ ] [ ]
– Got to have you back / That's the way love is / Whispers (gettin' louder) / Tell it's just a rumour baby / One too many heartaches / It's out of the question / Why when love is gone / Save me from the misery / Little Miss Sweetness / Good things / Catching up on time / Behind a painted smile.

Apr 68. (7") *(TMG 652) <54164>* **TAKE ME IN YOUR ARMS (ROCK ME A LITTLE WHILE). / WHY WHEN LOVE IS GONE** [ ] [ ]

1968. (7") *<54175>* **BEHIND A PAINTED SMILE. / ALL BECAUSE I LOVE YOU** [–] [ ]

1968. (7") *<54182>* **TAKE SOME TIME OUT FOR LOVE. / JUST AIN'T ENOUGH LOVE** [–] [ ]

Major Minor — T-Neck

Jun 69. (7") *(MM 621) <901>* **IT'S YOUR THING. / DON'T GIVE IT AWAY** [ ] Feb69 [2]

Jul 69. (lp) *(SMLP 59) <3001>* **IT'S OUR THING** [ ] Apr69 [22]
– This old heart of mine (is weak for you) / Who could ever doubt my love / I guess I'll always love you / That's the way love is / One too many heartaches / Why when love is gone / Just ain't enough love / Got to have you back / There's no love left / I hear a symphony / Take me in your arms (rock me for a while) / Take some time out for love.

Jul 69. (7") *<903>* **TURN ON, TUNE IN, DROP OUT. / (part 2)** [–] [ ]

Aug 69. (7") *<906>* **BLACK BERRIES. / (part 2)** [–] [79]

Sep 69. (7") *(MM 631) <902>* **I TURNED YOU ON. / I KNOW WHO YOU BEEN SOCKING IT TO** [ ] May69 [23]

— RONNIE, RUDOLPH and O'KELLY (who was now just KELLY) with brass section added **ERNIE ISLEY** (b. 7 Mar'52) – guitar, percussion, guitar (later EVERETT COLLINS – drums) / **MARVIN ISLEY** (b.18 Aug'53) – bass, percussion / **CHRIS JASPER** – keyboards

Stateside — T-Neck

Dec 69. (7") *<912>* **BLESS YOUR HEART. / GIVE THE WOMEN WHAT THEY WANT** [–] [ ]

Feb 70. (7") *(SS 2162) <908>* **WAS IT GOOD TO YOU. / I GOT TO GET MYSELF TOGETHER** [ ] Sep69 [83]

Feb 70. (7") *<914>* **KEEP ON DOIN'. / SAVE ME** [–] [75]

Apr 70. (7") *<919>* **IF HE CAN, YOU CAN. / HOLDIN' ON** [–] [ ]

Jun 70. (lp) *(SSL 10300)* **THE BROTHERS: ISLEY** [ ] Oct69 [ ]
– Black berries / Vacuum cleaner / I turned you on / Was it good to you / She's my girl / Get down off the train / Gotta get myself together / Feel like the world / Holdin' on.

Jul 70. (7") *<921>* **GIRLS WILL BE GIRLS, BOYS WILL BE BOYS. / GET DOWN OFF THE TRAIN** [–] [75]

Sep 70. (7") *<924>* **GET INTO SOMETHING. / (part 2)** [–] [89]

Sep 70. (lp) *<3004>* **LIVE AT THE YANKEE STADIUM (live)** [–] Oct69 [ ]
– (shared with The Edwin Hawkins Singers + Brooklyn Bridge)

Dec 70. (7") *<927>* **FREEDOM. / I NEED YOU SO** [–] [72]

May 71. (7") *(SS 2188) <929>* **WARPATH. / I GOT TO FIND ME ONE** [ ] [ ]

Sep 71. (7") *<932>* **SPILL THE WINE. / TAKE INVENTORY** [–] [49]

Sep 71. (lp) **GIVIN' IT BACK** (all covers) [–] [71]
– Fire and rain / Ohio machine gun / Lay lady lay / etc

Oct 71. (7") *(SS 2193) <930>* **LOVE THE ONE YOU'RE WITH. / HE'S GOT YOUR LOVE** [ ] Jun71 [18]

Dec 71. (7") *<933>* **LAY LADY LAY. / VACUUM CLEANER** [–] [71]

Mar 72. (7") *<934>* **LAY AWAY. / FEEL LIKE THE WORLD** [–] [54]

Jun 72. (lp) *<3009>* **BROTHER, BROTHER, BROTHER** [–] [29]
– Brother, brother / Put a little love in your heart / Sweet seasons / Keep on walkin' / Work to do / Pop that thang / Lay away / It's too late / Love put me on the corner.

Jun 72. (7") *<935>* **POP THAT THANG. / I GOT TO FIND ME ONE** [–] [24]

Oct 72. (7") *<936>* **WORK TO DO. / BEAUTIFUL** [–] [51]

Mar 73. (lp) *<3010>* **ISLEY BROTHERS LIVE (live)** [–] [ ]
– Work to do / It's too late / It's your thing / Pop that thang / Love the one you're with / Lay lady lay / Lay away / Ohio / Machine gun.

May 73. (7") *<937>* **IT'S TOO LATE. / NOTHING TO DO BUT TODAY** [–] [ ]

Epic — T-Neck

Aug 73. (7") *(EPC 1704) <2251>* **THAT LADY. / THAT LADY (part 2)** [14] Jul73 [6]

Nov 73. (lp) *(EPC 65740) <32453>* **3 + 3** [ ] Sep73 [ ]
– That lady / Don't let me be lonely tonight / If you were there / You walk your way / Listen to the music / What it comes down to / Sunshine (go away today) / Summer breeze / The highways of my life. *(re-iss. Mar81 lp/c; EPC/40 32039) (cd-iss. Apr94 on 'Sony'; 962615-2) (cd re-iss. Jul97; 487937-2)*

Nov 73. (7") *<2252>* **WHAT IT COMES DOWN TO. / HIGHWAYS OF MY LIFE** [–] [55]

Dec 73. (7") *(EPC 1980)* **THE HIGHWAYS OF MY LIFE. / DON'T LET ME BE LONELY TONIGHT** [25] [–]

Apr 74. (7") *(EPC 2244) <2253>* **SUMMER BREEZE. / SUMMER BREEZE (part 2)** [16] Mar74 [60]

Aug 74. (7") *(EPC 2578) <2254>* **LIVE IT UP. / (part 2)** [ ] Jul74 [52]

Sep 74. (lp/c) *(EPC/40 80317) <33070>* **LIVE IT UP** [ ] [14]
– Live it up / Brown eyed girl / Need a little taste of love / Lover's eye / Midnight sky / Hello it's me / Ain't I been good to you.

Nov 74. (7") *(EPC 2803)* **NEED A LITTLE TASTE OF LOVE. / IF YOU WERE THERE** [ ] [–]

Feb 75. (7") *(EPC 3034) <2255>* **MIDNIGHT SKY. / (part 2)** [ ] Nov74 [73]

Jul 75. (7") *(EPC 3434) <2256>* **FIGHT THE POWER. / (part 2)** [ ] Jun75 [4]

Jul 75. (lp/c) *(EPC/40 69139) <33536>* **THE HEAT IS ON** [ ] Jun75 [1]
– Fight the power / The heat is on (pts.1 & 2) / Hope you feel better love (pts.1 & 2) / For the love of you (pts.1 & 2) / Sensuality (pts.1 &2) / Make me say it again girl (pts.1 & 2). *(cd re-mast.Sep01 +=; 504041-2)* – Fight the power.

Jan 76. (7") *(EPC 3865) <2259>* **FOR THE LOVE OF YOU. / YOU WALK YOUR WAY** [ ] Nov75 [22]

Jun 76. (7") *(EPC 4369)* **HARVEST FOR THE WORLD. / LET ME DOWN EASY** [10] [–]

Jun 76. (lp/c) *(EPC/40 81268) <33809>* **HARVEST FOR THE WORLD** [50] May76 [9]
– Harvest for the world (prelude) / Harvest for the world / People of today / Who loves you better / Let me down easy / (At your best) You are love / So you wanna stay down / You still feel the need. *(re-iss. Jun85 lp/c; EPC/40 32652) (cd re-mast.Sep01 +=; 50404-2)* – Summer breeze.

Aug 76. (7") *<2260>* **HARVEST FOR THE WORLD. / (part 2)** [–] [63]

Sep 76. (7") *(EPC 4373) <2260>* **WHO LOVES YOU BETTER. / WHO LOVES YOU BETTER (part 2)** [ ] May76 [47]

Apr 77. (lp/c) *(EPC/40 86027) <34432>* **GO FOR YOU GUNS** [46] [6]
– Livin' in the life / Go for your guns / Voyage to Atlantis / Footsteps in the dark (part 1 & 2) / Tell me when you need it again (part1 & 2) / The pride (part 1 & 2). *(re-iss. May93 on 'Sony Collectors')*

May 77. (7") *<2262>* **THE PRIDE. / (part 2)** [–] [63]

Jul 77. (7") *(EPC 5443)* **VOYAGE TO ATLANTIS. / TELL ME WHEN YOU NEED IT AGAIN** [ ] [–]

Apr 78. (7") *(EPC 6292)* **TAKE ME TO THE NEXT PHASE. / LIVIN' IN THE LIFE** [ ] [–]

Apr 78. (7") *<2264>* **LIVIN' IN MY LIFE. / GO FOR YOUR GUNS** [–] [40]

Apr 78. (lp/c) *(EPC/40 86039) <34930>* **SHOWDOWN** [46] [4]
– Showdown (part 1 & 2) / Groovin' with you / Ain't givin' up no love / Rockin' with fire (part 1 & 2) / Take me to the next phase (part 1 & 2) / Coolin' me out (part 1 & 2) / Fun and games / Love fever (part 1 & 2).

May 78. (7") *<2270>* **SO YOU WANNA STAY DOWN. / VOYAGE TO ATLANTIS** [–] [ ]

Jun 78. (7") *<2276>* **TAKE ME TO THE NEXT PHASE. / TELL ME WHEN YOU NEED IT AGAIN** [–] [ ]

Jul 78. (7") *(EPC 6481) <2277>* **GROOVE WITH YOU. / FOOTSTEPS IN THE DARK** [ ] [ ]

Jul 79. (d-lp/c) *(EPC/40 88460) <36077>* **WINNER TAKES ALL** [ ] [14]
– I wanna be with you / Liquid love / Winner takes all / Life in the city / It's a disco night (rock don't stop) / Let's fall in love / (Can't you see) What you do to me / How lucky I am / You're the key to my heart / You're beside me / Love comes and goes / Let me into your life / Go for what you know / Mind over matter.

Aug 79. (7") *(EPC 7757)* **LIFE IN THE CITY. / (part 2)** [ ] [–]

Oct 79. (7") *(EPC 7911) <2287>* **IT'S A DISCO NIGHT (ROCK DON'T STOP). / AIN'T GIVIN' UP ON LOVE** [14] [90]

Jan 80. (7") *(EPC 7795)* *<2284>* **WINNER TAKES ALL. / FUN AND GAMES** [ ] Aug79 [ ]
Apr 80. (lp/c) *(EPC/40 65740)* *<36035>* **GO ALL THE WAY** [ ] [8]
– Go all the way / Say you will / Pass it on / The belly dancer / Here we go again / Don't say goodnight (it's time for love).
Jun 80. (7") *(EPC 8664)* *<2290>* **DON'T SAY GOODNIGHT (IT'S TIME FOR LOVE). / (part 2)** [ ] Apr80 [39]
Apr 81. (7") *(EPCA 1122)* **TONIGHT IS THE NIGHT (IF I HAD YOU). / WHO SAID** [ ] [–]
Apr 81. (lp/c) *(EPC/40 84914)* *<37080>* **GRAND SLAM** [ ] Mar81 [28]
– Tonight is the night (if I had you) / Hurry up and wait / I once had your love (and I can't let go) / Young girls / Party night / Don't let go / Who said.
Apr 81. (7") *<02033>* **HURRY UP AND WAIT. / ('A' instrumental)** [–] [58]
Jul 81. (7") *<02179>* **I ONCE HAD YOUR LOVE (AND CAN'T LET GO). / ('A'instrumental)** [–] [ ]
Nov 81. (7") *<02531>* **INSIDE YOU. / (part 2)** [–] [ ]
Nov 81. (7") *(EPCA 1741)* **INSIDE YOU. / LOVE ZONE** [ ] [–]
Nov 81. (lp/c) *(EPC/40 85252)* *<37533>* **INSIDE YOU** [ ] Oct81 [45]
– Inside you (part 1 & 2) / Baby hold on / First love / Welcome into my heart / Don't hold back your love (part 1 & 2) / Love merry-go-round / Love zone.
Jan 82. (7") *<02705>* **WELCOME INTO MY HEART. / PARTY NIGHT** [–] [ ]
Sep 82. (7") *<02985>* **THE REAL DEAL. / ('A'instrumental)** [–] [ ]
Sep 82. (lp/c) *(EPC/40 85790)* *<38047>* **THE REAL DEAL** [ ] Aug82 [87]
– The real deal (part 1 & 2) / Are you with me / I'll do it all for you / Stone cold lover / It's alright with me / All in my lover's eyes / Under the influence.
Nov 82. (7") *<03281>* **IT'S ALRIGHT WITH ME. / ('A'instrumental)** [–] [ ]
Feb 83. (7") *<03420>* **ALL IN MY LOVER'S EYES. / I'LL DO IT ALL FOR YOU** [–] [ ]
Jun 83. (lp/c) *(EPC/40 25419)* *<38674>* **BETWEEN THE SHEETS** [ ] May83 [19]
– Choosey lover / Touch me / I need your body / Let's make love tonight / Between the sheets / Ballad for the fallen soldier / Slow down children / Way out love / Gettin' over you / Rock you.
Jun 83. (7") *<03797>* **BETWEEN THE SHEETS. / (part 2)** [–] [ ]
Jun 83. (7"/12") *(A/TA 3513)* **BETWEEN THE SHEETS. / THAT LADY** [52] [–]
Aug 83. (7"/12") *(A/TA 3690)* *<03994>* **CHOOSEY LOVER. / CHOOSEY LOVER (part 2)** [ ] [ ]
Nov 83. (7") *<04320>* **LETS MAKE LOVE TONIGHT. / ('A'instrumental)** [–] [ ]

—— Reverted to original trio when others formed ISLEY, JASPER, ISLEY

Warners Warners

Nov 85. (7") *<28860>* **COLDER ARE MY NIGHTS. / BREAK THIS CHAIN** [–] [ ]
Dec 85. (7"/12") *(WB 8860/+T)* **COLDER ARE MY NIGHTS. / ('A'instrumental)** [ ] [–]
Dec 85. (lp/c/cd) *(925347-1/-4/-2)* *<25347>* **MASTERPIECE** [ ] [ ]
– May I / My best was good enough / If leaving me is easy / You never know when you're gonna fall in love / Stay gold / Colder are my nights / Come to me / Release your love / The most beautiful girl.
Mar 86. (7") *<28764>* **MAY I. / ('A'instrumental)** [–] [ ]

—— Now a duo of RONNIE and RUDOLF, when O'KELLY died of a heart attack on the 31st of March '86

Jun 87. (7") *<28385>* **SMOOTH SAILIN' TONIGHT. / (part 2)** [–] [ ]
Jul 87. (lp/c/cd) *(925586-1/-4/-2)* *<25586>* **SMOOTH SAILIN'** [ ] Jun87 [64]
– Everything is alright / Pick it out / It takes a good woman / Send a message / Smooth sailin' tonight / Somebody I used to know / Come my way / I wish.
Sep 87. (7") *<28241>* **COME MY WAY. / (part 2)** [–] [ ]
Nov 87. (7") *<28129>* **I WISH. / ('A'instrumental)** [–] [ ]
Feb 88. (7") *<27954>* **IT TAKES A GOOD WOMAN. / (part 2)** [–] [ ]

ISLEY BROTHERS featuring RONALD ISLEY

—— **RONALD, ERNIE + MARVIN**

Jun 89. (7") *<22990>* **SPEND THE NIGHT (CE SOIR). / ('A'instrumental)** [–] [ ]
Jul 89. (lp/c/cd) *(925940-1/-4/-2)* *<25940>* **SPEND THE NIGHT** [ ] [89]
– Spend the night (ce soir) / You'll never walk alone / One of a kind / Real woman / Come together / If you ever need somebody / Baby come back home / One of a kind (reprise).
Oct 89. (7") *<22748>* **YOU'LL NEVER WALK ALONE. / ONE OF A KIND** [–] [ ]
Feb 90. (7") *<19910>* **IF YOU EVER NEED SOMEBODY. / ONE OF A KIND** [–] [ ]
May 90. (c-s) *<19814>* **COME TOGETHER /** [–] [ ]

—— In Mar 90, RONALD ISLEY backed ROD STEWART on a US Top 10 version of THIS OLD HEART OF MINE. ROD, of course, had earlier made UK No.4 with the song. ERNIE released his solo album, 'HIGH WIRE' early in 1990.

Jun 92. (cd/c) *<(7559 26620-2/-4)>* **TRACKS OF LIFE** [ ] [ ]
– Turn on the demon / Bedroom eyes / Morning love / Sensitive lover / Searching for a miracle / No axe to grind / Brazilian wedding song (setembro) / Dedicate this song / Got my licks in / I'll be there 4 u / Koolin' out / Lost in your love / Red hot.

4th & Broad Island

May 96. (c-s,cd-s) *<854586>* **LET'S LAY TOGETHER / ('A'instrumental)** [–] [93]
May 96. (cd/c) *<(524214-2/-4)>* **MISSION TO PLEASE** [ ] [31]
– Floatin' on your love / Whenever you're ready / Let's lay together / Can I have a kiss (for old time's sake)? / Mission to please you / Make your body sing / Let's het intimate / Show us the way / Tears . . . Ron crying alone.
Oct 96. (c-s) *(BRAC 338)* *<854738>* **FLOATIN' ON YOUR LOVE / ('A'remix)** [ ] Sep96 [47]
(12"+=/cd-s+=) *(12BRW/BRCD 338)* – ('A'remixes by LIL' KIM and 112).
Jan 97. (cd-s) *<854862>* **TEARS / TEARS (album) / MAKE YOUR BODY SING** [–] [55]

ISLEY BROTHERS featuring RONALD ISLEY AND MR. BIGGS

Dreamworks Dreamworks

Jul 01. (-) *<radio cut>* **CONTAGIOUS** [–] [19]
Aug 01. (cd) *<(450291-2)>* **ETERNAL** [ ] [3]
– Move your body / Contagious / Warm summer night / You deserve better / Just like this / Secret lover / You're all I need / Settle down / Eternal / If you leave me now / Said enough / You didn't see me / Ernie's jam / Think.
May 03. (-) *<radio cut>* **WHAT WOULD YOU DO?** [–] [49]
May 03. (cd) *<(450409-2)>* **BODY KISS** [ ] [1]
– Superstar / Lucky charm / What would you do? / Body kiss / Busted / Showdown Vol.1 / Keep it flowin' / Prize posession / Take a ride / I want that / I like / What would you do? (part 2 remix).

– (selective) compilations, etc. –

on 'Tamla Motown' until otherwise mentioned

Jan 69. (7") *(TMG 683)* **I GUESS I'LL ALWAYS LOVE YOU. / IT'S OUT OF THE QUESTION** [11] [ ]
Apr 69. (7") *(TMG 693)* **BEHIND A PAINTED SMILE. / ONE TOO MANY HEARTACHES** [5] [ ]
Aug 69. (7") *(TMG 708)* **PUT YOURSELF IN MY PLACE. / LITTLE MISS SWEETNESS** [13] [ ]
Sep 69. (lp) *(STML 1112)* **BEHIND A PAINTED SMILE** [ ] [ ]
– Behind a painted smile / Got to have you back / Take me in your arms (rock me a little while) / Catching up on a time / Save me from this misery / Little Miss Sweetness / Good things / All because I love you / That's the way love is / Tell me it's just a rumour baby / It's out of the question / Why when love is gone / One too many heartaches / Whispers (gettin' louder).
Oct 77. (lp) *Epic; (EPC 86040)* *<34452>* **FOREVER GOLD** [ ] [58]
(re-iss. Aug84 lp/c; EPC/40 32238) (cd-iss. Jan98; CD 32238)
1986. (lp/c) *Stateside; (SSL/TCSSL 6001)* **LET'S GO** [ ] [–]
(cd-iss. Apr02; 537514-2)
Mar 88. (lp/c/cd) *Telstar; (STAR/STAC/SCD 2306)* **GREATEST HITS** [41] [–]
Mar 90. (cd) *Charly; (CDCH 928)* **SHOUT AND TWIST WITH RUDOLPH, RONALD AND O'KELLY** [ ] [–]
Apr 91. (cd) *E.M.I.; (CZ 421)* **THE COMPLETE U.A. SESSIONS** [ ] [–]

May 91. (d-cd/d-c) *Rhino; <R2/R4 70908>* **ISLEY BROTHERS STORY VOL 1: ROCK'N'SOUL YEARS 1959-68** [–] [ ]
May 91. (d-cd/d-c) *Rhino; <R2/R4 70909>* **ISLEY BROTHERS STORY VOL.2: THE T-NECK YEARS 1969-85** [–] [ ]
Jul 96. (cd) *Spectrum; (552122-2)* **MOTOWN EARLY CLASSICS** [ ] [ ]
May 98. (cd) *Camden; (74321 57814-2)* **SHOUT** [ ] [ ]
Nov 99. (3xcd-box) *Legacy; (Z3K 65547)* **IT'S YOUR THING: THE STORY OF THE ISLEY BROTHERS** [ ] [ ]
Jul 00. (cd) *Epic; (498787-2)* **SUPER HITS** [ ] [ ]
Mar 01. (cd) *Spectrum; (544516-2)* **THE ESSENTIAL COLLECTION** [ ] [ ]
Feb 02. (cd) *R.C.A.; (07863 68059-2)* **SHOUT: THE RCA SESSIONS** [ ] [ ]
Nov 02. (cd) *(017190-2)* **THIS OLD HEART OF MINE / SOUL ON THE ROCKS** [ ] [ ]
Dec 02. (d-cd) *(509456-2)* **HARVEST FOR THE WORLD / THE HEAT IS ON** [ ] [ ]

□ ISOTOPE 217 (see under ⇒ TORTOISE)

□ IVEYS (see under ⇒ BADFINGER)

The JAM

Janet JACKSON

Born: 16 May'66, Gary, Indiana, USA. The baby sister of the precocious JACKSON clan, JANET began her showbiz career singing alongside the family in their 70's variety show before securing parts in US TV sitcoms, 'Good Times' and 'Diff'rent Strokes'. Aged only sweet sixteen, JANET signed up to 'A&M' for an eponymous 1982 debut album. Neither this nor its successor, 'DREAM STREET' (1984) made much of an impact on the pop chart although they did spawn a couple of respectable R&B hits. In the meantime she'd also appeared in the TV series of 'Fame' and become hitched to JAMES DeBARGE, a marriage that barely lasted a year. From this point on JACKSON began taking the initiative, hooking up with crack R&B production team Jimmy Jam and Terry Lewis for her definitive 'CONTROL' (1986) album. Boldly underlining her new independent woman stance (thanks to help from dance star-to-be PAUL ABDUL), the record scaled the US chart and spawned two million selling singles, 'WHEN I THINK OF YOU' and 'LET'S WAIT AWHILE' while Jam/Lewis' hard-assed funk production came into its own on the likes of 'WHAT HAVE YOU DONE FOR ME LATELY' and 'NASTY' (both US Top 5). To top the whole package off, the accompanying videos showcased JACKSON's hyperactive, highly choreographed dance moves and sassy new woman-of-the-world image. Encouraged by her success, she saddled a larger share of the writing duties on 'JANET JACKSON'S RHYTHM NATION 1814' (1989). The result was tracks such as 'STATE OF THE WORLD' and 'THE KNOWLEDGE', dealing with topics like racism, inequality etc. While not all critics were convinced by her newfound social conscience, there was no doubting the quality of another Jam/Lewis production and while her vocal prowess mightn't be top flight she made up for it with another gut-busting performance; the slinky pop of 'MISS YOU MUCH' made the US top spot as did 'ESCAPADE' and the throbbing 'BLACK CAT'. A glitzy sell-out tour ensued and JACKSON's lucrative market value was confirmed as 'Virgin' shelled out fifty million dollars on a two album deal in 1991. The resulting 'JANET' (1993) was a somewhat drawn-out affair spliced with interludes and presenting her in a new sexually mature mould. It was massive nevertheless, going straight in at No.1 on both the US and UK chart and featuring the US No.1 weepie, 'AGAIN'. A 1995 retrospective, 'DESIGN OF A DECADE' cemented her superstar position and aired a couple of new tracks, 'RUNAWAY' and 'TWENTY FOREPLAY'. While her early/mid 90's tours upped the ooer, missus ... factor with raunchy dance routines etc., JANET (now without the JACKSON tag) returned in 1997 with a new Afro-centric image. One of her funkiest, soulful singles to date, 'GOT TIL IT'S GONE' (based on JONI MITCHELL's famous 'Big Yellow Taxi') featured a great video in which JANET looked naturally sexy without trying too hard. 'THE VELVET ROPE' (1997) was her most explicit recording to date, a faux-concept set held together by dark sexual desires, between song interludes and a marked retro feel. Despite (or perhaps because of) its parental advisory sticker, the record topped the US chart, as did the single 'TOGETHER AGAIN' (UK Top 5). The lurid 'GO DEEP', meanwhile, made the British Top 20 but was conspicuous by its absence from the American charts. 1999 saw the starlet collaborating on hits by BLACKstreet, BUSTA RHYMES and SHAGGY while the sassy starlet kept up her penchant for steamy self indulgence on the marathon 'ALL FOR YOU' (2001). • **Songwriters:** Her pensmiths and collaborators from 1985 have been producers JIMMY JAM (JAMES HARRIS III) and TERRY LEWIS (both ex-The TIME). In 1989, she began to write and collaborate with both. • **Trivia:** In 1991, she signed new multi-million dollar contract with 'Virgin America'.

Album rating: JANET JACKSON (*4) / DREAM STREET (*3) / CONTROL (*7) / JANET JACKSON'S RHYTHM NATION 1814 (*7) / JANET. (*6) / DESIGN OF A DECADE 1986-1996 compilation (*8) / THE VELVET ROPE (*6) / ALL FOR YOU (*6)

JANET JACKSON – vocals (with session people)

		A&M	A&M
Nov 82.	(7") *<2440>* **YOUNG LOVE. / THE MAGIC IS WORKING**	–	64
Jan 83.	(lp/c) *(AMLH/+C 64907)* <4907> **JANET JACKSON** – Say you do / You'll never find (a love like mine) / Young love / Love and my best friend / Don't mess up this good thing / Forever yours / The magic is working / Come give your love to me.		Nov82 63
Jan 83.	(7") *<2522>* **COME GIVE YOUR LOVE TO ME. / FOREVER YOURS**	–	58
Feb 83.	(7"/12") *(AMS/AMX 8303)* **COME GIVE YOUR LOVE TO ME. / THE MAGIC IS WORKING**		–
May 83.	(7"/12") *(AM/+X 112)* **DON'T MESS UP THIS GOOD THING. / YOUNG LOVE**		
Sep 84.	(7"; JANET JACKSON & CLIFF RICHARD) *(AM 210)* **TWO TO THE POWER OF LOVE. / ROCK'N'ROLL** (12"+=) *(AMX 210)* – Don't mess up this good thing.		
Oct 84.	(lp/c/cd) <*(AMA/AMC/CDA 4962)*> **DREAM STREET** – Don't stand another chance / Two to the power of love / Pretty boy / Dream street / Communication / Fast girls / Hold back the tears / All my love to you / If it takes all night.		
Feb 86.	(7") *<2812>* **WHAT HAVE YOU DONE FOR ME LATELY. / HE DOESN'T KNOW I'M ALIVE**	–	4
Mar 86.	(7") *(AM 308)* **WHAT HAVE YOU DONE FOR ME LATELY. / YOUNG LOVE** (12"+=) *(AMX 308)* – ('A'dub).	3	–
Mar 86.	(lp/c/cd) <*(AMA/AMC/CDA 5106)*> **CONTROL** – Control / What have you done for me lately / You can be mine / The pleasure principle / When I think of you / He doesn't know why I'm alive / Let's wait awhile / Funny how time flies / Nasty. *(re-iss. Mar93)*	8	1
May 86.	(7") *(AM 316)* *<2830>* **NASTY. / YOU'LL NEVER FIND (A LOVE LIKE MINE)** (12"+=) (AMY 316) – ('A'instrumental).	19	3
Aug 86.	(7") *<2855>* **WHEN I THINK OF YOU. / PRETTY BOY**	–	1
Aug 86.	(7") *(AM 337)* **WHEN I THINK OF YOU. / COME GIVE YOUR LOVE TO ME**	10	–
Oct 86.	(7") *<2877>* **CONTROL. / FAST GIRLS**	–	5
Oct 86.	(7") *(AM 359)* **CONTROL. / PRETTY BOY**	42	–

(cd-s+=) (AMS 359) – Nasty (cool summer nix).
(12"++=) (AMY/AMX 359) – ('A'dub).

Breakout-A&M Breakout-A&M

Jan 87. (7") <2906> **LET'S WAIT AWHILE. / PRETTY BOY** – 2

Mar 87. (7"/7"pic-d) (USA/+P 601) **LET'S WAIT AWHILE. / NASTY (cool summer mix part 1)** 3 –
(12"+=) (USAT 601) – Nasty (cool summer mix part 2).
(d7"pic-d/clear+=) (USAD 601) – Nasty (original) / Control / ('A'version) / Nasty (cool summer mix part 1 fade).

— she guested on HERB ALPERT's 1987 album, 'Diamonds'

May 87. (7") <2927> **THE PLEASURE PRINCIPLE. / FAST GIRLS** – 14

Jun 87. (7") (USA 604) **THE PLEASURE PRINCIPLE (Shep Pettibone mix). / ('A'dub)** 24 –
(ext;12"+=/c-s+=) (USAT/+C 604) – ('A'-acapella).

Nov 87. (7") (USA 613) **FUNNY HOW TIME FLIES (WHEN YOU'RE HAVING FUN). / WHEN I THINK OF YOU** 59 –
(12"+=) (USAT 613) – Nasty (cool summer part 1).

Nov 87. (lp/c/cd) (MIX LP/MC/CD 1 – AMA/AMC/CDA 5169) **CONTROL – THE REMIXES** (remixes) 20 –

Aug 89. (7"/7"s/c-s) (USA/+S/TC 663) <1445> **MISS YOU MUCH. / YOU NEED ME** 25 1
(12"+=/cd-s+=) (USA 663 T/CD) – ('A'-Mama extended mix).

Sep 89. (lp/c/cd) <(CDA/AMC/AMA 3920)> **JANET JACKSON'S RHYTHM NATION 1814** 4 1
– (Pledge) / Rhythm nation /(TV) / State of the world / Race The knowledge / (Let's dance) Miss you much / (Come back interlude) / Love will never do (without you) / Livin' in a world (they didn't make) / Alright / (Hey baby) / Escapade / (No acid) / Black cat / Lonely / Come back to me / Someday is tonight / (Livin' in . . . complete darkness). *(note: interlude segments in brackets) (re-iss. Oct90 pic-lp/cd+=; AMAP/AMAD 3920)*

Oct 89. (7"/7"s/c-s) (USA/+S/TC 673) <1455> **RHYTHM NATION. / ('A'-C.H.R. remix)** 23 Nov89 2
(12"/12"pic-d/cd-s) (USA T/PD/CD 673) – ('A'mixes; 12" House Nation / 12" United / United dub).

Jan 90. (7"/7"box/c-s) (USA/+B/MC 681) **COME BACK TO ME. / ALRIGHT** 20 –
(12"+=/cd-s+=) (USA T/CD 681) – Alright (Hip Hop dub).

Mar 90. (7"/7"pic-d/c-s) (USA/+P/MC 684) <1490> **ESCAPADE. / ('A'-Housecapade)** 17 Jan90 1
(12"/cd-s) (USA T/D 684) – ('A'mixes; Shep's Housecapade / Housecapade dub / Shep's good time).

Mar 90. (7") <1479> **ALRIGHT. / (remix)** – 4

Jun 90. (7"/7"sha-pic-d/c-s) (USA/+S/MC 693) **ALRIGHT. / VUELVE A MI (COME BACK TO ME)** 20 –
(12") (USAT 693) – ('A'-hip hop mix) / ('A'extended house mix).
(cd-s+=) (USAD 693) – (all 4 tracks above).

Jun 90. (7") <1475> **COME BACK TO ME. / VUELVE A MI (COME BACK TO ME)** – 2

A&M A&M

Aug 90. (7"/c-s) (AM/+MC 587) **BLACK CAT. / 1814 MEGAMIX – ALRIGHT – ESCAPADE – RHYTHM NATION – MISS YOU MUCH** 15 –
(ext;12"+=/12"s+=/cd-s+=) (AM Y/X/CD 587) – ('A'-3 snaps up mix).

Sep 90. (7") <1477> **BLACK CAT. / (remix)** – 1

Oct 90. (7"/c-s) (AM/+MC 700) <1538> **LOVE WILL NEVER DO (WITHOUT YOU). / ('A'-The Love mix)** 34 Nov90 1
(12"/12"s/cd-s) (AM Y/X/CD 700) – ('A'mixes; Shep's work it out / Shep's work it out dub / U.K. funky).

— in Jun'92, she hit US No.10 with LUTHER VANDROSS on a duet of 'THE BEST THINGS IN LIFE ARE FREE'; it went on to hit No.2 in the UK

Virgin Virgin

Apr 93 (7"/c-s) (VS/+C 1460) <12650> **THAT'S THE WAY LOVE GOES. / (instrumental)** 2 1
(12"+=/cd-s+=) (VST/VSCDG 1460) – ('A'-CJ R&B mixes).

May 93. (cd/c/lp) (CD/TC+/V 2720) <87825> **JANET.** 1 1
– Morning / That's the way love goes / You want this / If / Throb / What'll I do / Funky big band / New agenda / Because of love / Again / Another lover / Where are you now / The body that loves you / Any time, any place / Are you still up. *(d-cd-iss. Dec93 w/ 'REMIXED'+=; CDVX 2720)* – Whoops now / That's the way love is / If (medley) / That's the way love goes (we aimsta win mix) / Again (French) / If (Brothers In Rhythm swing yo pants mix) / One more chance / That's the way love goes (CJ Mackintosh mix) / If (Todd Terry & Janet's jeep mix) / Again (piano-vocal). *(re-iss. Mar95; CDVY 2720)*

Jul 93. (7"/c-s) (VS/+C 1474) <12676> **IF. / ONE MORE CHANCE** 14 4
(12"/cd-s) (VST/VSCDT 1474) – ('A'mixes; Brothers In Rhythm swing yp pants / D&D 12" / extended / Tee's Freeze).

Nov 93. (7"/c-s) (VS/+C 1481) <38404> **AGAIN. / AGAIN (vocal/piano mix)** 6 Oct93 1
(cd-s+=) (VSCDG 1481) – ('A'instrumental) / Funky big band.
(cd-s+=) (VSCDX 1481) – ('A'-French) / That's the way love goes (We aimsta win mix).

Jan 94. (c-s,cd-s) <38422> **BECAUSE OF LOVE / FUNKY BIG BAND** – 10

Mar 94. (7"/c-s) (VS/+C 1488) **BECAUSE OF LOVE. / ('A'-Frankie & David mix)** 19 –
(12"+=/cd-s+=) (VST/VSCDG 1488) – ('A'mixes; Frankie & David classic / D&D Bentley radio / Muggs 7" w-bass intro / D&D slow).

Jun 94. (c-s/cd-s) (VSC/VSCDT 1501) <38435> **ANY TIME, ANY PLACE / THROB (David Morales remix) / AND ON AND ON** 13 May94 2
(12") (VST 1501) – ('A'-CJ's 12"mix) / Throb / ('A'-D&D house).
(cd-s) (VSCDG 1501) – ('A'-R Kelly mix) / ('A'-C.J. Mackintosh mix) / ('A'-D&D mix).

Nov 94. (c-s/cd-s) (VSC/VSCDG 1519) <38455> **YOU WANT THIS / 70's LOVE GROOVE / YOU WANT THIS (Mafia & Fluxy dancehall mix) / AND ON AND ON** 14 Oct94 8
(12") (VST 1519) – ('A'mixes; E-Smoove's house anthem / E-Smoove's anthem dub / underdub / disco theory / smoove soul 7").
(cd-s) (VSCDT 1519) – ('A'mixes; remix / E-Smoove's anthem / Mafia & Fluxy dancehall / Spoiled milk / Disco theory / funk extravaganza / Smoove soul 12").

Mar 95. (7"pic-d/c-s) (VSY/VSC 1533) **WHOOPS NOW / WHAT'LL I DO** 9 –
(12"pic-d+=/cd-s+=) (VSTY/CDG 1533) – ('B'-Dave Navarro mix) / The body that loves you.

— In Jun'95, JANET teamed up with brother MICHAEL to hit Top 3 with 'SCREAM'. In 1997, she was simply called JANET in the States only.

Sep 97. (7"/c-s; as JANET, Q-TIP & JONI MITCHELL) (VS HL/C 1666) **GOT TIL IT'S GONE / ('A'mix)** 6
(12"+=/cd-s+=) (VS T/CDG 1666) – ('A'mixes).

Oct 97. (cd/c/lp) (CD/TC+/V 2860) <44762> **THE VELVET ROPE** 6 1
– Interlude / The velvet rope / You / Got til it's gone / Go deep / Free zone / Memory / Together again / Online / Empty / Full / What about / Every time / Tonight's the night / I get lonely / Rope burn / Anything / Sad / Special / Can't be stopped.

Dec 97. (c-s) (VSC 1670) <38623> **TOGETHER AGAIN / ('A'-Tony Hum mix)** 4 1
(cd-s+=) (VSCDT 1670) – ('A'mixes; DJ Premier / Jimmy Jam).
(12") (VST 1670) – ('A'mixes; Tony Morales / Jimmy Jam).

Mar 98. (c-s) (VSC 1683) <38631> **I GET LONELY / ('A'-TNT remix)** 5 May98 3
(12"+=/cd-s+=) (BST/VSCDT 1683) – ('A'mixes; extended / Jam & Lewis / Jason vs. Janet).
(above was credited in the States to:- JANET featuring BLACKSTREET)

Jun 98. (c-s) (VSC 1680) **GO DEEP / ('A'-Teddy Riley funk mix)** 13
(12"+=/cd-s+=) (VST/VSCDT 1680) – ('A'mixes; Roni Size / Master At Work – 2).

Sep 98. (c-s/cd-s) (VSC/+DT 1713) **YOU / ACCEPT ME / GO DEEP** –

Dec 98. (c-s) (VSC 1720) **EVERY TIME / ACCEPT ME** 46
(12"+=/cd-s+=) (VST/VSCDT 1720) – ('A'mixes).

— in Apr'99, JANET featured on BLACKstreet's hit single, 'Girlfriend – Boyfriend' and also on BUSTA RHYMES chartbuster, 'What's It Gonna Be!?' and SHAGGY's 'Luv Me, Luv Me' (a little earlier).

Aug 00. (c-s) (562915-4) <562846> **DOESN'T REALLY MATTER / (album mix)** 5 Jun00 1
(cd-s) (562915-2) – ('A'mixes; dance all day extended / Jonathan Peters club / video).
(above issued on 'Mercury')

Apr 01. (c-s/12"/cd-s) (VSC/VST/VSCDT 1801) <97522> **ALL FOR YOU / ('A'-Thunderpuss club) / ('A'-Top heavy mix)** 3 Mar01 1
(12") (VSTX 1801) – ('A'-DK Quik remix) / ('A'-DJ Quik instrumental) / ('A'-rock mix) / ('A'-instrumental rock).

Apr 01. (cd/d-lp) (CD+/V 2590) <10144> **ALL FOR YOU** 2 1
– (intro) / You ain't right / All for you / 2wayforyou (interlude) / Come on get up / When we oooo / China love / Love scene (ooh baby) / Would you

mind / Lame (interlude) / Trust a try / Clouds (interlude) / Son of a gun (I betcha think this song is about you) (with CARLY SIMON) / Truth / Theory (interlude) / Someone to call my lover / Feels so right / Doesn't really matter / Better days / (outro).

Jul 01. (c-s) *(VSC 1813)* <38799> **SOMEONE TO CALL MY LOVER / (Hex Hector & Mac Quayle mix)** 11 Jun01 3
(12"+=/cd-s+=) *(VST/VSCDT 1813)* – ('A'-def & velvet mixes).

Dec 01. (c-s; by JANET featuring MISSY ELLIOTT, P. DIDDY & CARLY SIMON) *(VUSC 232)* <46171> **SON OF A GUN (I BETCHA THINK THIS SONG IS ABOUT YOU) / ('A'-original Flyte tyme & P. Diddy remixes)** 13 Oct01 28
(cd-s+=) *(VUSCD 232)* – ('A'-Route 80 remix).
(12"++=) *(VUST 232)* – ('A'-Cottonbelly dub).
(cd-s) *(VUSCDX 232)* – ('A'side) / ('A'-Cottonbelly remix) / ('A'-rock remix).

– compilations, others. –

—— on 'A&M' unless mentioned otherwise

Sep 95. (c-s) *(581 197-4)* <1194> **RUNAWAY / WHEN I THINK OF YOU (extended Morales house mix)** 6 Aug95 3
(12"+=/cd-s+=) *(581 209-1/197-2)* – ('A'mixes; Junior's Factory).
(d12"+=) *(581 243-1)* – ('A'mixes; Junior's unplugged) / When I think of you.

Oct 95. (cd/c) *(540 422-2/-4)* <0399> **DESIGN OF A DECADE – 1986-1996** (compilation) 2 3
– Runaway / What have you done for me lately / Nasty / When I think of you / Escapade / Miss you much / Love will never do (without you) / Alright / Control / Pleasure principle / Black cat / Rhythm nation / That's the way love goes / Come back to me / Let's wait awhile / Twenty foreplay.

Dec 95. (c-s; LUTHER VANDROSS & JANET JACKSON) *(581 309-4)* **THE BEST THINGS IN LIFE ARE FREE / ('A'mix)** 7 –
(cd-s+=) *(581 309-2)* – ('A'mixes).

Mar 96. (c-s) *(581 511-4)* **TWENTY FOREPLAY / ('A'mix)** 22 –
(cd-s+=) *(581 511-2)* – ('A'mixes).

Sep 96. (12"/cd-s) *(581 691-1/-2)* **WHEN I THINK OF YOU / (mixes)** –

Joe JACKSON

Born: 11 Aug'54, Burton-On-Trent, Staffordshire, England, although raised from a very early age in Gosport, near Portsmouth. He left school with top grade music honour and enrolled at The Royal College Of Music in 1973. After a spell in JOHNNY DANKWORTH's NATIONAL YOUTH JAZZ ORCHESTRA, he joined pub rock outfit, ARMS & LEGS; they released three flop singles for 'M.A.M.' between 1976-1977, before he quit. In 1977, he became a musical director for 'Opportunity Knocks' (TV talent show, hosted by Hughie Green) winners, COFFEE AND CREAM (yuk!). The following year, he moved away from the cabaret scene to London, where he recorded demo tape, which A&M's David Kershenbaum approved, producing first solo attempt, 'IS SHE REALLY GOING OUT WITH HIM?' (it took a re-issue of this single in Summer 1979 to break him into UK and US charts). The debut album, 'LOOK SHARP!' (1979), subsequently hit the US Top 20, its jazzy new-wave power-pop and acerbic lyrics inevitably drawing comparisons with ELVIS COSTELLO. 'I'M THE MAN' (1979), and its accompanying UK Top 5 hit single, the sly 'IT'S DIFFERENT FOR GIRLS', carried on in a similar vein although JACKSON veered off into more unsettling, eclectic musical textures with 1980's self-produced 'BEAT CRAZY'. Although credited to The JOE JACKSON BAND, the line-up remained identical to that which had played on the first two releases, namely GRAHAM MABY, GARY SANFORD and DAVE HOUGHTON. For 'JOE JACKSON'S JUMPIN' JIVE' (1981), only the former remained from the original formation, an array of jazz musicians employed in a fairly successful attempt to update the 40's swing style of LOUIS JORDAN and CAB CALLOWAY. The exotic musical landscape of New York was JACKSON's next stop; having relocated to the Big Apple following the breakdown of his marriage, he proceeded to soak up the spicy latin jazz/salsa influences for his 'NIGHT AND DAY' (1982) album. A transatlantic Top 5 hit, it spawned JACKSON's biggest hit single to date in the dancefloor friendly 'STEPPIN' OUT' and eventually went gold. JACKSON recruited another new group of musicians for 'BODY AND SOUL' (1984), while 'BIG WORLD' was an ambitious live double set featuring all-new material recorded over three successive nights. The vocal-free 'WILL POWER' (1987) set saw JACKSON dabbling in classical orchestration and accordingly failed to chart, while the autobiographical 'BLAZE OF GLORY' (1989) covered all JACKSON's stylistic bases to date. A change of label to 'Virgin', saw the man pen his most direct, accessible material in years with 'LAUGHTER AND LUST' (1991), a welcome diversion from his constant experimentation. 'HEAVEN & HELL' (1997) was another classically influenced work comprised of seven pieces relating to the biblical seven deadly sins, the likes of SUZANNE VEGA and JANE SIBERRY guesting. Even more straightforward in its classical intentions, 'SYMPHONY No.1' (1999) was conceived as a symphonic piece although with the likes of STEVE VAI on board, it never completely abandoned the realm of rock and jazz idioms. On a completely different note, 'SUMMER IN THE CITY: LIVE IN NEW YORK' (2000) documented a summer '99 gig wherein the breadth of JACKSON's musical reach was demonstrated in a choice of covers which ranged from Lovin' Spoonful and The Beatles ('ELEANOR RIGBY') to Duke Ellington's 'MOOD INDIGO'. Later the same year, JACKSON, always full of surprises, released 'NIGHT AND DAY II', a belated sequel to his early 80's classic. 2003's confusingly titled 'VOLUME 4', meanwhile, found JACKSON and BAND reunited for the first time in over twenty years. While any fan expecting a re-run of those late 70's glory years could only ever be in for a let-down, this was the most authentic and committed JACKSON had sounded for many a year, eclipsing most of his work since the early 80's. • **Covered:** OH WELL (Fleetwood Mac) / MAKING PLANS FOR NIGEL (Xtc). • **Trivia:** He also produced The KEYS in '81, and reggae outfits RASSES and The TOASTERS.

Album rating: LOOK SHARP! (*8) / I'M THE MAN (*7) / BEAT CRAZY (*7) / JUMPIN' JIVE (*7) / NIGHT AND DAY (*7) / BODY AND SOUL (*5) / BIG WORLD (*5) / WILL POWER (*4) / LIVE . . . 1980-1986 (*6) / BLAZE OF GLORY (*5) / STEPPIN' OUT – THE VERY BEST OF JOE JACKSON compilation (*8) / LAUGHTER AND LUST (*5) / NIGHT MUSIC (*3) / GREATEST HITS compilation (*8) / THIS IS IT! THE A&M YEARS compilation (*8) / HEAVEN & HELL (*3) / SYMPHONY NO.1 (*4) / SUMMER IN THE CITY – LIVE IN NEW YORK (*5) / NIGHT AND DAY II (*4) / JOE JACKSON BAND VOLUME 4 (*6)

ARMS AND LEGS

JOE JACKSON – piano, violin, vocals, harmonica / **MARK ANDREWS** – vocals / **GRAHAM MABY** – bass

M.A.M. not iss.

Apr 76. (7") *(MAM 140)* **JANICE. / SHE'LL SURPRISE YOU** –

Aug 76. (7") *(MAM 147)* **HEAT OF THE NIGHT. / GOOD TIMES** –

Feb 77. (7") *(MAM 156)* **IS THERE ANY MORE WINE. / SHE'LL SURPRISE YOU** –

JOE JACKSON

solo – lead vocals, piano with backing band **GRAHAM MABY** – bass / **GARY SANFORD** – guitar / **DAVE HOUGHTON** – drums

A&M A&M

Sep 78. (7") *(AMS 7392)* <2132> **IS SHE REALLY GOING OUT WITH HIM? / (DO THE) INSTANT MASH** May79 21

Jan 79. (lp/c) *(AMLH/CAM 64743)* <4743> **LOOK SHARP!** 40 20
– One more time / Sunday papers / Is she really going out with him? /

Happy loving couples / Throw it away / Baby stick around / Look sharp! / Fools in love / (Do the) Instant mash / Pretty girls / Got the time. *(re-iss. Aug79 on white-lp; same) (re-iss. Mar82; AMID 120) (re-iss. Sep84 on 'Hallmark' lp/c; SHM/HSC 3154) (cd-iss. Nov84; CDA 64743) (re-iss. 1988 lp/c; AMA/AMC 3187) (cd re-iss. Oct92; CDMID 115)*

Feb 79. (7") *(AMS 7413)* **SUNDAY PAPERS. / LOOK SHARP!** [ ] [–]

May 79. (7"/10"white) *(AMS/+P 7433)* **ONE MORE TIME. / DON'T ASK ME** [ ] [–]

Jul 79. (7") *(AMS 7459)* **IS SHE REALLY GOING OUT WITH HIM?. / YOU GOT THE FEVER** [13] [–]

Aug 79. (7") *<2186>* **IT'S DIFFERENT FOR GIRLS. / COME ON** [–] [ ]

Oct 79. (7") *(AMS 7479) <2209>* **I'M THE MAN. / COME ON (live)** [ ] [ ]

Oct 79. (lp/c)(5x7"box) *(AMLH/CAM 64794)(none) <4794>* **I'M THE MAN** [12] [22]
– On your radio / Geraldine and John / Kinda kute / It's different for girls / I'm the man / The band wore blue shirts / Don't wanna be like that / Amateur hour / Get that girl / Friday. *(cd-iss. 1988; CDA 3221) (cd re-iss. Oct92; CDMID 117)*

Dec 79. (7") *(AMS 7493)* **IT'S DIFFERENT FOR GIRLS. / FRIDAY** [5] [–]

Mar 80. (7") *(AMS 7513)* **KINDA KUTE. / GERALDINE AND JOHN** [ ] [–]

JOE JACKSON BAND

Jun 80. (7"/7"w-poster) *(AMS/+P 7536)* **THE HARDER THEY COME. / OUT OF STYLE / TILT** [ ] [–]

Oct 80. (7") *(AMS 7563)* **MAD AT YOU. / ENOUGH IS NOT ENOUGH** [ ] [–]

Oct 80. (lp/c) *(AMLH/CAM 64837) <4837>* **BEAT CRAZY** [42] [41]
– Beat crazy / One to one / In every dream home (a nightmare) / The evil eye / Mad at you / Crime don't pay / Someone up there / Battleground / Biology / Pretty boys / Fit. *(cd-iss. 1988; CDA 3241)*

Nov 80. (7") *<2276>* **ONE TO ONE. / ENOUGH IS NOT ENOUGH** [–] [ ]

Jan 81. (7") *(AMS 8100)* **BEAT CRAZY. / IS SHE REALLY GOING OUT WITH HIM?** [ ] [–]

Mar 81. (7") *(AMS 8116)* **ONE TO ONE. / SOMEONE UP THERE** [ ] [–]

JOE JACKSON'S JUMPIN' JIVE

JOE retained **GRAHAM MABY** plus **PETE THOMAS** – sax / **RAUOL OLIVERA** – trumpet / **DAVE BITELI** – wind instr. NICK WELDON – piano / **LARRY TOLFREE** – drums / **NICK WELDON** – piano

Jun 81. (7") *(AMS 8145) <2365>* **JUMPIN' JIVE. / KNOCK ME A KISS** [43] [ ]

Jun 81. (lp/c) *(AMLH/CAM 68530) <4871>* **JOE JACKSON'S JUMPIN' JIVE** [14] [42]
– Jumpin' with symphony Sid / Jack, you're dead / Is you or is you ain't my baby / We the cats will help ya / San Francisco fan / Five guys named Moe / Jumpin' jive / You run your mouth (and I'll run my business) / What's the use of getting sober (when you're gonna get drunk again) / You're my meat / Tuxedo junction / How long must I wait for you. *(cd-iss. 1988; CDA 3271) (re-iss. May93 on 'Spectrum' cd/c; 550062-2/-4)*

Aug 81. (7") *(AMS 8161)* **JACK, YOU'RE DEAD. / FIVE GUYS NAMED MOE** [ ] [–]

JOE JACKSON

—— **SUE HADJOPOULOS** – percussion, flute; repl. WELDON + horns

Jun 82. (7"pic-d) *(AMS 8231)* **REAL MEN. / CHINATOWN** [ ] [–]

Jun 82. (lp/c) *(AMLH/CAM 64906) <4906>* **NIGHT AND DAY** [3] [4]
– Another world / Chinatown / T.V. age / Target / Steppin' out / Breaking us in two / Cancer / Real men / A slow song. *(cd-iss. 1983; CDA 64906) (re-iss. Oct92 cd/c; CD/C MID 158)*

Aug 82. (7") *(AMS 8247)* **BREAKING US IN TWO. / EL BLANCO** [ ] [–]

Aug 82. (7") *<2428>* **STEPPIN' OUT. / CHINATOWN** [–] [6]

Oct 82. (7") *(AMS 8262)* **STEPPIN' OUT. / ANOTHER WORLD** [6] [–]

Jan 83. (7") *<2510>* **BREAKING US IN TWO. / TARGET** [–] [18]

Feb 83. (7") *(AM 101)* **BREAKING US IN TWO. / EL BLANCO** [59] [–]
(12"+=) *(AMX 101)* – T.V. age.

May 83. (7") *(AM 114)* **A SLOW SONG. / REAL MEN** [ ] [–]

Jul 83. (7") *<2548>* **ANOTHER WORLD. / ORTO MUNDO** [–] [ ]

—— added **JOY ASKEW** – synthesizers

Aug 83. (7") *(AM 134)* **COSMOPOLITAN. / BREAKDOWN** [ ] [–]

Sep 83. (lp/c) *(AMLX/CAM 64931) <4931>* **MIKE'S MURDER (soundtrack)** [ ] [64]
– Cosmopolitan / 1-2-3-go (this town's a fairground) / Laundromat Monday / Memphis / Moonlight / Zemeo / Breakdown / Moonlight theme.

Nov 83. (7") *<2601>* **MEMPHIS. / BREAKDOWN** [–] [85]

—— retained only **MABY** and brought in **GARY BURKE** – drums / **VINNIE ZUMMO** – guitar / **ED ROYNESDAL** – keyboards, violin / **TONY AIELLO** – sax, flute / **MICHAEL MORREALE** – wind

Mar 84. (lp/c) *(AMLX/CXM 65000) <5000>* **BODY AND SOUL** [14] [20]
– The verdict / Cha cha loco / Not here, not now / You can't get what you want ('till you know what you want) / Go for it / Loisaida / Be my number two / Heart of ice. *(cd-iss. Oct84; CXM 65000) (cd re-iss. Oct92; CDMID 118)*

Apr 84. (7"/12") *(AM/+X 186) <2635>* **HAPPY ENDING. / LOISAIDA** [58] Jul84 [57]

Jun 84. (7") *(AM 200)* **BE MY NUMBER TWO. / IS SHE REALLY GOING OUT WITH HIM?** [70] [–]
(7") *(AMX 200)* – ('A'side) / Heart of ice.

Sep 84. (7") *(AM 212) <2628>* **YOU CAN'T GET WHAT YOU WANT ('TILL YOU KNOW WHAT YOU WANT). / CHA CHA LOCO** [ ] Apr84 [15]
(12"+=) *(AMX 212)* – ('A' dub version).

—— **RICK FORD** – bass, guitar, vox repl. MABY, AIELLO, ROYNESDAL + MORREALE

Mar 86. (3.sided.d-lp/c/cd) *(JWA/JWC/JWD 3) <6021>* **BIG WORLD (live)** [41] [34]
– Wild west / Right and wrong / (It's a) Big world / Precious time / Tonight and forever / Shanghai sky / Fifty dollar love affair / We can't live together / Forty years / Survival / Soul kiss / The jet-set / Tango Atlantico / Hometown / Man in the street.

Apr 86. (7") *(AM 312) <2829>* **RIGHT OR WRONG. / BREAKING US IN TWO (live)** [ ] [ ]
(12"+=) *(AMY 312)* – I'm the man (live).

Jun 86. (7"/12") *(AM/+Y 324)* **HOME TOWN. / TANGO ATLANTICO** [ ] [–]

Jun 86. (7") *<2847>* **HOME TOWN. / I'M THE MAN (live)** [–] [ ]

Apr 87. (lp/c/cd) *(<AMA/AMC/CDA 3908>)* **WILL POWER** [ ] [ ]
– No Pasaran / Solitude / Will power / Nocturne / Symphony in one movement. *(cd re-iss. Apr89 on 'Mobile Fidelity'; UDCD 503)*

May 87. (7") *<2944>* **WILL POWER. / NOCTURNE** [–] [ ]

Apr 88. (7") *(AM 441)* **JUMPIN' JIVE (live). / MEMPHIS (live)** [ ] [ ]
(12"+=) *(AMY 441)* – You can't get what you want (till you know what you want).

May 88. (d-lp/c/cd) *(<AMA/AMC/CDA 6706>)* **LIVE 1980/86 (live)** [66] [91]
– One to one / I'm the man / Beat crazy / Is she really going out with him? / Cancer / Don't wanna be like that / On your radio / Fools in love / Cancer / Is she really going out with him? (acappella version) / Look sharp! / Sunday papers / Real men / Is she really going out with him? (acoustic) / Memphis / A slow song / Be my number two / Breaking us in two / It's different for girls / You can't get what you want ('till you know what you want) / Jumpin' jive / Steppin' out.

Jun 88. (7") *<1207>* **LOOK SHARP (live). / MEMPHIS (live)** [–] [ ]

Aug 88. (7") *(AM 481) <1228>* **(HE'S A) SHAPE IN A DRAPE. / SPEEDWAY** [ ] [ ]
(12"+=) *(AMY 481)* – Sometime in Chicago.

Nov 88. (lp/c/cd) *(<AMA/AMC/CDA 3917>)* **TUCKER – A MAN AND HIS DREAMS (Soundtrack)** [ ] [ ]
– Captain of industry / Car of tomorrow / No chance blues / (He's a) Shape in a drape / Factory / Vera / It pays to advertise / Tiger rag / Showtime in Chicago / Loan bank loan blues / Speedway / Marilee / Hangin' in Howard Hughes' hangar / The toast of the town / Abe's blues / The trial / Freedom swing / Rhythm delivery.

—— Now with 10-piece line-up, **MABY, ZUMMO, BURKE, ASKEW, AIELLO, FORD, ROYNESDAL, HADJOPOULOS + TOM TEELEY** – guitar / **ANTHONY COX** – bass

Apr 89. (lp/c/cd) *(<AMA/AMC/CDA 5249>)* **BLAZE OF GLORY** [36] [61]
– Tomorrow's child / Me and you (against the world) / Down to London / Sentimental thing / Acropolis now / Blaze of glory / Rant and rave /

Nineteen forever / The best I can do / Evil empire / Discipline / The uman touch.

May 89. (7") *(AM 506)* <1404> **NINETEEN FOREVER. / ACROPOLIS NOW (instrumental)** ☐ ☐
(cd-s+=) *(CDEE 506)* – ('A'extended).

Oct 89. (7") *(AM 512)* **DOWN TO LONDON. / YOU CAN'T GET WHAT YOU WANT (TIL YOU KNOW WHAT YOU WANT)** ☐ –
(cd-s+=) *(CDEE 512)* – Sunday papers.

Aug 90. (7"/c-s) *(AM/+MC 583)* **STEPPIN' OUT (re-mix). / SENTIMENTAL THING** ☐ –
(cd-s+=) *(AMCD 583)* – It's a big worth.

Sep 90. (cd/c/lp) *(397052-2/-4/-1)* **STEPPIN' OUT – THE VERY BEST OF JOE JACKSON** (compilation) 7 –
– Is she really going out with him? / Fools in love / I'm the man / It's different for girls / Beat crazy / Jumpin' jive / Breaking us in two / Steppin' out / Slow song (live) / You can't get what you want ('till you know what you want) / Be my number two / Right and wrong / Home town / Down to London / Nineteen forever.

Virgin America — Virgin America

Apr 91. (c-s) *(VUSC 40)* **STRANGER THAN FICTION. / DROWNING** ☐ –
(cd-s+=) *(VUSCD 40)* – It's different for girls (acoustic).

Apr 91. (cd/c/lp) *(CDVUS/VUSMC/VUSLP 34)* <91628> **LAUGHTER & LUST** 41 ☐
– Obvious song / Goin' downtown / Stranger than fiction / Oh well / Jamie G / Hit single / It's all too much / When you're not around / The other me / Trying to cry / My house / The old songs / Drowning.

Oct 94. (cd/c) *(CDVUS/VUSMS 78)* <39880> **NIGHT MUSIC** ☐ ☐
– Nocturne No.1 / Flying nocturne No.2 / Ever after / The man who wrote Danny Boy / Nocturne No.3 / Lullaby / Only the future / Nocturne No.4 / Sea of secrets.

Sony Classical — Sony Classical

Sep 97. (cd) *<60273>* **HEAVEN & HELL** – ☐
– Prelude / Fugue 1 – More is more (gluttony) / Angel (lust) / Tuzla (avarice) / Passacaglia – A bud and a slice (sloth) / Right (anger) / The bridge (envy) / Fugue 2 – Song of Daedalus (pride).

Oct 99. (cd) *(<SK 64435>)* **SYMPHONY NO.1** ☐ ☐
– First movement / Fast movement / Slow movement / Last movement.

Jun 00. (cd) *(<SK 89237>)* **SUMMER IN THE CITY: LIVE IN NEW YORK (live)** ☐ May00 ☐
– Summer in the city / Obvious song / Another world / Fools in love – For your love / Mood indigo / The crowd – Down to London / Eleanor Rigby / Be my number two / Home town / It's different for girls / King of the world / You can't get what you want / One more time.
(above also credited **GRAHAM MABY + GARY BURKE**

Sony Jazz — Sony Jazz

Oct 00. (cd) *(<SK 89261>)* **NIGHT AND DAY II** ☐ ☐
– Prelude / Hall of a town / Stranger than you / Why / Glamour and pain / Dear mom / Love got lost / Just because / Happyland / Stay.

Rykodisc — Rykodisc

Mar 03. (cd) *(<RCD 10639>)* **JOE JACKSON BAND VOLUME 4** ☐ ☐
– Take it like a man / Still alive / Awkward age / Chrome / Love at first light / Fairy dust / Little bit stupid / Blue flame / Dirty martini / Thugz 'R' us / Bright grey. *(<ltd-d-cd iss.+=; RCD 10638>)* – live:- One more time / Is she really going out with him? / On your radio / Got the time / It's different for girls / I'm the man.

Jul 03. (cd-s) *(RCD 51074)* **CHROME / IS SHE REALLY GOING OUT WITH HIM? (live) / COULDN'T I JUST TELL YOU** ☐ –

– compilations, etc. –

Oct 93. (d-cd) *A&M; (CDA 24121)* **NIGHT AND DAY / LOOK SHARP!** ☐ –
Mar 96. (cd-s) *A&M; (581396)* **STEPPIN' OUT** ☐ –
May 96. (cd) *A&M; <540524>* **GREATEST HITS** – ☐
Feb 97. (d-cd) *A&M; (540402-2)* **THIS IS IT! THE A&M YEARS** ☐ ☐
Jul 00. (cd) *Universal; (E 497277-2)* **UNIVERSAL MASTERS COLLECTION** ☐ –
Feb 01. (cd) *Spectrum; (<544513-2>)* **THE COLLECTION** ☐ Apr01 ☐

Michael JACKSON (& The JACKSONS)

Born: 29 Aug'58, Indiana, USA. Brought up in a family of child prodigies guided by musician father, JOE (no, not that one!), MICHAEL was groomed for a lead vocal spot from an early age, soon taking pole position alongside his brothers (JACKIE, TITO, JERMAINE and MARLON) in the all singing, all dancing JACKSON 5. Musically inspired by legendary 'Godfather' of soul, JAMES BROWN, along with the choreographed moves of Motown's best acts, this youthful posse initially recorded a couple of tracks for small local label, 'Steeltown', having proved themselves in the prestigious talent contests of The Apollo Theater in New York. Inevitably, the group were subsequently signed up by 'Motown' in 1968, the label quick to spot the potential of a group who were perfect for moulding and developing in their established style. Label guru Berry Gordy moved the family en masse to Hollywood, got the crack in-house team of writers on the job (it's rumoured 'Motown' initially refused to use the group's own material) and sharpened up their moves before eventually releasing a debut single in late '69, 'I WANT YOU BACK'. The label had struck gold yet again and the single became the first of four consecutive US No.1 hits, its pre-pubescent naivety and sugary charm a winning formula (and a treasure trove for hip hop samplers) which saw the classic 'ABC', 'THE LOVE YOU SAVE' and 'I'LL BE THERE' all topping the charts in quick succession. Like many soul outfits, The JACKSON 5 were primarily a singles venture and while albums such as 'DIANA ROSS PRESENTS THE JACKSON 5' (1970), 'ABC' (1970) and 'THE THIRD ALBUM' (1971) had more than their fair share of filler, the emotional charge of the early hits can still get a dancefloor grinning ear to ear. After another clutch of Top 20 singles in '71 (including the timeless 'NEVER CAN SAY GOODBYE'), MICHAEL was singled out for a solo career, debuting with the ballad, 'GOT TO BE THERE' early the following year. The single was a transatlantic Top 5 smash, MICHAEL JACKSON the pop star had arrived; the album of the same name hit the American Top 20, while a sassy cover of Bobby Day's 'ROCKIN' ROBIN' repeated the success of the debut. His most famous hit of the era, however, arrived in the shape of the syrupy 'BEN', an unlikely ode to a pet rat! Although the track gave MICHAEL the first No.1 of his illustrious career, the ensuing few years would see commercial fortunes take a bit of a back seat, both for him and his brothers (with whom he was maintaining a parallel career in The JACKSON 5). From the heady heights of starring in their very own cartoon series, The JACKSON 5 began to struggle as they made the transistion from using 'Motown'-penned material to writing their own stuff, the proto-disco of the 'DANCING MACHINE' (1974) album rejuvenating them somewhat despite it being their penultimate set for the label. They (all but JERMAINE who stayed with 'Motown' and was replaced by younger brother RANDY) finally jumped ship for 'Epic' in 1975 (presumably procuring a better royalty rate than the whopping 2.7% they'd been getting at 'Motown'), although GORDY sued them for alleged breach of contract the following year and they were obliged to change their name to The JACKSONS; the case was finally settled at the turn of the decade with the siblings paying GORDY a tidy sum and giving up the rights to the JACKSON 5 name. Ensconced at 'Epic', the brothers enjoyed almost instant succes in 1976 with Top 10 hit, 'ENJOY YOURSELF', while the second single lifted from the eponymous major label debut album, 'SHOW YOU THE

WAY TO GO', became the family's first UK No.1. In line with the burgeoning disco craze, The JACKSON's adopted a tougher, more mature sound as the decade wore on, the 'DESTINY' (1979) album spawning such enduring glitterball favourites as 'BLAME IT ON THE BOOGIE' and 'SHAKE YOUR BODY (DOWN TO THE GROUND)'. MICHAEL was also developing his stunning vocal prowess, his seminal solo set, 'OFF THE WALL' (released the same year) seeing the singer reinvented as a boogie-down pop powerhouse, sophisticated yet gloriously loose limbed. Seasoned producer/arranger QUINCY JONES was JACKSON's creative foil for the project, the pair having met while working on 'The Wiz', a commercially disastrous attempt at revamping the 'Wizard Of Oz' musical in an Afro-American stylee. JONES' expertise seemingly freed MICHAEL up to put in a career best performance on such electric material as 'DON'T STOP 'TIL YOU GET ENOUGH' (a massive transatlantic hit and a US No.1), 'ROCK WITH YOU' (another to top the American charts) and tear-jerker 'SHE'S OUT OF MY LIFE'. The album itself – a milestone in pop/soul – went on to become a multi-million worldwide seller and secure a place in history as the first record by a solo artist to spawn four consecutive Top 10 hits. Its success also had a knock-on effect for the subsequent JACKSONS album, 'TRIUMPH' (1980), which sold in bucketloads and prompted a huge US tour, wherein MICHAEL took the opportunity to develop his solo material and work on the moves which would eventually flower into his celebrated stage show. The next phase in the singer's solo career came as he and JONES reunited in 1982 to work on an obscure spoken word set based on the 'E.T.' movie (the record was subsequently withdrawn due to legal problems) before beginning work on a follow-up proper, the legendary 'THRILLER'. Quite literally the biggest selling album in the world . . . ever (40-odd million and counting), JACKSON's second masterpiece was released in late '82, and despite its predecessor's plaudits, few could've predicted the stratospheric commercial heights it would scale. Previewed by the PAUL McCARTNEY duet, 'THE GIRL IS MINE' (which almost reached the US Top spot), the 'THRILLER' phenomenon only really kicked into gear with the release of 'BILLIE JEAN' early the following year, a huge UK/US No.1 which set an ice-cool, tightrope disco-pop groove to a blinding visual backdrop of fleet-footed, snake-hipped choreography and revolutionary effects. Next up was the compulsive 'BEAT IT', a throbbing dancefloor killer utilising the guitar wizardry of EDDIE VAN HALEN and, incredibly, the first video by a black artist to be aired on MTV. JACKSON was now at the cutting edge of the all-important video medium (still in relative infancy) as it mushroomed with the all-pervasive influence of the aforementioned MTV; not content with merely recording the greatest selling album in history, JACKSON went ahead and filmed the most popular, the most talked about, and possibly the most hyped video in history. The near quarter of an hour long promo for 'THRILLER' (the single) came with the added kudos of JOHN LANDIS (director) and VINCENT PRICE (spook voice-over), featuring JACKSON strutting his funky stuff (he'd already debuted his legendary 'moonwalk' on American TV) amid a cast of moonlit grotesqueries. The film's mildly controversial content also marked his first, but by no means his last, major encounter with critical pressure (this time around a fairly mild fracas with his fellow Jehovah's Witnesses). Nevertheless, the hits kept on coming, JACKSON scoring with a further three hits from the album, the jittering 'WANNA BE STARTIN' SOMETHING', 'HUMAN NATURE' and 'P.Y.T. (PRETTY YOUNG THING)'. At the tail end of '83, he also enjoyed a further extended run at the top of the charts with another PAUL McCARTNEY duet, 'SAY SAY SAY' (from the latter's 'Pipes Of Peace' album), the singer's newfound superstar status netting him a record breaking sponsorship deal with Pepsi. While recording a commercial for the company, an accident led to JACKSON suffering second-degree burns requiring scalp and facial treatment. Much has since been made of JACKSON's alleged cosmetic surgery, and while the singer has constantly denied it, the evidence that he's become progressively "whiter" is in-your-face as it were, or indeed his face. While a whole book could probably be devoted to JACKSON's more colourful behaviour, surely any sentient being would struggle to cope with the pressure of following up such a colossal artistic and commercial feat. In the immediate aftermath of 'THRILLER's success, JACKSON recorded a further album with his brothers, 'VICTORY' (1984), and reluctantly undertook an ecstatically received, yet turbulent tour, the last time he'd perform/record with The JACKSONS as a group. Although the singer subsequently helped pen the huge USA For Africa famine-relief single, 'WE ARE THE WORLD', more controversy followed as he snapped up the rights to the catalogue of music publishers, ATV. This included the bulk of BEATLES material penned by LENNON/McCARTNEY, and, surprisingly enough, no further JACKSON/McCARTNEY collaborations ensued. Instead, JACKSON once again hooked up with QUINCY JONES to record a belated follow-up album, 'BAD' (1987). Previewed by a duet with SIEDAH GARRETT, 'I JUST CAN'T STOP LOVING YOU' (another transatlantic No.1), the album once again topped the charts in too many countries to mention and spawned a further four US No.1's, 'THE WAY YOU MAKE ME FEEL', 'MAN IN THE MIRROR', 'DIRTY DIANA' and the title track. Inevitably, the record paled in comparison to what had gone before, both commercially and artistically, even though its sales figures would've counted as blockbusting had they been enjoyed by almost any other artist. He did manage to break one record though, with the accompanying world tour, a gargantuan feat of logistical mastery which was touted as the biggest operation of its kind so far. The late 80's also saw the publication of JACKSON's autobiography, 'Moonwalker', though if fans were hoping for any juicy insights into what made the man tick, they were sorely disappointed. More newsworthy was his record breaking new contract with 'Sony', a multi-media billion dollar deal in which the singer negotiated, amongst other things, a sizable royalty rate, humungous advances and his own label (MJJ) to play around with. The first release under the new agreement was 1991's 'DANGEROUS' opus, JACKSON partially opting for a more street smart sound on tracks such as 'WHY YOU WANNA TRIP ON ME' and 'IN THE CLOSET', the pared-back style courtesy of New Jack Swing maestro, Teddy Riley. The biggest hits, however, 'BLACK OR WHITE' (a transatlantic No.1 addressing the controversy over his skin colour), 'HEAL THE WORLD' etc., were in the patented JACKSON style. The resulting world tour was plagued with misfortune and bad press; JACKSON attracted flak for his alleged arrogance during the African leg of the jaunt, while persistent poor health forced the singer to cancel a number of European shows after collapsing onstage at Wembley Stadium in London. The following year proved even worse, the tabloid machine going into overkill following allegations of sexual impropriety with a 13-year old boy. JACKSON strenuously denied the charge, although, bearing in mind the singer's family appeal, the controversy looked set to wreak havoc on his career. His love of children was already well publicised; the singer regularly invited underprivileged kids to his Neverland theme home, while he'd also set up the 'Heal The World Foundation' to tackle child-based issues. Opinion was understandably split although the press had a field day with the reclusive star, endlessly speculating on the reality behind the accusations. The pressure became too much and the exhausted JACKSON subsequently sought help for an addiction to painkillers before returning to the US to face the music; in the event, he reputedly paid off a sum of between 13 and 30 million dollars to the boy and his family, the LAPD also finally dropping a rumoured criminal case. Though some saw the settlement as a tacit admission of guilt, JACKSON emerged relatively unscathed (commercially at least) from the scandal; while he lost his Pepsi sponsorship, sales of 'DANGEROUS' didn't suffer too badly and he signed a new multi-million dollar deal with 'E.M.I' to handle his ATV catalogue. More surprises were in store as JACKSON announced his marriage to Lisa Marie Presley (ELVIS' daughter) in late '94, doubters proved correct when the relationship hit the rocks less than two years later. On the recording front, he was back in the news again by summer '95, an astronomically expensive video for the 'SCREAM' single (a duet with sister JANET) and a semi-retrospective double set, 'HIStory – PAST, PRESENT AND FUTURE, BOOK 1' ensuring media hyperbole. The latter set predictably topped the charts everywhere, while two new tracks, 'YOU ARE NOT ALONE' and 'EARTH SONG' (his best song ever!?) both topped the UK charts, another unprecedented feat for the veteran pop star. While JACKSON, in all his egocentric, asexual eccentricity, continues to be adored by fanatical fans the world over, some remain less impressed; just ask PULP's JARVIS COCKER, who took such a dislike to JACKSON's Christ-like appearance (rather unadvisedly with 'beggar' children in tow) during his 1997 Brit Awards performance that he invaded the stage and caused another press beano, this time with JACKSON as the victim rather than the villain. Despite everything, MICHAEL JACKSON remains a mythic figure, his increasingly rare recorded output unlikely to yield any clues and even more unlikely to match the towering standards of his early 80's heyday. The optimistically titled 'INVINCIBLE' (2001) opened yet another decade in the MICHAEL JACKSON saga although this time around, in a surprising lack of bad press, the music was forced to do the talking. Another US and UK No.1, the record benefitted from a raft of outside writing talent although apart from sounding convincingly modern, it was hardly the great comeback effort his career needed. In fact, JACKSON's career took a massive nosedive (so to speak) when, from a surgical mask, he revealed what was left of his nose due to cosmetic surgery. Days later, the phantom JACKO horrified even his most ardent fans and certainly the press by dangling his 11-month baby son over the balcony on the 7th floor of a German hotel – who's bad indeed. A subsequent Martin Bashir special TV report also didn't show the King Of Pop at his best and, with MICHAEL stating some children slept with him in his room at his Neverland ranch, police were called into action. In November 2003, with a compilation of his best work (entitled 'NUMBER ONES') at No.1 in the charts, the California police raided Neverland and in turn charged him with child molestation. The case and verdict will be forthcoming in the next year or so. • **Songwriters:** JACKSON 5 singles covered NEVER CAN SAY GOODBYE (Clifton Davis) / LITTLE BITTY PRETTY ONE (Thurston Harris) / DOCTOR MY EYES (Jackson Browne) / FOREVER CAME TODAY (Supremes) / etc. The JACKSONS:- BLAME IT ON THE BOOGIE (Mick Jackson; no relation). MICHAEL covered ROCKIN' ROBIN (Bobby Day) / AIN'T NO SUNSHINE (Bill Withers) / GIRLFRIEND (Paul McCartney; who he also had two Top 3 duets with) / COME TOGETHER (Beatles). • **Miscellaneous:** In the late 80's, the Jackson family was at the centre of a controversial allegation by daughter/singer LaTOYA, who stated in a book and on US TV, that she was beaten as a child by her/their father. This divided the family into either defending their father or saying nothing. LaTOYA, of course had recently shocked them all by baring herself in the centre spread of Playboy magazine.

Album rating: GOT TO BE THERE (*5) / BEN (*6) / MUSIC AND ME (*4) / FOREVER MICHAEL (*4) / THE BEST OF MICHAEL JACKSON compilation (*6) / OFF THE WALL (*8) / THRILLER (*10) / BAD (*7) / DANGEROUS (*6) / HIStory: PAST, PRESENT AND FUTURE – BOOK 1 part compilation (*8) / BLOOD ON THE DANCE FLOOR: HIStory In The Mix (*5) / INVINCIBLE (*5) / NUMBER ONES compilation (*8) / THE ULTIMATE COLLECTION the best Jackson 5/Jacksons compilation (*8)

JACKSON 5

MICHAEL JACKSON – lead vocals / **JACKIE JACKSON** (b.SIGMUND, 4 May'51) – vocals / **TITO JACKSON** (b.TORIANO, 15 Oct'53) – vocals / **JERMAINE JACKSON** (b.11 Dec'54) – vocals / **MARLON JACKSON** (b.12 Mar'57) – vocals

		not iss.		Steeltown
1968.	(7") *<681>* **BIG BOY. / YOU'VE CHANGED**	–		
1969.	(7") *<684>* **SOME GIRLS WANT ME FOR THEIR LOVE. / YOU DON'T HAVE TO BE 21 TO FALL IN LOVE** *<re-iss. 1980s on 'Dynamo'; 146>*	–		
		Tamla Motown		Motown
Jan 70.	(7") *(TMG 724) <1157>* **I WANT YOU BACK. / WHO'S LOVING YOU** *(re-iss. Oct81)*	2	Nov69	1
Mar 70.	(7") *<1163>* **ABC. / IT'S ALL IN THE GAME**	–		1
Apr 70.	(lp) *(STML 11142) <700>* **DIANA ROSS PRESENTS THE JACKSON 5** – Zip-a dee doo-dah / Nobody / I want you back / Can you remember / Standing in the shadows of love / You've changed / My Cherie amour / Who's loving you / Chained / I'm losing you / Stand / Born to save you. *(re-iss. Aug81)*	16	Jan70	5
May 70.	(7") *(TMG 738)* **ABC. / THE YOUNG FOLKS**	8		–
Jul 70.	(7") *(TMG 746) <1166>* **THE LOVE YOU SAVE. / I FOUND THAT GIRL**	7	May70	1
Aug 70.	(lp) *(STML 11156) <709>* **ABC** – The love you save / One more chance / ABC / Come round here (I'm the one you need) / Don't know why I love you / Never had a dream come true / True love can be beautiful / La la means I love you / I'll bet you / I found that girl / The young folks. *(re-iss. Jun82)*	22	May70	4
Nov 70.	(7") *(TMG 758) <1171>* **I'LL BE THERE. / ONE MORE CHANCE**	4	Sep70	1
Dec 70.	(7") *<1174>* **SANTA CLAUS IS COMING TO TOWN. / CHRISTMAS WON'T BE THE SAME THIS YEAR**	–		
Dec 70.	(lp) *(STML 11168) <713>* **THE JACKSON 5 CHRISTMAS ALBUM** (festive – hit No.1 US Xmas chart) *(cd-iss. Nov94 on 'Spectrum')*			
Feb 71.	(lp) *(STML 11174) <718>* **THE THIRD ALBUM** – I'll be there / Ready or not here I come / Oh how happy / Bridge over troubled water / Can I see you in the morning / Goin' back to Indiana / How funky is your chicken / Mama's pearl / Reach in / The love I saw in you was just a mirage / Darling dear. *(re-iss. Mar82) (cd-iss. Sep93)*		Sep70	4
Apr 71.	(7") *(TMG 769) <1177>* **MAMA'S PEARL. / DARLING DEAR**	25	Jan71	2
Jun 71.	(7") *(TMG 778) <1179>* **NEVER CAN SAY GOODBYE. / SHE'S GOOD**	33	Mar71	2
Jul 71.	(7") *<1186>* **MAYBE TOMORROW. / I WILL FIND A WAY**	–		20
Oct 71.	(lp) *(STML 11188) <735>* **MAYBE TOMORROW** – Maybe tomorrow / She's good / Never can say goodbye / The wall / Petals / 16 Candles / (We've got) blue skies / My little baby / It's great to be here / Honey chile / I will find a way. *(cd-iss. Aug93)*		Apr71	11
Oct 71.	(lp) *<742>* **GOIN' BACK TO INDIANA (TV Soundtrack)** – (contained live hits from TV show)	–		16
Mar 72.	(7") *(TMG 809) <1194>* **SUGAR DADDY. / I'M SO HAPPY**		Dec71	10
Sep 72.	(lp) *(STML 11212) <741>* **THE JACKSON 5 GREATEST HITS** (compilation) *(re-iss. Mar 82, re-iss. +cd.Feb88)*	26	Jan72	12

MICHAEL JACKSON

started solo career as well on same label.

Jan 72. (7") *(TMG 797) <1191>* **GOT TO BE THERE. / MARIA (YOU WERE THE ONLY ONE)** 5 Oct71 4

May 72. (7") *(TMG 816) <1197>* **ROCKIN' ROBIN. / LOVE IS HERE AND NOW YOU'RE GONE** 3 Mar72 2

May 72. (lp) *(STML STML 11205) <747>* **GOT TO BE THERE** 37 Feb72 14
– Ain't no sunshine / I wanna be where you are / Girl don't take your love from me / In our small way / Got to be there / Rockin' robin / Wings of my love / Maria (you were the only one) / Love is here and now / You're gone / You've got a friend. *(re-iss. Aug81 & May84) (cd-iss. Jun89) (re-iss. cd Aug93)*

May 72. (7") *<1202>* **I WANNA BE WHERE YOU ARE. / WE GOT A GOOD THING GOIN'** – 16

Jul 72. (7") *(TMG 826)* **AIN'T NO SUNSHINE. / I WANNA BE WHERE YOU ARE** 8 –
(re-iss. Oct81)

Nov 72. (7") *(TMG 834) <1207>* **BEN. / YOU CAN CRY ON MY SHOULDER** 7 Aug72 1
(re-iss. Oct81)

Dec 72. (lp) *(STML 11220) <755>* **BEN** 17 Sep72 5
– Ben / Greatest show on Earth / People make the world go round / We've got a good thing going / Everybody's fool / My girl / What goes around comes around / In our small way / Shoo-be-doo-be-doo-da-day / You can cry on my shoulder. *(re-iss. Oct81 + May84) (cd-iss. Feb90) (cd re-iss. Sep93)*

May 73. (7") *<1218>* **WITH A CHILD'S HEART. / MORNING GLOW** – 50

Jul 73. (lp) *(STML 11235) <767>* **MUSIC AND ME** Apr73 92
– With a child's heart / Up again / All the things you are / Happy / Too young / Doggin' around / Johnny Raven / Euphoria / Morning glow / Music and me. *(re-iss. Nov84) (re-iss. cd/c May93 on 'Spectrum')*

Jul 73. (7") *(TMG 863)* **MORNING GLOW. / MY GIRL** –

May 74. (7") *(TMG 900)* **MUSIC AND ME. / JOHNNY RAVEN** –

Feb 75. (7") *<1341>* **WE'RE ALMOST THERE. / TAKE ME BACK** – 54

Mar 75. (lp) *(STMA 8022) <825>* **FOREVER MICHAEL**
– We're almost there / Take me back / One day in your life / Cinderella stay awhile / We've got forever / Just a little bit of you / You are there / Dapper Dan / Dear Michael / I'll come home to you. *(re-iss. Jun83 + Jun88) (cd-iss. Mar90)*

Apr 75. (7") *(TMG 946)* **ONE DAY IN YOUR LIFE. / WITH A CHILD'S HEART** –

Oct 75. (7") *(TMG 1006) <1349>* **JUST A LITTLE BIT OF YOU. / DEAR MICHAEL** Jun75 23

Oct 75. (lp) *(STML 12005) <851>* **THE BEST OF MICHAEL JACKSON** (compilation)
(re-iss. Mar80 + May84) (Jul81 saw it hit UK No.11)

JACKSON 5

MICHAEL had continued as the group's main singer

Apr 72. (7") *<1199>* **LITTLE BIT PRETTY ONE. / IF I HAVE TO MOVE A MOUNTAIN** – 13

Sep 72. (7") *(TMG 825)* **LITTLE BITTY PRETTY ONE. / MAYBE TOMORROW** –

Oct 72. (lp) *(STML 11214) <750>* **LOOKIN' THROUGH THE WINDOWS** 16 Jun72 7
– Ain't nothing like the real thing / Lookin' through the windows / Don't let your baby catch you / To know / Doctor my eyes / Little bitty pretty one / E-ne-me-ne-mi-ne-moe / I'll have to move a mountain / Don't want to see you tomorrow / Children of the light / I can only give you love. *(re-iss. Feb83)*

Oct 72. (7") *(TMG 833) <1205>* **LOOKIN' THROUGH THE WINDOWS. / LOVE SONG** 9 Jul72 16

Nov 72. (7") *<1214>* **CORNER OF THE SKY. / TO KNOW** – 18

Dec 72. (7"m) *(TMG 837)* **SANTA CLAUS IS COMING TO TOWN. / SOMEDAY AT CHRISTMAS / CHRISTMAS WON'T BE THE SAME THIS YEAR** 43 –

Feb 73. (7") *(TMG 842)* **DOCTOR MY EYES. / MY LITTLE BABY** 9 –

Mar 73. (7") *<1224>* **HALLELUJAH DAY. / YOU MAKE ME WHAT I AM** – 16

May 73. (7") *(TMG 856)* **HALLELUJAH DAY. / TO KNOW** 20 –

Jul 73. (lp) *(STML 11231) <761>* **SKYWRITER** Apr73 44
– Skywriter / Hallelujah day / Boogie man / Touch / Corner of the sky / I can't quit your love / Uppermost / World of sunshine / Ooh, I'd love to be with you / You made me what I am. *(re-iss. Nov84) (cd-iss. Aug93)*

Aug 73. (7") *(TMG 865)* **SKYWRITER. / AIN'T NOTHING LIKE THE REAL THING** 25 –

Nov 73. (7") *(TMG 878) <1277>* **GET IT TOGETHER. / TOUCH** Sep73 28

Nov 73. (lp) *(STML 11243) <783>* **GET IT TOGETHER** 100
– Dancing machine / Get it together / Don't say goodbye again / Reflections / Hum along and dance / Mama I gotta brand new thing (don't say no) / It's too late to change the time / You need love like I do (don't you).

Apr 74. (7") *(TMG 895)* **THE BOOGIE MAN. / DON'T LET YOUR BABY CATCH YOU** –

Jun 74. (7") *(TMG 904) <1286>* **DANCING MACHINE. / IT'S TOO LATE TO CHANGE THE TIME** Mar74 2

Nov 74. (lp) *(STML 11275) <780>* **DANCING MACHINE** Oct74 16
– Dancing machine / I am love / Whatever you got, I want / She's a rhythm child / The life of the party / What you don't know / If I don't love you this way / It all begins and ends with love / The mirrors of my mind.

Nov 74. (7") *<1308>* **WHATEVER YOU GOT, I WANT. / I CAN'T QUIT YOUR LOVE** – 38

Nov 74. (7") *(TMG 927)* **WHATEVER YOU GOT, I WANT. / THE LIFE OF THE PARTY** –

Mar 75. (7") *(TMG 942) <1310>* **I AM LOVE. / (Part 2)** Feb75 15

Jun 75. (7") *<1356>* **FOREVER CAME TODAY. / ALL I DO IS THINK OF YOU** – 60

Jul 75. (lp) *(STML 11290) <829>* **MOVING VIOLATION** 36
– Forever came today / Moving violation / (You were made) Especially for me / Honey love / Body language (do the love dance) / All I do is think of you / Breezy / Call of the wild / Time explosion.

Sep 75. (7") *(TMG 1001)* **FOREVER CAME TODAY. / I CAN'T QUIT YOUR LOVE** –

JACKSONS

RANDY JACKSON (b.29 Oct'62) – vocals repl. JERMAINE who is having own solo career. Temporarily added sisters **LaTOYA** (b.29 May'56) – vocals / **REBBIE** (b. MAUREEN, 29 May'50) – vocals. In 1976, another sister **JANET** also appeared on tours.

Epic Epic

Feb 77. (7") *(EPC 4708) <50289>* **ENJOY YOURSELF. / STYLE OF LIFE** 42 Oct76 6

Feb 77. (lp/c) *(EPC/40 86009) <34229>* **THE JACKSONS** 54 Nov76 36
– Enjoy yourself / Think happy / Good times / Keep on dancing / Blues away / Show you the way to go / Living together / Strength of one man / Dreamer / Style of life. *(also on pic-lp US) (re-iss. cd Jun94 on 'Sony')*

May 77. (7") *(EPC 5266) <50350>* **SHOW YOU THE WAY TO GO. / BLUES AWAY** 1 Apr77 28

Jul 77. (7") *(EPC 5458)* **DREAMER. / GOOD TIMES** 22 –

Oct 77. (7") *(EPC 5732) <50454>* **GOIN' PLACES. / DO WHAT YOU WANNA** 26 52

Oct 77. (lp/c) *(EPC/40 86035) <34835>* **GOIN' PLACES** 45 63
– Music's takin' over / Goin' places / Different kind of lady / Even though you're gone / Jump for joy / Heaven knows I love you girl / Man of war / Do you wanna / Find me a girl. *(also iss.pic-lp US) (re-iss. cd Jun94 on 'Sony')*

Jan 78. (7") *<50496>* **FIND ME A GIRL. / DIFFERENT KIND OF LADY** –

Jan 78. (7") *(EPC 5919)* **EVEN THOUGH YOU'RE GONE. / DIFFERENT KIND OF LADY** 31 –

Apr 78. (7") *(EPC 6263)* **MUSIC'S TAKING OVER. / MAN OF WAR** –

Sep 78. (7") *(EPC 6683)* **BLAME IT ON THE BOOGIE. / DO WHAT YOU WANNA** 8 –

Oct 78. (7") *<50595>* **BLAME IT ON THE BOOGIE. / EASE ON DOWN THE ROAD** – 54

Dec 78. (7") *(EPC 6983)* **DESTINY. / THAT'S WHAT YOU GET** 39 –
(12"+=) *(EPC13 6983)* – Blame it on the boogie.

Apr 79. (lp/c) *(EPC/40 83200) <35552>* **DESTINY** 33 Dec78 11
– Blame it on the boogie / Push me away / Things I do for you / Shake your body (down to the ground) / Destiny / Bless his soul / All night dancin' / That's what you get. *(re-iss. 1984)*

Mar 79. (7"/12") *(EPC/+13 7181)* **SHAKE YOUR BODY (DOWN TO THE GROUND). / ALL NIGHT DANCIN'** 4 –

Mar 79. (7") *<50656>* **SHAKE YOUR BODY (DOWN TO THE GROUND). / THAT'S WHAT YOU GET (FOR BEING POLITE)** [–] [7]

MICHAEL JACKSON

solo again. In Oct78, he duetted with DIANA ROSS ⇒ on 'MCA' Top 50 US/UK single 'EASE ON DOWN THE ROAD'. (re-iss. May84)

Epic Epic

May 79. (7"pic-d/12") *(EPC/+13 7135)* **YOU CAN'T WIN. / (Part 2)** [ ] Feb79 [81]

Aug 79. (7") *(EPC 7763) <50654>* **DON'T STOP 'TIL YOU GET ENOUGH. / I CAN'T HELP IT** [3] [1]

Aug 79. (lp/c) *(EPC/40 83458) <35745>* **OFF THE WALL** [5] [3]
– Don't stop 'til you get enough / Rock with you / Working day and night / Get on the floor / Off the wall / Girlfriend / She's out of my life / I can't help it / It's the falling in love / Burn this disco out. *(re-dist.1980 w / free 7" YOU CAN'T WIN) (re-iss. Nov86) (cd-iss. 1983 & Dec95) (re-iss. Aug92, hit UK No.48)*

Oct 79. (7") *<50797>* **ROCK WITH YOU. / WORKING DAY AND NIGHT** [–] [1]

Nov 79. (7") *(EPC 8045)* **OFF THE WALL. / WORKING DAY AND NIGHT** [7] [–]

Feb 80. (7") *<50838>* **OFF THE WALL. / GET ON THE FLOOR** [–] [10]
(re-iss. Apr82)

Feb 80. (7")(12") *(EPC 8206)* **ROCK WITH YOU. / GET ON THE FLOOR** [7] [–]
(re-iss. Apr82)

Apr 80. (7") *(EPC 8384)* **SHE'S OUT OF MY LIFE. / Jacksons: PUSH ME AWAY** [3] [–]

Apr 80. (7") *<50871>* **SHE'S OUT OF MY LIFE. / GET ON THE FLOOR** [–] [10]

Jul 80. (7") *(EPC 8782)* **GIRLFRIEND. / Jacksons: BLESS HIS SOUL** [41] [–]

JACKSONS

—— returned to the fold

Oct 80. (7") *<50938>* **LOVELY ONE. / BLESS HIS SOUL** [–] [12]

Oct 80. (7") *(EPC 9302)* **LOVELY ONE. / THINGS I DO FOR YOU** [29] [–]

Oct 80. (lp/c) *(EPC/40 86112) <36424>* **TRIUMPH** [13] [10]
– Can you feel it / Lovely one / Your ways / Everybody / Heartbreak hotel / Time waits for no one / Walk right now / Give it up / Wondering who.

Dec 80. (7") *<50959>* **HEARTBREAK HOTEL. / THINGS I DO FOR YOU** [–] [22]

Dec 80. (7") *(EPC 9391)* **HEARTBREAK HOTEL. / DIFFERENT KIND OF LADY** [44] [–]

Feb 81. (7") *(EPC 9554)* **CAN YOU FEEL IT. / WONDERING WHO** [6] [–]

Apr 81. (7") *<01032>* **CAN YOU FEEL IT. / EVERYBODY** [–] [77]

Jun 81. (7") *(EPC 1294) <02132>* **WALK RIGHT NOW. / YOUR WAYS** [7] [73]

Sep 81. (7") *(EPC 1579)* **TIME WAITS FOR NO ONE. / GIVE IT UP** [ ] [–]

Nov 81. (7") *<02720>* **THE THINGS I DO FOR YOU (live). / WORKING DAY AND NIGHT (live)** [–] [ ]

Nov 81. (d-lp/d-c) *(EPC/40 88562) <37545>* **THE JACKSONS – LIVE! (live)** [53] [30]
– Opening: Can you feel it? Things I do for you / Off the wall / Ben / Heartbreak hotel / She's out of my life / Movie and rap medley (a) I want you back, (b) Never can say goodbye, (c) Got to be there / The love you save / I'll be there / Rock with you / Lovely one / Working day and night / Don't stop 'til you get enough / Shake your body (down to the ground).

Nov 81. (7") *(EPC 1902)* **THINGS I DO FOR YOU (live). / DON'T STOP 'TIL YOU GET ENOUGH (live)** [ ] [–]

MICHAEL JACKSON

returned to solo work again

Epic Epic

Nov 82. (7"/7"pic-d; by MICHAEL JACKSON & PAUL McCARTNEY) *(EPCA/+11 2729) <03288>* **THE GIRL IS MINE. / CAN'T GET OUT OF THE RAIN** [10] [2]

—— (Nearly a year later they had another hit, 'SAY SAY SAY' a No.2 UK / No.1 US)

Dec 82. (lp/c/cd) *(EPC/40/CD 85930) <38112>* **THRILLER** [1] [1]
– Wanna be startin' something / Baby be mine / The girl is mine / Thriller / Beat it / Billie Jean / Human nature / P.Y.T. (Pretty Young Thing) / The lady in my life. *(pic-lp.Jul83; EPC11 85930) (re-iss. Aug92 hit UK No.17)*

Jan 83. (7") *<03509>* **BILLIE JEAN. / CAN'T GET OUT OF THE RAIN** [–] [1]

Jan 83. (7") *(EPC 3084)* **BILLIE JEAN. / IT'S FALLING IN LOVE** [1] [–]
(12"+=) *(EPC/+13 3084)* – ('A'extended).

Mar 83. (7") *<03759>* **BEAT IT. / GET ON THE FLOOR** [–] [1]

Mar 83. (7"/12") *(EPC/+13 3258)* **BEAT IT. / BURN THIS DISCO OUT** [3] [–]

May 83. (7") *<03914>* **WANNA BE STARTIN' SOMETHING. / (part 2)** [–] [5]

May 83. (7") *(A 3427)* **WANNA BE STARTIN' SOMETHING. / Jacksons: ROCK WITH YOU** [8] [–]
(12"+=) *(TA 3427)* – ('A'instrumental).

Jul 83. (7") *<03914>* **HUMAN NATURE. / BABY BE MINE** [–] [7]

Oct 83. (7") *<04165>* **P.Y.T. (PRETTY YOUNG THING). / WORKING DAY AND NIGHT** [–] [10]

Nov 83. (7"/12") *(EPCA/TA 3643)* **THRILLER. / THE THINGS I DO FOR YOU** [10] [–]

Jan 84. (7") *<04364>* **THRILLER. / CAN'T GET OUTTA THE RAIN** [–] [4]

Mar 84. (7") *(A 4136)* **P.Y.T. (PRETTY YOUNG THING). / HEARTBREAK HOTEL** [11] [–]
(12"+=) *(TA 4136)* – Thriller (instrumental).

JACKSONS

—— now 6-piece when **JERMAINE** returned to join the 5 brothers.

Jun 84. (7"pic-d/12") *(A/TA 4431)* **STATE OF SHOCK. / YOUR WAYS** [14] [3]
(above featured MICK JAGGER on dual vocals with MICHAEL)

Jul 84. (pic-lp/c) *(EPC/40 86303) <38946>* **VICTORY** [3] [4]
– Torture / Wait / One more chance / Be not always / State of shock / We can change the world / The hurt / Body. *(cd-iss. May87) (cd-iss. Dec94)*

Aug 84. (7") *(A 4675) <04575>* **TORTURE. / ('A'instrumental)** [26] [17]
(12"+=) *(TA 4675)* – Show you the way to go / Blame it on the boogie.

Nov 84. (7"/12") *(A/TA 4883) <04673>* **BODY. / ('A'instrumental)** [ ] [47]

Feb 85. (7"/12") *(A/TA 6105)* **WAIT. / SHE'S OUT OF MY LIFE** [ ] [–]

MICHAEL JACKSON

Jul 87. (7"/7"s/12") *(650 202-7/-0/-6) <07253>* **I JUST CAN'T STOP LOVING YOU. / BABY BE MINE** [1] [1]
(above featured duet with SIEDAH GARRETT)

Sep 87. (7") *<07418>* **BAD. / I CAN'T HELP IT** [–] [1]

Sep 87. (7") *(651 155-7)* **BAD. / ('A'instrumental)** [3] [–]
(12"+=) *(651 155-6)* – ('A'acappella mix) / ('A'dub version).
(c-s+=) *(651 155-4)* – ('A'extended).

Sep 87. (lp/c/cd) *(450 290-1/-4/-2) <40600>* **BAD** [1] [1]
– Bad / The way you make me feel / Speed demon / Liberian girl / Just good friends / Another part of me / Man in the mirror / I just can't stop loving you / Dirty Diana / Smooth criminal. *(pic-lp Nov87; 450 290-0) (re-iss. Jul88 as 5x7"box; 450 290-9) (re-iss. Aug92, hit UK No.14)*

Nov 87. (7") *(651 275-7) <07645>* **THE WAY YOU MAKE ME FEEL. / ('A'instrumental)** [3] [1]
(12"+=) *(651 275-0)* – ('A'dance mix) / ('A'dub mix).
(cd-s+=) *(651 275-2)* – ('A'acappella mix).

Feb 88. (7"/7"sha-pic-d) *(651 388-7/-9) <07668>* **MAN IN THE MIRROR. / ('A'instrumental)** [21] [1]
(12"+=/cd-s+=) *(651 388-6/-2)* – ('A'mix).

—— (In Apr'88, he did a duet single, 'GET IT', with STEVIE WONDER which hit UK Top40 & US No.80)

Jul 88. (7") *(651 546-7) <07739>* **DIRTY DIANA. / ('A'instrumental)** [4] [1]
(12"+=/cd-s+=) *(651 546-6/-9)* – Bad (extended dance).
(3"cd-s+=) *(651 546-2)* – ('A'-album version).

Sep 88. (7"/7"s) *(652 844-7/-9) <07962>* **ANOTHER PART OF ME. / ('A'instrumental)** [15] [11]
(12"+=/cd-s+=) *(652 844-6/-2)* – ('A'acappella) / ('A'radio).
(3"cd-s+=) *(653 004-2)* – ('A'drum mix) / ('A'acappella).

Nov 88. (7"/7"s) *(653 026-7/-0) <08044>* **SMOOTH CRIMINAL. / ('A'instrumental)** [8] [7]
(12"+=/cd-s+=) *(653 026-1/-2)* – ('A'extended) / ('A'acappella) / ('A'dance dub).
(cd-s++=) *(653 026-2)* – ('A'Annie mix).

Feb 89. (7"/7"s) *(654 672-7/-0)* **LEAVE ME ALONE. / HUMAN NATURE** 2 –
(c-s+=/3"cd-s+=) *(654 672-4/-3)* – Don't stop 'til you get enough.
(cd-s++=) *(654 672-2)* – Wanna be startin' something (extended).

Jul 89. (7"/7"s/c-s) *(654 947-7/-0/-4)* **LIBERIAN GIRL. / GIRLFRIEND** 13 –
(3"cd-s+=) *(654 947-3)* – Get on the floor.
(cd-s++=) *(654 947-2)* – The lady in my life.

JACKSONS

Apr 89. (7"/c-s) *(654 808-7/-4)* <68688> **NOTHIN' (THAT COMPARES 2 U). / HEARTBREAK HOTEL / ALRIGHT WITH ME** [ ] 77
(12"+=/cd-s+=) *(654 808-6/-2)* – ('A'choice dub extended).

Jun 89. (lp/c/cd) *(463 352-1/-4/-2)* <40911> **2300 JACKSON STREET** [ ] 59
– Art of madness / Nothin' (that compares 2 U) / Maria / Private affair / 2300 Jackson Street / Harley / She / Alright with me / Play it up / Midnight rendezvous / If you'd only believe.

Aug 89. (7"/c-s) *(655 206-7/-4)* <69022> **2300 JACKSON STREET. / WHEN I LOOK AT YOU** [ ] [ ]
(12"+=) *(655 206-6)* – Please come back to me.
(cd-s++=) *(655 206-2)* – ('A'lp version) / Keep her.

MICHAEL JACKSON

Nov 91. (7"/c-s) *(657 598-7/-4)* <74100> **BLACK OR WHITE. / ('A'instrumental)** 1 1
(12"+=) *(657 598-6)* – Bad / Thriller.
(cd-s+=) *(657 598-2)* – Smooth criminal.
(12"+=/cd-s+=) – (other mixes by and 1 by C&C MUSIC FACTORY)

Dec 91. (cd/c/lp) *(465 802-2/-4/-1)* <45400> **DANGEROUS** 1 1
– Jam / Why you wanna trip on me / In the closet / She drives me wild / Remember the time / Can't let her get away / Heal the world / Black or white / Who is it / Give in to me / Will you be there / Keep the faith / Gone too soon / Dangerous.

Jan 92. (c-s) <74200> **REMEMBER THE TIME / BLACK OR WHITE (Clivilies & Cole mix)** – 3

Feb 92. (7"/c-s/12"/cd-s) *(657 774-7/-4/-6/-2)* **REMEMBER THE TIME. / COME TOGETHER** 3 –

Apr 92. (7"/c-s) *(658 018-7/-4)* <74266> **IN THE CLOSET. / ('A'remix)** 8 6
(12"+=/cd-s+=) *(658 018-6/-2)* – (other 'A'mixes).

Jul 92. (7"/c-s) *(658 179-7/-4)* **WHO IS IT. / ROCK WITH YOU (mix)** 10 –
(12"+=/cd-s+=) *(658 179-6/-2)* – Don't stop 'til you get enough (remix).

Jul 92. (c-s) <74333> **JAM / ROCK WITH YOU (remix)** – 26

Sep 92. (7"/c-s) *(658 360-7/-4)* **JAM. / BEAT IT (Moby mix)** 13 –
(12"+=) *(658 360-6)* – Wanna be starting something (Brothers In Rhythm house mix).
(cd-s) *(658 360-2)* – ('A'side) / ('A'-Roger's Jeep mix) / ('A'-Atlanta techno mix) / Wanna be startin' something (Brothers In Rhythm house mix).

Nov 92. (7"/c-s) *(658 488-7/-4)* <74708> **HEAL THE WORLD. / SHE DRIVES ME WILD** 2 Dec92 27
(12"+=) *(658 488-6)* – Man in the mirror.
(cd-s) *(658 488-2)* – ('A'side) / Wanna be starting something / Don't stop till you get enough / Rock with you.

Feb 93. (7"/c-s) *(659 069-7/-4)* **GIVE IN TO ME. / DIRTY DIANA** 2 –
(cd-s+=) *(659 069-2)* – Beat it.

Apr 93. (c-s) <74406> **WHO IS IT / (Oprah Winfrey intro)** – 14

Jun 93. (7"/c-s) *(659 222-7/-4)* <77060> **WILL YOU BE THERE. / GIRLFRIEND** 9 7
(cd-s+=) *(659 222-2)* – Keep the faith.

Dec 93. (7"/c-s) *(659 976-7/-4)* **GONE TOO SOON. / ('A'instrumental)** 33 –
(12"/cd-s) *(659 976-6/-2)* – ('A'side) / Human nature / She's out of my life / Thriller.

Jun 95. (7"/c-s/cd-s; MICHAEL JACKSON & JANET JACKSON) *(662 022-7/-4/-2)* <78000> **SCREAM / CHILDHOOD** 3 5
(cd-s/12"/12") *(662 022-2/-6/-8)* – ('A'album version) / ('A'-Pressurized dub pt.1 & 2) / ('A'-Naughty By Nature pretty-pella mix) / ('A'-N.B.N. acappella).
(12") – ('A'-classic club mix) / ('A'-David Morales R&B extended mix) / ('A'-Def radio mix). / ('A'-Naughty By Nature main mix) / ('A'-Naughty By Nature main mix no rap) / ('A'-Dave "Jam" Hall's extended urban remix). *(note the above 4th & 5th formats hit UK No.43)*

Jun 95. (d-cd/d-c/t-lp) *(474 709-2/-4/-1)* <59000> **HIStory: PAST, PRESENT AND FUTURE – BOOK 1** 1 1
– Billie Jean / The way you make me feel / Black or white / Rock with you / She's out of my life / Bad / I just can't stop loving you / Man in the mirror / Thriller / Beat it / The girl is mine / Remember the time / Don't stop 'til you get enough / Wanna be startin' somethin' / Heal the world. // Scream / They don't care about us / Stranger in Moscow / This time around / Earth song / DS / Money / Come together / You are not alone / Childhood / Tabloid junkie / 2 bad / History / Little Susie / Smile.

Aug 95. (c-s) *(662 310-4)* <78002> **YOU ARE NOT ALONE / SCREAM LOUDER (Flyte Tyme mix with JANET JACKSON)** 1 1
(cd-s/12") *(662 310-2/-8)* – ('A'-Frankie Knuckles remix) / ('A'-Jon B remix).
(cd-s) *(662 310-5)* – ('A'-R Kelly remix) / Rock with you (Masters At work remix) / Rock with you (Frankie Knuckles remix).

Nov 95. (c-s) *(662 695-4)* **EARTH SONG / ('A'-Hani's extended radio experience)** 1 –
(cd-s) *(662 695-2)* – ('A'side) / ('A'-Hani's club experience) / Michael Jackson DMC megamix.
(cd-s) *(662 695-5)* – ('A'side) / Wanna be startin' somethin' / ('A'-Brothers In Rhythm mix) / ('A'-Tommy D's main mix).

Apr 96. (c-s/cd-s) *(662 950-4/-2)* <78060> **THEY DON'T CARE ABOUT US / ROCK WITH YOU / EARTH SONG** 4 Jun96 30
(cd-s) *(662 950-2)* – ('A'mixes) / Beat it.

—— In Aug'96, MICHAEL featured on nephews 3T (offspring of TITO) Top 3 hit 'Why'.

Nov 96. (c-s) *(663 787-4)* **STRANGER IN MOSCOW / ('A'-Tee's radio mix)** 4 Aug97 91
(cd-s) *(663 787-2)* – ('A'-side) / ('A'-Todd Terry mix) / ('A'-Charles 'The Mixologist' Roane mix).
(cd-s) *(663 787-5)* – ('A'side) / ('A'-Hani mix) / ('A'-Basement Boys mix).

Apr 97. (c-s/12"/cd-s) *(664 462-4/-0/-2)* **BLOOD ON THE DANCEFLOOR / (mixes)** 1 42
(12"/12"/cd-s) *(664 462-6/-8/-5)* – ('A'remixes).

May 97. (cd/c) *(487 500-2/-4)* <68000> **BLOOD ON THE DANCEFLOOR** (remixes) 1 24
– Blood on the dancefloor / Morphine / Superfly sister / Ghosts / Is it scary / Scream louder / Money / 2 bad / Stranger in Moscow / This time around / Earth song / You are not alone / History.

Jul 97. (c-s/cd-s) *(664 796-4/-2)* **HISTORY / GHOSTS** 5 –
(cd-s) *(664 796-5)* – ('A'mixes).

Oct 01. (c-s) *(672029-4)* *<radio cut>* **YOU ROCK MY WORLD / (mix)** 2 Sep01 10
(12"+=) *(672029-6)* – ('A'-instrumental) / ('A'-acappella).
(cd-s++=) *(672029-2)* – ('A'-video).

Oct 01. (cd/c/d-lp) *(495174-2/-4/-1)* <69400> **INVINCIBLE** 1 1
– Unbreakable / Heartbreaker / Invincible / Break of dawn / Heaven can wait / You rock my world / Butterflies / Speechless / 2000 watts / You are my life / Privacy / Don't walk away / Cry / The lost children / Whatever happens / Threatened.

Nov 01. (-) *<radio cut>* **BUTTERFLIES** – 19

Dec 01. (12"/c-s) *(672182-4/-6)* **CRY. / SHOUT / STREETWALKER** 25 –
(cd-s+=) *(672182-2)* – ('A'-video).

Nov 03. (cd/d-lp) *(513800-2/-1)* <88998> **NUMBER ONES** (compilation) 1 13
– Don't stop 'til you get enough / Rock with you / Billie Jean / Beat it / Thriller / I just can't stop loving you (with SIEDAH GARRETT) / Bad / Smooth criminal / The way you make me feel / Man in the mirror / Dirty Diana / Black or white / You are not alone / Earth song / You rock my world / Break of dawn / One more chance / Ben (live).

Nov 03. (12"/cd-s) *(674480-6/-2)* *<radio>* **ONE MORE CHANCE (mixes; incl. Paul Oakenfold)** 5 83
(cd-s) *(674480-5)* – ('A'mixes; Oakenfold / Metro / Ron G club).

– (MICHAEL JACKSON) compilations, others –

Note; All below on 'Motown' unless stated.

Apr 80. (7") **BEN. / ('B'by MARVIN GAYE)** [ ] [ ]
(re-iss. Oct81)

Oct 80. (7") *(TMG 973)* **GOT TO BE THERE. / ('B'by MARV JACKSON)** [ ] [ ]
(re-iss. Oct81)

Apr 81. (7") *(TMG 976)* **ONE DAY IN YOUR LIFE. / TAKE ME BACK** [1] [55]
(re-iss. Oct81)

Jul 81. (lp/c) *(STML 12158/CSTML 12158)* **ONE DAY IN YOUR LIFE** [29] [ ]
– One day in your life / We're almost there / You're my best friend, my love / Don't say goodbye again / Take me back / It's too late to change the time / We've got a good thing going / You are there / Doggin' around / Dear Michael / Girl, don't take your love from me / I'll come home to you.
(re-iss. Mar85)

Jul 81. (7"/12") *(TMG/+T 977)* **WE'RE ALMOST THERE. / WE GOT A GOOD THING GOING** [46] [ ]

Jul 83. (7"pic-d/12"/7") *(TMG P/T 986/TMG 986)* **HAPPY (LOVE THEME FROM 'LADY SINGS THE BLUES'). / WE'RE ALMOST THERE** [52] [ ]

Jul 83. (c-ep) *(CTME 2035)* **FLIPHITS** [ ] [–]
– One day in your life / Got to be there / Ben / Ain't no sunshine.

May 84. (7"/12") *TMG/+T 1342)* **FAREWELL MY SUMMER LOVE. / CALL ME** [7] [38]

Aug 84. (lp/c) *(Z L/K 72227)* **FAREWELL MY SUMMER LOVE** [9] [46]
– Don't let it get you down / You've really got a hold on me / Melodie / Touch the one you love / Girl you're so together / Farewell my summer love / Call on me / Here I am / To make my father proud.
(re-iss. Jun88, cd-iss. Oct89)

Aug 84. (7") *(TMG 1355)* **GIRL YOU'RE SO TOGETHER. / TOUCH THE ONE YOU LOVE** [ ] [ ]
(12"+=) – Ben / Ain't no sunshine.

Nov 84. (lp/c) *(W L/K 72289)* **THE GREAT LOVE SONGS OF MICHAEL JACKSON** [ ] [ ]

May 86. (lp/c) *(W L/K 72424)* **LOOKING BACK TO YESTERDAY** [ ] [ ]

Apr 87. (d-cd) *(ZD 72530)* **MICHAEL JACKSON ANTHOLOGY** [ ] [ ]
– Got to be there / Rockin' Robin / Ain't no sunshine / Maria (you were the only one) / I wanna be where you are / Girl don't take your love from me / Love is here and now you're gone / Ben / People make the world go 'round / Shoo-be-doo-be-doo-da-day / With a child's heart / Everybody's somebody's fool / In our small way / All the things you are / You can cry on my shoulder / Maybe tomorrow / I'll be there / Never can say goodbye / It's too late to change the time / Dancing machine / When I come of age / Dear Michael / Music and me / You are there / One day in your life / Love's gone bad / That's what love is made of / Who's looking for a lover / Lonely teardrops / We're almost there / Take me back / Just a little bit of you / Melodie / I'll come home to you / If'n I was God / Happy / Don't let it get you down / Call on me / To make my father proud / Farewell my summer love. – (w/ JACKSON 5 tracks) *(re-iss. d-cd Apr93)*

1987. (7") **25 MILES. / UP ON THE HOUSETOP** [–] [ ]

Feb 92. (cd/c/lp) *(530014 – 2/-4/-1)* **MOTOWN'S GREATEST HITS** [ ] [ ]

Apr 82. (7") *Epic; (EPC 8046)* **OFF THE WALL. / DON'T STOP 'TIL YOU GET ENOUGH** [ ] [ ]

Dec 82. (c-ep) *Epic; (EPC 2906)* **GREATEST ORIGINAL HITS** [ ] [–]
(re-iss. Mar83 as 7"ep)

Nov 83. (9x7"red-pack) *Epic; (MJ 1)* **SINGLES PACK** [66] [ ]
(re-iss. Jul88)

Sep 86. (c-ep) *Epic; (4501274)* **THE 12" TAPE** [ ] [ ]
– Billie Jean / Beat it / Wanna be startin' something / Thriller.

Jul 88. (singles pack) *Epic; (MJ 5)* **SOUVENIR SINGLES PACK** [91] [–]

Jul 92. (4xpic-cd-ep's) *Epic; (MJ 4)* **TOUR SOUVENIR PACK** [32] [ ]
– (3 tracks on each disc)

Jul 82. (lp/c) *Pickwick; (2/4 0038)* **AIN'T NO SUNSHINE** [ ] [–]
(re-iss. Nov84 on 'Astan')

Jul 83. (lp/c/cd) *Telstar; (STA R/C 2232/TCD 2232)* **18 GREATEST HITS (by MICHAEL JACKSON / JACKSON 5)** [1] [ ]
(re-iss. Jun88)

May 84. (cd) *Motown; (MCD 06070MD)* **COMPACT COMMAND PERFORMANCES: 18 GREATEST HITS** [ ] [ ]
(re-iss. Oct87)

Nov 86. (d-cd) *Motown; (ZD 72468)* **GOT TO BE THERE / BEN** [ ] [ ]

Oct 87. (lp/c/cd) *Telstar;* **LOVE SONGS (w / DIANA ROSS)** [15] [ ]

Nov 87. (lp/c/cd) *Stylus; (SM R/C/D 745)* **THE MICHAEL JACKSON MIX** [27] [ ]

Nov 95. (3xcd-box) *Motown;* **FOREVER MICHAEL / MUSIC & ME / BEN** [ ] [–]

Jun 97. (cd/c) *Polygram TV; (530804-2/-4)* **THE BEST OF MICHAEL JACKSON & THE JACKSON 5** [5] [–]
– I want you back / ABC / Love you save / I'll be there / Mama's pearl / Never can say goodbye / Got to be there / Rockin' robin / Ain't no sunshine / Looking through the windows / Ben / Doctor my eyes / We're almost there / Farewell my summer love / Girl you're so together.

Nov 01. (cd) *MJJ Music; (501869-2) <85250>* **GREATEST HITS: HISTORY VOL.1** [68] [85]

– (JACKSONS) compilations, others. –

Note; All on 'Motown' unless stated.

Apr 74. (7") *(TMG 895)* **BOOGIE MAN. / DON'T LET YOUR BABY TOUCH YOU** [ ] [ ]

Dec 76. (lp/c) *(STML 12046/)* **JOYFUL JUKEBOX MUSIC** [ ] [ ]

Jan 77. (d-lp/d-c) *(TMSP 6004/)* **THE JACKSON 5 ANTHOLOGY** [ ] Aug 76 [84]
(cd-iss. Jun87)(re-iss. d-cd. Apr93)

Mar 77. (lp) *(STMX 6006)* **MOTOWN SPECIAL – JACKSON 5** [ ] [ ]

Aug 77. (7") **SKYWRITER. / I WANT YOU BACK / THE LOVE YOU SAVE** [ ] [ ]

Sep 79. (c/lp) *(CSTML 12121/STML 12121)* **20 GOLDEN GREATS** [ ] [ ]
(re-iss. Oct81 & Apr84)

Mar 82. (c/lp) *(CSTMS 5038/STMS 5038)* **GREATEST HITS** [ ] [ ]

Jul 83. (c-ep) *(CTME 2034)* **FLIP HITS** [ ] [–]
– I want you back / I'll be there / ABC / Lookin' through any window.

Nov 84. (lp/c) *(W L/K 72290)* **GREAT LOVE SONGS OF THE JACKSON 5** [ ] [ ]

Nov 86. (cd) *(ZD 72483)* **DIANA ROSS PRESENTS . . . / ABC** [ ] [ ]

Nov 87. (12") *(ZXT 41656)* **I SAW MOMMY KISSING SANTA CLAUS / SANTA CLAUS IS COMING TO TOWN. / UP ON THE HOUSE TOP / FROSTY THE SNOWMAN** [ ] [–]

Feb 88. (lp/c/cd) **THE ORIGINAL SOUL OF . . .** [ ] [ ]

Apr 88. (7"/12") **I WANT YOU BACK ('88 remix – Stock Aitken Waterman). / NEVER CAN SAY GOODBYE** [8] [ ]

Jan 79. (lp/c) *M.F.P.; (MFP 50418)* **ZIP-A-DEE-DOO-DAH** [ ] [–]

Aug 80. (7"/12") *Epic;* **SHAKE YOUR BODY (DOWN TO THE GROUND). / BLAME IT ON THE BOOGIE** [ ] [–]

1984. (d-c) *Epic;* **GOIN' PLACES / DESTINY** [ ] [ ]

Jul 84. (7") *Epic;* **SHOW YOU THE WAY TO GO. / BLAME IT ON THE BOOGIE** [ ] [ ]

Sep 82. (lp/c) *Pickwick; (TM S/C 3503)* **THE JACKSON 5** [ ] [–]

Mar 90. (lp/cd/c) *S.D.E.G.; (SDE/+CD/+MC 4018)* **BEGINNING YEARS 1965-67** [ ] [ ]

Mar 90. (cd/c/lp) *S.D.E.G.; (CD/MC SDE 4018/SDE 4018)* **THE JACKSON 5 AND JOHNNY** [ ] [ ]

May 93. (cd/c) *Spectrum; (550076 – 4/-2)* **CHILDREN OF THE NIGHT ("JACKSON 5")** [ ] [–]

Sep 93. (cd) *Stardust; (STACD 081)* **THE JACKSON 5 FEATURING MICHAEL JACKSON ("JACKSON 5")** [ ] [–]

Jul 95. (cd) *Charly; (CPCD 8122)* **THE HISTORIC EARLY RECORDINGS** [ ] [–]

Jul 95. (cd) *Wisepack;* **SOUL LEGENDS** [ ] [–]

Jul 95. (4xcd-box) *Motown; (5304892)* **SOULSATION** [ ] [–]

Nov 95. (3xcd-box) *Motown;* **MAYBE TOMORROW / SKYWRITER / THE THIRD ALBUM** [ ] [–]

—— JERMAINE, JACKIE, LaTOYA and more successfully JANET, had own solo hits.

□ Mick JAGGER (see under ⇒ ROLLING STONES)

JAM

Formed: Woking, Surrey, England . . . late '73 by PAUL WELLER, BRUCE FOXTON, RICK BUCKLER and 4th member STEVE BROOKS – guitar. This quartet first gigged mid-74, progressing to the likes of London's Marquee, 101 Club & Red Cow in late '76, by which time BROOKS had departed. Peddling amphetamine charged retro R&B, the band rode in on the first wave of punk's brave new musical world. Incendiary live performances had generated a loyal following and considerable record company interest, the band signing with 'Polydor' early the following year via A&R man Chris Parry. In Spring '77, their debut, 'IN THE CITY', cracked the UK Top 40, an album of the same name following a month later. Image wise, the band were kitted out in unashamed allegiance to the mod masterplan of yore; sharp suits, parkas, scooters etc., another factor that set the band apart from the anti-fashion of punk. Something WELLER did share with his glue-sniffing peers was anger; yep, before WELLER the 'red-wedge' soul smoothie and WELLER the patron of 'Dad Rock' came WELLER the angry young man, so angry in fact, that he professed to voting conservative. Politics aside, 'IN THE CITY' was a cut above the average three chord punk thrash, bristling with adolescent fury yet possessed of an irresistible melodic verve. 'THIS IS THE MODERN WORLD' (1977) was a hastily recorded follow-up, and it showed. Only the pounding title track (the single backed with a cover of Arthur Conley's 'SWEET SOUL MUSIC') really hit the target, the rest of the album pointlessly recycling WHO riffs ad nauseam. With 'ALL MOD CONS' (1978), however, The JAM were onto something big, WELLER's cutting social reportage and songwriting genius translating into such gems as 'DOWN IN THE TUBE-STATION AT MIDNIGHT', a cover of The Kinks' 'DAVID WATTS' indicating the heights he was aiming for. Come 'SETTING SONS' (1979), and with the bile-spewing 'ETON RIFLES', in particular, WELLER came pretty damn close to updating RAY DAVIES' class-conscious agenda for a harsh new age. The single gave the band their first Top 5 success and the album achieved a similar feat upon its release a month later. In February of the following year, the band went straight in at No.1 with 'GOING UNDERGROUND', a snarling critique of the establishment. The band followed this up with 'START!', a virtual remake (well, intro definitely) of George Harrison/Beatles' 'TAXMAN', quite why there's never been a court case over the matter remains a mystery. Still, the single marked a move into more ambitious musical territory, WELLER penning his most accomplished tune to date in the lilting, understated ennui of 'THAT'S ENTERTAINMENT'. The album, 'SOUND AFFECTS' (1980), confirmed the shift away from powerchord aggression with the use of horns and more obviously black music-derived rhythms. By this point, THE JAM were one of, if not the, biggest band in Britain although, despite repeated attempts, the American market was apparently impossible for the band to crack. Then again, it's not hard to see that their defiantly British sound just didn't translate in the States, in much the same way as, more recently, BLUR's idiosyncratic Englishness has precluded US recognition. Back home though, the band were No.1 again in early 1982 with the heavily Motown-influenced 'TOWN CALLED MALICE', 'THE GIFT' album being released the following month. It was to be the band's swansong as WELLER, at the peak of the band's fame later that summer, announced he was to break the group up to explore his soul fixation with The STYLE COUNCIL. After a final kiss-off with 'THE BITTEREST PILL' and the brilliant 'BEAT SURRENDER', the band were no more. While WELLER went on to a undergo many musical rebirths, there was no such joy for FOXTON, who later joined aging punks STIFF LITTLE FINGERS. BUCKLER, meanwhile, forsook the evils of the music business for furniture restoration. Thankfully, with no reunion so far, and the possibility of one rather slim, the legend of The JAM remains intact. • **Songwriters:** WELLER penned except; BACK IN MY ARMS AGAIN (Holland-Dozier-Holland) / DAVID WATTS (Kinks) / MOVE ON UP (Curtis Mayfield). • **Trivia:** In Oct'81, WELLER started own record company 'Respond', and signed acts The QUESTIONS and TRACIE.

Album rating: IN THE CITY (*6) / THIS IS THE MODERN WORLD (*5) / ALL MOD CONS (*8) / SETTING SONS (*8) / SOUND EFFECTS (*8) / THE GIFT (*6) / DIG THE NEW BREED live collection (*6) / SNAP! compilation (*10) / GREATEST HITS compilation (*8) / DIRECTION REACTION CREATION boxed compilation (*9) / THE VERY BEST OF THE JAM compilation (*8) / THE SOUND OF THE JAM compilation (*8)

PAUL WELLER (b. JOHN WELLER, 25 May'58) – vocals, guitar / **BRUCE FOXTON** (b. 1 Sep'55) – bass, vocals / **RICK BUCKLER** (b. PAUL RICHARD BUCKLER, 6 Dec'55) – drums

		Polydor	Polydor
Apr 77.	(7") *(2058 866)* **IN THE CITY. / TAKIN' MY LOVE**	40	–
	(re-iss. Apr80) – hit No.40 *(re-iss. Jan83)* – hit No.47 *(re-iss. Apr02; 587611-7)* – hit No.36		
May 77.	(lp) *(2383 447)* *<6110>* **IN THE CITY**	20	
	– Art school I've changed my address / Slow down / I got by in time / Away from the numbers / Batman / In the city / Sounds from the street / Non stop dancing / Time for truth / Takin' my love / Bricks and mortar. *(re-iss. Aug83 lp/c; SPE LP/MC 27) (re-iss. Jul90 cd/c/lp; 817124-2/-4/-1) (cd re-iss. Jul97; 537417-2)*		
Jul 77.	(7") *(2058 903)* **ALL AROUND THE WORLD. / CARNABY STREET**	13	–
	(re-iss. Apr80) – hit No.43 *(re-iss. Jan83)* – hit No.38		
Oct 77.	(7"m) *(2058 945)* **THE MODERN WORLD. / SWEET SOUL MUSIC (live) / BACK IN MY ARMS AGAIN (live) / BRICKS AND MORTAR (live)**	36	–
	(re-iss. Apr80) – hit No.52 *(re-iss. Jan83)* – hit No.51		
Nov 77.	(lp) *(2383 475)* *<6129>* **THIS IS THE MODERN WORLD**	22	
	– The modern world / London traffic / Standards / Life from the window / The combine / Don't tell them you're sane / In the street today / London girl / I need you / Here comes the weekend / Tonight at noon / In the midnight hour. *(re-iss. Aug83 lp/c; SPE LP/MC 66) (re-iss. Jul90 cd/c/lp; 823281-2/-4/-1) (cd re-iss. Jul97; 537418-2)*		
Feb 78.	(7") *<14462>* **I NEED YOU. / IN THE CITY**	–	
Mar 78.	(7"m) *(2058 995)* **NEWS OF THE WORLD. / AUNTIES AND UNCLES / INNOCENT MAN**	27	–
	(re-iss. Apr80) – hit No.53 *(re-iss. Jan83)* – hit No.39		
Aug 78.	(7") *(2059 054)* **DAVID WATTS. / 'A' BOMB IN WARDOUR STREET**	25	–
	(re-iss. Apr80) – hit No.54 *(re-iss. Jan83)* – hit No.50		
Oct 78.	(7"m) *(POSP 8)* **DOWN IN THE TUBE STATION AT MIDNIGHT. / SO BAD ABOUT US / THE NIGHT**	15	–
	(re-iss. Apr80) (re-iss. Jan83) – hit No.30		
Nov 78.	(lp/c) *(POLD/+C 5008)* *<6218>* **ALL MOD CONS**	6	
	– All mod cons / To be someone (didn't we have a nice time) / Mr. Clean / David Watts / English rose / In the crowd / Billy Hunt / It's too bad / Fly 3.18 / The place I love / 'A' bomb in Wardour Street / Down in the tube station at midnight. *(cd-iss. 1989; 823282-2) (cd re-iss. Jul97; 537419-2) (lp re-iss. Aug99 on 'Simply Vinyl'; SVLP 108)*		
Mar 79.	(7") *(POSP 34)* *<14553>* **STRANGE TOWN. / THE BUTTERFLY COLLECTOR**	15	
	(re-iss. Apr80) – hit No.44 *(re-iss. Jan83)* – hit No.42		
Jun 79.	(7") *<14566>* **DOWN IN THE TUBE STATION AT MIDNIGHT. / MR. CLEAN**	–	
Aug 79.	(7") *(POSP 69)* **WHEN YOU'RE YOUNG. / SMITHERS-JONES**	17	–
	(re-iss. Jan83) – hit No.53		
Oct 79.	(7") *(POSP 83)* **THE ETON RIFLES. / SEE-SAW**	3	–
	(re-iss. Jan83) – hit No.54		
Nov 79.	(lp/c) *(POLD/+C 5028)* *<6249>* **SETTING SONS**	4	
	– Girl on the phone / Thick as thieves / Private hell / Little boy soldiers / Waste land / Burning sky / Smithers-Jones / Saturday's kids / The Eton rifles / Heat wave. *(cd-iss. May88; 831314-2) (cd re-iss. Jul97; 537420-2) (lp re-iss. May00 on 'Simply Vinyl'; SVLP 209) (cd re-iss. Nov01 on 'Collectors Choice'+=; CCM 0247-2)* – Strange town / When you're young / Smithers-Jones / See saw / Going underground / Dreams of children / So sad about us / Hey mister / Start.		
Dec 79.	(7") *<2051>* **THE ETON RIFLES. / SMITHERS-JONES**	–	
Feb 80.	(7") *(POSP 113)* **GOING UNDERGROUND. / DREAMS OF CHILDREN**	1	–
	(d7"+=) *(POSPJ 113 – 2616 024)* – The modern world (live) / Away from the numbers (live) / Down in the tube station at midnight (live). *(re-iss. Jan83)* – hit No.21		
Apr 80.	(7") *<2074>* **SATURDAY'S KIDS. / (LOVE IS LIKE A) HEATWAVE**	–	

Aug 80. (7") *(2059 266)* **START! / LIZA RADLEY** [1] [–]
(re-iss. Jan83) – hit No.60

Sep 80. (7") *<2155>* **START! / WHEN YOU'RE YOUNG** [–] [ ]

Nov 80. (lp/c) *(POLD/+C 5035)* *<6315>* **SOUND AFFECTS** [2] [72]
– Pretty green / Monday / But I'm different now / Set the house ablaze / Start! / That's entertainment / Dreamtime / Man in the cornershop / Music for the last couple / Boy about town / Scrape away. *(re-iss. Apr90 cd/c/lp; 823284-2/-4/-1) (cd re-iss. Jul97; 537421-2)*

Jan 81. (7") *(0030 364)* **THAT'S ENTERTAINMENT. / DOWN IN THE TUBE STATION AT MIDNIGHT (live)** [21] [–]
(above 45, was actually imported into Britain by German 'Metrognome') *(re-iss. Jan83 on 'Polydor'; 2059 482)* – hit No.60

May 81. (7") *(POSP 257)* **FUNERAL PYRE. / DISGUISES** [4] [ ]
(re-iss. Jan83)

Oct 81. (7") *(POSP 350)* **ABSOLUTE BEGINNERS. / TALES FROM THE RIVERBANK** [4] [ ]
(re-iss. Jan83)

Dec 81. (m-lp) *<503>* **THE JAM** [–] [ ]
– Absolute beginners / Funeral pyre / Liza Radley / Tales from the riverbank / Disguises.

Feb 82. (7"/12") *(POSP/+X 400)* **TOWN CALLED MALICE. / PRECIOUS** [1] [ ]
(re-iss. Jan83) – hit No.73

Mar 82. (lp/c) *(POLD/+C 5055)* *<6349>* **THE GIFT** [1] [82]
– Happy together / Ghosts / Precious / Just who is the 5 o'clock hero? / Trans-global express / Running on the spot / Circus / The planner's dream goes wrong / Carnation / Town called Malice / The gift. *(re-iss. Apr90 cd/c/lp; 823285-2/-4/-1) (cd re-iss. Jul97; 537422-2)*

Jun 82. (7") *(2059 504)* **JUST WHO IS THE 5 O'CLOCK HERO?. / THE GREAT DEPRESSION** [6] [ ]
(12"+=) *(2141 558)* – War.

Sep 82. (7") *(POSP 505)* **THE BITTEREST PILL (I EVER HAD TO SWALLOW). / PITY POOR ALFIE / FEVER – PITY POOR ALFIE** [2] [ ]
<US-iss.Nov82 as 12"m-lp> – Great depression.

Nov 82. (7") *(POSP 540)* **BEAT SURRENDER. / SHOPPING** [1] Mar83 [ ]
(d7"+=)<m-lp> *(POSPJ 540 – JAM 1)* *<810751>* – Move on up / War / Stoned out of my mind.

Dec 82. (lp/c) *(POLD/+C 5075)* *<6365>* **DIG THE NEW BREED (live 77-82)** [2] [ ]
– In the city / All mod cons / To be someone / It's too bad / Start! / Big bird / Set the house ablaze / Ghosts / Standards / In the crowd / Going underground / Dreams of children / That's entertainment / Private hell. *(re-iss. Jun87 lp/c; SPE LP/MC 107) (re-iss. Jun90 cd/c/lp; 810041-2/-4/-1) (cd re-iss. Sep95)*

—— They split late '82. WELLER formed The STYLE COUNCIL, before making it huge as a solo star. FOXTON, meanwhile, went solo, delivering a solitary solo album, 'TOUCH SENSITIVE' (May 1984) for 'Arista'; the Top 75 breaker contained his only Top 30 hit, 'FREAK', released a year earlier. BUCKLER formed TIME UK who had one minor hit, 'THE CABARET' (Sep'83), before he and FOXTON teamed up with TIME UK singer, JIMMY EDWARDS, to become mid-late 80's outfit, SHARP.

– compilations, etc. –

on 'Polydor' unless mentioned otherwise

Sep 80. (d-lp) *(2683 074)* **IN THE CITY / THIS IS THE MODERN WORLD** [ ] [–]
(re-iss. Jan91 cd/c; 847730-2/-4)

Jan 83. (d-c) *(TWOMC 1)* **SOUND AFFECTS / THE GIFT** [ ] [–]

Feb 83. (d-c) *(1574 098)* **ALL MOD CONS / SETTING SONS** [ ] [–]

Oct 83. (d-lp/d-c) *(SNAP/+C 1)* **SNAP!** [2] [–]
– In the city / Away from the numbers / All around the world / The modern world / News of the world / Billy Hunt / English Rose / Mr. Clean / David Watts / 'A' bomb in Wardour Street / Down in the tube station at midnight / Strange town / The butterfly collector / When you're young / Smithers-Jones / Thick as thieves / The Eton rifles / Going underground / Dreams of children / That's entertainment / Start! / Man in the cornershop / Funeral pyre / Absolute beginners / Tales from the riverbank / Town called Malice / Precious / The bitterest pill (I ever had to swallow) / Beat surrender. *(d-lp.with free 7"ep)* **LIVE AT WEMBLEY (live)** – The great depression / But I'm different now / Move on up / Get yourself together. *(cd-iss. Sep84 as 'COMPACT SNAP'; 821712-2)* – omits 8 tracks. *(re-iss. Jun90 cd/c/lp; 815537-2/-4/-1)*

Mar 90. (7") *Old Gold; (OG 9894)* **TOWN CALLED MALICE. / ABSOLUTE BEGINNERS** [ ] [–]

Mar 90. (7") *Old Gold; (OG 9895)* **BEAT SURRENDER. / THE BITTEREST PILL (I EVER HAD TO SWALLOW)** [ ] [–]

Mar 90. (7") *Old Gold; (OG 9896)* **THE ETON RIFLES. / DOWN IN THE TUBE STATION AT MIDNIGHT** [ ] [–]

Mar 90. (7") *Old Gold; (OG 9897)* **GOING UNDERGROUND. / START!** [ ] [–]

Sep 90. (12"ep/cd-ep) *Strange Fruit; (SFPS/+CD 080)* **THE PEEL SESSIONS** (26.4.77) [ ] [–]
– In the city / Art school / I've changed my address / The modern world. *(cd-ep re-iss. Sep96; same)*

Jun 91. (7"/c-s) *(PO/+CS 155)* **THAT'S ENTERTAINMENT. / DOWN IN THE TUBE-STATION AT MIDNIGHT (live)** [57] [–]
(12"+=/cd-s+=) *(PZ/+CD 155)* – Town called Malice (live).

Jul 91. (cd/c/lp) *(849554-2/-4/-1)* **GREATEST HITS** [2] [–]
– In the city / All around the world / Modern world / News of the world / David Watts / A bomb in Wardour Street / Down in the tube-station at midnight / Strange town / When you're young / Eton rifles / Going underground / Dreams of children / Start / That's entertainment / Funeral pyre / Absolute beginners / A town called Malice / Precious / Just who is the 5 o'clock hero / The bitterest pill (I ever had to swallow) / Beat surrender.

Mar 92. (7"/c-s) *(PO/+CS 199)* **THE DREAMS OF CHILDREN. / AWAY FROM THE NUMBERS (live)** [ ] [–]
(12"+=/cd-s+=) *(PZ/+CD 199)* – This is the modern world (live).

Apr 92. (cd/c/lp) *(513177-2/-4/-1)* **EXTRAS: A COLLECTION OF RARITIES** [ ] [–]

Oct 92. (cd/c) *Pickwick; (PWK S/MC 4129P)* **WASTELAND** [ ] [–]

Oct 93. (cd/c/d-lp) *(519667-2/-4/-1)* **LIVE JAM (live)** [28] [ ]
– The modern world / Billy Hunt / Thick as thieves / Burning sky / Mr. Clean / Smithers-Jones / Little boy soldiers / The Eton Rifles / Away from the numbers / Down in the tube station at midnight / Strange town / When you're young / 'A' Bomb In Wardour Street / Pretty green / Boy about town / Man in the cornershop / David Watts / Funeral pyre / Move on up / Carnation / The butterfly collector / Precious / Town called Malice / Heatwave. *(cd re-iss. Apr02; same)*

Jul 96. (d-cd/d-c/d-lp) *(531493-2/-4/-1)* **THE JAM COLLECTION** [58] [–]

May 97. (5xcd-box) *(537143-2)* **DIRECTION REACTION CREATION** [8] [–]

Sep 97. (7"/c-s) *(571598-7/-4)* **THE BITTEREST PILL (I EVER HAD TO SWALLOW). / THE BUTTERFLY COLLECTOR** [30] [–]
(cd-s+=) *(571598-2)* – That's entertainment / ('A'version).

Oct 97. (cd/c) *(537423-2/-4)* **THE VERY BEST OF THE JAM** (all the singles 1977-1982) [9] [–]
– (see 'GREATEST HITS' for track details).

Nov 98. (cd/c) *Spectrum; (550006-2/-4)* **BEAT SURRENDER** [ ] [–]

Apr 01. (9xcd-s-box) *(587610-2)* **THE SINGLES 1977-1979** [ ] [–]

Apr 01. (9xcd-s-box) *(587620-2)* **THE SINGLES 1980-1982** [ ] [–]

May 02. (cd/d-lp) *(589781-2/-1)* **THE SOUND OF THE JAM** [3] [–]

Jun 02. (3xcd-box) *(589690-2)* **THE JAM AT THE BBC** [33] [–]

JAMES

Formed: Manchester, England ... 1982 by JIM GLENNIE, TIM BOOTH, LARRY GOTT and GAVAN WHELAN. In 1983 they signed to Tony Wilson's 'Factory' label, issuing a debut 3-track, the 'JIMONE EP'. Their folksy idiosyncracy and wilful weirdness was beloved of the music press almost from the off and their cult standing increased considerably after their 2nd classic 45, 'HYMN FROM A VILLAGE', topped the indie chart early in '85. They were soon snapped up by Seymour Stein's 'Sire', legendary underground mover and shaker Lenny Kaye producing the debut album, 'STUTTER'. BOOTH's overtly accented vocals were the primary focus of the band's often erratic and unorthodox, cerebral, improvisation-driven indie rock/folk and this bizarre combination made the band a compelling live act. However, financial difficulties led to the band moving label to WEA subsidiary 'Blanco Y Negro', where they released 'STRIP MINE' (1988). In 1990, after a change of personnel and a spell on 'Rough Trade', JAMES had their first

Top 40 hit on 'Fontana' with 'HOW WAS IT FOR YOU?'. It was soon followed by a Top 20 album, 'GOLD MOTHER', that when re-promoted early 1991 with No.2 hit, the outrageously anthemic and subsequently tediously annoying 'SIT DOWN', also hit No.2. Suddenly the band were riding on the frayed, flared coat-tails of the baggy scene alongside fellow Manchester bands like The HAPPY MONDAYS and The STONE ROSES. Their obstinately obscure sound of old had now been bolstered by chant-along choruses of almost terrace proportions and the ubiquitous JAMES t-shirt was de rigeur for fresher students up and down the country. The band were now playing to stadium-sized audiences and they made their follow-up, 'SEVEN' (1992), to match, all big production and bombast that went down like a lead balloon with critics. With 'LAID' (1993), the band roped in BRIAN ENO, and went for a more opaque, stripped-down sound that recalled their experimental, earlier work. Lyrically, the album was as complex and as vivid as ever while the gorgeous 'SOMETIMES' gave the band their first Top 20 hit since early '92. The ENO sessions also provided the material for the 'WAH WAH' (1994) album, a collection of ambient improvisations with the aging electronic wizard. Of late, TIM BOOTH teamed up with ANGELO BADALAMENTI (he of 'Twin Peaks' fame') and ex-SUEDE guitarist, BERNARD BUTLER to release one-off set, 'BOOTH AND THE BAD ANGEL' (1996). Last year (1997), JAMES were again in the UK Top 10, the single 'SHE'S A STAR' and its parent album, 'WHIPLASH', both achieving the feat. Of late, a stop-gap 'best of' package was treated well by the fans (who made it UK No.1) but 'MILLIONAIRES' (1999) fell short of requirements. Although the near chart-topping record featured hit singles, 'I KNOW WHAT I'M HERE FOR' and 'JUST LIKE FRED ASTAIRE', it had none of the zip and lyrical sparkle of old. Ten albums in and JAMES were showing little sign of middle age spread although 'PLEASED TO MEET YOU' (2001) imparted the wisdom of maturity rather than the arrogance of youth. Although the album didn't quite make the Top 10 and 'GETTING AWAY WITH IT' should've been a bigger hit, the veteran Mancunians proved that mid-life musical crisis is all in the mind. Unfortunately, a few months later, JAMES were no more. • **Songwriters:** TIM BOOTH penned, except SUNDAY MORNING (Velvet Underground) / CHINA GIRL (Iggy Pop & David Bowie).

Album rating: STUTTER (*6) / STRIP MINE (*6) / ONE MAN CLAPPING (*6) / GOLD MOTHER (*8) / SEVEN (*8) / LAID (*7) / WAH WAH (*6) / WHIPLASH (*6) / THE BEST OF JAMES compilation (*8) / MILLIONAIRES (*5) / PLEASED TO MEET YOU (*6) / ULTRA: B-SIDES collection (*5) / GETTING AWAY WITH IT . . . LIVE (*5) / Booth & The Bad Angel: BOOTH & THE BAD ANGEL (*5)

TIM BOOTH (b. 4 Feb'60) – vocals / **LARRY GOTT** (b. JAMES GOTT) – guitar / **JIM GLENNIE** (b.10 Oct'63) – bass / **GAVAN WHELAN** – drums

Factory / not iss.

Sep 83. (7") *(FAC 78)* **JIMONE** [ ] [–]
– What's the world / Fire so close / Folklore.

Feb 85. (7") *(FAC 119)* **JAMES II** [ ] [–]
– Hymn from a village / If things were perfect.

Jun 85. (12"ep) *(FAC 138)* **VILLAGE FIRE** [ ] [–]
– What's the world / Fire so close / Folklore / Hymn from a village / If things were perfect.

Sire / Warners

Feb 86. (7") *(JIM 3)* **CHAIN MAIL. / HUP STRINGS** [ ] [–]
(12"+=) *(JIM 3T)* **SIT DOWN EP** – Uprising.

Jul 86. (7") *(JIM 4)* **SO MANY WAYS. / WITHDRAWN** [ ] [–]
(12"+=) *(JIM 4T)* – Just hipper.

Jul 86. (lp/c) *(JIM LP/C 1)* **STUTTER** [68] [–]
– Skullduggery / Scarecrow / So many ways / Just hip / Johnny Yen / Summer song / Really hard / Billy's shirts / Why so close / Withdrawn / Black hole. *(cd-iss. Nov91; 7599 25437-2)*

Blanco Y Negro / Sire

Sep 87. (7") *(NEG 26)* **YAHO. / MOSQUITO** [ ] [–]
(12"+=) *(NEG 26T)* – Left out of her will / New nature.

Mar 88. (7") *(NEG 31)* **WHAT FOR. / ISLAND SWING** [ ] [–]
(c-s+=/12"+=) *(NEG 31 C/T)* – Not there.

Sep 88. (lp/c)(cd) *(JIM LP/C 2)(925657-2)* **STRIP MINE** [90] [ ]
– What for / Charlie Dance / Fairground / Are you ready / Yaho / Medieval / Not there / Riders / Vulture / Strip mining / Refrain. *(re-iss. Jul91; same) (cd re-iss. Feb95; 925657-2)*

Rough Trade / not iss.

Mar 89. (lp/c/cd) *(ONEMAN 001/+C/CD)* **ONE MAN CLAPPING (live in Bath)** [ ] [–]
– Chain mail / Sandman (hup strings) / Whoops / Riders / Why so close / Leaking / Johnny Yen / Scarecrow / Are you ready / Really hard / Burned / Stutter. *(cd+=)* – Yaho.

—— **DAVE BAYNTON-POWER** – drums repl. WHELAN / added **SAUL DAVIS** – violin, percussion, guitar / **MARK HUNTER** – keyboards

Jun 89. (7") *(RT 225)* **SIT DOWN. / SKY IS FALLING** [ ] [–]
(12"+=/3"cd-s+=) *(RTT 225/+CD)* – Goin' away / Sound investment.

—— added **ANDY DIAGRAM** – trumpet (ex-PALE FOUNTAINS, ex-DIAGRAM BROS)

Nov 89. (7") *(RT 245)* **COME HOME. / PROMISED LAND** [ ] [–]
(12"+=/cd-s+=) *(RTT 245/+CD)* – ('A'extended) / Slow right down (demo).

Fontana / Mercury

May 90. (7") *(JIM 5)* **HOW WAS IT FOR YOU? / WHOOPS (live)** [32] [–]
(12") *(JIM 5-12)* – ('A'side) / Hymn from a village (live) / Lazy.
(cd-s) *(JIMCD 5)* – ('A'side) / Hymn from a village (live) / Undertaker.
(12") *(JIMM 5-12)* – ('A'side) / ('A'different mix) / Lazy / Undertaker.

Jun 90. (cd/c/lp) *(<846189-2/-4/-1>)* **GOLD MOTHER** [16] Aug90 [ ]
– Come home / Government walls / God only knows / You can tell how much suffering (on a face that's always smiling) / How was it for you? / Crescendo / Hang on / Walking the ghost / Gold mother / Top of the world. *(re-iss. Apr91 cd/c/lp; 848595-2/-4/-1); hit No.2) (cd+=)* – Sit down / Lose control. *(cd re-iss. Dec01 ++; 548785-2)* – Come home (skunk weed skank mix) / Lose control (live) / Sit down (live) / Gold mother (remix).

Jul 90. (7"/c-s) *(JIM/+C 6)* **COME HOME (Flood mix). / DREAMING UP TOMORROW** [32] [–]
(12") *(JIM 6-12)* – ('A'extended) / Stutter (live) / Fire away.
(cd-s) *(JIMCD 6)* – ('A'side) / ('A'extended) / Gold mother (remix) / Fire away.
(12") *(JIMM 6-12)* – ('A'live) / Gold mother (Warp remix) / ('A'-Andy Weatherall Boys own remix).

Nov 90. (7"/c-s) *(JIM/+C 7)* **LOSE CONTROL. / SUNDAY MORNING** [38] [–]
(ext.12"+=/ext.cd-s+=) *(JIM 7-12/CD7)* – Out to get you.

Mar 91. (7"/c-s) *(JIM/+C 8)* **SIT DOWN. / ('A'live)** [2] [ ]
(12"+=/cd-s+=) *(JIM 8-12/CD8)* – Tonight.

Nov 91. (7"/c-s) *(JIM/+C 9)* **SOUND. / ALL MY SONS** [9] [ ]
(12"+=/cd-s+=) *(JIM 9-12/CD9)* – ('A'extended) / Come home (Youth mix).

Jan 92. (7"/c-s) *(JIM/+C 10)* **BORN OF FRUSTRATION. / BE MY PRAYER** [13] [ ]
(12"+=/cd-s+=) *(JIM 10-12/CD10)* – Sound (mix).

Feb 92. (cd/c/lp) *(<510932-2/-4/-1>)* **SEVEN** [2] Mar92 [ ]
– Born of frustration / Ring the bells / Sound / Bring a gun / Mother / Don't wait that long / Live a life of love / Heavens / Protect me / Seven. *(cd+=/c+=)* – Next lover. *(re-iss. Aug98; same) (cd re-iss. Dec01 +=; 548786-2)* – live:- Protect me (acoustic) / Sound / Heavens / Don't wait that long.

Mar 92. (7"/c-s) *(JIM/+C 11)* **RING THE BELLS. / FIGHT** [37] [ ]
(12"+=/cd-s+=) *(JIM 11-12/CD11)* – The skunk weed skank / Come home (live dub version).
(12"++=) *(JIM 11-122)* – Once a friend.

Jul 92. (7"ep/c-ep/cd-ep) *(JIM/+C/CD 12)* **SEVEN (remix) / GOALIES BALL. / WILLIAM BURROUGHS / STILL ALIVE** [46] [–]

Sep 93. (7"/c-s) *(JIM/+C 13)* **SOMETIMES. / AMERICA** [18] [ ]
(12"+=/cd-s+=) *(JIM 13-12/CD13)* – Building a charge.

Sep 93. (cd/c/lp) *(<514943-2/-4/-1>)* **LAID** [3] Oct93 [72]
– Out to get you / Sometimes (Lester Piggott) / Dream thrum / One of the three / Say something / Five-o / P.S. / Everybody knows / Knuckle too far / Low, low / Laid / Lullaby / Skindiving. *(re-iss. Aug98; same) (cd re-iss. Dec01 +=; 548787-2)* – live at the BBC:- Laid / Sometimes / Five-O / Say something (live).

Nov 93. (7"/c-s) *(JIM/+C 14) <858217>* **LAID. / WAH WAH KITS** [25] Jan94 [61]
(cd-s+=) *(JIMCD 14)* – The lake / Seconds away.
(cd-s) *(JIMDD 14)* – ('A'live) / Five-O / Say something / Sometimes.

Mar 94. (c-s) *(JIMMC 15)* **JAM J / SAY SOMETHING** [24] [ ]
(12"+=)(cd-s+=) *(JIMX 15)(JMCD 15)* – Assassin / ('B'-version).
(cd-s) *(JIMCD 15)* – JAM J – James vs The Sabres Of Paradise (i) Arena dub (ii) Amphetamine pulsate / JAM J – James vs The Sabres Of Paradise (i) Sabresonic tremelo dub (ii) Spaghetti steamhammer.

Sep 94. (cd/c/d-lp;ltd) *(<314 526 408-2/-4/-1>)* **WAH WAH** (w / BRIAN ENO) [11] Oct94 [ ]
– Hammer strings / Pressure's on / Jam J / Frequency dip / Lay the law down / Burn the cat / Maria / Low clouds (1) / Building a fire / Gospel oak / DVV / Say say something / Rhythmic dreams / Dead man / Rain whistling / Low clouds (2) / Bottom of the well / Honest Joe / Arabic agony / Tomorrow / Laughter / Sayonara.

— **ADRIAN OXAAL** – repl. DIAGRAM

Feb 97. (cd-s) *(JIMED 16)* **SHE'S A STAR / STUTTER (live) / JOHNNY YEN (live)** [9] [–]
(cd-s) *(JIMDD 16)* – ('A'side) / Chunney chops / Fishknives / Van Gogh's dog.
(cd-s) *(JIMCD 16)* – ('A'-Dave Angel mix) / ('A'-Biosphere mix) / Come home (Weatherall mix).

Mar 97. (cd/c/lp) *(<534354-2/-4/-1>)* **WHIPLASH** [9] [ ]
– Tomorrow / Lost a friend / Waltzing along / She's a star / Greenpeace / Go to the bank / Play dead / Avalanche / Homeboy / Watering hole / Blue pastures. *(cd re-iss. Dec01 +=; 548788-2)* – LOst a friend (live) / Greenpeace (live) / Homeboy (live) / Waltzing along (Flytronic mix).

Apr 97. (cd-ep) *(JIMCD 17)* **TOMORROW / GONE TOO FAR / HONEST PLEASURE / ALL ONE TO ME** [12] [–]
(cd-s) *(JIMDD 17)* – ('A'side) / Lost a friend (session) / Come home (session) / Greenpeace (session).
(cd-s) *(JIMED 17)* – ('A'mixes; Fila Brazilia / Archive / Dirty Beatnik).

Jun 97. (cd-s) *(JIMCD 18)* **WALTZING ALONG / ('A'mix)** [23] [–]
(cd-s) *(JIMED 18)* – ('A'side) / ('A'live) / (live).
(cd-s) *(JIMDD 18)* – ('A'remixes by; Midfield General & Flytronix).

Mar 98. (cd-ep) *(JIMCD 19)* **DESTINY CALLING / GOALIE'S BALL / ASSASSIN / THE LAKE** [17] [–]
(cd-ep) *(JIMDD 19)* – ('A'side) / Jam J (live) / Honest Joe (live) / Sound (live).
(cd-s) *(JIMED 19)* – ('A'side) / She's a star (CD-Rom video).

Mar 98. (cd/c) *(<536898-2/-4>)* **THE BEST OF** (compilation) [1] [ ]
– Come home / Sit down / She's a star / Laid / Waltzing along / Say something / Tomorrow / Born of frustration / Destiny calling / Out to get you / Runaground / Lose control / How was it for you? / Seven / Sound / Ring the bells / Sometimes / Hymn from a village.
(also d-cd-iss. ; 558173-2)

May 98. (cd-ep) *(JIMCD 20)* **RUNAGROUND / CRESCENDO / HANG ON / BE MY POWER** [29] [–]
(cd-ep) *(JIMDD 20)* – ('A'side) / Say something (live) / Laid (live) / Lose control (live).
(cd-ep) *(JIMED 20)* – ('A'side) / ('A'remix) / Egoiste / Lost a friend (Aloof remix).

Nov 98. (c-s/cd-s) *(JIM MC/CD 21)* **SIT DOWN (1998 remix) / ('A'-Apollo 440 remix)** [7] [–]
(cd-s) *(JIMDD 21)* – China girl (radio 1 Iggy Pop tribute).

Jul 99. (c-s) *(JIMC 22)* **I KNOW WHAT I'M HERE FOR / ALL GOOD BOYS** [22] [ ]
(cd-s+=) *(JIMCD 22)* – Imagine ourselves.
(cd-s) *(JIMDD 22)* – ('A'side) / Downstairs / Stolen horses.

Oct 99. (c-s) *(JIMC 23)* **JUST LIKE FRED ASTAIRE / I DEFEAT** [17] [ ]
(cd-s+=) *(JIMCD 23)* – Long to see.
(cd-s) *(JIMDD 23)* – ('A'side) / Mary / Goal, goal, goal.

Oct 99. (cd/c) *(<546386-2/-4>)* **MILLIONAIRES** [2] [ ]
– Crash / Just like Fred Astaire / I know what I'm here for / Shooting my mouth off / We're going to miss you / Strangers / Hello / Afro lover / Surprise / Dumb jam / Someone's got it in for me / Vervaceous. *(also d-cd+=; 546789-2)* – (live):- I know what I'm here for / Crash / Destiny calling / Someone's got it in for me / Just like Fred Astaire / I know what I'm here for (video) / Just like Fred Astaire (video).

Dec 99. (c-s) *(JIMMC 24)* **WE'RE GOING TO MISS YOU / WISDOM OF THE THROAT** [48] [ ]
(cd-s+=) *(JIMCD 24)* – Top of the world (live).
(cd-s) *(JIMDD 24)* – ('A'side) / Pocketful of lemons ('A'-Eno's version).

— now without OXAAL

Jun 01. (cd-s) *(JIMCD 25)* **GETTING AWAY WITH IT (ALL MESSED UP) / MAKE IT ALRIGHT / SO SWELL (ambient mix)** [22] [–]
(cd-s) *(JIMDD 25)* – ('A'side) / Stand / Shining (live).

Jul 01. (cd) *(<586146-2>)* **PLEASED TO MEET YOU** [11] [ ]
– Space / Falling down / English beefcake / Junkie / Pleased to meet you / The shining / Senorita / Give it away / Fine / Getting away with it (all messed up) / Alaskan pipeline.

— JAMES disbanded in December 2001

– compilations, etc. –

Dec 01. (cd) *Fontana; (<548440-2>)* **ULTRA: B-SIDES** [ ] Jan02 [ ]
– Gone too far / Honest pleasure / Sunday morning / China girl / Still alive / The lake / I defeat / Goalie's ball / Chunny pops / Tonight / Dream up tomorrow / William Burroughs / Assassin / Stolen horse / Undertaker / Egoiste / Van Gogh's dog / Where you gonna run?

Jun 02. (d-cd) *Sanctuary; (SANDD 119) <84557>* **GETTING AWAY WITH IT . . . LIVE (live)** [ ] [ ]
– Say something / Waltzing along / Sometimes / Laid / I know what I'm here for / God only knows / Someone's got it in for me / Vervaceous / Protect me / Out to get you / Hymn from a village / Johnny Yen / Getting away with it / Tomorrow / Born of frustration / Ring the bells / Top of the world / Sound / Space / She's a star / Come home / Sit down.

BOOTH AND THE BAD ANGEL

— **TIM BOOTH / ANGELO BADALAMENTI / + BERNARD BUTLER** (ex-Suede)

Fontana Mercury

Jun 96. (c-s) *(BBMC 1)* **I BELIEVE (edit) / I BELIEVE (long version)** [25] [–]
(cd-s+=) *(BBCD 1)* – When you smiled.
(cd-s+=) *(BBDD 1)* – Melting away.

Jul 96. (cd/c) *(<526 852-2/-4>)* **BOOTH AND THE BAD ANGEL** [35] [ ]
– I believe / Dance of the bad angels / Hit parade / Fall in love with me / Old ways / Life gets better / Heart / Rising / Butterfly's dream / Stranger / Hands in the rain.
(below lifted from the film 'Martha Meet Franky, Daniel & Laurence'.

Jun 98. (c-s) *(MERMC 503)* **FALL IN LOVE WITH ME (live) / I BELIEVE (live)** [57] [–]
(cd-s+=) *(MERCD 503)* – Hit parade (live).
(cd-s) *(MERDD 503)* – ('A'side) / Butterfly's dream (live) ('A'live).

Elmore JAMES

Born: 27 January 1918, Richland, Mississippi, USA. Although his recording career spanned only ten years, he will always be remembered for his first hit, 'DUST MY BROOM', a bombshell of a song based on a composition by ROBERT JOHNSON, (whom he had met in 1937 and taught how to play bottleneck), featuring his trademark powerful slide guitar. After a stint in the US Navy (between 1943 and 1945), his formative years were spent in the company of RICE MILLER (SONNY BOY WILLIAMSON II), who was a regular on Radio KFFA's 'King Biscuit Time' show (JAMES played on the programme in 1947). They travelled together for several years, JAMES securing his first contract in 1951 with LILLIAN McMURRAY's 'Trumpet' label through MILLER'S contacts, initially appearing on disc as a backing musician on cuts by WILLIAMSON. After these sessions, WILLIAMSON convinced ELMO (as he was credited then) to record the aforementioned 'DUST MY BROOM' (with WILLIAMSON on harmonica), the record subsequently going on to hit the Top 10 in the R&B chart in 1952. JAMES then moved to Chicago where he formed The BROOMDUSTERS and signed to Joe Bihari's 'Modern' label with further recordings (variations on his initial hit) 'I BELIEVE' and 'DUST MY BLUES' building on that success. Other compositions were to prove influential on future artists with 'BLEEDING HEART', 'SHAKE YOUR MONEYMAKER' and 'DONE SOMEBODY WRONG' being taken up by FLEETWOOD

MAC, JIMI HENDRIX and DUANE ALLMAN respectively. His bottleneck style of guitar resurfaced in numerous British R&B bands and in particular, JEREMY SPENCER of FLEETWOOD MAC and BRIAN JONES (early stage name ELMO LEWIS in respect of JAMES) of the ROLLING STONES paid homage to him although his greatest recognition came when B.B. KING admitted to adopting areas of JAMES' style. After heavy drinking affected his recording schedules he was dropped by his record company in 1956 and was blacklisted by the American Foundation of Musicians for using non union backing players. He went into semi-retirement after a mild heart attack which caused him to reflect on his life, returning to Chicago in 1957 to record with Mel London's 'Mel' records (with backing from WAYNE BENNETT, EDDIE TAYLOR, WILLIE DIXON and FRED BELEW). By the end of the 50's, JAMES was tempted to return to club gigs, subsequently spotted by 'Fire' Records boss, Bobby Robinson, who duly signed him and released the single, 'THE SKY IS CRYING' (which became another R&B success) in 1960. JOHN MAYALL's 'MR. JAMES' was a tribute to the man who sadly didn't live to bask in the acclaim; on the 23rd of May 1963, on the verge of a comeback, he suffered a third, and this time fatal, heart attack after a concert at the Copa Cabana in Chicago. ELMORE died at the home of his cousin, HOMESICK JAMES, who along with J.B. HUTTO, took on his mantle of 'King of the slide guitar'. He only released one album during his lifetime, the 1961 offering, 'BLUES AFTER HOURS' although many more were released after his death, including 'THE IMMORTAL ELMORE JAMES: KING OF THE BOTTLENECK BLUES' which is crammed full of JAMES's best with the wonderful, 'IT HURTS ME TOO' along with his own compositions 'DUST MY BROOM', 'THE SKY IS CRYING', 'SHAKE YOUR MONEYMAKER', 'DONE SOMEBODY WRONG', 'LOOK ON YONDER WALL', 'CAN'T STOP LOVING' and 'BLEEDING HEART'.

Best CD compilation: ROLLIN' AND TUMBLIN': THE BEST OF . . . (*8)

ELMORE JAMES – vocals, acoustic guitar / with **JOHNNY JONES** – piano / **J.T. BROWN** – tenor sax / **ODIE PAYNE** – drums / **RANSOM KNOWLING** – bass

not iss. Trumpet

1952. (78; as ELMO JAMES) *<146>* **DUST MY BROOM. / Bobo Thomas: CATFISH BLUES** [–] [ ]
<re-iss. 1954 on 'Ace'; 508>

not iss. Meteor

1953. (78) *<5000>* **I BELIEVE. / I HELD MY BABY LAST NIGHT** [–] [ ]

1953. (78) *<5003>* **BABY WHAT'S WRONG. / SINFUL WOMAN** [–] [ ]

not iss. Checker

1953. (78) *<777>* **COUNTRY BOOGIE. / SHE JUST WON'T DO RIGHT** [–] [ ]

not iss. Flair

1953. (78) *<1011>* **HAWAIIAN BOOGIE. / EARLY IN THE MORNING** [–] [ ]

1953. (78) *<1014>* **CAN'T STOP LOVIN'. / MAKE A LITTLE LOVE** [–] [ ]

1954. (78) *<5016>* **SAXONY BOOGIE. / DUMB WOMAN BLUES** [–] [ ]
(above single on 'Meteor')

1954. (78) *<1022>* **PLEASE FIND MY BABY. / STRANGE KINDA BABY** [–] [ ]

1954. (78) *<1031>* **MAKE MY DREAMS COME TRUE. / HAND IN HAND** [–] [ ]

1954. (78) *<1039>* **SHO'NUFF I DO. / 1839 BLUES** [–] [ ]

— now with new line-up **WILLARD McDANIEL** – piano / **CHUCK HAMILTON** – bass / **JESSE SAILES** – drums / **MAXWELL DAVIES** – tenor sax / **JAMES PARR** – trumpet / **JEWEL GRANT** – baritone sax

1955. (78) *<1048>* **DARK AND DREARY. / ROCK MY BABY RIGHT** [–] [ ]

1955. (78) *<5024>* **SAX SYMPHONY BOOGIE. / FLAMING BLUES** [–] [ ]
(above single on 'Meteor')

1955. (78) *<1057>* **SUNNY LAND. / STANDING AT THE CROSSROADS** [–] [ ]
<re-iss. 1966 on 'Kent'; 465>

1955. (78) *<1062>* **LATE HOURS AT MIDNIGHT. / THE WAY YOU TREAT ME** [–] [ ]

1955. (78) *<1069>* **HAPPY HOME. / NO LOVE IN MY HEART** [–] [ ]

1955. (78) *<1074>* **DUST MY BLUES. / I WAS A FOOL** [–] [ ]

1955. (78) *<1079>* **BLUES BEFORE SUNRISE. / GOODBYE BABY** [–] [ ]

not iss. Modern

1956. (7") *<983>* **LONG TALL WOMAN. / WILD ABOUT YOU** [–] [ ]

— returned to his original line-up + added **HOMESICK JAMES** – guitar

not iss. Mel-Chief

1957. (7") *<7001>* **THE TWELVE-YEAR OLD BOY. / COMING HOME** [–] [ ]

1957. (7") *<7004>* **IT HIRTS ME TOO. / ELMORE'S CONTRIBUTION TO JAZZ** [–] [ ]

1957. (7") *<7006>* **CRY FOR ME BABY. / TAKE ME WHERE YOU GO** [–] [ ]
(above also on 'S&M' and 'M-Pac')(re-iss. 1966 on 'USA')

1958. (7") *<7020>* **KNOCKING AT YOUR DOOR. / CALLING ALL BLUES** [–] [ ]

not iss. Fire

1959. (7") *<1011>* **MAKE MY DREAMS COME TRUE. / BOBBY'S ROCK** [–] [ ]

1959. (7"; as ELMORE JAMES and THE BROOM DUSTERS) *<331>* **DUST MY BLUES (I BELIEVE). / HAPPY HOME** [–] [ ]
<above single issued on 'Kent'; 331> <re-iss. 1963 on 'Kent'; 394> (UK-iss.Oct64 on 'Sue' records; WI 335)

1960. (7") *<1016>* **THE SKY IS CRYING. / HELD MY BABY LAST NIGHT** [–] [ ]

1960. (7") *<1756>* **I CAN'T HOLD OUT. / THE SUN IS SHINING** [–] [ ]
(above single on 'Chess')

1960. (7") *<1024>* **ROLLIN' AND TUMBLIN'. / I'M WORRIED** [–] [ ]

1960. (7") *<1031>* **DONE SOMEBODY WRONG. / FINE LITTLE MAMA** [–] [ ]

1961. (lp) *<102>* **BLUES AFTER HOURS** [–] [ ]
– Dust my blues / Sunnyland / Mean and evil / Dark and dreamy / Standing at the crossroads / Happy home / No love in my heart for you / Blues before sunrise / I was a fool / Goodbye baby. *<re-iss. 1963 on 'Crown'; CLP 5168> <re-iss. 1964 as 'THE ORIGINAL FOLK BLUES' on 'Kent'; KLP 522> <re-iss. 1968 as 'ELMORE JAMES' on 'Kent'; KLP 5022> <re-iss. 1969 as 'BLUES IN MY HEART, RHYTHM IN MY SOUL' on 'United'; 7716> <& again on 'Custom'; 1054>*

— retained **HOMESICK JAMES** + recruited **SPRUCE JOHNSON** – guitar

1961. (7") *<1503>* **STRANGER BLUES. / ANNA LEE** [–] [ ]

1961. (7") *<504>* **LOOK ON YONDER WALL. / SHAKE YOUR MONEYMAKER** [–] [ ]
<re-iss. 1965 on 'Enjoy'; 2022>

— His 1962 line-up were **JOHNNY ACEY** – piano / **RIFF RUFFIN** – guitar / **DANNY MOORE** – trumpet / **WILLIAMS** – drums

1963. (7") *<2020>* **PICKIN' THE BLUES. / IT HURTS ME TOO** [–] [ ]

— ELMORE died of a heart attack on the 23rd of May '63

– (selective) compilations, etc. –

1966. (lp) *Sue; (ILP 918)* **THE BEST OF ELMORE JAMES** [ ] [–]
– Dust my blues / Fine little mama / The sky is crying / Shake your moneymaker / Anna Lee / I'm worried / Stranger blues / Rollin' and tumblin' / Look on yonder wall / Happy home / Bobby's rock / Held my baby last night / Done somebody wrong / Make my dreams come true. *(re-iss. 1981 on 'Ace'; CH 31)*

1967. (lp) *Sue; (ILP 927)* **ELMORE JAMES MEMORIAL ALBUM** [ ] [–]
– Standing at the crossroads / The twelve year old boy / One way out / It hurts me too (part 1) / Elmore's contribution to jazz / Take me where you go / I can't stop lovin' you / It hurts me too (part 2) / Dust my broom / Knocking at your door / Coming home / Pickin' the blues / Bleeding heart / Cry for me baby.

1969. (lp) *Sphere Sound; <7002>* **THE SKY IS CRYING** [–] [ ]

Nov 86.	(lp/cd) *Ace; (CH/CDCH 192)* **LET'S CUT IT: THE VERY BEST OF ELMORE JAMES** *(re-iss. Nov93; same)*		–
Dec 86.	(cd) *Charly; (CDCHARLY 34)* **SHAKE YOUR MONEYMAKER** *(cd-iss. Nov01 on 'B.M.G.'; 74465 99781-2)*		–
Apr 92.	(cd) *Charly; (CDBM 12)* **THE SKY IS CRYING: CHARLY BLUES MASTERWORKS VOL.12**		
Dec 92.	(4xcd-box) *Charly; (CDREDBOX 4)* **KING OF THE SLIDE GUITAR**		
Oct 93.	(3xcd-box) *Ace; (ABOXCD 4)* **THE CLASSIC EARLY RECORDINGS (1951-1956)**		–
Jun 95.	(cd) *Ace; (CDCHD 563)* **THE BEST OF ELMORE JAMES – THE EARLY YEARS**		–
Feb 97.	(cd) *Charly; (CPCD 8205)* **COME GO WITH ME** *(re-iss. May03 on 'Snapper'; SNAP 121CD)*		
Feb 97.	(cd) *Blue Nite; (BN 023)* **ELMORE JAMES**		
Jun 97.	(cd) *Crown; (CWNCD 2033)* **RAW BLUES POWER**		
Sep 97.	(cd) *Camden; (74321 52376-2)* **THE SKY IS CRYING**		
Aug 99.	(d-cd) *Snapper; (SMDCD 231)* **THE BEST OF ELMORE JAMES**		
May 00.	(cd) *Play..; (PBCD 20503)* **PLAY ME THE BLUES VOL.3: THE LEGENDARY BLUES SINGERS**		
Feb 03.	(d-cd) *Black Box; (BB 254)* **DUST MY BROOM**		
Apr 03.	(d-cd) *Excellence; (EXCEL 2112)* **BLUES EVERGREENS**		
Apr 03.	(3xcd-box) *Snapper; (SNAJ 722CD)* **THE KING OF THE SLIDE GUITAR: THE COMPLETE CHIEF & FIRE SESSIONS**		
Aug 03.	(cd) *Tomato; (TOM 2097)* **DUST MY BROOM**		

Etta JAMES

Born: JAMESETTA HAWKINS, 25 Jan'38, Los Angeles, California, USA; an illegitimate daughter of a black mother and a father of Italian extraction. She was initially raised by step-parents under the name of ROGERS, until they died and she returned to her real mother. Discovered by JOHNNY OTIS in 1954 while she sang in vocal group The CREOLETTES. OTIS soon nicknamed her PEACHES, after her lighter-than-brown complexion and red-ish hair. Their /her first recording for 'Modern' was 'THE WALLFLOWER', which was originally recorded as 'ROLL WITH ME BABY', but this was censored. This song was quickly snatched by white pop singer GEORGIA GIBBS, who took it to No.1 in the US charts, much to the annoyance of ETTA, OTIS and her group. It did however make Top 3 for her in the R&B charts, although she fell out with OTIS over the next decade, due to non-payment of royalties. Her second solo venture in 1955 'I HOPE YOU'RE SATISFIED', was first to feature duet with HARVEY FUQUA, with backing from musician MAXWELL DAVIS. In the early 60's, her contract was bought by 'Chess' subsidiary 'Argo' records, who quickly rushed out 'ALL I COULD DO WAS CRY', which was her first crossover into pop Top 40. Many hits followed but by the mid-60's it was clear her increasing drug habit (heroin) was taking over. In 1967 she recorded what was to become her greatest song 'I'D RATHER GO BLIND', which 2 years later was a massive UK hit for CHICKEN SHACK (who featured at the time CHRISTINE PERFECT (McVIE), later of FLEETWOOD MAC). In the 70's, she recorded sporadically, although her choice of standards didn't return her to former glory. In the late 80's, she was signed to 'Island', who kept her name alive and hip-shakin' by releasing solo comeback sets, 'SEVEN YEAR ITCH' (1989) and 'STICKIN' TO MY GUNS' (1990). A brief contract with 'Elektra', brought forth her umpteenth long-player c/o, 'THE RIGHT TIME' (1992), although it would be a TV-advert for a certain cola early '96 (for her classic 'I JUST WANT TO MAKE LOVE TO YOU') that would give ETTA her long-awaited British breakthrough; she has since maintained her profile by releasing a handful of albums for 'Private-BMG'. • **Covered:** BABY WHAT YOU WANT ME TO DO (Jimmy Reed) / NO PITY (Jackie Wilson) / STRANGE MAN (Dorothy Love Coates) / ONLY WOMEN BLEED (Alice Cooper) / PIECE OF MY HEART (Bert Berns) / TAKE IT TO THE LIMIT (Eagles) / 99 AND A HALF WON'T DO (Wilson Pickett) / etc. • **Trivia:** West Coast producer JERRY WEXLER worked on her return 1978 album (see below).

Album rating (original): AT LAST! (*7) / THE SECOND TIME AROUND (*5) / ETTA JAMES (*5) / SINGS FOR LOVERS (*4) / ETTA JAMES TOP TEN compilation (*6) / ROCKS THE HOUSE (*7) / QUEEN OF SOUL (*6) / CALL MY NAME (*5) / TELL MAMA (*8) / SINGS FUNK (*4) / LOSERS WEEPERS (*4) / ETTA JAMES (*5) / PEACHES compilation (*7) / COME A LITTLE CLOSER (*5) / ETTA IS BETTER THAN EVVAH! (*4) / DEEP IN THE NIGHT (*6) / CHANGES (*4) / BLUES IN THE NIGHT with Eddie 'Cleanhead' Vinson (*5) / R&B DYNAMITE compilation (*6) / SEVEN YEAR ITCH (*6) / STICKIN' TO MY GUNS (*5) / THE RIGHT TIME (*5) / MYSTERY LADY: SONGS OF BILLIE HOLIDAY (*5) / THE ESSENTIAL ETTA JAMES compilation (*8) / TIME AFTER TIME (*5) / THE GENUINE ARTICLE: THE BEST OF ETTA JAMES compilation (*8) / LOVE'S BEEN ROUGH ON ME (*5) / LIFE, LOVE AND THE BLUES (*5) / THE HEART OF A WOMAN (*5) / MATRIARCH OF THE BLUES (*5) / BLUE GARDENIA (*5) / BURNIN' DOWN THE HOUSE (*6) / LET'S ROLL (*6)

ETTA JAMES – vocals; with session people/etc

		not iss.	Modern
Jan 55.	(7",78; as ETTA JAMES and "THE PEACHES") *<947>* **THE WALLFLOWER (ROLL WITH ME HENRY). / HOLD ME, SQUEEZE ME** *<re-iss. as 'THE WALLFLOWER'> <re-iss. as '. . .(DANCE WITH..)'>*	–	
Apr 55.	(7",78; with the Maxwell Davis Orchestra) *<957>* **HEY, HENRY (DOIN' FINE, HENRY). / BE MINE (BE MY LOVE)**	–	
Jul 55.	(7",78; with the Dreamers) *<962>* **GOOD ROCKIN' DADDY. / CRAZY FEELING**	–	
Oct 55.	(7",78; with the Maxwell Davis Orchestra) *<972>* **THAT'S ALL. / W-O-M-A-N**	–	
Jan 56.	(7",78; with the Flairs) *<984>* **NUMBER ONE (MY ONE AND ONLY). / I'M A FOOL (HOW BIG A FOOL)**	–	
Apr 56.	(7",78) *<988>* **TEARS OF JOY. / SHORTIN' BREAD ROCK**	–	
Jul 56.	(7",78) *<998>* **FOOLS WE MORTAL BE. / TOUGH LOVER**	–	
Oct 56.	(7",78) *<1007>* **THEN I'LL CARE. / GOOD LOOKIN'**	–	
May 57.	(7",78) *<1016>* **THE MARKET PLACE. / THE PICK UP**	–	
Apr 57.	(7",78) *<1022>* **COME WHAT MAY. / BY THE LIGHT OF THE SILVERY MOON**	–	

		not iss.	Kent
Sep 57.	(7",78; with the Flairs) *<304>* **SUNSHINE OF LOVE. / BABY, BABY, EVERY NIGHT**	–	

— In Feb'58, ETTA featured on BETTY & DUPREE's single, 'I Hope You're Satisfied' / 'If It Ain't One Thing' *Kent; <318>*

		not iss.	Kent
Jun 58.	(7") *<345>* **ROLL WITH ME, HENRY. / GOOD ROCKIN' DADDY** *(UK-iss.Feb65 on 'Sue'; WI 359)*	–	
Oct 58.	(7") *<352>* **HOW BIG A FOOL. / GOOD ROCKIN' DADDY**	–	
Feb 59.	(7") *<370>* **GOOD ROCKIN' DADDY. / DO SOMETHING CRAZY**	–	

		London	Argo
Apr 60.	(7") *<5359>* **ALL I COULD DO WAS CRY. / GIRL (BOY) OF MY DREAMS**	–	33
Jun 60.	(7") *(HLM 9139)* **ALL I COULD DO WAS CRY. / TOUGH MARY**		–
Sep 60.	(7") *<5268>* **MY DEAREST DARLING. / TOUGH MARY**	–	34
Nov 60.	(7") *(HLM 9234)* **MY DEAREST DARLING. / GIRL (BOY) OF MY DREAMS**		–

		not iss.	Chess
Jul 60.	(7"; as ETTA & HARVEY) *<1760>* **IF I CAN'T HAVE YOU. / MY HEART CRIES**	–	52
Dec 60.	(7"; as ETTA & HARVEY) *<1771>* **SPOONFUL. / IT'S A CRYING SHAME**	–	78

— HARVEY = HARVEY FUQUA of The MOONGLOWS

Pye Int. Argo

Apr 61. (7") *(7N 25079)* <5380> **AT LAST. / I JUST WANT TO MAKE LOVE TO YOU** [ ] Jan61 [47]

May 61. (7") *(7N 25080)* <5385> **TRUST IN ME. / ANYTHING TO SAY YOU'RE MINE** [ ] Mar61 [30]

Aug 61. (lp; mono/stereo) <LP/+S 4003> **AT LAST!** [–] [68]
– Something's got a hold on me / My dearest darling / At last / Fool that I am / Sunday kind of love / Pushover / All I could do was cry / Stop the wedding / Trust in me / Would it make any difference. *(UK-iss.1967 on 'Chess' diff.tracks; CRL 4524) (re-iss. Oct87 on 'Charly' lp/c; GCH/+K7 8036) (re-iss. Jul90 on 'Chess-MCA' lp/c/cd; CH/+C/D 9266) (cd re-iss. Nov91 as 'AT LAST – THE ORIGINAL CHESS MASTERS' on 'Chess-MCA'; CHLD 19168) (cd re-iss. Mar93 on 'Charly'; CDCD 1053) (cd re-iss. Apr00 on 'Chess'; 112017-2)*

Jun 61. (7") <5390> **FOOL THAT I AM. / DREAM** [–] [50] [55]
(UK-iss.Oct61; 7N 25113)

Jul 61. (7") <5393> **DON'T CRY, BABY. / A SUNDAY KIND OF LOVE** [–] [39]

Oct 61. (7") <5402> **IT'S TOO SOON TO KNOW. / SEVEN DAY FOOL** [–] [54] [95]

Dec 61. (lp; mono/stereo) *(LP/+S 4011)* **THE SECOND TIME AROUND** [–] [ ]
– Plum nuts / I'll dry my tears / Seven day fool / In my diary / Dream / Don't cry baby / Fool that I am / One for my baby / It's too soon to know / Don't get around much more.

Apr 62. (7") *(7N 25131)* <5409> **SOMETHING'S GOT A HOLD ON ME. / WAITING FOR CHARLIE TO COME HOME** [ ] Feb62 [37]

May 62. (lp; mono/stereo) *(LP/+S 4013)* **ETTA JAMES** [–] [ ]
– Let me know / My heart cries / Spoonful / Nobody but you / You can count on me / My dear / Lover's mourn / Waiting for my Charlie to come home / Guess again.

Sep 62. (7") *(7N 25162)* <5418> **STOP THE WEDDING. / STREET OF TEARS** [ ] Jul62 [34]

Nov 62. (7") <5424> **FOOLS RUSH IN. / NEXT DOOR TO THE BLUES** [–] [87] [71]

Dec 62. (lp; mono/stereo) <LP/+S 4018> **SINGS FOR LOVERS** [–] [ ]
– Don't take your love from me / How do you speak to an angel / Fools rush in / Don't blame me / Someone to watch over me / Again / I want to be loved / It could happen to you / These foolish things / Prisoner of love.

Jan 63. (7") <5430> **WOULD IT MAKE ANY DIFFERENCE TO YOU. / HOW DO YOU TALK TO AN ANGEL** [–] [64]

Jun 63. (7") *(7N 25205)* <5437> **PUSHOVER. / I CAN'T HOLD IT ANY MORE** [ ] Apr63 [25]

Aug 63. (7") <5445> **PAY BACK. / BE HONEST WITH ME** [–] [78]

Aug 63. (lp; mono/stereo) <LP/+S 4025> **ETTA JAMES TOP TEN** (compilation) [–] [ ]
– All I could do was cry / My dearest darling / A Sunday kind of love / At last / Fool that I am / Something's got a hold on me / Stop the wedding / Pushover / Would it make any difference to you.

Sep 63. (7") <5452> **TWO SIDES (TO EVERY STORY). / I WORRY BOUT YOU** [–] [63]

Jan 64. (7") <5459> **BABY WHAT YOU WANT ME TO DO. / WHAT I SAY** [–] [82]

Jan 64. (lp; mono/stereo) <LP/+S 4032> **ETTA JAMES ROCKS THE HOUSE (live)** [–] [96]
– Something's got a hold on me / Baby what you want me to do / What I say / Money / Seven day fool / Sweet little angel / Ooh poo pah doo / Woke up this morning. *(UK-iss.1965 on 'Chess'; CRL 4502) (re-iss. 1987 on 'Charly' lp/c; GCH/+K7 8030) (cd-iss. 1992 on 'Chess-MCA'; CHD 9184)*

Apr 64. (7") <5465> **LOVING YOU MORE EVERY DAY. / LOOK WHO'S BLUE** [–] [65]

Jun 64. (7") <5477> **THAT MAN BELONGS BACK HERE WITH ME. / BREAKING POINT** [–] [ ]

Dec 64. (7") <5485> **MELLOW FELLOW. / BOBBY IS HIS NAME** [–] [ ]

Jan 65. (lp; mono/stereo) <LP/+S 4040> **QUEEN OF SOUL** [–] [ ]
– Flight 101 / You better do right / I worry 'bout you / Lovin' you more every day / I wish someone would care / That man belongs back here with me / Breaking point / Somewhere out there / Mellow fellow / Bobby is his name.

Chess Cadet

Dec 65. (7"; with Sugar Pie DeSanto) *(CRS 8025)* <5519> **DO I MAKE MYSELF CLEAR. / SOMEWHERE DOWN THE LINE** [ ] [96]

Feb 66. (7") <5526> **ONLY TIME WILL TELL. / I'M SORRY FOR YOU** [–] [ ]

Aug 66. (7"; with Sugar Pie DeSanto) <5539> **IN THE BASEMENT (part 1). / (part 2 by DeSANTO)** [–] [97]

Jan 67. (7") *(CRS 8052)* <5552> **I PREFER YOU. / I'M SO GLAD** [ ] Nov66 [ ]

Feb 67. (lp; mono/stereo) <LP/+S 4055> **CALL MY NAME** [–] [ ]
– Happiness / I prefer you / I'm so glad (I found love in you) / Nobody like you / That's all I want from you / It must be your love / Have faith in me / 842-3089 (Call my name) / Nobody loves me / Don't pick me for your fool / It's all right / You are my sunshine.

Apr 67. (7") <5564> **IT MUST ME YOUR LOVE. / DON'T TAKE ME FOR YOUR FOOL** [–] [ ]

Sep 67. (7") <5568> **842-3089 (CALL MY NAME). / HAPPINESS** [–] [ ]

Nov 67. (7") *(CRS 8063)* <5578> **TELL MAMA. / I'D RATHER GO BLIND** [ ] [23]

Feb 68. (7") *(CRS 8069)* <5594> **SECURITY. / I'M GONNA TAKE WHAT HE'S GOT** [ ] [35]

May 68. (lp) *(CRL 4536)* <802> **TELL MAMA** [ ] Aug67 [82]
– Tell mama / I'd rather go blind / Watchdog / The love of my man / I'm gonna take what he's got / The same rope / Security / Steal away / My mother in law / Don't lose your good thing / It hurts me so much / Just a little bit. *(cd-iss. Oct88 on 'Charly'; CDRED 7) (re-iss. May90 on 'Chess-MCA' lp/c/cd; CH/+C/D 9269) (cd re-iss. Apr92 on 'Chess-MCA'; CHLD 19035)*

Jul 68. (7") *(CRS 8076)* <5606> **I GOT YOU BABE. / I WORSHIP THE GROUND YOU WALK ON** [ ] May69 [69]

Sep 68. (7") *(CRS 8082)* <5620> **YOU GOT IT. / FIRE** [ ] [ ]

Jan 69. (7") <5630> **ALMOST PERSUADED. / STEAL AWAY** [–] [79]

Aug 69. (7") <5655> **MISS PITIFUL. / BOBBY IS HIS NAME** [–] [ ]

Jan 70. (7") <5664> **WHAT FOOLS WE MORTALS BE. / TIGHTEN UP YOUR OWN THING** [–] [ ]

Jan 70. (lp) <832> **ETTA JAMES SINGS FUNK** [–] [ ]
– Tighten up your own thing / Quick reaction and satisfaction / Nothing from nothing leaves nothing / Your replacement / The sound of love / What fools we mortals be / My man is together / Sweet memories / The man I love / Are my thoughts with you / When I stop dreaming.

Mar 70. (7") <5671> **THE SOUND OF LOVE. / WHEN I STOP DREAMING** [–] [ ]

Oct 70. (7") <5676> **LOSERS WEEPERS – PART 1. / WEEPERS** [–] [94]

Jan 71. (lp) <847> **LOSERS WEEPERS** [–] [ ]
– Losers weepers / I got it bad / For all we know / Someone / You're the fool / Ease away a little bit at a time / Take out some insurance / I think it's you / Hold back my tears / Look at the rain / Love of my man / Weepers.

Chess Chess

1971. (7") <2100> **THE LOVE OF MY MAN. / NOTHING FROM NOTHING LEAVES NOTHING** [–] [ ]

1971. (7") <2112> **I THINK IT'S YOU. / TAKE OUT SOME INSURANCE** [–] [ ]

May 72. (7") <2125> **I FOUND A LOVE. / NOTHING FROM NOTHING LEAVES NOTHING** [–] [ ]

Aug 72. (7") <2128> **TELL IT LIKE IT IS. / W.O.M.A.N.** [–] [ ]

1972. (7"m) *(6145 016)* **TELL MAMA. / I'D RATHER GO BLIND / I FOUND A LOVE** [ ] [–]

Sep 73. (7") <2144> **ALL THE WAY DOWN. / LAY BACK DADDY** [–] [ ]

Sep 73. (lp) <50042> **ETTA JAMES** [–] [ ]
– All the way down / God's song / Only a fool / Down so low / Leave your hat on / Sail away / Yesterday's music / Lay back daddy / Just one more day.

Mar 74. (7") <2148> **LEAVE YOUR HAT ON. / ONLY A FOOL** [–] [ ]

Aug 74. (7") *(6145 033)* <2153> **OUT ON THE STREET, AGAIN. / COME A LITTLE CLOSER** [ ] [ ]

Aug 74. (lp) <60029> **COME A LITTLE CLOSER** [–] [ ]
– Power play / Feeling uneasy / St. Louis blues / Gonna have some fun tonight / Sooki sooki / Out on the street again / Mama told me / You give me what I want / Come a little closer / Let's burn down the cornfield. *(UK-iss.May88 on 'Charly' lp/c; GCH/+K7 8047) (cd-iss. Apr97 on 'Chess-MCA'; MCD 91509)*

Dec 75. (7") <2171> **LOVIN' ARMS. / TAKE OUT SOME INSURANCE** [–] [ ]

Dec 75. (lp) *<19003>* **ETTA IS BETTA THAN EVVAH!** [–] [ ]

Jul 76. (7") *<30001>* **JUMP INTO LOVE. / I'VE BEEN A FOOL** [–] [ ]

Warners Warners

Jul 78. (7") *(K 17173) <8545>* **PIECE OF MY HEART. / LOVESICK BLUES** [ ] May78 [ ]

Jul 78. (lp/c) *(K/K4 56492) 3156>* **DEEP IN THE NIGHT** [ ] [ ]
– Laying beside you / Piece of my heart / Only women bleed / Take it to the limit / Lovesick blues / Strange man / Sugar on the floor / Sweet touch of love / I'd rather go blind. *(cd-iss. Jun96 on 'Bullseye'; CDBB 9579)*

Sep 78. (7") *(K 17224)* **TAKE IT TO THE LIMIT. / STRANGE MAN** [ ] [–]

Jan 79. (7") *<8611>* **SUGAR ON THE FLOOR. / LOVESICK BLUES** [–] [ ]

not iss. T-Electric

1980. (7") **MEAN MOTHER. / IT TAKES LOVE TO KEEP A WOMAN** [–] [ ]

not iss. M.C.A.

1980. (lp) *<3244>* **CHANGES** [–] [ ]
– Mean mother / Donkey / Changes / Don't stop / Who's getting your love / Night by night / It takes love to keep a woman / Wheel of fire / Night people / With you in mind.

Fantasy not iss.

Nov 86. (lp/c; by ETTA JAMES & EDDIE 'CLEANHEAD' VINSON) *(F/SF 9647)* **BLUES IN THE NIGHT (live at Maula's club, LA)** [ ] [–]
– Kidney stew / Railroad porter blues / Something's got a hold on me / At last – Trust in me – Sunday kind of love / I just want to make love to you / Please send me someone to love / Lover man (oh where can you be) / Misty. *(cd-iss. Apr94 as 'BLUES IN THE NIGHT VOL.1 – THE EARLY SHOW'; FCD 9647-2)*

Island Island

Mar 89. (lp/c/cd) *(ILPS/ICT/CID 9923)* **SEVEN YEAR ITCH** [ ] [ ]
– I got the will / Jump into fire / Shakey ground / Come to mama / Damn your eyes / Breakin' up somebody's home / The jealous kind / How strong is a woman? / It ain't always what you do (it's who you let see you do it) / One night.

—— In May'89, she was credited on DAVID A. STEWART's single 'Avenue D'

Jul 89. (7") *(IS 418)* **I GOT THE WILL. / ONE NIGHT** [ ] [–]
(10"+=/cd-s+=) *(10IS/CID 418)* – Come to mama.

Apr 90. (cd/c/lp) *(CID/ICT/ILPS 9955)* **STICKIN' TO MY GUNS** [ ] [ ]
– Whatever gets you through the night / Love to burn / The blues don't care / Your good thing (is about to end) / Get funky / Beware / Out of the rain / Stolen affection / A fool in love / I've got dreams to remember. *(re-iss. cd Aug94; IMCD 191)*

—— next featured STEVE CROPPER + STEVE WINWOOD + STEVE FERRONE

Elektra Elektra

Oct 92. (cd) *<(7559 61347-2)>* **THE RIGHT TIME** [ ] [ ]
– Give it up / Down home blues / Love and happiness / I sing the blues / Evening of love / Wet match / You're taking up another man's place / Let it rock / Ninety-nine and a half (won't do) / You've got me / Night time is the right time (with ERIC BURDON).

Private Private

Apr 94. (cd) *<(1005 82114-2)>* **MYSTERY LADY – THE SONGS OF BILLIE HOLIDAY** [ ] [ ]
– Don't explain / You've changed / I don't stand a ghost of a chance (with you) / Embraceable you / How deep is the ocean / (I'm afraid) The masquerade is over / Body and soul / The very thought of you / Lover man (oh where can you be) / I'll be seeing you.

Jun 95. (cd) *<1005 82128-2>* **TIME AFTER TIME** [–] [ ]
– Don't go to strangers / Teach me tonight / Love is here to stay / The nearness of you / Time after time / My funny valentine / Everybody's somebody's fool / Fool that I am / Willow weep for me / Imagination / Night and day / Someone to watch over me.

Apr 97. (cd) *<(1005 82140-2)>* **LOVE'S BEEN ROUGH ON ME** [ ] [ ]
– The rock / Cry like a rainy day / Love's been rough on me / Love it or leave it alone / Don't touch me / Hold me / If I had any pride left at all / I can give you everything / I've been loving you too long / Done in the dark.

Jul 98. (cd) *<(1005 82162-2)>* **LIFE, LOVE AND THE BLUES** [ ] [ ]
– Born under a bad sign / I want to ta ta you baby / Running out of lies / Inner city blues / Spoonful / Life, love and the blues / Hoochie coochie gal / Cheating in the nest room / If you want to stay / Love you save me be your own / I'll take care of you / Here I am (come and take me).

Oct 98. (cd) *<1005 82166-2>* **12 SONGS OF CHRISTMAS** (festive) [–] [ ]

Jun 00. (cd) *<1005 82180-2>* **HEART OF A WOMAN** [–] [ ]
– You don't know what love is / Good morning heartache / My old flame / Say it isn't so / At last / Tenderly / I only have eyes for you / I got it bad and that ain't good / You go to my head / Sunday kind of love / If it's the last thing I do / Only women bleed.

Jun 01. (cd) *<(74321 85860-2)>* **MATRIARCH OF THE BLUES** [ ] Dec00 [ ]
– Gotta serve somebody / Don't let my baby ride / Rhymes / Try a little tenderness / Miss you / Hawg for ya / You're gonna make me cry / Walking the back streets / Let's straighten it out / Born on the bayou / Come back baby / Hound dog.

Aug 01. (cd) *<01934 11580-2>* **BLUE GARDENIA** [–] [ ]
– The bitter earth / He's funny that way / In my solitude / There is no greater love / Don't let the sun catch you crying / Love letters / These foolish things / Come rain or come shine / Don't worry 'bout me / Cry me a river / Don't blame me / My man / Blue gardenia. *(UK-iss.Jun03; same as US)*

May 02. (cd; as ETTA JAMES & THE ROOTS BAND) *<01934 11633-2>* **BURNIN' DOWN THE HOUSE (live December 2001)** [–] [ ]
– Introduction / Come to mama / I just want to make love to you – Born to be / I'd rather go blind / All the way down / At last / You can leave your hat on / Something's got a hold on me / Your good thing (is about to end) / Rock me baby / Love and happiness – Take me to the river – My funny valentine / Sugar on the floor.

May 03. (cd) *<01934 11646-2>* **LET'S ROLL** [–] [ ]
– Somebody to love / The blues is my business / Leap of faith / Strongest weakness / Wayward saints of Memphis / Lie no better / Trust yourself / A change is gonna do me good / Old weakness / Stacked deck / On the 7th day / Please, no more.

– (selective) compilations, etc. –

1961. (lp) *Crown; <CLP 5209>* **MISS ETTA JAMES** [–] [ ]
<re-iss. 1962; same diff cover> <re-iss. 1964 mono/stereo; red on 'Kent'; KLP 5000 / KST 500>

1962. (lp) *Crown; <CLP 5234>* **THE BEST OF ETTA JAMES** [–] [ ]
<re-iss. 1963 on 'United'; 7727>

1962. (lp) *Crown; <CLP 5250>* **TWIST WITH ETTA JAMES** [–] [ ]

1962. (lp) *United; <7712>* **ETTA JAMES SINGS** [–] [ ]

1973. (d-lp) *Chess; (6671 003) <2CH 60004>* **PEACHES** [ ] [ ]
– Lovin' you more every day / I'd rather go blind / Only time will tell / At last / All I could do was cry / Stop the wedding / Two sides (to every story) / Pushover / Losers weepers / Security / Tell mama / Something's got a hold on me / A Sunday kind of love / Next door to the blues / Trust in me / Would it make any difference to you / My dearest darling / 842-3089 (call my name) / Baby what you want me to do / Don't take me for your fool / Pay back / You got it / Tighten up your own thing.

Feb 94. (cd) *Charly; (CPCD 8017)* **THE SOULFUL MISS PEACHES** [ ] [–]

Apr 94. (cd) *Fantasy; (FCD 9655)* **BLUES IN THE NIGHT VOL.2 – THE LATE SHOW WITH EDDIE 'CLEANHEAD' VINSON** [ ] [–]
– Cleanhead blues / Old maid boogie / Home boy / Cherry red / Baby what you want me to do / Sweet little angel / I'd rather go blind / Teach me tonight / Only women bleed / He's got the whole world in his hands.

Apr 94. (cd) *That's Soul; (TS 21)* **MISS PEACHES SINGS THE SOUL** [ ] [–]

Apr 94. (cd) *Charly; (CDRB 3)* **SOMETHING'S GOT A HOLD** [ ] [–]

Jul 94. (cd) *Tomato; (598.1099.20) <R2 7174-2>* **ETTA JAMES LIVE (live)** [ ] [ ]

Feb 95. (cd) *Private Music; <(1005 82125-2)>* **LIVE FROM SAN FRANCISCO (live 1981)** [ ] [ ]

Jun 95. (cd) *Chess-MCA; <(CHD 9354)>* **THESE FOOLISH THINGS – THE CLASSIC BALLADRY OF ETTA JAMES** [ ] [ ]

Nov 95. (cd) *<(SFWCD 45045)>* **MULTI-CULTURAL CHILDREN'S SONGS** [ ] [ ]

Jan 96. (c-s) *Chess-MCA; (MCSC 48003)* **I JUST WANT TO MAKE LOVE TO YOU / TELL MAMA** [5] [ ]
(cd-s+=) *(MCSTD 48003)* – Stormy weather.

Feb 96. (cd) *Chess-MCA; (CHD 9361)* **THE GENUINE ARTICLE – THE BEST OF ETTA JAMES** [ ] [ ]
– I just want to make love to you / Sunday kind of love / I just want to be loved / I'd rather go blind / Tell mama / Stormy weather / Do right woman do right man / Security / Miss Pitiful / You got it / It's alright / I found a love / At last / All I could do was cry / Spoonful (with HARVEY FUQUA) /

Don't blame me / 842 3089 (call my name) / These foolish things / If I can't have you (with HARVEY FUQUA) / Something's got a hold on me / Tell it like it is / W-O-M-A-N / I never meant to love him / Loving arms / My dearest darling.

Apr 96. (cd) *I.M.P.; (IMP 304)* **RESPECT YOURSELF** –
Jul 97. (cd) *Chess-MCA; (MCD 09367)* **HER BEST**
Mar 98. (cd) *Ace-Charly; (CDCHM 680)* **HICKORY DICKORY DOCK** –
Jul 00. (3xcd-box) *Universal; <(AA 88112288-2)>* **THE CHESS BOX**

JAMES GANG

Formed: Cleveland, Ohio, USA . . . 1967 by JIM FOX, TOM KRISS and GLENN SCHWARTZ, taking the name from the legendary outlaw gang. When the latter left to join the group, PACIFIC GAS & ELECTRIC, he was replaced by guitarist JOE WALSH (future EAGLES strummer). Late in '69, the JAMES GANG debut set, 'YER' ALBUM', was complete, the record breaking into the US Top 100. A wholesome serving of earthy mid-Western hard-rock revered by PETE TOWNSHEND, the "Pinball Wizard" was so impressed by WALSH's PAGE-esque axe-grinding, he invited them to support The WHO on a European tour. On his return to the States, WALSH witnessed the killings of four students on the campus of his old university of Kent State, Ohio (4th of May, 1970 – he was later to campaign vigorously for a memorial). With DALE PETERS replacing KRISS, they released their follow-up album, 'RIDES AGAIN', which boasted a minor hit single, 'FUNK 49', a sequel to 'FUNK NO.48', from the first album. Two more Top 30 gold-selling sets followed in quick succession, before WALSH took his not inconsiderable talents to an extremely fruitful solo career. It took two people to replace him, Canadians DOMENIC TROIANO on guitar and ROY KENNER on vocals. The resulting WALSH-less output was found lacking, two albums 'STRAIGHT SHOOTER' (1972) and 'PASSIN' THRU' (1973) not a patch on their earlier work. Following the subsequent departure of TROIANO, guitar prodigy TOMMY BOLIN was secured as a replacement on the recommendation of WALSH. Despite BOLIN's talent, a further two lacklustre albums continued to disappoint all but the most loyal fans, the guitarist soon poached by the revamped DEEP PURPLE. This finally brought about the 'GANG's demise, although FOX and PETERS resurrected the band with two newcomers, BUBBA KEITH and RICHARD SHACK for a couple of forgettable albums. • **Songwriters:** WALSH – KRISS to WALSH-PETERS to group compositions. Covered; CAST YOUR FATE TO THE WIND (Guaraldi-Werber) / STOP (Ragavoy-Schean) / YOU'RE GONNA NEED ME (B.B. King) / LOST WOMAN (Yardbirds) / BLUEBIRD (Buffalo Springfield) / etc.

Album rating: YER' ALBUM (*6) / THE JAMES GANG RIDES AGAIN (*8) / THIRDS (*6) / JAMES GANG LIVE IN CONCERT (*5) / STRAIGHT SHOOTER (*4) / PASSIN' THRU (*4) / THE BEST OF THE JAMES GANG FEATURING JOE WALSH compilation (*7) / 16 GREATEST HITS compilation (*7) / BANG (*4) / MIAMI (*4) / NEWBORN (*4) / JESSE COME HOME (*3) / THE TRUE STORY OF THE JAMES GANG compilation (*7)

JOE WALSH (b.20 Nov'47, Wichita, Kansas, USA) – guitar, vocals; repl. GLEN SCHWARTZ who joined PACIFIC GAS & ELECTRIC / **TOM KRISS** – bass, vocals / **JIM FOX** – drums, vocals

Stateside Bluesway

Sep 69. (7") *<61027>* **I DON'T HAVE THE TIME. / FRED** –
Nov 69. (lp) *(SSL 10295) <6034>* **YER' ALBUM** Oct69 83
– Tuning part one / Take a look around / Funk #48 / Bluebird / Lost woman / Stone rap / Collage / I don't have the time / a) Wrapcity in English, b) Fred / Stop. *(re-iss. Oct90 on 'Beat Goes On'; BGOCD 60)*

Jan 70. (7") *(SS 2158) <61030>* **FUNK #48. / COLLAGE** Nov69
Jun 70. (7") *(SS 2173) <61033>* **STOP. / TAKE A LOOK AROUND**

— **DALE PETERS** – bass, vocals repl. KRISS

Probe A.B.C.

Aug 70. (7") *(PRO 502) <11272>* **FUNK #49. / THANKS** 59
Oct 70. (lp) *(SPBA 6253) <711>* **JAMES GANG RIDES AGAIN** Jul70 20
– Funk #49 / Asshtonpark / Woman / The bomber: (a) Closet queen – (b) Cast your fate to the wind / Tend my garden / Garden gate / There I go again / Thanks / Ashes the rain and I. *(re-iss. Oct74; 5009) <cd-iss. Jun88; 31145> (cd-iss. Sep91 on 'Beat Goes On'; BGOCD 121)*
Apr 71. (7") *(PRO 533) <11301>* **WALK AWAY. / YADIG?** 51
Jul 71. (lp) *(SPB 1038) <721>* **THIRDS** Apr71 27
– Walk away / Yadig? / Things I could be / Dreamin' in the country / It's all the same / Midnight man / Again / White man – black man / Live my life again. *(cd-iss. Sep91 on 'Beat Goes On'; BGOCD 119)*
Oct 71. (7") *<11312>* **MIDNIGHT MAN. / WHITE MAN – BLACK MAN** – 80
Dec 71. (lp) *(SPB 1045) <733>* **JAMES GANG LIVE IN CONCERT (live)** Sep71 24
– Stop / You're gonna need me / Take a look around / Tend my garden / Ashes, the rain & I / Walk away / Lost woman. *(cd-iss. Sep91 on 'Beat Goes On'; BGOCD 120)*

— **DOMENIC TROIANO** (b. Canada) – guitar, vocals repl. WALSH went solo / added **ROY KENNER** – vocals

Apr 72. (7") *<11325>* **LOOKING FOR MY LADY. / HAIRY HYPOCHONDRIAC** –
Jul 72. (lp) *(SPB 1056) <741>* **STRAIGHT SHOOTER** Mar72 58
– Madness / Kick back man / Get her back again / Looking for my lady / Getting old / I'll tell you why / Hairy hypochondriac / Let me come home / My door is open.
Jul 72. (7") *<11336>* **KICK BACK MAN. / HAD ENOUGH** –
Oct 72. (lp) *(SPB 1065) <760>* **PASSIN' THRU** 72
– Ain't seen nothin' yet / One way street / Had enough / Up to yourself / Every day needs a hero / Run, run, run / Things I want to say to you / Out of control / Drifting girl.

Atlantic Atco

Dec 73. (lp) *(K 50028) <SD 7039>* **BANG**
– Standing in the rain / The Devil is singing our song / Must be love / Alexis / Ride the wind / Got no time for trouble / Rather be alone with you / From another time / Mystery.
Jan 74. (7") *(K 10432) <6953>* **MUST BE LOVE. / GOT NO TIME FOR TROUBLES** 54
Apr 74. (7") *<6966>* **STANDING IN THE RAIN. / FROM ANOTHER TIME** –

— **TOMMY BOLIN** (b.1951, Sioux City, Iowa) – guitar (ex-ENERGY, ex-ZEPHYR) repl. TROIANO (to GUESS WHO)

Aug 74. (7") *<7006>* **CRUISIN' DOWN THE HIGHWAY. / MIAMI TWO-STEP** –
Sep 74. (lp) *(K 50028) <9739>* **MIAMI** 97
– Cruisin' down the highway / Do it / Wildfire / Sleepwalker / Miami two-step / Red skies / Spanish lover / Summer breezes / Head above the water.

— **PETERS + FOX** recruited **RICHARD SHACK** – guitar repl. KENNER **BUBBA KEITH** – vocals, guitar repl. BOLIN who joined DEEP PURPLE, then went solo (he died on the 4th December '76)

— added **DAVID BRIGGS** – keyboards

May 75. (7") *<7021>* **MERRY GO ROUND. / RED SATIN LOVER** –
May 75. (lp) *(K 50148) <36112>* **NEWBORN**
– Merry-go-round / Gonna get by / Earthshaker / All I have / Watch it / Driftin' dreamer / Shoulda' seen your face / Come with me / Heartbreak Hotel / Red satin lover / Cold wind.

— **BOB WEBB** – vocals, guitar / **PHIL GIALLOMARDO** – keyboards, vocals / **FLACO PADRON** – percussion repl. BUBBA, RICHARD + DAVID

Feb 76. (7") *<7067>* **I NEED LOVE. / FEELIN' ALRIGHT** –
Feb 76. (lp) *<36141>* **JESSE COME HOME** –
– I need love / Another year / Feelin' alright / Pleasant song / Hollywood dream / Love hurts / Pick up the pizzas / Stealin' the show / When I was a sailor.

— Disbanded later in 1976.

– compilations, others –

Jan 73. (lp) *Probe; (1070) / A.B.C.; <774>* **THE BEST OF THE JAMES GANG FEATURING JOE WALSH** [ ] [79]
– Walk away / Funk #49 / Midnight man / The bomber: (a) Closet queen – (b) Cast your fate to the wind / Yadig? / Take a look around / Funk No.48 / Woman / Ashes the rain and I / Stop. *(re-iss. Oct74; 5027) (re-iss. Oct81 on 'M.C.A.'; 1615) (cd-iss. Nov02 on 'Repertoire'; REP 4671)*

Dec 73. (d-lp) *A.B.C.; <801-2>* **16 GREATEST HITS** [-] [ ]

Mar 87. (lp) *See For Miles; (SEE 88)* **THE TRUE STORY OF THE JAMES GANG** [ ] [-]
(cd-iss. Mar93; SEECD 367) – (with . . . PLUS tracks)

—— (also some JAMES GANG tracks on May'94 release, 'ALL THE BEST' by JOE WALSH & THE JAMES GANG)

□ JAMIE WEDNESDAY (see under ⇒ CARTER THE UNSTOPPABLE SEX MACHINE)

JAMIROQUAI

Formed: /based Ealing, London . . . early 1991, by the youthful, JASON KAY (aka JAY K). After scoring a minor hit on Eddie Pillar's 'Acid Jazz' label, with his debut single, 'WHEN YOU GONNA LEARN?', JAMIROQUAI switched labels to 'Sony Soho Square', the label no doubt hoping to cash in on the super-hip Acid Jazz scene which had already seen The BRAND NEW HEAVIES reap financial rewards for 'London' records, especially in the lucrative American market. And cash in on it they did; where Acid Jazz had once been the preserve of a London clique, JAY K sold the concept nationwide. The image was calculated but perfect; Adidas Gazelles, 70's cords, ethnic hats and funky soul-boy footwork. Vocally, the comparisons with STEVIE WONDER were unavoidable, all 'doo-doo-da-doo-doo' flourishes which seemed irreconcilable with a skinny white kid from London. 'TOO YOUNG TO DIE', his first effort for 'Sony', went Top 10, the debut album, 'EMERGENCY ON PLANET EARTH' (1993) reaching No.1 later that summer. Spontaneous, irresistibly funky and musically accomplished, what the record lacked in originality, it made up for with brazen charm. The only thing that indicated the album had been recorded in the 90's was the lavish use of digeridoo, although this added novelty value rather then any real innovation. Lyrically, the record was a platform for JAY's unceasingly positive guide to life and his often naive, if well meaning, political and ecological diatribes. In interviews and on stage, JAY's charisma was undeniable, rebuffing charges of being contrived with a cocksure cheekiness. By 'THE RETURN OF THE SPACE COWBOY' (1994) the image was still intact, it was just a case of different album, different hat. As well as cornering the money-spinning pop/teen market, the DAVID MORALES mix of the title track was a massive European club hit, further boosting sales of the album. Musically, the record more or less stuck to the same formula although there were signs of a growing maturity in JK's songwriting and lyrics. 'TRAVELLING WITHOUT MOVING' (1996) saw JAMIROQUAI consolidate their position as purveyors of reliable, chart-friendly pop-funk while JK has become as much of a 90's icon as OASIS, if a bit more stylish. Now "lord of the manor" in a Buckinghamshire country estate (he also owns a number of sports cars, etc.) and the beau of Big Breakfast starlet, Denise Van Outen, JASON KAY was back to what he knows best, writing songs; a new song from the 'Godzilla' movie, 'DEEPER UNDERGROUND' was his return to No.1. 'SYNKRONIZED' (1999) was JAMIROQUAI's fourth album in six years, although the slickness of JAY K's retro persona was wearing a little thin. Nevertheless, the album shot to the top of the UK charts (his first since his debut!) and produced three further hits, 'CANNED HEAT', 'SUPERSONIC' and 'KING FOR A DAY'. The man in the silly hat returned in 2001 with 'A FUNK ODYSSEY', sounding more and more like STEVIE WONDER with each album. The set, mostly based on the group's strained attempts at disco/funk, entered the UK charts at No.1 and the US Billboard's Top 50. It also reaped in the cash for JK and Co via the singles 'LITTLE L' and the estranged, break-up track 'YOU GIVE ME SOMETHING' both reaching the UK Top 10 and being shoved down the public's throats by repeated plays on MTV, etc. • **Songwriters:** JAY and TOBY are main writers, although ZENDER, McKENZIE and others contribute. • **Trivia:** Pronounced JAM-EAR-OH-KWAI, they took name from a tribe of Native Americans.

Album rating: EMERGENCY ON PLANET EARTH (*9) / RETURN OF THE SPACE COWBOY (*7) / TRAVELLING WITHOUT MOVING (*7) / SYNKRONIZED (*6) / A FUNK ODYSSEY (*5)

JAY K (b. JASON KAY, 30 Sep'69, Stretford, Lancashire, England) – vocals / **TOBY SMITH** (b. TOBY GRAFFETY-SMITH, 29 Oct'70) – keyboards / **NICK VAN GELDER** – drums / **STUART ZENDER** (b.18 Mar'74, Philadelphia, Pennsylvania, USA) – bass / **WALLIS BUCHANAN** (b.29 Nov'65) – didgeridoo / plus **KOFI KARIKARI** – percussion / **MAURIZIO RAVALIO** – percussion / **GLENN NIGHTINGALE + SIMON BARTHOLOMEW** – guitars / **D-ZIRE** – DJ / **GARY BARNACLE** – sax, flute / **JOHN THIRKELL** – trumpet, flugel horn / **RICHARD EDWARDS** – trombone

Acid Jazz — not iss.

Oct 92. (12") *(JAZID 46T)* **WHEN YOU GONNA LEARN (JK mix & instrumental). / WHEN YOU GONNA LEARN (mixes; Cante Hondo / original demo / Digeridoo instrumental)** [52] [-]
(re-iss. Feb93 hit No.69)
(cd-s+=) *(JAZID 46CD)* – ('A'-digeridon't mix).

Sony S2 — Epic

Mar 93. (12") *(659011-6)* **TOO YOUNG TO DIE (mixes; extended / original / instrumental)** [12] [-]
(cd-s+=) *(659011-2)* – ('A'edit).

May 93. (c-s) *(659297-4)* **BLOW YOUR MIND (part 1) / HOOKED UP** [10] [-]
(12"+=) *(659297-6)* – Blow your mind (part 2).
(cd-s++=) *(659297-2)* – When you gonna learn (JK mix).

Jun 93. (cd/c/lp) *(474069-2/-4/-2)* **EMERGENCY ON PLANET EARTH** [1] [ ]
– When you gonna learn (digeridoo) / Too young to die / Hooked up / If I like it, I do it / Music of the mind / Emergency on Planet Earth / Whatever it is, I just can't stop / Blow your mind / Revolution 1993 / Didgin' out.

Aug 93. (12"/c-s/cd-s) *(659578-6/-4/-2)* **EMERGENCY ON PLANET EARTH. / IF I LIKE IT, I DO IT (MTV acoustic) / REVOLUTION 1993 (demo)** [32] [ ]

Sep 93. (c-s) *(659695-6)* **WHEN YOU GONNA LEARN (Digeridoo). / DIDGIN' OUT (live at the Milky Way, Amsterdam)** [28] [ ]
(cd-s+=) *(659695-2)* – Too young to die (live) / ('A'-Cante Hondo mix).
(12") *(659695-6) <74925>* – ('A'mixes from 'Acid Jazz').

—— **DERRICK McKENZIE** (b.27 Mar'62, Islington, London) – drums; repl. VAN GELDER

Sep 94. (12") *(660851-6)* **SPACE COWBOY. / JOURNEY TO ARNHEMLAND / SPACE COWBOY – STONED AGAIN** [17] [ ]
(cd-s) *(660851-2)* – (first two tracks) / Kids / ('A'demo).
(cd-s/12") *<77827+1>* – (6-'A'versions).

Oct 94. (cd/c/d-lp) *(477813-2/-4/-1)* **THE RETURN OF THE SPACE COWBOY** [2] [ ]
– Just another story / Stillness in time / Half the man / Light years / Manifest destiny / The kids / Mr. Moon / Scam / Journey to Arnhemland / Morning glory / Space cowboy. *(cd re-iss. Dec01; same)*

Nov 94. (c-s) *(661003-4)* **HALF THE MAN / SPACE CLAV** [15] [-]
(12"+=/cd-s+=) *(661003-6/-2)* – Emergency on Planet Earth.
(cd-s) *(661003-5)* – ('A'side) / Jamiroquai's Greatest Hits: When you gonna learn? / Too young to die / Blow your mind.

Feb 95. (c-s) *(661256-4)* **LIGHT YEARS / JOURNEY TO ARNHEMLAND (live)** [ ] [-]
(ext-12"+=) *(661256-6)* – Light years (live).
(cd-s+=) *(661256-2)* – Scan / We gettin' down.

Jun 95. (12"/cd-s) *(662025-6/-2)* **STILLNESS IN TIME. / SPACE COWBOY (mix)** [9] [ ]
(cd-s+=) *(662025-5)* – Emergency on Planet Earth / Light years.

— In Jun'96, JAMIROQUAI featured on M-BEAT's No.12 hit version of 'DO U KNOW WHERE YOU'RE COMING FROM'.

Aug 96. (7") *(663613-7)* **VIRTUAL INSANITY. / ('A'-Unreality mix)** [3] [–]
(c-s+=) *(663613-4)* – ('A'-album mix).
(12"/cd-s) *(663613-6/-2)* – ('A'side) / Do you know where you're coming from / Bullet / ('A'-album version).
(cd-s) *(663613-5)* – ('A'side) / Space cowboy (classic radio) / Emergency on Planet Earth (London-Rican mix) / Do you know where you're coming from.

Sep 96. (cd/c/lp) *(483999-2/-4/-1)* *<67903>* **TRAVELLING WITHOUT MOVING** [2] [24]
– Virtual insanity / Cosmic girl / Use the force / Everyday / Alright / High times / Drifting along / Didjerama / Didjital vibrations / Travelling without moving / You are my love / Spend a lifetime. *(cd+=)* – (bonus track).

Nov 96. (7"/c-s) *(663829-7/-4)* **COSMIC GIRL / SLIPIN 'N' SLIDIN'** [6] [ ]
(cd-s+=) *(663829-2)* – Didjital vibrations / ('A'-classic radio).
(12"/cd-s) *(663829-6/-5)* *<78501-2>* – ('A'mixes; radio / classic / Quasar / dub).

May 97. (cd-s) *(664235-2)* *<78703>* **ALRIGHT (mixes; radio / vocal version / dub vocal / DJ version excursion)** [6] Sep97 [78]
(cd-s) *(664235-5)* – ('A'mixes; extended / Tee's In House / Tee's Digital club / Tee's radio Jay).
(12") *(664235-6)* – ('A'-version vocal & Tee's In House mix) / Space cowboy (classic club) / Cosmic girl (classic mix).
(d12") *<786591>* – (7 version incl. above stuff).

Dec 97. (12"/cd-s) *(665370-6/-2)* **HIGH TIMES (mixes; original / Bionic Supachronic / Doobie dub / album or Jamiroquai dub)** [20] [ ]
(cd-s+=) *(665370-5)* – ('A'mixes; incl. Sanchez radio edit).

Jul 98. (c-s) *(666218-4)* **DEEPER UNDERGROUND / DEEPER UNDERGROUND (the metro mix)** [1] [ ]
(cd-s+=) *(666218-2)* – ('A'-instrumental).
(cd-s) *(666218-5)* – ('A'side & mixes; Ummah & S-Man Meets Da Northface Killa dub).
(cd-s+=) *<79032>* – (all above) / High times (album & Doobie dub).

May 99. (c-s) *(667302-4)* *<79189-4/-7>* **CANNED HEAT / WOLF IN SHEEP'S CLOTHING** [4] [ ]
(cd-s+=) *(667302-2)* – ('A'radio edit).
(cd-s) *(667302-5)* – ('A'versions) / Deeper underground (Chillington mix).
(cd-s) *<79162>* – (all above tracks).

Jun 99. (cd/c/lp) *(494517-2/-4/-1)* *<69973>* **SYNKRONIZED** [1] [28]
– Canned heat / Planet home / Black Capricorn day / Soul education / Falling / Destitute illusions / Supersonic / Butterfly / Where do we go from here? / King for a day. *(cd+=)* – Deeper underground. *(cd re-iss. Sep01; same)*

Sep 99. (c-s) *(667839-4)* **SUPERSONIC / SUPERSONIC (album version)** [22] [ ]
(cd-s) *(667839-32)* *<79320><12"=79307>* – ('A'side) / ('A'-Pete Heller – the love mix) / ('A'-Harvey's Fuel altered mix).
(cd-s) *(667839-5)* – ('A'side) / ('A'-Restless Soul main vocal) / ('A'-Sharp Razor remix).

Nov 99. (c-s) *(667973-4)* **KING FOR A DAY / PLANET HOME (Trabant Brothers Inc. remix)** [20] [–]
(cd-s+=) *(667973-2)* – Supersonic (Dirty Rotten Scoundrels mix).
(cd-s) *(667973-5)* – ('A'side) / Canned heat (Shanks & Bigfoot – extended master mix) / Supersonic (edit) / Supersonic (CD-Rom version).

— in Feb'01, JAMIROQUAI featured on JOOLS HOLLAND's UK hit, 'I'm In The Mood For Love'

Aug 01. (c-s) *(671718-4)* **LITTLE L / LITTLE L (wounded buffalo mix)** [5] [–]
(12"+=) *(671718-6)* – ('A'-Bob Sinclair mix) / ('A'-Boris Dlugosch mix).
(cd-s++=) *(671718-2)* – ('A'-video).

Sep 01. (cd/c/lp) *(504069-2/-4/-1)* *<85954>* **A FUNK ODYSSEY** [1] [44]
– Feel so good / Little L / You give me something / Corner of the earth / Love foolosophy / Stop don't panic / Black crow / Main vein / Twenty zero one / Picture of my life. *(UK+=)* – So good to feel real.

Nov 01. (c-s) *(672007-4)* **YOU GIVE ME SOMETHING / DO IT LIKE WE USED TO** [16] [–]
(cd-s) *(672007-2)* – ('A'side) / ('A'-mixes; Blacksmith R&B / Full intention / Cosmos / King Unique).

Feb 02. (cd-s) *(672325-2)* **LOVE FOOLOSOPHY / (Knee Deep remix) / (Bini & Martini's ocean remix) / (original video)** [14] [–]
(cd-s) *(672325-2)* – ('A'side) / (twin club remix) / (Blaze remix) / (alternate video).

Jul 02. (cd-s) *(672788-2)* **CORNER OF THE EARTH / MAIN VEIN (knee deep remix) / MAIN VEIN (deep swing jazzy thumper mix)** [31] [–]
(12"+=) *(672821-6)* – Main vein (knee deep vocal dub).
(cd-s) *(672788-5)* – ('A'side) / Bad girls (with ANASTACIA live at The Brits) / Little L (the making of the video).

JANE'S ADDICTION

Formed: Los Angeles, California, USA . . . 1984 by Miami-raised PERRY FARRELL. The band's debut effort was a self-financed eponymous live album on 'Triple XXX', the record's naked intensity going some way towards capturing FARRELL's skewed musical vision. More successful was the band's debut for 'Warner Brothers', 'NOTHING'S SHOCKING' (1988), a wilfully perverse and eclectic blend of thrash, folk and funk that, musically and lyrically, made L.A.'s cock-rock brigade look like school boys. FARRELL's creepy shrill was something of an acquired taste, although it complemented the abrasive, mantra-like music perfectly, from the juddering 'PIGS IN ZEN' to the bleakly beautiful 'JANE SAYS'. The record courted controversy almost immediately, with its cover art depicting naked siamese twins strapped to an electric chair. Live, the band were just as confrontational, FARRELL stalking the stage like some transexual high priest. 'RITUAL DE LO HABITUAL' (1990) was JANE'S' masterstroke, combining the compelling musical dynamics of the debut with more rhythm and melody. The result was a UK Top 40 hit for 'BEEN CAUGHT STEALING', a funky paeon to the delights of shoplifting. Inevitably, JANE'S ADDICTION incurred, yet again, the wrath of America's moral guardians and the record was banned from several US retail chains. The band replied by re-releasing it in a plain white sleeve with only the First Amendment printed on it. The following year, FARRELL organised the first Lollapalooza tour, a travelling festival of indie, rap and alternative acts. It was while headlining this jaunt that the band reached its messy conclusion, FARRELL eventually coming to blows with guitarist NAVARRO and splitting soon after. While NAVARRO subsequently joined the RED HOT CHILI PEPPERS, FARRELL formed PORNO FOR PYROS with PERKINS and a cast of likeminded musicians. The 1993 eponymous debut was like a more aggressive, less mysterious JANE'S ADDICTION, reaching the Top 5. Following personal problems and a drug bust, the band eventually released a follow-up three years later, 'GOOD GOD'S URGE', a more heavy-lidded, narcotic-centric affair which even featured NAVARRO on one track, 'FREEWAY'. JANE'S ADDICTION have since reformed (with the 'CHILI's FLEA on bass), initially for some live work in 1997, although a handful of new tracks surfaced on the odds'n'sods collection, 'KETTLE WHISTLE'. Towards the end of the millennium, PERRY was back in a solo capacity, the album 'REV' receiving some tender reviews for his er, carnival of sound. The zen-like figure of FARRELL was back in 2001 with the second instalment of his solo career, 'SONG YET TO BE SUNG', a diversion into electronica which almost succeeds in capturing the spirit of global musical enlightenment FARRELL was so obviously after. While fans expecting a return to the serrated alchemy of yore would have been disappointed by 'STRAYS' (2003), JANE'S' first full length studio album in more than a decade, the warped genius of FARRELL was still evident in fits and starts. Hazy and unfocused, the album seemed unable to shake off the sense that it was a continuation of FARRELL's intermittent solo career, especially bearing in mind that AVERY was missing. • **Songwriters:** Group penned, except SYMPATHY FOR THE DEVIL (Rolling Stones). Perry solo covered WHOLE LOTTA LOVE (Led Zeppelin) / TONIGHT (from 'West Side Story') / SATELLITE OF LOVE (Lou Reed) / RIPPLE (Grateful Dead).

Album rating: JANE'S ADDICTION (*7) / NOTHING'S SHOCKING (*8) / RITUAL DE LO HABITUAL (*9) / KETTLE WHISTLE part compilation (*6) / Porno For Pyros: PORNO FOR PYROS (*6) / GOOD GOD'S URGE (*8) / Perry Farrell: REV (*7) / SONG YET TO BE SUNG (*5) / Jane's Addiction: STRAYS (*6)

PERRY FARRELL (b. PERRY BERNSTEIN, 29 Mar'59, Queens, N.Y.) – vocals / **DAVE NAVARRO** (b. 6 Jun'67, Santa Monica, Calif.) – guitar / **ERIC AVERY** (b.25 Apr'65) – bass / **STEPHEN PERKINS** (b.13 Sep'67) – drums

not iss. Triple X

Aug 87. (lp) *<XXX 51004>* **JANE'S ADDICTION (live)** [–] [ ]
– Trip away / Whores / Pigs in Zen / 1% / I would for you / My time / Jane says / Rock'n'roll / Sympathy / Chip away. *<re-iss. Dec88 lp/c/cd; TX 510041 LP/MC/CD> (UK-iss.Dec90 on 'WEA' cd/c/lp; 7599 26599-2/-4/-1)*

Warners Warners

Sep 88. (lp/c)(cd) *(WX 216/+C)(925727-2) <25727>* **NOTHING'S SHOCKING** [ ] [ ]
– Up the beach / Ocean size / Had a dad / Ted, just admit it . . . / Standing in the shower . . . thinking / Summertime rolls / Mountain song / Idiots rule / Jane says / Thank you boys. *(cd+=)* – Pigs in Zen.

Mar 89. (7") *<27520>* **MOUNTAIN SONG. / STANDING IN THE SHOWER . . . THINKING** [–] [ ]

May 89. (7") *(W 7520)* **MOUNTAIN SONG. / JANE SAYS** [ ] [–]
(12"ep+=) **THE SHOCKING EP** *(W 7520T)* – Had a dad (live).

—— added guest **MORGAN** (a female) – violin

Aug 90. (cd)(lp/c) *(7599 25993-2)(WX 306/+C) <25993>* **RITUAL DE LO HABITUAL** [37] [19]
– Stop / No one's leaving / Ain't no right / Obvious / Been caught stealing / Three days / Then she did . . . / Of course / Classic girl.

Aug 90. (7"/c-s) *(W 9584/+C)* **THREE DAYS. / (part 2)** [ ] [ ]
(12"/cd-s) *(W 9584 T/CD)* – ('A'side) / I would for you (demo) / Jane says (demo).

Mar 91. (7"/c-s) *(W 0011/+C) <19574>* **BEEN CAUGHT STEALING. / HAD A DAD (demo)** [34] [ ]
(12"+=/12"box+=/cd-s+=) *(W 0011 T/TB/CD)* – ('A'remix) / L.A. medley:- L.A. woman / Nausea / Lexicon devil.

May 91. (7"/c-s) *(W 0031/+C)* **CLASSIC GIRL. / NO ONE'S LEAVING** [60] [ ]
(12"pic-d+=/cd-s+=) *(W 0031 TP/CD)* – Ain't no right.

—— Had already disbanded when FARRELL looked liked heading into film acting. NAVARRO had briefly filled in for IZZY STRADLIN in GUNS N' ROSES, before joining RED HOT CHILI PEPPERS.

PORNO FOR PYROS

—— **FARRELL + PERKINS** with **PETER DISTEFANO** (b.10 Jul'65) – guitar, samples, vocals / **MARTYN LE NOBLE** (b.14 Apr'69, Vlaardingen, Netherlands) – bass (ex-THELONIUS MONSTER) / and guest **DJ SKATEMASTER TATE** – keyboards, samples

Warners Warners

Apr 93. (cd/c/lp) *<(9362 45228-2/-4/-1)>* **PORNO FOR PYROS** [13] [3]
– Sadness / Porno for pyros / Meija / Cursed female – cursed male / Pets / Badshit / Packin' / • 25 / Black girlfriend / Blood rag / Orgasm.

Jun 93. (7"/c-s) *(W 0177/+C) <18480>* **PETS. / TONIGHT (from 'West Side Story')** [53] [67]
(12"pic-d+=/cd-s+=) *(W 0177 T/CD)* – Cursed female – cursed male (medley).

1994. (cd-s) *<41449>* **SADNESS / A LITTLE SADNESS / COOK THE RICE (live) / PETS (live) / PETE'S DAD (live)** [–] [ ]

—— **MIKE WATT** – bass (ex-fIREHOSE, ex-MINUTEMEN, ex-CICCONE YOUTH) repl. MARTYN (on most)

—— added **THOMAS JOHNSON** – samples, engineer and co-producer

May 96. (cd/c/lp) *<(9362 46126-2/-4/-1)>* **GOOD GOD'S URGE** [40] [20]
– Porpoise head / 100 ways / Tahitian moon / Kimberly Austin / Thick of it all / Good God's:// Urge! / Wishing well / Dogs rule the night / Freeway / Bali eyes.

JANE'S ADDICTION

—— re-formed **PERRY FARRELL / DAVE NAVARRO / STEPHEN PERKINS + FLEA**

Dec 97. (cd/c) *<(9362 46752-2/-4)>* **KETTLE WHISTLE** (4 new + live, demos & out-takes) [ ] Nov97 [21]
– Kettle whistle / Ocean size / Maceo / Hadadad / So what! / Jane says / Mountain song / Slow divers / Three days / Ain't no right / Up the beach / Stop / Been caught stealing / Whores / City.

Sep 99. (cd-s) *<44709-2>* **SO WHAT! (The Deep Red remixes)** [–] [ ]

PERRY FARRELL

with **STEPHEN PERKINS, KARL LEIKER + BRENDAN HAWKINS**

Warners Warners

Nov 99. (cd/c) *<(9362 47544-2/-4)>* **REV** (part comp) [ ] [ ]
– Rev / Whole lotta love / Been caught stealing / Jane says / Stop / Mountain song / Summertime rolls / Kimberley Austin / Tonight / Tahitian moon / Pets / Cursed male / 100 ways / Hard charger / Ripple / Satellite of love.

Virgin Virgin

Jul 01. (cd) *(CDVUS 197) <50030>* **SONG YET TO BE SUNG** [ ] [ ]
– Happy birthday jubilee / Song yet to be sung / Did you forget / Shekina / Our song / Say something / Seeds / King Z / To me / Nua nua / Admit I / Happy birthday jubilee (reprise).

JANE'S ADDICTION

FARRELL, NAVARRO, PERKINS plus **ERIC AVERY** – bass

Capitol Capitol

Jul 03. (7"/cd-s) *(CL/CDCL 847) <552637>* **JUST BECAUSE. / SUFFER SOME (live)** [14] [72]

Jul 03. (cd)(lp) *(592197-2)(590186-1) <90186>* **STRAYS** [14] [4]
– True nature / Strays / Just because / Price I pay / The riches / Superhero / Wrong girl / Everybody's fool / Suffer some / Hypersonic / To match the sun.

Oct 03. (7"/cd-s) *(CL/CDCL 850)* **TRUE NATURE. / BEEN CAUGHT STEALING (live)** [41] [ ]
(cd-s) *(CDCLS 850)* – ('A'side) / Just because (live) / Stop (Westwood One session) / ('A'-video).

□ Bill JANOVITZ (see under ⇒ BUFFALO TOM)

□ Bert JANSCH (see under ⇒ PENTANGLE)

JAPAN

Formed: Catford / Lewisham, London, England . . . mid-70's by DAVID SYLVIAN, his brother STEVE JANSEN, MICK KARN and RICHARD BARBIERI. In 1977, they added a second guitarist, ROB DEAN, subsequently signing to 'Ariola-Hansa' after winning a talent competition run by the label. They released a debut album, 'ADOLESCENT SEX', in the Spring of '78, followed six months later by 'OBSCURE ALTERNATIVES'. Basically pop music at the more accessible end of the avant-garde spectrum, JAPAN's proto-New Romantic image contrasted with SYLVIAN's (FERRY-esque) monotone croon. The following year, JAPAN scored a major hit in (of all places) Japan, with the GIORGIO MORODER-produced single, 'LIFE IN TOKYO'; a year on they finally gained a UK chart placing with 'QUIET LIFE'. By the turn of the decade, they'd secured a deal with 'Virgin', releasing the John Porter-produced Top 50 album, 'GENTLEMEN TAKE POLAROIDS'. The next year, after three minor hits in Britain, they went overground with a top selling classic album, 'TIN DRUM'. The record subsequently spawned the spectral 'GHOSTS' single in early '82, which hit the UK Top 5 after their former label had initiated a string of re-issues with 'EUROPEAN SON'; these exploitation releases graced the charts over the course of the next eighteen months while

JAPAN officially folded. All band members went on to other projects, DAVID SYLVIAN enjoying most success. After a 1982 collaboration with RYUICHI SAKAMOTO ('BAMBOO HOUSES' and 'FORBIDDEN COLOURS' from the movie, 'Merry Xmas Mr. Lawrence'), the immaculately fringed frontman released his debut solo album, 'BRILLIANT TREES' (1984). The Top 5 album utilised the talents of world trumpeter, JON HASSELL, while JAPAN cohorts JANSEN and BARBIERI also helped to sculpt its sophisticated ambience. On future albums such as 'GONE TO EARTH' (1986), 'SECRETS OF THE BEEHIVE' (1987), 'PLIGHT AND PREMONITION' (1988) and 'FLUX AND MUTATION' (1989) – the latter two were collaborations with HOLGER CZUKAY (ex-CAN) – he worked with left-field luminaries like BILL NELSON and ROBERT FRIPP. In 1991, JAPAN re-formed as RAIN TREE CROW, although it became clear this set-up was only temporary, as all members (especially SYLVIAN), continued to pursue solo careers. SYLVIAN briefly returned to the charts in 1993 with the ROBERT FRIPP collaboration, 'THE FIRST DAY', a more accessible yet still inventive set. Although MICK KARN began a solo career at the same time as SYLVIAN (the bassist's work reminiscent of ENO or BILL NELSON), he went on to work as a sculptor; his track, 'TRIBAL DAWN' (from the album, 'TITLES' – 1982), was used on Channel 4's arty TV programme, 'Altered States'. SYLVIAN was still gaining respect in some quarters of the music world when he turned up courtesy of a fresh set of scrumptious solo songs entitled 'DEAD BEES ON A CAKE' (1999), his aura and presence still on show when this returned him to the Top 40 (as did single, 'I SURRENDER').
• **Songwriters:** SYLVIAN lyrics / group compositions except; DON'T RAIN ON MY PARADE (Rogers-Hammerstein) / AIN'T THAT PECULIAR (Marvin Gaye) / I SECOND THAT EMOTION (Smokey Robinson) / ALL TOMORROW'S PARTIES (Velvet Underground).

Album rating: ADOLESCENT SEX (*6) / OBSCURE ALTERNATIVES (*6) / QUIET LIFE (*6) / GENTLEMEN TAKE POLAROIDS (*7) / TIN DRUM (*9) / ASSEMBLAGE compilation (*7) / OIL ON CANVAS live (*6) / EXORCISING GHOSTS compilation (*9) / Rain Tree Crow: RAIN TREE CROW (*4) / David Sylvian: BRILLIANT TREES (*8) / GONE TO EARTH (*6) / SECRETS OF THE BEEHIVE (*7) / PLIGHT AND PREMONITION with Holger Czukay (*7) / FLUX AND MUTABILITY with Holger Czukay (*6) / THE FIRST DAY with Robert Fripp (*6) / DEAD BEES ON A CAKE (*8) / APPROACHING SILENCE (*5) / EVERYTHING AND NOTHING compilation (*8) / CAMPHOR collection (*4) / BLEMISH (*7) / Mick Karn: TITLES (*7) / DREAMS OF REASON PRODUCE (*6) / BESTIAL CLUSTER (*5) / POLLYTOWN (*5) / THE TOOTH MOTHER (*5) / Jansen & Barbieri: CATCH THE FALL (*5) / STORIES ACROSS THE BORDER (*5) / BEGINNING TO MELT with Karn (*5) / SEED with Karn (*5) / STONE TO FLESH (*5) / OTHER WORLDS IN A SMALL ROOM (*4)

DAVID SYLVIAN (b. DAVID BATT, 23 Feb'58) – vocals, guitar, keyboards / **RICHARD BARBIERI** (b.30 Nov'57) – keyboards, synthesizers / **ROB DEAN** – guitar, mandolin / **MICK KARN** (b. ANTHONY MICHAELIDES, 24 Jul'58) – bass, saxophone / **STEVE JANSEN** (b. STEVE BATT, 1 Dec'59) – drums, percussion

Ariola Hansa — Ariola

Mar 78. (7") *(AHA 510)* **DON'T RAIN ON MY PARADE. / STATELINE** [ ] [–]

Apr 78. (lp) *(AHAL 8004)* *<50037>* **ADOLESCENT SEX** [ ] [ ]
– Transmission / The unconventional / State line / Wish you were black / Performance / Lovers on Main Street / Don't rain on my parade / Suburban love / Adolescent sex / Communist China / Television. *(re-iss. Sep82; same) (re-iss. Sep84 on 'Fame' lp/c; FA41 3108-1/-4) (cd-iss. 1989 on 'Hansa Germany'; VDP 1153)*

Aug 78. (7") *(AHA 525)* **THE UNCONVENTIONAL. / ADOLESCENT SEX** [ ] [–]

Nov 78. (lp) *(AHAL 8007)* *<50047>* **OBSCURE ALTERNATIVES** [ ] [ ]
– Automatic gun / Rhodesia / Love is infectious / Sometimes I feel so low / Obscure alternatives / Deviation / Suburban Berlin / The tenant. *(re-iss. Sep82; same) (re-iss. Apr84 on 'Fame' lp/c; FA41 3098-1/-4) (cd-iss. 1989 on 'Hansa Germany'; CDP 1154)*

Nov 78. (7",7"blue) *(AHA 529)* *<7727>* **SOMETIMES I FEEL SO LOW. / LOVE IS INFECTIOUS** [ ] [ ]

May 79. (7"red/ext.12"red) *(AHA/+D 540)* **LIFE IN TOKYO. / LIFE IN TOKYO (part 2)** [ ] [–]

Jul 79. (12") *<7756>* **LIFE IN TOKYO. / LOVE IS INFECTIOUS** [–] [ ]

Jan 80. (lp) *(AHAL 8011)* **QUIET LIFE** [53] [–]
– Quiet life / Fall in love with me / Despair / In-vogue / Halloween / All tomorrow's parties / Alien / The other side of life. *(re-iss. Sep82 on 'Fame' lp/c; FA/TCFA 3037) (cd-iss. 1989 on 'Hansa Germany'; VDP 1155)*

Feb 80. (7",7"maroon) *(AHA 559)* **I SECOND THAT EMOTION. / QUIET LIFE** [ ] [–]

Virgin — not iss.

Oct 80. (7") *(VS 379)* **GENTLEMEN TAKE POLAROIDS. / THE EXPERIENCE OF SWIMMING** [60] [–]
(d7"+=) *(VS 379)* – The width of a room / Burning bridges.

Oct 80. (lp/c) *(V/TCV 2180)* **GENTLEMEN TAKE POLAROIDS** [45] [–]
– Gentlemen take polaroids / Swing / Some kind of fool / My new career / Methods of dance / Ain't that peculiar / Night porter / Taking islands in Africa. *(re-iss. Aug88 lp/c; OVED/+C 138) (cd-iss. Jun88; CDV 2180) <US cd-iss. 1991 on 'Caroline'; CAROL 1829-2>*

—— Trimmed to quartet when ROB DEAN left, to later form ILLUSTRATED MAN

Apr 81. (7"/12") *(VS 409/+12)* **THE ART OF PARTIES. / LIFE WITHOUT BUILDINGS** [48] [–]

Oct 81. (7") *(VS 436)* **VISIONS OF CHINA. / TAKING ISLANDS IN AFRICA** [32] [–]
(12"+=) *(VS 436-12)* – Swing. *(re-iss. Dec84; same)*

Nov 81. (lp/c) *(V/TCV 2209)* **TIN DRUM** [12] [–]
– The art of parties / Talking drum / Ghosts / Canton / Still life in mobile homes / Visions of China / Sons of pioneers / Cantonese boy. *(re-iss. Apr86 lp/c; OVED/+C 158) (cd-iss. Jun88; CDV 2209) <US cd-iss. 1991 on 'Caroline'; CAROL 1830-2>*

Jan 82. (7"/7"pic-d/12") *(VS/+Y 472)(VS 472-12)* **GHOSTS. / THE ART OF PARTIES (version)** [5] [–]

Feb 82. (7") **VISIONS OF CHINA. / CANTON** [–] [ ]

May 82. (d7") *(VS 502)* **CANTONESE BOY. / BURNING BRIDGES // GENTLEMEN TAKE POLAROIDS / THE EXPERIENCE OF SWIMMING** [24] [–]

—— They had earlier in the year quietly branched out into new projects. DAVID SYLVIAN went solo after a brief collaboration with RYUICHI SAKAMOTO. MICK KARN went solo, had one-off single with MIDGE URE, then went into sessions before forming DALI'S CAR with PETE MURPHY in '84. BARBERI and JANSEN produced Swedes LUSTAN LAKEJER. The pair formed their own duo (The DOLPHIN BROTHERS) before joining DAVID SYLVIAN again.

– compilations, exploitation releases etc. –

—— on 'Hansa-Ariola' unless otherwise mentioned

Apr 81. (7"/12") *(HANSA/+12 4)* **LIFE IN TOKYO. / EUROPEAN SON** [ ] [–]

Aug 81. (7"/12") *(HANSA/+12 6)* **QUIET LIFE. / A FOREIGN PLACE / FALL IN LOVE WITH ME** [19] [–]

Sep 81. (lp)(c) *(HANLP 1)(ZCHAN 003)* **ASSEMBLAGE** [26] [–]
– Adolescent sex / State line / Communist China / Rhodesia / Suburban Berlin / Life in Tokyo / European son / All tomorrow's parties / Quiet life / I second that emotion. *(c+=)* – (12"extended versions). *(re-iss. Sep85 on 'Fame' lp/c; FA41 3136-1/-4)*

Jan 82. (7"/12") *(HANSA/+12 10)* **EUROPEAN SON. / ALIEN** [31] [–]

Jun 82. (7"/12") *(HANSA/+12 12)* **I SECOND THAT EMOTION. / HALLOWEEN** [9] [–]

Sep 82. (7"/12") *(HANSA/+12 17)* **LIFE IN TOKYO. / THEME** [28] [–]

—— now on 'Virgin' unless mentioned otherwise

Nov 82. (7") *(VS 554)* **NIGHT PORTER. / AIN'T THAT PECULIAR** [29] [–]
(12"+=) *(VS 554-12)* – Methods of dance.

Feb 83. (7"/12") *Hansa; (HANSA/+12 18)* **ALL TOMORROW'S PARTIES. / IN VOGUE** [38] [–]

May 83. (7") *(VS 581)* **CANTON (live). / VISIONS OF CHINA (live)** [42] [–]

Jun 83. (d-lp/c) *(VD/TCVD 2513)* **OIL ON CANVAS (live)** [5] [ ]
– Oil on canvas / Sons of pioneers / Gentlemen take polaroids / Swing / Cantonese boy / Visions of china / Ghosts / Voices raised in welcome, hands held in prayer / Night porter / Still life in mobile homes / Methods

of dance / Quiet life / The art of parties / Canton / Temple of dawn. *(cd-iss. Apr85; CDVD 2513)*

Aug 83. (d-c) *(XTWO 24)* **ADOLESCENT SEX / OBSCURE ALTERNATIVES** [ ] [-]

Nov 84. (d-lp/c/cd) *(VGD/+C/CD 3510)* **EXORCISING GHOSTS** [45] [ ]
– Methods of dance / Swing / Gentlemen take polaroids / Quiet life / A foreign place * / Night porter / My new career / The other side of life / Visions of China / Sons of pioneers * / Talking drum / The art of parties / Taking islands in Africa / Voices raised in welcome, hands held in prayer / Life without buildings / Ghosts. *(cd-omits *)*

Jun 88. (3"cd-ep) *(CDT 11)* **GHOSTS / THE ART OF PARTIES / VISIONS OF CHINA** [ ] [ ]

Nov 88. (3"cd-ep) *(CDT 32)* **GENTLEMEN TAKE POLAROIDS / CANTONESE BOY / METHODS OF DANCE** [ ] [ ]

Sep 87. (7") *Old Gold; (OG 9666)* **I SECOND THAT EMOTION. / ALL TOMORROW'S PARTIES** [ ] [-]
(12"+=) *(OG 4020)* – Life in Tokyo.

Nov 87. (7") *Old Gold; (OG 4031)* **QUIET LIFE. / LIFE IN TOKYO** [ ] [-]

Nov 88. (7") *Old Gold; (OG 9817)* **GHOSTS. / CANTONESE BOY** [ ] [-]

Dec 89. (c/cd) *R.C.A.; (410/260 360)* **A SOUVENIR FROM JAPAN** [ ] [-]

Nov 90. (3xcd-box) *(TPAK 6)* **COLLECTOR'S EDITION** [ ] [ ]
– (GENTLEMEN TAKE POLAROIDS / TIN DRUM / OIL ON CANVAS)

Nov 92. (cd-ep) *Old Gold; (OG 6187)* **I SECOND THAT EMOTION / QUIET LIFE / LIFE IN TOKYO** [ ] [-]

Oct 91. (cd/c) *Receiver; (RR CD/MC 150)* **THE OTHER SIDE OF JAPAN** [ ] [-]

Aug 96. (cd) *B.M.G.; (74321 39338-2)* **IN VOGUE** [ ] [ ]

DAVID SYLVIAN

- vocals, instruments (ex-JAPAN) / **RYUICHI SAKAMOTO** – synthesizers (ex-YELLOW MAGIC ORCHESTRA)

Virgin Caroline

Jul 82. (7"/ext.12"; by SYLVIAN / SAKAMOTO) *(VS 510)* **BAMBOO HOUSES. / BAMBOO MUSIC** [30] [-]
(below from the the film soundtrack 'Merry Christmas Mr.Lawrence')

Jun 83. (7"; by DAVID SYLVIAN & RYUICHI SAKAMOTO) *(VS 601)* **FORBIDDEN COLOURS. / THE SEED AND THE SOWER (by RYUICHI SAKAMOTO)** [16] [ ]
(12"+=) *(VS 601-12)* – Last regrets.
(3"/5"cd-ep of SYLVIAN tracks was iss.Aug88; CDT 18)

— now solo – vocals, keyboards, guitar, percussion, with **RICHARD BARBIERI** and **STEVE JANSEN** (ex-JAPAN) / **RYUICHI SAKAMOTO** – synthesizers / **HOLGER CZUKAY** – tapes / **DANNY THOMPSON** – upright bass / **KENNY WHEELER** – horns

May 84. (7"/7"pic-d)(12") *(VS/+Y 633)(VS 633-12)* **RED GUITAR. / FORBIDDEN COLOURS (version)** [17] [-]

Jun 84. (lp/c/cd) *(V/TCV/CDV 2290)* <CAROL 1812> **BRILLIANT TREES** [4] [ ]
– Pulling punches / The ink in the well / Nostalgia / Red guitar / Weathered wall / Backwaters / Brilliant trees. *(re-iss. Apr90 lp/c; OVED/+C 239)*

Aug 84. (7"/12") *(VS 700/+12)* **THE INK IN THE WELL (remix). / WEATHERED WALL (instrumental)** [36] [-]

Oct 84. (7"/ext.12") *(VS 717/+12)* **PULLING PUNCHES. / BACKWATERS (remix)** [56] [-]

— now with **JOHN HASSELL** and **ROBERT FRIPP** – guitar / **HOLGER CZUKAY** – tapes / **KENNY WHEELER** – horns

Nov 85. (12"ep) *(VS 835-12)* **WORDS WITH THE SHAMEN** [72] [-]
– Part 1:- Ancient evening / Part 2:- Incantation / Part 3:- Awakening.

Dec 85. (c) *(SLY 1)* **ALCHEMY (AN INDEX OF POSSIBILITIES)** [ ] [-]
– WORDS WITH THE SHAMEN / Preparations for a journey / Steel cathedrals.

— now with **ROBERT FRIPP** and **BILL NELSON** – guitar / **PHIL PALMER** – accoustic guitar / **MEL COLLINS** – soprano sax. / **KENNY WHEELER** – flugel horn

Virgin Virgin

Jul 86. (7"/7"sha-pic-d) *(VS/+Y 815)* **TAKING THE VEIL. / ANSWERED PRAYERS** [53] [-]
(remix-12"+=) *(VS 815-12)* – Bird of prey vanishes into a bright blue sky.

Aug 86. (d-lp)(c)(cd) *(VDL/TCVDL/CDVDL 1)* <96003> **GONE TO EARTH** [24] [ ]
– Taking the veil / Laughter and forgetting / Before the bullfight / Gone to earth / Wave / River man / Silver moon / The healing place / Answered prayers * / Where the railroad meets the sea / The wooden cross * / Silver moon over sleeping steeples * / Campfire: Coyote country * / A bird of prey vanishes into a blue cloudless sky * / Sunlight seen through the towering trees * / Upon this Earth. *(cd-omits tracks *)*

Sep 86. (7"/s7") *(VS/+P 895)* **SILVER MOON. / GONE TO EARTH** [ ] [-]
(12"+=) *(VS 895-12)* – Silver moon over sleeping steeples.

— DAVID was also credited on VIRGINIA ASTLEY's Feb87 'Some Small Hope'.

— now with **SAKAMOTO, PALMER, JANSEN** plus **DANNY CUMMINGS** – percussion / **DAVID TORN** – guitar / **DANNY THOMPSON** – d. bass / **MARK ISHAM** – trumpet

Oct 87. (lp)(c)(cd) *(V/TCV/CDV 2471)* <86028> **SECRETS OF THE BEEHIVE** [37] [ ]
– September / The boy with the gun / Maria / Orpheus / The Devil's own / When poets dreamed of angels / Mother and child / Let the happiness in / Waterfront.

Oct 87. (7") *(VS 1001)* **LET THE HAPPINESS IN. / BLUE OF MOON** [66] [ ]
(12"+=) *(VS 1001-12)* – Buoy (remix).

Apr 88. (7") *(VS 1043)* **ORPHEUS. / THE DEVIL'S OWN** [ ] [ ]
(12"+=) *(VS 1043-12)* – Mother and child.

— His touring band **JANSEN, BARBIERI, TORN, ISHAM** plus **IAN MAIDMAN** – bass, percussion / **ROBBY ALEDO** – guitar

DAVID SYLVIAN & HOLGER CZUKAY

with **JAKI LIEBEZEIT** – drums (ex-CAN)

Venture Virgin

Mar 88. (lp/c/cd) *(VE/TCVE/CDVE 11)* <86053> **PLIGHT AND PREMONITION** [71] [ ]
– Plight (the spiralling of winter ghosts) / Premonition (giant empty iron vessel).

— with **LIEBEZEIT, MICHAEL KAROLI** – guitar / **MARKUS STOCKHAUSEN** – flugel horn / **MICHI** – vocals

Venture Caroline

Sep 89. (lp/c/cd) *(VE/TCVE/CDVE 43)* <CAROLCD 1602> **FLUX AND MUTABILITY** [ ] [ ]
– Flux (a big, bright, colourful world) / Mutability ("a new beginning is in the offing").

DAVID SYLVIAN

Virgin not iss.

Nov 89. (7") *(VS 1221)* **POP SONG. / A BRIEF CONVERSATION ENDING IN DIVORCE** [ ] [-]
(12"+=/cd-s+=) *(VST/VSCDX 1221)* – ('A'remix).
(cd-s+=) *(VSCD 1221)* – Stigmas of childhood.

Nov 89. (5-cd-box) *(DXCD 1)* **WEATHERBOX** [ ] [-]
– (BRILLIANT TREES / GONE TO EARTH / GONE TO EARTH (instrumental) / SECRETS OF THE BEEHIVE / ALCHEMY – AN INDEX OF POSSIBILITIES)

Nov 91. (cd) *(DSRM 1)* **EMBRE GLANCE (THE PERMANENCE OF MEMORY)** [ ] [-]
– The beekeeper's apprentice / Epiphany.

— JAPAN had reformed quartet in 1990, but as . . .

RAIN TREE CROW

Virgin Virgin

Mar 91. (7"/c-s) *(VS/+C 1340)* **BLACK WATER. / RAIN TREE CROW / I DRINK TO FORGET** [62] [-]
(12") *(VST 1340)* – (1st + 3rd track) / Red Earth (as summertime ends).
(cd-s) *(VSCD 1340)* – (all above 4).

Apr 91. (cd/c/lp) *(CD/TC+/V 2659)* <91774> **RAIN TREE CROW** [24] [ ]
– Big wheels in Shanty town / Every colour you are / Rain tree crow / Red Earth (as summertime ends) / Rocket full of charge / Boat's for burning / New Moon Red Deer wallow / Black water / A reassuringly dull Sunday / Blackcrow hats shoe shine city.

SYLVIAN – SAKAMOTO

— next with **INGRID CHAVEZ**

		Virgin America	Virgin Am.
Jun 92.	(7"/c-s) *(VUS/+C 57)* **HEARTBEAT (TAINAI KAIKI II) RETURNING TO THE WOMB. / NUAGES**	58	–
	(cd-s+=) *(VUSCD 57)* – The lost emperor.		
	(cd-s) *(VUSCDG 57)* – ('A'side) / Forbidden colours / Heartbeat.		

DAVID SYLVIAN & ROBERT FRIPP

with **FRIPP** – guitar (of-KING CRIMSON & solo artist) / **TREY GUNN** – synthesizers, vocals, co-writer plus band **DAVID BOTTRILL** – synthesizers / **JERRY MAROTTA** – drums, percussion / **MARC ANDERSON** – percussion / **INGRID CHAVEZ** – backing vocals

		Virgin	Virgin
Jul 93.	(cd/c/lp) *(CD/TC+/V 2712)* *<88208>* **THE FIRST DAY**	21	
	– God's monkey / Jean the birdman / Firepower / Brightness falls / 20th century dreaming (a shaman's song) / Darshan (the road to Graceland).		
Aug 93.	(c-ep/cd-ep) *(VSC/DG 1462)* **JEAN THE BIRDMAN / EARTHBOUND – STARBLIND / ENDGAME**	68	–
	(cd-ep) *(VSCDT 1462)* – ('A'side) / Tallow moon / Dark water / Gone to Earth.		
Dec 93.	(cd/c/lp) *(SYL CD/MC/LP 1)* **DARSHAN** (mixes)		–
	– Darshan (the road to Graceland) (remixed by The GRID & others).		
Sep 94.	(cd) *(DAMAGE 1)* *<39905>* **DAMAGE (live)**		
	– Damage / God's monkey / Brightness falls / Every colour you are / Firepower / Gone to Earth / 20th century dreaming (a shaman's song) / Wave / Riverman / Darshan (the road to Graceland) / Blinding light of Heaven / The first day. *(re-iss. Nov01 on 'Venture'; CDVE 958)*		

— In 1996, SYLVIAN was credited on soundtrack of 'Marco Polo' film alongside NICOLA ALESINI & PIER LUIGI ANDREONI. It was released on 'Materiali Sonori'; *MASOCD 90069)*

DAVID SYLVIAN

Mar 99.	(cd-s) *(VSCDT 1722)* **I SURRENDER / LES FLEURS DU MAL / STARRED AND DREAMING**	40	–
	(cd-s) *(VSCDX 1722)* – ('A'side) / Whose trip is this / Remembering Julia.		
Mar 99.	(cd/c) *(CDV/TCV 2876)* *<47071>* **DEAD BEES ON A CAKE**	31	
	– I surrender / Dobro #1 / Midnight sun / Thalhelm / Godman / Alphabet angel / Krishna blue / Shining of things / Cafe Europe / Pollen path / All of my mother's name / Wanderlust / Praise / Darkest dreaming.		
		Venture	Virgin
Sep 99.	(cd-s) *(VEND 8)* **GODMAN (mixes) / SHADOWLAND (mixes)**		–
Sep 99.	(m-cd) *(CDVE 943)* *<848177>* **APPROACHING SILENCE**		Oct99
	– The beekeeper's apprentice / Epiphany / Approaching silence.		

– compilations, etc. –

Oct 00.	(d-cd/d-c) *Virgin; (CDVD/TCVD 2897)* *<50017>* **EVERYTHING AND NOTHING**	57	
	– The scent of magnolia / Heartbeat (Tainai kaiki II) / Blackwater / Albuquerque (dobro No.6) / Ride / The golden way / Ghosts / Pop song / Every colour you are / Wanderlust / God's monkey / Let the happiness in / I surrender / Thoroughly lost to logic / Jean the birdman / Cover me with flowers / The boy with the gun / Riverman / Aparna and Nimisha (dobro No.5) / Midnight sun / Orpheus / Some kind of fool / Cries and whispers / Godman / Laughter and forgetting / Buoy / Weathered wall / Bamboo houses / Come morning. *(3xcd-box+=; CDVDX 2897)* – Scent of magnolia (edit) / Blinding light of Heaven / Scent of magnolia (Portobello mix) / Brilliant trees (version 2000).		
May 02.	(cd/d-cd) *Venture; (CDVE/+X 962) / E.M.I.; <812201>* **CAMPHOR** (out-takes)		

Jean-Michel JARRE

Born: 24 Aug'48, Lyon, France. In the late 60's, having played lead guitar for a few rock bands, he enrolled at Pierre Schaeffer's Musical Research Group, studying ethnic music. His love of free-form conflicted with MRG and he left to work in his own studio with a new synthesizer. He released three lp's in France at the turn of the decade, but chose to write jingles for radio and TV etc. In 1971, JARRE had become the youngest composer to appear at the Palais Garnier Opera House, while in 1973, he scored the soundtrack for the film, 'Les Granges Brulee'. In 1977, JEAN-MICHEL was signed to 'Polydor', who issued 'OXYGENE', a record which was earlier released in France on the 'Disques Motors' imprint. The album soon rose to No.2 in the UK charts, helped by a surprise Top 5 single 'OXYGENE (part 4)', JARRE's multi-layered electro-rock/pop muzak was conceptually similar to MIKE OLDFIELD, minus the instrumental dexterity of course. Later the following year, JARRE's next album, 'EQUINOXE', traced the same formulated pattern without quite the same effect. The record nevertheless matched its predecessor's sales, his subsequent works continuing to triumph commercially throughout the world during the 80s. In April '86, he set a record when playing live to over one million people at Houston, Texas. Two and a half years later, JARRE appeared in front of around three million people at Docklands, London, recorded over two separate nights (due to earlier Newham Council objection). HANK MARVIN, guitarist of The SHADOWS, featured on JARRE's 'LONDON KID' hit, the veteran guitar twanger performing the track alongside JARRE at the aforementioned concert. Not exactly the trendiest of the electronic pioneers, JARRE belatedly gained a smattering of instant credibility in the early 90's with the 'CHRONOLOGIE' series of dance remixes. The reworking by Glasgow's SLAM, in particular, was highly sought after on promo, changing hands for ridiculous sums of money. • **Trivia:** He married actress Charlotte Rampling, after meeting her at 1976 Cannes film festival. In 1983, he released a solitary copy of his lp, 'MUSIC FOR SUPERMARKETS', and after auctioning it for around £10,000, destroyed the master disc.

Album rating: OXYGENE (*8) / EQUINOXE (*6) / MAGNETIC FIELDS (*5) / THE CONCERTS IN CHINA (*4) / THE ESSENTIAL JEAN-MICHAEL JARRE compilation (*6) / ZOOLOOK (*5) / RENDEZ-VOUS (*5) / IN CONCERT: LYON – HOUSTON (*4) / REVOLUTIONS (*5) / JARRE LIVE (*3) / WAITING FOR COUSTEAU (*3) / IMAGES – THE BEST OF JEAN-MICHEL JARRE compilation (*7) / CHRONOLOGIE (*4) / OXYGENE 7-13 (*4) / DESTINATION DOCKLANDS (*4) / HONG KONG (*4) / ODYSSEY THROUGH OXYGEN (*3) / METAMORPHOSES (*4) / SESSIONS 2000 (*5)

JEAN-MICHEL JARRE – synthesizers, keyboards

		EMI-Pathe	not iss.
1971.	(lp) *(C006-11739)* **LA CAGE / EROS MACHINE**	– France	–
		Disques Motors	not iss.
1972.	(lp; unreleased) **DESERTED PALACE**	– France	–
1973.	(7") *(MT 043)* **HYPNOSE. / DESERTED PALACE**	– France	–
		Polydor	Polydor
Jul 77.	(lp)(c) *(2310 555)(3100 398)* *<6112>* **OXYGENE**	2	78
	– Oxygene (Parts 1 – 6). *(cd-iss. 1983; 800 015-2) (re-iss. Jun97 on 'Epic' cd/c; 487375-2/-4)*		
Aug 77.	(7") *(2001 721)* **OXYGENE (part 4). / OXYGENE (part 6)**	4	
Dec 78.	(lp/c) *(POLD/+C 5007)* *<6175>* **EQUINOXE**	11	
	– Equinoxe (Parts I – VIII). *(cd-iss. 1983; 800 025-2) (re-iss. Jan93;) (re-iss. Jun97 on 'Epic' cd/c; 487376-2/-4)*		
Dec 78.	(7") *(POSP 20)* **EQUINOXE (part V). / EQUINOXE (part I)**	45	
Jul 79.	(7") *(2001 896)* **EQUINOXE (part IV remix). / EQUINOXE (part III)**		

Feb 80. (7") *(2001 968)* **EQUINOXE (part VII) (live). / EQUINOXE (part VIII) (live)**

May 81. (lp/c) *(POLS/+C 1033)* <6325> **MAGNETIC FIELDS** 6 98
– Magnetic fields (parts 1 – 5) / The last rumba. *(cd-iss. 1983; 800 024-2) (re-iss. Jan93;)*

Jun 81. (7") *(POSP 292)* **MAGNETIC FIELDS (part 2 remix). / MAGNETIC FIELDS (part 1 excerpt)**

Nov 81. (7") *(POSP 363)* **MAGNETIC FIELDS (part 4 remix). / MAGNETIC FIELDS (part 1 excerpt)**

—— added **DOMINIQUE PERRIER + FREDERIC ROUSSEAU** – synthesizers / **ROGER RIZZITELLI** – percussion, drums

May 82. (d-lp/d-c) *(PODV/+C 3)* <811551> **THE CONCERTS IN CHINA (live)** 6
– The overture / Arpegiator / Equinoxe IV / Fishing junks at sunset / Band in the rain / Equinoxe VII / Laser harp / Orient express / Magnetic fields I, III & IV / Night in Shanghai / The last rumba / Magnetic fields II Souvenir of China. *(d-cd-iss. 1983; 811 551-2) (re-iss. Jan93;)*

May 82. (7") *(POSP 430)* **ORIENT EXPRESS. / FISHING JUNKS AT SUNSET** –

Oct 83. (lp/c) *(PRO LP/MC 3)* **THE ESSENTIAL JEAN-MICHEL JARRE** (compilation) 14 –
– Oxygene 2, 4 & 6 / Equinoxe 1, 3, 4 & 5 / Magnetic fields 1, 2, 4 & 5 / Orient express / Fishing junks at sunset / Overture. *(cd-iss. Sep84; 817 003-2)*

Polydor Polydor

Nov 84. (lp/c)(cd) *(POLH/+C 15)(<823 763-2>)* **ZOOLOOK** 47
– Ethnicolour / Diva / Zoolook / Wooloomooloo / Zoolookologie / Blah-blah cafe / Ethnicolour II. *(cd+=)* – Zoolook (remix) / Zoolookologie (remix).

—— retained **FREDERIC** and recruited **ADRIAN BELEW + IRA SIEGEL** – guitar / **MARCUS MILLER** – bass / **YOGI HORTON** – drums, percussion / **LAURIE ANDERSON** – vocals

Nov 84. (7") *(POSP 718)* **ZOOLOOK. / WOOLOOMOOLOO** –
(remix.12"+=) *(POSPX 718)* – ('A'-effects) / ('A'extended).

Mar 85. (7") *(POSP 740)* **ZOOLOOKOLOGIE (remix). / ETHNICOLOUR** –
(12"+=) *(POSPX 740)* – ('A'extended remixed).
(d7"+=) *(POSPG 740)* – Oxygene (part 4) / Oxygene (part 6).

—— w / **PERRIER / MICHEL GEISS** – synth / **JO HAMMER** – electro drums / **DAVID JARRE** – keyboards

Apr 86. (lp/c)(cd) *(POLH/+C 27)(<829 125-2>)* **RENDEZ-VOUZ** 9 52
– First rendez-vous / Second rendez-vous (part I / II / III / IV) / Third rendez-vous / Fourth rendez-vous / Fifth rendez-vous (part I / II / III) / Last rendez-vous – Ron's piece.

Aug 86. (7") *(POSP 788)* **RENDEZ-VOUS IV. / FIRST RENDEZ-VOUS** 65 –
(12") *(POSPX 788)* – ('A'side) / Rendez-vous (special + original mix) / Moon machine.

—— with **GEISS** – synthesizers / **FRANCIS LIMBERT** – keyboards, synth. / **PASCAL LEBOURG** – keyboards, synth. / **SYLVIAN DURAND** – keyboards, synthesizers / **PERRIER** – keys, synth (HOUSTON only) / **CHRISTINE DURAND** – soprano / **HAMMER** – drums / **KIRK WHALUM** – sax / **GUY DELACROIX** – bass (LYON only) / **DINO LUMBROSO** – percussion (LYON only) / also used choirs & orchestra, etc.

Jul 87. (lp/c)(cd) *(POLH/+C 36)(<833 170-2>)* **IN CONCERT – LYON / HOUSTON (live)** 18
– Oxygene V / Ethnicolour / Magnetic fields I / Souvenir of China / Equinoxe 5 / Rendez-vous III / Rendez-vous II / Ron's piece / Rendez-vous IV. *(re-iss. Jun97 on 'Epic' cd/c; 487377-2/-4)*

—— with **DOMINIQUE, MICHAEL, JO** and **GUY,** plus guests **SYLVIAN** – synth / & **HANK MARVIN** – guitar (of SHADOWS) on track – *

Aug 88. (lp/c)(cd) *(POLH/+C 45)(<837 098-2>)* **REVOLUTIONS** 3
– Industrial revolution: (overture – part 1 – part 2 – part 3) / London kid * / Revolutions / Tokyo kid / Computer weekend / September / The emigrant.

Oct 88. (7") *(PO 25)* **REVOLUTIONS. / INDUSTRIAL REVOLUTION 2** 52 –
(12"+=) *(PZ/+CD 25)* – ('A'extended).

Dec 88. (7") *(PO 32)* **LONDON KID. / INDUSTRIAL REVOLUTION 3** 48 –
(12"+=/cd-s+=) *(PZ/+CD 32)* – Revolutions (remix).

Sep 89. (7") *(PO 55)* **OXYGENE IV (remix). / INDUSTRIAL REVOLUTION OVERTURE** 65 –
(12"+=/cd-s+=) *(PZ/+CD 55)* – ('A'live version) / September.

Oct 89. (lp/c/cd) *(841 258-1/-4/-2)* **JARRE LIVE (live)** 16 –
– Introduction (revolution) / Industrial revolution: (Overture – part I – part II – part III) / Magnetic fields II / Oxygene IV / Computer weekend / Revolutions / Rendez-vous IV / Rendez-vous II / The emigrant. *(cd+=)* – (2 extra).

—— Retained **PERRIER and GEISS,** plus introduced The **AMACO RENEGADES** – steel drums / guests **GUY DELACROIX** – bass / **CHRISTOPHE DESCHAMPS** – drums

Jun 90. (cd/c/lp) *(843 614-2/-4/-1)* **WAITING FOR COUSTEAU** –
– Calypso / Calypso (pt.2) / Calypso (pt.3, finale side) / Waiting for Cousteau. *(cd+=)* – (extra music).

May 93. (cd/c/lp) *(519 373-2/-4/-1)* <36152> **CHRONOLOGIE** 11
– (part.1 – part.4) / (part.5 – part.8). *(re-iss. Jun97 & Jan00 on 'Epic' cd/c; 487379-2/-4)*

Jun 93. (c-s/12"/cd-s) *(POCS/PO/POCD 274)* **CHRONOLOGIE (part 4). / ('A'part)** 55 –
(re-mixed re-iss. Oct93; same); hit UK 56)

May 94. (cd/c/lp) *(519 373-2/-4/-1)* **CHRONOLOGIE VI (mixes)** –
– (slam mix) / (slam mix 2) / (main mix) / (alternative mix) / (original mix).

Dreyfus-Epic Dreyfus-Epic

Feb 97. (cd/c) *(EPC 486984-2/-4)* <68009> **OXYGENE 7-13** 11 May97
– Oxygene 7 (part 1 – part 2 – part 3) / Oxygene 8 / Oxygene 9 (part 1 – part 2 – part 3) / Oxygene 10 / Oxygene 11 / Oxygene 12 / Oxygene 13.

Mar 97. (c-s) *(664323-4)* **OXYGENE 8 / ('A'mix)** 17 –
(12"+=/cd-s+=) *(664 323-6/-2)* – ('A'mixes).

Jun 97. (c-s/cd-s) *(664715-4/-2)* **OXYGENE 10 / ('A'mix)** 21 –
(cd-s) *(664715-5)* – ('A'side) / Transcengenics 1 & 2.

Sep 97. (cd) *(488143-2)* **DESTINATION DOCKLANDS (live)** –
– Introduction (Revolutions) / Overture / Revolution industrielle (parts 1-3) / Magnetic fields II / Oxygene IV / Computer weekend / Revolutions / London kid / Rendevous IV / Rendezvous II / September / The emigrant.

Sep 97. (cd) *(488145-2)* **HONG KONG (live)** –
– Countdown / Chronologie (pt.2) / Chronologie (pt.3) / How old are you / Equinoxe (pt.4) / Souvenir of China / Qu est ce que l'amour / Chronologie (pt.6) / Chronologie (pt.8) / Where are you going / Oxygene (pt.4) / Fishing junks at sunset / Sale of the century / Digi sequencer / Magnetic fields (pt.2) / Band in the rain / Rendez-vous (pt.4) / Chronologie (pt.4).

May 98. (cd/c) *(489764-2/-4)* **ODYSSEY THROUGH OXYGEN** 50 –
– Odyssey overture / Oxygene 10 / Oxygene 7 / Oxygene 8 / Oxygene (Hani's 303) / Odyssey (phase 2) / Oxygene 8 (Sunday club) / Oxygene 10 (440 dub) / Odyssey 11 / Oxygene 11 / Oxygene 12 / Oxygene 8 (Takkyu Ishino) / Odyssey finale / Rendezvous '98 / Oxygene 13.

Jun 98. (c-s; JEAN-MICHEL JARRE & APOLLO 440) *(666110-4)* **RENDEZVOUS (1998 mix) /** 12 –
(cd-s+=) *(666110-2)* – ('A'mixes).

Jan 00. (cd/c) *(496022-2/-4)* **METAMORPHOSES** –
– Je me souviens / C'est la vie / Rendez-vous a Paris / Hey gagarin / Million of stars / Tout est bleu / Love love love / Bells / Miss Moon / Give me a sign / Gloria, lonely boy / Silhouette.

Feb 00. (10"/cd-s; by JEAN-MICHEL JARRE featuring NATACHA ATLAS) *(668930-6/-2)* **C'EST LA VIE (mixes)** 40 –
(cd-s) *(668930-3)* – ('A'mixes).

Oct 02. (cd) *(<FDM 36165-2>)* **SESSIONS 2000** Jan03
– January 24 / March 23 / May 1 / June 21 / September 14 / December 17.

– compilations, etc. –

on 'Polydor' unless mentioned otherwise

1981. (d-c) *(2683 077)* **OXYGENE / EQUINOXE** –

Dec 87. (8xcd-box) *(833 737-2)* **CD BOX SET** –
– (OXYGENE / EQUINOXE / MAGNETIC FIELDS / THE CONCERTS IN CHINA / ZOOLOOK / RENDEZ-VOUS / JARRE IN CONCERT; Houston / Lyon)

Feb 88. (7") *Old Gold; (OG 9780)* **OXYGENE (part IV). / EQUINOXE (part 5)** –

Oct 91. (cd/c/lp) *(511 306-2/-4/-1)* **IMAGES – THE BEST OF JEAN MICHEL JARRE** 16
– Oxygene 4 / Equinoxe 5 / Magnetic fields 2 / Oxygene 2 / Computer weekend / Equinoxe 4 / Band in the rain / Rendez-vous 2 / London kid / Ethnicolor 1 / Orient express / Calypso 1 / Calypso 3 (fin de siecle) / Rendez-vous 4 / Moon machine / Eldorado / Globe trotter. *(re-iss. Jun97 on 'Epic' cd/c; 487378-2/-4)*

Jan 93. (cd/c/lp) *(815 686-2/-4/-1)* **MUSIK AUS ZEIT UND RAUM** [ ] [ ]
Oct 95. (cd) **JARREMIX** (dance mixes compilation) [ ] [–]

JA RULE

Born: JEFFREY ATKINS, 29 Feb'76, Queens, New York, USA. JA RULE got his first break in the late 90's when 'Def Jam' producer IRV GOTTI took the young man under his 'Murder Inc.' associated wing. Hardcore gangsta rap with a leaning to DMX and The RUFF RYDERS crew, JA found his particular branding of his genre a hit with the East Coast public via debut single, 'HOLLA HOLLA' and US Top 3 album, 'VENNI VETTI VECCI' (1999). Featuring the likes of ERICK SERMON, JAY-Z, CASE, RONALD ISLEY and the aforementioned DMX, the long-player set the tone for a future post-millennium supergroup project, The MURDERERS. Together with JAY-Z and DMX on initial recordings, JA and IRV also introduced new rappers such as BLACK CHILD, TAH MURDAH and VITA for their collaborative one-off 'IRV GOTTI PRESENTS . . .' (2000). To end what was to be a very busy year for JA, the man also despatched a follow-up chart-topping solo set, 'RULE 3:36' (2000), featuring no less than three further hits, 'PUT IT ON ME' (with VITA), 'BETWEEN ME AND YOU' (with CHRISTINA MILIAN) and 'I CRY' (with LIL' MO). However, it wasn't until 2001's 'PAIN IS LOVE' album that JA became the critically acclaimed superstar and household name (well, at least in the US). Another to peak at No.1, his collaborative R&B divas this time around included ASHANTI (on the chart-topping 'ALWAYS ON TIME'), JENNIFER LOPEZ and MISSY ELLIOTT. With this hit formula JA RULE continued to expand his risky musical horizons on his fourth solo set, 'THE LAST TEMPTATION' (2002), although this only reached the Top 5 (Top 20 in Britain). Whether his choice of pop-friendly collaborations with the likes of BOBBY BROWN (on 'THUG LOVIN'') and the aforementioned ASHANTI again (on major smash 'MESMERIZE') was a little diverse to say the least, JA RULE and his GOTTI-produced mates made their mark once more. However, fall-outs with DMX and newcomer 50 CENT (the latter saw him as a 2PAC impersonator), saw JA RULE subsequently crack under the strain. This was evident on the poor showing both critically and chartwise for 2003's 'BLOOD IN MY EYE', an album that took a swipe at most of his rivals including 50 CENT and EMINEM – it was time to get real!

Album rating: VENNI VETTI VECCI (*5) / IRV GOTTI PRESENTS . . . THE MURDERERS (by The Murderers; *5) / RULE 3:36 (*5) / PAIN IS LOVE (*7) / THE LAST TEMPTATION (*6) / BLOOD IN MY EYE (*4)

JA RULE – vocals / with various session people

Def Jam Def Jam

Mar 99. (c-s/12"/cd-s; by JA RULE, DMX & JAY-Z) *<566959>* **HOLLA HOLLA (mixes)** [–] [35]
May 99. (cd) *<538920-2>* **VENNI VETTI VECCI** [ ] [3]
– The March prelude / We here now / World's most dangerous (with NEMESIS) / Let's ride / Holla holla / Kill 'em all (with JAY-Z) / I hate nigguz (skit) / Nigguz theme / Suicide freestyle (with CASE) / Story to tell / Chris Black (skit) / Count on your nigga / It's murda (with DMX & JAY-Z) / E-dub & Ja (with ERICK SERMON) / 187 murda baptiss church (skit) / Murda 4 life (with MEMPHIS BLEEK) / Daddy's little baby (with RONALD ISLEY) / Race against time / Only begotten son / The murderers (with BLACK CHILD & TAH MURDAH).

—— The MURDERERS: **JA RULE + VITA + BLACK CHILD + TAH MURDAH + 0-1 + RONNIE BUMPS**

Feb 00. (12"; as The MURDERERS) *<56266-1>* **VITA, VITA, VITA (mixes)** [–] [ ]
Mar 00. (cd; as The MURDERERS) *<(542258-2)>* **IRV GOTTI PRESENTS . . . THE MURDERERS** [ ] [15]
– Intro / Murderers / Dem niggaz / We don't give a fuck / Clowns (skit) / Shit gets ugly / We Murderers baby / Interview with Vita (skit) / Vita, Vita, Vita / How many wanna die / Fuck parole (skit) / We getting high tonight / Tales from the darkside / I love the Yankees (skit) / Get it right / We different / Remo (skit) / Rebels symphony / Black or white / The 187 murda baptist church picknicing / If you were my bitch / 96R-0709 / Crime scene / Somebody's gonna die tonight / Holla holla (remix).

Oct 00. (cd) *<(542934-2)>* **RULE 3:36** [ ] [1]
– Intro / Watching me / Between me and you (with CHRISTINA MILIAN) / Put it on me (with VITA) / 6 feet underground / Love me, hate me / Die (with TAH MURDAH, BLACK CHILD & DAVE BING) / Fuck you (with 01 & VITA) / I'll fuck you girl (skit) / Grey box (skit with TAH MURDAH & BLACK CHILD) / Extasy (with TAH MURDAH & BLACK CHILD) / It's your life (with SHADE SHEIST) / I cry (with LIL' MO) / One of us / Chris Black (skit) / The rule won't die.

Nov 00. (12") *<572701>* **6 FEET UNDERGROUND (mixes)** [–] [ ]
Dec 00. (12"; with LIL' MO & VITA) *<572751>* **PUT IT ON ME** [–] [8]
Feb 01. (12"/cd-s; by JA RULE & CHRISTINA MILIAN) *<(572740-2)>* **BETWEEN ME AND YOU (mixes)** [26] Jan01 [11]
Apr 01. (12"; with LIL' MO) *<572856>* **I CRY (mixes)** [–] [40]
Oct 01. (cd/d-lp) *<(586437-2/-1)>* **PAIN IS LOVE** [17] Sep01 [1]
– Pain is love (skit) / Dial M for murder / Livin' it up (with CASE) / The Inc. (with CADDILLAC TAH & BLACK CHILD) / Always on time (with ASHANTI) / Down ass bitch (with CHUCK) / Never again / Worldwide gangsta (with CADDILLAC TAH & BLACK CHILD) / Leo (skit) / I'm real (with JENNIFER LOPEZ) / Smokin' and ridin' (with JODIE MACK & 0-1) / X (with MISSY ELLIOTT & TWEET) / Big Remo (skit) / Lost little girl / So much pain (with2PAC) / Pain is love. *(re-iss. Oct02; same)* – hit UK No.3

Oct 01. (c-s/12"/cd-s; JA RULE featuring CASE) *(588814-4/-1/-2) <588741>* **LIVIN' IT UP (mixes)** [27] Aug01 [6]
Jan 02. (c-s; JA RULE & ASHANTI) *(588946-4) <588795>* **ALWAYS ON TIME / I CRY (with Lil' Mo)** [6] Oct01 [1]
(12"+=) *(588946-1)* – ('A'-radio version).
(cd-s++=) *(588946-2)* – ('A'-video).
Feb 02. (12"/cd-s) *<588941-1/-2>* **DOWN ASS CHICK. / SMOKIN' & RIDIN'** [–] [21]

—— in Mar'02, JA RULE & CADDILLAC TAH featured on J.LO's Top 5 hit 'Ain't It Funny'

Jul 02. (c-s; JA RULE featuring CASE) *(063978-4)* **LIVIN' IT UP / LIVIN' IT UP (live at the London Astoria)** [5] [–]
(12"+=) *(063978-1)* – Always on time (Agent X mix) / Always on time (delight camp dub).
(cd-s+=) *(063978-2)* – Always on time (Agent X mix) / ('A'-video).
Nov 02. (cd/d-lp) *<(063487-2/-1)>* **THE LAST TEMPTATION** [14] [4]
– Intro / Thug lovin' (with BOBBY BROWN) / Mesmerize (with ASHANTI) / Pop niggas / The pledge (remix with ASHANTI, NAS & 2PAC) / Murder reigns / Last temptation (with CHARLI BALTIMORE) / Murder me (with CADDILLAC TAH & ALEXI) / The warning / Connected (with EASTWOOD & CROOKED I) / Emerica (with YOUNG LIFE & CHINK SANTANA) / Rock star / Destiny (outro).
Dec 02. (c-s; by JA RULE & BOBBY BROWN) *(63787-4) <63770>* **THUG LOVIN' / THE PLEDGE** [15] Nov02 [42]
(12"+=) *(63787-4)* – ('A'-remix) / The pledge (remix).
(cd-s++=) *(63787-2)* – ('A'-video).
Mar 03. (c-s; by JA RULE & ASHANTI) *(077958-4) <063773>* **MESMERIZE / (instrumental)** [12] Jan03 [2]
(12"+=) *(077958-1)* – Between you and me (explicit) / Pop niggaz (explicit).
(cd-s++=) *(077958-2)* – ('A'-video).
Nov 03. (cd) *(9861329) <015770-2>* **BLOOD IN MY EYE** [51] [6]
– Murder intro / The life (with HUSSEIN FATAL & CADDILLAC TAH) / Clap back / The crown (with SIZZLA) / Kay slay / Things gon' change – 2 punk ass quarter (by I. GOTTI) / Race against time II / Bobby creep / Niggas & bitches / The INC is back (with SHADOW, SEKOU 720 & BLACK CHILD) / Remo / Blood in my eye (with HUSSEIN FATAL). *(bonus +=)* – It's murda (with HUSSEIN FATAL) / The wrap (with HUSSEIN FATAL).
Nov 03. (12") *(9814619) <981461>* **REIGNS. / MURDER REIGNS (by Jay-Z) / CLAP BACK (instrumental)** [9] [44]
(cd-s+=) *(9814618)* – ('A'-video) / Murder reigns (video).

□ JAYBIRDS (see under ⇒ TEN YEARS AFTER)

JAYHAWKS

Formed: Minneapolis, Minnesota, USA . . . 1985 by MARK OLSON and GARY LOURIS, who formed the core of the band through an ever changing series of line-ups. After two American-only albums of rough-hewn country rock, 'THE JAYHAWKS' (1986) and 'BLUE EARTH' (1989), the band were taken under the wing of producer GEORGE DRAKOULIAS. In a well-thumbed tale, they were signed to Rick Rubin's 'Def American' label after roots maestro DRAKOULIAS allegedly phoned 'Twintone' mainman DAVE AYERS and heard a JAYHAWKS tape playing in the background. He was immediately spellbound, as were the country rock faithful among the record buying public when they heard the band's debut for 'Def American', the seminal 'HOLLYWOOD TOWN HALL' (1992). While many fans were under the impression this was the band's first album, the pristine harmonies of OLSON and LOURIS suggested otherwise. Like a fine malt whisky, The JAYHAWKS's songwriting and harmonising had been maturing over almost a decade and the result was something to savour. There wasn't a duff track in sight, and with veteran piano player NICKY HOPKINS on board, this was an essential purchase. Following its release, the band embarked on a heavy round of touring, sparking, along with peers like UNCLE TUPELO, a mini country-rock revival. Expectations were high for the follow-up, 'TOMORROW THE GREEN GRASS' (1995), the band bypassing the dilemma of matching 'HOLLYWOOD's perfection by going for a more eclectic approach. The crystal clear harmonising was still intact, the single 'BLUE' perhaps the JAYHAWKS' finest moment, as affecting a piece of resigned melancholy as ever graced a slab of vinyl. After a further tour, OLSON left and, after a long period of uncertainty and personal crisis, The JAYHAWKS re-emerged, albeit in a radically altered form. 'THE SOUND OF LIES' (1997) was a decidedly low-key affair and despite receiving a 'Masterpiece' award from retro music mag Mojo, the record has largely gone unnoticed. Something of a departure musically and lyrically, the album was downbeat and edgy, not as immediate as the older material but well worth persevering with; the likes of 'TROUBLE' and 'DYING ON THE VINE' the sound of a band exorcising their demons, coming through bruised but wiser. 'SMILE' (2000), meanwhile, suggested that The JAYHAWKS also wanted to exorcise some of their deep running country roots, opting instead for a more contemporary percussive kick and power pop sheen which strived to shake off the melancholy of their last album without leaving longtime fans in the lurch. Reduced once more to a core trio of LOURIS, PERLMAN and O'REAGAN, with the addition of new guitarist STEPHEN McCARTHY (ex-LONG RYDERS), the band once again overhauled their sound for the Ethan Johns-produced 'RAINY DAY MUSIC' (2003). This time around, The JAYHAWKS – not unwisely given the record's keening harmonies and engaging jangle – chose to channel their creative energies through classic folk-rock, while retaining just enough of a country edge to keep their root identity. • **Songwriters:** OLSON-LOURIS except; REASON TO BELIEVE (Tim Hardin). In 1996 LOURIS co-wrote with other members after OLSON left. • **Trivia:** OLSON and LOURIS can also be heard on sessions for MARIA McKEE, COUNTING CROWS and former stablemates SOUL ASYLUM. The latter's DAN MURPHY and DAVE PIRNER (latter part-time) were in the offshoot band, GOLDEN SMOG, which featured LOURIS and PERLMAN.

Album rating: THE JAYHAWKS (*6) / BLUE EARTH (*6) / HOLLYWOOD TOWN HALL (*8) / TOMORROW THE GREEN GRASS (*7) / THE SOUND OF LIES (*6) / SMILE (*5) / RAINY DAY MUSIC (*5)

MARK OLSON – vocals, guitar, harmonica / **GARY LOURIS** – vocals, electric guitar / **MARC PERLMAN** – bass / **NORM ROGERS** – drums

not iss. Bunkhouse

1986. (lp) <*7001*> **THE JAYHAWKS** [–] [ ]
– Falling star / Tried and true / Let the critics wonder / Let the last night be the longest / Behind bars / Cherry pie / The liquor store came first / People in this place on every side / Misery tavern / (I'm not in) Prison / King of kings / Good long time / Six pack on the dashboard. *<US cd-iss. 2001>*

THAD SPENCER – drums; repl. NORM who joined The COWS

not iss. Twin/Tone

Oct 89. (lp/cd) <*TTR 89151-1/-2*> **THE BLUE EARTH** [–] [ ]
– Two angels / She's not alone anymore / Will I be married / Dead end angel / Commonplace streets / Ain't no end / Five cups of coffee / The Baltimore sun / Red firecracker / Sioux City / I'm still dreaming now I'm yours / Martin's song. *(UK-iss.cd Jul95; same) (cd re-iss. Sep98 on 'R.C.A.'; 74321 60575-28)*

—— **KEN CALLAHAN** – drums; repl. THAD

—— session **NICKY HOPKINS** – keyboards (ex-JEFF BECK GROUP, etc)

Def American / Def American

Sep 92. (cd/c/lp) *(512 986-2/-4/-1)* <*26829*> **HOLLYWOOD TOWN HALL** [ ] [ ]
– Waiting for the sun / Crowded in the wings / Clouds / Two angels / Take me with you / Sister cry / Settled down like rain / Wichita / Nevada, California / Martin's song. *(re-iss. cd Apr95 on 'American-RCA'; 74321 23994-2) (cd re-iss. Apr00 on 'Columbia'; 491794-2)*

Aug 93. (7"/c-s) *(DEF A/MC 28)* **SETTLED DOWN LIKE RAIN. / SISTER CRY** [ ] [–]
(cd-s+=) *(DEFCD 28)* – Live medley: Settled down like rain – Martin's song.

Nov 93. (7"/c-s) *(DEF A/MC 25)* **WAITING FOR THE SUN. / MARTIN'S SONG** [ ] [–]
(cd-s+=) *(DEFCD 25)* – Up above my head / Keith & Quentin.
(cd-s+=) *(DEFCDX 25)* – Reason to believe / Sister cry / Medley: Martin's song – Settled down like rain.
(cd-s) *(DEFCDXX 25)* – ('A'side) / Up above my head.

—— added **KAREN GROTBERG** – keyboards

American-RCA / American-RCA

—— drummers **DON HEFFINGTON** (studio) / **TIM O'REAGAN** (tour); repl. KEN

Feb 95. (cd/c) *(74321 23680-2/-4)* <*43006*> **TOMORROW THE GREEN GRASS** [41] [92]
– Blue / I'd run away / Miss Williams' guitar / Two hearts / Real light / Over my shoulder / Bad time / See him on the streets / Nothing left to borrow / Ann Jane / Pray for me / Red's song / Ten little kids. *(cd re-iss. Jan99 on 'Columbia'; 491795-2)*

Feb 95. (7"/c-s) *(74321 25797-7/-4)* **BLUE. / TOMORROW THE GREEN GRASS** [ ] [–]
(cd-s+=) *(74321 25797-2)* – Darling today.

Jul 95. (7"/c-s) *(74321 29163-7/-4)* **BAD TIME. / LAST CIGARETTE** [70] [–]
(cd-s+=) *(74321 29163-2)* – Get the load out / Sing me back home.

—— now without OLSON (later 2 sets, 'My Own Jo Ellen' and December's Child') / new line-up **LOURIS, PERLMAN, GROTBERG + O'REAGAN** plus **KRAIG JOHNSON + JESSY GREENE**

Apr 97. (cd/c) <*(74321 46406-2/-4)*> **SOUND OF LIES** [61] [ ]
– The man who loved life / Think about it / Trouble / It's up to you / Stick in the mud / Big star / Poor little fish / Sixteen down / Haywire / Dying on the vine / Bottomless cup / Sound of lies / I hear you cry. *(cd re-iss. Jan99 on 'Columbia'; 491796-2)*

Jun 97. (c-s) *(74321 48755-4)* **BIG STAR / SLEEPYHEAD** [ ] [–]
(cd-s+=) *(74321 48677-2)* – Dying on the vine / I'd run away.

—— now without GREENE

Columbia / Columbia

May 00. (cd) *(497971-2)* <*69522*> **SMILE** [60] [ ]
– Smile / I'm gonna make you love me / What led me to this town / Somewhere in Ohio / A break in the clouds / Queen of the world / Life floats by / Broken harpoon / Pretty thing / Mr. Wilson / (In my) Wildest dreams / Better days / Baby, baby, baby. *(re-iss. Aug01; same)*

Jul 00. (m-cd) *(669689-2)* **I'M GONNA MAKE YOU LOVE ME** [ ] [–]
– I'm gonna make you love me / Somewhere in Ohio / What led me to

this town / Waiting for the sun / Take me with you (when you go) / Blue / The man who loved life.

—— **STEPHEN McCARTHY** – guitar (ex-LONG RYDERS); repl. JOHNSON

Lost Highway | Lost Highway

Apr 03. (cd)<lp> *<(077137-2)><0800-1>* **RAINY DAY MUSIC** [70] [51]
– Stumbling through the dark / Tailspin / All the right reasons / Save it for a rainy day / Eyes of Sarah Jane / One man's problem / Don't let the world get in your way / Come to the river / Angelyne / Madman / You look so young / Tampa to Tulsa / Will I see you in Heaven / Stumbling through the dark (reprise).

– compilations, etc. –

Sep 00. (cd) *Columbia; (499876-2)* **TOMORROW THE GREEN GRASS / HOLLYWOOD TOWN** [ ] [–]

JAY-Z

Born: SHAWN CARTER, 4 Dec'70, Brooklyn, New York, USA. Despite being one of the most lauded yet egotistical rappers in the game, JAY-Z, who worked his way up from the slums of Brooklyn, had become one of the richest young entrepreneurs in the music industry thanks to his booming 'Roc-a-Fella' imprint. Raised in the Marcy projects of Brooklyn, the young JAY-Z (then known as 'Jazzy') began hustling on the streets in his teens until he met the aspiring rapper BIG JAZ, who was signed to a small label. Influenced by JAZ, JAY-Z decided to launch his own record label with just a few well-known rap artists around Brooklyn instead of trying to break into the already expanding rap industry. He enlisted DAMON DASH and KAREEM BURKE, and together they established 'Roc-a-Fella' records in 1995, just one year before JAY-Z issued his fantastic debut set 'REASONABLE DOUBT'. Critically acclaimed and pretty successful for an independent release, the set charted in the Billboard charts at number 23 but became a cult record amongst the fledgling rapsters on the East Coast scene. The album also boasted a fine line-up of guests (soon to become a common thing on JAY-Z records) such as MARY J BLIGE and the tragic NOTORIOUS B.I.G. The following year JAY-Z ditched his gangsta efforts and went for a more pop orientated direction for his subsequent release 'IN MY LIFE: VOL 1'. The usual guest stars appeared (PUFF DADDY, TEDD RILEY) but with an entourage of singles such as 'SUNSHINE' and 'THE CITY IS MINE', JAY-Z proved to a mainstream audience that he was no ghetto thug – but a sound producer with a lot to offer to the overground. Not surprisingly, the set entered the Billboard charts at Number 3, a huge climb from the self-produced debut. 'VOL 2: HARD KNOCK LIFE' (1998) surfaced the following year boasting the huge single 'HARD KNOCK LIFE (GHETTO ANTHEM)' which cleverly and bizarrely enough sampled the 'Annie' song, with piano and a chorus of orphaned children respectively. Other singles 'JIGGA WHAT?' and 'MONEY AIN'T A THING' climbed the charts but didn't possess the strangeness and quirkiness of the album's title track. By this point JAY-Z had turned his record company into a "dynasty", by producing his own clothing line and representing a huge host of New York's finest talents. Like usual, he unfettered another two albums over the next two years; vanity project 'VOL 3: LIFE AND TIMES OF S. CARTER' (1999) truly for only the most avid collector, and a sort of label sampler (but not quite) 'DYNASTY ROC LA FAMILIA' (2000), which included a whole host of in-house artists like MEMPHIS BLEEK and AMIL. These two albums were literally nothing compared to the excellent 'THE BLUEPRINT' album, issued in 2001 and heavily compared by critics to Z's breakthrough 'REASONABLE DOUBT'. It featured the track 'TAKEOVER', a vicious attack on East Coasters NAS and MOBB DEEP. Although the feud continued for many months after the release of the set – nobody is very clear why JAY-Z launched such a tirade on two very respected members of the hip-hop scene. The album spawned two other hit singles 'GIRLS, GIRLS, GIRLS' and 'JIGGA THAT NIGGA' and went on to rank high on many album-of-the-year polls. After sharing an album with R. KELLY, 'THE BEST OF BOTH WORLDS' (2002), New York's shrewdest cut double set, 'THE BLUEPRINT: THE GIFT & THE CURSE' (2002). A sprawling, near 2-hour trawl through contemporary hip hop featuring everyone from the NEPTUNES and DR. DRE to LENNY KRAVITZ and BEYONCe, the album represented an opportunity for JAY-Z to pander to his artistic whims without the editorial discipline required of a conventional set. While he's certainly not the first artist to do a 'BLACK ALBUM' (2003), JAY-Z is perhaps the first to instill the title with such meaning. And while his lyrics cut to the quick on the travails of the black experience, more often than not it was, as usual, from a strictly personal viewpoint. Which, of course, is what made the likes of 'DECEMBER 4' and the Russell Crowe-sampling 'WHAT MORE CAN I SAY', so compelling.

Album rating: REASONABLE DOUBT (*6) / IN MY LIFETIME, VOL.1 (*7) / VOL.2 . . . HARD KNOCK LIFE (*8) / VOL.3 . . . LIFE AND TIMES OF S. CARTER (*7) / THE DYNASTY ROC DA FAMILIA (2000) (*6) / THE BLUEPRINT (*8) / MTV UNPLUGGED (*5) / CHAPTER ONE compilation (*7) / THE BLUEPRINT 2: THE GIFT & THE CURSE (*6) / THE BLACK ALBUM (*7)

JAY-Z – vocals / with various artists

not iss. | ffrr

Jul 95. (12"/cd-s) *<120072>* **IN MY LIFETIME (mixes; original ski / original ski street / skitrumental / big jazz radio / big jazmental) / CAN'T GET WITH THAT (DJ Clark Kent version)** [–] [ ]

Feb 96. (12"/cd-s) *<53233>* **DEAD PRESIDENTS (mixes; clean / album instrumental) / AIN'T NO NIGGA (album / instrumental)** [–] [ ]

Northwest – Arista | Roc-a-fella

Feb 97. (c-s; by JAY-Z featuring MARY J. BLIGE) *(74321 44719-4) <53242>* **CAN'T KNOCK THE HUSTLE (mixes; clean / dirty)** [30] [73]
(cd-s+=) *(74321 44719-2)* – (instrumental / acappella).

Mar 97. (cd/c/d-lp) *(74321 44720-2/-4/-1) <50592>* **REASONABLE DOUBT** [ ] Jul96 [23]
– Can't knock the hustle (with MARY J. BLIGE) / Politics as usual / Brooklyn's finest (with NOTORIOUS B.I.G.) / Dead presidents II Feelin' it (with MECCA) / D'Evils / 22 two's / Can I live / Ain't no nigga (with FOXY BROWN) / Friend or foe / Coming of age (with MEMPHIS BLEEK) / Cashmere thoughts / Bring it on (with BIG JAZ) / Regrets / Can I live II. *(re-iss. May99 cd/c; same)*

Apr 97. (12"/cd-s; by JAY-Z with FOXY BROWN) *(74321 47484-1/-2)* **AIN'T NO PLAYA/NIGGA (mixes; clean / original radio / Ganjo Kru / Fresh to Def / New York street / original)** [31] [50]

—— JAY-Z returned the favor to FOXY by featuring on her hit, 'I'll Be'

Aug 97. (12"/cd-s) *(W 0411 T/CD) <43883>* **WHO YOU WIT (mixes; clean / album / instrumental / acappella)** [65] [84]
(above issued on 'Qwest-Warners')

Oct 97. (c-s; by JAY-Z featuring BABYFACE & FOXY BROWN) *(74321 52870-4) <574923>* **(ALWAYS BE MY) SUNSHINE / DEAD PRESIDENTS II** [25] [95]
(12"+=/cd-s+=) *(74321 52870-1/-2)* – ('A'-mixes; radio / album / clean / TV acappella).

Feb 98. (c-s; by JAY-Z featuring GWEN DICKEY) *(74321 55463-4)* **WISHING ON A STAR (mixes; radio / masters / D Influence)** [13] [–]
(12"+=/cd-s+=) *(74321 55463-1/-2)* – Brooklyn's finest (featuring NOTORIOUS B.I.G.).

Feb 98. (cd/c)(t-lp) *(74321 55989-2/-4)(52869-1) <536392>* **IN MY LIFETIME, VOL.1** [ ] Nov97 [3]
– intro / A million and one questions / Rhyme no more / The city is mine (with BLACKstreet) / I know what girls like (with PUFF DADDY & LIL' KIM) / Imaginary player / Streets is watching / Friend or foe '98 / Lucky me / (Always be my) Sunshine (with BABYFACE & FOXY BROWN) /

Who you wit – Face off / Real niggaz (with TOO SHORT) / Rap game – Crack game / Where I'm from / You must love me.

Jun 98. (c-s; by JAY-Z featuring BLACKstreet) *(74321 58801-4)* **THE CITY IS MINE / (version)** [38] Jan98 [52]
(12"+=/cd-s+=) *(74321 58801-1/-2)* – A million and one questions.

— mid'98, JAY-Z had a US hit (w/ MEMPHIS BLEEK), 'It's Alright'

Nov 98. (c-s) *(74321 63533-4)* *<566977>* **HARD KNOCK LIFE (GHETTO ANTHEM) / CAN'T KNOCK THE HUSTLE** [2] [15]
(12"+=/cd-s+=) *(74321 63533-1/-2)* – ('A'mixes).

Jan 99. (cd/c/lp) *(74321 62555-2/-4/-1)* *<558902>* **VOL.2 . . . HARD KNOCK LIFE** [ ] Oct98 [1]
– intro / Hand it down (w/ MEMPHIS BLEEK) / Hard knock life (ghetto anthem) / If I should die / Ride or die / Nigga what, nigga who (originator 99) (with BIG JAZ) / Money cash hoes (with DMX) / A week ago (with TOO SHORT) / Coming of age (da sequel) (with MEMPHIS BLEEK) / Can I get a . . . (with AMIL & JA RULE) / Paper chase (with FOXY BROWN) / Reservoir dogs / It's like that (with KID CAPRI) / It's alright (with MEMPHIS BLEEK) / Money ain't a thing (with JERMAINE DUPRI).

Feb 99. (12") *<566893>* **MONEY CASH HOES (mixes)** [–] [ ]

Mercury Roc-A-Fella

Mar 99. (12"/cd-s; by JAY-Z featuring AMIL & JA RULE) *(566847-1/-2)* *<567688>* **CAN I GET A . . . (mixes)** [24] Oct98 [19]

Mar 99. (-; by JAY-Z featuring BIG JAZ) *<radio>* **JIGGA WHAT, JIGGA WHO / AIN'T NO NIGGA / BRING IT ON** [–] [84]

— in Apr'99, JAY-Z featured ANOTHER LEVEL's hit, 'Be Alone No More'

— in Jun'99, he also featured on TIMBALAND's hit, 'Lobster & Scrimp'

Jun 99. (cd-s) *<562201>* **JIGGA MY NIGGA / MEMPHIS BLEEK IS / WHEN WILL U SEE / WHAT A THUG ABOUT** [–] [28]

Aug 99. (cd-s) *<668138>* **GIRLS' BEST FRIEND** [–] [52]

— in Nov'99, the rapper appeared on MARIAH CAREY's Top 5 'Heartbreaker'

— a month later, JAY-Z featured on yet another collaboration single (with MEMPHIS BLEEK), 'What You Think Of That'

Roc-A-Fella Roc-A-Fella

Dec 99. (cd-s; by JAY-Z featuring BEANIE SIGEL & AMIL) *<562575>* **DO IT AGAIN (PUT YA HANDS UP) (mixes) / SO GHETTO / JIGGA MY NIGGA** [–] [65]

Feb 00. (c-s) *(562650-4)* *<562670>* **ANYTHING / GO GHETTO** [18] [55]
(cd-s+=) *(562650-2)* – There's been a murder.

Jun 00. (c-s/12"; JAY-Z featuring UGK) *(562833-4/-1)* *<562774>* **BIG PIMPIN'. / ANYTHING** [29] Apr00 [18]
(cd-s+=) *(562774-2)* – ('A'mixes).

Jun 00. (cd/c/lp) *(546815-2/-4/-1)* *<546822>* **VOL.3 . . . LIFE AND TIMES OF S. CARTER** [ ] Jan00 [1]
– Hova song (intro) / So ghetto / Do it again (put ya hands up) (with BEANIE SIGEL & AMIL) / Dope man (with SERENA ALTSHUL) / Things that U do (with MARIAH CAREY) / It's hot (some like it hot) / Snoopy track (with JUVENILE) / S. Carter / Pop 4 roc (with BEANIE SIGEL, MEMPHIS BLEEK & AMIL) / Hove interlude / Big pimpin' (with UGK) / Is that yo bitch (with TWISTA & MISSY) / Come and get me (with TWISTA & MISSY) / N.Y.M.P. (with TWISTA & MISSY) / Hova song (outro). *(UK+=)* – Anything. *(clean cd version; 546814-2)*

Aug 00. (cd-s; by JAY-Z featuring MEMPHIS BLEEK) *<562862>* **HEY PAPI (mixes)** [–] [76]

Nov 00. (cd/lp) *<(548203-2/-1)>* **ROC LA FAMILIA – THE DYNASTY** [ ] [1]
– (intro) / Change the game / I just wanna love U (give it 2 me) / Streets is talking / This can't be life (with SCARFACE) / Get your mind right mami (with SNOOP DOGG) / Stick 2 the script / You, me, him and her / Guilty until proven innocent (with R. KELLY) / Parking lot pimpin' / Holla / 1-900 hustler / The R.O.C. / Soon you'll understand / Squeeze 1st / Where have you been.

Dec 00. (c-s) *(572746-4)* *<572666>* **I JUST WANNA LOVE U (GIVE IT 2 ME) / PARKING LOT PIMPIN' (radio)** [17] Oct00 [11]
(12"+=) *(572746-1)* – Hey papi.
(cd-s++=) *(572746-2)* – ('A'video).

Jan 01. (cd-s; by JAY-Z featuring BEANIE SIGEL & MEMPHIS BLEEK) *<572761>* **CHANGE THE GAME (mixes; radio / instrumental / research hook)** [–] [86]

— in Mar'01. JAY-Z featured on R KELLY's hit, 'Fiesta'

Apr 01. (cd-s; by JAY-Z & R KELLY) *<572809>* **GUILTY UNTIL PROVEN INNOCENT (radio / album) / CHANGE THE GAME** [–] [82]

Sep 01. (cd/d-lp) *<(586396-2/-1)>* **THE BLUEPRINT** [30] [1]
– The ruler's back / Takeover / Izzo (H.O.V.A.) / Girls, girls, girls / Jigga that n**** / U don't know / Hola' hovita / Heart of the city (ain't no love) / Never change / Song cry / All I need / Renegade / Blueprint (momma loves me).

Oct 01. (c-s) *(588815-4)* *<588701>* **IZZO (H.O.V.A.) / (album)** [21] Jul01 [8]
(12"+=/cd-s+=) *(588815-1/-2)* – (instrumental).

Jan 02. (c-s) *(588906-4)* *<588793>* **GIRLS, GIRLS, GIRLS / (part 2)** [11] Oct01 [17]
(12"+=) *(588906-1)* – Big pimpin' (with UGK).
(cd-s++=) *(588906-2)* – ('A'video).

Mar 02. (cd) *<(586614-2)>* **MTV UNPLUGGED (live)** [ ] Dec01 [34]
– Izzo (H.O.V.A.) / Takeover / Girls, girls, girls / Jigga what, jigga who / Big pimpin' / Heart of the city (ain't no love) / Can I get a . . . / Hard knock life (ghetto anthem) / Ain't no / Can't knock the hustle – Family affair / Song cry / I just wanna love U (give it 2 me) / Jigga that nigga.

— in Mar'02, JAY-Z collaborated with R. KELLY on the album, 'THE BEST OF BOTH WORLDS' and the single, 'HONEY'; both hits.

Nov 02. (d-cd/q-lp) *<(63381-2/-1)>* **THE BLUEPRINT 2: THE GIFT & THE CURSE** [23] [1]
– A dream (with FAITH EVANS & The NOTORIOUS B.I.G.) / Hovi baby / The watcher 2 (with DR. DRE & TRUTH HURTS) / '03 Bonnie & Clyde (with BEYONCE KNOWLES) / Excuse me miss / What they gonna do (with SEAN PAUL) / All around the world (with LaTOIYA WILLIAMS) / Poppin' tags (with BIG BOI, KILLER MIKE & TWISTA) / Fuck all nite / The bounce / I did it my way / Diamond is forever / Guns & roses (with LENNY KRAVITZ) / U don't know (remix) (with M.O.P.) / Meet the parents / Some how some way (with BEANIE SIGEL & SCARFACE) / Some people hate / Blueprint2 / Nigga please (with YOUNG CHRIS) / 2 many hoes / As one (with MEMPHIS BLEEK, FREEWAY & YOUNG GUNS) / A ballad for the fallen soldier / Show you how / Bitches & sisters / What they gonna do, pt.II. *<(re-iss. Apr03 as 'BLUEPRINT 2.1'; 077344-2)>* – <hit US No.17>

Jan 03. (c-s; by JAY-Z & BEYONCE KNOWLES) *(077010-4)* *<063843>* **'03 BONNIE & CLYDE / (explicit album version)** [2] Nov02 [4]
(12") *(077010-1)* – ('A'side) / U don't know (explicit remix) / ('A'-instrumental).
(cd-s++=) *(077010-2)* – ('A'-video).

Apr 03. (12"/cd-s) *(077912-1/-2)* *<63717>* **EXCUSE ME MISS. / ('A'-instrumental) / Heart of the city (ain't no love) (live)** [17] Feb03 [8]

— in Jul'03, JAY-Z featured on PANJABI MC's hit 'Jogi' + also PHARRELL WILLIAMS' Top 10 smash, 'Frontin''

Nov 03. (cd/d-lp) *(9861121)* *<15280-2/-1>* **THE BLACK ALBUM** [40] [1]
– Interlude / December 4th / What more can I say / Encore / Change clothes / Dirt off your shoulder / Threat / Moment of clarity / 99 problems / Public service announcement (interlude) / Justify my thug / Lucifer / Allure / My 1st song.

Dec 03. (cd-s) *(981522-5)* *<165111>* **CHANGE CLOTHES / WHAT MORE CAN I SAY** [32] Nov03 [10]
(12"/cd-s) *(981522-7/-6)* – ('A'side) / Excuse me miss / I just wanna love U (give it 2 me) / Excuse me miss again.

– compilations, etc. –

Mar 02. (cd/lp) *B.M.G.; (74321 92046-2/-1)* *<86098>* **CHAPTER ONE** [65] [ ]
– Hard knock life (the ghetto anthem) / Wishing on a star / Sunshine (with FOXY BROWN & BABYFACE) / The city is mine / Can't knock the hustle / Ain't no nigga / Imaginary prayer / Money ain't a thang (with JERMAINE DUPRI) / Can I get a . . . (with AMIL & JA RULE) / Streets is watching / Money, cash, hoes (with DMX) / I know what girls like / Feelin' it / Dead presidents II / Wishing on a star / Can't knock the hustle (with MELISSA MORGAN) / Ain't no nigga (with FOXY BROWN).

Oct 03. (cd) *Camden-BMG; (82876 56697-2)* **BRING IT ON: THE BEST OF JAY-Z** [ ] [–]

☐ Wyclef JEAN & The REFUGEE ALLSTARS (see under ⇒ FUGEES)

☐ JEEVAS (see under ⇒ KULA SHAKER)

JEFFERSON AIRPLANE

Formed: San Francisco, California, USA . . . early 1965 by MARTY BALIN and PAUL KANTNER. They recruited others and signed to 'RCA' in late '65, releasing a flop debut single, 'IT'S NO SECRET'. In September '66, their first album, ' . . . TAKES OFF', was finally issued, a competent hybrid of folk-rock and blues notable for the powerful singing of second vocalist SIGNE ANDERSON. By the time of the album's release, however, ANDERSON had left to have a baby and was replaced by GRACE SLICK (formerly of The GREAT SOCIETY). SKIP SPENCE also left and the drum stool was filled by SPENCER DRYDEN. The potential of this all-playing, all-writing group was fulfilled on the follow-up lp, 'SURREALISTIC PILLOW' (1967). A psychedelic classic, the record spawned two top 10 singles in the U.S., 'SOMEBODY TO LOVE' (1967) and 'WHITE RABBIT' (967), SLICK having brought both songs with her from her previous band. Her vocals were even stronger than ANDERSON's and her commanding clarity stamped itself indelibly on every song, particularly 'WHITE RABBIT', a neo classical, lysergic nursery rhyme (inspired by the Lewis Carroll book 'Alice In Wonderland') that managed to sound at once sinister and insidiously catchy. Even KAUKONEN's blistering guitar work and newcomer JACK CASADY's relentlessly inventive bass playing sounded more assured, the album going on to sell half a million copies. The band then took psychedelic experimentation ever further with 'AFTER BATHING AT BAXTER'S' (1968). Comprising a number of free-form song 'suites', the album was hard going; the melodies were still in there, they were just harder to find among the wilful weirdness and extended instrumental jams. 'R.C.A.' must have breathed a sigh of relief when the band came up with the relatively more accessible 'CROWN OF CREATION' (1968). A more conventional set of songs, it featured the scary 'THE HOUSE AT POOH CORNER', SLICK's haunting 'LATHER' and a cover of DAVID CROSBY's menage-a-trois elegy, 'TRIAD'. After a thundering live set, 'BLESS ITS POINTED LITTLE HEAD' (1969), the band recorded the last album to feature the classic JEFFERSON line-up, 'VOLUNTEERS' (1970). It featured the unflinching politicism of 'WE CAN BE TOGETHER' and though the title track was used in the 'Woodstock' movie, the band's own performance wasn't filmed. Soon after the album's release, DRYDEN left to join The NEW RIDERS OF THE PURPLE SAGE and was replaced by JOEY COVINGTON. BALIN also departed around this time after a prolonged period of tension with SLICK, violinist PAPA JOHN CREACH (was this the man behind MADONNA's 'Papa Don't Preach' we ask ourselves?) taking up the slack. The subsequent 'BARK' (1971) and 'LONG JOHN SILVER' (1972) albums (released on the band's newly formed 'Grunt' label) bore none of the intensity of The 'AIRPLANE's earlier work and the band's final effort, the live 'THIRTY SECONDS OVER WINTERLAND' (1973) was similarly underwhelming. By this point, JOHN BARBATA had replaced sticksman COVINGTON while DAVID FRIEBERG (ex-QUICKSILVER MESSENGER SERVICE) had been recruited on vocals. While CASSADY and KAUKONEN went full-time with their side project, HOT TUNA, SLICK and KANTNER formed JEFFERSON STARSHIP with the remaining 'AIRPLANE members. The name was taken from an earlier, KANTNER sci-fi inspired project that released one album, 1971's '(IT'S A FRESH WIND THAT) BLOWS AGAINST THE NORTH'. The debut JEFFERSON STARSHIP album, 'DRAGONFLY' (1974), was well written and skillfully executed but it was clear the band were headed towards the mainstream and with 'RED OCTOPUS' (1975), the band's sleek sound was crystallised, the album shifting a cool four million copies. MARTY BALIN was also back in the fold by this point and his song, 'MIRACLES', went Top 3 later the same year. Disillusioned with the new direction, SLICK soon left for a low key solo career while JEFFERSON STARSHIP continued to notch up hit albums. She later rejoined, although by 1984 even KANTNER had become tired of the group's commercial sound, leaving and taking the JEFFERSON part of the name with him. As STARSHIP, the SLICK fronted band went on to even bigger success, reeling off hits like 'WE BUILT THIS CITY ON ROCK 'N' ROLL' (1985) and the nauseous pop slush of 'NOTHING'S GONNA STOP US NOW' (1987). Incredibly/inevitably there was a full reunion of the classic JEFFERSON AIRPLANE line-up in 1989 which produced an eponymous album. A pointless exercise in crusty nostalgia, it was almost as dull as the dishwater STARSHIP were peddling.

Album rating: JEFFERSON AIRPLANE TAKES OFF (*5) / SURREALISTIC PILLOW (*8) / AFTER BATHING AT BAXTER'S (*7) / CROWN OF CREATION (*7) / VOLUNTEERS (*6) / THE WORST OF JEFFERSON AIRPLANE compilation (*6) / BLOWS AGAINST THE EMPIRE (*5; as PAUL KANTNER & JEFFERSON STARSHIP) / SUNFIGHTER (*5; by Paul Kantner & Grace Slick) / BARK (*6) / LONG JOHN SILVER (*5) / THIRTY SECONDS OVER WINTERLAND (*5) / BARON VON TOLBOOTH & THE CHROME NUN (*4; by Paul Kantner, Grace Slick & David Freiberg) / EARLY FLIGHT early stuff (*4) / Grace Slick: MANHOLE (*4) / DREAMS (*4) / WELCOME TO THE WRECKING BALL (*5) / Jefferson Starship: DRAGON FLY (*6) / RED OCTOPUS (*7) / SPITFIRE (*6) / FLIGHT LOG 1966-1976 compilation (*6; Jefferson Airplane & Starship) / EARTH (*4) / GOLD compilation (*7) / FREEDOM AT POINT ZERO (*5) / MODERN TIMES (*5) / WINDS OF CHANGE (*4) / NUCLEAR FURNITURE (*4) / Starship: KNEE DEEP IN THE HOOPLA (*4) / 2400 FULTON STREET – AN ANTHOLOGY remastered early collection (*7) / NO PROTECTION (*4) / LOVE AMONG THE CANNIBALS (*4) / JEFFERSON AIRPLANE (*3; as Jefferson Airplane) / DEEP SPACE – VIRGIN SKY (*3) / GREATEST HITS (TEN YEARS AND CHANGE 1979-1991) compilation (*6; by Starship)

MARTY BALIN (b. MARTYN JEREL BUCHWALD, 30 Jan'43, Cincinnati, Ohio, USA) – vocals, guitar (ex-solo) / **PAUL KANTNER** (b.12 Mar'42, San Francisco) – guitar, vocals / **JORMA KAUKONEN** (b.23 Dec'40, Washington, D.C.) – lead guitar / **SIGNE TOLY ANDERSON** (b.15 Sep'41, Seattle, Wash.) – vocals / **JACK CASADY** (b.13 Apr'44, Washington, D.C.) – bass repl. BOB HARVEY / **SKIP SPENCE** (b.18 Apr'46, Ontario, Canada) – drums (ex-QUICKSILVER MESSENGER SERVICE) repl. JERRY PELOQUIN

		R.C.A.	R.C.A.
Feb 66.	(7") *<8679>* **IT'S NO SECRET. / RUNNIN' ROUND THIS TABLE**	–	
May 66.	(7") *<8848>* **COME UP THE YEARS. / BLUES FROM AN AEROPLANE**	–	
Sep 66.	(lp) *<LSP 3584>* **JEFFERSON AIRPLANE TAKES OFF**	–	

– Blues from an airplane / Let me in / It's no secret / Bringing me down / Tobacco road / Coming up the years / Run around / Let's get together / Don't slip away / Chauffeur blues / And I like it. *(UK-iss.Oct71; SF 8195) (re-iss. Jun74;) <(cd re-mast.Aug03 +=; 82876 50352-2)>* – Runnin' 'round this world / High flyin' bird / It's alright / Go to her / Let me in (alt.) / Run around (alt.) / Chauffeur blues (alt.) / And I like it (alt.).

Sep 66.	(7") *<8967>* **BRINGING ME DOWN. / LET ME IN**	–	

— **GRACE SLICK** (b. GRACE BARNETT WING, 30 Oct'39, Chicago, Illinois) – vocals (ex-GREAT SOCIETY) repl. SIGNE who left to look after her baby / **SPENCER DRYDEN** (b. 7 Apr'38, New York City) – drums (ex-PEANUT BUTTER CONSPIRACY, ex-ASHES) repl. SKIP who formed MOBY GRAPE

Dec 66.	(7") *<9063>* **MY BEST FRIEND. / HOW DO YOU FEEL**	–	
Sep 67.	(lp; mono/stereo) *(RD/SF 7889) <LSP 3766>* **SURREALISTIC PILLOW**		Feb67 3

– She has funny cars / Somebody to love / My best friend / Today / Comin' back to me / How do you feel / 3/5 mile in 10 seconds / D.C.B.A. – 25 / Embryonic journey / White rabbit / Plastic fantastic lover. *(UK-rel.had different tracks) (cd-iss. Sep84; PD 83766) (cd re-iss. Oct87; ND 83738) <(cd re-mast.Aug03 +=; 82876 50351-2)>* – In the morning / J.P.P. McStep B. blues / Go to her / Come back baby / Somebody to love / White rabbit.

May 67. (7") *(RCA 1594)* *<9140>* **SOMEBODY TO LOVE. / SHE HAS FUNNY CARS** [ ] Feb67 [5]
Sep 67. (7") *(RCA 1631)* *<9248>* **WHITE RABBIT. / PLASTIC FANTASTIC LOVER** [ ] Jun67 [8]
Nov 67. (7") *(RCA 1647)* *<9297>* **BALLAD OF YOU AND ME AND POONEIL. / TWO HEADS** [ ] Sep67 [42]
Jun 68. (lp; mono/stereo) *(RD/SF 7926)* *<LSP 1511>* **AFTER BATHING AT BAXTER'S** [ ] Dec67 [17]
– (Streetmasse): / Ballad of you and me and Pooneil – A small package of value will come to you, shortly – Young girl Sunday blues / (The war is over): / Martha – Wild thyme / (Hymn to an older generation): / The last wall of the castle – Rejoyce / How sweet it is:- Watch her ride – Spare chaynge / Shizoforest love suite: Two heads – Won't you try – Saturday afternoon. *(re-iss. Dec88 lp/c; NL/NK 84718) (cd-iss. May98; ND 84718) <(cd re-mast.Aug03 +=; 82876 53225-2)>* – The ballad of you and me and Pooneil (live) / Martha (version) / Two heads (alt.) / Things are better in the east (demo).
Jan 68. (7") *<9389>* **WATCH HER RIDE. / MARTHA** [–] Dec67 [61]
Jun 68. (7") *(RCA 1711)* *<9496>* **GREASY HEART. / SHARE A LITTLE JOKE** [ ] Mar68 [98]
Sep 68. (7") *(RCA 1736)* **IF YOU FEEL LIKE CHINA BREAKING. TRIAD** [ ] [–]
Oct 68. (7") *<9644>* **CROWN OF CREATION. / TRIAD** [–] [64]
Dec 68. (lp; mono/stereo) *(RD/SF 7976)* *<LSP 4058>* **CROWN OF CREATION** [ ] Sep68 [6]
– Lather / In time / Triad / Star track / Share a little joke / Chushingura / If you feel / Crown of creation / Ice cream Phoenix / Greasy heart / The house at Pooh Corner. *(re-iss. Oct85 lp/c; NL/NK 83797) (cd-iss. Jun88 & Jan98; ND 83660) <(cd re-mast.Aug03 ++; 82876 53226-2)>* – Ribump ba bap dum dum / Would you like a snack? / Share a little joke / The saga of Sydney Spacepig.
Jun 69. (lp; mono/stereo) *(RD/SF 8019)* *<LSP 4133>* **BLESS ITS POINTED LITTLE HEAD (live)** [38] Feb69 [17]
– Clergy / 3/5 of a mile in 10 seconds / Somebody to love / Fat angel / Rock me baby / The other side of this life / It's no secret / Plastic fantastic lover / Turn out the lights / Bear melt.
Jul 69. (7") *<0150>* **PLASTIC FANTASTIC LOVER (live). / THE OTHER SIDE OF THIS LIFE (live)** [–] [ ]
Feb 70. (lp) *(SF 8164)* *<LSP 4238>* **VOLUNTEERS** [34] Nov69 [13]
– We can be together / Good shepherd / The farm / Hey Frederick / Turn my life down / Wooden ships / Eskimo blue day / A song for all seasons / Meadowlands / Volunteers. *(re-iss. Oct85)*
Mar 70. (7") *(RCA 1933)* *<0245>* **VOLUNTEERS. / WE CAN BE TOGETHER** [ ] Nov69 [65]

—— **JOEY COVINGTON** – drums repl. DRYDEN who joined NEW RIDERS OF THE PURPLE SAGE (above new with **SLICK, CASADY, BALIN** and **KAUKONEN)** (note also DRYDEN played on below 'A' side)

Aug 70. (7") *(RCA 1989)* *<0343>* **MEXICO. / HAVE YOU SEEN THE SAUCERS?** [ ] [ ]

—— At this time various members, mainly KAUKONEN and CASADY side-lined HOT TUNA. PAUL KANTNER then recorded album with what was then p/t JEFFERSON STARSHIP (see further below and his late '71 co-credit with GRACE SLICK)

—— **PAPA JOHN CREACH** (b.28 May 1917, Beaver Falls, Pennsylvania) – violin (of HOT TUNA) finally repl. BALIN who left earlier.

Grunt Grunt

Oct 71. (lp) *<(FTR 1001)>* **BARK** [42] Sep71 [11]
– When the Earth moves again / Feel so good / Crazy Miranda / Pretty as you feel / Wild turkey / Law man / Rock and roll island / Third week in Chelsea / Never argue with a German if you're tired or European song / Thunk / War movie. *(re-iss. Jul84; NL 84386)*
Oct 71. (7") *<(65-0500)>* **PRETTY AS YOU FEEL. / WILD TURKEY** [ ] [60]

—— **JOHN BARBATA** – drums (ex-CROSBY & NASH, ex-TURTLES) repl. JOEY

Jun 72. (lp) *<(FTR 1007)>* **LONG JOHN SILVER** [30] [20]
– Long John Silver / Aerie (gang of eagles) / Twilight double leader / Milk train / Son of Jesus / Easter? / Trial by fire / Alexander the medium / Eat starch mom.
Sep 72. (7") *<(65-0506)>* **LONG JOHN SILVER. / MILK TRAIN** [ ] [ ]
1972. (7") *<(65-0511)>* **TWILIGHT DOUBLE DEALER. / TRIAL BY FIRE** [ ] [ ]

—— **DAVID FREIBERG** (b.24 Aug'38, Boston, Mass.) – vocals (ex-QUICKSILVER MESSENGER SERVICE) (They made last album recorded between 71-72)

Apr 73. (lp) *<(FTR 0147)>* **30 SECONDS OVER WINTERLAND (live)** [ ] [52]
– Have you seen the saucers / Feel so good / Crown of creation / When the Earth moves again / Milk train / Trial by fire / Twilight double leader. *(re-iss. Oct85 lp/c; NL/NK 83867)*

—— Now non-recording quintet of SLICK, KANTNER, FREIBERG, BARBATA and CREACH. CASADY and KAUKONEN made HOT TUNA their full-time band.

PAUL KANTNER & JEFFERSON STARSHIP

with JERRY GARCIA, DAVID CROSBY, GRAHAM NASH, MICKEY HART

R.C.A. R.C.A.

Jan 71. (7") *<0426>* **A CHILD IS COMING. / LET'S GO TOGETHER** [–] [ ]
Apr 71. (lp) *(SF 8163)* *<LSP 4448>* **(IT'S A FRESH WIND THAT) BLOWS AGAINST THE NORTH** [ ] Nov70 [20]
– Mau mau (Amerikon) / The baby tree / Let's go together / A child is coming / Sunrise / Hijack / Home / Have you seen the stars tonite / X-M / Starship.

PAUL KANTNER & GRACE SLICK

Grunt Grunt

Dec 71. (lp) *<(FTR 1002)>* **SUNFIGHTER** [ ] [89]
– Silver spoon / Diana (part 1) / Sunfighter / Titanic / Look at the wood / When I was a boy I watched the wolves / Million / China / Earth mother / Diana (part 2) / Universal Copernican mumbles / Holding together. *(re-iss. Apr89 on 'Essential' lp/cd; ESS LP/CD 001)*
Jan 72. (7") *<0503>* **SUNFIGHTER. / CHINA** [–] [ ]

—— KANTNER later released a US only album 'THE PLANET EARTH ROCK AND ROLL ORCHESTRA iss.Aug83. After leaving JEFFERSON STARSHIP he formed KBC with BALIN and CASADY (ex-AIRPLANE members). They released a single and album early '83.

PAUL KANTNER, GRACE SLICK, DAVID FREIBERG

with guests **JORMA KAUKONEN** – guitar / **JACK CASADY** – bass / **CHAQUICO** – guitar / **JERRY GARCIA** ('Grateful Dead') / **DAVID CROSBY** ('Crosby, Stills & Nash')

Grunt Grunt

Jun 73. (lp) *<(BFL 1-0148)>* **BARON VON TOLBOOTH & THE CHROME NUN** [ ] [ ]
– Ballad of the chrome nun / Fat / Flowers of the night / Walkin' / Your mind has left your body / Across the board / Harp tree lament / White boy (transcaucasian airmachine blues) / Fishman / Sketches of China.
Jun 73. (7") *<0094>* **BALLAD OF THE CHROME NUN. / SKETCHES OF CHINA** [–] [ ]

JEFFERSON STARSHIP

(new name re-formed) **SLICK, KANTNER, FREIBERG, CREACH + BARBATA** recruited **CRAIG CHAQUICO** (b.26 Sep'54, Sacramento, Calif.) – guitar (ex-STEELWIND) repl. JORMA / **PETE SEARS** (b. England) – bass, keyboards, vocals repl. PETER KAUKONEN, who had repl. JACK

Grunt Grunt

Nov 74. (7") *<FB 10080>* **RIDE THE TIGER. / DEVIL'S DEN** [–] [84]
Dec 74. (lp) *<(BFL 1-0717)>* **DRAGONFLY** [ ] Oct74 [11]
– Ride the tiger / That's for sure / Be young you / Caroline / Devil's den / Come to life / All fly away / Hyperdrive.
1975. (7") *<FB 10206>* **BE YOUNG YOU. / CAROLINE** [–] [ ]

—— added the returning **MARTY BALIN** – vocals, guitar

Jul 75. (lp) *(FTR 2002)* *<BFL 1-0999>* **RED OCTOPUS** [ ] [1]
– Fast buck Freddie / Miracles / Git fiddler / Al Garimasu (there is love) / Sweeter than honey / Play on love / Tumblin' / I want to see another world / Sandalphon / There will be love. *(re-iss. Feb81 on 'RCA International' lp/c; INT S/K 5069) (re-iss. Oct84 on 'RCA' lp/c/cd; PL/PK/PD 80999) (re-iss. Jun86 on 'Fame' lp/c; FA/TC-FA 3156) (cd-iss. Oct87 & Jun88; ND 83464 & ND 83660)*
Sep 75. (7") *<(FB 10367)>* **MIRACLES. / AL GARIMASU (THERE IS LOVE)** [ ] Aug75 [3]
Nov 75. (7") *<FB 10456>* **PLAY ON LOVE. / I WANT TO SEE ANOTHER WORLD** [–] [49]

—— Trimmed to sextet when PAPA JOHN CREACH then GRACE SLICK went solo

Jul 76. (lp) *<(BFL 1-1557)>* **SPITFIRE** 30 3
– Hot water / Big city / Switchblade / Cruisin' / Love lovely love / St. Charles / Dance with the dragon / St. Charles / With your love / Song to the sun / Ozymandias / Don't let it rain. *(cd-iss. Jun97 on 'R.C.A.'; 0786366876-2)*

Aug 76. (7") *<(FB 10746)>* **WITH YOUR LOVE. / SWITCHBLADE** Jul76 12

Nov 76. (7") *<FB 10791>* **ST. CHARLES. / LOVE LOVELY LOVE** – 64

Feb 78. (7") *<(FB 11196)>* **COUNT ON ME. / SHOW YOURSELF** 8

Mar 78. (lp/c) *(FL/FK 12515) <2515>* **EARTH** 5
– Love too good / Count on me / Take your time / Crazy feelin' / Skateboard / Fire / Show yourself / All nite long. *(cd-iss. Jun97 on 'R.C.A.'; 0786366878-2)*

Jun 78. (7") *<(FB 11274)>* **RUNAWAY. / HOT WATER** May 78 12

Aug 78. (7") *<FB 11374>* **CRAZY FEELIN' / LOVE TOO GOOD** – 54

Nov 78. (7"/12") *<FB 11426/11469>* **LIGHT THE SKY ON FIRE. / HYPERDRIVE** – 66

—— **MICKEY THOMAS** (b. Cairo, Georgia) – vocals (ex-ELVIN BISHOP) repl. BALIN who went solo / **AYNSLEY DUNBAR** (b.10 Jan'46, Liverpool, England) – drums (ex-JOURNEY ex-KGB) repl. BARBATA (above 2 joining **KANTNER, FREIBERG, CHAQUICO** and **SEARS**) / **GRACE SLICK** also guested uncredited on the next album (she joined full-time Feb81.)

Jan 80. (7") *<(FB 11750)>* **JANE. / FREEDOM AT POINT ZERO** 21 Nov79 14

Jan 80. (lp) *(FL 13452) <3452>* **FREEDOM AT ZERO POINT** 22 Nov79 10
– Girl with hungry eyes / Freedom at Zero Point / Fadiing lady night / Lightning Rose / Things to come / Just the same / Rock music / Awakening / Jane. *(re-iss. Sep81 lp/c; RCA LP/K 3038) (re-iss. Jun89; NL 89912) (cd-iss. Feb90; ND 89912)*

Apr 80. (7") *<(FB 11921)>* **GIRL WITH THE HUNGRY EYES. / JUST THE SAME** 55

Jun 80. (7") *<FB 11961>* **ROCK MUSIC. / LIGHTNING ROSE** –

R.C.A. Grunt

May 81. (7"/12") *(RCA 66) <FB 1221-1/-3>* **FIND YOUR WAY BACK. / MODERN TIMES** Apr81 29

Jun 81. (lp) *(3050) <BZL 1-3848>* **MODERN TIMES** Apr81 26
– Find your way back / Stranger / Wild eyes / Save your love / Modern times / Mary / Free / Alien / Stairway to Cleveland. *(re-iss. Sep81 lp/c; RCA LP/K 3050)*

Jul 81. (7") *<12275>* **STRANGER. / FREE** – 48

Oct 81. (7"/12") *<1233-2/-3>* **SAVE YOUR LOVE. / WILD EYES** –

Oct 82. (7") *<13350>* **BE MY LADY. / OUT OF CONTROL** – 28

Feb 83. (lp/c) *(RCA LP/K 6060) <BXL 1-4372>* **WINDS OF CHANGE** Oct82 26
– Winds of change / Keep on dreamin' / Be my lady / I will stay / Out of control / Can't find love / Black widow / I came back from the jaws of the dragon / Quit wasting time. *(re-iss. Oct84 lp/c/cd; FL/FK/FD 84372)*

Jan 83. (7") *<13439>* **WINDS OF CHANGE. / BLACK WIDOW** – 38

Apr 83. (7") *<13531>* **CAN'T FIND LOVE. / I WILL STAY** –

—— **DON BALDWIN** – drums (ex-ELVIN BISHOP BAND) repl. DUNBAR

Jun 84. (7") *(RCA 424) <13811>* **NO WAY OUT. / ROSE GOES TO YALE** May84
(12"+=) *(RCA 424T) <13812>* – Be my lady.

Jun 84. (lp/c/cd) *(FL/FK/FD 84921) <4921>* **NUCLEAR FURNITURE** 28
– Layin' it on the line / No way out / Sorry me, sorry you / Live and let live / Connection / Nuclear furniture / Rose goes to Vale / Magician / Assassin / Shining in the moonlight / Showdown / Champion.

Sep 84 (7") *<13872>* **LAYIN' IT ON THE LINE. / SHOWDOWN** – 66

STARSHIP

was the name they were allowed to use after KANTNER left. Now **GRACE SLICK, MICKEY THOMAS, CRAIG CHAQUICO, PETE SEARS** and **DON BALDWIN**

Oct 85. (7") *(FB 49929) <14170>* **WE BUILT THIS CITY. / PRIVATE ROOM** 12 Sep85 1
(12"+=) *(FT 49930)* – ('A'extended).

Nov 85. (lp/c/cd) *(FL/FK/FD 85488) <5488>* **KNEE DEEP IN THE HOOPLA** Oct85 7
– We built this city / Sara / Tomorrow doesn't matter tonight / Rock myself to sleep / Desperate heart / Private room / Before I go / Hearts of the world (will understand) / Love rusts. *(re-iss. Sep89 lp/c/cd; NL/NK/ND 90367)*

Jan 86. (7") *(FB 49893) <14253>* **SARA. / HEARTS OF THE WORLD (WILL UNDERSTAND)** Dec85 1
(12"+=) *(FT 49894)* – Jane.

May 86. (7") *(FB 49855) <14332>* **TOMORROW DOESN'T MATTER TONIGHT. / LOVE RUSTS** Apr86 26
(12"+=) *(FT 49856)* – No way out / Layin' it on the line.

Jun 86. (7",12") *<14393>* **BEFORE I GO. / CUT YOU DOWN** – 68

—— now w/out SEARS

R.C.A. RCA-Grunt

Mar 87. (7") *(FB 49757) <5109>* **NOTHING'S GONNA STOP US NOW. / LAYING IT ON THE LINE** 1 Jan87 1
(12"+=) *(FT 49757)* – We built this city / Tomorrow doesn't matter tonight.

Jul 87. (lp/c/cd) *(FL/FK/FD 86413) <6413>* **NO PROTECTION** 26 12
– Beat patrol / Nothing's gonna stop us now / It's not over ('til it's over) / Girls like you / Wings of a lie / The children / I don't know why / Transatlantic / Babylon / Set the night to music.

Aug 87. (7") *(RCA 5001) <5225>* **IT'S NOT OVER ('TIL IT'S OVER). / BABYLON** Jun87 9
(12"+=)<US-cd-s> *(RCAT 5000)* – Jane / Sara.

Nov 87. (7") *(RCA 5002) <5308>* **BEAT PATROL. / GIRLS LIKE YOU** Sep87 46
(12"+=) *(RCAT 5002)* – ('A'extended).

Feb 88. (7") *<6964>* **SET THE NIGHT TO MUSIC. / I DON'T KNOW WHY** –
(12"+=) *<6964>* – ('A'dub version) / ('A'instrumental).

—— STARSHIP in the 90's were: – **MICKEY THOMAS, DONNY BALDWIN, CRAIG CHAQUICO** plus **MARK MORGAN** – keyboards / **BRETT BLOOMFIELD** – bass

Feb 89. (7") *(EKR 88) <69349>* **WILD AGAIN. / LAYIN' IT ON THE LINE** Dec88 73
(12"+=) *(EKR 88T)* – Tutti Frutti.
(above was from the film 'Cocktail' on label 'Elektra')

R.C.A. R.C.A.

Sep 89. (7"/c-s) *(PB/PK 49357) <9032>* **IT'S NOT ENOUGH. / LOVE AMONG THE CANNIBALS** Jul89 12
(12"+=) *(PT 49358)* – Wild again.
(cd-s++=) *(PD 49356)* – Nothing's gonna stop us now.

Sep 89. (lp/c/cd) *(PL/PK/PD 90387) <9693>* **LOVE AMONG THE CANNIBALS** Aug89 64
– The burn / It's not enough / Trouble in mind / I didn't mean to stay all night / Send a message / Love among the cannibals / We dream in colour / Healing waters / Blaze of love / I'll be there. *(cd+=)* – Wild again.

Nov 89. (c-s) *(9109)* **I DIDN'T MEAN TO STAY ALL NIGHT / WE DREAM IN COLOR** – 75

Apr 91. (c-s) *<2796>* **GOOD HEART / (3 album excerpts)** – 81

Aug 91. (cd/c/lp) *(PD/PK/PL 82423)* **GREATEST HITS (TEN YEARS AND CHANGE 1979-1991)** (compilation) –
– Jane / Find your way back / Stranger / No way out / Layin' it on the line / Don't lose any sleep / We built this city / Sara / Nothing's gonna stop us now / It's not over ('til it's over) / It's not enough / Good heart. *(re-iss. cd Oct95)*

JEFFERSON AIRPLANE

were reformed with **SLICK, KANTNER, KAUKONEN, CASADY and BALIN.** Augmented by **KENNY ARONOFF** – drums / **PETER KAUKONEN and RANDY JACKSON** – guitar (ex-ZEBRA)

Epic Epic

Oct 89. (lp/c/cd) *(465 659-1/-4/-2) <45271>* **JEFFERSON AIRPLANE** 85
– Planes / Solidarity / Summer of love / The wheel / True love / Now is the time / Panda / Freedom / Ice age / Madeleine Street / Common market madrigal / Upfront blues / Too many years.

Oct 89. (7") *<73044>* **SUMMER OF LOVE. / PANDA** –

Jan 90. (c-s) *<73080>* **TRUE LOVE /** –

—— JEFFERSON STARSHIP ("the next generation") were formed after above.

JEFFERSON STARSHIP ("the next generation")

KANTNER / CASADY / BALIN + SLICK (repl. CREACH) / **TIM GORMAN** – keyboards, vocals (ex-KBC BAND) / **PRAIRIE PRINCE** (b. 7 May'50, Charlotte, New Connecticut) / **MARK AUGUILAR** – guitar, vocals (ex-KBC BAND) / **DARBY GOULD** – vocals

		Essential	Intersound
Jul 95.	(cd/c) *(ESM CD/MC 493) <9151>* **DEEP SPACE – VIRGIN SKY** – Shadowlands / Ganja of love / Dark ages / I'm on fire / Papa John / Women who fly / Gold / The light / Crown of creation / Count on me / Miracles / Intro to lawman / Lawman / Wooden ships / Somebody to love / White rabbit.		

– (AIRPLANE) compilations, etc.

on 'R.C.A.' unless mentioned otherwise

Jun 70.	(7") *(RCA 1964)* **WHITE RABBIT. / SOMEBODY TO LOVE**		
Nov 70.	(lp) *(SF 8164) <4459>* **THE WORST OF JEFFERSON AIRPLANE** *(re-iss. Sep86 on 'Fame' lp/c; FA/TC-FA 3167)*		12
Apr 74.	(lp) *Grunt; <(APL 1-0437)>* **EARLY FLIGHT**		
Apr 76.	(7"m) *(RCA 2676)* **WHITE RABBIT. / SOMEBODY TO LOVE / CROWN OF CREATION**		
Dec 76.	(d-lp) *(SF 7889) <1255>* **FLIGHT LOG** (1966-76 work)		37
Apr 79.	(12") *RCA Gold; (GOLD 4)* **WHITE RABBIT. / SOMEBODY TO LOVE**		–
Jul 80.	(lp/c) *(INT S/K 5030) <42727>* **THE BEST OF JEFFERSON AIRPLANE** *(re-iss. 1984 lp/c; NL/NK 89186)*		
Nov 86.	(7") *Old Gold; (OG 9631)* **WHITE RABBIT. / SOMEBODY TO LOVE**		–
1987.	(7") *<5156>* **WHITE RABBIT. / PLASTIC FANTASTIC LOVER**		–
May 87.	(7") *Ariola; (JEFF 1)* **WHITE RABBIT. / SOMEBODY TO LOVE** (12"+=) *(JEFFT 1)* – She has funny cars / Third week in Chelsea.		
Jul 87	(d-lp/c/d-cd) *(NL/NK/ND 90036) <5724>* **2400 FULTON STREET – AN ANTHOLOGY** – It's no secret / Come up the years / My best friend / Somebody to love / Comin' back to me / Embryonic journey / She has funny cars / Plastic fantastic lover / Wild tyme / The ballad of you & me & Pooneil – A small package of value will come to you, shortly / White rabbit / Won't you try Saturday afternoon / Lather / We can be together / Crown of creation / Mexico / Wooden ships / Rejoyce / Volunteers / Pretty as you feel / Martha / Today / Third week in Chelsea. *(d-cd+=)* – Let's get together / Blues from an airplane / J.P.P. McStep B. Blues / Fat angel / Greasy heart / We can be together / Have you seen the saucers / Eat starch mom / Good shepherd / Eskimo blue day / The Levi commercials. *(re-iss. d-cd.1992;)*		
Oct 88.	(d-lp/c/cd) *Castle; (CCS LP/MC/CD 200)* **THE COLLECTION** *<US cd-iss. Oct92; >*		–
1989.	(3"cd-ep) *(PD 49463)* **WHITE RABBIT / PLASTIC FANTASTIC LOVER / SOMEBODY TO LOVE / SHE HAS FUNNY CARS**		–
May 90.	(cd/lp) *Thunderbolt; (CDTB/THBL 074)* **LIVE AT THE MONTEREY FESTIVAL (live)**		–
Nov 92.	(3xcd-box) **JEFFERSON AIRPLANE LOVES YOU**		
Apr 93.	(cd) *Pulsar;* **WOODSTOCK REVIVAL**		–
Sep 93.	(cd/c) *Remember; (RMB 7/4 5065)* **WHITE RABBIT (featuring GRACE SLICK)**		–
Aug 96.	(cd) *B.M.G. Special; <74321 40057-2>* **JOURNEY (THE BEST OF JEFFERSON AIRPLANE)**		–
Sep 96.	(cd; w-free pic-cd) *Experience; (EXP 021)* **JEFFERSON AIRPLANE LIVE**		–
Jan 97.	(cd) *Stampa Alternativa; (SB 03)* **WE ARE ALL ONE**		

– (STARSHIP) compilations etc. –

Mar 79.	(lp/c) *Grunt-RCA; (FL/FK 13247) <3247>* **GOLD** *(with free 7")* – LIGHT THE SKY ON FIRE. / HYPERDRIVE		Feb79 20
1979.	(7") *Grunt-RCA;* **MIRACLES. / WITH YOUR LOVE**	–	
Nov 92.	(cd-ep) *Old Gold;* **NOTHING'S GONNA STOP US NOW / WE BUILT THIS CITY / SARA**		–

GRACE SLICK

solo, all featuring JEFFERSON's and session people

		Grunt	Grunt
Jan 74.	(7") *<0183>* **THEME FROM MANHOLE. / COME AGAIN? TOUCAN**	–	
Jan 74.	(lp) *<(BFL 1-0347)>* **MANHOLE** – Jay / Theme from 'Manhole' / Come again? Toucan / It's only music / Better lying down / Epic (#38).		

		R.C.A.	R.C.A.
May 80.	(7") *<11939>* **SEASONS. / ANGEL OF NIGHT**	–	
May 80.	(7") *(PB 9534)* **DREAMS. / ANGEL OF NIGHT**	50	–
May 80.	(lp/c) *<(PL/PK 1-3544)>* **DREAMS** – Dreams / El Diablo / Face to the wind / Angel of night / Seasons / Do it the hard way / Full Moon man / Let it go / Garden of man. *(re-iss. Sep81 lp/c; RCA LP/K 3040) (re-iss. Sep91 on 'Great Expectations' cd/c/lp; PIP CD/MC/LP 030)*	28	32
Jul 80.	(7",12") *<1204-1/-2>* **DREAMS. / DO IT THE HARD WAY**	–	
Feb 81.	(7") *(RCA 33)* **MISTREATER. / FULL MOON MAN**		
Feb 81.	(lp/c) *(RCA LP/K 5007) <3851>* **WELCOME TO THE WRECKING BALL** – Wrecking ball / Mistreater / Shot in the dark / Round & round / Shooting star / Just a little love / Sea of love / Lines / Right kind / No more heroes. *(re-iss. Sep91 on 'Great Expectations' cd/c/lp; PIP CD/MC/LP 029)*		48
May 81.	(7") *<12171>* **SEA OF LOVE. / FULL MOON MAN**	–	
Mar 84.	(lp/c) *(PL/PK 84791)* **SOFTWARE** – Call it right call it wrong / Me and me / All the machines / Fox face / Through the window / It just won't stop / Habits / Rearrange my face / Bikini Atoll.		–
Mar 84.	(12") *<13708>* **ALL THE MACHINES. / ('A'long version)**	–	
May 84.	(7") *<13764>* **THROUGH THE WINDOWS. / HABITS**	–	

—— (see also under GREAT SOCIETY for other SLICK material)

☐ JENNIFERS (see under ⇒ SUPERGRASS)

JESUS & MARY CHAIN

Formed: East Kilbride, Scotland . . . 1983 by brothers WILLIAM and JIM REID, who took their name from a line in a Bing Crosby film. After local Glasgow gigs, they moved to Fulham in London, having signed for Alan McGhee's independent 'Creation' label in May'84. Their debut SLAUGHTER JOE-produced 45, 'UPSIDE DOWN', soon topped the indie charts, leading to WEA subsidiary label, 'Blanco Y Negro', snapping them up in early 1985. They hit the UK Top 50 with their next single, 'NEVER UNDERSTAND', and they were soon antagonising new audiences, crashing gear after 20 minutes on set. Riots ensued at nearly every major gig, and more controversy arrived when the next 45's B-side 'JESUS SUCKS', was boycotted by the pressing plant. With a new B-side, the single 'YOU TRIP ME UP', hit only No.55, but was soon followed by another Top 50 hit in October, 'JUST LIKE HONEY'. A month later they unleashed their debut album, 'PSYCHOCANDY', and although this just failed to breach the UK Top 30, it was regarded by many (NME critics especially) as the album of the year. Early in '86, BOBBY GILLESPIE left to concentrate on his PRIMAL SCREAM project and soon after, JAMC hit the Top 20 with the softer single, 'SOME CANDY TALKING'. In 1987 with new drummer JOHN MOORE, the single 'APRIL SKIES' and album 'DARKLANDS' both went Top 10. Later that year, they remixed The SUGARCUBES' classic 'Birthday' single.'BARBED WIRE KISSES' (1988) was a hotch-potch of B-sides and unreleased material, essential if only for the anarchic trashing of The Beach Boys' 'SURFIN' U.S.A.'. By the release of the 'AUTOMATIC' album in 1989, the Reid brothers had become the core of the band, enlisting additional musicians as needed. The record sounded strangely muted and uninspired although the 'ROLLERCOASTER' EP and subsequent tour (alongside MY BLOODY VALENTINE and a pre-'PARKLIFE' BLUR) were an improvement. True to controversial style, the band returned to the singles chart in 1992 with the radio un-friendly, post-industrial mantra, 'REVERENCE'. Perhaps the last great piece of venom-spewing noise the 'MARY CHAIN produced, the follow-up album, 'HONEY'S DEAD', was tame in comparison. No surprise then, that it received mixed reviews although there were a few low key highlights, notably the melodic bubblegum grunge of 'FAR GONE AND OUT'. After 1993's 'SOUND OF SPEED' EP, the band hooked up with MAZZY STAR'S Hope Sandoval for 'STONED AND DETHRONED', a mellow set of feedback free strumming. While still echoing the brooding portent of the THE VELVETS, the style of the record was more 'PALE BLUE EYES' than 'SISTER RAY'. Predictably, the band were seen as having 'sold out' by Indie-Rock dullards and a 1995 single, 'I HATE ROCK'N'ROLL', didn't even scrape the Top 50. 1998's comeback set, 'MUNKI', peaked at only No.47 in the charts; tension had been reported from other band members as WILLIAM and JIM fought out their differences. With the latter working on something solo (and Alan McGee's label coming to a close) it was inevitable that the brothers would split the 'CHAIN late in '99. WILLIAM had already delivered his first solo outing a year earlier, 'TIRED OF FUCKING' very low key. LAZYCAME's 'SATURDAY THE FOURTEENTH' finally featured his rejected penis sleeve (from creation days) and FREEHEAT (JIM's project) comprised of BEN LURIE (guitar), ROMI MORI (bass & ex-GUN CLUB) and NICK SANDERSON (drums of EARL BRUTUS) • **Songwriters:** All written by JIM and WILLIAM except; VEGETABLE MAN (Syd Barrett) / SURFIN' USA (Beach Boys) / WHO DO YOU LOVE (Bo Diddley) / MY GIRL (Temptations) / MUSHROOM (Can) / GUITAR MAN (Jerry Lee Hubbard) / TOWER OF SONG (Leonard Cohen) / LITTLE RED ROOSTER (Willie Dixon) / (I CAN'T GET NO) SATISFACTION (Rolling Stones) / REVERBERATION (13th Floor Elevators) / GHOST OF A SMILE (Pogues) / ALPHABET CITY (Prince) / NEW KIND OF KICK (Cramps). • **Trivia:** Their 1986 single 'SOME CANDY TALKING' was banned by Radio 1 DJ Mike Smith, due to its drug references. The following year in the States, they were banned from a chart show due to their blasphemous name.

Album rating: PSYCHOCANDY (*9) / DARKLANDS (*8) / BARBED WIRE KISSES collection (*7) / AUTOMATIC (*7) / HONEY'S DEAD (*8) / THE SOUND OF SPEED compilation (*7) / STONED AND DETHRONED collection (*6) / I HATE ROCK N ROLL (*5) / MUNKI (*5) / 21 SINGLES compilation (*9) / Lazycame: FINBEGIN (*8)

JIM REID (b.29 Dec'61) – vocals, guitar / **WILLIAM REID** (b.28 Oct'58) – guitar, vocals / **MURRAY DALGLISH** – drums (bass tom & snare) / **DOUGLAS HART** – bass

Creation — not iss.

Nov 84. (7") *(CRE 012)* **UPSIDE DOWN. / VEGETABLE MAN** [ ] [–]
(12"+=) *(CRE 012T)* – ('A' demo).

— **BOBBY GILLESPIE** – drums (ex-WAKE, of PRIMAL SCREAM) repl. DALGLISH who formed BABY'S GOT A GUN

Blanco Y Negro — Reprise

Feb 85. (7") *(NEG 8)* **NEVER UNDERSTAND. / SUCK** [47] [–]
(12"+=) *(NEGT 8)* – Ambition.

Jun 85. (7") *(NEG 13)* **YOU TRIP ME UP. / JUST OUT OF REACH** [55] [–]
(12"+=) *(NEGT 13)* – Boyfriend's dead.

Oct 85. (7") *(NEG 017)* **JUST LIKE HONEY. / HEAD** [45] [–]
(12"+=) *(NEGT 17)* – Just like honey (demo) / Cracked.
(d7"+=) *(NEGF 17)* – ('A'demo) / Inside me.

Nov 85. (lp/c) *(BYN/+C 11)* *<25383>* **PSYCHOCANDY** [31] [ ]
– Just like honey / The living end / Taste the floor / Hardest walk / Cut dead / In a hole / Taste of Cindy / Never understand / It's so hard / Inside me / Sowing seeds / My little underground / You trip me up / Something's wrong. *(cd-iss. Aug86 & Jan97 +=; K 242 000-2)* – Some candy talking.

— **JOHN LODER** – drums (on stage when BOBBY was unavailable)

Jul 86. (7") *(NEG 19)* **SOME CANDY TALKING. / PSYCHO CANDY / HIT** [13] [–]
(12"+=) *(NEGT 19)* – Taste of Cindy.
(d7"+=) *(NEGF 19)(SAM 291)* – Cut dead (acoustic) / You trip me up (acoustic) / Some candy talking (acoustic) / Psycho candy (acoustic).

— now basic trio of **JIM, WILLIAM** and **DOUGLAS** brought in **JOHN MOORE** (b.23 Dec'64, England) – drums repl. GILLESPIE (who was busy with PRIMAL SCREAM) / **JAMES PINKER** – drums (ex-DEAD CAN DANCE) repl. MOORE now on guitar

Apr 87. (7") *(NEG 24)* **APRIL SKIES. / KILL SURF CITY** [8] [–]
(12"+=) *(NEGT 24)* – Who do you love.
(d7"+=) *(NEGF 24)* – Mushroom / Bo Diddley is Jesus.

Aug 87. (7") *(NEG 25)* **HAPPY WHEN IT RAINS. / EVERYTHING IS ALRIGHT WHEN YOU'RE DOWN** [25] [–]
(ext.12"+=) *(NEGT 25)* – Happy place / F-Hole.
(ext.10"+=) *(NEGTE 25)* – ('A'demo) / Shake.

— trimmed to basic duo of REID brothers.

Sep 87. (lp/c)(cd) *(BYN/+C 25)(K 242 180-2)* *<25656>* **DARKLANDS** [5] [ ]
– Darklands / Deep one perfect morning / Happy when it rains / Down on me / Nine million rainy days / April skies / Fall / Cherry came too / On the wall / About you. *(cd re-iss. Nov94; K 242 180-2)*

Oct 87. (7"/7"g-f) *(NEG/+F 29)* **DARKLANDS. / RIDER / ON THE WALL (demo)** [33] [–]
(12"+=/12"g-f+=) *(NEGTF 29)* – Surfin' U.S.A.
(10"+=/cd-s+=) *(NEG TE/CD 29)* – Here it comes again.

— **DAVE EVANS** – rhythm guitar repl. MOORE who formed EXPRESSWAY

Mar 88. (7") *(NEG 32)* **SIDEWALKING. / TASTE OF CINDY (live)** [30] [–]
(12"+=) *(NEGT 32)* – ('A'extended) / April skies (live).
(cd-s++=) *(NEGCD 32)* – Chilled to the bone.

Apr 88. (lp/c)(cd) *(BYN/+C 29)(K 242 331-2)* *<25729>* **BARBED WIRE KISSES** (part compilation) [9] [ ]
– Kill Surf City / Head / Rider / Hit / Don't ever change / Just out of reach / Happy place / Psychocandy / Sidewalking / Who do you love / Surfin' USA / Everything's alright when you're down / Upside down / Taste of Cindy / Swing / On the wall. *(c+=/cd+=)* – Cracked / Here it comes again / Mushroom / Bo Diddley is Jesus. *(cd re-iss. Jan97; same)*

— In Nov'88, DOUGLAS HART moonlighted in The ACID ANGELS, who released 7"promo 'SPEED SPEED ECSTASY' on 'Product Inc.'; *FUEL 1)*

Nov 88. (7") *<27754>* **KILL SURF CITY. / SURFIN' USA (summer mix)** [–] [ ]

— Basically REID brothers, HART and EVANS. (added **RICHARD THOMAS** – drums) / **BEN LURIE** – rhythm guitar repl. EVANS

Sep 89. (7") *(NEG 41)* **BLUES FROM A GUN. / SHIMMER** [32] [–]
(10"+=) *(NEG 41TE)* – Break me down / Penetration.
(12"+=/c-s+=) *(NEG 41 T/C)* – Penetration / Subway.
(3"cd-s+=) *(NEG 41CD)* – Penetration / My girl.

Oct 89. (lp/c)(cd) *(BYN/+C 20)(K 246 221-2)* *<26015>* **AUTOMATIC** [11] [ ]
– Here comes Alice / Coast to coast / Blues from a gun / Between planets / UV ray / Her way of praying / Head on / Take it / Halfway to crazy / Gimme hell. *(cd re-iss. Jan97; same)*

Nov 89. (7") *(NEG 42)* **HEAD ON. / IN THE BLACK** [57] [–]
(12"+=) *(NEG 42T)* – Terminal beach.
(3"cd-s++=) *(NEG 42CD)* – Drop (acoustic re-mix).
(7") *(NEG 42XB)* – ('A'side). / DEVIANT SLICE
(7") *(NEG 42Y)* – ('A'side). / I'M GLAD I NEVER
(7") *(NEG 42Z)* – ('A'side). / TERMINAL BEACH

Mar 90. (7") *<19891>* **HEAD ON. / PENETRATION** [–] [ ]

Aug 90. (7") *(NEG 45)* **ROLLERCOASTER. / SILVER BLADE** [46] [–]
(12"+=) *(NEG 45T)* – Tower of song.
(7"ep++=/cd-ep++=) *(NEG 45 D/CD)* – Low-life.

— Trimmed again, when THOMAS joined RENEGADE SOUNDWAVE on U.S.tour. HART became video director. The **REID** brothers and **BEN** recruited **MATTHEW PARKIN** – bass + **BARRY BLACKER** – drums (ex-STARLINGS)

Blanco Y Negro — American

Feb 92. (7") *(NEG 55)* **REVERENCE. / HEAT** [10] [–]
(12"+=/cd-s+=) *(NEG 55 T/CD)* – ('A'radio remix) / Guitar man.

Mar 92. (cd/c/lp) *(9031 76554-2/-4/-1)* *<26830>* **HONEY'S DEAD** [14] [ ]
– Reverence / Teenage lust / Far gone and out / Almost gold / Sugar Ray / Tumbledown / Catchfire / Good for my soul / Rollercoaster / I can't get enough / Sundown / Frequency. *(cd re-iss. Jan97; same)*

Apr 92. (7") *(NEG 56)* **FAR GONE AND OUT. / WHY'D DO YOU WANT ME** [23] [–]
(12"+=/cd-s+=) *(NEG 56 T/CD)* – Sometimes you just can't get enough.

Jun 92. (7") *(NEG 57)* **ALMOST GOLD. / TEENAGE LUST (acoustic)** [41] [–]

(12"+=) *(NEG 57T)* – Honey's dead.
(gold-cd-s+=) *(NEG 57CD)* – Reverberation (doubt) / Don't come down.

Jun 93. (7"ep/c-ep/10"ep/cd-ep) *(NEG 66/+C/TE/CD)* **SOUND OF SPEED EP** [30] [–]
– Snakedriver / Something I can't have / White record release blues / Little red rooster.

Jul 93. (cd/c/lp) *(4509 93105-2/-4/-1)* **THE SOUND OF SPEED** (part comp '88-'93) [15] [–]
– Snakedriver / Reverence (radio mix) / Heat / Teenage lust (acoustic version) / Why'd you want me / Don't come down / Guitar man / Something I can't have / Sometimes / White record release blues / Shimmer / Penetration / My girl / Tower of song / Little red rooster / Break me down / Lowlife / Deviant slice / Reverberation / Sidewalking (extended version). *(cd re-iss. Jan97; same)*

— next album feat. guest vox HOPE SANDOVAL (Mazzy Star) + SHANE MacGOWAN / **STEVE MONTI** – drums repl. BLACKER

Jul 94. (7"/c-s) *(NEG 70/+C)* **SOMETIMES ALWAYS. / PERFECT CRIME** [22] [–]
(10"+=/cd-s+=) *(NEG 70 TE/CD)* – Little stars / Drop.

Aug 94. (cd/c/lp) *(4509 93104-2/-4/-1)* *<45573>* **STONED AND DETRONED** [13] [98]
– Dirty water / Bullet lovers / Sometimes always / Come on / Between us / Hole / Never saw it coming / She / Wish I could / Save me / Till it shines / God help me / Girlfriend / Everybody I know / You've been a friend / These days / Feeling lucky. *(cd re-iss. Jan97; same)*

Oct 94. (c-s) *<18078>* **SOMETIMES ALWAYS / DROP** [–] [96]

Oct 94. (7"/c-s) *(NEG 73/+C)* **COME ON. / I'M IN WITH THE OUT-CROWD** [52] [–]
(cd-s+=) *(NEG 73CD)* – New York City / Taking it away.
(cd-s) *(NEG 73CD)* – ('A'side) / Ghost of a smile / Alphabet city / New kind of kick.

Jun 95. (c-ep/12"ep/cd-ep) *(NEG 81 C/TEX/CD)* **I HATE ROCK N ROLL / BLEED ME. / 33 1-3 / LOST STAR** [61] [–]

Sep 95. (cd,c) *<43043>* **HATE ROCK N ROLL** (compilation of B-sides & rarities) [–] [ ]
– I hate rock'n'roll / Snakedriver / Something I can't have / Bleed me / Thirty three and a third / Lost star / Penetration / New York City / Taking it away / I'm in with the out crowd / Little stars / Teenage lust / Perfect crime.

— **JIM, WILLIAM + BEN** were joined by **NICK SANDERSON** – drums / **TERRY EDWARDS** – horns / + guests vocalists **HOPE SANDOVAL** + **SISTER VANILLA** (PAUL KING was also a member late '97)

Creation / Sub Pop

Apr 98. (7") *(CRE 292)* **CRACKING UP. / ROCKET** [35] [–]
(cd-s+=) *(CRESCD 292)* – Hide myself / Commercial.

May 98. (7"/c-s) *(CRE/+CS 296)* **I LOVE ROCK N ROLL. / EASYLIFE, EASYLOVE** [38] [–]
(cd-s+=) *(CRESCD 296)* – 40,000k / Nineteen 666.

Jun 98. (cd/c/d-lp) *(CRECD/CCRE/CRELP 232)* *<SP 426>* **MUNKI** [47] [ ]
– I love rock n roll / Birthday / Stardust remedy / Fizzy / Moe Tucker / Perfume / Virtually unreal / Degenerate / Cracking up / Commercial / Supertramp / Never understood / I can't find the time for times / Man on the moon / Black / Dream lover / I hate rock n roll. *(cd re-iss. Jan01; same)*

— they disbanded in October '99

– compilations, etc. –

Sep 91. (m-lp/m-c/m-cd) *Strange Fruit; (SFP MA/MC/CD 210)* **THE PEEL SESSIONS (1985-86)** [ ] [–]
– Inside me / The living end / Just like honey / all / Hapy place / In the rain.

Jun 94. (cd+book) *Audioglobe;* **LIVE (live)** [ ] [–]

Jul 01. (lp) *Strange Fruit; (SFRSLP 092)* **THE COMPLETE JOHN PEEL SESSIONS** [ ] [–]

May 02. (cd) *Blanco Y Negro; (0927 46141-2) / Rhino; <78256>* **21 SINGLES** [ ] Jul02 [ ]

LAZYCAME

WILLIAM REID – solo

Creation / not iss.

Apr 98. (cd-ep; as WILLIAM) *(CRESCD 295)* **TIRED OF FUCKING EP** [ ] [–]
– Tired of fucking / Lucibelle / Kissaround / Hard on.

Hot Tam / not iss.

Oct 99. (7"ep) *(HTAM 001)* **TASTER EP** [ ] [–]
– Muswileclouds / Stevinik / Dement / Engine8.
(cd-ep+=) *(HTAM 001CD)* – God / Complicated.

Dec 99. (cd) *(HOTTAMCD 002)* **FINBEGIN** [ ] [–]
– God / Complicated / Five one zero lovers / Rokit / Go get find / Fornicate / Unfinished business / Blue June / Naturallow / McIntosh lost.

May 00. (cd) *(HOTTAMCD 003)* **SATURDAY THE FOURTEENTH** [ ] [–]
– Drizzle / Last days of Creation / Lo Fi Li / Fuck you genius / You don't belong / Kill kool kid / Kissaround / Muswil clouds / Tired of fucking / Mayhem / Everyone knows / Dement / Unamerican.

Guided Missile / not iss.

Apr 00. (7"ep) *(GUIDE 41)* **YAWN! EP** [ ] [–]
– Drizzle / K to be lost.
(cd-ep+=) *(GUIDE 41CD)* – Who killed Manchester? / Male wife / Commercial.

FREEHEAT

JIM REID – vocals, guitar / **BEN LURIE** – guitar / **ROMI MORI** – bass (ex-GUN CLUB) / **NICK SANDERSON** – drums (ex-EARL BRUTUS)

Outafocus / Hall Of Records

Nov 00. (cd-ep) *<1104>* **DON'T WORRY, BE HAPPY** [–] [ ]
– Two of us / Facing up to the facts / Shine on little star / Nobody's gonna trip my wire.

Feb 02. (cd-ep) *(OUTA 4CD)* **RETOX** [ ] [–]
– DON'T WORRY, BE HAPPY + / Long goodbye.

□ JESUS LOVES YOU (see under ⇒ BOY GEORGE)

JET

Formed: Melbourne, Australia ... mid-90's as MOJO FILTER by NICK CESTER and CAMERON MUNCEY. NICK's younger brother CHRIS completed the core of a band hailed as Australia's great white hopes. Never tiring in their defence of "real" rock (which apparently means The ROLLING STONES, The BEATLES, LED ZEPPELIN etc etc etc ad nauseam) over almost anything else but particularly dance music, they even resurrected that essential piece of late 70's fashion, the 'Disco Sucks' t-shirt which, let's face it, wasn't even funny first time round. Aside from spouting tired, tedious musical fascism they made half decent attempts at approximating their beloved "real" music after being picked up by 'Elektra' amidst an A&R scramble in late 2002. With bass player MARK WILSON now completing the line-up, they released the limited edition 'DIRTY SWEET' EP in their home territory (then the UK) before 2003's 'GET BORN' album had critics namechecking about every classic rock influence in the book. The stand-out track on the Top 20 set was easily the classy hit single, 'ARE YOU GONNA BE MY GIRL'. • **Covered:** THAT'S ALRIGHT MAMMA (Elvis Presley).

Album rating: GET BORN (*7)

NIC CESTER – vocals, guitar / **CHRIS CESTER** – vocals, drums / **CAMERON MUNCEY** – vocals, guitar / **MARK WILSON** – bass

Elektra / not iss.

May 03. (12"ep) *(7559 62886-1)* **DIRTY SWEET EP** [ ] [–]
– Take it or leave it / Cold hard bitch / Move on / Rollover D.J.

Aug 03. (12") *(E 7456T)* **ARE YOU GONNA BE MY GIRL. / HEY KIDS / THAT'S ALRIGHT MAMMA** [23] [–]
(cd-s) *(E 7456CD1)* – ('A'side) / Hey kids / You were right (demo) / ('A'video).
(cd-s) *(E 7456CD2)* – ('A'-alt version) / That's alright mamma (live) / Take it or leave it (video).

Sep 03. (cd/lp) *(7559 62892-2/-1)* **GET BORN** [17] [–]
– Last chance / Are you gonna be my girl / Rollover D.J. / Look what you've

done / Get what you need / Move on / Radio song / Get me outta here / Cold hard bitch / Come around again / Take it or leave it / Lazy gun / Timothy.

Nov 03. (cd-s) *(E 7486CD1)* **ROLLOVER D.J. / SGT. MAJOR / ARE YOU GONNA BE MY GIRL (live)** [34] [–]
(cd-s) *(E 7486CD2)* – ('A'side) / You don't look the same / Cold hard bitch (live) / ('A'-video).

JETHRO TULL

Formed: London, England ... late 1967 by Scots-born IAN ANDERSON and GLENN CORNICK, who had both been in Blackpool band, JOHN EVANS' SMASH for four years alongside school friends EVANS and JEFFREY HAMMOND-HAMMOND. IAN and GLENN brought in former McGREGORY'S ENGINE members MICK ABRAHAMS plus CLIVE BUNKER, adopting the 18th century name of an English agriculturist/inventor, JETHRO TULL. It was often mistaken by the uninitiated as the name of the lead singer, IAN ANDERSON. Early in 1968, through agents Terry Ellis & Chris Wright, 'M.G.M.' issued their debut single, 'SUNSHINE DAY', mistakenly credited as JETHRO TOE at the pressing plant (it has since changed hands for over £100 at record fairs). On the 29th of June '68, after a residency at the Marquee Club, they supported PINK FLOYD at a free rock concert in Hyde Park, London. Following another enthusiastically received concert at Sunbury's Jazz & Blues Festival in August, they signed to 'Island'. By the end of the year, their debut album, 'THIS WAS', had cracked the UK Top 10, even managing to break into the American Top 75. Early in '69, they hired TONY IOMMI (future BLACK SABBATH) and DAVID O'LIST (of The NICE), for a few gigs following the departure of ABRAHAMS. In May '69, with the addition of MARTIN BARRE, they secured a UK Top 3 placing with the classic 'LIVING IN THE PAST' single. This was quickly followed by the UK No.1 album, 'STAND UP', which also made the Top 20 in the States. They then signed to associate label, 'Chrysalis', scoring two more UK Top 10 singles in 'SWEET DREAM' and 'THE WITCH'S PROMISE'. By this juncture, the band were moving away from their early blues-orientated sound into the murky waters of progressive rock, ANDERSON's songwriting voice becoming more vocal with each successive release. With his fevered, one-legged flute playing and laughably outlandish vagrant garb, ANDERSON gave the group its visual trademark, for many people he was *JETHRO TULL*. After a series of line-up changes and continued success in America, the band released 'AQUALUNG' (1971), a million selling concept album through which ANDERSON expressed his contempt for organised religion. This was nothing, however, compared to the contempt which ANDERSON himself would be subject to from a volatile music press whose patience was wearing thin. If the ambitious 'THICK AS A BRICK' (1972) received a less than enthusiastic response from the press, then 'PASSION PLAY's whimsical self-indulgence was met with a critical mauling. As is often the case, the public ignored the reviews and queued up in droves for a copy, especially in America. 'WAR CHILD' and 'MINSTREL IN THE GALLERY' heralded a return to more traditional song structures but by this time, the critics had it in for the band. 'TULL did little to improve the situation by releasing the execrable 'TOO OLD TO ROCK'N'ROLL, TOO YOUNG TO DIE' (1976). Cast into the ghetto of eternal unhipness with the onslaught of punk, JETHRO TULL carried on unhindered, their live shows attracting hordes of die-hard fans. While their recorded output took on a more folky bent with 'SONGS FROM THE WOOD' and 'HEAVY HORSES', the beast that was the 'TULL live phenomenon was beamed around the world by satellite from a show at New York's Madison Square Garden in 1978. ANDERSON began working on a solo album in 1980 with ex-members of ROXY MUSIC and FAIRPORT CONVENTION, the finished article, "A", eventually being released as an official JETHRO TULL album. While the record was greeted with enthusiasm from fans, the follow-up ANDERSON solo LP, 'WALK INTO THE LIGHT' (1983) and subsequent group project 'UNDER WRAPS' (1984) tested even the most ardent 'TULL devotees with their cod-electronica. After a few years break, the band released 'CREST OF A KNAVE' (1987), a harder rocking affair and a return to form of sorts. 'ROCK ISLAND' (1989) and 'CATFISH RISING' (1991) were disappointing in comparison while the live 1992 album, 'A LITTLE LIGHT MUSIC', saw the band in refreshing semi-acoustic mode. 1995 marked a fair solo effort by ANDERSON and a well received 'TULL album, 'ROOTS TO BRANCHES'. While the band's studio output continues to be inconsistent at best, the prospect of a JETHRO TULL live show still has old prog die-hards parting with their hard-earned cash. 'J-TULL.COM' (1999) found the band dragging themselves kicking and screaming into the Net era, in theory if not in actual musical practice. While song titles like 'HOT MANGO FLUSH' and 'BLACK MAMBA' might have suggested a deepening of the world music ties which characterised this album's predecessor, it was a remarkably pedestrian effort from ANDERSON and Co. Even the entirely predictable and highly polished live splurge, 'LIVING WITH THE PAST' (2002), was more engrossing. • **Songwriters:** ANDERSON lyrics / group compositions, except BOUREE (J.S.Bach) / JOHN BARLEYCORN (trad.) / CAT'S SQUIRREL (Cream). • **Trivia:** ANDERSON still controls his trout-farming business in Northern Scotland. In 1974, he produced STEELEYE SPAN's 'Now We Are Six' album.

Album rating: THIS WAS (*6) / STAND UP (*7) / BENEFIT (*6) / AQUALUNG (*8) / THICK AS A BRICK (*6) / LIVING IN THE PAST part compilation/live (*7) / A PASSION PLAY (*7) / WAR CHILD (*6) / MINSTREL IN THE GALLERY (*6) / M.U. – THE BEST OF JETHRO TULL compilation (*8) / TOO OLD TO ROCK'N'ROLL, TOO YOUNG TO DIE (*4) / SONGS FROM THE WOOD (*7) / REPEAT – THE BEST OF JETHRO TULL, VOL.II compilation (*6) / HEAVY HORSES (*6) / JETHRO TULL LIVE – BURSTING OUT (*5) / STORMWATCH (*4) / "A" (*4) / THE BROADSWORD AND THE BEAST (*4) / UNDER WRAPS (*3) / CREST OF A KNAVE (*6) / 20 YEARS OF JETHRO TULL boxed-set compilation (*8) / ROCK ISLAND (*4) / CATFISH RISING (*5) / A LITTLE LIGHT MUSIC (*3) / THE BEST OF JETHRO TULL: THE ANNIVERSARY COLLECTION compilation (*7) / NIGHTCAP rare material (*4) / ROOTS TO BRANCHES (*4) / J-TULL DOT COM (*3) / LIVING WITH THE PAST (*5) / Ian Anderson: WALK INTO LIGHT (*3)

IAN ANDERSON (b.10 Aug'47, Edinburgh, Scotland) – vocals, flute / **GLENN CORNICK** (b.24 Apr'47, Barrow-in-Furness, England) – bass / **MICK ABRAHAMS** (b. 7 Apr'43, Luton, England) – guitar, vocals (ex-McGREGORY'S ENGINE) / **CLIVE BUNKER** (b.12 Dec'46) – drums (ex-McGREGORY'S ENGINE)

M.G.M. | not iss.

Mar 68. (7"; as JETHRO TOE) *(MGM 1384)* **SUNSHINE DAY. / AEROPLANE** [ ] [–]

Island | Reprise

Aug 68. (7") *(WIP 6043)* **A SONG FOR JEFFREY. / ONE FOR JOHN GEE** [ ] [–]

Oct 68. (lp; mono/stereo) *(ILP/+S 9805)* <6336> **THIS WAS** [10] Feb69 [62]
– My Sunday feeling / Some day the sun won't shine for you / Beggar's farm / Move on alone / Serenade to a cuckoo / Dharma for one / It's breaking me up / Cat's squirrel / A song for Jeffrey / Round. *(re-iss. Jan74 lp/c; CHR/ZCHR 1041) (cd-iss. 1986; CCD 1041) (lp re-iss. Apr99; 499468-1) (<cd re-mast.Sep01 on 'EMI-Capitol'+=; 5 35459-2>)* – One for John Gee / Love story / Christmas song.

Dec 68. (7") *(WIP 6048)* **LOVE STORY. / A CHRISTMAS SONG** [29] [–]

Mar 69. (7") *<0815>* **LOVE STORY. / A SONG FOR JEFFREY** [–] [ ]

— **MARTIN BARRIE** (b.17 Nov'46) – guitar; repl. MICK ABRAHAMS who formed BLODWYN PIG

May 69. (7") *(WIP 6056)* **LIVING IN THE PAST. / DRIVING SONG** [3] [–]

Jul 69. (lp) *(ILPS 9103) <6360>* **STAND UP** [1] Oct69 [20]
– A new day yesterday / Jeffrey goes to Leicester Square / Bouree / Back to the family / Look into the sun / Nothing is easy / Fat man / We used to know / Reasons for waiting / For a thousand mothers. *(re-iss. Nov83 on 'Fame' lp/c; FA/TCFA 413086-1/-4) (cd-iss. Jan89; CCD 1042) (re-iss. Feb97 on 'E.M.I.'; LPCENT 8) (<cd re-mast.Sep01 on 'EMI-Capitol'+=; 5 35458-2>)* – Living in the past / Driving song / Sweet dream / 17.

Chrysalis Reprise

Oct 69. (7") *(WIP 6070)* **SWEET DREAM. / 17** [9] [–]

Oct 69. (7") *<0886>* **SWEET DREAM. / REASONS FOR WAITING** [–] [ ]

Jan 70. (7") *(WIP 6077) <0899>* **THE WITCH'S PROMISE. / TEACHER** [4] [ ]

— augmented by **JOHN EVAN** (b.28 Mar'48) – keyboards (he later joined full-time)

Apr 70. (lp) *(ILPS 9123) <6400>* **BENEFIT** [3] [11]
– With you there to help me / Nothing to say / Alive and well and living in / Son / For Michael Collins, Jeffrey and me / To cry you a song / A time for everything / Inside / Play in time / Sossity; you're a woman. *(re-iss. Jan74 lp/c; CHR/ZCHR 1043) (cd-iss. Jun87; CPCD 1043) (<cd re-mast.Oct01 on 'EMI-Capitol'+=; 5 35457-2>)* – Singing all day / Witch's promise / Just trying to be / Teacher.

May 70. (7") *(WIP 6081)* **INSIDE. / ALIVE AND WELL AND LIVING IN** [ ] [–]

Jul 70. (7") *<0927>* **INSIDE. / A TIME FOR EVERYTHING** [–] [ ]

— **JEFFREY HAMMOND-HAMMOND** (b.30 Jul'46) – bass repl. CORNICK who formed WILD TURKEY

Mar 71. (lp) *(ILPS 9145) <2035>* **AQUALUNG** [4] Apr71 [7]
– Aqualung / Cross-eyed mary / Cheap day return / Mother goose / Wond'ring aloud / Up to me / My God / Hymn #43 / Slipstream / Locomotive breath / Wind up. *(re-iss. Jan74 lp/c; CHR/ZCHR 1044) (cd-iss. 1988; CCD 933-2) (re-iss. cd Mar94; CD25CR 08) (cd re-iss. Jun96 +=; CD25CR 08)* – (sessions):- Lick your fingers clean / Wind up (quad version) / (Ian Anderson interview) / Song for Jeffrey / Fat man / Bouree. *(<cd re-mast.Jun98 +=; 495401-2>)* – Lick your fingers clean / Wind up (quad) / (excerpts from the Ian Anderson interview) / A song for Jeffrey / Fat man / Bouree. *(lp re-iss. Aug00 on 'D.C.C.'; LPZ 2030)*

Jul 71. (7") *<1024>* **HYMN #43. / MOTHER GOOSE** [–] [91]

— **ANDERSON, BARRE, HAMMOND-HAMMOND** and **EVAN** were joined by **BARRIEMORE BARLOW** (b.10 Sep'49) – drums (ex-JOHN EVAN'S SMASH) who repl. BUNKER who joined BLODWYN PIG

Sep 71. (7"ep) *(WIP 6106)* **LIFE IS A LONG SONG / UP THE POOL. / DR. BOGENBROOM / FOR LATER / NURSIE** [11] [–]

Oct 71. (7") *<1054>* **LOCOMOTIVE BREATH. / WIND** [–] [ ]

Chrysalis Reprise

Mar 72. (lp) *(CHR 1003) <2071>* **THICK AS A BRICK** [5] May72 [1]
– Thick as a brick (side 1) / Thick as a brick (side 2). *(re-iss. Jan74 lp/c; CHR/ZCHR 1003) (cd-iss. 1986; ACCD 1003) (cd-re-iss. Apr89 on 'Mobile Fidelity'; UDCD 510) (cd re-iss. Jun98 as part of 25th Anniversary on 'E.M.I.'+=; CDCNTAV 5)* – Thick as a brick (live at Madison Square Gardens 1978) / (interview).

Apr 72. (7") *<1153>* **THICK AS A BRICK (edit #1). / HYMN #43** [–] [ ]

Chrysalis Chrysalis

Jul 72. (d-lp) *(CJT 1) <2106>* **LIVING IN THE PAST** (live / studio compilation) [8] Nov72 [3]
– A song for Jeffrey / Love story / Christmas song / Teacher / Living in the past / Driving song / Bouree / Sweet dream / Singing all day / Witches promise / Teacher / Inside / Just trying to be / By kind permission of / Dharma for one / Wond'ring again / Locomotive breath / Life is a long song / Up the pool / Dr. Bogenbroom / For later / Nursie. *(cd-iss. Oct87; CCD 1035) (re-iss. Mar94 cd/c; ZCJTD 1)*

Oct 72. (7") *<2006>* **LIVING IN THE PAST. / CHRISTMAS SONG** [–] [11]

May 73. (7") *<2012>* **A PASSION PLAY (edit #8). / A PASSION PLAY (edit #9)** [–] [80]

Jul 73. (lp) *(<CHR/ZCHR 1040>)* **A PASSION PLAY** [13] [1]
– A passion play (part 1; including 'The story of the hare who lost his spectacles' part 1)- /- (part 2) / A passion play (part 2). *(cd-iss. Jan89; CCD 1040) (<cd re-mast.Apr03 on 'EMI-Capitol'+=; 5 815690>)* – (enhanced video track).

Aug 73. (7") *<2017>* **A PASSION PLAY (edit #6). / A PASSION PLAY (edit #10)** [–] [ ]

Oct 74. (7") *(CHS 2054) <2101>* **BUNGLE IN THE JUNGLE. / BACK-DOOR ANGELS** [ ] [12]

Oct 74. (lp/c) *(<CHR/ZCHR 1067>)* **WAR CHILD** [14] [2]
– Warchild / Queen and country / Ladies / Back-door angels / Sealion / Skating away on the thin ice of a new day / Bungle in the jungle / Only solitaire / The third hooray / Two fingers. *(cd-iss. Apr99 on 'Mobile Fidelity'; UDCD 745) (cd re-iss. Aug00; CCD 1067) (<cd re-mast.Oct02 on 'EMI-Capitol'+=; 5 41571-2>)* – Warchild waltz / Quartet / Paradise steakhouse / Sealion (part 2) / Rainbow blues / Glory row / Saturation.

Jan 74. (7") *<2103>* **SKATING AWAY ON THE THIN ICE OF A NEW DAY. / SEALION** [–] [ ]

Sep 75. (lp/c) *(<CHR/ZCHR 1082>)* **MINSTREL IN THE GALLERY** [20] [7]
– Minstrel in the gallery / Cold wind to Valhalla / Black satin dancer / Requiem / One white duck / 0x10 = Nothing at all – Baker St. Muse (including Pig-me and the whore – Nice little tune – Crash barrier waltzer – Mother England reverie) / Grace. *(cd-iss. 1986; CCD 1082) (<cd re-mast.Oct02 on 'EMI-Capitol'+=; 5 41572-2>)* – Summerday sands / March the mad scientist / Pan dance / Minstrel in the gallery (live) / Cold wind to Valhalla (live).

Oct 75. (7") *(CHS 2075) <2106>* **MINSTREL IN THE GALLERY. / SUMMER DAY SANDS** [ ] [79]

— **JOHN GLASCOCK** (b.1953) – bass (ex-CHICKEN SHACK, ex-TOE FAT) repl. HAMMOND-HAMMOND

Mar 76. (7") *(CHS 2086)* **TOO OLD TO ROCK'N'ROLL, TOO YOUNG TO DIE. / RAINBOW BLUES** [ ] [–]

Apr 76. (7") *<2114>* **TOO OLD TO ROCK'N'ROLL, TOO YOUNG TO DIE. / BAD-EYED AND LOVELESS** [–] [ ]

May 76. (lp/c) *(<CHR/ZCHR 1111>)* **TOO OLD TO ROCK'N'ROLL: TOO YOUNG TO DIE** [25] [14]
– Quizz kid / Crazed institution / Salamander / Taxi grab / From a dead beat to an old greaser / Bad-eyed and loveless / Big dipper / Too old to rock'n'roll: too young to die / Pied piper / The chequered flag (dead or alive). *(cd-iss. Nov86 & Aug00; CCD 1111) (<cd re-mast.Oct02 on 'EMI-Capitol'+=; 541573-2>)* – A small cigar / Strip cartoon.

— added **DAVID PALMER** – keyboards (He had been their past orchestrator)

Nov 76. (7"ep) *(CXP 2)* **RING OUT, SOLSTICE BELLS / MARCH THE MAD SCIENTIST. / A CHRISTMAS SONG / PAN DANCE** [28] [–]

Jan 77. (7") *(CHS <2135>)* **THE WHISTLER. / STRIP CARTOON** [ ] Apr77 [59]

Feb 77. (lp/c) *(<CHR/ZCHR 1132>)* **SONGS FROM THE WOOD** [13] [8]
– Songs from the wood / Jack-in-the-green / Cup of wonder / Hunting girl / Ring out, solstice bells / Velvet green / The whistler / Pibroch (cap in hand) / Fire at midnight. *(cd-iss. 1986; ACCD 1132) (<cd re-mast.Apr03 on 'EMI-Capitol'+=; 581570-2>)* – Beltane / Velvet green (live).

Apr 78. (7") *(CHS 2214)* **MOTHS. / LIFE IS A LONG SONG** [ ] [–]

Apr 78. (lp/c) *(<CHR/ZCHR 1175>)* **HEAVY HORSES** [20] [19]
– . . .And the mouse police never sleeps / Acres wild / No lullaby / Moths / Journeyman / Rover / One brown mouse / Heavy horses / Weathercock. *(cd-iss. 1986; CCD 1175) (<cd re-mast.Apr03 on 'EMI-Capitol'+=; 581571-2>)* – Living in these hard times / Broadford bazaar.

Oct 78. (d-lp/c) *(CJT/ZCJT 4) <1201>* **LIVE – BURSTING OUT (live)** [17] [21]
– No lullaby / Sweet dream / Skating away on the thin ice of a new day / Jack in the green / One brown mouse / A new day yesterday / Flute solo improvisation – God rest ye merry gentlemen – Bouree / Songs from the wood / Thick as a brick / Hunting girl / Too old to rock'n'roll: too young to die / Conundrum / Cross-eyed Mary / Quatrain / Aqualung / Locomotive breath / The dambusters march.

Nov 78. (7",7"white) *(CHS 2260)* **A STITCH IN TIME. / SWEET DREAM (live)** [ ] [–]

Sep 79. (7") *(CHS 2378)* **NORTH SEA OIL. / ELEGY** [ ] [ ]

Sep 79. (lp/c) *(<CDL/ZCDL 1238>)* **STORMWATCH** [27] [22]
– North Sea oil / Orion / Home / Dark ages / Warm sporran / Something's on the move / Old ghosts / Dun Ringill / Flying Dutchman / Elegy. *(cd-iss. Jan89; CCD 1238)*

Nov 79. (7") *<2387>* **HOME. / WARM SPORRAN** [–] [ ]

Nov 79. (7"ep) *(CHS 2394)* **HOME / KING HENRY'S MADRIGAL (THEME FROM MAINSTREAM). / WARM SPORRAN / RING OUT SOLSTICE BELLS** [ ] [–]

— ANDERSON for what was supposed to be a solo album retained **BARRE** / plus new **DAVE PEGG** (b. 2 Nov'47, Birmingham, England) – bass (ex-FAIRPORT CONVENTION) repl. GLASCOCK who died. / **EDDIE JOBSON** (b.28 Apr'55, England) – keyboards (ex-ROXY MUSIC, ex-CURVED AIR, etc) repl. EVANS and PALMER who took up session work /

MARK CRANEY (b. Los Angeles, Calif.) – drums repl. BARLOW who went solo.

Aug 80. (lp/c) *(<CDL/CDC 1301>)* **"A"** [25] Sep 80 [30]
– Crossfire / Fylingdale flyer / Working John, working Joe / Black Sunday / Protect and survive / Batteries not included / 4.W.D. (low ratio) / The Pine Marten's jig / And further on. *(<cd re-mast.Oct02 on 'EMI-Capitol'; 321301-2>)*

Oct 80. (7") *(CHS 2468)* **WORKING JOHN, WORKING JOE. / FYLINGDALE FLYER** [ ] [–]

— **PETER JOHN VITESSE** – keyboards repl. JOBSON who went solo / **GERRY CONWAY** – drums (ex-STEELEYE SPAN) repl. CRANEY

Apr 82. (lp/c) *(<CDL/CDC 1380>)* **THE BROADSWORD AND THE BEAST** [27] May82 [19]
– Beastie / Clasp / Fallen on hard times / Flying colours / Slow marching band / Broadsword / Pussy willow / Watching me watching you / Seal driver / Cheerio. *(cd-iss. Apr83; CCD 1380)*

May 82. (7") *<2613>* **PUSSY WILLOW. / FALLEN ON HARD TIMES** [–] [ ]

May 82. (7"/7"pic-d) *(CHS/+P 2616)* **BROADSWORD. / FALLEN ON HARD TIMES** [ ] [–]

— **DOANNE PERRY** – drums repl. CONWAY

Sep 84. (lp/pic-lp/c/cd) *(CDL/CDLP/ZCDL/CCD 1461) <1-/0-/4-/2-1461>* **UNDER WRAPS** [18] [76]
– Lap of luxury / Under wraps #1 / European legacy / Later that same evening / Saboteur / Radio free Moscow / Nobody's car / Heat / Under wraps #2 / Paparazzi / Apogee. *(c+=/cd+=)* – Automatic engineering / Astronomy / Tundra / General crossing. *(<cd re-mast.Oct02; same>)*

Sep 84. (7") *(TULL 1)* **LAP OF LUXURY. / ASTRONOMY** [70] [ ]
(d7"+=/12"+=) *(TULL D/X 1)* – Tundra / Automatic engineering.

Jun 86. (7") *(TULL 2)* **CORONIACH. / JACK FROST AND THE HOODED CROW** [ ] [ ]
(12"+=) *(TULLX 2)* – Living in the past / Elegy.

— **ANDERSON, BARRE, PEGG** and **PERRY** recruited new member **MARTIN ALLCOCK** – keyboards (ex-FAIRPORT CONVENTION) repl. VITESSE

Sep 87. (lp/c/cd) *(CDL/ZCDL/CCD 1590) <1-/4-/2-1590>* **CREST OF A KNAVE** [19] [32]
– Steel monkey / Farm on the freeway / Jump start / Said she was a dancer / Dogs in midwinter * / Budapest / Mountain men / The waking edge * / Raising steam. *(cd+= *) (cd re-iss. Aug00; same)*

Oct 87. (7"/7"pic-d) *(TULL/+P 3)* **STEEL MONKEY. / DOWN AT THE END OF YOUR ROAD** [ ] [ ]
(12"+=)(c-s+=) *(TULLX/ZTULL 3)* – Too many too / I'm your gun.

Dec 87. (7"/7"pic-d) *(TULL/+P 4)* **SAID SHE WAS A DANCER. / DOGS IN MIDWINTER** [55] [ ]
(12"+=) *(TULLX 4)* – The waking edge.
(cd-s+=) *(TULLCD 4)* – Down at the end of your road / Too many too.

Aug 89. (lp/pic-lp/c/cd) *(CHR/CHRP/ZCHR/CCD 1708) <1-/0-/4-/2-21708>* **ROCK ISLAND** [18] [56]
– Kissing Willie / The rattlesnake trail / Ears of tin / Undressed to kill / Rock Island / Heavy water / Another Christmas song / The whalers dues / Big Riff and Mando / Strange avenues.

Aug 89. (c-s) **KISSING WILLIE. / EARS OF TIN** [–] [ ]

Nov 89. (7") *(TULL 5)* **ANOTHER CHRISTMAS SONG. / SOLSTICE BELLS** [ ] [ ]
(12"+=) *(TULLX 5)* – Jack Frost.
(12"+=/cd-s) *(TULL EX/CD 5)* – ('A'side) / Intro – A Christmas song (live) / Cheap day return – Mother goose / Outro – Locomotive breath (live).

— **ANDY GIDDINGS** – keyboards (3) / **MATT PEGG** – bass (3) / etc. repl. ALLCOCK

Aug 91. (7"/c-s) *(TULL/+XMC 6)* **THIS IS NOT LOVE. / NIGHT IN THE WILDERNESS** [ ] [ ]
(12"+=/cd-s+=) *(TULL X/CD 6)* – Jump start (live).

Sep 91. (cd/c/lp) *(CCD/ZCHR/DCHR 1886) <2-/4-/1-1863>* **CATFISH RISING** [27] [88]
– This is not love / Occasional demons / Rocks on the road / Thinking round corners / Still loving you tonight / Doctor to my disease / Like a tall thin girl / Sparrow on the schoolyard wall / Roll yer own / Gold-tipped boots, black jacket and tie. *(free 12"ep)* – WHEN JESUS CAME TO PLAY. / SLEEPING WITH THE DOG / WHITE INNOCENCE

— **DAVID MATTACKS** – drums, percussion, keyboards repl. PERRY and guests

Mar 92. (12"pic-d) *(TULLX 7)* **ROCKS ON THE ROAD. / JACK-A-LYNN (demo) / AQUALUNG – LOCOMOTIVE BREATH (live)** [47] [ ]
(c-s) *(TULLMC 7)* – ('A'side) / Bouree (live) / Mother goose – Jack-a-Lyn (live).
(2xbox-cd-s++=) *(TULLCD 7)* – Tall thin girl (live) / Fat man (live).

Sep 92. (cd/c/d-lp) *(CCD/ZCHR/CHR 1954) <2-/4/-1-1954>* **A LITTLE LIGHT MUSIC (live in Europe '92)** [34] [ ]
– Someday the sun won't shine for you / Living in the past / Life is a long song / Rocks on the road / Under wraps / Nursie / Too old to rock and roll, too young to die / One white duck / A new day yesterday / John Barleycorn / Look into the sun / A Christmas song / From a dead beat to an old greaser / This is not love / Bouree / Pussy willow / Locomotive breath.

— **PERRY** returned to repl. MATTACKS; bass playing was provided by **DAVE PEGG / STEVE BAILEY**

Sep 95. (cd/c/d-lp) *(CCD/ZCHR/CHR 6109) <2-/4-/1-6109>* **ROOTS TO BRANCHES** [20] [ ]
– Roots to branches / Rare and precious chain / Out of the noise / This free will / Valley / Dangerous veils / Beside myself / Wounded old and treacherous / At last, forever / Stuck in the August rain / Another Harry's bar.

— **ANDERSON, BARRE, GIDDINGS + PERRY** were joined by **JONATHAN NOYCE** – bass

Papillon Varese

Aug 99. (cd) *(BTFLYCD 0001) <1043>* **J-TULL DOT COM** [44] [ ]
– Spiral / Dot com / Awol / Nothing @ all / Wicked windows / Hunt by numbers / Hot mango flush / El Nino / Black mamba / Mango surprise / Bends like a willow / Far Alaska / The dog-ear years / A gift of roses.

Nov 99. (cd-s) *(BTFLYS 0001)* **BENDS LIKE A WILLOW / BENDS LIKE A WILLOW (version) / IT ALL TRICKLES DOWN** [ ] [–]

Eagle Fuel 2000

May 02. (cd) *(EAGCD 231) <061199>* **LIVING WITH THE PAST (live 2001)** [ ] [ ]
– (intro) / My Sunday feeling / Roots to branches / Jack in the green / The Habanero reel / Sweet dream / In the grip of stronger stuff / Aqualung / Locomotive breath / Living in the past / Protect and survive / Nothing is easy / Wond'ring aloud / Life is a long song / A Christmas song / Cheap day return / Mother goose / Dot com / Fat man / Dome day the sun won't shine for you / Cheerio.

– compilations, others, etc. –

on 'Chrysalis' unless mentioned otherwise

Jan 76. (7") *(CHS 2081)* **LIVING IN THE PAST. / REQUIEM** [ ] [ ]

Jan 76. (lp/c) *(<CHR/ZCHR 1078>)* **M.U. – THE BEST OF JETHRO TULL** [44] [13]
– Teacher / Aqualung / Thick as a brick (edit #1) / Bungle in the jungle / Locomotive breath / Fat man / Living in the past / A passion play (#8) / Skating away on the thin ice of a new day / Rainbow blues / Nothing is easy. *(cd-iss. Dec85; ACCD 1078)*

Feb 76. (7") *<2110>* **LOCOMOTIVE BREATH. / FAT MAN** [–] [62]

Nov 77. (lp/c) *(<CHR/ZCHR 1135>)* **REPEAT – THE BEST OF JETHRO TULL VOL.2** [ ] [94]
– Minstrel in the gallery / Cross-eyed Mary / A new day yesterday / Bouree / Thick as a brick (edit #1) / War child / A passion play (edit #9) / To cry you a song / Too old to rock'n'roll, too young to die / Glory row. *(cd-iss. Apr86; CCD 1135)*

Dec 82. (d-c) *(ZCDP 105)* **M.U. / REPEAT** [ ] [–]

Oct 85. (lp/c/cd) *(JTTV/ZJTTV/CCD 1515)* **ORIGINAL MASTERS** [63] [ ]

Aug 87. (7") *Old Gold; (OG 9637)* **LIVING IN THE PAST. / THE WITCHES' PROMISE** [ ] [–]

Jun 88. (5xlp-box/3xc-box/3xcd-box) *(T/MC/CD BOX 1) <41653>* **20 YEARS OF JETHRO TULL** [78] [97]
– THE RADIO ARCHIVES:- A song for Jeffrey / Love story * / Fat man / Bouree / Stormy Monday blues * / A new day yesterday * / Cold wind to Valhalla / Minstrel in the gallery / Velvet green / Grace * / The clasp / / Pibroch (pee-break) – Black satin dancer (instrumental) * / Fallen on hard times // THE RARE TRACKS:- Jack Frost and the hooded crow / I'm your gun / Down at the end of your road / Coronach * / Summerday sands * / Too many too / March the mad scientist * / Pan dance / Strip cartoon / King Henry's madrigal / A stitch in time / 17 / One for John Gee / Aeroplane / Sunshine day // FLAWED GEMS:- Lick your fingers clean * / The Chateau Disaster Tapes: Scenario – Audition – No rehesal / Beltane / Crossword * / Saturation * / Jack-A-Lynn * / Motoreyes * / Blues instrumental (untitled) / Rhythm in gold // THE OTHER SIDES OF TULL:- Part of the machine * / Mayhem, maybe * / Overhang * / Kelpie * / Living in these hard times / Under wraps II * / Only solitaire / Cheap day return / Wond'ring aloud * / Dun Ringill * / Salamander / Moths / Nursie * / Life is a long song * / One white duck – 0x10 = Nothing at all // THE

ESSENTIAL TULL:- Songs from the wood / Living in the past * / Teacher * / Aqualung * / Locomotive breath * / The witches promise * / Bungle in the jungle / Farm on the freeway / Thick as a brick / Sweet dream. *(re-iss. Aug88 as d-lp/d-c/d-cd; tracks *; CHR/ZCHR/CCD 1655)*

Jun 88. (pic-cd) *(TULLPCD 1)* **PART OF THE MACHINE / STORMY MONDAY BLUES (live) / LICK YOUR FINGERS CLEAN (live) / MINSTREL IN THE GALLERY (live) / FARM ON THE FREEWAY (live)** [ ] [-]

Jan 91. (cd/c/lp) *Raw Fruit; (FRS CD/MC/LP 004)* **LIVE AT HAMMERSMITH 1984 (live)** [ ] [-]

Apr 93. (4xcd-box) *(CDCHR 60044)* **25th ANNIVERSARY BOXED SET** [ ] [ ]
– REMIXED (CLASSIC SONGS) / CARNEGIE HALL N.Y. (RECORDED LIVE NEW YORK CITY 1970) / THE BEACON'S BOTTOM (TAPES) / POT POURRI (LIVE ACROSS THE WORLD AND THROUGH THE YEARS)

May 93. (7") *(CHS 3970)* **LIVING IN THE PAST. / HARD LINER** [32] [ ]
(12") *(12CHS 3970)* – ('A'side) / ('A'club)/ ('A'dub ravey master) / ('A'dub N.Y. mix).
(d-cd-s) *(23970-1)* – Living in the (slightly more recent) past (live) / Silver river turning / Rosa on the factory floor / I don't want to be me / ('A'side) / Truck stop runner / Piece of cake / Man of principle.

May 93. (d-cd/d-c) *(CDCHR/ZCHR 6001)* **THE VERY BEST OF JETHRO TULL – THE ANNIVERSARY COLLECTION** [ ] [ ]
– A song for Jeffrey / Beggar's farm / A Christmas song / A new day yesterday / Bouree / Nothing is easy / Living in the past / To cry you a song / Teacher / Sweet dream / Cross-eyed Mary / Mother goose / Aqualung / Locomotive breath / Life is a long song / Thick as a brick (extract) / Skating away on the thin ice of a new day / Bungle in the jungle/ / Minstrel in the gallery / Too old to rock'n'roll / Songs from the wood / Jack in the green / The whistler / Heavy horses / Dun Ringill / Fylingdale flyer / Jack-a-Lynn / Pussy willow / Broadsword / Under wraps II / Steel monkey / Farm on the freeway / Jump start / Kissing Willie / This is not love.

Nov 93. (d-cd) *(CDCHR 6057)* **NIGHTCAP – THE UNRELEASED MASTERS 1973-1991** [ ] [ ]
– CHATEAU D'ISASTER – First post / Animelee / Tiger Moon / Look at the animals / Law of the bungle / Law of the bungle part II / Left right / Solitaire / Critique oblique / Post last / Scenario / Audition / No rehearsal/ / UNRELEASED & RARE TRACKS – Paradise steakhouse / Sealion II / Piece of cake / Quartet / Silver river turning / Crew nights / The curse / Rosa on the factory floor / A small cigar / Man of principle / Commons brawl / No step / Drive on the young side of life / I don't want to be me / Broadford bazaar / Lights out / Truck stop runner / Hard liner.

Apr 95. (cd) *Windsong; (WINCD 070)* **IN CONCERT (live)** [ ] [-]

Feb 97. (cd) *EMI Gold; (CDGOLD 1079)* **THROUGH THE YEARS** [ ] [-]
(re-iss. Apr00 on 'Disky'; SI 99195-2)

Mar 97. (cd) *Disky; (DC 87861-2)* **THE JETHRO TULL COLLECTION** [ ] [-]

Apr 97. (3xcd-box) *(CDOMB 021)* **THE ORIGINALS** [ ] [-]
– (THIS WAS / STAND UP / BENEFIT) *(re-iss. Sep00 on 'EMI'; 528364-2)*

Feb 98. (cd) *Strange Fruit; (SFRSCD 051)* **BBC LIVE IN CONCERT** [ ] [-]

Mar 03. (d-cd) *(5 82353-2)* **STAND UP / THIS WAS** [ ] [-]

Mar 03. (cd) *EMI-Capitol; (582145-2)* **THE ESSENTIAL** [ ] [-]

Oct 03. (cd) *R&M; (RAMCD 004) / Fuel 2000; <061340>* **THE JETHRO TULL CHRISTMAS ALBUM** (festive recordings) [ ] [ ]

IAN ANDERSON

solo album augmented by **PETER JOHN VITESSE** – synth, keyboards

Chrysalis Chrysalis

Nov 83. (7") *(CHS 2746)* **FLY BY NIGHT. / END GAME** [ ] [-]

Nov 83. (lp/c) *<CDL/ZCDL 1443>* **WALK INTO LIGHT** [78] [ ]
– Fly by night / Made in England / Walk into light / Trains / End game / Black and white television / Toad in the hole / Looking for Eden / User-friendly / Different Germany. *(cd-iss. 1988; CCD 1443) (cd re-iss. Jun97 on 'Beat Goes On'; BGOCD 350)*

E.M.I. E.M.I.

Sep 98. (cd) *(<CDC 555262-2>)* **DIVINITIES (12 DANCES WITH GOD)** [ ] May95 [ ]
– In a stone circle / In sight of a minaret / In a black box / In the grip of stronger stuff / In material grace / In the moneylender's temple / At their father's knee / En Afrique / In the olive garden / In the pay of Spain / In times of India (Bombay valentine).

Papillion Varese

Mar 00. (cd) *(BTFLYCD 2000) <061053>* **THE SECRET LANGUAGE OF BIRDS** [ ] [ ]
– The secret language of birds / Little flower girl / Montserrat / Postcard day / Water carrier / Set-aside / Better Moon / Sanctuary / Jasmine corridor / Habanero reel / Panama freighter / The secret language of birds, pt.2 / Boris dancing / Circular breathing / Stormont shuffle.

JEWEL

Born: JEWEL KILCHER, 23 May'74, Payson, Utah, USA, daughter of a struggling farmer in Homer, Alaska. She had an equally tough time as a waitress in San Diego, California for over two years, while residing in her car and tirelessly working her way through California's seedier nightspots. She was signed to 'Atlantic' in 1994, recording her debut set, 'PIECES OF YOU' at NEIL YOUNG's studio (another rock veteran, DYLAN is also apparently a fan). The album stiffed upon its 1995 release, however, a year later, after much airplay for the hit single, 'WHO WILL SAVE YOUR SOUL', sales of the re-issued debut began to pick up (it has since sold over five million copies hitting Top 5 in the process). Fortuitously, the currently buoyant American female singer/songwriter scene (i.e. SHERYL CROW, ALANIS MORISSETTE and JOAN OSBORNE), has given JEWEL a platform for her rootsy, intelligent folk-pop; of course, her stunning blonde looks haven't hindered her any. Her not inconsiderable charms have recently attracted the romantic attentions of actor, Sean Penn (once the husband of MADONNA), while Bill Clinton invited her to one of his 1996 inaugural balls (ooh er!). Her album was still riding high in the US charts in 1997, although Britain has only began to take note, the single 'YOU WERE MEANT FOR ME' hitting the Top 40 by the end of the year. Sophomore effort, 'SPIRIT' (1998), made the US Top 3, a more professionally highly tuned effort than her debut and a stepping stone to 'THIS WAY' (2001) wherein the blonde songstress arguably came of age as a singer/songwriter. Another US Top 10 success, the album's worthy but only occasionally dull coffee table folk-rock marked a progression from youthful experimentation to twenty-something self-possession. So self-possessed in fact, that she did a volte-face with '0304' (2003), following her creative whims and making a kind of grown-up dance album, as lyrically involved as her best work but stylistically all over the map. Written in the mind-set of of a singer-songwriter but utilising dance rhythms, while intertwining various strands of urbane folk and even touches of jazz, the album succeeded on its own terms, however unpredictable those may have been. • **Trivia:** In 1995, JEWEL played Dorothy in the TV concert production of 'The Wizard Of Oz'.

Album rating: PIECES OF YOU (*7) / SPIRIT (*5) / THIS WAY (*6) / 0304 (*6)

JEWEL – vocals, acoustic guitar

Atlantic Atlantic

May 96. (c-s) *<87151>* **WHO WILL SAVE YOUR SOUL / NEAR YOU ALWAYS** [-] [11]

Jun 96. (cd/c) *<7567 82700-2/-4>* **PIECES OF YOU** [ ] May96 [4]
– Who will save your soul / Pieces of you / Little sister / Foolish games / Near you always / Painters / Morning song / Adrian / I'm sensitive / You were meant for me / Don't / Daddy / Angel standing by / Amen / Foolish games edit.

Feb 97. (c-s) *(A 8514C)* **WHO WILL SAVE YOUR SOUL / PIECES OF YOU** [ ] [-]
(cd-s+=) *(A 8514CD)* – Emily.
(re-iss. May97; same)

Nov 96. (c-s) *<87021>* **YOU WERE MEANT FOR ME / FOOLISH GAMES** [-] [2]

Jul 97. (c-s) *(A 5463C)* **YOU WERE MEANT FOR ME / COLD SONG** [52] [–]
(cd-s+=) *(A 5463CD)* – Rocker girl.
(re-iss. Nov97, hit UK No.32)

Jan 98. (c-s) *(A 0022C)* <85421> **FOOLISH GAMES / ANGEL NEEDS A RIDE** [ ] Jun98 [7]
(cd-s+=) *(A 0022CD)* – Everything breaks.

Nov 98. (c-s/cd-s) *(AT 0055 C/CD1)* *<radio play>* **HANDS / INNOCENCE MAINTAINED** [41] [6]
(cd-s) *(AT 0055CD2)* – ('A'side) / Who will save your soul (live) / You were meant for me (live).

Nov 98. (cd/c) *<(7567 82950-2/-4)>* **SPIRIT** [54] [3]
– Deep water / What's simple is true / Hands / Kiss the flame / Down so long / Innocence maintained / Jupiter / Fat boy / Enter from the east / Barcelona / Life uncommon / Do you / Abscence of fear.

Jun 99. (c-s) *(AT 0069C)* **DOWN SO LONG / DEEP WATER** [38] Apr99 [59]
(cd-s) *(AT 0069CD)* – Emily.

Nov 99. (cd/c) *<83250>* **JOY: A HOLIDAY COLLECTION** (festive) [–] [32]

Feb 02. (cd/c) *<(7567 83519-2/-4)>* **THIS WAY** [34] Nov01 [9]
– Standing still / Jesus loves you / Everybody needs someone sometime / Break me / Do you want to play? / Till we run out of road / Serve the ego / This way / Cleveland / I won't walk away / Love me, just leave me alone / The new wild west. *<cd+=>* – Grey matter (live) / Sometimes it be that way (live).

Mar 02. (cd-s) *(AT 0123CD)* *<85164>* **STANDING STILL / A LONG SLOW SLIDE (live)** [ ] Nov01 [25]

Aug 03. (cd-s) *(W 619CD)* *<88110>* **INTUITION (mixes; album / Todd Terry in house / Ford's radio / Tee's kat dub / video)** [52] May03 [20]

Sep 03. (cd) *(7567 93209-2)* *<83638>* **0304** [ ] Jun03 [2]
– Stand / Run 2 U / Intuition / Leave the lights on / 2 find U / Fragile heart / Doin' fine / 2 become 1 / Haunted / Sweet temptation / Yes U can / U and me = love / America / Becoming.

JIMMY EAT WORLD

Formed: Tempe, Arizona, USA . . . 1993 by JIM ADKINS, TOM LINTON, MITCH PORTER and ZACH LIND. Having begun life as a METALLICA covers band, the quartet soon developed a more lugubrious, melodic post-grunge sound as evidenced on their independently released debut 7". An eponymous album quickly followed as did a slew of split singles with the likes of CHRISTIE FRONT DRIVE and BLUEPRINT. Subsequently signed to 'Capitol', the group released 'STATIC PREVAILS' as their major label debut in 1996. Their contract nevertheless allowed for indie releases and they issued an eponymous five track EP in 1998 as a taster for the acclaimed 'CLARITY' (1999), a blinding, infused album of pure rock energy. Hailed by music journos as "the official Emo boys", the group settled on playing their abrasive, no bullshit, straight up rock'n'roll. But this wasn't three-chord idiot rock, oh no! JIMMY EAT WORLD incorporated intelligent lyrics and swirling, prolonged instrumentals, akin to the good ol' days of FUGAZI and straight-edged punk. After a split mini-album with Australian rockers JEBEDIAH, the group were dropped by majors 'Capitol'. They headed back into the studio and self-financed their sophomore set 'BLEED AMERICAN', later to be re-titled 'JIMMY EAT WORLD' (2001), after the 9/11 terrorists attacks. With runaway single 'The MIDDLE' blasted all over MTV, and the growing popularity of emo-core, the 'EAT WORLD found themselves a distribution deal with Geffen/Spielberg label 'Dreamworks'. The album subsequently catapulted them into the mainstream and they are said to be currently recording its long-awaited follow-up. • **Covered:** NEW RELIGION (Duran Duran) / SPANGLE (Wedding Present) / LAST CHRISTMAS (Wham) / FIRSTARTER (Prodigy).

Album rating: JIMMY EAT WORLD (*4) / STATIC PREVAILS (*5) / CLARITY (*6) / SINGLES compilation (*6) / BLEED AMERICAN (*7)

JIM ADKINS – vocals, guitar / **TOM LINTON** – vocals, guitar / **MITCH PORTER** – bass / **ZACH LIND** – drums

not iss. / Wooden Blue

1994. (7"ep) **ONE, TWO, THREE, FOUR** [–] [ ]
– What would I say to you now / Speed read.

1994. (cd) **JIMMY EAT WORLD** [–] [ ]
– Chachi / Patches / Amphibious / Splat out of luck / House arrest / Usery / Wednesday / Crooked / Reason 346 / Scientific / Cars.

1995. (7") **OPENER. / 77 SATELLITES** [–] [ ]
<re-iss. 1995 on 'Jimmy Eat World'; >

1995. (7") **DIGITS. / (other by CHRISTIE FRONT DRIVE)** [–] [ ]

not iss. / Ordinary

Nov 95. (7") **BETTER THAN OH. / (other by EMERY)** [–] [ ]

not iss. / Abridged

Dec 95. (7"ep) **CHRISTMAS CARD / UNTITLED. / (other 2 by BLUEPRINT)** [–] [ ]

—— **RICK BURCH** – bass; repl. PORTER

not iss. / Capitol

Jul 96. (cd/c) *<32404>* **STATIC PREVAILS** [–] [ ]
– Thinking, that's all / Rockstar / Claire / Call it in the air / Seventeen / Episode IV / Digits / Caveman / World is static / In the same room / Robot factory / Anderson Mesa. *(UK cd-iss. Jul02 on 'E.M.I.'+=; 539615-2)* – Rockstar (video).

1996. (7"ep) **LESS THAN JAKE / JIMMY EAT WORLD split** [–] [ ]
– Rockstar / Call it in the air / Seventeen / (other 3 by LESS THAN JAKE).

—— in 1997, the track 'CRUSH' featured on a 7" split alongside SENSEFIELD + MINERAL

1998. (7"ep) **JIMMY EAT WORLD / JEJUNE split** [–] [ ]
– What I would say to you now / Speed read / (other 2 by JEJUNE).
(above issued on 'Big Wheel Recreation') (below on 'Fueled By Ramen')

Oct 98. (cd-ep) *<FBR 020CD>* **JIMMY EAT WORLD** [–] [ ]
– Lucky Denver mint / For me this is heaven / Your new aesthetic (demo) / Softer / Roller queen. *(UK-iss.Apr99; same as US)*

Feb 99. (cd) *<55950>* **CLARITY** [–] [ ]
– Table for glasses / Lucky Denver mint / Your new aesthetic / Believe in what you want / Sunday / Crush / 12.23.95 / Ten / Just watch the fireworks / For me this is Heaven / Blister / Clarity / Goodbye sky harbor. *(UK-iss.Jul02 on 'E.M.I.'+=; 539616-2)* – Lucky Denver mint (video).

Big Wheel / Big Wheel

Oct 00. (3x7"/cd-ep) *<(BWR 0232/+CD)>* **JEBEDIAH & JIMMY EAT WORLD** [ ] [ ]
– The most beautiful things / No sensitivity / Cautioners / (other 3 by JEBEDIAH).

Universal / Dreamworks

Aug 01. (cd) *(450348-2)* *<450334>* **BLEED AMERICAN** [ ] Jul01 [54]
– Bleed American / A praise chorus / The middle / Your house / Sweetness / Hear you me / If you don't, don't / Get it faster / Cautioners / The authority song / My sundown / Splash, turn, twist *[UK+lp-only]*. *<lp-iss.on 'Grand Royal'; GR 99> <(re-prom.Nov01 & Feb02 as 'JIMMY EAT WORLD'; same)* – hit No.62 *(lp-iss.Mar03 on 'I.M.S.'; E 450334-1) (lp re-iss. Jun03 on 'Western Tread'; WT 002)*

Oct 01. (cd-s) *(450897-2)* **BLEED AMERICAN / SPLASH, TURN, TWIST / YOUR HOUSE (demo) / THE AUTHORITY SONG (demo) / BLEED AMERICAN (video)** [ ] [–]

Nov 01. (7") *(450878-7)* **SALT SWEAT SUGAR. / YOUR HOUSE (demo)** [60] [–]
(c-s) *(450878-4)* – ('A'side) / Splash, turn, twist.
(cd-s+=) *(450878-2)* – ('A'-video).

Dec 01. (7") **LAST CHRISTMAS. / FIRESTARTER** [–] [ ]
(above issued on 'Better Looking' records)

Jan 02. (7"/c-s) *(450848-7/-4)* **THE MIDDLE. / A PRAISE CHORUS** [26] [–]
(cd-s) *(450848-2)* – ('A'side) / If you don't, don't / Game of pricks / ('A'video).

Jun 02. (7") *(450832-7)* **SWEETNESS. / CLARITY (live)** [38] [–]
(cd-s) *(450833-2)* – ('A'side) / Blister (live) / Your new acoustic (live).
(cd-s) *(450834-2)* – ('A'side) / A praise chorus (live) / Lucky Denver mint (live).

– compilations, etc. –

Aug 01. (cd) *Big Wheel; <(BWR 0230CD)>* **SINGLES** [ ] [ ]
– Opener / 77 satellites / What would I say to you now / Speed read / Spangle / H Ramina / Christmas card / Untitled / Carbon scoring / Digits. *(cd re-iss. Oct01 on 'Golf'+=; CDGOLF 049)* – If model / Most beautiful things / Cautioners.

JJ72

Formed: Dublin, Ireland ... 1997 by MARK GREANEY and percussionist FERGAL MATTHEWS. The pair met whilst attending Belvedere College and struck up a friendship after MATTHEWS complimented GREANEY on his "cool" coat. They also shared a similar intrest in music: NIRVANA, MUDHONEY and JOY DIVISION are cited as primary influences. The only thing missing was a bassist, and after sifting through Dublin's directory of musicians, young actress HILARY WOODS was quickly recruited. The newly formed trio subsequently cut a demo tape entitled 'OXYGEN' and sent it to assorted radio stations and record companies. Progress was undoubtably slow, but surely the group (and their ubiquitous name) started making waves within the music industry. They signed to 'Lakota' records mid 1999 and issued the single 'OCTOBER SWIMMER', a swirling hybrid of indie guitar, pop punk and fuzz grunge all backed by GREANEY's melodic vocals. Comparisons to ASH were obvious, although there was definitely a hint of R.E.M. (strictly their 'Monster' period) in there too, although GREANEY would deny this in the NME. Various other singles emerged over the next couple of years, notably 'SNOW' and a re-issue of the demo 'OXYGEN' before the release of their eponymous debut album in 2000. Although the album boasted many delicious tracks, the group seemed to be hiding in their rehearsal room for now. JJ72 followed their critically acclaimed debut with the not-so-strong 'I TO SKY', a pop record bursting with radio-friendly melodies and a keen eye for intrumentation and production. GREANEY, once again did his best BONO impression and the album's producer, FLOOD, gave a clean, crisp sound that detracted from the group's heavier, more abrasive rock. Still, tracks 'I SAW A PRAYER' and 'HALF THREE' managed to keep within the JJ72 mould.

Album rating: JJ72 (*7) / I TO SKY (*6)

MARK GREANEY – vocals, guitar / **HILARY WOODS** – bass, vocals / **FERGAL MATTHEWS** – drums

		Lakota	Sony
Nov 99.	(cd-s) *(LAK 0011CD)* **OCTOBER SWIMMER / IMPROV / GHERKIN**		–
Feb 00.	(7")(cd-s) *(LAK7 0014)(LAK 0014CD)* **SNOW. / WILLOW / FRESH WATER**		–
May 00.	(7")(cd-s) *(LAK7 0015)(LAK 0015CD)* **LONG WAY SOUTH. / SNOW (acoustic) / EARTHLY DELIGHTS**	68	–
Aug 00.	(7")(cd-s) *(LAK7 0016)(LAK 0016CD1)* **OXYGEN. / ASTORIA / OXYGEN (live)**	23	–
	(cd-s) *(LAK 0016CD2)* – ('A'side) / Desertion / Long way south (live).		
Aug 00.	(cd/lp) *(LAK CD/LP 017) <85825>* **JJ72** – October swimmer / Undercover angel / Oxygen / Willow / Surrender / Long way south / Snow / Broken down / Improv / Not like you / Algeria / Bumble bee.	16	
Oct 00.	(7")(cd-s) *(LAK7 0018)(LAK 0018CD1)* **OCTOBER SWIMMER. / GUIDANCE / BLACK-EYED DOG**	29	–
	(cd-s) *(LAK 0018CD2)* – ('A'side) / Blood tests / Bumble bee (live).		
Jan 01.	(7")(cd-s) *(LAK7 0019)(LAK 0019CD1)* **SNOW / WOUNDED / SURRENDER (original demo)**	21	–
	(cd-s) *(LAK 0019CD2)* – ('A'side) / Gherkin / Oxygen (CD-Rom).		
		Columbia	Columbia
Sep 02.	(7") *(673159-7)* **FORMULAE. / DREAM'D IN A DREAM**	28	–
	(cd-s+=) *(673159-2)* – ('A'demo) / ('A'video).		
	(cd-s) *(673159-5)* – ('A'side) / Alabaster ocean / Higher than gods.		
Oct 02.	(cd) *(<509529-2>)* **I TO SKY** – Nameless / Formulae / I saw a prayer / Serpent sky / Always and forever / Brother sleep / Sinking / 7th wave / Half three / Glimmer / City / Olche mhaith.	20	
Feb 03.	(7"green) *(673432-7)* **ALWAYS AND FOREVER. / WICKED GAME**	43	–
	(cd-s+=) *(673432-5)* – Nameless Dave Fanning (2FM session).		
	(cd-s) *(673432-2)* – ('A'-John Leckie version) / Dog (demo 2000 version) / City (live at POD Dublin) / ('A'-video).		

— now with HILARY who left just after above

Billy JOEL

Born: WILLIAM MARTIN JOEL, 9 May'49, Hicksville, Long Island, New York, USA. In 1965, the classically trained JOEL played piano in his first group, The ECHOES, having been a welterweight boxing champ for local Long Island boys' club. In 1967, he joined The HASSLES who signed to 'United Artists' and released a couple of albums, after an initial SAM & DAVE cover version 45, 'YOU GOT ME HUMMIN''. In 1969, JOEL became a rock critic for 'Changes' art-magazine and formed his own hard-rock duo, ATTILA, with JON SMALL. They issued one 1970 album for 'Epic', before disbanding. JOEL then suffered a bout of depression and entered Meadowbrook mental hospital, with psychiatric problems. In 1971 he was back in circulation to sign a solo contract with Family Productions' Artie Ripp (allegedly known as 'Ripp-off' to his employees, due to his large percentage of artist royalties). JOEL's debut solo effort, 'COLD SPRING HARBOR' was soon issued but, due to a mixing fault, was pressed at the wrong speed!! Embarrassingly for JOEL, who had been well-received by live audiences, this version hit the shops without being corrected, and it made him sound slightly Chipmunk-ish (an 80's re-release rectified matters). Nevertheless, JOEL's piano playing was faultless and with the ballad, 'SHE'S GOT A WAY', he proved his songwriting calibre. He subsequently moved to Los Angeles, soon marrying the ex-wife of JON SMALL, Elizabeth Weber. Culled from JOEL's experiences of playing incognito in piano bars, the 'PIANO MAN' (1973) opus gave him a deserved break with 'Columbia', after his 'CAPTAIN JACK' track was played on FM radio. The following year, the album made the US Top 30, as did its title track. 'STREETLIFE SERENADE' (1974) carried on in much the same vein, JOEL at his strongest on ballad material like 'ROBERTA'. 'TURNSTILES' (1976) sounded more assured, 'NEW YORK STATE OF MIND' JOEL's most accomplished track of his career up to that point. This promise was realised with 'THE STRANGER' (1977), which reached No.2 in the US chart and spawned such enduring candlelight smoochers as 'JUST THE WAY YOU ARE' (written for Elizabeth) and 'SHE'S ALWAYS A WOMAN'. The hits were coming thick and fast, '52nd STREET' (1978) giving JOEL another No.1 album, while the rollicking piano pop/rock of 'MY LIFE' hit NO.3 in the American singles chart and furnished the singer with his biggest UK hit single to date. 'GLASS HOUSES' (1980) kept up the momentum, the retro pastiche of 'IT'S STILL ROCK'N'ROLL TO ME' giving JOEL his first No.1 single (US) while proving he could still be relied upon for cringe-inducing lyrics. With 'THE NYLON CURTAIN' (1982), however, JOEL turned his attention to more pressing concerns, addressing, SPRINGSTEEN style, such issues as Vietnam veterans ('GOODNIGHT SAIGON') and unemployment ('ALLENTOWN'). 'AN INNOCENT MAN' (1984), on the other hand, saw JOEL revisiting his musical roots. By far the biggest success of his career, the record was a highly listenable blend of doo-wop, soul and early rock'n'roll. It was also packed with hits; 'UPTOWN GIRL' (his first UK No.1), 'TELL HER ABOUT IT' and the title track all went Top 10 on both sides of the Atlantic, JOEL enjoying his greatest UK success to date. 'THE BRIDGE' (1986) carried on in a vaguely similar, if not so successful vein, while 'STORM FRONT' (1989) rose to the top of the US charts on the back of the 'WE DIDN'T

START THE FIRE' single, an uncharacteristically ballsy rocker which set the tone for the rest of the album, a partially successful attempt at stadium bombast. Employing a new cast of seasoned musicians, JOEL recorded 'RIVER OF DREAMS' (1993), another big selling opus. While the doo-wop influenced title track went Top 5, the other singles failed to make any headway. Nevertheless, over almost three decades, JOEL has proved himself a consistent writer and performer, an elder statesman of pop/rock who pays little heed to constant press barbs. '2000 YEARS: THE MILLENNIUM CONCERT' (2000) only partly lived up to its grandiose, overblown title, the record a document of JOEL's New Year's Eve '99 bash at New York's Madison Square Garden. Although the veteran pianist had ostensibly retired from the music biz, he hammed it up one more time with a crowd pleasing run through his back catalogue, even wheeling out the obligatory 'AULD LANG SYNE' at the bells. The pianist subsequently invested his creative energies in composing classical music, or rather classical music with populist flourishes. 'FANTASIES & DELUSIONS' (2001) was a collection of solo piano works written by JOEL but performed by RICHARD JOOS. While it might be argued that the record was not, strictly speaking, a BILLY JOEL album, the man's trademark, strident melodicism was neatly stamped over most of the material, making it a pleasurable listen even for pop fans not normally taken to buying classical pieces. • **Covered:** BACK IN THE USSR + I'LL CRY INSTEAD (Beatles) / THE TIMES THEY ARE A CHANGIN' + TO MAKE YOU FEEL MY LOVE (Bob Dylan) / LIGHT AS THE BREEZE (Leonard Cohen) / and a few more. • **Trivia:** Divorced from his wife (Elizabeth) in July '82, he soon married supermodel and star of his 'UPTOWN GIRL' promo video; Christine Brinkley. In 1989, he fired his manager ex-brother-in-law Frank Weber, after an audit of the accounts showed nearly $100 million missing. The following year, JOEL was awarded $2 million by the courts, and a countersuit by Weber for $30 million was thrown out.

Album rating: COLD SPRING HARBOR (*4) / PIANO MAN (*5) / STREETLIFE SERENADE (*5) / TURNSTILES (*6) / THE STRANGER (*8) / 52ND STREET (*7) / GLASS HOUSES (*6) / SONGS IN THE ATTIC (*6) / THE NYLON CURTAIN (*7) / AN INNOCENT MAN (*6) / GREATEST HITS, VOLUME 1 & 2 compilation (*8) / THE BRIDGE (*5) / KOHU,EPT (LIVE IN LENINGRAD) (*4) / STORM FRONT (*5) / RIVER OF DREAMS (*6) / GREATEST HITS, VOLUME III compilation (*6) / 2000 YEARS – THE MILLENNIUM CONCERT (*4) / THE ULTIMATE COLLECTION compilation (*8) / FANTASIES & DELUSIONS (*5)

Philips Family

May 72. (7") *(6078 001) (0900>* **SHE'S GOT A WAY. / EVERYBODY LOVE YOU NOW** [ ] [ ]

Jun 72. (lp) *(6269 150) <2700>* **COLD SPRING HARBOUR** [ ] Nov71 [ ]
– She's got a way / You can make me free / Everybody loves you now / Why Judy why / Falling of the rain / Turn around / You look so good to me / Tomorrow is today / Nocturne / Got to begin again. *(re-iss. re-mixed Jan84 on 'C.B.S.' lp/c; CBS/40 32400)* – hit UK No.95 *(cd-iss. Jan84; CD 26108) (re-iss. Sep91 on 'Pickwick' cd/c; 982637-2/-4)*

Jan 73. (7") *<0906>* **TOMORROW IS TODAY. / EVERYBODY LOVES YOU NOW** [–] [ ]

Apr 74. (7") *(6078 018)* **THE BALLAD OF BILLY THE KID. / IF I ONLY HAD THE WORDS (TO TELL YOU)** [ ] [–]

—— Stage band around this time were **DON EVANS** – guitar / **PAT McDONALD** – bass / **TOM WHITEHORSE** – steel guitar, banjo / **RHYS CLARK** – drums

C.B.S. Columbia

Jun 74. (7") *<46055>* **WORSE COMES TO THE WORST. / SOMEWHERE ALONG THE LINE** [–] [80]

Aug 74. (7") *<10015>* **TRAVELIN' PRAYER. / AIN'T NO CRIME** [–] [77]

Apr 75. (lp/c) *(CBS/40 80719) <32544>* **PIANO MAN** [ ] Nov73 [27]
– Travelin' prayer / Piano man / Ain't no crime / You're my home / The ballad of Billy The Kid / Worse comes to the worst / Stop in Nevada / If I only had the words (to tell you) / Somewhere along the line / Captain Jack. *(re-iss. Mar81 lp/c; CBS/40 32002)* – hit UK No.98 in Jun84 *(cd-iss. Sep85; CD 80719) (cd re-iss. Apr89; CD 32002) (cd re-iss. Jul97 on 'Columbia'; 487938-2)*
(above should have been released May74 by 'Philips' – withdrawn)

Nov 74. (7") *<10064>* **THE ENTERTAINER. / THE MEXICAN CONNECTION** [–] [34]

Apr 75. (7") *(CBS 3183) <45963>* **PIANO MAN. / YOU'RE MY HOME** [ ] Feb74 [25]

Sep 75. (7") *(CBS 3469)* **IF I ONLY HAD THE WORDS (TO TELL YOU). / STOP IN NEVADA** [ ] [–]

Jul 75. (lp/c) *(CBS/40 80766) <33146>* **STREETLIFE SERENADE** [ ] Nov74 [35]
– Streetlife serenader / Los Angelenos / The great suburban showdown / Root beer rag / Roberta / Last of the big time spenders / Weekend song / Souvenir / The Mexican connection. *(re-iss. Mar81 lp/c; CBS/40 32035) (cd-iss. Mar87; CD 80766) (cd re-iss. Feb97 on 'Columbia'; 484461-2)*

—— band now incl. **NIGEL OLSSON + DEE MURRAY** (both ex-ELTON JOHN)

Jul 76. (lp/c) *(CBS/40 81195) <33848>* **TURNSTILES** [ ] Jun76 [ ]
– Say goodbye to Hollywood / Summer, Highland falls / All you wanna do is dance / New York state of mind / James / Prelude / Angry young man / I've loved these days / Miami 2017 (seen the lights go on Broadway). *(re-iss. Nov81 lp/c; CBS/40 32057) (cd-iss. Mar87; Cd 81195) (re-iss. Nov89 on 'Pickwick' lp/c/cd; 902197-1/-4/-2) (cd re-iss. Feb97 on 'Columbia'; 474681-2)*

Jul 76. (7") *<10412>* **SUMMER, HIGHLAND FALLS. / JAMES** [–] [ ]

Oct 76. (7") *<10562>* **I'VE LOVED THESE DAYS. / SAY GOODBYE TO HOLLYWOOD** [–] [ ]

Nov 76. (7") *(CBS 4686)* **SAY GOODBYE TO HOLLYWOOD. / STOP IN NEVADA** [ ] [ ]

Sep 77. (7") *<10624>* **MOVIN' OUT (ANTHONY'S SONG). / SHE'S ALWAYS A WOMAN** [–] [ ]

Dec 77. (lp/c) *(CBS/40 82311) <34987>* **THE STRANGER** [25] Oct77 [2]
– Movin' out (Anthony's song) / The stranger / Just the way you are / Scenes from an Italian restaurant / Vienna / Only the good die young / She's always a woman / Get it right the first time / Everybody has a dream. *(re-iss. May87 lp/c; 450914-1/-4) (cd-iss. Dec85; CD 82311) (cd re-iss. Jun89; 450914-2)*

Jan 78. (7") *(CBS 5872) <10646>* **JUST THE WAY YOU ARE. / GET IT RIGHT THE FIRST TIME** [19] Nov77 [3]

Mar 78. (7") *<10708>* **MOVIN' OUT (ANTHONY'S SONG). / EVERYBODY HAS A DREAM** [–] [17]

Apr 78. (7") *(CBS 6266)* **SHE'S ALWAYS A WOMAN. / EVERYBODY HAS A DREAM** [ ] [–]

May 78. (7") *<10750>* **ONLY THE GOOD DIE YOUNG. / GET IT RIGHT THE FIRST TIME** [–] [24]

Jun 78. (7") *(CBS 6412)* **MOVIN' OUT (ANTHONY'S SONG). / VIENNA** [35] [–]

Aug 78. (7") *<10788>* **SHE'S ALWAYS A WOMAN. / VIENNA** [–] [17]

Nov 78. (lp/c) *(CBS/40 83181) 35609>* **52nd STREET** [10] Oct78 [1]
– Big shot / Honesty / My life / Zanzibar / Stiletto / Rosalind's eyes / Half a mile away / Until the night / 52nd Street. *(re-iss. Nov85 lp/c; CBS/40 32693) (cd-iss. Nov87; CD 83181) (cd re-iss. Feb95 on 'Columbia'; CK 64412)*

Nov 78. (7") *(CBS 6821) <10853>* **MY LIFE. / 52nd STREET** [12] [3]

Feb 79. (7") *<10913>* **BIG SHOT. / ROOT BEER BAG** [–] [14]

Mar 79. (7") *(CBS 7242)* **UNTIL THE NIGHT. / ROOT BEER RAG** [50] [–]

Jun 79. (7") *(CBS 7422) <10959>* **HONESTY. / THE MEXICAN CONNECTION** [ ] Apr79 [24]

Feb 80. (7") *<11229>* **SOUVENIR. / ALL FOR LENYA** [–] [ ]

Mar 80. (lp/c) *(CBS/40 86108) <36384>* **GLASS HOUSES** [9] [1]
– You may be right / Sometimes a fantasy / Don't ask me why / It's still rock'n'roll to me / All for Lenya / I don't want to be alone / Sleeping with the television on / C'Etait toi (you were the one) / Close to the borderline / Through the long night. *(cd-iss. Dec85; CD 86108) (re-iss. Nov86 lp/c; 450087-1/-4) (cd-iss. Mar91; 450087-2) (re-iss. May94 on 'Columbia' cd/c; 450067-2/-4)*

Mar 80. (7") *(CBS 8325)* **ALL FOR LEYNA. / CLOSE TO THE BORDERLINE** [40] [–]

Mar 80. (7") *<11231>* **YOU MAY BE RIGHT. / CLOSE TO THE BORDERLINE** [–] [7]

May 80. (7") *(CBS 8643)* **YOU MAY BE RIGHT. / THROUGH THE LONG NIGHT** [ ] [–]

Jul 80. (7") *(CBS 8753) <11276>* **IT'S STILL ROCK'N'ROLL TO ME. / THROUGH THE LONG NIGHT** [14] May80 [1]

Oct 80. (7") *(CBS 9031) <11331>* **DON'T ASK ME WHY. / C'ETAIT TOI (YOU WERE THE ONE)** [ ] Aug80 [19]

Oct 80. (7") *<11379>* **SOMETIMES A FANTASY. / ALL FOR LEYNA** – 36

Jan 81. (7") *(CBS 9419)* **SOMETIMES A FANTASY. / SLEEPING WITH THE TELEVISION ON** [ ] –

Sep 81. (7") *(CBS 1642) <02518>* **SAY GOODBYE TO HOLLYWOOD (live). / SUMMER, HIGHLAND FALLS (live)** [ ] 17

Sep 81. (lp/c) *(CBS/40 85273) <37461>* **SONGS IN THE ATTIC (live)** 57 8
– Miami 2017 (seen the lights go out on Broadway) / Summer, Highland Falls / Streetlife serenader / Los Angelenos / She's got a way / Everybody loves you now / Say goodbye to Hollywood / Captain Jack / You're my home / The ballad of Billy The Kid / I've loved these days. *(re-iss. Nov83 lp/c; CBS/40 32364) (cd-iss. May87; CD 85273) (cd re-iss. Jun89; CD 32364)*

Nov 81. (7") *(A 1808)* **YOU'RE MY HOME (live). / THE BALLAD OF BILLY THE KID (live)** [ ] –

Jan 82. (7") *(A 2002) <02628>* **SHE'S GOT A WAY (live). / THE BALLAD OF BILLY THE KID (live)** [ ] Nov81 23

Sep 82. (7") *(A 2730) <03244>* **PRESSURE. / LAURA** [ ] 20

Sep 82. (lp/c) *(CBS/40 85959) <38200>* **THE NYLON CURTAIN** 27 7
– Allentown / Laura / Pressure / Goodnight Saigon / She's right on time / A room on your own / Surprises / Scandinavian skies / Pressure / Where's the orchestra. *(cd-iss. Jan83; CD 85959) (re-iss. Mar88 lp/c; 460186-1/-4)*

Nov 82. (7") *(A 2981) <03413>* **ALLENTOWN. / ELVIS PRESLEY BOULEVARD** [ ] 17

Feb 83. (7") *(A 3029)* **GOODNIGHT SAIGON. / WHERE'S THE ORCHESTRA** [ ] –

Feb 83. (7") *<03780>* **GOODNIGHT SAIGON. / A ROOM OF OUR OWN** – 56

Aug 83. (7") *(A 3655) <04012>* **TELL HER ABOUT IT. / EASY MONEY** [ ] Jul83 1

Sep 83. (lp/c) *(CBS/40 25554) <38837>* **AN INNOCENT MAN** 2 Aug83 4
– Easy money / An innocent man / The longest time / This night / Tell her about it / Uptown girl / Careless talk / Christie Lee / Leave a tender moment alone / Keeping the faith. *(cd-iss. Aug84; CD 25554)*

Oct 83. (7") *(A 3775) <04149>* **UPTOWN GIRL. / CARELESS TALK** 1 Sep83 3
(12"+=) *(TA 3775)* – Just the way you are / It's still rock'n'roll to me.

Dec 83. (7") *(A 3655)* **TELL HER ABOUT IT. / EASY MONEY** 4 –
(12"+=) *(TA 3655)* – You got me hummin' (live).

Dec 83. (7") *<04259>* **AN INNOCENT MAN. / I'LL CRY INSTEAD** – 10

Feb 84. (7") *(A 4142)* **AN INNOCENT MAN. / YOU'RE MY HOME (live)** 8 –
(12"+=) *(TA 4142)* – She's always a woman / Until the night.

Apr 84. (7") *(A 4280) <0440>* **THE LONGEST TIME. / CHRISTIE LEE** 25 Mar84 14
(12"+=) *(TA 4280)* – Captain Jack (live) / The ballad of Billy the kid (live).

Jun 84. (7") *(A 4521)* **LEAVE A TENDER MOMENT ALONE. / GOODNIGHT SAIGON** 29 –
(12"+=) *(TA 4521)* – Movin' out (Anthony's song) / Big shot / You may be right.

Jul 84. (7") *<04514>* **LEAVE A TENDER MOMENT ALONE. / THIS NIGHT** – 27

Nov 84. (7") *(A 4884)* **THIS NIGHT. / I'LL CRY INSTEAD (live)** [ ] –

Jan 85. (7") *<04681>* **KEEPING THE FAITH. / SHE'S RIGHT ON TIME** – 18

—— featured on the 'USA FOR AFRICA' single, 'WE ARE THE WORLD'.

Jun 85. (7") *(A 6378) <05417>* **YOU'RE ONLY HUMAN. / SURPRISES** [ ] 9
(12"+=) *(TA 6378)* – Keeping the faith / Scenes from an Italian restaurant.

Oct 85. (7") *(A 6622) <05657>* **THE NIGHT IS STILL YOUNG. / SUMMER, HIGHLAND FALLS** [ ] 34

Jul 86. (7") *(A 7247) <06118>* **MODERN WOMAN. / SLEEPING WITH THE TELEVISION ON** [ ] Jun86 10
(d7"+=) *(DA 7247)* – Uptown girl / All for love.
(12"+=) *(TA 7247)* – The night is still young / You're only human.

Aug 86. (lp/c/cd) *(CBS/40/CD 86323) <40402>* **THE BRIDGE** 38 7
– Running on ice / This is the time / A matter of trust / Modern woman / Baby grand (w/ RAY CHARLES) / Big man on Mulberry Street / Temptation / Code of silence (w/ CYNDI LAUPER) / Getting closer. *(re-iss. Oct89 lp/c; 465 561-1/-4) (re-iss. Feb94 on 'Columbia' cd/c; 465561-2)*

Sep 86. (7") *(650057-7) <06108>* **A MATTER OF TRUST. / GETTING CLOSER** 52 Aug86 10
(12"+=) *(650057-6)* – An innocent man / Tell her about it.

Nov 86. (7") *<06526>* **THIS IS THE TIME. / CODE OF SILENCE (with CYNDI LAUPER)** – 18

Mar 87. (7"; BILLY JOEL featuring RAY CHARLES) *<06994>* **BABY GRAND. / BIG MAN ON MULBERRY STREET** – 75

Nov 87. (d-lp/c/cd) *(460407-1/-4/-2) <40996>* **KOHU.EPT – LIVE IN LENINGRAD (live)** 92 38
– Odoya / Angry young man / Honesty / Goodnight Saigon / Stiletto / Big man on Mulberry Street / Baby grand / An innocent man / Allentown / A matter of trust / Only the good die young / Sometimes a fantasy / Uptown girl / Big shot / Back in the U.S.S.R. / The times they are a-changin'. *(cd re-iss. Oct90 on 'Columbia'; 467448-2)*

Nov 87. (7") *(651206-7) <07626>* **BACK IN THE U.S.S.R. (live). / BIG SHOT (live)** [ ] [ ]
(12"+=)(cd-s+=) *(651206-6)(CDEWF 1)* – A matter of trust (live) / The times they are a-changin' (live).

Feb 88. (7") *<07664>* **THE TIMES THEY ARE A-CHANGIN' (live). / BACK IN THE U.S.S.R. (live)** – [ ]

—— new band **MINDY JOSTIN** – rhythm guitar, violin, harp / **DAVID BROWN** – guitar / **MARK RIVIERA** – sax / **LIBERTY DeVITO** – drums / **SCHUYLER DEALE** – bass / **JEFF JACOBS** – synthesizers / **CRYSTAL TALIEFERO** – vocals, percussion

Sep 89. (7"/c-s) *(JOEL/+M 1) <73021>* **WE DIDN'T START THE FIRE. / HOUSE OF BLUE LIGHT** 7 Oct89 1
(12"+=/cd-s+=) *(JOEL T/C 1)* – Just the way you are.

Oct 89. (lp/c/cd) *(465658-1/-4/-2) <44366>* **STORM FRONT** 5 1
– That's not her style / We didn't start the fire / The downeaster "Alexa" / I go to extremes / Shameless / Storm front / Leningrad / State of Grace / When in Rome / And so it goes. *(cd re-iss. Mar96 on 'Columbia'; 4656583)*

Dec 89. (7"/c-s) *(JOEL/+M 3)* **LENINGRAD. / THE TIMES THEY ARE A-CHANGIN' (live)** 53 –
(cd-s+=) *(CDJOEL 3)* – Uptown girl (live) / Back in the USSR (live).
(3"cd-s+=) *(JOELC 3)* – Goodnight Saigon / Vienna / Scandinavian skies.

Mar 90. (7"/c-s) *(JOEL/+M 2) <73091>* **I GO TO EXTREMES. / WHEN IN ROME** 70 Jan90 6
(12"+=/cd-s+=) *(JOEL T/C 2)* – Uptown girl / All for Leyna.
(7"ep+=) *(JOELEP 2)* – Prelude / Angry young man / Tell her about it / Leave a tender moment alone.

Apr 90. (c-s) *<73333>* **THE DOWNEASTER "ALEXA" / AND SO IT GOES** – 57

May 90. (7"/c-s) *(JOEL/+M 4)* **THE DOWNEASTER "ALEXA". / AND SO IT GOES / STREETLIFE SERENADE** [ ] –
(12"+=/cd-s+=) *(JOELT/CDJOEL 4)* – I've loved these days / An innocent man.
(pic-cd-s+=) *(JOELC 4)* – Say goodbye to Hollywood / Allentown / Only the good die young.

Jul 90. (c-s) *<73602>* **THAT'S NOT HER STYLE / AND SO IT GOES** – 77

Oct 90. (7"ep/cd-ep) **THAT'S NOT HER STYLE / WE DIDN'T START THE FIRE / UNTIL THE NIGHT / JUST THE WAY YOU ARE** [ ] –

Oct 90. (c-s) *<73602>* **AND SO IT GOES / THE DOWNEASTER ALEXA / SHAMELESS / STATES OF GRACE** – 37

Jan 92. (c-s) *<74188>* **SHAMELESS / STORM FRONT (live)** – [ ]
(below from film 'Honeymoon In Las Vegas' on 'Epic records')

Aug 92. (7"/c-s) *(658343-7/-4) <74422>* **ALL SHOOK UP. / (b-side by Ricky Van Shelton)** 27 92
(cd-s+=) *(658343-2)* – (other artist).
other musicians; **DAN KORTCHMAR, TOMMY BYRNES, LESLIE WEST** – guitar / **T.H. STEVENS, LONNIE HILLER** – bass / **STEVE JORDAN, ZACHARY ALFORD, LIBERTY DeVITTO** – drums

Jul 93. (7"/c-s) *(659543-7/-4) <77086>* **THE RIVER OF DREAMS. / NO MAN'S LAND** 3 3
(cd-s+=) *(659543-2)* – The great wall of China.

Aug 93. (cd/c/lp) *(473872-2/-4/-1) <53003>* **RIVER OF DREAMS** 3 1
– No man's land / The great wall of China / Blonde over blue / A minor variation / Shades of grey / All about soul / Lullabye (goodnight, my angel) / The river of dreams / Two thousand years / Famous last words.

Oct 93. (7"/c-s) *(659736-7/-4) <77254>* **ALL ABOUT SOUL. / YOU PICKED A REAL BAD TIME** 32 29
(cd-s+=) *(659736-2)* – (2-'A'mixes).

Feb 94. (7"/c-s) *(659920-7/-4)* **NO MAN'S ISLAND. / SHADES OF GREY (live)** 50 –
(cd-s+=) *(659920-2)* – ('A'mix).

Mar 94. (c-s) *<77363>* **LULLABYE (GOODNIGHT MY ANGEL) / TWO THOUSAND YEARS** [–] [77]

Aug 97. (cd-s) *<78641>* **TO MAKE YOU FEEL MY LOVE / (bare bones version) / GOODBYE YELLOW BRICK ROAD / A HARD DAY'S NIGHT** [–] [50]
(cd-s) *<78660>* – (first 2 tracks) / House of blue lights / Intro – Summer, Highland falls (live) / Goodbye yellow brick road (live).

Oct 97. (cd/c) *(488236-2/-4) <67347>* **GREATEST HITS – VOLUME III** (compilation) [23] Aug97 [9]
– Keeping the faith / An innocent man / A matter of trust / Baby grand / This is the time / Leningrad / We didn't start the fire / I go to extremes / And so it goes / Downeaster Alexa / Shameless / All about soul / Lullabye / River of dreams / To make you feel my love / Hey girl / Light as a breeze.

May 00. (d-cd/d-c) *(497981-2/-4) <63792-2>* **2000 YEARS – THE MILLENNIUM CONCERT (live 31st December, 1999)** [68] [40]
– Beethoven's ninth symphony / Big shot / Movin' out (Anthony's song) / Summer, Highland falls / The ballad of Billy The Kid / Don't ask me why / New York state of mind / I've loved these days / My life / Allentown / Prelude – Angry young man / Only the good die young / I go to extremes / Goodnight Saigon / We didn't start the fire / Big man on Mulberry street / 2000 years / Auld lang syne / River of dreams / Scenes from an Italian restaurant / Dance to the music / Honky tonk woman / It's still rock'n'roll to me / You may be right / This night / This is the time.

Sony Classical — Sony Classical

Nov 01. (cd) *<(SK 85397)>* **FANTASIES & DELUSIONS (MUSIC FOR SOLO PIANO)** [ ] Sep01 [83]
– Opus 3: Reverie (villa d'este) / Opus 2: Waltz #1 (Nunley's carousel) / Opus 7: Aria (grand canal) / Opus 6: Invention in C minor / Opus 1: Soliloquy (on a separation) / Opus 8: Suite for piano (star-crossed) I/II/III / Opus 5: Waltz #2 (Steinway hall) / Opus 9: Waltz #3 (for Lola) / Opus 4: Fantasy (film noir) / Opus 10: Air (Dublinesque).

– compilations, etc. –

on 'CBS' UK / 'Columbia' US unless mentioned otherwise

Oct 79. (3-lp-box) *(CBS 66352)* **3-LP BOX SET** [ ] [–]
– 'TURNSTILES' / 'THE STRANGER' / '52nd STREET'

1980. (7") *Columbia;* **DOWN IN THE BOONDOCKS. / 21ST CENTURY MAN** [–] [ ]

Feb 83. (7"ep) *Epic; (EPCA 2619)* **GREATEST ORIGINAL HITS** [ ] [–]
– Just the way you are / Movin' out (Anthony's song) / My life / She's a woman. *(c-iss.Aug82)*

Jul 84. (7") *(A 4591)* **JUST THE WAY YOU ARE. / MY LIFE** [ ] [–]

Jul 85. (d-lp/c/cd) *(CBS/40/CD 88666)* **GREATEST HITS VOL.1 & VOL.2** [7] [6]
– Piano man / Say goodbye to Hollywood / New York state of mind / The stranger / Just the way you are / Movin' out (Anthony's song) / Only the good die young / She's always a woman / My life / Big shot / Honesty / You may be right / It's still rock and roll to me / Pressure / Allentown / Goodnight Saigon / Tell her about it / Uptown girl / The longest time / You're only human (second wind) / The night is still young. *(d-cd-iss. Sep92 on 'Columbia'; CD 88666)*

Feb 86. (7") *(A 6862)* **SHE'S ALWAYS A WOMAN. / JUST THE WAY YOU ARE** [53] [–]

Apr 86. (lp/c) *Showcase; (SHLP/SHTC 114)* **CALIFORNIA FLASH** [ ] [–]

Jul 87. (d-lp) *(BJ 241)* **THE STRANGER / AN INNOCENT MAN** [ ] [–]

1988. (d-c) *(4022143)* **PIANO MAN / STREETLIFE SERENADE** [ ] [–]

Aug 88. (3"cd-ep) *<38K 07950>* **IT'S STILL ROCK'N'ROLL TO ME. / JUST THE WAY YOU ARE** [–] [ ]

Nov 91. (4xcd-box/4xc-box) *Columbia; (469174-2/-4)* **THE BILLY JOEL SOUVENIR – THE ULTIMATE COLLECTION INTERVIEW WITH BILLY JOEL** [ ] [–]
– (GREATEST HITS VOL.1 & 2 / STORM FRONT / LIVE AT THE YANKEE STADIUM plus 50 minute interview)

Jun 92. (c/cd) *Tring; (MC+/JHD 004)* **FURTHER THAN HEAVEN** [ ] [–]

Sep 92. (d-cd) *Columbia;* **THE BRIDGE / GLASS HOUSES** [ ] [ ]

Mar 93. (d-cd) *(471604-2)* **AN INNOCENT MAN / THE STRANGER** [ ] [ ]
(re-iss. Feb95; 478478-2)

Oct 96. (3xcd-box) *(485320-2)* **AN INNOCENT MAN / STORM FRONT / THE STRANGER** [ ] [–]

Jun 98. (3xcd-box) *(491274-2)* **THE GREATEST HITS COLLECTION VOLUMES I, II & III** [33] [ ]

Mar 01. (d-cd/d-c) *Sony TV; (SONYTV 98 CD/MC)* **THE ULTIMATE COLLECTION** [4] [–]
– Just the way you are / My life / It's still rock & roll to me / An innocent man / Piano man / You're my home / Everybody loves you now / The entertainer / Streetlife serenader / New York state of mind / Say goodbye to Hollywood / She's got a way / Movin' out (Anthony's song) / She's always a woman / Honesty / You may be right / Don't ask me why / Miami 2017 / Uptown girl / Tell her about it / The river of dreams / The longest time / We didn't start the fire / Goodnight SAigon / Allentown / All for Leyna / This is the time / Leave a tender moment alone / A matter of trust / Modern woman / Baby grand / I go to extremes / Leningrad / The downeaster "Alexa" / You're only human (second wind) / All about soul (remix).

Oct 01. (4xcd-box) *(504502-2)* **THE COMPLETE HITS COLLECTION (BILLY JOEL'S GREATEST HITS 1973-1997)** [ ] [–]

Oct 01. (d-cd) *<86005>* **THE ESSENTIAL BILLY JOEL** [–] [29]

Elton JOHN

Born: REGINALD KENNETH DWIGHT, 25 Mar'47, Pinner, Middlesex, England. After learning piano at an early age, he attained a scholarship from Royal Academy Of Music. In the early 60's, he joined BLUESOLOGY, and by 1965 had written his first 45, 'COME BACK BABY' for 'Fontana', the band subsequently touring in the UK as back-up to American acts (i.e. MAJOR LANCE, The BLUE BELLES with PATTI LaBELLE, etc). Late in 1966, the group were joined by five others including singer LONG JOHN BALDRY, who virtually took over show, much to the dislike of the young REG DWIGHT. In 1967, he left BLUESOLOGY and auditioned for 'Liberty', but after failure found other writer BERNIE TAUPIN (b.22 May'50, Lincolnshire). They wrote LONG JOHN BALDRY's b-side, 'Lord You Made The Night Too Long', for his UK No.1 'Let The Heartaches Begin'. DWIGHT of course became ELTON JOHN, taking names from BLUESOLOGY members ELTON DEAN and LONG JOHN BALDRY. In 1968, ELTON and BERNIE joined the Dick James Music Publishing (later D.J.M.) stable, and earned around £10 a week each. With CALEB QUAYE (ex-BLUESOLOGY) on production, ELTON released debut solo single 'I'VE BEEN LOVING YOU TOO LONG' for 'Philips'. Early in '69, he gained needed airplay for 'LADY SAMANTHA', but when this failed, he tried to join KING CRIMSON, to no avail. The pair then wrote a number for the Eurovision Song Contest, 'I CAN'T GO ON LIVING WITHOUT YOU', which was heard but rejected by LULU for eventual winner, 'Boom Bang A Bang'. Early in 1969, ELTON signed to 'DJM', and flopped with both 45 'IT'S ME THAT YOU NEED' & lp 'EMPTY SKY'. To make ends meet, ELTON played on HOLLIES 'He Ain't Heavy . . . ' session, and worked for budget labels 'Pickwick' & 'MFP', on some pop covers. In 1970 after more HOLLIES sessions, he released 'BORDER SONG', which, when picked up by 'Uni', broke into US Top 100. The accompanying eponymous album (the first of many to be produced by Gus Dudgeon) made the American Top 5 and the UK Top 20, ELTON finally setting out on the road to superstardom that would see him become one of the most unlikely pop icons of the 70's. With the liltingly effective 'YOUR SONG', the JOHN/TAUPIN writing partnership also stepped up a gear, the chemistry obvious from the beginning despite TAUPIN's often impenetrable lyrics. Later that year, ELTON made his US stage debut (along with guitarist CALEB QUAYE – yes, part of the same clan as FINLAY – and the rhythm section of NIGEL OLSSON and DEE MURRAY) at the Troubadour in L.A., giving the Americans a taste of the flamboyant showmanship which would become ever more OTT as the decade wore on and which subsequently resulted in the LIBERACE comparisons. A relatively successful attempt at retro Americana, 'TUMBLEWEED CONNECTION' (1970) was another big seller and included the rustic beauty of 'COUNTRY COMFORT', later covered in memorable style by ROD STEWART, although 'MADMAN ACROSS THE WATER' (1971) saw Paul Buckmaster's overbearing string arrangements come in for some critical flak. With DAVY JOHNSTONE replacing QUAYE, 'HONKY CHATEAU' (1972) was the first album to be credited to the ELTON JOHN GROUP; a more robust affair and his first No.1 (US), it saw ELTON begin to adopt the musical maverick approach which would characterise most of his 70's albums, spawning a massive hit in the soaring 'ROCKET MAN'. 'DON'T SHOOT ME I'M ONLY THE PIANO PLAYER' (1973) consolidated his commercial appeal, a transatlantic No.1 which saw him flirting gamely with bubblegum pop on 'CROCODILE ROCK' (his first No.1 single) and adult balladry on 'DANIEL'. The pinnacle of JOHN's early career, however, came with 'GOODBYE YELLOW BRICK ROAD' (1973) a massive selling double set which saw ELTON's chameleon-like talent embrace a dazzling, occasionally over ambitious, array of styles, from the musclebound piano assault of 'SATURDAY'S ALRIGHT FOR FIGHTING' and the cloying bombast of 'BENNIE AND THE JETS' to his poignant Marilyn Monroe tribute, 'CANDLE IN THE WIND'. The same year, ELTON did the obligatory rock star thing and formed his own label, 'Rocket', KIKI DEE and NEIL SEDAKA being two of his more prominent signings, JOHN also working with JOHN LENNON the following year on his comeback single, 'Whatever Gets You Thru The Night'. 'CAPTAIN FANTASTIC AND THE BROWN DIRT COWBOY' (1975) was a concept affair documenting the development of the JOHN/TAUPIN partnership through the years, the soul baring 'SOMEONE SAVED MY LIFE TONIGHT' ranking among the pair's best. As well as making a cameo appearance in Ken Russell's screen version of The WHO's 'Tommy' (sporting one of the rather more erm, exotic models from his famed sunglasses collection), JOHN let go longstanding sidemen, MURRAY and OLSON, revamping his band prior to recording 'ROCK OF THE WESTIES' (1975), his last No.1 album for almost fifteen years. The latter half of the decade saw JOHN retire from performing, and, to a large extent, from recording; 1976's lengthy double-set, 'BLUE MOVES', marked the end of his partnership with TAUPIN, and JOHN subsequently busied himself with chairing his beloved Watford F.C. Though it spawned the Top 5 'SONG FOR GUY', 'A SINGLE MAN' (1978) was hardly a convincing return and the early 80's marked a creative nadir as ELTON fumbled his way through a series of confused albums and ill-advised musical experiments. Only a reunion with TAUPIN halted the slide on 1983's 'TOO LOW FOR ZERO' and its defiant hit single, 'I'M STILL STANDING'. 'BREAKING HEARTS' (1984) continued the renaissance with insidiously catchy 'PASSENGERS' and the cheesy but gorgeous 'SAD SONGS (SAY SO MUCH)', Top 10 hits both. Nevertheless, like many of his contemporaries, JOHN was now a card carrying member of the glossy, MOR brigade whose airbrushed, MTV sterility partly defined the 80's. But as his music became smoother, his personal life was in turmoil; an ill-fated marriage to Renate Blauer, well documented drug/alcohol problems and throat surgery all gave the gutter press hours of speculative fun. JOHN had the last laugh, however, when he successfully sued The Sun newspaper in October '88. Openly gay, JOHN increasingly devoted his time and money into AIDS care and research, founding the Elton John AIDS Foundation in 1992 and announcing that, from 'THE ONE' onwards, he'd donate all future royalties from singles sales. 1993 saw the release of the 'DUETS' album, featuring JOHN in tandem with everyone from TAMMY WYNETTE to LEONARD COHEN, while a suitably camp run through of 'DON'T GO BREAKING MY HEART' with RuPAUL hit the UK Top 10. The bland 'MADE IN ENGLAND' (1995) has been only the singer's second set of new material in the 90's, its embarrassingly awful title track incredibly/unsurprisingly hitting the UK Top 20. However, by far the most high profile of ELTON's more recent activities was his rendition of 'CANDLE IN THE WIND' at the funeral of Diana, Princess Of Wales, the single subsequently re-issued and a hysterical public pushing it to the top of the charts. Coincidentally, JOHN released his latest solo set, 'THE BIG PICTURE' (1997) the following month, a transatlantic Top 10 which spawned a couple of minor hits. More successful was another high profile duet (with LeANN RIMES), 'WRITTEN IN THE STARS', a prelude to a whole album's worth of coffee table bonhomie, 'ELTON JOHN AND TIME RICE'S AIDA' (1999). Credited to ELTON JOHN & FRIENDS, the record boasted a "galaxy" of stars in the mould of STING, SHANIA TWAIN, JANET JACKSON etzzzz . . . Come the new millennium, the ubiquitous star decided to resurrect a raft of his old classics for 'ONE NIGHT ONLY' (2000), treating paying guests in New York's Madison Square Garden to a final, definitive rendering of the hits that made ELTON the man he is today. All this nostalgia seemed to rub off on him, inspiring a belated return to the rollicking, expansive musical sweep of his best 70's era recordings with 'SONGS FROM THE WEST COAST' (2001). • **Covered:** GET BACK + LUCY IN THE SKY WITH DIAMONDS + I SAW HER STANDING THERE (Beatles; on which ELTON did duet with JOHN LENNON) / PINBALL WIZARD (Who; from the film 'Tommy', in which he featured) / JOHNNY B. GOODE (Chuck Berry) / WHERE HAVE ALL THE GOOD TIMES GONE (Kinks) / I HEARD IT THROUGH THE GRAPEVINE (hit; Marvin Gaye) / I'M YOUR MAN (Leonard Cohen) / etc.

Album rating: EMPTY SKY (*4) / ELTON JOHN (*7) / TUMBLEWEED CONNECTION (*8) / "FRIENDS" soundtrack (*3) / 11-17-70 (*4) / MADMAN ACROSS THE WATER (*7) / HONKY CHATEAU (*8) / DON'T SHOOT ME I'M ONLY THE PIANO PLAYER (*8) / GOODBYE YELLOW BRICK ROAD (*9) / CARIBOU (*4) / GREATEST HITS compilation (*9) / CAPTAIN FANTASTIC AND THE BROWN DIRT COWBOY (*7) / ROCK OF THE WESTIES (*5) / HERE AND THERE (*4) / BLUE MOVES (*6) / GREATEST HITS, VOL.II compilation (*8) / A SINGLE MAN (*6) / VICTIM OF LOVE (*3) / 21 AT 33 (*5) / THE FOX (*4) / JUMP UP! (*5) / TOO LOW FOR ZERO (*6) / BREAKING HEARTS (*5) / ICE ON FIRE (*5) / LEATHER JACKETS (*5) / LIVE IN AUSTRALIA (*4) / GREATEST HITS, VOL.III, 1979-1987 compilation (*6) / REG STRIKES BACK (*5) / SLEEPING WITH THE PAST (*5) / THE VERY BEST OF ELTON JOHN compilation (*8) / THE ONE (*5) / DUETS (*4) / MADE IN ENGLAND (*6) / LOVE SONGS compilation (*6) / BIG PICTURE (5) / ELTON JOHN AND TIM RICE'S AIDA (*3) / ONE NIGHT ONLY – THE GREATEST HITS compilation (*6) / SONGS FROM THE WEST COAST (*7) / GREATEST HITS 1970-2002 compilation (*9)

BLUESOLOGY

REG DWIGHT – vocals, piano / **STUART BROWN** – guitar, vocals / **REX BISHOP** – bass / **MICK INKPEN** – drums

		Fontana	not iss.
Jul 65.	(7") *(TF 594)* **COME BACK BABY. / TIME'S GETTING TOUGHER THAN TOUGH**	☐	–
Feb 66.	(7") *(TF 668)* **MISTER FRANTIC. / EVERYDAY (I HAVE THE BLUES)**	☐	–

— added **LONG JOHN BALDRY** – vocals / **CALEB QUAYE** – guitar / **ELTON DEAN** – sax / **PETE GAVIN, NEIL HUBBARD + MARK CHARIG** – wind

		Polydor	not iss.
Oct 67.	(7"; as STU BROWN & BLUESOLOGY) *(56195)* **SINCE I FOUND YOU BABY. / JUST A LITTLE BIT**	☐	–

ELTON JOHN

(solo) – vocals, piano with session people, incl.**NIGEL OLSSON** (note most of BLUESOLOGY later joined SOFT MACHINE)

Philips Congress

Mar 68. (7") *(BF 1643)* **I'VE BEEN LOVING YOU TOO LONG. / HERE'S TO THE NEXT TIME** [ ] [–]

Jan 69. (7") *(BF 1739)* **LADY SAMANTHA. / ALL ACROSS THE HEAVENS** [ ] [–]

1969. (7") *<6017>* **LADY SAMANTHA. / IT'S ME THAT YOU NEED** [–] [ ]

1969. (7") *<6022>* **BORDER SONG. / BAD SIDE OF THE MOON** [–] [ ]

—— In 1969, ELTON was part of BREAD & BEER BAND, who issued 1 'Decca' single 'THE DICK BARTON THEME. / BREAKDOWN BLUES. (re-iss. 1972)

D.J.M. Uni

May 69. (7") *(DJS 205)* **IT'S ME THAT YOU NEED. / JUST LIKE STRANGE RAIN** [ ] [–]

Jun 69. (lp; mono/stereo) *(DJMLP/DJLPS 403) <2130>* **EMPTY SKY** [ ] [ ]
– Empty sky / Valhalla / Western Ford gateway / Hymn 2000 / Lady what's tomorrow / Sails / The scaffold / Skyline pigeon / Gulliver – Hay chewed – Reprise. *<US re-iss. Jan75 on 'M.C.A.'; 2130>* – reached No.6 *(re-iss. May81 lp/c; DJM 2/-4 2086) (cd-iss. Oct86; DJMCD 13) (re-iss. May87 lp/c; PRICE/PRIMC 97) (cd re-iss. Jun87; 823017-2) <US cd-iss. Jun88; 31000> (cd re-iss. May95 on 'Rocket';)*

—— now with band **NIGEL OLSSON** (b.10 Feb'49, Merseyside) – drums / **DEE MURRAY** (b.DAVID MURRAY OATES, 3 Apr'46, Southgate, London) – bass / **CALEB QUAYE** – guitar (ex-BLUESOLOGY)

Mar 70. (7") *(DJS 217) <55246>* **BORDER SONG. / BAD SIDE OF THE MOON** [ ] Jul70 [92]

Apr 70. (lp/c) *(DJLPS 2/4 0406) <73090>* **ELTON JOHN** [11] Sep70 [4]
– Your song / I need you to turn to / Take me to the pilot / No shoestrings on Louise / First episode at Heinton / Sixty years on / Border song / Greatest discovery / The cage / The king must die. *(re-iss. May81 lp/c; DJM 2/4 2087) (re-iss. Apr87 lp/c; PRICE/PRIMC 98) (cd-iss. Jun87; 827689-2) (cd re-iss. May95 on 'Rocket';)*

Jun 70. (7") *(DJS 222)* **ROCK AND ROLL MADONNA. / GREY SEAL** [ ] [–]

Oct 70. (lp/c) *(DJLPS 2/4 0410) <73096>* **TUMBLEWEED CONNECTION** [6] Jan71 [5]
– Ballad of well-known gun / Come down in time / Country comfort / Son of your father / My father's gun / Where to now St. Peter / Love song / Amoreena / Talking old soldiers / Burn down the mission. *(re-iss. May81 lp/c; DJM 2/4 2088) (re-iss. Apr87 lp/c; PRICE/PRIMC 99) (cd-iss. Jun87; 829248-2) (cd re-iss. May95 on 'Rocket')*

Nov 70. (7") *<55265>* **YOUR SONG. / TAKE ME TO THE PILOT** [–] [8]

Jan 71. (7") *(DJS 233)* **YOUR SONG. / INTO THE OLD MAN'S SHOES** [7] [–]

Apr 71. (7") *(DJS 244) <55277>* **FRIENDS. / HONEY ROLL** [ ] Mar 71 [34]

Apr 71. (lp/c) *(DJLPS 2/4 0414) <93105>* **17.11.70 (live)** [20] May71 [11]
– Take me to the pilot / Honky tonk women / Sixty years on / Can I put you on / Bad side of the Moon / Burn down the mission: My baby left me – Get back. *(re-iss. Mar78 on 'Hallmark' lp/c; SHM 942/HSC 314) (cd-iss. Sep95 on 'Rocket')*

Nov 71. (lp/c) *(DJH 2/4 0420) <93120>* **MADMAN ACROSS THE WATER** [41] [8]
– Tiny dancer / Levon / Razor face / Madman across the water / Indian sunset / Holiday inn / Rotten Peaches / All the nasties / Goodbye. *(re-iss. May81 lp/c; DJM 2/4 2089) (re-iss. Apr87 lp/c; PRICE/PRIMC 100) (cd-iss. Jun87; 825487-2) (cd re-iss. Aug95 on 'Rocket')*

Dec 71. (7") *<55314>* **LEVON. / GOODBYE** [–] [24]

Feb 72. (7") *<55318>* **TINY DANCER. / RAZOR FACE** [–] [41]

—— **DAVEY JOHNSTONE** (b. 6 May'51, Edinburgh, Scotland) – guitar (ex-MAGNA CARTA) repl. QUAYE. Added **RAY COOPER** – percussion

Apr 72. (7"m) *(DJX 501)* **ROCKET MAN. / HOLIDAY INN / GOODBYE** [2] [–]

May 72. (7") *<55328>* **ROCKET MAN. / SUZIE (DREAMS)** [–] [6]

May 72. (lp/c) *(DJLPH 2/4 0423) <93135>* **HONKY CHATEAU** [2] Jun72 [1]
– Honky cat / Mellow / I think I'm going to kill myself / Susie (dramas) / Rocket man / Salvation / Slave / Amy / Mona Lisas and mad hatters / Hercules. *(re-iss. May81 lp/c; DJM 2/4 2090) (re-iss. Apr87 lp/c; PRICE/PRIMC 101) (cd-iss. Jun87; 829249-2) (cd re-iss. Aug95 on 'Rocket')*

Aug 72. (7"m) *(DJS 269)* **HONKY CAT. / LADY SAMANTHA / IT'S ME THAT YOU NEED** [31] [–]

Aug 72. (7") *<55343>* **HONKY CAT. / SLAVE** [–] [8]

D.J.M. M.C.A.

Oct 72. (7") *(DJS 271) <40000>* **CROCODILE ROCK. / ELDERBERRY WINE** [5] Dec72 [1]

Jan 73. (7") *(DJS 275) <40046>* **DANIEL. / SKYLINE PIGEON** [4] Apr73 [2]

Feb 73. (lp/c) *(DJLPH 2/4 0427) <2100>* **DON'T SHOOT ME I'M ONLY THE PIANO PLAYER** [1] [1]
– Daniel / Teacher I need you / Elderberry wine / Blues for my baby and me / Midnight creeper / Have mercy on the criminal / I'm going to be a teenage idol / Texan love song / Crocodile rock / High flying bird. *(re-iss. May81 lp/c; DJM 2/4 2091) (re-iss. Apr87 lp/c; PRICE/PRIMC 105) (cd-iss. Jun87; 827690-2) (cd re-iss. May95 on 'Rocket')*

Jun 73. (7"m) *(DJX 502) <40105>* **SATURDAY NIGHT'S ALRIGHT FOR FIGHTING. / JACK RABBIT / WHEN YOU'RE READY (WE'LL GO STEADY AGAIN)** [7] Jul73 [12]

Sep 73. (7") *(DJS 285) <40148>* **GOODBYE YELLOW BRICK ROAD. / SCREW YOU** [6] [–]

Oct 73. (7") *<40148>* **GOODBYE YELLOW BRICK ROAD. / YOUNG MAN'S BLUES** [–] [2]

Oct 73. (d-lp/d-c) *(DJE 2/4 9001) <10003>* **GOODBYE YELLOW BRICK ROAD** [1] [1]
– Funeral for a friend / Love lies bleeding / Bennie and the jets / Candle in the wind / Goodbye yellow brick road / This song has no title / Grey seal / Jamaica jerk off / I've seen that movie too / Sweet painted lady / The ballad of Danny Bailey (1909-34) / Dirty little girl / All the girls love Alice / Your sister can't twist (but she can rock'n'roll) / Saturday night's alright for fighting / Roy Rogers / Social disease / Harmony. *(re-iss. Nov87 lp/c; PRICE/PRIMC 13) (cd-iss. Nov87; DJMCD 2) (cd re-iss. May95 on 'Rocket')*

Nov 73. (7") *(DJS 290) <65018>* **STEP INTO CHRISTMAS. / HO! HO! HO! WHO'D BE A TURKEY AT CHRISTMAS** [24] [ ]

Feb 74. (7") *<40198>* **BENNY AND THE JETS. / HARMONY** [–] [1]

Feb 74. (7") *(DJS 297)* **CANDLE IN THE WIND. / BENNIE AND THE JETS** [11] [–]

May 74. (7") *(DJS 302) <40259>* **DON'T LET THE SUN GO DOWN ON ME. / SICK CITY** [16] Jun74 [2]

Jun 74. (lp/c) *(DJLH 2/4 0439) <2116>* **CARIBOU** [1] [1]
– The bitch is back / Pinky / Grimsby / Dixie Lily / Solar prestige a gammon / You're so static / I've seen the saucers / Stinker / Don't let the sun go down on me / Ticking. *(re-iss. May81 lp/c; DJM 2/4 2092) (re-iss. Nov87 lp/c; PRICE/PRIMC 106) (cd-iss. Nov87; DJMCD 6) (cd re-iss. May95 on 'Rocket')*

Sep 74. (7") *(DJS 322) <40297>* **THE BITCH IS BACK. / COLD HIGHWAY** [15] [4]

Nov 74. (7") *(DJS 340) <40344>* **LUCY IN THE SKY WITH DIAMONDS. / ONE DAY AT A TIME** [10] [1]

Feb 75. (7"; ELTON JOHN BAND) *(DJS 354) <40364>* **PHILADELPHIA FREEDOM. / I SAW HER STANDING THERE (with JOHN LENNON)** [12] [1]

May 75. (lp/c) *(DJX 1) <2142>* **CAPTAIN FANTASTIC AND THE BROWN DIRT COWBOY** [2] [1]
– Captain Fantastic and the brown dirt cowboy / Tower of Babel / Bitter fingers / Tell me when the whistle blows / Someone saved my life tonight / (Gotta get a) Meal ticket / Better off dead / Writing / We fall in love sometimes / Curtains. *(re-iss. pic-disc '78; DJLPX 1) (re-iss. May81 lp/c; DJM 2/4 2094) (re-iss. Nov87 lp/c; PRICE/PRIMC 108) (cd-iss. Nov87; 821746-2) (cd re-iss. Aug95 on 'Rocket')*

Jun 75. (7") *(DJS 385) <40421>* **SOMEONE SAVED MY LIFE TONIGHT. / HOUSE OF CARDS** [22] [4]

—— ELTON now w/ others, after firing MURRAY and OLSSON (to BILLY JOEL)

Sep 75. (7") *(DJS 610) <40461>* **ISLAND GIRL. / SUGAR ON THE FLOOR** [14] [1]

Nov 75. (lp/c) *(DJH 2/4 0464) <2163>* **ROCK OF THE WESTIES** [5] [1]
– Medley: Yell help – Wednesday night – Ugly / Dan Dare (pilot of the future) / Island girl / Grow some funk of your own / I feel like a bullet (in the gun of Robert Ford) / Street kids / Hard luck story / Billy Bones and the white bird. *(re-iss. May81 lp/c; DJM 2/4 2093) (re-iss. Nov87 lp/c; PRICE/PRIMC 107) (cd-iss. Nov87; DJMCD 9) (cd re-iss. Aug95 on 'Rocket')*

Jan 76. (7") *(DJS 629) <40505>* **GROW SOME FUNK OF YOUR OWN. / I FEEL LIKE A BULLET (IN THE GUN OF ROBERT FORD)** [ ] [14]

Mar 76. (7") *(DJS 652)* **PINBALL WIZARD. / HARMONY** [7] [–]

May 76. (lp/c) *(DJH 2/4 0473) <2197>* **HERE AND THERE (live)** [6] [4]
– Skyline pigeon / Border song / Honky cat / Love song / Crocodile rock /

Funeral for a friend / Love lies bleeding / Rocket man / Bennie and the jets / Take me to the pilot. *(re-iss. Sep78 as 'LONDON AND NEW YORK' on 'Hallmark' lp/c; SHM 942/HSC 333) (cd-iss. Sep95 on 'Rocket')*

Rocket | M.C.A.

Jun 76. (7"; ELTON JOHN & KIKI DEE) *(ROKN 512)* <40585> **DON'T GO BREAKING MY HEART. / SNOW QUEEN** | 1 | 1

Oct 76. (d-lp/d-c) *(ROLL/TC2ROLL 12)* <11004> **BLUE MOVES** | 3 | 3
– Your starter for . . . / Tonight / One horse town / Chameleon / Boogie pilgrim / Cage the songbird / Crazy water / Shoulder holster / Sorry seems to be the hardest word / Out of the blue / Between seventeen and twenty / The wide-eyed and laughing / Someone's final song / Where's the shoorah / If there's a God in Heaven (what's he waiting for) / Idol / Theme from a non-existant TV series / Bite your lip (get up and dance!). *(re-iss. Sep84 d-lp/d-c; PRID/+C 2) (cd-iss. Jun89; 822818-2)*

Oct 76. (7") *(ROKN 517)* <40645> **SORRY SEEMS TO BE THE HARDEST WORD. / SHOULDER HOLSTER** | 11 | 6

Feb 77. (7") <40677> **BITE YOUR LIP (GET UP AND DANCE!). / CHAMELEON** | – | 28

Feb 77. (7") *(ROKN 521)* **CRAZY WATER. / CHAMELEON** | 27 | –

May 77. (7")(12") *(RU 1)* **BITE YOUR LIP (GET UP AND DANCE!). / CHICAGO** | 28 | –

Apr 78. (7") *(ROKN 538)* <40892> **EGO. / FLINTSTONE BOY** | 34 | 34

Oct 78. (7") *(XPRES 1)* <40973> **PART-TIME LOVE. / I CRY AT NIGHT** | 15 | 22

Oct 78. (lp/c) *(TRAIN/SHUNT 1)* <3027> **A SINGLE MAN** | 8 | 15
– Shine on through / Return to Paradise / I don't care / Big dipper / Georgia / It ain't gonna be easy / Part-time love / Georgia / Shooting star / Madness / Reverie / Song for Guy. *(re-iss. Jun83 lp/c; PRICE/PRIMC 24) (cd-iss. Jun83; 826805-2)*

Dec 78. (7") *(XPRES 5)* <40993> **SONG FOR GUY. / LOVESICK** | 4 |

May 79. (7") *(XPRES 13)* **ARE YOU READY FOR LOVE (part 1). / (part 2)** | 42 | –
(12"+=) *(XPRES 13-12)* – Three way love affair / Mama can't buy you love.

Jun 79. (12"m) <13921> **THE THOM BELL SESSIONS** (recorded 1977) | – | 51
– Are you ready for love / Three way love affair / Mama can't buy you love.

Jun 79. (7") <41042> **MAMA CAN'T BUY YOU LOVE. / THREE WAY LOVE AFFAIR** | – | 9

Sep 79. (7") *(XPRES 21)* <41126> **VICTIM OF LOVE. / STRANGERS** | | 31

Oct 79. (lp/c) *(HISPD/REWND 125)* M5104> **VICTIM OF LOVE** | 41 | 35
– Johnny B. Goode / Warm love in a cold climate / Born bad / Thunder in the night / Spotlight / Street boogie / Born Bad / Victim of love. *(re-iss. Jul84 lp/c; PRICE/PRIMC 70)*

Dec 79. (7") <41159> **JOHNNY B. GOODE. / GEORGIA** | – |

Dec 79. (7"/12") *(XPRES 24/+12)* **JOHNNY B. GOODE. / THUNDER IN THE NIGHT** | | –

May 80. (7") *(XPRES 32)* <41236> **LITTLE JEANNIE. / CONQUER THE SUN** | 33 | 3

May 80. (lp/c) *(HISPD/REWND 126)* <5121> **21 AT 33** | 12 | 13
– Chasing the crown / Little Jeannie / Sartorial eloquence / Two rooms at the end of the world / White lady, white powder / Dear God / Never gonna fall in love again / Take me back / Give me the love. *(re-iss. Jul84 lp/c; PRICE/PRIMC 71) (cd-iss. Jun89; 800055-2)*

Aug 80. (7") *(XPRES 41)* <41293> **SARTORIAL ELOQUENCE. / WHITE MAN DANCER; CARTIER** | 44 | 39

Nov 80. (7") *(XPRESS 45)* **DEAR GOD. / TACTICS** | | –
(d7") *(XPRESS 45 – ELTON 1)* – Steal away child / Love so cold.

Rocket | Geffen

May 81. (7") *(XPRES 54)* <49722> **NOBODY WINS. / FOOLS IN FASHION** | 42 | 21

May 81. (lp/c) *(TRAIN/SHUNT 016)* <2002> **THE FOX** | 12 | 21
– Breaking down barriers / Heart in the right place / Just like Belgium / Nobody wins / Fascist faces / Carla etude / Fanfare / Chloe / Heels of the wind / Elton's song / The fox. *(re-iss. Jul84 lp/c; PRICE/PRIMC 72) (cd-iss. Jun89; 800063-2)*

Jul 81. (7") *(XPRESS 59)* **JUST LIKE BELGIUM. / CAN'T GET OVER LOSING YOU** | | –

Jul 81. (7") <49788> **CHLOE. / TORTURED** | – | 34

Mar 82. (7") *(XPRES 71)* <29954> **BLUE EYES. / HEY PAPA LEGBA** | 8 | Jul82 12

Apr 82. (lp/c) *(HISPD/REWND 127)* <2013> **JUMP UP!** | 13 | 17
– Dear John / Spiteful child / Ball and chain / Legal boys / I am your robot / Blue eyes / Empty garden /Princess / Where have all the good times gone? / All quiet on the western front. *(cd-iss. 1983; 800037-2)*

May 82. (7"/7"pic-d) *(XPRES/XPPIC 77)* <50049> **EMPTY GARDEN. / TAKE ME DOWN TO THE OCEAN** | 51 | Mar82 13

Sep 82. (7") *(XPRES 85)* **PRINCESS. / THE RETREAT** | | –

Nov 82. (7") *(XPRES 88)* **ALL QUIET ON THE WESTERN FRONT. / WHERE HAVE ALL THE GOOD TIMES GONE?** | | –

Nov 82. (7") <29846> **BALL AND CHAIN. / WHERE HAVE ALL THE GOOD TIMES GONE?** | – |

Apr 83. (7") *(XPRES 91)* **I GUESS THAT'S WHY THEY CALL IT THE BLUES. / LORD CHOC ICE GOES MENTAL** | 5 | –

May 83. (7") <29639> **I'M STILL STANDING. / LOVE SO COLD** | – | 12

Jun 83. (lp/c)(cd) *(HISPD/REWND 24)(811052-2)* <4006> **TOO LOW FOR ZERO** | 7 | 25
– Cold at Christmas / I'm still standing / Too low for zero / Religion / I guess that's why they call it the blues / Crystal / Kiss the bride / Whipping boy / Saint / One more arrow. *(cd re-mast.Jun98; 558475-2)*

Jul 83. (7"/7"sha-pic-d)(12") *(EJ S/PIC 1)(EJS 1-12)* **I'M STILL STANDING. / EARN WHILE YOU LEARN** | 4 | –

Aug 83. (7") <29568> **KISS THE BRIDE. / LORD CHOC ICE GOES MENTAL** | – | 25

Oct 83. (7"/12") *(EJS 2/+12)* **KISS THE BRIDE. / DREAMBOAT** | 20 | –
(d7"+=) *(EJS 2 – FREEJ 2)* – Ego / Song for Guy.

Oct 83. (7") <29460> **I GUESS THAT'S WHY THEY CALL IT HTE BLUES. / THE RETREAT** | – | 4

Dec 83. (7") *(EJS 3)* **COLD AT CHRISTMAS. / CRYSTAL** | 33 | –
(12"+=) *(EJS 3-12)* – J'veux de la tendresse.
(d7"+=) *(EJS 3-2)* – Don't go breaking my heart / Snow queen.

May 84. (7"/7"sha-pic-d)(12") *(PH/+PIC 7)(PH 7-12)* <29292> **SAD SONGS (SAY SO MUCH). / SIMPLE MAN** | 7 | 5

Jun 84. (lp/c)(cd) *(HISPD/REWND 25)(882088-2)* <24031> **BREAKING HEARTS** | 2 | 20
– Restless / Slow down Georgie (she's poison) / Who wears these shoes? / Breaking hearts (ain't what it used to be) / Li'l fridgerator / Passengers / In neon / Burning bridges / Did he shoot her? / Sad songs (say so much).

Aug 84. (7"/12") *(EJS 5/+12)* **PASSENGERS (remix). / LONELY BOY** | 5 | –

Sep 84. (7") <29189> **WHO WEARS THESE SHOES? / LONELY EYES** | – | 16

Oct 84. (7") *(EJS 6)* **WHO WEARS THESE SHOES? / TORTURED** | 50 | –
(12"+=) *(EJS 6-12)* – I heard it through the grapevine.

Nov 84. (7") <29111> **IN NEON. / TACTICS** | – | 38

Feb 85. (7") *(EJS 7)* **BREAKING HEARTS (AIN'T WHAT IT USED TO BE). / IN NEON** | 59 | –

Jun 85. (7"; ELTON JOHN & MILLIE JACKSON) *(EJS 8)* <28956> **ACT OF WAR (part 1). / (part 2)** | 32 |
(12"+=) *(EJS 8-12)* – (part 3) / (part 4).

Sep 85. (7") *(EJS 9)* **NIKITA. / THE MAN WHO NEVER DIED** | 3 | –
(12"+=)(d7"+=) *(EJS 9-12)(EJSD 9)* – Sorry seems to be the hardest word (live) / I'm still standing (live).

Oct 85. (7") <28873> **WRAP HER UP. / THE MAN WHO NEVER DIED** | – |

Nov 85. (lp/c)(cd) *(HISPD/REWND 26)(826213-2)* <24077> **ICE ON FIRE** | 3 | 48
– Wrap her up / Satellite / Tell me what the papers say / Candy by the pound / Shoot down the Moon / This town / Cry to heaven / Soul glove / Nikita / Too young. *(c+=/cd+=)* – Act of war (with MILLIE JACKSON). *(cd re-mast.Jun98; 558476-2)*

Nov 85. (7"/7"sha-pic-d) *(EJ SC/PIC 10)* **WRAP HER UP. / RESTLESS (live with GEORGE MICHAEL)** | 12 | –
(ext.d12"+=) *(EJS 10-12 – EJS 9-12)* – Nikita / The man who never died / Sorry seems to be the hardest word (live) / I'm still standing (live).

Jan 86. (7") <28800> **NIKITA. / RESTLESS** | – | 7

Feb 86. (7") *(EJS 11)* **CRY TO HEAVEN. / CANDY BY THE POUND** | 47 | –
(12"+=) *(EJS 11-12)* – Rock'n'roll medley.
(d7"++=) *(EJSD 11)* – Your song.

Sep 86. (7") *(EJS 12)* <28578> **HEARTACHES ALL OVER THE WORLD. / HIGHLANDER** | 45 | 55
(12"+=) *(EJS 12-12)* – ('A'version).
(d7"+=) *(EJSD 12)* – Passengers / I'm still standing.

Nov 86. (lp/c)(cd) *(EJLP/EJMC 1)(830487-2) <24114>* **LEATHER JACKETS** 24 91
– Leather jackets / Hoop of fire / Go it alone / Don't trust that woman / Gypsy heart / Slow rivers / Heartache all over the world / Angeline / Memory of love / Paris / I fall apart.

Nov 86. (7"pic-d/c-s; ELTON JOHN & CLIFF RICHARD) *(EJS P/C 13)* **SLOW RIVERS. / BILLY AND THE KIDS** 44 –
(12"+=) *(EJS 13-12)* – Lord of the flies.

Rocket M.C.A.

Jun 87. (7") *(EJS 14)* **YOUR SONG (live). / DON'T LET THE SUN GO DOWN ON ME (live)** [ ] –
(12"+=) *(EJS 14-12)* – I need you to turn to / The greatest discovery.

Sep 87. (d-lp/d-c/cd) *(EJBX L/C/D 1) <8022>* **LIVE IN AUSTRALIA (live)** 43 Jul87 24
– Sixty years on / I need you to turn to / The greatest discovery / Tonight / Sorry seems to be the hardest word / The king must die / Take me to the pilot / Tiny dancer / Have mercy on the criminal / Madman across the water / Candle in the wind / Burn down the mission / Your song / Don't let the Sun go down on me. *(cd re-mast.Jun98; 558477-2)*

Dec 87. (7"/7"pic-d) *(EJS/+P 15) <53196>* **CANDLE IN THE WIND (live). / SORRY SEEMS TO BE THE HARDEST WORD (live)** 5 Nov87 6
(12"+=)(cd-s+=) *(EJS 15-12)(EJSCD 15)* – Your song (live) / Don't let the sun go down on me (live).

Mar 88. (7") **TONIGHT. / TAKE ME TO THE PILOT** – [ ]

May 88. (7"/7"pic-d) *(EJS/+IP 16) <53345>* **I DON'T WANT TO GO ON WITH YOU LIKE THAT. / ROPE AROUND A FOOL / (interview)** 30 Jun88 2
(12"+=)(cd-s+=) *(EJS 16-12)(EJSCD 16)* – ('A'-Shep Pettibone mix).

Jun 88. (lp/c)(cd) *(EJLP/EJMC 3)(834701-2) <6240>* **REG STRIKES BACK** 18 16
– Town of plenty / A word in Spanish / Mona Lisas and mad hatters (part 2) / I don't want to go on with you like that / Japanese hands / Goodbye Marlon Brando / The camera never lies / Heavy traffic / Poor cow / Since God invented girls. *(cd re-mast.Jun98; 558478-2)*

Sep 88. (7") *(EJSLB 17)* **TOWN OF PLENTY. / WHIPPING BOY** 74 –
(12"+=) *(EJS 17-12)* – My baby's a saint.
(cd-s++=) *(EJSCD 17)* – I guess that's why they call it the blues.

Nov 88. (7") *(EJS 18) <53408>* **A WORD IN SPANISH. / HEAVY TRAFFIC** [ ] Sep88 19
(12"+=) *(EJS 18-12)* – Live in Australia medley: Song for Guy – I guess that's why they call it the blues – Blue eyes.
(cd-s++=) *(EJSCD 18)* – Daniel.

— In Apr'89, he was credited on 'THROUGH THE STORM' UK No.41 / No.16 single with ARETHA FRANKLIN.

Aug 89. (7"/c-s) *(EJS/+MC 19) <53692>* **HEALING HANDS. / DANCING IN THE END ZONE** 45 13
(12"+=)(cd-s+=) *(EJS 19-12)(EJCD 19)* – ('A'version).

Sep 89. (lp/c/cd) *(838839-1/-4/-2) <6321>* **SLEEPING WITH THE PAST** 1 23
– Durban deep / Healing hands / Whispers / Club at the end of the street / Sleeping with the past / Stone's throw from hurtin' / Sacrifice / I never knew her name / Amazes me / Blue avenue. *(cd re-mast.Jun98; 558479-2)*

Oct 89. (7"/c-s) *(EJS/+MC 20) <53750>* **SACRIFICE. / LOVE IS A CANNIBAL** 55 Jan90 18
(12"+=)(cd-s+=) *(EJS 20-12)(EJSCD 20)* – Durban deep.

Apr 90. (7") *<53818>* **CLUB AT THEN END OF THE STREET. / SACRIFICE** – 28

Jun 90. (7"/c-s) *(EJS/+MC 22)* **SACRIFICE. / HEALING HANDS** 1 –
(12"+=)(cd-s+=) *(EJS 22-12)(EJSCD 22)* – Durban deep.

Aug 90. (7"/c-s) *(EJS/+MC 23)* **CLUB AT THE END OF THE STREET. / WHISPERS** 47 –
(12"+=) *(EJS 23012)* – I don't wanna go on with you like that.
(cd-s+=) *(EJSCD 23)* – Give peace a chance.

Oct 90. (7"/c-s) *(EJS/+MC 24) <53953>* **YOU GOTTA LOVE SOMEONE. / MEDICINE MAN** [UK-only] 33 Nov90 43
(12"+=)(cd-s+=) *(EJS 24-12)(EJSCD 24)* – ('B'-Adamski version).

Nov 90. (7"/c-s) *(EJS/+MC 25)* **EASIER TO WALK AWAY. / SWEAR I HEARD THE NIGHT TALKING** 63 –
(12"+=)(cd-s+=) *(EJS 25-12)(EJSCD 25)* – Made for me.

— DEE MURRAY died of a heart attack, after suffering from cancer

May 92. (7"/c-s) *(EJS/+MC 28) <54423>* **THE ONE. / SUIT OF WOLVES** 10 Jun92 9
(cd-s+=) *(EJSCD 28)* – Fat boys and ugly girls.

Jun 92. (cd/c/lp) *(512360-2/-4/-1) <10614>* **THE ONE** 2 8
– Simple life / The one / Sweat it out / Runaway train / Whitewash county / The North / When a woman doesn't want you / Emily / On dark street / Understanding women / The last song. *(cd re-mast.Jun98; 558477-2)*

Jul 92. (7"/c-s; ELTON JOHN & ERIC CLAPTON) *(EJS/+MC 29)* **RUNAWAY TRAIN. / UNDERSTANDING WOMEN** 31 –
(cd-s+=) *(EJSCD 29)* – Made for me.
(cd-s) *(EJSCDX 29)* – ('A'side) / Through the storm (with ARETHA FRANKLIN) / Don't let the sun go down on me (with GEORGE MICHAEL) / Slow rivers (with CLIFF).

Oct 92. (7"/c-s) *(EJS/+MC 30) <54510>* **THE LAST SONG. / THE MAN WHO NEVER DIED / SONG FOR GUY** 21 23
(cd-s) *(EJSCD 30)* – ('A'side) / Are you ready / Three way love affair / Mama can't buy you love.

Feb 93. (c-s) *<54581>* **SIMPLE LIFE / THE NORTH** – 30

May 93. (7"/c-s) *(EJS/+MC 31)* **SIMPLE LIFE. / THE LAST SONG** 44 –
(cd-s+=) *(EJSCD 31)* – The north.

Nov 93. (7"/c-s; ELTON JOHN & KIKI DEE) *(EJS/+MC 32)* **TRUE LOVE. / THE SHOW MUST GO ON** 2 –
(cd-s+=) *(EJSCD 32)* – Runaway train.
(cd-s) *(EJSCDX 32)* – ('A'side) / Wrap her up / That's what friends are for / Act of war.

Nov 93. (c-s; ELTON JOHN & KIKI DEE) *<54762>* **TRUE LOVE / RUNAWAY TRAIN (with ERIC CLAPTON)** – 56

Nov 93. (cd/c/d-lp) *(516478-2/-4/-1) <10926>* **DUETS** (with other artists) 5 25
– Teardrops (k.d.LANG) / When I think about love (I think about you) (P.M.DAWN) / The power (LITTLE RICHARD) / Shakey ground (DON HENLEY) / True love (KIKI DEE) / If you were me (CHRIS REA) / A woman's needs (TAMMY WYNETTE) / Don't let the Sun go down on me (GEORGE MICHAEL) / Old friend (NIK KERSHAW) / Go on and on (GLADYS KNIGHT) / Don't go breaking my heart (RuPAUL) / Ain't nothing like the real thing (MARCELLA DETROIT) / I'm your puppet (PAUL YOUNG) / Love letters (BONNIE RAITT) / Born to lose (LEONARD COHEN) / Duets for one (ELTON JOHN solo).

Feb 94. (7"/c-s; ELTON JOHN & RuPAUL) *(EJS/+MC 33) <54813>* **DON'T GO BREAKING MY HEART. / DONNER POUR DONNER** 7 92
(cd-s+=) *(EJCD 33)* – A woman's needs.
(cd-s) *(ERJMX 33)* – ('A'side) / (5-'A'mixes).

— In May 94, he & MARCELLA DETROIT (ex-SHAKESPEAR'S SISTER) hit UK No.24 with 'AIN'T NOTHIN' LIKE THE REAL THING'.

Jun 94. (7"/c-s) *(EJS/+MC 34) <64543>* **CAN YOU FEEL THE LOVE TONIGHT? / ('A'mix)** 14 May94 4
(cd-s+=) *(EJCD 34)* – (other artists).
(above & below from the animated 'Hollywood' movie 'The Lion King')

Sep 94. (c-s) *(EJSMC 35) <64516>* **THE CIRCLE OF LIFE / ('A'-other artist)** 11 Aug94 18
(cd-s+=/pic-cd-s+=) *(EJS CD/CX 35)* – I just can't wait to be king / (other artist).

— with **GUY BABYLON** – keyboards/ **BOB BIRCH** – bass/ **DAVEY JOHNSTONE** – guitar, mandolin, banjo/ **CHARLIE MORGAN** – drums/ **RAY COOPER** – percusion

Feb 95. (c-s) *(EJSMC 36)* **BELIEVE / SORRY SEEMS TO BE THE HARDEST WORD (live)** 15 –
(cd-s+=) *(EJCD 36)* – Believe (live).
(cd-s) *(EJCDX 36)* – ('A'side) / The one / The last song.

Rocket Rocket

Mar 95. (c-s) *<856014>* **BELIEVE / THE ONE (live)** – [ ]

Mar 95. (cd/c/lp) *(<526185-2/-4/-1>)* **MADE IN ENGLAND** 3 13
– Believe / Made in England / House / Cold / Pain / Belfast / Latitude / Please / Man / Lies / Blessed.

May 95. (c-s) *(EJSMC 37) <852092>* **MADE IN ENGLAND / DANIEL (live) / CAN YOU FEEL THE LOVE TONIGHT** 18 52
(cd-s+=) *(EJSCD 37)* – Your song / Don't let the sun go down on me.
(cd-s) *(EJCDX 37)* – ('A'side) / Whatever gets you thru the night / Lucy in the sky with diamonds / I saw her standing there.

Oct 95. (c-s) *(EJSMC 38) <852394>* **BLESSED / LATITUDE** [ ] 34
(cd-s) *(EJSCD 38)* – ('A'side) / Made in England (mixes).
(cd-s) *(EJSDD 38)* – ('A'side) / Honky cat (live) / Take me to the pilot (live) / The bitch is back (live).

Nov 95. (cd/c) *(528788-2/-4) <11481>* **LOVE SONGS** (compilation) 7 Sep96 24
– Sacrifice / Candle in the wind / I guess that's why they call it the blues / Don't let the sun go down on me (with GEORGE MICHAEL) / Sorry

seems to be the hardest word / Blue eyes / Daniel / Nikita / Your song / The one / Someone saved my life tonight / True love (with KIKI DEE) / Can you feel the love tonight / Circle of life / Blessed / Please / Song for Guy.

Jan 96. (c-s) *(EJSMC 40)* **PLEASE / LATITUDE** [33] [–]
(cd-s+=) *(EJSCD 40)* – Made in England (mixes).
(cd-s) *(EJSCDX 40)* – ('A'side) / Honky cat (live) / Take me to the pilot (live) / The bitch is back (live).

Oct 96. (c-s) *<55222>* **YOU CAN MAKE HISTORY (YOUNG AGAIN) / SONG FOR GUY** [–] [70]

Rocket Mercury

Dec 96. (c-s; by ELTON JOHN & LUCIANO PAVAROTTI) *(LLHMC 1)* **LIVE LIKE HORSES / ('A'live finale)** [9] [ ]
(cd-s+=) *(LLHCD 1)* – ('A'solo studio) / I guess that's why they call it the blues.
(cd-s) *(LLHDD 1)* – ('A'side) / Step into Christmas / Blessed.

Sep 97. (c-s) *(EJSMC 41)* **SOMETHING ABOUT THE WAY YOU LOOK TONIGHT / I KNOW I'M IN LOVE** [ ] [ ]
(cd-s+=) *(EJSCD 41)* – No valentines ('A'extended).
(cd-s+=) *(EJSCX 41)* – You can make history (young again) / ('A'extended).
(above was withdrawn after the events below)

Sep 97. (c-s/cd-s) *(PT MC/CD 1)* **CANDLE IN THE WIND 1997 / SOMETHING ABOUT THE WAY YOU LOOK TONIGHT** [1] [1]
(cd-s+=) *(568108-2)* – You can make history (young again).
(above double 'A'side was a tribute to Princess Diana who recently died in a car crash)

Oct 97. (cd/c) *<(536266-2/-4>)* **THE BIG PICTURE** [3] [9]
– Long way from happiness / Live like horses / The end will come / I can bend / Love's got a lot to answer for / Something about the way you look tonight / If the river can bend / The big picture / Recover your soul / January / I can't steer my heart / Wicked dreams.

Feb 98. (c-s) *(EJSMC 42) <568762>* **RECOVER YOUR SOUL / I KNOW WHY I'M IN LOVE** [16] Apr98 [55]
(cd-s+=) *(EJSCD 42)* – Big man in a little suit / ('A'mix).
(cd-s+=) *(EJSCX 42)* – No valentines.

Jun 98. (c-s) *(EJSMC 43)* **IF THE RIVER CAN BEND / BENNIE AND THE JETS** [32] [ ]
(cd-s+=) *(EJSCD 43)* – Saturday night's alright for fighting / ('A'original).
(cd-s) *(EJSDD 43)* – ('A'side) / Don't let the sun go down on me (live) / I guess that's why they call it the blues (live) / Sorry seems to be the hardest word (live).

Feb 99. (c-s; ELTON JOHN & LeANN RIMES) *(EJSMC 45) <566918>* **WRITTEN IN THE STARS / (alternative version)** [10] [29]
(cd-s+=) *(EJSCD 45)* – Recover your soul.

—— next with "friends" **STING, LENNY KRAVITZ, TINA TURNER, SHANIA TWAIN, the SPICE GIRLS, JAMES TAYLOR, JANET JACKSON, LeANN RIMES + HEATHER HEADLEY**

Mar 99. (cd/c; ELTON JOHN & FRIENDS) *<(524628-2/-4)>* **ELTON JOHN AND TIM RICE'S AIDA** [29] [41]
– Another pyramid / Written in the stars / Easy as life / My strongest suit / I know the truth / Not me / Amneris' letter / A step too far / Like father like son / Elaborate lives / How I know you / The messenger / Gods love Nubia / Enchantment passing through / Orchestral finale.

Rocket DreamWorks

Apr 00. (cd-s) *<459039>* **SOMEDAY OUT OF THE BLUE / CHELDORADO** [–] [49]

Jun 00. (cd) *(<4 50219-2>)* **THE ROAD TO EL DORADO** (soundtrack) [ ] Mar00 [63]
– El Dorado / Someday out of the blue (theme) / Without question / Friends never say goodbye / The trail we blaze / 16th century man / Panic in me / It's tough to be a god / (with RANDY NEWMAN) / Trust me / My heart dances / Queen of cities / Cheldorado / The brig / Wonders of the new world.

Rocket Universal

Nov 00. (cd/c) *(548334-2/-4) <013050>* **ONE NIGHT ONLY – THE GREATEST HITS (live)** [7] [65]
– Goodbye yellow brick road / Philadelphia freedom / Don't go breaking my heart (with KIKI DEE) / Rocket man / Daniel / Crocodile rock / Sacrifice / Can you feel the love tonight / Bennie and the jets / Your song (with RONAN KEATING) / Sad songs (say so much) (with BRYAN ADAMS) / Candle in the wind / The bitch is back / Saturday night's alright for fighting (with ANASTACIA) / I'm still standing / Don't let the sun go down on me / I guess that's why they call it the blues (with MARY J. BLIGE).

Sep 01. (c-s) *(588706-4)* **I WANT LOVE / NORTH STAR** [9] [ ]
(cd-s+=) *(588706-2)* – Tiny dancer (live) / ('A'video).
(cd-s) *(588706-5)* – ('A'side) / God never came there / One (live).

Oct 01. (cd) *(<586330-2>)* **SONGS FROM THE WEST COAST** [2] [15]
– The emperor's new clothes / Dark diamond / Look ma, no hands / American triangle / Original sin / Birds / I want love / The wasteland / Ballad of the boy in the red shoes / Love her like me / Mansfield / This train don't stop there anymore. *(special cd+=; 063194-2)* – Your song (with ALESSANDRO SAFINA) / Teardrops (with LULU) / Northstar (with LULU) / Original sin (Junior Earth's mix) / I want love (video) / This train don't stop there anymore (video) / Your song (video with ALESSANDRO SAFINA).

—— in Dec'01, ELTON featured on BLUE's No.1 version of his 'Sorry Seems To Be The Hardest Word'

Jan 02. (c-s) *(588896-4)* **THIS TRAIN DON'T STOP THERE ANYMORE / DID ANYONE SLEEP WITH JOAN OF ARC** [24] [ ]
(cd-s+=) *(588896-2)* – I want love (live).
(cd-s) *(588897-2)* – ('A'side) / American triangle (live) / Philadelphia freedom (live).

Apr 02. (c-s) *(588999-4)* **ORIGINAL SIN / I'M STILL STANDING (live)** [39] [ ]
(cd-s+=) *(588999-2)* – This train don't stop there anymore (live) / This train don't stop there anymore (video).
(cd-s) *(582850-2)* – ('A'side) / ('A'live) / All the girls love Alice (live) / ('A'video).

Jul 02. (c-s; by ELTON JOHN & ALESSANDRO SAFINA) *(063997-4)* **YOUR SONG / (instrumental)** [4] [ ]
(cd-s+=) *(063997-2)* – ('A'video).

Nov 02. (d-cd/d-c) *(63499-2/-4) <865570>* **GREATEST HITS 1970-2002** (compilation) [3] [12]
– Your song / Tiny dancer / Honky cat / Rocket man (I think it's going to be a long long time) / Crocodile rock / Daniel / Saturday night's alright for fighting / Goodbye yellow brick road / Candle in the wind / Bennie and the jets / Don't let the sun go down on me / The bitch is back / Philadelphia freedom / Someone saved my life tonight / Island girl / Don't go breaking my heart (with KIKI DEE) / Sorry seems to be the hardest word / Blue eyes / I'm still standing / I guess that's why they call it the blues / Sad songs (say so much) / Nikita / Sacrifice / The one / Kiss the bride / Can you feel the love tonight? / Circle of life / Believe / Made in England / Something about the way you look tonight / Written in the stars (with LeANN RIMES) / I want love / This train don't stop there anymore / Song for Guy / Levon / Border song / Lucy in the sky with diamonds / Pinball wizard / True love (with KIKI DEE) / Live like horses (with LUCIANO PAVAROTTI) / I don't wanna go on with you like that / Don't let the sun go down on me (with GEORGE MICHAEL) / Your song (with ALESSANDRO SAFINA) / Sorry seems to be the hardest word (with BLUE) / Are you ready for love.

—— late in 2002, ELTON and BLUE hit No.1 with 'SORRY SEEMS TO BE THE HARDEST WORD'

Aug 03. (c-s/cd-s) *(ECB 50 MCS/CDS) / Ultra; <1177>* **ARE YOU READY FOR LOVE (1979 radio edit) / (full length version) / THREE WAY LOVE AFFAIR** [1] [ ]
(12") *(ECB 50)* – ('A'side) / ('A'-Freeform Five reform mix).
(above issued on 'Southern Fried')

– compilations, others, etc. –

on 'DJM' UK / 'MCA' in the US unless mentioned otherwise

Apr 71. (lp) *Paramount; (SPFL 269) <6004>* **FRIENDS (soundtrack)** [ ] [36]

Nov 74. (lp/c) *(DJH 2/4 0442) <2128>* **ELTON JOHN'S GREATEST HITS** (compilation) [1] [1]
– Your song / Daniel / Honky cat / Goodbye yellow brick road / Saturday night's alright for fighting / Rocket man / Candle in the wind / Don't let the Sun go down on me / Border song / Crocodile rock / The bitch is back / Lucy in the sky with diamonds / Sorry seems to be the hardest word / Don't go breaking my heart / Someone saved my life tonight / Philadelphia freedom / Island girl / Grow some funk of your own / Benny & the jets / Pinball wizard. *(cd-iss. Oct84; DJMCD 3)*

Sep 76. (7") *(DJS 10705)* **BENNIE AND THE JETS. / ROCK AND ROLL MADONNA** [37] [–]

May 77. (7"ep) *(DJR 18001)* **FOUR FROM FOUR EYES** [ ] [–]
– Your song / Rocket man / Saturday night's alright for fighting / Whenever you're ready (we'll go steady again).

Sep 77. (lp/c) *(DJH 2/4 0520) <3027>* **GREATEST HITS VOL.2** [6] [21]

Sep 78. (12"ep) *(DJT 15000)* **FUNERAL FOR A FRIEND; LOVE LIES BLEEDING / CURTAINS / WE ALL FALL IN LOVE SOMETIMES** □ –

Sep 78. (12x7"box) *(EJ 12)* **THE ELTON JOHN SINGLES COLLECTION** □ □
(also available separately as below)

Sep 78. (7") *(DJS 10901)* **LADY SAMANTHA. / SKYLINE PIGEON** □ □

Sep 78. (7") *(DJS 10902)* **YOUR SONG. / BORDER SONG** □ □

Sep 78. (7") *(DJS 10903)* **HONKY CAT. / SIXTY YEARS ON** □ □

Sep 78. (7") *(DJS 10904)* **CROCODILE ROCK. / COUNTRY COMFORT** □ □

Sep 78. (7") *(DJS 10905)* **ROCKET MAN. / DANIEL** □ □

Sep 78. (7") *(DJS 10906)* **GOODBYE YELLOW BRICK ROAD. / SWEET PAINTED LADY** □ □

Sep 78. (7") *(DJS 10907)* **DON'T LET THE SUN GO DOWN ON ME. / SOMEONE SAVED MY LIFE** □ □

Sep 78. (7") *(DJS 10908)* **CANDLE IN THE WIND. / I FEEL LIKE A BULLET (. . .** □ □

Sep 78. (7") *(DJS 10909)* **THE BITCH IS BACK. / GROW SOME FUNK OF YOUR OWN** □ □

Sep 78. (7") *(DJS 10910)* **ISLAND GIRL. / SATURDAY NIGHT'S ALRIGHT FOR FIGHTING** □ □

Sep 78. (7") *(DJS 10911)* **PHILADELPHIA FREEDOM. / BENNIE AND THE JETS** □ □

Sep 78. (7") *(DJS 10912)* **PINBALL WIZARD. / BENNIE AND THE JETS** □ □

Feb 79. (d-lp/d-c) *Pickwick; (PDA/PDC 047)* **THE ELTON JOHN LIVE COLLECTION** □ –
– (live albums of Apr71 + May76) *(re-iss. Nov88 as 'THE COLLECTION'; PWKS 551)*

Aug 79. (5xlp-box) *(DJV 2300)* **ELTON JOHN** □ □
(originally released in US contains 'EARLY YEARS', 'ELTON ROCKS', 'MOODS', 'SINGLES' & 'CLASSICS')

Oct 80. (lp/c) *(DJM 2/4 2085)* **LADY SAMANTHA** (rare 'B's) 56 □

Nov 80. (7") *(DJS 10961)* **HARMONY. / MONA LISA AND THE MAD HATTERS** □ –

Mar 81. (7") *(DJS 10965)* **I SAW HER STANDING THERE. / WHATEVER GETS YOU THROUGH THE NIGHT / LUCY IN THE SKY WITH DIAMONDS (with JOHN LENNON)** 30 –

1988. (d-c) **ROCK OF THE WESTIES / ELTON JOHN'S GREATEST HITS** □ □

1988. (d-c) **EMPTY SKY / GREATEST HITS VOL.2** □ □

1988. (d-c) **CAPTAIN FANTASTIC AND THE BROWN DIRT COWBOY / ELTON JOHN** □ □

1988. (d-c) **DON'T SHOOT ME I'M ONLY THE PIANO PLAYER / TUMBLEWEED CONNECTION** □ □

1988. (d-c) **GREATEST HITS / ROCK OF THE WESTIES** □ □
Note; All 'Rocket' releases were issued on 'MCA' in the US.

Apr 77. (7"mail-order) *Rocket; (GOALD 1)* **THE GOALDIGGER SONG. / (spoken)** □ –

Mar 81. (7") *Rocket; (XPRESS 49)* **DON'T GO BREAKING MY HEART. / SNOW QUEEN** □ –

Sep 87. (cd,c,lp) *<24153>* **ELTON JOHN'S GREATEST HITS, VOLUME III, 1979-1987** – 84

Oct 90. (cd/c/d-lp) *Rocket; (846947-2/-4/-1)* **THE VERY BEST OF ELTON JOHN** 1 –
– Your song / Rocket man / Crocodile rock / Daniel / Goodbye yellow brick road / Saturday night's alright for fighting / Candle in the wind / Don't let the Sun go down on me / Lucy in the sky with diamonds / Philadelphia freedom / Someone saved my life tonight / Don't go breaking my heart / Bennie and the jets / Sorry seems to be the hardest word / Song for Guy / Part time love / Blue eyes / I guess that's why they call it the blues / I'm still standing / Kiss the bride / Sad songs / Passengers / Nikita / Sacrifice / You gotta love someone. *(cd+=/c+=)* – Pinball wizard / The bitch is back / I don't wanna go on with you like that / Easier to walk away. *(re-iss. Nov91 hit UK No.29)*

Feb 91. (7"/c-s) **DON'T LET THE SUN GO DOWN ON ME. / SONG FOR GUY** □ –
(12"+=/cd-s+=) – Sorry seems to be the hardest word.

Nov 91. (cd-box/c-box) *<10110>* **TO BE CONTINUED . . .** – 82

Jan 78. (lp) *St.Michael; (2094 0102)* **CANDLE IN THE WIND** □ –

Oct 80. (lp) *K-Tel; (NE 1094)* **THE VERY BEST OF ELTON JOHN** 24 –

Sep 81. (lp/c) *Hallmark; (SHM/HSC 3088)* **THE ALBUM** □ –

Nov 82. (lp/c) *T.V.; (TVA/TVC 3)* **LOVE SONGS** □ –
(re-iss. Feb84 on 'Rocket' lp/c/cd; 814 085-2)

Jun 83. (lp/c) *Premier; (CBR/KCBR 1027)* **THE NEW COLLECTION** □ –

1984. (lp/c) *Premier; (CBR/KCBR 1036)* **THE NEW COLLECTION VOL.2** □ –

1983. (d-c) *Cambra; (CRT 003)* **ELTON JOHN (hits)** □ –

May 84. (d-c) *Cambra; (CRT 130)* **SEASONS . . . THE EARLY LOVE SONGS** □ –

Oct 84. (cd) *(DJMCD 4)* **THE SUPERIOR SOUND OF . . .** □ –

Feb 88. (7") *Old Gold; (OG 9776)* **NIKITA. / I'M STILL STANDING** □ –

Jun 88. (7") *Old Gold; (OG 9789)* **DON'T GO BREAKING MY HEART. / I GOT THE MUSIC IN ME (Kiki Dee)** □ –

Jun 88. (7") *Old Gold; (OG 9791)* **SONG FOR GUY. / BLUE EYES** □ –

1988. (cd) *Starr; (825 173-2)* **BIGGEST** □ –
below, a guest spot w/**KIKI DEE.**

Apr 81. (7") *Ariola; (ARO 269)* **LOVING YOU IS SWEETER THAN EVER. / 24 HOURS** □ –

May 87. (7") *CBS; (650865-7/-6) / Epic; <07119>* **FLAMES OF PARADISE. / CALL ON ME** □ 36
above JENNIFER RUSH & ELTON JOHN single

Mar 94. (cd/c) *Spectrum; (550213-2/-4)* **ROCK & ROLL MADONNA** □ –

Feb 95. (cd-s) *D.J.;* **UNITED WE STAND / NEANDERTHAL MAN** □ –
(above credited to REG DWIGHT) (early recordings)

Apr 95. (cd) *RPM; (RPM 142)* **CHARTBUSTERS GOES POP** □ –

□ JOHN AND MARY (see under ⇒ 10,000 MANIACS)

□ JOHNNY & THE SELF-ABUSERS (see under ⇒ SIMPLE MINDS)

□ Holly JOHNSON (see under ⇒ FRANKIE GOES TO HOLLYWOOD)

Linton Kwesi JOHNSON

Born: 1952, Chapelton, Jamaica, West Indies. Following his parents to England in 1963, he was introduced to the politics, history and literature that would inspire him to write poetry through membership of the Black Panthers, discovering whilst there the mighty 'Souls Of Black Folk' by W.E.B. DuBois. His first band, RASTA LOVE, formed in the early seventies, accompanied poetry with rasta drummers and was to form the foundation of his unique style of dub poetry. After studying Sociology at Goldsmith's College and becoming writer-in-residence for the London Borough of Lambeth in 1977, the Brixton based journal 'Race Today' published two collections of poetry in 1974/75; 'VOICES OF THE LIVING AND THE DEAD' and 'DREAD BEAT AN' BLOOD', the latter collection used as the title of his debut album on 'Virgin' in 1978. Featuring the musicianship of The DENNIS BOVELL DUB BAND, a partnership that was continue throughout the 80's and 90's, it confronted the reality of living in a racist society, with songs like 'FIVE NIGHTS OF BLEEDING' and 'SONG OF BLOOD' graphically capturing the increasingly apocalyptic mood of disenfranchised Black London. In 1980, 'Race Today' published his third collection, 'INGLAN IS A BITCH', a track featured on his album of the same year, 'BASS CULTURE'. Two more albums followed on the 'Island' label, 'LKJ IN DUB', which mixed tracks off the previous two albums to great effect, especially the anti-sus poem, 'SONNY'S LETTAH', and 'MAKING HISTORY'. By 1981, JOHNSON had launched his own label, the logo for the label being the sharp-suited image first seen on the 'BASS CULTURE' LP sleeve.

Two singles from the Jamaican poet Michael Smith, 'Mi Cyan Believe It' and 'Roots', were issued in the first year, with later releases by jazz trumpeter Skake Keane and writer Jean Binta Breeze to follow in the early 80's. Regularly touring with The DENNIS BOVELL DUB BAND and putting together a radio series about Jamaican popular music for Radio One, as well as reporting for Channel 4's The Bandung File, 'LKJ LIVE IN CONCERT WITH THE DUB BAND' was independently released in 1985. 'TINGS AN' TIMES' followed in 1991, and for the first time tackled issues outside of Britain in the song 'MI REVOLUTIONARY FRIEN', focusing on the dramatic changes taking place in Eastern Europe. The selected poems of LKJ were co-published in the same year by Bloodaxe Books and LKJ Music Publishers and in 1992, 'LKJ IN DUB: VOLUME TWO' was released, again combining the talents of BOVELL and JOHNSON. Now performing more frequently without a band, his most recent album, 'LJK A CAPELLA LIVE', reflects the emphasis on his poetry as a social conscience with a potent challenge to those in power.

Album rating: DREAD BEAT AN' BLOOD (*5; as Poet & The Roots) / FORCES OF VICTORY (*8) / BASS CULTURE (*8) / LKJ IN DUB (*6) / MAKING HISTORY (*7) / LINTON KWESI JOHNSON (*6) / IN CONCERT WITH THE DUB BAND (*5) / TINGS AN' TIMES (*6) / A CAPPALLA LIVE (*4)

POET & THE ROOTS

aka LINTON KWESI JOHNSON, plus DENNIS BOVELL of MATUMBI

Virgin — not iss.

Dec 77. (12"ep) *(VS 190-12)* **DREAD BEAT AND BLOOD. / ALL WE DOIN' IS DEFENDING / ('A'dub version)** [ ] [-]

LINTON KWESI JOHNSON

Island — not iss.

Apr 79. (lp) *(ILPS 9566)* **FORCES OF VICTORY** [66] [ ]
– Want fi goh rave / It noh funny / Sonny's lettah (anti-sus poem) / Independant intavenshan / Fite dem back / Forces of viktry / Time come. *(re-iss. Oct86 lp/c; ILPM/ICM 9566) (re-iss. Sep91 on 'Reggae Refreshers' cd/c; RR CD/CT 32)*

May 79. (7"/12") *(WIP/12XWIP 6494)* **WANT FI GOH RAVE. / REALITY POEM** [ ] [-]

Sep 79. (7"ep) *(WIP 6528)* **SONNY'S LETTAH (ANTI-SUS POEM). / IRON BAR DUB / TEK CHANCE / FUNNY DUB** [ ] [-]

Jan 80. (7") *(WIP 6554)* **DI BLACK PETTY BOSSHWAH. / STRAIGHT TO MADRAY'S HEAD** [ ] [-]
(12"+=) *(12WIP 6554)* – Action line / Action (dub).

Apr 80. (lp) *(ILPS 9605)* **BASS CULTURE** [46] [-]
– Bass culture / Street 66 / Reggae fi Peach / Di black petty booshwah / Inglan is a bitch / Loriane / Reggae sounds / Two sides of silence. *(re-iss. Jan91 on 'Reggae Refreshers' cd/c; RR CD/CT 26)*

Nov 80. (lp) *(ILPS 9650)* **LKJ IN DUB** [ ] [-]
– Victorious dub / Reality dub / Peach dub / Shocking dub / Iron bar dub / Bitch dub / Cultural dub / Brain smashing dub. *(re-iss. Sep91 on 'Reggae Refreshers' cd/c; RR CD/CT 34)*

Feb 84. (lp) *(ILPS 9770)* **MAKING HISTORY** [73] [-]
– Di eagle an' di bear / Wat about di workin' class? / Di great insoreckshan / Making history / Reggae fi Radni / Reggae fi Dada / New craas massahkah.

Rough Trade — Shanachie

Oct 84. (d-lp) *(ROUGH 78)* **LINTON KWESI JOHNSON IN CONCERT (live with The DUB BAND)** [ ] 1986 [ ]
– Five nights of bleeding / Dread beat an' blood / Intro / All wi doin' is defendin' / It dread inna Inglan / Man free / Wnat fi goh rave / It noh funny / Forces of viktry / Independant intavenshan / Reggae fi Peach / Di black petty booshwah / New craas Massahkah / Reality poem / Wat about di workin' claas / Di great insohreckshan / Making history. *(re-iss. May88 on 'Shanachie' d-lp/d-c/d-cd; SHAN/+C/CD 43034) (cd-iss. Apr95 & Feb02 on 'LKJ'; LKJCD 03)*

not iss. — Sterns

1980's. (7") **HISTORY REPEATS ITSELF** [-] [ ]

LKJ — not iss.

Jun 91. (cd/lp) *(LKJ CD/LP 001)* **TINGS AN' TIMES** [ ] [-]
– Story / Sense outta nansense / Tings an' times / Mi revalueshanary fren / Di good life / Di anfinish revalueshan / Dubbing for life. *(re-iss. Nov95 cd/lp; LKJ CD/LP 013)*

Apr 95. (cd/lp) *(LKJ CD/LP 009)* **LKJ IN DUB VOLUME 2** [ ] [-]
– Historic dub / Cold war dub / Guyanese dub / Timeless dub / Sensical dub / Sensical dubrise / Face card dub / Dub tale / Dubbin di revalueshan.

Oct 96. (cd) *(LKJCD 016)* **LKJ ACAPPELLA LIVE (live)** [ ] [-]

Jun 98. (cd/lp) *(LKJ CD/LP 018)* **MORE TIME** [ ] [-]

Aug 02. (cd/lp) *(LKJ CD/LP 021)* **LKJ IN DUB VOLUME 3** [ ] [-]
– Dirty langwidge dub / Rootikal dub / Liesense fe dub / Dubbin di tradition / Time fi dub / Row man tik dub / Mensch dub / Afro-German dub / Dubbin di diaspora / Poetic dub.

– compilations, etc. –

Jul 81. (lp) *Virgin; (VX 1002)* **DREAD BEAT 'N' BLOOD** (1978 material) [ ] [-]
– Dread beat 'n' blood / Five nights of bleeding / Down de road / Song of blood / It dread inna Inglan (for George Lindo) / Come wi goh dung deh / Man free (for Darcus Howe) / All wi doin' is defending. *(c-iss.1987; TCVX 1002) (cd-iss. 1988 on 'Heartbeat'; HBCD 01) (cd re-iss. Sep90 as POET & THE ROOTS on 'Frontline'; CDFL 9009) (cd re-iss. Sep00; CDFL 12)*

May 85. (lp/c) *Island; (IRG/+C 6)* **REGGAE GREATS** [ ] [-]
(cd-iss. Apr88; CIDRG 6) (cd re-iss. 1989; IMCD 14) (c re-iss. 1990; ICM 2033) (cd re-iss. Jul97 on 'Spectrum'; 552881-2)

Nov 98. (d-cd) *Island; (524573-2)* **ANTHOLOGY** [ ] [ ]

Jun 03. (cd) *Island; (IMCD 296)* **STRAIGHT TO INGLAN'S HEAD: AN INTRODUCTION TO LINTON KWESI JOHNSON** [ ] [ ]

Robert JOHNSON

Born: 8 May, 1911, Hazlehurst (a small industrialised railway town in the deep South of) Mississippi, USA. The seminal blues and Delta slide hero spent the early part of his life in a migrant labour camp after a fleeting affair with a W.A.P. worker (Noah Johnson) had forced ROBERT's mother, Julia Dodds, to flee to Memphis. After moving back with her original husband, Charles Spencer, Dodds was incapable of raising young ROBERT due to the struggles of parenthood and his increasingly disturbing and arrogant behaviour. ROBERT and his mother subsequently moved to Robinsonville, a sleepy Northern cotton community 40 miles out of Memphis, where she married Willie Willis in 1916 and settled down to raise ROBERT properly. Throughout his teenage years ROBERT became fascinated with music and instruments: he experimented with his new found Jews Harp before moving onto harmonica and then finally the guitar. His friend R.L. WINDUM occasionally accompanied him on Harp while RJ played the popular blues on his guitar, but this relationship was very short-lived due to ROBERT's subsequent attendance at the Indiana Creek School. In the early 20's he left school when his eyesight frequently failed him during exams and important lectures. Heading nowhere, he acquired the help of WILLIE BROWN, a talented local musician who introduced ROBERT to a string of "Jook" houses (blues venues) throughout the decade, enabling the talented bluesman a valid chance to broaden and advance his musical horizons. In 1929 and rumoured to be somewhat of a ladies man, 18-year old ROBERT married 16-year old Virginia Travis and they subsequently bought a farmhouse when she fell pregnant. Then tragedy struck the following April: Virginia and the baby died during childbirth. This catapulted ROBERT into extreme depression. The only way he felt he could cure his melancholia was to play raw edged Delta blues which displayed a degree of fiery passion, not heard since BLIND WILLIE JOHNSON's (no relation) 'DARK WAS THE NIGHT . . .'. It was said that he sat alone at night in the forest, engulfed in his own thoughts, strumming his guitar with an eerie, but beautiful prowess.

Two months later he followed the advice of his mentor, WILLIE BROWN, and set off to Wisconsin to record for 'Paramount'. There he created his most vivid and stripped-down recordings with preacher-cum-bluesman SON HOUSE, a remarkable pioneer who altered ROBERT's perception on standard blues playing. After a short stint on the road, he returned back to his home town of Hazlehurst, where he met IKE ZINNERMAN, an eccentric gothic blues guitarist, who claimed that he had self taught himself the blues whilst sitting on gravestones in the local crematorium in the dead of night! ROBERT remarried in 1931 to Calletta Craft who was 10 years his senior, although he abandoned her after she had a nervous breakdown. He began playing the "Jook" houses in the early 30's and enjoyed acclaim from a huge group of people who packed out venues wherever he played. However, this attraction made ROBERT deranged and paranoid; he would never reveal the chords or notes to any of his songs and he could be seen frequently leaving the stage midway through a set because he claimed the audience were eyeing him too closely! He continued travelling and after a brief residency in Arkansas he was approached by Ernie Oertle, a talent scout for the deep south who took him to San Antonio to record, during which time he produced the awesome 'TERRAPLANE BLUES'. A feast of slide and fast-handed guitar, with ROBERT's falsetto ramblings a highlight, the song became a huge success in America, providing this new found blues hero with instant fortune and a mass following. Tours of dancehalls, camps and "Jook" houses followed, along with the arrival of no less than eleven single 78 rpm records: a total of 41 recordings. The tour path led ROBERT through Detroit, New York City, New Jersey, St. Louis, Canada, Windsor and back to the south. By this time he had grown fond of drinking and was said to be the "life of a party" when drunk. His final excursion came in the summer of 1938 when he stopped off in Greenwood County to play in a bar called Three Forks. According to sources, ROBERT had become infatuated with the owner's wife, which caused a bad atmosphere within the joint. He was handed an open bottle of whiskey by the proprieter which was immediately slapped out of his hand by a friend who told him: "Don't ever take a drink from an open bottle, you don't know what could be in it!". ROBERT took another bottle and less than an hour later he was struggling to sing on stage. Leaving halfway through his set, he was found outside vomiting violently. It was then evident that he had been poisoned by the jealous barman. He lay sick that night in bed, contracting pneumonia before he finally passed away three day later on August the 16th, 1938. Remembered as one of the great blues guitarists of his time, ROBERT JOHNSON's influence still remains to this day. Among BOB DYLAN, MUDDY WATERS, KEITH RICHARDS and ERIC CLAPTON, the inexplicable artist has never failed to wow audiences and musicians alike; his warped interpretation of blues guitar and his haunting vocals have provided a catalyst for many inspired guitarists and vocalists who could not shake the sound of ROBERT JOHNSON's exploding originality from their mind. KEITH RICHARDS wrote in the booklet which accompanied 'THE COMPLETE RECORDINGS OF ROBERT JOHNSON' (1991): "I have never heard anybody before or since use the form and bend so much to make it work for himself . . . he came out with such compelling themes . . . it was almost like listening to Bach, you know, you think you can handle the blues until you've heard ROBERT JOHNSON . . ."

Best CD compilations: THE BEST OF THE DELTA BLUES SINGERS (*9) / THE BEST OF THE DELTA BLUES SINGERS VOL.2 (*8) / THE COMPLETE RECORDINGS (*9)

ROBERT JOHNSON – vocals, acoustic guitar

original very limited & rare singles below had a first and second pressing and are worth over £2,500 each! – the 4th one over £6,000

not iss. / Vocalion – Arc

Feb 37. (78) *<03416> – <7-03-56>* **TERRAPLANE BLUES. / KINDHEARTED WOMAN BLUES** –

Mar 37. (78) *<03445> – <7-04-60>* **32-20 BLUES. / LAST FAIR DEAL GONE DOWN** –
<re-iss. 1937 on 'Oriole'; 7-04-60>

Apr 37. (78) *<03475> – <7-04-81>* **I BELIEVE I'LL DUST MY BROOM. / DEAD SHRIMP BLUES** –
<re-iss. 1937 on 'Conqueror'; 8871>

May 37. (78) *<03519> – <7-05-81>* **CROSS ROAD BLUES. / RAMBLING ON MY MIND** –

Jun 37. (78) *<03563> – <7-07-57>* **COME ON IN MY KITCHEN. / THEY'RE RED HOT** –

Jul 37. (78) *<03601>* **SWEET HOME CHICAGO. / WALKIN' BLUES** –

Aug 37. (78) *<03623> – <7-09-56>* **HELL HOUND ON MY TRAIL. / FROM FOUR UNTIL LATE** –

Sep 37. (78) *<03665> – <7-10-65>* **MILKCOW'S CALF BLUES. / MALTED MILK** –
<re-iss. 1937 on 'Conqueror'; 8944>

Nov 37. (78) *<03723> – <7-12-57>* **STONES IN MY PASSWAY. / I'M A STEADY ROLLIN' MAN** –
<re-iss. 1937 on 'Conqueror'; 8973>

Jan 38. (78) *<04002>* **STOP BREAKIN' DOWN BLUES. / HONEYMOON BLUES** –

Feb 38. (78) *<04108>* **ME AND THE DEVIL BLUES. / LITTLE QUEEN OF SPADES** –

May 38. (78) *<04630>* **LOVE IN VAIN BLUES. / PREACHING BLUES** –

—— Tragically, on the 16th of August, 1938, JOHNSON was dead after being poisoned (see above).

– (selective) compilations, etc. –

1962. (lp) *Philips; (BBL 7539)* **ROBERT JOHNSON 1936-1937** –

1966. (lp) *C.B.S.; (BPG 62456) / Columbia; <CL 1654>* **KING OF THE DELTA BLUES SINGERS** 1961
– Cross road blues / Terraplane blues / Come on in my kitchen / Walkin' blues / Last fair deal gone down / 32-20 blues / Kind hearted woman blues / If I had possession over judgement day / Preaching blues / When you got a good friend / Rambling on my mind / Stones on my passway / Traveling riverside blues / Milkcow's calf blues / Me and the Devil blues / Hell hound on my trail. *<US re-iss. Dec87; same>* – hit No.34 *<(cd-iss. Nov94; CK 52944)> (cd re-iss. Sep96 on 'Columbia'; 484419) <(cd re-iss. Jan99 on 'Sony Jazz;; 493006-2)>*

Apr 90. (lp/c/cd) *Aldabra; <(ALB 1003/+MC/CD)>* **DELTA BLUES – THE ALTERNATE TAKES**

Nov 90. (d-cd/d-c) *Columbia; (467246-2) <46222>* **THE COMPLETE RECORDINGS** Oct00 80
(re-iss. May94 d-cd/d-c; CD/40 46222) (d-cd-iss. Sep99 on 'Definitive'; DRCD 11147)

Apr 92. (cd/c) *Charly; (CDBM/TCBM 13)* **DELTA BLUES LEGEND** –

Aug 92. (cd)(c) *Blues Encore; (CD 52019)(BEMC 1519)* **TRAVELLING RIVERSIDE BLUES** –

Dec 92. (cd/c) *Deja Vu; (D2CD/D2MC 14)* **THE GOLD COLLECTION** –

Mar 93. (cd) *Charly; (CHCD 1049)* **THE LEGENDARY BLUES SINGER** –

1993. (cd) *Blues Collection; <BLVC 006>* **RED HOT BLUES** –

Mar 95. (cd) *Indigo; (IGOCD 2017)* **HELL HOUND ON MY TRAIL** –

Apr 95. (cd) *Deja Vu; (DVBC 905-2)* **ROBERT JOHNSON: COLLECTOR'S EDITION** –

Jun 95. (cd) *Nectar; (NTMCD 504)* **CROSS ROAD BLUES: THE BEST OF ROBERT JOHNSON** –
(re-iss. Feb98 on 'Reactive'; REMCD 504)

Jan 96. (d-cd) *Deja Vu; (R2CD 4014)* GOLD –

Feb 96. (d-cd) *Fremeaux; (FA 251)* **THE BLUES (SAN ANTONIO / DALLAS)** –

Oct 96. (cd) *Music Memoria; (842027-2)* **ALL-TIME BLUES CLASSICS** –

Oct 97. (cd) *Legacy-Columbia; <(487844-2)>* **KING OF THE DELTA**

Nov 97.	(cd) *Eagle; (EABCD 067)* **THE MASTERS**		–
Apr 98.	(cd/c) *Hallmark; (30567-2/-4)* **LOVE IN VAIN**		–
May 98.	(cd) *Summit; (SUMCD 4194)* **I WENT DOWN TO THE CROSSROADS**		–
Jun 98.	(3xcd-box; with Various Artists) *Catfish; <(KATCD 107)>* **BEG, BORROW OR STEAL**		
Nov 98.	(3xcd-box; with SON HOUSE & MUDDY WATERS) *Sony Jazz; (492740-2)* **KING OF THE DELTA BLUES**		–
Mar 99.	(3xcd-box; with MUDDY WATERS & RAY CHARLES) *Summit; (SDCDBX 3668)* **PREACHING THE BLUES**		–
Jun 99.	(cd) *A.B.M.; (ABMMCD 1047)* **THE LAST OF THE GREAT BLUES SINGERS**		
Aug 99.	(d-cd) *Snapper; (SMCD 234)* **THE BIRTH OF BLUES**		–
Oct 99.	(cd) *Delta; (4701-2)* **HELLHOUND ON MY TRAIL**		
Jan 01.	(cd) *Arpeggio; (ARB 006)* **DEAL WITH THE DEVIL, VOL.1**		
Apr 01.	(cd) *Zircon Bleu; (BLEU 515)* **THE R.L. SPENCER LEGACY**		
May 01.	(cd) *Arpeggio; (APB 010)* **DEAL WITH THE DEVIL, VOL2: THE DALLAS RECORDINGS**		
Jul 01.	(cd) *Jasmine; (JASMCD 3001)* **HIS RECORDED LEGACY: 29 SONGS**		
Aug 02.	(cd) *Sony; (509010-2)* **CONTRACTED TO THE DEVIL**		

☐ JON & VANGELIS (see under ⇒ VANGELIS)

☐ John Paul JONES (see under ⇒ LED ZEPPELIN)

Norah JONES

Born: 30 Mar'79, New York City, New York, USA. Daughter of RAVI SHANKER (which possibly accounts for her alluringly exotic looks), JONES moved to Dallas, Texas aged only four. Displaying a precocious musical talent, she entered the city's Booker T Washington High School for the Performing and Visual Arts in her mid-teens, graduating to local performances and collecting armfuls of student music awards. A degree in jazz piano from the University of North Texas was the next addition to her burgeoning CV, while valuable work experience came with funk outfit WAX POETIC. Stepping out in her own right, JONES recruited longtime sidemen JESSE HARRIS, DAN RIESER and LEE ALEXANDER, eventually signing to 'Blue Note' on the strength of her demos. Blue Note jazz guitarist CHARLIE HUNTER was graced with NORAH's silky vocals on his 'Songs From The Analogue Playground' set, while sessions for her own debut album were eventually handled by legendary producer Arif Mardin. The result was the multi-platinum 'COME AWAY WITH ME' (2002), a tasteful, mellifluous set of songs, performed with a smoky sophistication beyond her years. Covers of J.D. Loudermilk's 'TURN ME ON', Hank Williams' 'COLD COLD HEART' and Hoagy Carmichael's 'THE NEARNESS OF YOU', pretty much gave a flavour of the various rootsy influences at work although the seamless contributions of the jazz-tested sessions hands and JONES' elegant delivery kept proceedings firmly in the adult/jazz/Grammy contemporary mould.

Album rating: COME AWAY WITH ME (*8)

NORAH JONES – vocals, piano / with **JESSE HARRIS** – guitar / **LEE ALEXANDER** – bass / **DAN REISER** – drums / + others

		Parlophone	Blue Note
Nov 01.	(cd-ep) *<none>* **FIRST SESSIONS** – Don't know why / Come away with me / Something is calling you / Turn me on / Lonestar / Peace.	–	
Mar 02.	(cd) *(538609-2) <32088>* **COME AWAY WITH ME** – Don't know why / Seven years / Cold cold heart / Feelin' the same way / Come away with me / Shoot the moon / Turn me on / Lonestar / I've got to see you again / Painter song / One flight down / Nightingale / The long day is over / The nearness of you. *(re-iss. Jun03 +=; 581880-2)* – Ruler of my heart / Cold cold heart (live) / I'll be your baby tonight / Peace / Come away with me (video). *(re-iss. Sep03; 541747-2)*	1	Feb02 1
May 02.	(cd-s) *(CDCL 836)* **DON'T KNOW WHY / LONESTAR (live) / PEACE (live)**	59	–
Aug 02.	(cd-s) *(CDCL 838)* **FEELIN' THE SAME WAY / I'LL BE YOUR BABY TONIGHT / RULER OF MY HEART**	72	–
Oct 02.	(cd-s) *(CDCL 839)* **COME AWAY WITH ME / TURN ME ON (live) / COLD COLD HEART (live)**		–
Sep 03.	(cd-s) *(CDCL 848)* **DON'T KNOW WHY / I'LL BE YOUR BABY TONIGHT / CRAZY (live)**	67	30

Rickie Lee JONES

Born: 8 Nov'54, Chicago, Illinois, USA. A rebellious child, JONES and a friend ran away from home at the age of fifteen, stealing a car in the process; she was later expelled from a number of schools in Olympia, Washington, where she grew up. Relocating to L.A. in 1973, JONES took waitressing work while writing and performing in her spare time; with her beat-poet jazz influences and West Coast, piano-tinkling cool, JONES found a musical soulmate in TOM WAITS (she's allegedly the dame on the cover of WAITS' 'Blue Valentine' album), while the late, great LOWELL GEORGE (of LITTLE FEAT) recorded one of her songs, 'EASY MONEY', on his 1979 solo album. With such notable references, it was only a matter of time before she was signed up, 'Warners' releasing her eponymous debut set in summer '79. Eventually reaching the US Top 5 following the success of the classic 'CHUCK E.'S IN LOVE' single, the album established JONES as a unique talent within L.A.'s musical elite; her swinging boho narratives also divided opinion, there were few waverers. The more ambitious 'PIRATES' (1981) set failed to spawn any hits, although her cult appeal again saw the album making the US Top 5. 1983's 'GIRL AT HER VOLCANO' was a mini-set comprised largely of jazz covers, while 'THE MAGAZINE' (1984) found JONES veering too close to synth-centric electro-rock for comfort. Never the most prolific of artists, it would be a further five years before a fourth set appeared, the more accessible and grounded 'FLYING COWBOYS'. Produced by WALTER BECKER (STEELY DAN) and featuring contributions from Scots mood masters, The BLUE NILE, the album's release found JONES enjoying her most praiseworthy reviews in years. More ill-advised was 'POP POP' (1991), a confused collection of unlikely torch ballad cover versions, while 'TRAFFIC FROM PARADISE' (1993) saw her working with an array of star names including LYLE LOVETT and LEO KOTTKE. More convincing, insightful and downright entertaining than her earlier covers set, 'IT'S LIKE THIS' (2000) encompassed a broader range of material. Everything from Traffic's 'LOW SPARK OF HIGH HEELED BOYS' to Marvin Gaye's 'TROUBLE MAN' was given the inimitable RICKIE LEE treatment, with guest contributions from the likes of BEN FOLDS, JOE JACKSON and TAJ MAHAL. In a similar companion piece type vein, 'LIVE AT RED ROCKS' (2001) made an interesting comparison to her mid 90's acoustic concert set. In 'EVENING OF MY BEST DAY' (2003), meanwhile, JONES had come up with one of her most satisfying and convincing sets in years. With a huge casts of session musicians and guests – including ROB WASSERMAN, BILL FRISELL and GRANT LEE PHILLIPS – the album spliced fragments of blues, jazz, soul, gospel, folk, pop and rock into the kind of luminous, free spirited musical poetry which JONES has long made her natural environment and which would overwhelm lesser talents. Fired up by righteous indignation, the singer took a rare – if celebratory rather than berating – potshot at

President Bush and his cronies on the testifying 'TELL SOMEBODY (REPEAL THE PATRIOT ACT NOW)', while in general, her lyrical weave was more lucid, candid and compassionate than it had ever been. • **Songwriters:** Co-wrote with PASCAL NABAT-MAYER in '89. She covered; WALK AWAY RENEE (Four Tops) / ANGEL WINGS (Tom Waits) / ON BROADWAY (Drifters) / DON'T LET THE SUN CATCH YOU CRYING (Gerry & The Pacemakers) / FRIDAY ON MY MIND (Easybeats) / SHOWBIZ KIDS (Steely Dan) / FOR NO ONE (Beatles) / SMILE (Chaplin-Parsons-Philips) / ON THE STREET WHERE YOU LIVE (Lerner-Loewe) / I CAN'T GET STARTED (Duke-Gershwin) / UP A LAZY RIVER (Hoagy Carmichael) / SOMEONE TO WATCH OVER ME (Gershwin) / CYCLES (. . .Caldwell) / ONE HAND, ONE HEART (Bernstein-Sondheim).

Album rating: RICKIE LEE JONES (*8) / PIRATES (*6) / GIRL AT HER VOLCANO mini (*5) / THE MAGAZINE (*6) / FLYING COWBOYS (*6) / POP POP (*5) / TRAFFIC FROM PARADISE (*5) / NAKED SONGS – LIVE AND ACOUSTIC (*4) / GHOSTYHEAD (*5) / IT'S LIKE THIS (*5) / LIVE AT RED ROCKS (*5) / THE EVENING OF MY BEST DAY (*6)

RICKIE LEE JONES – vocals, keyboards, guitar / with session people

Warners Warners

Jun 79. (lp/c) *(K/K4 56628) <3296>* **RICKIE LEE JONES** 18 Apr79 3
– Chuck E.'s in love / On Saturday afternoons in 1963 / Night train / Young blood / Easy money / Last chance Texaco / Danny's all star joint / Coolsville / Weasel and the white boys cool / Company / After hours (twelve bars past goodnight). *(cd-iss. 1989; K2 56628)*

Jun 79. (7") *(K 17390) <8825>* **CHUCK E.'S IN LOVE. / ON SATURDAY AFTERNOONS IN 1963** 18 Apr79 4

Aug 79. (7") *(K 17445) <49018>* **YOUNG BLOOD. / COOLSVILLE** Jul79 40

Oct 79. (7") *<49100>* **DANNY'S ALL-STAR JOINT. / LAST CHANCE TEXACO** –

Nov 79. (7") *(K 17477)* **DANNY'S ALL-STAR JOINT. / NIGHT TRAIN** –

Jan 80. (7") *(K 17556)* **EASY MONEY. / COMPANY** –

Jul 81. (lp/c) *(K/K4 56816) <3432>* **PIRATES** 37 5
– We belong together / Living it up / Skeletons / Woody and Dutch on the slow train to Peking / Pirates / Traces of the western slopes / Returns. *(cd-iss. Jan86; K2 56816)*

Aug 81. (7") *<49816>* **A LUCKY GUY. / SKELETONS** – 64

Sep 81. (7") *(K 17851)* **WOODY AND DUTCH ON THE SLOW TRAIN TO PEKING. / SKELETONS** –

Oct 81. (7") *<49871>* **WE BELONG TOGETHER. / THE RETURNS** –

Jan 82. (7") *<50046>* **PIRATES. / SKELETONS** –

Jun 83. (10"m-lp/c) *(923805-1/-4) <23805>* **GIRL AT HER VOLCANO** 51 39
– Lush life / Walk away Renee / Hey, Bub / My funny valentine / Under the boardwalk / Rainbow sleeves / So long. *(c+=)* – Something cool / Letters from the 9th ward.

Aug 83. (7") *(W 9559) <29559>* **UNDER THE BOARDWALK. / SO LONG**

Oct 84. (lp/c) *(925117-1/-4) <25117>* **THE MAGAZINE** 40 44
– (prelude to gravity) / Gravity / Juke box fury / It must be love / Magazine / The real end / Deep space / Runaround / Rorschachs – Theme for the Pope – The unsigned painting – The weird beast. *(cd-iss. Mar86; 925117-2)*

Sep 84. (7") *<29191>* **THE REAL END. / WOODY AND DUTCH ON A SLOW TRAIN TO PEKING** – 83

Oct 84. (7"/12") *(W 9191/+T)* **THE REAL END. / MAGAZINE** –

Apr 85. (7") *<29059>* **IT MUST BE LOVE. / MAGAZINE** –

Geffen Geffen

Sep 89. (lp/c)(cd) *(WX 309/+C)(924249-2) <24246>* **FLYING COWBOYS** 50 39
– The horses / Just my baby / Ghetto of my mind / Rodeo girl / Satellites / Ghost train / Flying cowboys / Don't let the sun catch you crying / Love is gonna bring us back alive / Away from the sky / Atlas' marker. *(cd re-iss. Nov91 & Sep97; GEFD 24246)*

Sep 89. (7") *(GEF 64)* **SATELLITES. / GHOST TRAIN** –
(12"+=/cd-s+=) *(GEF 64 T/CD)* – Friday on my mind.

Aug 91. (cd/c/lp) *<(GED/GEC/GEF 24426)>* **POP POP**
– My one and only love / Spring can really hang you up the most / Hi-li hi-lo / Up from the skies / Second time around / Dat dere / I'll be seeing you / Bye bye blackbird / The ballad of the sad young men / I won't grow up / Love junkyard / Come back to me. *(re-iss. cd Oct95; GFLD 19293)*

— with **JOHN LEFTWICH** – bass, cello, vocals / **LEO KOTTKE** – guitars, vocals / **SAL BERNARDI** – acoustic guitar, vocals / **JIM KELTNER** – drums / **BOBBY BRUCE** – violin / **BRAD DUTZ** – percussion / **DOUG LYONS** – French horn / + guest guitarists on 1 track each **DAVID HIDALGO, BRIAN SETZER, DEAN PARKS + DAVID BAERWALD**

Sep 93. (cd/c) *<(GED/GEC 24602)>* **TRAFFIC FROM PARADISE**
– Pink flamingos / Alter boy / Stewart's coat / Beat angels / Tigers / Rebel rebel / Jolie Jolie / Running from mercy / A stranger's car / The albatross. *(cd re-iss. Sep97; GED 24602)*

Reprise Reprise

Oct 95. (cd/c) *<(9362 45950-2/-4)>* **NAKED SONGS – LIVE AND ACOUSTIC (live)**
– The horses / Weasel and the white boy's cool / Altar boy / It must be love / Young blood / The last chance Texaco / Skeletons / Magazine / Loving it up / We belong together / Coolsville / Flying cowboys / Stewart's coat / Chuck E.'s in love / Autumn leaves.

Sep 97. (c-s) *(W 0418C)* **FIREWALKER / ('A'mix)**
(12"+=/cd-s+=) *(W 0418 T/CD)* – ('A'mixes).

Sep 97. (cd/c) *<(9362 46557-2/-4)>* **GHOSTYHEAD**
– Little yellow town / Road kill / Matters / Firewalker / Howard / Ghostyhead / Sunny afternoon / Scary Chinese movie / Cloud of unknowing / Vessel of light.

Epic Artemis

Sep 00. (cd) *(499582-2) <751054>* **IT'S LIKE THIS**
– Showbiz kids (with JOE JACKSON) / Trouble man / For no one / Smile / Low spark of high-heeled boys / On the street where you live / I can't get started / Up a lazy river / Someone to watch over me / Cycles / One hand, one heart (with JOE JACKSON).

Dec 01. (cd) *(505359-2) <751101>* **LIVE AT RED ROCKS (live)** Nov01
– Rodeo girl / Satellites / We belong together / Coolsville / Weasel and the white boys cool / Chuck E's in love / Just my baby / Flying cowboys / Youngblood / Don't let the sun catch you crying / Love is gonna bring us back alive / Gloria.

V2 V2

Oct 03. (cd) *(VVR 102473-2) <27171>* **THE EVENING OF MY BEST DAY**
– Ugly man / Second chance / Bitchenostrophy / Little mysteries / Lap dog / Tell somebody (repeal the patriot act now) / Sailor song / A tree on Allenford / It takes you there / Mink coat at the bus stop / The evening of my best day / A face in the crowd.

Tom JONES

Born: THOMAS JONES WOODWARD, 7 Jun'40, Pontypridd, Wales. After a hard-bitten working class upbringing (his dad was a coal miner), the 16-year old JONES moved on from juvenile troublemaking to a marriage that would subsequently be kept separate from his public ladies man persona. Cutting his teeth as a part-time pub singer, he eventually formed his own combo under the pseudonymous moniker of TOMMY SCOTT & THE SENATORS. In 1963, he was spotted by fellow countryman, Gordon Mills, who, in turn, became both his manager and co-writer. By mid '64, he'd become TOM JONES (after the success of the British comedy movie of the same name) and having secured a deal with London label 'Decca', released a cover of Ronnie Love's 'CHILLS AND FEVER' as his debut in August '64. Although it was a flop, JONES made his name early the following year with the classic 'IT'S NOT UNUSUAL'. A chart topper in the UK, the single showcased JONES' powerful, versatile vocal prowess while his charismatic TV appearances wowed the ladies with a hip-swiveling stage style influenced by the likes of JERRY LEE LEWIS, SOLOMON BURKE and ELVIS "The Pelvis" PRESLEY. A fully-fledged Welsh "sex bomb", medallion man JONES became a regular fixture in both the UK and US charts with such timeless pop nuggets as 'WHAT'S

NEW PUSSYCAT' (a Bacharach & David-penned title theme to the 1965 movie), 'GREEN, GREEN GRASS OF HOME' (a UK No.1 in '66), 'I'LL NEVER FALL IN LOVE AGAIN' (No.2 in Britain), 'I'M COMING HOME' (also a No.2) and his piece de resistance, 'DELILAH' (yet another to narrowly miss out on prime position, the song was taken into the Top 10 seven years on by ALEX HARVEY!). His golden period was extended into the early 70's with further full-scale hits in the shape of 'I (WHO HAVE NOTHING)', 'SHE'S A LADY', 'TILL' and 'THE YOUNG NEW MEXICAN PUPPETEER'. Yet as his flares grew wider, the hits became thinner on the ground with the advent of "glam-rock" and JONES decamped to the glitzy cabaret circuit of Las Vegas having earlier moved to California. Having achieved a certain degree of mid-80's success in the US country charts, JONES made his UK comeback in '87 with the aptly titled near chart-topper 'A BOY FROM NOWHERE'. This served as a springboard from which he went on to re-establish himself as a credible crooner via a collaboration with the ART OF NOISE on a hit cover of Prince's 'KISS'. JONES' critical rehabilitation continued well into the 90's when – after the success of singles, 'ALL YOU NEED IS LOVE' (for the Childline appeal) and 'IF I ONLY KNEW' (a No.11 hit in '94) – the cream of the latter day alt-pop scene (save for a few oldsters like VAN the man!) queued up to work with him on the massively successful 'RELOAD' (1999). Among the collaborations featured were Talking Heads' 'BURNING DOWN THE HOUSE' (with the CARDIGANS), Ray Charles' 'BABY, IT'S COLD OUTSIDE' (with CERYS from CATATONIA) and Randy Newman's 'MAMA TOLD ME NOT TO COME' (with other Welsh youngsters, STEREOPHONICS) alongside duets with ROBBIE WILLIAMS (whom he'd appeared with in 1998's Brit awards), DIVINE COMEDY, SPACE, JAMES DEAN BRADFIELD, MOUSSE T, HEATHER SMALL, PRETENDERS, PORTISHEAD, SIMPLY RED, NATALIE IMBRUGLIA, BARENAKED LADIES and ZUCCHERO. A further bid for credibility came in the shape of 'MR. JONES' (2002), an unlikely – and for some hilarious – WYCLEF JEAN-produced affair which married the latter's ubiquitous production skills with JONES' near-septuagenarian sexiness. The result? A wildly eclectic album which sometimes works (as on the cover of 'BLACK BETTY') and sometimes falls flat on its face-'TJ INTERNATIONAL'. JONES is never going to be the next P. DIDDY but there aren't many – if any – men his age with the balls to try something like this. • **Songwriters:** Outside writers and covers (singles only and er, selective):- WITH THESE HANDS (Billy Eckstine) / PROMISE HER ANYTHING (Burt Bacharach) / THUNDERBALL (John Barry) / GREEN, GREEN GRASS OF HOME (Curly Putnam) / DETROIT CITY (Bobby Bare) / I'LL NEVER FALL IN LOVE AGAIN (Lonnie Donegan) / SIXTEEN TONS (Tennessee Ernie Ford) / DELILAH (Les Reed & Barry Mann) / WITHOUT LOVE (Clyde McPhatter) / I (WHO HAVE NOTHING) (Ben E.King) / PUPPET MAN (Neil Sedaka) / TILL (Angels) / A BOY FROM NOWHERE (Mike Leander) / MOVE CLOSER (Phyllis Nelson) / COULDN'T SAY GOODBYE (Diane Warren & Albert Hammond) / CARRYING A TORCH (Van Morrison) / BLACK BETTY (Leadbelly) / THE LETTER (Box Tops) / I WHO HAVE NOTHING (hit; Shirley Bassey). He also interpreted many Italian language tunes, and covered more than 100 others on his lp's. • **Trivia:** In 1988, he appeared with other Welsh artists in the musical version of Dylan Thomas' 'Under Milk Wood'. A year later, Katherine Berkeley won a paternity suit against TOM and the court made him pay £200 a week for the child's maintenence. He is still married, much to the dismay of his largely female knicker-throwing fans.

Album rating (selective): CARRYING A TORCH (*5) / THE COMPLETE TOM JONES compilation (*7) / THE LEAD AND HOW TO SWING IT (*5) / RELOAD (*7) / MR. JONES (*4) / GREATEST HITS compilation (*7)

TOM JONES – vocals with session people

Decca — Parrot

Aug 64. (7") *(F 11966)* **CHILLS AND FEVER. / BREATHLESS** [ ] [ ]

Jan 65. (7") *(F 12062) <9737>* **IT'S NOT UNUSUAL. / TO WAIT FOR LOVE (IS TO WASTE YOUR LIFE AWAY)** [1] Mar65 [10]

Apr 65. (7") *(F 12121)* **ONCE UPON A TIME. / I TELL THE SEA** [32] [ ]

May 65. (lp) *(LK 4693)* **ALONG CAME JONES** [11] [–]
– Some other guy / I've got a heart / It takes a worried man / Spanish Harlem / Autumn leaves / Skye boat song / Memphis Tennessee / Watcha gonna do / I need your loving / If you need me / Endlessly / It's just a matter of time / When the world was beautiful.

Jun 65. (7") *<9765>* **WHAT'S NEW PUSSYCAT? / ONCE UPON A TIME** [–] [3]

Jun 65. (7") *(F 12191)* **WITH THESE HANDS. / UNTRUE** [13] [–]

Jun 65. (lp) *<71004>* **IT'S NOT UNUSUAL** [–] [54]

Aug 65. (7") *<9787>* **WITH THESE HANDS. / SOME OTHER GUY** [–] [27]

Aug 65. (7") *(F 12203)* **WHAT'S NEW PUSSYCAT? / ROSE** [11] [–]

Sep 65. (lp) *<71006>* **WHAT'S NEW PUSSYCAT?** [–] [ ]
(UK-iss.on cd Jun88 on 'London', 4 extra tracks)

Jan 66. (7") *(F 12292) <9801>* **THUNDERBALL. / KEY TO MY HEART** [35] Nov65 [25]

Jan 66. (lp; mono/stereo) *(LK/SKL 4743)* **A-TOM-IC JONES** [ ] [ ]
– Doctor Love / Face of a loser / It's been a long time coming / In a woman's eyes / More / I'll never let you go / The loser / To make a big man cry / Key to my heart / True love comes only once in a lifetime / You're so good to me / Where do you belong / These things you don't forget / Stop breaking my heart. *(cd-iss. Nov88 on 'London'+=; 820556-2)* – Hide and seek / Not responsible / This and that / Promise her anything / Thunderball.

Feb 66. (7") *<9809>* **PROMISE HER ANYTHING. / A LITTLE YOU** [–] [74]

Feb 66. (7") *(F 12349)* **STOP BREAKING MY HEART. / NEVER GIVE AWAY LOVE** [ ] [–]

May 66. (7") *(F 12390)* **NOT RESPONSIBLE. / ONCE THERE WAS A TIME** [18] Jun66 [58]

Aug 66. (7") *(F 12461)* **THIS AND THAT. / CITY GIRL** [44] [ ]

Sep 66. (lp; mono/stereo) *(LK/SKL 4815)* **FROM THE HEART** [23] [–]
– You came a long way from St. Louis / Kansas City / Someday (you'll want me to want you) / If ever I would leave you / Georgia on my mind / A taste of honey / The nearness of you / My foolish heart / When I fall in love / Begin the beguine / Hello young lovers / It's magic / My prayer / That old black magic. *(cd-iss. Apr89 on 'London'+=; 820557-2)* – (4 extra).

Nov 66. (7") *(F 12511)* **GREEN, GREEN GRASS OF HOME. / PROMISE HER ANYTHING** [1] [–]

Dec 66. (7") *<40009>* **GREEN, GREEN GRASS OF HOME. / IF I HAD YOU** [–] [11]

Feb 67. (7") *(F 22555)* **DETROIT CITY. / IF I HAD YOU** [8] [–]

Mar 67. (7") *<40012>* **DETROIT CITY. / TEN GUITARS** [–] [27]

Mar 67. (lp; mono/stereo) *(LK/SKL 4855) <71009>* **GREEN, GREEN GRASS OF HOME** [3] Feb67 [65]
– Green, green grass of home / My mother's eyes / He'll have to go / Riders in the sky / Funny familiar forgotten feelings / Sixteen tons / Two brothers / Ring of fire / Field of yellow daisies / Wish I could say no to you / All I get from you is heartaches / Mohair Sam / Cool water / Detroit City. *(cd-iss. Sep88 on 'London'; 820182-2)*

Apr 67. (7") *(F 12599) <40014>* **FUNNY FAMILIAR FORGOTTEN FEELINGS. / I'LL NEVER LET YOU GO** [7] May67 [49]

Jun 67. (lp; mono/stereo) *(LK/SKL 4874) <71014>* **LIVE! AT THE TALK OF THE TOWN (live)** <US-title 'TOM JONES LIVE!> [6] Jul67 [ ]
– The star theme / Ain't that good news / Hello young lovers / I can't stop loving you / What's new pussycat? / Not responsible / I believe / My Yiddish momma / Shake / That lucky old Sun / Thunderball / Green, green grass of home / It's not unusual / Land of a 1000 dances. *<US re-iss. Mar69; same>* – hit No.13

Jul 67. (7") *(F 12639)* **I'LL NEVER FALL IN LOVE AGAIN. / THINGS I WANNA DO** [2] [–]

Aug 67. (7") *<40016>* **SIXTEEN TONS. / THINGS I WANNA DO** [–] [68]

Sep 67. (7") *<40018>* **I'LL NEVER FALL IN LOVE AGAIN. / ONCE UPON A TIME** – 49
<US re-iss. Jul69; same> – hit No.6

Nov 67. (7") *(F 12693) <40024>* **I'M COMING HOME. / THE LONELY ONE** 2 Dec67 57

Dec 67. (lp; mono/stereo) *(/LK/SKL 4909)* **13 SMASH HITS** 5
– Don't fight it / You keep me hangin' on / Hold on I'm coming / I was made to love her / Keep on running / Get ready / I'll never fall in love again / I know / I wake up crying / Funny how time slips away / Danny boy / It's a man's man's man's world / Yesterday. *(cd-iss. Jun88 on 'London'; 820524-2)*

Feb 68. (7") *(F 12747) <40025>* **DELILAH. / SMILE AWAY YOUR BLUES** 2 Mar68 15

Jul 68. (lp; mono/stereo) *(LK/SKL 4946)* **DELILAH** <US-title 'TOM JONES FEVER ZONE'> 1 Jun68 14
– Delilah / You can't stop love / Only a fool breaks his own heart / Take me / My elusive dreams / Make this heart of mine smile again / Weeping Annaleah / Just out of reach (of my empty arms) / Why can't I cry / Lingering on / One day soon / Laura (what's he got that I ain't got). *(cd-iss. Sep88 on 'London'; 820486-2)*

Jul 68. (7") *(F 12812) <40029>* **HELP YOURSELF. / DAY BY DAY** 5 Aug68 35

Nov 68. (7") *(F 12854) <40035>* **A MINUTE OF YOUR TIME. / LOOKING OUT MY WINDOW** 14 Dec68 48

Nov 68. (lp; mono/stereo) *(LK/SKL 4982) <71025>* **HELP YOURSELF** 4 Jan69 5
– Help yourself / I can't break the news to myself / The bed / Isadora / Set me free / I get carried away / This house (the house song) / So afraid / If I promise / If you go away / My girl Maria / All I can say is goodbye / Ten guitars / What a party. *(cd-iss. Jan89 on 'London'+=; 820559-2)* – Looking out my window / Can't stop loving you / Let there be love / Without love.

May 69. (7") *(F 12924) <40038>* **LOVE ME TONIGHT. / HIDE AND SEEK** 9 13

Jun 69. (lp; mono/stereo) *(LK/SKL 5007) <71028>* **THIS IS TOM JONES** 2 4
– Fly me to the moon / Little green apples / Wichita lineman / (Sittin' on) The dock of the bay / Dance of love / Hey Jude / Without you (non che lei) / That's all any man can say / That wonderful sound / Only once / I'm a fool to want you / Let it be me. *(cd-iss. Nov88 on 'London'; 820234-2)*

Nov 69. (lp; mono/stereo) *(LK/SKL 5032) <71031>* **LIVE IN LAS VEGAS – AT THE FLAMINGO (live)** <US-title 'TOM JONES LIVE IN LAS VEGAS'> 3 3
– Turn on your love light / The bright lights and you girl / I can't stop loving you / Hard to handle / Delilah / Danny boy / (It looks like) I'll never fall in love again / Help yourself / Yesterday / Hey Jude / Love me tonight / It's not unusual / Twist and shout. *(cd-iss. Jun88 on 'London'; 820318-2)*

Dec 69. (7") *(F 12990) <40045>* **WITHOUT LOVE (THERE IS NOTHING). / THE MAN WHO KNOWS TOO MUCH** 10 5

Apr 70. (7") *(F 13013) <40048>* **DAUGHTER OF DARKNESS. / TUPELO MISSISSIPPI FLASH** 5 13

Apr 70. (lp; mono/stereo) *(LK/SKL 5045) <71037>* **TOM** 4 6
– I can't turn you loose / Polk salad Annie / Proud Mary / Sugar, sugar / Venus / I thank you / Without love / You've lost that lovin' feeling / If I ruled the world / Can't stop loving you / Impossible dream / Let there be love.

Aug 70. (7") *(F 13061) <40051>* **I (WHO HAVE NOTHING). / STOP BREAKING MY HEART** 16 14

Nov 70. (lp; mono/stereo) *(LK/SKL 5072) <71039>* **I, WHO HAVE NOTHING** 10 23
– Daughter of darkness / I have dreamed / Love's been good to me / Lodi / Try a little tenderness / I (who have nothing) / What the world needs now is love / With one exception / To love somebody / Brother, can you spare a dime / See-saw.

Nov 70. (7") *<40056>* **CAN'T STOP LOVING YOU. / NEVER GIVE AWAY LOVE** – 25

Jan 71. (7") *(F 13113) <40058>* **SHE'S A LADY. / MY WAY** 13 2

May 71. (lp) *(SKL 5089) <71046>* **TOM JONES SINGS SHE'S A LADY** 9 17
– She's a lady / Do what you gotta do / In dreams / Nothing rhymed / 'Til I can't take it anymore / Resurrection shuffle / Puppet man / It's up to the woman / Eb tide / (I ain't no) One night only love maker / You're my world. *(re-iss. Nov77 on 'E.M.I.'; EMC 3205)*

May 71. (7") *(F 13183) <40062>* **PUPPET MAN. / EVERY MILE** 49 26

Jun 71. (7") *<40064>* **RESURRECTION SHUFFLE. / PUPPET MAN** – 38

Oct 71. (7") *(F 13236)* **TILL. / THE SUN DIED** 2 –

Oct 71. (7") *<40067>* **TILL. / ONE DAY SOON** – 41

Nov 71. (d-lp) *(DKL 1/1-1/2) <71049>* **TOM JONES LIVE AT CAESARS PALACE, LAS VEGAS (live)** 27 Oct71 43
– I'll never fall in love again – Daughter of darkness – Love me tonight – It's not unusual – Hi-heel sneakers (hits medley) / Dance of love / Cabaret / Soul man / I (who have nothing) / Delilah / Bridge over troubled water / My way / God bless the children / Resurrection shuffle / She's a lady / Till / Rock'n'roll medley: Johnny B. Goode – Bony moronie – Long tall Sally. *(re-iss. Oct77 on 'M.F.P.'; 5035-1) (cd/c-iss.Oct91; CD/TC MFP 5931)*

Mar 72. (7") *(F 13298) 40070>* **THE YOUNG NEW MEXICAN PUPPETEER. / ALL THAT I NEED IS SOME TIME** 6 Apr72 80

Jun 72. (lp) *(SKL 5132) <71055>* **CLOSE UP** 17 64
– Witch queen of New Orleans / Tired of being alone / Woman, you took my life / Young New Mexican puppeteer / All I ever need is you / You've got a friend / Time to get it together / I won't be sorry to see Suzanne again / Kiss an angel good mornin'.

Mar 73. (7") *(F 13393) <40074>* **LETTER TO LUCILLE. / THANK THE LORD** 31 May73 60

Jun 73. (lp) *(SKL 5162) <71060>* **THE BODY AND SOUL OF TOM JONES** 31 60
– Runnin' bear / Ain't no sunshine when she's gone / (If loving you is wrong) I don't want to be right / Since I loved you last / Lean on me / Letter to Lucille / Today I started loving you again / I'll share my world with you / I still love you enough (to love you all over again) / Ballad of Billie Joe.

Jul 73. (7") *(F 13434)* **TODAY I STARTED LOVING YOU AGAIN. / I STILL LOVE YOU ENOUGH** –

Nov 73. (7") *(F 13471)* **GOLDEN DAYS. / GOODBYE, GOD BLESS YOU BABY** –

Feb 74. (7") *(F 13490)* **LA LA LA (JUST HAVING YOU HERE). / LOVE LOVE LOVE** –

Aug 74. (7") *(F 13550)* **SOMETHIN' 'BOUT YOU BABY I LIKE. / KEEP A-TALKING 'BOUT LOVE** 36 –

Nov 74. (lp) *(SKL 5197)* **SOMETHIN' 'BOUT YOU BABY I LIKE**
– Somethin' 'bout you baby I like / You make me smile / Till I get it right / Rainin' in my heart / It never hurts to be nice to somebody / Run Cleo run / Make believe world / Which way home / Sing for the good times / Right place, wrong time.

Nov 74. (7") *(F 13564)* **PLEDGING MY LOVE. / I'M FAR TOO GONE (TO TURN AWAY)** –

Apr 75. (7") *(F 13575)* **AIN'T NO LOVE. / WHEN THE BAND GOES HOME**

Jul 75. (7") *(F 13590)* **I GOT YOUR NUMBER. / THE PAIN OF LOVE** –

Sep 75. (7") *(F 13598)* **MEMORIES DON'T LEAVE LIKE PEOPLE DO. / MY HELPING HAND** –

Oct 75. (lp) *(SKL 5214)* **MEMORIES DON'T LEAVE LIKE PEOPLE DO**
– Memories don't leave like people do / I got your number / Pain of love / Mr. Helping hand / City life / Lusty lady / We got love / Son of a fisherman / You inspire me / Us.

E.M.I. Epic

Jan 77. (7") *<50308>* **SAY YOU'LL STAY UNTIL TOMORROW. / LADY LAY** – 15

Jan 77. (7") *(EMI 2583)* **SAY YOU'LL STAY UNTIL TOMORROW. / NOTHING RHYMED** 40 –

Apr 77. (lp) *(EMC 3178) <34468>* **SAY YOU'LL STAY UNTIL TOMORROW** Feb77 76
– Say you'll stay until tomorrow / One man woman, one woman man / Anniversary song / When it's just you and me / Papa / Take me tonight / At every end there's a beginning / Come to me / We had it all / Have you ever been lonely.

Jul 77. (7") *(EMI 2662)* **HAVE YOU EVER BEEN LONELY. / ONE MAN WOMAN, ONE WOMAN MAN**

Feb 78. (7") *(EMI 2756)* **NO ONE GAVE ME LOVE. / THAT'S WHERE I BELONG**

Feb 78. (lp) *(EMC 3221)* **WHAT A NIGHT**
– What a night / We don't live here / No one gave me love / Day to day affair / If this is love / I wrote this song to send my love to you / That's where I belong / Easy to love / The heart / Ramblin' man.

Lotus not iss.

Sep 78. (lp/c) *<WH 5/6 001)* **I'M COMING HOME** 12 –
– (It looks like) I'll never fall in love again / To wait for love (is to waste your life away) / I can't stop loving you / Once there was a time / Untrue / Someday (you'll want me to want you) / To make a big man cry / (Won't you give him) One more chance / He'll have to go / Some other guy / Field of yellow daisies / I wake up crying / Autumn leaves / Funny familiar forgotten feelings. *(cd/c-iss.May93 on 'Spectrum'; 550020-2/-4)*

Columbia Columbia

Jul 79. (7") *(DB 9098)* **DO YOU TAKE THIS MAN. / IF I SING YOU A LOVE SONG** [ ] [ ]

Sep 79. (lp/c) *(SCX/TC-SCX 6620)* **DO YOU TAKE THIS MAN** [ ] [ ]
– Do you take this man / How deep is the ocean / Out of mercy / Baby as you turn away / Go easy lady / Love is in the air / You're so good / Going through the motions / Lady put the light out / If I sing you a love song / But if you'd ever leave me / Hey love it's a feeling.

Jun 80. (lp/c) *(SCX/TC-SCX 6628)* **RESCUE ME** [ ] [ ]
– Rescue me / Never had a lady before / Somebody out there will / Dancing endlessly / Dark storm on the horizon / What becomes of the broken hearted? / Once you hit the road / Flashback / Don't cry for me Argentina.

Polydor Mercury

Oct 81. (lp/c) *(2480/3194 622)* *<4010>* **DARLIN'** [ ] May81 [ ]
– Darlin' / But I do / Lady lay down / No guarentee / What in the world's come over you? / One night / A daughter's question / I don't want to know you that well / Dime queen of Nevada / Things that matter most to me / Come home Rhondda boy. *<re-iss. Aug87 lp/c/cd; 818898-1/-4/-2>*

Nov 81. (7") *(POSP 371)* **COME HOME RHONDDA BOY. / WHAT IN THE WORLD'S COME OVER YOU?** [ ] [ ]

Feb 82. (7") *(POSP 410)* **BUT I DO. / ONE NIGHT WITH YOU** [ ] [ ]

Apr 83. (7") **TOUCH ME (I'LL BE YOUR FOOL ONCE MORE). /** [–] [ ]

Sep 83. (7") **IT'LL BE ME. /** [–] [ ]

Nov 83. (lp) **DON'T LET OUR DREAMS DIE YOUNG** [–] [ ]
– You've got a right / The one I sing my love songs to / This ain't Tennessee and she ain't you / I've been rained on too / You are no angel / Don't let our dreams die young / This time / That old piano / Loving arms of Tennessee / You lay a whole lot of love on me.

Jan 84. (7") **I'VE BEEN RAINED ON TOO. /** [–] [ ]

May 84. (7") **THIS TIME. /** [–] [ ]

Nov 84. (lp) **LOVE IS ON THE RADIO** [–] [ ]
– My kind of girl / All the love is on the radio / That runaway woman of mine / Give her all the roses (don't wait until tomorrow) / Bad love / A picture of you / The moonlight hours / Still a friend of mine / Only my heart knows / I'm an old rock and roller (dancin' to a different beat).

Dec 84. (7") **I'M AN OLD ROCK'N'ROLLER (DANCING TO A DIFFERENT BEAT). /** [–] [ ]

RCA Camden Mercury

Mar 85. (lp/c) *(CDS/CAM 2074)* **THE COUNTRY SIDE OF TOM JONES** [ ] [–]
– (his US-only releases from 1983-85)

1986. (lp) **TENDER LOVING CARE** [–] [ ]

1986. (7") **IT'S FOUR IN THE MORNING. /** [–] [ ]

Epic Epic

Apr 87. (7") *(OLE 1)* **A BOY FROM NOWHERE. / (excerpts from I'LL DRESS YOU IN MOURNING + DANCE WITH DEATH + TO BE A MATADOR)** [2] [ ]
(12"+=) *(OLET 1)* – (full B-side versions).

Apr 87. (lp/c/cd) *(VIVA/+MC/CD 1)* **MATADOR – THE MUSICAL LIFE OF EL CORDOBES** [26] [ ]
– Overture / There's no way out of here / To be a matador / I was born to be me / Only other people / Manolete! Belmonte! Joselito! / A boy from nowhere / Wake up Madrid / I'll take you out to dinner / This incredible journey / Don't be deceived / I'll dress you in mourning / Dance with death / A Panama hat.

Nov 87. (7"/7"s) *(OLE/+Q 4)* **I WAS BORN TO BE ME. / A PANAMA HAT** [ ] [ ]
(12"+=) *(OLET 4)* – A boy from nowhere.

— In Oct'88, JONES collaborated with The ART OF NOISE on a joint single, 'KISS', which hit UK No.5 & US No.31.

Jive Jive

Apr 89. (7") *(JIVE 203)* **MOVE CLOSER. / 'TIL THE END OF TIME** [49] [ ]
(12"+=/cd-s+=) *(JIVET 203)* – ('A'instrumental).

Apr 89. (lp/c/cd) *(TOM TV/TC/CD 1)* **AT THIS MOMENT** [34] [–]
– Kiss / Move closer / Who's gonna take you home tonight / I'm counting on you / 'Til the end of time / What you been missing / After the tears / I can't get no satisfaction / Touch my heart.

Sep 89. (7") *(JIVE 209)* **AT THIS MOMENT. / AFTER THE TEARS** [ ] [ ]
(12") *(JIVEX 209)* – ('A'side) / Green, green grass of home (live) / It's not unusual (live).
(cd-s) *(JIVECD 209)* – ('A'side) / Help yourself (live) / I'll never fall in love again (live) / Delilah (live).

Dover-Chrysalis Chrysalis

Jan 91. (7") *(ROJ 10)* **COULDN'T SAY GOODBYE. / ZIP IT UP** [51] [ ]
(12"+=/cd-s+=) *(ROJ T/CD 10)* – Kiss (Art Of Noise remix).

Mar 91. (7") *(ROJ 12)* **CARRYING A TORCH. / WALK TALL (VALLEY OF THE SHADOWS)** [ ] [ ]
(12"+=/cd-s+=) *(ROJ T/CD 12)* – ('A'mix).

Mar 91. (cd/c/lp) *(CCD/ZDD/ADD 20)* **CARRYING A TORCH** [44] [ ]
– Carrying a torch / Some peace of mind / Stage boat / I'm not feelin' it anymore / Do I ever cross your mind / Fool for rock'n'roll / Only in America / Couldn't say goodbye / Killer in the sheets / Give me a chance / Zip it up / It must be you / Old flame blue.

Childline not iss.

Jan 93. (c-s/cd-s) *(CHILD C/CD 93)* **ALL YOU NEED IS LOVE / ('A'mixes; with DAVE STEWART)** [19] [–]

Z.T.T. Interscope

Oct 94. (7"/c-s) *(ZANG 59/+C)* **IF I ONLY KNEW. / (version)** [11] [–]
(12"+=/cd-s+=) *(ZANG 59 T/CD)* – ('A'-Fade out version).

Nov 94. (cd/c/lp) *(6544 92498-2/-4/-1)* *<IND 92498>* **THE LEAD AND HOW TO SWING IT** [55] [ ]
– If I only knew / A girl like you / I wanna get back with you / Situation / Something for your head / Fly away / Love is on our side / I don't think so / Life me up / Show me / I'm ready / Changes. *(cd re-iss. Sep97 on 'Interscope'; IND 92498)*

Mar 95. (7"/c-s) *(ZANG 64/+C)* **I WANNA GET BACK WITH YOU (featuring TORI AMOS). / IF I ONLY KNEW** [ ] [–]
(12"+=/cd-s+=) *(ZANG 64 T/CD)* – Situation / I don't think so.

Gut Mushroom

Sep 99. (c-s; TOM JONES & The CARDIGANS) *(CAGUT 026)* **BURNING DOWN THE HOUSE / (Delakota mix) / (Pepe Deluxe mix)** [7] [–]
(cd-s+=) *(CDGUT 026)* – ('A'-DJ Scissorkicks instrumental).
(cd-s) *(CXGUT 026)* – ('A'live) / Unbelievable (live) / Come together (live).

Sep 99. (cd/c) *(GUT CD/MC 009)* *<33251>* **RELOAD** [1] Nov99 [ ]
– Burning down the house (with the CARDIGANS) / Mama told me not to come (with STEREOPHONICS) / Are you gonna go my way (with ROBBIE WILLIAMS) / All mine (with the DIVINE COMEDY) / Sunny afternoon (with SPACE) / I'm left, you're right, she's gone (with JAMES DEAN BRADFIELD) / Sex bomb (with MOUSSE T.) / You need love like I do (with HEATHER SMALL) / Looking out of my window (with JAMES TAYLOR QUARTET) / Sometimes we cry (with VAN MORRISON) / Lust for life (with the PRETENDERS) / Little green bag (with BARENAKED LADIES) / Ain't that a lot of love (with SIMPLY RED) / She drives me crazy (with ZUCCHERO) / Never tear us apart (with NATALIE IMBRUGLIA) / Baby, it's cold outside (with CERYS from CATATONIA) / Motherless child (with PORTISHEAD). *(cd+=)* – Green green grass of home / (It looks like) I'll never fall in love again.

Dec 99. (c-s; TOM JONES & CERYS from CATATONIA) *(CAGUT 029)* **BABY, IT'S COLD OUTSIDE / (part 2)** [17] [–]
(cd-s+=) *(CDGUT 029)* – ('A'-At the Speakeasy).

Mar 00. (c-s/cd-s; TOM JONES & STEREOPHONICS) *(CA/CD GUT 031)* **MAMA TOLD ME NOT TO COME / Tom Jones & James Taylor Quartet: LOOKING OUT OF MY WINDOW** [4] [–]
(cd-s) *(CXGUT 031)* – ('A'mixes).

May 00. (c-s/cd-s; TOM JONES & MOUSSE T) *(CA/CD GUT 033)* **SEX BOMB / (peppermint disco mix)** [3] [–]
(12"+=/cd-s+=) *(12/CX GUT 033)* – (mixes; strike / sounds of..)

Nov 00. (c-s/cd-s; TOM JONES & HEATHER SMALL) *(CA/CD GUT 036)* **YOU NEED LOVE LIKE I DO / (fused mix) / Kiss (live)** [24] [–]
(cd-s+=) *(CXGUT 036)* – (double click mix).

V2 V2

Oct 02. (c-s) *(VVR 502108-5)* **INTERNATIONAL / (mix)** [31] [–]
(cd-s) *(VVR 502108-3)* – ('A'mixes).

Nov 02. (cd/c) *(<VVR 102107-2/-4>)* **MR. JONES** [36] Dec02 [ ]
– International / Younger days / Holiday / Whatever it takes / Heaven's been a long time comin' / Black Betty / Jezebel / The letter (with ALLURE) / This is my life / We've got tonight / Feel the rain / I who have nothing.

Feb 03. (cd-s) *(VVR 502176-3)* *<2321-3>* **BLACK BETTY / I WHO HAVE NOTHING / BLACK BETTY (mixes)** [50] Dec02 [ ]

– (selective) compilations, etc. –

May 65. (7") *Columbia; (DB 7566) / Tower; <126>* **LITTLE LONELY ONE. / THAT'S WHAT WE'LL DO** [ ] [42]

Dec 73. (lp) *Decca; (SKL 5176) / Parrot; <71062>* **TOM JONES' GREATEST HITS** [15] [ ]

Mar 75. (d-lp/d-c) *Decca; (TJD 1-1/1-2)* **20 GREATEST HITS** [1] [–]

May 87. (lp/c/cd) *Telstar; (STAR/STAC/TCD 2296)* **TOM JONES – THE GREATEST HITS** [16] [–]

May 87. (7") *London; (F 103)* **IT'S NOT UNUSUAL. / DELILAH** [17] [–]
(12"+=) *(FX 103)* – ('A'extended) / Land of a 1000 dances (live).

Jul 87. (lp/c)(cd) *Decca; (TOM/KTOM 2)(820544-2)* **IT'S NOT UNUSUAL – HIS GREATEST HITS** [ ] [–]

Jun 89. (lp/c/cd) *Stylus; (SMR/SMC/SMD 978)* **AFTER DARK** [46] [–]

Jun 92. (cd/c/lp) *London; 844286-2/-4/-1)* **THE COMPLETE TOM JONES** [8] [–]
– It's tot unusual / Delilah / Kiss / (It looks like) I'll never fall in love again / She's a lady / Green green grass of home / Love me tonight / Without love / Daughter of darkness / A boy from nowhere / What's new pussycat? / I'm coming home / Help yourself / I (who have nothing) / Move closer / Detroit city / Couldn't say goodbye / Till / Something 'bout you baby I like / The young New Mexican puppeteer.

Apr 98. (cd) *Repertoire; (REP 4694)* **I, WHO HAVE NOTHING / SHE'S A LADY** [ ] [–]

Apr 98. (cd) *Repertoire; (REP 4695)* **THE YOUNG NEW MEXICAN PUPPETEER / THE BODY AND SOUL OF TOM JONES** [ ] [–]

Feb 03. (cd) *Universal TV; (8828623) <068608>* **GREATEST HITS** [2] [ ]
– It's not unusual / What's new pussycat? / Green green grass of home / Delilah / Funny familiar feelings / I'll never fall in love again / I'm coming home / Help yourself / Love me tonight / She's a lady / Thunderball / Without love / Daughter of darkness / If I only knew / Till / The young New Mexican puppeteer / The boy from nowhere / Kiss / Burning down the house (with CARDIGANS) / Baby it's cold outside (with CERYS MATTHEWS) / Mama told me not to come (with STEREOPHONICS) / Sex bomb (with MOUSSE T) / The Full Monty medley (with ROBBIE WILLIAMS).

Janis JOPLIN

Born: 19 Jan'43, Port Arthur, Texas, USA. In the early 60's, she hitched to California and San Francisco, where she sang in The WALLER CREEK BOYS trio alongside future 13th FLOOR ELEVATORS member R.POWELL ST.JOHN. In 1963, she subsequently appeared opposite JORMA KAUKONEN (later JEFFERSON AIRPLANE) at local night spots. In 1966, after nearly giving up singing and her hippy drug-taking ways for a life of domesticity, she returned to Texas where she briefly rehearsed with The 13th FLOOR ELEVATORS. That same year, she again ventured to San Francisco, this time joining BIG BROTHER & THE HOLDING COMPANY. They released two albums, the second of which, 'CHEAP THRILLS', stayed at the top of the US charts for 8 weeks. When they temporarily folded late in '68, she went solo, although her alcohol and drug abuse was becoming increasingly pronounced. After three major concerts; London's Royal Albert Hall, Newport Festival and New Orleans Pop Festival, she unleashed her 1969 solo debut, 'I GOT DEM OL' KOSMIC BLUES AGAIN', which made the US Top 5. In May '70, she formed her new backing group, The FULL-TILT BOOGIE BAND, beginning work on an album in the Autumn of 1970. Before it was completed, however, on the 4th of October 1970, JANIS was found dead in her Hollywood hotel room. The coroner's verdict reported that her death was due to an accidental drug overdose. Early in 1971, her last recording, 'PEARL' was issued, topping the US charts for 9 weeks, also giving her a first taste of UK chart action. She again hit pole position in the States with a great version of KRIS KRISTOFFERSON's 'ME AND BOBBY McGEE'. But for her death, she would probably have become the greatest female singer of all-time, her powerful 3-octave vocals having the capacity to transform the most run-of-the-mill tune into a tour de force. • **Songwriters:** She used many outside writers, including JERRY RAGAVOY, and covered; PIECE OF MY HEART (hit; Erma Franklin) / MAYBE (Chantells) / TO LOVE SOMEBODY (Bee Gees) / etc. • **Trivia:** In 1979, a film, 'The Rose', was released based on her life, featuring BETTE MIDLER in her role.

Album rating: I GOT DEM OL' KOSMIC BLUES AGAIN MAMA (*6) / PEARL (*7) / JOPLIN IN CONCERT posthumous (*5) / JANIS JOPLIN'S GREATEST HITS compilation (*8) / JANIS early stuff (*4) / FAREWELL SONG (*4) / 18 ESSENTIAL SONGS compilation (*8)

JANIS JOPLIN – vocals (ex-BIG BROTHER & THE HOLDING COMPANY) / **SAM ANDREW** – guitar (ex-BIG BROTHER & THE HOLDING COMPANY) / others in her KOZMIC BLUES BAND were **BRAD CAMPBELL** (aka KEITH CHERRY) – bass / **TERRY CLEMENTS** – saxophone / **RICHARD KERMODE** – organ repl. BILL KING (Feb69) / **LONNIE CASTILLE** – drums repl. ROY MARKOWITZ (Apr69) / **TERRY HENSLEY** – trumpet repl. MARCUS DOUBLEDAY (Apr69) / added **SNOOKY FLOWERS** – saxophone (Feb69)

—— (Jul69) **JOHN TILL** – guitar, vocals repl. SAM ANDREW / **MAURY BAKER** – drums repl. CASTILLE / **DAVE WOODWARD** – trumpet repl. GASCA who repl. HENSLEY

C.B.S. Columbia

Oct 69. (lp) *(CBS 63546) <9913>* **I GOT DEM OL' KOZMIC BLUES AGAIN MAMA!** [ ] [5]
– Try (just a little bit harder) / Maybe / One good man / As good as you've been to this world / To love somebody / Kozmic blues / Little girl blue / Work me, Lord. *(re-iss. 1983 lp/c; CBS/40 32063) (cd-iss. 1988; CD 63546) (cd re-iss. Jan91;)*

Nov 69. (7") *<45023>* **KOZMIC BLUES. / LITTLE GIRL BLUE** [–] [41]

Dec 69. (7"w-drawn) *(CBS 3683)* **TURTLE BLUES. / PIECE OF MY HEART** [–] [–]

Jan 70. (7") *<45080>* **TRY (JUST A LITTLE BIT HARDER). / ONE GOOD MAN** [–] [ ]

Apr 70. (7") *<45128>* **MAYBE. / WORK ME, LORD** [–] [ ]

—— JANIS JOPLIN & THE FULL TILT BOOGIE BAND retained **CAMPBELL** and **TILL** / added **RICHARD BELL** – piano / **KEN PEARSON** – organ / **CLARK PIERSON** – drums/ On the 4th Oct70, JANIS died of a drug overdose. She had just recorded below album

Jan 71. (lp) *(CBS 64188) <30322>* **PEARL** [50] [1]
– Move over / Cry baby / A woman left lonely / Half Moon / Buried alive in the blues / My baby / Me and Bobby McGee / Mercedes Benz / Trust me / Get it while you can. *(re-iss. Jan84 lp/c; CBS/40 32064) (cd-iss. 1988; CD 64188) (cd re-iss. Jan91 & Jul95 on 'Columbia'; 480415-2)*

Jan 71. (7") *(CBS 7019) <45314>* **ME AND BOBBY McGEE. / HALF MOON** [ ] [1]

May 71. (7") *(CBS 7217) <45379>* **CRY BABY. / MERCEDES BENZ** [ ] [42]

Sep 71. (7") *<45433>* **GET IT WHILE YOU CAN. / MOVE OVER** [–] [78]

– other posthumous JANIS JOPLIN releases –

on 'CBS' UK / 'Columbia' US unless mentioned otherwise

Oct 71. (7"ep) *(CBS 9136)* **MOVE OVER / CRY BABY. / TRY (JUST A LITTLE BIT HARDER) / PIECE OF MY HEART** [ ] [ ]

Jul 72. (d-lp) *(CBS 67241) <31160>* **JANIS JOPLIN IN CONCERT (live half with BIG BROTHER & THE HOLDING COMPANY / half with FULL TILT BOOGIE BAND)** [30] May72 [4]
– Down on me / Bye, bye baby / All is loneliness / Piece of my heart / Road block / Flower in the sun / Summertime / Ego rock / Half moon / Kozmic blues / Move over / Try (just a little bit harder) / Get it while you can / Ball and chain. *(re-iss. Sep87; 460128-1/4) (cd-iss. Aug93; 466838-2)*

Jul 72. (7") *(CBS 8241) <45630>* **DOWN ON ME (live). / BYE, BYE BABY (live)** [ ] [91]

Jul 73. (lp) *(CBS 65470) <32168>* **JANIS JOPLIN'S GREATEST HITS** [ ] [37]
– Piece of my heart / Summertime / Try (just a little bit harder) / Cry baby / Me and Bobby McGee / Down on me / Get it while you can / Bye, bye baby / Move over / Ball and chain. *(re-iss. Sep82 & May90 lp/c; CBS/40 32190) (cd-iss. 1988; 831 726-2) (cd re-iss. Oct94 on 'Sony'; 476555-2)*

May 75. (d-lp) *(CBS 88115) <33345>* **JANIS (soundtrack)** [ ] [54]
(includes rare 1963-65 material)

1975. (7") *(13-33205)* **ME AND BOBBY McGHEE. / GET IT WHILE YOU CAN** [ ] [–]

Mar 76. (7") *(CBS 3960)* **PIECE OF MY HEART. / KOZMIC BLUES** [ ] [–]

Jul 80. (d-lp) <*(CBS 88492)*> **ANTHOLOGY**
(d-cd-iss. Jun97 on 'Columbia'; 467 405-2)
Feb 82. (lp) *(CBS 85354)* **FAREWELL SONG**
Nov 84. (d-c) **PEARL / CHEAP THRILLS**
Jun 86. (lp/c) *(CBS/40 54731)* **GOLDEN HIGHLIGHTS OF JANIS JOPLIN** | | – |
Dec 90. (3xcd-box) *(467387-2)* **CHEAP THRILLS / PEARL / I GOT DEM OL' KOZMIC BLUES AGAIN** | | – |
Sep 92. (d-cd) *Sony; (4610202)* **PEARL / I GOT DEM OL' KOZMIC BLUES AGAIN!**
Nov 92. (cd) *I.T.M.; (ITM 960001)* **MAGIC OF LOVE** | | – |
Sep 93. (cd) *I.T.M.; (ITM 960007)* **LIVE AT WOODSTOCK, 1969 (live)**
Jan 94. (3xcd-box) *Legacy; (CD 48845-2)* **JANIS**
Dec 94. (cd) *Columbia;* **THE BEST**
Apr 95. (cd) *Legacy; (478515-2)* **18 ESSENTIAL SONGS** | | – |
Aug 98. (cd) *Sony; (491683)* **THE ULTIMATE COLLECTION** | 26 | |

JOURNEY

Formed: San Francisco, California, USA . . . early 1973, originally as The GOLDEN GATE BRIDGE by NEAL SCHON, GEORGE TICKNER, ROSS VALORY and PRAIRIE PRINCE. Due to manager Walter Herbert auditioning through a radio station for the group name, they settled with JOURNEY. They made their live debut on the 31st of December 1973 in front of over 10,000 people at San Francisco's 'Wonderland' venue. Prior to the recording of their eponymous first album in 1975, (the group had secured a deal with 'Columbia'), another SANTANA veteran, GREGG ROLIE, was added, while English-born AYNSLEY DUNBAR replaced the TUBES-bound PRINCE. The debut, and subsequent releases, 'LOOK INTO THE FUTURE' (1976) and 'NEXT' (1977), focused on jazzy art-rock, although major changes were afoot by 1978's 'INFINITY'. With the addition of ex-ALIEN PROJECT vocalist, STEVE PERRY, the group were transformed from noodling jam-merchants into sleek AOR-pomp exponents set for American FM radio domination. Produced by Roy Thomas Baker (QUEEN), the album saw PERRY's strident, impressively dynamic vocals given free rein over a new improved pop-friendly format, gleaming synths and irresistible hooks now the order of the day. The record also gave JOURNEY a near brush with the Top 20, a feat they'd achieve with 'EVOLUTION' (1979). By this juncture, DUNBAR had departed for JEFFERSON STARSHIP, his replacement being STEVE SMITH on a set which provided JOURNEY with their biggest hit single to date (Top 20) in 'LOVIN', TOUCHIN', SQUEEZIN'. The following year's 'DEPARTURE' album performed even better, JOURNEY finally nearing their ultimate destination, i.e. the top of the US charts. Enhanced by the polished pop instincts of ex-BABYS' frontman JONATHAN CAIN (a replacement for ROLIE, who went solo, later forming The STORM with VALORY and SMITH), JOURNEY scored their first (and only) No.1 album with the massively successful 'ESCAPE' (1981). The record spawned an unprecedented three US Top 10 hits, namely 'WHO'S CRYING NOW', 'OPEN ARMS' and the swooning 'DON'T STOP BELIEVIN'. Despite almost universal critical derision from the more elitist factions of the music press, JOURNEY continued to capture the lucrative middle ground between pop and tasteful metal, even breaking into the previously impenetrable UK Top 10 with 'FRONTIERS' (1983). The same month, SCHON released his second solo collaboration with keyboard wizard, JAN HAMMER, 'HERE TO STAY', while PERRY subsequently launched his solo career to huge success with the melodramatic 'OH SHERRIE' single and 'STREET TALK' (1984) album. JOURNEY eventually regrouped in the mid-80's, the band now comprising the core trio of PERRY, SCHON and CAIN, augmented by RANDY JACKSON and LARRIE LONDIN. The resulting album, 'RAISED ON RADIO' (1986) proved to be JOURNEY's end, the group bowing out on a high point. Following an official split in early '87, CAIN (along with VALORY) joined MICHAEL BOLTON, while SCHON eventually hooked up with JOHN WAITE in BAD ENGLISH, before forming HARDLINE in '92 with ROLIE and SMITH. With reunion fever all the rage in the 90's, JOURNEY finally got back together in 1996 for the successful 'TRIAL BY FIRE' album. Fans were disappointed, however, with the subsequent departure of PERRY and his replacement with STEVE AUGERI. Although a relative soundalike, AUGERI couldn't quite match PERRY's charisma on 'ARRIVAL' (2001), a blatant attempt to capture the spirit of the band's early 80's golden period. • **Trivia:** A couple of JOURNEY tracks, featured on the 1980 & 1981 film soundtracks of 'Caddyshack' & 'Heavy Metal'.

Album rating: JOURNEY (*3) / LOOK INTO THE FUTURE (*4) / NEXT (*3) / IN THE BEGINNING compilation (*4) / INFINITY (*6) / EVOLUTION (*5) / DEPARTURE (*4) / CAPTURED (*7) / ESCAPE (*8) / FRONTIERS (*6) / RAISED ON RADIO (*7) / THE BEST OF JOURNEY compilation (*8) / TIME 3 compilation (*7) / TRIAL BY FIRE (*4) / ARRIVAL (*5) / THE ESSENTIAL JOURNEY compilation (*8)

NEAL SCHON (b.27 Feb'54, San Mateo, Calif.) – lead guitar, vocals (ex-SANTANA) / **GREGG ROLIE** (b.17 Jun'47) – vocals, keyboards (ex-SANTANA) / **GEORGE TICKNER** – guitar, vocals / **ROSS VALORY** (b. 2 Feb'49) – bass, vocals (ex-STEVE MILLER BAND) / **AYNSLEY DUNBAR** (b.1946, Liverpool, England) – drums (ex-FRANK ZAPPA, ex-JOHN MAYALL, ex-JEFF BECK) repl. PRAIRIE PRINCE who joined The TUBES

C.B.S. | Columbia

Apr 75. (lp/c) *(CBS/40 80724)* <*33388*> **JOURNEY**
– Of a lifetime / In the morning day / Kohoutek / To play some music / Topaz / In my lonely feeling – Conversations / Mystery mountain. *(cd-iss. Oct93 on 'Sony Collectors'; 983313-2) (cd re-iss. Oct94 on 'Columbia'; 477854-2)*
Jun 75. (7") <*10137*> **TO PLAY SOME MUSIC. / TOPAZ** | – | |
— (Apr'75) reverted to a quartet when TICKNER departed
Jan 76. (lp/c) *(CBS/40 69203)* <*33904*> **LOOK INTO THE FUTURE** | | 100 |
– On a Saturday nite / It's all too much / Anyway / She makes me (feel alright) / You're on your own / Look into the future / Midnight dreamer / I'm gonna leave you. *(re-iss. Mar82; CBS 32102)*
Mar 76. (7") <*10324*> **ON A SATURDAY NIGHT. / TO PLAY SOME MUSIC** | – | |
Jul 76. (7") <*10370*> **SHE MAKES ME (FEEL ALRIGHT). / IT'S ALL TOO MUCH** | – | |
Feb 77. (7") <*10522*> **SPACEMAN. / NICKEL AND DIME** | – | |
Feb 77. (lp/c) *(CBS/40 81554)* <*34311*> **NEXT** | | 85 |
– Spaceman / People / I would find you / Here we are / Hustler / Next / Nickel & dime / Karma.
— (Jun'77) added **ROBERT FLEISCHMAN** – lead vocals
— (Oct77) **STEVE PERRY** (b.22 Jan'53, Hanford, Calif.) – lead vocals; repl. FLEISCHMAN
Mar 78. (7") *(CBS 6238)* <*10700*> **WHEEL IN THE SKY. / CAN DO** | | 57 |
May 78. (lp/c) *(CBS/40 82244)* <*34912*> **INFINITY** | | Feb78 21 |
– Lights / Feeling that way / Anytime / La do da / Patiently / Wheel in the sky / Somethin' to hide / Winds of March / Can do / Opened the door. *(cd-iss. 1988; CD 82244) (cd re-iss. Nov96 on 'Columbia'; 486665-2)*
Jun 78. (7") <*10757*> **ANYTIME. / CAN DO** | – | 83 |
Aug 78. (7") *(CBS 6392)* **LIGHTS. / OPEN THE DOOR** | | – |
Aug 78. (7") <*10800*> **LIGHTS. / SOMETHIN' TO HIDE** | – | 68 |
— (Nov'78) **STEVE SMITH** – drums repl. DUNBAR who joined JEFFERSON STARSHIP (above now alongside SCHON, ROLIE, PERRY and VALORY)
Apr 79. (lp/c) *(CBS/40 83566)* <*35797*> **EVOLUTION** | 100 | 20 |
– Sweet and simple / Just the same way / Do you recall / City of angels / Lovin', touchin', squeezin' / Daydream / When you're alone (it ain't easy) / Lady luck / Too late / Lovin' you is easy / Majestic. *(re-iss. Jul83 lp/c; CBS/40 32342) (cd-iss. Oct93 on 'Sony Collectors'; 982737-2) (cd re-iss. Nov96 on 'Columbia'; 486666-2)*
Apr 79. (7") <*10928*> **JUST THE SAME WAY. / SOMETHIN' TO HIDE** | – | 58 |

Sep 79. (7") *(CBS 7890) <11036>* **LOVIN', TOUCHIN', SQUEEZIN'. / DAYDREAM** Jul79 16
Dec 79. (7") *<11143>* **TOO LATE. / DO YOU RECALL** – 70
Feb 80. (7") *<11213>* **ANY WAY YOU WANT IT. / WHEN YOU'RE ALONE (IT AIN'T EASY)** – 23
Mar 80. (lp/c) *(CBS/40 84101) <36339>* **DEPARTURE** 8
– Any way you want it / Walks like a lady / Someday soon / People and places / Precious time / Where were you / I'm cryin' / Line of fire / Departure / Good morning girl / Stay awhile / Homemade love. *(re-iss. Feb86 lp/c; CBS/40 32714) (cd-iss. 1987; CD 84101) (cd re-iss. Nov96 on 'Columbia'; 486667-2)*
May 80. (7"/12") *(CBS/12 8558)* **ANY WAY YOU WANT IT. / DO YOU RECALL** –
May 80. (7") *<11275>* **WALKS LIKE A LADY. / PEOPLE AND PLACES** –
Aug 80. (7") *<11339>* **GOOD MORNING GIRL. / STAY AWHILE** – 55
Feb 81. (d-lp) *(CBS 88525) <37016>* **CAPTURED (live)** 9
– Majestic / Where were you / Just the same way / Line of fire / Lights / Stay awhile / Too late / Dixie highway / Feeling that way / Anytime / Do you recall / Walks like a lady / La do da / Lovin', touchin', squeezin' / Wheel in the sky / Any way you want it / The party's over (hopelessly in love). *(re-iss. Sep87 d-lp/d-c/cd; 451132-1/-4/-2) (cd re-iss. Jun89; CD 88525) (cd re-iss. Nov96 on 'Columbia'; 486661-2)*
Mar 81. (7") *(CBS 9578) <60505>* **THE PARTY'S OVER (HOPELESSLY IN LOVE) (live). / WHEEL IN THE SKY (live)** Feb81 34

—— (Apr'81) **JONATHAN CAIN** (b.26 Feb'50, Chicago, Illinois) – keyboards, guitar, vocals (ex-BABYS) repl. ROLIE who went solo, and later formed The STORM with VALORY and SMITH

Aug 81. (lp/c) *(CBS/40 85138) <37408>* **ESCAPE** 32 1
– Don't stop believin' / Stone in love / Who's crying now / Keep on runnin' / Still they ride / Escape / Lay it down / Dead or alive / Mother, father / Open arms. *(cd-iss. May87; CD 85138) (re-iss. Feb88 lp/c; 460185-1/-4) (cd re-iss. Apr89; 460285-2) (cd re-iss. Nov96 on 'Columbia'; 486662-2)*
Jul 81. (7") *<02241>* **WHO'S CRYING NOW. / MOTHER, FATHER** – 4
Aug 81. (7"/12") *(A/TA 1467)* **WHO'S CRYING NOW. / ESCAPE** –
Dec 81. (7"/12"/12"pic-d) *(A/+13/11 1728) <02567>* **DON'T STOP BELIEVIN'. / NATURAL THING** 62 Oct81 9
Apr 82. (7") *(A 2057) <02687>* **OPEN ARMS. / LITTLE GIRL** Jan82 2
May 82. (7") *<02883>* **STILL THEY RIDE. / RAZA DEL SOL** – 19
Aug 82. (7") *(A 2725)* **WHO'S CRYING NOW. / DON'T STOP BELIEVIN'** 46 –
(12") *(TA 2725)* – ('A'side) / The Journey story (14 best snips).
Oct 82. (7") *(A 2890)* **STONE IN LOVE. / ONLY SOLUTIONS** –
Feb 83. (lp/c) *(CBS/40 25261) <38504>* **FRONTIERS** 6 2
– Separate ways (worlds apart) / Send her my love / Chain reaction / After the fall / Faithfully / Edge of the blade / Troubled child / Back talk / Frontiers / Rubicon. *(cd-iss. 1988; CD 25261) (cd re-iss. Nov96 on 'Columbia'; 486663-2)*
Feb 83. (7"/12") *(A/+13 3077) <03513>* **SEPARATE WAYS (WORLDS APART). / FRONTIERS** 8
Apr 83. (7") *<03840>* **FAITHFULLY. / FRONTIERS** – 12
Apr 83. (7") *(A 3358)* **FAITHFULLY. / EDGE OF THE BLADE** –
Jul 83. (7") *<04004>* **AFTER THE FALL. / OTHER SOLUTIONS** – 23
Jul 83. (7") *(A 3692)* **AFTER THE FALL. / RUBICON** –
(12"+=) *(TA 3692)* – Any way you want me / Don't stop believin'.
Sep 83. (7") *<04151>* **SEND HER MY LOVE. / CHAIN REACTION** –

—— (the band take on some solo projects, see further below)

Feb 85. (7") *(A 6058) <29090>* **ONLY THE YOUNG. / (B-side by Sammy Hagar)** Jan85 9
(above songs from the film 'Vision Quest' on 'Geffen' records)

—— **PERRY, SCHON and CAIN** regrouped and added **RANDY JACKSON** – bass (ex-ZEBRA) / **LARRIE LONDIN** – drums

Apr 86. (7") *(A 7095) <05869>* **BE GOOD TO YOURSELF. / ONLY THE YOUNG** 9
(12"+=) *(TA 7095)* – Any way you want it / Stone in love.
(d7"+=) *(DA 7095)* – After the fall / Rubicon.
May 86. (lp/c/cd) *(CBS/40/CD 26902) <39936>* **RAISED ON RADIO** 22 4
– Girl can't help it / Positive touch / Suzanne / Be good to yourself / Once you love somebody / Happy to give / Raised on radio / I'll be alright without you / It could have been you / The eyes of a woman / Why can't this night go on forever. *(re-iss. Apr91 on 'Columbia' cd/c; 467992-2/-4) (cd re-iss. Nov96 on 'Columbia'; 486664-2)*
Jul 86. (7") *(A 7265) <06134>* **SUZANNE. / ASK THE LONELY** Jun86 17
(12"+=) *(TA 7265)* – Raised on radio.

—— (Aug'86) **MIKE BAIRD** – drums repl. LONDIN

Oct 86. (7") *(650116-7) <06302>* **GIRL CAN'T HELP IT. / IT COULD HAVE BEEN YOU** Aug86 17
Dec 86. (7") *<06301>* **I'LL BE ALRIGHT WITHOUT YOU. / THE EYES OF A WOMAN** – 14
Apr 87. (7") *<07043>* **WHY CAN'T THIS NIGHT GO ON FOREVER. / POSITIVE TOUCH** – 60

—— split early '87. CAIN and VALORY joined MICHAEL BOLTON. SCHON joined BAD ENGLISH in '89, then HARDLINE in '92 with ROLIE and SMITH.

NEAL SCHON / JAN HAMMER

collaboration with HAMMER – keyboards (solo)

C.B.S. Columbia

Nov 81. (lp/c) *(CBS/40 85355) <37600>* **UNTOLD PASSION** (instrumental) Oct81
– Wasting time / I'm talking to you / The ride / I'm down / Arc / It's alright / Hooked on love / On the beach / Untold passion.
Feb 83. (lp/c) *(CBS/40 25229) <38428>* **HERE TO STAY**
– No more lies / Don't stay away / (You think you're) So hot / Turnaround / Self defence / Long time / Time again / Sticks and stones / Peace of mind / Covered by midnight.
Mar 83. (7") *<03785>* **NO MORE LIES. / SELF DEFENCE** –

—— **NEAL SCHON** collaborated next (May'84) on album 'THROUGH THE FIRE' with **SAMMY HAGAR, KENNY AARONSON & MIKE SHRIEVE.**

STEVE PERRY

C.B.S. Columbia

May 84. (7") *(A 4342) <04391>* **OH SHERRIE. / DON'T TELL ME WHY YOU'RE LEAVING** Mar84 3
(12"+=) *(TA 4342)* – I believe.
May 84. (lp/c) *(CBS/40 25967) <39334>* **STREET TALK** Apr84 12
– Oh Sherrie / I believe / Go away / Foolish heart / It's only love / She's mine / You should be happy / Running alone / Captured by the moment / Strung out.
Jul 84. (7") *(A 4638) <04496>* **SHE'S MINE. / YOU SHOULD BE HAPPY** Jun84 21
Sep 84. (7") *<04598>* **STRUNG OUT. / CAPTURED BY THE MOMENT** – 40
Jan 85. (7") *(A 6017) <04693>* **FOOLISH HEART. / IT'S ONLY LOVE** Nov84 18

—— STEVE PERRY released solo recordings between 88-89. In Aug'94, 'Columbia' issued his album 'FOR THE LOVE OF STRANGE MEDICINE' (it hit UK No.64), the record included US hits, 'YOU BETTER WAIT' and 'MISSING YOU'.

The STORM

ROLIE – vocals, keyboards / **ROSS VALORY** – bass / **STEVE SMITH** – drums) with **KEVIN CHALFANT** – vocals (ex-707) / **JOSH RAMOS** – guitar (ex-LE MANS)

East West Interscope

Oct 91. (c-s) *<98726>* **I'VE GOT A LOT TO LEARN ABOUT LOVE / GIMME LOVE** – 26
Nov 91. (cd/c/lp) *<(7567 91741-2/-4/-1)>* **THE STORM**
– You got me waiting / I've got a lot to learn about love / In the raw / You're gonna miss me / Call me / Show me the way / I want you back / Still loving you / Touch and go / Gimme love / Take me away / Can't live without your love.

—— **RON WIKSO** – drums; repl. SMITH

not iss. Miramar

Mar 98. (cd) *<23102>* **EYE OF THE STORM** –
– Don't give up / Waiting for the world to change / I want to be the one / To have and to hold / Livin' it up / Love isn't easy / Fight for the right / Give me tonight / Soul of a man / What ya doing tonight? / Come in out of the rain / Long time coming.

HARDLINE

NEAL SCHON – lead guitar, vocals / **JOHNNY SCHON** – vocals / **JOEY GIOELLI** – guitar / **TODD JENSEN** – bass (ex-DAVID LEE ROTH) / **DEAN CASTRONOVO** – drums (ex-BAD ENGLISH)

M.C.A. M.C.A.

May 92. (cd) *<(MCAD 10586)>* **DOUBLE ECLIPSE** [ ] [ ]
– Life's a bitch / Dr. love / Red car / Change of heart / Everything / Taking me down / Hot Cheri / Bad taste / Can't find my way / I'll be there / 31-91 / In the hands of time.

Jun 92. (c-s) *<54548>* **CAN'T FIND MY WAY / HOT CHERIE / TAKIN' ME DOWN / I'LL BE THERE** [–] [ ]

JOURNEY

re-formed the quintet in 1996:- **PERRY, SCHON, CAIN, VALORY + SMITH**

Columbia Columbia

Oct 96. (cd/c) *(485264-2/-4) <67514>* **TRIAL BY FIRE** [ ] [3]
– Message of love / One more / When you love a woman / If he should break your heart / Forever in blue / Castles burning / Don't be down on me baby / Still she cries / Colours of the spirit / When I think of you / Easy to fall / Can't tame the lion / It's just the rain / Trial by fire / Baby I'm leaving you. *(cd re-iss. Jan00; same)*

Oct 96. (c-s) *<78428>* **WHEN YOU LOVE A WOMAN / MESSAGE OF LOVE / OPEN ARMS** [–] [12]

—— **DEAN CASTRONOVO** – drums (ex-BAD ENGLISH) repl. SMITH

Apr 01. (cd) *(498479-2) <69864>* **ARRIVAL** [ ] [56]
– Higher piece / All the way / Signs of life / All the things / Loved by you / Livin' to do / I got a reason / With your love / Lifetime of dreams / Live and breathe / Nothin' comes close / To be alive again / Kiss me softly / I'm not that way / We will meet again.

– compilations, others, etc. –

on 'CBS' UK / 'Columbia' US, unless mentioned otherwise

Sep 80. (d-lp) *(CBS 22073) <36324>* **IN THE BEGINNING** (from first 3 albums) [ ] Jan80 [ ]

Dec 82. (c-ep) *(40 2908)* **CASSETTE EP** [ ] [–]
– Don't stop believin' / Who's crying now / Open arms / Lovin' touchin' squeezin'.

Aug 82. (7") *<03133>* **OPEN ARMS. / THE PARTY'S OVER** [–] [ ]

Aug 82. (7") *<03134>* **DON'T STOP BELIEVIN'. / WHO'S CRYING NOW** [–] [ ]

Feb 83. (d-c) *(EPC-40 22150)* **INFINITY / NEXT** [ ] [–]

Aug 87. (d-lp) *(CBSJ 241)* **FRONTIERS / ESCAPE** [ ] [–]

Nov 88. (lp/c/cd) *(463149-1/-4/-2) <44493>* **GREATEST HITS** [ ] [10]
– Only the young / Don't stop believin' / Wheel in the sky / Faithfully / I'll be alright with you / Any way you want it / Ask the lonely / Who's crying now / Separate ways (worlds apart) / Lights / Lovin', touchin', squeezin' / Open arms / Girl can't help it / Send her my love / Be good to yourself. *(cd re-iss. Apr96 & Apr00 on 'Columbia'; 463149-2)*

Jan 89. (7") *(654541-7)* **WHO'S CRYING NOW. / OPEN ARMS** [ ] [–]
(12"+=/cd-s+=) *(654541-6/-2)* – Suzanne / Don't stop believing.

—— (now on 'Columbia' unless mentioned otherwise)

Dec 92. (t-cd/t-c) *(472810-2/-4) <48937>* **TIME 3** [ ] [90]
(re-iss. Apr98; C3K 65159)

Jan 93. (c-s) *<74842>* **LIGHTS (live) / (6 album excerpts)** [–] [74]

Apr 98. (cd/c) *(489703-2/-4) <69139>* **GREATEST HITS LIVE (live)** [ ] [ ]

Nov 00. (3xcd-box) *(492658-2)* **INFINITY / ESCAPE / FRONTIERS** [ ] [ ]

Mar 01. (cd) *Sony; <2416>* **THE JOURNEY CONTINUES . . .** [–] [–]

Nov 01. (cd) *<86080>* **THE ESSENTIAL JOURNEY** [–] [47]

JOY DIVISION

Formed: Salford, Manchester, England . . . mid '77 initially as The STIFF KITTENS by IAN CURTIS, BERNARD ALBRECHT, PETER HOOK and STEPHEN MORRIS. By the time they were ready to take the stage for the first time, the group were going under the WARSAW moniker, finally settling on JOY DIVISION later that year. A term used by the Nazis for Jewish prostitutes, the band had taken the name from the book, 'House Of Dolls'; unsurprisingly, they ran into a little media trouble, the press subsequently speculating about their supposedly fascistic tendencies and unfairly branding them little Adolfs. Particularly controversial was the track, 'AT A LATER DATE', included on the 'Virgin' various artists punk sampler, 'Short Circuit: Live At The Electric Circus'. A vinyl debut proper came with the limited EP, 'AN IDEAL FOR LIVING', although it was through manager Rob Gretton and a subsequent deal with the emerging 'Factory' records that JOY DIVISION's career really got off the ground. Their first recordings for the label were a couple of tracks, 'GLASS' and 'DIGITAL', featured on a 'Factory' sampler (in mid-'79, a further two tracks, 'AUTO-SUGGESTION' and 'FROM SAFETY TO WHERE', surfaced on the 'Fast' records compilation EP, 'Earcom 2'), while their legendary Martin Hannett-produced debut album, 'UNKNOWN PLEASURES' was finally released later that summer. Groundbreaking in its bass-heavy, skeletal sound and evocation of urban alienation, isolation and despair, the record ensured CURTIS's position as a latter day messiah of existential angst; while his lyrics trawled the underbelly of the human psyche with disturbing clarity, his sub-JIM MORRISON ruminations were a blueprint for every pasty-faced goth pretender of the next decade. Tony Wilson's faith in the band was such that he contributed his life savings of over £8,000 towards the album's cost, the 'Factory' supremo's investment rewarded as the record topped the indie charts and JOY DIVISION became the foremost post-punk cult act. Yet even as the hypnotic rhythms of sublime new single, 'TRANSMISSION', hinted at an equally compelling new direction, CURTIS's robotic contortions and trance-like stage presence were giving way to epileptic fits as the singer struggled to cope with the increasing demands of live work. Tragically, on the 18th May, 1980, depressed with the break-up of his marriage and his worsening illness, CURTIS hanged himself. Ironically, JOY DIVISION scored their first chart hit a month later with the seminal 'LOVE WILL TEAR US APART'; the loss of such a fiercely individual talent was underlined as the track suggested a singer (and indeed, band) at the very apex of their creative potential. CURTIS had actually recorded a full album's worth of material before his death, released that summer as 'CLOSER'; even more lyrically unsettling, the record's bleak vision nevertheless pre-empted rock's dancefloor embrace on the synth-laced likes of 'ISOLATION', as well as forming the basis for NEW ORDER's experiments in cross-genre innovation. The latter act were formed later that year from JOY DIVISION's ashes, while further CURTIS-era material was posthumously released in late '81 as 'STILL'. The band remain one of the most revered and certainly one of the most influential outfits to emerge from the punk 'revolution', the best of NEW ORDER's work an indication as to what musical heights JOY DIVISION might have scaled had CURTIS prolonged the battle with his personal demons.

Album rating: UNKNOWN PLEASURES (*10) / CLOSER (*10) / STILL part compilation/live (*8) / SUBSTANCE compilation (*9) / PERMANENT: JOY DIVISION 1995 remixes (*6)

IAN CURTIS (b.15 Jul'56, Macclesfield, England) – vocals / **BERNARD ALBRECHT** (b. BERNARD DICKEN, 4 Jan'56) – guitar, vocals / **PETER HOOK** (b.13 Feb'56, Salford, Manchester) – bass / **STEPHEN MORRIS** (b.28 Oct'57, Macclesfield) – drums

Enigma not iss.

Jun 78. (7"ep) *(PSS 139)* **AN IDEAL FOR LIVING** [ ] [–]
– An ideal for living / Warsaw / Leaders of men / No love lost / Failures. *(re-iss. Jul78 on 'Anonymous' 12"ep; ANON 1)*

Factory not iss.

Aug 79. (lp) *(FACT 10)* **UNKNOWN PLEASURES** [ ] [–]
– Disorder / Day of the lords / Candidate / Insight / New dawn fades / She's lost control / Shadowplay / Wilderness / Interzone / I remember

nothing. *(re-dist.Jul80, hit No.71) (re-iss. Jul82; same) (c-iss.Nov84; FACT 10C) (cd-iss. Apr86; FACD 10) (re-iss. Jul93 on 'Centredate-London' cd/c; 520016-2) <US-iss.1989 on 'Qwest' lp/c/cd; 1-/4-/2-25840> (cd re-iss. Jan00; 3984 28223-2)*

Oct 79. (7") *(FAC 13)* **TRANSMISSION. / NOVELTY** [ ] [–]
(re-iss. Oct80 as 12"; FAC 13-12)

Mar 80. (7") *(SS 33-002)* **ATMOSPHERE. / DEAD SOULS** [–] France [–]
(above single released on 'Sordide Sentimentale' & now worth lots)

Jun 80. (7") *(FAC 23)* **LOVE WILL TEAR US APART. / THESE DAYS** [13] [–]
(re-iss. Oct80 as 12"+=; FAC 23-12) – ('A'version). *(re-iss. Oct83; same); hit UK No.19)*

Jul 80. (lp) *(FACT 25)* **CLOSER** [6] [–]
– Heart and soul / 24 hours / The eternal / Decades / Atrocity exhibition / Isolation / Passover / Colony / Means to an end. *(c-iss.Jul82; FACT 25C) (cd-iss. Apr86; FACD 25) (re-iss. Jul93 on 'Centredate-London' cd/c; 520015-2) <US-iss.1989 on 'Qwest' lp/c/cd; 1-/4/-2-25841> (cd re-iss. Sep99 on 'Factory Too'; 3984 28219-2)*

—— After another fit of depression, IAN CURTIS hanged himself 18th May 1980. The others became NEW ORDER

– compilations, others, etc. –

Sep 80. (12") *Factory Benelux; (FACTUS 2)* **ATMOSPHERE. / SHE'S LOST CONTROL** [ ] [–]

Apr 81. (free 7"flexi) *Factory; (FAC 28)* **KOMAKINO. / INCUBATION** [–] [–]

May 81. (7"ep/12"ep; as WARSAW) *Enigma; (PSS 138)* **THE IDEAL BEGINNING** [ ] [–]
– Inside the line / Gutz / At a later date.

Oct 81. (d-lp) *Factory; (FACT 40)* **STILL (live & rare)** [5] [–]
– Exercise one / Ice age / The sound of music / Glass / The only mistake / Walked in line / The kill / Something must break / Dead souls / Sister Ray / Ceremony / Shadowplay / Means to an end / Passover / New dawn fades / Transmission / Disorder / Isolation / Decades / Digital. *(c-iss.Dec86; FACT 40C) (cd-iss. Mar90; FACD 40) (re-iss. Jul93 on 'Centredate-London' cd/c; 520014-2/-4) <US-iss.1989 on 'Qwest' lp/c/cd; 26495> (cd re-iss. Jan00 on 'Factory Too'; 3984 28222-2)*

Nov 86. (12"ep) *Strange Fruit; (SFPS 013)* **THE PEEL SESSIONS (31.1.79)** [ ] [–]
– Exercise one / Insight / She's lost control / Transmission. *(re-iss. Jul88 cd-ep; SFPSCD 013)*

Sep 87. (12"ep) *Strange Fruit; (SFPS 033)* **THE PEEL SESSIONS 2 (26.11.79)** [ ] [–]
– Love will tear us apart / 24 hours / Colony / The sound of music. *(re-iss. Jul88 cd-ep; SFPSCD 033)*

1987. (7"ep+book) *Stampa; (SCONIC 001)* **YOU'RE NO GOOD FOR ME / KOMAKINO / INCUBATION / INCUBATION (version)** [–] Italy [–]

Jun 88. (7") *Factory; (FAC 213-7)* **ATMOSPHERE. / THE ONLY MISTAKE** [34] [–]
(12"+=) *(FAC 213)* – The sound of music.
(cd-s) *(FACD 213)* – ('A'side) / Love will tear us apart / Transmission.

Jul 88. (lp/c/dat)(cd) *Factory; (FACT 250/+C/D)(FACD 250) / Qwest; <1-/4-/2-25747>* **SUBSTANCE** (The best of..) [7] [ ]
– She's lost control / Dead souls / Atmosphere / Love will tear us apart / Warsaw / Leaders of men / Digital / Transmission / Auto-suggestion. *(cd+=)* – (7 extra tracks). *(re-iss. Jul93 on 'Centredate-London' cd/c; 520 014-2/-4) (cd re-iss. Sep99 on 'Factory Too'; 3984 28224-2)*

Sep 90. (cd/c) *Strange Fruit; (SFR CD/MC 111)* **COMPLETE PEEL SESSIONS** [ ] [–]

Jun 95. (c-s) *London; (YOJC 1)* **LOVE WILL TEAR US APART (radio version) / ('A'-original version)** [19] [ ]
(12"+=/cd-s+=) *(YOJ T/CD 1)* – These days / Transmission.

Jun 95. (cd/c/d-lp) *London; (828 624-2/-4/-1) / Warners; <45979>* **PERMANENT: JOY DIVISION 1995** (remixes) [16] Aug95 [ ]
– Love will tear us apart / Transmission / She's lost control / Shadow play / Day of the lords / Isolation / Passover / Heart and soul / 24 hours / These days / Novelty / Dead souls / The only mistake / Something must break / Atmosphere / Love will tear us apart (Permanent mix). *(cd re-iss. Sep99; 3984 28221-2)*

Jan 98. (4xcd-box) *London; (<828 968-2>)* **HEART AND SOUL** (all material) [70] [ ]
(re-iss. Sep99; 3984 29040-2)

Feb 98. (cd+book) *Sonic Book; (SB 10)* **ALL THE LYRICS** [ ] [–]

Jul 00. (cd) *Fractured: (FACD 260)* **PRESTON – THE WAREHOUSE 28/2/80 (live)** [ ] [ ]
(lp-iss.Oct00 on 'Get Back'; GET 69)

Aug 00. (cd) *Strange Fruit; (SFRSCD 094)* **THE COMPLETE RADIO ONE RECORDINGS** [ ] [ ]
(lp-iss.Apr01; SFRSCD 084)

Apr 01. (cd) *Fractured; (FACD 261)* **LES BAINS DOUCHES** [ ] [–]
(d-lp-iss.Jun01 on 'Get Back'; GET 79)

JUDAS PRIEST

Formed: Birmingham, England . . . 1969 by KK DOWNING and IAN HILL. In 1971, they completed the line-up with vocalist AL ATKINS – who named the band after a BOB DYLAN track, 'The Ballad Of Frankie Lee And Judas Priest' – and drummer JOHN ELLIS; the latter was replaced by ALAN MOORE then CHRIS CAMPBELL. In 1973, both CAMPBELL and ATKINS bailed out (the latter went solo in the 90's releasing 'Victim Of Changes') as the 'PRIEST recruited singer ROB HALFORD and drummer JOHN HINCH. Three years later, with a few hundred gigs behind them, they brought in second guitarist GLENN TIPTON. Signed to 'Decca' off-shoot label 'Gull', they unleashed a debut album, 'ROCKA ROLLA', the same year. The record made little impact and after replacing HINCH with the returning ALAN MOORE, the band surfaced again in '76 with the excellent 'SAD WINGS OF DESTINY'. Following a resoundingly triumphant appearance at that year's Reading Festival, they signed to 'C.B.S.' in early '77. They soon had a UK Top 30 album with the ROGER GLOVER (Deep Purple)-produced 'SIN AFTER SIN', another metal masterpiece which included an unlikely, but effective cover of Joan Baez's 'DIAMONDS AND RUST'. While the leather clad JUDAS PRIEST weren't exactly original in their steadfast adherence to the leaden riffing and helium overdose of heavy metal, they helped to shape the genre's increasing preoccupation with all things grim 'n' nasty. 'STAINED CLASS' (1978), another Top 30 UK album, proferred such lyrical delights as 'SAINTS IN HELL', 'SAVAGE' and 'BEYOND THE REALMS OF DEATH', plus a cover of SPOOKY TOOTH's 'BETTER BY YOU, BETTER THAN ME', the record later having serious repercussions for the band (see below). Coming at the height of the NWOBHM explosion, 'BRITISH STEEL' (1980) was the band's biggest critical and commercial success to date, the Top 20 success of the 'LIVING AFTER MIDNIGHT' and 'BREAKING THE LAW' singles showing the more accessible, hook-driven face of the band. This was to be one of the most fertile periods of the 'PRIEST's career with a trio of consistent Top 20 albums; 'POINT OF ENTRY' (1981), 'SCREAMING FOR VENGEANCE' (1982) and 'DEFENDERS OF THE FAITH' (1984) were all testosterone-saturated howlers, the kind of British metal that just doesn't exist anymore. The latter housed the PMRC-baiting 'EAT ME ALIVE', securing the band's position as perceived deviant enemy of the nation's lank-haired youth alongside the equally wholesome W.A.S.P. Late in 1985, two of their fans shot themselves while listening to a track off the 'STAINED CLASS' album, prompting the boys' parents to sue both JUDAS PRIEST and their label, 'Columbia'. They alleged the record contained subliminal satanic messages hidden in the lyrics, thus forcing the boys to commit suicide. This fiasco finally got to court in July '90, the judge ruling against the dead boys' parents, although he did fine the label a 5-figure sum for withholding the master tapes!!? Despite the controversy, fans were less enamoured with 'TURBO' (1986), PRIEST's attempts at guitar synthesized innovation cutting no ice with the band's metal diehards. 'RAM IT DOWN' (1988) was a return to harder fare while the band underwent a critical rebirth of sorts with the thrash-y 'PAINKILLER' (1990), their status acknowledged as grandaddies of heavy metal and a glaring influence on the likes of METALLICA and SLAYER. ROB HALFORD has since left the band after forming side-project, FIGHT, the group soon turning into a full-time affair. 'PRIEST returned in 1997 with a new frontman, the cornily-monikered "RIPPER" OWENS lending his eardrum rupturing shriek over the tuneless assault of the poorly-received comeback set, 'JUGULATOR'. • **Songwriters:** TIPTON, HALFORD & DOWNING on most, except extra covers; THE GREEN MANALISHI (Fleetwood Mac) / JOHNNY B. GOODE (Chuck Berry).

Album rating: ROCKA ROLLA (*2) / SAD WINGS OF DESTINY (*8) / SIN AFTER SIN (*7) / STAINED CLASS (*6; recommended only to those without access to a gun, a bazooka, a tank or any tactical nuclear weapon) / KILLING MACHINE (*6) / UNLEASHED IN THE EAST (*7) / BRITISH STEEL (*8) / POINT OF ENTRY (*4) / SCREAMING FOR VENGEANCE (*8) / DEFENDERS OF THE FAITH (*6) / TURBO (*5) / PRIEST . . . LIVE! (*6) / RAM IT DOWN (*6) / PAINKILLER (*8) / METAL WORKS compilation (*8) / JUGULATOR (*3) / MELTDOWN LIVE '98 (*4) / DEMOLITION (*4)

ROB HALFORD (b.25 Aug'51, Walsall) – vocals; repl. ALAN ATKINS / **KK DOWNING** (b. KENNETH, 27 Oct'51, West Midlands) – guitars / **GLENN TIPTON** (b.25 Oct'48, West Midlands) – guitar, vocals (ex-FLYING HAT BAND) / **IAN HILL** (b.20 Jan'52, West Midlands) – bass / **JOHN HINCH** – drums; repl. CHRIS CAMPBELL who'd repl. ALAN MOORE who'd repl. JOHN ELLIS

Gull / Janus

Aug 74. (7") *(GULS 6)* **ROCKA ROLLA. / NEVER SATISFIED** [ ] [–]

Sep 74. (lp) *(GULP 1005)* **ROCKA ROLLA** [ ] [–]
– One for the road / Rocka rolla / Winter / Deep freeze / Winter retreat / Cheater / Never satisfied / Run of the mill / Dying to meet you / Caviar and meths. *(re-iss. Sep77; same) <US-iss.Oct82 on 'Visa'; 7001> (re-iss. Nov85 on 'Fame' lp/c; FA41 3137-2/-4) (cd-iss. Nov87 on 'Line'; LICD 900101) (cd-iss. Mar93 on 'Repertoire'; RR 4305) (cd re-iss. Aug98 on 'Snapper'; SMMCD 562)*

— **ALAN MOORE** – drums (who had been 1971 member) returned to repl. HINCH

Mar 76. (7") *(GULS 31)* **THE RIPPER. / ISLAND OF DOMINATION** [ ] [–]

Apr 76. (lp) *(GULP 1015) <7019>* **SAD WINGS OF DESTINY** [ ] [ ]
– Prelude / Tyrant / Genocide / Epitaph / Island of domination / Victim of changes / The ripper / Epitaph / Dreamer deceiver. *(pic-lp.Sep77; PGULP 1015) (re-iss. 1984 on 'Line' white-lp; LILP 4.00112) (cd-iss. Nov87; LICD 9.00112) (re-iss. cd May95 on 'Repertoire';) (cd re-iss. Aug98 on 'Snapper'; SMMCD 562)*

— **SIMON PHILLIPS** – drums repl. MOORE

C.B.S. / Columbia

Apr 77. (7") *(CBS 5222)* **DIAMONDS AND RUST. / DISSIDENT AGGRESSOR** [ ] [–]

Apr 77. (lp/c) *(CBS/40 82008) <34587>* **SIN AFTER SIN** [23] [ ]
– Sinner / Diamonds and rust / Starbreaker / Last rose of summer / Let us prey / Call for the priest – Raw deal / Here come the tears / Dissident aggressor. *(re-iss. Mar81; CBS 32005) (re-iss. cd.Nov93 on 'Sony Collectors'; 983286-2) (cd re-iss. Feb97 on 'Epic'; 474684-2)*

— **LES BINKS** – drums repl. PHILLIPS

Jan 78. (7") *(CBS 6077)* **BETTER BY YOU, BETTER BY ME. / INVADER** [ ] [–]

Feb 78. (lp/c) *(CBS/40 82430) <35296>* **STAINED CLASS** [27] [ ]
– Exciter / White heat, red hot / Better by you, better by me / Stained class / Invader / Saints in Hell / Savage / Beyond the realms of death / Heroes end. *(re-iss. Nov81; CBS 32075) (re-iss. May91 on 'Columbia' cd/c; CD/40 32075)*

Sep 78. (7") *(CBS 6719)* **EVENING STAR. / STARBREAKER** [ ] [–]

Nov 78. (red-lp/c) *(CBS/40 83135) <36179>* **KILLING MACHINE** <US-title 'HELL BENT FOR LEATHER'> [32] [ ]
– Delivering the goods / Rock forever / Evening star / Hell bent for leather / Take on the world / Burnin' up / Killing machine / Running wild / Before the dawn / Evil fantasies. *(re-iss. red-lp.Sep82; CBS 32218)*

Oct 78. (7") *(CBS 6794)* **BEFORE THE DAWN. / ROCK FOREVER** [ ] [ ]

Jan 79. (7") *(CBS 6915)* **TAKE ON THE WORLD. / STARBREAKER (live)** [ ] [14]
(12"+=) *(CBS12 6915)* – White heat red hot (live).

Apr 79. (7") *(CBS 7312)* **EVENING STAR. / BEYOND THE REALMS OF DEATH** [53] [ ]
(12"clear+=) *(CBS12 7312)* – The green Manalishi.

May 78. (7") *<11000>* **ROCK FOREVER. / THE GREEN MANALISHI (WITH THE TWO-PRONGED CROWN)** [–] [ ]

Sep 79. (lp/c) *(CBS/40 83852) <36179>* **UNLEASHED IN THE EAST (live)** [10] [70]
– Exciter / Running wild / Sinner / The ripper / The green manalishi (with the two-pronged crown) / Diamonds and rust / Victim of changes / Genocide / Tyrant. *(free 7"w.a.)* **ROCK FOREVER / HELL BENT FOR LEATHER. / BEYOND THE REALMS OF DEATH** *(cd-iss. 1988; CD 83852) (re-iss. May94 on 'Columbia' cd/c; 468604-2/-4)*

Dec 79. (7") *<11135>* **DIAMONDS AND RUST (live). / STARBREAKER (live)** [–] [ ]

— **DAVE HOLLAND** – drums repl. BINKS

Mar 80. (7") *(CBS 8379)* **LIVING AFTER MIDNIGHT. / DELIVERING THE GOODS (live)** [12] [–]
(12"+=) *(CBS12 8379)* – Evil fantasies (live).

Apr 80. (lp/c) *(CBS/40 84160) <36443>* **BRITISH STEEL** [4] [34]
– Rapid fire / Metal gods / Breaking the law / Grinder / United / You don't have to be old to be wise / Living after midnight / The rage / Steeler. *(re-iss. Jan84 lp/c; CBS/40 32412) (cd-iss. 1988; CD 32412) (cd re-iss. Jun94 on 'Sony'; 982725-2)*

May 80. (7") *<11308>* **LIVING AFTER MIDNIGHT. / METAL GODS** [–] [ ]

May 80. (7") *(CBS 8644)* **BREAKING THE LAW. / METAL GODS** [12] [ ]

Aug 80. (7") *(CBS 8897) <11396>* **UNITED. / GRINDER** [26] [ ]

Feb 81. (7") *(CBS 9520)* **DON'T GO. / SOLAR ANGELS** [51] [–]

Feb 81. (lp/c) *(CBS/40 84834) <37052>* **POINT OF ENTRY** [14] [39]
– Heading out to the highway / Don't go / Hot rockin' / Turning circles / Desert plains / Solar angels / You say yes / All the way / Troubleshooter / On the run. *(cd-iss. Apr01 on 'Columbia'; 502132-2)*

Apr 81. (7") *(A 1153)* **HOT ROCKIN' / BREAKING THE LAW (live)** [60] [–]
(12") *(A12 1153)* – ('A'side) / Steeler / You don't have to be old to be wise.

Apr 81. (7") *<02083>* **HEADING OUT TO THE HIGHWAY. / ROCK FOREVER** [–] [ ]

Jul 82. (lp/c) *(CBS/40 85941) <38160>* **SCREAMING FOR VENGEANCE** [11] [17]
– The hellion / Electric eye / Riding on the wind / Bloodstone / (Take these) Chains / Pain and pleasure / Screaming for vengeance / You've got another thing comin' / Fever / Devil's child. *(re-iss. Feb86 lp/c; CBS/40 32712)*

Aug 82. (7"/7"pic-d) *(A/+11 2611)* **YOU'VE GOT ANOTHER THING COMIN'. / EXCITER (live)** [66] [–]

Oct 82. (7") *<03168>* **YOU'VE GOT ANOTHER THING COMIN'. / DIAMONDS AND RUST** [–] [67]

Oct 82. (7") *(A 2822)* **(TAKE THESE) CHAINS. / JUDAS PRIEST AUDIO FILE** [ ] [ ]

Jan 84. (7") *(A 4054)* **FREEWHEEL BURNING. / BREAKING THE LAW** [42] [–]
(12"+=) *(TA 4054)* – You've got another thing comin'.

Jan 84. (lp/c) *(CBS/40 25713) <39219>* **DEFENDERS OF THE FAITH** [19] [18]
– Freewheel burning / Jawbreaker / Rock hard ride free / The sentinel / Love bites / Eat me alive / Some heads are gonna roll / Night comes down / Heavy duty / Defenders of the faith. *(cd-iss. Jul84; CD 25713)*

Feb 84. (7") *<04371>* **SOME HEADS ARE GONNA ROLL. / BREAKING THE LAW (live)** [–] [ ]

Mar 84. (7") *(A 4298)* **SOME HEADS ARE GONNA ROLL. / THE GREEN MANALISHI (WITH THE TWO-PRONGED CROWN)** [ ] [–]
(12"+=) *(TA 4298)* – Jawbreaker.

Apr 84. (7") *<04436>* **JAWBREAKER. / LOVE BITES** [–] [ ]

Apr 86. (lp/c/cd) *(CBS/40/CD 26641) <40158>* **TURBO** [33] [17]
– Turbo lover / Locked in / Private property / Parental guidance / Rock you all around the world / Out in the cold / Wild night, hot and crazy days / Hot for love / Reckless. *(re-iss. Feb89 lp/c/cd; 463365-1/-4/-2)*

Apr 86. (7") *(A 7048)* **TURBO LOVER. / HOT FOR LOVE** [ ] [–]

May 86. (7") *(A 7144)* **LOCKED IN. / RECKLESS** [ ] [–]
(ext.12"+=) *(QTA 7144)* – Desert plains (live) / Free wheel burning (live).

May 86. (7") *<05856>* **LOCKED IN. / HOT FOR LOVE** [–] [ ]

Aug 86. (7") *<06142>* **TURBO LOVER. / RESTLESS** [–] [ ]

Nov 86. (7") *<06281>* **PARENTAL GUIDANCE. / ROCK YOU AROUND THE WORLD** [–] [ ]

Jun 87. (d-lp/c/cd) *(450639-1/-4/-2) <40794>* **PRIEST . . . LIVE! (live)** [47] [38]
– Out in the cold / Heading out to the highway / Metal gods / Breaking

the law / Love bites / Some heads are gonna roll / The sentinel / Private property / Rock you all around the world / Electric eye / Turbo lover / Free wheel burning / Parental guidance / Living after midnight / You've got another thing comin'. *(cd+=)* – Shout – Oh yeah!

Atlantic Columbia

Apr 88. (7") *(A 9114) <89114>* **JOHNNY B. GOODE. / ROCK YOU ALL AROUND THE WORLD (live)** [64] [ ]
(12"+=) *(AT 9114)* – Turbo lover (live).
(3"cd-s++=) *(A 9114CD)* – Living after midnight (live).

May 88. (lp/c/cd) *(461108-1/-4/-2)* **RAM IT DOWN** [24] [31]
– Ram it down / Heavy metal / Love zone / Come and get it / Hard as iron / Blood red skies / I'm a rocker / Johnny B. Goode / Love you to death / Monsters of rock.

— **SCOTT TRAVIS** – drums (ex-RACER-X) repl. HOLLAND

C.B.S. Columbia

Sep 90. (7"/c-s) *(656273-7/-4)* **PAINKILLER. / UNITED** [74] [ ]
(12"+=/cd-s+=) *(656273-6/-2)* – Better by you, better than me.

Sep 90. (cd/c/lp) *(467290-2/-4/-1) <46891>* **PAINKILLER** [24] [26]
– Painkiller / Hell patrol / All guns blazing / Leather rebel / Metal meltdown / Night crawler / Between the hammer and the anvil / A touch of evil / Battle hymn (instrumental) / One shot at glory.

Columbia Columbia

Mar 91. (7"/7"sha-pic-d/c-s) *(656589-7/-0/-4)* **A TOUCH OF EVIL. / BETWEEN THE HAMMER AND THE ANVIL** [58] [ ]
(12"+=/cd-s+=) *(656589-6/-2)* – You've got another thing comin' (live).

— In Oct'92, HALFORD left after already forming FIGHT in 1991, taking with him SCOTT TRAVIS.

Apr 93. (7"/c-s) *(659097-7/-4)* **NIGHT CRAWLER (Edit) / BREAKING THE LAW** [63] [ ]
(cd-s+=) *(659097-2)* – Living after midnight.

Apr 93. (d-cd/d-c/t-lp) *(473050-2/-4/-1) <53932>* **METAL WORKS '73-'93** (compilation) [37] [ ]
– The hellion / Electric eye / Victim of changes / Painkiller / Eat me alive / Devil's child / Dissident aggressor / Delivering the goods / Exciter / Breaking the law / Hell bent for leather / Blood red skies / Metal gods / Before the dawn / Turbo lover / Ram it down / Metal meltdown/ / Screaming for vengeance / You've got another thing comin' / Beyond the realms of death / Solar angels / Bloodstone / Desert plains / Wild nights, hot & crazy days / Heading out to the highway / Living after midnight / A touch of evil / The rage / Night comes down / Sinner / Freewheel burning / Night crawler.

— **"RIPPER" OWENS** – vocals; completed the line-up

S.P.V. C.M.C.

Nov 97. (cd/c/lp) *(SPV 085 1878-2/-4/-1) <86224>* **JUGULATOR** [ ] [82]
– Jugulator / Blood stained / Dead meat / Death row / Decapitate / Burn in hell / Brain dead / Abductors / Bullet train / Cathedral spires.

Oct 98. (d-cd) *(SPV 0891954-2) <86261>* **MELTDOWN (live '98)** [ ] [ ]
– The hellion / Electric eye / Metal gods / Grinder / Rapid fire / Blood stained / The sentinnel / Touch of evil / Burn in hell / The ripper / Bullet train / Beyond the realms of death / Death row / Metal meltdown / Night crawler / Abductors / Victim of changes / Diamonds and rust / Breaking the law / The green manalishi (with the two-pronged crown) / Painkiller / You've got another thing comin' / Hell bent for leather / Living after midnight.

S.P.V. Atlantic

Jun 01. (cd-s) *(0567245-2)* **MACHINE MAN / SUBTERFUGE / BURN IN HELL (video)** [ ] [–]

Jul 01. (cd/lp) *(0857242-2/-1) <83480>* **DEMOLITION** [ ] [ ]
– Machine man / One on one / Hell is home / Jekyll and Hyde / Close to you / Devil digger / Bloodsuckers / In between / Feed on me / Subterfuge / Lost and found / Cyberface / Mental messiah.

– compilations, etc. –

Feb 78. (pic-lp/lp) *Gull; (P+/GULP 1026)* **THE BEST OF JUDAS PRIEST** (early work) [ ] [–]
(cd-iss. May87 +=; GUCD 1026) – (2 extra tracks).

Aug 80. (7") *Gull; (GULS 71)* **THE RIPPER. / VICTIMS OF CHANGE** [ ] [–]
(12"+=) *(GUL 71-12)* – Never satisfied.

Jun 83. (12"white) *Gull; (GULS 76-12)* **TYRANT. / ROCKA ROLLA / GENOCIDE** [ ] [–]

Jan 83. (c-ep) *C.B.S.; (A40 3067)* **CASSETTE EP** [ ] [–]
– Breaking the law / Living after midnight / Take on the world / United.

Aug 83. (d-c) *C.B.S.; (22161)* **SIN AFTER SIN / STAINED GLASS** [ ] [–]

Sep 83. (7"ep/c-ep) *(7SR/ 5018)* **6 TRACK HITS** [ ] [–]
– Sinner / Exciter / Hell bent for leather / The ripper / Hot rockin' / The green manalishi.

Aug 86. (pic-lp) *Shanghai; (PGLP 1026)* **JUDAS PRIEST** [ ] [–]

Nov 87. (cd) *Line; (LICD 900414)* **HERO HERO** [–] German [–]
(re-iss. 1988 on 'Gull' c/lp; ZC+/GUD 2005-6) (cd re-iss. Jul95 on 'Connoisseur'; CSAPCD 119)

Feb 89. (7") *Old Gold; (OG 9864)* **LIVING AFTER MIDNIGHT. / BREAKING THE LAW** [ ] [–]

May 89. (lp/c/cd) *Castle; (CCS LP/MC/CD 213)* **THE COLLECTION** [ ] [–]
– (first two albums)

Mar 93. (3xcd-box) *Columbia; (468328-2)* **BRITISH STEEL / SCREAMING FOR VENGEANCE / STAINED GLASS** [ ] [–]

Apr 97. (cd) *Columbia; (487242-2)* **LIVING AFTER MIDNIGHT** [ ] [–]

Jun 98. (cd) *Ranch Life; (CRANCH 3)* **CONCERT CLASSICS (live)** [ ] [–]

Nov 98. (3xcd-box) *Columbia; (492657-2)* **BRITISH STEEL / POINT OF ENTRY / SCREAMING FOR VENGEANCE** [ ] [–]

Jan 99. (cd) *Columbia; (493008-2) / Sony; <7713>* **LIVE AND RARE** [ ] Sep99 [ ]

Jul 99. (cd) *Eureka; (EURCD 401)* **TYRANT (THE ORIGINAL MASTERS)** [ ] [–]

Feb 00. (d-cd) *Snapper; (<SMDCD 273>)* **GENOCIDE** [ ] [ ]

Feb 01. (cd) *Koch; <8071>* **THE BEST OF JUDAS PRIEST** [–] [ ]

JURASSIC 5

Formed: Los Angeles, California, USA ... 1993 by MARK 7EVEN, SOUP (ZAAKIR), CUT CHEMIST, DJ NU-MARK, AKIL and frontman CHALI 2NA; all from local groups REBELS OF RYHTHM and UNITY COMMITTEE. Protagonists CHALI and CUT CHEMIST met while struggling DJ, WILL-DOG, was still working at a job centre organising jams and gigs with local musicians that would subsequently play at his socialist benefit concerts. Through the revered DJ, the two met several other rappers and hip-hop influenced artists, forming JURASSIC 5 while dedicating their time to offshoot group OZOMATLI. The er . . . 6-piece embarked on a righteous pilgrimage to Brooklyn where they wrote and released their eponymous debut mini-set (full-set in UK), 'JURASSIC 5' (1997) to much critical acclaim. The most interesting thing about this ensemble was that they weren't the usual run-of-the-mill angry lads; they didn't have any enemies within the hip-hop circle, their lyrics weren't about "bitches" or the current state of gangland America, the J5 were basically a bunch of hedonists who were just out to "P.A.R.T.Y." From the brilliant cut'n'paste 'LESSON 6' to the infectious Top 40 hit, 'CONCRETE SCHOOLYARD', the debut set was a beautifully controlled, laid back hip-hop and funk album, mixing (like OZOMATLI) rap, scratching, blaxploitation and weird samples. After the word-of-mouth success of J5's debut, the group began working on the follow up, eventually to be released as 'QUALITY CONTROL' (2000). Mixed and produced again by NU-MARK and CUT CHEMIST, the album was more definite in tone and structure, with the MC's rhymes turning into total tongue-twisting poems from the old-school and the music standards deeply rooted in the funky organic sounds of flutes, big brash drum-loops and, in 'CONTRIBUTION', even an old forties two-step jazz sample. It was certainly clear with this in tow that JURASSIC 5 were becoming one of the most lauded of underground groups. Their pioneering stance (even if some samples used in this album could be heard on their debut), became clear on tracks such as 'CONTACT' and the title track (which was also issued as a single). A fantasic release from a band that will hopefully cross the line between underground and mainstream without losing an ounce of their dignity. Hip-hop's tightest crew issued their third set in 2002, aptly titled 'POWER IN NUMBERS'. As always, CUT CHEMIST and DJ NU-MARK were forefront on the production and turntables, but massive credit was due to the five MC's whom really pulled the whole thing together. We're in 'Paul's Boutique' territory once again, only with the production values a little more refined. Guests included BIG DADDY KANE and, shudder, NELLY FURTADO, but it's J5's gig here, with subjects as diverse as Third World poverty and urban impoverishment under the microscope. The breakneck beats, fantastic scratching (from, let's face it, two very immensely talented professionals) and DOUBLE-TROUBLE esque rhythms were all still as fresh and as funky as they were back whenever.

Album rating: JURASSIC 5 (*8) / QUALITY CONTROL (*8) / POWER IN NUMBERS (*6)

CHALI 2NA (b. CHARLES STEWART, 1971, Chicago, Illinois) – MC / **MARK 7EVEN** (b. MARK STUART, New Jersey) – MC / **SOUP / ZAAKIR** (b. COURTNAY HENDERSON) – MC / **AKIL** (b. DANTE GIVENS, 1971) – MC / **CUT CHEMIST** (b. LUCAS McFADDEN, 1973) – DJ / **NU-MARK** (b. MARK POTSIC, 1971) – DJ

not iss. | T.V.T.

Aug 95. (c-s/12"/cd-s) *<5811>* **UNIFIED REBELLION** [–] [ ]

Pan | Rumble – Pickininny

Jun 98. (cd/c/lp) *(PAN 015 CD/MC/LP)* *<001>* **JURASSIC 5** [70] Oct97 [ ]
– In the flesh / Quality control part II / Jayou / Lesson 6: the lecture / Concrete schoolyard / Setup / Action satisfaction / Sausage gut. *(UK+=)* – Improvise / Blacktop beat / Without a doubt / Lesson 6 (reprise) / Action satisfaction (dub). *<cd re-iss. Jun99 on 'Interscope'; 90289>*

Jul 98. (12"/c-s/cd-s) *(PAN 018/+MC/CD)* **JAYOU. / JAYOU (instrumental) / WITHOUT A DOUBT** [56] [–]

Oct 98. (cd-s) *(PAN 020CD)* **CONCRETE SCHOOLYARD / RUBBER TYRES CONCRETE SCHOOLYARD (mixes)** [35] [–]
(12"+=) *(PAN 020)* – Improvise.
(cd-s) *(PAN 020CDX)* – ('A'mixes) / Lesson 6 (the lecture).

Interscope | Rawkus

Jul 99. (cd-s) *<97119>* **IMPROVISE / CONCRETE SCHOOLYARD / CONCRETE AND CLAY** [–] [ ]

Jun 00. (cd/d-lp) *(490710-2/-1)* *<490664>* **QUALITY CONTROL** [23] [43]
– How we get along – intro / The influence / Great expectations / Quality control – intro / Quality control / Contact / Lausd / World of entertainment (W.O.E. is me) / Monkey bars / Jurass finish first / Contribution / One two / The game / Swing set.

Jul 00. (12")(cd-s) *<256><1009-2>* **QUALITY CONTROL (mixes; clean / instrumental / acappella) / TWELVE (mixes; clean / dirty / instrumental)** [–] [ ]

Oct 02. (cd/d-lp) *<(493437-2/-1)>* **POWER IN NUMBERS** [46] [15]
– This is / Freedom / If you only knew / Break / React / A day at the races (with PERCY P & BIG DADDY KANE) / Remember his name / What's golden / Thin line (with NELLY FURTADO) / After school special / High fidelity / Sum of us / DDT (with KOOL KEITH) / One of them (with JUJU) / Hey (with BOY WONDER) / I am somebody (with BOY WONDER) / Acetate prophets.

— in Mar'03, CHALI 2NA & AKIL featured on DJ FORMAT's single, 'We Know Something You Don't Know'

☐ JUSTIFIED ANCIENTS OF MU MU (see under ⇒ KLF)

KISS

KANSAS

Formed: Topeka, Kansas, USA . . . 1970 initially as WHITE CLOVER, by KERRY LIVGREN, DAVE HOPE and PHIL EHART. With the addition of classically trained ROBBY STEINHARDT, RICH WILLIAMS and frontman STEVE WALSH, the group adopted the KANSAS moniker during 1972. Two years of constant touring later, they signed to 'Kirshner' (the new label set up by industry guru, Don Kirshner) and hit the US Top 200 with their eponymous debut set. A windswept American answer to the British art-rock scene of the early 70's, KANSAS combined progressive, harmony laden muscle (somewhat akin to the likes of BOSTON or STYX) with ambitiously intricate 'suites'. Throughout the 70's, the band enjoyed increasing commercial success, the Jeff Glixman-produced 'LEFTOVERTURE' (1976) taking them into the US Top 5 for the first time on the back of the grandiose Top 10 smash, 'CARRY ON WAYWARD SON. For many fans, the subsequent triple-platinum 'POINT OF KNOW RETURN' (1977) marked the peak of the group's career, its string-laden pseudo-classical pretensions providing another Top 10 hit with 'DUST IN THE WIND'. KANSAS' more indulgent tendencies were glaringly evident on the rambling live set, 'TWO FOR THE SHOW' (1978), although as the 70's turned into the 80's, the group increasingly pursued a more accessible approach. Disillusioned with this direction, WALSH had already recorded a solo debut, 'SCHEMER-DREAMER' in 1980, eventually leaving the band following the 'AUDIO-VISIONS' (1980) set and forming a harder rocking outfit, STREETS. LIVGREN, meanwhile, had become a born-again Christian, the inspiration for his solo debut, 'SEEDS OF CHANGE' (1980). With JOHN ELEFANTE now in place as frontman, KANSAS cut a further couple of albums, 'VINYL CONFESSIONS' (1982) and 'DRASTIC MEASURES' (1983), before splitting in late '83. While LIVGREN and ELEFANTE both went on to successful careers in the Christian music field, EHART and WILLIAMS subsequently reformed KANSAS with former vocalist STEVE WALSH, fellow ex-STREETS man, BILLY GREER, and guitar maestro STEVE MORSE. Now signed to 'M.C.A.', the new improved KANSAS enjoyed middling chart success with 'POWER' (1986), an album which bore the stamp of WALSH's heavier work with STREETS. A follow-up set, 'IN THE SPIRIT OF THINGS' (1988), was a commercial failure, however, and the band found themselves without a record deal. Ploughing on, they re-introduced violin to their sound in 1991 courtesy of DAVID RAGSDALE, MORSE having left by the independently released concert set, 'LIVE AT THE WHISKY' (1993). A belated studio set, 'FREAKS OF NATURE' (1995) finally appeared in summer '95, KANSAS retaining a core fanbase despite their absence from the charts. Things became more interesting in 1998 with the release of 'ALWAYS NEVER THE SAME', an album recorded at Abbey Road and utilising the LONDON SYMPHONY ORCHESTRA. Hardly an original idea but one which breathes new life into KANSAS chestnuts alongside a trio of competent new tracks and a bombastic cover of The Beatles' 'ELEANOR RIGBY'. 'SOMEWHERE TO ELSEWHERE' (2000), meanwhile, heralded a new decade and a new millennium with an album recorded by the original line-up. Based on a WWII concept, the record captured at least some of the band's early flair and dynamism with a clutch of near-10 minute epics tailor made for longtime fans.

Album rating: KANSAS (*6) / SONG FOR AMERICA (*6) / MASQUE (*5) / LEFTOVERTURE (*7) / POINT OF KNOW RETURN (*6) / TWO FOR THE SHOW (*5) / MONOLITH (*6) / AUDIO-VISIONS (*6) / VINYL CONFESSIONS (*5) / DRASTIC MEASURES (*4) / THE BEST OF KANSAS compilation (*7) / POWER (*5) / IN THE SPIRIT OF THINGS (*5) / LIVE AT THE WHISKY (*2) / FREAKS OF NATURE (*3) / ALWAYS NEVER THE SAME (*4) / SOMEWHERE TO ELSEWHERE (*5)

STEVE WALSH (b.1951, St. Joseph, Missouri) – vocals, keyboards, synthesizer / **KERRY LIVGREN** (b.18 Sep'49) – guitar, piano, synthesizer / **ROBBY STEINHARDT** (b.1951, Mississippi) – violin / **RICH WILLIAMS** (b.1951) – guitar / **DAVE HOPE** (b. 7 Oct'49) – bass / **PHIL EHART** (b.1951) – drums

		UK: Kirshner	US: Kirshner
Nov 74.	(7") *<4253>* **CAN I TELL YOU. / THE PILGRIMAGE**	–	
Feb 75.	(7") *<4256>* **BRINGING IT ALL BACK. / LONELY WIND**	–	
Apr 75.	(lp) *(KIR 80174) <32817>* **KANSAS** – Can I tell you / Bringing it back / Lonely wind / Belexes / Journey from Mariabronn / The pilgrimage / Apercu / Death of Mother Nature suite. *(cd-iss. Apr92 on 'Sony Collectors'; 982733-2) (cd re-iss. Feb97 on 'Epic'; 468883-2)*		Jun74
Apr 75.	(7") *<4258>* **SONG FOR AMERICA. / (part 2)**	–	
Aug 75.	(lp) *(KIR 80740) <33385>* **SONG FOR AMERICA** – Down the road / Song for America / Lamplight symphony / Lonely street / The Devil game / Incomudro – hymn to the Atman.		Mar75 57
Feb 76.	(7") *<4259>* **IT TAKES A WOMAN'S LOVE (TO MAKE A MAN). / IT'S YOU**	–	
May 76.	(lp) *(KIR 81180) <33806>* **MASQUE** – It takes a woman's love (to make a man) / Two cents worth / Icarus – borne on wings of steel / All the world / Child of innocence / It's you / Mysteries and mayhem / The pinnacle.		Dec75 70
Dec 76.	(lp) *(KIR 81728) <34224>* **LEFTOVERTURE** – Carry on wayward son / The wall / What's on my mind / Miracles out of nowhere / Opus insert / Questions of my childhood / Cheyenne anthem / Magnus opus: Father Padilla meets the gnat – Howling at the Moon – Man overboard – Industry on parade – Release the beavers – Gnat attack. *(re-iss. Nov92 on 'Sony Collectors' cd/c; 982837-2/-4)*		Nov76 5
Dec 76.	(7") *<4267>* **CARRY ON WAYWARD SON. / QUESTIONS OF MY CHILDHOOD**	–	11
May 77.	(7") *<4270>* **WHAT'S ON MY MIND. / LONELY STREET**	–	
Nov 77.	(lp)*<US-pic-lp> (KIR 82234) <34929>* **POINT OF KNOW RETURN** – Point of know return / Paradox / The spider / Portrait (he knew) / Closet chronicles / Lightning's hand / Dust in the wind / Sparks of the tempest / Nobody's home / Hopelessly human. *(cd-iss. Jul89 on 'C.B.S.'; CD 32361)*		Oct77 4
Dec 77.	(7") *(S-KIR 5820) <4273>* **POINT OF KNOW RETURN. / CLOSET CHRONICLES**		Oct77 28
Mar 78.	(7") *(S-KIR 6205) <4274>* **DUST IN THE WIND. / PARADOX**		Jan78 6

Jun 78. (7") *(S-KIR 4932)* **CARRY ON WAYWARD SON. / QUESTIONS OF MY CHILDHOOD** [51] [–]
Jun 78. (7") *<4276>* **PORTRAIT (HE KNEW). / LIGHTNING'S HAND** [–] [64]
Dec 78. (d-lp) *(KIR 88318) <PZ2 35560>* **TWO FOR THE SHOW (live)** [ ] Nov78 [32]
– Songs for America / Point of know return / Paradox / Icarus – borne on wings of steel / Portrait (he knew) / Carry on wayward son / Journey from Mariabronn / Dust in the wind / Lonely wind / Mysteries and mayhem / Lamplight symphony / The wall / Closet chronicles / Magnum opus: Father Padilla meets the gnat – Howling at the Moon – Man overboard – Industry on parade / Release the beavers – Gnat attack.
Jan 79. (7") *<4280>* **LONELY WIND (live). / SONG FOR AMERICA (live)** [–] [60]
Jun 79. (7") *(S-KIR 7426) <4284>* **PEOPLE OF THE SOUTH WIND. / STAY OUT OF TROUBLE** [ ] [23]
Jul 79. (lp) *(KIR 83644) <36000>* **MONOLITH** [ ] May79 [10]
– On the other side / People of the south wind / Angels have fallen / How my soul cries out for you / A glimpse of home / Away from you / Stay out of trouble / Reason to be.
Sep 79. (7") *<4285>* **REASON TO BE. / HOW MY SOUL CRIES OUT FOR YOU** [–] [52]
Sep 80. (7") *<4291>* **HOLD ON. / DON'T OPEN YOUR EYES** [–] [40]
Oct 80. (lp) *(KIR 84500) <36588>* **AUDIO-VISIONS** [ ] Sep80 [26]
– Relentless / Anything for you / Hold on / Loner / Curtain of iron / Got to rock on / Don't open your eyes / No one together / No room for a stranger / Back door. *(cd-iss. Mar96 on 'Epic'; 481161-2)*
Dec 80. (7") *<4292>* **GOT TO ROCK ON. / NO ROOM FOR A STRANGER** [–] [76]

—— **JOHN ELEFANTE** (b.1958, Levittown, N.Y.) – vocals, keyboards repl. WALSH who continued on recent solo work

Jul 82. (7") *(S-KIR 2408) <02903>* **PLAY THE GAME TONIGHT. / PLAY ON** [ ] May82 [17]
Jul 82. (lp) *(KIR 85714) <38002>* **VINYL CONFESSIONS** [ ] Jun82 [16]
– Play the game tonight / Right away / Fair exchange / Chasing shadows / Diamonds and pearls / Face it / Windows / Borderline / Play on / Crossfire. *(cd-iss. Mar96 on 'Epic'; 481162-2)*
Aug 82. (7") *<03084>* **RIGHT AWAY. / WINDOWS** [–] [73]

—— now w/out STEINHARDT

Epic CBS Assoc.

Aug 83. (7") *<04057>* **FIGHT FIRE WITH FIRE. / INCIDENT ON A BRIDGE** [–] [58]
Sep 83. (lp) *(EPC 25561) <38733>* **DRASTIC MEASURES** [ ] [41]
– Fight fire with fire / Everybody's my friend / Mainstream / Andi / Going through the motions / Get rich / Don't take your love away / End of the age / Incident on a bridge. *(cd-iss. Mar96 on 'Epic'; 481163-2)*
Sep 83. (12"m) *(TA 3696)* **FIGHT FIRE WITH FIRE. / CARRY ON WAYWARD SON / DUST IN THE WIND** [ ] [–]
Nov 83. (7") **EVERYBODY'S MY FRIEND. / END OF THE AGE** [–] [ ]

—— Disbanded late 1983. Re-formed 1986 but without LIVGREN, HOPE & ELEFANTE. Past members **EHART & WILLIAMS** brought back **STEVE WALSH.** They recruited **STEVE MORSE** (b.28 Jul'54, Hamilton, Ohio) – guitar (ex-DIXIE DREGS) / **BILLY GREER** – bass (ex-STREETS)

M.C.A. M.C.A.

Dec 86. (lp/c) *(MCG/+C 6021) <5838>* **POWER** [ ] Nov86 [35]
– Silhouettes in disguise / Power / All I wanted / Secret service / We're not alone anymore / Musicatto / Taking in the view / Three pretenders / Tomb 19 / Can't cry anymore.
Jan 87. (7"/12") *(MCA/+S 1116) <52958>* **ALL I WANTED. / WE'RE NOT ALONE ANYMORE** [ ] Oct86 [19]
Feb 87. (7") *<53027>* **POWER. / TOMB 19** [–] [84]
Apr 87. (7") *<53070>* **CAN'T CRY ANYMORE. / THREE PRETENDERS** [–] [ ]
Oct 88. (lp/c/cd) *<(MCA/MCAC/DMCA 6254)>* **IN THE SPIRIT OF THINGS** [ ] [ ]
– Ghosts / One big sky / Inside of me / One man, one heart * / House on fire / Once in a lifetime * / Stand beside me / I counted on love * / The preacher / Rainmaker / T.O. Witcher * / Bells of Saint James. *(cd+= *)*
Nov 88. (7") *<53425>* **STAND BESIDE ME. / HOUSE ON FIRE** [–] [ ]

—— In 1991, they added **DAVID RAGSDALE** – violin

—— **WALSH / LIVGREN / EHART / RAGSDALE**

Essential Intersound

Jul 93. (cd) *<9107>* **LIVE AT THE WHISKY (live)** [–] [ ]
– Introduction / Howlin' at the moon from Magnum Opus / Paradox / Point of know return / Song for America / The wall / Hold on / Dust in the wind / Miracles out of nowhere / Mysteries and mayhem / Portrait (he knew) / Carry on wayward son / Down the road. *(hidden track+=)* – Lonely street.
Jul 95. (cd/c) *(ESS CD/MC 299) <9148>* **FREAKS OF NATURE** [ ] [ ]
– I can fly / Desperate times / Hope once again / Black fathom four / Under the knife / Need / Freaks of nature / Cold grey morning / Peaceful and warm.

—— next with the London Symphony Orchestra

not iss. River North

May 98. (cd) *<161384>* **ALWAYS NEVER THE SAME** [–] [ ]
– Eleanor Rigby / Dust in the wind / Preamble / Song for America / In your eyes / Miracles out of nowhere / Hold on / The sky is falling / Cheyenne anthem / Prelude & introduction / The wall / Need to know / Nobody's home.

—— reverted to the original sextet of **WALSH, WILLIAMS, STEINHARDT, HOPE, LIVGREN + EHART** plus **GREER** (to make seven)

S.P.V. Magna Carta

Jul 00. (cd) *(SPV 0857101-2) <9050>* **SOMEWHERE TO ELSEWHERE** [ ] [ ]
– Icarus II / When the world was young / Grand fun alley / The coming down (Thanatopsis) / Myriad / Look at the time / Disappearing skin tight blues / Distant vision / Byzantium / Not man bag. *(hidden+=)* – (untitled).

– compilations, others –

Sep 84. (lp/c) *Epic; (EPC/40 26065) / CBS Assoc; <39283>* **THE BEST OF KANSAS** [ ] [ ]
– Carry on wayward son / The point of know return / Fight fire / No one together / Play the game tonight / The wall. *(cd-iss. Nov85; CD 26065) (cd re-iss. Aug90; 461036-2)*
Jul 94. (d-cd) *Legacy; (CD 47364)* **THE KANSAS BOXED SET** [ ] [ ]
Jul 98. (cd) *Epic; (487592-2)* **THE DEFINITIVE COLLECTION** [ ] [–]
Nov 98. (cd) *King Biscuit; <(KBFHCD 024)>* **KING BISCUIT PRESENTS . . .** [ ] [ ]

—— STEVE WALSH and KERRY LIVGREN both issued solo releases, although they were of the soft-rock/AOR variety.

□ Paul KANTNER & Grace SLICK
(see under ⇒ JEFFERSON AIRPLANE)

□ KATASTROPHY WIFE
(see under ⇒ BABES IN TOYLAND)

□ John KAY (see under ⇒ STEPPENWOLF)

KELIS

Born: KELIS ROGERS, 21 Aug'80, Harlem, New York, USA. Raised by her soul-singing mother and minister father, KELIS was attracted to music from a very early age, thanks to the efforts of both her parents. She fled the nest in 1996 and subsequently found herself with a lucrative recording contract via 'Virgin' a few years later, after A&R men were impressed by her backing vocals on WU-TANG's most troubled member OL' DIRTY BASTARD's 'GOT YOUR MONEY'. She issued the hip-hop themed album 'KALEIDOSCOPE' early in 2000 (and possibly titled after her freaky, rainbow-coloured afro), backed by UK Top 10 single 'CAUGHT OUT THERE', a raging anthem for disgruntled women everywhere; 'GOOD STUFF' was to follow into the British charts. The rockier, less subdued but disappointing second set, 'WANDERLAND', was issued in 2001 and featuring a whole host of guests from the bizarre, ever-expanding world of Rock and Hip Hop. NO DOUBT's GWEN STEFANI lent her talents to the track 'PERFECT DAY', while BRIAN HEAD WELCH donated his guitar playing, er talents to 'EASY COME, EASY GO'. Super producers the NEPTUNES, meanwhile, supplied the lazy beats to an album that paled in comparison to its predecessor. 'TASTY' (2003) also featured the production talents of The NEPTUNES (i.e. N*E*R*D). The album was a slow-burner at first – being released at Xmas time didn't help – although it did manage to climb the charts the following year due her mouth-wateringly suggestive 'MILKSHAKE' hit single.

Album rating: KALEIDOSCOPE (*7) / WANDERLAND (*5) / TASTY (*8)

KELIS – vocals / with various backing

Virgin Virgin

Feb 00. (c-s) *(VUSC 158)* *<38677>* **CAUGHT OUT THERE / SUSPENDED** [4] Nov99 [54]
(12"+=/cd-s+=) *(VUS T/CD 158)* – ('A'mixes).
(above originally hit UK No.52 as an import!)

Feb 00. (cd/d-lp) *(CDVUS/VUSLP 167)* *<47911>* **KALEIDOSCOPE** [54] Jan00 [ ]
– Intro / Good stuff / Caught out there / Get along with you / Mafia / Game show / Suspended / Mars / Ghetto children / I want your love / No turning back / Roller pink / In the morning / Wouldn't you agree.

Jun 00. (c-s) *(VUSC 164)* **GOOD STUFF / (Junior's radio mix)** [19] [–]
(12"+=/cd-s+=) *(VUS T/CD 164)* – ('A'-Forces of nature radio edit) / ('A'-Cd-Rom).

— in Jul'00, KELIS featured on OL' DIRTY BASTARD's hit single, 'Got Your Money'

Oct 00. (c-s/cd-s) *(VUS C/CD 174)* **GET ALONG WITH YOU / mixes:- Soul inside / Bump & Flex / Morales)** [51] [–]
(12") *(VUST 174)* – ('A'-Bump & Flex club) / ('A'-Morales club).
(12") *(VUSTX 174)* – ('A'-Soul inside funk) / ('A'-Bump & Flex dub) / ('A'-Morales dub).

Oct 01. (c-s/12"/cd-s) *(VUS C/T/CD 212)* **YOUNG FRESH 'N' NEW / (Timo Maas remix) / (So Solid Crew vocal remix)** [32] [–]
(12") *(VUSTX 212)* – ('A'-Timo Maas dub) / ('A'-Timo Maas instrumental).

Oct 01. (cd) *(CDVUS 205)* **WANDERLAND** [ ] [–]
– Intro / Young fresh 'n' new / Flash back / Popular thug (with PUSHA T) / Daddy (with MALICE) / Scared money / Shooting stars / Digital world (with ROSCOE) / Perfect day / Easy come easy go / Junkie / Get even / Mr UFO man (with JOHN OSTBY) / Little Suzie.

— in Oct'02, KELIS feat. on TIMO MAAS single, 'Help Me'

— in Aug'03, KELIS feat. on a hit single, 'Let's Get Ill' with P. DIDDY plus a further one with RICHARD X, 'Finest Dreams'

Virgin Arista

Dec 03. (cd/d-lp) *(CD+/V 2978)* *<52132>* **TASTY** [ ] [27]
– Intro / Trick me / Milkshake / Keep it down / In public / Flashback / Protect my heart / Millionaire / Glow / Sugar honey iced tea / Attention / Rolling through the hood / Stick up / Marathon.

— (the album will hit UK No.11 in Jan'04)

Alicia KEYS

Born: 25 Jan'81, Harlem, New York, USA. From the tender age of five, KEYS began to show signs of her musical promise, later enrolling in classical piano tuition at the age of seven. Her secondary school education at the Professional Performing Arts High School in New York further helped to hone her blossoming talent. It was here she met Conrad Robinson, a major inspirational force in her life, who assisted her in vocal training, and whose brother Jeff became her manager. By the age of fourteen, KEYS had already written the song 'BUTTERFLYZ', a track which was later to appear on her debut album. After secondary school KEYS graduated to Columbia University, which she subsequently dropped out of to pursue her musical career full-time. Originally inking an unfruitful deal with 'Columbia', she almost immediately signed to 'Arista' in 1998. Her debut album, 'songs in A minor' finally came out in 2001 on former Arista boss, Clive Davis's newly formed 'J' records. From the album's intro, 'PIANO & I', the listener was greeted with the mixing of musical styles; this opening track began with her playing a rendition of Beethoven's 'MOONLIGHT SONATA' overlaid with a hip hop beat. KEYS early years growing up in Harlem heavily influenced her music; the album was awash with soul, funk and jazz stylings, combined with her classical training, which set her as an individual amongst already huge female R&B and soul singers of the time such as ARETHA FRANKLIN and LAURYN HILL. Although the album was full of proficient songwriting (similar in some respects to the great STEVIE WONDER), the real stand-out track was 'FALLIN', which rocketed her to pole position in the US charts in 2001. Later in the year saw the release of another hit single, 'A WOMAN'S WORTH', massive respect gaining her no less than five grammys and the promise of a prolific career. Following the release of single 'YOU DON'T KNOW MY NAME', nu-soul's renaissance lady didn't disappoint with sophomore set, 'DIARY OF ALICIA KEYS' (2003). Again revealing a sophistication way beyond her years, the record's flawless marriage of classic and contemporary black music, pure pop and singer-songwriter self examination suggested that KEYS' talent was more long term than some of her peers.

Album rating: songs in A minor (*9) / THE DIARY OF ALICIA KEYS (*6)

ALICIA KEYS – vocals, piano, etc / with **KRUCIAL BROTHERS** (production) & various session people

J – Arista J – Arista

Jul 01. (cd) *<(80813 20002-2)>* **songs in A minor** [6] [1]
– Piano & I / Girlfriend / How come you don't call me / Fallin' / Troubles / Rock wit U / A woman's worth / Jane Doe / Goodbye / The life / Mr. Man (duet with JIMMY COZIER) / Never felt this way (interlude) / Butterflyz / Why do I feel so sad / Caged bird / Lovin U. *(re-iss. Oct02; 74321 96962-2)*

Oct 01. (c-s) *(74321 90369-4)* *<21041>* **FALLIN' / REAR VIEW MIRROR** [3] Jun01 [1]
(cd-s+=) *(74321 90369-2)* – Rampage / ('A'version with Busta Rhymes) / ('A'video).
(12") *(74321 90369-1)* – ('A'album mix) / ('A'instrumental).

— in Mar'02, ALICIA and EVE featured on ANGIE STONE's hit single, 'Brotha Part II'

Mar 02. (c-s) *(74321 92869-4)* *<21112>* **A WOMAN'S WORTH / (remix)** [18] Oct01 [7]
(12"+=) *(74321 92869-1)* – ('A'-instrumental).
(cd-s++=) *(74321 92869-2)* – ('A'-video).

Jul 02. (c-s) *(74321 94312-4)* **HOW COME YOU DON'T CALL ME / (Neptunes remix)** [26] [59]
(12"+=) *(74321 94312-1)* – (live version).
(cd-s++=) *(74321 94312-2)* *<94289>* – Butterflyz (Roger's mix).

— in Oct'02, ALICIA featured on EVE's hit single, 'Gangsta Lovin'

Nov 02. (c-s) *(74321 97497-4)* **GIRLFRIEND / (Brat pac mix)** [24] [–]
(12"+=/cd-s+=)) *(74321 97497-1/-2)* – ('A'-Troubles Jay-J & Chris Lum bootleg mix).

J-Records J-Records

Dec 03. (cd/lp) *<(82876 58620-2/55712-1)>* **THE DIARY OF ALICIA KEYS** [13] [1]
– Harlem's nocturne / Karma / Heartburn / If I was your woman – Walk on by / You don't know my name / If I ain't got you / Diary (with TONY! TONI! TONE!) / Dragon days / Wake up / So simple / When you really love someone (with LELLOW) / Feeling U, feeling me (interlude) / Slow down / Samsonite man / Nobody not really (interlude). *(UK+=)* – Streets of New York. *(ltd-cd+=)* – Diary (documentary).

Dec 03. (cd-s) *(82876 58865-2)* **YOU DON'T KNOW MY NAME / FALLIN' (All soundtrack version)** [19] Nov03 [3]
(cd-s) *(82876 58161-2)* – ('A'side) / Butterflyz (Roger's release mix) / ('A'-video).
(12") *(82876 57460-1)* *<56599>* – ('A'side) / ('A'-instrumental) / Streets of New York.

☐ K.G.B. (see under ⇒ ELECTRIC FLAG)

Johnny KIDD (& The PIRATES)

Born: FREDERICK HEATH, 23 Dec'39, Willesden, London, England. In 1956, together with ALAN CADDY, he formed skiffle combo, FREDDIE HEATH & THE NUTTERS, although they never made it onto vinyl. Early in 1959, after toying with calling himself CAPTAIN KIDD, the singer adopted the stage name of JOHNNY KIDD. Signing for 'H.M.V.', his debut single, 'PLEASE DON'T TOUCH' (written w/ manager Gus Robinson), hit the UK Top 30, attitude-laden rock'n'roll to match America's GENE VINCENT. KIDD borrowed his limp follow-up, 'IF YOU WERE THE ONLY GIRL IN THE WORLD', from the music hall tradition and unsurprisingly it bombed. In 1960, a new approach was needed, KIDD enlisting back-up band, The PIRATES (i.e. MICK GREEN – guitar, JOHNNY SPENCE – bass, FRANK FARLEY – drums) in an attempt to beef up his sound (they even dressed as pirates!). Now trading under the moniker of JOHNNY KIDD & THE PIRATES, they returned to the UK Top 30 with a rendition of Marv Johnson's 'YOU GOT WHAT IT TAKES'. With the classic 'SHAKIN' ALL OVER', however, the band introduced a dirty, reverb-heavy R&B sound which became a template for the more basic, riff-centric bands of the UK beat boom. Although the track topped the UK charts, their subsequent 45's failed to generate the same level of interest. Although these were still rockin', KIDD was another to be taken over by the aforementioned British Invasion (c. 1963/64). Still without an album to his name, KIDD formed his new PIRATES, who included DEEP PUPLE-bound NICK SIMPER. Tragically, on the 7th of October 1966, JOHNNY was killed after his tour van collided with a lorry on the M1. He was only 26 years of age and would have certainly enjoyed a renewed acquaintance with success following the advent of hard rock towards the end of the decade. • **Songwriters:** Although not prolific, JOHNNY wrote/co-wrote some fine gems. Also covered; LINDA LU (Ray Sharpe) / THE BIRDS AND THE BEES (Jewel Atkins) / I CAN TELL (Bo Diddley) / A SHOT OF RHYTHM AND BLUES (Arthur Alexander) / MY BABE (Little Walter) / ALWAYS AND EVER (Latin-American standard) / WHOLE LOTTA WOMAN (Marvin Rainwater) / etc. • **Trivia:** NICK SIMPER, later an early member of DEEP PURPLE, was also injured in the crash.

Best CD compilation: THE COMPLETE JOHNNY KIDD & THE PIRATES (*8)

JOHNNY KIDD – vocals (solo with session people)

		H.M.V.	not iss.
May 59.	(7") *(POP 615)* **PLEASE DON'T TOUCH. / GROWL**	25	–
Dec 59.	(7") *(POP 674)* **IF YOU WERE THE ONLY GIRL IN THE WORLD. / FEELIN'**		–

JOHNNY KIDD & THE PIRATES

(still session men) His live line-up **ALAN CADDY** – guitar / **TONY DOHERTY** – rhythm guitar / **JOHNNY GORDON** – bass / **KEN McKAY** – drums / **MIKE WEST** and **TOM BROWN** – backing vocals

Feb 60.	(7") *(POP 698)* **YOU GOT WHAT IT TAKES. / LONGIN' LIPS**	25	–

— **KIDD** retained only **CADDY** (JOE MORETTI – lead guitar on below 1 only) with **BRIAN GREGG** – bass (ex-BEAT BOYS) / **CLEM CATTINI** – drums (ex-BEAT BOYS)

		H.M.V.	Capitol
Jun 60.	(7") *(POP 753)* **SHAKIN' ALL OVER. / YES SIR, THAT'S MY BABY** *(re-iss. Feb76 on 'EMI')*	1	
Sep 60.	(7") *(POP 790)* **RESTLESS. / MAGIC OF LOVE**	22	
Mar 61.	(7") *(POP 853)* **LINDA LU. / LET'S TALK ABOUT US**	47	

— KIDD now reverted to session men

Sep 61.	(7") *(POP 919)* **PLEASE DON'T BRING ME DOWN. / SO WHAT**		

— KIDD completely changed his PIRATES line-up; **JOHNNY PATTO** – guitar / **JOHNNY SPENCE** – bass / **FRANK FARLEY** – drums (all ex-CUDDLY DUDLEY) repl. ALAN, BRIAN + CLEM who all joined COLIN HICKS' Band

Jan 62.	(7") *(POP 978)* **HURRY ON BACK TO LOVE. / I WANT THAT**		

— **MICK GREEN** – guitar repl. PATTO

Nov 62.	(7") *(POP 1088)* **A SHOT OF RHYTHM AND BLUES. / I CAN TELL**	48	–
Jun 63.	(7") *(POP 1173)* **I'LL NEVER GET OVER YOU. / THEN I GOT EVERYTHING**	4	Oct63
Nov 63.	(7") *(POP 1228)* **HUNGRY FOR LOVE. / ECSTACY**	20	–
Apr 64.	(7") *(POP 1269)* **ALWAYS AND EVER. / DR. FEELGOOD**	46	–

— added **VIC COOPER** – organ

Jun 64.	(7") *(POP 1309)* **JEALOUS GIRL. / SHOP AROUND**		–

— **JOHN WIEDER** – guitar (ex-TONY MEEHAN) repl. MICK to BILLY KRAMER

Oct 64.	(7") *(POP 1353)* **WHOLE LOTTA WOMAN. / YOUR CHEATIN' HEART**		–
Feb 65.	(7") *(POP 1397)* **THE BIRDS AND THE BEES. / DON'T MAKE THE SAME MISTAKE AS I DID**		–
May 65.	(7") *(POP 1424)* **SHAKIN' ALL OVER '65. / I GOTTA TRAVEL ON**		–

— KIDD, SPENCE, FARLEY and COOPER recruited **JON MORSHEAD** – guitar repl. WIEDER who later joined ERIC BURDON

Apr 66.	(7"; by JOHNNY KIDD) *(POP 1520)* **IT'S GOT TO BE YOU. / I HATE TO GET UP IN THE MORNING**		–

— JOHNNY KIDD brought in completely new musicians **MICK STEWART** – guitar repl. MORSHEAD / **NICK SIMPER** – bass (ex-SIMON RAVEN CULT) repl. SPENCE / **ROGER TRUTH** – drums (ex-SIMON RAVEN CULT) repl. FARLEY / also **RAY SOAPER** – keyboards (left before recording below). First three that left became band The PIRATES.

— JOHNNY KIDD was killed in a car crash on the 7th October '66. Below released posthumously

Nov 66.	(7") *(POP 1559)* **THE FOOL. / SEND FOR THAT GIRL**		–

— without KIDD the new PIRATES continued until May67. SIMPER to DEEP PURPLE

– (selective) compilations, etc. –

Apr 78.	(lp) *EMI Nut; (NUTM 12)* **THE BEST OF JOHNNY KIDD & THE PIRATES** – A shot of rhythm & blues / Shakin' all over / Longing lips / Restess / Growl / I want that / Linda Lu / You've got what it takes / Your cheatin' heart / I'll never get over you / Hungry for love / I can tell / Jealous girl / Shop around / Please don't touch / Always and ever. *(re-iss. Feb87 on 'E.M.I.' lp/c; EMS/TC-EMS 1120)*		–
May 87.	(lp) *See For Miles; (SEE 120)* **RARITIES** *(cd-iss. Oct89 & Jan97; SEECD 120)*		–
Feb 90	(lp/cd) *See For Miles; (SEE/+CD 287)* **CLASSIC AND RARE** *(cd re-iss. Aug93; same)*		–
Aug 92.	(d-cd/d-c) *E.M.I.; (CD/TC KIDD 11)* **THE COMPLETE JOHNNY KIDD & THE PIRATES**		–
Jul 95.	(cd/c) *E.M.I.; (CD/TC SL 8256)* **THE VERY BEST OF JOHNNY KIDD & THE PIRATES**		–
Feb 98.	(cd) *Disky; (WB 88587-2)* **SHAKIN' ALL OVER**		
Jul 98.	(cd) *EMI Gold; (495480-2)* **25 GREATEST HITS**		–
Feb 01.	(cd) *EMI Plus; (5761990)* **THE STORY**		–
Mar 03.	(cd) *Beat Goes On; (BGOCD 580)* **THE JOHNNY KIDD MEMORIAL ALBUM**		

KID ROCK

Born: ROBERT RITCHIE, 17 Jan'71, Dearborn, Michigan, USA. This white rapper-cum-metalist debuted with the depthless 'GRITS SANDWICHES FOR BREAKFAST' (1990) before his stab at major label success via the even weaker 'THE POLYFUZE METHOD' (1993). The baseball clad, cigar smoking MC shot to notoriety in 1997 – one year after the release of the single 'EARLY MORNING STONED PIMP' – when a leading radio station in Motor City played his infamous 'YODELING IN THE VALLEY' track (from the debut album) and were subsequently fined for obscene broadcasting. KID ROCK signed to 'Atlantic' in 1997 and issued his third set 'DEVIL WITHOUT A CAUSE' the following year. Like the string of white suburban metal bands, ROCK relied heavily on bad language, songs about drugs (and "bitches") and endless references to the degenerate culture, which somehow made this album sound like a bit of a charlatan. The entertainer (who's now going down a storm with WWF mob!) spent much of his time prancing around on stage in a pair of horrible silver MC HAMMER-esque baggy trousers – with a dwarf and two lap dancers in tow – proving he could yet become a novelty act for juvenile teens after all – sadly one of his MC's, JOE C, died in November 2000. Now a multi-platinum super anti-star, The KID pretty much repeated his formula on the indulgently titled 'COCKY' (2001), mashing up the usual lashings of redneck rock'n'roll with white trash hip-hop and twisted humour. Britain still failed to take him on board and the man in the hat had to settle for a US Top 10 placing. The oldest KID in town was back with the 'KID ROCK' album in 2003, its simple title and austere sleeve suggesting some kind of artistic renewal. Following the huge success of his countrified duet with SHERYL CROW, 'PICTURE', that renewal took the shape of southern-fried, country-tempered roots rock replacing much of the pseudo-hip hop of yore. It was still obnoxious, still foot-stomping and still determinedly un-PC but it somehow succeeded in placing the KID in the unlikely context of Great American Music without sounding too contrived.

Album rating: GRITS SANDWICHES FOR BREAKFAST (*4) / THE POLYFUZE METHOD (*3) / DEVIL WITHOUT A CAUSE (*6) / COCKY (*6) / KID ROCK (*7)

KID ROCK – rapper, bass, guitar / with various friends

not iss. — Novus-Jive

Oct 90. (c-s/12") *<1349/+1>* **YO-DA-LIN IN THE VALLEY** [–] [ ]

Nov 90. (cd/c/lp) *<1409-2/-4/-1>* **GRITS SANDWICHES FOR BREAKFAST** [–] [ ]
– Yo-da-lin in the valley / Genuine article / Cramp ya style / New York's not my home / Super rhyme maker / With a one two / Wax the booty / Pimp of the nation / Abdul Jabar cut / Step in stride / Upside / Style of X pression / Trippin' over a rock. *(cd re-iss. Jun01 on 'Jive'; 922025-2)*

Continuum — Continuum

1992. (c-s/12"/cd-s) *<19255>* **BACK FROM THE DEAD (extended). / ('A'-short) / ('A'-instrumental)** [–] [ ]

Aug 93. (12"/cd-s) *(12/CD CTUM 101) <12205>* **U DON'T KNOW ME /** [ ] Feb93 [ ]

Sep 93. (cd/lp) *(CD+/CTUM 2) <19205-2/-4>* **THE POLYFUZE METHOD** [ ] [ ]
– Fred / Killin' brain cells / Prodigal son / Cramper / 3 sheets to the wind / Fuck U blind / Desperate (radio) / Back from the dead / My Oedipus complex / Balls in your mouth / Trippin' with Dick Vitale / TV dinner / Pancake breakfast / Blow me / In so deep / U don't know me.

Dec 93. (m-cd/m-c) *<15205>* **FIRE IT UP** [–] [ ]
– I am the bullgod / My Oedipus complex / Country boy can survive / Balls in your mouth / Cramper / Rollin' on the island.

not iss. — Top Dog

Jan 96. (c-ep/cd-ep) *<50001>* **EARLY MORNIN' STONED PIMP** [–] [ ]

—— now backed by band, TWISTED BROWN TRUCKER:- **KENNY OLSON** – guitar / **STEFANIE EULINBERG** – drums / **TWEEDS KRACKER** – turntables / **JIMMY BONES** – keyboards / **JASON KRAUSE** – guitar / **MISTY LOVE + SHIRLEY HAYDEN** – backing vocals

Lava – Atlantic — Lava – Atlantic

Jun 99. (cd/c) *<(7567 83119-2/-4)>* **DEVIL WITHOUT A CAUSE** [ ] Aug98 [4]
– Bawitdaba / Cowboy / Devil without a cause / I am the bullgod / Roving gangster (rollin') / Wasting time / Welcome 2 the party (ode 2 the old skool) / I got one for ya / Somebody's gotta feel this / Fist of rage / Only God knows why / Fuck off (w/ EMINEM) / Where U at Rock (w/ EMINEM) / Black chick, white guy (w/ EMINEM). *<clean version-iss.Oct98; 83152>*

Oct 99. (c-s/cd-s) *(AT 0076 C/CD) <84520>* **COWBOY / COWBOY (album version) / I AM THE BULLGOD (live)** [36] [82]

Feb 00. (-) *<radio cut>* **ONLY GOD KNOWS WHY** [–] [19]

May 00. (cd/c) *<(7567 83314-2/-4)>* **THE HISTORY OF ROCK** [73] [2]
– Intro / American bad ass / Prodigal son / Paid / Early mornin' stoned pimp (by KID ROCK & JOE C) / Tino / Dark and grey / 3 sheets to the wind (what's my name) / Abortion / I wanna go back / Ya' keep on / Fuck that / Fuck you blind / Born to be a hick / My oedipus complex (KID ROCK & TWISTED BROKEN TRUCKER).

Aug 00. (c-s) *(AT 0085C)* **AMERICAN BAD ASS (clean version) / 3 SHEETS TO THE WIND (live) / COWBOY (live)** [25] [ ]
(cd-s+=) *(AT 0085CD)* – ('A'-promo video).

Apr 01. (cd-s) *(AT 0098CD1)* **BAWITDADA / MY OEDIPUS COMPLEX (father edit) / MY OEDIPUS COMPLEX (Son edit) / ('A'video)** [41] [–]
(cd-s) *(AT 0098CD2)* – ('A'side) / Cowboy / Prodigal son / Cowboy (video).
(cd-s) *(AT 0098CD3)* – ('A'side) / I am the the bullgod / Paid / I am the bullgod (video).

Jan 02. (cd/c) *<(7567 83482-2/-4)>* **COCKY** [ ] Nov01 [7]
– Trucker anthem / Forever / Lay it on me / Cocky / What I learned out on the road / I'm wrong, but you ain't right / Lonely road of faith / You never met a motherfucker quite like me / Picture (with SHERYL CROW) / I'm a dog / Midnight train to Memphis / Baby come home / Drunk in the morning. *(cd+=)* – WCSR (with SNOOP DOGG).

Nov 03. (cd) *<(7567 83685-2)>* **KID ROCK** [ ] [8]
– Rock n' roll pain train / Cadillac pussy / Feel like makin' love / Black Bob / Jackson, Mississippi / Cold and empty / Intro / Rock n' roll / Hillbilly stomp / I am / Son of Detroit / Do it for you / Hard night for Sarah / Run off to L.A. *(bonus track+=)* – Single father.

☐ KILBURN & THE HIGH ROADS (see under ⇒ DURY, Ian)

KILLING JOKE

Formed: Notting Hill, London, England ... 1979 by JAZ COLEMAN and PAUL FERGUSON, who subsequently added GEORDIE (K. WALKER) and YOUTH (MARTIN GLOVER). After borrowing money to finance a debut EP (contained three tracks including 'TURN TO RED'), the band were the subject of some interest to DJ John Peel who championed their alternative rock sound. This immediately led to KILLING JOKE signing a deal with 'Island', who virtually re-issued the aforementioned single/EP in abbreviated 7" form (A-side, 'NERVOUS SYSTEM'), adding a fourth track on the 12". While supporting the likes of JOY DIVISION and The RUTS, they released a follow-up double A-sided single, 'WARDANCE' / 'PSYCHE', resurrecting their own 'Malicious Damage' label in the process. The left-field 'E.G.' operation were quick to spot the group's potential, taking on both KILLING JOKE and their label. The first results of this partnership came in the form of 'REQUIEM', the single taken from their pioneering eponymous UK Top 40 album. Replacing the anger of punk with apocalyptic doom mongering, KILLING JOKE were akin to a sonically disturbing, industrialised BLACK SABBATH. Now regarded as a catalystic classic in metal circles, the album also inspired many US hardcore acts, as well as such big guns as METALLICA, MINISTRY, SOUNDGARDEN and NIRVANA. By the release of follow-up set, 'WHAT'S THIS FOR' (1981), KILLING JOKE had taken their occult punk-like chants/anthems to extreme new dimensions. Nevertheless, they retained a strange accessibility which saw the single, 'FOLLOW THE LEADERS' attaining a minor UK chart placing and incredibly, a hit on the American dancefloors! A third set, 'REVELATIONS' (1982), eased up a little on the intensity factor, although it peaked at No.12 having already spawned another hit single, 'EMPIRE SONG'. Convinced of imminent world destruction, the occult-fixated COLEMAN remained in Iceland after a tour, YOUTH initially returning home but later following his lead to the frozen north. He subsequently flew back to England, teaming up with FERGUSON and newfound friend, PAUL RAVEN to form BRILLIANT. However, both FERGUSON and RAVEN soon departed from YOUTH's group, taking off for Iceland in search of the missing COLEMAN. Eventually locating their frontman, all three returned to UK shores and re-entered the studio (GEORDIE also in tow) with a view to recording new KILLING JOKE material. The resulting album, 'FIRE DANCES' (1983), only managed to scrape into the Top 30, its lack of bite and experimentation possibly a hangover from their northern treks. The following year, KILLING JOKE released only two 45's, although one of them, 'EIGHTIES' (a minor hit), was showcased in all its eccentric glory on Channel 4's new pop show, 'The Tube'. Having overcome the mental obstacle of 1984 (and all of its apocalyptic implications), COLEMAN and Co. unleashed their most focused work to date in 'NIGHT TIME' (a near Top 10 album), the 'LOVE LIKE BLOOD' single preceding the set and breaking into the Top 20 in early '85. The latter half of the eighties weren't so kind, both critically and commercially, the albums, 'BRIGHTER THAN A THOUSAND SUNS' (1986) and 'OUTSIDE THE GATE' (1988), taking a more self-indulgent keyboard-orientated approach. Following major personnel upheavals, KILLING JOKE decided to take a brief sabbatical, COLEMAN finding time to release a collaborative album with ANNE DUDLEY (ex-ART OF NOISE), 'SONGS FROM THE VICTORIOUS CITY' (1990). The same year, COLEMAN, GEORDIE, RAVEN and newcomer MARTIN ATKINS, returned with the acclaimed 'EXTREMITIES, DIRT AND VARIOUS REPRESSED EMOTIONS' album. Having spent most of the early 90's globetrotting in various exotic locations, KILLING JOKE (now COLEMAN, GEORDIE and the returning YOUTH), were back with a vengeance on 1994's 'PANDEMONIUM'. Their biggest selling album to date, the record and the 'PANDEMONIUM' single from it both made the Top 30 (the previous 'MILLENNIUM' made Top 40), while also seeing an American release on the 'Zoo' label. Another, increasingly metallic/industrial set, 'DEMOCRACY' followed in 1996, although COLEMAN now spends the bulk of his time in New Zealand, where he is composer in residence for the country's Symphony Orchestra. After almost a decade, COLEMAN, GEORDIE, YOUTH (and DAVE GROHL on drums!) were back with the eponymous 'KILLING JOKE' (2003). If the stark title harked back to their classic 1980 debut, the uncompromising likes of 'TOTAL INVASION' and 'ASTEROID' – sharpened by an Andy Gill production – indeed seemed to suggest they'd come full circle, updating the steamrolling sound which initially made their name.

Album rating: KILLING JOKE (*9) / WHAT'S THIS FOR ...! (*7) / REVELATIONS (*5) / HA! KILLING JOKE LIVE (*5) / FIRE DANCES (*7) / NIGHT TIME (*7) / BRIGHTER THAN A THOUSAND SUNS (*6) / OUTSIDE THE GATE (*6) / EXTREMITIES, DIRT AND VARIOUS REPRESSED EMOTIONS (*7) / LAUGH? I NEARLY BOUGHT ONE! compilation (*8) / PANDEMONIUM (*8) / DEMOCRACY (*6) / KILLING JOKE (*7)

JAZ COLEMAN (b. JEREMY, 26 Feb'60, Cheltenham, England; raised Egypt) – vocals, keyboards / **GEORDIE** (b. K. WALKER, 18 Dec'58, Newcastle-upon-Tyne, England) – guitar, synthesizers / **YOUTH** (b. MARTIN GLOVER, 27 Dec'60, Africa) – bass, vocals (ex-RAGE) / **PAUL FERGUSON** (b.31 Mar'58, High Wycombe, England) – drums

Malicious Damage | not iss.

Oct 79. (10"ep) *(MD 410)* **ARE YOU RECEIVING ME. / TURN TO RED / NERVOUS SYSTEM** [ ] [–]

Island | not iss.

Nov 79. (7") *(WIP 6550)* **NERVOUS SYSTEM. / TURN TO RED** [ ] [–]
(12"+=) *(12WIP 6550)* – Almost red / Are you receiving me.

Malicious Damage | not iss.

Mar 80. (7") *(MD 540)* **WARDANCE. / PSYCHE** [ ] [–]

E.G. – Malicious Damage | Editions

Sep 80. (7") *(EGMD 1.00)* **REQUIEM. / CHANGE** [ ] [–]
(12"+=) *(EGMX 1.00)* – Requiem 434 / Change (version).

Oct 80. (lp/c) *(EGMD/+C 545)* **KILLING JOKE** [39] [–]
– Requiem / Wardance / Tomorrow's world / Bloodsport / The wait / Complications / S.O. 36 / Primitive. *(re-iss. Jan87 lp/c/cd; EG LP/MC/CD 57) <US cd-iss. 1987 on 'Caroline'; 1538>*

May 81. (7") *(EGMDS 1.01)* **FOLLOW THE LEADERS. / TENSION** [55] [–]
(10"+=) *(EGMDX 1.010)* – Follow the leaders – dub.

Jun 81. (lp/c) *(EGMD/+C 550)* *<111>* **WHAT'S THIS FOR...!** [42] [ ]
– The fall of Because / Tension / Unspeakable / Butcher / Follow the leaders / Madness / Who told you how? / Exit. *(re-iss. Jan87 lp/c/cd; EG LP/MC/CD 58) <US cd-iss. 1987 on 'Caroline'; 1539>*

E.G. | Caroline

Mar 82. (7") *(EGO 4)* **EMPIRE SONG. / BRILLIANT** [43] [–]

— **GUY PRATT** – bass; repl. YOUTH who formed BRILLIANT

Apr 82. (lp/c) *(EGMD/+C 3)* **REVELATIONS** [12] [–]
– The hum / Empire song / We have joy / Chop chop / The Pandys are coming / Chapter III / Have a nice day / Land of milk and honey / Good samaritan / Dregs. *(re-iss. Jan87 lp/c/cd; EG LP/MC/CD 59) <US cd-iss. 1987 on 'Caroline'; 1540>*

Jun 82. (7") *(EGO 7)* **CHOP CHOP. / GOOD SAMARITAN** [ ] [–]

Oct 82. (7") *(EGO 10)* **BIRDS OF A FEATHER. / FLOCK THE B-SIDE** [64] [–]
(12"+=) *(EGOX 10)* – Sun goes down.

Nov 82. (10"m-lp/m-c) *(EGMD T/C 4)* **HA – KILLING JOKE LIVE (live)** [66] [–]
– Psyche / Sun goes down / The Pandys are coming / Take take take / Unspeakable / Wardance.

— **PAUL RAVEN** – bass (ex-NEON HEARTS) repl. PRATT who joined ICEHOUSE

Jun 83. (7") *(EGO 11)* **LET'S ALL GO (TO THE FIRE DANCES). / DOMINATOR (version)** [51] [–]
(12"+=) *(EGOX 11)* – The fall of Because (live).

Jul 83. (lp/c) *(EGMD/+C 5)* **FIRE DANCES** [29] [–]
– The gathering / Fun and games / Rejuvenation / Frenzy / Harlequin / Feast of blaze / Song and dance / Dominator / Let's all go (to the fire dances) / Lust almighty. *(re-iss. Jan87 lp/c/cd; EG LP/MC/CD 60) <US cd-iss. 1987 on 'Caroline'; 1541>*

Oct 83. (7") *(EGOD 14)* **ME OR YOU?. / WILFUL DAYS** [57] [–]
(with free 7") *(KILL 1-2)* – ('A'side) / Feast of blaze.
(d12"++=) *(EGOXD 14)* – Let's all go (to the fire dances) / The fall of Because (live) / Dominator (version).

Mar 84. (7") *(EGO 16)* **EIGHTIES. / EIGHTIES (Coming mix)** [60] [–]
(12"+=) *(EGOX 16)* – ('A'-Serious dance mix).

Jun 84. (7") *(EGO 17)* **A NEW DAY. / DANCE DAY** [56] [–]
(12"+=) *(EGOX 17)* – ('A'dub).

Jan 85. (7") *(EGO 20)* **LOVE LIKE BLOOD. / BLUE FEATHER** [16] [–]
(12"+=) *(EGOY 20)* – ('A'-Gestalt mix).
(12"++=) *(EGOX 20)* – ('A'instrumental).

Feb 85. (lp/c) *(EGMD/+C 6)* *<1531>* **NIGHT TIME** [11] [ ]
– Night time / Darkness before dawn / Love like blood / Kings and queens / Tabazan / Multitudes / Europe / Eighties. *(re-iss. Jan87 lp/c/cd; EG LP/MC/CD 61)*

Mar 85. (7") *(EGO 21)* **KINGS AND QUEENS. / THE MADDING CROWD** [58] [–]
(12"+=) *(EGOX 21)* – ('A'-Right Royal mix).
(12"+=) *(EGOY 21)* – ('A'-Knave mix).

Aug 86. (7") *(EGO 27)* **ADORATIONS. / EXILE** [42] [–]
(d7"+=) *(EGOD 27)* – Ecstacy / ('A'instrumental).

E.G. Virgin

Oct 86. (7") *(EGO 30)* **SANITY. / GOODBYE TO THE VILLAGE** 70 –
(free c-s with-7") *(above tracks)* – Wardance (remix).
(12"+=) *(EGOX 30)* – Victory.

Nov 86. (lp/c/cd) *(EG LP/MC/CD 66) <90568-1/-4/-2>* **BRIGHTER THAN A THOUSAND SUNS** 54
– Adorations / Sanity / Chessboards / Twilight of the mortal / Love of the masses / A southern sky / Wintergardens / Rubicon. *(c+=/cd+=)* – Goodbye to the village / Victory.

E.G. Caroline

Apr 88. (7") *(EGO 40)* **AMERICA. / JIHAD (Beyrouth edit)** –
(12"+=) *(EGOX 40)* – ('A'extended).
(cd-s++=) *(EGOCD 40)* – Change (original 1980 mix).

Jun 88. (lp/c/cd) *(EG LP/MC/CD 73) <1378>* **OUTSIDE THE GATE** 92
– America / My love of this land / Stay one jump ahead / Unto the ends of the Earth / The calling / Obsession / Tiahuanaco / Outside the gate. *(cd+=)* – America (extended) / Stay one jump ahead (extended).

Jul 88. (7") *(EGO 43)* **MY LOVE OF THIS LAND. / DARKNESS BEFORE DAWN** –
(12"+=) *(EGOX 43)* – Follow the leaders (dub) / Psyche.
(10"+=) *(EGOT 43)* – Follow the leaders (dub) / Sun goes down.

— **JAZ + GEORDIE** brought in new members **MARTIN ATKINS** (b. 3 Aug'59, Coventry, England) – drums (ex-PUBLIC IMAGE LTD.) repl. FERGUSON / **TAFF** – bass repl. ANDY ROURKE (ex-SMITHS) who had repl. RAVEN. Early 1990, **JAZ COLEMAN** teamed up with ANNE DUDLEY (see; ART OF NOISE)

— **KILLING JOKE** reformed (**COLEMAN, GEORDIE, ATKINS + RAVEN**)

Noise Int. R.C.A.

Nov 90. (cd/c/lp) *(AGR 054-2/-4/-1) <4828-2/-4>* **EXTREMITIES, DIRT AND VARIOUS REPRESSED EMOTIONS**
– Money is not our god / Age of greed / Beautiful dead / Extremities / Inside the termite mound / Intravenus / Solitude / North of the border / Slipstream / Kalijuga struggle. *(cd re-iss. Sep98 on 'F.A.D.'; FAD 5054)*

Jan 91. (12"/cd-s) *(AG 054-6/-3)* **MONEY IS NOT OUR GOD. / NORTH OF THE BORDER** –

Invisible Invisible

Jul 93. (d-lp) *(<INV 004>)* **THE COURTHOLD TALKS**
– (spoken word with JAZ, GEORDIE & JAFF SCANTLEBURY on percussion)

— **YOUTH** returned to repl. RAVEN

— **GEOFF DUGMORE** – drums (ex-ART OF NOISE) repl. ATKINS (to PIGFACE, etc)

Butterfly Volcano-Zoo

Mar 94. (10"ep/cd-ep) *(BFL T/D 11)* **EXORCISM. / ('A'live) / ('A'-German mix) / WHITEOUT (Ugly mix) / ANOTHER CULT GOES DOWN (mix) / ('A'-Bictonic revenge mix)** –

Apr 94. (7"clear/c-s) *(BFL/+C 12)* **MILLENNIUM. / ('A'-Cybersank remix)** 34 –
(12"+=/cd-s+=) *(BFL T/D 12)* – ('A'-Drum Club remix) / ('A'Juno Reactor remix).

Jul 94. (12"/c-s/cd-s) *(BFL T/C/D 17) <14178>* **PANDEMONIUM. / ('A'mix)** 28 Oct94
(cd-s) *(BFLD 17)* – ('A'side) / Requiem (Kris Weston & Greg Hunter remix).

Jul 94. (cd/c/d-lp) *(BFL CD/MC/LP 9) <31085>* **PANDEMONIUM** 16 Aug94
– Pandemonium / Exorcism / Millenium / Communion / Black Moon / Labyrinth / Jana / Whiteout / Pleasures of the flesh / Mathematics of chaos.

— re-united originals **JAZ COLEMAN / GEORDIE + YOUTH**

Jan 95. (cd-ep) *(BFLDA 21)* **JANA (Youth remix) / JANA (Dragonfly mix) / LOVE LIKE BLOOD (live) / WHITEOUT** 54 –
(12"ep/cd-ep+=) *(BFL T/DB 21)* – Jana (live) / Wardance (live) / Exorcism (live) / Kings and queens (live).

Mar 96. (cd-s) *(BFLDA 33) <34262>* **DEMOCRACY / DEMOCRACY (Rooster mix by Carcass) / MASS** 39
(cd-s) *(BFLDB 33)* – ('A'-United Nations mix) / ('A'-Russian tundra mix) / ('A'-Hallucinogen mix).

Apr 96. (cd/c) *(BFL CD/MC 17) <31127>* **DEMOCRACY** 71
– Savage freedom / Democracy / Prozac people / Lanterns / Aeon / Pilgrimage / Intellect / Medicine wheel / Absent friends / Another bloody election. *(cd re-iss. Aug99; same)*

— added guest **DAVE GROHL** – drums (of FOO FIGHTERS) + **YOUTH**

Zuma Zuma

Jul 03. (12"/cd-s) *(ZUMA/+D 004)* **LOOSE CANNON. / LOOSE CANNON (full version) / WARDANCE (the ultimate version)** 25 –

Jul 03. (cd) *(ZUMACD 002) <6365>* **KILLING JOKE** 43 Aug03
– The death & resurrection show / Total invasion / Asteroid / Implant / Blood on your hands / Loose cannon / You'll never get to me / Seeing red / Dark forces / The house that pain built. *(bonus track+=)* – Wardance.

Oct 03. (cd-s) *(ZUMAD 005)* **SEEING RED (mixes; radio / full version / Jagz Kooner / Jagz Kooner instrumental)** –

– compilations, etc. –

on 'Virgin' unless mentioned otherwise

Sep 92. (12"/c-s) *(VST/VSC 1432)* **CHANGE. / REQUIEM** –
(cd-s) *(VSCDT 1432)* – ('A'spiral tribe mix). / ('B'trash Greg Hunter mix).
(cd-s) *(VSCDX 1432)* – ('A'-Youth mix). / ('B'-Youth mix).

Oct 92. (cd/c) *(CDV/TCV 2693) / Caroline; <1596>* **LAUGH? I NEARLY BOUGHT ONE!**
– Turn to red / Psyche / Requiem / Wardance / Follow the leaders / Unspeakable / Butcher / Exit / The hum / Empire song / Chop-chop / The Sun goes down / Eighties / Darkness before dawn / Love like blood / Wintergardens / Age of greed.

May 95. (cd) *(CDOVD 440) / Caroline; (1884>* **WILFUL DAYS** (remixes)

Oct 95. (cd) *Windsong; (WINCD 068)* **BBC LIVE IN CONCERT** (live) –

Apr 98. (12") *Dragonfly; <48>* **LOVE LIKE BLOOD. / INTELLECT** –

Aug 99. (cd) *Butterfly; (BFLCD 9) <114151>* **WAR DANCE** (remix album) – Aug98

Apr 01. (d-cd) *Burning Airlines; <(PILOT 085)>* **NO WAY OUT BUT FORWARD GO (live 1985)** May01

Nov 02. (cd) *Brilliant; (BT 33087)* **LOVE LIKE BLOOD** –

Albert KING

Born: ALBERT NELSON, 23rd of April 1923, Indianola, Mississippi, USA. Although overshadowed by his namesake, B.B. KING (no relation, although ALBERT's PR men would later try to claim that they were half brothers), he was one of the finest blues/soul performers to come out of the south, citing his main influence to be T-BONE WALKER. He took off to Chicago in the early fifties, where he and JIMMY REED auditioned for the SPANIELS (KING on drums), his first solo recording being, 'BAD LUCK BLUES' (released by 'Parrot' Records in 1953). He didn't start his full time career, however, until the end of the decade when he was picked up by the St. Louis based label, 'Bobbin'. These early recordings were heavily influenced by the big band sound and were leased to KING Records, who issued the album 'THE BIG BLUES' in 1962, while three years later he cut tracks for 'Countree'. KING'S first successful single was 'DON'T THROW YOUR LOVE ON ME TOO STRONG', although he found his true style when he signed for the 'Stax' label in 1966, releasing his real debut lp, 'BORN UNDER A BAD SIGN', to critical acclaim, (due to the strong R&B tracks 'CROSSCUT SAW' ,'LAUNDROMAT BLUES' and 'PERSONAL MANAGER') in 1967. The guitarist also started working with BOOKER T & THE MGs, who supplied the perfect rhythm, allied to horn power, for KING'S burgeoning guitar. 'COLD FEET' (which included references to many of his 'Stax' stablemates) and 'I LOVE LUCY', dedicated to his Flying V guitar (which he played left hand, without a pick and upside down (ie: the high strings were at the top) are among his best recordings from this period although he is best remembered for 'BORN UNDER A BAD SIGN' (1967) and 'THE HUNTER' (1968), two songs that became standards and were included in the sets of

CREAM and FREE. KING became a central part of the late sixties blues boom, touring the college and concert circuits, his classic 1968 album, 'LIVE WIRE/BLUES POWER', (recorded at San Francisco's Fillmore Audotorium, as support to JIMI HENDRIX and JOHN MAYALL), introducing his music to a white rock audience. Further excellent albums followed, including, 'KING DOES THE KING'S THING' (a tribute collection of ELVIS PRESLEY songs) and 'YEARS GONE BY'. KING'S seventies work didn't stray too much from the successful formula although 'THAT'S WHAT THE BLUES IS ALL ABOUT' contained just about enough contemporary influences to give him a Top 20 R&B single and he left 'Stax' for GIORGIO GOMELSKY'S 'Utopia', cutting three albums, starting with 'TRUCKLOAD OF LOVIN', before moving again, this time to 'Tomato'. He took a recording break between 1978 and 1983, only recording sparsely after that, (two forgettable albums for FANTASY, 'SAN FRANCISCO 83' in 1983 and 'I'M IN A PHONE BOOTH BABY' in 1984), due to ill health, his final album, 'RED HOUSE' being a slight anti-climax although it contained an excellent version of JIMI HENDRIX'S title track. ROBERT CRAY, FREE, PAUL BUTTERFIELD, and STEVIE RAY VAUGHAN all acknowledged his influence and this was reinforced when KING guested on GARY MOORE'S album, 'STILL GOT THE BLUES'. For proof of his influence, just listen to CREAM'S 'STRANGE BREW' for an almost exact copy of 'OH PRETTY WOMAN' and to MARK KNOPFLER and STEVIE RAY VAUGHAN paying homage on BOB DYLAN'S, 'SLOW TRAIN COMING' and DAVID BOWIE'S, 'LET'S DANCE' respectively. He died at home on the 21st of December 1992. • **Songwriters:** Self-penned mainly. In 1969 he released an lp of ELVIS covers 'KING, DOES THE KING'S THINGS'. Also interpreted HONKY TONK WOMAN (Rolling Stones) / CORINA CORINA (Bob Dylan) / THE SKY IS CRYING (Elmore James) / I CAN'T STAND THE RAIN (Ann Peebles; hit) / FEEL THE NEED IN ME (Detroit Emeralds) / etc.

Album rating (selective): BORN UNDER A BAD SIGN (*8) / KING OF THE BLUES GUITAR (*7) / LIVE WIRE – BLUES POWER (*7) / YEARS GONE BY (*7) / I'LL PLAY THE BLUES FOR YOU – BEST OF.. compilation (*7) / HARD BARGAIN (*6)

ALBERT KING – vocals, guitar

not iss. Parrot

1954. (7",78) <798> **BAD LUCK (BLUES). / (BE ON YOUR) MERRY WAY** –

not iss. Bobbin

1958. (7",78) <114> **WHY ARE YOU SO MEAN TO ME. / OOH-EE BABY** –

1959. (7",78) <119> **THE TIME HAS COME. / NEED YOU BY MY SIDE** –

1959. (7",78) <126> **BLUES AT SUNRISE. / LET'S HAVE A NATURAL BALL** –

1960. (7",78) <129> **I WALKED ALL NIGHT LONG. / I'VE MADE NIGHTS BY MYSELF** –

1960. (7",78) <131> **DON'T THROW YOUR LOVE ON ME SO STRONG. / THIS MORNING** –

1960. (7",78) <5588> **TRAVELIN' TO CALIFORNIA. / DYNAFLOW** –

(above + below singles also issued on 'King'.

1961. (7") <135> **I GET EVIL. / WHAT CAN I DO TO CHANGE YOUR MIND** –

1962. (7") <141> **GOT TO BE SOME CHANGES MADE. / I'LL DO ANYTHING YOU SAY** –

1962. (7") <143> **OLD BLUE RIBBON. / I'VE HAD NIGHTS BY MYSELF** –

not iss. King

1962. (lp) <852> **THE BIG BLUES** –
– Let's have a natural ball / What can I do to change your mind? / I get evil / Had you told it like it was (it wouldn't be like it is) / The morning / I walked all night long / The big blues / Don't throw your love on me so strong / Travelin' to California / I've made nights by myself / This funny feeling / Oo-ee baby / Dynaflow. *(UK cd-iss. Sep92; KCD 852)*

1963. (7") <5751> **HAD YOU TOLD IT LIKE IT WAS. / THIS FUNNY FEELING** –

— now w / **STEVE CROPPER** – guitar / **DONALD 'Duck' DUNN** – bass / **AL JACKSON** – drums

Atlantic Stax

1966. (7") <190> **LAUNDROMAT BLUES. / OVERALL JUNCTION** –

1966. (7") <197> **OH PRETTY WOMAN (CAN'T MAKE YOU LOVE ME). / FUNK-SHUN** –

Feb 67. (lp) <7723> **BORN UNDER A BAD SIGN** –
– Laundromat blues / Oh, pretty woman / Crosscut saw / Down don't bother me / Born under a bad sign / Personal manager / Kansas City / The very thought of you / The hunter / Almost lost my mind / As the years go passing by.

Feb 67. (7") *(584 099)* <201> **CROSSCUT SAW. / DOWN DON'T BOTHER ME**

Stax Stax

Jul 67. (7") *(601 015)* <217> **BORN UNDER A BAD SIGN. / PERSONAL MANAGER**

Feb 68. (7") *(601 029)* <241> **COLD FEET. / YOU SURE DRIVE A HARD BARGAIN** Jan68 67

Jul 68. (7") *(601 042)* <252> **(I LOVE) LUCY. / YOU'RE GONNA NEED ME**

Nov 68. (lp) *(2363 003)* <2003> **LIVE WIRE / BLUES POWER**
– Watermelon man / Blues power / Night stomp / Blues at sunrise / Please love me / Lookout. *<re-iss. 1980> (cd-iss. Nov89 cd/lp; CD+/STX 022)*

Jan 69. (7") <0020> **BLUES POWER. / NIGHT STOMP (instrumental)** –

Jan 69. (lp) *(SXATS 1017)* <2015> **KING, DOES THE KING'S THINGS** –
– Hound dog / That's all right / All shook up / Jailhouse rock / Heartbreak hotel / Don't be cruel / One night / Blue suede shoes / Love me tender. *(re-iss. 1983 as 'BLUES FOR ELVIS'; MPS 8504) (cd-iss. Sep92; CDSXE 073)*

May 69. (lp) *(SXATS 1022)* <2010> **YEARS GONE BY**
– Wrapped up in love again / You don't love me / Cockroach / Killing floor / Lonely man / If the washing don't get you, the rinsing will / Drowning on dry land / Drowning on dry land (instrumental) / Heart fixing business / You threw your love on me too strong / The sky is crying. *(cd-iss. Apr92 +=; CDSXE 045)*

Jun 69. (7") <0034> **DROWNING ON DRY LAND. / ('A'instrumental)** –

Jul 69. (lp; ALBERT KING, STEVE CROPPER & POP STAPLES) <2020> **JAMMED TOGETHER**
– What'd I say / Tupelo / Opus de soul / Baby, what you want me to do / Big bird / Homer's theme / Trashy dog / Don't turn your heater down / Water / Knock on wood.

Aug 69. (7"; ALBERT KING, STEVE CROPPER & POP STAPLES) <0047> **TUPELO. / (part 2)** –

Oct 69. (7"; ALBERT KING, STEVE CROPPER & POP STAPLES) <0048> **WATER. / OPUS DE SOUL** –

Mar 70. (7") <0058> **COCKROACH. / WRAPPED UP IN LOVE AGAIN** –

1970. (7") <0069> **COLD SWEAT. / CAN'T YOU SEE WHAT YOU'RE DOING TO ME** –

— now w / **session people JESSE ED DAVIS, TIPPY ARMSTRONG, WAYNE PERKINS, MICHAEL TOLES** – guitar / **JOHN GALLIE, BARRY BECKETT** – keyboards / **DUNN, DAVID HOOD** – bass / **ROGER HAWKINS, JIM KELTNER** – drums / **SANDY KONIKOFF** – percussion

Jul 71. (7") <0101> **EVERYBODY WANTS TO GET TO HEAVEN. / LOVEJOY** –

Jul 71. (lp) *(2325 042)* <2040> **LOVEJOY**
– Honky tonk woman / Bay Area blues / Corina Corina / She caught the Katy & left me a mule to ride / For the love of a woman / Lovejoy / Everybody wants to get to Heaven / Going back to Luka / Like a road leading home.

Feb 72. (7") <0121> **ANGEL OF MERCY. / FUNKY LONDON** –

Sep 72. (7") <0135> **I'LL PLAY THE BLUES FOR YOU. / (part 2)** –

Oct 72. (lp) *(2325 089)* <3009> **I'LL PLAY THE BLUES FOR YOU**
– I'll play the blues for you (parts 1 & 2) / Little brother / Breaking up somebody's home / High cost of loving / I'll be doggone / Answer to the laundromat blues / Don't burn down the bridge (cause you might wanna come back) / Angel of mercy. *(cd-iss. Mar95; CDSXE 007)*

Apr 73. (7") *(2025 162)* <0147> **BREAKING UP SOMEBODY'S HOME. / LITTLE BROTHER** Feb73 91

Sep 73. (7") *<0166>* **PLAYIN' ON TIME. / HIGH COST OF LOVING**

Nov 73. (7") *<0189>* **I WANNA GET FUNKY. / THAT'S WHAT THE BLUES IS ALL ABOUT**

Dec 73. (lp) *(STX 1003) <5505>* **I WANNA GET FUNKY**
– I wanna get funky / Playin' on me / Walkin' the back streets and cryin' / Till my back ain't got no bone / Flat tire / I can't hear nothing but the blues / Travelin' man / Crosscut saw / That's what the blues is all about. *(cd-iss. Jul93; CDSXE 081)*

Aug 74. (7") *<0217>* **FLAT TIRE. / I CAN HEAR NOTHING BUT THE BLUES**

Oct 74. (7") *<0228>* **CROSSCUT SAW. / DON'T BURN DOWN THE BRIDGES**

1975. (lp) *<5520>* **MONTREUX FESTIVAL (live)**
– CHICO HAMILTON: In view / LITTLE MILTON: Let me down easy / We're gonna make it / ALBERT KING: Don't make no sense / Stormy Monday / For the love of a woman. *(cd-iss. Nov92; CDSXE 070)*

— now w / **BERT DE COTEAUX, JOE SAMPLE, JERRY PETERS** – keyboards / **CHUCK RAINEY, HENRY DAVIS** – bass / **WAH WAH WATSON, GREG POREE, BILL FENDER** – guitar / **JAMES GADSON** – drums / **KING ERRISON** – percussion / + backing vocalists: DEE IRVIN, MAXINE WILLARD, LANI GROVES, JULIA TILMAN, DENIECE WILLIAMS, JEANIE ARNOLD

Utopia-RCA Utopia-RCA

Mar 76. (lp) *(UTS 602) <1387>* **TRUCKLOAD OF LOVIN'**
– Cold women with warm hearts / Gonna make it somehow / Sensation, communication, together / I'm your mate / Truckload of lovin' / Hold hands with one another / Cadillac assembly line / Nobody wants a loser. *(re-iss. Apr88 on 'Charly' lp/c; CRB/TCCRB 1180) (cd-iss. Apr88; CDCHARLY 112) (cd re-iss. Feb97 on 'Charly'; CPCD 8201)*

Apr 76. (7") *<10544>* **NOBODY WANTS A LOSER. / CADILLAC ASSEMBLY LINE**

Jun 76. (7') *<10682>* **GONNA MAKE IT SOMEHOW. / SENSATION, COMMUNICATION, TOGETHER**

— **MARVIN JENKING** – keyboards repl. PETERS / **JOE CLAYTON** – congas repl. ERRISON

— **ROY GAINES + JAY GRAYDON** – guitar repl. WATSON + FENDER /

— **HAROLD MASON + PAUL HUMPHREY** – drums repl. GADSON / **ALEX BROWN** – vocals repl. JEANIE / **SCOTT EDWARDS + WILLIAM UPCHURCH** – bass repl. RAINEY /

— added **ERNIE FIELDS + HERMAN RILEY** – sax, flute / **BOB ZIMMITTI** – percussion / etc

Jan 77. (7") *<10770>* **GUITAR MAN. / RUB MY BACK**

Jan 77. (lp) *<1731>* **ALBERT**
– Guitar man / I'm ready / Ain't nothing you can do / I don't care what my baby do / Change of pace / My babe / Running out of steam / Rub my back / (Ain't it) A real good sign. *(UK-iss.Mar88 on 'Charly' lp/c; CRB/TCCRB 1173) (cd-iss. Mar88; CDCHARLY 103) (cd re-iss. Jun93 on 'Tomato'; 598002520)*

Mar 77. (7") *<10879>* **AIN'T NOTHIN' YOU CAN DO. / I DON'T CARE WHAT MY BABY DO**

Mar 77. (d-lp) *<2205>* **ALBERT LIVE (live)**
– Watermelon man / Don't burn down the bridge / Blues at sunrise / That's what the blues is all about / Stormy Monday / Kansas city / I'm gonna call you as soon as the Sun goes down / Matchbox / Jam in a flat / As the years go passing by / Overall junction / I'll play the blues for you. *(re-iss. Nov88 on 'Charly' lp/c; CDX/TCCDX 35) (cd-iss. Nov88; CDCHARLY 136)*

not iss. Tomato

1977. (lp) *<6002>* **GREAT KING ALBERT**
– Love shock / You upset me baby / Chump chance / Let me rock you easy / Boot lace / Love mechanic / Call my job / Good time Charlie. *(UK-iss.May88 on 'Tomato' lp/c/cd; 269603-1/-4/-2)*

— returned **DUNN, JACKSON + The MEMPHIS HORNS** to the fold, and recruited **BOBBY MANUEL, MICHAEL TOLES + VERNON BURCH** – guitar / **LESTER SNELL, MARVEL THOMAS + WINSTON STEWART** – keyboards / **WILLIE HALL** – drums / **EARL THOMAS** – bass

Stax Stax

Dec 77. (7") *<0234>* **SANTA CLAUS WANTS SOME LOVIN'. / DON'T BURN DOWN THE BRIDGES**
<re-iss. Dec79; 3225>

1978. (7") *<3203>* **THE PINCH PAID OFF. / (part 2)**

1978. (lp) *(3001) <4101>* **THE PINCH**
– The blues don't change / I'm doing fine / Nice to be nice / Oh, pretty woman / King of kings / Feel the need in me / Firing line / The pinch paid off (parts 1 & 2) / I can't stand the rain / Ain't it beautiful.

— now w / **ALLEN TOUSSAINT, ROBERT DABON + WARDELL QUEZERQUE** – piano / **GEORGE PORTER** – bass / **LEROY BREAUX, CHARLES WILLIAMS + JUNE GARDNER** – drums / **LEO NOCENTELLI** – guitar / **KENNETH WILLIAMS** – percussion

1979. (lp) *<7022>* **NEW ORLEANS HEAT**
– Get out of my life woman / Born under a bad sign / The feeling / We all wanna boogie / The very thought of you / I got the blues / I get evil / Angel of mercy / Flat time. *(re-iss. Aug87; CRB 1066) (cd-iss. Jan87; CDCHARLY 49)*

Fantasy not iss.

Nov 83. (lp) *(F 9627)* **SAN FRANCISCO '83 (live)**

— ALBERT died on the 21st of December, 1992

– (selective) compilations, etc. –

Nov 67. (lp) *Polydor; (2343 026) / Stax; <1060>* **TRAVELIN' TO CALIFORNIA**
– Travelin' to California / What can I do to change your mind / I get evil / Had I told you like it was / This morning / I walked all night long / Don't throw your love on me so strong / Let's have a natural ball / I've had nights by myself / This funny feeling / Ooh-lee baby / Dynaflow. *(re-iss. Jun88 on 'Bellaphon'; BID 8016)*

Apr 69. (lp) *Atlantic; (588 173) <SD 8213>* **KING OF THE BLUES GUITAR**
– Cold feet / You're gonna need me / Born under a bad sign / (I love) Lucy / Crosscut saw / You sure drive a hard bargain / Oh, pretty woman / Overall junction / Funk-shun / Laundromat blues / Personal manager. *(cd-iss. Mar93; 7567 82017-2)*

1986. (lp) *Stax; (MPS 8534)* **THE LAST SESSION** (rec.1971)
– She won't gimme no loving / Cold in hand / Stop lying / All the way down / Tell me what true love is / Down the road I go / Money lovin' women / Sun gone down (take 1) / Brand new razor / Sun gone down (take 2).
above featured **JOHN MAYALL** – producer, keyboards, harmonica, guitar / **ERNIE WATTS** – tenor sax / **RON SELICO** – drums / **LARRY TAYLOR** – bass / **LEE KING** – guitar / **CLIFF SOLOMON** – saxophones / **BLUE MITCHELL** – trumpet / **KEVIN** – keyboards

Mar 88. (lp/c) *Stax; (SX/+C 007)* **I'LL PLAY THE BLUES FOR YOU – THE BEST OF . . .**
– Born under a bad sign / Answer to the laundromat blues / You threw your love on me too strong / Crosscut saw / I'll play the blues for you (part 1) / Angel of mercy / Heart fixing business / Killing floor / The sky is crying / Going back to Luka / (I think I'm) Drowning on dry land (part 1) / That's what the blues is all about / Left hand woman (get right with me) / Driving wheel. *(cd-iss. Jan90 +=; CDSX 007)* – Firing line / Don't burn the bridge (cause you might wanna come back) / Can't you see what you're doing to me.

Sep 90. (cd) *Stax; (CDSXE 031)* **WEDNESDAY NIGHT IN SAN FRANCISCO (live)**
(re-mast.Feb01; SDD24 8556)

Oct 90. (cd) *Stax; (CDSXE 032)* **THURSDAY NIGHT IN SAN FRANCISCO (live)**
(re-mast.Feb01; SCD24 8557)

May 91. (cd) *Stax; (CDSXD 969)* **I'LL PLAY THE BLUES FOR YOU / LOVEJOY**

Jun 92. (cd/c) *Charly; (CD/TC BM 18)* **LIVE (CHARLY BLUES MASTERWORKS) VOL.18**

Jul 92. (cd) *Stax; (CDSXE 017)* **BLUES AT SUNRISE (LIVE AT MONTREAUX)**

Oct 92. (cd) *Stax; (CDSXE 076)* **CROSSCUT SAW**

Apr 93. (cd) *Stax; (CDSXE 085)* **THE BLUES DON'T CHANGE** (rec.1973-74)

Aug 94. (cd) *Tomato; (598.1096.20)* **THE TOMATO YEARS**

Sep 94. (cd) *Charly; (CDBL 754)* **LIVE, VOL.5 CHICAGO 1978**

Oct 95. (cd) *Stax; (CDSXD 120)* **BLUES FOR YOU: THE BEST OF ALBERT KING**

Nov 95. (cd) *Charly; (CDCBL 755)* **LIVE IN CANADA (live)**

Oct 96. (cd) *Stax; (SCD 8586)* **FUNKY LONDON**

Oct 96. (cd) *Stax; (SCD 8594)* **HARD BARGAIN**

Jan 97. (d-cd) *Charly; (CPCD 82652)* **I'M READY (BEST OF THE TOMATO YEARS)**

B.B. KING

Born: RILEY B. KING, 16 Sep'25, Indianola, Mississippi, USA, the cousin of respected country bluesman, BUKKA WHITE. A self-taught guitarist (earliest influences being jazz players CHARLIE CHRISTIAN and DJANGO REINHARDT, although T-BONE WALKER would become his future idol), KING initiated a blues style that became a cornerstone of rock music. The son of a sharecropper, as a young man he picked cotton (through the depression) for around 20 dollars a week; the chances of buying a $200-$300 guitar were remote, not to mention the fact that his town didn't have any electricity! KING performed with The ELKHORN SINGERS in his teens and moved to Memphis in 1946 to look for work as a musician, linking up with SONNY BOY WILLIAMSON and initially playing a residency at the 16th Avenue Grill. Subsequently talent-spotted, he won his own, regular 10-minute spot (The Sepia Swing Show) on a black music radio station, WDIA, and word of his prowess spread; the station's PR man dubbed him 'The BEALE STREET BLUES BOY' which was shortened to 'BLUES BOY' and eventually 'BB'. Towards the end of 1949, KING signed to the 'Bullett' label and debuted with 'MISS MARTHA KING', while the following year, he inked a deal with the 'Kent/Modern/RPM' group of labels through their talent scout, IKE TURNER, remaining there until 1962 (he also formed his own, short-lived 'Blue Boy' label during the 50's). BB developed his own sound on his Gibson guitar, LUCILLE (so named because of an incident after a gig in Twist, Arkansas during which a fight – caused by a woman named Lucille – ended up in the venue being evacuated). In February 1952, KING hit US number 1 for fifteen weeks in the R&B charts with 'THREE O'CLOCK BLUES' (written by LOWELL FULSON), while in November, 'YOU DIDN'T WANT ME', repeated the feat. KING was to enjoy regular R&B chart success over the next five years, including two more chart toppers, 'PLEASE LOVE ME' (1953) and 'YOU UPSET ME BABY' (1954). The big man achieved his first national chart success in 1957 via 'BE CAREFUL WITH A FOOL' and followed it with 'I NEED YOU SO BAD' which also broke into the US Top 100. KING subsequently left 'Kent' in 1962 for the larger 'A.B.C.' label, with whom he was to record until their absorption into 'M.C.A.' in 1979. His first ABC release was a version of Louis Jordan's 'HOW BLUE CAN YOU GET', while in May '62, 'ROCK ME BABY' (written by ARTHUR 'BIG BOY' CRUDUP and recorded for 'Kent' before his move) was his first recognised pop hit, entering the US Top 40 and becoming the subject of countless cover versions by UK R&B bands. 'LIVE AT THE REGAL' recorded at the Regal Theatre, Chicago in 1960 and released in 1965, captured him at his best playing songs that were to be mainstays of his set for years to come – Memphis Slim's 'EVERYDAY I HAVE THE BLUES', 'HOW BLUE CAN YOU GET' and 'IT'S MY OWN FAULT' (written by JOHN LEE HOOKER). 'LIVE IN COOK COUNTY JAIL' (1971) was in the same vein featuring 'WORRY WORRY', 'THREE O'CLOCK BLUES' and the unmistakeable 'THE THRILL IS GONE' (his only US Top 20 single). At the end of the decade (after achieving his second US Top 40 hit with 'PAYING THE COST TO BE THE BOSS'), he left his long term manager, Lou Zito, after an argument over money, his accountant, Sidney Siedenberg, took over. On the 4th of April 1968 (the night that MARTIN LUTHER KING was assassinated) KING, BUDDY GUY and JIMI HENDRIX played an all-night blues session, passing the hat round to collect money for the Southern Leadership fund. The following year, after the release of albums, 'LUCILLE' and 'BLUES ON TOP OF BLUES', he made his first trip to Europe, appeared at numerous festivals including the Newport Jazz Festival and opened for The ROLLING STONES on their sixth US tour. KING's manager subsequently encouraged him to widen his fan base and steered him away from his traditional (although declining) black audience towards the middle class white kids involved in the R&B/blues revival. In December that year, his version of Roy Hawkins' 'THE THRILL IS GONE' gave him his biggest hit single so far, reaching the US Top 20, with the accompanying album, 'COMPLETELY WELL' achieving similar results. His next album, 'HUMMINGBIRD' and the jazzy Top 30 set, 'INDIANOLA MISSISSIPPI SEEDS' were both released at the turn of the decade, while 1971 brought him a Grammy for 'THE THRILL IS GONE'; a string of minor hits followed, both singles and albums. In August 1979, 'TAKE IT HOME', gave him his first UK album chart success (reaching No.60), although it struggled to achieve a similar position in the States. 'THERE MUST BE A BETTER WORLD SOMEWHERE' (1981), with music and lyrics by DR. JOHN and DOC POMUS, was one of his finest studio albums, cuts such as 'THE VICTIM' and the ironic 'LIFE AIN'T NOTHING BUT A PARTY' enduring highlights. In 1982, KING demonstrated what a thoroughly generous guy he was when he donated his entire record collection (20,000 discs including 7,000 rare blues 78's) to the Mississippi University Centre For The Study Of Southern Culture. His second Grammy came in February for 'THERE MUST BE A BETTER WORLD SOMEWHERE' and on September the 16th (his 57th birthday), he recorded 'BLUES N JAZZ' which won him another Grammy in 1984. He added yet another one to the trophy cabinet in 1986 with 'MY GUITAR SINGS THE BLUES', a track taken from his 50th album, 'SIX SILVER STRINGS'. In 1988, he surprisingly recorded a one-off track with U2, 'WHEN LOVE COMES TO TOWN' making the UK Top 10 for the first and only time in his chequered history. Meanwhile, KING continued with his charity work, performing at a concert for the National Coalition For The Homeless and a Dallas based group for the homeless, Common Ground (later performing at the Roy Orbison All Star Benefit Tribute and helping to raise $500,000 for homeless charities). In December 1989, he featured on the album, 'HAPPY ANNIVERSARY CHARLIE BROWN' which commemorated the 40th year of the Peanuts cartoon strip (he later continued his association with cartoon characters by playing guitar on 'BORN UNDER A BAD SIGN' for the 'SIMPSONS SINGS THE BLUES' album in 1990 and 'MONDAY MORNING BLUES' for 'AM I COOL, OR WHAT?', a homage to Garfield the cat in 1991). KING went into hospital in April 1990 because of problems relating to his diabetes, resulting in the cancellation of some concerts although he soon got back to his intensive recording and touring schedule (he averages 300 one-nighters a year – mainly to pay for his compulsive gambling habit). February 1991 brought him another Grammy, this time for 'LIVE AT SAN QUENTIN' (recorded 20 years earlier!) and in May that year he opened his own restaurant and night club (BB KING's MEMPHIS BLUES CLUB) on Beale Street, Memphis. This busy year continued in October with the release of his best studio album in a decade, 'THERE IS ALWAYS ONE MORE TIME', highlights being 'I'M MOVIN' ON' and 'THE BLUES COME OVER ME'. In 1992, he received a Grammy for 'LIVE AT THE APOLLO', reached UK Top 60 with GARY MOORE on 'SINCE I MET YOU BABY' and in December performed at the Gainsville Drug Treatment Centre in Florida before 300 prison inmates including his daughter, PATTY, who was serving a 3-year term for trafficking. March 1993 saw him headline a benefit concert in Chattanooga, raising $90,000 for the Bessie Smith Hall (opened later in the year) and in September, 'BLUES SUMMIT' (recorded with ROBERT CRAY, ALBERT COLLINS, ETTA JAMES, JOHN LEE HOOKER, BUDDY GUY and IRMA THOMAS) breached the US Top 200. The legend of US urban blues subsequently teamed up with the legend of white boy English blues, ERIC CLAPTON, for 'RIDING WITH THE KING' (2000). The two guitarists amicably trading licks on a bevvy of KING nuggets – 'TEN LONG YEARS', 'THREE O'CLOCK BLUES', 'WHEN MY HEART BEATS LIKE A HAMMER' etc.- and other assorted blues favourites such as 'KEY TO THE HIGHWAY'. Well into his 70's come the new millennium, KING kept on trucking with 'MAKIN' LOVE IS GOOD FOR YOU' (2000), perhaps a hint as to this blues colossus' longevity. Whatever it is, he still has that musical virility missing in many players half his age and on the likes of the title track and the cover of Barbara George's 'I KNOW', he proved he can still cut is a soul-man as well. 'REFLECTIONS' (2003), as its title suggests, was more of a taking stock affair, winding casually and unashamedly nostalgically back through the decades with readings of 'ALWAYS ON MY MIND', 'WHAT A WONDERFUL WORLD' and '(I LOVE YOU) FOR SENTIMENTAL REASONS' alongside straight-up blues cuts. KING returns to his old neighbourhood each year and puts on a weekend of free concerts; a tireless ambassador for the blues, he succeeded in bringing the form into the mainstream and remains one of the most well-known artists in the genre's near hundred year history. • **Covered:** LOVE ME TENDER (hit; Elvis Presley) / ONE OF THOSE NIGHTS (Conway Twitty) / DON'T CHANGE ON ME (James Holiday & Edward Reeves) / LEGEND IN MY TIME (Don Gibson) / YOU'VE ALWAYS GOT THE BLUES + TIME IS A THIEF (Mickey Newbury) / NIGHTLIFE (Willie Nelson) / PLEASE SEND ME SOMEONE TO LOVE (Percy Mayfield) / YOU AND ME, ME AND YOU (Will Jennings) / YOU SHOOK ME (Willie Dixon) / PLAYIN' WITH MY FRIENDS (Robert Cray & T-Bone Walker) / YOU'RE THE BOSS (Lieber-Stoller) / etc. • **Trivia:** He gave his "Lucille" guitar a cameo role in the 1985 movie, 'Into The Night' and two years later appeared in 'Amazon Women On The Moon'.

Album rating (selective): ROCK ME BABY (*7) / LIVE AT THE REGAL (*8) / BLUES IS KING (*7) / LUCILLE (*7) / LIVE AND WELL (*7) / COMPLETELY WELL (*6) / INDIANOLA MISSISSIPPI SEEDS (*7) / LIVE IN COOK COUNTY JAIL (*7) / B.B. KING IN LONDON (*6) / L.A. MIDNIGHT (*6) / GUESS WHO (*6) / THE BEST OF B.B. KING compilation (*7) / TO KNOW YOU IS TO LOVE YOU (*6) / FRIENDS (*6) / TOGETHER FOR THE FIRST TIME . . . LIVE with Bobby Bland (*7) / LUCILLE TALK BACK (*6) / TOGETHER AGAIN . . . LIVE with Bobby Bland (*6) / KING SIZE (*6) / MIDNIGHT BELIEVER (*6) / TAKE IT HOME (*6) / NOW APPEARING AT OLE MISS (*6) / THERE MUST BE A BETTER WORLD SOMEWHERE (*7) / BLUES 'N' JAZZ (*6) / BLUES SUMMIT (*7) / HEART & SOUL: A COLLECTION OF BLUES BALLADS compilation (*6) / RIDING WITH THE KING with Eric Clapton (*6) / MAKIN' LOVE IS GOOD FOR YOU (*5) / REFLECTIONS (*6)

B.B. KING – vocals, guitar

		not iss.	Bullet
1949.	(78) <*309*> **MISS MARTHA KING. / WHEN YOUR BABY PACKS UP AND GOES**	–	

Note: All release dates in the 50's & 60's are approximate guesses, through working out dates / years of session recordings relating to catalogue numbers.

1949.	(78) <*315*> **GOT THE BLUES. / TAKE A SWING WITH ME**	–	

		not iss.	R.P.M.
Oct 50.	(78) <*304*> **MISTREATED WOMAN. / B.B.'S BOOGIE**	–	
Jan 51.	(78) <*311*> **THE OTHER NIGHT BLUES. / WALKIN' AND CRYIN'**	–	

B.B.KING & HIS ORCHESTRA

Mar 51.	(78) <*318*> **MY BABY'S GONE. / DON'T YOU WANT A MAN LIKE ME**	–	
Jun 51.	(78) <*323*> **SHE'S DYNAMITE. / B.B.'S BLUES**	–	
Sep 51.	(78) <*330*> **SHE'S A MEAN WOMAN. / HARD WORKING WOMAN**	–	
Dec 51.	(78) <*339*> **3 O'CLOCK BLUES. / THAT AIN'T THE WAY TO DO IT**	–	
Mar 52.	(78) <*348*> **SHE DON'T MOVE ME NO MORE. / FINE LOOKING WOMAN**	–	
May 52.	(78) <*355*> **MY OWN FAULT DARLIN'. / SHAKE IT UP AND GO**	–	
Jul 52.	(78) <*360*> **SOME DAY SOME WHERE. / GOTTA FIND MY BABY**	–	
Sep 52.	(78) <*363*> **YOU KNOW I LOVE YOU. / YOU DIDN'T WANT ME**	–	
Nov 52.	(78) <*374*> **STORY FROM MY HEART AND SOUL. / BOOGIE WOOGIE WOMAN**	–	
Jan 53.	(78) <*380*> **DON'T HAVE TO CRY (PAST DAY). / WOKE UP THIS MORNING (MY BABY WAS GONE)**	–	
Mar 53.	(78) <*386*> **PLEASE LOVE ME. / HIGHWAY BOUND**	–	
May 53.	(78) <*391*> **NEIGHBORHOOD AFFAIR. / PLEASE HURRY HOME**	–	
Jul 53.	(78) <*395*> **WHY DID YOU LEAVE ME. / BLIND LOVE (WHO CAN YOUR GOOD MAN BE)**	–	
Sep 53.	(78) <*403*> **PRAYING TO THE LORD. / PLEASE HELP ME**	–	

B.B. "BLUES BOY" KING & HIS ORCHESTRA

(same label)

Nov 53.	(78) <*408*> **I LOVE YOU BABY. / THE WOMAN I LOVE**	–	
Jan 54.	(78) <*411*> **EVERYTHING I DO IS WRONG. / DON'T YOU WANT A MAN LIKE ME**	–	
Feb 54.	(78) <*412*> **WHEN MY HEART BEATS LIKE A HAMMER. / BYE! BYE! BABY**	–	
1954.	(78) <*416*> **YOU UPSET ME BABY. / WHOLE LOT OF LOVIN'**	–	
1955.	(78) <*421*> **EVERYDAY I HAVE THE BLUES. / SNEAKIN' AROUND**	–	
1955.	(78) <*425*> **JUMP WITH YOU BABY. / LONELY AND BLUE**	–	
1955.	(78) <*430*> **SHUT YOUR MOUTH. / I'M IN LOVE**	–	
1955.	(78) <*435*> **WHAT CAN I DO (JUST SING THE BLUES). / TEN LONG YEARS (I HAD A WOMAN)**	–	
Feb 56.	(78) <*450*> **I'M CRACKING UP OVER YOU. / RUBY LEE**	–	
Mar 56.	(78) <*451*> **SIXTEEN TONS. / CRYING WON'T HELP YOU**	–	
May 56.	(78) <*457*> **DID YOU EVER LOVE A WOMAN. / LET'S DO THE BOOGIE**	–	
Jun 56.	(78) <*459*> **DARK IS THE NIGHT. / (part 2)**	–	
Sep 56.	(78) <*468*> **SWEET LITTLE ANGEL. / BAD LUCK**	–	
Feb 57.	(78) <*479*> **ON MY WORD OF HONOUR. / BIM BAM**	–	
Apr 57.	(78) <*486*> **EARLY IN THE MORNING. / YOU DON'T KNOW**	–	
May 57.	(78) <*490*> **HOW DO I LOVE YOU. / YOU CAN'T FOOL MY HEART**	–	
Jun 57.	(78) <*492*> **I WANT TO GET MARRIED. / TROUBLES TROUBLES (TROUBLES)**	–	
Jul 57.	(78) <*494*> **BE CAREFUL WITH A FOOL. / (I'M GONNA) QUIT MY BABY**	–	95
Oct 57.	(78) <*498*> **I NEED YOU SO BAD. / I WONDER**	–	85
Dec 57.	(78) <*501*> **THE KEY TO MY KINGDOM. / MY HEART BELONGS TO YOU**	–	

		not iss.	Kent/Crown
1958.	(lp) <*5020*> **SINGING THE BLUES** (compilation)	–	

– 3 o'clock blues / You know I love you / Woke up this morning / Please love me / You upset me baby / Everyday I have the blues / Ten years long (I had a woman) / Did you ever love a woman / Crying won't help you / Sweet little angel / Bad luck.

1958.	(lp) <*5063*> **THE BLUES** (compilation)	–	

– Boogie woogie woman / Don't have to cry (past day) / Don't you want a man like me / When my heart beats like a hammer / What can I do (just sing the blues) / Ruby Lee / Early in the morning / I want to get married / Troubles troubles / Why does everything happen to me.

Sep 58. (7") *<301>* **WHY DOES EVERYTHING HAPPEN TO ME. / YOU KNOW I GO FOR IT**

Nov 58. (7") *<307>* **DON'T LOOK NOW, BUT I'VE GOT THE BLUES. / DAYS OF OLD**

Feb 59. (7"; by B.B.KING & THE VOCAL CHORDS) *<315>* **PLEASE ACCEPT MY LOVE. / YOU'VE BEEN AN ANGEL**

1959. (lp) *<5115>* **WAILS**
– Tomorrow is another day / We can't make it / I've got papers on you baby (do what I say) / Sweet thing / Treat me right (oh baby) / Time to say goodbye / I love you so / The woman I love / The fool (a fool too long) / Come by here.

B.B. KING

(same label)

Aug 59. (7") *<317>* **I AM. / WHY WORRY**

Sep 59. (7") *<319>* **COME BY HERE. / THE FOOL (A FOOL TOO LONG)**

Oct 59. (7") *<325>* **A LONELY LOVER'S PLEA. / THE WOMAN I LOVE**

Nov 59. (7") *<327>* **EVERYDAY I HAVE THE BLUES. / TIME TO SAY GOODBYE**
(above 'A'side featured members of The COUNT BASIE BAND)

Dec 59. (7") *<329>* **MEAN OLE FRISCO. / SUGAR MAMA**

Jan 60. (7") *<5>* **SWEET SIXTEEN. / (part 2)**
(above on 'Modern' records)

Feb 60. (lp) *<568>* **SWEET SIXTEEN** (compilation)
– Sweet sixteen (parts 1 & 2) / Days old old / Be careful with a fool / (I'm gonna) Quit my baby / What can I do (just sing the blues) / Ten long years (I had a woman) / I was blind / Whole lotta lovin' / Someday baby.

Feb 60. (7") *<333>* **(I'VE) GOT A RIGHT TO LOVE MY BABY. / MY OWN FAULT**

Mar 60. (7") *<336>* **CRYING WON'T HELP YOU. / PLEASE LOVE ME**

Apr 60. (7") *<337>* **BLIND LOVE (WHO CAN YOUR GOOD MAN BE). / YOU UPSET ME BABY**

May 60. (7") *<338>* **TEN LONG YEARS (I HAD A WOMAN). / EVERYDAY I HAVE THE BLUES**

May 60. (7") *<339>* **THREE O'CLOCK BLUES. / DID YOU EVER LOVE A WOMAN**

Jun 60. (7") *<340>* **YOU DONE LOST YOUR GOOD THING NOW. / SWEET LITTLE ANGEL**
(above 4 singles were recorded between 1953-56)

Jul 60. (7") *<346>* **GOOD MAN GONE BAD. / PARTIN' TIME**

Aug 60. (lp) *<5167>* **KING OF THE BLUES**
– (I've) Got a right to love my baby / Good man gone bad / Partin' time / Long nights (the feeling they call the blues) / I'll survive / What a way to go / Feel like a million / If I lost you / You're on top / I'm king. *(UK-iss.1976 on 'Music For Pleasure'; 50259)*

Sep 60. (7") *<350>* **YOU DONE LOST YOUR GOOD THING NOW. / WALKING DR.BILL**

Oct 60. (7") *<351>* **THINGS ARE NOT THE SAME. / FISHIN' AFTER ME (CATFISH BLUES)**

Nov 60. (7") *<353>* **GET OUT OF HERE. / BAD LUCK SOUL**

Jan 61. (lp) *<5188>* **MY KIND OF BLUES**
– You done lost your good thing now / Walking Dr. Bill / Fishin' after me (catfish blues) / Hold that train / Understand / Someday baby / Mr. Pawnbroker / Driving wheel / My own fault (baby) / Please set a date.

Feb 61. (7") *<358>* **HOLD THAT TRAIN. / UNDERSTAND**

Jun 61. (7") *<360>* **PEACE OF MIND. / SOMEDAY BABY**

Jul 61. (lp) *<5230>* **MORE B.B.KING**
– My reward / Don't cry anymore / You're breaking my heart / Blues for me (groovin' twist) / Just like a woman (rockin' twist) / Bad case of love / Bad luck soul / Get out of here / Shut your mouth.

Oct 61. (7") *<362>* **BAD CASE OF LOVE. / YOU'RE BREAKING MY HEART**

Nov 61. (lp) *<5248>* **TWIST WITH B.B.KING** (compilation recent & old)

Feb 62. (lp) *<5286>* **EASY LISTENING BLUES**
– Hully gully (twist) / Easy listening (blues) / Blues for me / Slow walk (slow burn) / Shoutin' the blues / Night long / Confessin' / Don't touch / Rambler / Walkin'.

Mar 62. (7") *<372>* **HULLY GULLY (TWIST). / GONNA MISS YOU AROUND HERE**

1962. (lp) *<7708>* **BLUES FOR ME**
– Got 'em bad / I can't explain / You're gonna miss me / Troubles don't last / Strange things / Down hearted / So many days / I need you baby / The wrong road / The letter / You never know / Sundown / You won't listen.
<above issued on 'United'>

H.M.V. — ABC Paramount

Apr 62. (7") *<10316>* **YOU ASK ME. / I'M GONNA SIT IN TILL YOU GIVE IN**

Jun 62. (7") *<10334>* **BLUES AT MIDNIGHT. / MY BABY'S COMIN' HOME**

Sep 62. (7") *<10361>* **SNEAKIN' AROUND. / CHAINS OF LOVE**

Nov 62. (7") *<10367>* **TOMORROW NIGHT. / A MOTHER'S LOVE**

1963. (lp) *<456>* **MR. BLUES**
– Young dreamers / By myself / Chains of love / A mother's love / Blues at midnight / Sneakin' around / On my word of honor / Tomorrow night / My baby's comin' home / Guess who / You ask me / I'm gonna sit in 'til you give in.

Mar 63. (7") *<10390>* **GUESS WHO. / BY MYSELF**

Jun 63. (7") *<10455>* **YOUNG DREAMERS. / ON MY WORD OF HONOR**

Oct 63. (7") *<10486>* **HOW DO I LOVE YOU. / SLOWLY LOSING MY MIND**

Feb 64. (7") *<10527>* **HOW BLUE CAN YOU GET. / PLEASE ACCEPT MY LOVE** — 97

May 64. (7") *<10552>* **HELP THE POOR. / I WOULDN'T HAVE IT ANY OTHER WAY** — 98

Jul 64. (7") *<10576>* **THE HURT. / WHOLE LOTTA LOVIN'**

Oct 64. (7") *<10599>* **NEVER TRUST A WOMAN. / WORRYIN' BLUES** — 90

Dec 64. (7") *<10616>* **WORST THING IN MY LIFE. / PLEASE SEND ME SOMEONE TO LOVE**

Feb 65. (7") *<10634>* **IT'S MY OWN FAULT. / EVERYDAY I HAVE THE BLUES**

Apr 65. (7") *<10675>* **TIRED OF YOUR JIVE. / NIGHT OWL**

Jun 65. (7") *<10724>* **ALL OVER AGAIN. / THE THINGS YOU PUT ME THROUGH**

Jul 65. (lp) *(CLP 1870)* *<ABCD 509>* **LIVE AT THE REGAL (live in Chicago 1964)**
– Everyday (I have the blues) / Sweet little angel / It's my own fault / How blue can you get / Please love me / You upset me baby / Worry, worry / Woke up this mornin' / You done lost you good thing / Help the poor. *<re-iss. Sep71; ABCS 724> (re-iss. Oct83 on 'Charly'; CH 86) (cd-iss. Dec94 on 'Beat Goes On'; BGOCD 235)*

Aug 65. (7") *<10754>* **I'D RATHER DRINK MUDDY WATER. / GOIN' TO CHICAGO BLUES**

Mar 66. (lp) *(CLP 3514)* *<528>* **CONFESSIN' THE BLUES**
– See see rider / Do you call that a buddy / Wee baby blues / I'd rather drink muddy water / In the dark / Confessin' the blues / Goin' to Chicago blues / I'm gonna move to the outskirts of town / World of trouble / How long blues / Cherry red / Please send me someone to love.

Jun 66. (7") *<10766>* **TORMENTED. / YOU'RE STILL A SQUARE**

Dec 66. (7") *<10856>* **DON'T ANSWER THE DOOR. / (part 2)** — Oct66 72

Jan 67. (lp) *(CLP 3608)* *<704>* **BLUES IS KING**
– Waitin' on you / Gambler's blues / Tired of your jive / Night life / Buzz me / Don't answer the door / Blind love / I know what you're puttin' down / Baby get lost / Gonna keep on loving you. *(re-iss. Nov87 on 'See For Miles'; SEE 216) (cd-iss. Jul92; SEECD 216)*

1967. (7") *(POP 1580)* *<10889>* **NIGHT LIFE. / WAITIN' ON YOU**

Stateside — Bluesway

Jul 67. (lp) *(SSL 10238)* *<BLS 6011>* **BLUES ON TOP OF BLUES**
– Heartbreaker / Losing faith in you / Dance with me / That's wrong little mama / Having my say / I'm not wanted anymore / Worried dream / Paying the cost to be the boss / Until I found you / I'm gonna do what they do to me / Raining in my heart / Now that you've lost me. *(re-iss. 1989 on 'B.G.O.' lp/cd; BGO/+CD 69)*

1967. (7") *<61004>* **THINK IT OVER. / MEET MY HAPPINESS**

1967. (7") *(POP 1594)* **I DON'T WANT YOU CUTTIN' YOUR HAIR. / THINK IT OVER**

1967. (7") *<61007>* **WORRIED DREAM. / THAT'S WRONG LITTLE MAMA**

1967. (7") *<61011>* **HEARTBREAKER. / RAINING IN MY HEART**

1968. (7") *<61012>* **SWEET SIXTEEN. / (part 2)**

May 68. (7") *(SS 2112)* <61015> **PAYING THE COST TO BE THE BOSS. / HAVING MY SAY** Feb68 39

Jun 68. (7") <61018> **I'M GONNA DO WHAT THEY DO TO ME. / LOSING FAITH IN YOU** – 74

Sep 68. (7") <61019> **THE B.B. JONES. / YOU PUT IT ON ME** 98 82

Dec 68. (7") <61021> **DANCE WITH ME. / PLEASE SEND ME SOMEONE TO LOVE** –

—— (below feat. musicians **The MAXWELL DAVIS BAND**

Jan 69. (lp) *(SSL 10272)* <6016> **LUCILLE** Oct68

– Lucille / You move me so / Country girl / No money no luck / I need your love / Rainin' all the time / I'm with you / Stop putting the hurt on me / Watch yourself *(re-iss. 1977 on 'A.B.C.'; 712) (cd-iss. Feb89 on 'Beat Goes On' lp/cd; BGO/+CD 36)*

Feb 69. (7") *(SS 2141)* <61022> **DON'T WASTE MY TIME. / GET MYSELF SOMEBODY**

Mar 69. (lp) *(SSL 10284)* <6022> **THE ELECTRIC B.B.KING** (compilation)

– Tired of your jive / Don't answer the door / B.B.Jones / All over again / Paying the cost to the boss / Think it over / I done got wise / Meet my happiness / Sweet sixteen / You put it on me / I don't want you cuttin' off your hair. *(re-iss. Jan89 on 'Beat Goes On' lp/cd; BGO/+CD 37)*

Apr 69. (7") <61024> **WHY I SING THE BLUES. / FRIENDS** – 61

Jun 69. (7") <61026> **GET OFF MY BACK WOMAN. / I WANT YOU SO BAD** – 74

Jun 69. (lp) *(SSL 10297)* <6031> **LIVE AND WELL (half live)** 56

– Don't answer the door / Just a little love / My mood / Sweet little angel / Please accept my love / I want you so bad / Friends / Get off my back woman / Let's get down to business / Why I sing the blues. *<cd-iss. Jun88 on 'M.C.A.'; 31191> (cd-iss. Jul94 on 'Beat Goes On'; BGOCD 233)*

Sep 69. (7") *(573161)* <57-3161> **EVERYDAY I HAVE THE BLUES. / FIVE LONG YEARS** –

—— (above iss.UK on 'Blue Horizon')

Oct 69. (7") <61029> **JUST A LITTLE LOVE. / MY MOOD** – 76

Feb 70. (7") *(SS 2161)* <61032> **THE THRILL IS GONE. / YOU'RE MEAN** Jan70 15

Feb 70. (lp) *(SSL 10299)* <6037> **COMPLETELY WELL** Dec69 38

– The thrill is gone / So excited / No good / You're losing me / What happened / Confessin' the blues / Key to my kingdom / Crying won't help you now / You're mean. *(cd-iss. Jul87 on 'M.C.A.'; CMCAD 31039)*

May 70. (7") *(SS 2169)* <61035> **SO EXCITED. / CONFESSIN' THE BLUES** Mar70 54

Probe A.B.C.

Aug 70. (7") *(SS 2176)* <11268> **HUMMINGBIRD. / ASK ME NO QUESTIONS** Jun 70 48

Oct 70. (7") *(PRO 516)* <11280> **CHAINS AND THINGS. / KING'S SPECIAL** – 45

Nov 70. (lp) *(SPBA 6255)* <713> **INDIANOLA MISSISSIPPI SEEDS** Oct70 26

– Nobody loves me but my mother / You're still my woman / Ask me no questions / Until I'm dead and cold / King's special / Ain't gonna worry my life anymore / Chains and things / Go underground / Hummingbird. *(re-iss. May88 on 'Castle' lp/c/cd; CLA LP/MC/CD 141) (cd re-iss. Apr95 on 'Beat Goes On'; BGOCD 237)*

Feb 71. (7") <11268> **ASK ME NO QUESTIONS. / NOBODY LOVES ME BUT MY MOTHER** – 40

Mar 71. (7") *(PRO 528)* **ASK ME NO QUESTIONS. / HELP THE POOR / HUMMING BIRD** –

Mar 71. (lp) *(SPB 1032)* <723> **LIVE IN COOK COUNTY JAIL (live)** Feb71 25

– Every day I have the blues / How blues can you get / Worry, worry, worry / 3 o'clock blues / Darlin' you know I love you / Sweet sixteen / The thrill is gone / Please accept my love. *(re-iss. Oct87 on 'M.C.A.'; IMCA 27005) <US cd-iss. Jun88 on 'M.C.A.'; 31080> (d-cd-iss. Jul96 on 'M.C.A.'; MCD 33007)*

Jun 71. (7") <11302> **HELP THE POOR. / LUCILLE'S GRANNY** – 90

Aug 71. (7") <11310> **GHETTO WOMAN. / SEVEN MINUTES** – 68

below feat. **RINGO STARR, DR.JOHN, ALEXIS KORNER + STEVE MARRIOTT**

Oct 71. (lp) *(SPB 1041)* <730> **B.B. KING IN LONDON** 57

– Introduction / Every day I have the blues / Night life / Love the life I'm living / When it all comes down (I'll still be around) / I've got a right to give up livin' / Encore. *(re-iss. 1977 on 'A.B.C.'; ABC 5015) (re-iss. Oct88 on 'Beat Goes On' lp/cd; BGO/+CD 42)*

Oct 71. (7") <11316> **AIN'T NOBODY HOME. / ALEXI'S BOOGIE** – 46

Feb 72. (7") <11319> **SWEET SIXTEEN. / I'VE BEEN BLUE TOO LONG** – 93

Feb 72. (lp) *(SPB 1051)* <743> **L.A. MIDNIGHT** 53

– I got some help I don't need help / The poor / Can't you hear me talking to you / Midnight / Sweet sixteen / I believe (I've been blue too long) / Lucille's granny.

May 72. (7") <11321> **I GOT SOME HELP I DON'T NEED IT. / LUCILLE'S GRANNY** – 92

Aug 72. (7") <11330> **GUESS WHO. / BETTER LOVIN' MAN** – 62

Aug 72. (lp) *(SPB 1063)* <759> **GUESS WHO** 65

– Summer in the city / Just can't please you / Any other way / You don't know nothin' about love / Found what I need / Neighborhood affair / It takes a young girl / Better lovin' man / Guess who / Shouldn't have left me / Five long years *<re-iss. 1974 on 'A.B.C.'; 5021> (re-iss. May89 on 'Beat Goes On' lp/cd; BGO LP/CD 71)*

Oct 72. (7") <11339> **FIVE LONG YEARS. / SUMMER IN THE CITY** –

Nov 72. (7") *(PRO 573)* **SUMMER IN THE CITY. / FOUND WHAT I NEED** –

Jul 73. (7") *(PRO 603)* <11373> **TO KNOW YOU IS TO LOVE YOU. / I CAN'T LEAVE** 38

Aug 73. (lp) *(SPB 1083)* <794> **TO KNOW YOU IS TO LOVE YOU** 71

– I like to live the love / Respect yourself / Who are you / Love / I can't leave / To know you is to love you / Thank you for loving the blues / Oh to me. *(re-iss. Oct74 on 'A.B.C.'; 5083> (cd-iss. Feb02 on 'M.C.A.'; MCD 10414)*

Jan 74. (7") *(PRO 613)* <11406> **I LIKE TO LIVE THE LOVE. / LOVE** 28

A.B.C. A.B.C.

Aug 74. (7") *(ABC 4005)* <11433> **WHO ARE YOU. / OH TO ME** Jun 74 78

Aug 74. (lp) *(ABCL 5051)* <825> **FRIENDS**

– Friends / I got them blues / Baby I'm yours / Up at 5 a.m. / Philadelphia / When everything else is gone / My song. *(cd-iss. Sep91 on 'Beat Goes On'; BGOCD 125)*

Oct 74. (7") *(ABC 4017)* <12029> **PHILADELPHIA. / UP AT 5 P.M.** 64

Nov 74. (d-lp; B.B. KING & BOBBY BLAND) *Anchor; (ABCD 605) / Dunhill; <751096>* **TOGETHER FOR THE FIRST TIME . . . LIVE (live)** 43

– Introduction / 3 o'clock in the morning / It's my own fault baby / Driftin' blues / That's the way love is / I'm sorry / I'll take care of you / Don't cry no more / Don't want a soul hangin' around / Medley / Everybody wants to know why I sing the blues / Goin' down slow / I like to live the love. *(cd-iss. Jun94 on 'Beat Goes On'; BGOCD 161)*

Jan 75. (7") <12053> **FRIENDS. / MY SONG** –

Sep 75. (7") <12158> **HAVE FAITH. / WHEN I'M WRONG** –

Oct 75. (lp) *(5149)* <898> **LUCILLE TALKS BACK**

– Lucille talks back (copulation) / Breaking up somebody's home / Reconsider baby / Don't make me pay for his mistakes / When I'm wrong / I know the price / Have faith / Everybody lies a little.

Jul 76. (lp; BOBBY BLAND & B.B. KING) *Impulse; (IMPL 8027) <9317>* **TOGETHER AGAIN . . . LIVE (live)** 73

– Let the good times roll / Strange things happen / Feel so bad / Mother-in-law blues / Mean old world / Everyday (I have the blues) / The thrill is gone / I ain't gonna be the first to cry. *(re-iss. Jan90 on 'M.C.A.' lp/cd; MCA/+D 4160) (cd re-iss. Feb93 on 'Beat Goes On'; BGOCD 162)*

1976. (7") *Impulse; <31006>* **LET THE GOOD TIMES ROLL. / STRANGE HINGS HAPPEN** –

1976. (7") *Impulse; <31009>* **EVERYDAY (I HAVE THE BLUES). / THE THRILL IS GONE** –

Feb 77. (lp) *(95148)* <977> **KINGSIZE**

– Confessin' the blues / Paying the cost to be the boss / Think it over / You move me so / Heartbreaker / I'm gonna do what they do to me / What happened / By myself / That's wrong little mama / How long, how long blues / I'm not wanted anymore / My baby's comin' home.

1977. (7") <12247> **I WONDER WHY. / SLOW AND EASY** –

1977. (7") <12380> **LET ME MAKE YOU CRY A LITTLE LONGER. / NEVER MADE A MOVE TOO SOON** –

Mar 78. (7") <12412> **I JUST CAN'T LEAVE YOUR LOVE ALONE. / ?**

Apr 78. (lp) *(ABCL 5246)* <1061> **MIDNIGHT BELIEVER**

– When it all comes down / Midnight believer / I just can't leave your love alone / Hold on (I feel our love is changing) / Never make a move too soon / A world full of strangers / Let me make you cry a little longer.

(re-iss. Jun84 on 'M.C.A.' lp/c; MCL/+C 1802) (cd-iss. May90; DMCL 1802) (re-iss. Jan93 cd/c; MCL D/C 19170)

Jun 78. (7") *(ABC 4236)* **HOLD ON (I FEEL OUR LOVE IS CHANGING). / MIDNIGHT BELIEVER** [ ] [–]

M.C.A. M.C.A.

Aug 79. (7") *(MCA 515) <41062>* **BETTER NOT LOOK DOWN. / HAPPY BIRTHDAY BLUES** [ ] [ ]

Aug 79. (lp) *(MCF 3010) <3151>* **TAKE IT HOME** [60] [ ]
– Better not look down / Same old story / Happy birthday blues / I've always been lonely / Second hand woman / Tonight I'm gonna make you a star / The beginning of the end / A story everybody knows / Take it home. *(re-iss. Feb84 lp/c; MCL/+C 1784)*

Oct 79. (7") *(MCA 535)* **TAKE IT HOME. / SAME OLD STORY** [ ] [ ]

Apr 80. (d-lp) *<2-8016>* **NOW APPEARING AT OLE MISS (live)** [ ] [ ]
– B.B. King theme / Caledonia / Don't answer the door / You done lost your good thing now / I need love so bad / Nobody loves me but my mother / Hold on (I feel our love is changing) / I got some outside help (I don't really need) / Darlin' you know I love you / When I'm wrong / The thrill is gone / Never made a move too soon / Three o'clock in the morning / Rock me baby / Guess who / I just can't leave your love alone. *(UK-iss.Feb86 d-lp/d-c; MCDL/+C 601)*

May 80. (7") *(MCA 588)* **CALEDONIA (live). / ROCK ME BABY (live)** [ ] [–]

Feb 81. (7") *<51101>* **THERE MUST BE A BETTER WORLD SOMEWHERE. / YOU'RE GOING WITH ME** [–] [ ]

Feb 81. (lp) *(MCF 3095) <5162>* **THERE MUST BE A BETTER WORLD SOMEWHERE** [ ] [ ]
– Life ain't nothing but a party / Born again human / There must be a better world somewhere / The victim / More, more, more / You're going with me. *(cd-iss. Sep91 on 'Beat Goes On'; BGOCD 124)*

Apr 82. (7") *(MCA 772)* **LEGEND IN MY TIME. / LOVE ME TENDER** [ ] [ ]

Apr 82. (lp) *(MCF 3139) <5307>* **LOVE ME TENDER** [ ] [ ]
– One of these nights / Love me tender / Don't change on me / (I'd be) A legend in my time / You've always got the blues / Please send me someone to love / You and me, me and you / Since I met you baby / Time is a thief / A world I never made.

Jun 82. (7") *(MCA 788) <52057>* **ONE OF THESE NIGHTS. / SINCE I MET YOU BABY** [ ] [ ]

—— augmented The CRUSADERS and The Royal Philharmonic Orchestra on the 'Street Life' single.

Sep 82. (7") *<52125>* **LOVE ME TENDER. / THE WORD I NEVER MADE** [–] [ ]

Jul 83. (7") *<52218>* **INFLATION BLUES. / SELL MY MONKEY** [–] [ ]

Jul 83. (lp) *(MCF 3170) <5413>* **BLUES 'N' JAZZ** [ ] Jun83 [ ]
– Inflation blues / Broken hearted / Sell my monkey / Heed my warning / Teardrops from my eyes / Rainbow riot / Darlin' you know I love you / I can't let you go. *(re-iss. Oct87 lp/c; MCL/+C 1836)*

Jul 85. (7") *(MCA 947) <52530>* **INTO THE NIGHT. / CENTURY CITY CHASE** [ ] [ ]
(12"+=) *(MCAT 947)* – Midnight believer.

Sep 85. (lp/c) *(MCF/+C 3281) <5616>* **SIX SILVER STRINGS** [ ] [ ]
– Strings / Big boss man / In the midnight hour / Into the night / My Lucille / Memory lane / My guitar sings the blues / Double trouble.

Sep 85. (7") *<52574>* **MY LUCILLE. / Keep It Light (by Thelma Houston)** [–] [ ]

Nov 85. (7") *<53675>* **BIG BOSS MAN. / MY GUITAR SINGS THE BLUES** [–] [ ]

Feb 86. (7") *<52751>* **SIX SILVER STRINGS. / MEMORY LANE** [–] [ ]

Mar 87. (7") *(MCA 1124)* **STANDING ON THE EDGE OF LOVE. / DON'T TELL ME NOTHNG** [ ] [–]
(12"+=) *(MCAT 1124)* – Let yourself in for it.

Sep 87. (7") *(MCA 1196)* **IN THE MIDNIGHT HOUR. / HEED MY WARNING** [ ] [–]

Jan 89. (7") *<53872>* **GO ON. / LAY ANOTHER LOG ON THE FIRE** [–] [ ]

Feb 89. (lp/c/cd) *(MCG/MCGC/DMCG 6038) <42183>* **KING OF THE BLUES 1989** [ ] [ ]
– (You've become a) Habit to me / Drowning in the sea of love / Can't get enough / Standing on the edge / Go on / Let's straighten it out / Change in your lovin' / Undercover man / Lay another log on the fire / Business with my baby tonight.

—— Apr'89, BB was credited on U2's Top 10 hit 'WHEN LOVE COMES TO TOWN'

Aug 89. (7") *(MCA 1354)* **AIN'T NOBODY HOME. / LAY ANOTHER LOG ON THE FIRE** [ ] [–]
(cd-s+=/12"+=) *(D+/MCAT 1354)* – Standing on the edge.

Oct 91. (lp/c/cd) *<(MCA/+C/D 10295)>* **THERE IS ALWAYS ONE MORE TIME** [ ] [ ]
– I'm moving on / Back in L.A. / The blues come over me / Fool me once / The lowdown / Mean and evil / Something up my sleeve / Roll, roll, roll / There is always one more time.

Feb 92. (c-s) *<54339>* **THE BLUES COME OVER ME (wild & bluesy club mix) / ('A'-integrity mix)** [–] [ ]

Jul 93. (cd/c) *<(MCD/MCC 10710)>* **BLUES SUMMIT** [ ] [ ]
– Playin' with my friends / Since I met you baby / I pity the fool / You shook me / Something you got / There's something on your mind / Call it stormy Monday / You're the boss / We're gonna make it / Medley: I gotta move out of this neighborhood – Nobody loves me but my mother / Little by little / Everybody had the blues.

Nov 93. (cd-s; by B.B.KING / PHILIP BENT & TONY REMY / DIANE SCHUUR) **MERRY CHRISTMAS BABY. /** [ ] [ ]
(above on 'G.R.P.')

Nov 97. (cd) *<(MCD 1172-2)>* **DEUCES WILD** [ ] [73]
– If you love me / The thrill is gone / Rock me baby / Please send me someone to love / Baby I love you / Ain't nobody home / There must be a better world somewhere / Confessin' the blues / Paying the cost to be the boss / Dangerous mood / Keep it coming / Crying won't help you / Night life.

May 00. (cd) *<(112299-2)>* **MAKIN' LOVE IS GOOD FOR YOU** [ ] Apr00 [ ]
– I got to leave this woman / Since I fell for you / I know / Peace of mind / Monday woman / Ain't nobody like my baby / Makin' love is good for you / Don't go no farther / Actions speak louder than words / What you bet / You're on top / Too good to you baby / I'm in the wrong business / She's my baby.

Reprise Reprise

Jun 00. (cd/c/lp; by B.B. KING & ERIC CLAPTON) *<(9362 47612-2/-4/-1)>* **RIDING WITH THE KING** [15] [3]
– Riding with the king / Ten long years / Key to the highway / Marry you / 3 o'clock blues / Help the poor / I wanna be / Worried life blues / Days of old / When my heart beats like a hammer / Hold on! I'm coming / Come rain or shine.

not iss. M.C.A.

Nov 01. (cd) *<112756>* **A CHRISTMAS CELEBRATION OF HOPE** (festive) [–] [ ]

Jun 03. (cd) *<53202>* **REFLECTIONS** [–] [ ]
– Exactly like you / On my word of honor / I want a little girl / I'll string along with you / I need you / A mother's love / (I love you) For sentimental reasons / Neighborhood affair / Tomorrow night / There I've said it again / Always on my mind / Cross my heart / What a wonderful world.

– (selective) compilations, etc. –

May 64. (7") *Kent; <393>* **ROCK ME BABY. / I CAN'T LOSE** [ ] [34]
(also iss.US on 'Modern')

Apr 64. (7") *<421>* **PLEASE LOVE ME. / BABY LOOK AT YOU** [–] [ ]
note all below released on 'Kent'

Oct 64. (7") *<403>* **BEAUTICIAN BLUES. / I CAN HEAR MY NAME** [–] [82]

Jun 65. (7") *<426>* **BLUE SHADOWS. / AND LIKE THAT** [–] [97]

Mar 67. (7") *<462>* **THE JUNGLE. / LONG GONE BABY** [–] [94]

Sep 68. (7") *Blue Horizon; (57-3144) <492>* **THE WOMAN I LOVE. / YOU PUT IT ON ME** [ ] [94]

Apr 71. (7") *<4542>* **THAT EVIL CHILD. / HELP THE POOR** [–] [97]

Sep 71. (lp) *A.B.C.; (ABCD 509)* **LIVE AT THE REGAL live 1964)** [ ] [78]

Jan 87. (lp/c/cd) *Ace; (C H/HC/DCH 199)* **THE BEST OF B.B.KING VOLUME 2** [ ] [–]

Apr 87. (lp) *Ace; (CHD 201)* **ONE NIGHTER BLUES** [ ] [–]

Aug 89. (lp/cd) *Ace; (CHD 271)* **LUCILLE HAD A BABY** [ ] [–]

Sep 90. (cd/c/lp) *M.C.A.; (DMCG/MCGC/MCG 6103)* **LIVE AT SAN QUENTIN (live 1970)** [ ] [ ]
(re-iss. cd+c Sep94)

Aug 91. (cd/c) *Ace; (CDFAB/FABC 004)* **THE FABULOUS B.B.KING** [ ] [–]

Jul 92. (cd) *Ace; (CDCHD 300)* **MY SWEET LITTLE ANGEL** [ ] [–]

Nov 92. (4xcd-box/4xc-box) *M.C.A.; (E 112418-2)* **KING OF THE BLUES** [ ] [ ]

Aug 93. (cd/c) *MCA; (MCL D/C 19214)* **KING OF THE BLUES 1989**

Feb 95. (cd) *Castle; (CCSCD 412)* **THE COLLECTION** – –

Jul 95. (cd) *M.C.A.; (MCD 33008)* **LUCILLE / FRIENDS** – –

May 97. (cd) *A-Play; (10033-2)* **THE BLUES COLLECTION**

Jul 98. (cd) *Ace; (CDCHK 691)* **HE'S DYNAMITE**

Oct 98. (cd) *M.C.A.; (MCD 11879)* **BLUES ON THE BAYOU**

Nov 98. (cd/c) *Castle Pulse; (PLS CD/MC 298)* **THE GREAT B.B. KING**

Dec 98. (cd) *GP Records; (GP 2035)* **THE BEST**

Mar 99. (cd) *Ace; (CHCHD 712)* **THE RPM HITS 1951-1957**

Apr 99. (cd/c) *Universal TV; (547340-2/-4)* **HIS DEFINITIVE GREATEST HITS** 24

Aug 99. (cd) *Castle Pie; (PIESD 051)* **ROCK ME BABY**

Oct 99. (cd) *M.C.A.; (112042-2)* **LET THE GOOD TIMES ROLL: THE MUSIC OF LOUIS JORDAN**

Jun 00. (cd) *Ace; (CDCHD 760)* **THE BEST OF THE KENT SINGLES 1958-1971**

Jul 00. (cd) *M.C.A.; (MCBD 1905)* **THE VERY BEST OF B.B. KING**

Jun 01. (cd) *Castle Select; (SELCD 581)* **BB'S BLUES**

Apr 02. (d-cd) *Ace; (CDCHM2 835)* **THE MODERN RECORDINGS 1950-1951**

Jun 02. (4xcd-box) *Ace; (ABOXCD 8)* **THE VINTAGE YEARS**

Mar 03. (cd) *King Biscuit; (KBCCD 114)* **IN CONCERT**

Mar 03. (cd) *Universal; (AAMCAD 11939)* **20TH CENTURY MASTERS**

May 03. (cd) *Ace; (CDCHM 881)* **MY KIND OF BLUES**

Ben E. KING

Born: BENJAMIN EARL NELSON, 23 Sep'38, Henderson, North Carolina, USA. Relocating to Harlem with his family in 1947, KING began singing in gospel choirs. He subsequently played with high school doo-wop group The FOUR B's before moving on to join his first full-time band, The FIVE CROWNS, in his late teens. Although they cut a series of unsuccessful records, The 'CROWNS eventually struck lucky in summer 1958 when DRIFTERS manager, George Treadwell, fired his entire band and recruited KING & Co as replacements. Teamed up with crack writers JERRY LEIBER and MIKE STOLLER, the new look DRIFTERS were rejuvenated by a string of US Top 20 hits including 'THERE GOES MY BABY', 'DANCE WITH ME', 'THIS MAGIC MOMENT', 'SAVE THE LAST DANCE FOR ME' and 'I COUNT THE TEARS'; KING's emotive balladeering was at the epicentre of the group's appeal, flanked by lush strings and lilting latin rhythms. In May 1960, however, a complaint about low wages contributed to their star vocalist departing for a solo career. The partnership with LEIBER & STOLLER endured (alongside writers DOC POMUS and MORT SHUMAN), the pair even using new apprentice PHIL SPECTOR to help them pen KING's first solo Top 10, 'SPANISH HARLEM', later that year. Yet the song that marked the definitive chapter in his career was penned by KING himself; a goose-bump hymn to the endurance of love amid impending catastrophe, 'STAND BY ME' was KING's masterpiece and a deserved US Top 5 in summer '61. Ironically enough, the track didn't make much headway in the UK chart (No.27!) until 1987 when it climbed to No.1 after being used in the film of the same name (a poignant tale of boyhood coming-of-age starring a young River Phoenix). Over the ensuing two years, the man had a further couple of major hits with 'DON'T PLAY THAT SONG (YOU LIED)' and 'I (WHO HAVE NOTHING)' although his success thereafter was largely confined to the R&B chart. The late 60's and early 70's proved a particularly tough time but a return to 'Atlantic' in 1975 found him back in the US Top 5 with 'SUPERNATURAL THING'. The accompanying Top 40 album, 'SUPERNATURAL' (1975), spawned a further minor hit with 'DO IT IN THE NAME OF LOVE' although that was to be his last chart action for over a decade. In mid '77, he teamed up with transplanted Scottish funksters The AVERAGE WHITE BAND for the 'BENNY & US' album, resulting in two R&B hits. Following 1981's 'STREET TOUGH' album, KING cut his losses and rejoined The DRIFTERS although he later briefly resurrected his solo career after the success of the aforementioned 'STAND BY ME' re-issue. • **Trivia:** KING gave a very brief cameo performance on the 1974 GENESIS album, 'The Lamb Lies Down on Broadway'; the soul legend was drafted in to sing two closing words, "On Broadway" in the style of the original DRIFTERS hit which ironically he hadn't originally performed!

Best CD compilation: STAND BY ME (THE ULTIMATE COLLECTION) (*7)

BEN E. KING – vocals with session players

London / Atco

Oct 60. (7") *<6166>* **SHOW ME THE WAY. / BRACE YOURSELF** –

Dec 60. (7") *(HLK 9258) <6185>* **FIRST TASTE OF LOVE. / SPANISH HARLEM** 27 53 / 10

Jun 61. (7") *(HLK 9358) <6194>* **STAND BY ME. / ON THE HORIZON** 27 Apr61 4

Sep 61. (7") *(HLK 9416) <6203>* **AMOR. / SOUVENIR OF MEXICO** 38 Jul61 18

Nov 61. (lp; mono/stereo) *(HA-K 2395/SAH-K 6195) <33133>* **SPANISH HARLEM** Jul61 57
– Amor / Sway / Come closer to me / Perfidia / Granada / Sweet and gentle / Quizas, quizas, quizas (Perhaps, perhaps, perhaps) / Frenesi / Souvenir of Mexico / Besame mucho / Love me, love me / Spanish Harlem. *(UK re-iss. Jun67 on 'Atlantic'; 590 001)* – hit No.30 *(cd-iss. Sep96 on 'Sequel'; RSACD 837)*

Nov 61. (7") *(HLK 9457) <6207>* **HERE COMES THE NIGHT. / YOUNG BOY BLUES** 81 / Oct61 66

Mar 62. (7") *(HLK 9517) <6215>* **ECSTASY. / YES** Feb62 56

May 62. (7") *(HLK 9544) <6222>* **DON'T PLAY THAT SONG (YOU LIED). / THE HERMIT OF MISTY MOUNTAIN** Apr62 11

Aug 62. (7") *(HLK 9586) <6231>* **TOO BAD. / MY HEART CRIES FOR YOU** 88

Oct 62. (lp) *(HA-K 8012) <33142>* **DON'T PLAY THAT SONG**
– Don't play that song (you lied) / Ecstasy / On the horizon / Show me the way / Here comes the night / First taste of love / Stand by me / Yes / Young boy blues / The hermit of misty mountain / I promise love / Brace yourself. *(cd-iss. Sep96 on 'Sequel'; RSACD 839)*

Nov 62. (7") *(HLK 9631) <6237>* **I'M STANDING BY. / WALKING IN THE FOOTSTEPS OF A FOOL**

Jan 63. (7") *<6246>* **TELL DADDY. / AUF WIEDERSEHEN** –

Mar 63. (7") *(HLK 9691) <6256>* **HOW CAN I FORGET. / GLORIA, GLORIA** 85

Sep 63. (7") *(HLK 9778) <6267>* **I (WHO HAVE NOTHING). / THE BEGINNING OF TIME** Jun63 29

Dec 63. (7") *(HLK 9819) <6275>* **I COULD HAVE DANCED ALL NIGHT. / GYPSY** Oct63 72

Jan 64. (lp; mono/stereo) *(HA-K/SH-K 8026) <333137>* **SONGS FOR SOULFUL LOVERS** Oct63
– My heart cries for you / He will break your heart / Dream lover / Will you love me tomorrow / My foolish heart / Fever / Moon River / What a difference a day made / Because of you / at last / On the street where you live / It's all in the game. *(cd-iss. Sep96 on 'Sequel'; RSACD 838)*

Jan 64. (7") *<6284>* **WHAT NOW MY LOVE. / GROOVIN'** –

Feb 64. (7") *(HLK 9840)* **AROUND THE CORNER. / GROOVIN'** –

Atlantic / Atco

1964. (lp) *(ATL 5016) <33165>* **GREATEST HITS** (compilation)
– Stand by me / Don't play that song (you lied) / Amor / Young boy blues / Goodnight my love / Spanish Harlem / How can i forget / It's all over / I (who have nothing) / Save the last dance for me / I Count the tears / This magic moment. *(re-iss. 1973 on 'Atlantic') (re-iss. cd+c May93 on 'Prestige')*

Mar 64. (7") *<6288>* **THAT'S WHEN IT HURTS. / AROUND THE CORNER** – 63

Jun 64. (7") *<6303>* **WHAT CAN A MAN DO. / SI SENOR** –

Oct 64. (7") *(AT 4007)* *<6315>* **IT'S ALL OVER. / LET THE WATER RUN DOWN** Sep64 72

Jan 65. (7") *(AT 4018)* *<6328>* **SEVEN LETTERS. / RIVER OF TEARS** Dec64 45

Jan 65. (lp) *<33174>* **SEVEN LETTERS** –
– Seven letters / River of tears / I'm standing by / Jamaica / Down home / Si senor / It's all over / Let the water run down / This is my dream / It's no good for me / In the middle of the night / Don't drive me away. *(UK-iss.1968; 588 125) (cd-iss. Nov96 on 'Sequel'; RSACD 853)*

Apr 65. (7") *(AT 4025)* *<6343>* **THE RECORD (BABY I LOVE YOU). / THE WAY YOU SHAKE IT** 84

Jun 65. (7") *<6357>* **NOT NOW (I'LL TELL YOU WHEN). / SHE'S GONE AGAIN** –

Sep 65. (7") *(AT 4043)* *<6371>* **CRY NO MORE. / THERE'S NO PLACE TO HIDE**

Nov 65. (7") *<6390>* **GOODNIGHT MY LOVE, PLEASANT DREAMS. / I CAN'T BREAK THE NEWS TO MYSELF** – 91

Jan 66. (7") *(AT 4065)* **GOODNIGHT MY LOVE, PLEASANT DREAMS. / TELL DADDY** –

May 66. (7") *(584 008)* *<6413>* **SO MUCH LOVE. / DON'T DRIVE ME AWAY** 96

Oct 66. (7") *(584 046)* *<6431>* **I SWEAR BY THE STARS ABOVE. / GET IN A HURRY**

Jan 67. (7") *(584 069)* *<6454>* **WHAT IS SOUL? / THEY DON'T GIVE MEDALS TO YESTERDAY'S HEROES**

Feb 67. (lp) *(587 072)* **WHAT IS SOUL?** –
– The record (baby I love you) / She's gone again / There's no place to hide / Cry no more / Goodnight my love / Katherine / I can't break the news to myself / I swear by stars above / Get in a hurry / They don't give medals to yesterday's heroes / Teeny weeny little bit / What is soul? *(cd-iss. Nov96 on 'Sequel'; RSACD 854)*

Apr 67. (7") *(584 106)* *<6472>* **TEARS, TEARS, TEARS. / MAN WITHOUT A DREAM** – 93

Jul 67. (7") *<6493>* **TEENY WEENIE LITTLE BIT. / KATHERINE** –

Oct 67. (7") *<6527>* **SHE KNOWS WHAT TO DO FOR ME. / DON'T TAKE YOUR SWEET LOVE AWAY** –

Jan 68. (7"; as BEN E. KING & DEE DEE SHARPE) *<6557>* **WE GOT A THING GOING ON. / WHATCHA GONNA DO** –

Apr 68. (7") *(584 184)* *<6571>* **DON'T TAKE YOUR LOVE FROM ME. / FORGIVE THIS FOOL**

Aug 68. (7") *(584 205)* *<6596>* **IT'S AMAZING. / WHERE'S THE GIRL**

Feb 69. (7") *(584 238)* *<6637>* **TIL I CAN'T TAKE ANYMORE. / IT AIN'T FAIR**

May 69. (7") *<6666>* **WHEN YOU LOVE SOMEBODY. / HEY LITTLE ONE** –

Crewe Maxwell

1970. (7") *(CRW 2)* **GOODBYE MY OLD GIRL. / I CAN'T TAKE IT LIKE A MAN**

1970. (lp) *(CRWS 203)* *<88001>* **ROUGH EDGES**
– She lets her hair down (early in the morning) / Little green apples / Wishing for tomorrow / If you've gotta make a fool of somebody / Come together / One man / In the midnight hour / Lay lady lay / Don't let me down / Tonight I'll be staying here with you.

C.B.S. Mandala

Feb 72. (7") *(CBS 7785)* *<2512>* **TAKE ME TO THE PILOT. / I GUESS IT'S GOODBYE**

Feb 72. (lp) *(CBS 64570)* *<3007>* **THE BEGINNING OF IT ALL**
– Take me to the pilot / I guess it's goodbye / Travellin' woman / Love is / Into the mystic / White moon / Love is gonna get you / Beginning of it all / Only you and I know / All of your tomorrows / She does it right.

May 72. (7") *<2513>* **INTO THE MYSTIC. / WHITE MOON** –

Aug 72. (7") *<2518>* **SPREAD MYSELF AROUND. /** –

Atlantic Atlantic

Apr 75. (7") *(K 10565)* *<3241>* **SUPERNATURAL THING. / (part 2)** Feb75 5

Apr 75. (lp/c) *(K/K4 50118)* *<18132>* **SUPERNATURAL** 39
– Supernatural thing (part 1 & 2) / You're lovin' ain't good enough / Drop my heart off (on your way to the door) / Do it in the name of love / Happiness is where you find it / Do you wanna do a thing / Imagination / What do you want me to do. *(cd-iss. Nov96 on 'Sequel'; RSACD 855)*

Jun 75. (7") *(K 10618)* **HAPPINESS IS WHERE YOU FIND IT. / DROP MY HEART OFF (ON YOUR WAY TO THE DOOR)** –

Jul 75. (7") *(K 10636)* *<3274>* **DO IT IN THE NAME OF LOVE. / IMAGINATION** May75 60

Jan 76. (7") *(K 10708)* *<3308>* **I HAD A LOVE. / WE GOT LOVE**

Apr 76. (lp/c) *(K/K4 50264)* *<18169>* **I HAD A LOVE**
– I had a love / I betcha didn't know that / Smooth sailing / No danger ahead / Everybody plays the fool / Standing in the wings of heartache / We got love / Tower of strength / You're stepping on my heart.

May 76. (7") *<3337>* **I BETCHA DIDN'T KNOW THAT. / SMOOTH SAILING** –

Dec 76. (7") *<3359>* **SOMEBODY'S KNOCKING. / ONE MORE TIME** –

Apr 77. (7") *<3402>* **GOT IT UP FOR LOVE. / KEEPIN' IT TO MYSELF** –

— (mid'77) KING teamed up with AVERAGE WHITE BAND on LP, 'BENNY & US' *(cd-iss. Nov96 on 'Sequel'; RSACD 856)*

Jan 79. (lp/c) *(K/K4 50527)* *<19200>* **LET ME LIVE IN YOUR LIFE**
– Fifty years / Tippin' / Spoiled / Wonder woman / Let me live in your life / I see the light / Fly away (to my wonderland) / Dark storm on the horizon / Family jewels / Sweet rhapsody / Fifty years.

Feb 79. (7") *<3494>* **TIPPIN'. / I SEE THE LIGHT** –

Apr 79. (7") *<3535>* **SPOILED. / FLY AWAY TO MY WONDERLAND** –

Nov 79. (7") *(K 11407)* *<3635>* **MUSIC TRANCE. / AND THIS IS LOVE**

May 80. (lp/c) *(K/K4 50713)* *<19269>* **MUSIC TRANCE**
– And this is love / Music trance / Touched by your love / You've only got one chance to be young / Hired gun / Work that body.

Jun 80. (7") *(K 11495)* **YOU'VE ONLY GOT ONE CHANCE TO BE YOUNG. / MUSIC TRANCE**

May 81. (lp/c) *(K/K4 50787)* *<19300>* **STREET TOUGH**
– Street tough / Staying power / Souvenirs of love / Stay a while with me / Something to be loved / Made for each other / Why is the question / You made the difference to my life.

May 81. (7") *<3808>* **STREET TOUGH. / WHAT IS THE QUESTION** –

Oct 81. (7") *<3839>* **SOUVENIRS OF LOVE. / YOU MADE THE DIFFERENCE TO MY LIFE** –

— In 1982, he rejoined The DRIFTERS. By the late 80's, he had resurrected solo career after hitting No.1 w / 'STAND BY ME'.

Bold Reprieve not iss.

May 87. (7"/12") *(BRM 003/+T)* **SPREAD MYSELF AROUND. / DO IT NOW** –

Syncopate not iss.

Jun 87. (7"/12") *(SY/12SY 3)* **DANCING IN THE NIGHT. / ('A'version)** –

Manhattan Manhattan

Jun 87. (7"/12") *(MT/12MT 25)* **SAVE THE LAST DANCE FOR ME. / WHEEL OF LOVE** 69

Nov 87. (7") *(MT 33)* **LOVER'S QUESTION. / BECAUSE OF LAST NIGHT**
(12"+=) *(12MT 33)* – Stand by me (1987 version).

Nov 87. (cd/c/lp) *<(CD/TC+/MT 1013)>* **SAVE THE LAST DANCE FOR ME** Apr88
– Wheel of love / Save the last dance for me / Because of last night / Lover's question / Whatever this is (it ain't true love) / Halfway to Paradise / Let a man do it for you / I cry for you / Test of time / Two lovers.

— semi-retired from the studio

– (selective) compilations, etc. –

on 'Atlantic' unless mentioned otherwise

May 84. (lp) *Edsel; (ED 131)* **HERE COMES THE NIGHT** –

Jan 87. (7") *(A 9361)* *<89361>* **STAND BY ME. / Coasters: YAKETY YAK** 1 Sep86 9
(12"+=) *(A 9361T)* – Music trance.

Feb 87. (lp/c)(cd) *(WX 90/+C)(780213-2)* **STAND BY ME (THE ULTIMATE COLLECTION)** 14
– Stand by me / Save the last dance for me / I (who have nothing) / That's when it hurts / I could have danced all night / First taste of love / Dream lover / Moon river / Spanish Harlem / Amor / I count the tears / Don't play

that song / This magic moment / Young boy blues / It's all in the game / Supernatural thing (pt.1).
(above & below also featured DRIFTERS tracks)

Oct 90.	(cd/c/d-lp) *Telstar; (STCD/STAC/STAR 2373)* **THE BEST OF BEN E. KING & THE DRIFTERS**	15	–
Oct 93.	(d-cd) *<(8122 71215-2)>* **ANTHOLOGY**		
May 98.	(cd) *Rhino; <(8122 72970-2)>* **THE VERY BEST OF BEN E. KING**		
Aug 98.	(cd) *Collectables; (CCLCD 62102)* **SPANISH HARLEM / DON'T PLAY THAT SONG**		–
Nov 98.	(d-cd/d-c) *Global TV; (RAD CD/MC 108)* **THE BEST OF BEN E. KING & THE DRIFTERS**	41	–
Aug 02.	(cd) *Castle; (CMRCD 549)* **THE BEGINNING OF IT ALL**		

Carole KING

Born: CAROLE KLEIN, 9 Feb'40, Brooklyn, New York, USA. Taught to play piano and sing by her mother from an early age, CAROLE's first serious forays into songwriting were with PAUL SIMON in 1958. She then met lyricist (and future husband) GERRY GOFFIN at college, the pair subsequently forming one of the most prolific and successful writing partnerships the music business has ever seen. Setting up shop in New York's famed 'Brill Building' (working for AL NEVINS and DON KIRSHNER's 'Aldon Music'), the duo scored their first success in 1961 when 'WILL YOU STILL LOVE ME TOMORROW' (by the SHIRELLES) and 'TAKE GOOD CARE OF MY BABY' (by BOBBY VEE), both hit the US top spot. The following year, 'THE LOCOMOTION' (by LITTLE EVA), gave them their third No.1, a track they also arranged, conducted and produced for the young singer. The hits kept on coming and meanwhile, KIRSHNER had persuaded CAROLE to release her solo version of 'IT MIGHT AS WELL RAIN UNTIL SEPTEMBER', which subsequently went UK Top 3 and US Top 30. The hit was a one-off though, and KING wasn't to resume her recording career until the late 60's. A relatively lean spell ensued (during which CAROLE and GERRY were divorced, although they kept the writing partnership going) before STEVE LAWRENCE took a GOFFIN-KING number back to the top of the US charts, 'GO AWAY LITTLE GIRL' (also a hit for DONNY OSMOND). Nor were the duo fazed by the onset of psychedelia, scoring hits for the ANIMALS ('DON'T BRING ME DOWN), THE MONKEES ('PLEASANT VALLEY SUNDAY', they also recorded 'TAKE A GIANT STEP') and The BYRDS (a brilliant version of 'GOIN' BACK', they also transformed 'WASN'T BORN TO FOLLOW' into a psych-country classic). At the height of the hippy scene in 1967, GOFFIN, KING and columnist, AL ARONOWITZ, founded their own label, 'Tommorrow', signing up flower power outfit, The MYDDLE CLASS. The project flopped, although the band's bass player, CHARLES LARKEY (ex-FUGS) would soon become KING's second husband. He and KING subsequently formed their own band, The CITY, with DANNY 'KOOTCH' KORTCHMAR (guitar, ex-FUGS) and JIM GORDON (drums). The outfit released one poor selling album, 'NOW THAT EVERYTHING'S BEEN SAID' (1969) on LOU ADLER's 'Ode' label, KING soon striking out on her own for a solo career. Encouraged to pen her own lyrics by fellow Laurel Canyon singer/songwriter JAMES TAYLOR (for whom CAROLE had played piano on his debut 'Apple' album, 'Sweet Baby James'), the first hesitant results came in the form of the 'WRITER' album in 1970, KING remaining with 'Ode' records. A breakthrough came with 'TAPESTRY' in 1971, a multi-million seller that became the biggest album in recording history up to that point. From the opening shimmy of 'I FEEL THE EARTH MOVE', to the melancholy reflection of 'SO FAR WAY' and 'HOME AGAIN', KING sounded more confident and self-possessed, her unpretentious vocal style and straight talking, confessional lyrics proving a winning combination. The record also benefitted from the midas touch of Lou Adler's production and the backing of 'The Section', the semi-legendary session team of KORTCHMAR, LELAND SKLAR (bass), RUSS KUNKEL (drums) and CRAIG DOERGE (keyboards), creating a highly commercial pop/rock/white soul fusion making up in melody what it lacked in earthiness. The album not only set the tone for the MOR dominated American music of the 70's, but initiated a slew of similar releases by songwriters desperate to get out from behind a desk. Sales of 'TAPESTRY' were further boosted when JAMES TAYLOR had a US No.1 in the summer of '71 with a cover of 'YOU'VE GOT A FRIEND'. KING's follow-up albums, 'MUSIC' (1971), 'RHYMES AND REASONS' (1972), 'FANTASY' (1973) and 'WRAP AROUND JOY (1974) all carried on in much the same vein, going gold and spawning such reliable AOR fare as 'SWEET SEASONS' (Top 10 in 1971) and 'JAZZMAN' (No.2 in 1974). The latter album employed the lyric-writing services of DAVID PALMER, later of STEELY DAN. None of the records, however, achieved the consistency of 'TAPESTRY', although they did cement KING's position as a fully paid-up superstar member of the L.A. elite. She eventually reunited with GOFFIN in 1976 for 'THOROUGHBRED' , her last album for 'Ode', subsequently signing for 'Capitol'. Her first release for the company, 'SIMPLE THINGS' (1977) saw her hooking up with backing band NAVARRO who numbered KING's future husband, RICK EVERS among their ranks. Tragedy struck the following year, however, when EVERS died of a drug overdose. It marked the beginning of a relatively barren period for KING, only her 'PEARLS – SONGS OF GOFFIN AND KING' (1980) album making any impact on the charts, and even that consisted of rehashed past glories. A brief move to 'Atlantic' and the return of KORTCHMAR and KUNKEL failed to resurrect her career and KING hasn't had a hit album or single since. She remains a respected figure within the business, however, and continues to tour and record, releasing material on her own 'King's X' label, finally receiving the dubious honour of being inducted into the Rock'n'roll Hall Of Fame in 1990. KING returned with a millennial comeback of sorts in the shape of 'LOVE MAKES THE WORLD' (2001), a partly successful attempt at recapturing the singer/songwriter grace of yore. Pared-down ballad fare such as 'YOU WILL FIND ME THERE' and 'THIS TIME' came closest to realising that early 70's magic, while guest spots from the likes of k.d. LANG and WYNTON MARSALIS kept things interesting.

Album rating: WRITER: CAROLE KING (*6) / TAPESTRY (*8) / MUSIC (*7) / RHYMES & REASONS (*6) / FANTASY (*7) / WRAP AROUND JOY (*7) / REALLY ROSIE (*6) / THOROUGHBRED (*6) / SIMPLE THINGS (*4) / HER GREATEST HITS compilation (*7) / WELCOME HOME (*4) / TOUCH THE SKY (*4) / PEARLS – SONGS OF GOFFIN AND KING (*5) / ONE TO ONE (*4) / SPEEDING TIME (*3) / CITY STREETS (*4) / IN CONCERT (*3) / COLOR OF YOUR DREAMS (*3) / NATURAL WOMAN – THE VERY BEST OF . . . compilation (*8) / LOVE MAKES THE WORLD (*5)

CAROLE KING – vocals, piano (with session people)

		not iss.	ABC-Paramount
Jan 59.	(7") *<9921>* **GOIN' WILD. / THE RIGHT GIRL**	–	
Mar 59.	(7") *<9986>* **BABY SITTIN'. / UNDER THE STARS**	–	
		not iss.	RCA Victor
May 59.	(7") *<7560>* **QUEEN OF THE BEACH. / SHORT MORT**	–	
		not iss.	Alpine
Nov 59.	(7") *<57>* **OH NEIL!. / A VERY SPECIAL BOY**	–	

—— She keeps on writing for others husband GERRY GOFFIN. After two and a half years she returned to solo work for . . .

London Dimension

Aug 62. (7") *(HLU 9591) <2000>* **IT MIGHT AS WELL RAIN UNTIL SEPTEMBER. / NOBODY'S PERFECT** [3] [22]
<first issued in US on 'Companion'; 2000> (re-iss. Sep72; HL 10391) (reached No.43 UK)

Nov 62. (7") *<1004>* **SCHOOL BELLS ARE RINGING. / I DIDN'T HAVE ANY** [–] [ ]

Apr 63. (7") *<1009>* **HE'S A BAD BOY. / WE GROW UP TOGETHER** [–] [94]

— Soon divorced her husband GERRY, although they still carried on writing.

London Tomorrow

Apr 66. (7") *(HL 10036) <7502>* **SOME OF YOUR LOVIN'. / ROAD TO NOWHERE** [ ] [ ]

The CITY

CAROLE KING with **CHARLES LARKEY** – bass (of FUGS) / **DANNY 'KOOTCH' KORTCHMAR** – guitar / **JIM GORDON** – drums

A & M Ode

Jan 69. (lp) *<244012>* **NOW THAT EVERYTHING'S BEEN SAID** [–] [ ]
– Snow queen / I wasn't born to follow / Now that everything's been said / Paradise alley / Man without a dream / Victim of circumstance / Why are you leaving / Lady / My sweet home / I don't believe it / That old sweet roll (hi-de-do) / All my time.

Feb 69. (7") *<113>* **PARADISE ALLEY. / SNOW QUEEN** [–] [ ]

May 69. (7") *<119>* **THAT OLD SWEET ROLL. / WHY ARE YOU LEAVING** [–] [ ]

CAROLE KING

— solo, with session people

May 70. (lp) *(AMLS 996) <77006>* **WRITER: CAROLE KING** [ ] [ ]
– Spaceship races / No easy way down / Child of mine / Goin' back / To love / What have you got to lose / Eventually / Raspberry jam / Can't you be real / I can't hear you no more / Sweet sweetheart / Up on the roof. *<re-prom.Apr71 hit US No.84> (re-iss. Feb79 on 'Epic'; EPC 82318)*

Mar 70. (7") **EVENTUALLY. / UP ON THE ROOF** [–] [ ]

— now again with regulars LARKEY and KORTCHMAR plus **RUSS KUNKEL** – drums and guest **JAMES TAYLOR** – guitar, backing vocals (solo artist)

Nov 70. (lp/c) *(AMLS/CAM 2025) <77009>* **TAPESTRY** [4] [1]
– I feel the earth move / So far away / It's too late / Home again / Beautiful / Way over yonder / You've got a friend / Where you lead / Will you still love me tomorrow / Smackwater Jack / Tapestry / (You make me feel like) A natural woman. *(re-iss. 1977 on 'Epic'; EPC 82308) (re-iss. Aug84 on 'Epic' lp/c; EPC/40 32110) (cd-iss. May84 on 'Polydor'; 821 194-1) (cd re-iss. 1988 on 'C.B.S.'; CDCBS 82308) (cd re-iss. Jun89; CD 32110) (cd re-iss. Sep95 on 'Epic'; 480422-2)*

Apr 71. (7") *(AMS 849) <66015>* **IT'S TOO LATE. / I FEEL THE EARTH MOVE** [6] [1]

Jul 71. (7") *(AMS 867) <66019>* **SO FAR AWAY. / SMACKWATER JACK** [ ] [14]

Dec 71. (lp/c) *(AMLH/CAM 67013) <77013>* **MUSIC** [18] [1]
– Brother, brother / Song of long ago / Brighter / Surely / Some kind of wonderful / It's going to take some time / Music / Sweet seasons / Carry your load / Growing away from me / Too much rain / Back to California. *(re-iss. Feb79 on 'Epic'; EPC 82319) (re-iss. 1983 on 'C.B.S.' lp/c; CBS/40 32066) (cd-iss. Jun91 on 'Pickwick'; 982595-2) (cd re-iss. Feb97 on 'Epic'; 484462-2)*

Jan 72. (7") *(AMS 887) <66022>* **SWEET SEASONS. / POCKET MONEY** [ ] [9]

Mar 72. (7") **BROTHER, BROTHER. / IT'S GOING TO TAKE SOME TIME** [–] [ ]

Ode Ode

Oct 72. (7") *<(ODS 66031)>* **BEEN TO CANAAN. / BITTER WITH THE SWEET** [ ] [24]

Nov 72. (lp/c) *<(77016)>* **RHYMES AND REASONS** [40] Oct72 [2]
– Come down easy / My my she cries / Peace in the valley / Feeling sad tonight / The first day in August / Bitter with the sweet / Goodbye don't mean I'm gone / Stand behind me / Gotta get through another day / I think I can hear you / Ferguson Road / Been to Canaan.

Jun 73. (7") *<(ODS 66035)>* **YOU LIGHT UP MY LIFE. / BELIEVE IN HUMANITY** [ ] [28] [67]

Jul 73. (lp/c) *<(77018)>* **FANTASY** [ ] Jun73 [6]
– Fantasy beginning / You've been around too long / Being at war with each other / Directions / That's how things go down / Weekdays / Haywood / A quiet place to live / Welfare symphony / You light up my life / Corazon / Believe in humanity / Fantasy end. *(cd-iss. Oct93 on 'Sony Collectors'; 983307-2) (cd re-iss. Jul97 on 'Epic'; 487939-2)*

Oct 73. (7") *<ODS 66039>* **CORAZON. / THAT'S HOW THINGS GO DOWN** [–] [37]

— added guest **TOM SCOTT** – saxophone

Jul 74. (7") *<(ODS 66101)>* **JAZZMAN. / YOU GO YOUR WAY, I'LL GO MINE** [ ] [2]

Oct 74. (lp/c) *<(77024)>* **WRAP AROUND JOY** [ ] Sep74 [1]
– Nightingale / Change in mind, change of heart / Jazzman / You go your way, I'll go mine / You're something new / We are all in this together / Wrap around joy / You gentle me / My lovin' eyes / Sweet Adonis / A night this side of dying / The best is yet to come. *(cd-iss. May92 on 'Thunderbolt'; CDTB 137)*

Jan 75. (7") *<(ODS 66106)>* **NIGHTINGALE. / YOU'RE SOMETHING NEW** [ ] [9]

Mar 75. (lp) *<77027>* **REALLY ROSIE** (children's TV) [–] [20]
– Really Rosie / One was Johnny / Alligators all around / Pierre / Screaming and yelling / The ballad of chicken soup / Chicken soup and rice / Ave. P / My simple humble neighborhood / The awful truth / Such suffer / Really Rosie. *(cd-iss. Sep93 on 'Sony Collectors'; 983257-2)*

Jul 75. (7") *<>* **PIERRE. / CHICKEN SOUP WITH RICE** [–] [ ]

Jan 76. (7") *<ODS 66119>* **ONLY LOVE IS REAL. / STILL HERE THINKING OF YOU** [–] [37]

Jan 76. (lp/c) *<(77034)>* **THOROUGHBRED** [ ] [3]
– So many ways / Daughter of light / High out of time / Only love is real / There's a space between us / I'd like to know you better / We all have to be alone / Ambrosia / Still here thinking of you / It's gonna work out fine. *(re-iss. Jul84 on 'C.B.S.' lp/c; CBS/40 31841)*

Jul 76. (7") *<(ODS 66123)>* **HIGH OUT OF TIME. / I'D LIKE TO KNOW YOU BETTER** [ ] May76 [76]

— She now worked with backing band NAVARRO, which included new 3rd husband **RICK EVERS** – guitar

Capitol Capitol

Jul 77. (7") *(CL 15934) <4455>* **HARD ROCK CAFE. / TO KNOW THAT I LOVE YOU** [ ] [30]

Aug 77. (lp/c) *<(EA-ST 11667)>* **SIMPLE THINGS** [ ] [17]
– Simple things / Hold on / In the name of love / Labyrinth / You're the one who knows / Hard rock cafe / Time alone / God only knows / To know that I love you / One.

Oct 77. (7") *<4497>* **HOLD ON. / SIMPLE THINGS** [–] [ ]

Nov 77. (7") *(CL 15949)* **LABYRINTH. / SIMPLE THINGS** [ ] [–]

Apr 78. (lp/c) *<(EA-ST 11785)>* **WELCOME HOME** [ ] [ ]
– Main Street Saturday night / Sunbird / Venusian diamond / Changes / Morning sun / Disco tech / Ways of love / Ride the music / Everybody's got the spirit / Welcome home.

Apr 78. (7") *<4593>* **MAIN STREET SATURDAY NIGHT. / CHANGES** [–] [ ]

Aug 78. (7") *<4649>* **MORNING SUN. / SUNBIRD** [–] [ ]

Aug 78. (7") *(CL 16009)* **DISCO TECH. / VENUSIAN DIAMOND** [ ] [–]

— Her husband RICK died Mar78 of a drug overdose. She recorded next album with ex-JERRY JEFF WALKER's musicians.

Jul 79. (lp/c) *<(EA-ST 11953)>* **TOUCH THE SKY** [ ] Jun79 [ ]
– Time gone by / Move lightly / Dreamlike I wander / Walk with me / Good mountain people / You still want her / Passing of the days / Crazy / Eagle / Seeing red.

Aug 79. (7") *(CL 16093) <4718>* **MOVE LIGHTLY. / WHISKEY** [ ] [ ]

Oct 79. (7") *<4766>* **TIME GONE BY. / DREAMLIKE I WANDER** [–] [ ]

— ex-husband **LARKEY** returned on bass and **CHRISTOPHER CROSS** – guitar

Jun 80. (lp/c) *<(EA-ST 12073)>* **PEARLS – SONGS OF GOFFIN AND KING** (new versions old songs) [ ] [44]
– Dancin' with tears in my eyes / Locomotion / One fine day / Hey girl / Snow queen / Chains / Oh no not my baby / Hi de ho / Wasn't born to follow / Goin' back.

Jun 80. (7") *(CL 16152) <4864>* **ONE FINE DAY. / RULERS OF THE WORLD** [ ] May80 [12]

Aug 80. (7") *<4911>* **LOCOMOTION. / OH NO NOT MY BABY** [–] [ ]

Oct 80. (7") *<4941>* **CHAINS. / HEY GIRL** [–] [ ]

— Now with new session people

Atlantic Atlantic

Mar 82. (lp/c) *(K/K4 50880)* *<19344>* **ONE TO ONE**
– One to one / It's a war / Lookin' out for number one / Life without love / Golden man / Read between the lines / Love is like (a boomerang) / Goat Annie / Someone you never met before / Little prince.

Mar 82. (7") *<4026>* **ONE TO ONE. / GOAT ANNIE** – 45

Apr 82. (7") *(K 11725)* **READ BETWEEN THE LINES. / GOLDEN MAN** –

May 82. (7") *<4062>* **READ BETWEEN THE LINES. / LIFE WITHOUT LOVE** –

Jun 82. (7") *(K 11738)* **LITTLE PRINCE. / SOMEONE YOU NEVER MET BEFORE** –

—— **KUNKEL** and **KORTCHMAR** returned to line-up

Dec 83. (lp/c/cd) *<(780 118-1/-4)>* **SPEEDING TIME**
– Computer eyes / Small voice / Crying in the rain / Sacred heart of stone / Speeding time / Standin' on the border line / So ready for love / Chalis Borealis / Dancing / Alabaster lady.

Dec 83. (7") *<89756>* **CRYING IN THE RAIN. / A SACRED HEART OF STONE** –

Feb 84. (7") *<89694>* **SPEEDING TIME. /** –

In 1985, she and JOHN SEBASTIAN wrote songs for the "Care Bears" film

Capitol Capitol

Apr 89. (7") *<44336>* **CITY STREETS. / TIME HEALS ALL WOUNDS** –

Apr 89. (7") *(CL 527)* **CITY STREETS. / I CAN'T STOP THINKING ABOUT YOU** –
(12"+=/cd-s+=) *(12/CD CL 527)* – Time heals all wounds.

Apr 89. (cd/c/lp) *(CD/TC+/EST 2092)* *<90885>* **CITY STREETS**
– City streets / Sweet life / Down to the darkness / Lovelight / I can't stop thinking about you / Legacy / Ain't that the way / Midnight flyer / Homeless heart / Someone who believes in you.
(above featured ERIC CLAPTON – guitar / MAX WEINBERG – drums)

Jul 89. (7") *<44444>* **SOMEONE WHO BELIEVES IN YOU. / CITY STREETS** –

Quality Rhythm Safari

Mar 93. (cd) *<57197>* **COLOR OF YOUR DREAMS** –
– Lay down my life / Hold out for love / Standing in the rain / Now and forever / Wishful thinking / Color of your dreams / Tears falling down on me / Friday's tie-dye nightmare / Just one thing / Do you feel love / It's never too late.

Mar 94. (cd/c) *(CKING CD/MC 01)* *<53878>* **IN CONCERT – THE GREATEST HITS LIVE (live)**
– Hard Rock Cafe / Up on the roof / Smackwater Jack / So far away / Beautiful / A natural woman (you make me feel like) / Hold out for love / Will you love me tomorrow / Jazzman / It's too late / Chains / I feel the earth move / You've got a friend / The locomotion / You've got a friend.
above was recorded at LA's Amphitheater, with guest spots for CROSBY & NASH, plus SLASH of GUNS N' ROSES playing guitar on 'The Locomotion'.

not iss. Koch Int.

Sep 01. (cd) *<8346>* **LOVE MAKES THE WORLD** –
– Love makes the world / You can do anything / The reason / I wasn't gonna fall in love / I don't know / Oh no, not my baby / It could have been anyone / Monday without you / An uncommon love / You will find me there / Safe again / This time.

– compilations etc. –

Note; All below releases on 'Epic' were issued on 'Ode' US.

May 78. (lp/c) *Epic; (EPC 86043) / Ode; <34967>* **HER GREATEST HITS** Mar78 47
– Jazzman / So far away / Sweet seasons / I feel the Earth move / Brother, brother / Only love is real / It's too late / Nightingale / Smackwater Jack / Been to Canaan / Corazon / Believe in humility. *(re-iss. Jul83 lp/c; EPC/40 32345) (cd-iss. Mar87 on 'C.B.S.'; CD 86043) (cd re-iss. Mar91; CD 32345)*

Jun 79. (7") *Epic; (EPC 7067)* **IT'S TOO LATE. / YOU'VE GOT A FRIEND** –

Oct 83. (7") *Old Gold; (OG 9355)* **IT MIGHT AS WELL RAIN UNTIL SEPTEMBER. / THE ROAD TO NOWHERE** –

Jul 94. (cd) *Connoisseur; (VSOPCD 199)* **PEARLS / TIME GONE BY** –

Oct 94. (d-cd/d-c) *Legacy-Epic; (E2K/E2T 48833)* **A NATURAL WOMAN – THE ODE COLLECTION 1968-1976** –

Nov 96. (cd) *Epic; (485104-2)* **LIVE AT CARNEGIE HALL (live)** –

Jun 97. (cd) *Marginal; (MAR 010)* **HITS AND RARITIES** –

Sep 00. (cd/c) *Sony TV; (SONYTV 93 CD/MC)* **NATURAL WOMAN – THE VERY BEST OF . . .** 31 –

□ KING BISCUIT TIME (see under ⇒ BETA BAND)

KING CRIMSON

Formed: Bournemouth, England . . . summer 1967 by ROBERT FRIPP, plus brothers MIKE and PETE GILES, who formed the soft-rock trio BRAIN, then GILES, GILES & FRIPP. After signing to 'Deram' early in '68 and adding couple, IAN McDONALD and JUDY DYBLE, they issued flop album, 'THE CHEERFUL INSANITY OF . . .', in September of that year. With IAN now replacing PETE, the trio soon became KING CRIMSON, adding new vocalist GREG LAKE, who debuted at The Speakeasy in London on the 9th of April 1969. Three months later, they supported The ROLLING STONES at Hyde Park's free concert, a performance which attracted the attention of the 'Island' label. Subsequently signed up, they unleashed 'IN THE COURT OF THE CRIMSON KING' in October '69, a masterful debut album which made UK Top 5 and US Top 30. At this stage, the group were basically a prog-rock neo-classical outfit, their initial MOODY BLUES' mellotron-sound soon swapped for experimental, occasionally self-indulgent guitar-mastery of FRIPP. KING CRIMSON found themselves in turmoil when a couple of group members departed, leaving FRIPP and lyricist/road manager, PETE SINFIELD, to work things out. Eventually, with augmentation from session men and ex-members, they recorded the 1970 follow-up album, 'IN THE WAKE OF POSEIDON'. An aggregation of KING CRIMSON members had earlier performed the weird 'CAT FOOD' single on 'Top Of The Pops'; this release signalled a move towards avant-jazz territory, a sound they'd develop over the course of early 70's albums, 'LIZARD', 'ISLANDS' and 'LARKS' TONGUES IN ASPIC'. Throughout this turbulent period, FRIPP and Co. went through even more upheavals, although they still scored with astounding album successes ('STARLESS AND BIBLE BLACK' and 'RED' – both 1974) until they disbanded for the first time late in '74. FRIPP had already been a prolific session man for the likes of VAN DER GRAAF GENERATOR and (BRIAN) ENO, and together with the latter was co-credited on two experimental budget lp's, 'NO PUSSYFOOTIN' (1973) and 'EVENING STAR' (1975). He then moved to New York in 1977 and worked with PETER GABRIEL on his first three albums, at the same time lending his expertise to BOWIE's 'Heroes'. In 1979, FRIPP released his debut solo album, 'EXPOSURE', which featured many of his close friends handling vocals (GABRIEL, HAMILL, etc). The following year, his instrumental set, 'GOD SAVE THE QUEEN / UNDER HEAVY MANNERS' developed his patented brand of electro-experimentation, dubbed "Frippertronics", the record trailed by a short-lived project/band, The LEAGUE OF GENTLEMEN. In 1981, he reformed KING CRIMSON with BILL BRUFORD, ADRIAN BELEW and TONY LEVIN, recording a clutch of slightly more accessible albums, before FRIPP was again left contemplating a revived solo career. During the period, 1982-84, the guitarist collaborated on two albums, 'I ADVANCE MASKED' and 'BEWITCHED', with ANDY SUMMERS (POLICE guitarist). Like many of their contemporaries, KING CRIMSON reformed in 1994, issuing a series of studio and live sets. Come the new millennium, KING CRIMSON were still going strong, embracing the fad for treated vocals on 'HAPPY WITH WHAT YOU HAVE

TO BE HAPPY WITH' (2002), a record which also featured some of the most aggressive material of the band's career. 'THE POWER TO BELIEVE' (2003) meanwhile, collected the cream of their more recent releases – including the startling 'EYES WIDE OPEN' – with new material. • **Trivia:** In the mid-80's, FRIPP married singer/actress, TOYAH WILLCOX, even collaborating on an album, 'THE LADY OR THE TIGER', in 1987.

Album rating: Giles, Giles & Fripp: THE CHEERFUL SANITY OF . . . (*5) / King Crimson: IN THE COURT OF THE CRIMSON KING (*9) / IN THE WAKE OF POSEIDON (*6) / LIZARD (*6) / ISLANDS (*7) / EARTHBOUND (*4) / LARKS' TONGUES IN ASPIC (*8) / STARLESS & BIBLE BLACK (*8) / RED (*8) / U.S.A. (*5) / A YOUNG PERSON'S GUIDE TO KING CRIMSON compilation (*8) / DISCIPLINE (*6) / BEAT (*6) / THREE OF A PERFECT PAIR (*5) / FRAME BY FRAME – THE ESSENTIAL KING CRIMSON compilation (*8) / VROOOM (*5) / THRAK (*5) / B'BOOM: OFFICIAL SOUNDTRACK – LIVE IN ARGENTINA (*5) / THRaKaTTaK (*4) / THE CONSTRUCKTION OF LIGHT (*6) / HAPPY WITH WHAT YOU HAVE TO BE HAPPY WITH mini (*6) / THE POWER TO BELIEVE (*6) / Robert Fripp: EXPOSURE (*7) / GOD SAVE THE QUEEN – UNDER HEAVY MANNERS (*7) / LET THE POWER FALL (FRIPPERTRONICS) (6) / LEAGUE OF GENTLEMEN (*5) / NETWORK collection (*6) / GOD SAVE THE KING (*5) / ROBERT FRIPP AND THE LEAGUE OF CRAFTY GUITARISTS!: LIVE (*5) / THE BRIDGE BETWEEN (*5) / 1995 SOUNDTRACKS, VOLUME 2 – LIVE IN CALIFORNIA (*5) / RADIOPHONICS: 1995 SOUNDSCAPES VOLUME 1 (*5) / INTERGALACTIC BOOGIE EXPRESS – LIVE IN EUROPE 1991 (*5) / THAT WHICH PASSES (*5)

GILES, GILES & FRIPP

PETE GILES – bass / **MICHAEL GILES** (b.1942)– drums / **ROBERT FRIPP** (b.16 May'46, Wimbourne, Dorset, England)– guitar, mellotron

C.B.S. not iss.

May 67. (7"; as BRAIN) *(R 5595)* **NIGHTMARES IN RED. / KICK THE DONKEY** [ ] [-]

Deram not iss.

Jun 68. (7") *(DM 188)* **ONE IN A MILLION. / NEWLY-WEDS** [ ] [-]

— added **IAN McDONALD** (b.25 Jun'46, London) – keyboards / and guest **JUDY DYBLE** – vocals (ex-FAIRPORT CONVENTION) also featured as did KING CRIMSON lyricist **PETE SINFIELD**

Sep 68. (lp; mono/stereo) *(DML/SML 1022)* **THE CHEERFUL INSANITY OF GILES, GILES & FRIPP** [ ] [-]
– The Saga of Rodney Toady / One in a million / Just George / Thursday morning / North meadow / Call tomorrow / Newly-weds / Digging my lawn / Suite No.1 / Little children / The crukster / How do you know / The sun is shining / Brudite eyes / Elephant song. *(re-iss. 1970; SPA 423) (re-iss. Apr82 on 'Editions-EG'; EGED 16) (re-iss. Aug93 cd/c+=; 820 965-2/-4)* – (extra versions).

— IAN now on vocals (JUDY left to join TRADER HORNE)

Sep 68. (7") *(DM 210)* **THURSDAY MORNING. / ELEPHANT SONG** [ ] [-]

KING CRIMSON

ROBERT, IAN + MIKE recruited **GREG LAKE** (b.10 Nov'48) – vocals, bass (ex-GODS)

Island Atlantic

Oct 69. (7") *(WIP 6071) <2703>* **THE COURT OF THE CRIMSON KING (part 1). / (part 2)** [ ] Dec69 [80]

Oct 69. (lp) *(ILPS 9111) <8245>* **IN THE COURT OF THE CRIMSON KING** [5] Dec69 [28]
– 21st century schizoid man (including; Mirrors) / I talk to the wind / Epitaph (including; March for no reason – Tomorrow and tomorrow) / Moonchild (including; The dream – The illusion) / The court of the Crimson King (including: The return of the fire witch – The dance of the puppets). *<US re-iss. 1970; SD 19155> (re-iss. Mar77 on 'Polydor' lp)(c; 2302 057)(3100 357) (cd-iss. May83 on 'Polydor'; 800 030-2) (re-iss. Jan87 & Nov91 on 'E.G.' lp/c/cd; EG LP/MC/CD 1)*

— **PETE GILES** – bass (ex-GILES, GILES & FRIPP) repl. IAN who with MIKE had formed McDONALD & GILES. IAN later formed FOREIGNER. MIKE appeared below. Added **KEITH TIPPET** – piano (other two were FRIPP & LAKE)

Mar 70. (7") *(WIP 6080)* **CAT FOOD. / GROON** [ ] [-]

— added **MEL COLLINS** – saxophone (ex-CIRCUS) / plus guest on 1 track **GORDON HASKELL** – vocals

May 70. (lp) *(ILPS 9127) <8266>* **IN THE WAKE OF POSEIDON** [4] Sep70 [31]
– Peace – a beginning / Pictures of a city (including; 42nd at Treadmill) / Cadence and cascade / In the wake of Poseidon (including; Libra's theme) / Peace – a theme / Cat food / The Devil's triangle: Merday morn – Hand of Sceiron – Garden of worm / Peace – an end. *(re-iss. Mar77 on 'Polydor' lp)(c; (2302 058)(3100 358) (re-iss. Jan87 & Nov91 on 'E.G.' lp/c/cd; EG LP/MC/CD 2)*

— **GORDON HASKELL** (now full-time) repl. GREG who formed EMERSON, LAKE & PALMER (earlier). FRIPP had also retained **MEL COLLINS / ANDY McCULLOCH** – drums repl. MIKE

Dec 70. (lp) *(ILPS 9141) <8278>* **LIZARD** [30] [ ]
– Cirkus (including; Entry of the chameleons) / Indoor games / Happy family / Lady of the dancing water / Lizard suite: Prince Rupert awakes – Bolero-The peacock's tale – The battle of glass tears; (a) Dawn song – (b) Last skirmish – (c) Prince Rupert's lament / Big top. *(re-iss. Apr77 on 'Polydor' lp)(c; 2302 059)(3100 359) (re-iss. Jan87 & Nov91 on 'E.G.' lp/c/cd; EG LP/MC/CD 4)*

— **BOZ BURRELL** (b. RAYMOND, 1946, Lincoln, England) – vocals, bass repl. HASKELL who went solo / **IAN WALLACE** (b.29 Sep'46, Bury, England) – drums repl. McCULLOCH who joined GREENSLADE

Dec 71. (lp) *(ILPS 9175) <7212>* **ISLANDS** [30] [76]
– Formentera lady / The sailor's tale / Letters / (prelude) / Song of the gulls – Islands / Ladies of the road. *(re-iss. Apr77 on 'Polydor' lp)(c; 2302 060)(3100 360) (re-iss. Jan87 on 'E.G.' lp/c/cd; EG LP/MC/CD 5)*

— FRIPP was sole survivor (lyricist PETE SINFIELD left early '72, to go into production for ROXY MUSIC's debut and be lyricist for Italians P.F.M.) / **JOHN WETTON** (b.12 Jul'49, Derby, England) – vocals, bass (ex-FAMILY) repl. BOZ who formed BAD COMPANY / **BILL BRUFORD** (b.17 May'48, London, England) – drums (ex-YES) repl. WALLACE who joined STREETWALKERS / **DAVID CROSS** (b.1948, Plymouth, England) – violin, flute repl. COLLINS who later joined CAMEL + sessions / added **JAMIE MUIR** – percussion and new lyricist **RICHARD PALMER-JAMES**

Mar 73. (lp) *(ILPS 9230) <7263>* **LARKS' TONGUES IN ASPIC** [20] [61]
– Larks' tongues in aspic (part one) / Book of Saturday / Exiles / Easy money / The talking drum / Larks' tongues in aspic (part two). *(re-iss. Apr77 on 'Polydor' lp)(c; 2302 061)(3100 361) (re-iss. Jan87 & Nov91 on 'E.G.' lp/c/cd; EG LP/MC/CD 7)*

— Reverted to a quartet when JAMIE became a Tibetan monk

Feb 74. (7") *(WIP 6189) <3016>* **THE NIGHT WATCH. / THE GREAT DECEIVER** [ ] [ ]

Feb 74. (lp) *(ILPS 9275) <7298>* **STARLESS AND BIBLE BLACK** [28] [64]
– The great deceiver / Lament / We'll let you know / The night watch / Trio / The mincer / Starless and bible black / Trio / Fracture. *(re-iss. Apr77 on 'Polydor' lp)(c; 2302 065)(3100 365) (re-iss. Jan87 & Nov91 on 'E.G.' lp/c/cd; EG LP/MC/CD 12)*

— now just basically a trio of FRIPP, WETTON and BRUFORD with old guests **MEL COLLINS, IAN McDONALD** and the departing **CROSS** augmenting on a track

Oct 74. (lp) *(ILPS 9308) <18110>* **RED** [45] [66]
– Red / Fallen angel / One more red nightmare / Providence / Starless. *(re-iss. Apr77 on 'Polydor' lp/c; 2302 066)(3100 366) (re-iss. Jan87 & Nov91 on 'E.G.' lp/c/cd; EG LP/MC/CD 15)*

— Split just before last album. Next live album was recorded with DAVID CROSS

Apr 75. (lp) *(ILPS 9316) <18136>* **U.S.A. (live)** [ ] [ ]
– Larks' tongues in aspic (part II) / Lament / Exiles / Asbury park / Easy money / 21st century schizoid man. *(re-iss. Dec79 on 'Polydor'; 2302 067) (re-iss. Jan87 on 'E.G.' lp/c/cd; EG LP/MC/CD 18)*

— JOHN WETTON joined BRIAN FERRY, then URIAH HEEP and later ASIA etc. As above BILL BRUFORD went solo and formed UK, after GONG stints.

ROBERT FRIPP

solo adding keyboards and a number of friends **PETER GABRIEL, PETER HAMILL & DARYL HALL** on vox, plus **PHIL COLLINS, BARRY ANDREWS, TONY LEVIN & MICHAEL NARADA WALDEN** – other instruments

E.G. E.G.-Polydor

Apr 79. (lp/c) *(EG LP/MC 101) <6201>* **EXPOSURE** [71] [79]
– (prelude) / You burn me up I'm a cigarette / Breathless / Disengage / North star / Chicago / NY3 / Mary / Exposure / Haaaden two / Urban landscape / I may not have had enough of me but I've had enough of you / (first inaugural address to the J.A.C.E. Sherborne House) / Water music

I / Here comes the flood / Water music II / Postscript. *(cd-iss. Jan87 & Apr89; EGCD 41)*

Mar 80. (lp/c) *(EG LP 105)* *<PL 6266>* **GOD SAVE THE QUEEN / UNDER HEAVY MANNERS (instrumental)**
– Under heavy manners / The zero of the signified / Red two scorer / God save the Queen / 1983. *(re-iss. Jan87 lp/c/cd; EG LP/MC/CD 45)*

E.G.-Editions not iss.

Apr 81. (lp/c) *(EGED/+C 10)* **LET THE POWER FALL (FRIPPERTRONICS)** –
– 1984 / 1985 / 1986 / 1987 / 1988 / 1989. *(cd-iss. Jan87; EEGCD 10)*

LEAGUE OF GENTLEMEN

FRIPP retained **BARRY ANDREWS** adding **SARA LEE** – bass (ex-JANE AIRE) / **JOHNNY TOOBAD** – drums

E.G.-Editions Polydor

Dec 80. (7") *(EGEND 1)* **HEPTAPARAPARSHINOKH. / MARRIAGEMUZIC** –

Mar 81. (lp) *(EGED 9)* *<16317>* **LEAGUE OF GENTLEMEN (instrumental)**
– Indiscreet / Inductive recurrance / Minor man / Heptaparaparshinokh / Dislocated / Pareto optimum 1 / Eye needles / Indiscreet II / Pareto optimum 2 / Cognitive dissonance / H.G. Wells / Trap / Ochre / Indiscreet III.

Mar 81. (7") *(EGEND 2)* **DISLOCATED. / 1984** –

KING CRIMSON

FRIPP along with past member BRUFORD recruits newcomers **ADRIAN BELEW** (b. ROBERT STEVEN BELEW, 23 Dec'49, Covington, Kentucky) – guitar, vocals (ex-TOM TOM CLUB) / **TONY LEVIN** (b. 6 Jun'46, Boston, Mass.) – bass (ex-session man including PETER GABRIEL)

E.G. Warners

Sep 81. (lp/c) *(EG LP/MC 49)* *<BSK 3629>* **DISCIPLINE** 41 45
– Elephant talk / Frame by frame / Matte Kudasai / Indiscipline / Thelahun ginjeet / The sheltering sky / Discipline. *(re-iss. Jan87 & Nov91 lp/c/cd; EG LP/MC/CD 49)*

Nov 81. (7") *(EGO 2)* **MATTE KUDASAI. / ELEPHANT TALK** –

Jun 82. (lp/c) *(EG LP/MC 51)* *<23692-1>* **BEAT** 39 52
– Neal and Jack and me / Heartbeat / Sartori in Tangier / Waiting man / Neurotica / Two hands / The howler / Requiem. *(cd-iss. Apr84 on 'Polydor'; 821 194-2) (re-iss. Jan87 & Nov91 lp/c/cd; EG LP/MC/CD 51)*

Jun 82. (7") *(EGO 6)* *<29964>* **HEARTBEAT. / REQUIEM (excerpt)**

Feb 84. (7") *(EGO 15)* *<29309>* **SLEEPLESS. / NUAGES**
(12") *(EGOX 15)* – ('A'side) / ('A'instrumental & dance mixes).

Mar 84. (lp/c/cd) *(EG LP/MC/CD 55)* *<25071>* **THREE OF A PERFECT PAIR** 30 58
– Three of a perfect pair / Model man / Sleepless / Man with an open heart / Nuages (that which passes, passes like clouds) / Industry / Dig me / No warning / Lark's tongues in aspic (part three). *(re-iss. Jan87 & Nov91; same)*

— FRIPP disbanded KING CRIMSON project for a decade

– compilations, others, etc. –

Jun 72. (lp) *Help-Island; (HELP 6)* **EARTHBOUND (live)** –
– 21st century schizoid man / Peoria / The sailor's tale / Earthbound / Groon. *(re-iss. Oct77 on 'Polydor' lp)(c; 2343 092)(3192 385) (re-iss. Apr82 on 'EG')*

Feb 76. (d-lp) *Island; (ISLP 7)* **A YOUNG PERSON'S GUIDE TO KING CRIMSON** –
– Epitaph (including; (a) March for no reason – (b) Tomorrow and tomorrow / Cadence and cascade / Ladies of the road / I talk to the wind / Red / Starless / The night watch / Book of Saturday / Peace – a beginning / Cat food / Groon / Coda from Larks' tongues in aspic part 2 / Moonchild; (a) Mirrors – (b) The illusion / Trio / The court of the crimson king (including; (a) The return of the fire witch – (b) Dance of the puppets / 21st century schizoid man. *(re-iss. Mar77 on 'Polydor' d-lp/c; 2612 035)(3500 123) (cd-iss. 1986 on 'E.G.'; EGCD 22)*

Feb 76. (7") *Island; (WIP 6274)* **21st CENTURY SCHIZOID MAN. / EPITAPH** –

Dec 80. (d-lp) *Polydor;* **IN THE COURT OF THE CRIMSON KING / LARKS' TONGUES IN ASPIC** –

Dec 86. (cd/d-lp/d-c) *E.G.; (EG CD/MC/LP 68)* **THE COMPACT KING CRIMSON**

Apr 87. (7"; by BRAIN) *Bam Caruso; (OPRA 63)* **NIGHTMARES IN RED. / (other artist)** –

Dec 89. (3xcd-box/3xc-box/3xlp-box) *E.G.; (EGBC/EGBM/EGBL 6)* **KING CRIMSON BOXED SET** –
– (IN THE COURT OF THE CRIMSON KING / LARKS' TONGUES IN ASPIC / DISCIPLINE)
(above 3 albums were packaged with other 'Island' artists)

1991. (cd-ep) *Virgin;* **THE ABBREVIATED KING CRIMSON – HEARTBEAT (medley)** –
– The King Crimson barber shop – 21st century schizoid man (abbreviated) – In the court of the crimson king (abbreviated) – Elephant talk (edit) – Matte Kudesai – Heartbeat (edit).

Dec 91. (4xcd-box) *Virgin; (KCBOX 1)* **FRAME BY FRAME: THE ESSENTIAL KING CRIMSON** –

Nov 92. (4xcd-box) *Virgin; (KCDIS 1)* **THE GREAT DECEIVER** –

Sep 93. (cd/c) *Virgin; (CDV/TCV 2721)* **SLEEPLESS: THE CONCISE KING CRIMSON**
– 21st century schizoid man / Epitaph / In the court of the crimson king / Cat food / Ladies of the road / Starless (abridged) / Red / Fallen angel / Elephant talk / Frame by frame / Matte Kudasai / Heartbeat / Three of a perfect pair / Sleepless.

Dec 93. (3xcd-box) *Virgin;* **IN THE COURT OF THE CRIMSON KING / IN THE WAKE OF POSEIDON / LIZARD** –

Apr 97. (d-cd) *Discipline; (DGM 9607)* **EPITAPH (live in 1969)** –

ROBERT FRIPP / LEAGUE OF GENTLEMEN

EG-Editions E.G.

Jun 85. (lp/c) *(EGED/+C 9)* **GOD SAVE THE KING**
– God save the King / Under heavy manners / Heptaparparshinokh / Inductive resonance / Cognitive dissonance / Dislocated / HG Wells / Eye needles / Trap. *(cd-iss. Jan87; EEGCD 9)*

Nov 86. (lp/c/cd) *(EGED/+C 43)* **ROBERT FRIPP AND THE LEAGUE OF CRAFTY GUITARISTS: LIVE! (live)**
– Guitar craft theme 1: Invocation / Tight muscle party at Love Beach / The chords that bind / Guitar craft theme 3: Eye of the needle / All or nothing II / Guitar craft theme 2: Aspiration / All or nothing I / Circulation / A fearful symmetry / The new world / Crafty march. *(cd-iss. Jan87; EEGCD 43)*

— Late 1988, FRIPP / FRIPP (TOYAH) toured augmented by **TREY GUNN** – stick bass / **PAUL BEAVIS** – percussion, drums

— In mid'93, ROBERT FRIPP collaborated with ex-JAPAN singer DAVID SYLVIAN on near UK Top 20 album 'THE FIRST DAY'.

— In Aug'94, FRIPP was part of FFWD alongside THOMAS FEHLYN, KRIS WESTON + Dr.ALEX PATTERSON of The ORB. In Sep'94, FRIPP again teamed up with DAVID SYLVIAN on album 'DAMAGE'.

KING CRIMSON

FRIPP / BRUFORD / BELEW / LEVIN / GUNN / PAT MASTELOTTO

Discipline Virgin

Dec 94. (cd) *(DGM 0004)* **VROOOM**
– Vrooom / Sex, sleep, eat, drink, dream / Cage / Thrak / When I say stop, continue / One time.

Apr 95. (cd/cd/c) *(KC CDX/CDY/MC 1)* *<40313>* **THRAK** 58 83
– Vrooom / Coda: Marine 475 / Dinosaur / Walking on air / B'boom / Thrak / Inner garden I / People / Radio I / One time / Radio II / Inner garden II / Sex, sleep, eat, drink, dream / Vrooom vrooom / Vrooom vrooom coda.

Aug 95. (d-cd) *(<DGM 9503>)* **B'BOOM: OFFICIAL SOUNDTRACK – LIVE IN ARGENTINA (live**
– Vrooom / Frame by frame / Sex, sleep, eat, drink, dream / Red / One time / B'boom / Thrak / Improv – Two sticks / Elephant talk / Indiscipline // Vrooom vrooom / Matte Kudesai / The talking drum / Lark's tongues in aspic (part 2) / Heartbeat / Sleepless / People / B'boom / Thrak.

May 96. (cd) *(<DGM 9604>)* **THRaKaTTaK (live 1995)** Jun96
– Thrak / Fearless and highly thrakked / Mother hold the candle steady while I shave the chicken's lips / Thrakattak (pt.1) / The slaughter of the innocents / This night wounds time / Thrakattk (pt.2) / Thrak reprise.

Sep 96. (cd) *(DGMVC 1)* **LIVE IN JAPAN 1995 (live)** –
– Frame by frame / Dinosaur / One time / Red / B'room / Thrak / Matte kudasai / Three of a perfect pair / Vroom vroom / Sex, sleep, eat, drink, dream / Elephant talk / Indiscipline / Talking drum / Larks' tongues in aspic part II / People / Walking on air.

— **FRIPP, BELEW, GUNN + MASTELOTTO**

King Crimson Virgin

May 00. (cd) *(KCCDX2) <49261>* **THE CONSTRUCkTION OF LIGHT** [ ] [ ]
– ProzaKc blues / The construcKtion of light (2 parts) / Into the frying pan / FraKctured / The world's my oyster soup kitchen floor wax museum / Larks' tongues in aspic – part IV / Coda: I have a dream / ProjeKct X: Heaven and Earth.

Sanctuary Sanctuary

Nov 02. (m-cd) *(SANEP 123) <84580>* **HAPPY WITH WHAT YOU HAVE TO BE HAPPY WITH** [ ] Oct02 [ ]
– Bude / Happy with what you have to be happy with / Mie gakure / She shudders / Eyes wide open / Shoganai / I ran / Potato pie / Larks' tongues in aspic (pt.IV) / Clouds.

Feb 03. (cd) *(SANCD 155) <84585>* **THE POWER TO BELIEVE** [ ] Mar03 [ ]
– The power to believe I: a cappella / Level five / Eyes wide open / Elektrik / Facts of life (intro) / Facts of life / The power to believe II / Dangerous curves / Happy with what you have to be happy with / The power to believe III / The power to believe IV: Coda (live).

ROBERT FRIPP

Discipline Virgin

Nov 94. (cd; ROBERT FRIPP STRING QUARTET) *(DGM 9303)* **THE BRIDGE BETWEEN** [ ] [ ]

Feb 95. (cd) *(DGM 9402-2)* **1999 SOUNDSCAPES – LIVE IN ARGENTINA (live)** [ ] [–]
– 1999 (part one) / 2000 / 2001 / Interlude / 2002.

Oct 95. (cd) *(DGM 9502)* **INTERGALACTIC BOOGIE EXPRESS – LIVE IN EUROPE 1991** (live with The LEAGUE OF CRAFTY GUITARISTS) [ ] [–]
– A Connecticut Yankee in the court of King Arthur / Rhythm of the universe / Lark's hrak / Circulation 1 / Intergalactic boogie express / G force / Eye of the needle / Corrente / Driving force / Groove penetration / Flying home / Circulation II / Fireplace / Fragments of skylab / Asturias / Prelude circulation / Cheeseballs / Prelude in c minor / Wabash cannonball / Fractual Jazn / Ashesis. *(re-iss. Mar97; same)*

Mar 96. (cd) *(DGM 9505)* **RADIOPHONICS: 1995 SOUNDSCAPES VOL.1 (live in Argentina)** [ ] [–]
– Radiophonic I / Radiophonic II / Buenos Aires suite: I- Atmosphere, II- Elegy (for mothers and children), III- Streets, IV- Sky.

Sep 96. (cd) *(DGM 9506)* **A BLESSING OF TEARS: 1995 SOUNDSCAPES – VOLUME TWO (live in California)** [ ] [–]
– The cathedral of tears / First light / Midnight blue / Reflection 1 / Second light / A blessing of tears / Returning I / Returning II.

May 96. (cd; LEAGUE OF GENTLEMEN) *(DGM 9602)* **THRANG THRANG GOZINBULX** [ ] [ ]

Sep 96. (cd) *(DGM 9507)* **THAT WHICH PASSES** [ ] [ ]
– On acceptance / On the approach of doubt / Worm in Paradise / New worlds / On triumph / On awe / This too shall pass / Fear of light / Time to die.

Jun 97. (cd-ep) *(<DGM 9704>)* **PIE JESU EP** [ ] Sep97 [ ]
– Pie Jesu / Midnight blue / Abandonment to divine providence / Sometimes God hides.

Apr 98. (cd) *(DGM 9608)* **GATES OF PARADISE** [ ] [ ]
– Outer darkness: the outer darkness / Gates of Paradise: Abandonment to divine / Outer darkness: In fear of trembling / Gates of Paradise: Sometimes God hides.

– FRIPP compilations, etc. –

Jan 87. (10"m-lp/c) *E.G.; (EGM LP/MC 4)* **NETWORK** [ ] [ ]
– North star / (i) Water music 1 – (ii) Here comes the flood / God save the king / Under heavy manners.

May 91. (cd; ROBERT FRIPP & LEAGUE OF CRAFTY GUITARISTS) *E.G.; (EEG 21022)* **SHOW OF HANDS** [ ] [ ]

KINGSMEN

Formed: Portland, Oregon, USA ... 1958 by schoolboys LYNN EASTON and JACK ELY, who soon enlisted MIKE MITCHELL, BOB NORDBY and DON GALLUCCI. In May '63, after tours supporting PAUL REVERE & THE RAIDERS, they gained studio time, recording a classic garage cover of Richard Berry's 'LOUIE LOUIE'. This was soon given a release on 'Jerden', becoming a hit in Boston before it was re-issued on 'Wand'. Although banned in certain states, it soared to No.2 in the American charts, becoming a standard for many future rock/pop groups. At the time of its success, the group went through turmoil when EASTON took over both the leadership and vocals of the group (this led to his friend ELY departing). On American TV, EASTON was seen miming to ELY's raunchy vocals. They continued in the same vein covering many standards in their inimitable garage-punk style. • **Covers:** LOUIE LOUIE (Richard Berry) / MONEY (Barrett Strong) / LITTLE LATIN LUPE LU (Righteous Brothers) / KILLER JOE (Rocky Fellers) / etc.

Best CD compilation: THE BEST OF THE KINGSMEN (*7)

LYNN EASTON – saxophone, vocals / **JACK ELY** – vocals, guitar / **MIKE MITCHELL** – lead guitar / **BOB NORDBY** – bass / **DON GALLUCCI** – organ

not iss. Jalynne

1962. (7") *<108>* **DIG THIS. / LADY'S CHOICE** [–] [ ]

not iss. Jerden

Jun 63. (7") *<712>* **LOUIE LOUIE. / HAUNTED CASTLE** [–] [ ]

Pye Inter Wand

Jan 64. (7") *(7N 25231) <143>* **LOUIE LOUIE. / HAUNTED CASTLE** [26] Sep63 [2]
<US re-iss. May66; same>; hit No.97>

— (Aug'63) **EASTON** took over vox from **ELY** who moved to drums! just before he departed / **GARY ABBOTT** – drums repl. ELY. **NORM SUNDHOLM** – bass repl. NORDBY

Jan 64. (lp) *(NPL 28050) <657>* **LOUIE LOUIE: THE KINGSMEN IN PERSON (live Portland)** [ ] [20]
– Louie Louie / The waiting / Mojo workout / Fever / Money / Bent scepter / Long tall Texan / You can't sit down / Twist & shout / J.A.J. / Night train / Mashed potatoes. *<(cd-iss. Jan94 on 'Sundazed'+=; SC 6004)>* – Haunted castle / The krunch / You got the gamma coochee.

Mar 64. (7") *<150>* **MONEY. / BENT SCEPTER** [–] [16]

— **BARRY CURTIS** – organ repl. **DON DICK PETERSON** – drums repl. GARY

Jul 64. (7") *(7N 25262) <157>* **LITTLE LATIN LUPE LU. / DAVID'S MOOD** [ ] [46]

Sep 64. (7") *(7N 25273) <164>* **DEATH OF AN ANGEL. / SEARCHING FOR LOVE** [ ] [42]

Feb 65. (7") *(7N 25292) <172>* **THE JOLLY GREEN GIANT. / LONG GREEN** [ ] Jan65 [4]

Feb 65. (lp) *(NPL 28054) <659>* **THE KINGSMEN, VOLUME II (live)** [ ] Sep64 [15]
– Kingsmen introduction / Little Latin Lupe Lu / Long green / Do you love me / New Orleans / Walking the dog / David's mood / Something's got a hold on me / Come on baby, let the good times roll / Ooh poo pah doo / Great balls of fire / Linda Lou / Death of an angel. *<(cd-iss. Jan94 on 'Sundazed'+=; SC 6005)>* – And you believed him / Give her lovin'.

Feb 65. (lp) *<662>* **THE KINGSMEN, VOLUME 3 (live)** [–] [22]
– The jolly green giant / Over you / That's cool, that's trash / Don't you just know it / I go crazy / La-do-dada / Long green / Mother-in-law / Shout / Searching for love / Tall cool one / Comin' home baby. *<(cd-iss. Jan94 on 'Sundazed'+=; SC 6006)>* – Since you've been gone / It's only the dog / Wolf of Manhattan / I'll go crazy.

Jun 65. (7") *(NPL 25311) <183>* **THE CLIMB. / WAITING** [ ] May65 [65]

Jul 65. (7") *<189>* **ANNIE FANNY. / GIVE HER LOVIN'** [–] [47]

Aug 65. (7") *(NPL 25322)* **ANNIE FANNY. / SOMETHING'S GOT A HOLD ON ME** [ ] [–]

Feb 66. (7") *<1107>* **(YOU GOT) THE GAMMA GOOCHE. / IT'S ONLY THE DOG** [–] [ ]

Mar 66. (lp) *(NPL 28068) <670>* **THE KINGSMEN ON CAMPUS (live)** [ ] Oct65 [68]
– Annie Fanny / Rosalie / A hard day's night / I like it like that / Stand by me / Little green thing / The climb / Sticks and stones / Peter Gunn / Some

times / Shotgun / Genevieve. *<cd-iss. Jan94 on 'Sundazed'+=; SC 6014>* – Get out of my life woman / Don't say no / My wife can't cook (mono).

Jun 66. (7") *(7N25370)* <1115> **KILLER JOE. / LITTLE GREEN THING** Mar66 77

Jun 66. (7") **THE KRUNCH. / THE CLIMB** –

Sep 66. (lp) *(NPL 28085)* <674> **THE KINGSMEN'S GREATEST HITS** <US-title '15 GREAT HITS'> (compilation & new) Aug66 87
– Killer Joe / Good lovin' / Jenny take a ride / Ooh poo pah doo / Fever / Quarter to three / Poison Ivy / Satisfaction / Twist and shout / Money / Searchin' / Hang on Sloopy / Do you love me / Shout / New Orleans.

Sep 66. (7") *<1127>* **LITTLE SALLY TEASE. / MY WIFE CAN'T COOK** –

Nov 66. (7") *<1137>* **IF I NEEDED SOMEONE. / THE GRASS IS GREEN** –

Jan 67. (7") *(7N 25406)* *<1147>* **DAYTIME SHADOWS. / TROUBLE**

Wand Wand

Jan 67. (lp) *<(WNS 6)>* **UP AND AWAY**
– Trouble / If I needed someone / Grass is green / Tosin' and turnin' / Under my thumb / Wild thing / (I have found) Another girl / Daytime shadows / Shake a tailfeather / Children's caretaker / Land of a thousand dances / Mustang Sally / Little Sally tease / Hushabye. *<cd-iss. Jan94 on 'Sundazed'+=; SC 6015>* – Killer Joe.

Mar 67. (7") *<1154>* **THE WOLF OF MANHATTAN. / CHILDREN'S CARETAKER** –

Jul 67. (7") *<1157>* **DON'T SAY NO. / ANOTHER GIRL (I HAVE FOUND)** –

— In Jul'67, EASTON left group as they soon dissolved.

1968. (7") *<1164>* **BO DIDDLEY BACH. / JUST BEFORE THE BREAK OF DAY** –

1968. (7") *<1174>* **GET OUT OF MY LIFE WOMAN. / SINCE YOU'VE BEEN GONE** –

1968. (7") **I GUESS I WAS DREAMIN'. / ON LOVE** –

— split in Sep'68. Re-formed in 1972 with **FREDDIE DENNIS** – bass / **STEVE FRIEDSON** – keyboards (added to MIKE MITCHELL, DICK PETERSON + BARRY CURTIS)

– compilations, etc. –

on 'Pye International'; unless mentioned otherwise

1964. (7"ep) *(NEP 44023)* **THE KINGSMEN**

1965. (7"ep) *(NEP 44040)* **MOJO WORKOUT**

1966. (7"ep) *(NEP 44063)* **FEVER**

Apr 66. (7") *(7N 25366)* **LITTLE LATIN LUPE LU. / LOUIE LOUIE** –

1969. (lp) *Marble Arch; (MAL 829)* **THE KINGSMEN'S GREATEST HITS** –

1971. (7") *Wand; (WN 14)* **LOUIE LOUIE. / IF I NEEDED SOMEONE** –

1972. (lp) *Scepter; <18002>* **THE BEST OF THE KINGSMEN** –
(re-iss. Jan86 on 'Rhino'; RNLP 126) (cd-iss. Sep91)

1980. (lp) *Piccadilly; <3329>* **A QUARTER TO THREE** –

1980. (lp) *Piccadilly; <3330>* **YA YA** –

1980. (lp) *Piccadilly; <3346>* **HOUSE PARTY** –

1980. (lp) *Piccadilly; <3348>* **GREAT HITS** –

Jul 81. (7") *Old Gold; (OG 9054)* **LOUIE LOUIE. / THE JOLLY GREEN GIANT** –

Jan 87. (lp) *Decal; (LIK 6)* **LOUIE LOUIE – GREATEST HITS** –
– Louie Louie / Money (that's what I want) / The jolly green giant / Death of an angel / The climb / Get out of my life woman / Little Latin lupe lu / Killer Joe / Annie Fanny / Long green / Little Sally tease / Trouble / If I needed someone.

1989. (cd) *Rhino; <70745>* **THE BEST OF THE KINGSMEN** –
– Louie, Louie / Money / Little Latin lupe lu / Death of an angel / Jolly green giant / Climb / Rosalie / Haunted castle / Long green / That's cool, that's trash / J.A.J. / Genevieve / Annie Fanny / Little green thing / Killer Joe / Give her lovin' / Little Sally tease / Trouble.

Jan 94. (cd) *Sundazed; <(SC 6010)>* **JERK & TWINE TIME**

Jan 94. (cd) *Sundazed; <(SC 6011)>* **LIES**

Jan 96. (cd) *Instant; (CPCD 8160)* **LOUIE LOUIE** –

Jul 97. (cd) *Magic; (52327-2)* **THE 1960s FRENCH EP COLLECTION**

Apr 02. (lp) *Munster; (MR 203)* **LIVE AND UNRELEASED**
(cd-iss. Jan03 on 'Jerden'; JRCD 7004)

KINGS OF LEON

Formed: Nashville, Tennessee, USA . . . 2000 by brothers CALEB, JARED and NATHAN FOLLOWILL; cousin MATTHEW FOLLOWILL was recruited in a matter of months. Somewhat akin to The ALLMAN BROTHERS in their earliest incarnation, plaid shirts, drain-pipe jeans, et al, The KINGS OF LEON were like preacher's sons gatecrashing a porn movie. After playing as a backing band in churches for their father and moving from one trailer park to the next when they were young 'uns, they decided the best route for their homegrown garage blues was to keep it strictly in the family (another cousin is their road manager). Swinging like The BAND meeting GRAM PARSONS' wandering ghost at a CREEDENCE CLEARWATER REVIVAL concert, The KINGS OF LEON issued their southern fried debut EP 'HOLY ROLLER NOVOCAINE' (featuring superb lead track 'MOLLY'S CHAMBERS') early in 2003 and followed into the charts a few months later via 'WHAT I SAW', both lifted from their groundbreaking first set, 'YOUTH & YOUNG MANHOOD', Top 5 in Britain. Thanks to some hype from the NME, etc., their label ('Down') finally launched 'MOLLY'S CHAMBERS' into the UK charts in its own right and set up a possible challenge in their homelands. Elsewhere on the album, we heard songs of redemption, cross-dressing cowboys and tequila-stained bedsheets from a band of ex-religious nuts who had a penchant for the days of NEIL YOUNG and MC5.

Album rating: YOUTH & YOUNG MANHOOD (*8)

CALEB FOLLOWILL – vocals, rhythm guitar / **MATTHEW FOLLOWILL** – lead guitar / **JARED FOLLOWILL** – bass / **NATHAN FOLLOWILL** – drums, percussion, vocals

Handmedown R.C.A.

Feb 03. (cd-ep) *<7863 60614-2>* **HOLY ROLLER NOVOCAINE** –
– Molly's chambers / Wasted time / California waiting / Wicker chair / Holy roller novocaine.

Feb 03. (10"red-ep/cd-ep) *(HMD 20/21)* **HOLY ROLLER NOVOCAINE EP** 53 –
– Molly's chambers / California waiting / Holy roller novocaine.

Jun 03. (10"blue-ep) *(HMD 22)* **WHAT I SAW EP** 22 –
– Red morning light / Wicker chair.
(cd-ep+=) *(HMD 23)* – Talihina sky.
(dvd-ep) *(HMD 24)* – Red morning light (+ live video clips).

Jul 03. (cd)(d10"lp) *(HMD 27JC)(HMD 26)* *<52394>* **YOUTH & YOUNG MANHOOD** 5 Aug03
– Red morning light / Happy alone / Wasted time / Joe's head / Trani / California waiting / Spiral staircase / Molly's chambers / Genius / Dusty / Holy roller novocaine. *(hidden track+=/d10"lp+=)* – Talihina sky.

Aug 03. (10") *(HMD 28)* **MOLLY'S CHAMBERS. / CALIFORNIA WAITING (live)** 23 –
(cd-s) *(HMD 29)* – ('A'side) / Wasted time (live) / Spiral staircase (live).
(cd-s) *(HMD 30)* – ('A'live) / Red morning light (live).

Oct 03. (10") *(HMD 31)* **WASTED TIME. / MOLLY'S HANGOVER** 51 –
(cd-s) *(HMD 32)* – ('A'side) / Joe's head (live from LA) / ('A'-video).

KINKS

Formed: Muswell Hill, London, England . . . 1963 by brothers RAY and DAVE DAVIES, who recruited PETER QUAIFE from The RAVENS. With help from managers Robert Wace and Grenville Collins, they met Larry Page who gave them the name KINKS late '63. He also arranged demos, which were soon heard by American SHEL TALMY, securing them a deal with 'Pye' early '64. Two singles flopped, but the third, 'YOU REALLY GOT ME', stormed the top spot in the UK, soon breaking into US Top 10. With its scuzzy, propulsive guitar riff, the song is oft cited as one of the first real "heavy rock" records, although it's debatable whether RAY DAVIES would admit to inspiring a multitude of poodle-maned Van Halen soundalikes. A top selling eponymous lp followed, as did a series of Top 10 sixties singles, including two more UK No.1's, 'TIRED OF WAITING FOR YOU' and 'SUNNY AFTERNOON'. As RAY's songwriting developed, the band moved to a quieter, more reflective sound, his camp, semi-detached vocals complementing the wry observations and quintessential Englishness of the lyrical themes. Come 1967, when every band worth their weight in spiked sugarcubes were looking towards the 'East', Davies looked no further than his proverbial back garden. 'SOMETHING ELSE', with its heartfelt eulogies to a mythical England past, still stands as the Kinks' greatest moment, the aching melancholy of 'WATERLOO SUNSET' its crowning glory. Davies' nostalgic bent continued on 1968's 'THE KINKS ARE THE VILLAGE GREEN PRESERVATION SOCIETY', an enchanting concept album that reached ever further into a faded history of rural simplicity. It also included the KINKS' sole dalliance with psychedelia, 'WICKED ANNABELLA', a Brothers Grimm-like fairytale come nightmare fantasy. DAVIES' lyrical obsessions were given centre stage once more on 'ARTHUR (OR THE DECLINE OF THE ROMAN EMPIRE)' (1969) wherein the rosy hue of the past was contrasted with the grey decline of modern day Britain. The mood lightened somewhat with 1970's surprise No.2 hit single, 'LOLA', a tongue in cheek tribute to a male cross-dresser and the standout track from the subsequent album, 'LOLA VERSUS POWERMAN AND THE MONEYGOROUND PART 1'. 1971's 'MUSWELL HILLBILLIES' echoed 'VILLAGE GREEN's collection of storybook vignettes although the band were beginning to lose their focus and the hits were about to dry up. 'SUPERSONIC ROCKETSHIP' went top 20 in 1972 but the follow-up, 'CELLULOID HEROES', failed to chart. Both songs were taken from the album, 'EVERYBODY'S IN SHOWBIZ', and were high points in an otherwise unremarkable affair. The remainder of the 70's saw the KINKS become bogged down in ill-advised concept albums and self-parody although while the band were virtually ignored in the UK, they still had a sizeable following in America, hitting the US Top 30 with the patchy 'SLEEPWALKER' album in 1977. With the release of the harder rocking 'LOW BUDGET' a couple of years later, the band were embraced fully by the US rock fraternity and hitched a lucrative ride on the stadium rock circuit as well as gaining a sizeable piece of chart action. While the early 80's albums, 'GIVE THE PEOPLE WHAT THEY WANT' and 'STATE OF CONFUSION' were competent albeit largely uninspired, the Americans lapped them up and the band even found themselves back in the UK Top 20 with the classic 'COME DANCING' single. Throughout the 80's the band once again descended into inconsistency and commercial wilderness, their live shows being the sole factor in keeping the KINKS' spirit intact. Fast forward to 1995 and BLUR were riding high on the 'Britpop' wave with their heavily KINKS-influenced 'Parklife' album. Overrated and trailing in the KINKS shadows, the album's success nevertheless gave Blur mainman DAMON ALBORN the opportunity to express his admiration for his hero RAY DAVIES and perform a poignant TV duet with the great man on 'WATERLOO SUNSET'. The renewed interest also resulted in a TV documentary on the KINKS and a solo tour by RAY, not to mention autobiographies by both RAY and DAVE. RAY's 1998 'THE STORYTELLER', meanwhile, was his first solo effort since 1985's low-key 'RETURN TO WATERLOO' soundtrack. Inspired by the the promotional tour he undertook after the release of his book, the album's appeal lay in its witty, intimate dialogue revealing the often amusing stories behind the songs – many of which were culled from the KINKS back catalogue. • **Songwriters:** RAY DAVIES wrote all of work, except covers; LONG TALL SALLY (Ernie Johnson) / TOO MUCH MONKEY BUSINESS (Chuck Berry) / GOT LOVE IF YOU WANT IT (Slim Harpo) / MILK COW BLUES (Elvis Presley) / etc. • **Trivia:** RAY produced 1969 lp 'Turtle Soup' for The TURTLES. He was married on the 12th December '64 to Rasa Dicpetri, but later divorced her (see KINKS biography by Johnny Rogan). In 1981, he divorced his second wife Yvonne. (RAY had a relationship with CHRISSIE HYNDE of The PRETENDERS for three years). She gave him a daughter, Natalie, in February '83, although they separated when she started dating JIM KERR (of SIMPLE MINDS). In 1986, RAY appeared in the film musical, 'Absolute Beginners'.

Album rating: THE KINKS – YOU REALLY GOT ME (*6) / KINDA KINKS (*5) / KINKS-SIZE (*6) / THE KINK KONTROVERSY (*5) / KINKS KINKDOM (*5) / THE KINKS GREATEST HITS! compilation (*8) / FACE TO FACE (*8) / LIVE AT KELVIN HALL (*5) / SOMETHING ELSE BY THE KINKS (*7) / VILLAGE GREEN PRESERVATION SOCIETY (*8) / ARTHUR (OR THE DECLINE AND FALL OF THE BRITISH EMPIRE) (*8) / LOLA VERSUS POWERMAN AND THE MONEYGOROUND, PART ONE (*7) / PERCY soundtrack (*4) / MUSWELL HILLBILLIES (*7) / EVERYBODY'S IN SHOW-BIZ (*6) / THE GREAT LOST KINKS ALBUM early (*6) / PRESERVATION ACT I (*6) / PRESERVATION ACT II (*6) / SOAP OPERA (*4) / SCHOOLBOYS IN DISGRACE (*5) / SLEEPWALKER (*6) / MISFITS (*7) / LOW BUDGET (*6) / ONE FOR THE ROAD (*5) / GIVE THE PEOPLE WHAT THEY WANT (*6) / STATE OF CONFUSION (*6) / WORD OF MOUTH (*5) / THINK VISUAL (*4) / COME DANCING WITH THE KINKS – THE BEST OF . . . 1977-1986 compilation (*7) / THE ROAD (*4) / THE ULTIMATE COLLECTION compilation (*9) / UK JIVE (*4) / PHOBIA (*5) / TO THE BONE (*6) / THE ULTIMATE COLLECTION double compilation (*9) / Ray Davies: RETURN TO WATERLOO (*5) / THE STORYTELLER (*6)

RAY DAVIES (b.21 Jun'44) – vocals, guitar / **DAVE DAVIES** (b. 3 Feb'47) – guitar, vocals / **PETER QUAIFE** (b.31 Dec'43, Tavistock, Devon) – bass with session drummers

Pye — Cameo

Mar 64. (7") *(7N 15611)* <308> **LONG TALL SALLY. / I TOOK MY BABY HOME** [ ] Apr64 [ ]
<US re-iss. Nov64; 345>

May 64. (7") *(7N 15636)* **YOU STILL WANT ME. / YOU DO SOMETHING TO ME** [ ] [–]

Pye — Reprise

Aug 64. (7") *(7N 15673)* <0306> **YOU REALLY GOT ME. / IT'S ALRIGHT** [1] Sep64 [7]

—— **MICK AVORY** (b.15 Feb'44) – drums was now used although he joined 9 months previously

Oct 64. (lp) *(NPL 18096)* <6143> **THE KINKS** <US-title 'YOU REALLY GOT ME'> [3] Dec64 [29]
– Beautiful Delilah / So mystifying / Just can't go to sleep / Long tall Shorty / You really got me / Cadillac / Bald headed woman / Revenge / Too much monkey business / I've been driving on Bald mountain / Stop your sobbing / Got love if you want it. *(re-iss. Jan67 on 'Golden Guinea'; GGL 0357) (re-iss. May80 as 'YOU REALLY GOT ME'; NSPL 18615) (re-iss. Oct87 on 'P.R.T.' lp/c/cd; PYL/PYM/PYC 6002) (cd re-iss. Dec89 on 'Castle'; CLACD 155) (cd re-mast.Mar98 on 'Essential'+=; ESMCD 482)* – I took my baby home / I'm a lover not a fighter / You still want me / I don't need you any more.

Oct 64. (7") *(7N 15714)* <0334> **ALL DAY AND ALL OF THE NIGHT. / I GOTTA MOVE** [2] Dec64 [7]
(re-iss. Oct84 on 'P.R.T.'; KIS 003) (re-iss. Jan88 on 'P.R.T.'; PYS 4)

Jan 65. (7") *(7N 15759)* <0347> **TIRED OF WAITING FOR YOU. / COME ON NOW** [1] Mar65 [6]

Mar 65. (lp) <6158> **KINKS-SIZE** [–] [13]
– Tired of waiting for you / Louie Louie / I've got that feeling / Revenge / I gotta move / Things are getting better / I gotta go now / I'm a lover not a fighter / Come on now / All day and all of the night.

Mar 65. (lp) *(NPL 18112)* <6173> **KINDA KINKS** [3] Aug65 [60]
– Look for me baby / Got my feet on the ground / Nothin' in the world can stop me worryin' 'bout that girl / Naggin' woman / Wonder where my

baby is tonight / Tired of waiting for you / Dancing in the street / Don't ever change / Come on now / So long / You shouldn't be sad / Something better beginning. *(re-iss. Oct87 on 'P.R.T.' lp/c/cd; PYL/PYM/PYC 6003) (cd re-iss. Dec89 on 'Castle'; CLACD 156) (cd re-mast.Mar98 on 'Essential'+=; ESMCD 483)* – I need you / See my friends / Never met a girl like you before / I go to sleep.

Mar 65. (7") *(7N 15813) <0366>* **EVERYBODY'S GONNA BE HAPPY. / WHO'LL BE THE NEXT IN LINE** [11] Apr65 [ ]
<above 45 flipped over in the States with B-side hitting No.34>

May 65. (7") *(7N 15854) <0379>* **SET ME FREE. / I NEED YOU** [9] Jun65 [23]

Jul 65. (7") *(7N 15919) <0409>* **SEE MY FRIENDS. / NEVER MET A GIRL LIKE YOU BEFORE** [10] [ ]

Nov 65. (7") *<0420>* **A WELL RESPECTED MAN. / MILK COW BLUES** [–] [13]

Nov 65. (7") *(7N 15981) <0454>* **TILL THE END OF THE DAY. / WHERE HAVE ALL THE GOOD TIMES GONE** [6] Mar66 [50]

Nov 65. (lp) *(NPL 18131) <6197>* **THE KINK KONTROVERSY** [9] Apr66 [95]
– Milk cow blues / Ring the bells / Gotta get the first plane home / When I see that girl of mine / Till the end of the day / The world keeps going round / I'm on the island / Where have all the good times gone / It's too late / What's in store for me / You can't win. *(re-iss. Oct87 on 'P.R.T.' lp/c/cd; PYL/PYM/PYC 6004) (cd re-iss. Dec89 on 'Castle'; CLACD 157) (cd re-mast.Mar98 on 'Essential'+=; ESMCD 507)* – Dedicated follower of fashion / Sittin' on my sofa.

Dec 65. (lp) *<6184>* **KINKS KINKDOM** [–] [47]
– A well respected man / Such a shame / Wait 'til the summer comes along / Naggin' woman / Who'll be the next in line / Don't you fret / I need you / It's all right / Louie Louie.

Feb 66. (7") *(7N 17064) <0471>* **DEDICATED FOLLOWER OF FASHION. / SITTING ON MY SOFA** [4] May66 [36]

—— **JOHN DALTON** – bass deputised on tour for QUAIFE while injured

Jun 66. (7") *(7N 17125) <0497>* **SUNNY AFTERNOON. / I'M NOT LIKE EVERYBODY ELSE** [1] Aug66 [14]

Aug 66. (lp) *<6217>* **THE KINKS GREATEST HITS** (compilation) [–] [9]
– Dedicated follower of fashion / Tired of waiting for you / All day and all of the night / You really got me / A well respected man / Who'll be the next in line / Everybody's gonna be happy / Till the end of the day / Set me free / Something better beginning.

—— **JOHN DALTON** sessioned between 66-69, QUAIFE's photo on covers

Oct 66. (lp; mono/stereo) *(NPL/NSPL 18145) <6228>* **FACE TO FACE** [12] Feb67 [ ]
– Party line / Rosy won't you please come home / Dandy / Too much on my mind / Session man / Rainy day in June / House in the country / Sunny afternoon / Holiday in Waikiki / Most exclusive residence for sale / Fancy / Little Miss Queen of Darkness / You're looking fine / I'll remember. *(re-iss. Oct87 on 'P.R.T.' lp/c/cd; PYL/PYM/PYC 6005) (cd re-iss. Dec89 on 'Castle'; CLACD 158) (cd re-mast.Mar98 on 'Essential'+=; ESMCD 479)* – I'm not like everybody else / Dead end street / Big black smoke / Mr. Pleasant / This I where I belong. *(cd re-iss. Aug01 on 'Castle'; CMTCD 302)*

Nov 66. (7") *(7N 17125) <0540>* **DEAD END STREET. / BIG BLACK SMOKE** [5] Jan67 [73]

May 67. (7") *(7N 17321)* **WATERLOO SUNSET. / ACT NICE AND GENTLE** [2] [–]

May 67. (lp; mono/stereo) *(NPL/NSPL 18191) <6260>* **LIVE AT KELVIN HALL (live in Glasgow)** <US-title 'THE LIVE KINKS'> [ ] Sep67 [ ]
– Till the end of the day / I'm on an island / You really got me / All day and all of the night / A well respected man / You're looking fine / Sunny afternoon / Dandy / Come on now / Milk cow blues – Batman theme – Tired of waiting for you. *(re-iss. Oct87 on 'P.R.T.' lp/c/cd; PYL/PYM/PYC 6007) (cd re-iss. Dec89 on 'Castle'; CLACD 160) (cd re-mast.May98 on 'Essential'; ESMCD 508) (cd re-iss. Sep01 on 'Castle'; CMTCD 323)*

Jun 67. (7") *<0587>* **MR. PLEASANT. / HARRY RAG** [–] [80]

Sep 67. (7") *<0612>* **WATERLOO SUNSET. / TWO SISTERS** [–] [ ]

Oct 67. (lp; mono/stereo) *(NPL/NSPL 18193) <6279>* **SOMETHING ELSE BY THE KINKS** [35] Feb68 [ ]
– David Watts / Death of a clown / Two sisters / No return / Harry Rag / Tin soldier man / Situation vacant / Love me till the sun shines / Lazy old sun / Afternoon tea / Funny face / End of the season / Waterloo sunset. *(re-iss. Oct87 on 'P.R.T.' lp/c/cd; PYL/PYM/PYC 6006) (cd re-iss. Dec89 on 'Castle'; CLACD 159) (cd re-mast.Mar98 on 'Essential'+=; ESMCD 480)* – Susannah's still alive / Autumn almanac / Act nice and gentle / Wonderboy / Pretty Polly / Lincoln County / There's no life without love. *(cd re-iss. Aug01 on 'Castle'; CMTCD 303)*

Oct 67. (7") *(7N 17400) <0647>* **AUTUMN ALMANAC. / MR. PLEASANT** [3] [ ]

Apr 68. (7") *(7N 17468) <0691>* **WONDERBOY. / POLLY** [37] [ ]

Jul 68. (7") *(7N 17573) <0762>* **DAYS. / SHE'S GOT EVERYTHING** [12] [ ]

Jul 68. (lp; mono/stereo) *(NPL/NSPL 18233) <6327>* **THE KINKS ARE THE VILLAGE GREEN PRESERVATION SOCIETY** [ ] [ ]
– Village green preservation society / Do you remember Walter / Picture book / Johnny Thunder / The last of the steam powered trains / Big sky / Sitting by the riverside / Animal farm / Village green / Starstruck / Phenomenal cat / All my friends were there / Wicked Annabella / Monica / People take pictures of each other. *(re-iss. Nov85 on 'Flashback-PRT'; FBLP 8091) (re-iss. Oct87 on 'P.R.T.' lp/c/cd; PYL/PYM/PYC 6008) (cd re-iss. Oct89 on 'Castle'; CLACD 161) (cd re-iss. Feb97 on 'Original Recordings'; ORRLP 005) (cd re-mast.Mar98 on 'Essential'; ESMCD 481) (cd re-iss. Sep01 on 'Castle'; CMTCD 319)*

Apr 69. (7") *(7N 17724) <0743>* **PLASTIC MAN. / KING KONG** [31] [ ]

Apr 69. (7") *<0806>* **STARSTRUCK. / PICTURE BOOK** [–] [ ]

—— **JOHN DALTON** (b.21 May'43) – bass officially repl. QUAIFE

Jun 69. (7") *<0847>* **WALTER. / VILLAGE GREEN PRESERVATION SOCIETY** [–] [ ]

Jun 69. (7"; b-side by KINKS featuring DAVE DAVIES) *<7N 17776)* **DRIVIN'. / MINDLESS CHILD OF MOTHERHOOD** [ ] [–]

Sep 69. (7") *(7N 17812)* **SHANGRI-LA. / THIS MAN HE WEEPS TONIGHT** [ ] [–]
(above initially had 'LAST OF THE STEAM-POWERED TRAINS' on B-side)

Oct 69. (lp) *(NSPL 18317) <6366>* **ARTHUR (OR THE DECLINE AND FALL OF THE BRITISH EMPIRE** [ ] [ ]
– Victoria / Yes sir, no sir / Some mother's son / Brainwashed / Australia / Shangri-la / Mr. Churchill says / She bought a hat like Princess Marina / Young and innocent days / Nothing to say / Arthur. *(re-iss. Oct87 on 'P.R.T.' lp/c/cd; PYL/PYM/PYC 6009) (cd re-iss. Oct89 on 'Castle'; CLACD 162) (cd re-mast.May98 on 'Essential'; ESMCD 511) (cd re-iss. Sep01 on 'Castle'; CMTCD 322)*

Dec 69. (7") *(7N 17865)* **VICTORIA. / MR. CHURCHILL SAYS** [33] [–]

Jan 70. (7") *<0863>* **VICTORIA. / BRAINWASHED** [–] [62]

Jun 70. (7") *(7N 17961)* **LOLA. / BERKELEY MEWS** [2] [–]

Aug 70. (7") *<0930>* **LOLA. / MINDLESS CHILD OF MOTHERHOOD** [–] [9]

Nov 70. (lp) *(NSPL 18359) <6423>* **LOLA VERSUS POWERMAN & THE MONEYGOROUND, PART ONE** [ ] [35]
– The contenders / Strangers / Denmark Street / Get back in line / Lola / Top of the pops / The moneygoround / This time tomorrow / A long way from home / Rats / Apeman / Powerman / Got to be free. *(re-iss. Oct87 on 'P.R.T.' lp/c/cd; PYL/PYM/PYC 6010) (cd re-iss. Oct89 on 'Castle'; CLACD 163) (cd re-mast.May98 on 'Essential'; ESMCD 509) (cd re-iss. Sep01 on 'Castle'; CMTCD 320)*

Nov 70. (7") *(7N 45016) <0979>* **APEMAN. / RATS** [5] Jan71 [45]

Mar 71. (lp) *(NSPL 18365)* **(SOUNDTRACK FROM THE FILM) "PERCY"** [ ] [–]
– God's children / Lola / The way love used to be / Completely / Running round town / Moments / Animals in the zoo / Just friends / Helga / Willesden Green / God's children – end. *(re-iss. Oct87 on 'P.R.T.' lp/c/cd; PYL/PYM/PYC 6011) (cd re-iss. Oct89 on 'Castle'; CLACD 164) (cd re-mast.May98 on 'Essential'; ESMCD 510) (cd re-iss. Sep01 on 'Castle'; 321)*

Apr 71. (7") *(7N 8001)* **GOD'S CHILDREN. / MOMENTS** [ ] [–]
(7"m+=) *(7NX 8001)* – The way love used to be / Dreams.

Apr 71. (7") *<1017>* **GOD'S CHILDREN. / THE WAY LOVE USED TO BE** [–] [ ]

—— added **JOHN GOSLING** – keyboards (he guested on 'LOLA' album), plus **LAURIE BROWN** – trumpet / **JOHN BEECHAM** – trombone / **ALAN HOLMES** – saxophone recruited from The MIKE COTTON SOUND. The three became full-time members '73, adding to **R. DAVIES, D. DAVIES, AVORY and DALTON**

R.C.A. R.C.A.

Nov 71. (lp) *(SF 8243) <LSP 4644>* **MUSWELL HILLBILLIES** [ ] [100]
– 20th century man / Acute schizophrenia paranoia blues / Holiday / Skin and bone / Alcohol / Complicated life / Here come the people in the grey / Have a cuppa tea / Holloway jail / Oklahoma U.S.A. / Uncle son / Muswell hillbilly.

Feb 72. (7") *<74-0620>* **20th CENTURY MAN. / SKIN AND BONE** [–] [ ]

May 72. (7") *(RCA 2211) <74-0807>* **SUPERSONIC ROCKET SHIP. / YOU DON'T KNOW MY NAME** [16] [ ]

Aug 72. (d-lp) *(DPS 2035) <6065>* **EVERYBODY'S IN SHOWBIZ** [ ] [70]
– Here comes yet another day / Maximum consumption / Unreal reality / Hot potatoes / Sitting in my hotel / You don't know my name / Supersonic rocket ship / Look a little on the sunny side / Celluloid heroes / Motorway. / **EVERYBODY'S A STAR (live)** – Top of the pops / Brainwashed / Mr. Wonderful / Acute schizophrenia paranoia blues / Holiday / Muswell Hillbilly / Alcohol / Banana boat song / Skin and bone / Baby face / Lola.

Nov 72. (7") *(RCA 2299) <74-0852>* **CELLULOID HEROES. / HOT POTATOES** [ ] [ ]

Jun 73. (7") *<74-0940>* **ONE OF THE SURVIVORS. / SCRAPHEAP CITY** [–] [ ]

Jun 73. (7") *(RCA 2387)* **SITTING IN THE MIDDAY SUN. / ONE OF THE SURVIVORS** [ ] [–]

Sep 73. (7") *(RCA 2418)* **SWEET LADY GENEVIEVE. / SITTING IN MY HOTEL** [ ] [–]

Sep 73. (7") *<5001>* **SWEET LADY GENEVIEVE. / SITTING IN THE MIDDAY SUN** [–] [ ]

Dec 73. (d-lp) *(SF 8392) <LPL 5002>* **PRESERVATION ACT I** [ ] [ ]
– Morning song / Daylight / Sweet Lady Genevieve / There's a change in the weather / Where are they now / One of the survivors / Cricket / I am your man / Here comes Flash / Sitting in the midday Sun / Demolution.

—— next 45 only contained **RAY & DAVE DAVIES**, before full 5 + 3 again

Apr 74. (7") *(RCA 5015)* **MIRROR OF LOVE. / CRICKET** [ ] [–]

Jun 74. (7") *<0275>* **MONEY TALKS. / HERE COMES FLASH** [–] [ ]

Jun 74. (d-lp) *<(LPL2 5040)>* **PRESERVATION ACT II** [ ] [ ]
– (announcement) / Introduction to solution / When a solution comes / Money talks / (announcement) / Shepherds of the nation / Scum of the Earth / Secondhand car spiv / He's evil / Mirror of love / (announcement) / Nobody gives / Oh where oh where is love? / Flash's dream / Flash's confession / Nothing lasts forever / (announcement) / Artificial man / Scrapheap city / (announcement) / Salvation Road.

Jul 74. (7") *(RCA 5042) <APBO 10019>* **MIRROR OF LOVE. / HE'S EVIL** [ ] [ ]

Oct 74. (7") *(RCA 2478)* **HOLIDAY ROMANCE. / SHEPHERDS OF THE NATION** [ ] [–]

Oct 74. (7") *<APBO 10121>* **PRESERVATION. / SALVATION** [–] [ ]

Apr 75. (7") *<APBO 10251>* **ORDINARY PEOPLE. / STAR MAKER** [–] [ ]

Apr 75. (7") *(RCA 2546)* **DUCKS ON THE WALL. / RUSH HOUR BLUES** [ ] [–]

May 75. (lp) *(SF 8411) <LPI 5081>* **SOAP OPERA** [ ] [51]
– Everybody's a star (starmaker) / Ordinary people / Rush hour blues / Nine to five / When work is over / Have another drink / Underneath the neon sign / Holiday romance / You make it all worth while / Ducks on the wall / Face in the crowd / You can't stop the music. *(re-iss. Jul84)*

May 75. (7") *(RCA 2567)* **YOU CAN'T STOP THE MUSIC. / HAVE ANOTHER DRINK** [ ] [–]

Nov 75. (lp) *(RS 1028) <FLI 5102>* **SCHOOLBOYS IN DISGRACE** [ ] [45]
– Schooldays / Jack the idiot dunce / Education / The first time we fall in love / I'm in disgrace / Headmaster / The hard way / The last assembly / No more looking back / (finale).

Nov 75. (7") *<10551>* **THE HARD WAY. / I'M IN DISGRACE** [–] [ ]

Jan 76. (7"m) *(RCM 1)* **NO MORE LOOKING BACK. / JACK THE IDIOT DUNCE / THE HARD WAY** [ ] [–]

—— Now down to basic 5-piece after the 3 brass section members departed

Arista Arista

Feb 77. (lp/c) *(SP/TC ARTY 1002) <AL 4106>* **SLEEPWALKER** [ ] [21]
– Life on the road / Mr. Big man / Sleepwalker / Brother / Juke box music / Sleepless night / Stormy sky / Full moon / Life goes on.

Mar 77. (7") *(ARIST 97) <0240>* **SLEEPWALKER. / FULL MOON** [ ] [48]

Jun 77. (7") *(ARIST 114)* **JUKE BOX MUSIC. / SLEEPLESS NIGHT** [ ] [–]

Jun 77. (7") *<0247>* **JUKE BOX MUSIC. / LIFE GOES ON** [–] [ ]

—— **ANDY PYLE** – bass (ex-BLODWYN PIG, ex-SAVOY BROWN, etc) repl. DALTON

Dec 77. (7") *(ARIST 153) <0296>* **FATHER CHRISTMAS. / PRINCE OF THE PUNKS** [ ] [ ]

May 78. (lp/c) *(SP/TC ART 1055) <AL 4167>* **MISFITS** [ ] [40]
– Misfits / Hay fever / Live life / Rock'n'roll fantasy / In a foreign land / Permanent waves / Black Messiah / Out of the wardrobe / Trust your heart / Get up.

May 78. (7") *(ARIST 189) <0342>* **ROCK'N'ROLL FANTASY. / ARTIFICIAL LIGHT** [ ] Jul78 [30]

Jul 78. (7") *(ARIST 199)* **LIVE LIFE. / IN A FOREIGN LAND** [ ] [–]

Jul 78. (7") *<0372>* **LIVE LIFE. / BLACK MESSIAH** [–] [ ]

Sep 78. (7") *(ARIST 210)* **BLACK MESSIAH. / MISFITS** [ ] [–]

—— RAY DAVIES, DAVE DAVIES and MICK AVORY recruited new members **GORDON EDWARDS** – keyboards (ex-PRETTY THINGS) repl. GOSLING (to NETWORK) / **JIM RODFORD** (b. 7 Jul'45, St. Albans, England) – bass (ex-ARGENT, ex-PHOENIX) repl. PYLE (to NETWORK)

Jan 79. (7"/12") *(ARIST/+12 240)* **(WISH I COULD FLY LIKE) SUPERMAN. / LOW BUDGET** [ ] [–]

—— **IAN GIBBON** – keyboards repl. EDWARDS

Apr 79. (7") *<0409>* **(WISH I COULD FLY LIKE) SUPERMAN. / PARTY LINE** [–] [41]

Sep 79. (7") *(ARIST 300)* **MOVING PICTURES. / IN A SPACE** [ ] [–]

Sep 79. (lp/c) *(SP/TC ART 1099) <AB 4240>* **LOW BUDGET** [ ] Jul79 [11]
– Attitude / Catch me now I'm falling / Pressure / National health / (I wish I could fly like) Superman / Low budget / In a space / Little bit of emotion / Gallon of gas / Misery / Moving pictures. *(cd-iss. Apr88; 251 146)*

Sep 79. (7") *<0448>* **GALLON OF GAS. / LOW BUDGET** [–] [ ]

Nov 79. (7") *<0458>* **CATCH ME NOW I'M FALLING. / LOW BUDGET** [–] [ ]

Nov 79. (7") *(ARIST 321)* **PRESSURE. / NATIONAL HEALTH** [ ] [–]

Jul 80. (d-lp) *(DARTY 6) <8401>* **ONE FOR THE ROAD (live)** [ ] Jun80 [14]
– The hard way / Catch me now I'm falling / Where have all the good times gone / Lola / Pressure / All day and all of the night / 20th century man / Misfits / Prince of the punks / Stop your sobbing / Low budget / Attitude / (Wish I could fly like) Superman / National health / Till the end of the day / Celluloid heroes / You really got me / Victoria / David Watts.

Jul 80. (7"ep) *(ARIST 360)* **WHERE HAVE ALL THE GOOD TIMES GONE (live)** [ ] [–]
– Where have all the good times gone / Victoria / Attitude / David Watts.

Aug 80. (7") *<0541>* **LOLA (live). / CELLULOID HEROES (live)** [–] [81]

Oct 80. (7") *<0577>* **YOU REALLY GOT ME (live). / ATTITUDE (live)** [–] [ ]

Jun 81. (lp/c) *(SP/TC ART 1171) <9567>* **GIVE THE PEOPLE WHAT THEY WANT** [ ] [15]
– Around the dial / Give the people what they want / Killer's eyes / Predictable / Add it up / Destroyer / Yo-yo / Back to front / Art lover / A little bit of abuse / Better things.

Jun 81. (7") *(ARIST 415)* **BETTER THINGS. / MASSIVE REDUCTIONS** [46] [–]
(d7"+=) *(KINKS 1)* – Lola / David Watts.

Oct 81. (7",7"pic-d) *(ARIST 426)* **PREDICTABLE. / BACK TO FRONT** [ ] [–]

Oct 81. (7") *<0619>* **DESTROYER. / BACK TO FRONT** [–] [85]

Nov 81. (7") *<0649>* **BETTER THINGS. / YO-YO** [–] [92]

Jun 83. (lp/c) *(205/405 275) <8018>* **STATE OF CONFUSION** [ ] [12]
– State of confusion / Definite maybe / Labour of love / Come dancing / Property / Don't forget to dance / Young Conservatives / Heart of gold / Cliches of the world (B movie) / Bernadette. *(cd-iss. 1988 on 'Ariola')*

Jul 83. (7"/12") *(ARIST/+12 502) <1054/9016>* **COME DANCING. / NOISE** [12] May83 [6]

Aug 83. (7") *<9075>* **DON'T FORGET TO DANCE. / YOUNG CONSERVATIVES** [–] [29]

Sep 83. (7",12") *(ARIST 524)* **DON'T FORGET TO DANCE. / BERNADETTE** [58] [–]

Mar 84. (7") *(ARIST 560)* **STATE OF CONFUSION. / HEART OF GOLD** [ ] [–]
(12"+=) *(ARIST12 560)* – 20th century man (live) / Lola (live).

Jul 84. (7") *(ARIST 577)* **GOOD DAY. / TOO HOT** [ ] [ ]
(ext.12"+=) *(ARIST12 577)* – Don't forget to dance.

Nov 84. (lp/c) *(206/406 685) <8264>* **WORD OF MOUTH** [ ] [57]
– Do it again / Word of mouth / Good day / Living on a thin line / Sold me out / Massive reductions / Guilty / Too hot / Missing persons / Summer's gone / Going solo. *(cd-iss. Jun88; 259 047)*

Apr 85. (7") *(ARIST 617) <9309>* **DO IT AGAIN. / GUILTY** [ ] Dec84 [41]
(12"+=) *(ARIST12 617)* – Summer's gone.

Apr 85. (7") *<9334>* **SUMMER'S GONE. / GOING SOLO** [–] [ ]

Oct 86. (d-lp/c) *(302/502 778)* *<8428>* **COME DANCING WITH THE KINKS – THE BEST OF THE KINKS 1977-1986** (compilation) [ ] Jul86 [ ]

—— Returned to original line-up of **RAY, DAVE + MICK,** plus sessioners. (RODFORD and GIBBONS departed).

London | M.C.A.

Nov 86. (7") *<52960>* **ROCK'N'ROLL CITIES. / WELCOME TO SLEAZY TOWN** [–] [ ]

Nov 86. (lp/c)(cd) *(LON LP/C 27)(828 030-2)* *<5822>* **THINK VISUAL** [ ] [81]
– Working at the factory / Lost and found / Repetition / Welcome to Sleazy Town / The video shop / Rock'n'roll cities / How are you / Think visual / Natural gift / Killing time / When you were a child.

Dec 86. (7") *(LON 119)* **HOW ARE YOU. / KILLING TIME** [ ] [–]
(12"+=) *(LONX 119)* – Welcome to Sleazy town.

Mar 87. (7") *(LON 132)* *<53015>* **LOST AND FOUND. / KILLING TIME** [ ] [ ]
(12"+=) *(LONX 132)* – (Ray Davies interview).

May 87. (7") *<53093>* **HOW ARE YOU. / WORKING AT THE FACTORY** [–] [ ]

Feb 88. (7") *(LON 165)* **THE ROAD. / ART LOVER** [ ] [ ]
(ext.12"+=) *(LONX 165)* – Come dancing.

May 88. (lp/c)(cd) *(LON LP/C 49)(828 078-2)* *<42107>* **THE ROAD (live / studio *)** [ ] Feb88 [ ]
– The road * / Destroyer / Apeman / Come dancing / Art lover / Cliches of the world (B-movie) / Living on a thin line / Lost and found / It * / Around the dial / Give the people what they want.

—— **BOB HENRIT** (b. 2 May'45)- drums repl. AVORY / added **MARK HALEY** – keyboards, vocals

Sep 89. (7") *(LON 239)* **DOWN ALL THE DAYS (TILL 1992). / YOU REALLY GOT ME (live)** [ ] [–]
(12"+=/cd-s+=) *(LON X/CD 239)* – Entertainment.

Oct 89. (lp/c/cd) *(828 165-1/-4/-2)* *<6337>* **UK JIVE** [ ] [ ]
– Aggravation / How do I get close / UK jive / Now and then / What are we doing / Entertainment / War is over / Down all the days (till 1992) / Loony balloon / Dear Margaret. *(c+=/cd+=)* – Bright lights / Perfect strangers. *(re-iss. Apr91;)*

Feb 90. (7") *(LON 250)* **HOW DO I GET CLOSE. / DOWN ALL THE DAYS (TILL 1992)** [ ] [–]
(12"+=/cd-s+=) *(LON X/CD 250)* – War is over.

Mar 90. 7") *<53699>* **HOW DO I GET CLOSE. / WAR IS OVER** [–] [ ]

Columbia | Columbia

Mar 93. (cd/c) *(472489-2/-4)* *<48724>* **PHOBIA** [ ] [ ]
– Opening / Wall of fire / Drift away / Still searching / Phobia / Only a dream / Don't / Babies / Over the edge / Surviving / It's alright (don't think about it) / The informer / Hatred (a duet) / Somebody stole my car / Close to the wire / Scattered. *(cd+=)* – Did ya.

Jul 93. (cd-s) **SCATTERED. / HATRED (A DUET) / DAYS** [ ] [–]

Nov 93. (7") *(659922-7)* **ONLY A DREAM (Radio Version) / SOMEBODY STOLE MY CAR** [ ] [ ]
(cd-s+=) *(659922-2)* – Babies.

Konk | not iss.

Oct 94. (cd/c/lp) *(KNK CD/MC/LP 1)* **TO THE BONE (live)** [ ] [–]
– All day and all of the nigt / Apeman / Tired of waiting for you / See my friend / Death of a clown / Waterloo sunset / Muswell hillbillies / Better things / Don't forget to dance / Autumn almanac / Sunny afternoon / Dedicated follower of fashion / You really got me.

Oct 94. (cd-ep) *(KNKD 2)* **WATERLOO SUNSET E.P. (live)** [ ] [–]
– Waterloo sunset / You really got me / Elevator man / On the outside.

When! | not iss.

Jan 97. (c-ep/cd-ep) *(WEN M/X 1016)* **DAYS EP** [35] [–]
– Days / You really got me / Dead end street / Lola.

– (selective) compilations, etc. –

on 'Pye' UK / 'Reprise' US, unless mentioned otherwise

Jun 66. (lp) *Marble Arch; (MAL 612)* **WELL RESPECTED KINKS** [5] [–]

Sep 67. (lp) *Marble Arch; (MAL 716)* **SUNNY AFTERNOON** [9] [–]

Oct 71. (lp) *Golden Hour; (GH 501)* **THE GOLDEN HOUR OF THE KINKS** [21] [–]
(cd-iss. Apr89 on 'Castle'; GHCD 1)

Apr 72. (lp) *<6454>* **THE KINK KRONICLES** [–] [94]

Oct 78. (d-lp) *Ronco-Pye; (RPL 2031)* **THE KINKS 20 GOLDEN GREATS** [19] [–]

Oct 83. (d-lp) *P.R.T.; (KINK 1)* **KINKS' GREATEST HITS – DEAD END STREET** [96] [–]

Oct 83. (7"/7"pic-d) *P.R.T.; (KD/KPD 1)* **YOU REALLY GOT ME. / MISTY WATER** [47] [–]
(12"pic-d+=) *(DKL 1)* – All day and all of the night.

Sep 89. (lp/c/cd) *Castle; (CTV LP/MC/CD 001)* **THE ULTIMATE COLLECTION** [35] [–]
– You really got me / All day and all of the night / Tired of waiting for you / Everybody's gonna be happy / Set me free / Till the end of the day / Dedicated follower of fashion / Sunny afternoon / Dead end street / Waterloo sunset / Autumn almanac / Wonder boy / Days / Plastic man / Victoria / Lola / Apeman / David Watts / Where have all the good times gone / A well respected man / I'm not like everybody else / End of the season / Death of a clown (DAVE DAVIES) / Suzannah's still alive (DAVE DAVIES).

Jun 90. (lp/c/cd) *See For Miles; (SEE/+K/CD 295)* **THE EP COLLECTION** [ ] [–]

Feb 92. (cd/c) *See For MIles; (SEE CD/K 329)* **THE EP COLLECTION VOL.2** [ ] [–]

Sep 93. (cd/c) *Polygram TV; (516 465-2/-4)* **THE DEFINITIVE COLLECTION – THE KINKS' GREATEST HITS** [18] [–]
(re-iss. Mar97; same)

Apr 97. (cd/c) *Polygram TV; (537554-2/-4)* **THE VERY BEST OF THE KINKS** [42] [–]

Sep 97. (d-cd) *Essential; (ESSCD 592)* **THE SINGLES COLLECTION / WATERLOO SUNSET** [ ] [ ]

Nov 98. (10xcd-ep;box) *Essential; (ESFCD 667)* **THE KINKS EP COLLECTION VOL.1** [ ] [–]

Oct 99. (cd) *Castle Pie; (PIESD 134)* **IT'S THE KINKS** [ ] [ ]

Jan 00. (cd/c) *Castle Select; (SEL CD/MC 560)* **YOU REALLY GOT ME: THE BEST OF THE KINKS** [ ] [ ]

Jul 00. (10xcd-ep;box) *Essential; (ESFCD 904)* **THE KINKS EP COLLECTION VOL.2** [ ] [–]

Mar 01. (d-cd/3xlp) *Sanctuary; (SAN DD/TV 010)* **BBC SESSIONS 1964-1977** [ ] [ ]

Mar 01. (d-cd) *Essential; (CMEDD 018)* **LIVE AT THE BBC: SONGS WE SANG FOR AUNTIE 1964-1994** [ ] [ ]

Jun 01. (cd) *Castle; (CMRCD 212)* **THE SINGLES COLLECTION** [ ] [ ]

Jul 01. (3xcd-box) *Castle; (CMGBX 318)* **THE MARBLE ARCH YEARS** [ ] [ ]
– (WELL RESPECTED KINKS / SUNNY AFTERNOON / KINDA KINKS)

May 02. (d-cd) *Sanctuary; (SANDD 109)* **THE ULTIMATE COLLECTION** [32] [–]
– You really got me / All day and all of the night / Tired of waiting for you / Everybody's gonna be happy / Set me free / See my friend / Till the end of the day / Dedicated follower of fashion / Sunny afternoon / Dead end street / Waterloo sunset / Death of a clown (DAVE DAVIES) / Autumn almanac / Susannah's still alive (DAVE DAVIES) / Wonderboy / Days / Plastic man / Victoria / Lola / Apeman / Supersonic rocket ship / Better things / Come dancing / Don't forget to dance / David Watts / Stop your sobbing / Dandy / Mr. Pleasant / I gotta move / Who'll be the next in line / I need you / Where have all the good times gone / Sittin' on my sofa / A well respected man / I'm not like everybody else / Love me till the sun shines / She's got everything / Starstruck / Shangr-la / God's children / Celluloid heroes / Wish I could fly like Superman / Do it again / Living on a thin line.

DAVE DAVIES

Pye | Reprise

Jul 67. (7") *(7N 17356)* *<0614>* **DEATH OF A CLOWN. / LOVE ME TILL THE SUN SHINES** [3] Aug67 [ ]

Nov 67. (7") *(7N 17429)* *<0660>* **SUSANNAH'S STILL ALIVE. / FUNNY FACE** [21] [ ]

Aug 68. (7") *(7N 17514)* **LINCOLN COUNTY. / THERE IS NO LOVE WITHOUT LIFE** [ ] [ ]

Jan 69. (7") *(7N 17678)* **HOLD MY HAND. / CREEPING JEAN** [ ] [ ]

R.C.A. | R.C.A.

Sep 80. (7") *<PB 12089>* **IMAGINATION'S REAL. / WILD MAN** [–] [ ]

Sep 80. (lp/c) *(PL/PK 13603)* *<AFL-1-3603; the US title>* **DAVE DAVIES** [ ] Jul80 [42]
– Where do you come from / Doing the best for you / Move over / Visionary dreamer / Nothin' more to lose / Imagination real /

In you I believe / See the beast / Run / The world is changing hands.

Nov 80. (7") *<PB 12147>* **DOING THE BEST FOR YOU. / NOTHING MORE TO LOSE** [-] [ ]

Dec 80. (7") *(PB 9620)* **DOING THE BEST FOR YOU. / WILD MAN** [ ] [-]

Oct 81. (lp/c) *(RCA LP/K 6005) <AFL-1-4036>* **GLAMOUR** [ ] Jul81 [ ]
– Is this the only way / Reveal yourself / World of our own / Two serious / Glamour / 7th channel / Body / Eastern eyes / Body.

Warners Warners

Sep 83. (lp/c) *(92-3917-1/-4) <23917-1/-4>* **CHOSEN PEOPLE** [ ] Aug 83 [ ]
– Mean disposition / Love gets you / Take one more / True story / Danger zone / Tapes / Freedom lies / Fire burning / Cold winter / Matter of decision / Is it any wonder / Charity / Chosen people.

Sep 83. (7") *<7-29509>* **LOVE GETS YOU. / ONE NIGHT WITH YOU** [-] [ ]

Nov 83. (7") *<7-29425>* **MEAN DISPOSITION. / COLD WINTER** [-] [ ]

– (DAVE DAVIES) compilations, etc. –

Apr 68. (7"ep) *Pye; (NEP 24289)* **DAVE DAVIES HITS** [ ] [ ]

Aug 82. (7") *Old Gold; (OG 9128)* **DEATH OF A CLOWN. / SUSANNAH'S STILL ALIVE** [ ] [-]

Feb 88. (lp/c) *P.R.T.; (PYL/PYK 6012)* **DAVE DAVIES – THE ALBUM THAT NEVER WAS** [ ] [-]
– (1960's singles)

Jul 92. (cd) *Mau Mau; (MAUDCD 617)* **DAVE DAVIES / GLAMOUR** [ ] [-]

RAY DAVIES

not iss. Pioneer

Jan 85. (lp) *<8380>* **RETURN TO WATERLOO** (soundtrack) [-] [ ]
– Intro / Return to Waterloo / Going solo / Missing persons / Sold me out / Lonely hearts / Not far away / Expectations / Voices in the dark.
(below was from the film 'Absolute Beginners')

Virgin not iss.

May 86. (7"/12") *(VS 865/+12)* **QUIET LIFE. / VOICES IN THE DARK** [ ] [-]

E.M.I. Capitol

Mar 98. (cd) *(<494168-2>)* **THE STORYTELLER** [ ] Apr98 [ ]
– Storyteller / Introduction / Victoria / My name (dialogue) / 20th century man / London song / My big sister (dialogue) / That old black magic / Tired of waiting / Set me free (instrumental) / Dad and the green amp (dialogue) / Set me free / The front room (dialogue) / See my friends / Autumn almanac / Hunchback (dialogue) / X-ray / Art school (dialogue) / Art school babe / Back in the front room / Writing the song (dialogue) / When big Bill speaks – The man who knew a man / It's alright (dialogue) / It's alright (dialogue) / It's alright (dialogue) / Julie Finkle (dialogue) / The ballad of Julie Finkle / The third single (dialogue) / You really got me / London song (studio).

☐ KIPPINGTON LODGE
(see under ⇒ BRINSLEY SCHWARZ)

KISS

Formed: New York City, New York, USA . . . late '71 by ex-WICKED LESTER members GENE SIMMONS and PAUL STANLEY, who recruited guitarist ACE FREHLEY and drummer PETER CRISS. After a year of touring in '73, they were signed to the new 'Casablanca' label, hitting the US Top 100 with an eponymous debut album in early '74. This, together with subsequent follow-up albums, 'HOTTER THAN HELL' (1974) and 'DRESSED TO KILL' (1975) set the greasepainted scene for what was to follow; low-rent glitter-metal so tacky it almost stuck to the speakers. Though these early albums sound like they were recorded on a cheap walkman in a sawmill, they contained some of KISS' finest groin-straining moments; 'STRUTTER', 'DEUCE' and 'ROCK AND ROLL ALL NITE' were anthemic shout-alongs for white college kids who could pretend to be rebellious for three minutes. But KISS undoubtedly built their reputation on a garish image and the sensory overkill of their live show, ALICE COOPER-style make-up and onstage schlock the order of the day. Accordingly, it was the double live album, 'ALIVE' (1975) that finally powered the band into the US Top 10 and the stadium major league. With 'DESTROYER' (produced by COOPER mentor, BOB EZRIN), the band refined their sound slightly, even recording a ballad, the PETER CRISS-penned/crooned teen heartbreaker, 'BETH' which furnished the band with their biggest ever hit single. This mid-70's career peak also saw a further three releases achieve platinum status, 'ROCK AND ROLL OVER' (1976), 'LOVE GUN' (1977) and 'ALIVE II'. KISS had struck a resounding chord in some back alley of the American consciousness and now boasted a merchandise line almost as long as SIMMONS' grotesque tongue, a perverted, proto-SPICE GIRLS marketing job from the dark side. And you couldn't get a much better marketing coup than releasing four solo albums on the same day, which is exactly what KISS did (one by each member), probably because they knew they could get away with it. Unsurprisingly, most of the material was self-indulgent rubbish and, with the threat of punk never far away, the band began to falter. Although the 'DYNASTY' (1979) album went Top 10 and provided a massive hit with 'I WAS MADE FOR LOVIN' YOU', CRISS soon bowed out, the drum stool filled by session man ANTON FIG for the 'UNMASKED' (1980) album. A permanent replacement was found in ERIC CARR who made his debut on the ill-advised concept nonsense of 'THE ELDER' (1981), though the new musical direction was just too much for FREHLEY to take and he wisely departed the following year. His place was filled by VINNIE VINCENT, who played on the back to basics 'CREATURES OF THE NIGHT'. When this album failed to revive their commercial fortunes, the band did the unthinkable, removing their make-up for the 'LICK IT UP' album. Perhaps as a result of the public discovering they weren't blood sucking ghouls after all but (relatively) normal looking people, the album went Top 30. Ironically, the band had just started to re-establish themselves in Britain, where 'LICK IT UP' made the Top 10, no doubt giving them heart in their struggle back to world domination. KISS then went through more line-up changes, with VINCENT being replaced first by MARK ST. JOHN, then BOB KULICK. With the unashamedly commercial 'CRAZY CRAZY NIGHTS' single and 'CRAZY NIGHTS' (1987) album, the band enjoyed their biggest success since their 70's heyday, both releases reaching No.4 in the UK. After another reasonably successful album, 'HOT IN THE SHADE' (1989), tragedy struck the band in the early 90's when CARR died following heart problems and cancer. Shaken but unbowed the band carried on with ERIC SINGER on drums, going back to the hoary sound of old with the 'REVENGE' (1992) opus, an album that saw them showing the young bucks who had patented the moves. It had to happen of course; 1996 marked a money-spinning, full-blown reunion tour with the original line-up and re-applied warpaint, the perfect KISS-off to those who had written them off for dead. Of course, this now meant that KULICK and SINGER were surplus to requirement; the pair were duly given their marching orders and the KISS album they'd just worked on, 'CARNIVAL OF SOULS: THE FINAL SESSIONS' was shelved. With bootleggers having a field day, the album was eventually given a belated release in 1997 although critics were generally agreed that its lacklustre contents should've been kept on the mastertape. Still, KISS were flying high after the runaway success of the reunion tour and even decided to record a full album together. The resulting 'PSYCHO CIRCUS' (1998) made the US

Top 3 to incredibly become the highest charting album of their near three decade career! This despite the fact it offered nothing new or even compared to their glory days. Then again, when the mainstream modern alternatives are so bland is it any wonder people consistently cling to retro fantasies? The band proceeded to indulge in perhaps one of heavy metal's most annoying and consistently dull fantasies, that of classical orchestra meets rock band. 'KISS SYMPHONY: ALIVE IV' (2003) was as dire as anything they've done and that's saying something. A double set of preposterous, string-backed rehashes, minus FREHLEY (who'd wisely bailed out by this point, to be replaced by former BLACK 'N' BLUE man TOMMY THAYER) and plus a musical non-connection between KISS and the MELBOURNE SYMPHONY ORCHESTRA did not Grammy material make. • **Songwriters:** Most by STANLEY or SIMMONS, with some ballads by CRISS. Covered; THEN (S)HE KISSED ME (Crystals) / GOD GAVE ROCK'N'ROLL TO YOU (Argent). MICHAEL BOLTON co-wrote with STANLEY their minor hit ballad 'FOREVER'. GENE SIMMONS solo covered; WHEN YOU WISH UPON A STAR (Judy Garland). • **Trivia:** In 1977, Marvel Comics started a KISS feature series in their monthly mag. In 1984, SIMMONS starred as a villain in the film 'Runaway' alongside Tom Selleck. Two years later 'The Bat-Winged Vampire' featured in films 'Never Too Young To Die', 'Trick Or Treat' & 'Wanted Dead Or Alive'. In 1994, a tribute album 'KISS MY ASS' was released by 'Mercury'. It featured star cover versions by LENNY KRAVITZ, GARTH BROOKS, ANTHRAX, GIN BLOSSOMS, TOAD THE WET SPROCKET, SHANDI's ADDICTION, DINOSAUR JR., EXTREME, LEMONHEADS, etc.

Album rating: KISS (*7) / HOTTER THAN HELL (*7) / DRESSED TO KILL (*7) / ALIVE! (*8) / DESTROYER (*8) / ROCK AND ROLL OVER (*6) / LOVE GUN (*6) / ALIVE II (*7) / DOUBLE PLATINUM compilation (*8) / DYNASTY (*6) / UNMASKED (*5) / (MUSIC FROM) THE ELDER (*4) / KILLERS compilation (*5) / CREATURES OF THE NIGHT (*6) / LICK IT UP (*6) / ANIMALIZE (*5) / ASYLUM (*6) / CRAZY NIGHTS (*5) / SMASHES, THRASHES AND HITS compilation (*7) / HOT IN THE SHADE (*6) / REVENGE (*6) / ALIVE III (*7) / MTV UNPLUGGED (*5) / CARNIVAL OF SOULS (*5) / PSYCHO-CIRCUS (*4) / THE BOX SET collection (*6) / THE VERY BEST OF KISS compilation (*6) / KISS SYMPHONY: ALIVE IV (*3)

GENE SIMMONS (b. GENE KLEIN, 25 Aug'49, Haifa, Israel) – vocals, bass / **PAUL STANLEY** (b. STANLEY EISEN, 20 Jan'52, Queens, N.Y.) – guitar, vocals / **ACE FREHLEY** (b. PAUL FREHLEY, 22 Apr'51, Bronx, N.Y.) – lead guitar, vocals / **PETER CRISS** (b. PETER CRISSCOULA, 27 Dec'47, Brooklyn, N.Y.) – drums, vocals

Casablanca Casablanca

Feb 74. (7") *<0004>* **NOTHIN' TO LOSE. / LOVE THEME FROM KISS** [–] [ ]

Feb 74. (lp) *<9001>* **KISS** [–] [87]
– Strutter / Nothin' to lose / Fire house / Cold gin / Let me know / Kissin' time / Deuce / Love theme from Kiss / 100,000 years / Black diamond. *(UK-iss.Feb75; CBC 4003) (re-iss. May77 red-lp; CAL 2006) (re-iss. Feb82 lp/c; 6399/7199 057) (re-iss. Jul84 lp/c; PRICE/PRIMC 68) (cd-iss. Aug88; 824146-2)*

May 74. (7") *<0011>* **KISSIN' TIME. / NOTHIN' TO LOSE** [–] [83]

Aug 74. (7") *<0015>* **STRUTTER. / 100,000 YEARS** [–] [ ]

Nov 74. (lp) *<7006>* **HOTTER THAN HELL** [–] [100]
– Got to choose / Parasite / Goin' blind / Hotter than Hell / Let me go, rock'n roll / All the way / Watchin' you / Mainline / Comin' home / Strange ways. *(UK-iss.May77 red-lp; CAL 2007) (re-iss. Feb82 lp/c; 6399/7199 058) (cd-iss. Aug88; 824147-2)*

Jan 75. (7") *(CBX 503)* **NOTHIN' TO LOSE. / LOVE THEME FROM KISS** [ ] [–]

Mar 75. (7") *<823>* **LET ME GO ROCK'N'ROLL. / HOTTER THAN HELL** [–] [ ]

Aug 75. (lp) *(CBC 4004) <7016>* **DRESSED TO KILL** [ ] Mar75 [32]
– Room service / Two timer / Ladies in waiting / Getaway / Rock bottom / C'mon and love me / Anything for my baby / She / Love her all I can / Rock and roll all nite. *(re-iss. May77 red-lp; CAL 2008) (re-iss. Feb82 lp/c; 6399/7199 059) (cd-iss. Aug88; 824148-2)*

May 75. (7") *<829>* **ROCK AND ROLL ALL NITE. / GETAWAY** [–] [68]

Jun 75. (7") *(CBX 510)* **ROCK AND ROLL ALL NITE. / ANYTHING FOR MY BABY** [ ] [–]

Oct 75. (7") *<841>* **C'MON AND LOVE ME. / GETAWAY** [–] [ ]

Nov 75. (7") *<850>* **ROCK AND ROLL ALL NITE (live). / ('A'studio mix)** [–] [12]

Apr 76. (7") *(CBX 516) <854>* **SHOUT IT OUT LOUD. / SWEET PAIN** [ ] Mar76 [31]

May 76. (lp) *(CBC 4008) <7025>* **DESTROYER** [22] Mar76 [11]
– Detroit rock city / King of the night time world / God of thunder / Great expectations / Flaming youth / Sweet pain / Shout it out loud / Beth / Do you love me. *(re-iss. May77 red-lp; CAL 2009) (re-iss. Feb82 lp/c; 6399/7199 064) (cd-iss. Apr87; 824149-2)*

Jun 76. (7") *<858>* **FLAMING YOUTH. / GOD OF THUNDER** [–] [74]

Jun 76. (d-lp) *(CBC 4011+2) <7020>* **ALIVE! (live)** [49] Oct75 [9]
– Deuce / Strutter / Got to choose / Hotter than Hell / Firehouse / Nothin' to lose / C'mon and love me / Parasite / She / Watchin' you / 100,000 years / Black diamond / Rock bottom / Cold gin / Rock and roll all nite / Let me go, rock'n'roll. *(re-iss. May77 red-lp; CALD 5001) (re-iss. Feb82; 6640 064) (re-iss. Sep84 d-lp/d-c; PRID/+C 3) (cd-iss. Apr87; 822780-2)*

Aug 76. (7") *<863>* **BETH. / DETROIT ROCK CITY** [–] [7]

Jul 76. (7") *(CBX 519)* **BETH. / GOD OF THUNDER** [ ] [–]

Feb 77. (red-lp) *(CALH 2001) <NBLP 7037>* **ROCK AND ROLL OVER** [ ] Nov76 [11]
– I want you / Take me / Calling Dr. Love / Ladies room / Baby driver / Love 'em and leave 'em / Mr. Speed / See you in your dreams / Hard luck woman / Makin' love. *(re-iss. Feb82 lp/c; 6399/7199 060) (cd-iss. Aug88; 824150-2)*

Dec 76. (7") *<873>* **HARD LUCK WOMAN. / MR. SPEED** [–] [15]

Mar 77. (7") *<880>* **CALLING DR. LOVE. / TAKE ME** [–] [16]

May 77. (7"m) *(CAN 102)* **HARD LUCK WOMAN. / CALLING DR. LOVE / BETH** [ ] [–]

Jun 77. (lp) *(CALH 2017) <7057>* **LOVE GUN** [ ] [4]
– I stole your love / Christine sixteen / Got love for sale / Shock me / Tomorrow and tonight / Love gun / Hooligan / Almost human / Plaster caster / The she kised me. *(re-iss. Feb82 lp/c; 6399/7199 063) (re-iss. Jul84 lp/c; PRICE/PRIMC 69) (cd-iss. Aug88; 824151-2)*

Jul 77. (7") *<889>* **CHRISTINE SIXTEEN. / SHOCK ME** [–] [25]

Aug 77. (7"m/12"m) *(CAN/L 110)* **THEN SHE KISSED ME. / HOOLIGAN / FLAMING YOUTH** [ ] [–]

Sep 77. (7") *<895>* **LOVE GUN. / HOOLIGAN** [–] [61]

Nov 77. (d-lp/d-c) *(CALD/+C 5004) <7076>* **KISS ALIVE II** [60] [7]
– Detroit rock city / King of the night time world / Ladies room / Makin' love / Love gun / Calling Dr. Love / Christine sixteen / Shock me / Hard luck woman / Tomorrow and tonight / I stole your love / Beth / God of thunder / I want you / Shout it out loud / All American man / Rockin' in the U.S.A. / Larger than life / Rocket ride / Anyway you want it. *(re-iss. Feb82 d-lp)(d-c; 6685 043)(7599 512) (cd-iss. May89; 822781-2)*

Jan 78. (7") *<906>* **SHOUT IT OUT LOUD (live). / NOTHIN' TO LOSE (live)** [–] [54]

Feb 78. (7") *<915>* **ROCKET RIDE. / TOMORROW AND TONIGHT** [–] [39]

Mar 78. (7") *(CAN 117)* **ROCKET RIDE. / LOVE GUN (live)** [ ] [–]
(12"+=) *(CANL 117)* – Detroit rock city (live).

Jun 78. (7") *(CAN 126)* **ROCK AND ROLL ALL NITE. / C'MON AND LOVE ME** [ ] [–]

—— Took time to do solo projects (all same label on below)

GENE SIMMONS

Sep 78. (lp/pic-lp) *<NBLP/NBPIX 7120>* **GENE SIMMONS** [–] [22]
– Radioactive / Burning up with fever / See you tonite / Tunnel of love / True confessions / Living in sin / Always near you – Nowhere to hide / Man of 1000 faces / Mr. Make Believe / See you in your dreams / When you wish upon a star. *<re-iss. 1987 pic-lp; NBLPP 7120> <cd-iss. 1997 (UK Mar03) on 'Universal'; 532384-2>*

Oct 78. (7") *<NB 951>* **RADIOACTIVE. / SEE YOU IN YOUR DREAMS** [–] [ ]

Jan 79. (7",7"red) *(CAN 134)* **RADIOACTIVE. / WHEN YOU WISH UPON A STAR** [41] [–]

ACE FREHLEY

Sep 78. (lp/pic-lp) *<NBLP/NBPIX 7121>* **ACE FREHLEY** [–] [26]
– Rip it out / Speedin' back to my baby / Snow blind / Ozone / What's on your mind / New York groove / I'm in need of love / Wiped-out / Fractured

mirror. *<re-iss. 1987 pic-lp; NBLPP 7121> (cd-iss. May88; 826916-2) <cd re-iss. 1997 (UK Mar03) on 'Universal'; 532385-2>*

Nov 78. (7"blue) *(CAN 135) <NB 941>* **NEW YORK GROOVE. / SNOW BLIND** [ ] Sep78 [13]

PETER CRISS

Sep 78. (lp/pic-lp) *<NBLP/NBPIX 7122>* **PETER CRISS** [–] [43]
– I'm gonna love you / You matter to me / Tossin' and turnin' / Don't you let me down / That's the kind of sugar papa likes / Easy thing / Rock me, baby / Kiss the girl goodbye / Hooked on rock'n'roll / I can't stop the rain. *<re-iss. 1987 pic-lp; NBLPP 7122> (cd-iss. Nov91; 826917-2) (re-iss. Aug94 cd+red-lp+book on 'Megarock') <cd re-iss. 1997 (UK Mar03) on 'Universal'; 532386-2>*

Dec 78. (7") *(NB 952)* **DON'T YOU LET ME DOWN. / HOOKED ON ROCK AND ROLL** [–] [ ]

Feb 79. (7"green) *(CAN 139)* **YOU MATTER TO ME. / HOOKED ON ROCK AND ROLL** [ ] [–]

PAUL STANLEY

Sep 78. (lp/pic-lp) *<NBLP/NBPIX 7123>* **PAUL STANLEY** [–] [40]
– Tonight you belong to me / Move on / Ain't quite right / Wouldn't you like to know / Take me away (together as one) / It's alright / Hold me, touch me (think of me when we're apart) / Love in chains / Goodbye. *(re-iss. 1987 pic-lp; NBLPP 7123> (cd-iss. Nov91; 826918-2) <cd re-iss. 1997 (UK Mar03) on 'Universal'; 532387-2>*

Feb 79. (7",7"purple) *(CAN 140)* **HOLD ME TOUCH ME. / GOODBYE** [ ] [–]

KISS

—— returned to studio

Casablanca Casablanca

Jun 79. (7") *(CAN 152) <983>* **I WAS MADE FOR LOVIN' YOU. / HARD TIMES** [50] May79 [11]
(12") *(CANL 152)* – ('A'side) / Charisma.

Jun 79. (lp/c) *(CALH/+C 2051) <7152>* **DYNASTY** [50] [9]
– I was made for lovin' you / 2,000 man / Sure know something / Dirty livin' / Charisma / Magic touch / Hard times / X-ray eyes / Save your love. *(re-iss. Oct83 lp/c; PRICD/PRIMC 42) <cd-iss. 1988; > (cd-iss. Aug88; 812770-2)*

Aug 79. (7") *(CAN 163) <2205>* **SURE KNOW SOMETHING. / DIRTY LIVIN'** [ ] [47]

Feb 80. (7"m/12"m) *(NB/+L 1001)* **2000 MAN. / I WAS MADE FOR LOVIN' YOU / SURE KNOW SOMETHING** [ ] [–]

Mercury Casablanca

Jun 80. (7") *<2282>* **SHANDI. / SHE'S SO EUROPEAN** [–] [47]

Jun 80. (7") *(MER 19)* **TALK TO ME. / SHE'S SO EUROPEAN** [ ] [–]

Jun 80. (lp/c) *(6302 032) <7225>* **UNMASKED** [48] [35]
– Is that you / Shandi / Talk to me / Naked city / What makes the world go 'round / Tomorrow / Two sides of the coin / She's so European / Easy as it seems / Torpedo girl / You're all that I want. *(cd-iss. May83; 800041-2)*

Aug 80. (7") *(KISS 1)* **WHAT MAKES THE WORLD GO 'ROUND. / NAKED CITY** [ ] [–]

Aug 80. (7") *<2299>* **TOMORROW. / NAKED CITY** [–] [ ]

—— (May'80) **ERIC CARR** (b.12 Jul'50) – drums, producer repl. CRISS who went solo (early 80's pop albums; 'OUT OF CONTROL' / 'LET ME ROCK YOU')

Nov 81. (lp/c) *(6302/7144 163) <7261>* **MUSIC FROM 'THE ELDER'** [51] [75]
– The oath / Fanfare / Just a boy / Dark light / Only you / Under the rose / A world without heroes / Mr. Blackwell / Escape from the island / Odyssey / I. *(cd-iss. Jun89; 825153-2)*

Nov 81. (7") *<2343>* **A WORLD WITHOUT HEROES. / DARK LIGHT** [–] [56]

Jan 82. (7"/7"pic-d) *(KISS/+P 2)* **A WORLD WITHOUT HEROES. / MR. BLACKWELL** [55] [–]

—— **VINNIE VINCENT** (b. VINCENT CUSANO) – guitar repl. BOB KULICK who had repl. FREHLEY (he formed FREHLEY'S COMET)

Casablanca Casablanca

Oct 82. (7") *<2365>* **DANGER. / I LOVE IT LOUD** [–] [ ]

Oct 82. (7") *(KISS 3)* **KILLER. / I LOVE IT LOUD** [ ] [–]
(12"+=) *(KISS 3-12)* – I was made for lovin' you.

Oct 82. (lp/c) *(6302/7144 219) <7270>* **CREATURES OF THE NIGHT** [22] [45]
– Creatures of the night / Saint and sinner / Keep me comin' / Rock and roll Hell / Danger / I love it loud / I still love you / Killer / War machine. *(cd-iss. Aug88; 824154-2)*

Mar 83. (7") *(KISS 4)* **CREATURES OF THE NIGHT. / ROCK AND ROLL ALL NITE (live)** [34] [–]
(12"+=) *(KISS 4-12)* – War machine.

Vertigo Mercury

Oct 83. (7") *<814 671-7>* **LICK IT UP. / DANCE ALL OVER YOUR FACE** [–] [66]

Oct 83. (7"/7"sha-pic-d) *(KISS 5/+P)* **LICK IT UP. / NOT FOR THE INNOCENT** [34] [–]
(12"+=) *(KISS 5-12)* – I still love you.

Oct 83. (lp/c) *(VERL/+C 9) <814 297>* **LICK IT UP** [7] [24]
– Exciter / Not for the innocent / Lick it up / Young and wasted / Gimme more / All Hell's breakin' loose / A million to one / Fits like a glove / Dance all over your face / And on the 8th day. *(cd-iss. Dec89 on 'Mercury'; 814297-2)*

Jan 84. (7") *<818 216-2>* **ALL HELL'S BREAKIN' LOOSE. / YOUNG AND WASTED** [–] [ ]

—— **MARK (NORTON) ST. JOHN** – guitar repl. VINCENT who formed VINNIE VINCENT'S INVASION

Sep 84. (7") *(VER 12) <880 205-7>* **HEAVEN'S ON FIRE. / LONELY IS THE HUNTER** [43] [49]
(12"+=) *(VERX 12)* – All hell's breakin' loose.

Sep 84. (lp/c) *(VERL/+C 18) <822 495>* **ANIMALIZE** [11] [19]
– I've had enough (into the fire) / Heaven's on fire / Burn bitch burn / Get all you can take / Lonely is the hunter / Under the gun / Thrills in the night / While the city sleeps / Murder in high-heels. *(cd-iss. Dec89 on 'Mercury'; 822 495-2)*

Nov 84. (7") *<880 535-2>* **THRILLS IN THE NIGHT. / BURN BITCH BURN** [–] [ ]

—— **BRUCE KULICK** – guitar repl. MARK who became ill

Oct 85. (lp/c) *(VERH/+C 32) <826 099>* **ASYLUM** [12] [20]
– King of the mountain / Any way you slice it / Who wants to be lonely / Trial by fire / I'm alive / Love's a deadly weapon / Tears are falling / Secretly cruel / Radar for love / Uh! All night. *(cd-iss. May89 on 'Mercury'; 826 303-2)*

Oct 85. (7") *<884 141-7>* **TEARS ARE FALLING. / ANY WAY YOU SLICE IT** [–] [51]

Oct 85. (7") *(KISS 6)* **TEARS ARE FALLING. / HEAVEN'S ON FIRE (live)** [57] [–]
(12"+=) *(KISS 6-12)* – Any way you slice it.

Sep 87. (7"/7"s) *(KISS 7/+P) <888 796-7>* **CRAZY CRAZY NIGHTS. / NO, NO, NO** [4] [65]
(12"+=) *(KISS 7-12)* – Lick it up / Uh! All night.
(12"pic-d+=) *(KISSP 7-12)* – Heaven's on fire / Tears are falling.

Oct 87. (lp/c) *(VERH/+C 49) <832626>* **CRAZY NIGHTS** [4] [18]
– Crazy crazy nights / I'll fight Hell to hold you / Bang bang you / No, no, no / Hell or high water / My way / When your walls come down / Reason to live / Good girl gone bad / Turn on the night / Thief in the night. *(cd-iss. Feb91; 832 626-2)*

Dec 87. (7"/7"s) *(KISS/+P 8) <870 022-7>* **REASON TO LIVE. / THIEF IN THE NIGHT** [33] [64]
(c-s+=) *(KISSMC 8)* – Who wants to be lonely.
(12"++=) *(KISS 8-12)* – Thrills in the night.
(12"pic-d++=) *(KISSP 8-12)* – Secretly cruel.
(cd-s+=) *(KISCD 8)* – Tears are falling / Crazy crazy nights.

Feb 88. (7"/7"s) *(KISS/+P 9) <870 215-7>* **TURN ON THE NIGHT. / HELL OR HIGH WATER** [41] [ ]
(12"+=/12"pic-d+=) *(KISS/+P 9-12)* – King of the mountain / Any way you slice it.
(cd-s+=) *(KISCD 9)* – Heaven's on fire / I love it loud.

Oct 89. (7"/7"red/c-s) *(KIS S/R/MC 10) <876 146-7>* **HIDE YOUR HEART. / BETRAYED** [59] [66]
(12"+=/cd-s+=) *(KIS SX/CD 10)* – Boomerang.
(10"pic-d) *(KISP 10-10)* – ('A'side) / Lick it up / Heaven's on fire.

Oct 89. (lp/c/cd) *<(838 913-2/-4/-1)>* **HOT IN THE SHADE** [35] [29]
– Rise to it / Betrayed / Hide your heart / Prisoner of love / Read my body / Love's a slap in the face / Forever / Silver spoon / Cadillac dreams / King of hearts / The street giveth and the street taketh away / You love me to hate you / Somewhere between Heaven and Hell / Little Caesar / Boomerang.

Mar 90. (7"/7"s) *(KISS/+P 11) <876 716-7>* **FOREVER (remix). / THE STREET GIVETH AND THE STREET TAKETH AWAY** [65] Feb90 [8]
(12"white+=) *(KISS 12-12)* – Deuce (demo) / Strutter (demo).
(12"/12"g-f) *(KIS SX/XG 11)* – ('A'side) / All American man / Shandi / The Oath.

(cd-s) *(KISCD 11)* – ('A'side) / Creatures of the night / Lick it up / Heaven's on fire.

Jun 90. (c-s) *<875096>* **RISE TO IT. / SILVER SPOON** [–] [81]

— In May'91, ERIC CARR underwent open heart surgery. He was admitted to hospital again but they found malignant cancer growth. He died on the 24th Nov'91. In Jan'92, KISS hit UK No.4 with 'GOD GAVE ROCK'N'ROLL TO YOU II' from the film 'Bill & Ted's Bogus Journey'. On the same single issued on 'Interscope' were tracks by 'KINGS X' & 'SLAUGHTER'.

— **ERIC SINGER** – drums (ex-BADLANDS, ex-BLACK SABBATH) repl. CARR

May 92. (7"/c-s) *(KISS/KISMC 12)* **UNHOLY. / GOD GAVE ROCK'N'ROLL TO YOU II** [26] [ ]
(12"+=/12"pic-d+=)(cd-s+=) *(KISS/+P 12-12)(KISCD 12)* – Partners in crime / Deva / Strutter (demos).

May 92. (cd/c/lp) *(848 037-2/-4/-1)* *<48037>* **REVENGE** [10] [6]
– Unholy / Take it off / Tough love / Spit / God gave rock'n'roll to you II / Domino / Heart of chrome / Thou shalt not / Every time I look at you / Paralyzed / I just wanna / Carr jam 1981.

May 93. (cd/c) *<(514 827-2/-4)>* **KISS ALIVE III (live)** [24] [9]
– Creatures of the night / Deuce / I just wanna / Unholy / Heaven's on fire / Watchin' you / Domino / I was made for lovin' you / I still love you / Rock'n'roll all nite / Lick it up (featuring BOBBY WOMACK) / Take it off / I love it loud / Detroit rock city / God gave rock'n'roll to you / Star spangled banner.

Mar 96. (cd/c/lp) *<(528 950-2/-4/-1)>* **MTV UNPLUGGED (live)** [74] [15]
– Comin' home / Plaster caster / Goin' blind / Do you love me / Domino / Sure know something / A world without heroes / Rock bottom / See you tonight / I still love you / Every time I look at you / 2,000 man / Beth / Nothin' to lose / Rock and roll all nite.

Oct 97. (cd/c) *<(536 323-2/-4)>* **CARNIVAL OF SOULS** [ ] [27]
– Hate / Rain / Master and slave / Childhood's end / I will be there / Jungle / In my head / It never goes away / Seduction of the innocent / I confess / In the mirror / I walk alone.

— originals were back again (**SIMMONS, STANLEY, FREHLEY + CRISS**)

Sep 98. (cd/c) *<(558 992-2/-4)>* **PSYCHO-CIRCUS** [47] [3]
– Psycho-circus / Within / I pledge allegience (to the state of rock & roll) / Into the void / We are one / You wanted the best / Raise your glasses / I finally found my way / Dreamin' / Journey of 1,000 years.

— **TOMMY THAYER** – guitar (ex-BLACK 'N' BLUE) repl. FREHLEY

— next with the MELBOURNE SYMPHONY ORCHESTRA

Sanctuary Sanctuary

Jul 03. (cd/t-lp) *(SAN DD/TV 195)* *<84617>* **KISS SYMPHONY: ALIVE IV (live)** [ ] [ ]
– Deuce / Strutter / Let me go rock & roll / Lick it up / Calling Dr. Love / Psycho circus / Beth / Forever / Goin' blind / Sure know something / Shandi / Detroit rock city / King of the night time world / Do you love me / Shout it out loud / God of thunder / Love gun / Black diamond / Great expectations / I was made for lovin' you / Rock and roll all nite.

– compilations etc. –

Aug 76. (t-lp) *Casablanca; <7032>* **THE ORIGINALS** (first 3 albums) [–] [ ]

May 78. (d-lp) *Casablanca; (CALD 5005) <7100 1-2>* **DOUBLE PLATINUM** [ ] [24]
(re-iss. Feb82; 6641 907) (re-iss. May85 d-lp/d-c; PRID/+C 8) cd-iss. Jun87; 824 148-2)

Jan 81. (lp) *Casablanca; (6302 060)* **THE BEST OF THE SOLO ALBUMS** [ ] [–]

Jun 82. (lp) *Casablanca; (CANL 1)* **KILLERS** [42] [–]

Nov 88. (7") *Mercury; <872 246-7>* **LET'S PUT THE 'X'. / CALLING DR. LOVE** [–] [97]

Nov 88. (lp/c/cd) *Vertigo / Mercury; <(836 759-1/-4/-2)>* **SMASHES, THRASHES AND HITS** [62] [21]
– Let's put the X in sex / Crazy, crazy nights / (You make me) Rock hard / Love gun / Detroit rock city / I love it loud / Reason to live / Lick it up / Heavens on fire / Strutter / Beth / Tears are falling / I was made for lovin' you / Rock and roll all nite / Shout it out loud.

Oct 88. (5"vid-cd) *Vertigo; (080 232-2)* **CRAZY, CRAZY NIGHTS. / NO, NO, NO / WHEN YOUR WALLS COME DOWN / THIEF IN THE NIGHT** [ ] [–]

1989. (7") *Mercury; <814 303-7>* **BETH. / HARD LUCK WOMAN** [–] [ ]

1989. (7") *Mercury; <814 304-7>* **ROCK AND ROLL ALL NITE. / I WAS MADE FOR LOVIN' YOU** [–] [ ]

Sep 89. (5"vid-cd) *Vertigo; (080 044-2)* **LICK IT UP. / DANCE ALL OVER YOUR FACE / GIMME MORE / FITS LIKE A GLOVE** [ ] [–]

Sep 89. (5"vid-cd) *Vertigo; (080 058-2)* **TEARS ARE FALLING. / ANY WAY YOU SLICE IT / WHO WANTS TO BE LONELY / SECRETLY CRUEL** [ ] [–]

— (all lp's were released as pic-lp's in Europe)

Jul 96. (cd/c) *Mercury: <(532 741-2/-4)>* **YOU WANTED THE BEST, YOU GOT THE BEST (live compilation)** [ ] [17]

Jul 97. (cd/c) *Polygram TV; <(536 159-2/-4)>* **GREATEST HITS** [58] Apr97 [77]

Dec 01. (5xcd-box) *<(586561-2)>* **THE BOX SET** [ ] Nov01 [ ]

Sep 02. (cd) *Universal; <(E 063122-2)>* **THE VERY BEST OF KISS** [ ] Aug02 [52]
– Strutter / Deuce / Got to choose / Hotter than hell / C'mon and love me / Rock and roll all nite / Detroit rock city / Shout it out loud / Beth / I want you / Calling Dr. Love / Hard luck woman / I stole your love / Christine sixteen / Love gun / New York groove / I was made for lovin' you / I love it loud / Lick it up / Forever / God gave rock & roll to you II.

KLF

Formed: KOPYRIGHT LIBERATION FRONT. Based; London, England . . . 1986 by BILL DRUMMOND and JIM CAUTY. Raised in Clydebank, Scotland, DRUMMOND was already a seasoned music industry veteran when he teamed up with CAUTY, having helped to form the pivotal 'Zoo' label in the late 70's, initially home to such Merseyside legends as TEARDROP EXPLODES and ECHO & THE BUNNYMEN. DRUMMOND also worked as an A&R bod for 'WEA', signing up the band BRILLIANT with whom CAUTY played guitar. Eventually, the pair ditched their existing music industry responsibilities with the intention of subverting the notion of the 'pop star' and began working on their first project, JUSTIFIED ANCIENTS OF MU MU. Under that improbably titled moniker, the pair released their first album, '1987 – WHAT THE FUCK IS GOING ON' (1987), a question one might well have asked oneself in those dark, RICK ASTLEY-dominated days. The JAMMS answer was to desecrate the works of such revered musical greats as The BEATLES, LED ZEPPELIN and ABBA, the latter taking great offence to this and demanding that the band destroy the offending copies . . . all 500 of them. The JAMS went on to bigger and better things with their dancefloor-friendly Dr. Who/GARY GLITTER pastiche, 'DOCTORIN' THE TARDIS' (released under The TIMELORDS moniker) at the height of the first house explosion in 1988. The record went to No.1, prompting the group to make their ninth official release a mock-guide book to the music industry, detailing how to make No.1 with the minimum of effort. Next was the pair's most famous incarnation as the KLF, DRUMMOND and CAUTY experimenting with house and ambient music to create a string of tracks that were massive club hits as well as Top 5 singles, at the turn of the decade. 'WHAT TIME IS LOVE?', 'LAST TRAIN TO TRANSCENTRAL' and '3 A.M. ETERNAL' were all collected on 'THE WHITE ROOM' (1991) album, the latter single even reaching the US Top 5 in 1990. The album went to No.3 in Britain, becoming a consistent seller until the band deleted it the following year. A fertile period for the KLF, the outfit also released the highly regarded ambient album, 'CHILL OUT' (1990), while CAUTY played a major part in the formation of The ORB. Taking the opportunity to resurrect the JAMMS, the duo released 'IT'S GRIM UP NORTH', a hilarious run through of dismal English towns, as well as roping in TAMMY WYNETTE for an improbable duet on 'JUSTIFIED AND ANCIENT (STAND BY THE JAMMS)'. While the single was a massive cross-Atlantic hit, the lines were becoming blurred as to who was taking the piss out of who. But the KLF had yet to play their trump card, and after a suitably overwrought version of 'WHAT TIME IS LOVE' went Top 5, they decided enough was enough and set out to sabotage the success they'd created. Invited to play at the annual Brit awards ceremony in 1992, the KLF proceeded to obliterate 'WHAT TIME IS LOVE' with the help of hardcore punk/thrash merchants 'EXTREME NOISE TERROR'. The numerous rumours about the duo mutilating a dead sheep on stage never materialised although they created enough of a furore to keep the press speculating for weeks. A couple of months later the duo announced that the KLF was officially no more, the back catalogue promptly deleted. CAUTY and DRUMMOND subsequently turned their guerilla tactics on the art world, and under the guise of the mysterious K Foundation, awarded Rachel Whiteread a £40,000 prize for the worst art piece of the year. The Foundation's shortlist for the prize was identical to that of the shortlist for the Turner prize, an annual award for the best piece of non-mainstream art which Whiteread had also scooped. The K Foundation further bemused a sceptical art world when they exhibited £1,000,000 in banknotes, profits from their hit making which they nailed to a board for a private viewing. CAUTY and DRUMMOND then made the most radical statement of their career and one of the most radical "art" statements in history when they literally torched the money in a farmhouse on a remote Scottish island, even filming the event for posterity. Roundly condemned as a highly irresponsible waste of cash that could have been donated to charity etc, etc, the questions that the duo raised were predictably ignored. CAUTY was allegedly cautioned by police after scaring cows with high freqency electronic sound waves (!), while the duo contributed a suitably bizarre track to the 1995 'HELP' Warchild charity album. The K Foundation also released a single, 'F**K THE MILLENNIUM', in late '97, asking people to phone in and cast their 'vote' on the matter. Towards the end of a tiring decade (for some of us!) CAUTY was unmasked as the man behind that novelty hit by the SOLID GOLD CHARTBUSTERS, '1-2-1'; I hate mobile phones even worse now.

Album rating: WHO KILLED THE JAMMS? (*6) / SHAG TIMES (*6) / WHAT TIME IS LOVE STORY (*6) / CHILL OUT (*7) / THE WHITE ROOM (*8)

JUSTIFIED ANCIENTS OF MU MU

(aka J.A.M.M.s) **KING BOY D** (aka BILL DRUMMOND) (b. WILLIAM BUTTERWORTH, 29 Apr'53, South Africa) – synths (ex-BIG IN JAPAN, ex-LORI & THE CHAMELEONS) / **ROCKMAN ROCK** (aka JIM CAUTY) (b.1954) – guitar (ex-BRILLIANT, etc.)

KLF Comm. — not iss.

May 87. (one-sided-12") *(JAMS 23)* **ALL YOU NEED IS LOVE** [ ] [–]
(12"+=) *(JAMS 23T)* – Ivum naya / Rap, rhyme and scratch yourself.
(7") *(JAMS 23s)* – ('A'-Me Ru Con mix) / ('A'-Ibo version).

Jun 87. (lp; w-drawn) *(JAMS LP1)* **1987 (WHAT THE FUCK IS GOING ON?)** [–] [–]

Sep 87. (one-sided-12") *(JAMS 24T)* **WHITNEY JOINS THE JAMS (120 bpm)** [–] Scots [–]

Nov 87. (12") *(JAMS 25T)* **1987 – THE 45 EDITS** [ ] [–]
– (excerpts from the unissued lp)

Dec 87. (12") *(JAMS 27)* **DOWN TOWN (A-side mix). / DOWN TOWN (B-side mix)** [ ] [–]
(above also available as 2 one-sided-12"; same)
(7"/ext.12") *(JAMS 27 s/T)* – Down town (118 bpm) / Down town.

Dec 87. (12"; as DISCO 2000) *(D 2000)* **I GOTTA CD. / I LOVE DISCO 2000** [ ] [–]

Feb 88. (lp) *(JAMS LP2)* **WHO KILLED THE JAMS?** [ ] [–]
– The candy store / The candy man / Disaster fund collection / King boy's dream / The porpoise song / The Prestwich prophet's grin / Burn the bastards. *(w/ free KLF 1987 COMPLETIST LIST discography; KLF 001)*

Mar 88. (export-12"ep) *(JAMS 26T)* **BURN THE BEAT EP** [–] [–]
– Burn the bastards / Burn the beat (I) / Prestwich prophet's grin (dance mix 90 bpm) / The porpoise song (dance mix 114 bpm).

Mar 88. (one-sided-12"grey) *(JAMS 28T)* **IT'S GRIM UP NORTH** [ ] [–]

K.L.F.

— just a justified change of name

KLF Comm. — TVT

Mar 88. (7") *(KLF 002)* **BURN THE BEAT (II). / THE PORPOISE SONG** [ ] [–]
(12") *(KLF 002T)* – ('A'side) / Burn the bastards.

Apr 88. (12"; as DISCO 2000) *(D 2002)* **ONE LOVE NATION. / ('A'edit) / ('A'instrumental)** [ ] [–]

May 88. (7"/7"sha-pic-d; as TIMELORDS) *(KLF 003 s/P)* *<4025>* **DOCTORIN' THE TARDIS. / ('A'-minimal version)** [1] Nov88 [66]
(12"+=) *(KLF 003T)* – ('A'club version).
(video-cd-s++=) *(KLFCD 003)* – ('A'-video mix).
(12"+=) *(KLF 003R)* – ('A'-with Gary Glitter).

Jan 89. (7"; as DISCO 2000) *(D 2003)* **UPTIGHT (EVERYTHING'S ALRIGHT (Banana 2000 mix). / MR. HOTTY LOVES YOU (edit)** [ ] [–]
(12") *(D 2003)* – ('A'-discorama mix) / ('B'side).

— JIM CAUTY released eponymous album under **SPACE** banner mid-1990 on 'Space-Rough Trade'; *LP/CD 1.*

Jun 89. (12") *(KLF 004T)* **WHAT TIME IS LOVE? (trance). / ('A'mix 2)** [ ] [–]
(12") *(KLF 004R)* – ('A'-primal remix) / ('A'-Techno slam) / ('A'-Trance mix).

Sep 89. (12") *(KLF 005T)* **3 A.M. ETERNAL. / ('A'-Break for love mix) / ('A'-Pure trance mix)** [ ] [–]
(remix.12") *(KLF 005R)* – ('A'original) / ('A'-Blue Danube Orbital mix) / ('A'-Moody Boy mix).

Oct 89. (lp/cd) *(JAMS LP/CD 4)* **THE WHAT TIME IS LOVE STORY** [ ] [–]
– What time is love? (original) / Relax your body / What time is love? (Italian) / Heartbeat / No limit (dance mix) / What time is love? (live at the Land of Oz).

Dec 89. (12"; not issued) *(KLF 008R)* **LAST TRAIN FROM TRANCENTRAL** [–] [–]

Mar 90. (cd/lp) *(JAMS CD/LP 5)* **CHILL OUT** [ ] [–]

Jul 90. (7"/ext.12") *(KLF 010 s/PT)* **KYLIE SAID TO JASON. / KYLIE SAID TRANCE** [ ] [–]
(cd-s+=) *(KLF 010CD)* – Madrugaral eternal.

— added **MAXINE HARVEY** – vocals

KLF — Arista

Aug 90. (7"/12"/c-s) *(KLF 004/+X/C)* **WHAT TIME IS LOVE (live at Trancentral). / ('A'-Techno gate mix)** [5] [ ]
(12") *(KLF 004P)* – ('A'side) / ('A'-Wandafull mix).
(cd-s) *(KLF 004CD)* – ('A'radio) / ('A'side) / ('A'-Trance).
(remix.12") *(KLF 004Y)* – ('A'-Moody Boys vs. the KLF) / ('A'-Echo & The Bunnymen mix) / ('A'-Virtual reality mix).

Jan 91. (7"/12"/c-s) *(KLF 005 R/X/C)* *<2230>* **3 A.M. ETERNAL (live at SSL). / ETERNAL (GUNS OF MU MU)** [1] Jun91 [5]
(12"+=/cd-s+=) *(KLF 005 Y/CD)* – ('A'-Break for love mix).

Mar 91. (cd/c/lp) *(JAMS CD/MC/LP 6)* *<8657>* **THE WHITE ROOM** [3] Jun91 [39]
– What time is love? / Make it rain / 3 a.m. eternal (live at the S.S.L.) / Church of the KLF / Last train to Transcentral / Build a fire / The white room / No more tears / Justified and ancient.

Apr 91. (7"/12"/c-s) *(KLF 008/+X/C)* **LAST TRAIN TO TRANSCENTRAL. / THE IRON HORSE** [2] [ ]
(12"+=) *(KLF 008T)* – Live from the Lost Continent.
(cd-s++=) *(KLF 008CD)* – ('A'-Pure trance version '89).

Oct 91. (c-s,cd-s) *<2365>* **WHAT TIME IS LOVE? / BUILD A FIRE** [–] [57]

Nov 91. (7"/12"/c-s; as JUSTIFIED ANCIENTS OF MU MU) *(JAMS 028/+T/C)* **IT'S GRIM UP NORTH. / (part 2)** [10] [ ]
(cd-s+=) *(JAMS 028CD)* – Jerusalem on the Moors.

Nov 91. (7"/c-s; as The KLF featuring THE FIRST LADY OF COUNTRY: TAMMY WYNETTE) *(KLF 099/+C)* *<12401>* **JUSTIFIED AND ANCIENT (STAND BY THE JAMS). / ('A'original version)** [2] Jan92 [11]
(12"+=/cd-s+=) *(KLF 099 T/CD)* – Let them eat ice-cream / Make mine a 99 / All bound for Mu Mu land (with MAXINE).

Jan 92. (7"/c-s) **P.O. 3 A.M. ETERNAL / ('A'-Guns of MuMu mix)** [ ] [–]
(12"+=/cd-s+=) – ('A'diff.versions).

Feb 92. (7"/c-s) *(KLFUSA 004/+C)* *<12366>* **AMERICA: WHAT TIME IS LOVE. / AMERICA NO MORE** [4] [ ]
(12"+=/cd-s+=) *(KLFUSA 004 T/CD)* – (other 'A'mixes).

— both now used KLF as art movement, causing controversy with their large inner city billboards nearly gaining Turner prize. Late in 1993, they collaborated on EXTREME NOISE TERROR version of '3 A.M. ETERNAL'.

Blast First | not iss.

Oct 97. (12"/cd-s; as 2K) *(BFFP 146 TK/CDK)* *****K THE MILLENNIUM (mixes)** [28] [–]

– compilations, etc. –

Jan 89. (d-lp/cd; as JUSTIFIED ANCIENTS OF MU MU) *KLF; (DLP/DCD 3)* **SHAG TIMES** [ ] [–]
– All you need is love / Don't take five (take what you want) / Whitney joins the JAMS / Downtown / Candyman / Burn the bastards / Doctorin' the tardis / 114 BPM / 90 BPM / 118 BPM / 125 BPM / 120 BPM / 118 BPM / 120 BPM (all releases, from all aliases)

☐ Terry KNIGHT & THE PACK (see under ⇒ GRAND FUNK RAILROAD)

☐ Mark KNOPFLER (see under ⇒ DIRE STRAITS)

KOOL AND THE GANG

Formed: Jersey City, New Jersey, USA … 1964 as high school band The JAZZIACS by ROBERT 'KOOL' BELL, his brother RONALD and a cast of classmates that included ROBERT 'SPIKE' MICKENS, DENNIS 'DEE TEE' THOMAS, RICKY WESTFIELD and GEORGE 'FUNKY' BROWN. Jazz blood ran through the BELL brothers' veins, what with their father being an old acquaintance of THELONIOUS MONK and the boys themselves being on first name terms with the likes of LEON THOMAS. A couple of name changes and shift towards funky R&B over the latter half of the decade finally saw the group make their vinyl debut on the small 'De-Lite' label in 1969 with the eponymous single, 'KOOL & THE GANG' and subsequent album of the same name. A rigorous live schedule – documented on early 70's sets, 'LIVE AT THE SEX MACHINE' and 'LIVE AT P.J.'s' – honed their skintight, abruptly funky yet fluid approach and with the release of 1973's 'WILD AND PEACEFUL' album, KOOL & THE GANG had written one of the definitive chapters in the book of 70's funk. Characterised by BELL's butt-funking bass, raucous horn blasts and in-yer-face chorus chants, the sound of prime K&tG can still tear up the tamest dancefloor almost 30 years on; if 'JUNGLE BOOGIE' (subsequently given a very welcome 90's resurrection courtesy of 70's connoisseur Quentin Tarantino and his peerless 'Pulp Fiction') was perhaps the best example of their killer formula from a musical point of view, from a party point of view, 'FUNKY STUFF' was downright wild. The former made the US Top 5 in 1974 and established KOOL & THE GANG as pop stars, the Top 10 'HOLLYWOOD SWINGING' cementing their position the same year. Nevertheless, the chart action was shortlived and over the next half-decade, BELL & Co had to make do with success on the US R&B charts, scoring with material from spiritually-inclined (several members had converted to the Muslim faith) albums like 'LIGHT OF WORLDS' (1974) and 'SPIRIT OF THE BOOGIE' (1975). Although the 'OPEN SESAME' single (from the 1976 album of the same name) featured on 1977's seminal 'Saturday Night Fever' soundtrack, KOOL & THE GANG – like many black funk acts who'd reached a musical peak in the early-mid 70's – struggled to find their place as disco became king of New York. Finally, with the addition of balladeer JAMES 'J.T.' TAYLOR (sadly not he of 'Fire & Rain' fame, now that would've been interesting!) and the studio wizardry of fusion-cheesemeister EUMIR DEODATO, the group were commercially and musically reborn with 'LADIES NIGHT' (1979). The title track became their biggest selling US hit of the 70's while the album itself went platinum, spawning a further Top 10 in 'TOO HOT'. The new decade brought even bigger success as the group moved even further into the emasculated sphere of MOR soul-pop with feel-good anthem, 'CELEBRATION', a US chart-topping single that also reached the UK Top 10. The host album, 'CELEBRATE' (1980), was another radio-friendly unit shifter destined for platinum status, as was 'SOMETHING SPECIAL' (1981), which spawned a slew of easy-boogieing dancefloor fodder like 'GET DOWN ON IT'. If fans of their vintage 70's funk heyday had long since tuned out, they certainly weren't given cause to tune back in with cloying, saccharine ballads like 'JOANNA' and 'CHERISH', both massive transatlantic hits from 'IN THE HEART' (1983) and 'EMERGENCY' (1984) respectively. The latter half of the 80's were less kind to the now seriously uncool KOOL & THE GANG, TAYLOR eventually parting company with BELL and Co in 1989. Despite drafting in former DAZZ BAND man, SKIP MARTIN (alongside GARY BROWN and DEAN MAYS) as a replacement, subsequent TAYLOR-less albums, 'SWEAT' (1989) and 'UNITE' (1993) attracted little interest. With the former singer and the band still on good terms, he eventually returned in the mid-90's for the 'STATE OF AFFAIRS' album.

Album rating: KOOL AND THE GANG (*5) / LIVE AT THE SEX MACHINE (*5) / MUSIC IS THE MESSAGE – GOOD TIMES (*5) / WILD AND PEACEFUL (*6) / KOOL JAZZ compilation (*5) / LIGHT OF WORLDS (*6) / GREATEST HITS! compilation (*6) / SPIRIT OF THE BOOGIE (*6) / LOVE & UNDERSTANDING (*5) / OPEN SESAME (*5) / THE FORCE (*5) / SPIN THEIR TOP HITS compilation (*6) / LADIES' NIGHT (*6) / CELEBRATE! (*7) / SOMETHING SPECIAL (*6) / AS ONE (*6) / TWICE AS KOOL compilation (*6) / IN THE HEART (*6) / EMERGENCY (*6) / FOREVER (*5) / EVERYTHING'S KOOL & THE GANG: GREATEST HITS & MORE compilation (*7) / THE SINGLES COLLECTION compilation (**8**) / SWEAT (*4) / UNITE (*4) / THE BEST OF KOOL & THE GANG compilation (*7) / STATE OF AFFAIRS (*4)

ROBERT 'Kool' BELL (b. 8 Oct'50, Youngstown, Ohio) – bass / **RONALD BELL** (b. 1 Nov'51, Youngstown) – saxophone / **GEORGE BROWN** (b. 5 Jan'49) – drums / **ROBERT 'Spike' MICKENS** – trumpet / **DENNIS 'Dee Dee' THOMAS** – saxophones / **RICK WESTFIELD** – keyboards / CLAYDES SMITH – guitar; repl. WOODY SPARROW

London | De-Lite

Aug 69. (7") *<519>* **KOOL AND THE GANG. / RAW HAMBURGERS** [–] [59]

Dec 69. (7") *<523>* **THE GANGS BACK AGAIN. / KOOLS BACK AGAIN** [–] [85]

Jan 70. (lp) *<2003>* **KOOL AND THE GANG** (instrumental) [–] [ ]

Apr 70. (7") *(HLZ 10308)* **KOOL AND THE GANG. / RAW HAMBURGER** [ ] [–]

— now lead members added vocals

Jun 70. (7") *<529>* **LET THE MUSIC TAKE YOUR MIND. / CHOCOLATE BUTTERMILK** [–] [78]

Sep 70. (7") *<534>* **FUNKY MAN. / 1-2-3-4-5-6-7-8** [–] [87]

Feb 71. (lp) *<DE 2008>* **LIVE AT THE SEX MACHINE (live/instrumental)** [–] [ ]
– Medley: What would the world be like without music – Let the music take your mind / Walk on by / Chocolate buttermilk / Trying to make a fool of me / Who's gonna take the weight (part 1 & 2) / Pneumonia / Wichita lineman / I want to take you higher / Funky man / Touch of you. *(UK-iss.Mar72 on 'Mojo'; 2347 003) (re-iss. Mar76 on 'Polydor'; 2343 083) (cd-iss. Nov99; DE 2008)*

Sep 71. (lp) *<DE 2009>* **THE BEST OF KOOL AND THE GANG** (compilation) [–] [ ]
– Kool and the gang / Raw hamburger / The gangs back again / Kools back again / Let the music take your mind / Chocolate buttermilk / Funky man / Kool it (here comes the fuzz) / Give it up / Who's gonna take the weight (parts 1 & 2). *(UK-iss.Dec71 on 'Mojo'; 2347 002)*

Mojo De-Lite

Nov 71. (7"m) *(2027 005)* **FUNKY MAN. / KOOL AND THE GANG / LET THE MUSIC TAKE YOUR MIND** [ ] [–]

Jan 72. (7") *(2027 006)* **LOVE THE LIFE YOU LIVE. / THE PENGUIN** [ ] [–]

Jun 72. (lp) *(2347 001)* *<DE 2010>* **LIVE AT P.J.'S (live/instrumental 29 May'71, Hollywood)** [ ] Dec71 [ ]
– The penguin / Ricksonata / Sombrero Sam / Ronnie's groove / Ike's mood – You've lost that lovin' feeling / Lucky for me / Dujii.

Mar 73. (lp) *(2347 004)* *<DE 2012>* **MUSIC IS THE MESSAGE** <US title 'GOOD TIMES'> [ ] [ ]
– Music is the message / Electric frog (part 1 & 2) / Soul vibrations / Love the life you live (part 1 & 2) / Stop, look and listen (to your heart) / Blowin' with the wind / Funky granny. *<(lp re-iss. Feb00; same)>*

Polydor De-Lite

Nov 73. (7") *(2001 474)* *<557>* **FUNKY STUFF. / MORE FUNKY STUFF** [ ] Aug73 [29]

Jan 74. (lp) *(2310 299)* *<DE 2013>* **WILD AND PEACEFUL** [ ] Oct73 [33]
– Funky stuff / More funky stuff / Jungle boogie / Heaven at once / Hollywood swinging / This is you, this is me / Life is what you make it / Wild and peaceful. *(cd-iss. Sep98 on 'Mercury'; 522082-2)*

Jan 74. (lp) *<DE 4001>* **KOOL JAZZ** (instrumental compilation) [–] [ ]
– I remember John W. Coltrane / Sombrero Sam / Blowin' with the wind / Duji / Lucky for me / North, East, South, West / Breeze & soul / Wild is love / Sea of tranquility.

Apr 74. (7") *(2001 500)* *<559>* **JUNGLE BOOGIE. / NORTH, EAST, SOUTH, WEST** [ ] Nov73 [4]

Jul 74. (7") *(2001 530)* *<561>* **HOLLYWOOD SWINGING. / DUJI** [ ] Apr74 [6]

Sep 74. (7") *(2001 541)* *<1562>* **HIGHER PLANE. / WILD IS LOVE** [ ] Aug74 [37]

Nov 74. (lp) *(2310 357)* *<DE 2014>* **LIGHT OF WORLDS** [ ] Aug74 [63]
– Street corner symphony / Fruitman / Rhyme tyme people / Light of worlds / Whiting H&G / You don't have to change / Higher plane / Summer madness / Here after. *(cd-iss. Sep98 on 'Motown'; 532194-2) (lp re-iss. Feb00; DE 2014)*

Jan 75. (7") *(2001 558)* *<1563>* **RHYME TYME PEOPLE. / FATHER FATHER** [63] Dec74

Mar 75. (7") *<1567>* **SPIRIT OF THE BOOGIE. / SUMMER MADNESS** [–] [35]

Mar 75. (7") *(2001 566)* **SPIRIT OF THE BOOGIE. / JUNGLE JAZZ** [ ] [–]

Oct 75. (7") *<1573>* **CARIBBEAN FESTIVAL. / (disco version)** [–] [55]

— added **OTHA NASH** – trombone + **LARRY GITTENS** – trumpet

Mar 76. (7") *(2058 645)* *<1579>* **LOVE AND UNDERSTANDING (COME TOGETHER). / SUNSHINE AND LOVE** [ ] [77]

May 76. (lp) *(2310 441)* *<DE 2018>* **LOVE & UNDERSTANDING** (some live) [ ] Mar76 [68]
– Love and understanding / Sugar / Do it right now / Cosmic energy / Hollywood swinging / Summer madness / Universal sound / Come together.

Cooltempo De-Lite

Oct 76. (7") *<1586>* **OPEN SESAME (part 1). / (part 2)** [–] [55]

Nov 76. (lp) *<DE 2023>* **OPEN SESAME** [–] [ ]
– Open sesame / Gift of love / Little children / All night long / Whisper softly / Super band / L-O-V-E / Sunshine.

Apr 77. (7"/12") *(CS/12CS 1001)* **SUPER BAND. / OPEN SESAME** [ ] [–]

— **KEVIN LASSITER** – keyboards; repl. RICK (he died in 1986) + GITTENS

Mercury De-Lite

Jan 78. (lp) *(6372 700)* *<9501>* **THE FORCE** [ ] [ ]
– The force / Free / Slick superchick / Place in space / Life's a song / Mighty, mighty high / Just be true.

— added **JAMES "J.T." TAYLOR** (b.16 Aug'53, South Carolina) – vocals / **EARL TOON JR.** – keyboards; repl. LASSITER + NASH

Sep 79. (7") *<801>* **LADIES NIGHT. / IF YOU FEEL LIKE DANCIN'** [–] [8]

Oct 79. (7") *(KOOL 7)* **LADIES NIGHT. / (version)** [9] [–]

Nov 79. (lp) *(6372 763)* *<9513>* **LADIES' NIGHT** [ ] Sep79 [13]
– Ladies night / Got you into my life / If you feel like dancin' / Hangin' out / Tonight's the night / Too hot. *(re-iss. Dec83 lp/c; PRICE/PRIMC 52) (cd-iss. Feb88; 822537-2)*

Jan 80. (7") *(KOOL 8)* *<802>* **TOO HOT. / TONIGHT'S THE NIGHT** [23] [5]

De-Lite De-Lite

Jun 80. (7") *(KOOL 9)* **HANGIN' OUT. / OPEN SESAME (part 1)** [52] [–]

Oct 80. (7"/12") *(KOOL 10/+12)* *<807>* **CELEBRATION. / MORNING STAR** [7] [1]

Dec 80. (lp) *(6359 029)* *<9518>* **CELEBRATE!** [ ] Oct80 [10]
– Celebration / Jones vs Jones / Take it to the top / Morning star / Love festival / Just friends / Night people / Love affair. *(re-iss. Dec83 lp/c; PRICE/PRIMC 53) (cd-iss. Feb88; 822538-2)*

Feb 81. (7") *(KOOL 11)* **JONES VS JONES. / SUMMER MADNESS** [17] [–]
(d7"+=)(12"+=) *(GANG 11)(KOOL 11-12)* – Funky stuff / Hollywood swinging.

May 81. (7") *<813>* **JONES VS JONES. / NIGHT PEOPLE** [–] [39]

May 81. (7") *(DE 2)* **TAKE IT TO THE TOP. / CELECREMOS** [15] [–]

— EARL TOON departed

Oct 81. (7") *<815>* **TAKE MY HEART (YOU CAN HAVE IT IF YOU WANT IT). / JUST FRIENDS** [–] [17]

Oct 81. (7") *(DE 4)* **STEPPIN' OUT. / JUST FRIENDS** [12] [–]

Nov 81. (lp/c) *(DSR/DCR 001)* *<8502>* **SOMETHING SPECIAL** [10] Oct81 [12]
– Steppin' out / Good time tonight / Take my heart / Be my lady / Get down on it / Pass it on / Stand up and sing / No show. *(re-iss. Mar85 on 'Mercury'; PRICE/PRIMC 81) (cd-iss. Feb88; 822534-2)*

Dec 81. (7") *(DE 5)* **GET DOWN ON IT. / SUMMER MADNESS** [3] [–]

Jan 82. (7") *<816>* **STEPPIN' OUT. / LOVE FESTIVAL** [–] [89]

Feb 82. (7") *<818>* **GET DOWN ON IT. / STEPPIN' OUT** [–] [10]

Feb 82. (7") *(DE 6)* **TAKE MY HEART (YOU CAN HAVE IT IF YOU WANT IT). / CARIBBEAN FESTIVAL** [29] [–]

Jul 82. (7") *(DE 7)* **BIG FUN. / GET DOWN ON IT** [14] [–]

Aug 82. (7") *<822>* **BIG FUN. / NO SHOW** [–] [21]

Sep 82. (lp/c) *(DSR/DCR 3)* *<8505>* **AS ONE** [49] [29]
– Street kids / Big fun / As one / Hi de hi, hi de ho / Ooh la la la (Let's go dancin') / Pretty baby / Think it over. *(cd-iss. Feb88; 822535-2)*

Oct 82. (7") *(DE 9)* **OOH LA LA LA (LET'S GO DANCIN'). / STAND UP AND SING** [6] [–]

Oct 82. (7") *<824>* **LET'S GO DANCIN' (OOH LA, LA, LA). / BE MY LADY** [–] [30]

Nov 82. (7") *(DE 14)* **HI DE HI, HI DE HO. / NO SHOW** [29] [–]

May 83. (d-lp/d-c) *(PRO LP/MC 2)* **TWICE AS KOOL** (compilation) [4] [–]
– Ladies night / Big fun / Celebration / Take it to the top / Get down on it / Hi de hi, hi de ho / Funky stuff / Hollywood swinging / Summer madness / Open sesame / Steppin' out / Night people / Street kids / Ooh la la la (let's go dancing) / Jones vs Jones / Too hot / Take my heart (you can have it if you want it) / Hangin' out.

Oct 83. (7") *<829>* **JOANNA. / PLACE FOR US** [–] [2]

Dec 83. (7"/12") *(DE/+X 15)* **STRAIGHT AHEAD. / PLACE FOR US** [15] [–]

Dec 83. (lp/c) *(DSR/DCR 4)* *<8508>* **IN THE HEART** [18] [29]
– In the heart / Joanna / Tonight / Rollin / Place for us / Straight ahead / Home is where the heart is / You can do it / September love. *(re-iss. 1988 on 'Phonogram' lp/c/cd; 814351-1/-4/-2)*

Feb 84. (7") *(DE 16)* **JOANNA. / TONIGHT** [2] [–]
(12"+=) *(DEX 16)* – You can do it.

Feb 84. (7") *<830>* **TONIGHT. / HOME IS WHERE THE HEART IS** [–] [13]

Apr 84. (7"/12") *(DE/+X 17)* **(WHEN YOU SAY YOU LOVE SOMEBODY) IN THE HEART. / SEPTEMBER LOVE** [7] [–]

Nov 84. (7"/12") *(DE/+X 18)* **FRESH. / HOME IS WHERE THE HEART IS** [11] [–]

Dec 84. (lp/c)(cd) *(DSR/DCR 6)<(822943-2)>* **EMERGENCY** [47] [13]
– Emergency / Fresh / Misled / Cherish / Surrender / Bad woman / You are the one.

Feb 85. (7") *(DE 19)* *<880431>* **MISLED. / ROLLIN'** [28] Nov84 [10]
(12"+=) *(DEX 19)* – Ladies night (remix).

Mar 85. (7") *<880623>* **FRESH. / IN THE HEART** [–] [9]

May 85. (7") *(DE 20)* **CHERISH. / CELEBRATION** [4] [–]
(12"+=) *(DEX 20)* – Fresh (U.S. remix).
(d7"+=) *(GANG 20)* – Cherish (instrumental) / Joanna.

Jun 85. (7") *<880869>* **CHERISH. / (instrumental)** [–] [2]

Oct 85. (7") *<884199>* **EMERGENCY. / YOU ARE THE ONE** [–] [18]

Oct 85. (7") *(DE 21)* **EMERGENCY. / OOH LA LA LA (LET'S GO DANCIN') / FRESH** [50] [–]
(12"+=) *(DEX 21)* – Misled / Cherish.
(12"+=) *(DEXR 21)* – ('A'remix).

— **BELL, BELL, TAYLOR, BROWN, SMITH, THOMAS + MICKENS** added **CURTIS WILLIAMS** – keyboards / **CLIFFORD ADAMS** – trombone / **MICHAEL RAY** – trumpet

Club Mercury

Nov 86. (7"/c-s/12"/cd-s) *(JAB/+M/X/D 44)* *<888074>* **VICTORY. / BAD WOMAN** 30 Oct86 10
(12"+=) *(JABXR 44)* – Throwdown mix medley:- Get down on it – Ladies night – Fresh – Big fun – Celebration.

Dec 86. (lp/c)(cd) *(JABH/+C 23)<(830398-2)>* **FOREVER** Nov86 25
– Victory / I.B.M.C. / Stone love / Forever / Holiday / Peace maker / Broadway / Special way / God's country.

Feb 87. (7"/12") *(JAB/+X 47)* *<888292>* **STONE LOVE. / DANCE CHAMPION** 45 Jan87 10
(d7"+=) *(JABXD 47)* – Get down on it (extended) / Ladies night (remix).

Jun 87. (7") *<888712>* **HOLIDAY. / (jam mix)** – 66

Oct 87. (7") *<888867>* **SPECIAL WAY. / GOD'S COUNTRY** – 72

— when TAYLOR went solo he was repl. by **GARY BROWN + SKIP MARTIN** (ex-DAZZ BAND) + **ODEEN MAYS** – vocals

Jul 88. (7") **RAGS TO RICHES. /** –

Aug 88. (lp/c/cd) *<834780>* **EVERYTHING'S KOOL & THE GANG: GREATEST HITS & MORE** (compilation & 3 new) –
– Rags to riches / Strong / Money and power / Stone love / Joanna / Too hot / Fresh (remix) / Jungle boogie (remix) / Hollywood swinging (remix) / Funky stuff (remix) / Open sesame (remix) / Cherish / Celebration.

Dec 88. (7") *(JAB 78)* **CELEBRATION (SAW remix). / RAGS TO RICHES** 56 –
(12"+=/cd-s+=) *(JAB X/CD 78)* – Celebration (original).

Mercury Mercury

Aug 89. (7"/c-s) *(MER/+MC 293)* **RAINDROPS. / AMORE AMORE**
(12"+=/cd-s+=) *(MER X/CD 293)* – ('A'extended) / ('A'dub mix).

Sep 89. (lp/c/cd) *<(838233-1/-4/-2)>* **SWEAT**
– I sweat / This is what love can do / Never give up / You got my heart on fire / Someday / Raindrops / In your company / I'll follow you anywhere / All she wants to do is dance / Now can I get close to you / You are the meaning of friend.

Jun 91. (7") *(MER 346)* **GET DOWN ON IT (remix). /** 69 –
(12"+=/cd-s+=) *(MER X/CD 346)* – ('A'mixes).

Jul 91. (cd/c/lp) *(84860-2/-4/-1)* **GREAT AND REMIXED '91** –
– Ladies night / Get down on it / Celebration / Victory / Tonight / Big fun / Funky stuff / Jungle boogie / The megamix.

— **ODEEN MAYS** was now on lead vocals

JRS-Mogull JRS-Mogull

Oct 92. (7"/12") *(JRS/12JRS 101)* **(JUMP UP ON THE) RHYTHM & RIDE. / (version)** –
(cd-s+=) *(CDJRS 101)* – ('A'version).

Nov 92. (cd) *<(JRSCD 1002)>* **UNITE**
– (Jump up on the) Rhythm & ride / I think I love you / Love comes down / Sexy Miss / Better late than never / Heart / My search is over / Summer / Brown / Give right now / The weight / Show us the way / Unite / God will find you. *(re-iss. Oct93 on 'Charly'; CDUNITE 1) (re-iss. Jan94 as 'N.Y.C. COOL' on 'Magnum'; MDCD 4) (re-iss. Apr95 on 'Star Collection'; ST 5010)*

Charly not iss.

Oct 93. (7") *(UNITE 1)* **UNITE. / (version)** –
(12"+=/cd-s+=) *(12/CD UNITE 1)* – ('A'mixes).

— **JT** returned on vocals (+ was co-credited)

Curb Curb

May 96. (c-s/12"/cd-s) *(CUB C/T/Z 12)* **IN THE HOOD (mixes; Gyp style / Boss 2 / unplugged)**

Jun 96. (cd/c) *<(CUR CD/MC 21)>* **STATE OF AFFAIRS** May96
– Salute to the ladies / In the hood / Color line / Second thoughts / Crabs in a barrel / Woman, lover, friend / Game of love / 90's news / Live in the 90's / Friends / My body / Reunited.

– compilations, etc. –

1978. (lp) *De-Lite; <9507>* **SPIN THEIR TOP HITS** –

1979. (lp) *De-Lite; <9509>* **EVERYBODY'S DANCIN'** –

Nov 82. (lp/c) *De-Lite; (MIP/+4 19318)* **KOOL KUTS** –

Feb 88. (7") *Old Gold; (OG 9766)* **CELEBRATION. / LADIES NIGHT** –

Feb 88. (7") *Old Gold; (OG 9777)* **JOANNA. / CHERISH** –

Oct 88. (lp/c)(cd) *De-Lite; (KGTV/+C 1)(836636-2)* **THE SINGLES COLLECTION** 28 –
– Celebration / Ladies night / Too hot / Get down on it / Joanna / Jones vs Jones / Straight ahead / Fresh / Ooh la la la (let's go dancing) / Big fun / Cherish / In the heart / Hi de hi, hi de ho / Take it to the top / Victory / Steppin' out.

Dec 88. (cd) *Polydor; (810877-2)* **AT THEIR BEST** –

Mar 90. (12") *Old Gold; (OG 4160)* **LADIES NIGHT. / GET DOWN ON IT** –

May 90. (12") *Old Gold; (OG 4167)* **CELEBRATION. /** –

May 90. (lp/c)(cd) *Arcade; (01440-22/-41)(0143561)* **KOOL & THE GANG** –

Aug 90. (cd) *Mercury; (842519-2)* **THE BALLAD COLLECTION** –

Aug 90. (cd) *Mercury; (842520-2)* **THE DANCE COLLECTION** –

Oct 90. (cd/c/lp) *Telstar; (TCD/STAC/STAR 2435)* **KOOL LOVE** 50 –

Nov 91. (cd/c) *Connoisseur; (VSOP CD/MC 168)* **ANTHOLOGY** –

May 92. (cd-s) *Old Gold; (OG 6517)* **GET DOWN ON IT / CELEBRATION / STEPPIN' OUT** –

Jul 92. (cd-s) *Old Gold; (OG 6519)* **LADIES NIGHT / FRESH / BIG FUN** –

Sep 92. (cd/c) *Pickwick; (PWK S/MC 4109P)* **STEPPIN' OUT** –

Jun 93. (cd/c) *Mercury; <(514822-2/-4)>* **THE BEST OF KOOL & THE GANG 1969-1976**
(re-iss. Sep98; 522458-2)

Mar 94. (cd) *Freestyle; (FG 2808)* **GREATEST HITS LIVE** –
(re-iss. Oct96 on 'Milan'; 74321 40063-2) (re-iss. Nov98 on 'Creole'; CP 1013)

Aug 94. (cd/c) *Spectrum; (550198-2/-4)* **NIGHT PEOPLE** –

Nov 94. (cd) *Start; (HP 9347-2)* **IN CONCERT (live)** –

Nov 94. (cd) *Music De-Luxe; (MSCD 7)* **LIVE ON STAGE (live)** –

Oct 95. (cd) *Laserlight; (12607)* **KOOL AND THE GANG** –

Mar 96. (cd/c) *Spectrum; (551635-2/-4)* **THE COLLECTION** –

Jun 96. (cd) *Emporio; (EMPRCD 657)* **TOO HOT – LIVE HITS EXPERIENCE (live)** –

Jul 97. (cd) *Going For a Song; (GFS 067)* **KOOL & THE GANG** –

Aug 98. (cd) *Curb; (CURCD 058)* **ALL THE BEST** –

Jan 00. (cd) *Exceed; (50029-2)* **LIVE** –

Al KOOPER

Born: 5 Feb'44, Brooklyn, New York, USA. After leaving school at 15, he formed his first pro-band, The ROYAL TEENS, for whom he played guitar. They scored a minor US novelty hit with 'SHORT SHORTS', before he became a noted session man for first half of the 60's. He also set up a writing partnership with IRWIN LEVINE and BOBBY BRASS, penning hits for GARY LEWIS & THE PLAYBOYS ('This Diamond Ring'), GENE PITNEY ('I Must Be Seeing Things') and ROCKIN' BERRIES ('Water Is Over My Head'). In 1965, he was asked by producer TOM WILSON to sit in on a BOB DYLAN session, which led him to play organ accompaniment to MIKE BLOOMFIELD's guitar. Their electric sound was noteably highlighted on DYLAN's 'Like A Rolling Stone' from the classic 'Highway 61 Revisited' album. The following year, he stayed for 'Blonde On Blonde', while sessioning for other folk stars TOM RUSH plus PETER, PAUL & MARY. That year (1966) saw him join his first rock band, BLUES PROJECT, with whom he recorded three albums, 'LIVE AT THE CAFE AU GO GO', 'PROJECTIONS' and 'LIVE AT THE TOWN HALL'. His departure in 1967, was due to his formation of R&B brass-laden hitmakers, BLOOD, SWEAT & TEARS, however arguments over direction led him to depart after only one 1968 album, 'CHILD IS FATHER TO THE MAN'. His next project was inspired by MOBY GRAPE's 'Grape Jam' and he decided to do the same on a collaboration with MIKE BLOOMFIELD (ex-ELECTRIC FLAG) and STEVE STILLS (ex-BUFFALO SPRINGFIELD). The subsequent album, 'SUPER SESSION', was a massive hit in the States, resulting in label 'Columbia' asking AL and MIKE to do another. Early in

1969, their live in the studio, self-indulgent double-lp, 'THE LIVE ADVENTURES OF MIKE BLOOMFIELD & AL KOOPER' was complete and this also made US Top 20 lists. Later in the year, KOOPER released his solo debut 'I STAND ALONE' but this failed to emulate predecessors. During these releases, KOOPER had kept up his session work for the likes of JIMI HENDRIX EXPERIENCE ('Electric Ladyland' lp) and The ROLLING STONES ('Let It Bleed' lp). For the next decade KOOPER continued as a solo artist, although session and production work for LYNYRD SKYNYRD, NILS LOFGREN and The TUBES took up most of his time. In the early 70's, he re-united for concerts with past group BLUES PROJECT and set up own label 'Sounds Of The South'. The early 80's saw him complete a new album 'CHAMPIONSHIP WRESTLING', superseding his involvement in ad hoc outfit SWEET MAGNOLIA. In 1991, he came out of semi-retirement in Nashville to produce GREEN ON RED's 'Scapegoats'. Over the last three decades or so, KOOPER has become an accomplished blues musician although his singing voice was questioned by critics of the day. • **Songwriters:** Self-penned some with others. He covered many classics including; PARCHMAN FARM (Mose Allison) / 59th STREET BRIDGE SONG (Simon & Garfunkel) / DEAR MR. FANTASY (Traffic) / GREEN ONIONS (Booker T & The MG's) / BLUE MOON OF KENTUCKY (Bill Monroe) / BABY PLEASE DON'T GO (. . .Williams) / CHANGES (Phil Ochs) / PACK UP YOUR SORROWS (Richard Farina) / etc. • **Trivia:** In the 80's, he also produced EDDIE & THE HOT RODS ('Fish & Chips') / LEO SAYER ('Here') / DAVID ESSEX ('Be-Bop The Future') and an album for JOHNNY VAN ZANDT.

Album rating: (see ELECTRIC FLAG n' MIKE BLOOMFIELD for early stuff) / I STAND ALONE (*5) / YOU NEVER KNOW WHO YOUR FRIENDS ARE (*4) / KOOPER SESSION – WITH SHUGGIE OTIS (*4) / EASY DOES IT (*7) / NEW YORK CITY (YOU'RE A WOMAN) (*5) / A POSSIBLE PROJECTION OF THE FUTURE – CHILDHOOD'S END (*3) / NAKED SONGS (*4) / AL'S BIG DEAL (UNCLAIMED FREIGHT) compilation (*7) / ACT LIKE NOTHING'S WRONG (*4) / CHAMPIONSHIP WRESTLING (*3) / REKOOPERATION collection (*5) / SOUL OF A MAN: LIVE (*6) / YOU NEVER KNOW WHO (*4)

AL KOOPER – vocals, keyboards, guitar (with sessioners)

Mercury | Verve Folkways

Nov 65. (7"; as ALAN KOOPER) *(MF 885)* **PARCHMAN FARM. / YOU'RE THE LOVING END** [ ] [–]

—— became a session man for BOB DYLAN, etc.

1967. (7") *<5026>* **CHANGES. / PACK UP YOUR SORROWS** [–] [ ]

—— Joined The BLUES PROJECT then BLOOD, SWEAT & TEARS before returning solo. Also see under ELECTRIC FLAG (albums with MIKE BLOOMFIELD)

C.B.S. | Columbia

Mar 69. (lp) *(63596)* *<CS 9718>* **I STAND ALONE** [ ] Feb69 [54]
– Overture / I stand alone / Camille / One / Coloured rain / Soft landing on the Moon / I can love a woman / Blue Moon of Kentucky / Toe hold / Right now for you / Hey, Western Union man / Song and dance for the unborn, frightened child.

Apr 69. (7") *(4011)* *<44748>* **YOU NEVER KNOW WHO YOUR FRIENDS ARE. / SOFT LANDING ON THE MOON** [ ] Dec68 [ ]

Jul 69. (7") *(4160)* *<44811>* **HEY, WESTERN UNION MAN. / I STAND ALONE** [ ] [ ]

1969. (lp) *(63651)* *<CS 9855>* **YOU NEVER KNOW WHO YOUR FRIENDS ARE** [ ] Oct69 [ ]
– Magic in my socks / Lucille / Too busy thinking about my baby / First time around / Loretta (Union turnpike eulogy) / Blues part IV / You never know who your friends are / The great American marriage – Nothing / I don't know why I love you / Mourning glory story / Anna Lee (what can I do for you) / Never gonna let you down.

—— next with SHUGGIE OTIS – guitar / STU WOODS – bass / WELLS KELLY – drums

1970. (lp) *(63697)* *<CS 9951>* **KOOPER SESSION – WITH SHUGGIE OTIS** [ ] Jan70 [ ]
– Bury my body / Double or nothing / One room country shack / Lookin' for a home / The blues:- 12:15 Slow goonbash blues – Shuggie's old time dee-di-lee-di-leet-deet slide boogie – Shuggie's shuffle.

1970. (7") *<45093>* **BURY MY BODY. / ONE ROOM COUNTRY SHACK** [–] [ ]

—— Reverted to numerous session people

1970. (d-lp) *(66252)* *<G 30031>* **EASY DOES IT** [ ] Sep70 [ ]
– Brand new day (main theme from 'The Landlord') / I got a woman / Country road / I bought you the shoes (you're walking away with it) / Easy does it / Buckskin boy / Love theme from 'The Landlord' / Sad, sad sunshine / Let the Duchess know / She gets me where I live / A rose and a baby Ruth / Baby please don't go / God sheds his grace on thee.

1970. (7") *<45148>* **GOD SHEDS HIS GRACE ON THEE. / SHE GETS ME WHERE I LIVE** [–] [ ]

Mar 71. (7") *(5146)* *<45179>* **BRAND NEW DAY. / LOVE THEME FROM THE LANDLORD** [ ] [ ]

1971. (7") *<45243>* **I GOT A WOMAN. / EASY DOES IT** [–] [ ]

—— a few of above tracks appeared on 1971 'United Artists' UK film soundtrack of 'THE LANDLORD' (UAS 29120), which also featured The STAPLE SINGERS and LORRAINE ELLISON.

Jul 71. (lp) *(64340)* *<C 30506>* **NEW YORK CITY (YOU'RE A WOMAN)** [ ] Jun71 [ ]
– New York City (you're a woman) / John The Baptist (Holy John) / Can you hear it now (500 miles) / The ballad of the hard rock kid / Going quietly mad / Medley: Oo wee baby, I love you- Love is a man's friend / Back on my feet / Come down in time / Dearest darling / Nightmare No.5 / The warning (someone's on the cross again).

Jul 71. (7") *(7376)* *<45412>* **JOHN THE BAPTIST. / BACK ON MY FEET** [ ] [ ]

1972. (7") *<45566>* **THE MONKEY TIME. / BENDED KNEES (PLEASE DON'T LEAVE ME NOW)** [–] [ ]

Jul 72. (lp) *(64208)* *<KC 31159>* **A POSSIBLE PROJECTION OF THE FUTURE / CHILDHOOD'S END** [ ] Apr72 [ ]
– Bended knees (please don't leave me now) / Possible projection of the future / Childhood's end / The man in me / Please tell me why / Love trap / The monkey time / Let your love shine / Swept for you baby.

1972. (7") *<45691>* **SAM STONE. / BE REAL** [–] [ ]

1973. (lp) *(65193)* *<KC 31793>* **NAKED SONGS** [ ] [ ]
– Be real / As the tears go passing by / Jolie / Blend baby / Been and gone / Sam Stone / Peacock lady / Touch the hem of his garment / Where were you when I needed you / Unrequited.

1973. (7") *<45735>* **JOLIE. / BE REAL** [–] [ ]

1975. (d-lp) *(88093)* *<KG 33169>* **AL'S BIG DEAL (UNCLAIMED FREIGHT)** (compilation) [ ] [ ]
– I can't quit her / I love you more than you'll ever know / My days are numbered / Without her / So much love – Underture / Albert's shuffle / Season of the witch / If dogs run free / The 59th Street Bridge song (fellin' groovy) / The weight / Bury my body / Jolie / I stand alone / Brand new day / Sam Stone / New York City (you're a woman) / I got a woman.

U.A. | U.A.

Dec 76. (7") *<879>* **HOLLYWOOD VAMPIRE. / THIS DIAMOND RING** [–] [ ]

Jan 77. (lp) *(UAG 30020)* *<LA 702-G>* **ACT LIKE NOTHING'S WRONG** [ ] Dec76 [ ]
– Is we on the downbeat? / This diamond ring / She don't ever lose her groove / I forgot to be your lover / Missing you / Out of left field / (Please not) One more time / In my own sweet way / Turn my head towards home / A visit to the Rainbow bar & grill / Hollywood vampire.

C.B.S. | Columbia

1982. (7"; with VALERIE CARTER) *<38-03312>* **TWO SIDES (TO EVERY SITUATION). / SNOWBLIND** [–] [ ]

1982. (lp) *<KC 38137>* **CHAMPIONSHIP WRESTLING** [–] [ ]
– I wish you would / Two sides / Wrestless with this / Lost control / I'd rather be an old man's sweetheart / The heart is a lonely hunter / Bandstand / Finders keepers / Snowblind.

—— returned to production work before . . .

Limelight | Limelight

Jun 94. (cd) *(844 400-2)* **REKOOPERATION** [ ] [ ]
– Downtime / After the lights go down low / When the spell is broken / How am I ever gonna get over you / Sneakin' round the barnyard / Soul twist-ed / Looking for clues / Honky tonk / Clean up woman / Don't be cruel / Alvino Johnson's shuffle / Johnny B Goode / I wanna little girl.

—— next featured backing by The BLUES PROJECT, The REKOOPERATORS + BLOOD, SWEAT & TEARS

Music Masters / Music Masters

Jan 97. (d-cd) *<(MM 65113)>* **SOUL OF A MAN: LIVE (live February 1994)** [ ] 1995 [ ]
– Somethin' goin' on / Can't keep from cryin' sometimes / I stand alone medley / Flute thing / Don't tell (repo man) / Two trains running / Heartbeat / Sleepwalk / Just one smile // I can't quit her / I want a little girl / My days are numbered / I love you more than you'll ever know / (spoken intro) / Made in the shade / Downtime / Violets of dawn / Albert's shuffle / Closing medley: You can't always get what you want – Seasons of the witch – Al's witch hunt.

– compilations, etc. –

Jan 02. (d-cd) *Sony Jazz; (504721-2) <62153>* **RARE AND WELL DONE** [ ] Sep01 [ ]
Apr 03. (cd; with MIKE BLOOMFIELD) *Legacy; <(506034-2)>* **FILLMORE EAST: THE LOST CONCERT TAPES 12/13/68 (live)** [ ] Mar03 [ ]

KORN

Formed: Bakersfield / Huntington Beach, California, USA . . . 1993 out of CREEP, by JONATHAN DAVIS, J MUNKY SHAFFER, BRIAN 'HEAD' WELCH, FIELDY and DAVID. Signed to 'Epic' the following year, they unleashed to the public their eponymous US Top 75 debut. A barrage of aural psychosis, DAVIS' tortured performance more than lived up to the hype surrounding the record's release. Among its schizophrenic highs and lows were the disturbing but cathartic ten minute (+) emotional minefield, 'DADDY', which cried out from the core of DAVIS' very soul. Bizarrely, DAVIS turned his hand (and elbow) to the bagpipes on the nursery rhyme parody, 'SHOOTS AND LADDERS', a track that even GAVIN FRIDAY might have disowned in his VIRGIN PRUNES heyday! Consolidating this seminal meisterwork, KORN toured the world, resurfacing in 1996 with another primal scream of sinuous, bass-heavy angst-metal in the shape of 'LIFE IS PEACHY'. The album contained no less than three UK Top 30 hits, 'NO PLACE TO HIDE', 'A.D.I.D.A.S.' (which stands for "All Day I Dream About Sex"; nothing to do with the sports company) and 'GOOD GOD', the set also featuring covers of Oshea Jackson's 'WICKED' and War's 'LOWRIDER'. A US Top 3, the record also cracked the UK Top 40, due largely to the strong Kerrang! support only rivalled in 1997 by DAVIS's more attention-seeking contemporary, MARILYN MANSON. Two further chart-topping albums, 'FOLLOW THE LEADER' (1998) and the concept 'ISSUES' (1999), didn't sell quite so well in Britain, the grim storytelling of KORN's leader beginning to get short shrift from some of his gloomy disciples. While DAVIS' lyrical agenda continued in this brooding, navel-gazing vein for 'UNTOUCHABLES' (2002), KORN continued to forge a distinctively dense mesh of sound which further distanced them from the incestuous nu-metal scene, almost completely paring back the rap pretensions for an altogether more intimidating sound. 'TAKE A LOOK IN THE MIRROR' (2003), meanwhile, trimmed off any sonic excess they'd been accumulating over the years with an album which concentrated the essence of their root sound while still taking them a tad forward. • **Covered:** EARACHE MY EYE (Cheech & Chong) / SHOULD I STAY OR SHOULD I GO (Clash) / ONE (Metallica).

Album rating: KORN (*9) / LIFE IS PEACHY (*8) / FOLLOW THE LEADER (*5) / ISSUES (*6) / UNTOUCHABLES (*5) / TAKE A LOOK IN THE MIRROR (*4)

JONATHAN DAVIS – vocals, bagpipes / **J MUNKY SHAFFER** (b. JAMES) – guitar, vocals / **BRIAN 'HEAD' WELCH** – guitar, vocals / **FIELDY** – bass, vocals / **DAVID** – drums, vocals

Epic / Immortal

Jul 95. (cd/c) *(478080-2/-4) <66633>* **KORN** [ ] Nov94 [72]
– Blind / Ball tongue / Need to / Clown / Divine / Faget / Shoots and ladders / Predictable / Fake / Lies / Helmet in the bush / Daddy.
Oct 95. (10"ep) *(KORN 1)* **BLIND** [ ] [ ]
Oct 96. (7"white) *(663845-0)* **NO PLACE TO HIDE. / PROUD** [26] [ ]
(cd-s+=) *(663845-2)* – Sean Olsen.
(cd-s) *(663845-5)* – ('A'side) / Shoots and ladders (Dust Brothers industrial mix) / Shoots and ladders (Dust Brothers hip-hop mix).
Oct 96. (cd/c/lp/cd-rom) *(485369-2/-4/-1/-6) <67554>* **LIFE IS PEACHY** [32] [3]
– Twist / Chi / Lost / Swallow / Porno creep / Good God / Mr. Rogers / K"£o%! / No place to hide / Wicked / A.D.I.D.A.S. / Lowrider / Ass itch / Kill you.
Feb 97. (10"white-ep) *(664204-0)* **A.D.I.D.A.S. / CHI (live). / LOWRIDER – SHOOTS AND LADDERS (live)** [22] [ ]
(cd-ep+=) *(664204-2)* – Ball tongue (live).
(cd-ep) *(664204-5)* – ('A'side) / Faget / Porno creep / Blind.
Jun 97. (cd-ep) *(664658-2)* **GOOD GOD / GOOD GOD (Mekon mix) / GOOD GOD (Dub Pistols mix) / WICKED (Tear The Roof Off mix)** [25] [ ]
(cd-ep) *(664658-5)* – ('A'side) / A.D.I.D.A.S. (Synchro dub) / A.D.I.D.A.S. (Under Pressure mix) / A.D.I.D.A.S. (The Wet Dream mix).
(12"ep) *(664658-6)* – ('A'-Mekon mix) / ('A'-Dub Pistols mix) / A.D.I.D.A.S. (Synchro dub) / A.D.I.D.A.S. (Under Pressure mix).
Aug 98. (ltd-cd-s) *(666391-2)* **GOT THE LIFE / (12"mixes by DeeJay Punk-Roc and D.O.S.E.)** [23] [ ]
(cd-s) *(666391-5)* – ('A'side) / I can remember / Good god (oomph! vs such a surge mix).
Aug 98. (cd/c/lp) *(491221-2/-4/-1) <69001>* **FOLLOW THE LEADER** [5] [1]
– It's on / Freak on a leash / Got the life / Dead bodies eveywhere / Children of the korn / B.B.K. / Pretty / All in the family / Reclaim my place / Justin / Seed / Cameltosis / My gift to you.
Apr 99. (cd-s) *(667252-2)* **FREAK ON A LEASH / FREAK ON A LEASH (Dante Ross mix) / FREAK ON A LEASH (Josh A's beast on a leash mix)** [24] [ ]
(cd-s) *(667252-5)* – ('A'-Freakin' bitch mix) / ('A'-Josh A's beast on a leash mix) / ('A'-Dante Ross mix).
(12") *(667252-6)* – ('A'mixes; above).
Nov 99. (cd/c/lp) *(496359-2/-4/-1) <63710>* **ISSUES** [37] [1]
– Dead / Falling away from me / Trash / 4U / Beg for me / Make me bad / It's gonna go away / Wake up / Am I going crazy / Hey daddy / Somebody someone / No way / Let's get this party started / Wish you could be me / Counting / Dirty. *(re-iss. Apr00 cd/cd/cd; 497850-2/-6/-9)*
Jan 00. (7"orange) *(668869-7)* **FALLING AWAY FROM ME. / JINGLE BALLS** [24] [ ]
(cd-s+=) *(668869-2)* – ('A'-Krust remix) / ('A'-CD-Rom).
(cd-s) *(668869-5)* – ('A'side) / ('A'-Mantronik Beatdown formula) / Got the life (Josh Abraham remix).
May 00. (7") *(669433-7)* **MAKE ME BAD. / DIRTY (live)** [25] [ ]
(cd-s+=) *(669433-2)* – ('A'-live).
(cd-s) *(669433-5)* – ('A'side) / ('A'mixes; Kornography / Sickness In Salvation / Sybil / Danny Saber).
May 02. (cd-s) *(672742-2) <radio>* **HERE TO STAY / (T-Ray's mix) / (T-Ray's instrumental) / (video)** [12] Jun02 [72]
(cd-s) *(672742-5)* – ('A'side) / (T-Ray's mix) / (BT's managed anger mix).
Jun 02. (cd/d-lp) *(501770-2/-1) <61488>* **UNTOUCHABLES** [4] [2]
– Here to stay / Make believe / Blame / Hollow life / Bottled up inside / Thoughtless / Hating / One more time / Alone I break / Embrace / Beat it upright / Wake up hate / I'm hiding / No one's there. *(ltd-cd+=; 501770-2)* – Here to stay (T-Ray's mix) / Here to stay (video).
Sep 02. (cd-s) *(673157-2)* **THOUGHTLESS / (DJ Cooley remix) / (Dante Ross remix) / (video)** [37] [–]
(cd-s) *(673157-5)* – ('A'side) / Here to stay (mindless self indulgence mix) / Here to stay (Tone Toven & sleep remix).
Aug 03. (cd-s) *(674142-2)* **DID MY TIME / (greyedout mix) / ONE (live from MTV ICON: Metallica)** [15] [–]
Nov 03. (cd) *(513325-2) <90335>* **TAKE A LOOK IN THE MIRROR** [53] [9]
– Right now / Break some off / Counting on me / Here it comes again / Deep inside / Did my time / Everything I've known / Play me (with NAS) / Alive / Let's do this now / I'm done / Y'all want a single / When will this end. *(cd w/dvd+=; 513325-3)* – One (live) / Korn kut up / Right now (mirror mix video) / (Untouchables 2002 tour documentary).

KRAFTWERK

Formed: Dusseldorf, Germany . . . 1969 as ORGANISATION by RALF HUTTER, FLORIAN SCHNEIDER-ESLEBEN and three others, namely BUTCH HAUF, FRED MONICKS and BASIL HAMMOND. After one CONRAD PLANK-produced album, 'TONE FLOAT', for 'R.C.A.' in 1970, the pair broke away to form KRAFTWERK (German for POWERPLANT), with KLAUS DINGER and THOMAS HOMANN. After one album for 'Philips', RALF & FLORIAN became KRAFTWERK, releasing the 1973 album (titled after their Christian names) for 'Vertigo' in the process. In 1974, they added KLAUS ROEDER & WOLFGANG FLUR, issuing their magnus-opus 'AUTOBAHN'. This UK & US Top 5 album contained a 22-minute title track, which, edited into 3 minutes, also became a hit. The next album, 'RADIO ACTIVITY' (which was also issued on their own 'Kling Klang' label in Germany), disappointed most and failed to secure a Top 50 placing. In 1978, they were back in the UK Top 10 at least, with an excellent return to form, 'THE MAN MACHINE'. In the early 80's, they enjoyed another hit album, 'COMPUTER WORLD', and a run of UK hit singles, one of which, 'THE MODEL' (from 1978 lp) made the top spot. A projected album by the name of 'TECHNOPOP', was pencilled in for release in 1983 and allegedly 'E.M.I.' were even supplied with artwork. The record never appeared, and of course, given KRAFTWERK's reclusive reticence, no explanation was offered. The same year, however, the band did release a one-off 12" single, 'TOUR DE FRANCE', no doubt inspired by HUTTER's preoccupation with cycling. It was to be another three years before the band released a full album, the disappointing 'ELECTRIC CAFE'. By this point the band were starting to tread water, an assumption that seemed to be confirmed when fans had to wait another five years for 'new' material. 'THE MIX', released in 1991, was actually an album of reworkings of old tracks, a bit of a hit and miss affair which failed to deliver any original pieces per se. Both BARTOS and FLUR had left the band before the album's release, allegedly sick of the laboriously slow and detailed recording process and the band's reclusive inertia. Despite a reputation for a disciplined working ethos, the band remain defiantly distant from the music industry. Their studio apparently possesses neither fax nor phone, they've no management and they've turned down all offers of remix work and collaborations. Whether they can remain on the cutting edge in such a vacuum remains to be seen and for the moment, their Guru-like status is based on past glories, sounds that continue to permeate almost all strands of pop culture, now more than ever. It's testament to their towering influence that despite releasing no new material for more than a decade, they headlined the Tribal Gathering dance festival in the late 90's. This robotic electronic rock act with minimalist synth-tunes, being at times (on stage!) twiddled by dummies, were more inspirational than their contemporaries TANGERINE DREAM. KRAFTWERK became a major influence for ULTRAVOX!, GARY NUMAN, DAVID BOWIE '77, JEAN-MICHEL JARRE, SIMPLE MINDS, OMD, etc. Back on the musical autobahn for the new millennium, KRAFTWERK released a single, 'EXPO 2000'. Their first album in two decades, incredible but true, followed in summer 2003. 'TOUR DE FRANCE SOUNDTRACKS', as its title might suggest, was inspired by the band's love of cycling. Preceded by an update of the track they originally released in 1983, the album was quintessential KRAFTWERK, as disciplined and precision-crafted as the race itself. • **Songwriters:** RALF & FLORIAN. • **Trivia:** They have been sampled by many, including AFRIKA BAMBAATAA on his single, 'Planet Rock'.

Album rating: Organisation: TONE FLOAT (*4) / Kraftwerk: KRAFTWERK (HIGHRAIL) (*4) / KRAFTWERK 2 (VAR) (*4) / RALF AND FLORIAN (*5) / AUTOBAHN (*8) / RADIOACTIVITY (*4) / TRANS-EUROPE EXPRESS (*8) / THE MAN MACHINE (*8) / COMPUTER WORLD (*7) / ELECTRIC CAFE (*4) / THE MIX remixes (*5) / TOUR DE FRANCE SOUNDTRACKS (*6)

ORGANISATION

RALF HUTTER (b.1946, Krefeld, Germany) – electric organ, strings / **FLORIAN SCHNEIDER-ESLEBEN** (b.1947, Dusseldorf)– flute, echo unit, strings / **BUTCH HAUF** – bass, percussion / **FRED MONICKS** – drums / **BASIL HAMMOND** – percussion, vocals

R.C.A. | not iss.

Aug 70. (lp) *(SF 8111)* **TONE FLOAT** [ ] [–]
– Tone float / Milk float / Silver forest / Rhythm salad / Noitasinagro.

KRAFTWERK

HUTTER + SCHNEIDER with **KLAUS DINGER** – guitar, keyboards / **THOMAS HOMANN** – percussion

Philips | not iss.

1971. (lp) *(6305 058)* **KRAFTWERK** [–] German [–]
– Ruckzuck / Stratowargius / Megaherz / Vom Himmel hoch.

— **HUTTER + SCHNEIDER** trimmed to a duo. (DINGER and HOMANN formed NEU!)

1972. (lp) *(6305 117)* **KRAFTWERK 2** [–] German [–]
– Klingklang / Atem / Strom / Spule 4 / Wellenlange / Harmonika.

Vertigo | Vertigo

Nov 72. (d-lp) *(6641 077)* **KRAFTWERK** (2 German lp's combined) [ ] [–]
Nov 73. (lp) *(6360 616)* **RALF & FLORIAN** [ ] [–]
– Elektrisches roulette (Electric roulette) / Tongebirge (Mountain of sound) / Kristallo (Crystals) / Heimatklange (The bells of home) / Tanzmusik (Dance music) / Ananas symphonie (Pineapple symphony). *<US-iss.Sep75; 2006>*

— added **KLAUS ROEDER** – violin, guitar / **WOLFGANG FLUR** – percussion

Nov 74. (lp/c) *(6360/ 620) <2003>* **AUTOBAHN** [4] [5]
– Autobahn / Kometenmelodie 1 & 2 (Comet melody) / Mitternacht (Midnight) / Morgenspaziergang (Morning walk). *(re-iss. Mar82 on 'E.M.I.' lp/c; EMC/TC-EMC 3405); hit 61 UK) (re-iss. Jun85 on 'Parlophone' lp/c; AUTO/TCAUTO 1) (cd-iss. Jun87 & Aug95 on 'E.M.I.'; CDP 746153-2)*
Feb 75. (7") *(6147 012)* **AUTOBAHN. / KOMETENMELODIE** [11] [–]
Feb 75. (7") *<203>* **AUTOBAHN. / MORGENSPAZIERGANG** [–] [25]
Jul 75. (7") *(6147 015)* **KOMETENMELODIE 2. / KRISTALLO** [ ] [–]
Jul 75. (7") *<204>* **KOMETENMELODIE 2. / MITTERNACHT** [–] [ ]

— In Oct'75, **KARL BARTOS** – percussion repl. ROEDER

Capitol | Capitol

Nov 75. (lp/c) *(<EST/TC-EST 11457>)* **RADIO-ACTIVITY** [ ] [ ]
– Geiger counter / Radio-activity / Radioland / Airwaves / (intermission) / News / The voice of energy / Antenna / Radio stars / Uran / Transistor / Ohm sweet ohm. *(re-iss. Jun84 on 'Fame' lp/c; FA 413103-1/-4) (re-iss. 1985 on 'E.M.I.' lp/c; EMS/TC-EMS 1256) (cd-iss. May87 on 'E.M.I.'; CDP 746474-2) (re-iss. Aug87 on 'E.M.I.' lp/c; ATAK/TCATAK 104) (re-iss. cd Apr94 on 'Cleopatra';) (re-iss. cd Apr95 on 'E.M.I.';)*
Feb 76. (7") *(CL 15853) <4211>* **RADIO-ACTIVITY. / ANTENNA** [ ] [ ]
Apr 77. (lp/c) *(<EST/TC-EST 11603>)* **TRANS-EUROPE EXPRESS** [ ] [ ]
– Europe endless / The hall of mirrors / Showroom dummies / Trans-Europe express / Metal on metal / Franz Schubert / Endless endless. *(in Feb82, they hit UK No.49 Feb82) (re-iss. 1985 on 'E.M.I.' lp/c; ATAK/TCATAK 5) (re-iss. Jun86 on 'Fame' lp/c; FA 413151-1/-4) (cd-iss. May87 on 'E.M.I.'; CDP 746473-2) (re-iss. cd Apr94 on 'Cleopatra';)*
Apr 77. (7") *(CL 15917)* **TRANS-EUROPE EXPRESS. / EUROPE ENDLESS** [ ] [–]
Aug 77. (7") *(CLX 104)* **SHOWROOM DUMMIES. / EUROPE EXPRESS** [ ] [ ]
May 78. (7") *<4460>* **TRANS-EUROPE EXPRESS. / FRANZ SCHUBERT** [–] [67]
May 78. (lp/c) *(<EST/TC-EST 11728>)* **THE MAN MACHINE** [9] [ ]
– The robots / Spacelab / Metropolis / The model / Neon lights / The man

machine. *(re-iss. Mar85 on 'Fame' lp/c; 413118-1/-4) (re-iss. Jul88 on 'Fame' cd/c/lp; CD/TC+/FA 3118) (re-iss. cd Apr94 on 'Cleopatra'; CLEO 5877CD) (re-iss. cd/c Apr95 on 'E.M.I.'; CD/TC EMS 1520) (cd re-iss. Jun97 on 'E.M.I.'; CDCNTAV 4)*

May 78. (7") *(CL 15981)* **THE ROBOTS (edit). / SPACELAB** [ ] [ ]
Jun 78. (7") *<4620>* **NEON LIGHTS. / THE ROBOTS** [-] [ ]
Sep 78. (7"/12"luminous) *(CL/12CL 15998)* **NEON LIGHTS. / TRANS-EUROPE EXPRESS / THE MODEL** [53] [ ]
Nov 78. (12"m) *(CL 16098)* **SHOWROOM DUMMIES. / EUROPE ENDLESS / SPACELAB** [ ] [-]

E.M.I. Warners

Apr 81. (7") *(EMI 5175) <49723>* **POCKET CALCULATOR. / DENTAKU** [39] [ ]
(12"+=) *(12EMI 5175)* – Numbers.
(c-s) *(TCEMI 5175)* – ('A'extended) / ('A'side) / Numbers.
May 81. (lp/c) *(EMC/TC-EMC 3370) <3549>* **COMPUTER WORLD** [15] [72]
– Pocket calculator / Numbers / Computer-world / Computer love / Home computer / It's more fun to compute. *(re-iss. Apr95 cd/c; CD/TC EMS 1547)*
Jun 81. (7"/12") *(EMI/12EMI 5207)* **COMPUTER LOVE. / THE MODEL** [36] [-]
(Dec81; flipped over, hit UK No.1) (re-iss. May84; G45 16)
Jun 81. (7") *<49795>* **COMPUTER LOVE. / NUMBERS** [-] [ ]
Feb 82. (7") *(EMI 5272)* **SHOWROOM DUMMIES. / NUMBERS** [25] [-]
(12"+=) *(12EMI 5272)* – Pocket calculator.

—— (In May'83, they had album 'TECHNO POP' cancelled)

Jul 83. (7") *(EMI 5413) <29342>* **TOUR DE FRANCE. / TOUR DE FRANCE (instrumental)** [22] [ ]
(c-s+=/12"+=) *(TC/12 EMI 5413)* – ('A'version).
Aug 84. (7") *(EMI 5413)* **TOUR DE FRANCE (remix). / TOUR DE FRANCE** [24] [-]
(12"+=) *(12EMI 5413)* – ('A'instrumental).
Oct 86. (7"/ext.12") *(EMI/12EMI 5588)* **MUSIQUE NON-STOP. / MUSIQUE NON STOP (version)** [ ] [ ]
Nov 86. (lp/c)(cd) *(EMD/TC-EMD 3370)(CDP 746416-2) <25525>* **ELECTRIC CAFE** [58] [ ]
– Boom boom tschak / Techno pop / Musique non stop / The telephone call / Sex object / Techno pop / Electric cafe. *(cd re-iss. Aug95; CDEMS 1546)*
Feb 87. (7") *(EMI 5602) <28441>* **THE TELEPHONE CALL. / DER TELEFON ANRUF** [ ] [ ]
(12"+=) *(12EMI 5602)* – House phone.

—— **FRITZ HIJBERT** repl. WOLFGANG FLUR

May 91. (c-s/7") *(TC+/EM 192)* **THE ROBOTS (re-recorded). / ROBOTRONIK** [20] [ ]
(12"+=) *(12EM 192)* – ('A'album version).
(cd-s+=) *(CDEM 192)* – Robotnik.
Jun 91. (cd/c/d-lp) *(CD/TC+/EM 1408)* **THE MIX** ('91 remixes) [15] [ ]
– The robots / Computer love / Pocket calculator / Dentaku / Autobahn / Radioactivity / Trans-Europe express / Abzug / Metal on metal / Homecomputer / Musique non-stop. *(cd re-iss. Aug95; CDEM 1408)*
Oct 91. (c-s/7") *(TC+/EM 201)* **RADIOACTIVITY (Francois Kevorkian remix). / ('A'-William Orbit mix)** [43] [ ]
(12"+=/cd-s+=) *(12/CD EM 201)* – ('A'extended).

—— In Jul'91, BARTOS and FLUR formed their own project, ELEKTRIC

Oct 99. (12"/cd-s) *(887421-0/-6)* **TOUR DE FRANCE (mixes)** [61] [-]
Dec 99. (12"/cd-s) *(EXPO 1/+CD)* **EXPO 2000 (mixes)** [ ] [-]
(above issued on German 'Kling Klang')

E.M.I. Astralwerks

Mar 00. (12"/cd-s) *(12EM/CDEM 562)* **EXPO 2000 (mixes)** [27] [-]
Nov 00. (2x12"/m-cd) *(EMP/CDEM 583) <38768>* **EXPO REMIX** [ ] Oct01 [ ]
– (remixes: Orbital / Francois K & Rob Rives / DJ Rolando / Underground resistance / UR infiltrated / UR thought 3).
Jul 03. (2x12") *(552689-6) <52989>* **TOUR DE FRANCE 2003** [20] [ ]
– (version 1 / version 2 / version 3 / long distance version).
Aug 03. (cd)(d-lp) *(cd/d-lp) <91708> (CDEM 591710-2)(591 708-1)* **TOUR DE FRANCE SOUNDTRACKS** [21] [ ]
– Prologue / Tour de France etape 1 / Tour de France etape 2 (continued) / Tour de FRance etape 3 (continued) / Chrono / Vitamin / Aero dynamik / Titanium / Elektro kardiogramm / La forme / Regeneration / Tour de FRance.

– compilations, others, etc. –

on 'Vertigo' unless mentioned otherwise

Oct 75. (lp) *(6360 629)* **EXCELLER 8** [ ] [-]
Oct 80. (7") *(CUT 108)* **AUTOBAHN. / (b-side by BEGGAR'S OPERA)** [ ] [-]
Apr 81. (lp) *(6449 066)* **ELEKTRO KINETIC** [ ] [-]
May 81. (7") *(VER 3)* **KOMETENMELODIE 2. / VON HIMMEL HOCH** [ ] [-]

—— <In the US compilation lp 'THE ROBOTS' on 'Capitol'; 9445>

Apr 94. (cd) *Cleopatra; (CLEO 6843CD)* **SHOWROOM DUMMIES** [ ] [-]
(re-iss. May97; same)
Apr 94. (cd) *Cleopatra; (CLEO 5761-2)* **THE MODEL (The Best Of Kraftwerk 1975-1978)** [ ] [-]
Mar 97. (12") *Discopromo; (D 762)* **NUMBERS** [ ] [-]
Mar 97. (12") *Discopromo; (D 801)* **TOUR DE FRANCE** [ ] [-]
May 97. (d-cd) *Cleopatra; (CLEO 9416-2)* **THE CAPITOL YEARS** [ ] [-]

☐ Wayne KRAMER (see under ⇒ MC5)

Lenny KRAVITZ

Born: 26 May'64, New York City, New York, USA, son of a Russian Jew and black Bahamas-born actress. As a teenager, he moved with his family to Los Angeles, where he joined the local boys' choir and taught himself to play guitar and piano. In 1987, KRAVITZ formed his own one-man band, ROMEO BLUE, marrying girlfriend of two years, 'Cosby Show' actress Lisa Bonet. Over the course of the ensuing two years, he recorded demos which were soon heard by Henry Hirsch, who recommended them to 'Virgin'. In October '89, after many arguments with the record company over production techniques, etc., KRAVITZ finally released a debut album and single, 'LET LOVE RULE'. A back to basics operation of luddite proportions, the record slavishly imitated KRAVITZ's paisley-shirted heroes of yesteryear (HENDRIX, CURTIS MAYFIELD, DYLAN) in much the same fashion as The BLACK CROWES paid homage to The FACES and The ALLMAN BROTHERS. Yet, despite charges of plagiarism from critics, much like The 'CROWES debut, 'LET LOVE RULE' was consistently listenable. Unsurprisingly then, the album subsequently notched up sales of half a million copies in the US, eventually reaching Top 60 in the UK. In 1990, the title track became KRAVITZ's first Top 40 success in Britain, tempting MADONNA into requesting his writing skills (along with INGRID CHAVEZ) for her controversial 'Justify My Love' single. Quite a celebrity in his own right, KRAVITZ played up the part of Hollywood socialite to the max, immaculately decked out in nouveau-retro clobber (a la PRINCE) and de rigueur dreadlocks. Later that year, he also appeared in Liverpool at YOKO ONO's tribute to her late husband JOHN LENNON. 'MAMA SAID' (1991) was a more accomplished, soulful affair which fleshed out the sound with brass and strings, songs alternating between introspective mood pieces (he'd recently split with his wife) and gritty funk-rock. Early in '92, LENNY settled out of court over royalties owing to INGRID CHAVEZ from the MADONNA collaboration, although the whole thing seemed a bit of a sham bearing in mind that the main thrust of the song was highly reminiscent of PUBLIC ENEMY's 'Security Of The First World'. Nevertheless, KRAVITZ could well afford to pay, 'MAMA SAID' notching up considerable American and British sales, while the single, 'IT AIN'T OVER 'TIL IT'S OVER' was a US No.2. After writing a passable album for sexy French goddess, VANESSA PARADIS, KRAVITZ re-emerged in thundering rock-God mode (replete with red leather trousers, no less) for 'ARE YOU GONNA GO MY WAY', a HENDRIX-esque song that made the UK Top 5. The album of the same name was KRAVITZ's biggest success to date, scaling the album charts in Britain, although it was clear the singer was running out of fresh ideas (or at least fresh ways of presenting old ideas). 'CIRCUS' (1995) carried on in much the same vein, successful but stale. The imaginatively titled '5' (1998) hardly broke the mould although, with the UK No.1 success of the 'FLY AWAY' single (aided at least in part by its use on a UK TV ad), the album was a resounding transatlantic success. A pointless cover of The Guess Who's 'AMERICAN WOMAN' (for the 'Austin Powers' soundtrack and a 'GREATEST HITS' package) suggested that KRAVITZ was approaching creative meltdown. All the more surprising then, that 'LENNY' (2001), if being equally imaginatively titled, offered a return to his more varied, soulful palate of yesteryear. Never highly original, but certainly his most engaging work in almost a decade. • **Covered;** COLD TURKEY + GIVE PEACE A CHANCE (John Lennon) / IF SIX WAS NINE (Jimi Hendrix) / DEUCE (Kiss) / AMERICAN WOMAN (Guess Who). • **Trivia:** SLASH of GUNS N' ROSES played guitar on 2 tracks from 'MAMA SAID'.

Album rating: MAMA SAID (*8) / LET LOVE RULE (*7) / ARE YOU GONNA GO MY WAY (*7) / CIRCUS (*5) / 5 (*5) / GREATEST HITS compilation (*8) / LENNY (*5)

LENNY KRAVITZ – vocals, guitar, piano, bass, drums with on session / **HENRY HIRSCH** – keyboards / **KARL DENSON** – sax / + guests

Virgin Virgin

Oct 89. (7"/7"w-poster) *(VUS/+P 10)* *<99166>* **LET LOVE RULE. / EMPTY HANDS** [ ] [89]
(12"+=/cd-s+=) *(VUS T/CD 10)* – Blues for Sister Someone / Flower child.

Nov 89. (lp/c/cd) *(VUSLP/VUSMC/CDVUS 10)* *<91290>* **LET LOVE RULE** [56] [61]
– Sitting on top of the world / Let love rule / Freedom train / My precious love / I build this garden for us / Fear / Does anybody out there even care / Mr. Cab driver / Rosemary / Be. *(c+=)* – Blues for Sister Someone / Flower child. *(cd++=)* – Empty hands.

Jan 90. (7"/c-s) *(VUS/+C 17)* **I BUILT THIS GARDEN FOR US. / FLOWER CHILD** [81] [–]
(12"+=/cd-s+=) *(VUS T/CD 17)* – Fear.

May 90. (7"/c-s) *(VUS/+C 20)* **MR. CAB DRIVER. / BLUES FOR SISTER SOMEONE (live) / DOES ANYBODY OUT THERE EVEN CARE (live)** [58] [ ]
(12"/cd-s) *(VUS T/CD 20)* – (first 2 tracks) / Rosemary (live).
(10") *(VUSA 20)* – ('A'side) / Rosemary (live) / Let love rule (live).

Jul 90. (7"/c-s) *(VUS/+C 26)* **LET LOVE RULE. / COLD TURKEY (live)** [39] [–]
(12"+=) *(VUSTG 26)* – Flower child (live).
(cd-s+=) *(VUSCD 26)* – My precious love (live).
(10") *(VUSA 26)* – ('A'side) / If six was nine (live) / My precious love (live).

Mar 91. (7"/c-s) *(VUS/+C 34)* **ALWAYS ON THE RUN. / ('A'instrumental)** [41] [–]
(12"+=/12"box+=) *(VUST/+X 34)* – Light skin girl from London.
(cd-s++=) *(VUSCD 34)* – Butterfly.

Apr 91. (cd)(c/lp) *(CDVUS 31)(VUS MC/LP 31)* *<91610>* **MAMA SAID** [8] [39]
– Fields of joy / Always on the run / Stand by my woman / It ain't over 'til it's over / More than anything in this world / What goes around comes around / The difference is why / Stop draggin' around / Flowers for Zoe / Fields of joy (reprise) / All I ever wanted / When the morning turns to night / What the . . .. are we saying? / Butterfly.

May 91. (7"/c-s) *(VUS/+C 43)* **IT AIN'T OVER 'TIL IT'S OVER. / THE DIFFERENCE IS WHY** [11] [–]
(12"+=/cd-s+=) *(VUST 43)* – I'll be around.
(12"pic-d) *(VUSTY 43)* – ('A'side) / (interview).

May 91. (c-s) *<98795>* **IT AIN'T OVER 'TIL IT'S OVER / I'LL BE AROUND** [–] [2]

Sep 91. (7"/c-s) *(VUS/+C 45)* **STAND BY MY WOMAN. / FLOWERS FOR ZOE** [55] [–]
(12"+=) *(VUST 45)* – Stop dragging around (live).
(cd-s+=) *(VUSCD 45)* – What the . . .. are we saying? (live) / Always on the run (live).

Oct 91. (c-s) *<98736>* **STAND BY MY WOMAN / LIGHT SKIN GIRL FROM LONDON** [–] [76]

—— now with **CRAIG ROSS** – electric guitar (co-writes some music) / **TONY BRETT** – bass / **MICHAEL HUNTER** – flugel horn

Feb 93. (7"/c-s) *(VUS/+C 65)* **ARE YOU GONNA GO MY WAY. / MY LOVE** [4] [–]
(cd-s) *(VUSCD 65)* – ('A'side) / Always on the run / It ain't over 'til it's over / Let love rule.

Mar 93. (cd)(c/lp) *(CDVUS 60)(VUS MC/LP 60)* *<86984>* **ARE YOU GONNA GO MY WAY** [1] [12]
– Are you gonna go my way / Believe / Come on and love me / Heaven help / Just be a woman / Is there any love in your heart / Black girl / My love / Sugar / Sister / Eleutheria.

May 93. (7"/c-s) *(VUS/+C 72)* *<12662>* **BELIEVE. / FOR THE FIRST TIME** [30] [60]
(10"pic-d+=/cd-s+=) *(VUS T/CD 72)* – ('A'acoustic) / Sitar (acoustic).

Aug 93. (7"/c-s) *(VUS/+C 73)* **HEAVEN HELP. / ELEUTHERIA** [21] [–]
(cd-s+=) *(VUSDG 73)* – Ascension / Brother.

Nov 93. (7"pic-d/12") *(VUS P/T 76)* **IS THERE ANY LOVE IN YOUR HEART. / ALWAYS ON THE RUN (live)** [52] [ ]
(cd-s+=) *(VUSDG 76)* – What goes around comes around (live) / Freedom train (live).

Mar 94. (c-s) *<38412>* **HEAVEN HELP. / SPINNING AROUND OVER YOU** [–] [80]

Aug 95. (c-s) *(VUSC 93)* **ROCK AND ROLL IS DEAD / ANOTHER LIFE** [22] [–]
(10"+=/cd-s+=) *(VUS AB/CD 93)* – Confused / Is it me or is it you.

Sep 95. (c-s) *<38514>* **ROCK AND ROLL IS DEAD / ANOTHER LIFE / ARE YOU GONNA GO MY WAY (live)** [–] [75]

Sep 95. (cd/c/lp) *(CDVUS/VUSLP/MUSMC 86)* *<40696>* **CIRCUS** [5] [10]
– Rock and roll is dead / Circus / Beyond the 7th sky / Tunnel vision / Can't get you off my mind / Magdalene / God is love / Thin ice / Don't go and put a bullet in your head / In my life today / The resurrection.

Dec 95. (c-s) *(VUSC 96)* **CIRCUS / ('A'acoustic)** [54] [ ]
(10"+=/cd-s+=) *(VUS A/CD 96)* – Tunnel vision (live) / Are you gonna go my way (live).

Feb 96. (7"/c-s) *(VUS A/C 100)* *<38535>* **CAN'T GET YOU OFF MY MIND. / EMPTY HANDS** [54] [62]
(cd-s+=) *(VUSCD 100)* – Stand by my woman.

Sep 96. (10"/cd-s) *(VUS A/CD 107)* **THE RESURRECTION (live). /** [–] w-drawn [–]

May 98. (c-s) *(VUSC 130)* **IF YOU CAN'T SAY NO / WITHOUT YOU** [48] [ ]
(12"+=/cd-s+=) *(VUS T/CD 130)* – ('A'-Zero & BT . . . mixes).

May 98. (cd/c) *(CDVUS/VUSMC 140)* *<47758>* **5** [18] [28]
– Live / Supersoulfighter / I belong to you / Black velveteen / If you can't say no / Thinking of you / Take time / Fly away / It's your life / Straight cold player / Little girl's eyes / You're my flavor / Can we find a reason? *(cd re-iss. Jun99; CDVUSX 140)*

Sep 98. (c-s) *(VUSC 138)* **I BELONG TO YOU / IF YOU CAN'T SAY NO (Flunky in the attic mix)** [75] [ ]
(cd-s+=) *(VUSCD 138)* – If you can't say no (BT twilo dub).

Feb 99. (c-s/cd-s) *(VUSC/+D 141)* *<radio cut>* **FLY AWAY / FLY AWAY (live acoustic) / BELIEVE (live acoustic)** [1] Nov98 [12]

Jun 99. (c-s) *(VUSC 146)* **BLACK VELVETEEN / LIVE / FLY AWAY** [ ] [–]
(cd-s) *(VUSCD 146)* – (first 2 tracks) / Supersoulfighter.
(cd-s) *(VUSCDX 146)* – (first & third tracks) / Straight cold player. *(re-iss. Dec99; same)*

Aug 99. (c-s) *(VUSC 153)* *<radio cut>* **AMERICAN WOMAN / THINKING OF YOU (Nick Hexam's dancehall mix)** [ ] Jul99 [49]
(cd-s+=) *(VUSCD 153)* – Straight cold player (live) / Fields of joy (live).

Mar 00. (-) *<album cut>* **I BELONG TO YOU** [–] [71]

Oct 00. (cd/c) *(CDVUSX/VUSMCX 183)* *<50316>* **GREATEST HITS** (compilation) [12] [2]
– Are you gonna go my way / Fly away / Rock and roll is dead / Again / It ain't over 'til it's over / Can't get you off my mind / Mr. Cab driver / American woman / Stand by my woman / Always on the run / Heaven help / I belong to you / Believe / Let love rule / Velveteen.

Nov 00. (c-s) *(VUSC 187)* *<radio play>* **AGAIN / FLY AWAY (live) / ARE YOU GONNA GO MY WAY (live)** [ ] [4]
(cd-s) *(VUSCD 187)* – (first two tracks) / Always on the run (live).
(cd-s) *(VUSCDG 187)* – (first & third tracks) / Let love rule (live).

Oct 01. (cd/lp) *(CDVUS/VUSLP 213)* *<11233>* **LENNY** [55] [12]
– Battlefield of love / If I could fall in love / Yesterday is gone (my dear

Kay) / Stillness of heart / Believe in me / Pay to play / A million miles away / God save us all / Dig in / You were in my heart / Bank robber man / Let's get high.

Nov 01. (cd-s) *(VUSCD 229)* <*radio cut*> **DIG IN / ROSEMARY / CAN'T GET YOU OFF MY MIND** — Sep01 **31**

Mar 02. (cd-s) *(VUSCD 236)* **STILLNESS OF HEART / STILLNESS OF HEART (acoustic) / FLOWERS FOR ZOE (acoustic)** — **44**

– compilations, etc. –

Oct 01. (d-cd) *(810873-2)* **LET LOVE RULE / MAMA SAID** — –

□ KRAYZIE BONE
(see under ⇒ BONE THUGS-N-HARMONY)

Kris KRISTOFFERSON

Born: 22 Jun'36, Brownsville, Texas, USA. A PhD student who won a Rhodes scholarship to Oxford in 1958, KRISTOFFERSON was also a budding songwriter and after a brief spell in the army he relocated to Nashville where he continued writing while holding down various jobs (including a spell as a janitor at the Columbia studios). Having befriended country legend JOHNNY CASH, his first break came in 1969 when CASH handed KRISTOFFERSON's 'ME AND BOBBY McGHEE' to country maverick ROGER MILLER who in turn, took it into the country charts. CASH himself hit with KRIS's definitive 'SUNDAY MORNIN' COMIN' DOWN' later that year and the lanky, bearded songwriter secured a deal with the 'Monument' imprint. Titled simply 'KRISTOFFERSON' (1970), his debut album caught the attention of both rock and country critics as the fabled "outlaw" movement began to coalesce around CASH, WAYLON JENNINGS, WILLIE NELSON etc. 1971 proved a pivotal year as friend JANIS JOPLIN took 'ME AND BOBBY McGHEE' to No.1. (US). While SAMMI SMITH scored a US Top 10 hit with 'HELP ME MAKE IT THROUGH THE NIGHT' (a track that has since, like much of his material, become a country standard), at the same time KRISTOFFERSON's second album, 'THE SILVER TONGUED DEVIL AND I' (1971) finally saw him racking up sales in his own right. Literate, laconic and liberal, he helped steer country music away from the middle of the road and on to a far more interesting path. While hardly the most gifted of singers, his laid-back style was perfect for the kind of freewheeling rebel image he liked to portray (he certainly wins top prize for references to getting stoned, hardly a typical Nashville topic) and, like his hero BOB DYLAN, KRIS's songs were ripe for interpretation. Branching out into acting in the early 70's, he made his film debut in Dennis Hopper's (another close friend) 'The Last Movie' before going on to star in cult classics, 'Cisco Pike' and 'Pat Garrett And Billy The Kid' (alongside James Coburn and BOB DYLAN, who penned the sublime soundtrack). Singer RITA COOLIDGE also appeared in the latter, KRISTOFFERSON marrying her the same year (1973). In the meantime – although his stock with the critics had gone down – he'd scored his first US No.1 with 'WHY ME', from 1972's 'JESUS WAS A CAPRICORN' album. As well as recording duets with his new wife, he continued cutting his own albums to diminishing critical returns, among them 'FULL MOON' (1973), 'BREAKAWAY' (1974), 'WHO'S TO BLESS AND WHO'S TO BLAME' (1975) and 'THIRD WORLD WARRIOR' (1976). KRISTOFFERSON's biggest success of the decade came with a remake of 'A Star Is Born' (1976), in which he co-starred with Barbra Streisand. The accompanying soundtrack (written and sung by the man himself) sold millions and spawned his last major hit of the decade, 'WATCH CLOSELY NOW'. While his recordings dried up in the 80's he continued to concentrate on acting, appearing in everything from 'Heaven's Gate' (1980) to John Sayles' 'Lone Star' (1986). The mid-80's also found him hooking up with veteran outlaw mates JOHNNY CASH, WAYLON JENNINGS and WILLIE NELSON for the acclaimed 'HIGHWAYMEN' (1985) album. The quartet went on to record a sequel, 'HIGHWAYMEN II' (1990) as well as 1995's 'ROAD GOES ON FOREVER'. KRISTOFFERSON himself did win back the critics to a certain extent in the 90's, recording comeback set, 'A MOMENT OF FOREVER' for Texas label, 'Justice', in 1995. The close of the millennium meanwhile, found KRISTOFFERSON in fine fettle with 'THE AUSTIN SESSIONS' (1999), featuring new versions of his many classic tunes. 'BROKEN FREEDOM SONG: LIVE FROM SAN FRANCISCO' (2003) was an oddity of a live album, an ad hoc collection of stripped down songs gathered from the more obscure corners of his huge song vault. Accompanied only by mandolin and bass, KRISTOFFERSON performed an intimate, politically slanted set dusting down the likes of 'SKY KING', 'THE CIRCLE' and 'SANDINISTA'.

Best CD compilation: THE VERY BEST OF KRIS KRISTOFFERSON (*7)

KRIS KRISTOFFERSON – vocals; with numerous session people

Monument Monument

Apr 70. (7") <*1210*> **SUNDAY MORNIN' COMIN' DOWN. / TO BEAT THE DEVIL** — –

May 70. (7") *(MON 1050)* **BLAME IT ON THE STONES. / HELP ME MAKE IT THRU' THE NIGHT** — –

Jun 70. (lp) <*(SMO 5042)*> **KRISTOFFERSON**
– Blame it on the stones / To beat the Devil / Me and Bobby McGee / The best of all possible worlds / Help me make it thru' the night / The law is for protection for the people / Casey's last ride / Just the other side of nowhere / Darby's castle / For the good times / Duvalier's dream / Sunday mornin' comin' down. <*US re-iss. Sep71 as 'ME AND BOBBY McGEE'; 30817*> – hit No.43 *(re-iss. Oct71 as 'ME AND BOBBY McGEE'; MNT 64631)* <*(cd-iss. Apr01 +=; 501543-2)*> – Shadow of your mind / Lady's not for sale / Junkie and the juicehead / Come sundown.

Jun 71. (lp) *(MNT 64636)* <*30679*> **THE SILVER-TONGUED DEVIL AND I** — **21**
– The silver-tongued devil and I / Jody and the kid / Billy Dee / Good Christian soldier / Breakdown / Loving her was easier (than anything I'll ever do again) / The taker / When I love her / The pilgrim: chapter 33 / Epitaph. *(re-iss. 1974; same)*

Oct 71. (7") *(MNT 7523)* <*8525*> **LOVING HER WAS EASIER (THAN ANYTHING I'LL EVER DO AGAIN). / EPITAPH** — Aug71 **26**

Dec 71. (7") <*8531*> **THE TAKER. / THE PILGRIM: CHAPTER 33** — –

Mar 72. (7") <*8536*> **JOSIE. / BORDER LORD** — – **63**

Apr 72. (lp) *(MNT 64963)* <*31302*> **BORDER LORD** — Mar72 **41**
– Josie / Burden of freedom / Stagger mountain tragedy / Border Lord / Somebody nobody knows / Little girl lost / Smokey put the sweet on me / When she's wrong / Gettin' by high and strange / Kiss the world goodbye.

1972. (7"m) *(MNT 9154)* **BREAKDOWN./ THE PILGRIM CHAPTER 33/ LOVING HER WAS EASIER** — –

Dec 72. (lp) *(MNT 65391)* <*31909*> **JESUS WAS A CAPRICORN** — Nov72 **31**
– Jesus was a Capricorn / Nobody wins / It sure was / Enough for you / Help me Lord / Jesse Younger / Give it time to be tender / Out of mind, out of sight / Sugar man / Why me.

Feb 73. (7") *(MNT 1188)* <*8558*> **JESUS WAS A CAPRICORN. / ENOUGH FOR YOU** — Dec72 **91**

Feb 73. (7") <*8564*> **JESSE YOUNGER. / GIVE IT TIME TO BE TENDER** — –

May 73. (7") *(MNT 1461)* **IT SURE WAS. / NOBODY WINS** — –

—— in Sep73, 'A&M' issued his collaboration album 'FULL MOON' with new wife RITA COOLIDGE. It hit US No.26 and contained two US hit singles 'A SONG I'D LIKE TO SING' and 'LOVING ARMS'.

Oct 73. (7") *(MNT 1482)* <*8571*> **WHY ME. / HELP ME LORD** — Mar73 **16**

Jun 74. (lp) *(MNT 69074)* <*32914*> **SPOOKY LADY'S SIDESHOW** — May74 **78**
– Same old song / Broken freedom song / Shandy / Starspangled bummer /

Lights of Magdala / I may smoke too much / One for the money / Late again / Stairway to the bottom / Rescue mission / Smile at me again / Rock and roll time.

Jun 74. (7") *<8618>* **LIGHTS OF MAGDALA. / I MAY SMOKE TOO MUCH** –

KRIS KRISTOFFERSON & RITA COOLIDGE

Dec 74. (lp) *(MNT 80547) <33278>* **BREAKAWAY**
– Lover please / We must have been out of our minds / Dakota / What'cha gonna do / The thing I might have been / Slow down / Rain / Sweet Susannah / I've got to have you / I'd rather be sorry / Crippled crow.

Jan 75. (7") *(MNT 2871) <8630>* **RAIN. / WHAT'CHA GONNA DO**

Mar 75. (7") *<8636>* **SLOW DOWN. / LOVER PLEASE** –

May 75. (7") *<8646>* **SWEET SUSANNAH. / WE MUST HAVE BEEN OUT OF OUR MINDS** –

KRIS KRISTOFFERSON

Nov 75. (lp) *(MNT 69158) <33379>* **WHO'S TO BLESS . . . AND WHO'S TO BLAME**
– The year 200 minus 25 / If it's all the same to you / Easy, come on / Stallion / Rocket to stardom / Stranger / Who's to bless . . . and who's to blame / Don't cuss the fiddle / Silver.

Nov 75. (7") *<8658>* **ROCKET TO STARDOM. / EASY, COME ON** –

Feb 76. (7") *<8679>* **IF IT'S ALL THE SAME TO YOU. / THE YEAR 2000 MINUS 25** –

Aug 76. (lp) *(MNT 81496) <34254>* **SURREAL THING**
– You show me yours / Killing time / The prisoner / Eddie the eunuch / It's never gonna be the same again / I got a life of my own / The stranger I love / The golden idol / Bad love story / If you don't like Hank Williams.

Aug 76. (7") *<8707>* **IT'S NEVER GONNA BE THE SAME AGAIN. / THE PRISONER** –

— Late in '76 the 'Columbia' soundtrack of the film re-make of 'A STAR IS BORN', which starred BARBRA STREISAND and KRIS. The No.1 album (also UK No.1 Apr'77; (CBS 86021), featured duets from both as well as 3 solo tracks from KRIS including 'C.B.S.' single below . . .

Jun 77. (7") *(CBS 5336) <10525>* **WATCH CLOSELY NOW. / CRIPPLED CROW** May77 52

Apr 78. (lp) *(MNT 86056) <35310>* **EASTER ISLAND** Mar78 86
– Risky bizness / How do you feel / Forever in your love / The sabre and the rose / Spooky lady's revenge / Easter Island / The bigger the fool / Lay me down / The fighter / Living legend.

Jun 78. (7") *(MNT 6474)* **LOVER PLEASE. / SLOW DOWN** –

— In 1978, 'A&M' released KRIS lp alongside RITA COOLIDGE; 'NATURAL ACT' <(AMLH 64690)>

Sep 79. (lp/c) *(MNT/40 83793) <36135>* **SHAKE HANDS WITH THE DEVIL**
– Shake hands with the Devil / Prove it to you one more time again / Whiskey whiskey / Lucky in love / Seadream / Killer barracuda / Come sundown / Michoacan / Once more with feeling / Fallen angel.

Mar 81. (lp/c) *(MNT/40 84818) <36885>* **TO THE BONE**
– Magdalene / Star-crossed / Blessing in disguise / The Devil to pay / Daddy's song / Snakebit / Nobody loves anybody anymore / Maybe you heard / The last time / I'll take any chance I can with you.

Jan 83. (d-lp/d-c; by KRIS KRISTOFFERSON, WILLIE NELSON, DOLLY PARTON & BRENDA LEE) *(MNT/40 88611) <38389>* **KRIS, WILLIE, DOLLY & BRENDA . . . THE WINNING HAND**
– You're gonna love yourself (in the morning) / Ping pong / You'll always have someone / Here comes that rainbow again / The bigger the fool, the harder the fall / Help me make it through the night / Happy happy birthday baby / You left me a long, long time ago / To make a long story short, she's gone / Someone loves you honey / Everything's beautiful (in it's own way) / Bring on the sunshine / Put it off until tomorrow / I never cared for you / Casey's last ride / King of a lonely castle / The little things / The bandits of Beverly Hills / What do you think about lovin' / Born to love me.

Jan 83. (7") *<21000>* **HERE COMES THAT RAINBOW AGAIN. /** –

— In Oct'84, 'Columbia' US <39531> released WILLIE NELSON and KRIS lp 'MUSIC FROM THE SONGWRITER' in which they co-starred together. On the same label, the same pair plus JOHNNY CASH and WAYLON JENNINGS, released lp 'THE HIGHWAYMAN' in August '85.

Mercury Mercury

Mar 87. (lp/c)(cd; as KRIS KRISTOFFERSON & THE BORDERLORDS) *(MERH/+C 103)<(830460-2)>* **REPOSSESSED**
– Mean old man / Shipwrecked in the eighties / They killed him / What about me / El Gavilan (the hawk) / El coyote / Anthem / The heart / This old road / Love is the way.

Jan 90. (cd/c/lp) *<(834629-2/-4/-1)>* **THIRD WORLD WARRIOR**
– The eagle and the bear / Third World warrior / Aquila del norte / The hero / Don't let the bastards (get you down) / Love of money / Third World war / Jesse Jackson / Mal sacate / Sandinista.

— The HIGHWAYMEN released the set, 'THE ROAD GOES ON FOREVER' in Apr'95

Transatla. Justice

Apr 96. (cd) *(TRACD 220)* **A MOMENT OF FOREVER** Aug95
– A moment of forever / Worth fighting for / Johnny Lobo / The promise / Shipwrecked in the eighties / Slouching towards the millennium / Between Heaven and here / Casey's last ride / Good love (shouldn't feel so bad) / A new game now / New mister me / Under the gun / Road warrior's lament / Sam's song (ask any working girl).

Warner ESP Warner ESP

Oct 99. (cd) *<(7567 83208-2)>* **THE AUSTIN SESSIONS**
– Me and Bobby McGee / Sunday morning coming down / For the good times / The silver tongued devil and I / Help me make it through the night / Loving her was easier (than anything I'll ever do again) / To beat the Devil / Who's to bless and who's to blame / Why me? / Nobody wins / The pilgrim: chapter 33 / Please don't tell how the story ends.

Oh Boy Oh Boy

Nov 03. (cd) *<(OBR 025CD)>* **BROKEN FREEDOM SONG / LIVE FROM SAN FRANCISCO (live)** Jul03
– Shipwrecked in the eighties / Darby's castle / Broken freedom song / Shandy (the perfect disguise) / What about me / Here comes that rainbow again / Nobody wins / The race / The captive / live:- The circle (song for Layla Al-Attar) / Sky king / Sandinista / Moment of forever / Don't let the bastards get you down / Road warrior's lament.

– compilations, others, etc. –

1975. (7") *Monument; (ZS 88920)* **WHY ME. / JESUS WAS A CAPRICORN** –

May 77. (lp) *Monument; (82002) <34687>* **SONGS OF KRISTOFFERSON** 45
(re-iss. Nov82 lp/c; MNT/40 32106)

1984. (lp/c) *CBS-Embassy; (EMB/40 31839)* **HELP ME MAKE IT THROUGH THE NIGHT** –

1988. (lp/c/cd) *Country Store; (CST/CSTK/CDCST 5)* **KRIS KRISTOFFERSON** –

Apr 90. (cd/c/d-lp) *Connoisseur; (KKVSOP CD/MC/LP 141)* **THE LEGENDARY YEARS** –

Apr 98. (cd) *Spectrum; (554009-2)* **THE COUNTRY COLLECTION** –

Jun 99. (cd/c) *Columbia; (494188-2/-4)* **THE VERY BEST OF KRIS KRISTOFFERSON**

□ KUKL (see under ⇒ BJORK)

KULA SHAKER

Formed: Highgate, London, England . . . mid 90's out of mods The KAYS by CRISPIAN MILLS. They initially played down the fact his mother was the famous English actress Hayley Mills (daughter of Sir John Mills) and father being director, Roy Boulting. In the late 80's, CRISPIAN and ALONZA BEVIN set up a school group, The LOVELY LADS, later becoming The OBJECTS. In 1995, after jointly winning the 'In The City' new band competition and a Glastonbury appearance, KULA SHAKER (now with PAUL WINTER-HART and JAY DARLINGTON) signed to 'Columbia', through A&R man Ronnie Gurr. They debuted that Xmas with the limited edition single, 'TATTVA'. Their first single proper,

'GRATEFUL WHEN YOU'RE DEAD', was a tribute of sorts to the late, great JERRY GARCIA and earned them their first Top 40 hit. Their follow-up, a re-vamped version of 'TATTVA', fared even better, making the Top 5. 'HEY DUDE', the next single, kept up the momentum, reaching No.2 following a blinding 'T In The Park' appearance in Scotland (they returned there in 1997 as headliners). CRISPIAN MILLS' songwriting was heavily influenced by a combination of classic 60's psychedelia and grandiose 70's rock, much in evidence on their debut album 'K' (1996). Relying on similar Eastern influences as 'TATTVA', 'GOVINDA' was another slice of elaborate, but cliched psychedelia, while 'HUSH' (1997) was workman-like in its similarity to the DEEP PURPLE version of the JOE SOUTH original. KULA SHAKER continued to musically spar with their tried and tested cod-mod/psychedelia, a Top 3 single in '98, 'SOUND OF DRUMS', testament to just that. The track was also included on their Bob Ezrin-produced sophomore set, 'PEASANTS, PIGS & ASTRONAUTS' (1999), a pretentious set of good-time cosmic rock'n'roll that gave ammunition to the gun-toting music journos all ready to shoot them down at any opportunity. Two further Top 20 singles, 'MYSTICAL MACHINE GUN' and 'SHOWER YOUR LOVE', marked the end for CRISPIAN and his chums as the band split that September. The frontman was expected to go solo but chose instead to form trad-rock trio, the JEEVAS who released a few singles prior to their debut album, '1 2 3 4' (2002). • **Covered:** BALLAD OF A THIN MAN (Bob Dylan).

Album rating: K (*7) / PEASANTS, PIGS & ASTRONAUTS (*5) / Jeevas: 1 2 3 4 (*4)

CRISPIAN MILLS (b.18 Jan'73) – vocals, guitars / **ALONZA BEVIN** (b.24 Oct'70) – bass, piano, tabla, vocals / **JAY DARLINGTON** (b. 3 May'69, Sidcup, England) – keyboards / **PAUL WINTER-HART** (b.19 Sep'71) – drums

Columbia Columbia

Dec 95. (ltd; 7"/cd-s) *(KULA 71/CD1)* **TATTVA (Lucky 13 mix)/ HOLLOW MAN (part II)** [ ] [–]

Apr 96. (c-s) *(KULAMC 2)* **GRATEFUL WHEN YOU'RE DEAD – JERRY WAS THERE. / ANOTHER LIFE** [35] [–]
(cd-s+=) *(KULACD 2)* – Under the hammer.

Jun 96. (7") *(KULA 3)* **TATTVA. / TATTVA ON ST. GEORGE'S DAY / DANCE IN YOUR SHADOW** [4] [–]
(cd-s) *(KULACD 3)* – (first & third tracks) / Moonshine / Tattva (lucky 13).
(cd-s) *(KULACD 3K)* – (second & third tracks) / Red balloon (Vishnu's eyes).

Aug 96. (7"/c-s) *(KULA/+MC 4)* **HEY DUDE. / TROUBLED MIND** [2] [–]
(cd-s+=) *(KULACD 4)* – Grateful when you're dead (Mark Radcliffe session) / Into the deep (Mark Radcliffe session).
(cd-s) *(KULACD 4K)* – ('A'side) / Tattva / Drop in the sea / Crispian reading from the Mahabharata.

Sep 96. (cd/c/lp) *(SHAKER CD/MC/LP 1)* <67822> **K** [1] Oct96 [ ]
– Hey dude / Knight on the town / Temple of the everlasting light / Govinda / Smart dogs / Magic theatre / Into the deep / Sleeping jiva / Tattva / Grateful when you're dead – Jerry was there / 303 / Start all over / Hollow man (parts 1 & 2). *(also ltd-cd; SHAKER CD1K)*

Nov 96. (c-s) *(KULAMC 5)* **GOVINDA / GOKULA** [7] [–]
(cd-s+=) *(KULACD 5)* – Hey dude (live) / Alonza Bevan's The Leek.
('A'-Hari & St.George mix-cd-s+=) *(KULACD 5K)* – ('A'-Monkey Mafia Pigsy's vision) / ('A'-Monkey Mafia Ten to ten version).
(7"mail-order+=) *(KULA 75)* – Temple of everlasting light.

Feb 97. (c-s) *(KULAMC 6)* **HUSH / RAAGY ONE (WAITING FOR TOMORROW)** [2] [–]
(cd-s+=) *(KULACD 6)* – Knight on the town (live) / Smart dogs (live).
(cd-s+=) *(KULACD 6K)* – Under the hammer (hold on to the magical key) / Govinda (live).

—— (all above cd-singles were re-iss. Jul98; *KULA 71-76CD)*

Jul 97. (cd-ep) *<68514>* **SUMMER SUN EP** [–] [ ]
– Govinda / Gokula / Dance in your shadow / Raagy one (waiting for tomorrow) / Moonshine / Troubled mind.

Apr 98. (c-s) *(KULA 21MC)* **SOUND OF DRUMS / HURRY ON SUNDOWN (HARI OM SUNDOWN)** [3] [–]
(cd-s+=) *(KULA 21CD)* – Reflections of love / Fairyland (featuring DON PECKER).
(cd-s+=) *(KULA 21CDX)* – The one that got away / Smile.

Feb 99. (c-s) *(KULA 22MC)* **MYSTICAL MACHINE GUN / GUITAR MAN** [14] [–]
(cd-s+=) *(KULA 22CD)* – Prancing bride.
(cd-s) *(KULA 22CDX)* – ('A'side) / Avalanche / Holy river.

Mar 99. (cd/c/lp) *(SHAKER 2 CD/MC/LP)* **PEASANTS, PIGS & ASTRONAUTS** [9] [ ]
– Great Hosannah / S.O.S. / Mystical machine gun / Radhe radhe / I'm still here / Shower your love / 108 battles / Sound of drums / Timeworn / Last farewell / Golden avatar / Namami nanda nandana.

May 99. (c-s) *(KULA 23MC)* **SHOWER YOUR LOVE / GOODBYE TIN TERRIERS** [14] [–]
(cd-s+=) *(KULA 23CD)* – Sound of drums (live).
(cd-s) *(KULA 23CDX)* – ('A'side) / The dancing flea / Light of the day.

—— disbanded in September '99

JEEVAS

CRISPIAN MILLS / DAN McKINNA / ANDY NIXON

Cowboy Epic

Jul 02. (7"m) *(COW 001)* **SCARY PARENTS. / SHE SPEAKS / MEET THE JEEVAS** [ ] [–]

Sep 02. (7"m) *(COW 002)* **VIRGINIA. / TEENAGE BREAKDOWN (acoustic) / MEET THE JEEVAS (part 2)** [ ] [–]
(cd-s) *(COWCD 002)* – ('A'side) / Stoned love / Old friends new faces (live).

Sep 02. (cd) *(COWCD 003)* *<150>* **1 2 3 4** [ ] Oct02 [ ]
– Virginia / Ghost cowboys in the movies / You got my number / What is it for? / Once upon a time in America / Don't say the good times are over / Scary parents / Teenage breakdown / Silver apples / She speaks / Edge of the world / America (demo).

Nov 02. (7") *(COW 004)* **GHOST (COWBOYS IN THE MOVIES). / MEET THE JEEVAS (part 3)** [ ] [–]
(cd-s) *(COWCD 004)* – ('A'side) / It could only happen to you / It's not what you do.

Mar 03. (7") *(COW 005)* **ONCE UPON A TIME IN AMERICA. / SILVER APPLES (Brighton rocks live)** [61] [–]
(cd-s) *(COWCDA 005)* – ('A'side) / She speaks / 303 (Brighton rocks live).
(cd-s) *(COWCDB 005)* – ('A'side) / Hush (Brighton rocks live) / ('A'-original acoustic version).

Sep 03. (7") *(COW 006)* **THE WAY YOU CARRY ON. / ENDLESS NIGHT** [ ] [–]
(cd-s+=) *(COWCD 006)* – How much do you suck.

□ KYUSS (see under ⇒ QUEENS OF THE STONE AGE)

LED ZEPPELIN

☐ Greg LAKE (see under ⇒ EMERSON, LAKE & PALMER)

LAMBCHOP

Formed: Nashville, Tennessee, USA ... 1992 initially as POSTERCHILD by KURT WAGNER, the 90's country-lounge answer to 60's icons, CAT STEVENS and TIM HARDIN. His hesitant but heavy-lidded vocal monotone sat perfectly against the lethargic drowsiness of the country-jazz played by his large backing ensemble. Although they could hardly be termed rock, LAMBCHOP emerged from the flourishing alternative roots scene with an album on 'Merge' ('City Slang' UK) 'I HOPE YOU'RE SITTING DOWN' (1995). A post-modern cousin of CHET ATKINS (although at times at least twice removed!), the record revealed WAGNER's love of vintage string-laden production and his penchant for beer-soaked, meandering tales of ordinary madness. Early the following year, KURT and LAMBCHOP delivered another collection of near comatose country vignettes, 'HOW I QUIT SMOKING', this time around wrapped up in a classic 70's Nashville production sheen courtesy of arranger, John Mock. One of the record's highlights, 'THE MAN WHO LOVED BEER', was issued as the first LAMBCHOP single and has since been adopted as author, Martin C. Strong's theme tune. Joking aside, 1996 also saw the release of a third set, the critically acclaimed live/festival (1995) recorded 'HANK', relaxzzzed audiences no doubt giving WAGNER and Co the first ever horizontal standing ovation. A third studio album, meanwhile, sauntered onto the scene in 1997, the LAMBCHOP man surely being just a tad ironic in naming it 'THRILLER', although opening cuts, 'MY FACE YOUR ASS' and 'YOUR SUCKING FUNNY DAY', raised the pulse a little. Prolific as ever, WAGNER and his entourage (they had all worked on VIC CHESNUTT's 'The Salesman & Bernadette') returned in 1998 with possibly his/their best album to date, 'WHAT ANOTHER MAN SPILLS', featuring croonsome classic, 'THE SATURDAY OPTION', alongside a few covers by F.M. CORNOG (i.e. EAST RIVER PIPE) and one by Curtis Mayfield, 'GIVE ME YOUR LOVE'. The country-soul meets disco connection carried on to the acclaimed 'NIXON' (2000) wherein WAGNER's impenetrable songwriting was transformed into (relatively) more intelligible but no less fascinating observations on life's essential minutiae. As for the album title, it was apparently inspired by the infamous ex-American President, LAMBCHOP kindly supplying a reading list of related material on the sleeve. Take for instance minor hit, 'UP WITH PEOPLE' – complete with their hilarious and overlooked "Nixon" video – and opener 'THE OLD GOLD SHOE'; surely this was truly the album that set WAGNER and Co apart from anything remotely similar. LAMBCHOP returned with their most intimate and mature album to date, the breezy 'IS A WOMAN' in early 2002. If 'NIXON' was a Saturday night out on the town, then 'IS A WOMAN' was most certainly the sleepy Sunday morning afterwards. WAGNER muted the soul-thang to give us soft croaky songs, reminiscent of 70's RANDY NEWMAN. The tracks, all recorded bare-bones, like delicate little ornaments, also displayed WAGNER's impending talent which makes you wonder if this man was writing songs thirty years ago, he would be a living legend by now. MARK NEVER's production and spacey guitar was impeccable, with the last track even sliding into a reggae riff. Bloody marvellous.

Album rating: I HOPE YOU'RE SITTING DOWN (*6) / HOW I QUIT SMOKING (*7) / HANK (*7) / THRILLER (*6) / WHAT ANOTHER MAN SPILLS (*7) / NIXON (*9) / IS A WOMAN (*8)

KURT WAGNER – vocals, guitar / **BILL KILLEBREW** – guitar / **MARC TROVILLION** – bass / **STEVE GOODHUE** – drums / **ALLEN LOWREY** – percussion / **JONATHAN MARX** – clarinet, trumpet / **SCOTT CHASE** – washboard, maracas

		not iss.	Thump Audio
1992.	(7"ep; as POSTERCHILD) *<1>* **AN OPEN FRESCA / A MOIST TOWELETTE / (other two by Crop Circle Hoax)**	–	
		City Slang	Merge
1992.	(7") *<MRG 048>* **NINE. / MOODY FUCKER**	–	
1994.	(7") *<02>* **MY CLICHE. / LORETTA LUNG** *(re-iss. 1999 on Spanish label 'Elefant'; ER 15913-69>*	–	
——	<above on 'Sunday Driver'>		
Aug 94.	(7") *<MRG 066>* **SOAKY IN THE POOPER. / TWO KITTENS DON'T MAKE A PUPPY**	–	
1994.	(7") **IT'S IMPOSSIBLE. / (other track by NONPAREILS AND BARTLEBEES)**	–	
	(above on 'Contrast International') <below on 'Bloodsucker'>		
1995.	(7"ep) *<19846>* **I CAN HARDLY SPELL MY NAME / THE SCARY CAROLER. / (other tracks by CYOD)**	–	

—— line-up **WAGNER, CHASE, MARX, TROVILLION, LOWREY, KILLEBREW + GOODHUE** added **PAUL NIEHAUS** – lap steel guitar, trombone, vocals / **JOHN DELWORTH** – organs / **DEANNA VARAGONA** – vocals, alto sax, banjo, cello / **MIKE DOSTER** – bass (on 1)

Mar 95.	(cd/d-lp) *(efa 04953-2/-1) <MRG 70>* **I HOPE YOU'RE SITTING DOWN / JACK'S TULIPS** – Begin / Betweemus / Soaky in the pooper / Because you are the very air he breathes / Under the same moon / I will drive slowly / Oh, what a disappointment / Hellmouth / Bon soir, bon soir / Hickey / Breathe deep / So I hear you're moving / Let's go bowling / What was he wearing? / Cowboy on the moon / The pack-up song. *(cd re-iss. May00; 8403530)*		Sep94
1995.	(7") *<7003-7>* **YOUR LIFE AS A SEQUEL. / SMUCKERS**	–	
——	<above on 'Mute America'> <below issued for 'I-sore 5" club'>		
1996.	(5") *<#1>* **SCARED OUT OF MY SHOES. / (other track by Spent)**	–	
Jan 96.	(cd/d-lp) *(efa 04969-2/-1) <MRG 97>* **HOW I QUIT SMOKING** – For which we are truly thankful / The man who loved beer / The militant / We never argue / Life's little tragedy / Suzieju / All smiles and mariachi / The scary caroler / Smuckers / The militant / Garf / Your life as a sequel / Theone / Again.		
Apr 96.	(7"m)(cd-s) *(efa 04974-45)(efa 04977-03)* **THE MAN WHO LOVED BEER. / ALUMNI LAWN / BURLY & JOHNSON**		–

—— added guest **HANK TILBURY** – banjo

Jul 96. (m-cd/10"m-lp) *(efa 04979-2/-1)* <MRG 108> **HANK (live)** [ ] [ ]
– I'm a stranger here / Blame it on the brunettes / The tin chime / Randi / Doak's need / Poor bastard. *(cd+=)* – I sucked my boss's dick.

below by VIC CHESNUTT, DAVE LOWERY, KURT WAGNER + PAUL NIEHAUS

1996. (7") *<25075>* **A LOOSE CONFEDERATION OF SATURDAY CITY-STATES** [–] [ ]
– Plagarism / How can I face tomorrow.

—— added **PAUL BIRCH JR., MARKY NEVERS, ALEX McMANUS + JOHN CATCHINGS**; to repl. STEVE + BILL

Jul 97. (7") *<(MRG 124)>* **CIGARETTIQUETTE. / MR. CRABBY** [ ] [ ]
(above & below 45's released on 'Merge' only)

Sep 97. (7") *<(MRG 126)>* **WHITEY. / PLAYBOY, THE SHIT** [ ] [ ]

Sep 97. (cd/lp) *(efa 04998-2/-1)* *<MRG 130>* **THRILLER** [ ] [ ]
– My face your ass / Your fucking sunny day / Hey, where's your girl / Crawl away / Gloria Leonard / Thriller / The old fat robin / Superstar in France.

Nov 97. (cd-ep) *(efa 0870-03)* **YOUR SUCKING FUNNY DAY / THE PETRIFIED FLORIST / THE THEME FROM THE NEAL MILLER SHOW** [ ] [–]

—— added **DENNIS CRONIN, MIKE GRIFFITH, VIC CHESNUTT + TONY CROW**

Sep 98. (cd/lp) *(efa 08711-2/-1)* *<MRG 146>* **WHAT ANOTHER MAN SPILLS** [ ] [ ]
– Interrupted / The Saturday option / Shucks / Give me your love (love song) / Life #2 / Scamper / It's not alright / N.O. / I've been lonely for so long / Magnificent obsession / King of nothing never / The theme from the Neil Miller show.

Nov 98. (ltd-12") *<fu 003>* **GIVE ME YOUR LOVE (LOVE SONG) – Dopperganger remix. / ('A'-album & Doppelganger instrumental)** [–] [ ]

—— <above on City Slang's 'For Us' records, below on own label>

Dec 98. (cd-s) *<none>* **CHRISTMAS TIME IS HERE / CHRISTMAS TIME IS HERE** [–] radio [–]

Apr 99. (ltd-7") *<(ER 198)>* **LA DISTANCIA DESCE ELLA HASTA ALLI (THE DISTANCE FROM HER TO THERE). / THE BOOK I HAVEN'T READ** [ ] [–]
(above issued on Spanish 'Elefant 6') (below on 'Third Gear')

—— **MATT SWANSON** – bass + **DENNIS CRONIN** – trumpet, cornet; repl. KILLEBREW + CATCHINGS + CHESNUTT + GRIFFITH

Nov 99. (7") *(3G 23)* **UP WITH PEOPLE. / Dump: Die For The Memory** [ ] [–]

—— Nov'99, KURT WAGNER was credited on an EP, 'Chester' with JOSH ROUSE

Feb 00. (cd/lp) *(20152-2/-1)* *<MRG 175>* **NIXON** [60] [ ]
– The good old shoe / Grumpus / You masculine you / Up with people / Nashville parent / What else could it be? / The distance from her to there / The book I haven't read / The petrified florist / The butcher boy.

May 00. (7") *(20165-7)* **UP WITH PEOPLE. / MISS PRISSY** [66] [–]
(cd-s+=) *(20159-2)* – ('A'-remix by Zero 7).
(12") *(20159-6)* – ('A'side) / ('A'-remix by Zero 7) / ('A'-reprise by Zero 7).

Feb 02. (cd/d-lp) *(20190-2/-1)* *<MRG 504>* **IS A WOMAN** [38] [ ]
– The daily growl / The new cobweb summer / My blue wave / I can hardly spell my name / Autumn's vicar / Flick / Caterpillar / D. Scott Parsley / Bugs / The old matchbook trick / Is a woman.

May 02. (cd-s) *(20196-0)* **IS A WOMAN / THE NEW COBWEB SUMMER (Schneider TM Lanzarote remix) / IS A WOMAN (Alpha remix) / IS A WOMAN (Maxwell implosion rework) / IS A WOMAN (video)** [ ] [–]

☐ Mark LANEGAN (see under ⇒ SCREAMING TREES)

k.d. LANG

Born: KATHRYN DAWN LANG, 2 Nov'61, Consort, Alberta, Canada. A genuine cowgirl, LANG was raised in a remote rural town, developing her impressive voice from the age of 5 and picking up a guitar at age 10. Her infatuation with country, and more specifically with PATSY CLINE, began when LANG played a 'CLINE-type' character in a play at college. Hooking up with backing band The RECLINES, LANG toured her sensual, often campy, stage show around Canada, releasing a debut album, 'A TRULY WESTERN EXPERIENCE' (1984) on the Canadian independent label, 'Bumstead'. Her live reputation brought LANG to the attention of 'Sire' head, SEYMOUR STEIN, and with a revamped RECLINES: HAROLD BRADLEY (bass), JIMMY CAPPS (rhythm guitar), BUDDY HARMAN (drums), PETE WADE (guitar), HAL RUGG (stee guitar), HENRY STRZELECKI (bass), ROB HAJACOBS (fiddle), MARCUS 'PIG' ROBBINS (piano), TONY MIGLIORE (piano), BUDDY EMMONS (pedal steel) and BEN MINK (co-writer and violin), LANG set about recording her major label debut, 'ANGEL WITH A LARIAT' (1987). Produced by DAVE EDMUNDS, the record was tougher and more considered than the debut with LANG at her best on cover material, whether the effervescent swirl of Lynn Anderson's 'ROSE GARDEN' or the dark introspection of Eddie Miller & W.S. Stevenson's 'THREE CIGARETTES IN AN ASHTRAY'. Mooted as a bid to prove her credentials, 'SHADOWLAND' (1988) saw LANG in stone country mode, teaming up with Nashville production maestro, OWEN BRADLEY and even rounding up the likes of BRENDA LEE, KITTY WELLS and LORETTA LYNN for vocal contributions. Early the following year, she notched up further kudos by duetting with ROY ORBISON on his classic 'CRYING', released as the B-side to his hit, 'YOU GOT IT'. The performance subsequently netted the pair a Grammy award, LANG again working with ORBISON later that summer on 'BLUE BAYOU' (released as the B-side to his 'California Blue' single) as well as guesting on DION's 'Yo Frankie' album. LANG's third opus, 'ABSOLUTE TORCH AND TWANG' (1989) was more adventurous, consolidating her status as one of country music's most versatile and original performers. Whether poring over lovelorn laments like 'TRAIL OF BROKEN HEARTS' or tearing through Willie Nelson & Faron Young's 'THREE DAYS', LANG injected her music with a sass and style that the cobwebbed corners of Nashville hadn't glimpsed since EMMYLOU HARRIS emerged in the mid-70's. The record won LANG another Grammy, although as the 80's turned into the 90's, increasing column inches were dedicated to personal matters rather than praise for her music. While LANG had long been adopted as an icon by lesbians, the style press jumped on her quiffed, smouldering tomboy looks when she officially admitted her homosexuality in gay publication, 'The Advocate'. Surprisingly, this revelation didn't seem to affect sales of 'INGENUE' (1992), presumably because LANG's fanbase was now far wider than the conservative confines of country. Her most accessible release to date, the record found LANG inflecting her country with a subtle pop nous and silky sophistication, the album becoming a UK Top 30 hit while the gorgeously languid 'CONSTANT CRAVING' eventually made the Top 40. Following her appearance in the 1991 Percy Adlon film, 'Salmonberries', LANG continued her dalliance with the movie world by scoring the soundtrack to GUS VAN SANT's 'EVEN COWGIRLS GET THE BLUES' (1993). Her next album proper came with 'ALL YOU CAN EAT' (1995), a more playful affair that saw LANG more at ease with her sexuality (she was once press fodder for her association with tennis star, Martini Navratilova) and moving even further from her country roots. Of recent times, the album 'DRAG' has kept the buying public in awe of her capability to turn basic tunes into joyful torch ballads. The singer entered the new decade with 'INVINCIBLE SUMMER' (2000), a record which suggested life might well begin at 40 after all. A supremely contented sounding LANG sashayed her way through a set of luxuriously produced pop, letting the vintage wine-smoothness of her voice linger on all the right notes. If it was all a bit too MOR for longtime fans, they could at least content themselves with 'LIVE BY REQUEST' (2001), a trawl through the cream of her catalogue as recorded for an American cable TV channel. The Canadian ingratiated herself further into the realms of super-smooth sophistication via a collaborative set with TONY BENNETT. Produced by T-BONE BURNETT, 'A WONDERFUL WORLD' (2003) was perhaps the logical next step for LANG, a labour (if that's not too strong a word for the record's easy charm) of love which not only put a deliciously different spin on some well worn LOUIS ARMSTRONG standards but hopefully began a beautiful musical friendship. • **Songwriters:** LANG collaborates with BEN MINK. Covered; CRAZY + I FALL TO PIECES (Patsy Cline) / LOCK, STOCK AND TEARDROPS (Roger Miller) / WESTERN STARS (Chris Isaak) / JOHNNY GET ANGRY (Carol Deene) / SO IN LOVE (Cole Porter) / FULL MOON FULL OF LOVE (Jeannie Smith & Leroy Preston) / BIG BIG LOVE (Wynn Stewart) / WHAT'S NEW PUSSYCAT? (Bacharach-David) / etc. The 'DRAG' album featured covers THEME FROM THE VALLEY OF THE DOLLS (Dory & Andre Previn) / HAIN'T IT FUNNY (Jane Siberry) / THE JOKER (Steve Miller) / MY LAST CIGARETTE (Boo Hewerdine).

Album rating: A TRULY WESTERN EXPERIENCE (*4) / ANGEL WITH A LARIAT (*6) / SHADOWLAND (*6) / ABSOLUTE TORCH AND TWANG (*6) / INGENUE (*8) / EVEN COWGIRLS GET THE BLUES (*4) / ALL YOU CAN EAT (*6) / DRAG (*6) / INVINCIBLE SUMMER (*6) / LIVE BY REQUEST (*6)

k.d. LANG – vocals, acoustic guitar with / **STEWART MacDOUGALL** – keyboards repl. MIKE CREBER + TED BOROWIECKI / **JOHN DYMOND** – bass repl. DENNIS MARCENKO + FARLEY SCOTT / **MICHEL POULIOT** – drums repl. DAVE BARNSON / **GORDIE MATTHEWS** – guitar (other early members **GARY KOLIGER** – slide guitar / **JAMIE KIDD** – organ)

not iss. Bumstead

1983. (7"ltd.) *<none>* **DAMNED OLD DOG. / FRIDAY DANCE PROMENADE** [–] Canada [–]

Feb 84. (lp) *<none>* **A TRULY WESTERN EXPERIENCE** [–] Canada [–]
– Bopatena / Pine and stew / Up to me / Tickled pink / Hanky Panky / There you go / Busy being blue / Stop, look and listen / Hooked on junk.

— **k.d. LANG & The RECLINES,** with in 1986 **HAROLD BRADLEY** – bass / **JIMMY CAPPS** – rhythm guitar / **BUDDY HARMAN** – drums / **PETE WADE** – guitar / **HAL RUGG** – steel guitar / **HENRY STRZELECKI** – bass / **ROB HAJACOBS** – fiddle / **MARCUS 'Pig' ROBBINS** – piano / **TONY MIGLIORE** – piano / **BUDDY EMMONS** – steel / **BEN MINK** – violin

Sire Sire

Jan 87. (7") *(W 8465) <28465>* **ROSE GARDEN. / HIGH TIME FOR A DETOUR** [ ] [ ]

Feb 87. (lp/c) *(K 92544-1/-4)* **ANGEL WITH A LARIAT** [ ] [ ]
– Turn me around / High time for detour / Diet of strange places / Got the bull by the horns / Watch your step polka / Tune into my wave / Rose garden / Angel with a lariat / Pay dirt / Three cigarettes in an ashtray.

Apr 88. (7") *<27919>* **I'M DOWN TO MY LAST CIGARETTE. / WESTERN STARS** [–] [ ]

Apr 88. (lp/c/cd) *(WX 171/+C/CD) <25724>* **SHADOWLAND** [ ] [73]
– Western stars / Lock, stock and teardrops / Sugar moon / I wish I didn't love you so / Once again around the dancefloor / Black coffee / Shadowland / Don't let the stars get in your eyes / Tears don't care who cries them / I'm down to my last cigarette / Too busy, being blue / Honky tonk angel's medley: In the evening (when the Sun goes down) – You nearly lose your mind – Blues stay away from me.

Jun 88. (7") *<27813>* **LOCK, STOCK AND TEARDROPS. / DON'T LET THE STARS GET IN YOUR EYES** [–] [ ]

Jun 88. (7") *(W 7841)* **SUGAR MOON. / HONKY TONK ANGELS MEDLEY** [ ] [ ]
(12"+=) *(W 7841T)* – I'm down to my last cigarette.
(below 'A'side featured in the soundtrack to 'Shag' film.

Nov 88. (7") *(W 7697)* **OUR DAY WILL COME. / THREE CIGARETTES IN AN ASHTRAY (live)** [ ] [ ]
(12"+=) *(W 7697T)* – Johnny get angry (live).

— Jan'89, she duetted on ROY ORBISON's 'Crying', a B-side to 'You Got It'. The same song featured on his B-side to Mar'89 single 'She's A Mystery To Me'. In Jul89, she again sang with the recently deceased ROY on 'Blue Bayou', which was a B-side to his 'California Blue'. The song had originally featured in the 1987 film 'Hiding Out'. In Jun'89, she guested on DION's album 'Yo Frankie'.

— Her band still included **MINK, POULIOT, DYMOND, MATTHEWS, CREBER** plus **GREG LEISZ** – steel guitar / **GRAHAM BOYLE** – perc. / **DAVID PILTCH** – fretless bass

May 89. (7") *<22932>* **WALLFLOWER WALTZ. / FULL MOON OF LOVE** [–] [ ]

May 89. (lp/c/cd) *(WX 259/+C/CD) <25877>* **ABSOLUTE TORCH AND TWANG** [ ] [69]
– Luck in my eyes / Three days / Trail of broken hearts / Big boned gal / Didn't I / Wallflower waltz / Full Moon full of love / Pullin' back the reins / Big big love / It's me / Walkin' in and out of your arms / Nowhere to stand.

Nov 89. (7") *<22734>* **TRAIL OF BROKEN HEARTS. / THREE DAYS** [–] [ ]

— In Jul'90, she guested on WENDY & LISA's album 'Eroica'.

Oct 90. (7") *(W 9535)* **RIDIN' THE RAILS. / (track by Darlene Love)** [ ] [ ]

— (above single appeared on 'Warners' and the soundtrack to 'Dick Tracy') Late in 1991, she guested on JANE SIBERRY's song 'Calling All Angels'.

— She is now credited solo, but still retaining some or most of band.

Mar 92. (cd/c/lp) *<(7599 26840-2/-4/-1)>* **INGENUE** [3] [18]
– Save me / The mind of love (where is your head Kathryn?) / Miss Chatelaine / Wash me clean / So it shall be / Still thrives this love / Season of hollow soul / Outside myself / Tears of love's recall / Constant craving.

May 92. (7"/c-s) *(W 0100/+C)* **CONSTANT CRAVING. / BAREFOOT** [52] [–]
(12"+=/cd-s+=) *(W 0100 T/CD)* – Season of hollow soul.

Jul 92. (c-s) *<18942>* **CONSTANT CRAVING / SEASON OF HOLLOW SOUL** [–] [38]

— CRYING was re-issued by 'Virgin' Aug'92 as 'A'side and hit UK No.13. 2 months later it again featured as a 'B'side. This time on his 'Heartbreak Radio'.

Sep 92. (7"/c-s) *(W 0135/+C)* **MISS CHATELAINE. / ('A'-St.Tropez edit)** [ ] [ ]
(cd-s+=) *(W 0135CD)* – Wash me clean / The mind of love.
(12"+=) *(W 0135TW)* – (2-'A'-St.Tropez mixes).

Feb 93. (7"/c-s) *(W 0157/+C)* **CONSTANT CRAVING. / MISS CHATELAINE** [15] [–]
(cd-s+=) *(W 0157CD)* – Wash me clean (live) / The mind of love (live).
(cd-s) *(W 0157CDX)* – ('A'side) / Big boned gal (live) / Outside myself (live).

Apr 93. (7"/c-s) *(W 0170/+C)* **THE MIND OF LOVE (WHERE IS YOUR HEAD KATHRYN?). / THE MIND OF LOVE (live)** [72] [ ]
(cd-s+=) *(W 0170CD1)* – Pullin' back the reins.
(cd-s) *(W 0170CD2)* – ('A'side) / Three cigarettes in a ashtray / Trail of broken hearts / Busy being blue.

Jun 93. (7"/c-s) *(W 0181/+C)* **MISS CHATELAINE. / ('A'mix)** [68] [ ]
(cd-s) *(W 0181CD)* – ('A'side) / ('A'-St.Tropez mix) / ('A'-Paris 92 mix).

Nov 93. (cd/c) *<(9362 45433-2/-4)>* **EVEN COWGIRLS GET THE BLUES (soundtrack)** [36] [82]
– Just keep me moving / Much finer place / Or was I / Hush sweet lover / Myth / Apogee / Virtual vortex / Lifted by love / Overture / Kundalini yoga waltz / In perfect dreams / Curious soul astray / Ride of Bonanza Jellybean / Don't be a lemming polka / Sweet little Cherokee / Cowgirl pride.

Dec 93. (7"/c-s) *(W 0227/+C)* **JUST KEEP ME MOVING. / IN PERFECT DREAMS** [59] [ ]
(12"/cd-s) *(W 0227 T/CD)* – ('A'side) / ('A'wild planet mixes) / ('A'moving mixes).

Warners Warners

Sep 95. (c-s) *(W 0319C)* **IF I WERE YOU / WHAT'S NEW PUSSYCAT** [53] [ ]
(cd-s+=) *(W 0319CD)* – Get some.

Oct 95. (cd/c) *<(9362 46034-2/-4)>* **ALL YOU CAN EAT** [7] [37]
– If I were you / Maybe / You're ok / Sexuality / Get some / Acquiesce / This / World of love / Infinite and unforeseen / I want it all.

May 96. (c-s) *(W 0332C)* **YOU'RE OK / IF I WERE YOU** [44] [–]
(12"+=/cd-s+=) *(W 0332 T/CD)* – If I were you (smokin' lounge + Junior's X-beat mixes).

Jul 97. (cd/c) *<(9362 46623-2/-4)>* **DRAG** [19] [29]
– Don't smoke in bed / The air that I breathe / Smoke dreams / My last cigarette / The joker / Theme from the Valley Of The Dolls / Your smoke screen / My old addiction / Till the heart caves in / Smoke rings / Hain't it funny? / Love is like a cigarette.

Jul 00. (cd/c) *<(9362 24706-2/-4)>* **INVINCIBLE SUMMER** [17] [58]
– Consequences of falling / Summerfling / Suddenly / It's happening with you / Extraordinary thing / Love's great ocean / Simple / What better said / When we collide / Curiosity / Only love.

Jul 00. (cd-s) *(W 528CD)* **SUMMERFLING (mixes; Victor Calderone extended vocal / Wamdue's summer bliss extended / Anando's sweet bird of summer extended / Victor Calderone dub / Wamdue's makin' me high dub / Anando's sweet dub of summer / album)** [ ] [–]

Oct 00. (c-s) *(W 536C)* **THE CONSEQUENCES OF FALLING / (love to infinity radio mix)** [ ] [–]
(cd-s+=) *(W 536CD)* – ('A'-love to infinity master & funk mixes).

Sep 01. (cd) *<9362 48108-2>* **LIVE BY REQUEST (live December 14, 2000)** [ ] Aug01 [94]
– Summerfling / Big boned gal / Black coffee / Trail of broken hearts / Crying / Don't smoke in bed / The consequences of falling / Miss Chatelaine / Three cigarettes in an ashtray / Barefoot / Constant craving / Wash me clean / Pullin' back the reins / Simple.

— Late in 2002 (mid 2003 UK), k.d. LANG teamed up with TONY BENNETT for the album, 'A WONDERFUL WORLD'; US No.41 + UK No.33

LA'S

Formed: Liverpool, England ... 1984 by songwriters MIKE BADGER (ex-KINDERGARTEN PAINTSET) and LEE MAVERS, along with drummer JOHN TIMSON; a limited V/A sampler 'A Secret Liverpool' exists of these times. When an inexperienced young bass player JOHN POWER joined the well-touted LA'S (alongside brief member PAUL HEMMINGS), things began to change, friction also set-in between BADGER and MAVERS, the former bailing out and disappearing into the world of sculpture and painting (he had been a great fan of CAPTAIN BEEFHEART!). Signing to 'Go! Discs' early in 1987, the new LA'S (with MAVERS at the helm) released the charming retro-pop debut single, 'WAY OUT'. The record was well received but failed to chart and replacing TIMSON with CHRIS SHARROCK, the band followed up the single with the seminal BYRDS-like pop genius of 'THERE SHE GOES', all soaring melodies and youthful vigour. Incredibly, the single failed to chart, although it later reached the Top 20 when it was re-released in 1990 at the same time as the eponymous debut. Over the two year period it took to record the album, MAVERS' friend BARRY SUTTON replaced SHARROCK on the drum stool while JAMES JOYCE was recruited for the departing POWER (who went on to form the highly successful CAST). CAMMY, another guitarist, was also added. Part of the problem was the notoriously perfectionist MAVERS who obsessed over every tiny detail of the recording process in his search for an 'authentic' sound. 'Go! Discs' became increasingly worried about the escalating cost of the project and decided to go ahead and release the album against MAVERS' wishes. He retaliated by criticising the company in press interviews and dismissed the debut as a collection of demos. In reality, the album was a seamless collection of post-baggy guitar pop, drawing comparisons with the STONE ROSES and garnering almost universal acclaim. After a tour of America and Japan in 1991, the band went to ground and little has been heard from them since, save a brief, disastrous appearance supporting PAUL WELLER in 1994. While rumours continue to abound, the band remain one of the greatest modern day musical enigmas. BADGER finally emerged as a solo artist (he had worked for SPACE on the cover of 'Tin Planet') at the beginning of 1999, an album 'VOLUME' (on his SPACE mate TOMMY SCOTT's new 'Viper' imprint and produced by now LIGHTNING SEEDS man PAUL HEMMINGS) was the missing piece in The LA's troubled rock'n'roll history. A subsequent tabloid grouch by the equally reclusive MAVERS on the worthiness of CAST frontman JOHN POWER was given short shrift – meanwhile SIXPENCE NONE THE RICHER (how well named) were high in the US charts with the LA'S classic, 'THERE SHE GOES'.

Album rating: THE LA'S (*8) / BREAKLOOSE (LOST LA'S 1983-86) (*6) / Mike Badger: VOLUME (*6)

LEE MAVERS (b. 2 Aug'62) – vocals, guitar / **JOHN TIMSON** – drums / added **JOHN POWER** (b.14 Sep'67) – bass

— (late '86) MIKE BADGER was repl. by **PAUL HEMMINGS** – guitar / **JOHN 'BOO' BYRNE** – guitar

Go! Discs London

Oct 87. (7") *(GOLAS 1)* **WAY OUT. / ENDLESS** [ ] [ ]
(12"+=) *(GOLAS 1-12)* – Knock me down.
(12"++=) *(GOLAR 1-12)* – Liberty ship (demo) / Freedom song (demo).

— **CHRIS SHARROCK** – drums (ex-ICICLE WORKS) repl. TIMSON

Nov 88. (7") *(GOLAS 2)* **THERE SHE GOES. / COME IN, COME OUT** [59] [ ]
(12"+=)(cd-s+=) *(GOLAS 2-12)(LASCD 2)* – Who knows / Man I'm only human.
(7"ep+=) *(LASEP 2)* – Who knows / Way out (new version).

May 89. (7";w-drawn) *(GOLAS 3)* **TIMELESS MELODY. / CLEAN PROPHET** [–] [–]
(10"+=; w-drawn) *(LASEP 3)* – All by myself / There she goes.
(cd-s+=; w-drawn) *(LASCD 3)* – All by myself / Ride yer camel.

— **NEIL MAVERS** (b. 8 Jul'71) – drums repl. SHARROCK / **JAMES JOYCE** (b.23 Sep'70) – bass repl. POWER who formed CAST / added **CAMMY** (b.PETER JAMES CAMELL, 30 Jun'67) – guitar (ex-MARSHMALLOW)

Sep 90. (7"/c-s) *(GOLAS/LASMC 4)* **TIMELESS MELODY. / CLEAN PROPHET** [57] [ ]
(12"purple+=)(cd-s+=) *(GOLAS 4-12)(LASCD 4)* – Knock me down / Over.

Oct 90. (cd/c/lp) *(<828 202-2/-4/-1>)* **THE LA'S** [30] [ ]
– Son of a gun / I can't sleep / Timeless melody / Liberty ship / There she goes / Doledrum / Feelin' / Way out / I.O.U. / Freedom song / Failure / Looking glass. *(cd re-iss. Sep99 on 'Polydor'; same) (cd re-mast.Jan01 on 'Universal'+=; 549566-2)* – All by myself / Clean prophet / Knock me down / Over (live) / IOU (alt.take).

Oct 90. (7"/c-s) *(GOLAS/LASMC 5)* **THERE SHE GOES (new version). / FREEDOM SONG** [13] [–]
(12"+=)(cd-s+=) *(GOLAS 5-12)(LASCD 5)* – All by myself.

Feb 91. (7"/c-s) *(GOLAS/LASMC 6)* **FEELIN'. / DOLEDRUM** [43] [ ]
(12"+=)(cd-s+=)(7"ep+=) *(GOLAS 6-12)(LASCD 6)(GOLAB 6)* – I.O.U. (alt.version) / Liberty ship.

Jun 91. (c-s) *<869 370-4>* **THERE SHE GOES / ALL BY MYSELF** [–] [49]

— had already disbanded just prior to above. In Apr'97 a various artists EP (taken from the movie, 'Fever Pitch', featured 'THERE SHE GOES' (issued on 'Blanco Yo Negro'; *NEG 104 C/T/CD)*

– compilations, etc. –

Sep 99. (cd-s) *Polydor; (561403-2)* **THERE SHE GOES / COME IN COME OUT / WHO KNOWS** [65] [–]

Oct 99. (cd/lp) *Viper; (VIPER 2 CD/LP)* **BREAKLOOSE (LOST LA'S 1984-1986)** [ ] [–]
– Breakloose (live) / Open your heart / Sweet 35 / Trees and plants / Red deer stalk / Dovecot dub / Walk / Get down over / What do you do / I did the painting / My girl sits like reindeer / Money in your talk / You blue / Moonlight.

Jul 01. (cd/lp) *Viper; (VIPER 8 CD/LP)* **CALLIN' ALL (LOST LA'S 1986-1987)** [ ] [–]

LAST POETS

Formed: Harlem, New York, USA . . . May '69 by DAVID NELSON, GYLAN KAIN and CHUCK DAVIS (aka ABIODUN OYEWOLE). Coming together via an impromptu poetry performance at a Malcolm X birthday celebration in a Harlem park, the trio subsequently set up the East Wind cultural center/poetry workshop where they were joined by FELIPE LUCIANO. The collective's ranks were swelled by the addition – in quick succession – of JALAL MANSUR NURIDDIN, OMAR BIN HASSAN and ALAFIA PUDIM, taking the name The LAST POETS from a poem DAVIS had written after being inspired by the work of South African writer,

K. William Kokafili. Although they'd set out to promote black unity, internal divisions soon led to a split with NELSON, KAIN and LUCIANO forming one group and OYEWOLE, NURRIDIN, BIN HASSAN and PUDIM forming another. Both camps soon got down to recording, OYEWOLE's bunch emerging with 1970's acclaimed 'THE LAST POETS' on 'Douglas' (the label owned by jazz man, Alan Douglas, who also produced the album), while NELSON and Co took a little longer on their debut long-player, 'RIGHT ON!' (1971). The former set boasted stark, uncompromising material – with the deliberate use of the derogatory term 'nigger' – intended to both rouse Afro-Americans from their torpor and act as a metaphorical call to arms. Recorded with minimal percussive accompaniment, the likes of 'NIGGERS ARE SCARED OF REVOLUTION' and 'WHEN THE REVOLUTION COMES' were heavily influential on the young GIL SCOTT-HERON who'd record in a similar style on his 1972 debut, 'Small Talk At 125th & Lennox' (125th Street, incidentally, being the location of the East Wind workshop). OYEWOLE & Co enjoyed the greatest success with 'THE LAST POETS' album even entering the US Top 30, largely by word of mouth sales. OYEWOLE, meanwhile subsequently found himself behind bars for armed robbery and was therefore absent from the recording of Spring 1971's equally militant follow-up set, 'THIS IS MADNESS'; the record's scathing criticisms of the Nixon administration allegedly landed them on an FBI counter-intelligence black list. At the same time the aforementioned 'RIGHT ON!' (billed as The ORIGINAL LAST POETS) was displaying similar sentiments, bubbling under the US Top 100 in tandem with their Muslim counterparts. HASSAN subsequently left for a religious sect (replaced by SULIAMAN EL-HADI) prior to 1972's 'CHASTISEMENT', a more musically dense affair utiilising back-up singers. The following year saw the release of perhaps the best-loved LAST POETS-related album, 'HUSTLER'S CONVENTION'. A jive-talkin' concept affair based on the real life 1959 hustler's convention at Hamhock's Hall, the album was recorded by JALAL (who'd now taken over the reins of the 'POETS) under the alias LIGHTNIN' ROD and told the story of Sport and his buddy Spoon, two hustler's who eventually go straight after a series of misadventures. Superfunk musical backing was provided by KOOL & THE GANG, BILLY PRESTON and BROTHER GENE DINWIDDIE amongst others, the album going on to become a minor legend and influencing the styles of rap progenitors such as KOOL HERC and MELLE MEL. The free-jazz stylings of 1976's 'AT LAST' served as the next LAST POETS release, heralding a lay-off of three years before 'DELIGHTS OF THE GARDEN' (1977). Issued on 'Casablanca', the latter set featured the EL-HADI penned jazz-funk floorfiller, 'IT'S A TRIP' as well as JALAL's epic 'BEYONDER', both tracks backed by the drums of veteran BERNARD PURDIE. As rap and hip-hop revolutionised black music in the late 70's/early 80's, The LAST POETS were conspicuous by their absence from the recording front. They eventually re-emerged in 1984 on Bill Laswell's 'Celluloid' imprint with the album, 'OH MY PEOPLE', less frenetic than of old but still as committed as ever; P-funk man, BERNIE WORRELL guested on two tracks, the electro-influenced 'GET MOVIN' and 'HOLD FAST'. Another four years ensued before 'FREEDOM EXPRESS' (1988) while the early 90's saw JALAL working with London's premier acid-jazzers, GALLIANO. In 1995, there arose yet another situation whereby two groups released material as The LAST POETS; OYEWOLE and HASSAN re-emerged with the HOLY TERROR album while JALAL and SULIAMAN released the 'SCATTERAP / HOME' CD. Despite the schism, The LAST POETS remain one of the most influential black music formations of the last thirty years, their militant stance echoed in the work of PUBLIC ENEMY while their records remain highly prized collectors items sampled by the likes of A TRIBE CALLED QUEST amongst others.

Album rating: THE LAST POETS (*8) / RIGHT ON!; by The Original Last Poets (*7) / THIS IS MADNESS (*6) / CHASTISEMENT (*6) / AT LAST (*4) / HUSTLER'S CONVENTION as Lightnin' Rod – aka Jalal (*8) / DELIGHTS OF THE GARDEN (*7) / OH, MY PEOPLE (*5) / FREEDOM EXPRESS (*4) / SCATTERAP – HOME (*4) / HOLY TERROR (*5) / THE BEST OF THE LAST POETS compilation (*8) / REAL RAP compilation (*8)

ABIODUN OYEWOLE (aka CHUCK DAVIS) – vocals / **GYLAN KAIN** – vocals / **DAVID NELSON** – vocals / **FELIPE LUCIANO** – vocals / **JALAL MANSUR NURIDDIN** – vocals / **OMAR BIN HASSAN** – vocals / **ALAFIA PUDIM** – vocals

— the departing NELSON, LUCIANO and KAIN went on to release one album, 'RIGHT ON!' in Feb'71 for 'Juggernaut' <8802>

Douglas Douglas

Jun 70. (lp) <*3*> **THE LAST POETS** [–] [29]
– Run nigger / On the subway / Niggers are scared of revolution / Black thighs / Gashman / Wake up, niggers / New York, New York / Jones comin' down / Just because / Black wish / When the revolution comes / Two little boys / Surprises. *(cd-iss. Dec93 on 'Celluloid'; CELD 6101) (cd re-iss. Jun96 on 'Charly'; CPCD 8184) (lp re-iss. Nov01 on 'Get Back'; GET 8005) (cd re-iss. Apr02 on 'Sunspot'; SPOT 502)*

— now without OYEWOLE who was imprisoned

— added **NILAJA** – percussion

1972. (lp) *(DGL 69012)* <*30583*> **THIS IS MADNESS** [ ] Mar71 [ ]
– True blues / Related to what / Black is / Time / Mean machine / White man's got a God complex / Opposites / Black people what y'all gon' do / O.D. / This is madness. *(cd-iss. Dec93 on 'Celluloid'; CELD 6105) (cd re-iss. Nov95 on 'Charly'; CPCD 8154) (cd re-iss. Aug02 on 'Sunspot'; SPOT 512) (lp re-iss. Apr02 on 'Get Back'; GET 8009) (lp re-iss. Sep02 on 'Vampi Soul'; VAMPI 010)*

— added **SULIAMAN EL-HADI** – drums / plus **OBABI, OMIYINKA + OMONIDE** – congas / **JOHN HART** – bass / **SAM HARKNESS** – sax

not iss. Blue Thumb

1972. (lp) <*BTS 39*> **CHASTISEMENT** [–] [ ]
– Tribute to Obabi (Ogun) / Jazzoetry / Black soldier / E pluribus unum / Before the white man came / Hands off / Bird's word. *(cd-iss. Dec93 on 'Celluloid'; CELD 6209) (cd re-iss. Apr97 on 'Charly'; CPCD 822)*

— In 1973, JALAL (under the moniker of LIGHTNIN' ROD) issued the album, 'HUSTLER'S CONVENTION'.

1976. (lp) <*BTS 52*> **AT LAST** [–] [ ]
– Tranquility / Reflections / Uncle Sam's lament / The African slave / Ode to Saphcallah / In search of knowledge / In time and space / The courtroom / Death row / Picture of blue.

— (NILAJA left) **JALAL + SULIAMAN** added **BERNARD PURDIE** – drums / **ALEX BLAKE** – bass / **ABU MUSTAPHA** – vocals, percussion

not iss. Casablanca

1977. (lp) <*NBLP 7051*> **DELIGHTS OF THE GARDEN** [–] [ ]
– It's a trip / Ho Chi Minh / Blessed are those who struggle / The pill / Delights of the garden / Beyonder: 1. Be – 2. Yond – 3. Er. *(cd-iss. Dec93 on 'Celluloid'; CELD 6136) (cd re-iss. Sep96 on 'Charly'; CPCD 8191)*

— the pair were joined by **BERNIE WORRELL** – synthesizer / **BILL LASWELL** – percussion, electric drums / **AIYB DIENG** – percussion, drums / **JAMAL ABDUS SABUR** – bass / **KENYATTI ABDUR RAHMAN** – synthesizer / **PHILIP WILSON** – percussion

Celluloid Celluloid

Apr 85. (lp) <*(CELL 6108)*> **OH, MY PEOPLE** [ ] [ ]
– Get movin' / This is your life / What will you do / Oh, my people / Hold fast / Parting comany. *(cd-iss. Nov92 on 'Mau Mau'; MAUCD 627) (cd re-iss. Dec93 on 'Celluloid'; CELD 6108) (cd re-iss. Mar96 on 'Charly'; CPCD 8174)*

Jul 85. (12") <*(CEL 703)*> **GET MOVIN'. / MEAN MACHINE** [ ] [ ]

Acid Jazz Celluloid

Jan 89. (lp/cd) *(JAZID 8 LP/CD)* <*CELL 6172*> **FREEDOM EXPRESS** [ ] Nov88 [ ]
– Tough enough / Woodshed walk / Freedom express / Geronimo / Unholy alliance. *(cd re-iss. Dec93 on 'Celluloid'; CELD 6172) (cd re-iss. Jan97 on 'Movieplay Gold'; MPG 74040) (cd re-iss. Feb98 on 'Charly'; CPCD 8329)*

— JALAL also issued three other solo releases, the 10" for 'On-U-Sound' 'MANKIND' (1993), 'ON THE ONE' (1996) and 'FRUITS OF RAP' (1997).

— **JALAL + SULIAMAN** were the LAST POETS who released . . .

		Bond Age	not iss.
Aug 94.	(cd) <9471> **SCATTERAP / HOME** – See / Hear / Taste / Touch / Smell / Reasoning / Choice / Minority of one (under the shadow of the . . . .) / Mystery man / You can do it / The drama / Way over due's blues.	– French	–

— **OYEWOLE + HASSAN** reclaimed The LAST POETS moniker also (guests included BOOTSY COLLINS, GEORGE CLINTON + GRANDMASTER MELLE MEL)

		Black Arc – Rhino	Black Arc – Rhino
May 95.	(cd) <*(RCD 10319)*> **HOLY TERROR** – Invocation / Homesick / Black rage / Men-tality / Late rite / Talk show / Illusion of self / If only we knew / Funk / Phelhourinho. *(re-iss. Mar97; same)*		
Jul 95.	(12") <*(RA 121048)*> **BLACK & STRONG (HOMESICK). / (instrumental)**		

– compilations, etc. –

Dec 93.	(cd) *Celluloid; <(CELD 6208)>* **RETRO FIT**		
Apr 95.	(cd/c) *On The One; (SPOA 22/21)* **THE BEST OF THE PRIME TIME RHYME VOL.1**		
Nov 95.	(cd/lp) *On The One; (SPOA 32/31)* **THE BEST OF THE PRIME TIME RHYME**		
Mar 97.	(cd) *Charly; (CDNEW 105)* **THE BEST OF THE LAST POETS** *(cd re-iss. Feb03 on 'Snapper'; SNAP 110CD)*		–
Sep 97.	(cd) *Music Club; (MCCD 311)* **BEATS RHYME AND REVOLUTION**		–
Mar 99.	(d-cd) *Snapper; (SMDCD 183)* **REAL RAP**		–
Sep 02.	(d-cd) *Vampi Soul; (VAMPI 011CD)* **THE LAST POETS / THIS IS MADNESS**		–
May 03.	(lp) *Get Back; (GET 8028)* **JAZZOETRY**		–

Avril LAVIGNE

Born: 27 Sep'84, Napanee, Ontario, Canada. A self-confessed tomboy who couldn't wait to swap small town life for stardom, LAVIGNE made a name for herself in local church choirs and talents contests before being picked up by 'Arista' records. Plunged into the high wire environment of NYC's music industry, LAVIGNE was initially paired with a crack team of songwriters although it took a move to L.A. and a link-up with producer Clif Magness to really get her creative cogs turning. With Magness and the Matrix production crew overseeing recording, the teenager cut the songs which would make up debut album, 'LET'S GO' (2002). Propelled by the success of the 'COMPLICATED' single (Top 3 on both sides of the Atlantic), the album presented LAVIGNE as the latest teen prodigy, although her adolescent-lite (MORISSETTE) lyrical fare and derivative "skater" chic was just a little bit tiresome. As for the so-called "wild child" label, LAVIGNE's music was about as wild as MARIE OSMOND's, and almost as subversive. • **Covered:** KNOCKIN' ON HEAVEN'S DOOR (Bob Dylan).

Album rating: LET GO (*7)

AVRIL LAVIGNE – vocals, guitar / + session people

		Arista	Arista
Jun 02.	(cd) <*(07822 14740-2)*> **LET GO** – Losing grip / Complicated / Sk8er boi / I'm with you / Mobile / Unwanted / Tomorrow / Anything but ordinary / Things I'll never say / My world / Nobody's fool / Too much to ask / Naked.	1	2
Sep 02.	(c-s) *(74321 96596-4)* <94577> **COMPLICATED / I DON'T GIVE / WHY** (cd-s+=) *(74321 96596-2)* – ('A'video).	3 Jul02	2
Dec 02.	(c-s) *(74321 98070-4)* <97785> **SK8ER BOI / GET OVER IT / NOBODY'S FOOL** (cd-s+=) *(74321 98070-2)* – ('A'video).	8 Nov02	10
Mar 03.	(c-s) *(82876 51575-4)* **I'M WITH YOU / I'M WITH YOU (live) / UNWANTED (live)** (cd-s+=) *(82876 51575-2)* – ('A'video).	7	4
Jul 03.	(c-s) *(82876 53454-4)* **LOSING GRIP / LOSING GRIP (live) / NAKED (live)** (cd-s+=) *(82876 53454-2)* – ('A'video).	22	64

□ LAZYCAME (see under ⇒ JESUS & MARY CHAIN)

□ L-BURNA A.K.A. LAYZIE BONE (see under ⇒ BONE THUGS-N-HARMONY)

LEADBELLY

Born: HUDSON WILLIAM LEDBETTER, 29th of January, 1889, Mooringsport, Los Angeles, USA. A blues legend in his own right, HUDDIE LEDBETTER displayed a unique musical talent at an early age and had ambition beyond range or scope. When he was 13, he had managed to learn to read and write (a very difficult thing to achieve for a black man at the start of the century) and had a substantial grasp on the ethics of guitar playing and performing. The teenager spent most of his nights wandering aimlessly through the red light districts and town squares on his home turf, attracting an audience with his own take-on of popular blues and spiritual music. After his marriage soured in the first decade of the 20th century, LEADBELLY changed his guitar format from 6-string to 12-string, a choice that bettered his career and enabled him to broaden his musical style. He re-worked a traditional song called 'IRENE', which became one of his most treasured songs, and impressed BLIND LEMON JEFFERSON so much that he decided to teach LEADBELLY slide guitar. However, sucess was not forthcoming, and due to his violent outbursts LEADBELLY constantly found himself on the wrong side of the law. In 1917, he was given a life sentence for murder and was sent to Texas State prison, where, ironically, he wrote his best material. His songs became increasingly popular with the prison inmates and governers, and in 1925, the man performed for one particular Texas governer who subsequently pardoned the enigmatic guitarist. When he was released from prison, LEADBELLY tried his best to keep on a straight path by doing odd and regular jobs. He was arrested again in 1930 and sentenced to life imprisonment for attempted murder. In Louisiana prison he met John Lomax (a travelling researcher for the Library of Congress) who was gathering Americana and blues related music with his son. Lomax was more than impressed with LEADBELLY's talents and managed to record material on his small portable studio in prison. In 1934, Lomax persuaded the Congress to free the bluesman, and with the aid of father and son, he became a minor hero in the white community. Lomax subsequently booked LEADBELLY for sessions at the "American record company", which brought coherence to his creations with smooth, clean and professionally recorded songs. However, LEADBELLY's relationship with Lomax was on the rocks due to manipulative and manufactured concerts where he was forced to dress up in a striped prison uniform; ultimately a gimmick to spread LEADBELLY's notoriety. Their partnership expired with LEADBELLY subsequently flitting to New York City in search of a more respectful audience – and that he found. Members of the Bohemian intelligentsia and folk/roots fans created a huge and almost cult following which attracted the attention of Moe Asch, manager of 'Folkway' records. It was here that perhaps the man's finest works were drawn: songs depicting the horrors of World War II were particularly ahead of their time. He continued to record for Asch and 'Capitol' records throughout the 40's although inevitably he fell ill and died on the 6th of December 1949. In his final encore at Texas University he promised the audience he would return explaining his new doctor would help him make a speedy recovery. Sadly, this was untrue as LEADBELLY died a month later. Like many blues legends, fame came to LEADBELLY in death: The WEAVERS had a hit single with their rendition of 'GOODNIGHT IRENE' in 1951, while skiffle-king LONNIE DONEGAN also had a hit with 'ROCK ISLAND LINE' in 1957. Most memorably and most recent was when KURT COBAIN performed a poignant, gut-wrenching version of 'WHERE DID YOU SLEEP LAST NIGHT'. As always, the legend lives on . . .

Best CD compilation: THE VERY BEST OF LEADBELLY (*8)

LEADBELLY – vocals, acoustic guitar

not iss. Mus

1939. (78) *<223>* **FRANKIE AND ALBERT. / unknown**
1939. (78) *<224>* **FRANKIE AND ALBERT. / unknown**
1939. (78) *<225>* **FANNIN STREET. / unknown**
1939. (78) *<226>* **DE KALB BLUES. / THE BOLL WEEVIL**
1939. (78) *<227>* **THE GALLIS POLE. / THE BOURGEOIS BLUES**

not iss. Victory

1940. (78) *<27266>* **HAM AN' EGGS. / MIDNIGHT SPECIAL**
1940. (78) *<27267>* **GREY GOOSE. / STEW-BALL**
1940. (78) *<27268>* **ALABAMA BOUND. / PICK A BALE OF COTTON**
(UK-iss.1955 on 'H.M.V.'; MH 190)

not iss. Bluebird

1940. (78) *<B 8550>* **DON'T YOU LOVE YOUR DADDY NO MORE? / SAIL ON, LITTLE GIRL, SAIL ON**
1940. (78) *<B 8559>* **T.B. BLUES. / ALBERTA**
1940. (78) *<B 8570>* **WORRIED BLUES. / EASY RIDER**
1941. (78) *<B 8709>* **RED CROSS STORE BLUES. / ROBERTA**
1941. (78) *<B 8750>* **YOU CAN'T LOSE-A ME CHOLLY. / NEW YORK CITY**
1941. (78) *<B 8791>* **GOOD MORNING BLUES. / LEAVING BLUES**
1941. (78) *<B 8981>* **I'M ON MY LAST GO ROUND. /**

not iss. Asch

1941. (78) *<SC 26/27>* **HA HA THISAWAY. / LITTLE SALLY WALKER**
1941. (78) *<SC 32/34>* **REDBIRD. / CHRISTMAS SONG**
1941. (78) *<SC 79/80>* **SKIP TO MY LOU. / YOU CAN'T LOSE ME CHOLLY**
1942. (78) *<101>* **TAKE THIS HAMMER. / CORN BREAD ROUGH**
1942. (78) *<102>* **ROCK ISLAND LINE. / OL' RILEY**
1942. (78) *<103>* **OLD MAN. / HAUL AWAY, JOE**
1943. (78) *<343-1>* **HOW LONG BLUES. / GOOD MORNING BLUES**
(UK-iss.1951 on 'Melodisc'; 1140)
1943. (78) *<343-2>* **IRENE. / AIN'T YOU GLAD**
(UK-iss.1951 on 'Melodisc'; 1151) – 'A'side 'GOODNIGHT IRENE'
1943. (78) *<343-3>* **ON A MONDAY. / JOHN HENRY**
(UK-iss.1951 on 'Melodisc'; 1187)
1944. (78) *<561-1>* **MEETING AT THE BUILDING. / BRING ME A LIL' WATER SYLVIE**
1944. (78) *<561-2>* **PLAYING WITH YOUR POODLE. / FIDDLER'S DRAM**
1944. (78) *<561-3>* **BIG FAT WOMAN. / JOHN HARDY**

not iss. Musicraft

1944. (78> *<310>* **YELLOW GAL. / WHEN THE BOYS WERE ON THE WESTERN PLAIN**
1944. (78) *<311>* **ROBERTA. / JOHN HARDY**
1944. (78) *<312>* **IN NEW ORLEANS. / (BLACK GIRL) WHERE DID YOU SLEEP LAST NIGHT**
1944. (78) *<313>* **BILL BRADY. / PRETTY FLOWER IN MY BACKYARD**

not iss. Asch

1944. (78) *<331-1>* **LITTLE SALLY WALKER. / MO' YET**
1944. (78) *<331-2>* **HOW DO YOU KNOW. / SKIP TO MY LOU**
1944. (78) *<331-3>* **(WHAT ARE) LITTLE BOYS (MADE OF). / MOTHER'S BLUES**

Capitol not iss.

1945. (78) *<40038>* **SWEET MARY BLUES. / GRASSHOPPERS IN MY PILLOW**
1945. (78) *<40130>* **BACKWATER BLUES. / IRENE**
1945. (78) *<15628>* **ROCK ISLAND LINE. / Nappy Lamare: HIGH SOCIETY**
1945. (78) *<15629>* **EAGLE ROCK RAG. / Nappy Lamare: AT THE JAZZ BAND BALL**

not iss. Disc

1945. (78) *<6043>* **MIDNIGHT SPECIAL. / HAM AND EGGS**
1945. (78) *<6044>* **YELLOW GAL. / GRAY GOOSE**
1945. (78) *<6045>* **STEW BALL. / ALABAMY BOUND**

— LEADBELLY continued to record until he died on the 6th of Dec'49

– (selective) compilations, etc. –

1966. (d-lp) *Elektra; <(EKL 301-2)>* **THE LIBRARY OF CONGRESS RECORDINGS**
Oct 86. (lp/c) *Deja Vu; (DVLP/DVMC 2072)* **THE COLLECTION: 20 BLUES GREATS**
Nov 91. (cd/c) *Columbia; <(467893-2/-4)>* **KING OF THE TWELVE STRING GUITAR**
Feb 92. (cd) *Rounder; <(ROUCD 1044)>* **MIDNIGHT SPECIAL (LIBRARY OF CONGRESS RECORDINGS VOL.1)**
Feb 92. (cd) *Rounder; <(ROUCD 1045)>* **GWINE DIG A HOLE TO PUT THE DEVIL IN (LIBRARY OF CONGRESS RECORDINGS VOL.2)**
Mar 92. (cd) *Rounder; <(ROUCD 1046)>* **LET IT SHINE ON ME (LIBRARY OF CONGRESS RECORDINGS VOL.3)**
May 93. (cd) *Music Club; (MCCD/MCTC 106)* **THE VERY BEST OF LEADBELLY**
– Midnight special / Sylvie / Matchbox blues / You must have that pure religion, halleloo / Fannin' street / Green corn / Bourgeois blues / When I was a cowboy / Cow cow yicky yicky yea / CC rider / Rock island line / Governor o.k. Allen / De kalb blues / Leavin' blues / Roberta / Frankie and Albert / Alberta / Gray goose / Careless love / Goodnight Irene.
Nov 93. (cd) *Blues Encore; (CD 52028)* **IRENE GOODNIGHT**
Mar 94. (lp/c/cd) *Aldabra; (ALB 1007/+MC/CD)* **CONGRESS BLUES**
Apr 94. (cd) *Document; (DOCD 5226)* **COMPLETE RECORDED WORKS VOL.1: 1939-40**
Apr 94. (cd) *Document; (DOCD 5227)* **COMPLETE RECORDED WORKS VOL.2: 1940-43**
Apr 94. (cd) *Document; (DOCD 5228)* **COMPLETE RECORDED WORKS VOL.3: 1943-44**
Apr 94. (cd) *Rounder; <(ROUCD 1097)>* **THE TITANIC (LIBRARY OF CONGRESS RECORDINGS VOL.4)**
Apr 94. (cd) *Rounder; <(ROUCD 1098)>* **NOBODY KNOWS THE TROUBLE I'VE SEEN (LIBRARY OF CONGRESS RECORDINGS VOL.5)**
Apr 94. (cd) *Rounder; <(ROUCD 1099)>* **GO DOWN OLD HANNAH (LIBRARY OF CONGRESS RECORDINGS, VOL.6)**
Oct 94. (4xcd-set/4xc-box) *Smithsonian Folkways; <(SFW CD/MC 40068)>* **THE LAST SESSIONS**
Dec 94. (cd) *Document; (DOCD 5310)* **COMPLETE RECORDED WORKS VOL.4: 1944**
Dec 94. (cd) *Document; (DOCD 5311)* **COMPLETE RECORDED WORKS VOL.5: 1944-46**
Oct 95. (cd) *Aim; (COLLECT 4CD)* **THE LEGENDARY MASTERS SERIES**
Feb 96. (cd) *Tradition; (TCD 1006)* **GOODNIGHT IRENE**
Apr 96. (cd/c) *Smithsonian Folkways; (SFW CD/MC 40044)* **WHERE DID YOU SLEEP LAST NIGHT (THE LEADBELLY LEGACY VOL.1)**
May 96. (cd) *Tradition; (TCD 1018)* **IN THE SHADOWS OF THE GALLOW'S POLE**
Jun 96. (cd) *Document; (DOCD 5461)* **LEADBELLY & JOSH WHITE / PEETIE WHEATSTRAW 1924 – MID 1940's**
Sep 96. (cd) *Blue Moon; (CDBM 119)* **THE MASTERS**
Oct 96. (cd) *Music Memoria; (842032-2)* **ALL TIME BLUES CLASSICS**
Nov 96. (cd) *I.M.P.; (IMP 310)* **GOODNIGHT IRENE**

May 97. (cd) *Smithsonian Folkways; (SFWCD 40045)* **BOURGEOIS BLUES (THE LEADBELLY LEGACY VOL.2)**
Jun 97. (cd; shared with BLIND WILLIE McTELL) *Biograph; (BCD 144)* **MASTERS OF THE COUNTRY BLUES**
Sep 97. (cd) *Document; (DOCD 5568)* **COMPLETE RECORDED WORKS VOL.6: 1947**
Dec 97. (3xcd-box; shared with SONNY BOY WILLIAMSON & ROBERT JOHNSON) *Indigo; (IGOBCD 001)* **THE ESSENTIAL BLUES GREATS**
Feb 98. (cd) *Document; (DOCD 5591)* **REMAINING LIBRARY OF CONGRESS RECORDINGS VOL.1: 1934-1935**
Feb 98. (cd) *Document; (DOCD 5592)* **REMAINING LIBRARY OF CONGRESS RECORDINGS VOL.2: 1935**
Feb 98. (cd) *Document; (DOCD 5593)* **REMAINING LIBRARY OF CONGRESS RECORDINGS VOL.3: 1935**
Feb 98. (cd) *Document; (DOCD 5594)* **REMAINING LIBRARY OF CONGRESS RECORDINGS VOL.4: 1935-1938**
Feb 98. (cd) *Document; (DOCD 5595)* **REMAINING LIBRARY OF CONGRESS RECORDINGS VOL.5: 1938-1942**
Mar 98. (cd) *Beat Goes On; (BGOCD 403)* **HUDDIE LEDBETTER'S BEST**
Apr 98. (cd) *Smithsonian Folkways; (SFWCD 40105)* **SHOUT ON (THE LEADBELLY LEGACY VOL.3)**
Feb 99. (cd) *Members Edition; (UAE 30282)* **LEADBELLY**
Mar 99. (cd) *Smithsonian Folkways; (SFWCD 45047)* **LEADBELLY SINGS FOR CHILDREN**
May 99. (cd/c) *Platinum; (PLA TCD/C 290)* **MIDNIGHT SPECIAL**
May 99. (cd; shared with JOSHUA WHITE) *Document; (DOCD 1018)* **THE BLACK FOLK SINGERS**
Jun 99. (cd) *A.B.M.; (ABMMCD 1055)* **LEADBELLY VOL.1**
Jul 99. (cd) *Document; (DOCD 5640)* **THE COMPLETE RECORDED WORKS VOL.7: 1947-1949**
Oct 99. (cd) *Catfish; (KATCD 131)* **EASY RIDER**
Oct 99. (cd) *A.B.M.; (ABMMCD 1173)* **LEADBELLY VOL.2**
Nov 99. (d-cd) *Snapper; (SMDCD 240)* **MY LAST GO ROUND**
Dec 99. (cd) *Rounder; (ROUCD 1151)* **BRIDGING LEADBELLY**
Jun 02. (cd) *Document; (DOCD 5664)* **PRIVATE PARTY MINNEAPOLIS, MINNESOTA 1948**
Jun 02. (cd) *Fabulous; (FABCD 113)* **YOU DON'T KNOW MY MIND**
Sep 02. (cd) *Tradition; (TCD 1086)* **THE TRADITION MASTERS**
Jan 03. (d-cd) *Classic Blues; (CBL 200003)* **THE ESSENTIAL**
Jun 03. (cd) *B.M.G.; (82876 50957-2)* **TAKE THIS HAMMER: THE COMPLETE RCA VICTOR RECORDINGS**

□ LEAGUE OF GENTLEMEN
(see under ⇒ KING CRIMSON)

LED ZEPPELIN

Formed: London, England . . . mid '68 out of The NEW YARDBIRDS, by guitar wizard JIMMY PAGE, session bassist JOHN PAUL JONES and frontman ROBERT PLANT. Another session musician, drummer JOHN BONHAM, completed the line-up, arriving in time for their live debut at Surrey University on the 15th October '68. Taking the group name from one of KEITH MOON's catchphrases, "going down like a lead zeppelin", the band came under the wing of PETER GRANT, one of the most notoriously shrewd managers in the history of rock and an integral part of the 'ZEPPELIN legend. Following some early dates in Scandinavia and the UK, GRANT secured a lucrative worldwide deal with 'Atlantic', the group subsequently touring America with fellow proto-metallers, VANILLA FUDGE. Universally saddled with the dubious honour of inventing heavy metal, the group nevertheless started out as a power-blues outfit, as evidenced on their blistering 1969 debut set, the eponymous 'LED ZEPPELIN'. From the beginning it was obvious 'ZEPPELIN had a musical chemistry more electric than any rock'n'roll band that had gone before; in spite of, or perhaps as a result of, the fact that BONHAM and JONES came from a soul background while PLANT and PAGE were coming from the heavy blues/R&B angle, the group had an almost superhuman grasp of dynamics. Whether negotiating the climactic blues of 'BABE I'M GONNA LEAVE YOU' or ripping out the power drill rhythms of 'COMMUNICATION BREAKDOWN', each musician wielded their instrument like a weapon, deadly accurate and timed to perfection. PLANT, meanwhile, had one of the most distinctive, orgasmic blues wails in rock, bringing it down to a rustic canter on the folkier numbers. These would come later, though, the sole folk song on the blues-dominated debut being the trad-based instrumental, 'BLACK MOUNTAIN SIDE'. The album's centrepiece was the tortured 'DAZED AND CONFUSED', PAGE's guitar trawling the depths of black despair, while PLANT put in one of his career best performances over a track which would become a mainstay of the LED ZEPPELIN live extravaganza. These were marathon events, with solos and improvisation aplenty, albeit in a more focussed way than the likes of the GRATEFUL DEAD. The shows were also concentrated, initially at least, in America, where GRANT was intent upon breaking the band. While the debut was a transatlantic Top 10 success, the follow-up, 'LED ZEPPELIN II' (1969), scaled both the UK and US charts later that year. Cited by many as the birthdate of British heavy metal, the sledgehammer, divebombing riff of 'WHOLE LOTTA LOVE' ushered in a new era for rock, blasting the competition out of the water. Recorded on the road, the album was graced with more than a little of the improvisatory tension of the live show; the grungy groove of 'MOBY DICK' panned out to a marathon display of BONHAM's rhythmic alchemy, while the middle part of 'WHOLE LOTTA LOVE' lingered in a kind of suspended animation as PAGE engendered all manner of bizarre effects and PLANT got himself all hot and bothered. 'THANK YOU' and 'RAMBLE ON' indicated the direction 'ZEPPELIN would follow on subsequent releases while 'LIVING LOVING MAID (SHE'S JUST A WOMAN)' and 'BRING IT ON HOME', were itchy, funky blues/metal barnstormers, the latter boasting one of the most effective intros and majestic, f***-off riffs in the 'ZEP pantheon. Prepared at 'Bron-Y-Aur' cottage in rural Wales, 'LED ZEPPELIN III' (1970) was something of a departure, at least in its equal billing for the gentler acoustic folk numbers such as 'THAT'S THE WAY' and 'TANGERINE'. Nevertheless, proceedings opened with the lumbering battlecry of 'IMMIGRANT SONG', while PAGE performed one of his most endearingly rocking solos midway through 'CELEBRATION DAY'. Though the album again topped the British and US charts (without the aid of any UK singles; LED ZEPPELIN famously never released any British singles, all part of GRANT's masterplan), critics were sceptical of the change in emphasis. They soon changed their tune with the arrival of the group's fourth effort, an untitled affair with four mystical runes adorning the cover. This immersion in myth and mysticism (PAGE had even purchased the notoriously haunted 'Boleskine Lodge' on the shores of Loch Ness, previously home to occult figurehead, Aleister Crowley) was reflected in the material contained within; the epic 'STAIRWAY TO HEAVEN' remains the most (in)famous LED ZEPPELIN song, its pseudo-hippie musings and acoustic strumming leading into one of the most revered guitar solos of all time. Basically, if you want to spank your plank, this is where you're supposed to start. 'MISTY MOUNTAIN HOP' was another hippie fantasy, while 'THE BATTLE OF EVERMORE' was a folk-rock epic blessed by the golden tonsils of SANDY DENNY. 'BLACK DOG' and 'ROCK AND ROLL' were funky, chunky riffathons, the album's heaviest track surprisingly placed at the end of side two, the wailing, harmonica driven, rolling thunder of 'WHEN THE LEVEE BREAKS', arguably 'ZEPPELIN's most hauntingly effective update of the delta blues tradition. BONHAM's drumming didn't get get much better than this, his molten rhythms subsequently sampled by arch-rappers The BEASTIE BOYS on their massive selling debut album. At the other end of the spectrum, the sun-bleached warmth of 'GOING TO CALIFORNIA' was 'ZEPPELIN at their folky, laidback best, PLANT adopting a mellow, down-home drawl. And this was exactly what the group did, spending most of their time on the road and a fair portion of it in America. With British bands not exactly known for their good manners abroad, LED ZEPPELIN had the most infamous reputation by far. Chief suspects were BONHAM and road manager RICHARD COLE, their alleged appetite for groupies and general debauchery the stuff of rock'n'roll legend; any reader with an interest in such matters will no doubt find the gory details in any of the many books written on 'ZEPPELIN's antics. The embodiment of 70's excess, the band even leased their own jet, nicknamed 'The Starship', which reportedly turned into a 'flying brothel'. With LED ZEPPELIN having released their most successful album to date, one of the most successful albums ever, in fact, they were now riding high as probably the biggest group on the planet. They knew they could get away with anything they wanted and with 'HOUSES OF THE HOLY' (1973), they clearly fancied a bit of experimentation. The majority of critics remained unimpressed with their half-baked attempts at funk ('THE CRUNGE') and reggae ('D'YER MAKER'), 'ZEPPELIN sounding more at home on familiar ground, especially the evocative 'OVER THE HILLS AND FAR AWAY' and JONES' scathing 'NO QUARTER'. Regardless of what commentators might've thought, 'ZEPPELIN remained the crown kings of rock, the album predictably topping the charts and the group undertaking their biggest US tour to date. Subsequently activating their own record label, 'Swan Song', the group took artistic control into their own hands, releasing the ambitious double set, 'PHYSICAL GRAFFITI' in Spring '75. While the quality control was spread rather thin in places, there were some unforgettable moments, obviously the exultant 'KASHMIR', but also the affecting 'CUSTARD PIE', the booty-shaking 'TRAMPLED UNDERFOOT' and the obligatory blues odyssey, 'IN MY TIME OF DYING'. Although the group's popularity ensured massive sales, 'PRESENCE' (1976) saw major cracks appearing in the LED ZEPPELIN armoury; in a set which sounded merely slung together, only 'ACHILLES LAST STAND' put up a fight. The double live set, 'THE SONG REMAINS THE SAME' (1976), was also overblown, the album a soundtrack to a rockumentary/movie of the same name featuring live footage from '73 spliced with dodgy 'dream sequences'. Having recovered from a car crash in 1975, PLANT was dealt another blow when his young son, KARAC, died from a viral infection in the summer of '77. Amid much speculation that the group would finally call it a day, LED ZEPPELIN re-emerged in 1979 with 'IN THROUGH THE OUT DOOR', another patchy effort which nevertheless initiated a comeback tour. Following UK dates at Knebworth and a European jaunt, the group went into rehearsals for a full-scale US tour. It never happened. On the 25th of September 1980, BONHAM was found dead after another sizeable drinking session and the group officially split shortly before Christmas. A posthumous collection of outtakes, 'CODA', was issued in late '82, while more recently, the celebrated 'REMASTERS' (1990) set brought together the cream of 'ZEPPELIN's material on shiny, remastered compact disc. While PLANT went on to record solo material in the early 80's, the transatlantic Top 5, 'PICTURES AT ELEVEN' (1982) and the equally fine 'THE PRINCIPLE OF MOMENTS' (1983), PAGE recorded a sole soundtrack effort, 'DEATH WISH II' (1982). PAGE and PLANT finally got back together in 1984 via the mediocre HONEYDRIPPERS R&B/soul project along with JEFF BECK. Then came The FIRM, PLANT and PAGE hooking up with veteran BAD COMPANY frontman, PAUL RODGERS. Despite the expectation, both 'THE FIRM' (1985) and 'MEAN BUSINESS' (1986) were disappointing, suffering from turgid supergroup syndrome. Much more worthy of attention were PLANT's 'SHAKEN 'N' STIRRED' (1985), 'NOW AND ZEN' (1988), and 'MANIC NIRVANA' (1990), the singer maintaining his experimental spirit throughout, dabbling with everything from hip hop rhythms to metallic blues. Even better was 1993's 'FATE OF NATIONS', the likes of '29 PALMS' and a delicate cover of TIM HARDIN's 'IF I WERE A CARPENTER' seeing PLANT in wistfully reflective, folky mood. Save a one-off collaboration with his old mucker, ROY HARPER ('Whatever Happened To Jugula?' 1985), PAGE's only solo outing proper came with 1988's 'OUTRIDER', a competent, if hardly rivetting set of hard rocking blues (vocals courtesy of seasoned hands JOHN MILES and CHRIS FARLOWE). In 1993 however, PAGE teamed up with WHITESNAKE frontman DAVID COVERDALE to record the highly successful but rather derivative album, 'COVERDALE – PAGE'. While PLANT and PAGE teamed up once more in the mid-90's for a startling album of ethnically reworked 'ZEPPELIN classics (including four new tracks), 'NO QUARTER – UNLEDDED' (1994), the prospect of a LED ZEPPELIN reunion looks as improbable as ever and with the death of PETER GRANT (of a heart attack) on the 21st November 1995, another part of the 'ZEPPELIN legend was laid to rest. Still, fans could console themselves with the release of the acclaimed 'BBC SESSIONS' at Christmas '97, featuring a couple of electrifying performances from the earliest part of their career. Early the following year, PAGE & PLANT were back again with a complete set of new recordings, 'WALKING INTO CLARKSDALE' (1998), the material on the album being close to LED ZEPPELIN standard. JOHN PAUL JONES, meanwhile, was working on his solo project, although why the appropriately titled 'ZOOMA' (1999) was ever issued is beyond me; "What is and what should never have been" are words that spring to mind. When PLANT finally returned with 'DREAMLAND' (2002), his first studio set in a decade, critics were fairly unanimous in piling on the plaudits. Never mind that there were only a couple of original tunes, the choice of covers was as peerless as the quality of the interpretations. In the same way that he brought out the pathos in Tim Hardin's 'IF I WERE A CARPENTER' (on 'FATE OF NATIONS'), his ability to tap into the root emotions and psychological strata of relatively unsung classics like Bob Dylan's 'ONE MORE CUP OF COFFEE' and The Youngbloods' brooding 'DARKNESS DARKNESS' again demonstrated why he's perhaps still the most accomplished interpreter in rock. Anthology 'SIXTY SIX TO TIMBUKTU' (2003), only added further weight to that theory, gathering together startling, long forgotten covers from his pre-ZEP days as well as a comprehensive overview of his solo career in all its freewheeling glory. PAGE, meanwhile, wasn't exactly twiddling his thumbs, rather he was compiling a belated live album culled from American concerts recorded during the band's early 70's peak. 'HOW THE WEST WAS WON' (2003) was as exalted and regal as its title suggested, lining up a clean sweep of the band's most dynamic compositions performed in all their thundering, hammer-of-the-gods glory. • **Songwriters:** PAGE + PLANT wrote nearly all with some help from JONES and/or BONHAM. They also covered; I CAN'T QUIT YOU BABY (Otis Rush) / YOU SHOOK ME (Willie Dixon) / BRING IT ON HOME (Sonny Boy Williamson) / GALLOW'S POLE + HATS OFF TO

HARPER (trad.) / etc. JIMMY PAGE covered; HUMMINGBIRD (B.B. King). The HONEYDRIPPERS;- SEA OF LOVE (Phil Phillips with the Twilights). ROBERT PLANT: LET'S HAVE A PARTY (Elvis Presley). • **Trivia:** In the early 70's, C.C.S. (aka. ALEXIS KORNER) had a Top 10 hit with 'WHOLE LOTTA LOVE' (later adopted for the Top Of The Pops theme). In 1985, with PHIL COLLINS on drums, LED ZEPPELIN played LIVE AID. JOHN BONHAM's drumming son, JASON, formed his own band, BONHAM in the late 80's. Around the same time, a kitsch mickey-take outfit DREAD ZEPPELIN, hit the music scene, playing reggae adaptations of the group's classics. In 1992, Australian 60's hitmaker and TV personality ROLF HARRIS destroyed 'STAIRWAY TO HEAVEN', hitting the charts in the process. It was even worse than 1985's FAR CORPORATION version, which also hit the UK Top 10. **Early work:** As well as session work with many (THEM, etc.), JIMMY PAGE released a solo single in early '65 ('SHE JUST SATIFIES' / 'KEEP MOVIN') for 'Fontana' (TF 533) – it's now worth 250 quid! He had earlier played on 45's by NEIL CHRISTIAN & THE CRUSADERS, plus CARTER-LEWIS & THE SOUTHERNERS. JOHN PAUL JONES played in The TONY MEEHAN COMBO, before issuing a solo 45 in April '64 ('A FOGGY DAY IN VIETNAM' / 'BAJA'), for 'Pye' label. ROBERT PLANT had been part of LISTEN, who released one 45 in November '66; ('YOU'D BETTER RUN' / 'EVERYBODY'S GOTTA SAY') (CBS; 202456). He stayed with the label for two solo releases in March '67; ('OUR SONG' / 'LAUGHING, CRYING, LAUGHING') (202656), and July '67 ('LONG TIME COMING' / 'I'VE GOT A SECRET') (2858). He subsequently teamed up that year with BONHAM, to form Birmingham-based group, BAND OF JOY. All these rare singles now fetch upwards of 100 quid.

Album rating: LED ZEPPELIN (*9) / LED ZEPPELIN II (*10) / LED ZEPPELIN III (*9) / UNTITLED (LED ZEPPELIN IV) (*10) / HOUSES OF THE HOLY (*8) / PHYSICAL GRAFFITI (*10) / PRESENCE (*6) / THE SONG REMAINS THE SAME (*6) / IN THROUGH THE OUT DOOR (*6) / CODA (*5) / REMASTERS double compilation (*10) / EARLY DAYS AND LATTER DAYS – THE VERY BEST OF ... double compilation (*10) / HOW THE WEST WAS WON live compilation (*8) / Robert Plant: PICTURES AT ELEVEN (*6) / PRINCIPLE OF MOMENTS (*7) / MANIC NIRVANA (*7) / FATE OF NATIONS (*7) / Jimmy Page: OUTRIDER (*6) / Page & Plant: UNLEDDED (*7) / WALKING INTO CLARKSDALE (*7) / John Paul Jones: ZOOMA (*3) / Robert Plant: DREAMLAND (*6) / SIXTY SIX TO TIMBUKTU compilation (*7)

ROBERT PLANT (b.20 Aug'48, West Bromwich, England) – vocals (ex-LISTEN) / **JIMMY PAGE** (b. JAMES PATRICK PAGE, 9 Jan'44, Heston, England) – lead guitars (ex-YARDBIRDS) / **JOHN PAUL JONES** (b. JOHN BALDWIN, 3 Jun'46, Sidcup, Kent, England) – bass / **JOHN BONHAM** (b.31 May'48, Redditch, England) – drums

Atlantic Atlantic

Mar 69. (lp) *(588 171) <8216>* **LED ZEPPELIN** 6 Feb69 10
– Good times bad times / Babe I'm gonna leave you / You shook me / Dazed and confused / Your time is gonna come / Black mountain side / Communication breakdown / I can't quit you baby / How many more times. *(re-iss. Mar72 lp/c; K/K4 40031) (cd-iss. Jan87 & 1989 special; 240031) (re-iss. Jul94 & Aug97 cd/c; 7567 82632-2) (lp re-iss. Oct99 on 'Classic'; SD 19126)*

Mar 69. (7") *<2613>* **GOOD TIMES BAD TIMES. / COMMUNICATION BREAKDOWN** – 80

Oct 69. (lp) *(588 198) <8236>* **LED ZEPPELIN II** 1 1
– Whole lotta love / What is and what should never be / The lemon song / Thank you / Heartbreaker / Livin' lovin' maid (she's just a woman) / Ramble on / Moby Dick / Bring it on home. *(re-iss. Mar72 lp/c; K/K4 40037) (cd-iss. Jan87 & 1989 special; 240037) (re-iss. Jul94 & Aug97 cd/c; 7567 82633-2)*

Nov 69. (7") *<2690>* **WHOLE LOTTA LOVE. / LIVING LOVING MAID (SHE'S JUST A WOMAN)** – 4 / 65

Oct 70. (lp) *(2401 002) <7201>* **LED ZEPPELIN III** 1 1
– Immigrant song / Friends / Celebration day / Since I've been loving you / Out on the tiles / Gallows pole / Tangerine / That's the way / Bron-y-aur stomp / Hats off to (Roy) Harper. *(re-iss. Mar72 lp/c; K/K4 50002) (cd-iss. Jan87 & 1989 special; 250002) (cd-iss. Aug97; 7567 82678-2)*

Nov 70. (7") *<2777>* **IMMIGRANT SONG. / HEY HEY WHAT CAN I DO** – 16

Nov 71. (lp) *(2401 012) <7208>* **(UNTITLED – 4 SYMBOLS)** 1 2
– Black dog / Rock and roll / The battle of Evermore / Stairway to Heaven / Misty mountain hop / Four sticks / Going to California / When the levee breaks. *(re-iss. Mar72 lp/c; K/K4 50008) (lilac-lp Nov78; K 50008) (cd-iss. Jul83; 250008) (cd-iss. Jan87 & 1989 special; 250008) (re-iss. Jul94 & Aug97 cd/c; 7567 82638-2/-4)*

Dec 71. (7") *<2849>* **BLACK DOG. / MISTY MOUNTAIN HOP** – 15

Mar 72. (7") *<2865>* **ROCK AND ROLL. / FOUR STICKS** – 47

Apr 73. (lp/c) *(K/K4 50014) <7255>* **HOUSES OF THE HOLY** 1 1
– The song remains the same / The rain song / Over the hills and far away / The crunge / Dancing days / D'yer mak'er / No quarter / The ocean. *(cd-iss. Jan87; 250014) (re-iss. Jul94 & Aug97 cd/c; 7567 82639-2/-4)*

Jun 73. (7") *<2970>* **OVER THE HILLS AND FAR AWAY. / DANCING DAYS** – 51

Oct 73. (7") *<2986>* **D'YER MAK'ER. / THE CRUNGE** – 20

Swan Song Swan Song

Mar 75. (d-lp/d-c) *(SSK/SK4 89400) <200>* **PHYSICAL GRAFFITI** 1 1
– Custard pie / The rover / In my time of dying / Houses of the holy / Trampled underfoot / Kashmir / In the light / Bron-y-aur / Down by the seaside / Ten years gone / Night flight / The wanton song / Boogie with Stu / Black country woman / Sick again. *(d-cd-iss. Jan87; 294800) (re-iss. Oct94 & Aug97 on 'Atlantic' cd/c; 7567 92442-2)*

Mar 75. (7") *<70102>* **TRAMPLED UNDERFOOT. / BLACK COUNTRY WOMAN** – 38

Apr 76. (lp/c) *(SSK/SK4 59402) <8416>* **PRESENCE** 1 1
– Achilles last stand / For your life / Royal Orleans / Nobody's fault but mine / Candy store rock / Hots on for nowhere / Tea for one. *(cd-iss. Jun87; 259402) (re-iss. Oct94 Aug97 on 'Atlantic' cd/c; 7567 92439-2/-4)*

May 76. (7") *<70110>* **CANDY STORE ROCK. / ROYAL ORLEANS** –

Oct 76. (d-lp/d-c) *(SSK/SK4 89402) <201>* **The soundtrack from the film 'THE SONG REMAINS THE SAME' (live)** 1 2
– Rock and roll / Celebration day / The song remains the same / Rain song / Dazed and confused / No quarter / Stairway to Heaven / Moby Dick / Whole lotta love. *(d-cd-iss. Feb87; 289402) (cd re-iss. Aug97 on 'Atlantic'; SK2 89402)*

—— Above was also a film from concerts at Madison Square Gardens in 1973. It featured some dream sequences / fantasies of each member.

Aug 79. (lp/c) *(SSK/SK4 59410) <16002>* **IN THROUGH THE OUT DOOR** 1 1
– In the evening / South bound Saurez / Fool in the rain / Hot dog / Carouselambra / All my love / I'm gonna crawl. *(cd-iss. Jan87; 259410) (re-iss. Oct94 & Aug97 on 'Atlantic' cd/c: 7567 92443-2)*

Dec 79. (7") *<71003>* **FOOL IN THE RAIN. / HOT DOG** – 21

—— Disbanded when JOHN BONHAM died after a drinking session 25 Sep'80.

—— JOHN PAUL JONES was already a top producer. In 1992, he contributed string arrangements to R.E.M.'s classic album 'Automatic For The People'. ROBERT PLANT went solo and teamed up with JIMMY PAGE in The HONEYDRIPPERS. PAGE also went solo and formed The FIRM.

—— In Aug 94; JOHN PAUL JONES turned up on an unusual collaboration (single 'Do You Take This Man') between himself and loud punk-opera diva DIAMANDA GALAS.

– compilations, others, etc. –

on 'Atlantic' unless mentioned otherwise

Nov 82. (lp/c) *Swan Song; (A 0051/+4) <90051>* **CODA** (demos from 68-79) 4 Dec82 6
– We're gonna groove / Poor Tom / I can't quit you baby / Walter's walk / Ozone baby / Darlene / Bonzo's Montreaux / Walter's walk / Wearing and tearing. *(cd-iss. Jul87; 790051) (cd re-iss. Aug97 on 'Atlantic'; 7567 92444-2)*

Oct 90. (4xcd/4xc/5xlp) *(<7567 82144-2/-4/-1>)* **LED ZEPPELIN: THE REMASTERS BOX** 48 18

Nov 90. (d-cd/d-c/t-lp) *(ZEP/+C/CD 1) <82371>* **REMASTERS** 10 Mar92 47
– Communication breakdown / Babe I'm gonna leave you / Good times bad times / Dazed and confused / Whole lotta love / Heartbreaker / Ramble on / Immigrant song / Celebration day / Since I've been loving you / Black dog / Rock and roll / The battle of Evermore / Misty mountain hop / Stairway to Heaven / The song remains the same / The rain song / D'yer

mak'er / No quarter / Houses of the holy / Kashmir / Trampled underfoot / Nobody's fault but mine / Achilles last stand / All my love / In the evening. *(re-iss. cd Sep92; 7567 80415-2) (cd re-iss. Aug97 hit UK No.27; as last)*

Sep 93. (2xcd-box/2xc-box) *(<7567 82477-2/-4>)* **BOXED SET II** [56] [87]

Oct 93. (10xcd-box) *(<7567 82526-2>)* **REMASTERS 2** [ ] [ ]

Nov 96. (cd) *Tring; (QED 107)* **WHOLE LOTTA LOVE (Bootleg Zep)** [ ] [–]

Sep 97. (cd-s) *(AT 0013CD)* **WHOLE LOTTA LOVE / BABY COME ON HOME / TRAVELLING RIVERSIDE BLUES** [21] [–]

Nov 97. (d-cd/d-c) *(<7567 83061-2/-4>)* **BBC SESSIONS** [23] [12]
– You shook me / I can't quit you baby / Communication breakdown / Dazed and confused / The girl I love / What is and what should never be / Communication breakdown / Travelling riverside blues / Whole lotta love / Something else / Communication breakdown / I can't quit you baby / You shook me / How many more times / Immigrant song / Heartbreaker / Since I've been loving you / Black dog / Dazed and confused / Stairway to Heaven / Going to California / That's the way / Whole lotta love / Thank you.

Nov 99. (cd/c) *(<7567 83268-2/-4>)* **EARLY DAYS: THE BEST OF LED ZEPPELIN VOLUME ONE** [55] [71]
(<d-lp iss.Feb03; 83268-1>)

Mar 00. (cd/c) *(<7567 83278-2/-4>)* **LATTER DAYS: THE BEST OF LED ZEPPELIN VOLUME TWO** [40] [81]
(<d-lp iss.Feb03; 83278-1>)

May 00. (cd) *Thunderbolt; (CDTB 210)* **ROCK AND ROLL HIGHWAY** [ ] [–]

Feb 03. (d-cd) *(<7567 83619-2>)* **EARLY DAYS AND LATTER DAYS: THE VERY BEST OF LED ZEPPELIN** [11] Nov02 [ ]
– Good times bad times / Babe I'm gonna leave you / Dazed and confused / Communication breakdown / Whole lotta love / What is and what should never be / Immigrant song / Since I've been loving you / Black dog / Rock and roll / The battle of evermore / When the levee breaks / Stairway to Heaven // The song remains the same / No quarter / Houses of the holy / Trampled underfoot / Kashmir / Ten years gone / Achilles last stand / Nobody's fault but mine / All my love / In the evening.

May 03. (t-cd) *(<7567 83587-2>)* **HOW THE WEST WAS WON** (live at the L.A. Forum & Long Beach Arena, 25 & 27th June 1972) [5] [1]
– (L.A. drone) / Immigrant song / Heartbreaker / Black dog / Over the hills and far away / Since I've been loving you / Stairway to Heaven / Going to California / That's the way / Bron-y-aur stomp // Dazed and confused / What is and what should never be / Dancing days / Moby Dick // Whole lotta love / Rock and roll / The ocean / Bring it on home.

ROBERT PLANT

— with **BOBBIE BLUNT** – guitar / **JEZZ WOODRUFFE** – keyboards / **PAUL MARTINEZ** – bass / **COZY POWELL** – drums / guest **PHIL COLLINS** – drums, percussion

Swan Song Swan Song

Jul 82. (lp/c) *(SSK/+4 59418) <8512>* **PICTURES AT ELEVEN** [2] [5]
– Burning down one side / Moonlight in Samosa / Pledge pin / Slow dancer / Worse that Detroit / Fat lip / Like I've never been gone / Mystery title. *(cd-iss. 1984; SSK2 59418)*

Sep 82. (7") *(SSK 19429) <99979>* **BURNING DOWN ONE SIDE. / MOONLIGHT IN SAMOSA** [73] [44]
(12"+=) *(SSK 19429T)* – Far post.

Nov 82. (7") *<99952>* **PLEDGE PIN. / FAT LIP** [–] [74]

— **RITCHIE HAYWARD** – drums (ex-LITTLE FEAT) repl. COZY /

— added **BOB MAYO** – keyboards, guitar

Es Paranza Es Paranza

Jul 83. (lp/c) *(790101-1/-4) <90101>* **THE PRINCIPLE OF MOMENTS** [7] [8]
– Other arms / In the mood / Messin' with the Mekon / Wreckless love / Thru with the two-step / Horizontal departure / Stranger here . . .than over there / Big log. *(cd-iss. 1984; 790101-2)*

Jul 83. (7") *(B 9848)* **BIG LOG. / MESSIN' WITH THE MEKON** [11] [–]
(12"+=) *(B 9848T)* – Stranger here . . . than over there.

Sep 83. (7") *<99844>* **BIG LOG. / FAR POST** [–] [20]

Nov 83. (7") *<99820>* **IN THE MOOD. / HORIZONTAL DEPARTURE** [–] [39]

Jan 84. (7") *(B 6970)* **IN THE MOOD. / PLEDGE PIN (live)** [ ] [–]
(12"+=) *(B 6970T)* – Horizontal departure.

May 85. (7") *(B 9640)* **PINK AND BLACK. / TROUBLE YOUR MONEY** [ ] [–]

May 85. (7") *<99644>* **LITTLE BY LITTLE. / TROUBLE YOUR MONEY** [–] [36]

May 85. (lp/c/cd) *(790265-1/-4/-2) <90265>* **SHAKEN 'N' STIRRED** [19] [20]
– Hip to hoo / Kallalou Kallalou / Too loud / Trouble your money / Pink and black / Little by little / Doo doo a do do / Easily led / Sixes and sevens.

Jul 85. (7") *<99622>* **TOO LOUD. / KALLALOU KALLALOU** [–] [ ]

Aug 85. (7") *(B 9621)* **LITTLE BY LITTLE (remix). / DOO DOO A DO DO** [ ] [–]
(ext.12"+=) *(B 9621T)* – Easily led (live).
(d7"++=) *(B 9621F)* – Rockin' at midnight (live).

— now with **DOUG BOYLE** – guitars / **PHIL SCRAGG** – bass / **PHIL JOHNSTONE** – keyboards, co-writer / **JIMMY PAGE** – guitar / **CHRIS BLACKWELL** – drums, percussion / **MARIE PIERRE, TONI HALLIDAY + KIRSTY MacCOLL** – backing vocals

Jan 88. (7") *(A 9373) <99373>* **HEAVEN KNOWS. / WALKING TOWARDS PARADISE** [33] [ ]
(ext.12"+=/ext.3"cd-s+=) *(A 9373 T/CD)* – Big log.
(ext.12"box+=) *(A 9373TB)* – ('A'-Astral mix).

Feb 88. (lp/c)(cd) *(WX 149/+C)(790863-2) <90863>* **NOW AND ZEN** [10] [6]
– Heaven knows / Dance on my own / Tall cool one / The way I feel / Helen of Troy / Billy's revenge / Ship of fools / Why / White, clean and neat. *(cd+=)* – Walking towards Paradise.

Apr 88. (7") *(A 9348) <99348>* **TALL COOL ONE (remix). / WHITE, CLEAN AND NEAT** [ ] [25]
(12"+=) *(A 9348T)* – ('A'extended).
(3"cd-s++=) *(A 9348CD)* – Little by little.

Aug 88. (7") *(A 9281)* **SHIP OF FOOLS. / HELEN OF TROY** [ ] [–]
(12"+=/12"w-poster+=) *(A 9281 T/TF)* – Heaven Knows (live).
(3"cd-s+=/3"box-cd-s+=) *(A 9281 CD/+B)* – Dimples (live).

Aug 88. (7") *<99333>* **SHIP OF FOOLS. / BILLY'S REVENGE** [–] [84]

— **PAT THORPE** – drums repl. BLACKWELL who became ill

— now with **BLACKWELL, CHARLIE JONES, JOHNSTONE and BOYLE**

Mar 90. (lp/c/cd) *(WX 229/+C/CD) <91336>* **MANIC NIRVANA** [15] [13]
– Hurting kind (I've got my eyes on you) / Big love / S S S & Q / I cried / She said / Nirvana / The dye on the highway / Your ma said you cried in your sleep last night / Anniversary / Liars dance / Watching you.

Mar 90. (7") *<98985>* **HURTING KIND (I'VE GOT MY EYES ON YOU). / I CRIED** [–] [46]

Apr 90. (7") *(A 8985)* **HURTING KIND (I'VE GOT MY EYES ON YOU). / OOMPAH (WATERY BINT)** [45] [–]
(12"+=) *(A 8985T)* – I cried / One love.
(cd-s+=) *(A 8985CD)* – Don't look back / One love.

Jun 90. (7"/c-s) *(A 8945/+C)* **YOUR MA SAID YOU CRIED IN YOUR SLEEP LAST NIGHT. / SHE SAID** [ ] [ ]
(12"/cd-s) *(A 8945 T/CD)* – ('A'side) / ('A'version) / One love.

— with **KEVIN SCOTT MACMICHAEL** – guitar / **PHIL JOHNSTONE** – electric piano / **CHARLIE JONES** – bass / **MICHAEL LEE** – drums / **CHRIS HUGHES** – drums, co-producer / plus guests **FRANCIS DUNNERY, MAIRE BRENNAN, NIGEL KENNEDY + RICHARD THOMPSON**

Fontana Es Paranza

Apr 93. (7") *(FATE 1)* **29 PALMS. / 21 YEARS** [21] [ ]
(c-s+=) *(FATEM 1)* – Dark moon.
(cd-s++=) *(FATEX 1)* – Whole lotta love (you need love).

May 93. (cd/c/lp) *(<514 867-2/-4/-1>)* **FATE OF NATIONS** [6] [34]
– Calling to you / Down to the sea / Come into my life / I believe / 29 palms / Memory song (hello, hello) / If I were a carpenter / Colours of a shade / Promised land / The greatest gift / Great spirit / Network news.

Jun 93. (7"/c-s) *(FATE/+M 2)* **I BELIEVE. / GREAT SPIRIT (acoustic mix)** [64] [ ]
(cd-s+=) *(FATEX 2)* – Hey Jayne.
(12"pic-d++=) *(FATETP 2)* – Whole lotta love (you need love).

Aug 93. (c-s) *(FATEM 3)* **CALLING TO YOU. / NAKED IF I WANT TO** [ ] [ ]
(12"+=/cd-s+=) *(FATE/+X 3)* – 8.05.

Dec 93. (c-s) *(FATEM 2)* **IF I WERE A CARPENTER / I BELIEVE (live)** [63] [ ]
(cd-s+=) *(FATED 4)* – Going to California (live).
(cd-s) *(FATEX 4)* – ('A'side) / Ship of fools (live) / Tall cool one (live).

JIMMY PAGE

— solo with **CHRIS FARLOWE** – vocals / **DAVE LAWSON + DAVID SINCLAIR WHITTAKER + GORDON EDWARDS** – piano / **DAVE PATON** – bass / **DAVE MATTACKS** – drums

Swan Song Swan Song

Feb 82. (lp) *(SSK 59415) <8511>* **DEATH WISH II (Soundtrack)** 40 Mar82 50
– Who's to blame / The chase / City sirens / Jam sandwich / Of Carole's theme / The release / Hotel rats and photostats / Shadow in the city / Jill's theme / Prelude / Big band, sax and violence / Hypnotizing ways (oh mamma).

— In 1985, PAGE collaborated with friend ROY HARPER on dual album 'WHATEVER HAPPENED TO JUGULA', which hit UK Top 50.

— In 1987, he released soundtrack blue-lp 'LUCIFER RISING' for 'Boleskine House'; *<BHR 666>*

— now guest vocals – **JOHN MILES, ROBERT PLANT, CHRIS FARLOWE JASON BONHAM** – drums / **DURBAN LEVERDE** – bass / **FELIX KRISH, TONY FRANKLIN, BARRYMORE BARLOW** – drums

Geffen Geffen

Jun 88 (lp/c)(cd) *(WX 155/+C)(924188-2) <24188>* **OUTRIDER** 27 26
– Wasting my time / Wanna make love / Writes of winter / The only one / Liquid mercury / Hummingbird / Emerald eyes / Prison blues / Blues anthem (if I cannot have your love . . .). *(re-iss. Feb91 & Aug99 cd/c; GEFD/GEFC 24188)*

Jun 88. (7"w-drawn) *(GEF 41)* **WASTING MY TIME. / WRITES OF WINTER** –

T.V.T. T.V.T.

Jul 00. (d-cd; by JIMMY PAGE and BLACK CROWES) *(TVT 61214) <2140>* **LIVE AT THE GREEK (live)** 39 64
– Celebration day / Custard pie / Sick again / What is and what should never be / Woke up this morning / Shapes of things / Sloppy drunk / Ten years gone / In my time of dyin' / Your time is gonna come / The lemon song / Nobody's fault but mine / Heartbreaker / Hey hey what can I do / Mellow down easy / Oh well / Shake your money maker / You shook me / Out on the tiles / Whole lotta love. *(d-cd iss.Jul00 on 'S.P.V.'; SPV 0917202-2)*

– other recordings, etc –

Jan 82. (lp; JIMMY PAGE, SONNY BOY WILLIAMSON & BRIAN AUGER) *Charly; (CR 30193)* **JAM SESSION** (rec.1964) –
– Don't send me no flowers / I see a man downstairs / She was so dumb / The goat / Walking / Little girl, how old are you / It'a a bloody life / Getting out of town.
below featured on session; **JOHN PAUL JONES / ALBERT LEE / NICKY HOPKINS + CLEM CATTINI**

Sep 84. (lp/c/cd; by JIMMY PAGE & FRIENDS) *Thunderbolt; (THBL/THBC/CDTB 007)* **NO INTRODUCTION NECESSARY** –
– Lovin' up a storm / Everything I do is wrong / Think it over / Boll Weevil song / Livin' lovin' wreck / One long kiss / Dixie friend / Down the line / Fabulous / Breathless / Rave on / Lonely weekends / Burn up. *(re-iss. cd May93;)*
below from early 70's featuring; **JOHN BONHAM, JEFF BECK, NOEL REDDING + NICKY HOPKINS** + actually a re-issue of LORD SUTCH AND HEAVY FRIENDS album.

May 85. (lp/c) *Thunderbolt; (THB L/C 2002)* **SMOKE AND FIRE** –
– Wailing sounds / 'Cause I love you / Flashing lights / Gutty guitar / Would you believe / Smoke and fire / Thumping beat / Union Jack car / One for you baby / L-O-N-D-O-N / Brightest lights / Baby come back. *(cd-iss. Aug86; CDTB 2002)*
below featured him in session with:- JET HARRIS & TONY MEEHAN / MICKIE MOST / DAVE BERRY / The FIRST GEAR / MICKEY FINN / solo / etc.

Jan 90. (lp/cd) *Archive Int.; <AIP/+CD 10041>* **JAMES PATRICK PAGE SESSION MAN VOLUME 1** –

Jul 90. (lp/cd) *Archive Int.; <AIP/+CD 10053>* **JAMES PATRICK PAGE SESSION MAN VOLUME 2** –

Aug 92. (cd) *Sony; <AK 52420>* **JIMMY'S BACK PAGES: THE EARLY YEARS** –
In the US, 'EARLY WORKS ' was issued on 'Springboard' <SPB 4038>

HONEYDRIPPERS

ROBERT PLANT – vocals / **JIMMY PAGE** – guitar / **JEFF BECK** – guitar (solo artist) / **NILE RODGERS** – producer, etc.

Es Paranza Es Paranza

Oct 84. (7") *<99701>* **SEA OF LOVE. / I GET A THRILL** – 3

Nov 84. (10"m-lp/c) *(790220-2/-4) <90220>* **VOLUME 1** 56 Oct84 4
– I get a thrill / Sea of love / I got a woman / Young boy blues / Rockin' at midnight. *(cd-iss. Feb93; 7567 90220-2)*

Jan 85. (7") *(YZ 33)* **SEA OF LOVE. / ROCKIN' AT MIDNIGHT** 56 –

Mar 85. (7") *<99686>* **ROCKIN' AT MIDNIGHT. / YOUNG BOY BLUES** – 25

The FIRM

JIMMY PAGE – guitar / **PAUL RODGERS** – vocals (ex-FREE, ex-BAD COMPANY) / **TONY FRANKLIN** – bass, keys / **CHRIS SLADE** – drums (ex-MANFRED MANN'S EARTH BAND)

Atlantic Atlantic

Feb 85. (lp/c/cd) *(781 239-1/-4/-2) <81239>* **THE FIRM** 15 17
– Closer / Make or break / Someone to love / Together / Radioactive / You've lost that lovin' feeling / Money can't buy satisfaction / Satisfaction guarenteed / Midnight moonlight.

Feb 85. (7"/7"sha-pic-d) *(A 9586/+P) <89586>* **RADIOACTIVE. / TOGETHER** 28
(12") *(A 9586T)* – ('A'-special mix) / City sirens (live) / Live in peace (live).
(12") *(A 9586TE)* – (all 4 above).

Apr 85. (7") *<89561>* **SATISFACTION GUARENTEED. / CLOSER** – 73

Apr 86. (lp/c)(cd) *(WX 43/+C)(781628-2) <81628>* **MEAN BUSINESS** 46 Feb86 22
– Fortune hunter / Cadillac / All the King's horses / Live in peace / Tear down the walls / Dreaming / Free to live / Spirit of love.

Apr 86. (7") *(A 9458) <89458>* **ALL THE KING'S HORSES. / FORTUNE HUNTER** 61

Jun 86. (7") *<89421>* **LIVE IN PEACE. / FREE TO LIVE** –

— In 1993, JIMMY collaborated with DAVID COVERDALE (of WHITESNAKE) to make one hit album 'COVERDALE • PAGE'.

JIMMY PAGE & ROBERT PLANT

— with **CHARLIE JONES** – bass, percussion / **PORL THOMPSON** – guitar, banjo / **MICHAEL LEE** – drums, percussion / **NAJMA AKHTAR** – vocals / **JOE SUTHERLAND** – mandolin, bodhran / **NIGEL EASTON** – hurdy gurdy / **ED SHEARMUR** – hammond organ & orchestral arrangements for (large) English + Egyptian Ensemble + London Metropolitan Orchestra

Fontana Atlantic

Nov 94. (cd/c/d-lp) *(526362-2/-4/-1) <82706-2/-4/-1>* **NO QUARTER – UNLEDDED** 7 4
– Nobody's fault but mine / Thank you / No quarter / Friends / Yallah / City don't cry / Since I've been loving you / The battle of Evermore / Wonderful one / Wah wah / That's the way / Gallows pole / Four sticks / Kashmir.

Dec 94. (7") *(PP 2)* **GALLOWS POLE. / CITY DON'T CRY** 35 –
(pic-cd-s+=) *(PPCD 2)* – The rain song.
(pic-cd-s) *(PPDD 2)* – ('A'side) / Four sticks / What is and what should never be.

Mar 95. (cd-ep) *<CD5 85591-2>* **WONDERFUL ONE (2 versions) / WHAT IS AND WHAT SHOULD NEVER BE / WHEN THE LEVEE BREAKS** –

— **PLANT & PAGE** were actually a 4-piece with other rhythm section & co-writers, **CHARLIE JONES** – bass / **MICHAEL LEE** – drums

Mercury Atlantic

Mar 98. (7") *(PP 3)* **MOST HIGH. / THE WINDOW** 26
(cd-s+=) *(PPCD 3)* – Upon a golden horse.

Apr 98. (cd/c/lp) *(558025-2/-4/-1) <83092>* **WALKING INTO CLARKSDALE** 3 8
– Shining in the light / When the world was young / Upon a golden horse / Blue train / Please read the letter / Most high / Heart in your hand / Walking into Clarksdale / Burning up / When I was a child / House of love / Sons of freedom.

Jun 98. (7") *(MER 506)* **SHINING IN THE LIGHT. / MOST HIGH (guitar mix)**
(cd-s+=) *(MERDD 506)* – How many more times (live).

(cd-s) *(MERCD 506)* – ('A'side) / Walking into Clarksdale (live) / No quarter (live).

JOHN PAUL JONES

Discipline Discipline

Sep 99. (cd) <*(DGM 9909)*> **ZOOMA** [ ] [ ]
– Zooma / Grind / Smile of your shadow / Bass'n'drums / B fingers / Snake eyes / Nosumi blues / Tidal.

ROBERT PLANT

with **JUSTIN "SCARECROW" ADAMS** – guitar / **PORL THOMPSON** – guitar / **CHARLIE JONES** – bass / **CLIVE DEAMER** – drums / **JOHN BAGGOT** – drums, percussion, string arrangements

Mercury Universal

Jun 02. (cd-s) *(582958-2)* **MORNING DEW / A HOUSE IS NOT A MOTEL (live) / (interview video) / MORNING DEW (video)** [ ] [–]

Jun 02. (cd)(lp) *(<586963-2>)(63094-1)* **DREAMLAND** [20] [40]
– Funny in my mind (I believe I'm fixin' to die) / Morning dew / One more cup of coffee / Last time I saw her / Song to the siren / Win my train fare home (if I ever get lucky) / Darkness, darkness / Red dress / Hey Joe / Skip's song. *(d-cd-iss. Oct02 +=; 063465-2)* – Dirt in a hole / Song to the siren (alpha mix) / Morning dew (BBC Radio 2 session) / Funny in my mind (I believe I'm fixin' to die) / Darkness, darkness (video).

Mar 03. (cd-s) *(77933-2)* **THE LAST TIME I SAW HER / SONG TO THE SIREN** [ ] [–]

Nov 03. (d-cd) *(981319-9)* <*83626*> **SIXTY SIX TO TIMBUKTU** (compilation) [27] [ ]
– Tie dye on the highway / Upside down / Promised land / Tall cool one / Dirt in a hole / Calling to you / 29 palms / If I were a carpenter / Sea of love / Darkness, darkness / Big log / Ship of fools / I believe / Little by little / Heaven knows / Song to the siren / You'd better run / Our song / Hey Joe (demo with BAND OF JOY) / For what it's worth (demo with BAND OF JOY) / Operator / Road to the sun / Philadelphia baby (with CRAWLING KINGSNAKES) / Red is for danger / Let's have a party / Hey Jayne / Louie, Louie / Naked if I want to / 21 years / If it's really got to be this way / Rude world (PLANT & PAGE) / Little hands / Life begin again (with AFRO CELT SOUND SYSTEM) / Let the boogie woogie roll / Win my train fare home.

☐ Alvin LEE (see under ⇒ TEN YEARS AFTER)

☐ Arthur LEE (see under ⇒ LOVE)

☐ Geddy LEE (see under ⇒ RUSH)

LEFTFIELD

Formed: London, England . . . 1990 by ex-teacher of English NEIL BARNES and PAUL DALEY, formerly of Balearic housers A MAN CALLED ADAM. Barnes had previously released the 'Mississippi Burning'-sampling 'NOT FORGOTTEN' on dance indie Outer Rhythm and when the single became an underground club hit, contractual problems ensued. Undeterred, the duo kept a high profile with remix work (including David Bowie and Inner City) before setting up the Hard Hands label and cutting two singles in 1992, 'RELEASE THE PRESSURE' and 'SONG OF LIFE', the latter a slow building progressive house epic which further enhanced their dancefloor reputation and nudged into the lower regions of the pop charts. But the song that really branded LEFTFIELD into the musical consciousness of the nation was the pounding crossover hit, 'OPEN UP'. A collaboration with P.I.L.'s JOHN LYDON, his blood curdling wail of 'BURN HOLLYWOOD BURN' was scarier than Michael Bolton's mullet cut and was enough to have the video banned from ITV's Chart Show. Spookily enough, the song was released at the same time as a spate of Californian fires . . . The single was a corking tune into the bargain and climbed to No.13 in the charts. The debut album, 'LEFTISM' was greeted with critical plaudits galore upon its release in 1995, reaching No.3 in the U.K. and even being nominated for The Mercury Music Prize . An exhilarating cross-fertilisation of musical stylings, the album took pumping techno trance as its base ingredient, interspersing this with everything from cerebral sonic tapestries ('MELT') to dark, foreboding drum 'n' bass ('STORM 3000'). It contained all the aforementioned singles (save the earlier 'NOT FORGOTTEN') as well as a vocal-led collaboration with goth goddess Toni Halliday. LEFTFIELD enjoyed further chart success with tracks and remixes from the album and contributed material to both the 'Shallow Grave' and 'Trainspotting' film soundtracks. A nationwide tour and a series of legendary festival appearances in 1996 cemented their position as one of the key players in the new techno vanguard alongside UNDERWORLD, PRODIGY et al. 'PHAT PLANET' (from that Guinness ad with the white horses riding the waves) was LEFTFIELD's first musical/video venture for some time, the duo finally releasing (in September '99) the excellent bass-heavy track on the B-side of another CHRIS CUNNINGHAM-directed single/promo, 'AFRIKA SHOX' (with of course, the man BAMBAATAA). Around the same time, the duo finally unleashed their (chart-topping) second album proper, 'RHYTHM AND STEALTH', an enjoyable journey through four years of hard toil in the studio; had their contemporaries beaten them to the prizes though? LEFTFIELD went their separate ways in March 2002. • **Songwriters:** BARNES / DALEY / guests and some samples. • **Trivia:** Their label 'Hard Hands' run by manager LISA HORRAN, also included acts VINYL BLAIR, DELTA LADY, DEE PATTEN and SCOTT HARRIS.

Album rating: BACKLOG compilation (*6) / LEFTISM (*9) / RHYTHM AND STEALTH (*7)

NEIL BARNES – DJ, percussion, synthesizers / **PAUL DALEY** – samples (ex-A MAN CALLED ADAM)

Outer Rhythm not iss.

Mar 90. (12") *(FOOT 003)* **NOT FORGOTTEN. / PATELL'S ON THE CASE / ('A'version)** [ ] [–]

Feb 91. (12") *(FOOT 009)* **NOT FORGOTTEN (Hard Hands mix). / MORE THAN I KNOW** [ ] [–]
(12") *(FOOT 009R)* – ('A'&'B'remixes).

Hard Hands Medicine

Aug 92. (12"ltd.; featuring EARL SIXTEEN) *(HAND 001T)* **RELEASE THE PRESSURE (3 track vocal)** [ ] [–]
(12"ltd.) *(HAND 001R)* – Release the dubs (instrumental mixes). *(re-iss. Mar99; same)*

Nov 92. (12"ltd.) *(HAND 002T)* **SONG OF LIFE. / FANFARE OF LIFE / DUB OF LIFE** [59] [ ]
(12") *(HAND 002R)* – ('A'-3 Underworld mixes).
(cd-s) *(HAND 002CD)* – ('A'side) / Fanfare of life / Release the dub. *(re-iss. Mar99; same)*

Dec 92. (cd) *(OUTERCD 001)* **BACKLOG** (compilation of above material on 'Outer Rhythm') [ ] [–]

below single with JOHN LYDON (of PUBLIC IMAGE LTD) on vocals

Nov 93. (7"/c-s; as LEFTFIELD / LYDON) *(HAND 009/+MC)* <*42232*> **OPEN UP (radio edit). / ('A'instrumental)** [13] Feb94 [ ]
(12"+=)(cd-s+=) *(HAND 009 T/CD)* – ('A'vocal 12"mix) / ('A'-Dervish overdrive mix) / ('A'-Andrew Weatherall mix) / ('A'-Dust Brothers mix). *(re-iss. Mar99; same)*
(12") *(HAND 9R)* – ('A'remixes).

Hard Hands Sony-Columbia

Jan 95. (cd/c/d-lp) *(HAND CD/MC/LP 002/+D)* <*67231-2/-4/-1*> **LEFTISM** [3] [ ]
– Release the pressure / Afro-left / Melt / Song of life / Original / Black flute / Space shanty / Inspection (check one) / Storm 3000 / Open up / 21st century poem. *(iss.Apr95, 3x12"+=) (HANDLP 2T)* – Half past dub. *(cd w/ bonus disc)* – Afro-left (Afro-ride) / Release the pressure (release one) / Original (live dub) / Filter fish / Afro-left (Afro-Central) / Release the pressure (release four).

below single as featured TONI HALLIDAY (ex-CURVE) on vocals

Mar 95. (c-ep/cd-ep; as LEFTFIELD & HALLIDAY) *(HAND 018 MC/CD)* **ORIGINAL / ('A'-live mix) / ('A'jam mix) / FILTER FISH** [18] [–]
(12"ep) *(HAND 018T)* – ('A'-Drift version) – repl. ('A'live)

Jul 95. (12"ep/c-ep/cd-ep; LEFTFIELD featuring DJUM DJUM) *(HAND 023 T/MC/CD)* <78045> **AFRO-LEFT EP** [22] [ ]
– Afro left / Afro ride / Afro sol / Afro central.

Jan 96. (c-s) *(HAND 029MC)* **RELEASE THE PRESSURE (remix 96 vocal): RELEASE ONE / RELEASE TWO** [13] [ ]
(12"+=) *(HAND 029T)* – Release four.
(cd-s++=) *(HAND 029CD)* – Release three.

Sep 99. (12"/cd-s; as LEFTFIELD. BAMBAATAA) *(HAND 057 T/CD1)* **AFRIKA SHOX. / PHAT PLANET (Dave Clarke mix) / AFRIKA SHOX (Jedis elastic bass mix)** [7] [ ]
(cd-s) *(HAND 057CD2)* – ('A'mixes; VX / etc).

Sep 99. (cd/c/d-lp) *(HAND CD/MC/LP 004)* <68529> **RHYTHM AND STEALTH** [1] [ ]
– Dusted / Phat planet / Chant of a poor man / Double flash / El Cid / Afrika shox / Dub gussett / Swords / 6-8 war / Rhino's prayer. *(cd re-mixed; May00; HANDCD 4X)*

Nov 99. (12"/cd-s; as LEFTFIELD w/ ROOTS MANUVA) *(HAND 058 T/CD)* **DUSTED (mixes)** [28] [ ]
(cd-s) *(HAND 058CD2)* – ('A'mixes).

—— split March 2002

LEMONHEADS

Formed: Boston, Massachusetts, USA . . . 1983 by EVAN DANDO. Raised by middle-class parents (they were divorced when he was 12), the singer was originally the band's drummer and in March '86 he was joined by one-time school-friend, jazz-bassist JESSE PORETZ. With BEN DEILY completing the line-up, this early incarnation of The LEMONHEADS released their debut EP, the amateurish indie squall of 'LAUGHING ALL THE WAY TO THE CLEANERS' on the recently formed Boston label, 'Taang!'. The band stayed with the label for their first three releases, belting out spirited melodic punk (drawing comparisons with DINOSAUR JR, HUSKER DU, REPLACEMENTS etc,) on 'HATE YOUR FRIENDS' (1987), 'CREATOR' (1988) and 'LICK' (1989), the latter the pick of the bunch with a beguiling cover of Suzanne Vega's 'LUKA'. 'Atlantic' records were sufficiently confident in the band's pop-grunge abilities to offer them a deal, the initial fruits of which, the well received 'LOVEY' (1990), saw DANDO take more of a leading role following the departure of DEILY. From this point on he steered the band in an increasingly mellow, country-flavoured direction (an area he'd already explored on his 1990 solo EP, 'FAVOURITE SPANISH DISHES') with a brilliant cover of Mike Nesmith's 'DIFFERENT DRUM', while 'LOVEY' featured a fairly faithful rendition of his hero Gram Parson's 'BRASS BUTTONS'. Yet the ever unpredictable DANDO split the band up after the major label debut, eventually reforming with the help of girlfriend JULIANA HATFIELD and DAVE RYAN, the latter having played on 'LOVEY'. A spell in Australia seemed to have further mellowed the singer and the resultant album, 'IT'S A SHAME ABOUT RAY', was the most accessible LEMONHEADS release to date, heavy on harmonies and melody. Despite a favourable critical reception, the album lingered in the lower reaches of the album chart and it was only when 'Atlantic' issued the band's power pop cover of Simon & Garfunkel's 'MRS. ROBINSON', that The LEMONHEADS became a household name. Re-released to include the track, 'IT'S A SHAME ABOUT RAY' enjoyed a commercial comeback, eventually making it into the UK Top 40. Suddenly DANDO's long-haired, slacker-extraordinaire visage was staring out from every magazine cover from NME to The FACE, although this sudden thrust into the limelight seemed to drive DANDO further into drug abuse, a follow-up album, 'COME ON FEEL THE LEMONHEADS', eventually surfacing in late 1993. The record was another mellow beauty, powering into the UK Top 5 on the back of a successful Love Positions' cover, 'INTO YOUR ARMS', and even featuring contributions from legendary pedal steel player, SNEAKY PETE KLEINOW. Predictably, the Yanks just didn't get it, preferring the bluster of PEARL JAM instead. Lack of success in his home country sent DANDO spiralling further into drug use, although he had apparently cleaned up by the end of the year, undertaking a solo acoustic tour of the US. However, after a much criticised appearance at the 1995 Glastonbury festival, DANDO went to ground, spending much of his time in Australia strung out on heroin and LSD. A shorn, torn and frayed DANDO eventually surfaced in October 1996 with 'CAR BUTTON CLOTH', the first LEMONHEADS album in four years, finding DANDO in reflective and world weary mood, the melancholy side of his songwriting more pronounced than ever. After a seemingly interminable wait, DANDO came in from the wilderness with 'LIVE AT THE BRATTLE THEATRE / GRIFFITH SUNSET' (2001), a half live/half studio covers affair which revisited old favourites like 'DOWN ABOUT IT' and 'MY DRUG BUDDY'. If it was hardly a high profile comeback, we shouldn't be too surprised; thankfully DANDO still sounds as if he's doing it all off the cuff with the kind of haphazard enthusiasm his druggy days might well have leached out of him. It was a wiser, cleaned-up DANDO which eventually resurfaced in early 2003 with 'BABY I'M BORED', his debut studio album and his first collection of new material in years. Although the wiry angst of old was gone completely, the singer had unsurprisingly honed the poignant, bittersweet essence of his more reflective work, resulting in the least immediate but perhaps most rewarding album of his career thus far. While his voice betrayed the trials of recent years it had lost none of its melancholy charm and while his songs remained as deceptively basic as ever, they were permeated with the wisdom of encroaching middle age. • **Songwriters:** DANDO, although DELLY or MADDOX were contributors early on. Covered; I AM A RABBIT (Proud Scum) / HEY JOE + AMAZING GRACE (trad.) / MOD LANG (Big Star) / STRANGE (Patsy Cline) / YOUR HOME IS WHERE YOU ARE HAPPY (C. MANSON / PLASTER CASTER (Kiss) / SKULLS (Misfits) / GONNA GET ALONG WITHOUT YA NOW (Hoagy Carmichael) / STEP BY STEP (New Kids On The Block) / FRANK MILLS (from 'Hair' musical) / KITCHEN (Hummingbirds) / MISS OTIS REGRETS (Cole Porter) / FADE TO BLACK (Metallica) / LIVE FOREVER (Oasis) / KEEP ON LOVING YOU (Reo Speedwagon) / TENDERFOOT (Tom Morgan / Adam Young) / GALVESTON (Jimmy Webb) / PIN YR HEART (Jacobites). Between 1994-1996, he co-wrote 'PURPLE PARALLELOGRAM' with Noel Gallagher (Oasis) + 'IF I COULD TALK I'D TELL YOU' with Eugene Kelly (Eugenius). • **Trivia:** DANDO and JOHN STROHM appeared on BLAKE BABIES lp, 'Slow Learners'.

Album rating: HATE YOUR FRIENDS (*4) / CREATOR (*4) / LICK (*7) / LOVEY (*5) / IT'S A SHAME ABOUT RAY (*8) / COME ON FEEL THE LEMONHEADS (*7) / CAR BUTTON CLOTH (*6) / THE BEST OF THE LEMONHEADS compilation (*8) / Evan Dando: LIVE AT THE BRATTLE THEATRE . . . (*5) / BABY I'M BORED (*7)

EVAN DANDO (b. 4 Mar'67) – vocals, guitar + some drums / **JESSE PERETZ** – bass / **BEN DEILY** – guitar, + some drums

not iss. ArmoryArms

Jul 86. (7"ep) *<1-2-Huh-Bag 1>* **LAUGHING ALL THE WAY TO THE CLEANERS** [–] [ ]
– Glad I don't know / I like to / I am a rabbit / So I fucked up.

— added **DOUG TRACHTON** – drums

World Service / Taang!

May 88. (lp)<US-lp some colrd> *(SERVM 001)* <*T 15*> **HATE YOUR FRIENDS** [ ] Jun87 [ ]
– I don't wanna / 394 / Nothing time / Second change / Sneakyville / Amazing Grace / Belt / Hate your friends / Don't tell yourself it's ok / Uhhh / Fed up / Rat velvet. *(US-cd 1989; same +=)* – Glad I don't know / I like to / I am a rabbit / So I fucked up / Ever / Sad girl / Buried alive / Gotta stop. *(re-iss. cd Mar93 with the extra tracks)*

— **EVAN,** on bass, also joined BLAKE BABIES in 1988, alongside girlfriend JULIANA HATFIELD. **JOHN STROHM** – drums (ex-BLAKE BABIES) repl. DOUG.

Sep 88. (lp)(c) *(SERV 001)* <*T 23*> **CREATOR** [ ] [ ]
– Burying ground / Sunday / Clang bang clang / Out / Your home is where you're happy / Falling / Die right now / Two weeks in another town / Plaster caster / Come to my window / Take her down / Postcard / Live without. *(US-cd 1989; same +=)* – Luka (live) / Interview / Mallo cup. *(re-iss. Sep92 on 'Taang!', with 6 extra live tracks included) (re-iss. cd Mar93 with all re-issued tracks + 2 acoustic)*

— **COREY LOOG BRENNAN**– guitar (ex-BULLET LAVOLTA) repl. JOHN STROHM

Apr 89. (7"colrd) <*T 31*> **LUKA. / STRANGE / MAD** [ ] [–]
(scheduled UK Nov89 unissued 12"/cd-s; SEVS 010/+CD)
(UK-iss. 7"/12"/cd-s Apr93)

May 89. (lp/cd) *(SERV/+CD 007)* <*T 32*> **LICK** [ ] [ ]
– Mallo cup / Glad I don't know / 7 powers / A circle of one / Cazzo di ferro / Anyway / Luka / Come back D.A. / I am a rabbit / Sad girl / Ever. *(US-cd+=)* – Strange / Mad. *(re-iss. cd Mar93)*

— **MARK "BUDOLA"** – drums, toured until he checked out mid '89. (COREY also left to concentrate on his PhD)

Roughneck / not iss.

Jun 90. (7") *(HYPE 3)* **DIFFERENT DRUM. / PAINT** [ ] [–]
(12"+=)(cd-s+=) *(12 HYPE 3)(HYPE 3CD)* – Ride with me. *(re-iss. Feb93 12"ep/cd-ep; HYPE 3 T/CD)*

Atlantic / Atlantic

Jun 90. (cd-ep) <*786088-2*> **FAVORITE SPANISH DISHES EP** [–] [ ]
– Different drum / Paint / Ride with me / Skulls / Step by step.

— **DAVID RYAN** (b.20 Oct'64, Fort Wayne, Indiana) – drums repl. DEILY

Oct 91. (cd/c/lp) <*(7567 82137-2/-4/-2)*> **LOVEY** [ ] Aug90 [ ]
– Ballarat / Half the time / Year of the cat / Ride with me / Li'l seed / Stove / Come downstairs / Left for dead / Brass buttons / (The) Door. *(re-iss. cd/c/lp Nov93)*

— In Sep'90, **DANDO** recruited **BEN DAUGHTY** – drums (ex-SQUIRREL BAIT) repl. RYAN / **BYRON HOAGLAND** – bass (ex-FANCY PANTS) repl. PERETZ.

Sep 91. (7") *(A 7709)* **GONNA GET ALONG WITHOUT YA NOW. / HALF THE TIME** [ ] [–]
(12"ep+=) *(TA 7709)* – PATIENCE AND PRUDENCE EP: Stove (remix) / Step by step.

— **DANDO, RYAN + JULIANA HATFIELD** (b. 2 Jul'67, Wiscasset) – bass, vocals (ex-BLAKE BABIES)

Jul 92. (cd/c/lp) <*(7567 82137-2/-4/-1)*> **IT'S A SHAME ABOUT RAY** [69] [68]
– Rockin' stroll / Confetti / Rudderless / My drug buddy / The turnpike down / Bit part / Alison's starting to happen / Hannah and Gaby / Kitchen / Ceiling fan in my spoon / Frank Mills. *(album hit UK No.33 Jan'93) (re-iss. Feb95)*

Oct 92. (7"/c-s) *(A 7423/+C)* **IT'S A SHAME ABOUT RAY. / SHAKEY GROUND** [70] [–]
(10"+=/cd-s+=) *(A 7423 TE/CD)* – Dawn can't decide / The turnpike down.

Nov 92. (7"/c-s) *(A 7401/+C)* **MRS. ROBINSON. / BEING AROUND** [19] [–]
(10"+=/cd-s+=) *(A 7401 TE/CD)* – Divan / Into your arms.

— 1993 line-up: **DANDO, RYAN, NIC DALTON** (b.14 Jun'64, Australia) although she did provide b.vox for 1993 releases. – bass HATFIELD formed own trio)

Jan 93. (7"/c-s) *(A 7430/+C)* **CONFETTI (remix). / MY DRUG BUDDY** [44] [–]
(10"+=/cd-s+=) *(A 7430 TE/CD)* – Ride with me (live) / Confetti (acoustic).

Mar 93. (c-s) *(A 5764C)* **IT'S A SHAME ABOUT RAY / ALISON'S STARTING TO HAPPEN** [31] [–]
(cd-s+=) *(A 5764CD)* – Different drum (Evan acoustic) / Stove (Evan acoustic).
(10"+=) *(A 5764TE)* – Different drum (acoustic) / Rockin' stroll (live).
(cd-s) *(A 5764CDX)* – ('A'live) / Confetti / Mallo cup / Rudderless (all 4 live).

Oct 93. (7"/c-s) *(A 7302/+C)* <*87294*> **INTO YOUR ARMS. / MISS OTIS REGRETS** [14] [67]
(10"+=/cd-s+=) *(A 7302 TE/CD)* – Little black egg / Learning the game.

Oct 93. (cd/c/lp) <*(7567 82537-2/-4/-1)*> **COME ON FEEL THE LEMONHEADS** [5] [56]
– The great big no / Into your arms / It's about time / Down about it / Paid to smile / Big gay heart / Style / Rest assured / Dawn can't decide / I'll do it anyway / Rick James style / Being around / Favourite T / You can take it with you / The jello fund. *(lp+=)* – Miss Otis regrets.

Nov 93. (7"/c-s) *(A 7296/+C)* **IT'S ABOUT TIME. / RICK JAMES ACOUSTIC STYLE** [57] [–]
(10"+=/cd-s+=) *(A 7296 TE/CD)* – Big gay heart (demo) / Down about it (acoustic).
(above 'A'side was written about JULIANA. I'LL DO IT ANYWAY for BELINDA CARLISLE)

May 94. (c-ep/10"ep/cd-ep) *(A 7259 C/TE/CD)* **BIG GAY HEART / DEEP BOTTOM COVE. / HE'S ON THE BEACH / FAVORITE T (session)** [55] [–]

— Offending lyrics to above 'A'side, were changed; with Stroke & Brick.

— DALTON departed Sep '94

— **PATRICK MURPHY** – drums (ex-DINOSAUR JR) repl. RYAN

— other members with DANDO; **BILL GIBSON** – bass, guitar / **DINA WAXMAN** – bass / **KENNY LYON** – guitar / **RICH GILBERT** – pedal steel / **BRYCE GOGGIN** – vocals, keyboards / etc.

Sep 96. (c-s) *(A 5495C)* **IF I COULD TALK I'D TELL YOU /** [39] [–]
(cd-s) *(A 5495CD)* – ('A'side) / How will I know (acoustic & electric version) / I don't want to go home / Seagulls aren't free.
(cd-s) *(A 5495CDX)* – ('A'side) / It's all true (acoustic – no drums) / Sexual bryceulidge.

Oct 96. (cd/c) <*(7567 92726-2/-4)*> **CAR BUTTON CLOTH** [28] [ ]
– It's all true / If I could talk I'd tell you / Break me / Hospital / The outdoor type / Losing your mind / Something's missing / Knoxville girl / 6ix / C'mon daddy / One more time / Tenderfoot / Secular rockulidge.

Nov 96. (c-s) *(A 5635C)* **IT'S ALL TRUE / LIVE FOREVER** [61] [–]
(10"+=/cd-s+=) *(A 5635 TE/CD)* – Fade to black / Keep on loving you.

Mar 97. (c-s) *(A 5620C)* **THE OUTDOOR TYPE (remix) / PIN YR HEART** [ ] [–]
(cd-s+=) *(A 5620CD)* – Losing your mind (live acoustic).

Aug 97. (7") *(AT 0012)* **BALANCING ACTS. / GALVESTON** [ ] [–]

– compilations, etc. –

1990. (cd) *Taang!;* <*T 15/T23*> **CREATE YOUR FRIENDS** [–] [ ]
– (HATE YOUR FRIENDS / CREATOR / LAUGHING E.P.)

Aug 98. (cd/c) *Atlantic;* <*(7567 80851-2/-4)*> **THE BEST OF THE LEMONHEADS** [ ] [ ]
– Confetti / Into the arms / Mrs. Robinson / Rudderless / It's a shame about Ray / The great big no / Ride with me (acoustic) / My drug buddy / Big gay heart / It's about time / The outdoor type / It's all true / If I could talk I'd tell you / Hospital / Rudy with a flashlight / Into your arms (acoustic) / Down about it (acoustic) / Being around / Rick James acoustic style.

EVAN DANDO

Modular / Modular

Dec 01. (d-cd) <*(MODCD 017)*> **LIVE AT THE BRATTLE THEATRE / GRIFFITH SUNSET (live)** [ ] Nov01 [ ]
– Down about it / The turnpike down / The outdoor type / My drug buddy / The same thing you thought hard about is . . . . / Ride with me / Frying pan / Excuse me mister / Thirteen / Stove / Half the time / Ba-de-da / Fraulein / Sam Stone / Nothin / My baby's gone / Tribute to Hank Williams / (untitled).

— next with **JON BRION, BROKAW, JOEY BURNS, JOHN COVERTINO, HOWE GELB, ROYSTON LANGDON + SIM CAIN**

Setanta / Bar/None

Mar 03. (cd) *(SETCD 114)* <*141*> **BABY I'M BORED** [?] Feb03 [ ]
– Repeat / My idea / Rancho Santa Fe / Waking up / Hard drive / Shots is fired / It looks like you / The same thing you thought hard about is the same part I can live without / Why do you do this to yourself? / Stop my head / In the grass all wine colored. *(lp-iss.Apr03; SETLP 114)*

May 03. (7"red) *(SET 127)* **STOP MY HEAD. / THRASHER** [38] [–]
(cd-s) *(SETCDA 127)* – ('A'side) / Shots is fired / Tongue tied.
(cd-s) *(SETCDB 127)* – ('A'side) / Things have gone to pieces / Au bord la Seine / ('A'-video).

Dec 03. (7") *(SET 130)* **IT LOOKS LIKE YOU. / WHOOPS / THE TODD KILLINGS** [68] [–]
(cd-s) *(SETCDA 130)* – ('A'side) / The same thing you thought hard about is the same part I can live without (live) / Hannah and Gabi (live).

□ LEMON INTERRUPT (see under ⇒ UNDERWORLD)

John LENNON

Born: JOHN WINSTON LENNON, 9 Oct'40, Liverpool, England. While still a member of The BEATLES (late 1968), he teamed up with his new girlfriend at the time, YOKO ONO, to record the controversial, 'UNFINISHED MUSIC NO.1: TWO VIRGINS'. The cover-shot displayed a full-frontal nude photo of the couple and the album was subsequently sold in brown paper wrapping to apparently save embarrassment to both the customers and the retailers! During Spring next year, its follow-up, 'UNFINISHED MUSIC NO.2: LIFE WITH THE LIONS', hit the shops and continued their anti-commercial, free-form direction, the songs mainly recorded on a small cassette player. Now divorced from his wife CYNTHIA, JOHN married YOKO on the 20th March '69, even changing by deed poll, his middle name from WINSTON to ONO. After the LENNON's completed an 8-day peace protest by publicly lying/sitting in a hotel bed, they released The PLASTIC ONO BAND's debut hippy anthem, 'GIVE PEACE A CHANCE'. This gave JOHN his first non-BEATLES hit, rising into the UK Top 3 and US Top 20. Later that year, 'COLD TURKEY' (a drug withdrawal song), also gave him a Top 30 smash on both sides of the Atlantic. Late 1969, he unveiled two albums, one, another avant-garde collaboration with YOKO, 'THE WEDDING ALBUM', and the other a more standard commercial product from The PLASTIC ONO BAND, 'LIVE IN TORONTO 1969', a record which breached the US Top 10. They also scored with another UK/US Top 5 hit, 'INSTANT KARMA', which was produced by PHIL SPECTOR early in 1970. In May that year, The BEATLES officially split prior to the release of another No.1 album, 'Let It Be'. JOHN then concentrated wholly on his solo career, returning with the album, 'JOHN LENNON: PLASTIC ONO BAND'. This was followed by another Top 20 anthem, 'POWER TO THE PEOPLE'. On the 3rd of September '71, he went to New York to live with YOKO and a month later, his classic album, 'IMAGINE', topped the charts in both the US and the UK (its US-only released title track, hitting No.3). In 1971, he failed in a bid to have a Christmas hit in the States with 'HAPPY XMAS (WAR IS OVER)', although this reached the UK Top 5 a year later. During the next three years, during which he released three albums, he fought to stay in America after being ordered by immigration authorities to leave. During this period, in which he temporarily split from YOKO, he went through drinking bouts with his buddy HARRY NILSSON, the pair recording an album, 'PUSSY CATS', together. On the 9th of October '75, YOKO gave birth to their first child, SEAN. LENNON then went into retirement to look after the boy in their Manhattan apartment, leaving behind a charting greatest hits, 'SHAVED FISH'. He was soon to receive his green card, allowing him to permanently reside in the States. However, in 1980 he returned to the studio once again, David Geffen offering to release an album on his self-titled label. In November that year, 'DOUBLE FANTASY' was released, soon topping both US and UK album charts. There was also a return to the singles chart, when the appropriately titled '(JUST LIKE) STARTING OVER' made the Top 10. Tragically on the 8th of December 1980, JOHN was shot five times by a deranged fan, Mark Chapman, outside the LENNON's apartment block. He died shortly afterwards at Roosevelt hospital. Not surprisingly, his previous 45 climbed back up the charts and peaked at No.1, with a re-issue of 'IMAGINE' following it to the top early in 1981. His killer was sent to a mental institution for the rest of his life, and we can only ponder what the 40-year-old might have achieved in the 80's & 90's had he lived. He remains a much revered genius, an artist who attempted to alienate the pop industry with non-conventional music styles. He was also a peaceful man, whose outbursts and human faults seemed to be portrayed falsely by the media, especially in his BEATLES days. His love of YOKO was undoubtably a turning point, finding both himself and the world around him a happier place to live. Although some of his songs exploded into frenetic rock anthems of anti-war and anti-government sentiments, his music, in its many facets, showed a poetic beauty and untouched romance. • **Songwriters:** LENNON, except covers album 'ROCK'N'ROLL' which contained;- BE-BOP-A-LULA (Gene Vincent) / STAND BY ME (Ben E.King) / PEGGY SUE (Buddy Holly) / AIN'T THAT A SHAME (Fats Domino) / SWEET LITTLE SIXTEEN + YOU CAN'T CATCH ME (Chuck Berry) / BONY MORONIE (Larry Williams) / BRING IT HOME TO ME + SEND ME SOME LOVIN' (Sam Cooke) / JUST BECAUSE (Lloyd Price) / YA YA (Lee Dorsey) / RIP IT UP + SLIPPIN' AND SLIDIN' + READY TEDDY (Little Richard) / DO YOU WANT TO DANCE (Bobby Freeman). • **Trivia:** In 1967, JOHN acted in the movie, 'How I Won The War', also appearing in many zany films with The BEATLES. In 1975, he co-wrote 'Fame' with DAVID BOWIE, which topped the US charts. His son from his first marriage, JULIAN, has previously enjoyed chart action, while SEAN has also been more visible, appearing at benefits, etc.

Album rating: UNFINISHED MUSIC NO.1: TWO VIRGINS (*3) / UNFINISHED MUSIC NO.2: LIFE WITH THE LIONS (*3) / THE WEDDING ALBUM (*2) / THE PLASTIC ONO BAND – LIVE PEACE IN TORONTO 1969 (*5) / JOHN LENNON – PLASTIC ONO BAND (*8) / IMAGINE (*9) / SOMETIME IN NEW YORK CITY (*5) / MIND GAMES (*7) / WALLS AND BRIDGES (*6) / ROCK'N'ROLL (*5) / SHAVED FISH compilation (*8) / DOUBLE FANTASY (*7) / THE JOHN LENNON COLLECTION compilation (*10) / MILK & HONEY posthumous (*4) / LIVE IN NEW YORK CITY early stuff (*4) / MENLOVE AVE. (*4) / LENNON LEGEND boxed-set (*9)

JOHN LENNON & YOKO ONO

JOHN LENNON – vocals, guitar, etc. / **YOKO ONO** (b.18 Feb'33, Tokyo, Japan) – wind, vocals

Apple Apple

Nov 68. (lp; stereo/mono) *(S+/APCOR 2) <5001>* **UNFINISHED MUSIC NO.1: TWO VIRGINS** [ ] [ ]
– Section 1, 2, 3, 4, 5, 6 / Side 2. *(cd-iss. Jan93 on'Rock Classics';) (cd re-iss. Jun97 on 'Rykodisc'; RCD 10411)*

Zapple Zapple

May 69. (lp) *(ZAPPLE 01) <3357>* **UNFINISHED MUSIC NO.2: LIFE WITH THE LIONS (1/2 live)** [ ] [ ]
– Cambridge 1969 / No bed for Beatle John / Baby's heartbeat / Two minutes silence / Radio play. *(cd-iss. Jun97 on 'Rykodisc'; RCD 10412)*

The PLASTIC ONO BAND

Apple Apple

Jul 69. (7") *(APPLE 13) <1809>* **GIVE PEACE A CHANCE. / REMEMBER LOVE** [2] [14]
(re-iss. Jan81, reached UK No.33)

Oct 69. (7") *(APPLES 1001) <1813>* **COLD TURKEY. / DON'T WORRY KYOKO (MUMMY'S ONLY LOOKING FOR A HAND IN THE SNOW)** [14] Dec69 [30]

Dec 69. (lp; as JOHN ONO LENNON & YOKO ONO LENNON) *(SAPCOR 11) <3361>* **WEDDING ALBUM** [ ] [ ]
– John and Yoko / Amsterdam. *(cd-iss. Jun97 on 'Rykodisc'; RCD 10413)*

—— JOHN and YOKO hired the following musicians **ERIC CLAPTON** – guitar (ex-YARDBIRDS, ex-CREAM, ex-BLUESBREAKERS) / **KLAUS VOORMAN** – bass (ex-MANFRED MANN) / **ALAN WHITE** – drums

Dec 69. (lp) *(CORE 2001)* *<3362>* **THE PLASTIC ONO BAND – LIVE PEACE IN TORONTO 1969 (live 13 Sep'69)** [ ] Jan70 [10]
– Blue Suede shoes / Money (that's what I want) / Dizzy Miss Lizzy / Yer blues / Cold turkey / Give peace a chance / Don't worry Kyoko / John John (let's hope for peace).

Feb 70. (7"; LENNON / ONO WITH PLASTIC ONO BAND) *(APPLES 1003)* *<1818>* **INSTANT KARMA!. / Yoko Ono: WHO HAS SEEN THE WIND?** [5] [3]

JOHN LENNON & THE PLASTIC ONO BAND

— The **LENNON's** retained only **KLAUS / RINGO STARR** – drums (ex-BEATLES) repl. WHITE who later joined YES

Dec 70. (lp) *(SAPCOR 17)* *<3372>* **JOHN LENNON: PLASTIC ONO BAND** [11] [6]
– Mother / Hold on / I found out / Working class hero / Isolation / Remember / Love / Well well well / Look at me / God / My mummy's dead. *(re-iss. Jul84 on 'Fame' lp/c; 41-3102-1/-4) (cd-iss. Apr88 on 'E.M.I.'; CDP 746770-2) (cd re-iss. Dec94 on 'Fame'; CDFA 3310) (cd re-iss. Oct00 on 'Parlophone'+=; 528740-2)* – Power to the people / Do the oz.

Dec 70. (7") *<1827>* **MOTHER. / WHY (Yoko Ono)** [–] [43]

— next single also credited with **YOKO ONO**

Mar 71. (7") *(R 5892)* **POWER TO THE PEOPLE. / OPEN YOUR BOX** [7] [–]

Mar 71. (7") *<1830>* **POWER TO THE PEOPLE. / Yoko Ono: TOUCH ME** [–] [11]

Oct 71. (lp) *(PAS 10004)* *<3379>* **IMAGINE** [1] Sep71 [1]
– Imagine / Crippled inside / Jealous guy / It's so hard / I don't want to be a soldier / Give me some truth / Oh my love / How do you sleep? / How? / Oh Yoko!. *(also on quad-lp Jun72; Q4PAS 10004) (cd-iss. May87 on 'Parlophone'; CDP 746641-2) (re-iss. Nov97; LPCENT 27) (re-mast.Feb00 cd/c/lp; 524858-2/-4/-1)* – hit UK No.51

Oct 71. (7") *<1840>* **IMAGINE. / IT'S SO HARD** [–] [3]

May 72. (7") *<1848>* **WOMAN IS THE NIGGER OF THE WORLD. / Yoko Ono: SISTERS, OH SISTERS** [–] [57]

— with ELEPHANT'S MEMORY & FLUX / INVISIBLE STRINGS and lots of guests including **FRANK ZAPPA, ERIC CLAPTON,** etc.

Sep 72. (d-lp; JOHN & YOKO / PLASTIC ONO BAND) *(PCSP 7161)* *<3392>* **SOMETIME IN NEW YORK CITY (live)** [11] [48]
– Woman is the nigger of the world / Sisters o sisters / Attica state / Born in a prison / New York City / Sunday bloody Sunday / The luck of the Irish / John Sinclair / Angela / We're all water / (w/ CAST OF THOUSANDS); Cold turkey / Don't worry Kyoko / (w/ The MOTHERS); Jamrag / Scumbag / Au. *(re-iss. Feb86 on 'Parlophone'; see LIVE IN NEW YORK CITY')*

— Next single credited as **JOHN & YOKO / PLASTIC ONO BAND** with **The HARLEM COMMUNITY CHOIR**

Nov 72. (7",7"green) *(R 5970)* **HAPPY XMAS (WAR IS OVER). / LISTEN THE SNOW IS FALLING** [4] Nov71 [ ]
(re-iss. Dec74; same); hit No.48) (re-iss. Dec80; same); No.2) (re-iss. Dec81; same); No.28) (re-iss. Dec82; ; hit 56)

JOHN LENNON

Nov 73. (7") *(R 5994)* *<1868>* **MIND GAMES. / MEAT CITY** [26] [18]

Nov 73. (lp/c; JOHN LENNON & PLASTIC U.F.ONO BAND) *(PCS/TC-PCS 7165)* *<3414>* **MIND GAMES** [13] [9]
– Mind games / Tight a $ / Aisumasen (I'm sorry) / One day (at a time) / Bring on the Lucie (freda people) / Nutopian international anthem / Intuition / Out of the blue / Only people / I know (I know) / You are here / Meat city. *(re-iss. Oct80 on 'Music For Pleasure' lp/c; MFP/TCMFP 50509) (cd-iss. Aug87 & Sep91 on 'Parlophone'; CDP 746769-2) (cd re-mast.Oct02 +=; 542425-2)* – home versions:- Aisumasen (I'm sorry) / Bring on the Lucie (freda people) / Meat city.

Oct 74. (7"; JOHN LENNON & THE PLASTIC ONO NUCLEAR BAND featuring ELTON JOHN) *(R 5998)* *<1874>* **WHATEVER GETS YOU THRU' THE NIGHT. / BEEF JERKY** [36] Sep74 [1]

Oct 74. (lp/c) *(PC/+TC 253)* *<3416>* **WALLS AND BRIDGES** [6] [1]
– Going down on love / Whatever gets you thru the night / Old dirt road / What you got / Bless you / #9 dream / Surprise surprise (sweet bird of Paradise) / Steel and glass / Beef jerky / Nobody loves you (when you're down and out) / Ya-ya / Scared. *(re-iss. Jan85 on 'Parlophone' lp/c; ATAK/TC-ATAK 43) (cd-iss. Jul87; CDP 746768-2)*

Jan 75. (7") *(R 6003)* *<1878>* **#9 DREAM. / WHAT YOU GOT** [23] [9]

Feb 75. (lp/c) *(PCS/TC-PCS 7169)* *<3419>* **ROCK'N'ROLL** [6] [6]
– Be-bop-a-lula / Stand by me / Medley: Rip it up – Ready Teddy / You can't catch me / Ain't that a shame / Do you want to dance / Sweet little sixteen / Slippin' and slidin' / Peggy Sue / Medley: Bring it on home to me – Send me some lovin' / Ya ya / Just because. *(re-iss. Nov81 on 'Music For Pleasure' lp/c; MFP/TCMFP 50522) (cd-iss. Jul87 on 'Parlophone'; CDP 746 707-2) (re-iss. Feb97 on 'E.M.I.'; LPCENT 9)*

Apr 75. (7") *(R 6005)* *<1881>* **STAND BY ME. / MOVE OVER MS. L** [30] Mar75 [20]
(re-iss. Apr81; same)

Oct 75. (7") *(R 6009)* **IMAGINE. / WORKING CLASS HERO** [6] [–]
(re-iss. Dec80; same); hit No.1)

Nov 75. (lp/c) *(PCS 7173)* *<3421>* **SHAVED FISH** (compilation) [8] [12]
– Give peace a chance / Cold turkey / Instant karma / Power to the people / Mother / Woman is the nigger of the world / Imagine / Whatever gets you thru the night / Mind games / #9 dream / Happy Xmas (war is over) / Give peace a chance (reprise). *(cd-iss. May87 on 'E.M.I.'; CDP 746642-2)*

— JOHN was also credited on a few singles by ELTON JOHN – Feb75 'I Saw Her Standing There' which was also realeased Mar81 with 2 other. In Jul71 a rare single 'GOD SAVE US'/'DO THE OZ' was released by him and Plastic Ono Band backing 'BILL ELLIOT AND THE ELASTIC OZ BAND'

JOHN LENNON & YOKO ONO

returned after a long break

Geffen Geffen

Oct 80. (7") *(K 79186)* *<49604>* **(JUST LIKE) STARTING OVER. / KISS KISS KISS (Yoko Ono)** [1] [1]

Nov 80. (lp/c) *(K/K4 99131)* *<2001>* **DOUBLE FANTASY** [1] [1]
– (Just like) Starting over / Every man has a woman who loves him (YOKO ONO) / Clean up time / Give me something (YOKO ONO) / I'm losing you / I'm moving on (YOKO ONO) / Beautiful boy (darling boy) / Watching the wheels / I'm your angel (YOKO ONO) / Dear Yoko / Beautiful boys (YOKO ONO) / Kiss kiss kiss (YOKO ONO) / Woman / Hard times are over (YOKO ONO). *(re-iss. Jan89 on 'Capitol' cd)(c/lp; CDP 791 425-2)(TC+/EST 2083) (cd re-iss. Oct00 on 'Parlophone'+=; 528739-2)* – Help me to help myself / Walking on thin ice / Central Park stroll (dialogue).

Jan 81. (7"/c-s) *(K/MK 79195)* *<49644>* **WOMAN. / Yoko Ono: BEAUTIFUL BOYS** [1] [2]

Mar 81. (7"/c-s) *(K/MK 79207)* *<49695>* **WATCHING THE WHEELS. / Yoko Ono: YES, I'M YOUR ANGEL** [30] [10]

— His last two singles were released after his tragic murder 8th Dec'80

JOHN & YOKO

had recorded one more album prior to his death.

Polydor Polydor

Jan 84. (lp) *(<817 238-1>)* **A HEART PLAY: UNFINISHED DIALOGUE** (interview with Playboy) [ ] [ ]

Jan 84. (7") *(POSP 700)* *<817254>* **NOBODY TOLD ME. / O SANITY** [6] [5]

Jan 84. (lp/pic-lp/c)(cd) *(POLH/+P/C 5)(<817160-2>)* **MILK AND HONEY** [3] [11]
– I'm stepping out / Sleepless night (YOKO ONO) / I don't wanna face it / Don't be scared (YOKO ONO) / Nobody told me / O'sanity (YOKO ONO) / Borrowed time / Your hands (YOKO ONO) / (Forgive me) My little flower princess / Let me count the ways (YOKO ONO) / Grow old with me / You're the one (YOKO ONO). *(cd re-mast.Oct01 on 'Parlophone'+=; 535959-2)* – Every man has a woman who loves him / I'm moving on (home demo) / I'm stepping out (home demo) / (interview).

Mar 84. (7") *(POSP 701)* **BORROWED TIME. / YOUR HANDS (Yoko Ono)** [32] [ ]
(12"+=) *(POSPX 701)* – Never say goodbye.

Jul 84. (7") *(POSP 702)* *<821107>* **I'M STEPPING OUT. / SLEEPLESS NIGHT (Yoko Ono)** [ ] [55]
(12"+=) *(POSPX 702)* – Loneliness.

Nov 84. (7") *(POSP 712)* **EVERY MAN HAS A WOMAN WHO LOVES HIM. / IT'S ALRIGHT** [ ] [ ]
(above from various compilation 'B'-side by his son SEAN ONO LENNON)

– posthumous releases, etc. –

on 'Parlophone' UK /'Capitol' US, unless mentioned otherwise

Jun 81. (8xlp-box) *Apple; (JLB 8)* **JOHN LENNON (BOXED)** [ ] [ ]
– (all lp's from LIVE PEACE – SHAVED FISH) *(4xcd-box-iss.Oct90; LENNON 1)*

Nov 82. (lp/c) *E.M.I.; (EMTV/TC-EMTV 37) / Geffen; <GHSP 2023>* **THE JOHN LENNON COLLECTION** [1] [33]
– (nearly as 'SHAVED FISH') *(re-iss. Jun85; same) (cd-iss. Oct89; CDEMTV 37)* – (2 extra tracks).

Nov 82. (7") *(R 6059)* **LOVE. / GIVE ME SOME TRUTH** [41] [ ]

Mar 84. (7") *EMI Gold; (G45 2)* **GIVE PEACE A CHANCE. / COLD TURKEY** [ ] [–]

Nov 85. (7") *(R 6117)* **JEALOUS GUY / GOING DOWN ON LOVE** [65] [ ]
(12"+=) *(12R 6117)* – Oh Yoko!

Feb 86. (lp/c)(cd) *(PCS/TC-PCS 7301)(CDP 746 196-2) <12451>* **LIVE IN NEW YORK CITY (live)** [55] [41]

Nov 86. (lp/c/cd) *(PCS/TCPCS/CDPCS 7308) <12533>* **MENLOVE AVE.** (sessions 74-75) [ ] [ ]
– Here we go again / Rock'n'roll people / Angel baby / Since my baby left me / To know her is to love her / Steel and glass / Scared / Old dirt road / Nobody loves you (when you're down and out).

May 87. (7") *Antar;* **TWO MINUTES SILENCE. / TWO MINUTES SILENCE (dub!)** [ ] [ ]

Aug 87. (cd) **LIVE JAM** (half of SOMETIME lp) [ ] [ ]

Oct 88. (cd/d-c/d-lp) *(CD/TC+/PCSP 722) <90803>* **IMAGINE: THE MOVIE** (Music from the Motion Picture; with some songs by The BEATLES) [64] [31]
– Real love / Twist and shout / Help! / In my life / Strawberry fields forever / A day in the life / Revolution / The ballad of John & Yoko / Julia / Don't let me down / Give peace a chance / How? / Imagine (rehearsal) / God / Mother / Stand by me / Jealous guy / Woman / Beautiful boy (darling boy) / (Just like) Starting over / Imagine.

Oct 88. (cd-s) *<44230>* **JEALOUS GUY** [–] [80]

Nov 88. (7"/7"pic-d) *(R/RP 6199)* **IMAGINE. / JEALOUS GUY** [45] [–]
(12"+=/12"pic-d+=) *(12R/+P 6199)* – Happy Xmas (war is over).
(cd-s+=) *(CDR 6199)* – Give peace a chance.

Oct 97. (cd/c/lp) *(<8 21954-2/-4/-1>)* **LENNON LEGEND – THE VERY BEST OF JOHN LENNON** [4] Mar98 [65]
– Imagine / Instant karma / Mother / Jealous guy / Power to the people / Cold turkey / Love / Mind games / Whatever gets you thru the night / No.9 dream / Stand by me / (Just like) Starting over / Woman / Beautiful boy / Watching the wheels / Nobody told me / Borrowed time / Working class hero / Happy Xmas (war is over) / Give peace a chance. *(cd re-iss. Oct03; 595067-2)*

Sep 98. (3xcd-box) *Dressed To Kill; (DTKBOX 92)* **IN MY LIFE** [ ] [–]

Nov 98. (4xcd-box+book) *(<8 30614-2>)* **JOHN LENNON ANTHOLOGY** (alt.takes, live rarities and home recordings) [62] [99]
– ASCOT / NEW YORK CITY / THE LOST WEEKEND / DAKOTA)

Nov 98. (cd/c) *(497639-2/-4)* **WONSAPONATIME** (above highlights) [ ] [ ]

Dec 99. (c-s/cd-s) *(TCR/CDR 6534)* **IMAGINE / HAPPY XMAS (WAR IS OVER) / GIVE PEACE A CHANCE** [3] [–]

Dec 03. (7") *(R 6627)* **HAPPY XMAS (WAR IS OVER). / IMAGINE** [33] [–]
(cd-s+=) *(CDR 6627)* – Instant karma (version) / Imagine (instrumental).

□ Annie LENNOX (see under ⇒ EURYTHMICS)

□ Deke LEONARD (see under ⇒ MAN)

LEVELLERS

Formed: Brighton, England . . . early '88 by MARK CHADWICK, JEREMY CUNNINGHAM, CHARLIE HEATHER, JON SEVINK and ALAN MILES. Taking their name from the English political radicals of the 17th Century, The LEVELLERS were one of the most successful and consistent bands to emerge from the free festival/crusty scene, building up a loyal grassroots fanbase with their raggle-taggle blend of folk and punk. After Phil Nelson took over as manager the following year, he released a couple of raw EP's on his own 'Hag' imprint, before the band signed to European label, 'Musidisc', and began work on a debut album with WATERBOYS producer, Phil Tennant. While 'A WEAPON CALLED THE WORD' helped introduce their rootsy assault to a larger audience, the band subsequently broke from their contract and signed to 'China', while MILES was replaced by songwriter/guitarist, SIMON FRIEND. Another hectic UK tour followed and by Autumn '91, The LEVELLERS' popularity was such that the 'LEVELLING THE LAND' album made the Top 20 with only the support of minor hit single, 'ONE WAY'. With a more accessible anthemic rock/folk approach, the album took the band's defiantly pro-earth, pro-equality philosophy overground and into the mainstream, 'BATTLE OF THE BEANFIELD' commemorating the famous festival stand-off between hippies and police. In spring '92, The LEVELLERS scored their biggest hit to date with the 'FIFTEEN YEARS' EP, almost making the Top 10, while they chose to end the year with a series of 'Freakshows' combining the likes of fellow agit-poppers, CHUMBAWAMBA with such established crusty pastimes as juggling and fire-eating. The following year's eponymous album missed the No.1 spot by a whisker, spawning a trio of Top 20 singles in 'BELARUSE', 'THIS GARDEN' and the lovely 'JULIE'; although The LEVELLERS were now rather unlikely but fully fledged pop stars, they also became embroiled in a war of words with the music press and fellow musicians. Not that this affected their popularity one iota, the band finally topping the UK charts with 'ZEITGEIST' (1995) as they found themselves surfing the new wave of enthusiasm for British music in general. 'MOUTH TO MOUTH' (1997) – their final output for 'China' – and 'HELLO PIG' (2000) – their first on 'East West' – kept the fans reletively happy for a while, and even 2002's 'GREEN BLADE RISING' – on punk's final outpost, 'Eagle', kept the wolf from the door. Certainly one of the UK's more conscientious bands, The LEVELLERS are sadly part of a dying breed who still believe that music and politics are a feasible combination. • **Songwriters:** Group compositions except; THE DEVIL WENT DOWN TO GEORGIA (Charlie Daniels Band) / TWO HOURS (McDermott) / GERM FREE ADOLESCENCE (X-Ray Spex) / PRICE OF LOVE (Everly Brothers) / HANG ON TO YOUR EGO (Pixies). • **Trivia:** The FENCE released one single in May '87 on 'Flag'; FROZEN WATER / EXIT.

Album rating: A WEAPON CALLED THE WORD (*7) / LEVELLING THE LAND (*8) / THE LEVELLERS (*6) / ZEITGEIST (*5) / HEADLINES, WHITE LINES, BLACK TAR RIVERS – BEST LIVE (*6) / MOUTH TO MOUTH (*5) / ONE WAY OF LIFE (THE BEST OF . . .) compilation (*8) / HELLO PIG (*5) / GREEN BLADE RISING (*5)

MARK CHADWICK – vocals, guitar, banjo (ex-FENCE) / **JEREMY CUNNINGHAM** – bass, bazouki / **CHARLIE HEATHER** – drums / **JON SEVINK** – violin (ex-FENCE) / **ALAN MILES** – vocals, guitar, mandolin, harmonica

Hag — not iss.

May 89. (12"ep) *(HAG 005)* **CARRY ME** [ ] [–]
– Carry me / What's in the way / The lasy days of winter / England my home.

Oct 89. (12"ep) *(HAG 006)* **OUTSIDE INSIDE. / HARD FIGHT / I HAVE NO ANSWERS / BARREL OF A GUN** [ ] [–]

Musidisc — not iss.

Apr 90. (7") *(105 577)* **WORLD FREAK SHOW. / BARREL OF A GUN (acoustic)** [ ] [–]
(12"+=) *(108 936)* – What you know.

Apr 90. (cd/c/lp) *(10557-2/-4/-1)* **A WEAPON CALLED THE WORD** [ ] [–]
– World freak show / Carry me / Outside-inside / Together all the way / Barrel of a gun / Three friends / I have no answers / No change / Blind faith / The ballad of Robbie Jones / England my home / What you know. *(cd re-iss. Jan01 on 'Universal'; E 15397-2)*

Oct 90. (7") *(106897)* **TOGETHER ALL THE WAY. / THREE FRIENDS (re-mix) (Arfa mix short version)** [ ] [–]
(12"+=) *(106896)* – Cardboard box city / Social insecurity.

— **SIMON FRIEND** – guitars, vocals repl. ALAN.

China Elektra

Sep 91. (7"/c-s) *(WOK/+MC 2008)* **ONE WAY. / HARD FIGHT (acoustic) / THE LAST DAYS OF WINTER** [51] [–]
(12"+=/cd-s+=) *(WOK T/CD 2008)* – ('A'-Factory mix) / The Devil went down to Georgia.

Oct 91. (lp/c/cd) *(WOL/+MC/CD 1022)* *<61325-1/-4/-2>* **LEVELLING THE LAND** [14] May92 [ ]
– One way / The game / The boatman / The liberty song / Far from home / Sell out / Another man's cause / The road / The riverflow / Battle of the beanfield. *(cd re-iss. Jul99; 4509 96100-2)*

Nov 91. (7"/c-s) *(WOK/+MC 2010)* **FAR FROM HOME. / WORLD FREAK SHOW (live)** [71] [–]
(12"+=/cd-s+=) *(WOK T/CD 2010)* – Outside inside (live) / The boatman (live) / Three friends (live).

May 92. (c-ep/10"pic-d-ep/12"ep/cd-ep) *(WOK MC/X/T/CD 2020)* **15 YEARS / DANCE BEFORE THE STORM. / RIVERFLOW (live) / PLASTIC JEEZUS** [11] [–]

Jun 93. (c-s) *(WOKMC 2034)* **BELARUSE / SUBVERT (live at Trancentral) / BELARUSE RETURN** [12] [–]
(12"+=/cd-s+=) *(WOK T/CD 2034)* – Is this art?

Sep 93. (lp/c/cd) *(WOL/+MC/CD 1034)* *<61532>* **THE LEVELLERS** [2] [ ]
– Warning / 100 years of solitude / The likes of you and I / Is this art? / Dirty Davey / This garden / Broken circles / Julie / The player / Belaruse. *(cd re-iss. Jul99; 4509 95908-2)*

Oct 93. (7"pic-d/c-s) *(WOK P/MC 2039)* **THIS GARDEN. / LIFE (acoustic)** [12] [–]
(12"+=/cd-s+=) *(WOK T/CD 2039)* – ('A'-Marcus Dravs remix) / ('A'-Banco De Gaia remix).

May 94. (7"clear-ep/c-ep/10"pic-d-ep/cd-ep) *(WOK/+MC//CD 2042)* **THE JULIE EP** [17] [–]
– Julie (new version) / English civil war / Warning (live) / 100 years of solitude / The lowlands of Holland.

Jul 95. (7"pic-d) *(WOKP 2059)* **HOPE ST. / LEAVE THIS TOWN** [12] [–]
(7"pic-d) *(WOKPX 2059)* – ('A'side) / Miles away.
(cd-s++=/c-s++=) *(WOK CD/MC 2059)* – Busking on Hope Street.

Aug 95. (lp/c/cd) *(WOL/+MC/CD 1064)* *<61887>* **ZEITGEIST** [1] [ ]
– Hope St. / The fear / Exodus / Maid of the river / Saturday to Sunday / 4.am / Forgotten ground / Fantasy / P.C. Keen / Just the one / Haven't made it / Leave this town / Men-an-tol. *(cd re-iss. Jul99; 0630 11597-2)*

Oct 95. (7"/c-s/cd-s) *(WOK/+MC/CD 2067)* **FANTASY. / SARA'S BEACH / SEARCHLIGHTS (extended)** [16] [–]
(below featured JOE STRUMMER (ex-CLASH) on piano)

Dec 95. (7"ep/c-ep/cd-ep) *(WOK/+MC/CD 2076)* **JUST THE ONE / A PROMISE. / YOUR 'OUSE / DRINKING FOR ENGLAND** [12] [–]

Jul 96. (7"ep/c-ep/cd-ep) *(WOK/+MC/CD 2082)* **EXODUS – LIVE (live)** [24] [–]
– Exodus / Another man's cause / Leave this town / P.C. Keen.

Aug 96. (cd/c) *(WOL CDX/MC 1074)* **HEADLIGHTS, WHITE LINES, BLACK TAR RIVERS – BEST LIVE (live)** [13] [–]
– Sell out / Hope St. / 15 years / Exodus / Carry me / The boatman / 3 friends / Men-an-tol / The road / One way / England my home / England my home / Battle of the beanfield / Liberty / The riverflow. *(cd re-iss. Jul99; 0630 15783-2)*

Aug 97. (c-s/cd-s) *(WOK MC/CD 2088)* **BEAUTIFUL DAY / BAR ROOM JURY / ALL YOUR DREAMS** [13] [–]
(cd-s) *(WOKCDX 2088)* – ('A'side) / Germ free adolescence / Price of love / Hang on to your ego.

Aug 97. (lp/c/cd) *(WOL/+MC/CD 1084)* **MOUTH TO MOUTH** [5] [–]
– Dog train / Beautiful day / Celebrate / Rain and snow / Far away / C.C.T.V. / Chemically free / Elation / Captains' courageous / Survivors / Sail away / Too real. *(cd re-iss. Jul99; 0630 19856-2)*

Oct 97. (c-ep/cd-ep) *(WOK MC/CD 2089)* **CELEBRATE / RAIN & SNOW (The White Mountain Yarn mix) / SEA OF PAIN / SURVIVORS** [28] [–]
(cd-s) *(WOKCDX 2089)* – ('A'side) / Men-an-tol (live acoustic) / 4 + 20 / Ring of fire.

Dec 97. (12"ep/c-ep/cd-ep) *(WOK/+MC/CD 2090)* **DOG TRAIN / LAST DAYS OF WINTER. / CARRY ME / WHAT'S IN THE WAY** [24] [–]

Mar 98. (12"ep/c-ep/cd-ep) *(WOK/+MC/CD 2091)* **TOO REAL (mixes; Steve Osborne / Morcheeba / Indian Rope Man / Lean Fiddler / Morcheeba instrumental / Bliss)** [46] [–]

Oct 98. (7"/c-s) *(WOK/+MC 2096)* **BOZOS. / DON'T YOU GRIEVE** [44] [–]
(cd-s) *(WOKCD 2096)* – Plastic factory.
(cd-s) *(WOKCDR 2096)* – ('A'side) / New York mining disaster 1941 / Supercharger (heavy mental mix).

Oct 98. (cd/c) *(052173-2/-4)* **ONE WAY OF LIFE (THE BEST OF . . .)** (compilation) [15] [–]
– One way / What a beautiful day / Fifteen years / Shadow on the sun / Hope street / Belaruse / Celebrate / Too real (12"mix) / Bozos / This garden / Carry me / Fantasy / Julie / Dog train / Far from home / Just the one. *(ltd.d-cd+=)* – Far from home / Just the one / PC Keen / Sell out / Hope Street / 15 years / Men-an-to. *(cd re-iss. Jun02; 3984 25099-2)*

Jan 99. (c-s) *(WOKMC 2102)* **ONE WAY (new version). / ANGEL** [33] [–]
(cd-s+=) *(WOKCD 2102)* – Windows.
(cd-s) *(WOKCDX 2102)* – ('A'side) / England my home / I have no answers.

East West not iss.

Aug 00. (c-s) *(EW 218C)* **HAPPY BIRTHDAY REVOLUTION / SURPRISINGLY EASY!** [57] [–]
(cd-s+=) *(EW 218CD)* – Best part of the day.

Sep 00. (cd/c/lp) *(8573 84339-2/-4/-1)* **HELLO PIG** [28] [–]
– Happy birthday revolution / Invisible / The weed that killed Elvis / Edge of the world / Do it again tomorrow / Walk lightly / Voices on the wind / Sold England / Modern day tragedy / Dreams / 61 minutes of pleading / Red sun burns / Gold and silver.

Eagle Eagle

Sep 02. (7") *(EHAG7 001)* **COME ON. / WELCOME TO TOMORROW** [44] [–]
(cd-s+=) *(EHAGXA 001)* – Vanished.
(cd-s) *(EHAGXS 001)* – ('A'side) / Hooligan / Tranquil blue.

Sep 02. (cd) *(EHAGCD 002)* *<20000>* **GREEN BLADE RISING** [ ] Feb03 [ ]
– Four winds / Falling from the tree / Pretty target / Come on / Pour / Aspects of spirit / Wild as angels / Believers / A chorus line / Not what we wanted / Wake the world. *(other cd+=; EHAGLT 002)* – Come on (dub).

Jan 03. (7"ep/cd-ep) *(EHAG 7/XS 003)* **WILD AS ANGELS EP** [34] [–]
– Wild as angels / Galahad / Adulterer's blues / Wild as angels (video).
(cd-s) *(EHAGXA 003)* – ('A'side) / American air do / Burn.

– compilations, etc. –

Jan 92. (7") *Musidisc; (105 557)* **WORLD FREAK SHOW (remix). / WHAT YOU KNOW** [ ] [–]
(12"+=/cd-s+=) *(10893 6/2)* – Barrel of a gun / What you know.

Mar 93. (lp/c/cd) *China; (WOL 1035/+MC/CD)* **SEE NOTHING, HEAR NOTHING, DO SOMETHING** (early material) [ ] [–]

May 01. (cd) *Hag; (HAG 005)* **SPECIAL BREW** [ ] [–]

☐ LEVON & THE HAWKS (see under ⇒ BAND)

Jerry Lee LEWIS

Born: 29 Sep'35, Ferriday, Louisiana, USA. In 1949, his parents mortgaged their house to buy him a piano which the young JERRY mastered in two weeks! A few years later, after being expelled from a religious school that taught music, he married a preacher's daughter; he soon deserted her however, bigamously marrying another girl in true shotgun style. In 1956, LEWIS went to Memphis, Tennessee with his father and through perseverance, set up recording time in Sam Phillips' 'Sun' studios. The following year, after his debut, 'CRAZY ARMS', was banned from airplay, LEWIS secured a couple of appearances on the Steve Allen TV Show, the exposure leading to massive sales of his second single, 'WHOLE LOTTA SHAKIN' GOIN' ON'. Although LEWIS didn't actually write any of his material, his demented rock'n'roll performances (he even pummelled the piano with his feet!) earned him the rather unfortunate nickname, "The Killer". Later in '57, JERRY bigamously married again!, this time secretly to his 13 year-old second cousin, Myra Gale Brown. Perhaps inspired by his recent activities, LEWIS scored two enormous worldwide classics in the appropriately titled 'GREAT BALLS OF FIRE' and 'BREATHLESS'. Meanwhile, he divorced his second wife and brought the wrath of the religious establishment and moral majority when his questionable lifestyle was disclosed; LEWIS' UK arrival (in May '58) caused uproar and near tour cancellation after newspapers had a field day over his "minor" misdemeanours. Although JERRY LEE made a few more sporadic returns to the charts, his career had been severely dented by this late 50's hysteria. While Myra gave birth to his second son, Steve Allen, in February '59, LEWIS's intake of alcohol and pills was increasing every month. Tragedy struck in April '62, when his aforementioned son drowned in a swimming pool accident. Around a year and a half later, coinciding with LEWIS' signature for new imprint 'Smash', Myra produced another child, this time a daughter, Phoebe Allen. In the early 70's, Myra finally divorced him, claiming neglect, etc. It didn't stop him marrying a fourth time, although this time he did it legally in late '71. With his career enjoying something of a resurrection in 1973 (by which time he'd traded in his blue suede shoes for Stetson-styled country-pop), tragedy struck again when his son (his drummer on tour) JERRY LEE JR was killed in a motoring accident. In 1976, LEWIS was involved in two gun incidents, one when he accidently shot his bassman, NORMAN OWENS, the other occurring outside Gracelands (Elvis Presley's home) hours after being charged with drunk driving. He signed to 'Elektra' in 1978, although a few albums and a serious stomach ulcer operation later, he sued the label. In 1982, his estranged fourth wife, Jaren Gunn Lewis (ne Pate), drowned in a mysterious swimming pool incident just prior to their divorce settlement. The following year, coming up for his 50th birthday, the irrepressible LEWIS tied the knot yet again, this time to a 25 year-old, Shawn Michelle Stevens; just over two months later, she was to be found dead in their home. Although suspected of foul play, no case was brought and LEWIS, proving that he was a family man at heart, went on to marry his sixth wife, the 22 year-old, Kerrie McCarver, who, in early '87, gave birth to a son, Jerry Lee Lewis III. A few years later, his biopic film story appeared (Nick Tosches' celebrated biography, 'Hellfire', had previously hit the shelves in 1982) featuring re-recordings of his oldies, his part played by actor, Dennis Quaid. • **Songwriters:** Wrote own material, except CRAZY ARMS (Ray Price) / WHOLE LOTTA SHAKIN' GOIN' ON (D.Williams & Sunny Dave) / YOU WIN AGAIN + SETTIN' THE WOODS ON FIRE (Hank Willliams) / WHAT'D I SAY + HIT THE ROAD JACK (Ray Charles) / BREAK UP + I'LL MAKE IT ALL UP TO YOU (Charlie Rich) / SWEET LITTLE SIXTEEN + LITTLE QUEENIE (Chuck Berry) / GOOD GOLLY MISS MOLLY + LONG TALL SALLY (Little Richard) / ME AND BOBBY McGEE (Kris Kristofferson) / GREEN GREEN GRASS OF HOME (Curly Putnam) / CHANTILLY LACE (Big Bopper) / JACK DANIELS (Heads, Hands & Feet) / DRINKIN' WINE SPO . . . (Stick McGhee) / RITA MAE (Bob Dylan) etc. • **Trivia:** His sister, LINDA GAIL LEWIS, also issued solo recordings between 1965 and 74. Another unlikely cousin of JERRY LEE is the TV evangelist, Jimmy Swaggart!

Best CD compilation: THE VERY BEST OF JERRY LEE LEWIS (*8)

JERRY LEE LEWIS – vocals, piano + sessions

London — Sun

Dec 56. (7") *<259>* **CRAZY ARMS. / END OF THE ROAD** [–] [ ]

Jul 57. (7",78) *(HLS 8457) <267>* **WHOLE LOTTA SHAKIN' GOIN' ON. / IT'LL BE ME** [8] Jun57 [3]

Nov 57. (7") *<281>* **GREAT BALLS OF FIRE. / YOU WIN AGAIN** [–] [2] [95]

Dec 57. (7",78) *(HLS 8529)* **GREAT BALLS OF FIRE. / MEAN WOMAN BLUES** [1] [–]

Feb 58. (7",78) *(HLS 8559)* **YOU WIN AGAIN. / I'M FEELIN' SORRY** [ ] [–]

Apr 58. (7",78) *(HLS 8592) <288>* **BREATHLESS. / DOWN THE LINE** [8] Feb58 [7]

Jun 58. (7") *<301>* **THE RETURN OF JERRY LEE. / LEWIS BOOGIE** [–] [ ]

Sep 58. (7",78) *(HLS8700) <303>* **BREAK-UP. / I'LL MAKE IT ALL UP TO YOU** [ ] [52] Aug58 [85]

Jan 59. (lp) *(HAS 2138) <1230>* **JERRY LEE LEWIS** [ ] Dec57 [ ]
– Don't be cruel / Goodnight Irene / Put me down / It all depends / Ubangi stomp / Crazy arms / Jambalaya / Fools like me / High school confidential / Where the saints go marching in Matchbox / It'll be me. *(re-iss. May82 on 'Mercury' lp/c; 6463/7145 042) (cd-iss. Apr86 on 'Pickwick'; PCD 814)*

Jan 59. (7",78) *(HLS 8780) <296>* **HIGH SCHOOL CONFIDENTIAL. / FOOLS LIKE ME** [12] May58 [12]

Apr 59. (7",78) *(HLS 8940) <317>* **LOVIN' UP A STORM. / BIG BLON' BABY** [28] [ ]

Sep 59. (7",78) *(HLS 8941) <324>* **LET'S TALK ABOUT US. / THE BALLAD OF BILLY JOE** [ ] [ ]

Nov 59. (7",78) *(HLS 8993) <330>* **LITTLE QUEENIE. / I COULD NEVER BE ASHAMED OF YOU** [ ] [ ]

Mar 60. (7") *(HLS 9083) <312>* **I'LL SAIL MY SHIP ALONE. / IT HURT ME SO** [–] Dec 58 [93]

May 60. (7") *(HLS 9131) <337)* **BABY, BABY, BYE, BYE. / OLD BLACK JOE** [47] [ ]

Oct 60. (7") *(HLS 9202) <344>* **JOHN HENRY. / HANG UP MY ROCK'N'ROLL SHOES** [ ] [ ]

Dec 60. (7") *<352>* **WHEN I GET PAID. / LOVE MADE A FOOL OF ME** [–] [ ]

Apr 61. (7") *(HLS 9335) <356>* **WHAT'D I SAY. / LIVIN' LOVIN' WRECK** [10] [30]

1961. (lp) *<1265>* **JERRY LEE'S GREATEST** (part compilation) [–] [ ]

Sep 61. (7") *(HLS 9414) <364>* **IT WON'T HAPPEN WITH ME. / COLD COLD HEART** [ ] [ ]

Oct 61. (7") *(HLS 9446)* **AS LONG AS I LIVE. / WHEN I GET PAID** [ ] [–]

Oct 61. (7") *<367>* **SAVE THE LAST DANCE FOR ME. / AS LONG AS I LIVE** [–] [ ]

Dec 61. (7") *<371>* **MONEY. / BONNIE B** [–] [ ]

Mar 62. (7") *(HLS 9526) <374>* **I'VE BEEN TWISTIN'. / RAMBLING ROSE** [ ] [ ]

May 62. (lp) *(HAS 2440)* **JERRY LEE LEWIS VOL.2** [14] [ ]
– Money / As long as I live / Country music is here to stay / Frankie and Johnny / Home / Hello baby / Let's talk about us / What'd I say Breakup / Great balls of fire / Cold, cold heart / Hello Josephine *(cd-iss. Apr86 on 'Pickwick'; PCD 840)*

Aug 62. (7") *(HLS 9584) <379>* **SWEET LITTLE SIXTEEN. / HOW'S MY EX TREATING YOU** [38] [95]

Feb 63. (7") *(HLS 9688) <382>* **GOOD GOLLY MISS MOLLY. / I CAN'T TRUST ME (IN YOUR ARMS ANYMORE)** [31] Dec62 [ ]

May 63. (7") *(HLS 9722) <384>* **TEENAGE LETTER. ("& LINDA GAIL LEWIS") / SEASONS OF MY HEART** [ ] Feb63 [ ]

Philips — Smash

1963. (7") *(AMT 1216) <1857>* **HIT THE ROAD JACK. / PEN AND PAPER** [–] [ ]

Mar 64. (7") *(BF 1324) <1886>* **I'M ON FIRE. / BREAD AND BUTTER MAN** [ ] [98]

1964. (7") *<1906>* **SHE WAS MY BABY. / THE HOLE HE SAID HE'D DIG FOR ME** [–] [‘]

Oct 64. (7") *(BF 1371) <1930>* **HI HEAL SNEAKERS. / YOU WENT BACK ON YOUR WORD** [ ] [91]

Dec 64. (7") **WHOLE LOTTA SHAKIN' GOIN' ON (live). / BREATHLESS (live)** [–] [ ]

Feb 65. (7") **GREAT BALLS OF FIRE (live). / HIGH SCHOOL CONFIDENTIAL (live)** [–] [ ]

Apr 65. (7") *(BF 1407) <1969>* **BABY HOLD ME CLOSE. / I BELIEVE IN YOU** [ ] [ ]

May 65. (lp) *(SBL 7650) <67650>* **THE GREATEST LIVE SHOW ON EARTH (live)** [ ] Dec64 [71]
– Jenny Jenny / Who will the next fool be / Memphis Tennessee / Hound

dog / Mean woman blues / Hi-heel sneakers / No particular place to go / Together again / Long tall Sally / Whole lotta shakin' goin' on / Little Queenie (intro) / How's my ex treating you / Johnny B. Goode / Green, green grass of home / What'd I say (part 2) / You win again / I'll sail my ship alone / Cryin' time / Money / Roll over Beethoven.

Jul 65. (7") *(BF 1425)* **ROCKIN' PNEUMONIA AND THE BOOGIE WOOGIE FLU. / THIS MUST BE THE PLACE** [ ] [ ]

Jul 65. (lp) *(SBL 7668) <67063>* **THE RETURN OF ROCK** [ ] May65 [ ]
– I believe in you / Maybeline / Flip, flop and fly / Roll over Beethoven / Baby, hold me close / Herman the hermit / Don't let go / You went back on your word / Corrine, Corrina / Sexy ways / Johhny B.Goode / Got you on my mind.

1965. (7") *<2006>* **GREEN GREEN GRASS OF HOME. ("& LINDA GAIL LEWIS") / BABY, YOU'VE GOT WHAT IT TAKES** [–] [ ]

Jan 66. (lp) *(SBL 7688) <67071>* **COUNTRY SONGS FOR CITY FOLKS** [ ] [ ]
– Green green grass of home / Wolverton mountain Funny how time slips away North to Alaska / The wild side of life / Ray of fire / Detroit city / Crazy arms King of the road / Seasons of my heart.

1966. (7") *<2027>* **STICKS AND STONES. / WHAT A HECK OF A MESS** [–] [ ]

May 66. (lp) *(SBL 7706) <67079>* **MEMPHIS BEAT** [ ] [ ]
– Memphis beat / Mathilda / Darlin' wine spo-dee-o-dee / Hallelujah, I love her so / She thinks I still care / Just because / Sticks and stones / Whenever you're ready / Lincoln limousine / Big boss man / Too young / The urge.

Oct 66. (7") *(BF 1521) <2053>* **MEMPHIS BEAT. / IF I HAD TO DO IT OVER** [ ] [ ]

Jan 67. (lp) *(SBL 7746) <67086>* **BY REQUEST – MORE GREATEST LIVE SHOW ON EARTH (live)** [ ] [ ]
– Introduction / Little Queenie / How's my ex treating you / Johnny B.Goode / Green green grass of home / What'd I say / You win again / I'll sail my ship alone / Crying time / Money / Roll over Beethoven.

Jul 67. (7") *(BF 1594) <2103>* **IT'S A HANG-UP BABY. / HOLDIN' ON** [ ] [ ]

Mercury Smash

Mar 68. (7") *(MF 1020) <2146>* **ANOTHER TIME ANOTHER PLACE. / WALKING THE FLOOR OVER YOU** [ ] [97]

Jul 68. (lp) *(MCL 20117) <67097>* **SOUL MY WAY** [ ] [ ]
– Turn on your love light / It's a hang-up baby / Dream baby (how long must I dream / Just dropped in Wedding bells / He took it like a man / Hey baby / Treat her right / Holdin' on Shotgun man I bet you're gonna like it.

Aug 68. (7") *(MF 1045) <2164>* **WHAT MADE MILWALKEE FAMOUS. / ALL THE GOOD IS GONE** [ ] [94]

1968. (7") *<2186>* **SHE STILL COMES AROUND. / SLIPPIN' AROUND** [–] [ ]

Jan 69. (lp) *(SMWL 21011) <67104>* **ANOTHER PLACE ANOTHER TIME** [ ] Jun68 [ ]
– What made Milwaukee famous Play me a song I can cry to / On the back row / Walking the floor over you All night long / I'm a lonesome fugitive Another place, another time / Break my mind / Before the next teardrop falls / All the good is gone / We live in two different worlds (w/ Linda)

Mar 69. (7") *(MF 1088) <2202>* **TO MAKE LOVE SWEETER FOR YOU. / LET'S TALK ABOUT US** [ ] Dec68 [ ]

May 69. (lp) *(SMCL 20147) <67112>* **SHE STILL COMES AROUND (TO LOVE WHAT'S LEFT OF ME)** [ ] Feb69 [ ]
– To make love sweeter for you / Let's talk about us / I can't get over you / Out of my mind / Today I started loving you again / She still comes around (to love what's lkeft of me) / Louisiana man / Release me / Listen, they're playing my song / There stands the glass / Echoes.

May 69. (7") *(MF 1105)* **LONG TALL SALLY. / JENNY JENNY** [ ] [–]

1969. (7") *<2220>* **DON'T LET ME CROSSOVER. / WE LIVE IN TWO DIFFERENT WORLDS** [–] [ ]

1969. (7"; JERRY LEE LEWIS & LINDA GAIL LEWIS) *<2224>* **ONE HAS MY NAME. / I CAN'T STOP LOVING YOU** [–] [ ]

Feb 70. (lp; JERRY LEE LEWIS & LINDA GAIL LEWIS) *(SMCL 20172) <67126>* **TOGETHER** [ ] Nov69 [ ]
– Milwaukee here I come / Jackson / Don't take it out on me / Cryin' time / Sweet thing / Secret places / Don't let me cross over / Gotta travel on / We live in two different worlds / Earth up above / Roll over Beethoven.

1970. (7") *<2224>* **SHE EVEN WOKE ME UP TO SAY GOODBYE. / ECHOES** [–] [ ]

Jun 70. (lp) *(6338 010) <67128>* **SHE EVEN WOKE ME UP TO SAY GOODBYE** [ ] Feb70 [ ]
– Once more with feeling / Working man blues / Waiting for a train / Brown eyed handsome man / My only claim to fame / Since I met you baby / She woke me up to say goodbye / Wine me up / When the grass grows over me / You went out of your way / Echoes.

Aug 70. (7") *<2257>* **ONCE MORE WITH FEELING. / YOU WENT OUT OF YOUR WAY** [–] [ ]

Nov 70. (7") *<73155>* **I CAN'T HAVE A MERRY CHRISTMAS MARY (WITHOUT YOU). / IN LOVING MEMORIES** [–] [ ]

1971. (7") *<73099>* **THERE MUST BE MORE TO LOVE THAN THIS. / HOME AWAY FROM HOME** [–] [ ]

Jun 71. (lp) *(6338 045) <61323>* **THERE MUST BE MORE TO LOVE THAN THIS** [ ] Jan71 [ ]
– There must be more to love than this / Bottles and barstools / Rueben James / I'd be talkin' / All the time / One more time / Sweet Georgia Brown / Woman, woman / I forget more than you'll ever know / Foolaid / Home away from home / Life's little ups and downs.

Jul 71. (7") *<73192>* **TOUCHING HOME. / WOMAN, WOMAN** [–] [ ]

Jul 71. (lp) *<61343>* **TOUCHING HOME** [–] [ ]

1971. (7") *<73227>* **WHEN HE WALKS ON YOU. / FOOLISH KIND OF MAN** [–] [ ]

Feb 72. (lp) *(6338 071) <61346>* **WOULD YOU TAKE ANOTHER CHANCE ON ME?** [ ] Nov71 [ ]

Jan 72. (7") *(6052 117) <73248>* **ME AND BOBBY McGEE. / WOULD YOU TAKE ANOTHER CHANCE ON ME** [ ] [40]

Apr 72. (7") *(6502 141) <73273>* **CHANTILLY LACE. / THINK ABOUT IT DARLIN'** [33] [43]

Jun 72. (7") *<73296>* **TURN ON YOUR LOVELIGHT. / LONELY WEEKENDS** [–] [95]

Jun 72. (7") *(6052 162)* **TURN ON YOUR LOVELIGHT. / I'M WALKIN'** [ ] [–]

1972. (7"; JERRY LEE LEWIS & LINDA GAIL LEWIS) *<73328>* **WHO'S GONNA PLAY THIS OLD PIANO. / NO HONKY TONKS IN HEAVEN** [–] [ ]

Mar 73. (7") *(6052 260) <73374>* **DRINKIN' WINE SPO-DEE O'DEE. / ROCK & ROLL MEDLEY** [ ] [41]

Apr 73. (d-lp) *(6672 008) <803>* **THE SESSION** [ ] Mar73 [37]
– Johnny B. Goode / Trouble in mind / Early morning rain / No headstone on my grave / Pledgin' my love / Memphis / Drinkin' wine spo-dee o'dee / Music to the man / Bad Moon rising / Sea cruise / Sixty minute man / Moving on down the line / What'd I say / Medley: Good golly Miss Molly – Long tall Sally – Jenny . . . – Tutti frutti – Whole lotta shakin' goin' on. *(cd-iss. May85; 822751-2)*
(above recorded with PETER FRAMPTON, ALBERT LEE, RORY GALLAGHER, ALVIN LEE)

1973. (7") *<73361>* **NO MORE HANGING ON. / THE MERCY OF A LETTER** [–] [ ]

1973. (7") *<73402>* **NO HEADSTONE ON MY GRAVE. / JACK DANIELS (OLD No.7)** [–] [ ]

Jul 73. (lp) *(6338 148) <61278>* **LIVE AT THE INTERNATIONAL, LAS VEGAS (live)** [ ] Oct70 [ ]
– Mean woman blues / High school confidential / Money / Matchbox / What'd I say / What'd I say (pt.2) / Great balls of fire / Good golly Miss Molly / Lewis boogie / Your cheating heart / Hound dog / Long tall Sally / Whole lotta shakin' goin' on.

Sep 73. (7") *(6052 378)* **TAKING MY MUSIC TO THE MAN. / JACK DANIELS** [ ] [–]

1973. (7") *<73423>* **SOMETIMES A MEMORY AIN'T ENOUGH. / I NEED TO PRAY** [–] [ ]

1974. (7") *<73462>* **JUST A LITTLE BIT. / MEAT MAN** [–] [ ]

Mar 74. (lp) *(6338 452) <SRM-1 690>* **SOUTHERN ROOTS** [ ] [ ]
– Meat man / When a man loves a woman / Hold on I'm coming / Just a little bit / Born to be a loser / The haunted house / Blueberry hill The revolutionary man / Big blue diamond / That Old Bourbon Street church.

1974. (7") *<73491>* **TELL TALE SIGNS. / COLD, COLD MORNING LIGHT** [–] [ ]

1974. (7") *<73518>* **HE CAN'T FILL MY SHOES. / TOMORROW'S TAKING BABY AWAY** [–] [ ]

1974. (7") *<73661>* **I CAN STILL HEAR THE MUSIC IN THE RESTROOM. / REMEMBER ME I'M THE ONE WHO LOVES YOU** [–] [ ]

1975. (7") *<73685>* **BOOGIE WOOGIE COUNTRY MAN. / I'M STILL JEALOUS OF YOU** [–] [ ]

1975. (7") *<73729>* **A DAMN GOOD COUNTRY SONG. / WHEN I TAKE MY VACATION IN HEAVEN** [–] [ ]

Nov 75.	(lp) *(6338 602)* **I'M A ROCKER**		–
1976.	(7") *<73763>* **DON'T BOOGIE WOOGIE. / THAT KIND OF FOOL**	–	
1976.	(7") *<73822>* **LET'S PUT IT BACK TOGETHER AGAIN. / JERRY LEE'S ROCK'N' ROLL REVIVAL SHOW**	–	
1976.	(7") *<73872>* **THE CLOSEST THING TO YOU. / YOU BELONG TO ME**	–	
1977.	(7") *<55011>* **MIDDLE-AGE CRAZY. / GEORGIA ON MY MIND**	–	
1978.	(7") *<55021>* **COME ON IN. / WHO'S SORRY NOW**	–	
1978.	(7") *<55028>* **I'LL FIND IT WHERE I CAN. / DON'T LET THE STARS GET IN YOUR EYES**	–	
Nov 78.	(d-lp) *(6641 869)* **BACK TO BACK**		–
1979.	(7") *<76146>* **I'M SO LONESOME I COULD CRY. / PICK ME UP ON THE WAY DOWN**	–	
		Elektra	Elektra
May 79.	(7") *<46030>* **ROCKIN' MY LIFE AWAY. / I WISH I WAS EIGHTEEN AGAIN**	–	
May 79.	(7") *(K 12351)* **DON'T LET GO. / I WISH I WAS EIGHTEEN AGAIN**		–
Apr 79.	(lp/c) *(K/K4 52132) <184>* **JERRY LEE LEWIS** – Don't let go / Rita May / Every day I have to cry / I like it like that / Number one lovin' man / Rockin' my life away / Who will the next fool be (you've got) / Personality / I wish I was eighteen again / Rockin' little angel. *(re-iss. Apr90 as 'ROCKIN' MY LIFE AWAY' on 'Tomato' lp/c/cd; 269661-1/-4/-2)*		
Aug 79.	(7") *(K 12374)* **ROCKIN' MY LIFE AWAY. / RITA MAE**		–
1979.	(7") *<46067>* **WHO WILL THE NEXT FOOL BE? / RITA MAE**	–	
Nov 79.	(7") *(K 12399)* **EVERYDAY I HAVE TO CRY. / WHO WILL THE NEXT FOOL BE?**		–
Feb 80.	(7") *(K 12432) <46642>* **ROCKIN' JERRY LEE. / GOOD TIME CHARLIE'S GOT THE BLUES**		
Apr 80.	(7") *<46591>* **WHEN TWO WORLDS COLLIDE. / GOOD NEWS TRAVELS FAST**	–	
Apr 80.	(lp) *(K 52113) <254>* **WHEN TWO WORLDS COLLIDE** – Rockin' Jerry Lee / Who will buy the wine / Love game / Alabama jubilee / Goodtime Charlie's got the blues / When two worlds collide / Good news travels fast / I only want a buddy not a sweetheart / Honky tonk stuff / Toot toot Tootsie.		
1980.	(7") *<46642>* **HONKY TONK STUFF. / ROCKIN' JERRY LEE**	–	
Jan 81.	(7") *<47026>* **FOLSAM PRISON BLUES. / OVER THE RAINBOW**	–	
May 81.	(lp) *(K 52246) <291>* **KILLER COUNTRY** – Folsam prison blues / I'll do it all over again / Jukebox junkie / Too weak to fight / Late night lovin' man / Change places with me / Let me on / Thirty-nine and holding / Mama, this one's for you / Over the rainbow. *(re-iss. Feb87; ED 250)*		
May 81.	(7") *<47095>* **THIRTY-NINE AND HOLDING. / CHANGE PLACES WITH ME**	–	
Aug 81.	(7") *<69962>* **I'D DO IT ALL AGAIN. / WHO WILL BUY THE WINE**	–	

—— On Apr'82, he was one of the stars alongside JOHNNY CASH & CARL PERKINS to feature on 'THE SURVIVORS' album, recorded in Germany 1981 for 'CBS-Columbia'.

		M.C.A.	M.C.A.
Jan 83.	(7") *(MCA 808) <52151>* **MY FINGERS DO THE TALKIN'. / FOREVER FORGIVING**		
May 83.	(lp) *(MCF 3162)* **MY FINGERS DO THE TALKING** – My fingers do the talkin' / She sure makes leaving look easy / Why you been gone so long / She sings Amazing Grace / Better not look down / Honky tonk rock and roll piano man / Come as you were / Circumstantial evidence / Forever forgiving / Honky tonk Heaven.		
May 83.	(7") *<52188>* **CIRCUMSTANTIAL EVIDENCE. / COME AS YOU WERE**	–	
Aug 83.	(7") *<52233>* **SHE SINGS AMAZING GRACE. / WHY YOU BEEN GONE SO LONG**	–	
Jun 84.	(7") *<52369>* **I AM WHAT I AM. / THAT WAS THE WAY IT WAS THEN**	–	
Jul 84.	(lp) *(MCL 1810)* **I AM WHAT I AM** – I am what I am / Only you (and you alone) / Get out your big roll daddy / Have I got a song for you / Careless hands / Candy kisses / I'm looking over a four leaf clover / Send me the pillow that you dream on / Honky tonk heart / That was the way it was then. *(re-iss. May85 lp/c; MCL/+C 1810) (re-iss. Aug89 on 'Instant' cd/c/lp; CD/TC+/INS 5008)*		
		not iss.	Sire
Jun 90.	(7") *<19809>* **IT WAS THE WHISKEY TALKIN' (NOT ME). / ('A'-Rock'n'roll version)**	–	
		Warners	Warners
Jun 95.	(cd/c) *<(7559 61795-2/-4)>* **YOUNG BLOOD** – House of blue lights / Young blood / Things / It was the whiskey talkin' (not me) / Goosebumps / Crown Victoria custom '51 / Restless heart / High school pressure / One of them old things / Poison love / Down the road apiece / Gotta travel on / Miss the Mississippi and you / I'll never get out of this world alive.		
		Fabulous	Fabulous
Sep 03.	(cd) *<(FABCD 189)>* **MIDDLE AGED CRAZY** – Whole lotta shakin' goin' on / Middle aged crazy / Roll over Beethoven / Little Queenie / Crazy arms / She even woke me up to say goodbye / You win again / Sweet little sixteen / What'd I say / Great balls of fire / Hadacol boogie / High school confidential / Boogie woogie country man – Rockin' my life away / I'll find it where I can / Come on in / Who will the next fool be? / Would you take another chance on me / No headstones on my grave.		

– (selective) compilations, others, etc. –

Nov 65.	(lp) *London; (HA-S 8251)* **WHOLE LOTTA SHAKIN' GOIN' ON** *(re-iss. +c.Oct74) (re-iss. 10"lp.Jul82 on 'Charly') (re-iss. Jul86 on 'Sun')*		–
Jun 67.	(lp) *London; (HAS 8323)* **BREATHLESS**		–
Dec 87.	(cd) *Bear Family; (BCD 15408)* **UP THROUGH THE YEARS 1956-1963**		
May 89.	(cd) *Magnum Force; (CDMF 071)* **LIVE IN ITALY (live)**		–
Jul 89.	(cd/c/lp) *Polydor; (839516-2/-4/-1)* **GREAT BALLS OF FIRE: ORIGINAL MOTION PICTURE SOUNDTRACK**		62
Sep 89.	(8xcd-box) *Sun; (CDSUNBOX 1)* **THE SUN YEARS**		
Dec 90.	(lp/cd) *See For Miles; (SEE/+CD 307)* **THE EP COLLECTION**		–
Apr 91.	(cd) *Ace; (CDCH 326)* **LIVE AT THE VAPORS CLUB (live)**		–
Dec 91.	(cd) *Ace; (CDCH 332)* **HONKY TONK ROCK'N'ROLL PIANO MAN**		–
Apr 92.	(cd) *Ace; (CDCH 348)* **PRETTY MUCH COUNTRY**		–
May 92.	(cd) *See For Miles; (SEECD 397)* **THE EP COLLECTION . . . PLUS: VOLUME 2**		–
Sep 92.	(cd) *Music Club; (MCCD 081)* **THE BEST OF JERRY LEE LEWIS** – Great balls of fire / Whole lotta shakin' goin' on / Drinkin' wine spo-dee-o-dee / Lewis boogie / Mean woan blues / You win again / Jailhouse rock / Lovin' up a storm / Pumpin' piano rock / High school confidential / Fools like me / Down the line / Breathless / Wild one / Milkshake mademoiselle / Pink pedal pushers / I could never be ashamed of you / In the mood / Let's talk about us / What'd I say.		–
Jun 93.	(d-cd) *Tomato; (2696742)* **THE COMPLETE PALOMINO CLUB RECORDINGS**		
Feb 94.	(cd) *Javelin; (HADCD 124)* **SPOTLIGHT ON . . .**		
Dec 94.	(9xcd-box) *Bear Family; (BCD 15783)* **LOCUST YEARS & THE RETURN TO THE PROMISED LAND**		
Aug 95.	(cd) *Charly; (CPCD 8121)* **WHOLE LOTTA HITS**		–
Oct 96.	(d-cd) *Charly; (CPCD 8243-2)* **THE VERY BEST OF JERRY LEE LEWIS**		
Feb 97.	(cd) *Charly; (CPCD 8206)* **GREAT BALLS OF FIRE**		
May 97.	(cd/c) *A-Play; (10041-2/-4)* **IN CONCERT**		
May 97.	(cd) *Koch; (399538)* **JERRY LEE LEWIS**		
Jan 98.	(cd) *Summit; (SUMCD 4167)* **THE DEFINITIVE COLLECTION**		
Aug 99.	(cd) *Castle Pie; (PIESD 053)* **COUNTRY CONCERT**		
Jan 00.	(cd) *Platinum; (PLATCD 512)* **GREAT BALLS OF FIRE**		
Jan 00.	(cd) *Castle Pie; (PIESD 185)* **GREAT BALLS OF FIRE**		
May 00.	(cd) *Music; (CD 41001)* **THE SUN YEARS VOL.1**		
Jun 00.	(cd) *Warners; <(7599 26689-2)>* **ROCKIN' MY LIFE AWAY: THE JERRY LEE LEWIS COLLECTION**		
Jul 00.	(cd) *Spectrum; (554379-2)* **THE COUNTRY COLLECTION: THE VERY BEST OF JERRY LEE LEWIS**		
Jul 00.	(cd) *Music; (CD 41002)* **THE SUN YEARS VOL.2**		
Jul 00.	(cd) *Music; (CD 41003)* **THE SUN YEARS VOL.3**		

Jul 00. (cd) *Spectrum; (554193-2)* **THE KILLER COLLECTION**

Jul 00. (cd) *Spectrum; (554765-2)* **THE KILLER VOL.3: 1973-1977**

Feb 01. (cd) *EMI Plus; (5760220)* **THE STORY**

Oct 01. (cd) *Disky; (GO 64017-2)* **GREAT BALLS OF FIRE**

Jul 02. (cd) *Stomper Time; (STCD 2)* **THAT BREATHLESS CAT**

Aug 02. (cd) *Beat Goes On; (BGOCD 561)* **SINGS THE COUNTRY MUSIC HALL OF FAME HITS VOL.1 & 2**

Sep 02. (4xcd-box) *Snapper; (SNAB 904CD)* **SUN ESSENTIALS**

Oct 02. (cd) *Raven; (RVCD 155)* **ANOTHER PLACE ANOTHER TIME / SHE EVEN WOKE ME UP TO SAY GOODBYE**

Jan 03. (cd) *King Biscuit; (KBCCD 106)* **IN CONCERT**

Mar 03. (d-cd) *Ember; (EMBCD 505)* **BY INVITATION ONLY** (live in Dalton, Ga., 31 December 1972)

Jun 03. (cd) *Charly; (SNAP 124CD)* **HEARTBREAK**

Jul 03. (d-cd) *Gemini; (22040130-2)* **ROCK RIGHT NOW WITH THE PIANO MAN**

Jul 03. (cd) *Rock'n'roll Heroes; (RR 001)* **ROCK'N'ROLL HERO**

LIBERTINES

Formed: Bethnal Green, London, England . . . 2001 by CARL BARAT, PETE DOHERTY, both of whom shared guitar and vocal duties, along with the rhythm section of JOHN HASSALL on bass guitar and GARY POWELL on drums. Having secured a deal with 'Rough Trade', The LIBERTINES arrived on the music scene in 2002 by way of their debut single 'WHAT A WASTER'. Instantly they were compared with other groups such as The STROKES, The WHITE STRIPES and The HIVES who were, jointly, seen as the frontrunners in an emerging garage rock scene. The group were quickly recognised as serious contenders with the release of another, assured, single 'I GET ALONG', almost immediately followed by the debut album 'UP THE BRACKET' (2002). A blend of aggressive, catchy, melodies that THE JAM would be proud of and a scuzzy guitar sound not unlike The STOOGES, the band's first long player demanded that you pay attention. The entire album brims with confidence and attitude; however, 'BOYS IN THE BAND', 'TIME FOR HEROES', and, third single and title track, 'UP THE BRACKET' are particularly rousing. It is no coincidence that the album was produced by MICK JONES of The CLASH as like their punk classics 'London Calling' and 'Give 'Em Enough Rope' this is music for trouble makers. Summer 2003 saw some weird goings-on in the LIBERTINES camp as according to the tabloids PETE and CARL split the band into two factions. It was later revealed that PETE had actually been charged with burglary and that his victim was noneother than bandmate CARL! Drug addict PETE plead guilty and was subsequently sentenced to six months in Wandsworth prison, although this was reduced to two after an appeal that led to him being released in October. Both CARL and PETE put the past behind them and reunited the band; The LIBERTINES had already chalked up another major UK hit via 'DON'T LOOK BACK INTO THE SUN'.

Album rating: UP THE BRACKET (*7)

CARL BARAT – vocals, guitar / **PETE DOHERTY** – vocals, guitar / **JOHN HASSALL** – bass / **GARY POWELL** – drums

Rough Trade Sanctuary

Jun 02. (7") *(RTRADES 054)* **WHAT A WASTER. / I GET ALONG** 37 –
(cd-s+=) *(RTRADESCD 054)* – Mayday.

Sep 02. (7") *(RTRADES 064)* **UP THE BRACKET. / BOYS IN THE BAND** 29 –
(cd-s+=) *(RTRADESCD 064)* – Skag & bone man.
(cd-s) *(RTRADESCD 064X)* – ('A'side) / The Delaney / Plan A.

Oct 02. (cd/lp) *(RTRADE CD/LP 065)* <83213> **UP THE BRACKET** 35
– Vertigo / Death on the stairs / Horror show / Time for heroes / Boys in the band / Radio America / Up the bracket / Tell the king / The boy looked at Johnny / Begging / The good old days / I get along. *<US cd+=>* – What a waster / Mayday. *(re-iss. cd Sep03 w/dvd+=; RETRADECD 065)* – Up the bracket (video) / Time for heroes (video) / I get along (video). *(hit No.51)*

Jan 03. (7") *(RTRADES 074)* **TIME FOR HEROES. / 7 DEADLY SINS** 20 –
(cd-s+=) *(RTRADESCD 074)* – ('A'side) / General smuts / Bangkok.
(cd-s) *(RTRADESCD 074X)* – ('A'side) / Mr Finnegan / Sally Brown.

Aug 03. (7") *(RTRADES 119)* **DON'T LOOK BACK INTO THE SUN. / DEATH ON THE STAIRS** 11 –
(cd-s+=) *(RTRADESCD 119)* – Tell the king (original version).
(cd-s) *(RTRADESCDS 120)* – ('A'side) / Skint and minted / Mockingbird.

LIFEHOUSE

Formed: Malibu, California, USA . . . 1996 originally as BLYSS by singer/songwriter JASON WADE who recruited SERGIO ANDRADE, RICK WOOLSTENHULME and STUART MATHIS. The group toured the West Coast (including Seattle and Portland) before moving to L.A., performing there for a further two years. Their mix of heavy PEARL JAM-meets-MATCHBOX TWENTY-inspired songs duly got them noticed by a talent scout working for Steven Spielberg's label 'Dreamworks'. LIFEHOUSE subsequently issued their inaugural, Brendon O'Brien-mixed set, 'NO NAME FACE', late in 2000, a record which received wide critical and commercial acclaim, well . . . in America anyway. The debut featured strong performances, especially from WADE, who at a mere twenty years of age, showed maturity and emotion in his lyrics. However, the music aspect did falter in places and sometimes LIFEHOUSE sounded like a sub-SOUL ASYLUM tribute band. 'STANLEY CLIMBFALL' (2002) failed to reverse that situation, lumbering under the weight of hoary vocals, stodgy chords, claustrophobic lyrics and an overweening production, again courtesy of O'Brien.

Album rating: NO NAME FACE (*6) / STANLEY CLIMBFALL (*4)

JASON WADE – vocals, guitar / **SERGIO ANDRADE** – bass / **RICK WOOLSTENHULME** – drums

Dreamworks Dreamworks

Mar 01. (cd) <(450231-2)> **NO NAME FACE** Nov00 6
– Hanging by a moment / Sick cycle carousel / Unknown / Somebody else's song / Trying / Only one / Simon / Cling and clatter / Breathing / Quasimodo / Somewhere in between / Everything. *(re-iss. Jul01; same)*

Aug 01. (c-s) *(450913-4)* *<radio cut>* **HANGING BY A MOMENT / FAIRY TALES SAND CASTLES** 25 Jan01 2
(cd-s+=) *(450913-2)* – ('A'acoustic) / ('A'-CD-Rom).

Sep 02. (cd) *<(450404-2)>* **STANLEY CLIMBFALL** 7
– Spin / Wash / Sky is falling / Anchor / Am I ever going to find out / Stanley Climbfall / Out of breath / Just another name / Take me away / My precious / Empty space / The beginning (acoustic). *(UK+=)* – How long / Sky is falling (acoustic).

Jan 03. (c-s) *(450796-4)* *<radio cut>* **SPIN / WASH (acoustic)** Sep02 71
(cd-s+=) *(450797-2)* – Hanging by a moment / ('A'-video).

Gordon LIGHTFOOT

Born: 17 Nov'38, Orillia, Ontario, Canada. At 19, having just spent 18 months at the Westlake School of Music in L.A., LIGHTFOOT returned to Canada equipped with composition and sight-reading skills. He moved to Toronto, 80 miles south east of his place of birth and sunk his way deep into the mid-60's folk-club scene attracting attention for his low, smooth voice and melodious blend of folk and country. He subsequently caught the attention of folkies IAN & SYLVIA (TYSON) who introduced his music to the American audiences with their recordings of 'FOR LOVIN' ME' and 'EARLY MORNING RAIN'. A number of American musicians began picking up on Lightfoot's songs including Grand Ole Opry ole timer MARTY ROBBINS who took 'RIBBON OF DARKNESS' to the top spot in the country charts in '65. PETER, PAUL & MARY, meanwhile, had success with 'FOR LOVIN' ME' two months earlier (No.30 in the Hot 100). GORDON duly signed to 'United Artists', showcasing his DYLAN aspirations with a debut cover of 'JUST LIKE TOM THUMB'S BLUES' taken from his debut LP, 'LIGHTFOOT' (1965). 'THE WAY I FEEL' (1967) included 'CANADIAN RAILROAD TRILOGY', the first of many songs he wrote harking back to the birth of his nation. Three more albums followed before 1970's $1,000,000 label switch to 'Reprise', where he was paired up with producer LENNY WARONKER. LIGHTFOOT's first outing for the company, 'IF YOU COULD READ MY MIND' (1970), acquainted the man with singer songwriter RANDY NEWMAN (at his peak), JOHN SEBASTIAN and blues scholar RY COODER. Recorded in Nashville, 'SUMMER SIDE OF LIFE' (1972) was one of LIGHTFOOT's most melodic and beautiful albums but it wasn't until the million selling title track of 'SUNDOWN' (1974) that he scored his second major commercial success ('IF YOU COULD . . .' had already made Top 5). Yet another US Top 10 hit followed hot on its heels, 'CAREFREE HIGHWAY'. 'THE WRECK OF THE EDMUND FITZGERALD' from the 1976 album, 'SUMMERTIME DREAM' resurrected the traditional purpose of folk music by telling a story of an event of the times rather than from a history book. LIGHTFOOT had been a major figure in the folk scene from its mid 60's dawn to mid 70's dusk, and although he scored a minor US chart entry with 1982's 'SHADOWS' LP, the man faded into folk cultdom. Stop press:- Late in '98, GORDIE's 'IF YOU COULD READ MY MIND' was given the STARS on 54 (yes, 54!) treatment by 'Tommy Boy' hip hop acts ULTRA NATE, AMBER and JOCELYN ENRIQUEZ; it hit US No.52.

Album rating: LIGHTFOOT (*6) / THE WAY I FEEL (*7) / DID SHE MENTION MY NAME (*7) / BACK HERE ON EARTH (*5) / SUNDAY CONCERT (*6) / SIT DOWN YOUNG STRANGER (*7) / SUMMER SIDE OF LIFE (*5) / DON QUIXOTE (*5) / OLD DAN'S RECORDS (*4) / SUNDOWN (*7) / COLD ON THE SHOULDER (*4) / GORD'S GOLD compilation (*7) / SUMMERTIME DREAM (*6) / ENDLESS WIRE (*4) / DREAM STREET ROSE (*4) / SHADOWS (*4) / SALUTE (*5) / EAST OF MIDNIGHT (*5) / WAITING FOR YOU (*5) / A PAINTER PASSING THROUGH (*5)

GORDON LIGHTFOOT – vocals, acoustic guitar / with at first TWO TONES collaborator TERRY WHELAN

Decca Chateau

Oct 62. (7"; as GORD LIGHFOOT) *(F 11527) <142>* **(REMEMBER ME) I'M THE ONE. / DAISY-DOO** [ ] [ ]
<re-iss. 1965 on 'ABC Paramount'; 10352>

Fontana Chateau

1963. (7"; as GORDIE LIGHTFOOT) *(267275 TF) <148>* **NEGOTIATIONS. / IT'S TOO LATE, HE WINS** [ ] [ ]
<re-iss. 1965 on 'ABC Paramount'; 10373>

1963. (7"; as GORDIE LIGHTFOOT) *(TF 405)* **THE DAY BEFORE YESTERDAY. / TAKE CARE OF YOURSELF** [ ] [–]

1964. (7"; as GORDIE LIGHTFOOT) *<152>* **I'LL MEET YOU IN MICHOOAN. / IS MY BABY BLUE TONIGHT** [–] [ ]

—— now with **DAVID REA + BRUCE LANGHORNE** – guitar / **BILL LEE** – bass

U.A. U.A.

Oct 65. (7") *(UP 1109) <929>* **JUST LIKE TOM THUMB'S BLUES. / RIBBON OF DARKNESS** [ ] [ ]

Jan 66. (lp) *<UAS 6487>* **LIGHTFOOT** [–] [ ]
– Rich man's spiritual / Long river / The way I feel / For lovin' me / The first time / Changes / Early morning rain / Steel rail blues / Sixteen miles / I'm not sayin' / Pride of man / Ribbon of darkness / Oh, Linda / Peaceful waters.

1966. (7") *<50055>* **FOR LOVIN' ME. / SPIN, SPIN** [–] [ ]

—— now with **RED SHEA** – guitar / **JOHN STOCKFISH** – bass

1967. (lp) *<UAS 6587>* **THE WAY I FEEL** [–] [ ]
– Walls / If you got it / Softly / Crossroads / A minor ballad / Go-go round / Rosanna / Home from the forest / I'll be alright / Song for a winter's night / Canadian railroad trilogy / The way I feel. *(UK-iss.1971 on 'Sunset'; SLS 50231) (cd-iss. Dec95 on 'Beat Goes On'; BGOCD 296)*

1967. (7") *<50114>* **GO-GO ROUND. / I'LL BE ALRIGHT** [–] [ ]

1967. (7") *<50152>* **THE WAY I FEEL. / PEACEFUL WATERS** [–] [ ]

Apr 68. (7") *(UP 2216) <50281>* **BLACK DAY IN JULY. / PUSSY WILLOWS, CAT-TAILS** [ ] [ ]

May 68. (lp) *(SULP 1199) <6649>* **DID SHE MENTION MY NAME** [ ] [ ]
– The last time I saw her / Black day in July / May I / Magnificent outpouring / Does your mother know / The mountain and Maryann / Pussy willows, cat-tails / I want to hear it from you / Something very special / Boss man / Did she mention my name.

Mar 69. (7") *(UP 2272)* **THE CIRCLE IS SMALL. / DOES YOUR MOTHER KNOW** [ ] [–]

Mar 69. (7") *<50447>* **BITTER GREEN. / DOES YOUR MOTHER KNOW** [–] [ ]

May 69. (7") *(UP 35020)* **BITTER GREEN. / MAY I** [ ] [–]

Jun 69. (lp) *(SULP 1239) <6672>* **BACK HERE ON EARTH** [ ] [ ]
– Long way back home / Unsettled ways / Long thin dawn / Bitter green / The circle is small / Marie Christine / Cold hands from New York / Affair on 8th Avenue / Don't beat me down / The gypsy / If I could / Wherefore and why.

Sep 69. (7") *(UP 35036)* **EARLY MORNING RAIN. / THE GYPSY** [ ] [–]

Feb 70. (lp) *(UAS 29040) <6714>* **SUNDAY CONCERT (live at Massey Hall, Toronto)** [ ] Nov69 [ ]
– Canadian railroad trilogy / Pussy willows, cat-tails / Boss man / Softly / Ballad of Yarmouth Castle / Bitter green / Apology / Medley: Ribbon of darkness / I'm not sayin' / The lost children / In a windowpane / Peaceful waters / Oh, Linda. *(cd-iss. Mar93 on 'Bear Family'+=; BCD 15691)*

—— **RICK HAYNES** – bass; repl. JOHN

Reprise Reprise

Nov 70. (7") *<0926>* **ME AND BOBBY McGEE. / THE PONY MAN** [–] [ ]

Jan 71. (lp) *(K 44091) <6392>* **SIT DOWN YOUNG STRANGER** [ ] May70 [12]
– Minstrel of the dawn / Me and Bobby McGee / Approaching Lavender / Saturday clothes / Cobweb and dust / Poor little Alison / Sit down young stranger / If you could read my mind / Baby it's alright / Your love's return / The pony man. *(re-titled.Jun71 'IF YOU COULD READ MY MIND') (cd-iss. Feb93; 7599 27451-2)*

May 71. (7") *(K 20974) <0974>* **IF YOU COULD READ MY MIND. / POOR LITTLE ALISON** [30] Dec70 [5]

Jun 71. (7") *<1020>* **TALKING IN YOUR SLEEP. / NOUS VIVONS ENSEMBLE** [–] [64]

—— now w /diff. session people.

Jun 71. (lp) *(K 44132) <2037>* **SUMMER SIDE OF LIFE** [ ] May71 [38]
– 10 degrees and getting colder / Miguel / Go my way / Summer side of life / Cotton Jenny / Talking in your sleep / Nous vivons ensemble / Same old loverman / Redwood Hill / Love and maple syrup / Cabaret.

Aug 71. (7") *<1035>* **SUMMER SIDE OF LIFE. / LOVE AND MAPLE SYRUP** [–] [98]

—— the above 1970 personnel added **TERRY CLEMENTS** – guitar

Mar 72. (7") *<1088>* **BEAUTIFUL. / DON QUIXOTE** [–] [58]

Apr 72. (lp) *(K 44166) <2056>* **DON QUIXOTE** [44] Mar72 [42]
– Don Quixote / Christian Island / Alberta bound / Looking at the rain / Ordinary man brave mountaineers / Ode to big blue second cup of coffee / Beautiful / On Susan's floor / The patriot's dream.

May 72. (7") *(K 14176)* **BEAUTIFUL. / CHRISTIAN ISLAND** [ ] [–]

Nov 72. (7") *<1128>* **THE SAME OLD OBSESSION. / YOU ARE WHAT I AM** [–] [ ]

Nov 72. (lp) *(K 44219) <2116>* **OLD DAN'S RECORDS** [ ] [95]
– Old Dan's records / Farewell to Annabelle / That same old obsession / Lazy mornin' / You are what I am / Can't depend on love / My pony won't go / It's worth believin' / Mother of a miner's child / Hi way songs.

Jan 73. (7") *(K 14251) <1145>* **CAN'T DEPEND ON LOVE. / IT'S WORTH BELIEVIN'** [ ] [ ]

—— brought back **JOHN STOCKFISH** – bass

May 74. (7") *(K 14327) <1194>* **SUNDOWN. / TOO LATE FOR PRAYIN'** 33 Apr74 1

Jun 74. (lp) *(K 44258) <2177>* **SUNDOWN** 45 Jan74 1
– Sundown / Somewhere U.S.A. / High and dry / Seven Island suite / Circle of steel / Is there anyone home / The watchman's gone / Carefree highway / The list / Too late for prayin'. *<US re-iss. 1980 on 'Mobile'> (cd-iss. Feb93; 7599 27211-2)*

Nov 74. (7") *(K 14370) <1309>* **CAREFREE HIGHWAY. / SEVEN ISLAND SUITE** Aug74 10

Mar 75. (lp) *(K 54033) <2206>* **COLD ON THE SHOULDER** Feb75 10
– Rainy day people / Bells of the evening / Rainbow trout / Cold on the shoulder / A tree to weak to stand / All the lovely ladies / Fine as can be / Now and then / Slide on over / Bend with the water / Soul is the rock / Cherokee band.

Apr 75. (7") *(K 14389) <1328>* **RAINY DAY PEOPLE. / CHEROKEE BAND** Mar75 26

—— live band now **RED SHEA + TERRY CLEMENTS** – guitar / **RICK HAYNES** – bass / **PEE WEE CHARLES** – steel guitar / **JIM GORDON** – (studio) drums

Dec 75. (d-lp) *(K 64033) <2237>* **GORD'S GOLD** (remixed compilation) Nov75 34
– I'm not sayin' – Ribbon of darkness / Song for a winter's night / Canadian railroad trilogy / Softly / For lovin' me – Did she mention my name / Affair on 8th Avenue / Steel rail blues / Wherefore and why / Bitter green / Early morning rain / Minstrel of the dawn / Sundown / Beautiful / Summer side of life / Rainy day people / Cotton Jenny / Don Quixote / Circle of steel / Old Dan's records / If you could read my mind / Cold on the shoulder / Carefree highway.

Aug 76. (lp/c) *(K/K4 54067) <2246>* **SUMMERTIME DREAM** Jun76 12
– The wreck of the Edmund Fitzgerald / Race among the ruins / I'm not supposed to care / I'd do it again / Never too close / Protocol / The house you live in / Summertime dream / Spanish moss / Too many clues in the room.

Nov 76. (7") *(K 14451) <1369>* **THE WRECK OF THE EDMUND FITZGERALD. / THE HOUSE YOU LIVE IN** 40 Aug76 2

Feb 77. (7") *<1380>* **RACE AMONG THE RUINS. / PROTOCOL** – 65

Warners Warners

Feb 78. (lp/c) *(K/K4 56444) <3149>* **ENDLESS WIRE** Jan78 22
– Endless wire / If there's a reason / Daylight Katy / The circle is small (I can see it in your eyes) / Sweet Guinevere / Hangdog hotel room / Dreamland / Songs of the minstrel / Sometime I don't mind / If children had wings.

Feb 78. (7") *<8518>* **THE CIRCLE IS SMALL (I CAN SEE IT IN YOUR EYES). / SWEET GUINEVERE** – 33

Jul 78. (7") *(K 17214) <8579>* **DAYLIGHT KATY. / HANGDOG HOTEL ROOM** 41

Nov 78. (7") *<8644>* **DREAMLAND. / SONGS THE MINISTER SANG** –

Jun 80. (lp/c) *(K/K4 56802) <3426>* **DREAM STREET ROSE** Mar80 60
– Sea of tranquility / Ghosts of Cape Horn / Dream street Rose / On the high seas / Whisper my name / If you need me / Hey you / Make way for the lady / Mister rock of ages / Auctioneer.

Jun 80. (7") *(K 17637) <49230>* **DREAM STREET ROSE. / MAKE WAY FOR THE LADY**

Feb 82. (lp/c) *(K/K4 56970) <3633>* **SHADOWS** 87
– 14 karat gold / In my fashion / Shadows / Blackberry wine / Heaven help the Devil / Thank you for the promises / Baby step back / All I'm after / Triangle / I'll do anything / She's not the same.

May 82. (7") *(K 17945) <50012>* **BABY STEP BACK. / THANK YOU FOR THE PROMISES** Mar82 50

Sep 83. (lp/c) *<(9 23901-1/-4)>* **SALUTE** Jul83
– Salute (a lot more livin' to do) / Gotta get away / Whispers of the north / Someone to believe in / Romance / Knotty pine / Biscuit city / Without you / Tattoo / Broken dreams.

Sep 86. (7") *<28553>* **STAY LOOSE. / MORNING GLORY** –

Oct 86. (lp/c) *<(K9 25482-1/-4)>* **EAST OF MIDNIGHT** Aug86
– Stay loose / Morning glory / East of midnight / A lesson in love / Anything for love / Let it ride / Ecstasy made easy / You just gotta be / A passing ship / I'll tag along.

Nov 86. (7") *<28222>* **ECSTASY MADE EASY. / MORNING GLORY** –

—— LIGHTFOOT's band now incl. **TERRY CLEMENTS** – guitar / **RICK HAYNES** – bass / **MIKE HEFFERNAN** – keyboards / **BARRY KEANE** – drums

Nov 88. (d-lp/c/cd) *<(K9 25784-1/-4/-2)>* **GORD'S GOLD, VOLUME II** (remixed compilation)
– If it should please you / Endless wire / Hangdog hotel room / I'm not supposed to care / High and dry / The wreck of the Edmund Fitzgerald / The pony man / Race among the ruins / Christian Island / All the lovely ladies / Alberta bound / Cherokee band / Triangle / Shadows / Make way (for the lady) / Ghosts of Cape Horn / Baby step back / It's worth believin'.

not iss. Reprise

Apr 93. (cd) *<45208>* **WAITING FOR YOU** –
– Restless / Ring them bells / Fading away / Only love would know / Welcome to try / I'll prove my love / Waiting for you / Wild strawberries / I'd rather press on / Drink yer glasses empty.

May 98. (cd) *<46949>* **A PAINTER PASSING THROUGH** –
– Drifters / My little love / Ringneck loon / I used to be a country singer / Boathouse / Much to my surprise / A painter passing through / On Yonge Street / Red velvet / Uncle Toad said.

– compilations, etc. –

1966. (7") *Warners; <(WB 5621)>* **I'M NOT SAYIN'. / FOR LOVIN' ME**

1968. (7") *President; (PT 138)* **ADIOS ADIOS. / MY BABY IS BLUE TONIGHT** –

Sep 69. (lp) *United Artists; <UAS 29012>* **EARLY LIGHTFOOT** –

Jul 71. (lp) *United Artists; <(UAS 5510)>* **CLASSIC LIGHTFOOT (THE BEST OF GORDON LIGHTFOOT, VOL.2)** Jun71

1972. (7"ep) *Reprise; (K 14210)* **IF YOU COULD READ MY MIND / ME AND BOBBY McGEE. / SUMMER SIDE OF LIFE / TALKING IN YOUR SLEEP** –

1974. (7"ep) *Reprise;* **IF YOU COULD READ MY MIND / CHRISTIAN ISLAND. / ODE TO BIG BLUE SECOND CUP OF COFFEE / ME AND BOBBY McGEE** –

Jul 74. (d-lp) *United Artists; <LA 243>* **THE VERY BEST OF GORDON LIGHTFOOT VOL.I & II** –

1975. (d-lp) *Reprise; (K 64022)* **TWO ORIGINALS OF . . .** –
– (albums 'DON QUIXOTE' + 'SUMMER SIDE OF LIFE')

May 81. (lp/c) *Reprise; (K/K4 56915)* **THE BEST OF GORDON LIGHTFOOT** –
– Early morning rain / The wreck of Edmund Fitzgerald / Carefree highway / Minstrel / Rainy day people / Sundown / Summer side of life / Cold on the shoulder / Endless wire / If you could read my mind / Canadian railroad trilogy / If there's a reason / Cotton Jenny / Song for the winters night / Daylight Katy / Old Dan's records / Me and Bobby McGee / The circle is small.

Nov 76. (lp) *Sunset; (SLS 50398)* **EARLY MORNING RAIN** –

Mar 86. (7") *Old Gold; (OG 9572)* **IF YOU COULD READ MY MIND. / SUNDOWN** –

Feb 92. (cd) *Bear Family; <(BCD 15576)>* **LIGHTFOOT! / THE WAY I FEEL**

Apr 93. (cd) *Beat Goes On; (BGOCD 166)* **EARLY LIGHTFOOT / SUNDAY CONCERT** –

Apr 93. (cd) *Beat Goes On; (BGOCD 167)* **DID SHE MENTION MY NAME / BACK HERE ON EARTH** –

LIGHTNING SEEDS

Formed: by IAN BROUDIE, 4 Aug'58, Liverpool, England. This seasoned Scouser had previously been an integral part of BIG IN JAPAN (Autumn 77-78), before joining The SECRETS and then London-based band, ORIGINAL MIRRORS, in late '78. The latter outfit cut one eponymous album (c. early 1980) for 'Mercury', although BROUDIE left soon after to go into production work, chosen by ECHO & THE BUNNYMEN, The WAH!, The FALL and ICICLE WORKS, amongst the many to request his services. He subsequently helped form The CARE in 1983, with ex-WILD SWANS leader PAUL SIMPSON, although they disbanded after around a year and three singles; one of them, 'MY FLAMING SWORD', hit No.48 in the UK charts. After production work (mainly Merseyside bands), BROUDIE resurfaced in 1989, when he and a few session people formed The LIGHTNING SEEDS. The group signed to new indie label 'Ghetto', immediately scoring with surely one of the most fey, quintessentially indie-pop yet swoonsomely gorgeous singles ever, 'PURE'. This and its parent album, 'CLOUDCUCKOOLAND' (1990), surprised many by also making the US lists in '91 and BROUDIE garnered enough interest for 'Virgin' to sign him up for 1992's 'SENSE' album. Despite another batch of pristine, gilt-edged pop nuggets, the album hung around tentatively on the fringes of the album chart like a shy kid at the playground gates. Only 'THE LIFE OF RILEY' single managed to dent the Top 30. Perhaps as a response, 'JOLLIFICATION' (1994) was more blatantly commercial. The change was very subtle, but it was definitely there; in the way every track sounded like a muso rerun of 'PURE', in the way BROUDIE's little-boy-lost vocals now seemed to grate rather than soothe and in the way that the whole shebang continually teetered on the verge of self-parody. The resultant live shows, with their cack-handed rock approach, confirmed that BROUDIE was now writing for 20-something couples who had grown too old to go down the indie disco. The final nail in the coffin was the utterly nauseating England Euro '96 football theme, 'THREE LIONS', a track that sounded even more limp-wristed than NEW ORDER's World Cup effort two years previously. They think it's all over . . . it is now (we live in hope!?). The LIGHTNING SEEDS were back in the music game by 1999, although their comeback album of-sorts, 'TILT', did nothing to seriously shake up the indie-pop world. • **Songwriters:** BROUDIE obviously, except SOMETHING IN THE AIR (Thunderclap Newman) / HANG ON TO A DREAM (Tim Hardin) / LUCIFER SAM (Pink Floyd) / HERE TODAY (Beach Boys) / ANOTHER GIRL, ANOTHER PLANET (Only Ones) / WHOLE WIDE WORLD (Wreckless Eric) / OUTDOOR MINER (Wire) / YOU SHOWED ME (Byrds; minor hit Turtles). LUCKY YOU + FEELING LAZY + MY BEST DAY were co-written & sung w/ TERRY HALL + IAN McNABB + ALISON MOYET respectively. The track OPEN GOALS sampled; LOOK KA PY PY (Meters). • **Trivia:** The track 'PERSUASION' featured IAN McCULLOCH (ex-ECHO & THE BUNNYMEN). He has also produced NORTHSIDE, PRIMITIVES and TERRY HALL.

Album rating: CLOUDCUCKOOLAND (*7) / SENSE (*6) / JOLLIFICATION (*6) / PURE LIGHTNING SEEDS compilation (*7) / DIZZY HEIGHTS (*7) / LIKE YOU DO . . . THE BEST OF compilation (*7) / TILT (*5)

IAN BROUDIE – vocals, keyboards, guitar / with **PETER COYLE** + **PAUL SIMPSON** (ex-LOTUS EATERS + WILD SWANS)

Ghetto M.C.A.

Jun 89. (7") *(GTG 004)* *<53816>* **PURE. / FOOLS** 16 Apr90 31
(12"+=) *(GTGT 004)* – God help them.
(cd-s++=) *(GTG 004CD)* – All I want.

Aug 89. (lp/c/cd) *(GHETT/+C/CD 3)* *<MCA/+C/D 6404>* **CLOUDCUCKOOLAND** 50 46
– All I want / Bound in a nutshell / Pure / Sweet dreams / The nearly man / Joy / Love explosion / Don't let go / Control the flame / The price / Fools / Frenzy. *(c+=/cd+=)* – God help them. *(re-iss. cd May92; CDOVD 436)*

Oct 89. (7") *(GTG 6)* **JOY. / FRENZY** □ □
(12"+=/cd-s+=) *(GTGT/CDGTG 6)* – Control The Flame.
(US cd-ep+=) – Hang on to a dream.

Apr 90. (7") *(GTG 9)* *<24054>* **ALL I WANT. / PERSUASION** □ Aug90 □
(12"+=/cd-s+=) *(GTGT/CDGTG 9)* – ('A'extended).

—— BROUDIE made appearance on WILD SWANS non-UK album 'SPACE FLOWER'.

Virgin M.C.A.

Mar 92. (7"/c-s) *(VS/VSC 1402)* *<54195>* **THE LIFE OF RILEY. / SOMETHING IN THE AIR** 28 98
(12"+=/cd-s+=) *(VST/VSCDG 1402)* – Marooned.
(US c-s) *<54195>* – ('A'side) / excerpts: Blowing bubbles – Sense – A cool place.

Apr 92. (cd/c/lp) *(CDV/TCV/V 2690)* *<MCA D/C 10388>* **SENSE** 53 □
– Sense / The life of Riley / Blowing bubbles / A cool place / Where flowers fade / A small slice of heaven / Tingle tangle / Happy / Marooned / Thinking up, looking down.

May 92. (7"/c-s) *(VS/VSC 1414)* *<54431>* **SENSE. / FLAMING SWORD** 31 Jun92 □
(12"+=/cd-s+=) *(VST/VSCDT 1414)* – The life of Riley (remix) / Hang on to a dream.

May 92. (c-s) *<54425>* **SENSE / TINGLE TANGLE** – □
(cd-s) *<54431>* – ('A'side) / The life of Riley / Flaming sword / Lucifer Sam.

—— **BROUDIE** added **SIMON ROGERS** – instruments, co-producer / **CLIVE LAYTON** – Hammond organ / **MARINA VAN RODY** – vocals (Why Why Why). The live band **BROUDIE** – vocals, guitar / with **ALI KANE** – keyboards / **MARTYN CAMPBELL** – bass / **CHRIS SHARROCK** – drums

Epic Trauma-Interscope

Aug 94. (7"/c-s) *(660 628-8/-4)* *<51002>* **LUCKY YOU. / ('A'lunar mix)** 43 □
(12"/cd-s) *(660 628-6/-2)* – ('A'hard luck mix) / ('A'lucky devil mix) / ('A'lunar cabaret mix).

—— Above was co-written w / **TERRY HALL.** They are now best known for contributing football theme to Match of the Day's 'Goal Of The Month'. ALISON MOYET wrote a track for the next album.

Sep 94. (cd/c/lp) *(477237-2/-4/-1)* *<71008>* **JOLLIFICATION** 12 Dec94 □
– Perfect / Lucky you / Open goals / Change / Why why why / Marvellous / Feeling lazy / My best day / Punch & Judy / Telling tales.

Jan 95. (7")(c-s) *(660 986-7/-4)* **CHANGE. / SAY YOU WILL** 13 –
(cd-s+=) *(660 986-5)* – Dust.
(cd-s) *(660 986-2)* – ('A'side) / The life of Riley (instrumental) / Lucky you (live).

Apr 95. (c-s) *(661 426-4)* **MARVELLOUS / LUCIFER SAM** 24 –
(cd-s+=) *(661 426-5)* – I met you.
(cd-s) *(661 426-2)* – ('A'side) / ('A'club mix) / ('A'dub mix) / All I want.

Jul 95. (c-s) *(662 179-4)* **PERFECT / HOWL** 18 –
(cd-s+=) *(662 179-2)* – ('A'acoustic) / Blowing bubbles (extended remix).
(cd-s) *(662 179-5)* – ('A'side) / Change (live) / Flaming sword (live).

Oct 95. (c-s) *(662 518-4)* **LUCKY YOU / LUCKY YOU (Lunar mix)** 15 –
(cd-s) *(662 518-2)* – ('A'side) / Life of Riley (live) / Pure (live) / Here today (live).
(cd-s) *(662 518-5)* – ('A'side) / Open your eyes / The likely lads.

Feb 96. (c-s) *(662 967-4)* **READY OR NOT / PUNCH AND JUDY (electric '96 version)** 20 –
(cd-s+=) *(662 967-5)* – Outdoor miner.
(cd-s) *(662 967-2)* – ('A'side) / Another girl, another planet / Whole wide world.

May 96. (7"/c-s; BADDIEL & SKINNER & The LIGHTNING SEEDS) *(663 273-7/-4)* **THREE LIONS (The Official Song Of The England Football Team) / ('A'-Karaoke version)** 1 –
(cd-s+=) *(663 273-2)* – ('A'-Jules Rimet extended version).
(the '98 World Cup version returned to No.1 in Jun'98)

Epic Sony

Oct 96. (c-s) *(663863-4)* **WHAT IF . . . / HERE TODAY (live)** 14 –
(cd-s) *(663863-2)* – ('A'side) / Never / The crunch / ('A'-Leuroj's slo'n'easy mix).
(cd-s) *(663863-5)* – ('A'side) / Lightning Seeds mix'n'match / ('A'-Leuroj's easy disco dub mix).

Nov 96. (cd/c) *(486640-2/-4)* *<68054>* **DIZZY HEIGHTS** 11 □
– Imaginary friends / You bet your life / Waiting for today to happen / What if . . . / Sugar coated iceberg / Touch and go / Like you do / Wishaway / Fingers and thumbs / You showed me / Ready or not / Fishes on the line.

Jan 97. (c-s) *(664043-4)* **SUGAR COATED ICEBERG / THIS POWER** 12 □
(cd-s+=) *(664043-2)* – S.F. sorrow is born / Porpoise song.
(cd-s) *(664043-5)* – ('A'side) / Why why why / Telling tales.

Apr 97. (cd-s) *(664328-2)* **YOU SHOWED ME (mixes by Attica Blues / The Wiseguys & DJ Pulse)** 8 □
(c-s+=) *(664328-4)* – (Todd Terry mix).
(cd-s) *(664328-5)* – (Todd Terry mixes).

Nov 97. (cd/c) *(<489034-2/-4>)* **LIKE YOU DO . . . THE BEST OF** (compilation) 5 □
– What you say / Life of Riley / Lucky you / You showed me / Change / Waiting for today to happen ('97 mix) / Pure / Sugar coated iceberg / Ready or not / All I want / Perfect / What if? / Sense / Marvellous / Three lions.

Epic Alex

Nov 97. (c-s) *(665367-4)* **WHAT YOU SAY / BE MY BABY** 41 Apr98 □
(cd-s+=) *(665367-2)* *<6090>* – Weirdaway / Blue.
(cd-s) *(665367-5)* *<6050>* – ('A'-Psyche Beach trip pts.1-3) / ('A'mixes by Ballistic Brothers & Wiseguys).

Nov 99. (c-s) *(668150-4)* **LIFE'S TOO SHORT / EVERYDAY AND EVERYNIGHT** 27 –
(cd-s+=) *(668150-2)* – ('A'-ATFC remix).
(cd-s) *(668150-5)* – ('A'mixes by; 3 Jays & Way Out West).
Nov 99. (cd/c) *(496263-2/-4)* **TILT** 46 –
– Life's too short / Sweetest soul sensations / If only / City bright lights / I wish I was in love / Happy satellite / Get it right / Cigarettes and lies / Crowdpleaser / Tales of the riverbank / Pussyfoot: reprise / All the things.
Mar 00. (c-s/cd-s) *(668942-4/-2)* **SWEETEST SOUL SENSATIONS / LIFE'S TOO SHORT – remix / SWOOSH** 67 –
(cd-s) *(668942-5)* – ('A'side) / ('A'mixes; Underwolves mind games / Terminalhead).

—— in June 2002, The LIGHTNING SEEDS were again involved with the Top 20 re-issued of '3 Lions '98'.

– compilations, etc. –

on 'Virgin' unless otherwise mentioned
May 96. (cd/c/lp) *(CDV/TCV/V 2805)* **PURE LIGHTNING SEEDS** 27 –
May 96. (c-s) *(VSC 1586)* **LIFE OF RILEY / SOMETHING IN THE AIR** [ ] –
(cd-s+=) *(VSCDT 1586)* – Marooned.
(cd-s) *(VSCDX 1586)* – ('A'side) / Control the flame / ('A'remix).
Sep 00. (cd) *Epic; (500511-2)* **JOLLIFICATION / DIZZY HEIGHTS** [ ] –
Aug 03. (cd) *EMI Gold; (591570-2)* **LIFE OF RILEY: THE LIGHTNING SEEDS COLLECTION** [ ] –

LIL' KIM

Born: KIMBERLY JONES, 11 Jul'75, Bedford-Stuyvesant, Brooklyn, New York, USA. Raised in the small Bedford area of Brooklyn's projects, tragedy struck when, as a teenager, LIL' KIM's parents split, forcing her to live with her father who eventually threw her out on to the streets. She became a regular street MC, rapping with her friends on the sidewalk until she was noticed by the NOTORIOUS B.I.G.. He persuaded KIM to appear on JUNIOR M.A.F.I.A.'s single 'Player's Anthem' – a huge hit Stateside – and guest on their 1995 debut album 'Conspiracy'. Her name was now synonymous with hip hop. LIL' KIM was soon to go where no female rapper had gone before after she issued the B.I.G. co-produced 'HARD CORE' in 1996. A sex-riddled and highly controversial set, KIM literally turned the tables on misogynistic gangster rap with explicit lyrics, bouncing bass and an all-round raunchy image. 'NO TIME', the first single from the album (and featuring PUFF DADDY) became a Top 20 smash, KIM was looking set to become hip hop's best crossover act. However, when close friend and collaborator B.I.G. was killed in 1997, she reacted badly, only release of note being a hit duet with MISSY ELLIOTT ('Hit 'Em With Da Hee'). The new millennium saw yet another collaboration, this time with PINK, MISSY ELLIOTT and CHRISTINA AGUILERA on a jazzed-up version of the 70's disco hit 'LADY MARMALADE'. Her eagerly awaited sophomore effort 'THE NOTORIOUS K.I.M.' was in the shops (and in the US Top 5) the same year, the feisty temptress' voice had lost none of its raw and uncut style. If that album had played for the crossover dollar, 'LA BELLA MAFIA' (2003) restored the "Queen Bee" to her rightful throne amid the hard nuts of hip-hop, holding up her x-rated image against beat collages put together by the like of TIMBALAND and KAYNE WEST, and performed alongside the likes of MISSY ELLIOTT and 50 CENT.

Album rating: HARD CORE (*6) / THE NOTORIOUS K.I.M. (*6) / LA BELLE MAFIA (*7)

LIL' KIM – vocals / with various friends and guests

Atlantic Undeas

Apr 97. (c-s; as LIL' KIM featuring PUFF DADDY) *(AT 5594C)* *<98044>* **NO TIME / (instrumental)** 45 Nov96 18
(cd-s+=) *(AT 5594CD)* – (mixes).
Jun 97. (c-s) *(AT 0002C)* **CRUSH ON YOU / (instrumental)** 36 –
(cd-s+=) *(AT 0002CD)* – (mixes).
(re-iss. Oct97; same) – No.23
Aug 97. (c-s) *(AT 0007C)* *<98019>* **NOT TONIGHT / (instrumental)** 11 6
(cd-s+=) *(AT 0007CD)* *<95574>* – ('A'side) / Crush on you (remix) / Drugs / ('A'version).

—— <above also credited DA BRAT, LEFT EYE, MISSY ELLIOTT & ANGIE MARTINEZ in US-only>

Sep 97. (cd) *(7567 92789-2)* *<92733>* **HARD CORE** [ ] Nov96 11
– Intro in A-minor / Big momma thang (with JAY-Z) / No time / Spend a little doe / Take it! (by LIL' CEASE & TRIFE & NOTORIOUS B.I.G.) / Crush on you / Drugs / Scheamin' / Queen b"#$h / Dreams / M.A.F.I.A. land / We don't need it / Not tonight / Player haters / **** you.

—— in Aug'98, LIL' KIM featured on MISSY 'MISDEMEANOR' ELLIOTT's Top 30 hit, 'Hit 'Em Wit Da Hee'

—— early in 2000, LIL' KIM featured on NOTORIOUS B.I.G.'s eponymous hit

Jun 00. (cd/c/lp) *<(7567 92840-2/-4/-1)>* **THE NOTORIOUS K.I.M.** 67 4
– Lil' drummer boy (with CEE-LO & REDMAN) / Custom made (give it to you) / Who's number one? / Suck my d**k / Single black female (with MARIO "YELLOWMAN" WINANS) / Revolution (with GRACE JONES & LIL' CEASE) / How many licks? (with SISQO) / Notorious Kim / No matter what they say / She don't love you / Queen bitch pt.2 / Don't mess with me / Do what you like (with JUNIOR M.A.F.I.A.) / Off the wall (with LIL' CEASE) / Right now (with CARL THOMAS) / Aunt Dot (with LIL' SHANICE) / Hold on (with MARY J. BLIGE) / I'm human.
Aug 00. (c-s) *(7567 84697-4)* *<84703>* **NO MATTER WHAT THEY SAY / (instrumental)** 35 Jun00 60
(12"+=/cd-s+=) *(7567 84697-2)* – (mixes; album / a cappella).
Nov 00. (12"; by LIL' KIM & SISQO) *<85032>* **HOW MANY LICKS? (mixes)** – 75
Sep 01. (c-s; by LIL' KIM & PHIL COLLINS) *(WEA 331C)* **IN THE AIR TONITE / (stargate remix)** 26 –
(12"+=/cd-s+=) *(WEA 331 T/CD)* – (mixes; Mintman's floorfiller / Boogieman's album / True Busyness).
Mar 03. (cd/lp) *<(7567 83572-2/-1)>* **LA BELLE MAFIA** [ ] 5
– Intro / Hold it now (with HAVOC) / Doing it way big / Can't fuck with Queen Bee (with GOVERNOR & SHELENE THOMAS) / (Hollyhood skit) / Shake ya bum bum (with LIL' SHANICE) / This is who I am (with SWIZZ BEATZ & MASHONDA) / The jump off (with MR. CHEEKS) / This is a warning / (When Kim say) Can you hear me now? (with MISSY ELLIOTT) / Thug luv (with TWISTA) / Magic stick (with 50 CENT) / Get in touch with us (with STYLES P) / Heavenly father (with BIG HILL) / Tha beehive (with REEKS, BUNKY S.A., VEE & SAINT) / Came back for you.
Apr 03. (12"/cd-s; by LIL' KIM & MR. CHEEKS) *(AT 015 T/CD)* *<88055>* **THE JUMP OFF (mixes)** 16 Feb03 17
Nov 03. (-; with 50 CENT) *<radio cut>* **MAGIC STICK** – 2

LIMP BIZKIT

Formed: Jacksonville, Florida, USA . . . 1994 by FRED DURST, WES BORLAND, SAM RIVERS, JOHN OTTO and DJ LETHAL, the latter snatched from the recently defunct, HOUSE OF PAIN. Drawing inevitable comparisons to KORN and RAGE AGAINST THE MACHINE, the band thrust their bass-chunky metal funk/rap into the melting pot of 90's rock with favourable results. Of a generally more sprightly disposition than the aforementioned bands, this goatee-bearded fly-shaded posse released their 'Interscope' debut, 'THREE DOLLAR BILL, Y'ALL$' in the summer of '97. Not content with BIZKIT's minor breakthrough, DURST also guested for COLD, SOULFLY and KORN on their early 1998 sets. With METHOD MAN from WU-TANG CLAN (on the track,

'N 2 GETHER NOW') and a celebrity feast of stars courtesy of KORN, STONE TEMPLE PILOTS and PRIMUS all on show, how could their follow-up album, 'SIGNIFICANT OTHER', fail. In fact, its MTV-friendly hardcore rap was all the rage with trendy young teenagers who helped it get all the way to No.1 on its first week of release. However, the more discerning Brit was not quite convinced (it only reached No.26). The new millennium got off to a flyer via a $2 million deal with Napster which was soon followed by a breakthrough Top 3 single in the UK, 'TAKE A LOOK AROUND' (the theme to 'MI:2'). Better still was when their 3rd set, 'CHOCOLATE STARFISH AND THE HOT DOG FLAVORED WATER' smashed in at No.1 in the US charts that Autumn; it finally reached peak spot in Britain after the 'ROLLIN' single did the same. In the unlikely event that you hadn't had your fill of LIMP BIZKIT's one dimensional rap-metal, 'NEW OLD SONGS' (2001) offered up remixes from the likes of TIMBALAND and DJ PREMIER. Just prior to this (October 2001), WES BORLAND had opted to bail out from the band. His departure had a resounding effect on the band as the long awaited 'RESULTS MAY VARY' (2003) testified. Having recorded and scrapped sessions more than once, DURST and Co finally released an unfocused, creatively bankrupt set of songs – only Top 3 in US – which actually varied very little in their sheer monotony, notable only for the frontman's incoherent, vitriolic lyrical outbursts.

Album rating: THREE DOLLAR BILL, Y'ALL$ (*7) / SIGNIFICANT OTHER (*5) / CHOCOLATE STARFISH AND THE HOT DOG FLAVORED WATER (*7) / NEW OLD SONGS (*5) / RESULTS MAY VARY (*4)

FRED DURST – vocals / **WES BORLAND** – guitar / **SAM RIVERS** – bass / **JOHN OTTO** – drums / **DJ LETHAL** (b. LEOR DiMANT, 18 Dec'72, Latvia) – turntables (ex-HOUSE OF PAIN)

not iss. — Flip

Jun 96. (c-s) *<24894>* **COUNTERFEIT / POLLUTION / STUCK** [–] [ ]

Interscope — Interscope

Jul 97. (cd) *<(IND 90124)>* **THREE DOLLAR BILL, Y'ALL$** [ ] [22]
– Intro / Pollution / Counterfeit / Stuck / Nobody loves me / Sour / Stalemate / Clunk / Faith / Stinkfinger / Indigo flow / Leech / Everything. *(hit UK No.68 in Aug00 & No.50 in Jun01)*

Jul 99. (cd/c/d-lp) *(IND/INC/INT2 90335) <490335>* **SIGNIFICANT OTHER** [26] [1]
– Intro / Jusy like this / Nookie / Break stuff / Re-arranged / I'm broke / Nobody like you / Don't go off wandering / 9 teen 90 nine / N 2 gether now / Trust? / No sex / Show me what you got / A lesson learned / Outro. *(cd re-iss. Sep00+=; 490788-2)* – Re-arranged (live) / Nookie (live) / N 2 gether now / Break stuff (video).

Jul 99. (cd-s) *<497139-2>* **NOOKIE / COUNTERFEIT / COUNTERFEIT (mix)** [–] [80]

Nov 99. (c-s/cd-s; as LIMP BIZKIT featuring METHOD MAN) *<497183>* **N 2 GETHER NOW** [–] [73]

Nov 99. (cd-s) *<497138-2>* **RE-ARRANGED / FAITH** [–] [88]

Apr 00. (cd-s) *<497309-2>* **BREAK STUFF / CRUSHED / N 2 GETHER** [–] [ ]

Jul 00. (cd-s) *(497368-2)* **TAKE A LOOK AROUND (THEME FROM MI:2) / FAITH** [3] [ ]
(cd-s) *(497369-2)* – ('A'side) / N 2 gether now (live) / Break stuff (CD-Rom video) / ('A'-CD-Rom video).

Oct 00. (cd/d-lp) *(490770-2) <490759>* **CHOCOLATE STARFISH AND THE HOT DOG FLAVORED WATER** [1] [1]
– Intro / Hot dog / My generation / Full nelson / My way / Rollin' (air raid vehicle) / Livin' it up / One / Getcha groove on / Take a look around / It'll be ok / Boiler / Hold on / Rollin' (urban assault vehicle) / Outro. *(special d-cd+=; 490793-2)* – Crushed / Faith / Counterfeit (Lethal Dose mix) / Faith (video) / Nookie (video) / Re-arranged (video) / N2 gether now (video).

Oct 00. (7"pic-d) *(497447-7)* **MY GENERATION. / IT'S LIKE THAT Y'ALL** [15] [–]
(cd-s+=) *(497447-2)* – Snake in your face.
(cd-s) *(497448-2)* – ('A'side) / Back on da bus / My generation (US mix) / My generation (video).

Jan 01. (c-s) *(INC 97474) <radio play>* **ROLLIN' (AIR RAID VEHICLE) / ROLLIN' (URBAN ASSAULT VEHICLE)** [1] Oct00 [65]
(cd-s+=) *(IND 97474)* – Take a look around (live) / My generation (live) / ('A'-CD-ROM).

— also in early 2001, FRED DURST teamed up with AARON LEWIS of STAIND to have a US hit single, 'OUTSIDE'

Jun 01. (c-s) *(497574-4) <radio play>* **MY WAY / ROLLIN' (Air Raid Vehicle remix)** [6] [75]
(cd-s) *(497573-2)* – ('A'side) / ('A'-William Orbit mix) / ('A'-DJ Premier remix).
(cd-s) *(497574-2)* – ('A'side) / ('A'-Dub Pistols remix) / ('A'-Dancehall dub remix) / ('A'-Dub Pistols remix instrumental).

Oct 01. (cd-s) *(497636-2)* **BOILER / FAITH / MY WAY (P Diddy remix) / BOILER (video)** [18] [ ]

— WES BORLAND was now no longer a member

Dec 01. (cd/d-lp) *<(493192-2/-1)>* **NEW OLD SONGS** (remixes) [ ] [26]
– Nookie – for the nookie / Take a look around (Timbaland) / Break stuff (DJ Lethal mix) / My way (P Diddy mix) / Crushed (Bosko mix) / N2gether now (all in together now) / Rearranged (Timbaland mix) / Getcha groove on (DJ Premier dirt road mix) (with XZIBIT) / Faith – Fame (mix) / My way (DJ Lethal mix) / Nookie (Androids vs. Las Putas mix) / Counterfeit (Lethal Dose extreme guitar mix) / Rollin' (DJ Monk vs. The Track Mack mix). *(cd+=)* – My way (DJ Premier mix) / My way (William Orbit mix) / My way (Dub Pistols dancehall mix).

Sep 03. (7") *(9811758)* **EAT YOU ALIVE. / SHOT** [10] [ ]
(cd-s+=) *(9811757) <11013>* – Just drop dead / ('A'-video).

Sep 03. (cd) *(9860971) <12350-2>* **RESULTS MAY VARY** [7] [3]
– Re entry / Eat you alive / Gimme the mic / Underneath the gun / Down another day / Almost over / Build a bridge / Red light – green light / The only one / Let me down / Lonely world / Phenomenon / Creamer (radio is dead) / Behind blue eyes / Drown. *(UK+=)* – Let it go.

Nov 03. (7") *(9814743) <radio>* **BEHIND BLUE EYES. / JUST DROP DEAD** [18] [71]
(cd-s+=) *(9814744)* – Rollin' (DJ Monk-vs-The track Mack remix) / ('A'-video).

LINDISFARNE

Formed: Newcastle-upon-Tyne, England . . . 1969 as BRETHREN by SIMON COWE (guitar, mandolin), RAY JACKSON (guitar, mandolin, mouth harp), JEFF SANDLER (guitar), ROD CLEMENTS (bass, violin, vocals) and ROY LAIDLAW (drums) (The latter two had earlier been part of Newcastle band The DOWNTOWN FACTION). With singer/songwriter ALAN HULL (who released a solo credited single in 1969, 'WE CAN SWING TOGETHER' / 'OBADIAH'S GRAVE' for 'Transatlantic') soon replacing SANDLER, the band took a more mellow folk approach, adopting the name LINDISFARNE. Initially gaining some support on the college circuit, the band had soon secured a contract on Tony Stratton-Smith's 'Charisma' label. The 1970 debut, 'NICELY OUT OF TUNE', was a folky gem, featuring the atmospheric 'LADY ELEANOR' and introducing the band's impressive use of harmony. For the follow-up, 'FOG ON THE TYNE', the band hooked up with Nashville producer Bob Johnston. Released in late '71, the album scaled the UK charts the following year, aided by the Top 5 success of the exquisitely melodic 'MEET ME ON THE CORNER' single and a re-issued 'LADY ELEANOR'. The band retained JOHNSTON for the 'DINGLY DELL' (1972) album, although this time the pairing was a recipe for commercial and critical failure. In summer 1973, the band split; COWE, CLEMENTS and LAIDLAW going off to form JACK THE LAD while ALAN HULL released a solo effort, 'PIPEDREAM'. Later that year, HULL resurrected the band along with JACKSON, recruiting a new line-up of CHARLIE HARCOURT (guitar), KENNY CRADDOCK (keyboards), TOMMY DUFFY (bass) and PAUL NICHOLS (drums). After a couple of flop albums, 'ROLL ON RUBY' (1973) and 'HAPPY DAZE' (1974), the band once again called it a day, HULL releasing a solo follow-up, 1975's 'SQUIRE'. Three years later, the original line-up re-formed, scoring a new deal with 'Mercury' and a Top 10 UK hit with the harmony-laden classic, 'RUN FOR HOME'. The cringe-ingly titled 'BACK AND FOURTH' album made the British Top 30, although subsequent releases foundered and the band were once again confined to the margins. Not content with churning out rock'n'roll medleys, the band teamed up with PAUL GASCOIGNE (former Rangers and England footballer) in 1990 for a 'hilarious' run through of 'FOG ON THE TYNE'. While the single made No.2, it's doubtful if it won the band any new admirers outside their loyal Geordie fanbase. Tragically, mainman ALAN HULL died of a heart attack on the 17th of November, 1995. LINDISFARNE (CLEMENTS and LAIDLAW) returned in 1998 with a new frontman, BILLY MITCHELL, releasing new set, 'HERE COMES THE NEIGHBOURHOOD'. • **Songwriters:** HULL, JACKSON plus others contributed.

Album rating: NICELY OUT OF TUNE (*7) / FOG ON THE TYNE (*8) / DINGLY DELL (*6) / LINDISFARNE LIVE (*5) / ROLL ON RUBY (*4) / HAPPY DAZE (*5) / BACK AND FOURTH (*6) / MAGIC IN THE AIR (*4) / THE NEWS (*4) / SLEEPLESS NIGHTS (*4) / LINDISFARNETASTIC (*4) / LINDISFARNETASTIC VOLUME 2 (*3) / DANCE YOUR LIFE AWAY (*3) / THE BEST OF LINDISFARNE compilation (*7) / AMIGOS (*4) / CAUGHT IN THE ACT live collection (*7) / ELVIS LIVES ON THE MOON (*4) / ANOTHER FINE MESS (*4) / HERE COMES THE NEIGHBOURHOOD (*5)

ALAN HULL (b.20 Feb'45) – vocals, guitar (ex-CHOSEN FEW, solo artist) / **RAY JACKSON** (b.12 Dec'48, Wallsend, England) – guitar, mandolin, mouth harp / **SIMON COWE** (b. 1 Apr'48, Tynemouth, England) – guitar, mandolin / **ROD CLEMENTS** (b.17 Nov'47, North Shields, England) – bass, violin, vocals / **ROY LAIDLAW** (b.28 May'48, North Shields) – drums

Charisma / Elektra

Sep 70. (7") *(CB 137)* **CLEAR WHITE LIGHT – PART 2. / KNACKERS YARD BLUES** [ ] [–]

Nov 70. (lp) *(CAS 1025)* **NICELY OUT OF TUNE** [ ] [ ]
– Lady Eleanor / Road to kingdom come / Winter song / Turn a deaf ear / Clear white light (part II) / We can swing together / Alan in the river with flowers / Down / The things I should have said / Jackhammer blues / Scarecrow song. *(re-dist.Jan 72, hit No.8) (re-iss. Aug86 lp/c; CHC/+MC 31) (cd-iss. Aug88 on 'Virgin'; CASCD 1025) (+=)* – Knackers yard blues / Nothing but the marvellous is beautiful.

Jan 71. (7") *(CB 153)* **LADY ELEANOR. / NOTHING BUT THE MARVELLOUS IS BEAUTIFUL** [ ] [–]
(re-iss. May72, hit UK No.3)

Sep 71. (7") **LADY ELEANOR. / DOWN** [–] [ ]
<re-iss. US; Aug72, hit No.82>

Oct 71. (lp) *(CAS 1050)* **FOG ON THE TYNE** [1] [ ]
– Meet me on the corner / Alright on the night / Uncle Sam / Together forever / January song / Peter Brophy don't care / City song / Passing ghosts / Train in G major / Fog on the Tyne. *(re-iss. Oct86 lp/c; CHC/+MC 52) (cd-iss. Aug88 + Feb91 on 'Virgin'; CASCD 1050) (+=)* – Scotch mist / No time to lose.

Feb 72. (7"m) *(CB 173)* **MEET ME ON THE CORNER. / SCOTCH MIST / NO TIME TO LOSE** [5] [–]

Mar 72. (7") **MEET ME ON THE CORNER. / FOG ON THE TYNE** [–] [ ]

Sep 72. (7") *(CB 191)* **ALL FALL DOWN. / WE CAN SWING TOGETHER (live)** [34] [ ]

Sep 72. (lp/c) *(CAS 1057/)* **DINGLY DELL** [5] [ ]
– All fall down / Plankton's lament / Bring down the government / Poor old Ireland / Don't ask me / Oh, no not again / Dingle regatta / Wake up little sister / Go back / Court in the act / Mandolin king / Dingly dell. *(cd-iss. Aug88 on 'Virgin'; CASCD 1057) (+=)* – We can swing together (live).

Dec 72. (7") *(CB 199)* **COURT IN THE ACT. / DON'T ASK ME** [ ] [ ]

Jul 73. (lp/c) *(CLASS 2/)* **LINDISFARNE LIVE (live)** [25] [–]
– No time to lose / Meet me on the corner / All right on the night / Train in G major / Fog on the Tyne / We can swing together / Jackhammer blues. *(re-iss. Sep83 lp/c; CHC/+MC 7)*

—— COWE, CLEMENTS and LAIDLAW bailed out to form JACK THE LAD. Made 4 albums **JACK THE LAD** (1974) / **OLD STRAIGHT TRACK** (1974) / **ROUGH DIAMONDS** (1975) . **The 4th JACKPOT** (1976) on 'United Art' was without CLEMENTS, COWE or LAIDLAW.

ALAN HULL

Charisma / Warners

Jun 73. (7"m) *(CB 208)* **NUMBERS (TRAVELLING BAND). / DRINKING SONG / ONE OFF PAT** [ ] [–]

Jul 73. (lp/c) *(CAS 1069/)* **PIPEDREAM** [29] [ ]
– Breakfast / Monkey game / Country gentleman's wife / Just another sad song / Numbers (travelling band) / For the bairns / Drinking song / Song for a windmill / United States of mind / I hate to see you cry / Blue murder. *(re-iss. Mar83 lp/c; CHC/+MC 16) (cd-iss. Feb91 & Mar94 on 'Virgin'; CASCD 1069)*

Sep 73. (7") *(CB 211)* **JUST ANOTHER SAD SONG. / WAITING** [ ] [–]

LINDISFARNE

re-formed Autumn 1973. Same label. **HULL & JACKSON** brought in **CHARLIE HARCOURT** – lead guitar / **KENNY CRADDOCK** – keyboards / **TOMMY DUFFY** – bass / **PAUL NICHOLS** – drums

Dec 73. (lp/c) *(CAS 1076/)* **ROLL ON RUBY** [ ] [ ]
– Taking care of business / North Country boy / Steppenwolf / Nobody loves you anymore / When the war is over / Moonshine / Lazy / Roll on river / Tow the line / Goodbye.

Mar 74. (7") *(CB 228)* **TAKING CARE OF BUSINESS. / NORTH COUNTRY BOY** [ ] [ ]

Warners / Asylum

Oct 74. (lp/c) *(K/K4 56070)* **HAPPY DAZE** [ ] [ ]
– Tonight / In yer head / River / You put the laff on me / No need to tell me / I'm juiced / Up to lose / Dealer's choice / Nellie / The man down there / Gin and tonic all round / Tomorrow.

Jan 75. (7") *(K 16489)* **TONIGHT. / NO NEED TO TELL ME** [ ] [ ]

—— Disbanded again.

ALAN HULL

returned with own studio work.

Warners / Warners

May 75. (7") *(K 16561)* **DAN THE PLAN. / ONE MORE BOTTLE OF WINE** [ ] [–]

May 75. (lp/c) *(K/K4 56121)* **SQUIRE** [ ] [ ]
– Squire / Dan the plan / Picture a little girl / Nuthin' shakin' / One more bottle of wine / Golden oldies / I'm sorry squire / Waiting / Bad side of town / Mr.Inbetween.

Aug 75. (7") *(K 16599)* **SQUIRE. / ONE MORE BOTTLE OF WINE** [ ] [–]

Dec 75. (7") *(K 16643)* **CRAZY WOMAN. / GOLDEN OLDIES** [ ] [–]

LINDISFARNE

—— the original 1970 line-up re-formed

Mercury / Atco

May 78. (7") *(6007 177)* **RUN FOR HOME. / STICK TOGETHER** [10] Sep 78 [33]

Jun 78. (lp) *(9109 609)* **BACK AND FOURTH** [22] [ ]
– Juke box gypsy / Warm feeling / Woman / Only alone / Run for home / Kings X blues / Get wise / You and me / Marshall Riley's army / Angels at eleven / Make me want to stay. *(re-iss. Dec83 lp/c; PRICE/PRIMC 54) (cd-iss. 1991; 848 226-2)*

Sep 78. (7") *(6007 187)* **JUKE BOX GYPSY. / WHEN IT GOES THE HARDEST** [56] [–]

Nov 78. (7") *(6007 195)* **BRAND NEW DAY. / WINTER SONG** [ ] [–]

Dec 78. (7") **WARM FEELING. / WOMAN** [–] [ ]

Dec 78. (d-lp) *(6641 877)* **MAGIC IN THE AIR (live)** [ ] [–]
– Lady Eleanor / Road to kingdom come / Turn a deaf ear / January song / Court in the act / Meet me on the corner / Bye bye birdie / Train in G-major / Scarecrow song / Dingly dell / Scotch mist / No time to lose / Winter song / Uncle Sam / Wake up little sister / All fall down / We can swing together / Fog on the Tyne / Clear white light.

Feb 79. (7") *(6007 205)* **WARM FEELING. / CLEAR WHITE LIGHT (live)** [ ] [–]

Aug 79. (7") *(NEWS 1)* **EASY AND FREE. / WHEN FOREVER COMES ALONG** [ ] [ ]

Sep 79. (lp)(c) *(9109 626)(7231 439)* **THE NEWS** [ ] [–]
– Call of the wild / People say / 1983 / Log on your fire / Evening / Easy and free / Miracles / When Friday comes along / Dedicated hound / This has got to end / Good to be here.

Oct 79. (7") *(6007 241)* **CALL OF THE WILD. / DEDICATED HOUND** ☐ –

Subterranean not iss.

Jun 80. (7") *(SUB 1)* **FRIDAY GIRL. / 1983** ☐ –

Hangover not iss.

Nov 81. (7") *(HANG 9)* **I MUST STOP GOING TO PARTIES. / SEE HOW THEY RUN** ☐ –

L.M.P. not iss.

Jun 82. (7") *(LM 1)* **SUNDERLAND BOYS. / CRUISING TO DISASTER** ☐ –

Sep 82. (7") *(FOG 1)* **NIGHTS. / DOG RUFF** ☐ –

Oct 82. (lp/c) *(GET/ZCGET 1)* **SLEEPLESS NIGHTS** ☐ –
– Nights / Start again / Cruising to disaster / Same way down / Winning the game / About you / Underland boys / Love is a pain / Do what I want / Never miss the water / I must stop going to parties / Stormy weather. *(cd-iss. May93 on 'Castle'; CLACD 382)*

Jan 83. (7") *(FOG 2)* **DO WHAT I WANT. / SAME WAY DOWN** ☐ –

Sep 84. (lp) *(GET 2)* **LINDISFARNTASTIC LIVE (live)** ☐ –

Nov 84. (lp/c) *(GET/ZCGET 3)* **LINDISFARNTASTIC VOL.2 (live)** ☐ –

Jun 85. (7") *(FOG 3)* **I REMEMBER THE LIGHTS (acappella version). / DAY OF THE JACKAL** ☐ –

Dec 85. (7"; at concerts) *(FOG 4)* **CHRISTMAS EP (live)** ☐ –
– Warm feeling / Red square dance / Run for home / Nights (acappella version).

— **HULL** + **JACKSON** added **MARTY CRAGGS** – saxophone / + 4th member/producer **STEVE DAGGETT** – keyboards

River City not iss.

Sep 86. (7"m) *(LIND 1)* **SHINE ON. / HEROES / DANCE YOUR LIFE AWAY (Gogo mix)** ☐ –

Oct 86. (lp/c) *(LIND LP/C 1)* **DANCE YOUR LIFE AWAY** ☐ –
– Shine on / Love on the run / Heroes / All in the same boat / Dance your life away / Beautiful day / Broken doll / One hundred miles to Liverpool / Take your time / Song for a stranger. *(cd-iss. 1988; LINCD 1) (re-iss. cd May93 on 'Castle'; CLACD 383)*

Feb 87. (7") *(LIND 2)* **LOVE ON THE RUN. / ONE HUNDRED MILES TO LIVERPOOL** ☐ –
(w/ free 7") *(LIND 2A)* – Save our ales. / Save our ales (sub mix).

Honeybee not iss.

Dec 87. (7"/ext.12") *(HONEY 3/+12)* **PARTY DOLL. / Medley; C'MON EVERYBODY – DO YOU WANNA DANCE – TWIST AND SHOUT – DO YOU LOVE ME** ☐ –

Virgin not iss.

Nov 88. (7") *(LADY 1)* **LADY ELEANOR '88. / MEET ME ON THE CORNER** ☐ –
(12"+=) *(LIND 1-12)* – Lost in space.
(3"cd-s++=) *(LADYCD 1)* – Reason to be.

Black Crow not iss.

Nov 89. (lp/cd) *(CRO/+CD 224)* **AMIGOS** ☐ –
– One world / Everything changes / Working for the man / Roll on that day / You're the one / Wish you were here / Do it like this / Any way the wind blows / Strange affair / When the night comes down / Don't say goodnight / Another world. *(re-iss. cd May93 on 'Castle'; CLACD 384)*

— Below w/ Geordie England footballer GAZZA (aka PAUL GASCOIGNE)

Best not iss.

Nov 90. (7"/7"pic-d/c-s; by GAZZA & LINDISFARNE) *(ZB/ZA/ZK 44083)* **FOG ON THE TYNE (REVISITED). / ('A'instrumental)** 2 –
(ext.12"+=/cd-s+=) *(ZT/ZD 44083)* – ('A'extended).

— now without JACKSON; repl. by **KENNY CRADDOCK** – multi

Essential not iss.

May 93. (7"/12") *(ESS/+T 2026)* **DAY OF THE JACKAL. / DEMONS** ☐ –
(cd-s+=) *(ESSX 2026)* – So lonely / ('A'extended).

Jun 93. (cd/c) *(ESS CD/MC 197)* **ELVIS LIVES ON THE MOON** ☐ –
– Day of the jackal / Soho Square / Old peculiar feeling / Mother Russia / Demons / Don't leave me tonight / Elvis lives on the Moon / Keeping the rage / Heaven waits / Spoken like a man / Think.

Sep 94. (cd-s) *(ESSX 2044)* **WE CAN MAKE IT / WALK IN THE SEA (live)** ☐ –

Sep 94. (cd) *(ESSCD 214)* **ON TAP: A BARREL FULL OF HITS** (compilation) ☐ –
– Run for home / Lady Eleanor / Meet me on the corner / We can make it / All fall down / Warm feeling / Winter song / Road to kingdom come / Fog on the tyne / Miracles / No time to lose / Running man / Elvis lives on the Moon / Juke box gypsy / Dance your life away / Evening / Roll on that day / Clear white light II.

— line-up **HULL / CLEMENTS / CRAGGS / LAIDLAW / + DAVE DENHOLM** – guitars / **IAN THOMSON** – bass

Grapevine not iss.

Jul 96. (cd) *(GRACD 211)* **ANOTHER FINE MESS (live 2 July '95)** ☐ –
– Clear white light (part 2) / Squire / Lady Eleanor / Meet me on the corner / Evening / City song / One world / All fall down / Winter song / This heart of mine / We can make it / Road to kingdom come / Money / Run for home / Fog on the Tyne.

— sadly, ALAN HULL died of a heart attack on 17th of November '95

— **BILLY MITCHELL** – vocals (was added to **LAIDLAW** + **CLEMENTS**)

Park Park

Sep 98. (cd) *(PRKCD 47)* **HERE COMES THE NEIGHBOURHOOD** ☐ Nov98 ☐
– Born at the right time / Ghost in blue suede shoes / Jubilee corner / Can't do right for doing wrong / Working my way back home / Wejibeleng / Unmarked car / Devil of the north / Uncle Henry / One day / Driftin' through.

– compilations, others –

on 'Charisma' unless mentioned otherwise

1974. (7") *(CB 232)* **FOG ON THE TYNE. / MANDOLIN KING** ☐ –

Oct 75. (lp) *(lp/c) (CAS 1108)* **FINEST HOUR** 55 –
(re-iss. Sep83; same)

Nov 75. (7") *(CB 266)* **LADY ELEANOR. / FOG ON THE TYNE** ☐ –

Aug 77. (lp/c) *Hallmark; (SHM/SHC 919)* **LADY ELEANOR** ☐ –

May 81. (7") *(CB 409)* **CLEAR WHITE LIGHT. / THE TRAVELLER** ☐ –

May 81. (lp/c) *(BG/+C 5)* **REPEAT PERFORMANCE: THE SINGLES ALBUM** ☐ –

Jul 82. (7") *Old Gold; (OG 9005)* **MEET ME ON THE CORNER. / LADY ELEANOR** ☐ –

Mar 83. (d-c) **FOG ON THE TYNE / NICELY OUT OF TUNE** ☐ –

Oct 87. (d-lp/d-c/d-cd) *Stylus; (SMR/SMC/SMD 738)* **C'MON EVERYBODY** ☐ –

Nov 88. (12"ep/cd-ep) *Strange Fruit; (SFPS/+CD 059)* **THE PEEL SESSION** (8.5.72) ☐ –
– Mandolin king / Poor old Ireland / Lady Eleanor / Road to kingdom come.

Sep 89. (lp/c/cd) *VIP-Virgin; (VVIP/+C/D 103)* **THE BEST OF LINDISFARNE** ☐ –
(re-iss. cd Dec93; CDVIP 103)

Aug 92. (cd) *Castle; (CCSCD 346)* **CAUGHT IN THE ACT** ☐ –
– Moving house / Taxman / Lady Eleanor / Nights / Mr.Inbetween / Brand new day / Mystery play / Lover not a fighter / Day of the jackal / Stormy weather / I must stop going to parties / Marshall Riley's army / Warm feeling / Fog on the tyne / Run for home / Meet me on the corner / Clear white light.

Nov 92. (cd) *Virgin; (CDVM 9012)* **BURIED TREASURES VOLUME 1** ☐ –

Nov 92. (cd) *Virgin; (CDVM 9013)* **BURIED TREASURES VOLUME 2** ☐ –

Jun 93. (cd) *Code 90; (NINETY 5)* **LIVE – 1990 (live)** ☐ –

Jun 96. (cd) *Mooncrest; (CRESTCD 020)* **THE OTHER SIDE OF . . .** ☐ –
– Meet me on the corner / Lady Eleanor / Fog on the Tyne / Run for home / Warm feeling / Clear white light / Love you more than I can say / Oh Donna / Keep your hands off my baby / Rhythm of the rain / Speedy Gonzales / Little darling / Dreamin' / La bamba.

Oct 97. (cd) *Mooncrest; (CRESTCD 024)* **THE CROPREDY CONCERT** (live at Cropredy 1994) ☐ –

ALAN HULL

Rocket not iss.

Apr 79. (7") *(XPRES 12)* **I WISH YOU WELL. / LOVE IS THE ANSWER** ☐ –

May 79. (lp) *(TRAIN 6)* **PHANTOMS** ☐ –
– Anywhere is everywhere / Corporation rock / Dancin' / I wish you well /

Love is an alibi / Love is the answer / Madman and loonies / Make me want to stay / Somewhere out there / A walk in the sea.

Jul 79. (7") *(XPRES 19)* **A WALK IN THE SEA. / CORPORATION ROCK** [ ] [–]

Black Crow — not iss.

Oct 83. (7") *(CROS 2)* **MALVINAS MELODY. / ODE TO A TAXMAN** [ ] [–]

Nov 83. (lp) *(CRO 206)* **ON THE OTHER SIDE** [ ] [–]

Jun 88. (lp) *(CRO 219)* **ANOTHER LITTLE ADVENTURE** [ ] [–]

Mooncrest — not iss.

Jul 94. (cd) *(CRESTCD 017)* **BACK TO BASICS** [ ] [–]
– United states of mind / Poor old Ireland / All fall down / Lady Eleanor / Wintersong / Walk in the sea / Mother Russia / This heart of mine / Mister inbetween / January song / Breakfast / Day of the jackal / Oh no not again / Run for home / Fog on the Tyne.

[LINKIN PARK]

Formed: Los Angeles, California, USA . . . 1999 as HYBRID THEORY by high school friends BRAD DELSON, MIKE SHINODA and ROB BOURDON together with JOSEPH HAHN and CHESTER BENNINGTON. Influenced by the likes of NINE INCH NAILS, APHEX TWIN and The ROOTS, [LINKIN PARK] are yet another act to muscle in on the heavily saturated rap-metal market. Offered a publishing deal after their very first gig at L.A.'s Whisky, the band subsequently signed with 'Warners' for their debut album, '[HYBRID THEORY]' (2000). While admittedly pretty fly for white guys, [LINKIN PARK], like most bands of their ilk, possess neither the fluid funk of the 'CHILI PEPPERS nor the wiry conviction of RATM. Like most bands of their ilk, however, they seem to have found an audience willing to part with their hard earned cash and are, at the time of writing, racing up the charts. Remix set, '[REANIMATION]' (2002), found a posse of rappers, producers and DJ's making brave attempts at sprucing up tracks from the band's debut. Makeovers from the likes of PHAROAH MONCH and ALCHEMIST certainly improved on the originals although that wasn't exactly difficult. In fact, the LINKIN lads could've done with similar treatment on 'METEORA' (2003), where it was back to lumpen nu-metal business for the masses. There was little discernible creative progress from the debut but it was admittedly slick and professional enough to rely on cruise control, something which couldn't be said for 'LIVE IN TEXAS' (2003) which perhaps showed up more of LP's non-studio shortcomings than they might've liked.

Album rating: [HYBRID THEORY] (*6) / [REANIMATION] (*5) / METEORA (*5) / LIVE IN TEXAS (*4)

CHESTER BENNINGTON – vocals / **MIKE SHINODA** – vocals/MC / **BRAD DELSON** – guitar / **JOSEPH HAHN** – DJ, vocals / **ROB BOURBON** – drums / with **SCOTT KOZIOL** – bass

Warners — Warners

Oct 00. (cd) *<(9362 47755-2)>* **[HYBRID THEORY]** [4] Apr00 [7]
– Papercut / One step closer / With you / Points of authority / Crawling / Runaway / By myself / In the end / A place for my head / Forgotten / Cure for the itch / Pushing me away. *(lp-iss.Oct01; 9362 47755-1)*

—— **PHOENIX** – bass; repl. part-timer SCOTT

Jan 01. (10"/c-s) *(W 550 TE/MC) <radio play>* **ONE STEP CLOSER. / MY DECEMBER** [24] [75]
(cd-s+=) *(W 550CD)* – High voltage / ('A'-CD-ROM).

Apr 01. (c-s) *(W 556MC) <radio cut>* **CRAWLING / PAPERCUT (live)** [16] Aug01 [79]
(cd-s+=) *(W 556CD)* – (CD-Rom video footage).
(dvds) *(W 556DVD)* – ('A'side) / ('A'live snippets).

Jun 01. (c-s) *(W 562C)* **PAPERCUT / POINTS OF AUTHORITY (live)** [14] [ ]
(cd-s+=) *(W 562CD)* – Papercut (live).

Oct 01. (cd-s) *(W 569CD) <42411>* **IN THE END / A PLACE FOR MY HEAD (live) / STEP UP** [8] [2]
(cd-s) *(W 569CDX)* – ('A'side) / ('A'live) / Points of authority (live).

Jul 02. (c-s; as LINKIN PARK & EVIDENCE featuring PHAROAHE MONCH & DJ BABU) *(W 588C) <24247>* **H! VLTG3 / PTS.OF.ATHRTY (with JAY GORDON)** [9] Aug02 [ ]
(cd-s+=) *(W 588CD)* – Buy myself (with MARILYN MANSON).

Jul 02. (cd/c) *<(9362 48326-2/-4)>* **[REANIMATION]** (remixes) [3] [2]
– (Opening) / Pts.of.athrty (with JAY GORDON) / Enth e nd (with KAMASTA KURT & MOTION MAN) / (Chali) / Frgt-10 (with CHALI 2NA & ALCHEMIST) / P5hng me a*wy (with STEPHEN RICHARDS) / Plc.4 mie haed (with AMP LIVE & ZION) / X-ecutioner style (with BLACK THOUGHT) / H! Vltg3 (with EVIDENCE featuring PHAROAHE MONCH & DJ BABU) / (Riff raff) / Wth you (with CHAIRMAN HAHN & ACEYALONE) / (Ntr-mssion) / Ppr: kut (with CHEAPSHOT & JUBACCA) / Rnw@y (with BACKYARD BANGERS & PHOENIX ORION) / My (with MICKEY P. & KELLI ALI) / (Stef) / By myslf (with JOSH ABRAHAM) / Kyur4 th ich (with CHAIRMAN HAHN) / 1 stp klosr (with HUMBLE BROTHERS & JONATHAN DAVIS) / Krwlng (with AARON LEWIS) / Untitled (dub).

Mar 03. (7") *(W 602) <radio>* **SOMEWHERE I BELONG. / STEP UP (live)** [10] [32]
(cd-s+=) *(W 602CD)* – My December (live).

Mar 03. (cd/lp) *<(9362 48443-2/48186-1)>* **METEORA** [1] [1]
– (Foreword) / Don't stay / Somewhere I belong / Lying from you / Hit the floor / Easier to run / Faint / Figure.09 / Breaking the habit / From the inside / Nobody's listening / Session / Numb. *<(cd w/dvd+=; 9362 48461-2)>* – (the making of Meteora).

Jun 03. (7"pic-d) *(W 610) <16652>* **FAINT. / LYING FROM YOU (live)** [15] Oct03 [48]
(cd-s+=) *(W 610CD1)* – Somewhere I belong (video).
(cd-s) *(W 610CD2)* – ('A'side) / One step closer (live) / ('A'-video).

Sep 03. (cd-s) *(W 622CD1)* **NUMB / FROM THE INSIDE (live) / NUMB (video)** [14] [–]
(cd-s) *(W 622CD2)* – ('A'side) / Easier to run (live) / Faint (video).

Nov 03. (cd) *(9362 48638-2)* **LIVE IN TEXAS (live)** [47] [–]
– Somewhere I belong / Lying from you / Paper cut / Points of authority / Runaway / Faint / From the inside / Pushing me away / Numb / Crawling / In the end / One step closer.

LIT

Formed: Orange County, California, USA . . . 1990 by songwriting brothers, JEREMY and A. JAY POPOFF; the line-up being completed by KEVIN BALDES and ALLAN SHELLENBERGER. The band, who looked, but didn't sound like the "SINATRA" rat pack, took their influences primarily from COSTELLO and PRESLEY. An EP, 'FIVE SMOKIN' TRACKS FROM LIT' was released in 1996 and didn't really do much for the rap-metal/pop punk quartet, neither did the debut, 'TRIPPING THE LIGHT FANTASTIC', which bagged some excellent reviews. It wasn't until 1999 that LIT unleashed 'MY OWN WORST ENEMY', the single that predictably sent melodramatic US teens into hyper mode, proving to be just as successful on British shores too. The song was a darkly comic cartoon punk (can you feel the ghosts of early GREEN DAY) track about a white trash alcoholic's misadventures with his argument-happy girlfriend. The album that followed, 'A PLACE IN THE SUN' didn't even graze the US billboard charts and hardly reached boiling-point selling figures in Europe. This could possibly be blamed on the band's rivals, SUGAR RAY, who sounded familiarly similar. 2001's 'ATOMIC' was hardly designed to remedy that situation with another feisty if ultimately faceless set of high octane hormone-pop, gurning amid the kind of frat-house lyrics which could've been plucked from an 80's American teen "comedy".

Album rating: FIVE SMOKIN' TRACKS FROM LIT mini (*5) / TRIPPING THE LIGHT FANTASTIC (*6) / A PLACE IN THE SUN (*6) / ATOMIC (*5)

A. JAY POPOFF – vocals / **JEREMY POPOFF** – guitar / **KEVIN BALDES** – bass / **ALLAN SHELLENBERGER** – drums

Date	Release	not iss.		Malicious Vinyl
Dec 96.	(m-cd) *<MV 5001>* **FIVE SMOKIN' TRACKS FROM LIT** – Bitter / Fireman / No big thing / Beginning / Stain.	–		
Apr 97.	(cd) *<MV 5016>* **TRIPPING THE LIGHT FANTASTIC** – Beginning / My world / Fuel / No big thing / Habib / Explode / Bitter / Amount to nothing / Dozer / Fireman / Cadillac / I don't get it.	–		
		R.C.A.		R.C.A.
Jun 99.	(7"/c-s) *(74321 61265-7/66999-4) <radio cut>* **MY OWN WORST ENEMY. / BITTER** (cd-s) *(74321 66999-2)* – ('A'side) / Money / Lovely day.	16	Apr99	51
Jun 99.	(cd/c/lp) *(74321 67859-2/-4/-1) <07863 67775-2/-4>* **A PLACE IN THE SUN** – Four / My own worst enemy / Down / Miserable / No big thing / Zip-lock / Lovely day / Perfect one / Quicksand / Happy / The best is yet to come undone / A place in the sun.	55	Feb99	31
Sep 99.	(c-s) *(74321 70185-4)* **ZIP-LOCK / QUICKSAND** (cd-s+=) *(74321 70185-2)* – ('A'album version).	60		
Aug 00.	(c-s) *(888953-4)* **OVER MY HEAD / (other tracks by BLISS and KARMA SLAVE** (above from the movie, 'Titan A.E.', issued on 'E.M.I.')	37		–
Feb 02.	(cd) *(74321 91611-2) <68086>* **ATOMIC** – Something to someone / The last time again / Addicted / Lipstick and bruises / Everything's cool / Happy in the meantime / Drop D / Sunny weather / Next time around / Slip / She comes / Live for this. *(bonus+=)* – Over my head.		Oct01	36

LITTLE FEAT

Formed: Los Angeles, California, USA . . . late 1969 out of The FACTORY, by ex-ZAPPA cohorts LOWELL GEORGE and ROY ESTRADA, plus BILL PAYNE and RICHIE HAYWARD, both recent members of cult act The FRATERNITY OF MAN. Having all previously played together in the aforementioned outfits, the formation of LITTLE FEAT was more of a natural progression, GEORGE bailing out of ZAPPA's band after playing on 'Hot Rats' and 'Weasels Ripped My Flesh'. Signed to 'Warners' on the strength of three demo tracks ('WILLIN'', 'TRUCK STOP GIRL' and 'BRIDES OF JESUS'), the band began work on their eponymous debut with producer RUSS TITELMAN. Eventually surfacing in late 1970, 'LITTLE FEAT' announced the arrival of a major force in American music; the aforementioned 'WILLIN' was GEORGE's statement of intent, a much covered nugget that gave LITTLE FEAT more exposure than was ever afforded their overlooked debut. In its earliest incarnation, the song was a lean sliver of poor-boy country blues, GEORGE on resolutely unadorned vocal form with RY COODER carving out shards of wiry slide guitar. Just as raggedly affecting was 'TRUCK STOP GIRL'; closer in spirit to traditional country heartbreak than anything GEORGE would subsequently write, the song was given a wonderfully sympathetic reading by CLARENCE WHITE the same year on The BYRDS self-titled, half live/half studio opus. The 'FORTY FOUR BLUES/HOW MANY MORE YEARS' medley called to mind the mutant blues of CAPTAIN BEEFHEART while 'SNAKES ON EVERYTHING' and 'STRAWBERRY FLATS' were by turns, swaggering and shambling R&B. Though the record was met with ecstatic reviews, LITTLE FEAT didn't appear to be high on 'Warners' list of priorities, a bottom of the bill slot on a BEEFHEART/RY COODER double header more or less the only exposure the band were afforded. Returning to the studio, they cut 'SAILIN' SHOES' (1972), an album that more successfully melted LITTLE FEAT's eclectic Americana into a rich, gumbo stew. 'WILLIN' had been lovingly refashioned into a work of resonant, almost transcendent beauty, embellished by wisps of pedal steel (courtesy of 'SNEAKY' PETE KLEINOW) and PAYNE's graceful piano. 'EASY TO SLIP' was as commercial as LITTLE FEAT got, and that was part of the problem, at least in terms of widespread commercial acceptance. There was a brilliantly gritty surreallism and warped humour to GEORGE's lyrics at odds with the prevailing Californian decadence of The EAGLES/DOOBIE BROTHERS axis and the hippie utopianism of CROSBY, STILLS and NASH. This skewed vision of modern America's seedy underbelly also touched the music, the likes of 'TRIPE FACE BOOGIE' and 'TEENAGE NERVOUS BREAKDOWN' highly original, blistering slabs of rock'n'roll while the title track was a subversive slice of gospel blues. 'SAILIN' SHOES' was also the first record to feature the gaudy, surrealist artwork of NEON PARK, a regular fixture for the remainder of the band's career. Although the record again sold poorly and ROY ESTRADA left for CAPTAIN BEEFHEART's MAGIC BAND, LITTLE FEAT regrouped with extra members KENNEY GRADNEY, SAM CLAYTON (both from DELANEY & BONNIE) and PAUL BARRERE, entering the studio in late '72 to begin work on 'DIXIE CHICKEN' (1973). The pinnacle of LITTLE FEAT's career, this release represented the band's most consistent and complete body of work. Rooted in the swamp funk of New Orleans, the album was a swaggering, intoxicating masterpiece. LOWELL had developed into a frighteningly good slide player, his soaring, smoking runs interlocking with PAYNE's piano and CLAYTON's percussion to create a vibe that many have since tried and failed to imitate. The title track, 'TWO TRAINS' and 'FAT MAN IN THE BATHTUB' were anthemic stuff, BONNIE BRAMLETT and LOWELL's close friend BONNIE RAIT providing suitably soulful backing vocals. Elsewhere, LOWELL navigated a cover of ALLEN TOUSSAINT's 'ON YOUR WAY DOWN' with trenchant ease, his gilt-edged gravel/molasses vocals oozing class. The PAYNE/BARRERE-penned 'WALKIN' ALL NIGHT', meanwhile, strutted like a catwalk model. Sensual, sexy and insidiously funky, it remains a mystery why 'Warners' failed to make any commercial headway with 'DIXIE CHICKEN'. Subsequent low sales led to tension in the ranks and the band briefly split up. In the interim, GEORGE worked on ROBERT PALMER's 'Sneakin' Sally Through The Alley' and BONNIE RAITT's 'Takin' My Time' amongst other session work while PAYNE toured with labelmates, The DOOBIE BROTHERS. By May '74, the band were back together, ensconced in their Maryland studio and working on a fourth album, 'FEATS DON'T FAIL ME NOW' (1974). While the record gave them belated success, it marked a turning point in LITTLE FEAT's musical evolution. The opening salvo of 'ROCK AND ROLL DOCTOR' and 'OH ATLANTA' were skintight R&B numbers, entertaining but hardly possessed of the trademark LITTLE FEAT genius. The VAN DYKE PARKS-produced 'SPANISH MOON' was more like it, slinky and sexy with a louche, after-midnight feel. Elsewhere on the album, there was a worrying move towards jazz fusion noodling, PAYNE and BARRERE muscling in on the songwriting as GEORGE took a backseat. This was partly due to his belief in band deomcracy and increasingly due to his immersion in more hedonistic pleasures rendering the ever more girthsome GEORGE unable to exert full control over the band's direction. Ironically, just as LOWELL began to retreat, Warner Brothers began to show some support, sending the band on a European package tour with The DOOBIE BROTHERS, MONTROSE, TOWER OF POWER etc., early in 1975. The London show became the stuff of legend, GEORGE and Co. receiving a rapturous reception that lasted well into the DOOBIE's set. 'THE LAST RECORD ALBUM' (1975) confirmed the worst, however,

PAYNE/BARRERE collaborations dominating proceedings. While the likes of 'ALL THAT YOU DREAM' was charming, its jazz-pop sound strayed far from the path of LITTLE FEAT's original vision. Of GEORGE's contributions, 'LONG DISTANCE LOVE' saw him at his bittersweet best while 'DOWN BELOW THE BORDERLINE' and 'MERCENARY TERRITORY' showed his songwriting had lost none of its bite. 'TIME LOVES A HERO' (1977) continued the descent into WEATHER REPORT territory while the double concert set, 'WAITING FOR COLUMBUS' (1978) was met with mixed reviews, revealing little of the fire and spark that marked the numerous live bootlegs on the market. GEORGE had already released his solo album, 'THANKS, I'LL EAT IT HERE' (1979) by the time the band embarked on recording sessions for 'DOWN ON THE FARM' (1979). By the time the latter had been completed, LOWELL had left the band completely although a number of his compositions featured, notably the lovely 'KOKOMO'. Bloated and tired, LOWELL's heart finally packed in on him that summer (29th June) while promoting his album. Tragically cut down in his prime (aged just 34), GEORGE may have suffered a typical rock'n'roll death, but he was no ordinary musician; revered by everyone from MICK JAGGER to JIMMY PAGE, the man was a one-off, a troubled genius whose music had the rare power to move hearts, minds and feet and whose ultimate potential will sadly never be realised. LITTLE FEAT was subsequently reformed in the mid-80's by ESTRADA, PAYNE and HAYWARD together with past collaborator FRED TACKET and CRAIG FULLER (ex-PURE PRAIRIE LEAGUE). The new-look 'FEAT released a string of listenable, if ultimately forgettable albums in 'LET IT ROLL' (1988), 'SHAKE ME UP' (1991) and 'AIN'T HAD ENOUGH FUN' (1995), succeeding in keeping the name alive if not exactly adding to the legacy. The addition of sandpaper-throated female vocalist SHAUN MURPHY lent 'UNDER THE RADAR' (1998) an extra dimension, with the likes of 'CALLING THE CHILDREN HOME' attempting to reprise the old New Orleans magic with at least some degree of success. 'CHINESE WORK SONGS' (2000) was another worthy if hardly essential chapter in the band's second coming, turning in a rootsy cover of Bob Dylan's 'IT TAKES A LOT TO LAUGH, IT TAKES A TRAIN TO CRY'. • **Covered:** HOW MANY MORE YEARS (Howlin' Wolf) / ON YOUR WAY DOWN (Allen Toussaint) / etc. LOWELL solo:- EASY MONEY (Rickie Lee Jones) / + a few more.

Album rating: LITTLE FEAT (*6) / SAILIN' SHOES (*8) / DIXIE CHICKEN (*9) / FEATS DON'T FAIL ME NOW (*8) / THE LAST RECORD ALBUM (*7) / TIME LOVES A HERO (*7) / WAITING FOR COLOMBUS (*6) / DOWN ON THE FARM (*5) / HOY-HOY collection (*7) / AS TIME GOES BY – THE BEST OF LITTLE FEAT compilation (*9) / LET IT ROLL (*5) / REPRESENTING THE MAMBO (*4) / SHAKE ME UP (*4) / AIN'T HAD ENOUGH FUN (*5) / LIVE FROM NEON PARK (*4) / UNDER THE RADAR (*5) / CHINESE WORK SONGS (*5) / Lowell George: THANKS, I'LL EAT IT HERE (*6)

LOWELL GEORGE (b.13 Apr'45) – vocals, guitar (ex-MOTHERS OF INVENTION/**ZAPPA**) / **ROY ESTRADA** (b. Santa Ana) – bass, vocals (ex-MOTHERS OF INVENTION/ZAPPA) / **BILL PAYNE** (b.12 Mar'49, Waco, Texas) – keyboards, vocals (ex-FRATERNITY OF MAN) / **RICHIE HAYWARD** – drums (ex-FRATERNITY OF MAN)

Warners Warners

May 70. (7") *<7431>* **STRAWBERRY FLATS. / HAMBURGER MIDNIGHT** [–] [ ]

Nov 70. (lp) *(K 46072) <1890>* **LITTLE FEAT** [ ] [ ]
– Snakes on everything / Strawberry flats / Truck stop girl / Brides of Jesus / Willin' / Hamburger midnight; (a) Forty four blues, (b) How many more years / Crack in your door / I've been the one / Takin' my time / Crazy Captain Gunboat Willie. *<(cd-iss. Dec93; 7599 27189-2)>*

May 72. (7") *<7553>* **EASY TO SLIP. / CAT FEVER** [–] [ ]

May 72. (lp) *(K 46156) <2600>* **SAILIN' SHOES** [ ] [ ]
– Easy to slip / Cold cold cold / Trouble / Tripe face boogie / Willin' / Apolitical blues / Sailin' shoes / Teenage nervous breakdown / Got no shadows / Cat fever / Texas rose cafe. *<(cd-iss. 1988; K2 46156)> <(cd re-iss. May95; 7599 27258-2)>*

— **KENNY GRADNEY** (b. New Orleans) – bass (ex-DELANEY AND BONNY) repl. ESTRADA who joined CAPTAIN BEEFHEART & HIS MAGIC BAND / added **PAUL BARRERE** (b. 3 Jul'48, Burbank, California) – guitar, vocals / **SAM CLAYTON** – congas / **BONNIE BRAMLETT** – guest vocals

Nov 72. (7") *<7689>* **DIXIE CHICKEN. / LAFAYETTE RAILROAD** [–] [ ]

Feb 73. (lp) *(K 46200) <2686>* **DIXIE CHICKEN** [ ] [ ]
– Dixie chicken / Two trains / Roll um easy / On your way down / Kiss it off / Fool yourself / Walkin' all night / Fat man in the bathtub / Juliette / Lafayette railroad. *(cd-iss. Jul88; K2 46200)*

— Band split for 6 months (Oct '73-May '74). BILL joined DOOBIE BROTHERS and others, mainly LOWELL went into sessions. The sextet re-formed May74

Jul 74. (7") *<8054>* **OH ATLANTA. / DOWN THE ROAD** [–] [ ]

Sep 74. (7") *<8091>* **SPANISH MOON. / DOWN THE ROAD** [–] [ ]

Sep 74. (lp) *(K 56030) <2784>* **FEATS DON'T FAIL ME NOW** [ ] [36]
– Rock and roll doctor / Cold cold cold / Tripe face boogie / The fan / Oh Atlanta / Skin it back / Down the road / Spanish moon / Down the road / Feats don't fail me now. *(cd-iss. Jan89; K2 56030)*

Feb 75. (7") *(K 16524)* **DIXIE CHICKEN. / OH ATLANTA** [ ] [–]

Nov 75. (lp/c) *(K/K4 56156) <3015>* **THE LAST RECORD ALBUM** [36] [36]
– Romance dance / All that you dream / Long distance love / Day or night / One love / Down below the borderline / Somebody's leavin' / Mercenary territory. *(cd-iss. Jul88; K2 56156)*

Feb 76. (7") *(K 16689)* **LONG DISTANCE LOVE. / ROMANCE DANCE** [ ] Oct75 [ ]

Feb 76. (7") *<8219>* **ALL THAT YOU DREAM. / ONE LOVE** [–] [ ]

May 77. (lp/c) *(K/K4 56349) <3140>* **TIME LOVES A HERO** [8] [34]
– Time loves a hero / Hi roller / New elhi freight train / Old folks boogie / Red streamliner / Keepin' up with the Joneses / Rocket in my pocket / Missin' you / Day at the dog races. *(cd-iss. Jul88; K2 56349)*

Jun 77. (7") *<8420>* **TIME LOVES A HERO. / SAILIN' SHOES** [–] [ ]

Jul 77. (7") *(K 16694)* **TIME LOVES A HERO. / ROCKET IN MY POCKET** [ ] [–]

Mar 78. (d-lp/d-c) *(K/K4 66075) <3140>* **WAITING FOR COLUMBUS (live)** [43] [18]
– Join the band / Fat man in the bathtub / All that you dream / Oh Atlanta / Old folks boogie / Time loves a hero / Day or night / Mercenary territory / Spanish moon / Dixie chicken / Tripe face boogie / Rocket in my pocket / Don't bogart that joint / Willin' / Apolitical blues / Sailin' shoes / Feats don't fail me now. *<(cd-iss. Dec93; 7599 2734-2)> <(d-cd-iss. Apr02 on 'Rhino'+=; 8122 78274-2)>* – One love stand / Rock & roll doctor / Skin it back / On your way down / Walkin' all night / Cold, cold, cold / Day at the dog races / Skin it back / Red streamliner / Teenage nervous breakdown.

Jul 78. (7") *<8566>* **WILLIN' (live). / OH ATLANTA (live)** [–] [ ]

Oct 79. (lp/c) *(K/K4 56667) <3345>* **DOWN ON THE FARM** [46] [29]
– Down on the farm / Six feet of snow / Perfect imperfection / Kokomo / Be one now / Straight from the heart / Front page news / Wake up dreaming / Feel the groove. *(cd-iss. Jul88; K2 56667)*

— They had by this time split (Apr79). BARRERE and CLAYTON joined NICOLETTE LARSON. BARRERE went solo '83 and released 'ON MY OWN TWO FEET'. The others went into sessions.

LOWELL GEORGE

— - solo (vocals, guitar) with **FRED TACKETT** – guitar / **EDDIE ZIP** – keyboards,vocals / **PETER WASNER** – keyboards / **JERRY JUMONVILLE** – saxophone / **LEE THORNBERG** – trumpet / **MAXINE DIXON** – b. vocals / **ARMANDO COMPION** – bass / **DON HEFFINGTON** – drums

Warners Warners

Apr 79. (7") *<8847>* **WHAT DO YOU WANT THE GIRL TO DO. / 20 MILLION THINGS** [–] [ ]

Apr 79. (lp/c) *(K/K4 56487) <3194>* **THANKS, I'LL EAT IT HERE** [ ] [71]
– What do you want the girl to do / Honest man / Two trains / Can't stand the rain / Cheek to cheek / Easy money / 20 million things / Find a river / Himmler's ring. *(cd-iss. Dec93; 7599 26755-2)*

Jul 79. (7") *(K 17379)* **CHEEK TO CHEEK. / HONEST MAN** [ ] [–]

— Tragically LOWELL died 29th June '79 of a drug induced heart attack. He had gigged the night before. In 1983, PAUL BARRERE issued his debut album 'ON MY OWN TWO FEET' for 'Mirage'; *25-0093-1/-4)*

LITTLE FEAT

—— re-formed 1988. (**BARRERE, PAYNE, HAYWARD & FRED TACKETT**) plus **CRAIG FULLER** – vocals (ex-PURE PRAIRIE LEAGUE) / **KENNY GRADNEY** – bass / **SAM CLAYTON** – percussion, vocals

Warners Warners

Jul 88. (lp/c)(cd) *(WX 192/+C)(925750-2) <25750>* **LET IT ROLL** [ ] [36]
– Hate to lose your lovin' / One clear moment / Cajun girl / Hangin' on to the good times / Listen to your heart / Let it roll / Long time till I get over you / Business as usual / Changin' luck / Voices on the wind.

Jul 88. (7") *<27728>* **HATE TO LOSE YOUR LOVIN'. / CAJUN GIRL** [–] [ ]

Sep 88. (7") *<27684>* **ONE CLEAR MOMENT. / CHANGIN' LUCK** [–] [ ]

Apr 90. (cd/c/lp) *<(7599 26163-2/-4/-1)>* **REPRESENTING THE MAMBO** [ ] [45]
– Texas twister / Daily grind / Representing the mambo / Woman in love / Rad gumbo / Teenage warrior / That's her, she's mine / Feelin's all gone / Those feet'll steer ya wrong sometimes / The ingenue / Silver screen.

Polydor Morgan Creek

Sep 91. (c-s) *<23005>* **SHAKE ME UP** [–] [ ]

Oct 91. (cd/c/lp) *(511310-2/-4/-1) <20005>* **SHAKE ME UP** [ ] [ ]
– Spider's blues (might need it sometime) / Shake me up / Things happen / Mojo haiku / Loved and lied to / Don't try so hard / Boom boy car / Fast & furious / Livin' on dreams / Clownin' / Down in flames.

Oct 91. (c-s) *<3007>* **THINGS HAPPEN** [–] [ ]

—— **SHAUN MURPHY** – vocals; repl. FULLER

Zoo Zoo

Jun 95. (cd/c/lp) *<(72445 11097-2/-4/-1)>* **AIN'T HAD ENOUGH FUN** [ ] [ ]
– Drivin' blind / Blue jean blues / Cadillac hotel / Romance without finance / Big bang theory / Cajun rage / Heaven's where you find it / Borderline blues / All that you can stand / Rock & roll every night / Shakeytown / Ain't had enough fun / That's a pretty good love.

Jun 96. (d-cd) *<11129>* **LIVE FROM NEON PARK (live)** [–] [ ]
– (introductions) / Two trains / Spanish moon – Skin it back / Rock & roll every night / Down on the farm / Willin' / Hate to lose / Can't be satisfied – They're red hot / Cadillac hotel / Changin' luck / You're taking up another man's place / Oh, Atlanta / Texas twister / Fat man in the bathtub / Representing the mambo / Long distance love / Rad gumbo / Dixie chicken / Feats don't fail me now / Sailin' shoes / Let it roll – High roller.

S.P.V. C.M.C.

Aug 98. (cd) *(SPV 0852924-2) <86253>* **UNDER THE RADAR** [ ] Jun98 [ ]
– Home ground / Eden's wall / A distant thunder / Hoy hoy / Under the radar / Vale of tears / Loco motives / Ferocious morning / Voiceless territory (intro to Falling through the worlds) / Falling through the worlds / The blues don't tell it all / I got happiness / Calling the children home.

Jun 00. (cd) *(SPV 0857100-2) <607686295-2>* **CHINESE WORK SONGS** [ ] [ ]
– Rag mama rag / Evla / Bed of roses / Sample in a jar / Just another Sunday / Gimme a stone / Rio Esperenza / Tattoo heart / Marginal creatures / Chinese work songs / It takes a lot to laugh, it takes a train to cry.

– compilations, etc. –

on 'Warners' unless otherwise mentioned

Oct 75. (d-lp) *(K 66038)* **TWO ORIGINALS OF LITTLE FEAT** [ ] [–]
– (LITTLE FEAT / DIXIE CHICKEN).

Aug 81. (d-lp/d-c) *(K/K4 66100) <3538>* **HOY-HOY!** (remixes of rare material) [76] [39]
– Rocket in my pocket / Rock and roll doctor / Skin it back / Easy to slip / Red streamliner / Lonesome whistle / Front page news / The fan / Forty-four blues: How many more years / Teenage nervous breakdown (live) / Framed / Strawberry flats / Gringo / Over the edge / Two trains / China white / All that you dream / Feats don't fail me now. *<(cd-iss. Jul02; WB 3538)>*

Aug 81. (7") *<49801>* **EASY TO SLIP. / FRONT PAGE NEWS** [–] [ ]

Oct 81. (7") *<49841>* **GRINGO. / STRAWBERRY FLATS** [–] [ ]

Aug 86. (lp/c)(cd) *(WX 36/+C)(240 863-2)* **THE BEST OF LITTLE FEAT – AS TIME GOES BY** [ ] [–]
– Dixie chicken / Willin' / Rock and roll doctor / Two trains *[cd-only *]* / Truck stop girl *[cd-only *]* / Fat man in the bathtub *[cd-only *]* / Trouble / Sailin' shoes / Spanish moon / Feats don't fail me now / Oh, Atlanta *[cd-only *]* / All that you dream / Long distance love / Mercenary territory / Rocket in my pocket *[cd-only *]* / Texas twister *[cd-only*]* / Let it roll *[cd-only *]* / Hate to lose your lovin' *[cd-only *]* / Old folks boogie / Twenty million things. *(cd re-iss. Aug93 * <US Feb94 *>; 9548 32247-2)*

Oct 00. (4xcd-box) *Rhino; <(8122 79912-2)>* **HOTCAKES & OUTTAKES** [ ] Sep00 [ ]

Aug 01. (d-cd) *Burning Airlines; (PILOT 110)* **LATE NIGHT TRUCK STOP (live from Denver 1973)** [ ] [–]
(d-lp-iss.Nov02 on 'Fruit Tree'; FT 823)

Nov 01. (d-cd) *S.P.V.; <(31071180)>* **UNDER THE RADAR / CHINESE WORK SONGS** [ ] [ ]

Jul 02. (d-cd) *Hot Tomato; <(HTR 0203)>* **RAW TOMATOS: VOLUME ONE (live and rare)** [ ] Jun02 [ ]

Jul 02. (d-cd) *Hot Tomato; <(HTR 0204)>* **RIPE TOMATOS: VOLUME ONE** (live and rare) [ ] Jun02 [ ]

Nov 02. (d-cd) *Hot Tomato; <(HTR 0205)>* **LIVE AT THE RAMS HEAD (live)** [ ] [ ]

Jan 03. (12"/cd-s) *S.P.V.; <293-9/-0>* **A DISTANT THUNDER / HOME GROUND** [–] [ ]

Sep 03. (d-cd) *Hot Tomato; <(HTR 0206)>* **DOWN UPON THE SUWANNEE RIVER** [ ] Jul03 [ ]

Nov 03. (cd) *Hot Tomato; <(HTR 0208)>* **KICKIN' IT AT THE BARN** [ ] [ ]

LITTLE RICHARD

Born: RICHARD WAYNE PENNIMAN, 5 Dec'35, Macon, Georgia, USA, raised in a large family by preacher parents who schooled him in the ways of gospel singing. Aged 16, the petite RICHARD was given the opportunity (through singer, BILLY WRIGHT) to record for 'RCA-Victor'. After four flop singles for the imprint, LITTLE RICHARD subsequently moved on to Don Robey's 'Peacock' label in 1953, where he sessioned for doo-wop group, The TEMPO-TOPPERS. After fronting The JOHNNY OTIS ORCHESTRA in 1955, the man signed a solo deal with 'Specialty'. His first single for the label, 'TUTTI FRUTTI', gave him his maiden entry into the US Top 20. Outrageously attired in flamboyant pink body-suits, this eccentric, clowning pioneer of rock'n'roll, was like nothing the white music establishment had ever encountered; in both his image and his hollering, tongue-in-cheek assault, the effeminate RICHARD borrowed nothing from his contemporaries. Over the course of the next few years, he flounced his way through a series of classic hits which would subsequently become standards:- 'LONG TALL SALLY', 'RIP IT UP', 'THE GIRL CAN'T HELP IT' (exposure from the rock'n'roll movie of the same name gave him yet another UK hit), 'LUCILLE', 'JENNY, JENNY', 'KEEP A KNOCKIN' and 'GOOD GOLLY, MISS MOLLY'. At the height of his fame, RICHARD was to publicly renounce his "evil" rock'n'roll music/lifestyle, reverting back to gospel and pledging his life to Jeeesus. In 1960, the now Rev. LITTLE RICHARD spent a couple of years under the production of QUINCY JONES, returning to rock'n'roll in 1964. Although he had a few minor hits, including 'BAMA LAMA BAMA LOO', his new material was overshadowed by British acts covering his earlier work. In the 70's, RICHARD released a few albums, while collaborating with the likes of CANNED HEAT and DELANEY & BONNIE, swinging back and fourth between rock'n'roll and God, homosexuality and heterosexuality. By the mid 80's, the veteran showman was back in the limelight when he took up the offer to appear in the movie, 'Down And Out In Beverley Hills'. From then on in, LITTLE RICHARD has successfully kept his profile high via guest spots in TV series including 'Miami Vice', while also fraternising with top named celebrities such as ELTON JOHN, TANYA TUCKER and er, KERMIT THE FROG!

Best CD compilation: 20 CLASSIC CUTS (*8)

LITTLE RICHARD – vocals, piano + sessions

not iss. | RCA Victor

1952. (7") *<4392>* **EVERY HOUR. / TAXI BLUES** [–] [ ]
1952. (7") *<4582>* **GET RICH QUICK. / THINKIN' 'BOUT MY MOTHER** [–] [ ]
1952. (7") *<4772>* **WHY DID YOU LEAVE. / AIN'T NOTHIN' HAPPENIN'** [–] [ ]
1953. (7") *<5025>* **I BROUGHT IT ALL ON MYSELF. / PLEASE HAVE MERCY ON ME** [–] [ ]

The TEMPO-TOPPERS featuring LITTLE RICHARD

not iss. | Peacock

1953. (7") *<1616>* **AIN'T THAT GOOD NEWS. / FOOL AT THE WHEEL** [–] [ ]
1954. (7") *<1628>* **ALWAYS. / RICE, RED BEANS & TURNIP GREENS** [ ] [ ]

—— On the same label, he joined The JOHNNY OTIS BAND in 1955. They released 2

1955. (7") *<1658>* **LITTLE RICHARD BOOGIE. / DIRECTLY FROM MY HEART TO YOU** [–] [ ]
1955. (7") *<1673>* **MAYBE I'M RIGHT. / I LOVE MY BABY** [–] [ ]

LITTLE RICHARD

went solo again, backed by **RED TYLER** – saxophone / **LEE ALLEN** – saxophone / **FRANK FIELDS** – bass / **ERNEST McLEAN & JUSTIN ADAMS** – guitar / **EARL PALMER** – drums / plus pianists **HUEY SMITH, EDWARD FRANK, LITTLE BOOKER & SALVADOR DOUCHETTE.**

London | Specialty

Dec 55. (7") *<561>* **TUTTI FRUTTI. / I'M JUST A LONELY GUY** [–] [17]
Mar 56. (7") *<572>* **LONG TALL SALLY. / SLIPPIN' AND SLIDIN' (PEEPIN' AND HIDIN')** [–] [6] [33]
Jul 56. (7",78) *(HLO 8336) <579>* **RIP IT UP. / READY TEDDY** [30] [17] [44]
1956. (7") *<584>* **SHE'S GOT IT. / HEEBIE JEEBIES** [–] [ ]
Jan 57. (7",78) *(HLO 8366)* **LONG TALL SALLY. / TUTTI FRUTTI** [3] [–] [29]
Feb 57. (7") *<591>* **THE GIRL CAN'T HELP IT. / ALL AROUND THE WORLD** [–] [49]
Feb 57. (7",78) *(HLO 8382)* **SHE'S GOT IT. / THE GIRL CAN'T HELP IT** [15] [–] [9]
Jun 57. (7",78) *(HLO 8446) <598>* **LUCILLE. / SEND ME SOME LOVIN'** [10] [21] Mar57 [54]
Jul 57. (lp) *(HA-O 2055) <2100>* **HERE'S LITTLE RICHARD** [ ] [13]
– Tutti frutti / True fine mama / Ready Teddy / Baby / Slippin' and slidin' (peepin' and hidin') / Long tall Sally / Miss Ann / Oh why / Rip it up / Jenny, Jenny / She's got it / Can't believe you wanna leave. *(re-iss. Feb85 on 'Ace'; CH 128) (cd-iss. Jun89; CDCHM 128)*
Aug 57. (7",78) *(HLO 8470) <606>* **JENNY, JENNY. / MISS ANN** [11] [14] Jun57 [56]
Nov 57. (7",78) *(HLO 8509) <611>* **KEEP A KNOCKIN'. / CAN'T BELIEVE YOU WANNA LEAVE** [21] Sep57 [8]
Feb 58. (7",78) *<HLU 8560) <624>* **GOOD GOLLY MISS MOLLY. / HEY HEY HEY HEY** [8] [10]
Jun 58. (7",78) *(HLO 8647) <633>* **OOH! MY SOUL. / TRUE FINE MAMA** [22] [31] [68]
Dec 58. (7",78) *(HLU 8770) <645>* **BABY FACE. / I'LL NEVER YOU GO** [2] Sep58 [41]
Dec 58. (lp) *(HA-U 2126) <2103>* **LITTLE RICHARD 2** [ ] [ ]
– Keep a knocking / Send me some lovin' / I'll never let you go / All around the world / By the light of the silvery Moon / Good golly Miss Molly / Baby face / Hey hey hey hey / Ooh my soul / Lucille / The girl can't help it. *(re-iss. Feb85 on 'Ace'; CH 131) (cd-iss. Jul89; CDCHM 131)*
Jan 59. (7") *<652>* **SHE KNOWS HOW TO ROCK. / EARLY ONE MORNING** [ ] [–]
Mar 59. (7") *<660>* **BY THE LIGHT OF THE SILVERY MOON. / WONDERING** [–] [ ]
Mar 59. (7",78) *(HLU 8831)* **BY THE LIGHT OF THE SILVERY MOON. / EARLY ONE MORNING** [17] [–]
May 59. (7",78) *(HLU 8868) <664>* **KANSAS CITY. / LONESOME AND BLUE** [26] [95]
1959. (lp) *(HA-U 2193) <2104>* **THE FABULOUS LITTLE RICHARD** [ ] [ ]
– Shake a hand / Chicken little baby / All night long / Most I can offer / Lonesome and blue / Wonderin' / Whole lotta shakin' goin' on / She knows how to rock / Kansas City / Directly from my heart / Maybe I'm right / Early one morning / I'm just a lonely girl. *(re-iss. Jul80 on 'Sonet'; SNTF 5027) (re-iss. Feb85 on 'Ace'; CH 133) (cd-iss. Aug89; CDCHM 133) (cd re-iss. Aug91 on 'Ace'; CDFAB 001)*
1959. (7") *<670>* **SHAKE A HAND. / ALL NIGHT LONG** [–] [ ]
1959. (7") *<680>* **WHOLE LOTTA SHAKIN' GOIN' ON. / MAYBE I'M RIGHT** [–] [ ]
Feb 60. (7",78) *(HLU 9065) <681>* **BABY. / I GOT IT** [ ] Dec 59 [ ]
1960. (7") *<686>* **DIRECTLY FROM MY HEART. / THE MOST I CAN OFFER** [–] [ ]

not iss. | Coral

1960. (7") *<62366>* **NEED HIM. / MILKY WHITE WAY** [–] [ ]

Mercury | Mercury

1961. (7") *(AMT 1165) <71884>* **HE'S NOT JUST A SOLDIER. / JOY JOY JOY** [ ] [ ]
1962. (7") *<71911>* **DO YOU CARE. / RIDE ON KING JESUS** [–] [ ]
Sep 62. (7") *(AMT 1189) <71965>* **HE GOT WHAT HE WANTED. / WHY DON'T YOU CHANGE YOUR WAYS** [38] [ ]

London | Woodman

Apr 63. (7") *(HLK 9708) <2181>* **CRYING IN THE CHAPEL. / HOLE IN THE WALL** [ ] [ ]
(re-dist.US 1963 on 'Atlantic')

London | Atlantic

Jul 63. (7") *(HLK 9756) <2192>* **TRAVELLIN' SHOES. / IT IS NO SECRET** [ ] [ ]
1964. (lp) *(LVA 9220) <757446>* **COMING HOME** [ ] [ ]
– ust a closer walk with thee / Coming home / Search me Lord / I want Jesus to walk with me / Milky white way / Need him / Every time I feel the spirit / Does Jesus care / God is real / I'm trampin' / Jesus walked this lonesome valley / Precious Lord.

London | Specialty

Apr 64. (7") *<692>* **BAMA LAMA BAMA LOO. / ANNIE'S BACK** [–] [82]
May 64. (7") *(HL 9896)* **BAMA LAMA BAMA LOO. / KEEP A KNOCKIN'** [20] [–]

Stateside | Vee-Jay

Sep 64. (7") *(SS 340) <612>* **WHOLE LOTTA SHAKIN' GOIN' ON. / GOODNIGHT IRENE** [ ] [ ]
1964. (7") *(SON 5001) <699>***POOR BOY PAUL. / WONDERIN'** [–] [ ]
(UK-iss.1976 on 'Specialty')

Stateside | 20th Century

1964. (lp) *(SL 10054)* **LITTLE RICHARD SINGS GOSPEL** [ ] [–]
– Every time I feel the spirit / I'm trampin' / Milky white way / Does Jesus care / Coming home / I know the Lord / I've just come from the fountain / God is real / Troubles of the world / Certainly Lord / Tell God my troubles / Precious Lord. *(re-iss. Jul82 on 'Bulldog')*

Mercury | Mercury

Jan 65. (7") *(MF 841)* **PEACE IN THE VALLEY. / JOY JOY JOY** [ ] [ ]
Jan 65. (lp) *(MCL 20036)* **IT'S REAL** [ ] [ ]
– It's real / Joy, joy, joy / Do you care / The captain calls for you / In times like these / Do Lord, remember me / Ride on King Jesus / (There'll be) Peace in the valley (for me) / He's not just a soldier / My desire / He's my star / It takes everything to serve the Lord.

Fontana | Vee-Jay

Jan 65. (7") *(H 519) <625>* **BLUEBERRY HILL. / CHERRY RED** [ ] [ ]
Feb 65. (lp) *(TL 5235) <1107>* **LITTLE RICHARD IS BACK!** [ ] [ ]
– A whole lotta shakin' goin' on / Going home tomorrow / Money honey / Only you ./ Hound dog / Goodnight Irene / Lawdy Miss Clawdy / Groovy little Suzy / Short Fat Fanny / Cherry red / Memories are made of this / Blueberry hill. *<re-iss Jul68 on 'Joy'; 100>*
Oct 65. (7") *(H 652) <698>* **I DON'T KNOW WHAT YOU'VE GOT BUT IT'S GOT ME. / (Part 2)** [ ] [92]

Sue — Vee-Jay

Feb 66. (7") *(SR 4001)* <665> **WITHOUT LOVE. / DANCE WHAT YOU WANNA** [ ] [ ]

Jul 66. (7") *(WI 4015)* <652> **CROSS OVER. / IT AIN'T WHAT'CHA DO** [ ] [ ]

Stateside — Modern

May 66. (7") *(SS 508)* <1018> **HOLY MACKERAL. / BABY DON'T YOU WANT A MAN LIKE ME** [ ] [ ]

1966. (7") <1019> **DO YOU FEEL IT. / (Part 2)** [–] [ ]

1966. (7") <1022> **DIRECTLY FROM THE HEART. / I'M BACK** [–] [ ]

1966. (7") <1043> **BABY WHAT YOU WANT ME TO DO. / (Part 2)** [–] [ ]
<re-iss. Feb69 on 'Action'>

not iss. — Kent

1966. (7") <4567> **IN THE NAME. / DON'T YOU KNOW I** [–] [ ]

Columbia — Okeh

1966. (7") *(DB 7974)* <7251> **POOR DOG (WHO CAN'T WAG HIS TAIL). / WELL** [ ] [ ]

1966. (7") *(DB 8058)* <7262> **I NEED LOVE. / THE COMMANDMENTS OF LOVE** [ ] [ ]

Jan 67. (7") *(DB 8116)* **GET DOWN WITH IT. / ROSEMARY** [ ] [–]

Apr 67. (7") *(DB 8263)* <7271> **HURRY SUNDOWN. / I DON'T WANT TO DISCUSS IT** [–] [ ]

May 67. (lp) *(6136)* <14117> **THE EXPLOSIVE LITTLE RICHARD** [ ] [ ]
– I don't want to discuss it / Land of a 1000 dances / Commandments of love / Money / Poor dog / I need love / Never gonna let you go / Don't deceive me / Function at the junction / Well. *(cd-iss. Nov97 on 'Beat Goes On'; BGOCD 368)*

1967. (7") <7278> **DON'T DECEIVE ME (PLEASE DON'T GO). / NEVER GONNA LET YOU GO** [–] [ ]

Jul 67. (7") *(DB 8240)* **LITTLE BIT OF SOMETHING. / MONEY** [ ] [ ]

Aug 67. (lp) <14121> **LITTLE RICHARD'S GREATEST HITS (live)** [–] [ ]
<re-iss. Jul68 on 'Joy'; 100>

1967. (7") <7325> **LUCILLE. / WHOLE LOTTA SHAKIN' GOIN' ON** [–] [ ]

M.C.A. — Brunswick

Mar 68. (7") *(MU 1006)* <55362> **TRY SOME OF MINE. / SHE'S TOGETHER** [ ] [–]

1968. (7") <55377> **TEAR MY CLOTHES. / STINGY JENNY** [–] [ ]

1968. (7") <55386> **SOUL TRAIN. / CAN I COUNT ON YOU** [–] [ ]

Reprise — Reprise

Jun 70. (7") *(RS 20907)* <0907> **FREEDOM BLUES. / DEW DROP INN** [ ] [47]

Aug 70. (7") <0942> **GREENWOOD MISSISSIPPI. / I SAW HER STANDING THERE** [–] [85]

1970. (lp) <(RSLP 6406)> **THE RILL THING** [ ] [ ]
– Freedom blues / Greenwood, Mississippi / Two-time loser / Dew Drop Inn / Somebody saw you / Spreadin' Natta, what's the matter / The rill thing / Lovesick blues / I saw her standing there.

1971. (7") <1005> **SHAKE A HAND. / SOMEBODY SAW YOU** [–] [ ]

Nov 71. (lp) *(K 44156)* <6462> **THE KING OF ROCK AND ROLL** [ ] [ ]
– King of rock'n'roll / Joy to the world / Brown sugar / In the name / Dancing in the street / Midnight special / The way you do the things you do / Green power / I'm so lonesome I could die / Settin' the woods on fire / Born on the bayou. *(re-iss. Jul88 on 'Entertainers' lp/c; ENT LP/MC 13044) (cd-iss. same; ENTCD 264)*

Dec 71. (7") **SHAKE A HAND. / SOMEBODY SAW YOU** [ ] [–]

Feb 72. (7") *(K 14150)* <1062> **MONEY RUNNER. / MONEY IS** [ ] [ ]

1972. (7") *(K 14915)* **MOCKINGBIRD SALLY. / ROCKIN' ROCKIN' BOOGIE** [ ] [ ]

1972. (lp) *(K 44024)* <2107> **THE SECOND COMING** [ ] [ ]
– Mockingbird Sally / It ain't what you do, it's the way that you do it / The saints / Nuki Suki / Rockin' rockin' boogie / Prophet of peace / Thomasine / Sanctified, satisfied toe-tapper.

— (Around this time, he teamed up with CANNED HEAT on lp, 'ROCKIN' WITH THE KING')

not iss. — Green Mountain

1973. (7") <413> **IN THE MIDDLE OF THE NIGHT. / WHERE WILL I FIND A PLACE TO SLEEP THIS EVENING** [–] [ ]

Reprise — not iss.

1974. (7"ep) *(K 14343)* **ROCKIN' ROLLIN' BOOGIE / KING OF THE ROCK'N'ROLL / SAINTS / MOCKINGBIRD SALLY** [ ] [–]

not iss. — Atlantic

1976. (7") *<7007>* **CALL MY NAME. / STEAL MISS LIZA** [ ] [ ]

not iss. — Mainstream

1979. (lp) **GOD'S BEAUTIFUL CITY** [–] [ ]

1980. (7") <5572> **TRY TO HELP YOUR BROTHER. / (part 2)** [ ] [ ]

— Next from film 'Down And Out In Beverley Hills'

M.C.A. — M.C.A.

Feb 86. (7") *(MCA 1049)* <52780> **GREAT GOSH A'MIGHTY (IT'S A MATTER OF TIME). / THE RIDE** [ ] [42]
(12"+=) *(MCAT 1049)* – Down and out in Beverley Hills.

W.E.A. — Warners

Oct 86. (7"/12") *(YZ 89/+T)* **OPERATOR. / BIG HOUSE REUNION** [ ] [ ]

Oct 86. (lp/c)(cd) *(WX 72/+C)(242018-2)* <42018> **LIFETIME FRIEND** [ ] [ ]
– Great gosh a'mighty (it's a matter of time) / Operator / Somebody's comin' / Destruction / I found my way / The world can't do me / One ray of sunshine / Someone cares / Big house reunion.

Jan 87. (7") *(YZ 98)* **SOMEBODY'S COMIN'. / ONE RAY OF SUNSHINE** [ ] [ ]

Atco — Atco

Nov 87. (7"pic-d/12"pic-d; LITTLE RICHARD & The BEACH BOYS) *(B 9392/+TP)* <99392> **HAPPY ENDING. / CALIFORNIA GIRLS** [ ] [ ]

— collaborated with PHILIP BAILEY (Earth, Wind & Fire) on the the single, 'TWINS', which was from the film of the same name

not iss. — Disney

1992. (cd/c) <60849-2/-4> **SHAKE IT ALL ABOUT** (childrens) [–] [ ]

– (selective) compilations, etc. –

1974. (lp) *Ember; (EMB 3434)* **FRIENDS FROM THE BEGINNING (with JIMI HENDRIX)** [ ] [–]
(cd-iss. Mar98; EMBCD 3434)

Jun 77. (7"m) *Creole; (CR 140)* **GOOD GOLLY MISS MOLLY. / RIP IT UP / BY THE LIGHT OF THE SILVERY MOON** [37] [–]

Oct 77. (lp) *Creole; (CRLP 510)* **LITTLE RICHARD – NOW** [ ] [–]
(cd-iss. Jun93 & Aug01 on 'Rhino'; RNCD 1007)

1980. (lp) *Charly; (CR 30190)* **GEORGIA PEACH** [ ] [–]

Dec 86. (lp) *Ace; (CH 195)* **20 CLASSIC CUTS** [ ] [–]
– Long tall Sally / Ready Teddy / The girl can't help it / Rip it up / Miss Ann / She's got it / Lucille / Keep a knockin' / Good golly Miss Molly / Send me some lovin' / Hey-hey-hey-hey / Slippin' and slidin' / Tutti frutti / Heeby jeebies / Baby face / Jenny Jenny / By the light of the silvery Moon / Ooh! my soul / True fine mama / Bama lama bama loo. *(re-iss. Jul90 +=; CDCH/CCH 195)* – Can't believe you leave / I'll never let you go.

Oct 89. (8xlp-box/6xc-box/6xcd-box) *Ace; (ABOX LP/MC/CD 1)* **THE SPECIALITY SESSIONS** [ ] [–]
(3xcd-box re-iss. Aug02 on 'Speciality'; 3SPCD 8508)

Jul 90. (cd) *Ace; (CDCHD 109)* **HIS GREATEST RECORDINGS** [ ] [ ]

Oct 90. (3xcd-box) *Ace; (ABOXCD 2)* **HERE'S LITTLE RICHARD / VOLUME 2 / THE FABULOUS LITTLE RICHARD** [ ] [ ]

Feb 93. (cd) *Charly; (CDCD 1014)* **THE WILDEST** [ ] [–]

Mar 93. (cd) *See For Miles; (SEECD 366)* **THE E.P. COLLECTION** [ ] [–]

Jun 95. (cd) *Collection; (COL 006)* **LITTLE RICHARD COLLECTION** [ ] [ ]

Oct 96. (cd) *Summit; (SUMCD 4019)* **THE VERY BEST OF LITTLE RICHARD** [ ] [–]

May 97. (cd/c) *A-Play; (10154-2/-4)* **HITS COLLECTION** [ ] [–]

Aug 01. (cd) *Ace; (CDCHM 729)* **THE ORIGINAL BRITISH HIT SINGLES** [ ] [ ]

Feb 01. (cd) *R.P.M.; (RPMSH 217)* **TALKING 'BOUT SOUL** [ ] [ ]

Jul 02. (d-cd) *Snapper; (SMDCD 413)* **ROCKIN' WITH THE GEORGIA PEACH** [ ] [ ]

Nov 02. (cd) *Repertoire; (REP 4876)* **THE BEST OF LITTLE RICHARD: KEEP A KNOCKIN'** [ ] [ ]

Nov 02. (cd) *Planet Media; (PML 1125)* **GOOD GOLLY MISS MOLLY** [ ] [–]

Aug 03. (cd) *Castle Pulse; (PLS CD/MC 625)* **ROCKIN' WITH LITTLE RICHARD** [ ] [ ]

☐ LITTLE VILLAGE (see under ⇒ LOWE, Nick)

LIVE

Formed: York, Pennsylvania, USA ... early 90's by EDWARD KOWALCZYK, CHAD TAYLOR, PATRICK DAHLHEIMER and CHAD GRACEY. Coming up with a moniker that both displayed a complete lack of imagination and confused prospective fans, they nevertheless released a competent neo-grunge debut, 'MENTAL JEWELRY' (1991). Produced by JERRY HARRISON (ex-TALKING HEADS), the record (on MCA subsidiary, 'Radioactive') found a large US audience with its rather derivative hybrid of PEARL JAM and R.E.M. Three years in the making, 'THROWING COPPER' eventually scaled the US charts, largely due to a clutch of harder-edged tracks/singles such as, 'SELLING THE DRAMA' and the MTV fave, 'I ALONE'. These semi-classics also cracked the British charts, setting the scene for a show-stealing (LIVE!) slot at the 1995 Glastonbury Fest. A third album, 'SECRET SAMADHI' (1997), repeated the winning formula, although the more discerning fans considered the album overproduced. In October '99, LIVE were back to their near best, the fourth set 'THE DISTANCE TO HERE' winning back most of the fans. While 'V' (2001) displayed as much of a talent for naming albums as the band wielded when trying to hit upon a name, the album itself was another progression in their high minded (a la KINGS X) alt-pop/rock, rewarded with their lowest US chart placing for some time (No.22). The rather ridiculously titled 'BIRDS OF PRAY' (2003) dealt with loftier themes in the wake of 9/11, often buckling under the weightiness of the lyrical topics and the sheer po-faced plod of the music. • **Covered:** LOVE MY WAY (Psychedelic Furs) / SUPERNATURAL (Vic Chesnutt).

Album rating: MENTAL JEWELRY (*6) / THROWING COPPER (*7) / SECRET SAMADHI (*5) / THE DISTANCE TO HERE (*6) / V (*5) / BIRDS OF PRAY (*5)

EDWARD KOWALCZYK – vocals, guitar / **CHAD TAYLOR** – guitar, vocals / **PATRICK DAHLHEIMER** – bass / **CHAD GRACEY** – drums, vocals

Radioactive Radioactive

Jan 92. (7") *<54387>* **PAIN LIES ON THE RIVERSIDE. / HEAVEN WORE A SHIRT** [–] [ ]

Apr 92. (lp/c/cd) *<(RAR/+C/D 10346)>* **MENTAL JEWELRY** [ ] Jan92 [73]
– Pain lies on the riverside / Operation spirit (the tyranny of tradition) / The beauty of Gray / Brothers unaware / Tired of me / Mirror song / Waterboy / Take my anthem / You are the world / Good pain / Mother Earth is a vicious crowd / 10,000 years (peace is now).

Apr 92. (cd-ep) *<54442>* **OPERATION SPIRIT (THE TYRANNY OF TRADITION) (live) / THE BEAUTY OF GRAY (live) / GOOD PAIN / LIES ON THE RIVERSIDE (live)** [–] [ ]

Jun 92. (7") *(RAX 1)* **OPERATION SPIRIT. / HEAVEN WORE A SKIRT** [ ] [–]
(12"+=/cd-s+=) *(RAX T/TD 1)* – Negation / Good pain.

May 94. (c-s) *<54816>* **SELLING THE DRAMA / LIGHTNING CRASHES** [–] [43]

Sep 94. (c-s/cd-s) *(RAX C/TD 11)* **SELLING THE DRAMA. / ('A'acoustic) / WHITE DISCUSSION** [ ] [–]

Oct 94. (cd/c) *<(RAD/RAC 10997)>* **THROWING COPPER** [37] May94 [1]
– The dam at Otter Creek / Selling the drama / I alone / Iris / Lightning crashes / Top / All over you / Shit towne / T.B.D. / Stage / Waitress / Pillar of Davidson / White discussion. *(cd hidden track +=)* – Horse.

Feb 95. (7"clear/c-s) *(RAX/+C 13)* **I ALONE. / PAIN LIES ON THE RIVERSIDE** [48] [–]
(cd-s+=) *(RAXTD 13)* – ('A'mix).

Jun 95. (c-s/cd-s) *(RAX C/TD 17)* **SELLING THE DRAMA / THE DAN AT OTTER CREEK** [30] [–]
(cd-s+=) *(RAXXD 17)* – ('A'acoustic).

Sep 95. (c-s) *(RAXC 20)* **ALL OVER YOU / SHIT TOWNE** [48] [–]
(cd-s+=) *(RAXTD 20)* – ('A'live at Glastonbury).
(cd-s) *(RAXXD 20)* – ('A'side) / Waitress (live) / Iris (live at Glastonbury).

Jan 96. (c-s/cd-s) *(RAX C/TD 23)* **LIGHTNING CRASHES / THE BEAUTY OF GRAY (bootleg) / TBD (acoustic)** [33] [–]
(cd-s) *(RAXXD 23)* – ('A'side) / ('A'-live at Glastonbury) / White discussion (live at Glastonbury).

Mar 97. (7"silver) *(RAX 28)* **LAKINI'S JUICE. / SUPERNATURAL (remix)** [29] [–]
(cd-s+=) *(RAXXD 28)* – White discussion (remix).
(cd-s) *(RAD 49023)* – ('A'side) / Pain lies on the riverside (remix) / Selling the drama (acoustic).

Mar 97. (cd/c/d-lp) *<(RAD/RAC/RAR2 11590)>* **SECRET SAMADHI** [31] [1]
– Rattlesnake / Lakini's juice / Graze / Century / Ghost / Unsheathed / Insomnia and the hole in the universe / Turn my head / Heropsychodreamer / Freaks / Merica / Gas Hed goes west.

Jun 97. (7") *(RAX 29)* **FREAKS. / LOVE MY WAY (live)** [60] Apr99 [ ]
(cd-s+=) *(RAXTD 29)* – Freaks (Labor, Labor, Labor remix).
(cd-s) *(RAXD 29) <49032>* – ('A'side) / Lakini's juice (live) / Freaks (live).

Oct 99. (cd) *(RAD 11966) <111966>* **THE DISTANCE TO HERE** [56] [4]
– The dolphin's cry / The distance / Sparkle / Run to the water / Sun / Voodoo lady / Where fishes go / Face and ghost (The children's song) / Feel the quiet river rage / Meltdown / They stood up for love / We walk in the dream / Dance with you.

Jan 00. (cd-s) *(RAXTD 39) <radio cut>* **THE DOLPHIN'S CRY / VINE STREET / LAKINI'S JUICE** [62] Nov99 [78]
(cd-s) *(RAXXD 39)* – ('A'side) / Sun (remix) / Turn my head (live) / The dolphin's cry (video).

Jul 00. (cd-s) *<155761>* **THEY STOOD UP FOR LOVE / RUN TO THE WATER (acoustic) / THE DISTANCE (acoustic) / ('A'-acoustic)** [–] [ ]
(cd-s) – ('A'side) / I alone (live acoustic) / The dolphin's cry (live acoustic) / ('A'-live acoustic).

Sep 01. (cd) *<(112485-2)>* **V** [ ] [22]
– Intro / Simple creed / Deep enough / Like a soldier / People like you / Transmit your love / Forever may not be long enough / Call me a fool / Flow / The ride / Nobody knows / OK? / Overcome / Hero of love. *(UK bonus+=)* – Deep enough (remix) / Simple creed (video).

Sep 01. (cd-s; as LIVE & TRICKY) *<155870>* **SIMPLE CREED / SHIT TOWN (live)** [–] [ ]

Dec 01. (cd-s) *<155915>* **OVERCOME / OVERCOME (acoustic)** [–] [ ]

May 03. (cd) *(RARW 32029) <37402>* **BIRDS OF PRAY** [ ] [28]
– Heaven / She / The sanctity of dreams / Run away / Life marches on / Like I do / Sweet release / Everytime I see your face / Lighthouse / River town / Out to dry / Bring the people together / What are we fighting for? *(UK+=)* – Forever may not be long enough / Overcome (live).

Nov 03. (cd-s) *<981246>* **SWEET RELEASE / LIGHTHOUSE / BEAUTY OF GRAY / THEY STOOD UP FOR LOVE / HEAVEN (video)** [–] [ ]

LIVING COLOUR

Formed: New York, USA ... 1984 by English-born guitarist VERNON REID, who had studied performing arts at Manhattan community college. 1986 saw the arrival of COREY GLOVER (vocals) and WILL CALHOUN (drums), with MUZZ SKILLINGS (bass) completing the line-up the following year. After MICK JAGGER clocked the band at a CBGB's gig, he invited the outfit to play on his 'Primitive Cool' album. The 'STONES frontman also produced two demos for the group, helping to secure them a deal with 'Epic'. LIVING COLOUR's debut album, 'VIVID' (1988) attracted a lot of attention if only because the band were an all-black outfit playing hard rock, not so surprising, and in reality a very interesting prospect. Leaving most of their junk-headed contemporaries at the starting post, LIVING COLOUR played rock with the invention of jazz and the spontaneity of funk. 'CULT OF PERSONALITY' was the album's highlight, a masterful blend of cutting political commentary and driving, spiralling riffs while 'GLAMOUR BOYS' was a playful piece of funk-pop vaguely reminiscent of PRINCE. But it was socially and politically aware material that formed the main thrust of the band's output, 'OPEN LETTER (TO A LANDLORD)' and 'WHICH WAY TO AMERICA' pointedly addressing the oppression of African-Americans to an eclectic, always soulful hard rock backing. The band became critical darlings, figureheads for the loose funk-rock movement that included The RED HOT CHILI PEPPERS and latterly FAITH NO MORE. They also won respect from many fellow musicians, REID contributing to KEITH RICHARDS' 'Talk Is Cheap' album, while the likes of LITTLE RICHARD, CARLOS SANTANA and MACEO PARKER all offered their services for LIVING COLOUR's follow-up effort, 'TIME'S UP' (1990). A wildly eclectic range of styles encompassed everything from hardcore thrash ('TYPE') to the PAUL SIMON ('GRACELAND'-era)-like 'SOLACE OF YOU', even spawning a UK Top 20 single with the meandering blues of 'LOVE REARS ITS UGLY HEAD'. Again the critics frothed although the album failed to match the commercial success of its predecessor. The 'BISCUITS' EP (1991) was a stop gap affair, hardly essential but worth hearing for inspired takes on JAMES BROWN's 'TALKIN' LOUD AND SAYING NOTHING' and HENDRIX's 'BURNING OF THE MIDNIGHT LAMP'. Shortly after the record's release, SKILLINGS departed, his replacement being ex-'Sugarhill' session man and TACKHEAD bassist DOUG WIMBISH. A third album, 'STAIN' (1993), a decidedly harder affair, failed to break any new ground or spark any increase in sales, the band eventually splitting two years later when founder REID decided to pursue solo projects (i.e. the 1996 album, 'MISTAKEN IDENTITY'). REID finally resurfaced with veteran sparring partner DJ LOGIC (both were founder members of the Black Rock Coalition) under the alias YOHIMBE BROTHERS. The pair's oblique, cerebral meeting of minds was showcased on 2002's 'FRONT END LIFTER'. LIVING COLOUR themselves returned in 2003 with the coruscating 'COLLIDEOSCOPE' album, railing at human bankruptcy and media manipulation with an unprecedented ferocity, and focusing on the blank terror of 9/11 with a numbing, dispassionate gaze. • **Covers:** SHOULD I STAY OR SHOULD I GO (Clash) / FINAL SOLUTION (Pere Ubu) / MEMORIES CAN'T WAIT (Talking Heads) / BURNING OF THE MIDNIGHT LAMP (Jimi Hendrix) / TALKING LOUD AND SAYING NOTHING (James Brown) / LOVE AND HAPPINESS (Al Green) / SUNSHINE OF YOUR LOVE (Cream). • **Trivia:** COREY played a smart-assed soldier in the Vietnam film, 'Platoon'.

Album rating: VIVID (*7) / TIME'S UP (*7) / STAIN (*6) / PRIDE: THE GREATEST HITS compilation (*7) / COLLIDEOSCOPE (*6) / Vernon Reid: MISTAKEN IDENTITY (*4)

COREY GLOVER (b. 6 Nov'64) – vocals / **VERNON REID** (b.22 Aug'58, London, England) – guitar / **MANUEL 'MUZZ' SKILLINGS** (b. 6 Jan'60, Queens, N.Y.) – bass / **WILLIAM CALHOUN** (b.22 Jul'64) – drums

Epic Epic

May 88. (7"/7"sha-pic-d) *(LCL/+P 1)* **MIDDLE MAN. / DESPERATE PEOPLE** [ ] [ ]
(12"+=/pic-cd-s+=) *(LCLT/CPLCL 1)* – Funny vibe.

May 88. (lp/c/cd) *(460 758-1/-4/-2) <44099>* **VIVID** [ ] [6]
– Cult of personality / I want to know / Middle man / Desperate people / Open letter (to a landlord) / Funny vibe / Memories can't wait / Broken hearts / Glamour boys / What's your favourite colour? / Which way to America?

Jul 88. (7"/7"g-f)(7"pic-d) *(LCL/+G 2)(CTLCL 2)* **GLAMOUR BOYS. / WHICH WAY TO AMERICA?** [ ] [ ]
(12"+=/cd-s+=) *(LCLT/CDLCD 2)* – Middle man / Rap track (conversation with LIVING COLOUR).

Sep 88. (7"/7"s) *(LCL/+B 3)* **CULT OF PERSONALITY. / OPEN LETTER (TO A LANDLORD)** [ ] [ ]
(12"+=/cd-s+=) *(LCLT/CDLCL 3)* – Middle Man (live).

Dec 88. (7"/7"s) *(LCL/+Q 4)* **OPEN LETTER (TO A LANDLORD). / CULT OF PERSONALITY (live)** [ ] [–]
(12"+=/cd-s+=) *(LCLT/CDLCL 4)* – Talkin' 'bout a revolution (live).

Feb 89. (7") *<68611>* **CULT OF PERSONALITY. / FUNNY VIBE** [–] [13]

Apr 89. (7") *(LCL 5)* **CULT OF PERSONALITY. / SHOULD I STAY OR SHOULD I GO** [ ] [–]
(12"+=/cd-s+=) *(LCLT/CDLCL 5)* – What's your favourite colour.

Jun 89. (7") *<68934>* **OPEN LETTER (TO A LANDLORD). / TALKIN' 'BOUT A REVOLUTION** [–] [82]

Oct 89. (7"/7"g-f) *(LCL/+G 6) <68548>* **GLAMOUR BOYS (remix). / CULT OF PERSONALITY (live)** [ ] Aug89 [31]
(12"+=) *(LCLT 6)* – Memories can't wait.
(pic-cd-s++=) *(CDLCL 6)* – I don't want to know.
(cd-s+=) *(LCLC 6)* – Middle man (live) / Open letter (to a landlord).

Oct 89. (7") *<73010>* **FUNNY VIBE. / ('A'instrumental)** [–] [ ]

Aug 90. (7") *<73575>* **TYPE. / SHOULD I STAY OR SHOULD I GO** [–] [ ]

Aug 90. (7"/c-s) *(LCL/+M 7)* **TYPE. / FINAL SOLUTION** [75] [–]
(12"+=/cd-s+=) *(LCLGT/CDLCL 7)* – Should I stay or should I go? / Middleman (live).

Sep 90. (cd/c/lp) *(466 920-2/-4/-1) <46202>* **TIME'S UP** [20] [13]
– Time's up / History lesson / Pride / Love rears its ugly head / New Jack theme / Someone like you / Elvis is dead / Type / Information overload / Undercover of darkness / Olozy I / Fight the fight / Tag team partners / Solace of you / This is the life. *(cd+=)* – Final solution (live) / Middle man (live) / Love rears its ugly head (soul power mix).

Jan 91. (7"/7"sha-pic-d/c-s) *(656 593-7/-0/-4) <73677>* **LOVE REARS IT'S UGLY HEAD. / ('A'-Soul power mix)** [12] [ ]
(12"+=) *(656 593-6)* – Type (remix).
(cd-s+=/pic-cd+=) *(656 593-2/-5)* – ('A'version) / Love and happiness.

May 91. (c-s,cd-s) *<73800>* **SOLACE OF YOU / SOMEONE LIKE YOU** [–] [ ]

May 91. (7"/c-s) *(656 908-7/-4)* **SOLACE OF YOU. / NEW JACK THEME** [33] [–]
(12"+=) *(656 908-8)* – Elvis is dead (mix).
(cd-s+=) *(656 908-9)* – ('A'live) / Type (live) / Information overload (live) / Desperate people (live).

Jul 91. (7"/12"/cd-ep) **BURNING OF THE MIDNIGHT LAMP / MEMORIES CAN'T WAIT / TALKING LOUD AND SAYING NOTHING** [–] [ ]

Aug 91. (m-cd) *<47988>* **BISCUITS (live)** [–] [ ]
– Burning of the midnight lamp / Memories can't wait (live) / Talking loud and saying nothing / Desperate people (live) / Money talks / Love and happiness.

Oct 91. (7"/c-s) *(657 535-7/-4)* **THE CULT OF PERSONALITY. / LOVE REARS IT'S UGLY HEAD (live)** [67] [–]
(12"+=) *(657 535-6)* – ('A'live) / Pride (live).
(cd-s+=) *(657 535-2)* – Talkin' loud and saying nothing / Burning of the midnight lamp.

— MUZZ SKILLINGS departed Nov'91, and was replaced (Jun'92) by **DOUG WIMBUSH** (b.22 Sep'56, Hartford, Connecticut) – bass (ex-GEORGE CLINTON, ex-TACKHEAD)

Feb 93. (7") *(658 976-7)* **LEAVE IT ALONE. / 17 DAYS** [34] [ ]
(12"pic-d+=/cd-s+=) *(658 976-6/-2)* – T.V. news / Hemp (extended).

Feb 93. (cd/c/lp) *(472856-2/-4/-1) <52780>* **STAIN** [19] [26]
– Go away / Ignorance is bliss / Leave it alone / B1 / Mind your own business / Auslander / Never satisfied / Nothingness / Postman / W.T.F.F. / This little pig / Hemp / Wall / T.V. news / Love rears its ugly head (live).

Apr 93. (7"pic-d) *(659 173-7)* **AUSLANDER (remix). / AUSLANDER (Dublander mix)** [53] [ ]
(12"colrd+=/pic-cd-s+=) *(659 173-6/-2)* – Auslander (Radio Days mix) / New Jack theme.

May 93. (7"colrd) *(659 300-7)* **NOTHINGLESS. / 17 DAYS** [ ] [ ]
(cd-s+=) *(659 300-2)* – ('A'remix) / ('A'acoustic mix).

Jan 94. (c-ep) *(660 780-4)* **SUNSHINE OF YOUR LOVE / AUSLANDER (overload mix) / ('A'-Adrian Sherwood & S. McDonald mix)** [ ] [ ]
(cd-ep) *(660 780-2) – (first 2 tracks) / ('A'remix) / Love rears its ugly head (extended).*

— they disbanded early '95 after poor sales

Nov 95. (cd/c) *(481 021-2/-4) <57698>* **PRIDE – THE GREATEST HITS** (compilation) [ ] [ ]
– Pride / Release the pressure / Sacred ground / Visions / Love rears it's ugly head (soul power remix) / These are happy times / Memories can't wait / Cult of personality / Funny vibe / WTFF / Glamour boys / Open letter (to

a landlord) / Solace of you / Nothingless / Type / Time's up / What's your favourite colour? (theme song).

Mayan Sanctuary

Oct 03. (cd) *(MYNCD 014)* <84638> **COLLIDEOSCOPE**
– Song without sin / A ? of when / Operation: mind control / Flying / In your name / Back in black / Nightmare city / Lost halo / Holy roller / Great expectation / Choices mash up / Pocket of tears / Sacred ground / Tomorrow never knows / Nova.

– compilations, etc. –

Jul 00. (cd) *Epic; (498784-2) <65276>* **SUPER HITS** Jan98

VERNON REID

—— with various personnel

Jul 96. (cd/c) *<(483921-2/-4)>* **MISTAKEN IDENTITY**
– C.P. time / Mistaken identity / You say he's just a psychic friend / Who are you (mutation 1) / Lightnin' / Projects / Uptown drifter / Saint Cobain / Important safety instructions (mutation 2) / What's my name / Signed ficticious / Call waiting to exhale (mutation 3) / My last nerve / Freshwater coconut / Mysterious power / Unborne embrace / Who invited you (mutation 4).

—— VERNON subsequently founded the YOHIMBE BROTHERS with DJ LOGIC (ex-EYE & I), releasing 'FRONT END LIFTER' for 'Rope-a-dope' records in '02

LL COOL J

Born: JAMES TODD SMITH, 14 Jan'68, Bayshore, Long Island, New York, USA. Cocksure from the start, L.(ADIES) L.(OVE) COOL J(AMES) began making demos while still at school, one of these picked up by a young RICK RUBIN for his new 'Def Jam' label. Released in 1984, 'I NEED A BEAT' kickstarted not only the career of young JAMES but the 'Def Jam' empire, selling 100,000 copies and leading to L.L. prematurely abandoning his school career. Following up with the seminal B-Boy holler of 'I CAN'T LIVE WITHOUT MY RADIO', the rapper established himself as one of the key players in the new hip hop mafia alongside RUN D.M.C. and subsequently The BEASTIE BOYS. With RUBIN revving up L.L.'s solid arrangements via his trademark metal grind, 'RADIO' (1986) was the first in a string of groundbreaking 'Def Jam' albums, boasting such heavyweight knockouts as 'ROCK THE BELLS' alongside the first two singles. Live, L.L. could go twenty rounds with just about any other act on the scene, sleek with sweat from his gold-chained, bare-chested torso and stalking the stage like a panther. It came as something of a surprise, then, when L.L. played the sensitive, doomed romantic card with the rather limp ballad, 'I NEED LOVE' and although it broke him into both the UK Top 10 and the US Top 20, the track wasn't exactly representative of his street tough style. The accompanying concept album, 'BIGGER AND DEFFER' (1987) was also a bit of a disappointment to many, lacking the headstrong focus of the debut while the US Top 10 'WALKING WITH A PANTHER' (1989) alienated him from the more grassroots element of his fanbase with its overtly commercial sound, typified by the likes of 'I'M THAT TYPE OF GUY'. Its saving grace was the bizarre minimalism of 'GOIN' BACK TO CALI', a track featured on the 'Def Jam' soundtrack to cult film 'Less Than Zero' alongside metal acts like SLAYER and AEROSMITH. L.L.'s passport back to some kind of credibility came with the aid of veteran producer MARLEY MARL, the pair working together on the Grammy-winning 'MAMA SAID KNOCK YOU OUT' (1990), L.L.'s biggest selling and most consistently rounded release to date. In the early to mid 90's, COOL J again lost his way somewhat, taking vague aim at gangsta rap with '14 SHOTS TO THE DOME' (1993) and descending into self-parody and cliche with 'MR. SMITH' (1995). Ironically, it was via heavy metal, or rather heavy metal goons BEAVIS & BUTT-HEAD, that COOL J stormed his way back into the charts, collaborating with the gruesome twosome on a cover of CHAKA KHAN's 'AIN'T NOBODY' for the BEAVIS & BUTT-HEAD movie. The single was a UK No.1 in early '97, paving the way for L.L.'s re-invention as red-leather clad funk grinder on the brilliant 'PHENOMENON' single, another UK Top 10 later that year. Along with the likes of BUSTA RHYMES' scorching 'Put Your Hands Where My Eyes Can See', the track saw rap pared down to raw, minimalist funk, a visceral departure from the snooze-core, weed-obsessed hip hop of recent years. 'PHENOMENON' (1997) the album saw L.L. back in the US Top 10, back on form and working with some of the most respected artists in the game, including the aforementioned RHYMES, REDMAN and the WU TANG's METHOD MAN. His third decade in the business and the ladies were still loving cool James, at least going by the rap-meister's ever self regarding lyrics on 'G.O.A.T. FEATURING JAMES T. SMITH: THE GREATEST OF ALL TIME' (2000). Long winded as the title was, the record was basically another helping of occasionally tough talking, occasionally witty, often overtly sexual and almost always smooth and slick rap. Now in his 30's, LL shows no signs of growing old gracefully which, really, is something we should probably be thankful for. No surprise then that '10' (2002) was, incredibly perhaps, the man's tenth album of his career. While all the top name producers of the day showed their face, the record's half-hearted bluster and sweet talk served only to underline the fact that those halcyon recordings of the mid-80's are unlikely to be matched anytime soon.

Album rating: RADIO (*7) / BIGGER AND DEFFER (*6) / WALKING WITH A PANTHER (*7) / MAMA SAID KNOCK YOU OUT (*8) / 14 SHOTS TO THE DOME (*5) / MR. SMITH (*6) / ALL WORLD: GREATEST HITS compilation (*8) / PHENOMENON (*5) / G.O.A.T. FEATURING JAMES T. SMITH THE GREATEST OF ALL TIME (*5) / 10 (*5)

L.L. COOL J – vocals (with various back-up)

Def Jam-CBS Def Jam

Jan 86. (7") *(A 6684)* **I CAN'T LIVE WITHOUT MY RADIO. / I CAN'T GIVE YOU MORE**
(12"+=) *(TA 6684)* – ('A'instrumental).

Feb 86. (lp/c) *(DEF/40 26745) <40239>* **RADIO** 71 Jan86 46
– I can't live without my radio / You can't dance / Dear Yvette / I can give you more / Dangerous / Rock the bells / I need a beat / You'll rock / I want you. *(cd-iss. Jul95; 527352-2)*

Mar 86. (7") *(A 7003)* **ROCK THE BELLS. / EL SHABAZZ**
(12"+=) *(TA 7003)* – ('A'original mix).
(d7"+=) *(DA 7003)* – I can't live without my radio / I can give you more.

Sep 86. (7") *(650113-7)* **I CAN'T LIVE WITHOUT MY RADIO. / ROCK THE BELLS**
(12"+=) *(650113-6)* – You'll rock / El shabazz.

Jun 87. (7") *(650856-7) <07120>* **I'M BAD. / GET DOWN** 71 May87 84
(12"+=) *(650856-6)* – Dangerous.
(7"pic-d) *(650856-8)* – ('A'side) / Rock the bells / I can't live without my radio.

Jun 87. (lp/c) *(450515-1/-4) <40793>* **BIGGER AND DEFFER** 54 3
– I'm bad / Get down / The Bristol hotel / The rhyme ain't done / 357 – Break it on down / Go cut creator go / Breakthrough / I need love / Ahh, let's get ill / The doo-wop / On the ill tip. *(cd-iss. 1991; 450515-2) (cd re-iss. Jul95; 527353-2)*

Aug 87. (7") *(651101-7) <07350>* **I NEED LOVE. / MY RHYME AIN'T DONE** 8 Jul87 14
(12"+=) *(651101-6)* – ('A'mixes).

Nov 87. (7"/7"pic-d) *(LLCJ/+P 1)* **GO CUT CREATOR GO. / I NEED LOVE** 66
(10"+=/12"+=/cd-s+=) *(LL CJQ/CJT/CD 1)* – The Bristol hotel / Kandy.

Feb 88. (7") *(LLCJ 2) <07679>* **GOIN' BACK TO CALI. / JACK THE RIPPER** 37 31
(10"+=/12"+=) *(LLCJ Q/T 2)* – I can't live without my radio.

May 89. (7"/c-s) *(LLCJ/+M 3) <68902>* **I'M THAT TYPE OF GUY. / IT GETS NO ROUGHER** 43 15
(12"+=) *(LLCJT 3)* – Rock the bells.
(cd-s+=) *(CDLLCJ 3)* – ('A'mixes).

Jun 89. (lp/c/cd) *(465112-1/-4/-2)* *<45172>* **WALKING WITH A PANTHER** 43 6
– Droppin' em / Smokin' dopin' / Fast peg / Clap your hands / Nitro / You're my heart / I'm that type of guy / Why do you think they call it dope? / It gets no rougher / Big ole butt / One shot at love / 1-900 LL Cool J / Two different worlds / Jealous / Jingling baby / Def jam in the motherland. *(cd+=)* – Goin' back to Cali / Crime stories. *(c++=)* – Change your ways / Jack the ripper. *(cd re-iss. Jul95; 527355-2)*

Sep 90. (c-s) *<73457>* **THE BOOMIN' SYSTEM / ('A'-Underground mix)** – 48

Oct 90. (cd/c/lp) *(467315-2/-4/-1)* *<46888>* **MAMA SAID KNOCK YOU OUT** 49 Sep90 16
– Boomin' system / Around the way girl / Eat 'em up L. Chill / Mr. Good bar / Murdergram (live at Rapmania) / Cheesy rat blues / Farmers boulevard (our anthem) / Mama said knock you out / Milky cereal / Jingling baby / To da break of dawn / 6 minutes of pleasure / Illegal search / Power of God. *(cd re-iss. Jul95; 523477-2)* *(cd re-iss. May00; 542428-2)*

Nov 90. (c-s) *<73609>* **AROUND THE WAY GIRL / ('A'remix)** – 9

Nov 90. (7") *(6564470-7)* **AROUND THE WAY GIRL. / MAMA SAID KNOCK YOU OUT** 41 –
(12"+=/cd-s+=) *(6564470-6/-2)* – ('A'mixes).
(re-iss. Mar91; hit UK No.36)

Apr 91. (c-s) *<73706>* **MAMA SAID KNOCK YOU OUT / ('A'-Hot mix)** – 17

Sep 91. (c-s) *<73820>* **6 MINUTES OF PLEASURE / EAT EM UP L CHILL** – 95

Mar 93. (7") *(659169-7)* *<74811>* **HOW I'M COMIN'. / BUCKIN 'EM DOWN** 37 57
(12"+=/cd-s+=) *(659169-6/-2)* – ('A'mixes).

Apr 93. (cd/c/lp) *(473678-2/-4/-1)* *<53325>* **14 SHOTS TO THE DOME** 74 5
– How I'm comin' / Buckin' em down / Stand by your man / Little somethin' / Pink cookies in a plastic bag getting crushed by buildings / Straight from Queens / Funkadelic relic / All we got left is the beat / (NFA) No frontin' allowed / Back seat / Soul survivor / Ain't no stoppin' this / Diggy down / Crossroads. *(cd re-iss. Jan96; 523488-2)*

Jun 93. (c-s) *<74984>* **BACK SEAT (OF MY JEEP) / PINK COOKIES IN A PLASTIC BAG GETTING CRUSHED BY BUILDINGS** – 42 96

Nov 95. (cd/c) *(529724-2/-4)* *<529583>* **MR. SMITH** 20
– Make it hot / Hip hop / Hey lover (featuring BOYZ II MEN) / Doin' it / Life as / I shot ya / Mr. Smith / No aerplay / Loungin' / Hollis to Hollywood / God bless / Get the drop on 'em.

Jan 96. (c-s; LL COOL J featuring BOYZ II MEN) *(DEFMC 14)* *<577494>* **HEY LOVER / ('A'instrumental)** 17 Nov95 3
(12"+=/cd-s+=) *(12DEF/DEFCD 14)* – ('A'mix).
below featured guest vocals by LeSHAUN

May 96. (c-s) *(DEFMC 15)* *<576120>* **DOIN' IT / HEY LOVER (street version)** 15 Feb96 9
(12"+=/cd-s+=) *(12DEF/DEFCD 15)* – ('A'-unarmed mix) / Hey lover (street instrumental).

Sep 96. (c-s) *(DEFMC 30)* *<575062>* **LOUNGIN' / SUMMER LUV** 7 Jun96 3
(12"+=/cd-s+=) *(12DEF/DEFCD 30)* – ('A'-who do ya luv featuring TOTAL mix).

Nov 96. (cd/c/d-lp) *<(534125-2/-4/-1)>* **ALL WORLD: GREATEST HITS** (compilation) 23
– I can't live without my radio / Rock the bells / I'm bad / I need love / Goin' back to Cali / Jack the ripper / Jingling baby / Big ole butt / Boomin' system / Around the way girl / Mama said knock you out / Back seat / I need a beat / Doin' it / Loungin' (who do ya luv) / Hey lover (with BOYZ II MEN).

Dec 96. (c-s) *<19410>* **AIN'T NOBODY / (track by Madd Head)** – 46

Jan 97. (c-s) *(GFSC 22195)* **AIN'T NOBODY / (track by Beavis & Butt-Head)** 1 –
(12"+=/cd-s+=) *(GFST/+T 22195)* – ('A'mix).
(above single on 'Geffen' & lifted from the animated movie 'Beavis & Butt-Head Do America')

— in Apr'97, COOLIO was one of a bunch of rap stars who featured on the UK Top 10 single, 'HIT EM HIGH (THE MONSTARS' ANTHEM)'

Oct 97. (cd/c/lp) *<(539186-2/-4/-1)>* **PHENOMENON** 37 7
– Phenomenon / Candy (with RALPH TRESVANT & RICKY BELL) / Starsky and Hutch (with BUSTA RHYMES) / Another dollar / Nobody can freak with you (with KEITH SWEAT & LeSHAUN) / Hot hot hot / 4,3,2,1 (with METHOD MAN, REDMAN, DMX, CANIBUS & MASTER P) / Wanna get paid (with LOST BOYZ) / Father / Don't be late don't come too soon (with TAMIA).

Oct 97. (c-s) *(568116-4)* *<568081>* **PHENOMENON / ('A'mix)** 9 56
(12"/cd-s) *(568117-1/-2)* – ('A'mix) / Wanna get paid / Mama said knock you out.

Dec 97. (cd-s; LL COOL J featuring METHOD MAN, REDMAN, DMX, CANIBUS & MASTER P) *<568321>* **4,3,2,1 /** – 75

Mar 98. (c-s) *(568117-4)* *<568332>* **FATHER / (instrumental)** 10 Jan98 18
(cd-s+=) *(568117-2)* *<568333>* – 4,3,2,1 (E-dub remix 6) (radio).

— In Jul'98, COOL J was credited on DR DRE's hit, 'Zoom'

— In Nov'98, he also appeared on 'Incredible' hit with KEITH MURRAY

Nov 99. (c-s/cd-s) *(W 512 C/CD)* **DEEPEST BLUEST (SHARK'S FIN) (mixes; album / instrumental / acappella)**
(above issued on 'Warners')

Jun 00. (cd-s) *<562827>* **IMAGINE THAT (mixes; radio / explicit / instrumental)** – 98

Sep 00. (cd) *(542997-2)* *<546819>* **G.O.A.T. FEATURING JAMES T. SMITH THE GREATEST OF ALL TIME** 29 1
– (intro) / Imagine that / Back where I belong / LL Cool J / Take it off / (skit) / Fuhgidabowdit / Farmers / This is us / Can't think / Hello / You and me / Homicide / U can't fuck with me / Queen is / The G.O.A.T.

— In Nov'01, LL COOL J was credited on the LUDACRIS hit, 'Fatty Girl'

Oct 02. (c-s) *(63872-4)* *<063956>* **LUV U BETTER / FA-HA** 7 Aug02 4
(12") *(63872-1)* – ('A'-instrumental).
(cd-s+=) *(63872-2)* – ('A'-video).

Oct 02. (cd) *<(63219-2)>* **10** 26 2
– (intro) / Born to love you / Luv U better / Paradise (with AMERIE) / Fa ha / Niggy nuts / Amazin' (with KANDICE LOVE) / Clockin' G's / Lollipop / After school (with P. DIDDY) / Throw ya L's up / U should / 10 million stars / Mirror mirror / Big mama (unconditional love) (with DRU HILL).

Feb 03. (c-s; by LL COOL J featuring AMERIE) *(63703-4)* *<063820>* **PARADISE / PARADISE (James Yarde mix with TERRI WALKER)** 18 Nov02 36
(12"+=) *(63703-1)* – ('A'-instrumental).
(cd-s++=) *(63703-2)* – ('A'-video).

— in Mar'03, LL COOL J featured on JENNIFER LOPEZ's hit, 'All I Have'

– compilations, etc. –

Mar 93. (cd/c) *Def Jam; (473043-2/-4)* **12" TAPE** (versions)
– Rock the bells / I need love / I can't live without my radio / Boomin' system / Around the way girl.

Los LOBOS

Formed: Los Angeles, California, USA ... 1974 by DAVID HIDALGO, LUIS PEREZ, CESAR ROSAS and CONRAD LOZANO, all members of L.A.'s Chicano community. Although they initially set out playing chart covers at local clubs, weddings etc., the group subsequently began exploring their musical roots in a traditional acoustic framework before going on to combine this approach with more popular American musical idioms. The 1978 debut set, 'JUST ANOTHER BAND FROM EAST L.A.', was a self-financed affair sold at gigs, the wider listening public not introduced to the LOS LOBOS sound until 1983 and the release of a mini-set, 'AND A TIME TO DANCE'. The first fruits of a new deal with 'Slash', the T-BONE BURNETT-produced set included a Grammy winning rendition of the traditional Mexican folk anthem, 'ANSELMA'. Moving into more adventurous territory with the acclaimed 'HOW WILL THE WOLF SURVIVE' (1984), LOS LOBOS proved themselves to be one of America's most authentically eclectic roots-rock purveyors. Inspired by the likes of RY COODER and FLACO JIMINEZ, the group moved effortlessly through Tex-Mex, country, norteno, R&B and rock without sacrificing their unique appeal. The record also saw LOS LOBOS make the US Top 50, its title track a minor hit in Britain. Although 'BY THE LIGHT OF THE MOON' (1987) featured arguably one of LOS LOBOS' finest ballads in 'RIVER OF FOOLS', the album was considered a disappointing follow-up by both fans and critics alike, its more politically aware mantle sitting uneasily on the shoulders of a band at their best on celebratory dance tunes. A cult attraction up to this point, LOS LOBOS became overnight pop stars via their contributions to the soundtrack for RICHIE VALENS biopic, 'LA BAMBA'; the strum 'n' shimmy of the title track was a massive transatlantic No.1 while the album itself (also featuring performances by the likes of MARSHALL CRENSHAW and BO DIDDLEY) topped the US charts. No doubt loathe to be bracketed as a rock'n'roll covers outfit, LOS LOBOS' next studio set, 'LA PISTOLA EL Y CORAZON' (1988) saw them returning squarely and convincingly to their Mexican roots (and chart oblivion). With this out of their system, the group resumed their innovative rock hybrid with 'THE NEIGHBOURHOOD' (1990), a solid set benefitting from the muscular backbeat of session veteran JIM KELTNER and featuring guest vocals from JOHN HIATT. Following a period of collaboration with The BAND on material for their comeback album, LOS LOBOS penned what many regard as their most accomplished and rewarding album, 'KIKO' (1992); by turns gutsy, instinctive, subtle and atmospheric, the record's shifting latin pop/rock/folk textures effectively transformed the band's experimentation into something with a completely separate and unique musical identity. LOS LOBOS filled in time until their next studio outing with a fine 1993 compilation set, 'JUST ANOTHER BAND . . . – THE BEST OF . . .', also collaborating with LALO GUERRERO on low-key album, 'PAPA'S BREATH', in 1995. The following year, the band from East L.A. issued their first album for 'Warners', 'COLOSSAL HEAD', the record scoring their highest chart placing at No.81 US since the heady days of 'LA BAMBA'. 1999's 'THIS TIME' was very much a continuation of the band's previous two studio efforts, gathering up the creative threads of those works and attempting to apply a little more discipline. In fact, the magnitude of the creative journey the band had made since their mid-70's inception was only put into the proper context with the release of 'EL CANCIONERO: MAS Y MAS' (2000). A boxed set covering the many and varied musical bases the LOS LOBOS have covered during their long career, the most encouraging aspect of this release is the feeling that the hispanic mavericks have still got a lot more music to make. Ending their recent partnership with Mitchell Froom and hooking up instead with the legendary John Leckie seemed to have done the band no end of good in the early years of the new millennium. 'GOOD MORNING AZTLAN' (2002) was perhaps the most solid LOS LOBOS effort in a decade, vibing off unadorned rock, soul, funk and R&B with that latin flair which sets them apart from the competition. • **Songwriters:** Group penned except; RIP IT UP (Little Richard) / CRYING, WAITING, HOPING (Buddy Holly) / and some trad. • **Trivia:** Country star, WAYLON JENNINGS, later covered 'HOW WILL THE WOLF SURVIVE'. HIDALGO and ROSAS featured on RY COODER's 1985 lp, 'Alamo Bay', with the former guesting on albums (King Of America) by ELVIS COSTELLO and (Gracelands) by PAUL SIMON, alongside other LL members.

Album rating: JUST ANOTHER BAND FROM L.A. mini (*5) / . . . AND A TIME TO DANCE mini (*6) / HOW WILL THE WOLF SURVIVE? (*8) / BY THE LIGHT OF THE MOON (*7) / LA BAMBA soundtrack (*5) / LA PISTOLA Y EL CORAZON (*6) / THE NEIGHBORHOOD (*7) / KIKO (*7) / JUST ANOTHER BAND FROM L.A. – THE BEST OF compilation (*8) / COLOSSAL HEAD (*4) / THIS TIME (*5) / EL CANCIONERO – MAS Y MAS boxed set (*6) / GOOD MORNING AZTLAN (*7)

DAVID HIDALGO (b. 6 Oct'54) – vocals, guitar, accordion / **CESAR ROSAS** (b.26 Sep'54) – vocals, guitar / **CONRAD LOZANO** (b.21 Mar'51) – bass, vocals, guitar / **LUIS PEREZ** (b.21 Mar'51) – drums, guitar

not iss. — New Vista

1978. (m-lp) **JUST ANOTHER BAND FROM L.A.** [-] [ ]
– El canelo / El pescando nadador (ranchera) / Sabor a mi / Flor de huevo / Cielito lindo (cancion Mexicano) / La iguana (son Jarocho) / El cuchipe / Imploracion (bolero ranchero) / Guantanamera / La fer. *<US cd-iss. Sep00 as 'DEL ESTE DE LOS ANGELES'; 162242>*

Rough Trade — Slash

Jan 84. (m-lp) *(ROUGH 71) <SLMP 1>* **AND A TIME TO DANCE** [ ] 1983 [ ]
– Let's say goodnight / Walking song / Anselma / Come on, let's go / How much can I do? / Why do you do / Ay te dejo en San Antonio. *(re-iss. Jan87 on 'Slash' lp/c; SLM P/C 17)*

—— added **STEVE BERLIN** (b.14 Sep'55, Philadelphia, Pennsylvania) – saxophone, soprano vocals (ex-BLASTERS)

Slash-London — Slash-Warners

Nov 84. (lp/c) *(SLMP/SMMC 3) <25177>* **HOW WILL THE WOLF SURVIVE?** [77] [47]
– Don't worry baby / A matter of time / Corrida #1 / Our last night / The breakdown / I got loaded / Serenata Nortena / Evageline / I got to let you know / Lil' king of everything / Evangeline / Will the wolf survive?. *(re-iss. Jan87; same) (cd-iss. Apr89; 820184-2)*

Mar 85. (7"/12") *(LASH/+X 4) <29093>* **WILL THE WOLF SURVIVE? / DON'T WORRY BABY** [57] [78]
(10"+=) *(LASHT 4)* – ('A'live).

Jan 87. (lp/c)(cd) *(SLA P/C 13)(828033-2) <25523>* **BY THE LIGHT OF THE MOON** [77] [47]
– One time one night / Shakin' shakin' shakes / Is this all there is? / Prenda del Alma / All I wanted to do was dance / Set me free (Rosa Lee) / The hardest time / My boy's gone / River of fools / The mess we're in / Tears of God.

Feb 87. (7"m) *(LASH 10)* **SET ME FREE (ROSA LEE). / SHAKIN' SHAKIN' SHAKES / PREUDEABELALAMA** [ ] [-]
(12"+=) *(LASHX 10)* – Will the wolf survive?

Mar 87. (7") *<28464>* **ONE TIME ONE NIGHT. / ALL I WANTED TO DO WAS DANCE** [-] [ ]

Apr 87. (7") *(LASH 11)* **ONE TIME ONE NIGHT. / RIVER OF FOOLS** [ ] [-]
(12"+=) *(LASHX 11)* – Anselma / Don't worry baby.

Jul 87. (7"/c-s) *(LASH/LASCS 13) <28336>* **LA BAMBA. / CHARLENA** [1] [1]
(12"+=) *(LASHX 13)* – Rip it up.
(below album released on 'London'; Slash's UK paymaster

Aug 87. (lp/c)(cd) *(LON LP/C 36)(828058-2) <25605>* **LA BAMBA (soundtrack)** [24] [1]
– La Bamba / Come on, let's go / Ooh! my head / We belong together / Framed / Donna / Lonely teardrops (HOWARD HUNTSBERRY) / Crying, waiting, hoping (MARSHALL CRENSHAW) / Summertime blues (BRIAN SETZER) / Who do you love (BO DIDDLEY) / Charlena / Goodnight my love.

Sep 87. (7") *(LASH 14) <28186>* **COME ON, LET'S GO. / OOH! MY HEAD** [18] [21]
(10"+=/12"+=) *(LASH T/X 14)* – (track by MARSHALL CRENSHAW).

Nov 87. (7") *(LASH 16)* **DONNA. / FRAMED** [ ] [-]
(12"+=)(10"+=) *(LASHX 16)(HL 8803)* – Goodnight my love.

Oct 88. (lp/c/cd) *(828 121-1/-4/-2) <25790>* **LA PISTOLA Y EL CORAZON** [ ] [ ]
– La Guacamaya / Las amarillas / Si yo quisiera / (Sonajas) Mananitas Michoacanas / Estoy sentado aqui / El gusto / Que nadie sepa mi sufrir / El Canelo / La pistola y el corazon.

—— guests **JIM KELTNER** – drums / **JOHN HIATT** – vocals / **ALEX ACUNA** – percussion

Sep 90. (cd/c/lp) *(828 190-2/-4/-1) <26131>* **THE NEIGHBOURHOOD** [ ] [ ]
– Down on the riverbed / Emily / I walk alone / Angel dance / Little John of God / Deep dark hole / Georgia slop / I can't understand / The giving tree / Take my hand / Jenny's got a pony / Be still / The neighbourhood.

May 92. (cd/c/lp) *(828 298-2/-4/-1) <26786>* **KIKO** [ ] [ ]
– Dream in blue / Wake up Dolores / Angels with dirty faces / That train don't stop here / Kiko and the lavender Moon / Saint behind the glass / Reva's house / When the circus comes / Arizona skies / Short side of

nothing / Two Janes / Wicked rain / Whiskey trail / Just a man / Peace / Rio de Tenampa.

Sep 93. (d-cd/d-c) *(828 400-2/-4)* *<45367>* **JUST ANOTHER BAND FROM EAST L.A. THE BEST OF LOS LOBOS** (compilation)
– Volver, volver / El cuchipe / La feria de la flores / Saborami / Let's say goodnight / Anselma / Will the wolf survive? / A matter of time / I got to let you know / Don't worry baby / One time one night / Shakin' shakin' shakes / River of fools / Carabina 30-30 / Tears of God / Set me free (Rosa Lee) / Come on, let's go / La bamba / El gusto / Estoy sentado aqui / La pistola y el corazon / I wanna be like you (the monkey song) / Some day / Down on the riverbed / Be still / The neighbourhood / I can't understand / Angel dance / Bertha / Saint behind the glass / Angels with dirty faces / Wicked rain / Kiko and the lavender Moon / When the circus comes / Peace / Bella Maria de mi alma / What's going on / Wrong man theme / Blue moonlight / Politician / New Zandu.

— Early in 1995, LOS LOBOS collaborated on an album, 'PAPA'S DREAM' with LALO GUERRERO on the label 'Music For Little People' (94256-2)

WEA Warners

Mar 96. (cd) *<(9362 46172-2)>* **COLOSSAL HEAD** [81]
– Revolution / Everybody loves a train / Mas y mas / Maricela / Can't stop the rain / Little Japan / Life is good / Buddy Ebsen loves the night time / This bird's gonna fly / Colossal head / Manny's bones.

Hollywood Hollywood

Sep 99. (cd) *<(0121852HWR)>* **THIS TIME** Jul99
– This time / Oh yeah / Viking / High places / Cumbia raza / Run away with you / Corazon / Some say, some do / Turn around / La playa / Why we wish. *(re-iss. Jun02; 0927 45490-2)*

Mammoth Mammoth

Jun 02. (cd) *(HLL 65518)* *<11501>* **GOOD MORNING AZTLAN**
– Done gone blue / Hearts of stone / Luz de mi vida / Good morning Aztlan / The big ranch / The word / Malaque / Tony and Maria / Get to this / Maria Christina / What in the world / Round and round. *<(d-cd+=)* – Can't stop the rain (live) / Manny's bones – Good morning Aztlan (live). *(re-iss. Oct02 on 'WEA'; 0927 47740-2)*

– compilations, etc. –

Feb 01. (4xcd-box) *Rhino; <8122 76670-2>* **EL CANCIONERO – MAS Y MAS** [–]

Nils LOFGREN

Born: 21 Jun'51, Chicago, Illinois, USA. Raised in Maryland, Washington DC by Italian/Swedish parents, he formed PAUL DOWELL & THE DOLPHIN in 1969; two flop singles later he folded the outfit and formed the harder-edged GRIN. While building up their live reputation, LOFGREN sessioned for NEIL YOUNG & CRAZY HORSE on 'After The Goldrush', CRAZY HORSE also employing him the following year as a part-time writer and session man on their brilliant eponymous debut. Meanwhile, GRIN signed to 'Spindizzy' (distributed by 'Columbia') and issued their self-titled debut lp in late summer '71. The record only managed to scrape into the US Top 200, as did their follow-ups, '1 + 1' and 'ALL OUT' (the latter added NILS' younger brother TOM). In 1973, the group signed to 'A&M', although they subsequently split when NILS joined NEIL YOUNG & CRAZY HORSE for the sublime 'Tonight's The Night' (1975). As well as contributing haunting piano and vocals to the likes of 'Albuquerque' and 'Tired Eyes', LOFGREN offered up some searing guitar licks on 'Speakin' Out' and the title track, his precocious talent confirmed with an eponymous 'A&M' solo debut. Released the same year as 'Tonight ...', the album found LOFGREN finally hitting his groove with an irrepressible verve and a rock solid set of songs, from the brawny KEITH RICHARDS tribute, 'KEITH DON'T GO (ODE TO THE GLIMMER TWIN)' and the sensitive rendition of Carole King's 'GOIN' BACK' (also recorded by The BYRDS amongst others) to the infectious pop/rock of single, 'BACK IT UP'. Although the record failed to chart, LOFGREN enjoyed some belated chart success with the Al KOOPER-produced 'CRY TOUGH' (1976). A more guitar-orientated affair, it made the UK Top 10 and the US Top 40, briefly elevating NILS to the level of recognition enjoyed by most of his peers. It wasn't to last though, the disappointing 'I CAME TO DANCE' (1977) failing to maintain the momentum, while the much improved 'NILS' (1979) sold even less despite the lyrical suss of guest, LOU REED. A new deal with 'Backstreet-M.C.A.' failed to turn things around and early 80's sets, 'NIGHT FADES AWAY' (1981) and 'WONDERLAND' (1983) made little impact. While 1983 had seen NILS again working with NEIL YOUNG (on the 'Trans' tour), LOFGREN initiated his marathon stint with BRUCE SPRINGSTEEN's E-STREET BAND the following year. Independently released in the UK, 'FLIP' (1985) was LOFGREN's final studio release of the decade, a frenetic set of high octane rockers which went down well with fans but again failed to cross over or break any new ground. The early 90's saw the singer/guitarist return with a new band (including ex-BAND man, LEVON HELM) and a couple of albums in the space of two years, an uncharacteristically prolific burst of creativity no doubt fuelled by his long years as a sideman. 1994 saw LOFGREN's first foray into soundtrack work for the movie 'Every Breath', while a further studio album, 'DAMAGED GOODS', and the obligatory unplugged set, 'ACOUSTIC LIVE', appeared in '95 and '97 respectively. The Mr. Nice of the rock establishment, LOFGREN remains one of the most respected, highly praised and in-demand guitarists around; the fact that his solo career never really took off only serves to fuel his cult status. LOFGREN returned in 2002 with 'BREAKAWAY ANGEL', a largely acoustic set featuring the axemeister in unfamiliar but satisfying terrain, amid dobro, mandolin, upright bass and fiddle, and even covering Boudleaux Bryant classic, 'ALL I HAVE TO DO IS DREAM'. • **Songwriters:** Self-penned except covers; FOR YOUR LOVE (Yardbirds) / ANYTIME AT ALL (Beatles) / IT'S ALL OVER NOW (Valentinos) / etc.

Album rating: NILS LOFGREN (*7) / BACK IT UP authorized bootleg (*6) / CRY TOUGH (*7) / I CAME TO DANCE (*5) / NIGHT AFTER NIGHT (*5) / NILS (*6) / NIGHT FADES AWAY (*4) / WONDERLAND (*6) / FLIP (*6) / CODE OF THE ROAD (*5) / THE BEST OF NILS LOFGREN – DON'T WALK . . . ROCK compilation (*7) / SILVER LINING (*4) / CROOKED LINE (*4) / EVERYBREATH (*4) / DAMAGED GOODS (*5) / ACOUSTIC LIVE (*5) / BREAKAWAY ANGEL (*5) / NILS LOFGREN BAND LIVE (*5)

PAUL DOWELL & THE DOLPHIN

NILS LOFGREN – lead guitar, keyboards, / and **BOB GORDON** (b.1951, Oklahoma)– bass, vocals / unknown drummer

not iss. Sire

1968. (7") *<4107>* **THE LAST TIME I SAW YOU. / IT'S BETTER TO KNOW YOU** [–]

GRIN

(NILS + BOB)plus **BOB BERBERICH** (b.1949, Maryland)– drums (ex-REEKERS)

C.B.S. Spindizzy

Jul 71. (7") *(CBS 5239)* **WE ALL SUNG TOGETHER. / SEE WHAT A LOVE CAN DO** Oct70

Aug 71. (lp) *(CBS 64272)* *<30321>* **GRIN** Jun71
– Like rain / See what a love can do / Everybody's missin' the sun / 18 faced lover / Outlaw / We all sung together / If I were a song / Take you to the movies tonight / Direction / Pioneer Mary / Open wide / I had too much (Miss Dazi). *(re-iss. 1975 on 'Spindizzy')*

Sep 71. (7") *(CBS 7405)* *<7405>* **EVERYBODY'S MISSIN' THE SUN. / 18 FACED LOVER**

Mar 72. (7") *(CBS 7757)* *<4005>* **WHITE LIES. / JUST TO HAVE YOU** Jan72 [75]

Jun 72. (lp) *(CBS 64652)* *<31038>* **1 + 1** Jan72
– White lies / Please don't hide / Slippery fingers / Moon tears / End

unkind / Sometimes / Lost a number / Hi, hello home / Just a poem / Soft fun. <(cd-iss. Jan98; 489446-2)>

— added **TOM LOFGREN** – rhythm guitar

Epic Spindizzy

May 73. (lp) *(EPC 65166)* <31701> **ALL OUT** Mar73
– That letter / Heavy Chevy / Don't be long / Love again / She ain't right / Love or else / Ain't love nice / Hard on fire / All out / Rusty gun. *(cd-iss. Oct94; 477847-2)*

May 73. (7") *(EPC 1463)* **AIN'T LOVE NICE. / LOVE OR ELSE**

A&M A&M

Nov 73. (lp) <4415> **GONE CRAZY** –
– You're the weight / Boy and girl / What about me / One more time / True thrill / Beggar's day / Nightmare / Believe / Ain't for free. *(UK-iss.Jan76; AMLH 64415)*

Feb 74. (7") **YOU'RE THE WEIGHT. / BEGGAR'S DAY** –

— NILS joined NEIL YOUNG & CRAZY HORSE (Aug73-Mar74, on 'Tonight's The Night')

– (GRIN) compilations, others, etc. –

C.B.S. Columbia

Jun 76. (d-lp) *(88024)* **GRIN FEATURING NILS LOFGREN**
– ('GRIN' & '1 + 1' albums)

Jun 76. (7") *(4339)* **SOFT FUN. / SLIPPERY FINGERS**

Oct 79. (lp) *(31770)* **THE BEST OF NILS LOFGREN AND GRIN**
(re-iss. Feb86; 32717)

NILS LOFGREN

with **WORNELL JONES** – bass / **AYNSLEY DUNBAR** – drums

A&M A&M

Apr 75. (lp/c) *(AMLH/CAM 64509)* <4509> **NILS LOFGREN** Mar75
– Be good tonight / Back it up / One more Saturday night / If I say it, it's so / I don't want to know / Keith don't go (ode to the Glimmer twin) / Can't buy a break / Duty / The sun hasn't set on this boy yet / Rock and roll crook / Two by two / Goin' back. *(cd-iss. Apr97; 540 702-2)*

Jun 75. (7") *(AMS 7175)* **BACK IT UP. / IF I SAY IT, IT'S SO**

Nov 75. (7") *(AMS 7197)* **I DON'T WANT TO KNOW. / ONE MORE SATURDAY NIGHT**

Jan 76. (ltd.lp) **BACK IT UP!! NILS LOFGREN LIVE – AN AUTHORIZED BOOTLEG** (live radio show)

— added **TOM LOFGREN** – rhythm guitar, vocals (ex-GRIN)

Mar 76. (lp/c) *(AMLH/CAM 64573)* <4573> **CRY TOUGH** 8 32
– Cry tough / It's not a crime / Incidentally . . . it's over / For your love / Share a little / Mud in your eye / Can't get closer (WCGC) / You lit a fire / Jailbait. *(re-iss. Jul83 on 'Fame' lp/c; FA/TCFA 3070) (cd-iss. Oct92; CDMID 122)*

May 76. (7") *(AMS 7229)* **CRY TOUGH. / SHARE A LITTLE**

Aug 76. (7") *(AMS 7252)* **IT'S NOT A CRIME. / SHARE A LITTLE**

— **ANDY NEWMARK** – drums repl. ZACK

— added **PATRICK HENDERSON** – keyboards

Mar 77. (lp/c) *(AMLH/CAM 64628)* <4628> **I CAME TO DANCE** 30 36
– I came to dance / Rock me at home / Home is where your hurt is / Code of the road / Happy ending kids / Goin' south / To be a dreamer / Jealous gun / Happy.

May 77. (7") *(AMS 7288)* **I CAME TO DANCE. / CODE OF THE ROAD**

— **DAVID PLATSHON** – drums repl. NEWMARK

Oct 77. (d-lp/d-c) *(AMLH/CLM 64839)* <3707> **NIGHT AFTER NIGHT (live)** 38 44
– Take you to the movies / Back it up / Keith don't go (ode to the Glimmer twin) / Like rain / Cry tough / It's not a crime / Goin' back / You're the weight / Beggars day / Moon tears / Code of the road / Rock and roll crook / Goin' south / Incidentally . . . it's over / I came to dance.

— now used mainly session people except TOM (on next only)

Jun 79. (lp/c) *(AMLH/CAM 64756)* <4756> **NILS** 54
– No mercy / I'll cry tomorrow / Baltimore / Shine silently / Steal away / Kool skool / A fool like me / I found her / You're so easy. <(cd-iss. Jan97; 540707-2)>

Jul 79. (7") **NO MERCY. / KOOL SKOOL** –

Jul 79. (7",7"colrd) *(AMS 7455)* **SHINE SILENTLY. / KOOL SKOOL** –

Sep 79. (7") **SHINE SILENTLY. / BALTIMORE** –

Oct 79. (7") *(AMS 7486)* **NO MERCY. / A FOOL LIKE ME** –

Backstreet-MCA Backstreet

Sep 81. (lp/c) *(MCF/+C 3121)* <5251> **NIGHT FADES AWAY** 50 99
– Night fades away / I go to pieces / Empty heart / Don't touch me / Dirty money / Sailor boy / Anytime at all / Ancient history / Streets again / In motion. *(re-iss. Feb84 on 'M.C.A.' lp/c; MCL/+C 1786)*

Sep 81. (7") **NIGHT FADES AWAY. / ANCIENT HISTORY** –

Sep 81. (7"/12") *(MCA/+T 749)* **NIGHT FADES AWAY. / ANYTIME AT ALL** –

Nov 81. (7") *(MCA 757)* **I GO TO PIECES. / ANCIENT HISTORY**

Aug 83. (lp/c) *(MCF/+C 3182)* **WONDERLAND**
– Across the tracks / Into the night / It's all over now / I wait for now / Daddy dream / Wonderland / Room without love / Confident girl / Lonesome ranger / Everybody wants / Deadline. *(re-iss. Jun87 lp/c; MCL/+C 1851)*

Oct 83. (7") *(MCA 834)* **ACROSS THE TRACKS. / DADDY DREAM**

— Split his own band to join BRUCE SPRINGSTEEN & THE E-STREET SHUFFLE between 1984-1985. He returned to solo work, bringing back **NEWMARK + JONES** plus **TOMMY MANDELS + T. LAVITZ** – synthesizers

Towerbell Columbia

May 85. (7"/12") *(TOW/+T 68)* **SECRETS IN THE STREET. / FROM THE HEART** 53
(d7"+=) *(TOWG 68)* – Message / Little bit of time.
(12"+=) *(TOWRT 68)* – ('A'extended).

Jun 85. (lp/c) *(TOWLP/ZCTOW 11)* <39982> **FLIP** 36
– Flip ya flip / Secrets in the street / From the heart / Delivery night / King of the rock / Sweet midnight / New holes in old shoes / Dreams die hard / Big tears fall. *(cd-iss. 1988; CDTOW 11) (re-iss. cd Dec92 on 'Castle'; CLACD 312) (cd re-iss. May99 on 'Essential'; ESMCD 721)*

Aug 85. (7"/ext.12") *(TOW/+T 73)* **FLIP YA FLIP. / NEW HOLES IN OLD SHOES** –
(12"pic-d) *(TOWTX 73)* – ('A'extended) / Message (11 minute).

Aug 85. (7") **FLIP YA FLIP. / DELIVERY NIGHT** –

Nov 85. (7") *(TOW 76)* **DELIVERY NIGHT. / DREAMS DIE HARD**
(12") *(TOWT 76)* – ('A'side) / Keith don't go (live).

— Live band = **JONES, TOM LOFGREN, STEWART SMITH, JOHNNY 'BEE' BADANJEK**

Mar 86. (d-lp/c) *(TOWDLP/ZCTOWD 17)* **CODE OF THE ROAD (live)** 86 –
– Beggars day / Secrets in the street / Across the tracks / Delivery night / Cry tough / Dreams die hard / Believe / The sun hasn't set on this boy yet / Code of the road / Moon tears / Back it up / Like rain / Sweet midnight / No mercy / Anytime at all / New holes in old shoes / Keith don't go / Shine silently / I came to dance. *(cd-iss. Dec92 on 'Castle'; CLACD 311) (cd re-iss. May99 on 'Essential'; ESMCD 719)*

Mar 86. (7") *(TOW 86)* **ANYTIME AT ALL (live). / NEW HOLES IN OLD SHOES (live)**

— He decided to re-join BRUCE SPRINGSTEEN, mainly for stage work. Returned in '91 with main band **SCOTT THURSTON** – keyboards / **ANDY NEWMARK** – drums / **KEVIN McCORMICK** – bass, keyboards, percussion / + **LEVON HELM** – harmonica, vocals

Essential Rykodisc

May 91. (cd/c/lp) *(ESS CD/MC/LP 145)* <10170> **SILVER LINING** 61 Mar91
– Silver lining / Valentine / Walkin' nerve / Live each day / Sticks and stones / Trouble's back / Little bit of time / Bein' angry / Gun and run / Girl in motion. *(cd re-iss. Apr96; same)*

1991. (cd-s) **VALENTINE / ('A'-album version) / ('A'-original)** –

1991. (cd-s) **WALKIN' NERVE / KEITH DON'T GO** –

Jul 92. (cd/c/lp) *(ESS CD/MC/LP 183)* <RCD 10238> **CROOKED LINE**
– A child could tell / Blue skies / Misery / You / Shot at you / Crooked line / Walk on me / Someday / New kind of freedom / Just a little / Drunken driver / I'll fight for you.

Jul 92. (cd-s) <51026> **JUST A LITTLE / NO MERCY (live) / ACROSS THE TRACKS (live)** –

Permanent not iss.

Oct 94. (d-cd) *(PERMCD 28)* **EVERYBREATH (soundtrack)** –
– No return / Tender love / Take me home / No tomorrow / Dreams come

true / Rainy nights / Alone / Tryin' not to fall / Good day for goodbyes / Lions wake (instrumental) / Out of the grave / A. Lefty (instrumental) / Fallen into his hands. *(with free cd-s)*
(above featured LOU GRAMM)

— next with **ANDY NEWMARK** – drums / **ROGER GREENAWALT** – bass, percussion, samples / **MICHAEL MATOUSEK** – production coordinator

Essential Pure

Oct 95. (cd/c) *(ESS CD/MC 337)* <2230> **DAMAGED GOODS** [ ] [ ]
– Damaged goods / Only five minutes / Alone / Trip to Mars / Here for you / Black books / Setting Sun / Life / Heavy hats / In the room / Nothin's fallin' / Don't be late for yesterday.

Demon Capitol

Aug 97. (cd) *(FIENDCD 934)* <95736> **ACOUSTIC LIVE (live)** [ ] [ ]
– You / Sticks and stones / Some must dream / Little on up / Keith don't go / Wonderland / Big tears fall / Believe / Black books / To your heart / Man in the moon / I'll arise / Blue skies / Tears on ice / All out / Mud in your eye / No mercy.

Hypertension Vision

May 02. (cd) *(HYP 2215)* <1009> **BREAKAWAY ANGEL** [ ] Jan02 [ ]
– Puttin' out fires / I found you / Love a child / Tears ain't enough / I can't fly / All I have to do is dream / Driftin' man / Love you most / Cryin' tonight / Heaven's answer to blue / Seize love / The hill / Without you / Open road.

— the band:- **PAUL BERRY** – guitar / **WADE MATTHEWS** – bass / **TIMM BIERY** – drums

May 03. (d-cd) *(HYP 3220)* <1011> **NILS LOFGREN BAND LIVE (live)** [ ] Mar03 [ ]
– Puttin' out fires / Daddy dream / Too many miles / Driftin' man / Damaged goods / Two by two / White lies / (band introduction) / Shot at you / Tears ain't enough / I'm buyin' / I don't wanna talk about it / Like rain / I found you / Can't get closer / Lost a number / Slippery fingers / Message / Girl in motion / Bass and drum intro / Gun and run / The star spangled banner. *(bonus+=)* – The first time ever I saw your face.

– compilations, others, etc. –

on 'A&M' unless mentioned otherwise

Apr 82. (lp/c) *(AMLH/CAM 68543)* **A RHYTHM ROMANCE** [100] [ ]
Apr 82. (7") *(AMS 8211)* **SHINE SILENTLY. / KEITH DON'T GO (ODE TO THE GLIMMER TWIN)** [ ] [ ]
Jun 85. (7") *(AM 262)* **SHINE SILENTLY. / I CAME TO DANCE** [ ] [ ]
(12"+=) *(AMY 262)* – No mercy.
Jun 90. (cd/c/d-lp) *Connoisseur; (VSOP CD/MC/LP 152)* **THE BEST OF NILS LOFGREN – DON'T WALK . . . ROCK** [ ] [–]
– Moon tears (live) / Back it up / Keith don't go (ode to the Glimmer twin) / The sun hasn't set on this boy yet / Goin' back / Cry tough / Jailbait / Can't get closer (WCGC) / Mud in your eye / I came to dance / To be a dreamer / No mercy / Steal away / Baltimore / Shine silently / Secrets in the street / Flip ya flip / Delivery night / Anytime at all (live).
Jun 94. (cd) *Windsong; (WHISCD 001)* **LIVE ON THE TEST (live)** [ ] [–]
May 95. (cd) *Spectrum; (5507502)* **SHINE SILENTLY** [ ] [–]
Jul 95. (cd) *Raven; (RVCD 44)* **SOFT FUN, TOUGH TEARS 1971-79** [ ] [–]
Mar 96. (d-cd) *(540 411-2)* **STEAL YOUR HEART AWAY (THE BEST OF NILS LOFGREN)** [ ] [–]
Aug 97. (d-cd) *Snapper; (SMDCD 106)* **ACROSS THE TRACKS** [ ]
May 98. (cd) *Connoisseur; (NSPCD 517)* **ARCHIVE ALIVE: LIVE AT THE STONE PONY, ASBURY PARK, NEW JERSEY)** [ ] [–]
Nov 98. (cd) *Hux; <(HUX 010)>* **NEW LIVES** (BBC sessions) [ ] Aug98 [ ]
Jan 00. (cd) *Columbia; (495249-2) / Epic; <65697>* **THE VERY BEST OF GRIN FEATURING NILS LOFGREN** [ ] Jun99 [ ]
– Everybody's missin' the sun / See what a love can do / Like rain / We all sung together / Nobody / Sing for happiness / White lies / Hi, hello home / Slippery fingers / Lost a number / Moon tears / Soft fun / Just to have you / Love or else / Sad letter / Ain't love nice / All out / Rusty gun / You're the weight.

LO-FIDELITY ALLSTARS

Formed: London, England . . . mid 90's by THE WREKKED TRAIN (aka DAVE RANDALL), SHERIFF JOHN STONE (aka MATT), THE ALBINO PRIEST (aka PHIL), THE SLAMMER (aka JOHNNY), A ONE MAN CROWD CALLED GENTILEE (aka ANDY) and THE MANY TENTACLES (aka MARTIN); DAVE and MATT were brought up in Sussex, while JOHNNY and engineer MARTIN hail from Leeds. Having met while working in Tower Records, PHIL and MATT found that they had similar tastes, i.e. FUNKADELIC, BOOTSY COLLINS and late, great writer, CHARLES BUKOWSKI. Signed to trendy Big Beat label, 'Skint', they debuted in 1997 with the 'KOOL ROC BASS' EP, the music press heralding them as leaders of the new skool skunk-rock brigade that would also include The REGULAR FRIES. As well as creating a bastard 90's fusion of HAPPY MONDAYS, FLOWERED UP and trippy electro, these bands also shared a greasy haired, dishevelled druggy image. Later the same year, they scored their first Top 50 entry with 'DISCO MACHINE GUN', followed by an even bigger success (Top 30) with 'VISION INCISION', both lifted from their excellent sampletastic Top 20 debut set, 'HOW TO OPERATE WITH A BLOWN MIND' (1998); the record also featured a cover/collaboration of Pigeonhed's 'BATTLEFLAG', which became another hit single later in the year. By this point, DAVE RANDALL had quit the show due to musical differences. Skint's mainmen subsequently delivered a compilation mix born from Brighton's Big Beat Boutique, entitled 'ON THE FLOOR AT THE BOUTIQUE' (2000), featuring a non-stop mix of 17 tracks ranging from JUNGLE BROTHERS, KRS-ONE, TROUBLE FUNK, ARMAND VAN HELDEN, etc, "giving it large" on what must've been one of the most eclectic compilations of the year.

Album rating: HOW TO OPERATE WITH A BLOWN MIND (*8) / ON THE FLOOR AT THE BOUTIQUE various artists (*7)

THE WREKKED TRAIN (aka DAVE RANDALL) – vocals / **THE ALBINO PRIEST** (aka PHIL) – decks, samples / **A ONE MAN CROWD CALLED GENTILEE** (aka ANDY) – bass / **THE SLAMMER** (aka JOHNNY) – drums / **SHERIFF JOHN STONE** (aka MATT) – keyboards / plus **THE MANY TENTACLES** (aka MARTIN) – engineering, keyboards

Skint Sub Pop

Jun 97. (12"ep/cd-ep) *(skint 24/+cd)* **KOOL ROC BASS EP** [ ] [–]
– Kool roc bass (radio) / Kool roc bass / One man's fear / Taking fear from behind. *(re-iss. Jun98; same)*
Sep 97. (12"ep/cd-ep) *(skint 30/+cd)* **DISCO MACHINE GUN EP** [50] [–]
– (mixes; radio / original / II) / Puppy Phat Number One.
(withdrawn after 3 days due to a sample of The BREEDERS 'Cannonball')
Apr 98. (12"ep/cd-ep) *(skint 33/+cd)* **VISION INCISION EP** [30] [–]
– (mixes; radio / 12 inch) / Midfield General shorter / Gringo's return.
(12"ep) *(skint 33x)* – ('A'remixes).
Apr 98. (cd/c/d-lp) *(brassic 8 cd/mc/lp)* <69654> **HOW TO OPERATE WITH A BLOWN MIND** [15] May98 [ ]
– Warming up the brain farm / Kool roc bass / Kasparov's revenge / Blisters on my brain / How to operate with a blown mind / I used to fall in love / Battleflag (feat. Pigeonhed) / Lazer sheep dip funk / Will I get out of jail / Vision incision / Nightime story.
Nov 98. (12"/cd-s; featuring PIGEONHED) *(skint 38/+cd)* *<41551>* **BATTLEFLAG / PONY PRESSURE / BONUS BEATS** [36] [ ]
(cd-s) *(SKINT 38XCD)* – ('A'edit) / ('A'-Space Raiders mix) / ('A'live).
— (Dec'98) DAVE RANDALL left the band
Jun 99. (cd/c; with Various Artists) *(brassic 16 cd/mc)* <63951> **ON THE FLOOR AT THE BOUTIQUE** [ ] Feb00 [ ]
Nov 00. (12"ep/cd-ep) *(skint 59/+cd)* **GHOSTMUTT EP** [ ] [–]
– The all, the all / Voodoo house / Just enough / The all, the all (instrumental).
Oct 01. (12"/cd-s) *(skint 72/+cd)* **LO-FI'S IN IBIZA / LO-FI IN IBIZA (dub) / ZIP . . . JUST GONE** [ ] [–]

Jan 02. (12"/cd-s) *(SKINT 75/+CD)* **SLEEPING FASTER / SLEEPING FASTER (laid mix) / SLEEPING WITH BYRON (hotbed remix) (feat BYRON STINGILY) / ('A'-video)** [ ] [-]

□ LONE JUSTICE (see under ⇒ McKEE, Maria)

LONG RYDERS

Formed: Paisley, Los Angeles, California, USA . . . March '82, out of The UNCLAIMED by SID GRIFFIN, BARRY SKANK, MATT ROBERTS and STEVE WYNN. The latter soon formed his own band, The DREAM SYNDICATE and was superseded by STEPHEN McCARTHY. This revised line-up made an EP for 'Moxie', which included the tracks, 'Time to Time' and 'Deposition Central'. As The LONG RYDERS (named so after the Walter Hill film, 'The Long Riders), they issued a debut album, '10-5-60' (a mini-set), on their own 'Jem' label, a distinctive hybrid of jagged garage rock, psychedelia and country. While the band were lumped in with their mates under the catch-all term, "Paisley Underground", The LONG RYDERS always wore their country influences more proudly. 'NATIVE SONS' (1984), their debut for 'Zippo', marked the fruition of that experimentation, a finely hewn tapestry of alternative country which featured GENE CLARK on the keening 'IVORY TOWER'. Heralded by the critics, the band signed to 'Island' in 1985 and recorded a further two albums, 'STATE OF OUR UNION' (1985) and 'TWO FISTED TALES' (1987). More overtly country and lyrically politically pointed than their previous efforts, the latter proved to be the band's swansong and they split the following year. SID GRIFFIN subsequently relocated to London where he concentrated on his band The COAL PORTERS. The man has also helped to keep the 'Cosmic American Music' flame burning by penning a GRAM PARSONS biog and he continues to write for various music mags. Of late, GRIFFIN initiated a new project, WESTERN ELECTRIC, who released one eponymous set at the turn of the millennium. • **Songwriters:** GRIFFIN-McCARTHY compositions, except YOU'RE GONNA MISS ME (13th Floor Elevators) / I SHALL BE RELEASED + MASTERS OF WAR (Bob Dylan) / DIRTY OLD TOWN (Ewan MacColl) / PRISONERS OF ROCK'N'ROLL (Neil Young) / ANARCHY IN THE UK (Sex Pistols) / PUBLIC IMAGE (P.I.L. w/ STEVE MACK of THAT PETROL EMOTION on vox). • **Trivia:** Will Birch produced them in 1985. SID, STEPHEN + TOM featured on 'Zippo' lp THE LOST WEEKEND by DANNY & DUSTY. They also guested on DREAM SYNDICATE album 'Medicine Show'.

Album rating: 10-5-60 (*6) / NATIVE SONS (*8) / STATE OF OUR UNION (*7) / TWO-FISTED TALES (*5) / METALLIC B.O. early stuff (*4) / Coal Porters: REBELS WITHOUT APPLAUSE (*6) / THE LAND OF HOPE AND CROSBY (*7) / LOS LONDON (*5) / THE GRAM PARSONS TRIBUTE CONCERT (*6) / THE CHRIS HILLMAN TRIBUTE CONCERTS (*6) / Sid Griffin: LITTLE VICTORIES (*5) / Western Electric: WESTERN ELECTRIC (*7)

SID GRIFFIN (b.18 Sep'55, Louisville, Kentucky) – vocals, guitar / **STEPHEN McCARTHY** (b.12 Feb'58, Richmond, Virginia) – steel guitar, vocals; repl. STEVE WYNN (to DREAM SYNDICATE) / **DES BREWER** – bass; repl. BARRY SKANK / **MATT ROBERTS** – drums

not iss. P.V.C.

1983. (m-lp) *<PVC 5906>* **10-5-60** [-] [ ]
– Join my gang / I don't care what's right, I don't care what's wrong / 105-60 / And she rides / Born to believe in you. *(UK-iss.1985 on 'P.V.C.'; PVC 50) (re-iss. Nov85 on 'Zippo'+=; ZANE 004)* – The trip. *(cd-iss. Aug87 on 'Zippo'; CMCAD 31038)*

—— **TOM STEVENS** (b.17 Sep'56, Elkhart, Indiana) – drums repl. DON McCALL who had repl. DES BREWER

—— **GREG SOWDERS** (b.17 Mar'60, La Jolla, Calif.) – drums, repl. ROBERTS

Zippo Frontier

Nov 84. (lp) *(ZONG 004) <4606-1>* **NATIVE SONS** [ ] 1983 [ ]
– Final wild sun / Still by / Ivory tower / Run Dusty run / (Sweet) Metal revenge / Fair game / Tell it to the judge on Sunday / Too close to the light / Wreck of the 809 / Never get to meet the man / I had a dream. *(cd-iss. Jan88; ZONGCD 003)* – (w/ last m-lp tracks). *(cd re-iss. Jun96 on 'Diablo'; DIAB 821) <(cd re-iss. Jul02 on 'Frontier'; FR 31013CD)>*

Apr 85. (7") *(ZIPPO 45-2)* **I HAD A DREAM. / TOO CLOSE TO THE LIGHT (Buckskin mix)** [ ] [ ]

Island Island

Sep 85. (7") *(IS 237)* **LOOKING FOR LEWIS & CLARK. / CHILD BRIDE** [59] [ ]
(d7"+=/10"+=) *(ISD/10IS 237)* – Southside of the story / If I were a bramble and you were a rose.

Oct 85. (lp/c) *(ILPS/ICT 9802) <422842863-1>* **STATE OF OUR UNION** [66] [ ]
– Looking for Lewis & Clark / Lights of downtown / WDIA / Mason-Dixon line / Here comes that train again / Years long ago / Good times tomorrow, hard times today / Two kinds of love / You just can't ride the boxcars anymore / Capturing the flag / State of my union. *<(cd-iss. Mar95 on 'Prima'+=; SID 003)>* – If I were a bramble and you were a rose / Southside of the story / Child bride / Christmas in New Zealand.

Jun 87. (lp/c/cd) *(ILPS/ICT/CID 9869) <422842864-1>* **TWO FISTED TALES** [ ] [ ]
– Gunslinger man / I want you bad / A stitch in time / The light gets in the way / Prairie fire / Baby's in toyland / Long short story / Man of misery / Harriet Tubman's gonna carry me home / For the rest of my life / Spectacular fall. *<(cd re-iss. cd Mar96 on 'Prima'+=; SID 005)>* – Ring bells / Time keeps travelling / State of our union (live) / Baby we've all got to go down (live).

Jun 87. (7") *(IS 330)* **I WANT YOU BAD. / RING BELLS** [ ] [ ]
(12"+=) *(12IS 330)* – State of our union.

—— They split New Year '88. In Spring '90, GRIFFIN formed country-rock band The COAL PORTERS, who released first album 'REBELS WITHOUT APPLAUSE' in 1992. McCARTHY later appeared in GUTTERBALL with STEVE WYNN.

– compilations, others, etc. –

Jan 91. (cd) *Overground; (OVER 16CD)* **METALLIC B.O.** (covers) [ ] [-]
– You're gonna miss me / Route 66 / Brand new headache / Prisoners of rock'n'roll / Dirty old town / Billy Jean / Circle round the sun / Six days on the road / Anarchy in the U.K. / Masters of war / Sandwich man / Blues theme / P.I.L. theme / I shall be released. *(re-iss. Dec94; same) (re-iss. Mar00 on 'Prima'; SID 001)*

May 94. (cd) *Windsong; (WINCD 058)* **BBC RADIO 1 LIVE IN CONCERT (live)** [ ] [-]

COAL PORTERS

SID GRIFFIN – vocals, guitar / **BILLY BLOCK** – drums; repl. GREG SOWDERS / **CHRIS BUESSEM** – guitar / **IAN THOMSON** – bass / added **ANDY KAULKIN** – keyboards

Rubber Rubber

Aug 92. (cd) *<(RUB 17)>* **REBELS WITHOUT APPLAUSE** [ ] [ ]
– Roll Columbia roll / I tell her all the time / The light that shines within / Rhythm and blues angel / Stealin' horses / Sittin' in an isle of palms (live). *(UK+=)* – Stuck on an island / John F. Kennedy blues (live) / March of the tap-dancing rats.

—— **GRIFFIN** retained **THOMSON** and added **PAT McGARVEY** – bass + **BOB STONE** – keyboards / (wife **KATE ST. JOHN** (ex-DREAM ACADEMY) guested

Prima Prima

Sep 94. (cd) *<(SID 002)>* **THE LAND OF HOPE AND CROSBY** [ ] [ ]
– Imperial beach / Death like a valentine / She loved me / What am I doing? (in this thing called love) / How did we get this far? / You can see them there / Windy city / Playing dumb #1 / Everybody's fault but mine / What about tomorrow / All the colours of the world / The pipsqueaks theme.

Sep 95. (cd) *<(SID 004)>* **LOS LONDON** [ ] [ ]
– Me, here at the door / Crackin' at the seams / Chasing rainbows / A woman to love / Apple tree / It happened to me / Santa Mira / After it's broken / A Jacobite at heart / Someone's gonna love you too / Help me / Ain't no way I'll be your cowboy.

Oct 98. (cd-ep) *<SID 008>* **EP ROULETTE** –
– Everything / Emily in ginger / Who'll stop the rain / Help me / Don't fence me in / Me, here at your door (live).

Mar 99. (cd) *<(SID 010)>* **THE GRAM PARSONS TRIBUTE CONCERT (live)**
– Luxury liner / Hickory wind / One hundred years from now / Drug store truck driving man / Sweet mental revenge / Sin city / Return of the grevious angel / Wheels / In my hour of darkness / Older guys / Hot burrito #2 / Six days on the road / Apple tree.

Jul 01. (cd) *<(SID 013)>* **THE CHRIS HILLMAN TRIBUTE CONCERTS (live)**
– (introduction) / My uncle / When the ship comes in / Summer wind / Draft morning / Older guys / Tim between / Wheels / The lost highway / Sin city / Cody, Cody / Brand new heartache / The girl with no name / I am a pilgrim / The fallen eagle / So you want to be a rock'n'roll star? / You ain't goin' nowhere.

SID GRIFFIN

May 97. (cd) *<(SID 007)>* **LITTLE VICTORIES**
– When I'm out walking with you / Jimmy Reed / Good times tomorrow, hard times today / Rate of exchange / I wish I was a mountain / Distant trains / Sailors and soldiers / Man who invented the blues / Monk's moods / Flak jacket / Alma mater / Jerusalem road.

WESTERN ELECTRIC

GRIFFIN + McGARVEY with a few others

Munich Gadfly

May 00. (cd) *(MRCD 199) <261>* **WESTERN ELECTRIC** Mar01
– Everything / The power of glory / When I'm out walking with you / Emily in ginger / 10-4 faithless disciplewhirlwind / Memory captures time / Carousel days / Straight from the heart / (untitled) / (untitled).

□ LOOSE FUR (see under ⇒ WILCO)

LOSTPROPHETS

Formed: Pontypridd, Cardiff, Wales . . . summer 1997 from the ashes of PUBLIC DISTURBANCE by MIKE LEWIS and IAN WATKINS, who duly recruited MIKE CHIPLIN and LEE GAZE. After paying their dues on the local gig circuit, the so called boy band of nu-metal bolstered their line-up and pin-up factor with the addition of bass player STUART RICHARDSON, while JAMIE OLIVER (that's DJ – not celeb chef) wasn't far behind. A deal with indie label 'Visible Noise' and a slow-burning debut album, 'THE FAKE SOUND OF PROGRESS' (2001) ensued amid encouraging reviews and mounting sales. While they contributed little to the advancement of their chosen genre and stood little chance of stealing the MANICS', or even the SUPER FURRY's Welsh rock crown, their spirited racket made them the darlings of the metal press. Watch out in 2004. • **Covered:** A VIEW TO A KILL (Duran Duran).

Album rating: THE FAKE SOUND OF PROGRESS (*6)

IAN WATKINS – vocals / **MIKE LEWIS** – guitar / **LEE GAZE** – guitar / **STUART RICHARDSON** – bass / **BIG MIKE CHIPLIN** – drums / **STEPZAK** – DJ, samples

Visible Noise Columbia

Nov 97. (demo-cd-s) **HERE COMES THE PARTY** –

1998. (demo-cd-s) **PARA TODAS LAS PUTAS CE LOSAS** –

Oct 00. (cd) *(TORMENT 5CD) <85955>* **THE FAKE SOUND OF PROGRESS**
– Shinobi vs. Dragon Ninja / The fake sound of progress / Five is a four letter word / . . .And she told me to leave / Kobrakai / The handsome life of swing / A thousand apologies / Still laughing / For sure / Awkward / Ode to summer. *(re-mast.Feb02; TORMENT 10CD)* – hit UK No.44

Nov 01. (7") *(TORMENT 18)* **SHINOBI VS. DRAGON NINJA. / MILES AWAY FROM NOWHERE** 41 –
(cd-s+=) *(TORMENT 17)* – Still laughing (BBC Radio 1 session).
(cd-s) *(TORMENT 16)* – ('A'side) / Directions / The lesson part 1.

Mar 02. (7") *(TORMENT 21)* **THE FAKE SOUND OF PROGRESS. / HAPPY NEW YEAR, HAVE A GOOD 1985** 21 –
(cd-s+=) *(TORMENT 19)* – A view to a kill.
(cd-s) *(TORMENT 20)* – ('A'side) / Shoulder to the wheel / Need you tonight.

—— **JAMIE OLIVER** – keyboards, samples; repl. STEPZAK

Nov 03. (7") *(TORMENT 31)* **BURN BURN. / OUR BROKEN HEARTS (SCENE FROM TOP GUN 2)** 17 –
(cd-s+=) *(TORMENT 29)* – Like a fire.
(cd-s) *(TORMENT 30)* – ('A'side) / Lucky you / Push out the jive, bring in the love.

LOVE

Formed: Los Angeles, California, USA . . . early '65 originally as The GRASS ROOTS, by ARTHUR LEE and former BYRDS roadie BRYAN MacLEAN. The contrasting songwriters recruited JOHN ECHOLS, KEN FORSSI and DON CONKA (the latter being replaced by SNOOPY PFISTERER). When another band of the same name made the US charts, they became LOVE, soon signing to Jac Holzman's 'Elektra' records. In 1966, they released a snarling cover of Burt Bacharach's 'MY LITTLE RED BOOK', nearly breaking it into the US Top 50. With The LEAVES beating them to the US Top 40 on a cover of 'HEY JOE', LOVE opted instead for a British release, although it failed to chart. Soon after, an eponymous album hit the shops, a fairly competent folk-rock set that nevertheless contained the classics, 'SIGNED D.C.', 'CAN'T EXPLAIN' and the two singles. Around the same time, the band scored their only Top 40 success with the galloping HENDRIX-like psych-out of '7 AND 7 IS'. Early in 1967, they followed up with the classic, 'DA CAPO' album, containing the ambitious 20-minute 'REVELATION' alongside such timeless jewels, 'ORANGE SKIES', 'SHE COMES IN COLORS', 'STEPHANIE KNOWS WHO', 'THE CASTLE' and the previous 45. Shacked-up in LEE's Hollywood mansion, the band eventually emerged with 'FOREVER CHANGES', often cited as one of the greatest albums of all-time. A psychedelic tour de force, it combined acoustic musings, Latin rhythms and the eerily surreal LEE-penned lyrics. Almost every track was flawless and it remains one of rock's great mysteries why the album's two singles, 'ALONE AGAIN OR' and 'ANDMOREAGAIN', failed to chart. Equally baffling was the fact that the album only made the highest position of No.154, while in Britain it hit the Top 30. The band recorded a further brilliant single, 'YOUR MIND AND WE BELONG TOGETHER', before LEE sacked the rest of the group "cause they couldn't cut it". He subsequently formed a "new" LOVE with JAY DONELLAN, JIM HOBSON, FRANK FAYAD, GEORGE SURANOVICH and some additional members. This line-up cut a fourth album, the disappointing 'FOUR SAIL', following it up with two others in the early 70's, 'OUT HERE' and 'FALSE START'. Eventually LEE was again left on his own, leading him to carve out a solo career, the album 'VINDICATOR' (1972) being released to a lukewarm reception. He re-created yet another LOVE in 1974, fans again bitterly disappointed with a commercial set that even unadvisedly touched on disco! After various other re-unions in the late 70's, LEE released a self-titled solo effort in 1981, before going AWOL again. In the early 90's, with renewed LOVE interest, LEE re-formed the group for a re-union album, 'ARTHUR LEE AND LOVE'. The 90's weren't exactly kind to this revered eccentric, LEE being diagnosed with Parkinson's Disease and, more recently, receiving a 12-year sentence for firearms offences. His former partner, born-again christian BRYAN MacLEAN (who had virtually retired in 1970, although he did pen songs for his half-sister MARIA McKEE and country-star PATTY LOVELESS) tragically died of a suspected heart attack on Christmas Day, 1998. ARTHUR LEE quietly re-formed LOVE for a series of live concerts in the late 90's, 'ELECTRICALLY SPEAKING' (2001), was document of some of these. Following LEE's release from prison, he eventually got a serious band together and began touring again to increasing UK acclaim and often sold out shows. The reverence afforded the wayward genius was such that he was able to stage a performace of 'FOREVER CHANGES' in its entirety at London's Royal Festival Hall in January 2003. The resulting live document, titled simply 'THE FOREVER CHANGES CONCERT' (2003), was testament to both the album's timeless appeal and LEE's enduring genius. • **Trivia:** In 1970, LEE was about to initiate a supergroup, BAND AID (not the charity) with STEVE WINWOOD and HENDRIX, but JIMI died on September '70. In 1973, he recorded an album, 'BLACK BEAUTY' for 'Buffalo' records. This was shelved, although illegal bootlegs did surface.

Album rating: LOVE (*6) / DA CAPO (*8) / FOREVER CHANGES (*10) / FOUR SAIL (*6) / OUT HERE (*4) / FALSE START (*4) / REEL TO REAL (*4) / LOVE LIVE (*4) / ARTHUR LEE AND LOVE (*4) / COMES IN COLOURS compilation (*8) / LOVE STORY 1966-1972 compilation (*8) / ELECTRICALLY SPEAKING: LIVE IN CONCERT (*5) / FIVE STRING SERENADE (*6) / THE FOREVER CHANGES CONCERT (*7) / Bryan MacLean: IFYOUBELIEVEIN (*6) / posthumous CANDY'S WALTZ (*5)

ARTHUR LEE (b. ARTHUR TAYLOR PORTER, 1945, Memphis, Tennessee) – vocals, guitar (ex-LAG'S, ex-AMERICAN FOUR) / **BRYAN MacLEAN** (b.1947) – guitar, vocals / **JOHN ECHOLS** (b.1945, Memphis) – lead guitar (ex-LAG'S) / **KEN FORSSI** (b.1943, Cleveland, Ohio) – bass (ex-SURFARIS) / **ALBAN 'SNOOPY' PFISTERER** (b.1947, Switzerland) – drums; repl. DON CONKA

London Elektra

Mar 66. (7") *<45603>* **MY LITTLE RED BOOK. / A MESSAGE TO PRETTY** [–] [52]

Jun 66. (7") *(HLZ 10053)* **HEY JOE. / MY LITTLE RED BOOK** [ ] [–]

Sep 66. (7") *(HLZ 10073) <45605>* **7 AND 7 IS. / NO. FOURTEEN** [ ] Aug66 [33]

Elektra Elektra

Sep 66. (lp; mono/stereo) *<(EKL/EKS 7-4001)>* **LOVE** [ ] Jul66 [57]
– My little red book / A message to Pretty / Softly to me / Emotions / Gazing / Signed D.C. / Mushroom clouds / Can't explain / My flash on you / No matter what you do / You I'll be following / Hey Joe / Coloured bells falling / And more. *(re-iss. Jan72 lp/c; K/K4 42068) (re-iss. Feb87 on 'Edsel'; ED 218) (cd-iss. Feb93 & Dec93; 7559 74001-2) <cd re-iss. Sep01 +=; 8122 73567-2>* – LOVE (stereo). *<(lp re-iss. Jan02 on 'Sundazed'; SCLP 5100)>*

— added **MICHAEL STUART** – drums (ex-SONS OF ADAM) ('SNOOPY' now on keyboards) + **TJAY CANTRELLI** – saxophone

Dec 66. (7") *(EKSN 45010) <45608>* **SHE COMES IN COLOURS. / ORANGE SKIES** [ ] [ ]

Feb 67. (lp; mono/stereo) *<(EKL/EKS 7-4005)>* **DA CAPO** [ ] [80]
– Stephanie knows who / Orange skies / Que vida / 7 and 7 is / The castle / She comes in colors / Revelation. *(re-iss. Jan72 lp/c; K/K4 42011) (cd-iss. 1989 on 'WEA'; 974005-2) <(lp re-iss. Jan02 on 'Sundazed';* **SCLP 5101**)>

Mar 67. (7") *<45613>* **QUE VIDA (edit). / HEY JOE** [–] [ ]

Sep 67. (7") *(EKSN 45016)* **THE CASTLE. / SOFTLY TO ME** [ ] [–]

— Reverted to a quintet when 'SNOOPY' and TJAY left. (latter to DOMINIC TROIANO)

Jan 68. (7") *<45629>* **ALONE AGAIN OR (edit). / A HOUSE IS NOT A MOTEL** [–] [ ]

Jan 68. (7") *(EKSN 45024)* **ALONE AGAIN OR. / BUMMER IN THE SUMMER** [ ] [–]
(re-iss. Oct70; 2101-019)

Feb 68. (lp; mono/stereo) *<(EKL/EKS 7-4013)>* **FOREVER CHANGES** [24] Jan68 [ ]
– Alone again or / A house is not a motel / Andmoreagain / The daily planet / Old man / The red telephone / Maybe the people would be the times or between Clark and Hilldale / Live and let live / Good honor man he sees everything like this / Bummer in the summer / You set the scene. *(re-iss. Jan72 lp/c; K/K4 42015) (cd-iss. Jul88 on 'WEA'; 7559 60656-2) <cd re-mast.Feb01 +=; 8122 73537-2>* – Hummingbirds (demo) / Wonder people (I do wonder) (alt.) / Alone again or (alt.) / You set the scene (alt.) / Your mind and we belong together (alt.) / Your mind and we belong together (single) / Laughing stock (single). *<(lp re-iss. Jan02 on 'Sundazed'; SCLP 5102)>*

Mar 68. (7") *(EKSN 45024)* **ANDMOREAGAIN. / THE DAILY PLANET** [ ] [–]

Sep 68. (7") *(EKSN 45038) <45633>* **YOUR MIND AND WE BELONG TOGETHER. / LAUGHING STOCK** [ ] [ ]

— ARTHUR LEE dismissed others and recruited new people below **JAY DONELLAN** (LEWIS) – guitar / **JIM HOBSON** – keyboards / **FRANK FAYAD** – bass / **GEORGE SURANOVICH** – drums

— augmented by **PAUL MARTIN** and **GARY ROWLES** – guitar plus **DRACKEN THEAKER** – keyboards (ex-CRAZY WORLD OF ARTHUR BROWN)

Nov 69. (lp) *<(EKS 74049)>* **FOUR SAIL** [ ] Sep69 [ ]
– August / Your friend and mine – Neil's song / I'm with you / Good times / Singing cowboy / Dream / Robert Montgomery / Nothing / Talking in my sleep / Always see your face. *(re-iss. Jan72 lp/c; K/K4 42030) (re-iss. Nov87 on 'Thunderbolt'; THBL 047) (cd-iss. Jun88; CDBT 047) <(cd re-mast.Nov02; 8122 73640-2)>*

Mar 70. (7") *(EKSN 45086)* **I'M WITH YOU. / ROBERT MONTGOMERY** [ ] [–]

Harvest Blue Thumb

May 70. (d-lp) *(SHDW 3-4) <BTS 9000>* **OUT HERE** [29] Dec69 [ ]
– I'll pray for you / Abalony / Signed D.C. / Listen to my song / I'm down / Stand out / Discharged / Doggone / I still wonder / Love is more than words or better late than never / Nice to be / Car lights on in the day time blues / Run to the top / Willow willow / Instra-mental / You are something / Gather round. *(re-iss. Jul88 on 'Big Beat' lp; WIKA 69) (cd-iss. Jul90; CDWIKA 69)*

May 70. (7") *<BLU-7 106>* **I'LL PRAY FOR YOU. / STAND OUT** [–] [ ]

Nov 70. (7") *(HAR 5030) <BLU-7 116>* **KEEP ON SHINING. / THE EVERLASTING FIRST** [ ] [ ]

— **GARY ROWLES** now full time; repl. JAY

Jan 71. (lp) *(SHVL 787) <BTS 8822>* **FALSE START** [ ] Dec 70 [ ]
– The everlasting first / Flying / Gimi a little break / Stand out / Keep on shining / Anytime / Slick Dick / Love is coming / Feel daddy feel good / Ride that vibration. *(cd-iss. Jul92 on 'Beat Goes On'; BGOCD 127) (cd re-iss. Apr94 on 'One Way'; MCAD 22029)*

Mar 71. (7") *(HAR 5014)* **STAND OUT. / DOGGONE** [ ] [–]

ARTHUR LEE

— a solo venture with BAND AID: **FAYAD** and new men **CHARLES KARP** – guitar / **CRAIG TARWATER** – guitar / **CLARENCE McDONALD** – keyboards / **DON PONCHA** – drums / + guest **DAVID HULL** – bass

A&M A&M

Aug 72. (lp) *(AMLS 64356) <SP 4356>* **VINDICATOR** [ ] [ ]
– Sad song / You can save up to 50% / Love jumped through my window / Find somebody / He said she said / Everytime I look up / Everybody's gotta live / He knows a lot of good women / You want change for your re-run / Hamburger breath stinkfinger / Ol' morgue mouth / Busted feet. *(cd-iss. Apr97; 540697-2)*

Aug 72. (7") *<1361>* **EVERYBODY'S GOT TO LIVE. / LOVE JUMPED THROUGH MY WINDOW** [–] [ ]

Nov 72. (7") *<1381>* **SAD SONG. / YOU WANT TO CHANGE FOR YOUR RE-RUN** [–] [ ]

LOVE

— **ARTHUR LEE** recruited **MELVIN WHITTINGTON + JOHN STERLING** – guitar / **SHERWOOD AKUNA + ROBERT ROZENO** – bass / **JOE BLOCKER** – drums

R.S.O. R.S.O.

Dec 74. (7") *<SO 502>* **TIME IS LIKE A RIVER. / WITH A LITTLE ENERGY** [–] [ ]

Jan 75. (7") *(2090 151)* **TIME IS LIKE A RIVER. / YOU SAID YOU WOULD** [ ] [–]

Jan 75. (lp) *(2394 145) <SO 4804>* **REEL TO REAL** [ ] [ ]
– Time is like a river / Stop the music / Who are you? / Good old fashioned love / Which witch is which / With a little energy / Singing cowboy / Be thankful for what you got / You said you would / Busted feet / Everybody's gotta live.

Mar 75. (7") *<SO 506>* **YOU SAID YOU WOULD. / GOOD OLD FASHIONED DREAM** [–] [ ]

ARTHUR LEE

— solo again, using loads of session people

Da Capo / not iss.

1977. (7"ep) *(CAP 001)* **I DO WONDER / JUST US. / DO YOU KNOW THE SECRET? / HAPPY YOU** — / –

Beggars Banquet / Rhino

Jul 81. (lp) *(BEGA 26)* <*RNLP 020*> **ARTHUR LEE**
– One / I do wonder / Just us / Happy you / Do you know the secret / One and one / Seven and seven is / Mr. Lee / Bend down / Stay away from evil / Many rivers to cross.

— LOVE re-formed in Autumn '91, with **ARTHUR LEE, DON CONKA, SHUGGIE OTIS** – guitar / **MELLAN WHITTINGTON** – guitar / **SHERWOOD AKUNA** – bass

New Rose / not iss.

May 92. (cd/lp) *(ROSE CD/LP 288)* **ARTHUR LEE AND LOVE** — / –
– Five string serenade / Somebody's watching you / Twenty on my way / You're the prettiest song / I believe in you / Ninety miles away / Seventeen / Love saga / The watcher / Passing by. *(re-iss. May94; 422214)*

— ARTHUR was diagnosed with Parkinson's Disease in the early 90's (see biog above)

LOVE

ARTHUR LEE – vocals, guitar / **MELVAN WHITTINGTON** – guitar / **SHERWOOD AKUNA** – bass / **GARY STERN** – drums

Yeaah / Yeaah

Jun 01. (cd) <*(YEAAH 49)*> **ELECTRICALLY SPEAKING: LIVE IN CONCERT (live)** — / Nov01
– Alone again or / My little red book / 7 and 7 is / Orange skies / Signed DC / The everlasting first / Andmoreagain / Hey Joe / She comes in colors / Everybody's gotta live – Instant karma / That's the way it goes / Signed DC / Andmoreagain / Little wing.

Last Call / Last Call

Oct 01. (cd; as ARTHUR LEE & LOVE) <*(306986-2)*> **FIVE STRING SERENADE**
– Five string serenade / Somebody's watching you / Twenty on my way / You're the prettiest song / I believe in you / Nonety miles away / Seventeen / Love saga / Watcher / Passing by.

Snapper / Snapper

Jul 03. (d-cd) <*(SMACD 868/869)*> **THE FOREVER CHANGES CONCERT (live at The Royal Festival Hall)** — / Sep03
– Alone again or / A house is not a motel / Andmoreagain / The daily planet / Old man / The red telephone / Maybe the people would be the times (or between Clark and Hilldale) / Live and let live / The good humor man he sees everything like this / Bummer in the summer / You set the scene / Seven and seven is / Your mind and we belong together / Signed D.C. / My little red book / Alone again or.

– LOVE compilations etc. –

on 'Elektra' unless mentioned otherwise

Aug 70. (7") <*45700*> **ALONE AGAIN OR. / GOOD TIMES** – / 99
Dec 70. (lp) *(2469 009)* <*EKS 74049*> **LOVE REVISITED** — / Aug70
(re-iss. Jan72 lp/c; K/K4 42091) <*(re-iss. Jan02 on 'Sundazed'; SCLP 5104)*>
Feb 73. (lp/c) *(K/K4 32002)* **LOVE MASTERS** — / –
– My little red book / Signed D.C. / Hey Joe / 7 and 7 is / Stephanie knows who / Orange skies / Que vida / The castle / She comes in colours / Laughing stock / Your mind / And we belong together / Old man / The Daily Planet / A house is not a motel / Andmoreagain / Alone again or.
Jul 73. (7") *(K 12113)* **ALONE AGAIN OR. / ANDMOREAGAIN** — / –
(re-iss. Apr84; E 9740)
Sep 76. (7") *(K 12231)* **ALONE AGAIN OR. / THE CASTLE**
1980. (lp) *Rhino;* <*RNLP 800*> **THE BEST OF LOVE** – / —
1981. (pic-lp) *Rhino;* <*RNDF 251*> **LOVE LIVE (live)** – / —
1982. (lp) *M.C.A.;* <*27025*> **STUDIO / LIVE** – / —
(UK cd-iss. Apr94 on 'One Way'; MCAD 22036)
1986. (lp) *Rhino;* <*RNLP 70175*> **GOLDEN ARCHIVE** – / —
Jan 93. (cd) *Raven; (RVCD 29)* **COMES IN COLOURS** — / –
– My little red book / Can't explain / Message to pretty / Softly to me / Hey Joe / Signed D.C. / And more / 7 and 7 is / No.14 / Stephanie knows who / Orange skies / Que vida / The castle / She comes in colors / Alone again or / Andmoreagain / Old man / A house is not a motel / Daily planet / Live and let live / Laughing stock / Your mind and we belong together / August / (Arthur Lee interview). *(re-iss. Feb99; same)*
May 00. (cd/lp; by ARTHUR LEE & SHACK) *Viper;* <*(VIPER 3 CD/LP)*> **LIVE IN LIVERPOOL 1992 (live)**

BRYAN MacLEAN

— solo recordings between 1966-82 + 1970's respectively

Sundazed / Sundazed

Nov 97. (cd) <*(SC 11051)*> **IFYOUBELIEVEIN**
– Barber John / Fresh hope / Kathleen / Orange skies / Strong commitment / Alone again or / Tired of sitting / Blues singer / Friday's party / People / Claudia / If you believe in / Orange skies (2nd version) / Alone again or (2nd version) / She looks good / Old man.
Oct 00. (cd) <*SC 11076*> **CANDY'S WALTZ** – / —
– I can't remember / Most of us / Special joy / Love will be here / Candy's waltz / Always I wanted / Castle waltz / Hip-hip hooray / Claudia / Husband and father / If this is love / Claudine's samba / Candy's waltz (live) / Kathleen (live) / You could be here / Soon / Darlin / Love in the end / We'll be together again / (Bryan MacLean interview).

☐ LOVE AND ROCKETS (see under ⇒ BAUHAUS)

☐ LOVE SCULPTURE (see under ⇒ EDMUNDS, Dave)

☐ LOVE SPIT LOVE (see under ⇒ PSYCHEDELIC FURS)

LOVIN' SPOONFUL

Formed: Greenwich Village, New York, USA ... early '65 by JOHN SEBASTIAN and ZAL YANOVSKY. They had been part of the N.Y. folk scene during '63-'64 and had played in bands The HALIFAX THREE and The MUGWUMPS, the latter featuring DENNY DOHERTY and CASS ELLIOT (future MAMAS & THE PAPAS). Via producer ERIK JACOBSEN, they secured a deal with the 'Kama Sutra' label, issuing debut 45, 'DO YOU BELIEVE IN MAGIC', which hit the US Top 10. A string of hits followed, including a 1966 US No.1, 'SUMMER IN THE CITY'. Its jaunty momentum was preceded by the meandering 'DAYDREAM', a No.2 on both sides of the Atlantic and the perfect soundtrack for "rolling a fat one" on a lazy midsummer's afternoon. Unfortunately for the band and especially YANOVSKY, the LOVIN' SPOONFUL had a renowned penchant for doing just that, amid other more serious narcotic dabblings. After a bust, he was allegedly sent packing by the rest of the band in 1967 for informing on his dealer. The next album, 'EVERYTHING PLAYING', lacked the effervescent sparkle of their previous material and stiffed big style. With nary a hit single in sight, the band struggled on with, ironically, YANOVSKY replacing the recently departed SEBASTIAN for a final lacklustre album. While the band's vaguely psychedelic pop was fine in 1966, by the following year's 'Summer of love' the 'SPOONFUL's happy go lucky ditties appeared a bit lukewarm in contrast to the cosmic soul searching of many other bands, especiallly their L.A. counterparts THE BYRDS and LOVE. Nevertheless, their jug-band pop/rock still has the power to put a smile on the glummest of faces and as well as the hits there were more than a few sweetly charming tracks like 'DARLIN' COMPANION' tucked away on their albums. SEBASTION was the only member to have any kind of solo success although the band regrouped fleetingly in 1980 for a guest appearance on Paul Simon's 'One Trick Pony'. • **Songwriters:** SEBASTIAN (with some traditional arrangements of 30's songs) until his departure when BUTLER was virtually going solo under

LOVIN' SPOONFUL banner, although using pensmiths BONNER and GORDON. Covered; YOU BABY (Ronettes) / OTHER SIDE OF THIS LIFE (Fred Neil) / ALMOST GROWN (Chuck Berry) / SEARCHIN' (Coasters) / NEVER GOING BACK (John Stewart) / etc.

Album rating: DO YOU BELIEVE IN MAGIC (*7) / DAYDREAM (*6) / WHAT'S UP, TIGER LILY? soundtrack (*4) / HUMS OF THE LOVIN' SPOONFUL (*7) / THE BEST OF THE LOVIN' SPOONFUL compilation (*8) / YOU'RE A BIG BOY NOW (*5) / EVERYTHING PLAYING (*5) / REVELATION: REVOLUTION '69 (*3) / ANTHOLOGY compilation (*8)

JOHN SEBASTIAN (b.17 Mar'44, New York City, N.Y.) – vocals, guitar, harmonica, autoharp / **ZALMAN YANOVSKY** (b.19 Dec'44, Toronto, Canada) – guitar, vocals / **STEVE BOONE** (b.23 Sep'43, Camp Lejeune, New Connecticut) – bass, vocals / **JOE BUTLER** (b.16 Sep'43, Long Island, N.Y.) – drums, vocals

Pye Inter | Kama Sutra

Oct 65. (7") *(7N 25327)* <201> **DO YOU BELIEVE IN MAGIC. / ON THE ROAD AGAIN** [ ] Jul65 [9]

Jan 66. (7") *(7N 25344)* <205> **YOU DIDN'T HAVE TO BE SO NICE. / MY GAL** [ ] Nov65 [10]

Mar 66. (lp; mono/stereo) *(NPL 28069)* <*KLP/+S 8050*> **DO YOU BELIEVE IN MAGIC** [ ] Nov65 [32]
– Do you believe in magic / Blues in the bottle / Sportin' life / My gal / You baby / Fishin' blues / Did you ever have to make up your mind / Wild about my lovin' / Other side of this life / Younger girl / On the road again / Night owl blues. <*(cd-iss. Jul02 on 'R.C.A.'+=; 74465 99730-2)*> – Alley oop / Younger girl (demo) / Blues in the bottle (alt.) / Wild about my lovin' (alt.) / Other side of this life (alt.). <*(lp re-iss. Jul02 on 'Sundazed'+=; SCLP 5159)*>

Apr 66. (7") *(7N 25361)* <208> **DAYDREAM. / NIGHT OWL BLUES** [2] Feb66 [2]

May 66. (lp; mono/stereo) *(NPL 28078)* <*KLP/+S 8051*> **DAYDREAM** [8] Mar66 [10]
– Daydream / There she is / It's not time now / Warm baby / Day blues / Let the boy rock and roll / Jug band music / Didn't want to have to do it / You didn't have to be so nice / Bald headed Lena / Butchie's tune / Big noise from Speonk. *(re-iss. 1990 on 'Castle' lp/cd; CLA/+CD 194)* <*(cd re-iss. Jul02 on 'R.C.A.'+=; 74465 99731-2)*> – Fishin' blues / Didn't want to have to do it / Jug band music / Daydream (demo) / Night owl blues (alt.). <*(lp re-iss. Jul02 on 'Sundazed'+=; SCLP 5160)*>

May 66. (7") <209> **DID YOU EVER HAVE TO MAKE UP YOUR MIND. / DIDN'T WANT TO HAVE TO DO IT** [–] [2]

Kama Sutra | Kama Sutra

Jul 66. (7") <211> **SUMMER IN THE CITY. / BUTCHIE'S TUNE** [–] [1]

Jul 66. (7") *(KAS 200)* **SUMMER IN THE CITY. / BALD HEADED LENA** [8] [–]

Sep 66. (lp; mono/stereo) <*KLP/+S 8053*> **WHAT'S UP, TIGER LILY (Soundtrack)** [–] [ ]
– (introduction to Flick) / POW / Gray prison blues / POW revisited / Unconscious minuet / Fishin' blues / Respoken / A cool million / Speakin' of spoken / Lookin' to spy / Phil's love theme / (end title).

Oct 66. (7") <216> **RAIN ON THE ROOF. / POW** [–] [10]

Oct 66. (7") *(KAS 201)* **RAIN ON THE ROOF. / WARM BABY** [ ] [–]

Dec 66. (lp; mono/stereo) *(KLP 401)* <*KLP/+S 8054*> **HUMS OF THE LOVIN' SPOONFUL** [ ] Nov66 [14]
– Sittin' here lovin' you / Bes' friends / Voodoo in the basement / Darlin' companion / Henry Thomas / Full measure / Rain on the roof / Coconut grove / Nashville cats / 4 eyes / Summer in the city. *(re-iss. 1990 on 'Castle' lp/cd; CLA/+CD 195)* <*(cd re-iss. Apr03 on 'R.C.A.'+=; 74465 99732-2)*> – Darlin' companion (alt.) / Rain on the roof (alt.) / 4 eyes (alt.) / Full measure (alt.) / Voodoo in the basement (alt.) / Darlin' companion (alt.). <*(lp re-iss. Apr03 on 'Sundazed'; SCLP 5166)*>

Dec 66. (7") *(KAS 204)* <219> **NASHVILLE CATS. / FULL MEASURE** [26] [8] [87]

Feb 67. (7") *(KAS 207)* <220> **DARLING BE HOME SOON. / DARLIN' COMPANION** [44] [15]

Apr 67. (7") <225> **SIX O'CLOCK. / YOU'RE A BIG BOY NOW** [–] [18]

May 67. (lp; mono/stereo) *(KLP 402)* <*KLP/+S 8058*> **YOU'RE A BIG BOY NOW (Soundtrack)** [ ] Apr67 [ ]
– You're a big boy now / Lonely (Amy's theme) / Wash her away / Kite chase / Try and be happy / Peep show percussion / Girl, beautiful girl / Darling be home soon / Dixieland big boy / Letter to Barbara / Barbara's theme / Miss Thing's thang / March / The finale.

May 67. (lp; mono/stereo) *(KLP 403)* <*KLP/+S 8056*> **THE BEST OF THE LOVIN' SPOONFUL** (compilation) [ ] Mar67 [3]
– Do you believe in magic / Did you ever have to make up your mind / Butchie's tune / Jug band music / Night owl blues / You didn't have to be so nice / Daydream / Blues in the bottle / Didn't want to have to do it / Wild about my lovin' / Younger girl / Summer in the city. *(re-iss. Mar69 on 'Marble Arch'; MAL 1115)*

May 67. (7") *(KAS 208)* **SIX O'CLOCK. / THE FINALE** [ ] [–]

Jul 67. (7") <231> **YOU'RE A BIG BOY NOW. / LONELY (AMY'S THEME)** [–] [ ]

— **JERRY YESTER** – guitar, vocals (ex-MODERN FOLK QUARTET) repl. YANOVSKY who was ostracized by rest, after reportedly being busted for drugs and incriminating others to avoid prosecution and deportation back to Canada.

Oct 67. (7") *(KAS 210)* <239> **SHE IS STILL A MYSTERY. / ONLY PRETTY, WHAT A PITY** [ ] [27]

Nov 67. (7") *(KAS 211)* <241> **MONEY. / CLOSE YOUR EYES** [ ] [48]

Mar 68. (lp) *(KLP 404)* <*KLPS 8061*> **EVERYTHING PLAYING** [ ] Jan68 [ ]
– She is still a mystery / Priscilla millionaira / Boredom / Six o'clock / Forever / Darling be home soon / Younger generation / Money / Old folks / Only pretty, what a pity / Try a little bit / Close your eyes. *(cd-iss. Feb97 on 'Wooden Hill'; (HILLCD 11)* <*(cd re-iss. Apr03 on 'R.C.A.'+=; 74465 99733-2)*> – She is still a mystery (alt.) / Only pretty, what a pity (alt.) / Try a little bit (alt.).

May 68. (lp; mono/stereo) *(KLP/+S 405)* <*KLPS 8064*> **THE BEST OF THE LOVIN' SPOONFUL VOL. 2** (compilation) [ ] Mar68 [ ]
– Money / She is still a mystery / Younger generation / Six o'clock / Darling be home soon / lovin' you / Boredom / Full measure / Nashville cats / Rain on the roof / Darlin' companion. *(re-iss. Mar69 on 'Marble Arch'; MAL 1116)*

— Now a trio (BUTLER now vocals) after SEBASTIAN left to go solo.

Oct 68. (7") *(KAS 213)* <250> **NEVER GOING BACK. / FOREVER** [ ] Jul68 [73]

Oct 68. (7") <251> **(TIL I) RUN WITH YOU. / REVELATION** [–] [ ]

Jan 69. (7") <255> **ME ABOUT YOU. / AMAZING AIR** [–] [91]

Jun 69. (lp; by The LOVIN' SPOONFUL featuring JOE BUTLER) *(620 009)* <8073> **REVELATION: REVOLUTION '69** [ ] Mar69 [ ]
– Amazing air / Never going back / The prophet / Only yesterday / War games / (Til I) Run with you / Jug of wine / Revelation: revolution '69 / Me about you / Words.

— BUTLER was virtually solo, with BONNER & GORDON the main songwriters.

— In 1969, BUTLER packed in group name. 20 years later BUTLER, BOONE, JERRY YESTER and brother JIM YESTER re-formed for US concerts.

– (selective) compilations, etc. –

May 88. (lp/c/cd) *See For Miles; (SEE/+K/CD 229)* **THE EP COLLECTION** [ ] [–]

Aug 88. (d-lp/c/cd) *Castle; (CCS LP/MC/CD 187)* **THE COLLECTION** [ ] [–]
– Do you believe in magic / Did you ever have to make up your mind / Younger girl / Jug band music / Didn't want to have to do it / Daydream / You're a big boy now / Wash her away / Girl beautiful girl (Barbara's theme) / Bespoken / Darling be home soon / Lookin' to spy / You didn't have to be so nice / Sittin' here lovin' you / Darlin' companion / Rain on the roof / Coconut grove / Summer in the city / She is still a mystery / Boredom / Six o'clock / Younger generation / Till I run with you / Never going back.

Nov 88. (d-lp/d-c/d-cd) *That's Original; (TFO LP/MC/CD 12)* **DO YOU BELIEVE IN MAGIC / EVERYTHING PLAYING** [ ] [–]

Apr 94. (cd) *Disky; (DISK 4503)* **HIT SINGLE COLLECTABLES** [ ] [ ]

Sep 97. (d-cd) *Magic; (51778-2)* **THE 1960'S FRENCH EP COLLECTION** [ ] [ ]

Jan 98. (cd) *Camden; (74321 55849-2)* **THE VERY BEST OF THE LOVIN' SPOONFUL** [ ] [ ]

Sep 99. (cd) *Camden; (74321 69952-2)* **WHAT'S UP TIGER LILY? / YOU'RE A BIG BOY NOW** [ ] [ ]

May 00. (d-cd) *Buddha; (74465 99716-2)* **GREATEST HITS** [ ] [ ]

Nov 02. (cd-ep) *Magic; (3930243)* **DO YOU BELIEVE IN MAGIC** [ ] [ ]

Jul 03. (cd) *Paradiso; (PA 7712)* **THE BEST OF THE LOVIN' SPOONFUL** [ ] [ ]

LOW

Formed: Duluth, Minnesota, USA ... late 1993 by Mormons ALAN SPARHAWK, his wife MIMI PARKER and third member, JOHN NICHOLS (replaced by ZAK SALLY after debut). Their early efforts, 'I COULD LIVE IN HOPE' (1994) and 'LONG DIVISION' (1995), were more or less ignored, although critics pricked up their ears for the low-key Lo-Fi/ambient classic, 'THE CURTAIN HITS THE CAST' (1996). LOW subsequently completed a few UK gigs to promote it during that summer and later cut a single for the legendary 'Sub Pop', 'VENUS'. The trio delivered a further two sets, namely 'SONGS FOR A DEAD PILOT' (1997) and 'ONE MORE REASON TO FORGET' (1998), described as "sad-core" in the music tabloids; it also featured 17-minute track, 'DO YOU KNOW HOW TO WALTZ?'). 1999 saw the return of the trio and the release of their 5th and best work to date, the bruised and ultra sensitive 'SECRET NAME' album. Recorded over a 7-day period with West Coast rock throwback and ex-BIG BLACK frontman STEVE ALBINI riding the faders, the band had hit a new creative peak with this warm and whispering alternative classic. Tracks such as 'SOON' and the harmonic 'MISSOURI' evoked blissful sensation and echoed tingling country heir to GRAM PARSONS. Others like 'TWO-STEP' and 'I REMEMBER' could easily be compared to a CARPENTERS ballad or something reminising GALAXIE 500. Meanwhile, ZAK SALLY moonlighted with another minimalist trio, ENEMYMINE (along with MIKE KUNKA of GODHEADSILO and DANNY SASAKI), recording an eponymous mini-set for Calvin Johnson's 'K' imprint. Towards the end of the millennium, LOW came up with 'THE CHRISTMAS EP', which featured four brand new tracks and cover of four traditional hymns that would peacefully send the children off to sleep by the fire come the festive season. Prolific as always, LOW returned in 2001 with their most accessible album to date, the haunting 'THINGS WE LOST IN THE FIRE'. The album, produced by Steve Albini once again, saw the group head towards a more uptempo, song-based direction, although tracks such as 'WHITETAIL', 'JULY' and 'CLOSER' still upheld the LOW watermark. But songs 'DINOSAUR ACT' (issued as a single) and 'WHORE' stepped towards a rockier area, with fuzz guitar being used in the latter, in amongst the soaring vocals of PARKER, SPARHAWK and the crashing drums. Not as poignant or as beautiful as 'SECRET NAME' (every track was a classic), 'THINGS WE LOST IN THE FIRE' demonstrated the group's abilities to write great compositions, while still maintaining the sad-core motif that had became so synonymous with the group. A split EP was issued in April the same year with underground artist K and although LOW were on top form (produced by WARN DeFEVER), it was really K's tremendous contribution that shone most on the set. In another bizarre but brilliant twist in LOW's direction, the band issued a cover single of the Smiths' 'LAST NIGHT I DREAMT THAT SOMEBODY LOVED ME', which could've almost been better than the original, with strings fusing into crashing crescendos and PARKER's and SPARHAWK's vocals sounding as strange and as powerful as always. It's also worth mentioning the B-side track 'BECAUSE YOU STOOD STILL'; how did something so incredible get omitted from an album? LOW returned in September of 2002 with the delicately crafted 'TRUST', a slightly unadorned set, from the usually consistently reliable group. The album, which saw LOW delve deeper into sparse and darker terrain, may have been saved from droning obscurity by PARKER's light vocals and the group's undeniable knack for writing beautiful songs, no matter how dark and eerie. • **Songwriters:** Group except SUNSHINE (Mitchell – Davis) / JACK SMITH (Supreme Dicks) / Transmission (Joy Division) / LONG LONG LONG (George Harrison) / DOWN BY THE RIVER (Neil Young) / LAST NIGHT I DREAMT THAT SOMEBODY LOVED ME (Smiths) / LITTLE DRUMMER BOY + BLUE CHRISTMAS + SILENT NIGHT + TAKING DOWN THE TREE (trad).

Album rating: I COULD LIVE IN HOPE (*7) / LONG DIVISION (*8) / THE CURTAIN HITS THE CAST (*7) / SECRET NAME (*8) / THINGS WE LOST IN THE FIRE (*8) / TRUST (*6)

ALAN SPARHAWK – vocals, guitar / **JOHN NICHOLS** – bass / **MIMI PARKER** – vocals, drums

Quigley Quigley

Aug 94. (cd) <*(QUIGD 5)*> **I COULD LIVE IN HOPE**
– Words / Fear / Cut / Slide / Lazy / Lullaby / Sea / Down / Drag / Rope / Sunshine.

not iss. Summershine

1994. (cd-ep) <*shine 48CD*> **LOW** [–]
– Below & above / Lazy / Words / Caroline / Tired.

—— **ZAK SALLY** – bass; repl. NICHOLS

Vernon Yard Vernon Yard

1995. (cd) <*YARDCD 014*> **LONG DIVISION** [–]
– Violence / Below and above / Shame / Throw out the line / Swingin' / See-through / Turn / Caroline / Alone / Streetlight / Stay / Take. *(UK-iss.Feb97; same)*

Feb 96. (cd-ep) *(FLATSCD 24)* **TRANSMISSION EP** [–]
– Transmission / Bright / Cardine / Hands / Jack Smith / Untitled.
(above issued on 'Vernon Yard' UK)

May 96. (cd-ep) <*(YARD 022CD)*> **FINALLY**
– Anon / Tomorrow one / Prisoner / Turning over.

Aug 96. (d-lp/cd) *(YARD/+CD 018)* **THE CURTAIN HITS THE CAST**
– Anon / The plan / Over the ocean / Mom says / Coat tails / Standby / Laugh / Lust / Stars gone out / Same / Do you know how to waltz / Dark. *(d-lp+=)* – Prisoner / Tomorrow one.

Nov 96. (7"/cd-s) <*(YARD 024/+CD)*> **OVER THE OCEAN. / CIOLENCE / BE THERE**

Sub Pop Sub Pop

Sep 97. (7") <*(SP 392)*> **VENUS. / BOYFRIEND**

Wurlitzer Jukebox not iss.

Oct 97. (7") *(WJ 44)* **IF YOU WERE BORN TODAY (A SONG FOR LITTLE BABY JESUS). / BLUE CHRISTMAS**

Kranky Kranky

Oct 97. (m-lp/m-cd) <*(KRANKY 021/+CD)*> **SONGS FOR A DEAD PILOT**
– Will the night / Condescend / Born by the wires / Be there / Landlord / Hey Chicago.

Tugboat Kranky

May 98. (7") *(TUG 001)* **JOAN OF ARC. / LONG LONG LONG** [–]
(re-iss. Aug99 on 'Tugboat'; same)

Jul 98. (cd) *(INR 1040CD)* **ONE MORE REASON TO FORGET**
– Be there / Venus / Condescend / Landlord / Over the ocean / Do you know how to waltz? / Shame / If you were born today (song for the little baby Jesus).
(above issued on 'Bluesanct Musak')

Feb 99. (7") *(TUGS 006)* **IMMUNE. / I REMEMBER** [–]

Apr 99. (cd/d-lp) *(TUG CD/LP 007)* <*KRANKY 035*> **SECRET NAME**
– I remember / Starfire / 2-step / Weight for water / Missouri / Don't understand / Soon / Immune / Lion – Lamb / Days of . . . / Will the night / Home.

Nov 99. (m-cd) <*(TUGCD 014 – LOWXMASD 1)*> **CHRISTMAS**
– Just like Christmas / Long way around the sea / Little drummer boy / If you were born today / Blue Christmas / Silent night / Taking down the tree / One special gift.

May 00. (12"/cd-s; with SPRINHEEL JACK) *(TUGS/+CD 017)* **BOMBSCARE EP** [–]
– Bombscare / Hand so small / So easy (so far) / The way behind.

Oct 00. (7") *(TUGS 024)* **DINOSAUR ACT. / OVERHEAD** [–]
(cd-s+=) (TUGSCD 024) – Don't carry it all.

Feb 01. (cd/lp) *(TUG CD/LP 027)* <*KRANKY 046*> **THINGS WE LOST IN THE FIRE**
– Sunflower / Whitehall / Dinosaur act / Medicine magazines / Laser

beam / July / Embrace / Whore / Kind of girl / Like a forest / Closer / Funny noise / In metal. *(lp+=)* – Overhead / Don't carry it all.

not iss. | Tiger Style

Apr 01. (7"ep; shared w/ K) *<15>* **THOSE GIRLS** [–] [ ]
– (track by K) / Those girls / Venus / (track by K).

Rough Trade | Chairkicker's Music

Oct 01. (7") *(RTRADES 033) <CKM 003>* **LAST NIGHT I DREAMT THAT SOMEBODY LOVE ME. / BECAUSE YOU STOOD STILL** [ ] [ ]
(cd-s+=) *(RTRADESCD 033)* – Dinosaur act (dub).

Mar 02. (7") *<(MM 01)>* **split w/ VIBRACATHEDRAL** [ ] [ ]
(above issued on 'Misplaced') *(re-iss. Sep02; same)*

Rough Trade | Kranky

Sep 02. (cd/d-lp) *(RTRADE CD/LP 061) <KRANKY 52>* **TRUST** [ ] [ ]
– (That's how you sing) Amazing grace / Canada / Candy girl / Time is the diamond / Tonight / The lamb / In the drugs / Last snowstorm of the year / John Prine / Little argument with myself / La la la song / Point of disgust / Shots & ladders.

Oct 02. (7"/cd-s) *(RTRADES/+CD 058)* **CANADA. / FEARLESS** [ ] [–]

– compilations, etc. –

Jul 98. (cd) *Vernon Yard; <YARD 27>* **OWL** (LOW remixes by other artists) [–] [ ]
– Down / Annon (spore) / Over the ocean / Laugh / Anon (pollen) / Do you know how to waltz / Over the ocean / Words.

May 01. (cd/lp; shared with DIRTY THREE) *In The Fishtank; (FISH 7 CD/LP)* **IN THE FISHTANK** [ ] [–]
– I hear . . . goodnight / Down by the river / Invitation day / When I called upon your seed / Cody / Lordy.

Nick LOWE

Born: 24 Mar'49, Woodchurch, Suffolk, England. In 1963, LOWE formed his first semi-serious musical enterprise, SOUND 4 PLUS 1, with schoolfriend, BRINSLEY SCHWARZ. This subsequently evolved into KIPPINGTON LODGE, a pseudo-psychedelic outfit which released a series of flop singles before re-launching in 1969 under the BRINSLEY SCHWARZ banner. Despite a disastrous beginning (see separate entry), the band became one of the leading lights of the 70's pub-rock scene and released a clutch of fine, rootsy albums before their eventual demise in 1975. As well as handling bass and vocal duties, LOWE had penned the bulk of the band's material, finally embarking on a solo career the following year. Although his first releases were a couple of pseudonymous, tongue-in-cheek singles (TARTAN HORDE – 'Bay City Rollers We Love You' / 'Rollers Theme' and DISCO BROTHERS – 'Let's Go To The Disco' / 'Everybody Dance'), LOWE was also making a name for himself as a producer (GRAHAM PARKER & THE RUMOUR, DR. FEELGOOD etc.) and in 1976 had a hand in setting up Jake Rivera's seminal 'Stiff' label. His debut single, 'SO IT GOES', was also Stiff's very first release, LOWE helping to shape both the operation's identity and the careers of its artists i.e. The DAMNED, IAN DURY, ELVIS COSTELLO amongst others. LOWE joined the latter in late '77 at Rivera's new venture, 'Radar', where he recorded the UK Top 10 single, 'I LOVE THE SOUND OF BREAKING GLASS', and Top 30 album, 'THE JESUS OF COOL' (1978). Released in America under the title, 'PURE POP FOR NOW PEOPLE', the album saw LOWE's writing take a distinctly more sardonic turn although his lyrical barbs were rarely as razor sharp as those of labelmate COSTELLO. He nevertheless proved himself to be witty, articulate and intelligent as well as a consummate musical chameleon capable of traversing rock'n'roll boundaries while injecting his songs with a rootsy authenticity. 1979's 'LABOUR OF LUST' spawned a second major hit single in 'CRUEL TO BE KIND', the song also making the American Top 20. From the summer of '77 onwards, LOWE had also been a member of DAVE EDMUND's band, ROCKPILE (EDMUNDS and other band members played on LOWE's solo material), the outfit graduating from live work to releasing an album, 'Seconds Of Pleasure', in 1980. Although the record was a minor success, the group folded shortly after and LOWE divided his time between production (working with The PRETENDERS, PAUL CARRACK, FABULOUS THUNDERBIRDS and JOHN HIATT amongst others) and solo work. The turn of the decade also saw him marrying CARLENE CARTER (daughter of JOHNNY CASH), a successful country singer in her own right who numbered among LOWE's production clients. Recorded with new backing band, The CHAPS (subsequently NOISE TO GO), 'NICK THE KNIFE' (1980) was his first album for 'Columbia' and his last to enjoy any kind of chart success. The 80's were a difficult period for LOWE; increasingly countrified sets such as 'THE ABOMINABLE SHOWMAN' (1983) and 'NICK LOWE & HIS COWBOY OUTFIT' (1984) were enjoyable enough if never threatening to break him into the mainstream. Towards the end of the decade, he sunk into depression and considered retiring from the music business before making a convincing return to form with 1990's 'PARTY OF ONE', an infectious, invigorating album which saw him reunited with EDMUNDS and featured the likes of JIM KELTNER and RY COODER. The latter two hooked up with LOWE and JOHN HIATT in a kind of critics' supergroup, LITTLE VILLAGE (the same formation that played on HIATT's 1987 album, 'Bring The Family'), releasing an eponymous, one-off album in 1992. A fairly average affair, the album nevertheless saw LOWE back in the UK Top 30 for the first time in more than a decade. Yet this success failed to have a knock-on effect in terms of his solo career, 'THE IMPOSSIBLE BIRD' (1994) failing to cross over to a wider audience despite widespread critical acclaim. It's typical of LOWE's career, the man remaining something of an unsung, backroom hero when at the very least, he deserves some kind of recognition for his contributions to popular music over a career spanning more than thirty years. While 1998's 'DIG MY MOOD' found LOWE in balladeering mode, the equally laid back musings of 'CONVINCER' (2001) proved that, if his muse flows as easily as it does on this record, then he doesn't actually need to convince anybody at all, least of all his fans. • **Songwriters:** Self-penned except; PEACE, LOVE & UNDERSTANDING (Brinsley Schwarz) / HALFWAY TO PARADISE (Billy Fury) / ENDLESS SLEEP (Joey Reynolds) / I KNEW THE BRIDE (Dave Edmunds) / etc.

Album rating: JESUS OF COOL (aka PURE POP FOR NOW PEOPLE) (*8) / LABOUR OF LUST (*7) / NICK THE KNIFE (*6) / THE ABOMINABLE SHOWMAN (*4) / NICK LOWE AND HIS COWBOY OUTFIT (*6) / THE ROSE OF ENGLAND (*6) / PINKER AND PROUDER THAN PREVIOUS (*5) / BASHER: THE BEST OF NICK LOWE compilation (*7) / PARTY OF ONE (*4) / THE WILDERNESS YEARS early stuff (*5) / THE IMPOSSIBLE BIRD (*6) / DIG MY MOOD (*6) / THE CONVINCER (*5) / Little Village: LITTLE VILLAGE (*5)

NICK LOWE – vocals, bass, guitar (ex-BRINSLEY SCHWARZ) He was also a member of DAVE EDMUNDS' ROCKPILE group between Jul77-Feb81. His solo band included **EDMUNDS** – guitar and other ROCKPILE members **BILLY BREMNER** – guitar and **TERRY WILLIAMS** – drums (ex-MAN, etc.) used mainly on 2 albums below.

Stiff | not iss.

Aug 76. (7") *(BUY 1)* **SO IT GOES. / HEART OF THE CITY** [ ] [–]

May 77. (7"ep) *(LAST 1)* **BOWI** [ ] [–]
– Born a woman / Shake that rat / Marie Provost / Endless sleep.

Oct 77. (7") *(BUY 21)* **HALFWAY TO PARADISE. / I DON'T WANT THE NIGHT TO END** [ ] [–]

Radar | Columbia

Feb 78. (7") *(ADA 1)* **I LOVE THE SOUND OF BREAKING GLASS. / THEY CALLED IT ROCK** [7] [–]

Feb 78. (lp/c) *(RAD/RAC 1) <35329>* **THE JESUS OF COOL** <US-title 'PURE POP FOR NOW PEOPLE'> [22] [ ]
– Music for money / I love the sound of breaking glass / Little Hitler / Shake & pop / Tonight / So it goes / No reason / 36 inches high / Marie Provost / Nutted by reality / Heart of the city. *(re-iss. Oct88 & Aug00 on 'Demon' lp/c/cd; FIEND/+CASS/CD 131)*

May 78. (7") *(ADA 12)* **LITTLE HITLER. / CRUEL TO BE KIND** [ ] [–]

Jul 78. (7") *<10734>* **HEART OF THE CITY. / SO IT GOES** [–] [ ]

Sep 78. (7") *<10844>* **I LOVE THE SOUND OF BREAKING GLASS. / ENDLESS SLEEP** [–] [ ]

Nov 78. (7") *(ADA 26)* **AMERICAN SQUIRM. / Nick Lowe & His Sound: (WHAT'S SO FUNNY 'BOUT) PEACE, LOVE AND UNDERSTANDING** [ ] [–]

May 79. (7") *(ADA 34)* **CRACKING UP. / BASING STREET** [34] [–]

Jun 79. (lp/c) *(RAD/RAC 21) <36087>* **LABOUR OF LUST** [43] [31]
– Cruel to be kind / Cracking up / Big kick, plain scrap / Born fighter / You make me / Skin deep / Switchboard Susan / Grey ribbon / Without love / Dose of you / Love so fine. *<US cd-iss. Jun88; CK 36087> (cd-iss. Apr90 & Aug00 on 'Demon'; FIENDCD 182)*

Aug 79. (7") *(ADA 43) <11018>* **CRUEL TO BE KIND. / ENDLESS GREY RIBBON** [12] Jul79 [12]

Dec 79. (7") *<11131>* **SWITCHBOARD SUSAN. / BASING STREET** [–] [ ]

— After he split from ROCKPILE in Feb'81, LOWE formed his own band, **NICK LOWE & THE CHAPS**

(They became NOISE TO GO early '82) **MARTIN BELMONT** – guitar / **PAUL CARRACK** – keyboards / **BOBBY IRWIN** – drums

F-Beat Columbia

Feb 82. (7") *(XX 20)* **BURNING. / ZULU KISS** [ ] [–]

Feb 82. (lp/c) *(XX LP/MC 14) <37932>* **NICK THE KNIFE** [99] [50]
– Burning / Heart / Stick it where the sun don't shine / Queen of Sheba / My heart hurts / Couldn't love you (any more than I do) / Let me kiss ya / Too many teardrops / Ba doom / Raining raining / One's too many / Zulu kiss. *(cd-iss. Apr90 & Aug00 on 'Demon'; FIENDCD 183)*

Apr 82. (7") *(XX 23)* **MY HEART HURTS. / PET YOU AND HOLD YOU** [ ] [–]
(d7"+=) *(XX 23F – SAM 147)* – Cracking up / (What's so funny 'bout) Peace, love and understanding.

Apr 82. (7") *<02813>* **MY HEART HURTS. / STICK IT WHERE THE SUN DON'T SHINE** [–] [ ]

— added **JAMES ELLER** – bass

Apr 83. (7") *(XX 31)* **RAGIN' EYES. / TANGUE-RAE** [ ] [–]
(12"+=) *(XX 31T)* – Cool reaction.

Jun 83. (lp/c) *(XX LP/MC 18)* **THE ABOMINABLE SHOWMAN** [ ] [ ]
– We want action / Ragin' eyes / Cool reaction / Time wounds all heels / Man of a fool / Tanque-Rae / Wish you were here / Chicken and feathers / Paid the price / Mess around with love / Saint beneath the paint / How do you talk to an angel. *(cd-iss. Apr90 & Aug00 on 'Demon'; FIENDCD 184)*

Jun 83. (7") *<03837>* **HOW DO YOU TALK TO AN ANGEL / I WISH YOU WERE HERE** [–] [ ]

NICK LOWE AND HIS COWBOY OUTFIT

— with **PAUL CARRACK**, etc

F-Beat/ RCA Columbia

May 84. (7") *(XX 340)* **HALF A BOY AND HALF A MAN. / AWESOME** [53] [–]
(12"+=) *(XX 34T)* – Cruel to be kind.

May 84. (lp/c) *(ZL/ZK 79338) <39371>* **NICK LOWE & HIS COWBOY OUTFIT** [ ] [ ]
– Half a boy and half a man / You'll never get me up / (in one of those) / Maureen / God's gift to women / The Gee and the Rick and the three card trick / (Hey big mouth) Stand up and say that / Awesome / Breakaway / Love like a glove / Live fast, love hard, die young / L.A.F.S. *(cd-iss. Aug00 on 'Demon'; FIENDCD 185)*

Aug 84. (7") *(XX 36)* **L.A.F.S. / (HEY BIG MOUTH) STAND UP AND SAY THAT** [ ] [–]
(12"+=) *(XX 36T)* – Baby it's you.

Jul 85. (7") *(ZB 40303)* **I KNEW THE BRIDE (WHEN SHE USE TO ROCK AND ROLL). / DARLIN' ANGEL EYES** [ ] [–]
(12"+=) *(ZT 40303)* – Seven nights to rock.

Aug 85. (lp/c) *(ZL/ZK 70765) <39958>* **THE ROSE OF ENGLAND** [ ] [ ]
– Darlin' angel eyes / She don't love nobody / 7 nights to rock / Long walk back / The rose of England / Lucky dog * / I knew the bride (when she use to rock and roll) / Indoor fireworks / (Hope to God) I'm right / I can be the one you love / Everyone * / Bobo ska diddle daddle. *(re-iss. Dec88 & Aug00 on 'Demon' lp/c/cd; FIEND/+CASS/CD 73)* – (omits tracks *)

Nov 85. (7") *<05570>* **I KNEW THE BRIDE (WHEN SHE USE TO ROCK AND ROLL). / LONG WALK BACK** [–] [77]

NICK LOWE

Demon Columbia

Jan 88. (7") **CRYING IN MY SLEEP. / LOVER'S JAMBOREE** [–] [ ]

Feb 88. (lp/c/cd) *(FIEND/+CASS/CD 99)* **PINKER AND PROUDER THAN PREVIOUS** [ ] [ ]
– (You're my) Wildest dream / Crying in my sleep / Big hair / Love gets strange / I got the love / Black Lincoln Continental / Cry it out / Lover's jambouree / Geisha girl / Wishing well / Big big love.

— now with **DAVE EDMUNDS, PAUL CARRACK, JIM KELTNER** / plus **BILL KIRCHEN** – electric guitar / **AUSTIN DE LONE** – piano, guitar / **RY COODER** – steel guitar

Warners Reprise

Apr 90. (7") *(W 9821)* **ALL MEN ARE LIARS. / GAI-GIN MAN** [ ] [–]
(12"+=/cd-s+=) *(W 9821 T/CD)* – I love the sound of breaking glass / Cruel to be kind.

Apr 90. (cd)(lp/c) *(<7599 26132-2>)(WX 337/+C)* **PARTY OF ONE** [ ] [ ]
– You got the look I like / (I want to build a) Jumbo ark / Gai-gin man / Who was that man? / What's shakin' on the hill / Shting-shtang / All men are liars / Rocky road / Refrigerator white / I don't know why you keep me on / Honeygun. *(cd re-iss. Nov95 on 'Demon'; FIENDCD 767)* – (extra tracks)

LITTLE VILLAGE

were another amalgamation of near superstars; **NICK LOWE** – vocals, bass / **RY COODER** – vocals, guitar / **JOHN HIATT** – vocals, guitar / **JIM KELTNER** – drums, percussion, guitar, composer

Reprise Reprise

Feb 92. (cd)(lp/c) *(<7599 26713-2>)(WX 462/+C)* **LITTLE VILLAGE** [23] [66]
– Solar sex panel / The action / Inside job / Big love / Take another look / Do you want my job / Don't go away mad / Fool who knows / She runs hot / Don't think about her when you're trying to drive / Don't bug me when I'm working.

Mar 92. (7"/c-s) **SOLAR SEX PANEL. / DO WITH ME WHAT YOU WANT TO DO** [ ] [ ]
(12"+=/cd-s+=) – Haunted house.

May 92. (7"/c-s) **DON'T GO AWAY MAD. / BIG LOVE** [ ] [ ]
(12"+=/cd-s+=) – Do with me what you want to do.

NICK LOWE

Demon Upstart

Nov 94. (cd-s) *(NICKA 315)* **TRUE LOVE TRAVELS ON A GRAVEL ROAD EP** [ ] [–]
– I am the cancer / Two seater / Rag doll / Laying blame.

Nov 94. (cd) *(FIENDCD 757) <13>* **THE IMPOSSIBLE BIRD** [ ] [ ]
– Soulful wind / The beast in me / True love travels on a gravel road / Trail of tears / Shelly my love / Where's my everything / 12-step program / Lover don't go / Drive-thru man / Withered on the vine / I live on a battlefield / 14 days / I'll be there.

Jul 95. (cd-ep) *<21>* **LiVe! ON THE BATTLEFIELD (live)** [–] [ ]
– I live on a battlefield / 36 inches high / Without love / Dream girl / In the middle of it all.

Jan 98. (cd) *(FIENDCD 939) <38>* **DIG MY MOOD** [ ] [ ]
– Faithless lover / Lonesome reverie / You inspire me / What lack of love has done / Time I took a holiday / Failed Christian / The man that I've become / Freezing / High on a hilltop / Lead me not / I must be getting over you / Cold grey light of dawn.

Jun 98. (cd-ep) *(VEXCD 17)* **YOU INSPIRE ME EP** [ ] [–]
– You inspire me / Soulful win (live) / She don't love nobody (live) / Cruel to be kind (live) / Half a boy and half a man (live).

Proper Yep Roc

Sep 01. (cd) *(PRPCD 12) <2027>* **THE CONVINCER** [ ] Oct01 [ ]
– Homewrecker / Only a fool breaks his own heart / Lately I've let things slide / She's got soul / Cupid must be angry / Indian queens / Poor side of town / I'm a mess / Between dark and dawn / Bygones (won't go) / Has she got a friend? / Let's stay in and make love.

Nov 01. (cd-s) *(DDTB 1)* **LATELY I'VE LET THINGS SLIDE / SHE'S GOT SOUL / THERE WILL NEVER BE ANY PEACE** –

– compilations etc. –

on 'Demon' unless mentioned otherwise

Sep 84. (lp/c) *(FIEND/+CASS 20)* **16 ALL-TIME LOWES** –
– Born fighter / Marie Provost / American squirm / Skin deep / When I write the book / Little Hitler / Cruel to be kind / Heart of the city / Switchboard Susan / (I love the sound of) Breaking glass / Big kick plain scrap / Cracking up / Without love / Nutted by reality / So it goes / They called it rock. *(cd-iss. 1986 as '20 ALL-TIME LOWES'; FIENDCD 20)* – (4 extra tracks). *(cd re-iss. Oct93 on 'Diablo'; DIAB 801)*

Mar 86. (lp/c/cd) *(FIEND/+CASS/CD 59)* **NICK'S NACK** –

Aug 89. (d-lp/c/cd) *(FIEND/+CASS/CD 142)* **BASHER: THE BEST OF NICK LOWE** –

Jun 91. (cd) *(FIENDCD 203)* **THE WILDERNESS YEARS** –
– (rare material 1974-1977)

Jan 94. (4xcd-box) *(NICK 1)* **BOXED SET** –
– (JESUS OF COOL / ROSE OF ENGLAND / NICK LOWE AND HIS COWBOY OUTFIT / PINKER AND PROUDER THAN PREVIOUS)

Jul 99. (4xcd-box) *Demon; (LOWE 50)* **THE DOINGS** –

LOWGOLD

Formed: London, England . . . 1998 by main songwriter DARREN FORD and DAN SYMONS. If Britain had a thriving alt country scene then it was quite certain that LOWGOLD, a group who almost didn't see their debut album make it onto the shop floor, were the driving force. Named after the brief translation of a Nordic word meaning 'of hidden worth', FORD and SYMONS met in a university bar and after two tracks were quickly recorded, the pair sent the demo tape to 'Nude' records (home of SUEDE). 'Nude' asked them to perform live and the duo had to quickly recruit MILES WILLEY and SCOTT SIMON for one weeks rehearsal. Luckily for them, the record company virtually signed the group on the spot. Unluckily for the record company, however, they were experiencing major finanical difficulties and LOWGOLD's dreamy debut 'JUST BACKWARDS OF SQUARE' was shelved. It appeared some two years later with mixed reactions from the British music press, although it did hit the Top 40 (as did the single, 'BEAUTY DIES YOUNG'). Some tipped the band to go on to do great things in the new year, others just saw them as imitators of "cool" American Lo-Fi. Whatever, the ensemble still managed to be compared to BADLY DRAWN BOY, GRANDADDY and The RED HOUSE PAINTERS and were far more interesting than some tabloid-y music-journos made them out to be. • **Covers:** SHE DARKED THE SUN (Dillards).

Album rating: JUST BACKWARDS OF SQUARE (*7)

DARREN FORD – vocals, guitar / **DAN SYMONS** – guitar / **MILES WILLEY** – bass / **SIMON SCOTT** – drums

Nude / not iss.

Jul 00. (10"ep/cd-ep) *(NUD 50 T/CD)* **THE 108 EP** –
– In amber / Can't say no / The feelings / God willing.

Sep 00. (7"/cd-s) *(NUD 52 S/CD1)* **BEAUTY DIES YOUNG. / PLEASE BE GOOD TO ME / SILVER OCEAN** 67 –

Jan 01. (7"/cd-s) *(NUD 53 S/CD1)* **MERCURY. / EDDIE LEJEUNE / IF PEOPLE WERE VINYL (featuring TUX)** 48 –

Feb 01. (cd/lp) *(NUDE 17 CD/LP)* **JUST BACKWARDS OF SQUARE** 33 –
– Golden ratio / Beauty dies young / Mercury / Out of reach / Back here again / Counterfeit / Never alone / In amber / Open the airwaves / Less I offer / Into the void.

Apr 01. (7") *(NUD 55S)* **COUNTERFEIT. / WHATEVER YOU THINK, YOU'RE WRONG** 52 –
(cd-s+=) *(NUD 55CD1)* – Atlantic Pacific.
(cd-s) *(NUD 55CD2)* – ('A'side) / She darked she sun / Remission time.

Aug 01. (7") *(NUD 59)* **BEAUTY DIES YOUNG. / END OF THE MATTER** 40 –
(cd-s) *(NUD 59CD1)* – ('A'side) / Can't say no / Coming strong.
(cd-s) *(NUD 59CD2)* – ('A'-Graham Coxon mix) / Make over, make up / I'd rather fuck up than miss out.

L7

Formed: Los Angeles, California, USA . . . 1986 by DONITA SPARKS (guitar/vocals) and SUZI GARDNER (guitar/vocals). Recruiting seasoned L.A. punk veteran JENNIFER FINCH on bass and drummer ANNE ANDERSON, the band signed for the small 'Epitaph' label. The feisty punk-metal noise of their 1988 eponymous debut attracted the attention of the now-famous 'Sub Pop' label the following year, DEE PLAKAS replacing ANDERSON and 'SMELL THE MAGIC' (1990) fuelling the band's growing cult reputation. 1990 also saw the girls touring with a relatively unknown NIRVANA, L7's infamous onstage antics almost causing as much of a stir as the headliners. The band were soon snapped up by 'Slash', hitting the UK Top 20 in 1992 with the pop-grunge of the 'PRETEND WE'RE DEAD' single. This was closely followed by the 'BRICKS ARE HEAVY' album, a hard hitting collision of girl power grunge and ultra hard line, often humorous, post-feminist lyrics. The band caused further uproar later that year when DONITA exposed her womanly charms on 'The Word', having already blessed that year's Reading Festival audience with a used tampon. Irreverent yet committed, L7 also formed 'Rock For Choice', a pro-abortion pressure group which won unprecedented support in the male-dominated environs of the music business. 'HUNGRY FOR STINK' (1994) was equally blistering, the frenetic 'FUEL MY FIRE' later covered by The PRODIGY on their landmark 'THE FAT OF THE LAND' album. 'THE BEAUTY PROCESS: TRIPLE PLATINUM' (1997) marked FINCH's final fling with the band before she left to form LYME, the record's move into harder rocking territory signalling a new era for L7 as they attempted to chart the uncertain waters of the post-grunge era. With first GRETA BRINKMAN and then GAIL GREENWOOD at the helm, they went on to record 'SLAP-HAPPY' (1999), an album which came in for some critical flak for sounding too one dimensional. More satisfying for longtime fans was the live set, 'OMAHA TO OSAKA', a visceral aural document culled from various Japanese club dates. • **Songwriters:** Group or SPARKS penned except THREE DAYS (Willie Nelson).

Album rating: L7 (*6) / SMELL THE MAGIC mini (*6) / BRICKS ARE HEAVY (*8) / HUNGRY FOR STINK (*6) / THE BEAUTY PROCESS: TRIPLE PLATINUM (*6) / FROM OSAKA TO OMAHA (*6) / SLAP-HAPPY (*6) / THE BEST OF L7 compilation (*7)

DONITA SPARKS (b. 8 Apr'63, Chicago, Illinois) – vocals, guitar / **SUZI GARDNER** (b. 1 Aug'60, Altus, Oklahoma) – guitar, vocals / **JENNIFER FINCH** (b. 5 Aug'66) – bass, vocals / **ANNE ANDERSON** (b.Chicago) – drums repl.by **ROY KOUTSKY**

not iss. / Epitaph

Dec 88. (lp/c/cd) <*E 86401-1/-4/-2*> **L7** –
– Bite the wax tadpole / Cat-o'-nine-tails / Metal stampede / Let's rock tonight / Uncle Bob / Snake handler / Runnin' from the law / Cool out / It's not you / I drink / Ms. 45. *(UK-iss.Jun92; same)*

— **(DEMETRA) DEE PLAKAS** (b. 9 Nov'60, Chicago) – drums repl. ROY

Glitterhouse / Sub Pop

Jan 90. (7",7"green) <*SP 58*> **SHOVE. / PACKIN' A ROD** –
(UK-iss.Jan91 on 'Sub Pop'; EFA 08105)

Nov 90. (12"ep,12"purple-ep) <*(SP 79)*> **SMELL THE MAGIC** Aug90
– Shove / Til the wheels fall off / Fast'n'frightening / (Right on) Thru / Deathwish / Broomstick. *(cd-ep Oct95+= ; SPCD 79)* – Packin' a rod / Just like me / American society.

Slash | Slash

Mar 92. (7"red/c-s) *(LASH/LACS 34)* **PRETEND WE'RE DEAD. / SHIT LIST** [21] [ ]
(12"+=/cd-s+=) *(LASHX/LASCD 34)* – Lopsided head / Mr. Integrity.

Apr 92. (cd/c/lp) *(828 307-2/-4/-1)* *<26784>* **BRICKS ARE HEAVY** [24] [ ]
– Wargasm / Scrap / Pretend we're dead / Diet pill / Everglade / Slide / One more thing / Mr. Integrity / Monster / Shit list / This ain't pleasure.

May 92. (7"green) *(LASH 36)* **EVERGLADE. / FREAK MAGNET** [27] [ ]
(12"+=/cd-s+=) *(LASHXP/LASHCD 36)* – Scrap.

Sep 92. (7"/c-s) *(LASH/LACS 38)* **MONSTER. / USED TO LOVE HIM** [33] [ ]
(12"+=/cd-s+=) *(LASHX/LASCD 38)* – Diet pill.

Nov 92. (7"/c-s) *(LASH/LACS 42)* **PRETEND WE'RE DEAD. / FAST 'N' FRIGHTENING (live)** [50] [–]
(cd-s+=) *(LASCD 42)* – (Right on) Thru / Shove / Shit list / Diet pill.

— L7 appeared as CAMEL LIPS group in the film 'Serial Mom'.

Jun 94. (7"colrd/12"colrd) *(LASH/LASCS 48)* **ANDRES. / BOMB** [34] [ ]
(cd-s+=) *(LASCD 48)* – (KRXT radio interview).

Jul 94. (cd/c/lp) *<(828 531-2/-4/-1)>* **HUNGRY FOR STINK** [26] [ ]
– Andres / Baggage / Can I run / The bomb / Questioning my sanity / Riding with a movie star / Stuck here again / Fuel my fire / Freak magnet / She has eyes / Shirley / Talk box.

— After recording 1996 album, FINCH left to form LYME. She was repl. by **GRETA BRINKMAN** who appeared on next album, before **GAIL GREENWOOD** (ex-BELLY) took over

Feb 97. (cd/c) *<(828 868-2/-4)>* **THE BEAUTY PROCESS: TRIPLE PLATINUM** [ ] [ ]
– Beauty process / Drama / Off the wagon / I need / Moonshine / Bitter wine / Masses are asses / Bad things / Must have more / Non existant Patricia / Me, myself and I / Lorenza, Giada, Alessandra / Guera.

Feb 97. (c-s/cd-s) *<17403/43834>* **OFF THE WAGON / GUERA / PUNK BROKE (MY HEART)** [–] [ ]

Man's Ruin | Man's Ruin

Jan 99. (cd) *<(MR 146CD)>* **FROM OSAKA OR OMAHA** [ ] Dec98 [ ]
– L7 medley – Overture: Fast and frightening / Bad things / Must have more / Deathwish / Slide / Bitter wine / Drama / Non-existant Patricia / Pattylean / El Whatusi / Shitlist / Andres / Fast and frightening / Off the wagon / Little one / Lorenza, Giada, Allesandra.

Bongload | Bongload

Aug 99. (cd/lp) *<(BL 43 CD/V)>* **SLAP-HAPPY** [ ] [ ]
– Crackpot baby / On my rockin' machine / Lackey / Human / Livin' large / Freeway / Stick to the plan / War with you / Long green / Little one / Freezer burn / Mantra down.

– compilations, etc. –

Mar 00. (cd) *Slash; <(8573 82064-2)>* **THE BEST OF L7: THE SLASH YEARS** [ ] May00 [ ]
– Pretend we're dead / Mr Integrity / Monster / Everglade / Andres / Fuel my fire / Freak magnet / Can I run / Bad things / Off the wagon / Moonshine / Bitter wine.

☐ LUCKY PIERRE (see under ⇒ ARAB STRAP)

LUDACRIS

Born: CHRIS BRIDGES, 11 Sep'77, Atlanta, Georgia, USA. Having already honed his patter and his industry chops as a popular Atlanta-based radio DJ, LUDACRIS made his debut in 2000 with the wittily titled, independently released 'INCOGNEGRO'. With the album increasing his local fame to fever pitch, 'Def Jam' talent scout SCARFACE subsequently snapped up LUDACRIS as the flagship act on the newly created 'Def Jam South' imprint (itself created to get a piece of the increasingly hot hip hop action in America's deep south). Shrewdly (but no doubt annoyingly for fans who'd already bought the debut), the label re-packaged the album later the same year, re-issuing it with four new big name tracks (and soon to be hits) including a revamped version of his TIMBALAND collabo 'FAT RABBIT' (which had originally appeared on the producer's 1998 album, 'Tim's Bio'), the NEPTUNES floor filler 'SOUTHERN HOSPITALITY' and a FOXY BROWN-enhanced version of the risqué 'WHAT'S YOUR FANTASY', the song which had gotten LUDACRIS noticed in the first place and which became his national breakthrough hit. Not quite as enticingly underground but studded with an array of name talent, 'WORD OF MOUF' (2001) made the US Top 3 on the strength of larger than life singles 'ROLLOUT (MY BUSINESS)' and 'SATURDAY (OOOH OOOH!)'. From its wonderfully tacky cover to its razor-witted raps, 'CHICKEN-N-BEER' (2003) was roundly hailed as LUDACRIS' crowning achievement, a raucous round-up of Dirty South attitude, humour and street smart philosophy.

Album rating: BACK FOR THE FIRST TIME (*6) / WORD OF MOUF (*7) / CHICKEN-N-BEER (*7)

LUDACRIS – vocals / with session people

not iss. | Disturbing The Peace

May 00. (cd) *<911>* **INCOGNEGRO** [–] [ ]
– (intro) / U got a problem? / Game got switched / 1st and 10 (with INFAMOUS 2-D & F.A.T.E.) / It wasn't us / (Come on over – skit) / Hood stuck / Get off me / Mouthing off / Midnight train (with CHIMERE) / (Ho – skit) / Ho / (Tickets sold out – skit) / Catch up (with INFAMOUS 2-D & F.A.T.E.) / What's your fantasy (with SHAWNA) / Rock and a hard place.

Def Jam | Def Jam

Oct 00. (cd) *<(548138-2)>* **BACK FOR THE THE FIRST TIME** [ ] [4]
– U got a problem? / Game got switched (with INFAMOUS 2.0 & FATE WILSON) / 1st and 10 / What's your fantasy (with SHAWNA) / (Come on over – skit) / Hood stuck / Get off me (with PASTOR TROY) / Mouthing off (with 4-IZE) / Stick 'em up (with UGK) / (Ho – skit) / Ho / Tickets sold out – skit) / Catch up (with INFAMOUS 2.0 & FATE WILSON) / Southern hospitality (with PHARRELL) / What's your fantasy (remix with TRINA, SHAWNA & FOXY BROWN) / Phat rabbit.

May 01. (12"; as LUDACRIS featuring SHAWNA) *(572948-1)* *<562944>* **WHAT'S YOUR FANTASY / (mixes)** [19] Sep00 [21]
(cd-s+=) *(572948-2)* – ('A'video).

— in Aug'01, he featured on MISSY ELLIOTT's single, 'One Minute Man'

Sep 01. (c-s; as LUDACRIS featuring NATE DOGG) *(588772-4)* *<588671>* **AREA CODES / SOUTHERN HOSPITALITY** [25] [24] [23]
(12"+=/cd-s+=) *(588772-1/-2)* – ('A'mixes).

Nov 01. (cd/d-lp) *<(586446-2/-1)>* **WORD OF MOUF** [ ] [3]
– Coming 2 America / Rollout (my business) / Go 2 sleep (with I-20, LIL' WILSON & THREE 6 MAFIA) / Cry babies (oh no) / She said (with FATE WILSON) / (Howhere – skit) / Area codes (with NATE DOGG) / Growing pains (with FATE WILSON & KEON BRYCE) / (Greatest hits – skit) / Move bitch (with MYSTIKAL & I-20) / (Stop lying – skit) / Saturday (oooh oooh!) (with SLEEPY BROWN) / Keep it on the hush (with JAZZE PHA) / Word of mouf (freestyle) (with 4-IZE) / Get the fuck back (with SHAWNA, I-20 & FATE WILSON) / Freaky thangs (with TWISTA & JAGGED EDGE) / Cold outside / Block lockdown (with I-20). *(re-iss. Jun02; same)* – hit No.57

Dec 01. (cd-s) *<15531>* **FATTY GIRL** [–] [87]

Jun 02. (c-s) *(582963-4)* *<588914>* **ROLLOUT (MY BUSINESS) / (album version)** [20] Jan02 [17]
(12"+=) *(582963-1)* – ('A'-Wiley Cat instrumental).
(cd-s++=) *(582963-2)* – What's your fantasy (explicit version with SHAWNA) / ('A'-video).

May 02. (12") *<582948>* **MOVE B***H. / KEEP IT ON THE HUSH (with Jazze Pha)** [–] [10]

Sep 02. (c-s; as LUDACRIS featuring SLEEPY BROWN) *<(063914-4)>* **SATURDAY (OOOH! OOOH!) / (Southern hospitality remix with MS. DYNAMITE)** [31] [22]
(12"+=) *(063914-1)* – Move b***h (with MYSTIKAL).
(cd-s++=) *(063914-2)* – ('A'-video).

May 03. (12") *<053911>* **ACT A FOOL. / BLOCK REINCARNATED** [–] [32]

Oct 03. (cd) *(9861137)* *<93002>* **CHICKEN-N-BEER** [44] [1]
– Southern fried intro / Blow it out / Stand up (with SHAWNA) / (Rob quarters skit) / Splash waterfalls / Hard times (with 8 BALL, MJG & CARL THOMAS) / Diamond in the back / Screwed up / (T baggin' skit) / P-

poppin' (with SHAWNA & LIL' FATE) / Hip hop quotables / (Black man's struggles skit) / Hoes in my room (with SNOOP DOGG) / Teamwork / (Interactive skit) / We got (with CHINGY, I-20 & TITY BOI) / Eyesbrows down (with TITY BOI & DOLLA BOY).

Nov 03. (12") *(981400-1)* **STAND UP. / WHAT'S YOUR FANTASY (with TRINA, SHAWNA & FOXY BROWN)** [14] [–]
(cd-s+=) *(981400-2)* – ('A'-video).

LUSH

Formed: Camberwell, London, England . . . October '88 by girls MIKI BERENYI (half-Japanese / half-Hungarian) and EMMA ANDERSON, plus lads STEVE RIPPON and CHRIS ACLAND. After supports slots to DARLING BUDS, etc, they signed to top independent label '4.a.d.' in 1989 (MERIEL BARHAM was also a member before she joined The PALE SAINTS). A 1989 debut EP, 'SCAR', introduced the band's delicate wash of sound, all hazy guitar effects and celestial harmonies; immediately hailed by the press as one of the front runners in the 'shoegazing' scene, the band even attracted the attentions of ROBIN GUTHRIE (of 'shoegazing' forebears, COCTEAU TWINS) who produced a follow-up, the 'MAD LOVE' EP. Along with MY BLOODY VALENTINE, RIDE etc., LUSH were now the toast of the UK indie scene, while also enjoying minor success in Europe and America. A further EP, 'BLACK SPRING', followed in Autumn '91 prior to the departure of RIPPON. With former NME employee, PHIL KING (ex-FELT, SERVANTS etc.) drafted in as a replacement, the band eventually completed work on a debut album, 'SPOOKY'. Issued to a mixed critical reaction in early '92, the record reached the UK Top 10 despite complaints about the suffocating GUTHRIE production. Nevertheless, the scene which had spawned LUSH was dying on its feet (still staring at its shoes, presumably) with the influx of American grunge and the group took time out to reconsider their approach. The resultant follow-up, 'SPLIT' (1994), was well received by fans but failed to break the band out of the indie margins. Finally, with the advent of Brit-pop, LUSH re-emerged with a more straightforward, spiky pop sound, the fey vocal affectations of old giving way to unashamed cockney wide-girl attitude on the 'LADYKILLERS' single while 'SINGLE GIRL' was as breezy as anything they'd ever recorded. An album, 'LOVELIFE', made the Top 10 later that summer and although older fans might've mourned the haunting textures of old, the simple approach suited them down to the ground. Yet this mini-revival in the band's fortunes was tragically marred later that year when the 30-year old CHRIS ACLAND took his own life. • **Songwriters:** MIKI and EMMA, except HEY HEY HELEN (Abba) / FALLIN' IN LOVE (Dennis Wilson) / OUTDOOR MINER (Wire) / LOVE AT FIRST SIGHT (Young Marble Giants) / I WANNA BE YOUR GIRLFRIEND (Rubinoos). • **Trivia:** In 1990, they all posed topless for an NME cover shot, although they were given the body paint treatment.

Album rating: SPOOKY (*8) / GALA (*7) / SPLIT (*6) / LOVELIFE (*8) / CIAO! 1989-1996 compilation (*7)

MIKI BERENYI (b.18 Mar'67) – vocals, guitar / **EMMA ANDERSON** (b.10 Jun'67) – guitar, vocals / **STEVE RIPPON** – bass / **CHRIS ACLAND** (b. 7 Sep'66, Lancaster, England) – drums

4 a.d. / Nesak

Oct 89. (m-lp/m-c/m-cd) *(JAD/+C 911/+CD)* <911> **SCAR** [ ] [ ]
– Baby talk / Thoughtforms / Scarlet / Bitter / Second sight / Etheriel.

Feb 90. (12"ep/c-ep/cd-ep) *(BAD/+C 0003/+CD)* **MAD LOVE EP** [55] [–]
– De luxe / Leaves me cold / Downer / Thoughtforms.

4 a.d. / 4 a.d.-Reprise

Oct 90. (7"/c-s) *(AD/+C 0013)* **SWEETNESS AND LIGHT. / BREEZE** [47] [–]
(12"+=/cd-s+=) *(BAD 0013/+CD)* – Sunbathing.

Dec 90. (lp/c/cd) *(CAD/+C 0017/+CD)* <26463> **GALA** [ ] [ ]
– Sweetness and light / Sunbathing / Breeze / De luxe / Leaves me cold / Downer / Baby talk / Thoughtforms / Scarlet / Bitter / Second light / Etheriel / Hey hey Helen / Scarlet (alt.take).

Sep 91. (7"/c-s) *(AD/+C 1016)* <40231> **NOTHING NATURAL. / GOD'S GIFT** [43] [ ]
(12"ep+=/cd-ep+=) *(BAD 1016/+CD)* – 'BLACK SPRING EP' – Fallin' in love / Monochrome.

Dec 91. (12"ep/10"ep/c-ep)(cd-ep) *(BAD/+D/C 2001)(BAD 2001CD)* **FOR LOVE / STARLUST. / OUTDOOR MINER / ASTRONAUT** [35] [–]

—— Although on above + below recording RIPPON had left Oct'91.

Jan 92. (lp/d-10"lp/c)(cd)(s-cd) *(CAD/+D/C 2002)(CAD/+D 2002CD)* <26798> **[SPOOKY]** [7] [ ]
– Stray / Nothing natural / Tiny smiles / Covert / Ocean / For love / Superblast! / Untogether / Fantasy / Take / Laura / Monochrome.

—— RIPPON was replaced by **PHIL KING** (b.29 Apr'60) – bass (ex-SEE SEE RIDER, ex-APPLE BOUTIQUE, ex-FELT)

4 a.d. / Warners

May 94. (7") *(AD 4008)* **HYPOCRITE. / LOVE AT FIRST SIGHT** [52] [–]
(12"+=/cd-s+=) *(BAD 4008/+CD)* – Cat's chorus / Undertow.

May 94. (7") *(AD 4010)* **DESIRE LINES. / WHITE WOOD** [60] [–]
(12"+=)(cd-s+=) *(BAD 4010/+CD)* – Girl's world / Lovelife (suga bullit remix).

Jun 94. (lp/c/cd) *(CAD/+C 4011/+CD)* <45578> **SPLIT** [19] [ ]
– Light from a dead star / Kiss chase / Blackout / Hypocrite / Lovelife / Desire lines / The invisible man / Undertow / Never-never / Lit up / Stardust / When I die.

Jan 96. (7"clear) *(AD 6001)* **SINGLE GIRL. / SWEETIE** [21] [–]
(cd-s) *(BAD 6001CD)* – ('A'side) / Tinkerbell / Outside world / Cul de sac.
(cd-s) *(BADD 6001CD)* – ('A'side) / Pudding / Demystification / Shut up.

Feb 96. (7"green) *(AD 6002)* **LADYKILLERS. / I WANNA BE YOUR GIRLFRIEND** [22] [–]
(cd-s) *(BAD 6002CD)* – ('A'side) / Matador / Ex / Dear me.
(cd-s) *(BADD 6002CD)* – ('A'side) / Heavenly / Carmen / Plums and oranges.

Mar 96. (clear-lp/c/cd) *(CAD/+C 6004/+CD)* *<46170>* **LOVELIFE** [8] [ ]
– Ladykillers / Heavenly nobodies / 500 / I've been here before / Papasan / Single girl / Ciao! / Tralala / Last night / Runaway / The childcatcher / Olympia.

—— JARVIS COCKER (Pulp) featured vox with MIKI on the track 'Ciao!'.

Jul 96. (7"red) *(AD 6009)* **500 (SHAKE BABY SHAKE). / I HAVE THE MOON** [21] [–]
(cd-s+=) *(BAD 6009CD)* – Piledriver / Olympia (acoustic).
(cd-s) *(BADD 6009CD)* – ('A'side) / I'd like to walk around your mind / Kiss chase (acoustic) / Last night (hexadecimal dub mix).

—— Sadly on the 17th of October '96, 30 year-old ACLAND committed suicide after returning from the States and splitting with his girlfriend. LUSH virtually gave up with the group after that. A dance group of the same name issued a single, 'GOLD', late '97 (nothing to do with the real LUSH). In 1998, EMMA teamed up with vocalist, LISA O'NEILL, to form SING-SING, debuting that year with a single, 'FEELS LIKE SUMMER'. It was released on the indie label, 'Bella Union' (with help of COCTEAU TWINS' ROBIN GUTHRIE and SIMON RAYMONDE), when EMMA couldn't find a new one after severing her association with '4 a.d.'.

– compilations, etc. –

Mar 01. (cd) *4 a.d.; (GAD 2K22CD)* <70022> **CIAO! 1989-1996** [ ] [ ]
– Ladykillers / Single girl / Ciao! / 500 (shake baby shake) / Light from a dead star / Hypocrite / Desire lines / Lovelife / When I die / Nothing natural / Untogether / For love / Monochrome / De-luxe / Sweetness and light / Thoughtforms / Etheriel.

☐ LUXURIA (see under ⇒ MAGAZINE)

☐ John LYDON (see under ⇒ PUBLIC IMAGE LTD.)

☐ Jeff LYNNE
(see under ⇒ ELECTRIC LIGHT ORCHESTRA)

☐ Phil LYNOTT (see under ⇒ THIN LIZZY)

LYNYRD SKYNYRD

Formed: Jacksonville, Florida, USA ... 1966 initially as MY BACKYARD, by RONNIE VAN ZANT (vocals) who carefully hand picked a line-up of GARY ROSSINGTON (guitar), ALLEN COLLINS (guitar), BOB BURNS (drums) and LARRY JUNSTROM (bass) to realise his boyhood dream of creating an American equivalent to The ROLLING STONES. The band were blown away after witnessing an early incarnation of The ALLMAN BROTHERS, vowing to conquer the world with their own unique take on the roots music of the South. Continually brought to task for having long hair by gym teacher, Leonard Skinner, VAN ZANT and co. packed in school at the earliest opportunity, spending up to sixteen hours a day honing the sound of the band they'd eventually dub LYNYRD SKYNYRD after their schoolhouse nemesis (name slightly changed to protect themselves from enforced circuit training). At the time, the band's home town of Jacksonville boasted a thriving and eclectic music scene that saw the likes of future ALLMAN's DICKY BETTS and BERRY OAKLEY paying their dues, as well as a young TOM PETTY amongst a slew of others. SKYNYRD's first victory in their campaign to resurrect the glory of the South was winning a support slot to psychedelic one-hit wonders, STRAWBERRY ALARM CLOCK. By 1970, the band had almost notched up a mind boggling 1,000 gigs and the real touring hadn't even started. Record wise, they had a limited issue single, 'NEED ALL MY FRIENDS', (released in 1968 by the local 'Shadetree' label) under their belts and in 1971, they issued a second single, 'I'VE BEEN YOUR FOOL', the cut taken from sessions the band had recorded at the famed Muscle Shoals studio in Sheffield, Alabama. Over the course of the sessions, the septet laid down early versions of the tracks that would later become their acclaimed debut, 'PRONOUNCED LEH-NERD SKIN-NERD' (1974), bassist LEON WILKINSON joining the band midway through the sessions, while future BLACKFOOT man, RICKY MEDLOCKE, contributed some drum and vocal parts. Manager ALAN WALDEN touted the demos around various companies to no avail, opportunity eventually knocking in the form of industry mover and shaker extraordinaire, AL KOOPER (ex-BLUES PROJECT), who was in the process of setting up the Atlanta-based 'Sounds Of The South' label with the backing of 'M.C.A.'. The purpose of this venture was to capitalise on the booming Southern music scene and in SKYNYRD, KOOPER knew he'd found a band to take Southern Rock to a new plateau. As Intense and driven as the band themselves, KOOPER constantly clashed with them during the recording of the debut which he had taken upon himself to produce. Nevertheless, KOOPER functioned like an extra member of the group, playing and singing on many of the tracks, his input pivotal in creating one of rock's great debut albums. A simmering gumbo stew that drew influences from the likes of The 'STONES, FREE and CREAM yet was also haunted by the spectre of raw country blues, the album's flagbearer and breathtaking finale was 'FREE BIRD', the song most people think of at the mention of SKYNYRD's name. From BILLY POWELL's piano-led intro (which, after writing, resulted in the former roadie being taken up as a full time member of the band), the song led into a gorgeously melancholy DUANE ALLMAN-style (whom the band would dedicate the song to after he was killed in a motorcycle crash) slide guitar part, eventually building up to a blistering triple guitar climax. The band achieved the latter by overdubbing an extra guitar part by COLLINS, authentically replicating the song live as LEON WILKINSON (who'd left prior to recording the album) later returned, allowing ED KING (who'd filled in as a bass player on the debut) to become a permanent member, switching to guitar and cementing the three-pronged attack of the classic 'SKYNYRD line-up. Alongside 'FREE BIRD', the album contained some of the finest songs of the band's career in the mournful 'TUESDAY'S GONE', VAN ZANT's normally commanding voice sounding as forlorn as hero's MERLE HAGGARD and WAYLON JENNINGS. 'SIMPLE MAN' was another earthy ballad, RONNIE's lyrics as succinct and unpretentious as ever. 'THINGS GOIN' ON', meanwhile, was a biting criticism of underhand political dealings set to a rollicking honky tonk backing. KOOPER secured the band a support slot on The WHO's 1973 American tour, and immediately the band were thrown in at the deep end, playing to stadium sized audiences. Incredibly, at almost every show, the band had won the normally fiercely partisan WHO crowd over by the end of their set and when 'SWEET HOME ALABAMA' (a rousing, tongue-in-cheek rebuke to NEIL YOUNG's 'Southern Man') made the US Top 10 the following year, the band were well on the way to becoming major league stars. 'SECOND HELPING' (1974) almost matched the power of the debut, the vicious sting of 'WORKIN' FOR M.C.A.' contrasting with the strum and slide of 'THE BALLAD OF CURTIS LOWE', a tribute to a black bluesman. And thus lay the contradiction with LYNYRD SKYNYRD; denounced as reactionary rednecks, their music was haunted by the music of black immigrants. As many commentators have noted, SKYNYRD didn't have any defined politics; VAN ZANT was fiercely proud of his upbringing, attempting in his own blunt way to speak out for a part of America that had been discredited after the civil war; charges of racism, however, were way off the mark. Similarly, an anti-firearms song, 'SATURDAY NIGHT SPECIAL', didn't exactly fit with the archetype of the rifle-toting redneck. The song formed the centrepiece of the band's third effort, 'NUTHIN' FANCY' (1975), a harder rockin' affair that nevertheless failed to break any new ground or capture the excitement of the band's live show. The album also marked the first of LYNYRD SKYNYRD's many casualties as BOB BURNS was replaced with ARTIMUS PYLE after freaking out on tour. The band had been on the road almost constantly from their inception and things began coming to a head, the trek that followed the release of 'NUTHIN' FANCY' coming to be dubbed the 'Torture Tour'. The tales of sex, drugs, violence and madness are legendary, VAN ZANT's infamous violent outbreaks particularly nauseating. While ED KING departed, the rest of the band soldiered on under the auspices of the notoriously unpredictable VAN ZANT, his dedication winning unfaltering loyalty despite his temper. KING's replacement was STEVE GAINES, brother of backing singer CASSIE. Though he was only featured on a handful of the tracks on the live 'ONE MORE FROM THE ROAD' (1976), his visceral playing re-energised a flagging 'SKYNYRD, helping to make 'STREET SURVIVORS' (1977) their best release since 'SECOND HELPING'. Inspired by the 'Outlaw' movement that saw country stars like WILLIE NELSON and TOMPALL GLASER moving away from the polished Nashville sound, 'STREET SURVIVORS' was more countrified than any previous release, right down to a cover of MERLE HAGGARD's 'HONKY TONK NIGHT TIME MAN'. It also included VAN ZANT's heartfelt anti-heroin track, 'THAT SMELL'. The song's lyrics and the album's cover art (featuring the band surrounded by flames) were to take on a chilling new resonance when, on October 20, en route to Baton Rouge, the aircraft carrying band and crew plummeted from the sky after both its engines failed. VAN ZANT was killed on impact, as were STEVE and CASSIE GAINES, and assistant road manager DEAN KILPATRICK. The remaining passengers were all seriously injured and the details of the crash were horrific, the effects of the tragedy still resonating to this day. The remaining members decided to disband LYNYRD SKYNYRD, even although 'STREET SURVIVORS' had become their biggest selling album ever, the remnants of 'SKYNYRD forming the ROSSINGTON-COLLINS BAND, who released two forgettable albums at the turn of the decade, COLLINS later forming his own band after the death of his wife KATHY. This wasn't the end to his strife; COLLINS was involved in a serious car accident in 1986 which killed his girlfriend and left him paralysed from the waist down (he died of pneumonia four years later). COLLINS wasn't the only one to suffer in the aftermath of the band's tragedy; suicide, drug addiction and even alleged child abuse dogged the survivors of the plane crash for years to come. In the late 80's, the remaining members regrouped for a memorial tour and subsequent live album, 'SOUTHERN BY THE GRACE OF GOD' (1988), RONNIE's brother, JOHNNY, fronting the band. Another reformation in 1991 resulted in the eponymous 'LYNYRD SKYNYRD 1991', a credible comeback that saw the return of ED KING. The band released a further three albums during the 90's, 'THE LAST REBEL' (1993), the unplugged 'ENDANGERED SPECIES' (1994) and 1997's 'TWENTY', the latter featuring BLACKFOOT man RICKY MEDLOCKE, who'd played on sessions for the debut over a quarter of a century previously. Of late, LYNYRD SKYNYRD have delivered three more sets, 'LYVE FROM STEEL TOWN' (1998), 'EDGE OF FOREVER' (1999) and the ill-advised 'CHRISTMAS TIME AGAIN' (2000). None of these albums captured the intensity of the original line-up, however, and those looking for a comprehensive musical history lesson are pointed in the direction of the 1991 'M.C.A.' boxed set. Alongside all the essential album cuts, the collection includes a spectral demo version of 'FREE BIRD' as well as unreleased gems like the impassioned 'HE'S ALIVE' and the spine-tingling 'ALL I CAN DO IS WRITE ABOUT IT', as revealing a song as to what drove the late VAN ZANT as the man ever penned. The new millennium saw the death of yet another longtime member when LEON WILKESON passed away as a result of natural causes on 27th July 2001. With EAN EVANS coming in to replace him, the group bounced back with one of their better latter day releases, 'VICIOUS CYCLE' (2003), with KID ROCK even turning up for a raucous run through 'GIMME BACK MY BULLETS'. • **Songwriters:** Bulk by VAN ZANT + COLLINS or VAN ZANT + GAINES after '75. When they re-formed in '87, ROSSINGTON, KING and the new VAN ZANDT contributed all. Covered; SAME OLD BLUES + CALL ME THE BREEZE (J.J. Cale) / CROSSROADS (Robert Johnson) / NONE OF US ARE FREE (Mann-Weil-Russell) / etc.

Album rating: PRONOUNCED LEH-NERD SKIN-NERD (*8) / SECOND HELPING (*8) / NUTHIN' FANCY (*6) / GIMME BACK MY BULLETS (*6) / ONE MORE FROM THE ROAD (*8) / STREET SURVIVORS (*7) / SKYNYRD'S FIRST AND.. LAST posthumous (*6) / GOLD AND PLATINUM compilation (*9) / LEGEND rare live (*6) / SOUTHERN BY THE GRACE OF GOD: LYNYRD SKYNYRD TRIBUTE TOUR – 1987 (*5) / LYNYRD SKYNYRD 1991 (*5) / THE LAST REBEL (*5) / LYNYRD SKYNYRD boxed set (*9) / FREEBIRD – THE VERY BEST OF . . . compilation (*8) / ENDANGERED SPECIES (*4) / TWENTY (*4) / LYVE FROM STEEL TOWN (*5) / EDGE OF FOREVER (*5) / CHRISTMAS TIME AGAIN (*2) / VICIOUS CYCLE (*6) / THYRTY: 30th ANNIVERSARY COLLECTION (*8)

RONNIE VAN ZANT (b.15 Jan'48) – vocals / **GARY ROSSINGTON** (b. 4 Dec'51) – guitar / **ALLEN COLLINS** (b.19 Jul'52) – guitar / **GREG WALKER** (or) **LEON WILKESON** (b. 5 Apr'52) – bass / **RICKY MEDLOCKE** (or) **BOB BURNS** – drums

not iss. — Shade Tree

1971. (7") **I'VE BEEN YOUR FOOL. / GOTTA GO** [–] [ ]
(UK-iss.Oct82 on 'M.C.A.'; 799)

— **ED KING** – bass (ex-STRAWBERRY ALARM CLOCK) repl. LEON & GREG / added **BILLY POWELL** (b. 3 Jun'52) – piano (RICKY MEDLOCKE had now formed BLACKFOOT, after contributing vox + drums on 2 tracks 'White Dove' & 'The Seasons')

M.C.A. — M.C.A.

Nov 73. (7") *<40158>* **GIMME THREE STEPS. / MR. BANKER** [–] [ ]
Jan 74. (lp/c) *(MCG/+C 3502) <363>* **PRONOUNCED LEH-NERD SKIN-NERD** [ ] Sep73 [27]
– I ain't the one / Tuesday's gone / Gimme three steps / Simple man / Things goin' on / Mississippi kid / Poison whiskey / Free bird. *(re-iss. Jun84 lp/c; MCL/+C 1798) (cd-iss. Jul88; DMCL 1798) (cd re-iss. Nov91; MCLD 19072) (lp re-iss. Nov98 on 'Simply Vinyl'; SVLP 52)*

— added returning **LEON WILKESON** – bass (ED KING now 3rd guitarist)

May 74. (7") *(MCA 136) <40231>* **DON'T ASK ME NO QUESTIONS. / TAKE YOUR TIME** [ ] Jan74 [ ]
Oct 74. (lp/c) *(MCF/+C 2547) <413>* **SECOND HELPING** [ ] Apr74 [12]
– Sweet home Alabama / I need you / Don't ask me no questions / Workin' for MCA / The ballad of Curtis Loew / Swamp music / The needle and the spoon / Call me the breeze. *(re-iss. 1983 lp/c; MCL/+C 1746) (re-iss. Oct87 on 'Fame' lp/c; FA/TC-FA 3194) (cd-iss. Aug89; DMCL 1746) (cd re-iss. Oct92; MCLD 19073)*
Oct 74. (7") *(MCA 160) <40258>* **SWEET HOME ALABAMA. / TAKE YOUR TIME** [ ] Jul74 [8]
Nov 74. (7") *<40328>* **FREE BIRD (edit). / DOWN SOUTH JUKIN'** [–] [19]

— (Dec74) **ARTIMUS PYLE** (b. 15 Jul'48, Spartanburg, South Carolina) – drums repl. BURNS

May 75. (lp/c) *(MCF/+C 2700) <2137>* **NUTHIN' FANCY** [43] Apr75 [9]
– Saturday night special / Cheatin' woman / Railroad song / I'm a country boy / On the hunt / Am I losin' / Made in the shade / Whiskey rock-a-roller. *(re-iss. 1983 lp/c; MCL/+C 1760) (cd-iss. Aug87; CMCAD 31003) (cd re-iss. Nov94; MCLD 19074) (cd re-iss. Nov99; MCD 12024)*
Jul 75. (7") *(MCA 199) <40416>* **SATURDAY NIGHT SPECIAL. / MADE IN THE SHADE** [ ] May75 [27]

— Reverted to six-piece, when ED KING departed / added backing vocalists **CASSIE GAINES, LESLIE HAWKINS + JO JO BILLINGSLEY**

Feb 76. (7") *(MCA 229) <40532>* **DOUBLE TROUBLE. / ROLL GYPSY ROLL** [ ] [80]
Mar 76. (lp/c) *(MCF/+C 2744) <2170>* **GIMME BACK MY BULLETS** [34] Feb76 [20]
– Gimme back my bullets / Every mother's son / Trust / (I got the) Same old blues / Double trouble / Roll gypsy roll / Searching / Cry for the bad man / All I can do is write about it. *(re-iss. Feb82 lp/c; MCL/+C 1653) (cd-iss. Nov99; MCD 12023)*
Jun 76. (7") *<40565>* **GIMME BACK MY BULLETS. / ALL I CAN DO IS WRITE ABOUT IT** [–] [ ]
Aug 76. (7"ep) *(MCA 251)* **FREE BIRD. / SWEET HOME ALABAMA / DOUBLE TROUBLE** [31] [–]
(re-iss. Nov79, hit No.43) (re-iss. May82 hit No.21) (re-iss. Dec83 12"/12"pic-d; MCAT/+P 251)

— added **STEVE GAINES** (b.14 Sep'49, Seneca, Missouri) – 3rd guitar (ex-SMOKEHOUSE)

Oct 76. (7") *<40647>* **TRAVELIN' MAN (live). / GIMME THREE STEPS (live)** [–] [ ]
Oct 76. (d-lp/d-c) *(MCSP/+C 279) <6001>* **ONE MORE FROM THE ROAD (live)** [17] Sep76 [9]
– Workin' for MCA / I ain't the one / Searching / Tuesday's gone / Saturday night special / Travelin' man / Whiskey rock-a-roller / Sweet home Alabama / Gimme three steps / Call me the breeze / T for Texas / The needle and spoon / Crossroads / Free bird. *<US cd-iss. 1991 with edited applause> (d-cd-ss.Dec92; MCLDD 19139)*
Nov 76. (7") *<40665>* **FREE BIRD (live). / SEARCHING (live)** [–] [38]
Jan 77. (7") *(MCA 275)* **FREE BIRD (live edit). / GIMME THREE STEPS (live)** [ ] [–]
Oct 77. (lp/c) *(MCG/+C 3525) <3029>* **STREET SURVIVORS** [13] [5]
– What's your name / That smell / One more time / I know a little / You got that right / I never dreamed / Honky tonk night time man / Ain't no good life. *(re-iss. Jul82 lp/c; MCL/+C 1694) (cd-iss. Oct94; MCLD 19248)*

— On 20th Oct'77, a few days after release of above album, the band's tour plane crashed. RONNIE VAN ZANT, STEVE & CASSIE GAINES plus roadie DEAN KILPATRICK were all killed. The remainder all suffered other injuries, but would recover. ARTIMUS went solo, the rest became ROSSINGTON-COLLINS BAND

Jan 78. (7") *(MCA 342)* *<40819>* **WHAT'S YOUR NAME. / I KNOW A LITTLE** [ ] Nov77 [13]

Mar 78. (7") *<40888>* **YOU GOT THAT RIGHT. / AIN'T NO GOOD LIFE** [-] [69]

ROSSINGTON-COLLINS BAND

— formed 1979 by **GARY & ALLEN** with **BILLY POWELL** – keyboards / **LEON WILKESON** – bass / **DALE KRANTZ** – vocals / **BARRY HAREWOOD** – guitars, slide / **DEREK HASS** – drums, percussion

M.C.A. M.C.A.

Jul 80. (lp/c) *(MCG/+C 4011)* *<5130>* **ANYTIME, ANYPLACE, ANYWHERE** [ ] [13]
– Prime time / Three times as bad / Don't misunderstand me / Misery loves company / One good man / Opportunity / Getaway / Winners and losers / Sometimes you can put it out. *(re-iss. Jun87 lp/c; MCL/+C 1748)* *<US cd-iss. Jun88; 31220>*

Aug 80. (7") *(MCA 636)* *<41284>* **DON'T MISUNDERSTAND ME. / WINNERS AND LOSERS** [ ] [55]

Oct 80. (7") *<51023>* **GETAWAY. / SOMETIMES YOU CAN PUT IT OUT** [-] [ ]

Oct 80. (7") *(MCA 648)* **ONE GOOD MAN. / MISERY LOVES COMPANY** [ ] [-]

Jun 81. (7") *<51218>* **GOTTA GET IT STRAIGHT. / DON'T STOP ME NOW** [-] [ ]

Oct 81. (lp/c) *(MCF/+C 4018)* *<5207>* **THIS IS THE WAY** [ ] [24]
– Gotta get it straight / Teshauna / Gonna miss it when it's gone / Pine box / Fancy ideas / Don't stop me now / Seems like every day / I'm free today / Next phone call / Means nothing to you.

Oct 81. (7") *(MCA 752)* **TESHAUNA. / GONNA MISS IT WHEN IT'S GONE** [ ] [-]
(12"+=) *(MCAT 572)* – Don't stop me now.

ROSSINGTON

— with **GARY** & his wife **DALE** with **HASS** – drums / **JAY JOHNSON** – guitar / **TIM LINDSAY** – bass

not iss. Atlantic

Nov 86. (lp) *<81672>* **RETURNED TO THE SCENE OF THE CRIME** [-] [ ]
– Turn it up / Honest hearts / God luck to you / Wounded again / Waiting in the shadows / Dangerous love / Can you forget about my love / Returned to the scene of the crime / Are you leaving me / Path less chosen.

Nov 86. (7") *<89364>* **TURN IT UP. / PATH LESS CHOSEN** [-] [ ]

— now with **TIM LINDSEY** – bass / **TIM SHARPTON** – keyboards / **RONNIE EADES** – sax / **MITCH RIGER** – drums

M.C.A. M.C.A.

Jul 88. (lp/c/cd; as The ROSSINGTON BAND) *<(MCA/+C/D 42166)>* **LOVE YOUR MAN** [ ] [ ]
– Losin' control / Welcome me home / Call it love / Holdin' my own / Rock on / Love your man / Stay with me / Nowhere to run / Say it from the heart / I don't want to leave you.

ALLEN COLLINS BAND

— with **COLLINS, HAREWOOD, POWELL, WILKESON, HESS,** plus **JIMMY DOUGHERTY** – vocals / **RANDALL HALL** – guitar

not iss. M.C.A.

1983. (lp) *<39000>* **HERE THERE AND BACK** [-] [ ]
– Just trouble / One known soldier / Hangin' judge / Time after time / This ride's on me / Ready to move / Chapter one / Commitments / Everything you need. *<US cd-iss. 1990's; MCAD 31324>*

— After a spell in prison, POWELL joined Christian band VISION. Also in 1986, ALLEN COLLINS was involved in a car crash which killed his girlfriend, and paralized himself from the waist down. On the 23rd Jan'90 he died of pneumonia.

LYNYRD SKYNYRD

— re-formed Autumn 1987 with **ROSSINGTON, POWELL, PYLE, WILKESON, KING** plus **DALE KRANTZ ROSSINGTON, RANDALL HALL + JOHNNY VAN ZANT** – vocals (ex-• 38 SPECIAL)

M.C.A. M.C.A.

Apr 88. (d-lp/d-c/cd) *(DCMDMCMDC/DMCMD 7004)* *<8027>* **SOUTHERN BY THE GRACE OF GOD (live)** [ ] [68]
– Workin' for MCA / That smell / I know a little / Comin' home / You got that right / What's your name / Gimme back my bullets / Swamp music / Call me the breeze / Dixie – Sweet home Alabama / Free bird.

— **LYNYRD SKYNYRD** re-formed again in 1991 with **ROSSINGTON, KING** and **HALL** – guitars / **JOHNNY VAN ZANT** – vocals / **POWELL** – keyboards / **WILKESON** – bass / **PYLE** – percussion, drums / **CUSTER** – drums, percussion

Atlantic Atlantic

Jun 91. (cd/c/lp) *<(7567 82258-2/-4/-1)>* **LYNYRD SKYNYRD 1991** [ ] [64]
– Smokestack lightning / Keeping the faith / Southern women / Pure & simple / I've seen enough / Good thing / Money man / Backstreet crawler / It's a killer / Mama (afraid to say goodbye) / End of the road.

— extended members **JERRY JONES** – bass, guitar / **DALE KRANTZ-ROSSINGTON** – backing vocals repl. ARTIMUS PYLE

Mar 93. (cd/c) *<(7567 82447-2/-4)>* **THE LAST REBEL** [ ] [64]
– Good lovin's hard to find / One thing / Can't take that away / Best things in life / The last rebel / Outta Hell in my Dodge / Kiss your freedom goodbye / South of Heaven / Love don't always come easy / Born to run. *(re-iss. cd Feb95; same)*

not iss. Capricorn

Aug 94. (cd/c) *<42028-2>* **ENDANGERED SPECIES** [-] [ ]
– Down south jukin' / Heartbreak hotel / Devil in the bottle / Things goin' on / Saturday night special / Sweet home Alabama / I ain't the one / Am I losin' / All I have is a song / Poison whiskey / Good luck, bad luck / The last rebel / Hillbilly blues.

S.P.V. S.P.V.

Jul 96. (d-cd) *(SPV 0874419-2)* **SOUTHERN KNIGHTS (live)** [ ] [ ]
– Working for MCA / Ain't the one / Saturday night special / Down south jukin' / Double trouble / T for Texas / Devil in the bottle / That smell / Simple man / Whiskey rock and roller / What's your name / Gimme three steps / Sweet home Alabama / Free bird.

— line-up now **ROSSINGTON, VAN ZANT, WILKESON, POWELL** plus **RICKEY MEDLOCKE** – guitars, vocals (ex-BLACKFOOT) / **HUGHIE THOMASSON** – guitars, vocals (ex-OUTLAWS) / **OWEN HALE** – drums, percussion

May 97. (cd) *(SPV 0854439-2)* **TWENTY** [ ] [97]
– We ain't much different / Bring it on / Voodoo lake / Home is where the heart is / Travelin' man / Talked myself right into it / Never too late / O.R.R. / Blame it on a sad song / Berneice / None of us are free / How soon we forget.

— **MICHAEL CARTELLONE** – drums (ex-DAMN YANKEES) repl. HALE

S.P.V. CMC Int.

Jun 98. (d-cd) *(SPV 0852916-2)* *<607686147>* **LYVE FROM STEEL TOWN (live)** [ ] Apr98 [ ]
– We ain't much different / Saturday night special / What's your name? / On the hunt / You got that right / Voodoo lake / That smell / Bring it on / Simple man / I know a little / Berneice / Gimme three steps / Sweet home Alabama / Travelin' man / Free bird / (interview pt.1 & 2).

Aug 99. (cd) *(SPV 0852964-2)* *<86272>* **EDGE OF FOREVER** [ ] [96]
– Workin' / Full moon night / Preacher man / Mean streets / Tomorrow's goodbye / Edge of forever / Gone fishin' / Through it all / Money back guarentee / G.W.T.G.G. / Rough around the edges / Fla.

Oct 00. (cd) *(SPV 0857102-2)* *<86298>* **CHRISTMAS TIME AGAIN** (festive) [ ] Sep00 [ ]

— **EAN EVANS** – bass; repl. WILKESON who died 21st July 2001

Sanctuary Sanctuary

May 03. (cd) *(SANCD 180)* *<84607>* **VICIOUS CYCLE** [ ] [30]
– That's how I like it / Pick 'em up / Dead man walkin' / The way / Red white and blue / Sweet mama / All funked up / Hell or Heaven / Mad hatter / Rockin' little town / Crawl / Jake / Life's lessons / Lucky man / Gimme back my bullets (with KID ROCK).

– compilations, others, etc. –

All 'M.C.A.' unless otherwise stated.

Oct 78. (lp/c) *(MCG/+C 3529)* *<3047>* **SKYNYRD'S FIRST AND . . .LAST** (rec.1970-72) [50] Sep78 [15]
– Down south jukin' / Preacher's daughter / White dove / Was I right or wrong / Lend a helpin' hand / Wino / Comin' home / The seasons / Things goin' on. *(re-iss. Aug81 lp/c; MCL/+C 1627)*

Oct 78. (7") *<40957>* **DOWN SOUTH JUKIN'. / WINO** [–] [ ]

Oct 78. (7"ep) *(MCEP 101)* **DOWN SOUTH JUKIN' / THAT SMELL. / LEND A HELPIN' HAND / CALL ME THE BREEZE** [ ] [–]

Jan 80. (d-lp/d-c) *(MCSP/+C 308)* *<11008>* **GOLD & PLATINUM** [49] Dec79 [12]
– Down south jukin' / Saturday night special / Gimme three steps / What's your name / You got that right / Gimme back my bullets / Sweet home Alabama / Free bird / That smell / On the hunt / I ain't the one / Whiskey rock-a-roller / Simple man / I know a little / Tuesday's gone / Comin' home. *(re-iss. Jul82 lp/c; MCDW/+C 456)*

Apr 82. (d-c) *(MCA2 107)* **PRONOUNCED LEH-NERD SKIN-NERD / SECOND HELPING** [ ] [–]

Nov 82. (lp) *<5370>* **THE BEST OF THE REST** [–] [ ]

Jul 84. (7") *Old Gold; (OG 9421)* **FREE BIRD (edit). / SWEET HOME ALABAMA** [ ] [–]
(re-iss. Aug95 on cd-s;)

Sep 86. (d-c) *(MCA2 111)* **NUTHIN' FANCY / GIVE ME BACK MY BULLETS** [ ] [–]

Mar 87. (d-lp/c) *Raw Power; (RAW LP/TC 031)* **ANTHOLOGY** [ ] [–]

Nov 87. (7") *<53206>* **WHEN YOU GOT GOOD FRIENDS. / TRUCK DRIVIN' MAN** [–] [ ]

Nov 87. (lp/c) *(MCF/+C 3405)* *<42084>* **LEGEND** (rare live) [ ] Oct87 [41]
– Georgia peaches / When you got good friends / Sweet little Missy / Four walls of Raiford / Simple man / Truck drivin' man / One in the sun / Mr. Banker / Take your time.

Jan 89. (7"/12") *(MCA/+T 1315)* **FREE BIRD. / SWEET HOME ALABAMA** [ ] [–]

Apr 89. (lp/c/cd) *(MCG/MCGC/DMCG 6046)* *<42293>* **SKYNYRD'S INNYRDS** [ ] [ ]

1990. (c-s) *<54306>* **FREE BIRD. / SWEET HOME ALABAMA** [–] [ ]

Feb 92. (3xcd-box) *(MCA3 10390)* **THE DEFINITIVE LYNYRD SKYNYRD COLLECTION** [ ] [ ]

Mar 94. (cd/c) *Nectar; (NTR CD/C 015)* **FREEBIRD – THE VERY BEST** [ ] [–]
– Saturday night special / Whiskey rock & roller / Workin' for MCA / I ain't the one / Sweet home Alabama / Ballad of Curtis Loew / Tuesday's gone / Gimme 3 steps / The needle & the spoon / Free bird / Call me the breeze / What's your name / Swamp music / Gimme back my bullets / That smell / You got that right.

Sep 94. (cd) *(MCLD 19248)* **STREET SURVIVORS / SKYNYRD'S FIRST AND . . . LAST** [ ] [–]

Sep 96. (cd) *(MCD 1147-2)* **FREEBIRD – THE MOVIE** (live at Knebworth 1976) [ ] [ ]

Jun 97. (d-cd) *Repertoire; (RR 4637)* **OLD TIME GREATS** [ ] [–]

Nov 98. (cd) *B.M.G.; <44845>* **EXTENDED VERSIONS** [–] [ ]

Nov 98. (cd) *<MCD 11888>* **SKYNYRD'S FIRST** [–] [ ]

Jan 99. (d-cd) *<(MCD 11807)>* **THE ESSENTIAL LYNYRD SKYNYRD** [ ] Aug98 [ ]

Mar 99. (cd) *<MCD 11941>* **THE MILLENNIUM COLLECTION: THE BEST OF LYNYRD SKYNYRD** [–] [ ]

Oct 99. (cd) *<MCD 12041>* **SOLO FLYTES** [–] [ ]

Jan 00. (cd) *Universal; (E 112173-2)* **UNIVERSAL MASTERS COLLECTION** [ ] [ ]

Mar 00. (cd) *<112229>* **ALL TIME GREATEST HITS** [–] [ ]

Mar 00. (cd) *Calamari; <12606>* **THE COMPLETE LYNYRD SKYNYRD LIVE** [–] [ ]

Jul 00. (cd) *S.P.V.; (SPV 0762994-2) / C.M.C.; <86293>* **THEN AND NOW** [ ] Apr00 [ ]

Aug 00. (cd) *Universal; <112341>* **DOUBLE TROUBLE** [–] [ ]

Oct 00. (3xcd-box) *Universal; (E 132182-2)* **NUTHIN' FANCY / SECOND HELPING / STREET SURVIVORS** [ ] [–]

Dec 00. (cd) *Universal; (AA 88112429-2) / M.C.A.; <429>* **COLLECTYBLES** [ ] Nov00 [ ]

Apr 00. (cd) *B.M.G.; <45721>* **YESTERDAY AND TODAY** [–] [ ]

Apr 01. (cd) *Spectrum; (544451-2)* **THE ESSENTIAL COLLECTION** [ ] [–]

Aug 03. (d-cd) *Universal TV; <2840-2>* **THYRTY: 30th ANNIVERSARY COLLECTION** [–] [16]

BOB MARLEY

Kirsty MacCOLL

Born: 10 Oct'59, London, England. Being the daughter of semi-legendary folk singer EWAN MacCOLL, KIRSTY no doubt had music in her blood and began her career in punk outfit, The DRUG ADDIX (as MANDY DOUBT!). Striking out on her own in 1979, she joined the fashionable 'Stiff' roster and released a debut single that summer, 'THEY DON'T KNOW'. Although TRACY ULLMAN would later take the track into the upper regions of the chart, MacCOLL made little headway with it and parted company with 'Stiff' after a second single, 'YOU CAUGHT ME OUT', was withdrawn. Netting a major label deal with 'Polydor', she had her first taste of success in summer '81 with the Top 20 rockabilly-style novelty hit, 'THERE'S A GUY WORKS DOWN THE CHIPSHOP SWEARS HE'S ELVIS'. Despite the exposure, an accompanying debut album, 'DESPERATE CHARACTER' (1981) did nothing and MacCOLL's confidence was further dented after a bout of stage fright on tour in Ireland. Nevertheless, the singer refused to throw in the towel and in 1983, made the first of many guest appearances by augmenting rockabilly revivalists, MATCHBOX on a single, 'I Want Out'. After a one-off single, 'BERLIN', for the tiny 'North Of Watford' label, MacCOLL moved back to 'Stiff' the same year, subsequently marrying top indie producer Steve Lillywhite (they divorced around ten years later). Another high profile guest slot came in early '84 when she appeared on SIMPLE MINDS' classic single, 'Speed Your Love To Me'. Early the following year, MacCOLL's dogged determination was finally rewarded as her bittersweet rendition of Billy Bragg's 'NEW ENGLAND' made the UK Top 10. Disappointingly, the follow-up, 'HE'S ON THE BEACH', again failed to consolidate her success and over the ensuing four years she concentrated on her backing vocal prowess, enhancing the recordings of everyone from The HAPPY MONDAYS and The SMITHS to London-Irish rabble rousers The POGUES. MacCOLL's earthy, folksy voice sat particularly well with the latter outfit and as well as touring with the band, she locked horns with the inimitable SHANE MacGOWAN on The POGUES' 1987 Christmas lullaby from hell, 'FAIRYTALE OF NEW YORK'. With her profile now higher that at any point in her career, MacCOLL finally released a follow-up album, 'KITE' (1989), proving herself a subtle, skillful and politically aware songwriter with a strong sense of humour and a gift for interpreting emotive neo-folk ballads like 'DAYS' (the old KINKS number), a Top 20 hit that summer. Yet again, though, follow-up tracks, 'INNOCENCE' and the droll 'DON'T COME THE COWBOY WITH ME SONNY JIM' failed to chart and MacCOLL took a radically different approach with her next single, 'WALKING DOWN MADISON'. A near-Top 20 collaboration with JOHNNY MARR, the record married urban folk-pop to electronic dance beats, echoing the likes of SUZANNE VEGA's 'Tom's Diner' remix. The accompanying album, 'ELECTRIC LANDLADY' (1991) found her experimenting with different sounds and collaborators including MARSHALL CRENSHAW and FAIRGROUND ATTRACTION's MARK E. NEVIN. Although the record made the Top 20 and received encouraging reviews sales could've been better and KIRSTY moved on to 'Z.T.T.' for 1994's 'TITANIC DAYS', recorded with a cast of veterans including NEVIN, DAVID RUFFY and GARY TIBBS. While that record didn't even make the Top 40, 1995's 'GALORE' retrospective became her biggest selling release to date, collecting the cream of both her original material and the slew of covers (everyone from The SMITHS to MARTY ROBBINS) she's recorded over the years. With a new album, 'TROPICAL BRAINSTORM' (2000), receiving her best reviews for years, it looked like MacCOLL was back to her best. South America was the theme, bright and happy tunes played to a celebratory samba/mambo rhythm, her divorce of several years ago well behind her. Tragically, just as things looked on the up for KIRSTY, she was killed on the 18th of December 2000, when a speedboat hit her while she was swimming off the coast of Cozumel, Mexico. • **Songwriters:** Writes / co-writes material. In 1990, she collaborated with MARK NEVIN (ex-FAIRGROUND ATTRACTION). She has covered many songs including; JUST ONE LOOK (Hollies) / TERRY (Twinkle) / YOU JUST HAVEN'T EARNED IT YET BABY (Smiths) / DON'T GO NEAR THE WATER (Beach Boys) / WALK RIGHT BACK (Everly Brothers) / PERFECT DAY (Lou Reed) / EL PASO (Marty Robbins). • **Trivia:** The DRUG ADDIX released one EP for 'Chiswick' in 1978; THE DRUG ADDIX MAKE A RECORD. Her brothers are NEIL of The BIBLE and CALLUM of MacCOLL & SEEGER.

Album rating: DESPERATE CHARACTER (*5) / KIRSTY MacCOLL compilation (*5) / KITE (*6) / ELECTRIC LANDLADY (*6) / TITANIC DAYS (*5) / GALORE (THE BEST OF KIRSTY MacCOLL) compilation (*7) / TROPICAL BRAINSTORM (*6)

KIRSTY MacCOLL – vocals with various members of ROCKPILE

		Stiff	not iss.
Jun 79.	(7"/7"pic-d) *(BUY/+P 47)* **THEY DON'T KNOW. / TURN MY MOTOR ON**		–
Oct 79.	(7"; w-drawn) *(BUY 57)* **YOU CAUGHT ME OUT. / BOYS**	–	–
		Polydor	Polydor
Feb 81.	(7") *(POSP 225)* **KEEP YOUR HANDS OFF MY BABY. / I DON'T NEED YOU**		–
May 81.	(7") *(POSP 250)* **THERE'S A GUY WORKS DOWN THE CHIPSHOP SWEARS HE'S ELVIS. / HARD TO BELIEVE**	14	–
Jul 81.	(7") **THERE'S A GUY WORKS DOWN THE CHIPSHOP SWEARS HE'S ELVIS. / OVER YOU**	–	
Jul 81.	(lp/c) *(POLS/+C 1035)* **DESPERATE CHARACTER** – Clock goes round / See that girl / There's a guy works down the chipshop swears he's Elvis / Teenager in love / Mexican sofa / Until the night / Falling for faces / Just one look / The real ripper / Hard to believe / He thinks I still care / There's a guy works down the chipshop swears he's Elvis (country version).		–

Sep 81. (7") *(POSP 326)* **SEE THAT GIRL. / OVER YOU** [ ] [-]
Nov 81. (7") *(POSP 368)* **YOU STILL BELIEVE IN ME. / QUEEN OF THE HIGH TEAS** [ ] [-]

— early 1983, she guested for MATCHBOX on the single 'I Want Out'

North Of Watford — not iss.

Aug 83. (7"/12") *(NOW/+X 100)* **BERLIN. / RHYTHM OF THE REAL THING** [ ] [-]

Stiff — not iss.

Oct 83. (7"/12") *(BUY/+IT 190)* **TERRY. / QUIETLY ALONE** [ ] [-]

— in early '84, she guested on SIMPLE MINDS hit 'Speed Your Love To Me'

Jan 85. (7"pic-d) *(SBUY 216)* **A NEW ENGLAND. / PATRICK** [7] [ ]
(12"+=) *(BUYIT 216)* – I'm going out with an 80 year old millionaire.
Jun 85. (7"/12") *(BUY/+IT 225)* **HE'S ON THE BEACH. / PLEASE GO TO SLEEP** [ ] [-]

— In 1986-87, she guested on tours & in studio for The POGUES

Virgin — Charisma

Feb 89. (7") *(KMA 1)* **FREE WORLD. / CLOSER TO GOD?** [43] [-]
(12"+=) *(KMAT 1)* – You just haven't earned it yet, baby.
(3"cd-s++=) *(KMACD 1)* – La floret de mimosas.
(10"+=) *(KMAN 1)* – The end of a perfect day.
Apr 89. (lp/c/cd) *(KMLP/TCKM/CDKM 1)* <91232> **KITE** [34] [ ]
– Innocence / free world / Mother's ruin / Days / No victims / Fifteen minutes / Don't come the cowboy with me Sonny Jim / Tread lightly / What do pretty girls do? / Dancing in limbo / The end of a perfect day / You and me baby.
Jun 89. (7"/c-s/3"cd-s) *(KMA/+C/CDX 2)* **DAYS. / HAPPY** [12] [-]
(10"++=) *(KMAN 2)* – Still life / El Paso.
(cd-s+=) *(KMACD 2)* – Please help me, I'm falling / Still life.
Sep 89. (7"/c-s) *(KMA/+C 3)* **INNOCENCE. / CLUBLAND** [ ] [-]
(10"+=) *(KMAN 3)* – Don't run away from me now.
(12"+=/3"cd-s+=) *(KMA T/CDX 3)* – ('A'-guilt mix) / ('A'-guitar mix) / No victims (mix).
Mar 90. (7"/c-s) *(KMA/+C 4)* **DON'T COME THE COWBOY WITH ME SONNY JIM. / OTHER PEOPLES HEARTS** [ ] [-]
(12"+=) *(KMAT 4)* – Complainte pourste Catherine.
(cd-s++=) *(KMACD 4)* – Am I right?
May 91. (7"/c-s) *(VS/+C 1348)* **WALKING DOWN MADISON. / ONE GOOD THING** [23] [-]
(12"+=/cd-s+=) *(VST/VSCDT 1348)* – ('A'club mix) / ('A'ambient mix).
(cd-s) *(VSCDX 1348)* – ('A'side) / ('A'-Urban mix) / Days / Darling let's have another baby (duet with BILLY BRAGG).
Jun 91. (cd/c/lp) *(CD/TC+/V 2663)* <91688> **ELECTRIC LANDLADY** [17] [ ]
– Walking down Madison / All I ever wanted / Children of the revolution / Halloween / My affair / Lying down / He never mentioned love / We'll never pass this way again / The hardest word / Maybe it's imaginary / My way home / The one and only.
Jul 91. (7"/c-s) *(VS/+C 1354)* **MY AFFAIR. / ALL THE TEARS I CRIED** [68] [-]
(cd-s+=) *(VSCDT 1354)* – Don't go near the water / ('A' olive groove mix).
(12") *(VST 1354)* – ('A'-Ladbroke mix) / ('A'-bass sexy mix) / ('A'-olive groove).
Oct 91. (7"/c-s) *(VS/+C 1373)* **ALL I EVER WANTED. / THERE'S A GUY WORKS DOWN THE CHIPSHOP SWEARS HE'S ELVIS (live)** [ ] [-]
(cd-s+=) *(VSCDT 1373)* – Walk right back (live) / A new England (live with BILLY BRAGG).
(12"+=) *(VST 1373)* – What do pretty girls do? / Walk right back (live).

— In 1991, she helped present BBC2's TV consumer programme 'Byline' and featured vox on WONDER STUFF's hit single 'Welcome To The Cheap Seats'

Z.T.T. — I.R.S.

Dec 93. (7"/c-s) *(ZANG 46/+C)* **ANGEL. / ('A'-Jay's edit)** [ ] [-]
(12"+=) *(ZANG 46T)* – ('A'-Apollo 440 remix) / ('A'-Stuart Crichton remix).
(cd-s++=) *(ZANG 46CD)* – ('A'-Into the light mix).

— with **MARK NEVIN** – guitars, co-writer (ex-FAIRGROUND ATTRACTION, ex-MORRISSEY) / **DAVID RUFFY** – drums (ex-AZTEC CAMERA) / **GARY TIBBS** – bass (ex-ADAM & THE ANTS) / **PETE GLENISTER** – guitars / **STEVE NIEVE** – keyboards / etc.

Feb 94. (cd/c) *(450 994711-2/-4)* <27214> **TITANIC DAYS** [46] [ ]
– You know it's you / Soho Square / Angel / Last days of Summer / Bad / Can't stop killing you / Titanic days / Don't go home / Big boy on a Saturday night / Just woke up / Tomorrow never comes.
Feb 95. (7"/c-s) *(VS/+C 1517)* **CAROLINE. / IRISH COUSIN** [58] [-]
(cd-s+=) *(VSCDT 1517)* – A new England / The butcher boy.
(cd-s) *(VSCDX 1517)* – ('A'side) / El Paso / My affair (Ladbroke Grove mix).
Mar 95. (cd/c) *(CDV/TCV 2763)* <30257> **GALORE (THE BEST OF KIRSTY MacCOLL)** (compilation) [6] [ ]
– They don't know / A new England / There's a guy works down the chip shop swears he's Elvis / He's on the beach / Fairytale of New York (w/ POGUES) / Miss Otis regrets / Free world / Innocence / You just haven't earned it yet baby / Don't come the cowboy with me Sonny Jim / Walking down Madison / My affair / Angel / Titanic days / Can't stop killing you / Caroline / Perfect day.
Jun 95. (c-s; as KIRSTY MacCOLL & EVAN DANDO) *(VSC 1552)* **PERFECT DAY / TERRY** [75] [-]
(cd-s+=) *(VSCDT 1552)* – Tread lightly / He's on the beach.
Jul 95. (c-s) *(VSC 1558)* **DAYS / STILL LIFE (extended)** [42] [-]
(cd-s+=) *(VSCDT 1558)* – Happy / Walking down Madison (club mix).

V2 — Instinct

Nov 99. (cd-s) *(VVR 501097-3)* **MAMBO DE LA LUNA (mixes; album / Mint Royale x2) / GOLDEN HEART / THINGS HAPPEN** [ ] [-]
(cd-s) *(VVR 501097-8)* – ('A'mixes).
Feb 00. (cd-s) *(VVR 501218-3)* **IN THESE SHOES? / GOOD FOR ME / MY AFFAIR (live)** [ ] [-]
(cd-s) *(VVR 501218-8)* – ('A'side) / ('A'-Le Rosbifs mix) / ('A'-P.mix).
Mar 00. (cd/c) *(VVR 100987-2/-4)* <557> **TROPICAL BRAINSTORM** [39] Apr01 [ ]
– Mambo de la luna / In these shoes? / Treachery / Here comes that man again / Autumngirlsoup / Celestine / England 2 Columbia 0 / Nao esperando / Alegria / Us Amazonians / Wrong again / Designer life / Head. <US+=> – Golden heart / Things happen / Good for me / Mambo de la luna (video).
Sep 00. (cd-s) *(VVR 501428-3)* **IN THESE SHOES? (UR crazy remixes) / MY AFFAIR (live)** [ ] [-]
(cd-s) *(VVR 501428-8)* – ('A'mixes).

— KIRSTY died on the 18th of December, 2000

– compilations, etc. –

Mar 85. (lp/c) Polydor; *(SPE LP/MC 95)* **KIRSTY MacCOLL** [ ] [-]
– There's a guy works down the chipshop swears he's Elvis / See that girl / You still believe in me / Roman gardens / Man with no name / Annie / Keep your hands off my baby / Hard to believe / Berlin / Falling for faces / Clock goes round / Sleepless nights.
Aug 96. (cd) Disky; *(STIFFCD 17)* **THE ESSENTIAL COLLECTION** [ ] [-]
Feb 98. (cd) Hux; *(HUX 001)* **WHAT DO PRETTY GIRLS DO** [ ] [-]

Shane MacGOWAN & THE POPES

Formed: King's Cross, London, England ... early 1994 by ex-NIPPLE ERECTORS (1978), ex-NIPS (1978-'81) and ex-POGUES (1983-1991) frontman/legend, SHANE MacGOWAN (b.25 Dec'57, Kent, England), along with PAUL McGUINESS, BERNIE FRANCE, DANNY POPE and TOM McMANAMON. Following his messy departure from The POGUES in the early 90's, the Irish KEITH RICHARDS (though even RICHARDS' mythical debauchery would struggle to match MacGOWAN's self-destructiveness in terms of sheer dogged determination) threatened to form his own outfit, The POPES; sceptics who doubted the man could even form an opinion were at least partly silenced by MacGOWAN's late '92 duet with fellow maverick, NICK CAVE, on a brilliantly skewed cover of Louis Armstrong's 'WONDERFUL WORLD'. Two years on and much press rumination later, The POPES' debut single, 'THE CHURCH OF THE HOLY SPOOK', finally put an end to the speculation and announced that MacGOWAN's muse was as darkly fertile as ever.

Released on 'Z.T.T.', the song's uptempo thrash recalled the unholy spirit of The POGUES' classic 'SICK BED OF CUCHULAINN', scraping into the UK Top 75. Follow-up single, 'THAT WOMAN'S GOT ME DRINKING' (excuses, excuses), made the Top 40, while Hollywood hearthrob, JOHNNY DEPP, played guitar on their debut Top Of The Pops appearance. The accompanying album, 'THE SNAKE', was the best album The POGUES never recorded in the last decade, finding MacGOWAN back at his cursing, doomed romantic best. Alongside the obligatory traditional songs ('THE RISING OF THE MOON' and 'NANCY WHISKEY'), the record featured an amusingly appropriate cover of Gerry Rafferty's 'HER FATHER DIDN'T LIKE ME ANYWAY', while 'HAUNTED' was a collaboration with SINEAD O'CONNOR which made the Top 30 when released as a single in Spring '95. CLANNAD's MAIRE BRENNAN also hooked up with MacGOWAN for 'YOU'RE THE ONE', underlining the depth of respect afforded the wayward genius, even among his more conventional peers. The live appearances which followed the record's release mightn't have matched the ferocious abandon of The POGUES in full flow but came damn near it, while MacGOWAN followed in SID VICIOUS' footsteps (the man's love of the SEX PISTOLS was revealed to the nation via a barely coherent admission on Jo Whiley's Channel 4 TV show) by recording a version of 'MY WAY' in gloriously two-fingered style. 1997 saw the release of a disappointing follow-up set, 'THE CROCK OF GOLD', a record that was at times easier on the ear but hardly threatened to set the pulse racing. Surely only SHANE MacGOWAN could perform at two St. Patrick's Day shows on the trot, given that they took place on opposite sides of the Atlantic Ocean. Yet, due to a quirk of fate, that was exactly what he did, the cream of both performances collected together on 'ACROSS THE BROAD ATLANTIC: LIVE ON PADDY'S DAY' (2002). As anticipated, the atmosphere is raucous, the banter paints the air blue and the set list is primed for maximum, whiskey-soaked celebration. • **Songwriters:** MacGOWAN except CRACKLIN' ROSIE (Neil Diamond) / THE RISING OF THE MOON + NANCY WHISKEY (trad). • **Trivia:** Their/his debut album also featured guest appearances from ex-POGUES; SPIDER and FINER, plus DUBLINERS musician/friend BARNEY McKENNA. 'VICTORIA' was written about his writer girlfriend at the time, VICTORIA CLARKE. MacGOWAN is still a reader & fan of writer JAMES JOYCE and Spanish poet LORCA.

Album rating: THE SNAKE (*8) / THE CROCK OF GOLD (*5) / THE RARE OUL' STUFF (*5) / ACROSS THE BROAD ATLANTIC (*4)

SHANE McGOWAN – vocals (ex-POGUES, ex-NIPS) / **PAUL McGUINNESS** – guitar / **BERNIE FRANCE** – bass / **DANNY POPE** – drums / **TOM NcMANAMON** – banjo

Z.T.T. Warners

Sep 94. (7"/c-s/cd-s) *(ZANG 57/+C/CD)* **THE CHURCH OF THE HOLY SPOOK. / RAKE AT THE GATES OF HELL** 74 –
(cd-s+=) *(ZANG 57CDX)* – King of the bop / Nancy Whiskey.

Oct 94. (c-s) *(ZANG 56C)* **THAT WOMAN'S GOT ME DRINKING / HER FATHER DIDN'T LIKE ME ANYWAY** 34 –
(12"+=/cd-s+=) *(ZANG 56 T/CD)* – Roddy McCorley / Minstrel boy.

Oct 94. (cd/c/lp) *(4509 98104-2/-4/-1)* <45821> **THE SNAKE** 37 Jan95
– The church of the holy spook / That woman's got me drinking / The song with no name / Aisling / I'll be your handbag / Her father didn't like me anyway / A Mexican funeral in Paris / The snake with the eyes of Garnet / Donegal express / Victoria / The rising of the moon / Bring down the lamp. *(re-iss. Jun95 cd/c; 0630 10402-2/-4)* – Haunted (with SINEAD O'CONNOR) / You're the one (with MAIRE BRENNAN) / Cracklin' Rosie / Bring down the lamp. *(cd re-iss. Nov98; MACG 004CD)*

Dec 94. (c-s) *(ZANG 60C)* **THE SONG WITH NO NAME / NANCY WHISKEY** –
(12"+=/cd-s+=) *(ZANG 60 T/CD)* – Cracklin' Rosie.

Apr 95. (c-s; SHANE MacGOWAN & SINEAD O'CONNOR) *(ZANG 65C)* **HAUNTED. / THE SONG WITH NO NAME** 30 –
(cd-s+=) *(ZANG 65CD)* – Bring down the lamp / Cracklin' Rosie.

Jun 95. (c-s; SHANE MacGOWAN & MAIRE BRENNAN) *(ZANG 68C)* **YOU'RE THE ONE / AISLING** –
(cd-s) *(ZANG 68CD)* – Victoria.

Apr 96. (c-s; SHANE MacGOWAN) *(ZANG 79C)* **MY WAY / SONG WITH NO NAME** 29 –
(cd-s+=) *(ZANG 79CD)* – Aisling / My way (your way).

— **LUCKY DOWLING** – bass; repl. BERNIE

— added **KIERAN KIELY** – accordions, whistles, vocals + **JOHN MYERS** – fiddle, whistle, guitar

Oct 97. (cd-s) *(MACG 001CD)* **LONESOME HIGHWAY /** –

Oct 97. (cd/c) *(MACG 002 CD/C)* **THE CROCK OF GOLD** 59 –
– Paddy rolling stone / Rock'n'roll Paddy / Paddy public enemy No.1 / Back in County Hell / Lonesome highway / Come to the bower / Ceilidh cowboy / More pricks than kicks / Truck drivin' man / Joey's in America / B&I ferry / Mother mo chroi / Spanish lady / St. John of gods / Skipping rhymes / Maclennan / Wanderin' star.

Mar 98. (cd-s) *(MACG 003CD)* **ROCK'N'ROLL PADDY / SHE MOVES THROUGH THE FAIR** –

Jan 02. (cd) *(ZTT 178CD)* <18036> **THE RARE OUL' STUFF** Feb 02
– You're the one / The song with no name / Nancy Whiskey / Roddy McCorley / Rock'n'roll Paddy / Christmas lullaby / Danny boy / Monstrel boy / Rake at the gates of Hell / Victoria / Donegal express / Ceilidh cowboy / Paddy rolling stone / Paddy public enemy No.1 / Back in the county hell / The snakes with eyes of garnet / Cracklin' Rosie / Aisling / Spanish lady / Come to the bower / St. John of gods.

Eagle Red Ink

Feb 02. (cd; as SHANE MacGOWAN'S POPES) *(EAGCD 192)* *<57068>* **ACROSS THE BROAD ATLANTIC: LIVE ON PADDY'S DAY – NEW YORK – DUBLIN (live)**
– If I should fall from grace with God / Rock & roll Paddy / Nancy Whiskey / A rainy night in Soho / Poor Paddy works on the railway / The broad majestic Shannon / Popes' instrumental:- My Ballyvourney love – The limpin' general – Bag of chips / Dirty old town / Mother MO Chroi / Body of an American / Granuaille / More pricks than kicks / Aisling / A pair of brown eyes / Streams of whiskey / Lonesome highway / Angel of death / Sick bed of Cuchulainn / The Irish rover / Fairytale of New York.

MACHINE HEAD

Formed: Oakland, California, USA . . . mid '92 by ex-VIOLENCE frontman ROBB FLYNN, LOGAN MADER, ADAM DUCE and CHRIS KONTOS. Dragging the flagging spirit of heavy metal kicking and screaming into the 90's, MACHINE HEAD roared into life with the universally acclaimed, COLIN RICHARDSON-produced debut album, 'BURN MY EYES' (1994). Rupturing eardrums with a bass-heavy bludgeon of mogadon guitars and a vocal style that alternated between CHRIS CORNELL (Soundgarden) and JAMES HETFIELD (Metallica), MACHINE HEAD became the ace in 'Roadrunner's (their label) pack, hitting the UK Top 30. Although they were signed to 'Interscope' in their native land, the group concentrated more on the British metal scene, especially after Kerrang! proclaimed them to be the best machine since ZAK DE LA ROCHA and Co (RATM). In 1995, one of the tracks from the album, 'OLD', was a surprise gatecrasher into the UK Top 50, the single backed by covers of POISON IDEA and CRO-MAGS material. With newcomer DAVE McCLAIN on the drumstool, their much-anticipated second set, 'THE MORE THINGS CHANGE . . .', was finally delivered early in 1997, the UK Top 20 album again proving that no frills, heavy-duty metal was still viable. Another round of ear-bashing was just what the doctor ordered, although not my doctor. Now without guitarist MADER (replaced by AHRUE LUSTER), MACHINE HEAD spurted out their third album, 'THE BURNING RED' (1999). The record entered the US Top 100 (their first to do so!) and the UK Top 20, although what the metal pundits from Kerrang! thought of their version of the Police's 'MESSAGE IN A BOTTLE', I dread to think. – take them away STING. 'SUPERCHARGER' (2001) laid off the dodgy covers but hardly lived up to its MONSTER MAGNET-style title, offering up too many metal cliches that were more short circuit than electric shock.

Album rating: BURN MY EYES (*8) / THE MORE THINGS CHANGE . . . (*6) / THE BURNING RED (*4) / SUPERCHARGER (*5) / HELLALIVE (*5)

ROBB FLYNN – vocals, guitar (ex-VIOLENCE) / **LOGAN MADER** -guitar / **ADAM DUCE** – bass, vocals / **CHRIS KONTOS** – drums

Roadrunner Roadrunner

Aug 94. (cd) *<(RR 9016-9)>* **BURN MY EYES** [25] [ ]
– Davidian / Old / A thousand lies / None but my own / The rage to overcome / Death church / A nation on fire / Blood for blood / I'm your god now / Real eyes, realize, real lies / Block. *(re-iss. May95 cd/c/lp; RR 9016-2/-4/-1)*

Oct 94. (12") **INFECTED. / PROTOPLAN** [ ] [-]

May 95. (10"pic-d-ep) *(RR 23408)* **OLD / A NATION ON FIRE (demo) / REAL LIES – FUCK IT ALL (demo) / OLD (demo)** [43] [-]
(cd-ep) *(RR 23403)* – ('A'side) / Davidian (live) / Hard times (live) / Death church (demo).
(cd-s) *(RR 23405)* – ('A'side) / Death church (convent mix) / Old (eve of apocalypse mix) / The rage to overcome.

Aug 95. (10"pic-d) **DEATH CHURCH. / A NATION ON FIRE (demo)** [ ] [-]
(cd-s+=) – Fuck it all (demo) / Old (demo).
(cd-s) – ('A'side) / Old (mix) / The rage to overcome (demo).

— **DAVE McCLAIN** – drums (ex-SACRED REICH) repl. KONTOS

Roadrunner Interscope

Mar 97. (cd/c/lp) *(RR 8860-2/-4/-1)* *<INT 846.371>* **THE MORE THINGS CHANGE . . .** [16] [ ]
– Ten ton hammer / Take my scars / Struck a nerve / Down to none / The frontlines / Spine / Bay of pigs / Violate / Blistering / Blood of the zodiac.

Nov 97. (cd-ep) *(RR 2257-3)* **TAKE MY SCARS / NEGATIVE CREEP / TAKE MY SCARS (live) / BLOOD FOR BLOOD (live)** [73] [-]
(cd-ep) *(RR 2257-5)* – (first 2 tracks) / Ten ton hammer (demo) / Struck a nerve (demo).

— now without LOGAN MADER who was repl. by **AHRUE LUSTER**

Roadrunner Roadrunner

Aug 99. (cd) *<(RR 8651-2)>* **THE BURNING RED** [13] [88]
– Enter the phoenix / Desire to fire / Nothing left / The blood, the sweat, the tears / Silver / From this day / Exhale the vile / Message in a bottle / Devil with the king's card / I defy / Five / The burning red.

Dec 99. (cd-s) *(RR 2138-3)* **FROM THIS DAY / ALCOHOLOCAUST / HOUSE OF SUFFERING** [74] [-]

Jul 00. (cd-ep) *(RR 2093-3)* **YEAR OF THE DRAGON EP** [ ] [-]
– The blood, the sweat, the tears / Desire to fire (live) / The blood, the sweat, the tears (live) / From this day (live) / New resistance (demo).

Oct 01. (cd) *<(120 8500-2)>* **SUPERCHARGER** [34] [ ]
– Declaration / Bulldozer / White-knuckle blackout! / Crashing around you / Kick you when you're down / Only the names / All in your head / American high / Brown acid / Sick of you / Nausea / Blank generation / Trephination / Deafening silence / Supercharger. *(ltd-cd+=; 1208500-5)* – Ten fold / Rat race / Hole in the sky / The blood, the sweat, the tears (live).

Dec 01. (cd-s) *(2320470-3)* **CRASHING AROUND YOU / TEN TON HAMMER (live) / SILVER (live) / ('A'video)** [ ] [-]

Mar 03. (cd) *<(RR 8437-2)>* **HELLALIVE (live)** [ ] [ ]
– Bulldozer / The blood, the sweat, the tears / Ten ton hammer / Old / Crashing around you / Take my scars / I'm your god now / None but my own / From this day / American high / Nothing left / Burning red / Davidian / Supercharger.

☐ Billy MACKENZIE (see under ⇒ ASSOCIATES)

☐ Bryan MacLEAN (see under ⇒ LOVE)

MADNESS

Formed: Camden, London, England . . . early '79, out of Kentish Town ska outfit, The INVADERS. In its earliest incarnation MADNESS comprised MIKE BARSON (keyboards), LEE THOMPSON (saxaphone, vocals) CHRIS FOREMAN (guitar), CHAS SMASH (horns, vocals, 'nutty' dancing), GRAHAM 'SUGGS' McPHERSON (vocals, equally 'nutty' dancing), MARK BEDFORD (bass) and DAN WOODGATE (drums). MADNESS were one of the leading lights of the ska revivalist '2-Tone' movement, the most exciting musical phenomenon since the advent of punk a few years earlier. Becoming friends with The SPECIAL AKA, MADNESS signed a one-off singles deal with JERRY DAMMERS' (the SPECIALS mainman) '2-Tone' label, releasing 'THE PRINCE' in August '79. An irrepressible dancefloor shuffle embellished with loose-limbed piano courtesy of BARSON, the track was a tribute to blue beat legend PRINCE BUSTER, whose song 'MADNESS' inspired the group's name and which they covered in their own inimitable style on the B-side. The track powered into the Top 20 and after a '2-Tone' tour with The SPECIALS and The SELECTER, MADNESS signed to 'Stiff', embarking upon an impressive run of chart domination. The follow-up single was 'ONE STEP BEYOND', its famous 'Hey you, don't watch that, watch this . . .' intro leading into a largely instrumental, sax-driven epic. The album of the same name reached No.2, confirming MADNESS had arrived. The group's "nutty boy" postures, madcap humour, cockney patois and unerringly catchy hooks won them a wide cross section of fans, from primary school kids and grannys to style-conscious teenagers, a far cry from their early audience of hardcore NF skinheads, most of whom they thankfully managed to shake off. As the band progressed from the likes of 'BAGGY TROUSERS' to the mordant social commentary of the '7' (1981) album, they moved away slightly from their ska roots, developing a highly original pop sound. After nine Top 10 hits, the band scored their first No.1 in 1982 with 'HOUSE OF FUN', a colourful coming of age yarn that contrasted with the increasing sense of melancholy that would come to mark their later work. Even earlier tracks like the brilliant 'BED AND BREAKFAST MAN' (from ONE STEP BEYOND) possessed a kind of bittersweet poignancy, as did the band's final single as a 7-piece, 'THE SUN AND THE RAIN'. MADNESS were still capable of a good old rave up of course, as they illustrated with their previous effort, the celebratory calypso vibe of 'WINGS OF A DOVE', a No.2 hit in the summer of '83. With the departure of MIKE BARSON (one the band's main writers), the band began to lose their trademark sound. Songs likes 'MICHAEL CAINE' were interesting but not the MADNESS fans knew and loved, their declining popularity marked by increasingly lower chart positions. In 1984, the band formed their own label, 'Zarjazz', releasing work by FEARGAL SHARKEY as well as their own material which was, by this point, largely uninspired, coming to a juddering anti-climax with a cover of Scritti Politti's 'SWEETEST GIRL' and 'WELCOME TO THE GHOST TRAIN'. The band had already decided to split by the time of the latter's release in October '86, BEDFORD and WOODFORD subsequently joining VOICE OF THE BEEHIVE. In 1988, McPHERSON, THOMPSON, FOREMAN and SMASH re-fromed the band as THE MADNESS, an eponymous album not even breaching the Top 50. They had split for good by the end of the year, SUGGS going on to become a suitably "nutty" TV presenter as well as inflicting The FARM upon an unsuspecting music world at the turn of the decade. SMASH became an A&R man for 'Go! Discs', while THOMPSON and FOREMAN went back to ska basics with a new outfit, The NUTTY BOYS, releasing an album, 'CRUNCH!', in 1990. Back by popular demand, the original line-up reformed in 1992 for two sell-out shows in London's Finsbury Park where an army of 20-something's donned their pork pie hats and relived their days down the youth centre disco. The event was such a triumph that MADNESS repeated it in successive years. Not content with merely presenting Top Of The Pops now and again, SUGGS released a solo album, 'THE LONE RANGER', in 1995, subjecting innocent pop kids to an awful cod-reggae version of Simon & Garfunkel's 'CECILIA'. Maybe he's finally lost it. No, SUGGS was back to give us a second helping of his nutty pop songs, 'THE THREE PYRAMIDS CLUB' in 1998 was followed a year later by a re-formed MADNESS set, 'WONDERFUL' (1999) – well, if you like that sort of thing. • **Songwriters:** Either McPHERSON-THOMPSON or BARSON or BEDFORD-FOREMAN. Covered; ONE STEP BEYOND (Cornell Campbell) / SWAN LAKE (Tchaikovski) / IT MUST BE LOVE (Labi Siffre) / THE HARDER THEY COME (Jimmy Cliff). SUGGS covered; I'M ONLY SLEEPING (Beatles). • **Trivia:** Early in 1982, SUGGS married singer and fellow 'Stiff' artist, BETTE BRIGHT.

Album rating: ONE STEP BEYOND (*8) / ABSOLUTELY (*6) / 7 (*6) / THE RISE AND FALL (*7) / COMPLETE MADNESS compilation (*9) / KEEP MOVING (*5) / MAD NOT MAD (*4) / UTTER MADNESS compilation (*6) / THE MADNESS (*6) / DIVINE MADNESS compilation (*9) / MADSTOCK (*5) / WONDERFUL (*5) / Suggs: THE LONE RANGER (*5) / THREE PYRAMIDS CLUB (*4)

GRAHAM 'SUGGS' McPHERSON (b.13 Jan'61, Hastings, England) – vocals / **MIKE BARSON** (b.21 May'58) – keyboards / **CHRIS 'CHRISSIE BOY' FOREMAN** (b. 8 Aug'58) – guitar / **LEE 'KIX' THOMPSON** (b. 5 Oct'57) – saxophone, vocals / **MARK 'BEDDERS' BEDFORD** (b.24 Aug'61) – bass / **DAN 'WOODY' WOODGATE** (b.19 Oct'60) – drums repl. JOHN HASLER / **CHAS SMASH** (b. CATHAL SMYTH, 14 Jan'59) – horns, vocals, dancer

2-Tone-Chrysalis | not iss.

Aug 79. (7") *(CHS TT3)* **THE PRINCE. / MADNESS** [16] [–]
(re-iss. Feb87 on 'Old Gold'; OG 9685)

Stiff | Sire

Oct 79. (lp/c) *(SEEZ/CSEEZ 17)* *<6085>* **ONE STEP BEYOND . . .** [2] [ ]
– One step beyond / My girl / Night boat to Cairo / Believe me / Land of hope & glory / The prince / Tarzan's nuts / In the middle of the night / Bed and breakfast man / Razor blade alley / Swan Lake / Rockin' in Ab / Mummy's boy / Chipmunks are go. *(re-iss. Aug88 on 'Virgin' lp/c; OVED/+C 133) (cd-iss. Apr90; CDOVED 133)*

Oct 79. (7") *(BUY 56)* **ONE STEP BEYOND. / MISTAKES** [7] [ ]
(12"+=) *(BUYIT 56)* – Nutty theme.
(re-iss. Jun85 on 'Virgin' 7"; VS 780)

Dec 79. (7") *(BUY 62)* **MY GIRL. / STEPPING INTO LINE** [3] [ ]
(12"+=) *(BUYIT 62)* – In the rain.
(re-iss. Jun85 on 'Virgin' 7"; VS 781)

Mar 80. (7"ep) *(BUY 71)* **WORK, REST & PLAY EP** [6] [ ]
– Night boat to Cairo / Deceives the eye / The young and the old / Don't quote me on that. *(re-iss. Jun85 on 'Virgin' 7"ep; VS 782)*

Sep 80. (7") *(BUY 84)* **BAGGY TROUSERS. / THE BUSINESS** [3] [ ]
(re-iss. Jun85 on 'Virgin' 7"; VS 783)

Sep 80. (lp/c) *(SEEZ/CSEEZ 29)* *<6094>* **ABSOLUTELY** [2] [ ]
– Baggy trousers / Embarrassment / E.R.N.I.E. / Close escape / Not home today / On the beat Pete / Solid gone / Take it or leave it / Shadow of fear / Disappear / Overdone / In the rain / You said / The return of the Los Palmas 7. *(re-iss. Aug88 on 'Virgin' lp/c; OVED/+C 134) (cd-iss. Nov89; CDOVED 134)*

Nov 80. (7") *(BUY 102)* **EMBARRASSMENT. / CRYING SHAME** [4] [ ]

Jan 81. (7") *(BUY 108)* **THE RETURN OF THE LOS PALMAS 7. / THAT'S THE WAY TO DO IT** [7] [ ]
(12"+=) *(BUYIT 108)* – My girl (demo) / Swan Lake (live).

Apr 81. (7"/c-s) *(BUY/ZBUY 112)* **GREY DAY. / MEMORIES** [4] [–]

Sep 81. (7") *(BUY 126)* **SHUT UP. / A TOWN WITH NO NAME** [7] [–]
(12"+=) *(BUYIT 126)* – Never ask twice.

Oct 81. (lp/c) *(SEEZ/CSEEZ 39)* **7** [5] [–]
– Cardiac arrest / Shut up / Sign of the times / Missing you / Mrs. Hutchinson / Tomorrow's dream / Opium eaters / Grey day / Pac-amac / Promises promises / Benny bullfrog / When dawn arrives / The opium eaters / Aeroplane. *(re-iss. Aug88 on 'Virgin' lp/c; SEEZ/CSEEZ 135) (cd-iss. Nov89; CDOVED 135)*

Stiff | Geffen

Nov 81. (7"/12") *(BUY/S'BUY 134)* **IT MUST BE LOVE. / SHADOW ON THE HOUSE** [4] [–]

Feb 82. (7"/ext.12") *(BUY/+IT 140)* **CARDIAC ARREST. / IN THE CITY** [14] [ ]

Apr 82. (lp/c) *(HITTV/ZHITV 1)* **COMPLETE MADNESS** (compilation) [1] [–]
– Embarrassment / Shut up / My girl / Baggy trousers / It must be love / The prince / Bed and breakfast man / Night boat to Cairo / One step beyond / House of fun / Cardiac arrest / Take it or leave it / Madness / The return of the Los Palmas 7 / In the city. *(cd-iss. Jul 86 on 'Virgin'; HITCD 1)*

May 82. (7"/7"pic-d) *(BUY/P-BUY 140)* **HOUSE OF FUN. / DON'T LOOK BACK** [1] [ ]
(re-iss. Jun85 on 'Virgin' 7"; VS 784)

Jul 82. (7"/7"pic-d) *(BUY/P-BUY 153)* **DRIVING IN MY CAR. / ANIMAL FARM** [4] [ ]
(12"+=) *(S'BUY 153)* – Riding on my bike.
(re-iss. Jun85 on 'Virgin' 7"; VS 785)

Oct 82. (7"/7"pic-d) *(BUY/P-BUY 163)* **OUR HOUSE. / WALKING WITH MR WHEEZE** [5] [–]
(12"+=) *(BUYIT 163)* – ('A'extended).
(re-iss. Jun85 on 'Virgin' 7"; VS 786)

Nov 82. (lp/c) *(SEEZ/CSEEZ 46)* **PRESENTS THE RISE AND FALL** [10] [ ]
– Rise and fall / Tomorrow's (just another day) / Blue skinned beast / Primrose hill / Mr. Speaker (gets the word) / Sunday morning / Our house / Tiptoes / New Delhi / That face / Calling cards / Are you coming (with me) / Madness (is all in the mind). *(re-iss. Aug88 on 'Virgin' lp/c; OVED/+C 190) (cd-iss. Nov89; CDOVED 190)*

Feb 83. (7"/7"pic-d) *(BUY/P-BUY 169)* **TOMORROW'S (JUST ANOTHER DAY). / MADNESS (IS ALL IN THE MIND)** [8] [ ]
(ext.12"+=) *(BUYIT 169)* – Blue beast / ('A'version with ELVIS COSTELLO).
(re-iss. Jun85 on 'Virgin' 7"; VS 787)

Mar 83. (lp) *<4003>* **MADNESS** [–] [41]
– It must be love / Shut up / Rise and fall / Tomorrow's just another day / Primrose Hill / Madness (is all in the mind) / Grey day / House of fun / Blue skinned beast / Cardiac arrest / Night boat to Cairo / Shadow of fear.

May 83. (7")(12") *<29668>* **OUR HOUSE. / CARDIAC ARREST** [–] [7]

Aug 83. (7") *<29562>* **IT MUST BE LOVE. / CALLING CARDS** [–] [33]

Aug 83. (7"/7"pic-d) *(BUY/P-BUY 181)* **WINGS OF A DOVE. / BEHIND THE 8 BALL** [2] [ ]
('A'-Blue train mix-12"+=) *(BUYIT 181)* – One's second thoughtlessness.
(re-iss. Jun85 on 'Virgin' 7"; VS 788)

Oct 83. (7"/7"pic-d) *(BUY/P-BUY 192)* **THE SUN AND THE RAIN. / FIREBALL XL5** [5] [–]
(ext.12"+=) *(BUYIT 192)* – My girl (live).
(re-iss. Jun85 on 'Virgin' 7"; VS 789)

Jan 84. (7") *<29350>* **THE SUN AND THE RAIN. / TIME FOR TEA** [–] [72]

—— trimmed to a 6-piece, when BARSON went to stay in Holland with his Dutch wife.

Jan 84. (7"/7"pic-d) *(BUY/P-BUY 196)* **MICHAEL CAINE. / IF YOU THINK THERE'S SOMETHING** [11] [ ]
(12"+=) *(BUYIT 196)* – ('A'extended).
(re-iss. Jun85 on 'Virgin' 7"; VS 790)

Feb 84. (lp/pic-lp/c) <4022> *(SEEZ/PSEEZ/CSEEZ 53)* **KEEP MOVING** [6] [ ]
– Keep moving / Michael Caine / Turning blue / One better day / March of the gherkins / Waltz into mischief * / Brand new beat / Victoria Gardens. *<US repl. * w/)* – Wings of a dove (a celebratory song) / The sun and the rain / Prospects / Samantha. *(re-iss. Aug88 on 'Virgin' lp/c; OVED/+C 191) (cd-iss. Nov89; CDOVED 191)*

May 84. (7"/7"pic-d) *(BUY/P-BUY 201)* **ONE BETTER DAY. / GUNS** [17] [ ]
(12"+=) *(BUYIT 201)* – Victoria Gardens / Sarah.
(re-iss. Jun85 on 'Virgin' 7"; VS 791)

Zarjazz Virgin

Aug 85. (7") *(JAZZ 5)* **YESTERDAY'S MEN. / ALL I KNEW** [18] [ ]
(ext.12") *(JAZZ 5-12)* – ('A'demo).
(7"square-pic-d/incl.free-7"+=) *(JAZZ D5)* – YESTERDAY'S MEN (harmonica mix) / IT MUST BE LOVE (live)
Oct 85. (lp/c) *(JZ LP/MC 1)* **MAD NOT MAD** [16] [ ]
– I'll compete / Yesterday's men / Uncle Sam / White heat / Mad not mad / Sweetest girl / Burning the boats / Tears you can't hide / Time / Coldest day. *(cd-iss. Jul87; JZCD 1)*
Oct 85. (7"/s7") *(JAZZ/+F 7)* **UNCLE SAM. / PLEASE DON'T GO** [21] [ ]
(7"pic-d+=) *(JAZZY 7)* – Inanity over Christmas.
(ext.12"+=) *(JAZZ 7-12)* – ('A'demo).
Jan 86. (7"/one-sided-7"pic-d) *(JAZZ/+Y 8)* **SWEETEST GIRL. / JENNIE (A PORTRAIT OF)** [35] [ ]
(ext.12"+=) *(JAZZ 8-12)* – ('A'dub).
(d7"+=) *(JAZZ D8)* – Tears you can't hide / Call me.

—— **BARSON** returned for swan-song

Oct 86. (7"/7"square-pic-d) *(JAZZ/+S 9)* **(WAITING FOR) THE GHOST TRAIN. / MAYBE IN ANOTHER LIFE** [18] [ ]
(12"+=/12"w-booklet+=) *(JAZZ/+B 9-12)* – Seven year scratch.
Nov 86. (lp/c/cd) *(JZ LP/MC/CD 2)* **UTTER MADNESS** (compilation) [29] [ ]
– Our house / Driving in my car / Michael Caine / Wings of a dove / Yesterday's men / Tomorrow's (just another day) / I'll compete / (Waiting for) The ghost train / Uncle Sam / The sun and the rain / Sweetest girl / One better day / Victoria Gardens. *(cd+=)* – Seven year scratch (hit megamix). *(re-iss. Apr90 on 'Virgin' lp/c; OVED/+C 287)*

—— Had already split Sep'86. BEDDERS and WOODY joined VOICE OF THE BEEHIVE. They had recently backed female duo STRAWBERRY SWITCHBLADE.

THE MADNESS

—— **McPHERSON, THOMPSON, FOREMAN + SMYTH,** re-formed Feb'88, with slight change of name (allowed to just prefix THE), bringing in some session people; **JERRY DAMMERS, STEVE NIEVE + BRUCE THOMAS**

Virgin Virgin

Mar 88. (7") *(VS 1054)* **I PRONOUNCE YOU. / PATIENCE** [44] [ ]
(d7"+=/12"+=/cd-s+=) *(VS X/T/CD 1054)* – 4 BF / 11th hour.
May 88. (lp/c/cd) *(V/TCV/CDV 2507)* **THE MADNESS** [65] [ ]
– Nail down the days / What's that / I pronounce you / Oh / In wonder / Song in red / Nightmare nightmare / Thunder and lightning / Beat the bride / Gabriel's horn. *(cd+=)* – 11th Hour / 4BF / Be Good Boy / Flashings.
May 88. (7"/7"sha-pic-d) *(VS/+S 1078)* **WHAT'S THAT. / BE GOOD BOY.** [ ] [ ]
(7"sha-pic-d) *(VSJ 1078)* – WHAT'S THAT. / FLASHINGS
(12"+=) *(VST 1078)* – Be good boy.

—— Disbanded again in 1988. SUGGS became a TV presenter and the manager of The FARM, who he produced in 1985, and CHAS became A&R man for 'Go! Discs'. They were encouraged to re-unite for a one-off gig on 8 Aug'92 at Finsbury Park, after old hits re-charted (see further below).

MADNESS

(original line-up, see above)

Go! Discs London

Oct 92. (cd/c/lp) *(828367-2/-4/-1)* **MADSTOCK (live)** [22] [ ]
– One step beyond / The Prince / Embarrassment / My girl / The Sun and the rain / Grey day / It must be love / Shut up / Driving in my car / Bed and breakfast man / Close escape / Wings of a dove / Our house / Night boat to Cairo / Madness / House of fun / Baggy trousers / The harder they come.
Nov 92. (7"/c-s) *(GOD/+C 93)* **THE HARDER THEY COME (live). / TOMORROW'S JUST ANOTHER DAY (live) / TAKE IT OR LEAVE IT (live)** [44] [ ]
(cd-s+=) *(GODCD 93)* – Land of hope & glory.

STARVATION

MADNESS with other ska-groups (for charity)

Zarjazz not iss.

Feb 85. (7") *(JAZZ 3)* **STARVATION. / TAM-TAM POUR L'ETHIOPIE** [33] [–]
(12"+=) *(JAZZ 3-12)* – Haunted / ('B'-part 2).

SUGGS

WEA not iss.

Aug 95. (c-s) *(YZ 975C)* **I'M ONLY SLEEPING / OFF ON HOLIDAY** [7] [–]
(cd-s+=) *(YZ 975CD)* – Off on holiday (instrumental).
(cd-s+=) *(YZ 975CDX)* – Animal / When you came.
Oct 95. (7"/c-s) *(WEA 019/+C)* **CAMDEN TOWN. / BEDAZZLED** [14] [–]
(cd-s+=) *(WEA 019CD)* – ('A'-Chili pepper dub) / ('A'-Ragga in London mix).
Oct 95. (cd/c) *(0630 12478-2/-4)* **THE LONE RANGER** [14] [–]
– I'm only sleeping / Camden Town / Alcohol / 4 am / The tune / Cecilia / Haunted / Off on holiday / Green eyes / Fortune fish / She's gone.
Dec 95. (7") *(WEA 031)* **THE TUNE. / ALRIGHT** [33] [–]
(c-s+=/cd-s+=) *(WEA 031 C/CD)* – Sleigh ride.
Apr 96. (c-s/cd-s) *(WEA 042 C/CD)* **CECILIA / I FEEL GOOD** [4] [–]
(cd-s+=) *(WEA 052CDX)* – The tune.
above featured LOUCHIE LOU and MICHIE ONE, as did below
Sep 96. (c-s/cd-s) *(WEA 065 C/CD1)* **NO MORE ALCOHOL / FORTUNE FISH** [24] [–]
(cd-s+=) *(WEA 065CD2)* – ('A'mix).
May 97. (c-s/cd-s; as SUGGS & CO. featuring CHELSEA TEAM) *(WEA 112 C/CD)* **BLUE DAY / ALRIGHT** [22] [–]
(cd-s+=) *(WEA 112CD2)* – ('A'versions).
Aug 98. (c-s) *(WEA 174C)* **I AM / SAME AGAIN** [38] [–]
(cd-s+=) *(WEA 174CD)* – It really would be nice.
Sep 98. (cd/c) *(3984 23815-2/-4)* **THE THREE PYRAMIDS CLUB** [ ] [–]
– I am / So tired / Straight banana / Invisible man / Sing / Girl / The greatest show on earth / Our man / On drifting sand / The three pyramids club.

MADNESS

re-formed yet again

Virgin E.M.I.

Jul 99. (c-s) *(VSC 1737)* **LOVESTRUCK. / WE ARE LOVE** [10] [–]
(cd-s+=) *(VSCDT 1737)* – ('A'-CD-Rom).
(12") *(VSLH 1737)* – ('A'side) / Round & round / Maddley (album medley).
Oct 99. (cd-s) *(VSCDT 1740)* **JOHNNY THE HORSE / YOU'RE WONDERFUL (remix)** [44] [–]
(c-s/cd-s) *(VSC/+DX 1740)* – ('A'side) / I was the one / Dreaming man.
Oct 99. (cd/c) *(CDV/TCV 2889)* <848406> **WONDERFUL** [17] Dec99 [ ]
– Lovestruck / Johnny the horse / Communicator / 4 a.m. / Wizard / Drip fed Fred / Going to the top / Elysium / Saturday night Sunday morning / If I didn't care / No money.
Feb 00. (c-s; by MADNESS featuring IAN DURY) *(VSC 1768)* **DRIP FED FRED / WE WANT FREDDIE** [55] [–]
(cd-s+=) *(VSCDT 1768)* – Elysium.
(cd-s) *(VSCDX 1768)* – ('A'side) / Light of the way.

– compilations, etc. –

on 'Virgin' unless otherwise stated

Oct 86. (12"ep) *Strange Fruit; (SFPS 007)* **THE PEEL SESSIONS (27.8.79)** [ ] [–]
– The prince / Bed and breakfast man / Land of hope & glory / Stepping into line. *(c-ep.Jun87; SFPSC 007) (cd-ep.Jul88; SFPSCD 007)*
Nov 88. (7") *Old Gold; (OG 9821)* **BAGGY TROUSERS. / EMBARRASSMENT** [ ] [ ]
Nov 88. (7") *Old Gold; (OG 9826)* **IT MUST BE LOVE. / MY GIRL** [ ] [ ]
May 89. (7") *(VS 1197)* **IT MUST BE LOVE. / THE RETURN OF THE LOS PALMAS 7** [6] [–]
Sep 90. (lp/c/cd) *Pickwick;* **IT'S . . . MADNESS** [ ] [–]
(re-iss. May94 on 'Virgin-VIP' cd/c; VVIP D/C 107)
Oct 90. (3xcd-box) *(TPAKJ 8)* **ONE STEP BEYOND / ABSOLUTELY / THE RISE AND FALL** [ ] [–]
Jul 91. (cd) *Pickwick; (cd)* **IT'S MADNESS . . . TOO** [ ] [–]
(re-iss. Oct94 on 'Virgin-VIP' cd/c; VVIP D/C 115)
Jan 92. (7"/c-s) *(VS/+C 1405)* **IT MUST BE LOVE. / BED AND BREAKFAST MAN** [6] [–]
(cd-s+=/pic-cd-s+=) *(VSCD T/P 1405)* – Airplane / Don't quote me on that.
Feb 92. (cd/c/d-lp) *(CD/TC+/V 2692)* **DIVINE MADNESS** [1] [ ]
– The Prince / One step beyond / My girl / Night boat to Cairo / Baggy trousers / Embarrassment / The return of Los Palmas 7 / Grey day / Shut up / It must be love / Cardiac arrest / House of fun / Driving in my car /

Our house / Tomorrow's just another day / Wings of a dove / The sun and the rain / Michael Caine / One better day / Yesterday's men / Uncle Sam / (Waiting for) The ghost train.

Apr 92. (7"/c-s) *(VS/+C 1413)* **HOUSE OF FUN. / UN PASO ADELAINTE (ONE STEP BEYOND – Spanish version)** [40] [ ]
(12"+=/cd-s+=) *(VS T/CD 1413)* – Yesterday's men / Gabriel's horn (demo).

Aug 92. (7"/c-s) *(VS/+C 1425)* **MY GIRL. / MADNESS** [27] [ ]
(cd-s) *(VSCD 1425)* – ('A'side) / E.R.N.I.E. / Embarrassment / Tomorrow's dream.
(cd-s) *(VSCDX 1425)* – ('A'side) / Precious one (live) / My girl (live) / Disappear (live).

Feb 93. (7"/c-s) *(VS/+C 1447)* **NIGHT BOAT TO CAIRO. / ('A'mix)** [56] [ ]
(12"+=/cd-s+=) *(VS T/CD 1447)* – ('A'mixes).

Nov 93. (3xcd-box) *(MADBOX 1)* **THE BUSINESS – THE DEFINITIVE SINGLES COLLECTION** [ ] [–]

—— In Oct'93, 'THE PRINCE' alongside other ska-revival bands on '2-TONE EP' hit UK No.30.

Jun 98. (cd/c) *(CDV/TCV 2862) / E.M.I.; <846040>* **THE HEAVY HEAVY HITS** [19] Feb99 [ ]
– Grey day / The sweetest girl / Michael Caine / Embarrassment / Night boat to Cairo / House of fun / Yesterday's men / It must be love / Driving in my car / (Waiting for the) Ghost train / Uncle Sam / Shut up / Cardiac arrest / Our house / My girl / The sun and the rain / Baggy trousers / Wings of a dove / Tomorrow's just another day / One better day / Return of the Los Palmas 7 / The prince / One step beyond.

Mar 99. (cd) *Goldenvoice; (GVC 0440-2)* **UNIVERSAL MADNESS (live)** [ ] [–]

Nov 99. (6xcd-box) *(MADBOX 2)* **THE LOT** [ ] [–]

Oct 02. (cd) *(CDV 2965)* **OUR HOUSE – THE ORIGINAL SONGS** [45] [–]
– House of fun / Our house / Simple equation / My girl / Baggy trousers / Prospects / Embarrassment / Driving in my car / Grey day / Shut up / The return of Los Palmas 7 / The sun and the rain / Tomorrow's just another day / Night boat to Cairo / Wings of a dove / One better day / Rise and fall / Sarah's song / White heat / Michael Caine / It must be love (remix).

MADONNA

Born: MADONNA LOUISE VERONICA CICCONE, 16 Aug'59, Rochester, Michigan, USA. After winning a scholarship to her local university (where she also learned ballet), the budding singer subsequently dropped out in the late 70's and headed for New York where she supported herself with waitressing and part-time model work (nude photos were later published in 1985 by top shelf mags, 'Penthouse' and 'Playboy'). To make ends meet (as they say), she also acted in a budget soft-porn flick, 'A Certain Sacrifice', later (1988) released on video without her consent; on first name terms with controversy from the beginning, MADONNA would nevertheless prove herself to be one of the 80's most deft media manipulators and arguably one of the most driven women in the history of the music business. Her first real experience of professional performance was as a touring dancer/backing singer for Hi-NRG legend, PATRICK HERNANDEZ (when will 'Born To Be Alive' ever get a re-release?!!!), although she soon returned to the Big Apple and began writing with ex-boyfriend, STEVE BRAY. Local DJ Mark Kamins was sufficiently impressed with the resulting material to help secure MADONNA a deal with 'Sire', the label releasing her debut single, 'EVERYBODY', late in '82. The track became a dancefloor favourite, as did US-only 12", 'BURNING UP', the singer subsequently hooking up with DJ 'Jellybean' Benitez to work on a whole albums worth of material. 'MADONNA' the album, hit the shelves in Autumn '83, its pilot single, 'HOLIDAY', finally making the jump from clubland to the charts (Top 20) a few months later. The track's unpretentious dance-pop and naive appeal served MADONNA well throughout this early period; the song also hit the UK Top 20 and prompted the re-issue of second single, 'LUCKY STAR', while the teen-love poignancy of 'BORDERLINE' gave the singer her first US Top 10 early the following year. The album itself was well on its way to becoming a multi-million seller and, in late summer '84, MADONNA firmly imprinted herself on public consciousness with US No.1 (album and single), 'LIKE A VIRGIN' and its attendant video. Through a winning combination of coy sexuality, pouting girlishness, Nile Rodgers-enhanced rhythmic backing and pop savvy, MADONNA had invented herself as an icon for not only the 80's 'MATERIAL GIRL', but legions of gay men and hormonal adolescents. Accordingly, manager Freddie DeMann was quick to break the singer into a parallel acting career, helping her secure a minor part in the film 'Vision Quest' and a more high profile role alongside Rosanna Arquette in 'Desperately Seeking Susan'. While these didn't exactly present a case for Oscar nominations, their soundtracks did provide MADONNA with two further No.1 singles in 'CRAZY FOR YOU' and 'INTO THE GROOVE'. More transatlantic hits followed in 'DRESS YOU UP', 'ANGEL' and 'GAMBLER', although it was only with the 'TRUE BLUE' (1986) album and preceding No.1 singles, 'LIVE TO TELL' and 'PAPA DON'T PREACH', that MADDY began to win the grudging respect of the rock press and fully blossom as a powerful vocalist. The latter track, in particular, showed a quantum leap in songwriting ability, its controversial, teenage pregnancy subject matter seeing MADONNA finally spark debate for something other than her risqué videos/stage show. Successive singles 'OPEN YOUR HEART' and the sultry 'LA ISLA BONITA' saw her top the charts yet again, while the album became her biggest selling to date. Summer '87 saw more movie action, her title track from the 'Who's That Girl' (in which she starred alongside Griffin Dunne) soundtrack scaling the charts on both sides of the Atlantic. Though the ensuing couple of years were a bit quieter on the recording front (save for a dodgy remix compilation, 'U CAN DANCE'), MADONNA's massive international superstar status and stormy marriage to actor Sean Penn (with whom she starred in 1986's 'Shanghai Surprise') ensured she was never far from the tabloid gossip columns. The more self-appointedly moralistic elements of the press had a field day with the video for 1989's 'LIKE A PRAYER', the sight of MADONNA making lewd advances to a black priest not going down (oops!) too well with the Vatican either. In the resulting furore, the pointy-bra'd one saw her sponsorship deal with 'Pepsi' go flat, although the intense interest guaranteed humungous sales of the accompanying album (also called 'LIKE A PRAYER'). Incidentally, the record was her most mature and fully realised piece of work to date, candidly exploring her favourite themes of religion and sex in a more frankly personal fashion than ever. The turn of the decade saw another feverish burst of activity with the release of two albums, 'I'M BREATHLESS' (as the sleeve states, 'Music Inspired By The Film Dick Tracy') and an impressive greatest hits set, wittily entitled 'THE IMMACULATE COLLECTION'. By far the most controversial offering of the year, however, was the 'JUSTIFY MY LOVE' single, its X-rated video (banned just about everywhere, it nevertheless enjoyed an airing on Channel 4's infamous ambassador of tack, 'The Word') and pre-orgasmic panting taking up almost as much column inches as the ensuing row over the writing credits (LENNY KRAVITZ and INGRID CHAVEZ at loggerheads). MADONNA took the increasingly overt sexuality angle to its ultimate conclusion with the simultaneous release of the 'EROTICA' (1992) album and 'Sex' book. The latter was MADONNA's first

venture into publishing and possibly her last; the explicit soft-porn poses and woefully weak thematic thread saw the expensive (25 quid a throw, and you weren't even allowed to peruse the damn thing before you bought it!) panned by critics. Still, 1992 wasn't all bad as the singer signed a multi-million dollar agreement with 'Warners', giving added commercial oomph to her developing 'Maverick' label. Over the next five years, MADONNA was more often featured in the music press in connection with her business acumen (amongst others, she's secured the signatures of ALANIS MORISSETTE) than her recorded output, 1994's 'BEDTIME STORIES' album offering up a limp R&B sound. Nevertheless, MADONNA's longtime blonde ambition was fulfilled in 1996 as she played the lead part of Eva Peron in the screen version of 'Evita', the singer finally winning unreserved critical plaudits from all quarters and even acquiring a fair degree of respectability among her moralising detractors. If her 90's output had been spotty overall, 1998's 'RAY OF LIGHT' album opened up a whole new chapter of creative birth and rebirth for the ageing (but seemingly ageless) pop chameleon. The recruitment of electronica sculptor WILLIAM ORBIT was a shrewd move yet few could have predicted how well the pairing's flawless marriage of star glamour and contemporary club sounds would imprint itself on the transatlantic musical consciousness. MADONNA had sculpted her singing style to suit this brave new style while her newfound spirituality permeated the album's surging grooves. The ballad, 'FROZEN', topped the UK chart, as did the album itself, a feat almost repeated on her home territory. While not incuded on the album, 'BEAUTIFUL STRANGER' became one of the singer's biggest UK hits in years, providing a stop gap and a musical link for her next album. Come the new millennium, MADONNA had subtly reinvented herself yet again, an urban cowgirl image complementing the electro panorama of 'MUSIC' (2000). ORBIT again supplied the deftest of touches while co-writer Mirwais Ahmadzai made a significant contribution to the record's post-modern digi-pop. The insistent, sensual, stuttering throb of the title track secured MADONNA yet another massive transatlantic hit while the album itself topped both the US and UK charts. MADDY was once again at the forefront of pop culture while her celebrity knew no bounds, a massively publicised marriage to ('Lock, Stock & Two Smoking Barrels') director Guy Ritchie in a Scottish Castle giving the tabloids material to chew on for weeks. If compilation set, 'GHV2' (2001) didn't sound as consistent and cohesive as 'IMMACULATE COLLECTION', it was due to the glaring gap between her average early 90's pop and her millennial revisionism. Few then, would've predicted the critical and commercial backwards step of 'AMERICAN LIFE' (2003), an uncharacteristically muted and sterile affair seemingly hung up on style over substance despite the weighty lyrical matter. Subsequent musical attempts to repair the damage via a Gap commercial with MISSY ELLIOTT and an MTV Video Music Awards performance of 'LIKE A VIRGIN – HOLLYWOOD' (with BRITNEY SPEARS, AGUILERA and ELLIOTT) were compressed into the equally dispensible 'REMIXED AND REVISITED' EP.
• **Songwriters:** She collaborated on most material, the bulk with ex-boyfriend STEVE BRAY. Others & covers; PHYSICAL ATTRACTION (Reggie Lucas) / HOLIDAY (Jellybean Benitez) / LOVE DON'T LIVE HERE ANYMORE (Rose Royce; hit) / LIKE A VIRGIN (Tom Kelly & Billy Steinberg) / CRAZY FOR YOU (Jon Lind & John Bettis) / JUSTIFY MY LOVE (Lenny Kravitz & Ingrid Chavez) / FEVER (Peggy Lee) / LOVE SONG (co-w/ PRINCE) / BEDTIME STORY (Bjork) / GUILT BY ASSOCIATION with Joe Henry (Vic Chesnutt) / I WANT YOU (Marvin Gaye).

Album rating: MADONNA (*6) / LIKE A VIRGIN (*6) / TRUE BLUE (*7) / YOU CAN DANCE remixes (*5) / LIKE A PRAYER (*8) / THE IMMACULATE COLLECTION compilation (*9) / I'M BREATHLESS soundtrack (*4) / EROTICA (*6) / BEDTIME STORIES (*7) / SOMETHING TO REMEMBER compilation (*7) / EVITA soundtrack (*5) / RAY OF LIGHT (*8) / MUSIC (*8) / GHV2 compilation (*7) / AMERICAN LIFE (*5)

MADONNA – vocals with session people, producers, etc.

Date	Release	Sire		Sire
Dec 82.	(7"/12") *(W 9899/+T)* *<29841>* **EVERYBODY. / EVERYBODY (dub version)**			
May 83.	(7") *<29609>* **BURNING UP. / PHYSICAL ATTRACTION**	–		
Oct 83.	(7") *<29478>* **HOLIDAY. / I KNOW IT**	–		16
Oct 83.	(7"/ext.12") *(W 9522/+T)* *<29177>* **LUCKY STAR. / I KNOW IT**		Aug84	4
	(12") *(W 9522TV)* – ('A'-U.S.remix) / I know it.			
	(re-prom.Mar84 hit UK No.14)			
Sep 83.	(lp/c) *(923867-1/-4)* *<23867>* **MADONNA**	6	Aug83	8
	– Lucky star / Borderline / Burning up / I know it / Holiday / Think of me / Physical attraction / Everybody. *(re-iss. Sep85 as 'THE FIRST ALBUM'; WX 22)*			
Nov 83.	(7"/ext.12") *(W 9405/+T)* **HOLIDAY. / THINK OF ME**	6		–
	(re-prom.Jul85, hit UK-No.2; also 12"pic-d; W 9405P)			
Mar 84.	(7") *<29354>* **BORDERLINE. / THINK OF ME**	–		10
May 84.	(7") *(W 9260)* **BORDERLINE. / PHYSICAL ATTRACTION**	56		–
	(d7"+=) *(W 9260F)* – Holiday / Think of me.			
	(12") *(W 9260T)* – ('A'-U.S.remix) / ('A'dub remix) / ('B'side).			
	(re-Prom.Jan86, hit UK No.2 – also 7"sha-pic-d; W 9260P)			
Nov 84.	(7") *(W 9210)* *<29210>* **LIKE A VIRGIN. / STAY**	3		1
	(12") *(W 9210T)* *<20239>* – ('A' US dance remix) / ('B'side).			
Nov 84.	(lp/c)(cd)) *(WX 20/+C)(925157-2)* *<25157>* **LIKE A VIRGIN**	1		1
	– Material girl / Angel / Like a virgin / Over and over / Love don't live here anymore / Dress you up / Shoo-be-doo / Stay / Pretender. *(re-iss. Aug85 pic-lp)(cd+=; WX 20P)(925181-2)* – Into the groove.			
Feb 85.	(7") *(W 9083)* *<29083>* **MATERIAL GIRL. / PRETENDER**	3		2
	(12") *(W 9083T)* *<20304>* – ('A'-Jellybean dance mix) / ('B'side).			
	(below single issued on 'Geffen' from the film 'Vision Quest')			
Mar 85.	(7")(12") *<29051><26325>* **CRAZY FOR YOU. / (B-side by Berlin)**	–		1
Apr 85.	(7") *<29008>* **ANGEL. / (dance mix)**	–		5
	(12") *<20335>* – Angel (extended dance mix) / Into the groove.			
Jun 85.	(7"/7"sha-pic-d) *(A/WA 6323)* **CRAZY FOR YOU. / (B-side by Sammy Hagar)**	2		–
	(below from the film 'Desperately Seeking Susan')			
Jul 85.	(7"/7"sha-pic-d) *(W 8934/+P)* **INTO THE GROOVE. / SHOO-BE-DOO**	1		–
	(12"+=) *(W 8934T)* – Everybody.			
Aug 85.	(7") *<28919>* **DRESS YOU UP. / SHOO-BEE-DOO**	–		5
	(12"+=) *<20369)* – ('A'-Casual instrumental mix).			
Sep 85.	(7"/7"sha-pic-d) *(W 8881/+P)* **ANGEL. / BURNING UP**	5		–
	(12") *(W 8881T)* – ('A'-12"extended dance mix) / ('B'side).			
	(below single issued on 'Geffen' from the film 'Vision Quest')			
Oct 85.	(7"/7"+poster) *(A/QA 6585)* **GAMBLER. / (B-side by Black 'n' Blue)**	4		–
	(12") *(TA 6585)* – ('A'extended dance mix) / ('A'instrumental) / ('B'side).			
Nov 85.	(7"/7"sha-pic-d) *(W 8848/+P)* **DRESS YOU UP. / I KNOW IT**	5		–
	(12"/12"+poster) *(W 8848T/+F)* – ('A'-instrumental).			
Apr 86.	(7") *(W 8717)* *<28717>* **LIVE TO TELL. / ('A'instrumental)**	2		1
	(12"+=/12"+poster) *(W 8717T/+W)* *<20461>* – ('A'version).			
Jun 86.	(7")(ext.12") *<28660><20492>* **PAPA DON'T PREACH. / PRETENDER**	–		1
Jun 86.	(7") *(W 8636)* **PAPA DON'T PREACH. / AIN'T NO BIG DEAL**	1		–
	(12"+=/12"+poster+=/12"pic-d+=) *(W 8636T/+W/P)* – ('A'extended).			
Jul 86.	(lp/c)(cd) *(WX 54/+C)(925442-2)* *<25442>* **TRUE BLUE**	1		1
	– Papa don't preach / Open your heart / White heat / Live to tell / Where's the party / rue blue / La Isla Bonita / Jimmy Jimmy / Love makes the world go round.			
Sep 86.	(7") *(W 8550)* **TRUE BLUE (remix). / HOLIDAY (lp version)**	1		–

(12"/12"pic-d) *(W 8550T/+P)* – ('A'extended version version) / Holiday (full length).

Sep 86. (7",7"blue) *<28591>* **TRUE BLUE. / AIN'T NO BIG DEAL** [–] [3]
(12"+=) *<20533>* – ('A'Colour mix) / ('A'instrumental).

Dec 86. (7") *<28508>* **OPEN YOUR HEART. / WHITE HEAT** [–] [1]
(ext.12"+=) *<20597>* – ('A'dub version).

Dec 86. (7") **(W 8480) OPEN YOUR HEART. / LUCKY STAR** [4] [–]
(ext.12"+=/ext.12"pic-d+=) *(W 8480T/+P)* – ('A'dub mix).

Mar 87. (7") *(W 8378) <28425>* **LA ISLA BONITA (remix). / ('A'instrumental)** [1] [4]
(12"/12"pic-d) *(W 8378T/+P) <20633>* – ('A'extended remix) / ('A'extended instrumental).

Jul 87. (7"/ext.12"/ext.12"pic-d) *(W 8341/+T/TP) <28341>* **WHO'S THAT GIRL. / WHITE HEAT** [1] [1]
(ext.12") *(W 8341TX) <20692>* – ('A'dub version).
(above A-side from the film 'Who's That Girl') (the Various Artists Soundtrack hit UK 4 + US 7 in Aug'87)

Sep 87. (7") *(W 8224) <28224>* **CAUSING A COMMOTION (Silver Screen mix). / JIMMY JIMMY** [4] [2]
(12"+=/12"pic-d+=/c-s+=) *(W 8224 T/TP/C) <20762>* – ('A'-movie house mix).

Nov 87. (lp/c)(cd) *(WX 76/+C)(925535-2) <25535>* **U CAN DANCE** (remixes) [5] [14]
– Spotlight / Holiday / Everybody / Physical attraction / Over and over / Into the groove / Where's the party / Spotlight (dub) / Holiday (dub) / Into the groove (dub) / Over and over (dub). *(re-iss. cd/c Feb95;)*

Dec 87. (7") *(W 8115)* **THE LOOK OF LOVE. / I KNOW IT** [9] [–]
(12"+=/12"pic-d+=) *(W 8115T/+P)* – Love don't live here anymore.

Mar 89. (7") *(W 7539) <27539>* **LIKE A PRAYER. / ACT OF CONTRITION** [1] [1]
(ext.12"+=/ext.12"pic-d+=/c-s+=) *(W 7539 T/TP/C)* – ('A'club mix).
(12") *(W 7539TX) <21170>* – ('A'dance mix) / ('A'-Churchapella mix) / ('A'side).
(3"cd-s) *(W 7539CD)* – ('A'extended remix) / ('A'club mix).

Mar 89. (lp/c)(cd) *(WX 239/+C)(925844-2) <25844>* **LIKE A PRAYER** [1] [1]
– Like a prayer / Express yourself / Love song / Till death us do part / Promise to try / Cherish / Dear Jessie / Oh father / Keep it together / Spanish eyes / Act of contrition.

May 89. (7"s/7"s/c-s) *(W 2948 X/W/C) <22948>* **EXPRESS YOURSELF. / THE LOOK OF LOVE** [5] [2]
(c-s/cd-s/12"pic-d) *(W 2948 CX/CD/TP)* – ('A'side) / ('A'-Non-stop mix) / ('A'-Stop & go mix).

Aug 89. (7"/c-s) *(W 2883/+C) <22883>* **CHERISH. / SUPERNATURAL** [3] [2]
(12"pic-d+=/cd-s+=) *(W 2883 TP/CD)* – ('A'extended).

Nov 89. (7"/7"pic-d/c-s) *(W 2668/+P/C)* **DEAR JESSIE. / TILL DEATH US DO PART** [5] [–]
(12"+=/cd-s+=/pic-cd-s+=) *(W 2668 TW/CD/CDX)* – Holiday (12"mix).

Nov 89. (7"/c-s) *<22723-7/-4>* **OH FATHER. / PRAY FOR SPANISH EYES** [–] [20]

Jan 90. (7"/c-s) *<19986-7/-4>* **KEEP IT TOGETHER. / (instrumental)** [–] [8]

Mar 90. (7"/7"pic-d/c-s) *(W 9851/+P/C)* **VOGUE. / KEEP IT TOGETHER** [1] [–]
(12"+=/cd-s+=) *(W 9851 TX/CD)* – ('A'-Strike-a-pose dub mix).
(12"pic-d+=) *(W 9851TW)* – ('A'Bette Davis dub).

Apr 90. (7"/c-s) *<19863-7/-4>* **VOGUE. / ('A'-Bette Davis dub)** [–] [1]
(12"+=/c-s+=/cd-s+=) *<21513-0/-4/-2>* – ('A'-Stike-a-pose dub).

May 90. (cd)(lp/c) *<(7599 26209-2)>(WX 351/+C)* **I'M BREATHLESS** (music inspired by the film 'Dick Tracy') [2] [2]
– He's a man / Sooner or later / Hanky panky / I'm going bananas / Cry baby / Something to remember / Back in business / More / What can you lose / Now I'm following you (pt.1 & 2) / Vogue.

Jul 90. (7"/c-s) *(W 9789/+C) <19789>* **HANKY PANKY. / MORE** [2] Jun90 [10]
('A'-Bare Bottom mix;12"+=/12"pic-d+=/cd-s+=) *(W 9789 T/TP/CD) <21577>* – ('A'-Bare Bones mix).

Nov 90. (7"/c-s) *(W 9000/+C) <19485-7/-4>* **JUSTIFY MY LOVE. / EXPRESS YOURSELF** [2] [1]
(12"pic-d+=/cd-s+=) *(W 9000 TP/CD)* – ('A'-William Orbit mix).

Nov 90. (cd)(lp/c) *<(7599 26440-2)>(WX 370/+C)* **THE IMMACULATE COLLECTION** (compilation) [1] [5]
– Spotlight / Holiday / Everybody / Physical attraction / Over and over / Into the groove / Where's the party / Spotlight (dub) / Holiday (dub) / Into the groove (dub) / Over and over (dub).

Feb 91. (7"/7"sha-pic-d) *(W 0008/+P)* **CRAZY FOR YOU (remix). / KEEP IT TOGETHER** [2] [–]
(12"pic-d+=/c-s+=/cd-s+=) *(W 0008 TP/C/CD)* – Into the groove.

Feb 91. (c-s) *<19490-4>* **RESCUE ME (remix) / RESCUE ME (alternate mix)** [–] [9]

Apr 91. (7"/c-s) *(W 0024/+C)* **RESCUE ME (remix). / SPOTLIGHT (version)** [3] [–]
(cd-s+=) *(W 0024CD)* – ('A'-Titanic mix).

May 91. (7"/7"pic-d) *(W 0037/+P)* **HOLIDAY. / TRUE BLUE** [5] [–]
(cd-s+=/c-s+=) *(W 0037 CD/CT)* – Causin' a commotion / Who's that girl.
(12") *(W 0037T)* – ('A'side) / Where's the party / Everybody (remix).

—— Below from the film, 'A League Of Their Own'.

Jul 92. (7"/c-s) *(W 0122/+C) <18822>* **THIS USED TO BE MY PLAYGROUND. / (long version)** [3] [1]
(12"+=/cd-s+=) *(W 0122 T/CD)* – ('A'mixes).

Maverick-Sire Maverick-Sire

Oct 92. (7"/7"pic-d/c-s) *(W 0138/+P/C) <18782>* **EROTICA. / (instrumental)** [3] [3]
(12"+=/12"pic-d+=/cd-s+=) *(W 0138 T/TP/CD) <40585>* – ('A'mixes; William Orbit / Jeep beats / Underground club / Kenlou B-boy / etc).

Oct 92. (cd/c/lp) *<(9362 45031-2/-4/-1)>* **EROTICA** [2] [2]
– Erotica / Fever / Where life begins / Bye bye baby / Bad girl / Waiting / Deeper and deeper / Thief of hearts / Words / Rain / Why it's so hard / In this life / Did you do it / Secret garden.

Dec 92. (7"/c-s) *(W 0146/+C) <18639>* **DEEPER AND DEEPER. / ('A'instrumental)** [6] [13]
(12"pic-d+=/cd-s+=) *(W 0146 TP/CD) <40722>* – ('A'mixes; Shep's deep beats / David's deeper dub / David's klub mix / etc).

Feb 93. (c-s/cd-s) *<18650-4/-2>* **BAD GIRL / FEVER** [–] [36]
(c-s+=/cd-s+=) *<40793-4/-2>* – ('A'mixes; Murk Boys Deep South mix / Oscar G's dope mix / Shep's remedy mix / etc.)

Feb 93. (7"/c-s) *(W 0145/+C)* **BAD GIRL. / EROTICA (William Orbit mix)** [10] [–]
(12"pic-+=/cd-s+=) *(W 0145 TP/CD)* – ('A'mixes; (see US above).

Mar 93. (7"pic-d/c-s) *(W 0168 P/C)* **FEVER. / ('A'remix)** [6] [–]
(12"pic-d+=/cd-s+=) *(W 0168 TP/CD)* – ('A'mixes).

Jul 93. (c-s/cd-s) *<18505-4/-2>* **RAIN / WAITING** [–] [14]
(12"+=/c-s+=/cd-s+=) *<40988-0/-4/-2>* – Up down suite / ('A'album version).

Jul 93. (7"/c-s) *(W 0190/+C)* **RAIN. / OPEN YOUR HEART** [7] [–]
(12"pic-d+=/cd-s+=) *(W 0190 TP/CD)* – Up down suite (dub).

—— her backing; **DALLAS AUSTIN** – drums, keyboards, co-writer / **TOMMY MARTIN** – guitar / **ME'SHELL NDEGEOCELLO + COLIN WOLFE** – bass / **MARCUS DeVRIES** – prog. / **BABYFACE** – synth, drum prog / etc.

Mar 94. (7"/c-s) *(W 0240/+C) <18247>* **I'LL REMEMBER. / SECRET GARDEN** [7] [2]
(12"pic-d/cd-s) *(W 0240 TP/CD) <41355>* – ('A'-Orbit + Guerilla Beach mixes) / Why is it so hard? (live).

Sep 94. (c-s/cd-s) *<18035-4/-2>* **SECRET / (instrumental)** [–] [3]
(12"+=/cd-s+=) *<41772-0/-2>* – ('A'mixes; Junior Luscious various).

Sep 94. (7"pic-d/c-s) *(W 0268 P/C)* **SECRET. / LET YOUR GUARD DOWN (rough mix edit)** [5] [–]
(12"pic-d+=) *(W 0268TP)* – ('A'instrumental) / ('A'other version).
(cd-s) *(W 0268CD)* – ('A'side) / ('A'-Junior mixes).

Oct 94. (cd/c/lp) *<(9362 45767-2/-4/-1)>* **BEDTIME STORIES** [2] [3]
– Survival / Secret / I'd rather be your lover / Don't stop / Inside of me / Human nature / Forbidden love / Love tried to welcome me / Sanctuary / Bedtime story / Take a bow.

Dec 94. (7"pic-d/c-s) *(W 0278 T/C) <18000>* **TAKE A BOW. / ('A'-InDaSoul mix)** [17] [1]
(cd-s+=) *(W 0278CD) <41887>* – ('A'mixes; instrumental / Silky Soul).

—— Above single co-written w /BABYFACE as was 7th track. The singular title track was written by NELLEE HOOPER, BJORK & MARCUS DeVRIES. DAVE HALL co-wrote 5th, 6th & 8th track. Many samples included The ISLEYS (written) / AALIYAH / GAP BAND / GUTTERSNYPES / MAIN SOURCE / GRANT GREEN / HERBIE HANCOCK.

Feb 95. (c-s) *(W 0285C)* **BEDTIME STORY / ('A'-Junior's mix)** [4] Apr95 [42]
(12"pic-d/cd-s) *(W 0285 TP/CD)* – ('A'side) / ('A'-Junior's wet dream mix) / ('A'-Junior's Dreamy drum dub) / ('A'-Orbital mix) / ('A'-Junior's sound factory mix).
(cd-s) *(W 0285CDX)* – ('A'-Junior's mix) / Secret (Allstar mix) / Secret (Some Bizarre mixes).

Apr 95. (c-s/cd-s) *<17924-4/-2>* **BEDTIME STORY / SURVIVAL** [–] [42]
(12"+=/cd-s+=) *<41895-0/-2>* – (see Junior mixes above).

Jul 95. (c-s/cd-s) *<17882-4/-2>* **HUMAN NATURE / SANCTUARY** [–] [46]
(12"/cd-s) *<41880-0/-2>* – ('A'mixes; I'm Not Your Bitch / Bottom Heavy dub / Love Is The nature / Runway Club / etc)

Aug 95. (c-s) *(W 0300C)* **HUMAN NATURE / ('A'-Chorus door slam mix)** [8] [–]
(cd-s+=) *(W 0300CD)* – ('A'club mix) / ('A'-Runway club mix) / I'm not your bitch.
(12"pic-d) *(W 0300TP)* – (all above except 'A'side).

Oct 95. (c-s) *(W 0324C)* *<17719>* **YOU'LL SEE / (instrumental)** [5] [6]
(cd-s+=) *(W 0324CD)* – Rain.
(cd-s) *(W 0324CDX)* – ('A'side) / Secret (Junior Luscious club mix) / Sooner or later / Bad girl.

Nov 95. (cd/c/lp) *<(9362 46100-2/-4/-1)>* **SOMETHING TO REMEMBER** (compilation) [3] [6]
– I want you / I'll remember (theme from "With Honors") / Take a bow / You'll see / Crazy for you / This used to be my playground / Live to tell / Love don't live here anymore (remix) / Something to remember / Forbidden love / One more chance / Rain / Oh father / I want you (orchestral).

Dec 95. (c-s) *(W 0326C)* **OH FATHER / LIVE TO TELL (live)** [16] [–]
(cd-s+=) *(W 0326CD)* – Why it's so hard (live).

Mar 96. (c-s) *(W 0337C)* **ONE MORE CHANCE / ('A'-Spanglish version)** [11] [–]
(cd-s+=) *(W 0337CD)* – You'll see (Spanish version).

Apr 96. (c-s/cd-s) *<17714-4/-2>* **LOVE DON'T LIVE HERE ANYMORE / ('A'-album version)** [–] [79]

Oct 96. (c-s/cd-s) *(W 0378 C/CD)* *<17495-4/-2>* **YOU MUST LOVE ME / RAINBOW HIGH** [10] [18]

Dec 96. (c-s/cd-s) *(W 0384 C/CD)* **DON'T CRY FOR ME ARGENTINA / SANTA EVITA** [3] [–]
(cd-s+=) *(W 0384CDX)* – Latin chant.

Feb 97. (c-s/cd-s) *<43809-4/-2>* **DON'T CRY FOR ME ARGENTINA / ('A'mixes; Spanlish / Miami dub & instrumental / etc).** [–] [ ]
(above singles from the 'Warner Bros.' film 'EVITA', which she finally starred in. The various artists soundtrack hit UK No.7)

Mar 97. (c-s) *(W 0388C)* **ANOTHER SUITCASE IN ANOTHER HALL / DON'T CRY FOR ME ARGENTINA** [7] [–]
(cd-s+=) *(W 0388CDX)* – Waltz for Eva and Che.
(cd-s) *(W 0388CD)* – ('A'dance mix) / Hello and goodbye / You must love me.

Feb 98. (c-s/cd-s) *(W 0433C)* *<17244>* **FROZEN / SHANTI-ASHTANGI** [1] [2]
(12") *(W 0433T)* ('A'extended) / ('A'-Stereo Mc's mix) / ('A'-Meltdown mix).
(cd-s+=) *(W 0433T)* – ('A'-Widescreen mix).

Mar 98. (cd/c/lp) *<(9362 46847-2/-4/-1)>* **RAY OF LIGHT** [1] [2]
– Drowned world – Substitute for love / Swim / Ray of light / Candy perfume girl / Skin / Nothing really matters / Sky fits Heaven / Shanti – Ashtangi / Frozen / The power of good-bye / To have and not to hold / Little star / Mer girl.

Apr 98. (c-s) *(W 0444C)* *<17206>* **RAY OF LIGHT / HAS TO BE** [2] Jun98 [5]
(12"+=/cd-s+=) *(W 0444 T/CD)* – ('A'mixes).
(cd-s) *(W 0444CD2)* – ('A'side) / ('A'-Sasha mix) / ('A'-Victor Calderone mix) / ('A'-William Orbit mix).

Aug 98. (c-s/cd-s) *(W 0453 C/CD2)* **DROWNED WORLD – SUBSTITUTE FOR LOVE / SKY FITS HEAVEN (Victor Calderone & Sasha remix)** [10] [–]
(cd-s) *(W 0453CD1)* – ('A'mixes by BT & Sasha).

Nov 98. (c-s/cd-s) *(W 0459 C/CD)* *<17160>* **THE POWER OF GOOD-BYE / LITTLE STAR** [6] Oct98 [11]
(12") *(W 0459T)* – ('A'mixes) / Mer girl.

Mar 99. (c-s) *(W 471C)* *<17102>* **NOTHING REALLY MATTERS / TO HAVE AND NOT TO HOLD** [7] Apr99 [93]
(cd-s) *(W 471CD1)* – ('A'mixes; album / club 69 / club 69 vocal / Kruder & Dorfmeister).
(cd-s+=) *(W 471CD2)* – ('A'-Vikram mix).
(12") *(W 471T)* – ('A'mixes).

Jun 99. (c-s) *(W 495C)* *<radio cut>* **BEAUTIFUL STRANGER / ('A'-Calderone radio mix)** [2] [19]
(cd-s+=) *(W 495CD)* – ('A'mixes; Calderone club).
(cd-s) *(W 495T)* – ('A'mixes).

Mar 00. (c-s) *(W 519C)* *<radio cut>* **AMERICAN PIE / (Calderone filter dub)** [1] Feb00 [29]
(cd-s+=) *(W 519CD1)* – ('A'-Richard 'Humpty' vission mix).
(cd-s) *(W 519CD2)* – ('A'-Victor Calderone & Richard 'Humpty' mixes).
(12") *(W 519T)* – ('A'mixes).

Aug 00. (c-s) *(W 537C)* *<16826>* **MUSIC / (Calderone mix)** [1] [1]
(cd-s+=) *(W 537CD1)* – ('A'-Deep dish / Groove Armada / HQ2 mixes).
(cd-s) *(W 537CD2)* – ('A'mixes).

Sep 00. (cd/c/lp) *(9362 47865-2/-4/-1)* *<47598>* **MUSIC** [1] [1]
– Music / Impressive instant / Runaway lover / I deserve it / Amazing / Nobody's perfect / Don't tell me / What it feels like for a girl / Paradise (not for me) / Gone / American pie.

Nov 00. (c-s) *(W 547C)* *<16825>* **DON'T TELL ME / (Thunderpuss' hands in the air radio mix)** [4] Dec00 [4]
(cd-s+=) *(W 547CD1)* – ('A'-Tracy Young club & Vission mixes).
(cd-s+=) *(W 547CD2)* – ('A'-Victor Calderone sensory mix).

Apr 01. (c-s) *(W 553C)* *<42372>* **WHAT IT FEELS LIKE FOR A GIRL / (Calderone & Quayle dark side mix)** [7] [23]
(cd-s+=/12") *(W 553 CD1/T1)* – ('A'mixes; above & beyond / Paul Oakenfold Perfecto / Richard Vission).
(cd-s/12") *(W 553 CD2/T2)* – ('A'mixes; above & beyond / Spanish / Richard Vission velvet / Tracy Young club) / Lo que siente la muyer.

Nov 01. (cd/c) *<(9362 48000-2/-4)>* **GHV2 (GREATEST HITS VOL.2)** (compilation) [2] [7]
– Deeper and deeper / Erotica / Human nature / Secret / Don't cry for me Argentina / Bedtime story / The power of good-bye / Beautiful stranger / Frozen / Take a bow / Ray of light / Don't tell me / What it feels like for a girl / Drowned world – Substitute for love / Music.

Oct 02. (c-s) *(W 595C)* **DIE ANOTHER DAY / (Dirty Vegas main mix)** [3] [8]
(cd-s+=) *(W 595CD2)* *<42492>* – (Deepsky remix).
(cd-s) *(W 595CD1)* – ('A'side) / (Thunderpuss mix) / (Felix Da Housecat thee retroelectro mix).
(d12"+=) *(W 595T)* – (Dirty Vegas dub).

Apr 03. (cd-s) *(W 603CD1)* *<16658>* **AMERICAN LIFE / (Missy Elliott remix) / (Peter Rauhofer's American anthem)** [2] [37]
(cd-s) *(W 603CD2)* – ('A'side) / (Oakenfold downtempo remix) / (Felix Da Housecat Devin dazzle club mix).
(12") *(W 603T)* – ('A'side) / Die another day (Calderone & Quayle afterlife mix).
(d12"/cd-s) *(W 603 T2/CDX)* – (all above).

Apr 03. (cd/d-lp) *(9362 48454-2)* *<48439>* **AMERICAN LIFE** [1] [1]
– American life / Hollywood / I'm so stupid / Love profusion / Nobody knows me / Nothing fails / Intervention / X-static process / Mother and father / Die another day / Easy ride. *(special cd; 9362 48440-2)*

Jul 03. (cd-s) *(W 614CD1)* *<42638>* **HOLLYWOOD / (Oakenfold full remix) / (Deepsky HSH vocal mix)** [2] [ ]
(cd-s) *(W 614CD2)* – ('A'side) / (Jacques Lu Cont's Thin White Duck mix) / (Micronauts remix).
(12") *(W 614T)* – ('A'side) / (Micronauts remix) / (Oakenfold full remix).
(d12"/cd-s) *(W 614 T2/CDX)* – (all above tracks).

—— In Nov'03, MADONNA feat. on BRITNEY SPEARS' hit, 'Me Against The Music'

Nov 03. (m-cd) *(W 631CD)* *<48624>* **REMIXED AND REVISITED** [ ] [ ]
– Nothing fails / Love profusion / Nobody knows me / American life / Like a virgin – Hollywood (live medley with CHRISTINA AGUILERA & BRITNEY SPEARS) / Into the Hollywood groove (with MISSY ELLIOTT) / Your honesty.

Dec 03. (cd-s) *(W 634CD1)* **LOVE PROFUSION / NOTHING FAILS / LOVE PROFUSION (passengerz club mix)** [11] [–]
(cd-s) *(W 634CD2)* – ('A'side) / (Ralph Rosario house vocal mix) / Nobody knows me (above and beyond 12" mix).
(12") *(W 634T)* *<42682>* – ('A'-Passengerz club mix) / Nobody knows me (above & beyond 12" mix).

– compilations, others, etc. –

on 'Replay' unless mentioned otherwise (many with OTTO WERNHERR)

Feb 87. (12") *(3006)* **WILD DANCING. / ('A'dance mix)** [ ] [–]
(re-iss. cd-s Sep93 & Apr95)

Apr 89. (12") *(3000)* **COSMIC CLUB (extended dance mix). / WE ARE THE GODS** [ ] [–]
(re-iss. cd-s Sep93)

May 89. (12") *(3007)* **TIME TO DANCE (extended). / (instrumental) / (radio mix)** [ ] [–]
(cd-s-iss.Oct95; RRSCD 3007)
Sep 89. (12") *(3008)* **ON THE STREET (edit). / (extended mix)** [ ] [–]
(cd-s-iss.Oct95; RRSCD 3008)
May 90. (12") *(3009)* **OH MY!!! (edit). / ('A'disco mix)** [ ] [–]
Aug 90. (cd/c) *Action Replay; (CDAR/ARLC 1005)* **THE BEST & THE REST OF MADONNA AND OTTO WERNKERR** [ ] [–]
Sep 90. (12") *(3010)* **SHAKE (extended). / ('A'mix) / ('A'instrumental)** [ ] [–]
(cd-iss. Oct95; RRSCD 3010)
now on 'Receiver' unless mentioned otherwise
1989. (cd/c/lp) *(CD/TC+/KNOB 1)* **IN THE BEGINNING** [ ] [–]
(cd re-iss. Oct98 on 'Gravity'; GTY 2001-2) (cd re-iss. Feb99; same as original)
Oct 89. (lp/c/cd) *(RR LP/LC/CD 118)* **THE EARLY YEARS** [ ] [–]
Jul 91. (cdlp) *(RR CD/LP 144)* **GIVE IT TO ME** [ ] [–]
Apr 92. (7"/12"pic-d/pic-cd-s) **SHINE A LIGHT. / ON THE GROUND / LITTLE BOY** [ ] [–]
Jul 93. (cd/c) *(CDAR/ARLC 1033)* **BEST OF THE REST VOLUME II** [ ] [–]

□ MAD SEASON (see under ⇒ ALICE IN CHAINS)

MAGAZINE

Formed: Manchester, England . . . spring 1977 by former BUZZCOCKS frontman HOWARD DEVOTO and guitarist JOHN McGEOGH, who recruited the rhythm section of BARRY ADAMSON and MARTIN JACKSON along with keyboard player, BOB DICKINSON. After six months of rehearsals, they played their debut gig on the final night of legendary Manchester punk club, The Electric Circus, subsequently signing to 'Virgin' on the strength of a demo. A classic debut single, 'SHOT BY BOTH SIDES' established MAGAZINE's post-punk credentials, its stark, uncompromising approach and lyrical despair paving the way for countless gaggles of miserable young men in trenchcoats. Although DICKINSON had left prior to recording the single, the band had recruited a replacement, DAVE FORMULA, in time for the debut album, 'REAL LIFE' (1978). Its icy keyboard textures and spiky sonic artistry announced the arrival of a unique talent although DEVOTO's hyper-intelligent wayward genius was nothing new for fans who'd admired the punk maverick since his BUZZCOCKS days. With major radio support from John Peel and a growing cult fanbase, the album made the UK Top 30, while JACKSON was replaced with JOHN DOYLE following the obligatory tour. A follow-up set, 'SECONDHAND DAYLIGHT' (1979), was even more liberal in its use of keyboards although MAGAZINE's leftfield approach could hardly be accused of straying into New Romantic territory (some of MAGAZINE did dip a toe into these waters when they guested for VISAGE). Although a further three singles (including the unsettling 'A SONG FROM UNDER THE FLOORBOARDS' and an unlikely cover of Sly Stone's 'THANK YOU') failed to chart, a third album, 'THE CORRECT USE OF SOAP' (1980), became their most successful to date. DEVOTO wasn't happy with the direction the band were headed, however, and the defection of McGEOGH to SIOUXSIE & THE BANSHEES led to a slow decline and a patchy final effort in 'MAGIC, MURDER AND THE WEATHER' (1981). By the time of the album's release, DEVOTO had already announced his departure, effectively ending MAGAZINE's limited shelf life. The singer went on to release a solo set, 'JERKY VERSIONS OF THE DREAM' before forming LUXURIA with NOKO. He subsequently quit the music business; BARRY ADAMSON has enjoyed greater recognition, initially with NICK CAVE & The BAD SEEDS and latterly with his acclaimed solo career. • **Songwriters:** DEVOTO penned all except; I LOVE YOU BIG DUMMY (Captain Beefheart). LUXURIA covered JEZEBEL (Marty Wilde).

Album rating: REAL LIFE (*9) / SECONDHAND DAYLIGHT (*6) / THE CORRECT USE OF SOAP (*8) / PLAY (*4) / MAGIC, MURDER AND THE WEATHER (*6) / AFTER THE FACT compilation (*8) / RAYS AND HAIL compilation (*8) / Howard Devoto: JERKY VERSIONS OF THE DREAM (*5) / Luxuria: THE UNANSWERABLE LUST (*5) / BEAST BOX (*4)

HOWARD DEVOTO (b. HOWARD TROTTER, 1955) – vocals (ex-BUZZCOCKS) / **JOHN McGEOGH** – guitar / **BARRY ADAMSON** – bass / **MARTIN JACKSON** – drums / **BOB DICKINSON** – keyboards (latter left before debut recording)

Virgin Int

Jan 78. (7") *(VS 200)* **SHOT BY BOTH SIDES. / MY MIND AIN'T SO OPEN** [41] [–]
Apr 78. (7") *(VS 207)* **TOUCH AND GO. / GOLDFINGER** [ ] [–]

— added **DAVE FORMULA** – keyboards

Jun 78. (lp/c) *(V/TCV 2100)* **REAL LIFE** [29] [ ]
– Definitive gaze / My tulpa / Shot by both sides / Recoil / Burst / Motorcade / The great beautician in the sky / The light pours out of me / Parade. *(re-iss. Mar84; OVED 62) (cd-iss. Oct88; CDV 2100)*

— **JOHN DOYLE** – drums repl. JACKSON (to CHAMELEONS, then SWING OUT SISTER)

Nov 78. (7") *(VS 237)* **GIVE ME EVERYTHING. / I LOVE YOU, YOU BIG DUMMY** [ ] [–]
Feb 79. (7") *(VS 251)* **RHYTHM OF CRUELTY. / T.V. BABY** [ ] [–]
Mar 79. (lp/c) *(V/TCV 2121)* **SECONDHAND DAYLIGHT** [38] [ ]
– Feed the enemy / Rhythm of cruelty / Cut-out shapes / Talk to the body / I wanted your heart / The thin air / Back to nature / Believe that I understand / Permafrost. *(re-iss. 1987 lp/c; OVED/+C 84) (cd-iss. Oct88; CDV 2121)*
Feb 80. (7") *(VS 321)* **A SONG FROM UNDER THE FLOORBOARDS. / TWENTY YEARS AGO** [ ] [–]
Mar 80. (7") *(VS 328)* **THANK YOU (FALETTINME BE MICE ELF AGIN). / THE BOOK** [ ] [–]
Apr 80. (7") *(VS 334)* **UPSIDE DOWN. / THE LIGHT POURS OUT OF ME (live)** [ ] [–]
May 80. (lp/c) *(V/TCV 2156) <13144>* **THE CORRECT USE OF SOAP** [28] [ ]
– Because you're frightened / Model worker / I'm a party / You never knew me / Philadelphia / I want to burn again / Thank you (falettinme be mice elf agin) / Sweetheart contract / Stuck / A song from under the floorboards. *(re-iss. 1988 lp/c; OVED/+C 116) (cd-iss. Oct88; CDV 2156)*
Jul 80. (d7/12"ep) *(VS 368/+12)* **SWEETHEART CONTRACT. / FEED THE ENEMY (live) // TWENTY YEARS AGO. / SHOT BY BOTH SIDES (live)** [54] [–]

— **ROBIN SIMON** – guitar (ex-ULTRAVOX) repl. McGEOGH who joined SIOUXSIE . . . (above now alongside **DEVOTO, ADAMSON, FORMULA** and **DOYLE**)

Virgin I.R.S.

Nov 80. (lp/c) *(V/TCV 2184) <70015>* **PLAY (live at Melbourne Festival Hall)** [69] [ ]
– Give me everything / A song from under the floorboards / Permafrost / The light pours out of me / Model worker / Parade / Thank you (falettinme be mice elf agin) / Because you're frightened / Twenty years ago / Definitive gaze. *(re-iss. 1988 lp/c; OVED/+C 117) (cd-iss. Oct88; CDV 2184)*

— **BEN MANDELSON** – guitar (ex-AMAZORBLADES) repl. ROBIN.

May 81. (7") *(VS 412)* **ABOUT THE WEATHER. / IN THE DARK** [ ] [–]
(12"+=) *(VS 412-12)* – The operative.
Jun 81. (lp/c) *(V/TCV 2200) <70020>* **MAGIC, MURDER AND THE WEATHER** [39] [ ]
– About the weather / So lucky / The honeymoon killers / Vigilante / Come alive / The great man's secrets / This poison / Naked eye / Suburban Rhonda / The garden. *(re-iss. 1988 lp/c; OVED/+C 141) (cd-iss. Oct88; CDV 2200)*

— They split mid '81. DEVOTO went solo with help from FORMULA (see below). BEN MANDELSON joined The MEKONS, JOHN DOYLE later joined ARMOURY SHOW. BARRY ADAMSON joined PETE SHELLEY then later NICK CAVE & THE BAD SEEDS. FORMULA had also joined the group DESIGN FOR LIVING.

– compilations, etc. –

on 'Virgin' unless mentioned otherwise

May 82. (lp/c) *(VM/+C 1)* **AFTER THE FACT** (best of) – –

May 83. (12"ep) *(VS 592-12)* **SHOT BY BOTH SIDES** – –
– Shot by both sides / Goldfinger / Give me everything / A song from under the floorboards.

May 87. (cd) *(COMCD 5)* **RAYS AND HAIL 1978-81** (best of) – –
– Shot by both sides / Definitive gaze / Motorcade / The light pours out of me / Feed the enemy / Rhythm of cruelty / Back to nature / Permafrost / Because you're frightened / You never knew me / A song from under the floorboards / I want to burn again / About the weather / Parade. *(re-iss. Jul93; CDVM 9020)*

Jul 90. (cd) *(CDOVD 312)* **SCREE** (rarities 76-81) –

Aug 93. (cd) *Windsong; (WINCD 040)* **BBC RADIO 1 LIVE IN CONCERT** –

Oct 00. (cd) *(CDV 2924)* **MAGAZINE: WHERE THE POWER IS** –

Oct 00. (3xcd-box) *(MAGBOX 1)* **MAGAZINE: MAYBE IT'S RIGHT TO BE NERVOUS NOW** –
(above two releases were B-sides, out-takes, Peel sessions)

HOWARD DEVOTO

— went solo, with **DAVE FORMULA** – keyboards / **PAT AHORN** – drums / **ALAN ST. CLAIR** – guitar / **NEIL PYZER** – keyboards,synth / **MARTIN HEATH** – bass

Virgin I.R.S.

Jun 83. (7"/12") *(VS 598/+12)* **RAINY SEASON. / RAIN FOREST** –

Aug 83. (lp/c) *(V/TCV 2272)* *<SP 70036>* **JERKY VERSIONS OF THE DREAM** 57
– Cold imagination / Topless / Rainy season / I admire you / Way out of shape / Some will pay (for what others pay to avoid) / Waiting for a train / Out of shape with me / Taking over Heaven / Seeing is believing. *(re-iss. Aug88; OVED 129) (cd-iss. Apr90; CDV 2272)*

Aug 83. (7"/12") *(VS 642/+12)* **COLD IMAGINATION. / OUT OF SHAPE WITH ME** –

— PYZER and ST.CLAIR joined SPEAR OF DESTINY. HEATH and AHORN joined DAVE HOWARD SINGERS, DEVOTO guested for B.SZAJNER a French electronic wizard. He then took 4 years off before his new venture . . .

LUXURIA

DEVOTO with **NOKO** (b. Liverpool) – guitar, co-composer

Beggars Banquet Beggars Banquet

Jan 88. (7") *(BEG 204)* **REDNECK. / SHE'S YOUR LOVER NOW (pt.1)** –
(12"+=) *(BEG 204T)* – She's your lover now (pt.2).

Feb 88. (lp/c)(cd) *(BEGA/BEGC 90)(BEGA 90CD)* *<6990>* **THE UNANSWERABLE LUST**
– Redneck / Flesh / Public highway / Pound / Lady 21 / Celebrity / Rubbish / Mile / Luxuria.

May 88. (7") *(BEG 211)* **PUBLIC HIGHWAY (Short cut) / SICKLY THUG AND I** –
(12"+=) *(BEG 211T)* – Luxuria (The wilderness mix).

Mar 90. (7"ep/12"ep/cd-ep) *(BEG 233/+T/CD)* **THE BEAST BOX IS DREAMING / BEAST BOX / USELESS LOVE** –

Apr 90. (cd)(c/lp) *(BEGA 106CD)(BEGC/BEGA 106)* *<2233-2/-4/-1>* **BEAST BOX**
– The beast box is dreaming / Stupid blood / Against the past / Our curious leader / We keep on getting there / Ticket / Animal in the mirror / Dirty beating heart / Smoking mirror / I've been expecting you / Karezza / Beast box / Jezebel.

May 90. (7") *(BEG 242)* **JEZEBEL. / SMOKING MIRROR (instrumental)** –
(12"+=) *(BEG 242T)* – Sickly thug and I (live).
(cd-s++=) *(BEG 242CD)* – Luxuria (live).

— after their split, NOKO went to ground for a while, re-emerging later in the 90's with hard techno act, APOLLO 440. DEVOTO re-joined the BUZZCOCKS temporary in 2002

□ MAGICK (see under ⇒ BOND, Graham)

□ MAHAVISHNU ORCHESTRA (see under ⇒ McLAUGHLIN, John)

□ MAKAVELI (see under ⇒ 2PAC)

□ Stephen MALKMUS (see under ⇒ PAVEMENT)

MAMAS AND THE PAPAS

Formed: St. Thomas, Virgin Islands, USA . . . 1964 as The NEW JOURNEYMAN by DENNY DOHERTY, and two JOURNEYMEN; JOHN PHILLIPS and MICHELLE GILLIAM. They soon brought in the larger-than-life CASS ELLIOT, relocating to California where they became The MAMAS & THE PAPAS (Mama being Hell's Angels slang for girlfriend). They were introduced to producer and owner of 'Dunhill' records Lou Adler, by 'Eve Of Destruction'-man, BARRY McGUIRE. He contracted them initially as backing singers for McGUIRE's 1965 album, 'Precious Time', which included PHILLIPS' 'CALIFORNIA DREAMIN''. The following year, this classic piece of harmony-orientated folk-pop became their debut 45, hitting the US Top 5. Their follow-up, 'MONDAY MONDAY', topped the charts (No.3 in the UK), succeeded by a string of hits, abruptly halted by the split of the group in '68. This was the result of the eventual marriage break-up of JOHN and MICHELLE, as well as drug busts and alleged record company rip-offs. All subsequently took off on solo ventures, often re-uniting for one-off concerts, etc. Tragically, on the 29th of July '74, CASS ELLIOT died of a heart attack while choking on food. In 1982, the three remaining members re-grouped with a new singer, SPANKY McFARLANE (ex-SPANKY & HER GANG). MICHELLE had already begun an acting career, that has since seen her in US TV dramas such as 'Knot's Landing'. Sadly, great songwriter, extraordinaire, JOHN PHILLIPS, died of a heart attack in March 2001. • **Covered:** DANCING IN THE STREET (Martha & The Vandellas) / DEDICATED TO THE ONE I LOVE (Shireles) / DO YOU WANNA DANCE (Bobby Freeman) / I CALL YOUR NAME (Beatles) / etc. In 1967, PHILLIPS wrote No.1 smash, 'SAN FRANCISCO', for late 80's PAPA-to-be SCOTT McKENZIE. Twenty years later, JOHN co-wrote US No.1, 'Kokomo', with The BEACH BOYS. • **Trivia:** On the 31st October 1970, MICHELLE, now divorced from JOHN, married cult actor DENNIS HOPPER (but only for a week!).

Album rating: IF YOU CAN BELIEVE YOUR EYES AND EARS (*7) / THE MAMAS & THE PAPAS (*7) / THE MAMAS AND THE PAPAS DELIVER (*6) / FAREWELL TO THE FIRST GOLDEN ERA compilation (*7) / THE PAPAS & THE THE MAMAS (*6) / GOLDEN ERA, VOL.2 compilation (*6) / 16 OF THEIR GREATEST HITS compilation (*8) / PEOPLE LIKE US (*3) / CREEQUE ALLEY: HISTORY OF THE MAMAS & THE PAPAS compilation (*8) / Mama Cass: DREAM A LITTLE DREAM (*5) / BUBBLE GUM, LEMONADE & . . . SOMETHING FOR MAMA (*5) / MAMA'S BIG ONES compilation (*6) / John Phillips: JOHN, THE WOLFKING OF L.A. (*8)

JOHN PHILLIPS (b.30 Aug'35, Parris Island, South Carolina) – vocals / **CASS ELLIOT** (b. ELLEN NAOMI COHEN, 19 Sep'41, Baltimore, Maryland) – vocals / **MICHELLE GILLIAM** (b. HOLLY MICHELLE GILLIAM, 4 Jun'45, Long Beach, Calif.) – vocals (ex-JOURNEYMEN, with PHILLIPS) (ELLIOT ex-MUGWUMPS with DOHERTY) / **DENNY DOHERTY** (b.29 Nov'41, Halifax, Nova Scotia, Canada) – vocals

R.C.A. Dunhill

Jan 66. (7") *(1503)* *<4020>* **CALIFORNIA DREAMIN'. / SOMEBODY GROOVY** 23 Dec65 4

May 66. (7") *(1516)* *<4026>* **MONDAY MONDAY. / GOT A FEELIN'** 3 Apr66 1

Jun 66. (lp; mono/stereo) *(RD 7803)* *<D/DS 50001>* **IF YOU CAN BELIEVE YOUR EYES AND EARS** 3 Feb66 1

– Do you wanna dance / Go where you wanna go / California dreamin' / Spanish harlem / Somebody groovy / Hey girl / You baby / In crowd / Monday, Monday / Straight shooter / Got a feelin' / I call your name. *(cd-iss. 1990 on 'MCA';)*

Jul 66. (7") *(1533) <4031>* **I SAW HER AGAIN. / EVEN IF I COULD** 11 Jun66 5

— **JILL GIBSON** – vocals repl. MICHELLE for a while

Oct 66. (7") *(1551) <4050>* **LOOK THRU MY WINDOW. / ONCE THERE WAS A TIME I THOUGHT** 24

— **MICHELLE** returned when she reconciled with husband JOHN

Jan 67. (lp; mono/stereo) *(RD/SF 7834) <D/DS 50010>* **CASS JOHN MICHELLE DENNY** 24 Sep66 4
– No salt on her tail / Trip, stumble and fall / Dancing bear / Words of love / My heart stood still / Dancing in the street / I saw her again / Strange young girl / I can't wait / Even if I could / That kind of girl / Once was a time I thought.

Jan 67. (7") *(1564) <4057>* **WORDS OF LOVE. / DANCING IN THE STREET** 47 5 Nov66 75

Mar 67. (7") *(1576) <4077>* **DEDICATED TO THE ONE I LOVE. / FREE ADVICE** 2 Feb67 2

Apr 67. (7") *<4083>* **CREEQUE ALLEY. / NO SALT IN HER TAIL** – 5

Jun 67. (lp; mono/stereo) *(RD/SF 7880) <D/DS 50014>* **DELIVER** 4 Mar67 2
– Dedicated to the one I love / My girl / Creeque Alley / Sing for your supper / Twist and shout / Free advice / Look through any window / Boys and girls together / String man / Frustration / Did you ever want to cry / John's music box.

Jul 67. (7") *(1613)* **CREEQUE ALLEY. / DID YOU EVER WANT TO CRY** 9 –

Sep 67. (7") *(1630) <4099>* **12:30 (YOUNG GIRLS ARE COMING TO THE CANYON). / STRAIGHT SHOOTER** Aug67 20

Dec 67. (7") *(1649) <4107>* **GLAD TO BE UNHAPPY. / HEY GIRL** Oct67 26

Dec 67. (lp; mono/stereo) *<D/DS 50025>* **FAREWELL TO THE FIRST GOLDEN ERA** (compilation) Oct67 5
– Dedicated to the one I love / Go where you wanna go / Words of love / Look through any window / Dancing in the street / Monday Monday / Creeque Alley / Got a feelin' / 12:30 (young girls are coming to the canyon) / I call your name / I saw her again last night / California dreamin'.

Dec 67. (7") *<4113>* **DANCING BEAR. / JOHN'S MUSIC BOX** – 51

Jun 68. (7") *(1710) <4125>* **SAFE IN MY GARDEN. / TOO LATE** May68 53

Sep 68. (lp; mono/stereo) *(RD/SF 7960) <DS 50031>* **. . .PRESENTING THE PAPAS AND THE MAMAS** May68 15
– Dream a little dream of me / Gemini child / Ivy / Mansions / Meditation mama (transcendental woman travels) / Midnight voyage / Nothing's too good for my little girl / Rooms / Safe in my garden / The right somebody to love / Too late / Twelve thirty.

Sep 68. (7") *(1744) <4150>* **FOR THE LOVE OF IVY. / STRANGE YOUNG GIRLS** 81

Nov 68. (7") *<4171>* **DO YOU WANNA DANCE. / MY GIRL** – 76

— (Jul68) Disbanded, when JOHN and MICHELLE broke up. JOHN PHILLIPS later went solo, as did DENNY and MICHELLE.

MAMA CASS

had already gone solo.

R.C.A. Dunhill

Aug 68. (7") *(1726) <4145>* **DREAM A LITTLE DREAM OF ME (live). / MIDNIGHT VOYAGE** 11 Jul68 12
(above also credited with The MAMAS AND THE PAPAS)

Stateside Dunhill

Nov 68. (7") *(SS 8002) 4166>* **CALIFORNIA EARTHQUAKE. / TALKIN' TO YOUR TOOTHBRUSH** Oct68 67

Dec 68. (lp; stereo/mono) *(S+/SL 5004) <DS 50040>* **DREAM A LITTLE DREAM** Oct68 87
– Dream a little dream of me / California earthquake / The room nobody lives in / Talkin' to your toothbrush / Blues for breakfast / You know who I am / Rubber band / Long time loving you / Jane, the insane dog lady / What was I thinking of / Burn your hatred / Sweet believer.

Feb 69. (7") *<4184>* **MOVE IN A LITTLE BIT CLOSER. / ALL FOR ME** – 58

Mar 69. (7") *(SS 8014)* **MOVE IN A LITTLE BIT CLOSER. / I CAN DREAM, CAN'T I** –

Jul 69. (7") *(SS 8021) <4195>* **IT'S GETTING BETTER. / WHO'S TO BLAME** 8 May69 30

Nov 69. (lp; stereo/mono) *(S+/SL 5014) <DS 50055>* **BUBBLEGUM, LEMONADE AND . . . SOMETHING FOR MAMA** Jun69 91
– Blow me a kiss / It's getting better / Easy come, easy go / I can dream, can't I / Welcome to the world / Lady Love / He's a runner / Move in a little closer, baby / When I just wear my smile / Who's to blame / Sour grapes. *<US re-iss. Nov69 as 'MAKE YOUR OWN KIND OF MUSIC'; DS 50071>* – Make your own kind of music.

MAMA CASS ELLIOT

Nov 69. (7") *(SS 8031) <4114>* **MAKE YOUR OWN KIND OF MUSIC. / LADY LOVE** Oct69 36

Mar 70. (7") *(SS 8039) <4225>* **NEW WORLD COMING. / BLOW ME A KISS** Jan70 42

Mar 70. (7") *<4226>* **SOMETHING TO MAKE YOU HAPPY. / NEXT TO YOU** –

Sep 70. (7") *(SS 8057) <4244>* **A SONG THAT NEVER COMES. / I CAN DREAM, CAN'T I?** Jul70 99

Nov 70. (7") *(4253>* **DON'T LET THE GOOD TIMES PASS YOU BY. / A SONG THAT NEVER COMES** –

Mar 71. (lp) *(SPB 1020) <DS 50093>* **MAMA'S BIG ONES** (compilation)
– Dream a little dream of me / Make your own kind of music / It's getting better / Easy come, easy go / Words of love / Move in a little closer, baby / Song that never comes / One way ticket / Ain't nobody else like you / Don't let the good life pass you by / The good times are coming / New world coming. *(re-iss. Oct74 on 'A.B.C.'; ABCL 5011)*

— Late 1970-early 1971, MAMA CASS teamed up with DAVE MASON on some releases.

MAMAS AND THE PAPAS

re-united.

Probe Dunhill

Nov 71. (lp) *(SPB 1048) <DS 50106>* **PEOPLE LIKE US** Oct 71 84
– Dream a little dream of me / Make your own kind of music / It's getting better / Easy come, easy go / Words of love / Move in a little closer, baby / Song that never comes / One way ticket / Ain't nobody else like you / Don't let the good life pass you by / The good times are coming / New world coming. *(re-iss. Oct74 on 'A.B.C.'; ABCL 5017) (re-iss. Nov76 on 'Music For Pleasure'; 50299)*

Jan 72. (7") *<4301>* **STEP OUT. / SHOOTING STAR** – 81

Feb 72. (7") *(PRO 552)* **SHOOTING STAR. / NO DOUGH** –

— Break-up, once again for final time. All try-out solo careers.

CASS ELLIOT

went solo again.

R.C.A. R.C.A.

1972. (7") *(2179) <74-0644>* **BABY I'M YOURS. / CHERRIES JUBILEE**

Feb 72. (lp) *<(LSP 4619)>* **CASS ELLIOT**
– Introduction – Dream a little dream of me / Extraordinary / I think a lot about you / Don't call me Mama anymore / My love / I'm coming to the best part of my life / The torchsong medley: I came here to sing a torchsong – I got a right to sing the blues – I've got it bad and that ain't good – Mean to me – Why was a born – I came here to sing a torchsong (reprise) / The night before / I like what I like / I'll be seeing you / Closing – I don't call me Mama anymore (reprise).

1972. (7") *<74-0693>* **THAT SONG. / WHEN IT DOESN'T WORK OUT** –

1972. (7") *<74-0764>* **DISNEY GIRLS (1957). / BREAK ANOTHER HEART** –

1973. (7") *<74-0830>* **DOES ANYBODY LOVE YOU. / THE ROAD IS NO PLACE FOR A LADY** –

1973. (lp) *(SF 8306) <LSP 4753>* **THE ROAD IS NO PLACE FOR A LADY**
– (If you're gonna) Break another heart / Saturday suit / Does anybody love you / Walk beside me / All my life – Say hello / Who in the world / Love was not a word / Oh babe, what would you say / The road is no place for a lady.

1973. (7") *<74-0957>* **LISTEN TO THE WORLD. / I THINK A LOT ABOUT YOU** [–] [ ]

Jul 74. (7") *(LPB 07521)* **IF YOU'RE GONNA BREAK ANOTHER HEART. / DON'T CALL ME MAMA ANYMORE** [ ] [–]

Jul 74. (lp) *<(APL1-0303)>* **DON'T CALL ME MAMA ANYMORE** [ ] [ ]
– Introduction – Dream a little dream of me / Extraordinary / I think a lot about you / Don't call me Mama anymore / My love / I'm coming to the best part of my life / The torchsong medley: I came here to sing a torchsong – I got a right to sing the blues – I've got it bad and that ain't good – Mean to me – Why was a born – I came here to sing a torchsong (reprise) / The night before / I like what I like / I'll be seeing you / Closing – I don't call me Mama anymore (reprise).

—— on July '74, CASS ELLIOT died of a heart attack

– (MAMAS & PAPAS) compilations, etc. –

below on 'Stateside' UK / 'Dunhill' US unless mentioned otherwise

Dec 68. (lp; stereo/mono) *(S+SL 5002) <DS 50038>* **GOLDEN ERA, VOL.2** [ ] Sep68 [53]

Apr 69. (lp; stereo/mono) *(S+/SL 5007)* **HITS OF GOLD** [7] [–]
(re-iss. Oct74 on 'A.B.C.'; ABCL 5003) (re-iss. Aug81 on 'M.C.A.'; MCL 1614)

Sep 69. (lp) *<DS 50064>* **16 OF THEIR GREATEST HITS** [–] [61]

May 77. (lp) *Arcade; (ADEP 30)* **THE BEST OF THE MAMAS AND THE PAPAS** [6] [–]

May 91. (d-cd) *M.C.A.; (MCAD2-10195)* **CREEQUE ALLEY: THE HISTORY OF THE MAMAS & PAPAS** [ ] [ ]
– Wild women / Winken', blinkin' and nod / I'll remember tonight / I don't wanna know / This precious time / (John Phillips dialogue) / California dreamin' / Go where you wanna go / Monday, Monday / You baby / Do you wanna dance / I call your name / Spanish harlem / Straight shooter / Got a feelin' / I saw her again last night / Look through my window / Words of love / Dancing in the street / (Mama Cass dialogue) / Once was a time I thought / No salt in her tail / Trip, stumble and fall / Dancing bear / Dedicated to the one I love / Creeque Alley / My girl / Twist and shout / I call your name / Twelve thirty (young girls are coming to the canyon) / Glad to be unhappy / For the love of Ivy / Safe in my garden / Midnight voyage / Dream a little dream of me / California earthquake / It's getting better / Mississippi / Watcha gonna do / (Mama Cass dialogue) / Step out / The achin' kind.

Jun 92. (cd/c) *See For Miles; (SEE CD/K 333)* **THE EP COLLECTION** [ ] [–]

Dec 94. (cd/c) *Polygram TV; (523 973-2/-4)* **CALIFORNIA DREAMING – THE VERY BEST OF THE MAMAS & THE PAPAS** [14] [–]
(re-dist.Aug97; hit No.30)

Jul 97. (c-s/cd-s) *M.C.A.; (MCS C/TD 48058)* **CALIFORNIA DREAMIN' / DREAM A LITTLE DREAM OF ME / MONDAY MONDAY / MAKE YOUR OWN KIND OF MUSIC** [9] [–]

Aug 99. (cd) *Beat Goes On; (BGOCD 462)* **DELIVER / THE PAPAS & THE MAMAS** [ ] [ ]

Jan 00. (cd) *Universal; (E 112175-2)* **UNIVERSAL MASTERS COLLECTION** [ ] [ ]

Oct 00. (cd/c) *M.C.A.; (MCBD/MCBC 19519)* **THE BEST OF THE MAMAS & THE PAPAS** [ ] [ ]

Aug 01. (d-cd) *Universal; (AA88 112653-2)* **ALL THE LEAVES ARE BROWN** [ ] [ ]

Feb 02. (d-cd) *BR Music; (BS 8125-2)* **THE SINGLES PLUS** [ ] [–]

Mar 03. (cd) *Universal; (AAMCAD 11739)* **IF YOU CAN BELIEVE YOUR EYES** [ ] [ ]

Mar 03. (cd) *Universal; (AAMCAD 11740)* **GREATEST HITS** [ ] [ ]

Mar 03. (cd) *Universal; (AAMCAD 11945)* **20TH CENTURY MASTERS** [ ] [ ]

MAN

Formed: Merthyr Tydfil, Wales ... 1964 as The BYSTANDERS by MICKY JONES, CLIVE JOHN, RAY WILLIAMS and JEFFREY JONES. They released many 45's during a 4-year period, one of them, '98.6', hitting the Top 50 in early '67. The following year, they amalgamated with another Welsh group, The DREAM, locating singer/guitarist DEKE LEONARD. Signing to 'Pye' in 1969, MAN released their debut album, 'REVELATION', a conceptual affair which contained the European hit, 'EROTICA' (banned in the UK for its simulated orgasm sounds). Their subsequent effort, '2 OZS. OF PLASTIC WITH A HOLE IN THE MIDDLE', was another to embrace the West Coast sound of bands like QUICKSILVER MESSENGER SERVICE. Early in 1970, MARTIN ACE and TERRY WILLIAMS were drafted in to replace RAY and JEFFREY, the new line-up featuring on their eponymous third, rather self-indulgent set. Already established as a consummate live act, they released a fourth album, 'DO YOU LIKE IT HERE NOW, ARE YOU SETTLING IN?', which contained the acid-tinged classic, 'MANY ARE CALLED, BUT FEW GET UP'. The 1972 set (which didn't include the departed DEKE), 'BE GOOD TO YOURSELF AT LEAST ONCE A DAY', boasted yet another lengthy jewel, 'BANANAS'. They finally reached the Top 30 in 1973, with 'BACK TO THE FUTURE', before DEKE returned for an equally successful follow-up, 'RHINOS, WINOS AND LUNATICS'. During the first half of the 70's, MAN were continually dogged by personnel changes, the most recent member, MALCOLM MORLEY, leaving after the aforementioned album. The most astonishing of these personnel upheavals came with the addition of QUICKSILVER MESSENGER SERVICE figurehead/hero, JOHN CIPPOLINA. He stayed for only one album, the Top 30 live-set, 'MAXIMUM DARKNESS'. In 1976, they charted for the final time, with the disappointing, 'WELSH CONNECTION'. They split soon after, DEKE continuing a solo career (with MAN members) until he, MICKEY JONES, MARTIN ACE and JOHN WEATHER reformed the group in 1983. In 1995, they were still going strong, an album, 'CALL DOWN THE MOON, testament to their longevity. Always a band for sniggering titles, 'UNDRUGGED' (2002) was MAN's take on the 'unplugged' generation with an acoustic revision of past classics and a few covers, among them a middling rendition of the Beach Boys' 'SAIL ON SAILOR' and an unnecessary run through Hoagy Carmichael's 'GEORGIA ON MY MIND'. • **Songwriters:** Group penned from the 70's, except covers; CODINE (Buffy Sainte-Marie) / I'M GONNA LEAVE YOU (Quicksilver Messenger Service) / LET THE GOOD TIMES ROLL (Shirley & Lee) / etc. • **Trivia:** MAN also featured on the live Various Artists albums, 'GREASY TRUCKERS PARTY VOL.1' and 'CHRISTMAS AT THE PATTI', both on the 'United Artists' label (1972 + 1973).

Album rating: REVELATION (*6) / 2 ozs. OF PLASTIC WITH A HOLE IN THE MIDDLE (*6) / MAN (*5) / DO YOU LIKE IT HERE NOW, ARE YOU SETTLING IN? (*7) / AT THE PADGET ROOMS, PENARTH (*6) / BE GOOD TO YOURSELF AT LEAST ONCE A DAY (*6) / BACK INTO THE FUTURE (*5) / RHINOS, WINOS AND LUNATICS (*6) / SLOW MOTION (*5) / MAXIMUM DARKNESS (*6) / THE WELSH CONNECTION (*4) / ALL'S WELL THAT ENDS WELL (*4) / FRIDAY THE 13th (*4) / THE TWANG DYNASTY (*4) / CALL DOWN THE MOON (*4) / PERFECT TIMING (THE U.A. YEARS 1970-75) compilation (*8) / ENDANGERED SPECIES (*4) / UNDRUGGED (*4)

BYSTANDERS

VIC OAKLEY – vocals / **MICKY JONES** (b. 7 Jun'46) – guitar, vocals / **CLIVE JOHN** – keyboards, vocals / **RAY 'TAFF' WILLIAMS** – bass (ex-EYES OF BLUE) / **JEFFREY JONES** – drums

Pylot / not iss.

1965. (7") *(WD 501)* **THAT'S THE END. / THIS TIME** [ ] [–]

Piccadilly / not iss.

Jun 66. (7") *(7N 35330)* **(YOU'RE GONNA) HURT YOURSELF. / HAVE I OFFENDED THE GIRL** [ ] [–]

Oct 66. (7") *(7N 35351)* **MY LOVE – COME HOME. / IF YOU WALK AWAY** [ ] [–]

Dec 66. (7") *(7N 35363)* **98.6. / STUBBORN KIND OF FELLOW** [45] [–]

Jun 67. (7") *(7N 35382)* **ROYAL BLUE SUMMER SUNSHINE DAY. / MAKE UP YOUR MIND** –
Aug 67. (7") *(7N 35399)* **PATTERN PEOPLE. / GREEN GRASS** –

Pye not iss.

Feb 68. (7") *(7N 17476)* **WHEN JEZAMINE GOES. / CAVE OF CLEAR LIGHT** –
May 68. (7") *(7N 17540)* **THIS WORLD IS MY WORLD. / PAINTING THE TIME** –

— (disbanded 1968)

MAN

DEKE LEONARD (b.18 Dec'44, Llanelli, Wales) – guitar, vocals (ex-The DREAM) / **MICKY JONES** / plus **CLIVE, RAY + JEFFREY**

Pye Philips

Jan 69. (7") *(7N 17684)* **SUDDEN LIFE. / LOVE** –
Jan 69. (lp) *(NSPL 18275)* **REVELATION** (US-title 'MANPOWER')
– And in the beginning . . . / Sudden life / Empty room / Puella! Puella! (woman! woman!) / Love / Erotica / Blind man / And castles rise in children's eyes / Don't just stand there (come in out of the rain) / The missing pieces / The future hides its face. *(re-iss. Oct89 on 'See For Miles' lp/cd; SEE/+CD 274) (cd re-iss. Aug91 on 'Repertoire'; REP 4024WZ) (lp re-iss. Feb00 on 'Get Back'; GET 563)*

Dawn Philips

Sep 69. (lp) *(DNLS 3003)* **2 OZS OF PLASTIC WITH A HOLE IN THE MIDDLE**
– (prelude) – The storm / It is as it might be / Spunk box / My name is Jesus Smith / Parchment and candles / Brother Arnold's red and white striped tent. *(re-iss. Oct89. on 'See For Miles' lp/cd; SEE/+CD 273) (lp re-iss. Jan01 on 'Get Back'; GET 585)*

— **MARTIN ACE** – bass (ex-The DREAM) repl. RAY who joined The BIG SLEEP / **TERRY WILLIAMS** (b.11 Jan'48, Swansea, Wales) – drums (ex-The DREAM) repl. JEFFREY

Liberty U.A.

Oct 70. (lp) *(LBG 83464)* *<9803>* **MAN**
– Romain / Country girl / Would the Christians wait five minutes? the lions are having a draw / Daughter of the fireplace / The alchemist. *(re-iss. Feb76 as 'MAN 1970' on 'Sunset'; SLS 50380) (cd-iss. Nov98 on 'Point'; PNTVP 117CD) (<cd re-iss. Nov02 on 'Repertoire'+=; REP 4969>)* – Daughter of the fireplace (single version) / Country girl (single version).
Mar 71. (7") *(LBF 15448)* **DAUGHTER OF THE FIREPLACE. / COUNTRY GIRL** –

U.A. U.A.

Nov 71. (lp) *(UAS 29236)* *<1032>* **DO YOU LIKE IT HERE NOW, ARE YOU SETTLING IN?**
– Angel easy / All good clean fun / We're only children / Many are called but few get up / Manillo / Love your life. *(re-iss. Aug80 on 'Liberty'; LBR 16-032) (cd-iss. Oct97 on 'Point'; PNTVP 107CD) (cd re-iss. Jan99 on 'Eagle'; EAMCD 077)*

— now a quartet when CLIVE joined IORWITH PRITCHARD & THE NEUTRONS

Sep 72. (lp) *(USP 100)* **AT THE PADGET ROOMS, PENARTH (live)** –
– Many are called but few get up / Daughter of the fireplace / H. Samuel (jam). *(cd-iss. Sep97 on 'Beat Goes On'; BGOCD 365)*

— **MICKY + TERRY** + the returning **CLIVE** – guitar / recruited **PHIL RYAN** – keyboards (ex-EYES OF BLUE, PIBLOKTO) repl. DEKE who went solo / **MICHAEL 'WILL' YOUATT** – bass (ex-QUICKSAND, ANCIENT GREASE) repl. MARTIN

Oct 72. (lp) *(UAG 29417)* *<077>* **BE GOOD TO YOURSELF AT LEAST ONCE A DAY**
– C'mon / Keep on crinting / Bananas / Life on the road. *(re-iss. May88 & Apr97 on 'Beat Goes On'; BGOLP 14) (cd-iss. Feb92; BGOCD 14)*

— **ALAN 'TWEKE' LEWIS** – keyboards (ex-WILD TURKEY) repl. RYAN (in studio)

Sep 73. (d-lp) *(UAD 60053-4)* *<170>* **BACK INTO THE FUTURE** (half live / half studio) 23
– A night in dad's bag / Just for you / Back into the future / Don't go away / Ain't their fight / Never say nups to Nepalese / Sospan fack (featuring The Gwalia male choir) / C'mon / Jam up jelly tight. *(cd-iss. Dec93 on 'Beat Goes On'+=; BGOCD 211)* – Oh no, not again (spunk rock '73).
Sep 73. (7") *<341>* **DON'T GO AWAY. / BACK TO THE FUTURE** –

— **MICKY & TERRY** added the returning **DEKE LEONARD** – guitar, vocals / **MALCOLM MORLEY** – keyboards (ex-HELP YOURSELF) repl. WILL (to NEUTRONS) / **KEN WHALEY** – bass (ex-HELP YOURSELF, ex-BEES MAKE HONEY) repl. CLIVE and TWEKE

May 74. (lp) *(UAG 29631)* *<247>* **RHINOS, WINOS AND LUNATICS** 24
– Taking the easy way out again / The thunder and lightning kid / California silks and satins / Four day Louise / Intro / Kerosene / Scotch corner / Exit. *(cd-iss. Nov93 on 'Beat Goes On'; BGOCD 208)*
Jul 74. (7") *(UP 35703)* *<505>* **TAKING THE EASY WAY OUT AGAIN. / CALIFORNIA SILKS AND SATINS**

— trimmed to a quartet when MALCOLM departed.

Oct 74. (7") *(UP 35739)* **DAY AND NIGHT. / HARD WAY TO LIVE (live)**
Nov 74. (lp) *(UAG 29675)* *<345>* **SLOW MOTION**
– Hard way to die / Grasshopper / Rock & roll you out / You don't like us / Bedtime bone / One more chance / Rainbow eyes / Day and night. *(cd-iss. Nov93 on 'Beat Goes On'; BGOCD 209)*
Nov 74. (7") *<611>* **DAY AND NIGHT. / RAINBOW EYES** –

— **MARTIN ACE** – bass returned to replace KEN who joined TYLA GANG. added American **JOHN CIPPOLINA** – guitar (ex-QUICKSILVER MESSENGER SERVICE)

Sep 75. (lp) *(UAG 29872)* **MAXIMUM DARKNESS (live)** 25 –
– Codine / 7171-551 / Babe I'm gonna leave you / Many are called, but few get up / Bananas. *(re-iss. Mar89 & Apr 97 on 'Beat Goes On'; BGOLP 43) (cd-iss. Feb92; BGOCD 43)*

— **PHIL RYAN** – keyboards returned to replace CIPPOLINA / **JOHN McKENZIE** – bass (of GLOBAL VILLAGE TRUCKING CO.) repl. MARTIN ACE who joined The MOTORS

M.C.A. M.C.A.

Mar 76. (lp) *(MCF 2753)* *<2190>* **THE WELSH CONNECTION** 40
– The ride and the view / Out of your head / Love can find a way / The Welsh connection / Something is happening / Cartoon / Born with a future. *(cd-iss. JUl97 on 'Turning Point'; PNTVP 102CD) (cd re-iss. Jan99 on 'Eagle'; EAMCD 063)*
Mar 76. (7") *(MCA 236)* *<40539>* **OUT OF YOUR HEAD. / I'M A LOVE TAKER**

— (disbanded Spring '76)

Nov 77. (lp) *(MCF 2815)* **ALL'S WELL THAT ENDS WELL (live farewell gigs)** –
– Let the good times roll / The Welsh connection / The ride and the view / A hard way to live / Born with a future / Spunk Rock / Romain. *(cd-iss. May98 on 'Turning Point'; PNTVP 103CD) (cd re-mast.Mar99 on 'Eagle'; EAMCD 068)*

— TERRY WILLIAMS continued in DAVE EDMUNDS' ROCKPILE, before joining The MOTORS and later DIRE STRAITS. PHIL RYAN joined PETE BROWN Band.

DEKE LEONARD

— solo with ICEBERG at times with MAN members **MICKY JONES, MARTIN ACE, KEN WHALEY + TERRY WILLIAMS** / Others incl. **TOMMY RILEY** – drums, etc.

U.A. U.A.

Feb 73. (7") *(UP 35494)* **DIAMOND ROAD. / CIRCLES AND SQUARES**
Jul 73. (lp) *(UAG 29464)* **ICEBERG**
– Razor blade and rattlesnake / I just can't win / Lisa / Nothing is happening / Looking for a man / A hard way to live / Broken ovation / Jesse / Ten thousand takers / The ghost of Musket flat / Jesse / Crosby (second class citizen blues) / 7171 551. *(re-iss. Dec80 on 'Liberty'; LBR 1042) (cd-iss. Nov95 on 'Beat Goes On'+=; BGOCD 288)* – KAMIKAZE
Sep 73. (7") *(UP 35556)* **A HARD WAY TO LIVE. / THE ACHING IS SO SWEET** –
Oct 73. (7") **A HARD WAY TO LIVE. / JESSE (live)** –
Mar 74. (lp) *(UAG 29544)* **KAMIKAZE** 50
– Cool summer rain / Jayhawk special / Sharpened claws / Taking the easy way out / The black gates of death / Stacia / Broken glass and limejuice / April the third / Louisiana hoedown / In search of Sarah and twenty-six horses / The Devil's gloves.
Apr 74. (7") *(UP 35668)* **LOUISIANA HOEDOWN. / SHE'S A CAR**
Feb 79. (7") *(UP 36488)* **MAP OF INDIA. / LADY IN THE BLUE TUXEDO** –
Mar 81. (lp) *(UAG 30240)* **BEFORE YOUR VERY EYES** –
– Someone is calling / Fools like me / Marlene / Oh / When am I coming back / Get off the line / Hiding in the darkness / Big hunk of love / I feel

like a pill / The world exploded in my face / What am I gonna do when the money runs out / Bad luck. *(cd-iss. Sep98 on 'Point'+=; PNTVP 114CD)* – Map of India / Hey there (lady in the blue tuxedo).

Jun 81. (7") *(BP 400)* **BIG HUNK OF LOVE. / MARLENE** [ ] [–]

MAN

— re-formed briefly 1983. **MICKY JONES, DEKE LEONARD, MARTIN ACE** plus **JOHN WEATHERS** – drums (ex-EYES OF BLUE, ex-GENTLE GIANT)

Picasso not iss.

Dec 83. (lp/c) *(PIK/+C 001)* **FRIDAY THE 13th (live Marquee, May '83)** [ ] [–]
– C'mon / Talk about a morning / Kerosene / A hard way to die / Back into the future / The ride and the view / Romain. *(cd-iss. Aug93 on 'Great Expectations';) (cd re-iss. Ovt97 on 'Point'; PNTVP 106CD) (cd re-mast.Mar99 on 'Eagle'; EAMCD 062)*

Omox-ROR. not iss.

1984. (7") **WHAT A NIGHT. / THE LAST BIRTHDAY PARTY** [–] German [–]

— (1987 reformed again but only to do gigs) **TERRY WILLIAMS** – drums had returned to replace WEATHERS.

Road Goes On Forever not iss.

Feb 93. (cd/c) *(RGF CD/MC 1003)* **THE TWANG DYNASTY** [ ] [–]
– A feather on the scales of justice / Mad on her / Jumpin' like a kangaroo / The chimes at midnight / Circumstances / The price / Women / The Chinese cut / Out of the darkness / Fast and dangerous / The wings of Mercury. *(cd re-mast.Mar99 on 'Eagle'; EAMCD 067)*

Hypertension Griffin

May 95. (cd) *(HYCD 200154)* *<480>* **CALL DOWN THE MOON** [ ] [ ]
– Call down the Moon / If I were you / Dream away / Blackout / The man with x-ray eyes / Heaven and Hell / The girl is trouble / Drivin' around / Burn my workin' clothes. *(re-iss. Aug98 on 'Point'; PNTVP 116CD)*

— line-up:- **LEONARD, ACE, JONES + RYAN**

Evangeline Evangeline

Jun 00. (cd) *(<GEL 4001>)* **ENDANGERED SPECIES** [ ] Sep00 [ ]
– Conflict of interest / Stuck behind the popemobile / Saints and sinners / Face to face / Hangin' on / Tie up the wind / Victim of love / Love isn't love.

Point not iss.

May 02. (cd) *(PNTVP 121CD)* **UNDRUGGED** [ ] [–]
– Scotch corner / Babe, I'm gonna leave you / I always thought the walrus was protected / Dream away / Manillo / Asylum / Trying to get to you / Listen to me, sister / Georgia on my mind / SAil on sailor / Day and night.

– compilations, others, etc. –

Oct 73. (lp) *Pye; (GH 569)* **GOLDEN HOUR OF MAN** [ ] [–]
Nov 76. (7"ep) *United Artists; (REM 408)* **BANANAS (part 1). / BANANAS (part 2)** [ ] [–]
Nov 86. (lp) *Latymer; (DLATE 1)* **GREEN FLY** [ ] [–]
Aug 90. (lp/cd; BYSTANDERS) *See For Miles; (SEE/+CD 301)* **BIRTH OF MAN** [ ] [–]
Feb 91. (cd) *Worldwide;* **LIVE AT THE RAINBOW 1972 (live)** [ ] [–]
(re-iss. Jan99 on 'Eagle'; EAMCD 060)
Jun 91. (cd/c/lp) *E.M.I.; (CD/TC+/EMS 1403)* **PERFECT TIMING (THE U.A. YEARS: 1970-1975)** [ ] [–]
(cd+=/c+=) – (3 extra tracks).
Mar 93. (cd) *Raw Fruit; (FRSCD 010)* **LIVE AT READING '83 (live)** [ ] [–]
Oct 93. (cd; 1-side by DEKE LEONARD'S ICEBERG) *Windsong; (WNDSNG 45)* **BBC RADIO 1 LIVE IN CONCERT** (live) [ ] [–]
Nov 93. (cd) *Great Expectations; (PIPCD 055)* **LIVE AT THE MARQUEE (live)** [ ] [–]
Apr 97. (cd) *Think Progressive; (EFA 035052)* **LIVE OFFICIAL BOOTLEG (live at Glastonbury 1994)** [ ] [–]
(re-iss. May98 on 'Point'; PNTVP 109CD) (cd re-mast.Mar99 on 'Eagle'; EAMCD 066)
Jul 97. (cd) *Point; (<PNTVP 101CD>)* **LIVE IN LONDON 1975** [ ] [ ]
(re-iss. Jan99 on 'Eagle'; EAMCD 061>)
Jul 97. (cd) *Point; (<PNTVP 104CD>)* **GREASY TRUCKERS PARTY** [ ] [ ]
(re-iss. Jan99 on 'Eagle'; EAMCD 064)
Sep 97. (cd) *Point; (PNTVP 110CD)* **CHRISTMAS AT THE PATTI (live)** [ ] [–]
Apr 98. (cd) *Point; (<PNTVP 108CD>)* **TO LIVE FOR TO DIE** [ ] Sep99 [ ]
(re-iss. Jan99 on 'Eagle'; EAMCD 067)
Mar 99. (cd) *Point; (<PNTVP 120CD>)* **RARE MAN** [ ] [ ]
Mar 99. (cd) *Eagle; (EAMCD 069)* **THE 1999 PARTY TOUR** (live in Chicago, March 21st, 1974) [ ] [ ]
Feb 00. (d-cd) *Eagle; (EAMCD 099)* **THREE DECADES OF MAN** [ ] [–]
Jul 00. (d-cd) *Essential; (<ESACD 917>)* **THE DEFINITIVE COLLECTION** [ ] [ ]
May 01. (cd) *Receiver; (RRDCD 312)* **MANY ARE CALLED BUT FEW GET UP** [ ] [–]
Apr 02. (cd; by DEKE LEONARD) *Road Goes On Forever; (RGFDL 501)* **UNFINISHED BUSINESS** [ ] [–]
Mar 03. (cd) *Altrichter; (AM 310556)* **LEGAL BOOTLEG '99 (live)** [ ] [–]
Mar 03. (cd) *Altrichter; (AM 310559)* **DOWN TOWN LIVE (live)** [ ] [–]
(re-iss. Nov03 on 'Point'; PNTVP 130CD)
Aug 03. (d-cd) *Point; (PNTVP 129CD)* **1998 STAR CLUB (live)** [ ] [–]
Aug 03. (d-cd) *Snapper; (<SMDCD 478>)* **MAN ALIVE (live)** [ ] Nov03 [ ]
Oct 03. (d-cd) *Voiceprint; (VP 241022CD)* **THE 1999 PARTY TOUR / THE TWANG DYNASTY** [ ] [–]

MANIC STREET PREACHERS

Formed: Blackwood, Caerphilly, Wales . . . 1988 by JAMES DEAN BRADFIELD (vocals, guitar) and cousin SEAN MOORE (drums). With the addition of former school friends NICKY WIRE (bass) and RICHEY EDWARDS (rhythm guitar), the line-up was complete and the band set about recording their self-financed debut single, 'SUICIDE ALLEY'. The group began to attract attention with the release of the 'NEW ART RIOT' EP (1990), derivative but impassioned neo-punk which drew interest more for the band's defiant slurs on a range of targets (fellow musicians were shown no mercy) than its musical content. While the band looked the part (low rent glamour chic) and namechecked all the right people (RIMBAUD, The CLASH, etc.), their philosophy of kill your idols and then burn out, smacked of contrivance to say the least. When journalist STEVE LAMACQ said as much in an interview with EDWARDS in 1991, the guitarist proceeded to carve '4 REAL' into his arm with a razor, upping the ante in the band's already precarious relationship with the music press and causing furious debate between doubters and obsessive fans. The group proceeded to release a couple of raging singles on 'Heavenly', 'MOTOWN JUNK' and the stinging 'YOU LOVE US' (aimed at the press), before signing to 'Columbia' in 1991. After a couple of minor hits, 'STAY BEAUTIFUL' and 'LOVE'S SWEET EXILE', the MANICS cracked the Top 20 with a re-released 'YOU LOVE US', their much anticipated debut album, 'GENERATION TERRORISTS' following in February 1992. A sprawling double set, it kicked convincingly against the pricks, lashing out at such deserving targets as high street banks ('NAT WEST-BARCLAYS-MIDLAND-LLOYDS') and our beloved monarch ('REPEAT'). The band also proved they had a way with melody and songwriting in the soaring melancholy of 'MOTORCYCLE EMPTINESS'. Despite their original well intentioned claims to break up after the debut, the band rather predictably toured the album and began work on a new collection, 'GOLD AGAINST THE SOUL' (1993). Lacking the vicious kick of the debut, the record nevertheless contained some fine moments in the likes of 'LA TRISTESSE DURERA (SCREAM TO A SIGH)' and 'LIFE BECOMING A LANDSLIDE', reaching No.8 in the album charts. The MANIC STREET PREACHERS continued to court controversy with NICKY WIRE making his infamous comments about MICHAEL STIPE at the 1993 Reading Festival. The following year RICHEY EDWARDS' depression, self-mutilation and anorexia reached a head, the guitarist eventually admitted to a clinic for several weeks. His trauma was detailed in the harrowing '4st 7lb' from their third album, 'The HOLY BIBLE' (1994), a dark night of the soul which centred on such grim topics as Nazi genocide. Then, on 1st February '95, with EDWARDS apparently recovered, he went AWOL from his London hotel. A fortnight later, his abandoned car was found at the Severn Bridge, and rumours of suicide abounded. Even after a protracted police search, there was no trace of the guitarist and at the time of writing , he is still missing. Numerous sightings have since been reported, most notably in Goa, India although the Police have continued to draw a blank. The remaining members eventually decided to carry on, contributing a poignant 'RAIN DROPS KEEP FALLING ON MY HEAD' to the 1995 Warchild charity album, 'HELP', and releasing their fourth album, 'EVERYTHING MUST GO' (1996). The group's most accomplished work to date, the record was preceded by their biggest hit single (No.2), the bitter 'A DESIGN FOR LIFE'. Embellished with soaring strings and lavish arrangements, the band scored with a succession of brilliant songs including 'AUSTRALIA' and the title track, compositions that were almost transcendant in their emotive power, the memory of EDWARDS never far away. It seemed that at last the MANIC STREET PREACHERS had lived up to their early boasts and in early 1997 their talent was recognised when 'EVERYTHING MUST GO' won the coveted Mercury Music Award. The top of the singles chart was the only place the MANICS hadn't been. This was remedied late summer '98 when 'IF YOU TOLERATE THIS YOUR CHILDREN WILL BE NEXT' made No.1, a taster from their massive selling parent album, 'THIS IS THE TRUTH TELL ME YOURS' (1998). Classic anthems such as 'THE EVERLASTING', 'YOU STOLE THE SUN FROM MY HEART', and 'TSUNAMI', also became top selling in the UK charts, although what was happening to their records in America? Not that the staunchly socialist MANICS gave a fig for their Stateside oblivion, content to become the first Western rock band to play in Communist Cuba, that longtime thorn in Uncle Sam's bloated side. No need to ask then, what 'BABY ELIAN' was all about given the Cuba vs USA tussle of summer 2000. The latter track was served up for 'KNOW YOUR ENEMY' (2001), the band's sixth album and one of their most accomplished to date. The almost STOOGES-style savagery of 'FOUND THAT SOUL' (a dual Top 10 single released simultaneously with 'SO WHY SO SAD') set the tone, a blistering punk/garage track that put many of the so called American nu-metal/punk groups to shame and served as a timely reminder of how good angry rock music can be when it comes from the gut and not the marketing strategy. 'OCEAN SPRAY', in contrast, was a poignant homage to JAMES' mum's battle with cancer, Ocean Spray being a brand of cranberry juice used to combat the disease. Yet this album was primarily a politicised affair, again railing against the evils of the USA in the likes of 'FREE SPEECH WON'T FEED MY CHILDREN' and 'LET ROBESON SING', a tribute to the forgotten entertainer/political activist. They may be guilty of naivety, bombast and even double standards but few bands of the modern era write, play and perform with the emotional and political intensity, the dignity and the humbleness of The MANIC STREET PREACHERS; Britain's anaemic music scene (never mind the USA) needs this band now more than ever. In the absence of any new material, the inevitable greatest hits and B-sides collections were released in 2002 and 2003 respectively. While 'FOREVER DELAYED' made a fair stab at charting their fascinating career curve, the dearth of representative material from the traumatic 'HOLY BIBLE' era meant it didn't tell the whole story. 'LIPSTICK TRACES', meanwhile, told a slightly different story, its disc of covers giving an often intimate insight into the roots and influences that made them the singular artists they are. • **Covered:** IT'S SO EASY (Guns N' Roses) / UNDER MY WHEELS (Alice Cooper) / SUICIDE IS PAINLESS (Theme from 'M.A.S.H.') / WE ARE BOURGEOIS NOW + CHARLES WINDSOR (McCarthy) / THE DROWNERS (Suede) / STAY WITH ME (Faces) / WROTE FOR LUCK (Happy Mondays) / RAINDROPS KEEP FALLING ON MY HEAD (Bacharach-David) / VELOCITY GIRL (Primal Scream) / TAKE THE SKINHEADS BOWLING (Camper Van Beethoven) / BEEN A SON (Nirvana) / OUT OF TIME (Rolling Stones) / BRIGHT EYES (Mike Batt) / I CAN'T TAKE MY EYES OFF YOU (hit; Andy Williams) / TRAIN IN VAIN + WHAT'S MY NAME (Clash) / LAST CHRISTMAS (George Michael) / DIDN'T MY LORD DELIVER DANIEL (trad.) / ROCK AND ROLL MUSIC (Chuck Berry).

Album rating: GENERATION TERRORISTS (*8) / GOLD AGAINST THE SOUL (*9) / THE HOLY BIBLE (*9) / EVERYTHING MUST GO (*9) / THIS IS MY TRUTH TELL ME YOURS (*8) / KNOW YOUR ENEMY (*7) / FOREVER DELAYED – GREATEST HITS compilation (*8) / LIPSTICK TRACES: A SECRET HISTORY OF . . . double compilation (*5)

JAMES DEAN BRADFIELD (b.21 Feb'69, Newport) – vocals, guitar / **RICHEY JAMES EDWARDS** (b.27 Dec'69) – rhythm guitar / **NICKY WIRE** (b. NICHOLAS JONES, 20 Jan'69, Tredegar) – bass / **SEAN MOORE** (b.30 Jul'70, Pontypool) – drums

S.B.S. | not iss.

Aug 89. (7") *(SBS 002)* **SUICIDE ALLEY. / TENNESSEE (I FEEL SO LOW)** [ ] [–]

Damaged Goods | not iss.

Jun 90. (12"ep) *(YUBB 4)* **NEW ART RIOT** [ ] [–]
– New art riot / Stip it down / Last exit on yesterday / Teenage 20-20. *(re-iss. Dec91, Jul93 + Sep96, 12"pink-ep/cd-ep; YUBB 4 P/CD)*

Heavenly | not iss.

Jan 91. (12"ep/cd-ep) *(HVN8 12/CD)* **MOTOWN JUNK. / SORROW 16 / WE HER MAJESTY'S PRISONERS** [92] [–]

May 91. (7") *(HVN 10)* **YOU LOVE US. / SPECTATORS OF SUICIDE** [62] [–]
(12"+=/cd-s+=) *(HVN 10 12/CD)* – Starlover / Strip it down (live).

Caff | not iss.

Jul 91. (7") *(CAFF 15)* **FEMININE IS BEAUTIFUL: NEW ART RIOT. / REPEAT AFTER ME** [ ] [–]

Columbia | Columbia

Jul 91. (7") *(657337-7)* **STAY BEAUTIFUL. / R.P. McMURPHY** [40] [ ]
(12"+=/12"w-poster/cd-s+=) *(657337-6/-8/-2)* – Soul contamination.
(US-cd-ep+=) – Motown junk / Sorrow 16 / Star lover.
(cd-ep re-iss. Sep97 on 'Epic' hit No.52; MANIC 1CD)

Nov 91. (7") *(657582-7)* **LOVE'S SWEET EXILE. / REPEAT** [26] [–]
(12"+=/cd-s+=) *(657582-6/-2)* – Democracy coma.
(12"ltd.++=) *(657582-8)* – Stay beautiful (live).
(cd-ep re-iss. Sep97 on 'Epic' hit No.55; MANIC 2CD)

Jan 92. (7"/c-s) *(657724-7/-4)* **YOU LOVE US. / A VISION OF DEAD DESIRE** [16] [–]
(12"+=) *(657724-6)* – It's so easy (live).
(cd-s++=) *(657724-2)* – We her majesty's prisoners.
(cd-ep re-iss. Sep97 on 'Epic' hit No.49; MANIC 3CD)

Feb 92. (pic-cd/cd/d-c/d-lp/pic-d-lp) *(471060-0/-2/-4/-1/-9)* *<52474>* **GENERATION TERRORISTS** [13] [ ]
– Slash 'n' burn / Nat West-Barclays-Midland-Lloyds / Born to end / Motorcycle emptiness / You love us / Love's sweet exile / Little baby nothing / Repeat (stars and stripes) / Tennessee / Another invented disease / Stay beautiful / So dead / Repeat (UK) / Spectators of suicide / Damn dog / Crucifix kiss / Methadone pretty / Condemned to rock'n'roll. *(cd re-iss. Jan99; same)*

Mar 92. (7"/c-s) *(657873-7/-4)* **SLASH 'N' BURN. / AIN'T GOING DOWN** [20] [–]
(12"+=) *(657873-6)* – Motown junk.
(cd-s++=/gold-cd-s++=) *(657873-2/-0)* – ('A'version).

(cd-ep re-iss. Sep97 on 'Epic' hit No.54; MANIC 4CD)

Jun 92. (7"/c-s) *(658083-7/-4)* **MOTORCYCLE EMPTINESS. / BORED OUT OF MY MIND** [17] [–]
(12"pic-d+=) *(658083-8)* – Under my wheels.
(cd-s++=/s-cd-s++=) *(658083-2/-9)* – Crucifix kiss (live).
(cd-ep re-iss. Sep97 on 'Epic' hit No.41; MANIC 5CD)

Sep 92. (7"/cd-s) *(658382-7/-2)* **THEME FROM M.A.S.H. (SUICIDE IS PAINLESS). / ('b'side by 'Fatima Mansions' – Everything I Do (I Do It For You)** [7] [–]

Nov 92. (7") *(658796-7)* **LITTLE BABY NOTHING. / SUICIDE ALLEY** [29] [–]
(12"+=/cd-s+=) *(658796-6/-2)* – Yankee drawl / Never want again.
(cd-ep re-iss. Sep97 on 'Epic' hit No.50; MANIC 6CD)

Jun 93. (c-s) *(659337-4)* **FROM DESPAIR TO WHERE. / HIBERNATION** [25] [–]
(12"+=) *(659337-6)* – Spectators of suicide (Heavenly version).
(cd-s+=) *(659337-2)* – Star lover (Heavenly version).

Jun 93. (cd/c/lp/pic-lp) *(474064-2/-4/-1/-9)* *<57386>* **GOLD AGAINST THE SOUL** [8] [ ]
– Sleepflower / From despair to where / La tristesse durera (scream to a sigh) / Yourself / Life becoming a landslide / Drug drug druggy / Roses in the hospital / Nostalgic pushead / Symphony of tourette / Gold against the soul.

Jul 93. (7"/c-s) *(659477-7/-4)* **LA TRISTESSE DURERA (SCREAM TO A SIGH). / PATRICK BATEMAN** [22] [–]
(12"+=) *(659477-6)* – Repeat (live) / Tennessee.
(cd-s+=) *(659477-2)* – What's my name (live) / Slash'n'burn (live).

Sep 93. (7"/c-s) *(659727-7/-4)* **ROSES IN THE HOSPITAL. / US AGAINST YOU / DONKEY** [15] [–]
(cd-s+=) *(659727-2)* – Wrote for luck.
(12") *(659727-6)* – ('A'side) / (5-'A' mixes).

Epic Epic

Feb 94. (c-s) *(660070-4)* **LIFE BECOMING A LANDSLIDE / COMFORT COMES** [36] [–]
(12"+=) *(660070-6)* – Are mothers saints.
(cd-s++=) *(660070-2)* – Charles Windsor.

Jun 94. (7"/c-s) *(660447-7/-4)* **FASTER. / P.C.P.** [16] [–]
(10"+=) *(660447-0)* – Sculpture of man.
(cd-s++=) *(660447-2)* – New art riot (in E-minor).

Aug 94. (10"/c-s) *(660686-0/-4)* **REVOL. / TOO COLD HERE** [22] [–]
(cd-s+=) *(660686-2)* – You love us (original Heavenly version) / Love's sweet exile (live).
(cd-s) *(660686-5)* – ('A'side) / (3 live at Glastonbury tracks).

— RICHEY booked himself into a health clinic, after wasting himself down to 5 stone.

Aug 94. (cd/c/pic-lp) *(477421-2/-4/-0)* *<66967>* **THE HOLY BIBLE** [6] [ ]
– Yes / Ifwhiteamericatoldthetruthforonedayit'sworldwouldfallapart / Of walking abortion / She is suffering / Archives of pain / Revol / 4st 7lb / Mausoleum / Faster / This is yesterday / Die in the summertime / The intense humming of evil / P.C.P.

Oct 94. (10"/c-s) *(660895-0/-4)* **SHE IS SUFFERING. / LOVE TORN US UNDER (acoustic)** [25] [–]
(cd-s+=) *(660895-2)* – The drowners / Stay with me (both live w/ BERNARD BUTLER).
(cd-s) *(660895-5)* – ('A'side) / La tristesse durera (scream to a sigh) / Faster (Dust Brothers remixes).

— RICHEY was now fully recuperated . . . but on 1st Feb '95, he went AWOL again after walking out of London's Embassy Hotel at 7 that morning. Two weeks later, his car was found abandoned and after police frogmen searched the Severn, it was believed he might be dead. By the end of 1995, with RICHEY still missing, the group carried on as a trio.

— Meanwhile, BRADFIELD produced the debut of NORTHERN UPROAR.

Apr 96. (c-s) *(663070-4)* **A DESIGN FOR LIFE / BRIGHT EYES (live)** [2] [–]
(cd-s) *(663070-2)* – ('A'side) / Mr Carbohydrate / Dead passive / Dead trees and traffic islands.
(cd-s) *(663070-5)* – ('A'side) / ('A'-Howard Grey remix) / ('A'-Apollo 440 remix) / Faster (Chemical Brothers remix).

May 96. (cd/c/lp) *(483930-2/-4/-1)* *<67709>* **EVERYTHING MUST GO** [2] [ ]
– Elvis impersonator: Blackpool pier / A design for life / Kevin Carter / Enola – alone / Everything must go / Small black flowers that grow in the sky / The girl who wanted to be God / Removables / Australia / Interiors (song for Willem De Kooning) / Further away / No surface at all.

Jul 96. (c-s) *(663468-4)* **EVERYTHING MUST GO / RAINDROPS KEEP FALLING ON MY HEAD (live)** [5] [–]
(cd-s) *(663468-2)* – ('A'side) / Hanging on / Black garden / No-one knows what it's like to be me.
(cd-s) *(663468-5)* – ('A'side) / ('A'-Stealth Sonic Orchestra remix) / ('A'-Chemical Brothers remix).

Sep 96. (c-s) *(663775-4)* **KEVIN CARTER / EVERYTHING MUST GO (acoustic)** [9] [–]
(cd-s) *(663775-2)* – ('A'side) / Horses under starlight / Sepia / First republic.
(cd-s) *(663775-5)* – Kevin Carter busts loose (Jon Carter remix) / ('A'-Stealth Sonic Orchestra mixes).

Dec 96. (c-s) *(664044-4)* **AUSTRALIA / A DESIGN FOR LIFE (live)** [7] [–]
(cd-s) *(664044-2)* – ('A'side) / Velocity girl / Take the skinheads bowling / I can't take my eyes off you (acoustic).
(cd-s) *(664044-5)* – ('A'side) / ('A'-Lionrock remix) / Motorcycle emptiness (Stealth Sonic Orchestra version).

Epic Virgin

Aug 98. (c-s) *(666345-4)* **IF YOU TOLERATE THIS YOUR CHILDREN WILL BE NEXT / KEVIN CARTER (live)** [1] [–]
(cd-s) *(666345-2)* – ('A'side) / Prologue to history / Montana Autumn '78.
(cd-s) *(666345-5)* – ('A'side) / ('A'-Massive Attack remix) / ('A'-The Class Reunion Of The Sunset Marquis mix; aka David Holmes).

Sep 98. (cd/c/lp) *(491703-2/-4/-1)* *<47579>* **THIS IS MY TRUTH TELL ME YOURS** [1] [ ]
– The everlasting / If you tolerate this your children will be next / You stole the sun from my heart / Ready for drowning / Tsunami / My little empire / I'm not working / You're tender and you're tired / Born a girl / Be natural / Black dog on my shoulder / Nobody loved you / S.Y.M.M. *(cd re-iss. Nov02; 491703-6)*

Nov 98. (c-s) *(666686-4)* **THE EVERLASTING / SMALL BLACK FLOWERS THAT GROW IN THE SUN (live at Nunex)** [11] [–]
(cd-s) *(666686-2)* – ('A'side) / Blackholes for the young / Valley boy.
(cd-s) *(666686-5)* – ('A'extended) / ('A'-Deadly Avenger's Psalm 315) / ('A'-Stealth Sonic Orchestra mix).

Mar 99. (c-s) *(666953-4)* **YOU STOLE THE SUN FROM MY HEART / IF YOU TOLERATE THIS YOUR CHILDREN WILL BE NEXT (live)** [5] [–]
(cd-s) *(666953-2)* – ('A'side) / Socialist serenade / Train in vain (live).
(cd-s) *(666953-5)* – ('A'side) / ('A'mixes by David Holmes & Mogwai).

Jul 99. (c-s) *(667411-4)* **TSUNAMI / MOTOWN JUNK (live)** [11] [–]
(cd-s) *(667411-2)* – ('A'side) / Buildings for dead people / A design for life (video).
(cd-s) *(667411-5)* – ('A'mixes by Cornelius & Stereolab).

Jan 00. (c-s) *(668530-4)* **THE MASSES AGAINST THE CLASSES / CLOSE MY EYES** [1] [–]
(10"+=/cd-s+=) *(668530-6/-2)* – Rock and roll music.

Feb 01. (c-s) *(670832-4)* **SO WHY SO SAD / YOU STOLE THE SUN FROM MY HEART (live from Cardiff Millennium Stadium 31st December 1999)** [8] [–]
(cd-s) *(670832-2)* – ('A'side) / ('A'-Avalanche remix) / Pedestal.

Feb 01. (7") *(670833-7)* **FOUND THAT SOUL. / THE MASSES AGAINST THE CLASSES (live)** [9] [–]
(cd-s) *(670833-2)* – ('A'side) / Locust valley / Ballad of the Bangkok Novotel.

Mar 01. (cd/c/lp) *(501880-2/-4/-1)* *<10113>* **KNOW YOUR ENEMY** [2] [ ]
– Found that soul / Ocean spray / Intravenus agnostic / So why so sad / Let Robeson sing / The year of purification / Wattsville blues / Miss Europa disco dancer / Dead martyrs / His last painting / My Guernica / The convalescent / Royal correspondent / Epicentre / Baby Elian / Freedom of speech won't feed my children. *(untitled hidden track+=) (cd re-iss. Nov01; same)*

Jun 01. (c-s) *(671253-4)* **OCEAN SPRAY / OCEAN SPRAY (Ellis Island mix)** [15] [–]
(cd-s) *(671253-2)* – ('A'side) / The groundhog days / Just a kid.
(cd-s) *(671253-5)* – ('A'side) / ('A'-Medicine mix) / ('A'-Kinobe mix).

Sep 01. (12") *(671773-6)* **LET ROBESON SING. / ('A'-Ian Brown mix) / ('A'-thee glitz mix by Felix Da Housecat)** [19] [–]
(cd-s+=) *(671773-5)* – ('A'video).
(cd-s) *(671773-2)* – ('A'-side) / Masking tape / Didn't my Lord deliver Daniel / ('A'-video).

Oct 02. (cd-s) *(673166-2)* **THERE BY THE GRACE OF GOD / AUTOMATIK TEKNICOLOUR / IT'S ALL GONE / ('A'video)** [6] [–]
(cd-s) *(673166-5)* – ('A'-side) / Unstoppable salvation / Happy ending.

Oct 02. (cd/lp) *(509551-2/-1) <87029>* **FOREVER DELAYED – GREATEST HITS** (compilation) [4] [ ]
– A design for life / Motorcycle emptiness / If you tolerate this your children will be next / La tristesse durera (scream to a high) / There by the grace of God / You love us / Australia / You stole the sun from my heart / Kevin Carter / Tsunami / Masses against the classes / From despair to where / Door to the river / Everything must go / Faster / Little baby nothing / M.A.S.H. (suicide is painless) / So why so sad / Everlasting / Motown junk. *(d-cd+=; 509551-9)* – (remixes).

Jul 03. (d-cd/t-lp) *(512386-2/-1) <862000>* **LIPSTICK TRACES: A SECRET HISTORY OF . . .** (compilation) [11] [ ]
– Prologue to history / 4 ever delayed / Sorrow 16 / Judge yr'self / Socialist serenade / Donkeys / Comfort comes / Mr. Carbohydrate / Dead trees and traffic islands / Horses under starlight / Sepia / Sculpture of man / Spectators of suicide / Democracy coma / Strip it down (live) / Bored out of my mind / Just a kid / Close my eyes / Valley boy / We her Majesty's prisoners / We are all bourgeoise now / Rock and roll music / It's so easy (live) / Take the skingheads bowling / Been a son / Out of time / Raindrops keep falling on my head / Bright eyes (live) / Train in vain (live) / Wrote for luck / What's my name (live) / Velocity girl / Can't take my eyes off you / Didn't my Lord deliver Daniel / Last Christmas (live).

Aimee MANN

Born: 9 Aug'60, Richmond, Virginia, USA. After moving to Boston to attend the Berklee School of Music, one of MANN's rather unlikely initial musical forays was working with AL JOURGENSEN / MINISTRY. This group, the YOUNG SNAKES (one 1982 EP exists) were around prior to her forming pop/rock outfit, 'TIL TUESDAY along with ROBERT HOLMES, JOEY PESCE and MICHAEL HAUSMANN. While many of the songs on the debut set, 'VOICES CARRY' (1985), sprang from MANN's break-up with former lover, HAUSMANN, the group's critically acclaimed third set, 'EVERYTHING'S DIFFERENT NOW' (1989), was largely inspired by MANN's relationship with co-writer, JULES SHEAR. In spite of, or perhaps because of this 'Rumours'-style emotional entanglement, the album was a compelling stepping stone to MANN's solo career and saw her developing into an accomplished and affecting songwriter. Yet the record sold poorly and the band dissolved amid record company hassles, MANN spending the next few years attempting to disentangle herself before embarking upon a solo career. She eventually emerged in Autumn '93 with a new deal ('Imago') and album, 'WHATEVER', her eclectic, BEATLES/PRETENDERS-like pop/rock drawing praise from such legendary songwriters as ELVIS COSTELLO, a personal friend and sometime collaborator. The record also provided her with her first major UK success, nudging into the Top 40, although just when it seemed as if MANN was finally beginning to establish herself as an artist in her own right, 'Imago' went bust. The ensuing hassles almost persuaded MANN to give it all up, 'Geffen' finally releasing a follow-up, 'I'M WITH STUPID', in 1995. With an array of guests including BERNARD BUTLER (who co-wrote 'SUGARCOATED'), JULIANA HATFIELD and the SQUEEZE songwriting axis of GLENN TILBROOK and CHRIS DIFFORD, the album was another critical success, its more acerbic lyrical bile no doubt a result of MANN's industry tribulations. She subsequently found herself without a recording contract, although some of her new material (including the Academy Award-winning 'SAVE ME' track) did surface on the 'Magnolia' movie soundtrack in 1999. A year later, AIMEE finally delivered her third solo set, 'BACHELOR No.2 – OR THE LAST REMAINS OF THE DODO' (2000), a melancholy record which saw her back to her best.
'LOST IN SPACE' (2002) was another poignant study in dislocation and emotional drift, rich in aural imagery and subtle, uneasy atmospherics. While the writing was as sharp, as barbed and as unrelentingly reflective as any of her past efforts, the widescreen tension of the instrumentation lent 'LOST . . .' a depth realised only fleetingly in the past. • **Covers:** ONE (Harry Nilsson). • **Trivia:** In 1987, she guested on RUSH's hit single, 'Time Stand Still'.

Album rating: 'Til Tuesday: VOICES CARRY (*6) / WELCOME HOME (*5) / EVERYTHING'S DIFFERENT NOW (*4) / COMING UP CLOSE retrospective (*6) / Aimee Mann: WHATEVER (*7) / I'M WITH STUPID (*6) / BACHELOR No.2 – OR THE LAST REMAINS OF THE DODO (*7) / THE ULTIMATE COLLECTION compilation (*7) / LOST IN SPACE (*6)

'TIL TUESDAY

AIMEE MANN – vocals, bass / **ROBERT HOLMES** (b.31 Mar'59, Hampton, England) – guitar, vocals / **JOEY PESCE** (b.14 Apr'62, Bronx, N.Y.) – synthesizers, piano, vocals / **MICHAEL HAUSMANN** (b.12 Jun'60, Philadelphia, Pennsylvania) – drums, percussion

Epic Epic

Apr 85. (7") *(EPCA 6120) <04795>* **VOICES CARRY. / ARE YOU SERIOUS?** [ ] [8]

Jun 85. (lp/c) *(EPC/40 26434) <39458>* **VOICES CARRY** [ ] Apr85 [19]
– Love in a vacuum / Looking over my shoulder / I could get used to this / No more crying / Voices carry / Winning the war / You know the rest / Maybe Monday / Don't watch me bleed / Sleep. *(cd-iss. 1988; CDEPC 26434)*

Aug 85. (7") *<04935>* **LOOKING OVER MY SHOULDER. / DON'T WATCH ME BLEED** [–] [61]

Oct 85. (7") **LOVE IN A VACUUM. / NO MORE CRYING** [–] [ ]

Jan 87. (lp/c/cd) *(EPC/40/EPCCD 57094) <40314>* **WELCOME HOME** [ ] Oct86 [49]
– What about love / Coming up close / On Sunday / Will she just fall down / David denies / Lover's day / Have mercy / Sleeping and walking / Angels never call / No one is watching you now.

Feb 87. (7") *(650125-7) <06289>* **WHAT ABOUT LOVE. / WILL SHE JUST FALL DOWN** [ ] Sep86 [26]
(12"+=/ext.12"+=) *(650125-6/-8)* – Voices carry.

Apr 87. (7") *<06571>* **COMING UP CLOSE. / ANGELS NEVER CALL** [–] [59]

—— **MICHAEL MONTES** – keyboards / **JON BRION** + **CLAYTON SCOBEL** – guitar; repl. PESCE

Jan 89. (7"/7"poster) *(653064-7/-0) <08059>* **(BELIEVED YOU WERE) LUCKY. / LIMITS TO LOVE** [ ] [95]
(12"+=/cd-s+=) *(653064-6/-2)* – Voices carry / What about love.

Mar 89. (lp/c/cd) *(460737-1/-4/-2) <44041>* **EVERYTHING'S DIFFERENT NOW** [ ] Nov88 [ ]
– Everything's different now / R.I.P. in Heaven / Why must I / J for Jules / (Believed you were) Lucky / Limits to love / Long gone (buddy) / The other end (of the telescope) / Crash and burn / How can you give up.

Jul 89. (7") **R.I.P. IN HEAVEN. / HOW CAN YOU GIVE UP** [–] [ ]

—— disbanded after above album

– compilations, etc. –

Sep 96. (cd) *Epic; <64944>* **COMING UP CLOSE – A RETROSPECTIVE** [–] [ ]
– Love in a vacuum / I could get used to this / Voices carry / You know the rest / No one is watching you now / On Sunday / Coming up close / Will she just fall down / David denies / What about love / Why must I / The other end of the telescope / J for Jules / Believed you were lucky / Limits to love / Long gone buddy / Do it again. *(UK-iss.Jun99; 485113-2)*

Apr 98. (cd) *Sony; <28466>* **ALL ABOUT LOVE** [–] [ ]

AIMEE MANN

solo with **DAVE GREGORY** – guitar (of XTC)

Imago Imago

Aug 93. (7"/c-s) *(72787 25048-7/-4)* **I SHOULD'VE KNOWN. / JIMMY HOFFA JOKES** [55] [ ]
(cd-s+=) *(72787 25048-2)* – Jacob Marley's chains.

Sep 93. (cd/c/lp) *<(72787 21017/-2/-4/-1)>* **WHATEVER** [39] [ ]

– I should've known / Fifty years after the fair / 4th of July / Could've been anyone / Put me on top / Stupid thing / Say anything / Jacob Marley's chain / Mr. Harris / I could hurt you now / I know there's a word / I've had it / Way back when. *(cd re-iss. Jul96 on 'Geffen'; GFLD 19319)*

Nov 93. (7"/c-s) *(72787 25043-7/-4)* **STUPID THING. / I'VE HAD IT** [47] [–]
(cd-s) *(72787 25043-2)* – ('A'side) / Baby blue / Other end (of the telescope) (live) / Say anything (live).
(cd-s) *(72787 25043-5)* – ('A'side) / Put me on top (live) / Fourth of July (live) / I should've known (live).

Nov 93. (cd-s) *<72787 25032-2>* **I SHOULD'VE KNOWN / TAKE IT BACK** [–] [ ]

Feb 94. (7"/c-s) *(72787 25060-7/-4)* **I SHOULD'VE KNOWN. / TRUTH ON MY SIDE (demo)** [45] [–]
(cd-s+=) *(72787 25060-2)* – Fifty years after the fair (demo) / Put on some speed (demo).
(10") *(72787 25060-0)* – ('A'side) / 4th of July / Stupid thing / The other end (of the telescope).

— with **JON BRION** – guitars, drums, co-writer (some) / **JOHN SANDS** – drums / guests **BERNARD BUTLER** (co-writer SUGARCOATED) / **GLENN TILBROOK + CHRIS DIFFORD / JULIANA HATFIELD / MICHAEL PENN**

Geffen Imago

Jan 95. (c-s) *<25086>* **THAT'S JUST WHAT YOU ARE / I SHOULD'VE KNOWN** [–] [93]

Nov 95. (cd/c) *<(GED/GEC 24951)>* **I'M WITH STUPID** [51] [82]
– Long shot / Choice in the matter / Sugarcoated / You could make a killing / Superball / Amateur / All over now / Par for the course / You're with stupid now / That's just what you are / Frankenstein / Ray / It's not safe.

Apr 96. (c-s) *(GFSC 22133)* **LONG SHOT / YOU'RE WITH STUPID NOW** [ ] [ ]
(cd-s+=) *(GFSTD 22133)* – Driving with one hand on the wheel.

— several AIMEE MANN tracks also surfaced on the s-track to 'Magnolia'

Superego Superego

Jun 00. (cd) *<(SE 002)>* **BACHELOR No.2 – OR THE LAST REMAINS OF THE DODO** [ ] [ ]
– How am I different / Nothing is good enough / Red vines / The fall of the world's own optimist / Satellite / Deathly / Ghost world / Calling it quits / Driving sideways / Just like anyone / Susan / It takes all kinds / You do. *(re-iss. Apr01 on 'V2'; VVR 101587-2)*

V2 Superego

May 01. (cd-s) *(72278)* **CALLING IT QUITS / ONE / GHOST WORLD (acoustic version) / NOTHING IS GOOD ENOUGH (instrumental)** [ ] [–]

Sep 02. (cd) *(VVR 102088-2) <SE 007>* **LOST IN SPACE** [72] Aug02 [35]
– Humpty Dumpty / High on Sunday 51 / Lost in space / This is how it goes / Guys like me / Pavlov's bell / Real bad news / Invisible ink / Today's the day / The moth / It's not.

– compilations, etc. –

Sep 00. (cd) *Hip-O; <524760>* **THE ULTIMATE COLLECTION** [–] [ ]
– That's just what you are / You could make a killing / You're with stupid now / Wise up / Driving with one hand on the wheel / Long shot / Choice in the matter / Voices carry / Take it back / Say anything / Jacob Marley's chain / Amateur / All over now / Baby blue / Everything's different now / Sign of love / The other end of the telescope (live) / Jimmy Hoffa jokes / Stupid thing / I should've known.

Manfred MANN

Formed: London, England ... late '62, initially as The MANN-HUGG BLUES BAND, subsequently naming themselves MANFRED MANN after the band's keyboard player. MANN and HUGG then recruited DAVE RICHMOND, PAUL JONES and MIKE VICKERS, playing local gigs which secured them a deal with the 'H.M.V.' label. Early in 1964, after two flop singles, they had their first chart success, hitting the Top 5 with the harmonica-fuelled R&B classic, '5-4-3-2-1'. They continued to storm the charts throughout the 60's, reaching pole position three times with 'DOO WAH DIDDY DIDDY' (1964), 'PRETTY FLAMINGO' (1966) and 'THE MIGHTY QUINN' (1968). The latter was fronted by MIKE D'ABO, who had replaced the solo bound PAUL JONES. In 1969, MANN and HUGG churned out commercial jingles for Michelen tyres and Ski yogurt before forming the heavier jazz-rock outfit, MANFRED MANN CHAPTER THREE. They delivered a couple of albums for 'Vertigo', soon reverting back to their original name in 1971. The following year, they re-emerged minus HUGG, with the more ambitious and progressive MANFRED MANN'S EARTH BAND. They struggled initially, although they created their own take on GUSTAV HOLST's "Jupiter suite" (from 'The Planets') in the form of 'JOYBRINGER' (a top 10 hit in 1973). A dry period of three years ensued, during which time they released three accessible rock albums, 'SOLAR FIRE', 'THE GOOD EARTH' and 'NIGHTINGALES AND BOMBERS'. The band saw a return to chart action with a cover of BRUCE SPRINGSTEEN's, 'BLINDED BY THE LIGHT', which also hit No.1 in America. Their albums fared a lot better from this point on, another SPRINGSTEEN re-hash, 'SPIRIT IN THE NIGHT', denting the US Top 40 in 1977. In the 80's (and 90's!), his EARTH BAND continued to tread the same ground, releasing a plethora of mediocre cover versions for the coffee-table set. One particular song, 'THE RUNNER', saw them sprinting back into the US Top 30 early in 1984. Over the course of the decade or so, MANFRED MANN delivered the odd pop-rock album, although it was in 1999, that he would return to some kind of press coverage, albeit over the sample/use of his song 'TRIBUTE' on MASSIVE ATTACK's 'Black Mark'; the Bristol posse settled out of court. • **Songwriters:** MANN-HUGG until latter's departure in '71. Covered; DOO WAH DIDDY DIDDY (Exciters) / SHA LA LA (Shirelles) / OH NO NOT MY BABY (Goffin-King) / SMOKESTACK LIGHTNING (Howlin' Wolf) / MY LITTLE RED BOOK (Bacharach-David) / WITH GOD ON OUR SIDE + IF YOU GOTTA GO, GO NOW + JUST LIKE A WOMAN + THE MIGHTY QUINN + PLEASE, MRS.HENRY + others (Bob Dylan) / SWEET PEA (Tommy Roe) / SO LONG DAD + LIVING WITHOUT YOU (Randy Newman) / MY NAME IS JACK (John Simon) / etc. His EARTH BAND covered FATHER OF DAY, FATHER OF NIGHT + YOU, ANGEL YOU + SHELTER FROM THE STORM (Bob Dylan) / SPIRIT IN THE NIGHT + BLINDED BY THE LIGHT + FOR YOU (Bruce Springsteen) / DON'T KILL IT CAROL (Mike Heron) / REDEMPTION SONG (Bob Marley) / DO ANYTHING YOU WANNA DO (Eddie & The Hot Rods) / GOING UNDERGROUND (Jam) / BANQUET (Joni Mitchell) / PLAY WITH FIRE (Rolling Stones) / NOTHING EVER HAPPENS (Del Amitri) / PLEASURE + PAIN (Chapman-Knight) / TUMBLING BALL (M. Spiro) / THE PRICE I PAY (Robert Cray) / LOSE THE TOUCH (C. Schumann) / THE COMPLETE HISTORY OF SEXUAL JEALOUSY (Momus) / 99 LBS (D Bryant) / etc. • **Trivia:** MIKE HUGG wrote 'SHAPES OF THINGS' in 1966 for fellow R&B hitmakers, The YARDBIRDS. MANFRED played Moog synthesizer on URIAH HEEP's 1971 album, 'Look At Yourself'. The 'GLORIFIED MAGNIFIED' track was used for the theme to Radio 1's 'Sound Of The 70's'.

Best CD compilation(s): AGES OF MANN (22 CLASSICS OF THE 60s) (*7) / 20 YEARS OF MANFRED MANN'S EARTH BAND (*6)

MANFRED MANN (b. MANFRED LUBOWITZ, 21 Oct'40, Johannesburg, South Africa) – keyboards / **PAUL JONES** (b.PAUL POND, 24 Feb'42, Portsmouth, England) – vocals, harmonica / **MIKE VICKERS** (b.18 Apr'41, Southampton, England) – guitar / **DAVE RICHMOND** – bass / **MIKE HUGG** (b.11 Aug'42, Andover, England) – drums

H.M.V. Prestige

Jul 63. (7") *(POP 1189)* **WHY SHOULD WE NOT. / BROTHER JACK** [ ] [–]

Oct 63. (7") *(POP 1225)* **COCK-A-HOOP. / NOW YOU'RE NEEDING ME** [ ] [–]

— **TOM McGUINESS** (b. 2 Dec'41, Wimbledon, London, England) – bass (ex-ROOSTERS) repl. RICHMOND

Jan 64. (7") *(POP 1252)* **5-4-3-2-1. / WITHOUT YOU** [5] Mar64 [ ]

H.M.V. Ascot

Apr 64. (7") *(POP 1282) <2151>* **HUBBLE BUBBLE TOIL AND TROUBLE. / I'M YOUR KINGPIN** [11] [ ]

Jul 64. (7") *(POP 1320) <2157>* **DOO WAH DIDDY DIDDY. / WHAT YOU GONNA DO** [1] Aug64 [1]
(re-iss. Oct82; PMS 1003)

Sep 64. (lp) *(CLP 1731)* **THE FIVE FACES OF MANFRED MANN** [3] [–]
– Smokestack lightning / Don't ask me what I say / It's gonna work out fine / Sack of wool / What you gonna do / I'm your kingpin / Hoochie coochie / Down the road apiece / I've got my mojo working / Mr. Analles / Untie me / Bring it to Jerome / Without you / You've got to take it. *(cd-iss. Jun97 on 'E.M.I.'; DORIG 121)*

Oct 64. (7") *(POP 1346) <2165>* **SHA LA LA. / JOHN HARDY** [3] Nov64 [12]

Nov 64. (lp) *<16015>* **THE MANFRED MANN ALBUM** [–] [35]
– Do wah diddy diddy / Sack o' woe / Don't ask me what I say / What you gonna do / Got my mojo working / I'm your hoochie coochie man / Smokestack lightning / It's gonna work out fine / Down the road apiece / Untie me / Bring it to Jerome / Without you.

Jan 65. (7") *(POP 1381) <2170>* **COME TOMORROW. / WHAT DID I DO WRONG** [4] Feb65 [50]

Mar 65. (lp) *<ALS 16018>* **THE FIVE FACES OF MANFRED MANN** [–] [ ]
– Sha la la / Come tomorrow / She / Can't believe it / John Hardy / Did you have to do that / Watermelon man / I'm your kingpin / Hubble bubble (toil and trouble) / You've got to take it / Dashing away with the smoothing iron / Groovin'.

Apr 65. (7") *(POP 1413)* **OH NO NOT MY BABY. / WHAT AM I DOING WRONG** [11] [–]

Apr 65. (7") *<2181>* **POISON IVY. / I CAN'T BELIEVE WHAT YOU SAY** [–] [ ]

Jun 65. (7") *<2184>* **MY LITTLE RED BOOK. / WHAT AM I DOING WRONG** [–] [ ]
<re-iss. 1966; 2241>

Jul 65. (lp) *<ALS 16201>* **MY LITTLE RED BOOK OF WINNERS** [–] [ ]
– My little red book / Oh no, not my baby / What am I to do / One in the middle / You gave me somebody to love / You're for me / Poison Ivy / Without you / Brother Jack / Love like yours / I can't believe what you say / With God on your side.

Sep 65. (7") *(POP 1466)* **IF YOU GOTTA GO, GO NOW. / STAY AROUND** [2] [–]

Oct 65. (lp) *(CLP 1911) <ALS 16024>* **MANN MADE** [7] [ ]
– Since I don't have you / You're for me / Look away / L.S.D. / The abominable snowman / Watch your step / The way you do the things you do / Stormy Monday blues / Hi lili hi lo / I really do believe / Bear Hugg / You don't know me / I'll make it up to you. *(re-iss. Nov69 on 'Regal Starline'; SRS 5007)*

Oct 65. (7") *<2194>* **IF YOU GOTTA GO, GO NOW. / THE ONE IN THE MIDDLE** [–] [ ]

Jan 66. (7") *<2210>* **HI LILI, HI LO. / SHE NEEDS COMPANY** [–] [ ]

— (PETE BURFORD and DAVID HYDE deputised for VICKERS on tour until) / **JACK BRUCE** (b.14 May'43, Lanarkshire, Scotland) – bass (ex-JOHN MAYALL, ex-GRAHAM BOND) repl. VICKERS / added **LYN DOBSON** – saxophone / **HENRY LOWTHER** – trumpet (McGUINESS now guitar)

H.M.V. U.A.

Apr 66. (7") *(POP 1523) <50040>* **PRETTY FLAMINGO. / YOU'RE STANDING BY** [1] Jun66 [29]

— **MANN, HUGG** and **McGUINESS** added new members **MIKE D'ABO** (b. 1 Mar'44, Bethworth, England) – vocals (ex-BAND OF ANGELS) repl. JONES who went solo, etc. / **KLAUS VOORMAN** (b.29 Apr'42, Berlin, Germany) – bass repl. JACK BRUCE who formed CREAM.

Jun 66. (7") *(POP 1541)* **YOU GAVE ME SOMEBODY TO LOVE. / POISON IVY** [36] [–]

Sep 66. *<50066>* **DO YOU HAVE TO DO THAT. / WHEN WILL I BE LOVED** [–] [ ]

Fontana Mercury

Jul 66. (7") *(TF 730) <72607>* **JUST LIKE A WOMAN. / I WANNA BE RIGHT** [10] [ ]

Oct 66. (7") *(TF 757) <72629>* **SEMI-DETACHED SUBURBAN MR. JAMES. / MORNING AFTER THE PARTY** [2] [ ]

Oct 66. (lp; stereo/mono) *(S+/TL 5377)* **AS IS** [22] [–]
– Trouble and tea / A now and then thing / Each other's company / Box office draw / Dealer dealer / Morning after the party / Another kind of music / As long as I have lovin' / Autumn leaves / Superstitious guy / You're my girl / Just like a woman.

Dec 66. (lp) *<6549>* **PRETTY FLAMINGO** [–] [ ]
– Pretty flamingo / Let's go get stoned / Tired of trying / Bored with living / Scared of dying / I put a spell on you / It's getting late / You're standing by / Machines / Stay around / Tennessee waltz / Drive man / Do you have to do that.

Mar 67. (7") *(TF 812) <72676>* **HA! HA! SAID THE CLOWN. / FEELING SO GOOD** [4] [ ]

May 67. (7") *(TF 828)* **SWEET PEA. / ONE WAY** [36] [–]

Sep 67. (7") *(TF 862)* **SO LONG DAD. / FUNNIEST GIG** [ ] [–]

Jan 68. (lp) *(TL 5460)* **UP THE JUNCTION (Soundtrack)** [ ] [–]
– Up the junction (vocal) / Sing songs of love / Walking around up the junction (instrumental) / Love theme (instrumental) / Up the junction (vocal & instrumental) / Just for me / Love theme (instrumental) / Sheila's dance / Belgravia / Wailing horn / I need your love / Up the junction (vocal). *(re-iss. 1970; 6852 005) (cd-iss. Nov99 on 'R.P.M.'++; RPM 189)* – Sleepy hollow.

Fontana Mercury

Jan 68. (7") *(TF 897) <72770>* **MIGHTY QUINN. / BY REQUEST EDWIN GARVEY** [1] [10]
(re-iss. Jun82 on 'Old Gold'; OG 9252)

Mar 68. (lp) *(SFL 13003)* **WHAT A MANN** (compilation) [ ] [–]
– Funniest gig / Sunny / Get away / With a girl like you / Sweet pea / Wild thing / The morning after the party / Feeling so good / One way / So long dad.

Mar 68. (7") *(TF 908)* **THEME – UP THE JUNCTION. / SLEEPY HOLLOW** [ ] [–]

May 68. (lp) *<61168>* **MIGHTY QUINN** [–] [ ]
– Mighty Quinn / Ha! ha! said the clown / Every day another hair turns grey / It's so easy falling / Big Betty / Cubist town / Country dancing / Semi-detached suburban Mr. James / The vicar's daughter / Each and every day / No better, no worse.

Jun 68. (lp; stereo/mono) *(S+/TL 5470)* **MIGHTY GARVEY!** [ ] [–]
– Happy families / No better, no worse / Each and every day / Country dancing / It's so easy falling / Happy families / Mighty Quinn / Big Betty / The vicar's daughter / Every day another hair turns grey / Cubist town / Ha! ha! said the clown / Harry the one-man band / Happy families.

Jun 68. (7") *(TF 943) <72872>* **MY NAME IS JACK. / THERE IS A MAN** [8] [ ]

Dec 68. (7") *(TF 985) <72879>* **FOX ON THE RUN. / TOO MANY PEOPLE** [5] [97]

May 69. (7") *(TF 1013) <72921>* **RAGAMUFFIN MAN. / A 'B' SIDE** [8] [ ]

— split mid 69. TOM formed McGUINESS FLINT. D'ABO went solo, and VOORMAN joined JOHN LENNON's PLASTIC ONO BAND

MANFRED MANN'S CHAPTER III

MANFRED retained **MIKE HUGG** – vocals, electric piano. — Recruited **BRIAN HUGG** – guitar / **STEVE YORK** – bass plus session singers, drummers and wind section

Vertigo Polydor

Nov 69. (lp) *(VO 3) <4013>* **MANFRED MANN CHAPTER THREE** [ ] [ ]
– Travelling lady / Snakeskin garter / Konekuf / Sometimes / Devil woman / Time / One way glass / Mister you're a better man than I / Ain't it sad / A study in inaccuracy / Where am I going. *(cd-iss. Feb94 on 'Cohesion'; MFMCD 14)*

Mar 70. (7") *<14026>* **SNAKESKIN GARTER. / SOMETIMES** [–] [ ]

— on session **CHRIS SLADE** – drums (alongside others)

Sep 70. (7") *(6059 012)* **HAPPY BEING ME. / DEVIL WOMAN** [ ] [–]

Oct 70. (lp) *(6360 012)* **MANFRED MANN CHAPTER III, VOL.2** [ ] [–]
– Lady Ace / I ain't laughing / Poor sad Sue / Jump before you think / It's good to be alive / Happy being me / Virginia. *(cd-iss. Feb94 on 'Cohesion'; MFMCD 15) (cd re-mast.Dec99 on 'Cohesion'; MANN 002)*

MANFRED MANN'S EARTH BAND

— His new band now featured **CHRIS SLADE** – drums (now a full time member) / **MICK ROGERS** – vocals, guitar repl. MIKE HUGG / **COLIN PATTENDEN** – bass repl. STEVE YORK and BRIAN HUGG

Philips Polydor

Jun 71. (7"; as MANFRED MANN; w-drawn) *<14074>* **CALIFORNIA COASTLINE. / PART TIME** [–] [ ]

Jun 71. (7"; as MANFRED MANN) *(6006 122) <14113>* **LIVING WITHOUT YOU. / TRIBUTE** [ ] Jan72 [69]

Sep 71. (7"; as MANFRED MANN) *(6006 251)* **MRS HENRY. / PRAYER** [ ] [ ]

Feb 72. (lp) *(6308 086) <5015>* **MANFRED MANN'S EARTH BAND** [ ] [ ]
– California coastline / Captain Bobby Stout / Sloth / Living without you / Tribute / Mrs Henry / Jump sturdy / Prayer / Part time man / I'm up and leaving. *(re-iss. Apr77 & 1981 on 'Bronze'; BRON 252) (re-iss. Jan90 on 'Castle' lp/cd; CLA LP/CD 150) (re-iss. Jan91 on 'Cohesion' lp/c/cd; COMME/+T/CD 6) (cd re-mast.Aug99 on 'Cohesion'; MANN 003)*

Mar 72. (7") *<14130>* **PART TIME MAN. / I'M UP AND LEAVING** [–] [ ]

Sep 72. (lp) *(6308 125) <5031>* **GLORIFIED MAGNIFIED** [ ] [ ]
– Meat / Look around / One way glass / I'm gonna have you all / Down home / Our friend George / Ashes to the wind / It's all over now, baby blue / Glorified magnified. *(re-iss. Apr77 & 1981 on 'Bronze') (cd-iss. Dec93 on 'Cohesion'; MFMCD 11) (cd re-mast.Dec99 on 'Cohesion'; MANN 004)*

Nov 72. (7") *(6006 251)* **MEAT. / GLORIFIED MAGNIFIED** [ ] [–]

Feb 73. (7") *<14164>* **IT'S ALL OVER NOW, BABY BLUE. / ASHES TO THE WIND** [–] [ ]

Vertigo Polydor

Apr 73. (7"; as EARTH BAND) *(6059 078)* **GET YOUR ROCKS OFF. / SADJOY** [ ] [–]

Jun 73. (lp) *(6360 087) <5050>* **MESSIN'** <US-title 'GET YOUR ROCKS OFF'> [ ] [ ]
– Buddah / Messin' / Cloudy eyes / Get your rocks off / Sadjoy / Black and blue / Mardi Gras day. *(re-iss. Apr77 & 1981 on 'Bronze'; BRON 261) (re-iss. Jan90 on 'Castle' lp/cd; CLA LP/CD 151) (re-iss. Jan91 on 'Cohesion' lp/c/cd; COMME/+T/CD 7)*

Jun 73. (7") *<14173>* **MARDI GRAS DAY. / SADJOY** [–] [ ]

Aug 73. (7") *<14191>* **GET YOUR ROCKS OFF. / ASHES TO THE WIND** [–] [ ]

Aug 73. (7") *(6059 083)* **JOYBRINGER. / CAN'T EAT MEAT** [9] [–]

Sep 73. (7") *<14205>* **JOYBRINGER. / CLOUDY EYES** [–] [ ]

Bronze Polydor

Nov 73. (lp) *(ILPS 9265) <6019>* **SOLAR FIRE** [ ] [96]
– Father of night, in the beginning / Pluto the dog / Solar fire / Saturn (Mercury) / Earth the circle (pts.1 & 2). *(re-iss. Apr77 & 1981; BRON 265) (re-iss. Nov87 on 'Legacy' lp/c/cd; LLP/LLK/LLCD 121) (re-iss. Jan91 on 'Cohesion' lp/c/cd; COMME/+T/CD 1)*

Mar 74. (7") **FATHER OF DAY, FATHER OF NIGHT. / SOLAR FIRE 2** [ ] [–]

Bronze Warners

Oct 74. (7") *(BRO 13)* **BE NOT TOO HARD. / EARTH HYMN (part 2a)** [ ] [–]

Oct 74. (lp/c) *(ILPS/ICT 9306) <BS 2826>* **THE GOOD EARTH** [ ] [ ]
– Give me the good earth / Launching place / I'll be gone / Earth hymn (pts.1 & 2) / Sky high / Be not too hard. *(re-iss. Apr77 + 1981; BRON 306) (cd-iss. Dec93 on 'Cohesion'; MFMCD 12) (cd re-mast.Mar99 on 'Cohesion'; MANN 007)*

Jul 75. (7") *(BRO 18) <8152>* **SPIRIT IN THE NIGHT. / AS ABOVE SO BELOW (part 2)** [ ] [ ]

Aug 75. (lp/c) *(ILPS/ICT 9337) <BS 2877>* **NIGHTINGALES AND BOMBERS** [ ] [ ]
– Spirit in the night / Countdown / Time is right / Crossfade / Visionary mountains / Nightingales and bombers / Fat Nelly / As above so below. *(re-iss. Apr77 + 1981; BRON 337) (re-iss. 1987 on 'Castle' lp/cd; CLA LP/CD 137) (re-iss. Jan91 on 'Cohesion' lp/c/cd; COMME/+T/CD 8)*

Feb 76. (7") *<8176>* **SPIRIT IN THE NIGHT. / AS ABOVE SO BELOW** [–] [97]

— **CHRIS THOMPSON** – vocals repl. ROGERS who later formed AVIATOR / added **DAVE FLETT** – guitar

Aug 76. (7") *(BRO 29) <8252>* **BLINDED BY THE LIGHT. / STARBIRD No.2** [6] [1]

Aug 76. (lp/c) *(ILPS/ICT 9357) <BS 3055>* **THE ROARING SILENCE** [10] [10]
– Blinded by the light / Singing the dolphin through / Waiter, there's a yawn in my ear / The road to Babylon / This side of Paradise / Starbird / Questions. *(re-iss. Apr77 + 1981; BRON 357) (re-iss. Nov87 on 'Legacy' lp/c/cd; LLP/LLK/LLCD 122) (re-iss. Jan91 on 'Cohesion' lp/c/cd; COMME/+T/CD 2)*

Nov 76. (7") *(BRO 34)* **QUESTIONS. / WAITER, THERE'S A YAWN IN MY EAR No.2** [ ] [–]

Dec 76. (7") *<8355>* **QUESTIONS. / SPIRIT IN THE NIGHT** [–] [ ]

— **PAT KING** – bass (ex-SHANGHAI, etc.) repl. PATTENDEN (to TERRA NOVA)

Jun 77. (7") *<8355>* **SPIRIT IN THE NIGHT (remix). / ROAD TO BABYLON** [–] [40]

Nov 77. (7") *(BRO 48)* **CALIFORNIA. / CHICAGO INSTITUTE** [ ] [–]

Feb 78. (lp/c) *(BRON/+C 507) <BS 3157>* **WATCH** [33] [83]
– Circles / Drowning on dry land / Fish soup / California / Chicago institute / Davy's on the road again / Martha's madman / The mighty Quinn. *(re-iss. 1981; same) (re-iss. Nov87 on 'Legacy'; LLCD 123) (re-iss. Jan91 on 'Cohesion' lp/c/cd; COOME/+T/CD 3)*

Mar 78. (7") *(BRO 51)* **THE MIGHTY QUINN. / TINY** [ ] [–]

Apr 78. (7") *(BRO 52) <8620>* **DAVY'S ON THE ROAD AGAIN. / BOUILLABAISE** [6] Sep78 [ ]

Jul 78. (7") *<8574>* **CALIFORNIA. / BOUILLABAISE** [–] [ ]

— After a short split, MANN reformed band retaining **THOMPSON + KING / STEVE WALLER** – guitar (ex-GONZALES) repl. FLETT / **GEOFF BRITTON** – drums (ex-EAST OF EDEN, ex-WINGS, ex-ROUGH DIAMOND, ex-CHAMPION) repl. CHRIS SLADE who joined URIAH HEEP. He later joined The FIRM (see; LED ZEPPELIN)

Feb 79. (7") *(BRO 68)* **YOU ANGEL YOU. / OUT IN THE DISTANCE** [54] [–]

Mar 79. (lp/c) *(BRON/+C 516) <3302>* **ANGEL STATION** [30] [ ]
– Don't kill it Carol / You angel you / Hollywood town / Belle of the Earth / Platform end / Angels at my gate / You are I am / Waiting for the rain / Resurrection. *(re-iss. Nov87 on 'Legacy' lp/c/cd; LLP/LLK/LLCD 124) (re-iss. Jan91 on 'Cohesion' lp/c/cd; COMME/+T/CD 4) (cd re-mast.Aug99 on 'Cohesion'; MANN 011)*

May 79. (7") *<8850>* **YOU ANGEL YOU. / BELLE OF THE EARTH** [–] [58]

Jun 79. (7"/7"pic-d) *(BRO/BPO 77)* **DON'T KILL IT CAROL. / BLINDED BY THE LIGHT** [45] [ ]

— **JOHN LINGWOOD** – drums repl. BRITTON who became ill. / guests included **PETER MARSH, WILLY FINLAYSON.** (vocals – **CHRIS THOMPSON**)

Oct 80. (lp/c) *(BRON/+C 529) <BSK 3498>* **CHANCE** [ ] [87]
– Lies (through the 80's) / On the run / For you / Adolescent dream / Fritz the blank / Stranded / This is your heart / No guarentee / Heart on the street. *(re-iss. 1987 on 'Castle' lp/cd; CLA LP/CD 133) (re-iss. Jan91 on 'Cohesion' lp/c/cd; COMME/+T/CD 9) (cd re-mast.Aug99 on 'Cohesion'; MANN 012)*

Nov 80. (7") *(BRO 103) <49762>* **LIES (THROUGH THE 80'S). / ADOLESCENT DREAM** [ ] Jun81 [ ]

Jan 81. (7") *(BRO 113) <49678>* **FOR YOU. / A FOOL I AM** [ ] [ ]

— **MATT IRVING** – bass (ex-DREAM POLICE, ex-BABYS, ex-LONGDANCER) repl. KING

Nov 81. (7") *(BRO 137)* **I (WHO HAVE NOTHING). / MAN IN JAM** [ ] [–]

Bronze Arista

Feb 82. (7") *(BRO 141)* **EYES OF NOSTRADAMUS. / HOLIDAY'S END** [ ] [–]
(12"+=) *(BROX 141)* – Man in jam.

Jun 82. (7") *(BRO 150)* **REDEMPTION SONG (NO KWAZULU). / WARDREAM** [ ] [–]

Nov 82. (7") *(BRO 157)* **TRIBAL STATISTICS. / WHERE DO THEY SEND THEM** [ ] [–]

Jan 83. (lp/c) *(BRON/C 543) <8194>* **SOMEWHERE IN AFRIKA** [87] Mar84 [40]
– Tribal statistics / Eyes of Nostradamus / Third world service / Demolition man / Brothers and sisters of Azania:- (a) Afrika suite – (b) Brothers and sisters of Afrika – (c) To ban Tustan – (d) Koze Kobenini (how long must we wait?) / Lalela / Redemption song (no Kwazulu) / Somewhere in Afrika. *(re-iss. Nov87 on 'Legacy' lp/c/cd; LLP/LLK/LLCD 125) (re-iss. Jan91 on 'Cohesion' lp/c/cd; COMME/+T/CD 1) (cd re-mast.Aug99 on 'Cohesion'; MANN 013)*

Jan 83. (7") *(BRO 161)* **DEMOLITION MAN. / IT'S STILL THE SAME** [ ] [–]

Feb 84. (7") *(BRO 177)* **DAVY'S ON THE ROAD AGAIN (live). / THE MIGHTY QUINN (live)** [ ] [–]
(12"+=) *(BROX 177)* – Don't kill it Carol (live).

Feb 84. (lp/c) *(BRON/+C 550)* **BUDAPEST (live)** [ ] [ ]
– Spirits in the night / Demolition man / For you / Davy's on the road again / Lies (through the 80's) / Blinded by the light / Redemption song (no Kwazulu) / The mighty Quinn. *(cd-iss. 1988 on 'Ariola'; ACD 610163) (re-iss. Jan91 on 'Cohesion' lp/c/cd; COMME/+T/CD 10) (cd re-mast.Dec99 on 'Cohesion'; MANN 014)*

— **MICK RODGERS** – vocals, guitar returned to repl. WALLER (MANN, THOMPSON, LINGWOOD) also still in band. (IRVING left to join LORDS OF THE NEW CHURCH. He later joined PAUL YOUNG band).

Jan 84. (7") *(BRO 180)* **(THE) RUNNER. / NO TRANSKEI** [ ] [–]
(12"+=) *(BROX 180)* – Lies (through the 80's).

Jan 84. (7") *<9143>* **(THE) RUNNER. / WHERE DO THEY SEND THEM** [–] [22]

Jun 84. (7") *<9203>* **REBEL. / FIGURES ON A PAGE** [–] [ ]

10-Virgin not iss.

Mar 86. (7"/12") *(TEN 115/+12)* **DO ANYTHING YOU WANNA DO. / CROSSFIRE** [ ] [–]

May 86. (7"/12") *(TEN/+T 121)* **GOING UNDERGROUND. / I SHALL BE RESCUED** [ ] [–]

Jun 86. (lp/c/cd) *(XID/CXID/DIXCD 17)* **CRIMINAL TANGO** [ ] [–]
– Going underground / Who are the mystery kids / Banquet / Killer on the loose / Do anything you wanna do / Rescue / You got me through the heart / Hey bulldog / Crossfire. *(cd re-iss. Aug99 on 'Cohesion'+=; MANN 015)* – Going underground (alt.) / Do anything you wanna do (alt.) / (The) Runner / Rebel.

— **MAGGIE RYDER** – vocals repl. CHRIS THOMPSON who went solo (guests incl.**FRANK MEAD** – saxophone / **DENNY NEWMAN** – bass, vocals on 1)

Oct 87. (7"/12") *(TEN/+T 196)* **GERONIMO'S CADILLAC. / TWO FRIENDS** [ ] [–]

Nov 87. (lp/c/cd) *(DIX/CDIX/DIXCD 69)* **MASQUE** [ ] [–]
– Joybringer (from 'Jupiter') / Billies orno bounce (including Billies bounce) / What you give is what you get (start) / Rivers run dry / Planets schmanets / Geronimo's Cadillac / Sister Billies bounce (including Sister Sadie & Billies bounce) / Telegram to Monica / A couple of mates (from 'Mars' & 'Saturn') / Neptune *Icebringer) / The hymn (from 'Jupiter) / We're going wrong. *(cd re-mast.Dec99 on 'Cohesion'; MANN 016)*

Kaz Priority

Aug 92. (cd) *(KAZCD 902) <57123>* **MANFRED MANN'S PLAIN MUSIC** [ ] [ ]
– Kiowa / Medicine song / Wounded Knee / Sikelele / Hunting bow / Salmon fishing / Laguna / Instrumedicine song / Sikelele II. *(cd re-mast.Mar99 on 'Cohesion'; MANN 017)*

— **MANFRED MANN** with **CHRIS THOMPSON + NOEL McCALLA** – vocals / **MICK ROGERS** – guitars / **STEVE KINCH** – bass / **CLIVE BUNKER + DAVID FARMER** – drums / + guests

Grapevine not iss.

Jun 96. (cd/c) *(GRA CD/MC 213)* **SOFT VENGEANCE** [ ] [–]
– SOFT: Pleasure and pain / Play with fire / Nothing ever happens / Shelter from the storm / Tumbling ball / The price I pay / Lose the touch / Adults only / Wherever love drops (part one) / (interval 10 seconds) / VENGEANCE: The complete history of sexual jealousy / 99 lbs / Miss you / Nature of the beast / Wherever love drops (part two).

– compilations, others, etc. –

Jul 77. (lp) *Vertigo; (9199 107)* **MANFRED MANN'S EARTH BAND 1971-73** [ ] [–]

Oct 90. (7") *Cohesion;* **DAVY'S ON THE ROAD AGAIN. / BLINDED BY THE LIGHT** [ ] [–]

Jan 91. (cd/c/lp) *Cohesion; (BOMME 1 CD/MC/LP)* **20 YEARS OF MANFRED MANN'S EARTH BAND 1971-1991** [ ] [–]
– Blinded by the light / California / Joybringer / Tribal statistics / Somewhere in Africa / Davy's on the road again / You angel you / The runner / Questions / The mighty Quinn / Angels at the gate / For you / Demolition man.

Nov 92. (10xlp-box/10xc-box/10xcd-box) *Cohesion; (COMME/+T/CD 6)* **MANFRED MANN'S EARTH BAND** [ ] [–]
– (albums from 1972-1986) *(free-12"+=)*

Oct 99. (cd) *Cohesion; (MANN 018)* **THE BEST OF MANFRED MANN'S EARTH BAND REMASTERED VOL.1** [ ] [ ]

Mar 00. (cd) *Music Club; (MCCD 414)* **BLINDIN': A STUNNING COLLECTION OF POWERFUL MASTERPIECES 1973-1982** [ ] [–]

Apr 02. (cd) *Brilliant; (BT 33085)* **ON THE ROAD** [ ] [–]

– (early MANN selective) compilations, etc. –

on 'H.M.V.' unless otherwise mentioned

Jul 65. (7"ep) *(7EG 8908)* **ONE IN THE MIDDLE** [6] [–]
– With God on our side / Watermelon man / What am I to do / One in the middle.

Sep 66. (lp) *(CLP 3559)* **MANN MADE HITS** [11] [–]
– Pretty flamingo / The one in the middle / Oh no not my baby / John Hardy / Spirit feel / Come tomorrow / Do wah diddy diddy / With God on our side / There's no living without your loving / Groovin' / I'm your kingpin / Sha la la / 5-4-3-2-1 / If you gotta go, go now.

Jan 67. (lp; mono/stereo) *(CLP/CSD 3594)* **SOUL OF MANN** (instrumentals) [40] [–]
– I got you babe / Bare Hugg / Spirit feel / Why should we not / L.S.D. / (I can't get no) Satisfaction / God rest ye merry gentlemen / My generation / Mr. Anello / Still I'm sad / Tengo tango / Brother Jack / The abominable snowman / Sack o' woe. *(re-iss. Jul85 on 'See For Miles'; SEE 52) (cd-iss. Jan99 on 'E.M.I.'; 498935-2)*

Sep 79. (d-lp/c) *E.M.I.; (EMTV/TC-EMTV 19)* **SEMI-DETACHED SUBURBAN (20 GREAT HITS OF THE SIXTIES)** [9] [–]
– Do wah diddy diddy / 5-4-3-2-1 / Sha la la / Hubble bubble, toil and trouble / Hi lili hi lo / One in the middle / Got my mojo working / With God on our side / Come tomorrow / If you gotta go, go now / Pretty flamingo / Semi-detached suburban Mr. James / There's no living without your loving / Just like a woman / Oh no not my baby / Ha ha said the clown / My name is Jack / Fox on the run / Ragamuffin man / Mighty Quinn.

Jun 89. (lp/c/cd) *E.M.I.; (SEE/+K/CD 252)* **THE EP COLLECTION** [ ] [–]
(re-iss. cd Nov94; same)

Jul 90. (cd/c/d-lp) *Castle; (CCS CD/MC/LP 245)* **THE COLLECTION** [ ] [–]

Jan 93. (cd/c/lp) *Polygram TV; (514362-2/-4/-1)* **AGES OF MANN (22 CLASSICS OF THE 60's)** [23] [–]
(re-iss. Sep95 cd/c; same)

Aug 94. (cd/c) *Arcade; (ARC 31001-62/-74)* **THE VERY BEST OF MANFRED MANN'S EARTH BAND** [69] [–]

Jun 95. (cd) *Disky; (BA 86009-2)* **BASIC ORIGINALS** [ ] [–]

Oct 97. (cd) *E.M.I.; (CDABBEY 101)* **AT ABBEY ROAD 1963-1966** [ ] [ ]

Oct 97. (cd) *BR Music; (BX 5152)* **SINGLES IN THE 60'S** [ ] [–]

Mar 98. (cd; as The MANFREDS) *Camden; (74321 56663-2)* **5-4-3-2-1** [ ] [–]

Aug 98. (cd) *Music For Pleasure; (CDMFP 6381)* **THE VERY BEST OF MANFRED MANN** [ ] [–]

Nov 98. (d-cd) *Disky; (HR 85300-2)* **ORIGINAL GOLD** [ ] [ ]

Nov 99. (cd) *Spectrum; (552375-2)* **THE WORLD OF MANFRED MANN** [ ] [–]

Apr 00. (cd) *Disky; (SI 25075-2)* **THE BEST OF THE 60'S** [ ] [ ]

Aug 00. (cd) *E.M.I.; (528496-2)* **THE BEST OF MANFRED MANN** [ ] [ ]

Feb 01. (d-cd) *Raven; (RVCD 102)* **ALL MANNER OF MENN 1963-1969** [ ] [ ]

Feb 01. (cd) *EMI Plus; (5760350)* **THE STORY** [ ] [ ]

Apr 02. (cd) *Disky; (GO 79346-2)* **5-4-3-2-1** [ ] [–]

Feb 03. (d-cd) *Creature; (MANFRED 1)* **THE EVOLUTION OF MANN** [ ] [–]

Mar 03. (cd) *E.M.I.; (583112-2)* **A'S, B'S & EP'S** [ ] [ ]

Marilyn MANSON

Formed: Fort Lauderdale, South Florida, USA ... early 90's by the once pneumonia-crippled MANSON (real name BRIAN WARNER), an ordained minister in the Church Of Satan (run by Anton LeVey), provoking the wrath of conservative America. MANSON had begun his infamous career as a music journalist, simultaneously forming MARILYN MANSON & THE SPOOKY KIDS and taking inspiration from schlock-meisters like ALICE COOPER, KISS and surprisingly, veteran UK goth throwbacks, ALIEN SEX FIEND. After interviewing TRENT REZNOR, he/they secured a support slot with Reznor's NINE INCH NAILS, ultimately resulting in a record deal with TRENT's 'Nothing' records. Although the ghoulish Edward Scissorhands lookalike MANSON dated porn-star TRACII LORDS, he caused uproar at a hometown show when he allegedly mouthed ROBIN FINCK's (NIN) "pink oboe". The piercingly contact-lensed MANSON, whose onstage regalia usually included surgical corset and stockings, completed his OTT persona by routinely mutilating himself with knives, light-bulbs and indeed anything that came to hand. Like ALICE COOPER before him, he overshadowed the rest of his band (who comprised DAISY BERKOWITZ, MADONNA WAYNE GACY, SARA LEE LUCAS and smackhead GIDGET GEIN – the latter was deposed by TWIGGY RAMIREZ). Typically subtle as the proverbial sledgehammer, the band members' names were stitched together from glamorous icons and serial killers! As for the music, MANSON's vinyl/cd freakshow began with 1994's sub-goth posturing of 'PORTRAIT OF AN AMERICAN FAMILY'. GINGER took over drum duties for their second set, a collection of remixes entitled 'SMELLS LIKE CHILDREN', which included gruesome versions of SWEET DREAMS (Eurythmics), I PUT A SPELL ON YOU (Screamin' Jay Hawkins) and ROCK'N'ROLL NIGGER (Patti Smith) – he had previously covered Gary Numan's 'DOWN IN THE PARK'. Later that year, MANSON and Co. finally launched a full-scale assault on the moral majority/minority (delete as appropriate) with the inflammatory 'ANTICHRIST SUPERSTAR', which crucified the Billboard chart at No.3. They finally drove a stake through England's conservative heart in 1997, when MANSON (at that time the beau of MTV babe Julia Valet) wowed audiences at secret gigs around the country. By this point, they had also introduced new guitarist ZIM ZUM, who replaced DAISY for the UK Top 20 single, 'BEAUTIFUL PEOPLE', the unholy climax of MANSON's bizarre career to date. Whatever else he is, MANSON is a consummate showman, enticing ghoulish audiences with threats of onstage suicide, the ultimate in 90's entertainment, presumably ? (that's if the Christian extremists don't get 'im first). MANSON (BRIAN) re-invented himself and became a BOWIE-clone/freak "undressed" eunuchoid-fashion on the cover of the band's 1998 US chart-topping set, 'MECHANICAL ANIMALS', "Aladdin INsane" you could say! The Manson who fell to Earth indeed, it looked like we'd have to wait even longer before his "Rock'n'roll Suicide". Earlier in the year, his first book, the autobiographical, 'The Long Hard Road Out Of Hell', was published and contained insights into how WARNER/MANSON's deranged brain evolved. With controversy never a light year away, the man's "evil-metal" music was even brought into question when two MARILYN MANSON-obsessed kamikaze teenagers gunned down thirteen people (12 students and a teacher – another 28 were injured) inside Columbine High School, near Denver. MANSON immediately cancelled the rest of the band's tour and sent his sympathies to the bereaved while answering Right-wing politicians who were intent on blaming MANSON and the world of Heavy Metal – they should ask themselves how easy it was for "easily-led" youngsters (and anyone with that constitution) to obtain firearms and does any other music genre such as Country or Pop get the same media furore when one of its klan goes haywire. Down but not out, the beleaguered scapegoat attempted a resurrection of sorts with 'HOLY WOOD' (2000), summoning up the darker forces which informed 'ANTICHRIST . . .' while retaining the more accessible textures of 'MECHANICAL . . .'. The question is whether MANSON's carefully manicured goth-horror schtick actually has the power to shock anymore. With a career so reliant on image, can the music exist independently once that image has become a cliche? Answers on the back of an inverted cross to the usual address. Judging by the lofty ambitions and even loftier concept of 'THE GOLDEN AGE OF GROTESQUE' (2003), MANSON's not content to become a caricature just yet. A barbed, twisted synthesis of pre-war European theatrics and his continuing obsession with the darker side of Hollywood, the record mightn't have restored him to his public enemy number one status but it at least demonstrated his willingness to at least try for some originality. • **Covers:** TAINTED LOVE (Soft Cell) / BIZARRE LOVE TRIANGLE (New Order) / SUICIDE IS PAINLESS (from 'M.A.S.H.') / PLEASE, PLEASE, PLEASE, LET ME GET WHAT I WANT (Smiths).

Album rating: PORTRAIT OF AN AMERICAN FAMILY (*6) / SMELLS LIKE CHILDREN (*6) / ANTICHRIST SUPERSTAR (*8) / MECHANICAL ANIMALS (*7) / THE LAST TOUR ON EARTH (*5) / HOLY WOOD (*7) / THE GOLDEN AGE OF GROTESQUE (*7)

REVEREND MARILYN MANSON (b. BRIAN WARNER, 5 Jan'69, Canton, Ohio) – vocals / **MADONNA WAYNE GACY** (b. STEPHEN) – keyboards, organ, theremin, saxophone, samples / **DAISY BERKOWITZ** (b. SCOTT MITCHELL PUTESKY) – guitars / **TWIGGY RAMIREZ** – bass; repl. GIDGET GEIN (b.BRAD STEWART) / **SARA LEE LUCAS** (b. FREDDY STREITHORST) – drums

Nothing-Interscope | Nothing-Interscope

Jun 94. (cd-ep) *<INTDM 95902>* **GET YOUR GUNN / MISERY MACHINE / MOTHER INFERIOR GOT HER GUNN / REVELATION No.9** [–] [ ]

Dec 94. (cd/c/d-lp) *<(IND 92344)>* **PORTRAIT OF AN AMERICAN FAMILY** [ ] [ ]
– Prelude (the family trip) / Cake and sodomy / Lunchbox / Organ grinder / Cyclops / Dope hat / Get your gunn / Wrapped in plastic / Dogma / Sweet tooth / Snake eyes and sissies / My monkey / Misery machine. *(re-iss. cd Jul96 on 'Nothing-Interscope'; same) (lp re-iss. Sep99 on 'Simply Vinyl'; SVLP 121)*

Feb 95. (cd-ep) *<INTDM 95806>* **LUNCHBOX / NEXT MOTHERFUCKER (remix) / DOWN IN THE PARK / BROWN BAG (remix) / METAL (remix)** [–] [ ]

— **GINGER FISH** – drums; repl. SARA LEE

Aug 96. (cd-ep) *(IND 95504)* **SWEET DREAMS (ARE MADE OF THIS) / DANCE OF THE DOPE HATS (remix) / DOWN IN THE PARK / LUNCHBOX (NEXT MOTHERF****R)** [ ] [ ]

Aug 96. (cd) *<(IND 92641)>* **SMELLS LIKE CHILDREN** [ ] Oct95 [31]
– The hands of small children / Diary of a dope fiend / S****y chicken gang bang / Kiddie grinder (remix) / Sympathy for the parents / Sweet dreams (are made of this) / Everlasting c***sucker (remix) / F*** Frankie / I put a spell on you / May cause discoloration of the urine or feces / Scatos, guns and peanut butter / Dance of the dope hats (remix) / White trash (remixed by Tony F. Wiggins) / Dancing with the one-legged . . . / Rock'n'roll nigger. *(cd re-iss. Aug98; same) (lp-iss.May00 on 'Simply Vinyl'; SVLP 208)*

— **ZIM ZUM** – guitar; repl. DAISY after below recording (he subsequently turned up with JACK OFF JILL in '98)

Oct 96. (cd/c) *<(IND 90006-2/-4)>* **ANTICHRIST SUPERSTAR** [73] [3]
– Irresponsible hate anthem / The beautiful people / Dried up, tied up and dead to the world / Tourniquet / Little horn / Cryptorchid / Deformography / Wormboy / Mister Superstar / Angel with the scabbed wings / Kinderfeld / Antichrist superstar / 1996 / Minute of decay / The reflecting God / Man that you fear. *(lp-iss.Nov98 on 'Simply Vinyl'; SVLP 55)*

Jun 97. (cd-ep) *(IND 95541)* **THE BEAUTIFUL PEOPLE / THE HORRIBLE PEOPLE (Danny Sabre remix) / SWEET DREAMS (lp version) / CRYPTORCHID** [18] [ ]
(cd-ep) *(INDX 95541)* – ('A'side) / The not so beautiful people (Jim Thirlwell remix) / Snake eyes and sissies / Deformography.
(10"pic-d) *(INVP 95541)* – The horrible people (Danny Sabre remix) / The not so beautiful people (Jim Thirlwell remix).

Sep 97. (10"pic-d) *(INVP 95552)* **TOURNIQUET. / TOURNIQUET (Prosthetic dance mix)** [28] [ ]
(cd-s+=) *(IND 95552)* – ('A'-Prosthetic dance mix edit).
(cd-s) *(INDX 95552)* – ('A'side) / Lunchbox / Next MF (remix).

Apr 98. (m-cd) *<(IND 95017)>* **REMIX & REPENT** [ ] Dec97 [ ]
– The horrible people (remixed by Danny Saber) / Tourniquet (prosthetic dance mix) / Dried up, tied and dead to the world (live in Utica, NY) / Antichrist superstar (live in Hartford, CT) / Man that you fear (acoustic requiem for Antichrist Superstar).

— **JOHNNIE 5** – guitar; repl. ZIM ZUM

Sep 98. (cd/c) *<(IND/INC 98273)>* **MECHANICAL ANIMALS** [8] [1]
– Great big white world / The dope show / Mechanical animals / Rock is dead / Disassociative / The speed of pain / Posthuman / I want to disappear / I don't like the drugs (but the drugs like me) / New model No.15 / User friendly / Fundamentally loathsome / The last day on earth / Coma white. *(ltd-cd-iss. Jun99; IND 90394) (lp-iss.Apr00 on 'Simply Vinyl'; SVLP 195)*

Nov 98. (one-sided-10"pic-d) *(INVP 95610)* **THE DOPE SHOW** [12] [ ]
(cd-s+=) *(IND 95610)* – Sweet dreams (live) / Apple of Sodom (live).
(cd-s+=) *(INDX 95610)* – The beautiful people (live) / ('A'-CD-rom video).

— now without the sacked ZIM ZUM; **JOHN LOWERY** was his replacement

Jun 99. (10"pic-d) *(W 486TE)* **ROCK IS DEAD. / I DON'T LIKE DRUGS (BUT THE DRUGS LIKE ME) (every day mix)** [23] [ ]
(cd-s) *(W 486CD)* – ('A'side) / Man that you fear (acoustic requiem for Antichrist Superstar) / Baxter (television radio edit).
(cd-s) *(W 486CDX)* – ('A'side) / I don't like the drugs (but the drugs like me) (absinthe makes the heart grow fonder mix) / Baxter (I can't see why album version) / ('A'-CD-ROM video).

Nov 99. (d-cd) *<(490524-2)>* **THE LAST TOUR ON EARTH (live)** [61] [ ]
– Inauguration of the mechanical Christ / The reflecting God / Great big white world / Get your gunn / Sweet dreams (are made of this) / Hell outro / Rock is dead / The dope show / Lunchbox / I don't like the drugs (but the drugs like me) / Antichrist superstar / The beautiful people / The irresponsible hate anthem / The last day on Earth. *(UK d-cd+=)* – Coma white / Get off my rocks / Coma white / A rose and a baby Ruth.

Nov 00. (12"pic-d) *(497458-1)* **DISPOSABLE TEENS. / WORKING CLASS HERO / FIVE TO ONE** [12] [–]
(cd-s) *(497437-2)* – (first two tracks) / Diamonds & pollen.
(cd-s) *(497438-2)* – (first & third tracks) / Astonishing panorama of the endtimes.

Nov 00. (cd/d-lp) *(490829-2/-1) <490790>* **HOLY WOOD** [23] [13]
– Godeatgod / The love song / The fight song / Disposable teens / Target audience (Narcissus narcosis) / President dead / In the valley of the shadow of Earth / Cruci-fiction in space / A place in the dirt / The nobodies / The death song / Lamb of God / Born again / Burning flag / Coma black: Eden eye – The apple of discord / Valentine's day / The fall of Adam / King kill 33 / Count to six and die.

Feb 01. (12"pic-d) *(497491-1)* **THE FIGHT SONG. / THE FIGHT SONG (Slipknot remix) / LOVE SONG (remix)** [24] [–]
(cd-s) *(497490-2)* – (first two tracks) / Disposable teens (CD-Rom video).
(cd-s) *(497491-2)* – (first & third tracks) / Disposable teens (remix).

Sep 01. (cd-s) *(497604-2)* **THE NOBODIES / THE NOBODIES (live) / DEATH SONG (with bible speech live) / (Cd-Rom)** [34] [–]

Mar 02. (cd-s) *(W 579CD1)* **TAINTED LOVE / MEST – I MELT WITH YOU / STABBING WESTWOOD – BIZARRE LOVE TRIANGLE** [5] [–]
(cd-s) *(W 579CD2)* – ('A'side) / Suicide is painless / Muse – Please, please, please, let me get what I want.

May 03. (cd)(d-lp) *(980008-2)(980108-9) <37002>* **THE GOLDEN AGE OF GROTESQUE** [4] [1]
– Thaeter / This is the new shit / Mobscene / Doll-dagga buzz-buzz ziggety-zag / Use your fist and not your mouth / The golden age of grotesque / (S)aint / Ka-boom ka-boom / Slutgarden / Spade / Para-noir / The bright young things / Vodevil / Obsequey (the death of art). *(UK+=)* – Tainted love / Baboon rape party.

Jun 03. (7") *(9807728)* **mOBSCENE. / PARANOIAC** [13] [–]
(cd-s) *(9807726)* – ('A'side) / Tainted love (re-Tainted interpretation) / ('A'-Flint & Youth's overnight mix) / ('A'-video).

Sep 03. (10"pic-d) *(9810794)* **THIS IS THE NEW SHIT. / THIS IS THE NEW SHIT (Marilyn Manson vs. Goldfrapp)** [29] [–]
(cd-s+=) *(9810793)* – Mind of a lunatic / ('A'-video).

– others, etc. –

Dec 96. (cd-ep) *Interscope; <(INTDM 95806)>* **LUNCHBOX** [ ] [ ]
Dec 96. (cd-ep) *Interscope; <(INTDM 95902)>* **GET YOUR GUN** [ ] [ ]
Nov 97. (cd+book) *UFO; (UFOCD 15BX)* **SMELLS LIKE WHITE TRASH** [ ] [–]
Jun 99. (cd-book) *Hallmark; (8086)* **STAR PROFILE** [ ] [–]
Mar 01. (cd; as MARILYN MANSON & THE SPOOKY KIDS) *Nightingale; <(ILLUSIONCD 2001)>* **BIRTH OF THE ANTI-CHRIST** [ ] [ ]
Mar 01. (cd; as MARILYN MANSON & THE SPOOKY KIDS) *Illusion; <(ILLUSIONCD 2002)>* **LIVE** [ ] [ ]
Mar 01. (d-cd/CD-Rom; as MARILYN MANSON & THE SPOOKY KIDS) *Illusion; <(ILLUSIONCD 2003)>* **THE WORD ACCORDING TO MANSON** [ ] [ ]
Jul 01. (lp/cd) *Megarock; <(COTP 7/+CD)>* **GENESIS OF THE DEVIL** [ ] [ ]
Apr 02. (cd; as MARILYN MANSON & THE SPOOKY KIDS) *Eastworld; <(EWO 012CD)>* **DANCING WITH THE ANTICHRIST** [ ] [ ]

MANSUN

Formed: Chester, England ... 1995 originally as MANSON by songwriter PAUL DRAPER, DOMINIC CHAD (both from Wales), STOVE, THE HIB and MARK STENT. After one single under this moniker ('TAKE IT EASY CHICKEN'), they caused a minor rumpus with the legal team of notorious killer CHARLES MANSON. The band claimed their name was taken from a VERVE b-side, 'A MAN CALLED SUN', deliberately slightly altering it to avoid court action. With name change now complete, they issued their follow-up, 'SKIN UP PIN UP'. A month later with the help of A&R man, Keith Wozencroft, they were part of Parlophone's enviable roster. Their blend of melodic, alternative rock, was described as a 90's indie update of TEARS FOR FEARS. Two UK Top 40 hits appeared as the EP's, 'ONE' & 'TWO' in 1996, paving the way for further successes, 'STRIPPER VICAR' and 'WIDE OPEN SPACE'. The year 1997, began on a high note with a Top 10 hit, the charmingly titled 'SHE MAKES MY NOSE BLEED' and a No.1 album, 'ATTACK OF THE GREY LANTERN'. Ambitious in its stylistic diversity, it contained additional Top 20 hits, 'TAXLO$$' and 'CLOSED FOR BUSINESS'. In the summer of '98, MANSUN were back in the hit parade with two EP's, 'LEGACY' (their eighth in the series) and 'NINE' (leading in with 'BEING A GIRL'), both taken from their pseudo-concept follow-up album, 'SIX', which, spookily enough, reached the same number in the charts. MANSUN returned in summer 2000 with their new set, the very average 'LITTLE KIX'. An overly produced, post-Britpop disappointment, MANSUN seemed content with not only isolating fans, but isolating their music itself with cringeworthy tracks such as 'UNTIL THE NEXT LIFE' and 'WE ARE THE BOYS'. The orchestral aspect remained, but after the melancholy dabblings of 'ATTACK OF THE GREY LANTERNS', 'LITTLE KIX' seemed like the metaphorical difference between a limousine and a horse and cart. Rumour had it that the group were planning to work with Ibiza dance guru PAUL OAKENFOLD. MANSUN split in May 2003. • **Covers:** RAILINGS (Howard Devoto). Everyone Must Win was co-written with the ex-MAGAZINE frontman.

Album rating: ATTACK OF THE GREY LANTERN (*8) / SIX (*7) / LITTLE KIX (*5)

PAUL DRAPER (b. Flint, Wales) – vocals, guitars, piano, synthesizer / **DOMINIC CHAD** (b. Bangor, Wales) – lead guitar, piano, vocals, synthesizer / **STOVE KING** – bass / **THE HIB** – drums / **MARK 'SPIKE' STENT** – beatbox

Regal — not iss.

Sep 95. (7"; as MANSON) *(REG 2)* **TAKE IT EASY CHICKEN. / ('A'version)** [ ] [–]
(above also issued on own 'Sci Fi Hi Fi' label; MANSON 1)
Nov 95. (7"white) *(REG 3)* **SKIN UP PIN UP. / FLOURELLA** [ ] [–]
(cd-s+=) *(REG 3CD)* – Take it easy chicken.

— early '96, MARK suddenly departed

Parlophone Sony

Mar 96. (cd-ep/c-ep/7"ep) *(CDRS/TCR/R 6430)* **MANSUN – ONE** 37 –
– Egg shaped Fred / Ski jump nose / Lemonade secret drinker / Thief.

Jun 96. (cd-ep/c-ep/7"ep) *(CD/TC+/R 6437)* **MANSUN – TWO** 32 –
– Take it easy chicken / Drastic sturgeon / The greatest pain / Moronica.

— lost another member when THE HIB quit

— **ANDIE RATHBONE** – drums; repl. temp. JULIAN (ex-KINKY MACHINE)

Sep 96. (7"clear) *(R 6447)* **STRIPPER VICAR. / NO ONE KNOWS US** 19 –
(cd-ep+=) *(CDR 6447)* **THREE EP** – An open letter to the lyrical trainspotter / Things keep falling off buildings.
(cd-ep) *(CDRS 6447)* **THREE EP** – ('A'side) / The edge / Duchess.

Nov 96. (7"white) *(R 6453)* **WIDE OPEN SPACE. / REBEL WITHOUT A QUILT** 15 –
(cd-s+=) *(CDR 6453)* **FOUR EP** – Vision impaired / Skin up pin up.
(cd-s) *(CDRS 6453)* **FOUR EP** – ('A'side) / The gods of not very much / Moronica (acoustic) / Lemonade secret drinker (acoustic).

Feb 97. (7"red) *(R 6458)* **SHE MAKES MY NOSE BLEED. / THE HOLY BLOOD AND THE HOLY GRAIL** 9 –
(cd-s+=) *(CDRS 6458)* **FIVE EP** – Live open space / Drastic sturgeon (live).
(cd-s) *(CDR 6458)* **FIVE EP** – ('A'side) / The most to gain / Flourella / ('A'acoustic).

Feb 97. (cd/c/d-lp) *(CD/TC+PCS 3787)* *<67935>* **ATTACK OF THE GREY LANTERN** 1
– The Chad who loved me / Mansun's only love song / Taxloss / You, who do you hate? / Wide open space / Stripper vicar / Disgusting / She makes my nose bleed / Naked twister / Egg shaped Fred / Dark Mavis.

May 97. (cd-ep) *(CDR 6465)* **SIX EP** 15 –
– Taxloss / Grey lantern / Taxloss (Lisa Marie Experience remix).
(cd-ep) *(CDRS 6465)* – ('A'side) / The impending collapse od it all / Ski jump nose (live) / Wide open space (acoustic).
(12"ep) *(12R 6465)* – ('A'mixes:- John '00' Fleming remix / album version / Slam remix / Gaudi remix).

Oct 97. (7"clear) *(R 6482)* **CLOSED FOR BUSINESS. / EGG SHAPED FRED (acoustic)** 10 –
(cd-s) *(CDR 6482)* **SEVEN EP** – ('A'side) / K.I.Double.S.I.N.G. / Everyone must win / The world's still open.
(cd-s) *(CDRS 6482)* **SEVEN EP** – ('A'side) / Dark Mavis (acoustic) / Stripper vicar (live) / Taxloss (video for PC or Mac).

Jun 98. (c-ep) *(TCR 6497)* *<57396>* **LEGACY EP (EIGHT EP)** 7 Aug98
– Legacy / Wide open space (the Perfecto remix) / The acoustic collapse of it all / Ski jump nose (acoustic).
(cd-ep) *(CDR 6497)* – ('A'side) / Wide open space (the Perfecto remix) / GSOH / Face in the crowd.
(cd-ep) *(CDRS 6497)* – ('A'side) / Can't afford to die / Spasm of identity / Check under the bed.

Aug 98. (c-ep) *(TCR 6503)* **NINE EP** 13 –
– Being a girl (part 1) / Wide open space (Trouse Enthusiasts mix) / Mansun's only acoustic song.
(cd-ep) *(CDR 6503)* – ('A'side) / Railings / Been here before.
(cd-ep) *(CDRS 6503)* – ('A'side) / Hideout / Wide open space (Trouser Enthusiasts mix).

Sep 98. (cd/c/d-lp) *(96723-2/-4/-1)* *<69748>* **SIX** 6 Apr99
– (Part one):- Six / Negative / Shotgun / Inverse Midas / Anti-everything / Fall out / Serotonin / Cancer / (interlude) / Witness to a murder (part two) / (Part two):- Television / Special – Blown it (delete as appropriate) / Legacy / Being a girl.

Oct 98. (7") *(R 6508)* **NEGATIVE. / MANSUN'S ONLY LIVE SONG** 27 –
(cd-s) *(CDR 6508)* – ('A'side) / I deserve what I get / Take it easy chicken (live).
(cd-s) *(CDRS 6508)* – ('A'side) / When the wind blows / King of beauty.

Feb 99. (7") *(R 6511)* **SIX. / BEING A GIRL (parts 1 & 2) / LIVE TELEVISION** 16 –
(cd-s) *(CDR 6511)* – ('A'side) / But the trains run on time / What's it like to be hated.
(cd-s) *(CDRS 6511)* – ('A'side) / Church of the drive thru Elvis / But the trains run on time.

Jul 00. (c-s) *(TCR 6544)* **I CAN ONLY DISAPPOINT U / REPAIR MAN / MY IDEA OF FUN** 8 –
(cd-s) *(CDR 6544)* – (first 2 tracks) / Decisions decisions.
(cd-s) *(CDRS 6544)* – (first & third tracks) / Golden stone.

Aug 00. (cd/c/d-lp) *(527782-2/-4/-1)* **LITTLE KIX** 12 –
– Butterfly (a new beginning) / I can only disappoint U / Comes as no surprise / Electric man / Love is . . . / Soundtrack 4 2 lovers / Forgive me / Until the next life / Fool / We are the boys / Goodbye.

Nov 00. (c-s/cd-s) *(TCR/CDRS 6550)* **ELECTRIC MAN / I CAN ONLY DISAPPOINT U (Perfecto mix) / ELECTRIC MAN (acoustic)** 23 –
(cd-s) *(CDCHS 6550)* – ('A'side) / Drifters / Apartment.

Jan 01. (c-s) *(TCR 6553)* **FOOL / I'VE SEEN THE TOP OF THE MOUNTAIN** 28 –
(cd-s+=) *(CDRS 6553)* – Promises.
(cd-s) *(CDR 6553)* – ('A'side) / Fade in time / Black infinite space.

— in May '03, MANSUN disbanded

– compilations, etc. –

Oct 02. (d-cd) *Parlophone; (543150-2)* **ATTACK OF THE GREY LATTERN / LITTLE KIX** –

□ MARC & THE MAMBAS (see under ⇒ ALMOND, Marc)

MARILLION

Formed: Aylesbury, Buckinghamshire, England . . . late '78 initially as SILMARILLION, by MICK POINTER and DOUG IRVINE. Taking their name from a J.R.R. Tolkien novel, they soon shortened it to MARILLION the following year. By this point, the all-instrumental outfit had added STEVE ROTHERY and BRIAN JELLIMAN, subsequently recruiting Scots vocalist, FISH (and DIZ MINNITT), after IRVINE departed late in 1980. By March '82, FISH (aka DEREK WILLIAM DICK), POINTER and ROTHERY, finally completed the line-up with Irishman MARK KELLY and PETE TREWAVAS. The band had now been gigging for almost four years and had built up a sizeable following, something that 'E.M.I.' had noticed before securing them a major deal. Soon after, the company issued 'MARKET SQUARE HEROES', the single denting the UK Top 60. Surprisingly, given their prog-rock pretensions, they were voted the best newcomer in the rock-centric (now defunct) Sounds magazine early in 1983. A second single, 'HE KNOWS, YOU KNOW', hit the Top 40, preceding the release of a debut album, 'SCRIPT FOR A JESTER'S TEAR'. Featuring one of their best-loved tracks, 'GARDEN PARTY' (also a UK Top 20 hit), the record reached the Top 10. With GENESIS pursuing a more commercial direction, MARILLION were perfectly poised to fill the gap in the market; a giant of a man, the enigmatic FISH updated PETER GABRIEL's early 70's vocal mannerisms over a keyboard-dominated backing. Like punk never happened, FISH and the lads took us back a decade, sporting ornate lyrical concepts masterminded by the hulking frontman. A harder-edged affair, the follow-up album, 'FUGAZI' strengthened the band's reputation among British rock fans looking for a genuine alternative to AOR-brushed material churning out of America. In the summer of '85, after a rather unnecessary live mini-set, 'REAL TO REEL', they wooed the mainstream with the wistful love song, 'KAYLEIGH', a near chart topper and an integral part of the conceptual yet accessible 'MISPLACED CHILDHOOD' opus. A UK No.1, the album also featured another top selling ballad, 'LAVENDER' and transformed MARILLION into a stadium-filling live proposition (although America proved impenetrable, 'KAYLEIGH' only scraping into their Hot 100). By 1987's top selling 'CLUTCHING AT STRAWS', FISH was uncomfortable with his newfound pop star status, his drink/drug problems fuelling speculation of an imminent split. The rumours proved all too true, when, just prior to the release of a double live set, 'THE THIEVING MAGPIE', the big man bailed out. While he contemplated a solo career, MARILLION decided to carry on, having found a worthy replacement in STEVE HOGARTH. An unknown quantity to many (although he had fronted minor chart group The EUROPEANS), HOGARTH's fluid, unassuming style nevertheless won over the majority of MARILLION fans, taking the band into unknown territory with the album, 'SEASON'S END' (1989). A competent set, the album's sole weak point was the Top 30 single, 'HOOKS IN YOU'. In 1992, they tried in vain to carry off a cover of Rare Bird's 'SYMPATHY', although this still managed a Top 20 placing, as did a singles collection. MARILLION found it hard to recapture the momentum of their halycon days, that is, until 1994's brilliant return to their conceptual roots with the album, 'BRAVE'. This fusion of folky melodic-rock and quasi-ambient atmospherics was their first to hit the Top 10 for some time, although two albums ('AFRAID OF SUNLIGHT' and the live 'MADE AGAIN') down the line, they finally parted company with 'E.M.I.'. Now on 'Raw Power' (rock's retirement stable), MARILLION subsequently released their 1997 set, 'THIS STRANGE ENGINE', a more accessible outing than previously. Its acoustic musings stood in contrast to 'RADIATION' (1998), a return to meatier, more conceptual waters which nevertheless retained an oblique pop edge. To their credit, MARILLION seemed unwilling to sit on their laurels and churn out music specifically created for their cult fanbase, instead making a concerted effort to update their influences for the new millennium as witnessed on 'MARILLION.COM' (1999). The wittily titled 'ANORAKNOPHOBIA' followed in 2001.

Album rating: SCRIPT FOR A JESTER'S TEAR (*8) / FUGAZI (*6) / REAL TO REEL (*5) / MISPLACED CHILDHOOD (*7) / CLUTCHING AT STRAWS (*6) / THE THIEVING MAGPIE (*5) / SEASON'S END (*5) / A SINGLES COLLECTION 1982-1992 compilation (*8) / HOLIDAYS IN EDEN (*6) / BRAVE (*7) / AFRAID OF SUNLIGHT (*5) / THIS STRANGE ENGINE (*6) / RADIATION (*5) / MARILLION.COM (*4) / ANORAKNOPHOBIA (*5)

FISH (b. DEREK WILLIAM DICK, 25 Apr'58, Dalkeith, Scotland) – vocals / **MARK KELLY** (b. 9 Apr'61, Dublin, Eire) – keyboards repl. BRIAN JELLIMAN / **MICK POINTER** (b.22 Jul'56) – drums / **STEVE ROTHERY** (b.25 Nov'59) – guitar / **PETER TREWAVAS** (b.15 Jan'59) – bass repl. DOUG IRVINE

E.M.I. Capitol

Oct 82. (7") *(EMI 5351)* **MARKET SQUARE HEROES. / THREE BOATS DOWN FROM THE CANDY** [60] [–]
(12"+=/12"pic-d+=) *(12EMI 5351/+P)* – Grendel. *(re-entered.Apr83; hit No.53)*

Jan 83. (7") *(EMI 5362)* **HE KNOWS, YOU KNOW. / CHARTING THE SINGLE** [35] [–]
(12"+=) *(12EMI 5362)* – ('A'extended).

Mar 83. (lp/c) *(EMC/TC-EMC 3429)* <12269> **SCRIPT FOR A JESTER'S TEAR** [7] [ ]
– Script for a jester's tear / He knows, you know / The web / Garden party / Chelsea Monday / Forgotten sons. *(pic-lp.Jun84; EMCP 3429) (cd-iss. Feb87; CDP 746237-2) (re-iss. May90 on 'Fame' cd/c/lp; CD/TC+/FA 3235) (re-iss. Mar96 on 'EMI Gold' cd/c; CD/TC GOLD 1012) (cd re-mast.Sep97 +=cd; REMARIL 001)* – Market Square heroes (battle priest version) / Three boats down from the candy / Grendel (fair deal studios version) / Chelsea Monday (demo) / He knows you know (demo) / Charting the single / Market Square heroes (alt.). *(cd re-iss. Aug00; 527115-2)*

Jun 83. (7"/7"sha-pic-d) *(EMI/+P 5393)* **GARDEN PARTY. / MARGARET (live)** [16] [–]
(ext.12"+=/ext.12"w-poster+=) *(12EMI/+P 5393)* – Charting the single (live).

— **ANDY WARD** – drums (ex-CAMEL) replaced POINTER / **IAN MOSLEY** (b.16 Jun'53) – drums (ex-STEVE HACKETT, ex-CURVED AIR) repl. WARD

Jan 84. (7") *(MARIL 1)* **PUNCH AND JUDY. / MARKET SQUARE HEROES (new version)** [29] [–]
(12"+=/12"pic-d+=) *(12MARIL/+P 1)* – Three boats down from the candy (new version).

Mar 84. (lp/pic-lp)(c) *(MRL/+P 1)(TC-MRL 1)* <46027> **FUGAZI** [5] [ ]
– Assassing / Punch and Judy / Jigsaw / Emerald lies / She chameleon / Incubus / Fugazi. *(re-iss. May88 on 'Fame' cd/c/lp; CD/TC+FA 3196) (cd re-iss. May94; CDEMS 1516) (cd re-mast.Mar98 +=cd; 493369-2)* – Cinderella search (12" version) / Assassing (alt.) / Three boats down from the candy / Punch and JUdy (demo) / She chameleon (demo) / Emerald lies (demo) / Incubus (demo).

Apr 84. (7")(ext;12"+=/12"pic-d+=) *(MARIL 2)(12MARIL/+P 2)* **ASSASSING. / CINDERELLA SEARCH** [22] [–]

Nov 84. (m-lp/c) *(JEST/TC-JEST 1)* **REAL TO REEL (live)** [8] [ ]
– Assassing / Incubus / Cinderella search / Forgotten sons / Garden party / Market square heroes. *(pic-lp.Jan85; EG 2603036) (re-iss. Nov85 on 'Fame' lp/c/cd+=; FA/TC-FA/CD-FA 3142)* – Emerald lies. *(cd re-iss. Oct87; CDM 752 021-2)*

May 85. (7"/7"pic-d) *(MARIL/+P 3)* **KAYLEIGH. / LADY NINJA** [2] [–]
(ext.12"+=/ext.12"pic-d+=) *(12MARIL/+P 3)* – ('A'-alternative).

Jun 85. (lp/pic-lp)(c)(cd) *(MRL/+P 2)(TC-MRL 2)(CDP 746160-2)* <12431> **MISPLACED CHILDHOOD** [1] [47]
– The pseudo silk kimono / Kayleigh / Lavender / Bitter suite – Heart of Lothian / Waterhole (expresso bongo) / Lords of the backstage / Blind curve / Childhood's end? / White feather. *(cd re-iss. May94; CDEMS 1518) (cd re-mast.Oct98 +=cd; 497034-2)* – Lady Nina / Freaks / Kayleigh (alt.) / Lavender blue / Heart Of Lothian (extended) / Pseudo silk komono (demo) / Kayleigh (demo) / Lavender (demo) / Bitter suite – Brief encounter – Lost weekend (demo) / LOrds of the backstage (demo) / Blue angel (demo) / Misplaced rendezvous / Heart of LOthian – Wide boy – Curtain call (demo) / Waterhole (express bongo) (demo) / Passing strangers – Mylo – Perimeter walk threshold (demo) / Childhood's end? (demo) / White feather (demo). *(cd re-iss. Aug00; 527116-20*

Aug 85. (7") *(MARIL 4)* <5539> **LAVENDER. / FREAKS** [5] [ ]
(12"+=/12"pic-d+=) *(12MARIL/+P 4)* – ('A'remix).

Sep 85. (7") <5493> **KAYLEIGH. / HEART OF LOTHIAN** [–] [74]

Nov 85. (7") *(MARIL 5)* **HEART OF LOTHIAN. / CHELSEA MONDAY (live)** [29] [–]
(12"+=/12"pic-d+=) *(12MARIL/+P 5)* – ('A'extended).

— Early 1986, FISH teamed up with TONY BANKS (GENESIS) on a single.

Dec 85. (7") <5561> **HEART OF LOTHIAN. / LADY NINJA** [–] [ ]

Mar 86. (m-lp) <15023> **BRIEF ENCOUNTER** (3 live early '86) [–] [67]
– Freaks / Fugazi / Kayleigh / Lady Ninja / Script for a jester's tear.

May 87. (7") *(MARIL 6)* <44043> **INCOMMUNICADO. / GOING UNDER** [6] [ ]
(12"pic-d+=)(cd-s+=) *(12MARILP 6)(CDMARIL 6)* – ('A'alternate).

Jun 87. (lp/pic-lp)(c/cd) *(EMD/+P 1002)(TC/CD EMD 1002)* <12539> **CLUTCHING AT STRAWS** [2] [ ]
– Hotel hobbies / Warm wet circles / That time of the night (the short straw) / Going under * / Just for the record / White Russian / Incommunicado / Torch song / Slainte Mhath / Sugar mice / The last straw: happy ending. *(cd+= *) (re-iss. 1989 cd)(c/lp; CZ 214)(TC+/ATAK 135) (cd re-mast.Mar99 +=cd; 498611-2)* – Incommunicado (alt.) / Tux on / Going under (extended) / Beaujolais day / Story from a thin wall / Shadows on the barley / Sunset hill / Tic-tac-toe / Voice in the crowd / Exile on Princes Street / White Russians (demo) / Sugar mice in the rain. *(cd re-iss. Aug00; 527117-2) (cd re-iss. Feb01; 527117-2)*

Jul 87. (7"/7"pic-d) *(MARIL/+P 7)* <44060> **SUGAR MICE. / TUX ON** [22] [ ]
(12"+=/12"pic-d+=) *(12MARIL/+P 7)* – ('A'extended).

Oct 87. (7") *(MARIL 8)* **WARM WET CIRCLES. / WHITE RUSSIAN (live)** [22] [–]
(12"+=/12"pic-d+=) *(12MARIL/+P 8)* – Incommunicado (live).
(cd-s++=) *(CDMARIL 8)* – Up on top of a rainbow.

Nov 88. (d-cd/c/d-lp) *(CD/TC+/MARL 1)* <C 191463> **THE THIEVING MAGPIE (live)** [25] [ ]
– (intro) / La gazza ladra / Slainte mhath / He knows, you know / Chelsea Monday / Freaks / Jigsaw / Punch and Judy / Sugar mice / Fugazi / Script for a jester's tear / Incommunicado / White Russian / Misplaced childhood part 1:- Pseudo silk kimono – Kayleigh – Lavender – Bitter suite – Heart of Lothian. *(d-cd+=)* – Misplaced childhood part 2:- Waterhole (expresso bongo) – Lords of the backstage – Blind curve – Childhood's end? – White feather.

Nov 88. (7"/7"sha-pic-d) *(MARIL/+P 9)* **FREAKS (live). / KAYLEIGH (live)** [24] [–]
(12"+=/cd-s+=) *(12/CD MARIL 9)* – Childhood's end (live) / White feather (live).

— **STEVE HOGARTH** – vocals (ex-HOW WE LIVE, ex-EUROPEANS, ex-LAST CALL) finally repl. FISH. (He had left to go solo Sep'88).

Aug 89. (c-s/7") *(TC+/MARIL 10)* **HOOKS IN YOU. / AFTER ME** [30] [–]
(12"+=/12"pic-d+=) *(12MARIL 10/+P)* – ('A'-meaty mix).
(cd-s+=) *(CDMARIL 10)* – ('A'-seven mix).

Sep 89. (cd/c/lp) *(CD/TC+/EMD 1011) <C 192877>* **SEASON'S END** [7] [ ]
– King of sunset town / Easter / The uninvited guest / Season's end / Holloway girl / Berlin / After me / Hooks in you / The space. *(c+=/cd+=)* – After me. *(pic-lp.Dec89; EMDPD 1011) (cd re-mast.Sep97 +=cd; REMARIL 005)* – The uninvited guest (12" version) / The bell in the sea / The release / The king of sunset town / Holloway girl / Season's end / The uninvited guest / Berlin / The bell in the sea. *(cd re-iss. Aug00; 527118-2)*

Nov 89. (7"/7"sha-pic-d)(c-s) *(MARIL/+PD 11)(TC-MARIL 11)* **THE UNINVITED GUEST. / THE BELL IN THE SEA** [53] [–]
(12"+=/12"pic-d+=)(cd-s+=) *(12MARIL/+P 11)(CDMARIL 11)* – ('A'extended).

Mar 90. (7"/7"pic-d)(c-s) *(MARIL/+P 12)(TC-MARIL 12)* **EASTER. / THE RELEASE** [34] [–]
(12"+=/12"g-f+=)(cd-s+=) *(12MARIL/+G 12)(CDMARIL 12)* – ('A'extended) / The uninvited guest (live).

Jun 91. (c-s/7") *(TC+/MARIL 13)* **COVER MY EYES (PAIN AND HEAVEN). / HOW CAN IT HURT** [34] [–]
(12"+=/cd-s+=) *(12/CD MARIL 13)* – The party.

Jul 91. (cd/c/lp) *(CD/TC+/EMD 1022) <13138>* **HOLIDAYS IN EDEN** [7] [ ]
– Splintered heart / Cover my eyes (pain and Heaven) / The party / No one can / Holidays in Eden / Dry land / Waiting to happen / This town / The rakes progress / 100 nights. *(cd re-mast.Mar98 +=cd; 493372-2)* – Sympathy / How can it hurt / A collection / Cover my eyes (acoustic) / Sympathy (acoustic) / I will walk on water (acoustic) / You don't need anyone / No one can / The party / This town / Waiting to happen / Eric / The epic (fairground).

Jul 91. (7"/7"box)(c-s) *(MARIL/+S 14)(TC-MARIL 14)* **NO ONE CAN. / A COLLECTION** [33] [–]
(cd-s+=) *(CDMARIL 14)* – Splintered heart (live).

Sep 91. (c-s/7") *(TC+/MARIL 15)* **DRY LAND. / HOLLOWAY GIRL / AFTER ME** [34] [–]
(12"+=) *(12MARIL 15)* – Substitute.
(10"clear+=) *(10MARIL 15)* – Waiting to happen.
(cd-s+=) *(CDMARIL 15)* – Easter / Sugar mice.
(12"pic-d+=) *(12MARILP 15)* – King of Sunset town.

May 92. (c-s/7") *(TC+/MARIL 16)* **SYMPATHY. / KAYLEIGH (live)** [17] [–]
(cd-s+=) *(MARILS 16)* – I will walk on water.
(12"pic-d+=)(cd-s+=) *(12MARILPD 16)(CDMARIL 16)* – Dry land (live).

Jun 92. (cd/c/d-lp) *(CD/TC+/EMD 1033)* **A SINGLES COLLECTION 1982-1992** (compilation) [27] [–]
– Cover my eyes (pain & Heaven) / Kayleigh / Easter / Warm wet circles / Uninvited guest / Assassing / Hooks in you / Garden party / No one can / Incommunicado / Dry land / Lavender / I will walk on water / Sympathy.

Jul 92. (c-s/7") *(TC+/MARIL 17)* **NO ONE CAN. / A COLLECTION** [26] [–]
(cd-s+=) *(CDMARIL 17)* – Splintered heart.

Feb 94. (cd/c/d-lp) *(CD/TC+/EMD 1054) <28032>* **BRAVE** [10] [ ]
– Bridge / Living with the big lie / Runaway / Goodbye to all that (i) Wave (ii) Mad (iii) The opium den (iv) The slide (v) Standing in the swing / Hard as love / The hollow man / Alone again in the lap of luxury (i) Now wash your hands / Paper lies / Brave / The great escape (i) The last of you (ii) Fallin' from the Moon / Made again. *(cd re-mast.Oct98 +=cd; 497038-2)* – The great escape (orchestral) / Marouatte jam / The hollow man (acoustic) / Winter trees / Alone again in the lap of luxury (acoustic) / Runaway (acoustic) / Hard as love (acoustic) / Living with the big lie (demo) / Alone again in the lap of luxury (demo) / Dream sequence / The great escape (remix).

Mar 94. (c-s/7") *(TC+/EM 307)* **THE HOLLOW MAN. / BRAVE** [30] [–]
(cd-s+=) *(CDEMS 307)* – Marouatte jam.
(cd-s) *(CDEM 307)* – ('A'side) / The last of you – Falling from the Moon (the great escape) / Winter trees.

Apr 94. (c-s) *(TCEM 318)* **ALONE AGAIN IN THE LAP OF LUXURY / LIVING WITH THE BIG LIE (live)** [53] [–]
(12"pic-d+=) *(12EMPD 318)* – The space (live).
(cd-s+=) *(CDEMS 318)* – River (live) / Bridge (live).
(cd-s) *(CDEM 318)* – ('A'side) / Cover my eyes / Slainte Mhath / Uninvited guest (all live).

Jun 95. (c-s/cd-s) *(TC/CD MARIL 18)* **BEAUTIFUL / AFRAID OF SUNRISE / ICON** [29] [–]
(cd-s) *(CDMARILS 18)* – ('A'side) / Live forever / Great escape (demo) / Hard as love (demo).

Jun 95. (cd/c/lp) *(CD/TC+/EMD 1079) <33874>* **AFRAID OF SUNLIGHT** [16] [ ]
– Gazpacho / Cannibal surf babe / Beautiful / Afraid of sunrise / Out of this world / Afraid of sunlight / Beyond you / King. *(cd re-mast.Mar99 +=cd; 498614-2)* – Icon / Live forever / Second chance (aka Beautiful) / Beyond you (demo) / Cannibal surf babe / Out of this world / Bass frenzy / Mirages (demo) / Afraid of sunlight (acoustic demo).

E.M.I. Castle

Mar 96. (d-cd/d-c) *(CD/TC EMD 1094) <117>* **MADE AGAIN (live)** [37] [ ]
– Splintered heart / Easter / No one can / Waiting to happen / Cover my eyes / The space / Hooks in you / Beautiful / Kayleigh / Lavender / Afraid of sunlight / King // Brave (live in Paris):- Bridge / Living with the big life / Runaway / Goodbye to all that / Wave / Mad / The opium den / Slide / Standing in the swing / Hard as love / Hollow man / Alone again in the lap of luxury / Now wash your hands / Paper lies / Brave / The great escape / The last of you / Falling from the Moon / Made again. *(d-cd re-iss. Feb01 on 'Castle'; CMDDD 123)*

Raw Power Velvel

May 97. (cd/c/pic-lp) *(RAW CD/MC/DP 121) <79791>* **THIS STRANGE ENGINE** [27] Jul97 [ ]
– Man of 100 faces / One fine day / Eighty days / Estonia / Memory of water / An accidental man / Hope for the future / This strange engine. *(cd re-iss. Feb01 on 'Castle'; CMRCD 071)*

May 97. (cd-s) *(RAWX 1044)* **MAN OF 1000 FACES / BEAUTIFUL / MADE AGAIN / ('A'mix)** [ ] [–]

Oct 97. (cd-s) *(RAWX 1049)* **EIGHTY DAYS / THIS STRANGE ENGINE (extended – live) / BELL IN THE SEA (live)** [ ] [–]

Sep 98. (cd-s) *(RAWX 1051)* **THESE CHAINS / FAKE PLASTIC TREES (live) / MEMORY OF WATER (Big Beat mix)** [ ] [–]

Sep 98. (cd) *(RAWCD 126) <79760>* **RADIATION** [35] Oct98 [ ]
– Costa del Slough / Under the sun / The answering machine / Three minute boy / Now she'll never know / These chains / Born to run / Cathedral wall / Few words for the dead. *<US+=>* – Estonia / Memory of water. *(re-iss. Feb01 on 'Castle'; CMRCD 113)*

Raw Power Never

Oct 99. (cd) *(RAWCD 144) <4505>* **MARILLION.COM** [53] Nov99 [ ]
– A legacy / Deserve / Go / Rich / Enlightened / Built-in bastard radar / Tumble down the years / Interior Lulu / House.

Liberty Sanctuary

May 01. (cd) *(532321-2) <84506>* **ANORAKNOPHOBIA** [ ] [ ]
– Between you and me / Quartz / Map of the world / When I grow old / Fruit of the wild rose / Separated out / This is the 21st century / If my heart were a ball it would roll uphill.

Capitol Capitol

Apr 02. (cd) *(<538727-2>)* **ANORAK IN THE UK (live)** [ ] [ ]
– Separated out / Quartz / Map of the world / Out of this world / Between you and me / The great escape / King / If my heart were a ball it would roll uphill / Waiting to happen / Easter.

– compilations etc. –

on 'E.M.I.' unless mentioned otherwise

Jan 88. (cd)(lp) *(CZ 39)(EMS 1295)* **B SIDES THEMSELVES (rare flips)** [64] [–]

Nov 95. (3xcd-box) *(CDOMB 015)* **THE ORIGINALS** [ ] [–]
– (SCRIPT FOR A JESTER'S TEAR / FUGAZI / MISPLACED CHILDHOOD). *(re-iss. Apr97; same)*

Oct 96. (cd) *EMI Gold; (CDGOLD 1058)* **THE COLLECTION** [ ] [–]

Feb 97. (d-cd) *(CDEMC 3761)* **THE BEST OF BOTH WORLDS** [ ] [–]

Apr 97. (d-pic-lp) *(EMCF 3761)* **THE BEST OF BOTH WORLDS 1982-88** [ ] [–]

Apr 97. (d-pic-lp) *(EMCH 3761)* **THE BEST OF BOTH WORLDS 1989-PRESENT** [ ] [–]

Jun 97. (d-cd) *(CDEM 1603)* **REAL TO REEL / BRIEF ENCOUNTER** [ ] [–]

Mar 99. (cd) *Disky; (DC 86718-2)* **KAYLEIGH** [ ] [–]

Jan 00. (cd/c) *Eagle; (EAG CD/MC 033)* **TALES FROM THE ENGINE ROOM** [ ] [–]
– (THIS STRANGE ENGINE remixed + MARILLION & THE POSITIVE LIGHT)

Jul 00. (12xcd-s) *(<888667-2>)* **THE CD SINGLES VOL.1: 1982-1988** [ ] [ ]

Oct 02. (12xcd-s) *(<550821-2>)* **THE CD SINGLES VOL.2: 1989-1995** [ ] [ ]

Mar 03. (cd) *Disky; (SI 90523-2)* **WARM WET CIRCLES** [ ] [–]

☐ MARK FOUR (see under ⇒ CREATION)

Bob MARLEY

Born: ROBERT NESTA MARLEY, 2 Feb'45, Rhoden Hall, St. Ann's, Jamaica, the son of an English sailor/captain and a Jamaican woman. By the early 60's, in common with most other Jamaicans (save older Calypso fans), he became influenced by ska and bluebeat, cutting his debut single, 'JUDGE NOT (UNLESS YOU JUDGE YOURSELF)' with the help of producer LESLIE KING. Another 7", 'ONE CUP OF COFFEE', followed early in '63, MARLEY subsequently forming vocal quintet, The WAILIN' WAILERS (shortened to The WAILERS after the first single) the following year. The outfit consisted of MARLEY (vocals, later also guitar), PETER TOSH (vocals, later also guitar), BUNNY LIVINGSTONE (vocals, percussion), JUNIOR BRAITHWAITE (vocals) and BEVERLEY KELSO (vocals) with instrumental backing by The SOUL BROTHERS and subsequently The SKATELITES. Teaming up with legendary producer COXSONE DODD, their first single, 'SIMMER DOWN', was a massive hit in Jamaica, the outfit recording a further string of 45's for DODD's seminal 'Studio One' and 'Coxsone' labels. MARLEY's career was put on hold, however, when he married RITA and subsequently spent a year in America visiting his mother who had moved there in 1963. He returned to his homeland in 1967, setting up his own 'Wailin' Soul' label with JOHNNY NASH and duly re-uniting with The WAILERS. Although their releases during this period met with little success, the group immersed themselves in the Rastafari religion which would subsequently influence much of their later work. In 1969, the outfit began working with pivotal songwriter/producer, LEE 'SCRATCH' PERRY, and over the course of the ensuing three years, developed from a soul/ska/R&B vocal outfit to form one of the cornerstones of reggae. With the addition of ASTON BARRETT on bass and brother CARLTON on drums (the former rhythm section of PERRY's UPSETTERS), the newly expanded WAILERS cut a further series of 7" singles under the guiding hand of PERRY, including such enduring tracks as 'KAYA', 'TRENCHTOWN ROCK' and 'SMALL AXE', as well as a debut album, 'SOUL REBEL' (1970). By 1971, The WAILERS had formed their own label, 'Tuff Gong', and had begun producing their own material. The following year, after JOHNNY NASH had taken MARLEY's 'STIR IT UP' into the UK Top 20, The WAILERS signed to 'Island', CHRIS BLACKWELL having previously distributed their early releases in the UK. He provided financial muscle for the outfit to record their major label debut in Jamaica, their first release to be promoted and widely available outside their home country. 'CATCH A FIRE' (1973) was scorching, bass-heavy vibrations providing a platform for impassioned, challenging lyrics on the likes of 'CONCRETE JUNGLE' and '400 YEARS', while the superior WAILERS version of 'STIR IT UP' glowed with laid back positivity. 'BURNIN' (1973) followed soon after, an even fierier set of spiritually and politically motivated songs that featured 'GET UP, STAND UP', a call for individual liberty powered by a knotty, insistent rhythm, as well as the plea for justice, 'I SHOT THE SHERIFF', a US No.1 for ERIC CLAPTON in the summer of '74. By the end of the year, however, PETER TOSH and BUNNY LIVINGSTONE (later renaming himself BUNNY WAILER) had both departed for solo careers, MARLEY recruiting the The I-THREES (a female vocal trio consisting of JUDY MOWAT, MARCIA GRIFFITHS and his wife, RITA) as a replacement as well as bringing in extra backing musicians. Under the revised moniker, BOB MARLEY & THE WAILERS, the outfit toured extensively for the first time in Europe, America and Africa, subsequently releasing the exceptional 'NATTY DREAD' (1975). A landmark roots reggae album, the set featured a studio version of the subsequent live hit, 'NO WOMAN NO CRY', a sublime love song with the I-THREES providing celestial harmonies and MARLEY putting in one of the most moving vocal performances of his career. Elsewhere, 'THEM BELLY FULL (BUT WE HUNGRY)' and 'REVOLUTION' were as politically charged as ever while 'SO JAH SEH' and the title track were ardent professions of MARLEY's rastafarian beliefs. 'LIVE!' was issused later that year, documenting an electric WAILERS performance in London the previous year, while 'RASTAMAN VIBRATION' (1976) gave The WAILERS their biggest commercial success to date, reaching Top 20 in the UK and Top 10 in the US on the back of the 'ROOTS, ROCK, REGGAE' single's Stateside success. Though 'EXODUS' (1977) made the US Top 20, it was the last release to make any significant commercial impact in America, the group's most vociferous fans residing in the UK, Europe, Africa and of course, Jamaica, where MARLEY was revered as if he was royalty. In general a more relaxed set than its predecessor, other highlights from 'EXODUS' included the gentle 'WAITING IN VAIN' and the hooky pop-reggae of 'THREE LITTLE BIRDS'. 'KAYA' (1978) carried on in a similar vein with the spliffed-out 'EASY SKANKING', the mellow 'SATISFY MY SOUL' and the meditative 'TIME WILL TELL' (later covered by The BLACK CROWES). After another live release, 'BABYLON BY BUS' (1978), the group recorded 'SURVIVAL' (1979), probably the most overtly political release of their career with MARLEY addressing the plight of his African brethren on 'ZIMBABWE' and 'AFRICA UNITE'. 'UPRISING' (1980) was released the same year as MARLEY was diagnosed with cancer, lending a new poignancy to tracks like 'REDEMPTION SONG', a beautiful, stripped down piece of African folk and arguably the singer's most spiritually resonant work. It also proved to be his epitaph, the final WAILERS release before MARLEY's death on the 11th of May '81. Later that summer, a Sunsplash Reggae Festival was dedicated to MARLEY and was attended by over 20,000 fans as well as his children, The MELODY MAKERS. More tragedy was to follow in 1987 when Ex-Wailers, CARLTON BARRETT and PETER TOSH, were both murdered in separate incidents, reflecting the inherently violent nature of Jamaican culture (MARLEY himself had earlier survived an attempt on his life in 1976 when gunmen broke into his Kingston home, shooting and injuring him, his wife and manager Don Taylor). Further controversy followed when RITA was ousted by the remaining WAILERS amid calls for an investigation into the MARLEY estate. Nevertheless, the legend of BOB MARLEY remains untarnished, the singer still a hero to countless Rastafarians and ordinary music fans alike. The singer's massive popularity was further illustrated in 1992 when 'SONGS OF FREEDOM', a collection of newly discovered demos, made the UK Top 10, a single culled from the set, 'IRON ZION LION', reaching No.5; MARLEY's has been hitting the charts in one way or another ever since (i.e. with LAURYN HILL). Original WAILERS singer, JUNIOR BRAITHWAITE, was sadly gunned down (in his hometown of Kingston, Jamaica) by an unknown assailant on the 2nd of June, 1999.

Album rating (selective): CATCH A FIRE (*8) / BURNIN' (*8) / NATTY DREAD (*9) / LIVE! (*6) / RASTAMAN VIBRATION (*7) / EXODUS (*8) / KAYA (*8) / BABYLON BY BUS (*6) / SURVIVAL (*8) / UPRISING (*8) / CONFRONTATION posthumous (*6) / LEGEND compilation (*10) / SONGS OF FREEDOM boxed collection (*6) / NATURAL MYSTIC collection (*6) / ONE LOVE: THE VERY BEST OF . . . compilation (*8)

ROBERT MARLEY

Island not iss.

Dec 62. (7") *(WI 088)* **JUDGE NOT (UNLESS YOU JUDGE YOURSELF). / DO YOU STILL LOVE ME?**

1963. (7") *(WI 128)* **ONE CUP OF COFFEE. / (B-side by Ernest Ranglin)**

The WAILERS

were formed by **MARLEY** (-vocals, +later guitar) plus **PETER TOSH** (b.WINSTON HUBERT MacINTOSH, 19 Oct'44, Westmoreland, Jamaica) – vocals, +later guitar / **BUNNY LIVINGSTONE** (b.NEVILLE O'RILEY LIVINGSTONE, 10 Apr'47, Kingston, Jamaica) – vocals, percussion / **JUNIOR BRAITHWAITE** – vocals / **BEVERLEY KELSO** – vocals / plus occasionally **RITA MARLEY** (b. ALPHARITA CONSTANTIA ANDERSON) – backing vocals / Instruments by SOUL BROTHERS then SKATELITES

Ska Beat not iss.

Jan 65. (7"; as WAILIN' WAILERS) *(JB 186)* **SIMMER DOWN. / I DON'T NEED YOUR LOVE**

— Released in Jamaica earlier, UK in batches

Island not iss.

Mar 65. (7") *(WI 188)* **IT HURTS TO BE ALONE. / MR.TALKATIVE**

Apr 65. (7") *(WI 206)* **PLAY BOY. / YOUR LOVE**

— added **CHERRY SMITH** – backing vocals

May 65. (7") *(WI 211)* **HOOT NANNY ROLL. / DO YOU REMEMBER**

(above A-side was actually credited to PETER TOUCH, the B-side BOB MARLEY, although all featured MARLEY, TOSH and The WAILERS

May 65. (7") *(WI 212)* **HOOLIGAN. / MAGA DOG**

Jun 65. (7"; as PETER TOSH & THE WAILERS) *(WI 215)* **SHAME AND SCANDAL. / THE JERK**

Jun 65. (7") *(WI 216)* **DON'T EVER LEAVE ME. / DONNA**

Dec 65. (7") *(WI 254)* **WHAT'S NEW PUSSYCAT. / WHERE WILL I FIND**

Mar 66. (7") *(WI 260)***JUMBIE JAMBOUREE. / (B-side by The Skatelites)**

Apr 66. (7") *(WI 268)* **PUT IT ON (FEEL THE SPIRIT). / LOVE WON'T BE MINE**

Ska Beat not iss.

Aug 65. (7") *(JB 211)* **LONESOME FEELINGS. / THERE SHE GOES**

Oct 65. (7") *(JB 226)* **I MADE A MISTAKE. / (B-side by The SOUL BROTHERS)**

(above A-side was probably by The WAILIN' RUDEBOYS)

1966. (7") *(JB 228)* **LOVE AND AFFECTION. / TEENAGER IN LOVE**

1966. (7") *(JB 230)* **AND I LOVE HER. / DO IT RIGHT**

1966. (7") *(JB 249)* **LONESOME TRACK. / SINNER MAN**

— (below might be without MARLEY)

Rio not iss.

1966. (7") *(R 116)* **DANCING SHOES. / DON'T LOOK BACK**

— MARLEY left Feb'66, to marry RITA but soon returned. CHERRY also left. LIVINGSTONE was imprisoned in 1966.

Doctor Bird not iss.

1966. (7") *(DB 1013)* **RUDE BOY. / (B-side by Roland Al & The Soul Brothers)**

1966. (7") *(DB 1021)* **GOOD GOOD RUDIE. / (B-side by City Slickers)**

Nov 66. (7") *(DB 1039)* **RASTA PUT IT ON. / (B-side by Roland Al & The Soul Brothers)**
(re-iss. Apr67 on 'Island')

— (below iss.Jamaica on 'Rocksteady')

1967. (7") *(DB 1091)* **NICE TIME. / HYPOCRITE**

— (below 2 without MARLEY)

Island not iss.

Nov 66. (7") *(WI 3001)* **HE WHO FEELS IT KNOWS IT. / SUNDAY MORNING**

Dec 66. (7") *(WI 3009)* **LET HIM GO (RUDE BOY GOT BAIL). / SINNER MAN**

Apr 67. (7") *(WI 3035)* **BABY I NEED YOU. / (B-side by Ken Boothe)**

— Now a trio of **MARLEY, TOSH & BUNNY.** (KELSO and BRAITHWAITE departed)

Apr 67. (7") *(WI 3043)* **BEND DOWN LOW. / FREEDOM TOWN**

Apr 67. (7"; PETER TOSH & THE WAILERS) *(WI 3042)* **I AM THE TOUGHEST. / (B-side by Marcia Griffiths)**

Studio One not iss.

1967. (7") *(SO 2010)* **I STAND PREDOMINANT. / (B-side by Norma Fraser)**

Trojan not iss.

Oct 68. (7") *(TR 617)* **STIR IT UP. / THIS TRAIN**

Bamboo not iss.

1970. (7") *(BAM 55)* **JAILHOUSE. / (B-side by John Holt)**

Escort not iss.

1970. (7") *(ERT 842)* **RUN FOR COVER. / TO THE RESCUE**

BOB MARLEY & THE WAILERS

— added **ASTON BARRETT** (b.22 Nov'46, KIngston) – bass / **CARLTON BARRETT** (b.17 Dec'50, Kingston) – drums

Upsetter Shelter

1970. (7") *(US 340)* **MY CUP. / SON OF THUNDER (by "LEE PERRY & THE WAILERS")**

1970. (7"; by The WAILERS) *(US 342)* **VERSION OF CUP. / (B-side by The Upsetters)**

Dec 70. (7") *(US 348)* **DUPPY CONQUEROR. / (B-side by The Upsetters)**

Jan 71. (7") *(US 354)* **MR. BROWN. / (B-side by The Upsetters)**

Feb 71. (7") *(US 356)* **KAYA. / (version by The Upsetters)**

Feb 71. (7") *(US 357)* **SMALL AXE. / ALL IN ONE**

1971. (7"; as The WAILERS) *(US 351)* **DREAMLAND. / (B-side by The Upsetters)**

1971. (7") *(US 372)* **MORE AXE. / (B-side by The Upsetters)**

1971. (7"; as RAS DAWKINS & THE WAILERS) *(US 368)* **PICTURE ON THE WALL. / (B-side by The Upsetters)**

Trojan not iss.

Sep 70. (7") *(TR 7759)* **SOUL SHAKEDOWN PARTY. / (B-side by The Beverley All-Stars)**

Dec 70. (lp) *(TBL 126)* **SOUL REBEL**
– There she goes / Put it on / How many times / Mellow mood / Changes are / Hammer / Tell me / Touch me / Treat you right / Soul rebel. *(re-iss. Sep81 on 'New Cross'; NC 001) (c-iss.Jan82 on 'Sun'; CFK 1020) (re-iss. Jun84 on 'Blue Moon' lp/c; BMLP/BMC 1018) (re-iss. Oct86 on 'Receiver' lp/c; RRLP/RRLC 106) (cd-iss. Jan90; RRCD 106) (re-iss. Apr90 on 'Action Replay' cd/c; CDAR/ARLC 1013)*

Jackpot not iss.

1971. (7") *(JP 730)* **MR. CHATTERBOX. / WALK THROUGH THE WORLD**

Punch not iss.

1971. (7") *(PH 69)* **MORE AXE. / (B-side by Dave Berber)**

1971. (7"; as The WAILERS) *(PH 77)* **DOWN PRESSER. / (B-side by Junior Byles)**

1972. (7") *(PH 101)* **SCREW FACE. / FACE MAN**

Bullet not iss.

1971. (7") *(BU 464)* **SOULTOWN. / LET THE SUN SHINE ON ME**

1971. (7") *(BU 493)* **LICK SAMBA. / SAMBA**

Summit not iss.

1971. (7") *(SUM 8526)* **STOP THE TRAIN. / CAUTION**

1971. (7") *(SUM 8530)* **FREEDOM TRAIN. /**

Green Door Tuff Gong

1971. (7") *(GD 4002)* **LIVELY UP YOURSELF. / (B-side by Tommy McCook)**

Nov 71. (7") *(GD 4005)* **TRENCHTOWN ROCK. / GROOVING KINGDOM**

1972. (7") *(GD 4025)* **GUAVA JELLY. / REDDER THAN RED**

— (below was 1968 demo)

C.B.S. not iss.

May 72. (7") *(CBS 4902)* **REGGAE ON BROADWAY. / OH LORD I GOT TO GET THERE**

Trojan / not iss.

Sep 72. (7") *(US 392)* **KEEP ON MOVING. / AFRICAN HERBSMAN** [ ] [–]

1972. (lp) *(TRL 62)* **AFRICAN HERBSMAN** [ ] [–]
– Lively up yourself / Small axe / Duppy conqueror / African herbsman / Trenchtown rock / Keep on moving / Fussing and fighting / Stand alone / All in one / Don't rock the boat / Put it on / Sun is shining / Kaya / Riding high / 400 years / Brain washing. *(re-iss. Jul84 lp/c; TRLS/ZCTRL 62) (cd-iss. Jun88; CDTRL 62) (re-iss. Nov83 on 'Fame' lp/c; FA/TCFA 41-3082-1/-4) (cd re-iss. Mar94 on 'Trojan'; same)*

The WAILERS

Blue Mountain / not iss.

Jan 73. (7") *(1021)* **BABY WE'VE GOT A DATE (ROCK IT BABY). / STOP THAT TRAIN** [ ] [–]

Island / Island

Apr 73. (7") *<1211>* **STOP THAT TRAIN. / ROCK IT BABY** [–] [ ]

Apr 73. (lp/c) *(<ILPS/ICT 9241>)* **CATCH A FIRE** [ ] [ ]
– Concrete jungle / Slave driver / 400 years / Stop that train / Baby we've got a date (rock it baby) / Stir it up / Kinky reggae / No more trouble / Midnight ravers. *(re-iss. Oct86 lp/c; ILPM/ICM 9241) (re-iss. Jun90 on 'Tuff Gong' cd/c; RRCD/RRCT 1) (cd re-iss. Jun01 +=; 548893-2)* – High tide or low tide / All day all night.

Jun 73. (7") *(WIP 6164)* **CONCRETE JUNGLE. / REINCARNATION SOUL** [ ] [–]

Jul 73. (7") *<1215>* **CONCRETE JUNGLE. / NO MORE TROUBLE** [–] [ ]

Sep 73. (7") *(WIP 6167) <1218>* **GET UP, STAND UP. / SLAVE DRIVER** [ ] [ ]

Nov 73. (lp/c) *(<ILPS/ICT 9256>)* **BURNIN'** [ ] [ ]
– Get up, stand up / Hallelujah time / I shot the sheriff / Burnin' and lootin' / Put it on / Small axe / Pass it on / Duppy conqueror / One foundation / Rastaman chant. *(re-iss. Mar87; ILPM 9256) (re-iss. Jun90 on 'Tuff Gong' cd/c; RRCD/RRCT 2) (cd re-iss. Jun01 +=; 548894-2)* – Reincranated soul / No sympathy / Oppressed song.

Feb 74. (7") *<005>* **I SHOT THE SHERIFF. / PUT IT ON** [–] [ ]

— added **The I-THREES** (female backers **JUDY MOWAT, MARCIA GRIFFITHS,** and **RITA**). They replaced PETER TOSH and BUNNY WAILER who both went solo.

BOB MARLEY & THE WAILERS

— **MARLEY, ASTON** and **BARRETT** added **EARL LINDO** – keyboards / **BERNARD HARVEY** – keyboards / **AL ANDERSON** – guitar.

May 75. (lp/c) *(<ILPS/ICT 9281>)* **NATTY DREAD** [43] [92]
– Lively up yourself / No woman no cry / Them belly full (but we hungry) / Rebel music (3 o'clock road block) / So jah seh / Natty dread / Bend down low / Talkin' blues / Revolution. *(re-iss. May87 lp/c/cd; ILPM/ICM/CID 9281) (re-iss. Jun90 on 'Tuff Gong' cd/c; RRCD/RRCT 3) (cd re-iss. Jul01 +=; 548895-2)* – Am a do.

Jun 75. (7") *(WIP 6212)* **NATTY DREAD. / SO JAH SEH** [ ] [–]

Jun 75. (7") *<027>* **LIVELY UP YOURSELF. / SO JAH SEH** [–] [ ]

— **TYRONE DOWNIE** – keyboards repl. HARVEY / **ALVIN 'SHECO' PATTERSON** – percussion repl. LINDO / added **JULIAN 'JUNIOR' MURVIN** – guitar

Aug 75. (7") *(WIP 6244) <037>* **NO WOMAN NO CRY (live). / KINKY REGGAE** [22] [ ]

Dec 75. (lp/c) *(<ILPS/ICT 9376>)* **LIVE! (live)** [38] [90]
– Trenchtown rock / Burnin' and lootin' / Them belly full (but we hungry) / Lively up yourself / No woman no cry / I shot the sheriff / Get up, stand up. *(re-iss. Jul81 + Sep86 as 'LIVE AT THE LYCEUM' lp/c; ILPM/ICM 9376) (cd-iss. Jan87; CID 9376) (re-iss. Nov90 on 'Tuff Gong' cd/c; RRCD/RRCT 4) (cd re-iss. Jul01 +=; 548896-2)* – Kinky reggae.

Jan 76. (7") *(WIP 6265)* **JAH LIVE. / CONCRETE JUNGLE (live)** [ ] [–]

Apr 76. (7") *(WIP 6296)* **JOHNNY WAS (WOMAN HANG HER HEAD AND CRY). / CRY TO ME** [ ] [–]

Apr 76. (lp/c) *(<ILPS/ICT 9383>)* **RASTAMAN VIBRATION** [15] [8]
– Positive vibration / Roots, rock, reggae / Johnny was / Cry to me / Want more / Crazy baldhead / Who the cap fit / Night shift / War / Rat race. *(re-iss. Apr87 lp/c/cd; ILPM/ICM/CID 9383) (re-iss. Nov90 on 'Tuff Gong' cd/c; RRCD/RRCT 5) (cd re-iss. Jul01 +=; 548897-2)* – Jah live.

Jun 76. (7") *(WIP 6309)* **ROOTS ROCK REGGAE. / STIR IT UP** [ ] [–]

Jun 76. (7") *<061>* **ROOTS ROCK REGGAE. / CRY TO ME** [–] [51]

Nov 76. (7") *<072>* **WHO THE CAP FIT. /** [–] [ ]

May 77. (lp/c) *(<ILPS/ICT 9498>)* **EXODUS** [8] Jun77 [20]
– Natural mystic / So much things to say / Guiltiness / The heathen / Exodus / Jamming / Waiting in vain / Turn your lights down low / Three little birds / One love – People get ready. *(re-iss. Mar87 lp/c/cd; ILPM/ICM/CID 9498) (re-iss. Nov90 on 'Tuff Gong' cd/c; RRCD/RRCT 6) (cd re-mast.Nov01 +=; 548898-2)* – Jammin' (long version) / Punky reggae party (long version).

Jun 77. (7") *(WIP 6390) <089>* **EXODUS. / EXODUS (dub)** [14] [ ]

Aug 77. (7") *(WIP 6402) <092>* **WAITING IN VAIN. / ROOTS** [27] [ ]

Dec 77. (7") *(WIP 6410)* **JAMMING. / PUNKY REGGAE PARTY** [9] [–]

— added the returning **EARL 'WIRE' LINDO** – keyboards

Feb 78. (7") *(WIP 6420) <099>* **IS THIS LOVE. / CRISIS (version)** [9] [ ]
(12"-iss.Jun81;)

Mar 78. (lp/c) *(<ILPS/ICT 9517>)* **KAYA** [4] [50]
– Easy shanking / Kaya / The sun is shining / Is this love / Satisfy my soul / She's gone / Misty morning / Crisis / Running away / Time will tell. *(re-iss. Feb87 lp/c/cd; ILPM/ICM/CID 9517) (re-iss. Nov90 on 'Tuff Gong' cd/c; RRCD/RRCT 7) (cd re-mast.Aug01 +=; 548899-2)* – Smile (Jamaica version).

May 78. (7") *(WIP 6440)* **SATISFY MY SOUL. / SMILE JAMAICA** [21] [–]

Dec 78. (d-lp/c) *(<ISLD/ICT 9542>)* **BABYLON BY BUS (live)** [40] [ ]
– Positive vibration / Punky reggae party / Exodus / Stir it up / Rat race / Concrete jungle / Kinky reggae / Lively up yourself / Rebel music (3 o'clock road block) / War / No more trouble / Is this love / The heathen / Jammin'. *(cd-iss. Feb87; CIDD 11) (re-iss. Nov90 on 'Tuff Gong' cd/c; RRCD/RRCT 8) (cd re-mast.Aug01 +=; 548900-2)* –

Jan 79. (7"; w-drawn) *(WIP 6478)* **STIR IT UP (live). / RAT RACE (live)** [–] [–]
(12") *(WIP12 6478)* – ('A'side) / War (live) / No more trouble (live).

Jul 79. (7") *<49080>* **WAKE UP AND LIVE. / (part 2)** [–] [ ]

Sep 79. (7") *(WIP 6510)* **SO MUCH TROUBLE IN THE WORLD. / ('A'instrumental)** [56] [–]

Oct 79. (lp/c) *(<ILPS/ICT 9542>)* **SURVIVAL** [20] [70]
– So much trouble in the world / Zimbabwe / Top ranking / Babylon system / Survival / Africa unite / One drop / Ride Natty ride / Ambush in the night / Wake up and live. *(re-iss. Mar87 lp/c/cd; ILPM/ICM/CID 9542) (re-iss. Nov90 on 'Tuff Gong' cd/c; RRCD RRCT 9) (cd re-mast.Aug01 +=; 548901-2)* – Ride Natty ride (12" mix) / Wake up and live (pt.1 & 2 – single version).

Nov 79. (7") *<49156>* **ONE DROP. / KAYA** [–] [ ]

Nov 79. (7") *(WIP 6553)* **SURVIVAL. / WAKE UP AND LIVE** [ ] [–]

Mar 80. (7") *(WIP 6597)* **ZIMBABWE. / SURVIVAL** [ ] [–]
(12") *(WIP12 6597)* – ('A'side) / Africa unite / Wake up and live.

May 80. (7") *(WIP 6610)* **COULD YOU BE LOVED. / ONE DROP** [5] [–]
(12"+=) *(12WIP 6610)* – Ride natty ride.

May 80. (7") *<49547>* **COULD YOU BE LOVED. / RIDE NATTY RIDE** [–] [ ]

Jun 80. (lp/c) *(<ILPS/ICT 9596>)* **UPRISING** [6] [45]
– Coming in from the cold / Real situation / Bad card / We and them / Work / Zion train / Pimper's paradise / Could you be loved / Forever loving Jah / Redemption song. *(cd-iss. Feb87; CID 9596) (re-iss. Nov90 on 'Tuff Gong' cd/c; RRCD/RRCT 10) (cd re-mast.Aug01 +=; 548902-2)* – Redemption song (band version) / Could you be loved (12" mix).

Aug 80. (7") *(WIP 6641)* **THREE LITTLE BIRDS. / EVERY NEED GOT AN EGO FEED** [17] [–]

Oct 80. (7"/12") *(WIP/12WIP 6653)* **REDEMPTION SONG. / ('A'-Band version)** [ ] [–]

Nov 80. (7") *<49636>* **REDEMPTION SONG. / COMING IN FROM THE COLD** [–] [ ]

— in Oct'80, BOB was diagnosed with lung cancer and died 11th May '81

– (selective) compilations, etc. –

Jul 74. (lp) *Trojan; (TRLS 89)* **RASTA REVOLUTION** [ ] [–]
(re-iss. 1981 + Jul84 lp/c; TRLS/ZCTRL 89) (cd-iss. Jun88; CDTRL 89) (re-iss. Jul85 on 'Fame' lp/c; FA/TCFA 41 3127) (cd re-iss. Mar94)

Jun 81. (12") *Island; (12WIP 6244) <49755>* **NO WOMAN NO CRY (live). / JAMMIN'** [8] [ ]

Sep 81. (lp/c) *Warners; (K/K4 99183) / Cotillion; <5228>* **CHANCES ARE** [ ] [ ]

1982. (9xlp-box) *Island; (EMSP 100)* **BOB MARLEY – THE BOXED SET** [ ] [–]

1982. (lp/c) *Island; (ISTDA 1)* **COUNTRYMAN** (Soundtrack with 8 MARLEY songs) [ ] [–]

Apr 83. (7"/12") *(IS/12IS 108)* **BUFFALO SOLDIER. / BUFFALO (dub)** [4] [ ]

May 83. (lp/c) *(ILPS/ICT 9760)* <90085> **CONFRONTATION** [5] [55]
– Chant down Babylon / Buffalo soldier / Jump Nyabinghi / Mix up, mix up / Give thanks and praises / Blackman redemption / Trenchtown / Stiff neked fools / I know / Rastaman live up!. *(re-iss. Mar87) (cd-iss. 1988 on 'Mango') (re-iss. cd+c Jun90 on 'Tuff Gong')*

Apr 84. (7") *Island; (IS 169)* **ONE LOVE. / PEOPLE GET READY** [5] [ ]
(12"+=/12"pic-d+=) *(12IS/+P 169)* – Keep on moving / So much trouble.

May 84. (lp/c) *Island; (BMW/+C 1)* <90169> **LEGEND** [1] [54]
– Is this love / Jamming / No woman no cry / Stir it up / Get up, stand up / Satisfy my soul / I shot the sheriff / One love / People get ready / Buffalo soldier / Exodus / Redemption song / Could you be loved / Want more. *(cd-iss. Aug85; CID 103) (cd re-iss. May91 on 'Tuff Gong' hit UK No.11, Mar92 No.18 / Jul92 No.25)*

Jun 84. (7") *Island; (IS 180)* **WAITING IN VAIN. / BLACK MAN REDEMPTION** [31] [ ]
(12"+=) *(12IS 180)* – Marley mix-up.

Nov 84. (7"/7"pic-d) *(IS/+P 210)* **COULD YOU BE LOVED. / NO WOMAN NO CRY** [71] [ ]
(12"+=) *(12IS 210)* – Jamming / Coming in from the cold.

Jun 86. (lp/c/cd) *Island; (ILPS/ICT/CID 9843)* <90169> **REBEL MUSIC** [54] [ ]
(re-iss. cd+c.Jun90 on 'Tuff Gong')

Mar 91. (cd/c/lp) *Tuff Gong; (TGL CD/MC/LP 12)* <848243> **TALKIN' BLUES** [ ] [–]
– (radio sessions 1973 + interviews 1975)

May 91. (c-s/7") *Tuff Gong; (TC+/TGX 1)* **ONE LOVE – PEOPLE GET READY. / SO MUCH TROUBLE IN THE WORLD** [42] [–]
(12"+=/cd-s+=) *(12/CD TGX 1)* – ('A'extended) / Keep on moving.

Sep 92. (c-s/7") *Tuff Gong; (TC+/TGX 2)* **IRON ZION LION ('74 track). / COULD YOU BE LOVED** [5] [ ]
(12"/cd-s) *(12/CD TGX 2)* – ('A'side) / Smile Jamaica / Three little birds.

Sep 92. (4xcd-box/4xc-box) *Tuff Gong; (TGCBX/TGMBX 1)* <512280> **SONGS OF FREEDOM** (discovered demos) [10] [86]
(re-iss. May93 as 8xlp-box; TGLBX 1)

Nov 92. (c-s/7") *Tuff Gong; (TC+/TGX 3)* **WHY SHOULD I. / ('A'-Kindread Spirit mix)** [42] [ ]
(cd-s+=) *(CDTGX 3)* – Exodus (rebel the remix)

May 95. (c-s) *Tuff Gong; (TCTGX 4)* **KEEP ON MOVING / PIMPER'S PARADISE** [17] [ ]
(12+=/cd-s+=) *(12/CD TGX 4)* – ('A'mixes).

May 95. (lp/c/cd) *Tuff Gong; (BMW/+C/CD 2)* <524103> **NATURAL MYSTIC** [5] [67]

Jun 96. (c-s) *Tuff Gong; (ANACA 002)* **WHAT GOES AROUND COMES AROUND** [42] [ ]
(12"+=/cd-s+=) *(ANA12/ANACD 002)* –

Sep 99. (c-s/12"/cd-s; as BOB MARLEY VS FUNKSTAR DE LUXE) *Club Tools; (0066895 9/0/5 CLU)* **THE SUN IS SHINING (mixes)** [3] [–]

Nov 99. (c-s/cd-s; by BOB MARLEY & LAURYN HILL) *Ruffhouse; (668436-4/-2)* **TURN YOUR LIGHTS DOWN LOW / (mixes)** [15] [ ]

Nov 99. (cd/lp) *Tuff Gong; (<546404-2/-1>)* **CHANT DOWN BABYLON** (remixed with modern artists) [ ] [60]

Jan 00. (12"/cd-s; by BOB MARLEY Vs FUNKSTAR DE LUXE) *Club Tools; (006722 0/5 CLU)* **RAINBOW COUNTRY** [11] [–]

Jun 00. (c-s/12"/cd-s; as BOB MARLEY featuring MC LYTE) *Tuff Gong; (12TGX/TGXCT/TGXCD 9)* **JAMMIN'** [42] [–]

Nov 00. (cd) *Prestige; (CDSGP 056)* **LIVELY UP YOURSELF** [ ] [–]
(re-dist.Jun01) – hit No.75

May 01. (cd) *Tuff Gong; (BMWCD 3) / Universal TV; <542855>* **ONE LOVE: THE VERY BEST OF BOB MARLEY** [5] [60]

Oct 01. (d-cd) *Universal TV; (586551-2)* **ONE LOVE – THE VERY BEST OF BOB MARLEY & THE WAILERS** [24] [–]

☐ Steve MARRIOTT (see under ⇒ HUMBLE PIE)

☐ MARS VOLTA (see under ⇒ AT THE DRIVE-IN)

John MARTYN

Born: IAIN McGEACHY, 11 Sep'48, New Malden, Surrey (he was partly brought up on a houseboat by his English mother, the other six months of the year by his father in Glasgow after they separated just after he was born – his grandmother subsequently brought him up in Scotland). Having learned guitar techniques from folk singer HAMISH IMLACH, MARTYN moved to London in 1967 after being the first white solo artist to secure a deal with Chris Blackwell's 'Island' label. His early albums, 'LONDON CONVERSATION' (1968) and 'THE TUMBLER' (1968) were competent folk sets, the latter revealing the first glimmers of MARTYN's nascent jazz/blues leanings, employing the services of respected flautist HAROLD McNAIR. Following MARTYN's marriage to Coventry girl, BEVERLEY KUTNER, the pair began recording together in 1969, releasing two albums, 'STORMBRINGER' and 'THE ROAD TO RUIN' the following year. The latter set was the first of many MARTYN albums to feature the double bass work of friend (and then PENTANGLE member) DANNY THOMPSON, the only musical collaborator who would become a fairly permanent fixture in the singer's career. Following the birth of the MARTYN's second child in 1971, JOHN resumed his solo career with 'BLESS THE WEATHER'. His most heavily jazz-influenced set to date, the record was a blueprint for much of MARTYN's subsequent work; here were the first signs of the singer's trademark lounge lizard slur (a defiantly unique hybrid of ERIC CLAPTON, LOWELL GEROGE and TOM WAITS) with which he'd dextrously negotiate the grey area where jazz, blues, folk and rock meet. With RICHARD THOMPSON on additional guitar (he also played on 'BLESS..') and a rhythm section courtesy of FAIRPORT CONVENTION (bassist DAVE PEGG and drummer DAVE MATTACKS), 'SOLID AIR' (1973) was the pivotal early MARTYN album. Pioneering use of acoustic guitar echo lent the album a uniquely haunting quality, the set featuring some of MARTYN's most affecting material. The title track was a drifting, twilight tribute to NICK DRAKE while among the more conventional, folk-ish numbers, 'OVER THE HILL' and lovely 'MAY YOU NEVER' (later covered by ERIC CLAPTON on his 'Slowhand' album) were soul stirring highlights. The album considerably widened his large cult following which numbered musicians like STEVE WINWOOD, a collaborator on the follow-up, 'INSIDE OUT' (1973). The record traced the same nebulous path as its predecessor, as did 'SUNDAY'S CHILD' (1975), the latter employing the services of the late PAUL KOSSOFF (ex-FREE and latterly BACKSTREET CRAWLER). In the two year gap prior to his next studio project, MARTYN released a limited (10,000) mail-order only (from his Sussex home) live album, the acclaimed 'LIVE AT LEEDS' (1975). The speed at which the pressing sold out indicated the extent of MARTYN's fanbase. Nevertheless, the singer was yet to make an overt attempt to turn his standing into commercial success; 'ONE WORLD' (1977) was as esoteric as ever. Extending his range of influences to include dub and oblique ambience, the record was another key release in MARTYN's career featuring both the gorgeous 'COULDN'T LOVE YOU MORE' and the sly, insidious skank of 'BIG MUFF', a collaboration with Jamaican legend LEE PERRY. The ensuing three years saw MARTYN split with wife BEVERLEY, this harrowing period providing much of the impetus for 1980's 'GRACE AND DANGER'. While the album was a relatively sombre affair, the emergence of PHIL COLLINS (here contributing percussion, vocals and production) signalled a move towards a more mainstream sound. Inevitably, then, his 1981 album, 'GLORIOUS FOOL' (a political assault on newly elected US president Ronald Reagan) made the UK Top 30, the follow-up, 'WELL KEPT SECRET' (1982) reaching No.20. Since then, however, he's failed to consolidate this brief flurry of chart action, conceivably because MARTYN's albums rarely include any glaring hit singles. Though the 80's were a fairly fallow period for MARTYN, he returned in fine style at the turn of the decade with 'THE APPRENTICE' (1990) and the sophisti-jazz of 'COOLTIDE' (1991). The latter set surfaced on 'Permanent' for whom he'd revisit a batch of old material on two studio sets and a live album over the course of the early-mid 90's. A surprise move to 'Go Discs!', resulted in his first Top 40 entry of the decade with 'AND' (1996). Upon the label's demise, MARTYN joined the new 'Independiente' stable (alongside TRAVIS!) and cut a low-key covers set, 'THE CHURCH WITH ONE BELL' (1998); he subsequently used the profits generated to help him procure the church pictured on the album sleeve(!). MARTYN's body of work remains unique, a rich seam of inspiration for the uninitiated; it's just a pity his talents aren't more widely acknowledged. The millennial 'GLASGOW WALKER' (2000) wasn't much of a departure from the kind of vapourous, jazz-inflected atmospherics with which he's constructed much of his latter day output although that wasn't such a bad thing, especially bearing in mind the oblique allure which MARTYN's vocal still holds, even on material like 'CRY ME A RIVER' and 'YOU DON'T KNOW WHAT LOVE IS'. The hard-living legend was to subsequently undergo a partial amputation (below the knee) of his right leg after a cyst burst and became infected. Laid up after the operation, financial necessity became the driving force behind some new recordings scheduled for 2004. • **Covered:** COCAINE BLUES (trad.) / I'D RATHER BE THE DEVIL (Skip James) / JOHNNY TOO BAD (Slickers) / TIGHT CONNECTION TO MY HEART (Bob Dylan) / NEVER LET ME GO (Joe Scott) / HE'S GOT ALL THE WHISKEY (Bobby Charles) / GOD'S SONG (Randy Newman) / HOW FORTUNATE THE MAN WITH NONE (Dead Can Dance; words Bertholt Brecht) / SMALL TOWN TALK (Bobby Charles & Rick Danko) / EXCUSE ME MISTER (Ben Harper) / STRANGE FRUIT (Billie Holiday) / THE SKY IS CRYING (Elmore James) / GLORY BOX (Portishead) / FEEL SO BAD (S. Hopkins) / DEATH DON'T HAVE NO MERCY (Reverend Gary Davis). • **Trivia:** He has also guested on albums by CLAIRE HAMMILL, BURNING SPEAR and BACK STREET CRAWLER, to mention but a few.

Album rating: LONDON CONVERSATION (*5) / THE TUMBLER (*5) / STORMBRINGER (*6) / THE ROAD TO RUIN (*6) / BLESS THE WEATHER (*7) / SOLID AIR (*8) / SUNDAY'S CHILD (*6) / LIVE AT LEEDS (*6) / INSIDE OUT (*6) / SO FAR SO GOOD compilation (*7) / ONE WORLD (*7) / GRACE & DANGER (*7) / GLORIOUS FOOL (*6) / THE ELECTRIC JOHN MARTYN compilation (*6) / WELL KEPT SECRET (*6) / PHILENTROPHY (*5) / SAPPHIRE (*5) / PIECE BY PIECE (*6) / FOUNDATIONS (*5) / THE APPRENTICE (*6) / COOLTIDE (*6) / NO LITTLE BOY (*5) / COULDN'T LOVE YOU MORE (*6) / SWEET LITTLE MYSTERIES compilation (*9) / AND. (*5) / THE CHURCH WITH ONE BELL (*6) / GLASGOW WALKER (*6)

JOHN MARTYN – vocals, acoustic guitar

Island Warners

Oct 67. (lp) *(ILP 952)* **LONDON CONVERSATION** –
– Fairy tale lullaby / Sandy grey / London conversation / Ballad of an elder woman / Cocaine blues / Run honey run / Back to stay / Rolling home / Who's grown up now / Golden girl / This time / Don't think twice. *(re-iss. Aug91 cd)(c; IMCD 134)(ICM 2074)*

— added **HAROLD McNAIR** – flute / **PAUL WHEELER** – guitar / **DAVE MOSES** – bass

Dec 68. (lp) *(ILPS 9091)* **THE TUMBLER** –
– Sing a song of summer / The river / Goin' down to Memphis / The gardeners / A day at the sea / Fishin' blues / Dusty / Hello train / Winding boy / Fly on home / Knuckledy crunch and slipp ledee slee song / Seven black roses. *(cd-iss. Apr94; IMCD 173)*

JOHN & BEVERLEY MARTYN

(as BEVERLEY, she recorded solo 45's) **BEVERLEY** nee KUTNER – vocals, with + **LEVON HELM** – drums (The BAND) / **PAUL HARRIS** – piano / **HARVEY BROOKS** – bass / **BIUX MUNDI + HERBIE LOVELL** – drums

Jan 70. (7") *(WIP 6076)* **JOHN THE BAPTIST. / THE OCEAN** –
Feb 70. (lp) *(ILPS 9113) <1854>* **STORMBRINGER**
– Go out and get it / Can't get the one I want / Stormbringer / Sweet honesty / Woodstock / John the baptist / The ocean / Traffic light lady / Tomorrow time / Would you believe me. *(re-iss. Aug91 cd)(c; IMCD 131)(ICM 9113)*

Apr 70. (7") **GO OUT AND GET IT. / CAN'T GET THE ONE I WANT** –

— with **DANNY THOMPSON** – bass (of PENTANGLE) / **WELLS KELLY** – drums, bass + **PAUL HARRIS**

Nov 70. (lp) *(ILPS 9133) <1882>* **THE ROAD TO RUIN**
– Primrose hill / Parcels / Auntie aviator / New day / Give us a ring / Sorry to be so long / Tree garden / Say what you can / The road to ruin. *(cd-iss. Mar93; IMCD 165)*

JOHN MARTYN

went solo again, with **DANNY THOMPSON** – double bass / **RICHARD THOMPSON** – guitar (solo artist) / **TONY REEVES** – (of COLOSSEUM) / **IAN WHITEMAN** and **ROGER POWELL** (of MIGHTY BABY)

Island Island

Nov 71. (lp) *(ILPS 9167) <9311>* **BLESS THE WEATHER**
– Go easy / Bless the weather / Sugar lump / Walk to the water / Just now / Head and heart / Let the good times come / Back down the river / Glistening Glyndebourne / Singing in the rain. *(re-iss. Aug91 cd)(c; IMCD 135)(ICM 9167)*

— retained **DANNY, RICHARD** and brought in **JOHN 'RABBIT' BUNDRICK** – keyboards / **DAVE PEGG** – bass / **DAVE MATTACKS** – drums / and **SPEEDY** (NEEMOI ACQUAYE) – congas / (all of FAIRPORT CONVENTION).

Nov 72. (7") *(WIP 6116)* **MAY YOU NEVER. / JUST NOW** –
Feb 73. (lp) *(ILPS 9226) <9325>* **SOLID AIR**
– Over the hill / Don't want to know / I'd rather be with the Devil / Go down easy / Dreams by the sea / May you never / The man in the station / Easy blues / Solid air. *(re-iss. Nov86 lp/c; ILPM/ICM 9226) (cd-iss. Feb87; CID 9226) (cd re-mast.Oct00; IMCD 274)*

Mar 73. (7") **MAY YOU NEVER. / DON'T WANT TO KNOW ABOUT EVIL** –

— retained **DANNY,** and brought in **BOBBY KEYES** and **REMI KABAKA** plus **STEVE WINWOOD** and **CHRIS WOOD** (both of TRAFFIC)

Oct 73. (lp) *(ILPS 9253) <9335>* **INSIDE OUT**
– Fine lines / Eibhli ghail ghiuin ni chearbhaill / Ain't no saint / Outside in / The glory of love / Look in / Beverley / Make no mistake / Ways to cry / So much in love with you. *(cd-iss. Apr94; IMCD 172)*

— with **DANNY THOMPSON / JOHN STEVENS** – drums / **PAUL KOSSOFF** – guitar (ex-FREE) and guests **BEVERLEY MARTYN** – vocals

Jan 75. (lp) *(ILPS 9296) <9396>* **SUNDAY'S CHILD**
– One day without you / Lay it all down / Root love / My baby girl / Sunday's child / Spencer the rover / Clutches / The message / Satisfied mind / You can discover / Call me crazy. *(cd-iss. Mar93; IMCD 163)*

Sep 75. (lp; ltd-mail order) *(ILPS 9343)* **LIVE AT LEEDS (live)** – –
– Outside in / Solid air / Make no mistake / Bless the weather / The man in the station / I'd rather be the Devil. *(re-iss. Jun87 on 'Cacophony'; SKELP 001) (cd-iss. May92 on 'Awareness'; AWCD 1036) (re-iss. cd Jul95 on 'Hypertension'; HYCD 200114) (cd re-iss. Aug98 on 'Blueprint'; OW 107CD)*

Feb 77. (7") *(WIP 6385)* **OVER THE HILL. / HEAD AND HEART**

Mar 77. (lp) *(<ILPS 9484>)* **SO FAR SO GOOD** (compilation) –
– May you never / Bless the weather / Head and heart / Over the hill / Spencer the rover / Glistening Glyndebourne / Solid air / One day without you / I'd rather be the Devil.

— with guests **STEVE WINWOOD** – keyboards / **MORRIS PERT** – percussion.

Nov 77. (lp/c) *(ILPS/ZCI 9492)* **ONE WORLD** 54 –
– Couldn't love you more / Certain surprise / Dancing / Small hours / Dealer / One world / Smiling stranger / Big Muff. *(re-iss. Sep86 lp/c/cd; ILPM/ICM/CID 9492)*

Jan 78. (7") *(WIP 6414)* **DANCING. / DEALER (version)** –

— with **PHIL COLLINS** – drums,vocals / **JOHN GIBLIN** – bass (both of

BRAND X) / **TOMMY EYRE** – keyboards (GREASE BAND) / **DAVE LAWSON** – keyboards (ex-GREENSLADE).

Island — not iss.

Oct 80. (lp/c) *(ILPS/ICT 9560)* **GRACE AND DANGER** 54 –
– Some people are crazy / Grace and danger / Lookin' on / Johnny too bad / Sweet little mystery/ Hurt in your heart / Baby please come home / Save some for me / Our love. *(cd-iss. May87; CID 9560)*

Oct 80. (7") *(WIP 6495)* **JOHNNY TOO BAD. / ('A'instrumental)** –

Mar 81. (7") *(WIP 6547)* **JOHNNY TOO BAD. / ('A'version)** –
(12") *(IPR 2046)* – ('A'ext. dub version) / Big Muff (ext.mix).

May 81. (7") *(WIP 6718)* **SWEET LITTLE MYSTERY. / JOHNNY TOO BAD** –

— with **PHIL COLLINS** – drums, vocals, producer / **ALAN THOMSON** – bass / **MAX MIDDLETON** – keyboards / **DANNY CUMMINGS** – percussion / **DICK CUTHELL** – horns 2.

WEA — Duke

Aug 81. (7") *(K 79243)* **PLEASE FALL IN LOVE WITH ME. / DON'T YOU GO** –

Sep 81. (lp/c) *(K/K4 99178)* **GLORIOUS FOOL** 25 –
– Couldn't love you more / Amsterdam / Hold on my heart / Perfect hustler / Hearts and keys / Glorious fool / Never say never / Oascanel (get back home) / Didn't do that / Please fall in love with me / Don't you go.

Feb 82. (7") **COULDN'T LOVE YOU MORE. /** –

— with **DANNY** and **ALAN** plus **JEFFREY ALLEN** – drums / **JIM PRIME** – keyboards / **MEL COLLINS** – sax / **MARTIN DROVER** – trumpet / **LEE KOSMIN** and **STEVE LANGE** – harmony.

Aug 82. (lp/c) *(K/K4 99255)* **WELL KEPT SECRET** 20 –
– Could've been me / You might need a man / Hung up / Gun money / Never let me go / Love up / Changes her mind / Hiss on the tape / Back with a vengeance / Livin' alone.

Sep 82. (7") *(K 79336)* **HISS ON THE TAPE. / LIVIN' ALONE** –

Nov 82. (7") *(259987-7)* **GUN MONEY (US remix). / HISS ON THE TAPE (live)**

— touring line-up **ALAN THOMSON** – bass / **JEFFREY ALLEN** – drums / **DANNY CUMMINGS** – percussion / **RONNIE LEAHY** – keyboards

Body Swerve — not iss.

Nov 83. (lp) *(JMLP 001)* **PHILENTHROPY (live)** –
– Sunday's child / Don't want to know / Johnny too bad / Make no mistake / Root love / Lookin' on / Hung up / Smiling stranger. *(re-iss. Mar86 on 'Dojo' lp/c/cd; DOJO LP/TC/CD 26)*

— **MARTYN** retained **JIM** and **ALAN** plus **BARRY REYNOLDS** add. guitar / **JACK WALDMAN** – keyboards / **ROBIN RANKIN** – keyboards / **JAMES HOOKER** – keyboards / **STEVEN STANLEY** – linn drums / **ANDY LYDEN** – linn drums / **UZZIAH 'STICKY' THOMPSON** – percussion / **COLIN TULLY** – saxophone / harmony by **MORWENNE LAIDLAW, TERRY NELSON** and **LORNA BROOKS**

Island — Island

Oct 84. (7") *(IS 209)* **OVER THE RAINBOW. / ROPE SOUL'D** –

Nov 84. (lp/c) *(ILPS/ICT 9779)* **SAPPHIRE** 57 –
– Sapphire / Over the rainbow / You know / Watching her eyes / Fisherman's dream / Acid rain / Mad dog days / Climb the walls / Coming in on time / Rope soul'd. *(cd-iss. Mar93; IMCD 164)*

— with **ALAN THOMSON** – fretless bass / **DANNY CUMMINGS** – percussion / **COLIN TULLY and FOSTER PATTERSON** – keyboards, vocals.

Feb 86. (lp/c/cd) *(ILPS/ICT/CID 9807)* **PIECE BY PIECE** 28 –
– Nightline / Lonely love / Angeline / One step too far / Piece by piece / Serendipity / Who believes in angels / Love of mine / John Wayne. *(cd+=)* – Tight connection to my heart / Solid air / One world / May you never.

Feb 86. (7") *(IS 265)* **ANGELINE. / TIGHT CONNECTION TO MY HEART** –
(12"+=) *(12IS 265)* – May you never / Certain surprise / One day without you.
(cd-ep+=) *(CID 265)* – May you never / Solid air / Glistening Glyndebourne.

May 86. (7") *(IS 272)* **LONELY LOVE. / SWEET LITTLE MYSTERY (live)** –
(12"+=) *(12IS 272)* – Fisherman's dream (live).

— **DAVID BALL** – bass repl. THOMPSON / added **ARRAN ABMUN** – drums + **JEFF CASTLE** – keyboards

Oct 87. (lp/c/cd) *(ILPS/ICT/CID 9884)* **FOUNDATIONS (live)** –
– Mad dog days / Angeline / The apprentice / May you never / Deny this love / Send me one line / John Wayne / Johnny too bad / Over the rainbow. *(re-iss. cd Apr94; IMCD 180)*

Permanent — not iss.

Mar 90. (cd/c/lp) *(PERM CD/MC/LP 1)* **THE APPRENTICE** –
– Live on love / Look at that gun / Send me one line / Hold me / The apprentice / The river / Income town / Deny this love / UPO / Patterns in the rain. *(cd+=)* – The moment. *(cd re-iss. Apr98 on 'Indelible'; INDELCD 1)*

Aug 90. (7") *(PERM S12)* **DENY THIS LOVE (remix). / THE APPRENTICE (live)** –
(cd-s+=) *(CDPERM 1)* – ('A'-lp version).

Nov 91. (cd/c/lp) *(PERM CD/MC/LP 4)* **COOLTIDE** –
– Hole in the rain / Annie says / Jack the lad / Number nine / The cure / Same difference / Father Time / Call me / Cooltide.

Apr 92. (cd-s) *(CDPERM 3)* **JACK THE LAD / ?** –

Sep 92. (7") *(PERM 6)* **SWEET LITTLE MYSTERY. / HEAD AND HEART** –
(12"+=/cd-s+=) *(12/CD PERM 6)* – Never let me go.

Oct 92. (cd/c/lp) *(PERM CD/MC/LP 9)* **COULDN'T LOVE YOU MORE** 65 –
– Lonely love / Couldn't love you more / Sweet little mystery / Head & heart / Could've been me / One day without you / Over the hill / Fine lines / May you never / One world / Way's to cry / Angeline / Man in the station / Solid air / Never let me go.

Jan 93. (cd-s; w-drawn) **LONELY LOVE** –

— with on next album **SPENCER COZENS** or **CHRIS CAMERON** – keyboards / **GERRY CONWAY** or **WAYNE STEWART** – drums / **ALAN THOMPSON** or **JOHN GIBLIN** – bass / **MILES BOULD** or **MARK WALKER** – percussion / **DAVE GILMOUR** or **ALAN DARBY** or **BILL RUPERT** – guitar / **ANDY SHEPHERD** or **GERRY UNDERWOOD** – sax / **FRED NELSON** – piano / **LEVON HELM** – guest / and of course **PHIL COLLINS** – b.vocals, etc.

Jul 93. (cd/c) *(PERM CD/MC 14)* **NO LITTLE BOY** (old songs re-worked) –
– Solid air / Ways to cry / Could've been me / I don't wanna know / Just now / One day without you / Sweet little mystery / Pascanel / Sunday's child / Head and heart / Fine lines / Bless the weather / Man in the station / One world / Rock salt and nails / Hole in the rain.

— with **PHIL COLLINS, JOHN GIBLIN + ALAN THOMPSON, JERRY UNDERWOOD, SPENCER COZENS,** etc

Go! Discs — not iss.

Aug 96. (cd/c) *(828 798-2/-4)* **AND.** 32 –
– Sunshine's better / Suzanne / The downward pull of human nature / All in your favour / A little strange / Who are they? / Step it up / Carmine / She's a lover.

— now with **GIBLIN, COZENS** / + **ARRAN AHMUN** – drums, percussion

Blueprint — not iss.

Dec 97. (cd-ep) *(BP 276CD)* **SNOOO . . . / SHE'S A LOVER / ALL IN YOUR FAVOUR / STEP IT UP / A LITTLE STRANGE** –

Independiente — Thirsty Ear

Mar 98. (cd) *(ISOM 3CD)* <57053> **THE CHURCH WITH ONE BELL** 51
– He's got all the whiskey / God's song / How fortunate the man with none / Small town talk / Excuse me mister / Strange fruit / The sky is crying / Glory box / Feel so sad / Death don't have no mercy.

Jun 98. (cd-s) *(ISOM 14MS)* **EXCUSE ME MISTER / GOD'S SONG (live) / ROCK, SALT AND NAIL (live) / JOHN WAYNE (live)** –

May 00. (cd) *(ISOM 15CD)* **GLASGOW WALKER** 66 –
– So sweet / Wildflower / The field of play / Cool in the life / Feel so good / Cry me a river / Mama T / Can't live without / The cat won't work tonight / You don't know what love is.

— in Mar'01, MARTYN was credited on the SISTER BLISS (of FAITHLESS) UK No.31 single, 'Deliver Me'

– compilations, etc. –

on 'Island' unless otherwise mentioned

Oct 82. (lp/c) *(ILPS/ICT 9715)* **THE ELECTRIC JOHN MARTYN**
(cd-iss. Apr88; CID 9715)

May 92. (cd) *Windsong; (WINCD 012)* **BBC RADIO 1 LIVE IN CONCERT (live)** –

Nov 92. (d-cd) *(ITSCD 2)* **SOLID AIR / ONE WORLD** –

Jun 94. (d-cd) *(CRNCD 4)* **SWEET LITTLE MYSTERIES – THE ISLAND ANTHOLOGY**

Jul 95. (d-cd/d-c) *Permanent; (PERM CD/MC 33) / Resurgent;* *<1122>* **LIVE (live at the Shaw Theatre, London, 31st March, 1990)** <US-title 'DIRTY, DOWN & LIVE'> Nov99
– Easy blues / May you never / Dealer / Outside in / Never let me go / Sapphire / Couldn't love you more / Deny this love / Fisherman's dream / Big Muff / Angeline / Sweet little mystery / The river / Income town / The apprentice / John Wayne / Look at the girl / Looking on / Johnny too bad / One world.

Mar 98. (cd) *Artful; (ARTFULCD 13)* **THE REST OF THE BEST** –

Mar 00. (d-cd) *Artful; (ARTFULCD 31)* **CLASSICS** –
(re-iss. Apr02; same)

Jul 00. (d-cd) *Eagle; (EDMCD 102)* **THE MASTERS (live '91)** –

Nov 00. (cd) *One World; (OW 113CD)* **THE NEW YORK SESSION** –

Apr 01. (cd) *Mooncrest; (<CRESTCD 065>)* **PATTERNS IN THE RAIN (some live)**

Jul 01. (cd; by JOHN MARTYN & DANNY THOMPSON) *One World; (OW 118CD)* **LIVE IN GERMANY 1986 (live)** –

Aug 01. (cd; by JOHN MARTYN & DANNY THOMPSON) *One World; (OW 115CD)* **LIVE AT THE BREWERY ARTS CENTRE KENDAL 1986 (live)** –

Aug 01. (cd) *One World; (OW 109CD)* **LIVE AT THE TOWN & COUNTRY CLUB 1986 (live)** –

Nov 01. (cd) *One World; (OW 116CD)* **LIVE AT THE BOTTOM LINE, NEW YORK 1983 (live)** –

Nov 01. (cd) *One World; (OW 119CD)* **SWEET CERTAIN SURPRISE (live)** –

May 02. (cd) *One World; (OW 117CD)* **LIVE IN MILAN (live)** –

□ J. MASCIS (see under ⇒ DINOSAUR JR.)

□ Nick MASON (see under ⇒ PINK FLOYD)

MASSIVE ATTACK

Formed: Bristol, England ... 1987 by 3-D, MUSHROOM and DADDY G. Having founded their own label, 'Wild Bunch' (named after the loose Bristol collective of DJ's, producers and musicians of which MASSIVE ATTACK were an integral part) five years earlier, they were subsequently snapped up by Virgin subsidiary, 'Circa' in 1990 and with only their second single, 'UNFINISHED SYMPATHY' – released under the revised moniker of MASSIVE (to distance themselves from any affiliation with the UN Gulf War policy) – crashed into the Top 20. Featuring the velvet tones of SHARA NELSON and luxuriant string arrangements to die for, this hypnotically beautiful track is oft cited as one of the most perfect singles ever crafted. While not boasting anything quite as tantalising, the classic debut album, 'BLUE LINES', hit the the Top 20 in Spring '91, a darkly sensual, spliff-heavy cocktail of sampladelic dub, hip-hop, funk and soul that can quite possibly lay claim to be the Big Daddy of that much-maligned genre, trip-hop. Alongside the aforementioned NELSON, the record featured guest vocalists, TRICKY (soon to carve out his own career in paranoid beats) and dub reggae veteran, HORACE ANDY. NELSON subsequently departed for a solo career and all was quiet from the MASSIVE' camp until the Autumn of '94, when they re-surfaced with the NELLEE HOOPER (Soul II Soul)-produced 'PROTECTION' album. An even darker, slinkier creature, it featured an array of guest vocalists, most effectively employing TRACEY THORN on the aching 'BETTER THINGS' and the title track; TRICKY, meanwhile, sounded almost catatonic on the spellbinding voodoo bass-psyche of 'KARMACOMA' while the exotic tones of NICOLETTE graced a couple of tracks. More cohesive soundwise, the record was characterised by a haunting dub-reggae feel and while it was perhaps pushing it a bit to revamp a Doors track ('LIGHT MY FIRE'), the claustrophobic brilliance of 'SPYING GLASS' (featuring HORACE ANDY in peerless form) more than made up for it. London dub producer, The MAD PROFESSOR, later gave it a bowel quaking, full-on dub reworking early in '95, the results surfacing as the mind scrambling 'NO PROTECTION'. Stunningly original and defiantly self-sufficient, MASSIVE ATTACK continue to shrug off any labels hopeful journos may pin on them (and woe betide anyone who mentions tr*p h*p), and while their perfectionism means lengthy periods between new material, fans have learned to be patient. In the summer of '97, the trio returned with their darkest, scariest track to date, 'RISINGSON', a solitary taster for the following year's long-awaited UK chart-topper, 'MEZZANINE'. Yet again cleaning up across the critical board, MASSIVE ATTACK had created a work many regarded as the pinnacle of their career, an unflinchingly bleak, downbeat and introspective record mired in paranoia, despair and apocalytic pre-millennium tension. Nevertheless, 3-D, MUSHROOM and DADDY-G explored more musical possibilities than most bands of their ilk put together, even hooking up with LIZ FRASER (of the COCTEAU TWINS) on the track, 'TEARDROPS', subsequently a Top 10 hit. 1999 started a little painfully for the trio when MANFRED MANN threatened a lawsuit against them for the use of his song 'Tribute' on their track 'BLACK MARK'; an out of court settlement was soon agreed on. However, that was the least of their problems, MUSHROOM opting to bail out in July that year. With DADDY G also departing on domestic duty, it was left to 3D to complete '100th WINDOW' (2003), the band's fourth album and the only one not to develop significantly from its predecessor. That said, its brooding, stifling atmospherics were almost as compelling as 'MEZZANINE', with SINEAD O'CONNOR taking up the role that SHARA NELSON, TRACEY THORN and LIZ FRASER filled with such grace in the past. Unsurprisingly, the Irish singer brought a different dimension to that role, illuminating the album's darker corners with her burning vision, and nowhere more so than 'WHAT YOUR SOUL SINGS'. HORACE ANDY also reported for duty once again, airing his timeless, genderless vocal chords on 'NAME TAKEN' and 'EVERYWHEN'. • **Songwriters:** Group except; BE THANKFUL FOR WHAT YOU'VE GOT (William DeVaughn) / LIGHT MY FIRE (Doors) / MAN NEXT DOOR (John Holt) / EXCHANGE (Bob Hilliard & Mort Garson). Sampled JAMES BROWN, PIECES OF A DREAM, YOUNG HOLT TRIO. • **Trivia:** Remixed PETER GABRIEL, LES NEGRESSES VERTES.

Album rating: BLUE LINES (*9) / PROTECTION (*9) / NO PROTECTION (*8; Massive Attack Vs. The Mad Professor) / MEZZANINE (*9) / 100th WINDOW (*6)

3-D (b. ROBERT DEL NAJA, 21 Jan'65, Brighton, England) – vocals / **MUSHROOM** (b. ANDREW VOWLES, 10 Nov'67) – keyboards / **DADDY-G** (b. GRANT MARSHALL, 18 Dec'59) – keyboards

Warners / Warners

Jul 88. (12") *(MASS 001)* **ANY LOVE. / ('A'mix)**

—— w/ **SHARA NELSON** – vocals / **NELLEE HOOPER** – programmer / arranger

Wild Bunch-Circa / Virgin

Nov 90. (7"/c-s) *(WBR S/C 1)* **DAYDREAMING. / ('A'instrumental)** –
(12"+=/cd-s+=) *(WBR T/X 1)* – Any love (2).
(12") *(WBR TX 1)* – ('A'-luv it mix) / ('A'-Brixton bass mix) / ('A'-luv it dub).

Feb 91. (7"/c-s; as MASSIVE) *(WBR S/C 2)* **UNFINISHED SYMPATHY. / ('A'-Nellee Hooper mix)** 13 –
(12"/cd-s) *(WBR T/X 2)* – ('A'side) / ('A'-Paul Oakenfold mix) / ('A'-P.O. instrumental) / ('A'instrumental).

—— Below also featured **HORACE ANDY** – vox

Apr 91. (cd/c/2x12"lp) *(WBR CD/MC/LP 1)* *<91685>* **BLUE LINES** 13 Aug91
– Safe from harm / One love / Blue lines / Be thankful for what you've got /

Five man army / Unfinished sympathy / Daydreaming / Lately / Hymn of the big wheel. *(re-iss. Sep96; same); hit UK 21)*

May 91. (7"/c-s) *(WBR S/C 3) <96332>* **SAFE FROM HARM. / ('A'version)** [25] [ ]
(cd-s+=) *(WBRX 3)* – ('A'-Perfecto mix).
(12") *(WBRT 3)* – ('A'-Perfecto mix) / ('A'dub mix) / ('A'instrumental).

Feb 92. (7"ep/c-ep/12"ep/cd-ep) *(WBR S/C/T/X 4)* **MASSIVE ATTACK** [27] [–]
– Hymn of the big wheel / Home of the whale / Be thankful / Any love.

— now w / **TRACEY THORN** (Everything But The Girl) / **NICOLETTE / TRICKY + HORACE ANDY** – vocals. **CRAIG ARMSTRONG** – piano / **CHESTER KAMEN** – guitar / **ROB MERRIL** – drums

Sep 94. (cd/c/lp) *(WBR CD/MC/LP 2) <39883>* **PROTECTION** [4] [ ]
– Protection / Karmacoma / Three / Weather storm / Spying glass / Better things / Eurochild / Sly / Heat miser / Light my fire (live).

Oct 94. (c-s/cd-s) *(WBR C/X 5) <38465>* **SLY / ('A'mix by UNDERDOG) / ('A'-Mad Professor mix) / ('A'-Tim Simenon mix)** [24] Nov94 [ ]
(12"s+=/cd-s+=) *(WBR T/DX 5)* – (extra-'A'mix).

Jan 95. (cd-s; by MASSIVE ATTACK with TRACEY THORN) *(WBRDX 6) <38471>* **PROTECTION / ('A'-J.Sw!ft mix) / THREE (Don T's house mix)** [14] Feb95 [ ]
(c-s/cd-s) *(WBR C/X 6)* – (1st 2 tracks) / ('A'-Radiation for the nation mix) / ('A'-Eno mix).
(12"+=) *(WBRT 6)* – ('A'-Mad Professor mix).

Feb 95. (cd/c/lp; as MASSIVE ATTACK VS MAD PROFESSOR) *(WBR CD/MC/LP 3)* **NO PROTECTION** [10] [–]
– Radiation ruling the nation (Protection) / Bumper ball dub (Karmacoma) / Trinity dub (Three) / Cool monsoon (Weather storm) / Eternal feedback (Sly) / Moving dub (Better things) / I spy (Spying glass) / Backward sucking (Heat miser).

Mar 95. (12"ep) *(WBRT 7)* **KARMACOMA. / ('A'-Napoli trip mix) / ('A'-Unkle mix) / BLACKSMITH – DAYDREAMING** [28] Jul95 [ ]
(cd-ep+=) *(WBRX 7)* – ('A'-Portishead experience mix) / ('A'-Bumper ball mix).
(c-ep++=/cd-ep++=) *(WBR C/DX 7)* – ('A'-Portishead mix).

— next album/releases saw the addition of vocalists **HORACE ANDY, ELIZABETH FRASER, SARA JAY, ROBERT DEL NAJA + GRANT MARSHALL** / guitars – **ANGELO BRUSCHINI** / bass – **JOHN HARRIS, BOB LOCKE + WINSTON** / drums – **ANDY GANGADEEN**

Jul 97. (12"/cd-s) *(WBR T/X 8)* **RISINGSON. / SUPERPREDATORS** [11] [ ]

Apr 98. (cd/c/lp) *(WBR CD/MC/LP 4) <45599>* **MEZZANINE** [1] May98 [60]
– Angel / Risingson / Teardrop / Inertia creeps / Exchange / Dissolved girl / Man next door / Black milk / Mezzanine / Group four / (Exchange).
(below single featured LIZ FRAZER on vocals)

Apr 98. (c-s) *(WBRC 9)* **TEARDROP / EURO ZERO HERO** [10] [–]
(12"+=/cd-s+=) *(WBR T/X 9)* – ('A'mixes).

Jul 98. (c-s) *(WBRC 10)* **ANGEL / GROUP 4** [30] [–]
(12"+=/cd-s+=) *(WBR T/X 10)* – ('A'mixes by Blur & the Mad Professor).

Oct 98. (d12"ep/cd-ep) *(WBR TD/DDX 11)* **INERTIA CREEPS** [–] non [–]
– (mixes:- Manic Street Preachers / State of Bengal / Alpha / Back she comes – Inertia mixed by Mad Professor / Reflection).

— now without MUSHROOM who left mid-'99

Virgin Astralwerks

Feb 03. (cd/t-lp) *(CD+/V 2967) <81239>* **100th WINDOW** [1] [69]
– Future proof / What your soul sings / Everywhen / Special cases / Butterfly caught / A prayer for England / Small time shot away / Name taken / Antistar.

Feb 03. (cd-s) *(VSCDT 1839)* **SPECIAL CASES / SPECIAL CASES (Akufen remix) / I AGAINST I (featuring MOS DEF) / SPECIAL CASES (version 2)** [15] [–]
(12") *(VST 1839)* – (Akufeb remix) / Luono's casing.

Jun 03. (cd-s) *(VSCDT 1853)* **BUTTERFLY CAUGHT (mixes; Paul Daley / Octave One / RJD2 / Jagz Kooner / Version Point / video)** [ ] [–]
(d12") *(VST 1853)* – (some above mixes).

matchbox20

Formed: Florida, USA . . . 1993 by singer/songwriter and ROB THOMAS and his army of rock-heavy cohorts, BRIAN YALE and drummer PAUL DOUCETTE. The chieftain of these south-coast rock exhibitionists, THOMAS, formed the group after dropping out of high school at the age of seventeen and performing in a number of local outfits where he met YALE and DOUCETTE. Polishing off the line-up with rhythm guitarist ADAM GAYNOR and KYLE COOK (who were both previously employees of 'Criteria recording studios' in Miami), the band subsequently recruited COLLECTIVE SOUL producer Matt Serletic and recorded several demo tapes which soon fell into the hands of 'Lava' (an offshoot of 'Atlantic'). The band issued 'YOURSELF OR SOMEONE LIKE YOU' (1996), continuing their tour to the farthest reaches of America after the album was slandered a lame PEARL JAM rip-off by critics. It's not difficult to see why the band received this reaction: from the outset, the album displays a neat array of complex guitar solos, meaningful lyrics and soulful EDDIE VEDDER meets JOE COCKER-style vocals. 'LONG DAY' became the first single to be taken from the album and, despite its failure to attract any constructive attention, was heavily played on rotation from major American radio stations and MTV alike, carving the way for matchbox20's second and more successful single. After its release in America, 'PUSH' also began its rounds on national radio and televison, steadily climbing up the alternative/rock charts until it reached the Top Ten in the summer of 1997. The 'YOURSELF OR . . .' album was catapulted into the Billboard Top 40 after it had gone gold due to the popularity of 'PUSH'. Before the beginning of 1998, the album had gone double-platinum, with three more hit singles ('REAL WORLD', 'BACK 2 GOOD' and '3 AM) in the bag and a momentous following in Australia and Canada. More recently and significantly was ROB THOMAS moonlighting on SANTANA's 'Smooth' single (a track taken from 1999 Grammy-hit album, 'Supernatural') which also became a gigantic MTV/FM-friendly success worldwide. Meanwhile, matchbox20, were already getting set to unleash their sophomore set. When it arrived, 'MAD SEASON' (2000) proved that THOMAS' sterling performance on the SANTANA album had been no fluke, his vocal prowess having matured along with the band's sound. A more inclusive, pop-friendly approach to millennial alt-rock suggested a bright future. All the more surprising then that 'MORE THAN YOU THINK YOU ARE' (2002) failed to build on that promise, proffering a strangely faceless set of songs lacking in either the band's killer instinct for hooky alt-rock or the suave self awareness of THOMAS' SANTANA collaborations. • **Covered:** DON'T LET ME DOWN (Beatles).

Album rating: YOURSELF OR SOMEONE LIKE YOU (*6) / MAD SEASON (*6) / MORE THAN YOU THINK YOU ARE (*4)

ROB THOMAS – vocals / **KYLE COOK** – lead guitar / **ADAM GAYNOR** – rhythm guitar / **BRIAN YALE** – bass / **PAUL DOUCETTE** – drums

Lava – Atlantic Lava – Atlantic

Mar 98. (7"/c-s) *(AT 0021/+C)* **PUSH. / TIRED** [38] [ ]
(cd-s+=) *(AT 0021CD)* – Busted (acoustic).

Apr 98. (cd/c) *<(7567 92721-2/-4)>* **YOURSELF OR SOMEONE LIKE YOU** [50] Feb97 [5]
– Real world / Long day / 3 a.m. / Push / Girl like that / Back 2 good / Damn / Argue / Kody / Busted / Shame / Hang.

Jun 98. (7"/c-s) *(AT 0034/+C)* **3 A.M. / PUSH (acoustic)** [64] [–]
(cd-s+=) *(AT 0034CD)* – Shame.

Oct 98. (7"/c-s) *(EW 773/+C) <radio play>* **REAL WORLD. / LONG DAY (live)** [ ] [38]
(cd-s+=) *(EW 773CD)* – 3 a.m. (live).

Dec 98. (-) *<radio cut>* **BACK 2 GOOD** [-] [24]

Jun 99. (cd-s) *(AT 0052CD)* **REAL WORLD / LONG DAY (live) / 3 A.M. (live)** [ ] [-]

— they were now slightly changed to **MATCHBOX TWENTY**

May 00. (cd/c) *<(7567 83302-2/-4)>* **MAD SEASON** [31] [3]
– Angry / Black & white people / Crutch / Last beautiful girl / If you're gone / Mad season / Rest stop / The burn / Bent / Bed of lies / Leave / Stop / You won't be mine.

Jul 00. (c-s/cd-s) *(AT 0082 C/CD) <84704>* **BENT / DON'T LET ME DOWN (live) / BUSTED (live)** [ ] Apr00 [1]

Feb 01. (c-s/cd-s) *(AT 0090 C/CD) <radio cut>* **IF YOU'RE GONE / IF YOU'RE GONE (edit) / BENT (live)** [50] Oct00 [5]

Jun 01. (c-s) *(AT 0105C) <radio cut>* **MAD SEASON / LONG DAY (live)** [ ] Apr01 [48]
(cd-s+=) *(AT 0105CD)* – Back 2 good (live).

Feb 03. (cd-s) *(AT 0145CD) <radio>* **DISEASE / PUSH (country version – from VH1 Storytellers) / CRUTCH (from VH1 Storytellers)** [50] Sep02 [29]

Feb 03. (cd) *(7567 93170-2) <83612>* **MORE THAN YOU THINK YOU ARE** [31] Nov02 [6]
– Feel / Disease / Bright lights / Unwell / Cold / All I need / Hand me down / Could I be you / Downfall / Soul / You're so real / The difference. *(hidden track+=)* – So lonely / If you are gone (live AOL session).

Apr 03. (cd-s) *(AT 0150CD) <88058>* **UNWELL / ALL I NEED (live) / UNWELL (live acoustic)** [ ] [-]

Sep 03. (cd-s) *(AT 0164CD)* **BRIGHT LIGHTS / DISEASES (live) / BRIGHT LIGHTS (live)** [ ] [-]

Nov 03. (cd-ep) *<83701>* **EP** [-] [43]
– Crutch / Push (live) / All I need (live) / If you're gone (live) / Disease (live) / Suffer me.

☐ MATCHING MOLE (see under ⇒ WYATT, Robert)

☐ Cerys MATTHEWS (see under ⇒ CATATONIA)

Dave MATTHEWS BAND

Formed: Charlottesville, Virginia, USA ... 1991/92 by South African born MATTHEWS. A New Yorker since a very early age, the singer moved back to Johannesburg with his mother following the death of his father. Back in America, DAVE gathered together a multi-racial bunch of eclectic musicians (CARTER BEAUFORD, LEROI MOORE and FULLARTON) to back him on his 1993 self-financed debut, 'REMEMBER TWO THINGS'. A live acoustic-based jazz-tinged rock set, it caught the attention of 'R.C.A.' who he signed to later that year. The band's debut for the label, 'UNDER THE TABLE AND DREAMING' (1995), slowly but steadily scaled the US Top 20, selling three million copies in the process. The following year, MATTHEWS and Co. delivered another set of well-crafted rock tunes on 'CRASH', a record which shot straight in to No.2 with relatively little press or TV exposure (certainly none in the UK, where he is still a non-entity to this day). Of late, even a concert album, 'LIVE AT RED ROCKS' (1997), managed a similar feat, although we tentatively await its UK release. Like The GRATEFUL DEAD before them, DAVE MATTHEWS and co are essentially an American phenomenon that can never hope to make a full cultural translation to the UK. Not that this fact is likely to bother them too much, especially when they can top the US chart with an album as downright average as 'BEFORE THESE CROWDED STREETS' (1998). Nor when they can cash in on their hardcore 'DEAD-like audience by releasing uninspired, official bootleg-type affairs like 'LISTENER SUPPORTED' (1999). Another US No.1 studio set 'EVERYDAY' (2001) utilised the production skills of Glen Ballard, after original recordings with Steve Lilywhite were aborted. This lack of resolve filtered through to the final version, a partially successful effort to rein in the group's inherent jamming impulse for a leaner, more focused sound. At least one highlight was 'THE SPACE BETWEEN', a classy single which made the Top 40 on both sides of the Atlantic. Those abandoned sessions became such an albatross round the band's neck that they eventually decided to dust down the tapes, spruce them up a bit and re-record them with a different producer (Stephen Harris). The result was 'BUSTED STUFF' (2002), at the same time the most emotionally raw and unaffected, and the most compelling album of their career. There was precious little jamming for jamming's sake to be found, as MATTHEWS, for once, let his songwriting really do the talking. In fact, the band leader was presumably so glad to have belatedly embraced these cast-offs that he carried the concept and vibe over to his debut solo set, 'SOME DEVIL' (2003).

Album rating: REMEMBER TWO THINGS (*5) / UNDER THE TABLE AND DREAMING (*8) / CRASH (*7) / LIVE AT RED ROCKS 8-15-95 (*6) / BEFORE THESE CROWDED STREETS (*6) / LIVE AT LUTHER COLLEGE (*5) / LISTENER SUPPORTED (*4) / EVERYDAY (*4) / LIVE IN CHICAGO 12.19.98 (*5) / BUSTED STUFF (*7) / SOME DEVIL (*5)

DAVE MATTHEWS (b.1967) – vocals, acoustic guitar / **CARTER BEAUFORD** – drums, percussion, vocals / **LEROI MOORE** – saxes, vocals / **BOYD TINSLEY** – violin, vocals / **STEFAN LESSARD** – bass; repl. bassist FULLARTON

not iss. | Bama Rags

1993. (cd) *<001>* **REMEMBER TWO THINGS (live)** [-] [ ]
– Ants marching / Tripping Billies / Recently / Satellite / One sweet world / Song that Jane likes / Minarets / Seek up / I'll back you up / Christmas song. *<re-iss. 1994 cd/c; 720-2/-4> (re-iss. 1997 on 'R.C.A.'; 67547>*

R.C.A. | R.C.A.

Mar 95. (cd/c) *<(7863 66449-2/-4)>* **UNDER THE TABLE AND DREAMING** [ ] Jul94 [11]
– The best of what's around / What would you say / Satellite / Rhyme and reason / Typical situation / Dancing Nancies / Ants marching / Lover lay down / Jimi thing / Warehouse / Pay for what you get / No.34. *(cd re-iss. Sep01; same)*

Jun 96. (7") *(74321 39483-7)* **TOO MUCH. / JIMI THING (acoustic)** [ ] [-]
(cd-s+=) *(74321 39483-2)* – Ants marching.

Jul 96. (cd/c) *<(7863 66904-2/-4)>* **CRASH** [ ] May96 [2]
– So much to say / Two step / Crash into me / Too much / No.34 / Say goodbye / Drive in, drive out / Let you down / Lie in our graves / Cry freedom / Tripping billies / Proudest monkeys. *(cd re-iss. Sep01; same)*

Nov 97. (d-cd/d-c) *<67587>* **LIVE AT RED ROCKS 8-15-95 (live)** [-] [2]
– Seek up / Proudest monkey / Satellite / Two step / Best of what's around / Recently / Lie in our graves / Dancing nancies / Warehouse / Tripping billies / Drive in, drive out / Lover lay down / Rhyme and reason / #36 / Ants marching in / Typical situation / All along the watchtower.

May 98. (cd) *<(07863 67660-2)>* **BEFORE THESE CROWDED STREETS** [ ] [1]
– Pantala naga pampa / Rapunzel / Last stop / Don't drink the water / Stay (wasting time) / Halloween / Stone / Crush / Dreaming tree / Pig / Spoon. *(re-iss. Sep01; same)*

Jan 99. (cd; by DAVE MATTHEWS & TIM REYNOLDS) *<67755>* **LIVE AT LUTHER COLLEGE (live)** [-] [2]
– One sweet world / #41 / Tripping billies / Jimi thing / Satellite / Crash into me / The deed is done / Lover lay down / What would you say / Minarets / Cry freedom / Dancing nancies / Typical situation / Stream / Warehouse / Christmas song / Seek up / Say goodbye / Ants marching / Little thing / Halloween / Granny / Two step.

Feb 99. (-) *<radio cut>* **CRUSH** [-] [75]

Jun 00. (d-cd) *<(07863 67898-2)>* **LISTENER SUPPORTED** [ ] Nov99 [15]
– Intro / Pantala naga pampa / Rapunzel / Rhyme & reason / Stone / #41 / Crash into me / Jimi thing / #36 / Warehouse / Too much / True reflections / Two step / Granny / Stay / #40 / Long black veil / Don't drink the water / All along the watchtower.

Jan 01. (-) *<radio cut>* **I DID IT** [-] [71]

Aug 01. (cd/c) *<(07863 67988-2/-4)>* **EVERYDAY** [ ] Feb01 [1]
– I did it / When the world ends / The space between / Dreams of our fathers / So right / If I had it all / What you are / Angel / Fool to think / Sleep to dream her / Mother father / Everyday.

Nov 01. (cd-s) *(74321 88319-2) <radio cut>* **THE SPACE BETWEEN / WHAT YOU ARE / I DID IT (video)** [35] May00 [22]
(cd-s) *(74321 88310-2)* – ('A'side) / Fool to think / ('A'video).

Jan 02. (d-cd) <*(0786 69317-2)*> **LIVE IN CHICAGO 12/19/98 (live)** [ ] Oct01 [6]
– (intro) / The last stop / Don't drink the water / #41 / #40 / Lie in our graves / What would you say / Pantala intro / Pantala naga-pampa / Rapunzel / Stay (wasting time) / The maker / Crash into me / Jimi thing / So much to say / Too much / Christmas song / Watchtower intro / All along the watchtower.

Jul 02. (d-cd) <*(68117)*> **BUSTED STUFF** (rec.2000) [ ] [1]
– Busted stuff / Grey Street / Where are you going / You never know / Captain / Raven / Grace is gone / Kit kat jam / Digging a ditch / Big eyed fish / Bartender.

Sep 03. (cd) *(82876 56276-2)* <*55167*> **SOME DEVIL** [ ] [2]
– Dodo / So damn lucky / Gravedigger / Some devil / Trouble / Grey blue eyes / Save me / Stay or leave / An' another thing / Oh / Baby / Up and away / Too high / Gravedigger (acoustic).

Eric MATTHEWS

Born: 12 Jan'69, Gresham, Portland, Oregon, USA. A one time student of the San Francisco Conservatory classical music college, MATTHEWS' first love was trumpet although his penchant for classic orchestral pop and his decision to take up the guitar eventually led him to the thriving alternative music scene in Boston, Massachusetts. There, he hooked up with SEBADOH's LOU BARLOW and BOB FAY, with whom he cut an obscure EP in 1993 under the name of BELT BUCKLE. Subsequently finding a musical foil in Australian ex-MOLES leader, RICHARD DAVIES, MATTHEWS found an outlet for his lush arranging/instrumental talent as one-half of the acclaimed duo, The CARDINAL. Although they only lasted one album – an eponymous 1994 effort – the publicity generated helped MATTHEWS secure a solo deal with Seattle label, 'Sub Pop'. Hardly a typical signing for the former bastion of grunge, MATTHEWS surpassed all expectations with his 1995 solo debut, 'IT'S HEAVY IN HERE', a darkly luxuriant sequence of equisitely arranged and executed orchestral pop. Showcasing a breathy, wistful vocal style that frequently brought comparisons with NICK DRAKE, MATTHEWS showed himself to be a master pop craftsman, layering trumpets, chiming guitars and melancholy string flourishes in a manner reminiscent of past masters like BRIAN WILSON, VAN DYKE PARKS and the largely unsung ROBERT KIRBY (NICK DRAKE's string arranger on his first two albums). Despite boasting a more extensive array of guest musicians, follow-up set, 'THE LATENESS OF THE HOUR' (1997) lost little of the debut's focus or sense of continuity, consolidating MATTHEWS' position as grand master of modern baroque pop for the thinking indie fan. • **Covered:** A CERTAIN KIND (Soft Machine).

Album rating: IT'S HEAVY IN HERE (*8) / THE LATENESS OF THE HOUR (*7)

ERIC MATTHEWS – on usual instruments & vocals (also conducts orchestra & produces) musicians mostly **JASON FALKNER** – guitars, bass / **STEVE HANFORD** – drums

Sub Pop Sub Pop

Nov 95. (lp/c/cd) <*(SP/+MC/CD 312)*> **IT'S HEAVY IN HERE** [ ] [ ]
– Fanfare / Forging plastic pain / Soul nation select them / Faith to clay / Angels for crime / Fried out broken girl / Lust takes time / Hop and tickle / Three-cornered moon / Distant mother reality / Flight and lion / Poison will pass me / Sincere sensation / Fanfare (reprise).

Feb 96. (7") <*(SP 319)*> **FANFARE. / LIDS, NAILS, SCREWS** [ ] [ ]
(cd-s+=) <*(SPCD 319)*> – A certain kind / Distant mother reality (S H mix).

—— now with **JASON FALKNER** – guitar, bass, piano, drums / **WES MATTHEWS** – guitar, bass, piano / **GREGG WILLIAMS** – drums, percussion / **TONY LASH** – drums, percussion, piano / **SPOOKEY RUBEN** – bass / plus others **DON SCHWARTZ** – bass / **ANDREW SHAW** – sax / **STEVEN HANFORD** – drums / **STEVEN MATTHEWS** – acoustic guitar

Nov 97. (lp/cd) <*(SP 404/+CD)*> **THE LATENESS OF THE HOUR** [ ] [ ]
– Ideas that died that day / My morning parade / Pair of cherry / To clear the air / Yes, everyone / Everything so real / Becomes dark blue / The pleasant kind / Gilded cages / dopeyness / Since the wheel free / Festival fun / No gnashing teeth.

—— ERIC has been a little conspicuous by his absence

☐ MAXIM (see under ⇒ PRODIGY)

☐ MAX Q (see under ⇒ INXS)

☐ Brian MAY (see under ⇒ QUEEN)

☐ Phil MAY & The FALLEN ANGELS (see under ⇒ PRETTY THINGS)

John MAYALL

Born: 29 Nov'33, Macclesfield, Cheshire, England. A National Service veteran from the Korean war in 1951-1955, he became a graphic artist (studying at Manchester Art College and working in an art studio attached to a local advertising agency) and picked up a taste for boogie from his trombone playing father. MAYALL started to master piano styles from boogie-woogie 78s by CRIPPLE CLARENCE LOFTON, PINETOP SMITH and others, before going on to learn the basics of harmonica and guitar. Although he initiated his first band, JOHN MAYALL's POWERHOUSE FOUR, in Manchester, he subsequently went to London at ALEXIS KORNER's request to form the BLUES SYNDICATE; this became the first of many BLUESBREAKERS featuring JOHN McVIE on bass, BERNIE WATSON on guitar and PETER WARD on drums (the latter was replaced by MARTIN HART when the band went full-time and gained a residency at the Scene, Great Windmill Street, London). Renowned for being a bit eccentric (he spent some time living in a self constructed tree-house), MAYALL was a strict bandleader and maintained an almost religious belief in blues purism. His songs were excellent pastiches of his heros' compositions, his voice being reminiscent of OTIS RUSH, BUDDY GUY and his ultimate idol, J.B. LENOIR. Signing a short term deal with 'Decca', he released his 1965 debut album, 'JOHN MAYALL PLAYS JOHN MAYALL', a badly recorded live set which nevertheless captured the initimate atmosphere of a sweaty R&B club. One of the record's tracks (which was duly released as a single), 'CRAWLING UP A HILL', showcased MAYALL's soft voice being over-run by a distorted harmonica and Hammond organ. The best BLUESBREAKERS line-ups were those that included ERIC CLAPTON, PETER GREEN and MICK TAYLOR, all of whom left the band with greatly enhanced reputations which enabled them to command vast amounts of money. CLAPTON joined in 1965, straight from The YARDBIRDS – bringing respectability to the band as fans flocked to see the guitar hero – and virtually dominated the classic UK Top 10 'BLUESBREAKERS' (1966) set. CLAPTON departed the following year to form CREAM and was replaced by PETER GREEN (he had earlier replaced him for a one-off 3-day period), who played on 'A HARD ROAD'. GREEN excelled on the instrumentals 'THE STUMBLE' (a Freddie King number) and his own 'THE SUPERNATURAL' as well as providing soulful vocals on the likes of 'YOU DON'T LOVE ME' and 'THE SAME

WAY'. GREEN eventually left in 1967, his replacement being a shy but exceptionally talented young guitarist by the name of MICK TAYLOR. Remaining with MAYALL until 1969 – before taking BRIAN JONES' slot in The ROLLING STONES – TAYLOR's tenure lasted up to and including 'BLUES FROM LAUREL CANYON' (a transatlantic Top 60 success), a period which also produced the brassier sounding 'CRUSADE' in 1967. 'DIARY OF A BAND VOLUMES 1 & 2' both hit the UK Top 30 in 1968 and featured the band's live sound from the previous year, the excellent work of KEEF HARTLEY and MICK TAYLOR a must to hear. 1968 also produced 'BARE WIRES', a record leaning towards jazz and featuring JON HISEMAN on drums and an experienced brass section of HENRY LOWTHER, CHRIS MERCER and DICK HECKSTALL-SMITH. Understandably, MAYALL became tired of running his band as a finishing school for aspiring megastars and disbanded The BLUESBREAKERS, subsequently signing to 'Polydor' and forming an acoustic band including guitarist JON MARK and saxophonist JOHNNY ALMOND. This formation recorded the live album, 'TURNING POINT' (his biggest seller, his only gold disc and a near UK Top 10) in 1969 at the Fillmore East, featuring his best known song, 'ROOM TO MOVE' (his finest harp solo) and 'THOUGHTS ABOUT ROXANNE'. MARK and ALMOND soon moved on (after 'EMPTY ROOMS', another UK Top 10'er which included MAYALL's only US chart single, 'DON'T WASTE MY TIME') to form their own group, MARK-ALMOND, while MAYALL moved to Los Angeles and formed his own record label, 'Crusade'. 'USA UNION' with a backing band of Americans, notably, HARVEY MANDEL, DON 'SUGARCANE' HARRIS and LARRY TAYLOR was another Top 50 success, although critics rounded on the insipid lyrics. Following the double set, 'BACK TO THE ROOTS', MAYALL's work-rate declined, his output over the next few years of poor quality. The struggling bluesman signed to 'ABC/Blue Thumb' in 1975, releasing 'NEW YEAR, NEW BAND, NEW COMPANY'; for the first time, MAYALL had employed a female vocalist, DEE McKIMMIE along with future FLEETWOOD MAC guitarist RICK VITO. The album was to be his last US chart entry for 15 years; a number of albums followed although their success was limited by inadequate exposure and MAYALL stopped recording, only playing the odd local gig near his home in California. MAYALL toured Europe in 1988 to small but enthusiastic audiences, signing to 'Island' Records and releasing a belated comeback album, 'CHICAGO LINE'. The man never regained his success of the 60's, although he's now recognised as the Father Of British Blues and is still nurturing the occasional rising blues star from his now reformed and ever-changing BLUESBREAKERS (WALTER TROUT being one of the most recent). The 90's were kinder to MAYALL, 1990's 'A SENSE OF PLACE' on 'Island' (which marked his return to the US charts) and the brilliant 'WAKE UP CALL' (1993) on 'Silvertone' (UK Top 75) – with guest appearances by ALBERT COLLINS, BUDDY GUY, MICK TAYLOR and MAVIS STAPLES – being his best albums in years. After a further trio of mid-late 90's efforts, of which 1999's 'PADLOCK ON THE DOOR' was the most successful, MAYALL rounded up a posse of pals and set to work on 'ALONG FOR THE RIDE' (2001). The list of collaborators read like a who's who of the 60's Brit blues scene, with the likes of MICK TAYLOR, JOHN McVIE and MICK FLEETWOOD lending their talents. The father-like figure of MAYALL even managed to coax PETER GREEN into making a contribution. 'STORIES' (2002) found MAYALL as undiminished by age as ever, the soon to be septuagenarian casting a knowing eye back over the history of his beloved blues with tributes such as 'OH LEADBELLY'. There aren't many men still cutting it in their 70's but then MAYALL was merely following the traditions of his chosen genre, and if there weren't many old time blues players afforded a bash as big as '70th BIRTHDAY CONCERT' (2003), then MAYALL made up for them all with a gutsy, heady trip down memory lane with guest spots by old friends MICK TAYLOR and ERIC CLAPTON. • **Songwriters:** Self-penned alongside covers; MY BABY IS SWEETER (Willie Dixon) / DOUBLE TROUBLE + ALL YOUR LOVE (Otis Rush) / BERNARD JENKINS (Eric Clapton) / WHAT'D I SAY (Ray Charles) / DOUBLE CROSSIN' TIME (w/ Clapton) / DUST MY BLUES (Elmore James) / THE SUPERNATURAL (Peter Green) / SO MANY ROADS (Paul) / LOOKING BACK (Johnny Guitar Watson) / ALL MY LIFE (Robinson) / RIDIN' ON THE L & N (Barley Hampton) / IT HURTS ME TOO (London) / OH, PRETTY WOMAN (Big Joe Williams) / MAN OF STONE (Eddie Kirkland) / NIGHT TRAIN / LUCILLE (Little Richard) / PARCHMAN FARM (Mose Allison) / STEPPIN' OUT (Charles Brackeen) / etc.

Album rating: JOHN MAYALL PLAYS JOHN MAYALL (*7) / BLUESBREAKERS WITH ERIC CLAPTON (*8) / A HARD ROAD (*7) / CRUSADE (*6) / THE BLUES ALONE (*6) / THE DIARY OF A BAND VOL.1 (*5) / THE DIARY OF A BAND VOL.2 (*5) / BARE WIRES (*8) / BLUES FROM LAUREL CANYON (*6) / THE TURNING POINT (*7) / EMPTY ROOMS (*7) / LOOKING BACK compilation (*7) / U.S.A. UNION (*5) / BACK TO THE ROOTS (*5) / MEMORIES (*5) / JAZZ BLUES FUSION (*5) / MOVING ON (*5) / TEN YEARS ARE GONE (*5) / THE LATEST EDITION (*4) / NEW YEAR, NEW BAND, NEW COMPANY (*4) / TIME EXPIRED, NOTICE TO APPEAR (*4) / A BANQUET OF BLUES (*4) / LOTS OF PEOPLE (*4) / A HARD CORE PACKAGE (*4) / BOTTOM LINE (*4) / NO MORE INTERVIEWS (*4) / ROAD SHOW BLUES (*4) / BEHIND THE IRON CURTAIN (*4) / CHICAGO LINE (*4) / A SENSE OF PLACE (*7) / LONDON BLUES compilation (*7) / ROOM TO MOVE compilation (*7) / WAKE UP CALL (*7) / SPINNING COIN (*4) / BLUES FOR THE LOST DAYS (*5) / PADLOCK ON THE BLUES (*6) / ALONG FOR THE RIDE (*5) / STORIES (*6) / 70th BIRTHDAY CONCERT (*7)

BLUESBREAKERS

JOHN MAYALL – vocals, keyboards, harmonica, guitar(ex-BLUES SYNDICATE) / **BERNIE WATSON** – guitar repl. JOHN GILBEY who had repl. SAMMY PROSSER / **JOHN McVIE** (b.26 Nov'45) – bass repl. PETE BURFORD who had repl. RICKY BROWN / **MARTIN HART** – drums repl. PETER WARD who had repl. KEITH ROBERTSON (note previous drummers early 1963 =BRIAN MYALL after SAM STONE.)

JOHN MAYALL'S BLUESBREAKERS

Decca — not iss.

Apr 64. (7"; as JOHN MAYALL & BLUES BREAKERS) *(F 11900)* **CRAWLING UP A HILL. / MR. JAMES** ☐ [-]

— MAYALL retained only McVIE, and recruited **ROGER DEAN** – guitar replaced WATSON **HUGHIE FLINT** – drums (ex-BLUES SYNDICATE) repl. HART

Feb 65. (7"; by JOHN MAYALL) *(F 12120)* **CROCODILE WALK. / BLUES CITY SHAKEDOWN** ☐ [-]

Mar 65. (lp; by JOHN MAYALL) *(LK 4680)* **JOHN MAYALL PLAYS JOHN MAYALL (live at Klook's Kleek)** ☐ [-]
– Crawling up a hill / I wanna teach you everything / When I'm gone / I need your love / The hoot owl / R&B time; Night train – Lucille / Crocodile walk / What's the matter with you / Doreen / Runaway / Heartache / Chicago line. *(cd-iss. Jun88 on 'London'; 820 536-2)*

— **ERIC CLAPTON** (b.30 Mar'45, Ripley, England) – guitar, vocals (ex-YARDBIRDS) repl. DEAN

Immediate — Immediate

Oct 65. (7") *(IM 012)* <502> **I'M YOUR WITCHDOCTOR. / TELEPHONE BLUES** ☐ ☐
(re-iss. Sep67 by JOHN MAYALL and the BLUESBREAKERS with ERIC CLAPTON; IM 051)

— (a month earlier CLAPTON departed to join The GONADS.) (he was repl. by ?) **JACK BRUCE** (b.14 May'43, Lanarkshire, Scotland) – bass (ex-GRAHAM BOND ORGANISATION) repl. McVIE

— MAYALL's band were now FLINT, McVIE and CLAPTON again. (BRUCE joined MANFRED MANN)

Decca London

Jul 66. (lp; mono/stereo; by JOHN MAYALL WITH ERIC CLAPTON) *(LK 4804)* *<LL3/PS 492>* **BLUES BREAKERS WITH ERIC CLAPTON** [6] [ ]
– All your love / Hideaway / Little girl / Another man / Double crossin' time / What'd I say / Key to love / Parchman farm / Have you heard / Ramblin' on my mind; (a) Steppin' out – (b) It ain't right. *(re-iss. 1969 mono/stereo; LK/SLK 4804) <US re-iss. 1985 on 'Mobile Fidelity'; MFSL 183> (cd-iss. Feb89; 800 086-2) (re-iss. Aug90 on 'Deram' cd/lp; 800 086-2/-1)*

Sep 66. (7"; A-side solo) *(F 12490)* *<20016>* **PARCHMAN FARM. / KEY TO LOVE** [ ] [ ]

Nov 66. (7") *<20024>* **ALL YOUR LOVE. / HIDEAWAY** [–] [ ]

—— (Jul66) **PETER GREEN** (b. PETER GREENBAUM, 29 Oct'46) – guitar(on above b-side) repl. CLAPTON who formed CREAM

—— (Sep66) **AYNSLEY DUNBAR** – drums (ex-MOJOS) repl. FLINT who later formed McGUINNESS FLINT

Oct 66. (7"; as JOHN MAYALL'S BLUESBREAKERS & PETER GREEN) *(F 12506)* **LOOKING BACK. / SO MANY ROADS** [ ] [–]

Oct 66. (7") *(F 12545)* **SITTING IN THE RAIN. / OUT OF REACH** [ ] [ ]

Feb 67. (lp; mono/stereo) *(LK/SKL 4853)* *<PS 502>* **A HARD ROAD** [10] [ ]
– A hard road / It's over / You don't love me / The stumble / Another kinda love / Hit the highway / Leaping Christine / Dust my blues / There's always work / The same way / The super natural / Top of the hill / Someday after a while (you'll be sorry) / Living alone.

Mar 67. (7"; as BLUESBREAKERS) *(F 12588)* **CURLY. / RUBBER DUCK** [ ] [ ]

Apr 67. (7"ep) *(DFE-R 8673)* **BLUESBREAKERS WITH PAUL BUTTERFIELD** [ ] [ ]

—— **MICK FLEETWOOD** (b.24 Jun'47, Redruth, England) – drums repl. MICKEY WALLER who had repl. DUNBAR (to JEFF BECK GROUP) (others still in band MAYALL, GREEN and McVIE)

Apr 67. (7") *(F 12621)* **DOUBLE TROUBLE. / IT HURTS ME TOO** [ ] [ ]

—— added **TERRY EDMONDS** – rhythm guitar, (for Jun67 only before he joined FERRIS WHEEL) / **MICK TAYLOR** (b.17 Jan'48, Welwyn Garden City, England) – guitar, vocals (ex-GODS) repl. PETER who formed FLEETWOOD MAC / **KEEF HARTLEY** (b. 8 Mar'44, Preston, England) – drums (ex-ARTWOODS) repl. MICK who formed FLEETWOOD MAC / added **CHRIS MERCER + RIP KANT** – saxophones

Sep 67. (lp; mono/stereo) *(LK/SKL 4890)* *<PS 529>* **CRUSADE** [8] [ ]
– Oh pretty woman / Stand back baby / My time after a while / Snowy wood / Man of stone / Tears in my eyes / Driving sideways / The death of J.B. Lenoir / I can't quit you baby / Streamline / Me and my woman / Checkin' up on my baby.

—— **MAYALL** retained **TAYLOR, HARTLEY** and **MERCER,** bringing in **PAUL WILLIAMS** – bass (ex-ZOOT MONEY) repl. McVIE who also joined FLEETWOOD MAC / **DICK HECKSTALL-SMITH** (b.26 Sep'34, Ludlow, England) – saxophone (ex-GRAHAM BOND) repl. KANT / added **HENRY LOWTHER** – trumpet

Sep 67. (7") *(F 12684)* **SUSPICIONS (part 1). / SUSPICIONS (part 2)** [ ] [–]

Sep 67. (7") *<20035>* **SUSPICIONS. / OH PRETTY WOMAN** [–] [ ]

—— **KEITH TILLMAN** – bass repl. WILLIAMS

Dec 67. (7"; solo) *(F 12732)* *<20037>* **JENNY. / PICTURES ON THE WALL** [ ] [ ]

Jan 68. (lp; mono/stereo) *(LK/SKL 4918)* *<PS 570>* **THE DIARY OF A BAND VOL.1** (live interviews & chat) [27] Feb70 [93]
– Blood on the night / (chat; Edmonton cooks Ferry Inn) / I can't quit you baby / (Keef Hartley interview x2) / Anzio Annie / (John Mayall interview x2) / Snowy wood / The lesson / My own fault / God save the queen.

Jan 68. (lp; mono/stereo) *(LK/SKL 4919)* *<PS 589>* **THE DIARY OF A BAND VOL.2** (live interviews & chat) <US-title 'JOHN MAYALL LIVE IN EUROPE'> [28] Apr71 [ ]
– (Gimme some lovin') / The train / Crying shame / (chat); local boy makes good / Help me / Blues in Bb / Soul of a short fat man.

Feb 68. (7") **BROKEN WINGS. / SONNY BOY BLUE** [–] [ ]

—— **TONY REEVES** – bass repl. ANDY FRASER (to FREE) who had repl. TILLMAN / **JON HISEMAN** (b.21 Jun'44) – drums (ex-GRAHAM BOND, ex-GEORGIE FAME) repl. HARTLEY (to solo)

Jun 68. (lp; mono/stereo) *(LK/SKL 4945)* *<PS 537>* **BARE WIRES** [3] [59]
– Where did I belong / I start walking / Open up a new door / Fire / I know now / Look in the mirror / I'm a stranger / Hartley quits / No reply / Killing time / She's too young / Sandy. *(cd-iss. Jun88 on 'London'; 820 538-2)*

Jun 68. (7") *(F 12792)* **NO REPLY. / SHE'S TOO YOUNG** [ ] [ ]

—— **MAYALL** only retained **MICK TAYLOR / COLIN ALLEN** – drums (ex-ZOOT MONEY) repl. HISEMAN who formed COLOSSEUM / **STEVE THOMPSON** – bass repl. REEVES. (he & HECKSTALL-SMITH also formed above) (also note MERCER left going into sessions and LOWTHER joined KEEF HARLEY BAND)

Nov 68. (7") *(F 12846)* **THE BEAR. / 2401** [ ] [ ]

Dec 68. (lp; mono/stereo) *(LK/SKL 4972)* *<PS 545>* **BLUES FROM LAUREL CANYON** [33] [68]
– Vacation / Walking on sunset / Laurel Canyon home / 2401 / Ready to ride / Medicine man / Somebody's acting like a child / The bear / Miss James / First time alone / Long gone midnight / Fly tomorrow. *(cd-iss. Jan88 on 'London'; 820 539-2)*

Dec 68. (7") **WALKING ON SUNSET. / LIVING ALONE** [–] [ ]

JOHN MAYALL

(his new band played without a drummer) **DUSTER BENNETT** – guitar, vocals repl. TAYLOR who joined ROLLING STONES / **JON MARK** (b. Cornwall, England) – guitar / **JOHNNY ALMOND** (b.20 Jul'46, Enfield, England) – saxophone repl. ALLEN who joined STONE THE CROWS / (after below lp **ALEX DMOCHOWSKI** – bass repl. THOMPSON who joined STONE THE CROWS)

Polydor Polydor

Oct 69. (lp; mono/stereo) *(582/583 571)* *<PD 4004>* **THE TURNING POINT (live 1969)** [11] Sep69 [32]
– The laws must change / Saw mill Gulch road / I'm gonna fight for you J.B. / So hard to share / California / Thoughts about Roxanne / California / Room to move. *(re-iss. May82 lp)(c; 2485 222)(3201 294) (cd-iss. Aug87; 823 305) (cd re-iss. Aug92 on 'Beat Goes On'; BGOCD 145)*

Oct 69. (7") *(56544)* *<14004>* **DON'T WASTE MY TIME. / DON'T PICK A FLOWER** [ ] [81]

Jan 70. (7") **ROOM TO MOVE. / SAW MILL GULCH ROAD** [–] [ ]

—— **LARRY TAYLOR** – bass deputised for the ill THOMPSON. (DMOCHOWSKI tour)

Mar 70. (lp) *(583 580)* *<PD 4010>* **EMPTY ROOMS** [9] [33]
– Don't waste my time / Plan your revolution / Don't pick a flower / Something new / People cling together / Waiting for the right time / Thinking of my woman / Counting the days / When I go / Many miles apart / To a princess / Lying in my bed.

May 70. (7") *(2066 021)* **THINKING OF MY WOMAN. / PLAN YOUR REVOLUTION** [ ] [–]

—— MAYALL's completely new band of US musicians **HARVEY MANDEL** (b.11 Mar'45, Detroit, Michigan) – guitar (ex-CANNED HEAT) repl. MARK who formed MARK-ALMOND / **DON 'SUGURCANE' HARRIS** – vocals (ex-FRANK ZAPPA) repl. ALMOND (as above) / **LARRY TAYLOR** – bass finally repl. DMOCHOWSKI

Dec 70. (lp) *(2425 020)* *<PD 4022>* **U.S.A. UNION** [50] Oct70 [22]
– Nature's disappearing / You must be crazy / Night flyer / Off the road / Possessive emotions / Where did my legs go / Took the car / Crying / My pretty girl / Deep blue sea.

Jan 71. (7") **NATURE'S DISAPPEARING. / MY PRETTY GIRL** [–] [ ]

—— Next reunified MAYALL with nearly all old BLUESBREAKERS + new US musicians

Jun 71. (d-lp) *(2657 005)* *<PD 3002>* **BACK TO THE ROOTS** [31] Apr71 [52]
– Prisons on the road / My children / Accidental suicide / Groupie girl / Blue fox / Home again / Television eye / Marriage madness / Looking at tomorrow / Dream with me / Full speed ahead / Mr. Censor man / Force of nature / Boogie Albert / Goodbye December / Unanswered questions / Devil's tricks / Travelling.

—— MAYALL retained only LARRY TAYLOR and recruited **JERRY McGEE** – guitar (ex-VENTURES) to replace MANDEL (who formed own band) and HARRIS

Nov 71. (lp) *(2425 085)* *<PD 5012>* **MEMORIES** [ ] [ ]
– Memories / Wish I knew a woman / Back from Korea / Home in a tree / Separate ways / The fighting line / Grandad / The city / Nobody cares / Play the harp.

Feb 72. (7") **NOBODY CARES. / PLAY THE HARP** [–] [ ]

—— **MAYALL** and **TAYLOR** brought in a drummer! – **RON SELICO / plus FREDDY ROBINSON** – guitar to repl. McGEE / added **BLUE MITCHELL** – trumpet / **CLIFFORD SOLOMON** – saxophone

May 72. (lp) *(2425 103)* *<PD 5027>* **JAZZ-BLUES FUSION (live)** [ ] [64]
– Country road / Mess around / Good time boogie / Change your ways /

Dry throat / Exercise in c-major for harmonica, bass and shufflers / Got to be this way.

— **VICTOR GASKIN** – bass repl. LARRY / **KEEF HARTLEY** – drums returned to repl. RON

— added on next **CHARLES OWEN** – flute / **FRED JACKSON** + **ERNIE WATTS** – saxophones

Jan 73. (lp) *(2391 047) <PD 5036>* **MOVING ON** Oct72
– (a brief introduction by Bill Cosby) / Worried mind / Keep our country green / Christmas 71 / Things go wrong / Do it / Moving on / Red sky / Reasons / High pressure living.

Jan 73. (7") **MOVING ON. / KEEP OUR COUNTRY GREEN** –

Nov 73. (d-lp) *(2683 036) <PD 3005>* **TEN YEARS ARE GONE** Sep73
– Ten years are gone / Driving till the break of day / Drifting / Better pass you by / California campground / Undecided / Good looking stranger / I still care / Don't hang me up / (introduction) / Sitting here thinking / Harmonica free form / Burning Sun / Dark of the night.

Nov 74. (7") **GASOLINE BLUES. / BRAND NEW BAND** –

Dec 74. (lp) *(2391 141) <PD 6030>* **THE LATEST EDITION**
– Gasoline blues / Perfect peace / Going to take my time / Deep down feelings / Troubled times / The pusher man / One of the few / Love song / Little kitchen / A crazy game.

Feb 75. (7") **LET ME GIVE. / PASSING THROUGH** –

— MAYALL brought back **LARRY TAYLOR** and **SUGERCANE HARRIS** plus new members **DEE McKINNIE** – vocals / **RICK VITO** – guitar / **JAY SPELL** – keyboards / **SOKO / RICHARDSON** – drums

A.B.C. A.B.C.

Mar 75. (lp) *(ABCL 5115) <6019>* **NEW YEAR, NEW BAND, NEW COMPANY**
– Sitting on the outside / Can't get home / Step in the sun / To match the wind / Sweet Scorpio / Driving on / Taxman blues / So much to do / My train time / Respectively yours.

Apr 75. (7") **STEP IN THE SUN. / AL GOLDSTEIN BLUES** –

— **MAYALL** now totally solo.

Nov 75. (lp) *(ABCL 5142) <ABCD 926>* **TIME EXPIRED, NOTICE TO APPEAR**
– Lil boogie in the afternoon / Mess of love / That love / The boy most likely to succeed / Who's next who's now / Hail to the man who lives alone / There will be a way / Just knowing you is a pleasure / A hard day's night / Oldtime blues. *(cd-iss. Apr94 on 'M.C.A.'; MCAD 22070)*

— His following albums feature session musicians.

Apr 76. (lp) *(ABCL 5187) <ABCD 958>* **A BANQUET OF BLUES**
– Sunshine / You can't put me down / I got somebody / Turn me loose / Seven days too long / Table top girl / Lady / Fantasyland. *(cd-iss. Apr94 on 'M.C.A.'; MCAD 22075)*

May 76. (7") *<12216>* **SUNSHINE. / TURN ME LOOSE** –

Apr 77. (lp) *(ABCL 5126) <ABCD 992>* **LOTS OF PEOPLE** (live)
– (spoken introduction by Red Holloway) / Changes in the wind / Burning down / Play the harp / A helping hand / I got to get down with you / He's a travelling man / Separate ways / Room to move. *(cd-iss. Apr94 on 'M.C.A.'; MCAD 22073)*

— now with **JAMES QUILL SMITH** – vocals, guitar / **STEVE THOMPSON** – bass / **SOKO RICHARDSON** – drums / and a brass section

Feb 78. (lp) *<ABCD 1039>* **A HARD CORE PACKAGE** –
– Rock and roll hobo / Do I please you / Disconnected line / An old sweet picture / The last time / Make up your mind / Arizona bound / Now and then / Goodnight dreams / Give me a chance. *(cd-iss. Apr94 on 'M.C.A.'; MCAD 22071)*

— now with loads of session people.

D.J.M. D.J.M.

May 79. (lp) *(DJF 20556) <23>* **BOTTOM LINE**
– Bottom line / Dreamboat / Desert flower / I'm gonna do it / Revival / Game of love / Celebration / Come with me.

Jul 79. (7") *(DJS 10918)* **BOTTOM LINE. / DREAMBOAT**

Dec 79. (lp) *(DJF 20564) <29>* **NO MORE INTERVIEWS**
– Hard going up / A bigger slice of pie / Falling / Take me home tonight / Sweet honey bee / Stars in the night / Consideration / Gypsy lady / Wild new lover.

— now with **SMITH, RICHARDSON** + **KEVIN McCORMICK** – bass / **MAGGIE PARKER** – vox

May 81. (lp) *(DJF2/DJH4 0570)* **ROAD SHOW BLUES**
– Why worry / Road show / Mama talk to your daughter / A big man / Lost and gone / Mexico City / John Lee boogie / Reaching for a mountain / Baby what you want me to do. *(re-iss. Jun88 on 'Thunderbolt' lp/cd; THBL/CDTB 060)*

Jun 81. (7") **JOHN LEE BOOGIE. / WHY WORRY. / MAMA TALK TO YOUR DAUGHTER**

— **MAYALL'S** new line-up featured **COCO MONTAYA** + **WALTER TROUT** – guitar / **BOBBY HAYNES** – bass / **JOE YUELE** – drums

P.R.T. GNP Crescendo

May 86. (lp/c) *(NCP/ZCNCP 709) <GNP S/5 2184>* **BEHIND THE IRON CURTAIN** (rec.1984) 1985
– Somebody's acting like a child / Rolling with the blues / The laws must change / Parchman farm / Have you heard / Fly tomorrow / Steppin' out. *(cd-iss. Dec95 on 'GNP Crescendo';)*

— After couple of years out of the studio he returned Spring '87. with famous guests **MICK TAYLOR, JOHN McVIE**, etc.

Charly Entente

Dec 88. (cd) *(CDCHARLY 202)* **CHICAGO LINE**
– Chicago line / Gimme one more day / One life to live / The last time / Dream about the blues / Fascination lover / Cold blooded woman / The dirty dozen / Tears came rollin' down / Life in the jungle.

— **FREEBO** – bass repl.HAYNES + TROUT

Island Island

Apr 90. (cd) *(CID/ICT/ILPS 9958) <842795>* **A SENSE OF PLACE**
– I want to go / Congo square / Send me down to Vicksburg / Without her / Sensitive kind / Jacksboro highway / Let's work together / I can't complain / Black cat moon / Sugarcane / All my life. *(cd re-iss. Mar93; IMCD 167)*

— **RICK CORTES** – bass repl. FREEBO

— guests; **MICK TAYLOR / BUDDY GUY** + **ALBERT COLLINS**

Silvertone Jive

Apr 93. (cd/c/lp) *(ORE CD/C/LP 527) <41518>* **WAKE UP CALL** 61
– Mail order mystics / Maydell / I could cry / Wake up call / Loaded dice / Undercover agent for the blues / Light the fuse / Anything I can say / Nature's disappearing / I'm a sucker for love / Not at home / Ain't that lovin' you baby.

1993. (cd-s) **WAKE UP CALL /** –

— the BLUESBREAKERS were MAYALL, MICK TAYLOR, COCO MONTOYA + DON McMINN

Sep 93. (cd/c) *(AIM CD/C 1004)* **RETURN OF THE BLUESBREAKERS** –
– An eye for an eye / The same old blues / Rock & roll kitchen / Rock it in the pocket / Keep on rollin' / My time after awhile (live) / Ridin' on the Santa Fe (live) / Howlin' moon (live) / You never can be trusted (live) / Lookin' for Willie (live) / My babe / A long long way / Black cat moan.
(above on 'Aim' records)

— **BUDDY WHITTINGTON** – guitar repl. MONTOYA

Feb 95. (cd/c/lp) *(ORE CD/C/LP 537) <41541>* **SPINNING COIN**
– When the Devil starts crying / Spinning coin / Ain't no brakeman / Double life feelings / Run / What passes for love / Fan the flames / Voodoo music / Long story short / No big hurry / Remember this. *(cd re-iss. Mar97; same)*

Apr 97. (cd) *(ORECD 547) <41605>* **BLUES FOR THE LOST DAYS**
– Dead city / Stone cold deal / All those heroes / Blues for the lost days / Trenches / One in a million / How can you live like that / Some other day / I don't mind / It ain't safe / Sen-say-shun / You are for real.

Eagle Red Ink

Apr 99. (cd; as JOHN MAYALL & THE BLUESBREAKERS) *(EAGCD 077) <597>* **PADLOCK ON THE BLUES**
– Don't turn your back / Padlock on the blues / Hard road / Somebody's watching / Always a brand new road / My country girl / The strip / I've got to talk to you / Dancing shoes / Bad dream catcher / When the blues are bad / Ain't no surrender / White line fever.

Apr 01. (cd; as JOHN MAYALL & FRIENDS) *(EAGCD 150) <18474>* **ALONG FOR THE RIDE** May01
– A world of hurt / Along for the ride / Put it right back / That's why I love you so / Yo yo man / If I don't get home / Testify / Early in the morning /

Something about my baby / So many roads / World war blues / California / She don't play by the rules.

Aug 02. (cd; as JOHN MAYALL & THE BLUESBREAKERS) *(EAGCD 223) <59669>* **STORIES**
– Southside story / Dirty water / Feels just like home / Kids got the blues / The witching hour / Oh, Leadbelly / Demons in the night / Pride and faith / Kokomo / Romance classified / I wished I had / Pieces and parts / I thought I heard the Devil / The mists of time.
below friends:- ERIC CLAPTON / CHRIS BARBER / MICK TAYLOR

Nov 03. (d-cd; as JOHN MAYALL & THE BLUESBREAKERS & FRIENDS) *(EAGCD 246) <20017>* **70th BIRTHDAY CONCERT**
– Grits ain't groceries / Jacksboro highway / Southside story / Kids got the blues / Dirty water / Somebody acting like a child / Blues for the lost days / Walking on sunset / Oh, pretty woman / No big hurry / Please Mr. Lofton / Hide away / All your love / Have you heard / (I'm your) Hoochie coochie man / I'm tore down / It ain't right / California / Talk to your daughter.

– (selective) compilations, etc. –

Aug 66. (7"ltd; by JOHN MAYALL and ERIC CLAPTON) *Purdah; (45-3502)* **LONELY HEARTS. / BERNARD JENKINS** –

Nov 67. (lp) *Ace Of Clubs; (SCL 1245) / London; <PS 543>* **THE BLUES ALONE** (nearly all instruments himself) 24
– Brand new start / Please don't tell / Down the line / Sonny Boy blow / Marsha's mood / No more tears / Catch that train / Cancelling out / Harp man / Brown sugar / Broken wings / Don't kick me. *(cd-iss. Jun88 on 'London'; 820 535-2)*

Aug 69. (lp; mono/stereo) *Decca; (LK/SKL 5010) / London; <562>* **LOOKING BACK** 14 79
– Mr. James / Blues city shakedown / They call it stormy Monday / So many roads / Looking back / Sitting in the rain / It hurts me too / Double trouble / Suspicions (part 2) / Jenny / Picture on the wall. *(cd-iss. Jan89 on 'London'; 820 331-2)*

Apr 86. (d-lp/c/cd) *Castle; (CCS LP/MC/CD 137)* **THE COLLECTION** –
– Key to love / Hideaway / Ramblin' on my mind / All your love / They call it stormy Monday / Hoochie coochie man / Crocodile walk (1st version) / Crawling up a hill / Marsha's mood / Sonny Boy blow / Looking back / A hard road / The supernatural / You don't love me / Leaping Christine / Suspicions (part 2) / Picture on the wall / The death of J.B. Lenoir / Sandy / The bear / Walking the sunset / Fly tomorrow.

Apr 86. (lp) *Decal; (LIK 1)* **SOME OF MY BEST FRIENDS ARE BLUES** –

Mar 92. (cd/c) *Charly; (CD/TC BM 4)* **LIFE IN THE JUNGLE** (rec.'84)

Apr 94. (cd) *One Way; (OW 30008)* **THE 1982 REUNION CONCERT (live)** –
(re-iss. Nov02 on 'Repertoire'; REP 4393)

Apr 99. (d-cd) *Eagle; (EDMCD 071)* **THE MASTERS**

Apr 99. (cd) *Indigo; (IGOXCD 102)* **ROCK THE BLUES TONIGHT** (live in Canada 1971)

Apr 99. (cd) *Eagle; (EAMCD 70)* **LIVE AT THE MARQUEE 1969**

Nov 99. (cd) *Deram; (844785-2)* **AS IT ALL BEGAN: THE BEST OF JOHN MAYALL & THE BLUESBREAKERS 1964-69**

May 00. (cd) *Beat Goes On; (BGOCD 492)* **NEW YEAR NEW BAND NEW COMPANY / LOTS OF PEOPLE**

Jun 00. (cd) *Beat Goes On; (BGOCD 493)* **A HARDCORE PACKAGE / THE LAST OF THE BRITISH BLUES**

Jun 00. (cd) *Beat Goes On; (BGOCD 495)* **NOTICE TO APPEAR / A BANQUET IN BLUES**

Mar 01. (cd) *Rialto; (RMCD 2322)* **THE JOHN MAYALL ARCHIVE**

Apr 01. (d-cd) *Universal; (AA314 549424-2)* **BACK TO THE ROOTS: A VERY SPECIAL DOUBLE ALBUM . . .**

May 01. (cd) *Silvertone; (059122-2)* **THE BEST OF JOHN MAYALL**

May 01. (cd) *Silvertone; (ORECD 547)* **BLUES FOR THE LOST DAYS**

Sep 01. (cd) *Deram; (882922-2)* **AN INTRODUCTION TO JOHN MAYALL AND THE BLUESBREAKERS: STEPPIN' OUT**

Jan 03. (d-cd) *Castle; (CMDDD 639)* **ROCKIN' THE ROADSHOW**

Apr 03. (cd) *Movieplay Gold; (MPG 74070)* **LOST AND GONE**

John MAYER

Born: 16 Oct'77, Atlanta, Georgia, USA. A graduate of the Berklee College of Music, MAYER cut his teeth in the clubs and bars of Atlanta before self-releasing the 'INSIDE WANTS OUT' in 1999. Showcasing spartan, acoustic-strummed musings chequered with MAYER's fondness for both jazzy elaboration and personal revelation, it was a promising debut. A solo acoustic performance at Austin's South by Southwest industry bash caught the attentions of 'Columbia' who subsequently signed him to their 'Aware' subsidiary, and, inevitably perhaps, had him re-record selections from the debut. These – along with a clutch of new tracks – became 'ROOM FOR SQUARES' (2001), which steadily climbed into the US Top 10 on the strength of the 'NO SUCH THING' single. The singer/songwriter found himself in the inevitable position of filling the worn but reliable sneakers of the ever rawer DAVE MATTHEWS, touring colleges to general acclaim and releasing the 'ANY GIVEN THURSDAY' (2003) concert set. Third album, 'HEAVIER THINGS' (2003) hit US top spot later the same year, confirming MAYER as the new don of sophisti-student songwriting. • **Covers:** LENNY (Stevie Ray Vaughan) / THE WIND CRIES MARY (Jimi Hendrix) / MESSAGE IN A BOTTLE (Police).

Album rating: INSIDE WANTS OUT (*5) / ROOM FOR SQUARES (*7) / ANY GIVEN THURSDAY (*5) / HEAVIER THINGS (*7)

JOHN MAYER – vocals, guitar / with session band

not iss. Sony

1999. (m-cd) *<86861>* **INSIDE WANTS OUT** –
– Back to you / No such thing / My stupid mouth / Neon / Victoria / Love soon / Comfortable / Quiet. *<re-iss. 2002>* – hit No.22

not iss. Aware

Jun 01. (cd) *<7121>* **ROOM FOR SQUARES** –
– No such thing / Why Georgia / My stupid mouth / Your body is a wonderland / Neon / City love / 83 / 3x5 / Love song for no one / Back to you / Great indoors / Not myself / St. Patrick's Day. *<re-iss. Sep01 on 'Sony'+=; 85293>* – Lenny / The wind cries Mary. *<hit No.8>* *(UK-iss.Oct02 on 'Columbia'; 508135-2)*

Columbia Sony

Aug 02. (cd-s) *<672918>* **YOUR BODY IS A WONDERLAND / NO SUCH THING (acoustic live XWPN) / ('A'-acoustic live from the X-Lounge) / NOT MYSELF (demo)** – 18

Oct 02. (cd-s) *(673232-2) <672635>* **NO SUCH THING / LENNY (live at the X-Lounge) / THE WIND CRIES MARY (live at the X-Lounge) / ('A'-video)** May02 13
(re-iss. Aug03; same) – hit UK No.42
(cd-s) *(673232-5)* – ('A'-acoustic – live from WXPN) / Your body is a wonderland (live in Birmingham).

Feb 03. (cd) *<87199>* **ANY GIVEN THURSDAY (live)** – 17
– 3x5 / No such thing / Back to you / City love / Something's missing / Lenny – Man on the side / Message in a bottle / Love song for no one / Why Georgia / Your body is a wonderland / My stupid mouth / Covered in rain / 83 / Comfortable / Neon.

Apr 03. (cd-s) *<673468>* **WHY GEORGIA / 3x5 (live from the X-Lounge) / NO SUCH THING (demo) / ('A'-live)** –

Oct 03. (cd) *(513472-2) <86185>* **HEAVIER THINGS** 74 Sep03 1
– Clarity / Bigger than my body / Something's missing / New deep / Come back to bed / Home life / Split screen sadness / Daughters / Only heart / Wheel.

Curtis MAYFIELD

Born: 3 Jun'42, Chicago, Illinois, USA. Immersed in music from an early age, MAYFIELD was a self-taught guitarist and lyricist, strongly influenced by the sounds of the Northern Jubilee Gospel Singers (a local group that included JERRY BUTLER). In 1957, BUTLER asked MAYFIELD to join a newly formed group, The ROOSTERS, who would soon evolve into The IMPRESSIONS under the management of Eddie Thomas. As a songwriter for the group, MAYFIELD had his first hit in '58 with 'FOR YOUR PRECIOUS LOVE', prior to BUTLER's departure. The IMPRESSIONS scored their first Top 20 hit in '60 with 'GYPSY WOMAN', MAYFIELD's prolific writing career taking off via a new contract with 'A.B.C.' records. During the 60's, he penned a wealth of hits, including 'WE'RE A WINNER', the lyrical content highlighting MAYFIELD's awareness of the civil rights movement and the increasing confidence and self-determination of the African-American community. The decade also saw the soul man writing for record labels such as Okeh and Veejay as well as Chicago based artists including GENE CHANDLER and MAJOR LANCE. This work inspired CURTIS to set up his own label, 'Curtom' (distributed through 'Buddah'), releasing material by a number of successful acts, among them DONNY HATHAWAY. Leaving The IMPRESSIONS to go solo in 1970, his critically acclaimed self-titled debut set was characterised by his trademark funky organic sounds blended with socially aware lyrics. This album was followed by 'ROOTS', a record which included the groove-laden, 'KEEP ON KEEPING ON'. The turning point from acclaimed artist to international stardom arrived in 1972 when MAYFIELD was asked to score and perform the soundtrack for the blaxploitation film, 'Superfly'. The movie was a massive hit, MAYFIELD's soundtrack complementing the film perfectly and producing hits in the form of the title track and 'FREDDIE'S DEAD'. Still regarded as one of contemporary black music's most momentous recordings, 'SUPERFLY' represented the pinnacle of MAYFIELD's solo career. Although the man released some above average albums in the 70's and continued to oversee the creative development of the 'Curtom' imprint (now distributed by 'Warners'), he didn't really come close to matching the soundtrack's power. Arguably his finest post-'Superfly' work, 'SHORT EYES' was another soundtrack, written for a movie in which MAYFIELD also had an acting role. The 80's saw MAYFIELD touring regularly and scoring intermittent hits, a reunion tour with The IMPRESSIONS seen the return of his old sparring partner, BUTLER. The beginning of the 90's saw tragedy strike when in August 1990, MAYFIELD was hit by a lighting rig that had been dislodged by high winds during an open air concert in Brooklyn; he was paralysed from the neck down. The next few years saw MAYFIELD elected into the Rock And Roll Hall Of Fame and various lifetime achievement awards bestowed on him, so it was all the more remarkable when his comeback album, 'NEW WORLD ORDER', was released in '96. The recording process involved was time consuming, although the result was worth the wait, MAYFIELD achieving his best solo work since the early 70's. Tragically, it would be CURTIS' swansong as the great man died of (a long suffering) cancer on Boxing Day, 1999.

Album rating: CURTIS (*7) / CURTIS/LIVE! (*6) / ROOTS (*7) / SUPERFLY (*8) / BACK TO THE WORLD (*7) / CURTIS IN CHICAGO (*6) / SWEET EXORCIST (*6) / GOT TO FIND A WAY (*5) / THERE'S NO PLACE LIKE AMERICA TODAY (*6) / GIVE, GET, TAKE AND HAVE (*5) / NEVER SAY YOU CAN'T SURVIVE (*4) / SHORT EYES soundtrack (*4) / DO IT ALL NIGHT (*5) / HEARTBEAT (*6) / THE RIGHT COMBINATION with Linda Clifford (*4) / SOMETHING TO BELIEVE IN (*4) / LOVE IS THE PLACE (*5) / HONESTY (*7) / WE COME IN PEACE WITH A MESSAGE OF LOVE (*4) / LIVE IN EUROPE (*5) / TAKE IT TO THE STREET (*4) / A MAN LIKE CURTIS – THE BEST OF compilation (*8) / NEW WORLD ORDER (*6)

CURTIS MAYFIELD – vocals, guitar, keyboards + live band

Date	Release	Buddah	Curtom
Nov 70.	(7") *(2011 055)* *<1955>* **(DON'T WORRY) IF THERE'S A HELL BELOW WE'RE ALL GOING TO GO. / THE MAKINGS OF YOU**		29
Feb 71.	(lp) *(2318 015)* *<8005>* **CURTIS** – (Don't worry) If there's a Hell below we're all going to go / The other side of town / The makings of you / We the people who are darker than blue / Move on up / Miss Black America / Wild and free / Give it up. *(re-iss. Oct74; BDLH 5005) (re-iss. Jun76 on 'Warners'; K 56252) (cd-iss. Nov93 on 'Movieplay Gold'; MPG 74026) (re-iss. Mar94 on 'Curtom' cd/c; CUR 2012 CD/MC)*		Sep70 19
May 71.	(7") *<1960>* **GIVE IT UP. / BEAUTIFUL BROTHER OF MINE**	–	
Jun 71.	(7"m) *(2011 080)* **MOVE ON UP. / GIVE IT UP / BEAUTIFUL BROTHER OF MINE**	12	–
Aug 71.	(d-lp) *(2659 004)* *<8008>* **CURTIS / LIVE! (live)** – Mighty mighty (spade and Whitey) / I plan to stay a believer / We're a winner (rap) / We've only just begun / Check out your mind / People get ready / Stare and stare / Gypsy woman / The makings of you / We the people who are darker than blue / (Don't worry) If there's a Hell below we're all going to go / Stone junkie. *(re-iss. Oct74; BDLP 2001) (re-iss. Jun76 on 'Warners'; K 66047) (d-cd-iss. Mar94 on 'Movieplay Gold'; MPG 74176) (d-cd-iss. Jun94 on 'Curtom'; CPCD 8038)*		May71 21
Sep 71.	(7") *<1963>* **MIGHTY MIGHTY (SPADE AND WHITEY) (live). /**	–	
Nov 71.	(7") *(2011 101)* **WE GOT TO HAVE PEACE. / PEOPLE GET READY**		–
Dec 71.	(7") *<1966>* **GET DOWN. / WE'RE A WINNER**	–	69
Jan 72.	(lp) *(2318 065)* *<8009>* **ROOTS** – Get down / Keep on keeping on / Underground / We got to have peace / Beautiful brother of mine / Now you're gone / Love to keep you in my mind. *(re-iss. Oct74; BDLH 5006) (re-iss. Jun76 on 'Warners'; K 56249) (cd-iss. Nov93 on 'Movieplay Gold'; MPG 74027) (cd re-iss. Jun94 on 'Charly'; CPCD 8037)*		Oct71 40
Feb 72.	(7") *<1968>* **WE GOT TO HAVE PEACE. / WE'RE A WINNER**	–	
Apr 72.	(7") *<1972>* **BEAUTIFUL BROTHER OF MINE. / LOVE TO KEEP YOU IN MY MIND**	–	
May 72.	(7") *(2011 119)* **KEEP ON KEEPING ON. / STONE JUNKIE**		–
Jun 72.	(7") *<1974>* **MOVE ON UP. / UNDERGROUND**	–	
Sep 72.	(7") *(2011 141)* *<1975>* **FREDDIE'S DEAD (theme from "Superfly"). / UNDERGROUND**		Aug72 4
Nov 72.	(lp) *(2318 065)* *<8014>* **SUPERFLY (Soundtrack)** – Little child runnin' wild / Freddie's dead / Give me your love / No thing on me (cocaine song) / Superfly / Pusherman / Junkie chase / Eddie you should know / Think. *(re-iss. Nov74; BDLH 4018) (re-iss. Aug79 on 'R.S.O.'; RSS 5) (re-iss. Jun88 on 'Curtom' cd/c/lp; CD/ZC+/CUR 2002) (cd re-iss. Jun94 on 'Charly'; CPCD 8039)*	26	Aug72 1
Nov 72.	(7") *<1978>* **SUPERFLY. / UNDERGROUND**	–	8
Feb 73.	(7") *(2011 156)* **SUPERFLY. / GIVE ME YOUR LOVE (LOVE SONG)**		–
Jul 73.	(7") *<1987>* **FUTURE SHOCK. / THE OTHER SIDE OF TOWN**	–	39
Sep 73.	(lp) *(2318 085)* *<8015>* **BACK TO THE WORLD** – Back to the world / Future shock / Right on for the darkness / If I were only a child again / Can't say nothin' / Keep on trippin' / Future song (love of a good woman, love of a good man). *(re-iss. Oct74; BDLH 5008) (re-iss. Jun76 on 'Warners'; K 56251) (cd-iss. Nov93 on 'Movieplay Gold'; MPG 74029) (cd re-iss. Jun94 on 'Charly'; CPCD 8040)*		Jun73 16
Oct 73.	(7") *(2011 187)* **BACK TO THE WORLD. / THE OTHER SIDE OF TOWN**		–
Oct 73.	(7") *<1991>* **IF I WERE ONLY A CHILD AGAIN. / THINK**	–	71
Jan 74.	(7") *<1993>* **CAN'T SAY NOTHIN'. / FUTURE SHOCK**	–	88
Mar 74.	(lp) *(2318 091)* *<8018>* **CURTIS IN CHICAGO (TV Soundtrack)** – Superfly / For your precious love / I'm so proud / Once in my life (IMPRESSIONS) / Preacher man (IMPRESSIONS) / Duke of Earl (GENE CHANDLER) / Love oh love (LEROY HUTSON) / Amen. *(re-iss. Oct74; BDLH 5009) (re-iss. Jun76 on 'Curtom'; K 56250) (cd-iss. Oct94 on 'Charly'; CPCD 8046)*		Nov73

Aug 74. (lp) *(2318 099)* *<8601>* **SWEET EXORCIST** [ ] May74 [39]
– Ain't got time / Sweet exorcist / To be invisible / Power to the people / Kung Fu / Suffer / Make me believe in you. *(re-iss. Oct74; BDLH 5001) (re-iss. Aug76 on 'Curtom'; K 56284) (cd-iss. Oct94 on 'Charly'; CPCD 8047)*

Aug 74. (7") *(BDS 402)* *<1999>* **KUNG FU. / RIGHT ON FOR THE DARKNESS** [ ] Jun74 [40]

Oct 74. (7") *<2005>* **SWEET EXORCIST. / SUFFER** [–] [ ]

Jan 75. (lp) *(BDLP 4029)* *<8604>* **GOT TO FIND A WAY** [ ] Nov74 [76]
– Love me (right in the pocket) / So you don't love me / A prayer / Mother's son / Cannot find a way / Ain't no love lost. *(cd-iss. Oct94 on 'Charly'; CPCD 8048)*

Mar 75. (7") *(BDS 426)* *<2006>* **MOTHER'S SON. / LOVE ME RIGHT IN THE POCKET** [ ] [ ]

Jun 75. (7") **STASH THAT BUTT, SUCKER. / ZANZIBAR** [–] [ ]
(above single issued on 'Columbia')

— His band from this period onwards **GARY THOMPSON** – guitar / **RICH TUFO** – keyboards / **LUCKY SCOTT** – bass / **QUINTON JOSEPH** – drums

Aug 75. (lp) *(BDLP 4033)* *<5001>* **THERE'S NO PLACE LIKE AMERICA TODAY** [ ] Jun75 [ ]
– Billy Jack / When seasons change / So in love / Jesus / Blue Monday people / Hard times / Love to the people. *(re-iss. Jan89 on 'Curtom' cd/c/lp; CD/ZC+/CUR 2003)*

Sep 75. (7") *<0105>* **SO IN LOVE. / HARD TIMES** [–] [67]

Jul 76. (7") *<0118>* **ONLY YOU BABE. / LOVE TO THE PEOPLE** [–] [ ]

Jul 76. (lp) *(BDLP 4042)* *<5007>* **GIVE, GET, TAKE AND HAVE** [ ] Jun76 [ ]
– In your arms again / This love is sweet / P.S. I love you / Party night / Get a little bit (give, get, take and have) / Soul music / Only you babe / Mr. Welfare you. *(re-iss. Mar94 on 'Curtom' cd/c; CUR 2011 CD/MC) (cd re-iss. Jun94 on 'Charly'; CPCD 8070)*

Sep 76. (7") *<0122>* **PARTY NIGHT. / P.S. I LOVE YOU** [–] [ ]

Curtom Curtom

Mar 77. (7") *<0125>* **SHOW ME LOVE. / JUST WANT TO BE WITH YOU** [–] [ ]

Mar 77. (lp) *(K 56352)* *<5013>* **NEVER SAY YOU CAN'T SURVIVE** [ ] [ ]
– Show me love / Just want to be with you / When we're alone / Never say you can't survive / I'm gonna win your love / All night long / When you used to be mine / Sparkle. *(re-iss. Mar94 on 'Curtom' cd/c; CUR 2010 CD/MC) (cd-iss. Oct94 on 'Charly'; CPCD 8049)*

Nov 77. (7") *<0131>* **DO DO WAP IS STRONG IN HERE. / NEED SOMEONE TO LOVE** [–] [ ]

Feb 78. (lp) *(K 56430)* *<5017>* **SHORT EYES (Soundtrack)** [ ] Nov77 [ ]
– Do do wap is strong in here / Back against the wall / Need someone to love / A heavy dupe / Short eyes / Break it down / Another fool in love / Father confessor. *(cd-iss. Jun96 on 'Charly'; CPCD 8183)*

Jul 78. (7") *<0135>* **YOU ARE, YOU ARE. / GET A LITLE BIT (GIVE, GET, TAKE AND HAVE)** [–] [ ]

Sep 78. (7") *<0141>* **DO IT ALL NIGHT. / PARTY PARTY** [–] [ ]

Oct 78. (lp) *<5022>* **DO IT ALL NIGHT** [–] [ ]
– Do it all night / No goodbyes / Party party / Keeps me loving you / In love, in love, in love / You are, you are. *(cd-iss. Oct94 on 'Charly'; CPCD 8050)*

Nov 78. (7") *<0142>* **IN LOVE, IN LOVE, IN LOVE. / KEEPS ME LOVING YOU** [–] [ ]

Atlantic not iss.

Dec 78. (12") *(LV 1)* **NO GOODBYES. / PARTY PARTY** [65] [–]

— With various session people

R.S.O. R.S.O.

Mar 79. (7") *(RSO 28)* *<919>* **THIS YEAR. / ('A'instrumental)** [ ] [ ]

Sep 79. (lp) *(RSS 4)* *<3053>* **HEARTBEAT** [ ] Aug79 [42]
– Tell me, tell me (how ya like to be loved) / What is my woman for? / Between you baby and me / Victory / Over the hump / You better stop / You're so good to me / Heartbeat. *(cd-iss. Jun94 on 'Charly'; CPCD 8071)*

Aug 79. (7"; by LINDA CLIFFORD & CURTIS MAYFIELD) *<RSO 43)* *<941>* **BETWEEN YOU BABY AND ME. / YOU'RE SO GOOD TO ME** [ ] [ ]

Jun 80. (lp; by LINDA CLIFFORD & CURTIS MAYFIELD) *(2394 269)* *<3084>* **THE RIGHT COMBINATION** [ ] [ ]
– Rock to your socks / The right combination / I'm so proud / Ain't no love lost / It's lovin' time / Love's sweet sensation / Between you baby and me. *(cd-iss. Jun94 on 'Charly'; CPCD 8072)*

1980. (7"; by LINDA CLIFFORD & CURTIS MAYFIELD) *<1029>* **LOVE'S SWEET SENSATION. / ('A'instrumental)** [–] [ ]

1980. (7") *<1036>* **LOVE ME, LOVE ME NOW. / IT'S ALRIGHT** [–] [ ]

Sep 80. (lp) *(2394 271)* *<3077>* **SOMETHING TO BELIEVE IN** [ ] Jul80 [ ]
– Something to believe in / Love me, love me now / Never let me go / Tripping out / People never give up / It's alright / Never stop loving me. *(re-iss. Oct89 on 'Curtom' lp/c/cd; CUR/+MC/CD 2005) (cd re-iss. Jun94 on 'Charly'; CPCD 8073) (cd re-iss. Oct94 on 'Curtom'; CUR 2005CD)*

Sep 80. (7") *<1046>* **TRIPPING OUT. / NEVER STOP LOVING** [–] [ ]

Oct 80. (7") *(RSO 68)* **IT'S ALRIGHT. / SUPERFLY** [ ] [–]

Epic Boardwalk

1981. (lp) *<2601 6012>* **LOVE IS THE PLACE** [–] German [–]
– She don't let nobody (but me) / Toot an' toot an' toot / Baby doll / Love is the place / Just ease my mind / You mean everything to me / You get all my love / Come free your people.

1981. (7") *<122>* **SHE DON'T LET NOBODY (BUT ME). / YOU GET ALL MY LOVE** [–] [ ]

1981. (7") *<132>* **COME FREE YOUR PEOPLE. / TOOT AN' TOOT AN' TOOT** [–] [ ]

Oct 82. (7") *<155>* **HEY BABY (GIVE IT ALL TO ME). / SUMMER HOT** [–] [ ]

Mar 83. (lp/c) *(EPC/40 25317)* *<2601 6022>* **HONESTY** [ ] German [–]
– Hey baby (give it all to me) / Still within your heart / Dirty laundry / Nobody but you / If you need me / What you gawn do? / Summer hot.

Mar 83. (7") *<169>* **DIRTY LAUNDRY. / NOBODY BUT YOU** [–] [ ]

not iss. C.R.C.

Sep 85. (lp) *<447>* **WE COME IN PEACE WITH A MESSAGE OF LOVE** [–] [ ]
(UK-iss.Feb91 on 'Curtom' lp/c/cd; CRC 2001/+MC/CD)

98.6 98.6

Nov 86. (7"/12") *(CURT 1/+T)* **BABY IT'S YOU. / BREAKIN' IN THE STREETS** [ ] [ ]

— In mid'87 he was credited on BLOW MONKEYS single 'Celebrate The Day'.

Capitol Capitol

1987. (lp; withdrawn) **LIVE IN LOS ANGELES (live)** [–] [–]

Ichiban Ichiban

Jun 88. (cd/c/lp) *(CD/ZC+/CUR 2901)* **LIVE IN EUROPE (live)** [ ] [ ]
– (intro) / Freddie's dead / We gotta have peace / People get ready / Move on up / Back to the world / Gypsy woman / Pusher man / We've only just begun / When seasons change / (Don't worry) If there's a Hell below we're all going to go.

Jul 88. (7"/12") *(CUR/12CUR 101)* **MOVE ON UP (live). / LITTLE CHILD RUNNIN' WILD (live)** [ ] [ ]

Curtom Arista

May 89. (7"; w/ FISHBONE) **HE'S A FLY GUY. / ('A'instrumental)** [–] [ ]

May 89. (7") *(7CUR 102)* **I MO GIT U SUCKA. / HE'S A FLY GUY** [ ] [–]
(12"+=/cd-s+=) *(12/CD CUR 102)* – ('A'extended).

Feb 90. (7"/12") *(7/12 CUR 106)* **HOMELESS. / PEOPLE NEVER GIVE UP** [ ] [ ]

Mar 90. (cd/c/lp) *(CD/ZC+/CUR 2008)* **TAKE IT TO THE STREET** [ ] [ ]
– Homeless / Got to be real / Do be down / Who was that lady / On and on / He's a fly guy / Don't push / I mo git u sucka. *(cd re-iss. Apr96 on 'Charly'; CPCD 8179)*

Jun 90. (7") *(7CUR 108)* **DO BE DOWN. / GOT TO BE REAL** [ ] [ ]
(12"+=) *(12CUR 108)* – ('A'extended) / ('A'-radio version).

— On the 13th August, 1990, while CURTIS prepared for a gig, a high wind brought down a lighting scaffold which struck him. This left him permanently paralysed from the neck downwards (his house subsequently burned down a month later!).

Capitol Capitol

Sep 90. (7"; as CURTIS MAYFIELD & ICE-T) *(CL 586)* **SUPERFLY 1990. / ('A'mix)** [48] [ ]
(12"+=/cd-s+=) *(12/CD CL 586)* – ('A'mixes).

— CURTIS returned to the studio 1995/96 with session backing

Warners WEA Int.

Jan 97. (cd/c) *<(9362 46348-2/-4)>* **NEW WORLD ORDER** [44] [ ]
– New world order / Ms. Martha / Back to living again / No one knows about a good thing (you don't have to cry) / Just a little bit of love / We people who are darker than blue / I believe in you / Here but I'm gone / It was love that we needed / The got dang song / The girl I find stays on my mind / Let's not forget / Oh so beautiful.

— on the 26th of December 1999, after suffering with cancer for a long time, CURTIS died in an Atlanta hospital

— posthumously, CURTIS was credited on BRAN VAN 3000's mid-2001 UK hit, 'Astounded'

– compilations, others, etc. –

Nov 74. (lp) *Buddah; (BDLP 4015)* **MOVE ON UP – THE BEST OF CURTIS MAYFIELD**

Nov 74. (7") *Buddah; (BDS 410)* **MOVE ON UP. / GIVE IT UP** -

Jan 83. (7") *Flashback; (FBS 23)* **MOVE ON UP. / (b-side by Melba Moore)** -

Feb 90. (cd/c) *Essential; (ESS CD/MC 003)* **PEOPLE GET READY (live At Ronnie Scott's)** -
(cd re-iss. 1993 on 'Castle'; CLACD 329)

Nov 90. (d-lp/c/cd) *Curtom; (CUR 22902/+MC/CD)* **OF ALL TIME – THE CLASSIC COLLECTION** -

Nov 92. (cd) *Music Collection; (MUSCD 007)* **A MAN LIKE CURTIS – THE BEST OF . . .** -
– Move on up / Superfly / (Don't worry) If there's a Hell below we're all gonna go / You are, you are / Give me your love / Never stop loving me / Tripping out / Soul music / This year / Ain't no love lost / Pusherman / Freddie's dead / Do do wop is strong in here / Hard times / In your arms again (shake it) / So in love.

Sep 93. (cd) *Traditional Line; (TL 001333)* **HARD TIMES** -

Jan 94. (cd) *Windsong; (WINDCD 052)* **BBC RADIO 1 LIVE IN CONCERT** -

May 94. (cd/c) *Laserlight; (1/7 2364)* **CURTIS MAYFIELD** -

Jun 94. (cd) *Charly; (CPCD 1211)* **POWER FOR THE PEOPLE** -

Aug 94. (cd) *Charly; (CPCD 8043)* **GROOVE ON UP** -

Nov 94. (cd) *Charly; (CPCD 8065)* **TRIPPING OUT** -

Feb 95. (d-cd) *Charly; (CPCD 8034)* **GET DOWN TO THE FUNKY GROOVE** -

Mar 96. (cd) *Sequel; (NEMCD 783)* **LOVE IS THE PLACE / HONESTY** -

Apr 96. (cd) *Audiophile; (APH 102802)* **MOVE ON UP** -

Apr 96. (cd) *Castle; (CCSCD 806)* **THE VERY BEST OF CURTIS MAYFIELD** -

— CURTIS also collaborated on other Film Soundtracks, 'CLAUDINE' in Aug74 with GLADYS KNIGHT & THE PIPS, 'LET'S DO IT AGAIN' in Sep76 with STAPLE SINGERS and 'SPARKLE' Oct76 with ARETHA FRANKLIN. There were also a few tribute cd's about the shops in the mid-90's.

☐ Paddy McALOON (see under ⇒ PREFAB SPROUT)

☐ McAULEY-SCHENKER GROUP (see under ⇒ SCHENKER, Michael)

Paul McCARTNEY

Born: JAMES PAUL McCARTNEY, 18 Jun'42, Liverpool, England. An integral part of The BEATLES throughout the 60's, he and JOHN LENNON were easily the greatest contemporary writing partnership of the 20th Century. The band officially split on the 11 April 1970, prior to issuing their final album, 'LET IT BE', (there was also a docu-film of the same name, detailing the last days of the fab four). Released three weeks previous was McCARTNEY's first solo outing, the eponymous 'McCARTNEY', which included backing from new wife, LINDA (who he married on the 12th of March '69). By virtue of its relative acoustic simplicity (PAUL played every instrument himself), the record remains one of the better releases from a time when self indulgence and wildly ambitious concepts were the order of the day. Though berated by critics at the time, the album contained one of PAUL's finer efforts in 'MAYBE I'M AMAZED', going on to top the American charts but being held off the UK No.1 by SIMON & GARFUNKEL's 'Bridge Over Troubled Water'. The following year, McCARTNEY scored a cross-Atlantic Top 5 with his debut solo single, 'ANOTHER DAY', and then took the unusual step of co-crediting his wife LINDA (though she did actually contribute keyboards, backing vocals and percussion) on the subsequent album, 'RAM' (1971). Sales wise, the album reversed the chart positions of its predecessor, spawning the whimsical US-only No.1 single, 'UNCLE ALBERT – ADMIRAL HALSEY'.'RAM' had also featured the drumming talents of DENNY SEIWELL who, together with ex-MOODY BLUES man, DENNY LAINE (guitar, vocals), would form one half of McCARTNEY's new group, WINGS, later that year. With the husband and wife duo of PAUL and LINDA completing the line-up, McCARTNEY hit an unprecedented critical low with WINGS's vaguely reggae-ish debut effort, 'WILDLIFE'. Unfazed, McCARTNEY took his band out on a low key colllege tour, beefing up the sound with the addition of HENRY McCULLOUGH (who had previously worked with JOE COCKER) on guitar and backing vocals. The next WINGS's release was the controversial (and surprisingly successful given its political sentiments) 'GIVE IRELAND BACK TO THE IRISH'. Annoyed at a radio ban, WINGS then put music to nursery rhyme with 'MARY HAD A LITTLE LAMB', a rather excessive anti-censorship statement that made the UK Top 10 but lost the band valuable credibility. The McCARTNEY's then underwent a series of drug busts and another pedantic BBC ban with their next hit, 'HI HI HI'. In Spring '73, PAUL McCARTNEY & WINGS topped the US charts with the single, 'MY LOVE', and another under par album, 'RED ROSE SPEEDWAY'. Following later that summer was the much more impressive 'LIVE AND LET DIE', a much covered McCARTNEY-penned theme song for the James Bond film of the same name. With the departure of SEIWELL and McCULLOUGH immediately prior to recording the fourth album, WINGS were reduced to a core of The McCARTNEY's and LAINE, one that endured for the remainder of the band's career. Going it alone, the trio surprisingly came up with the most successful album of their career, 'BAND ON THE RUN' (1973). Where before, McCARTNEY's compositions had been perfectly formed but lacking in substance, he silenced his critics with impassioned pop/rock of the highest calibre, notably on 'JET' and the title track. The album went on to sell over 6 million copies during its two year-plus stay in both the UK & US charts, PAUL finally proving his post-BEATLES mettle. The subsequent addition of JIMMY McCULLOCH and GEOFF BRITTON saw the band expanded to a 5-piece again, BRITTON only playing on one single, 'JUNIOR'S FARM'. His replacement was JOE ENGLISH, the new line-up recording the mediocre quasi-concept album, 'VENUS AND MARS' (1975). The album topped the American and British charts all the same, although the single 'LETTING GO' didn't even make the Top 40, a pattern that would continue into the late 70's and beyond. 'WINGS AT THE SPEED OF SOUND' (1976) gets points deducted for McCARTNEY's well intentioned but annoying insistence that each band member get a lead vocal although 'SILLY LOVE SONGS' and 'LET 'EM IN' were finely honed hit singles. The triple live set, 'WINGS OVER AMERICA' (1977), was impressive if overly long proof of the band's well deserved live reputation, showcasing McCARTNEY's vocal and multi-instrumentalist talents to often dazzling effect. In early 1977, the band were reduced to a trio once more following the departure of McCULLOCH and ENGLISH for The SMALL FACES and SEA LEVEL respectively. Incredibly, WINGS bounced back with their biggest single to date, the windswept sentimental indulgence that was 'MULL OF KINTYRE'. Blissfully oblivious to punk, McCARTNEY even employed a warts and all Scottish pipe band to give the song that 'authentic' Caledonian appeal. It obviously worked; the record stood proudly at the top of the UK charts for nine weeks, becoming the biggest selling UK single ever. Incredibly, given the yanks taste for anything remotely celtic, the single's B-side was promoted in the States, consequently stalling in the lower regions of the chart. WINGS had more US success via the single, 'WITH A LITTLE LUCK', a No.1 from the otherwise forgettable 'LONDON TOWN' (1978). The addition of LAURENCRE JUBER and STEVE HOLLY failed to prevent another critical pasting with 'BACK TO THE EGG' (1979). By the time WINGS had officially been laid to rest, PAUL had already released the Yuletide cutesiness of the 'WONDERFUL CHRISTMASTIME' single as well as the 'McCARTNEY II' (1980) album, a stripped down affair that heralded a new phase in his career. From the international chart topping 'EBONY AND IVORY' (a duet with STEVIE WONDER) onwards, the first half of the new decade saw McCARTNEY collaborating with the cream of the MOR elite. The results were sometimes intriguing, often downright dull. 'TUG OF WAR' (1982) and 'PIPES OF PEACE' (1983) kept the singer's profile high, the latter featuring 'SAY SAY SAY', a duet with buddy, MICHAEL JACKSON. While fans voted with their feet, critics were not so generous, although they saved their most vicious scorn for 'GIVE MY REGARDS TO BROAD STREET' (1984), McCARTNEY's own feature film and accompanying soundtrack. While 'NO MORE LONELY NIGHTS' was an affecting, if slight, ballad, the bulk of the project consisted of pointless BEATLES rehashes. It was two years before McCARTNEY surfaced again, although 'PRESS TO PLAY' (1986) failed to rectify matters. After finding a writing partner in ELVIS COSTELLO, McCARTNEY recroded his most committed and consistent work for more than a decade with 'FLOWERS IN THE DIRT' (1989). Recruiting a fairly permanent backing band: PAUL WICKENS (keyboards), CHRIS WHITTEN (drums), ROBBIE McINTOSH (guitar) and HAMISH STUART (guitar, bass), McCARTNEY set off on another world tour, documented on the fine 'TRIPPING THE LIVE FANTASTIC' (1990). An obligatory MTV unplugged set was released the following year, while an ambitious foray into classical music, 'LIVERPOOL ORATARIO' (1991) saw McCARTNEY working with the likes of CARL DAVIS and DAME KIRI TEKANEWA. His next album proper, 'OFF THE GROUND' (1993), failed to get that far, his solo career subsequently put on ice as he hooked up with his old chums, GEORGE HARRISON and RINGO STARR, to make the 'ANTHOLOGY' series of albums and videos tracing the history of The BEATLES. With his profile at its highest since the WINGS days, PAUL released 'FLAMING PIE' (1997), a work that even surpassed 'FLOWERS IN THE DIRT' and finally saw him live up to his reputation as one of the greatest songwriters popular music has ever known. However, tragedy was to strike the McCARTNEY's, when wife LINDA lost her battle against breast cancer on the 17th of April 1998 (PAUL was beside her to the end); a tribute album for her work, 'Wild Prairie' was issued that November while PAUL was inducted as a solo artist into the Rock And Roll Hall Of Fame – "about fucking time!" was fashion designer daughter STELLA's T-shirted opinion of the matter. On the music front, MACCA was back with a bluesy rock'n'roll covers set, 'RUN DEVIL RUN' (1999), although underneath all the showbiz glitz of a comeback tour, PAUL was still hurting inside. A long overdue WINGS anthology, 'WINGSPAN' (2001) was as fitting a tribute as any to LINDA's often unsung talents while the man himself was back with another solo set in the shape of 'DRIVING RAIN' later the same year. More adventurous and fresh sounding than much of the material he recorded in the previous decade, the record wasn't exactly a creative rebirth but suggested that the pioneering spirit of The BEATLES hadn't completely deserted him just yet. Meanwhile, PAUL had found a new love, thirty-something Heather Mills, whom he married on 12th June 2002. The double live 'BACK IN THE WORLD' (2003) – titled 'BACK IN THE US' in the States – was McCARTNEY back doing what he perhaps does best, entertaining a crowd and indulging that crowd with the kind of material they want to hear. Thus there was plenty LENNON/McCARTNEY material alongside WINGS and solo material although it was hard to avoid the impression of a man going through the motions. • **Songwriters:** 99% by PAUL, except some with group. Covered; MONY MONY (Tommy James & The Shandells) / GO NOW (Moody Blues) / RUDOLPH THE RED-NOSED REINDEER (Christmas trad.) / KANSAS CITY (Wilbert Harrison) / MATCHBOX (Carl Perkins) / TWENTY FLIGHT ROCK (Eddie Cochran) / LAWDY MISS CLAWDY + IT'S NOW OR NEVER + BLUE MOON OF KENTUCKY (Elvis Presley) / BE-BOP-A-LULA (Gene Vincent) / BACK ON MY FEET (co-with Elvis Costello) / HI-HEEL SNEAKERS (Tommy Tucker) / GIVE PEACE A CHANCE (John Lennon) / AIN'T THAT A SHAME (Fats Domino) / etc., and many past BEATLES songs live. • **Trivia:** The 'BAND ON THE RUN' album sleeve featured the group being caught escaping alongside celebrities; Michael Parkinson, Kenny Lynch, James Coburn, Clement Freud, Christopher Lee & John Conteh.

Album rating: McCARTNEY (*6) / RAM (*6) / WILD LIFE (*4) / RED ROSE SPEEDWAY (*5) / BAND ON THE RUN (*9) / VENUS AND MARS (*6) / WINGS AT THE SPEED OF SOUND (*4) / WINGS OVER AMERICA (*6) / LONDON TOWN (*5) / WINGS GREATEST compilation (*7) / BACK TO THE EGG (*5) / McCARTNEY II (*5) / TUG OF WAR (*5) / PIPES OF PEACE (*4) / GIVE MY REGARDS TO BROAD STREET (*3) / PRESS TO PLAY (*4) / ALL THE BEST! compilation (*8) / FLOWERS IN THE DIRT (*6) / TRIPPING THE LIVE FANTASTIC (*4) / UNPLUGGED (THE OFFICIAL BOOTLEG) (*6) / CHOBA B CCCP – THE RUSSIAN ALBUM (*4) / OFF THE GROUND (*4) / PAUL IS LIVE! (*4) / FLAMING PIE (*6) / RUN DEVIL RUN (*5) / WINGSPAN boxed compilation (*8) / DRIVING RAIN (*7) / BACK IN THE U.S./WORLD (*5)

PAUL McCARTNEY – vocals, bass, guitar, keyboards, drums (ex-BEATLES) with **LINDA McCARTNEY** (b. LINDA EASTMAN, 24 Sep'42, Scarsdale, New York, USA) – backing vocals

		Apple	Apple
Apr 70.	(lp/c) *(PCS/TC-PCS 7102)* *<3363>* **McCARTNEY**	2	1
	– The lovely Linda / That would be something / Valentine day / Every night / Hot as sun / Glasses / Junk / Man we was lonely / Momma miss America / Teddy boy / Singalong junk / Maybe I'm amazed / Kreen-Akrove. *(re-iss. May84 on 'Fame' lp/c; FA41 3100-1/-4) (cd-iss. Apr87; CDP 746 611-2) (re-iss. Apr90 lp/c; ATAK/TC-ATAK 152) (re-iss. Jun93 cd/c;)*		
Feb 71.	(7") *(R 5889)* *<1829>* **ANOTHER DAY. / OH WOMAN OH WHY**	2	5

— **PAUL** – vocals, guitar, bass / **LINDA** – keyboards, backing vocals, percussion / added **DENNY SEIWELL** – drums, vocals (plus various session people)

May 71.	(lp/c; PAUL & LINDA McCARTNEY) *(PAS/TC-PAS 10003)* *<3375>* **RAM**	1	2
	– Too many people / Three legs / Ram on / Dear boy / Uncle Albert – Admiral Halsey / Smile away / Heart of the country / Monkberry moon delight / Eat at home / Long-haired lady / Ram on / The back seat of my car. *(re-iss. Jan85 on 'Parlophone'; CDP 746 612-2) (re-iss. Jan88; ATAK/TC-ATAK 12) (re-iss. Jun93 cd/c;)*		
Aug 71.	(7"; PAUL & LINDA McCARTNEY) *(R 5914)* **THE BACK SEAT OF MY CAR. / HEART OF THE COUNTRY**	39	–
Aug 71.	(7"; PAUL & LINDA McCARTNEY) *<1837>* **UNCLE ALBERT – ADMIRAL HALSEY. / TOO MANY PEOPLE**	–	1

WINGS

— was the group the above trio formed; adding **DENNY LAINE** – guitar, vocals (ex-MOODY BLUES, ex-UGLYS, ex-BALLS, etc.)

Dec 71.	(lp/c) *(PCS/TC-PCS 7142)* *<3386>* **WILD LIFE**	8	10
	– Mumbo / Bip bop / Love is strange / Wild life / Some people never know / I am your singer / Tomorrow / Dear friend. *(re-iss. Apr84 on 'Fame' lp/c; FA/TCFA 3101) (cd-iss. Oct87 +=; CDFA 3101)* – Mary had a little lamb / Little woman love / Oh woman, oh why. *(re-iss. Jun93 cd/c;)*		

— added **HENRY McCULLOCH** – guitar, vocals (ex-JOE COCKER, etc.)

Feb 72. (7") *(R 5936)* <1847> **GIVE IRELAND BACK TO THE IRISH. / ('A'version)** 16 Mar72 21

May 72. (7") *(R 5949)* <1851> **MARY HAD A LITTLE LAMB. / LITTLE WOMAN LOVE** 9 Jun72 28

Dec 72. (7") *(R 5973)* <1857> **C MOON. / HI HI HI** 5 10

(above flipped over in the States)

PAUL McCARTNEY AND WINGS

Mar 73. (7") *(R 5985)* <1861> **MY LOVE. / THE MESS (live)** 9 Apr73 1

May 73. (lp/c) *(TC+/PCTC 251)* <3409> **RED ROSE SPEEDWAY** 5 1

– Big barn bed / My love / Get on the right thing / One more kiss / Little lamb dragonfly / Single pigeon / When the night / Hold me tight – Lazy dynamite – Hands of love – Power cut / Loup (1st Indian on the Moon). *(re-iss. Jan85 on 'Parlophone' lp/c; ATAK/TC-ATAK 16) (re-iss. Oct87 on 'Fame' lp/c/cd+=; FA/TCFA/CDFA 3193) (re-iss. Jun93)* – The mess (live) / I lie around / Country dreamer.

Jun 73. (7"; as WINGS) *(R 5987)* <1863> **LIVE AND LET DIE. / I LIE AROUND** 9 Jul73 2

— **PAUL, LINDA + DENNY LAINER. (McCULLOCH went solo, SEIWELL to sessions)**

Oct 73. (7") *(R 5993)* <1869> **HELEN WHEELS. / COUNTRY DREAMER** 12 Nov 73 10

Dec 73. (lp/c) *(PAS/TC-PAS 10007)* <3415> **BAND ON THE RUN** 1 1

– Band on the run / Jet / Bluebird / Mrs. Vanderbilt / Let me roll it / Mamunia / No words / Picasso's last words (drink to me) / Nineteen hundred and eighty-five. *<US pic-lp; > (re-iss. Jan85 on 'Parlophone' lp/c; ATAK/TC-ATAK 19) (cd-iss. Feb85 +=; CDP 746055-2)* – Helen wheels. *(re-iss. Jun93 cd/c;) (special 25th anniversary edition Mar99 d-cd/d-lp; 499176-2/-1)* – (extra versions). *(hit No.69)*

Feb 74. (7") *(R 5996)* <1871> **JET. / LET ME ROLL IT** 7 7

Apr 74. (7") <1873> **BAND ON THE RUN. / 1985** – 1

Jun 74. (7") *(R 5997)* **BAND ON THE RUN. / ZOO GANG** 3 –

— added **JIMMY McCULLOCH** (b. 4 Jun'53) – guitar, vocals (ex-THUNDERCLAP NEWMAN, ex-STONE THE CROWS) + **GEOFF BRITTON** – drums (ex-EAST OF EDEN)

Nov 74. (7") *(R 5999)* <1875> **JUNIOR'S FARM. / SALLY G** 16 3 / 17

WINGS

— **JOE ENGLISH** (b. Rochester, New York) – drums (ex-JAM FACTORY) repl. BRITTON who joined CHAMPION

Capitol Capitol

May 75. (7") *(R 6006)* <4091> **LISTEN TO WHAT THE MAN SAID. / LOVE IN SONG** 6 1

Jun 75. (lp/c) *(PCTC/TC-PCTC 254)* <11419> **VENUS AND MARS** 1 1

– Venus and Mars rock show / Love in song / You gave me the answer / Magneto and Titanium man / Letting go / Venus and Mars (reprise) / Spirits of ancient Egypt / Medicine jar / Call me back again / Listen to what the man said / Treat her gently – lonely old people / Crossroads theme. *(re-iss. Jan85 on 'Parlophone' lp/c; ATAK/TC-ATAK 14) (cd-iss. Nov88 cd+=/c/lp; CD/TC+/FA 3213)* – Zoogang / My carnival / Lunch box – odd socks. *(re-iss. Jun93 cd/c;)*

Sep 75. (7") *(R 6008)* <4145> **LETTING GO. / YOU GAVE ME THE ANSWER** 41 39

Nov 75. (7") *(R 6010)* <4175> **VENUS AND MARS ROCK SHOW. / MAGNETO AND TITANIUM MAN** 12

E.M.I. Capitol

Apr 76. (lp/c) *(PAS/TC-PAS 10010)* <11525> **WINGS AT THE SPEED OF SOUND** 2 1

– Let 'em in / The note you never wrote / She's my baby / Beware my love / Wino junko / Silly love songs / Cook of the house / Time to hide / Must do something about it / San Ferry Anne / Warm and beautiful. *(re-iss. Jan85 lp/c; ATAK/TCATAC 13) (cd-iss. Jul89 on 'Parlophone'; CDPAS 10010) (re-iss. Oct89 on 'Fame' cd/c/lp; CD/TC+/FA 3229) (re-iss. Jun93 cd/c;)*

May 76. (7") *(R 6014)* <4256> **SILLY LOVE SONGS. / COOK OF THE HOUSE** 2 Apr76 1

Jul 76. (7") *(R 6015)* <4293> **LET 'EM IN. / BEWARE MY LOVE** 2 3

Jan 77. (t-lp/d-c) *(PCSP/TC-PCSP 720)* <11593> **WINGS OVER AMERICA (live)** 8 Dec76 1

– Venus and Mars rock show / Jet / Let me roll it / Spirits of ancient Egypt / Medicine jar / Maybe I'm amazed / Call me back again / Lady Madonna / The long and winding road / Live and let die / Picasso's last words (drink to me) / Richard Cory / Bluebird / I've just seen a face / Yesterday / You gave me the answer / Magnet and Titanium man / Go now / My love / Listen to what the man said / Let 'em in / Time to hide / Silly love songs / Beware my love / Letting go / Band on the run / Hi hi hi / Soily. *(d-cd-iss. May87; CDS 746715-2) (re-iss. 1989 d-lp/d-c; ATAK/TC-ATAK 17)*

Feb 77. (7") *(R 6017)* <4385> **MAYBE I'M AMAZED (live). / SOILY (live)** 28 10

— cut to trio of **PAUL, LINDA** and **DENNY** when JIMMY joined SMALL FACES, and JOE joined SEA LEVEL (ex-ALLMANS).

Capitol Capitol

Nov 77. (7",7"blue) *(R 6018)* <4504> **MULL OF KINTYRE. / GIRLS SCHOOL** 1 33

(above flipped over in the States)

— added **STEVE HOLLY** – drums (on session but joined f/t Jul'78)

Parlophone Capitol

Mar 78. (7") *(R 6019)* <4559> **WITH A LITTLE LUCK. / CUFF LINK: BACKWARDS TRAVELLER** 5 1

Apr 78. (lp/c) *(PAS/TC-PAS 10012)* <11777> **LONDON TOWN** 4 2

– London town / Cafe on the Left Bank / I'm carrying / Backwards traveller – Cuff link / Children children / Girlfriend / I've had enough / With a little luck / Famous groupies / Deliver your children / Name and address / Don't let it bring you down / Morse Moose and the Grey Goose. *(re-iss. Jan85 lp/c; ATAK/TCATAK 18) (re-iss. Aug89 on 'Fame' cd/c/lp; CD/TC+/FA 3223) (re-iss. Jun93 cd/c;)*

Jun 78. (7") *(R 6020)* <4594> **I'VE HAD ENOUGH. / DELIVER YOUR CHILDREN** 42 25

Aug 78. (7") *(R 6021)* <4625> **LONDON TOWN. / I'M CARRYING** 60 39

Nov 78. (lp/c) *(PCTC/TC-PCTC 256)* <11905> **WINGS GREATEST** (compilation) 5 29

– Another day / Silly love songs / Live and let die / Junior's farm / With a little luck / Band on the run / Uncle Albert – Admiral Halsey / Hi hi hi / Let 'em in / My love / Mull of Kintyre. *(re-iss. Jan85 lp/c; ATAK/TCATAK 15) (cd-iss. 1989; CDP 746056-2) (re-iss. Aug93 cd/c;)*

— added **LAURENCE JUBER** – guitar, vocals

Parlophone Columbia

Mar 79. (7"/ext.12") *(R/12R 6023)* <10939> **GOODNIGHT TONIGHT. / DAYTIME NIGHTIME SUFFERING** 5 5

Jun 79. (7") *(R 6026)* **OLD SIAM, SIR. / SPIN IT ON** 35 –

Jun 79. (7") <11020> **GETTING CLOSER. / SPIN IT ON** – 20

Jun 79. (lp/c) *(PCTC/TC-PCTC 257)* <36057> **BACK TO THE EGG** 6 8

– Reception / Getting closer / We're open tonight / Spin it on / Again and again and again / Old Siam, sir / Arrow through me / Rockestra theme / To you / After the ball – Million miles / Winter rose – Love awake / The broadcast / So glad to see you here / Baby's request. *<US pic-lp promo, became worth $1,000; PCTCP 257) (cd-iss. Jul89; CDPCTC 257) (re-iss. Aug93 cd/c;)*

Aug 79. (7") *(R 6027)* **GETTING CLOSER. / BABY'S REQUEST** 60 –

Sep 79. (7") <11070> **ARROW THROUGH ME. / OLD SIAM, SIR** – 29

PAUL McCARTNEY

— went solo, augmented by LINDA plus session people

Parlophone Columbia

Nov 79. (7") *(R 6029)* <11162> **WONDERFUL CHRISTMASTIME. / RUDOLPH THE RED-NOSED REINDEER** 6

<US re-iss. Nov83; same>

Apr 80. (7") *(R 6035)* <11263> **COMING UP. / COMING UP (live) / LUNCH BOX – ODD SOX** 2 1

May 80. (lp/c) *(PCTC/TCPCTC 258)* <36511> **McCARTNEY II** 1 3

– Coming up / Temporary secretary / On the way / Waterfalls / Nobody knows / Front parlour / Summer's day song / Frozen Jap / Bogey music / Darkroom / One of these days. *(re-iss. Sep87 on 'Fame' cd+=/c/lp; CD/TC+/FA 3191)* – Secret friend / Check my machine. *(re-iss. Aug93 cd/c;)*

Jun 80. (7") *(R 6037)* <11335> **WATERFALLS. / CHECK MY MACHINE** 9

Sep 80. (12") *(12R 6039)* **TEMPORARY SECRETARY. / SECRET FRIEND** [ ] [–]

Apr 82. (7"; PAUL McCARTNEY & STEVIE WONDER) *(R 6054) <02860>* **EBONY AND IVORY. / RAINCLOUDS** [1] [1]
(12"+=) *(12R 6054)* – ('A'solo version).

Apr 82. (lp/c) *(PCTC/TC-PCTC 259) <37462>* **TUG OF WAR** [1] [1]
– Tug of war / Take it away / Somebody who cares / What's that you're doing? / Here today / Ballroom dancing / The pound is sinking / Wanderlust / Get it / Be what you see / Dress me up as a robber / Ebony and ivory. *(cd-iss. Jan85; CDP 746 057-2) (re-iss. Nov88 on 'Fame' cd/c/lp; CD/TC+/FA 3210) (re-iss. Aug93 cd/c;)*

Jun 82. (12"m) *(R 6056) <03018>* **TAKE IT AWAY. / I'LL GIVE YOU A RING / DRESS ME UP AS A ROBBER** [15] [10]

Sep 82. (7") *(R 6057) <03235>* **TUG OF WAR. / GET IT** [53] [53]

— (In Oct'82, duetted w/ MICHAEL JACKSON on 'THE GIRL IS MINE' Top 10)

Oct 83. (7"; by PAUL McCARTNEY & MICHAEL JACKSON) *(R 6062) <04168>* **SAY SAY SAY. / ODE TO KOALA BEAR** [2] [1]
(12"+=) *(12R 6062)* – ('A'instrumental).

Nov 83. (lp/c) *(PCTC/TCPCTC 1) <39149>* **PIPES OF PEACE** [4] [15]
– Pipes of peace / Say say say / The other me / Keep under cover / So bad / The man / Sweetest little show / Average person / Hey hey / Tug of peace / Through our love. *(cd-iss. Jan84; CDP 746 018-2) (re-iss. Aug93 cd/c;)*

Dec 83. (7") *(R 6064) <04296>* **PIPES OF PEACE. / SO BAD** [1] B-side [23]

Sep 84. (7") *(R 6080) <04581>* **NO MORE LONELY NIGHTS. / ('A' extended)** [2] [6]
(12"+=/12"pic-d+=) *(12R/+P 6080)* – Silly love songs.

Oct 84. (d-lp/c)(cd) *(PCTC/TCPCTC 2)(CDP 746043-2) <39613>* **GIVE MY REGARDS TO BROAD STREET – ORIGINAL SOUND TRACK** [1] [21]
– No more lonely nights (ballad) / Good day sunshine / Corridor music / Yesterday / Here, there and everywhere / Wanderlust / Ballroom dancing / Silly love songs (reprise) / Not such a bad boy / No values / No more lonely nights (reprise) / For no one / Eleanor Rigby – Eleanor's dream / The long and winding road / No more lonely nights (play out version). *(re-iss. Aug93 cd/c;)*

Nov 84. (7"/7"sha-pic-d; by PAUL McCARTNEY & THE FROG CHORUS) *(R/+P 6086)* **WE ALL STAND TOGETHER. / ('A'-Humming version)** [3] [–]
(re-iss. Dec85, reached No.34)

Parlophone Capitol

Nov 85. (7"/7"sha-pic-d) *(R/+P 6118) <5537>* **SPIES LIKE US. / MY CARNIVAL** [16] [7]
(12"+=/12"pic-d+=) *(12R/+P 6118)* – ('A'-party mix).

Jul 86. (7") *(R 6133) <5597>* **PRESS. / IT'S NOT TRUE** [25] [21]
(12"+=) *(12R 6133)* – Hanglide. / ('A' dub).
(10"++=) *(10R 6133)* – ('A'version).

Sep 86. (cd/c/lp) *(CD/TC+/PCSD 103) <12475>* **PRESS TO PLAY** [8] [30]
– Stranglehold / Good times coming – Feel the sun / Talk more talk / Footprints / Only love remains / Press / Pretty little head / Move over busker / Angry / However absurd. *(cd+=)* – Write away / It's not true / Tough on a tightrope. *(re-iss. Aug93 cd/c;)*

Oct 86. (7") *(R 6145)* **PRETTY LITTLE HEAD. / WRITE AWAY** [ ] [–]
(12"+=/c-s+=) *(12R/TCR 6145)* – Angry.

Nov 86. (7") *<5636>* **STRANGLEHOLD. / ANGRY (remix)** [–] [81]

Dec 86. (7"/12") *(R/12R 6148) <5672>* **ONLY LOVE REMAINS. / TOUGH ON A TIGHTROPE** [34] [ ]
(7" w-free 7') *(R 6018)* – Mull of Kinytre / Girls school.

Nov 87. (7") *(R 6170)* **ONCE UPON A LONG AGO. / BACK ON MY FEET** [10] [–]
(12"+=) *(12R 6170)* – Midnight special / Don't get around much anymore.
(12"+=) *(12RX 6170)* – Lawdy Miss Clawdy / Kansas City.
(cd-s+=) *(CDR 6170)* – Don't get around much anymore / Kansas City.

Nov 87. (cd/c/lp) *(CD/TC+/PMTV 1) <48287>* **ALL THE BEST!** (compilation) [2] [62]
– Coming up / Ebony and ivory (w/ STEVIE WONDER) / Listen to what the man said / No more lonely nights / Silly love songs / Let 'em in / C Moon / Pipes of peace / Live and let die / Another day / Maybe I'm amazed / Goodnight tonight / Once upon a long time ago / Say say say / With a little luck / My love / We all stand together / Mull of Kintyre / Jet / Band on the run. *<US slightly different tracks>*

— now with **LINDA** / **WIX** (PAUL WICKENS) – keyboards / **CHRIS WHITTEN** – drums / **ROBBIE McINTOSH** – guitar / **HAMISH STUART** – guitar, bass (ex-AVERAGE WHITE BAND)

May 89. (7") *(R 6213) <44367>* **MY BRAVE FACE. / FLYING TO MY HOME** [18] [25]
(12"+=/c-s+=/cd-s+=) *(12R/TCR/CDR 6213)* – I'm gonna be a wheel someday / Ain't that a shame.

Jun 89. (cd/c/lp) *(CD/TC+/PCSD 106) <91653>* **FLOWERS IN THE DIRT** [1] [21]
– My brave face / Rough ride / You want her too / Distractions / We got married / Put it there / Figure of eight / This one / Don't be careless love / That day is done / How many people / Motor of love. *(cd+=)* – Ou est le soleil. *(re-iss. Nov89 as 'FLOWERS . . . WORLD TOUR PACK' cd/lp; CD+/PCSDX 106) (w/free 7")* – PARTY PARTY *(free 3"cd-s.w/cd version) (re-iss. Aug93 cd/c;)*

Jul 89. (c-s/7") *(TC+/R 6223) <44438>* **THIS ONE. / THE FIRST STONE** [18] [94]
(12"+=/cd-s+=) *(12R/CDR 6223)* – I wanna cry / I'm in love again.

Nov 89. (c-s/7") *(TC+/R 6235) <44489>* **FIGURE OF EIGHT. / OU EST LE SOLEIL?** [42] [92]
(12"+=) *(12R 6235)* – ('B'dub mix).
(3"cd-s+=) *(CD3R 6235)* – Rough ride.
(12") *(12RX 6235)* – ('A'side) / This one (club mix).
(cd-s) *(CDR 6235)* – ('A'side) / Long and winding road / Loveliest thing.

Feb 90. (c-s/7") *(TC+/R 6246)* **PUT IT THERE. / MAMA'S LITTLE GIRL** [32] [–]
(12"+=/cd-s+=) *(12R/CDR 6246)* – Same time next year.

Oct 90. (c-s/7") *(TC+/R 6271)* **BIRTHDAY (live). / GOOD DAY SUNSHINE (live)** [29] [–]
(12"+=/cd-s+=) *(12R/CDR 6271)* – P.S. I love you (live) / Let 'em in (live).

Nov 90. (d-cd/d-c/t-lp) *(CD/TC+/PCST 7346) <94778>* **TRIPPING THE LIVE FANTASTIC (live)** [17] [26]
– Figure of eight / Jet / Rough ride / Got to get you into my life / Band on the run / Birthday / Ebony and ivory / we got married / Inner city madness / Maybe I'm amazed / The long and winding road / Cracking up / Fool on the hill / Sgt. Pepper's lonely hearts club band / Can't buy me love / Matchbox / Put it there / Together / Things we said today / Eleanor Rigby / This one / My brave face / I saw her standing there / Back in the USSR / Twenty flight rock / Coming up / Sally / Let it be / Ain't that a shame / Live and let die / If I were not upon the stage / Hey Jude / Yesterday / Get back / Golden slumbers – Carry that weight – The end / Don't let the Sun catch you crying.

Dec 90. (c-s/7") *(TC+/R 6278)* **ALL MY TRIALS (live). / C MOON (live)** [35] [–]
(12"+=) *(12R 6278)* – Mull of Kintyre / Put it there.
(cd-s+=) *(CDR 6278)* – Live medley:- Strawberry fields forever / Help / Give peace a chance.

— **BLAIR CUNNINGHAM** – drums (ex-LLOYD COLE) repl. WHITTEN

Jun 91. (cd/c/lp) *(CD/TC+/PCSD 116) <96413>* **UNPLUGGED – THE OFFICIAL BOOTLEG** [7] [14]
– Be-bop-a-lula / I lost my little girl / Here there and everywhere / Blue Moon of Kentucky / We can work it out / San Francisco Bay blues / I've just seen a face / Every night / She's a woman / Hi-heel sneakers / And I love her / That would be something / Blackbird / Ain't no sunshine / Good rockin' tonight / Singing the blues / Junk. *(re-iss. Aug91 as 'CHOBA B CCCP' cd/c/lp; CD/TC+/PCSD 117)* – hit UK No.63 *(re-iss. Sep94)*

Jan 93. (c-s/7") *(TC+/R 6330) <44904>* **HOPE OF DELIVERANCE. / LONG LEATHER COAT** [18] [83]
(12"/cd-s) *(12R/CDR 6330)* – ('A'side) / Big boys bickering / Deliverance (dub) / Kicked around no more.

Feb 93. (cd/c/lp) *(CD/TC+/PCSD 125) <80362>* **OFF THE GROUND** [5] [17]
– Off the ground / Looking for changes / Hope of deliverance / Mistress and maid / I owe it all to you / Biker like an icon / Peace in the neighbourhood / Golden Earth girl / The lovers that never were / Get out of my way / Winedark open sea / C'mon people.

Feb 93. (c-s/7") *(TC+/R 6338)* **C'MON PEOPLE. / I CAN'T IMAGINE** [41] [–]
(cd-s+=) *(CDR 6338)* – Down to the river / Keep coming back to love.
(cd-s) *(CDRS 6338)* – ('A'side) / Deliverance / Deliverance (dub).

Nov 93. (cd/c/lp) *(CD/TC+/PCSD 147) <27704>* **PAUL IS LIVE! (live)** [34] [78]
– Drive my car / Let me roll it / Looking for changes / Peace in the neighbourhood / All my loving / Robbie's bit / Good rocking tonight / We can work it out / Hope of deliverance / Michelle / Biker like an icon / Here there and everywhere / My love / Magical mystery tour / C'mon people / Lady Madonna / Paperback writer / Penny Lane / Live and let die / Kansas City / Welcome to Soundcheck / Hotel in Benidorm / I wanna be your man / A fine day.

— In 1995, PAUL had his biggest hit in a long time (No.19), when he was part of The SMOKIN' MOJO FILTERS ('Come Together') alongside PAUL WELLER and NOEL GALLAGHER (Oasis).

May 97. (7"pic-d) *(RP 6462)* **YOUNG BOY. / LOOKING FOR YOU** [19] [ ]
(cd-s+=) *(CDRS 6462)* – Oobu Joobu medley (part 1).
(cd-s) *(CDR 6462)* – ('A'side) / Broomstick / Oobu Joobu medley (part 2).

May 97. (cd/c/lp) *(CD/TC+/PCSD 171) <56500>* **FLAMING PIE** [2] [2]
– Song we were singing / The world tonight / If you wanna / Somedays / Young boy / Calico skies / Flaming pie / Heaven on a Sunday / Used to be bad / Souvenir / Little willow / Really love you / Beautiful night / Great day.

Jul 97. (7"pic-d) *(RP 6472)* **THE WORLD TONIGHT. / USED TO BE BAD** [23] May97 [64]
(cd-s+=) *(CDRS 6472)* – Oobu joobu (part 3).
(cd-s) *(CDR 6472)* – Oobu joobu (part 1).

Dec 97. (c-s/7") *(TC+/R 6489)* **BEAUTIFUL NIGHT. / LOVE COME TUMBLING DOWN** [25] [ ]
(cd-s+=) *(CDRS 6489)* – Oobu joobu (part 6).
(cd-s) *(CDR 6489)* – ('A'side) / Oobu joobu (part 6) / Same love.

Oct 99. (cd/c/lp) *(<5 22351-2/-4/-1>)* **RUN DEVIL RUN** [12] [27]
– Blue jean bop / She said yeah / All shook up / Run Devil run / No other baby / Lonesome town / Try not to cry / Movie mag / Brown eyed handsome man / What it is / Coquette / I got stung / Honey hush / Shake a hand / Party. *(8x7"box-iss.Nov99; 523229-1)*

Oct 99. (7") *(R 6527)* **NO OTHER BABY. / BROWN EYED HANDSOME MAN** [42] [ ]
(cd-s+=) *(CDRS 6527)* – Fabulous.
(cd-s) *(CDR 6527)* – (all three tracks in mono).

Oct 01. (7") *(R 6567)* **FROM A LOVER TO A FRIEND. / RIDING TO JALPUL** [45] [ ]
(c-s+=) *(TCR 6567)* – ('A'-David Kahne remix 2).
(cd-s) *(CDR 6567)* – ('A'side) / ('A'-David Kahne remix 1).

Nov 01. (cd/c/lp) *(<5 35510-2/-4>)* **DRIVING RAIN** [46] [26]
– Lonely road / From a lover to a friend / She's given up talking / Driving rain / I do / Tiny bubble / Magic / Your way / Spinning on an axis / About you / Heather / Back in the sunshine again / Your loving flame / Riding to Jaipur / Rinse the raindrops.

Dec 01. (cd-s) *<50291>* **FREEDOM / FROM A LOVER TO A FRIEND / FROM A LOVER TO A FRIEND (David Kahne remix 2)** [–] [97]

Mar 03. (d-cd) *(5 83005-2) <42318>* **BACK IN THE WORLD (live)** <US title 'BACK IN THE U.S.> [5] Nov02 [8]
– Hello goodbye / Jet / All my loving / Getting better / Coming up / Let me roll it / Lonely road / Driving rain / Your loving flame / Blackbird / Every night / We can work it out / Mother nature's son / Carry that weight / Fool on the hill / Here today / Something / Eleanor Rigby / Here, there and everywhere / Calico skies / Michelle / Band on the run / Back in the USSR / Maybe I'm amazed / Let 'em in / My love / She's leaving home / Can't buy me love / Live and let die / Let it be / Hey Jude / The long and winding road / Lady Madonna / I saw her standing there / Yesterday / Sgt. Pepper's lonely hearts club band / The end.

– compilations, etc. –

Feb 81. (lp) *E.M.I.; (CHAT 1) / Columbia; <36987>* **McCARTNEY INTERVIEW** [34] [ ]

May 01. (d-cd/d-c/q-lp) *Parlophone; (532850-2/-4/-1) / M.P.L.; <32946>* **WINGSPAN: HITS AND HISTORY** [5] [2]
– Listen to what the man said / Band on the run / Another day / Live and let die / Jet / My love / Silly love songs / Pipes of peace / C moon / Hi hi hi / Let 'em in / Goodnight tonight / Junior's farm / Mull of Kintyre / Uncle Albert – Admiral Halsey / With a little luck / Coming up / No more lonely nights / Let me roll it / Lovely Linda / Daytime nighttime suffering / Maybe I'm amazed / Helen wheels / Bluebird / Heart of the country / Every night / Take it away / Junk / Man he was lonely / Venus and Mars / Rockshow / Backseat of my car / Rockestra theme / Tomorrow / Too many people / Call me back again / Tug of war / Bip bop / Hey diddle / No more lonely nights (playout version).

– under an alias (various connections) –

—— PAUL's brother MIKE McGEAR with a sibling collaboration

Oct 74. (7"; COUNTRY HAMS) *E.M.I.; (EMI 2220)* **WALKING IN THE PARK WITH ELOISE. / BRIDGE OVER THE RIVER SUITE** [ ] [ ]

—— PAUL under a new moniker

Apr 77. (7"; as PERCY 'THRILLS' THRILLINGTON) *E.M.I.; (EMI 2594)* **UNCLE ALBERT, ADMIRAL HALSEY. / EAST AT HOME** [ ] [ ]
(also album, 'THRILLINGTON' lp/c; EMC/TC-EMC 3175)

—— next by LINDA McCARTNEY's band

Aug 79. (7"/7"yellow; by SUZY & THE RED STRIPES) *A&M; (AMS/+P 7461) / Epic; <50403>* **SEASIDE WOMAN. / B SIDE TO SEASIDE** [ ] Jun77 [59]
(re-iss. Jul80, 7"/7"pic-d; AMS/+P 7548) (re-iss. 1986 on 'E,M,I,' 7"12"; EMI/12EMI 5572)

—— PAUL had also guested on numerous singles and albums. DENNY LAINE has also had solo career, although with no commercial success.

☐ Ian McCULLOCH

(see under ⇒ ECHO & THE BUNNYMEN)

Country Joe McDONALD (& THE FISH)

Born: 1 Jan'42, Washington, D.C., USA. In the early 60's, McDONALD joined the navy, although he left after his service period was over. In 1964, he augmented fellow troubadour, BLAIR HARDIMAN, on his very rare 'GOODBYE BLUES' album, forming COUNTRY JOE & THE FISH the following year. The band cut a few EP's for the local 'Rag Baby' magazine, and, through its editor Ed Denson, they signed a recording contract with folk label, 'Vanguard'. In the summer of '67, after a much heralded Monterey Pop Festival outing, their debut album, 'ELECTRIC MUSIC FOR THE MIND AND BODY', breached the US Top 40. McDONALD was the quintessential urban folk-country star, whose satrical politico-drugs and anti-war themes induced many to identify with his anarchic outfit during the 60's. In 1968, they released a second set, 'I-FEEL-LIKE-I'M-FIXIN'-TO-DIE', which featured his ode to his ex-girlfriend, JANIS JOPLIN and the anti-nuke anthem, 'THE BOMB SONG'. The band issued a third album, 'TOGETHER', although this was their last to secure a major chart placing. Other albums followed, some solo, although in 1970, he was convicted and fined $500 for obscenity, inciting anti-social crowd behaviour after chanting 'Gimme a F.*.*.*.'. This 'Fish Cheer' had been an audience participation ritual since the mid-60's. In the 70's, he took the country element in his music to its natural conclusion, with a string of rootsy albums. • **Trivia:** In 1971, he joined actors JANE FONDA and DONALD SUTHERLAND, in a 'Free The Army' revue. In 1976, he campaigned to 'SAVE THE WHALES', even writing a single with that title.

Album rating: COUNTRY JOE AND BLAIR HARDMAN (*4) / ELECTRIC MUSIC FOR THE MIND AND BODY (*7) / I FEEL LIKE I'M FIXIN' TO DIE (*6) / TOGETHER (*5) / HERE WE ARE AGAIN (*4) / COUNTRY JOE & THE FISH – GREATEST HITS compilation (*6) / THINKING OF WOODY solo (*5) / C.J. FISH (*4) / TONIGHT I'M SINGING JUST FOR YOU solo (*5) / HOLD ON IT'S COMING (*4) solo / WAR, WAR, WAR solo (*4) / INCREDIBLE! LIVE! solo (*4) / THE LIFE AND TIMES OF COUNTRY JOE & THE FISH FROM HAIGHT-ASHBURY TO WOODSTOCK compilation (*6) / PARIS SESSIONS solo (*4) / COUNTRY JOE solo (*5) / PARADISE WITH AN OCEAN VIEW solo (*4) / LOVE IS A FIRE solo (*4) / REUNION (*4) / ROCK'N'ROLL MUSIC FROM PLANET EARTH solo (*4) / LEISURE SUITE solo (*4) / ON MY OWN solo (*4) / INTO THE FRAY (*4) / CHILDS PLAY (*4) / PEACE ON EARTH solo (*4) / VIETNAM EXPERIENCE solo (*4) / SUPERSTITIOUS BLUES solo (*4) / CARRY ON solo (*4) / THE COLLECTED COUNTRY JOE & THE FISH compilation (*7)

COUNTRY JOE & THE FISH

JOE McDONALD – vocals, guitar / **BARRY 'THE FISH' MELTON** (b.1947, Brooklyn, New York) – guitar, vocals / **CARL SHRAGER** – washboard / **BILL STEEL** – bass / **MIKE BEARDSLEE** – harp, vocals

not iss. | Rag Baby

Oct 65. (7"ep) *<1001>* **COUNTRY JOE & THE FISH** [–] [ ]
– I-feel-like-I'm-fixin'-to-die rag / Superbird. / PETER KRUG: Fire in the city / Johnny's gone to war.

—— **McDONALD + MELTON** introduced **BRUCE BARTHOL** (b.1947, Berkeley, Calif.) – bass / **DAVID COHEN** (b.1942, Brooklyn, N.Y.) – electric guitar / **CHICKEN HIRSCH** (b.1940, Calif.) – drums / **PAUL ARMSTRONG** – harp / **JOHN FRANCIS GUNNING** – drums

Jun 66. (7"ep) *<1002>* **RAG BABY** [–] [ ]
– Bass strings / Section 43 / (Thing called) Love.

—— **MARK RYAN** repl. BRUCE

Fontana | Vanguard

Jul 67. (7") *<35052>* **NOT SO SWEET MARTHA LORRAINE. / THE MASKED MARAUDER** [–] [95]

Oct 67. (lp; stereo/mono) *(S+/TFL 6081) <VSD 79244>* **ELECTRIC MUSIC FOR THE MIND AND BODY** [ ] Apr67 [39]
– Flying high / Not so sweet Martha Lorraine / Death sound blues / Porpoise mouth / Section 43 / Superbird / Sad and lonely times / Love / Bass strings / The masked marauder / Grace. *(re-iss. Mar69 & Feb72 on 'Vanguard'; SVRL 19026) (re-iss. Mar89 on 'Start' lp/c/cd; VM5/TC6/CD6 301) (cd re-iss. Oct95; VMD 79244)*

Nov 67. (7") *(TF 882)* **NOT SO SWEET MARTHA LORRAINE. / LOVE** [ ] [–]

Nov 67. (7") *<35059>* **JANIS. / JANIS (instrumental)** [–] [ ]

Jan 68. (7") *<35061>* **WHO AM I? / THURSDAY** [–] [ ]

Mar 68. (lp; stereo/mono) *(S+/TFL 6086) <VSD 79266>* **I-FEEL-LIKE-I'M-FIXIN'-TO-DIE** [ ] Nov67 [67]
– (the fish cheer) / I-feel-like-I'm-fixin'-to-die rag / Who am I / Pat's song / Rock coast blues / Magoo / Janis / Thought dream / Thursday / Eastern jam / Colors for Susan. *(re-iss. Mar69 & Feb72 on 'Vanguard'; SVRL 19029) (re-iss. Jul89 on 'Start' lp/c/cd; VM LP5/TC6/CD7 306) (cd re-iss. Oct95; VMD 79266)*

Vanguard | Vanguard

Jul 68. (7") *<35068>* **ROCK AND SOUL MUSIC. / (part 2)** [–] [ ]

Nov 68. (lp) *(SVRL 19006) <VSD 79277>* **TOGETHER** [ ] Jul68 [23]
– Rock and soul music / Susan / Mojo navigator / Bright suburban Mr. & Mrs. Clean machine / Good guys – bad guys cheer / The streets of your town / The fish moan / The Harlem song / Waltzing in the moonlight / Away bounce my bubbles / Cetacean / An untitled protest. *(cd re-iss. Oct95; VMD 79277)*

—— **JOE + BARRY** recruited new members **MARK KAPNER** – keyboards to replace COHEN (He joined BLUES PROJECT). **PETER ALBIN** – bass (ex-BIG BROTHER & THE HOLDING COMPANY) / **DAVID GETZ** – drums (ex-BIG BROTHER & THE HOLDING COMPANY) repl. others.

Jun 69. (7") *<35090>* **HERE I GO AGAIN. / BABY YOU'RE DRIVING ME CRAZY** [–] [ ]

Sep 69. (lp) *(STVL 19048) <VSD 79299>* **HERE WE ARE AGAIN** [ ] Jun69 [ ]
– Here I go again / Donovan's reef / It's nice to have love / Baby, you're driving me crazy / Crystal blues / For no reason / I'll survive / Maria / My girl / Doctor of electricity.

Oct 69. (7") *(VA 3)* **HERE I GO AGAIN. / IT'S SO NICE TO HAVE LOVE** [ ] [–]

—— **DOUG METZNER** – bass repl. ALBIN / **GREG DEWEY** – drums (ex-MAD RIVER) repl. GETZ who went solo.

Jun 70. (7") *<35112>* **I FEEL LIKE I'M FIXIN' TO DIE RAG. / JANIS** [–] [ ]

Jun 70. (7") *(6076 250)* **I FEEL LIKE I'M FIXIN' TO DIE RAG. / MARIA** [ ] [–]

Oct 70. (lp) *(6359 002) <VSD 6555>* **C.J. FISH** [ ] Apr70 [ ]
– Sing sing sing / She's a bird / Mara / Hang on / The baby song / Hey Bobby / Silver and gold / Rocking 'round the world / The love machine / The return of sweet Lorraine / Hand of man. *(re-iss. Feb72; same)*

—— They split Autumn 1970

COUNTRY JOE McDONALD

had solo releases between 69-71. with **HAROLD BRADLEY** – guitar, bass / **RAY EDENTON** – guitar / **GRADY MARTIN** – guitar / **NORMAN PUTMAN** – bass / **BUDDY HARMON** – drums / **HARGUS 'PIG' ROBBINS** – percussion

Vanguard | Vanguard

Apr 70. (lp; stereo/mono) *(S+/VRL 19057) <VSD 6546>* **THINKING OF WOODY GUTHRIE** [ ] Dec69 [ ]
– Pastures of plenty / Talkin' dust bowl / Blowing down that old dusty road / So long it's been good to know yuh / Tom Joad / The sinking of Rueben James / Roll on Columbia / Pretty Boy Floyd / When the curfew blows / This land is your land. *(re-iss. Feb72;) (re-iss. Sep89 on 'Start' cd/c; CDVMD/MCCV 6546)*

Jan 71 (lp) *(6359 004) <VSD 6557>* **TONIGHT I'M SINGING JUST FOR YOU** [ ] Mar70 [ ]
– Ring of fire / Tennessee stud / Heartaches by the number / Tiger by the tail / Crazy arms / You've done me wrong / All of me belongs to you / Oklahoma hills / Tonight I'm singing just for you / Friend, lover, woman, wife / Six days on the road. *(re-iss. Feb72;)*

—— solo releases now post-FISH, were augmented by some UK session men

Jan 71. (7") *<35133>* **HOLD ON IT'S COMING. / PLAYING WITH FIRE** [–] [ ]

Sep 71. (lp) *<(VSD 79314)>* **HOLD ON IT'S COMING** [ ] Apr71 [ ]
– Hold on it's coming / Air Algiers / Only love is worth this pain / Playing with fire / Travelling / Joe's blues / Mr. Big pig / Balancing on the edge of time / Jamila / Hold on it's coming No.2.

Sep 71. (7") *(6076 252)* **HOLD ON IT'S COMING. / (take 2)** [ ] [–]

—— with **ANNA RIZZO** – vocals / **GREG DEEY** – drums / **NACKO DEWEY** – harp / **JOHN REWIND** – guitar / **VIC SMITH** – bass

1971. (7"ep) *>1003>* **COUNTRY JOE McDONALD & GROOTNA** [–] [ ]
– Kiss my ass / Tricky Dicky / Free some day.
(above was issued in the States on his 'Rag Baby' label.

Jan 72. (lp) *<(VSD 79315)>* **WAR WAR WAR** [ ] Aug71 [ ]
– The call / Forward / Young fellow, my lad / The man from Aphabaska / The munition maker / The twins / Jean Desprez / War widow / The march of the dead.

1972. (7") *<35150>* **HANG ON. / HAND OF MAN** [–] [ ]

Jul 72. (lp) *<(VSD 79316)>* **INCREDIBLE! LIVE! COUNTRY JOE!** [ ] Feb72 [ ]
– Entertainment is my business / Sweet Marie / Kiss my ass / Living in the future in a plastic dome / Walk in Santiago / Tricky Dicky / You know what I mean / Fly so high / Deep down in our hearts / Free some day / I'm on the road again.

COUNTRY JOE

formed his ALL-STAR BAND with **PETER ALBIN** – bass / **DAVID GETZ** – drums / **TUCKI BAILEY** – saxophone / **DOROTHY MOSCOWITZ** – vocals, piano (ex-UNITED STATES OF AMERICA) / **PHIL MARSH** – guitar repl. BARRY MELTON / **ANNA RIZZO** – drums repl. SALLY HENDERSON – vocals / **SEBASTIAN NICHOLSON** – congas repl. **SUSAN LYDON** – vocals

Vanguard | Vanguard

Apr 73. (7") *<35161>* **FANTASY. / I SEE A ROCKET** [–] [ ]

Aug 73. (lp) *<(VSD 79328)>* **PARIS SESSIONS** [ ] [ ]
– Fantasy / Movieola / I'm so tired / Moving / I don't know why / Zombies in a house of madness / Sexist pig / Colorado Town / Coulene Anne / St. Tropez.

Oct 73. (7") *(VAN 1006)* **FANTASY. / HOLD ON IT'S COMING** [ ] [–]

—— **GINNY WHITTAKER** – drums, repl. GETZ, BAILEY, MARSH + NICHOLSON

—— (Feb'74) **COUNTRY JOE** toured as duo with BARRY MELTON. Still solo below.

Nov 74. (7") *<35181>* **DR. HIP. / SATISFACTORY** [–] [ ]

Apr 75. (lp) *<(VSD 79348)>* **COUNTRY JOE** [ ] Dec74 [ ]
– Dr. Hip / Old Joe Corey / Making money in Chile / You messed over me / Memories / Chile / Pleasin' / Jesse James / Satisfactory / It's finally over.

Apr 75. (7") *<35184>* **JESSE JAMES. / CHILE** [–] [ ]

COUNTRY JOE McDONALD

also augmented by ENERGY CRISIS (below) **PHIL MARSH** – guitar / **BRUCE BARTHOL** – bass / **JOHN BLAKELEY** – guitar / **PETER MILIO** – drums / **TED ASHFORD** – keyboards

Fantasy | Fantasy

Oct 75. (lp) *(FTA 3002) <9495>* **PARADISE WITH AN OCEAN VIEW** [ ] [ ]
– Tear down the walls / Holy roller / Lost my connection / The limit / Save the whales / Oh! Jamaica / Lonely on the road / Tricks / Breakfast for two.

Jan 76. (7") *(FTC 123) <758>* **BREAKFAST FOR TWO. / LOST MY CONNECTION** Nov75 92

Apr 76. (7") *(FTC 130) <765>* **SAVE THE WHALES. / OH! JAMAICA**

Aug 76. (lp) *(FTA 3005) <9511>* **LOVE IS A FIRE**
– It won't burn / You're the song / In love naturally / Oh no / Baby baby / True love at last / Who's gonna fry your eggs / Colortone / I need you (this and that) / Love is a fire.

Oct 76. (7") *<780>* **I NEED YOU. / LOVE IS A FIRE** –

Oct 76. (7") *(FT 135)* **IN LOVE NATURALLY. / WHO'S GONNA FRY YOUR EGGS** –

— next solo albums used BARRY MELTON and session people.

Apr 77. (lp) *(FT 529) <9525>* **GOODBYE BLUES**
– Copiapo / Thought dreams / Goodbye blues / Let's go ridin' in the car / Blood on the ice / Primitive people / TV blues / Dark clouds / Little blue whale / Wilderness trail.

Oct 77. (7") *(FT 143)* **LA DI DA. / RING OF FIRE** –

May 78. (lp) *(FT 539) <9544>* **ROCK'N'ROLL MUSIC FROM PLANET EARTH** Feb78
– Coyote / Bring back the sixties man / Sunshine through my window / Rock & roll again / Dark ship / Y.O.U. / Southern cross / Space patrol / U.F.O. / Get it together.

Mar 78. (7") *(FTC 154) <814>* **COYOTE. / SOUTHERN CROSS**

Jul 78. (7") *<822>* **SUNSHINE THROUGH MY WINDOW. / BRING BACK THE 60'S MAN** –

— (Sep78) **COUNTRY JOE** reformed THE FISH, with **BARRY MELTON** – guitar, vocals / **PETER ALBIN** – bass / **BOB FLURIE** – guitar / **HAROLD ACEVES** – drums

— continued solo work.

Dec 79. (lp) *(FT 565) <9586>* **LEISURE SUITE**
– Private parts / Take this time out / Doo-wop-oh / Hard work no play / La di da / Sure cure for the blues / Reaching for the stars. *(cd-iss. late'90 on 'Rag Baby'; RBCD900317)*

Dec 79. (7") **TAKE THIS TIME OUT. / PRIVATE PARTS** –

Rag Baby Rag Baby

Aug 81. (lp) *(RAG 1012) <147 406>* **ON MY OWN** (totally solo)
– Standing at the crossroads / Calamity Jane / Give some love, get some back / C-O-U-N-T-R-Y / The Halloween tree / Slide trombone blues / Your last few records just didn't make it / Power plant blues / A Vietnam veteran still alive / Yankee doodle / Darlin' Dan.

— now with ever-changing personnel.

Jun 82. (d-lp) *<RAG 2001>* **INTO THE FRAY (live)** –
– Kiss my ass / Quiet days in Clichy / Sexist pig / Here I go again / Breakfast for two / Love is a fire / Picks and lasers / Coyote / Hold on it's coming / Entertainment is my business / Holy roller / Not so sweet Martha Lorraine / Janis / Get it all together / A Vietnam veteran still alive / Breakfast for two / Fixin'-to-die-rag / Save the whales / Ring of fire. *(UK-iss.Feb89; same) (cd-iss. late'90; RBCD 900603)*

Oct 83. (lp) *<RAG 1018>* **CHILDS PLAY** –
– Not in a Chinese restaurant / Power plant blues / Picks and lasers / Ice pack / One more good year of good times / Vietnam never again / America my home / Star Yeck: Voyage of the good ship Undersize / Mi Corazon. *(UK-iss.Feb89; same)*

Line not iss.

Feb 85. (lp) *(RB 9.00068)* **PEACE ON EARTH** – German –
– Live in peace / Sunshine / Let it rain / You can get it if you really want / War hero / Feeling better / The girl next door / Darlin' man (the rocket man) / Pledging my love / Garden of Eden / Space lovin' / Peace on Earth. *(cd-iss. Feb89 & Oct94 on 'Rag Baby'; RBCD 9.00068)*

1986. (d-lp) *(LI 9.00418)* **VIETNAM EXPERIENCE** – German –
– I-feel-like-I'm-fixin'-to-die rag / Foreign policy blues / Agent Orange song / The girl next door (combat nurse) / Kiss my arse / Secret agent / Vietnam veteran still alive / Vietnam never again / Mourning blues / Welcome home / Vietnam requiem – part 1:- The beginning, part 2:- The end. *(cd-iss. Jun89; LICD 9.00418)*

— returned to the recording studio in 1990

Rykodisc Rykodisc

Jan 91. (cd) *(RBCD 90094-2) <10201>* **SUPERSTITIOUS BLUES**
– Standing at the crossroads / Eunicita / Superstitious blues / Tranquility / Starship ride / Cocaine (rock) / Blues for breakfast / Clara Barton / Blues for Michael.

Line Rykodisc

Jan 95. (cd) *(90130-2)* **CARRY ON**
– Picks and lasers / Lady with the lamp / Joe's blues / Hold on to each other / Stolen heart blues / Trilogy / Going home / Carry on / My last song.

– compilations, etc. (with the FISH *) –

Mar 70. (lp) *Vanguard; (SVRL 19058) <VSD 6545>* **COUNTRY JOE & THE FISH / GREATEST HITS** Dec69 74

Nov 73. (d-lp) *Vanguard; (VSD 27-28)* **THE LIFE AND TIMES OF COUNTRY JOE AND THE FISH FROM HAIGHT – ASHBURY TO WOODSTOCK** Oct71

Jul 76. (d-lp) *Vanguard; (VSD 85-86)* **THE ESSENTIAL COUNTRY JOE McDONALD**

Mar 77. (lp/c) *Golden Hour-Pye; (GH/ZCGH 865)* **THE GOLDEN HOUR OF COUNTRY JOE McDONALD** –

Jun 76. (lp) *Fantasy; <9530>* **REUNION** (live '67-'69 line-up) –

Jun 81. (lp) *Rag Baby; <AMR 3309>* **THE EARLY YEARS** –
– (tracks as below)

Jul 81. (lp) *Rag Baby; (RAG 1000)* **COLLECTOR'S ITEMS – THE FIRST THREE EP'S**
(re-iss. Mar87 on 'New World'; NEW 87) (re-iss. Apr87 on 'Decal'; LIK 8) (cd-iss. 1992 on 'Sequel';)

Aug 83. (lp) *Animus; (FEEL 1)* **ANIMAL TRACKS**

Sep 83. (7") *Animus; (TOUCH 1)* **BLOOD ON THE ICE. / (no b-side)**

— (also appeared on Various Artists compilations WOODSTOCK, QUIET DAY IN CLICHY, CELEBRATION – BIG SUE FESTIVAL (live), A TRIBUTE TO WOODY GUTHRIE, ZACHARIAH (Soundtrack).

Jun 91. (cd) *Pickwick; (VCD 111)* **COLLECTED COUNTRY JOE & THE FISH** –
– Superbird / Bass strings / Section 43 / Flying high / Not so sweet Martha Lorraine / Death sound blues / Porpoise mouth / Sad and lonely times / The fish cheer – I-feel-like-I'm-fixin'-to-die rag / Rock coast blues / Janis / Eastern jam / Good guys – bad guys cheer / Rock and roll music / An unlimited protest / Here I go again / Maria, my own / Crystal blues / Rockin' round the world.

Jul 92. (cd) *Big Beat; (CDWIK 108)* **CLASSICS** –

Aug 96. (cd) *Volt; (VCD 139)* **LIVE AT THE FILLMORE WEST 1969**

Aug 01. (4xcd-box) *Akarma; <(AK 171-2)>* **A REFLECTION OF CHANGING TIMES**

□ John McENTIRE (see under ⇒ TORTOISE)

MC5

Formed: Detroit, Michigan, USA . . . 1965 by ROB TYNER, FED 'SONIC' SMITH and WAYNE KRAMER. After two limited single releases, MC5 (MOTOR CITY FIVE) signed a contract with 'Elektra' in mid '68, helped by counter-cultural activist and DJ, John Sinclair. In addition to becoming the band's manager, he heavily influenced both their political extremism and warped takes on free jazz improvisation. Reflecting the harsher geographical and economic climate of Detroit, the band espoused revolution and struggle as opposed to the love and peace ethos of the sun-kissed Californian flower children. The riotous proto-punk of their legendary, acid-fuelled live show was captured on the controversial debut, 'KICK OUT THE JAMS'. Recorded in late October '68, it eventually hit the shops in May '69 and while the original uncensored pressings contained the line "Kick Out The Jams, Motherfuckers!", the offending word was later supplanted with the milder "Brothers And Sisters". Unfortunately, this wasn't enough to prevent some record stores from refusing to stock the lp, and after the band explicitly aired their views on one of the aforementioned dealers in a local newspaper, they were duly given the boot by Elektra. Nevertheless, the album reached No.30 in America and although it sounds a bit dated to modern ears, it was way radical for the time, remaining an inspiration to each new generation of noiseniks. After a split with Sinclair, the band signed with Atlantic and began to move away from the overtly subversive nature of their earlier material to a more straightahead rock approach, evidenced on their Jon Landau-produced follow-up album, 'BACK IN THE U.S.A.'. Wired rock'n'roll of an impeccable degree, the record didn't fare well in the laid-back, doped-up climate of the early 70's. An ambitious third album in 1971, 'HIGH TIME', featuring horns and even Salvation Army musicians, still failed to cut any commercial ice and the band split in 1972. KRAMER subsequently spent five years in jail for cocaine dealing before embarking on a low key solo career while former manager, Sinclair, was sentenced to ten years in the early 70's for a minor dope charge, serving only two after appeal. Tragically, ROB TYNER died from a heart attack in 1991 aged only 46. Pioneers in the true sense of the word, the MC5 together with the STOOGES were the first real punk bands, the originators who were never bettered. Although KRAMER released the odd obscure 7" throughout the late 70's/80's – during which time he teamed up with JOHNNY THUNDERS as GANG WAR and even worked with the mad, bad and dangerous to know G.G. ALLIN – his solo career only really got back on track via a mid-90's deal with hardcore/punk label 'Epitaph'. The first fruits of this partnership were unleashed in the shape of 'THE HARD STUFF' (1995), an abrasively unsentimental trawl through life's piss-stinking back alleys with guest support from the likes of HENRY ROLLINS and BAD RELIGION. The 'DANGEROUS MADNESS' album followed in 1996, KRAMER once again taking bitter lyrical inspiration from his school-of-hard-knocks background while kicking out the jams 90's style with more ferocity and bile than many of the young pretenders. The same year saw a collaborative effort with fellow Detroit veterans SCOTT MORGAN and DENIZ TEK entitled 'DODGE MAIN', while his rejuvenated solo career continued apace in 1997 with 'CITIZEN WAYNE'. 'LLMF (LIVE LIKE A MOTHERFUCKER' (1998) found KRAMER in his element while a further studio set, 'ADULT WORLD', appeared in 2002. KRAMER's post-millennial showcase displayed a fractured creative agenda, with half-realised spoken word passages bristling against timewarp nostalgia and recurring political motifs. • **Songwriters:** Group compositions, except; I CAN ONLY GIVE YOU EVERYTHING (Them) / TUTTI FRUTTI (Little Richard).

Album rating: KICK OUT THE JAMS (*9) / BACK IN THE USA (*7) / HIGH TIME (*5) / BABES IN ARMS collection (*5) / LOOKING AT YOU collection (*4) / POWER TRIP collection (*5) / THE BEST OF MC5 compilation (*9) / Wayne Kramer: DEATHTONGUE (*4) / THE HARD STUFF (*7) / DANGEROUS MADNESS (*5) / CITIZEN WAYNE (*5) / LLMF (*5) / ADULT WORLD (*5)

ROB TYNER (b. ROBERT DERMINER, 12 Dec'44) – vocals, harmonica / **WAYNE KRAMER** (b.30 Apr'48) – guitar, vocals, keyboards / **FRED 'SONIC' SMITH** (b. West Virginia) – guitar / **MICHAEL DAVIS** – bass / **DENNIS THOMPSON** – drums

not iss. A.M.G.

1966. (7") *<AMG 1001>* **I CAN ONLY GIVE YOU EVERYTHING. / I JUST DON'T KNOW** [–] [ ]
(above credited to MOTOR CITY FIVE)

not iss. A2.

Mar 68. (7") *<A2 333>* **LOOKING AT YOU. / BORDERLINE** [–] [ ]

—— added 6th member **Brother J.C.CRAWFORD** – rapper / narrative

Elektra Elektra

May 69. (7") *(EKSN 45056) <EK 45648>* **KICK OUT THE JAMS. / MOTOR CITY IS BURNING** [ ] Mar 69 82

May 69. (lp) *(mono/stereo; EKL/EKS 74042)* **KICK OUT THE JAMS** [ ] Mar 69 30
– Ramblin' rose / Kick out the jams / Come together / Rocket reducer No.62 (rama lama fa fa) / Borderline / Motor city is burning / I want you right now / Starship. *(re-iss. May77.) (re-iss. +cd.Nov91) (re-iss. cd+c Mar93 on 'Pickwick') (re-iss. cd/c Sep95 on 'Warners')*

Aug 69. (7") *(EKSN 45067)* **RAMBLIN' ROSE. / BORDERLINE** [ ] [–]

Atlantic Atlantic

Oct 70. (7") *<2678>* **TONIGHT. / LOOKING AT YOU** [–] [ ]

Nov 70. (lp) *(2400 016) <SD 8247>* **BACK IN THE U.S.A.** [ ] Feb 70 [ ]
– Tutti frutti / Tonight / Teenage list / Looking at you / Let me try / High school / Call me animal / The American ruse / Shakin' Street / The human being lawnmower / Back in the U.S.A. *(re-iss. Feb77.) (cd-iss. May93 on 'Rhino-Atlantic')*

1970. (7") *<2724>* **SHAKIN' STREET. / THE AMERICAN RUSE** [–] [ ]

Oct 71. (lp) *(2400 123) <SD 8285>* **HIGH TIME** [ ] [ ]
– Sister Anne / Baby won't ya / Miss X / Gotta keep movin' / Future – Now / Poison / Over nnd over / Skunk (sonically speaking). *(cd-iss. May93 on 'Rhino-Atlantic')*

—— (split early '72 when DAVIS departed) THOMPSON, SMITH and DAVIS formed short-lived ASCENSION. FRED SMITH married PATTI SMITH and later formed SONIC'S RENDEZVOUS BAND. TYNER was credited on HOT RODS single, late'77. (see ⇒ EDDIE & THE HOT RODS.

– compilations, etc. –

1969. (7") *A.M.G.; <AMG 1001>* **I CAN ONLY GIVE YOU EVERYTHING. / ONE OF THE GUYS** [–] [ ]

Jul 83. (c) *R.O.I.R.; <A 122>* **BABES IN ARMS** [–] [ ]
(re-iss. Apr90 & Dec92 on 'Danceteria' lp/cd; DAN LP/CD 031)

May 94. (cd) *Receiver; (RRCD 185)* **BLACK TO COMM** [ ] [–]

Oct 94. (10"lp/cd) *Alive; (ALIVE 005/+CD)* **POWER TRIP** [ ] [–]

Nov 94. (cd) *Receiver; (RRCD 193)* **LOOKING AT YOU** [ ] [–]

Feb 95. (10"lp/cd) *Alive; (NER/+CD 2001)* **THE AMERICAN RUSE** [ ] [–]

Mar 95. (10"lp) *Alive; (ALIVE 008)* **ICE PICK SLIM** [ ] [–]
(cd-iss. Feb97; ALIVECD 8)

Sep 95. (10"ep/cd) *Alive; (ALIVE 0010/+CD)* **FRIDAY, THE 13TH** [ ] [–]

Dec 96. (cd) *Dressed To Kill; (DTKLP 002)* **THUNDER EXPRESS – ONE DAY IN THE STUDIO** [ ] [–]

Mar 97. (lp) *Alive; (NER 3008)* **TEENAGE LUST** [ ] [–]

Feb 00. (cd) *Rhino; <(8122 79783-2)>* **BIG BANG – THE BEST OF MC5** [ ] [ ]

WAYNE KRAMER

—— went solo after spending 5 years in prison for cocaine dealing.

Stiff-Chiswick not iss.

Oct 77. (7") *(DEA-SUK 1)* **RAMBLIN' ROSE. / GET SOME** [ ] [–]

Radar not iss.

Jul 79. (7") *(ADA 41)* **THE HARDER THEY COME. / EAST SIDE GIRL** [ ] [–]

not iss. Pure&Easy

1983. (7") *<PE 017>* **NEGATIVE GIRLS. / STREET WARFARE** [–] [ ]

—— GANG WAR formed in 1980 with **JOHNNY THUNDERS** – vocals

Zodiac not iss.

1987. (7"ep; WAYNE KRAMER'S GANG WAR) *(800)* **GANG WAR (live at Max's May 1980)** [ ] [–]

May 90. (lp) *(LP 1001)* **GANG WAR** (live/studio) [ ] [–]

—— WAYNE had joined the DEVIANTS in 1984 for their album HUMAN GARBAGE.

Curio Progressive

1987. (7"; as WAYNE KRAMER'S DEATH TONGUE) **SPIKE HEELS EP** [–] [ ]

—— (WAYNE played late 80's with DAS DAMEN and G.G. ALLIN)

Nov 91. (d-cd/d-lp) *(ITEM 2 CD/LP) <PRO 023>* **DEATH TONGUE** [ ] [ ]
– Take your clothes off / Sike heels / Spend the rent / Negative girls / Death tongue / Leather skull / The scars never show / McArthur Park / Fun in the final days / Who shot you Dutch.

—— In Sep'91, ROB TYNER was found dead after suffering heart attack. He was 46.

—— with on first **KEITH MORRIS, BRETT REED, MATT FREEMAN, DALE CROVER, JOSH FREESE, BRETT GUREWITZ, CHRIS BAGAROZZI**, etc

Epitaph Epitaph

Jan 95. (cd/c/lp) *<(E 86447-2/-4/-1)>* **THE HARD STUFF** [ ] [ ]
– Crack in the universe / Junkie romance / Bad seed / Poison / Realm of

the pirate kings / Incident on Stock Island / Pillar of fire / Hope for sale / Edge of the switchblade / Sharkskin suit.

Feb 96. (cd/lp) *<(86458-2/-1)>* **DANGEROUS MADNESS** [ ] [ ]
– Dangerous madness / Back to DEtroit / Wild America / Something broken in the promised land / Take exit '97 / God's worst nightmare / The boy's got that look in their eyes / Dead man's vest / It's never enough / Rats of illusion / Dead movie stars.

May 97. (cd) *<(6488-2)>* **CITIZEN WAYNE** [ ] [ ]
– Stranger in the house / Back when dogs could talk / Revolution in apt.29 / Down on the ground / Shining Mr. Lincoln's shoes / Dope for democracy / No easy way out / You don't know my name / Count time / Snatched defeat / Doing the work / Farewell to whiskey.

—— MC5 were about to reform with KRAMER, DAVIS + THOMSON

—— next with rhythm **DOUGLAS LUNN + RIC PARNELL**

Nov 98. (cd/lp) *<(86539)>* **LLMF** (Live Like A Motherfucker) [ ] [ ]
– Bad seed / Stranger in the house / It's never enough / Something broken in the promised land / Take your clothes off / Down on the ground / Junkie romance / Poison / Count time / No easy way out / Crack in the universe / So long, Hank / Kick out the jams / Bomb day in Paris.

not iss. MuscleTone

Jul 02. (cd) <5> **ADULT WORLD** [–] [ ]
– Brought a knife to the gunfight / Great big amp / Adult world / Talkin' outta school / Nelson Algren stopped by / What about Laura? / Love, Fidel / The slime that ate Cleveland / Sundays in SAigon / The red arrow.

– others, etc. –

Nov 96. (cd; by WAYNE KRAMER – DENIZ TEK – SCOTT MORGAN) *Alive; <(ALIVE 25)>* **DODGE MAIN** [ ] [ ]
– City slang / 1.94 / Citizen of time / Future – Now / Fire comin' / 100 fools / The harder they come / Over and over / Better than that / I got a right.

Oct 00. (cd; by WAYNE KRAMER & PINK FAIRIES) *Table Of Elements; <(TOE 3028)>* **COCAINE BLUES 1974-1978** [ ] [ ]
(re-iss. Nov00 on 'Alive'; NER 3028 CD/LP)

☐ Roger McGUINN (see under ⇒ BYRDS)

Maria McKEE

Born: 17 Aug'64, Los Angeles, California, USA. The stepsister of BRYAN MACLEAN (of legendary L.A. band, LOVE, and whom she had previously sung with as a duo), McKEE had a more than a little to live up to when she formed country-rock outfit, LONE JUSTICE, in 1984. With RYAN HEDGECOCK (guitar), TONY GILKYSON (guitar), MARVIN ETZIONI (bass) and DON HEFFINGTON (drums) completing the line-up, the band soon secured a deal with 'Geffen'. An eponymous debut received rave reviews upon its Summer '85 release, the record featuring a number of songs co-penned with TOM PETTY while also drawing praise from luminaries like BOB DYLAN and U2, the latter inviting LONE JUSTICE onto their 'Joshua Tree' tour. McKEE's profile was further heightened when FEARGAL SHARKEY (ex-UNDERTONES) took one her songs, 'A GOOD HEART' to No.1 in the UK later that year. In 1986, she recruited an entire new line-up for the 'SHELTER' album, the second and final LONE JUSTICE release. When McKEE split for a solo career the following year, she took retained two of the new members, guitarists SHANE FONTAYNE and BRUCE BRODY, both of whom played on her acclaimed eponymous solo debut. Released in 1989, the album gave McKEE free reign with her doomed-romantic songwriting and diaphragm-rupturing vocal talent, the likes of 'I'VE FORGOTTEN WHAT IT WAS IN YOU (THAT PUT THE NEED IN ME)' and 'NOBODY'S CHILD' (co-written with ROBBIE ROBERTSON) reminding the Nashville pretenders what the term 'country' really meant. Despite the lack of any real success in America, McKEE scored a UK No.1 the following summer with 'SHOW ME HEAVEN', a fairly atypical number penned by the singer for the 'Days Of Thunder' film soundtrack. Another one-off venture came in the unlikely form of UK club hit, 'SWEETEST CHILD', a track recorded with the help of ubiquitous ex-KILLING JOKE man, YOUTH. She eventually began work on a follow-up album in 1992, teaming up with BLACK CROWES producer, GEORGE DRAKOULIAS. Ex-LONE JUSTICE members MARVIN ETZIONI and DON HEFFINGTON returned to the fold while the sessions also featured JAYHAWKS men MARK OLSEN and GARY LOURIS. Consequently, 'YOU GOTTA SIN TO GET SAVED' (1993) was tougher in a rootsy kind of way, McKEE surpassing herself on the gospel-rock of the title track and the bittersweet 'I CAN'T MAKE IT ALONE'. The following year, the tortured lament of 'IF LOVE WAS A RED DRESS (HANG ME IN RAGS)' saw McKEE featured on the ultra-hip 'Pulp Fiction' soundtrack, her female NICK CAVE-style voodoo country one of the record's highlights. On the album 'LIFE IS SWEET' (1996), however, McKEE comes over all post-modern, with decidedly mixed results. Never one to rush things on the recording front, McKEE finally re-emerged with 'HIGH DIVE' in 2003, once again confounding any rashly held expectations about her creative trajectory. Employing a raft of string and baroque brass arrangements, the ever ambitious singer contrived to approximate her own, passionately singular take on sweeping 60's pop/rock grandeur. That she in large part succeeded was down in no small part to her almost visionary production and arranging skills (along with those of musical compadre JIM AKIN) as well as an unsung lyrical prowess. • **Covered:** SWEET JANE (Velvet Underground) / HAS HE GOT A FRIEND FOR ME (Richard Thompson) / WICHITA LINEMAN (Jim Webb).

Album rating: Lone Justice: LONE JUSTICE (*7) / SHELTER (*5) / Maria McKee: MARIA McKEE (*6) / YOU GOTTA SIN TO GET SAVED (*7) / LIFE IS SWEET (*5) / THE ULTIMATE COLLECTION compilation (*7) / HIGH DIVE (*7)

LONE JUSTICE

MARIA McKEE – vocals / **RYAN HEDGECOCK** (b.27 Feb'61) – guitar / **TONY GILKYSON** – guitar / **MARVIN ETZIONI** (b.18 Apr'56, New York City, N.Y.) – bass / **DON HEFFINGTON** (b.20 Dec'50) – drums

Geffen Geffen

Apr 85. (7") *(A 6218)* *<29023>* **WAYS TO BE WICKED. / CACTUS ROSE** [ ] [71]
(12"+=) *(TX 6218)* – You are the light.

Jun 85. (lp) *(GEF 26288)* *<24060>* **LONE JUSTICE** [49] Apr85 [56]
– East of Eden / After the flood / Ways to be wicked / Don't toss us away / Working late / Sweet, sweet baby (I'm falling) / Pass it on / Wait 'til we get home / Soap, soup and salvation / You are the light. *(re-iss. Apr86 lp/c; GEF/40 32784) (re-iss. Mar91 lp/c/cd; GEF/+C/D 24060) (re-iss. Apr92 cd/c; GFL D/C 19058)*

Aug 85. (7") *(A 6426)* **SWEET, SWEET BABY (I'M FALLING). / PASS IT ON** [ ] [–]
(12"+=) *(TA 6426)* – Go 'way little boy.

Aug 85. (7") *<28965>* **SWEET, SWEET BABY (I'M FALLING). / DON'T TOSS US AWAY** [–] [73]

—— **MARIA McKEE** brought in entire new band, **SHANE FONTAYNE** – guitar (ex-STEVE FORBERT) who repl. HEDGECOCK / **BRUCE BRODY** (b.11 Dec'50) – guitar (ex-PATTI SMITH) who repl. GILYKSON / **GREG SUTTON** – bass who repl. ETZIONI / **RUDY RICHMAN** – drums who repl. HEFFINGTON

Oct 86. (7") *(GEF 16)* **SHELTER. / CAN'T LOOK BACK** [ ] [–]
(12"+=) *(GEF 16T)* – Belfry.

Nov 86. (lp/c)(cd) *(WX 73/+C)(924122-2)* *<24122>* **SHELTER** [84] [ ]
– I found love / Shelter / Reflected (on my side) / Beacon / Wheels / Belfry / Dreams come true (stand up and take it) / The gift / Inspiration / Dixie storms. *(re-iss. Mar91 lp/c/cd; GEF/+C/D 24122) (re-iss. Apr92 cd/c; GFL D/C 19059)*

Dec 86. (7") *<28520>* **SHELTER. / BELFRY** [–] [49]

Feb 87. (7") *(GEF 18)* **I FOUND LOVE. / IF YOU DON'T LIKE THE RAIN** [45] [ ]
(12"+=/12"pic-d+=) *(GEF 18 T/P)* – ('A'extended).
(d7"+=) *(GEF 18F)* – Sweet Jane (live) / Don't toss us away (live).

—— split after above. Past members – ETZIONI solo; released two albums for 'Restless' between 1992 and 1993; 'THE MANDOLIN MAN' and 'BONE'. HEDGECOCK solo in 1992; 'ECHO PARK' for 'Yellow Moon' UK.

MARIA McKEE

—— went solo, taking with her **FONTAYNE + BRODY** plus session people

Jun 89. (lp/c)(cd) *(WX 270/+C)(924229-2) <24229>* **MARIA McKEE** [49] [ ]
– I've forgotten what it was in you (that put the need in me) / To miss someone / Am I the only one (who's ever felt this way?) / Nobody's child / Panic beach / Can't pull the wool (over the little lamb's eyes) / More than a heart can hold / This property is condemned / Breathe / Has he got a friend for me? / Drinkin' in my Sunday dress. *(re-iss. Mar91 lp/c/cd; GEF/+C/D 24229) (re-iss. Mar93 cd/c; GFL D/C 19200)*

Aug 90. (7") *(656 303-7)* **SHOW ME HEAVEN. / (track by Hans Zimmer)** [1] [ ]
(12"+=/cd-s+=) *(656 303-6/-2)* – (track by Apollo Smile).
(above from the film, 'Days Of Thunder' on 'Epic')

Nov 90. (7"/c-s) *<22800>* **TO MISS SOMEONE. / PANIC BEACH** [ ] [ ]
(12"+=/cd-s+=) – Drinkin' in my Sunday dress.

Jan 91. (7"/c-s) *(GFS/+C 1)* **BREATHE. / PANIC BEACH** [59] [–]
(12"+=/cd-s+=) *(GFST/+D 1)* – Drinkin' in my Sunday dress.

Jul 92. (7"/c-s) *(GFS/+C 23)* **SWEETEST CHILD. / ('A'acappella remix)** [45] [–]
(12"+=/cd-s+=) *(GFST/+D 23)* – ('A'-Trans tribal ritual stomp mix).

—— FONTAYNE joined BRUCE SPRINGSTEEN in 1992. The JAYHAWKS' MARK OLSON and GARY LOURIS appeared on below album.

May 93. (c-s) *(GFSC 39)* **I'M GONNA SOOTHE YOU. / WHY WASN'T I MORE GRATEFUL (WHEN LIFE WAS SWEET)** [35] [–]
(cd-s+=) *(GFSTD 39)* – This thing (don't lead to Heaven).
(cd-s) *(GFSXD 39)* – ('A'side) / If love was a red dress (hang me in rags) / Show me Heaven (acoustic demo).

Jun 93. (cd/c/lp) *<(GED/GEC/GEF 24508)>* **YOU GOTTA SIN TO GET SAVED** [26] [ ]
– I'm gonna soothe you / My lonely sad eyes / My girlhood among the outlaws / One only / I forgive you / I can't make it alone / Precious time / The way young lovers do / Why wasn't I more grateful (when life was sweet) / You gotta sin to be saved. *(cd re-iss. Oct95; GFLD 19290)*

Aug 93. (c-s) *(GFSC 53)* **I CAN'T MAKE IT ALONE. / MY GIRLHOOD AMONG THE OUTLAWS** [74] [–]
(cd-s+=) *(GFSTD 53)* – I'm gonna soothe you / Wichita lineman (both acoustic).
(cd-s+=) *(GFSXD 53)* – I wish I was your mother.

Feb 96. (cd/c) *<(GED/GEC 24819)>* **LIFE IS SWEET** [ ] [ ]
– Searlover / This perfect dress / Absolutely barking stars / I'm not listening / Everybody / Smarter / What else you wanna know / I'm awake / Human carried / Life is sweet / Afterlife. *(cd re-iss. Jun03; 424819-2)*

Apr 96. (cd-s/cd-s) *(GFS C/TD 22134)* **THIS PERFECT DRESS / MAGDELAINE** [ ] [ ]
(cd-s+=) *(GFSXD 22134)* – Amnesia blues (sandpaper clues).

Viewfinder Viewfinder

Apr 03. (cd) *<(VFD 3000)>* **HIGH DIVE** [ ] [ ]
– To the open spaces / Life is sweet / After life / Be my joy / High dive / My friend foe / In your constellation / Love doesn't love / We pair off / No gala / Non religious building / Something similar / From our T.V. teens to the tomb / Worry birds.

– compilation, etc. –

Dec 93. (cd; LONE JUSTICE) *Windsong; (WINCD 048)* **BBC RADIO 1 LIVE IN CONCERT (live)** [ ] [–]

Sep 00. (cd) *Hip-O; <(AA314 541505-2)>* **THE ULTIMATE COLLECTION** [ ] Aug00 [ ]
– Ways to be wicked (LONE JUSTICE) / Sweet, sweet baby (I'm falling) (LONE JUSTICE) / Don't toss us away (LONE JUSTICE) / Shelter (LONE JUSTICE) / Wheels (LONE JUSTICE) / Panic beach / Only once / Absolutely barking stars / I'm awake / Scarlover / If love is a red dress (hang me in rags) / Show me heaven (version) / Sweetest child / Sweet Jane (LONE JUSTICE live) / Dixie storms (LONE JUSTICE) / Breathe / Am I the only one (who's ever felt this way).

Sarah McLACHLAN

Born: 28 Jan'68, Halifax, Nova Scotia, Canada. Professionally schooled in singing, guitar and piano as a child, McLACHLAN's first taste of the music business came with local band, OCTOBER GAME. After initially turning down a deal from 'Nettwerk' due to her art school studies, she later signed to the Canadian label as a solo artist and cut a 1988 debut album, 'TOUCH'. 'Arista' were sufficiently impressed to offer her a long term contract, re-issuing the record in 1989. A sophomore set, 'SOLACE' (1991), showcased a flowering songwriting talent within her trademark rootsy framework, the singer's Celtic heritage echoed in every chord. McLACHLAN would be profoundly inlfuenced by a subsequent trip to Asia where she worked on a Canadian documentary about poverty and exploitation, her experiences at least partly inspiring 1994's 'FUMBLING TOWARDS ECSTASY'. Generally regarded as her finest album, this immaculately produced record found her exploring more ambitious musical textures while putting in a compelling vocal performance. The club-influenced 'POSSESSION' single even scraped into the US Top 100 although she couldn't quite garner the same crossover audience enjoyed by her expanding bunch of female contemporaries. Nevertheless, McLACHLAN was instrumental in organising the 1997 'Lilith Fair' tour, an all-female affair featuring the likes of NATALIE MERCHANT. Later that year, her fourth set, 'SURFACING', surpassed all expectations by slowly rising into the US Top 3. It even broke her in Britain, albeit a year later when single 'ADIA' made the Top 20. Following the a pre-millennial live greatest hits set, 'MIRRORBALL' (1999), McLACHLAN ducked out of the music biz for serious domestic duties before making a low profile return with 'AFTERGLOW' (2003), a barely updated take on her signature singer/songwriter sound. • **Covered:** OL' 55 (Tom Waits) / SOLISBURY HILL (Peter Gabriel) / WEAR YOUR LOVE LIKE HEAVEN + BARABAJAGAL (Donovan) / BLUE (Joni Mitchell) / etc

Album rating: TOUCH (*5) / SOLACE (*6) / FUMBLING TOWARDS ECSTASY (*7) / SURFACING (*7) / MIRRORBALL (*6)

SARAH McLACHLAN – vocals, guitar, piano; with session people; plus **DAVID KERSHAW** – keyboards + **ASH SOOD**

Nettwerk Nettwerk

Jan 89. (lp/cd) *(NET/+CD 007) <8594>* **TOUCH** [ ] Oct88 [ ]
– Out of the shadows / Vox / Strange world / Trust / Touch / Steaming / Sad clown / Uphill battle / Ben's song. *(re-iss. Aug89 on 'Arista' lp/c/cd+=; 209/409/259 872)* – Vox (extended). *(cd re-iss. Jan99 on 'Arista'; 25987-2)*

Sep 89. (cd-s) *<3035>* **STEAMING / STEAMING (dance) / SOLISBURY HILL (live)** [–] [ ]

Jan 90. (7"/12") *<9804-5>* **VOX. / TOUCH** [–] [ ]

Jun 91. (cd-s) *<3056>* **THE PATH OF THORNS / (version) / SHELTER (violin version)** [–] [ ]

Sep 91. (cd-s) *<3063>* **INTO THE FIRE / SAD CLOWN / BLACK** [–] [ ]

Feb 92. (cd-s) *<3065>* **DRAWN TO THE RHYTHM / GLOOMY SUNDAY (live) / DRAWN TO THE RHYTHM (live acoustic)** [–] [ ]

Apr 92. (cd-s) *<3070>* **VOX / (instrumental) / INTO THE FIRE (extended mix)** [–] [ ]

Arista Arista

Mar 92. (cd/c/lp) *(261/411/211 955) <18631>* **SOLACE** [ ] Jun91 [ ]
– Drawn to the rhythm / Into the fire / The path of thorns (terms) / I will not forget you / Lost / Back door man / Shelter / Black / Home / Mercy / Wear your love like heaven. *(cd re-iss. Jan99; same)*

Jun 92. (cd-s) *<30075>* **ISLAND OF CIRCLES** [–] [ ]
– Wear your love like heaven / Barabajagal.

Oct 92. (m-cd) *<6313>* **LIVE EP** [–] [ ]
– Drawn to the rhythm / Back door man / Home / Lost / I will not forget you / Black / Ben's song.

Apr 94. (c-s) *<12662>* **POSSESSION / (version 2) / FEAR** [–] [73]

Sep 94. (c-s) <12690> **GOOD ENOUGH (album + live + remix) / BLUE** – 77

Oct 94. (cd/c) *(74321 19032-2/-4)* <18725> **FUMBLING TOWARDS ECSTASY** 50
– Possession / Wait / Plenty / Good enough / Mary / Elsewhere / Circle / Ice / Hold on / Ice cream / Fear / Fumbling towards ecstasy.

Apr 95. (m-cd+cd-rom) <*18784*> **THE FREEDOM SESSIONS** – 78
– Elsewhere / Plenty – Mary / Good enough / Hold on / Ice cream / Ice / Ol' 55. *(UK-iss.Aug98 on 'Rock The House' d-lp/cd; RTH 2000/+CD)*

Feb 96. (c-s) *(74321 33979-4)* <12893> **I WILL REMEMBER YOU / ICE CREAM** Oct95 65
(12"+=/cd-s+=) *(74321 33979-1/-2)* – ('A'full version).

Aug 97. (c-s,cd-s) <13395> **BUILDING A MYSTERY /** – 13

Oct 97. (cd/c) <*(18970-2/-4)*> **SURFACING** Jul97 2
– Building a mystery / I love you / Sweet surrender / Adia / Do what you have to do / Witness / Angel / Black & white / Full of grace / Last dance. *(re-prom.Oct98 hit UK No.47; same) (lp-iss.Oct99 on 'Rock The House'; RTH 18970)*

Feb 98. (c-s,cd-s) <13453> **SWEET SURRENDER (mixes)** – 28

Sep 98. (c-s) *(74321 61390-4)* <13497> **ADIA / ANGEL** 18 3
May98 56
(cd-s+=) *(74321 61390-2)* – Possession.

Nov 98. (cd-s) <13621> **ANGEL / ICE CREAM (live) / I WILL NOT FORGET YOU (live)** – 4

May 99. (cd-s) <13709> **I WILL REMEMBER YOU (live)** – 14

Jun 99. (cd) <*(07822 19049-2)*> **MIRRORBALL** (live: greatest hits) 3
– Building a mystery / Hold on / Good enough / I will remember you / Adia / I love you / Do what you have to do / Path of thorns / Fear / Posession / Sweet surrender / Ice cream / Fumbling towards ecstasy / Angel.

—— SARAH featured on the UK No.3 single, 'Silence', by DELIRIUM

Jan 01. (cd-s) *(74321 81963-2)* **SWEET SURRENDER (boilerhouse mix) / SWEET SURRENDER (DJ Tiesto radio mix) / ADIA (live)** –
(12") *(74321 81963-1)* – (2nd version) / Sweet surrender (Roni Size mix) / I love you (BT extended).
(cd-s) *(74321 82075-2)* – (extended versions of above).

Feb 04. (cd) *(82876 57575-2)* <50150> **AFTERGLOW** – Nov03 2
– Fallen / World on fire / Stupid / Drifting / Train wreck / Push / Answer / Time / Perfect girl / Dirty little secret.

– compilations, etc. –

on 'Nettwerk' unless mentioned otherwise

Jan 93. (cd) *(W 26313)* **SARAH McLACHLAN LIVE (live)**

Sep 97. (cd) *(30105)* **RARITIES B-SIDES AND OTHERS**

Aug 98. (d-lp/cd) *Rock The House; (RTH 2000/+CD)* **FUMBLING TOWARDS ECSTASY / THE FREEDOM SESSIONS** –

May 01. (12") *(33120)* **SWEET SURRENDER (BT mix). / SWEET SURRENDER (DJ Tiesto mix)**

Jul 01. (d12") *(333132-1)* **REMIXES** – Canada –
– Fear (Hybrid's super collider mix) / Hold on (BT mix) / Angel (Dusted mix) / Plenty (fade mix).

Nov 01. (cd/d-lp) *(30200-2/-1)* <30186> **REMIXED**
– Fear (Hybrid's super collider mix) / Sweet surrender (DJ Tiesto mix) / Angel (Dusted remix) / I love you (BT mix) / Silence (DJ Tiesto's in search of sunrise remix) / Black (William Orbit remix) / Possession (Rabbit In The Moon mix) / Hold on (BT mix) / Plenty (fade mix).

Jan 02. (cd-s) *(33148-2)* **ANGEL / SILENCE (fade sanctuary mix) / SWEET SURRENDER (DJ Tiesto remix).** 36
(12") *(33147-1)* <314719> – ('A'-Dusted remix) / Silence (Michael Woods mix) / Sweet surrender (DJ Tiesto remix).

John McLAUGHLIN / MAHAVISHNU ORCHESTRA

Born: 4 Jan'42, Yorkshire, England. Although he learned piano and violin at an early age, it was the guitar which vyed for his attention as a teenager. His first professional music business experience came in the mid-60's when he spent time in both the GRAHAM BOND ORGANISATION and the BRIAN AUGER TRINITY. His debut solo outing, 'EXTRAPOLATION' (1969), was evidence of McLAUGHLIN's increasing immersion in jazz, the virtuoso having been recruited by none other than the legendary MILES DAVIS. During his stint with the celebrated trumpeter, JOHN played on two of his most groundbreaking albums, 'In A Silent Way' and 'Bitches Brew'. During this prolific time for McLAUGHLIN at the turn of the decade, he also featured in TONY WILLIAMS' jazz-rock outfit, LIFETIME, who released two highly influential albums, 'Emergency' and 'Turn It Over'. This group featured JACK BRUCE, with whom he'd previously collaborated (alongside JON HISEMAN and DICK HECKSTALL-SMITH) on the 'THINGS WE LIKE' set in '69. By this point, McLAUGHLIN, who was now a practising vegetarian and convert to Sri Chimnoy, was taking his music in a more meditative Eastern-influenced direction. Another prolific period ensued during which he released three albums in quick succession, one of them, 'MY GOAL'S BEYOND' (1973), was issued under the banner of MAHAVISHNU JOHN McLAUGHLIN – the adopted name given him by his newfound guru. In turn, McLAUGHLIN was inspired to form The MAHAVISHNU ORCHESTRA, an exceptionally talented group of musicians who boasted the likes of BILLY COBHAM and JAN HAMMER. An American Top 100 entry, 'THE INNER MOUNTING FLAME' (1972), quickly established the group as one of the world's leading jazz-rock fusionists, while follow-up set, 'BIRDS OF FIRE', broke them through commercially. After a live set, 'LIVE – BETWEEN NOTHINGNESS AND ETERNITY' and a collaborative album with CARLOS SANTANA, McLAUGHLIN dissolved the original line-up and recruited a more string-orientated cast of musicians including JEAN-LUC PONTY. Two albums (the occasionally brilliant 'VISIONS OF THE EMERALD BEYOND' and 'INNER WORLDS') later, McLAUGHLIN abandoned the project completely, opting for a more overtly spiritual direction with Indian classical outfit, SHAKTI. Towards the end of the decade, the erstwhile fusion pioneer returned to electric guitar with the ONE TRUTH BAND before following a twin fusion/classical direction throughout the following two decades as a solo artist. The man's celebrated link-up with PACO DE LUCIA and AL DiMEOLA, 'FRIDAY NIGHT IN SAN FRANCISCO' (1981) remains one of the best selling items in his catalogue, a record which, along with follow-up, 'PASSION, GRACE AND FIRE' (1983), concentrated on acoustic, flamenco-based material. A reformed MAHAVISHNU ORCHESTRA – with newcomers MITCHELL FORMAN, BILL EVANS and DANNY GOTTLIEB – cut the eponymous 'MAHAVISHNU' in 1985, following it up with 'ADVENTURES IN RADIOLAND' two years later. The mid-80's also saw McLAUGHLIN making an appearance on the 'Round Midnight' jazz flick soundtrack. A new decade and McLAUGHLIN continued exploring new possibilities in jazz, performing 'MEDITERRANEAN GUITAR CONCERTO' (1990) with The London Symphony Orchestra and KATIA LABEQUE. The same TRIO (McLAUGHLIN, KAI ECKHARDT and TRILOK

GURTU) that recorded 1990's Royal Festival Hall live effort went into the studio for 1991's 'QUE ALEGRIA', the veteran fusion meister utilising a guitar synth to augment his acoustic playing. The death of his former colleague and formative influence BILL EVANS prompted the recording of tribute set 'TIME REMEMBERED: JOHN McLAUGHLIN PLAYS BILL EVANS' (1993), wherein JOHN worked with a classical guitar quintet. Older fans no doubt welcomed the man's return to electric guitar on 'TOKYO LIVE' (1994), a release billed as The FREE SPIRITS (McLAUGHLIN, JOEY DeFRANCESCO and DENNIS CHAMBERS), a blues-orientated gig which served as light relief from the intensity of its predecessor. 'THE PROMISE' (1995), meanwhile, took its inspiration from various strands of McLAUGHLIN's recent musical history, the guitarist working with a whole range of his favourite collaborators (including FRANCESCO, CHAMBERS, DE LUCIA, DiMEOLA and GURTU) and even some fresh faces in the shape of JEFF BECK and DAVID SANBORN. It was perhaps only a matter of time before McLAUGHLIN resurrected his SHAKTI project and so, more than two decades on from the original recordings, McLAUGHLIN once more joined forces with TH VINYAKRAM and ZAKIR HUSSEIN (along with new member HARIPRASAD CHAURASIA) for 'REMEMBER SHAKTI' (1999), a spiritually enriching set rooted in Indian classical music. The rejuvenated outfit travelled to Bombay in late 2000 for a show which was recorded and later released as 'SATURDAY NIGHT IN BOMBAY: REMEMBER SHAKTI' (2001). Sandwiched between these two releases was 'THE HEART OF THINGS' (2000), another fine electric set featuring CHAMBERS amongst others. 'THIEVES AND POETS' (2003) was a different beast altogether, an ambitious yet intimate and revealing collection of acoustic, classically influenced guitar work comprising both original compositions and a clutch of well-worn but – in McLAUGHLIN's masterful hands at least – still eminently listenable standards including 'STELLA BY STARLIGHT' and 'MY ROMANCE'. • **Songwriters:** McLAUGHLIN compositions except BLUES IN GREEN (Miles Davis) / PASHA'S LOVE (Gurtu – band member 1990) / THE WIND CRIES MARY (Jimi Hendrix) / etc.

Album rating: EXTRAPOLATION (*5) / DEVOTION (*5) / INNER MOUNTING FLAME (*6; as Mahavishnu Orchestra with John McLaughlin) / MY GOAL'S BEYOND (*4; as Mahavishnu John McLaughlin) / Mahavishnu Orchestra: BIRDS OF FIRE (*7) / BETWEEN NOTHINGNESS AND ETERNITY (*6) / APOCALYPSE (*5) / VISIONS OF THE EMERALD BEYOND (*5) / INNER WORLDS (*4) / Shakti with John McLaughlin: SHAKTI WITH JOHN McLAUGHLIN (*4) / A HANDFUL OF BEAUTY (*4) / NATURAL ELEMENTS (*4) / John McLaughlin: ELECTRIC GUITARIST (*5) / ELECTRIC DREAMS (*4; with the One Truth Band) / FRIDAY NIGHT IN SAN FRANCISCO (*5; with Al Di Meola & Paco De Lucia) / BELO HORIZONTE (*4) / PASSION, GRACE & FIRE (*4; with Al Di Meola & Paco Lucia) / MAHAVISHNU (*4) / AD VENTURES IN RADIOLAND (*4) / LIVE AT THE ROYAL FESTIVAL HALL (*4) / AFTER THE RAIN (*4) / THE PROMISE (*5) / REMEMBER SHAKTI (*6) / THE HEART OF THINGS (*6) / REMEMBER SHAKTI as Shakti (*5) / SATURDAY NIGHT IN BOMBAY as Remember Shakti (*5) / THIEVES AND POETS (*6)

JOHN McLAUGHLIN

solo with **JOHN SURMAN** – saxophone / **BRIAN ODGERS** – bass / **TONY OXLEY** – drums

Marmalade Polydor

1969. (lp) *(608 007) <5510>* **EXTRAPOLATION** [ ] Oct72 [ ]
– Extrapolation / It's funny / Argen's bag / Pete the poet / This is for us to share / Spectrum / Binky's beam / Really you know / Two for two / Peace piece. *(re-iss. 1974 on 'Polydor'; 2343 012) (re-iss. 1977 on 'Polydor'; 2310 018) (cd-iss. Oct90 on 'Polydor'; 841 498-2)*

— He was then credited on album 'THINGS WE LIKE' with JACK BRUCE, JON HISEMAN & DICK HECKSTAL-SMITH. McLAUGHLIN then went to America to join (TONY WILLIAM'S) LIFETIME, playing on 2 lp's 'EMERGENCY' + 'TURN IT OVER'. Around the same time MILES DAVIS gave him work on his 'IN A SILENT WAY' and 'BITCHES BREW'. Returned to solo work once more.

— Augmented by **BUDDY MILES** – drums / **JERRY GOODMAN** – violin (ex-FLOCK) / **BILLY RICH** – bass / **LARRY YOUNG** (aka KHALID YASIN) – keyboards

Douglas Columbia

Jan 71. (lp) *(DGL 65075) <31568>* **DEVOTION** [ ] 1972 [ ]
– Devotion / Dragon song / Marbles / Siren / Don't let the dragon eat your mother / Purpose of when. *<US cd-iss. Dec93 on 'Celluloid'; CELD 5010> (cd re-iss. Jan97 on 'Charly'; CPCD 8232)*

— **BILLY COBHAM** (b.16 May'44, Panama) – drums, percussion (ex-MILES DAVIS) repl. BUDDY MILES

1971. (lp; as MAHAVISHNU JOHN McLAUGHLIN) *(DGL 69014) <30766>* **MY GOAL'S BEYOND** [ ] [ ]
– Peace one / Peace two / Goodbye pork-pie hat / Something spiritual / Hearts and flowers / Philip Lane / Waltz for Bill Evans / Follow your heart / Song for my mother / Blue is green. *(re-iss. Mar82 on 'Elektra Musician'; K 52364) (cd-iss. May92 on 'Rykodisc'; RCD 10051)*

— next featured **JOHN SURMAN / KARL BERGER / STU MARTIN + DAVE HOLLAND**

Dawn not iss.

Mar 71. (lp) *(DNLS 3018)* **WHERE FORTUNES SMILES** [ ] [-]
– Glancing backwards (for Junior) / Earth bound hearts / Where fortune smiles / New place, old place / Hope. *(cd-iss. Jul93 on 'Beat Goes On'; BGOCD 191)*

MAHAVISHNU ORCHESTRA

JOHN McLAUGHLIN with **COBHAM + GOODMAN** and adding **RICK LAIRD** (b. 5 Feb'41, Dublin, Ireland) – bass / **JAN HAMMER** (b.17 Apr'48, Prague, Czech) – keyboards

C.B.S. Columbia

Jan 72. (lp/c) *(CBS/40 64717) <31067>* **THE INNER MOUNTING FLAME** [ ] [89]
– Meeting of the Spirits / Dawn / The noonward race / A lotus on Irish streams / Vital transformation / You know you know / The dance of Maya / Awakening. *<US cd-iss. 1989; CD 31067>*

Feb 73. (lp/c) *(CBS/40 65321) <31996>* **BIRDS OF FIRE** [20] [15]
– Birds of fire / Miles beyond (Miles Davis) / Celestial terrestrial commuters / Sapphire bullets of pure love / Thousand Island park / Hope / One word / Sanctuary / Open country joy / Resolution. *(quad-lp 1974; CQ 31996) (re-iss. Nov83 lp/c/cd; CBS/40/CD 32280) (re-iss. cd Jun89; CD 65321) (re-iss. Jan92 on 'Columbia-Legacy'; 468 224-2)*

May 73. (7") **OPEN COUNTRY BOY. / CELESTIAL COMMUTERS** [-] [ ]

— Mid'73, released collaboration Top 20 album 'LOVE DEVOTION SURRENDER' with CARLOS SANTANA. (see: SANTANA ⇒)

Jan 74. (lp/c) *(CBS/40 69046) <32766>* **LIVE – BETWEEN NOTHINGNESS & ETERNITY (live)** [ ] Dec73 [41]
– Trilogy / The sunlit path – La mere de la mer – Tomorrow's story not the same / Sister Andrea / Dream. *(cd-iss. 1988; CD 69046) (re-iss. Dec88 on 'Beat Goes On' lp/cd; BGO LP/CD 31) (cd re-iss. Dec91 on 'Columbia-Legacy'; 468 225-2)*

— (Jan74) McLAUGHLIN disbanded group, COBHAM went solo as did JAN HAMMER. Recruited new people **JEAN LUC-PONTY** – electric violin (ex-Solo, ex-ZAPPA) / **MICHAEL NARADA WALDEN** – drums / **GAYLE MORAN** – keyboards, vocals / **RALPHE ARMSTRONG** – bass / **STEVE FRANKOVITCH** – brass / **BOB KNAPP** – reeds / plus **PHILIP HIRSCHI** – cello / **MARSHA WESTBROOK** – viola / **CAROL SHIRE** – violin / **STEVE KINDLER** – violin also credited The LONDON SYMPHONY ORCHESTRA conducted by MICHAEL TILSON-THOMAS

Jun 74. (lp/c) *(CBS/40 69076) <32957>* **APOCALYPSE** [ ] May74 [43]
– Power of love / Vision of a naked sword / Smile of the beyond / Wings of Karma / Hymn to him. *<US cd-iss. Dec90 on 'Columbia-Legacy'; 467 092-2>*

Jan 75. (lp/c) *(CBS/40 69109) <33411>* **VISIONS OF THE EMERALD BEYOND** [ ] [68]
– Eternity's breath (part 1 & 2) / Lila's dance / Can't stand your funk / Pastoral / Faith / Cosmic strut / If I could see / Be happy / Earth ship / Pegasus / Opus 1 / On the way home to Earth. *<US cd-iss. Jun91 on 'Columbia-Legacy'; 467 904-2>*

Feb 75. (7") *(CBS 3007) <10134>* **CAN'T STAND YOUR FUNK. / ETERNITY'S BREATH (part 1)** [ ] [ ]

— Retained **WALDEN, PONTY, ARMSTRONG.** New **STU GOLDBERG** – keyboards

Feb 76. (lp/c; as MAHAVISHNU ORCHESTRA / JOHN McLAUGHLIN) *(CBS/40 69216) <33908>* **INNER WORLDS**
– All in the family / Miles out / In my life / Gita / Morning calls / The way of the pilgrim / River of my heart / Planetary citizen / Louis feet / Inner worlds (parts 1 & 2). *(cd-iss. Nov94 on 'Columbia-Legacy'; 476 905-2)*

SHAKTI

SHAKTI:- LEVI SHANKAR – violin / **JOHN McLAUGHLIN** – guitar / **TH VINYAKRAM** – percussion, vocals / **ZAKIR HUSSAIN** – percussion

C.B.S. Columbia

Jun 76. (lp) *(CBS 81388) <34162>* **SHAKTI (live)**
– Joy / Lotus feet / What need have I for this? – What need have I for that? / I am dancing at the feet of my Lord / All bliss – All bliss. *(cd-iss. 1990 on 'Columbia'; 46868)*

Mar 77. (lp) *(CBS 81664) <34372>* **A HANDFUL OF BEAUTY**
– La danse du bonheur / Lady L / India / Kriti / Isis / Two sisters.

Dec 77. (lp) *(CBS 82329) <34980>* > **NATURAL ELEMENTS**
– Mind ecology / Face to face / Come on baby dance with me / The daffodil and the eagle / Happiness is being together / Bridge of sighs / Get down and strut / Peace of mind.

– SHAKTI compilations –

Jun 91. (cd) *Sony; (467 905-2)* **SHAKTI WITH JOHN McLAUGHLIN**

Jan 95. (cd) *Koch Int.; (MRCD 1010)* **THE BEST OF SHAKTI** –

JOHN McLAUGHLIN

went solo again, using past band members, etc.

May 78. (lp/c) *(CBS/40 82702) <35326>* **ELECTRIC GUITARIST**
– New York on my mind / Friendship / Every tear from your eye / Do you hear the voices that you left behind / Are you the one? are you the one? / Phenomenon: Compulsion / My foolish heart. *(cd-iss. Jan92 on 'Columbia-Legacy'; 467 093-2)*

— Next with ONE TRUTH BAND, who were **SHANKER** – violin / **ANTHONY ALLEN SMITH** – drums / **STU GOLDBERG** – keyboards

May 79. (lp/c; JOHN McLAUGHLIN / ONE TRUTH BAND) *(CBS/40 83256)<35785>* **ELECTRIC DREAMS, ELECTRIC SIGHS** Apr79
– Guardian angels / Miles Davis / Electric dreams, electric sighs / Desire and the comforter / Love and understanding / Singing Earth / The dark prince / The unknown dissident. *(cd-iss. 1993 on 'Columbia-Legacy'; 476 905-2)*

Jun 81. (lp; by JOHN McLAUGHLIN with PACO DE LUCIA & AL DI MEOLA) *(CBS 84962) <37152>* **FRIDAY NIGHT IN SAN FRANCISCO: LIVE (live)** May81 97
– Mediterranean sundance – Rio Ancho / Short tales of the Black Forest / Frevo resgado / Fantasia suite / Guardian angels. *(cd-iss. 1988 on 'Philips'; 800 047-2) (re-iss. cd 1990 on 'Columbia'; 467 010-2)*

WEA Warners

Jan 82. (lp) *(K/K4 99185) <3619>* **BELO HORIZONTE** Dec81
– Belo horizonte / La baleine / Very early / One melody / Stardust on your sleeve / Waltz for Katia / Zamfir / Manita's d'aro (for Paco De Lucia).

1982. (lp) *(K 99254)* **MUSIC SPOKEN HERE** –
– Aspan / Blues for L.W. / The translators / Honky-tonk Heaven / Viene Clare Ando / David / Negative ions / Briese de coeur / Loro.

Mercury Columbia

Jun 83. (lp; by DiMELOA, McLAUGHLIN, DE LUCIA) *(MERL 24) <38645>* **PASSION, GRACE & FIRE**
– Aspen / Orient blue / Chiquito / Sichia / David / Passion, grace & fire. *(re-iss. 1990 on 'Philips'; 811 334-1)*

— with **MITCHELL FORMAN** – keyboards / **BILL EVANS** – saxophone / **JONAS HELLBORG** – bass / **DANNY GOTTLIEB** – drums

WEA WEA

Jan 85. (lp/c; as MAHAVISHNU) *(251 351-1/-4)* **MAHAVISHNU**
– Radio activity / Nostalgia / Nightriders / East side west side / Clarendon hills / Jazz / The unbeliever / Pacific express / When blue turns gold.

Polygram Intercord

Jul 87. (lp/c/cd; as JOHN McLAUGHLIN AND MAHAVISHNU) *(SOS/+MC/CD 2020) <88561 8081>* **AD VENTURES IN RADIOLAND**
– The wait / Just ideas / Jozy / Half man, half cookie / Florianapolis / Gotta dance / The wall will fall / Reincarnation / Mitch match / 20th century limited. *(re-iss. cd 1990's on 'Verve'; 519 397-2)*

— with **KAI ECKHARDT** – bass / **TRILOK GURTU** – percussion

J.M.T. J.M.T.

Apr 90. (cd/c/lp; by JOHN McLAUGHLIN TRIO) *(<834 436-2/-4/-1>)* **LIVE AT THE ROYAL FESTIVAL HALL (live)** Nov89
– Blue in green / Medley: Just ideas – Jozy / Florianapolis / Pasha's love / Mother tongues. *(c+=/cd+=)* – Blues for L.W.

— with **LONDON SYMPHONY ORCHESTRA & MICHAEL TILSON THOMAS / KATIA LABEQUE** – piano

C.B.S. Columbia

1990. (lp/cd; JOHN McLAUGHLIN with The LSO & KATIA LABEQUE) *(<MK/+CD 45578>)* **MEDITERRANEAN GUITAR CONCERTO**
– (I)- Rhythmic / (II)- Slow & sad / (III)- Animato / Briese de coeur / Montana / Two sisters / Until such time / Zakir.

Verve Verve

Jan 92. (cd; by JOHN McLAUGHLIN TRIO) *(<837 260-2>)* **QUE ALEGRIA**
– Belo horizonte / Baba (for Ramana Maharshi) / Reincarnation / 1 nite stand / Marie (bass solo) / Hijacked / Mila repa / Que alegria / 3 willows.

— with **JOEY DeFRANCESCO** – organ + **DENNIS CHAMBERS** – drums

Feb 94. (cd) *(<519 861-2>)* **TIME REMEMBERED: JOHN McLAUGHLIN PLAYS BILL EVANS**
– Prologue / Very early (homage to Bill Evans) / Only child / Waltz for Debby / Homage / My bells / Time remembered / Song for Helen / Turn out the stars / We will meet again / Epilogue.

— FREE SPIRITS:- **McLAUGHLIN, JOEY DeFRANCESCO** (organ), **DENNIS CHAMBERS** (drums)

May 94. (cd; by The FREE SPIRITS / JOHN McLAUGHLIN) *(<521 870-2>)* **TOKYO LIVE (live)**
– 1 nite stand / Hijacked / When love is far away / Little Miss Valley / Juju at the crossroads / Vuhovar / No blues / Mattinale.

— **ELVIN JONES** – drums; repl. CHAMBERS

Jun 95. (cd) *(<527 467-2>)* **AFTER THE RAIN**
– Take the Coltrane / My favorite things / Sing me softly of the blues / Encuentros / Naima / Tones for Elvin Jones / Crescent / Afro blue / After the rain.

Feb 96. (cd) *(<528 828-2>)* **THE PROMISE** Nov95
– Django / Thelonius melodius / Amy and Joseph / No return / El ciego / Jazz jungle / The wish / English jam / Tokyo decadence / Shin jin rui / The peacocks.

— later in '96, McLAUGHLIN teamed up once again with PACO DE LUCIA and AL DI MIELO on an eponymous set for 'Verve'; *(<533215-2>)*

— new SHAKTI line-up:- **McLAUGHLIN, ZAKIR HUSSEIN** (tabla), **T.H. VINAYAKRAM** (ghatam) + **HARIPRASAD CHAURASIA** (bansuri – flute)

Mar 99. (d-cd; as JOHN McLAUGHLIN & SHAKTI / HARIPRASAD CHAURASIA) *(<559945-2>)* **REMEMBER SHAKTI**
– Chandrakauns / The wish / Lotus feel / Mukti / Zakir.

Mar 00. (cd) *(<543536-2>)* **THE HEART OF THINGS: LIVE IN PARIS (live)**
– Seven sisters / Mother tongues / Fallen angels / The divide / Tony / Acid jazz.

Sep 00. (cd; as SHAKTI) *(<549044-2>)* **REMEMBER SHAKTI (THE BELIEVER)**
– 5 in the morning 6 in the afternoon / Ma po na / Lotus feel / Maya / Anna / Finding the way.

Jun 01. (cd; as REMEMBER SHAKTI) *(<014164-2>)* **SATURDAY NIGHT IN BOMBAY (live)**
– Luki / Shringar / Gringar / Bell' alla.

EmArcy Verve

Jan 04. (cd) *(9801075) <11370-2>* **THIEVES AND POETS** Oct03
– Thieves and poets (pt.1-3) / My foolish heart / The dolphin / Stella by starlight / My romance.

– compilations, others, etc. –

Oct 75. (d-lp) *Polydor; (2675 091)* **IN RETROSPECT** –

Jun 80. (lp/c) *C.B.S.; (CBS/40 84232)* **THE BEST OF THE MAHAVISHNU ORCHESTRA**
(cd-iss. Jan92 on 'Columbia-Legacy'; 468 226-2)

Jan 81. (lp/c) *C.B.S.; (CBS/40 84455)* **THE BEST OF JOHN McLAUGHLIN** [ ] [ ]
– A love supreme / New York on my mind / The dark prince / La danse du bonheur / Friendship / Face to face / The unknown dissident / Lotus feet.

1989. (cd) *Verve; (516 114-2)* **COMPACT JAZZ: JOHN McLAUGHLIN** [ ] [–]

Apr 91. (cd/c/lp) *Columbia; <467010-2/-4/-1>* **JOHN McLAUGHLIN – GREATEST HITS** [–] [ ]

Oct 91. (cd) *Castle; (CCSCD 305)* **JOHN McLAUGHLIN & THE MAHAVISHNU ORCHESTRA: THE COLLECTION** [ ] [–]

Don McLEAN

Born: 2 Oct'45, New Rochelle, New York, USA. Having been a club singer from 1963, he acquired a residency at Lena's bar in 1968, and was dubbed 'The Hudson River Troubadour'. The following year, he was invited to join PETE SEEGER on his expedition tour of the Hudson river. This 6-week journey involved over 25 concerts at various riverside destinations, and made people aware of the river's industrial pollution. In 1970, McLEAN's efforts were finally rewarded, when 'Mediarts' released his debut lp, 'TAPESTRY'. Although the album failed to chart, PERRY COMO scored with a cover of one of the tracks, 'AND I LOVE YOU SO', while McLEAN's soft, pastel-shaded style presumably inspired the songwriting team of Norman Gimbel and Charles Fox to pen the haunting 'Killing Me Softly' (a massive hit for ROBERTA FLACK and later The FUGEES) in his honour. Later that year, McLEAN's enduring BUDDY HOLLY tribute, 'AMERICAN PIE', almost provided him with a transatlantic No.1 while the album of the same name achieved similar success and spawned a UK No.1 hit in 'VINCENT', a tribute to another of McLEAN's heros, painter, Vincent Van Gogh. These two huge chart hits became something of an albatross round the singer's neck, McLEAN spending the rest of the decade attempting to distance himself from the success. 'DON McLEAN' (1973) and 'HOMELESS BROTHER' (1974) continued his socially aware balladeering, although his profile remained low for much of the 70's. A new deal with 'E.M.I.' ('Millennium' in the States) brought a brief period of chart action at the turn of the decade when he again topped the UK singles lists with a version of Roy Orbison's 'CRYING'. Since, then, however, McLEAN has moved increasingly into C&W and easy listening territory, his last recording to date being 1989's 'FOR THE MEMORIES'. • **Covered:** EVERYDAY (Buddy Holly) / CRYING IN THE CHAPEL (Elvis Presley) / MULE SKINNER BLUES (Fendermen) / SUNSHINE LIFE FOR ME (George Harrison) / FOOLS PARADISE (Linsley – Petty – LeGlaire) / GOING FOR THE GOLD (C.Bowder – J.W. Ryles) / MOUNTAINS OF MOURNE (P. French – H. Collinson) / SINCE I DON'T HAVE YOU (Skyliners) / LOVE HURTS (Everly Brothers) / etc. Albums 'PLAYIN' FAVOURITES', 'LOVE TRACKS' & 'FOR THE MEMORIES VOLUMES 1 & 2' were collections of other people's material.

Album rating: TAPESTRY (*5) / AMERICAN PIE (*8) / DON McLEAN (*6) / PLAYIN' FAVORITES (*4) / HOMELESS BROTHER (*5) / SOLO (*4) / PRIME TIME (*4) / CHAIN LIGHTNING (*5) / BELIEVERS (*4) / DOMINION (*3) / DON McLEAN'S GREATEST HITS – THEN AND NOW compilation (*6) / THE VERY BEST OF DON McLEAN compilation (*7) / FOR THE MEMORIES (*6) / HEADROOM (*3) / RIVER OF LOVE (*4) / AMERICAN PIE – THE GREATEST HITS compilation (*8)

DON McLEAN – vocals, guitar (with session people)

not iss. Mediarts

Feb 71. (7") *<108>* **CASTLES IN THE AIR. / AND I LOVE YOU SO** [–] [ ]

Feb 71. (lp) *<none>* **TAPESTRY** [–] [ ]
– Castles in the air / General store / Magdalene lane / Tapestry / Respectable / Orphans of wealth / Three flights up / And I love you so / Bad girl / Circus song / No reason for your dreams. *<US re-dist.Feb72 on 'United Artists'; 5522> (UK-iss.Jun72 on 'United Artists'; UAS 29350)* – hit No.16. *(re-iss. Sep84 on 'Fame'; FA41 3107-1) (cd-iss. Jul94 on 'Beat Goes On'; BGOCD 232)*

U.A. U.A.

Sep 71. (7") *<50796>* **AND I LOVE YOU SO. / CASTLES IN THE AIR** [–] [ ]

Nov 71. (7";w-drawn) *(UP 35323) <50856>* **AMERICAN PIE. / EMPTY CHAIRS** [–] [–]

Jan 72. (7") *(UP 35325) <50856>* **AMERICAN PIE (part 1). / (part 2)** [2] Nov71 [1]
(re-iss. Jan84 + Sep86)

Feb 72. (lp) *(UAS 29285) <5535>* **AMERICAN PIE** [3] Nov71 [1]
– American pie (parts 1 & 2) / Till tomorrow / Vincent / Crossroads / Winterwood / Empty chairs / Everybody loves me, baby / Sister Fatima / The grave / Babylon. *(re-iss. May81 on 'Greenlight'; GO 2004) (re-iss. May82 on 'Fame' lp/c; FA/TC-FA 3023) (cd-iss. May88; CDFA 3023)*

Apr 72. (7") *(UP 35359) <50887>* **VINCENT. / CASTLES IN THE AIR** [1] Mar72 [12]

Jan 73. (7") *(UP 35481) <51100>* **DREIDEL. / BRONCO BILL'S LAMENT** [ ] Dec72 [21]

Jan 73. (lp/c) *(UAS 29299) <5651>* **DON McLEAN** [ ] Dec72 [23]
– If we try / Narcisissma / Dreidel / Bronco Bill's lament / Birthday song / The pride parade / The more you pay / Falling through time / On the Amazon / Oh my what a shame. *(cd-iss. Mar95 on 'Beat Goes On'; BGOCD 246)*

Mar 73. (7") *(UP 35519)* **EVERYDAY. / THE MORE YOU PAY (THE MORE IT'S WORTH)** [38] [–]

Mar 73. (7") *<206>* **IF WE TRY. / THE MORE YOU PAY (THE MORE IT'S WORTH)** [–] [58]

Oct 73. (7"m) *(UP 35607)* **MOUNTAINS O' MOURNE. / MEDLEY (BILL CHEETHAM – OLD JOE CLARK)** [ ] [–]

Nov 73. (lp/c) *(UAG/UAC 29528) <LA 161>* **PLAYIN' FAVOURITES** [42] [ ]
– Sittin' on top of the world / Living with the blues / Mountains O'mourne / Fool's paradise / Love o love / Medley:- (Bill Cheetham – Old Joe Clark) / Ancient history / Over the mountains / Lovesick blues / New mule skinner blues / Happy trails. *(re-iss. 1989 on 'Beat Goes On'; BGO 21) (cd-iss. Jun95; BGOCD 21)*

Mar 74. (7") *(UP 35661)* **FOOL'S PARADISE. / HAPPY TRAILS** [ ] [–]

Jun 74. (7") *<541>* **NEW MULE SKINNER BLUES. / SITTIN' ON TOP OF THE WORLD** [–] [ ]

Nov 74. (lp/c) *(UAG/UAC 29646) <315>* **HOMELESS BROTHER** [ ] [ ]
– Winter has me in its grip / La la love you / Homeless brother / Sunshine life for me (sail away Raymond) / The legend of Andrew McCrew / Wonderful baby / We have lived / Great big man / Tangled (like a spider in her hair) / Crying in the chapel / Did you know. *(cd-iss. Nov94 on 'Beat Goes On'; BGOCD 247)*

Apr 75. (7") *<579>* **HOMELESS BROTHER. / LA LA I LOVE YOU** [–] [ ]

Jun 75. (7") *<614>* **WONDERFUL BABY. / BIRTHDAY SONG** [–] [93]

Jun 75. (7") *(UP 35764)* **WONDERFUL BABY. / HOMELESS BROTHER** [ ] [–]

Sep 76. (d-lp) *(UAD 60139) <LA 652>* **SOLO (live)** [ ] [ ]
– Magdalene lane / Masters of war / Wonderful baby / Where were you bany / Empty chairs / Geordie's lost his penker / Babylon / And I love you so / MacTavish is dead / Cripple creek / New mule skinner blues / Great big man / Bronco Bill's lament / Happy trails / Circus song / Birthday song / On the Amazon / American pie / Over the waterfall / Arkansas traveller / Homeless brother / Castles in the air / Three flights up / Lovesick blues / Winter has me in its grip / The legend of Andrew McCrew / Dreidel / Vincent / Till tomorrow. *(d-cd-iss. Nov95 on 'Beat Goes On'; BGOCD 300)*

EMI Int. Arista

Sep 77. (7") <> **PRIME TIME. / THE STATUE** [–] [ ]

Nov 77. (lp) *(INS 3011) <4149>* **PRIME TIME** [ ] Jun77 [ ]
– Prime time / The statue / Jump / Redwing / The wrong thing to do / The pattern is broken / When love begins / Colour TV blues / Building my body / Down the road / Sally Ann / When one good thing goes bad / South of the border (down Mexico way).

Nov 77. (7") **PRIME TIME. / REDWING** [ ] [–]

Jan 78. (7") *(INT 549)* **WHEN LOVE BEGINS. / COLOUR TV BLUES** [ ] [ ]

EMI Int. Millennium

Feb 79. (7") *(INT 575)* **IT DOESN'T MATTER ANYMORE. / IF WE TRY** [ ] [ ]

Mar 79. (lp) *(INS 3025)* <7756> **CHAIN LIGHTNING** [ ] [ ]
– Words and music / Crying / It's just the sun / Lotta lovin' / Your cheating heart / Wonderful night / It doesn't matter anymore / Since I don't have you / Genesis (in the beginning) / It's a beautiful life. *(UK re-dist.May80, hit No. 19) <US re-iss. Feb81, hit No.28>*

Apr 79. (7") *(INT 588)* **WORDS AND MUSIC. / YOUR CHEATING HEART** [ ] [–]

E.M.I. Millennium

Mar 80. (7") *(EMI 5051)* <11799> **CRYING. / GENESIS (IN THE BEGINNING)** [1] Jan81 [5]

Jul 80. (7") *(EMI 5094)* **SINCE I DON'T HAVE YOU. / IT'S A BEAUTIFUL LIFE** [ ] [–]

Apr 81. (7") <1804> **SINCE I DON'T HAVE YOU. / YOUR CHEATING HEART** [–] [23]

Jul 81. (7") <11809> **IT'S JUST THE SUN. / WORDS AND MUSIC** [–] [83]

Jan 82. (7") *(EMI 5258)* <11819> **CASTLES IN THE AIR. / CRAZY EYES** [47] Oct81 [36]

Jan 82. (lp/c) *(EMC/TC-EMC 3396)* <7762> **BELIEVERS** [ ] Nov81 [ ]
– Castles in the air / Love hurts / Jerusalem / Crazy eyes / Love letters / Sea cruise / I tune the world out / Isn't it strange / Left for dead on the road of love / Believers / Sea man.

Nov 82. (7") **JERUSALEM. / LEFT FOR DEAD ON THE ROAD OF LOVE** [–] [ ]

Nov 82. (7") *(EMI 5356)* **THE VERY THOUGHT OF YOU. / LEFT FOR DEAD ON THE ROAD OF LOVE** [ ] [–]

Feb 83. (d-lp/d-c) *(DOM/TC-DOM 82)* **DOMINION (live)** [ ] [–]
– It's just the sun / Building my body / Wonderful baby / The very thought of you / Fool's paradise / You're so square (baby I don't care) / You have lived / The statue / Prime time / American pie / Left for dead on the road of love / Believers / Sea man / It's a beautiful life / Chain lightning / Crazy eyes / La la I love you / Dream lover / Crying / Vincent.

Apr 87. (7") **HE'S GOT YOU. /** [–] [ ]

Apr 87. (cd) *(CDP 746586-2)* **DON McLEAN'S GREATEST HITS – THEN AND NOW** (part compilation) [ ] [–]
– He's got you / American pie / To have and to hold / Castles in the air / But she loves me / Superman's ghost / Vincent / And I love you so / Crying / Don't burn the bridge.

Capitol Capitol

Dec 87. (7") <44098> **YOU CAN'T BLAME THE TRAIN. / PERFECT LOVE** [–] [ ]

Jun 88. (7") <44186> **LOVE IN THE HEART. / EVERY DAY'S A MIRACLE** [–] [ ]

Sep 88. (7") <44258> **IT'S NOT YOUR FAULT. / EVENTUALLY** [–] [ ]

Nov 89. (lp/c/cd) *(1711330)* **FOR THE MEMORIES** [ ] [ ]
– Don't / Crazy / Travelin' man / You don't know me / Sittin' in the balcony / Wonderful world / I can't help it / Maybe baby / White sports coat / If I only had a match / But beautiful / Over the weekend / Someone to watch over me / Somebody loves me / Count your blessings / It had to be you / Not a moment too soon / Change partners / Nobody knows you when you're down and out / Stardust.

Curb Curb

Oct 91. (cd) *(469170-2)* <77427> **HEADROOM** [ ] [ ]
– Headroom / Fashion victim / 1967 / Infinity / One in a row / You who love the truth / Lady in waiting / Have you seen me / Siamese twins (joined at the heart) / Brand new world.

Nov 95. (cd) *(CURCD 19)* <77791> **THE RIVER OF LOVE** [ ] Oct95 [ ]
– The river of love / You're my little darlin' / If I hadn't met you / Better still / You got a way about you, baby / Angry words / This little girl (daddy-o) / Planet noise / From a beautiful star / Little cowboy / My love was true.

– compilations, others, etc. –

on 'United Artists' unless mentioned otherwise

1974. (7") **VINCENT. / DREIDEL** [–] [ ]

Jun 78. (7") **AND I LOVE YOU SO. / VINCENT** [ ] [ ]

Aug 80. (lp/c) *(UAG/UAC 30314)* **THE VERY BEST OF DON McLEAN** [4] [–]

Sep 88. (lp/c) *Music For Pleasure; (MFP/TC-MFP 5836)* **LOVE TRACKS** [ ] [–]

Oct 89. (cd/c/lp) *E.M.I.; (CD/TC+/EMS 1346)* **AND I LOVE YOU SO** [ ] [ ]

1990. (cd/c/lp) *Goldcastle;* **GREATEST HITS LIVE! (live 1980)** [ ] [ ]

Nov 91. (cd/c) *Manhattan; (CD/TC MTL 1065)* **THE BEST OF DON McLEAN** [ ] [ ]
– American pie / Castles in the air (1981 version) / Dreidel / Winterwood / Everyday / Sister Fatima / Empty chairs / The birthday song / Wonderful baby / La la I love you / Vincent / Crossroads / And I love you so / Fool's Paradise / If we try / Mountains of Mourne / The grave / Respectable / Going for the gold / Crying. *(cd+=)* – Bronco Bill's lament / Oh my what a shame / If we try / Babylon / Love in my heart.

Aug 91. (c-s/7") *Liberty;* **AMERICAN PIE. / VINCENT** [ ] [–]
(cd-s+=) – Castles in the air.

Nov 94. (cd) *BR Music; (BX 417-2)* **CRYING** [ ] [–]

Oct 97. (cd) *Hip-O;* <40074> **CHRISTMAS DREAMS** [–] [ ]

Apr 00. (cd/c) *Liberty; (525847-2/-4)* **AMERICAN PIE – THE GREATEST HITS** [30] [–]

□ G.W. McLENNAN (see under ⇒ GO-BETWEENS)

Ian McNABB

Born: ROBERT IAN McNABB, 3 Nov'60, Liverpool, England. After a spell with CITY LIGHTS, then SUNSET BOULEVARD, he formed The ICICLE WORKS in 1979 with CHRIS LAYHE and CHRIS SHARROCK. A cassingle appeared on 'Probe' in 1981, followed a year later by their vinyl debut 'NIRVANA', the single surfacing on manager Tony Barwood's 'Troll Kitchen' label. After their classy 45, 'BIRDS FLY' won over numerous indie legions, they moved upstairs in 1983 to 'Beggars Banquet' and immediately made an impact in the Top 20 with 'LOVE IS A WONDERFUL COLOUR'. A re-issue of 'BIRDS FLY (WHISPER TO A SCREAM)', didn't fare as well, although it surprisingly broke them into the US Top 40. Their eponymous debut album also cracked the American market having already gone Top 30 in the UK. Still sounding SCOTT WALKER-ish at this early stage, McNABB (complete with attached microphone gadget) was a compelling frontman for this college circuit power-rock trio. Follow-up set, 'THE SMALL PRICE OF A BICYCLE' (1985), featured a number of good reasons ('SEVEN HORSES' and 'ALL THE DAUGHTERS' for starters) why they deserved promotion from Rock's second division, while 'IF YOU WANT TO DEFEAT YOUR ENEMY SING HIS SONG' (1987) finally gave them a UK Top 30 album. The following year, 'BLIND' also scraped into the Top 40, although this was their final effort for the label having signed to 'Epic'. Major label status did them no favours, the disappointing 'PERMANENT DAMAGE' seeing a slide in their popularity and leading to them being dropped. McNABB was virtually left in the cold, that is until 'Way Cool' released his debut solo single, 'GREAT DREAMS OF HEAVEN' in 1991. This was closely followed by another independently released 45, McNABB's deserved break coming the following year when ANDREW LAUDER signed him to his 'This Way Up' label. Early in 1993, McNABB was back in the album charts, 'TRUTH & BEAUTY' nearly making the UK Top 50. He subsequently realised one of his longheld musical dreams when he secured the services of the legendary CRAZY HORSE, initially for live work before going into the studio to record a whole album together. The resulting 'HEAD LIKE A ROCK' (1994), was short-listed for a Mercury Music Award, his critical rehabilitation now complete. In 1996, McNABB released his third solo set, 'MERSEYBEAST', his second consecutive Top 30 achievement and a worthy addition to his increasingly impressive back catalogue. After the latter's full-frontal roots-pop assault, the singer/songwriter stripped things right down to basics for the cannily titled 'A PARTY POLITICAL BROADCAST ON BEHALF OF THE EMOTIONAL PARTY' (1998). McNABB's most skeletal recording to date, the album found the singer concentrating on affairs of the heart. Given that the crowd noise was dubbed out, 'LIVE AT LIFE' (2001), ostensibly recorded for a fan-club release, retains a slightly similar feel although the set list, unsurprisingly, is composed of tried and tested McNABB favourites stretching way back to the early days of The ICICLE WORKS. His next set proper (i.e. studio set) was 2001's 'WAIFS AND STRAYS' while 'IAN McNABB' (2002), as its title might imply, was, if not a creative rebirth as such, at least a return to the livewire pop/rock sound he'd made his name with. As ever, the scouse troubadour's guiding musical light is NEIL YOUNG/CRAZY HORSE although for many fans, that's no bad thing, bearing in mind the fact that he's tended to rein in his muse in recent years. • **Songwriters:** Mostly McNABB compositions for ICICLE WORKS except; SEA SONG (Robert Wyatt) / NATURE'S WAY (Spirit) / COLD TURKEY (John Lennon) / INTO THE MYSTIC (Van Morrison) / YOU AIN'T SEEN NOTHIN' YET (Bachman-Turner Overdrive) / SHOULD I STAY OR SHOULD I GO (Clash) / ROCK'N'ROLL (Led Zeppelin) / PRIVATE REVOLUTION (World Party) / ROADHOUSE BLUES (Doors) / TRIAD – CHESTNUT MARE (Byrds) / MR SOUL + FOR WHAT IT'S WORTH (Buffalo Springfield). McNABB covered UNKNOWN LEGEND + THE NEEDLE AND THE DAMAGE DONE (Neil Young) / CAROLINE NO (Brian Wilson). • **Trivia:** In Aug'85, an ICICLE WORKS off-shoot MELTING POT, were supposed to have had a single 'IT MAKES NO DIFFERENCE' issued.

Album rating: Icicle Works: THE ICICLE WORKS (*6) / THE SMALL PRICE OF A BICYCLE (*7) / IF YOU WANT TO DEFEAT YOUR ENEMY SING HIS SONG (*6) / BLIND (*5) / PERMANENT DAMAGE (*5) / THE BEST OF THE ICICLE WORKS compilation (*8) / Ian McNabb: TRUTH & BEAUTY (*6) / HEAD LIKE A ROCK (*8) / MERSEYBEAST (*6) / A PARTY POLITICAL BROADCAST ON BEHALF OF THE EMOTIONAL PARTY (*5) / LIVE AT LIFE (*4) / WAIFS & STRAYS (*5) / IAN McNABB (*5)

ICICLE WORKS

IAN McNABB – vocals, guitar, keyboards / **CHRIS LAYHE** – bass, keyboards, vocals / **CHRIS SHARROCK** – drums, percussion

Probe — not iss.

Mar 81. (c-ep) *(private)* **ASCENDING** [ ] [–]

Troll Kitchen — not iss.

Oct 82. (7"m) *(WORKS 001)* **NIRVANA. / LOVE HUNT / SIROCCO** [ ] [–]

Situation2 — not iss.

Jun 83. (7") *(SIT 22)* **BIRDS FLY (WHISPER TO A SCREAM). / REVERIE GIRL** [ ] [–]
(12"+=) *(SIT 22T)* – Gunboys.

Beggars Banquet — Arista

Oct 83. (7"/7"pic-d) *(BEG 99/+P)* **LOVE IS A WONDERFUL COLOUR. / WATERLINE** [15] [ ]
(ext.12"+=/ext.12"pic-d+=) *(BEG 99 T/TP)* – In the dance the Shamen led.
(d7"++=) *(BEG 99 + ICE 1)* – The Devil on horseback.

Mar 84. (7") *(BEG 108)* **BIRDS FLY (WHISPER TO A SCREAM). / IN THE CAULDRON OF LOVE** [53] [–]
(12"+=) *(BEG 108T)* – Ragweed campaign / Scarecrow.
(12"+=) *(BEG 108TD)* – ('A'-Frantic mix).

Mar 84. (lp/c) *(BEGA/BEGC 50)* *<8202>* **THE ICICLE WORKS** [24] [40]
– Chop the tree / Love is a wonderful colour / Reaping the rich harvest / As the dragonfly flies / Lover's day / In the cauldron of love / Out of season / A factory in the desert / Birds fly (whisper to a scream) / Nirvana. *(cd-iss. Jul86; BEGA 50CD) (re-iss. Jul88 lp/c/cd; BBL/+C 50/+CD)*

Mar 84. (7") *<9155>* **BIRDS FLY (WHISPER TO A SCREAM). / IN THE DANCE THE SHAMEN LED** [–] [37]

Sep 84. (7") *(BEG 119)* **HOLLOW HORSE. / THE ATHEIST** [ ] [–]
(12"+=) *(BEG 119T)* – Nirvana (live).
(12"+=) *(BEG 119TR)* – ('A'remix).

May 85. (7") *(BEG 133)* **ALL THE DAUGHTERS (OF HER FATHER'S HOUSE). / A POCKETFUL OF NOTHING** [ ] [–]
(12"+=) *(BEG 133T)* – Mr. Soul.

Jul 85. (7") *(BEG 142)* **SEVEN HORSES. / SLINGSHOT** [ ] [–]
(d7"+=) *(BEG 142D)* – Beggars legacy / Goin' back.
(12") *(BEG 142T)* – ('A'-American) / ('B'side) / Beggars legacy.

Sep 85. (lp/c) *(BEGA/BEGC 61)* **THE SMALL PRICE OF A BICYCLE** [55] [–]
– Hollow horse / Perambulator / Seven horses / Rapids / Windfall / Assumed sundown / Saint's sojourn / All the daughter's (of her father's horse) / Book of reason / Conscience of kings. *(re-iss. Jan89 lp/c/cd; BBL/+C 61/+CD)*

Oct 85. (7") *(BEG 151)* **WHEN IT ALL COMES DOWN. / (LET'S GO) DOWN TO THE RIVER** [ ] [–]
('A'unabridged-12"+=) *(BEG 151T)* – Cold turkey.

Feb 86. (m-lp/c) *(BEGA/BEGC 71)* **SEVEN SINGLES DEEP** (compilation) [52] [–]
– Hollow horse / Love is a wonderful colour / Birds fly (whisper to a scream) / All the daughters (of her father's house) / When it all comes down / Seven horses / Rapids. *(c+=)* – I never saw my hometown 'til I went around the world / (Let's go) Down to the river / Slingshot / The atheist / Into the mystic / A pocketful of nothing / Goin' back. *(re-iss. Sep88 lp/c/cd; BBL/+C 71/+CD) (cd+=)* – Perambulator / Lover's day / Out of season / Saints sojourn / Nirvana / Conscience of kings.

Beggars Banquet — Beggars Banquet

Jun 86. (7") *(BEG 160)* **UNDERSTANDING JANE. / I NEVER SAW MY HOMETOWN 'TIL I WENT AROUND THE WORLD** [52] [–]
(12"+=) *(BEG 160T)* – Into the mystic.
(d7"+=) *(BEG 160 + ICE 3)* – Hollow horse (live) / You ain't seen nothin' yet (live).
(c-s+=) *(BEG 160C)* – Seven horses (live) / Perambulator (live) / Rapids (live).

Sep 86. (7") *(BEG 172)* **WHO DO YOU WANT FOR YOUR LOVE. / UNDERSTANDING JANE (live)** [54] [–]
(w/ free c-s+=) *(BEG 172F)* – John Geoffrey Muir shopkeeper / Impossibly three lovers.
(12"+=) *(BEG 172T)* – Should I stay or should I go (live) / Roadhouse blues (live).

Dec 86. Situation2; (12"ep) *(SIT 45T)* **UP HERE IN THE NORTH OF ENGLAND. / SEA SONG (Ian McNabb) / NATURE'S WAY / IT MAKES NO DIFFERENCE / WAYLAID (Chis Layhe)** [ ] [–]

Jan 87. (7") *(BEG 181)* **EVANGELINE. / EVERYBODY LOVES TO PLAY THE FOOL** [53] [–]
(12"+=) *(BEG 181T)* – Waiting in the wings / ('A'demo).
(c-s+=) *(BEG 181C)* – It makes no difference / Nature's way / Sea song.

Mar 87. (lp/c)(cd) *(BEGA/BEGC 78)(BEGA 78CD)* *<6447>* **IF YOU WANT TO DEFEAT YOUR ENEMY SING HIS SONG** [28] [ ]
– Hope springs eternal / Travelling chest / Sweet Thursday / Up here in the north of England / Who do you want for your love / When you were mine / Evangeline / Truck driver's lament / Understanding Jane / Walking with a mountain. *(c+=)* – Everybody loves to play the fool / Don't let it rain on my parade. *(cd++=)* – I never saw my hometown 'til went around the world / Into the mystic. *(re-iss. Feb90 lp/c/cd; BBL/+C 78/+CD)*

Nov 87. (7"/s7") *(BEG 203/+S)* **HIGH TIME. / BROKEN HEARTED FOOL** [ ] [–]
(12"+=) *(BEG 203T)* – Travelling chest (live) / Private revolution (live).

Feb 88. (7") *(BEG 208)* **THE KISS OFF. / SURE THING** [ ] [–]
(12"ep/c-ep+=/cd-ep+=) *(BEG IW/+C/CD)* – THE NUMB EP – High time (acoustic) / Whipping boy.

Apr 88. (7") *(BEG 220)* **LITTLE GIRL LOST. / TIN CAN** [59] [–]
(12"+=/pic-cd-s+=) *(BEG 215 T/CD)* – Hot profit gospel / One time.

May 88. (lp/c)(cd) *(IWA/IWC 2)(IWA 2CD)* *<8424>* **BLIND** [40] [ ]
– (intro) Shit creek / Little girl lost / Starry blue-eyed wonder / One true love / Blind / Two two three / What do you want me to do? / Stood before Saint Peter / The kiss off / Here comes trouble / Walk a while with me.

Jun 88. (7") *(BEG 220)* **HERE COMES TROUBLE. / STARRY BLUE-EYED WONDER** [ ] [ ]
(12"+=)(12"box) *(BEG 220T)(IW 3)* – Rock'n'roll (live) / For what it's worth (medley live).

—— **ZAK STARKEY** (b.13 Sep'65, London, England, son of RINGO) – drums repl. LAYHE SHARROCK who joined WILD SWANS + The LA'S /

added **DAVE GREEN** – keyboards / **ROY CORKHILL** – bass (both ex-BLACK)

—— (1989) **IAN and ROY** brought in **DAVE BALDWIN** – keyboards / **MARK REVELL** – guitar, vocals / **PAUL BURGESS** – drums

Epic — Work-Epic

Mar 90. (7") *(WORKS 100)* **MOTORCYCLE RIDER. / TURN ANY CORNER** [73] [ ]
(12"+=/12"etched+=) *(WORKS T/E 100)* – People change.
(cd-s++=) *(WORKS C100)* – Victoria's ghost.
(12") *(WORKS Q100)* – ('A'side) / Let's get loaded / Red lightning.

May 90. (cd/c/lp) *(466 800-2/-4/-1)* **PERMANENT DAMAGE** [ ] [–]
– I still want you / Motorcycle rider / Melanie still hurts / Hope street rag / I think I'm gonna be OK / Baby don't burn / What she did to my mind / One good eye / Permanent damage / Woman on my mind / Looks like rain / Dumb angel.

May 90. (7") *(WORKS 101)* **MELANIE STILL HURTS. / WHEN THE CRYING'S DONE** [ ] [–]
(12"+=) *(WORKS T101)* – Mickey's blue.
(7"ep++=/cd-ep++=) *(WORKS Q/C 101)* – I dreamt I was a beautiful woman.

Jul 90. (7"/c-s) *(WORKS/+M 102)* **I STILL WANT YOU. / I WANT THAT GIRL** [ ] [–]
(12"+=) *(WORKST 102)* – It's gonna rain forever.
(10"++=/cd-ep++=) *(WORKS Q/C 102)* – Sweet disposition.

—— McNABB joined the WILD SWANS briefly before going solo.

– compilations, etc. –

Nov 88. (12"ep) *Nighttracks; (SFNT 015)* **THE EVENING SHOW SESSIONS** (14.11.82) [ ] [–]
– Birds fly (whisper to a scream) / Lover's day / Love hunt / As the dragonfly flies.

Jan 90. (7") *Old Gold; (OG 9918)* **LOVE IS A WONDERFUL COLOUR. / BIRDS FLY (WHISPER TO A SCREAM)** [ ] [–]

Aug 92. (cd)(c) *Beggars Banquet; (BEGA 124CD)(BEGC 124)* **THE BEST OF THE ICICLE WORKS** [60] [–]
– Hollow horse (long version) / Love is a wonderful colour / Birds fly (whisper to a scream) / Understanding Jane ('92 version) / Shit creek / High time (acoustic) / Who do you want for your love? / Evangeline / Little girl lost / When it all comes down ('92 version) / Starry blue eyed wonder / Out of season / The kiss off / Up here in the North of England / Firepower / Blind. *(ltd. w/ free cd 'BEST KEPT SECRET'; BEGA 124CD2) (re-iss. cd Sep95; BBL 124CD)*

Aug 92. (7") *Beggars Banquet; (BEG 262)* **UNDERSTANDING JANE '92. / LITTLE GIRL LOST** [ ] [–]
(12"+=) *(BEG 262T)* – When it all comes down '92 / Firepower.
(cd-s+=) *(BEG 262CD)* – Solid ground / Like weather.

Mar 94. (cd) *Windsong; (<WINCD 053>)* **BBC RADIO 1 LIVE IN CONCERT (live)** [ ] [ ]

Jul 97. (cd) *Dutch East India; <8004>* **THE PEEL SESSIONS** [–] [ ]

IAN McNABB

Way Cool — not iss.

Jun 91. (12"ep/cd-ep) *(WAYCOOL 14 T/CD)* **GREAT DREAMS OF HEAVEN / THAT'S WHY I BELIEVE. / MAKE LOVE TO YOU / POWER OF SONG** [ ] [–]

Fat Cat — not iss.

Oct 91. (12"ep/cd-ep) *(FC 001/+CD)* **THESE ARE THE DAYS. / TRAMS IN AMSTERDAM / GREAT DREAMS OF HEAVEN (acoustic)** [ ] [–]

This Way Up — not iss.

Jan 93. (7") *(WAY 211)* **IF LOVE WAS LIKE GUITARS. / TRAMS IN AMSTERDAM** [67] [–]
(cd-s+=) *(WAY 233)* – Great dreams of Heaven.

Jan 93. (cd/c/d-lp) *(514 378-2/-4/-1)* **TRUTH AND BEAUTY** [51] [–]
– (I go) My own way / These are the days / Great dreams of Heaven / Truth and beauty / I'm game / If love was like guitars / Story of my life / That's why I believe / Trip with me / Make love to you / Presence of the one. *(re-iss. cd/c Apr95; same)*

Mar 93. (7"/c-s) *(WAY 811/844)* **GREAT DREAMS OF HEAVEN. / UNKNOWN LEGEND** [ ] [–]
(12"+=/cd-s+=) *(WAY 822/833)* – I'm game / Caroline no.

Jun 93. (7") *(WAY 1211)* **I'M GAME. / A PIRATE LOOKS AT FORTY** [ ] [–]
(cd-s) *(WAY 1233)* – ('A'side) / What's it all about / ('A'version).

Sep 93. (7"/c-s/cd-s) *(WAY 1611/1644/1655)* **(I GO) MY OWN WAY / PLAY THE HAND THEY DEAL YOU** [ ] [–]
(10"+=/cd-s+=) *(WAY 1688/1633)* – If my daddy could see me now / For you, angel.

—— with **RALPH MOLINA + BILLY TALBOT** (of NEIL YOUNG's CRAZY HORSE) + **MIKE 'TONE' HAMILTON** (of SMITHEREENS)

Jun 94. (7"/c-s) *(WAY 3111/3144)* **YOU MUST BE PREPARED TO DREAM. / THAT'S WHY THE DARKNESS EXISTS** [54] [–]
(12"/cd-s) *(WAY 3122/3133)* – ('A'side) / Sometimes I think about you / Woo yer.
(cd-s) *(WAY 3199)* – ('A'side) / ('A'radio) / Love is a wonderful colour / When it all comes down (both acoustic).

Jul 94. (cd/c) *(522 298-2/-4)* **HEAD LIKE A ROCK** [29] [–]
– Fire inside my soul / You must be prepared to dream / Child inside a father / Still got the fever / Potency / Go into the light / As a life goes by / Sad strange solitary Catholic mystic / This time is forever / May you always. *(cd re-iss. Sep96 on 'Island'; IMCD 233)*

Aug 94. (c-s) *(WAY 3644)* **GO INTO THE LIGHT / TIME YOU WERE IN LOVE** [ ] [–]
(cd-s+=) *(WAY 3633)* – For you, angel.
(12") *(WAY 3622)* – ('A'side) / ('A'-Celestial dub mix) / For you, angel.
(cd-s) *(WAY 3699)* – ('A'side) / I stood before St.Peter / Rock / ('A'-Celestial dub mix).

Apr 96. (7"/c-s) *(WAY 5011/5044)* **DON'T PUT YOUR SPELL ON ME. / DON'T PATRONISE ME** [ ] [–]
(cd-s+=) *(WAY 5033)* – What she did to my mind.

May 96. (cd/c/d-lp) *(524 215-2/-4/-1)* **MERSEYBEAST** [30] [–]
– Merseybeast / Affirmation / Beautiful old mystery / Love's young dream / Camaraderie / Don't put your spell on me / Heydays / Little bit of magic / You stone my soul / Too close to the sun / They settled for less than they wanted / I'm a genius / Available light / Merseybeast (reprise). *(some cd's w/ free cd 'NORTH WEST COAST'; 524 240-2)*

Jun 96. (7") *(WAY 5211)* **MERSEYBEAST. / UP HERE IN THE NORTH OF ENGLAND (demo Jan 86)** [74] [–]
(cd-s+=) *(WAY 5233)* – Permanent damage (demo Sept 88) / Merseybeast (demo March 95).
(cd-s) *(WAY 5266)* – ('A'side) / Pretty boys with big guitars / The slider / Snaked.

—— next with **MIKE SCOTT, ANTHONY THISTLETHWAITE + DANNY THOMPSON**

Fairfield — not iss.

Oct 98. (cd) *(FAIRCD 1)* **A PARTY POLITICAL BROADCAST ON BEHALF OF THE EMOTIONAL PARTY** [ ] [–]
– Sex with someone you love / A guy like me (and a girl like you) / Loveless age / You only get what you deserve / Bloom / The man who can make a woman laugh / Liverpool girl / Absolutely wrong / Little princess / Girls are birds. *(<re+US-iss.Aug01 on 'Castle'; CMRCD 307>)*

Castle — Castle

Aug 01. (cd) *<CMRCD 306> <CMA 689>* **LIVE AT LIFE (live fan club rec. December '99)** [ ] Jan01 [ ]
– Hollow horse / Sex with someone you love / Great dreams of Heaven / Permanent damage / Little girl lost / I'm a genius / One true love / Why are the beautiful so sad? / When it all comes down / A guy like me (and a girl like you) / Fire inside my soul / What she did to my mind / Merseybeast / Camaraderie / Reaping the rich harvest.

—— next with **GEOFF DUGMORE, HENRY PRIESTMAN + DANNY STRITTMATTER**

Evangeline — Evangeline

Oct 01. (cd) *(<GEL 4034>)* **WAIFS & STRAYS** [ ] Nov01 [ ]
– Loveless age / Camaraderie / Fire inside my soul / Gak mummy No.1 / I'm a genius / Me and the Devil / Why are the beautiful so sad? / Misty meadows / Not lost enough to be rescued / Time of my time / Great dreams of Heaven / Nobody say nothin' to no one / You stole my soul / The new golden age.

Castle — not iss.

Apr 02. (cd) *(CMRCD 440)* **IAN McNABB** [ ] [–]
– Livin' proof (miracles can happen) / Whatever it takes / What you wanted / Liverpool girl / If we believe what love can do / Alright with me / Hollywood tears / Open air / Nothin' less than the very best / Hotel stationary / Rockin' for Jesus / Friend of my enemy / Moment in the sun / I wish I was in California.

☐ Tony McPHEE (see under ⇒ GROUNDHOGS)

☐ MC REN (see under ⇒ N.W.A.)

☐ MD.45 (see under ⇒ MEGADETH)

MEAT LOAF

Born: MARVIN LEE ADAY, 27 Sep'48, Dallas, Texas, USA, his nickname given to him after he trod on the toes of his school master. In 1966 he moved to Los Angeles and formed psychedelic-rock outfit POPCORN BLIZZARD, who opened for The WHO, AMBOY DUKES and The STOOGES, before disbanding in early 1969. That year, MEAT LOAF successfully auditioned for the 'Hair' musical, where he met female soul singer STONEY. In 1970, they made a self-titled lp together for 'Rare Earth', although he soon rejoined the 'Hair' tour in Cleveland, the behemoth subsequently taking the role of Buddha in the musical 'Rainbow'. A year and a half later, he starred in JIM STEINMAN's Broadway musical 'More Than You Deserve', a partnership that was to flower, both creatively and commercially, as the decade wore on. The following year, MEAT LOAF acted/sang in Richard O'Brien's Broadway musical 'The ROCKY HORROR PICTURE SHOW', which was soon made into a film with MEAT LOAF taking the part of EDDIE. He and STEINMAN went on to tour with the comedy show 'National Lampoon', MEAT LOAF playing the part of a priest in the 'Rockabye Hamlet' sketch. Keeping his finger in the rock'n'roll pie, he contributed vocals to TED NUGENT's 1976 set, 'Free For All'. Early the following year, the big man got together again in New York with STEINMAN, starting work on the 'NEVERLAND' project. They signed to 'R.C.A.', although the partnership changed stables (to 'Epic' affiliated label 'Cleveland International') after it was clear the label didn't want to work with producer TODD RUNDGREN. Late in 1977, they finally unleashed the finished article as 'BAT OUT OF HELL', and with heavy tours, the record eventually made the US Top 20 (also hitting the UK Top 10). A bombastic rock opera, the album shook up the punk/new wave dominated music scene, its heavyweight, anthemic choruses and vein-bursting vocal histrionics reclaiming the territory that "rock" had lost in the past few years. It crossed over to such an extent that it became part of nearly everyone's record collection, selling millions in the process and residing in the charts for over eight years. Songs such as 'YOU TOOK THE WORDS RIGHT OUT OF MY MOUTH', 'TWO OUT OF THREE AIN'T BAD', 'PARADISE BY THE DASHBOARD LIGHT' and the epic title track, took rock'n'roll to melodramatic new heights, its crescendos gripping and lulling the listener into submission. Sweating like a builder's arse crack, MEAT LOAF strained and contorted his way through each song with a theatrical passion as yet unwitnessed in rock. However, it wasn't without a price, the hairy one subsequently suffering throat and alcohol problems over the course of the next few years as the pressures of fame took their toll. Nevertheless, he starred in the film 'Roadie' (1980), alongside DEBBIE HARRY and her group BLONDIE. Impatient with MEAT LOAF's problems, STEINMAN released the 'BAD FOR GOOD' (May '81) album under his own name, although this was intended for MEAT. The long-awaited MEAT LOAF follow-up, 'DEAD RINGER FOR LOVE' was finally issued four months later, and although it hit the top of the charts, it only managed to scrape into US Top 50. Having used ELLEN FOLEY as a vocal foil on his last meisterwork, MEAT LOAF employed the powerful tonsils of CHER on the title track (also a hit single). With STEINMAN out of the picture, MEAT LOAF concentrated his activities in Britain, where he soon became a widely known celebrity, losing a few stone in the process. While mid 80's albums like 'MIDNIGHT AT THE LOST AND FOUND' (1983), 'BAD ATTITUDE' (1984) and 'BLIND BEFORE I STOP' (1986) did little to improve his critical standing, fans still came out in their droves for live appearances. Inevitably perhaps, MEAT LOAF and STEINMAN eventually got back together, 'Virgin' (having just lost MIKE OLDFIELD's massive selling 'Tubular Bells II' to 'Warners') being the lucky backer of a million-selling 1993 sequel, funnily enough called 'BAT OUT OF HELL II – BACK INTO HELL'. This provided the once 20-stone rocker with a return to transatlantic chart domination, the accompanying single 'I'D DO ANYTHING FOR YOU (BUT I WON'T DO THAT)'. This rejuvenated the singer's flagging career, a British beef ban unable to prevent MEAT LOAF (and new writer DIANE WARREN) once again making the UK Top 3 with the 'WELCOME TO THE NEIGHBORHOOD' album in 1995; a best of package hit the UK Top 20 late in 1998. MEAT was back in 2003 with 'COULDN'T HAVE SAID IT BETTER', MOTLEY CRUE's NIKKI SIXX (together with writing partner JAMES MICHAEL) surprisingly claiming the lion's share of the writing credits. The SIXX material most closely followed the hell-for-leather grandiloquence of MEAT in full flight, while the inclusion of Bob Dylan's 'FOREVER YOUNG' certainly made for interesting listening. • **Songwriters:** MEATLOAF co-wrote w/ PAUL CHRISTIE + others in 1983. P. JACOBS + S. DURKEE took the bulk of the load in 1984. Covered; MARTHA (Tom Waits) / OH WHAT A BEAUTIFUL MORNING (Rogers-Hammerstein) / WHERE ANGELS SING (Davis) / WHATEVER HAPPENED TO SATURDAY NIGHT (Richard O'Brien) / COME TOGETHER + LET IT BE (Beatles).

Album rating: BAT OUT OF HELL (*10) / DEAD RINGER (*6) / MIDNIGHT AT THE LOST AND FOUND (*5) / HITS OUT OF HELL compilation (*7) / BAD ATTITUDE (*6) / MEAT LOAF LIVE AT WEMBLEY (*5) / BLIND BEFORE I STOP (*5) / BAT OUT OF HELL II: BACK INTO HELL (*6) / WELCOME TO THE NEIGHBOURHOOD (*4) / THE VERY BEST OF MEAT LOAF compilation (*7) / COULDN'T HAVE SAID IT BETTER (*5)

STONEY AND MEATLOAF

STONEY – vocals (who later joined BOB SEGER)

Date	Release	Rare Earth	Rare Earth
Apr 71.	(7") *<5027-F>* **WHAT YOU SEE IS WHAT YOU GET. / LADY OF MINE**	–	71
Jun 71.	(7") *<5033-F>* **IT TAKES ALL KINDS OF PEOPLE. / THE WAY YOU DO THE THINGS YOU DO**	–	
Oct 71.	(7") *(RES 103)* **WHAT YOU SEE IS WHAT YOU GET. / THE WAY YOU DO THE THINGS YOU DO** *(re-iss. Mar79 on 'Prodigal'; PROD 10)*		–
Oct 72.	(lp) *(SRE 3005)* *<R 528-1>* **STONEY AND MEATLOAF** – Jimmy Bell / She waits by the window / It takes all kind of people / Stone heart / Who is the leader of the people / What you see is what you get / Kiss me again / Sunshine (where's Heaven) / Jessica White / Lady be mine / Everything under the sun. *<(re-iss. Oct78/Mar79 as 'MEATLOAF (FEATURING STONEY AND MEATLOAF)' on 'Prodigal'; P7 10029> (PDL 2010) (re-iss. Oct81 c; CPDL 2010) (re-iss. 1986 as 'MEAT LOAF' on 'Motown'; ZL 72217)*		Oct71

— Returned to feature in the musical 'Hair' (plus see above biography).

MEAT LOAF

Date	Release	not iss.	R.S.O.
1974.	(7") *<RS 407>* **MORE THAN YOU DESERVE. / PRESENCE OF THE LORD**	–	
		Ode	Ode
Oct 75.	(7"w-drawn) *(ODS 66304)* **CLAP YOUR HANDS AND STAMP YOUR FEET. / STAND BY ME** (above was recorded in 1973)		

— **MEAT LOAF** – vocals / **JIM STEINMAN** – composer, keyboards, percussion / **TODD RUNDGREN** – multi- / **ROY BITTAN** – piano, keyboards / **MAX WEINBERG** – drums / **KASIM SULTAN** – bass / **ROGER POWELL** – synth. / **ELLEN FOLEY + RORY DODD** – back.vox

Epic Epic

Jan 78. (lp/c)(pic-lp) *(EPC/40 82419)(EPC11 82419) <34974>* **BAT OUT OF HELL** 9 Oct77 14
– You took the words right out of my mouth (hot summer night) / Heaven can wait / All revved up with no place to go / Two out of three ain't bad / Bat out of hell / For crying out loud / Paradise by the dashboard light: (I)- Paradise, (II)- Let me sleep on it, (II)- Praying for the end of time. *(cd-iss. 1983; EPCCDEPC 82419) (re-iss. pic-cd Dec90; 467732-2) (re-iss. Jul91 lp/c+=; EPC/40 82419)* – Dread ringer for love. *(hit UK No.14, re-entered Jan92, peaked again at No.24-Jul92, returned to hit UK No.19 Autumn 1993) (cd re-iss. Jul95; 480411-2) (lp re-iss. Jun99 on 'Simply Vinyl'; SVLP 86)*

Mar 78. (7") *(SEPC 5980) <50467>* **YOU TOOK THE WORDS RIGHT OUT OF MY MOUTH. / FOR CRYING OUT LOUD** 33 Jan78

Jul 78. (7") *(SEPC 6281) <50513>* **TWO OUT OF THREE AIN'T BAD. / FOR CRYING OUT LOUD** 32 Mar78 11

Aug 78. (7") *<50588>* **PARADISE BY THE DASHBOARD LIGHT. / "BAT" OVERTURE** – 39

Sep 78. (7") *(SEPC 6797)* **PARADISE BY THE DASHBOARD LIGHT. / ALL REVVED UP WITH NO PLACE TO GO** –

Nov 78. (7") *<50634>* **YOU TOOK THE WORDS RIGHT OUT OF MY MOUTH. / PARADISE BY THE DASHBOARD LIGHT** – 39

Jan 79. (7"/ext.12"red) *(SEPC/+12 7018)* **BAT OUT OF HELL. / HEAVEN CAN WAIT** 15 –
(re-iss. Apr81)

—— MEAT LOAF now brought in many session people, including **CHER** on title track.

Sep 81. (lp/c)(pic-lp) *(EPC/40 83645)(EPC11 83645) <36007>* **DEAD RINGER** 1 45
– Peel out / I'm gonna love her for both of us / More than you deserve / I'll kill you if you don't come back / Read 'em and weep / Nocturnal pleasure / Dead ringer for love / Everything is permitted. *(re-iss. Nov85 lp/c; EPC 32692) (cd-iss. Nov87; EPCCD 83645)*

Sep 81. (7") *(EPCA 1580) <02490>* **I'M GONNA LOVE HER FOR BOTH OF US. / EVERYTHING IS PERMITTED** 62 84

Nov 81. (7"/7"pic-d) *(EPCA/+11 1697)* **DEAD RINGER FOR LOVE. / MORE THAN YOU DESERVE** 5 –
(re-iss. Aug88)

Mar 82. (7") *(EPCA 2012)* **READ 'EM AND WEEP. / EVERYTHING IS PERMITTED** –
(12"+=) *(EPCA 12-2012)* – (interview with MEAT LOAF).

Apr 82. (7") *<02607>* **READ 'EM AND WEEP. / PEEL OUT** –

1982. (12"ep-clear) *(EPCA 12-2251)* **MEAT LOAF IN EUROPE '82 (live)** –
– Two out of three ain't bad / You took the words right out of my mouth / I'm gonna love her for both of us / Dead ringer for love.

May 83. (lp)(c) *(EPC 25243)(450360-4)* **MIDNIGHT AT THE LOST AND FOUND** 7
– Razor's edge / Midnight at the lost and found / Wolf at your door / Keep driving / The promised land / You never can be too sure about the girl / Priscilla / Don't you look at me like that / If you really want to / Fallen angel. *(re-iss. Jan87 lp/c/cd; EPC 450360-1/-4/-2)*

May 83. (7") *(A 3357)* **IF YOU REALLY WANT TO. / KEEP DRIVING** 59 –
(12"+=/12"pic-d+=) *(TA/WA 3357)* – Lost love.

Jul 83. (7"/7"pic-d) *(A/WA 3511)* **RAZOR'S EDGE. / YOU NEVER CAN BE TOO SURE ABOUT THE GIRL** –
(12"+=) *(TA 3511)* – Don't look at me like that.

Sep 83. (7"/7"pic-d) *(A/WA 3748)* **MIDNIGHT AT THE LOST AND FOUND. / FALLEN ANGEL** 17 –
(d7"+=/12"+=) *(DA/TA 3748)* – Bat out of Hell (live) / Dead ringer for love (live).

Jan 84. (7") *(A 4080) <04028>* **RAZOR'S EDGE (remix). / PARADISE BY THE DASHBOARD LIGHT** 41
(12"+=) *(TA 4080)* – Read 'em and weep.

Arista R.C.A.

Sep 84. (7"/7"sha-pic-d) *(ARIS T/DP 585)* **MODERN GIRL. / TAKE A NUMBER** 17 –
(d7"/12")(12"pic-d) *(ARIST12 585/+D)(ARIPD12 585)* – ('A'-Freeway mix) / ('B'extended).

Nov 84. (lp)(c)(cd) *(206619)(406610)(610187) <5451>* **BAD ATTITUDE** 8 May85 74
– Bad attitude / Modern girl / Nowhere fast / Surf's up / Piece of the action / Jumpin' the gun / Cheatin' in your dreams / Don't leave your mark on me / Sailor to a siren. *(re-iss. May86 on 'Fame' lp/c; FA41/TCFA 3150) (cd re-iss. Jun88 & Feb94; 259049)*

Nov 84. (7"/7"s/7"g-f/7"sha-pic-d) *(ARI ST/PU/SG/SD 600)* **NOWHERE FAST. / CLAP YOUR HANDS** 67 –
(ext.12"+=) *(ARIST12 600)* – Stand by me.

Mar 85. (12") *<14050>* **MODERN GIRL. / ('A'long version)** –

Mar 85. (7"/7"sha-pic-d) *(ARIS T/D 603)* **PIECE OF THE ACTION. / SAILOR TO A SIREN** 47
(d7"+=) *(ARIST 603 + FS603)* – Bat out of Hell (live) / Modern Girl (US remix).
(ext.12"+=) *(ARIST12 603)* – Bad attitude.
(ext.d12"++=) *(ARIST12 603 + FS12 603)* – (see d7"above FS603).

May 85. (7") *<14101>* **(GIVE ME THE FUTURE WITH A) MODERN GIRL. / SAILOR TO A SIREN** –

Aug 85. (7") *<14149>* **SURF'S UP. / JUMPIN' THE GUN** –
(12") *<14141>* – ('A'extended) / ('A'side) / Bad attitude.

Aug 86. (7"/7"sha-pic-d/7"white-sha-pic-d/12"/12"pic-d; by MEAT LOAF and JOHN PARR) *(ARIST 666/+P/XP)* **ROCK'N'ROLL MERCENARIES. / REVOLUTIONS PER MINUTE** 31 –

Sep 86. (lp/c/cd) *(207/407/257 741)* **BLIND BEFORE I STOP** 28
– Execution day / Rock'n'roll mercenaries / Getting away with murder / One more kiss / Night of the soft parade / Blind before I stop / Burning down / Standing on the outside / Masculine / Man and a woman / Special girl / Rock'n'roll hero. *(re-iss. cd Feb94; 259741)*

Nov 86. (7"/7"sha-pic-d)(10") *(ARIST 683/+P)(ARIST10 683) <89340>* **GETTING AWAY WITH MURDER. / ROCK'N'ROLL HERO**
(12") *(ARIST12 683)* – ('A'-Scot free mix)/ ('B'extended).

Feb 87. (7"/12") *(RIS/+T 3)* **BLIND BEFORE I STOP. / EXECUTION DAY** –
(12"+=) *(RIST 3R)* – Dead ringer for love (live) / Paradise by the dashboard light (live).

Mar 87. (7") *<89303>* **ROCK'N'ROLL MERCENARY. / EXECUTION DAY** –

Apr 87. (7") *(RIS 14)* **SPECIAL GIRL. / ONE MORE KISS** –
(12"+=/cd-s+=) *(RIS T/CD 14)* – Dead ringer for love (live) / Paradise by the dashboard light (live).

Oct 87. (7"/ext.12") *(RIS/+T 41)* **BAT OUT OF HELL (live). / MAN AND A WOMAN** –

Nov 87. (lp/c/cd) *(208/408/258 599)* **LIVE AT WEMBLEY (live)** 60 –
– Blind before I stop / Rock & roll mercenaries / Took the words / Midnight at the lost and found / Modern girl / Paradise by the dashboard light / Two out of three ain't bad / Bat out of Hell. *(free 12"ep/cd+=)* – Masculine / Rock'n'roll medley: Johnny B. Goode – Slow down – Jailhouse rock – Blue suede shoes.

—— now with **MRS LOUD** – female vocal / **ROY BITTAN & BILL PAYNE** – piano / **TIM PIERCE & EDDIE MARTINEZ** – guitar / **KENNY ARONOFF & RICK MAROTTA & BRIAN MEAGHER & JIMMY BRALOWER** – drums / **STEVE BUSLOWE** – bass / **PAT THRALL** – guitar solo / **LENNY PICKETT** – sax / **JEFF BOVA** – synth. & prog. / **etc.**

Virgin M.C.A.

Sep 93. (cd/c/lp) *(CDV/TCV/V 2710) <10699>* **BAT OUT OF HELL II: BACK INTO HELL** 1 1
– I'd do anything for love (but I won't do that) / Life is a lemon and I want my money back / Rock and roll dreams come through / It just won't quit / Out of the frying pan (and into the fire) / Objects in the rear view mirror may appear closer than they are / Wasted youth / Everything louder than everything else / Good girls go to heaven (bad girls go everywhere) / Back into Hell / Lost boys and golden girls. *(ltd.pic-lp Dec93; VP 2710) (re-iss. Nov95; same)*

Sep 93. (c-s) *<54626>* **I'D DO ANYTHING FOR LOVE (BUT I WON'T DO THAT) / ('A'edit)** – 1

Oct 93. (7"/c-s) *(VS/+C 1443) <54626>* **I'D DO ANYTHING FOR LOVE (BUT I WON'T DO THAT). / BACK INTO HELL** 1 –
(cd-s+=) *(VSCDT 1443)* – Everything louder than everything else (live NYC).
(cd-s) *(VSCDG 1443)* – ('A'side) / You took the words right out of my mouth (live NYC) / Bat out of hell (live NYC).

Jan 94. (c-s) *<54757>* **ROCK AND ROLL DREAMS COME THROUGH / I'D DO ANYTHING FOR LOVE (BUT I WON'T DO THAT) (live)** – 13

Feb 94. (7"pic-d/c-s) *(VSP/VSC 1479)* **ROCK AND ROLL DREAMS COME THROUGH. / WASTED YOUTH** 11 –
(cd-s+=) *(VSCDT 1479)* – I'd do anything for love (but I won't do that) (live NYC).

(cd-s+=) *(VSCDG 1479)* – Heaven can wait (live) / Paradise by the dashboard light (live).

Apr 94. (7"/c-s) *(VS/+C 1492)* <54848> **OBJECTS IN THE REAR VIEW MIRROR MAY APPEAR CLOSER THAN THEY ARE. / TWO OUT OF THREE AIN'T BAD (live)** [26] [38]
(cd-s) *(VSCDT 1492)* – ('A'side) / Rock and roll dreams come through (live) / All revved up (live).

Oct 95. (c-s) *(VSC 1563)* <55134> **I'D LIE FOR YOU (AND THAT'S THE TRUTH). / I'D DO ANYTHING FOR LOVE (BUT I WON'T DO THAT)** [2] [13]
(cd-s+=) *(VSCDG 1563)* – Whatever happened to Saturday night.
(cd-s) *(VSCDT 1563)* – ('A'-Fountain Head mix) / Oh, what a beautiful mornin' / Runnin' for the red light (I gotta life).

Oct 95. (cd/c/d-lp) *(CD/TC+/V 2799)* <11341> **WELCOME TO THE NEIGHBOURHOOD** [3] Nov95 [17]
– When the rubber meets the road / I'd lie for you (and that's the truth) / Original sin / 45 seconds of ecstacy / Runnin' for the red light (I gotta life) / Fiesta de las Almas Perdidas / Left in the dark / Not a dry eye in the house / Amnesty is granted / If this is the last kiss (let's make it last all night) / Martha / Where angels sing.

Jan 96. (c-s) *(VSC 1567)* <55174> **NOT A DRY EYE IN THE HOUSE / I'D LIE TO YOU (AND THAT'S THE TRUTH) (live)** [7] [82]
(cd-s+=) *(VSCDT 1567)* – Where the rubber meats the road (live).
(cd-s) *(VSCDX 1567)* – ('A'side) / Come together / Let it be.

Apr 96. (c-s) *(VSC 1582)* **RUNNIN' FOR THE RED LIGHT (I GOTTA LIFE) / LIFE IS A LEMON AND I WANT MY MONEY BACK (live) / AMNESTY IS GRANTED** [21] [–]
(cd-s+=) *(VSCDX 1582)* – Dead ringer for love.
(12"pic-d) *(VSTP 1582)* – ('A'side) / Dead ringer for love (live) / All revved up (live) / Midnight at the lost and found (live).

Nov 98. (d-cd/d-c) *(CDV/TCV 2868)* <69335> **THE VERY BEST OF MEAT LOAF** (compilation) [14] [ ]
– Home by now – No matter what / Life is a lemon and I want my money back / You took the words right out of my mouth (hot summer night) / Two out of three ain't bad / Modern girl / Rock and roll dreams come through / Is nothing sacred / Paradise by the dashboard light / Heaven can wait / I'd do anything for love (but I won't do that) / A kiss is a terrible thing to waste / I'd lie for you (and that's the truth) / Not a dry eye in the house / Nocturnal pleasure / Dead ringer for love / Midnight at the lost and found / Objects in the rear view mirror may appear closer than they are / Bat out of Hell.

Apr 99. (c-s/cd-s; by MEAT LOAF featuring PATTI RUSSO) *(VSC/+DT 1734)* **IS NOTHING SACRED / NO MATTER WHAT / DEAD RINGER FOR LOVE (live)** [15] [–]
(cd-s) *(VSCDX 1734)* – ('A'side) / What you see is what you get (live) / Out of the frying pan (and into the fire) (live).

Mercury Sanctuary

Apr 03. (cd-s) *(065684-2)* **COULDN'T HAVE SAID IT BETTER / ('A'radio) / UNSAID / ('A'-video)** [31] [–]

Apr 03. (cd) *(076099-2)* <84653> **COULDN'T HAVE SAID IT BETTER** [4] Sep03 [85]
– Couldn't have said it better / Did I say that / Why isn't that enough / Love you out loud / Man of steel – Intermezzo / Testify / Tear me down / You're right, I was wrong / Because of you / Do it! / Forever young / Bat out of Hell (live). *<US+=>* – Couldn't have said it better (video) / Did I say that (video).

Nov 03. (cd-s) *(9815114)* **MAN OF STEEL / TEAR ME DOWN (live) / LOVE YOU OUT LOUD (live)** [21] [–]

– compilations, others, etc. –

on 'Epic' records (unless stated)

Aug 82. (c-ep) *(EPCA40 2621)* **GREATEST ORIGINAL HITS EP** [ ] [–]
– Bat out of Hell / Read 'em and weep / Dead ringer for love / I'm gonna love her for both of us. *(7"ep-iss.Mar83; EPCA 2621)*

Jan 85. (lp/c/cd) *(EPC/40/EPCCD 26156)* **HITS OUT OF HELL** [2] [ ]
– Bat out of Hell / Read 'em and weep / Midnight at the lost and found / Two out of three ain't bad / Dead ringer for love / Modern girl / I'm gonna love her for both of us / You took the words right out of my mouth (hot summer night) / Razor's edge / Paradise by the dashboard light. *(re-iss. Mar88 lp/c; 450447-1/-4) (re-iss. cd Mar91 & Jul99; EPC 450447-2)*

Sep 86. (c-ep) *(450131-4)* **MEAT LOAF** [ ] [–]
– Bat out of Hell / Dead ringer for love / Read 'em and weep / If you really want to / Razor's edge.

Aug 87. (d-lp) *(EPCML 241)* **BAT OUT OF HELL / HITS OUT OF HELL** [ ] [–]

Jan 88. (7") *Old Gold; (OG 9751)* **BAT OUT OF HELL. / DEAD RINGER FOR LOVE** [ ] [–]

Feb 89. (7") *Old Gold; (OG 9865)* **YOU TOOK THE WORDS RIGHT OUT OF MY MOUTH. / MIDNIGHT AT THE LOST AND FOUND** [ ] [–]

Nov 89. (lp/c/cd) *Arista; (210/410/260 363)* **PRIME CUTS** [ ] [ ]

Nov 89. (lp/c/cd; with tracks by BONNIE TYLER) *Telstar; (STAR/STAC/TCD 2361)* **HEAVEN AND HELL** [ ] [–]
(re-iss. cd-c.May93 & Dec95 on 'Columbia')

Jun 91. (7"/c-s) *(656982-7/-4)* **DEAD RINGER FOR LOVE. / HEAVEN CAN WAIT** [53] [ ]
(12"+=/cd-s+=) *(656982-6/-2)* – Bat out of Hell.

Jun 92. (7"/c-s) *(657491-7/-4)* **TWO OUT OF THREE AIN'T BAD. / MIDNIGHT AT THE LOST AND FOUND** [69] [ ]
(12"+=/cd-s+=) *(657491-6/-2)* – I'm gonna love her for both of us.

Jul 92. (c-s) *M.C.A.; <54557>* **PARADISE BY THE DASHBOARD LIGHT. /** [–] [ ]
(above from the 'Leap Of Faith' soundtrack starring Steve Martin)

Oct 92. (cd/c) *Pickwick; (PWK CD/S 4121)* **ROCK'N'ROLL HERO** [ ] [–]
(re-iss. May94; same)

Feb 93. (cd) *(CDX 82419)* **BAT OUT OF HELL – REVAMPED** [ ] [–]

Feb 93. (d-cd) *(CDX 82419D)* **DEAD RINGER / BAT OUT OF HELL** [ ] [–]

Apr 93. (d-cd) *(474032-2)* **DEAD RINGER / MIDNIGHT AT THE LOST AND FOUND** [ ] [–]
(re-iss. Feb95; 478486-2)

Sep 93. (cd/c) *Ariola; (74321 1528-2/-4)* **THE COLLECTION** [ ] [–]

Dec 93. (12"pic-d-ep/c-ep/pic-cd-ep) *(660006-6/-4/-2)* **BAT OUT OF HELL / READ 'EM AND WEEP. / OUT OF THE FRYING PAN (AND INTO THE FIRE) / ROCK AND ROLL DREAMS COME THROUGH (Jim Steinman)** [8] [ ]

Oct 94. (cd; with BONNIE TYLER) **THE BEST** [ ] [ ]

Oct 94. (cd/c/lp) *Pure Music; (PM CD/MC/LP 7002)* **ALIVE IN HELL (live)** [33] [–]
– (tracks on 'LIVE AT WEMBLEY' album) + (studio tracks;-) Piece of the action / Bad attitude / Surf's up.

Apr 95. (cd) *Arista; (74321 25957-2)* **BLIND BEFORE I STOP / BAD ATTITUDE** [ ] [–]

Jun 96. (cd/c) *Camden; (74321 39336-2/-4)* **ROCK'N'ROLL HERO** [ ] [–]

Jul 98. (cd) *(488674-2)* **THE DEFINITIVE COLLECTION** [ ] [–]

Sep 99. (cd) *Beyond; <78065>* **VH1 STORYTELLERS (live)** [–] [ ]

Nov 03. (d-cd) *Epic; (513743-2)* **THE VERY BEST OF MEAT LOAF** [ ] [ ]

MEAT PUPPETS

Formed: Tempe, Phoenix, Arizona, USA ... 1980 by brothers CURT and CRIS KIRKWOOD. They were soon snapped up by rising US indie label 'SST' in 1981, after a debut on their own label. Their first recording for the company, 'MEAT PUPPETS 1' (1982), was a demanding blast of howling noise and twisted country that barely hinted at the compelling sound they'd invent with the follow-up 'MEAT PUPPETS II' (1983). A hybrid of mystical GRATEFUL DEAD-like psychedelia that short-fused hardcore punk rock and the country-boy slur of CRIS, the record was the blueprint for most of their subsequent output. 'UP ON THE SUN' (1985) was slightly more polished and saw the band garner snowballing critical acclaim. By the release of 'MIRAGE' (1987), the band had fully realised their desert-rock vision with a collection of weather beaten, psychedelic country classics; tracks like 'BEAUTY' and 'CONFUSION FOG' rank among the MEAT PUPPETS' best. Yet the record failed to sell and the band returned to a rawer, ZZ TOP-influenced sound on 'HUEVOS'. This album, together with the more mainstream 'MONSTERS' (1989) and continuing critical praise led to a deal with 'London'. Their major label debut, 'FORBIDDEN PLACES' (1991) was accomplished but lacked the high-noon intensity of their earlier work. After a step-up from KURT COBAIN (see below), the raw 'NO JOKE' (1995) album at last saw The MEAT PUPPETS reaping some financial rewards, sales of the album going on to break the half million mark. Having relocated to Austin, Texas, KIRKWOOD finally re-emerged with a new-look MEAT PUPPETS – featuring ex-PARIAH members KYLE ELLISON and SHANDON SAHM along with ANDREW DUPLANTIS – and a belated album in the shape of 'GOLDEN LIES' (2000). MEAT-ier than most of the band's back catalogue, the album cranked up the amps for a set missing much of the sun-baked strangeness of old but at least partly making up for it with strong, memorable songwriting. Strong and memorable are two adjectives which wouldn't be much required in the context of EYES ADRIFT, the pseudo supergroup consisting of CRIS KIRKWOOD, FLOYD 'BUD' GAUGH (of SUBLIME) and KRIST NOVOSELIC (of NIRVANA fame). Formed in late 2001 after KIRKWOOD met both musicians on his solo tour, the trio undertook a live stint and finally released their eponymous debut in autumn 2002. Straying aimlessly into the margins of territory which the MEAT PUPPETS used to inhabit with much more presence, the record failed to convincingly fuse the capricious talents of its authors. • **Songwriters:** Most by CURT, some with CRIS or DERRICK. Covered TUMBLIN' TUMBLEWEEDS (Bob Nolan) / EL PASO CITY (Marty Robbins) / GOODNIGHT IRENE (Leadbelly) / PARANOID + SWEET LEAF (Black Sabbath). • **Trivia:** On 18 Nov'93, CURT & CRIS guested with NIRVANA's on an unplugged MTV spot. The tracks they performed were 'PLATEAU', 'OH ME' and 'LAKE OF FIRE'.

Album rating: MEAT PUPPETS mini (*5) / MEAT PUPPETS II (*8) / UP ON THE SUN (*9) / OUT MY WAY mini (*6) / MIRAGE (*8) / HEUVOS (*6) / MONSTERS (*7) / NO STRINGS ATTACHED compilation (*6) / FORBIDDEN PLACES (*6) / TOO HIGH TO DIE (*7) / NO JOKE! (*6) / LIVE IN MONTANA (*5) / GOLDEN LIES (*5) / LIVE (*6) / Eyes Adrift: EYES ADRIFT (*4)

CURT KIRKWOOD (b.10 Jan'59, Amarillo, Texas) – guitar, vocals / **CRIS KIRKWOOD** (b.22 Oct'60, Amarillo) – vocals, bass, rhythm guitar / **DERRICK BOSTROM** (b.23 Jun'60, Phoenix) – drums

not iss. / World Imitation

Sep 81. (7"ep) <PRC-1> **IN A CAR / BIG HOUSE. / DOLPHIN FIELD / OUT IN THE GARDENER / FOREIGN LAWNS** [–] [ ]
(cd-ep iss.Nov88 on 'S.S.T.'; SST 044CD)

S.S.T. / S.S.T.

Jan 82. (m-lp) <SST 009> **MEAT PUPPETS** [–] [ ]
– Reward / Love offering / Blue green god / Walking boss / Melons rising / Saturday morning / Our friends / Tumblin' tumbleweeds / Milo, Sorghum and maize / Meat puppets / Playing dead / Litterbox / Electromud / The goldmine. *(re-iss. May93 lp/c/cd; SST 009/+C/CD) <cd re-iss. Feb99 on 'Rykodisc'+=; RCD 10466>* – In a car / Big house / Dolphin field / Out in the gardner / Foreign lawns / Meat puppets / Everybody's talkin' / H Elenore / Hair / I got a tight / I am a child / Franklin's tower / Milo, Sorghum and maize / Electromud / Lover offering / Saturday morning / Magic toy missing / Unpleasant / Walking boss (video).

Apr 84. (lp) *<(SST 019)>* **MEAT PUPPETS II** [ ] 1983 [ ]
– Split myself in two / Magic toy missing / Lost plateau / Aurora Borealis / We are here / Climbing / New gods / Oh, me / Lake on fire / I'm a mindless idiot / The whistling song. *(re-iss. May93 lp/c/cd; SST 019/+C/CD) <cd re-iss. Feb99 on 'Rykodisc'+=; RCD 10467>* – Teenager / I'm not here / New gods / Lost / What to do / 100% of nothing / Aurora borealis / New gods (video).

Apr 85. (lp) *<(SST 039)>* **UP ON THE SUN** [ ] [ ]
– Up on the sun / Maiden's milk / Away / Animal kingdom / Hot pink / Swimming ground / Buckethead / Too real / Enchanted porkfist / Seal whales / Two rivers / Creator. *(cd-iss. Sep87; SST 039CD) (re-iss. May93 cd/c; SST 039 CD/C) <cd re-iss. Mar99 on 'Rykodisc'+=; RCD 10469>* – Hot pink / Up on the sun / Mother American marshmallow / Embodiment of evil / Hot pink / Swimming ground (video).

Aug 86. (m-lp) *<(SST 049)>* **OUT MY WAY** [ ] [ ]
– She's hot / Out my way / Other kinds of love / Not swimming ground / Mountain line / Good golly Miss Molly. *(cd-iss. Sep87; SST 049CD) (re-iss. May93 cd/c; SST 049 CD/C) <cd re-iss. Apr99 on 'Rykodisc'+=; RCD 10468>* – I just want to make love to you / On the move / Burn the honky tonk down / Boyhood home / Backwards drums / Everything is green / Other kinds of love / Little wing (video).

Apr 87. (lp/cd) *<(SST 100/+CD)>* **MIRAGE** [ ] [ ]
– Mirage / Quit it / Confusion fog / The wind and the rain / Mighty zero / Get on down / Leaves / I am a machine / Beauty / A hundred miles / Love your children forever / Liquified: Mighty zero – I am a machine – Liquified – Rubberneckin'. *(re-iss. May93 cd/c; SST 100 CD/C) <cd re-iss. May99 on 'Rykodisc'+=; RCD 10473>* – Grand intro.

Oct 87. (lp/cd) *<(SST 150/+CD)>* **HEUVOS** [ ] [ ]
– Paradise / Look at the rain / Bad love / Sexy music / Crazy / Fruit / Automatic mojo / Dry rain / I can't be counted on at all. *(re-iss. May93 cd/c; SST 150 CD/C) <cd re-iss. Apr99 on 'Rykodisc'+=; RCD 10470>* – Baby what you want me to do / I can't be counted on / Sexy music / Automatic mojo / Paradise / Fruit / Automatic mojo (video).

Oct 87. (12") *<(PSST 150)>* **I CAN'T BE COUNTED ON AT ALL. / PARADISE** [ ] [ ]

Oct 89. (lp/cd) *<(SST 253/+CD)>* **MONSTERS** [ ] [ ]
– Attacked by monsters / Light / Meltdown / In love / The void / Touchdown king / Party till the world obeys / Flight of the fire weasel / Strings on your heart / Like being alive. *<(cd re-iss. May99 on 'Rykodisc'+=; (RCD 10471)>* – Wish upon a storm / Flight of the fire weasel / Flight of the fire weasel / Light (video).

Nov 90. (d-lp/cd) *<(SST 265/+CD)>* **NO STRINGS ATTACHED** (compilation) [ ] [ ]
– Big house / In a car / Tumblin' tumbleweeds / Reward / The whistling song / New gods / Lost / Lake of fire / Split myself in two / Up on the Sun / Swimming ground / Maiden's milk / Bucket head / Out my way / Confusion fog / I am a machine / Quit it / Beauty / Look at the rain / I can't be counted on at all / Automatic mojo / Meltdown / Like being alive / Attacked by monsters.

London / London

Nov 91. (cd/c/lp) *<(828254-2/-4/-1)>* **FORBIDDEN PLACES** [ ] [ ]
– Sam / Nail it down / This day / Open wide / Another Moon / That's how it goes / Whirlpool / Popskull / No longer gone / Forbidden places / Six gallon pie.

Mar 94. (cd/c/lp) *<(828484-2/-4/-1)>* **TOO HIGH TO DIE** [ ] [62]
– Violet eyes / Never to be found / We don't exist / Severed goddess head / Flaming heart / Shine / Backwater / Roof with a hole / Station / Things / Why / Evil love / Comin' down / Lake of fire.

Jul 94. (cd-ep) *<857553>* **BACKWATER / OPEN WIDE / ANIMAL / UP ON THE SUN / WHITE SPORT COAT** [–] [47]

Dec 94. (10"ep) *<1109>* **RAW MEAT EP** [–] [ ]
– We don't exist / Up on the sun / El Paso city / White sport coat / Goodnight Irene.

Oct 95. (cd/c) *<(828665-2/-4)>* **NO JOKE!** [ ] [ ]
– Scum / Nothing / Head / Taste of the sun / Vampires / Predator / Poison arrow / Eyeball / For free / Cobbler / Inflamable / Sweet ammonia / Chemical garden.

—— **CURT** recruited entire new band **KYLE ELLISON** – guitar, vocals (ex-PARIAH) / **ANDREW DuPLANTIS** – bass / **SHANDON SAHM** – drums (ex-PARIAH)

Atlantic / Atlantic

Sep 00. (cd/c) *<(7567 83402-2/-4)>* **GOLDEN LIES** [ ] [ ]
– Intro / Armed and stupid / I quit / Lamp / Hercules / Batwing / Take off your clothes / You love me / Pieces of me / Push the button / Tarantula / Endless wave / Wipeout / Fat boy (Fat – Requiem).

not iss. / D.C.N.

Apr 02. (cd) *<1003>* **LIVE** (at Maxwell's 2.08.01) [–] [ ]
– Intro / Armed and stupid / Wipe out / I quit / Hercules / Oh, me / Push the button / Lamp / Pieces of me / Up on the sun / Take off your clothes / Fatboy – Fat – Requiem / Lake of fire / Way that it are / You love me / Plateau / Touchdown king.

– compilations, etc. –

Feb 99. (cd) *Rykodisc; <(RCD 1047-2)>* **LIVE IN MONTANA (live December '88)** [ ] [ ]
– Touchdown king / Cotton candy land / Automatic mojo / Plateau / Maiden's milk / Lake of fire / I can't be counted on / Liquified / Dough-rey-mi / S.W.A.T. (get down) – Attacked by monsters / Party till the world obeys / The small hours – Paranoid – Sweet leaf.

EYES ADRIFT

CURT KIRKWOOD – vocals, guitar / **KRIST NOVOSELIC** – bass, vocals (ex-NIRVANA, SWEET 75) / **BUD GAUGH** (b. FLOYD) – drums, percussion, synthesizer (ex-SUBLIME)

Cooking Vinyl SpinArt

Jan 03. (cd) *(COOKCD 249)* <*SPIN 115*> **EYES ADRIFT** ☐ Sep02 ☐
– Sleight of hand / Alaska / Inquiring minds / Untried / Blind me / Dottie Dawn and Julie Jewel / Solid / Pyramids / Telescope / Slow race / What I said / Pasted.

MEGADETH

Formed: San Francisco, California, USA ... 1983 by ex-METALLICA guitarist/vocalist, DAVE MUSTAINE, alongside DAVE ELLEFSON (bass), CHRIS POLAND (guitar) and GAR SAMUELSON (drums). MUSTAINE soon secured the band a deal with the small 'Combat' label, who released MEGADETH's breakneck debut album, 'KILLING IS MY BUSINESS ... AND BUSINESS IS GOOD' (1985). Taking the aural assault of METALLICA as a template, MUSTAINE and Co. had carved out an even more intense, speed-driven variation on heavy metal, but unlike many of their similarly speed-obsessed peers, MEGADETH had the instrumental prowess to pull it off. Signing to 'Capitol', the band followed up with 'PEACE SELLS ... BUT WHO'S BUYING?' (1986), after which MUSTAINE sacked both POLAND and SAMUELSON. Replacing them with JEFF YOUNG and CHUCK BEHLER respectively, the band returned in February '88 with a fierce cover of the SEX PISTOLS' 'ANARCHY IN THE U.K.' , complete with original 'PISTOLS' guitarist, STEVE JONES. 'SO FAR . . . SO GOOD . . . SO WHAT!' followed in March, the pinnacle of their career thus far and one of the finest metal albums of that year. Lyrically, MUSTAINE was as reliably pessimistic as ever, 'IN MY DARKEST HOUR' seeing the frontman wracked with bitterness and frustrated rage. Which possibly accounts for his headlong descent into substance abuse following the album's success, MUSTAINE again firing his musicians and not surfacing again until the cover of ALICE COOPER's 'NO MORE MR. NICE GUY' in late '89, his first Top 20 hit. Going on MUSTAINE's track record, there had never been a MR. NICE GUY, although new recruits MARTY FRIEDMAN (guitar) and NICK MENZA (drums) have been with the band now for an unprecedented eight years and MUSTAINE obviously had it together enough to record the critically acclaimed 'RUST IN PEACE' (1990). 'HOLY WARS . . . THE PUNISHMENT DUE' was the first single from the album, an uncannily prescient piece of writing in light of the Gulf War, the record made even more eerie by dint of its wailing Arab-esque embellishments. The whole set was more mature, both musically and lyrically, FRIEDMAN ripping out solo's at furious speed, note for perfect note while MUSTAINE tackled subjects from alien cover-ups ('HANGER 18', another Top 30 hit) to the threat of nuclear weapons ('RUST IN PEACE ...POLARIS'). COUNTDOWN TO EXTINCTION (1992) featured equally topical lyrical themes, mainly dealing with the danger to the earth's environment. Musically, the band had inevitably slowed the pace down somewhat; allowing more consideration for melody and structure, MEGADETH scored their biggest success to date, the album reaching No.2 in America, No.5 in Britain. 'SKIN O' MY TEETH' recounted MUSTAINE's brushes with death; rather than banging on about saving the planet, perhaps MUSTAINE should have dealt with his own affairs first as rumours began to surface about drug problems marring sessions for the 'YOUTHANASIA' (1994) album. Nevertheless, by the time of the album's release, MUSTAINE had apparently finally cleaned up and on the strength of the record, no one could really argue. It was another masterful effort, a transatlantic Top 10 that signalled MUSTAINE was hot on the heels of his old muckers METALLICA. After an odds'n'sods collection in '95, the band returned a few years later with 'CRYPTIC WRITINGS', a disappointing affair that should've served as MEGADETH's epitaph. However, they stood their ground for another cocktail of pitbull metal in the shape of 9th set, 'RISK' (1999); another transatlantic Top 30 entry. Having signed off (late in 2000) from 'Capitol' via an obligatory 'best of' package, 'CAPITOL PUNISHMENT: THE MEGADETH YEARS', the group signed a deal with 'Sanctuary' ('Metal-Is' in the UK), releasing the disappointing 'THE WORLD NEEDS A HERO' (2001). Following an arm injury MUSTAINE put the band on ice – apparently permanently – and fans had to be content with the limited thrills of double live set, 'RUDE AWAKENING' (2002), a fairly pedestrian summation of their helter skelter career if a better primer than ' . . .PUNISHMENT'. While its title harked back to the 80's glory years, 'STILL, ALIVE ...AND WELL?' (2002) was an unashamed cash-in released in the absence of new material and featuring both a batch of live cuts trimmed from 'RUDE AWAKENING' and another batch of previously released stuff from the disappointing ' . . .HERO'.

Album rating: KILLING IS MY BUSINESS . . . AND BUSINESS IS GOOD (*6) / PEACE SELLS . . . BUT WHO'S BUYING? (*8) / SO FAR . . . SO GOOD . . . SO WHAT? (*7) / RUST IN PEACE (*7) / COUNTDOWN TO EXTINCTION (*7) / YOUTHANASIA (*6) / HIDDEN TREASURES (*5) / CRYPTIC WRITINGS (*4) / RISK (*3) / CAPITOL PUNISHMENT compilation (*6) / THE WORLD NEEDS A HERO (*4) / RUDE AWAKENING (*5) / STILL ALIVE . . . AND WELL? (*4)

DAVE MUSTAINE (b.13 Sep'61, La Mesa, Calif.) – vocals, lead guitar (ex-METALLICA) / **CHRIS POLAND** – guitar / **DAVE ELLEFSON** (b.12 Nov'64, Minnesota) – bass / **GAR SAMUELSON** – drums

Music For Nations Combat

Jun 85. (lp) *(MFN 46)* <*970546*> **KILLING IS MY BUSINESS . . . AND BUSINESS IS GOOD** ☐ ☐
– Last rites – Loved to death / Killing in my business . . .and business is good / The skull beneath the skin / These boots / Rattlehead / Chosen ones / Looking down the cross / Mechanix. *(cd-iss. Aug87; CDMFN 46) (pic-lp May88; MFN 46P) (cd re-iss. Nov99 on 'Century Media'; 66034-2)*

—— POLAND was replaced by MIKE ALBERT (ex-KING CRIMSON) briefly until his return

Capitol Capitol

Nov 86. (lp/pic-lp)(c) *(EST/+P 2022)(TCEST 2022)* <*12526*> **PEACE SELLS . . . BUT WHO'S BUYING?** ☐ 76
– Wake up dead / The conjuring / Peace sells / Devils island / Good mourning – Black Friday / Bad omen / I ain't superstitious / My last words. *(cd-iss. Sep88; CDP 746148-2) (re-iss. Jul94 cd/c; CDEST 2022)*

Nov 87. (7"/7"pic-d) *(CL/+P 476)* **WAKE UP DEAD. / BLACK FRIDAY (live)** 65 ☐
(12"+=,12"w/7"pic-d) *(12CL 476)* – Devil's island (live).

—— **CHUCK BEHLER** – drums replaced SAMUELSON / **JEFF YOUNG**– guitar repl. JAY REYNOLDS who had briefly repl. POLAND

Feb 88. (7"/7"pic-d) *(CL/+P 480)* **ANARCHY IN THE U.K. / LIAR** 45 ☐
(12"+=) *(12CL 480)* – 502.

Mar 88. (lp/pic-lp)(c/cd) *(EST/+P 2053)(CD/TC EST 2053)* <*48148*> **SO FAR . . . SO GOOD . . . SO WHAT!** 18 Jan88 28
– Into the lungs of Hell / Set the world afire / Anarchy in the U.K. / Mary Jane / 502 / In my darkest hour / Liar / Hook in mouth.

May 88. (7"/7"pic-d) *(CL/+P 489)* **MARY JANE. / HOOK IN MOUTH** 46 ☐
(12"+=) *(12CL 489)* – My last words.

—— Late '88, YOUNG joined BROKEN SILENCE and BEHLER joined BLACK & WHITE

Nov 89. (7"/7"pic-d)(c-s) *(SBK/+PD 4)(TCSBK 4)* **NO MORE MR. NICE GUY. / DEAD ON: Different Breed** 13 ☐
(12"+=/cd-s+=) *(12/CD SBK 4)* – DANGEROUS TOYS: Demon bell (the ballad of Horace Pinker).
(above single released on 'S.B.K.')

— (Mar90) **MUSTAINE + ELLEFSON** bring in new members **MARTY FRIEDMAN** (b. 8 Dec'62, Washington, D.C.) – guitar (ex-CACOPHONY) / **NICK MENZA** (b.23 Jul'64, Germany) – drums

Sep 90. (c-s/7") *(TC+/CLP 588)* **HOLY WARS . . . THE PUNISHMENT DUE. / LUCRETIA** [24] [ ]
(12"+=/cd-s+=) *(12/CD CLP 588)* – Information.
(12"pic-d) *(12CLP 588)* – ('A'side) / (13-minute interview).

Oct 90. (cd/c)(lp/pic-lp) *(CD/TC EST 2132)(EST/+P 2132)* *<91935>* **RUST IN PEACE** [8] [23]
– Holy wars . . . the punishment due / Hangar 18 / Take no prisoners / Five magics / Poison was the cure / Lucretia / Tornado of souls / Dawn patrol / Rust in peace . . . Polaris. *(re-iss. Sep94 cd/c; same)*

Mar 91. (7"/7"sha-pic-d) *(CL/+PD 604)* **HANGAR 18. / THE CONJURING (live)** [26] [ ]
(cd-s+=) *(12/CD CLG 604)* – ('A'live) / Hook in mouth (live).

Jun 92. (7") *(CLS 662)* **SYMPHONY OF DESTRUCTION. / PEACE SELLS (live)** [15] [–]
(12"clear+=/cd-s+=) *(12CLS/CDCL 662)* – Go to Hell / Breakpoint.
(7"pic-d) *(CLPD 662) – ('A'side) / In my darkest hour (live).*

Jul 92. (cd/c/lp) *(CD/TC+/ESTU 2175) <98531>* **COUNTDOWN TO EXTINCTION** [5] [2]
– Skin o' my teeth / Symphony of destruction / Architecture of aggression / Foreclosure of a dream / Sweating bullets / This was my life / Countdown to extinction / High speed dirt / Psychotron / Captive honour / Ashes in your mouth.

Oct 92. (c-s) *<44886>* **SYMPHONY OF DESTRUCTION / SKIN O' MY TEETH** [–] [71]

Oct 92. (7"/7"pic-d)(c-s) *(CL/+P 669)(TCCL 669)* **SKIN O' MY TEETH. / HOLY WARS . . . THE PUNISHMENT DUE (General Norman Schwarzkopf)** [13] [ ]
(cd-s+=) *(CDCL 669)* – ('A'version) / Lucretia.
(10"+=) *(10CL 669)* – High speed drill / (Dave Mustaine interview).

May 93. (c-s/7") *(TC+/CL 692)* **SWEATING BULLETS. / ASHES IN YOUR MOUTH (live)** [26] [ ]
(12"/cd-s) *(12/CD CL 692)* – ('A'side) / Countdown to extinction (live '92) / Symphony of destruction (gristle mix) / Symphony of destruction (live).

Oct 94. (cd/c/blue-lp) *(CD/TC+/EST 2244) <29004>* **YOUTHANASIA** [6] [4]
– Reckoning day / Train of consequences / Addicted to chaos / A tout le monde / Elysian fields / The killing road / Blood of heroes / Family tree / Youthanasia / I thought I knew it all / Black curtains / Victory.

Dec 94. (7"clear) *(CL 730)* **TRAIN OF CONSEQUENCES. / CROWN OF WORMS** [22] [ ]
(cd-s+=) *(CDCL 730)* – Peace sells . . . but who's buying? (live) / Anarchy in the UK (live).
(laser-etched 12") *(12CL 730)* – ('A'side) / Holy wars . . . the punishment due (live) / Peace sells . . . but who's buying? (live) / Anarchy in the U.K. (live).

Aug 95. (d-cd) *(CDESTS 2244) <33670>* **HIDDEN TREASURES** [28] [90]
– No more Mr. Nice guy / Breakpoint / Go to Hell / Angry again / 99 ways to die / Paranoid / Diadems / Problems.

Jul 97. (cd/c/lp) *(CD/TC+/EST 2297) <38262>* **CRYPTIC WRITINGS** [38] [10]
– Trust / Almost honest / Use the man / Mastermind / The disintegrators / I'll get even / Sin / A secret place / Have cool, will travel / She-wolf / Vortex / FFF.

Sep 99. (cd) *(499130-2) <99134>* **RISK** [29] [16]
– Insomnia / Prince of darkness / Enter the arena / Crush 'em / Breadline / The doctor is calling / I'll be there / Wanderlust / Ecstasy / Seven / Time: the beginning / Time: the end.

Nov 00. (cd) *(525916-2) <25916>* **CAPITOL PUNISHMENT: THE MEGADETH YEARS** (compilation) [ ] Oct00 [66]
– Kill the king / Dread and the fugitive mind / Crush 'em / Use the man / Almost honest / Trust / A tout le monde / Train of consequences / Sweating bullets / Symphony of destruction / Hangar 18 / Holy wars . . . the punishment due / In my darkest hour / Peace sells. *(hidden tracks+=)*

Metal-Is — Sanctuary

May 01. (cd/lp) *(MIS CD/LP 006) <84503>* **THE WORLD NEEDS A HERO** [45] [16]
– Disconnect / The world needs a hero / Moto psycho / 1000 times goodbye / Burning bridges / Promises / Recipe for hate . . . warhorse / Losing my senses / Dread and the fugitive mind / Silent scorn / Return to Hangar / When.

Mar 02. (d-cd) *(MISDD 019) <84544>* **RUDE AWAKENING (live)** [ ] [ ]
– Dread and the fugitive mind / Kill the king / Wake up dead / In my darkest hour / Angry again / She wolf / Reckoning day / Devil's island / Train of consequences / A tout le monde / Burning bridges / Hangar 18 / Return to hangar / Hook in mouth / Almost honest / 1000 times goodbye / Mechanix / Tornado of souls / Ashes in your mouth / Sweating bullets / Trust / Symphony of destruction / Peace sells / Holy wars.

— disbanded in April 2002

Sep 02. (cd) *(MISCD 024) <84566>* **STILL ALIVE . . . AND WELL? (live & studio)** [ ] [ ]
– Time – Use the man / Conjuring / In my darkest hour / Sweating bullets / Symphony of destruction / Holy wars / Moto psycho / Dread and the fugitive mind / Promises / The world needs a hero / Burning bridges / Return to hangar.

– compilations, etc. –

Mar 97. (3xcd-box) *E.M.I.; (CDOMB 019)* **THE ORIGINALS** [ ] [–]
– (PEACE SELLS . . . BUT WHO'S BUYING / SO FAR . . . SO GOOD . . . SO WHAT / RUST IN PEACE). *(re-iss. Sep00; 528368-2)*

MD.45

DAVE MUSTAINE – guitar / **LEE VING** – vocals (ex-FEAR) / **KELLY LEMIEUX** – bass / **JAMES DE GRASSO** – drums

Capitol — Capitol

Jul 96. (cd/c) *(CD/TC EST 2286) <36616>* **THE CRAVING** [ ] [ ]
– Hell's motel / Day the music died / Fight hate / Designer behavior / Cartoon (segue) / The creed / My town / Voices / Nothing is something / Circus (segue) / Hearts will bleed / No pain / Roadman / Alley cat (segue).

☐ Melle MEL (see under ⇒ GRANDMASTER FLASH)

MELANIE

Born: MELANIE SAFKA, 3 Feb'47, Astoria, Long Island, New York, USA, of Ukrainian-Italian parentage. In 1966, while auditioning for a bit part in a play, she accidentally walked into a music publisher's office where she was asked to sing and play her guitar. Fortunately, they liked her and invited her back, the company in question being none other than 'Columbia' records. The budding singer/songwriter was assigned to producer, PETER SCHEKERYK, who was to become her husband and the father of her three children. After two flop singles, MELANIE signed to 'Buddah' late in 1968 and her first album, 'BORN TO BE', revealed her to be a child-like and coy vocalist inspired by LOTTE LENYA and EDITH PIAF. When this hit the shops in May '69, she was invited to play the 'Woodstock' festival later that year. In 1970, the folk-oriented SEEKERS had a US hit with one of her better known tracks, 'WHAT HAVE THEY DONE TO MY SONG, MA?', while she herself made the UK Top 10 with the melancholy 'RUBY TUESDAY' (from the pen of JAGGER-RICHARDS). Both songs were gleaned from the accompanying Top 5 album, 'CANDLES IN THE RAIN', this golden period seeing the release of three further successful albums, the last of which, 'GATHER ME', featured an American US No.1 (UK No.4), 'BRAND NEW KEY'. The aforementioned album appeared on her newly formed 'Neighborhood' label, an imprint she had initiated with her husband. Despite this venture, MELANIE's commercial clout dwindled as the 70's wore on. As her record sales fell away, so her label eventually went belly-up in the mid-70's. Help was at hand from 'Atlantic', however, who picked her up for 1979's 'PHOTOGRAPH'. While she couldn't quite manage to regain her former star status, MELANIE's cult following allowed her to go on releasing albums throughout the 80's, mainly on independent labels. Her only releases of the 90's to date has been 'SILENCE IS KING' (1995) – originally entitled 'FREEDOM KNOWS MY NAME' in Europe two years previously – and 'OLD BITCH WARRIOR'

(1996). The 60's flower child proved she hadn't wilted just yet on 2002's 'CRAZY LOVE', another unfailingly quixotic batch of songs featuring her son BEAU JARRED SCHEKERYK on guitar. • **Covered:** JIGSAW PUZZLE + WILD HORSES (Rolling Stones) / MR. TAMBOURINE MAN + SIGN ON THE WINDOW + LAY LADY LAY (Bob Dylan) / CAROLINA ON MY MIND (James Taylor) / LOVER'S CROSS (Jim Croce) / PRETTY BOY FLOYD (Woody Guthrie) / I THINK IT'S GOING TO RAIN TODAY (Randy Newman) / WILL YOU LOVE ME TOMORROW (Goffin-King) / CHORDS OF FAME (Phil Ochs) / MY FATHER (Judy Collins) / YOU CAN'T HURRY LOVE (Supremes) / etc. • **Trivia:** Her Neighborhood label also signed folky outfit, MIKE HERON'S REPUTATION (ex-INCREDIBLE STRING BAND) in 1973.

Album rating: BORN TO BE (*4) / AFFECTIONATELY MELANIE (*4) / CANDLES IN THE RAIN (*7) / LEFTOVER WINE (*5) / THE GOOD BOOK (*6) / GATHER ME (*7) / GARDEN IN THE CITY (*4) / STONEGROUND WORDS (*4) / MELANIE AT CARNEGIE HALL (*4) / MADRUGADA (*4) / AS I SEE IT NOW (*4) / SUNSET AND OTHER BEGINNINGS (*4) / PHOTOGRAPH (*4) / PHONOGENIC – NOT JUST A PRETTY FACE (*5) / BALLROOM STREETS (*4) / ARABESQUE (*4) / SEVENTH WAVE (*4) / AM I REAL OR WHAT? (*4) / COWABONGA – NEVER TURN YOUR BACK ON A WAVE (*4) / THE BEST OF MELANIE compilation (*7) / SILENCE IS KING (*4) / OLD BITCH WARRIOR (*4) / CRAZY LOVE (*5)

MELANIE – vocals, acoustic guitar

not iss. — Columbia

1967. (7") *<44349>* **BEAUTIFUL PEOPLE. / GOD'S ONLY DAUGHTER** [–] [ ]

1968. (7") *<45524>* **GARDEN IN THE CITY. / (WHY) DIDN'T MY MOTHER TELL ME?** [–] [ ]

Buddah — Buddah

Dec 68. (7") *(201 027)* **MR. TAMBOURINE MAN. / CHRISTOPHER ROBIN** [ ] [–]

Feb 69. (7") *(201 028) <113>* **BOBO'S PARTY. / I'M BACK IN TOWN** [ ] [ ]

May 69. (lp) *(203 019) <BDLH 5002>* **BORN TO BE** [ ] Jan69 [ ]
– In the hour / I'm back in town / Bobo's party / Mr. Tambourine man / Momma momma / I really loved Harold / Animal crackers / Christopher Robin (is saying his prayer) / Close to it all / Merry Christmas. *<re-pack Nov69 as 'MY FIRST ALBUM'; BDS 5074> (re-iss. Aug74; BDLH 5002) (cd-iss. Jul92 on 'C5'; C5CD 582)*

Sep 69. (7") *<135>* **BEAUTIFUL PEOPLE. / ANY GUY** [–] [ ]

Sep 69. (7") *(201 063)* **BEAUTIFUL PEOPLE. / UPTOWN DOWN** [ ] [–]

Dec 69. (lp) *(203 028) <BDLP 4016>* **AFFECTIONATELY MELANIE** [ ] Nov69 [ ]
– I'm back in town / Tuning my guitar / Soul sister Annie / Any guy / Uptown down again / Beautiful people / Johnny boy / Baby guitar / Deep down low / For my father / Take me home. *(re-iss. Aug74; BDLP 4016) (cd-iss. Nov93 on 'Sequel';)*

Feb 70. (7") *<161>* **TAKE ME HOME. /** [–] [ ]

Apr 70. (7") *(2011 013) <167>* **LAY DOWN (CANDLES IN THE RAIN). / ANIMAL CRACKERS** [ ] [–]

Aug 70. (7") *(2011 038)* **RUBY TUESDAY. / WHAT HAVE THEY DONE TO MY SONG MA?** [9] [–]
(above 45 was flipped over Jan71 with B-side reaching No.39 in UK)

Sep 70. (lp) *(2318 009) <BDLP 5003>* **CANDLES IN THE RAIN** [5] May70 [17]
– The good guys / Lovin' baby girl / Ruby Tuesday / Leftover wine / Lay down (candles in the rain) / Carolina in my mind / Citiest people / What have they done to my song ma. *(re-iss. UK-Aug74 diff.order tracks +=) (BDLH 2003)* – Alexander Beetle. *(cd-iss. Jan88 on 'Rock Machine';) (re-iss. Jul91 on 'Razor';)*

Nov 70. (7") *(2011 039) <186>* **PEACE WILL COME (ACCORDING TO PLAN). / CLOSE TO IT ALL** [ ] Aug70 [ ]

Nov 70. (7") *<202>* **RUBY TUESDAY. / MERRY CHRISTMAS** [–] [52]

— with **RONALD FRAGIPANE** – keyboards / etc, & onwards with sessioners

Nov 70. (lp) *(2318 011) <BDLH 5004>* **LEFTOVER WINE (live Carnegie Hall)** [22] Sep70 [33]
– Close to it all / Uptown and down / Momma momma / The saddest thing / Beautiful people / Animal crackers / I don't eat animals / Happy birthday / Tuning my guitar / Psychotherapy / Leftover wine / Peace will come (according to plan). *(re-iss. Aug74; BDLH 5004)*

Feb 71. (7") *(2011 064)* **STOP! I DON'T WANNA HEAR IT ANYMORE. / BEAUTIFUL PEOPLE** [ ] [–]

Feb 71. (7") *<224>* **THE GOOD BOOK. / WE DON'T KNOW WHERE WE'RE GOING** [–] [ ]

May 71. (lp) *(2322 001) <5006>* **THE GOOD BOOK** [9] Feb71 [80]
– The good book / Babe rainbow / Sign on the window / The saddest thing / Nickel song / Isn't it a pity / My father / Chords of fame / You can go fishin' / Birthday of the sun / The prize / Babe rainbow. *(cd-iss. Mar93 on 'C5'; C5CD 597)*

May 71. (7") *(2011 071)* **THE NICKEL SONG. / THE GOOD BOOK** [ ] [–]

Aug 71. (lp) *(2318 034)* **ALL THE RIGHT NOISES (Soundtrack)** [ ] Dec70 [ ]
– (basically orchestrated versions of her earlier work)

Buddah — N'bourhood

Nov 71. (7") *(2011 105) <4201>* **BRAND NEW KEY. / SOME SAY (I GOT DEVIL)** [4] Oct71 [1]

Dec 71. (lp) *(2322 002) <47001>* **GATHER ME** [14] Nov71 [15]
– Little bit of me / Some day I'll be a farmer / Ring around the Moon / Steppin' / Brand new key / Ring around the Moon / shine the living light (chant) – Ring the living bell – Shine the living light (chant reprise) / Railroad / Kansas / Some say (I got Devil) / Center of the circle / What wondrous love / Baby day / Tell me why. *(re-iss. Aug74; BDLP 4022) (cd-iss. Oct92 on 'C5'; C5CD 597)*

Mar 72. (7") *(2011 115) <4202>* **RING THE LIVING BELL. / RAILROAD** [ ] Jan72 [31]

Jul 72. (7") *<4204>* **SOMEDAY I'LL BE A FARMER. / STEPPIN'** [–] [ ]

Jul 72. (7") *(2011 136)* **SOMEDAY I'LL BE A FARMER. / LAY LADY LAY** [ ] [–]

N'bourhood — N'bourhood

Oct 72. (7") *<4207>* **TOGETHER ALONE. / CENTER OF THE CIRCLE** [–] [86]

Oct 72. (7") *(NBH 1)* **TOGETHER ALONE. / SUMMER WEAVING** [ ] [–]

Nov 72. (lp) *(NHTC 251) <47005>* **STONEGROUND WORDS** [ ] [70]
– Together alone / Between the road signs / Summer weaving / My rainbow race / Do you believe / I am not a poet (night song) / Stoneground words / Song of the south (based on a theme from song of the north, adapted from the original) / Maybe I was (a golf ball) / Here I am. *(re-iss. Jan75 on 'Anchor'; ABCL 5077)*

Jan 73. (7") *(NBH 5) <4209>* **DO YOU BELIEVE?. / STONEGROUND WORDS** [ ] [ ]

Feb 73. (7") *(NBH 6) <4210>* **BITTER BAD / DO YOU BELIEVE?** [ ] [36]

Jun 73. (7") *(NBH 8) <4212>* **SEEDS. / SOME SAY (I GOT DEVIL)** [ ] [ ]

Jul 73. (d-lp) *(NHLP 301) <49001>* **AT CARNEGIE HALL (live)** [ ] May73 [ ]
– Baby guitar / Lay your hands / Across the six strings / Pretty Boy Floyd / Someday I'll be a farmer / Baby rainbow / It's me again / Any guy / Brand new key / Some day / Bitter sad / Psycho therapy / Together alone / Beautiful people / Hearing the news / Seasons to change / Peace will come (according to plan) / My rainbow race / Poet / Ring the living bell – Shine the living light / The actress.

Nov 73. (7") *(NBH 9) <4213>* **WILL YOU LOVE ME TOMORROW?. / HERE I AM** [37] [82]

Mar 74. (7") *(NBH 10) <4214>* **LOVE TO LOSE AGAIN. / PINE AND FEATHER** [ ] [ ]

May 74. (7") *(NBH 11) <4215>* **LOVER'S CROSS. / HOLDING OUT** [ ] [ ]

May 74. (lp) *(NH 3003) <48001>* **MADRUGADA** [ ] [ ]
– Love to lose again / Lover's cross / Pretty Boy Floyd / Wild horses / Think it's going to rain today / Maybe not for a lifetime / Holding out / I am being guided / The actress / Pine and feather. *(re-iss. Jan75 on 'Anchor'; ABCL 5085)*

Jan 75. (7") *<10000>* **YOU'RE NOT A BAD GHOST, JUST AN OLD SONG. / EYES OF A MAN** [–] [ ]

Feb 75. (7") *(SNBH 2994)* **YOU'RE NOT A BAD GHOST, JUST AN OLD SONG. / MONOGAUELA RIVER** [ ] [–]

Feb 75. (lp) *(SNBH 80636) <3000>* **AS I SEE IT NOW** [ ] [ ]
– Yankee man / You're not a bad ghost / Just an old song / Record machine / Eyes of man / Stars up there / Don't think twice, it's alright / Sweet misery / Monongahela River / Yes sir, that's my baby / Autumn lady / Chart song / As I see it now.

Apr 75. (7") *(SNBH 3250)* **YES SIR, THAT'S MY BABY. / RECORD MACHINE** [ ] [–]

Jun 75. (7") *<10001>* **SWEET MISERY. / RECORD MACHINE**

Sep 75. (7") *(SNBH 3640)* **YOU CAN'T HURRY LOVE – MAMA SAID. / THE SUN AND THE MOON**

Oct 75. (lp) *(NBH 69168) <3001>* **SUNSET AND OTHER BEGINNINGS**
– Perceive it / Almost like being in love / Loving my children / You can't hurry love – Mama said / People are just getting ready / Ol' man river / I got my mojo working / Where's the band / Dream seller (meet me on the corner) / What do I keep / Sandman / The Sun and the Moon / Afraid of the dark.

Nov 75. (7") *(SNBH 3789)* **ALMOST LIKE BEING IN LOVE. / BEAUTIFUL PEOPLE (live)**

not iss. Atlantic

1976. (lp) *<18190>* **PHOTOGRAPH**
– Cyclone / If I needed you / The letter / Groundhog day / Nickel song / Photograph / I'm so blue / Secret of the darkness (I believe) / Save me / Raindance / Friends & co.

Jan 77. (7") *<3380>* **CYCLONE. / IF I NEEDED YOU**

R.C.A. Midsong

Sep 78. (7") *<40858>* **I'D RATHER LEAVE WHILE I'M IN LOVE. / RECORD PEOPLE**

Sep 78. (lp) *(XL 13056) <3033>* **PHONOGENIC – NOT JUST A PRETTY FACE**
– Knock on wood / Bon apetite / Spanky / Runnin' after love / We can work it out / I'd rather leave while I'm in love / Let it be me / Yankee man / Record people / California dreamin'.

Nov 78. (7") *<40903>* **KNOCK ON WOOD. / RECORD PEOPLE**

R.C.A. Tomato

Aug 79. (7") *<10007>* **RUNNIN' AFTER LOVE. / HOLDIN' OUT**

Aug 79. (d-lp) *(XL 03073) <9003>* **BALLROOM STREETS (live)**
– Runnin' after love / Holdin' out / Cyclone / Beautiful sadness / Do you believe? / Nickel song / Any guy / What have they done to my song, ma? / I believe / Poet / Save me / Together alone / Ruby Tuesday / Buckle down / Miranda / Brand new key / Groundhog day / Friends and company.

R.C.A. R.C.A.

Apr 82. (7") *<1>* **DETROIT OR BUFFALO. / IMAGINARY HEROES**

Apr 82. (7") *(RCA 253)* **DETROIT OR BUFFALO. / ROADBURN**

Aug 82. (lp) *(RCALP 3078)* **ARABESQUE**
– Detroit or Buffalo / It don't matter now / Anyway that you want me / Roadburn / Fooling yourself / Too late / Standing on the other side / Love you to loathe me / When you're dead and gone / Imaginary heroes / Chances.

Aug 82. (7") *<110>* **DETROIT OR BUFFALO. / WHEN YOU'RE DEAD AND GONE**

N'bourhood N'bourhood

Sep 83. (7"/7"pic-d) *(NB/+P 1)* **EVERY BREATH OF THE WAY. / LOVERS LULLABY** 70
(12"+=) *(NBT 1)* – Put a hat on your head.

Nov 83. (lp) *<(NBL 100)>* **SEVENTH WAVE**
– Every breath of the way / Apathy / Dance to the music / Lovers lullaby / If you go your way / Son of a rotten gambler / Lonesome eyes / The nickel song / Refrain from music, music, music / Lovin' the boy next door / Lay down Sally / Didn't you ever love somebody / What do I keep.

Nov 83. (7") *(NB 2)* **DIDN'T YOU EVER LOVE SOMEBODY. / DANCE TO THE MUSIC**

not iss. Amherst

1985. (7") *<300>* **WHO'S BEEN SLEEPING IN MY BED. / MAYBE I'M LONELY**

1985. (lp) **AM I REAL OR WHAT**
– Who's been sleeping in my bed / Maybe I'm lonely / Private parts / Cut the cord / Am I real to you / Crack seeks the edge / Abuse / Every breath of the way / Some buddy love.

Food For Thought not iss.

Mar 89. (7") *(YUM 117)* **RUBY TUESDAY ('89 version). / SHOW YOU**
(12"+=/cd-s+=) *(12/CD YUM 117)* – Rock'n'roll heart.

Apr 89. (c/lp) *(T+/GRUB 12)* **COWABONGA – NEVER TURN YOUR BACK ON A WAVE**
– Ruby Tuesday / Racing heart / Show you / To be a star / What have they done to the rain / On a lamb from a cow / Another lie / Window pain / Lovin' / Prematurely gay / Chosen few / The boy next door.

Hypertens not iss.

Feb 95. (cd) *(HYCD 200130)* **SILENCE IS KING**
– Estate sale / Silence is king / I will get over / In my rock'n'roll heart / A hard rain's a-gonna fall / Gone with the wind / Detroit or Buffalo / Fallen angel / Wear it like a flag / Undertow / Some day I'll be an old record.

R.C.A. R.C.A.

Feb 96. (cd) *<(74321 29357-2)>* **OLD BITCH WARRIOR**
– Rock in the road / No time to smell flowers / Something warm / Old bitch warrior / These nights / You don't know me / I don't know what love is / Beautiful people / Any time at all / Freedom knows my name / Summer of love / Ballerina / I will survive / Candles in the rain / Ruby Tuesday / Look what they've done to my song, ma.

not iss. Orpheus

2002. (cd) *<90213>* **CRAZY LOVE**
– And we fall / Jammin' alone / Punishment fits the crime / Smile / Till they all get home / This house / Right about now / Leftover emotion / You can find anything here / The wonderer / You don't know me / I can do this . . . / Crazy love / Prone to wander / Come away come go / Poet is king / Brand new key.

– compilations, etc. –

on 'Buddah' unless otherwise mentioned

Oct 71. (7"m) *(2011 093)* **ALEXANDER BEETLE. / CHRISTOPHER ROBIN. / ANIMAL CRACKERS**

Nov 71. (7") *<268>* **THE NICKEL SONG. / WHAT HAVE THEY DONE TO MY SONG, MA** 35

Mar 72. (lp) *(2318) <5095>* **GARDEN IN THE CITY** 19 Dec71
– Garden in the city / Love in my mind / We don't where we're going / Lay lady lay / Jigsaw puzzle / Don't you wait by the water / Stop I don't want to hear it anymore / Somebody loves me / People in the front row. *(re-iss. Aug74; BDLP 4017)*

Sep 72. (d-lp) *(2659 013)* **THE FOUR SIDES OF MELANIE** 23 Mar72
– Somebody loves me / Beautiful people / In the hour / I really loved Harold / Johnny boy / Any guy / I'm back in town / What have they done to my song, ma / Lay down / Peace will come (according to plan) / Good book / The nickel song / Babe rainbow / Mr.Tambourine man / Carolina on my mind / Ruby Tuesday / Sign in the window / Lay lady lay / Christopher Robin / Animal crackers / I don't eat animals / Psychotherapy / Leftover wine. *(re-iss. Aug74; BDLP 2002)*

Oct 72. (7") **JOHNNY BOY. / I'M BACK IN TOWN**

Apr 73. (7") *(2011 166)* **THE NICKEL SONG. / CLOSE TO IT ALL**

May 73. (lp) *(2318 080)* **THE VERY BEST OF MELANIE** *(re-iss. Aug74; BDLP 4001)*

Oct 73. (7"flexi) *Lyntone; (2673-4)* **A GIFT FROM HONEY**
– I am not a poet / Song of the south / Brand new key (live) / Seeds.

Dec 73. (lp) *(2318 090)* **PLEASE LOVE ME**

Apr 75. (lp) *A.B.C.; (ABCL 5124)* **FROM THE BEGINNING**

1976. (lp) *(BDLP 5705)* **BEST OF MELANIE** *(re-iss. Jul85; 2522 121)*

Feb 77. (lp) *Golden Hour-Pye; (GH 861)* **GOLDEN HOUR OF MELANIE**

Jun 77. (12"ep) *Buddah-Pye; (BD 104)* **LAY DOWN. / BRAND NEW KEY. / RUBY TUESDAY. / WHAT HAVE THEY DONE TO MY SONG, MA?**

Oct 82. (d-lp) *P.R.T.; (SPOT 1020)* **SPOTLIGHT ON . . .**

Jan 83. (7") *Flashback-Pye; (FBS 26)* **BRAND NEW KEY. / RUBY TUESDAY**

Jun 88. (d-lp/c/cd) *Castle; (CCS LP/C/CD 195)* **THE COLLECTION**

Jul 88. (lp/c) *Knight; (11007)* **EASY RIDING**

Dec 88. (lp/c/cd) *BR Music; (BR LP/MC/CD 23)* **VERY BEST OF MELANIE**

May 89. (cd) *Laserlight; (15120)* **MELANIE**

Oct 89. (lp/c/cd) *Mainline; (262 554-1/-4/-2)* **20 GREATEST HITS**

Mar 91. (cd/c) *Music Club; (MC CD/TC 011)* **THE BEST OF MELANIE**
– Ruby Tuesday / Brand new key / Animal crackers / Mr.Tambourine man / Baby day / Beautiful people / Save the night / Lay down (candles in the rain) / Close to it all / What have they done to my song ma / Lay lady lay / Some day I'll be a farmer / Good book / Peace will come according to my plan / Gardens in the city / Nickel song / Pebbles in the sand / Tell me why.

Mar 91. (cd/c) *O.N.O.; (ONN 83 CD/MC)* **CAROLINA ON MY MIND**

Jul 92. (cd) *Sequel; (NEXCD 205)* **THE BEST OF THE REST OF MELANIE: THE BUDDAH YEARS** ☐ -
May 93. (cd) *Royal Collection; (RC 83104)* **LOOK WHAT THEY'VE DONE** ☐ -
Aug 93. (cd/c) *Marble Arch; (MAT CD/MC 276)* **THE BEST OF MELANIE** ☐ -
Dec 93. (cd) *Gold; (GOLD 203)* **GOLD: GREATEST HITS** ☐ -
Feb 94. (d-cd) *Hypertension; (HYCD 200136)* **SILVER ANNIVERSARY** ☐ -
Apr 94. (cd) *Disky; (DISK 4505)* **HIT SINGLE COLLECTABLES** ☐ -
May 94. (cd/c) *Prima; (PMM 0571 2/4)* **RUBY TUESDAY** ☐ -
Nov 96. (d-cd) *Laserlight; (24337)* **HER GREATEST HITS LIVE & NEW (FROM WOODSTOCK TO THE WORLD)** ☐ -

John (Cougar) MELLENCAMP

Born: 7 Oct'51, Seymour, Indiana, USA. After graduating from high school, where he played in two bands, CREPE SOUL (!) and SNAKEPIT BANANA BARN, the young MELLENCAMP left home in 1970 and moved to Valonia where he married his pregnant girlfriend, Priscilla. Although he formed glam-rock outfit, TRASH (alongside LARRY CRANE) in the early 70's, it would be be another three years before MELLENCAMP made any serious inroads into the music business. By this point, he'd graduated from university, separated from his wife and child and secured a deal with 'M.C.A.' as well as management company 'Mainman' (home to DAVID BOWIE), after sending a demo to the latter's Tony DeFries. Released in 1976, his debut album, 'CHESTNUT STREET INCIDENT', was credited (reportedly unbeknownst to MELLENCAMP) to JOHN COUGAR, as DeFries had christened him. Not that many people noticed anyway, poor sales of both his debut and the follow-up, 'THE KID INSIDE' (1977) seeing him part company with the label and sign to 'Riva', an imprint run by ROD STEWART's manager, Billy Gaff, and indeed the recording home of the leopard-print trousered legend himself. At this stage, MELLENCAMP's recycled rock'n'roll struggled to even match the negligible quality of STEWART's airbrushed fodder and both the UK-only 'A BIOGRAPHY' (1978) and 'JOHN COUGAR' (1979) failed to come up with anything resembling originality although the latter set nevertheless spawned a minor US hit in 'I NEED A LOVER'. The apallingly titled, STEVE CROPPER-produced 'NOTHIN' MATTERS, & WHAT IF IT DID' (1981) continued in the same empty, rock-posturing vein although for the first time, saw MELLENCAMP in the (US) Top 40. Finally managing to combine hard-bitten authenticity with epic anthem-rock a la TOM PETTY, MELLENCAMP scored a surprise US No.1 with the MTV favourite, 'JACK & DIANE'. The accompanying album, 'AMERICAN FOOL' (1982) also topped the chart and almost spawned a further two No.1's in 'HURTS SO GOOD' and 'HAND TO HOLD ON TO'. Now commanding a bit of commercial leverage, the singer ensured that 'UH-HUH!' (1984) was issued under the JOHN COUGAR MELLENCAMP moniker, his newfound confidence evident on a set which consolidated the earlier success and convincingly announced the arrival of a major league contender. Placing MELLENCAMP's small-town ideology into the context of the American farming crisis, 'SCARECROW' (1985) was a work of seemingly heartfelt conviction with cast-iron rockouts to match; the record spawned five hit singles (including the Top 10 triple whammy of 'LONELY OL' NIGHT', 'SMALL TOWN' and 'R.O.C.K. IN THE U.S.A.'), its impact lent extra weight via MELLENCAMP's role in organising Farm Aid (alongside NEIL YOUNG and WILLIE NELSON). Expanding his troupe of backing musicians to include the likes of LISA GERMANO (here playing violin), the proletarian rocker embraced a more folky approach on 'THE LONESOME JUBILEE' (1987). Painting a bleak picture of contemporary life for the average down-at-heel American, the record included some of MELLENCAMP's most memorable songs, not least the bitter 'PAPER IN FIRE'. The latter track made the Top 10, as did the album itself and for the first time, MELLENCAMP began making an impact in Britain where the record almost went Top 30. Perversely enough, the singer's most introspective album to date, 'BIG DADDY' (1989) – he had recently become a grandad – was his most successful UK release; utilising a distinctively more subdued musical approach, the rootsy, melancholy backing echoed the more intensely personal lyrical fare. The late 80'/early 90's proved a difficult time for the artist as he re-evaluated his musical direction (meantime starring in the film, 'Falling From Grace'), suffered nervous exhaustion and saw his keyboard player, JOHN CASCELLA, meet an untimely death aged only 35. MELLENCAMP himself would come face to face with his own mortality in 1994 when his touring plans were abandoned following a heart attack. Ironically, that year's album, 'DANCE NAKED', was his finest of the decade so far, following on from the return to harder territory of 'WHATEVER WE WANTED' (1991) and 'HUMAN WHEELS' (1993). It also spawned the rather unlikely (US) Top 3 duet with ME'SHELL NDEGECELLO on a cover of Van Morrison's 'WILD NIGHT'. You'd be hard pushed to come up with a more bizarre choice of producer for a JOHN MELLENCAMP album than New York DJ Don, Junior Vasquez, yet that was exactly who took the helm for the Top 10 'MR. HAPPY GO LUCKY' (1996). While the likes of MADONNA can successfully change her spots at will, a man with such an honest rock'n'roll pedigree was never going to benefit to any great extent from such an ambitious pairing. Still, it did suggest a willingness to explore different avenues, something which didn't hamper the back to basics sound of 'JOHN MELLENCAMP' (1998), as straightforward an album as the title might suggest, perhaps too straightforward: it failed to reach the US Top 40, an affront he hadn't suffered since the late 70's. While the latter marked the beginning of the man's new deal with 'Columbia', 1999's 'ROUGH HARVEST' was an interesting hodge podge of covers and acoustic readings of old favourites, ostensibly released as a contractual obligation to 'Mercury'. MELLENCAMP found himself back in the chart fold (US Top 20) with 'CUTTIN' HEADS' (2001), an easy-going return to form with guest appearances as varied as CHUCK D and TRISHA YEARWOOD, proof if nothing else that the veteran troubadour is something of a minor American institution. Ostensibly inspired by a well received cover of Robert Johnson's 'STONES IN MY PASSWAY' at a tribute gig, 'TROUBLE NO MORE' (2003) was the man's first full-blown covers album. Unsurprisingly, the emphasis was squarely on great American songs, from blues (Willie Dixon's 'DOWN IN THE BOTTOM') to folk (Woody Guthrie's 'JOHNNY HART') to Tin Pan Alley standards (Hoagy Carmichael's 'BALTIMORE ORIOLE'), with the mood fairly downbeat and edgdy throughout. An interesting diverson from the man's usual fare, it made the US Top 40 and boaded well for further similar excursions. While he's never quite lived up to the "new SPRINGSTEEN" tag which greeted his 70's arrival, MELLENCAMP has earned his place as a pillar of trad US rock by dint of sheer hard graft, honesty and not a little talent. • **Songwriters:** Penned most himself, with collaborations mainly stemming from CRANE. Covered; KICKS (Paul Revere & The Raiders) / JAILHOUSE ROCK (Elvis Presley) / OH PRETTY WOMAN (Roy Orbison) / DO YOU BELIEVE IN MAGIC (Lovin'

Spoonful) / UNDER THE BOARDWALK (Drifters) / etc. • **Trivia:** Due to his height, he produced under the alias of The LITTLE BASTARD. His work in this field has included; MITCH RYDER (Never Kick A Sleeping Dog) / BLASTERS (Hard Line).

Album rating: CHESTNUT STREET INCIDENT (*3) / THE KID INSIDE (*3) / A BIOGRAPHY (*4) / JOHN COUGAR (*5) / NOTHIN' MATTERS AND WHAT IF IT DID (*5) / AMERICAN FOOL (*6) / UH-HUH (*6) / SCARECROW (*7) / THE LONESOME JUBILEE (*7) / BIG DADDY (*8) / WHENEVER WE WANTED (*6) / HUMAN WHEELS (*6) / DANCE NAKED (*6) / MR. HAPPY GO LUCKY (*5) / JOHN MELLENCAMP (*5) / THE BEST THAT I COULD DO compilation (*7) / ROUGH HARVEST compilation (*6) / CUTTIN' HEADS (*6) / TROUBLE NO MORE (*5)

JOHNNY COUGAR

JOHN MELLENCAMP – vocals, guitar; with session people

not iss. M.C.A.

Dec 76. (lp) *<2225>* **CHESTNUT STREET INCIDENT** [–] [ ]
– American dream / Oh pretty woman / Jailhouse rock / Dream killin' town / Supergirl / Chestnut street revisited / Good girls / Do you believe in magic / Twentieth century fox / Sad lady. *(UK-rel.Oct84 on 'MainMan'; MML 602) (re-iss. Apr86 on 'Castle' lp/c/cd; CLA LP/MC/CD 113) (cd re-iss. Feb98 on 'Snapper'; SMMCD 513)*

— his band **TIGER FORCE** were **LARRY CRANE** – guitars / **TOM WINCE** – keyboards / **DAVID PARMAN** – bass, guitar, violin, percussion / **TERENCE SALSA** – drums, percussion / **WAYNE HALL** – saxophone, flute, percussion

1977. (lp) **THE KID INSIDE** [–] [ ]
– Kid inside / Take what you want / Cheap shot / Side-walks and street lights / R.Gang / American son / Gearhead / Young genocides / Too young to live / Survive. *(UK-iss.May86 on 'Castle'; CLALP 112) (cd-iss. Nov86; CLACD 112) (cd re-iss. Feb98 on 'Snapper'; SMMCD 510)*

not iss. Gulcher

1977. (7"ep) **U.S. MALE** [–] [ ]
– 2000 a.d. / Lou-ser / Hot man / Kicks.

Riva Riva

Mar 78. (7") *(RIVA 14)* **I NEED A LOVER. / BORN RECKLESS** [ ] [–]
(re-iss. Nov79 as JOHN COUGAR; same)

Mar 78. (lp/c) *(RV LP/4 6)* **A BIOGRAPHY** [ ] [–]
– Born reckless / Factory / Night slumming / Taxi dancer / I need a lover / Alley of the angels / High "C" Cherie / Where the side walk ends / Let them run your lives / Goodnight.

Jun 78. (7") *(RIVA 16)* **FACTORY. / ALLEY OF THE ANGELS** [ ] [–]

JOHN COUGAR

Riva Riva

Jun 79. (7",7"pic-d) *(RIVA 20)* **MIAMI. / DO YOU THINK THAT'S FAIR** [ ] [–]

Jul 79. (lp/c) *(RV LP/4 9) <7401>* **JOHN COUGAR** [ ] [64]
– A little night dancin' / Small Paradise / Great mid-west / Miami / Take home pay / Sugar Marie / Welcome to Chinatown / Pray for me / Do you think that's fair / Taxi dancer. *(re-iss. Jun88 on 'Mercury'; PRICE 119) (cd-iss. Jan86; 814 995-2)*

Sep 79. (7") *<202>* **I NEED A LOVER. / WELCOME TO CHINATOWN** [–] [28]

Oct 79. (7") *(RIVA 21)* **TAXI DANCER. / SMALL PARADISE** [ ] [–]

Feb 80. (7") *<203>* **SMALL PARADISE. / SUGAR MARIE** [–] [87]

Apr 80. (7") *<204>* **PRAY FOR ME. / A LITTLE NIGHT DANCIN'** [–] [ ]

Sep 80. (7") *(RIVA 25) <RIVA 205>* **THIS TIME. / DON'T UNDERSTAND ME** [ ] [27]

Jan 81. (7") *<207>* **AIN'T EVEN DONE WITH THE NIGHT. / MAKE ME FEEL** [–] [17]

Feb 81. (lp/c) *(RV LP/4 10) <7403>* **NOTHIN' MATTERS AND WHAT IF IT DID** [ ] Sep80 [37]
– Hot night in a cold town / Ain't even done with the night / Don't understand me / This time / Make me feel / To M.G. (wherever she may be) / Tonight / Wild angel / Cheap shot. *(cd-iss. Jan86; 814 994-2)*

Feb 81. (7") *(RIVA 30)* **HOT NIGHT IN A COLD TOWN. / TONIGHT** [ ] [–]

May 81. (7") *(RIVA 31)* **AIN'T EVEN DONE WITH THE NIGHT. / TO M.G. WHEREVER SHE MAY BE** [ ] [–]

— his live band consisted of **LARRY CRANE** – guitar, vocals / **MIKE WANCHIC** – guitar, vocals / **TOBY MYERS** – bass, vocals / **KENNY ARONOFF** – drums, vocals

May 82. (7") *(RIVA 36) <207>* **HURTS SO GOOD. / CLOSE ENOUGH** [ ] Apr 82 [2]

Jul 82. (7") *<210>* **JACK & DIANE. / CAN YOU TAKE IT** [–] [1]

Nov 82. (lp/c) *(RV LP/4 16) <7501>* **AMERICAN FOOL** [37] May82 [1]
– Hurts so good / Jack & Diane / Hand to hold on to / Danger list / Can you take it / Thundering hearts / China girl / Close enough / Weakest moments. *(re-iss. Sep85 on 'Mercury' lp/c; PRICE/PRIMC 85) (cd-iss. Jan85; RVCD 7501) (re-iss. cd 1988; 814 993-2)*

Sep 82. (7") *(RIVA 37)* **JACK & DIANE. / DANGER LIST** [25] [–]
(12"+=) *(RIVA 37T)* – Need a lover.

Nov 82. (7") *<211>* **HAND TO HOLD ON TO. / SMALL PARADISE** [–] [3]

Jan 83. (7",7"pic-d/12") *(RIVA 38/+T)* **HAND TO HOLD ON TO. / HURTS SO GOOD** [ ] [–]

JOHN COUGAR MELLENCAMP

Nov 83. (7"/12") *(JCM 1/+12) <214>* **CRUMBLIN' DOWN. / GOLDEN GATES** [ ] Oct 83 [9]

Dec 83. (7") *<215>* **PINK HOUSES. / SERIOUS BUSINESS** [–] [8]

Feb 84. (lp/c) *(RIVL/+C 1) <7504>* **UH-HUH** [92] Oct83 [9]
– Crumblin' down / Pink houses / Authority song / Warmer place to sleep / Jackie O / Play guitar / Serious business / Lovin' mother fo ya / Golden Gates. *(cd-iss. Oct84; 814 485-2)*

Feb 84. (7") *(JCM 2)* **AUTHORITY SONG. / HURTS SO GOOD** [ ] [–]
(12"+=) *(JCM 212)* – Thundering hearts.

Mar 84. (7") *<216>* **AUTHORITY SONG. / PINK HOUSES (acoustic)** [–] [15]

Jun 84. (7") *(JCM 3)* **PINK HOUSES. / WARMER PLACE TO SLEEP** [ ] [–]

— added **JOHN CASCELLA** – keyboards plus others on session

Oct 85. (7") *(JCM 4) <880 984-7>* **LONELY OL' NIGHT. / JACK & DIANE** [ ] Aug 85 [6]
(12"+=) *(JCMX 4)* – Rumbleseat.

Nov 85. (lp/c)(cd) *(RIVH/+C 2)<(824865-2)>* **SCARECROW** [ ] Sep85 [2]
– Rain on the scarecrow / Grandma's theme / Small town / Minutes to memories / Lonely ol' night / The face of the nation / Justice and independence / Between a laugh and a tear / Rumbleseat / You've got to stand for somethin' / R.O.C.K. in the U.S.A. *(c+=)(cd+=)* – The kind of fella I am.

Jan 86. (7"/12") *(JCM/+X 5) <884 202-7>* **SMALL TOWN. / SMALL TOWN (acoustic)** [53] Oct 85 [6]
(d7"+=) *(JCMDP 5)* – Hurts so good / The kind of fella I am.
(d12"+=) *(JCMXD 5)* – Pink houses / Small town (acoustic).

Apr 86. (7") *(JCM 6) <884 455-7>* **R.O.C.K. IN THE U.S.A. / UNDER THE BOARDWALK** [67] Jan 86 [2]

Apr 86. (7") *<884 635-7>* **RAIN ON THE SCARECROW. / PRETTY BALLERINA** [–] [21]

Jun 86. (7") *<884 856-7>* **RUMBLESEAT. / COLD SWEAT** [–] [28]

Nov 86. (7") *(JCM 7)* **(as "CONSPIRACY OF HOPE"): PINK HOUSES. / (Howard Jones: No One Is To Blame)** [ ] [–]
(12"+=) *(JCMX 7)* – Pink houses (acoustic).

— added **LISA GERMANO** – violin / **PAT PETERSON** – backing vocals, percussion.

Mercury Mercury

Sep 87. (7") *(JCM 8) <888 763-7>* **PAPER IN FIRE. / NEVER TO OLD** [ ] Aug 87 [9]
(12"+=) *(JCMX 8)* – Cold sweat.

Sep 87. (lp/c)(cd) *(MERH/+C 109)<(832465-2)>* **THE LONESOME JUBILEE** [31] [6]
– Paper in fire / Down and out in paradise / Check it out / Real life / Cherry bomb / We are the people / Empty hands / Hard times for an honest man / Hot dogs and hamburgers / Rooty toot toot.

Nov 87. (7") *(JCM 9) <888 934-7>* **CHERRY BOMB. / SHAMA LAMA DING DONG** [ ] Oct87 [8]
(12"+=) *(JCMX 9)* – Under the boardwalk.
(cd-s++=) *(JCMCD 9)* – Pretty ballerina (live).

Feb 88. (7") *(JCM 10) <870 126-7>* **CHECK IT OUT. / WE ARE THE PEOPLE** [ ] [14]
(12"+=) *(JCMX 10)* – Shama lama ding dong / Pretty ballerina.
(cd-s+=) *(JCMCD 10)* – Pink houses (acoustic) / Check it out (live).

Jul 88. (7") *(JCM 11) <870 327-7>* **ROOTY TOOT TOOT. / CHECK IT OUT (live)** [ ] May 88 [61]
(12"+=) *(JCMX 11)* – Pretty ballerina / Like home (acoustic).
(cd-s+=) *(JCMCD 11)* – Never too old / Cold sweat.

Apr 89. (7") *(EKR 90)* **RAVE ON. / (Beach Boys: Kokomo)** [ ] [ ]
(12") *(EKRT 90)* – ('A'side) / (Fabulous Thunderbirds: Powerful Stuff) / (Starship: Wild Again).
(above single from the film 'Cocktail' on 'Elektra' label)

—— added **CRYSTAL TALIEFERO** – backing vocals, percussion

May 89. (lp/c/cd) *<(838220-1/-4/-2)>* **BIG DADDY** [25] [7]
– Big daddy of them all / To live / Martha say / Theo and weird Henry / Jackie Brown / Pop singer / Void in my heart / Mansions in Heaven / Sometimes a great notion / Country gentlemen / J.M.'s question. *(cd+=)* – Let it all hang out.

Jun 89. (7") *(JCM 12) <874 012-7>* **POP SINGER. / J.M.'S QUESTION** [ ] Apr 89 [15]
(12"+=) *(JCM 1212)* – Like a rolling stone (live).
(cd-s++=) *(JCMCD 12)* – Check it out (live).

Jul 89. (7") *<874 644-7>* **JACKIE BROWN. / JACKIE BROWN (acoustic)** [–] [48]

JOHN MELLENCAMP

Sep 91. (7") *(MER 354) <867890-7>* **GET A LEG UP. / WHENEVER WE WANTED** [ ] [14]
(c-s+=/12"+=/cd-s+=) *(MER MC/X/CD 354)* – Seventh son.

Oct 91. (cd/c/lp) *<(510151-2/-4/-1)>* **WHENEVER WE WANTED** [39] [17]
– Love and happiness / Now more than ever / I ain't ever satisfied / Get a leg up / Crazy ones / Last chance / They're so tough / Melting pot / Whenever we wanted / Again tonight. *(re-iss. cd Apr95)*

Jan 92. (7"/c-s) *(MER/+MC 362)* **LOVE AND HAPPINESS. / ('A'-L.A. rock dance mix)** [ ] [–]
(12") *(MERX 362)* – ('B'mix) / ('A'-Jezzard mix) / ('A'-dub).
(cd-s+=) *(MERCD 362)* – (all mixes + 'A'side above).

Feb 92. (c-s) *<866414-7>* **AGAIN TONIGHT / GET A LEG UP (live)** [–] [36]

Apr 92. (7") *(MER 368)* **NOW MORE THAN EVER. / JACK AND DIANE (live)** [ ] [ ]
(cd-s+=) *(MERCD 368)* – Check it out (live) / Martha say (live).
(c-s) *(MERMC 368)* – ('A'side) / Lonely ol' night.
(cd-s) *(MERCB 368)* – (above 2) / Small town / Pink houses.

—— Mid'92, MELLENCAMP suffered nervous exhaustion and cancelled gigs when his bassist MYERS severed a big toe in a boating accident. The 14th of November '92, also saw his keyboard player JOHN CASCELLA die. He was only 35, but still played on half of next album. He was replaced by **MALCOLM BURN** – organ, guitar, harmonica, synth.

—— **DAVID GRISSOM** – guitars, mandolin, bass repl. CRANE

Sep 93. (cd/c) *<(518088-2/-4)>* **HUMAN WHEELS** [37] [7]
– When Jesus left Birmingham / Junior / Human Wheels / Beige to beige / Case 795 (the family) / Suzanne and the jewels / Sweet evening breeze / What if I came knocking / French shoes / To the river. *(cd re-iss. Sep97; same)*

Oct 93. (c-s) *<862702-7>* **HUMAN WHEELS / ('A'edit)** [–] [48]

—— now w / **WANCHIC, MYERS, ARONOFF, ME'SHELL NDEGECELLO** (bass, vocals), **GERMANO, PETERSON + ANDY YORK** – guitar

Jun 94. (cd/c) *<(522428-2/-4)>* **DANCE NAKED** [ ] [13]
– Dance naked / Brothers / When Margaret comes to town / Wild night / L.U.V. / Another sunny day 12 / 25 / Too much to think about / The big jack / The breakout. *(cd re-iss. Sep97; same)*

Jun 94. (c-s) *<858738>* **WILD NIGHT / BROTHERS (live)** [–] [3]

Aug 94. (7"yellow/c-s) *(MER/+MC 409)* **WILD NIGHT. / HURTS SO GOOD** [34] [–]
(cd-s) *(MERCD 409)* – ('A'side) / Jack and Diane / Pink houses / R.O.C.K. in the U.S.A. (a salute to the 60's).
(cd-s) *(MERCX)* – ('A'side) / Dance naked (live) / When Jesus left Birmingham / Small town (acoustic).

Nov 94. (c-s) *<856346>* **DANCE NAKED / R.O.C.K. IN THE U.S.A.** [–] [41]
<with free live c-s> – Human wheels / Pink houses.

Aug 96. (c-s) *<578398>* **KEY WEST INTERMEZZO (I SAW YOU FIRST) / LIKE A ROLLING STONE** [–] [14]

Sep 96. (cd-ep) *(MERCD 474)* **KEY WEST INTERMEZZO (I SAW YOU FIRST) / WILD NIGHT (live) / WHAT IF I CAME KNOCKING (live) / SMALL TOWN (live acoustic)** [ ] [–]
(cd-ep) *(MERCX 474)* – ('A'side) / Cold sweat (live) / Check it out (live) / Like a rolling stone (live).

Oct 96. (cd/c) *<(532896-2/-4)>* **MR. HAPPY GO LUCKY** [ ] Sep96 [9]
– Overture / Jerry / Key west intermezzo (I saw you first) / Just another day / This may not be the end of the world / Emotional love / Mr. Bellows / The full catastrophe / Circling around the Moon / Large world turning / Jackamo road / Life is hard.

Feb 97. (cd-s) *<578816>* **JUST ANOTHER DAY / KEY WEST INTERMEZZO (I SAW YOU FIRST) / COLD SWEAT (live) / CRUMBLIN' DOWN (live)** [–] [46]

Columbia Columbia

Feb 99. (cd/c) *(491652-2/-4) <69602>* **JOHN MELLENCAMP** [ ] Oct98 [41]
– Fruit trader / Your life is now / Positively crazy / I'm not running anymore / Where the world began / It all comes true / Eden is burning / Chance meeting at the Tarantula / Miss Missy / Break me off some / Summer of love / Days of farewell.

Jan 02. (cd) *(503293-2) <85098>* **CUTTIN' HEADS** [ ] Oct01 [15]
– Cuttin' heads / Peaceful world / Deep blue heart / Crazy island / Just like you / The same way I do / Women seem / Worn out nervous condition / Shy / In our lives.

Columbia Best Buy Co.

Aug 03. (cd) *(512264-2) <2007201>* **TROUBLE NO MORE** [ ] Jun03 [31]
– Stones in my passway / Death letter / Johnny Hart / Baltimore oriole / Teardrops will fall / Diamond Joe / The end of the world / Down in the bottom / Lafayette / Joliet bound / John the revelator / To Washington.

– compilations, etc. –

Mar 86. (lp/c/cd; JOHN COUGAR) *Castle; (CCS LP/MC/CD 124)* **THE COLLECTION** (early) [ ] [–]

Jan 98. (cd/c) *Mercury; (536738-2/-4)* **THE BEST THAT I COULD DO** (1978-1988) [25] [33]
– Jack and Diane / R.O.C.K. in the U.S.A. / Hurts so good / I need a lover / Ain't even done with the night / Crumblin' down / Pink houses / Authority song / Lonely ol' night / Small town / Paper in fire / Cherry bomb / Check it out / Without expression.

Aug 99. (cd) *Mercury; <(558355-2)>* **ROUGH HARVEST** [ ] [99]
– Love and happiness / In my time of dying / Between a laugh and a tear / Human wheels / Rain on the scarecrow / Farewell Angelina / Key West intermezzo (I saw you first) / Jackie Brown / When Jesus left Birmingham / Full catastrophe of life / Minutes to memories / Under the boardwalk / Wild night.

Mar 00. (d-cd) *Snapper; (SMDCD 280)* **SKIN IT BACK** [ ] [–]

May 00. (3xcd-box) *Snapper; (SMXCD 108)* **THE BOX** [ ] [–]
– (CHESTNUT STREET INCIDENT / THE KID INSIDE / SKIN IT BACK).

☐ ME ME ME (see under ⇒ ELASTICA)

Natalie MERCHANT

Born: 26 Oct'63, Jamestown, New York, USA. Focal point with the 10,000 MANIACS since 1981, she embarked on a solo career in 1993. Spending over a year in the studio, she returned in fine style with her debut album, 'TIGERLILY' (1995), an emotive and eclectic collection of songs that stayed high in the American charts for some time. Three singles were lifted from it, 'CARNIVAL', 'WONDER' and 'JEALOUSY', all stirring up enough support for Top 30 placings; the latter's B-side featured a cover of The Rolling Stones' 'SYMPATHY FOR THE DEVIL'. Follow-up effort 'OPHELIA' (1998) was more oblique and impenetrable, a thing of nocturnal beauty enhanced by the likes of Zairean guitarist LOKUA KANZA and Tibetan devotional singer YUNGCHEN LIHAMO. Strikingly different to the wonderful performance MERCHANT put in on that year's WOODY GUTHRIE tribute set, 'Mermaid Avenue', the record made the US Top 10 but – perhaps unsurprisingly given its introspective depths – failed to make the critical or commercial impact of its predecessor. 'LIVE IN CONCERT' (1999) was made up largely of material from 'TIGERLILY' while NATALIE took a completely different tack via a collaboration with T-BONE BURNETT on The Top 30 'MOTHERLAND' (2001), a more solid album with arrangements that played to her vocal strengths. MERCHANT again surprised, confounded and delighted with 2003's 'THE HOUSE CARPENTER'S DAUGHTER'. While longtime fans – especially those who purchased the aforementioned 'Mermaid Avenue' – shouldn't have been too surprised to find the singer doing an album of full-blown folk covers, and while the arrangements allow breathing space for her rock roots, it was still a thrill to hear those distinctive, doleful tones carry the weight of traditional compositions like 'WEEPING PILGRIM' and 'POOR WAYFARING STRANGER', as well as covers of The Carter Family's 'BURY ME UNDER THE WEEPING WILLOW' and Fairport Convention's 'CRAZY MAN MICHAEL'. • **Other covers:** SPACE ODITTY (David Bowie) / AFTER THE GOLD RUSH (Neil Young) / THE GULF OF ARABY (Katell Keineg).

Album rating: TIGERLILY (*6) / OPHELIA (*6) / LIVE IN CONCERT (*6) / MOTHERLAND (*6) / THE HOUSE CARPENTER'S DAUGHTER (*5)

NATALIE MERCHANT – vocals / with **JENNIFER TURNER** -guitars, vocals / **BARRY MAGUIRE** – bass, guitar / **PETER YANOWITZ** – drums, percussion

Elektra Elektra

Jun 95. (cd/c) *<7559 61745-2/-4>* **TIGERLILY** 39 13
– San Andreas fault / Wonder / Beloved wife / River / Carnival / I may know the word / The letter / Cowboy romance / Jealousy / Where I go / Seven years.

Jul 95. (c-s) *(EKR 203C) <64413>* **CARNIVAL / I MAY KNOW THE WORD** 10
(cd-s+=) *(EKR 203CD)* – ('A'edit).

Nov 95. (cd-s) *<64376>* **WONDER / BABY I LOVE YOU – SON OF A PREACHER MAN (live medley) / ALL I WANT** – 20

Apr 96. (c-s/cd-s) *(EKR 217 C/CD1)* **WONDER / TAKE A LOOK (live) / THE WORK SONG (live)** –
(cd-s) *(EKR 217CD2)* – ('A'side) / Sympathy for the Devil – All I want (live medley).

May 96. (cd-s) *<64301>* **JEALOUSY / BABY I LOVE YOU – SON OF A PREACHER MAN (live) / SYMPATHY FOR THE DEVIL (live)** – 23

Jun 98. (cd/c) *<7559 62196-2/-4>* **OPHELIA** 52 May98 8
– Ophelia / Life is sweet / Kind & generous / Frozen Charlotte / My skin / Break your heart / King of May / Thick as thieves / Effigy / The living / When they ring the golden bells / Ophelia (reprise).

Nov 98. (cd-s) *(E 3831CD)* **KIND & GENEROUS / FROZEN CHARLOTTE / WONDER**

May 99. (cd-s) *(E 3786CD)* **BREAK YOUR HEART / BREAK YOUR HEART (version) / CARNIVAL (version)** –

Nov 99. (cd/c) *(7559 62479-2/-4) <62444>* **LIVE IN CONCERT (New York City – June 13, 1999)** 82
– Wonder / San Andreas fault / Beloved wife / Space oddity / Carnival / Dust bowl / After the gold rush / Gun shy / The gulf of Araby / Ophelia / Seven years.

Nov 01. (cd) *<(7559 62721-2)>* **MOTHERLAND** 30
– This house is on fire / Motherland / Saint Judas / Put the law on you / Build a levee / Golden boy / Henry Darger / The worst thing / Tell yourself / Just can't last / Not in this life / I'm not gonna beg.

not iss. Myth

Sep 03. (cd) *<1026>* **THE HOUSE CARPENTER'S DAUGHTER** –
– Sally Ann / Which side are you on? / Crazy man Michael / Diver boy / Weeping pilgrim / Soldier, soldier / Bury me under the weeping willow / House carpenter / Owensboro / Down on Penny's farm / Poor wayfaring stranger.

□ Freddie MERCURY (see under ⇒ QUEEN)

MERCURY REV

Formed: Buffalo, New York, USA ... 1988 by JONATHAN DONAHUE, DAVID BAKER, GRASSHOPPER (aka SEAN MACKIOWIAK), DAVE FRIDMANN, JIMY CHAMBERS and SUZANNE THORPE, who claimed they had all met while attending a psychiatric hospital. Admittedly, their sound, which came about by playing their own soundtrack to nature TV programmes! ('VERY SLEEPY RIVERS' indeed) was certainly deliciously deranged enough for this explanation of their secret history. Just over two years of rehearsals passed (DONAHUE, co-producer FRIDMANN and GRASSHOPPER were part-time members of FLAMING LIPS and utilised some spare studio time), before they finally surfaced with the mini-lp, 'YERSELF IS STEAM' (1991). Perhaps the most immaculate marriage of searing noise and crystalline pop ever committed to vinyl, this freaky guitar-angst rock classic mixed up psychedelia, noise, film dialogue and exhilarating experimentation in a way only previously matched by The FLAMING LIPS; other indie influences were also apparent (i.e. BIRTHDAY PARTY, STUMP, VERY THINGS and MY BLOODY VALENTINE). The inspired opening salvo of 'CHASING A BEE', 'SYRINGE MOUTH' and 'CONEY ISLAND CYCLONE', alone was enough to give the album a resounding thumbs-up by the British press and record buying public alike. Later that year, the 'CAR WASH HAIR' EP/track (recorded with DEAN WAREHAM of GALAXIE 500), further convinced commentators of MERCURY REV's volatile genius although squabbling and widely publicised, wildly unpredictable live shows led to break-up rumours. These were subsequently quashed when the band were snapped up by 'Beggars Banquet', a follow-up album, 'BOCES' (1993), carrying on in the established schizophrenic mould but too often straying into wanton self-indulgence at the expense of conventional tunes. However, it did satisfy some punters by becoming their first record to hit the UK Top 50. The following year, the band's infamous in-fighting reach a head as the proverbial time-honoured musical differences led to the wayward BAKER pursuing a noisier career of his own as SHADY. Although a solitary MERCURY REV single, 'EVERLASTING ARM', appeared in summer '94 (featuring ALAN VEGA of SUICIDE), it would be another long year before the release of 'SEE YOU ON THE OTHER SIDE' (1995), although by this time the first chapter of MERCURY REV's maverick career had already drawn to a close. While critics marvelled over the album's more accessible but wonderfully eclectic pop-jazz experiments, DONAHUE and GRASSHOPPER were in the process of completing a debut album, 'PARALYZED MIND OF THE ARCANGEL VOID' (1995) for their revamped side-project, HARMONY ROCKETS. A few years later, the pair resurrected the MERCURY REV moniker with a complete new cast (namely ADAM SNYDER, JUSTIN RUSSO, JASON RUSSO and JEFF MERCEL), although the subsequent return of THORPE, FRIDMANN and CHAMBERS (SNYDER was retained) resulted in a more fully-fledged reformation. V.I.P. HARMONY ROCKETS guests, LEVON HELM and GARTH HUDSON of The BAND, were also brought on board for the album no one thought was possible, 'DESERTER'S SONGS' (1998). Issued on Richard Branson's new imprint, 'V2' ('Epic' in the States), the record was widely hailed as THE album of the year as MERCURY REV enjoyed one of the critical rebirths of the decade. Older and wiser, the band (or THE BAND, take your pick!) had possibly stumbled upon what GRAM PARSONS really meant when he dreamt of his "cosmic American music", a wistful (in a far-out sort of way) melange of quixotic pop, spacey orchestration and

lullaby romanticism quite possibly unlike anything you've ever heard. If long-time fans were hoping to hear the anarchic spark of old they were in for a drastic shock, tracks such as 'TONITE IT SHOWS', 'OPUS 40', 'DELTA SUN BOTTLENECK BLUES' and 'ENDLESSLY', meandering to a more mature muse, the latter even incorporating their own heavy-lidded interpretation of traditional carol, 'Silent Night'. A couple of months previous to the album's release, GRASSHOPPER & His GOLDEN CRICKETS (including flautist, SUZANNE THORPE) had taken their own, more off-beat journey into the psychedelic musical galaxy with the album, 'THE ORBIT OF ETERNAL GRACE'. After recovering from the trailblazing glory of 'DESERTER'S SONGS', many fans and critics were pondering over the group's next release: how were they going to match the previous album? How would they write songs now that their woe and grief had disappeared thanks to their new found glory? MERCURY REV, however, answered both of these questions on the eve of the release of their fifth album, the epic 'ALL IS DREAM' (2001). A kaleidoscope of drifting thoughts, strange orchestral lulls, and dark, uncertain things that creeped around in the shadows, the set displayed all of the usual REV decorations, only with a brooding overtone. Darker than their last set, the record opened with the soaring, heart-wrenchingly poignant 'DARK IS RISING' (the unofficial sequel to 'HOLES') – a piano led wander into DONAHUE's subconscious, with aching violins and unnormally high choir voices that sounded like a collaboration between a broken-down NEIL YOUNG and a drunken SCOTT WALKER. Elsewhere on the album, 'DROP IN TIME', 'TIDES OF THE MOON' and 'HERCULES' were all fine demonstrations by the group that they hadn't lost any of their musical ambition (especially FRIDMANN, who was surely becoming the PHIL SPECTOR of the independent movement). If 'DESERTER'S SONGS' was the soundtrack to a sad children's Christmas movie, then 'ALL IS DREAM' was pitched somewhere between a classic romantic period drama and a high-tension adventure set in a faraway land.
• **Covered:** IF YOU WANT ME TO STAY (Sly Stone) / SHHH – PEACEFUL (Miles Davis) / DEADMAN (Alan Vega) / RAINDROPS KEEP FALLING ON MY HEAD (Bacharach & David) / HE WAS A FRIEND OF MINE (Bob Dylan) / SILVER STREET (Nikki Sudden) / MOTION PICTURES (Neil Young) / OBSERVATORY CREST (Captain Beefheart) / I KEEP A CLOSE WATCH (John Cale) / STREETS OF LAREDO (Marty Robbins) – The HARMONY ROCKETS covered I'VE GOT A GOLDEN TICKET (from 'Charlie & The Chocolate Factory') / L'APOCALYPSE DES ANIMAUX (Vangelis) / etc..

Album rating: YERSELF IS STEAM (*8) / BOCES (*6) / SEE YOU ON THE OTHER SIDE (*8) / DESERTER'S SONGS (*9) / ALL IS DREAM (*8) / Harmony Rockets: PARALYZED MIND OF THE ARCANGEL VOID (*6) / Grasshopper & The Golden Crickets: THE ORBIT OF ETERNAL GRACE (*7)

DAVID BAKER – vocals / **JONATHAN DONAHUE** – vocals, guitar (ex-FLAMING LIPS) / **SEAN 'Grasshopper' MACKIOWIAK** – guitar / **DAVID FRIDMANN** – bass / **JIMY CHAMBERS** – drums / **SUZANNE THORPE** – woodwind

Mint Films / Mint Films

Feb 91. (cd/c/blue-lp) <*(MINT CD/C/LP 4)*> **YERSELF IS STEAM**
– (Rocket): Chasing a bee / Syringe mouth / Coney Island cyclone / Blue and black / Sweet oddysee of a cancer cell t' th' center of yer heart / (Harmony): Frittering / Continuous trucks and thunder under a mother's smile / Very sleepy rivers. *(re-iss. Nov92 on 'Beggars Banquet' as d-cd+=/d-c+=/d-lp+=; BBQ CD/MC/LP 125)* **LEGO MY EGO** – If you want me to stay / Shhh – Peaceful – Very sleepy rivers / Frittering / Coney Island cyclone / Car wash hair / Syringe mouth / Blood on the moon / Chasing a girl (inside a car). *<US cd re-iss. Nov92 on 'Columbia'; 53030> (re-iss. Feb99 +=; same)* – Space patrol / Uh . . . it's out there / I better let my pants back on / My mom is coming over. *(d-cd-iss. Jul02; MINTCD 0045)*

Nov 91. (12"ep/cd-ep) <*(MINT 5 T/CD)*> **CAR WASH HAIR (The Bee's Chasing me) full pull / CHASING A BEE (demo) / CONEY ISLAND CYCLONE (demo)**

Rough Trade / not iss.

Apr 92. (7") *(45REV 6)* **IF YOU WANT ME TO STAY. / THE LEFT-HANDED RAYGUN OF PAUL SHARITS (RETIREMENT JUST LIKE THAT)** [ ] [–]

Beggars Banquet / Columbia

Nov 92. (12"/cd-s) *(BBQ 1/+CD)* *<74717>* **CHASING A BEE. / CONEY ISLAND CYCLONE**

Mar 93. (10"/cd-s) *(BBQ 5 T/CD)* *<74907>* **THE HUM IS COMING FROM HER. / SO THERE (with ROBERT CREELY)** [ ] Apr93 [ ]

May 93. (7") *(BBQ 14)* **SOMETHING FOR JOEY. / THREE SPIDER'S EGGS (live)** [ ] [–]
(12"+=) *(BBQ 14/+T)* – Suzanne peels out.
(cd-s++=) *(BBQ 14CD)* – Noise. *(re-iss. Jul93)*

Jun 93. (cd/c/lp) *(BBQ CD/MC/LP 140)* *<53217>* **BOCES** [43] [ ]
– Meth of a rockette's kick / Trickle down / Bronx cheer / Boys peel out / Downs are feminine balloons / Something for Joey / Snorry mouth / Hi-speed boats / Continuous drunks and blunders / Girlfren.

Jul 93. (cd-ep) *<CSK 5532>* **SOMETHING FOR JOEY / SO THERE / BOYS PEEL OUT / VERY SLEEPY RIVERS / (Ron Jeremy interview)** [–] [ ]

Feb 94. (cd-ep) *<77112>* **BRONX CHEER / THERE'S SPIDER EGGS IN BUBBLA YHUM / SUZANNE PEELS OUT** [–] [ ]

—— now without BAKER who re-surfaced as SHADY, releasing towards the end of '94, a solo album, 'WORLD' (for 'Beggars Banquet' UK, 'Atlantic' US), which included members of SWERVEDRIVER, ROLLERSKATE SKINNY, Th' FAITH HEALERS, SHARKBOY and BOO RADLEYS. A single, 'NARCOTIC CANDY' was taken from it with a subsequent single, 'PEARLS', coming out a year later.

Jun 94. (12"white/cd-s) *(BBQ 37 T/CD)* **EVERLASTING ARM. / DEADMAN** [ ] [–]

May 95. (cd/c/lp)(pic-lp) *(BBQ CD/MC/LP 176)(BBQ 176P)* *<64362>* **SEE YOU ON THE OTHER SIDE** [ ] Sep95 [ ]
– Empire state (Sun House in excelsis) / Young man's stride / Sudden ray of hope / Everlasting arm / Racing the tide / Close encounters of the 3rd grade / A kiss from an old flame (a trip to the Moon) / Peaceful night.

—— split late '94, as DONAHUE and GRASSHOPPER were already moonlighting as the HARMONY ROCKETS. The former and MERCURY REV collaborated on The CHEMICAL BROTHERS 'Dig Your Own Hole' track, 'Private Psychedelic Reel'.

HARMONY ROCKETS

—— **DONAHUE + GRASSHOPPER** plus **LEVON HELMS + GARTH HUDSON** (The BAND) (they also guested on MERCURY REV's comeback album) / **ZOOT ROLLO HORN** (ex-CAPTAIN BEEFHEART)

Rockville / Rockville

Jun 93. (7") *(ROCK 6113-7)* **SKELETON MAN. /**

Big Cat / Big Cat

Oct 95. (lp/cd) <*(ABB 90/+CD)*> **PARALYZED MIND OF THE ARCHANGEL VOID** [ ] Sep98 [ ]
– Paralyzed mind of the archangel void.

Big Cat / No.6

Oct 97. (cd-s) *(ABB 151SCD)* *<45>* **I'VE GOT A GOLDEN TICKET EP** [ ] Nov98 [ ]
– I've got a golden ticket / L'apocalypse des animaux / Tale scendeva l'etternale adore / I've got a golden ticket (version) / I've got a golden ticket (extended).

MERCURY REV

—— **JONATHAN + GRASSHOPPER** reformed the band in the summer of '97 with **ADAM SNYDER** – keyboards / **JUSTIN RUSSO** – keyboards / **JASON RUSSO** – bass / **JEFF MERCEL** – drums

—— by 1998, **SNYDER** was the only person that **JONATHAN + GRASSHOPPER** retained, bringing back **DAVE FRIDMANN, SUZANNE THORPE + JIMY CHAMBERS**

V2 / Epic

Oct 98. (cd/lp) *(VVR 100277-2/-1)* *<27027>* **DESERTER'S SONGS** [27] Sep98 [ ]
– Holes / Tonite it shows / Endlessly / I collect coins / Opus 40 / Hudson line / The happy end (the drunk room) / Goddess on a hiway / The funny

bird / Pick up if you're there / Delta sun bottleneck stomp. *(also on special cd; VVR 100379-2)*

Nov 98. (7") *(VVR 500332-7)* **GODDESS ON A HIWAY. / RAGTAG** 51 –
(cd-s+=) *(VVR 5000332-3)* – I only have eyes for you.

Jan 99. (12") *(VVR 500541-6)* **DELTA SUN BOTTLENECK STOMP. / ('A'-Chemical Brothers mix) / ENDLESSLY (instrumental)** 26 ☐
(cd-s) *(VVR 500541-3)* – (first two tracks) / Vampire blues (live).
(cd-s) *(VVR 500616-3)* – ('A'side) / Holes (live) / Isolation (live).

May 99. (7") *(VVR 500696-7)* **OPUS 40. / MOTION PICTURES (live)** 31 –
(cd-s) *(VVR 500697-3)* – ('A'side) / He was a friend of mine (live) / Raindrops keep falling on my head (live).
(cd-s) *(VVR 500696-3)* – ('A'side) / He was a friend of mine (live) / Tonite is shows (live).

Aug 99. (7") *(VVR 500849-7)* **GODDESS ON A HIWAY. / CAROLINE SAYS** 26 –
(cd-s) *(VVR 500849-3)* – ('A'side) / I don't wanna be a soldier / Car wash hair (live).
(cd-s) *(VVR 500849-8)* – ('A'side) / I dreamt / Very sleepy rivers (live).

Aug 01. (cd/lp) *(VVR 101752-2/-1)* <27106> **ALL IS DREAM** 11 ☐
– The dark is rising / Tides of the Moon / Chains / Lincoln's eyes / Nite and fog / Little rhymes / A drop in time / You're my queen / Spiders and flies / Hercules. *(cd re-iss. Apr02 w/free cd+=; VVR 101752-0)* – Saw song (live) / Hercules (live) / Little rhymes (live) / Nite and fog (video) / The dark is rising (video) / (interview documentary).

Sep 01. (7") *(VVR 501772-7)* **NITE AND FOG. / NITE AND FOG (demo)** 47 –
(cd-s) *(VVR 501772-3)* – ('A'side) / A drop in time (demo) / Serpentine.
(cd-s) *(VVR 501772-8)* – ('A'side) / Cool waves / Nite & fog (alt. version feat. boys choir).

Jan 02. (cd-s) *(VVR 501871-3)* **THE DARK IS RISING / NOCTURNE IN C# MINOR – OPUS 27 NO.1 / PLANET CARAVAN** 16 –
(cd-s) *(VVR 501871-8)* – ('A'side) / Spiders and flies (live) / Blues skies.

Jul 02. (cd-s) *(VVR 501978-3)* **LITTLE RHYMES / CHAINS (Peter Stillman mix) / I KEEP A CLOSE WATCH** 51 –
(cd-s) *(VVR 501978-8)* – ('A'side) / Observatory crest / Streets of Laredo.

GRASSHOPPER AND THE GOLDEN CRICKETS

with **SUZANNE THORPE** – flute, co-producer (of MERCURY REV) + others

Beggars Banquet | Beggars Banquet

Jul 98. (7") *(BBQ 325)* **SILVER BALLOONS. / SOLAR POWERED HORNET BEYOND THE SHADOWS OF OVERLOOK MOUNTAIN** ☐ –
(cd-s+=) *(BBQ 325CD)* – ('A'mix).

Aug 98. (cd/lp) *(BBQ CD/LP 201)* <80201> **THE ORBIT OF ETERNAL GRACE** ☐ ☐
– Silver balloons / The ballad of the one-eyed angelfish / O-ring (baby talk) / Nickel in a lemon / The orbit of eternal grace / September's fool / Univac bug track / Smpte for the Devil / N.Y. avenue playground / Sketches of Saturn (love in space) / Midnight express / N.Y. avenue playground (reprise).

☐ METALHEADZ (see under ⇒ GOLDIE)

METALLICA

Formed: Norvale, California, USA . . . 1981 by LARS ULRICH (this Danish-born drummer had previously filled the stool on a UK tour by DIAMOND HEAD, whose songs METALLICA would later cover) and JAMES HETFIELD (guitar vocals; ex-OBSESSION). Recruiting LLOYD GRAND on guitar, the band recorded their first demo, 'NO LIFE TILL LEATHER' and a one-off 7" single, 'LET IT LOOSE'. In early '82, LLOYD was replaced by future MEGADETH mainman DAVE MUSTAINE, while RON McGOVNEY was brought in on bass. After a brief period of relative stability, MUSTAINE was fired for drunkenness early the following year, being replaced by former EXODUS guitarist KIRK HAMMETT. By this point CLIFF BURTON (ex-TRAUMA) had already joined on bass following the departure of McGOVNEY. This was the classic early METALLICA line-up that played on the first three albums, redefining the boundaries of metal and touring constantly until the tragic death of BURTON in 1986. Moving to New Jersey in early '83, the band signed to John Zazula's 'Megaforce' label and unleashed their high octane debut, 'KILL 'EM ALL' (licensed to 'Music For Nations' for UK release). While it certainly wasn't without cliche, both lyrically and musically, there was a vibrancy in the speed and loudness of their sonic attack that drew on hardcore and punk, particularly in 'SEEK AND DESTROY', a track that would come to be a staple of the band's live set. The record also featured, horror of horrors, a track that consisted entirely of a bass solo! But METALLICA weren't trying to resurrect the indulgence of the 70's, their follow-up opus, 'RIDE THE LIGHTNING' (1984), confirming METALLICA's status as one of the most inventive, promising bands in the metal canon. The group had welded a keening sense of melody to their visceral thrash, alternating between grinding, bass heavy, mid-tempo uber-riffing (the title track and 'FOR WHOM THE BELL TOLLS') and all out pummelling ('FIGHT FIRE WITH FIRE' and 'TRAPPED UNDER ICE'). They even came close to ballad territory with the bleakly beautiful 'FADE TO BLACK', arguably one of the best tracks the band have ever penned. Then came 'MASTER OF PUPPETS' (1986), a masterful collection that rightfully saw METALLICA hailed as one of, if not the, foremost metal act in the world, at the heavier end of the spectrum at least. Opening with the relentless fury of 'BATTERY', followed by the epic, breathtaking dynamics of the title track, the album was almost flawless from start to finish, again using the combination of all-out thrashers alternated with bowel-quaking grinders ('THE THING THAT SHOULD NOT BE', 'WELCOME HOME (SANITARIUM)') to maximum effect. The album went Top 30 in the States without the help of a hit single or even radio play, eventually achieving platinum status. The band subsequently toured with metal godfather, OZZY OSBOURNE, playing to rapturous crowds wherever they went. Disaster struck, however, when the band's tour bus crashed on 27th September '86, BURTON losing his life in the accident. METALLICA decided to carry on, replacing BURTON with JASON NEWSTED (ex-FLOTSAM & JETSAM) and fulfilling their touring commitments. The following summer, the band released an EP of covers, '$5.98 EP – GARAGE DAYS REVISITED', a hotch potch of inspired reworkings from the likes of DIAMOND HEAD, BUDGIE and The MISFITS. The record made both the UK and US Top 30, the US edition containing an extra former KILLING JOKE track (see below). Their next album proper, ' . . .AND JUSTICE FOR ALL' (1988), was marred by overly ambitious structures and complex arrangements as well as a poor production, subduing the trademark gut intensity. Nevertheless, there were moments of brilliance, most notably with 'ONE', a distressing first person narrative of a soldier kept alive on a life support machine. The song almost made the UK Top 10, winning the band a Grammy the following year for Best Metal Performance. With the eponymous transatlantic No.1, 'METALLICA' (1991), the band entered the major league alongside the likes of U2 and R.E.M. as one of the biggest rock bands in the world. The aptly named Bob Rock had given the record a cleaner, 'big rock' sound that complemented the more melodic and accessible material contained within. Not that METALLICA had gone limp on the Beavis & Butthead element of their fanbase, 'ENTER SANDMAN' was as crunchingly heavy as ever, yet the single possessed a sufficiently strong melodic hook to see it go Top 5 in the UK. With 'NOTHING ELSE MATTERS', METALLICA really had penned a WISHBONE ASH-esque ballad, replete with strings (!) which saw the band notch up another Top 10 UK hit. After undertaking the biggest tour heavy rock has ever seen (obliterating co-headliners GUNS N' ROSES in the process), the band came back with another work of mature rock majesty, 'LOAD' (1996). From morbid metal to LYNYRD SKYNYRD-style rootsy acoustics, METALLICA once more developed and expanded their sonic palate, gaining widespread acclaim. The album went on to sell almost ten million copies, the band headlining the American Lollapolooza tour to promote it, again blowing most of the other acts away. Not exactly the most prolific of bands, METALLICA surpassed themselves by releasing a successor to 'LOAD' the following year, entitled, appropriately enough, 'RE-LOAD'. While other heavy rock acts flounder under the weight of 90's expectations, METALLICA continue to innovate and energise a tired genre, even, God forbid, cutting their hair(!) in line with their new standing as the post-modern kings of metal. In the Spring of '99, HETFIELD, ULRICH and Co were planning an orchestrated performance with composer MICHAEL KAMEN at the helm of the San Francisco Symphony Orchestra, a 'best of' live album, 'S&M' hitting the bemused public later in the year. Three years into the new millennium and more than two decades into a genre-defining career, the trio of HETFIELD, ULRICH and HAMMETT (together with longtime producer ROBERT TRUJILLO on bass, as a replacement for the departed NEWSTED) returned with all the sonic brutality and unalloyed rage that had perhaps been missing in their recent work. Judging by the fear and loathing within these pulverising grooves, HETFIELD's recent stint in rehab seemed to have unlocked a fearsome closet of skeletons, the frontman raging at the world and, in the process, unleashing a momentum that had his band members caged-in from the opening bars. • **Songwriters:** ULRICH-HETFIELD, bar other covers on record; BLITZKRIEG (Blitzkrieg) / CRASH COURSE IN BRAIN SURGERY + BREADFAN (Budgie) / AM I EVIL? + THE PRINCE + HELPLESS + IT'S ELECTRIC (Diamond Head) / LAST CARESS – GREEN HELL + DIE DIE MY DARLING (Misfits) / KILLING TIME (Sweet Savage) / THE SMALL HOURS (Holocaust) / THE WAIT (Killing Joke) / STONE COLD CRAZY (Queen) / SO WHAT (Anti-Nowhere League) / SABBRA CADABRA (Black Sabbath) / Medley: EVIL – CURSE OF THE PHARAOHS – SATAN'S FALL – A CORPSE WITHOUT SOUL – INTO THE COVEN (Mercyful Fate) / LOVERMAN (Nick Cave) / WHISKEY IN THE JAR (Thin Lizzy) / TURN THE PAGE (Bob Seger & The Silver Bullet Band) / TUESDAY'S GONE (Lynyrd Skynyrd) / OVERKILL + STONE DEAD FOREVER + DAMAGE CASE + TOO LATE, TOO LATE (Motorhead) / FREE SPEECH FOR THE DUMB + THE MORE I SEE (Discharge) / ASTRONOMY (Blue Oster Cult) / NOW I WANNA SNIFF SOME GLUE + CRETIN HOP (Ramones).

Album rating: KILL 'EM ALL (*7) / RIDE THE LIGHTNING (*8) / MASTER OF PUPPETS (*9) / . . . AND JUSTICE FOR ALL (*7) / METALLICA (*10) / LOAD (*8) / RE-LOAD (*6) / GARAGE INC. (*5) / S&M (*5) / ST. ANGER (*7)

JAMES HETFIELD (b. 3 Aug'63, Los Angeles) – vocals, rhythm guitar (ex-OBSESSION, etc) / **LARS ULRICH** (b.16 Dec'63, Gentoss, Copenhagen, Denmark) – drums / with **LLOYD GRAND** – guitar

not iss. Bootleg

Dec 81. (7") **LET IT LOOSE. / KILLING TIME** – [ ]

— (Jan'82) **DAVE MUSTAINE** (b.13 Sep'63, La Mesa, Calif.) – lead guitar, co-writer / **RON McGOVNEY** – bass repl. GRAND (JEF WARNER also played guitar in 1982)

— (early '83) **KIRK HAMMETT** (b.18 Nov'62, San Francisco) – lead guitar (ex-EXODUS) repl. MUSTAINE who was fired due to drunkenness. He was soon to form rivals MEGADETH.

— **CLIFF BURTON** (b.10 Feb'62) – bass (ex-TRAUMA) replaced McGOVNEY

Music For Nations Megaforce

Jul 83. (lp) *(MFN 7)* *<MRI-069>* **KILL 'EM ALL** [ ] [ ]
– Hit the lights / The four horsemen / Motorbreath / Jump in the fire / (Anesthesia) Pulling teeth / Whiplash / Phantom Lord / No remorse / Seek and destroy / Metal militia. *<US re-iss. Mar86; same> (pic-lp.Aug86; MFN 7P) (cd-iss. Apr87; CDMFN 7) <US re-iss. Feb88 on 'Elektra'+=; 60766>* – Am I evil? / Blitzkrieg. *(re-iss. Nov89 on 'Vertigo' lp/c/cd; 838 142-1/-4/-2)*

Jan 84. (12",12"red) *(12KUT 105)* *<MRS 04>* **JUMP IN THE FIRE /** *[us-only]* WHIPLASH (special neckbrace mix). / SEEK AND DESTROY (live) / PHANTOM LORD [ ] [ ]
(re-iss. Mar86, 7"sha-pic-d; PKUT 105)

Jul 84. (lp/c) *(MFN/TMFN 27)* *<769>* **RIDE THE LIGHTNING** 87 100
– Fight fire with fire / Ride the lightning / For whom the bell tolls / Fade to black / Trapped under ice / Escape / Creeping death / The call of Ktulu. *(re-iss. Sep86 cd/pic-lp; CDMFN 27/CDMFN 27P) <US re-iss. Oct84 on 'Elektra'; 60396> (re-iss. Nov89 on 'Vertigo' lp/c/cd; 838410-1/-4/-2) (cd re-iss. Apr00 on 'DCC'; GZS 1136)*

Music For Nations Elektra

Nov 84. (12"pic-d/12") *(P+/12KUT 112)* **CREEPING DEATH. / AM I EVIL. / BLITZKRIEG** [ ] [ ]
(re-iss. Jan87 12"gold/12"blue; GV/CV 12KUT 112)

Mar 86. (lp/pic-d-lp)(c/cd) *(MFN 60/+P)(T/CD MFN 60)* *<9-60439-1>* **MASTER OF PUPPETS** 41 29
– Battery / Master of puppets / The thing that should not be / Welcome home (sanitarium) / Disposable heroes / Leper messiah / Orion / Damage, Inc. *(re-iss. Dec87 d-lp; MFN 60DM) (re-iss. May89 on 'Vertigo' lp/c/cd; 838 141-1/-4/-2)*

— **JASON NEWSTEAD** (b. 4 Mar'63, Battle Creek, Missouri) – bass (ex-FLOTSAM AND JETSAM) repl. CLIFF who was killed in tour bus crash 27 Sep'86 Sweden.

Vertigo Elektra

Aug 87. (12"ep) *(METAL 1-12)* *<60757>* **$5.98 EP – GARAGE DAYS RE-REVISITED** 27 28
– Helpless / Crash course in brain surgery / The small hours / Last caress – Green hell. *<US+=>* – The Wait. *(re-iss. May90 lp/c/cd; 888 788-1/-4/-2)*

Sep 88. (7") *<69357>* **EYE OF THE BEHOLDER. / BREADFAN** – [ ]

Sep 88. (12"ep/cd-ep) *(METAL 2-12/CD2)* **HARVESTER OF SORROW. / BREADFAN. / THE PRINCE** 20 [ ]

Oct 88. (d-lp)(c)(cd) *(VERH/+C 61)(836 062-2)* *<60812>* **. . .AND JUSTICE FOR ALL** 4 Sep88 6
– Blackened / . . .And justice for all / Eye of the beholder / One / The shortest straw / Harvester of sorrow / The frayed ends of sanity / To live is to die / Dyers eve.

Feb 89. (7") *<69329>* **ONE. / THE PRINCE** – 35
(3"cd-s+=) – Eye of the beholder.

Mar 89. (7")(10"pic-d) *(MET 5)(METPD 5-10)* **ONE. / SEEK AND DESTROY (live)** 13 –
(12")(cd-s) *(MET 5-12)(METCD 5)* – ('A'demo) / For whom the bell tolls (live) / Welcome home (sanitarium) (live).
(12"g-f+=) *(METG 5-12)* – Creeping death (live).

Jul 91. (7"pic-d) *(METAL 7)* *<64857>* **ENTER SANDMAN. / STONE COLD CRAZY** 5 16
(12"+=/12"box+=)(cd-s+=) *(MET AL/BX 7-12)(METCD 7)* – Holier than thou.

Aug 91. (cd/c/d-lp) *(510022-2/-4/-1)* *<61113>* **METALLICA** 1 1
– Enter sandman / Sad but true / Holier than thou / The unforgiven / Wherever I may roam / Don't tread on me / Through the never / Nothing else matters / Of wolf and man / The god that failed / My friend of misery / The struggle within.

Nov 91. (7"/7"pic-d) *(METAL/METAP 8)* *<64814>* **THE UNFORGIVEN. / KILLING TIME** 15 35
(12"+=)(cd-s+=) *(METAL 8-12)(METCD 8)* – ('A'demo) / So what.

Apr 92. (7"/7"pic-d) *(META L/P 10)* *<64770>* **NOTHING ELSE MATTERS. / ENTER SANDMAN (live)** 6 Mar92 34
(12"+=)(cd-s+=) *(METAL 10-12)(METCD 10)* – Harvester of sorrow (live) / ('A'demo).
(live-cd-s+=) *(METCL 10)* – Stone cold crazy (live) / Sad but true (live).

— On tour only **JOHN MARSHALL (of METAL CHURCH)** repl. injured (burnt) HETFIELD

Oct 92. (7"/7"pic-d) *(METAL/METAP 9)* *<64741>* **WHEREVER I MAY ROAM. / FADE TO BLACK (live)** 25 Jul92 82

(pic-cd-s+=) *(METCD 9)* – ('A'demo).
(cd-s) *(METCB 9)* – ('A'side) / Last caress – Am I evil? – Battery (live medley).
(12"+=) *(METAL 9-12)* – ('A'demo).

Oct 92. (c-s) *<64696>* **SAD BUT TRUE / SO WHAT?** [–] [98]

Feb 93. (7") *(METAL 11) <64696>* **SAD BUT TRUE. / NOTHING ELSE MATTERS** [20] [–]
(12"+=,12"pic-d+=)(cd-s+=) *(METAL 11-12)(METCD 11)* – Creeping death (live) / ('A'demo).
(pic-cd-s) *(METCH 11)* – ('A'side) / ('B'live) / ('A'live).

Dec 93. (d-cd/d-c) *(518 726-2/-4) <61594>* **LIVE SHIT: BINGE & PURGE (live)** [54] [26]
– Enter sandman / Creeping death / Harvester of sorrow / Welcome home (sanitarium) / Sad but true / Of wolf and man / Guitar doodle / The unforgiven / And justice for all / Solos (bass/guitar) / Through the never / From whom the bell tolls / Fade to black / Master of puppets / Seek & destroy / Whiplash / Nothing else matters / Wherever I may roam / Am I evil? / Last caress / One / Battery. *(d-c+=)* – The four horsemen / Motorbreath / Stone cold crazy. *(also issued 3 videos + book, etc 'METALLICAN')*

May 96. (10"red-ep) *(METAL 12)* **UNTIL IT SLEEPS. / 2x4 (live) / UNTIL IT SLEPS (Moby remix)** [18] [–]
(cd-s) *(METCD 12)* – ('A'-Herman Melville mix) / 2x4 (live) / F.O.B.D. (aka; Until It Sleeps – demo).
(cd-s) *(METCX 12)* – (first & third tracks) / Kill – Ride (medley; Ride the lightning – No remorse – Hit the lights – The four horsemen – Phantom Lord – Fight fire with fire).

May 96. (c-s) *<64276>* **UNTIL IT SLEEPS / OVERKILL** [–] [10]

Jun 96. (cd/c/d-lp) *(532 618-2/-4/-1) <61923>* **LOAD** [1] [1]
– Ain't my bitch / 2 x 4 / The house Jack built / Until it sleeps / King Nothing / Hero of the day / Bleeding me / Cure / Poor twisted me / Wasting my hate / Mama said / Thorn within / Ronnie / The outlaw torn.

Sep 96. (12"ep) *(METAL 13)* **HERO OF THE DAY / MOULDY (aka HERO OF THE DAY – early demo version). / HERO OF THE DAY (outta b sides mix) / OVERKILL** [17] [–]
(cd-ep) *(METCD 13)* – ('A'side) / Overkill / Damage case / Hero of the day (outta b sides mix).
(cd-ep) *(METCX 13)* – ('A'side) / Stone dead forever / Too late too late / Mouldy (aka 'Hero Of The Day' – early demo version).
(cd-ep) *(METCY 13)* – ('A'side) / Overkill / Damage case / Stone dead forever / Too late too late.
(because of length of above, it also hit 47 in UK album charts)

Oct 96. (c-s) *<64248>* **HERO OF THE DAY / KILL – RIDE (medley)** [–] [60]

Nov 96. (7"pic-d) *(METAL 14)* **MAMA SAID. / AIN'T MY BITCH (live)** [19] [ ]
(cd-s) *(METCD 14)* – ('A'side) / King Nothing (live) / Whiplash (live) / ('A'edit).
(cd-s) *(METCX 14)* – ('A'side) / So what (live) / Creeping death (live) / ('A'-early demo).

Feb 97. (cd-s) *<64197>* **KING NOTHING / AIN'T MY BITCH (live)** [–] [90]

Nov 97. (7") *(METAL 15) <64126>* **THE MEMORY REMAINS. / FOR WHOM THE BELL TOLLS (Haven't Heard It Yet mix)** [13] [28]
(cd-s) *(METCD 15)* – ('A'side) / Fuel for fire / Memory (demo).
(cd-s) *(METDD 15)* – ('A'side) / The outlaw torn (Unencumbered By Manufacturing Restrictions version) / King Nothing (Tepid mix).

—— MARIANNE FAITHFULL supplied backing vocals on above single

Nov 97. (cd/c/d-lp) *(536409-2/-4/-1) <62126>* **RELOAD** [4] [1]
– Fuel / The memory remains / The Devil's dance / Unforgiven II / Better than you / Carpe diem baby / Prince Charming / Bad seed / Where the wild things are / Slither / Low man's lyric / Attitude / Fixxer.

Feb 98. (cd-ep) *(METCD 17) <64114>* **THE UNFORGIVEN II / HELPLESS (live) / The four horsemen (live) / Of wolf and man (live)** [15] Mar98 [59]
(cd-ep) *(METDD 17)* – ('A'side) / The thing that should not be (live) / The memory remains (live) / King nothing (live).
(cd-ep) *(METCX 17)* – ('A'side) / No remorse (live) / Am I evil? (live) / The unforgiven II (demo).

Jun 98. (cd-ep) *(METCD 16)* **FUEL / SAD BUT TRUE (live) / NOTHING ELSE MATTERS (live)** [31] [ ]
(cd-ep) *(METDD 16)* – ('A'side) / Wherever I roam (live) / One (live).
(cd-ep) *(METED 16)* – ('A'side) / Until it sleeps (live) / ('A'live) / ('A'demo).

Nov 98. (d-cd/d-c/d-lp) *(538351-2/-4/-1) <62323>* **GARAGE INC.** (the covers) [29] [2]
– Free speech for the dumb / It's electric / Sabba cadabra / Turn the page / Die die my darling / Loverman / Mercyful Fate medley:- Evil – Curse of the pharaohs – Satan's fall – A corpse without soul – Into the coven / Astronomy / Whiskey in the jar / Tuesday's gone / The more I see / Helpless / The small hours / The wait / Crash course in brain surgery / Last caress – Green hell / Am I evil? / Blitzkrieg / Breadfan / The prince / Stone cold crazy / So what? / Killing time / Overkill / Damage case / Stone dead forever / Too late, too late.

Nov 98. (cd-ep) *(566591-2)* **TURN THE PAGE / STONE COLD CRAZY (live) / THE WAIT (live) / BLEEDING ME (live)** [ ] [ ]

Feb 99. (cd-s) *(566855-2)* **WHISKEY IN THE JAR / BLITZKREIG (live) / THE PRINCE (live)** [29] [ ]
(cd-s) *(566857-2)* – ('A'side) / The small hours (live) / Killing time (live).
(cd-s) *(566859-2)* – ('A'side) / Last caress – Green hell (live) / Whiskey in the jar (live).

Jun 99. (cd-ep) *(METCD 20)* **DIE DIE MY DARLING / SABBRA CADABRA (live) / MERCYFUL FATE MEDLEY (live)** [ ] [ ]

Nov 99. (d-cd/d-c) *(546797-2/-4) <62463>* **S&M** (live with the San Francisco Symphony Orchestra) [33] [2]
– The ecstasy of gold / The call of the Ktulu / Master of puppets / Of wolf and man / The thing that should not be / Fuel / The memory remains / No leaf clover / Hero of the day / Devil's dance / Bleeding me / Nothing else matters / Until it sleeps / For whom the bell tolls / Human / Wherever I may roam / Outlaw torn / Sad but true / One / Enter sandman / Battery. *(re-iss. Apr00; same)*

Mar 00. (cd-s) *(562696-2) <album cut>* **NO LEAF CLOVER / ('A'-enhanced CD-Rom) / "S&M" Documentary (enhanced first 15 minutes)** [ ] Feb00 [74]
(cd-s) *(562697-2)* – ('A'side) / (photo gallery and album lyrics CD-Rom) / "S&M" Documentary (enhanced second 15 minutes).
(cd-s) *(562698-2)* – ('A'side) / (Metallica screensaver) / "S&M" Documentary (enhanced third 15 minutes).

Jul 00. (cd-s) *(0113875HWR) <album cut>* **I DISAPPEAR / I DISAPPEAR (instrumental)** [35] Feb00 [76]
(above iss.on 'Edel-Hollywood')

—— **ROBERT TRUJILLO** – bass; repl. NEWSTED (left in 2001)

Mercury Elektra

Jun 03. (cd/c/d-lp) *(986533-2/-4/-6) <62853>* **ST. ANGER** [3] [1]
– Frantic / St. Anger / Some kind of monster / Dirty window / Invisible kid / My world / Shoot me again / Sweet amber / The unnamed feeling / Purify / All within my hands.

Jun 03. (7") *(986541-1)* **ST. ANGER. / WE'RE A HAPPY FAMILY** [9] [–]
(cd-s) *(986541-2)* – ('A'side) / Commando / Today your love tomorrow the world.
(cd-s) *(986541-3)* ('A'side) / Now I wanna sniff some glue / Cretin hop / ('A'-video).

Sep 03. (12") *(981151-5)* **FRANTIC. / FRANTIC (UNKLE remix)** [16] [–]
(cd-s) *(981151-3)* – ('A'side) / Blackened (live) / Harvester of sorrow (live) / ('A'-video).
(cd-s) *(981151-4)* – ('A'side) / No remorse (live) / Welcome home – Sanitarium (live).

– compilations, others, etc. –

Aug 87. (7"ep/7"pic-ep) *Megaforce; <MRS 04/+P>* **WHIPLASH EP** [–] [ ]

Feb 90. (cd/c) *Vertigo; (642 219-2/-4)* **METALLICA** [ ] [ ]
– (JUMP IN THE FIRE + CREEPING DEATH singles).

May 90. (6x12"box) *Vertigo; (875 487-1)* **THE GOOD, THE BAD & THE LIVE – THE 6 1/2 YEARS ANNIVERSARY COLLECTION** [56] [–]

Apr 98. (cd) *Ranch Life; (CRANCH 1)* **BAY AREA THRASHERS** [ ] [ ]
(also pic-lp on 'Collectors Picture Disc Series'; CPD 014)

☐ METERS (see under ⇒ NEVILLE BROTHERS)

☐ METHOD MAN (see under ⇒ WU-TANG CLAN)

George MICHAEL

Born: GEORGIOS KYRIACOS PANAYIOTOU, 25 Jun'63, Finchley, Middlesex, England. After meeting and befriending ANDREW RIDGELEY (b.26 Jan'63, Windlesham, Surrey, England) at Bushey Meads comprehensive school, the pair left in 1979 to form ska band, The EXECUTIVE, with DAVID AUSTIN, ANDREW LEAVER and RIDGELEY's brother, PAUL. A couple of years later, the Adonis-like MICHAEL and the chiselled RIDGELEY broke away to form their own teen-dream duo, WHAM!, subsequently signing to Mark Dean's new 'Innervision' label. Disposable and contrived as they may have been, 'WHAM RAP (ENJOY WHAT YOU DO)' was as subversive as any po-faced post-punk outfit with its lyrical subtext of no work and all play, while 'YOUNG GUNS (GO FOR IT)' was in the same vein as The Special's 'TOO MUCH TOO YOUNG' (thematically, not musically!). With hit after hit of bouncy, sun-kissed lads-on-the-pull gleam-pop, WHAM! certainly brightened up the dour early 80's scene, their debut album, 'FANTASTIC' (1983), topping the UK charts. MICHAEL made his first inroads to America, meanwhile, when 'WAKE ME UP BEFORE YOU GO-GO' gave WHAM! a transatlantic No.1 in summer '84. Having finally broken free from 'Innervision' after a protracted legal battle, WHAM! were now signed to 'Epic', MICHAEL simultaneously making the first tentative steps towards a solo career via the moody 'CARELESS WHISPER', another UK/US No.1. With the breathless heartbreak of 'FREEDOM', WHAM! approached pop genius, going out on a high with a further couple of stellar No.1's ('I'M YOUR MAN' and 'THE EDGE OF HEAVEN'), a tour of China (!) and a knicker-wetting farewell concert at Wembley Stadium. The band split around the same time as MICHAEL scored his second No.1 solo hit with 'A DIFFERENT CORNER', and by now it was abundantly clear which one of the duo was destined for greater things. Having previously sung 'Don't Let The Sun Go Down On Me' at Live Aid with ELTON JOHN, MICHAEL teamed up with soul belter, ARETHA FRANKLIN in early '87 for a rendition of 'I KNEW YOU WERE WAITING (FOR ME)', another No.1 hit. His solo debut proper came later that summer with the deliberately controversial 'I WANT YOUR SEX', a semi-successful attempt at PRINCE-like raunch-funk which hardly warranted its BBC ban. Much more effective was the boot-tapping strum'n'roll of 'FAITH', MICHAEL desperate to prove his newly acquired 'adult' cred with the obligatory designer stubble, biker jacket, 501's and shades. The accompanying album of the same name was a transatlantic million seller, going down particularly well in the States where its streamlined pop/rock found a massive audience; out of an incredible four further hit singles, two ('ONE MORE TRY' and 'MONKEY') topped the US charts. MICHAEL's subsequent retreat from the glare of the media spotlight and a more introspective, soul baring follow-up in 'LISTEN WITHOUT PREJUDICE VOL.1' (1990) led to the GEORGE MICHAEL hit machine faltering somewhat; though it again made the No.1 spot, the record only spawned two major hits in 'PRAYING FOR TIME' and the mercifully more upbeat 'FREEDOM '90'. Freedom from the machinations of the music industry, that is, MICHAEL's grievances leading him into a marathon court battle with 'Sony'; the singer complained that the company had done little to promote his new direction, still wanting to present him as a sex symbol against his wishes. His restraint of trade action against the corporation was eventually thrown out of court in summer '94 when the judge upheld MICHAEL's multi-million pound contract, the singer duly vowing never to record for the company again. The whole sorry debacle was eventually resolved in summer '95 when 'Sony' released MICHAEL from his contract with a number of attached conditions (share of profits from future works etc.), 'Virgin' ('Dreamworks' in the States) signing the superstar in a multi-million pound deal. His absence from the charts certainly hadn't affected his popularity and his first single in almost four years, the delicate 'JESUS TO A CHILD', made the UK No.1 in early '96. A funkier follow-up, 'FASTLOVE', also topped the charts as did his comeback album, 'OLDER' (1996). Older and no doubt wiser, MICHAEL was nevertheless still seemingly troubled by the moody angst which had characterised 'LISTEN . . .', although this time around there was less navel contemplation and more melodic sophistication. Although he may have joined the ranks of the ultra-tasteful MOR brigade alongside ELTON JOHN, ERIC CLAPTON etc., MICHAEL continues to command a wide cross section of fans, not least the WHAM! teenyboppers who grew up with his music. However, tabloids were having a field day on the 7th of April, 1998, after GEORGE was arrested for lewd behavoir in a Beverly Hills park toilet; the undercover policeman we assume was not "taking the Michael". It was not a shock to most people that GEORGE was indeed gay, having admittedly never been intimate with a woman for over ten years. He was subsequently fined nearly $1000 and ordered to deliver meals to AIDS sufferers as part of an 80-hour community service order; the American TV cameras were of course there to interview GEORGE – he also appeared on the David Letterman show. The police officer in question, Marcello Rodriguez, was none too happy when GEORGE's next video for his single, 'OUTSIDE', allegedly depicted mock scenes of the arrest; the man would later sue. Meanwhile, a 'greatest hits' package, 'LADIES AND GENTLEMEN' (1998), was a success all over the world, although what the fans made of MICHAEL's end of the millennium covers album, 'SONGS FROM THE LAST CENTURY' (1999), is anyone's guess. Much more encouraging – not to mention hip – was the 'FREEEK' single, GEORGE's sybaritic, grindingly erotic return to the dancefloor after too long an absence. A UK Top 10 hit, it was followed up later that summer with 'SHOOT THE DOG', which scraped in at only No.12. • **The Covers:** BROTHER, CAN YOU SPARE A DIME? (hit; Bing Crosby) / ROXANNE (Police) / YOU'VE CHANGED (Carey-Fischer) / MY BABY JUST CARES FOR ME (hit; Nina Simone) / THE FIRST TIME EVER I SAW YOUR FACE (Ewan MacColl) / Miss Sarajevo (Passengers) / I REMEMBER YOU (Mercer-Schertzinger) / SECRET LOVE (hit; Doris Day) / WILD IS THE WIND (hit; Nina Simone) / WHERE OR WHEN – ITS ALRIGHT WITH ME (Hart-Rodgers – Cole Porter) / AS (Stevie Wonder) / THE LONG AND WINDING ROAD (Beatles).

Album rating: Wham!: FANTASTIC (*5) / MAKE IT BIG (*5) / THE FINAL (*4) / George Michael: FAITH (*8) / LISTEN WITHOUT PREJUDICE VOL.1 (*7) / OLDER (*6) / LADIES AND GENTLEMEN – THE BEST OF GEORGE MICHAEL compilation (*8) / SONGS FROM THE LAST CENTURY (*5)

WHAM!

GEORGE MICHAEL – vocals, bass / **ANDREW RIDGELEY** – guitar, keyboards

		Innervision		Columbia
Jun 82.	(7") *(IVLA 2442)* **WHAM RAP! (ENJOY WHAT YOU DO). / WHAM RAP! (unsocial mix)**		Feb83	
	(12"+=) *(IVLA13 2442)* – ('A'-Special US mix). *(re-act.Jan83, hit UK No.8)*			
Sep 82.	(7"/12") *(INVA/+13 2766)* **YOUNG GUNS (GO FOR IT). / GOING FOR IT**	3		–
May 83.	(7"/7"pic-d) *(INVA/INVWA 3143)* *<03932>* **BAD BOYS. / ('A'instrumental)**	2	Aug83	60
Jul 83.	(lp/c; US – as WHAM UK) *(INV/40 25328)* *<038911>* **FANTASTIC**	1		83
	– Bad boys / A ray of sunshine / Love machine / Wham rap (enjoy what			

you do) / Club Tropicana / Nothing looks the same in the light / Come on / Young guns (go for it). *(cd-iss. Jan84; CD 25328) (re-iss. Mar88 on 'Epic' lp/c; 450090-1/-4) (re-iss. +=)* – (extra instrumental).

Jul 83. (7"/7"pic-d) *(INVA/INVWA 3613)* **CLUB TROPICANA. / BLUE (ARMED WITH LOVE)** [4] [–]
(12"+=) *(INVA13 3613)* – ('A'instrumental).

Nov 83. (7") *(A 3586)* **CLUB FANTASTIC MEGAMIX. / A RAY OF SUNSHINE (instrumental)** [15] [–]
(12"+=) *(INVA13 3586)* – Come on / Love machine.

Epic Columbia

May 84. (7") *(A 4440)* *<04552>* **WAKE ME UP BEFORE YOU GO-GO. / ('A'instrumental)** [1] Sep84 [1]
(12"+=) *(TA 4440)* – A ray of sunshine.

— <in the US still credited to **WHAM featuring GEORGE MICHAEL**>

Jul 84. (7"/7"sha-pic-d/12"; by GEORGE MICHAEL) *(A/WA/TA 4603) <04691>* **CARELESS WHISPER. / ('A'instrumental)** [1] Dec84 [1]

Oct 84. (7"/7"sha-pic-d) *(A/QA 4743)* **FREEDOM. / (instrumental)** [1] [–]
(12"+=) *(TA 4743)* – ('A'extended).

Nov 84. (lp/c/cd) *(EPC/40/CD 86311) <39595>* **MAKE IT BIG** [1] [1]
– Wake me up before you go-go / Everything she wants / Heartbeat / Like a baby / Freedom / If you were there / Credit card baby / Careless whisper. *(re-iss. Oct89 lp/c; 465576-1/-4) <US pic-lp; >*

Dec 84. (7"/12") *(WHAM/+T 1)* **LAST CHRISTMAS. / EVERYTHING SHE WANTS** [2] [–]

Feb 85. (7") *<04840>* **EVERYTHING SHE WANTS. / LIKE A BABY** [–] [1]

Jul 85. (7") *<05409>* **FREEDOM. / HEARTBEAT** [–] [3]

— (In Jun'85, he dueted with ELTON JOHN for LIVE AID on his song 'DON'T LET THE SUN GO DOWN ON ME'). Also from same source Nov85, 'WRAP HER UP' again w / ELTON JOHN was issued as 45 and hit UK No.12, US No.20.

Nov 85. (7") *(A 6716) <05721>* **I'M YOUR MAN. / DO IT RIGHT (instrumental)** [1] [20]
(12"+=/12"pic-d+=) *(TA/WTA 6716)* – ('A'acappella version).

Dec 85. (7") *(re-issue)* **LAST CHRISTMAS. / BLUE (ARMED WITH LOVE) (live)** [6] [–]
(12"+=) *(re-issue)* – Everything she wants.

Mar 86. (7"/12"; by GEORGE MICHAEL) *(A/TA 7033) <05888>* **A DIFFERENT CORNER. / ('A'instrumental)** [1] [7]

Jun 86. (7") *(FIN 1)* **THE EDGE OF HEAVEN. / WHERE DID YOUR HEART GO?** [1] [–]
(d7"+=/12"+=) *(FIN/+T 1)* – Battlestations / Wham rap '86.

Jun 86. (7") *<06182>* **THE EDGE OF HEAVEN. / BLUE (live in China)** [–] [10]
(12"+=) *<40285>* – Where did your heart go? / Battlestations / Wham rap '86 / A different corner.

Oct 86. (7") *<06294>* **WHERE DID YOUR HEART GO?. / WHAM RAP '86** [–] [50]

— (WHAM! by this time had already split)

Oct 86. (d-lp/c/cd) *(EPC/40/CD 88681)* **THE FINAL** [1] [–]
– Wham! rap (enjoy what you do) / Young guns (go for it!) / Bad boys / Club Tropicana / Wake me up before you go-go / Careless whisper / Freedom / Last Christmas (pudding mix) / Everything she wants (remix) / I'm your man / A different corner / Battlestations / Where did your heart go? / The edge of Heaven. *(also iss.on 2 gold-lp's) (re-hit UK No.27 in Jun99)*

– compilations, etc. –

on 'Epic' unless mentioned otherwise

Sep 86. (c-ep) *(EPC 450 125-4)* **THE 12" TAPE** [ ] [–]
– Wham rap / Careless whisper / Freedom / Everything she wants / I'm your man.

Dec 86. (7") *(650 269-7)* **LAST CHRISTMAS. / WHERE DID YOUR HEART GO** [ ] [–]
(12"+=) *(650 269-6)* – ('A'&'B'extended).

Dec 86. (lp) *(WHAM 2)* **WHAM! BOXED SET** [ ] [–]

Nov 97. (cd/c) *(89020)* **THE BEST OF WHAM!** [4] [ ]
– If you were there / I'm your man / Everything she wants / Club Tropicana / Wake me up before you go-go / Like a baby / Freedom / The edge of Heaven / Wham rap! (enjoy what you do) / Young guns (go for it) / Last Christmas / Where did your heart go? / Everything she wants '97 / I'm your man.

GEORGE MICHAEL

Epic Columbia

Jan 87. (7"/12"; by ARETHA FRANKLIN & GEORGE MICHAEL) *(DUET/+T 2) <9559>* **I KNEW YOU WERE WAITING (FOR ME). / (instrumental)** [1] [3]
(above jointly issued on 'Arista':- ARETHA's label)

— GEORGE went solo, as did his WHAM! partner, ANDREW RIDGELEY

Jun 87. (7") *(LUST 1) <07164>* **I WANT YOUR SEX. / (instrumental)** [3] [2]
(c-s+=/12"+=/12"pic-d+=)(cd-s+=) *(LUST C/T/QT 1)(CDLUST 1)* – Rhythm 1 – Lust / Rhythm 2 – Brass in love / Rhythm 3 – A last request.

Oct 87. (7") *(EMU 3) <07623>* **FAITH. / HAND TO MOUTH** [2] [1]
(c-s+=/12"+=/12"pic-d+=) *(EMU C/T/P 3)* – ('A'instrumental).
(cd-s+=) *(CDEMU 3)* – Hard day (mix).

Nov 87. (lp/c/cd/pic-cd) *(460000-1/-4/-2/-9) <40867>* **FAITH** [1] [1]
– Faith / Father figure / I want your sex (part 1 & 2) / One more try / Hard day / Hand to mouth / Look at your hands / Monkey / Kissing a fool. *(re-iss. Sep90, hit UK 40)*

Dec 87. (7"/7"sha-pic-d) *(EMU/+P 4)* **FATHER FIGURE. / LOVE'S IN NEED OF LOVE TODAY** [11] [–]
(12"+=/cd-s+=) *(EMUT/CDEMU 4)* – ('A'instrumental).

Jan 88. (7") *<07682>* **FATHER FIGURE. / ('A'instrumental)** [–] [1]

Apr 88. (7"/7"s/12"/pic-cd-s) *(EMU/EMUB/EMYT/CDEMU 5) <07773>* **ONE MORE TRY. / LOOK AT YOUR HANDS** [8] [1]

Jul 88. (7") *(EMU 6) <07941>* **MONKEY. / MONKEY (acappella)** [13] [1]
(12"+=/cd-s+=) *(EMUT/CDEMU 6)* – ('A'extended versions).

Nov 88. (7") *(EMU 7) <08050>* **KISSING A FOOL. / (instrumental)** [18] Oct88 [5]
(12"+=/cd-s+=) *(EMUT/CDEMU 7)* – Rhythm 3 – A last request.

Aug 90. (7"/c-s) *(GEO/+M 1) <73512>* **PRAYING FOR TIME. / IF YOU WERE MY WOMAN** [6] [1]
(12"+=/cd-s+=) *(GEOT/CDGEO 1)* – Waiting (reprise).

Aug 90. (cd/c/lp) *(467 295-2/-4/-1) <46898>* **LISTEN WITHOUT PREJUDICE VOL.1** [1] [2]
– Praying for time / Freedom '90 / They won't go when I go / Something to save / Cowboys and angels / Waiting for that day / Mother's pride / Head the pain / Soul free / Waiting (reprise).

Oct 90. (7"/c-s/12") *(GEO/+M/T 2)* **WAITING FOR THAT DAY. / FANTASY** [23] [–]
(cd-s+=/pic-cd-d+=) *(GEOC/CDGEO 2)* – Kissing a fool / Father figure.

Oct 90. (c-s) *<73559>* **FREEDOM / FANTASY** [–] [8]

Dec 90. (7"/c-s) *(GEO/+M 3)* **FREEDOM '90. / FREEDOM (mix)** [28] [–]
(12"+=/cd-s+=) *(GEO T/C 3)* – Mother's pride.

Jan 91. (c-s) *<73663>* **MOTHER'S PRIDE. / WAITING FOR THAT DAY** [–] [46] [27]

Feb 91. (7"/c-s/12"/cd-s) *(656 647-7/-4/-6/-2)* **HEAL THE PAIN. / SOUL FREE** [31] [–]
(cd-s+=) *(656 647-5)* – Hand to mouth.

Mar 91. (7"/c-s/12"/cd-s) *(656 774-7/-4/-6/-2)* **COWBOYS AND ANGELS. / SOMETHING TO SAVE** [45] [–]

Nov 91. (7"/c-s; GEORGE MICHAEL & ELTON JOHN) *(657 646-7/-4) <74086>* **DON'T LET THE SUN GO DOWN ON ME. / I BELIEVE (WHEN I FALL IN LOVE IT WILL BE FOREVER)** [1] [1]
(12"+=) *(657 646-6)* – Last Christmas.
(cd-s+=) *(657 646-2)* – If you were my woman / Fantasy.

Jun 92. (7"/c-s/ext-12"/ext.cd-s) *(658 058-7/-4/-6/-2) <74353>* **TOO FUNKY. / CRAZYMAN DANCE** [4] [10]

— In Nov'92, GEORGE took 'Sony' to court for around $50m. In April '93, he teamed up with QUEEN on UK No.1 + US No.46 'FIVE LIVE EP'.

Virgin Dreamworks

Jan 96. (c-s/cd-s) *(VSC/+DG 1571) <59000>* **JESUS TO A CHILD / ONE MORE TRY (live gospel version)** [1] [7]
(cd-s+=) *(VSCDX 1571)* – Older (instrumental).

Apr 96. (12"/c-s) *(VST/VSC 1579) <59001>* **FASTLOVE / I'M YOUR MAN** [1] [8]
(cd-s+=) *(VSCD 1579)* – Fastlove (part II).

May 96. (cd/c/lp) *(CD/TC+/V 2802) <50000>* **OLDER** [1] [6]
– Jesus to a child / Fastlove / Older / Spinning the wheel / It doesn't really matter / The strangest thing / To be forgiven / Move on / Star people / You have been loved / Free. *(cd-iss. Dec97 as 'OLDER AND UPPER' +=; CDVX 2802)* – Fastlove (part II) / Spinning

the wheel / The strangest thing / You know what I want to do / Safe.

Aug 96. (7"/c-s) *(VSLH/VSC 1595)* **SPINNING THE WHEEL. / ('A'mix)** [2] [–]
(cd-s+=) *(VSCDG 1595)* – You know that I want to / Safe.
(cd-s) *(VSCDX 1595)* – ('A'-Forthright mix) / Fastlove (Forthright edit) / ('A'-Jon Douglas mix).

Jan 97. (7"ep/c-ep/cd-ep) *(VS LH/C/CDG 1626)* **OLDER / I CAN'T MAKE YOU LOVE ME. / DESAFINADO / THE STRANGEST THING (live)** [3] [–]
(cd-ep) *(VSCDE 1626)* – ('A'mixes).

May 97. (c-s/12"/cd-s) *(VSC/VSLH/VSCDG 1641)* **STAR PEOPLE '97. / EVERYTHING SHE WANTS** [2] [–]
(cd-s) *(VSCDX 1641)* – ('A'mixes).

—— In Jun'97, GEORGE was credited on the UK Top 10 single 'Waltz Away Dreaming' by TOBY BOURKE.

Sep 97. (c-s/cd-s) *(VSC/VSDG 1663)* **YOU HAVE BEEN LOVED / THE STRANGEST THING '97 / FATHER FIGURE** [2] [–]
(cd-s+=) *(VSCDX 1663)* – Praying for time.

Epic Epic

Oct 98. (c-s/cd-s) *(666562-4/-2)* **OUTSIDE / FANTASY 98 OUTSIDE (Jon Douglas remix)** [2] [ ]
(cd-s) *(666562-5)* – ('A'mixes; garage / house / K-Gee's cut).

Nov 98. (cd/c) *(491705-2/-4)* *<69635>* **LADIES AND GENTLEMEN – THE BEST OF GEORGE MICHAEL** (compilation) [1] [24]
– Jesus to a child / Father figure / Careless whisper / Don't let the sun go down on me / You have been loved / Kissing a fool / I can't make you love me / Heal the pain / A moment with you / Desafinado / Cowboys and angels / Praying for time / One more time / A different corner / Waltz away dreaming / Outside / As / Fastlove / Too funky / Freedom 90 / Star people 97 / Killer – Papa was a rollin' stone / I want your sex (pt.II) / Strangest thing 97 / Monkey / Spinning the wheel / Waiting for the day – You can't always get what you want / I knew you were waiting (for me) / Faith. *(c+=)* – Hard day / Somebody to love.

Mar 99. (c-s; by GEORGE MICHAEL & MARY J BLIGE) *(667012-4)* **AS / A DIFFERENT CORNER** [4] [ ]
(cd-s) *(667012-2)* – ('A'mixes; original / full crew / CJ Mackintosh x2).
(cd-s+=) *(667012-5)* – ('A'-CD-Rom).

Dec 99. (cd/c) *(CD TC/VX 2920)* *<48740>* **SONGS FROM THE LAST CENTURY** [2] [ ]
– Brother, can you spare a dime? / Roxanne / You've changed / My baby just cares for me / The first time ever I saw your face / Miss Sarajevo / I remember you / Secret love / Wild is the wind / Where or when. *(UK+=)* – It's alright with me (instrumental).

Mar 02. (c-s) *(570697-4)* *<570681>* **FREEEK! / THE LONG AND WINDING ROAD** [7] [ ]
(cd-s+=) *(570682-2)* – ('A'-Max Reich mix).
(cd-s) *(570681-2)* – ('A'side) / ('A'-Scumfrog mix) / ('A'-Moogymen mix).

Jul 02. (c-s) *(570924-4)* **SHOOT THE DOG / (Moogymen mix)** [12] [–]
(cd-s+=) *(570924-2)* – ('A'-Alex Kid shoot the club mix) / ('A'-video).

☐ MIKE + THE MECHANICS (see under ⇒ GENESIS)

Frankie MILLER

Born: 2 Nov'49, Bridgeton, Glasgow, Scotland. After serving his musical apprenticeship in a series of pub outfits during the late 60's, MILLER relocated to London in mid '71. Newly installed in the capital, he formed JUDE alongside guitar maestro ROBIN TROWER and a rhythm section of JIM DEWAR and CLIVE BUNKER. The project proved short-lived, however, as TROWER went solo early the following year, taking DEWAR with him. Teaming up with ex-members of the underrated BRINSLEY SCHWARZ (i.e. NICK LOWE, BOB ANDREWS, BILLY RANKIN and BRINSLEY SCHWARZ himself), MILLER proceeded to cut a debut solo album, 'ONCE IN A BLUE MOON' (1973) for 'Chrysalis'. The record failed to chart and the footloose singer-songwriter upped sticks for New Orleans where he hooked up with semi-legendary Crescent City soul guru, Allen Toussaint for the 'HIGHLIFE' (1974) album. Despite furnishing classic hits for Betty Wright ('SHOORAH SHOORAH') and Three Dog Night ('PLAY SOMETHING SWEET'), the album provided scant commercial pickings for MILLER himself. Returning to the UK, he amassed a band consisting of HENRY McCULLOUGH, MICK WEAVER, CHRISSY STEWART and STU PERRY, cutting a third album, 'THE ROCK' (1975). Again sales were disappointing and it was 1977 before MILLER scored a rare Top 30 hit with 'BE GOOD TO YOURSELF', the lead track on that year's 'FULL HOUSE' album. Released under the moniker FRANKIE MILLER'S FULL HOUSE, the record was recorded with a new band that lasted barely a year before MILLER again went solo. Augmented by such talents as PAUL CARRACK, 1978's 'DOUBLE TROUBLE' was another fine set of gravel-throated blues-rock that failed to notch up respectable sales. Retaining CARRACK and utilising a cast of session men, MILLER was finally rewarded for his efforts when the foot-tappin' parched-blues balladry of 'DARLIN' made the UK Top 10. Incredibly, the accompanying album 'FALLING IN LOVE . . . PERFECT FIT' (1979) still failed to chart, as did 1980's 'EASY MONEY' set, the latter representing his last release for 'Mercury'. Eventually picked up by 'Capitol', MILLER recorded 'STANDING ON THE EDGE' (1982) before cutting 'DANCING IN THE RAIN' (1986) for 'Vertigo' with a band that included such distinguished veterans as BRIAN ROBERTSON and SIMON KIRKE. Having already begun an acting career in 1979 with Peter McDougall's TV play, 'Just A Boy's Game' (for which he also penned/sung the theme tune, 'Playin' The Game'), MILLER increasingly concentrated his energies on thespian matters as the 80's wore on. Despite a brief moment of fame in the early 90's when Tennent's Lager used his version of 'CALEDONIA' in a TV ad, MILLER's career has of late been severely curtailed by serious illness after he suffered a brain aneurysm on the 25th August, 1994; it has robbed him of his speech. One of Scottish music's great underrated performers, MILLER remains almost universally respected among rock's elder statesmen. On the 7th September 2002, a plethora of stars including Joe Walsh, paid tribute to the man at Glasgow's Barrowland; all proceeds went to the Drake Project, a music therapy charity.

Album rating: ONCE IN A BLUE MOON (*6) / HIGH LIFE (*6) / THE ROCK (*6) / FULL HOUSE (*6) / DOUBLE TROUBLE (*6) / FALLING IN LOVE . . . PERFECT FIT (*5) / EASY MONEY (*5) / STANDING ON THE EDGE (*5) / DANCING IN THE RAIN (*4) / THE VERY BEST OF FRANKIE MILLER compilation (**7**)

FRANKIE MILLER – vocals (ex-JUDE) with ex-members of BRINSLEY SCHWARZ (aka NICK LOWE – bass / **BOB ANDREWS** – keyboards / **BRINSLEY SCHWARZ** – guitar / **BILLY RANKIN** – drums)

Chrysalis Chrysalis

Jan 73. (lp) *(<CHR 1036>)* **ONCE IN A BLUE MOON** [ ] [ ]
– You don't need to laugh (to be happy) / I can't change it / Candlelight sonata in f major / Ann Eliza Jane / It's all over / In no resistance / After all (I live my life) / Just like Tom Thumb's blues / Mail box / I'm ready. *(cd-iss. Oct98 on 'Repertoire'; REP 4725)*

—— brought in a number of session men to replace last band

Jan 74. (lp) *(<CHR 1052>)* **HIGH LIFE** [ ] [ ]
– High life / Play something sweet (brickyard blues) / Trouble / A fool / Little angel / With you in mind / The devil gun / I'll take a melody / Just a song / Shoorah shoorah / I'm falling in love again. *(cd-iss. Mar94; CD25CR 04) (cd re-iss. Oct98 on 'Repertoire'; REP 4724)*

FRANKIE MILLER BAND

—— with **HENRY McCULLOUGH** – guitar / **MICK WEAVER** – keyboards / **CHRISSY STEWART** – bass / **STU PERRY** – drums

Sep 75. (7") *(CHS 2074)* **A FOOL IN LOVE. / I KNOW WHY THE SUN DON'T SHINE** [ ] [–]

Dec 75. (lp) *(<CHR 1088>)* **THE ROCK** ☐ ☐
– A fool in love / The heartbreak / The rock / I know why the sun don't shine / Hard on the levee / Ain't got no money / All my love to you / I'm old enough / Bridgeton / Drunken nights in the city. *(cd-iss. Oct98 on 'Repertoire'; REP 4726)*
Jul 76. (7") *(CHS 2095)* **THE ROCK. / THE HEARTBREAK** ☐ [–]
Oct 76. (7") *(CHS 2103)* **LOVING YOU IS SWEETER THAN EVER. / I'M OLD ENOUGH** ☐ [–]
May 77. (7") *(CHS 2147)* **BE GOOD TO YOURSELF. /** [27] [–]

FRANKIE MILLER'S FULL HOUSE

— with **RAY MINHINNIT** – guitar / **JAMES HALL** – keyboards / **CHARLIE HARRISON** – bass / **GRAHAM DEACON** – drums
Jun 77. (lp/c) *(<CHR/ZCHR 1128>)* **FULL HOUSE** ☐ ☐
– Be good to yourself / The doodle song / Jealous guy / Searching / Love letters / Take good care of yourself / Down the Honky Tonk / The love of mine / Let the candlelight shine / (I'll never) Live in vain. *(cd-iss. Feb99 on 'Repertoire'; REP 4728)*
Jun 77. (7") *<CHS 2145>* **THE DOODLE SONG. / (I'LL NEVER) LIVE IN VAIN** [–] [71]
Aug 77. (7") *(CHS 2166)* **LOVE LETTERS. / LET THE CANDLELIGHT SHINE** ☐ [–]
Nov 77. (7"ep) *(CHS 2184)* **ALVERIC'S ELFLAND JOURNEY EP** ☐ [–]
– Jealous guy / A fool in love / Brickyard blues / Sail away.
— went solo again, augmented by **PAUL CARRACK** – keyboards / **RAY RUSSELL** – guitar / **MARTIN DROVER** – trumpet / **CHRIS MERCER** – saxophone / **B.J. WILSON** – drums
Apr 78. (lp) *(<CHR 1174>)* **DOUBLE TROUBLE** ☐ ☐
– Have you seen me lately Joan / Double heart trouble / The train / You'll be in my mind / Good time love / Love waves / (I can't) Breakaway / Stubborn kind of fellow / Love is all around / Goodnight sweetheart. *(cd-iss. Feb99 on 'Repertoire'; REP 4727)*
Jun 78. (7"colrd) *(CHS 2221)* **STUBBORN KIND OF FELLOW. / GOOD TIME LOVE** ☐ [–]

FRANKIE MILLER

— **FRANKIE** only retained **CARRACK,** and brought in **CHRIS HALL** – keyboards / **TIM RENWICK + STEVE SIMPSON + TERRY BRITTON** – guitar / **RON ASPERY** – horns / **TEX COMER + DAVE WINTOUR** – bass / **CHRIS SLADE + FRAN BYRNE** – drums
Oct 78. (7") *(CHS 2255)* **DARLIN'. / DRUNKEN NIGHTS IN THE CITY** [6] [–]
Jan 79. (7") *(CHS 2276)* **WHEN I'M AWAY FROM YOU. / AIN'T GOT NO MONEY** [42] [–]
Jan 79. (lp) *(CHR 1220)* **FALLING IN LOVE . . . PERFECT FIT** ☐ [–]
– When I'm away from you / Is this love / If I can love somebody / Darlin' / And it's your love / A woman to love / Falling in love with you / Everytime a teardrop falls / Pappa don't know / Good to see you. *(cd-iss. Feb99 on 'Repertoire'; REP 4729)*
Apr 79. (7") *(CHS 2299)* **GOOD TO SEE YOU. / COLD AND RAINY NIGHT** ☐ [–]
— his backing band were now **REGGIE YOUNG + BOBBY THOMPSON** – guitar / **JOE OSBOURNE** – bass / **LARRY LONDIN** – drums
Jun 80. (7") *(CHS 2436)* **SO YOUNG, SO YOUNG. / TEARS** ☐ [–]
Jul 80. (lp) *(<CHR 1268>)* **EASY MONEY** ☐ ☐
– Easy money / The woman in you / Why don't you spend the night / So young so young / Forget about me / Heartbreak radio / Cheap . . .thrills / No chance / Gimme love / Tears. *(cd-iss. Jun99 on 'Repertoire'; REP 4731)*
Jul 80. (7") *(CHS CHS 2448)* **WHY DON'T YOU SPEND THE NIGHT. / HEARTBREAK RADIO** ☐ [–]
— now with **BARRY BECKETT** – keyboards, producer / **DAVID HOOD** – bass / **ROGER HAWKINS** – drums / **CHRIS SPEDDING** – guitar
Capitol Capitol
Jun 82. (7") *(CL 253) <5131>* **TO DREAM THE DREAM. / DON'T STOP** ☐ [62]
Jun 82. (lp/c) *(<EST/TC-EST 12206>)* **STANDING ON THE EDGE** ☐ ☐
– Danger danger / Standing on the edge / Zap zap / To dream the dream / Don't stop / Angels with dirty faces / Firin' line / Jealousy / It's all coming down tonight / On my way. *(cd-iss. Feb00 on 'Repertoire'; REP 4837)*
Aug 82. (7") *(CL 259)* **ANGELS WITH DIRTY FACES. / JEALOUSY** ☐ [–]
Sep 82. (7") **DANGER DANGER. / ON MY WAY** [–] ☐
— brought in **BRIAN ROBERTSON** – lead guitar / **CHRISSIE STEWART** – bass / **SIMON KIRKE** – drums (ex-BAD COMPANY)
Vertigo not iss.
Mar 86. (7") *(VER 25)* **I'D LIE TO YOU FOR LOVE. / DANCING IN THE RAIN** ☐ [–]
(12"+=) *(VERX 25)* – Do it till we drop.
Apr 86. (lp/c)(cd) *(VERH/+C 34)(826647-2)* **DANCING IN THE RAIN** ☐ [–]
– I'd lie to you for love / Do it till we drop / That's how long my love is / How many tears can you hide / Dancing in the rain / Shakey ground / The boys and girls are doing it / Game of love / Gladly go blind / You're a puzzle I can't put down.
— FRANKIE concentrated more on acting in the mid 80's
M.C.S. not iss.
Mar 92. (7"/c-s/cd-s) *(MCS 2001/+C/CD)* **CALEDONIA. / I'LL NEVER BE THAT YOUNG AGAIN** [45] [–]
— since 1994, FRANKIE has suffered serious ill health due to a brain aneurysm

– compilations, etc. –

Feb 87. (7") *Old Gold; (OG 9688)* **DARLIN'. / BE GOOD TO YOURSELF** ☐ [–]
Mar 94. (cd/c) *Chrysalis; (CD/TC 1981)* **THE VERY BEST OF FRANKIE MILLER** ☐ [–]
– Darlin' When I'm away from you / Be good to yourself / I can't change it / High life / Brickyard blues / A fool in love / Have you seen me lately Joan / Love letters / Caledonia / Stubborn kind of fellow / Devil gun / Hard on the levee / Tears / I'm ready / Shoo-rah shoo-rah / Double heart trouble / So young, so young.
Apr 94. (cd) *Windsong; (WINDCD 54)* **BBC RADIO 1 LIVE IN CONCERT (live)** ☐ [–]
Mar 96. (cd) *Disky; (DC 86432-2)* **LOVE LETTERS** ☐ [–]

Steve MILLER

Born: 5 Oct'43, Milwaukee, Wisconsin, USA; raised in Dallas, Texas. After forming school band, The MARKSMAN COMBO, with BOZ SCAGGS, he later played for bluesman JIMMY REED at a 1957 gig. In the early 60's, he and SCAGGS joined The ARDELLS, who, along with BEN SIDRAN, became The FABULOUS NIGHT TRAIN. In 1964, after a brief spell in Denmark, he moved to Chicago, where he sessioned for MUDDY WATERS, HOWLIN' WOLF and PAUL BUTTERFIELD. The following year, he partnered BARRY GOLDBERG in the group, The WORLD WAR III BAND, who issued a one-off 45, 'THE MOTHER SONG' (Epic 9865) as The GOLDBERG-MILLER BAND. Late in '66, he moved to San Francisco and formed The MILLER BAND with JAMES 'Curly' COOKE, LONNIE TURNER and TIM DAVIS, later adding JIM PETERMAN, and replacing COOKE with SCAGGS. After a June appearance at The Monterey Pop Festival, they signed to 'Capitol', recording three songs for the 'Revolution' film soundtrack, which eventually hit the shops late in '69. Their debut album, 'CHILDREN OF THE FUTURE', was issued in the Spring of '68, making all of No.134 in the US charts. Its mild success, was overshadowed by the follow-up, 'SAILOR', which introduced his trademark 'GANGSTER OF LOVE' motif. The album gave them their first of many entries into US Top 30, although with each successive release, they moved further away from the neo-psychedelic experimentation which had characterised their earlier releases. In 1973, after a lean couple of years, they hit US No.1 with 'THE JOKER', a song that lyrically revived his "Gangster Of Love". Although it was regarded as a classic in the UK, it still failed to chart (that is, until 1990, when it topped the charts after being given fresh exposure on a Levi jeans TV ad). The single was the title track of the album, which became his biggest selling album to date, hitting US No.2 and staying in the chart for nine months. After a prolonged break, MILLER returned with his most accessible and commercial album to date, 1976's 'FLY LIKE AN EAGLE'. The record showcased a more straightforward approach with finely crafted songs and strong hooks, spawning a slew of hit singles that even reached the UK Top 20. Its title track was a return to the laid-back psychedelia MILLER had flirted with back in the 60's (more recently it was a hit for SEAL). The next effort, 'BOOK OF DREAMS', was almost as big; No.2 stateside and No.12 in Britain. Following another hiatus, the band released 'CIRCLE OF LOVE' (1981), a collection of radio-friendly rockers that stuck more or less to MILLER's proven formula. The title track of the band's 1982 album, 'ABRACADABRA' was a worldwide smash, its quirky jack-in-the-box feel making it a quintessential 80's record, although the album sounded somewhat laboured. After a live album and a disappointing couple of studio sets, MILLER went solo in 1988, going back to his roots on 'BORN 2 B BLUE' and releasing a further solo album in 1993, 'WIDE RIVER'. • **Songwriters:** MILLER and BEN SIDRAN compositions, except covers on 87 & 88 albums. • **Trivia:** On '69 song 'MY DARK HOUR', PAUL McCARTNEY played bass under pseudonym MARK RAMON.

Album rating: CHILDREN OF THE FUTURE (*7) / SAILOR (*7) / BRAVE NEW WORLD (*7) / YOUR SAVING GRACE (*6) / NUMBER FIVE (*6) / LIVING IN THE U.S.A. (*7) / ROCK LOVE (*3) / RECALL THE BEGINNING . . . (*5) / ANTHOLOGY: THE BEST OF STEVE MILLER BAND 1968-1973 compilation (*8) / THE JOKER (*6) / FLY LIKE AN EAGLE (*8) / BOOK OF DREAMS (*6) / GREATEST HITS 1974-1978 compilation (*7) / CIRCLE OF LOVE (*6) / ABRACADABRA (*6) / STEVE MILLER BAND – LIVE! (*4) / ITALIAN X-RAYS (*4) / LIVING IN THE 21st CENTURY (*4) / BORN 2B BLUE (*5) / WIDE RIVER (*4)

STEVE MILLER BAND

STEVE MILLER – vocals, guitar / **LONNIE TURNER** (b.24 Feb'47, Berkeley, Calif.) – bass, vocals / **BOZ SCAGGS** (b. 8 Jun'44, Ohio) – guitar / **JIM PETERMAN** – organ, vocals / **TIM DAVIS** – drums

Capitol Capitol

Apr 68. (7") *(CL 15539) <2156>* **SITTIN' IN CIRCLES. / ROLL WITH IT**

Sep 68. (lp; stereo/mono) *(S+/T 2920) <718>* **CHILDREN OF THE FUTURE** Apr68
– Children of the future / Pushed me to it / You've got the power / In my first mind / The beauty of time is that it's snowing / Baby's callin' me home / Steppin' stone / Roll with it / Junior saw it happen / Fanny Mae / Key to the highway. *<re-iss. 1980; SN 16262> (cd-iss. Apr97 on 'E.M.I.'; REPLAYCD 19)*

Oct 68. (7") *(CL 15564) <2287>* **LIVING IN THE U.S.A. / QUICKSILVER GIRL** 94

Jan 69. (lp; stereo/mono) *(S+/T 2984) <719>* **SAILOR** Oct68 24
– Song for our ancestors / Dear Mary / My friend / Living in the U.S.A. / Quicksilver girls / Lucky man / Gangster of love / You're so fine / Overdrive / Dime-a-dance romance. *(re-iss. Nov83 on 'Fame' lp/c; FA41/TCFA 3085-1/-4) (re-iss. Apr91 cd/c/lp; CD/TC+/FA 3254) (cd re-iss. Apr97 on 'E.M.I.'; REPLAYCD 17)*

Jan 69. (7") *<2447>* **DEAR MARY. / SITTIN' IN CIRCLES** –

— Trimmed to a trio of **MILLER, TURNER** and **DAVIS** with session men. (PETERMAN left just after SCAGGS who went solo) **BEN SIDRAN** – keyboards (joined briefly)

— (Mar69) **NICKY HOPKINS** – keyboards (ex-JEFF BECK GROUP) repl. SIDRAN

Sep 69. (lp) *<(E-ST 184)>* **BRAVE NEW WORLD** Jun69 22
– Brave new world / Space cowboy / Got love 'cause you need it / It's a midnight dream / Can't you hear daddy's heartbeat / Celebration song / Seasons / Kow kow calculator / My dark hour. *(re-iss. Feb84 on 'E.M.I.'; IC 038 80117) (cd-iss. Apr97 on 'E.M.I.'; REPLAYCD 20)*

Jul 69. (7") *(CL 15604) <2520>* **MY DARK HOUR. / SONG FOR OUR ANCESTORS**

Nov 69. (7") *(CL 15618) <2638>* **LITTLE GIRL. / DON'T LET NOBODY TURN YOU AROUND**

Mar 70. (lp) *<(E-ST 331)>* **YOUR SAVING GRACE** Nov69 38
– Little girl / Just a passin' fancy in a midnite dream / Don't let nobody turn you around / Baby's house / Motherless children / The last wombat in Mecca / Feel so glad / Your saving grace. *(cd-iss. May91 on 'E.M.I.'; CZ 434) (cd re-iss. Apr97 on 'E.M.I.'; REPLAYCD 21)*

— **BOBBY WINKLEMAN** – bass, vocals repl. TURNER and HOPKINS who joined QUICKSILVER MESSENGER SERVICE

Nov 70. (lp) *<(EA-ST 436)>* **NUMBER 5** Jul70 23
– Good morning / I love you / Going to the country / Hot chili / Tokin's / Going to Mexico / Steve Miller's midnight tango / Industrial military complex hex / Jackson-Kent blues / Never kill another man. *(cd-iss. Apr97 on 'E.M.I.'; REPLAYCD 18)*

Sep 70. (7") *(CL 15665) <2878>* **GOING TO THE COUNTRY. / NEVER KILL ANOTHER MAN** Aug70 69

Dec 70. (7") *<2945>* **GOING TO MEXICO. / STEVE MILLER'S MIDNIGHT TANGO** –

— **STEVE MILLER** recruited entire new band **ROSS VALORY** – bass, vocals repl. WINKLEMAN / **JACK KING** – drums, vocals repl. DAVIS who went solo

Sep 71. (7") *<3228>* **ROCK LOVE. / LET ME SERVE YOU** –

Nov 71. (lp) *<(EA-ST 748)>* **ROCK LOVE** Oct71
– The gangster is back / Blues without blame / Love shock / Let me serve you / Rock love / Harbor lights / Deliverance.

— **GERALD JOHNSON** – bass, vocals repl. VALORY who later joined JOURNEY / added **DICKY THOMPSON** – keyboards / **ROGER ALAN CLARK** – 2nd drummer

May 72. (lp) *<(EST 11022)>* **RECALL THE BEGINNING . . . A JOURNEY FROM EDEN** Mar72
– Welcome / Enter Maurice / High on you mama / Heal your heart / The sun is going down / Somebody somewhere help me / Love's riddle / Fandango / Nothing lasts / Journey from Eden. *(re-iss. Feb84 on 'E.M.I.'; IC 062 81099)*

May 72. (7") *<3344>* **FANDANGO. / LOVE'S RIDDLE** –

— (Mar72) **JOHN KING** – drums repl. JACK and ROGER / **LONNIE TURNER** – bass, vocals returned to repl. JOHNSON who joined BOZ SCAGGS

Oct 73. (7") *(CL 15765) <3732>* **THE JOKER. / SOMETHING TO BELIEVE IN** 1

Oct 73. (lp) *<(EST 11235)>* **THE JOKER** 2
– Sugar babe / Mary Lou / Loving cup / Shu ba da du ma ma / Your cash ain't nothin' but trash / The joker / Lovin' cup / Come on into my kitchen / Evil / Something to believe in. *(re-iss. Oct80; same) (re-iss. Jan83 on 'E.M.I.'; IC 062 81514) (re-iss. Oct90 on 'Fame' cd/c/lp; CD/TC+/FA 3250)*

Feb 74. (7") *<3837>* **YOUR CASH AIN'T NOTHIN' BUT TRASH. / EVIL** – 51

— (May74) **STEVE MILLER** retired for a while, when THOMPSON and KING departed.

— (Jul75) **MILLER** retained **TURNER** and recruited for Knebworth festival **LES DUDEK** – guitar, vocals / **DOUG CLIFFORD** – drums (ex-CREEDENCE CLEARWATER REVIVAL)

— (1976) **GARY MALLABER** (b.11 Oct'46, Buffalo, N.Y.) – drums repl. CLIFFORD and DUDEK

Mercury Capitol

May 76. (7") *(6078 800) <4260>* **TAKE THE MONEY AND RUN. / SWEET MARIE** Apr76 11

May 76. (lp)(c) *(9286 177)(7100 925) <11497>* **FLY LIKE AN EAGLE** 11 3
– (Space intro) / Fly like an eagle / Wild mountain honey / Serenade / Dance, dance, dance / Mercury blues / Take the money and run / Rock'n'me / You send me / Blue odyssey / Sweet Marie / The window. *(re-iss. Nov84 lp/c; PRICE/PRIMC 75) (re-iss. Jun92 on 'Arcade' cd/c; ARC 94710-2/-4)*

Aug 76. (7") *<4323>* **ROCK'N'ME. / LIVING IN THE U.S.A.** – 1

Aug 76. (7") *(6078 802)* **FLY LIKE AN EAGLE. / MERCURY BLUES** –

Oct 76. (7") *(6078 804)* **ROCK'N'ME. / THE WINDOW** 11 –

Dec 76. (7") *<4372>* **FLY LIKE AN EAGLE. / LOVIN' CUP** – 2

Jan 77. (7") *(6078 808)* **SERENADE. / DANCE, DANCE, DANCE** –

— (Oct76) added **DAVID DENNY** – guitar, vocals (ex-TERRY & THE PIRATES) / **BYRON ALLRED** – keyboards / **NORTON BUFFALO** – harmonica, vocals

Apr 77. (7") *(6078 811) <4424>* **JET AIRLINER. / BABES IN THE WOOD** 8

May 77. (lp)(c) *(9286 455)(7299 393) <11630>* **BOOK OF DREAMS** 12 2
– Threshold / Jet airliner / Winter time / Swingtown / True fine love / Wish upon a star / Jungle love / Electro lux imbroglio / Sacrifice / The stake /

My own space / Babes in the wood. *(re-iss. Jan85 lp/c; PRICE/PRIMC 78) (re-iss. Jun92 on 'Arcade' cd/c; ARC 94730-2/-4)*

Sep 77. (7") *(6078 812) <4466>* **JUNGLE LOVE. / WISH UPON A STAR** [ ] Jul77 [23]

Jan 78. (7") *(6078 813) <4496>* **SWINGTOWN. / WINTER TIME** [ ] Oct77 [17]

—— trimmed to a quintet of **MILLER, MALLABER, ALLRED, DOUGLAS** and **BUFFALO**

Oct 81. (lp/c) *(6302/7144 061) <ST 12121>* **CIRCLE OF LOVE** [ ] [26]
– Heart like a wheel / Get on home / Baby wanna dance / Circle of love / Macho city. *(re-iss. Jun92 on 'Arcade' cd/c; ARC 94730-2/-4)*

Oct 81. (7") *<5068>* **HEART LIKE A WHEEL. / TRUE FINE LOVE** [–] [24]

Nov 81. (7"m) *(STEVE 1)* **HEART LIKE A WHEEL. / JET AIRLINER / THRESHOLD** [ ] [–]

Jan 82. (7") *<5086>* **CIRCLE OF LOVE. / (part 2)** [–] [55]

Feb 82. (7") *(STEVE 2)* **MACHO CITY. / FLY LIKE AN EAGLE** [ ] [–]

—— **KENNY LEWIS** – guitar / **JOHN MASSARO** – guitar both repl. DOUGLAS

May 82. (7") *<5126>* **ABRACADABRA. / GIVE IT UP** [–] [1]

Jun 82. (7") *(STEVE 3)* **ABRACADABRA. / NEVER SAY NO** [2] [–]
(re-iss. Oct84;)

Jun 82. (lp/c) *(6302/7144 204) <ST 12216>* **ABRACADABRA** [10] [3]
– Keeps me wondering why / Abracadabra / Something special / Give it up / Never say no / Things I told you / Young girl's heart / Goodbye love / Cool magic / While I'm waiting. *(cd-iss. Jan83; 800090-2) (re-iss. Jun92 on 'Arcade' cd/c; ARC 94740-2/-4)*

Aug 82. (7") *(STEVE 4)* **KEEPS ME WONDERING WHY. / GET ON HOME** [52] [ ]
(12"+=) *(STEVE 4-12)* – Abracadabra.

Oct 82. (7") *(STEVE 5)* **GIVE IT UP. / ROCK'N'ME** [ ] [–]

Oct 82. (7") *<5162>* **COOL MAGIC. / YOUNG GIRL'S HEART** [–] [57]

Dec 82. (7") *<5194>* **GIVE IT UP. / HEART LIKE A WHEEL** [–] [60]

Mar 83. (7") *<5223>* **LIVING IN THE U.S.A. (live). / BUFFALO SERENADE** [–] [ ]

Apr 83. (lp/c)(cd) *(MERL/+C 18)(811020-2) <12263>* **THE STEVE MILLER BAND LIVE! (live)** [79] [ ]
– Gangster of love / Rock'n'me / Living in the U.S.A. / Fly like an eagle / Jungle love / The joker / Mercury blues / Take the money and run / Abracadabra / Jet airliner. *(cd+=)* – Buffalo serenade.

Apr 83. (7") *(STEVE 6)* **TAKE THE MONEY AND RUN (live). / THE JOKER (live)** [ ] [–]
(12"+=) *(STEVE 6-12)* – Buffalo serenade (live).

—— Now without MASSARO

Oct 84. (7") *(STEVE 7) <5407>* **SHANGRI-LA. / CIRCLE OF LOVE** [ ] [57]
(12"+=) *(STEVE 7-12)* – Abracadabra.

Nov 84. (lp/c)(cd) *(MERL/+C 50)(822823-2) <12339>* **ITALIAN X-RAYS** [ ] [ ]
– Radio 1 / Italian x-rays / Daybreak / Shangri-la / Who do you love / Harmony of the spheres 1 / Radio 2 / Bongo bongo / Out of the night / Golden opportunity / The Hollywood dream / One in a million / Harmony of the spheres 2. *(re-iss. Jun92 on 'Arcade' cd/c; ARC 94750-2/-4)*

Jan 85. (7") *(STEVE 8) <5442>* **BONGO BONGO. / GET ON HOME** [ ] [84]

Mar 85. (7") *<5476>* **ITALIAN X-RAYS. / WHO DO YOU LOVE** [–] [ ]

—— **MILLER** with **MALLABER** and **BUFFALO** bring back **LES DUDEK** – guitar

Capitol Capitol

Jan 87. (lp/c)(cd) *(EST/TC-EST 2027)(CDP 746326-2) <12445>* **LIVING IN THE 20TH CENTURY** [ ] Nov86 [65]
– Nobody but you baby / I want to make the world turn around / Slinky / Living in the 20th century / Maelstrom / I wanna be loved / My babe / Big boss man / Caress me baby / Ain't that lovin' you baby / Behind the barn.

Mar 87. (7"/12") *(CL/12CL 444) <5646>* **I WANT TO MAKE THE WORLD TURN AROUND. / SLINKY** [ ] Nov86 [97]

Apr 87. (7") *<5671>* **NOBODY BUT YOU BABY. / MAELSTROM** [–] [ ]

Jun 87. (7") *<5704>* **I WANNA BE LOVED. / (part 2)** [–] [ ]

STEVE MILLER

solo with **BEN SIDRAN** – keyboards / **BILLY PATERSON** – bass / **GORDY KNUDTSON** – drums

Sep 88. (7") *(CL 506)* **YA YA. / FILTHY McNASTY** [ ] [ ]
(12"+=) *(12CL 506)* – ('A'remix by Steve Weiss).

Sep 88. (cd/c/lp) *(CD/TC+/EST 2072) <48303>* **BORN 2B BLUE** [ ] [ ]
– Zip-a-dee-doo-dah / Ya ya / God bless the child / Filthy McNasty / Born to be blue / Mary Ann / Just a little bit / When Sunny gets blue / Willow weep for me / Red top.

Polydor Polydor

Jul 93. (cd/c) *<(519441-2/-4)>* **WIDE RIVER** [ ] [85]
– Wide river / Midnight train / Blue eyes / Lost in your eyes / Perfect world / Horse and rider / Circle of fire / Conversation / Cry cry cyr / Stranger blues / Walks like a lady / All your love (I miss loving).

Jul 93. (c-s/cd-s) *<85919-4/-2>* **WIDE RIVER / STRANGER BLUES** [ ] [64]

—— STEVE retired from the music biz after above

– compilations, etc. –

on 'Capitol' unless mentioned otherwise

Feb 72. (7"ep) *(33RPM 7)* **MY DARK HOUR. / SONG FOR OUR ANCESTORS / THE GANGSTER IS BACK** [ ] [–]

Mar 73. (d-lp) *(ESTSP 12) <11114>* **ANTHOLOGY** [ ] Nov72 [56]

1973. (d-lp) *(STBB 717)* **CHILDREN OF THE FUTURE / LIVING IN THE U.S.A.** [ ] [ ]

Jun 74. (7") *(CL 15786) <3884>* **LIVING IN THE U.S.A. / KOW KOW CALQULATOR** [ ] May74 [49]

Oct 75. (lp) *(VMP 1008)* **THE LEGEND** [ ] [–]

Mar 77. (lp) *(EST 24058)* **THE BEST OF THE STEVE MILLER BAND 1968-73** [ ] [ ]
– Living in the U.S.A. / I love you / Don't let nobody turn you around / Seasons / Shu ba da du ma ma ma / Kow kow calculator / The joker / Going to the country / My dark hour / Your saving grace / Celebration song / Space cowboy. *(re-iss. May82 on 'Fame' lp/c; FA/TC-FA 3030) (re-iss. Aug86 on 'E.M.I.' lp/c; ATAK/TCATAK 86) (re-iss. Sep90; EST 2133) (hit UK No.34)(cd+=)* – (4 extra).

Oct 78. (7") *(6078 815)* **THE JOKER. / THE STAKE** [ ] [ ]

Nov 78. (lp)(c) *(9199 916)(7299 883) <11822>* **GREATEST HITS 1974-78** [ ] [18]
– Swingtown / Jungle love / Take the money and run / Rock 'n me / Serenade / True fine love / The stake / The joker / Fly like an eagle / Threshold / Jet airliner / Dance, dance, dance / Winter time / Wild mountain honey. *(cd-iss. Jan83; 800 058-2) (re-iss. Aug85 on 'Mercury' lp/c; PRICE/PRIMC 86)*

Jan 83. (7") *(CL 258)* **THE JOKER. / MY DARK HOUR. / LIVING IN THE U.S.A.** [ ] [–]

May 87. (lp/c)(cd) *Mercury; (MERH/+C 105)(830978-2)* **GREATEST HITS – A DECADE OF AMERICAN MUSIC (1976-1986)** [ ] [ ]

Aug 90. (7"/c-s) *(CL/TCCL 583)* **THE JOKER. / DON'T LET NOBODY TURN YOU AROUND** [1] [ ]
(12"+=) *(12CL 583)* – Shu ba da du ma ma ma.
(cd-s++=) *(CDCL 583)* – Living in the U.S.A.

Oct 91. (7"/cd-s) *Arcade; (AR 91621-7/-2)* **SPACE INTRO. / FLY LIKE AN EAGLE** [ ] [–]

Sep 98. (cd/c) *Polygram TV; (559240-2/-4)* **GREATEST HITS** [58] [–]
– The joker / Space intro / Fly like an eagle / Jet airliner / Dance, dance, dance / Give it up / Keeps me wondering why / Abracadabra / Swingtown / Jungle love / Take the money and run / Rock 'n me / The stake / Heart like a wheel / Wide river / True fine love / Cry cry cry / Serenade / Winter time / Wild mountain honey.

MINISTRY

Formed: Chicago, Illinois, USA ... 1981 by ex-SPECIAL EFFECT member AL JOURGENSEN. The latter bunch included FRANKIE NARDIELLO (who'd replaced TOM HOFFMAN), MARTY SORENSON and HARRY RUSHAKOFF, this synth-pop aggregation releasing a couple of 7" singles and a soundtrack album at the turn of the decade. Continuing in this vein, JOURGENSEN co-formed the 'Wax Trax' label and issued a debut MINISTRY 12" in 1982, 'COLD LIFE'. A further string of limp electro singles and a debut album, 'WITH SYMPATHY' (1983; European title 'WORK FOR LOVE') followed, before JOURGENSEN adopted a decidedly harder electronic sound on 'TWITCH' (1986). Around the same time, the MINISTRY mainman initiated a number of offshoot projects, the most high profile being The REVOLTING COCKS, who included in the ranks RICHARD 23, LUC VAN ACKER (the former later replaced by CHRIS CONELLY of FINI TRIBE). JOURGENSEN was said to have described this bunch as "Disco For Psychopaths", the 12", 'NO DEVOTION' and the long-player, 'BIG SEXY LAND' were aural proof. Another single, 'YOU OFTEN FORGET' (1987) was equally controversial, having already annoyed the PMRC (Parental Music Resource Center) with their overtly blasphemous debut. A live album, 'GODDAMNED SON OF A BITCH' was The REVOLTING COCKS next release in 1988, drummer BILL RIEFLIN now a steady part of both JOURGENSEN's groups. Meanwhile, MINISTRY had recruited bassist PAUL BARKER (and brother ROLAND BARKER), the outfit consolidated their harsher industrial approach with the vicious 1989 set, 'LAND OF RAPE AND HONEY'. To end the decade, MINISTRY unleashed yet another uncompromisingly bleak set of industrial grinding, 'THE MIND IS A TERRIBLE THING TO TASTE', while four months later, The REVOLTING COCKS offered some light relief with a decidedly unsympathetic version of Olivia Newton John's '(LET'S GET) PHYSICAL'. This was lifted from parent album, 'BEERS, STEERS AND QUEERS', the title track a brilliant must-hear send-up of backwoods American perversion. The REVOLTING COCKS gained even more notoriety when a proposed tour (which was to include onstage strippers and livestock) was the subject of an outraged House Of Commons discussion. Having briefly collaborated with JELLO BIAFRA (ex-DEAD KENNEDYS) on a project entitled LARD, JOURGENSEN released a one-off single under the 1000 HOMO DJ's banner, the main track being a cover of Black Sabbath's 'SUPERNAUT'. With the addition of guitarist MIKE SCACCIA and the unhinged guest vocals of GIBBY HAYNES (Butthole Surfers), MINISTRY recorded arguably their finest moment to date, 'JESUS BUILT MY HOTROD'. This was closely followed by MINISTRY's breakthrough Top 40 (on both sides of the Atlantic!) album, 'PSALM 69: THE WAY TO SUCCEED AND THE WAY TO SUCK EGGS', a highly regarded set which saw the group veering towards searing sonic metal. A Top 50 single, 'N.W.O.' followed a successful near headlining slot on the Lollapalooza' 1992 tour, PAUL BARKER also moonlighting in yet another MINISTRY offshoot, LEAD INTO GOLD (releasing the 'AGE OF REASON' a follow-up to 1990's mini-cd 'CHICKS & SPEED'). A year later, The REVOLTING COCKS returned with their inimitably twisted brand of black humour, a version of Rod Stewart's 'DO YA THINK I'M SEXY' one of the highlights of their 1993 album, 'LINGER FICKEN' GOOD'. The two main MINISTRY men, AL JOURGENSEN and PAUL BARKER, replaced the departing RIEFLIN with RAY WASHAM and moved the operation to Texas (JOURGENSEN set up a country label). Late in 1995, after AL escaped a drugs bust, MINISTRY ventured even further into metal territory with the 'FILTH PIG' opus, a collection that contained a murderous version of Bob Dylan's 'LAY LADY LAY'. In 1999, AL, PAUL and the MINISTRY were growling once again at the music industry, 'DARK SIDE OF THE SPOON' (redneck punk, et AL), however the album failed to make its commercial impact – sadly, the release was around the same time as guitarist WILLIAM TUCKER committed suicide by slashing his throat. While it's been all quiet on the studio front of late, fans of popular music's baddest bad taste merchants were at least partly satiated by the release of the charmingly titled 'SPHINCTOUR' (2002), a live document culled from the band's mid-90's heyday and deriving the bulk of its content from 'PSALM . . .' and 'FILTHPIG'. Girding itself against the tide of posturing, sub-standard nu-metal, MINISTRY swaggered into the new millennium with the palindromical, tongue twisting 'ANIMOSITISOMINA' (2003). Their nastiest and hardest hitting slab of leadweight metal in over a decade, the album also took a backwards glance at the band's post-punk beginnings with a cover of the Magazine classic, 'THE LIGHT POURS OUT OF ME'.

Album rating: WORK FOR LOVE (aka WITH SYMPATHY) (*5) / TWITCH (*5) / LAND OF RAPE AND HONEY (*7) / THE MIND IS A TERRIBLE THING TO TASTE (*6) / IN CASE YOU DIDN'T FEEL LIKE SHOWING UP (*4) / PSALM 69: HOW TO SUCCEED AND HOW TO SUCK EGGS (*8) / FILTH PIG (*6) / DARK SIDE OF THE SPOON (*8) / GREATEST FITS compilation (*8) / SPHINCTOUR (*5) / ANIMOSITISOMNIA (*6) / Revolting Cocks: BIG SEXY LAND (*6) / YOU GODAMNED SON OF A BITCH (*5) / BEERS, STEERS & QUEERS (*7) / LINGER FICKEN' GOOD . . . AND OTHER BARNYARD ODDITIES (*6)

SPECIAL EFFECT

AL JOURGENSEN (b. 9 Oct'58, Havana, Cuba) – guitar / **FRANKIE NARDIELLO** – vocals; repl. TOM HOFFMAN / **MARTY SORENSON** – bass / **HARRY RUSHAKOFF** – drums

not iss. / Special Effect

1979. (7"ep) *<2955>* **MOOD MUSIC EP** [–] [ ]
– I know a girl / Vertigo feeling / Innocense / Dress me dolls.

1980. (lp; soundtrack) *<008028>* **TOO MUCH SOFT LIVING** [–] [ ]

—— also flexidisc from 'Praxis' magazine; HEADACHE. / NUCLEAR GLOOM

not iss. / Thermidor

Oct 81. (7") *<T 5>* **EMPTY HANDED. / THE HEAT** [–] [ ]

MINISTRY

AL JOURGENSEN – guitar, keyboards, synthesizers, vocals / **LAMONT WELTON** – bass / **STEVO** – drums

Situation 2 / Wax Trax

Mar 82. (12"m) *(SIT 17T) <110072X>* **COLD LIFE. / I'M FALLING / COLD LIFE (dub) / PRIMENTAL** [ ] [ ]

—— AL used musicians on next lp; **SHAY JONES** – vocals / **WALTER TURBETT** – guitar / **JOHN DAVIS** – keyboards / **ROBERT ROBERTS** – keyboards / **STEPHEN GEORGE** – drums / **MARTIN SORENSEN** – bass

Arista / Arista

Feb 83. (7"/12") *(ARIST/+12 510)* **WORK FOR LOVE. / FOR LOVE (instrumental)** [ ] [–]

Apr 83. (7"/12") *<9021>* **REVENGE (YOU DID IT AGAIN). / SHE'S GOT A CAUSE** [–] [ ]

Jun 83. (7") *(ARIST 533) <9068>* **I WANTED TO TELL HER. / A WALK IN THE PARK** [ ] [ ]
(12"+=) *(ARIST12 533) <9102>* – ('A'-Tongue Tied mix).

Sep 83. (lp/c) *(205/405 306) <6608>* **WORK FOR LOVE** <US title 'WITH SYMPATHY'> [ ] Jun83 [96]
– Work for love / Do the Etawa / I wanted to tell her / Say you're sorry / Here we go / Effigy / Revenge / She's got a cause / Should have known better. *(cd-iss. 1989 as 'WITH SYMPATHY'+=; ARCD 8016) (cd-iss. Mar93 +=; 255 306)* – What He Say.

Nov 83. (7") *(ARIST 549)* **REVENGE (YOU DID IT AGAIN). / EFFIGY** [ ] [–]
(12"+=) *(ARIST12 549)* – Work for love.

—— now basically AL solo

Wax Trax / Wax Trax

Oct 85. (12") *(WAXUK 009)* **NATURE OF LOVE. / ('A'-Cruelty mix)** [ ] [–]

Sire / Sire

Apr 86. (lp/c) *(925309-1/-4) <25309>* **TWITCH** [ ] [ ]
– Just like you / We believe / All day remix / The angel / Over the shoulder / My possession / Where you at now? / Crash and burn / Twitch (version II). *(cd+=)* – Over the shoulder (mix) / Isle Of Man.

—— added partner **PAUL BARKER** (b. 8 Feb'50, Palo Alto, Calif.) – bass, programming (ex-FRONT 242) + **WILLIAM RIEFLIN** (b.30 Sep'60, Seattle, Washington) – drums / **ROLAND BARKER** (b.30 Jun'57, Mountainview, Calif.) – keyboards

Jan 89. (lp/c/cd) *(925799-1/-4/-2) <25799>* **THE LAND OF RAPE AND HONEY** [ ] Nov88 [ ]
– Stigmata / The missing / Deity / Golden dawn / Destruction / The land

of rape and honey / You know what you are / Flashback / Abortive. *(cd+=)* – Hizbollah / I prefer. *(cd re-iss. Dec92; 7599 25799-2)*

Feb 90. (cd/c/lp) *<(7599 26004-2/-4/-1)>* **THE MIND IS A TERRIBLE THING TO TASTE** [ ] Dec89 [ ]
– Thieves / Burning inside / Never believe / Cannibal song / Breathe / So what / Test / Faith collapsing / Dream song. *(cd re-iss. Dec92)*

Sep 90. (cd/lp) *<7599 26266-2/-1>* **IN CASE YOU DIDN'T FEEL LIKE SHOWING UP (live)** [-] [ ]
– The missing / deity / So what / Burning inside / Seed / Stigmata. *(UK cd-iss. Dec92 on 'WEA'; same)*

—— next with guest **GIBBY HAYNES** (of BUTTHOLE SURFERS)

—— added **MIKE SCACCIA** (b.14 Jun'65, Babylon, N.Y.) – guitar

Apr 92. (7") *(W 0096)* **JESUS BUILT MY HOTROD. / TV SONG** [ ] [ ]
(12"+=/cd-s+=) *(W 0096 T/C)* – ('A'-Red line-white line version).

Jul 92. (cd/c/10"lp) *<(7599 26727-2/-4/-1)>* **PSALM 69: HOW TO SUCCEED AND HOW TO SUCK EGGS** [33] [27]
– N.W.O. / Just one fix / TV II / hero / Jesus built my hot rod / Scarecrow / Psalm 69 / Corrosion / Grace.

Jul 92. (10") *(W 0125)* **N.W.O. / F***ED (non lp version)** [49] [ ]
(cd-s+=) *(W 0125CD)* – ('A'extended dance mix).

—— **JOURGENSEN + PAUL BARKER + SCACCIA** recruited **RAY WASHAM** – drums (of JESUS LIZARD) / **DUANE BUFORD** – keyboards / **LOUIS SVITEK** – guitar (ex-MINDFUNK)

W.E.A. Warners

Dec 95. (c-s) *(W 0328C)* **THE FALL / RELOAD** [53] [ ]
(cd-s+=) *(W 0328CD)* – TV III.

Jan 96. (cd/c/lp) *<(9362 45838-2/-4/-1)>* **FILTHPIG** [43] [19]
– Reload / Filth pig / Crumbs / Useless / Lava / Dead guy / The face / Brick windows / Gane show / Lay lady lay / Reload (edit).

Feb 96. (c-s) *(W 0338C)* **LAY LADY LAY / LAY LADY LAY (album version)** [ ] [ ]
(cd-s+=) *(W 0338CD)* – Paisley / Scarecrow (live).

—— line-up **JOURGENSEN, BARKER, RAY WASHUM + LOUIS SVITEK**

Jun 99. (cd/c) *<(9362 47311-2/-4)>* **DARK SIDE OF THE SPOON** [ ] [92]
– Supermanbiac soul / Whip or the chain / Bad blood / Eureka pie / Step / Nursing home / Kaif / Vex ans siolence / 10-10.

—— now without guitarist E. WILLIAM TUCKER who committed suicide by slashing his throat (after taking pills) on the 14th May, 1999 (aged 38)

Mayan Sanctuary

Apr 02. (cd) *(MYNCD 005) <84540>* **SPHINCTOUR (live)** [ ] [ ]
– Psalm 69 / Crumbs / Reload / Filth pig / Just 1 fix / N.W.O. / Hero / Thieves / Scarecrow / Lava / The fall.

Feb 03. (cd) *(MYNCD 010) <84568>* **ANIMOSITISOMNIA** [ ] [ ]
– Animosity / Unsung / Piss / Lockbox / Broken / The light pours out of me / Shove / Impossible / Stolen / Leper.

– compilation, others, etc. –

1985. (lp) *Hot Trax; (WAXC 35)* **12" INCH SINGLES 1981-1984** [-] [ ]

Jun 01. (cd) *Warners; <(9362 48115-2)>* **GREATEST FITS** [ ] [ ]
– What about us? / Stigmata / The land of rape and honey / Thieves / So what (live) / N.W.O. / Just one fix / Jesus built my hotrod / Reload (12" mix) / Lay lady lay / Supermaniac soul / Bad blood / Supernaut.

REVOLTING COCKS

AL's studio outfit, with FRONT 242 members; LUC and RICHARD 23. The latter was soon replaced CHRIS CONNELLY of FINI TRIBE.

Wax Trax Wax Trax

Feb 86. (12"m) *(WAXUK 011)* **NO DEVOTION. / ATTACK SHIPS / ON FIRE** [ ] [-]

Nov 86. (lp)(cd) *(WAXUK 017)(WAX 017CD) <7017>* **BIG SEXY LAND** [ ] [ ]
– 38 / We shall cleanse the world / Attack ships on fire / Big sexy land / Union carbide (West Virginia version) / T.V. mind / No devotion / Union carbide (Bhopal version). *(re-iss. Mar92 on 'Devotion' cd/c/lp; CD/T+/DVN 6)*

Feb 87. (12") *(WAXUK 022)* **YOU OFTEN FORGET. / ('A'version)** [ ] Nov90 [ ]

AL now with **BARKER, VAN ACKER, RIEFLIN + CONNELLY** – vocals

Jun 88. (d-lp/cd) *(WAX UK/CD 037) <7037>* **LIVE! – YOU GODDAMNED SON OF A BITCH** (live + 2 studio) [ ] [ ]
– You Goddamned son of a bitch / Cattle grind / We shall cleanse the world / 38 / In the neck / You often forget / TV mind / Union carbide / Attack ships on fire / No devotion. *(re-iss. May92 on 'Devotion' cd/c/lp; CD/T+/DVN 8)*

Mar 89. (12") *(WAX 042) <7042>* **STAINLESS STEEL PROVIDERS. / AT THE TOP / TV MIND (remix)** [ ] [ ]

—— **AL + PHIL** were also part of JELLO BIAFRA's (Dead Kennedys) group LARD.

May 90. (cd/c/lp) *(WAX 063 CD/MC/LP) <7063>* **BEERS, STEERS + QUEERS** [ ] [ ]
– Beers, steers + queers / (Let's get) Physical / In the neck / Get down / Stainless steel providers / Can't sit still / Something wonderful / Razor's edge. *(cd+=)* – (Let's talk) Physical. *(re-iss. Feb92 on 'Devotion' cd/c/lp; CD/T+/DVN 4)*

May 90. (cd-s) *(WAX 086CD) <9086>* **(LET'S GET) PHYSICAL. / (LET'S TALK) PHYSICAL** [ ] [ ]

Mar 91. (12"/cd-s) *<9199>* **CRACKIN' UP. / ('A'-Amylnitrate mix) / GUACOPTER (version 2)** [-] [ ]
(UK-iss.Jun94 on 'Devotion' 12"/cd-s; 12/CD DVN 112)

—— now without RIEFLIN (on below only TRENT REZNOR of NINE INCH NAILS)

Apr 91. (12"ep/cd-ep; 1000 HOMO DJ'S) *<WAX 032>* **SUPERNAUT / HEY ASSHOLE / APATHY / BETTER WAYS** [ ] 1987 [ ]

Devotion Sire

Sep 93. (12"ep/cd-ep) *(12/CD DVN 111) <41088>* **DA YA THINK I'M SEXY? / SERGIO GUITAR / WRONG (sexy mix)** [61] [ ]

Sep 93. (cd/c/d-lp) *(CD/T+/DVN 22) <45407>* **LINGER FICKEN' GOOD . . . AND OTHER BARNYARD ODDITIES** [39] [ ]
– Gila copter / Creep / Mr.Lucky / Crackin' up / Sergio / Da ya think I'm sexy? / The rockabye / Butcher flower's woman / Dirt / Linger ficken' good.

Kylie MINOGUE

Born: 28 May'68, Melbourne, Australia. KYLIE didn't start her career with any preconceived notion of the pop stardom she would reach, although from an early age she got stuck into the entertainment world, although in the form of televison actress. By the age of eleven she had landed a role in Australian TV show, 'Skyways', after which she gained a more substantial part in the child-orientated soap, 'The Henderson Kids'. But massive fame in both Australia and Britain came with her leading role as Charlene in Aussie soap, 'Neighbours'. In this she acted alongside JASON DONOVAN, who also became a pop sensation in the late 80's. MINOGUE played the part of girlfriend, and later wife, to DONOVAN's character, Scott. This was an important marketing tool for the duo's pop career, as it led to much-loved speculation about their behind the limelight and real-life affection for each other. Her path to pop stardom began fairly accidentally when MINOGUE sang 'THE LOCO-MOTION' at a charity event. The popularity of this led 'Mushroom' records to release a studio recorded version, which rocketed to pole position in Australia. The success of this attracted the attention of British record producing/songwriting trio, STOCK, AITKEN and WATERMAN. They realised that if marketed correctly, the already popular KYLIE could also be re-fashioned into a popstar. They penned for MINOGUE the accessible, sing-along pop song, 'I SHOULD BE SO LUCKY', which became an instant number one in both Britain and Australia. Realising her own potential as a popstar, the teenager soon left 'Neighbours' to pursue her musical career full-time. STOCK, AITKEN and WATERMAN were also well aware of the money spinner they now had and worked the fledgling singer to her full potential; putting out an album a year from 1988 to 1991. Yet it was on her 1991 album, 'LET'S GO TO IT', that MINOGUE decided she wanted more artistic control of her output. The writing partnership of SA&W were reluctant to relinquish their control of her image and thus the album marked the end of their partnership. The next eight years saw a dearth for MINOGUE's chart success although she did release several hit singles and a handful of albums, but in a more experimental vein, notably the eponymous 'KYLIE MINOGUE' (1994). It was widely known that a romantic attachment between herself and MICHAEL HUTCHENCE (of Antipodean rock outfit INXS) had led to the more progressive/dance stance she took in her music – exemplified by her dueting with NICK CAVE on the track 'WHERE THE WILD ROSES GROW', and teaming up with members of the MANIC STREET PREACHERS to write material for her follow-up album, 'IMPOSSIBLE PRINCESS' – also entitled 'KYLIE MINOGUE' in the UK! Alhough an interesting piece, many critics viewed it as too much of an image shift for the popstar, and chart sales reflected this. The turn of the millennium saw the maturing and gorgeous MINOGUE back at No.1 with the release of the single 'SPINNING AROUND'; the album 'LIGHT YEARS' nearly copied its success. Her fame grew massively again the following year when she extended her sexy but sophisticated new image with the massive chart-topping hit, 'CAN'T GET YOU OUT OF MY HEAD' (complete with award-winning video – oh that dress!) from the massive selling album, 'FEVER' (2001). With this dancefloor friendly single she managed to extend her pop market to the clubbing set. By the end of the year MINOGUE's place in the pop-buying hearts of the European and Australian market was complete and seemed unalterable, a task only to be furthered by winning the same place on the other side of the Atlantic. Preceded by the No.1 single, 'SLOW', 2003's 'BODY LANGUAGE' confirmed her position among that coterie of ageing divas who manage to reinvent themselves to a degree necessary to keep both the public and themselves interested. This time around, the diminutive Aussie benefitted from a more experimental, cutting edge production and a team of savvy writers, enough to ensure a UK Top 10 placing and continuing street cred.

Album rating: KYLIE – THE ALBUM (*5) / ENJOY YOURSELF (*5) / RHYTHM OF LOVE (*4) / LET'S GET TO IT (*4) / GREATEST HITS compilation (*7) / KYLIE MINOGUE (*5) / IMPOSSIBLE PRINCESS (*5) / LIGHT YEARS (*5) / FEVER (*7) / GREATEST HITS 87-92 compilation (*6) / BODY LANGUAGE (*5)

KYLIE MINOGUE – vocals / with producers, etc.

P.W.L. Geffen

Jan 88. (7"/ext.12"/cd-s) *(PWL/+T/CD 8)* *<27922>* **I SHOULD BE SO LUCKY. / (instrumental)** [1] Apr88 [28]
(12") *(PWLT 8R)* – ('A'-Bicentennial mix) / (instrumental).

May 88. (7") *(PWL 12)* **GOT TO BE CERTAIN. / (instrumental)** [2] [–]
(12") *(PWLT 12)* – ('A'side) / ('A'-Out for a duck bill platter dub mix).
(cd-s+=) *(PWCD 12)* – I should be so lucky (extended).
(12") *(PWLT 12R)* – ('A'-extra beat boys mix) / ('A'side).

Jul 88. (lp/c/cd) *(HF/+C/CD 3)* *<24195>* **KYLIE – THE ALBUM** [1] Aug88 [53]
– I should be so lucky / The loco-motion / Je ne sais pas pourquoi / It's no secret / Got to be certain / Turn it into love / I miss you / I'll still be loving you / Look my way / Love at first sight.

Jul 88. (7"/12")(cd-s) *(PWL/+T 14)(PWCD 14)* *<27752>* **THE LOCO-MOTION. / I'LL STILL BE LOVING YOU** [2] Aug88 [3]
(12") *(PWLT 14R)* – ('A'-Sankie mix) / ('B'side).

Oct 88. (7") *(PWL 21)* **JE NE SAIS PAS POURQUOI. / MADE IN HEAVEN** [2] [–]
(12"/cd-s) *(PWLT/PWCD 21)* – ('A'-Moi non plus mix) / ('B'-Made in England mix).
(12") *(PWLT 21R)* – ('A'-Revolutionary mix) / ('B'side).

Nov 88. (7") *<27651>* **IT'S NO SECRET. / MADE IN HEAVEN** [–] [37]

Dec 88. (7"/12"/3"cd-s,5"cd-s; by KYLIE MINOGUE & JASON DONOVAN) *(PWL/+T 24)(PWCD 24)* **ESPECIALLY FOR YOU. / ALL I WANNA DO IS MAKE YOU MINE** [1] [–]

Apr 89. (7"/c-s) *(PWL/PWMC 35)* **HAND ON YOUR HEART. / JUST WANNA LOVE YOU** [1] [ ]
('A'-Aorta mix-12"+=) *(PWLT 35)* – ('A'-dub).
('A'-Aorta mix-3"cd-s+=,5"cd-s+=) *(PWCD 35)* – It's no secret.
(12") *(PWLT 35R)* – ('A'-Heartache mix) / ('B'side).

Jul 89. (7"/c-s) *(PWL/PWMC 42)* **WOULDN'T CHANGE A THING. / IT'S NO SECRET** [1] [ ]
(12") *(PWLT 42)* – ('A'-Your thang mix) / ('B'extended) / ('A'instrumental).
(3"cd-s,5"cd-s) *(PWCD 42)* – ('A'side) / ('A'-Your thang mix) / Je ne sais pas pourquoi (revolutionary mix).

Oct 89. (lp/c/cd) *(HF/+C/CD 9)* *<24272>* **ENJOY YOURSELF** [1] [ ]
– Wouldn't change a thing / Hand on your heart / Enjoy yourself / Tell tale signs / Tears on my pillow / Never too late / Nothing to lose / Heaven and Earth / I'm over dreaming (over you) / My secret heart. *<US cd re-iss. 1998 on 'Mushroom'; 32209>*

Oct 89. (7"/c-s) *(PWL/PWMC 45)* **NEVER TOO LATE. / ('a"-Kylie's smiley mix)** [4] [–]
(ext;12"+=/cd-s+=) *(PWLT/PWCD 45)* – ('A'-extended).

Jan 90. (7"/c-s) *(PWL/PWMC 47)* **TEARS ON MY PILLOW. / WE KNOW THE MEANING OF LOVE** [1] [–]
(12"+=/cd-s+=) *(PWLT/PWCD 47)* – ('A'extended).

May 90. (7"/c-s) *(PWL/PWMC 56)* **BETTER THE DEVIL YOU KNOW. / I'M OVER DREAMING OVER YOU** [2] [–]
(12"+=/cd-s+=) *(PWL/PWCD 56)* – ('A'-Mad March Hare mix).

Oct 90. (7"/c-s) *(PWL/PWMC 64)* **STEP BACK IN TIME. / (instrumental)** [4] [–]
(ext;cd-s+=) *(PWCD 64)* – ('A'-Walkin' rhythm mix).

Nov 90. (cd/c) *(HFCD/HFC 18)* **RHYTHM OF LOVE** [9] [–]
– Better the devil you know / Step back in time / What do I have to do / Secrets / Always find the time / The world still turns / Shocked / One girl boy / Things can always get better / Count the days / Rhythm of love. *(re-iss. Jun91 cd/c; HF CDL/CL 18)* *<US cd-iss. 1998 on 'Mushroom'; 32215>*

Jan 91. (7"pic-d/c-s) *(PWLP/PWMC 72)* **WHAT DO I HAVE TO DO. / (instrumental)** [6] [–]
(ext;cd-s+=) *(PWCD 72)* – ('A'-Pumpin Polly mix).

May 91. (7"pic-d/c-s) *(PWL/PWMC 81)* **SHOCKED. / SHOCKED (Harding Curnow mix)** [6] [–]
(ext;cd-s+=) *(PWCD 81)* – ('A'-DNA extended mix).

Aug 91. (7"/c-s) *(PWL/PWMC 204)* **WORD IS OUT / (instrumental)** [16] [–]
(cd-s+=) *(PWCD 204)* – Say the word – I'll be there.
(12"etched) *(PWLT 204R)* – ('A'-Summer breeze mix).

Oct 91. (cd/c) *(HFCD/HFC 21)* **LET'S GET TO IT** [15] [–]
– Word is out / Give me just a little more time / Too much of a good thing / Finer feelings / If you were with me now (with KEITH WASHINGTON) / Let's get to it / Right here, right now / Live and learn / No world without you / I guess I like it like that. *<US cd-iss. 1998 on 'Mushroom'; 29253>*

Oct 91. (7"/c-s; as KYLIE MINOGUE & KEITH WASHINGTON) *(PWL/PWMC 208)* **IF YOU WERE WITH ME NOW. / I GUESS I LIKE IT LIKE THAT** [4] [–]
(cd-s+=) *(PWCD 208)* – ('A'extended mix).

in Nov'91, she and TONY KING featured on the VISIONMASTERS Top 50 single, 'KEEP ON PUMPIN' IT' (PWL 207)

Jan 92. (7"/c-s) *(PWL/PWMC 212)* **GIVE ME JUST A LITTLE MORE TIME. / (extended)** [2] [–]
(cd-s+=) *(PWCD 212)* – Do you dare (new rave + NRG mixes).

Apr 92. (7"/c-s) *(PWL/PWMC 227)* **FINER FEELINGS. / CLOSER (the pleasure mix)** [11] [–]
(cd-s+=) *(PWCD 227)* – ('A'mixes).

Aug 92. (7"/c-s) *(PWL/PWMC 241)* **WHAT KIND OF FOOL (HEARD IT ALL BEFORE). / (instrumental)** [14] [–]
(cd-s+=) *(PWCD 241)* – ('A'-Brothers In Rhythm mixes).

Aug 92. (cd/c) *(HFCD/HFC 25)* **GREATEST HITS** (compilation) [1] [–]
– I should be so lucky / Got to be certain / The loco-motion / Je ne sais pas pourquoi / Especially for you / Turn it into love / It's no secret / Hand on your heart / Wouldn't change a thing / Never too late / Tears on my pillow / Better the devil you know / Step back in time / What do I have to do? / Shocked / Word is out / If you were with me now / Give me just a little more time / Finer feelings / What kind of fool (heard all that before) / Where in the world? / Celebration. *<US-iss.1999 on 'Mushroom'; 93366>*

Nov 92. (7"/c-s) *(PWL/PWMC 257)* **CELEBRATION. / LET'S GET TO IT** [20] [–]
(cd-s+=) *(PWCD 257)* – ('A'-Have a party mix).

Deconstr. Deconstr.

Sep 94. (c-s) *(74321 22748-4)* **CONFIDE IN ME / (master mix)** [2] [–]
(12"+=/cd-s+=) *(74321 22747-1/-2)* – ('A'-truth mix) / Where has all the love gone (Fire Island mix).
(cd-s) *(74321 22748-2)* – ('A'side) / Nothing can stop us / If you don't love me.

Sep 94. (cd/c) *(<74321 22749-2/-4>)* **KYLIE MINOGUE** [4] [ ]
– Confide in me / If I was your lover / Where is the feeling / Put yourself in my place / Dangerous games / Automatic love / Where has the love gone / Falling / Time will pass you by. *(re-iss. Jun96; same)*

Nov 94. (c-s) *(74321 24657-4)* **PUT YOURSELF IN MY PLACE / CONFIDE IN ME (Philip Damien mix)** [11] [–]
(cd-s+=) *(74321 24657-2)* – ('A'-Dan's quiet storm mixes).

Jul 95. (c-s) *(74321 29361-4)* **WHERE IS THE FEELING / (mix)** [16] [–]
(12"+=/cd-s+=) *(74321 29361-1/-2)* – ('A'-BIR mixes).

—— In Oct'95, KYLIE teamed up with NICK CAVE to have a near Top 10 UK hit, 'WHERE THE WILD ROSES GROW'

Sep 97. (c-s) *(74321 51725-4)* **SOME KIND OF BLISS / LIMBO** [22] [–]
(cd-s+=) *(74321 51725-2)* – ('A'-quiver mix).

Nov 97. (c-s/cd-s) *(74321 53570-4/-2)* **DID IT AGAIN / TEARS** [14] [–]
(cd-s) *(74321 53570-2)* – ('A'-Did it four times mix).

Mar 98. (c-s/cd-s) *(74321 57013-4/-2)* **BREATHE / (album mix)** [14] [–]
(cd-s+=) *(74321 57014-2)* – ('A'-mixes; Tee's freeze / Nalin & Kane).

Mar 98. (cd/c) *(74321 51727-2/-4) <33069>* **KYLIE MINOGUE** <US-title 'IMPOSSIBLE PRINCESS'> [10] [ ]
– Too far / Cowboy style / Some kind of bliss / Did it again / Breathe / Say hey / Drunk / I don't need anyone / Jump / Limbo / Through the years / Dreams. *(re-iss. May99; same)*

Aug 98. (d-cd/t-lp) *(74321 58715-2/-1)* **THE MIXES** [ ] [–]

—— In Oct'98, KYLIE featured on minor hit, 'GBI', with TOWA TEI

Parlophone Mushroom

Jun 00. (c-s/cd-s) *(TCR/CDRS 6542) <1957-2>* **SPINNING AROUND / (mixes)** [1] [ ]
(cd-s) *(CDR 6542) <1957-5>* – ('A'mix) / Cover me with kisses / Paper dolls.

Sep 00. (c-s) *(TCR 6546)* **ON A NIGHT LIKE THIS / (Bini & Martin mix) / (Motiv8 mix)** [2] [–]
(cd-s+=) *(CDR 6546)* – ('A'-Robe Searle mix).
(cd-s) *(CDRS 6546)* – ('A'side) / Ocean blue / Your disco needs you (almighty mix).

Sep 00. (cd/c) *(528400-2/-4)* **LIGHT YEARS** [2] [–]
– Spinning around / On a night like this / So now goodbye / Disco down / Loveboat / Coocachoo / Your disco needs you / Kids (w/ ROBBIE WILLIAMS) / Please stay / Bittersweet goodbye / Butterfly / Under the influence of love / I'm so high / Light years. *(d-cd re-iss. Mar01; 532129-2)* – TOUR PACK mixes. *<US-iss.Sep01 on 'E.M.I.'; 532129>*

—— In Oct'00, KYLIE collaborated with ROBBIE WILLIAMS on the UK No.2 single, 'KIDS'

Dec 00. (c-s/cd-s) *(TCR/CDRS 6551) <2004>* **PLEASE STAY / SANTA BABY / GOOD LIFE** [10] Feb01 [ ]
(cd-s) *(CDR 6551)* – ('A'side) / ('A'-7th District club mix) / ('A'-Hatrias dreamy vocal mix).

Parlophone Capitol

Sep 01. (c-s) *(TCR 6562) <879864>* **CAN'T GET YOU OUT OF MY HEAD / BOY** [1] Oct01 [7]
(cd-s+=) *(CDRS 6562)* – Rendezvous at sunset.
(cd-s) *(CDR 6562)* – ('A'-enhanced).

Oct 01. (cd/c) *(535804-2/-4) <37670>* **FEVER** [1] Feb02 [3]
– More more more / Love at first sight / Can't get you out of my head / Fever / Give it to me / Fragile / Come into my world / In your eyes / Dancefloor / Love affair / Your love / Burning up.

Feb 02. (c-s) *(TCR 6569)* **IN YOUR EYES / TIGHTROPE** [3] [–]
(cd-s+=) *(CDR 6569)* – Good like that.
(cd-s) *(CDRS 6569)* – ('A'side) / ('A'-Tha S Man release mix) / ('A'-Jean Jacques smoothie mix).
(12") *(12R 6569)* – ('A'-Saeed & Palash main mix) / ('A'-Powder spaced dub) / ('A'-Roger Sanchez release the dub mix).

Jun 02. (12") *(12R 6577) <77724>* **LOVE AT FIRST SIGHT. / CAN'T GET BLUE MONDAY OUT OF MY MIND / ('A'-Scumfrogs acappella mix)** [2] May02 [23]
(cd-s) *(CDR 6577)* – (first 2 tracks) / Baby / ('A'-video).
(cd-s) *(CDRS 6577)* – ('A'side) / ('A'-Ruff & Jam club mix) / ('A'-Scumfrogs vocal mix).

Nov 02. (cd-s)<12"> *(CDR 6590) <77829>* **COME INTO MY WORLD / (Ashtrax remix) / (Robbie Rivera's hard and sexy remix) / ('A'video)** [8] Oct02 [91]
(cd-s) *(CDRS 6590)* – ('A'side) / Love at first sight (live) / Fever (live).

Nov 03. (cd-s) *(CDR 6625) <53362>* **SLOW / SWEET MUSIC / SLOW (medicine 8 remix) / SLOW (video)** [1] [91]
(12") *(12R 6625)* – ('A'-Medicine 8 remix) / ('A'-extended) / ('A'-Radio Slave mix).
(cd-s) *(CDRS 6625)* – ('A'side) / Soul on fire.

Nov 02. (cd) *(595645-2) <595758>* **BODY LANGUAGE** [6] Feb04 [42]
– Slow / Still standing / Secret (take you home) / Promises / Sweet music / Red blooded woman / Chocolate / Obsession / I feel for you / Someday / Loving days / After dark.

– compilations, etc. –

Oct 00. (cd) *Global TV; (74321 78534-2)* **HITS** [41] [–]
– Confide in me / Put yourself in my place / Where is the feeling / Some kind of bliss / Did it again / Breathe / Where the wild roses grow / Tears / Take me with you / If you don't love me / Difficult by design / Gotta move on / Stay this way / Automatic love (acoustic) / Where has the love gone (Farley & Hellier mix).

Oct 00. (d-cd) *Mushroom; (MUSH 33183-2)* **INTIMATE AND LIVE (live)** [ ] [ ]

Nov 02. (cd) *Jive; (922468-2)* **GREATEST HITS 87-92** [20] [–]

□ MINOR THREAT (see under ⇒ FUGAZI)

MINUTEMEN

Formed: San Pedro, California, USA ... 1979 originally as The REACTIONARIES, by D BOON and MIKE WATT (third member GEORGE HURLEY replaced FRANK TONCHE). The band featured on Various Artists US lp's on indie labels 'Radio Tokyo', 'New Alliance' and 'Posh Boy', before signing for 'S.S.T.' (home base of BLACK FLAG and MEAT PUPPETS). For five years they committed many songs (mostly hardcore/jazz! around a minute long!) to EP and LP before having to disband late in 1985 after the untimely death of BOON. From 'PARANOID TIME' to '3-WAY TIE (FOR LAST)', MINUTEMEN showcased their politically leftfield attacks on the establishment including RONNIE REAGAN and JOE McCARTHY. In 1986 the remaining two, MIKE WATT and GEORGE HURLEY re-formed as fIREHOSE alongside guitarist ED CRAWFORD. This trio debuted with an album, 'RAGIN' FULL ON' (1987), their sound slightly mellowing. After an acclaimed 1989 third album 'fROMOHIO', they shifted to 'Columbia', where they scored minor hit albums in the early 90's. • **Covered:** HEY LAWDY MAMA (Steppenwolf) / HAVE YOU EVER SEEN THE RAIN + GREEN RIVER (Creedence Clearwater Revival) / DOCTOR WU (Steely Dan) / THE RED AND THE BLACK (Blue Oyster Cult). fIREHOSE covered WALKING THE COW (Daniel Johnston) / SLACK MOTHERFUCKER (Superchunk). DOS covered PACIFIC COAST HIGHWAY (Sonic Youth) + DON'T EXPLAIN (Billie Holiday).

Album rating: PARANOID TIME (*5) / THE PUNCH LINE mini (*4) / WHAT MAKES A MAN START FIRES? (*7) / DOUBLE NICKELS ON THE DIME (*8) / 3-WAY TIE (FOR LAST) (*6) / PROJECT: MERSH mini (*6) / BALLOT RESULTS (*7) / firehose: RAGIN', fULL-ON (*6) / fROMOHIO (*8) / FLYING THE FLANNEL (*6) / Mike Watt: BALL-HOG OR TUGBOAT? (*7) / CONTEMPLATING THE ENGINE ROOM (*6) / Dos: DOS (*6)

D BOON (b. DENNES DALE BOON, 1 Apr'58) – vocals, guitar / **MIKE WATT** (b.20 Dec'57, Portsmouth, Virginia) – bass (also of DOS) / **GEORGE HURLEY** (b. 4 Sep'58, Brockton, Massachusetts) – drums; repl. FRANK TONCHE

S.S.T. S.S.T.

Dec 80. (7"ep) *<SST 002>* **PARANOID TIME** [–] [ ]
– Untitled song for Latin America / Political song for Michael Jackson to sing / Validation / The maze / Definitions / Fascist / Joe McCarthy's ghost. *(UK-iss.Mar83, cd-ep iss.Nov88; same)*

Sep 81. (7"ep) *<NAR 004>* **JOY / BLACK SHEEP. / MORE JOY**

— <above issued on 'New Alliance'>

Nov 81. (m-lp) *<SST 004>* **THE PUNCH LINE**
– Search / Tension / Games / Boiling / Disguises / Struggle / Monuments / Ruins / Issued / The punch line / Song for El Salvador / History lesson / Fanatics / No parade / Straight jacket / Gravity / Warfare / Static. *<(cd/c-iss.May93; SST CD/C 004)>*

Feb 83. (lp) *<SST 014>* **WHAT MAKES A MAN START FIRES?**
– Bob Dylan wrote propaganda songs / One chapter in the book / Fake contest / Beacon sighted through fog / Mutiny in Jonestown / East wind – Faith / Pure joy / '99 / The anchor / Sell or be sold / Only minority / Split red / Colors / Plight / Tin roof / Life as rehearsal / This road / Polarity. *(UK-iss.Aug91 & May93 cd/c; SST 014 CD/C)*

Nov 83. (m-lp) *<SST 016>* **BUZZ OR HOWL UNDER THE INFLUENCE OF HEAT**
– Self-referenced / Cut / Dream told by Moto / Dreams are free, motherfucker! / Tow jam / I felt like a gringo / Product / Little man with a gun in his hand. *(UK-iss.May93 cd/c; SST 016 CD/C)*

Oct 84. (d-lp) *<(SST 028)>* **DOUBLE NICKELS ON THE DIME**
– D's car jam – Anxious Mo-Fo / Theatre is the life of you / Viet nam / Cohesion / It's expected I'm gone / #1 hit song / Two beads at the end / Do you want new wave or do you want the truth? / Don't look now / Shit from an old notebook / Nature without man / One reporter's opinion / Political song for Michael Jackson to sing / Maybe partying will help / Toadies / Retreat / The big foist / God bows to math / Corona / The glory of man / Take 5, D. / My heart and the real world / History lesson – part II / You need the glory / The roar of the masses could be farts / ***** Mr Robot's holy orders / West Germany. *<(cd-iss. Oct87 +=; SST 028CD)>* – THE POLITICS OF TIME lp – The politics of time / Themselves / Please don't be gentle with me / Nothing indeed / No exchange / There ain't shit on TV tonight / This ain't no picnic / Spillage / Untitled song for Latin America / Jesus and tequila / June 16th / Storm in my house / Martin's story / Doctor Wu / Ain't talkin' about love / Little man with a gun in his hand / The world according to nouns / Love dance.

Jun 85. (12"ep) *<(SST 034)>* **PROJECT: MERSH**
– Cheerleaders / King of the hill / Hey lawdy mama / Take our test / Tour-spiel / More spiel.

— tragedy struck on the 23rd December '85 when D BOON was killed in a car crash

Jan 86. (lp) *<(SST 058)>* **3 WAY TIE (FOR LAST)**
– The price of Paradise / Lost / The big stick / Political nightmare / Courage / Have you ever seen the rain? / The red and the black / Spoken word piece / No one / Stories / What is it? / Ack ack ack / Just another soldier / Situations at hand / Hittin' the bong / Bermuda. *(cd-iss. Aug87; SST 058CD)*

— Broke-up early 1986. WATT guested for CICCONE YOUTH (aka SONIC YOUTH).

– compilations, etc. –

1984. (lp/cd) *New Alliance;* **THE POLITICS OF TIME** (early REACTIONARIES material)

Apr 85. (7"ep) *Reflex; (REFLEX L)* **TOUR SPIEL (live)**

Dec 86. (d-lp/cd) *S.S.T.; <(SST 068)>* **BALLOT RESULTS**
– Little man with a black gun in his hand / Political song for Michael Jackson to sing / I felt like a gringo / Jesus and tequila / Courage / King of the hill / Bermuda / No one / Mr.Robot's holy orders / Ack ack ack / History lesson (part two) / This ain't no picnic / The cheerleaders / Time / Cut / Split red / Shit you hear at parties / Hell (second take) / Tour-spiel / Take our test / The punch line / Search / Bob Dylan wrote propaganda songs / Badges / Tension / If Reagan played disco / No! no! no! to draft and war – Joe McCarthy ghost. *(re-iss. May93)*

1987. (lp/cd) *S.S.T.; <SST 138/+CD>* **POST-MERSH, VOL.I**
– THE PUNCH LINE ep / WHAT MAKES A MAN START FIRES lp *(re-iss. May93)*

1987. (lp/cd) *S.S.T.; <SST 139/+CD>* **POST-MERSH, VOL.II**
– BUZZ OR HOWL UNDER THE INFLUENCE OF HEAT lp / PROJECT: MERSH ep *(re-iss. May93)*

Sep 87. (7"ep) *New Alliance;* **JOY / BLACK SHEEP. / MORE JOY**
(re-iss. Feb90 on 'S.S.T.' 10"colrd; SST 214)

May 89. (cd) *S.S.T.; <(SST 165)>* **POST-MERSH, VOL.III**

Aug 98. (cd) *S.S.T.; <(SST 363CD)>* **INTRODUCING THE MINUTEMEN**

MIRACLES

Formed: Detroit, Michigan, USA . . . 1957 as The MATADORS by 15-year old WILLIAM 'SMOKEY' ROBINSON together with school friends RONNIE WHITE, BOBBY ROGERS and his sister CLAUDETTE (whom SMOKEY married in late '59), PETE MOORE and MARVIN TARPLIN. Following a debut single, 'I LOVE YOU SO', on the 'Fury' label in 1958, the ROBINSON-penned 'GOT A JOB' (a response to The SILHOUETTES recent No.1 hit, 'Get A Job') caused a local stir, sold respectably and prompted BERRY GORDY Jnr. (whom the group had met a year earlier when auditioning for JACKIE WILSON's manager) to initiate the fledgling 'Motown'. The MATADORS' fourth single, 'BAD GIRL', was released on 'Chess' while GORDY distributed it locally and its minor chart success persuaded the budding mogul to expand his enterprise. In early '61, the newly renamed MIRACLES furnished 'Tamla/Motown' with the first of countless massive hits, 'SHOP AROUND' (US No.2). Again the track had been penned by ROBINSON and he went on to write for many of the label's artists, providing them with many of their biggest hits. For his troubles he was made company vice-president, becoming GORDY's right-hand man during his lifelong tenure at the label (he even named his kids BERRY and TAMLA!). A towering talent – he was famously named 'America's greatest living poet' by none other than BOB DYLAN – with a creamy falsetto vocal and a headful of lovestruck metaphors, he led The MIRACLES on a chart crusade throughout the 60's. While he could throw down footstomping R&B (a la 'MICKEY'S MONKEY' and 'GOING TO A GO-GO' – US Top 10 and 20 respectively) with the best of them, his forte was the tortured ballad and they don't come much more deliciously painful as 'THE TRACKS OF MY TEARS', a US Top 20 hit in summer '65 hot on the heels of 'OOH BABY BABY'. While the chart positions never really reflected the greatness of these songs, the sheer volume of Top 40 hits (well in excess of 20) at least partly made up for it. Ironically, SMOKEY's works became bigger hits in the hands of other 'Motown' artists, MARY WELLS taking 'MY GUY' to the top of the charts in 1964. His most favoured act upon which to lavish his writing/production skills, however, were The TEMPTATIONS, who hit No.1 with 'MY GIRL' while MARVIN GAYE and The MARVELETTES also scored with SMOKEY material. Prior to The MIRACLES' biggest hit to date, 'I SECOND THAT EMOTION' (No.4 in late '67 and one of the few tracks to make the UK Top 30), ROBINSON's pivotal role was recognised by prefixing the group's name with his own. Success was patchier in the late 60's/early 70's as artists like STEVIE WONDER and MARVIN GAYE pushed for more creative control and The TEMPTATIONS went psychedelic under the aegis of Norman Whitfield. Nevertheless, SMOKEY ROBINSON & THE MIRACLES hit paydirt one last time in 1970 with the pop perfection of 'TEARS OF A CLOWN', a transatlantic No.1. Aged 30, SMOKEY left for a solo career in 1972 and WILLIAM GRIFFIN was brought in as a replacement. While never recreating the magic of the SMOKEY years, the MIRACLES continued fairly successfully right up until the mid-70's when they scored a massive transatlantic hit with 'LOVE MACHINE (part 1)'. A move to 'Columbia' proved less successful and following a final, eponymous album in 1978, they disbanded.

Best CD compilation: THE ANTHOLOGY: OOO BABY BABY (*8)

SMOKEY ROBINSON (b. WILLIAM, 19 Feb'40) – lead vocals / **RONNIE WHITE** (b. 5 Apr'39) – vocals / **BOBBY ROGERS** (b.19 Feb'40) – vocals / **CLAUDETTE ROGERS** (b.1942) – vocals / **PETE MOORE** (b.19 Nov'39) – vocals / **MARVIN TARPLIN** – guitar, musical director not iss. Fury

1958. (7") <1001> **I LOVE YOU SO. / YOUR LOVE (IS ALL I NEED)** –

not iss. End

1958. (7") <1016> **GOT A JOB. / MY MAMA DONE TOLD ME** –

1959. (7") <1084> **I CRY. / MONEY** –

not iss. Chess

Sep 59. (7") <1734> **BAD GIRL. / I LOVE YOU BABY** – 93

Jan 60. (7") <1768> **I NEED A CHANGE. / ALL I WANT** –

London Tamla

Mar 60. (7"; by RON & BILL) **DON'T SAY BYE BYE. / IT** *<originally issued 1958 on 'Argo'>* –

Jun 60. (7") <74028> **WAY OVER THERE. / DEPEND ON ME** –

Feb 61. (7") *(HL 9276)* <54034> **SHOP AROUND. / WHO'S LOVIN' YOU** Dec60 2

Feb 61. (lp) *(PS 40044)* <220> **HI, WE'RE THE MIRACLES**
– Who's lovin' you / Depend on me / Heart like mine / Shop around / Won't you take me back / 'Cause I love you / Your love / After all / Way over there / Money / Don't leave me. *(UK-iss Jul 63 on 'Oriole')*

Apr 61. (7") *(HL 9366)* <54036> **AIN'T IT BABY. / THE ONLY ONE I LOVE** Mar61 49

Jul 61. (7") <54044> **MIGHTY GOOD LOVIN'. / BROKEN HEARTED** – 51

Oct 61. (7") <54048> **EVERYBODY'S GOTTA PAY SOME DUES. / I CAN'T BELIEVE** – 52

Nov 61. (lp) <223> **COOKIN' WITH THE MIRACLES** –
– Embraceable you / Everybody's gotta pay some dues / Mama / You never miss a good thing / That's the way I feel / Ain't it baby / Determination / Broken hearted / Only one I love / I can't believe.

Fontana Tamla

Mar 62. (7") *(H 384)* <54053> **WHAT'S SO GOOD ABOUT GOODBYE. / I'VE BEEN SO GOOD TO YOU** Dec61 35

May 62. (7") <54059> **I'LL TRY SOMETHING NEW. / YOU NEVER MISS A GOOD THING** – 39

Jun 62. (lp) <230> **I'LL TRY SOMETHING NEW** –
– I'll try something new / Speak low / What's so good about goodbye / I've got you under my skin / On the street where you live / Love that can never be / If your mother only knew / I've been good to you / He don't care about me / This I swear, I promise.

Sep 62. (7") <54069> **WAY OVER THERE. / IF YOUR MOTHER ONLY KNEW** – 94

Dec 62. (lp) <236> **CHRISTMAS WITH THE MIRACLES** (festive) –

Oriole Tamla

Jan 63. (7") *(CBA 1794)* <54073> **YOU'VE REALLY GOT A HOLD ON ME. / HAPPY LANDING** Nov62 8

Mar 63. (7") <54058> **A LOVE SHE CAN COUNT ON. / I CAN TAKE A HINT** – 31

Sep 63. (7") *(CBA 1863)* <54083> **MICKEY'S MONKEY. / WHATEVER MAKES YOU HAPPY** Jul63 8

Oct 63. (lp; mono/stereo) *(TML/STML 10055)* <241> **THE MIRACLES ON STAGE (live)**
– Mighty good lovin' / A love she can count on / Happy landing / I've been good to you / What's so good about goodbye / You've really got a hold on me / Way over there.

Dec 63. (lp) <245> **DOIN' MICKEY'S MONKEY** –
– Mickey's monkey / Dance what you wanna / The Wah-Watusi / The twist / Dancin' holiday / Land of a 1000 dances / I gotta dance to keep from crying / The monkey time / The groovey thing / Twist and shout / Do you love me.

Stateside Tamla

Feb 64. (7") *(SS 263)* <54089> **I GOTTA DANCE TO KEEP FROM CRYING. / SUCH IS LOVE, SUCH IS LIFE** Nov63 35

Apr 64. (7") *(SS 282)* <54092> **(YOU CAN'T LET THE BOY OVERPOWER) THE MAN IN YOU. / HEARTBREAK ROAD** Jan64 59

Aug 64. (7") *(SS 324)* <54098> **I LIKE IT LIKE THAT. / YOU'RE SO FINE AND SWEET** Jun64 27

Nov 64. (lp) *(SL 10099)* <238> **THE FABULOUS MIRACLES** Jun63
– The man in you / Such is love, such is life / I can take a hint / Heartbreak Road / Your love / He don't care about me / Speak low / I've been good to you / If your mother only knew / Won't you take me back / A love that can never be / On the street where you live.

Nov 64. (7") *(SS 353)* <54102> **THAT'S WHAT LOVE IS MADE OF. / WOULD I LOVE YOU** Sep64 35

Jan 65. (7") *(SS 377)* <54109> **COME ON DO THE JERK. / BABY DON'T YOU GO** Nov64 50

Tamla Motown Tamla

Mar 65. (7") *(TMG 503)* <54113> **OOH BABY BABY. / ALL THAT'S GOOD** 16

Apr 65. (lp) *(TML 11003)* **I LIKE IT LIKE THAT** Oct64

Jul 65. (7") *(TMG 522)* <54118> **THE TRACKS OF MY TEARS. / A FORK IN THE ROAD** Jun65 16

Nov 65. (7") *(TMG 540)* <54123> **MY GIRL HAS GONE. / SINCE YOU WON MY HEART** Sep65 14

Feb 66. (7") *(TMG 547)* <54127> **GOING TO A GO-GO. / CHOOSEY BEGGAR** 44 Dec65 11

Feb 66. (lp) *(TML 11024)* <267> **GOING TO A GO-GO** Nov65 8
– The tracks of my tears / Going to a go-go / Ooh baby baby / My girl has gone / In case you need love / Choosey beggar / Since you won my heart / From head to toe / All that's good / My baby changes like the weather / Let me have some / A fork in the road.

Jul 66. (d-lp) *(STML 11031)* <254> **GREATEST HITS FROM THE BEGINNING** (compilation) Apr65 21
– Get a job / I cry / Mama done told me / (I need some) Money / Bad girl / I love your baby / I need a change / All I want is you / (You can) Depend on me / Who's loving you / That's what love is made of / Mickey's monkey / I gotta dance to keep from crying / You've really got a hold on me / I like it like that / A love she can count on / Shop around / Way over there / I've been good to you / Would I love you / I'll try something new / What's so good about goodbye.

Jul 66. (7") *(TMG 569)* <54134> **WHOLE LOT OF SHAKIN' IN MY HEART (SINCE I MET YOU). / OH BE MY LOVE** May66 46

Dec 66. (7") *(TMG 584)* <54140> **(COME ROUND HERE) I'M THE ONE YOU NEED. / SAVE ME** 45 Oct66 17

Feb 67. (lp; mono/stereo) *(TML/STML 11044)* <271> **AWAY WE A GO-GO** Dec66 41
– Whole lot of shakin' in my heart (since I met you) / You don't have to say you love me / (Come 'round here) I'm the one you need / Save me / Oh be my love / Can you love a poor boy / Beauty is only skin deep / I just don't know what to do with myself / Baby, baby / Walk on by / Swept for you baby / More, more, more of your love.

SMOKEY ROBINSON & THE MIRACLES

Feb 67. (7") <54145> **THE LOVE I SAW IN YOU WAS JUST A MIRAGE. / COME SPY WITH ME** – 20

Mar 67. (7") *(TMG 598)* **THE LOVE I SAW IN YOU WAS JUST A MIRAGE. / SWEPT FOR YOU BABY** –

Jun 67. (7") *(TMG 614)* <54152> **MORE LOVE. / SWEPT FOR YOU BABY** – 23

Jul 67. (7") *(TMG 614)* **MORE LOVE. / COME SPY WITH ME** –

Nov 67. (7") *(TMG 631)* <54159> **I SECOND THAT EMOTION. / YOU MUST BE LOVE** 27 Oct67 4

Feb 68. (lp; mono/stereo) *(TML/STML 11067)* <276> **MAKE IT HAPPEN** Oct67 28
– Soulful shack / Love I saw in you was just a mirage / My love for you / I'm on the outside looking in / Don't think it's me / My love is your love (forever) / More love / After you put back the pieces / It's a good feeling / You must be love / Dancing's alright / Tears of a clown. *<US re-iss. Dec70 as 'TEARS OF A CLOWN'; 276>*

Mar 68. (7") *(TMG 648)* <54162> **IF YOU CAN WANT. / WHEN THE WORDS FROM YOUR HEART GET CAUGHT UP IN YOUR THROAT** 50 Feb68 11

Jun 68. (lp; mono/stereo) *(TML/STML 11233)* <280> **GREATEST HITS, VOL.2** (compilation) Feb68 7
– Going to a go go / The tracks of my tears / I second that emotion / Ooo baby baby / My girl has gone / Come on do the jerk / Whole lot of shakin' in my heart (since I met you) / The love I saw in you was just a mirage / (Come 'round here) I'm the one you need / More love / Choosey beggar / Save me. *(re-iss. Jul73)*

Jun 68. (7") *(TMG 661)* <54167> **YESTER LOVE. / MUCH BETTER OFF** May68 31

Oct 68. (7") *(TMG 673)* <54172> **SPECIAL OCCASION. / GIVE HER UP** Aug68 26

Jan 69. (lp; mono/stereo) *(TML/STML 11089)* <290> **SPECIAL OCCASION** Oct68 42
– Yester love / If you can wait / Special occasion / Everybody needs love /

Just losing you / Give her up / I heard it through the grapevine / Yesterday / Your mother's only daughter / Much better off / You only build me up to tear me down.

Feb 69. (7") *(TMG 687)* <54178> **BABY, BABY DON'T CRY. / YOUR MOTHER'S ONLY DAUGHTER** [ ] Jan69 [8]

Apr 69. (7") *(TMG 696)* **THE TRACKS OF MY TEARS. / COME ON DO THE JERK** [9] [–]

May 69. (lp; mono/stereo) *(TML/STML 11107)* <289> **LIVE! (live)** [ ] Feb69 [71]
– Once in a lifetime / You and the night and the music / I second that emotion / The tracks of my tears / Poinciana / Up, up and away / Theme from 'Valley of the Dolls' / Yester love / Walk on by / Yesterday / If you can wait / Mickey's monkey / Ooh baby baby / Going to a go-go.

Jul 69. (7") <54183> **DOGGONE RIGHT. / HERE I GO AGAIN** [–] [33] [37]

Jul 69. (7") <54184> **ABRAHAM, MARTIN AND JOHN. / MUCH BETTER OFF** [–] [33]

Dec 69. (7") <54189> **POINT IT OUT. / DARLING DEAR** [–] [37] [100]

Feb 70. (lp; mono/stereo) *(TML/STML 11129)* <295> **TIME OUT FOR SMOKEY ROBINSON AND THE MIRACLES** [ ] Aug69 [25]

Feb 70. (7") <54194> **WHO'S GONNA TAKE THE BLAME. / I GOTTA THING FOR YOU** [–] [ ]

Jul 70. (lp) *(STML 11151)* <297> **FOUR IN BLUE** [ ] Dec69 [78]
– You send me (with your good lovin') / Dreams, dreams / Tomorrow is another day / Hey Jude / California soul / A legend in his own time / You've lost that lovin' feelin' / We can make it if we can / When nobody cares / Don't say you love me / Wish I knew / My world is empty without you.

May 70. (lp) <301> **WHAT LOVE HAS JOINED TOGETHER** [–] [97]
– What love has joined together / My cherie amour / If this world were mine / You've made me so very happy / This guy's in love with you / And I love her.

Jul 70. (7") *(TMG 745)* **THE TEARS OF A CLOWN. / YOU MUST BE LOVE** [1] [–]

Oct 70. (7") <54199> **THE TEARS OF A CLOWN. / PROMISE ME** [–] [1] [46]

Oct 70. (lp) *(STML 11172)* <306> **A POCKETFUL OF MIRACLES** [–] [56]

Jan 71. (7") *(TMG 761)* **(COME ROUND HERE) I'M THE ONE YOU NEED. / WE CAN MAKE IT, WE CAN** [13] [–]

Feb 71. (lp) *(STML 11172)* **SMOKEY ROBINSON & THE MIRACLES** [ ] [ ]

May 71. (7") *(TMG 774)* <54205> **I DON'T BLAME YOU AT ALL. / THAT GIRL** [11] Mar71 [18]

Jun 71. (7") <54206> **CRAZY 'BOUT THE LA LA LA. / OH BABY BABY I LOVE YOU** [–] [56]

Sep 71. (lp) <312> **ONE DOZEN ROSES** [–] [92]

Nov 71. (7") <54211> **SATISFACTION. / FLOWER GIRL** [–] [49]

Apr 72. (7") *(TMG 811)* **CRAZY 'BOUT THE LA LA LA. / MY GIRL HAS GONE** [ ] [–]

Jun 72. (7") <54220> **WE'VE COME TOO FAR TO END IT NOW. / WHEN SUNDOWN COMES** [–] [46]

Jul 72. (lp) <318> **FLYING HIGH TOGETHER** [–] [46]
– I can't stand to see you cry / Love story / We've come too far to end it now / Flying high together / With you love came / It will be alright / Oh girl / You ain't livin' you're lovin' / We had a love so strong / Got to be there / Betcha by golly wow.

Dec 72. (7") <54225> **I CAN'T STAND TO SEE YOU CRY. / WITH YOUR LOVE CAME** [–] [45]

—— In Jul'72, SMOKEY ROBINSON had already left to concentrate on his solo career while The MIRACLES also continued on 'Tamla' until 1978

The MIRACLES

—— replaced him with **WILLIAM GRIFFIN** – vocals

Tamla Motown | Tamla

Jul 73. (7") <54237> **DON'T LET IT END ('TIL YOU LET IT BEGIN). / WIGS AND LASHES** [–] [56]

Oct 73. (lp) *(STMA 8010)* <325> **RENAISSANCE** [ ] May73 [ ]
– What is a heart good for / If you're ever in the neighbourhood / I wanna be with you / Wigs and lashes / Don't let it end (til you let it begin) / I love you secretly / I don't need no reason / Nowhere to go / I didn't realise the show was over.

Mar 74. (7") *(TMG 891)* **DON'T LET IT END (TIL YOU LET IT BEGIN). / I WANNA BE WITH YOU** [ ] [–]

Aug 74. (7") <54248> **DO IT BABY. / I WANNA BE WITH YOU** [–] [13]

Aug 74. (7") *(TMG 914)* **DO IT BABY. / WIGS AND LASHES** [ ] [–]

Dec 74. (lp) *(STML 11276)* <334> **DO IT BABY** [ ] Sep74 [41]
– Do it baby / Up again / Where are you going to my love / What is a heart good for / You are love / Give me just another day / We feel the same / Calling out your name / A foolish thing to say / Can't get ready for losing you.

Dec 74. (7") <54256> **DON'T CHA LOVE IT. / UP AGAIN** [–] [78]

Feb 75. (7") *(TMG 940)* **WHERE ARE YOU GOING TO MY LOVE. / UP AGAIN** [ ] [–]

Sep 75. (7") <54259> **YOU ARE LOVE. / GEMINI** [–] [ ]

Nov 75. (7") *(TMG 1015)* <54262> **LOVE MACHINE (part 1). / LOVE MACHINE (part 2)** [3] Oct75 [1]

Nov 75. (lp) *(STML 12010)* <339> **CITY OF ANGELS** [ ] Oct75 [33]
– Overture / City of angels / Free press / Ain't nobody straight in L.A. / Night life / Love machine / My name is Michael / Poor Charlotte / Waldo Roderick / Dehammersmith / Smog.

Feb 76. (7") <54268> **NIGHT LIFE. / SMOG** [–] [ ]

Feb 76. (7") *(TMG 1023)* **NIGHT LIFE. / THE MIRACLE WORKERS: OVERTURE** [ ] [–]

Apr 76. (lp) *(STML 12020)* <336> **LOVE MACHINE** <US-title 'DON'T CHA LOVE IT'> [ ] Jan75 [96]
– Love machine / Don't cha love it / Keep on keepin' on (doin' what you do) / Sweet sweet lovin' / Got me goin' (again) / You are love / Gemini / Take it all / Broken-hearted girl, broken-hearted boy / A little piece of Heaven / Gonna tell the world (wedding song).

Oct 76. (lp) *(STML 12038)* <344> **THE POWER OF MUSIC** [ ] [ ]
– The power of music / Love to make love / Can I pretend / Let the children play (overture) / gossip / Let the children play / Street of love / You need a miracle.

C.B.S. | Columbia

Jan 77. (7") *(CBS 4936)* <10464> **SPY FOR BROTHERHOOD. / THE BIRD MUST FLY AWAY** [ ] [ ]

Feb 77. (lp) *(CBS 881696)* <34910> **LOVE CRAZY** [ ] [ ]
– Love crazy – introductory / Love crazy – overture / Too young / Spy for brotherhood / A better way to live / Women (make the world go round) / The bird must fly away / I can touch the sky.

Jun 77. (7") *(CBS 5200)* <10517> **WOMEN (MAKE THE WORLD GO ROUND). / I CAN TOUCH THE SKY** [ ] [ ]

Jul 78. (lp) <34910> **MIRACLES** [–] [ ]
– I can't stand it / Love doctor / The magic of your eyes (Laura's eyes) / Freeway / Hot dance / Mean machine / Sad rain / Reach for the sky.

Jul 78. (7") <10706> **MEAN MACHINE. / THE MAGIC OF YOUR EYES (LAURA'S EYES)** [–] [ ]

—— disbanded around 1978

– (selective) compilations, etc. –

on 'Tamla Motown' until mentioned otherwise

Apr 73. (d-lp) *(STMA 8008)* <320> **1957-1972 (live)** [ ] Dec72 [75]

Mar 74. (t-lp) <793> **SMOKEY ROBINSON & THE MIRACLES' ANTHOLOGY** [ ] Feb74 [97]
(re-iss. +c.Sep82) (cd-iss. Jun87 & Apr89)

Sep 76. (7") *(TMG 1048)* **THE TEARS OF A CLOWN. / THE TRACKS OF MY TEARS** [34] [–]

Oct 86. (cd) *(ZD 72458)* **GOING TO A GO-GO / THE TEARS OF A CLOWN** [ ] [ ]

Oct 87. (cd) *(ZD 72419)* **COMPACT COMMAND PERFORMANCES (18 GREATEST HITS)** [ ] [ ]
– Shop around / You've really got a hold on me / I'll try something new / You can depend on me / Mickey's monkey / Tracks of my tears / Going to a go-go / I second that emotion / If you can wait / Baby, baby don't cry / Doggone right / Tears of a clown / I don't blame you at all / Baby come close / Baby that's backatcha / Quiet storm / Cruisin' / Being with you (last 3 SMOKEY ROBINSON solo).

Aug 89. (cd) *(ZD 72510)* **COMPACT COMMAND PERFORMANCES VOL.2** [ ] [ ]

Nov 92. (cd/c/lp) *(530121-2/-4/-1)* **THE GREATEST HITS** [ ] [ ]

May 93. (cd/c) *Spectrum; (550073-2/-4)* **TEARS OF A CLOWN** [ ] [–]

Jun 93. (cd/c) *WEA; (8122 71181-2/-4)* **WHATEVER MAKES YOU HAPPY: MORE BEST OF SMOKEY ROBINSON & THE MIRACLES 1961-1971** [ ] [ ]

Mar 96. (cd) *(530121-2)* **GREATEST HITS** [ ] [ ]

Jul 96. (cd) *Spectrum; (552125-2)* **MOTOWN EARLY CLASSICS** [ ] [-]
Aug 98. (cd) *(530857-2)* **THE ULTIMATE COLLECTION** [ ] [ ]
Aug 99. (cd) *Spectrum; (530794-2)* **TRACKS OF MY TEARS** [ ] [ ]
Jul 00. (cd) *(153869-2)* **MOTOWN LOST AND FOUND: ALONG CAME LOVE** [ ] [ ]
May 01. (cd) *(013183-2)* **MAKE IT HAPPEN / SPECIAL OCCASION** [ ] [ ]
May 01. (cd) *(013185-2)* **GOING TO A GO-GO / AWAY WE A GO-GO** [ ] [ ]
May 01. (cd) *(013186-2)* **TIME OUT / FOUR IN BLUE** [ ] [ ]
Jul 01. (cd) *Universal; (E 157525-2)* **UNIVERSAL MASTERS COLLECTION** [ ] [ ]
Jul 01. (cd) *Cleopatra; (CLP 1082CD)* **LOVE MACHINE: REMIXED HITS** [ ] [ ]
Nov 01. (4xcd-box) *(530286-2)* **THE 35TH ANNIVERSARY COLLECTION** [ ] [ ]
Apr 02. (cd) *Spectrum; (544681-2)* **COLLECTION** [ ] [ ]
Sep 02. (d-cd) *(064481-2)* **THE ANTHOLOGY: OOO BABY BABY** [ ] [ ]
Mar 03. (cd) *Universal; (AA121 53398-2)* **THE MILLENNIUM COLLECTION** [ ] [ ]
Mar 03. (cd) *Universal; (AA121 59449-2)* **20TH CENTURY MASTERS** [ ] [ ]

MISSION

Formed: Leeds, England . . . late 1985 by ex-SISTERS OF MERCY members WAYNE HUSSEY and CRAIG ADAMS. After falling out with the aforementioned band's singer ANDREW ELDRITCH, the pair recruited SIMON HINKLER (ex-ARTERY) and MICK BROWN (ex-RED LORRY YELLOW LORRY), forming a new band originally under The SISTERHOOD moniker. Calculated to annoy their former colleague, ELDRITCH retaliated by releasing a single under a similar name, HUSSEY and Co. subsequently switching to The MISSION. In Spring '86, the band signed to indie label, 'Chapter 22', releasing the enjoyably amateurish goth theatrics of the 'SERPENT'S KISS' single a couple of months later. Another single, 'GARDEN OF DELIGHT', appeared that summer before the band were snapped up by 'Mercury'. The debut album, 'GOD'S OWN MEDICINE', appeared towards the end of the year, almost making the UK Top 10. Given a bit of a rough ride by critics for its often overbearing goth pompousness, the record was nevertheless a fairly accomplished set of adult rock, a bit like what U2 might have sounded like had they been born in Leeds and developed a penchant for wearing pointy shoes and smearing their faces with flour. The grandiose 'WASTELAND' made No.11 when it was released as a single early the following year, staking The MISSION's claim as the new Goth messiahs and no doubt making ELDRITCH sick to his stomach. But much as they liked to be serious fellows on record, they liked to party hard behind the scenes, CRAIG ADAMS coming a cropper on a particularly gruelling US tour and briefly leaving the band. His temporary replacement was PETE TURNER who filled in for the remainder of the tour and also played at The MISSION's triumphant Reading Festival headlining appearance later that summer. With ADAMS back in the fold, the band began work on a new album with LED ZEPPELIN bassist JOHN PAUL JONES on production chores. The less than impressive result was 'CHILDREN' (1988), a No.2 hit despite its critical lashing. Preceded by the delicate 'BUTTERFLY ON A WHEEL', the 'CARVED IN SAND' album was eventually released to expectant fans in early 1990. More elegantly refined than their normal heavy handed approach, the set remains their most listenable effort, if not their most successful. The band resumed heavy touring following the album's release, HINKLER subsequently storming out on the American jaunt. His replacement for the remainder of the tour was another ex-RED LORRY YELLOW LORRY man, DAVID WOLFENDEN, the band eventually recruiting guitarist ETCH (PAUL ETCHELLS, ex-GHOST DANCE) as a semi-permanent fixture later that year. Following the ambitious 'MASQUE' (1992) set (which featured the violin playing of FAIRPORT CONVENTION's RIC SAUNDERS), MARK THWAITE (ex-SPEAR OF DESTINY) and RIK CARTER (ex-PENDRAGON) were brought in after the departure of ADAMS. Two further albums appeared on the band's own label, 'Equator', following the end of their tenure with 'Mercury', none making any substantial commercial headway. In 1996, The MISSION scraped into the charts with their new 'BLUE' set, although this was a sad swansong for a once enterprising outfit. HUSSEY and crew resurfaced in the late 90's to re-work many of their past faves via the album, 'RESURRECTION' (1999). Leeds' goth shock troops returned in 2001 with 'AURA', a reasonable attempt at reanimating the spell they held over the nation's black clad youth back in their 80's heyday. • **Songwriters:** HUSSEY penned, except LIKE A HURRICANE (Neil Young) / DANCING BAREFOOT (Patti Smith) / SHELTER FROM THE STORM (Bob Dylan) / OVER THE HILLS AND FAR AWAY (Led Zeppelin) / LOVE (John Lennon) / ATOMIC (Blondie). • **Trivia:** In 1991, HUSSEY was ushered off James Whale's late night TV show for being drunk and abusive to its ever-polite presenter!!

Album rating: GOD'S OWN MEDICINE (*7) / CHILDREN (*6) / CARVED IN SAND (*5) / GRAINS OF SAND out-takes (*5) / MASQUE (*5) / SUM AND SUBSTANCE compilation (*7) / NEVERLAND (*4) / BLUE (*4) / RESURRECTION – THE GREATEST HITS (*6) / AURA (*6)

WAYNE HUSSEY (b.26 May'59, Bristol, England) – vocals, guitar (ex-SISTERS OF MERCY, ex-DEAD OR ALIVE, ex-HAMBI & THE DANCE, ex-WALKIE TALKIES) / **CRAIG ADAMS** – bass (ex-SISTERS OF MERCY, ex-EXPELAIRES) / **SIMON HINKLER** – guitar (ex-ARTERY) / **MICK BROWN** – drums (ex-RED LORRY YELLOW LORRY)

Chapter 22 | not iss.

May 86. (7") *(CHAP 6-7)* **SERPENT'S KISS. / WAKE (R.S.V.)** [70] [-]
(12"+=) *(CHAP 6)* – Naked and savage.
Jul 86. (7") *(CHAP 7)* **GARDEN OF DELIGHT. / LIKE A HURICANE** [50] [-]
(12"+=) *(12CHAP 7)* – Over the hills and far away / The crystal ocean.
(12"+=) *(L12CHAP 7)* – Dancing barefoot / The crystal ocean.

Mercury | Mercury

Oct 86. (7") *(MYSG 1)* **STAY WITH ME. / BLOOD BROTHER** [30] [-]
(12"+=) *(MYSGX 1)* – Islands in a stream.
Nov 86. (lp/c)(cd) *(MERH/+C 102)(<830603-2>)* **GODS OWN MEDICINE** [14] [ ]
– Wasteland / Bridges burning / Garden of delight (hereafter) / Stay with me / Blood brother * / Let sleeping dogs lie / Sacrilege / Dance on glass / And the dance goes on / Severina / Love me to death / Island in a stream *. *(c+=/cd+= *)*
Jan 87. (7") *(MYTH 2)* **WASTELAND. / SHELTER FROM THE STORM** [11] [-]
(12"+=) *(MYTHX 2-1)* – Dancing barefoot (live).
('A'-Anniversary mix.12"+=) *(MYTHX 2-2)* – 1969 (live) / Wake (live).
(d7") *(MYTHB 2)* – 1969 (live) / Serpent's kiss (live).
Mar 87. (7"/7"s) *(MYTH/+P 3)* **SEVERINA. / TOMORROW NEVER KNOWS** [25] [-]
(12"+=) *(MYTHL 3)* – Wishing well.

—— **PETE TURNER** – bass; took over on tour while ADAMS recovered from illness

—— **CRAIG ADAMS** was soon back after a 4 month lay-off.

Jan 88. (7") *(MYTH 4)* **TOWER OF STRENGTH. / FABIENNE** [12] [-]
(ext.12"+=) *(MYTHX 4)* – Dream on / Breathe (instrumental).
(ext.cd-s+=) *(MTHCD 4)* – Dream on / Breathe (vocal).
Mar 88. (lp/c)(cd) *(MISH/+C 2)(<834263-2>)* **CHILDREN** [2] [ ]
– Beyond the pale / A wing and a prayer / Fabienne * / Heaven on Earth / Tower of strength / Kingdom come / Breathe / Child's play / Shamera kye / Black mountain mist / Dream on * / Heat / Hymn (for America). *(c+=/cd+= *)*

Jul 88. (7") *(MYTH 6)* **BEYOND THE PALE. / TADEUSZ (1912-1988)** [32] [–]
('A'-Armageddon mix.12"+=) *(MYTHX 6)* – Love me to death / For ever more.
('A'-Armageddon mix.cd-s+=) *(MTHCD 6-2)* – Tower of strength (Bombay edit).

Nov 88. (7") *(MYTH 7)* **KINGDOM COME. / CHILD'S PLAY (live)** [ ] [–]
(12"+=) *(MYTHX 7)* – The crystal ocean.
(cd-s++=) *(MTHCD 7)* – Garden of delight (live).

— (all formats on above single withdrawn)

Jan 90. (7"/c-s) *(MYTH/MTHMC 8)* **BUTTERFLY ON A WHEEL. / THE GRIP OF DISEASE** [12] [–]
(12"+=/cd-s+=/box-cd-s+=)(10"+=) *(MYTHX/MTHCD/MYCDB 8)(MYTH 8-10)* – ('A'-Magni-octopus) / Kingdom come (forever and again).

Feb 90. (cd/c/lp) *(<842251-2/-4/-1>)* **CARVED IN SAND** [7] [ ]
– Amelia / Into the blue / Butterfly on a wheel / Sea of love / Deliverance / Grapes of wrath / Belief / Paradise (will shine like the Moon) / Hungry as the hunter / Lovely.

Mar 90. (7"/c-s) *(MYTH/MTHMC 9)* **DELIVERANCE. / MR. PLEASANT** [27] [–]
(12"+=/cd-s+=/pic-cd-s+=)(10"+=) *(MYTHX/MTHCD/MYCDB 9)(MYTH 9-10)* – Heaven sends us.

May 90. (7"/c-s) *(MYTH/MTHMC 10)* **INTO THE BLUE. / BIRD OF PARADISE** [32] [–]
(12"+=/cd-s+=) *(MYTHX/MTHCD 10)* – Divided we fall.

— **DAVID WOLFENDEN** – guitar (ex-RED LORRY YELLOW LORRY) repl. HINKLER.

— (Oct'90) added **ETCH** – guitar (ex-GHOST DANCE)

Oct 90. (cd/c/lp) *(846937-2/-4/-1)* **GRAINS OF SAND** (out-takes) [28] [–]
– Hands across the ocean / The grip of disease / Divided we fall / Mercenary / Mr.Pleasant / Kingdom come (forever and again) / Heaven sends you / Sweet smile of a mystery / Love / Bird of passage. *(c+=/cd+=)* – Tower of strength (Casbah mix) / Butterfly on a wheel (Troubadour mix).

Nov 90. (7"/c-s) *(MYTH/MTHMC 11)* **HANDS ACROSS THE OCEAN. / AMELIA / LOVE** [28] [–]
(12"+=) *(MYTHX 11)* – Amelia (live) / Tower of strength (mix) / Mercenary.
(cd-s+=) *(MTHCD 11)* – Amelia (live) / Stay with me / Mercenary.

Vertigo Mercury

Apr 92. (7"/c-s) *(MYTH/MTHMC 12)* **NEVER AGAIN. / BEAUTIFUL CHAOS** [34] [–]
(12"+=/cd-s+=) *(MYTHX/MTHCD 12)* – ('A'-F1 mix) / ('A'-Zero G mix.

Jun 92. (cd/c/lp) *<(512121-2/-4/-1)>* **MASQUE** [23] [ ]
– Never again / Shades of green (part II) / Even you may shine / Trail of scarlet / Spider and the fly / She conjures me wings / Sticks and stones / Like a child again / Who will love me tomorrow? / You make me breathe / From one Jesus to another / Until there's another sunrise. *(re-is.cd/c Aug94; same)*

Jun 92. (7"/c-s) *(MYTH/MTHMC 13)* **LIKE A CHILD AGAIN (remix). / ALL TANGLED UP IN YOU** [30] [–]
(12"+=/cd-s+=) *(MYTHX/MTHCD 13)* – ('A'-Mark Saunders remix) / Hush a bye baby (child again) (Joe Gibbs remix).

Oct 92. (7"/c-s) *(MYTH/MTHMC 14)* **SHADES OF GREEN. / YOU MAKE ME BREATHE** [49] [–]
(cd-s) *(MTHCD 14)* – ('A'side) / Sticks and stones / Trail of scarlet / Spider and the fly.
(etched-12"+=) *(MYTHX 14)* – ('A'mix).

— (Nov'92) **MARK THWAITE** – guitar (ex-SPEAR OF DESTINY) repl. HINKLER + ADAMS. Note:- **RIC SAUNDERS** – violin (of FAIRPORT CONVENTION) on last lp

Jan 94. (7") *(MYTH 15)* **TOWER OF STRENGTH (Youth remix). / WASTELAND** [33] [–]
(12"+=) *(MYTHX 15)* – Serpent's kiss.
(cd-s) *(MYTCD 15)* – ('A'mixes) / ('A'-East India Cairo mix) / Deliverance.

Feb 94. (cd/c/d-lp) *<(518447-2/-4/-1)>* **SUM AND SUBSTANCE** (compilation) [49] [ ]
– Never again / Hands across the ocean / Shades of green / Like a child again / Into the blue / Deliverance / Tower of strength / Butterfly on a wheel / Kingdom come / Beyond the pale / Severina / Stay with me / Wasteland / Garden of delight / Like a hurricane / Serpent's kiss / Sour puss / Afterglow.

Mar 94. (7") *(MYTH 16)* **AFTERGLOW. / SOUR-PUSS** [53] [–]
(cd-s+=) *(MYTCD 16)* – Cold as ice / Valentine.

Equator not iss.

Oct 94. (7"ep/cd-ep) *(HOOK S/CD 001)* **MISSION 1 EP** [ ] [–]
– Raising Cain / Sway / Neverland.

Jan 95. (7"ep/cd-ep) *(HOOK S/CD 002)* **MISSION 2 EP** [73] [–]
– Swoon / Where / Wasting away.
(cd-ep+=) *(HOOKCDR 002)* – ('A'-Resurrection mix).

Feb 95. (cd/lp) *(SMEE CD/MC/LP 001)* **NEVERLAND** [58] [–]
– Raising Cain / Sway / Lose myself / Swoon / Afterglow (reprise) / Stars don't shine without you / Celebration / Cry like a baby / Heaven knows / Swim with the dolphins / Neverland / Daddy's going to Heaven now.

Jun 96. (cd/c/lp) *(SMEE CD/MC/LP 002)* **BLUE** [73] [–]
– Coming home / Get back to you / Drown in blue / Damaged / More than this / That tears shall drown the wind / Black & blue / Bang bang / Alpha man / Cannibal / Dying room / Evermore & again.

— HUSSEY and Co called it a day after above; he revived the band with **GEOFF READING** – drums, etc.

Eagle Cleopatra

Nov 99. (cd) *(EAGCD 055) <CLP 756>* **RESURRECTION – GREATEST HITS** (re-workings) [ ] [ ]
– Prelude: Anniversary / Wasteland / Severina / Love me to death / Interlude: Never forever / Beyond the pale / Deliverance / Without you / Like a child again / Sacrilege / You make me breathe / Crystal ocean / Interlude: Infection / Hands across the ocean / 1969 / Resurrection.

Playground Playground

Nov 01. (12"/cd-s) *(PGND/+CD 001)* **EVANGELINE / ANYONE BUT YOU. / MELT / SWOON (reprise)** [ ] [–]

Dec 01. (lp/cd) *(<PGND/+CD 002>)* **AURA** [ ] [ ]
– Evangeline / Shine like the stars / (Slave to) Lust / Mesmerised / Lay your hands on me / Dragonfly / Happy / To die by your hand / Trophy – It never rains . . . / The light pours from you / Burlesque / Cocoon / In denial. *(d-cd-iss. Dec01 +=; PGNDCDX 002)* – (bonus tracks).

Mar 02. (d7"red-ep/cd-ep) *(PGND/+CD 003)* **SHINE LIKE THE STARS. / NEVER LET ME DOWN // SPIDER & THE FLY (IN THE OINTMENT) / SORRY . . .** [ ] [–]

Oct 02. (cd) *(PGNDCD 004)* **AURAL DELIGHT** [ ] [–]
– Amelia / Even you may shine / Spider in the fly (in the ointment) / Sorry . . . / Anyone but you / Never let me down / Never again / Melt / Mesmerised (reprise) / Swoon / Dragonfly (demo) / Can't help falling in love with you.

– compilations, others, etc. –

Jun 87. (lp/c) *Mercury; (MISH/+C 1) <832527-1/-4>* **THE FIRST CHAPTER** [35] May88 [ ]
(cd-iss. May88; 832527-2)

Jul 94. (cd/lp) *Nighttracks; (CDNT/LPNT 005)* **SALAD DAZE** [ ] [–]

Aug 95. (d-cd) *Mercury; (528805-2)* **CHILDREN / CARVED IN SAND** [ ] [–]

Feb 00. (cd) *Spectrum; (544228-2)* **TOWER OF STRENGTH** [ ] [–]

Aug 00. (cd) *Receiver; (RRCD 294)* **EVER AFTER: LIVE** [ ] [–]
(<US + re-iss. Nov02 on 'Castle'; CMRCD 592>)

Oct 02. (cd) *Delta; (CD 47100)* **REVISITED** [ ] [–]

Oct 02. (cd) *Armoury; (ARMCD 070)* **SACRILEGE** [ ] [–]

Joni MITCHELL

Born: ROBERTA JOAN ANDERSON, 7 Nov'43, Fort MacLeod, Alberta, Canada. In 1964, she performed at the Mariposa Folk Festival in Ontario, and married CHUCK MITCHELL in June '65, although after they relocated to Detroit the following year, they divorced. She retained the surname and moved to New York, where her songs were gradually recorded by others, mainly JUDY COLLINS ('BOTH SIDES NOW' & 'MICHAEL FROM MOUNTAINS') and TOM RUSH ('THE CIRCLE GAME'). Her self-titled DAVID CROSBY-produced debut lp came out in Summer of '68 and managed to only scrape into US Top 200. In August 1969 on the advice of David Geffen, she pulled out of WOODSTOCK free festival, and instead wrote the classic song of that name. It was later a US hit for CROSBY, STILLS, NASH & YOUNG, and also a UK No.1 for MATTHEWS' SOUTHERN COMFORT. Her second lp, 'CLOUDS', broke through into US Top 40 after her non-appearance, another classic album of the late 60's. Her third outing, 'LADIES OF THE CANYON' contained the aforementioned hippie mysticism of 'WOODSTOCK' as well as the surprise UK hit 'BIG YELLOW TAXI', making MITCHELL a household name in Britain when the album went to No.8. The romanticism had all but vanished by 'BLUE', one of the starkest, most soul searching records of the singer/songwriter era. The autobiographical intensity of the record is borne out by the fact that MITCHELL allegedly allowed no one but the engineer into the studio during recording. Not quite so intense but arguably more introspective was her 1972 album, 'FOR THE ROSES', a more experimental edge creeping into the arrangements and the first signs of MITCHELL's increasing preoccupation with jazz stylings. A combination of glittering melody and a light jazz sheen created one of her most listenable and commercially successful albums, 1974's 'COURT AND SPARK'. The assured sophistication of MITCHELL's blossoming talent was also evident in her live work, 'MILES OF AISLES', matching 'COURT AND SPARK's No.2 position on the US chart. Her next two albums, 'THE HISSING OF SUMMER LAWNS' and 'HEJIRA' marked a significant move away from the relative simplicity of her earlier work into more sophisticated sonic textures, underscored by jazz and world-inflected rhythms while her lyrical musings followed suit, away from personal confession towards pointed observation and cultural commentary. Alienated from the rock community which had nurtured her and amid scathing reviews, she moved ever further into obscure jazz fusion throughout the latter half of the 70's with the double album 'DON JUAN'S RECKLESS DAUGHTER' (1977) and ultimately, her collaboration with jazz legend CHALES MINGUS, released in 1979 and simply titled, 'MINGUS'. Come the 80's, MITCHELL seemed to lose her focus. 'WILD THINGS RUN FAST', saw her treading water although 1985's THOMAS DOLBY-produced 'DOG EAT DOG' was an impassioned attack on the rampant materialism and hypocrisy of the 80's, singling out such worthy targets as the TV evangelists of the religious right. The insipid banality of 'CHALK MARK IN A RAINSTORM' (1988) is best passed over while 1991's 'NIGHT RIDE HOME' saw a return to from of sorts, combining the jazz textures and lyrical expaniveness of her earlier work. Around this time, MITCHELL exhibited some of her paintings in London and Edinburgh to critical acclaim while her most recent album to date, 'TURBULENT INDIGO' was a mature, accomplished set taking on such controversial issues as domestic violence. 1998's 'TAMING THE TIGER' was no exception, wherein MITCHELL expanded her sound with the use of guitar synthesizer, the jazzy arrangements and uncompromising lyrics (supplied, on 'The CRAZY CRIES OF LOVE', by boyfriend Don Freed) suggesting that the singer/songwriter was still restless despite her approaching 50th birthday. If not exactly likely to win many new converts, her loyal fanbase ensured the record a Top 75 placing on both sides of the Atlantic, a feat replicated by 'BOTH SIDES NOW' (2000). Directed and co-produced by former husband Larry Klein, the latter was a concept set based around the theme of romance and musically fleshed out by a 71-piece orchestra. Once more demonstrating MITCHELL's desire to push herself, the album found her interpreting pre-war songwriting in sympathetic and original style. 'TRAVELOGUE' (2002), announced as the coda to her long and ever winding music biz road, was perhaps the most ambitious and far sighted project of her near four decades of recording. Backed by a sizeable orchestra and accompanied by jazz luminaries like WAYNE SHORTER and HERBIE HANCOCK, MITCHELL took a long, unsentimental look at her back catalogue, re-imagining a choice selection of her compositions with often intoxicating results. Like her old musical sparring partner NEIL YOUNG, MITCHELL remains one of the few survivors of the hippy era to avoid falling in terminal self-parody, admirably still challenging herself and her fans with each successive release. • **Songwriters:** All self-penned except; TWISTED (Annie Ross) / WHY DO FOOLS FALL IN LOVE (Frankie Lymon) / BABY I DON'T CARE (hit; Elvis Presley) / SLOUCHING TOWARDS BETHLEHEM (poem; W.B.Yeats).

Album rating: JONI MITCHELL (*7) / CLOUDS (*7) / LADIES OF THE CANYON (*9) / BLUE (*9) / FOR THE ROSES (*7) / COURT AND SPARK (*9) / MILES OF AISLES (*6) / THE HISSING OF SUMMER LAWNS (*8) / HEJIRA (*9) / DON JUAN'S RECKLESS DAUGHTER (*5) / MINGUS (*6) / SHADOWS AND LIGHT (*6) / WILD THINGS RUN FAST (*6) / DOG EAT DOG (*5) / CHALK MARK IN A RAINSTORM (*7) / NIGHT RIDE HOME (*5) / TURBULENT INDIGO (*6) / JONI MITCHELL HITS compilation (*8) / TAMING THE TIGER (*5) / BOTH SIDES NOW (*5) / TRAVELOGUE (*6)

JONI MITCHELL – vocals, acoustic guitar, piano with **STEPHEN STILLS** – bass / etc (on first)

Reprise Reprise

Jun 68. (lp) *(RSLP 6293)* <6293> **JONI MITCHELL** [ ] Mar68 [ ]
– I CAME TO THE CITY:- I had a king / Michael from the mountains / Night in the city / Marcie / Nathan la Freneer / OUT OF THE CITY AND DOWN TO THE SEASIDE:- Sisotowbell Lane / The dawntreader / The pirate of penance / Song to a seagull / Cactus tree. *(cd-iss. Jan88; K2 44051)*

Jul 68. (7") *(RS 20694)* **NIGHT IN THE CITY. / I HAD A KING** [ ] [–]

Aug 69. (7") *(23402)* **CHELSEA MORNING. / BOTH SIDES NOW** [ ] [–]
<US-iss.Jun72; 1154>

Oct 69. (lp) *(RSLP 6341)* <6341> **CLOUDS** [ ] May69 [31]
– Tin angel / Chelsea morning / I don't know where I stand / That song about the Midway / Roses blue / The gallery / I think I understand / Songs to ageing children come / The fiddle and the drum / Both sides now. *(cd-iss. Jan88; K2 44070)*

— next guests **MILT HOLLAND** – percussion / **TERESSA ADAMS** – cello / **JIM HORN** – baritone sax / **PAUL HORN** – clarinet, flute

May 70. (lp) *(RSLP 6376)* <6376> **LADIES OF THE CANYON** [8] Apr70 [27]
– Morning Morgantown / For free / Conversation / Ladies of the canyon / Willy / The arrangement / Rainy night house / The priest / Blue boy / Big yellow taxi / Woodstock / The circle game. *(cd-iss. Jul88; K2 44085)*

Jun 70. (7") *(RS 20906)* <0906> **BIG YELLOW TAXI. / WOODSTOCK** [11] [67]

— with **STILLS + JAMES TAYLOR** – guitar / **SNEAKY PETE KLEINOW** – steel guitar / **RUSS KUNKEL** – drums / etc.

Jul 71. (lp) *(K 44128)* <2038> **BLUE** [3] Jun71 [15]
– All I want / My old man / Little green / Carey / Blue / California / This flight tonight / River / A case of you / The last time I saw Richard. *(cd-iss. Jan87; K2 44128)*

Aug 71. (7") <1029> **CAREY. / THIS FLIGHT TONIGHT** [–] [93]

Aug 71. (7") *(K 14099)* **CAREY. / MY OLD MAN** [ ] [–]

Apr 72. (7") *(K 14130)* <1049> **CALIFORNIA. / A CASE OF YOU** [ ] Oct71 [ ]

Jul 72. (7") <1155> **CAREY. / BIG YELLOW TAXI** [–] [ ]

— Her band now **STILLS + NASH** (her recent boyfriend) + **KUNKEL / WILTON FELDER / JAMES BURTON** – guitar / **TOM SCOTT** – wind

Asylum Asylum

Nov 72. (7") *(AYM 511)* <11010> **YOU TURN ME ON, I'M A RADIO. / URGE FOR GOING** [ ] [25]

Dec 72. (lp) *(SYLA 8753)* <5057> **FOR THE ROSES** [ ] Nov72 [11]
– Banquet / Cold blue steel and sweet fire / Barangrill / Lesson in survival / Let the wind carry me / For the roses / See you sometime / Electricity / You turn me on, I'm a radio / Blonde in the bleachers / Woman of heart and mind / Judgement of the Moon and stars (Ludwig's tune). *(cd-iss. Dec87; K2 53007)*

Mar 73. (7") *(AYM 515)* **COLD BLUE STEEL AND SWEET FIRE. / BLONDE IN THE BLEACHERS** [ ] [–]

— Retained **TOM SCOTT's L.A. EXPRESS** with new boyfriend **JOHN GUERIN** – drums / **WILTON FELDER** – bass / **LARRY CARLTON** – guitar / **CHUCK FINDLEY** – trumpet / **JOE SAMPLE** – keyboards / **ROBBIE ROBERTSON** – guitar

Jan 74. (7") *(AYM 524)* <11029> **RAISED ON ROBBERY. / COURT AND SPARK** [ ] Dec73 [65]

Mar 74. (lp) *(SYLA 8756)* <7E 1001> **COURT AND SPARK** [14] Feb74 [2]

– Court and spark / Help me / Free man in Paris / People's parties / The same situation / Car on a hill / Down to you / Just like this train / People's parties / Raised on robbery / Trouble child. *(re-iss. Jun76 lp/c; K/K4 53002) (cd-iss. May83; 253002-2)*

Mar 74. (7") *<11034>* **HELP ME. / JUST LIKE THIS TRAIN** – 7

Jul 74. (7") *<11041>* **FREE MAN IN PARIS. / PEOPLE'S PARTIES** – 22

Oct 74. (7") *(AYM 533)* **FREE MAN IN PARIS. / CAR ON A HILL** – –

Jan 75. (7") *(AYM 537) <45221>* **BIG YELLOW TAXI (live). / RAINY NIGHT HOUSE (live)** – Dec74 24

Jan 75. (d-lp) *(SYSP 902) <202>* **MILES OF AISLES** 34 Nov74 2

– You turn me on, I'm a radio / Big yellow taxi / Rainy night house / Woodstock / Cactus tree / Cold blue steel and sweet fire / Woman of heart and mind / A case of you / The circle game / People's parties / All I want / Real good for free / Both sides now / Carey / The last time I saw Richard / Jericho / Love or money. *(re-iss. Jun76 d-lp/d-c; K/K4 63001) (cd-iss. 1989; K2 63001)* – (omits some dialogue).

(above also with **TOM SCOTT & THE L.A. EXPRESS;- SCOTT / GUERIN** plus **ROBBEN FORD** – guitar / **LARRY NASH** – piano / **MAX BENNETT** – bass

Nov 75. (lp/c) *(K/K4 53018) <7E 1051>* **THE HISSING OF SUMMER LAWNS** 14 4

– In France they kiss on Main Street / The jungle line / Edith and the kingpin / Don't interrupt the sorrow / Shades of Scarlett conquering The hissing of summer lawns / The boho dance / Harry's house – Centerpiece / Sweet bird / Shadows and light. *(cd-iss. Nov87; K2 53018)*

Mar 76. (7") *(K 13035) <45296>* **IN FRANCE THEY KISS ON MAIN STREET. / BOHO DANCE** – Feb76 66

Nov 76. (lp/c) *(K/K4 53053) <7E 1087>* **HEJIRA** 11 13

– Coyote / Amelia / Furry sings the blues / A strange boy / Hejira / Song for Sharon / Black crow / Blue motel room / Refuge of the roads. *(cd-iss. Oct87; 253053-2)*

Feb 77. (7") *(K 13072) <45377>* **COYOTE. / BLUE MOTEL ROOM** – –

— now with **JACO PASTORIUS** – bass / **GLENN FREY** – vocals / **WAYNE SHORTER** – sax / **J.D.SOUTHER + CHAKA KHAN** – both backing vocals

Dec 77. (d-lp/d-c) *(K/K4 63003) <101>* **DON JUAN'S RECKLESS DAUGHTER** 20 25

– Overture – Cotton Avenue / Talk to me / Jericho / Paprika plains / Otis and Marlena / The tenth world / Dreamland / Don Juan's reckless daughter / Off night backstreet / The silky veils of Ardor. *(cd-iss. 1988; K2 63003)*

Feb 78. (7") *(K 13110)* **OFF NIGHT BACKSTREET. / JERICHO** – –

Feb 78. (7") *<45467>* **JERICHO. / DREAMLAND** – –

— now with **JACO PASTORIUS** – bass / **WAYNE SHORTER** – sax / **HERBIE HANCOCK** – keyboards / **PETER ERSKINE** – drums / **DON ALIAS + EMIL RICHARDS** – percussion

Jun 79. (7") *(K 13154) <46506>* **THE DRY CLEANER FROM DES MOINES. / GOD MUST BE A BOOGIE MAN** – –

Jul 79. (lp/c) *(K/K4 53091) <505>* **MINGUS** 24 Jun79 17

– Happy birthday 1975 (rap) / God must be a boogie man / Funeral (rap) / A chair in the sky / The wolf that lives in Lindsey / I's a muggin' (rap) / Sweet sucker dance / Coin in the pocket (rap) / The dry cleaner from Des Moines / Lucky (rap) / Goodbye pork pie hat. *(cd-iss. 1988; K2 53091)*

— now with **PAT METHENY** – lead guitar / **JACO PASTORUS** – bass / **LYLE MAYS** – keyboards / **DON ALIAS** – drums / **MICHAEL BRECKER** – saxophone

Sep 80. (d-lp/d-c) *(K/K4 62030) <704>* **SHADOWS AND LIGHT (live)** 63 38

– (introduction) / In France they kiss on Main Street / Edith and the kingpin / Coyote / Goodbye pork pie hat / The dry cleaner from Des Moines / Amelia / Pat's solo / Hejira / Black crow / Don's solo / Dreamland / Free man in Paris / (band introduction) / Furry sings the blues / Why do fools fall in love? / Shadows and light / God must be a boogie man / Woodstock.

Oct 80. (7") *(K 12478) <47038>* **WHY DO FOOLS FALL IN LOVE? (live). / BLACK CROW (live)** – –

— **LARRY KLEIN** – bass (she married him Nov'82) / **LARRY WILLIAMS** – keyboards / **LARRY CARLTON / JOHN GUERIN / VICTOR FELDMAN** / etc.

Geffen Geffen

Nov 82. (7") *(GEF 2950) <29849>* **(YOU'RE SO SQUARE) BABY, I DON'T CARE. / LOVE** – 47

Nov 82. (lp/c) *(GEF/40 25102) <GHS 2019>* **WILD THINGS RUN FAST** 32 25

– Chinese cafe – Unchained melody / Wild things run fast / Ladies man / Moon at the window / Solid love / Be cool / (You're so square) Baby, I don't care / You dream flat tyres / Man to man / Underneath the streetlight / Love. *(cd-iss. Jul88; GEFD 02019) (re-iss. Jul92 cd/c; GFLD/GFLC 19129)*

Feb 83. (7") *<29757>* **BE COOL. / UNDERNEATH THE STREETLIGHT** – –

Feb 83. (7") *(GEF 3122)* **CHINESE CAFE. / LADIES MAN** – –

(d7"+=) *(DA 3122)* – (interview).

Nov 85. (7") *(A 6740) <28840>* **GOOD FRIENDS. / SMOKIN' (EMPTY TRY ANOTHER)** – 85

— Above feat. guest duet **MICHAEL McDONALD**

— now with co-producer **THOMAS DOLBY** – synthesizers / etc.

Nov 85. (lp/c) *(GEF/GEC 26455) <24074>* **DOG EAT DOG** 57 63

– Good friends / Fiction / Three great stimulants / Tax free / Smokin' (empty, try another) / Dog eat dog / Shiny toys / Ethiopia / Impossible dreamer / Lucky girl. *(cd-iss. May86; K 924074-2) (re-iss. Oct87 lp/c; K 924074-1/-4) (re-iss. Mar93 cd/c; GFLD/GFLC 19198)*

Apr 86. (7"/12") *(A/TA 7124)* **SHINY TOYS. / THREE GREAT STIMULANTS** – –

— guests **THOMAS DOLBY, TOM PETTY, WILLIE NELSON, DON HENLEY, WENDY & LISA, BILLY IDOL, PETER GABRIEL, etc. KLEIN** co-produced, as was next

Mar 88. (lp/c)(cd) *(WX 141/+C)(924172-2) <24172>* **CHALK MARK IN A RAIN STORM** 26 45

– My secret place / Number one / Lakota / The tea leaf prophecy / Dancing clown / The beat of black wings / Snakes and ladders / The recurring dream / The bird that whistles. *(re-iss. Jan91 lp/c/cd; GEF/+C/D 24172) (re-iss. Mar93 cd/c; GFLD/GFLC 19199)*

Apr 88. (7") *<27887>* **MY SECRET PLACE. / LAKOTA** – –

May 88. (7") *(GEF 37)* **MY SECRET PLACE. / NUMBER ONE** – –

(12"+=/3"cd-s+=) *(GEF 37 T/CD)* – Chinese eyes – Unchained melody / Good friends.

— ('A'featured **PETER GABRIEL**)

— retained **KLEIN** with band **VINNIE COLAIUTA** – drums / **ALEX ACUNA** – percussion / **WAYNE SHORTER** – saxophone / **BILL DILLON + MICHAEL LANDAU** – guitars

Mar 91. (lp/c/cd) *<(GEF/+C/D 24302)>* **NIGHT RIDE HOME** 25 41

– Night ride home / Passion play (when all the slaves are free) / Cherokee Louise / The windfall (everything for nothing) / Slouching towards Bethlehem / Come in from the cold / Nothing can be done / The only joy in town / Ray's dad's cadillac / Two grey rooms.

Jul 91. (7") *(GFS 4)* **COME IN FROM THE COLD. / RAY'S DAD'S CADILLAC** – –

(cd-s+=/pic-cd-s+=) *(GFS 4CD/+P)* – ('A'extended).

Reprise Reprise

Oct 94. (cd/c) *<(9362 45786-2/-4)>* **TURBULENT INDIGO** 53 47

– Sunny Sunday / Sex kills / The Magdalene laundries / Turbulent indigo / How do you stop / Last chance lost / Not to blame / Borderline / Yvette in English / The sire of sorrow (Job's sad song).

Nov 94. (c-s/cd-s) *(W 0273 C/CD)* **HOW DO YOU STOP / THE SIRE OF SORROW / MOON AT THE WINDOW** – –

Sep 98. (cd/c) *<(9362 46451-2/-4)>* **TAMING THE TIGER** 57 75

– Harlem in Havana / Man from Mars / Love puts on a new face / Lead balloon / No apologies / Taming the tiger / The crazy cries of love / Stay in touch / Face lift / My best to you / Tiger bones.

Feb 00. (cd/c) *<(9362 47620-2/-4)>* **BOTH SIDES NOW** 50 Mar00 66

– You're my thrill / At last / Comes love / You've changed / Answer me, my love / A case of you / Don't go to strangers / Sometimes I'm happy / Don't worry 'bout me / Stormy weather / I wish I were in love again / Both sides now (version).

Nonesuch Warners

Nov 02. (d-cd) *(7559 79817-2) <47965>* **TRAVELOGUE** – –

– Otis and Marlena / Amelia / You dream flat tires / Love / Woodstock / Slouching towards Bethlehem / Judgement of the Moon and stars (Ludwig's tune) / The sire of sorrow (Job's sad song) / For the roses / Trouble child / God must be a boogie man / Be cool / Just like this train / Sex kills / Refuge of the roads / Jejira / Chinese cafe – Unchained melody / Cherokee Louise / The dawntreader / The last time I saw Richard / Borderline / The circle game.

– compilations, others, etc. –

May 74. (7"ep) *Reprise; (K 14345)* **CAREY / BOTH SIDES NOW. / BIG YELLOW TAXI / WOODSTOCK** –
Oct 82. (d-c) *Reprise; (K4 64046)* **CLOUDS / BLUE** –
Jul 76. (7") *Asylum; (K 13048)* **YOU TURN ME ON, I'M A RADIO. / FREE MAN IN PARIS** –
Nov 83. (d-c) *Asylum;* **FOR THE ROSES / COURT AND SPARK** –
Oct 96. (cd/c) *Reprise; <(9362 46326-2/-4)>* **HITS**
– Urge for going / Chelsea morning / Big yellow taxi / Woodstock / The circle game / Carey / California / You turn me on I'm a radio / Raised on robbery / Help me / Free man in Paris / River / Chinese cafe / – Unchained melody / Come in from the cold / Both sides, now.
Oct 96. (cd/c) *Reprise; <(9362 46358-2/-4)>* **MISSES**
May 97. (cd) *Experience; (EXP 025)* **JONI MITCHELL** –
Jun 97. (cd) *Metro; (OTR 1100027)* **GHOSTS** –
Nov 03. (4xcd-box) *Geffen; <(81902)>* **THE COMPLETE GEFFEN RECORDINGS** Sep03

MOBY

Born: RICHARD MELVILLE HALL, 11 Sep'65, New York City, New York, USA. After being raised by his middle-class mother in Darien, Connecticut, he joined hardcore outfit The VATICAN COMMANDOS, which led to him having a brief stint in the similar, FLIPPER. He didn't record anything with the band and moved back to New York to become a DJ, making hardcore techno/dance records under the guise of BRAINSTORM and UHF3, etc. He subsequently became a mixer for The PET SHOP BOYS, ERASURE and MICHAEL JACKSON, before and during his return into solo work in the early 90's. His UK debut, 'GO', hit the Top 10 in October '91, having just breached the charts 3 months earlier. Sampling the 'Twin Peaks' theme, the song was a compelling piece of techno-pop that remains a dancefloor favourite. Little was subsequently heard of him barring a few US imports, although this led to UK semi-indie, 'Mute', taking him on board in mid '93. First up was his near Top 20 single, 'I FEEL IT', beginning a series of hits, albeit sporadic. Early in 1995, his album 'EVERYTHING IS WRONG' had critics lavishing praise on the man for his combination of acid-dance and ambience. 'ANIMAL RIGHTS', the 1996 follow-up added a new dimension; heavy industrial punk-metal which gave him a new found Kerrang! audience. Towards the tail-end of '97, the shaven-headed Christian vegan released the James Bond Theme to 'TOMORROW NEVER DIES', and although it rocketed into the UK Top 10, the accompanying soundtracks album, 'I LIKE TO SCORE', failed to gain the same chart momentum. Eager to once more turn up his amps to number 11, MOBY this time took elements of Southern Blues (courtesy of BESSIE JONES' 'Sometimes') and threw it into his punk/dance melting pot for next single, 'HONEY'. Although it deserved a better chart placing than No.33, it did pave the way for a series of diverse releases kicking off with CANNED HEAT-esque 'RUN ON' (aka 'Run On For A Long Time' by BILL LANDFORD), a taster from his fourth 'Mute' album, 'PLAY' (1999). Opening with the aforementioned 'HONEY', the second track 'FIND MY BABY' took a similar trek back in time (via a sample of the BOY BLUE's 'Joe Lee's Rock') while further UK hit singles, 'BODYROCK' and 'WHY DOES MY HEART FEEL SO BAD', rattled and graced the dancefloors respectively. Following up the unprecedented success of 'PLAY' was always going to prove a difficult if not impossible task for MOBY, especially in light of his often radical musical departures. In the event, '18' (2002) was as warm and self-assured as its predecessor while pointedly not attempting to repeat that record's singular fusion. The spiritual residue of that record did remain, however, imbuing '18's more conventional electronica with an earthy worldliness lacking in his earlier work. • **Songwriters:** Himself, and a few with singer, MIMI GOESE:- 'Into The Blue' + 'When It's Cold I'd Like To Die'. Other singers on 1995 album; ROZZ MOREHEAD / MYIM ROSE / NICOLE ZARAY / KOOKIE BANTON / SAUNDRA WILLIAMS. Samples BADALAMENTI's 'Twin Peaks' on 'GO'. Covered NEW DAWN FADES (Joy Division) / THAT'S WHEN I REACH FOR MY REVOLVER (Mission Of Burma). • **Trivia:** In 1992, he remixed JAM & SPOON's club smash 'Stella', which had sampled his 'GO'. He also provided vox for RECOIL's 1992 album, 'Bloodline'. MOBY remixed The B-52's, ESKIMOS AND EGYPT, LFO, FORTRAN 5, ORBITAL, ENO, PET SHOP BOYS + The OTHER TWO.

Album rating: MOBY (*6) / EARLY UNDERGROUND compilation (*6) / THE STORY SO FAR compilation (*6) / AMBIENT (*5) / EVERYTHING IS WRONG (*9) / ANIMAL RIGHTS (*8) / I LIKE TO SCORE (*7) / PLAY (*9) / 18 (*7)

MOBY HALL – vocals, guitar, etc

not iss. — Pregnant Nun

1983. (7"ep; by VATICAN COMMANDOS) *<#1>* **HIT SQUAD FOR GOD** –
– Why must I follow / It's so scary / Housewives on valium / Hit squad for God / Your way / Wonder bread.

— now with **PAUL JOHNSON** – bass + **ANDREW DeARUAJO** – drums

not iss. — Purity

1984. (12"ep; by AWOL) *<#1>* **AWOL** –
– Heart flag / Happy now / Holy mountain / One more dance / More than ever.

— now with **PAUL YATES + J. HARRELL**

1985. (lp; by SHOPWELL) *<HF-01>* **PEANUTS** –

— **TARQUIN KATIS** repl. HARRELL in a band called the PORK GUYS (MOBY still played drums with them in 1997!)

not iss. — Instinct

Sep 00. (12"; as the BROTHERHOOD) *<EX 224>* **TIME'S UP (mixes; deep / dope / bonus beats / radio / dust / acapella)** –
Nov 90. (12"ep) *<EX 226>* **MOBILITY / MOBILITY (aquamix). / GO / TIME SIGNATURE** –
Feb 91. (12"ep; as VOODOO CHILD) *<EX 227>* **VOODOO CHILD (contracted) / PERMANENT GREEN. / VOODOO CHILD (expanded) / M-FOUR** –
Mar 91. (12") *<EX 229>* **GO (mixes; Woodtick / Low spirit / Analog / Night time)** –

Low Spirit — Instinct

Apr 91. (12"; as BRAINSTORM) *(12YOBR 24) <EX 231>* **BRAINSTORM – ROCK THE HOUSE**
– Rock the house / Move the colors / Help me to believe.
May 91. (12"; as VOODOO CHILD) *<EX 232>* **VOODOO CHILD REMIXES (Brainstorm / original / Poor in N.Y.) / NO BUTTONS TO PUSH** –

C.T. — Instinct

May 91. (12"ep; as BARRACUDA) *<EX 233>* **DRUG FITS THE FACE / DRUG FITS THE FACE (drug free). / PARTY TIME / BARRACUDA** –
Jun 91. (12"ep; as BARRACUDA) *(CTT 31)* **DRUG FITS THE FACE. / DRUG FITS THE FACE (drug free) / MAD LOVE** –

Outer Rhythm — Instinct

Jul 91. (c-s) *(FOOT 15C)* **GO (low spirit) / GO (Woodtick)** 46 –
(cd-s+=) *(FOOT 15)* – GO (voodoo child mix).
(cd-s+=) *(FOOT 15CD)* – GO (analog mix).
(12") *(FOOT 15R)* – ('A'side) / ('A'-video aux w/ LYNCH & BADALAMENTI) / ('A'-Rain forest mix).
(re-iss. Oct91, hit No.10; same)

X.L. — Sonic

Nov 91. (12"ep/cd-ep; as UHF) *(XLT/XLS 25/+CD) <SNC 2002/+CD>* **UHF**
– UHF / Peacehead / Everything / Protect write.

Outer Rhythm — Instinct

Dec 91. (d-lp/cd; by various) *<EX 236/+CD>* **INSTINCT DANCE** –
– BARRACUDA: Party time / Drug fits the face / Besame / MOBY: Go /

Mobility / BRAINSTORM: Rock the house / Move the colors / Drop a beat / VOODOO CHILD: Voodoo child (remix) / Have you seen my baby? *<cd+=>* – Permanent green.

Jan 92. (12") *<EX 237>* **GO (mixes; radio / rainforest / subliminal / woodtick)** [–] [ ]
(cd-s+=) *<EX 237CDS>* – Go (mixes; soundtrack / original).

Mar 92. (12") *<EX 240-1>* **DROP A BEAT / ELECTRICITY. / DROP A BEAT (deep mix)** [–] [ ]
(cd-s+=) *(EX 240-2>* – UHF 2.

Jul 92. (cd/c/lp) *<EX 241-2/-4/-1>* **MOBY** [–] [ ]
– Drop a beat / Everything / Yeah / Electricity / Next is the E / Mercy. *<cd re-iss. 1995 on 'Elektra'+=; 61838>* – Go / Help me to believe / Have you seen my baby / Ah ah / Slight return / Stream.

Oct 92. (12") *<EX 247-1>* **NEXT IS THE E (mixes; I feel it / synthe / edit / victory) / THOUSAND** [–] [ ]
(cd-s+=) *<EX 247-2>* – Next is the E (cool world mix).

Mar 93. (cd/c) *<EX 250-2/-4>* **EARLY UNDERGROUND** [–] [ ]
– Besame / Rock the house / Move the colors / UHF3 / Party time / Protect write / Go (original) / Permanent green / Voodoo child / Drug fits the face / Time signature / Peace head / Barracuda / Mobility / M-four. *(UK cd-iss. Nov98 & Mar00 on 'Pinnacle'; PLRCD 016)*

Equator Instinct

Jun 93. (12") *(AXIST 001)* **I FEEL IT / I FEEL IT (synthe mix). / THOUSAND / I FEEL IT (victory mix)** [38] [–]
(12"/cd-s) *(AXIS TM/CD 001)* – I feel it (mixes; contentious / synthe / THK Tekk) / Thousand..
(12") *(AXISTX 001)* – (remixes; synthe / THK / I feel it) / Thousand.

Jul 93. (cd/c/lp) *(ATLAS CD/MC/LP 1)* **THE STORY SO FAR** (compilation) [ ] [–]
– Ah ah / I feel it (I feel it mix) / Everything / Help me to believe / Mercy *[cd-only]* / Go (woodtick mix) / Yeah / Drop a beat (the new version) / Thousand / Slight return / Go (subliminal mix unedited version) / Stream. *(cd re-iss. Nov98 & Mar00 on 'Pinnacle'; PLRCD 014)*

Oct 93. (cd/c) *(ATLAS CD/LP 2)* *<EX 253-2/4>* **AMBIENT** [ ] Aug93 [ ]
– My beautiful blue sky / Heaven / Tongues / J Breas / Myopia / House of blue leaves / Bad days / Piano & string / Sound / Dog / 80 / Lean on me. *(re-iss. Nov98 & Mar00 on 'Pinnacle'; PLRCD 015)*

Mute Elektra

Sep 93. (c-s) *(CMUTE 158)* *<61568>* **MOVE (YOU MAKE ME FEEL SO GOOD). / ('A'-disco threat mix)** [21] [ ]
(12"/cd-s) *(12/CD MUTE 158)* – ('A'side) / ('A'-Subversion) / ('A'-xtra mix) / ('A'-MK-Blades mix).
(cd-s) *(LCDMUTE 158)* – ('A'side) / All that I need is to be loved / Unloved symphony / Rainfalls and the sky shudders.
(12") *(L12MUTE 158)* – (last track repl. by)- Morning dove.

May 94. (c-s) *(CMUTE 161)* **HYMN – THIS IS MY DREAM (extended) / ALL THAT I NEED IS TO BE LOVED (H.O.S. mix)** [31] [ ]
(cd-s+=) *(CDMUTE 161)* – ('A'-European edit) / ('A'-Laurent Garnier mix).
(12") *(12MUTE 161)* – ('A'extended) / ('A'-Laurent Garnier mix) / ('A'-Upriver mix)/ ('A'-Dirty hypo mix).
(cd-s) *(LCDMUTE 161)* – Hymn (alternate quiet version 33 mins).

Oct 94. (c-s) *(CMUTE 173)* *<66180>* **FEELING SO REAL. / NEW DAWN FADES** [30] [ ]
(cd-s+=) *(CDMUTE 173)* – ('A'-Unashamed ecstatic piano mix) / ('A'-Old skool mix).
(cd-s) *(LCDMUTE 173)* – ('A'-Westbam remix) / ('A'-Ray Keith remix) / ('A'dub mix) / Everytime you touch me (remix parts).
(12") *(12MUTE 173)* – ('A'side) / (4-versions from cd's above).

Feb 95. (c-s/7"dinked) *(C+/MUTE 176/+D)* *<66154>* **EVERYTIME YOU TOUCH ME / THE BLUE LIGHT OF THE UNDERWATER SUN** [28] [ ]
(cd-s+=) *(CDMUTE 176)* – ('A'-Beatmasters mix) / ('A'-competition winner; Jude Sebastian mix) / ('A'Freestyle mix).
(cd-s++=) *(LCDMUTE 176)* – ('A'-Uplifting mix).
(12") *(12MUTE 176)* – ('A'-Sound Factory mix) / ('A'-SF dub) / ('A'-Follow me mix) / ('A'-Tribal mix).

Mar 95. (cd/c/d-lp) *(CD/C+/Stumm 130)* *<61701>* **EVERYTHING IS WRONG** [21] [ ]
– Hymn / Feeling so real / All that I need is to be loved / Let's go free / Everytime you touch me / Bring back my happiness / What love? / First cool hive / Into the blue / Anthem / Everything is wrong / God moving over the face of the waters / When it's cold I'd like to die. *(cd/c w/free cd/c) (XLCD/XLC+/Stumm 130)* – Underwater (parts 1-5).

Jun 95. (c-s) *(CMUTE 179)* **INTO THE BLUE / ('A'-Shining mix)** [34] [ ]
(cd-s+=) *(LCDMUTE 179)* – ('A'-Summer night mix) / ('A'-Beastmasters mix).
(12"/cd-s) *(12/CD MUTE 179)* – ('A'-Beastmasters mix) / ('A'-Jnr Vasquez mix) / ('A'-Phil Kelsey mix) / ('A'-Jon Spencer Blues mix).

Jan 96. (cd/c) *(XLStumm 130)* **EVERYTHING IS WRONG – MIXED AND REMIXED** [25] [ ]

—— The track 'GOD MOVING OVER THE FACE OF THE WATERS' was used for the Rover 400 TV commercial. Toyota had earlier sampled his 'GO'.

Aug 96. (12") *(12MUTE 184)* **THAT'S WHEN I REACH FOR MY REVOLVER. / ('A'-Rollo & Si Star Bliss mix)** [50] [–]
(cd-s) *(CDMUTE 184)* – ('A'side) / Lovesick / Displaced / Sway.
(cd-s) *(LCDMUTE 184)* – ('A'side) / Every one of my problems / God moving over the face of the waters (dark mix).

Oct 96. (cd/c/d-lp) *(CD/C+/Stumm 150)* *<62031>* **ANIMAL RIGHTS** [38] [ ]
– Now I let it go / Come on baby / Someone to love / Heavy flow / You / My love will never die / Soft / Say it's all mine / That's when I reach for my revolver / Face it / Living / Love song for my mom. *(cd w/ free cd)* **LITTLE IDIOT** *(LCDStumm 150)* – Degenerate / Dead city / Walnut / Old / A season in Hell / Love song for my mom / The blue terror of lawns / Dead sun / Reject.

Nov 96. (12"ep) *(12MUTE 200)* **COME ON BABY / LOVE HOLE / WHIP IT / GO / ALL THAT I NEED TO BE IS LOVED / HYMN** [ ] [ ]
(cd-ep) *(CDMUTE 200)* – ('A'-Eskimos And Egypt mix) / ('A'-Crystal method mix) / ('A'-Eskimos And Egypt extended).

Jan 97. (7") *<SP 377>* **THAT'S WHEN I REACH FOR MY REVOLVER. / WHIP IT (death metal version)** [–] [ ]

—— <above issued on 'Sub Pop'>

May 97. (12") *<0-63953>* **THAT'S WHEN I REACH FOR MY REVOLVER (mixes; Moby / Psychotic VE-gun / Moby's 2 / The Rollo & Sister Bliss vocal)** [–] [ ]

Jul 97. (cd) *<62092-2>* **THE END OF EVERYTHING** [–] [ ]
– Patient love / Great lake / Gentle love / Honest love / Slow motion suicide / Dog heaven / Reject.

Nov 97. (c-s/12"/cd-s) *(C/12/CD MUTE 210)* *<040>* **JAMES BOND THEME: TOMORROW NEVER DIES** [8] [ ]
– (mixes:- extended dance / Grooverider's Jeep remix / Da Bomb remix / CJ Bolland remix / Dub Pistols remix / CJ Bolland – Dubble-oh Heaven remix).
(12") *(XL12MUTE 210)* – ('A'mixes; re-version / Grooverider / Danny Tenaglia dub).

Nov 97. (cd/c/lp) *(CD/C+/Stumm 168)* *<62094>* **I LIKE TO SCORE** [ ] [ ]
– Novio / James Bond theme (Moby's re-version) / Go / Ah-ah / I like to score / Oil 1 / New dawn fades / God moving over the face of the waters / First cool hive / Nash / Love theme / Grace.

Aug 98. (cd-s) *(CDMUTE 218)* *<2186>* **HONEY / HONEY (Mario Caldato Jnr. mix) / MICRONESIA / MEMORY GOSPEL** [33] [ ]
(cd-s) *(LCDMUTE 218)* – ('A'-Rollo & Sister Bliss blunt edit) / ('A'-Moby's 118 mix) / ('A'-Westbam & Hardy mix) / ('A'-Aphrodite & Micky Finn mix).
(12") *(12MUTE 218)* – ('A'-Rollo & Sister Bliss mix) / ('A'-Sharam Jey's sweet honey mix) / ('A'-Moby's low side mix).

Mute V2

Apr 99. (cd-s) *(CDMUTE 221)* **RUN ON / SPIRIT / RUNNING** [33] [ ]
(cd-s) *(LCDMUTE 221)* – ('A'extended) / Sunday / Down slow.
(12") *(12MUTE 221)* – ('A'mixes; Moby young & funky / Dave Clarke / extended).

May 99. (cd/c/d-lp) *(CD/C+/STUMM 172)* *<27049>* **PLAY** [1] [38]
– Honey / Find my baby / Porcelain / Why does my heart feel so bad? / South side / Rushing / Bodyrock / Natural blues / Machete / 7 / Run on / Down slow / If things were perfect / Everloving / Inside / Guitar flute & string / The sky is broken / My weakness. *(d-cd+=; LCDSTUMM 172 / <27085>)* – THE B-SIDES (hit UK No.24)

Jul 99. (cd-s) *(CDMUTE 225)* **BODYROCK / SUNSPOT / ARP** [38] [ ]
(12"/cd-s) *(12/LCD MUTE 225)* – ('A'-Olav Basoski da hot funk mix) / ('A'-Da freak funk mix) / ('A'-B&H Bodyrock mix) / ('A'-Dani Konig mix).

Oct 99. (cd-s) *(LCDMUTE 230)* **WHY DOES MY HEART FEEL SO BAD / FLYING FOXES / PRINCESS** [16] [ ]
(12"/cd-s) *(12/CD MUTE 230)* – ('A'mixes by ATB, FERRY CORSTEN, SHARP BOYS + SUBSONIC LEGACY).

Mar 00. (12"/cd-s) *(12/CD MUTE 251)* **NATURAL BLUES / WHISPERING WIND / SICK IN THE SYSTEM** [11] [ ]
(12"/cd-s) *(L12/LCD MUTE 251)* – ('A'mixes).

Jun 00. (c-s) *(CMUTE 252)* **PORCELAIN / SUMMER** [5] [ ]
(cd-s+=) *(CDMUTE 252)* – Flying over the dateline.
(cd-s) *(LCDMUTE 252)* – ('A'mixes).

Oct 00. (c-s) *(CMUTE 255)* **WHY DOES MY HEART FEEL SO BAD / HONEY (remix)** [17] [ ]
(cd-s+=) *(CDMUTE 255)* – Flower (w/ KELIS).
(cd-s) *(LCDMUTE 255)* – ('A'side) / Honey (Fafu's 12"mix) / ('A'-Red Jerry's string and breaks mix) / The sun never stops setting.

Jan 01. (cd-s; by MOBY featuring GWEN STEFANI) *<27665>* **SOUTH SIDE / (original & mixes)** [–] [14]

Apr 02. (c-s) *(CMUTE 268)* **WE ARE ALL MADE OF STARS / WE ARE ALL MADE OF STARS (DJ Tiesto full vocal mix) / LANDING** [11] [ ]
(cd-s+=) *(CDMUTE 268)* – Soul to love.
(cd-s) *(LCDMUTE 268)* – ('A'-Downtempo mix) / ('A'-Timo Maas dub).

May 02. (cd/c/d-lp) *(CD/C+/STUMM 202) <27172>* **18** [1] [4]
– We are all made of stars / In this world / In my heart / Great escape / Signs of love / One of these mornings / Another woman / Fireworks / Extreme ways / Jam for the ladies (with ANGIE STONE & MC LYTE) / Sunday (the day before my birthday) / 18 / Sleep alone / At least we tried / Harbour (with SINEAD O'CONNOR) / Look back in / Rafters / I'm not worried at all.

Aug 02. (cd-s) *(CDMUTE 270)* **EXTREME WAYS / LOVE OF STRINGS / LIFE'S SO SWEET / EXTREME WAYS (video)** [39] [–]
(12"/cd-s) *(CD/12 MUTE 270)* – ('A'-DJ Tiesto mix) / ('A'-Junior Jack club mix).
(12"/cd-s) *(LCD/L12 MUTE 270)* – ('A'-Creamer & K mix) / ('A'-Lee Coombes remix).

Nov 02. (cd-s) *(CDMUTE 276)* **IN THIS WORLD / PIANO AND STRINGS / DOWNHILL** [35] [–]
(cd-s) *(LCDMUTE 276)* – ('A'-T&F remix) / ('A'-AFTC deep south vocal mix) / ('A'-Push vocal club mix).
(12") *(12MUTE 276)* – ('A'-ATFC deep south club mix) / ('A'-Slacker's rain before carnival mix).

Mar 03. (cd-s) *(CDMUTE 280)* **SUNDAY (THE DAY BEFORE MY BIRTHDAY) / AND I KNOW / I.S.S. / ('A'-video)** [ ] [–]
(cd-s/12") *(LCD/12 MUTE 280)* – ('A'-West London deep club mix) / ('A'-Boris Dlugosch & Michi Lange headbanger session) / In my heart (Ferry Corsten remix).

– compilations, specials, etc

Nov 93. (12") *Mute; (12NEMY 2)* **ALL THAT I NEED IS TO BE LOVED. / (3 other 'A'mixes)** [ ] [–]

Sep 94. (c-s) *Mute; (CNOCAR 1)* **GO (woodtick mix). / ('A'-Low spirit mix)** [ ] [–]
(12"+=) *(12NOCAR 1)* – ('A'-Voodoo chile mix).
(12"+=) *(12LNOCAR 1)* – ('A'-Appathoski mix) / ('A'-Amphemetix mix).
(cd-s+=) *(CDNOCAR 1)* – ('A'-Delirium mix).

Mar 95. (10"ltd.) *Soapbar; (SBR 15)* **FEELING SO REAL (mixes)** [ ] [–]

Nov 98. (d-cd) *Pinnacle; (PLRCD 017)* **RARE** (collected B-sides) [ ] [–]
(re-iss. Mar00; same)

Jul 00. (cd) *Elektra; <62554>* **MOBYSONGS (1993-1998)** [–] [ ]

MOBY GRAPE

Formed: San Francisco, California, USA ... September '66 by manager/self-styled scenester MATTHEW KATZ (who'd previously worked with JEFFERSON AIRPLANE) and ex-'AIRPLANE drummer turned guitarist SKIP SPENCE. Unknowns PETER LEWIS, BOB MOSELEY, JERRY MILLER and DON STEVENSON were drafted in and the fledgling GRAPES apparently took their name from a (pathetic) joke doing the rounds at the time: 'What's purple and lives at the bottom of the sea?' (who said the Americans don't have a sense of humour?!) KATZ himself wasn't exactly a laugh a minute, allegedly harassing the band into signing an outrageous contract that gave him complete control over the personnel in the band as well as the name MOBY GRAPE. After signing to Columbia, the band released their self-titled debut just as the "summer of love" was fermenting in June 1967. The album showcased the distinctive guitar triumvirate of SPENCE, LEWIS and MILLER, a sound that enhanced the fertile songwriting and close-knit harmonies. So confident were the record company in the band's profit making potential, they released five singles simultaneously. All the tracks could've been hits in their own right, but this foolhardy gesture was seen as a blatant attempt to hype the band, the result being a severe dent in their credibility and a lowly No.88 chart placing for the classic 'OMAHA'. The other four singles stiffed without trace. It didn't help matters when three of the band were caught with under-age girls on the night of the album launch. Nevertheless, the album reached the US Top 30 and the band's psychedelic mesh of country, rock, folk and blues made them favourites on the Bay Area scene. The sessions for the unfortunately titled follow-up, 'WOW', were beset with problems, not least SKIP SPENCE running amok with an axe and being carted off to hospital in a straitjacket. Unsurprisingly, the record was a patchy affair bolstered with gimmicks like the 'GRAPE JAM' disc, given away free with the album. With SPENCE out of the picture, the band released another two albums that mined a rootsier seam, 'MOBY GRAPE '69' and 'TRULY FINE CITIZEN', although the absence of SPENCE's incendiary genius was glaringly apparent. The band called it a day in 1969 only to reform in 1971, a process that'd be repeated over the following decade amid ever shifting line-ups. Due to the dodginess of their aforementioned management contract, KATZ retained the MOBY GRAPE name and set up his own version of the band in the early 70's, all very confusing, and although some decent stuff was produced, none of the various incarnations met with any commercial success. SKIP SPENCE, meanwhile, released a one-off solo album of sublime psychedelic country in 1969, 'OAR', before fading into obscurity. All in all, yet another case of what might've been, had not drugs, bad luck and even worse deals not prematurely snuffed out their talent. Sadly, years of living on the streets of Santa Cruz (while attending the local Dominican hospital) took its toll on SKIP SPENCE, when he died of lung cancer on the 16th of April 1999, leaving behind four children; like MOSLEY, he was diagnosed a schizophrenic. • **Songwriters:** Individually penned, either SPENCE, MOSLEY, MILLER & STEVENSON or LEWIS. • **Trivia:** Watch out for a track on the original 'WOW' lp, which spins at 78 rpm (impossible to play on most modern turntables).

Album rating: MOBY GRAPE (*8) / WOW (*6) / MOBY GRAPE '69 (*6) / TRULY FINE CITIZEN (*5) / 20 GRANITE CREEK (*6) / LIVE GRAPE (*5) / MOBY GRAPE '84 (*5) / VINTAGE: THE VERY BEST OF MOBY GRAPE compilation (*8) / Alexander Skip Spence: OAR (*8)

SKIP SPENCE (b. ALEXANDER, 18 Apr'46, Windsor, Ontario, Canada) – vocals, guitar (ex-JEFFERSON AIRPLANE) / **PETER LEWIS** (b.15 Jul'45, Los Angeles, Calif.) – guitar, vocals (ex-CORNELLS) / **JERRY MILLER** (b.10 Jul'43, Tacoma, Washington) – guitar, vocals (ex-FRANTICS) / **BOB MOSELEY** (b. 4 Dec'42, Paradise Valley, Calif.) – bass (ex-MISFITS) / **DON STEVENSON** (b.15 Oct'42, Seattle, Washington) – drums (ex-FRANTICS) repl. KENT DUNBAR

C.B.S. / Columbia

Jun 67. (7") *<44170>* **CHANGES. / FALL ON YOU** [–] [ ]

Jun 67. (7") *<44171>* **SITTING BY THE WINDOW. / INDIFFERENCE** [–] [ ]

Jun 67. (7") *<44172>* **8:05. / MISTER BLUES** [–] [ ]

Jun 67. (7") *(CBS 2953) <44173>* **OMAHA. / HEY GRANDMA** [ ] [88]

Jun 67. (7") *<44174>* **COME IN THE MORNIG. / HEY GRANDMA** [–] [ ]
(above 5 singles released simultaneously)

Jun 67. (lp; stereo/mono) *(S+/BPG 63090) <9498/2698>* **MOBY GRAPE** [ ] [24]
– Hey grandma / Mr. Blues / Fall on you / 8:05 / Come in the morning / Omaha / Naked, if I want to / Someday / Ain't no use / Sitting by the window / Changes / Lazy me / Indifference. *(re-iss. Sep84 on 'Edsel'; ED*

137) (cd-iss. Apr89; EDCD 137) <(cd re-iss. Feb98 on 'San Francisco Sound'; SFS 04805)>

Jul 68. (lp) *(63271)* *<9613>* **WOW** Apr68 20
– The place and the time / Murder in my heart for the judge / Bitter wind / Can't be so bad / Just like Gene Autry; a foxtrot *[plays at 78 rpm]* / He / Motorcycle Irene / Three-four / Funky-tunk / Rose colored eyes / Miller's blues / Naked, if I want to. *<US +free live-lp>* **GRAPE JAM** *<CXS 3>* – Never / Boysenberry jam / Black currant jam / Marmalade / The lake. *<(cd-iss. Feb98 on 'San FRancisco Sound'; SFS 04801)>*
above featured AL KOOPER & MIKE BLOOMFIELD.

Jul 68. (7") *<44567>* **CAN'T BE SO BAD. / BITTER WIND** –

Jul 68. (7") *(CBS 3555)* **CAN'T BE SO BAD. / MURDER IN MY HEART FOR THE JUDGE** –

— SPENCE became a serious drug addict and left – he went into a mental hospital for six months. He went solo later in 1969, releasing OAR album (see further below). He was now under residential-care at his home in San Jose, California.

Feb 69. (lp) *(63430)* *<9696>* **MOBY GRAPE '69**
– Ooh mama ooh / Ain't that a shame / I am not willing / It's a beautiful day today / Hoochie / Trucking man / If you can't learn from my mistakes / Captain Nemo / What's to choose / Going nowhere / Seeing. *(re-iss. Aug76; same)*

Feb 69. (7") *<44789>* **TRUCKING MAN. / IF YOU CAN'T LEARN FROM MY MISTAKES** –

Feb 69. (7") *(CBS 3945)* **TRUCKING MAN. / OOH MAMA OOH** –

Jun 69. (7") *<44885>* **OOH MAMA OOH. / IT'S SO BEAUTIFUL TODAY** –

— session man **BOB MOORE** – bass repl. MOSLEY who joined the US marines. He issued a self-titled album for 'Reprise' in 1972.

Sep 69. (lp) *(63698)* *<9912>* **TRULY FINE CITIZEN**
– Changes, circles spinning / Looper / Truly fine citizen / Beautiful is beautiful / Love song / Right before my eyes / Open up your heart / Now I know high / Treat me bad / Tongue-tied / Love song (part 2).

— MOBY GRAPE had already split Spring 1969. For nearly 2 years, MILLER and STEVENSON joined The RHYTHM DUKES. Original quintet re-formed with newcomer **GORDON STEVENS** – viola, mandolin

Reprise Reprise

Sep 71. (7") *<1040>* **GYPSY WEDDING. / APOCAYPSE** –

Nov 71. (7") *<1055>* **GOIN' DOWN TO TEXAS. / ABOUT TIME** –

Jan 72. (lp) *(K 44152)* *<6460>* **20 GRANITE CREEK** Sep71
– Gypsy wedding / I'm the kind of man that baby you can trust / About time / Goin' down to Texas / Road to the Sun / Apocalypse / Chinese song / Roadhouse blues / Ode to the man at the end of the bar / Wild oats moan / Horse out in the rain. *(re-iss. May86 on 'Edsel' lp/c; ED/CED 176)*

Jul 72. (7"; as BOB MOSLEY & MOBY GRAPE) *<1096>* **GONE FISHING. / GYPSY WEDDING** –

— In the early 70's, their manager Matthew Katz had put together a fake **MOBY GRAPE** with **FRANK RECARD** – vocals, guitar / **TOMMY SPURLOCK** – guitar / **DANNY TIMMS** – keyboards / **BOB NEWKIRK** – drums. BOB MOSLEY had gone solo Mar'72 releasing eponymous album on 'Warner Bros.'. The real MOBY GRAPE re-formed late 1973-Spring'75 with **LEWIS, MILLER, MOSLEY,** plus **JEFF BLACKBURN** – guitar + JOHN CRAVIOTTA – drums. With no new record deal, they broke again and **LEWIS, MILLER, CRAVIOTTA** and **MICHAEL BEAN** – guitar (ex-H.P. LOVECRAFT) formed **FINE WINE**. They issued one eponymous album in Germany mid'75. With NEIL YOUNG; MOSLEY, CRAVIOTTA and BLACKBURN formed the shortly defunct DUCKS (mid'77).

— **MOBY GRAPE** re-formed again, this time with **SKIP SPENCE** returning with **MILLER + LEWIS,** plus newboys **CORNELIUS BUMPUS** – keyboards / **CHRISTIAN POWELL** – bass / **JOHN OXENDINE** – drums

not iss. Escape

Apr 78. (lp) *<JAM 95018>* **LIVE GRAPE (live)** –
– The last horizon / Here I sit / Honk tonk / Cuttin' in / Must be goin' now dear / Your rider / Up in the air / Set me down easy / Love you so much / You got everything I need. *(UK-iss.Jun87 on 'Line'; 400 335)*

— Finally let go around the late 70's, although some releases surfaced.

not iss. San Fran Sound

1984. (lp) *<4830>* **MOBY GRAPE '84** –
– Silver wheels / Better days / Hard road to follow / Sitting and watching / City lights / Queen of the crow / Lost horizon / I didn't lie to you / Suzzam / Too old to boogie / Think it over / American dream / Reprise. *<(cd-iss. Mar98 on 'San Francisco Sound'; SFS 04830)>*

1989. (cd; as MOSLEY GRAPE) *<4880>* **LIVE AT INDIGO RANCH (live)** –
– This time / Cold beer / Took it all away / Move down town / Struck out again / All over town / What's the use / Mojo man / This rut / Crazy money / Lonesome highway / Want to leave me / Cajun song / Theresa. *<(re-iss. Mar98 on 'San Francisco Sound'; SFS 04880)>*

not iss. Herman

Dec 90. (ltd-c; as The MELVILLES) *<none>* **THE MELVILLES** –
– All my life / Nighttime rider / Give it hell / On the dime / Lady of the night / Took it all away / Bitter wind in Tanganika / Talk about love (I'm talking about you) / You'll never know / You can depend on me. *<(UK+cd-re-iss. Apr03 by LEGENDARY GRAPE as 'PURPLE REIGN' on 'Dig'+=; DIG 108)>* – Changing / Further on up the road / It don't take much / Gettin' used to being treated wrong / Forty feet tall / Forbidden love / Telephone love / Rodeo.

— Line-up:- MILLER, LEWIS, MOSLEY, STEVENSON + DAN ABERTNATHY – guitar + KIRT TUTTLE – drums. In 1993, JERRY MILLER issued cassette 'NOW I SEE' for 'Herman'.

– compilations, others, etc. –

on 'CBS / Columbia' unless mentioned otherwise

Jun 74. (lp) *(64743)* *<31098>* **GREAT GRAPE**

Jun 76. (lp) *(53371)* **THE BEST OF MOBY GRAPE** – Europe –

Feb 86. (lp) *Edsel; (ED 171)* **MURDER IN MY HEART** (2nd-4th lp's) –
– Murder in my heart for the judge / He / Can't be so bad / Motorcycle Irene / Three-four / Rose coloured eyes / Bitter wind / I am not willing / It's a beautiful day today / If you can't learn from my mistakes / What's to choose / Seeing / Changes, circles spinning / Right before my eyes.

Nov 93. (d-cd) *Legacy; (CD 53041)* **VINTAGE: THE VERY BEST OF MOBY GRAPE**
(re-iss. Jun96 on 'Columbia; 483958-2)

ALEXANDER SKIP SPENCE

— solo (all instruments)

not iss. Columbia

Oct 69. (lp) *<CS 9831>* **OAR** –
– Little hands / Cripple creek / Diana / Margaret – Tiger rug / Weighted down (the prison song) / War in peace / Broken heart / All come to meet her / Book of Moses / Dixie peach promenade / Lawrence of euphoria / Grey / Afro. *(UK-iss.Sep88 on 'Edsel'; ED 282) (cd-iss. Feb91; EDCD 282) <(cd-iss. Jun00 on 'Sundazed'+=; SC 11075)>* – This time he has come / It's the best thing for you / Everything under your hat / Furry heroine (halo of God) / Givin' up things / You know / Doodle / Fountain / I think you and I. *(re-iss. Feb00 on 'Sundazed'; LP 5030)*

– compilations, others, etc. –

Jun 00. (7") *Sundazed; <(S 153)>* **LAND OF THE SUN. / ALL MY LIFE (I LOVE YOU)**

☐ MODERN LOVERS (see under ⇒ RICHMAN, Jonathan)

MOGWAI

Formed: Glasgow, Scotland . . . 1995 by DOMINIC AITCHISON, STUART BRAITHWAITE (also of ESKA) and MARTIN BULLOCH. In the Spring of '96, the band debuted with 'TUNER' / 'LOWER', a precursor to the band's double whammy NME Singles Of The Week, 'SUMMER' and 'NEW PATHS TO HELICON'. Early in 1997, they signed to the suffocatingly hip Glasgow-based 'Chemikal Underground' (home of BIS and friends, ARAB STRAP), the first outing being 'THE 4 SATIN EP'. A fine collection of their early singles was released a month later in June, although another label was responsible. That summer, the new 5-piece MOGWAI (complete with JOHN CUMMINGS and former TEENAGE FANCLUB member, BRENDON O'HARE) alternately bludgeoned/charmed the NME tent at Scotland's premier festival

'T In The Park' with their striking hybrid of SONIC YOUTH, METALLICA and pre-'Blue Monday' NEW ORDER! The feverishly anticipated "proper" debut album, 'MOGWAI YOUNG TEAM' was released late '97 to rave reviews, also scraping into the Top 75. Stunningly dynamic, the record shifted seamlessly from tranquil, bleakly beautiful soundscapes to brain scrambling white noise and sledgehammer riffing. Prime examples were 'LIKE HEROD', 'WITH PORTFOLIO' and 'MOGWAI FEAR SATAN', while 'TRACY' was a near 10-minute collage of drifting, childlike charm segueing into a taped phone conversation. Another track, 'R U STILL IN 2 IT', featured the mumbling vocal talents of ARAB STRAP's AIDAN MOFFAT. Prior to the album's release, O'HARE was summarily dismissed, apparently for yapping his way through an ARAB STRAP gig (tsk, tsk!). 1998 was indeed a busy year for the "young team", five releases hitting the shops between March and August and nearly all making the Top 75. The first of these, ' . . ... DO THE ROCK BOOGALOO' was a split affair with fellow noisemongers MAGOO, the title not an EP but the "un"-covering of two classic BLACK SABBATH tracks, MOGWAI having a laugh with 'SWEET LEAF'. 'FEAR SATAN' was then chosen for the remix treatment (MY BLOODY VALENTINE's the highlight), while a full album, 'KICKING A DEAD PIG: MOGWAI SONGS REMIXED', was all their best tunes reworked by others including ARAB STRAP, KID LOCO and ALEC EMPIRE. 'Chemikal Underground' put their two-pennith in by issuing the 'NO EDUCATION = NO FUTURE (FUCK THE CURFEW)' ep, while 'TEN RAPID' was an early singles collection. The following March (with newcomer pianist BARRY BURNS now a fully-fledged member) 'COME ON DIE YOUNG' was the gangland war cry they chose as the title of their more sedate second album proper. A hard album indeed, in the sense that it took time to "get into" (probably due to the slight omission of their characteristic sonic crescendos), it unearthed a softer, more delicate style which was rewarded with a Top 30 entry. Opening with 'PUNK ROCK:' (complete with IGGY POP archive interview as voiceover), the Slo-Fi 'CODY' and the sludgedelic 'HELP BOTH WAYS, the album proved the young MOGWAI were top of the class; 'EX-COWBOY' and the emotional MORRICONE-inspired finale 'PUNK ROCK / PUFF DADDY / ANtICHRISt' were also noteworthy. Towards the end of '99, they delivered a self-titled EP, attributing 'STANLEY KUBRICK' as the lead track. 'BURN GIRL PROM QUEEN', an excellent diversion from the 'WAI featured the Cowdenbeath Brass Orchestra to eerie effect. Perhaps the best career move a band of their status could make, 'ROCK ACTION' (2001), saw MOGWAI reach new musical heights with their first release on their own 'Southpaw' label. The album, named after the band's other record label, focused its attention on the subtler side of life. It gladly took advice from the DAVID PAJO (who appears on the record) school of experimental rock, evoking his recent PAPA M meanderings. With its harmonic use of banjos, lap-steel and orchestra, the album harked back to the aforementioned 'STANLEY KUBRICK' EP. 'SINE WAVE' was briefly melodic, with hints of warped guitar static and BULLOCH's tom-toms adding an abrasive edge to the mix. '2 RIGHTS MAKE A WRONG' is quietly SLINT-ish, with the odd-kilter signature tune thrown in for good measure. But it's 'DIAL: REVENGE' with SUPER FURRY ANIMALS vocalist GRUFF RHYS which makes the album. His lingering Welsh vocals proved to be a catalyst for the overall structure of the album, and the emotions that surface during the intensified verse-chorus-verse of the song. Preceding the album by a few weeks was an unusual and unique appearance at Rothesay in the Isle Of Bute for 500 lucky fans who could afford the ferry and the entrance fee. 'HAPPY SONGS FOR HAPPY PEOPLE' (2003) marked a slight departure for MOGWAI, downsizing on the "rock action" front. As MOGWAI albums went, this was certainly their weakest and most over-produced, but it was still bloody good! The solemn funereal pace of 'MOSES? I AMN'T' was something to make the late great JOY DIVISION proud; the riff at the end of epic 'RATTS OF THE CAPITAL' was pure grunge, and the chiming, symmetrical piano and programmed rhythmic structure of 'I KNOW YOU ARE BUT WHAT AM I?' was the band entering AERIAL-M territory. Elsewhere there was more fun to be had via the romantically-inclined 'GOLDEN PORSCHE' and the signature-like opening track 'HUNTED BY A FREAK' – vocoder vocals and everything! Happy songs for happy people? Happy MOGWAI fans in the knowledge that they had made another decent album, more like. • **Covered:** HONEY (Spacemen 3).

Album rating: MOGWAI YOUNG TEAM (*9) / KICKING A DEAD PIG: MOGWAI SONGS REMIXED (*7) / TEN RAPID compilation (*8) / COME ON DIE YOUNG (*10) / ROCK ACTION (*9) / HAPPY SONGS FOR HAPPY PEOPLE (*8)

pLasmatroN (b. STUART BRAITHWAITE, 30 Mar'76) – guitar, vocals (also of ESKA, until Autumn '86) / **DEMONIC** (b. DOMINIC AITCHISON) – bass / **bionic** (b. MARTIN BULLOCH) – drums

Rock Action / not iss.

Feb 96. (ltd-7") *(RAR 001)* **TUNER. / LOWER** [ ] [–]

Che / not iss.

May 96. (ltd-7"green) *(che 61)* **ANGELS VERSUS ALIENS. / (other side by DWEEB)** [ ] [–]

Love Train / not iss.

Sep 96. (ltd-7"; "CAMDEN CRAWL II") *(PUBE 011)* **A PLACE FOR PARKS. / (other artists)** [ ] [–]

Oct 96. (ltd-7"; "TEN DAY WEEKEND") *(PUBE 012)* **I AM NOT BATMAN. / (other artists)** [ ] [–]

Nov 96. (ltd-7") *(PUBE 014)* **SUMMER. / ITHICA 27 o 9** [ ] [–]

Wurlitzer Jukebox / not iss.

Jan 97. (ltd-7") *(WJ 22)* **NEW PATHS TO HELICON** [ ] [–]
– Helicon 1 / Helicon 2.

—— added **Cpt. Meat** (aka JOHN CUMMINGS) – guitar

Chemikal U/ground / Jetset

May 97. (12"ep/cd-ep) *(chem 015/+cd)* <TWA 14CD> **4 SATIN EP** [ ] [ ]
– Superheroes of BMX / Now you're taken / Stereo Dee. <US++> – Guardians of space. *(re-iss. Apr99; same)*

—— added **+the relic+** (aka BRENDAN O'HARE – piano (of-MACROCOSMICA, ex-TEENAGE FANCLUB, ex-TELSTAR PONIES)

Oct 97. (cd/d-lp) *(chem 018 cd/lp)* <7> **MOGWAI YOUNG TEAM** [75] [ ]
– Yes! I am a long way from home / Like Herod / Radar maker / Tracy / Summer (Priority version) / With portfolio / R u still in 2 it / A cheery wave from stranded youngsters / Mogwai fear Satan. *(re-iss. Apr99; same)*

Feb 98. (7") *(SHaG 13.05)* **Club Beatroot Part Four** [ ] [–]
– Stereo Dee (live) / (other side by Ph FAMILY)
(above issued on 'Flotsam & Jetsam – 13th Note')

—— now without O'HARE, who was sacked (see above)

Mar 98. (7"; split w/ MAGOO) *(NING 47CD)* **. . ... DO THE ROCK BOOGALOO** [60] [–]
– Black Sabbath (by MAGOO) / Sweet leaf.
(above issued on 'Fierce Panda', below 2 for 'eye q' / US 'Jetset')

Apr 98. (cd-ep) *(eyeuk 032cd)* **FEAR SATAN remixes** [57] [–]
– Mogwai remix / U-ziq remix / Surgeon remix / My Bloody Valentine remix. *(re-iss. Apr99; same)*

May 98. (cd/d-lp) *(eyeuk cd/lp)* <TWA 13 CD/LP> **KICKING A DEAD PIG: MOGWAI SONGS REMIXED** [ ] Jun98 [ ]
– Like Herod (Hood remix) / Helicon 2 (Max Tundra remix) / Summer (Klute's weird winter remix) / Gwai on 45 (Arab Strap remix) / A cheery wave from stranded youngsters (Third Eye Foundation tet offensive remix) / Like Herod (Alec Empire's face the future remix) / Mogwai fear Satan (Surgeon remix) / R U still in to it? (DJ Q remix) / Tracy (Kid Loco's playing with the young team remix) / Mogwai fear Satan (Mogwai remix). *(re-iss. Apr99; same) (cd re-iss. Sep01 on 'Chemikal Underground'; CHEM 057CD)*

Jun 98. (12"ep/cd-ep) *(chem 026/+cd) <111230>* **NO EDUCATION = NO FUTURE (FUCK THE CURFEW) e.p.** [68] [ ]
– Xmas steps / Rollerball / Small children in the background. *(re-iss. Apr99; same)*

— In Nov'98, their track 'I CAN'T REMEMBER' featured on the 'Glasgow' V/A EP along with EL HOMBRE TRAJEADO, the KARELIA and the YUMMY FUR

— added **BARRY BURNS** – piano, flute, guitar

Chemikal U/ground — Matador

Mar 99. (d-lp/cd) *(chem 033/+cd) <OLE 365>* **COME ON DIE YOUNG** [29] [ ]
– Punk rock: / Cody / Helps both ways / Year 2000 non-compliant cardia / Kappa / Waltz for Aidan / May nothing but happiness come through your door / Oh! how the dogs stack up / Ex-cowboy / Chocky / Christmas steps / Punk rock – Puff Daddy – ANtICHRISt.

Oct 99. (12"ep/cd-ep) *(chem 036/+cd) <OLE 412>* **MOGWAI e.p.** [ ] [ ]
– Stanley Kubrick / Christmas song / Burn girl prom-queen / Rage: man. *(re-iss. Sep01 as 'MOGWAI+6'+=; CHEM 056CD)* – Xmas steps / Rollerball / Small children in the background / Superheroes of BMX / Now you're taken / Stereodee.

Southpaw — Matador

Apr 01. (cd/lp) *(PAW CD/LP 001) <OLE 490>* **ROCK ACTION** [23] [ ]
– Sine wave / Take me somewhere nice / O I sleep / Dial: revenge / You don't know Jesus / Robot chant / 2 rights make 1 wrong / Secret pint.

May 01. (12"ep) *<OLE 522-1>* **D TO E / DRUM MACHINE. / (other 2 by Bardo Pond)** [–] tour [–]

Rock Action — Matador

Oct 01. (cd-s) *(ROCKACTCD 10) <OLE 538>* **MY FATHER MY KING** [ ] [ ]

Jun 03. (cd/lp) *(PIASX 035 CD/LP) <OLE 567>* **HAPPY SONGS FOR HAPPY PEOPLE** [47] [ ]
– Hunted by a freak / Moses? I amn't / Kids will be skeletons / Killing all the flies / Boring machines disturbs sleep / Ratts of the capital / Golden Porsche / I know you are but what am I? / Stop coming to my house.

– compilations, etc. –

Aug 98. (cd) *Rock Action; (ROCKACTCD 5) / Jetset; <TWA 05LP>* **TEN RAPID (collected recordings 1996-1997)** [ ] Aug97 [ ]
– Summer / Helicon 2 / Angels versus aliens / I am not Batman / Tuner / Ithica 27 o 9 / A place for parks / Helicon 1 / End.

MOLOKO

Formed: Sheffield, England ... 1994 by Irish vocalist ROISIN MURPHY and multi-instrumentalist MARK BRYDON, both veterans of the music biz. With the trip-hop bandwagon careering across the mid-90's musical map at a rate of knots, the pair hitched up for a ride with their eponymous debut album in '95. Trading in a self-consciously arty take on the craze for slo-mo beats, MOLOKO (Russian for Milk) were received with mixed reactions from the music press. While some critics were impressed with the outfit's Clockwork Orange-meets-ART OF NOISE-in-Bristol-approach, others were more wary of what they saw as an abundance of style covering up a lack of substance. Follow-up set, 'DO YOU LIKE MY TIGHT SWEATER?' (1996) was another clever-clever collection of off-the-wall trip-pop ditties, definitely something of an acquired taste, although the minor hits, 'DOMINOID' and 'FUN FOR ME' were the exception. MOLOKO returned in 1998 with their follow-up set, 'I AM NOT YOUR DOCTOR', which cracked the charts yet again and featured the slow-burning, 'SING IT BACK', finally a UK Top 5 hit in September 1999. The new millennium saw MOLOKO again break the charts, this time No.2 with 'THE TIME IS NOW', a record that featured on their top-selling third album, 'THINGS TO MAKE AND DO' (2000). A year later, the duo remixed the various artists/MOLOKO collection, 'ALL BACK TO THE MINE' (2001). After the massive success of 'SING IT BACK', MOLOKO entered the studio with the intention of creating an album completely different from 2000's 'THINGS . . .'. The result was 2003's 'STATUES', a delicate little set which caught regular fans of MOLOKO by surprise. Moving in a direction more akin with GOLDFRAPP than GOLDIE, MURPHY's vocal talents were properly highlighted on the chilled and breezy 'THE ONLY ONES' and 'OVER AND OVER', while her brilliant backing band (and producer MARK BRYDON) were still keeping it relatively funky with floor-fillers 'COME ON' and 'CANNOT CONTAIN THIS'.

Album rating: DO YOU LIKE MY TIGHT SWEATER? (*7) / I AM NOT A DOCTOR (*6) / THINGS TO MAKE AND DO (*7) / ALL BACK TO THE MINE compilation (*7) / STATUES (*7)

ROISIN MURPHY (b. Dublin, Ireland) – vocals (ex-AND TURQUOISE CAR CRASH) / **MARK BRYDON** (b. 1962, Sheffield, England) – multi (ex-CHAKK, ex-CLOUD 9)

Echo — Warners

Mar 95. (c-s) *(ECSMC 20)* **FUN FOR ME (mixes; radio / Mr Scruff vocal / Doctor Rockitt)** [ ] [–]
(ext-12"+=) *(ECSY 20)* – ('A'-Stepping mole mix).
(cd-s++=) *(ECSCD 20)* – ('A'-mixes; DJ Plankton's pond life / Mr Scruff instrumental / Loko mole). *(re-iss. May96; same)* – hit UK No.36

May 95. (12"ep) *(ECSY 8)* **THE MOLOKO EP** [ ] [–]
– Where is the what if the what is in why? / Party weirdo (wackdown mix) / Party weirdo / Where is the what if the what is in why? (wonderbook mix).
(cd-ep) *(ECSCD 8)* – ('A'-radio) repl. (wackdown mix).

Aug 95. (c-s) *(ECSMC 12)* **FUN FOR ME / FUN FOR ME (DJ Plankton's pond life mix)** [ ] [–]
(ext-12"+=) *(ECSY 12)* – Fe fi fungle fool (tadpole dub).
(cd-s) *(ECSCD 12)* – (all tracks above).

Oct 95. (cd/c/d-lp) *(ECH CD/MC/LP 7) <46532>* **DO YOU LIKE MY TIGHT SWEATER?** [ ] Feb96 [ ]
– Fun for me / Tight sweater / Day for night / I can't help myself / Circus / Lotus eaters / On my horsey / Dominoid / Party weirdo / Tubeliar / Ho humm / Butterfly 747 / Dirty monkey / Killa bunnies / Boo / Where is the what if the what is in . . . / Who shot the go go dancer? *(cd re-iss. Mar99; same)*

Jan 96. (c-s) *(ECSMC 16)* **DOMINOID / DOMINOID (panty sniffer mix)** [65] [–]
(cd-s+=) *(ECSCD 16)* – ('A'-mixes; Cynthia hi-fi's fuzzy logic / Baroque vapid / album).

Sep 96. (12"promo) *(ECSY 26)* **LOTUS EATERS. / ('A'mix)** [–] [–]
(12"promo) *(ECSYX 26)* – ('A'mixes).

Echo — Mushroom

Jun 98. (12") *(ECSY 54)* **THE FLIPSIDE (mixes; album / DJ Plankton / All seeing I upside / Aphrodite vocal)** [53] [–]
(cd-s) *(ECSCD 054)* – ('A'side & mixes; DJ Plankton / All Seeing I upside / Swag mocoder dub / All seeing I dubside).
(cd-s) *(ECSCX 054)* – ('A'side & mixes; Aphrodite vocal / Krust dub / Herbert's surround sound).

Aug 98. (cd/c/d-lp) *(ECH CD/MC/LP 21) <33143>* **I AM NOT A DOCTOR** [64] [ ]
– The flipside / Knee deepen / Blink / Stylophone / Downsized / Sorry / Sing it back / Pretty bridges / Be like you / Caught in a whisper / Dr. Zee / I.D. / Tatty Narja / Over my head / Should've been could've been.

Mar 99. (12") *(ECSY 71)* **SING IT BACK (Tee's freeze mix). / SING IT BACK (Boris' musical mix)** [45] [–]
(cd-s) *(ECSCD 71)* – ('A'mixes; radio / Booker T loco / DJ Plankton's dub featuring Maurice).
(cd-s) *(ECSCX 71)* – ('A'mixes; Boris' musical / Herbert's tasteful dub / Tee's freeze).

Aug 99. (d12") *(1926451C)* **SING IT BACK (remixes)** [ ] [–]
(above & below issued on 'Scorpio' & 'Peppermint Jam' respectively)

Aug 99. (12") *(PJMS 0041)* **SING IT BACK (remix)** [ ] [–]

Aug 99. (c-s/12"/cd-s) *(ECS MC/Y/CD 82)* **SING IT BACK (mixes; Boris Dlouglosch musical / Can 7 Supermarket / Tee's radio (or) Herbert's tasteful dub (or) album)** [4] [–]

Echo — Roadrunner

Mar 00. (c-s/cd-s) *(ECS MC/CD 88)* **THE TIME IS NOW / (mixes; Can 7 soulfood / Francoise K main vocal)** [2] [–]
(12") *(ECSY 88)* – ('A'-mixes; Francoise K main vocal / Can 7 jungle boogie / Matt Darey vocal).

Apr 00. (cd/c/lp) *(ECH CD/MC/LP 31)* <8550> **THINGS TO MAKE AND DO** [3] [ ]
– Radio Moscow / Pure pleasure seeker / Absent minded friends / Indigo / Being is bewildering / Remain the same / Drop in the ocean / Dumb inc / The time is now / Mother / It's your problem / It's nothing / Bingo massacre / Somebody somewhere / Just you and me dancing / If you have a cross to bare you may as well use a crutch / Keep stepping / Sing it back.

Jul 00. (c-s/cd-s) *(ECS MC/CD 99)* **PURE PLEASURE SEEKER / (mixes: Todd Edwards / Murk deep south)** [21] [–]
(12") *(ECSY 99)* – ('A'mixes; dub disco seeker / Oscar G deeper dub / Plankton vox poindexter).

Nov 00. (cd-s) *(ECSCD 104)* **INDIGO (mixes; radio / 2 step / Robbie Rivera's vocal)** [51] [–]
(cd-s) *(ECSCV 104)* – ('A'-Gus Gus mix) / ('A'-Robbie Rivera's rhythm banger mix) / Sing it back (Mousse T's feel love mix).
(12") *(ECSY 104)* – ('A'-glamoloko edit) / Sing it back (Mousse T's feel love mix) / ('A'-Robbie Rivera's dark mix).

— in Jun'01, ROISIN featured on BORIS DLUGOSCH's UK hit, 'Never Enough'

Jul 01. (d-cd) *(ECHCD 37)* **ALL BACK TO THE MINE** (compilation) [ ] [–]
– The time is now (DJ Plankton mix) / The flipside (Herbert's surround sound mix) / Pure pleasure seeker (Todd Edwards pleasure for life UK vocal) / Dominoid (panty sniffer mix) / Sing it back (Mousse T's feel love mix) / Indigo (Robbie Rivera's dark mix) / Pure pleasure seeker (Oscar G's cuba libre dub) / The flipside (Swag's mocoder dub) / Knee deepen (Salt City Orchestra edit) / Sing it back (Can 7 1930's mix) // The time is now (bambino casino mix) / Lotus eaters (Ashley Beedle's funk in your neighbourhood mix) / Party weirdo (wackdown mix) / Fun for me (Plankton's pondlife mix) / Indigo (All Seeing I glamoloko edit) / Lotus eaters (Luke Vibert's plug mix) / The flipside (DJ Krust dub) / Where is the what (wonderbook mix) / Pure pleasure seeker (Pizzicato mix) / Day for night (quarter master mix) / The time is now (FK's blissed out dub).

Feb 03. (12") *(ECSY 131)* **FAMILIAR FEELING (mixes; radio / Timo Maas main / Max Reich / Robbie Rivera's dark and sexy)** [10] [–]
(cd-s+=) *(ECSCD 131)* – (Martin Buttrich remix) / (video).

Mar 03. (cd/c/lp) *(ECH CD/MC/LP 44)* <01635> **STATUES** [18] [ ]
– Familiar feeling / Come on / Cannot contain this / Statues / Forever more / Blow x blow / 100% / The only ones / I want you / Over and over.

Jun 03. (12") *(ECSY 136)* **FOREVER MORE. / CANNOT CONTAIN THIS** [17] [–]
(cd-s+=) *(ECSCD 136)* – ('A'side) / ('A'-FKEK dub mix) / Take my hand.

☐ MONACO (see under ⇒ NEW ORDER)

MONKEES

Formed: Los Angeles, California, USA ... 1965, the brainchild of Hollywood TV producers, BOB RAFELSON and BERT SCHNEIDER. The pair had wanted to make a sit-com based around The BEATLES' film, 'A Hard Day's Night' and in September of that year, they ran a wanted ad for four boys aged between 17 and 21. Out of over four hundred applicants, they picked the lucky DAVY JONES, MICKEY DOLENZ, MIKE NESMITH & PETER TORK, signing them to the 'Colpix' label. All had fairly notable previous experience (see below), and were duly sent for acting/grooming lessons early in '66. Following difficulties on the songwriting front, BOB & BERT brought in pensmiths TOMMY BOYCE and BOBBY HART (on appointment from 'Screen Gems' top man, Don Kirshner), who also became the group's producers. Other writers were brought in, namely NEIL DIAMOND, GERRY GOFFIN & CAROLE KING, NEIL SEDAKA plus BARRY MANN & CYNTHIA WEIL. On the 12th of September 1966, "The MONKEES" TV show premiered on NBC, and although not an overnight success, became a teenage favourite. A month later, their debut 45, 'LAST TRAIN TO CLARKSVILLE', was released, showcasing their BEACH BOYS-style harmonies and soon climbing to US No.1. Their follow-up, 'I'M A BELIEVER' (penned by NEIL DIAMOND), also hit the top, and with their show now on BBC TV, it repeated the feat in Britain. Another DIAMOND composition, 'A LITTLE BIT ME, A LITTLE BIT YOU', made both Top 3's in March '67 (two of their albums also having amassed cross-Atlantic success). The aforementioned 45's virtually turned the group into an overnight pop phenomenon, their boyish good looks and "zany" antics endearing their bubblegum psychedelia to the nation's teenyboppers (although their music has surprisingly stood the test of time, giving them cult status). For the remainder of the 60's (with NESMITH increasingly dominating the songwriting), they carried on with further TV series' (one featuring ZAPPA, another with TIM BUCKLEY) and some major hits. Their show was axed towards the end of the decade, by which time they had gone into the movies, making the box-office disaster, 'HEAD', with writers BOB RAFELSON and JACK NICHOLSON (yes that one!). • **Covered;** DAYDREAM BELIEVER (John Sebastian) / D.W. WASHBURN (Leiber-Stoller) / etc. • **Trivia:** In 1967, their 'RANDY SCOUSE GIT' (taken from the character Alf Garnett in British sit-com 'Til Death Us Do Part') was banned by the BBC, and later given the 'ALTERNATIVE TITLE' motif.

Best CD compilation: HERE THEY COME – THE GREATEST HITS OF . . . (*8)

DAVY JONES (b.30 Dec'46, Manchester, England) – vocals, rhythm guitar (ex-apprentice jockey, actor UK TV 'Coronation Street' & 'Z Cars' / solo artist) / **MICKEY DOLENZ** (b. GEORGE MICHAEL DOLENZ JR., 8 Mar'45, Tarzana, Calif.) – drums, vocals (child actor 'Circus Boy' as Corky, 'Peyton Place', etc.) **/ MIKE NESMITH** (b. ROBERT MICHAEL NESMITH, 30 Dec'42, Houston, Texas) – guitar, vocals (ex-folk solo act as MICHAEL BLESSING on 'Colpix' label) **/ PETER TORK** (b. PETER THORKELSON, 13 Feb'44, Washington, D.C.) – bass, vocals (ex-AU GO GO SINGERS with RICHIE FURAY / recommended by STEPHEN STILLS)

Session men on discs were; JAMES BURTON, GLEN CAMPBELL, LEON RUSSELL, HAL BLAINE + DAVID GATES.

RCA Victor / Colgems

Oct 66. (7") *(RCA 1547)* <1001> **LAST TRAIN TO CLARKSVILLE. / TAKE A GIANT STEP** [ ] Sep66 [1]
(late Jan'67; – debut single hit UK No.23)

Dec 66. (7") *(RCA 1560)* <1002> **I'M A BELIEVER. / I'M NOT YOUR STEPPING STONE** [1] [1] [20]

Jan 67. (lp; mono/stereo) *(RD/SF 7844)* <101> **THE MONKEES** [1] Oct66 [1]
– Theme from The Monkees / Saturday's child / I wanna be free / Tomorrow's gonna be another day / Papa Gene's blues / Take a giant step / Last train to Clarksville / This just doesn't seem to be my day / Let's dance on / I'll be true to you / Sweet young thing / Gonna buy me a dog. *<re-iss. Aug86 on 'Rhino' hit No.92; 70140> (cd-iss. Apr88 on 'Arista'; 258773) (cd-iss. Dec94 on 'Warners'; 4509 97655-2)*

Mar 67. (7") *(RCA 1580)* <1004> **A LITTLE BIT ME, A LITTLE BIT YOU. / THE GIRL I KNEW SOMEWHERE** [3] [2] [39]

Apr 67. (lp; mono/stereo) *(RD/SF 7868)* <102> **MORE OF THE MONKEES** [1] Feb67 [1]
– When love comes knockin' (at your door) / She / Mary, Mary / Hold on girl / Your Auntie Grizelda / (I'm not you) Steppin' stone / Look out (here comes tomorrow) / The kind of girl I could love / The day we fell in love / Sometime in the morning / Laugh / I'm a believer. *<re-iss. Aug86 on 'Rhino' hit No.96; 70142> (cd-iss. Jun88 on 'Arista'; 259052) (cd-iss. Dec94 on 'Warners'; 4509 97658-2)*

Jun 67. (7") *(RCA 1604)* **ALTERNATIVE TITLE. / FORGET THAT GIRL** [2] [–]
(above was to have been called 'RANDY SCOUSE GIT')

Jul 67. (lp; mono/stereo) *(RD/SF 7868)* <103> **HEADQUARTERS** [2] Jun67 [1]
– You told me / I'll spend my life with you / Forget that girl / Band 6 / You just may be the one / Shades of grey / I can't get her off my mind / For Pete's sake / Mr. Webster / Sunny girlfriend / Zilch / No time / Early morning blues and greens / Randy Scouse git. *<re-iss. Aug86 on 'Rhino'; 70143> (cd-iss. Feb95 on 'Warners'; 4509 97662-2)*

Jul 67. (7") *(RCA 1620) 1007>* **PLEASANT VALLEY SUNDAY. / WORDS** [11] [3] [11]

Nov 67. (7") *(RCA 1645) <1012>* **DAYDREAM BELIEVER. / GOING DOWN** [5] [1]

Jan 68. (lp; mono/stereo) *(RD/SF 7912) <104>* **PISCES, AQUARIUS, CAPRICORN AND JONES LTD.** [5] Nov67 [1]
– Salesman / She hangs out / The door into summer / Love is only sleeping / Cuddly toy / Words / Hard to believe / What am I doing hangin' round? / Peter Percival Patterson's pet pig Porky / Pleasant Valley Sunday / Daily nightly / Don't call on me / Star collector. *<re-iss. Aug86 on 'Rhino'; 70141> (cd-iss. Feb95 on 'Warners'; 4509 97663-2)*

Mar 68. (7") *(RCA 1673) <1019>* **VALLERI. / TAPIOCA TUNDRA** [12] [3] [34]

May 68. (lp; mono/stereo) *(RD/SF 7948) <109>* **THE BIRDS, THE BEES & THE MONKEES** [ ] [3]
– Dream world / Auntie's municipal court / We were made for each other / Tapioca tundra / Daydream believer / Writing wrongs / I'll be back on my feet / The poster / P.O. Box 9847 / Magnolia Simms / Valleri / Zor and Zam. *<re-iss. Aug86 on 'Rhino'; 70144> (cd-iss. Dec94 on 'Warners'; 4509 97665-2)*

Jun 68. (7") *(RCA 1706) <1023>* **D.W. WASHBURN. / IT'S NICE TO BE WITH YOU** [17] [19] [51]

Sep 68. (7") *<1031>* **THE PORPOISE SONG. / AS WE GO ALONG** [–] [62]

—— now down to trio when TORK departed. (he still appeared on below s/track)

Mar 69. (7") *(RCA 1802) <5000>* **TEARDROP CITY. / A MAN WITHOUT A DREAM** [46] Feb69 [56]

May 69. (lp; mono/stereo) *(RD/SF 8016) <113>* **INSTANT REPLAY** [ ] Feb69 [32]
– Through the looking glass / Don't listen to Linda / I won't be the same without her / Me without you / Just a game / Don't wait for me / You and I / While I cry / Teardrop city / The girl I left behind me / Man without a dream / Shorty Blackwell. *<re-iss. Oct86 on 'Rhino'; 70147> (cd-iss. Feb95 on 'Warners'; 4509 97661-2)*

Jun 69. (7") *(RCA 1824) <5004>* **SOMEDAY MAN. / LISTEN TO THE BAND** [47] [81] [63]

Aug 69. (7") *(RCA 1862)* **DADDY'S SONG. / THE PORPOISE SONG** [ ] [ ]

Sep 69. (lp; mono/stereo) *(RD/SF 8051) <5008>* **HEAD (Soundtrack)** [ ] Dec68 [45]
– Opening ceremony / The porpoise song (theme from 'Head') / Ditty Diego – War chant / Circle sky / (Supplicio) / Can you dig it / (Gravy) / Superstitious / As we go along / (Dandruff?) / Daddy's song / (Poll) / Long title: Do I have to do this all over again / Swami – Plus strings. *<re-iss. Oct86 on 'Rhino'; 70146> (cd-iss. Dec94 on 'Warners'+=; 4509 97659-2) –* Ditty Diego – War chant / Circle sky / Happy birthday to you / Can you dig it / Daddy's song / Head radio spot.

Sep 69. (7") *(RCA 1887) <5005>* **GOOD CLEAN FUN. / MOMMY AND DADDY** [ ] [82]

Oct 69. (lp) *<117>* **THE MONKEES PRESENT . . .** [–] [100]
– Little girl / Good clean fun / If I knew / Bye bye baby bye bye / Never tell a woman yes / Looking for the good times / Ladies Aid Society / Listen to the band / French song / Mommy and daddy / Oklahoma backroom dancer / Pillow time. *<re-iss. Nov86 on 'Rhino'; 70147> (cd-iss. Dec94 on 'Warners'; 4509 97660-2)*

—— now down to **JONES + DOLENZ** duo when NESMITH left to go solo.

Jun 70. (7") *(RCA 1958) <5011>* **OH MY MY. / LOVE YOU BETTER** [ ] [98]

1970. (lp) *<119>* **CHANGES** [–] [ ]
– Oh my my / Ticket on a ferry ride / You're so good to me / It's got to be love / Acapulco sun / 99 pounds / Tell me love / Do you feel it too / I love you better / All alone in the dark / Midnight train / I never thought it peculiar. *<re-iss. Aug86 on 'Rhino'; 70148> (cd-iss. Dec94 on 'Warners'; 4509 97657-2)*

MONKEES

—— re-formed with **DOLENZ, JONES + TORK** and session people.

Arista Arista

Oct 86. (7"pic-d-4/7") *(ARIST 1/2/3/4+/673) <9505>* **THAT WAS THEN, THIS IS NOW. / THEME FROM THE MONKEES** [68] Jul86 [20]
(12"+=) *(ARIST 12-673)* – Pleasant valley Sunday / Last train to Clarksville.

Oct 86. (lp/c/cd) *(207/407/257 874) <8432>* **THEN & NOW . . . THE BEST OF THE MONKEES** (w/ 3 new) [ ] Jul86 [21]
– Then and now / Tripwire / Theme from The Monkees / Last train to Clarksville / Take a giant step / I'm a believer / I'm not your stepping stone / A little bit me, a little you / Anytime, anyplace, anywhere / That was then, this is now / The girl I knew somewhere / Pleasant valley Sunday / What am I doing hangin' 'round / Daydream believer / Valeri / Kicks.

Oct 86. (7") *<9532>* **DAYDREAM BELIEVER. / RANDY SCOUSE GIT** [–] [79]

Rhino Rhino

Aug 87. (7") *<74408>* **HEART AND SOUL. / M.G.B.G.T.** [–] [87]

Aug 87. (lp/c/cd) *<(RN IN/IC/CD 70706)>* **POOL IT!** [ ] [72]
– Heart and soul / (I'd go the) Whole wide world / Long way home / Secret heart / Gettin' in / (I'll) Love you forever / Every step of the way / Don't bring me down / Midnight / She's movin' in with Rico / Since you went away / Counting on you. *(cd-iss. Nov95;)*

Nov 87. (7") **EVERY STEP OF THE WAY. / I LOVE YOU FOREVER** [–] [ ]

—— the original four re-formed in 1996

Artful Artful

Jan 97. (cd/c) *(ARTFUL CD/MC 6) <72542>* **JUSTUS** [ ] [ ]
– Circle sky / Never enough / Oh what a night / You and I / Unlucky stars / Admiral Mike / Dyin' of a broken heart / Regional girl / Run away from life / I believe you / It's my life / If't not too late.

– (selective) compilations, etc. –

Jun 69. (lp) *Colgems; <115>* **GREATEST HITS** [–] [89]

Aug 76. (lp) *Arista; <4089>* **THE MONKEES' GREATEST HITS** [–] [58]

Feb 80. (7"ep) *Arista; (ARIST 326)* **THE MONKEES** [33] [ ]
– Daydream believer / Last train to Clarksville / I'm a believer / A little bit me, a little bit you.

Jun 81. (7"ep) *Arista; (ARIST 402)* **THE MONKEES VOL.2** [ ] [ ]
– I'm not your stepping stone / Pleasant valley Sunday / Alternative title (Randy Scouse git) / What am I doing.

Jun 81. (d-lp/d-c) *Arista; (DARTY/TCDAR 12)* **THE MONKEES** [99] [ ]

Oct 87. (lp/c/cd) *Rhino; (RN LP/C/CD 70139)* **LIVE 1967 (live)** [–] [ ]

Oct 87. (lp/c) *Rhino; (RN LP/C 70150)* **MISSING LINKS** (rare) [–] [ ]

Mar 89. (7"ep/3"cd-ep) *Arista; (112/662 157)* **THE MONKEES** [62] [ ]
– Daydream believer / A little bit me, a little bit you / Theme from The Monkees.

Apr 89. (7"ep/3"cd-ep) *Arista; (112/662 158)* **THE MONKEES VOL.2** [ ] [ ]
– Last train to Clarksville / I'm a believer / Pleasant valley Sunday.

Apr 89. (lp/c/cd) *K-Tel; (NE1/CD2/NCD3 432)* **HEY HEY IT'S THE MONKEES – GREATEST HITS** [12] [–]
– Theme from The Monkees / Pleasant valley Sunday / The girl I knew somewhere / D.W. Washburn / Last train to Clarksville / A little bit me, a little bit you / teardrop city / Some day man / What am I doing hangin' 'round / Daydream believer / I'm not your stepping stone / Alternative title (randy scouse git) / Words / I'm a believer / Listen to the band / Valeri / Tapioca tundra / That was then, this is now.

Mar 97. (cd/c) *Telstar; (954835218-2/-4)* **HERE THEY COME: THE GREATEST HITS OF THE MONKEES** [15] [–]

Mar 00. (cd) *Audiophile; (APH 102811)* **20 GREATEST HITS** [ ] [–]

Feb 01. (d-cd/d-c) *Warners ESP; (8573 86691-2/-4)* **THE DEFINITIVE MONKEES** [15] [–]

Mar 01. (4xcd-box) *Rhino; <(8122 76706-2)>* **THE MONKEES MUSIC BOX** [ ] [ ]

Apr 03. (cd) *King Biscuit; (KBCCD 131)* **IN CONCERT** [ ] [ ]

MOODY BLUES

Formed: Birmingham, England . . . May '64 by DENNY LAINE (who had just dissolved his DIPLOMATS band), MIKE PINDER, RAY THOMAS, CLINT WARWICK and GRAEME EDGE. They hooked up with manager, Tony Secunda, who subsequently secured them a deal with 'Decca' records. Their debut 45, 'LOSE YOUR MONEY', bombed, but by early '65 they were at the top spot with the BESSIE BANKS cover, 'GO NOW'. They tried desperately to emulate its success, and although they scored a few minor chart hits, they disbanded in October '66. The band quickly re-united a month later, after finding JUSTIN HAYWARD and JOHN LODGE to replace DENNY LAINE and recent member ROD CLARKE. Late in the summer of '67, they switched to the more adventurous 'Deram', immediately hitting with the concept album, 'DAYS OF FUTURE PASSED'. It broke from their mid-60's R&B/pop sound, to a more ambitious hybrid of rock and orchestral pop. A haunting piece from it, 'NIGHTS IN WHITE SATIN', became a massive seller and an all-time classic in the process. After a rare concert at London's Queen Elizabeth Hall, they issued a follow-up concept album, 'IN SEARCH OF THE LOST CHORD'. Another massive seller, it was succeeded by their first No.1 album, 'ON THE THRESHOLD OF A DREAM', in 1969. Later that year they founded their own label, 'Threshold', continuing the winning formula on a further clutch of early 70's albums, in addition to some finely crafted 45's, including 'QUESTION', 'ISN'T LIFE STRANGE' and 'I'M JUST A SINGER (IN A ROCK AND ROLL BAND)'. In the mid-70's, The MOODY BLUES was put on ice while they ventured into side projects. All had a relative degree of success, most notably the BLUE JAYS (aka HAYWARD & LODGE) who had a more mainstream sounding pop hit, 'BLUE GUITAR' (1975 & produced by 10cc). With new Swiss-born keyboard wizard PATRICK MORAZ on board (fresh from a spell with YES), they released the comeback album, 'OCTAVE', in 1978, the record subsequently returning them to platinum status. Although early 80's album, 'LONG DISTANCE VOYAGER', went Top 10 on both sides of the Atlantic (No.1 in the US), creatively, the band were becoming stale. • **Songwriters:** LAINE wrote most of material, until LODGE or HAYWARD took over late '66. Also covered; I DON'T WANT TO GO ON WITHOUT YOU (Drifters) / IT AIN'T NECESSARILY SO (Gershwin) / TIME IS ON MY SIDE (Rolling Stones) / BYE BYE BIRD (Sonny Boy Williamson) / etc.

Album rating: THE MAGNIFICENT MOODIES (*5) / DAYS OF FUTURE PASSED (*8) / IN SEARCH OF THE LOST CHORD (*7) / ON THE THRESHOLD OF A DREAM (*8) / TO OUR CHILDREN'S CHILDREN'S CHILDREN (*6) / A QUESTION OF BALANCE (*6) / EVERY GOOD BOY DESERVES FAVOUR (*7) / SEVENTH SOJOURN (*6) / THIS IS THE MOODY BLUES compilation (*8) / CAUGHT LIVE + 5 (*5) / OCTAVE (*5) / LONG DISTANCE VOYAGER (*7) / THE PRESENT (*5) / VOICES IN THE SKY – THE BEST OF THE MOODY BLUES compilation (*8) / THE OTHER SIDE OF LIFE (*6) / SUR LA MER (*4) / GREATEST HITS compilation (*7) / KEYS OF THE KINGDOM (*4) / A NIGHT AT RED ROCKS WITH THE COLORADO SYMPHONY ORCHESTRA (*4) / TIME TRAVELLER boxed-set (*8) / STRANGE TIMES (*4) / HALL OF FAME (*4) / THE VERY BEST OF THE MOODY BLUES + STRANGE TIMES part compilation (*7) / Justin Hayward & John Lodge: BLUE JAYS (*6)

DENNY LAINE (b. BRIAN HINES, 29 Oct'44, Jersey, England) – vocals, guitar (ex-DIPLOMATS) / **MIKE PINDER** (b.12 Dec'41) – keyboards, vocals (ex-CREWCATS) / **RAY THOMAS** (b.29 Dec'42, Stourport-on-Severn, England) – flute, vocals, harmonica / **CLINT WARWICK** (b. CLINTON ECCLES, 25 Jun'39) – bass, vocals / **GRAHAM EDGE** (b.30 Mar'42, Rochester, England) – drums (ex-GERRY LEVENE AND THE AVENGERS)

Decca London

Aug 64. (7"; as MOODYBLUES) *(F 11971)* **STEAL YOUR HEART AWAY. / LOSE YOUR MONEY (BUT DON'T LOSE YOUR MIND)** [ ] [–]

Nov 64. (7") *(F 12022)* **GO NOW! / IT'S EASY CHILD** [1] [–]

Feb 65. (7") *(F 12095)* **I DON'T WANT TO GO ON WITHOUT YOU. / TIME IS ON MY SIDE** [33] [ ]

Feb 65. (7") *<9726>* **GO NOW! / LOSE YOUR MONEY (BUT DON'T LOSE YOUR MIND)** [–] [10]

May 65. (7") *(F 12166) <9764>* **FROM THE BOTTOM OF MY HEART (I LOVE YOU). / AND MY BABY'S GONE** [22] [93]

Jul 65. (lp) *(LK 4711) <LP 428>* **THE MAGNIFICENT MOODIES** <US-title 'GO NOW! – THE MOODY BLUES'> [ ] [ ]
– I'll go crazy / Something you got / Go now! / Can't nobody love you / I don't mind / I've got a dream / Let me go / Stop! / Thank you baby / It ain't necessarily so / True story / Bye bye bird. *(cd-iss. Nov88 & Jan93; 820 758-2) (re-iss. Mar93 on 'Repertoire' +=;)–* Steal your heart away / Lose your money (but don't lose your mind) / It's easy child / I don't want to go on without you (come back) / Time is on my side / From the bottom of my heart (I love you) / And my baby's gone.

Oct 65. (7") *(F 12266)* **EVERYDAY. / YOU DON'T (ALL THE TIME)** [44] [ ]

Mar 66. (7") *<9810>* **STOP! / BYE BYE BIRD** [–] [98]

—— (Jul66) **ROD CLARKE** – bass repl. WARWICK

Oct 66. (7") *(F 12498)* **BOULEVARD DE LA MADELAINE. / THIS IS MY HOUSE (BUT NOBODY CALLS)** [ ] [ ]

—— (Nov'66) **JUSTIN HAYWARD** (b.14 Oct'46, Swindon, England) – vocals, guitar (ex-WILDE THREE, ex-solo artist) repl. DENNY who went solo (and later to WINGS) / **JOHN LODGE** (b.20 Jul'45) – bass, vocals (ex-EL RIOT & THE REBELS) repl. CLARKE

Jan 67. (7"; w-drawn after a day) *(F 12543)* **LIFE'S NOT LIFE. / HE CAN WIN** [–] [–]

May 67. (7") *(F 12607)* **FLY ME HIGH. / REALLY HAVEN'T GOT THE TIME** [ ] [ ]

Aug 67. (7") *(F 12670)* **LOVE AND BEAUTY. / LEAVE THIS MAN ALONE** [ ] [ ]

Deram Deram

Nov 67. (7") *(DM 161) <85023>* **NIGHTS IN WHITE SATIN. / CITIES** [19] [ ]
<re-iss. Jul72; same>; hit No.2> (re-iss. Nov72; same); hit No.9) (re-iss. Mar76; same) (re-iss. Oct79; same); hit No.14) (re-iss. Oct83 & Jun88 on 'Old Gold'; OG 9349)

Nov 67. (lp; mono/stereo) *(DML/SML 707) <18012>* **DAYS OF FUTURE PASSED** [27] Apr68 [3]
– The day begins / Dawn:- Dawn is a feeling / The morning:- Another morning / Lunch break:- Peak hour / The afternoon:- Forever afternoon (Tuesday) / Time to get away / Evening:- The sunset / Twilight time / The night:- Nights in white satin. *<US re-iss. Sep72 hit No.3> (cd-iss. 1983 on 'Threshold'; 800 082-2) (re-iss. Nov84 lp/c; DOA/KDOAC 6) (re-iss. Apr91 cd/c/lp; 820006-2/-4/-1) (cd re-iss. Apr00 on 'Polydor'; 844767-2)*

Jul 68. (7") *<85028>* **TUESDAY AFTERNOON (FOREVER AFTERNOON). / ANOTHER MORNING** [–] [24]

Jul 68. (7") *(DM 196)* **VOICES IN THE SKY. / DR. LIVINGSTONE, I PRESUME** [23] [–]

Jul 68. (lp; mono/stereo) *(DML/SML 711) <18017>* **IN SEARCH OF THE LOST CHORD** [5] Sep68 [23]
– Departure / Ride my see-saw / Dr. Livingstone, I presume / House of four doors (part 1) / Legend of a mind / House of four doors (part 2) / Voices in the sky / The best way to travel / Visions of paradise / The actor / The word / Om. *(re-iss. Nov84 lp/c; DOA/KDOAC 7) (cd-iss. Aug86 & Apr91 on 'London'; 820 168-2) (cd re-iss. Apr00 on 'Polydor'; 844768-2)*

Oct 68. (7") *<85033>* **RIDE MY SEE-SAW. / VOICES IN THE SKY** [–] [61]

Nov 68. (7") *(DM 213)* **RIDE MY SEE-SAW. / A SIMPLE GAME** [42] [–]

Apr 69. (7") *(DM 247) <85044>* **NEVER COMES THE DAY. / SO DEEP WITHIN YOU** [ ] [91]

Apr 69. (lp; mono/stereo) *(DML/SML 1035) <18025>* **ON THE THRESHOLD OF A DREAM** [1] May69 [20]
– In the beginning / Lovely to see you / Dear diary / Send me no wine / To share our love / So deep within you / Never comes the day / Lazy day / Are you sitting comfortably / The dream / Have you heard (part 1) / The voyage / Have you heard (part 2). *(cd-iss. Aug86 on 'London'; 820 170-2) (cd re-iss. Apr00 on 'Polydor'; 844769-2)*

Threshold Threshold

Oct 69. (7") *(TH 1)* **WATCHING AND WAITING. / OUT AND IN** [ ] [–]

Nov 69. (lp; mono/stereo) *(<THM/THS 1>)* **TO OUR CHILDREN'S CHILDREN'S CHILDREN** [2] Jan70 [14]
– Higher and higher / Eyes of a child (part 1) / Floating / Eyes of a child (part 2) / I never thought I'd live to be a hundred / Beyond / Out and in / Gypsy / Eternity road / Candle of life / Sun is still shining / I never thought I'd live to be a million / Watching and waiting. *(cd-iss. Aug86 on 'London'; 820 364-2) (cd re-iss. Apr00 on 'Polydor'; 844770-2)*

Apr 70. (7") *(TH 4) <67004>* **QUESTION. / CANDLE OF LIFE** [2] [21]
(re-iss. Oct83 on 'Old Gold'; OG 9348)

Aug 70. (lp) *(<TH 3>)* **A QUESTION OF BALANCE** [1] Sep70 [3]
– Question / How is it (we are here) / And the tide rushes in / Don't you feel small / Tortoise and the hare / It's up to you / Minstrel's song / Dawning is the day / Melancholy man / The balance. *(cd-iss. Aug86 & Jul92 on 'London'; 820 211-2) (cd re-iss. Apr00 on 'Polydor'; 844771-2)*

Jul 71. (lp) *(<TH 5>)* **EVERY GOOD BOY DESERVES FAVOUR** [1] Aug71 [2]
– Procession / The story in your eyes / Our guessing game / Emily's song /

After you came / One more time to live / Nice to be here / You can never go home / My song. *(cd-iss. Aug86 & Apr91 on 'London'; 820 160-2) (cd re-iss. Apr00 on 'Polydor'; 844772-2)*

Aug 71. (7") *<67006>* **THE STORY IN YOUR EYES. / MELANCHOLY MAN** [–] [23]

Apr 72. (7") *(TH 9) <67009>* **ISN'T LIFE STRANGE. / AFTER YOU CAME** [13] [29]

Nov 72. (lp) *(<TH 7>)* **SEVENTH SOJOURN** [5] [1]
– Lost in a lost world / New horizons / For my lady / Isn't life strange / You and me / The land of make-believe / When you're a free man / I'm just a singer (in a rock'n'roll band). *(cd-iss. Sep86 on 'London'; 820 159-2) (cd re-iss. Apr00 on 'Polydor'; 844773-2)*

Jan 73. (7") *(TH 13) <67012>* **I'M JUST A SINGER (IN A ROCK'N'ROLL BAND). / FOR MY LADY** [36] [12]

—— Split early '73 but only for a 5 year trial period, releasing own solos released (2) compilations while they split

Nov 74. (d-lp) *(MB 1-2) <2-12-13>* **THIS IS THE MOODY BLUES** [14] [11]
– Question / The actor / The word / Eyes of a child / Dear diary / Legend of a mind / In the beginning / Lovely to see you / Never comes the day / Isn't life strange / The dream / Have you heard / Voyage / Ride my see-saw / Tuesday afternoon / And the tide rushes in / New horizons / Simple game / Watching and waiting / I'm just a singer (in a rock'n'roll band) / For my lady / Story in your eyes / Melancholy man / Nights in white satin. *(d-cd-iss. Aug89; 820 007-2)*

Decca London

Apr 77. (d-lp) *(MB 3-4) <690-1>* **CAUGHT LIVE + 5** (live '69 +1 studio side) [ ] Jun77 [26]
– Gypsy / The sunset / Dr. Livingstone, I presume / Never comes the day / Peak hour / Tuesday afternoon / Are you sitting comfortably / Have you heard (part 1) / The voyage / Have you heard (part 2) / Nights in white satin / Legend of a mind / Ride my see-saw / Gimme a little somethin' / Please think about it / Long summer days / King and Queen / What am I doing here. *(cd-iss. Apr00; 820161-2)*

—— re-formed mid 1978; **(HAYWARD, LODGE, EDGE, PINDER** and **THOMAS)**

Decca London

Jun 78. (lp/blue-lp/c) *(TX/+S/C 129) <PS 708>* **OCTAVE** [6] [13]
– Steppin' in a slide zone / Under moonshine / Had to fall in love / I'll be level with you / Driftwood / Top rank suite / I'm your man / Survival / One step into the light / The day we meet again. *(cd-iss. Oct86 & Jan93 & Apr00; 820 329-2)*

Jul 78. (7") *(F 13790) <270>* **STEPPIN' IN A SLIDE ZONE. / I'LL BE LEVEL WITH YOU** [ ] [39]

Oct 78. (7") *(F 13809) <273>* **DRIFTWOOD. / I'M YOUR MAN** [ ] [59]

—— **PATRICK MORAZ** (b.24 Jun'48, Morges, Switzerland) – keyboards (ex-YES, solo artist, ex-REFUGEE) repl. PINDER

Threshold Threshold

May 81. (lp/c) *(TXS 139) <TRL-1 2901>* **LONG DISTANCE VOYAGER** [7] Jun81 [1]
– The voice / Talking out of turn / Gemini dream / In my world / Meanwhile / 22,000 days / Nervous / Painted smile / Reflective smile / Veteran cosmic rocker. *(cd-iss. Oct86 & Apr00; 820 105-2)*

Jun 81. (7") *(TH 27) <601>* **GEMINI DREAM. / PAINTED SMILE** [ ] [12]

Jul 81. (7") *(TH 33) <602>* **THE VOICE. / 22,000 DAYS** [ ] [15]

Nov 81. (7"/7"pic-d) *(TH/+PD 29) <603>* **TALKING OUT OF TURN. / VETERAN COSMIC ROCKER** [ ] [65]

Aug 83. (7") *(TH 30)* **BLUE WORLD. / GOING NOWHERE** [35] [–]

Sep 83. (lp/c)(cd) *(TXS/+C 140)(810119-2) <2902>* **THE PRESENT** [15] [26]
– Blue world / Meet me halfway / Sitting at the wheel / Going nowhere / Hole in the world / Under my feet / It's cold outside of your heart / Running water / I am / Sorry. *(cd re-iss. Apr91 on 'London'; same)*

Sep 83. (7") *<604>* **SITTING AT THE WHEEL. / GOING NOWHERE** [–] [27]

Oct 83. (7") *(TH 31)* **SITTING AT THE WHEEL. / SORRY** [ ] [–]
(12"+=) *(THX 31)* – Gemini dream.

Nov 83. (7") *<605>* **BLUE WORLD. / SORRY** [–] [62]

Feb 84. (7") *<606>* **UNDER MY FEET. / RUNNING WATER** [–] [ ]

Polydor Polydor

Mar 86. (7"/12") *(POSP/+X 787) <883906>* **YOUR WILDEST DREAMS. / TALKIN' TALKIN'** [ ] Apr86 [9]

May 86. (lp/c)(cd) *(POLD/+C 5190)(829179-2) <829179>* **OTHER SIDE OF LIFE** [24] [9]
– Your wildest dreams / Talkin' talkin' / Rock'n'roll over you / I just don't care / Running out of love / The other side of life / The spirit / Slings and arrows / It may be a fire. *(cd re-iss. Feb97; same)*

Aug 86. (7") *(POSP 830) <885201>* **THE OTHER SIDE OF LIFE. / NIGHTS IN WHITE SATIN (live)** [ ] [58]
(12"+=) *(POSPX 830)* – The spirit. *<US; b-side>*

May 88. (7") *(POSP 921) <887600>* **I KNOW YOU'RE OUT THERE SOMEWHERE. / MIRACLE** [52] [30]
(12"+=) *(POSPX 921)* – ('A'extended).
(cd-s+=) *(POCD 921)* – Rock'n'roll over you (live).

Jun 88. (lp/c)(cd) *(POLH/+C 43)(<835756-2>)* **SUR LA MER** [21] [38]
– I know you're out there somewhere / Want to be with you / River of endless love / No more lies / Here comes the weekend / Vintage wine / Breaking point / Miracle / Love is on the run / Deep. *(cd re-iss. Feb97; same)*

Dec 88. (7") *(PO 27)* **NO MORE LIES. / RIVER OF ENDLESS LOVE** [ ] [ ]
(12"+=) *(PZ 27)* – The other side of life.

Jun 91. (7"/c-s) **SAY IT WITH LOVE. / LEAN ON ME (TONIGHT)** [ ] [ ]
(12"+=/cd-s+=) – Highway.

Aug 91. (cd/c/lp) *(<849433-2/-4/-1>)* **KEYS OF THE KINGDOM** [54] [94]
– Say it with love / Bless the wings (that bring you back) / Is this Heaven? / Say what you mean (pt.1 & 2) / Lean on me (tonight) / Hope and pray / Shadows on the wall / Celtic sonant / Magic / Never blame the rainbows for the rain. *(cd+=/c+=)* – Once is enough. *(re-iss. Jan93; same)*

Mar 93. (cd/c) *(<517977-2/-4>)* **A NIGHT AT RED ROCKS (with The Colorado Symphony Orchestra live)** [ ] [ ]
– Overture / Late lament / Tuesday afternoon (forever afternoon) / For my lady / Lean on me (tonight) / Lovely to see you / I know you're out there somewhere / The voice / Your wildest dreams / Isn't life strange / The other side of life / I'm just a singer (in a rock and roll band) / Nights in white satin / Question / Ride my see-saw. *(cd re-iss. Feb97; 517977-2) (<deluxe d-cd-iss. Mar03; 065275-2>)*

Universal Universal

Sep 99. (cd) *(<1 53265-2>)* **STRANGE TIMES** [ ] [93]
– English sunset / Haunted / Sooner or later (walkin' on air) / Wherever you are / Foolish love / Love don't come easy / All that is real is you / Strange times / Words you say / My little lovely / Forever now / One / Swallow / Nothing changes.

Apr 00. (d-cd)(c) *(541424-2)(535800-4)* **THE VERY BEST OF THE MOODY BLUES** (compilation; cd w/ 'STRANGE TIMES') [19] [–]
– Go now / Tuesday afternoon (forever autumn) / Nights in white satin / Ride my see-saw / Voices in the sky / Question / The story in your eyes / Isn't life strange / I'm just a singer (in a rock and roll band) / Blue guitar / Steppin' in a slide zone / Forever autumn / The voice / Gemini dream / Blue world / Your wildest dream / I know you're out there somewhere.

Sep 00. (cd) *(159537-2) <810059>* **HALL OF FAME (live)** [ ] Aug00 [ ]
– Overture / Tuesday afternoon (forever afternoon) / English sunset / Words you say / The story in your eyes / I know you're out there somewhere / Haunted / Your wildest dreams / Isn't life strange / I'm just a singer (in a rock and roll band) / Nights in white satin / Legend of a mind / Question / Ride my see-saw.

– (selective) compilations, etc. –

Nov 84. (lp/c)(cd) *Threshold; (SKL/KSKC 5341) <820155>* **VOICES IN THE SKY – THE BEST OF THE MOODY BLUES** [ ] Mar85 [ ]
– Ride my see-saw / Talking out of turn / Driftwood / Never comes the day / I'm just a singer (in a rock and roll band) / Gemini dream / The voice / After you came / Question / Veteran cosmic rocker / Isn't life strange / Nights in white satin. *(cd re-iss. Apr91)*

Oct 79. (lp/c) *K-Tel; (NE/+C 1051)* **OUT OF THIS WORLD** [15] [–]

Nov 89. (lp/c/cd) *Polydor; (<840 659-1/-4/-2>)* **GREATEST HITS** [71] [ ]

Sep 94. (5xcd-box) *Polydor; (516436-2)* **TIME TRAVELLER** [ ] [ ]
(re-iss. Feb97; 535223-2)

Sep 96. (cd/c) *Polygram TV; (535 800-2/-4)* **THE VERY BEST OF THE MOODY BLUES** [13] [–]
– Go now / Tuesday afternoon (forever afternoon) / Nights in white satin / Ride my see-saw / Voices in the sky / Questions / The story in your eyes / Isn't life strange / I'm just a singer (in a rock'n'roll band) / Blue guitar / Steppin' on a slide zone / Forever autumn / The voice / Gemini dream / Blue world / Your wildest dreams / I know you're out there somewhere.

Oct 98. (d-cd) *Universal; (AA314 565430-2)* **ANTHOLOGY** [ ] [ ]

Jan 00. (cd) *Universal; (E 541088-2)* **UNIVERSAL MASTERS COLLECTION** ☐ ☐

Mar 01. (cd) *Ark 21; <810065>* **JOURNEY INTO AMAZING CAVES** (soundtrack with STEVE WOOD & DANIEL MAY) [-] ☐
– To extremes / Search for daylight / Arizona / Water / Crystal chamber / Blue cathedral / Frozen in time / Home of the Mayan gods / Horizons turn inward / We can fly.

Jul 01. (d-cd) *Deram; (560241-2)* **THE COLLECTION** ☐ ☐

Feb 02. (d-cd) *BR Music; (BS 8123-2)* **THE SINGLES PLUS** ☐ ☐

Apr 02. (d-cd) *Universal TV; (583344-2)* **THE VERY BEST OF THE MOODY BLUES / HALL OF FAME LIVE AT THE ROYAL ALBERT HALL** [27] [-]
– (see THE VERY BEST OF . . .) / Overture / Tuesday afternoon / English sunset / Words you say / The story in your eyes / I know you're out there somewhere / Haunted / Your wildest dreams / Isn't life strange / I'm just a singer (in a rock'n'roll band) / Nights in white satin / Legend of a mind / Question / Ride my see-saw.

☐ Keith MOON (see under ⇒ WHO)

Gary MOORE

Born: 4 Apr'52, Belfast, N.Ireland. In the late 60's, he joined psychedelic outfit, GRANNY'S INTENTIONS, a band that included NOEL BRIDGEMAN on drums. While they later went on to record the 'HONEST INJUN' album for 'Deram', GARY and NOEL formed SKID ROW with bassist BRENDAN SHIELDS. Relocating to London in 1970, the band signed to 'C.B.S.', releasing two albums of progressive blues rock, 'SKID' (1970) and '34 HOURS' (1971) before MOORE left to form his own outfit (during this time he'd also undertaken some live work with DR. STRANGELY STRANGE, as well as guesting on their 1970 album, 'HEAVY PETTIN''). With a line-up of JAN SCHELHAAS (keyboards, ex-NATIONAL HEAD BAND), JOHN CURTIS (bass), PEARCE KELLY (drums) and session man PHILIP DONNELLY on guitar, The GARY MOORE BAND cut one album in 1973, 'GRINDING STONE'. The group never actually got round to making a follow-up as MOORE joined THIN LIZZY (PHIL LYNOTT had been a brief member of SKID ROW in its earliest incarnation) for three months as a replacement for the departed ERIC BELL. MOORE was eventually succeeded by SCOTT GORHAM and BRIAN ROBERTSON, the guitarist joining COLOSSEUM II and recording three albums with the group, 'STRANGE NEW FLESH' (1976), 'ELECTRIC SAVAGE' (1977) and 'WARDANCE' (1977). In addition to his rapidly improving guitar playing, MOORE sang lead vocals on some tracks, the material significantly heavier than the band's earlier incarnation as a progressive jazz rock outfit. Leaving COLOSSEUM in 1977, MOORE filled in for an injured BRIAN ROBERTSON on THIN LIZZY's American tour, eventually going full time with the band in the summer of 1978. At the same time MOORE resumed his solo career with the help of friends DON AIREY (keyboards; of COLOSSEUM II), JOHN MOLE (bass), SIMON PHILIPS (drums), plus PHIL LYNOTT and BRIAN DOWNEY of THIN LIZZY. Together they recorded an album, 'BACK ON THE STREETS' (1979) and two singles, one of which was the classic 'PARISIENNE WALKWAYS'. Featuring LYNOTT on vocals, the track was an epic piece of emotive axe work, MOORE's undulating soloing among the best work of his career. A Top 10 hit upon its original release in 1979, the track remains the guitarist's most played and most purchased record. Although MOORE remained a member of THIN LIZZY long enough to feature on their seminal UK Top 3 album, 'BLACK ROSE (A ROCK LEGEND)' in 1979, he left the band midway through an American tour, eventually setting up his own outfit, G-FORCE, in 1980. After a solitary eponymous album the same year, the group came to nothing, MOORE joining the GREG LAKE BAND for a couple of years. At the same time he also worked on a solo career, recruiting CHARLIE HUHN (vocals, ex-JACK LANCASTER), TOMMY EYRE (keyboards, ex-GREG LAKE BAND), NEIL MURRAY (bass, ex-WHITESNAKE) and IAN PAICE (drums, ex-WHITESNAKE, ex-DEEP PURPLE, ex-PAICE, ex-ASHTON & LORD, phew!!). The first album, 'CORRIDORS OF POWER' (1982) made the UK Top 30, although it failed to spawn any hit singles. For 1984's 'VICTIMS OF THE FUTURE', MOORE recruited a whole new band again, numbering NEIL CARTER (keyboards, guitar, ex-UFO, ex-WILD HORSES), BOBBY CHOUINARD (drums, although PAICE contributed to the next two albums) and CRAIG GRUBER (bass, ex-BILLY SQIER, although MURRAY appeared on the album). The set almost made the Top 10, while the melancholy ballad-ish 'EMPTY ROOMS' was a minor hit single. Replacing GRUBER first with BOB DAISLEY and then GLENN HUGHES (ex-DEEP PURPLE) while PAUL THOMPSON (ex-ROXY MUSIC) and TED McKENNA (ex-SAHB) took over on drums, MOORE once again hooked up with PHIL LYNOTT for the blistering 'OUT IN THE FIELDS', a No. 5 hit in 1985. Later that summer, a re-issued 'EMPTY ROOMS' went to No.23, while the album, 'RUN FOR COVER' almost made the Top 10. At last MOORE seemed to be on a bit of a roll, hooking up with Irish folk legends, The CHIEFTAINS for 'OVER THE HILLS AND FAR AWAY', another Top 20 hit. 'WILD FRONTIER' (1987) was released early the following Spring and saw MOORE looking back to his Irish roots for inspiration, the cover art depicting a bleak Celtic landscape. On the title track, MOORE tackled the equally bleak Irish political landscape, his wailing riffs echoing his feelings of frustration. With COZY POWELL on drums, 'AFTER THE WAR' (1989) continued in a similar vein, again exploring the Irish question in songs like 'BLOOD OF EMERALDS'. Throughout the 90's, harder-edged rock took a back seat for more blues-orientated material, MOORE releasing the acclaimed 'STILL GOT THE BLUES' in 1990. Subsequent albums 'AFTER HOURS', 'BLUES ALIVE', 'BLUES FOR GREENY' (a tribute to PETER GREEN) and his swansong studio Virgin release 'DARK DAYS IN PARADISE' followed a similar direction. In 1999, MOORE was back in circulation for 'Raw Power' via new album, 'A DIFFERENT BEAT', while 2001's 'BACK TO THE BLUES' (for 'Sanctuary' records) even returned him to the UK Top 60. It was back to basics for MOORE on 2002's Chris Tsangarides-produced 'SCARS', a refreshing backwards glance to his heavy rock roots after one too many albums of straight-up blues. His sense of feel for that genre was still there of course, although it was leavened with an almost tangible sense of relief as if he'd been itching champing at the bit to let loose with some power chords. The veteran axe meister revisited his past more explicitly on 2003's 'LIVE AT MONSTERS OF ROCK', turning in emotional versions of Phil Lynott's 'DON'T BELIEVE A WORD' and the pair's collaborative classic 'PARISIENNE WALKWAYS', as well as sterling covers of Free's 'WISHING WELL' and the Yardbirds' 'SHAPES OF THINGS'. • **Covered:** DON'T LET ME BE MISUNDERSTOOD (hit; Animals) / SHAPES OF THINGS (Yardbirds) / FRIDAY ON MY MIND (Easybeats) / DON'T YOU TO ME (Hudson Whittaker) / THE BLUES IS ALRIGHT (Milton Campbell) / KEY TO LOVE (John Mayall) / JUMPIN' AT SHADOWS (Duster Bennett) / etc. • **Trivia:** MOORE also sessioned on 1975's 'Peter & The Wolf', and ANDREW LLOYD WEBBER's 1978 lp 'Variations'. In 1980, he was heard on ROD ARGENT's 'Moving Home' & COZY POWELL's 'Over The Top'.

Album rating: GRINDING STONE (*4) / BACK ON THE STREETS (*6) / G-FORCE with G-Force (*5) / CORRIDORS OF POWER (*6) / VICTIMS OF THE FUTURE (*6) / WE WANT MOORE (*6) / RUN FOR COVER (*6) / WILD FRONTIER (*6) / AFTER THE WAR (*6) / STILL GOT THE BLUES (*8) / AFTER HOURS (*7) / BLUES ALIVE (*7) / BLUES FOR GREENY (*7) / BALLADS AND BLUES 1982-1994 compilation (*8) / DARK DAYS IN PARADISE (*4) / OUT IN THE FIELDS – THE VERY BEST OF GARY MOORE compilation (*8) / A DIFFERENT BEAT (*5) / BACK TO THE BLUES (*6) / SCARS (*5) / LIVE AT MONSTERS OF ROCK (*6)

GARY MOORE BAND

GARY MOORE – guitar, vocals (ex-SKID ROW) with **JAN SCHELHAAS** – keyboards (ex-NATIONAL HEAD BAND) / **JOHN CURTIS** – bass / **PEARCE KELLY** – drums / plus session man **PHILIP DONNELLY** – guitar

C.B.S. — Peters

1973. (lp) *(CBS 65527)* <9004> **GRINDING STONE** ☐ ☐
– Grinding stone / Time to heal / Sail across the mountain / The energy dance / Spirit / Boogie my way back home. *(re-iss. Nov85 lp/c; CBS/40 32699) (re-iss. Oct90 cd/c/lp; 467449-2/-4/-1) (cd re-iss. Jul00 on 'Essential'; ESMCD 914)*

— In 1974 GARY joined THIN LIZZY ⇒ for 3 mths. May75 he joined COLOSSEUM II before returning to THIN LIZZY p/t for 5 mths early'77 and f/t Aug'78.

GARY MOORE

also started a new solo career at this time with friends **DON AIREY** – keyboards (of COLOSSEUM) / **JOHN MOLE** – bass / **SIMON PHILLIPS** – drums / plus THIN LIZZY'S – **PHIL LYNOTT** and **BRIAN DOWNEY**.

M.C.A. — Jet

Dec 78. (7") *(MCA 386)* **BACK ON THE STREETS. / TRACK NINE** ☐ ☐
Jan 79. (lp) *(MCF 2853)* *<JZ 36187>* **BACK ON THE STREETS** 70 ☐
– Back on the streets / Don't believe a word / Fanatical fascists / Flight of the snow moose / Hurricane / Song for Donna / What would you rather bee or wasp / Parisienne walkways. *(re-iss. Aug81 lp/c; MCL/MCLC 1622) (re-iss. Apr92 cd/c; MCL D/C 19011)*
Apr 79. (7") *(MCA 419)* *<5061>* **PARISIENNE WALKWAYS. / FANATICAL FASCISTS** 8 ☐
(above single featured PHIL LYNOTT – vocals (of THIN LIZZY)
Oct 79. (7") *MCA 534)* **SPANISH GUITAR. / SPANISH GUITAR (instrumental)** ☐ –
Oct 79. (7") *<5066>* **BACK ON THE STREETS. / SONG FOR DONNA** – ☐

G-FORCE

GARY MOORE – guitar, vocals / **TONY NEWTON** – vocals / **WILLIE DEE** – keyboards, bass, vocals / **MARK NAUSEEF** – drums, percussion (ex-THIN LIZZY, ex-ELF, ex-IAN GILLAN BAND)

Jet — Jet

Jun 80. (7") *(JET 183)* **HOT GOSSIP. / BECAUSE OF YOUR LOVE** ☐ ☐
Jun 80. (lp/pic-lp) *(JET/+PD 229)* **G-FORCE** ☐ ☐
– You / White knuckles – Rockin' & rollin' / She's got you / I look at you / Because of your love / You kissed me sweetly / Hot gossip / The woman's in love / Dancin'. *(re-iss. Feb91 on 'Castle' cd/c/lp; CLA CD/MC/LP 212) (cd re-iss. Oct00 on 'Castle'; CMRCD 034)*
Aug 80. (7") *(JET 194)* **YOU. / TRUST YOUR LOVIN'** ☐ ☐
Nov 80. (7") *(JET 7005)* **WHITE KNUCKLES – ROCKIN' & ROLLIN'. / I LOOK AT YOU** ☐ ☐

— In '81 and '83 he was part of the GREG LAKE BAND. Although he did continue his solo career

GARY MOORE

with **CHARLIE HUHN** – vocals (ex-JACK LANCASTER) / **TOMMY EYRE** – keyboards (ex-GREG LAKE BAND) / **NEIL MURRAY** – bass (ex-WHITESNAKE) / **IAN PAICE** – drums (ex-WHITESNAKE, ex-DEEP PURPLE, ex-PAICE, ex-ASHTON & LORD)

Jet — not iss.

Oct 81. (12"ep; as GARY MOORE & FRIENDS) *(JET12 016)* **NUCLEAR ATTACK. / DON'T LET ME BE MISUNDERSTOOD / RUN TO YOUR MAMA** ☐ –

Virgin — Mirage

Sep 82. (7"/7"pic-d) *(VS/+Y 528)* *<99896>* **ALWAYS GONNA LOVE YOU. / COLD HEARTED** ☐ Feb83 ☐
Oct 82. (lp/c) *(V/TCV 2245)* *<90077>* **CORRIDORS OF POWER** 30 Apr83 ☐
– Don't take me for a loser / Always gonna love you / Wishing well / Gonna' break my heart again / Falling in love with you / End of the world / Rockin' every night / Cold hearted / I can't wait until tomorrow. *(free live 7"ep) (VDJ 34)* – PARISIENNE WALKWAYS. / ROCKIN' EVERY NIGHT / BACK ON THE STREETS *(re-iss. Jun85 lp/c; OVED/+C 210) (cd-iss. Jul85; CDV 2245)*

— **JOHN SLOMAN** – vocals, keyboards repl. HUHN / **DON AIREY** – keyboards (see above) (ex-OZZY OSBOURNE) repl. EYRE

Feb 83. (7"/7"pic-d) *(VS/+Y 564)* *<99856>* **FALLING IN LOVE WITH YOU. / ('A'instrumental)** ☐ May83 ☐
(12"+=) *(VST 564)* – Wishing well.

— GARY MOORE recruited new personnel after SLOMAN departed / **NEIL CARTER** – keyboards, guitar (ex-UFO, ex-WILD HORSES) repl. AIREY / **BOBBY CHOUINARD** – drums 1/2 repl. PAICE (he appeared on most of next 2 lp's) / on tour Mar 84 **CRAIG GRUBER** – bass (ex-BILLY SQUIER) 1/2 replaced MURRAY (he appeared on lp) (note that all: MURRAY, AIREY and PAICE rejoined past bands WHITESNAKE, OZZY OSBOURNE and DEEP PURPLE respectively)

10-Virgin — Mirage

Jan 84. (7"/7"sha-pic-d) *(TEN/+S 13)* **HOLD ON TO LOVE. / DEVIL IN HER HEART** 65 –
(12"+=) *(TEN 13-12)* – Law of the jungle.
Feb 84. (lp/c/cd) *(DIX/+C/CD 2)* *<90154>* **VICTIMS OF THE FUTURE** 12 May84 ☐
– Victims of the future / Teenage idol / Shapes of things / Empty rooms / Murder in the skies / All I want / Hold on to love / Law of the jungle. *(re-iss. Jun88 on 'Virgin' lp/c; OVED/+C 206)*
Mar 84. (7"/7"sha-pic-d) *(TEN/+S 19)* **SHAPES OF THINGS. / BLINDER** ☐ –
(12"+=) *(TEN 19-12)* – (an interview with Alan Freeman).
Aug 84. (7") *(TEN 25)* **EMPTY ROOMS. / NUCLEAR ATTACK (live)** 51 –
(12"+=) *(TEN 25-12)* – ('A'extended).
Aug 84. (7") **EMPTY ROOMS. / MURDER IN THE SKIES** – ☐
Oct 84. (d-lp/d-c/d-cd) *(GMDL/CGMDL/GMDLD 1)* **WE WANT MOORE (live)** 32 –
– Murder in the skies / Shapes of things / Victims of the future / Cold hearted / End of the world / Back on the streets / So far away / Empty rooms / Don't take me for a loser / Rockin' and rollin'.

— **GLENN HUGHES** – bass (ex-DEEP PURPLE) repl. BOB DAISLEY who repl. GRUBER / **PAUL THOMPSON** (ex-ROXY MUSIC) and **TED McKENNA** (ex-SAHB) took over drums

May 85. (7"/7"sha-pic-d; GARY MOORE & PHIL LYNOTT) *(TEN/+S 49)* **OUT IN THE FIELDS. / MILITARY MAN** 5 –
(12"+=) *(TEN 49-12)* – Still in love with you.
(d7"+=) *(TEND 49)* – Stop messin' around (live).
Jul 85. (7") *(TEN 58)* **EMPTY ROOMS. / OUT OF MY SYSTEM** 23 –
(12"+=) *(TEN 58-12)* – Parisienne walkways (live) / Empty rooms (summer '85).
(d7"+=) *(TEND 58)* – Parisienne walkways (live) / Murder in the skies (live).
Sep 85. (lp/c) *(DIX/CDIX 16)* *<90482>* **RUN FOR COVER** 12 Feb86 ☐
– Run for cover / Reach for the sky / Military man / Empty rooms / Out in the fields / Nothing to lose / Once in a lifetime / All messed up / Listen to your heartbeat. *(cd-iss. Feb86 +=; DIXCD 16)* – Out of my system. *(pic-lp-iss.1986; DIXP 16) (re-iss. 1989 on 'Virgin' lp/c; OVED/+C 274)*

— **GARY** now used members of The CHIEFTAINS. Retained **CARTER** + **DAISLEY**

Dec 86. (7"/7"sha-pic-d) *(TEN/+S 134)* **OVER THE HILLS AND FAR AWAY. / CRYING IN THE SHADOWS** 20 –
(d7"+=) *(TEND 134)* – All messed up (live) / Out in the fields (live).
(12"+=) *(TENT 134)* – All messed up (live) / ('A'version).
Feb 87. (7") *(TEN 159)* **WILD FRONTIER. / RUN FOR COVER (live)** 35 –
(12"+=) *(TENT 159)* – ('A'live) / ('A'extended).

(d7"+=) *(TEND 159)* – Murder in the skies (live) / Wild frontier (live).
(cd-s+=) *(KERRY 159)* – Over the hills and far away / Empty rooms / Out in the fields / Shapes of things.

Mar 87. (lp/c/cd) *(DIX/CDIX/DIXCD 56) <90588>* **WILD FRONTIER** 8 May87
– Over the hills and far away / Wild frontier / Take a little time / The loner / Friday on my mind / Strangers in the darkness / Thunder rising / Johnny boy. *(cd+=)* – Crying in the shadows / Over the hills and far away (12"version) / Wild frontier (12"version) *(re-iss. Sep87. WILD FRONTIER (SPECIAL EDITION); DIXG 56) (incl.extra 12"ep) (pic-cd-iss. Jan89; DIXPCD 56) (re-iss. Apr90 on 'Virgin' lp/c; OVED/+C 285)*

Apr 87. (7"/7"pic-d) *(TEN/+P 164)* **FRIDAY ON MY MIND. / REACH FOR THE SKY (live)** 26 –
(12"+=) *(TENT 164)* – ('A'version).
(cd-s+=) *(KERRY 164)* – Parisienne walkways (live) / ('A'-Kool rap version).

Aug 87. (7"/ext.7"s) *(TEN/+C 178)* **THE LONER. / JOHNNY BOY** 53 –
(12"+=) *(TENT 178)* – ('A'live).

Nov 87. (7") *(TEN 190)* **TAKE A LITTLE TIME. / OUT IN THE FIELDS** 75 –
(d7"+=) *(TEND 190)* – All messed up (live) / Thunder rising (live).

— brought back **COZY POWELL** – drums

Virgin Virgin

Jan 89. (7"/7"g-f/7"pic-d) *(GMS/+G/Y 1)* **AFTER THE WAR. / THIS THING CALLED LOVE** 37
(12"+=) *(GMST 1)* – Over the hills and far away.
(3"cd-s+=) *(GMSCD 1)* – Emerald / Thunder rising.

Jan 89. (cd/c/lp) *(CD/TC+/V 2575) <91066>* **AFTER THE WAR** 23 Mar89
– After the war / Speak for yourself / Livin' on dreams / Led clones / Running from the storm / This thing called love / Ready for love / Blood of emeralds. *(c+=/cd+=)* – Dunlace (pt.1 & 2) / The messiah will come. *(re-iss. Sep90 lp/c; OVED/+C 335) (cd re-iss. Aug98 on 'VIP-Virgin'; CDVIP 212)*

Mar 89. (7") *(GMS 2)* **READY FOR LOVE. / WILD FRONTIER** 56 –
(12"+=/12"g-f+=/cd-s+=) *(GMS T/TG/CD 2)* – The loner (live).
(3"cd-s+=) *(GMSCDX 2)* – Military man (live).

Apr 89. (7") *<99211>* **SPEAK FOR YOURSELF. / LED CLONES** –

— **CHRIS SLADE** – drums (ex-MANFRED MANN'S EARTH BAND, ex-FIRM) repl. COZY POWELL

Oct 89. (7") *(VS 1219)* **LIVIN' ON DREAMS. / THE MESSIAH WILL COME AGAIN** –
(12"+=) *(VST 1219)* – ('A'extended).

— His band were now **DON AIREY** – keyboards / **BOB DAISLEY + ANDY PYLE** – bass / **GRAHAM WALKER + BRIAN DOWNEY** – drums / **FRANK MEAD** – tenor sax / **NICK PAYN** – sax

Mar 90. (7"/c-s) *(VS/+C 1233)* **OH PRETTY WOMAN. / KING OF BLUES** 48
(12"+=/12"s+=/cd-s+=) *(VS T/TP/CDT 1233)* – The stumble.

Mar 90. (cd/c/lp) *(CD/TC+/V 2612) <91369>* **STILL GOT THE BLUES** 13 Jun90 83
– Moving on / Oh pretty woman / Walking by myself / Still got the blues / Texas strut / Too tired / King of the blues / As the years go passing by / Midnight blues / That kind of woman / All your love / Stop messin' around.

May 90. (7"/c-s) *(VS/+C 1267) <98854>* **STILL GOT THE BLUES (FOR YOU). / LET ME WITH THE BLUES** 31 Jan91 97
(12"+=) *(VST 1267)* – ('A'extended) / The sky is crying.
(cd-s+=) *(VSCDT 1267)* – Further on up the road / The sky is crying.
(cd-s+=) *(VSCDX 1267)* – Mean cruel woman.

Aug 90. (7") *(VS 1281)* **WALKING BY MYSELF. / ALL YOUR LOVE** 48 –
(12"+=) *(VST 1281)* – ('A'live).
(cd-s++=) *(VSCDT 1281)* – Still got the blues (live).

Dec 90. (7"; GARY MOORE featuring ALBERT COLLINS) *(VS/+C 1306)* **TOO TIRED. / TEXAS STRUT** 71 –
(12"+=/cd-s+=) *(VS T/CDT 1306)* – ('A'live).
(cd-s) *(VSCDX 1306)* – ('A'side) / All your love (live) / The stumble.

— He featured on TRAVELING WILBURYS single 'She's My Baby'.

— **WILL LEE + JOHNNY B.GAYDON** – bass repl. PYLE / **ANTON FIG** – drums repl. DOWNEY / **TOMMY EYRE** – keyboards repl. AIREY / added on horns **MARTIN DROVER, NICK PENTELOW, ANDREW LOVE + WAYNE JACKSON RICHARD MORGAN** – oboe / backing vocals – **CAROLE KENYON + LINDA TAYLOR**

Feb 92. (7"/c-s; GARY MOORE & THE MIDNIGHT BLUES BAND) *(VS/+C 1393)* **COLD DAY IN HELL. / ALL TIME LOW** 24 –
(cd-s+=) *(VSCDT 1393)* – Stormy Monday (live) / Woke up this morning.

Mar 92. (cd/c/lp) *(CD/TC+/V 2684) <91825>* **AFTER HOURS** 4
– Cold day in Hell / Don't lie to me (I get evil) / Story of the blues / Since I met you baby / Separate ways / Only fool in town / Key to love / Jumpin' at shadows / The blues is alright / The hurt inside / Nothing's the same.

May 92. (7"/c-s) *(VS/+C 1412)* **STORY OF THE BLUES. / MOVIN' ON DOWN THE ROAD** 40 –
(cd-s+=) *(VSCDT 1412)* – King of the blues.
(cd-s+=) *(VSCDG 1412)* – Midnight blues (live).

Jul 92. (7"/c-s; GARY MOORE & B.B. KING) *(VS/+C 1423)* **SINCE I MET YOU BABY. / THE HURT INSIDE** 59 –
(cd-s+=) *(VSCDT 1423)* – Moving on (live) / Texas strut (live).
(cd-s+=) *(VSCDX 1423)* – Don't start me talking / Once in a blue mood (instrumental).

Oct 92. (7"/c-s) *(VS/+C 1437)* **SEPARATE WAYS. / ONLY FOOL IN TOWN** 59 –
(cd-s+=) *(VSCDT 1437)* – You don't love me (live) / The stumble (live).
(cd-s+=) *(VSCDX 1437)* – Further on up the road (live with ALBERT COLLINS) / Caledonia (live with ALBERT COLLINS).

Apr 93. (7"/c-s) *(VS/+C 1456)* **PARISIENNE WALKWAYS (live '93). / STILL GOT THE BLUES** 32 –
(cd-s+=) *(VSCDT 1456)* – Since I met you baby (live with B.B. KING) / Key to love.
(cd-s+=) *(VSCDX 1456)* – Stop messin' around / You don't love me.

Virgin Virgin

May 93. (cd/c/d-lp; as GARY MOORE & THE MIDNIGHT BLUES BAND) *(CD/TC+/V 2716) <87798>* **BLUES ALIVE** 8
– Cold day in Hell / Walking by myself / Story of the blues / Oh pretty woman / Separate ways / Too tired / Still got the blues / Since I met you baby / The sky is crying / Further on up the road / King of the blues / Parisienne walkways / Jumpin' at shadows.

— In Jun '94, MOORE teamed up with JACK BRUCE + GINGER BAKER (ex-CREAM, and both solo artists) to form BBM. They had UK Top10 album 'AROUND THE NEXT DREAM' for 'Virgin' records

Nov 94. (cd/c/lp) *(CD/TC+/V 2768) <40054>* **BALLADS AND BLUES 1982-1994** (compilation) 33 Mar95
– Always gonna love you / Still got the blues / Empty rooms / Parisienne walkways / One day / Separate ways / Story of the blues / Crying in the shadows / With love (remember) / Midnight blues / Falling in love with you / Jumpin' at shadows / Blues for Narada / Johnny boy.
below a tribute to PETER GREEN (ex-Fleetwood Mac) guitarist

— musicians:- **TOMMY EYRE** – keyboards / **ANDY PYLE** – bass / **GRAHAM WALKER** – drums / **NICK PENTELOW + NICK PAYN** – brass

May 95. (cd/c/lp) *(CD/TC+/V 2784) <40507>* **BLUES FOR GREENY** 14
– If you be my baby / Long grey mare / Merry go round / I loved another woman / Need your love so bad / The same way / The supernatural / Driftin' / Showbiz blues / Love that burns. *(cd+=)* – Looking for somebody.

Jun 95. (7"ep/c-ep/cd-ep) *(VS/+C/CD 1546)* **NEED YOUR LOVE SO BAD / THE SAME WAY (acoustic). / THE WORLD KEEPS ON TURNIN' (acoustic) / STOP MESSIN' AROUND (acoustic)** 48 –

— with **GUY PRATT** – bass / **GARY HUSBAND** – drums / **MAGNUS FIENNES + PAUL NICHOLAS** – keyboards

May 97. (c-s) *(VSC 1632)* **ONE GOOD REASON / BEAST OF BURDEN** –
(cd-s+=) *(VSCDT 1632)* – Burning in our hearts / There must be a way.

May 97. (cd/c) *(CDV/TCV 2826) <44165>* **DARK DAYS IN PARADISE** 43
– One good reason / Cold wind blows / I have found my love in you / One fine day / Like angels / What are we here for? / Always there for you / Afraid of tomorrow / Where did we go wrong? / Business as usual.

Jun 97. (c-s) *(VSC 1640)* **I HAVE FOUND MY LOVE IN YOU / MY FOOLISH PRIDE** –
(cd-s+=) *(VSCDT 1640)* – All the way from Africa.

Nov 97. (c-s) *(VSC 1674)* **ALWAYS THERE FOR YOU / RHYTHM OF OUR LIVES** –
(cd-s+=) *(VSCDT 1674)* – ('A'mixes).

Oct 98. (cd/c) *(CDV/TCV 2871) <46687>* **OUT IN THE FIELDS – THE VERY BEST OF GARY MOORE** (compilation) 54 Dec98
– After the war / Run for cover / Still in love with you / Parisienne walkways / Out in the fields / Empty rooms / The loner / Shapes of things / Still got the blues / Ready for love / Military man / Wild frontier / Wishing well / Friday on my mind / Cold day in Hell / Over the hills and far away. *(d-cd+=; CDVX 2871)* – Emerald / All messed up (live) / Livin' on dreams (remix) / Military man (live) / Thunder rising (live) / Devil in her heart / Blinder / Reach for the sky (live) / Over the hills and far away (live) / Stop messin' atound (live).

Raw Power Castle

Sep 99. (cd) *(RAWCD 142) <550>* **A DIFFERENT BEAT** Oct99
– Go on home / Lost in your love / Worry no more / Fire / Surrender / House full of blues / Bring my baby back / Can't help myself / Fat boy / We want love / Can't help myself (E-Z Rollers mix). *<re-iss. 2001 on 'Sanctuary'; 81102>*

Sanctuary Sanctuary

Mar 01. (cd) *(SANCD 072) <86302>* **BACK TO THE BLUES** 53
– Enough of the blues / You upset me baby / Cold black night / Stormy Monday / Ain't got you / Picture of the Moon / Looking back / The prophet / How many lies / Drowning in tears.

— **SCARS** is GARY MOORE, CASS LEWIS (bass), DARRIN MOONEY (drums)

Sep 02. (cd) *(SANCD 120) <84564>* **SCARS**
– When the sun goes down / Rectify / Wasn't born in Chicago / Stand up / Just can't let you go / My baby (she's so good to me) / World of confusion / Ball and chain / World keep turnin' round / Who knows (what tomorrow may bring)?

Aug 03. (cd) *(SANCD 215) <84642>* **LIVE AT MONSTERS OF ROCK (live)** Sep03
– Shapes of things / Wishing well / Rectify / Guitar intro / Stand up / Just can't let go on / Walking by myself / Don't believe a word / Out in the fields / Parisienne walkways.

– compilations, etc. –

Jun 84. (lp/c) *Jet; (JET LP/CA 241)* **DIRTY FINGERS** –
(cd-iss. Nov86; JETCD 007) (re-iss. Apr87 on 'Castle' lp/c/cd; CLA LP/MC/CD 131) (cd re-iss. Oct00 on 'Castle'; CMRCD 035)

Jun 84. (7") *Jet; (7043)* **DON'T LET ME BE MISUNDERSTOOD. / SHE'S GOT YOU (live)** –

Oct 85. (lp) *Raw Power; (RAWLP 006)* **WHITE KNUCKLES** –
(re-iss. Apr86 c/cd; RAW TC/CD 006)

Jun 86. (lp/c/cd) *10-Virgin; (XID/CXID/XIDCD 1)* **ROCKIN' EVERY NIGHT** (live in Japan) 99
(re-iss. cd.Jun88; ZIDCD 1) (cd re-iss. Aug97 on 'Disky'; VI 88238-2)

Sep 86. (d-lp/d-c) *Raw Power; (RAW LP/TC 033)* **ANTHOLOGY** –

Jun 87. (lp/c/cd) *Raw Power; (RAW LP/TC/CD 034)* **LIVE AT THE MARQUEE (live)**
(re-iss. Feb91 on 'Castle' cd/c/lp; CLA CD/MC/LP 211) (cd re-iss. Oct00 on 'Castle'; CMRCD 033)

Nov 87. (lp/c) *M.C.A.; (MCL/+C 1864)* **PARISIENNE WALKWAYS** –
(cd-iss. May90; DMCL 1864) (re-iss. Oct92 cd/c; MCL D/C 19076)

Mar 88. (d-lp/c/d-cd) *That's Original; (TFO LP/MC/CD 2)* **G-FORCE / LIVE AT THE MARQUEE** –

1988. (cd-ep) *Special Edition; (CD3-4)* **GARY MOORE E.P.** –
– Don't let me be misunderstood / Parisienne walkways (live) / White knuckles – Rockin' & rollin'.

Jun 90. (cd/c) *Nightriding; (KN CD/MC 10014)* **GOLDEN DECADE OF GARY MOORE** –

Sep 90. (cd/c/lp; by SKID ROW) *Essential; (ESS CD/MC/LP 025)* **GARY MOORE, BRUSH SHIELDS, NOEL BRIDGEMAN** –

Oct 90. (cd/c/d-lp) *Castle; (CCS CD/MC/LP 273)* **THE COLLECTION** –
– Nuclear attack / White knuckles – Rockin' & rollin' / Grinding stone / Spirit / Run to your mama / Don't let me be misunderstood / Bad news / I look at you / She's got you / Back on the streets (live) / Hiroshima / Parisienne walkways (live) / Dancin' / Really gonna rock tonight / Dirty fingers.

Nov 91. (cd-box) *Virgin; (TPAK 18)* **CD BOX SET** –
– (AFTER THE WAR / RUN FOR COVER / WILD FRONTIER)

Feb 92. (cd-box) *Castle; (CLABX 904)* **CD BOX SET** –

Sep 94. (cd/c) *Spectrum; (550 738-2/-4)* **WALKWAYS** –

May 97. (d-cd) *Snapper; (SMDCD 123)* **LOOKING AT YOU** –

Sep 98. (cd) *Essential; (ESMCD 655)* **THE GARY MOORE COLLECTION** –

Oct 00. (d-cd) *Axe Killer; (AXE 306331CD)* **CORRIDORS OF POWER / RUN FOR COVER** –

MORCHEEBA

Formed: London, England . . . 1995 by the GODFREY brothers, PAUL and ROSS, who subsequently recruited female singer, SKYE EDWARDS. Launched into musical orbit at roughly the same time as fellow trip-hoppers PORTISHEAD, TRICKY et al., MORCHEEBA offered up a London-centric take on what was still essentially a Bristol-based phenomenon. With a bit of Southern-fried slide guitar thrown in for good measure, MORCHEEBA's paranoid beat collages were even compared to LYNYRD SKYNYRD at one point! Before you start dusting down your old copy of 'Freebird', however, be rest assured that this bunch deal in a musical hybrid throughly 90's in make-up. Blessed with the satin-silk vocals of SKYE, the debut 'IndoChina' album, 'WHO CAN YOU TRUST?' (1996) enjoyed lavish praise among even the most bpm-hardened journos. Liable to lull the listener into a soporific sense of insecurity with its deceptively laid back grooves, MORCHEEBA's edgy trip-hop sound reflected the urban unease of its native environment. Yet this bunch retain a certain warmth and accessibility missing in their contemporaries, an obvious fondness for folk, blues and vintage hammond grooves occasionally melting the glacial veneer of icy coolness. Autumn '96 saw the band's first Top 40 success with a re-released 'TRIGGER HIPPIE', a series of festival appearances and a growing fanbase seeing follow-up album, 'BIG CALM' make the UK Top 20. Another consumate collection of sculptured soundscapes infused with a healthy helping of pastoral strumming, the album garnered universal praise and was high on the year-end lists of many critics and music fans alike. Third set 'FRAGMENTS OF FREEDOM' (2000) was disappointing in comparison as the trio attempted to transform their signature sound into something a little more contemporary. More interesting was PAUL's contribution to the celebrity DJ series 'Back To Mine' (2001), where the MORCHEEBA man unsurprisingly proved himself a man of impeccable musical taste. Offering up a far richer and more discerning choice than the average DJ comp, the record found GODFREY digging through his crates for cuts like Os Mutantes' 'Baby', Dr John's 'Gris-Gris Gumbo Ya Ya' and slinky Bollywood funk classic 'Baby Let's Dance Together' while slipping in MORCHEEBA's own 'ON THE RHODES AGAIN'. 'CHARANGO' (2002) wasn't so much a departure as a natural progression for the band as they embraced more of a post-modernist approach to their craft, enlisting the likes of LAMBCHOP's KURT WAGNER and old skool wizard SLICK RICK in their bid to finally free themselves from the trip-hop tag.

Album rating: WHO CAN YOU TRUST? (*7) / BIG CALM (*8) / FRAGMENTS OF FREEDOM (*5) / CHARANGO (*6) / PARTS OF THE PROCESS compilation (*8)

SKYE EDWARDS – vocals / **PAUL GODFREY** – programming, scratching, live drums, lyrics / **ROSS GODFREY** – guitars, sitar, keyboards, synthesizer, bass / plus **PETE NORRIS** – synthesizer programming

China not iss.

Nov 95. (12"ltd) **TRIGGER HIPPIE** –

Feb 96. (c-s) *(WOKMC 2081)* **TRIGGER HIPPIE / KILLER HIPPIE (mix)** –
(12"+=/cd-s+=) *(WOK T/CD 2081)* – ('A'&'B'-mixes).

Indochina Discovery

Apr 96. (12"/cd-s) *(INDO 44 T/CD)* **NEVER AN EASY WAY (apocalyptic mix) / NEVER AN EASY WAY (long mix). / OVER & OVER (demo) / BABY SITAR (drummer of your dreams mix)** [ ] [-]

Apr 96. (cd/c/lp) *(ZEN 009 CD/MC/LP)* *<77050>* **WHO CAN YOU TRUST?** [ ] Sep96 [ ]
– Moog Island / Trigger hippie / Post houmous / Tape loop / Never an easy way / Howling / Small town / Enjoy the wait / Col / Who can you trust? / Almost done / End theme. *(re-dist.Apr97 hit No.70) (cd re-iss. Nov97 / US=Dec98 on 'Sire'+= 'BEATS AND B-SIDES'; ZEN 009CDX)<31049>* – Killer hippie / On the Rhodes again / Tape loop / Dungeness / Baby sitar / Ray payola / Shoulder holster / Post houmous.

Jul 96. (c-s/cd-s) *(INDO 45 MC/CD)* **TAPE LOOP (shortcheeba mix) / TAPE LOOP (Diabolical Brothers mix) / MOOG ISLAND (live for GLR) / ON THE RHODES AGAIN** [42] [-]

Oct 96. (c-s/cd-s) *(INDO 52 MC/CD)* **TRIGGER HIPPIE / TRIGGER HIPPIE (newtheeba mix) / THE SEA (acoustic demo)** [40] [-]
(cd-s) *(INDO 52CDR)* – ('A'remixes).

Indochina China-Sire

Feb 97. (c-s) *(INDO 54MC)* *<35001>* **THE MUSIC THAT WE HEAR (MOOG ISLAND) / (Arthur Baker mix)** [47] Dec97 [ ]
(cd-s+=) *(INDO 54CD)* – ('A'-Omni Trio mix).
(cd-s) *(IDO 54CDR)* – ('A'remixes).

Sep 97. (c-s/cd-s) *(IDO 64 MC/CD)* **SHOULDER HOLSTER / ('A'-Diabolical Brothers mix) / ('A'instrumental) / Payola (Curly Wurly mix)** [53] [ ]
(cd-s) *(IDO 64CDX)* – ('A'side) / ('A'-DJ Swamp mix) / ('A'-Rolling Boulder mix) / ('A'-Nation Of Teflon Souls mix) / ('A'-Low Pressure mix).

Feb 98. (cd-s) *(IDO 66CD)* **THE SEA / BIG CALM** [ ] [-]

Mar 98. (cd/c/lp) *(ZEN 017 CD/MC/LP)* *<31020>* **BIG CALM** [18] [-]
– The sea / Shoulder holster / Part of the process / Blindfold / Let me see / Bullet proof / Over and over / Friction / Diggin' a watery grave / Fear and love / Big calm.

Mar 98. (ltd;12"ep/pic-cd-ep) *(IDO 70 T/CD)* **BLINDFOLD / THE SEA / THREE ORANGE WHIPS** [56] [-]

Indochina WEA

Jun 98. (c-s) *(IDO 76C)* *<42387>* **LET ME SEE / LET ME SEE (Magnus Fiennes mix) / DON'T LET IT GET YOU DOWN** [46] Nov98 [ ]
(cd-s+=) *(IDO 76CD)* – ('A'-Talvin Singh mix).
(cd-s) *(IDO 76CDX)* – (first & third track) / ('A'mix by Reflections Eternal, Circa 1963 & QD 111) / Trigger hippie (live CD-Rom).

China not iss.

Aug 98. (c-s) *(WOKMC 2097)* **PART OF THE PROCESS / THE DYSLEXIC PORN STAR WHO FUNKED IN HER SPACE** [38] [-]
(12"+=/cd-s+=) *(WOK T/CD 2097)* – ('A'-The Americruiser Morfeedback mix).

Dec 98. (c-s/cd-s) *(WOK MC/CD 2102)* **SUMMERTIME / SUMMERTIME (C12 mix)** [ ] [-]

East West Sire

Jul 00. (cd/c/d-lp) *(8573 83602-2/-4)* *<31137>* **FRAGMENTS OF FREEDOM** [6] Aug00 [ ]
– The world looking in / Rome wasn't built in a day / Love is rare / Let it go / A well deserved break / Love sweet love (with MR. COMPLEX) / In the hands of the gods (with BIZ MARKIE) / Shallow end / Be yourself / Coming down gently / Good girl down (with BAHAMADIA) / Fragments of freedom. *(special cd+=; 8573 84027-2)* – EPK / Rome wasn't built in a day (video) / (mix your own Morcheeba song).

Jul 00. (c-s/cd-s) *(EW 214 C/CD1)* **ROME WASN'T BUILT IN A DAY / FRAGMENTS OF FREEDOM (frogmarched to freedom) / IN THE HANDS OF THE GODS (tumbleweed gunslinger mix)** [34] [-]
(cd-s+=) *(EW214CD2)* – In the hands of the gods (cheeky cheeba chainsaw mix).

Oct 00. (c-s/cd-s) *(EW 221 CCD1)* **BE YOURSELF / (bloodshy remix)** [ ] [-]
(cd-s) *(EW 221CD2)* – ('A'-bloodshy remix) / ('A'-electro folk mix) / Part of the process (live at Glastonbury 2000).

Mar 01. (c-s/cd-s) *(EW 225 C/CD1)* **THE WORLD LOOKING IN / LOVE SWEET LOVE** [48] [-]
(cd-s) *(EW 225CD2)* – ('A'-side) / ('A'-Bent remix).

Jun 02. (12"/cd-s) *(EW 247 T/CD)* **OTHERWISE (mixes; radio / sunship / un-cut + dub)** [64] [-]

Jul 02. (cd/d-lp) *(0927 45829-2/-1)* *<48347>* **CHARANGO** [7] [ ]
– Slow down / Otherwise / Aqualung / Sao Paulo / Charango / What New York couples fight about / Undress me now / Way beyond / Women lose weight / Get along / Public displays of affection / The great London traffic warden massacre. *(ltd-d-cd; 0927 46963-2)* – (instrumentals).

Oct 02. (cd-s) *(EW 255)* **WAY BEYOND / SAO PAULO (live) / I'D RATHER KILL US (THAN WATCH YOU LEAVE)** [ ] [-]

East West Reprise

Jun 03. (cd) *(5046 65870-2)* *<48510>* **PARTS OF THE PROCESS** (compilation) [6] Aug03 [ ]
– The sea / Tape loop / Otherwise / Blindfold / Be yourself / Part of the process / Let me see / Undress me now / What's your name (with BIG DADDY KANE) / Trigger hippie / Rome wasn't built in a day / Over and over / What NY couples fight about / The world looking in / Moog Island / Way beyond / Never an easy way / Can't stand it. *(<ltd-cd w/ dvd+=; 5046 65869-2>)*

– compilations, etc. –

Jul 01. (cd/t-lp) *D.M.C.; (BACK CD/LP 7) / Ultra; <1094>* **BACK TO MINE** (MORCHEEBA remixes) [ ] Aug01 [ ]

Alanis MORISSETTE

Born: 1 Jun'74, Ottawa, Ontario, Canada, to a French-Canadian father and Hungarian mother, both schoolteachers. She began writing songs at age ten and subsequently became a regular on the American cable show, 'You Can't Do That On Television'. Her debut, self-financed single 'FATE STAY WITH ME' (on 'Lamor'), was released around the same time and by the age of sixteen, the budding singer/songwriter had cut two disco/pop albums ('ALANIS' and 'NOW IS THE TIME'). MORISSETTE then left her native Canada for the lure of Los Angeles, subsequently hawking her demo unsuccessfully around almost every major record company. Salvation came in the form of MADONNA who recognised her talent, signing ALANIS to her own 'Maverick' label. 'JAGGED LITTLE PILL' (1995) was duly released to major critical acclaim, climbing to No.1 in America and scooping four Grammys and a Brit Award the following year. Confrontational and uncompromising as well as evocative and emotional, MORISSETTE's singing demanded attention, her pent-up adolescent angst finding an outlet in the likes of 'PERFECT' , 'YOU OUGHTA KNOW' and 'ONE HAND IN MY POCKET', the latter two both fairly successful UK singles. Musically, the album was largely straightahead guitar rock, solid, if not exactly hard-edged, with ALANIS playing guitar while backed up by BENMONT TENCH (organ, ex-TOM PETTY), LANCE MORRISON (bass) and MATT LAUG (drums). Touting a decidedly more earthy strain of 'girl power' than the SPICE GIRLS, it remains to be seen whether MORISSETTE can keep the momentum going and achieve a similar career trajectory as comtemporaries like SHERYL CROW. A taster single from her new album, 'THANK U' became her biggest hit to date, reaching the US Top 5. Yet with its convoluted title and meandering feel, the album in question, 'SUPPOSED FORMER INFATUATION JUNKIE' (1998), was never likely to spawn any further hits or create the sensation of her debut despite its pole position on the American chart. Even in the stripped down 'ALANIS UNPLUGGED' (1999), where MORISSETTE attempted to reintroduce the material in a more palatable form, these songs retained an inscrutable edge. By 2002's 'UNDER RUG SWEPT', the singer had parted company with her longtime writing partner Glen Ballard, resulting in a more cohesive and accessible yet still relatively impenetrable set of songs. Heralded by the 'HANDS CLEAN' single, the album was, musically at least, a fair attempt at revising her mid-90's heyday, with all the restless tension which fuelled that era hardly having dissipated in the interim. • **Songwriters:** Writes all music with GLEN BALLARD, who also plays guitar and keyboards. • **Trivia:** Guests on her debut included FLEA (Red Hot Chilis) and DAVE NAVARRO (ex-Jane's Addiction).

Album rating: JAGGED LITTLE PILL (*9) / SUPPOSED FORMER INFATUATION JUNKIE (*6) / MTV UNPLUGGED (*5) / UNDER RUG SWEPT (*6)

ALANIS MORISSETTE – vocals / with **BENMONT TENCH** organ (ex-TOM PETTY) / **LANCE MORRISON** -bass / **MATT LAUG** -drums

Maverick Maverick

Jun 95. (cd/c/lp) *<(9362-45901-2/-4/-1)>* **JAGGED LITTLE PILL** [1] [1]
– All I really want / You oughta know / Perfect / Hand in my pocket / Right through you / Forgiven / You learn / Head over feet / Mary Jane / Ironic / Not the doctor / Wake up. *(cd+=)* – Your house.

Jul 95. (c-s) *(W 0307C)* **YOU OUGHTA KNOW (clean version) / PERFECT (version)** [22] [–]
(cd-s+=) *(W 0307CD)* – ('A'-Jimmy The Saint blend) / Wake up.

Oct 95. (c-s) *(W 0312C)* **HAND IN MY POCKET / HEAD OVER FEET (live acoustic)** [26] [–]
(cd-s+=) *(W 0312 CD1)* – Not the doctor (live acoustic).
(cd-s) *(W 0312 CD2)* – ('A'side) / Right through you (live acoustic) / Forgiven (live acoustic).

Feb 96. (c-s) *(W 0334C)* **YOU LEARN / YOUR HOUSE (live)** [24] [–]
(cd-s+=) *(W 0334CD)* – Wake up (modern rock live) / Hand in my pocket (version).

Mar 96. (c-s) *<17698>* **IRONIC / FORGIVEN (live) / NOT THE DOCTOR (live)** [–] [4]

Apr 96. (c-s) *(W 0343C)* **IRONIC / YOU OUGHTA KNOW (live acoustic)** [11] [–]
(cd-s+=) *(W 0343CD)* – Mary Jane (live) / All I really want (live).

Jul 96. (c-s) *<17644>* **YOU LEARN / YOU OUGHTA KNOW (live)** [–] [6]

Jul 96. (c-s) *(W 0355C)* **HEAD OVER FEET / HAND IN MY POCKET (live)** [7] [–]
(cd-s+=) *(W 0355CD)* – You learn (live) / Right through you (live).

Nov 96. (c-s) *(W 0382C)* **ALL I REALLY WANT / IRONIC (live from Sydney)** [59] [–]
(cd-s+=) *(W 0382CD)* – Hand in my pocket (live from Brisbane).

—— now with **BENMONT** (again) + **NICK LASHLEY** + **JOEL SHEARER** – guitar / **CHRIS CHANEY** – bass / **GARY NOVAK** – drums

Oct 98. (c-s) *(W 0458C)* *<radio play>* **THANK U / UNINVITED (demo)** [5] [17]
(cd-s+=) *(W 0458CD)* – Pollyanna flower.

Nov 98. (cd/c/lp) *<(9362 47094-2/-4/-1)>* **SUPPOSED FORMER INFATUATION JUNKIE** [3] [1]
– Front row / Baba / Thank U / Are you still mad / Sympathetic character / That I would be good / The couch / Can't not / UR / I was hoping / One / Would not come / Unsent / So pure / Joining you / Heart of the house / Your congratulations.

Jan 99. (-) *<radio cut>* **UNSENT** [–] [58]

Mar 99. (c-s) *(W 472C)* **JOINING YOU / YOUR HOUSE (live)** [28] [–]
(cd-s+=) *(W 472CD2)* – London (live).
(cd-s+=) *(W 472CD1)* – These are the thoughts (live).

Jul 99. (c-s) *(W 492C)* **SO PURE / I WAS HOPING (acoustic modern rock live)** [38] [–]
(cd-s+=) *(W 492CD1)* – ('A'-Pure ecstasy mix).
(cd-s+=) *(W 492CD2)* – Would not come (live).

Nov 99. (cd/c) *<(9362 47589-2/-4)>* **MTV UNPLUGGED (live)** [59] [63]
– You learn / Joining you / No pressure over cappuccino / That I would be good / Head over feet / Princess familiar / I was hoping / Ironic / These R the thoughts / King of pain / You oughta know / Uninvited.

Dec 99. (c-s/cd-s) *(W 509 C/CD)* **THAT I WOULD BE GOOD (MTV unplugged live) / WOULD NOT COME (reverb live) / FORGIVE (reverb live) / I WAS HOPING (99X live)** [ ] [–]

Feb 02. (c-s) *(W 574C)* **HANDS CLEAN / UNPRODIGAL DAUGHTER** [12] [23]
(cd-s+=) *(W 574CD1)* *<42431>* – Symptoms.
(cd-s) *(W 574CD2)* – ('A'side) / Fear of bliss / Sister blister.

Mar 02. (cd/c) *<(9362 47988-2/-4)>* **UNDER RUG SWEPT** [2] Feb02 [1]
– 21 things I want in a lover / Narcissus / Hands clean / Flinch / So unsexy / Precious illusions / That particular time / A man / You owe me vnothing in return / Surrendering / Utopia.

Aug 02. (c-s) *(W 582C)* **PRECIOUS ILLUSIONS / HANDS CLEAN** [53] [–]
(cd-s+=) *(W 582CD1)* – Sorry 2 myself.
(cd-s) *(W 582CD2)* – ('A'side) / Offer / Bent 4 U.

MORPHINE

Formed: Boston, Massachusetts, USA ... 1990 out of TREAT HER RIGHT by MARK SANDMAN and DANA COLLEY, who subsequently added drummer JEROME DUPREE. Certainly not your average Boston indie band, MORPHINE employed a musical set-up that defied standard rock convention; while SANDMAN offered up subtle, often treated vocals and a pioneering two-string bass played like a bottleneck guitar, COLLEY contributed breathless baritone/tenor sax over DUPREE's spare, jazzy backbeat. The trio quickly made their mark with an independently released US-only debut album, 'GOOD' (1992), the record drawing across the board praise from America's alternative media network and resulting in a long term deal with 'Rykodisc'. The label subsequently gave it a new lease of life as well as releasing the set in Britain where MORPHINE were also fast rising cult stars. Although new drummer BILLY CONWAY was soon to replace DUPREE, the musical chemistry was even stronger than ever on 1993's follow-up, 'CURE FOR PAIN', another inspired set of avant blues/jazz. Two years on, MORPHINE had the critics intoxicated yet again with, 'YES' (1995) a more spontaneous album that swung between low-key introspection and upfront affirmation. One of the few alt-rock acts to be honoured with a 'DreamWorks' contract (US-only), SANDMAN and Co finally eased their way into chart territory (Top 75) via their fourth album, 'LIKE SWIMMING' (1997). Just as MORPHINE looked to be on the verge of something big, tragedy struck on the 3rd of July 1999, when frontman SANDMAN had a fatal heart attack while onstage in Italy. At the time of his death, the band had almost completed work on a fourth album, 'THE NIGHT', which SANDMAN had largely produced. Finally released in early 2000, the record was a fitting epitaph to the man, employing more varied but no less haunting instrumentation which served to magnify MORPHINE's patented sense of unease. Another, wholly different tribute to SANDMAN was released in 2000 in the shape of 'BOOTLEG DETROIT'. Slightly different to the usual official bootleg favoured by some bands, this was actually recorded by a member of the audience during a Detroit show on MORPHINE's 'Cure For Pain' tour. While the quality was never going to match a professional live release, the original tapes were mastered by SANDMAN before his death and give an intimate insight into what made this band tick.

Album rating: GOOD (*7) / CURE FOR PAIN (*6) / YES (*8) / LIKE SWIMMING (*8) / B-SIDES AND OTHERWISE compilation (*7) / THE NIGHT (*5) / BOOTLEG DETROIT posthumous (*5) / THE BEST OF MORPHINE compilation (*8)

MARK SANDMAN (b. 1952) – vocals, 2-string bass (ex-TREAT HER RIGHT) / **DANA COLLEY** – saxophones / **JEROME DUPREE** – drums

not iss. Accurate-Distortion

Jan 92. (cd/c) *<1001-2/-4>* **GOOD** [–] [ ]
– Good / Saddest song / Have a lucky day / You speak my language / You look like rain / Do not go quietly unto your grave / Lisa / Only one / Test tube baby / Shoot'm down / Other side / I know you (pts.1 & 2). *<(cd re-iss. Sep92=US/Jul93=UK & Apr97 on 'Rykodisc'; RCD 10263)>*

Rykodisc Rykodisc

— **BILLY CONWAY** – drums (ex-TREAT HER RIGHT) repl. JEROME

Jan 94. (cd/c) *<(RCD/RACS 10262)>* **CURE FOR PAIN** Sep93
– Dawna / Buena / I'm free now / All wrong / Candy / Head with wings / In spite of me / Thursday / Cure for pain / Mary, won't you call my name / Let's take a trip together / Sheila / Miles Davis' funeral. *<(cd re-iss. Apr97; same)>*

Jan 94. (cd-s) *<RCD 51033>* **CURE FOR PAIN / DOWN LOVE'S TRIBUTARIES / SHAME / MY BRAIN** –

Mar 94. (cd-ep) *<(RCD 51035)>* **BUENA / SHAME / MORPHINE PROFILE – INTERVIEW**

Mar 94. (7") *<(RA7 1036)>* **THURSDAY. / MARY WON'T YOU CALL MY NAME? (live)**
(cd-s+=) *<(RCD5 1036)>* – You look like rain.

Mar 95. (7") *<(RA7 1046)>* **SUPERSEX. / I KNOW YOU**
(cd-s+=) *<(RCD5 1046)>* – All wrong.

Apr 95. (cd/c/lp) *<(RCD/RAC/RALP 10320)>* **YES**
– Honey white / Scratch / Radar / Whisper / Yes / All your way / Supersex / I had my chance / Jury / Sharks / Free love / Gone for good. *<(cd re-iss. Apr97; same)>*

Jun 95. (7"clear) *<(RA7 1047)>* **HONEY WHITE. / BIRTHDAY CAKE**
(cd-s+=) *<(RCD5 1047)>* – Lucky day / Sunday afternoon weightlessness.

Rykodisc DreamWorks

Mar 97. (cd/c) *(RCD/RAC 10362) <50009>* **LIKE SWIMMING** 67
– Lilah / Potion / I know you (part 3) / Early to bed / Wishing well / Like swimming / Murder for my money / French lines with pepper / Empty box / Eleven o'clock / Hanging on a curtain / Swing it low.

May 97. (cd-s) *(RCD5 1057)* **MURDER FOR MY MONEY / KEROUAC** –

Jan 99. (cd-s) *<RCD 1131>* **ELEVEN O'CLOCK / KEROUAC / ELEVEN O'CLOCK / VIRGIN BRIDE / ANITA** –

— disbanded when SANDMAN died on the 3rd of July '99

Jan 00. (cd) *(RCD 10499) <450056>* **THE NIGHT** Feb00
– The night / So many ways / Souvenir / Top floor, bottom buzzer / Like a mirror / A good woman is hard to find / Rope on fire / I'm yours, you're mine / The way we met / Slow numbers / Take me with you.

– compilations, etc. –

on 'Rykodisc' unless mentioned otherwise

Sep 97. (cd) *<(RCD 10387)>* **B SIDES AND OTHERWISE**
– Have a lucky day (live) / All wrong (live) / I know you (live) / Bo's veranda / Mile high / Shame / Down love's tributaries / Kerouac / Pulled over the car / Sunday afternoon weightlessness / Virgin bride / Mail / My brain.

Sep 00. (cd) *<(RCD 10495)>* **BOOTLEG DETROIT (live 1993)**
– Intro / Come along / Dana intro / Mary / Banter #1 / Candy / Sheila / Billy intro / Claire / My brain / Banter #2 / Head with wings / Cure for pain / You speak my language / Thursday / Banter #3 / You look like rain / Buena.

Sep 01. (cd; as ORCHESTRA MORPHINE) *Accurate; (OM 1)*
LIVE ON TOUR (live) –
– The night / So many ways / Souvenir / Good woman / The way we met / Not like that / I know you (part 3) / Rope / Top floor / Cook / Take me with you.

Feb 03. (cd) *(RCD 10665) <RCD 10623>* **THE BEST OF MORPHINE**
– Buena / Honey white / You speak my language / Cure for pain / Candy / Have a lucky day / I'm free now / Thursday / Super sex / Whisper / Radar / You look like rain / Jack and Tina / Pretty face / Shame / Sexy Christmas baby mine / Shame (dub).

Ennio MORRICONE

Born: 11 Oct'28, Rome, Italy. A graduate of Rome's Conservatory Of Santa Cecilia, MORRICONE initially worked in radio before he began scoring films in the early 60's. Although he'd already worked with other directors on various Italian westerns, it would be his subsequent partnership with "Spaghetti Western" king, Sergio Leone, which would both revolutionise the concept of the film soundtrack and transform him into a cult figure. While Leone's unshaven, existential gunslingers aimed point blank at the heart of the great Western myth, MORRICONE conjured up the striking soundtracks to their invariably short lives and the unforgiving, sun-parched terrain they roamed in. Masterfully arranging seemingly incongruous instrumentation into a dazzling, seamless whole, MORRICONE employed everything from rattlesnake castanets and heartbreaking mariachi horns to thundering church organ, ghostly harmonica, jews harp and grunting native indian-style chants. Add to this his basic recipe of sweeping orchestration and echo-soaked, DUANE EDDY-style guitar twang and you had a musical vista unparalleled in the history of film. What's more, the likes of 'A FISTFUL OF DOLLARS', 'FOR A FEW DOLLARS MORE' and the sublime 'ONCE UPON A TIME IN THE WEST' don't even need the visual accompaniment. As contemporary sounding today as they undoubtedly were back then, these records have such hauntingly potent imagery locked in their collective grooves you need only don a set of headphones and close your eyes. This fertile period also produced the theme MORRICONE is most readily identified with even today, 'THE GOOD, THE BAD AND THE UGLY' (1968). Originally released as 'IL BUONO, IL BRUTTO, IL CATTIVO' in 1966, the theme was subsequently covered by HUGO MONTENEGRO who took it to the top of the UK chart (US No.2) and was duly inspired to record a whole album's worth of classic MORRICONE material. The Italian's incredibly prolific output (even the man himself doesn't know how many films he's worked on though it's rumoured to be in excess of 500!) continued throughout the 70's as he moved away from Westerns and worked with the cream of the world's directors. In 1972, he composed the theme to a film version of Mikhail Bulgakov's brilliant satirical novel, 'The Master And Margarita' (by Yugoslav director, Aleksander Petrovic) while 1977 saw him scoring 'Exorcist' follow-up, 'THE HERETIC'. Yet serious mainstream recognition didn't arrive until 1981 when the BBC dug up an obscure single from three years previous, 'CHI MAI'. Used as the theme tune to their 'Life & Times Of David Lloyd George' period drama, the track was a surprise No.2 UK hit. Starring Robert De Niro in a lead role, 'ONCE UPON A TIME IN AMERICA' (1984) was another massive soundtrack success for MORRICONE, while he subsequently went on to win an Oscar for 'THE MISSION' (1986) which utilised Native Indian melodies to haunting effect. In addition to these high profile projects, he spent the 80's and 90's working on all manner of obscure and not so obscure films, many of them in his native Italy. A seismic influence on modern music, the spectre of MORRICONE can be heard in the work of artists as diverse as NICK CAVE, GALLON DRUNK, MORPHINE, PORTISHEAD, TINDERSTICKS and JOHN ZORN. For committed fans and new initiates alike, the problem is that the bulk of the man's work is out of print, although a large chunk of previously unavailable Italian-only material hit the shops in the late 80's & early 90's. While 'B.M.G.' have recently repackaged his classic trio of 60's Spaghetti Westerns on one double-CD set, there are rumours of a boxed set in progress from the same people so watch this space.

Album rating (selective): A FISTFUL OF DOLLARS (*8) / FOR A FEW DOLLARS MORE (*7) / THE GOOD, THE BAD AND THE UGLY (*8) / ONCE UPON A TIME IN THE WEST (*9) / BURN (*7) / EXORCIST II: THE HERETIC (*6) / ONCE UPON A TIME IN AMERICA (*6) / THE MISSION (*8) / THE UNTOUCHABLES (*6) / RAMPAGE (*6) / CASUALTIES OF WAR (*7) / CINEMA PARADISO (*6) / DISCLOSURE (*5) / WOLF (*7) / FILM MUSIC BY ENNIO MORRICONE compilation (*7)

ENNIO MORRICONE – composer / credited with ORCHESTRA

RCA Victor RCA Victor

Jun 67. (lp; mono/stereo) *(RD/SF 7875) <1135>* **A FISTFUL OF DOLLARS** (soundtrack)
– Titoli / Almost dead / Square dance / The chase / The result / Without pity / Theme from a fistful of dollars / "A Fistful Of Dollars" suite. *<cd-iss. 1998 on 'Razor & Tie'; 82171>*

1967. (7") *(RCA 1596)* **A FISTFUL OF DOLLARS. / THE MAN WITH NO NAME**

1967. (lp) **FOR A FEW DOLLARS MORE** (soundtrack) – Italian –
– La resa dei conti / Osservatori osservati / Il vizio di uccidere / Il colpo / Addio colonnello / Per qualche dollaro in piu / Poker d'assi / Carillion. *(UK-iss.1970 w/ 'A FISTFUL OF DOLLARS' on 'RCA Camden'; CDS 1052) (c-iss.May74; CAM 411)*

1967. (7") *(RCA 1634)* **FOR A FEW DOLLARS MORE. / LA RESA DEI CONTI**

U.A. U.A.

Oct 68. (lp; stereo/mono) *(S+/ULP 1197)* *<5172>* **THE GOOD, THE BAD AND THE UGLY** (soundtrack) Feb68 4
– The good, the bad and the ugly – main title (Il buono, il brutto, il cattivo)/ The sundown (Il tramonto) / The strong (Il forte) / The desert (Il deserto) / The carriage of the spirits (La carrozza dei fantasmi) / Marcia (Marcetta) / The story of a soldier (La storia de un soldato) / Marcia without hope (Marcetta senza speranza) / The death of a soldier (Morte de un soldato) / The ecstasy of gold (L'estasi dell'oro) / The trio – main title (Il triello). *(re-iss. May85 on 'E.G.' lp/c; EG 260582-1/-4) (<cd-iss. Sep88 on 'EMI Manhattan'; CDP7 48408-2>) (cd re-iss. Jul93 on 'Silva Screen'; 46408-2)*

— New York-born composer HUGO MONTENEGRO also went US Top 10 with a collection of the above three soundtracks – the man also took the title track to No.2 (Feb'68) & No.1 (Sep'68) in the US & UK respectively. Around the same time, HUGO also scored with another Clint Eastwood-starring movie, 'Hang 'Em High'.

1969. (7") *(UP 35004)* **PROFESSIONAL GUN. / PACO**

R.C.A. not iss.

1969. (lp) **ONCE UPON A TIME IN THE WEST** (soundtrack) – Italian –
– Once upon a time in the west / As a judgement / Farewell to Cheyenne / The transgression / The first tavern / The second tavern / Once upon a time in the west (reprise) / Man with a harmonica / A dimly lit room / Bad orchestra / The man / Jill's America / Death rattle / Finale. *(UK-iss.Jul78 lp/c; PL/PK 31387) (re-iss. Oct83 lp/c; NL/NK 70032) (cd – iss.Jun88; ND 71704) (cd re-iss. Feb90 on 'Silva Screen'; 4736.2)*

1969. (7") *(RCA 1892)* **ONCE UPON A TIME IN THE WEST. / FINALE**
(re-iss. Oct79; PB 6197)

Stateside not iss.

1970. (lp) *(SSL 10307)* **THE SICILIAN CLAN** (soundtrack) –

C.B.S. Columbia

1970. (lp) *(70067)* **LOVE CIRCLE**

not iss. U.A.

1970. (lp) *<LA 303>* **BURN** (soundtrack) –
– Abolicao / Jose Dolores / Queimada seconda / Preparazione / Verso il futuro / Jose' E Dolores / Osanna / Queimada prima / Studi per un finale / Titoli di testa / L'estasi Dell'oro / Il Triello / Titoli / Titoli / Titoli di testa / Resa / Titoli finiali. *<cd-iss. Nov96 as 'QUEIMADA (BURN)' on 'Varese Sarabande'; VCDS 7020>*

R.C.A. not iss.

Jan 72. (lp; with JOAN BAEZ) *(SF 8211)* **SACCO AND VANZETTI** –
– Hope for freedom / The ballad of Sacco and Vanzetti (introduction – part 1) / In prison / The ballad of Sacco and Vanzetti (part 2) / Sacco and his son / The ballad of Sacco and Vanzetti (part 3) / Freedom from hope / Sentenced to death / Electric chair / Here's to you. *(re-iss. Jan89 on 'Silva Screen'; NL 70231) <US cd-iss. 1990's on 'Omega'; OCD 3015>*

Paramount Paramount

1972. (lp) *(SPFL 275)* **THE RED TENT**
– Love theme / Do dreams go on / Death at the pole / Love like the snow / Message from Rome / They're alive / Farewell / Others, who will follow us. *(re-iss. Jan89 on 'Silva Screen'; 255064-1) (cd-iss. Aug94 on 'Legend'; LEGENDCD 15)*

Mar 72. (7") *(PARA 3018)* **RED TENT – LOVE THEME. / DO DREAMS GO ON** –

R.C.A. R.C.A.

1976. (lp/c) *(NL/NK 43738)* **1900** (soundtrack)

Pye Pye

Feb 77. (lp) *(NSPH 28503)* **MOSES** (original soundtrack) 43 –

not iss. Warners

Jun 77. (lp) *<3068>* **EXORCIST II: THE HERETIC** (soundtrack) –
– Regan's theme / Pazuzu / Interrupted melody / Rite of magic / Little Afro – Flemish mass / Great bird of the sky / Magic and ecstasy / Seduction and magic / Regan's theme / Dark revelation / Night flight / Interrupted melody / Exorcism.

Private Stock Private Stock

Mar 78. (7") *(PVT 148)* **CHI MAI. / COME MADDALENA**
(re-iss. Apr81 as BBC theme from the TV series 'The Life And Times Of David Lloyd George'; RESL 92) – hit No.2

Pye not iss.

Jun 78. (7") *(7N 46092)* **WORLD CUP ARGENTINA. / WORLD CUP MARCH '78** –

M.C.A. M.C.A.

Sep 82. (lp) *(MCF 3148)* **THE THING** (soundtrack)
– Humanity (part 1) / Shape / Contamination / Bestiality / Solitude / Eternity / Wait / Humanity (part 2) / Sterilization / Despair. *(re-iss. Oct85; MCA 6111) (cd/c-iss.Aug91 on 'Varese Sarabande'; VDS/VCS 5278)*

Red Bus not iss.

Mar 84. (7") *(RBUS 88)* **SAHARA. / (instrumental)** –

Mercury Mercury

Nov 84. (lp)(c)(cd) *(MERH 45)(PRIMC 121)(<822334-2>)* **ONCE UPON A TIME IN AMERICA** (soundtrack)
– Once upon a time in America / Poverty / Deborah's theme / Childhood memories / Amapola / Friends / Prohibition dirge / Cockeye's song / Amapola – part 2 / Childhood poverty / Photographic memories / Friends / Friendship and love / Speakeasy / Deborah's theme – Amapola. *<cd re-iss. Oct95 on 'Musicrama'; 4003>*

Virgin not iss.

Oct 86. (lp/c/cd; with the London Philharmonic Orchestra) *(V/TCV/CDV 2402)* *<90567>* **THE MISSION** (soundtrack) 73 Feb87
– On earth as it is in Heaven / Falls / Gabriel's oboe / Ava Maria Guarani / Brothers / Carlotta / Vita nostra / Climb / Remorse / Penance / The mission / River / Gabriel's oboe / Te deum guarani / Refusal / Asuncion / Alone / Guarani / The sword / Miserere.

Oct 86. (7") *(VS 909)* **ON EARTH AS IT IS IN HEAVEN. / (part 2)** –
(12"+=) *(VS 909-12)* – Gabriel's oboe.

A&M A&M

Oct 87. (lp/c/cd) *(<39 3909-1/-4/-2>)* **THE UNTOUCHABLES** (soundtrack)
– The untouchables / Al Capone / Waiting at the border / Death theme / On the rooftops / Victorious / The man with the matches / The strength of the righteous / Ness and his family / False alarm / The untouchables / Four friends / Machine gun lullaby.

Elektra Elektra

May 88. (lp/c/cd) *(<K9 60782-1/-4/-2>)* **FRANTIC** (soundtrack)
– I'm gonna lose you (by SIMPLY RED) / Frantic / On the roofs of Paris / One flugel horn / Six short interludes / Nocturne for Michel / In the garage / Paris project / Sadly nostalgic. *(cd re-iss. Oct93 on 'WEA'; 7559 60782-2)*

Virgin Fastlane

Jun 88. (lp/c/cd) *(V/TCV/CDV 2491)* *<42685>* **RAMPAGE** (soundtrack)
– Rampage / Son / Findings / Over to the jury / Run, run, run / Since childhood / Magma / Gruesome discovery / Carillion / District attorney / Mother / Recollections.

Dec 88. (lp/c/cd) *(V/TCV/CDV 2539)* **A TIME OF DESTINY** (soundtrack)
(re-iss. Jan89 on 'Silva Screen' lp/c/cd; 790938-1/-4/-2)

R.C.A. not iss.

Jan 89. (cd) *(BL/BK/BD 71559)* **SECRET OF THE SAHARA** (1987 soundtrack) –
– Secret of the Sahara / Red ghosts / Sholomon / Mountain / Kerim / Hawk / Golden door / Myth and the adventure / Anthea and the desert / Farewell Orso / Death od Tamameth / Saharan dram / Miriam and Philip / Second dedication / First dedication. *(<cd re-iss. Jun96; 74321 34226-2>)*

Virgin not iss.

Sep 89. (lp/c/cd) *(V/TCV/CDV 2602)* **THE ENDLESS GAMES** (soundtrack) –
– The endless games / Alec's journey / The game goes on / Summer solitude / Caroline's song / From Russia / The love game / Anif / Silvia's game / Just a game / Chess game.

C.B.S. Columbia

Jan 90. (cd/c/cd) *(466016-2/-4/-1)* *<CK/SCT 45359>* **CASUALTIES OF WAR** (1989 soundtrack) Feb90

S.B.L. not iss.

Jun 90. (cd/c) *(CDSBL/SBLC 12598)* **NUOVO CINEMA PARADISO** (1988 soundtrack)
(re-iss. Jul93 on 'D.R.G.' cd/c; DRG CD/MC 12598)

Virgin Virgin

Jun 91. (cd/c/lp) *(CD/TC+/VMM 3)* **HAMLET** (1990 soundtrack)

– Hamlet (version 1) / The king is dead / Ophelia (version 1) / What a piece of work is man / The prayer / The ghost / The play / The banquet / Dance for the queen / Ophelia (version 2) / Hamlet's madness / Hamlet (version 2) / Simulated madness / The closet / Second madness / To be or not to be / Solid flesh / The vaults. *(cd re-iss. Jan94 on 'Silva Screen'; 91600-2)*

M.C.A. M.C.A.

Jul 91. (cd/c) *(MCA D/C 10019)* **STATE OF GRACE** (1990 soundtrack)

Varese Sarabande not iss.

Dec 91. (cd/c) *(VSD/VSC 5326)* **CROSSING THE LINE** ('THE BIG MAN' soundtrack)
– Running in the park / Main titles / Beth says "no" / Road training 1 / Road training 3 / Rain in Gobi Desert / Journey to fight / Round four / Road training 2 / The wasteland / Round one / Round two / Round six / "There's blood on that money" / Danny runs home / End titles.

Epic Epic

Mar 92. (cd/c) *(469371-2/-4)* **BUGSY** (1991 soundtrack)

Nov 92. (cd) *(ACCD 1025)* *<EK 52750>* **CITY OF JOY** (soundtrack) Apr92
– City of joy / Family of the poor / One night, by chance / Crack down / Hope / In the labyrinth / Family of the poor / Surgeon in despair / One night, by chance / For a daughter's dowry / Godfather of the bustee / Monsoon / Calcutta / Bustee day / Birth / The worm turns / Labyrinth / To Calcutta / Family of the poor / To Roland.

Sep 93. (cd/c) *(474285-2/-4)* **IN THE LINE OF FIRE** (soundtrack)

Columbia Sony

Aug 94. (cd/c) *(476601-2/-4)* *<64231-2/-4>* **WOLF** (soundtrack)
– Wolf and love / Barn / Dream and the deer / Moon / Laura goes to join Wolf / Laura and Wolf united / First transition / Howl and the city / Animals and encounters / Laura transformed / Wolf / Second transition / Will's final goodbye / Chase / Confirmed doubts / Talisman / Third transition / Shock for Laura / Laura and Will / Laura.

Virgin Virgin

Feb 95. (cd) *(CDVMM 16)* *<40162>* **DISCLOSURE** (soundtrack) Jan95
– Serene family / Unusual approach / With energy and decision / Virtual reality / Preparation and victory / Disclosure / Sad family / Unemployed / Sex and computers / Computers and work / Sex and power / First passacaglia / Second passacaglia / Third passacaglia / Sex, power and computers.

B.M.G. Milan

Jul 98. (cd) *(<35840>)* **LOLITA** (soundtrack with also V/A)
– Lolita / Love in the morning / Take me to bed / Lolita on Humbert's lap / Lolita in my arms / Requiescant / Quilty / What about me? / Togetherness / She had nowhere else to go / Humbert's diary / Humbert on the hillside / Ladies and gentlemen of the jury / Lolita (finale).

RCA Victor RCA Victor

Nov 98. (cd) *(<09026 63253-2>)* **BULWORTH** (soundtrack) Jun98
– Suite one: Bulworth (part 1) / Suite two: Bulworth (part 2).

– belated soundtracks, etc. –

Jan 89. (lp) *Silva Screen; (SP 8013)* **MENAGE ALL'ITALIANA** (1965)
Jan 89. (lp) *Silva Screen; (SP 8016)* **EL GRECO** (1966 soundtrack)
Jan 89. (lp) *Silva Screen; (SP 8018)* **SVEGLIATI E UCCIDI** (1966; 'Hawks And Sparrows')
Jan 89. (lp) *Silva Screen; (SP 8020)* **COME IMPARAI AD AMARE LE DONNE** (1966)
Jan 89. (lp) *Silva Screen; (SP 8021)* **AD OGNI COSTO** (1967; 'Grand Slam')
Jan 89. (lp) *Silva Screen; (SP 8022)* **L'AVVENTURA** (1959; 'The Rover')
Jan 89. (lp) *Interior Music; (IM 004)* **FACCIA A FACCIA** (1967; 'Face To Face')
Jan 89. (lp/c) *M.C.A.; (MCA/+C 25103)* **GUNS FOR SAN SEBASTIAN** (1968)
Jan 89. (lp) *Cerebus; (CBUS 101)* **MY NAME IS NOBODY**
Jan 89. (lp) *Cerebus; (CBUS 102)* **LA CAGE AUX FOLLES** (1978 soundtrack)
Jan 89. (lp) *Cerebus; (CBUS 103)* **THE CHOSEN / HOLOCAUST 2000** (1978)
Jan 89. (lp) *Cerebus; (CBUS 106)* **TEPEPA** (1969)
Jan 89. (lp) *Cerebus; (CBUS 108)* **THE BIRD WITH THE CRYSTAL PLUMAGE** (soundtrack)
Jan 89. (lp) *Cerebus; (CBUS 111)* **SONNY AND JED / THE CANNIBALS**
Jan 89. (lp) *Cerebus; (CBUS 112)* **L'ASSOLUTO NATURALE** (1969)
Jan 89. (lp) *Cerebus; (CBUS 115)* **IL PRATO / LITTLE NUNS**
Jan 89. (lp) *Silva Screen; (803036)* **INVESTIGATION OF A CITIZEN ABOVE SUSPICION**
(re-iss. Jan93 on 'Cinevox'; CDCIA 5086)
Jan 89. (lp) *Varese Sarabande; (STV 81131)* **BLOODLINE** (1979)
Jan 89. (lp) *Varese Sarabande; (STV 81147)* **THE ISLAND** (1980)
Jan 89. (lp) *Silva Screen; (803026)* **LE PROFESSIONNEL** (1981 soundtrack)
Jan 89. (lp) *Cerebus; (CBUS 118)* **WHEN MAN IS THE PREY** (soundtrack)
Jan 89. (lp) *Cerebus; (CBUS 119)* **A TIME TO DIE** (1983 soundtrack)
Jan 89. (lp) *Cerebus; (CBUS 120)* **THE SCARLET AND THE BLACK** (1983 soundtrack)
Jan 89. (lp) *Varese Sarabande; (STV 81211)* **SAHARA** (1983 soundtrack)
(cd re-iss. Mar93 on 'Intrada'; MAF 7074D)
Jan 89. (lp/c) *Varese Sarabande; (STV/CTV 81248)* **RED SONJA** (1985 soundtrack)
Jan 92. (cd) *Alhambra; (A 8916)* **OCCHIO ALLA PENNA** (1981)
Feb 92. (cd) *Alhambra; (A 8919)* **REVOLVER** (1973)
Feb 92. (cd) *Alhambra; (A 8922)* **MACHINE GUN McCAIN**
Feb 92. (cd) *Alhambra; (A 8924)* **WITHOUT APPARENT MOTIVE**
Feb 92. (cd) *Alhambra; (A 8928)* **LA CALIFFA** (1970)
<US-iss.Feb99 on import w/extra tracks; 7305>
Mar 92. (cd) *Prometheus; (<PCD 115>)* **COSI' COME SEI** (1978; 'Stay As You Are') Jul95
Mar 92. (cd) *Prometheus; (<PCD 116>)* **LA DAME AUX CAMELIAS** (soundtrack; 'Lady Of The Camelias') Jul95
Apr 92. (cd) *Prometheus; (<PCD 119>)* **LA DONNA DELLA DOMENCIA / LA MOGLIE PIU BELLA** (?; 'Sunday Woman' & ? '?') Jul95
Jul 92. (cd) *Milano Dischi; (OST 122)* **LA CLASSE OPERAIA VA IN PARADISO**
Jan 93. (cd) *Milano Dischi; (OST 101)* **THE ACHILLE LAURO AFFAIR** (soundtrack; 'Voyage Of Terror')
Jan 93. (cd) *Milano Dischi; (OST 109)* **SHIPHUNTERS** (soundtrack)
Jan 93. (d-cd) *Milano Dischi; (OST 113)* **MOSES THE LAWGIVER**
Jan 93. (cd) *Prometheus; (PCD 107)* **HUNDRA** (1982)
Jan 93. (cd) *Prometheus; (<PCD 108>)* **BUTTERFLY** (1981) Jul95
Jul 93. (cd) *Legend; (LEGENDCD 10)* **ORCA – KILLER WHALE** (1977)
Nov 93. (cd) *Cam; (COS 1)* **STANNO TUTTI BENE** (1990; 'Everybody's Fine') Italian
Nov 93. (cd) *Cam; (COS 3)* **MIO CARO DOTTOR GRASLER** (1990; 'Dear Dr. Grasler') Italian
Nov 93. (cd; w/ GIUSEPPE TORNATORE & TULLIO) *Cam; (COS 6)* **LA DOMINICA SPECIALMENTE** (1991) Italian
Nov 93. (cd) *Cam; (CSE 48)* **SUN SPOTS / EAT IT** (1969) / MACCHIE SOLARI)
Nov 93. (cd) *Cam; (CSE 50)* **PROFESSIONE FIGLIO** (1980; 'Venetian Lies') Italian
Nov 93. (cd) *Cam; (CSE 51)* **GRAZIE ZIA** (1968; 'Thank You Aunt') Italian
Nov 93. (cd) *Cam; (CSE 52)* **COMANDAMENTI PER GANGST** (soundtrack; 'Commandment For Gangster') Italian
Nov 93. (cd) *Cam; (CSE 53)* **ESCALATION** (1968) Italian
Nov 93. (cd) *Cam; (CSE 55)* **I CANNIBALI** (1969; 'Cannibals' Italian
Nov 93. (cd) *Cam; (CSE 57)* **INCONTRO** (soundtrack; 'Meeting') Italian
Nov 93. (cd) *Cam; (CSE 58)* **MANI SPORACE** (soundtrack' 'Dirty Hands') Italian
Nov 93. (cd) *Cam; (CSE 59)* **LEREDITA FERRAMONTI** (soundtrack; 'Inheritance') Italian

Nov 93. (cd) *Cam; (CSE 66)* **SAI COSA FACEVA STALIN ALLE DONNE** (soundtrack; 'Stalin's Women') [–] Italian [–]
Nov 93. (cd) *Cam; (CSE 99)* **IL BANDITO DAGLI OCCHI AZZURRI** (1980; 'The Blue Eyed Bandit') [–] Italian [–]
Nov 93. (cd) *Cam; (CSE 101)* **QUANDSO LAMORE E SENSUALITA** (soundtrack; 'When Love Is Lust') [–] Italian [–]
1994. (cd) *Chameleon; (2259)* **L'EREDITA'FERRAMONTI / LIBERA AMORE MIO** (1976 & 1975) [–] Italian [–]
1994. (cd) *Chameleon; (2263)* **L'IMMORALITA'** (1978) [–] Italian [–]
1994. (cd) *Chameleon; (2265)* **IL PRATO** (1979; 'The Meadow') [–] Italian [–]
1994. (cd) *Chameleon; (7060)* **UNA VITA VENDUTA** (1976) [–] Italian [–]
1994. (cd) *P.N.T.; <101>* **IL GATTO A NOVE CODE** (1971) [–] [–]
Aug 94. (cd) *Tristar; (80952)* **LA SCORTA** (1993) [–] Italian [–]
1994. (cd) *Cam; (COS 14)* **IL LUNGO SILENZIO** (1993; 'The Long Silence') [–] Italian [–]
1994. (cd) *Cam; (COS 15)* **JONA CHE VISSE NELLA BALENA** (1993; 'Jonah And The Whale') [–] Italian [–]
Jan 95. (cd) *Preamble; (PRCD 107)* **PIAZZA DI SPAGNA** (1991) [ ] [–]
Apr 96. (cd) *Silva Screen; (HW 620562)* **THE STARMAKER** [ ] [–]
Apr 96. (cd) *Varese Sarabande; (VCDS 7018)* **IL MERCENARIO** (1968) [ ] [–]
Apr 96. (cd) *Preamble; (PRCD 116)* **LA DONNA INVISIBLE** (1969) [ ] [–]
1996. (cd) *D.R.G.; <DRGCD 32916>* **DRAMMI GOTICI** (GOTHIC DRAMAS [–] [ ]
1997. (cd) *Intermezzo Media; <136>* **PRIMA DELLA RIVOLUZIONE** [–] [ ]
Jul 98. (cd) *Intermezzo Media; <309>* **IL DESERTO DEI TARTARI** (1976; 'Desert Of The Tartars') [–] [ ]
Nov 98. (cd) *Intermezzo Media; <314>* **IMPUTAZIONE DI OMICIDIO PER UNO STUDENTE** ('Murder Charge For A Student') [–] [ ]
Mar 99. (cd) *Intermezzo Media; <312>* **VITE STROZZATE** (1996) [–] [ ]
1999. (cd) *B.M.G.; <9392>* **AD OGNI COSTO** [–] [ ]
Sep 99. (cd) *D.R.G.; <DRG 12620>* **PHANTOM OF THE OPERA** (1998; 'Il Fantasma Dell'opera') [–] [ ]
Sep 99. (cd) *D.R.G.; <DRG 12621>* **THE STENDHAL SYNDROME** (1996; 'La Sindrome Di Stendhal') [–] [ ]
Sep 99. (cd) *D.R.G.; <DRG 12622>* **THE FOURTH KING** (1997; 'Il Quarto Re') [–] [ ]
Dec 99. (cd) *Intermezzo Media; <319>* **IL GIORNO PRIMA** ('Control') [–] [ ]

– compilations, etc. –

Sep 71. (lp) *Sunset; (SLS 50248)* **WESTERN THEMES – ITALIAN STYLE** [ ] [–]
– (cuts from the soundtracks of 'THE GOOD, THE BAD AND THE UGLY', 'DEATH RIDES A HORSE', 'NAVAJO JOE' & 'THE BIG GUNDOWN')
Nov 80. (lp/c) *RCA Int.; (INT S/K 5059)* **FILM HITS** [ ] [–]
– Once upon a time in the west / For a few dollars more / Moses theme (main title) / Bye bye colonel / A fistful of dollars / A gun for Ringo / The ballad of Sacco and Vanzetti / Here's to you / The vice of killing / Paying off scores / The adventurer / What have you done to Solange / Violent city / Mertello. *(re-iss. Sep84 lp/c; NL/NK 70091)*
Apr 81. (lp) *E.M.I.; (THIS 33)* **THIS IS ENNIO MORRICONE** [23] [–]
Apr 81. (lp/c) *B.B.C.; (REH/ZCR 414)* **CHI MAI** [29] [–]
– Chi Mai / Lontano / A fistful of dynamite / Poem of a woman / The secret / Come Maddalena / Once upon a time in the west / Good luck Jack / Here's to you / My name is nobody.
Jun 81. (7") *B.B.C.; (RESL 93)* **ONCE UPON A TIME IN THE WEST. / THE SECRET** [ ] [–]
May 84. (7") *Old Gold; (OG 9413)* **CHI MAI. / Who Pays The Ferryman (by Yannis Markopoulos)** [ ] [–]
Jul 84. (lp) *R.C.A,; (CL 31559)* **MASTERPIECES** [ ] [–]
Oct 84. (lp) *R.C.A.; (PD 70324)* **BEST OF ENNIO MORRICONE** [ ] [–]
– For a few dollars more / A fistful of dynamite / My name is nobody / A fistful of dollars / Sacco and Vanzetti / Moses theme / Metello / God with us / Once upon a time in the west / 1900 / Death rides a horse / Life's tough, isn't it? / Ciribiribin / Scetate.
Jan 88. (d-cd/d-c/d-lp) *Virgin; (CD/TC+/VD 2516)* **FILM MUSIC BY ENNIO MORRICONE** [ ] [–]
– The good, the bad and the ugly / The Sicilian clan / Chi Mai / The man with the harmonica / La Califfa / Gabriel's oboe / A fistful of dynamite / Once upon a time in the west (main theme) / Cockey's song / The mission (remix) / Come Maddelena / Falls / My name os nobody / Le vent, le cri / Deborah's theme. *(re-iss. Sep93 on 'Virgin-VIP' cd/c; CD/TC VIP 123)*
Aug 88. (lp/c/cd) *Venture; (VE/TCVE/CDVE 24)* **CHAMBER MUSIC** [ ] [ ]
– Sestetto / Musica per 11 violini / 3 studi / Ricercare per pianoforte / 4 pezzi per chitarra / Suoni per dino / Distanze.
Jan 89. (cd) *Silva Screen; (T 8710)* **LIVE IN CONCERT (live)** [ ] [–]
Jan 89. (lp) *Silva Screen; (I-MGM 009)* **MUSIC FROM THREE SERGIO CORBUCCI WESTERNS** [ ] [–]
– ('Hellbenders', 'Companeros' & 'C'Entriamo Noi Con La Revolutione')
Jan 90. (cd) *R.C.A.; (039126)* **FOR A FEW DOLLARS MORE / A FISTFUL OF DOLLARS** [ ] [ ]
Jan 92. (cd) *R.C.A.; (ND 74021)* **THE GOOD, THE BAD AND THE UGLY / A FISTFUL OF DOLLARS / FOR A FEW DOLLARS MORE** [ ] [–]
Mar 92. (cd) *Milano Dischi; (OST 111)* **EL GRECO / GIORDANO BRUNO** [ ] [–]
Sep 92. (cd/c) *Music Club; (MCCD/MCTC 056)* **THE VERY BEST OF ENNIO MORRICONE** [ ] [–]
Jan 93. (cd/c) *Edel; (EDL 2549-2/-4)* **OCTOPUS / ALLE ORIGINI DELLA MAFIA** (? & 1976; 'All About The Mafia') [ ] [–]
Jan 93. (cd) *Milano Dischi; (OST 103)* **ALLONSANFAN / METELLO** (1974 & 1970) [ ] [–]
Jan 93. (cd) *Milano Dischi; (OST 107)* **DEATH RIDES A HORSE / A PISTOL FOR RINGO** [ ] [–]
Jan 93. (cd) *Milano Dischi; (OST 118)* **L'UMANOIDE / NIGHTMARE CASTLE** (1979; 'The Humanoid' & ?) [ ] [–]
Jan 93. (cd) *Milano Dischi; (OST 120)* **L'AVVENTURA / OCEANO** (1959 & 1971) [ ] [–]
Jan 93. (cd/c) *Cinevox; (AK/AT 47705)* **GUNS FOR SAN SEBASTIAN / HANG 'EM HIGH** (1970 & 1968) [ ] [–]
Jan 93. (cd) *Cinevox; (CDCIA 5087)* **FATTI DI GENTE PERBENE / DIVINA CREATURA** (1974; 'The Bird With The Crystal Plume' & 1975 'Divine Creature') [ ] [–]
Aug 93. (c) *Epic; (473802-4)* **HIS GREATEST THEMES: MOVIE SOUND** [ ] [ ]
(cd-iss. Nov95 on 'Accord'; 76>
Nov 93. (cd) *P.M.F.; (90.696-2)* **ENNIO MORRICONE** [ ] [–]
Jul 94. (cd) *Silva Screen; (CDCR 17)* **SEPOLTA VIVA / THE ANTICHRIST**
Jan 95. (cd) *Preamble; (PRCD 106)* **D'AMORE SI MUORE / LE DUE STAGIONI DELLA VITA** [ ] [–]
May 95. (cd) *R.C.A.; (<74321 26495-2>)* **SPAGHETTI WESTERN** [ ] [ ]
– (from the films 'A Gun For Ringo', 'At Times Life Is Very Hard, Isn't That Fate?', 'Guns For The McGregor's', 'Gunfight And Red Sands', 'Bullets Don't Argue', 'Seven Women For The McGregor's', 'Death Rides A Horse', 'We'll Be Back, Isn't That Fate' and 'The Return Of Ringo').
May 95. (cd) *Silva Screen; (MASKMK 701)* **FACCIA A FACCIA ('Face To Face') / LA RESA DEI CONTI ('The Big Gundown')** [ ] [–]
May 95. (cd) *Milano Dischi; (OST 127)* **CITTA VIOLENTA / SVEGLIATI E UCCIDI** [ ] [–]
Jul 95. (d-cd) *D.R.G.; (<DRGCD 32907>)* **AN ENNIO MORRICONE WESTERN QUINTET** [ ] [ ]
– ('A Fistful Of Dynamite', 'My Name Is Nobody', 'A Fist Goes West', 'Blood And Guns' and 'Campaneros')
Sep 95. (d-cd) *D.R.G.; (DRGCD 32908)* **AN ENNIO MORRICONE ANTHOLOGY** (film scores) [ ] [–]
Sep 95. (cd) *D.R.G.; (DRGCD 32911)* **AN ENNIO MOORICONE DARLO ARGENTO** [ ] [–]
– (THE BIRD WITH THE CRYSTAL PLUMAGE / FOUR FLIES ON GREY VELVET / CAT O'NINE TAILS).
Sep 95. (cd) *R.C.A,; <98732>* **ACTION THRILLERS** [–] [ ]
Oct 95. (cd) *D.R.G.; (DRGCD 32913)* **WITH LOVE** [ ] [–]
Nov 95. (cd) *Cameo; (CD 3509)* **THE MUSIC OF ENNIO MORRICONE** [ ] [–]
Dec 95. (cd) *Replay; <4063>* **AN HOUR WITH ENNIO MORRICONE** [–] [ ]
Feb 96. (cd) *R.C.A.; (74321 31551-2)* **TIME OF ADVENTURE** [ ] [ ]
Feb 96. (cd) *R.C.A.; (74321 31552-2)* **TV FILM MUSIC** [ ] [ ]
Apr 96. (cd) *Milano Dischi; (OST 130)* **THE MUSIC FROM THE FILMS OF PIER PAOLO PASOLINI** [ ] [–]
– (UCCELLACCI / LE STREGNE / TEOREMA)

Apr 96. (cd) *Preamble; (PRCD 117)* **LE FOTO PROHIBITE DI UNA SIGNORA PERBENE / IL SEGRETO** ☐ [–]
Apr 96. (cd) *Preamble; (PRCD 121)* **BLUEBEARD / LA MONACA DI MONZA** ☐ [–]
Apr 96. (cd) *Preamble; (PRCD 122)* **GIORNATA NERA PER L'ARIETE / LI OCCHI FREDDI DELLA PAURA** ☐ [–]
Apr 96. (cd) *Silva Screen; (DE 76)* **FIVE MAN ARMY / THE LINK** ☐ [–]
Oct 96. (cd) *Legend; (LEGENDCD 26)* **LA VIOLENZA: QUINTO POERA ('Sicilian Checkmate') / UNA BRAVA STAGIONE ('A Brief Season')** ☐ [–]
Dec 96. (d-cd) *D.R.G.; (DRGCD 32920)* **MAIN TITLES 1965-1996** ☐ [–]
Apr 99. (d-cd) *Camden; (74321 660402)* **A FISTFUL OF SOUNDS** ☐ [–]
– The Complete Soundtracks: A Fistful Of Dollars / For A Few Dollars More / Once Upon A Time In The West.
May 99. (lp) *Studio Uno; (STN 1007LP)* **CLUB MORRICONE** ☐ [–]
Sep 00. (cd) *Virgin; (CDV 2929)* **THE VERY BEST OF ENNIO MORRICONE** [48] [–]
– A fistful of dollars / For a few dollars more / The good, the bad and the ugly / Chi mai / The mission / Gabriel's oboe / Cinema paradiso / Cockey's song / Deborah's theme / Once upon a time in the west / The man with the harmonica / The battle of Algiers / Sicilian clan / Sacco and Vanzetti / Fidtful of dynamite / My name is nobody / Moses theme / Frantic / Hamlet / Heart beats in space.

Van MORRISON

Born: GEORGE IVAN MORRISON, 31 Aug'45, Belfast, N.Ireland. Reared on such eclectic musical fare as HANK WILLIAMS, JIMMIE RODGERS, LEADBELLY and DUKE ELLINGTON, the young VAN began his professional musical apprenticeship on the Irish showband circuit, mastering guitar, piano and saxophone and laying the fertile seed bed of vocal improvisation and innovation that would come to distinguish his career. A rough and tumble tour of Germany with The MONARCHS was followed by spells in the The MANHATTAN SHOWBAND, The GOLDEN EAGLES and finally, The GAMBLERS, who, in turn, evolved into THEM, the brooding R&B bovver boys with whom MORRISON first stamped his gutteral howl on a nations's musical consciousness. Along with The ANIMALS, The PRETTY THINGS and The ROLLING STONES, THEM formed an integral part of the mid-60's British R&B boom from whence came rock music as we now know and love (or loathe, as the case may be) it today. Though the band only released two official albums, 'THEM' (1965) and 'THEM AGAIN' (1966), their place in legend was assured as the garage leer of 'GLORIA' came to be one of the most covered songs in rock history. One of the few constants in their ramshackle approach and ever changing line-up was MORRISON; his dour, threatening demeanour and erratically electric live performances coupled with a precocious gift for songwriting indicated a star in the ascendant. When THEM finally disintegrated, VAN took up an invitation from BERT BERNS (composer of THEM's hit, 'HERE COMES THE NIGHT' – he had also produced the band) to lay down some tracks in New York for his fledgling 'Bang' label. The resulting sessions produced eight finished songs, among them the youthful exuberance of 'BROWN EYED GIRL' and the harrowing, churning claustrophobia of 'T.B. SHEETS', polar opposites between which MORRISON began to develop his songcraft. The former song edged its way into the US Top 10 during the summer of love in 1967, the label subsequently releasing all the tracks as an album, 'BLOWIN' YOUR MIND', in September (without the consent, and much to the annoyance, of MORRISON himself). Nevertheless, the singer entered the studio once again later that year to record another series of tracks, including early versions of 'BESIDE YOU' and 'MADAME GEORGE' (later appearing in their full glory on 'ASTRAL WEEKS'), some surfacing on the hopefully titled 1970 cash-in, 'The BEST OF VAN MORRISON', while the remainder were eventually unearthed on 1974's 'T.B. SHEETS'. Following the sudden death of BERNS in December '67, VAN moved north to Cambridge, Massachusetts, where he was eventually spotted and signed to a management deal with New York's 'Inherit Productions'. A contract was subsequently secured with 'Warners' and the cream of the Big Apple's jazz musicians were rounded up to back VAN on his solo debut proper, 'ASTRAL WEEKS'. As hotly debated, analysed, shrouded in myth and generally deified as any recording in the history of music, the enigmatic, ethereal allure of the album remains ultimately impenetrable. Recorded, quintessentially MORRISON-style, in two spontaneous four-hour sessions, the record transcended any notion of "rock" per se, nor could it be bracketed under jazz. A darkly intoxicating stream of inspired musical consciousness, 'ASTRAL WEEKS' traded in conventional verse/chorus song structures for freefrom exporations and fragments, languidly vivid imagery floating in and out of focus. From the yearning warmth and acoustic strum of the title track and 'SWEET THING' to the harpsichord tapestry of 'CYPRUS AVENUE' and the epic, dizzying 'MADAME GEORGE', MORRISON set out the blueprint for much of his later work, an eternal quest for spiritual enlightenment that both embraced and transcended hope and despair, contentment and restlessness. Fittingly, then, this music is timeless, the only indication of its 1968 birthdate the supple potency of VAN's young voice. An instrument in its own right, MORRISON's vocal faculty is arguably among the most powerful, seductive and ultimately healing to have emerged in the last thirty or so years, capable of everything from a primal grunt a la JAMES BROWN, to a child-like, awestruck breathlessness. An album that has grown in stature with each passing year, 'ASTRAL WEEKS' was met with mixed reviews upon its original release, and it initially sold relatively poorly. Undeterred, VAN moved to Woodstock with his new wife, Janet Planet (yep, she was a fully paid up hippy), where he penned most of the material for a follow-up album, 'MOONDANCE'. Released in early 1970, the record was a more solidly constructed affair, MORRISON reigning in his more abstract tendencies into tighter, shorter, brassy bursts. Much of the album reflected VAN's love of soul and R&B, punchy horn flourishes replacing the meandering acoustics of 'ASTRAL WEEKS'. The soporific 'AND IT STONED ME' and the classic 'INTO THE MYSTIC' were closest in spirit to the debut, the latter track condensing the albums theme of the redemptive power of love. By this point, the critics were catching on to the stocky Irishman's genius, lauding the album and heralding MORRISON as one of the rock worlds most talented visionaries. He was also arguably one of the few white musicians to interpret black music forms in such a way as to retain the spontaneity and richness while creating something completely original. In saying that, it could be argued that 'VAN MORRISON, HIS BAND AND THE STREET CHOIR' (1970) relied too heavily on a straight soul/R&B formula, lacking any real depth as a result. 'DOMINO' was the standout track, a driving, hedonistic slice of white R&B that gave VAN his biggest (US) hit to date. The album's inside cover showed a scene of communal domesticity, an apparent contentedness (only rarely glimpsed since) that continued with 'TUPELO HONEY' (1971), a country-tinged collection celebrating love and romance. The lush balladeering of the title track saw VAN putting in one of the sweetest vocal performances of his career thus far, most of the songs finding the singer in laid-back, family man mode. Entertaining as the album was, 'ST. DOMINIC'S PREVIEW' (1972) was far more compelling. Tellingly, by the time VAN came to record the album, his relationship with Janet was on the rocks. While the disc opened with the life-affirming soul shout of 'JACKIE WILSON SAID', the epic 'LISTEN TO THE LION' formed the album's centrepiece, a musical and spiritual marathon that set out VAN's agenda of personal quest more explicitly than ever before. The title track was equally inspiring while the almost gospel-like 'REDWOOD TREE' was manna for the soul, healing harmonies of hope and forgiveness. The billowing, hypnotic ambience of 'INDEPENDENCE DAY' closed the album in suitably enigmatic style, and bizarrely enough, recalled the PINK FLOYD of 'Wish You Were Here' (though don't let that put you off!). 'ST. DOMINIC'S PREVIEW' came at a time when VAN was regaining his confidence on stage after a period of relative withdrawal from live performance. To catalogue the ever shifting personnel of MORRISON's various bands would probably warrant a book in its own right although the general concensus is that the man reached a zenith of sorts with his CALEDONIA SOUL ORCHESTRA. Recorded for posterity on the double live album, 'IT'S TOO LATE TO STOP NOW' (1974), MORRISON's summer '73 shows are the stuff of legend. One of the classic live albums, MORRISON takes his songs to places they were probably never designed for, stretching, remoulding and re-inventing them in his inimitable R&B preacher/spiritual warrior fashion. The result is rarely less than breathtaking. Ironically enough, 'HARD NOSE THE HIGHWAY' (1973), MORRISON's studio effort of the time, lacked the intensity of the live work although 'THE GREAT DECEPTION' is probably VAN's angriest song, berating the showbusiness falsity that he's always made a point of distancing himself from. The remainder of the 70's were MORRISON's wilderness years as he seemingly struggled to focus on any kind of musical direction, taking time out to explore his spiritual journey on a personal level. 'VEEDON FLEECE' (1974), apparently inspired by a return to his native Ireland after years in exile, presaged this more intense period of searching. Arguably closest in spirit to VAN's cosmic debut than anything else he's since released, the record shared 'ASTRAL WEEKS' otherworldly sense of drifting in and out of consciousness, set against a backdrop of Ireland's rich heritage. The Celtic folk influence was most prominent on 'STREETS OF ARKLOW', haunting Irish pipes conjuring up images of brooding, silent faces peering from rain lashed doorways. The album remains a pivotal release, signalling the more overtly Celtic and spiritual direction MORRISON's music would take in the 80's and after completing this milestone, the Irishman didn't surface again until 1977 with the poorly received 'PERIOD OF TRANSITION'. 'WAVELENGTH' (1978) saw VAN back on track, although 'INTO THE MUSIC' (1979) was really the beginning of a new phase in his career. Joyously religious but never dogmatic, the album found MORRISON flirting with Christianity; 'FULL FORCE GALE' was a revelation, a rock of strength and deep seated conviction. A rich seam of hope and inspiration runs through the whole album, culminating in 'AND THE HEALING HAS BEGUN'. From here on in, MORRISON's albums were increasingly concerned with religious redemption, Celtic mysteries and ultimately the healing power of music (or navel-gazing nonsense, if you erred towards cynicism) . 'COMMON ONE' (1980) divided the critics with its esoteric New Age slant, while other early 80's efforts like 'BEAUTIFUL VISION' (1982) and 'INARTICULATE SPEECH OF THE HEART' (1983) introduced a kind of airbrushed, synthesizer sound that didn't sit particularly well with MORRISON's organic voice and approach. 'NO GURU, NO METHOD, NO TEACHER' (1986) was a convincing return to form, 'ONE IRISH ROVER' a taster for his other great work of the decade, 'IRISH HEARTBEAT' (1988), the triumphant collaboration with Irish traditionalists, The CHIEFTAINS. The record found MORRISON in boisterous form, the resulting tour inspiring some of the most positive reactions since his seminal live shows of the 70's. The devotional 'POETIC CHAMPIONS COMPOSE' (1987) was sandwiched between these two, another work of nomadic spiritual searching, MORRISON's singing his pain on the haunting 'SOMETIMES I FEEL LIKE A MOTHERLESS CHILD'. Incredibly, VAN's first Top 20 UK solo hit came with 'WHENEVER GOD SHINES HIS LIGHT', a duet with CLIFF RICHARD the following year. The success of the single helped to boost VAN's commercial clout, the mellow 'AVALON SUNSET' (1989) opus reaching No.13 while subsequent albums, 'ENLIGHTENMENT' (1990) and the heavily gospel-orientated 'HYMNS TO THE SILENCE' (1991) both reached the UK Top 5. The latter's title could be used to describe the music that has made up a large part of MORRISON career, songs of love and devotion unique in rock'n'roll. While more recent releases like 'TOO LONG IN EXILE' (1993) and 'DAYS LIKE THIS' (1995) have lacked just such inspiration, VAN's live work was again re-energised and the live 'A NIGHT IN SAN FRANCISCO' (1994) was roundly praised, one of the record's many highlights an electric run through of 'GLORIA' with old jamming mate, JOHN LEE HOOKER. VAN had also taken to playing with jazz maestro, GEORGIE FAME, a breezy live set recorded at Ronnie Scott's in Soho, released as 'HOW LONG HAS THIS BEEN GOING ON' (1996). 'THE HEALING GAME' in 1997 saw the man return to Top 10 territory and a subsequent tour with BOB DYLAN helped maintain his profile; a 'Basement Tapes'-type of double CD set 'THE PHILOSOPHER'S STONE' (1998) saw a slight connection still, while VAN recorded a cover of 'MULESKINNER BLUES' on DYLAN's new imprint, 'Egyptian'. VAN's final album of the 90's, 'BACK ON TOP' was his first for Virgin offshoot 'Pointblank', the transatlantic Top 30 long-player even supplying his first Top 40 single in years, 'PRECIOUS TIME'. A grumpy curmudgeon to some, a Celtic visionary to others, VAN MORRISON remains as much of an enigma as his best work. While that album occasionally offered glimpses of the pained soul searching we haven't heard from the man in years (especially 'HIGH SUMMER'), MORRISON relaxed back into the bonhomie of contented middle age with 'THE SKIFFLE SESSIONS: LIVE IN BELFAST 1998'. A glowing tribute to the music that inspired him, MORRISON lives it up with two of his oldest chums, LONNIE DONEGAN and CHRIS BARBER. You may have heard them a million times before but a sheer unbridled love of the music elevates the likes of 'ALABAMY BOUND', MIDNIGHT SPECIAL' and 'GOODNIGHT IRENE' to essential listening status. DR JOHN also guested on this knees-up tribute to skiffle and its component parts of folk, country, blues and jazz. 'YOU WIN AGAIN' (2000) was similar in spirit, a feelgood collaboration between VAN and LINDA GAIL LEWIS, JERRY LEE's kid sister. Again, this was all about the simple joys of playing music with friends, nothing more, nothing less. MORRISON has rarely sounded so at ease, knocking out vintage country, R&B and rock'n'roll with an infectious enthusiasm fired up by the pair's natural musical synergy. It seems the older VAN gets, the more he wants to resuscitate the music which inspired him in the first place, and who, after all, can really blame him. 'DOWN THE ROAD' (2002) continued his recent run of great records, an unashamed trip down memory lane, both musically and lyrically. While his songs have always been peppered with recurring autobiographical motifs, thinly veiled or otherwise, the Irishman indulges himself here, musing on his roots with candour and humour against a lovingly rendered patchwork of blues, jazz, R&B, country and folk. He namechecks the likes of PJ PROBY and SCOTT WALKER, even covering the Hoagy Carmichael chestnut, 'GEORGIA ON MY MIND'. Recording an album for 'Blue Note', 'WHAT'S WRONG WITH THIS PICTURE' (2003), meanwhile, was perhaps the logical next step for MORRISON, especially given the record's feel of an artist finally coming home, opening up his muse to the music which really fires him. And there is a definite sense of some sort of artistic unshackling: the ageing star hasn't cut such earthy blues, soul and jazz for years, whether sparring with tenor saxophonist MARTIN WINNING, or taking possession of Lightnin' Hopkins' 'STOP DRINKING'. • **Songwriters:** Self-penned except covers; CALEDONIA (Fleecie Moore) / HELP ME (Sonny Boy Williamson) / BRING IT HOME TO ME (Sam Cooke) / SANTA FE (co-written w / Jackie DeShannon) / LONELY AVENUE (Doc Pomus) / GOOD MORNING LITTLE SCHOOLGIRL (Sonny Boy Williamson) / THE LONESOME ROAD (N.Shikret – G.Austin) / MOODY'S MOOD FOR LOVE (James Moody) / I'LL TAKE CARE OF YOU (Brook Benton) / BEFORE THE WORLD WAS MADE (W.B.Yeats / music; Kenny Craddock) / YOU DON'T KNOW ME (hit; Ray Charles) / I'LL NEVER BE FREE (Benjamin-Weiss) / THAT OLD BLACK MAGIC (hit; Sammy Davis Jnr).

Album rating: BLOWIN' YOUR MIND (*5) / ASTRAL WEEKS (*10) / MOONDANCE (*9) / HIS BAND AND THE STREET CHOIR (*6) / TUPELO HONEY (*8) / SAINT DOMINC'S PREVIEW (*9) / HARD NOSE THE HIGHWAY (*7) / IT'S TOO LATE TO STOP NOW (*9) / VEEDON FLEECE (*9) / A PERIOD OF TRANSITION (*5) / WAVELENGTH (*7) / INTO THE MUSIC (*8) / COMMON ONE (*6) / BEAUTIFUL VISION (*6) / INARTICULATE SPEECH OF THE HEART (*6) / LIVE AT THE GRAND OPERA HOUSE, BELFAST (*7) / A SENSE OF WONDER (*6) / NO GURU, NO METHOD, NO TEACHER (*7) / POETIC CHAMPIONS COMPOSE (*7) / IRISH HEARTBEAT with the Chieftains (*8) / AVALON SUNSET (*7) / THE BEST OF VAN MORRISON compilation (*9) / ENLIGHTENMENT (*7) / HYMNS TO THE SILENCE (*7) / THE BEST OF VAN MORRISON, VOLUME TWO compilation (*6) / TOO LONG IN EXILE (*6) / A NIGHT IN SAN FRANCISCO (*7) / DAYS LIKE THIS (*6) / HOW LONG HAS THIS BEEN GOING ON with Georgie Fame & Friends (*4) / THE HEALING GAME (*6) / THE PHILOSOPHER'S STONE (THE UNRELEASED TAPES VOL.1) collection (*6) / BACK ON TOP (*6) / YOU WIN AGAIN with Linda Gail Lewis (*5) / DOWN THE ROAD (*7) / WHAT'S WRONG WITH THIS PICTURE? (*6)

VAN MORRISON – vocals, guitar, saxophone (ex-THEM) with loads of session persons.

London Bang

Jun 67. (7") *(HLZ 10150)* *<545>* **BROWN EYED GIRL. / GOODBYE BABY (BABY GOODBYE)** [ ] [10]
(re-iss. Mar71 on 'President'; PT 328) (re-iss. Apr74; HLM 10453)

Sep 67. (7") *<552>* **RO RO ROSEY. / CHICK-A-BOOM** [–] [ ]

Nov 67. (7") *<585>* **SPANISH ROSE / MIDNIGHT ROSE** [–] [ ]

Feb 68. (lp; mono/stereo) *(HA-Z 8346) <BLP/+S 218>* **BLOWIN' YOUR MIND** [ ] Sep67 [ ]
– Brown eyed girl / He ain't give you none / T.B. sheets / Spanish rose / Goodbye baby (baby goodbye) / Ro Ro Rosey / Who drove the red sports car? / Midnight special. *(cd-iss. Jul95 on 'Epic';) (re-iss. Nov98 on 'Simply Vinyl'; SVLP 49)*

— now with **LARRY FALLON** – conductor, arranger / **JAY BERLINER** – guitar / **RICHARD DAVIS** – bass / **CONNIE KAY** – drums / **JOHN PAYNE** – flute, sporano sax / **WARREN SMITH JR** – percussion, vibraphone

Warners Warners

Sep 69. (lp) *(<WS 1768>)* **ASTRAL WEEKS** [ ] Nov68 [ ]
– In the beginning: Astral weeks / Beside you / Sweet thing / Cypress avenue / Afterwards: Young lovers do / Madame George / Ballerina / Slim slow rider. *(re-iss. Aug 71; K 46024) (cd-iss. May87; K 246024)*

— now with **JOHN PLATANIA** – guitar / **JEFF LABES** – keys / **JACK SHROER** – sax / **GARY MALLABER** – drums / **JOHN KLINGBERG** – bass

Mar 70. (lp) *(<WS 1835>)* **MOONDANCE** [32] [29]
– And it stoned me / Moondance / Crazy love / Into the mystic / Caravan / Come running / These dreams of you / Brand new day / Everyone / Glad tidings. *(re-iss. Aug71; K 46040) (cd-iss. Jan86; K 246040)*

May 70. (7") *(WB <7383>)* **COME RUNNING. / CRAZY LOVE** [ ] Apr70 [39]

Dec 70. (lp) *(<WS 1884>)* **HIS BAND AND THE STREET CHOIR** [ ] Nov70 [32]
– Domino / Crazy face / I've been working / Call me up in Dreamland / I'll be your lover, too / Blue money / Virgo clowns / Gypsy queen / Sweet Janine / If I ever needed someone / Street choir. *(re-iss. Aug71; K 46066) (cd-iss. Feb93;)*

Dec 70. (7") *(WB <7434>)* **DOMINO. / SWEET JANINE** [ ] Oct70 [9]
(re-iss. Jul71; K 16044)

Feb 71. (7") *<7462>* **BLUE MONEY. / SWEET THING** [–] [23]

Apr 71. (7") *<7488>* **CALL ME UP IN DREAMLAND. / STREET CHOIR** [–] [95]

— now with **MALLABER, SHROER + BILL CHURCH** – bass / **RONNIE MONTROSE** – guitar / **RICK SCHLOSSER** – drums + **CONNIE KAY** – drums

Sep 71. (7") *<7518>* **WILD NIGHT. / WHEN THAT EVENING SUN GOES DOWN** [–] [28]

Nov 71. (lp) *(K 46114) <WS 1950>* **TUPELO HONEY** [ ] Oct 71 [27]
– Wild night / (Straight to your heart) Like a cannonball / Old old Woodstock / Starting a new life / You're my woman / Tupelo honey / I wonna roo you / When that evening sun goes down / Moonshine whiskey. *(re-iss. Aug89 & Feb94 on 'Polydor' lp/c/cd; 839161-1/-4/-2) (re-iss. Apr98 on 'Polydor'; 537450-2)*

Dec 71. (7") *(7543>* **TUPELO HONEY. / STARTING A NEW LIFE** [–] [47]

Mar 72. (7") *<7573>* **(STRAIGHT TO YOUR HEART) LIKE A CANNONBALL. / OLD OLD WOODSTOCK** [–] [ ]

— **LEROY VINNEGAR** – bass repl. CHURCH (who later joined MONTROSE) / **ROY ELLIOT** – guitar + **MARK NAFTALIN** – piano repl. SCHOSSLER + MALLABER

Jul 72. (7") *(K 16210) <7616>* **JACKIE WILSON SAID (I'M IN HEAVEN WHEN YOU SMILE). / YOU'VE GOT THE POWER** [ ] [61]

Aug 72. (lp) *(K 46172) <WS 2633>* **SAINT DOMINIC'S PREVIEW** [ ] [15]
– Jackie Wilson said (I'm in Heaven when you smile) / Gypsy / I will be there / Listen to the lion / Saint Dominic's preview / Redwood tree / Almost Independance day. *(re-iss. Aug89 on 'Polydor' lp/c/cd; 839162-1/-4/-2) (cd-iss. Apr95;)*

Oct 72. (7") *(7638>* **REDWOOD TREE. / SAINT DOMINIC'S PREVIEW** [–] [98]

Jan 73. (7") *<7665>* **GYPSY. / SAINT DOMINIC'S PREVIEW** [–] [ ]

— RONNIE now formed MONTROSE went through various session personnel: **DAVID HAYES** – bass and most of new band.

Jul 73. (7") *(K 16299) <7706>* **WARM LOVE. / I WILL BE THERE** [ ] Jun73 [ ]

Jul 73. (lp) *(K 46242) <WS 2712>* **HARD NOSE THE HIGHWAY** [22] [27]
– Snow in San Anselmo / Warm love / Hard nose the highway / Wild children / The great deception / Green / Autumn song / Purple heather. *(re-iss. Aug89 on 'Polydor' lp/c/cd; 839163-1/-4/-2) (cd-iss. Apr95;)*

Sep 73. (7") *<7744>* **GREEN. / WILD CHILDREN** [–] [ ]

Feb 74. (7") *<7797>* **AIN'T NOTHING YOU CAN DO. / WILD CHILDREN** [–] [ ]

Feb 74. (d-lp) *(K 86007) <WS 2760>* **IT'S TOO LATE TO STOP NOW (live)** [ ] [53]
– Ain't nothing you can do / Warm love / Into the mystic / These dreams of you / I believe to my soul / I've been working / Help me / Wild children / Domino / I just wanna make love to you / Bring it on home to me / Saint Dominic's preview / Take your hand out of my pocket / Listen to the lion / Here comes the night / Gloria / Caravan / Cypress Avenue. *(re-iss. Aug89 on 'Polydor' d-lp/d-c/d-cd; 839166-1/-4/-2) (cd-iss. Apr95;)*

May 74. (7") *(K 16392)* **CALDONIA (WHAT MAKES YOUR BIG HEAD HARD?). / WHAT'S UP, CRAZY PUP** [ ] [–]

Oct 74. (lp/c) *(K/K4 56068) <WS 2805>* **VEEDON FLEECE** [41] [53]
– Streets of Arklow / Country fair / Cul de sac / Linden Arden stole the highlights / Fair play / Bulbs / You don't pull no punches but you don't push the river / Comfort you / Come here my love / Who was that masked man. *(re-iss. Aug89 on 'Polydor' lp/c/cd; 839164-1/-4/-2) (cd-iss. Apr95;)*

Jul 74. (7") *<8029>* **BULBS. / CUL DE SAC** [–] [ ]

Nov 74. (7") *(K 16486)* **BULBS. / WHO WAS THAT MASKED MAN** [ ] [–]

below featured DR. JOHN – piano

Mar 77. (lp/c) *(K/K4 56322) <2987>* **A PERIOD OF TRANSITION** [23] [43]
– You gotta make it through the world / It fills you up / The eternal Kansas City / Joyous sound / Flamingoes fly / Heavy connection / Cold wind in August. *(re-iss. +cd.Aug89 on 'Polydor')*

Apr 77. (7") *(K 16939)* **THE ETERNAL KANSAS CITY. / JOYOUS SOUND** [ ] [–]

Jul 77. (7") *(K 16986)* **JOYOUS SOUND. / MECHANICAL BLISS** [ ] [ ]

Oct 77. (7") **COLD WIND IN AUGUST. / MOONDANCE** [–] [ ]

— **PETER VAN HOOKE** – drums / **HERBIE ARMSTRONG** – guitar etc

Oct 78. (lp/c) *(K/K4 56526) <3212>* **WAVELENGTH** [27] [28]
– Kingdom hall / Checkin' it out / Natalia / Venice U.S.A. / Lifetimes / Wavelength / Santa Fe / Beautiful obsession / Hungry for your love / Take it where you find it. *(re-iss. Aug89 & Feb94 on 'Polydor' lp/c/cd; 839169-1/-4/-2) (re-iss. Apr98 on 'Polydor';)*

Oct 78. (7") *(K 17254)* **WAVELENGTH. / CHECKIN' IT OUT** [ ] [42]

Feb 79. (7") *(K 17322)* **NATALIA. / LIFETIMES** [ ] [ ]

Apr 79. (7") **CHECKIN' IT OUT. /** [–] [ ]

— now with **HOOKE, ARMSTRONG, HAYES / + MARK JORDAN** – keyboards / **MARK ISHAM** – trumpet / **PEE WEE ELLIS** – saxophone

Mercury Warners

Aug 79. (lp/c) *(9102/? 852) <3390>* **INTO THE MUSIC** [21] [43]
– Bright side of the road / Full force gale / Stepping out queen / Troubadours / Rolling hills / You make me feel so free / Angeliou / And the healing has begun / It's all in the game / You know what they're writing about. *(re-iss. May83 lp/c; PRICE/PRIMC 2) (re-iss. Aug89 & Feb94 on 'Polydor' lp/c/cd; 839603-1/-4/-2) (re-iss. Apr98 on 'Polydor'; 537540-2)*

Sep 79. (7") *(6001 121)* **BRIGHT SIDE OF THE ROAD. / ROLLING HILLS** [63] [ ]

Dec 79. (7") **FULL FORCE GALE. / YOU MAKE ME FEEL SO FREE** [–] [ ]

— **JOHN ALLAIR** – keyboards + **MICK COX** – guitar repl. JORDAN + MARCUS

Sep 80. (lp/c) *(6302/7144 021) <3462>* **COMMON ONE** [53] [73]
– Haunts of ancient peace / Summertime in England / Satisfied / Wild honey / Spirit / When heart is open. *(re-iss. May83 lp/c; PRICE/PRIMC 1) (cd-iss. 1986; 800 043-2) (re-iss. Aug89 & Apr95 on 'Polydor' lp/c/cd; 839600-1/-4/-2) (cd re-iss. Apr98; 537541-2)*

— added **TOM DONLINGER** – drums

Feb 82. (lp/c) *(6302/7144 122) <3652>* **BEAUTIFUL VISION** [31] [44]
– Celtic Ray / Northern muse (solid sound) / Dweller on the threshold / Beautiful vision / She gives me religion / Cleaning windows / Vanlose stairway / Aryan mist / Scandinavia / Across the bridge where angels dwell / Scandinavia. *(re-iss. Mar85 lp/c; PRICE/PRIMC 82) (re-iss. Aug89 & Feb94 on 'Polydor' lp/c/cd; 839601-1/-4/-2) (re-iss. Apr98 on 'Polydor'; 537542-2)*

Mar 82. (7") **CLEANING WINDOWS. / SCANDINAVIA** [–] [ ]

Mar 82. (7") *(MER 99)* **CLEANING WINDOWS. / IT'S ALL IN THE GAME** [ ] [–]

Jun 82. (7") *(MER 110)* **DWELLER ON THE THRESHOLD. / SCANDINAVIA** [ ] [ ]

— **CHRIS MICHIE** – guitar repl. COX

Feb 83. (7") *(MER 132)* **CRY FOR HOME. / SUMMERTIME IN ENGLAND (live)** [ ] [ ]
(12"+=) *(MERX 132)* – All saints day.

Mar 83. (lp/c) *(MERL/+C 16) <23802>* **INARTICULATE SPEECH OF THE HEART** [14] [ ]
– Higher than the world / Connswater / River of time / Celtic swing / Rave on, John Donne / Inarticulate speech of the heart No.1 / Irish heartbeat / The street only knew your name / Cry for home / Inarticulate speech of the heart No.2 / September night. *(re-iss. Oct86 lp/c; PRICE/PRIMC 93) (cd-iss. May86; 811 140-2) (re-iss. Aug89 & Feb94 on 'Polydor'; 839604-1/-4/-2) (re-iss. Apr98 on 'Polydor'; 537543-2)*

May 83. (7") *(MER 141)* **CELTIC SWING. / MR. THOMAS** [ ] [ ]
(12"+=) *(MERX 132)* – Rave on, John Donne.

Feb 84. (lp/c) *(MERL/+C 36)* **LIVE AT THE GRAND OPERA HOUSE, BELFAST (live)** [47] [–]
– (intro) / Into the music / Inarticulate seech of the heart / Dweller on the threshold / It's all in the game – You know what they're writing about / She gives me religion / Haunts of ancient peace / Full force gale / Beautiful vision / Vanlose stairway / Rave on, John Donne – Rave on (part 2) / Northern muse (solid ground) / Cleaning windows. *(cd-iss. 1986; 818336-2) (re-iss. Aug89 on 'Polydor' lp/c/cd; 839602-1/-4/-2) (cd re-iss. Apr98 on 'Polydor'; 537544-2)*

Mar 84. (7") *(MER 159)* **DWELLER ON THE THRESHOLD (live). / NORTHERN MUSE (SOLID GROUND)** [ ] [ ]

Mercury Mercury

Nov 84. (7"/12") *(MER/+X 178)* **A SENSE OF WONDER. / HAUNTS OF ANCIENT PEACE (live)** [ ] [ ]

Feb 85. (lp/c)(cd) *(MERH/+C 54)(<822 895-2>)* **A SENSE OF WONDER** [25] [61]
– Tore down a La Rimbaud / Ancient of days / Evening meditation / The master's eyes / What would I do / A sense of wonder / Boffyflow and Spike / If you only knew / Let the slave / A new kind of man. *(re-iss. May90 & Apr95 on 'Polydor' cd/c/lp; 843116-2/-4/-1) (cd re-iss. Apr98; 537545-2)*

Jun 86. (7") *(MER 223)* **IVORY TOWER. / NEW KIND OF MAN** [ ] [ ]
(12"+=) *(MERX 223)* – A sense of wonder / Cleaning windows.

Jul 86. (lp/c)(cd) *(MERH/+C 94)(<830077-2>)* **NO GURU, NO METHOD, NO TEACHER** [27] [70]
– Got to go back / Oh the warm feeling / Foreign window / Town called Paradise / In the garden / Tir na nog / Here comes the night / Thanks for the information / One Irish rover / Ivory tower. *(re-iss. Sep91 & Feb94 on 'Polydor'; 849619-2/-4/-1) (re-iss. Apr98 on 'Polydor'; 537546-2)*

Aug 86. (7") *(MER 231)* **GOT TO GO BACK. / IN THE GARDEN** [ ] [ ]

— note: HOOKE + ISHAM left early '84 / **ELLIS + DONLINGER** in '85 / now new band

Sep 87. (lp/c)(cd) *(MERH/+C 110)(<832585-2>)* **POETIC CHAMPIONS COMPOSE** [26] [90]
– Spanish steps / The mystery / Queen of the slipstream / I forgot that love existed / Sometimes I feel like a motherless child / Celtic excavation / Someone like you / Alan Watts blues / Give me my rapture / Did ye get healed? / Allow me. *(cd re-iss. 1992 on 'Polydor'; 517217-2)*

Sep 87. (7") *(MER 254)* **DID YE GET HEALED?. / ALLOW ME** [ ] [ ]

Apr 88. (7") *(MER 261)* **QUEEN OF THE SLIPSTREAM. / SPANISH STEPS** [ ] [ ]

Jun 88. (lp/c)(cd; VAN MORRISON & THE CHIEFTAINS) *(MERH/+C 124)(<834496-2>)* **IRISH HEARTBEAT** [18] [ ]
– Star of the County Down / Irish heartbeat / Ta mo chleamhnas deanta / Raglan road / She moved through the fair / I'll tell me ma / Carrickfergus / Celtic Ray / My lagan love / Marie's wedding. *(cd re-iss. Apr98 on 'Polydor'; 537548-2)*

Jun 88. (7") *(MER 262)* **I'LL TELL ME MA. / TA MO CHLEAMHNAS DEANTA** [ ] [ ]
(12"+=/cd-s+=) *(MER X/CD 262)* – Carrickfergus.

Polydor Polydor

May 89. (lp/c/cd) *(<839262-1/-4/-2>)* **AVALON SUNSET** [13] [91]
– Whenever God shines his light / Contacting my angel / I'd love to write another love song / Have I told you lately (that I love you) / Coney Island / I'm tired Joey boy / When will I ever learn to live in God / Orangefield / Daring night / These are the days.

Jun 89. (7"/c-s) *(VAN S/CS 1)* **HAVE I TOLD YOU LATELY (THAT I LOVE YOU). / CONTACTING MY ANGEL** [74] [ ]
(12"+=) *(VANX 1)* – Listen to the lion.
(cd-s+=) *(VANCD 1)* – Irish heartbeat.

Nov 89. (7"/c-s; by VAN MORRISON & CLIFF RICHARD) *(VAN S/CS 2)* **WHENEVER GOD SHINES HIS LIGHT. / I'D LOVE TO WRITE ANOTHER LOVE SONG** [20] [ ]
(12"+=) *(VANX 2)* – Cry for home.
(cd-s++=) *(VANCD 2)* – ('A'-lp version).

Dec 89. (7") *(VANS 3)* **ORANGEFIELD. / THESE ARE THE DAYS** [ ] [ ]
(12"+=) *(VANX 3)* – And the healing has begun.
(cd-s++=) *(VANCD 3)* – Coney Island.

Feb 90. (7"/c-s) *(VAN S/CS 4)* **CONEY ISLAND. / HAVE I TOLD YOU LATELY THAT I LOVE YOU** [ ] [ ]
(12"+=) *(VANX 4)* – A sense of wonder.
(cd-s++=) *(VANCD 4)* – Spirit.

Mar 90. (cd/c/lp) *(<841970-2/-4/-1>)* **THE BEST OF VAN MORRISON** (compilation) [4] May90 [41]
– Bright side of the road / Gloria (THEM) / Moondance / Baby please don't go (THEM) / Have I told you lately / Brown eyed girl / Sweet thing / Warm love / Wonderful remark / Jackie Wilson said (I'm in Heaven when you smile) / Full force gale / And it stoned me / Here comes the night (THEM) / Domino / Did ye get healed / Wild night / Cleaning windows / Whenever God shines his light (w / CLIFF RICHARD). *(c+cd.iss.has extra tracks) (cd re-iss. Apr98; 537459-2)*

Jul 90. (7"/c-s) *(VANS/+C 5)* **GLORIA (by Them). / RAVE ON, JOHN DONNE** [ ] [ ]
(12"+=) *(VANX 5)* – Vanlose stairway.
(cd-s++=) *(VANCD 5)* – Bright side of the road.

Sep 90. (7"/c-s) *(VAN S/CS 6)* **REAL REAL GONE. / START ALL OVER AGAIN** [ ] [ ]
(12"+=/cd-s+=) *(VAN X/CD 6)* – Cleaning windows.

Oct 90. (cd/c/lp) *(<847 100-2/-4/-1>)* **ENLIGHTENMENT** [5] [62]
– Real real gone / Enlightenment / So quiet in here / Avalon of the heart / See me through / Youth of 1,000 summers / In the days before rock'n'roll / Start all over again / She's a baby / Memories. *(lp re-iss. Aug99 on 'Simply Vinyl'; SVLP 109)*

Nov 90. (7"/c-s) *(VAN S/CS 7)* **IN THE DAYS BEFORE ROCK'N'ROLL. / I'D LOVE TO WRITE ANOTHER LOVE SONG** [ ] [ ]
(12"+=/cd-s+=) *(VAN X/CD 7)* – Coney Island.

Jan 91. (7") *(VANS 8)* **ENLIGHTENMENT. / AVALON OF THE HEART** [ ] [ ]
(12"+=/cd-s+=) *(VAN X/CD 8)* – Jackie Wilson said.

—— (VAN is credited w/ TOM JONES on his Mar91 single 'CARRYING A TORCH')

May 91. (7"/c-s; by VAN MORRISON & THE CHIEFTAINS) *(VAN S/CS 9)* **I CAN'T STOP LOVING YOU. / ALL SAINTS DAY** [ ] [ ]
(12"+=/cd-s+=) *(VAN X/CD 9)* – Carrying a torch.

Aug 91. (7"/c-s) *(VAN S/CS 10)* **WHY MUST I ALWAYS EXPLAIN?. / SO COMPLICATED** [ ] [ ]
(12"+=/cd-s+=) *(VAN X/CD 10)* – Enlightenment.

Sep 91. (d-cd/d-c/d-lp) *(<849 026-2/-4/-1>)* **HYMNS TO THE SILENCE** [5] [99]
– Professional jealousy / I'm not feeling it anymore / Ordinary life / Some peace of mind / So complicated / I can't stop loving you / Why must I always explain? / Village idiot / See me through part II (just a closer walk with thee) / Take me back / By his Grace / All Saints day / Hymns to the silence / On Hyndford Street / Be thou my vision / Carrying a torch / Green mansions / Pagan streams / Quality Street / It must be you / I need your kind of loving.

Feb 93. (cd/c/lp) *(<517 760-2/-4/-1>)* **THE BEST OF VAN MORRISON VOLUME 2** (compilation) [31] [ ]
– Real real gone / When will I ever learn to live in God / Sometimes I feel like a motherless child / In the garden / A sense of wonder / I'll tell me ma / Coney Island / Enlightenment / Rave on John Donne – Rave on part two live / Don't look back / It's all over now, baby blue / One Irish Rover / The mystery / Hymns to the silence / Evening meditation.

May 93. (7"/c-s; by VAN MORRISON & JOHN LEE HOOKER) *(VAN S/CS 11)* **GLORIA. / IT MUST BE YOU (live)** [31] [ ]
(cd-s+=) *(VANCD 11)* – And the healing has begun (live) / See me through (live).
(cd-s) *(VANDR 11)* – ('A'side) / Whenever God shines his light (live) / It fills you up (live) / The star of County Down (live).

Jun 93. (cd/c/lp) *(<519 219-2/-4/-1>)* **TOO LONG IN EXILE** [4] [29]
– Too long in exile / Big time operators / Lonely avenue / Ball & chain / In the forest / Till we get the healing done / Gloria / Good morning little schoolgirl / Wasted years / The lonesome road / Moody's mood for love / Close enough for jazz / Before the world was made / I'll take care of you – Instrumental – Tell me what you want.

Apr 94. (d-cd/d-c) *(<521 290-2/-4>)* **A NIGHT IN SAN FRANCISCO (live)** [8] [ ]
– Did ya get healed? / It's all in the game / Make it real one more time / I've been working / I forgot that love existed / Vanlose stairway / Trans-Euro train / Fool for you / You make me feel so real / Beautiful vision / See me through / Soldier of fortune / Thankyoufalettinmebemiseldagain / Ain't that lovin' you baby / Stormy Monday / Have you ever loved a woman / No rollin' blues / Help me / Good morning little schoolgirl / Tupelo honey / Moondance / My funny valentine / Jumpin' with Symphony Sid / It fills you up / I'll take care of you / It's a man's man's man's world / Lonely avenue / 4 o'clock in the morning / So quiet in here / That's where it's at / In the garden / You send me / Allegheny / Have I told you lately that I love you / Shakin' all over / Gloria.

Jun 95. (cd-s) *(VANCD 12)* **DAYS LIKE THIS / YO** [65] [ ]
(7"+=/c-s+=/cd-s+=) *(VAN/+CS/CDX 12)* – I don't want to go on without you / That old black magic.

Jun 95. (cd/c/lp) *(<527 307-2/-4/-1>)* **DAYS LIKE THIS** [5] [33]
– Perfect fit / Russian roulette / Rain check / You don't know me / No religion / Underlying depression / Songwriter / Days like this / I'll never be free / Melancholia / Ancient highway / In the afternoon.

Sep 95. (c-s) *(577 014-4)* **PERFECT FIT / RAINCHECK** [ ] [–]
(cd-s+=) *(577 015-2)* – Cleaning windows.

Nov 95. (cd-s) *(577 488-4)* **NO RELIGION / HAVE I TOLD YOU LATELY** [54] [–]
(cd-s+=) *(577 489-2)* – Whenever God shines his light / Gloria.
(cd-s) *(577 579-2)* – ('A'side) / Days like this / Raincheck.

below credited as VAN MORRISON with GEORGIE FAME & FRIENDS

Oct 95. (cd/c/lp) *(<529 136-2/-4/-1>)* **HOW LONG HAS THIS BEEN GOING ON (live 3 May'95 at Ronnie Scott's)** [ ] Jan96 [55]
– I will be there / The new symphony Sid / Early in the morning / Who can I turn to? / Sack o'woe / Moondance / Centerpiece / How long has this been going on? / Your mind is on vacation / All saint's day / Blues in the night / Don't worry about a thing / That's life / Heathrow shuffle.

Feb 96. (c-s) *(576 204-4)* **THAT'S LIFE / MOONDANCE (live)** [ ] [–]
(cd-s+=) *(576 205-2)* – That's life (live).
(above two releases on 'Verve', as was a credit on the 1996 GEORGIE FAME with BEN SIDRAN, VAN MORRISON and MOSE ALLISON set 'SONGS OF MOSE ALLISON')

Feb 97. (c-s) *(573 390-4)* **THE HEALING GAME / FULL FORCE GALE '96** [46] [–]
(cd-s+=) *(573 391-2)* – Look what the good people done / Celtic Spring.
(cd-s) *(573 393-2)* – ('A'side) / Have I told you lately / Whenever God shines his light (with CLIFF RICHARD) / Gloria (with JOHN LEE HOOKER).

Mar 97. (cd/c/lp) *(<537 101-2/-4/-1>)* **THE HEALING GAME** [10] [32]
– Rough God goes riding / Fire in the belly / This weight / Waiting game / Piper at the gates of dawn / Burning ground / It once was my life / Sometimes we cry / If you love me / The healing game.

Apr 97. (c-s) *(573 933-4)* **ROUGH GOD GOES RIDING / THE HEALING GAME (alt. version)** [ ] [–]
(cd-s+=) *(573 933-2)* – At the end of the day.

Jun 98. (d-cd/d-c) *(<531 789-2/-4>)* **THE PHILOSOPHER'S STONE** (THE UNRELEASED TAPES – VOLUME ONE) [20] [87]
– Really don't know / Ordinary people / Wonderful remark / Not supposed to break down / Laughing in the wind / Madame Joy / Contemplation rose / Don't worry about tomorrow / Try for sleep / Lover's prayer / Drumshanbo hustle / Twilight zone / Foggy mountain top / Naked in the jungle / There there child // The street only knew your name / John Henry / Western plain / Joyous sound / I have finally come to realise / Flamingoes fly / Stepping out queen part 2 / Bright side of the road / Street theory / Real real gone / Showbusiness / For Mr. Thomas / Crazy Jane on God / Song of being a child / High spirits. *(re-iss. Jul99; same)*

Pointblank Pointblank

Feb 99. (cd-s) *(POBD 14)* **PRECIOUS TIME / JACKIE WILSON SAID (I'M IN HEAVEN WHEN YOU SMILE) (live) / CALL ME UP IN DREAMLAND (live)** [36] [–]
(cd-s) *(POBDX 14)* – ('A'side) / Naked in the jungle (live) / Give me a kiss (live).

Mar 99. (cd/c) *(VPB CD/TC 50)* <47148> **BACK ON TOP** [11] [28]
– Goin' down Geneva / Philosopher's stone / In the midnight / Back on top / When the leaves come falling down / High summer / Reminds me of you / New biography / Precious time / Golden autumn day.

May 99. (cd-s) *(POBD 15)* **BACK ON TOP / JOHN BROWN'S BODY / I'M READY** [69] [–]
(cd-s) *(POBDX 15)* – ('A'side) / Tell me / Sax instrumental No.1.

Aug 99. (cd-s) *(POBD 16)* **THE PHILOSOPHER'S STONE / THESE DREAMS OF YOU / RAINCHECK** [ ] [–]

—— in Jan'00, VAN MORRISON teamed up with LONNIE DONEGAN and CHRIS BARBER on the UK No.14 set, 'THE SKIFFLE SESSIONS – LIVE IN BELFAST' on 'Virgin' cd/lp; *CDVE/LPVE 945)*

Sep 00. (cd/c; by VAN MORRISON & LINDA GAIL LEWIS) *(VPB CD/TC 54)* <50258> **YOU WIN AGAIN** [34] Oct00 [ ]
– Let's talk about us / You win again / Jambalaya / Crazy arms / Old black Joe / Think twice before you go / No way Pedro / A shot of rhythm and blues / Real gone lover / Why don't you love me / Cadillac / Baby (you got what it takes) / Boogie chillen. *(lp re-iss. Oct00 on 'Simply Vinyl'; SVLP 251)*

Polydor Universal

May 02. (cd-s) *(570596-2)* **HEY MR. DJ / SOMEONE LIKE YOU / THE BRIGHT SIDE OF THE ROAD (re-recording)** [58] [–]

May 02. (cd/lp) *(<589177-2/-1>)* **DOWN THE ROAD** [6] [25]
– Down the road / Meet me in the Indian summer / Steal my heart away / Hey Mr. DJ / Talk is cheap / Choppin' wood / What makes the Irish heart beat / All work and no play / Whatever happened to PJ Proby? / The beauty of the days gone by / Georgia on my mind / Only a dream / Man has to struggle / Evening shadows / Fast train.

Date	Release	UK	US
Aug 02.	(cd-s) *(570891-2)* **MEET ME IN THE INDIAN SUMMER / IN THE AFTERNOON / RAINCHECK (live) / IN THE MIDNIGHT (live)**		–
		Blue Note	Blue Note
Oct 03.	(cd) *(<590167-2>)* **WHAT'S WRONG WITH THIS PICTURE?** – What's wrong with this picture? / Whinin boy moan / Evening June / Too many myths / Somerset / Meaning of loneliness / Stop drinking / Goldfish bowl / Once in a blue moon / Saint James infirmary / Little village / Fame / Get on with the show.	43	32
		Parlophone	not iss.
Dec 03.	(cd-s) *(CDR 6628)* **ONCE IN A BLUE MOON / WHEN YOU'RE SMILING (live) / WALKIN' MY BABY BACK HOME (live)**		–

– compilations, others, etc. –

Date	Release	UK	US
May 71.	(lp) *President; (PTLS 1045) / Bang; <BLPS 222>* **THE BEST OF VAN MORRISON** *(nearly a re-issue of debut '67 lp)*		1970
Mar 74.	(lp) *London; (HSM 5008) / Bang; <BLPS 400>* **T.B. SHEETS** (a near re-issue of debut 1967 lp) *(cd-iss. May91 on 'Columbia'; 467827-2)*		Jan74
Sep 77.	(lp) *Bang; (6467 625)* **THIS IS WHERE I CAME IN** *(nearly a re-issue of debut '67 lp)*		–
Oct 75.	(d-lp) *Warners; (K 86009)* **TWO ORIGINALS OF VAN MORRISON** – (VAN MORRISON, HIS BAND AND STREET CHOIR / TUPELO HONEY)		–
Oct 77.	(7") *Warners; <8450>* **MOONDANCE. / COLD WIND IN AUGUST**	–	92
Oct 82.	(d-c) *Warners; (K 466116)* **MOONDANCE / . . .HIS BAND AND STREET CHOIR**		–
Jan 92.	(c) *Moles; (MRILC 012)* **CUCHULAINN** (spoken word)		–
Mar 92.	(d-cd/c) *Columbia; (468309-2/-4)* **BANG MASTERS**		–
Jan 93.	(cd) *Movieplay Gold; (74012)* **THE LOST TAPES VOLUME 1**		–
Jan 93.	(cd) *Movieplay Gold; (74013)* **THE LOST TAPES VOLUME 2**		–
May 94.	(cd) *Charly; (CDP 8035-2)* **PAYIN' DUES (The Best Of The 1965 Studio Recordings)**		–
Apr 96.	(cd) *Audiophile; (APH 102805)* **BROWN EYED GIRL**		–
Mar 97.	(t-lp) *Get Back; (GET 501)* **NEW YORK SESSIONS 1967**		–
Mar 98.	(cd) *Squire; (GUV 1)* **BROWN EYED GIRL**		–
Apr 98.	(d-cd) *Multimedia; (7956 766664-2)* **BROWN EYED BEGINNINGS**		–
Nov 98.	(d-cd) *Double Classics; (DC 31014)* **BROWN EYED GIRL**		–

MORRISSEY

Born: STEPHEN PATRICK MORRISSEY, 22 May'59, Manchester, England. After his bust-up with SMITHS guitarist JOHNNY MARR in August '87, MORRISSEY, one of rock music's most intellectually incisive wordsmiths, hastily embarked upon a relatively successful solo career. Remaining with 'E.M.I.', his debut effort, 'VIVA HATE', was subsequently released on the re-activated 'H.M.V.' imprint in Spring '88. With the music co-written by his new producer, STEPHEN STREET, and a backing band that numbered VINI REILLY (guitar, keyboards; ex-DURUTTI COLUMN) and ANDREW PARESI (drums), the album was a strong start, reaching No.2 in the UK charts on the back of the catchy 'SUEDEHEAD' single (incredibly, the singer's first ever Top 5 hit single). Another stand-out track was the lavish melancholy of 'EVERYDAY IS LIKE SUNDAY', arguably his best solo track to date and a song which gave him another Top 10 hit later that summer. Though the album received a relatively warm critical reception, it was, as ever, not without controversy. 'BENGALI IN PLATFORMS' was an ambiguous address to immigrants which he later unsuccessfully attempted to play down while 'MARGARET ON THE GUILLOTINE' was self explanatory, no doubt meeting with a little more empathy. Recruiting a new band composed of NEIL TAYLOR (guitar) and ex-SMITHS', CRAIG GANNON, ANDY ROURKE and MIKE JOYCE, MORRISSEY returned the following year with another couple of fine singles, the playfully coy 'LAST OF THE INTERNATIONAL PLAYBOYS' and 'INTERESTING DRUG', both records going Top 10. The line-up didn't last, however, and he brought in a completely new cast for his next single 'OUIJA BOARD, OUIJA BOARD', a song that suffered scathing reviews in the music press and barely made the Top 20. The following year, a projected album was scrapped although its title, 'BONA DRAG', was retained for an impressive career resume that appeared in late 1990. The collection also contained some new material, notably the grim 'NOVEMBER SPAWNED A MONSTER' and the contentious narrative, 'PICCADILLY PALARE', both released as singles. With a fresh backing group that included ex-MADNESS bassist BEDDERS and MORRISSEY's new writing partner, MARK E. NEVIN (ex-FAIRGROUND ATTRACTION), the singer cut the 'KILL UNCLE' opus. Released in 1991 to mixed reviews, the album failed to deliver on the promise of the earlier singles, although MORRISSEY subsequently recruited a rockabilly backing band: ALAIN WHYTE (guitar), GARY DAY (bass), BOZ BOORER (guitar, ex-POLECATS) and SPENCER COBRIN (drums), touring the album around the world, his first live appearances since the prime of The SMITHS. The tour was largely a success and, enlivened and inspired, MORRISSEY cut the 'YOUR ARSENAL' (1992) set. Produced by MICK RONSON and co-penned with WHYTE, the album took the watered down glam-rock of 'KILL UNCLE' and kickstarted it with some raw rockabilly, resulting in MORRISSEY's highest chart placing for years (No.4). Though the record failed to spawn any major hits, it contained such thoughtful material as 'I KNOW IT'S GONNA HAPPEN SOMEDAY' and 'YOU'RE THE ONE FOR ME, FATTY', the former subsequently covered by DAVID BOWIE, another of MORRISSEY's idols. The same year, MORRISSEY hit the headlines with his scathing criticism of Johnny Rogan, author of the SMITHS biography, 'Morrissey & Marr: The Severed Alliance'. It wasn't the last time the 'Oscar Wilde of Rock' would be in the news, MORRISSEY subsequently losing a well publicised court battle with MIKE JOYCE over unpaid SMITHS royalties. More controversy surrounded the singer following his disastrous appearance at the 1993 'Madstock' concert in London's Finsbury Park. Supporting headliners MADNESS, MORRISSEY was given an extremely hostile reception after coming out draped in a Union Jack, further fuelling debate over the perceived ambiguity of his motivations. Following all this strife, 'VAUXHALL AND I' (1994) resurrected MORRISSEY's career, a sympathetic production by STEVE LILLYWHITE setting the scene for his most considered and consistent album to date. The record was also MORRISSEY's first No.1, a critically acclaimed opus that was marked by more emotionally-charged lyrics, laying off the trademark caustic barbs. Moving to 'R.C.A.', MORRISSEY released 'SOUTHPAW GRAMMER' almost a year later, a bizarre album that focussed on the singer's apparent boxing fixation. Unsurprisingly, the record met with bewilderment from critics, though it consolidated his position as one of rock's few genuine mavericks. In 1997, MORRISSEY once again shifted stables, this time to 'Island' who got their chance to showcase the bard on some new work, 'MALADJUSTED'. Without a contract for around five years, MORRISSEY looked to have retired to his L.A. bachelor pad, until that is, 'Sanctuary' records signed him for a return in 2003. • **Covered:** THAT'S ENTERTAINMENT (Jam) / SKIN STORM (Bradford) / MOON RIVER (Henry

Mancini). • **Trivia:** In the late 80's, MORRISSEY made a cameo appearance in Channel 4's 'Brookside' off-shoot, 'South'.

Album rating: VIVA HATE (*9) / BONA DRAG collection (*7) / KILL UNCLE (*8) / YOUR ARSENAL (*8) / BEETHOVEN WAS DEAF (*5) / VAUXHALL AND I (*9) / WORLD OF MORRISSEY part compilation (*7) / SOUTHPAW GRAMMAR (*6) / MALADJUSTED (86) / SUEDEHEAD (THE BEST OF . . .) compilation (*7)

MORRISSEY – vocals; with **STEPHEN STREET** – guitar, bass, producer, co-writer / **ANDREW PARESI** – drums / **VINI REILLY** – guitar, keyboards (of DURUTTI COLUMN)

H.M.V. Sire

Feb 88. (7") *(POP 1618)* **SUEDEHEAD. / I KNOW VERY WELL HOW I GOT MY NAME** 5 –
(12"+=) *(12POP 1618)* – Hairdresser on fire.
(c-s++=/cd-s++=) *(TC/CD POP 1618)* – Oh well, I'll never learn.

Mar 88. (cd/c/lp) *(CD/TC+/CDS 3787)* *<25699>* **VIVA HATE** 2 48
– Alsatian cousin / Little man, what now? / Everyday is like Sunday / Bengali in platforms / Angel, angel, down we go together / Late night, Maudlin Street / Suedehead / Break up the family / The ordinary boys / I don't mind if you forget me / Dial-a-cliche / Margaret on the guillotine. *(re-iss. Mar94 on 'Parlophone' cd/c; same) (cd re-iss. Mar97 on 'E.M.I.'+=; CDCNTAV 2)* – Let the right one slip in / Pashernate love / At amber / Disappointed (live) / Girl least likely to / I'd love to / Michael's bones / I've changed my plea to guilty. *(lp re-iss. Aug00 on 'Simply Vinyl'; SVLP 233)*

Jun 88. (7") *(POP 1619)* **EVERYDAY IS LIKE SUNDAY. / DISAPPOINTED** 9 –
(12"+=) *(12POP 1619)* – Sister I'm a poet.
(c-s++=/cd-s++=) *(TC/CD+/POP 1619)* – Will never marry.

— **MORRISSEY** only retained **STREET.** He brought in **NEIL TAYLOR** – guitar and re-united with (ex-SMITHS):- **CRAIG GANNON, ANDY ROURKE + MIKE JOYCE**

Feb 89. (7") *(POP 1620)* **THE LAST OF THE FAMOUS INTERNATIONAL PLAYBOYS. / LUCKY LIPS** 6 –
(12"+=/cd-s+=) *(12/CD POP 1620)* – Michael's bones.

Apr 89. (7"/etched-12") *(POP/12POPS 1621)* **INTERESTING DRUG. / SUCH A LITTLE THING MAKES SUCH A BIG DIFFERENCE** 9 –
(c-s+=/12"+=/cd-s+=) *(TC/12/CD POP 1621)* – Sweet and tender hooligan (live).

— He brought in complete new line-up:- **KEVIN ARMSTRONG** – guitar / **MATTHEW SELIGMAN** – bass / **STEVE HOPKINS** – drums and returning **ANDREW PARESI** – keyboards

Nov 89. (7") *(POP 1622)* **OUIJA BOARD, OUIJA BOARD. / YES, I AM BLIND** 18
(c-s+=/12"+=/cd-s+=) *(TC/12/CD POP 1622)* *<21424>* – East west.

— **ANDY ROURKE** returned to repl. SELIGMAN + HOPKINS / added guest **MARY MARGARET O'HARA** – vocals (up & coming solo artist)

Apr 90. (c-s/7") *(TC+/POP 1623)* **NOVEMBER SPAWNED A MONSTER. / HE KNOWS I'D LOVE TO SEE HIM** 12
(12"+=/cd-s+=) *(12/CD POP 1623)* *<21529>* – The girl least likely to.

Oct 90. (c-s/7") *(TC+/POP 1624)* **PICCADILLY PALARE. / GET OFF THE STAGE** 18 –
(12"+=/cd-s+=) *(12/CD POP 1624)* – At amber.

Oct 90. (cd/c/lp) *(CD/TC+/CSD 3788)* *<26221>* **BONA DRAG** 9 59
– Piccadilly palare / Interesting drug / November spawned a monster / Will never marry / Such a little thing makes such a big difference / The last of the famous international playboys / Ouija board, ouija board / Hairdresser on fire / Everyday is like Sunday / He knows I'd love to see him / Yes, I am blind / Lucky lisp / Suedehead / Disappointed. *(re-iss. Mar94 on 'Parlophone' cd/c; same)*

— He now retained **ANDREW PARESI.** Newcomers were **BEDDERS** – bass (ex-MADNESS) / **MARK E.NEVIN** – guitars, co-composer (ex-FAIRGROUND ATTRACTION) plus **STEVE HEART + SEAMUS BEAGHAN** – keyboards / **NAWAZISH ALI KHAN** – violin

Feb 91. (c-s/7") *(TC+/POP 1625)* **OUR FRANK. / JOURNALISTS WHO LIE** 26
(12"+=/cd-s+=) *(12/CD POP 1625)* *<40043>* – Tony the pony.

Feb 91. (cd/c/lp) *(CD/TC+/CSD 3789)* *<26514>* **KILL UNCLE** 8 Mar91 52
– Our Frank / Asian rut / Sing your life / Mute witness / King Leer / Found found found / Driving your girlfriend home / The harsh truth of the camera eye / (I'm) The end of the family line / There's a place in Hell for me and my friends.

— His tour band Spring '91; **ALAIN WHYTE** – guitar / **GARY DAY** – bass / **BOZ BOORER** – guitar (ex-POLECATS) / **SPENCER COBRIN** – drums

Apr 91. (c-s/7") *(TC+/POP 1626)* **SING YOUR LIFE. / THAT'S ENTERTAINMENT** 33
(12"+=/cd-s+=) *(12/CD POP 1626)* *<40084>* – The loop.

Jul 91. (c-s/7") *(TC+/POP 1627)* **PREGNANT FOR THE LAST TIME. / SKIN STORM** 25 –
(12"+=/cd-s+=) *(12/CD POP 1627)* – Cosmic dancer (live) / Disappointed (live).

Oct 91. (c-s/7") *(TC+/POP 1628)* **MY LOVE LIFE. / I'VE CHANGED MY PLEA TO GUILTY** 29
(12"+=/cd-s+=) *(12/CD POP 1628)* *<40163>* – There's a place in Hell for me and my friends.

Oct 91. (cd-ep) *<40184>* **AT KROQ (live)** –
– There's a place in Hell for my friends / My love life / Sing your life.

May 92. (c-s/7") *(TC+/POP 1629)* **WE HATE IT WHEN OUR FRIENDS BECOME SUCCESSFUL. / SUEDEHEAD** 17
(12"+=) *(12POP 1629)* – Pregnant for the last time.
(cd-s+=) *(CDPOP 1629)* *<40560>* – I've changed my plea to guilty.

Jul 92. (c-s/7") *(TC+/POP 1630)* **YOU'RE THE ONE FOR ME, FATTY. / PASHERNATE LOVE** 19 –
(12"+=/cd-s+=) *(12/CD POP 1630)* – There speaks a true friend.

Jul 92. (cd/c/lp) *(CD/TC+/CSD 3790)* *<26994>* **YOUR ARSENAL** 4 21
– You're gonna need someone on your side / Glamorous glue / We'll let you know / The National Front disco / Certain people I know / We hate it when our friends become successful / You're the one for me, Fatty / Seasick, yet still docked / I know it's gonna happen someday / Tomorrow. *(lp re-iss. Sep00 on 'Simply Vinyl'; SVLP 244)*

Sep 92. (cd-s) *<40580>* **TOMORROW / LET THE RIGHT ONE SLIP IN / PASHERNATE LOVE** –

Dec 92. (c-s/7") *(TC+/POP 1631)* **CERTAIN PEOPLE I KNOW. / JACK THE RIPPER** 35 –
(12"+=/cd-s+=) *(12/CD POP 1631)* – You've had her.

Parlophone E.M.I.

May 93. (cd/c/lp) *(CD/TC+/CSD 3791)* *<89061>* **BEETHOVEN WAS DEAF (live)** 13
– You're the one for me, Fatty / Certain people I know / National Front disco / November spawned a monster / Seasick, yet still docked / The loop / Sister I'm a poet / Jack the ripper / Such a little thing makes such a big difference / I know it's gonna happen someday / We'll let you know / Suedehead / He knows I'd love to see him / You're gonna need someone on your side / Glamorous glue / We hate it when our friends become successful. *(re-iss. Sep94 on 'Parlophone' cd/c; same)*

— **BOZ BOORER + ALAIN WHYTE** – guitars / **JONNY BRIDGEWOOD** – bass / **WOODIE TAYLOR** – drums

Parlophone Sire

Mar 94. (c-s/7") *(TCR/R 6372)* *<18207>* **THE MORE YOU IGNORE ME, THE CLOSER I GET. / USED TO BE A SWEET BOY** 8 46
(12"+=/cd-s+=) *(12R/CDR 6372)* – I'd love to.

Mar 94. (cd/c/lp) *(CD/TC+/PCSD 148)* *<45451>* **VAUXHALL AND I** 1 18
– Now my heart is full / Spring-heeled Jim / Billy Budd / Hold on to your friends / The more you ignore me, the closer I get / Why don't you find out for yourself / I am hated for loving / Lifeguard sleeping, girl drowning / Used to be a sweet boy / The lazy sunbathers / Speedway.

Jun 94. (c-s/7") *(TCR/R 6383)* **HOLD ON TO YOUR FRIENDS. / MOONRIVER** 47 –
(12"/cd-s) *(12R/CDR 6383)* – (extended versions).

Aug 94. (c-s/7"; by MORRISSEY and SIOUXSIE) *(TCR/R 6365)* **INTERLUDE. / ('A'extended)** 25 –
(12"+=/cd-s+=) *(12R/CDR 6365)* – ('A'mix).

Aug 94. (cd-s) *<41700>* **NOW MY HEART IS FULL / MOON RIVER / JACK THE RIPPER** –

Jan 95. (c-s/7") *(TC+/R 6400)* **BOXERS. / HAVE-A-GO MERCHANT** 23
(12"+=/cd-s+=) *(12/CD R 6400)* *<41914>* – Whatever happens, I love you.

Feb 95. (cd/c/lp) *(CD/TC+/PCSD 163)* *<45879>* **WORLD OF MORRISSEY** (part compilation) 15
– Whatever happens, I love you / Billy Budd / Jack the ripper (live) / Have-a-go merchant / The loop / Sister I'm a poet (live) / You're the one for me, Fatty (live) / Boxers / Moon river (extended) / My love life / Certain people I know / The last of the famous international playboys / We'll let you know / Spring-heeled Jim. *(cd re-iss. Mar99 on 'EMI Gold'; CDPCSD 163)*

— **SPENCER JAMES COBRIN** – drums; repl. WOODIE

		RCA Victor	RCA Victor
Aug 95.	(7"/c-s) *(74321 29980-7/-4)* **DAGENHAM DAVE. / NOBODY LOVES US**	26	–
	(cd-s+=) *(74321 29980-2)* – You must please remember.		
Aug 95.	(cd/c/lp) *(74321 29953-2/-4/-1)* <45939> **SOUTHPAW GRAMMAR**	4	66
	– The teachers are afraid of the pupils / Reader meet author / The boy racer / The operation / Dagenham Dave / Do your best and don't worry / Best friend on the payroll / Southpaw.		
Nov 95.	(7") *(74321 33294-7)* **THE BOY RACER. / LONDON (live)**	36	–
	(cd-s+=) *(74321 33295-2)* – Billy Budd (live).		
	(cd-s) *(74321 33294-2)* – ('A'side) / Spring heeled Jim (live) / Why don't you find out for yourself (live).		
		Parlophone	Capitol
Dec 95.	(c-s/7") *(TC+/R 6243)* **SUNNY. / BLACK-EYED SUSAN**	42	–
	(cd-s+=) *(CDR 6243)* – A swallow on my neck.		
		Island	Polygram
Jul 97.	(c-s/7") *(C+/IS 667)* **ALMA MATTERS. / I CAN HAVE BOTH**	16	–
	(12"+=/cd-s+=) *(12IS/CID 667)* – Heir apparent.		
Aug 97.	(cd/c/lp) *(CID/ICT/ILPS 8059)* <536036> **MALADJUSTED**	8	61
	– Maladjusted / Alma matters / Ambitious outsiders / Trouble loves me / Papa Jack / Ammunition / Wide to receive / Roy's keen / He cried / Satan rejected my soul.		
Oct 97.	(c-s/7") *(C+/IS 671)* **ROY'S KEEN. / LOST**	42	–
	(12"+=/cd-s+=) *(12IS/CID 671)* – The edges are no longer parallel.		
Dec 97.	(c-s/7") *(C+/IS 686)* **SATAN REJECTED MY SOUL. / NOW I AM I WAS**	39	–
	(cd-s+=/12"+=) *(CID/12IS 686)* – This is not your country.		

— MORRISSEY is about to make his comeback in 2004

– compilations, etc. –

on 'E.M.I.' unless mentioned otherwise

Sep 97.	(cd/c/lp) *(<CD/TC+/EMC 3771>)* **SUEDEHEAD (THE BEST OF MORRISSEY)**	26	–
	– Suedehead / Interesting drug / Boxers / Last of the famous international playboys / Sunny / Tomorrow / Interlude / Everyday is like Sunday / Hold on to your friends / My love life / Our Frank / Piccadilly palare / Ouija board, ouija board / You're the one for me, fatty / We hate it when our friends become successful / Pregnant for the last time / November spawned a monster / The more you ignore me, the closer I get / That's entertainment. *(special edition; CDEMCX 3771)*		
Jun 00.	(10xcd-s-box) *(887293-2)* **THE CD SINGLES 1988-1991**		–
Sep 00.	(3xcd-box) *(528376-2)* **BONA DRAG / KILL UNCLE / VAUXHALL AND I**		–
Sep 01.	(9xcd-s-box) *(879745-2)* **THE CD SINGLES 1991-1995**		–
Dec 01.	(cd) *Rhino/Warners-Sire; <R2 78375>* **THE BEST OF . . .**	–	
	– The more you ignore me, the closer I get / Suedehead / Everyday is like Sunday / Glamorous glue / Do your best and don't worry / November spawned a monster / The last of the famous international playboys / Sing your life / Hairdresser on fire / Interesting drug / We hate it when our friends become successful / Certain people I know / Now my heart is full / I know it's gonna happen someday / Sunny / Alma matters / Hold on to your friends / Sister I'm a poet / Disappointed / Tomorrow / Lost.		
Oct 02.	(d-cd) *(543151-2)* **BONA DRAG / YOUR ARSENAL**		–

☐ MOTHER LOVE BONE (see under ⇒ PEARL JAM)

☐ MOTHERS (OF INVENTION) (see under ⇒ ZAPPA, Frank)

☐ MO THUGS FAMILY (see under ⇒ BONE THUGS-N-HARMONY)

MOTLEY CRUE

Formed: Los Angeles, California, USA . . . early 1981 by NIKKI SIXX (bass, ex-LONDON) who recruited VINCE NEIL (vocals, ex-ROCK CANDY), TOMMY LEE (drums) and finally MICK MARS (guitar). In 1981, they issued their debut album, 'TOO FAST FOR LOVE', on their own US label, 'Leathur'. From its 'STICKY FINGERS'-esque, crotch-shot cover to the low-rent sleaze-rock contained within, the album announced MOTLEY CRUE's status as wannabe metal successors to the likes of AEROSMITH and The NEW YORK DOLLS. There were certainly worse reference points to have, and the record was an amateurish, minor classic, the title track and 'PIECE OF YOUR ACTION' pouting highlights. After being signed to 'Elektra', the record was re-issued the following year while the band began work on a follow-up with producer Tom Werman. 'SHOUT AT THE DEVIL' (1983) added cod-satanic imagery to their glam fixation while beefing up the guitars. But VENOM this band were not and songs like 'GOD BLESS THE CHILDREN OF THE BEAST' were downright ridiculous. If catchy pop-metal like 'TOO YOUNG TO FALL IN LOVE' was the work of the devil, then God certainly had nothing to fear. Nevertheless, after a nationwide tour supporting KISS, the album hit the US Top 20 and things were looking up for the band. However on the 8th of December '84, VINCE NEIL was involved in a serious car accident; NICK 'RAZZLE' DINGLEY (drummer with HANOI ROCKS) was killed in the crash while two others were injured. NEIL was subsequently ordered to pay $2.5 million compensation and sentenced to 20 days in jail, after being convicted of vehicle manslaughter. The tragedy overshadowed much of the 'THEATRE OF PAIN' (1985) album, a record that went on to sell more than two million copies after its cover of Brownsville Station's 'SMOKIN' IN THE BOYS ROOM' was a Top 20 hit. The album also boasted the surprisingly poignant power ballad, 'HOME SWEET HOME', an MTV favourite later that year. 'GIRLS, GIRLS, GIRLS' (1987) was a marked improvement; the lyrics cementing The 'CRUE's reputation as the 'bad' boys of metal, the music confident and cocksure. Tracks like 'WILD SIDE', showed a newfound adventurousness, the first signs that the band were capable of promotion from the metal second division. Early in 1988, MATTHEW TRIPPE sued the CRUE for royalties, alleging he masqueraded and wrote songs as NIKKI SIXX, while he recovered from a 1983 car crash. This was later proved to be false, although there is still much speculation on how SIXX's face was bloated on some mug pics. Having survived a near-death experience after a heroin o.d., SIXX and the newly cleaned up 'CRUE delivered another album, 'DR. FEELGOOD', which duly topped the US charts (while hitting Top 5 in the UK). It was to be NEIL's parting shot, the singer ousted in the early 90's following media overkill on his war of words with AXL ROSE. While he released a solo album in '93, the group recruited a new frontman, JOHN CORABI, although the subsequent album, 'MOTLEY CRUE' found few takers. NEIL and the group had patched up their differences by 1997, the album, 'GENERATION SWINE' giving them a return to the US Top 5. With VINCE back in the fold it must've seemed a good time to capture some of their rekindled stage fire; 'LIVE: ENTERTAINMENT OR DEATH' (1999) featured a clutch of latter day tracks and a far larger whack from the halcyon days of yore, we're talking early 80's here. If that wasn't enough to please the band's diehard fans then 'NEW TATTOO' (2000) saw MOTLEY CRUE returning to their bad old days in fine style. Out went the half-arsed attempts at alternative metal and serious subject matter; in came scuzz-rock and such time honoured lyrical themes as, well, sex, drugs and rock'n'roll basically, the nastier and filthier the better. They even signed off with a rendition of The Tubes' 'WHITE PUNKS ON DOPE', a somehow more appropriate choice of cover than 'HELTER SKELTER' . . . • **Covered:** HELTER SKELTER (Beatles) / JAILHOUSE ROCK (Leiber-Stoller). • **Trivia:** Late 1985, TOMMY LEE married actress Heather Lockear, although it did not last. He is now the spouse of Baywatch actress PAMELA ANDERSON, although in the mid-90's press speculation was rife about an impending split. Around the same time, she gave birth to their first child, although the domestic bliss was short-lived; the couple divorced while TOMMY faced a lengthy jail sentence for wife-beating. In December '87, MICK married one-time PRINCE girlfriend VANITY (star of 'Purple Rain'). In May '90, NIKKI was hitched to former Playboy centrefold Brandi Brandt.

Album rating: TOO FAST FOR LOVE (*5) / SHOUT AT THE DEVIL (*6) / THEATRE OF PAIN (*5) / GIRLS, GIRLS, GIRLS (*7) / DR. FEELGOOD (*5) / DECADE OF DECADENCE compilation (*7) / MOTLEY CRUE (*5) / GENERATION SWINE (*5) / THE BEST OF MOTLEY CRUE compilation (*6) / LIVE: ENTERTAINMENT OR DEATH (*4) / NEW TATTOO (*5) / Vince Neil: EXPOSED (*4) / CARVED IN STONE (*3) / GREATEST HITS compilation (*7)

VINCE NEIL (b. VINCENT NEIL WHARTON, 8 Feb'61, Hollywood, Calif.) – vocals (ex-ROCK CANDY) / **NIKKI SIXX** (b. FRANK FERRANNO, 11 Dec'58, San Jose, Calif.) – bass (ex-LONDON) / **MICK MARS** (b. BOB DEAL, 3 Apr'56, Huntington, Indiana) – guitar / **TOMMY LEE** (b. THOMAS LE BASS, 3 Oct'62, Athens, Greece) – drums (ex-SUITE 19)

not iss. Leathur

1981. (lp) *<R-123>* **TOO FAST FOR LOVE** [–] [ ]
– Live wire / Public enemy No.1 / Take me to the top / Merry-go-round / Piece of your action / Starry eyes / Come on and dance / Too fast for love / On with the show. *(UK-iss.Oct82 as 'MOTLEY CRUE' on 'Elektra' lp/c; K/K4 52425) <US re-iss. Nov83 on 'Elektra'; 60174> (cd-iss. Feb93 on 'Elektra'; 7559 60174-2)*

1982. (7"gig freebie) **TOAST OF THE TOWN. / STICK TO YOUR GUNS** [–] [ ]

Elektra Elektra

Sep 83. (lp/c) *(960 289-1/-4) <60289>* **SHOUT AT THE DEVIL** [ ] [17]
– In the beginning / Shout at the Devil / Looks that kill / Bastard / Knock 'em dead, kid / Danger / Too young to fall in love / Helter skelter / Red hot / Ten seconds 'til love / God bless the children of the beast. *(cd-iss. Jan89; 960 289-2)*

Jul 84. (7") *(E 9756) <69756>* **LOOKS THAT KILL. / PIECE OF YOUR ACTION** [ ] Jan84 [54]
(12"+=) *(E 9756T)* – Live wire.

Oct 84. (7"/12") *(E 9732/+T) <69732>* **TOO YOUNG TO FALL IN LOVE. / TAKE ME TO THE TOP** [ ] Jun84 [90]

Jul 85. (lp/c) *(EKT 8/+C) <60418>* **THEATRE OF PAIN** [36] [6]
– City boy blues / Smokin' in the boys' room / Louder than Hell / Keep your eye on the money / Home sweet home / Tonight (we need a lover) / Use it or lose it / Save our souls / Raise your hands to rock / Fight for your rights. *(cd-iss. Jul86; 960 418-2)*

Aug 85. (7"/7"sha-pic-d/12") *(EKR 16/+P/T) <69625>* **SMOKIN' IN THE BOYS' ROOM. / USE IT OR LOSE IT** [71] Jul85 [16]
<US-12"> – ('A'side) / Helter skelter / Piece of your action / Live wire.

Oct 85. (7") *<69591>* **HOME SWEET HOME. / RED HOT** [–] [89]

Jan 86. (7"/7"sha-pic-d) *(EKR 33/+P)* **SMOKIN' IN THE BOYS' ROOM. / HOME SWEET HOME** [51] [–]
(12"+=) *(EKR 33T)* – Shout at the Devil.

Jun 87. (lp/c)(cd) *(EKT 39/+C)(960 725-2) <60725>* **GIRLS, GIRLS, GIRLS** [14] [2]
– The wild side / Girls, girls, girls / Dancing on glass / Bad bad boogie / Nona / Five years dead / All in the name of . . . / Sumthin' for nuthin' / You're all I need / Jailhouse rock (live).

Jul 87. (7"/7"w-poster) *(EKR 59/+P) <69465>* **GIRLS, GIRLS, GIRLS. / SUMTHIN' FOR NUTHIN'** [26] May87 [12]
(12"+=/12"pic-d+=) *(EKR 59T)* – Smokin' in the boys' room.

Sep 87. (7") *<69449>* **THE WILD SIDE. / FIVE YEARS DEAD** [–] [ ]

Nov 87. (7") *<69429>* **YOU'RE ALL I NEED. / ALL IN THE NAME OF ROCK** [–] [83]

Jan 88. (7") *(EKR 65)* **YOU'RE ALL I NEED. / WILD SIDE** [23] [–]
(12"+=/12"pic-d+=/12"boxed+=) *(EKR 65 T/+P/B)* – Home sweet home / Looks that kill.

Jul 88. (m-lp/m-cd) *<25XD 1052>* **HOME SWEET HOME** (RAW TRACKS) [–] [ ]
– Live wire / Piece of your action / Too young to fall in love / Knock 'em dead, kid / Home sweet home.

Sep 89. (lp/c)(cd) *(EKT 59/+C)(960 829-2) <60829>* **DR. FEELGOOD** [4] [1]
– Same ol' situation (S.O.S.) / Slice of your pie / Rattlesnake shake / Kickstart my heart / Without you / Don't go away mad (just go away) / She goes down / Sticky sweet / Time for a change / T.N.T. (Terror 'n' Tinseltown) / Dr. Feelgood.

Oct 89. (7"/7"sha-pic-d/c-s) *(EKR 97/+P/C) <69271>* **DR. FEELGOOD. / STICKY SWEET** [50] Aug89 [6]
(ext.12"+=/ext.3"cd-s+=) *(EKR 97 T/CD)* – All in the name of rock.

Nov 89. (c-s) *<69248>* **KICKSTART MY HEART. / SHE GOES DOWN** [–] [27]

Feb 90. (c-s) *<64985>* **WITHOUT YOU. / SLICE OF YOUR LIFE** [–] [8]

Apr 90. (7"/7"pic-d/c-s) *(EKR 109/+P/C)* **WITHOUT YOU. / LIVE WIRE** [39] [–]
(12"+=/cd-s+=) *(EKR 109 T/CD)* – Girls, girls, girls / All in the name of rock.

May 90. (c-s) *<64962>* **DON'T GO AWAY MAD (JUST GO AWAY). / RATTLESNAKE SHAKE** [–] [19]

Aug 90. (c-s) *<64942>* **SAME OL' SITUATION (S.O.S.). / WILD SIDE** [–] [78]

Nov 90. (m-cd) *<WPCP 3462>* **RAW TRACKS II** [–] [ ]

Aug 91. (7"/c-s) *(EKR 133/+C) <64848>* **PRIMAL SCREAM. / DANCING ON GLASS** [32] [63]
(12"+=/cd-s+=) *(EKR 133 T/CD)* – Red hot (live) / Dr. Feelgood (live).

Oct 91. (cd)(lp/c) *<(7559 61204-2)>(EKT 95/+C)>* **DECADE OF DECADENCE** (compilation) [20] [2]
– Live wire / Piece of your action / Shout at the Devil / Looks that kill / Home sweet home / Smokin' in the boys' room / Girls, girls, girls / Wild side / Dr. Feelgood / Kickstart my heart / Teaser / Rock'n'roll junkie / Primal scream / Angela / Anarchy in the UK.

Dec 91. (7") *(EKR 136) <64818>* **HOME SWEET HOME '91. / YOU'RE ALL I NEED** [37] Nov91 [37]
(12"+=/12"pic-d+=/cd-s+=) *(EKR 136 T/TP/CD)* – Without you / ('A'original mix).

—— Had already split temporarily Apr'91 to do own projects. The group parted company with VINCE NEIL, who went solo early 1992.

—— brought in **JOHN CORABI** (b.26 Apr'59, Philadelphia, Pennsylvania) – vocals (ex-SCREAM)

Feb 94. (7"yellow) *(EKR 180)* **HOOLIGAN'S HOLIDAY. / HYPNOTIZED (demo)** [36] [ ]
(12"+=/cd-s+=/cd-s+=) *(EKR 180 T/CD/CDX)* – ('A'-Brown nose edit) / ('A'-album version a.k.a. The Dregs of Society – featuring – The Slime City Sinners & The Canadian Connection) / Hypnotized (demo).

Mar 94. (cd/c/d-lp) *<(7559 61534-2/-4/-1)>* **MOTLEY CRUE** [17] [7]
– Power to the music / Uncle Jack / Hooligan's holiday / Misunderstood / Loveshine / Poison apples / Hammered / 'Til death us do part / Welcome to the numb / Smoke the sky / Droppin' like flies / Drift away.

May 94. (7"w-drawn) *(EKR 183)* **MISUNDERSTOOD. /** [–] [–]

—— **VINCE NEIL** returned to repl. CORABI

Jun 97. (cd/c) *<(7559 61901-2/-4)>* **GENERATION SWINE** [ ] [4]
– Find myself / Afraid / Flush / Generation swine / Confessions / Beauty / Glitter / Anybody out there / Let us prey / Rocketship / Rat like me / Shout at the Devil '97 / Brandon.

Jul 97. (cd-s) *(E 3936CD1)* **AFRAID / AFRAID (Swine mix) / LUST FOR LIFE / WELCOME TO THE PLANET BOOM** [58] [ ]
(cd-s) *(E 3936CD2)* – ('A'side) / Generation swine / Father / Bittersweet.
(cd-s) *(E 3936CD3)* – ('A'-alternative rave mix) / Shout at the Devil '97 / All in the name of . . . (live) / Girls, girls, girls (live).

Virgin Beyond

Nov 98. (cd) *(CDVIR 77) <78002>* **THE BEST OF MOTLEY CRUE** <US-title 'GREATEST HITS'> (compilation & 2 new) [ ] [20]
– Bitter pill / Enslaved / Girls, girls, girls / Kickstart my heart / Wild side / Glitter (remix) / Dr. Feelgood / Same ol' situation / Home sweet home / Afraid / Don't go away mad (just go away) / Without you / Smokin' in the boys room / Primal scream / Too fast for love / Looks that kill / Shout at the Devil '97.

— **RANDY CASTILLO** – drums (ex-OZZY OSBOURNE) repl. TOMMY LEE who formed METHODS OF MAYHEM

Jul 00. (cd) *(CDVIR 117) <78120>* **NEW TATTOO** Jun00 41
– Hell on high heels / Treat me like the dog I am / New tattoo / Dragstrip superstar / 1st band on the Moon / She needs rock & roll / Punched in the teeth by love / Hollywood ending / Fake / Porno star / White punks on dope.

– compilations, etc. –

Jan 00. (d-cd) *Spitfire; (SPITCD 058) / Beyond; <63985 78034>*
LIVE: ENTERTAINMENT OR DEATH Nov99
– Looks that kill / Knock 'em dead, kid / Too young to fall in love / Live wire / Public enemy #1 / Shout at the Devil / Merry-go-round / Ten seconds to love / Piece of your action / Starry eyes / Helter skelter / Smokin' in the boys' room / Don't go away mad (just go away) / The wild side / Girls, girls, girls / Dr. Feelgood / Without you / Primal scream / Same ol' situation / Home sweet home / Kickstart my heart.

Jun 03. (cd) *Hip-O; <(038659-2)>* **GREATEST HITS** Mar03
– Bitter pill / Enslaved / Girls, girls, girls / Kickstart my heart / Wild side / Glitter (remix) / Dr. Feelgood / Same ol' situation / Home sweet home / Afraid / Don't go away mad (just go away) / Without you / Smokin' in the boys' room / Primal scream / Too fast for love / Looks that kill / Shout at the Devil '97.

MOTORHEAD

Formed: London, England ... June '75 by LEMMY (aka IAN KILMISTER; vocals, bass) who decided to form his own band when, after a five year stint with hyperspace hippies HAWKWIND, he was finally given the boot. His sharp exit came after he was briefly detained in Canada on drugs charges; a notorious speed freak, his penchant for amphetamines was directly translated into MOTORHEAD's music, a synapse-crunching racket that somehow lent itself to a tune or two (the title of the band's first single, 'WHITE LINE FEVER', said it all really). Following his departure from HAWKWIND, LEMMY toyed with the name BASTARD, before opting for the MOTORHEAD moniker, the title of the last song he'd penned for his previous band. He subsequently hooked up with LARRY WALLIS (guitar, vocals) of the PINK FAIRIES and LUCAS FOX (drums), although by early '76 these two had been replaced with 'FAST' EDDIE CLARKE and PHIL 'PHILTHY ANIMAL' TAYLOR respectively. The initial line-up had recorded a relatively laid back outing, 'ON PAROLE' for 'United Artists' in 1975, although this was shelved until 1979 when the label cashed in on the band's success. The aforementioned 'WHITE LINE FEVER' single was also held back, 'Stiff' only releasing it once MOTORHEAD's commercial credentials had been established. It was the 'Chiswick' label who finally had the balls to release something, the eponymous 'MOTORHEAD' album in 1977. It was the first opus from the definitive MOTORHEAD line-up, a combination that would become one of the most infamous in the history of heavy metal and create some of the most enduring material in the band's career. Yet while MOTORHEAD were the epitome of headbanging metal, their maniacal energy also attracted hardcore punks in the same way IRON MAIDEN's early performances had a foot in both camps. Over a series of shit kicking albums, 'OVERKILL' (1979), 'BOMBER' (1979) and 'ACE OF SPADES' (1980), MOTORHEAD became a legend, laying the foundations of thrash with testosterone saturated anthems. The latter album was the landmark MOTORHEAD release, its title track the ultimate outlaw anthem and a Top 20 hit to boot. The record went to No.4, illustrating how quickly the band had risen through the metal ranks. While CLARKE and TAYLOR provided the musical fuel, LEMMY was undoubtedly the beast's engine, his dirty, propulsive bass driving MOTORHEAD ever onwards like the aural equivalent of road rage. And crucially, like all genuine badass outlaws, LEMMY was 'orrible!, yet he still got the chicks, and he had style. In bucketloads. Decked out in his white cowboy boots, bullet belt and mutton chop sideburns, he stood centre stage, rooted to the spot, head stretched up to the mike (maybe LIAM GALLAGHER clocked a few shows) like he was summoning up the God of Thunder (possibly). LEMMY didn't sing in the conventional sense, or even in the heavy metal sense, rather he rasped like a piece of industrial strength sandpaper scraped across a blackboard. He also had more charisma than most of the preening queens that passed as frontmen, his sharp wit and biting sense of humour making him quite a celebrity in his own right and ensuring that his band never fell into parody. MOTORHEAD gained further press attention when they hooked up with rock chicks, GIRLSCHOOL, for the 'ST. VALENTINE'S DAY MASSACRE' EP, released, appropriately enough, in February '81. Credited to HEADGIRL (guffaw, guffaw), the assembled n'er do wells ran through a suitably leering version of Johnny Kidd's 'PLEASE DON'T TOUCH'. Their blistering live set was finally laid down on vinyl in the form of 'NO SLEEP 'TIL HAMMERSMITH' (1981), the band's first (and only) No.1 album and deservedly so. Surely the tightest rock band on the planet at that point, MOTORHEAD ran through a hair whipping frenzy of favourites, from 'STAY CLEAN' and '(WE ARE) THE ROAD CREW' to 'IRON HORSE', LEMMY's tribute to Hell's Angel leader, Tramp. This line-up recorded a further album, the slightly disappointing 'IRON FIST' (1982), before CLARKE left to from his own outfit, FASTWAY. His replacement was BRIAN ROBERTSON (ex-THIN LIZZY, ex-WILD HORSES) who played on only one album, 1983's 'ANOTHER PERFECT DAY'. His more subtle style didn't sit well with the trademark MOTORHEAD cacophony and he soon departed for the more appropriate FRANKIE MILLER BAND, PHIL CAMPBELL and MICHAEL BURSTON (aka WURZEL) replacing him. TAYLOR also departed, PETE GILL (ex-Saxon) being recruited to fill the drum stool and complete the new look four piece MOTORHEAD. The new band made their debut on 'NO REMORSE' (1984), a compilation that collected MOTORHEAD's meanest tracks and showcased four new ones, among them the uber-grind of 'KILLED BY DEATH', possibly LEMMY and Co.'s finest hour. The band almost made the Top 20 once again with the BILL LASWELL-produced 'ORGASMATRON' (1986), LEMMY sounding almost inhuman on the brilliant title track; part android, part wild beast. TAYLOR returned to the fold the following year for the 'ROCK 'N' ROLL' album, its 'EAT THE RICH' track used on the 'Comic Strip' film of the same name, in which LEMMY made his acting debut. Another live album followed, 'NO SLEEP AT ALL' (1988), although it failed to make the same commercial impact as its predecessor. Following a move to L.A. (it had to come sooner or later), the band were back in the charts and back on form with '1916' (1991), its title track an unprecedented show of emotion from LEMMY as he narrated the tale of a young soldier lost in battle. The wart-ridden one also indulged his war fixation on the title track to 'MARCH OR DIE' (1992), while the three most recent releases, 'BASTARDS' (1993) and 'SACRIFICE' (1995) have seen MOTORHEAD content to cruise rather than let rip. Still, as long as LEMMY dons his bass and rides into onstage battle, there'll be a willing bunch of masochists ready to have their ears bled dry by the some of the loudest, filthiest rock'n'roll on the face of the earth. After the relatively disappointing 'SNAKE BITE LOVE' (1998), the remorseless sonic abusers returned to restate their claim with 'WE ARE MOTORHEAD' (2000), as loud and obnoxious as anything they'd come up with in the preceding decade. Sadly, the fine classical violin playing with which LEMMY is currently gracing a high profile TV ad (would we kid you on?) is notably absent; maybe next time. No sign of it either on 'HAMMERED' (2002), MOTORHEAD's umpteenth release but perhaps a candidate for title of the year? With no concessions whatsoever to musical fashion, even metal fashion, LEMMY and his cohorts once again showed that where MOTORHEAD are concerned, age ain't nuthin' but a number. • **Covers:** LOUIE LOUIE (hit; Kingsmen) / TRAIN KEPT A-ROLLIN' (Johnny Burnette Trio) / PLEASE DON'T TOUCH (Johnny Kidd) / (I'M YOUR) HOOCHIE COOCHIE MAN (Willie Dixon) / CAT SCRATCH FEVER (Ted Nugent).

Album rating: MOTORHEAD (*5) / OVERKILL (*8) / BOMBER (*6) / ACE OF SPADES (*8) / NO SLEEP 'TIL HAMMERSMITH (*9) / IRON FIST (*5) / ANOTHER PERFECT DAY (*5) / NO REMORSE (*7) / ORGASMATRON (*6) / ROCK'N'ROLL (*5) / NO SLEEP AT ALL (*6) / 1916 (*7) / MARCH OR DIE (*5) / SACRIFICE (*5) / OVERNIGHT SENSATION (*6) / SNAKE BITE LOVE (*4) / EVERYTHING LOUDER THAN EVERYONE ELSE (*6) / WE ARE MOTORHEAD (*5) / HAMMERED (*5)

LEMMY (b. IAN KILMISTER, 24 Dec'45, Stoke-On-Trent, England) – vocals, bass (ex-HAWKWIND, ex-OPAL BUTTERFLY, ex-SAM GOPAL'S DREAM, ROCKIN' VICKERS) / **PHIL 'ANIMAL' TAYLOR** (b.21 Sep'54, Chesterfield, England) – drums / **FAST EDDIE CLARKE** – guitar, vocals (ex-BLUE GOOSE, ex-CURTIS KNIGHT & ZEUS) (below withdrawn)

Stiff — not iss.

Dec 76. (7") *(BUY 9)* **LEAVING HERE. / WHITE LINE FEVER** – –
(withdrawn but iss.Dec78 in 'Stiff' box set Nos.1-10)

Chiswick — not iss.

Jun 77. (7",12") *(S 13)* **MOTORHEAD. / CITY KIDS** –
(re-iss. Sep79 on 'Big Beat' 7"colrd/7"pic-d; NS/+P 13)

Aug 77. (lp) *(WLK 2)* **MOTORHEAD** 43 –
– Motorhead / Vibrator / Lost Johnny / Iron horse – Born to lose / White line fever / Keepers on the road / The watcher / Born to lose / Train kept a-rollin'. *(re-iss. white-lp 1978; CWK 3008) (re-iss. Sep81 red-lp,clear-lp; WIK 2) (cd-iss. Jun88 & Feb 91 on 'Big Beat'; CDWIK 2)*

Bronze — not iss.

Sep 78. (7") *BRO 60)* **LOUIE LOUIE. / TEAR YA DOWN** 68 –

Feb 79. (7"/12") *(BRO/12BRO 67)* **OVERKILL. / TOO LATE, TOO LATE** 39 –

Mar 79. (lp,green-lp) *(BRON 515)* **OVERKILL** 24 –
– Overkill / Stay clean / Pay your price / I'll be your sister / Capricorn / No class / Damage case / Tear ya down / Metropolis / Limb for limb. *(cd-iss. Jul87 on 'Legacy'; LLMCD 3011) (re-iss. Jul90 on 'Fame' cd/c/lp; CD/TC+/FA 3236) (re-iss. Feb91 on 'Castle' cd/c/lp; CLA CD/MC/LP 178) (re-iss. cd Aug96 on 'Essential'; ESMCD 310)*

Jun 79. (7") *(BRO 78)* **NO CLASS. / LIKE A NIGHTMARE** 61 –

Oct 79. (lp,blue-lp) *(BRON 523)* **BOMBER** 12 –
– Dead men tell no tales / Lawman / Sweet revenge / Sharpshooter / Poison / Stone dead forever / All the aces / Step down / Talking head / Bomber. *(cd-iss. Jul87 on 'Legacy'; LLMCD 3012) (re-iss. Apr91 on 'Castle' cd/c/lp; CLA CD/MC/LP 227) (re-iss. Aug96 on 'Essential'; ESMCD 311)*

Nov 79. (7",7"blue) *(BRO 85)* **BOMBER. / OVER THE TOP** 34 –

Apr 80. (7"ep/12"ep) *(BRO/12BRO 92)* **THE GOLDEN YEARS (live)** 8 –
– Leaving here / Stone dead forever / Dead men don't tell tales / Too late, too late.

Bronze — Mercury

Oct 80. (7"/12") *(BRO/+X 106)* **ACE OF SPADES. / DIRTY LOVE** 15

Oct 80. (lp/gold-lp) *(BRON/+G 531) <4011>* **ACE OF SPADES** 4
– Ace of spades / Love me like a reptile / Shoot you in the back / Live to win / Fast and loose / (We are) The road crew / Fire, fire / Jailbait / Dance / Bite the bullet / The chase is better than the catch / The hammer. *(cd-iss. Aug87 on 'Legacy'; LLMCD 3013) (re-iss. cd Aug96 on 'Essential'; ESMCD 312)*

Feb 81. (7"ep/10"ep; as HEADGIRL) *(BRO/+X 116)* **ST.VALENTINE'S DAY MASSACRE** 5 –
– Please don't touch (by MOTORHEAD & GIRLSCHOOL) / Emergency (by MOTORHEAD) / Bomber (GIRLSCHOOL).

Jun 81. (lp/gold-lp/c) *(BRON/+G/C 535)* **NO SLEEP 'TIL HAMMERSMITH (live)** 1 –
– Ace of spades / Stay clean / Metropolis / The hammer / Iron horse / No class / Overkill / (We are) The road crew / Capricorn / Bomber / Motorhead. *(cd-iss. Aug87 on 'Legacy'; LLMCD 3014) (re-iss. Feb90 on 'Castle' cd/c/lp; CLA CD/MC/LP 179) (re-iss. cd Aug96 on 'Essential'; ESMCD 313)*

Jul 81. (7"/7"pic-d) *(BRO/+P 124)* **MOTORHEAD (live). / OVER THE TOP (live)** 6
below, one-off (MOTORHEAD and The NOLANS)

Oct 81. (7"; as YOUNG AND MOODY BAND) *(BRO 130)* **DON'T DO THAT. / HOW CAN I HELP YOU TONIGHT** 63 –

Mar 82. (7",7"red,7"blue) *(BRO 146)* **IRON FIST. / REMEMBER ME, I'M GONE** 29 –

Apr 82. (lp/c) *(BRNA/+C 539) <4042>* **IRON FIST** 6
– Iron fist / Heart of stone / I'm the doctor / Go to Hell / Loser / Sex and outrage / America / Shut it down / Speedfreak / (Don't let 'em) Grind ya down / (Don't need) Religion / Bang to rights. *(re-iss. Mar87 on 'Castle' lp/c/cd; CLA LP/MC/CD 123) (cd re-iss. Aug96 on 'Essential'; ESMCD 372)*

Sep 82. (7"m; by LEMMY & WENDY) *(BRO 151)* **STAND BY YOUR MAN. / NO CLASS (Plasmatics) / MASTERPLAN (Motorhead)** –

— **BRIAN ROBERTSON** (b. 2 Feb'56, Clarkston, Scotland) – guitar, vocals (ex-THIN LIZZY, ex-WILD HORSES) repl. CLARKE who formed FASTWAY

May 83. (7") *(BRO 165)* **I GOT MINE. / TURN YOU AROUND AGAIN** 46
(12"+=) *(BROX 165)* – Tales of glory.

May 83. (lp/c) *(BRON/+C 546) <811365>* **ANOTHER PERFECT DAY** 20
– Back at the funny farm / Shine / Dancing on your grave / Rock it / One track mind / Another perfect day / Marching off to war / I got mine / Tales of glory / Die you bastard. *(re-iss. Feb91 on 'Castle' cd/c/lp; CLA CD/MC/LP 225) (re-iss. cd Sep96 on 'Essential'; ESMCD 438)*

Jul 83. (7") *(BRO 167)* **SHINE. / HOOCHIE COOCHIE MAN (live)** 59 –
(12"+=) *(BROX 167)* – (Don't need) Religion.

— LEMMY with **PHIL CAMPBELL** (b. 7 May'61, Pontypridd, Wales) – guitar / **WURZEL** (b. MICHAEL BURSTON, 23 Oct'49, Cheltenham, England) – guitar both replace ROBERTSON who joined FRANKIE MILLER BAND / **PETE GILL** (b.9 Jun'51, Sheffield, England) – drums (ex-SAXON) repl. TAYLOR

Aug 84. (7"/7"sha-pic-d) *(BRO/+P 185)* **KILLED BY DEATH. / UNDER THE KNIFE** 51 –
(12"+=) *(BROX 185)* – Under the knife (version).

Sep 84. (d-lp) *(PRO MOTOR 1)* **NO REMORSE** (compilation) 14
– Ace of spades / Motorhead / Jailbait / Stay clean / Killed by death / Bomber / Iron fist / Shine / Dancing on your grave / Metropolis / Snaggletooth / Overkill / Please don't touch / Stone dead forever / Like a nightmare / Emergency / Steal your face / Louie Louie / No class / Iron horse / (We are) The road crew / Leaving here / Locomotive. *(re-iss. 1988 on 'Castle' d-lp/c/cd+=; CLA LP/MC/CD 121)* – Too late, too late. *(re-iss. cd Aug96 on 'Essential'; ESDCD 371) (cd re-iss. Jul97; ESMCD 557)*

G.W.R. — GWR-Profile

Jun 86. (7") *(GWR 2)* **DEAF FOREVER. / ON THE ROAD (live)** 67 –
(12"+=) *(GWT 2)* – Steal your face (live).

Aug 86. (lp/c/cd) *(GW LP/TC/CD 1) <1223>* **ORGASMATRON** 21 Nov86
– Deaf forever / Nothing up my sleeve / Ain't my crime / Claw / Mean machine / Built for speed / Riding with the driver / Doctor Rock / Orgasmatron. *(pic-lp.Aug89; GWPD 1) (re-iss. cd Mar92; CLACD 283)*

— **PHIL CAMPBELL** – drums returned to repl. GILL

Aug 87. (lp/c/cd) *(GW LP/MC/CD 14) <1240>* **ROCK'N'ROLL** 43 Oct87
– Rock'n'roll / Eat the rich / Blackheart / Stone deaf in the USA / The wolf / Traitor / Dogs / All for you / Boogeyman.

Nov 87. (7") *(GWR 6)* **EAT THE RICH. / CRADLE TO GRAVE**
(12"+=) *(GWR 6)* – Power.
(above from the soundtrack of the film 'Eat The Rich')

Oct 88. (lp/c/cd) *(GW LP/MC/CD 31)* **NO SLEEP AT ALL (live)** 79
– Dr. Rock / Stay clean / Traitor / Metropolis / Dogs / Ace of spades / Eat the rich / Built for speed / Deaf forever / Just cos you got the power / Killed by death / Overkill. *(cd+=)* – (3 extra). *(re-iss. cd Mar92 on 'Castle' cd/c; CLA CD/MC 285)*

Epic — W.T.G.

Jan 91. (7"/7"sha-pic-d/c-s) *(656578-7/-0/-4)* **THE ONE TO SING THE BLUES. / DEAD MAN'S HAND** 45
(12"+=/cd-s+=) *(656578-6/-2)* – Eagle rock / Shut you down.

Jan 91. (cd/c/lp/pic-lp) *(467481-2/-4/-1) <46858>* **1916** 24 Mar91

– The one to sing the blues / I'm so bad (baby I don't care) / No voices in the sky / Going to Brazil / Nightmare – The dreamtime / Love me forever / Angel city / Make my day / Ramones / Shut you down / 1916.

—— **TAYLOR** returned but was soon repl. by **MIKEY DEE** (b.31 Oct'63, Olundby, Sweden) – drums

Aug 92. (cd/c/lp) *(471723-2/-4/-1)* **MARCH OR DIE** [60] [ ]
– Stand / Cat scratch fever / Bad religion / Jack the ripper / I ain't no nice guy / Hellraiser / Asylum choir / Too good to be true / You better run / Name in vain / March or die.

Nov 92. (12"ep/cd-ep) *(658809-6/-2)* **'92 TOUR (live)** [63] [ ]
– Hellraiser / You better run / Going to Brazil / Ramones.

—— Above 1st track co-written w / OZZY OSBOURNE

ZYX | not iss.

Nov 93. (cd/lp) *(20263-2/-1)* **BASTARDS** [–] German [–]
– On your feet or on your knees / Burner / Death or glory / I am the sword / Born to raise hell / Don't let daddy kiss me / Bad woman / Liar / Lost in the ozone / I'm your man / We bring the shake / Devils.

Arista | Arista

Nov 94. (7"/c-s; by MOTORHEAD with ICE-T & WHITFIELD CRANE) *(74321 23915-7/-4)* **BORN TO RAISE HELL. / ('A'mix)** [49] [ ]
(12"+=/cd-s+=) *(74321 23915-1/-2)* – ('A'mix).

S.P.V. | C.M.C.

Apr 95. (cd/c/lp) *(SPV 085-7694-2/-4/-1) <86231>* **SACRIFICE** [ ] [ ]
– Sacrifice / Sex & death / Over your shoulder / War for war / Order – Fade to black / Dog-face boy / All gone to hell / Make 'em blind / Don't waste your time / In another time / Out of the sun.

Oct 96. (cd/c) *(SPV 085-1830-2/-4) <86207>* **OVERNIGHT SENSATION** [ ] [ ]
– Civil war / Crazy like a fox / I don't believe a word / Eat the gun / Overnight sensation / Love can't buy you money / Broken / Them not me / Murder show / Shake the world / Listen to your heart.

Mar 98. (cd) *(SPV 0851889-2) <86238>* **SNAKE BITE LOVE** [ ] [ ]
– Love for sale / Dogs of war / Snake bite love / Assassin / Take the blame / Dead and gone / Night side / Don't lie to me / Joy of labour / Desperate for you / Better off dead.

Mar 99. (d-cd) *(SPV 087-2114-2) <86268>* **EVERYTHING LOUDER THAN EVERYONE ELSE (live)** [ ] [ ]
– Iron fist / Stay clean / On your feet or on your knees / Over your shoulder / Civil war / Burner / Metropolis / Nothing up my sleeves / I'm so bad, baby I don't care / Chase I better than the catch / Take the blame / No class / Overnight sensation / Sacrifice / Born to raise hell / Lost in the ozone / One to sing the blues / Capricorn / Love for sale / Orgasmatron / Going to Brazil / Killed by death / Bomber / Ace of spades / Overkill.

May 00. (cd/lp) *(SPV 0852182-2/-1) <86292>* **WE ARE MOTORHEAD** [ ] [ ]
– See me burning / Slow dance / Stay out of jail / God save the Queen / Out to lunch / Wake the dead / One more fucking time / Stagefright – Crash & burn / (Wearing your) Heart on your sleeve / We are Motorhead.

Jul 00. (cd-s) *(SPV 0602184-3)* **GOD SAVE THE QUEEN / ONE MORE F**KING TIME / GOD SAVE THE QUEEN (enhanced video)** [ ] [–]

S.P.V. | Metal-Is

Apr 02. (cd/lp) *(SPV 0857/0787 406-2) <85229>* **HAMMERED** [ ] [ ]
– Walk a crooked mile / Down the line / Brave new world / Voices from the war / Mine all mine / Shut your mouth / Kill the world / Dr. Love / No remorse / Red raw / Serial killer. *(ltd-cd+=; SPV 0897 406-0)* – The game / Overnight sensation (live).

– compilations, etc. –

Oct 79. (lp) *Liberty; (LBR 1004)* **ON PAROLE** [65] [–]
– Motorhead / On parole / Vibrator / Iron horse – Born to lose / City kids / Fools / The watcher / Leaving here / Lost Johnny. *(was to be have been released Dec75) (re-iss. May82 on 'Fame' lp/c; FA/TC-FA 3009) (cd-iss. Oct90; CD-FA 3251) (cd remastered Feb97 on 'EMI Gold'; CDGO 2070)*

Nov 80. (7"ep,7"blue-ep,7"pink-ep,7"orange-ep/12"ep,12"blue-ep,12"pink-ep,12"orange-ep) *Big Beatl (NS/SWT 61)* **BEER DRINKERS EP** [43] [–]
– Beer drinkers & hell raisers / On parole / Instro / I'm your witch doctor.

Mar 83. (lp/c) *Big Beat; (NED/+C 2)* **WHAT'S WORDS WORTH (live at the Roundhouse 18/2/78)** [71] [–]
– The watcher / Iron horse – Born to lose / On parole (in A) / White line fever / Keep us on the road / Leaving here / I'm your witchdoctor / The train kept a-rollin' / City kids. *(re-iss. Jan90; WIKM 49)*

Aug 82. (d-c) *Bronze; (3574 138)* **OVERKILL / BOMBER** [ ] [–]

Nov 84. (lp/c) *Astan; <2/4 0041>* **RECORDED LIVE (live)** [–] [ ]

Apr 86. (lp/c) *Raw Power; (RAW LP/MC 011)* **ANTHOLOGY** [ ] [–]
(cd-iss. Dec86; RAWCD 011)

Apr 86. (lp/c) *Dojo; (DOJO LP/TC 18)* **BORN TO LOSE** [ ] [–]

1986. (cd) *Legacy; (LLMCD 3004)* **ANTHOLOGY VOL.1** [ ] [–]

Apr 88. (lp/cd) *That's Original; (TFO LP/CD 8)* **OVERKILL / ANOTHER PERFECT DAY** [ ] [–]

1988. (3"cd-ep) *Special Edition; (CD3-10)* **ACE OF SPADES / BOMBER / MOTORHEAD / OVERKILL** [ ] [–]

Nov 89. (lp/cd) *Receiver; (RR LP/CD 120)* **BLITZKREIG ON BIRMINGHAM LIVE '77 (live)** [ ] [–]

Jan 90. (cd/lp) *Receiver; (RR CD/LP 123)* **DIRTY LOVE** [ ] [–]

Apr 90. (cd/d-lp) *Castle; (CCS CD/LP 237)* **WELCOME TO THE BEAR TRAP** [ ] [–]

Apr 90. (cd/c/d-lp) *That's Original; (TFO CD/MC/LP 024)* **BOMBER / ACE OF SPADES** [ ] [–]

Apr 90. (cd/c/lp) *G.W.R.; (GW CD/MC/LP 101)* **THE BIRTHDAY PARTY (live '85)** [ ] [–]
(cd+=) – (3 extra tracks). *(also on 'Roadrunner'; RR 9376-1)*

Jun 90. (cd/c/lp) *Receiver; (RR CD/MC/LP 130)* **LOCK UP YOUR DAUGHTERS (live 1977)** [ ] [–]

Jul 90. (cd) *Marble Arch; (cd)* **GRIND YA DOWN** [ ] [–]
(re-iss. Jul94 on 'Success';)

Jul 90. (cd/c) *Action Replay; (ARLC/CDAR 1014)* **THE BEST OF THE REST OF MOTORHEAD** [ ] [–]
(re-iss. Jul93 cd/c; CDAR/ARLC 1032)

Nov 90. (cd/c/lp) *Knight; (NEX CD/MC/LP 136)* **FROM THE VAULTS** [ ] [–]

Jul 91. (3xcd-box/3xlp-box) *Essential; (ESB CD/LP 146)* **MELTDOWN** [ ] [–]

Feb 92. (3xcd-box) *Castle; (CLABX 901)* **3 ORIGINALS** [ ] [–]
– (NO REMORSE / ACE OF SPADES / NO SLEEP 'TIL HAMMERSMITH)

Feb 92. (cd/lp) *Receiver; (RR CD/LP 005)* **LIVE JAILBAIT (live)** [ ] [–]

Sep 92. (cd/c/lp) *Roadrunner; (RR 9125-2/-4/-1)* **THE BEST OF MOTORHEAD** [ ] [–]

Apr 93. (c/cd) *Tring; (MC+/JHD 081)* **LIVE (live)** [ ] [–]

Jun 93. (4xcd-box) *Receiver; (RRZCD 501)* **MOTORHEAD BOX SET** [ ] [–]

Aug 93. (c-s/12"/cd-s) *W.G.A.F.; (MC/12/CD WGAF 101)* **ACE OF SPADES (THE C.C.N.remix). / ('A'mixes)** [23] [–]

Nov 93. (cd/c/lp) *Castle TV; (CTV CD/MC/LP 125)* **ALL THE ACES** [ ] [–]

Mar 94. (cd/c/lp) *Roadrunner; (RR 9009-2/-4/-1)* **LIVE AT BRIXTON ACADEMY (live)** [ ] [–]

Aug 94. (cd) *Spectrum; (550 724-2)* **ACES HIGH** [ ] [–]

Sep 94. (cd) *Cleopatra; (CLEO 94132)* **IRON FIST AND THE HORDES FROM HELL** [ ] [–]

May 95. (cd) *Spectrum; ()* **ULTIMATE METAL** [ ] [–]

Jul 95. (2xcd-box) *Griffin; (GCD 2192)* **FISTFUL OF ACES / THE BEST OF MOTORHEAD** [ ] [–]

Oct 95. (cd) *Elite; (ELITE 019CD)* **HEADBANGERS** [ ] [–]

Apr 96. (cd/c) *Hallmark; (30369-2/-4)* **MOTORHEAD – LIVE** [ ] [–]

Nov 96. (cd) *Emperio; (EMPRCD 692)* **LIVE** [ ] [–]

Nov 96. (cd) *Steamhammer; (CD 0857694-2)* **WE'RE MOTORHEAD AND WE'RE GONNA KICK YOUR ASS** [ ] [–]

Feb 97. (cd) *Receiver; (RRCD 238)* **STONE DEAD FOREVER** [ ] [–]

May 97. (d-cd) *Snapper; (SMDCD 127)* **TAKE NO PRISONERS** [ ] [–]

Jul 97. (cd) *Going For A Song; (GFS 073)* **MOTORHEAD** [ ] [–]

Aug 97. (4xcd-box) *Essential; (ESBCD 562)* **PROTECT THE INNOCENT** [ ] [–]

Nov 97. (cd) *Rialto; (RMCD 221)* **ARCHIVES** [ ] [–]

Mar 98. (cd/c) *Select-Castle; (SEL CD/MC 502)* **DEAF FOREVER – THE BEST OF MOTORHEAD** [ ] [–]

Apr 98. (cd) *Cleopatra; (<CLP 203>)* **THE SINGLES COLLECTION** [ ] [ ]

Apr 98. (cd) *King Biscuit; <(KBFHCD 002)>* **KING BISCUIT PRESENTS . . .** [ ] [ ]

Oct 98. (3xcd-box) *Essential; (ESMBX 304)* **OVERKILL / BOMBER / ACE OF SPADES** [ ] [ ]

Oct 98. (d-cd) *Essential; (ESSCD 668)* **ALL THE ACES – THE BEST OF MOTORHEAD / THE MUGGER'S TAPES** [ ] [ ]

Jun 99. (cd) *Cleopatra; <(CLP 0497-2)>* **GOLDEN YEARS: THE ALTERNATIVE VERSIONS** [ ] [–]

Jul 00. (cd) *S.P.V.; (06021843)* **GOD SAVE THE QUEEN** [ ] [–]

Aug 00. (d-cd/t-lp) *Metal-Is; (MIS DD/LP 002)* **THE BEST OF MOTORHEAD** [52] [–]

Oct 00. (cd; by LEMMY, SLIM JIM & DANNY B) *S.P.V.; (085-2198-2)* **LEMMY & SLIM JIM / DANNY B** [ ] [–]
Oct 00. (10xcd-box) *Raw Power; (RAWBX 140)* **BORN TO LOSE / LIVE TO WIN** [ ] [ ]

MOTT THE HOOPLE

Formed: Hereford, England . . . Jun '69 by OVEREND WATTS, DALE GRIFFIN, VERDEN ALLEN and MICK RALPHS, who were part of The SHAKEDOWN SOUND with singer STAN TIPPINS. With new manager and producer Guy Stevens placing an ad in a music paper, the group found a replacement frontman in IAN HUNTER (he had once guested on a 45 by CHARLIE WOLFE). Naming themselves MOTT THE HOOPLE (after a novel by Willard Manus), they signed to Chris Blackwell's burgeoning 'Island' label. Their eponymous debut gained a minor chart placing, the record introducing HUNTER's bluesy DYLAN-esque delivery over a tentative set of earthy rock'n'roll. Although three more lacklustre albums were completed in quick succession, the group split in 1972 after the last of them, 'BRAIN CAPERS' failed to match its predecessors' Top 50 status. Fortunately for them, a young DAVID BOWIE was re-establishing himself in the songwriting stakes, the ascending glamster offering the band a lifeline in the form of 'ALL THE YOUNG DUDES'. Securing a new contract with 'C.B.S.', MOTT THE HOOPLE roared into the UK Top 3 with a new lease of life, although VERDEN had departed soon after the recording of the similarily-titled hit parent album. Using the glam-rock craze as their launch pad, the band straddled the widening gap between the teen-pop market and the college circuit. A trio of Top 20 hits in 1973, 'HONALOOCHIE BOOGIE', 'ALL THE WAY FROM MEMPHIS' and 'ROLL AWAY THE STONE' proved that the group were no overnight sensations, although the last of these had been recorded without RALPHS who joined BAD COMPANY. Together with VERDEN's deputy MICK BOLTON, he was replaced by ARIEL BENDER and MORGAN FISHER, two veterans of the British music scene. Releasing 'THE HOOPLE' album as a follow-up to 1973's 'MOTT', the band once again hit the UK and US charts, although the critical tide was turning against glam and everyone connected with it (i.e. SWEET, SLADE, GLITTER, QUATRO, etc). With BENDER (aka LUTHER GROSVENOR) opting to join heavyweights WIDOWMAKER, the band (with ex-BOWIE sidekick, MICK RONSON, now taking on guitar duties) also opted for a harder-edged direction after a single, 'SATURDAY GIGS', failed to scrape into the Top 40. Suffering from exhaustion, HUNTER was eager to follow a less high-profile solo career, RONSON also taking the same route, the pair, in addition touring together as The HUNTER-RONSON BAND. The remainder (OVEREND, DALE and MORGAN) re-grouped in 1975 as MOTT, enlisting the services of new frontman NIGEL BENJAMIN and guitarist RAY MAJORS for a new album, 'DRIVE ON'. Another uninspiring set, 'SHOUTING AND POINTING' was to appear in 1976, the band soon giving up amid general disinterest, although they did resurface as the more overtly hard-rockin' BRITISH LIONS. • **Songwriters:** HUNTER or others wrote most except; YOU REALLY GOT ME (Kinks) / LAUGH AT ME (Sonny Bono) / CROSSROADS (Sir Douglas Quintet) / KEEP A KNOCKIN' (Little Richard) / WHOLE LOTTA SHAKIN' GOIN' ON (Jerry Lee Lewis) / LAY DOWN (Melanie) / COME ON BABY, LET'S GO DOWNTOWN (Crazy Horse) / YOUR OWN BACKYARD (Dion) / etc.

Album rating: MOTT THE HOOPLE (*6) / MAD SHADOWS (*5) / WILD LIFE (*4) / BRAIN CAPERS (*6) / ALL THE YOUNG DUDES (*7) / MOTT (*8) / THE HOOPLE (*7) / LIVE (*4) / DRIVE ON (*3) / SHOUTING AND POINTING (*2) THE BALLAD OF MOTT THE HOOPLE – A RETROSPECTIVE compilation (*8)

IAN HUNTER (b. 3 Jun'46, Shrewsbury, England) – vocals, guitar, piano / **MICK RALPHS** (b.31 May'44) – guitar, vocals / **VERDEN ALLEN** (b.26 May'44, Crynant, Neath, Wales) – organ / **OVEREND WATTS** (b.13 May'49, Birmingham, England) – bass, vocals / **DALE 'BUFFIN' GRIFFIN** (b.24 Oct'48, Hereford) – drums, vocals

Island Atlantic

Oct 69. (7") *(WIP 6072)* **ROCK AND ROLL QUEEN. / ROAD TO BIRMINGHAM** [ ] [–]
Nov 69. (lp) *(ILPS 9108) <8258>* **MOTT THE HOOPLE** [66] [ ]
– You really got me / At the crossroads / Laugh at me / Backsliding fearlessly / Rock and roll queen / Rabbit foot and Toby time / Half Moon Bay / Wrath and wroll. *(cd-iss. Jul97 on 'Going For A Song'; GFS 065) (cd re-iss. Sep03 on 'Angel Air'+=; SJPCD 157)* – Ohio / Find your way (backtrack demo).
Jan 70. (7") **ROCK AND ROLL QUEEN. / BACKSLIDING FEARLESSLY** [–] [ ]
Sep 70. (lp) *(ILPS 9119) <8272>* **MAD SHADOWS** [48] [ ]
– Thunderbuck ram / No wheels to ride / You are one of us / Walkin' with a mountain / I can feel / Threads of iron / When my mind's gone.
Feb 71. (lp) *(ILPS 9144) <8284>* **WILDLIFE** [44] [ ]
– Whisky woman / Angel of 8th avenue / Wrong side of the river / Waterloo / Lay down / It must be love / Original mixed-up lad / Home is where I want to be / Keep a knockin'.
Sep 71. (lp) *(ILPS 9178) <8304>* **BRAIN CAPERS** [ ] [ ]
– Death maybe your Santa Claus / Darkness darkness / Your own backyard / Journey / Sweet Angeline / Wheel of the quivering meat conception / Second love / Moon upstairs.
Oct 71. (7") *(WIP 6105)* **MIDNIGHT LADY. / THE DEBT** [ ] [ ]
Dec 71. (7") *(WIP 6112)* **DOWNTOWN. / HOME IS WHERE I WANT TO BE** [ ] [ ]

C.B.S. Columbia

Jul 72. (7") *(8271) <45673>* **ALL THE YOUNG DUDES. / ONE OF THE BOYS** [3] [37]
Sep 72. (lp/c) *(CBS/40 65184) <31750>* **ALL THE YOUNG DUDES** [21] Nov72 [89]
– Sweet Jane / Momma's little jewel / All the young dudes / Sucker / Jerkin' crocus / One of the boys / Soft ground / Ready for love – After lights / Sea diver. *(cd-iss. Aug98 on 'Columbia'; 491691-2)*
Jan 73. (7") *<45754>* **ONE OF THE BOYS. / SUCKER** [–] [96]
Mar 73. (7") *<45784>* **SWEET JANE. / JERKIN' CROCUS** [–] [ ]

— **MICK BOLTON** – keyboards filled in for departing VERDEN who went solo

May 73. (7") *(1530) <45882>* **HONALOOCHIE BOOGIE. / ROSE** [12] [ ]
Jul 73. (lp/c) *(CBS/40 69038) <32425>* **MOTT** [7] Aug73 [35]
– All the way from Memphis / Whizz kid / Hymn for the dudes / Honaloochie boogie / Violence / Drivin' sister / Ballad of Mott The Hoople (March 26, 1972 – Zurich) / I'm a Cadillac – El Camino Dolo Roso / I wish I was your mother. *(cd-iss. 1988 on 'Castle'; CLACD 138X) (cd-iss. Mar95 on 'Rewind'; 467402-2)*
Aug 73. (7") *(1764)* **ALL THE WAY FROM MEMPHIS. / BALLAD OF MOTT THE HOOPLE (MARCH 26, 1972 – ZURICH)** [10] [–]
Sep 73. (7") *<45920>* **ALL THE WAY FROM MEMPHIS. / I WISH I WAS YOUR MOTHER** [–] [ ]

— **ARIEL BENDER** (b. LUTHER GROSVENOR, 23 Dec'49, Evesham, England) – guitar (ex-SPOOKY TOOTH) replaced RALPHS who joined BAD COMPANY / **MORGAN FISHER** – keyboards (ex-LOVE AFFAIR) repl. BOLTON (above 2 with HUNTER, WATTS and GRIFFIN.)

Nov 73. (7") *(1895)* **ROLL AWAY THE STONE. / WHERE DO YOU ALL COME FROM** [8] [–]
Mar 74. (7") *(2177) <46035>* **THE GOLDEN AGE OF ROCK'N'ROLL. / REST IN PEACE** [16] May74 [96]
Mar 74. (lp/c) *(CBS/40 69062) <32871>* **THE HOOPLE** [11] Apr74 [28]
– The golden age of rock'n'roll / Marionette / Alice / Crash Street kidds / Born late '58 / Trudi's song / Pearl 'n' Roy (England) / Through the looking glass / Roll away the stone.
Apr 74. (7") *<46076>* **ROLL AWAY THE STONE. / THROUGH THE LOOKING GLASS** [–] [ ]
Jun 74. (7") *(2439)* **FOXY FOXY. / TRUDI'S SONG** [33] [–]

— **BLUE WEAVER** – organ on tour (ex-AMEN CORNER)

Nov 74. (lp/c) *(CBS/40 69093) <33282>* **LIVE** (live; Broadway – Nov73 / Hammersmith – May74) [32] [23]
– All the way from Memphis / Sucker / Rest in peace / All the young dudes /

Walkin' with a mountain / Sweet Angeline / Rose / Medley:- (a) Jerkin' crocus – (b) One of the boys – (c) Rock'n'roll queen – (d) Get back – (e) Whole lotta shakin' – (f) Violence.

— **MICK RONSON** – guitar, vocals (Solo artist, ex-DAVID BOWIE; SPIDERS FROM MARS) repl. ARIEL who formed WIDOWMAKER

Oct 74. (7") *(2754)* **SATURDAY GIGS. / MEDLEY; JERKIN' CROCUS – SUCKER (live)** 41 –

Dec 74. (7") *<10091>* **ALL THE YOUNG DUDES (live). / ROSE** –

— Split Dec'74. HUNTER and RONSON formed duo and went solo.

MOTT

(OVEREND, DALE and **MORGAN**) were joined by **NIGEL BENJAMIN** – vocals (ex-ROYCE) **/ RAY MAJORS** – guitar (ex-HACKENSHACK)

C.B.S. Columbia

Aug 75. (7") *(3528)* **MONTE CARLO. / SHOUT IT ALL OUT**

Sep 75. (lp/c) *(CBS/40 69154) <33705>* **DRIVE ON** 45

– By tonight / Monte Carlo / She does it / I'll tell you something / Stiff upper lip / Love now / Apologies / The great white wall / Here we are / It takes one to know one / I can show you how it is.

Oct 75. (7") *(3741)* **BY TONIGHT. / I CAN SHOW YOU HOW IT IS**

Feb 76. (7") *(4055)* **IT TAKES ONE TO KNOW ONE. / I'LL TELL YOU SOMETHING**

Jun 76. (lp/c) *(CBS/40 81289) <34236>* **SHOUTING AND POINTING**

– Shouting and pointing / Collision course / Storm / Career (no such thing as rock'n'roll) / Hold on, you're crazy / See you again / Too short arms (I don't care) / Broadside outcasts / Good times. *(cd-iss. Jan98 on 'Columbia'; SMDCD 312)*

– compilations, etc. –

Oct 72. (lp) *Island; (ILPS 9215) / Atlantic; <7297>* **ROCK'N'ROLL QUEEN** Jul74

Feb 76. (7") *C.B.S.; (3963)* **ALL THE YOUNG DUDES. / ROLL AWAY THE STONE** –

(re-iss. Apr83 on 'Old Gold'; OG 9312)

Mar 76. (lp/c) *C.B.S.; (CBS/40 81225) <34368>* **GREATEST HITS**

– All the way from Memphis / Honaloochie boogie / Hymn for the dudes / Born late '58 / All the young dudes / Roll away the stone / Ballad of Mott The Hoople / Golden age of rock'n'roll / Foxy lady / Saturday gigs. *(re-iss. Jun81 lp/c; CBS/40 32007) (cd-iss. Apr89; CD 32007)*

Mar 81. (lp) *Island; (IRSP 8)* **TWO MILES FROM HEAVEN** –

Mar 81. (lp/c) *Hallmark; (SHM 3055)* **ALL THE WAY FROM MEMPHIS** –

Jul 84. (7") *C.B.S.; (A 4581)* **ALL THE YOUNG DUDES. / HONALOOCHIE BOOGIE** –

1988. (cd) *Castle; (CCSCD 174)* **THE COLLECTION** –

Jun 90. (cd) *Island; (IMCD 87)* **WALKING WITH A MOUNTAIN (BEST OF 1969-1972)**

– Rock and roll queen / At the crossroads / Thunderbuck ram / Whiskey woman / Waterflow / The Moon upstairs / Second love / The road to Birmingham / Black scorpio (mama's little jewel) / You really got me / Walking with a mountain / No wheels to ride / Keep a knockin' / Midnight lady / Death may be your Santa Claus / Darkness darkness / Growing man blues / Black hills.

Jun 92. (7"/c-s) *Columbia; (658177-7/-4)* **ALL THE YOUNG DUDES. / ONCE BITTEN TWICE SHY (by Ian Hunter)**

(cd-s+=) *(658177-2)* – Roll Away The Stone.

Dec 92. (cd) *Edsel; (EDCD 361)* **MOOT THE HOOPLE / MAD SHADOWS** –

Jun 93. (cd) *See For Miles; (SEECD 7)* **MOTT THE HOOPLE FEATURING STEVE HYAMS** –

Nov 93. (d-cd) *Legacy; (CD 46973)* **THE BALLAD OF MOTT THE HOOPLE – A RETROSPECTIVE** –

(re-iss. Jun96 on 'Coulmbia'; 474420-2)

Jun 96. (cd-s) *Old Gold; (126236380-2)* **ALL THE YOUNG DUDES / ONE OF THE BOYS** –

Jul 96. (cd) *Windsong; (WINCD 064)* **THE ORIGINAL MIXED UP KIDS – THE BBC SESSIONS 1970-71** –

Apr 97. (cd) *BR Music; (RM 1547)* **ALL THE YOUNG DUDES** –

Sep 98. (cd) *Spectrum; (554600-2)* **THE BEST OF MOTT THE HOOPLE – THE ISLAND YEARS 1969-1972** –

Nov 98. (cd) *Angel Air; (<SJPCD 029>)* **ALL THE WAY FROM STOCKHOLM TO PHILADELPHIA (live 1971-1972)**

Jun 99. (d-cd; by MOTT) *Angel Air; <(SJPCD 025)>* **LIVE OVER HERE AND OVER THERE 1975-1976**

Oct 99. (d-cd; with Various Artists) *Eagle; (EDGCD 104)* **FRIENDS AND RELATIVES** –

Apr 00. (cd; with Various Artists) *Connoisseur; (VSOPCD 283)* **MOTT THE HOOPLE FAMILY ALBUM** –

Jul 00. (cd) *Angel Air; <(SJPCD 061)>* **ROCK'N'ROLL CIRCUS (live in Wolverhampton 6/4/72)**

Jul 00. (cd; by MOTT) *Angel Air; <(SJPCD 054)>* **THE GOOSEBERRY SESSIONS AND RARITIES**

Sep 00. (d-cd) *Recall; (SMDCD 312)* **A TALE OF TWO CITIES** –

Sep 02. (cd) *Angel Air; (SJPCD 121)* **HOOPLING (BEST OF LIVE)** –

— In Feb'80, MOTT THE HOOPLE tracks were included on double album 'SHADES OF IAN HUNTER – THE BALLAD OF IAN HUNTER & MOTT THE HOOPLE' on 'CBS'; *(88476)*

□ Bob MOULD (see under ⇒ SUGAR)

MOUNTAIN

Formed: The Bronx, New York, USA … 1969 by FELIX PAPPALARDI and guitarist LESLIE WEST. A veteran producer, PAPPALARDI had worked with the likes of LOVIN' SPOONFUL, JOAN BAEZ, The YOUNGBLOODS etc., as well as helping CREAM to achieve their groundbreaking power trio crunch. He first came into contact with the girthsome WEST after being landed with the job of producing some salesworthy product by Long Island popsters The VAGRANTS. In the event he failed and the band split; impressed by WEST's guitar skills, however, the natural next move was for the pair to hook up, PAPPALARDI producing WEST's first solo set, 'MOUNTAIN' (1969). The record's encouraging reception duly persuaded the duo to make MOUNTAIN a full-time concern, PAPPALARDI playing bass alongside drummer NORMAN D. SMART and new recruit, keyboard player STEVE KNIGHT. This was the line-up which no doubt caused more than a few bad trips at 'Woodstock' in August '69, the group blasting the hippies with their warp-factor blues/sludge-metal on only their fourth ever gig. The 'MOUNTAIN CLIMBING!' (1970) set was unleashed the following Spring, the rousing 'MISSISSIPPI QUEEN' single pushing the album into the US Top 20. 'NANTUCKET SLEIGHRIDE' (1971) was another sizable Stateside success, its dense title track later used as the theme tune for ITV's long running 'World In Action' series. A third set, 'FLOWERS OF EVIL' (1972) didn't fare so well, the rather predictable organ-dominated riff overkill beginning to grate. A concert set, then, 'MOUNTAIN LIVE – THE ROAD GOES ON FOREVER' (1972), was just what the doctor didn't order, especially one where 'NANTUCKET SLEIGHRIDE' was spun out over a sanity-defying two sides-plus of vinyl; the solo goes on forever, anyone?. Wisely perhaps, PAPPALARDI opted to resume production work and the first incarnation of MOUNTAIN was no more. Along with CORKY LAING, who had replaced SMART in the drum stool, WEST engaged the services of ex-CREAM bassist, JACK BRUCE to form WEST, BRUCE & LAING. The trio secured a deal with 'Columbia', achieving moderate success with the album 'WHY DON'CHA' (1972) and releasing a second set through MOUNTAIN's label, 'Windfall'. By the time a posthumous live album was issued in 1974, WEST had already rejoined PAPPALARDI in a revamped MOUNTAIN, the pair bringing in ALLEN SCHWARZBERG and ROBERT MANN. Worryingly, their first release was a live album, 'TWIN PEAKS' (1974), and a subsequent studio set, 'AVALANCHE' (1974) was met with a muted response. MOUNTAIN faded from view once more, PAPPALARDI recording two solo albums for 'A&M', 'FELIX PAPPALARDI AND CREATION' (1976) and 'DON'T WORRY MUM?' (1979), before retiring to Japan. WEST, meanwhile, released two solo sets for 'R.C.A.', the self-deprecatingly titled 'THE GREAT FATSBY' (1975) and 'THE LESLIE WEST BAND' (1976). Another MOUNTAIN reformation was probably inevitable, however, and it came in 1981, the project later overshadowed by the death of PAPPALARDI, shot dead on 17th April '83 by his wife, Gail Collins. Ex-RAINBOW and URIAH HEEP man, MARK CLARKE was eventually hired as a replacement and the group cut a disappointing album for 'Scotti Brothers', 'GO FOR YOUR LIFE' (1985). MOUNTAIN were finally buried and WEST once again hooked up with JACK BRUCE for 'THEME' (1988) and 'ALLIGATOR' (1989), the legend given something of a dusting down via the release of 1995's 'Sony' retrospective, 'OVER THE TOP'. Following the German-only mid-90's release, 'MAN'S WORLD', WEST and LAING again teamed up for the more widely available 'MYSTIC FIRE' (2002), hardly a return to the hoary greatness of old but a decent showcase for WEST's still smoking guitar playing. • **Songwriters:** WEST – PAPPALARDI penned except; THIS WHEEL'S ON FIRE (Bob Dylan) / ROLL OVER BEETHOVEN (Chuck Berry) / WHOLE LOTTA SHAKIN' GOIN' ON (Jerry Lee Lewis). LESLIE WEST solo covered; RED HOUSE (Jimi Hendrix) / SPOONFUL (Cream) / THE STEALER (Free) / I PUT A SPELL ON YOU (Screaming Jay Hawkins) / HALL OF THE MOUNTAIN KING (Grieg) / DREAM LOVER (Bobby Darin) / THEME FROM EXODUS (Gold) / SEA OF FIRE (Cintron). • **Trivia:** On their live double album 'TWIN PEAKS', they used 1 album and a bit for track 'NANTUCKET SLEIGHRIDE'.

Album rating: LESLIE WEST – MOUNTAIN (*6) / MOUNTAIN CLIMBING! (*7) / NANTUCKET SLEIGHRIDE (*6) / FLOWERS OF EVIL (*6) / THE ROAD GOES ON FOREVER – MOUNTAIN LIVE (*4) / THE BEST OF MOUNTAIN (FEATURING LESLIE WEST & FELIX PAPPALARDI) compilation (*8) / AVALANCHE (*5) / TWIN PEAKS (*4) / GO FOR YOUR LIFE (*4) / OVER THE TOP part compilation (*7) / MAN'S WORLD (*5) / MYSTIC FIRE (*4) / West, Bruce & Laing: WHY DONTCHA (*5) / WHATEVER TURNS YOU ON (*4) / LIVE 'N' KICKIN' (*4) / Leslie West: THE GREAT FATSBY (*4) / THE LESLIE WEST BAND (*3) / THEME (*3) / ALLIGATOR (*4) / DODGIN' THE DIRT (*4)

LESLIE WEST

(b. LESLIE WEINSTEIN, 22 Oct'45, Queens, N.Y.) – vocals, lead guitar (ex-VAGRANTS) / with **FELIX PAPPALARDI** (b.1939) – bass, keyboards / **NORMAN LANDSBERG** – keyboards / **NORMAN D.SMART** (b. Boston) – drums

Bell / Windfall

Sep 69. (lp) *<4500>* **MOUNTAIN** [–] [72]
– Blood of the sun / Long red / Better watch out / Blind man / Baby I'm down / Dreams of milk & honey / Storyteller man / This wheel's on fire / Look to the wind / Southbound train / Because you are my friend.

Oct 69. (7") *(BLL 1078) <530>* **DREAMS OF MILK AND HONEY. / THIS WHEEL'S ON FIRE** [ ] [ ]

Jan 70. (7") *<531>* **BLOOD OF THE SUN. / LONG RED** [–] [ ]

MOUNTAIN

named after last album. **STEVE KNIGHT** – keyboards (ex-DEVIL'S ANVIL) repl. LANDSBERG (This line-up appeared at 'Woodstock' festival)

—— **CORKY LAING** (b.26 Jan'48, Montreal, Canada) – drums repl. SMART

Mar 70. (lp) *(SBLL 133) <4501>* **MOUNTAIN CLIMBING!** [ ] [17]
– Mississippi queen / Theme for an imaginary western / Never in my life / Silver paper / For Yasgur's farm / To my friend / The laird / Sittin' on a rainbow / Boys in the band. *(re-iss. Aug91 on 'Beat Goes On' cd/c; BGO CD/MC 112) (cd re-iss. Mar95 on 'Columbia'; 472180-2)*

May 70. (7") *(BLL 1112) <532>* **MISSISSIPPI QUEEN. / THE LAIRD** [ ] Mar70 [21]

Jun 70. (7") *<533>* **FOR YASGUR'S FARM. / TO MY FRIEND** [–] [ ]

Oct 70. (7") *(BLL 1125)* **SITTIN' ON A RAINBOW. / TO MY FRIEND** [ ] [–]

Island / Windfall

May 71. (lp) *(ILPS 9148) <5500>* **NANTUCKET SLEIGHRIDE** [43] Jan71 [16]
– Don't look around / Taunta (Sammy's tune) / Nantucket sleighride / You can't get away / Tired angels / The animal trainer and the toad / My lady / Travellin' in the dark / The great train robbery. *(cd-iss. Jun89 on 'Beat Goes On'; BGOCD 32)*

Mar 71. (7") *<534>* **THE ANIMAL TRAINER AND THE TOAD. / TIRED ANGELS** [–] [76]

Jul 71. (7") *<535>* **TRAVELIN' IN THE DARK. / SILVER PAPER** [–] [ ]

Jan 72. (lp) *(ILPS 9179) <5501>* **FLOWERS OF EVIL** [ ] Dec71 [35]
– Flowers of evil / King's chorale / One last cold kiss / Crossroader / Pride and passion / (Dream sequence: Guitar solo) / Roll over Beethoven / Dreams of milk and honey – Variations – Swan theme / Mississippi queen. *(re-iss. Dec91 on 'Beat Goes On' cd/c; BGO CD/MC 113)*

Feb 72. (7") *(WIP 6119) <536>* **ROLL OVER BEETHOVEN. / CROSSROADER** [ ] [ ]

Jun 72. (lp) *(ILPS 9199) <5502>* **MOUNTAIN LIVE – THE ROAD GOES EVER ON (live)** [21] May71 [63]
– Long red / Waiting to take you away / Crossroader / Nantucket sleighride. *(re-iss. Dec91 on 'Beat Goes On' cd/c/lp; BGO CD/MC/LP 111)*

Jul 72. (7") *<537>* **WAITING TO TAKE YOU AWAY. / NANTUCKET SLEIGHRIDE (live excerpt)** [–] [ ]

Island / C.B.S.

Feb 73. (lp) *(ILPS 9236) <32079>* **THE BEST OF MOUNTAIN (FEATURING LESLIE WEST & FELIX PAPPALARDI)** (compilation) [ ] [72]
– Never in my life / Taunta (Sammy's tune) / Nantucket sleighride / Roll over Beethoven / For Yasgur's farm / The animal trainer and the toad / Mississippi queen / King's chorale / Boys in the band / Don't look around / Theme for an imaginary western / Crossroader. *(cd-iss. Apr89 on 'Beat Goes On'; BGOCD 33) (cd re-iss. Dec92 on 'Columbia'; 466335-2)*

—— Disbanded mid 1972

WEST, BRUCE & LAING

were formed by ex-MOUNTAIN men and **JACK BRUCE** – vocals, bass (ex-CREAM, etc)

C.B.S. / Columbia

Nov 72. (lp) *(CBS 65314) <31929>* **WHY DONTCHA** [ ] Oct72 [26]
– Why dontcha / Out in the fields / The doctor / Turn me over / Third degree / Shake ma thing (Rollin' Jack) / While you sleep / Pleasure / Love is worth the blues / Pollution woman. *(re-iss. Aug85 on 'R.S.O.';) (cd-iss. Apr93 on 'Sony Europe')*

Dec 72. (7") *<45751>* **SHAKE MA THING (ROLLIN' JACK). / THE DOCTOR** [–] [ ]

Mar 73. (7") *<45829>* **WHY DONTCHA. / MISSISSIPPI QUEEN** [–] [ ]

R.S.O. / Windfall

Jul 73. (7") *(2090 113)* **DIRTY SHOES. / BACKFIRE** [ ] [ ]

Jul 73. (lp) *(2394 107) <32216>* **WHATEVER TURNS YOU ON** [ ] [ ]
– Backfire / Token / Sifting sand / November song / Rock and roll machine / Scotch krotch / Slow blues / Dirty shoes / Like a plate. *(cd-iss. Apr93 on 'Sony Europe')*

May 74. (lp) *(2394 128) <32899>* **LIVE 'N' KICKIN' (live)** [ ] [ ]
– Play with fire / The doctor / Politician / Powerhouse sod. *(cd-iss. Apr93 on 'Sony Europe')*

MOUNTAIN

had already re-formed late in 1973 with **WEST** + **PAPPALARDI** bringing in **ALLEN SCHWARZBERG** – drums / **ROBERT MANN** – keyboards

C.B.S. / Columbia

Feb 74. (d-lp) *<32818>* **TWIN PEAKS** (live in Japan '73) [–] [ ]
– Never in my life / Theme for an imaginary western / Blood of the sun / Guitar solo / Nantucket sleigh ride / Nantucket sleigh ride (conclusion) / Crossroader / Mississippi queen / Silver paper / Roll over Beethoven. *(UK-iss.Nov77; CBS 88095) (cd-iss. Jan98 on 'Columbia'; 472183-2)*

—— **DAVID PERRY** – rhythm guitar repl. ALLEN + ROBERT (FELIX now + keyboards)

Epic / Epic

Nov 74. (lp) *(CBS 80492) <33088>* **AVALANCHE** [ ] [ ]
– Whole lotta shakin' goin' on / Sister justice / Alisan / Swamp boy /

Satisfaction / Thumbsucker / You better believe it / I love to see you fly / Back where I belong / Last of the sunshine days. *(re-iss. Feb88 on 'Castle' lp/cd; CLA LP/CD 136X)*

— Split again late in '74. FELIX PAPPALARDI signed to 'A&M' and released 2 albums **FELIX PAPPALARDI AND CREATION** (1976) and **DON'T WORRY MUM?** (1979). He retired to Japan, and later (17 Apr'83) was dead, shot by his wife GAIL COLLINS.

LESLIE WEST

went solo with band **CORKY LAING** – drums / **DON KRETMMAR** – bass / **FRANK VICARI** – horns / **etc.**

		R.C.A.	Phantom
Feb 75.	(7") *<10301>* **DON'T BURN UP. / E.S.P.**	–	
Mar 75.	(lp) *(RS 1009) <0954>* **THE GREAT FATSBY**		

– Don't burn me / House of the rising sun / High roller / I'm gonna love you thru the night / E.S.P. / Honky tonk women / If I still had you / Doctor Love / If I were a carpenter / Little bit of love.

Feb 76.	(7") *<10424>* **MONEY – DEAR PRUDENCE. / GET IT UP – SETTING SUN**	–	
Mar 76.	(lp) *(1258) <701>* **THE LESLIE WEST BAND**		

– Money (watcha gonna do) / Dear Prudence / Get it up (no bass – whatsoever) / Singapore sling / By the river / The twister / Setting sun / Sea of heartache / We'll find a way / We gotta get out of this place.

May 76.	(7") *<10522>* **WE GOTTA GET OUT OF THIS PLACE. / BY THE RIVER**	–	

— LESLIE WEST retired for a while, until . . .

MOUNTAIN

re-formed in 1981. (**WEST, PAPPALARDI, LAING** and 2 others). In 1984, after death of PAPPALARDI. added **MARK CLARKE** – bass, keyboards (ex-URIAH HEEP, ex-RAINBOW, etc)

		not iss.	Scotti Brothers
Apr 85.	(lp) *(40006)* **GO FOR YOUR LIFE**	–	

– Hard times / Spark / She loves her rock (and she loves it hard) / Bardot damage / Shimmy on the footlights / I love young girls / Makin' it in your car / Babe in the woods / Little bit of insanity.

LESLIE WEST

brought in **JACK BRUCE** – vocals, bass / **JOE FRANCO** – drums (ex-TWISTED SISTER)

		not iss.	Passport
Apr 88.	(lp/cd) *<PB 606-1/-2>* **THEME**	–	

– Talk dirty / Motherlode / Theme for an imaginary western / I'm crying / Red house / Love is forever / I ate it / Spoonful / Love me tender.

— In Apr '89, he appeared on Various Artists live cd,c,d-lp,video 'NIGHT OF THE GUITAR' on his next label.

		I.R.S.	I.R.S.
Oct 89.	(cd) *<(EIRSACD 1017)>* **ALLIGATOR**		

– Sea of fire / Waiting for the F change / Whiskey / Alligator / I put a spell on you / All of me / The stealer / Medley: Hall of the mountain king – Theme from Exodus / Dream lover.

		not iss.	BluesBureau
1994.	(cd) *<BB 2015>* **DODGIN' THE DIRT**	–	

– Whiskey train / Daddy are you angry / New York state of mind / Sambuca / Juke joint jumping / Easy street / One last lick / Crosscut saw / Hang me out to dry / Wasted years / My friend Sam / Thunderbird / Red house.

MOUNTAIN

— re-formed with **WEST, LAING + CLARKE**

		not iss.	Viceroy
Apr 96.	(cd) *<8033>* **MAN'S WORLD**	–	

– In your face / Nobody gonna steal my thunder / This is a man's world / So fine / Hotel happiness / I'm sorry / I look (power mix) / Is that okay? / Crest of a slump / You'll never be alone / I look (hit mix). *(UK-iss.Jan99 on 'Dream Catcher'; CRIDE 12)*

— **CHUCK HEARNE** – bass; repl. CLARKE

		not iss.	Lightyear
Jul 02.	(cd) *<54492>* **MYSTIC FIRE**	–	

– Immortal / Mystic fire / Fever / The sea / Mutant X / Better off with the blues / Mountain express (oh boy) / Marble peach – Rotten peach / Johnny comes marching home / Nantucket sleighride (redux).

– compilations, etc. –

Jun 95.	(d-cd) *Columbia; (483898-2)* **OVER THE TOP**		
Mar 96.	(cd; LESLIE WEST & MOUNTAIN) *Raven; (RVCD 49)* **BLOOD OF THE SUN**		–
Jul 00.	(cd) *Columbia; (498783-2)* **SUPER HITS**		Nov98

MOVE

Formed: Birmingham, England . . . early 1966 by ROY WOOD, CARL WAYNE, TREVOR BURTON, ACE KEFFORD and BEV BEVAN. By that summer, they had found manager Tony Secunda, who helped them sign to 'Deram'. Early the next year, their debut 45, 'NIGHT OF FEAR' (based on the 1812 Overture), had crashed into the UK Top 3. After another Top 5 hit, their third single, 'FLOWERS IN THE RAIN' (the first record to be played on the newly launched BBC Radio 1), was another to make the Top 3 in October '67 on the recently formed 'Regal Zonophone' label. Their fourth successive Top 5 hit arrived in early '68 with 'FIRE BRIGADE', quickly followed by the Top 20 self-titled album. The aforementioned singles were, for the most part, classy bubblegum psychedelia penned by the multi-talented WOOD. After a surprise flop, they scored their first No.1 early in '69 with the single, 'BLACKBERRY WAY'. They never emulated this, WOOD becoming increasingly involved with his new project, The ELECTRIC LIGHT ORCHESTRA, in 1970. He subsequently departed, JEFF LYNNE taking over the leadership, while he ended The MOVE on a high-note in mid-'72 with the Top 10 hit, 'CALIFORNIA MAN'. Remaining at 'Harvest' records, WOOD formed the 50's pastiche rock'n'roll/glam outfit, WIZZARD (the band making their live debut at Wembley's Rock'n'roll festival in June '72). They hit the Top 10 with their first 45, 'BALL PARK INCIDENT', following it with two chart toppers, 'SEE MY BABY JIVE' and 'ANGEL FINGERS'. Around the same time (mid-'73), WOOD disgarded his WIZZARD attire (tartan troosers, multi-coloured robe, tooped with face-paint and a multi-coloured hair-do), entering the album charts with his solo (in every sense of the word), 'BOULDERS' album. He continued to work on both projects simultaneously, scoring many Top 20 chart hits. Following his signed to the 'Jet' label in 1975, the hits (bar a few minor ones) duly dried up. • **Covered;** LOVELY RITA + POLYTHENE PAM (Beatles). • **Trivia:** ROY also produced and wrote for DARTS, etc.

Album rating: THE MOVE (*7) / SHAZAM! (*9) / LOOKING ON (*5) / MESSAGE FROM THE COUNTRY (*7) / GREAT MOVE! THE BEST OF THE MOVE compilation (*8) / Roy Wood: BOULDERS (*7) / MUSTARD (*7) / ON THE ROAD AGAIN (*5) / STARTING UP (*4) / THROUGH THE YEARS – THE BEST OF ROY WOOD compilation (*7) / Wizzard: WIZZARD BREW (*4) / INTRODUCING EDDY & THE FALCONS (*5) / SUPER ACTIVE WIZZO (*4)

ROY WOOD (b. ULYSSES ADRIAN WOOD, 8 Nov'46) – guitar, vocals (ex-MIKE SHERIDAN & NIGHTRIDERS, ex-GERRY LEVENE & THE AVENGERS) / **TREVOR BURTON** (b. 9 Mar'44) – guitar, vox (ex-DANNY KING & THE MAYFAIR SET) / **CARL WAYNE** (b.18 Aug'44) – vocals (ex-CARL WAYNE & THE VIKINGS) / **CHRIS "ACE" KEFFORD** (b.10 Dec'46) – bass, vox (ex-CARL WAYNE & THE VIKINGS) / **BEV BEVAN** (b.24 Nov'44) – drums (ex-CARL WAYNE & THE VIKINGS, ex-DENNY LAINE & THE DIPLOMATS)

		Deram	Deram
Dec 66.	(7") *(DM 109) <7504>* **NIGHT OF FEAR. / THE DISTURBANCE**	2	
Apr 67.	(7") *(DM 117) <7506>* **I CAN HEAR THE GRASS GROW. / WAVE THE FLAG, STOP THE TRAIN**	5	
		Regal Zonophone	A&M
Sep 67.	(7") *(RZ 3001)* **FLOWERS IN THE RAIN. / (HERE WE GO ROUND) THE LEMON TREE**	2	–

Feb 68. (7") *(RZ 3005)* **FIRE BRIGADE. / WALK UPON THE WATER** [3] [ ]

Mar 68. (lp; stereo/mono) *(S+/LRZ 1002)* **THE MOVE** [15] [–]
– Yellow rainbow / Kilroy was here / (Here we go round) The lemon tree / Weekend / Walk upon the water / Flowers in the rain / Useless information / Zing went the strings of my heart / The girl outside / Fire brigade / Mist on a Monday morning / Cherry blossom clinic. *(cd-iss. Nov92 & Feb98 on 'Repertoire'+=; REP 4690)* – Night of fear / The disturbance / I can hear the grass grow / Wave the flag, stop the train / Vote for me / (+ 3 others).

—— quartet, (**BURTON** – bass, vocals) when KEFFORD formed ACE KEFFORD STAND

Jul 68. (7") *(RZ 3012)* **WILD TIGER WOMAN. / OMNIBUS** [ ] [–]

Sep 68. (7"ep) *(TRZ 2001)* **SOMETHING ELSE FROM THE MOVE** [ ] [–]
– Stephanie knows who / So you want to be a rock 'n' roll star / Something else / It'll be me / Sunshine help me.

Sep 68. (7") *<966>* **SOMETHING. / YELLOW RAINBOW** [–] [ ]

—— added **RICHARD TANDY** – hapsicord, keyboards (of The UGLYS)

Jan 69. (7") *(RZ 3015) <1020>* **BLACKBERRY WAY. / SOMETHING** [1] [ ]

—— **RICK PRICE** (b.10 Jun'44) – bass (ex-SIGHT'N'SOUND) repl. BURTON + TANDY whom became part of The UGLYS

Aug 69. (7") *(RZ 3021) <1119>* **CURLY. / THIS TIME TOMORROW** [12] [ ]

Feb 70. (lp) *(SLRZ 1012) <SP 4259>* **SHAZAM** [ ] [ ]
– Hello Susie / Beautiful daughter / Cherry blossom clinic revisted / Fields of people / Don't make my baby blue / The last thing on my mind. *(re-iss. 1982 on 'Cube';) (cd-iss. Mar93 & Nov00 on 'Repertoire' +=; REP 4691)* – Stephanie knows who / So you want to be a rock'n'roll star / Something else / It'll be me / Sunshine help me.

—— now trio of **WOOD, PRICE + BEVAN** (WAYNE became a cabaret singer)

Mar 70. (7") *(RZ 3026) <1197>* **BRONTOSAURUS. / LIGHTNING NEVER STRIKES TWICE** [7] [ ]

—— added **JEFF LYNNE** (b.30 Dec'47) – vocals, guitar, keys (ex-IDLE RACE)

Fly Capitol

Sep 70. (7") *(BUG 2)* **WHEN ALICE COMES BACK TO THE FARM. / WHAT?** [ ] [ ]

Oct 70. (lp) *(HIFLY 1) <ST 658>* **LOOKING ON** [ ] [ ]
– Looking on / Turkish tram conductor blues / What? / When Alice comes back to the farm / Open up said the world at the door / Brontosaurus / Feel too good. *(cd-iss. Mar93 & Nov00 on 'Repertoire'+=; REP 4692)* – Blackberry way / Something / Curly / This time tomorrow / Lightning never strikes twice.

Harvest Capitol

May 71. (7"; unissued) *(HAR 5036)* **ELLA JAMES. / NO TIME** [–] [–]

Jun 71. (7") *(HAR 5038) <3126>* **TONIGHT. / DON'T MESS ME UP** [11] [ ]

Jul 71. (lp) *(SHSP 4013) <ST 811>* **MESSAGE FROM THE COUNTRY** [ ] [ ]
– Message from the country / Ella James / No time / Don't mess me up / Until your moma's gone / It wasn't my idea to dance / The minister / Ben Crawley Steel Company / The words of Aaron / My Marge. *(cd-iss. Jul94 on 'Beat Goes On'; BGOCD 238) (cd re-iss. Sep01 on 'E.M.I.'+=; 535212-2)* – Tonight / Chinatown / Down on the bay / Do ya / California man / Don't mess me up / Words of Aaron / Do ya (BBC version).

Harvest U.A.

Oct 71. (7") *(HAR 5043) <50876>* **CHINATOWN. / DOWN ON THE BAY** [23] [ ]

—— (Aug'71) now a trio when RICK PRICE left to go solo. The other three (WOOD, LYNNE and BEVAN) continued with The MOVE although they formed ELECTRIC LIGHT ORCHESTRA. The MOVE made one more single below before ROY WOOD also undertook solo career and formed WIZZARD.

May 72. (7"m) *(HAR 5050) <50928>* **CALIFORNIA MAN. / DO YA / ELLA JAMES** [7] [ ]

– (selective) compilations, etc. –

Mar 71. (lp) *Fly; (TON 3)* **THE BEST OF THE MOVE** [ ] [–]
(cd-iss. Nov00 on 'Repertoire'; REP 4686)

Sep 74. (7") *Harvest; (HAR 5086) / United Artists; <50928>* **DO YA. / NO TIME** [ ] Oct72 [93]

Oct 74. (lp) *Harvest; (SHSP 4035)* **CALIFORNIA MAN** [ ] [–]

Mar 91. (cd/c) *Music Club; (MC CD/TC 009)* **THE BEST OF THE MOVE** [ ] [–]

Mar 95. (cd) *Band Of Joy; (BOJCD 011)* **THE BBC SESSIONS** [ ] [–]
(re-iss. Jul98 on 'Strange Fruit'; SFRSCD 69)

Oct 99. (d-cd) *Repertoire; (REP 4665)* **SINGLES A'S & B'S** [ ] [ ]

Oct 00. (cd) *Metro; (METRCD 031)* **THE VERY BEST OF THE MOVE** [ ] [ ]

May 01. (cd) *Disky; (SI 64613-2)* **FLOWERS IN THE RAIN** [ ] [–]

Jun 03. (3xcd-box) *Westside; (WESX 302)* **MOVEMENTS: 30th ANNIVERSARY ANTHOLOGY** [ ] [–]

ROY WOOD

in two bands (MOVE and ELO) had also gone solo. ROY played mostly every instrument himself.

Harvest U.A.

Feb 72. (7") *(HAR 5058)* **WHEN GRAN'MA PLAYS THE BANJO. / WAKE UP** [ ] [ ]

—— ROY WOOD solo (although he continued with his new band WIZZARD, see below)

Jun 73. (lp) *(SHVL 803) <VALA 168>* **BOULDERS** [15] [ ]
– Songs of praise / Wake up / Rock down low / Nancy sing me a song / Dear Elaine / a) All the way over the hill, b) Irish loafer (and his hen) / Miss Clarke and the computer / When gran'ma plays the banjo / Rock medley: a) Rockin' shoes, b) She's too good for me, c) Locomotive. *(re-iss. Oct77; RI 2021) (cd-iss. Mar94 on 'Beat Goes On'; BGOCD 219)*

Sep 73. (7") *(HAR 5074)* **DEAR ELAINE. / SONGS OF PRAISE** [18] [ ]

Nov 73. (7") *(HAR 5078)* **FOREVER. / MUSIC TO COMMIT SUICIDE BY** [8] [ ]

Jun 74. (7") *(HAR 5083)* **GOING DOWN THE ROAD. / THE PREMIUM BOND THEME** [13] [ ]

Jet U.A.

May 75. (7") *(JET 754)* **OH WHAT A SHAME. / BENGAL JIM** [13] [ ]

Nov 75. (7") *(JET 761)* **LOOK THRU' THE EYES OF A FOOL. / STRIDER** [ ] [ ]

Dec 75. (lp) *(JETLP 12) <LA 575>* **MUSTARD** [ ] [ ]
– Mustard / Any old time will do / The rain came down on everything / You sure got it now / Why does such a pretty girl sing those sad songs / The song / Look thru' the eyes of a fool / Interlude / Get on down home / Rock'n'roll winter. *(re-iss. as 'THE WIZZARD – ROY WOOD')*

Mar 76. (7"; as ROY WOOD'S WIZZARD) *(JET 768)* **INDIANA RAINBOW. / THE THING IS THIS (THIS IS THE THING)** [ ] [–]

May 76. (7") *(JET 785)* **ANY OLD TIME WILL DO. / THE RAIN CAME DOWN ON EVERYTHING** [ ] [–]

May 76. (7") **ANY OLD TIME WILL DO. / WHY DOES SUCH A PRETTY GIRL SING THOSE SAD SONGS** [–] [ ]

—— In Oct77, ROY WOOD made a duo single with ANNIE HASLAM of RENAISSANCE 'I NEVER BELIEVED IN LOVE. / INSIDE MY LIFE'. (from HASLAM's lp 'ANNIE IN WONDERLAND')

WIZZARD

(were formed August 1972 by **ROY WOOD** with **RICK PRICE**, plus other ex-MONGREL musicians) **CHARLIE GRIMA** – drums and **KEITH SMART** – drums also **HUGH McDOWELL** – cello and **BILL HUNT** – keyboards (both ex-ELO) and **NICK PENTELOW** – saxophone and **MICK BURNEY** – saxophone (ex-DALTONS)

Harvest U.A.

Nov 72. (7") *(HAR 5062)* **BALL PARK INCIDENT. / THE CARLSBERG SPECIAL** [6] [ ]

Apr 73. (7") *(HAR 5070)* **SEE MY BABY JIVE. / BEND OVER BEETHOVEN** [1] [ ]

Apr 73. (lp) *(SHSP 4025) <LA 042>* **WIZZARD BREW** [29] [ ]
– You can dance the rock & roll / Meet me at the jailhouse / Jolly cup of tea / Buffalo station – Get down to Memphis / Gotta crush / Wear a fast gun.

Aug 73. (7") *(HAR 5076)* **ANGEL FINGERS. / YOU GOT THE JUMP ON ME** [1] [ ]

—— (Sep73) trimmed slightly when McDOWELL returned to ELECTRIC LIGHT ORCH. (Nov73) **BOB BRADY** – keyboards (ex-APPLEJACKS) repl. HUNT

Nov 73. (7") *(HAR 5173)* **I WISH IT COULD BE CHRISTMAS EVERY DAY. / ROB ROY'S NIGHTMARE** [4] [ ]

Warners U.A.

Apr 74. (7") *(K 16357)* **ROCK'N'ROLL WINTER. / DREAM OF UNWIN** [6] [ ]

Aug 74. (7") *(K 16434)* **THIS IS THE STORY OF MY LOVE (BABY). / MIXTURE** [34] [ ]

Aug 74. (lp) *(K 56029) <LA 219>* **INTRODUCING EDDY AND THE FALCONS** [19] [ ]
– (intro) / Eddy's rock / Brand new '88' / You got me runnin' / I dun lotsa cryin' over you / This is the story of my love / Everyday I wonder / Crazy jeans / Come back Karen / We're gonna rock & roll tonight.

Oct 74. (7") *(K 16466)* **YOU'VE GOT ME RUNNIN'. / IT'S JUST MY IMAGINATION** [ ] [ ]

Dec 74. (7") *(K 16497)* **ARE YOU READY TO ROCK. / MARATHON MAN** [8] [ ]

— (Feb75) **WOOD** was just left with **PRICE** and **BURNEY,** and sessioners. (BRADY joined FAIRPORT CONVENTION) (SMART joined ROCKIN' BERRIES)

Jet not iss.

Oct 75. (7") *(JET 758)* **RATTLESNAKE ROLL. / CAN'T HELP MY FEELINGS** [ ] [–]

ROY WOOD'S WIZZO BAND

(**ROY** only retained stalwart **RICK PRICE** now on pedal steel) also **GRAHAM GALLERY** – bass / **DAVE DONOVAN** – drums / **PAUL ROBBINS** – keyboards / **BILLY PAUL** – alto sax / **BOB WILSON** – trombone

Warners Warners

Aug 77. (7") *(WB 16961)* **THE STROLL. / JUBILEE** [ ] [ ]

Sep 77. (lp) *(K 56388) <3065>* **SUPERACTIVE WIZZO** [ ] [ ]
– Life is wonderful / Waitin' at the door / Another wrong night / Sneakin' / Giant footsteps (jubilees) / Earthrise.

ROY WOOD

Feb 78. (7") *(K 17094)* **DANCIN' AT THE RAINBOW'S END. / WAITING AT THE DOOR** [ ] [–]

Nov 78. (7") *(K 17248)* **KEEP YOUR HANDS ON THE WHEEL. / JUBILEE** [ ] [–]

May 79. (7"/7"pic-d) *(K/KP 17459)* **(WE'RE) ON THE ROAD AGAIN. / SAXMANIACS** [ ] [–]

Aug 79. (lp) *(BSK 3247)* **ON THE ROAD AGAIN** [ ] [ ]
– (We're) On the road again / Wings over the sea / Keep your hands on the wheel / Colourful lady / Road rocket / Backtown sinner / Jimmy lad / Dancin' at the rainbow's end / Another night / Way beyond the rain.

ROY WOOD'S HELICOPTERS

with **MIKE DEACON** (ex-DARTS) / + members of RENAISSANCE & MAGNUM

Cheapskate not iss.

Nov 80. (7") *(CHEAP 6)* **GIVIN' YOUR HEART AWAY. / ROCK CITY** [ ] [–]

E.M.I. not iss.

Mar 81. (7") *(EMI 5156)* **GREEN GLASS WINDOWS. / DRIVING SONG** [ ] [–]

ROY WOOD

Jun 81. (7") *(EMI 5203)* **DOWN TO ZERO. / OLYMPIC FLYER** [ ] [–]

Jan 82. (7") *(EMI 5261)* **IT'S NOT EASY. / MOONRISER** [ ] [–]

Cheapskate not iss.

Dec 82. (7") *(CHEAP 12)* **SING OUT THE OLD. / WATCH THIS SPACE** [ ] [–]

Legacy not iss.

May 85. (7"/12") *(LGY/+T 24)* **UNDERFIRE. / ON TOP OF THE WORLD** [ ] [–]

Nov 85. (7"/12") *(LGY/+T 32)* **SING OUT THE OLD . . . BRING IN THE NEW. / ('A'instrumental)** [ ] [–]

Oct 86. (7") *(LGY 53)* **RAINING IN THE CITY. / ('A'instrumental)** [ ] [–]

Feb 87. (lp/c) *(LLP/LLK 106)* **STARTING UP** [ ] [–]
– Red cars are after me / Raining in the city / Under fire / Turn your body to the light / Hot cars / Starting up / Keep it steady / On top of the world / Ships in the night. *(cd-iss. May93 on 'Castle'; CLACD 387)*

— WOOD had earlier (late '86) featured on DOCTOR & THE MEDICS Top 50 version of ABBA's 'Waterloo'.

Woody not iss.

Dec 95. (c-s/cd-s; as The ROY WOOD BIG BAND) *(WOODY 001 CD/MC)* **I WISH IT COULD BE CHRISTMAS EVERYDAY /** [ ] [–]

— late in 2000, ROY returned to the UK charts (albeit alongside the WOMBLES) with the song, 'I WISH IT COULD BE A WOMBLING CHRISTMAS'

– (selective WOOD) compilations, etc. –

Apr 76. (d-lp) *Harvest; (SHDW 408)* **THE ROY WOOD STORY** (solo unless stated) [ ] [–]
– Ball park incident (WIZZARD) / Until you moma's gone / Dear Elaine / Ella James (MOVE) / First movement (ELECTRIC LIGHT ORCHESTRA) / California man (MOVE) / Whisper in the night / Chinatown (MOVE) / You can dance your rock'n'roll / Forever / Angel fingers (WIZZARD) / Look at me now (ELECTRIC LIGHT ORCHESTRA) / Tonight (MOVE) / See me baby jive (WIZZARD). *(re-iss. 1979 as 'YOU CAN DANCE THE ROCK'N'ROLL (THE ROY WOOD YEARS 1971-73)' lp/c; SHSM/TC-SHSM 2030) (re-iss. Jul89; CZ 177)* – Wake up / It wasn't my idea to dance / Nancy, sing me a song / Songs of praise.

Jul 82. (lp) *Speed; (SPEED 1000)* **THE SINGLES** (all his bands' work) [37] [–]
– See my baby jive / Are you ready to rock / Oh what a shame / Fire brigade / Forever / I can hear the grass grow / O.T.T. / Blackberry way / Angel fingers / We're on the road again / Flowers in the rain / Green grass windows / Keep your hands on the wheel / Rock & roll winter / This is the story of my love (baby).

Oct 96. (cd) *EMI Gold; (CDGOLD 1070)* **THROUGH THE YEARS** [ ] [ ]

Nov 97. (cd) *Rialto; (RMCD 219)* **ROY WOOD & WIZZARD ARCHIVE** [ ] [–]

Sep 99. (d-cd) *Repertoire; (REP 4744)* **EXOTIC MIXTURE** [ ] [ ]

Aug 01. (cd) *Armoury; (ARMCD 44)* **ROY WOOD & WIZZARD** [ ] [–]

□ MOVING SIDEWALKS (see under ⇒ ZZ TOP)

Alison MOYET

Born: GENEVIEVE ALISON MOYET, 18 Jun'61, Basildon, Essex, England. Nicknamed ALF by her French father, the singer's first forays into the music business came with Southend R&B outfits, The VICARS and The SCREAMING ABDABS. Early in 1982, she was invited by ex-DEPECHE MODE mainman, VINCE CLARKE, to join him in synth-pop duo, YAZOO (YAZ in the US). Over the course of the ensuing 18 months, the pair were a regular feature in the UK Top 20 with classic singles such as 'DON'T GO'. Their partnership was relatively brief however and after only two albums, both CLARKE and MOYET went their separate ways; CLARKE initially to The ASSEMBLY and later ERASURE, MOYET to a fairly successful if patchy solo career. Signing a solo contract with 'CBS-Columbia' around the same time as marrying long-time boyfriend Malcolm Lee and setting up home in Hertfordshire, MOYET got off to a good start with a summer '84 Top 10 hit, 'LOVE RESURRECTION'. A big woman with an even bigger vocal range, MOYET used her No.1 debut album, 'ALF' (1984) as a platform for her rich, earthy blues-soaked voice. While the quality of the songs didn't always match the quality of the singer, when they did – as on the likes of 'ALL CRIED OUT' (another Top 10 hit) – MOYET was a diva to reckon with. Her smoky, sultry style definitely owed something of a debt to the golden era of jazz and with a graceful ease, MOYET applied her tonsils to Billie Holiday's 'THAT OLE DEVIL CALLED LOVE', narrowly missing the number one slot in Spring '85. Aiming straight for the coffee table pop-rock market, Top 10 hits 'IS THIS LOVE' and 'WEAK IN THE PRESENCE OF BEAUTY' were radically different, dividing critics but bolstering sales of another near No.1 album, 'RAINDANCING' (1987). More true to form was a cover of vintage standard, 'LOVE LETTERS', a Top 5 hit (not included on the album) later in the year. Taking time out in the latter half of the 80's, MOYET finally returned in Spring

'91 with the 'HOODOO' album, a stylistically diverse record that found her finally making the space to exercise her voice to the max. Critics marvelled but the public weren't so supportive, the album almost breaking the Top 10 but failing to produce any hit singles. She did make it back into the Top 20 with 1994's 'WHISPERING YOUR NAME' single although the accompanying album, 'ESSEX' made little headway. More successful was 1995's No.1 retrospective, 'SINGLES', gathering together for the first time the cream of both her YAZOO and solo careers. After a recording layoff almost as long as that of PETER GABRIEL, MOYET returned with an album every bit as mature, complex, painstakingly crafted and subtle as might have been expected. There was a widescreen, filmic quality to these lingering ballads with enough modern production touches to make them contemporary yet not so much as to smother that classicism which she's always strived for, and, for much of the album, attains. • **Songwriters:** TONY SWAIN and STEVE JOLLEY wrote, produced and played on her debut album. She also covered; INVISIBLE (Lamont-Dozier) / LOVE LETTERS (Ketty Lester) / ROCK AND ROLL (Led Zeppelin). • **Trivia:** Female comedy duo FRENCH & SAUNDERS featured on the video of 'LOVE LETTERS'.

Album rating: ALF (*7) / RAINDANCING (*5) / HOODOO (*5) / ESSEX (*4) / SINGLES compilation (*7) / THE ESSENTIAL compilation (*7) / HOMETIME (*6)

ALISON MOYET – vocals with session people

C.B.S. | Columbia

Jun 84. (7") *(A 4497) <05411>* **LOVE RESURRECTION. / BABY I DO** 10 Jul85 82
(12") *(TA 4497)* – ('A'-Love injected mix).

Sep 84. (7"/ext-12") *(A/TA 4757)* **ALL CRIED OUT. / STEAL ME BLIND** 8

Nov 84. (lp/c) *(CBS/40 26229) <39956>* **ALF** 1 Mar85 45
– Love resurrection / Honey for the bees / For you only / Invisible / Steal me blind / All cried out / Money mile / Twisting the knife / Where hides sleep. *(cd-iss. Feb85; CD 26229) (re-iss. Sep96 on 'Columbia' cd/c; 483836-2/-4)*

Nov 84. (7"/remix-12") *(A/TA 4930) <04781>* **INVISIBLE. / HITCH HIKE (with The DARTS)** 21 Feb85 31
(d7"+=) *(DA 4930)* – Love resurrection / Baby I do.

Mar 85. (7") *(A 6044)* **THAT OLE DEVIL CALLED LOVE. / DON'T BURN DOWN THE BRIDGES** 2
(12"+=) *(TA 6044)* – ('A'-Jazz version).
(d7"+=) *(DA 6044)* – ('A'live) / Twisting the knife (live).

Aug 85. (7") **MONEY MILE. / FOR YOU ONLY** –

Nov 86. (7") *(MOYET 1)* **IS THIS LOVE? / BLOW WIND BLOW** 3 –
(12"+=) *(MOYETT 1)* – ('A'-L.A. mix).
(12") *(MOYETX 1)* – ('A'side) / For you only (Europa mix).

Mar 87. (7") *(MOYET 2)* **WEAK IN THE PRESENCE OF BEAUTY. / TO WORK ON YOU** 6 –
(ext-12"+=) *(MOYETT 2)* – Take my imagination to bed.
(d7"+=) *(MOYETD 2)* – Is this love / Blow wind blow.

Apr 87. (lp/c/cd) *(450152-1/-4/-2) <40653>* **RAINDANCING** 2 Jun87 94
– Weak in the presence of beauty / Ordinary girl / You got me wrong / Without you / Sleep like breathing / Is this love? / Blow wind blow / Glorious love / When I say no (no giveaway) / Stay. *(re-iss. Mar90; same)*

May 87. (7") *(MOYET 3)* **ORDINARY GIRL. / PALM OF YOUR HAND (CLOAK AND DAGGER)** 43 –
(12"+=) *(MOYETT 3)* – ('A'-dance remix).

Sep 87. (7") *(MOYET 4)* **SLEEP LIKE BREATHING. / LOVE RESURRECTION (live)** –
(12"+=) *(MOYETT 4)* – Ne me quitte pas (live).

Nov 87. (7") *(MOYET 5)* **LOVE LETTERS. / THIS HOUSE** 4 –
(12"+=) *(MOYETT 5)* – ('A'extended).
(cd-s++=) *(MOYETC 5)* – Ne me quitte pas (live).

Columbia | Columbia

Mar 91. (7"/c-s) *(656757-7/-4)* **IT WON'T BE LONG. / MY RIGHT A.R.M.** 50 –
(12"+=/cd-s+=) *(656757-6/-2)* – Take of me.

Apr 91. (cd/c/lp) *(468272-2/-4/-1) <47841>* **HOODOO** 11 Aug91
– Footsteps / It won't be long / This house / Rise / Wishing you were here / (Meeting with my) Main man / Hoodoo / Back where I belong / My right A.R.M. / Never too late / Find me.

May 91. (7"/c-s) *(656939-7/-4)* **WISHING YOU WERE HERE. / BACK WHERE I BELONG** 72 –
(12"+=/cd-s+=/pic-cd-s+=) *(656939-6/-2/-5)* – ('B'mixes).

Oct 91. (7"/c-s) *(657515-7/-4)* **THIS HOUSE. / COME BACK HOME** 40 –
(cd-s+=) *(657515-2)* – Love letters / That ole Devil called love.

Oct 93. (7"/c-s) *(659596-7/-4)* **FALLING. / ODE TO A BOY** 44 –
(cd-s+=) *(659596-2)* – ('A'mix).

Feb 94. (c-s) *(660162-4)* **WHISPERING YOUR NAME / F.O.S.** 18 –
(12") *(660162-6)* – ('A'extended mixes) / ('A'-Vince Clarke mix).
(cd-s) *(660162-2)* – ('A'side) / Rise / Wishing you were here / Rock and roll (all live).
(12"/cd-s) *(660162-5/-0)* – ('A'side) / Hoodoo / Back where I belong.

Mar 94. (cd/c/lp) *(475955-2/-4/-1) <57448>* **ESSEX** 24
– Falling / Whispering your name / Getting into something / Dorothy / So am I / And I know / Ode to boy / Satellite / Another living day / Boys own / Take of me / Ode to boy II / Whispering your name (single mix).

May 94. (c-s) *(660356-4)* **GETTING INTO SOMETHING / ('A'mix)** 51 –
(12"+=/cd-s+=) *(660356-6/-2)* – Never too late.
(cd-s++=) *(660356-5)* – Ne me quitte pas.

Oct 94. (c-s) *(660795-4)* **ODE TO BOY / LIFE IN A HOLE** 59 –
(cd-s) *(660795-2)* – (2-'A'mixes) / Sunderland Glynn.
(12") *(660795-6)* – (5-'A'mixes).

May 95. (cd/c) *(480663-2/-4) <67278>* **SINGLES** (compilation) 1
– The first time ever I saw your face / Only you (YAZOO) / Nobody's diary (YAZOO) / Situation (YAZOO) / Love resurrection / All cried out / Invisible / That ole Devil called love / Is this love? / Weak in the presence of beauty / Ordinary girl / Love letters / It won't be long / Wishing you were here / This house / Falling / Whispering your name / Getting into somthing / Ode to boy II / Solid wood. *(d-cd-iss. Apr96 w/ 'LIVE'+=; 480663-9)* – Getting into something / Chain of fools / Love letters / All cried out / Dorothy / Ode to boy / Is this love? / Nobody's diary / Whispering your name / There are worse things I could do.

Jun 95. (c-s/cd-s) *(662117-4/-2)* **THE FIRST TIME EVER I SAW YOUR FACE / BLUE** –

Aug 95. (c-s) *(662326-4)* **SOLID WOOD / BLUE / ODE TO BOY** 44 –
(cd-s+=) *(662326-2)* – There are worse things I could do.
(cd-s+=) *(662326-5)* – Whispering your name / The first time ever I saw your face.

Sanctuary | Sanctuary

Aug 02. (cd) *(SANCD 128) <84570>* **HOMETIME** 18 Sep02
– Yesterday's flame / The train I ride / You don't have to go.

Sep 02. (cd-s) *(SANX 137)* **SHOULD I FEEL THAT IT'S OVER / TONGUE TIED / NOBODY'S DARLING** –

Nov 02. (cd-s) *(SANX 145)* **DO YOU EVER WONDER / YESTERDAY'S FLAME (Insects remix) / BILAN** –

– compilations, etc. –

1988. (d-cd) *C.B.S.; (CDAM 241)* **ALF / RAINDANCING** –

Sep 01. (cd) *Sony TV; (STVCD 123) / Columbia; <504638>* **THE ESSENTIAL COLLECTION** 16 Apr03
– Don't go (YAZOO) / Nobody's diary (YAZOO) / Winter kills (YAZOO) / Love resurrection / All cried out / Invisible / That ole devil called love / Is this love / Weak in the presence of beauty / Love letters / It won't be long / Wishing you were here / This house / Falling / Whispering your name / Getting into something / Our colander eyes / Blue / Ne me quitte pas / There are worse things I could do.

MS. DYNAMITE

Born: NIOMI McLEAN-DALEY, 18 Sep'80, North London, England. Daughter of white Scots-born mother (teacher) and oldest sister to 10 siblings, NIOMI grooved on her mother's sizeable collection of reggae and soul records from an early age, nurturing a love of music which would eventually lead to her MC'ing at raves. What began as a bit of fun subsequently resulted in the foregoing of a university place to focus on music professionally. Initially hooking up with garage maestro STICKY for the huge underground club track, 'BOOO!', MS DYNAMITE made an unexpected leap into the UK Top 20 in 2002 after this inimitable account of garage scene violence was licensed (from JASON KAYE's 'Social Circles' imprint) by 'London-ffrr'. Subsequently signed up by 'Universal', she changed tack completely, swapping her gritty garage persona for that of sophisticated, silky-voiced R&B chanteuse on acclaimed debut album, 'A LITTLE DEEPER' (2002). There were still traces of her furious MC delivery (on the likes of 'DANGER' for instance) but NIOMI had successfully reinvented herself as perhaps the first bonafide Brit-R&B diva capable of sparring with the sassy Stateside legions. As well as the likes of Salaam Remi, the album was partly produced by reggae duo TONY and DAVE KELLY, and NIOMI's love of reggae, ragga and dancehall grounded the record's airier neo-soul moments. Lyrically, meanwhile, MS DYNAMITE displayed an admirable and sorely needed preference for questions over self-satisfied statements, even on such radio-friendly fare as 'IT TAKES MORE'. She went on to win a couple of Brit awards while also being labelled Britain's answer to LAURYN HILL.

Album rating: A LITTLE DEEPER (*8)

MS. DYNAMITE – vocals / with session producers

Soul Kandy / not iss.

Jun 01. (12"; as STICKY & MS. DYNAMITE) *(SK 002)* **BOOO! (mixes)** [ ] [–]

ffrr / not iss.

Jun 01. (c-s/12"/cd-s; as STICKY & MS. DYNAMITE) *(FCS/FX/FCD 399)* **BOOO! (mixes)** [12] [–]

Polydor / Universal

May 02. (c-s) *(570798-4)* **IT TAKES MORE / DYNAMITE** [7] [ ]
(cd-s+=) *(570798-2)* – ('A'-Bloody main mix) / ('A'-dirty version) / ('A'-video).
(12") *(570798-1)* – ('A'side) / ('A'-dirty version).

Jun 02. (cd/lp) *(589955-2/-1)* **A LITTLE DEEPER** [10] [ ]
– Natural high / Dy-na-mi-tee / Anyway U want it / Put him out / Brother / It takes more / Sick 'n' tired / Afraid 2 fly / Watch over them / Seed will grow / Krazy krush / Now U want my love / Too experienced / Gotta let U know / All I ever / A little deeper.

Aug 02. (c-s) *(570978-4)* **DY-NA-MI-TEE / (Yoruba soul mix)** [5] [–]
(cd-s+=) *(570978-2)* – It takes more (live lounge Radio 1 version) / ('A'-video).
(12") *(570979-1)* – ('A'mixes).

Dec 02. (c-s) *(065893-4)* **PUT HIM OUT / (JD aka Dready mix)** [19] [–]
(cd-s+=) *(065893-2)* – ('A'-Curtis Lynch Jnr. danger mix) / ('A'video).
(12"+=) *(065893-1)* – ('A'-instrumental).

□ M.S.G. (see under ⇒ SCHENKER GROUP, Michael)

MUDHONEY

Formed: Seattle, Washington, USA … 1988 by MARK ARM (vocals, guitar), STEVE TURNER (guitar), MATT LUKIN (bass) and DAN PETERS (drums). A band boasting impeccable credentials, ARM and TURNER had both graduated from the seminal GREEN RIVER (and The THROWN UPS), while LUKIN had previously been a member of Seattle noisemongers, The MELVINS. With as much a claim to the 'Godfathers of Grunge' crown as labelmates NIRVANA, MUDHONEY released the definitive 'Sub Pop' single in 1988 with 'TOUCH ME I'M SICK'. Arguably one of the few tracks to ever match the primal howl of The STOOGES, the single was a revelation, a cathartically dumb three chord bludgeon with ARM shrieking over the top like a man who was, erm, very sick indeed. A mini-album followed shortly after, the wonderfully titled 'SUPERFUZZ BIGMUFF' (rather disappointingly named after STEVE TURNER's favourite effects pedals, apparently). Visceral, dirty, fuzz-drenched rock'n'roll, this was one of the seminal records of the 80's and the blueprint for "grunge", a term that would later become bastardised to represent a glut of snooze-worthy, sub-metal toss. There was also a deep, underlying sense of unease and melancholy to these songs (especially 'NO ONE HAS' and 'NEED') that gave MUDHONEY an edge over most of their contemporaries, a subsequent cover of SONIC YOUTH'S 'HALLOWEEN' (released as a split single with SONIC YOUTH covering 'TOUCH ME..') sounding positively evil. Given all this, then, the debut album proper, 'MUDHONEY', was regarded as something of a disappointment when it was finally released in late '89. Nevertheless, 'THIS GIFT' and 'HERE COMES SICKNESS' were worth the price of admission alone. By summer '91, MUDHONEY had modified their sound somewhat, releasing the 'LET IT SLIDE' EP as a taster for the forthcoming 'EVERY GOOD BOY DESERVES FUDGE' album (a UK Top 40 hit). The intensity of the EP harked back to 'SUPERFUZZ..', this time with more of a retro garage-punk feel on the blistering 'PAPERBACK LIFE' and 'OUNCE OF DECEPTION'. The album continued in this direction, adding funky (in the loosest sense of the term) hammond organ and harmonica to the mutant guitar buzz. Hell, they even came close to a pop song with 'GOOD ENOUGH'. Following a financial dispute with 'Sub Pop', MUDHONEY followed NIRVANA into the big league, signing with 'Reprise' and releasing the lacklustre 'PIECE OF CAKE' (1992). Having sold their souls to the corporate 'devil', it seemed MUDHONEY had had the life sucked out of them, the rough edges smoothed into a major production gloss. The mini-album, 'FIVE DOLLAR BOB'S MOCK COOTER STEW' (1993) was an improvement but it took Seattle legend, Jack Endino to summon forth the raw spontaneity of old on 'MY BROTHER THE COW' (1995), a return to form of sorts, notably on 'INTO YOUR SCHTIK' and 'GENERATION SPOKESMODEL'. MUDHONEY subsequently took a few years hiatus in which ARM went on tour with his side-project, BLOODLOSS, while TURNER continued with his label, 'Super-Electro' (MUDHONEY were allowed dual output for the imprint) and PETERS guested for solo MIKE JOHNSON (DINOSAUR JR). In the Autumn of '98, the quartet were back once again, although the album, TOMORROW HIT TODAY', disappointed most of their hardcore fanbase. Recorded in just over a week, emboldened by blasts of neo-free jazz horns and adrenalised by an undertow of twisted gutter-funk, 'SINCE WE'VE BECOME TRANSLUCENT' (2002) was the sound of MUDHONEY rediscovering that mutant garage gene that made them so seminal in the first place. • **Covers:** HATE THE POLICE (Dicks) / EVOLUTION (Spacemen 3) / OVER THE TOP (Motorhead) / PUMP IT UP (Elvis Costello) / TONIGHT I THINK I'M GONNA GO DOWNTOWN (Jimmie Dale Gilmore) / BUCKSKIN STALLION BLUES (Townes Van Zandt). MARK ARM solo:- MASTERS OF WAR (Bob Dylan).

Album rating: SUPERFUZZ BIGMUFF mini (*7) / MUDHONEY (*6) / BOILED BEEF & ROTTING TEETH (*6) / EVERY GOOD BOY DESERVES FUDGE (*7) / PIECE OF CAKE (*5) / MY BROTHER THE COW (*5) / TOMORROW TODAY (*5) / MARCH TO FUZZ compilation (*7) / SINCE WE'VE BECOME TRANSLUCENT (*6) / Monkeywrench: CLEAN AS A BROKE-DICK DOG (*6) / ELECTRIC CHILDREN (*7)

MARK ARM (b.21 Feb'62, California) – vocals, guitar (ex-GREEN RIVER, ex-THROWN UPS) / **STEVE TURNER** (b.28 Mar'65, Houston, Texas) – guitar (ex-GREEN RIVER, ex-THROWN UPS) / **MATT LUKIN** (b.16 Aug'64, Aberdeen, Washington) – bass (ex-MELVINS) / **DAN PETERS** (b.18 Aug'67) – drums

Glitterhouse Sub Pop

Aug 88. (7",7"brown) *<SP 18>* **TOUCH ME I'M SICK. / SWEET YOUNG THING AIN'T SWEET NO MORE** [–] [ ]

Oct 88. (12"ep) *(GR 0034)* *<SP 21>* **SUPERFUZZ BIGMUFF** [ ] [ ]
– No one has / If I think / In 'n' out of grace / Need / Chain that door / Mudride. *(cd-iss. Mar00; same as US)*

Jan 89. (7",7"clear) *<SP 26>* **('A'side by 'Sonic Youth'). / TOUCH ME I'M SICK** [–] [ ]

Jun 89. (7",7"white) *(GR 060)* *<SP 33>* **YOU GOT IT (KEEP IT OUTTA MY FACE). / BURN IT CLEAN / NEED (demo)** [ ] [ ]
(re-iss. May93; same)

Oct 89. (7",7"purple,12") *(GR 0070)* *<SP 44AA>* **THIS GIFT. / BABY HELP ME FORGET / REVOLUTION** [ ] [ ]
(re-iss. May93; same)

Oct 89 (lp/c/cd) *(GR 0069)* *<SP 44/+A/B>* **MUDHONEY** [ ] [ ]
– This gift / Flat out f***ed / Get into yours / You got it / Magnolia caboose babyshit / Come to mind / Here comes sickness / Running loaded / The further I go / By her own hand / When tomorrow hits / Dead love. *(cd re-iss. Mar00; same as US)*

Jun 90. (7",7"pink) *(GR 0102)* *<SP 63>* **YOU'RE GONE. / THORN / YOU MAKE ME DIE** [60] [ ]
(re-iss. May93; same)

Sub Pop Sub Pop

Jul 91. (7",12"grey) *(SP 15154)* *<SP 95>* **LET IT SLIDE. / OUNCE OF DECEPTION / CHECKOUT TIME** [60] [ ]
(cd-s+=) *(SP 95B)* – Paperback life / The money will roll right in.

Aug 91. (lp/c/cd) *<(SP 160/+A/B)>* **EVERY GOOD BOY DESERVES FUDGE** [34] [ ]
– Generation genocide / Let it slide / Good enough / Something so clear / Thorn / Into the drink / Broken hands / Who you drivin' now / Move out / Shoot the Moon / Fuzzgun '91 / Poking around / Don't fade IV / Check out time.

1991. (7") *<scale 36>* **MOD SHOWDOWN!** [–] [ ]
– She's just fifteen / (track by HALO OF FLIES)
(above issued on 'Amphetamine Reptile' + below on 'eMpTy')

1991. (7") *<MT 166>* **YOU STUPID ASSHOLE. / (w/ Gas HUFFER)** [–] [ ]

—— MARK + STEVE took up time in MONKEYWRENCH, and DAN joined SCREAMING TREES, after below album.

Warners Reprise

Oct 92. (7"/c-s) *(W 0137/+C)* **SUCK YOU DRY. / DECEPTION PASS** [65] [–]
(12"+=/cd-s+=) *(W 0137 T/CD)* – Underride / Over the top.

Oct 92. (cd/c) *<(4509 90073-2/-4)>* **PIECE OF CAKE** [39] [ ]
– No end in sight / Make it now / Suck you dry / Blinding sun / Thirteenth floor opening / Youth body expression explosion / I'm spun / Take me there / Living wreck / Let me let you down / Ritzville / Acetone.

Jan 93. (cd-ep) *<40741>* **BLIDING SUN / DECEPTION PASS / KING SANDBOX / BABY O BABY** [–] [ ]

Oct 93. (m-cd/m-c/m-lp) *<(9362 45439-2/-4)>* **FIVE DOLLAR BOB'S MOCK COOTER STEW** [ ] [ ]
– In the blood / No song III / Between you & me kid / Six two one / Make it now again / Deception pass / Underide.

—— In Mar'94, MUDHONEY released a collab with JIMMIE DALE GILMOUR; 7"yellow/cd-ep 'BUCKSKIN STALLION BLUES' for 'Sub Pop' *(SP 124/305/+CD)* Also a single, 'PUMP IT UP, was released by 'Fox' in April '94

Reprise Reprise

Mar 95. (cd/c/lp) *<(9362 45840-2/-4/-1)>* **MY BROTHER THE COW** [70] [ ]
– Judgement, rage, retribution and thyme / Generation spokesmodel / What moves the heart? / Today, is a good day / Into yer schtik / In my finest suit / F.D.K. (Fearless Doctor KIllers) / Orange ball-pen hammer / Crankcase blues / Execution style / Dissolve / 1995.

Apr 95. (7") *(SE 708)* **INTO YOUR SCHTIK. / YOU GIVE ME THE CREEPS** [ ] [ ]
(above single on 'Super Electro')

May 95. (7"colrd/c-s) *(W 0292/+C)* **GENERATION SPOKESMODEL. / NOT GOING DOWN THAT ROAD AGAIN** [ ] [ ]
(cd-s+=) *(W 0292CD)* – What moves the heart live) / Judgement, rage, retribution and thyme (live).

Amphetam. Reptile Amphetam. Reptile

Aug 95. (7") *<scale 76>* **GOAT CHEESE. / (w/ Strapping Fieldhands)** [–] [ ]
(above on 'Amphetamine Reptile' and below on 'Super Electro')

May 98. (ltd-7") *(SE 716)* **NIGHT OF THE HUNTED. / BRAND NEW FACE** [ ] [ ]

Sep 98. (cd) *<(9362 47054-2)>* **TOMORROW HIT TODAY** [ ] [ ]
– A thousand forms of mind / I have to laugh / Oblivion / Try to be kind / Poisoned water / Real low vibe / This is the life / Night of the hunted / Move with the wind / Ghost / I will fight no more forever / Beneath the valley of the underdog.

—— MATT LUKIN departed in '99; **GUY MADDISON** – bass (replaced him)

Sub Pop Sub Pop

Aug 02. (lp/cd) *<(SP 555/+CD)>* **SINCE WE'VE BECOME TRANSLUCENT** [ ] [ ]
– Baby, can you dig the light / The straight life / Where the flavor is / In the winner's circle / Our time is now / Dyin' for it / Inside job / Take it like a man / Crooked and wide / Sonic infusion.

Sep 02. (7") *(SP 603)* **SONIC INFUSION. / A LONG WAY TO GO** [ ] [–]

– compilations, etc. –

Nov 89. (cd-ep) *Tupelo; (TUPCD 009) / Sub Pop; <SP 62>* **BOILED BEEF AND ROTTING TEETH** [ ] [ ]

Jan 00. (cd) *Strange Fruit; (SFRSCD 090)* **THE RADIO SESSIONS** [ ] [–]

Mar 00. (t-lp/d-cd) *Sub Pop; <(SP/+CD 500)>* **MARCH TO FUZZ** [ ] [ ]
– In 'n' out of grace / Suck you dry / I have to laugh / Sweet young thing ain't sweet no more / Who you drivin' now / You got it / Judgement, rage, retribution and thyme / Into the drink / A thousand forms of mind / Generation genocide / If I think / Here comes sickness / Let it slide / Touch me I'm sick / This gift / Good enough / Blinding sun / Into your shtik / Beneath the valley of the underdog / When tomorrow hits / Make it now again / Hate the police / Hey sailor / Twenty four / Baby help me forget / Revolution / You stupid asshole / Who is who / Stab yor back / Pump it up / The money will roll right in / Fix me / Dehumanized / She's just 15 / Baby o baby / Over the top / You goive me the creeps / March to fuzz / Ounce of deception / Paperback life / Bushpusher man / Fuzzbeater / Overblown / Run shithead run / King sandbox / Tonight I think I'm gonna go downtown / Holden / Not going down that road again / Brand new face / Drinking for two / Butterfly stroke / Editions of you.

☐ MUGGS (see under ⇒ CYPRESS HILL)

MULL HISTORICAL SOCIETY

Formed: Glasgow, Scotland . . . early in the year 2000 by COLIN MacINTYRE (son of KENNY MacINTYRE, the late and much missed political reporter for BBC Scotland), a man born and raised on the isle of Mull (Tobermory, to be exact). Having learned the guitar at an early age, he honed up on the music world by reading about, rather than listening to records; it was hard for him to obtain anything decent outside the Top 40. Writing a barrelload of songs (artwork complimented each one, apparently!), COLIN crossed the water to Glasgow and er, wrote some more. Abandoning other late 90's projects such as LOVE SICK ZOMBIES, WESTERNIZED and 7/11 (good names!), COLIN met up with like-minded bassist ALAN MALLOY (also from his hometown) and formed the MULL HISTORICAL SOCIETY (is there such a thing that already exists?). Towards the end of the year, the quartet (recent additions being COLIN 'SLEEPY' MacPHERSON and TONY SOAVE) unveiled their debut single for 'Tugboat', 'BARCODE BYPASS', a fine blend of MERCURY REV, BEACH BOYS and AZTEC CAMERA – 'Mull Of MacIntyre' anyone? Indeed. Moving on slightly and come the release of the group's debut set 'LOSS' (2001) – a universally praised homage to Glasgow (that's where most of the tracks were written) and an all-round great album – MacINTYRE's vocals did become a tad taxing on some tracks, but it was nothing that the music didn't make up for. 'PUBLIC SERVICE ANNOUNCER' opened the album with bursting, full-on guitars, heightening the pop factor to 11, whereas 'INSTEAD' offered up a quaint ballad, with a children's choir thrown in for good measure. The press had a field day over the album (and a minor hit 45, 'WATCHING XANADU'), which prompted the band to tour with the likes of The STROKES, TRAVIS and The MOLDY PEACHES, as well as being faves on the Glastonbury and T In The Park festivals.

Album rating: LOSS (*7) / US (*7)

COLIN MacINTYRE – vocals, guitar / **ALAN MALLOY** – bass / **COLIN 'SLEEPY' MacPHERSON** – keyboards / **TONY SOAVE** – drums

Tugboat | not iss.

Nov 00. (7"/cd-s) *(TUGS/+CD 28)* **BARCODE BYPASS. / MULL HISTORICAL SOCIETY** [ ] [-]

Mar 01. (7"/cd-s) *(TUGS/+CD 29)* **I TRIED. / SOME YOU WIN, SOME YOU LOSE** [ ] [-]

Rough Trade | not iss.

Jul 01. (7"/cd-s) *(RTRADES/+CD 021)* **ANIMAL CANNABUS. / UGLY BUILDINGS ARE BEAUTIFUL / INDUSTRIAL HANGERS** [53] [-]

Blanco Y Negro | Beggars XL

Oct 01. (cd/d-lp) *(0927 41307-2/-1)* <85027> **LOSS** [43] [ ]
– Public service announcer / Watching Xanadu / Instead / I tried / This is not who we were / Barcode bypass / Only I / Animal cannabus / Strangeways inside / Mull Historical Society / Paper houses.

Jan 02. (7") *(NEG 138)* **WATCHING XANADU. / PIGEON LOVESONG** [36] [-]
(cd-s) *(NEG 138CD1)* – ('A'side) / Pigeon fancier (by correspondence) / Don't suffer.
(cd-s) *(NEG 138CD2)* – ('A'side) / Naked ambition at the E.P.A. / Sad old day to be down / ('A'-CD-Rom).

—— now just down to **MacINTYRE** + session people

Feb 03. (7") *(NEG 144)* **THE FINAL ARREARS. / SORRY (LEAVING)** [32] [-]
(cd-s) *(NEG 144CD)* – ('A'side) / Stay something / Citizen fame / ('A'-video).
(cd-s) *(NEG 144CD2)* – ('A'side) / Return to the grass point / Instead of breaking us (break me).

Mar 03. (cd/lp) *(0927 49758-2/-1)* <85034> **US** [19] [ ]
– The final arrears / Am I wrong / Oh mother / Asylum / Live like the automatics / Don't take your love away from me / Minister for genetics & insurance M.P. / 5 more minutes / Gravity / Can / The supermarket strikes back / Clones / Her is you / Us – Whiting of the people.

Jun 03. (7") *(NEG 146)* **AM I WRONG. / WITH YOU NOT IN THE WORLD** [51] [-]
(cd-s) *(NEG 146CD1)* – ('A'side) / Narrow escape at 2000 feet / It takes more / ('A'-video).
(cd-s) *(NEG 146CD2)* – ('A'side) / I knew you well / (Mull Historical Society (John Peel session).

☐ MURDERDOLLS (see under ⇒ SLIPKNOT)

☐ Peter MURPHY (see under ⇒ BAUHAUS)

MUSE

Formed: Teignmouth, Devon, England . . . 1997 by MATTHEW BELLAMY, CHRIS WOLSTENHOLME and drummer DOMINIC HOWARD. After playing dingey pubs and damp basements, the 3-piece from the south-west arose when they debuted at the 'In The City' A&R field day in 1998. HOWARD's THOM YORKE-esque vox impressed record pedallers so much that they took the group to America to showcase them for MADONNA's record label 'Maverik' – home to The DEFTONES, ALANIS MORISSETTE and, erm, WANK. The 20-something indie kids released a John Leckie (knob-twiddler for RADIOHEAD, STONE ROSES and somebody called JOHN LENNON) produced EP entitled 'MUSE' at the beginning of 1999, which was only pressed on 999 copies (it can nowadays fetch up to £30). The EP sounded like many earlier RADIOHEAD efforts, with a little MY BLOODY VALENTINE twist thrown in for good measure. MUSE proceeded with the 'MUSCLE MUSEUM' EP and two singles 'UNO' and 'CAVE' before unveiling their debut set 'SHOWBIZ' in late '99. The album boasted nothing special (bar say, the track 'SUNBURN'), except that it may have contained some of the most melodramatic tracks since OASIS's 'WHAT'S THE STORY . . .'. It unleashed a new brand of genre that had the same ideology as Brit Pop: MOR – where have I heard this before? – rock. 2001 saw MUSE go from strength to strength via two major UK hit singles, 'PLUG IN BABY' and 'NEW BORN', both taken from their celebrated Top 3 sophomore set, 'ORIGIN OF SYMMETRY'. 2002 saw the release of the obligatory live/B-sides collection, 'HULLABALOO SOUNDTRACK', documenting a French concert performance and collecting various odd'n'sods for obsessives and completists. BELLAMY and Co returned once again in September 2003 with UK chart-topper 'ABSOLUTION', a jaded, spiky rock affair that bore all of the usual MUSE trademarks, but this time with a change of production (Rich Costey replaced regular John Leckie). In turn, the set proved to be more clean-cut, but all of the recognisable traits still remained in the band's agit (sometimes angular) – BELLAMY's soaring falsetto at the forefront of the gloomy, doom-laden music. • **Note:** The MUSE who released the CD in '97 entitled 'Innocent Voices' were not the same band.

Album rating: SHOWBIZ (*7) / ORIGIN OF SYMMETRY (*7) / HULLABALOO SOUNDTRACK (*6) / ABSOLUTION (*7)

MATTHEW BELLAMY (b.20 Mar'80) – vocals, lead guitar, piano / **CHRIS WOLSTENHOLME** – bass / **DOMINIC HOWARD** (b. 7 Dec'80) – drums

Dangerous | not iss.

May 98. (cd-ep) *(DREXCDEP 103)* **MUSE EP** [ ] [-]
– Overdue / Cave / Coma / Escape.

Jan 99. (cd-ep) *(DREXCDEP 104)* **MUSCLE MUSEUM EP** [ ] [-]
– Muscle museum / Sober / Uno / Unintented / Instant messenger / Muscle museum #2.

Mushroom | Warners

Jun 99. (7"clear) *(MUSH 50S)* **UNO. / AGITATED** [73] [-]
(cd-s) *(MUSH 50CDS)* – ('A'side) / Jimmy Kane / Forced in.

Sep 99. (7"clear) *(MUSH 58S)* **CAVE / CAVE (instrumental remix)** [52] [ ]
(cd-s+=) *(MUSH 58CDS)* – Twin.
(cd-s) *(MUSH 58CDX)* – ('A'side) / Host / Coma.

Oct 99. (cd/md/c/lp) *(MUSH 59 CD/MC/LP)* <47382> **SHOWBIZ** [69] [ ]
– Sunburn / Muscle museum / Fillip / Falling down / Cave / Showbiz / Unintended / Uno / Sober / Escape / Overdue / Hate this & I'll love you. *(re-iss. Feb00; same)*

Nov 99. (7") *(MUSH 66S)* **MUSCLE MUSEUM. / ('A'live acoustic)** [43] [ ]
(cd-s+=) *(MUSH 66CDS)* – Do we need this?
(cd-s) *(MUSH 66CDSX)* – ('A'extended) / Pink ego box / Con-science.

Feb 00. (7") *(MUSH 68S)* **SUNBURN. / ('A'live)** [22] [ ]
(cd-s+=) *(MUSH 68CDS)* – Ashamed.
(cd-s) *(MUSH 68CDSX)* – ('A'side) / Yes please / Uno (live).

Jun 00. (7"/c-s) *(MUSH 72 S/MCS)* **UNINTENDED. / RECESS** [20] [ ]
(cd-s+=) *(MUSH 72CDS)* – Falling down (live acoustic) / ('A'-CD-ROM).
(cd-s) *(MUSH 72CDSX)* – ('A'side) / Nishe / Hate this & I'll love you (live).

Oct 00. (7") *(MUSH 84S)* **MUSCLE MUSEUM. / SOBER (The Saint remix)** [25] [-]
(cd-s+=) *(MUSH 84CDS)* – Sunburn (Timo Maas sunstroke remix).

Mushroom | Mushroom

Mar 01. (c-s) *(MUSH 89MCS)* **PLUG IN BABY / NATURE 1** [11] [-]
(cd-s+=) *(MUSH 89CDS)* – Execution commentary.
(cd-s) *(MUSH 89CDSX)* – ('A'side) / Spiral static / Bedroom acoustics.

Jun 01. (7") *(MUSH 92)* **NEW BORN. / SHRINKING UNIVERSE** [12] [-]
(cd-s+=) *(MUSH 92CDS)* – Piano thing / ('A'-video).
(cd-s) *(MUSH 92CDSX)* – ('A'side) / Map of your head / Plug in baby (live).

(12") *(MUSH 92T)* – ('A'-Perfecto remix) / Sunburn (Timo Maas sunstroke remix).

Jun 01. (cd/c/lp) *(MUSH 93 CD/MC/LP) <40093>* **ORIGIN OF SYMMETRY** [3] Jul01 [ ]
– New born / Bliss / Space dementia / Hyper music / Plug in baby / Citizen erased / Micro cuts / Screenager / Dark shines / Feeling good / Megalomania.

Aug 01. (7") *(MUSH 96S)* **BLISS. / THE GALLERY** [22] [–]
(cd-s+=) *(MUSH 96CDS)* – Screenager (live) / ('A'-CD-Rom).
(cd-s) *(MUSH 96CDSX)* – ('A'side) / Hyper chondriac music / New born (live) / ('A'-making of the video).

Nov 01. (7") *(MUSH 97S)* **HYPER MUSIC. / FEELING GOOD (live)** [24] [–]
(cd-s+=) *(MUSH 97CDS)* – Shine / ('A'-video).
(cd-s) *(MUSH 97CDSX)* – ('A'live) / ('B'studio) / Please, please, please let me get what I want / ('B'video).

Jun 02. (7") *(MUSH 104S)* **IN YOUR WORLD. / DEAD STAR** [13] [–]
(cd-s+=) *(MUSH 104CDS)* – Futurism / Dead star (video).
(cd-s+=) *(MUSH 104CDSX)* – Can't take my eyes off you / In your world (video).

Jul 02. (d-cd) *(MUSH 105CD) <65021>* **HULLABALOO SOUNDTRACK (compilation + live)** [10] [ ]
– Forced in / Shrinking universe / Recess / Yes please / Map of your head / Nature 1 / Shine acoustic / Ashamed / The gallery / Hyper chondriac music // Dead star / Micro cuts / Citizen erased / Showbiz / Megalomania / Dark shines / Screenager / Space dementia / In your world / Muscle museum / Agitated.

East West | Taste Media

Sep 03. (7"clear) *(EW 272)* **TIME IS RUNNING OUT. / THE GROOVE** [8] [–]
(cd-s+=) *(EW 272CD)* – Stockholm syndrome (video).

Sep 03. (cd/d-lp) *(5046 68587-2/-1) <48733>* **ABSOLUTION** [1] [ ]
– Intro / Apocalypse please / Time is running out / Sing for absolution / Stockholm syndrome / Falling away with you / Interlude / Hysteria / Blackout / Butterflies and hurricanes / The small print / Endlessly / Thoughts of a dying atheist / Ruled by secrecy.

Dec 03. (7"/cd-s) *(EW 278/+CD)* **HYSTERIA. / ETERNALLY MISSED** [17] [–]

MUSIC

Formed: Kippax, Leeds, England . . . 1999 by STUART COLEMAN, ADAM NUTTER, ROBERT HARVEY and PHIL JORDAN. Barely out of their teens, and with very little money, this impressive quartet issued a demo EP entitled 'TAKE THE LONG ROAD AND WALK IT' in 2001, which led Radio 1 DJ Steve Lamacq to give the group almost unlimited airtime on his evening shows. On the strengh of this demo, tiny label 'Fierce Panda' bought the rights to the EP and re-issued it on a limited run of 1,000 copies – they sold out in almost a fortnight. With COLEMAN's intense swagger and vocals to match, he seemed like the new generation's BEZ, only with a few more brain cells. The MUSIC's music, well, it wasn't as almighty as the ensemble's moniker would have you believe; rough, early VERVE came to mind along with, traces of JOY DIVISION and even MOGWAI on the track 'WALLS GET SMALLER' – basically a fusion of good old Northern glum. 'Hut' records eventually won the bidding war for the band in 2001, prompting them to issue their first EP proper 'YOU MIGHT AS WELL TRY TO FUCK ME', followed by 'THE PEOPLE' EP and eventually their cracking self-titled debut album in 2002.

Album rating: THE MUSIC (*8)

ROBERT HARVEY – vocals / **ADAM NUTTER** – guitar / **STUART COLEMAN** – bass / **PHIL JORDAN** – drums

Fierce Panda | not iss.

May 01. (ltd-7") *(NING 107)* **TAKE THE LONG ROAD AND WALK IT. / THE WALLS GET SMALLER** [ ] [–]

Hut | Capitol

Nov 01. (12"ep/cd-ep) *(HUT T/CD 145) <546066>* **YOU MIGHT AS WELL TRY TO FUCK ME EP** [ ] Jan02 [ ]
– You might as well try to fuck me / Karma / Treat me right on / Too high.

Apr 02. (12"ep/cd-ep) *(HUT T/CD 152)* **THE PEOPLE EP** [ ] [–]
– The people / Let love be the healer / Life / Jag tune.

Hut | Virgin

May 02. (cd-ep) *<68381>* **THE MUSIC** [–] [ ]
– Take the long road and walk it / The walls get smaller / You might as well try to fuck me / Karma / Too high / New instrumental (live).

Hut | Capitol

Aug 02. (7"pic-d) *(HUT 158) <546023>* **TAKE THE LONG ROAD AND WALK IT. / ALONE** [14] Jan02 [ ]
(cd-s+=) *(HUTCD 158)* – Raindance / ('A'-video).
(12"++=) *(HUTT 158)* – The walls get smaller.
(cd-s) *(HUTDX 158)* – ('A'side) / The walls get smaller / New instrumental / ('A'-original).

Sep 02. (cd/d-lp) *(CDHUT/HUTDLP 76)* **THE MUSIC** [4] [–]
– The dance / Take the long road and walk it / Human / The truth is no words / Float / Turn out the light / The people / Getaway / Disco / Too high.

Nov 02. (7"pic-d) *(HUT 162)* **GETAWAY. / DRAGON SONG** [26] [–]
(cd-s+=) *(HUTCD 162)* – ('A'-video).

Feb 03. (7"pic-d) *(HUT 164)* **THE TRUTH IS NO WORDS. / WHAT'S IT FOR** [18] [–]
(cd-s+=) *(HUTCD 164)* – Turn out the light (live) / ('A'-video).

MY BLOODY VALENTINE

Formed: Dublin, Ireland . . . 1984 by KEVIN SHIELDS and COLM O'CIOSOIG. Later the same year, the pair travelled to Germany where they hooked up with DAVE CONWAY and TINA to record a mini-lp, 'THIS IS YOUR BLOODY VALENTINE', for the small 'Tycoon' records. This was issued the following year although only 50 copies seem to have emerged (now very rare!). They subsequently moved to London, DEBBIE GOODGE replacing TINA for the recording of the 'GEEK!' EP on 'Fever'. After more 45's for 'Kaleidoscope' then 'Lazy' (home of The PRIMITIVES), the band really began to move away from their early twanging, IGGY POP-style sound following a move to 'Creation' in 1988 (masterminded by SLAUGHTER JOE FOSTER, ex-TV PERSONALITIES). With co-"vocalist", BILINDA BUTCHER now also on board, SHIELDS and Co. finally made the breakthrough in 1990 when the 'GLIDER' EP nearly went Top 40 in the UK, hot on the heels of the acclaimed 'ISN'T ANYTHING' (1988) album. The full extent of their pioneering guitar manipulation – responsible for a whole scene of "shoegazing" musical admirers, stand up RIDE, MOOSE, LUSH etc., etc. – was revealed as MBV released their most challenging and inventive track to date in 'TO HERE KNOWS WHEN' (from the Top 30 'TREMOLO' EP). Creating a whole new concept and language of sound, the song either enveloped the listener in blissful noise or just seemed out of bloody tune, there was no middle ground. 'LOVELESS' (1991), MBV's long awaited and much heralded follow-up, was a revelation. Its hypnotic, undulating noisescapes sounded not-of-this-earth and 'Creation' were saddled with an astronomical studio bill to match, almost going bankrupt as a result. They subsequently signed to 'Island' records, and 12(!!!) years on, fans are still awaiting some new product. Although MY BLOODY VALENTINE have arguably been the most influential indie band of the last decade and few doubt their potential to return with a masterpiece, their reclusive silence makes the late Stanley Kubrick appear prolific. Nevertheless, SHIELDS has surfaced occasionally as a remixer, notably for the single release of PRIMAL SCREAM's 'Stuka' and many more; he subsequently joined them in 2000. • **Songwriters:** SHIELDS writes most of material, with words after 1987 by BILINDA. Covered MAP REF 41 (Wire). • **Trivia:** A track, 'SUGAR', was given away free with 'The Catalogue' magazine of February '89.

Album rating: THIS IS YOUR BLOODY VALENTINE (*5) / ISN'T ANYTHING (*8) / ECSTASY AND WINE compilation (*7) / LOVELESS (*9)

KEVIN SHIELDS (b.21 May'63, Queens, New York) – guitar, vocals, occasional bass / **DAVE CONWAY** – vocals / **COLM CUSACK** (b. COLM MICHAEL O'CIOSOIG, 31 Oct'64) – drums / **TINA** – keyboards

Tycoon / not iss.

1985. (m-lp) *(ST 7501)* **THIS IS YOUR BLOODY VALENTINE** [–] German [–]
– Forever and again / Homelovin' guy / Don't cramp my style / Tiger in my tank / The love gang / Inferno / The last supper.

—— **DEBBIE GOOGE** (b.24 Oct'62, Somerset, England) – bass; repl. TINA

Fever / not iss.

Apr 86. (12"ep) *(FEV 5)* **GEEK!** [ ] [–]
– No place to go / Moonlight / Love machine / The sandman never sleeps.

Jun 86. (7") *(FEV 5X)* **NO PLACE TO GO. / MOONLIGHT** [ ] [–]

Kaleidoscope Sound / not iss.

Oct 86. (12"ep) *(KS 101)* **THE NEW RECORD BY MY BLOODY VALENTINE** [ ] [–]
– Lovelee sweet darlene / By the danger in your eyes / On another rainy Sunday / We're so beautiful.

Lazy / not iss.

Feb 87. (7") *(LAZY 04)* **SUNNY SUNDAE SMILE. / PAINT A RAINBOW** [ ] [–]
(12"+=) *(LAZY 04T)* – Kiss the eclipse / Sylvie's head.

—— **BILINDA BUTCHER** (b.16 Sep'61, London, England) – vocals, guitar; repl. CONWAY

Nov 87. (m-lp) *(LAZY 08)* **ECSTASY** [ ] [–]
– (Please) Lose yourself in me / The things I miss / I don't need you / Clair / (You're) Safe in your sleep / She loves you no less / Strawberry wine / Lovelee sweet darlene.

Nov 87. (12"m) *(LAZY 07)* **STRAWBERRY WINE. / NEVER SAY GOODBYE / CAN I TOUCH YOU** [ ] [–]

Creation / Relativity

Jul 88. (7") *(CRE 055)* **YOU MADE ME REALISE. / SLOW** [ ] [–]
(12"+=) *(CRE 055T)* – Thorn / Cigarette in your bed / Drive it all over me. *(re-iss. Mar90 as cd-ep; CRECD 55)*

Oct 88. (7") *(CRE 061)* **FEED ME WITH YOUR KISSES. / EMPTINESS INSIDE** [ ] [–]
(12"+=) *(CRE 061T)* – I believe / I need no trust. *(re-iss. Mar90 as cd-ep; CRECD 61)*

Nov 88. (lp/cd)(c) *(CRELP 040/+CD)(C-CRELP 040) <1006>* **ISN'T ANYTHING** [ ] [ ]
– Soft as snow (but warm inside) / Lose my breath / Cupid come / (When you wake) You're still in a dream / No more sorry / All I need / Feed me with your kiss / Sue is fine / Several girls galore / You never should / Nothing much to lose / I can see it (but I can't feel it). *(free 7"w/ lp)* – INSTRUMENTAL. / INSTRUMENTAL *<US cd re-iss. 1993 on 'Warners'; 45231> (cd re-iss. Jan01; same)*

Creation / Sire

Apr 90. (7"ep/12"ep)(cd-ep) *(CRE 73/+T)(CRESCD 73) <26313>* **GLIDER** [41] [ ]
– Soon / Glider / Don't ask why / Off your face.

Feb 91. (7"ep/12"ep)(cd-ep) *(CRE 085/+T)(CRESCD 085) <40024>* **TREMOLO** [29] Apr91 [ ]
– To here knows when / Swallow / Honey power / Moon song.

Nov 91. (cd/lp)(c) *(CRE CD/LP 060)(C-CRELP 060) <26759>* **LOVELESS** [24] [ ]
– Only shallow / Loomer / Touched / To here knows when / When you sleep / I only said / Come in alone / Sometimes / Blown a wish / What you want / Soon. *(cd re-iss. Jan01; same)*

—— During their long hiatus, KEVIN SHIELDS contributed (1996) to an album 'Beyond The Pale' by EXPERIMENTAL AUDIO RESEARCH. It also featured SONIC BOOM (ex-SPACEMEN 3), KEVIN MARTIN (of GOD) & EDDIE PREVOST (of AMM). Meanwhile, DEBBIE GOOGE teamed up with KATHERINE GIFFORD and MAX CORRADI to form SNOWPONY. In 2000, COLM finally reappeared in HOPE SANDOVAL & THE WARM INVENTIONS (she of MAZZY STAR fame).

– compilations, others, etc. –

Feb 89. (lp/cd) *Lazy; (LAZY 12/+CD)* **ECSTASY AND WINE** [ ] [–]
– Strawberry wine / Never say goodbye / Can I touch you / She loves you no less / The things I miss / I don't need you / Safe in your sleep / Clair / You've got nothing / Lose yourself in me.

MYSTIKAL

Born: MICHAEL ERNEST TYLER, 22 Sep'71, New Orleans, Louisiana, USA. Although a respected and often revered figure in the underground scene, MYSTIKAL didn't have a huge chart hit until the massive 'SHAKE YA ASS' was issued in 2000. A southern native, MYSTIKAL was often mentioned in the same breath as NELLY or JUVENILE, although he made a name for himself way before these new kids on the block emerged onto the scene. Signed to 'Bad Boy' in 1994, MYSTIKAL issued his debut album, 'MIND OF MYSTIKAL' in October '95. A record of gangsta tracks and bass-inspired G-Funk, it received wide critical underground acclaim and was a near Top 100 entry. The following year, MYSTIKAL attracted the attention of MASTER P and his 'No Limit' record crew. The two collaborated together on 1997's 'UNPREDICTABLE', again retracing the glamourised world of the hustler and mixing lyrics about "guns" and "bitches" with the usual bouncing bass, scratching and keyboard hooks. The album sold extremely well (hit US No.3) and enabled the man to grab a foothold in the ever-expanding rapping world. It also paved the way for another Top 5 success, the well-received 'GHETTO FABULOUS' (1999), a set featuring contributions from GUILLOTINE, MASTER P, SILKK THE SHOCKER, MIA X, SNOOP DOGGY DOGG, NAUGHTY BY NATURE and BUSTA RHYMES. The rapper's fourth outing, 'LET'S GET READY' (2000), spawned the hit single 'SHAKE YA ASS', an uptempo funk track peppered with JAMES BROWN-isms such as "Shake ya ass, show me what your working for". The song was a refreshing change from MYSTIKAL's usual misogynous overtones and more than a tongue-in-cheek nod to the great BROWN. The album also featured the fantasic female vs. male rap-battle, 'COME SEE ABOUT ME', where MYSTIKAL is given the once-around by a rival "pimptress". The transcendent one returned in 2001 with 'TARANTULA', keeping up the party, retro-funk vibe of his biggest hit with NEPTUNES once again working their quirky magic. Yet despite such refreshingly un-hip hop, un-preening lyrics like 'BIG TRUCK DRIVER' and winning productions from the likes of Scott Storch, the album only managed a US Top 30 placing.

Album rating: MIND OF MYSTIKAL (*6) / UNPREDICTABLE (*7) / GHETTO FABULOUS (*6) / LET'S GET READY (*8) / TARANTULA (*6)

MYSTIKAL – vocals / with others (see above)

Jive / Big Boy – No Limit

Sep 95. (c-s/12") *<42330>* **Y'ALL AIN'T READY FOR THIS (mixes)** [–] [ ]

Oct 95. (cd/c) *<41581>* **MIND OF MYSTIKAL** [–] [ ]
– Y'all ain't ready yet / Murderer / Beware / Mr. Hood critic / I'm / Out that boot camp clicc / Not that nigga / Smoke something / That nigga ain't shit! / Mind of Mystikal / Here I go / Never gonna bounce (the dream) / Y'all ain't ready yet / Not that nigga (remix) / Dedicated to Michelle Tyler.

Oct 97. (12") *<42492>* **AIN'T NO LIMIT (mixes)** [–] [ ]

Nov 97. (cd/c) *<41620>* **UNPREDICTABLE** [–] [3]
– Born 2 be a soldier (with MASTER P & SILKK THE SHOCKER) / Murder 2 / 13 years / Unpredictable / Ain't no limit (with SILKK THE SHOCKER) / Ghetto child (with MASTER P & SILKK THE SHOCKER) / Did I do it / Here we go (with B LEGIT, E FORTY & MASTER P) / We got the clout (with MIA X) / Still smokin' / U can't handle this / The man right Chea / Dick on the track / Sleepin' with me (with O DELL) / It yearns / Gangstas (with SNOOP DOGGY DOGG & MASTER P) / Shine.

Feb 99. (cd/c) *(052274-2/-4) <41655>* **GHETTO FABULOUS** [ ] Dec98 [5]
– Round out the tank / There he go (with GUILLOTINE) / Keep it hype / That's the nigga / Ghetto fabulous (with CHARLIE WILSON & SNOOP DOGG) / Life ain't cool (with SILKK THE SHOCKER & MASTER P) / I'm on fire / Whacha want, whacha need (with BUSTA RHYMES) / The stick up (with MIA X & FIEND) / I smell smoke / Respect my mind (with GUILLOTINE) / Stack yo chips (with MASTER P & C MURDER) / Dirty south, dirty jerz (with NAUGHTY BY NATURE) / Yaah! / Let's go do it (with SNOOP DOGG & SILKK THE SHOCKER) / What's your alias? (with FIEND & SILKK THE SHOCKER). *(cd re-iss. May01; same)*

Jive Jive

Nov 00. (c-s) *(925155-4) <42721>* **SHAKE YA ASS / SHAKE IT FAST (clean)** [30] Aug00 [13]
(12"/cd-s+=) *(925155-0/-2)* – Shake it fast (anonymous people remix) / Shake it fast (2 step remix).

Dec 00. (cd) *(922134-2) <41696>* **LET'S GET READY** [ ] Sep00 [1]
– Ready to rumble / Shake ya ass / Jump / Danger (been so long) (with NIVEA) / Come see about me (with DA BRAT & PETEY PABLO) / Big truck boys / I rock, I roll / U would if U could / Mystikal fever / Family / Ain't gonna see tomorrow / The braids / Smoked out / Murderer III / Neck uv da woods (with OUTKAST).

—— late 2000/early 2001, MYSTIKAL featured on JOE's Top 10, 'Stutter'

Feb 01. (c-s; by MYSTIKAL featuring NIVEA) *(925172-4) <42860>* **DANGER (BEEN SO LONG) / (breathing instrumental)** [28] Jan01 [14]
(12"+=/cd-s+=) *(925172-0/-2)* – Ghetto fabulous (with CHARLIE WILSON & SNOOP DOGGY DOGG).

Oct 01. (c-s/12"/cd-s) *(925269-4/-0/-2)* **JUMP / JUMP (Neptune remix & clean version) / JUMP (dirty)** [ ] [ ]

Feb 02. (c-s/12"/cd-s) *(925327-4/-0/-2) <42992>* **BOUNCIN' BACK (BUMPIN' ME AGAINST THE WALL) / (mixes)** [45] Dec01 [37]

Feb 02. (cd/d-lp) *(922290-2/-1) <41770>* **TARANTULA** [ ] Dec01 [25]
– Bouncin' back (bumpin' me against the wall) / Tarantula (with BUTCH CASSIDY) / If it ain't live, it ain't me / Settle the score (with JUVENILE) / Pussy crook / Ooooh yeah / Big truck driver / Smoke one / Alright / I get it started (with REDMAN & METHOD MAN) / Paper stack ((with SHONNIE, BEEZY BOY & DART) / Go 'head / The return / That's the shit.

MY VITRIOL

Formed: London, England ... 1998 by Sri Lankan-born singer/songwriter SOM WIJAY-WARDNER and his college mate RAVI KESAVARAM. Taking the name from Graham Greene's classic novel, 'Brighton Rock', the pair cut a 6-track demo EP entitled 'DELUSIONS OF GRANDEUR'. Although more than 200 CDR's were pressed up, less than a quarter were actually playable due to a technical hitch. Luckily, one of these found its way into the hands of Radio 1 DJ Steve Lamacq who duly aired a track on his Evening Session show. Further tracks appeared on compilation albums courtesy of the 'Org' and 'Abuse' labels while the former was to release a debut single proper, 'ALWAYS YOUR WAY' / 'PIECES' in late '99. By this point, the line-up had been completed by SETH TAYLOR and CAROLYN BANNISTER, the four-piece finally landing a deal with 'Infectious' amid much column inches and radio play. The new millennium began with a session for Radio One followed by a couple of live acoustic sessions for X-FM. A much anticipated debut album, 'FINELINES' (2000), hit the shelves in March to widespread acclaim with critics namechecking a host of US noise luminaries including SONIC YOUTH, DINOSAUR JR and SMASHING PUMPKINS. SOM, for his part, cited NIRVANA's 'Smells Like Teen Spirit' as the spark that ignited his much raved over musical bile. A subsequent series of single releases culminated in a Top 40 entry for a re-released 'ALWAYS ...' while the album nearly breached the Top 20. With a string of festival appearances lined up for summer 2001, MV look set to win over yet more punters with their self-confessed 'C.O.R.'; that's critic-orientated-rock to you ... • **Covers:** BREAKFAST (Kelly) / WAIT A MINUTE (Wipers) / OH FATHER (Madonna) / GAME OF PRICKS (Guided By Voices) / STATIC (Jawbox).

Album rating: FINELINES (*7)

SOM WIJAY-WARDNER (b.26 Dec'79) – vocals, guitar (ex-SHOCK SYNDROME) / **SETH TAYLOR** – guitar (ex-MINT 400) / **CAROLYN BANNISTER** – bass, vocals (ex-PRODUCT) / **RAVI KESAVARAM** – drums

Org not iss.

Dec 99. (cd-ep) **ALWAYS YOUR WAY / PIECES / GROUNDED (demo)** [ ] [–]

Infectious Epic

Apr 00. (7") *(INFECT 88S)* **LOSING TOUCH. / TONGUE TIED** [ ] [–]
(cd-s+=) *(INFECT 88CDS)* – Breakfast (live/BBC). *(re-iss. Jan01)*

Jul 00. (7") *(INFECT 89S)* **CEMENTED SHOES. / WAIT A MINUTE** [65] [–]
(cd-s+=) *(INFECT 89CDS)* – All of me. *(re-iss. Jan01)*

Oct 00. (cd-s) *(INFECT 94CDS)* **PIECES / SAFETY ZONES AND CRUMPLE ZONES** [56] [–]
(cd-s) *(INFECT 94CDSX)* – ('A'side) / Another lie / Cemented shoes (live).

Feb 01. (7") *(INFECT 95S)* **ALWAYS: YOUR WAY. / SPOTLIGHTS** [31] [–]
(cd-s+=) *(INFECT 095CDS)* – Game of pricks.
(cd-s) *(INFECT 095CDSX)* – ('A'side) / Losing touch (acoustic) / It came crashing.

Mar 01. (cd/lp) *(INFECT 96 CDX/LP) <85958>* **FINELINES** [24] [ ]
– Alpha waves / Always: your way / The gentle art of choking / Kohlstream / Cemented shoes / Grounded / C.O.R. / Infantile / Ode to the red queen / Tongue tied / Windows & walls / Taprobane / Losing touch / Pieces / Falling off the floor / Under the wheels. *(d-cd-iss. Jul02 +=; INFECT 96CDS)* – Deadlines / Wait a minute / Windows and walls (acoustic) / Safety zones and crumple zones / Vapour trails / Taproplane and losing touch (live) / Oh father / Spotlights / Moodswings / Game of pricks / Another lie / It came crashing / Static / Always your way (live) / Breakfast / All of me.

May 01. (cd-s) *(INFECT 97CDS)* **GROUNDED / OH FATHER / ALWAYS: YOUR WAY** [29] [–]
(cd-s) *(INFECT 97CDSX)* – ('A'side) / Deadlines / Windows and walls (piano).

Jul 02. (cd-s) *(INFEC 107CDS)* **MOODSWINGS / THE GENTLE ART OF CHOKING (misery lab remix) / VAPOUR TRAILS** [39] [–]
(cd-s) *(INFEC 107CDSX)* – ('A'mixes) / Vapour trails / ('A'-video).

NIRVANA

N

NAPALM DEATH

Formed: Ipswich, England . . . 1982 by "vocalist" LEE DORRIAN and guitarist BILL STEER. Building up a small but fiercely loyal grassroots following by constant gigging, 'DEATH finally made in onto vinyl with 'SCUM' in 1987. Released on the band's own 'Earache' label, the record was a proverbial tale of two halves with NICK BULLEN (bass, vocals), JUSTIN BROADRICK (guitar) and MICK HARRIS (drums) producing side one, while side two was the work of STEER, DORRIAN and JIM WHILTELY. Needless to say, both sides were cranium-shreddingly extreme, pioneering white-hot blasts of a thrash/death-metal/punk hybrid which was duly christened "grindcore". Taking punk's short, sharp shock technique to its ultimate conclusion, many of the tracks were under a minute in length. John Peel's favourite, meanwhile, 'YOU SUFFER', lasted less than a second! The influential and ever eclectic PEEL would subsequently invite the band to record a session that year, acknowledging the group's sonic innovation while large sections of the metal press mocked them. The vocals, particularly, came in for a lot of stick; almost wholly unintelligible sub-human growling is how they might be best described although it's a style that has since been ripped off wholesale by legions of death-metal bands. And while the "singing" may have been incomprehensible to anyone missing a lyric sheet, the growling actually belied a radical political and social agenda, not exactly a priority of your average metal band. By the release of the 54 track (a single lp!) 'ENSLAVEMENT TO OBLITERATION' (1988), if anything more extreme than the debut, SHANE EMBURY had replaced WHITELY on bass. Further line-up changes ensued the following year when DORRIAN and STEER both quit to form their own outfits, CATHEDRAL and CARCASS respectively. Replacements were found in vocalist MARK 'Barney' GREENWAY and Mexican guitarist JESSE PINTADO, the group subsequently heading out on the infamous 'Grindcrusher' European tour. With another American guitarist, MITCH HARRIS, recruited to bolster the group's sound, NAPALM DEATH recorded 'HARMONY CORRUPTION'. Released in late 1990, the opus betrayed a more conventional death/thrash metal sound with longer songs. Prior to the release of the 'UTOPIA BANISHED' (1992) album, MICK HARRIS departed for scary ambient outfit, SCORN, his seat on the drum stool filled by DANNY HERARRA. More heavy touring followed, playing to NAPALM DEATH fans in the most unlikely, furthest flung corners of the globe. A 1993 cover of the Dead Kennedys' 'NAZI PUNKS FUCK OFF' proved the band hadn't left their roots behind completely and with the acclaimed 'FEAR, EMPTINESS, DESPAIR' (1994), the band finally managed to incorporate their uncompromising vision into a consistent, coherent set of songs. The album was their most successful to date, winning them a support from the music press which was consolidated with subsequent releases 'GREED KILLING' (a mini album; 1995) and 'DIATRIBES' (1996). 'INSIDE THE TORN APART' in '97 and '98's 'BOOTLEGGED IN JAPAN' and 'WORDS FROM THE EXIT WOUND' rounded off their time with the 'Earache' imprint, the latter another brutal barrage of sound with industrial skirmishes thrown in. Signing to 'Dream Catcher', NAPALM DEATH returned to form with two Kerrang!-friendly sets, the mini of cover versions 'LEADERS NOT FOLLOWERS' (1999) and the mind-blowing 'ENEMY OF THE MUSIC BUSINESS' (2000). In addition to their boundary-busting music, NAPALM DEATH have also helped cultivate the more extreme end of the music spectrum via their groundbreaking 'Earache' label, home to such uneasy listening experiences as GODFLESH, MISERY LOVES CO. etc. As well as being involved in EXTREME NOISE TERROR, HARRIS initiated side project MEATHOOK SEED alongside EMBURY and OBITUARY moonlighters DONALD TARDY and TREVOR PERES. Following on from the grindcore dynamics of their 1993 debut album, 'EMBEDDED', the pair were back with new members CHRISTOPHE LAMOURET (of OUT fame), RUSS RUSSELL and IAN TRACEY. The resulting 'BASIC INSTRUCTIONS BEFORE LEAVING EARTH' (1999) was an apocalyptic clash of techno and metal, lyrically inspired by Michael Drosnin's book, 'The Bible Code'. NAPALM DEATH themselves were back in the new millennium with the brutal wake-up call, 'ORDER OF THE LEECH' (2002). If the title gave a flavour of the coruscating political diabtribes within, it offered little forewarning of the manically accelerated tempo relative to the band's latter day records. • **Trivia:** NAPALM DEATH recorded the shortest track ever released (the 1 second) 'YOU SUFFER', for a free 7", given away with an 'Earache' sampler, 'Grindcrusher'. SHANE EMBURY exchanged death threats with another teeth-grinding outfit SORE THROAT (mainly band member RICH MILITIA). • **Covered:** POLITICIANS (Raw Power) / DEMONIC POSSESSION (Pentagram) / MAGGOTS IN YOUR COFFIN (Repulsion) / NAZI PUNKS FUCK OFF (Dead Kennedys) / etc.

Album rating: SCUM (*5) / FROM ENSLAVEMENT TO OBLITERATION (*6) / HARMONY CORRUPTION (*5) / UTOPIA BANISHED (*6) / DEATH BY MANIPULATION compilation (*7) / FEAR, EMPTINESS, DESPAIR (*4) / GREED KILLING mini (*4) / DIATRIBES (*4) / INSIDE THE TORN APART (*5) / BOOTLEGGED IN JAPAN (*3) / WORDS FROM THE EXIT WOUND (*4) / LEADERS NOT FOLLOWERS mini (*6) / LEADERS NOT FOLLOWERS mini (*6) / ENEMY OF THE MUSIC BUSINESS (*8) / ORDER OF THE LEECH (*6) / Meathook Seed: EMBEDDED (*5) / BASIC INSTRUCTIONS BEFORE LEAVING EARTH (*6)

LEE DORRIAN – vocals (also runs own label 'Rise Above') / **BILL STEER** – guitar (also of CARCASS) / **SHANE EMBURY** – bass (also drummer of UNSEEN TERROR) / **MICK HARRIS** – drums (also vocals of EXTREME NOISE TERROR) repl. FRANK HEALEY (other early drummer JUS of HEAD OF DAVID)

Earache | Relativity

Jul 87. (lp) *(MOSH 003)* **SCUM** –
– Multinational corporations / Instinct of survival / The kill / Scum / Caught . . . in a dream / Polluted minds / Sacrificed / Siege of power / Control / Born on your knees / Human garbage / You suffer / Life? / Prison without walls / Point of no return / Negative approach / Success? / Deceiver / C.S. / Parasites / Pseudo youth / Divine death / As the machine rolls on / Common enemy / Moral crusade / Stigmatized / M.A.D. / Dragnet. *(c-iss.May89; MOSH 003MC) <US-iss.1991 on 'Relativity'; 1065> (re-iss. cd Sep94; MOSH 003CD)*

Nov 88. (lp/c/cd) *(MOSH 008/+MC/CD)* **FROM ENSLAVEMENT TO OBLITERATION** –
– Evolved as one / It's a man's world / Lueid fairytale / Private death / Impressions / Unchallenged hate / Uncertainty blurs the vision / Cock rock alienation / Retreat to nowhere / Think for a minute / Display to me . . . / From enslavement to obliteration / Blind to the truth / Social sterility / Emotional suffocation / Practise what you preach / Inconceivable / Worlds apart / Obstinate direction / Mentally murdered / Sometimes / Make way. *(pic-lp iss.Jul90; MOSH 008P) <US-iss.1991 on 'Relativity'; 1066> (re-iss. cd Sep94; same)*

Aug 89. (7") *(7MOSH 014)* **MENTALLY MURDERED. / CAUSE AND EFFECT** –
(12"+=) *(MOSH 014T)* – Rise above / Missing link – Mentally murdered / Walls of confinement / Cause and effect – No manual effort.

— (Aug'89) **MARK 'Barney' GREENWAY** – vocals (ex-BENEDICTION) repl. LEE (LEE was to join CATHEDRAL, another 'Earache' band) **MITCH HARRIS** (b.Las Vegas, USA) + **JESSE PINTADO** (b.Mexico) – guitars repl. BILL who went full-time with CARCASS)

Aug 90. (7") *(7MOSH 024)* **SUFFER THE CHILDREN. / SIEGE OF POWER** –
(12"+=) *(MOSHT 24)* – Harmony corruption.

Sep 90. (lp/c/cd) *(MOSH 019/+MC/CD)* <2020> **HARMONY CORRUPTION** 67
– Vision conquest / If the truth be known / Inner incineration / Malicious intent / Unfit Earth / Circle of hypocrisy / Suffer the children / The chains that bind us / Mind snare / Extremity retained. *(some w/free 12") (re-iss. cd Sep94; same)*

May 91. (7") *(7MOSH 046)* **MASS APPEAL MADNESS. / PRIDE ASSASSIN** –
(12"+=/cd-s+=) *(MOSH 046 T/CD)* – Unchallenged hate / Social sterility.

— MICK HARRIS was arrested for jewel shop robbery & he left to join SCORN. He was soon replaced by **DANNY HERARRA** – drums

May 92. (lp/c/cd) *(MOSH 053/+MC/CD)* <1127> **UTOPIA BANISHED** 58 Jun92
– Discordance / I abstain / Dementia access / Christening of the world / The world keeps turning / Idiosyncratic / Aryanisms / Cause and effect (pt.II) / Juidicial slime / Distorting the medium / Got time to kill / Upward and uninterested / Exile / Awake (to a life of misery) / Contemptious. *(free 4 track 7"ep) (re-iss. cd Sep94; same)*

Jun 92. (12"ep/cd-ep) *(MOSH 065 T/CD)* **THE WORLD KEEPS TURNING EP** –
– The world keeps turning / A means to an end / Insanity excursion.

Jul 93. (7"ep/cd-ep) *(MOSH 092/+CD)* **NAZI PUNKS FUCK OFF. / ARYANISMS / ('A'version) / CONTEMPTUOUS (xtreem mix)** –

Earache | Sony

May 94. (lp/c/cd) *(MOSH 109/+MC/CD)* <64361> **FEAR, EMPTINESS, DESPAIR**
– Twist the knife (slowly) / Hung / Remain nameless / Plague rages / More than meets the eye / Primed time / State of mind / Armageddon X7 / Retching on the dirt / Fasting on deception / Throwaway.

Earache | Earache

Nov 95. (10"m-lp/m-c/m-cd) *(<MOSH 146/+MC/CD>)* **GREED KILLING**
– Greed killing / My own worst enemy / Self betrayal / Finer truths, white lies / Antibody / All links severed / Plague rages (live).

Jan 96. (10"d-lp/c/cd) *(<MOSH 141/+MC/CD>)* **DIATRIBES** 73
– Greed killing / Glimpse into genocide / Ripe for the breaking / Cursed to crawl / Cold forgiveness / My own worst enemy / Just rewards / Dogma / Take the strain / Corrosive elements / Placate, sedate, eradicate / Diatribes / Take the strain.

— In Nov'96, BARNEY was dismissed and was replaced by vocalist **PHIL VANE** (ex-EXTREME NOISE TERROR). This was brief when **BARNEY** returned

Jan 97. (cd-ep) *(MOSH 168CD)* **IN TONGUES WE SPEAK EP** –
– Food chains / Upward and uninterested / (2 others by COALESCE).

Jun 97. (d-lp/c/cd) *(<MOSH 171/+MC/CD>)* **INSIDE THE TORN APART**
– Breed to breathe / Birth in regress / Section / Reflect on conflict / Down in the zero / Inside the torn apart / If systems persist / Prelude / Indispose / Purist realist / Low point / Lifeless alarm / Time will come / Bled dry / Ripe for the breaking.

Nov 97. (cd-rom;ep) *(MOSH 185CD)* **BREED TO BREATHE / ALL INTENSIVE PURPOSES / STRANGER NOW / BLED DRY / TIME WILL COME / SUFFER THE CHILDREN (by; Fatality)** –

Jun 98. (cd) *(<MOSH 209CD>)* **BOOTLEGGED IN JAPAN (live 5th August, 1997)** Jul98
– Antibody / My own worst enemy / More than meets the eye / Hung / Greed killing / Suffer the children / Mass appeal madness / Cursed to crawl / Glimpse into genocide / I abstain / Lucid fairytale / Plague rages / Cold forgiveness / Control / Diatribes / Life? / Siege of power / If the truth be known / Unchallenged hate / Nazi punks fuck off / From enslavement to obliteration / The kill / Scum / Ripe for the breaking.

Oct 98. (cd) *(<MOSH 212CD>)* **WORDS FROM THE EXIT WOUND**
– The infiltraitor / Repression out of uniform / Next of kin to chaos / Trio-degradable – Affixed by disconcern / Cleanse impure / Devouring depraved / Ulterior exterior / None the wiser? / Clutching at barbs / Incendiary incoming / Throw down a rope / Sceptic in perspective.

Dream Catcher | Relapse

Nov 99. (m-cd) *(CRIDE 19M)* <6452> **LEADERS NOT FOLLOWERS**
– Politicians / Incinerator / Demonic possession / Maggots in your coffin / Back from the dead / Nazi punks fuck off.

Dream Catcher | Spitfire

Sep 00. (cd) *(CRIDE 33)* <15164> **ENEMY OF THE MUSIC BUSINESS** Mar01
– Take the poison / Next on the list / Constitutional hell / Vermin / Volume of neglect / Thanks for nothing / Can't play, won't pay / Blunt against the cutting edge / Cure for the common people / Necessarily evil / C.S. (Conservative Shithead) pt.2 / Mechanics of deceit / (The public gets) What the public doesn't want / Fracture in the equation.

Slave | Spitfire

Nov 02. (cd) *(SLAVE 001CD)* <15172> **ORDER OF THE LEECH**
– Continuing war on stupidity / The icing on the hate / Forced to fear / Narcoleptic / Out of sight out of mind / To lower yourself (blind servitude) / Lowest common denominator / Forewarned is disarmed? / Per capita / Farce and fiction / Blows to the body / The great capitulator.

– compilations, others, etc. –

May 88. (12"ep) *Strange Fruit; (SFPS 049)* **THE PEEL SESSIONS** (13.9.87) –
– The kill / Prison without walls / Dead part one / Deceiver / Lucid fairytale / In extremis / Blind to the trash / Negative approach / Common enemy / Obstinate direction / Life? / You suffer (Part 2). *(re-iss. May89 c-ep/cd-ep; SFPDS MC/CD 049)*

Dec 89. (cd/c) *Strange Fruit; (SFP MCD/MC 201)* **THE PEEL SESSIONS** (13.9.87 & 8.3.88) –
– (above tracks) / Multi-national corporations / Instinct of survival / Stigatised / Parasites / Moral crusade / Worlds apart / M.A.D. / Divine death / C 9 / Control / Walls / Raging in Hell / Conform or die / S.O.B. *<US-iss.1991 on 'Dutch East India'; 8409>*

Feb 92. (lp/cd) *Earache; (MOSH 051/+CD) / Relativity; <1072>* **DEATH BY MANIPULATION**
– Mass appeal madness / Pride assassin / Unchallenged hate / Social sterilty / Suffer the children / Siege of power / Harmony corruption / Rise above / The missing link / Mentally murdered / Walls of confinement / Cause and effect / No mental effort / Multinational corporations / Re address the problem / Changing colours / From the ashes / Understanding / Stalemate / Unchallenged hate (live) / Mentally murdered (live) / Walls of confinement (live). *(with free cd-ep) (re-iss. Oct92 & Sep94; same)*

Apr 00. (cd) *Strange Fruit; (SFRSCD 91)* **THE BBC RADIO 1 SESSIONS** –

Jul 03. (d-cd) *Earache; (<MOSH 266CD>)* **NOISE FOR MUSIC'S SAKE** Aug03

NAS

Born: NASIR JONES, 14 Sep'73, Queensbridge, New York, USA. Raised by a jazz-performing father, he cut his rapping teeth at the age of ten, developing his lyrical skills in local hip-hop posse, The DEVASTIN' SEVEN. By the end of the 80's, having made attempts at TV work, he was introduced to MAIN SOURCE producer, LARGE PROFESSOR, for whom he made a demo tape. NAS subsequently featured on their debut album, 'Breaking Atoms', making a noted guest appearance on the track 'Live At The BBQ'. With his personal life in crisis (i.e. death of friend and shooting of his brother), NAS's recording career was put on hold for a few years in the early 90's. That is, until he contributed a track, 'HALF TIME' for the 'Zebra Head' movie late in 1992, 'Columbia' subsequently impressed enough to give the precocious young rapper a sizeable deal. Guided by some of New York's most respected producers (including Q-TIP – A Tribe Called Quest, PREMIER – Gang Starr and PETE ROCK), he crafted 1994's acclaimed 'ILLMATIC' album. Two years on, NAS smashed into the US chart at No.1 with his follow-up, 'IT WAS WRITTEN', which spawned the hit singles, 'IF I RULED THE WORLD' and the crossover Eurythmics-inspired 'STREET DREAMS'. In the Autumn of '97, he collaborated with FOXY BROWN, AZ & NATURE, releasing the chart-topping 'THE FIRM – THE ALBUM', although for American ears only (so far that is). Two sets of differing quality were released before the century was out, the hard-hitting and absorbing 'I AM . . .' (1999) and the below par, 'NAStradamus' (1999). NAS was back after a two-year hiatus from the music industry via the largely disappointing 'STILLMATIC' (2001). Not even a patch on his classic breakthrough set 'ILLMATIC' the NAS man concentrated solely on rhymes and beats, letting his music wander into dangerously 'Old-Skool' territory (without a deliberate hint of irony or retro-revival). Also, it seemed the self-styled 'King of New York' had a bit of an inferiority complex, no thanks to West Coast player JAY-Z, who dissed NAS onstage and issued the venomous 'Super Ugly'. NAS struck back, but missed his target due to shoddy aiming; the anti-JAY-Z track 'ETHER' just sounded like a feeble playground taunt. But there were moments of greatness on the set, with the fantastic Big-Up to Brooklyn 'DESTROY AND REBUILD', and the chilled-out loop of 'YOU'RE DA MAN'. But the fact remained that NAS, humbled by the multi-millionaire JAY-Z, was perhaps too angry to write and produce a clever response to the rapper's comments. The album still entered the US Top Ten in 2001. 'GOD'S SON' (2002), was something of a return to form, albeit an uncomfortably personal one, probing the depths of his soul and considerable ego. Informed in part by the death of his mother, the record found NAS rising above the humdrum to concentrate on the essential.

Album rating: ILLMATIC (*6) / IT WAS WRITTEN (*7) / I AM . . . (*8) / NAStradamus (*5) / STILLMATIC (*5) / GOD'S SON (*6)

NAS – rapping, etc (with various producers, etc)

not iss. — Sony

Nov 92. (c-s/12"; as NASTY NAS) *<74777>* **HALF TIME (mixes)** [–] [ ]

Columbia — Columbia

Apr 94. (cd/c/lp) *(475959-2/-4/-1) <57684>* **ILLMATIC** [ ] [12]
– The genesis / N.Y. state of mind / Life's a bitch / The world is yours / Halftime / Memory lane (sittin' in da park) / One love / One time 4 your mind / Represent / It ain't hard to tell.

May 94. (c-s) *(660470-4) <77385>* **IT AIN'T HARD TO TELL / ('A'instrumental)** [64] Mar94 [91]
(12"+=) *(660470-6)* – (2 other mixes).
(cd-s++=) *(660470-2)* – ('A'mixes).

1994. (c-s/12") *<77513>* **THE WORLD IS YOURS (mixes)** [–] [ ]

1995. (c-s/12"/cd-s) *<77673>* **ONE LOVE (mixes)** [–] [ ]

Jul 96. (c-s) *(663402-4) <78327>* **IF I RULED THE WORLD (IMAGINE THAT) / ('A'instrumental)** [12] Jun96 [53]
(12"/cd-s) *(663402-6/-2)* – ('A'mixes).

Jul 96. (cd/c/lp) *(484196-2/-4/-1) <67015>* **IT WAS WRITTEN** [38] [1]
– Intro / Message / Street dreams / I gave you power / Watch dem niggas / Take it in blood / Nas is coming / Affirmative action / Set up / Black girl lost / Suspect / Shootouts / Live nigga rap / If I ruled the world (imagine that).

Jan 97. (c-s/12"/cd-s) *(664130-4/-6/-2) <78409>* **STREET DREAMS / AFFIRMATIVE ACTION / (+ bonus mixes)** [12] Nov96 [22]

—— In Mar'97, NAS featured on ALLURE's Top 40 hit, 'Head Over Heels'

Jul 97. (12") *<6642>* **AFFIRMATIVE ACTION (mixes)** [–] [ ]

Dec 97. (cd-s) *<2303>* **ESCOBAR 97** [–] [ ]
(above lifted from the 'Men In Black' movie)

Mar 99. (12"/cd-s) *<79113>* **NAS IS LIKE / (+ 2 mixes) / DR. KNOCKABOOT (3 versions)** [–] [86]

Apr 99. (cd/c/lp) *(489419-2/-4/-1) <68773>* **I AM . . .** [31] [1]
– (intro) / N.Y. state of mind / Hate me now / Small world / Favor for a favor / We will survive / Ghetto prisoners / You won't see me tonight / I want to talk to you / Dr. Knockaboot / Life is what you make it / Big things / Nas is like / K-I-SS-I-N-G / Money is my bitch / Undying love. *(cd re-iss. Aug01; same)*

May 99. (c-s; NAS featuring PUFF DADDY) *(667256-4) <79070>* **HATE ME NOW / ('A'mix)** [14] Apr99 [62]
(cd-s) *(667256-2)* – ('A'mix) / If I ruled the world (with LAURYN HILL) / Street dreams (with R. KELLY).
(cd-s) *(667256-5)* – ('A'-side) / ('A'-Callout hook 1 & 2).

—— NAS featured on MISSY "MISDEMEANOR" ELLIOTT's hit single, 'Hot Boyz'

Aug 99. (12"/cd-s; as NAS & NATURE) *<79216>* **IN TOO DEEP / (+ 2 mixes) / THE SPECIALIST (2 mixes)** [–] [ ]

Nov 99. (cd/c/lp) *(495312-2/-4/-1) <63930>* **NAStradamus** [ ] [7]
– Prediction / Life we choose / NAStradamus / Angels intro / Some of us have angels / Project windows / Naheim / Big girl / Hydro drops / Shoot 'em up / Last words / Hustler's and killers / Science / God love us / Quiet niggas / Come get me / Count down to 2000 / New world / You owe me / Outcome. *(cd re-iss. Dec01; same)*

Jan 00. (12"/cd-s) *(668557-6/-2) <79299>* **NAStradamus / (clean) / (instrumental) / SHOOT 'EM UP (album + instrumental)** [24] Oct99 [92]

Mar 00. (cd-s; by NAS featuring GINUWINE) *<radio cut>* **YOU OWE ME** [–] [59]

—— in Apr'01, NAS featured on QB FINEST's hit, 'Oochie Wally'

Dec 01. (cd) *(504176-9) <85736>* **STILLMATIC** [ ] [5]
– Stillmatic (intro) / Ether / Got ur self a . . . / Smokin' / You're da man / Rewind / One mic / 2nd childhood / Destroy and rebuild / The flyest / Braveheart party / Rule / My country / What goes around. *(bonus track+=)* – Every ghetto.

Dec 01. (cd-s) *<79676>* **GOT UR SELF A . . . / YOU'RE DA MAN** [–] [87]

Jan 02. (cd-s) *(672302-2)* **GOT UR SELF A . . . / DOO RAGS / BLACK ZOMBIE / ('A'video)** [30] [–]
(12") *(672302-6)* – ('A'side) / Ether.

Apr 02. (12"/cd-s) *<79723>* **ONE MIC (remix with BRAINPOWER) / MADE YOU LOOK (clean version) / ONE MIC (instrumental) / MADE YOU LOOK (instrumental) / ONE MIC (album version)** [–] [43]

Dec 02. (cd/d-lp) *(509811-2/-1) <86930-2/-1>* **GOD'S SON** [67] [12]
– Get down / The cross / Made you look / Last real nigga alive / Zone out (with BRAVEHEARTS) / Hey Nas (with KELIS & CLAUDETTE ORTIZ) / I can / Book of rhymes / Thugz mansion (N.Y.) (with 2 PAC & J. PHOENIX) / Mastermind / Warrior song (with ALICIA KEYS) / Revolutionary warfare (with LAKE) / Dance / Heaven (with JULLY BLACK).

Jan 03. (12"/cd-s) *(673479-6/-2) <79845>* **MADE YOU LOOK / MADE YOU LOOK (instrumental without guns) / ONE MIC** [27] Feb03 [32]

Mar 03. (12"/cd-s) *(673738-6/-2) <673695>* **I CAN / I CAN (Juliano Creatror explicit mix) / I CAN (instrumental)** [19] [12]
(cd-s) *(673738-5)* – ('A'side) / If I ruled the world (imagine that) (with LAURYN HILL) / Street dreams (with R. KELLY).

– others, etc. –

Dec 01. (12"; by NAS & KOOL G RAP) *Archives; (ARC 778)* **FAST LIFE (remixes) / SILENT MURDER / LIFE'S A BITCH (mixes) / STREET DREAMS** □ –

Jan 02. (cd) *Sony; <71>* **THE BEST OF NAS** – □

Sep 02. (cd/d-lp) *Columbia; (509362-2/-1) <85275>* **THE LOST TAPES VOL.1** □ 10

□ Graham NASH
(see under ⇒ CROSBY, STILLS, NASH & YOUNG)

NAZARETH

Formed: Dunfermline, Scotland ... 1969 out of the ashes of The SHADETTES by DAN McCAFFERTY, PETE AGNEW and DARREL SWEET. With the addition of MANNY CHARLTON, the group turned pro and relocated to London, gaining a record contract with 'Pegasus' in the process. Already armed with a loyal homegrown support, the band released two earthy hard-rock albums for the label between late '71 and mid '72 before moving to 'Mooncrest'. This was the band's turning point, NAZARETH hitting immediately with a Top 10 smash, 'BROKEN DOWN ANGEL'. An obvious focal point for the Caledonian rockers was the mean-looking McCAFFERTY, his whisky-throated wail coming to define the band's sound. Their acclaimed third album, 'RAZAMANAZ' followed soon after, narrowly missing the UK Top 10 but nevertheless spawning another top selling rock classic, 'BAD, BAD BOY'. With ROGER GLOVER (ex-DEEP PURPLE) at the production desk, NAZARETH re-invented Joni Mitchell's classic, 'THIS FLIGHT TONIGHT', the band virtually claiming it as their own with a re-working startling in its stratospheric melodic power. The accompanying, appropriately-named 'LOUD 'N' PROUD' album (also released in '73!), followed the established formula by combining excellent cover versions with original material, thus its Top 10 placing. However, by the following year, only their fifth album, 'RAMPANT' had achieved any degree of success. America finally took NAZARETH to their hearts with the release of the much covered Boudleaux Bryant ballad, 'LOVE HURTS', the single making the US Top 10 in 1975 (JIM CAPALDI of Traffic had pipped them to the post in Britain). McCAFFERTY returned to the UK charts that year in fine fettle with yet another classy cover, Tomorrow's 'MY WHITE BICYCLE'. The frontman even found time to complete and release a full album's worth of covers, the big man and the band suffering a backlash from some of their more hardcore fans. Switching labels to 'Mountain' (home of The SENSATIONAL ALEX HARVEY BAND) late in 1975, the band suffered a dip in profile, although having signed to 'A&M' in America (in the heyday) they consolidated their earlier Stateside success. The ALEX HARVEY connection took another twist with the addition of the latter's clown-faced sidekick ZAL CLEMINSON on guitar. This helped to pull back some of NAZARETH's flagging support, the following JEFF 'Skunk' BAXTER (ex-DOOBIES)-produced set, 'MALICE IN WONDERLAND' hitting Top 30 in America. ZAL departed soon after, his surprising replacement being the American JOHN LOCKE, who in turn (after an album, 'THE FOOL CIRCLE' 1981) was superseded by Glaswegian BILLY RANKIN. For the remainder of the 80's, NAZARETH churned out a plethora of reasonable albums, the band still retaining a North American fanbase while gaining a foothold in many parts of Europe. Founder member MANNY CHARLTON subsequently departed at the turn of the decade, RANKIN returning for their best album for ten years, 'NO JIVE' (1991). Surprisingly, after nearly 30 years in the business, NAZARETH are still plugging away, their most recent effort being 1995's 'MOVE ME'. A host of modern day hard-rockers such as AXL ROSE, MICHAEL MONROE, etc, claim to have been influenced by both McCAFFERTY and his three wise rockers, GUNS N' ROSES even covering 'HAIR OF THE DOG'. With McCAFFERTY, AGNEW and SWEET (plus newcomers JIMMY MURRISON and RONNIE LEAHY) carrying NAZARETH towards the 21st Century, their final album of the millennium was 'BOOGALOO' (1998). Sadly, DARRELL was to die in New Albany, Indiana, USA on the 30th of April, 1999. • **Songwriters:** Group penned, except SHAPES OF THINGS (Yardbirds) / DOWN HOME GIRL (Leiber-Stoller) / I WANT TO DO EVERYTHING FOR YOU (Joe Tex) / TEENAGE NERVOUS BREAKDOWN (Little Feat) / THE BALLAD OF HOLLIS BROWN (Bob Dylan) / YOU'RE THE VIOLIN (Golden Earring) / WILD HONEY (Beach Boys) / SO YOU WANT TO BE A ROCK'N'ROLL STAR (Byrds) / I DON'T WANT TO GO ON WITHOUT YOU (Berns/Wexler). DAN McCAFFERTY solo covered OUT OF TIME (Rolling Stones) / WHATCHA GONNA DO ABOUT IT (Small Faces) / etc.

Album rating: NAZARETH (*6) / EXERCISES (*6) / RAZAMANAZ (*7) / LOUD 'N' PROUD (*6) / RAMPANT (*6) / HAIR OF THE DOG (*7) / CLOSE ENOUGH FOR ROCK'N'ROLL (*5) / PLAY 'N' THE GAME (*4) / GREATEST HITS compilation (*8) / EXPECT NO MERCY (*5) / NO MEAN CITY (*5) / MALCE IN WONDERLAND (*5) / THE FOOL CIRCLE (*4) / 'SNAZ (*4) / 2XS (*4) / SOUND ELIXIR (*4) / THE CATCH (*4) / CINEMA (*4) / SNAKES AND LADDERS (*4) / THE SINGLES COLLECTION compilation (**8**) / NO JIVE (*5) / MOVE ME (*4) / BOOGALOO (*4)

DAN McCAFFERTY – vocals / **MANNY CHARLTON** – guitar, vocals / **PETE AGNEW** (b.14 Sep'48) – bass / **DARRELL SWEET** (b.16 May'47, Bournemouth, England) – drums, percussion

Pegasus Warners

Nov 71. (lp) *(PEG 10) <BS 2615>* **NAZARETH** □ Feb73 □
– Witchdoctor woman / Dear John / Empty arms, empty heart / If I had a dream / Red light lady / Fat man / Country girl / Morning dew / King is dead. *(re-iss. Apr74 on 'Mooncrest'; CREST 10) (re-iss. Nov 75 & Apr80 on 'Mountain' lp/c; TOPC/TTOPC 5001) (cd-iss. May92 on 'Castle'; CLACD 286) (cd re-iss. Oct99 on 'Essential'; ESMCD 796) (cd re-iss. Jun02 on 'Eagle'; EAMCD 145)*

Jan 72. (7") *(PGS 2)* **DEAR JOHN. / FRIENDS** □ –

Jun 72. (7") *(PGS 4)* **MORNING DEW. / SPINNING TOP** □ –

Jun 72. (lp) *(PEG 14) <BS 2639>* **EXERCISES** □ Nov72 □
– I will not be led / Cat's eye, apple pie / In my time / Woke up this morning / Called her name / Fool about you / Love now you're gone / Madelaine / Sad song / 1692 (Glen Coe massacre). *(re-iss. Apr74 on 'Mooncrest'; CREST 14) (re-iss. Nov75 & Apr80 on 'Mountain' lp/c; TOPS/TTOPS 103) (re-iss. May85 on 'Sahara'; SAH 121) (cd-iss. Feb91 on 'Castle'; CLACD 220) (cd re-iss. Jun02 on 'Eagle'; EAMCD 146)*

Jul 72. (7") *<7599>* **MORNING DEW. / DEAR JOHN** – □

Sep 72. (7") *(PGS 5)* **IF YOU SEE MY BABY. / HARD LIVING** □ –

Mooncrest A&M

Apr 73. (7") *(MOON 1)* **BROKEN DOWN ANGEL. / WITCHDOCTOR WOMAN** 9 –

May 73. (lp/c) *(CREST 1) <SP 4396>* **RAZAMANAZ** 11 □
– Razamanaz / Alcatraz / Vigilante man / Woke up this morning / Night woman / Bad, bad boy / Sold my soul / Too bad, too sad / Broken down angel. *(re-iss. Nov75 & Apr80 on 'Mountain' lp/c; TOPS/TTOPS 104) (re-iss. Oct82 on 'NEMS' lp/c; NEL/NEC 6023) (re-iss. Dec89 on 'Castle' lp/cd; CLA LP/CD 173) (cd re-iss. Sep96 on 'Essential'; ESMCD 370) (cd re-iss. Sep01 on 'Eagle'; EAMCD 132)*

Jul 73. (7"m) *(MOON 9)* **BAD, BAD BOY. / HARD LIVING / SPINNING TOP** 10 –

Sep 73. (7") *<1453>* **BROKEN DOWN ANGEL. / HARD LIVING** – □

Oct 73. (7") *(MOON 14)* **THIS FLIGHT TONIGHT. / CALLED HER NAME** 11 –

Nov 73. (lp/c) *(CREST 4) <3609>* **LOUD 'N' PROUD** 10 □
– Go down fighting / Not faking it / Turn on your receiver / Teenage nervous breakdown / Freewheeler / This flight tonight / Child in the sun / The ballad of Hollis Brown. *(re-iss. Nov75 & Apr80 on 'Mountain' lp/c;*

TOPS/TTOPS 105) (re-iss. Dec89 on 'Castle' lp/cd; CLA LP/CD 174) (cd re-iss. Oct96 on 'Essential'; ESMCD 379) (cd re-iss. Sep01 on 'Eagle'; EAMCD 133)

Nov 73. (7") *<1469>* **BAD, BAD BOY. / RAZAMANAZ** [–] [ ]

Feb 74. (7") *<1511>* **THIS FLIGHT TONIGHT. / GO DOWN FIGHTING** [–] [ ]

Mar 74. (7") *(MOON 22)* **SHANGHAI'D IN SHANGHAI. / LOVE, NOW YOU'RE GONE** [41] [ ]

May 74. (lp/c) *(CREST 15) <3641>* **RAMPANT** [13] [ ]
– Silver dollar forger (parts 1 & 2) / Glad when you're gone / Loved and lost / Shanghai'd in Shanghai / Jet lag / Light my way / Sunshine / a) Shapes of things – b) Space safari. *(re-iss. Nov75 & Apr80 on 'Mountain' lp/c; TOPS/TTOPS 106) (cd-iss. Sep92 on 'Castle'; CLACD 242) (cd re-iss. May97 on 'Essential'; ESMCD 551) (cd re-iss. Sep01 on 'Eagle'; EAMCD 134)*

Jul 74. (7") *<1548>* **SUNSHINE. / THIS FLIGHT TONIGHT** [–] [ ]

Nov 74. (7") *(MOON 37) <1671>* **LOVE HURTS. / DOWN** [ ] Nov75 [8]

Mar 75. (7") *(MOON 44)* **HAIR OF THE DOG. / TOO BAD, TOO SAD** [ ] [–]

Apr 75. (lp/c) *(CREST 27) <4511>* **HAIR OF THE DOG** [ ] [17]
– Hair of the dog / Miss Misery / Guilty * / Changin' times / Beggars day / Rose in the heather / Whisky drinkin' woman / Please don't Judas me. *(In the US, track* repl. by 'Love hurts') (re-iss. Nov75 & Apr80 on 'Mountain' lp/c; TOPS/TTOPS 107) (re-iss. Oct82 on 'NEMS' lp/c; NEL/NEC 6024) (re-iss. May85 on 'Sahara'; SAH 124) (cd-iss. Feb92 on 'Castle'; CLACD 241) (cd re-iss. May97 on 'Essential'; ESMCD 550) (cd re-iss. Sep01 on 'Eagle'; EAMCD 127)*

May 75. (7") *<1671>* **HAIR OF THE DOG. / LOVE HURTS** [–] [ ]

May 75. (7") *(MOON 47)* **MY WHITE BICYCLE. / MISS MISERY** [14] [ ]
(re-iss. 1979 on 'Mountain'; NAZ 10)

Mountain A&M

Oct 75. (7") *(TOP 3)* **HOLY ROLLER. / RAILROAD BOY** [36] [–]

Nov 75. (lp/c) *(TOPS/TTOPS 108) <9020>* **GREATEST HITS** (compilation) [54] [ ]
– Razamanaz / Holy roller / Shanghai'd in Shanghai / Love hurts / Turn on your receiver / Bad bad boy / This flight tonight / Broken down angel / Hair of the dog / Sunshine / My white bicycle / Woke up this morning *(re-iss. Oct82 on 'NEMS' lp/c; NEL/NEC 6022) (re-iss. Apr89 on 'Castle' lp/c/cd; CLA LP/MC/CD 149)*

Feb 76. (7") *(TOP 8) <1819>* **CARRY OUT FEELINGS. / LIFT THE LID** [ ] [ ]

Mar 76. (lp/c) *(TOPS/TTOPS 109) <4562>* **CLOSE ENOUGH FOR ROCK'N'ROLL** [ ] [24]
– Telegram (part 1:- On your way / part 2:- So you want to be a rock'n'roll star / part 3:- Sound check / part 4:- Here we are again) / Vicki / Homesick again / Vancouver shakedown / Born under the wrong sign / Loretta / Carry out feelings / Lift the lid / You're the violin. *(re-iss. May85 on 'Sahara'; SAH 126) (re-iss. Jun90 on 'Castle' lp/c/cd; CLA LP/MC/CD 182) (cd re-iss. Feb02 on 'Eagle'; EAMCD 138)*

Jun 76. (7") *(TOP 14)* **YOU'RE THE VIOLIN. / LORETTA** [ ] [–]

Sep 76. (7") *<1854>* **LIFT THE LID. / LORETTA** [–] [ ]

Nov 76. (7") *(TOP 21)* **I DON'T WANT TO GO ON WITHOUT YOU. / GOOD LOVE** [ ] [–]

Nov 76. (lp/c) *(TOPS/TTOPS 113) <4610>* **PLAY 'N' THE GAME** [ ] [75]
– Somebody to roll / Down home girl / Flying / Waiting for the man / Born to love / I want to (do everything for you) / I don't want to go on without you / Wild honey / L.A. girls. *(re-iss. May85 on 'Sahara; SAH 131) (cd-iss. Feb91 on 'Castle'; CLACD 219) (cd re-iss. Feb02 on 'Eagle'; EAMCD 139)*

Dec 76. (7") *<18??>* **I WANT TO (DO EVERYTHING FOR YOU). / BLACK CATS** [–] [ ]

Jan 77. (7") *(TOP 22)* **SOMEBODY TO ROLL. / VANCOUVER SHAKEDOWN** [ ] [ ]

Feb 77. (7") *<1895>* **I DON'T WANT TO GO ON WITHOUT YOU. / I WANT TO DO (EVERYTHING FOR YOU)** [–] [ ]

Apr 77. (7") *<1936>* **SOMEBODY TO ROLL. / THIS FLIGHT TONIGHT** [–] [ ]

Jun 77. (lp) *<4643>* **HOT TRACKS** (compilation) [–] [ ]

Sep 77. (7"ep) *(NAZ 1)* **HOT TRACKS** (compilation) [15] [–]
– Love hurts / This flight tonight / Broken down angel / Hair of the dog. *(re-iss. Jul80; HOT 1) (re-iss. Jan83 on 7"pic-ep on 'NEMS'; NEP 2)*

Nov 77. (lp/c) *(TOPS/TTOPS 115) <4666>* **EXPECT NO MERCY** [ ] [82]
– Expect no mercy / Gone dead train / Shot me down / Revenge is sweet / Gimme what's mine / Kentucky fried blues / New York broken toy / Busted / A place in your heart / All the king's horses. *(re-iss. May85 on 'Sahara'; SAH 123) (re-iss. Jun90 on 'Castle' cd/lp; CLA CD/LP 187) (re-iss. cd Sep93 on 'Elite'; ELITE 022CD) (cd re-iss. Feb02 on 'Eagle'; EAMCD 140)*

Jan 78. (7"m) *(NAZ 2)* **GONE DEAD TRAIN. / GREENS / DESOLATION ROAD** [49] [–]

Apr 78. (7") *(TOP 37)* **A PLACE IN YOUR HEART. / KENTUCKY FRIED BLUES** [70] [–]

Apr 78. (7") *<2009>* **SHOT ME DOWN. / KENTUCKY FRIED BLUES** [–] [ ]

Jul 78. (7") *<2029>* **GONE DEAD TRAIN. / KENTUCKY FRIED BLUES** [–] [ ]

— added **ZAL CLEMINSON** (b. 4 May'49, Glasgow, Scotland) – guitar, synth. (ex-SENSATIONAL ALEX HARVEY BAND)

Jan 79. (7") *(NAZ 3) <2116>* **MAY THE SUNSHINE. / EXPECT NO MERCY** [22] [ ]

Jan 79. (lp/c) *(TOPS/TTOPS 123) <4741>* **NO MEAN CITY** [34] [88]
– Just to get into it / May the sun shine / Simple solution (parts 1 & 2) / Star / Claim to fame / Whatever you want babe / What's in it for me / No mean city (parts 1 & 2). *(re-iss. May85 on 'Sahara'; SAH 120) (re-iss. May91 on 'Castle' lp/c/cd; CLA LP/MC/CD 213) (cd re-iss. Feb02 on 'Eagle'; EAMCD 135)*

Apr 79. (7",7"purple) *(NAZ 4) <2130>* **WHATEVER YOU WANT BABE. / TELEGRAM (PARTS 1, 2 & 3)** [ ] [ ]

Jul 79. (7") *<2158>* **STAR. / EXPECT NO MERCY** [–] [ ]

Jul 79. (7") *(TOP 45)* **STAR. / BORN TO LOVE** [54] [–]

Jan 80. (7") *(TOP 50) <2219>* **HOLIDAY. / SHIP OF DREAMS** [ ] [87]

Jan 80. (lp/c) *(TOPS/TTOPS 126) <4799>* **MALICE IN WONDERLAND** [ ] [41]
– Holiday / Showdown at the border / Talkin' to one of the boys / Heart's grown cold / Fast cars / Big boy / Talkin' 'bout love / Fallen angel / Ship of dreams / Turning a new leaf. *(re-iss. Sep90 on 'Castle' cd/lp; CLA CD/LP 181) (cd re-iss. Feb02 on 'Eagle'; EAMCD 136)*

Apr 80. (7") *<2231>* **SHIP OF DREAMS. / HEARTS GROWN COLD** [–] [ ]

NEMS A&M

Dec 80. (d7") *(BSD 1)* **NAZARETH LIVE (live)** [ ] [–]
– Hearts grown cold / Talkin' to one of the boys / Razamanaz / Hair of the dog.

— added **JOHN LOCKE** (b.25 Sep'43, Los Angeles, Calif.) – keyboards (ex-SPIRIT)

Feb 81. (lp/c) *(NEL/NEC 6019) <4844>* **THE FOOL CIRCLE** [60] [70]
– Dressed to kill / Another year / Moonlight eyes / Pop the Silo / Let me be your leader / We are the people / Every young man's dream / Little part of you / Cocaine (live) / Victoria. *(re-iss. Feb91 on 'Castle' cd/lp; CLA CD/LP 214) (cd re-iss. Feb02 on 'Eagle'; EAMCD 137)*

Mar 81. (7") *(NES 301) <2324>* **DRESSED TO KILL. / POP THE SILO** [ ] [ ]

— **BILLY RANKIN** (b.25 Apr'59, Glasgow) – guitar; repl. ZAL who joined TANDOORI CASSETTE

Sep 81. (d-lp/c) *(NELD/NELC 102) <6703>* **'SNAZ (live)** [78] [83]
– Telegram (part 1:- On your way – part 2:- So you want to be a rock'n'roll star – part 3:- Sound check) / Razamanaz / I want to do everything for you / This flight tonight / Beggars day / Every young man's dream / Heart's grown cold / Java blues / Cocaine / Big boy / Holiday / Dressed to kill / Hair of the dog / Expect no mercy / Shape of things / Let me be your leader / Love hurts / Tush / Juicy Lucy / Morning dew. *(re-iss. Jan87 on 'Castle' lp/c/cd; CLA LP/MC/CD 130) (cd re-iss. May97 on 'Essential'; ESMCD 531) (cd re-iss. Sep01 on 'Eagle'; EAMCD 129)*

Sep 81. (7") *(NES 302) <2378>* **MORNING DEW (live). / JUICY LUCY (live)** [ ] [ ]

Dec 81. (7") *<2389>* **HAIR OF THE DOG (live). / HOLIDAY (live)** [–] [ ]

Jul 82. (7") *(NIS 101) <2421>* **LOVE LEADS TO MADNESS. / TAKE THE RAP** [ ] [ ]

Aug 82. (7") *<2444>* **DREAM ON. / TAKE THE RAP** [–] [ ]

— In 1982, RANKIN departed + later released one US hit, 'BABY COME BACK' taken from the 1984 set, 'GROWIN' UP TOO FAST'.

Jan 83. (7") *(NIS 102)* **GAMES. / YOU LOVE ANOTHER** [ ] [–]

Feb 83. (lp/c) *(NIN 001) <4901>* **2XS** [ ] Jun82 [ ]
– Love leads to madness / Boys in the band / You love another / Gatecrash / Games / Back to the trenches / Dream on / Lonely in the night / Preservation / Take the rap / Mexico. *(cd-iss. Feb91 on 'Castle'; CLACD 217) (cd re-iss. Feb02 on 'Eagle'; EAMCD 141)*

Jun 83. (7") *(NIS 103)* **DREAM ON. / JUICY LUCY** [ ] [–]

Vertigo Capitol

Jun 83. (lp) *(812396-1)* **SOUND ELIXIR** [–] German [ ]
– All nite radio / Milk and honey / Whippin' boy / Rain on the window / Backroom boys / Why don't you read the book / I ran / Rags to riches /

Local still / Where are you now. *(re-iss. Jul85 on 'Sahara'; SAH 130) (cd-iss. Feb91 on 'Castle'; CLACD 218) (cd re-iss. Jun02 on 'Eagle'; EAMCD 147)*

Jul 83. (7") *(812 544-7)* **WHERE ARE YOU NOW. / ON THE RUN** [-] German [-]

Sep 84. (lp/c) *(VERL/+C 20)* **THE CATCH**
– Party down / Ruby Tuesday / Last exit Brooklyn / Moondance / Love of freedom / This month's Messiah / You don't believe in us / Sweetheart tree / Road to nowhere. *(cd-iss. Feb02 on 'Eagle'; EAMCD 142)*

Sep 84. (7") *(VER 13)* **RUBY TUESDAY. / SWEETHEART TREE**
(12"+=) *(VERX 13)* – This month's messiah / Do you think about it.

Oct 84. (7"/12") *(880 085-1/+Q)* **PARTY DOWN. / DO YOU THINK ABOUT IT** [-] German [-]

1986. (lp/cd) *(830 300-1/-2)* **CINEMA** [-] Europe [-]
– Cinema / Juliet / Just another heartache / Other side of you / Hit the fan / One from the heart / Salty salty / White boy / A veterans song / Telegram / This flight tonight. *(cd-iss. Sep97 on 'Essential'; ESMCD 500) (cd re-iss. Aug01 on 'Eagle'; EAMCD 128)*

1986. (7") *(884 982-7)* **CINEMA. / THIS FLIGHT TONIGHT (live)** [-] Europe [-]
(12"+=) *(884 981-1)* – Telegram (live).

1989. (lp/cd) *(838 426-1/-2)* **SNAKES 'N' LADDERS** [-] Europe [-]
– We are animals / Lady luck / Hang on to a dream / Piece of my heart / Trouble / The key / Back to school / Girls / Donna – Get off that crack / See you, see you / Helpless. *(UK cd-iss. May97 on 'Essential'; ESMCD 501) (cd re-iss. Feb02 on 'Eagle'; EAMCD 143)*

1989. (cd-s) *(874 733-2)* **PIECE OF MY HEART / LADY LUCK / SEE YOU SEE ME** [-] German [-]

1989. (7") *(876 448-7)* **WINNER ON THE NIGHT. / TROUBLE** [-] German [-]
(12"+=/cd-s+=) *(876 448-1/-2)* – Woke up this morning (live) / Bad, bad boy (live).

—— **BILLY RANKIN** – guitar; now totally repl. CHARLTON

Mausoleum Griffin

Nov 91. (cd/c/lp) *(3670010.2/.4/.1)* <3932> **NO JIVE** 1993
– Hire and fire / Do you wanna play house / Right between the eyes / Every time it rains / Keeping our love alive / Thinkin' man's nightmare / Cover your heart / Lap of luxury / a.The Rowan tree (traditional) – b.Tell me that you love me / Cry wolf. *(cd+=)* – This flight tonight. *(cd re-iss. Sep97 on 'Essential'; ESMCD 502) (cd re-iss. Jun02 on 'Eagle'; EAMCD 148)*

Jan 92. (7") *(3670010.7)* **EVERY TIME IT RAINS / THIS FLIGHT TONIGHT 1991** [-]
(12"+=/cd-s+=) *(3670010.0/.3)* – Lap of Luxury.

Mar 92. (cd-ep) *(903005.3)* **TELL ME THAT YOU LOVE ME / RIGHT BETWEEN THE EYES / ROWAN TREE – TELL ME THAT YOU LOVE ME (extended)** [-]

Essential Mayhem

May 97. (cd) *(ESMCD 503)* <11076> **MOVE ME** Oct95
– Let me be your dog / Can't shake these shakes / Crack me up / Move me / Steamroller / Stand by your beds / Rip it up / Demon alcohol / You had it comin' / Bring it on home to mama / Burning down. *(re-iss. Jun02 on 'Eagle'; EAMCD 149)*

—— **McCAFFERTY, AGNEW + SWEET** added **JIMMY MURRISON** – guitar + **RONNIE LEAHY** – keyboards

S.P.V. C.M.C.

Sep 98. (cd) *(SPV 0851850-2)* <86263> **BOOGALOO** Jan99
– Lights come down / Cheerleader / Loverman / Open up woman / Talk talk / Nothing so good / Party in the Kremlin / God save the South / Robber and the roadie / Waiting / May Heaven keep you. *(re-iss. Feb02; SPV 2301850-2)*

—— on the 30th of April, 1999, DARRELL died

– compilations, others, etc. –

Jun 85. (d-lp) *Sahara; (SAH 137)* **20 GREATEST HITS** [-]

Jun 88. (d-lp/c/cd) *That's Original; (TFO LP/TC/CD 13)* **RAMPANT / HAIR OF THE DOG** [-]

Jul 88. (7") *Old Gold; (OG 9801)* **LOVE HURTS. / BAD BAD BOY** [-]

Jul 88. (7") *Old Gold; (OG 9803)* **THIS FLIGHT TONIGHT. / BROKEN DOWN ANGEL** [-]

Dec 88. (lp/c/cd) *Raw Power; (RAW LP/TC/CD 039)* **ANTHOLOGY** [-]

Jan 89. (cd-ep) *Special Edition; (CD3-17)* **THIS FLIGHT TONIGHT / BROKEN DOWN ANGEL / LOVE HURTS / BAD, BAD BOY** [-]

Jun 89. (cd) *Milestones; (MSSCD 102)* **MILESTONES** [-]

1990. (cd) *Ariola Express; (295969)* **BROKEN DOWN ANGEL** [-]

Jan 91. (cd/c/d-lp) *Castle; (CLA CD/MC/LP 280)* **THE SINGLES COLLECTION** [-]
– Broken down angel / Bad, bad boy / This flight tonight / Shanghai'd in Shanghai / Love hurts / Hair of the dog / My white bicycle / Holy roller / Carry out feelings / You're the violin / Somebody to roll / I don't want to go on without you / Gone dead train / A place in your heart / May the Sun shine / Star / Dressed to kill / Morning dew / Games / Love will lead to madness.

Oct 91. (3xcd-box) *Essential; (ESBCD 967)* **ANTHOLOGY** [-]

Nov 91. (cd) *Windsong; (WINDCD 005)* **BBC RADIO 1 LIVE IN CONCERT** [-]

Dec 91. (cd) *Dojo; (EARLCD 2)* **THE EARLY YEARS** [-]

Mar 92. (3xcd-box) *Castle; (CLABX 908)* **SNAZ / RAZAMANAZ / EXPECT NO MERCY** [-]

Apr 93. (cd) *Sequel; (NEMCD 639)* **FROM THE VAULTS** [-]

Jun 93. (cd/c) *Optima; (OPTM CD/C 009)* **ALIVE AND KICKING** [-]

Jun 94. (cd) *BR Music; (BRCD 1392)* **GREATEST HITS** [-]

Mar 96. (cd) *Disky; (CR 86711-2)* **CHAMPIONS OF ROCK** [-]

Oct 96. (cd) *Essential; (ESMCD 369)* **GREATEST HITS** [-]

Jul 98. (d-cd) *Reef; (SRDCD 707)* **LIVE AT THE BEEB** [-]
(d-cd re-iss. Feb00 on 'Snapper'; SMDCD 272)

Oct 98. (3xcd-box) *Essential; (ESMBX 308)* **RAZAMANAZ / LOUD 'N' PROUD / HAIR OF THE DOG** [-]

Apr 01. (d-cd)(t-lp) *Receiver; (RDPCD 016)(RRLT 009)* **BACK TO THE TRENCHES (live 1972-1984)** [-]

Aug 01. (cd) *Eagle; (EAGCD 141)* **THE VERY BEST OF NAZARETH** [-]

Jan 02. (d-cd) *Snapper; (SMDCD 387)* **NAZOLOGY** [-]

Mar 02. (cd) *Eagle; (EAGCD 204)* **HOMECOMING: GREATEST HITS LIVE IN GLASGOW (live)** [-]

Mar 02. (cd) *Music Club; (MCCD 486)* **LOVE HURTS – THE ROCK BALLADS** [-]

☐ NAZZ (see under ⇒ RUNDGREN, Todd)

☐ NEARLY GOD (see under ⇒ TRICKY)

Fred NEIL

Born: 1937, St. Petersburg, Florida, USA. Gravitating to New York in the late 50's, NEIL not only wrote for other artists (his most famous credit being 'CANDY MAN', the B-side of ROY ORBISON's 1961 hit, 'CRYING') but actually recorded a series of obscure solo tracks for various labels. At the same time he was also making a name for himself on the Greenwich Village folk scene as one of the most inventive, mesmeric and enigmatic singer/songwriters of the era. Captivating audiences with an oak-matured voice pitched right at the bottom end and lying somewhere between JOHNNY CASH and DAN PENN, NEIL's acolytes included the likes of JOHN SEBASTIAN and DAVID CROSBY, future folk-rockers both who regarded NEIL as their mentor. By 1964, he was working in tandem with VINCE MARTIN and the pair recorded a one-off album for 'Elektra', 'TEAR DOWN THE WALLS' (1965). Guests included a pre-LOVIN' SPOONFUL JOHN SEBASTIAN and future MOUNTAIN man, FELIX PAPPALARDI (incongruous as that may seem) on a set which paved the way for NEIL's solo debut proper, 'BLEECKER & MACDOUGAL' (1966). Featuring the oft-covered 'OTHER SIDE OF LIFE', the record was a bluesy affair which predated his flight into fully electrified folk-rock at 'Capitol'. 'FRED NEIL' (1967) was the man's definitive statement, an eddying stream of hazy, heavy-lidded folk/rock/blues A&R'd by L.A. whizzkid, Nik Venet and rooted in the unique, jazz-influenced style NEIL had developed. Leading off with the sublime 'THE DOLPHINS' (later the subject of an equally exquisite cover by TIM BUCKLEY), a haunting, bittersweet and almost otherworldly meditation on love gone wrong, the album also featured his ubiquitous escapist masterpiece, 'EVERYBODY'S TALKIN' alongside live staples 'THAT'S THE BAG I'M IN' and 'BA-DE-DA'. The fact that the former two tracks, especially 'EVERYBODY'S TALKIN' (HARRY NILSSON's 'Midnight Cowboy' version is just one of many), found greater fame with other artists sums up NEIL's career; content to guide, influence and lay down blueprints for fame-hungry young bucks, NEIL himself wanted no part in the fame game and subsequently withdrew completely from the music scene. Before he did, he released a further couple of albums for 'Capitol', the drawn-out studio jamming of 'SESSIONS' (1968) and 'THE OTHER SIDE OF THIS LIFE' (1971), a hotch potch of live cuts and unused studio tracks featuring an interesting GRAM PARSONS-enhanced cover of William Bell's 'YOU DON'T MISS YOUR WATER' (PARSONS also cut the track with The BYRDS on 1968's 'Sweetheart Of The Rodeo' album). The speed and effectiveness of NEIL's subsequent retreat from the music business was unequalled in the industry's history, the man's reclusiveness so complete that despite his contribution to modern music (NEIL's spirit permeates the work of TIM BUCKLEY and TIM HARDIN especially) he remains all but forgotten and unknown even among many 60's buffs, record collectors and musicians. While some of his recordings are occasionally re-issued in the States, little has been available in the UK since a 'VERY BEST OF..' in '86. The little in question was the 'MANY SIDES OF' (1999), a double-CD which contained virtually all the essential recordings of Mr. NEIL. Sadly, due to cancer, FRED died at his Florida home, 7th July, 2001.

Album rating: TEAR DOWN THE WALLS with Vince Martin (*5) / BLEECKER & MACDOUGAL (*7) / FRED NEIL (*8) / SESSIONS (*4) / THE OTHER SIDE OF THIS LIFE (*5) / THE VERY BEST OF FRED NEIL compilation (*7) / THE MANY SIDES OF FRED NEIL compilation (*8)

FRED NEIL – vocals, guitar

not iss. F.M.

1964. (lp; with Various Artists) *<309>* **HOOTENANNY LIVE AT THE BITTER END (live)** – □

1964. (lp; with Various Artists) *<319>* **WORLD OF FOLK MUSIC** – □

not iss. Elektra

Mar 65. (lp; by FRED NEIL & VINCE MARTIN) *<EKS 7246>* **TEAR DOWN THE WALLS** – □
– I know you rider / Red flowers / Tear down the walls / Weary blues / Toy balloon / Baby / Morning dew / I'm a drifter / Linin' track / Wild child in a world of trouble / Dade County jail / I got 'em / Lonesome valley. *(cd-iss. Mar02 on 'Collector's Choice'; CCM 02742)*

Mar 65. (7"; by FRED NEIL & VINCE MARTIN) *<EKSN 45009>* **TEAR DOWN THE WALLS. / I KNOW YOU RIDER** – □

—— next featured **PETE CHILDS** – guitar / **JOHN SEBASTIAN** – harmonica / **FELIX PAPPALARDI + DOUGLAS HATFIELD** – bass

Feb 66. (lp) *<EKS 7293>* **BLEECKER & MACDOUGAL** – □
– Bleecker & MacDougal / Blues on the ceiling / Sweet mama / Little bit of rain / Country boy / Other side of this life / Mississippi train / Travelin' shoes / The water is wide / Yonder comes the blues / Candy man / Handful of gimme / Gone again. *(UK-iss.1969; same as US) <re-iss. 1970 as 'LITTLE BIT OF RAIN'; EKS 74073> <US cd-iss. 1999 on 'WEA Int'; 2693> <(lp re-iss. Dec01 on 'Sundazed'; SCLP 5107)> <(cd re-iss. Mar02 on 'Collector's Choice'; CCM 0275-2)>*

Capitol Capitol

Jan 67. (7") *<5786>* **BADI-DA. / THE DOLPHINS** – □

Jan 67. (lp) *<ST 2665>* **FRED NEIL** – □
– The dolphins / I've got a secret (didn't we shake sugaree) / That's the bag I'm in / Everybody's talkin' / Everything happens / Sweet cocaine / Green rocky road / Cynicrustpetefredjohn raga. *<re-iss. 1969 as 'EVERYBODY'S TALKIN'; SM 294>* – Badi-da / Faretheewell (Fred's tune). *(UK-iss.of re-iss. Jan94 on 'Creation Rev-Ola'; C-REV 21CD)*

Sep 67. (7") *<2047>* **I'VE GOT A SECRET (DIDN'T WE SHAKE SUGAREE). / THE DOLPHINS** – □

Jan 68. (7") *<2091>* **FELICITY. / PLEASE SEND ME SOMEONE TO LOVE** – □

Feb 68. (lp) *<ST 2862>* **SESSIONS** – □
– Felicity / Please send me someone to love / Merry-go-round / Look over yonder / Fools are a long time coming / Looks like rain / Roll on Rosie.

Jul 68. (7") *<2256>* **EVERYBODY'S TALKIN'. / THAT'S THE BAG I'M IN** – □

Oct 69. (7") *(CL 15616) <2604>* **EVERYBODY'S TALKIN'. / BADI-DA** □ □

1971. (lp) *<(E-ST 657)>* **THE OTHER SIDE OF THIS LIFE (live)** □ □
– Other side of this life / Roll on Rosie / The dolphins / That's the bag I'm in / Sweet cocaine / Everybody's talkin' / Come back baby / Badi-da / Prettiest train / Ya don't miss your water / Felicity.

—— FRED had already retired from the music world in the late 60's; on the 7th of July, 2001, FRED died of cancer

– compilations, others, etc. –

1968. (7") *Elektra; (EKSN 45036)* **CANDY MAN. / THE WATER IS WIDE** □ □

Nov 86. (lp) *See For Miles; (SEE 77)* **THE VERY BEST OF FRED NEIL** □ –
– That's the bag I'm in / Badi-da / Faretheewell (Fred's tune) / Merry go round / Felicity / Everybody's talkin' / Everything happens / Sweet cocaine / Green rocky road / Cynicrustpetefredjohn raga / Please send me someone to love / Fools are a long time coming / The dolphins / I've got a secret (didn't we shake sugaree).

Mar 99. (d-cd) *Collector's; <(WSCCM 0070-2)>* **THE MANY SIDES OF FRED NEIL** □ □
– The dolphins / I've got a secret (didn't we shake sugaree) / That's the bag I'm in / Badi-da / Faretheewell (Fred's tune) / Everybody's talkin' / Everything happens / Sweet cocaine / Green rocky road / Cynicrustpetefredjohn raga / Felicity / Please send me someone to love / Merry go round / Look over yonder / Fools are a long time coming / Looks like rain / Roll on Rosie / Other side of this life / Roll on Rosie (long) / The dolphins / That's the bag I'm in / Sweet cocaine / Everybody's talkin' / Come back baby / Badi-da / Prettiest train / You don't miss your water / Felicity / Long black veil / Bottom of the glass / Sweet mama / Trouble in mind / December's dream / Ride stormy weather / How long blues – Drown in tears / Other side of this life.

Oct 01. (cd) *Elektra; <(8122 73563-2)>* **TEAR DOWN THE WALLS / BLEECKER & MACDOUGAL** □ □

Jul 03. (cd) *Rev-ola; <(CRREV 47)>* **DO YOU EVER THINK OF ME?** □ □
– (FRED NEIL + SESSIONS).

NELLY

Born: CORNELL HAYNES, 2 Nov'74, Travis, Texas. After growing up in St. Louis and being a keen basketballer and freestyler, NELLY and his crew of MC's (ST. LUNATICS) had a moderate local hit with their self-financed and produced single 'GIMME WHAT YOU GOT' in 1996. However, the group failed to find a suitable party to issue their material, so NELLY went off into the daunting world of commercial hip hop. His sharp lyrics and southern attitude impressed 'Universal' enough to sign him. The man's debut album 'COUNTRY GRAMMAR' was issued in the summer of 2000, around the same time as the massive success of single '(HOT S**T) COUNTRY GRAMMAR'. Two more hits followed in quick succession 'E.I.' and 'RIDE WIT ME', the latter a cool, lazy ghetto sing-a-long anthem that had people chanting its "Hey, must be tha money" hook repeatedly. The album, featuring the ST. LUNATICS collective of BIG LEE, KYJUAN, MURPHY LEE and CITY SPUD (plus guests LIL' WAYNE, TEAMSTERS and CEDRIC THE ENTERTAINER) peaked at the top of the US Billboard charts and didn't move for several weeks. Returning after the massive success of his debut, NELLY – still with his producer and musical cohort JASON "JAY E" EPPERSON in tow – issued the slightly disappointing 'NELLYVILLE' in 2002. Peppered with the same bass-laden bounce that made him a rich fella' two years previous, there was nothing that spectacular about this album, apart from perhaps the TIMBALAND produced 'HOT IN HERE', which went on to become a major club and chart hit and all-around overplayed song. Elsewhere NELLY could be seen pairing up with JUSTIN TIMBERLAKE on the frankly dire 'WORK IT', but on a positive note, the JUST BLAZE produced 'ROC THE MIC' was immensely impressive and demonstrated NELLY's capability to pull off something truly magical. A year later, a pointless remix album 'DA DERRTY VERSIONS: THE REINVENTION' (think Aguilera, Scouser or Harold Steptoe for "derrty") was issued to a lukewarm reception. Ditching his trademark face-plaster and recruiting producers Jermaine Dupri and David Banner (not to be confused with The Hulk), the album was basically a track-for-track remix of the aforementioned 'NELLYVILLE', with the man himself giving us some cringe-worthy interview stylee commentary on his creative process. Utterly useless and not much of an improvement on the original, file this under "for fans only", or, more accurately, "crap rap".

Album rating: COUNTRY GRAMMAR (*9) / NELLYVILLE (*6) / DA DERRTY VERSIONS: THE REINVENTION (*4)

NELLY – vocals / with CITY SPUD, etc.

M.C.A. Fo' Real

Sep 00. (cd) *(157743-2) <55743>* **COUNTRY GRAMMAR** [14] Jun00 [1]
– Intro (with CEDRIC THE ENTERTAINER) / St. Louie / Greed, hate, envy (with CITY SPUD) / Country grammar (hot shit) / Steal the show (with ST. LUNATICS) / interlude (with CEDRIC THE ENTERTAINER) / Ride wit me (with CITY SPUD) / E.I. / Thicky thick girl / For my / Utha side / Tho dem wrappas / Wrap sumden (with ST. LUNATICS) / Batter up (with LEE, MURPHY & ALI) / Never let 'em C U sweat (with TEAMSTERS) / Luven me (with CITY SPUD) / Outro (with CEDRIC THE ENTERTAINER). *(re-iss. Apr01; 013836-2)*

Oct 00. (c-s) *(MCSC 40242) <156800>* **(HOT S**T) COUNTRY GRAMMAR / (album)** [7] Feb00 [7]
(12"+=/cd-s+=) *(MCST/+D 40242)* – (mixes; superclean / 2 step).

Feb 01. (c-s) *(MCSC 40249) <158684>* **E.I. / GREED, HATE, ENVY** [11] Sep00 [15]
(cd-s+=) *(MCSTD 40249)* – ('A'-CD-Rom).
(12") *(MCST 40249)* – ('A'side) / ('A'instrumental).

May 01. (c-s; as NELLY featuring CITY SPUD) *(MCSC 40252) <158820>* **RIDE WIT ME / (stargate mix)** [3] Feb01 [3]
(cd-s+=) *(MCSTD 40252)* – Come on over / ('A'video).
(12") *(MCST 40252)* – ('A'mixes).

— In Jun'01, NELLY was credited on JAGGED EDGE's US Top 3 hit, 'Where The Party At'

Sep 01. (12"; as NELLY & ST. LUNATICS) *(MCST 40261) <015320>* **BATTER UP (full Phat remix) / BATTER UP / BATTER UP (instrumental)** [28] [ ]
(cd-s) *(MCSTD 40261)* – ('A'side) / Icey / ('A'-CD-Rom).

Jun 02. (c-s) *(MCSC 40289) <279>* **HOT IN HERRE / (X-Ecutioners remix)** [4] [1]
(cd-s+=) *(MCST 40289)* – Not in my house.
(12"+=) *(MCSTD 40289)* – ('A'-Third eye remix).

Jul 02. (cd) *(018690-2) <017747>* **NELLYVILLE** [2] [1]
– Nellyville / "Getting it started" (with CEDRIC THE ENTERTAINER & LA LA) / Hot in herre / Dem boyz (with MURPHY LEE, KYJUAN & ALI) / Oh Nelly (with MURPHY LEE) / Pimp juice / Air force ones (with KYJUAN, MURPHY LEE & ALI) / "In the store" (with CEDRIC THE ENTERTAINER & LA LA) / On the grind (with KING JACOB) / Dilemma (with KELLY ROWLAND) / Splurge / Work it (with JUSTIN TIMBERLAKE) / Roc the mic (with FREEWAY, BEANIE SIGEL & MURPHY LEE) / The gank (with WAIEL "WALLY" YAGHNAM) / "5000" / #1 / CG 2 (with ALI, KYJUAN & MURPHY LEE) / Say now / "**** it then" (with CEDRIC THE ENTERTAINER & LA LA).

Oct 02. (c-s; by NELLY & KELLY ROWLAND) *(MCSC 40299) <19447>* **DILEMMA / (Jason Nevins remix) / KINGS HIGHWAY** [1] [1]
(cd-s+=) *(MCSTD 40299)* – ('A'video).
(12") *(MCST 40299)* – ('A'-G-Force radio) / ('A'-Jason Nevins club remix).

Mar 03. (cd-s; by NELLY & JUSTIN TIMERLAKE) *(MCSTD 40312)* **WORK IT / PUT YOUR HANDS UP (with AIR FORCE ONES) / ('A'-video)** [7] [ ]
(12") *(MCST 40312)* – (first 2 tracks) / ('A'-Nevins universal).
(cd-s) *(MCSXD 40312)* – ('A'-DJ Swamp mix) / ('A'-Nevins universal dub) / Dilemma (G-Force full vocal mix).

Apr 03. (12") *<2391-1>* **PIMP JUICE (mixes)** [–] [58]

Sep 03. (cd-s; by NELLY featuring P. DIDDY & MURPHY LEE) *(MCSTD 40337) <radio>* **SHAKE YA TAILFEATHER / (main version) / (instrumental) / (video)** [10] [1]
(12") *(MCST 40337)* – ('A'-versions).

Nov 03. (cd) *(MCD 60091) <16650-2>* **DA DERRTY VERSIONS: THE REINVENTION** (remixes) [ ] [12]

Dec 03. (cd-s) *(MCSTD 40436) <18381-1>* **IZ U / HOT IN HERRE / HOT IN HERRE (video)** [36] [–]
(12") *(MCST 40436)* – ('A'side) / ('A'-instrumental).

– compilations, etc. –

Mar 02. (c-s) *Priority; (PTYC 146) <radio cut>* **#1 / #1 (album)** [ ] Oct01 [22]
(12"+=/cd-s+=) *(PTY T/CD 146)* – Training day (in my hood) (with ROSCOE) / #1 (instrumental).

Bill NELSON

Born: 18 Dec'48, Wakefield, Yorkshire, England. In the late 60's, after a job as a government officer, he joined local groups, GLOBAL VILLAGE TRUCKING COMPANY and GENTLE REVOLUTION. NELSON subsequently released an obscure and limited solo album, 'NORTHERN DREAM', on his own label in 1971, the record soon finding its way to Radio 1 DJ, John Peel, who gave it night-time airplay. That year, the singer/guitarist formed BE-BOP DELUXE alongside IAN PARKIN, ROBERT BRYAN, NICHOLAS CHATTERTON-DEW and RICHARD BROWN and after one single, they signed to 'Harvest'. Their first album, 'AXE VICTIM' (1974), showcased the talent of the gifted NELSON, a dextrous multi-instrumentalist whose talent for quirky glam/prog-rock won him an immediate cult following. The record's release was swiftly followed by a tour supporting COCKNEY REBEL, a group they were constantly compared with in the music press. In August '74, NELSON split the band up, subsequently re-forming the group with unhappy ex-REBELS, MILTON REAME-JAMES and PAUL AVRON JEFFRYS. The revamped line-up debuted on the well-received set, 'FUTURAMA' (1975), consolidating their critical standing early the next year with a UK Top 30 hit single, 'SHIPS IN THE NIGHT' (taken from follow-up album, 'SUNBURST FINISH'). BE-BOP DELUXE enjoyed a couple of years in the big league until NELSON decided to concentrate on another project, RED NOISE. After a promising 1979 album, 'SOUND ON SOUND', the man went solo, subsequently hitting the Top 10 with an adventurous, experimental double-set, 'QUIT DREAMING AND GET ON THE BEAM' (1981). Throughout the 80's and 90's, NELSON released a plethora of albums, mostly for his own obscure 'Cocteau' label. Having also worked with The SKIDS, The ASSOCIATES, YELLOW MAGIC ORCHESTRA and DAVID SYLVIAN, on collaborative efforts and production work, he subsequently released his best work for some time in 1996, 'AFTER THE SATELLITE SINGS'. His first work of the new millennium, 'WHIMSEY' (2003) was an ambitious but nevertheless accessible double set of sonic investigation from a past master of the genre, referring back to his BE-BOP DELUXE days but also boldly exploring new avenues with a refreshing solidity and focus. • **Trivia:** His younger brother IAN (of RED NOISE), also had a minor hit with FIAT LUX.

Album rating: NORTHERN DREAM (*4) / Be-Bop Deluxe: AXE VICTIM (*5) / FUTURAMA (*4) / SUNBURST FINISH (*7) / MODERN MUSIC (*6) / LIVE IN THE AIR AGE (*5) / DRASTIC PLASTIC (*5) / RAIDING THE DIVINE ARCHIVES compilation (*8) / Bill Nelson: SOUND ON SOUND with Red Noise (*7) / QUIT DREAMING AND GET ON THE BEAM (*9) / DAS KABINETT (THE CABINET OF DR. CAGLIARI) (*4) / LA BELLE ET LA BETE (THE BEAUTY AND THE BEAST) (*4) / THE LOVE THAT WHIRLS (*6) / CHIMERA (*7) / SAVAGE GESTURE FOR CHARMS SAKE (*6) / GETTING THE HOLY GHOST ACROSS (*6) / CHAMBER OF DREAMS (*5) / SUMMER OF GOD'S PIANO (*5) / MAP OF DREAMS (*5) / CHANCE ENCOUNTERS IN THE GARDEN OF LIGHT (*5) / OPTIMISM (*5) / PAVILLIONS OF THE HEART AND SOUL (*6) / CATALOGUE OF OBSESSIONS (*6) / DUPLEX: THE BEST OF BILL NELSON compilation (*7) / LUMINOUS (*6) / BLUE MOONS & LAUGHING GUITARS (*6) / CRIMSWORTH (FLOWERS, STONES, FOUNTAINS AND FLAMES) (*5) / CULTUREMIX (*6) / PRACTICALLY WIRED (*5) / AFTER THE SATELLITE SINGS (*7) / WHIMSY (*7)

BILL NELSON – vocals, lead guitar

Smile | not iss.

1971. (lp) *(LAF 2182)* **NORTHERN DREAM** [ ] [–]
– Photograph (a beginning) / Everyone's hero / House of sand / End of the seasons / Rejoice / Love's a way / Northern dreamer (1957) / Bloo blooz / Sad fellings / See it through / Smiles / Chymepeace (an ending). *(re-iss. Feb81, Mar82 & Aug86 on 'Butt'; BUTT 002) (cd-iss. Mar96 on 'Blueprint'; SM 777CD)*

BE-BOP DELUXE

were formed by **BILL NELSON** plus **IAN PARKIN** – rhythm guitar / **ROBERT BRYAN** – bass / **NICHOLAS CHATTERTON-DEW** – drums / **RICHARD BROWN** – keyboards

Smile | not iss.

Jan 73. (7") *(LAFS 001)* **TEENAGE ARCHANGEL. / JETS AT DAWN** [ ] [–]

—— became trio, when BROWN departed.

Harvest | Harvest

May 74. (7") *(HAR 5081)* **JET SILVER (AND THE DOLLS OF VENUS). / THIRD FLOOR HEAVEN** [ ] [–]

Jun 74. (lp) *(SHVL 813) <SM 11689>* **AXE VICTIM** [ ] [ ]
– Axe victim / Love is swift arrows / Jet Silver (and the dolls of Venus) / Third floor Heaven / Night creatures / Rocket cathedrals / Adventures in a Yorkshire landscape / Jets at dawn / No trains to Heaven / Darkness (l'immoralise). *(cd-iss. Feb91; CZ 327)* – (3 extra).

—— Aug74, **NELSON** recruited entire new line-up **MILTON REAME-JAMES** – keyboards (ex-COCKNEY REBEL) repl. IAN / **PAUL AVRON JEFFRYS** – bass (ex-COCKNEY REBEL) repl. ROBERT / **SIMON FOX** – drums (ex-HACKENSHACK) repl. NICHOLAS

—— (late 1974) **BILL** and **SIMON** were joined by **CHARLIE TUMAHAI** (b. New Zealand) – bass who repl. MILTON & PAUL

Feb 75. (7"; w-drawn) *(HAR 5091)* **BETWEEN THE WORLDS. / LIGHTS** [–] [–]

May 75. (lp) *(SHSP 4045) <ST 11432>* **FUTURAMA** [ ] [ ]
– Stage whispers / Love with the madman / Maid in Heaven / Sister seagull / Sound track / Music in Dreamland / Jean Cocteau / Between the worlds / Swan song. *(cd-iss. Feb91; CZ 328) (cd re-iss. Apr97 on 'E.M.I.'; REPLAYCD 27)*

Jun 75. (7") *(HAR 5098)* **MAID IN HEAVEN. / LIGHTS** [ ] [–]

Jul 75. (7") *<4151>* **MAID IN HEAVEN. / SISTER SEAGULL** [–] [ ]

—— added **ANDREW CLARKE** – keyboards

Jan 76. (7") *(HAR 5104) <4244>* **SHIPS IN THE NIGHT. / CRYING TO THE SKY** [23] [ ]

Jan 76. (lp/c) *(SHSP/TC-SHSP 4053) <St 11478>* **SUNBURST FINISH** [17] [96]
– Fair exchange / Heavenly homes / Ships in the night / Crying to the sky / Sleep that burns / Beauty secrets / Life in the air age / Like an old blues / Crystal gazing / Blazing apostles. *(re-iss. Mar82 on 'Fame' lp/c; FA/TC-FA 3004) (re-iss. Jun86 on 'Revolver' lp/c; REV LP/MC 71) (cd-iss. Feb91 +=; CZ 329)* – Shine / Speed of the wind / Blue as a jewel.

Aug 76. (7") *(HAR 5110)* **KISS OF THE LIGHT. / Funky Phaser Unearthly Merchandise: SHINE** [ ] [–]

Sep 76. (lp/c) *(SHSP/TC-SHSP 4058) <ST 11575>* **MODERN MUSIC** [12] [88]
– Orphans of Babylon / Twilight capers / Kiss of the light / The bird charmer's destiny / The gold at the end of my rainbow / Bring back the spark / Modern music / Dancing in the moonlight / Honeymoon on Mars / Lost in the neon world / Dance of the Uncle Sam humanoids / Modern music / Forbidden lovers / Down on Terminal street / Make the music magic. *(cd-iss. Feb91; CZ 330)* – (3 extra). *(cd re-iss. Apr97 on 'E.M.I.'; REPLAYCD 28)*

Jul 77. (white-lp) *(SHVL 816) <11666>* **LIVE IN THE AIR AGE (live)** [10] [65]
– Life in the air age / Ships in the night / Piece of mine / Fair exchange / Mill street junction / Adventures in a Yorkshire landscape / Blazing apostles. *(free-7"ep)* **SHINE. / SISTER SEAGULL / MAID IN HEAVEN** *(cd-iss. Feb91; CZ 331)* – (3 extra ep tracks).

Sep 77. (7") *(HAR 5135)* **JAPAN. / FUTURIST MANIFESTO** [ ] [–]

Feb 78. (7") *(HAR 5147) <4571>* **PANIC IN THE WORLD. / BLUE AS A JEWEL** [ ] [ ]

Feb 78. (lp/c) *(SHSP/TC-SHSP 4091) <ST 11750>* **DRASTIC PLASTIC** [22] [95]
– Electrical language / New precision / New mysteries / Surreal estate / Love in flames / Panic in the world / Dangerous stranger / Superenigmatix (lethal appliances for the home) / Islands of the dead / Visions of endless hopes / Possession / Islands of the dead. *(cd-iss. Feb91; CZ 332)* – (3 extra tracks). *(cd re-iss. Apr97 on 'E.M.I.'; REPLAYCD 29)*

May 78. (7") *(HAR 5158)* **ELECTRICAL LANGUAGE. / SURREAL ESTATE** [ ] [–]

—— Disbanded Spring 1978. TUMAHAI joined The DUKES, SIMON joined JACK GREEN. CLARKE joined NICO's band.

– compilations, others, etc. –

on 'Harvest' unless mentioned otherwise

Oct 76. (7"ep) *(HAR 5117)* **HOT VALVES** [36] [ ]
– Maid in Heaven / Blazing apostles / Jet Silver and the dolls of Venus / Bring back the spark.

Nov 78. (d-lp) *(SHDW 410)* **THE BEST OF AND THE REST OF BE-BOP DELUXE** [ ] [ ]
(cd-iss. May90; 794 158-2)

May 81. (lp/c) *(SHSM/TC-SHSM 2034)* **THE SINGLES A's & B's** [ ] [–]
(cd-iss. Feb92 on 'See For Miles'; SEECD 336)

Aug 83. (7"m) *Cocteau; (COQ 7)* **PANIC IN THE WORLD. / MAID IN HEAVEN / ELECTRICAL LANGUAGE** [ ] [–]
(re-iss. Jul85 as 12"m; COQT 7)

Sep 83. (d-lp) *(EDP 154 6793)* **AXE VICTIM / FUTURAMA** [ ] [–]

May 84. (7") *EMI Gold; (G45 21)* **SHIPS IN THE NIGHT. / MAID IN HEAVEN** [ ] [–]

Aug 86. (lp) *Dojo; (DOJOLP 42)* **BOP TO THE RED NOISE** [ ] [–]

Mar 87. (lp/c) *(EMS/TC-EMS 1130)* **RAIDING THE DIVINE ARCHIVES** [ ] [–]
– Jet silver (and the dolls of Venus) / Adventures in a Yorkshire landscape / Maid in Heaven / Ships in the night / Life in the air age / Kiss of light / Sister seagull / Modern music / Japan / Panic in the world / Bring back the spark / Forbidden lovers / Electrical language. *(re-iss. Apr90 on 'E.M.I.'+=; CDP 794 158-2)* – Fair exchange / Sleep that burns / Between the worlds / Music in Dreamland.

Sep 94. (cd) *Windsong; (WINCD 065)* **RADIOLAND – BBC RADIO 1 LIVE IN CONCERT (live)** [ ] [–]

BILL NELSON'S RED NOISE

BILL NELSON with **ANDREW CLARKE** – keyboards / **RICK FORD** – drums / brother **IAN NELSON** – saxophone / **STEVE PEER** – drums

Harvest | Harvest

Feb 79. (7"red) *(HAR 5176)* **FURNITURE MUSIC. / WONDERTOYS THAT LAST FOREVER / ACQUITTED BY MIRRORS** [59] [–]

Feb 79. (lp/c) *(SHSP/TC-SHSP 4095) <11931>* **SOUND ON SOUND** [33] [ ]
– Don't touch me, I'm electric / For young moderns / Stop – go – stop / Furniture music / Radar in my heart / Stay young / Out of touch / A better home in the phantom zone / Substitute flesh / The atom age / Art – Empire – Industry / Revolt into style. *(re-iss. Nov85 on 'Cocteau' lp/c; JC/CJC 14) (<cd-iss. Jul99; 521206-2>)*

Apr 79. (7"blue) *(HAR 5183)* **REVOLT INTO STYLE. / OUT OF TOUCH** [69] [–]

BILL NELSON

solo, with **TOM KELLICHAN** – drums / with sessioners

Cocteau — not iss.

Jun 80. (7"ep) *(COQ 1)* **DO YOU DREAM IN COLOUR?** 52 –
– Do you dream in colour? / Ideal homes / Instantly yours / Atom Man loves Radium Girl.

Crepescule — not iss.

Mar 81. (7") **ROOMS WITH BRITTLE VIEWS. / DADA GUITARS** – Belgium –

Mercury — P.V.C.

Mar 81. (7") *(WILL 1)* **BANAL. / MR. MAGNETISN HIMSELF** –
(12"+=) *(WILL 1-12)* – Turn to fiction.

May 81. (lp)(c) *(6359 055)(7557 010)* **QUIT DREAMIMG AND GET ON THE BEAM** 7 –
– Banal / Living in my limousine / Vertical games / Disposable / False alarms / Decline and fall / Life runs out like sand / A kind of loving / Do you dream in colour? / U.H.F. / Youth of nation on fire / Quit dreaming and get on the beam. *(w/ free-lp)* **SOUNDING THE RITUAL ECHO** – Annuciation / The ritual echo / Sleep / Near east / Emak bakia / My intricate image / Endless orchids / The heat in the room / Another willingly opened window / Vanishing parades / Glass fish (for the final aquarium) / Cubical domes / Ashes of roses / The shadow garden (opium). *(iss.on own.Jun85 on 'Cocteau'; JCS 12) (cd-iss. on own.Sep89; JCCD 12) (cd-iss. Jul86 on 'Cocteau'+=; JCCD 15)* – White sound. *<US cd-iss. 1989 on 'Enigma'; 73385-2>*

Jun 81. (7") *(BILL 2)* **YOUTH OF NATION ON FIRE. / BE MY DYNAMO** 73 –
(d7"+=) *(WILL 22)* – Rooms with brittle views / All my wives were iron.

Sep 81. (7") *(WILL 3)* **LIVING IN MY LIMOUSINE. / BIRDS OF TIME** –
(12"+=) *(WILL 3-12)* – Love in the abstract / White sound.

Apr 82. (7") *(WILL 4)* **EROS ARRIVING. / HAUNTING IN MY HEAD** –
(d7"+=) *(WILL 44)* – Flesh / He and sleep were brothers.

Jun 82. (d-lp/d-c) *(WHIRL/CURL 3) <101>* **THE LOVE THAT WHIRLS** 28
– Empire of the senses / Hope for the heartbeat / Waiting for the voices / Private view / Eros arriving / Bride of Christ in Autumn / When your dream of perfect beauty comes true / Flaming desire / Portrait of Jan with flowers / Crystal escalator in the palace of God department store / Echo in her eyes / October man. *(re-iss. Jul86 on 'Cocteau', cd+=)* – Flesh / He and sleep were brothers. *<US cd-iss. 1989 on 'Enigma'; 73386-2>*

Jul 82. (7"/12") *(WILL 5/+12)* **FLAMING DESIRE. / THE PASSION** –

May 83. (lp/c) *(MERB/+C 19)* **CHIMERA** 30 –
– The real adventure / Acceleration / Every day feels like another new drug / Tender is the night / Glow world / Another day, another ray of hope. *(cd-iss. Sep87 on 'Cocteau', re-iss. Apr89)*

Cocteau — Portrait

Aug 83. (7"m) *(COQ 10)* **TOUCH AND GLOW. / DANCING IN THE WILD / LOVE WITHOUT FEAR** –

Dec 83. (m-lp) *(JCM 3)* **SAVAGE GESTURES FOR CHARMS SAKE**
– The man in the exine suit / Watching my dream boat go down in flames / The meat room / Another happy thought (carved forever in your cortex) / Portrait of Jan with Moon and stars. *(re-iss. Feb85) <US cd-iss. 1989 on 'Enigma'; 73373>*

Aug 84. (7") *(COQ 15)* **ACCELERATION. / HARD FACTS FROM THE FICTION DEPARTMENT** –
(12"pic-d+=) *(COQT 15)* – ('A'short) / ('A'long).

Portrait — Portrait

Mar 86. (7"/12") *(A/TA 6928)* **WILDEST DREAMS. / SELF IMPERSONATION** –

Apr 86. (lp/c) *(PRT/40 26602) <R 40146>* **GETTING THE HOLY GHOST ACROSS** <US-title 'ON A BLUE WING'> 91
– Suvasini / Contemplation / Theology / Wildest dreams / Lost in your mystery / Rise like a fountain / Age of reason / Hidden flame / Because of you / Living for the spangled moment / Word for word / Illusions of you / Heart and soul / Finks and stooges of the spirit. *(cd-iss. 1988 on 'C.B.S.'; CDCBS 26602)*

Cocteau — Enigma

Jun 86. (lp) *(JC 7)* **CHAMBER OF DREAMS** –
– The blazing memory of innuendo / Into the luminous future / Dip in the swimming pool / Reactor / Tomorrowland (the threshold of 1947) / Listening to lizards / Endless torsion / My sublime perversion / Eros in Autumn / Sleeplessness / The latest skyline / Train of thought / Packs and fountains clouds and trees / Golden bough / Forever Orpheus / In arcadia / Sentimental / Autumn fires / Wild blue yonder. *(cd-iss. Aug89; JCCD 7) <US cd-iss. 1989 on 'Enigma'; 73377-2>*

Oct 86. (lp/c) *(JC/TCJC 6)* **SUMMER OF GOD'S PIANO** –
– Antennae two / N.B.C.97293 / The sleep of Hollywood / The celestial bridegroom / Under the red arch / Orient pearl / Sacrament / Falling blossoms / The difficulty of being / Zanoni / The Chinese nightingale / Soon September (another enchantment) / Rural shires / Perfido incanto / The lost years / The charm of transit / Night thoughts (twilight radio) / Wysteria / Swing / Snowfall / Real of dusk / Over ocean. *(cd-iss. Aug89; JCCD 6) <US cd-iss. 1989 on 'Enigma'; 73376-2>*

Jan 87. (lp/c/cd) *(JC/TCJC/JCCD 19)* **MAP OF DREAMS** –
– Legions of the endless night / Spinning creatures / At the gates of the singing garden / Heavenly message No.1, 2 & 3 / Fellini's picnic / Dark angel / Infernal regions / Dance of the fragrant woman / The alchemy of ecstasy / Aphrodite adorned / The wheel of fortune and the hand of fate / Forked tongues, mixed blessings / Another tricky mission for the celestial pilot / Water of life (transfiguration). *<US cd-iss. 1989 on 'Enigma'; 73389-2>*

May 87. (12"; by SCALA: BILL NELSON & DARYL RUNSWICK) *(COQT 21)* **SECRET CEREMONY (theme from 'BROND'). / WIPING A TEAR FROM THE ALL SEEING EYE** –

Nov 87. (d-lp/c/cd) *(JEAN/+TC/CD 20) <73337>* **CHANCE ENCOUNTERS IN THE GARDEN OF LIGHT**
– My dark demon / The dove consumed (the serpent slumbers) / Calling Heaven, calling Heaven overs / Path of return / Theurgia / Staircase to no place / Evocation of a radiant childhood / The kingdom of consequence / Divine raptures of a radiant childhood / Bright star (moonlight over the ocean blue) / A bird of the air shall earn the voice / Clothed in light amongst the stars / Hastening the chariot of my hearts desire / Transcendant conversation / West deep / The spirit cannot fail / Pilots of kite / Phantom gardens / The angel of hearth and home / Villefranche interior / Night tides / First memory / Azure extention / Radiant spires / Evening peal / Thremodia / Short drink for a certain fountain / Body of light / At the centre / Self-initiation / The word that became flesh / The hermetic garden / Revolving globes / The four square citadel / Orient of Memphis / Little daughters of light / Angel at the western window.

Sep 88. (lp/c/cd; as BILL NELSON ORCHESTRA ARCANA) *(JC/+TC/CD 21) <73344>* **OPTIMISM**
– Exactly the way you want it / Why be lonely / Everyday is a better day / The receiver and the fountain pen / Welcome home Mr. Kane / This is true / Greeting a new day / The breath in my father's saxophone / Our lady of apparations / The whole city between us / Deva dance / Always looking forward to tomorrow / Profiles, hearts, stars / Alchemia.

Dec 88. (7") *(COQ 22)* **LIFE IN YOUR HANDS. / DO YOU DREAM IN COLOUR** –
(12"+=/cd-s+=) *(COQ T/CD 22)* – Get out of that hole / Drean demon.

Aug 89. (lp/cd) *(JC/+CD 8) <73378>* **PAVILLIONS OF THE HEART AND SOUL**
– Gift of the August tide / Loving tongues / Blue nude / In the realms of bells / Your nebulous smile / The glance of a glittering stranger / Another kiss for your slender neck / The warmth of women's eyes / Seduction (ritual with roses) / Dreamed entrances / Four pieces for imaginary strings:- Herself with her shadow – The exquisite corpse – Ardent hands – Her laughing torso / Migrating angels / Les amoureaux / Meshes of the afternoon / Mountains of the heart / Willow silk / Tender encounters (states of grace) / Melancholia / The eternal female.

Aug 89. (lp/cd) *(JC/+CD 9) <73379>* **CATALOGUE OF OBSESSIONS**
– Sex party six / Tune in Tokyo / Promise of perfume / View from a balcony / Test of affection / Birds in two hemispheres / Wider windows for the walls / The boy pilots of Bangkok / Talk technique / Glass breakfast / Edge of tears / Erotikon.

Sep 90. (cd/c) *(JCCD/TCJC 24)* **CHIMES AND RINGS** –
– Lady you're a strange girl / Kiss goodbye / Call of the wild / Lost to me / Dangerous lady / Working man / Giving it all away / Ice and fire / Wonder where we go / Dreams of yesterday / Sell my soul / Back to dreams / I wait for you / Walk away from Paradise / Playing Jesus to her Judas / Something's going on / The miracle belongs to you.

Sep 90. (cd/c) *(JCCD/TCJC 25)* **NUDITY** –
– Feels like up to me / Prize of years / Still waiting / Lover boy at heart / The wonder of it all / Devil in me / A little more time / What's it all about / Thunder on the wing / Shake it up / Love to win / Running / If love were gold / I want you / Kiss it off / Angel like you / Crying all night / Only love can tell.

Sep 90. (cd/c) *(JCCD/TCJC 26)* **HEARTBREAKLAND** –
– You know how to hurt / Broken / You make me cry / Mess around / Why? / Insanity / Confused / Heartbreakland / Lucky star / Heartbreak thru' the telephone / One day at a time / Tip the wink / Shadow haunting me / Raining / Love's immortal shining angel.

Sep 90. (cd/c) *(JCCD/TCJC 27)* **DETAILS** –
– Maybe it's the future / Wondering / Wasted lives / The best of you / Stay with me / Love and a bucket full of holes / Prisoner of love / Don't wait / Man on fire / Visionary / The world to me / Strong enough / Everything permitted / Aeroplane wings / One for you / Let it all pass you by.

Imaginary — not iss.

Apr 91. (lp/cd) *(ILLUSION/+CD 24)* **LUMINOUS** –
– A luminous kind of guy / Tiny aeroplanes / Bright sparks / Is this academy? / Language of the birds / All I am is you / Life in reverse / Telepathic cats / Two hearts beating / Blood off the wall / She's got me floating / It's OK / Burning down / Her true perfect serpent / Wait for tomorrow.

Venture — Plan 9

Aug 92. (cd/c) *(CD/TC VE 912) <1878>* **BLUE MOONS & LAUGHING GUITARS**
– Ancient guitars / Girl from another planet / Spinnin' around / Shaker / God man slain / The dead we wake with upstairs drum / New moon rising / The glory days / Wishes / Angel in my system / Wings and everything / Boat to forever / The invisible man and the unforgettable girl / So it goes / Fires in the sky / Dream ships set sail.

All Saints — Gyroscope

Mar 95. (cd) *(ASCD 022) <6613>* **PRACTICALLY WIRED OR HOW I BECAME . . . GUITARBOY**
– Roses and rocketships / Spinning planet / Thousand fountain island / Piano 45 / Pink buddha blues / Kid with cowboy tie / Royal ghosts / Her presence in flowers / Big noise in Twangtown / Tiny little thing / Wild blue cycle / Every moment infinite / Friends from Heaven / Eternal for Eniko.

Resurgent — Resurgent

Feb 95. (cd) *(<RES 104CD>)* **CRIMSWORTH (FLOWERS, STONES, FOUNTAINS AND FLAMES)**
– (part 1) / (part 2). *(re-iss. Oct96 & Apr97; same)*

Nov 95. (cd; CULTUREMIX & BILL NELSON) *(<RES 113CD>)* **CULTUREMIX** Mar99
– Luna park / Radio head / Housewives on drugs / Dancematic / Four postcards home / Zebra / Exile / Tangram / Cave paintings. *(re-iss. Apr97; same)*

Resurgent — Gyroscope

Oct 96. (cd) *(RES 114CD) <6616>* **AFTER THE SATELLITE SINGS**
– Deeply dazzled / Tomorrow yesterday / Flipside / Streamliner / Memory babe / Skull baby cluster / Zoom sequence / Rocket to Damascus / Beautiful nudes / Old goat / Squirm / Wow it's scootercar sexkitten / Phantom sedan / Ordinary idiots / V-ghost / Blink agog. *(re-iss. Apr97; same)*

Fabled Quixote — Fabled Quixote

Jul 03. (d-cd) *(<USR 103CD>)* **WHIMSY** Aug03
– Nostalgia (for the future) / Slumberlite / Let flow the wine / Switch off that desert sunset / Magnetism made me do it / A simple thought flashes through my mind / Senor Mysterioso / Ocean full of wishes / Swept away / Islands in the sky / Always summer / The fundamental blues / My favourite urban chrome-green sky / Dizzy in the head / I looked at the sea / The girl who disappeared into a cloud / Whimsy / So far / The violins of autumn / Will / Showtime / Dumb palooka / Garage full of clouds (part 2) / Organola (instrumental) / Perfect bliss / Powder blue / Here we go / When we were young / Fairyland before the fire / Cowboy Christmas / Struck dumb by beauty again / Don't be a stranger / The light this universe attracts / Sing ye golden sunbeams, sing / Superslippy / The fabulous fountain of your savior faire / A star named Desire / Buzz was honey / Over the moon / Close your eyes (the sleepy town symphony) (instrumental).

– compilations, specials, others –

—— on 'Cocteau' unless mentioned otherwise

Nov 81. (lp) *(JC 2)* **DAS KABINET (OF DR. CAGLIARI)** –
– The asylum / Waltz / The fairground / Doctor Cagliari / Cesare the somnabulist / Murder / The funeral / The somnabulist and the children / The children / Cagliari disciplines Cesare / Cagliari opens the cabinet / Jane discovers Cesare / The attempted murder of Jane / The dream dance of Jane and the somnabulist / Escape over the rooftops / The unmasking / The shot / The cabinet closes. *(cd-iss. Jan85; JCCD 40*

Jun 82. (lp) *(WHIRL 2)* **LA BELLE ET LA BETE (THE BEAUTY AND THE BEAST)** –
– Overture / The family / Sisters and Sedan chairs / In the forest of storms / The castle / The gates / The corridor / The great hall / Dreams (the merchant sleeps) / The rose and the beast / Magnificent (the white horse) / Beauty enters the castle / The door / The mirror / Candelabra and the gargoyles / Beauty and the beast / Transition No.1, 2 – The gift / The garden / Transitions No.3, 4 – The tragedy / Transitions No.5 – The enchanted glove / Tears as diamonds (the gift reverses) / The beast in solitude / Return of the magnificent / Transition No.6-The journey / The pavillion of Diana / Transformation No.1 & 2 / The final . . . *(above 2 albums re-iss. Jun85; JCCD 4)*

Nov 82. (5x7"box) *(JEAN 1)* **PERMANENT FLAME** –

Oct 84. (lp) *Mercury; <BFR 39270>* **VISTAMIX** –
– The real adventure / Flaming desire / Acceleration / Empire of the senses / Everyday feels like another new drug / Do you dream in color? / A kind of loving / Tender is the night / Glow world / Another day, another ray of hope.

Jan 85. (4xlp-box) *(JEAN 2)* **TRIAL BY INTAMACY** –
– (DAS KABINET / BEAUTY & THE BEAST / CHAMBER OF DREAMS / SUMMER OF GOD'S PIANO)

Feb 85. (cd) *(JCCD 10)* **THE TWO-FOLD ASPECT OF EVERYTHING** –
(d-lp-iss.Sep89; JC 10) <US-iss.1989 on 'Enigma'; 73380>

Nov 86. (lp/c; as ORCHESTRA ARCANA) *(JC/TCJC 18)* **ACONOGRAPHY** –

Sep 87. (d-cd) *(JCCD 17)* **CHIMERA / SAVAGE GESTURES FOR CHARMS SAKE** –

Sep 89. (cd/c/d-lp) *(CD/TC+/JCD 22) <73375>* **DUPLEX: THE BEST OF BILL NELSON**
– Flaming desire / Acceleration (remix) / hope for the heartbeat (remix) / Here and now / Life in your hands / Glow world / The blazing memory of the innuendo / The angel at the western window / The man in the Rexine suit / Right then left / Half asleep in the hall of mirrors / Opening / Metaphysical jerks / Loving tongues / Radiant spires / Do you dream in clour / Living in my limousine (remix) / October man / Private view / Contemplation / Another day, another ray of hope / Another tricky mission / Portrait of Jan with flowers / Wiping a tear from the all-seeing eye / Secret ceremony (theme from 'Brond') / Broadcast news (from 'Right To Reply') / Loosening up with lady luck / The garden / Burning the groove of Satyre / Set me a seal upon thine heart.

Dec 89. (4xcd-box) *(JEANCD 89)* **DEMONSTRATIONS OF AFFECTION** –

Sep 90. (cd; mail order) *(JCCD 23)* **SIMPLEX** – –

Aug 92. (3xcd-box) *Magpie; (MAGPIE 3)* **QUIT DREAMING AND GET ON THE BEAM / CHIMERA – SAVAGE GESTURES / THE LOVE THAT WHIRLS** –

Dec 95. (4xcd-box) *Resurgence; (RES 111CD)* **BOX SET** –
(re-iss. Oct96; same)

below trio were special recordings between 1988-1992

Apr 97. (cd) *Populuxe; (POPU 003CD) / Resurgent; <4082>* **ELECTRICITY MADE US ANGELS** Sep97
– Begin to burn / Heaven's happy hemisphere / God in her eyes / Float away / Big blue day / Sweet is the mystery / If wishes were horses / Fair winds and flying boats / Ocean over blue / River of love / This is destiny / Wonders never cease / Nothing yet / God thundered boy / She sends me.

Apr 97. (cd) *Populuxe; (POPU 004CD) / Resurgent; <4097>* **BUDDHA HEAD** Sep97
– My philosophy / Killing my desires / Buddha head / Way / Big river / Karma kisses / We will rise / Signs and signals / Lotus in the stream / Enlightenment / Eternally / Duality / Perfect world / Heart has its reasons / Sun will rise / Big illumination / Life as we know it.

Jun 97. (cd) *Populuxe; (POPU 005CD) / Resurgent; <4098>* **DEEP DREAM DECODER** Sep98
– Things to come / God bless me / Rise (above these things) / Snowing outside / It's all true / Head full of lights and a hat full of haloes / Girls I've loved / Amazing things / Deep dream decoder / Disolve / Year 44 (the birthday song) / Wing and a prayer / Dreamnoise and angel / Tired eyes / Golden girl / Spark.

Jul 98. (cd) *Resurgent; <4047>* **WEIRD CRITTERS** –

Sep 98. (cd) *Discipline; (DGM 9806)* **ATOM SHOP** –

Sep 98. (d-cd) *Discipline; (DGM 9807)* **WHAT NOW? WHAT NEXT?** –

Nov 02. (6xcd-box) *Toneswoon; (<TONESWOON 002>)* **NOISE CANDY**

Dec 02. (cd) *Populuxe; (USR 101CD) / United States; <154>* **CHAMELEON** (rec.1981) Feb03

Dec 02. (cd) *Populuxe; (USR 102CD) / United States;* **ORCHESTRA ARKANA** Feb03

N*E*R*D

Formed: USA . . . late 90's by NEPTUNES men CHAD HUGO and PHARRELL WILLIAMS along with longtime buddy SHAY. Inevitably and irrevocably overshadowed by an avalanche of inspired NEPTUNES productions, the trio's solo project was nevertheless a fascinating diversion from their day jobs. Initially released on 'Virgin' in Europe, 'IN SEARCH OF . . .' (2001) plied the relatively uncharted waters of alternative hip hop, ingeniously salvaging and recycling the genre's root sources and cultural detritus with studied post-millennial cool and sly humour. Ever the sonic perfectionists, the N*E*R*D posse subsequently decided they didn't actually like it after all, re-recording the whole shebang with live instrumentation and finally issuing it for US and worldwide consumption in 2002. Lacking the profile and branding of the NEPTUNES' pop outings (although the trio no doubt hoped that some of that glamour would rub off), singles 'LAPDANCE' and 'ROCK STAR' made a great impact on the UK chart. The NEPTUNES production successes continued apace however, while PHARRELL released a solo, soul-centric single, 'FRONTIN', in summer 2003. At the time of writing, N.E.R.D. (No One Ever Really Dies) seemed set to return with a much anticipated sophomore set scheduled for 2004.

Album rating: IN SEARCH OF . . . (*7)

PHARRELL WILLIAMS – vocals, multi / **CHAD HUGO** – multi / **SHAY** – vocals

		Virgin	Astralwerks
May 01.	(c-s/cd-s; by N*E*R*D featuring LEE HARVEY & VITA) *(VUSC/+D 196)* **LAPDANCE / LIL' SUZY (with Kelis) / WHAT'S WRONG WITH ME**	33	–
	(12"+=) *(VUST 196)* – ('A'-instrumental).		
Aug 01.	(cd) *(CDVUS 192)* <12622> **IN SEARCH OF . . .**		Mar02 56
	– Lapdance (with LEE HARVEY & VITA) / Things are getting better / Brain / Provider / Truth or dare (with KELIS & PUSHA T) / Tape you / Run to the sun / Baby doll / Am I high (with MALICE) / Rock star / Bobby James. *(re-iss. Mar02 cd+=/d-lp+=; CDVUS/+LP 216)* – Stay together. *(cd re-iss. Aug02 +=; CDVUSX 216)* – Rock star (Nevins' classic blaster). *(hit UK No.42) (d-lp re-iss. Mar03 +=; VUSLPX 216)* – Run to the sun (original). *(cd re-dist.Jun03)* – (hit UK No.28)		
Jul 02.	(cd-s) *(VUSTD 253)* **ROCK STAR (original / Jason Nevins' remix / Jason Nevins' classic club blaster)**	15	–
	(12"+=) *(VUST 253)* – ('A'-Jason Nevins' classic instrumental).		
Mar 03.	(12") *(VUST 262)* **PROVIDER / PROVIDER (Zero 7 remix) / LAPDANCE (Freeform reform)**	20	–
	(cd-s+=) *(VUSCD 262)* – ('A'-video).		

PHARRELL WILLIAMS

		Arista	Arista
Aug 03.	(12"; as PHARRELL WILLIAMS & JAY-Z) *(82876 55333-1)* <53004> **FRONTIN'. / HOT DAMN (with Ab Liva) / ('A'-instrumental)**	6	Jun03
	(cd-s) *(82876 55333-2)* <58647> – (first 2 tracks) / Popular thug (by Kelis & Nas) / ('A'-video).		

NEU!

Formed: Dusseldorf, Germany . . .Autumn 1971 by breakaway KRAFTWERK members KLAUS DINGER and THOMAS HOMANN. The latter was soon deposed by MICHAEL ROTHER who appeared on NEU!'s classic eponymous 1972 debut, cut in a short space of time with legendary knob-twiddler, CONRAD PLANK; live gigs were augmented at the time by EBERHARD KRAHNEMANN, who had also guested for KRAFTWERK. After only three acclaimed underground albums, the aforementioned 'NEU!', the seminal 'NEU! 2' (1973) and 'NEU! '75', they split for a second time so that ROTHER could go solo; their first break was after 'NEU! 2' when ROTHER and the CLUSTER duo (of DIETER MOEBIUS and JOACHIM ROEDELIUS) created HARMONIA. Although ROTHER and DINGER went their respective separate ways (the latter to LA DUSSELDORF), they still found time to record one more set in the mid-80's, surprisingly titled 'NEU 4' – left in the can until 1996. Encompassing repetitive trance-rock and avant-garde improvisation, NEU! mined similar territory to early KRAFTWERK, AMON DUUL II or HAWKWIND (DAVE BROCK was a great fan). Along with the likes of CAN and FAUST, the band are held in high esteem by Krautrock connoisseurs, search out STEREOLAB records for examples.

Album rating: NEU! (*8) / NEU II (*8) / NEU '75 (*9) / BLACK FOREST GATEAU compilation (*9) / NEU! 4 (*5)

MICHAEL ROTHER (b. 2 Sep'50) – guitar, bass, keyboards, synths, percussion / **KLAUS DINGER** (b.24 Mar'46) – guitar, vocals, drums, keyboards (ex-KRAFTWERK)

		U.A.	Billingsgate
Oct 72.	(lp) *(UAS 29396)* <1001> **NEU!**		
	– Hallo Gallo / Sonderangebot / Weissensee / Jahresuebersicht / Im glueck / Negativland / Lieber honig. *(re-iss. May80 as 'HALLO GALLO' on 'Brain' Germany; 0040 145) (cd-iss. Jan98 on 'Germanofon'; 941025) (cd re-iss. May01 on 'E.M.I.'; 530780-2)*		
Jan 73.	(7") *(UP 35485)* **SUPER. / NEUSCHNEE**		–
Sep 73.	(lp) *(UAS 29500)* **NEU! 2**		–
	– Fur immer / Spitzenqualitat / Gedenkminute / Lila engel / Neuschnee / Super 16 / Neuschnee / Cassetto / Super 78 / Hallo exentrico / Super. *(cd-iss. Jan98 on 'Germanofon'; 941026) (cd re-iss. May01 on 'E.M.I.'; 530781-2)*		
——	ROTHER joined HARMONIA, with CLUSTER members MOEBIUS + ROEDELIUS. They made two albums 'MUSIK VON HARMONIA' *(Brain; 1044)* & 'HARMONIA DELUXE' *(Brain 1073)*, before he returned to NEU!		
——	added **HANS LAMPE + THOMAS DINGER** – drums (ex-KRAFTWERK)		
Jun 75.	(7") *(UP 35874)* **ISI. / AFTER EIGHT**		–
Jun 75.	(lp) *(UAS 29782)* **NEU! '75**		–
	– Isi / Seeland / Leb' wohl / Hero / E-Musik / After eight. *(cd-iss. May98 on Germanofon'; 941030) (cd re-iss. May01 on 'E.M.I.'; 530782-2)*		
——	split after above; the DINGER's + LAMPE formed LA DUSSELDORF while ROTHER subsequently released a plethora of albums		

– compilations, others, etc. –

Nov 82.	(lp) *Cherry Red; (BRED 27)* **BLACK FOREST GATEAU**		–
	– Hallo Gallo / Isi / E-Musik / Negativland / Seeland / Leb' wohl / After eight.		
Dec 96.	(cd) *Captain Trip; (CTCD 020)* **NEU! 4** (rec.mid-80's)		–
	– Nazionale / Crazy / Flying Dutchman / Schaine welle (nice wave) / Wave naturelle / Good life (random – rough) / 86 commercial trash / Fly Dutch II / Danzing / Quick wave machineue / Bush – drum / La bomba (stop aparthijd worldwide) / Good life / Elanoizan.		
Dec 96.	(cd) *Captain Trip; (CTCD 045)* **1972 LIVE! (live)**		–
Jun 97.	(cd) *Captain Trip; (CTCD 051)* **LA NEU DUSSELDORF**		–
Feb 98.	(cd) *Captain Trip; (CTCD 086)* **LA NEU ZEELAND LIVE 1997**		–
Apr 98.	(cd) *Captain Trip; (CTCD 087)* **REMBRANDT**		–
Jun 98.	(cd) *Captain Trip; (CTCD 098)* **DIE WITH DIGNITY**		–
Jun 98.	(d-cd) *Captain Trip; (CTCD 100-101)* **CHA CHA 2000 (live in Tokyo)**		–
Apr 99.	(cd) *Captain Trip; (CTCD 123)* **GOLD REGIN**		–
Apr 99.	(cd; as LA NEU) *Captain Trip; (CTCD 124)* **YEAR OF THE TIGER**		–
Sep 99.	(d-cd; as LA NEU) *Captain Trip; (CTCD 176/177)* **LIVE IN TOKYO 1996 VOL.2**		–
Sep 99.	(cd; as LA NEU) *Captain Trip; (CTCD 178)* **BLUE**		–
Oct 02.	(d-cd; as LA NEU) *Captain Trip; (CTCD 344)* **LIVE AT KUNSTHALLE DUSSELDORF (live)**		–

NEVILLE BROTHERS

Formed: New Orleans, Louisiana, USA ... mid-60's as The NEVILLE SOUNDS by ART and younger brother AARON, the former initiating the family's musical dynasty in 1955 when, as a member of seven-piece R&B outfit, The HAWKETTS, he recorded the seminal 'MARDIS GRAS GUMBO'. Adopted as an anthem for the annual New Orleans rave-up, the single's enduring popularity means that it still gets re-issued anually by the 'Chess' label. The late 50's saw ART augmenting his band work with a string of solo singles for 'Speciality' including 'ZING ZING' and 'CHA DOOKY-DOO' (both re-issued in 1976 as a double A-side), AARON taking his place (CHARLES NEVILLE also joined briefly) when he joined the US Navy in 1958. The HAWKETTS continued to record for 'Minit', while AARON scored his first solo hit at the turn of the decade with a cover of Sam Cooke's 'OVER YOU'. Blessed with one of the most affecting tenor quivers in the history of the crescent city, he finally hit the charts (narrowly missing the US No.1 spot) in 1966 with definitive soul classic, 'TELL IT LIKE IT IS'. By this point, ART had returned from his naval duties, hooking up with ARRON, younger brother CYRIL, JOSEPH ZIGGY MODELISTE, GEORGE PORTER JR. and LEO NOCENTELLI to form The NEVILLE SOUNDS. New Orleans production guru, ALLEN TOUSSAINT, subsequently took on ART, MODELISTE, PORTER and NOCENTELLI as his session band, the outfit eventually going under the METERS moniker; AARON and CYRIL, meanwhile, formed SOUL MACHINE, while the former continued to record for various labels with little success. Funking up recordings by the likes of DR. JOHN ('In The Right Place' and 'Desitively Bonaroo') and ROBERT PALMER ('Sneaking Sally Through The Alley') as well as LaBELLE and PAUL McCARTNEY, The METERS' reputation as lean'n'spicy R&B sessioners was matched only by Memphis' MG's. They also recorded in their own right, releasing a string of dance instrumental singles (scoring minor US charts hits in 1969 with 'SOPHISTICATED CISSY' and 'CISSY STRUT') for the 'Josie' label before signing to 'Reprise' in 1972. Albums such as 'REJUVENATION' (1974) and 'FIRE ON THE BAYOU' (1975) mixed up visceral 70's funk with down-home New Orleans rhythms to create some of the most compelling dancefloor hits of the era, not least the brilliant 'JUST KISSED MY BABY'. The latter album saw the addition of CYRIL NEVILLE, while AARON and CHARLES joined up for 'TRICK BAG' (1976); all back together again, albeit briefly, the brothers hooked up with relatives GEORGE and AMOS LANDRY (members of a Mardi Gras Indian tribe, the WILD TCHOUPITOULAS) for a one-off set of carnival-crazy funk on 'Island', taking its title from the name of the tribe. The METERS released one further album later that summer, 'NEW DIRECTIONS', before metamorphosing into harmony vocal group, The NEVILLE BROTHERS, all the family save CHARLES featuring on their lukewarm eponymous debut set. Despite its shortcomings, the album (released on 'Capitol') caught the attentions of BETTE MIDLER who encouraged her label, 'A&M', to sign them at the turn of the decade. With all four reunited once more, they cut the vastly improved 'FIYO ON THE BAYOU' (1981), a move back to their New Orleans roots with some revamped blasts from the past. Despite fervent critical acclaim, the record failed to sell, and again the brothers found themselves minus a record deal. An independently released home turf-recorded live set, 'NEVILLE-IZATION' (1984), demonstrated that the brothers' fearsome live reputation was more than justified, an electrifying set drawing on the cream of their career. As the 80's wore on it seemed The NEVILLE BROTHERS' commercial career was in terminal decline, the slide eventually stalled with the Daniel Lanois-produced 'YELLOW MOON' (1989). A haunting collection of inspired covers and new material, the record managed to reconcile the brothers' sound with a modern sensibility, even flirting with rap on the pro-civil rights track, 'SISTER ROSA'. Following the set's minor chart success, AARON scored one of his biggest commercial successes for years via his LINDA RONSTADT duet, 'DON'T KNOW MUCH'. The single's popularity rekindled interest in the eminently talented AARON, his subsequent solo set (co-produced by RONSTADT), 'WARM YOUR HEART' (1991), spawning another US Top 10 hit in 'EVERYBODY PLAYS THE FOOL'. The NEVILLE BROTHERS, meanwhile, had released the similarly impressive DAVE STEWART-produced 'BROTHER'S KEEPER' (1990), although they couldn't sustain the momentum with 'FAMILY GROOVE' (1992). The 90's have seen only one further release by the siblings, 1996's 'MITAKUYE OYASIN OYASIN', and while AARON tested his fans patience with 'AARON NEVILLE'S SOULFUL CHRISTMAS' (1993), he was forgiven with the excellent 'TATTOOED HEART' (1995). He scored another middling success with 1997's 'TO MAKE ME WHO I AM', again pitting his honeyed vocal against RONSTADT on a sterling version of Ewan MacColl's 'THE FIRST TIME EVER I SAW YOUR FACE'. 'VALENCE STREET' (1999), the brothers' 'Columbia' debut, meanwhile, was a trip down memory lane, both musically and lyrically, revisiting the kind of chitlin' New Orleans funk and soul which had made them so great in the first place. Self-produced and with shared writing chores, the album benefitted from a self-possession and rhythmic momentum missing on many of their latter day albums. The title track even harked back to the METERS school of kinetic funk. AARON began the new millennium with 'DEVOTION' (2000), an album of public domain spirituals complemented by a scattering of redemptive rock classics including Bob Dylan's 'I SHALL BE RELEASED' and Simon & Garfunkel's 'BRIDGE OVER TROUBLED WATER'. • **Songwriters:** Each contributed, collaborating with other writers including more brothers IVAN and GAYNEILLE. Also HAWK WOLINSKI was added in 1992 alongside DARYL JOHNSON. Other recent collective contributors PHIL ROY, BOB THEILE and BILLY VALENTINE. Covered; BIRD ON A WIRE (Leonard Cohen) / WITH GOD ON OUR SIDE + THE BALLAD OF HOLLIS BROWN (Bob Dylan) / FLY LIKE AN EAGLE (Steve Miller Band) / IN THE STILL OF THE NIGHT (Cole Porter) / IT FEELS LIKE RAIN (John Hiatt) / LOUISIANA 1927 (Randy Newman) / DON'T GO PLEASE STAY (Bacharach-Milliard) / WITH YOU IN MIND + THAT'S THE WAY SHE LOVES (Allen Toussant) / CLOSE YOUR EYES (. . .Willis) / AVE MARIA (Mozart) / LOVE THE ONE YOU'RE WITH (Stephen Stills) / YOU CAN'T ALWAYS GET WHAT YOU WANT (Rolling Stones) / LET MY PEOPLE GO + AMAZING GRACE (trad) / ONE LOVE – PEOPLE GET READY (Bob Marley). Aaron also covered: YOU NEVER CAN TELL (Chuck Berry) / SONG OF BERNADETTE + AIN'T NO CURE FOR LOVE (Leonard Cohen) / BETCHA BY GOLLY WOW (Stylistics). • **Trivia:** AARON's son IVAN NEVILLE, had a US Top 30 hit in 1988 with 'NOT JUST ANOTHER GIRL'.

Album rating: Aaron Neville: LIKE IT 'TIS (*6) / Meters: THE METERS (*5) / LOOK: KA PY PY (*7) / STRUTTIN' (*7) / CABBAGE ALLEY (*5) / REJUVENATION (*6) / FIRE ON THE BAYOU (*5) / TRICK BAG (*5) / THE WILD TCHOUPITOULAS as the Wild Tchoupitoulas (*6) / NEW DIRECTIONS (*4) / compilation FUNKIFY YOUR LIFE (*8) / Neville Brothers: THE NEVILLE BROTHERS (*5) / FIYO ON THE BAYO (*7) / NEVILLE-IZATION exploitation (*5) / TREACHEROUS: A HISTORY OF THE NEVILLE BROTHERS 1955-1985 compilation (*8) / YELLOW MOON (*7) / BROTHER'S KEEPER (*6) / TREACHEROUS TOO: A HISTORY OF THE NEVILLE BROTHERS VOL.2 (1955-1987) compilation (*6) / WARM YOUR HEART (*5; by Aaron Neville) /

FAMILY GROOVE (*5) / LIVE ON PLANET EARTH (*6) / MITAKUYE OYASIN OYASIN – ALL MY RELATIONS (*5) / THE VERY BEST OF THE NEVILLE BROTHERS compilation (*8) / TO MAKE ME WHO I AM (*5; Aaron Neville) / VALENCE STREET (*6)

The HAWKETTS

(7-piece New Orleans band with **ART NEVILLE** (b.17 Dec'37) – vocals / **GEORGE DAVIS** – / etc.

1955. (7") **MARDI GRAS MAMBO. /** [–] [ ]
<re-iss. annually by 'Chess' US>

— ART still performed with them, and released solo singles for 'Speciality' in 1957; ZING ZING + CHA DOOKY-DOO. Both re-issued 1976 as double 'A'side. A year later, ART joined the US Navy and was replaced by brother **AARON** (b.24 Jan'41) – vocals. He also issued duo 45 with ALLEN TOUSSAINT

AARON NEVILLE

Minit | Minit

Jun 60. (7") *<612>* **OVER YOU. / EVERY DAY** [–] [ ]
Dec 60. (7") *<618>* **GET OUT OF MY LIFE. / SHOW ME THE WAY** [–] [ ]
Mar 61. (7") *<624>* **DON'T CRY. / REALITY** [–] [ ]
Aug 61. (7") *<631>* **I FOUND ANOTHER LOVE. / LET'S LIVE** [–] [ ]
Feb 62. (7") *<639>* **HOW MANY TIMES. / I'M WAITIN' AT THE STATION** [–] [ ]
Aug 62. (7") *<650>* **SWEET LITTLE MAMA. / HUMDINGER** [–] [ ]
Jan 63. (7") *<657>* **WRONG NUMBER. / HOW COULD I HELP BUT LOVE YOU** [–] [ ]

— Early 1962, ART re-joined The HAWKETTS, releasing solo single, 'ALL THESE THINGS'. To end the year, they became The NEVILLE SOUNDS, who were an 8-piece band with ART, AARON & CYRIL (b.10 Oct'48), plus MODELISTE & PORTER. AARON

Stateside | Par-Lo

Dec 66. (7") *(SS 584) <101>* **TELL IT LIKE IT IS. / WHY WORRY** [ ] Nov66 [2]
(re-iss. Sep69 on 'B&C'; CB 107) (re-iss. Aug74 on 'Contempo'; CS 9009) (re-iss. 1976 on 'Island'; WIP 6332)
Mar 67. (7") *(103>* **SHE TOOK YOU FOR A RIDE. / SPACE MAN** [–] [92]

Liberty | Minit

May 67. (lp) *(LBY 3089) <24007>* **HERE 'TIS** [ ] [ ]
– Over you / Get out of my life / I found another love / Don't cry / Sweet little mama / I'm waitin' at the station / How many times / Let's live / Everyday / Reality / Wrong number (I'm sorry, goodbye) / How dould I help but love you. *(cd-iss. Jul91 on 'Music Club')*

not iss. | Bell

Nov 68. (7") *<746>* **WHERE IS MY BABY. / YOU CAN GIVE, BUT YOU CAn"T TAKE** [–] [ ]
Jun 69. (7") *<781>* **YOU DON'T LOVE ME ANYMORE. / SPEAK TO ME** [–] [ ]

— The NEVILLE SOUNDS break-up with AARON + CYRIL forming SOUL MACHINE.

The METERS

— were founded by ex-NEVILLE SOUNDS people **ART NEVILLE** – keyboards, vocals / **JOSEPH ZIGGY MODELISTE** – drums, vocals / **GEORGE PORTER JR.** – bass, vocals / **LEO NOCENTELLI** – guitar, vocals

Stateside | Josie

Feb 69. (7") *(SS 2140) <1001>* **SOPHISTICATED CISSY. / SEHORNS FARM** [ ] [34]
Apr 69. (7") *<1005>* **CISSY STRUT. / HERE COMES THE METER MAN** [–] [23]
Jun 69. (lp) *<JOS 4010>* **THE METERS** (instrumental) [–] [ ]
– Sophisticated Cissy / Ease back / Cardova / Sehorns farm / 6v6 LA / Stormy / Cissy strut / Art / Ann / Here comes the meter man / Live wire / Simple song.
Jul 69. (7") *<1008>* **EASE BACK. / ANN** [–] [61]

Direction | Josie

Oct 69. (7") *<1013>* **LOOK-KA PY PY. / DRY SPELL** [–] [ ]
Jan 70. (7") *(58-4751) <1015>* **LOOK-KA PY PY. / THIS IS MY LAST AFFAIR** [ ] [56]
Jan 70. (lp) *<JOS 4011>* **LOOK-KA PY PY** (instrumental) [–] [ ]
– Dry spell / Look-ka Py Py / Oh, Calcutta! / Rigor mortis / Yeah, you're right / This is my last affair / Thinking / Pungee / The mob / 9 'til 5 / Little old money maker / Funky miracle.
Apr 70. (7") *<1018>* **CHICKEN STRUT. / HEY! LAST MINUTE** [–] [50]
Jun 70. (lp) *<JOS 4012>* **STRUTTIN'** [–] [ ]
– Chicken strut / Liver splash / Wichita lineman / Joog / Go for yourself / Same old thing / Hand clapping song / Darlin' darlin' / Tippi-toes / Britches / Britches / Hey! last minute / Ride your pony.
Jun 70. (7") *<1021>* **HAND CLAPPING SONG. / JOOG** [–] [89]
Sep 70. (7") *<1024>* **A MESSAGE FROM THE METERS. / ZONY MASH** [–] [ ]
Feb 71. (7") *<1026>* **GROOVY LADY. / STRETCH YOUR RUBBER BAND** [–] [ ]
Apr 71. (7") *<1029>* **I NEED MORE TIME. / DOODLE OOP** [–] [ ]
Jul 71. (7") *<1031>* **SASSY LADY. / GOOD OLD FUNKY MUSIC** [–] [ ]

Reprise | Reprise

1972. (lp) *(K 44242) <MS 2076>* **CABBAGE ALLEY** [ ] [ ]
– You've got to change (You've got to reform) / Stay away / Birds / Flower song / Soul island / Do the dirt / Smiling / Lonesome and unwanted people / Gettin' funkier all the time / Cabbage alley.
1972. (7") *<1086>* **DO THE DIRT. / SMILING** [–] [ ]
1972. (7") *<1106>* **CABBAGE ALLEY. / THE FLOWER SONG** [–] [ ]
1973. (7") *<1135>* **CHUG CHUG CHUG-A-LUG. / (part 2)** [–] [ ]

— The METERS did session work for DR. JOHN and ROBERT PALMER

Jun 74. (7") *<1307>* **AFRICA. / HEY ROCK-A-WAY** [–] [ ]
Aug 74. (7") *<1314>* **PEOPLE SAY. / LOVING YOU IS ON MY MIND** [–] [ ]
Sep 74. (7") *(K 14367)* **PEOPLE SAY. / AFRICA** [ ] [–]
Oct 74. (lp) *(K 54027) <MS 2200>* **REJUVENATION** [ ] [ ]
– People say / Love is for me / Just kissed me baby / What'cha say / Jungle man / Hey rocky a-way / It ain't no use Loving you is on my mind / Africa.

— added **CYRIL NEVILLE** – percussion, vocals (ex-SOUL MACHINE)

Jul 75. (7") *<1338>* **THEY ALL ASKED FOR YOU. / RUNNING FAST** [–] [ ]
Aug 75. (lp) *(K 54044) <MS 2228>* **FIRE ON THE BAYOU** [ ] [ ]
– Out in the country / Fire in the bayou / Love slip upon ya / Talkin' about New Orleans / They all asked for you / Can you do without / Liar / You're a friend of mine / Middle of the road / Running fast / Mardi Gras mambo.
Nov 75. (7") *(K 14405)* **FIRE ON THE BAYOU. / THEY ALL ASKED FOR YOU** [ ] [–]

— added **AARON + CHARLES NEVILLE** (b.1939) – vocals

Sep 76. (7") *<1357>* **DISCO IS THE THING TODAY. / MISTER MOON** [–] [ ]
Sep 76. (lp) *(K 54078) <MS 2252>* **TRICK BAG** [ ] [ ]
– Disco is the thing today / Find your self / All these things / I want to be loved by you / Suite for 20 G / The world is a little bit under the weather / Trick bag / Mister Moon / Chug-a-lug / Hang 'em high / Honky tonk women.
Nov 76. (7") *<1372>* **TRICK BAG. / FIND YOURSELF** [–] [ ]

WILD TCHOUPITOULAS

aka The METERS

Island | Island

Feb 77. (7") **MEET DE BOYS ON THE BATTLEFRONT. / BIG CHIEF GOT A GOLDEN CROWN** [–] [ ]
Apr 77. (lp) *<(ILPS 9360)>* **THE WILD TCHOUPITOULAS** [ ] [ ]
– Brother John / Meet de boys on de battlefront / Here dey come / Hey pocky-a-way / Indian red / Big chief got a golden crown / Hey mama, hey hey. *(re-iss. Apr88 lp/c/cd; ILPS/ICT/CID 9360) (re-iss. Feb90 cd)(c; IMCD 89)(ICM 2067)*
May 77. (7") *<071>* **BROTHER JOHN. / HERE DEY COME** [–] [ ]

AARON NEVILLE

not iss. | Polydor

May 77. (7") *<14426>* **GREATEST LOVE. / PERFORMANCE** [–] [ ]

METERS

Reprise | Warners

Jun 77. (lp) *(K 56378) <MS 3042>* **NEW DIRECTIONS** [ ] [ ]
– No more okey doke / I'm gone / Be my lady / My name up in lights /

Funkify your life / Stop that train / we got the kind of love / Give it all you can.

Sep 77. (7") *<8434>* **BE MY LADY. / NO MORE OKEY DOKE** [–] [78]

The NEVILLE BROTHERS

(with all brothers except CHARLES)

Capitol Capitol

Oct 78. (7") *<4688>* **SPEED OF LIGHT. / IF IT TAKES ALL NIGHT** [–] [ ]

Mar 79. (lp/c) *<(EST/TC-EST 11865)>* **THE NEVILLE BROTHERS** [ ] Mar78 [ ]
– Dancing Jones / Washable ink / All nights all right / Audience for my pain / Break away / If it takes all night / Viclux carre rouge / Arianne / Speed of light.

— 4 brothers again (**AARON, ART, CYRIL + CHARLES**)

not iss. A&M

Aug 81. (lp) *<4866>* **FIYO ON THE BAYOU** [–] [ ]
– Hey pocky way / Sweet honey dripper / Fire on the bayou / The ten commandments of love / Sitting in limbo / Brother John / Iko Iko / Mona Lisa / Run Joe. *(UK-iss.Jul86 on 'Demon' lp/c; FIEND/+CASS 65) (cd-iss. 1987; FIENDCD 65) (re-iss. Mar93 cd/c;)*

Sep 81. (7") *<2358>* **WHY ME? / BROHER JOHN – IKO IKO** [–] [ ]

Nov 81. (7") *<2388>* **SWEET HONEY DRIPPER. / BROTHER JOHN – IKO IKO** [–] [ ]

Jan 82. (7") **FIRE ON THE BAYOU. / MONA LISA** [–] [ ]

Jun 84. (lp/c) *(FIEND/+CASS 31) <BT 1031/+C>* **NEVILLE-IZATION** (live '82 New Orleans) [ ] [ ]
– Fever / Woman's gotta have it / Mojo Hannah / Tell it like it is / Why you wanna hurt my heart? / Fear, hate, envy, jealousy / Caravan / Big chief / Africa. *(cd-iss. Nov86; FIENDCD 31)*
(above issued on 'Demon' UK / 'Black Top' US)

— Late in 1988, AARON teamed up with WAS (NOT WAS) and BONNIE RAITT on 'A&M' single, 'BABY MINE'.

Mar 89. (lp/c/cd) *<(AMA/AMC/CDA 5240)>* **YELLOW MOON** [ ] [66]
– My blood / Yellow Moon / Fire and brimstone / A change is gonna come / Sister Rosa / With God on our side / Wake up / Voodoo / The ballad of Hollis Brown / Will the circle be unbroken / Healing chant / Wild Injuns. *(re-iss. cd May95)*

Apr 89. (7"/12") *(USA/+T 656)* **A CHANGE IS GONNA COME. / SISTER ROSA** [ ] [ ]

Jun 89. (7") *(USA 657)* **YELLOW MOON. / WITH GOD ON OUR SIDE** [ ] [–]
(12"+=/cd-s+=) *(USA T/CD 657)* – Healing chant.

Jul 89. (7") *<1277>* **VOODOO. / SISTER ROSA** [–] [ ]

Oct 89. (7") *<1410>* **SISTER ROSA. / ('A'-long version)** [–] [ ]

Nov 89. (7") *(AM 545)* **WITH GOD ON OUR SIDE. / VOODOO** [47] [–]
(12"+=/cd-s+=) *(AMY/CDEE 545)* – Healing chant.

Nov 89. (7") *<1434>* **YELLOW MOON. / HEALING CHANCE** [–] [ ]

Jan 90. (7") *(AM 548)* **A CHANGE IS GONNA COME. / WAKE UP (live)** [ ] [–]
(12"+=/cd-s+=) *(AMY/CDEE 548)* – Sister Rosa (live).

— Late 1989 & early 1990, AARON duetted on 2 hit singles; 'DON'T KNOW MUCH' and 'ALL MY LIFE', with LINDA RONSTADT. Below 'A'side from film of same name.

— with band **WILLIE GREEN** – drums / **TONY HALL** – bass / **ERIC STRUTHERS** – guitar

Jun 90. (7") *(AM 568) <1499>* **BIRD ON A WIRE. / BLACK DIAMOND PEARL** [72] [ ]
(12"+=/cd-s+=) *(AMY/CDEE 568)* – ('A'version).

Aug 90. (cd/c/lp) *(395312-2/-4/-1) <5312>* **BROTHER'S KEEPER** [35] [60]
– Brother blood / Brother Jake / Steer me right / Fearless / Sons and daughters / Fallin' rain / Jah love / River of life / Witness / My brother's keeper / Sons and daughters (reprise) / Mystery train / Bird on a wire.

Aug 90. (7") **RIVER OF LIFE. / TELL IT LIKE IT IS (live)** [ ] [ ]
(12"+=/cd-s+=) – Sister Rosa.

Oct 90. (7") **FEARLESS. / SHAKE YOUR TAMBOURINE (live)** [ ] [ ]
(12"+=/cd-s+=) – A change is gonna come (live).

The METERS

— re-formed in 1990, ART NEVILLE, NOCENTELLI + PORTER + **RUSSELL BATISTE** – drums; repl. MODELISTE

Special Delivery Rounder

Mar 92. (c/cd) *(SPDC/+D 1041) <ROU 2105>* **THE METERS JAM** [ ] [ ]
– Stretch your rubber band / Come together / People get ready / Big chief / Groovy lady / It's too late / Bo Diddley / All I do every day / Trip / Meters jam.

— **BRIAN STOLTZ** – guitar; repl. NOCENTELLI (before folding again)

– compilations, etc. –

1974. (lp) *Island; (ILPS 9250)* **CISSY STRUT** [ ] [–]

Jan 76. (lp) *Reprise; (K 54076) / Virgo; <SV 12002>* **THE BEST OF THE METERS** [ ] [ ]

May 79. (lp) *Pye; (PKL 5578)* **GOOD OLD FUNKY MUSIC** [ ] [–]
(re-iss. Oct90 on 'Special Delivery' lp/c/cd; PSD/+C/CD 1039) (cd-iss. Jan95 on 'Rounder'; ROUCD 2104)

Jul 80. (7"ep) *Charly; (CTD 113)* **LOOK-KA PY PY. / TIPPI-TOES / CISSY STRUT** [ ] [–]

Nov 80. (lp) *Charly; (CRB 1009)* **SECOND LINE STRUT** [ ] [–]

Apr 86. (lp) *Charly; (CRB 1112)* **HERE COME THE METERMEN** [ ] [–]

Feb 87. (lp) *Charly; (CRB 1009)* **STRUTTIN'** (diff.) [ ] [–]

Mar 91. (cd) *Charly; (CDNEV 2)* **FUNKY MIRACLE** [ ] [–]

Sep 92. (cd) *Sequel; (NEXCD 220)* **UPTOWN RULERS: LIVE ON THE QUEEN MARY 1975 (live)** [ ] [–]

Nov 92. (cd) *Instant;* **THE ORIGINAL FUNKMASTERS** [ ] [–]
– Sophisticated Cissy / Funky miracle / Look-ka Py Py / Till 5 / Ease back / Ride your pony / Stormy / Dry spell / Cissy strut / Tippi-toes / Chicken strut / I need more time / Live wire / Hand clapping song / Message from the Metermen. *(re-iss. Sep96 on 'Charly'; CPCD 8229)*

Jun 94. (cd) *Charly; (CPCD 8044)* **FUNDAMENTALLY FUNKY** [ ] [–]

Nov 94. (cd) *Charly; (CPCD 8066)* **CRESCENT CITY GROOVE MERCHANTS** [ ] [–]

Aug 95. (cd; with The JB Horns) *Lakeside; (LAKE 2026)* **SECOND HELPING** [ ] [–]

1995. (d-cd) *Rhino;* **FUNKIFY YOUR LIFE: THE METERS ANTHOLOGY** [ ] [ ]

NEVILLE BROTHERS

A&M A&M

Sep 92. (cd/c) *(397180-2/-4) <5384>* **FAMILY GROOVE** [ ] [ ]
– Fly like an eagle / One more day / I can see it in your eyes / Day to day thing / Line of fire / Take me to heart / Maori chant / It takes more / Family groove / True love / On the other side of Paradise / Let my people go / Saxafunk / Good song.

Oct 92. (7"/c-s) **FLY LIKE AN EAGLE. / ('A'instrumental)** [ ] [ ]
(cd-s+=) – ('A'-3 dub mixes) / ('A'other mix).
(12"++=) – (1 extra dub mix).

Apr 94. (cd/c) *(540225-2/-4) <0225>* **LIVE ON PLANET EARTH (live)** [ ] [ ]
– Shake your tambourine / Voodoo / Dealer / Junk man / Brother Jake / Sister Rosa / Yellow Moon / Her African eyes / Sands of time / Congo Square / Love the one you're with / You can't always get what you want / Let my people go / Get up stand up / Amazing Grace / One love – People get ready. *(re-iss. cd May95; same)*

— In Jun 94, he duetted with TRICIA YEARWOOD on 'MCA' single, 'I FALL TO PIECES'.

May 96. (cd/c) *(540512-2/-4) <0512>* **MITAKUYE OYASIN OYASIN** [ ] [ ]
– Love spoken here / Sound / Holy spirit / Soul to soul / Whatever you do / Saved by the grace of your love / You're gonna make your momma cry / Fire on the mountain / Ain't no sunshine / Orisha dance / Sacred ground.

Columbia Columbia

Feb 99. (cd) *(491657-2) <68906>* **VALENCE STREET** [ ] [ ]
– Over Africa / Utterly beloved / Little piece of heaven / Valence Street / If I had a hammer / Until we meet again / The dealer / Mona Lisa (with WYCLEF JEAN) / Dimming of the day / Real funk / Give me a reason / Tears.

AARON NEVILLE

Jun 91. (7"/c-s) **EVERYBODY PLAYS THE FOOL. / ANGELA BOUND** [ ] [–]
(12"+=/cd-s+=) – ('A'-Lovin' Eyes mix) / Hard times come around no more.

Jul 91. (c-s,cd-s) *<1563>* **EVERYBODY PLAYS THE FOOL / HOUSE ON A HILL** – 8

Jul 91. (cd/c/lp) *(397148-2/-4/-1) <5354>* **WARM YOUR HEART** 44
– Louisiana 1927 / Everybody plays the fool / It feels like rain / Somewhere, somebody / Don't go, please stay / With you in mind / That's the way she looks / Angela bound / Close your eyes / La vie dansette / Warm your heart / I bid you goodnight / Ave Maria.

Aug 91. (7"/c-s) **SOMEWHERE SOMEBODY. / BROTHER JAKE**
(12"+=/cd-s+=) – Yellow moon.

Jan 92. (7") **LOUISIANA 1927. / HOUSE ON A HILL**
(12"+=/cd-s+=) – A change is gonna come (live).

May 93. (c-s,cd-s) *<0240>* **DON'T TAKE AWAY MY HEAVEN / THE ROADIE SONG** – 56

Aug 93. (cd/c) *(540100-2/-4) <0086>* **THE GRAND TOUR** 37
– Don't take away my Heaven / I owe you one / Don't fall apart on me tonight / My brother, my brother / Betcha by golly wow / Song of Bernadette / You never can tell / The bells / These foolish things / The roadie song / Ain't no way / The grand tour / The Lord's prayer / Ronnie-O.

Sep 93. (c-s) *<0312>* **THE GRAND TOUR / THE ROADIE SONG** – 90

Nov 93. (cd) *(540127-2) <0127>* **AARON NEVILLE'S SOULFUL CHRISTMAS** (festive) 53

Apr 95. (cd/c) *(540349-2/-4) <0349>* **THE TATTOOED HEART** 64
– Can't stop my heart from loving you (the rain song) / Show some emotion / Everyday of my life / Down into muddy water / Some days are made for rain / Try (a little harder) / Beautiful night / My precious star / Why should I fall in love / Use me / For the good times / In your eyes / Little thing called life / Crying in the chapel.

Jun 95. (c-s,cd-s) *<1038>* **CAN'T STOP MY HEART FROM LOVING YOU (THE RAIN SONG) / IN YOUR EYES** – 99

Oct 97. (cd) *(540784-2) <540784>* **TO MAKE ME WHO I AM**
– Say what's in my heart / Just to be with you / Sweet Amelia / . . .To make me who I am / The first time ever I saw your face / Yes, I love you / Your sweet and smiling eyes / I can't change the way you don't feel / Please remember me / What did I do (to deserve you) / God made you for me / Lovely lady dressed in blue.

Alliance Chordant

Oct 00. (cd) *<(8 20287-2)>* **DEVOTION** Aug00
– Mary don't you weep / Jesus is a friend of mine / Banks of the River Jordan / What would Jesus do? / Singing you a prayer (with IVAN NEVILLE) / There is still a dream (with RACHAEL LAMPA) / By heart, by soul / Bridge over troubled water / Morning has broken / Were you there? / Jesus loves me / I shall be released.

– (NEVILLE BROTHERS) comps, others. –

Feb 86. (d-lp/c) *Rhino; <(RNFP/RNFC 71494)>* **TREACHEROUS: A HISTORY OF THE NEVILLE BROTHERS 1955-1985** Apr87

Apr 86. (lp; AARON NEVILLE) *Demon; (VEX 6)* **ORCHID IN THE STORM** –
(cd-iss. May95 on 'Rhino'; 8122 70956-2)

Sep 86. (lp/c; AARON NEVILLE) *Stateside; (SSL/TCSSL 6011)* **HUMDINGER** –

Nov 86. (lp; ART NEVILLE) *Ace; (CHD 188)* **MARDI GRAS ROCK'N'ROLL** –
(cd-iss. Oct90; CDCHD 188)

Feb 87. (lp/c; AARON NEVILLE) *Charly; (CRB/TCCRB 1111)* **MAKE ME STRONG** –
(cd-iss. Feb87; CDCRB 1111)

Apr 87. (cd) *E.M.I.; (CDP 746754-2) <17249>* **UPTOWN** (special release with various star guests)
(re-iss. May91 on 'Fame' cd/c/lp; CD/TC+/FA 3255)

Jun 88. (lp) *Demon; (FIEND 121)* **LIVE AT TIPITINA'S VOL.II (live)** –
(re-iss. Aug90 on 'Essential' cd/c/lp; ESS CD/MC/LP 130) (cd re-iss. Jun94 on 'Castle'; CLACD 347)

Sep 88. (lp; ART NEVILLE) *Charly; (CRB 1177)* **ROCK'N'ROLL HOOTENANNY** –

Aug 89. (cd)(c/lp; AARON NEVILLE) *Charly; (CDCHARLY 162)(TC+/CRB 1217)* **SHOW ME THE WAY** –

Apr 90. (d-cd/d-c) *Charly; (CD/TC NEV 1)* **LEGACY (A HISTORY OF THE NEVILLES)** –

1990. (cd; AARON NEVILLE) *Curb;* **GREATEST HITS** –

1991. (cd; AARON NEVILLE) *Rounder;* **MY GREATEST GIFT** –

Jul 91. (cd) *Rhino;* **TREACHEROUS TOO!** –

Sep 91. (cd; ART NEVILLE, EDDIE BO, CHARLES BROWN & WILLIE TEE) *Rounder; <(ROUCD 2087)>* **KEYS TO THE CRESCENT**

Jan 93. (cd; ART NEVILLE) *Ace; (CDCHD 434)* **HIS SPECIALITY RECORDINGS: 1956-1958** –

Nov 93. (cd; AARON NEVILLE) *Charly; (CPCD 8016)* **HERCULES** –

May 94. (cd) *Traditional Line; (TL 1328)* **LIVE AT TIPITINA'S (live)** –

Nov 95. (cd) *One Way;* **THE NEVILLE BROTHERS** –

NEW FOUND GLORY

Formed: Coral Springs, Florida, USA . . . 1997 as A NEW FOUND GLORY by JORDAN PUNDIK, STEVE KLEIN, CHAD GILBERT, IAN GRUSHKA and CYRUS BOLOOKI. Fired by the success of their Xmas '97 sell-out debut EP, 'IT'S ALL ABOUT THE GIRLS', this Southern punk-pop quintet put all the twenty-something, hard earned wisdom and romantic regret they could muster into debut long player, 'NOTHING GOLD CAN STAY' (1999). 'M.C.A.' were impressed enough to offer them a major-label deal, promptly re-releasing the album later that year (1999), and following up with the rather contrived covers mini-set, 'FROM THE SCREEN TO YOUR STEREO' (2000). We really could have done without yet another airing of Aerosmith's 'I DON'T WANT TO MISS A THING' or Bryan Adams' EVERYTHING I DO..', and we most definitely could have done without tedious, pointless and gratingly upbeat American "punk" versions of already overplayed and overly saccaharine songs. The eponymous 'NEW FOUND GLORY' followed in 2000, another hackneyed if professional and listenable set of overly enthusiastic so-called punk. Ditto 2002's 'STICKS AND STONES' which nevertheless hit the Top 10 in the US and UK. Kids nowadays – what's it all about? • **Covered:** THAT THING YOU DO! (. . . Schlesinger) / THE NEVERENDING STORY THEME SONG (Limahl) / THE GOONIES 'R' GOOD ENOUGH (Cyndi Lauper) / THE GLORY OF LOVE (Peter Cetera) / MY HEART WILL GO ON (Celine Dion).

Album rating: NOTHING GOLD CAN STAY (*7) / FROM THE SCREEN TO YOUR STEREO mini (*5) / NEW FOUND GLORY (*6) / STICKS AND STONES (*6)

JORDAN PUNDIK – vocals / **STEVE KLEIN** – guitar / **CHAD GILBERT** – guitar / **IAN GRUSHKA** – bass / **CYRUS BOLOOKI** – drums

not iss. Fiddler

Dec 97. (cd-ep; as A NEW FOUND GLORY) *<FR 004CD>* **IT'S ALL ABOUT THE GIRLS E.P.** –
– Shadow / My solution / Scraped knees / J.B. / Standstill. *(UK-iss.May01; same as US)*

drive-thru drive-thru

Mar 00. (cd; as A NEW FOUND GLORY) *(DRIVETHRU 013CD) <112114>* **NOTHING GOLD CAN STAY** Oct99
– Hit or miss / Never snows in Florida / 3rd and long / You've got a friend in Pennsylvania / The blue stare / 2's and 3's / Tell-tale heart / Winter of '95 / Passing time / Broken sound / Never sometimes / The good-bye song. *(re-iss. Jul01; same)*

M.C.A. M.C.A.

Mar 00. (m-cd; as A NEW FOUND GLORY) *<112245CD>* **FROM THE SCREEN TO YOUR STEREO** –
– That thing you do! / Never ending story theme song / I don't want to miss a thing / The Goonies 'R' good enough / The glory of love / (Everything I do) I do it for you / My heart will go on. *(UK-iss.Jul01; same) (re-iss. Jul03 on 'Eat Sleep'; EAT 029CD)*

Apr 01. (cd) *<(112338-2)>* **NEW FOUND GLORY** Sep00
– Better off dead / Dressed to kill / Sincerely me / Hit or miss / Second to

last / Eyesore / Vegas / Sucker / Black and blue / Boy crazy / All about her / Ballad for the lost romantics.

Jun 01. (cd-s) *<(155823-2)>* **HIT OR MISS (WAITED TOO LONG) / SO MANY WAYS / YOU'VE GOT A FRIEND IN PENNSYLVANIA / HIT OR MISS (video)** [58] Aug01 [ ]

Jun 02. (cd) *<(112945-2)>* **STICKS AND STONES** [10] [4]
– Understatement / My friends over you / Sonny / Something I call personality / Head on collision / It's been a summer / Forget my name / Never give up / The great Houdini / Singled out / Belated / The story so far (joke skits). *(special cd+=; 112972-2)* – Anniversary / Forget everything / The story so far (acoustic). *(d-cd-iss. Nov02 +=; AA88113123-2)* – Head on collision / Forget everything / Pride war (FURTHER SEEMS FOREVER) / What it is to burn (FINCH) / Roundabout (TSUNAMI BOMB) / Static (H20) / Lonely man's wallet (The EXIT) / Best of me (The STARTING LINE) / On my own (DON'T LOOK NOW).

Jun 02. (cd-s) *<155965>* **MY FRIENDS OVER YOU / IT'S BEEN A SUMMER** [–] [85]

Jul 02. (7"pic-d) *(MCS 40286)* **MY FRIENDS OVER YOU. / SUCKER (live)** [30] [–]
(cd-s+=) *(MCSTD 40286)* – Hit or miss (live) / ('A'-video).
(cd-s) *(MCSXD 40286)* – ('A'side) / Eyesore (live) / Dressed to kill (live).

Oct 02. (cd-s) *(MCSTD 40298)* **HEAD ON COLLISION / EX-MISS / HEAD ON COLLISION (version)** [64] [–]
(cd-s) *(MCSXD 40298)* – ('A'side) / Something I call personality / Broken sound.

Randy NEWMAN

Born: RANDOLPH NEWMAN, 28 Nov'44, New Orleans, Louisiana, USA, although (at the age of 10) he moved with his Jewish family to Los Angeles. His uncle, Alfred Newman, had written over 200 scores for 20th Century Fox films, including 'Wuthering Heights'. In 1961, RANDY issued a one-off 45, 'GOLDEN GRIDIRON BOY' for 'Dot', which was produced by singer PAT BOONE. After its flop, he became a staff-writer for 'Liberty' records, writing hits for VIC DANA, GENE McDANIELS, CILLA BLACK!, GENE PITNEY, etc in the mid-60's. In 1967, ALAN PRICE started borrowing his songs, and he scored a hit with 'SIMON SMITH AND HIS AMAZING DANCING BEAR'. That year, NEWMAN became staff arranger/producer for 'Warners', working with the likes of VAN DYKE PARKS, The BEAU BRUMMELS and HARPER'S BIZARRE. In 1968, he finally issued his eponymous debut for Warners subsidiary 'Reprise', two years later, another solo artist, NILSSON, was to release a whole album of his songs as 'NILSSON SINGS NEWMAN'. In April 1970, NEWMAN issued his second album, '12 SONGS', which included 'MAMA TOLD ME NOT TO COME', a record that went on to become a US chart topper for THREE DOG NIGHT. A much improved affair, NEWMAN finally began to formulate his unique style against a backdrop of classy slide guitar (provided by RY COODER), the arrangements more economical; the brilliant 'MY OLD KENTUCKY HOME' (covered by COODER in fine style on his debut album) was a darkly comic tale of everyday family dysfunction, while the warped tragedy of 'SUZANNE' was NEWMAN at his subversive best. 1972's 'SAIL AWAY' was another early classic, its lavish title track finding NEWMAN in one of his most convincing character roles to date, that of a slave trader in Africa. By this point, the man's slyly ironic sense of humour and idiosyncratic musical orchestrations were garnering considerable critical acclaim and a cult following, if not exactly endearing him to folks who took his work a bit too literally. A case in point was his 1974 quasi-concept set weaving together a cast of characters from the American South, his adoption of a racist perspective for 'REDNECKS', for example, baiting liberals while simultaneously mocking the attitude's of the song. In 'LOUISIANA 1927', meanwhile, NEWMAN showed how affecting his writing could really be when he wasn't satirising. The album marked his first foray into the US Top 40, while 'LITTLE CRIMINALS' (1977), his poorest set to date, ironically made the Top 10 on the strength of the near-No.1 hit, 'SHORT PEOPLE'. Possibly the most controversial of NEWMAN's stabs at twisted humour, its blunt send-up of bigots was understandably misinterpreted by some; perhaps the end didn't justify the means in this case. 'BORN AGAIN' (1979) brought further criticism that NEWMAN was crossing the fine line between satire and self-satisfied condascension, his collaboration with members of the EAGLES marking a move towards a more typical L.A. sound. The 'City Of Angels' formed part of the inspiration for the semi-conceptual 'TROUBLE IN PARADISE' (1983), NEWMAN deconstructing the facade around the world's more exotic cities against a slick schmooze-rock backdrop. During the mid-80's, he concentrated on film work with a score for 'The Natural' (1984) and contributions to the 'Three Amigos' (1987), NEWMAN also co-writing the script for the latter as well as making a cameo appearance; his previous film credits included contributions to cult classic, 'Performance' (1970) and a score for 'Ragtime' (1982), while the 90's saw him scoring a further two major productions, 'Parenthood' and 'Awakenings'. His only other studio set proper to date was 1988's 'LAND OF DREAMS', a patchy affair which nevertheless found NEWMAN in unprecedented autobiographical form on 'DIXIE FLYER' and 'NEW ORLEANS WINS THE WAR', both tracks alone worth the price of admission. For the first half of the 90's, NEWMAN worked feverishly on his very own rock opera project, 'RANDY NEWMAN'S FAUST' (1995). An ambitious update of the German literary classic with the L.A. old guard (DON HENLEY, JAMES TAYLOR, LINDA RONSTADT etc.) in starring roles, the semi-successful results appeared on 'A&M' in 1995, while a Broadway performance has yet to come to fruition. On the Mitchell Froom & Chad Blake-produced 'BAD LOVE' (1999), NEWMAN finally returned to what he does best: pared down character sketches which rarely flinch from deadbeat, deadpan realism. Sure, there were chinks in his satirical armour with the likes of 'I MISS YOU' and 'EVERY TIME IT RAINS', but the bespectacled chronicler sounded more candid and convincing than he had done for years. A natural follow-on from the resumption of his songwriting career, 'THE RANDY NEWMAN SONGBOOK Vol.1' (2003) found the don of irony – on the cusp of his sixtieth birthday – taking a relaxed, lingering trip through his back catalogue, sketching the foibles of humanity with perhaps more grace and subtlety than any writer of his generation.

Album rating: RANDY NEWMAN (*7) / 12 SONGS (*8) / RANDY NEWMAN – LIVE (*6) / SAIL AWAY (*8) / GOOD OLD BOYS (*8) / LITTLE CRIMINALS (*6) / BORN AGAIN (*6) / RAGTIME soundtrack (*4) / TROUBLE IN PARADISE (*5) / THE NATURAL soundtrack (*4) / LONELY AT THE TOP – THE BEST OF RANDY NEWMAN compilation (*8) / LAND OF DREAMS (*6) / PARENTHOOD soundtrack (*4) / AWAKENINGS soundtrack (*4) / THE PAPER soundtrack (*4) / MAVERICK soundtrack (*5) / RANDY NEWMAN'S FAUST (*5) / GUILTY: 30 YEARS OF . . . boxed compilation (*7) / BAD LOVE (*5) / THE BEST OF RANDY NEWMAN compilation (*7) / THE RANDY NEWMAN SONGBOOK VOL.1 (*7)

RANDY NEWMAN – vocals, piano

not iss. Dot

1962. (7") **GOLDEN GRIDIRON BOY. / COUNTRY BOY** [–] [ ]

—— RANDY became semi-successful songwriter for other established acts. He eventually embarked on a long awaited solo career, after a US instrumental 1966 lp 'THE RANDY NEWMAN ORCHESTRA PLAYS MUSIC FROM THE HIT TELEVISION SERIES 'PEYTON PLACE' for 'Epic'. In 1968, he used over 30-piece orchestra.

Reprise Reprise

May 68. (7") *<0692>* **BEEHIVE STATE. / I THINK IT'S GOING TO RAIN TODAY** [–] [ ]

Jun 68. (lp) *<(RSLP 6286)>* **RANDY NEWMAN CREATES SOMETHING NEW UNDER THE SUN** [ ] [ ]
– Love story / Bet no one ever hurt this bad / Living without you / So long dad / I think he's hiding / Linda / Laughing boy / Cowboy / The beehive state / I think it's going to rain today / Davy the fat boy. *(cd-iss. May95 on 'Warners'; 7599 26705-2)*

Jul 68. (7") *(RS 20692)* **LOVE STORY. / I THINK IT'S GOING TO RAIN TODAY** [ ] [–]

Nov 68. (7") *<0771>* **I THINK HE'S HIDING. / LAST NIGHT I HAD A DREAM** [–] [ ]

—— his guests included **RY COODER** – slide guitar / **RON ELLIOTT** – guitar / **GENE PARSONS** – drums / **CLARENCE WHITE** – guitar / **AL McKIBBON** – bass / etc.

Apr 70. (lp) *<(RSLP 6373)>* **12 SONGS** [ ] [ ]
– Have you seen my baby / Let's burn the cornfield / Mama told me not to come / Suzanne / Lover's prayer / Lucinda / Underneath the Harlem moon / Yellow man / Old Kentucky home / Rosemary / If you need oil / Uncle Bob's midnight oil. *(re-iss. Nov71; K 44084) (cd-iss. Sep89; 927449-2)*

May 70. (7") *<0917>* **HAVE YOU SEEN MY BABY. / HOLD ON** [–] [ ]
(below from the soundtrack of the film 'Performance')

Nov 70. (7") *(RS 20945) <0945>* **GONE DEAD TRAIN. / HARRY FLOWERS** [ ] [ ]

—— **RANDY** – just vocals and piano only.

Nov 71. (lp) *(K 44151) <6459>* **RANDY NEWMAN LIVE (live)** [ ] Sep71 [ ]
– Mama told me not to come / Tickle me / I'll be home / So long dad / Living without you / Last night I had a dream / I think it's going to rain today / Lover's prayer / Maybe I'm doing it wrong / Yellow man / Old Kentucky home / Davy the fat boy / Lonely at the top. *(cd-iss. May95 on 'Warners'; 7599 26706-2)*

Mar 72. (7") *(K 14155)* **LONELY AT THE TOP (live). / MY OLD KENTUCKY HOME (live)** [ ] [–]

—— Reverted to solo / orchestra plus past and new session people. From then after he continued to employ famous musicians and singers.

Jul 72. (lp) *(K 44185) <2064>* **SAIL AWAY** [ ] Jun72 [ ]
– Political science / Burn on / Memo to my son / Dayton, Ohio – 1903 / You can leave your hat on / God's song (that's why I love mankind) / Sail away / Lonely at the top / He gives us all his love / Last night I had a dream / Simon Smith and his amazing dancing bear / Old man. *(cd-iss. Sep89; 927203-2)*

Jul 72. (7") *(K 14190) <1102>* **SAIL AWAY. / POLITICAL SCIENCE** [ ] [ ]

Sep 72. (7") *<1123>* **MEMO TO MY SON. / YOU CAN LEAVE YOUR HAT ON** [–] [ ]

Sep 74. (7") *<1324>* **NAKED MAN. / GUILTY** [–] [ ]

Oct 74. (lp/c) *(K/K4 54022) <2193>* **GOOD OLD BOYS** [ ] [36]
– Rednecks / Birmingham / Marie / Mr. President (have pity on the working man) / Guilty / Louisiana 1927 / Every man a king / Kingfish / Naked man / Wedding in Cherokee County / Back on my feet again / Rollin'. *(cd-iss. Sep89; 927214-2)*

Nov 75. (7") *<1387>* **LOUISIANA 1927. / MARIE** [–] [ ]

Warners Warners

Sep 77. (lp/c) *(K/K4 56404) <3079>* **LITTLE CRIMINALS** [ ] [9]
– Short people / You can't fool the fat man / Little criminals / Texas girl at the funeral of her father / Jolly coppers on parade / In Germany before the war / Sigmund Freud's impersonation of Albert Einstein in America / Baltimore / I'll be home / Rider in the rain / Kathleen / Old man on the farm. *(cd-iss. Jan88; K2 56349)*

Oct 77. (7") *(K 17034) <8492>* **SHORT PEOPLE. / OLD MAN ON THE FARM** [ ] [2]

Jun 78. (7") *(K 17205)* **RIDER IN THE RAIN. / LITTLE CRIMINALS** [ ] [–]

Aug 78. (7") *<8550>* **BALTIMORE. / YOU CAN'T FOOL THE FATMAN** [–] [ ]

Oct 78. (7") *<8630>* **RIDER IN THE RAIN. / SIGMUND FREUD'S IMPERSONATION OF ALBERT EINSTEIN IN AMERICA** [–] [ ]

Aug 79. (7") *(K 17477)* **THE STORY OF A ROCK AND ROLL BAND. / PRETTY BOY** [ ] [–]

Sep 79. (lp/c) *(K/K4 56663) <3346>* **BORN AGAIN** [ ] Aug79 [41]
– It's money that I love / The story of a rock and roll band / Mr. Sheep / Pretty boy / They just got married / Ghosts / Spies / The girls in my life (part 1) / Half a man / William Brown / Pants. *(cd-iss. Feb93; 7599 25917-2)*

Nov 79. (7") *(K 17489) <49088>* **IT'S MONEY THAT I LOVE. / GHOSTS** [ ] Sep79 [ ]

Nov 79. (7") *<49149>* **THE STORY OF A ROCK AND ROLL BAND. / HALF A MAN** [–] [ ]

Feb 80. (7") *<49223>* **SPIES. / POLITICAL SCIENCE** [–] [ ]

Feb 82. (lp/c) *(K/K4 52342) <5E 565>* **RAGTIME (Soundtrack)** [ ] [ ]
– Main title / Newsreel / I could love a million girls / Train ride / Tateh's picture book / Lower East Side / Delmonico polka / Coalhouse and Sarah / Waltz for Evelyn / One more hour / Sarah's responsibility / Change your way / Clef club No.1 / Atlantic City / Clef club No.2 / arah's funeral / Denouncement: Morgan Library takeover – Rhinelander Waldo / Coalhouse's prayer / Ragtime. *(re-iss. Jan89 on 'Screen')*
(above soundtrack released on 'Elektra')

Jan 83. (lp/c) *(923755-1/-4) <23755>* **TROUBLE IN PARADISE** [ ] [64]
– I love L.A. / Christmas in Capetown / The blues / Same girl / The Mikey's / My life is good / Miami / Real emotional girl / Take me back / There's a party at my house / I'm different / Song for the dead. *(re-iss. Mar89 on 'Edsel'; ED 305) (cd-iss. Nov93)*

Jan 83. (7"; RANDY NEWMAN & PAUL SIMON) *(W 9803) <29803>* **THE BLUES. / SAME GIRL** [ ] [51]
(12") *(W 9803T)* – ('A'side) / Simon Smith and the amazing dancing bear / Short people / Mama told me not to come.

Apr 83. (7") *(W 9687) <29687>* **I LOVE L.A. / SONG FOR THE DEAD** [ ] [ ]

Oct 84. (7") *<29241>* **THE NATURAL. / THE FINAL GAME – TAKE ME TO THE BALLROOM** [–] [ ]

Oct 84. (lp/c) *(925116-1/-4) <25116>* **THE NATURAL (Soundtrack)** [ ] [ ]
– The natural / Prologue 1915-1923 / The whammer strike out / The old farm 1939 / The Majors: the mind is a strange thing / Knock the cover off the ball / Memo / Wrigley field / Iris and Roy / Winning / A father makes a difference / Penthouse party / The end title / The final game – Take me to the ballroom.

Sep 88. (lp/c)(cd) *(WX 212/+C)(925773-2) <25773>* **LAND OF DREAMS** [ ] [80]
– Dixie flyer / New Orleans wins the war / Four eyes / Falling in love / Something special / Bad news from home / Roll with the punches / Masterman and Baby J. / Follow the flag / It's money that matters / I want you to hurt like I do.

Oct 88. (7") *(W 7709) <27709>* **IT'S MONEY THAT MATTERS. / ROLL WITH THE PUNCHES** [ ] [60]
(12"+=/3"cd-s+=) *(W 7709 T/CD)* – Short people.

Feb 89. (7") *(W 7578) <27586>* **FALLING IN LOVE. / BAD NEWS FROM HOME** [ ] [ ]
(12"+=/3"cd-s+=) *(W 7578 T/CD)* – Miami.
(above 'A'side from film of the same name)

Sep 89. (7") *<22798>* **I'D LOVE TO SEE YOU SMILE. / END TITLE (I LOVE TO SEE YOU SMILE)** [–] [ ]

Jun 90. (cd/c/lp) *(925001-2/-4/-1) <25001>* **PARENTHOOD** (soundtrack) [ ] Sep89 [ ]
– Introduction – I love to see you smile / Kevin's graduation / Helen and Julie / Kevin's party (cowboy Gil) / Gary's in trouble / Father and son / Drag race / Todd and Julie / Kevin comes through / Karen and Gil (montage) / End title (I love to see you smile).

Mar 91. (cd/c) *<(7599 26466-2/-4)>* **AWAKENINGS** (soundtrack) [ ] [ ]
– Leonard / Dr. Sayer / Lucy / Catch / Rilke's panther / L dopa / Awakenings / Outside / Escape attempt / Ward five / Dexter's tune / The reality of miracles / End title.

May 94. (cd) *<(9362 45616)>* **THE PAPER** (soundtrack) [ ] [ ]
– Opening – Clocks / Henry goes to work / The sun / Bernie calls Deanne / Busting the guys / Marty and Henry / The newsroom 7.00 p.m. / More clocks / Henry leaves with McDougal / Bernie finds Deanne / Bernie / Stop the presses / Henry's fired / Marty / Marty's in trouble / To the hospital / Little Polenta is born / A new day 7.00 a.m. / Make up your mind.

Jul 94. (cd/c) *(7567 82592-2/-4) <45816>* **MAVERICK** (soundtrack) [ ] May94 [ ]
– Opening / Annabelle / Fight / Coop / Money in the bank / In & out of trouble / Magic cards, maybe – Lucky shirt / Headed for the game / Runaway stage / Sneakin' around / Maverick / Joseph & the Russian / Oh Bret / A noble aims / Trap / The hanging / Bret escapes / Bret's card – Sore loser / Coop sails away / Annabelle toodleoo / The commodore / Pappy shuffle / Bath house / Tartine de merde.

—— now with guests BONNIE RAITT / DON HENLEY / RY COODER / JAMES TAYLOR / LINDA RONSTADT / ELTON JOHN

Sep 95. (cd/c) *<(9362 45672-2/-4)>* **RANDY NEWMAN'S FAUST** [ ] [ ]
– Glory train / Can't keep a good man down / How great our Lord / Best

little girl / Northern boy / Bless the children of the world / Gainesville / Relax, enjoy yourself / Life has been good to me / Little island / The man / My hero / I gotta be your man / Feels like home / Bleeding all over the place / Sandman's coming / Happy ending.

DreamWorks DreamWorks

Jun 99. (cd) <(DRD 50115)> **BAD LOVE** ☐ ☐
– My country / Shame / I'm dead (but I don't know it) / Every time it rains / The great nations of Europe / The one you love / The world isn't fair / Big hat, no cattle / Better off dead / I miss you / Going home / I want everyone to like me.

Nonesuch Nonesuch

Sep 03. (cd) <(7559 79689-2)> **THE RANDY NEWMAN SONGBOOK VOL.1** ☐ ☐
– Lonely at the top / God's song (that's why I love mankind) / Louisiana 1927 / Let me go / Rednecks / Avalon / Living without you / I think it's going to rain today / You can leave your hat on / It's money that I love / Marie / When she loved me / Sail away / The world isn't fair / Political science / The great nations of Europe / In Germany before the war / Ragtime.

– compilations, etc. –

May 84. (lp/c) *WEA; (WX 101/+C)* **LONELY AT THE TOP – THE BEST OF RANDY NEWMAN** ☐ ☐
– Love story / Living without you / I think it's going to rain today / Mama told me not to come / Sail away / Simon Smith and his amazing dancing bear / Political science / God's song (that's why I love mankind) / Rednecks / Birmingham / Louisiana 1927 / Marie / Baltimore / Jolly coppers on parade / Rider in the rain / Short people / I love L.A. / Lonely at the top. *(cd-iss. Jul87 +=; 241126-2)* – My life is good / In Germany before the war / Christmas in Capetown / My old Kentucky home. *(re-iss. cd/c Nov93)*

—— (the 1987 movie 'THREE AMIGOS' also including several NEWMAN songs)

Dec 98. (4xcd-box) *Rhino;* <(8122 75567-2)> **GUILTY: 30 YEARS OF RANDY NEWMAN** ☐ ☐

Sep 01. (cd) *Rhino;* <8122 74364> **THE BEST OF RANDY NEWMAN** ☐ ☐
– Mama told me not to come / You can leave your hat on / I think it's going to rain today / Sail away / Political science / Rednecks / Marie / Louisiana 1927 / Short people / Little criminal / It's money that I love / I love L.A. / Miami / Take me back / Same girl / Dixie flyer / Happy ending / You've got a friend in me / Feels like home (live) / Shame / I miss you.

NEW ORDER

Formed: Manchester, England . . . mid 1980, from the fragments of JOY DIVISION following the death of frontman IAN CURTIS on the 18th of May 1980. The remaining JOY DIVISION members, vocalist/guitarist BERNARD ALBRECHT (now SUMNER), bassist PETER HOOK and drummer STEPHEN MORRIS remained with 'Factory' records, subsequently adopting the NEW ORDER moniker at the suggestion of manager Rob Gretton. With SUMNER taking over vocal duties, the group gigged around Manchester, eventually releasing a debut single, 'CEREMONY' in 1981. This broke the Top 40, as did the Martin Hannett-produced follow-up, 'PROCESSION' / 'EVERYTHING'S GONE GREEN' although in reality, these releases weren't much of a departure from the rumbling, melodic bass sound of old, critics unimpressed with SUMNER's weak vocals. With their debut album, 'MOVEMENT' (1981), however, NEW ORDER were beginning to crystallise their own unique sound, new recruit GILLIAN GILBERT embellishing the music with cutting keyboard swathes. A subtle dance feel was also edging it's way in and with the release of 'TEMPTATION' the following year, NEW ORDER had begun experimenting openly with sequencing technology. The single married the raw cut 'n' thrust of alternative rock to danceable rhythms, echoing hip-hop's similar experimentation with European electronica (see AFRIKA BAMBAATAA's seminal KRAFTWERK-sampling 'Planet Rock') and creating sonic waves that are still rippling through the eclectic musical free-for-all of the 90's. Fittingly then, NEW ORDER's tour de force, 'BLUE MONDAY' was produced by cult US hip-hop producer, Arthur Baker. The best selling 12 inch single in the history of rock, the record was dominated by compelling, almost militaristic dancefloor beats behind SUMNER's moodily introspective, melancholy vocal musings and HOOK's insidious bass melody. A true crossover single, the record appealed to indie fans, B-boys and club posers alike, cementing NEW ORDER's reputation as one of the UK's most street-cred acts. The accompanying album (an inferior demo version of 'BLUE MONDAY', '5-8-6' was included at the expense of the original single), 'POWER, CORRUPTION AND LIES' (1983) made the Top 5, confirming NEW ORDER's commitment to electronic experimentation via a hypnotic, slightly hazy set. A further Arthur Baker-produced 12 inch single followed, 'CONFUSION', the New Yorker also collaborating on the 1984 follow-up, 'THIEVES LIKE US'. But it wasn't until the acclaimed 'LOW LIFE' the following year that NEW ORDER successfully integrated the various strands which made up their inimitable sound. Previewed by the affecting 'PERFECT KISS' single and arguably the most consistently listenable NEW ORDER long player, the record convincingly welded driving, bass-heavy rock onto dance rhythms as well as featuring some interesting stylistic diversions. 'BROTHERHOOD' (1986) was a harder-edged affair, enjoyable enough and boasting the brilliant 'BIZARRE LOVE TRIANGLE', although hardly breaking new ground. 'TRUE FAITH' was another landmark NEW ORDER single; co-written and produced by STEPHEN HAGUE (who'd worked wonders on the PET SHOP BOYS' early material), the single was a hauntingly infectious piece of dance-pop, possibly the most commercial material NEW ORDER had ever released. Following the release of the best selling compilation, 'SUBSTANCE (1980-1987)' later that summer, the band went to ground, finally resurfacing in 1989 with 'TECHNIQUE' and quashing rumours of an imminent split. Heavily influenced by the house explosion of the late 80's and partly recorded on the Balearic Island of Ibiza, the album fully indulged the band's dancier leanings with a verve and passion that's missing from much of their later work. Deservedly, the album rode into the No.1 spot on the back of the club zeitgeist, a scene NEW ORDER had a major hand in creating. The single, 'FINE TIME', almost made the Top 10, an uncharacteristically humorous ditty featuring parodic mock-medallion man, BARRY WHITE-esque vocal rumblings. The following year, NEW ORDER were back at No.1 with their World Cup theme tune, 'WORLD IN MOTION'. Nationalist prejudice aside, this song seemed to set the trend for the nauseous, 'Enger-land' limp-wristed crap that the LIGHTNING SEEDS would update six years later for the European championships. Maybe NEW ORDER felt the same way, as the various members soon drifted away to their respective side projects; HOOK to the muscular REVENGE (subsequently stiffing with the 'ONE TRUE PASSION' album), GILBERT and MORRIS to The OTHER TWO (1993's 'THE OTHER TWO AND YOU' album getting lost in the ether when 'Factory' went belly-up) and SUMNER hooking up with JOHNNY MARR (ex-SMITHS) and occasionally NEIL TENNANT (PET SHOP BOYS) to form ELECTRONIC. By far the most successful NEW ORDER-offshoot, the group scored three Top 20 hit singles, including the pop wistfulness of 'GETTING AWAY WITH IT'. They also narrowly missed No.1 with their 1991 eponymous album, their sound akin to a breezier NEW ORDER, fusing house and indie-pop with wry, intelligent lyrics. With 'Factory' going bust following HAPPY MONDAYS' bank-breaking 'SUNSHINE AND LOVE' debacle, a belated NEW ORDER follow-up, 'REPUBLIC' (1993), was subsequently released on 'London' records. A strangely muted collection, the record nevertheless spawned a succession of Top 30 singles including the aptly named Top 5 hit, 'REGRET'. Rumours of tensions within the group persisted and after a final appearance at the 1993 Reading Festival, the various members soon went off to do their own thing once more. ELECTRONIC charted with another set, 'RAISE THE PRESSURE' in 1996 and HOOK came up with the highly-NEW ORDER-esque MONACO project (with SUMNER-like DAVID POTTS) the following year. In 1999, ELECTRONIC returned with a third set, 'TWISTED TENDERNESS' – featuring the UK hit 'VIVID' – while MONACO again delighted the pop world with their eponymous follow-up in 2000. Few could've predicted NEW ORDER would return at all, never mind return with as good an album as 'GET READY' (2001). Rather than cater to the whims of contemporary club tastes, SUMNER, HOOK et al unashamedly made a record on their own terms. As a taster single, 'CRYSTAL' was perfect, a keening slice of classic NEW ORDER with the constituent parts (HOOKY's all-consuming bassline, SUMNER's little boy lost vocals, a melody to die for) all present and correct. Even the collaborative efforts of BOBBY GILLESPIE and BILLY CORGAN were subsumed under the record's driving focus. • **Songwriters:** All group compositions except; TURN THE HEATER ON (Keith Hudson). • **Trivia:** In 1987, they contributed some tracks to the movie, 'Salvation'.

Album rating: MOVEMENT (*8) / POWER, CORRUPTION AND LIES (*9) / LOW-LIFE (*8) / BROTHERHOOD (*8) / SUBSTANCE 1980-1987 compilation (*10) / TECHNIQUE (*9) / REPUBLIC (*6) / ? (THE BEST OF) compilation (*9) / THE REST OF NEW ORDER compilation (*7) / GET READY (*6) / Electronic: ELECTRONIC (*8) / RAISE THE PRESSURE (*6) / TWISTED TENDERNESS (*6) / Revenge: ONE TRUE PASSION (*5) / Monaco: MUSIC FOR PLEASURE (*6) / MONACO (*7) / Other Two: THE OTHER TWO AND YOU (*5) / SUPER HIGHWAYS (*5)

BERNARD SUMNER (b. BERNARD DICKEN, 4 Jan'56) – vocals, guitar / **PETER HOOK** (b.13 Feb'56) – bass / **STEPHEN MORRIS** (b.28 Oct'57, Macclesfield, England) – drums

Factory Streetwise

Mar 81. (7"/ext.12") *(FAC 33/+T)* **CEREMONY. / IN A LONELY PLACE** [34] [–]
(re-iss. Jul81 re-recorded; FAC 33-12)

— added **GILLIAN GILBERT** (b.27 Jan'61) – keyboards, synth.

Sep 81. (7") *(FAC 53)* **PROCESSION. / EVERYTHING'S GONE GREEN** [38] [–]

Nov 81. (lp) *(FACT 50)* **MOVEMENT** [30] [–]
– Dreams never end / Truth / Senses / Chosen time / I.C.B. / The him / Doubts even here / Denial. *(re-iss. Nov86 c)(cd; FACT 50C)(FACD 50) (re-iss. Jul93 on 'Centredate' cd/c; 520018-2/-4)*

Dec 81. Factory Benelux; (12"m) *(FBN 8)* **EVERYTHING'S GONE GREEN (extended). / MESH / CRIES AND WHISPERS** [–] Belg. [–]
(re-iss. cd-ep Jul90; FBN 8CD)

May 82. (7"/ext.12") *(FAC 63/+T)* **TEMPTATION. / HURT** [29] [–]

Nov 82. Factory Benelux; (m-lp) *(FACTUS 8)* **NEW ORDER 1981-82** (compilation) [–] Belg. [–]

Mar 83. (12") *(FAC 73)* **BLUE MONDAY. / THE BEACH** [9] [ ]

May 83. (lp)(c) *(FACT 75)(FACTUS 12C)* *<25308>* **POWER, CORRUPTION AND LIES** [4] [ ]
– Your silent face / Ultraviolence / Ecstasy / Leave me alone / Age of consent / We all stand / The village / 5-8-6. *(re-iss. Nov86 c)(cd; FACT 75C)(FAC 75CD)* – Blue Monday / The beach. *(re-iss. Jul93 on 'Centredate' cd/c; 520019-2/-4)*

Aug 83. (12"ep) *(FAC 93)* **CONFUSION. / CONFUSED BEATS / CONFUSION (instrumental & Rough mixes)** [12] [ ]

Apr 84. (12") *(FAC 103)* **THIEVES LIKE US. / LONESOME TONIGHT** [18] [ ]

May 84. Factory Benelux; (12") *(FBN 22)* **MURDER. / THIEVES LIKE US (instrumental)** [–] Belg. [–]

Factory Qwest

May 85. (7") *(FAC 123)* **THE PERFECT KISS. / THE KISS OF DEATH** [46] [–]
(12"+=) *(FAC 123-12)* – Perfect pit.

Jun 85. (7") **THE PERFECT KISS. / PERFECT PIT** [–] [ ]

May 85. (lp/c)(cd) *(FACT 100/+C)(FACD 100)* *<25289>* **LOW-LIFE** [7] [94]
– Sooner than you think / Sub-culture / Face up / Love vigilantes / Elegia / The perfect kiss / This time of the night / Sunrise. *(c+=)* – The perfect kiss / The kiss of death / Perfect pit. *(re-iss. Jul93 on 'Centredate' cd/c; 520020-2/-4)*

Nov 85. (7"/ext.12") *(FAC 133/+T)* **SUB-CULTURE. / DUB-CULTURE** [63] [–]

Mar 86. (7") *(FAC 143)* **SHELLSHOCK. / THIEVES LIKE US (instrumental)** [28] [–]
(12") *(FAC 143T)* – ('A'extended) / Shellshock (dub).

Sep 86. (ext.12"/7") *(FAC 153/+7)* **STATE OF THE NATION. / SHAME OF THE NATION** [30] [–]

Oct 86. (lp/c/s-lp)(cd) *(FACT 150/+C/SP)(FACD 150)* *<25511>* **BROTHERHOOD** [9] [ ]
– Paradise / Weirdo / As it was when it was / Broken promise / Way of life / Bizarre love triangle / All day long / Angel dust / Every little counts. *(cd+=)* – State of the nation. *(re-iss. Jul93 on 'Centredate' cd/c; 520021-2/-4)*

Nov 86. (ext.12"/7") *(FAC 163/+7)* **BIZARRE LOVE TRIANGLE. / BIZARRE DUB TRIANGLE** [56] [–]

Mar 87. (7") **BIZARRE LOVE TRIANGLE. / EVERY LITTLE COUNTS** [–] [ ]

Jul 87. (ext-12"/7") *(FAC 183/+7)* *<28271>* **TRUE FAITH. / 1963** [4] Oct87 [32]
(remix-12"+=) *(FAC 183R)* – True dub.

Aug 87. (d-lp/d-c)(d-cd) *(FACT 200/+C)(FACD 200)* *<25621>* **SUBSTANCE (1980-1987)** (compilation) [3] [36]
– Ceremony / Everthing's gone green / Temptation / Blue Monday / Confusion / Thieves like us / Perfect kiss / Subculture / Shellshock / State of the nation / Bizarre love triangle / True faith. *(d-c+=)* – Procession / Mesh / Hurt / In a lonely place / The beach / Confused / Murder / Lonesome tonight / Kiss of death / Shame of the nation / 1963. *(cd++=)* – Cries and whispers / Dub culture / Shellcock / Bizarre dub triangle. *(re-iss. Jul93 on 'Centredate' cd/c; 520008-2/-4); hit UK No.32) (d-cd re-iss. Jun98; 520008-2)*

Dec 87. (ext.12"/7") *(FAC 193/+7)* **TOUCHED BY THE HAND OF GOD. / TOUCHED BY THE HAND OF DUB** [20] [–]
(cd-s) *(FACD 193)* – ('A'extended) / Confusion (dub '87) / Temptation (original).

Mar 88. (7") **TOUCHED BY THE HAND OF GOD. / BLUE MONDAY 1988** [–] [ ]

Dec 88. (7") *(FAC 223-7)* **FINE TIME. / DON'T DO IT** [11] [ ]
(12"+=) *(FAC 223)* – Fine line.
(cd-s+=) *(FACCD 223)* – ('A'-Silk mix) / ('A'-Messed around mix).

Jan 89. (cd)(lp/c/dat) *(FACD 275)(FACT 275/+C/D)* *<25845>* **TECHNIQUE** [1] [32]
– Fine time / All the way / Love less / Round & round / Guilty partner / Run / Mr. Disco / Vanishing point / Dream attack. *(re-iss. Jul93 on 'Centredate' cd/c; 520011-2)*

Mar 89. (ext.12"/7") *(FAC 263/+7)* *<27524>* **ROUND & ROUND. / BEST AND MARSH** [21] [64]
(ext.& club-12"+=) *(FAC 263R)* – ('A'-Detroit mix).
(cd-s+=) *(FACD 263)* – Vanishing point (instrumental 'Making Out' mix) / ('A'-12"mix).
(3"cd-s) *(FACD 263R)* – ('A'-Detroit) / ('A'-12") / ('A'-club).

Sep 89. (7") *(FAC 273-7)* **RUN 2. / MTO** [49] [–]
(12"+=) *(FAC 273)* – ('A'extended) / ('B'-Minus mix).

May 90. (12"/7"/c-s; as ENGLAND / NEW ORDER) *(FAC 293/+7/C)* **WORLD IN MOTION. . . . / THE B SIDE** [1] [–]
(cd-s+=) *(FACD 293)* – No alla violenzia / ('A'-Subbuteo mix).
(12") *(FAC 293R)* – ('A'-Subbuteo mix) / ('A'-Subbuteo dub) / No alla violenzia mix / ('A'-Carabinieri mix).

— Around the late 80's/early 90's, all members splintered to do own projects

Centredate Qwest

Apr 93. (7"/c-s) *(NUO/+C 1)* *<18586>* **REGRET. / ('A'mix)** [4] [28]
(cd-s+=) *(NUOCD 1)* – ('A'-Fire Island mix) / ('A'-Junior's dub mix).
(12") *(NUOX 1)* – ('A'-Fire Island mix) / ('A'-Junior's dub mix) / (2-'A' Sabres mixes)

May 93. (cd/c/lp) *(828413-2/-4/-1)* *<45250>* **REPUBLIC** [1] [11]
– Regret / World / Ruined in a day / Spooky / Everyone everywhere / Young offender / Liar / Chemical / Times change / Special / Avalanche.

Jun 93. (7"/c-s) *(NUO/+C 2)* **RUINED IN A DAY. / VICIOUS CIRCLE (mix)** [22] [–]
(cd-s+=) *(NUOCD 2)* – ('A'mixes).
(cd-s) *(NUOCDX 2)* – ('A'mixes).
(12") *(NUOX 2)* – ('A'side) / World (the price of dub mix).

Aug 93. (c-s) *(NUOC 3)* *<18432>* **WORLD (THE PRICE OF LOVE) / ('A'mixes)** [13] [–]

(12"+=/cd-s+=) *(NUOX/NUOCD 3)* – ('A'-Perfecto + sexy club mixes).
(cd-s) *(NUOCDX 3)* – ('A'-Brothers in rhythm mix) / ('A'dubstramental mix) / ('A'-World in action mix) / ('A'-Pharmacy dub).

Sep 93. (c-s,cd-s) *<18432>* **WORLD (THE PRICE OF LOVE) / RUINED IN A DAY** [–] [92]

Dec 93. (c-s/12"/cd-s) *(NUO MC/X/CD 4)* **SPOOKY. / (3 'A' mixes-magimix-minimix-moulimix)** [22] [ ]
(cd-s) *(NUCDP 4)* – ('A'-Out of order mix) / ('A'-Stadium mix) / ('A'-In Heaven mix) / ('A'-Boo-dub mix) / ('A'-Stadium instrumental).

Nov 94. (7"/c-s) *(NUO/+MC 5)* **TRUE FAITH '94. / ('A'-Perfecto mix)** [9] [ ]
(12"+=) *(NUOX 5)* – ('A'-sexy disco dub mix) / ('A'-TWA Gim Up North mix).
(cd-s++=) *(NUOCD 5)* – ('A'radio mix).

Nov 94. (cd/c/d-lp) *(828 580-2/-4/-1) <45794>* **? (THE BEST OF)** (compilation) [4] [78]
– True faith '94 / Bizarre love triangle '94 / 1963 / Regret / Fine time / The perfect kiss / Shellshock / Thieves like us / Vanishing point / Run (2) / Round and round '94 / World (price of love) / Ruined in a day / Touched by the hand of God / Blue Monday '88 / World in motion.

Jan 95. (c-s) *(NUOMC 6)* **NINETEEN63 (Arthur Baker remix) / ('A'-'94 album version) / ('A'-Lionrock full throttle mix) / ('A'-Joe T Venelli remix)** [21] [ ]
(12") *(NUOX 6)* – ('A'-Lionrock & Joe T mixes / True faith (Eschreamer mix)/ ('A'-Eschreamer dub).
(cd-s) *(NUOCD 6)* – ('A'-Arthur Baker remix) / Let's go/ Spooky (Nightstripper mix)/ True faith '87 (Shep Pettibone mix).

Jul 95. (c-s) *(NUOMC 7)* **BLUE MONDAY '95 / ('A'-original)** [17] [–]
(12"+=/cd-s+=) *(NUO X/CD 7)* – ('A'-Hardfloor mix) / ('A'-Jam & Spoon mix).

Jul 95. (cd-ep) *<20546>* **BIZARRE LOVE TRIANGLE (2 mixes) / STATE OF THE NATION (2 mixes)** [–] [98]

Aug 95. (cd/c) *(828 661-2/-4)* **THE REST OF NEW ORDER** (remixes, etc) [5] [ ]

Aug 01. (cd-s) *(NUCDP 8)* **CRYSTAL / CRYSTAL (Digweed & Muir bedrock remixes)** [8] [–]
(cd-s/d12") *(NUO CD/X 8)* – ('A'-Lee Coombs remix & dub) / ('A'-John Creamer & Stephane K mixes) / Behind closed doors.
(12") *(NUOXX 8)* – (some 'A'-mixes above).
(12") *(NUOXXX 8)* – (some 'A'-mixes above).

Aug 01. (cd/c/lp) *(<8573 89621-2/-4/-1>)* **GET READY** [6] Oct01 [41]
– Crystal / 60 miles an hour / Turn my way / Vicious streak / Primitive notion / Slow jam / Rock the shack / Someone like you / Close range / Run wild.

Nov 01. (cd-s) *(NUOCD 9)* **60 MILES AN HOUR / SABOTAGE / SOMEONE LIKE YOU (Funk D'void mix)** [29] [ ]
(cd-s) *(NUODP 9)* – ('A'side) / ('A'-Supermen lovers remix) / Someone like you (James Holden dub) / Someone like you (Future Shock mix).

Dec 01. (12") *(NUOX 10)* **SOMEONE LIKE YOU (mixes; futureshock vocal / Gabriel & Dresden 911 vocal / futureshock stripdown / Gabriel & Dresden voco-tech dub)** [ ] [–]
(12") *(NUOXX 10)* – ('A'-mixes; James Holden heavy dub / Funk d'Void).

Apr 02. (cd-s; as NEW ORDER & THE CHEMICAL BROTHERS) *(NUOCD 11)* **HERE TO STAY / HERE TO STAY (mix) / PLAYER IN THE LEAGUE** [15] [–]
(cd-s) *(NUCDP 11)* – ('A'mixes; radio / Felix Da Housecat – thee extended glitz / the scumfrog dub).
(12") *(NUOX 11)* – ('A'mixes) / Crystal (original).

Jun 02. (cd-s; as ENGLAND NEW ORDER) *(NUOCD 12)* **WORLD IN MOTION (mixes) / SUCH A GOOD THING** [43] [–]

— in Sep'03, PETER HOOK feat. on HYBRID's 'True To Form' hit

– compilations, etc. –

Sep 86. (12"ep) *Strange Fruit; (SFPS 001)* **PEEL SESSIONS** (1.6.82.) [54] [–]
– Turn the heater on / We all stand / 586 / Too late. *(re-iss. Jul87 c-ep; SFPSC 001) (re-iss. Mar88 cd-ep; SFPSCD 001)*

Oct 87. (12"ep) *Strange Fruit; (SFPS 039)* **PEEL SESSIONS** (26.1.81.) [ ] [–]
– Truth / Senses / I.C.B. / Dreams never end. *(re-iss. May88 cd-ep; SFPSCD 039)*

Mar 88. (7"/12") *Factory; (FAC 73-7/R) / Qwest; <27979>* **BLUE MONDAY 1988. / BEACH BUGGY** [3] [68]
(cd-s+=) *(FACD 73)* – ('A'original).

Sep 90. (m-cd/m-c/m-lp) *Strange Fruit; (SFR CD/C/LP 110)* **PEEL SESSIONS** (2 ep's combined) [ ] [–]

Feb 92. (cd/c/lp) *Windsong; (WIN CD/MC/LP 011)* **BBC RADIO 1 LIVE IN CONCERT (live June '87)** [33] [–]
– Touched by the hand of God / Temptation / True faith / Your silent face / Every second counts / Bizarre love triangle / Perfect kiss / Age of consent / Sister Ray.

Sep 97. (12") *Touch; (502780314769)* **TOUCH TONE 7.1** [ ] [–]

— In Mar'89, they issued two 5"cd-vids of TRUE FAITH + BLUE MONDAY '88

Jul 02. (12") *Factory USA; (2054-6)* **BIZARRE LOVE TRIANGLE** [ ] [ ]

Nov 02. (12"; as BAKER vs. NEW ORDER) *Whacked; (WACKT 002)* **CONFUSION (2002 remixes; Koma & Bones / Larry T's)** [64] [–]
(12") *(WACKT 002R)* – ('A'mixes; Junior Sanchez vocal / Arthur Baker / Asto's).
(cd-s) *(WACKT 002CD)* – (all mixes above).

Dec 02. (4xcd-box) *London; (0927 49499-2) <73834>* **RETRO** [ ] [ ]

ELECTRONIC

BERNARD SUMNER – vocals, guitar / **JOHNNY MARR** – guitar (ex-SMITHS) + both programmers / also with **NEIL TENNANT** – vocals (of PET SHOP BOYS)

Factory Warners

Dec 89. (7"/c-s) *(FAC 257-7/-C) <19880>* **GETTING AWAY WITH IT. / LUCKY BAG** [12] [38]
(12"+=/cd-s+=) *(FAC 257 T/CD)* – ('A'extended).
(12"+=) *(FAC 257X)* – ('A'extra mixes).

— added further guests **CHRIS LOWE, DONALD JOHNSON, DAVID PALMER, DENISE JOHNSON, HELEN POWELL + ANDREW ROBINSON** (on same track)

Apr 91. (7"/c-s) *(FAC 287-7/-C)* **GET THE MESSAGE. / FREE WILL** [8] [ ]
(cd-s+=) *(FACD 287)* – ('A'-DNA groove mix).
(12"+=) *(FAC-12 287)* – ('A' 2 other mixes).

May 91. (cd)(lp/c) *(FACD 290)(FACT 290/+C) <26387>* **ELECTRONIC** [2] [ ]
– Idiot country / Reality / Tighten up / The patience of a saint / Gangster / Soviet / Get the message / Try all you want / Some distant memory / Feel every beat. *(re-iss. Feb94 on 'Parlophone' cd/c; CD/TC PRG 1012)*

Sep 91. (7"/c-s) *(FAC 328-7/-C)* **FEEL EVERY BEAT. / LEAN TO THE INSIDE** [39] [ ]
(12"+=) *(FAC-12 328)* – ('A'dub version).
(cd-s+=) *(FACD 328)* – Second to none / ('A' DNA mix)

— next with NEIL TENNANT again

Parlophone Warners

Jun 92. (c-s/7") *(TC+/R 6311)* **DISAPPOINTED. / IDIOT COUNTRY TWO** [6] [ ]
(12"+=/cd-s+=) *(12R/CDR 6311)* – ('A'-808 State mix) / ('B'-Ultimatum mix).

Jun 96. (c-s/7") *(TC+/R 6436)* **FORBIDDEN CITY. / IMITATION OF LIFE** [14] [ ]
(cd-s+=) *(CDR 6436)* – A new religion.

Jul 96. (cd/c) *(CD/TC+/PCS 7382) <45955>* **RAISE THE PRESSURE** [8] [ ]
– Forbidden city / For you / Dark angel / One day / Until the end of time / Second nature / If you've got love / Out of my league / Interlude / Freefall / Visit me / How long / Time can tell.

Sep 96. (c-s) *(TCR 6445)* **FOR YOU / ALL THAT I NEED** [16] [ ]
(cd-s+=) *(CDR 6445)* – I feel alright.
(cd-s) *(CDRS 6445)* – ('A'side) / Free will (12"mix) / Disappointed / Get the message (DNA mix).

Feb 97. (c-s) *(TCR 6455)* **SECOND NATURE / TURNING POINT** [35] [ ]
(cd-s+=) *(CDRS 6455)* – Feel every beat (12"remix).
(cd-s) *(CDR 6455)* – ('A'side) / ('A'-Plastik mix) / ('A'-Trance Atlantic dub) / ('A'-Sweet remix).

Apr 99. (12") *(12R 6514)* **VIVID. / PRODIGAL SON (mixes; Two Lone Swordsmen & Harvey's)** [17] [–]
(cd-s) *(CDR 6514)* – ('A'side) / Radiation / Prodigal son (inch mix).
(cd-s) *(CDRS 6514)* – ('A'side) / Haze (alternative mix) / Prodigal son (Harvey's a star in your mind mix).

Apr 99. (cd/c) *(<498345-2/-4>)* **TWISTED TENDERNESS** 9
– Make it happen / Haze / Vivid / Vivid / Breakdown / Can't find my way home / Twisted tenderness / Like no other / Late at night / Prodigal son / When she's gone / Flicker.

Jul 99. (12") *(12R 6519)* **LATE AT NIGHT. / MAKE IT HAPPEN / MAKE IT HAPPEN (Darren Price mix)** –
(cd-s) *(CDR 6519)* – ('A'side) / King for a day / Come down now (Cevin Fisher mix).
(cd-s) *(CDRS 6519)* – ('A'side) / Warning sign / Make it happen (Darren Price mix).

REVENGE

PETER HOOK – bass / with **DAVE HICKS** – words, vocals / **C. JONES**

Factory Capitol

Nov 89. (7") *(FAC 247-7)* **7 REASONS. / JESUS I LOVE YOU** –
(12"+=) *(FAC 247)* – Love you 2.
(cd-s+=) *(FACD 247)* – ('B'version) / Bleach boy.

May 90. (7"/c-s) *(FAC 267-7/-C)* **PINEAPPLE FACE. / 14K** –
(12"+=) *(FAC 267)* – ('A'-Revenge version).
(cd-s+=) *(FACD 267)* – ('A'-Last Lunge version).

Jun 90. (cd)(lp/c) *(FACD 230)(FAC 230/+C) <94053>* **ONE TRUE PASSION**
– Pineapple face / Big bang / Lose the chrome / Slave / Bleachman / Surf Nazi / Fag hag / It's quiet.

Sep 90. (7") *(FAC 279)* **(I'M NOT YOUR) SLAVE. / AMSTERDAM** –
(12"+=/cd-s+=) *(FAC 279 T/CD)* – ('A'-II version) / Slave.

—— DAVE HICKS departed Apr'91, replaced by **POTTSY**

Jan 92. (12"ep/cd-ep) *(FAC 327 T/CD) <98479>* **GUN WORLD PORN** Feb92
– Deadbeat (remix) / Cloud nine / State of shock / Little pig.

MONACO

PETER HOOK – bass (now departed from NEW ORDER) / **DAVID POTTS** – guitar, vocals

Polydor A&M

Mar 97. (7"/c-s) *(573 190-7/-4)* **WHAT DO YOU WANT FROM ME? / BICYCLE THIEF** 11 –
(cd-s+=) *(573 191-2)* – Ultra.

May 97. (c-s) *(571 054-4)* **SWEET LIPS / SHATTERED** 18 –
(cd-s+=) *(571 055-2)* – ('A'-Tony De Vit mix) / ('A'-arley & Heller mix).
(cd-s) *(571 057-1/-2)* – ('A'side) / ('A'-Farley & Heller mix) / ('A'-Joey Negro mix).

Jun 97. (cd/c/lp) *(<537 242-2/-4/-1>)* **MUSIC FOR PLEASURE** 11
– What do you want from me? / Shine (someone who needs me) / Sweet lips / Buzz gum / Blue / Junk / Billy Bones / Happy Jack / Tender / Sedona.

Sep 97. (7"/c-s) *(571 418-7/-4)* **SHINE (SOMEONE WHO NEEDS ME). / (instrumental)** 55 –
(cd-s+=) *(571 418-2)* – Comin' around again / Tender.

Papillion Papillion

Aug 00. (7") *(BTFLYS 0005)* **I'VE GOT A FEELING. / HEAVEN** –
(cd-s+=) *(BTFLYX 0005)* – Barfly.

Aug 00. (cd) *(<BTFLYCD 0005>)* **MONACO**
– I've got a feeling / A life apart / Kashmere / Bert's theme / Ballroom / See-saw / Black rain / It's a boy / End of the world / Marine.

The OTHER TWO

STEPHEN + GILLIAN

Parlophone Warners

Oct 91. (7"/c-s) *(FAC 329-7/-C)* **TASTY FISH (Pascal mix). / ('A'mix)** 41 –
(12"+=/cd-s+=) *(FAC/+D 329)* – ('A'-Almond slice mix).

London London

Oct 93. (7"/c-s) *(TWO/+CD 1)* **SELFISH. / SELFISH (that pop mix)** 46
(12"+=/cd-s+=) *(TWO X/CD 1)* – ('A'-East Village vocal mix) / ('A'-Waterfront mix).

Nov 93. (cd/c/lp) *(<520028-2/-4/-1>)* **THE OTHER TWO AND YOU**
– Tasty fish / The greatest thing / Selfish / Movin' on / Ninth configuration / Feel this love / Spirit level / Night voice / Innocence. *(cd+=)* – Love it.

Feb 99. (c-s/cd-s) *(TWO CS/CD 2)* **SUPER HIGHWAYS / YOU CAN FLY (Cevin Fisher mile high club mix)** –
(cd-s) *(TWCDP 2)* – ('A'-Andy Votel mix).

Mar 99. (cd/c) *(566018-2/-4)* **SUPER HIGHWAYS** –
– You can fly / Super highways / The river / One last kiss / Voytek / Unwanted / New horizons / Cold feet / The grave / Hello / Ripple / Weird woman. *(cd-bonus+=)* – Super highways (Andy Votel mix) / You can fly (Cevin Fisher's mile high mix).

□ NEW POWER GENERATION (see under ⇒ PRINCE)

NEW RIDERS OF THE PURPLE SAGE

Formed: San Francisco, California, USA ... 1969 when The GRATEFUL DEAD's JERRY GARCIA formed a loose country-rock outfit with guitarists/vocalists JOHN 'Marmaduke' DAWSON (ex-NEW DELHI RIVER BAND) and DAVID NELSON. The group were augmented by fellow 'DEAD stalwarts PHIL LESH and MICKEY HART, although the latter two had been replaced by DAVE TORBERT (ex-NEW DELHI RIVER BAND) and SPENCER DRYDEN (ex-JEFFERSON AIRPLANE) respectively by the time the group secured a deal with 'Columbia' in 1971. Initially a 'DEAD side project, opening for the infamous psychedelic rockers on their 1970 tours, the group soon became a sizable live draw in its own right. The 'RIDERS' eponymous debut made the American Top 40, a competent set of hippie-country reminiscent of The GRATEFUL DEAD's peerless 'American Beauty'. GARCIA bowed out soon after, the 'DEAD road monster taking up too much of his time. A new pedal steel player was found in BUDDY CAGE, the group introducing a driving country-rock sound reminiscent of a more commercial FLYING BURRITO BROTHERS, whose 'DIM LIGHTS, THICK SMOKE (AND LOUD, LOUD MUSIC) they covered on their follow-up album, 'POWERGLIDE' (1972). The group's followers were cut from the same hippy, tribal cloth as those of The GRATEFUL DEAD and, like that act, the band's live shows were more of an event than a concert. The flipside of this was that the 'RIDERS' record sales never reflected their popularity. 'THE ADVENTURES OF PANAMA RED' (1973) was the band's most commercially successful record, the early to mid-70's being their golden era. Ex-BYRD, SKIP BATTIN replaced TORBERT for a handful of albums before himself being succeeded by STEVE LOWE, an ex-member of fellow country rocker RICK NELSON'S STONE CANYON BAND. The late 70's albums appeared on 'M.C.A.', the band subsequently dropped at the turn of the decade and splitting after the poorly received 'FEELIN' ALRIGHT' (1981). While DAWSON later resurrected the band with new members, NELSON hooked up once more with JERRY GARCIA in his ACOUSTIC BAND, before forming his own outfit in the mid-90's. • **Songwriters:** DAWSON penned most on their debut, but all group shared duties on follow up. Covered; HELLO MARY LOU (Ricky Nelson) / WILLIE AND THE HAND JIVE (Johnny Otis) / LONESOME L.A.COWBOY (Peter Rowan) / KICK IN THE HEAD (Robert Hunter) / etc. • **Trivia:** ROBERT HUNTER of the 'DEAD, also initially wrote the band's lyrics.

Album rating: NEW RIDERS OF THE PURPLE SAGE (*7) / POWERGLIDE (*6) / GYPSY COWBOY (*4) / THE ADVENTURES OF PANAMA RED (*5) / HOME, HOME ON THE ROAD (*4) / BRUJO (*4) / OH, WHAT A MIGHTY TIME (*4) / NEW RIDERS (*4) / THE BEST OF . . . compilation (*6) / WHO ARE THOSE GUYS (*3) / MARIN COUNTY LINE (*2) / FEELIN' ALRIGHT (*2) / KEEP ON KEEPIN' ON (*3) / WASTED TASTERS 1971-1975 compilation (*7)

JOHN 'Marmaduke' DAWSON (b.1945, San Francisco) – acoustic guitar, vocals (ex-NEW DELHI RIVER BAND) / **DAVID NELSON** (b. San Francisco) – vocals, guitars, mandolin / **DAVE TORBERT** – bass, acoustic guitar, vocals (ex-NEW DELHI RIVER BAND) repl. PHIL LESH (of GRATEFUL DEAD) / with **SPENCER DRYDEN** (b. 7 Apr'43, New York City, N.Y.) – drums, percussion (ex-JEFFERSON AIRPLANE) repl. MICKEY HART (of GRATEFUL DEAD) except 2 tracks / **JERRY GARCIA** (b. 1 Aug'42, San Francisco) – guitars, banjo (of GRATEFUL DEAD) / **COMMANDER CODY** – piano (2)

C.B.S. Columbia

Oct 71. (lp) *(CBS 64557)* *<30888>* **THE NEW RIDERS OF THE PURPLE SAGE** Sep71 39
– I don't know you / Whatcha gonna do / Portland woman / Henry / Dirty business / Glendale train / Garden of Eden / All I ever wanted / Last lonely eagle / Louisiana lady. *(re-iss. Feb88 on 'Edsel'; ED 265) (cd-iss. Jul88; EDCD 265)*

Oct 71. (7") *<45469>* **LOUISIANA LADY. / LAST LONELY LADY** –

Jan 72. (7") *<45526>* **I DON'T KNOW YOU. / GARDEN OF EDEN** –

— Basic 4-piece (DAWSON, NELSON, TORBERT and **DRYDEN** – now full-time) / added **BUDDY CAGE** (b. Toronto, Canada) – pedal steel guitar

Jun 72. (lp) *(CBS 64843)* *<31284>* **POWERGLIDE** May72 33
– Dim lights, thick smoke (and loud, loud music) / Rainbow / California day / Sweet lovin' one / Lochinvar / I don't need no doctor / Contract / Runnin' back to you / Hello Mary Lou / Duncan and Brody / Willie and the hand jive.

Jun 72. (7") *<45607>* **I DON'T NEED NO DOCTOR. / RUNNIN' BACK TO YOU** – 81

Dec 72. (7") *(CBS 8035)* **I DON'T NEED NO DOCTOR. / CALIFORNIA DAY** –

Dec 72. (7") *<45682>* **DIM LIGHTS, THICK SMOKE (AND LOUD, LOUD MUSIC). / RAINBOW** –

Dec 72. (lp) *(CBS 65008)* *<31930>* **GYPSY COWBOY** 85
– Gypsy cowboy / Whiskey / Groupie / Sutter's mill / Death and destruction / Linda / On my way back home / Superman / She's no angel / Long black veil / Sailin'.

Feb 73. (7") *<45763>* **GROUPIE. / SHE'S NO ANGEL** –

Oct 73. (lp) *(CBS 65687)* *<32450>* **THE ADVENTURES OF PANAMA RED** 55
– Panamas red / It's alright with me / Lonesome L.A. cowboy / Important exportin' man / One too many stories / Kick in the head / You should have seen me running / L.A. lady / Thank the day / Cement, clay and glass. *(re-iss. Feb89 on 'Beat Goes On'; BGOLP 26) (cd-iss. Aug92; BGOCD 26)*

Feb 74. (7") *<45976>* **PANAMA RED. / CEMENT, CLAY AND GLASS** –

Jun 74. (lp) *(CBS 80060)* *<32870>* **HOME, HOME ON THE ROAD (live)** Apr74 68
– Hi, hello, how are you / She's no angel / Groupie / Sunday Susie / Kick in the head / Truck drivin' man / Hello Mary Lou / Sutter's mill.

— **SKIP BATTIN** (b. 2 Feb'34, Gallipolis, Ohio) – bass (ex-BYRDS, ex-Solo artist) repl. TORBERT to KINGFISH

Nov 74. (7") *<19967>* **YOU ANGEL YOU. / PARSON BROWN** –

Jan 75. (lp) *(CBS 80405)* *<33145>* **BRUJO** Oct74 68
– Old man Noll / Ashes of love / You angel you / Instant armadillo blues / Workingman's woman / On the Amazon / Big wheels / Singing cowboy / Crooked judge / Parson Brown / Neon rose.

Dec 75. (lp) *(CBS 69182)* *<33688>* **OH, WHAT A MIGHTY TIME** Nov75
– Mighty time / I heard you been layin' my old lady / Strangers on a train / Up against the wall Redneck / Take a letter to Maria / Little old lady / On top of old Smokey / Over and over / La bamba / Going round the Horn / Farewell Angelina.

M.C.A. M.C.A.

May 76. (7") **FIFTEEN DAYS UNDER THE HOOD. / DON'T PUT HER DOWN** –

Jul 76. (lp) *(MCF 2758)* *<2196>* **NEW RIDERS** Jun76
– Fifteen days under the hood / Annie May / You never can tell / Hard to handle / Dead flowers / Don't put her down / The honky tonkin' (I guess I done me some) / She's looking better after every beer / Can't get over you / The swimming song. *(cd-iss. Apr94; MCAD 22108)*

Aug 76. (7") *(MCA 248)* *<40591>* **DEAD FLOWERS. / SHE'S LOOKING BETTER AFTER EVERY BEER**

— **STEPHEN LOVE** (b. Indiana) – bass (ex-RICK NELSON's STONE CANYON BAND) repl. BATTIN who joined FLYING BURRITO BROTHERS.

Feb 77. (7") *<40715>* **JUST ANOTHER NIGHT IN RENO. / HOME GROWN** –

Apr 77. (lp) *(MCF 2793)* *<2248>* **WHO ARE THOSE GUYS**
– I can heal you / High rollers / Peggy Sue / Just another night in Reno / It never hurts to be nice to somebody / Love has strange ways / Hold on it's coming / By and by / When I need you / Home grown / Red hot woman and ice cold beer. *(cd-iss. Apr94; MCAD 22109)*

May 77. (7") *(MCA 299)* **LOVE HAS STRANGE WAYS. / RED HOT WOMAN AND ICE COOL BEER** –

Feb 78. (lp) *(MCF 2830)* *<2307>* **MARIN COUNTY LINE**
– Jasper / Twenty good men / Echoes / Take a red / Knights and queens / A good woman likes to drink with the boys / Turkeys in a straw / Green eyes a flashing / Little Miss Bad / Echoes / Till I met you / Oh what a night / Llywelyn. *(cd-iss. Apr94; MCAD 22107)*

— **ALLEN KEMP** – guitar, vocals / **PATRICK SHANAHAN** – drums / **MICHAEL WHITE** – bass repl. DRYDEN + LOVE

not iss. A&M

Feb 81. (lp) *<SP 4818>* **FEELIN' ALRIGHT** –
– Night for making love / No other love / The way she dances / Tell me / Fly right / Crazy little girl / Full moon at midnite / Pakalolo man / Daydreamin' girl / Saralyn.

Apr 81. (7") *<2327>* **NIGHT FOR MAKING LOVE. / FLY RIGHT** –

Jul 81. (7") *<2352>* **FULL MOON AT MIDNIGHT. / NO OTHER LOVE** –

— added **RUSTY GAUTHIER** – guitar, etc

not iss. M.U.

1982. (lp) *<MU 31109>* **KEEP ON KEEPIN' ON** –
– Keep on keepin' on / Now I call it love / It's o.k. to cry / Bounty hunter / Barbaric splendor / Senorita / Night of the living lonely / Rancher's daughter / Big Ed / Friend of the Devil.

— **DAWSON** + **NELSON** with **GARY VOGENSEN** – vocals, guitar; who repl. KEMP

not iss. Relix

1986. (lp; as NEW RIDERS) *<2024>* **BEFORE TIME BEGAN** –
– Henry / All I ever wanted / Last lonely eagle / Cecilia / Garden of Eden / Superman / Deh Rominap / Handful of brains / I'm through with the fish, Harve / Och tamale / Handful of brains (part 2) / Where discipline comes in.

1992. (cd) *<2050>* **MIDNIGHT MOONLIGHT** –
– Midnight moonlight / Sutter's mill / Charlie's garden / All I remember / Louisiana lady / Ballad of the deportees / Taking it hard / Glendale train / Change in the weather / Diesel on my tail / Lonesome L.A. cowboy.

— **EVAN MORGAN** – guitar; repl. VOGENSEN

— In 1994, NELSON, DAWSON + CAGE re-formed

Sep 94. (cd) *<2065>* **LIVE IN JAPAN (live)** –
– Henry / Dire wolf / Rainbow / Early in the morning / Keep on keepin' on / Ripple / I don't know you / Friend of the Devil / Portland woman.

– compilations, etc. –

Dec 76. (lp) *C.B.S.; (81742) / Columbia; <34367>* **THE BEST OF NEW RIDERS OF THE PURPLE SAGE**

1988. (lp) *Relix; <RRCD 2025>* **VINTAGE** –

May 94. (cd) *Raven; (RVCD 36)* **WASTED TASTERS 1971-1975** –
– Hebry / Glendale train / Louisiana lady / I don't know you / Last lonely eagle / I don't need no doctor / Contract / Rainbow / Sweet lovin' one / Dim light thick smoke / She's no angel / Sutter's mill / Sailin' / Panama Red / Lonesome L.A. cowboy / Kick in the head / Teardrops in my eyes / Hello Mary Lou / Dead flowers / You angel you / Singing cowboy / I heard you been layin' my old lady / Farewell Angelina.

Nov 99. (cd) *Relix; <(RRCD 2071)>* **THE BEST OF THE EARLY YEARS**

Jan 00. (cd) *Wagon Wheel; <71501>* **DRIFTING CLOUDS** –

Oct 00. (cd) *Beat Goes On; (<BGOCD 509>)* **GYPSY COWBOY / THE ADVENTURES OF PANAMA RED**

May 02. (cd) *Beat Goes On; (<BGOCD 551>)* **NEW RIDERS OF THE PURPLE SAGE / POWERGLIDE**

NEW YORK DOLLS

Formed: New York City, New York, USA . . . late '71 by JOHNNY THUNDERS, DAVID JOHANSEN, BILLY MURCIA, ARTHUR KANE and RICK RIVETS. In March the following year, RIVETS left to form The BRATS, being swiftly replaced by SYLVAIN SYLVAIN. After a promising start as support act on a FACES British tour, the 'DOLLS' first casualty was MURCIA who died on the 6th of November '72 after drowning in his own bath (not, as widely believed, from a drug overdose). With JERRY NOLAN as a replacement, they signed to 'Mercury' in March '73 and promptly began work on an eponymous debut album with TODD RUNDGREN producing. Released in the summer of that year, 'THE NEW YORK DOLLS' was a proto-punk revelation, a way cool schlock of visceral rock'n'roll which combined the more essential moments of MC5, The PRETTY THINGS, PINK FAIRIES and The SHANGRI-LAS. The ROLLING STONES were another obvious reference point, JOHANSEN a dead-ringer for MICK JAGGER in terms of both vocal style and mascara'd looks. Inevitably, then, THUNDERS was the glam-punk KEITH RICHARDS, Glitter Twins to the JAGGERS/RICHARDS Glimmer coupling. The 'DOLLS' trashy transvestite attire also borrowed heavily from the 'STONES (circa '66 'Have You Seen Your Mother . . .'), although being American they'd obviously taken it to almost cartoon-esque proportions. The likes of 'PERSONALITY CRISIS', 'TRASH' and 'JET BOY' were seminal squalls of guitar abuse, making up in attitude what they lacked in musical ability. Although the record had the critics salivating, commercial success wasn't forthcoming and, unhappy with the record's production, the band opted for SHANGRI-LA's producer, GEORGE MORTON to work on 'TOO MUCH TOO SOON' (1974). Though the album had its moments, again the band had been paired with the wrong producer and the music press were emphatically unimpressed. The lukewarm reviews heightened inter-band tension and the 'DOLLS demise was swift and inevitable. Early the following year, Londoner MALCOLM McLAREN made a last-ditch attempt to save the band, revamping their image to no avail. THUNDERS was the first to leave, departing in 1975 to form The HEARTBREAKERS, while JOHANSEN and SYLVAIN subsequently sacked KANE before finally calling it a day the following Christmas. While THUNDERS went on to most acclaim with his HEARTBREAKERS (dying from an overdose on 23rd April '91), JOHANSEN recorded a number of solo albums, 'DAVID JOHANSEN' (1978), 'IN STYLE' (1979) and 'HERE COMES THE NIGHT' (1981) as well as releasing a 1988 set under the pseudonym of BUSTER POINDEXTER. NOLAN also met an untimely death, almost a year on from THUNDERS (14th January, 1992), suffering a fatal stroke while undergoing treatment for meningitis and pneumonia. A pivotal reference point for not only punk, but the US sleaze/glam metal movement of the mid-80's (FASTER PUSSYCAT, L.A. GUNS, GUNS N' ROSES, et al), The NEW YORK DOLLS influence remains hugely disproportionate to their relatively slim recorded legacy. • **Songwriters:** JOHANSEN with THUNDERS or SYLVAIN. Covered PILLS (Bo Diddley) / DON'T START ME TALKIN' (Sonny Boy Williamson) / SHOWDOWN (Archie Bell) / SOMETHIN' ELSE (Eddie Cochran) / etc. • **Trivia:** Two songs 'PERSONALITY CRISIS' & 'WHO ARE THE MYSTERY GIRLS', appeared on the 1977 Various Artists compilation 'NEW WAVE'. **JOHANSEN's filmography:** 'Married To The Mob', 'Scrooged' and 'The Fisher King'.

Album rating: NEW YORK DOLLS (*8) / TOO MUCH TOO SOON (*7) / LIPSTICK KILLERS exploitation (*5) / ROCK & ROLL compilation (*7).
David Johansen: DAVID JOHANSEN (*6) / IN STYLE (*5) / HERE COMES THE NIGHT (*4) / LIVE IT UP (*5) / SWEET REVENGE (*5) / CRUCIAL MUSIC: THE DAVID JOHANSEN COLLECTION (*6)

DAVID JOHANSEN (b. 9 Jan'50, Staten Island, N.Y.) – vocals / **JOHNNY THUNDERS** (b. JOHN GENZALE, 15 Jul'52) – guitar, vocals / **SYLVAIN SYLVAIN** (b. SIL MIZRAHI) – guitar, vocals repl. RICK RIVETS / **ARTHUR KANE** (b. 3 Feb'51) – bass / **JERRY NOLAN** (b. 7 May'51) – drums repl. BILLY MURCIA who died.

Mercury / Mercury

Jul 73. (7") *<73414>* **TRASH. / PERSONALITY CRISIS** [–] [ ]
Aug 73. (lp) *(6338 270) <SRM 675>* **NEW YORK DOLLS** [ ] Jul73 [ ]
– Personality crisis / Looking for a kiss / Vietnamese baby / Lonely planet boy / Frankenstein / Trash / Bad girl / Subway train / Pills / Private world / Jet boy. *<US re-iss. 1984; same>*
Nov 73. (7") *(6052 402)* **JET BOY. / VIETNAMESE BABY** [ ] [–]
Jul 74. (lp) *(6338 498) <SRM 1001>* **TOO MUCH TOO SOON** [ ] May74 [ ]
– Babylon / Stranded in the jungle / Who are the mystery girls? / (There's gonna be a) Showdown / It's too late / Puss 'n' boots / Chatterbox / Bad detective / Don't start me talkin' / Human being. *<US re-iss. 1984; same>*
Jul 74. (7") *(6052 615) <73478>* **STRANDED IN THE JUNGLE. / WHO ARE THE MYSTERY GIRLS?** [ ] [ ]
Sep 74. (7") *<73615>* **(THERE'S GONNA BE A) SHOWDOWN. / PUSS 'N' BOOTS** [–] [ ]

not iss. / Trash

1974. (fan club-7"ep) *<TR 001>* **LOOKING FOR A KISS (live). / WHO ARE THE MYSTERY GIRLS? (live) / SOMETHIN' ELSE (live)** [–] [ ]

— **PETER JORDAN** – bass (the roadie filled in on stage when KANE was drunk)

— Disbanded mid-1975, after **BOBBY BLAIN** – keyboards repl. CHRIS ROBINSON who had repl. THUNDERS (he formed The HEARTBREAKERS with NOLAN). **TOMMY MACHINE** (was last drummer). The NEW YORK DOLLS reformed again with JOHANSEN and SYLVIAN but only toured until late '76. SYLVIAN later formed The CRIMINALS. DAVID JOHANSEN went solo in 1978.

– compilations, others, etc. –

Jun 77. (7"m) *Mercury; (6160 008)* **JET BOY. / BABYLON / WHO ARE THE MYSTERY GIRLS?** [ ] [–]
Jul 77. (d-lp) *Mercury; (6641 631)* **NEW YORK DOLLS / TOO MUCH TOO SOON** [ ] [–]
(re-iss. Apr86; PRID 12)
Nov 81. (c) *R.O.I.R.; <A 104>* **LIPSTICK KILLERS – MERCER ST. SESSIONS** [–] [ ]
(re-iss. May90 on 'Danceteria' cd/lp; DAN CD/LP 038) (re-iss. cd Feb95 & Jun97 on 'ROIR Europe'; 885615027-2) (cd re-iss. Aug00 on 'R.O.I.R.'; RUSCD 8266)
Sep 82. (12"ep) *Kamera; (ERA 13-12)* **PERSONALITY CRISIS / LOOKING FOR A KISS. / SUBWAY TRAIN / BAD GIRL** [ ] [–]
(re-iss. Jul90 on 'See For Miles' cd-ep; SEACD 3)
Sep 84. (red-m-lp) *Fan Club; (FC 007)* **RED PATENT LEATHER (rec. 75)** [–] France [–]
– Girls / Downtown / Private love / Personality crisis / Pills / Something else / Daddy rollin' stone / Dizzy Miss Lizzy. *(cd-iss. Oct88; FC 007CD) (UK cd-iss. Feb93 on 'Receiver'+=; RRCD 173) (cd re-iss. Apr97 on 'Last Call'; 42241-2)*
Oct 84. (7"white) *Fan Club; (NYD 1)* **PILLS (live). / DOWN, DOWN, DOWN TOWN (live)** [–] France [–]
1985. (lp) *Mercury; <8260 941>* **NIGHT OF THE LIVING DOLLS** [–] [ ]
Feb 86. (7",12"pic-d,12"red) *Antler; (DOLLS 1)* **PERSONALITY CRISIS. / SUBWAY TRAIN** [ ] [–]
Feb 86. (7",12"pic-d,12"blue) *Antler; (DOLLS 2)* **LOOKING FOR A KISS. / BAD GIRL** [ ] [–]
1986. (lp; one-side by SEX PISTOLS) *Receiver; (RRLP 102)* **AFTER THE STORM** [ ] [–]
(cd-iss. Jul93; RRCD 102)
Jul 93. (cd) *Receiver; <(RRCD 163)>* **SEVEN DAY WEEKEND** [ ] [ ]
Jul 93. (cd) *Receiver; <(RRCD 173)>* **IN NYC 1975** [ ] [ ]
Oct 94. (cd) *Mercury; (522 129-2)* **ROCK'N'ROLL** [ ] [ ]
Mar 96. (cd) *Skydog; <(62256-2)>* **PARIS BURNING** [ ] [ ]

Mar 96. (cd) *Skydog;* <*(62257-2)*> **NEW YORK TAPES 1972-1973**
<(re-iss. Feb00 on 'Munster'; MR 167/+CD)>
Oct 97. (cd) *Red Star;* <*(RS 7006)*> **TEENAGE NEWS**
Nov 98. (cd; shared w/ JOHNNY THUNDERS) *Recall;* <*(SMDCD 207)*> **STREET TRASH**
Nov 98. (cd) *Receiver;* <*(RRCD 260)*> **I'M A HUMAN BEING (live)**
Sep 98. (cd) *Red Star;* <*(RSR 7006)*> **LIVE IN CONCERT PARIS 1974**
<(re-iss. Jun99 on 'Essential'; ESMCD 734)>
Jul 99. (cd) *Big Ear; (109634022-2)* **GLAMOROUS LIFE – LIVE**
Apr 00. (lp/cd) *Get Back; (GET 60/+CD)* **THE BIRTH OF THE NEW YORK DOLLS**

NICE

Formed: London, England . . . Oct'67 by ex-GARY FARR & THE T-BONES members, KEITH EMERSON and LEE JACKSON, who, along with DAVID O'LIST and BRIAN DAVIDSON, had backed-up British black soul singer, P.P.ARNOLD. Being part of Andrew Loog Oldham's 'Immediate' label, they moved in a different musical direction with their first 45, 'THOUGHTS OF EMERLIST DAVJACK'. This flopped, as did the similarly titled 1968 debut album containing their show-stopper, 'RONDO'. That summer, they surprised many when their rendition of Leonard Bernstein's 'AMERICA' (from 'West Side Story'), nearly hit the UK Top 20. It was banned in the States, however, where offence was taken to their promotional poster featuring the recently deceased Martin Luther King, Bobby and John F.Kennedy. During a subsequent performance at The Royal Albert Hall, NICE burned an American flag, riling Bernstein enough to prevent the 45 being issued in the States. Although their follow-up album, 'ARS LONGA VITA BREVIS' (1968) failed, subsequent efforts, 'THE NICE' (1969) and 'FIVE BRIDGES SUITE' (1970) both went Top 5. Pioneers of orchestral rock, NICE deconstructed classical music, arranging new interpretations around the keyboard-stabbing showman, KEITH EMERSON. This esteemed ivory-tinkler subsequently went on to even greater success with EMERSON, LAKE & PALMER. • **Songwriters:** Group compositions, using first letters of forenames (aka 'EMERLIST DAVJACK' until O'LIST left in 1968). Covered; AMERICA (Sondheim / Bernstein) / INTERMEZZO FROM KARELIA SUITE (Sibelius) / HANG ON TO A DREAM (Tim Hardin) / SHE BELONGS TO ME + MY BACK PAGES + COUNTRY PIE (Bob Dylan) / and other classical re-inditions.

Album rating: THE THOUGHTS OF EMERLIST DAVJACK (*7) / ARS LONGA VITA BREVIS (*6) / THE NICE (*6) / FIVE BRIDGES SUITE (*7) / ELEGY (*4) / THE NICE COLLECTION compilation (*8)

KEITH EMERSON (b. 2 Nov'44, Todmorden, England) – keyboards / **DAVID O'LIST** – guitar, vocals / **BRIAN DAVIDSON** (b.25 May'42, Leicester, England) – drums / **LEE JACKSON** (b. 8 Jan'43, Newcastle-upon-Tyne, England) – vocals, bass

Immediate Immediate

Nov 67. (7") *(IM 059)* **THE THOUGHTS OF EMERLIST DAVJACK. / AZRIAL (ANGEL OF DEATH)**
Dec 67. (lp; mono/stereo) *(IMLP/IMSP 016)* <*52004*> **THE THOUGHTS OF EMERLIST DAVJACK**
– Flower king of flies / The thoughts of Emerlist Davjack / Bonnie K. / Rondo / War and peace / Tantalising Maggie / Dawn / The cry of Eugene / Angel of death / America: 1A (adapted from 'West Side Story') – 1B second amendment / The diamond hard apples of the Moon. *(re-iss. Jul68; same) (re-iss. 1978 on 'Charly'; CR 3000021) (cd-iss. 1988 on 'Line'; IMCD 900228) (cd re-iss. Feb94 on 'Charly'; CDIMM 010) (<cd re-mast.Aug98 on 'Essential'+=; ESMCD 647>)* – The thoughts of Emerlist Davjack (mono).
Jun 68. (7") *(IM 068)* **AMERICA (2nd Amendment). / THE DIAMOND HARD APPLES OF THE MOON** 21
(re-iss. Dec82; same)
—— now a trio, when O'LIST departed, later joining ROXY MUSIC
Dec 68. (lp) *(IMSP 020)* <*52020*> **ARS LONGA VITA BREVIS**
– Daddy, where did I come from? / Little Arabella / Happy Freuds / Intermezzo from Karelia / Don Edito el Gruva / Ars longa vita brevis – Prelude: 1st movement – Wakening ; 2nd movement – Realisation ; 3rd movement – Acceptance – Brandenburger ; 4th movement – Denial / Coda – Extention to the big note. *(re-iss. Dec86 on 'Castle' lp/c/cd; CLA LP/MC/CD 120) (cd re-mast.Aug98 on 'Essential'; ESMCD 646)*
Dec 68. (7") *(IM 072)* **BRANDENBURGER. / HAPPY FREUDS** –
Jul 69. (7") **SHE BELONGS TO ME. / ('A'version)** –
Aug 69. (lp) *(IMSP 026)* <*52022*> **THE NICE** 3
– Azrael revisited / Hang on to a dream / Diary of an empty day / For example / Rondo 69 / She belongs to me. *(cd-iss. 1990's on 'Repertoire';) (cd re-mast.Aug98 on 'Essential'+=; ESMCD 645)* – Hang onto a dream (mono) / Diary of an empty day (mono).

Charisma Mercury

Jun 70. (lp) *(CAS 1014)* <*SR 61295*> **FIVE BRIDGES SUITE** 2
– The five bridges suite:- Fantasia, 1st bridge – 2nd bridge – Choral, 3rd bridge – High level fugue, 4th bridge – Finale, 5th bridge / Intermezzo Karelia suite:- Pathetique, 'Symphony No.6. 3rd movement' / Country pie – Bach: Brandenburg concerto No.6 / One of those people. *(cd-iss. Feb91 +=; CASCD 1014)* – The thoughts of Emerlist Davjack / Flower king of the flies / Bonnie K / Diary of an empty day / America.
Jul 70. (7") *(CB 132)* <*73114*> **COUNTRY PIE. / ONE OF THOSE PEOPLE**
—— Disbanded mid 1970. KEITH formed EMERSON, LAKE & PALMER. LEE and BRIAN later surfaced as REFUGEE and made one eponymous album in 1974 for 'Charisma', which featured future YES man, PATRICK MORAZ.

– compilations, others, etc. –

Apr 71. (lp) *Charisma; (CAS 1030) / Mercury;* <*SR 61324*> **ELEGY (live)** 5
– Hang on to a dream / My back pages / 3rd movement – Pathetique / America (from 'West Side Story'). *(re-iss. Sep83 lp/c; CHC/+MC 1) (cd-iss. Feb91 & Jun93 +=; CASCD 1030)* – Diamonds blue apples of the Moon / Dawn / Tantalising Maggie / The cry of Eugene / Daddy, where did I come from? / Aziral.
Feb 72. (d-lp) *Mercury;* <*SRM2 6500*> **KEITH EMERSON WITH THE NICE** (4th + 5th albums) –
(cd-iss. UK 1988; 830 457-2)
Mar 72. (7"; as KEITH EMERSON & THE NICE) *Mercury;* <*73272*> **COUNTRY PIE – BRANDENBERG No.6. / FINALE – 5th BRIDGE** –
1972. (lp) *Charisma; (CS 1)* **AUTUMN 67 SPRING 68** –
Mar 76. (lp) *Immediate; (IML 1003)* **AMOENI REDIVI** –
Jan 78. (lp) *Immediate; (IML 2003)* **THE NICE GREATEST HITS** –
Mar 83. (d-c) *Charisma; (CASMC 163)* **FIVE BRIDGES SUITE / AUTUMN 67 AND SPRING 68** –
Nov 85. (d-lp/c/cd) *Castle; (CCS LP/MC/CD 106)* **THE NICE COLLECTION** –
– America 1A (adapted from 'West Side Story') – 1B Second amendment / Happy Freuds / The cry of Eugene / The thoughts of Emerlist Davjack / Rondo / Daddy, where did I come from? / Little Arabella / Intermezzo from Karelia / Hang on to a dream / The diamond hard apples of the Moon / Angel of death / Ars longa vita brevis – Prelude:- 1st movement – Wakening, 2nd movement – Realisation, 3rd movement – Acceptance, Brandenburger, 4th movement – Denial / Coda – Extention to the big note. *(re-iss. cd Apr94; same)*
Aug 87. (lp/c) *Seal; (SLP/SC 002)* **THE 20th ANNIVERSARY OF THE NICE** –
(re-iss. Apr88 on 'Bite Back' lp/c/cd; BTE L/C/CD 2)
Dec 93. (cd) *Immediate; (CSL 6032) / Griffin;* <*228*> **THE BEST OF THE NICE – AMERICA** Jun95
(re-iss. Oct98 on 'Essential'; ESMCD 629)
Mar 94. (cd) *Laserlight; (CD 12334)* **AMERICA** –
Nov 95. (3xcd-box) *Charly; (CDIMMBOX 2)* **THE IMMEDIATE YEARS** –
Jul 96. (cd) *Receiver; (RRCD 224)* **AMERICA – THE BBC SESSIONS** –
Nov 99. (d-cd) *Snapper; (SMDCD 203)* **THE IMMEDIATE COLLECTION** –
Feb 00. (d-cd) *Double Classics; (DC 31025)* **THE LONG VERSIONS** –

Oct 00. (3xcd-box) *Castle; (CMETD 055)* **HERE COMES THE NICE** [ ] [–]
Oct 01. (cd) *Castle; (CMRCD 349)* **THE SWEDISH RADIO SESSIONS** [ ] [–]
Sep 02. (cd) *Castle; (<CMFCD 457>)* **BBC SESSIONS** [ ] [ ]
Apr 03. (d-cd) *Excellence; (EXCEL 2111)* **CLASSIC ROCK STANDARDS** [ ] [–]

NICKELBACK

Formed: Hanna, Calgary, Canada . . . 1995 by CHAD KROEGER, who played in a covers band but got fed up and wrote a handful of songs before cutting a demo tape in Vancouver. He invited his brother MIKE KROEGER and a bassist friend RYAN VIKEDAL to play in the band and after a short time rehearsing, the group recorded and independently issued EP 'HERSHER' (1996) and managed to raise enough cash to fund a cross-country 'toilet' tour across Canada before releasing their debut set 'CURB' (1997). After two years of squabbling and disagreeing with their management, KROEGER decided that it would be best if the group managed themselves, thus adding pressure for the other members whose job it was to distribute and advertise their debut long-player. KROEGER came up with the ingenious way of creating airplay for themselves by getting friends and family members to phone up radio stations and request their songs. By this time NICKELBACK had quite a cult following in the US and in North America. They independently produced and distributed 'THE STATE' (2000), the sophomore album which held the group's hard-edged rock ethos intact but lacked the punch of their first. The set proved to be highly successful, with a sell-out tour and a growing popularity, the trio soon found themselves playing for larger audiences, supporting the likes of CREED and FUEL. Not surprisingly, 'THE STATE' was bought by various different companies for major distribution all over the globe; 'E.M.I.' for the Canadian release and 'Roadrunner' elsewhere. It also broke them into the US Top 200 later in the year. 'SILVER SIDE UP' was released the following year and spawned the massive hit single 'HOW YOU REMIND ME', a PEARL JAM-esque rock-out, with big riffs and an even bigger chorus. The soon-to-be Top 3 album and the single put NICKELBACK on the musical map, with the aforementioned single being officially claimed as 'The Most Played Song On American Radio'. It topped the charts in both America and Canada at the same time, a feat not accomplished since The GUESS WHO's 'American Woman' (me thinks?). Although whether people will still be listening to NICKELBACK three decades hence is open to question. 2002 brought another sizeable hit in 'HERO', a duet with SALIVA frontman JOSEY SCOTT which had previously appeared on the soundtrack to the 'Spiderman' movie. 'THE LONG ROAD' (2003) was another constipated collection of meat and potatoes hard rock, with just enough tortuous whining to have it labelled alternative. • **Covers:** SATURDAY NIGHT'S ALRIGHT (FOR FIGHTING) (Elton John).

Album rating: HESHER mini (*5) / CURB (*5) / THE STATE (*6) / SILVER SIDE UP (*7) / THE LONG ROAD (*4)

CHAD KROEGER (b.15 Nov'74) – vocals, guitar / **RYAN PEAKE** – guitar, vocals / **MIKE KROEGER** – bass / **RYAN VIKEDAL** – drums

not iss. — own label

1996. (m-cd) *<none>* **HESHER EP** [–] Canada [–]
– Where? / Windowshopper / Fly / Truck / Left / In front of me / D.C.

1997. (cd) *<none>* **CURB** [–] Canada [–]
– Little friend / Pusher / Detangler / Curb / Where? / Falls back on / Sea groove / Fly / Just four / Left / Windowshopper / I don't have. *<(re+UK-iss.Jun02; RR 8440-2)>*

Roadrunner — Roadrunner

Mar 00. (cd) *<8586>* **THE STATE** [–] [ ]
– Breathe / Cowboy hat / Leader of men / Old enough / Worthy to say / Diggin' this / Deep / One last run / Not leavin' yet / Hold out your hand. *<cd-bonus+=>* – Leader of men (acoustic) / Worthy to say (acoustic).

Sep 01. (cd) *(120 8485-2) <61 8485>* **SILVER SIDE UP** [ ] [2]
– Never again / How you remind me / Woke up this morning / Too bad / Just for / Hollywood / Money bought / Where do I hide / Hangnail / Good times now. *(UK re-dist.Jan02)* – hit No.1 *(lp-iss.Sep02 on 'Simply Vinyl'; S 160001)*

Oct 01. (cd-s) *(2320332-3) <012053>* **HOW YOU REMIND ME / LEADER OF MEN (acoustic)** [ ] Aug01 [1]

Feb 02. (c-s) *(2320332-4)* **HOW YOU REMIND ME / (acoustic)** [4] [–]
(cd-s+=) *(2320332-0)* – Learn the hard way / ('A'-video).
(cd-s) *(2320332-5)* – ('A'side) / (gold mix) / Yanking out my / Leader of men / Leader of men (video).

Jun 02. (c-s; as CHAD KROEGER & JOSEY SCOTT) *(RR 2046-4)* **HERO / HERO (superhero mix)** [4] May02 [3]
(cd-s+=) *(RR 2046-3)* – Invisible man (THEORY OF A DEADMAN) / ('A'-video).

— 'HERO' from the movie, 'Spider Man'

Aug 02. (c-s) *(RR 2037-4)* **TOO BAD / HOW YOU REMIND ME (live)** [9] Mar02 [42]
(cd-s+=) *(RR 2037-3) <2051-3>* – Woke up this morning (live) / ('A'video).
(cd-s) *(RR 2037-5)* – ('A'side) / Never again (live) / Leader of men (live) / ('A'-live video).

Nov 02. (cd-s) *(RR 2025-3)* **NEVER AGAIN / ONE LAST RUN (live) / WORTHY TO SAY (live) / ('A'-video)** [30] [–]
(cd-s) *(RR 2025-5)* – ('A'-full length) / Breathe (live) / Old enough (live).

Sep 03. (cd-s) *(RR 2008-8) <55302-5>* **SOMEDAY / SLOW MOTION / SOMEDAY (acoustic) / SOMEDAY (video)** [6] [7]

Sep 03. (cd) *(RR 8400-2) <RRD 618400>* **THE LONG ROAD** [5] [6]
– Flat on the floor / Do this anymore / Someday / Believe it or not / Feelin' way too damn good / Because of you / Figured you out / Should've listened / Throw yourself away / Another hole in the head / See you at the show. *(special-cd+=; RR 8400-5)* – Yanking out my heart / Learn the hard way / Saturday night's alright (for fighting).

Stevie NICKS

Born: STEPHANIE NICKS, 26 May'48, Phoenix, Arizona, USA. Raised in California, she made up one half of early 70's Bay Area duo, BUCKINGHAM NICKS, alongside guitarist and he of bouffant hair, LINDSEY BUCKINGHAM. The pair released one self-titled album in 1973 before BUCKINGHAM was invited to join the strife-torn FLEETWOOD MAC as a replacement for BOB WELCH. He accepted the offer with one proviso, that NICKS was also be taken on board. 'MAC agreed, one of the shrewdest decisions they'd make in their long and chequered career. The youthful pair added a bit of much needed Californian style and sass to the band, as well as some sharp songwriting; the self-titled 'Fleetwood Mac' (1975) duly reaching the top of the US charts while its follow-up, 'Rumours' (1977) became one of the biggest selling albums of all time. NICKS was a key element of the band's allure, her huskily intoxicating vocals and sexually magnetic presence fuelling countless teen fantasies. While it goes without saying that at one time, she was arguably the sexiest woman on the planet, NICKS also penned some of FLEETWOOD MAC's most enduring songs including 'Rhiannon' (in which she fashioned the enigmatic temptress persona that would form the basis of her career), 'Gold Dust Woman' and the beautiful 'Sara'. Parallel to her 'MAC work, NICKS has also carved out a fairly successful solo career, debutting in 1981 on the TOM PETTY duet, 'STOP DRAGGIN' MY HEART AROUND'. The single made the US Top 3 while her debut album, 'BELLA DONNA', made the US No.1 spot, showcasing an AOR sound not unlike FLEETWOOD MAC, although lacking that band's songwriting consistency. NICKS continued to hit the charts with varying degrees of success throughout the mid-80's with material from 'THE WILD HEART' (1983) and 'ROCK A LITTLE' (1985). A gap of four years ensued before the release of 'THE OTHER SIDE OF THE MIRROR' (1989), a less satisfying collection that nevertheless contained one of NICKS' most affecting solo works, the soaring 'ROOMS ON FIRE'. In the five year period that followed, NICKS fans had to make do with the 'TIMESPACE' (1991) best of, no new material surfacing until 'STREET ANGEL' in 1994. In the interim, NICKS had left FLEETWOOD MAC to concentrate solely on her own work, maybe a wise move considering the poor commerical showing of her last aforementioned album. After her extended absence during the late 90's, NICKS returned with 'TROUBLE IN SHANGRI-LA' (2001). A cast of mates that included SHERYL CROW, MACY GRAY and SARAH McLACHLAN helped enhance the record's contemporary appeal while NICKS herself sounded older but wiser, that ineffable sensuality still colouring her best efforts. While NICKS' material may sometimes let her down, her dreamy voice rarely fails to send a shiver up the spine (or a stirring in MC STRONG's loin!). • **Songwriters:** Writes herself except; covers MAYBE LOVE (Nowells-Stewart) / JUST LIKE A WOMAN (Bob Dylan) / DOCKLANDS (Trevor Horn- Betsy Cook).

Album rating: BELLA DONNA (*7) / THE WILD HEART (*6) / ROCK A LITTLE (*5) / THE OTHER SIDE OF THE MIRROR (*6) / TIMESPACE – THE BEST OF compilation (*7) / STREET ANGEL (*4) / ENCHANTED collection (*7) / TROUBLE IN SHANGRI-LA (*6)

W.E.A. / Modern

Jul 81. (7"; by STEVIE NICKS with TOM PETTY & THE HEARTBREAKERS) *(K 79231)* <7336> **STOP DRAGGIN' MY HEART AROUND. / KIND OF WOMAN** [50] [3]

Jul 81. (lp/c) *(K/K4 99169)* <139> **BELLA DONNA** [11] [1]
– The highwayman / Stop draggin' my heart around / Bella Donna / Edge of 17 / Kind of woman / Leather and lace / Outside the rain / After the glitter fades / Think about it / How still my love. *(cd-iss. Jan84; K2 99169) (re-iss. Aug89 & Mar91 on 'EMI' lp/c/cd; EMC/TCEMC/CDEMC 3562)*

Sep 81. (7"; by STEVIE NICKS with DON HENLEY) <7341> **LEATHER AND LACE. / BELLA DONNA** [–] [6]

Oct 81. (7") *(K 79265)* **LEATHER AND LACE. / OUTSIDE THE RAIN** [ ] [–]

Feb 82. (7") <7401> **EDGE OF SEVENTEEN (JUST LIKE THE WHITE WINGED DOVE). / ('A'live)** [–] [11]

May 82. (7") *(K 79264)* **EDGE OF SEVENTEEN. / OUTSIDE THE RAIN** [ ] [–]

Jun 82. (7") <7405> **AFTER THE GLITTER FADES. / THINK ABOUT IT** [–] [32]

Jun 83. (7") *(U 9870)* <99863> **STAND BACK. / GARBO** [ ] [5]
(12"+=) *(U 9870T)* – Wild heart.

Jun 83. (lp/c) *(250071-1/-4)* <90048> **THE WILD HEART** [28] [5]
– If anyone falls / Gate and garden / Enchanted / Sable on blond / Nightbird / Stand back / I will run to you / The wild heart / Nothing ever changes / Beauty and the beast. *(cd-iss. Jan84; 250071-2) (re-iss. Oct89 on 'EMI' lp/c/cd; EMC/TCEMC/CDEMC 3563) (cd re-iss. Mar96 on 'EMI Gold'; CDGOLD 1017) (cd re-iss. Feb01 on 'EMI Plus'; 576037-2)*

Aug 83. (7") <99832> **IF ANYONE FALLS. / WILD HEART** [–] [14]

Oct 83. (7") *(X 9590)* **IF ANYONE FALLS. / GATE AND GARDEN** [ ] [–]

Dec 83. (7"; by STEVIE NICKS with SANDY STEWART) <99799> **NIGHTBIRD. / GATE AND GARDEN** [–] [33]

Jan 84. (7") *(U 9690)* **NIGHTBIRD. / NOTHING EVER CHANGES** [ ] [–]

Parlophone / Modern

Dec 85. (lp/c)(cd) *(PCS/TCPCS 7300)(CDP 746201-2)* <90479> **ROCK A LITTLE** [30] [12]
– Sister honey / I can't wait / Rock a little / Imperial hotel / I sing for the things / Some become strangers / The nightmare / Has anyone ever written anything for you / If I were you / No spoken word / Talk to me.

Dec 85. (7"/12") *(R/12R 6110)* **I CAN'T WAIT. / ROCK A LITTLE** [54] [–]

— returned the compliment to TOM PETTY, when providing vocals on their US hit version of 'NEEDLES AND PINS'.

Feb 86. (7") <99565> **I CAN'T WAIT. / THE NIGHTMARE** [–] [16]

Mar 86. (7") *(R 6124)* <99582> **TALK TO ME . / ONE MORE BIG TIME ROCK'N'ROLL STAR** [68] Nov85 [4]
(12"+=) *(12R 6124)* – Imperial hotel.

E.M.I. / Modern

Aug 86. (7") <99532> **HAS ANYONE EVER WRITTEN ANYTHING FOR YOU. / IMPERIAL HOTEL** [–] [60]

Aug 86. (7") *(EMI 5574)* **HAS ANYONE EVER WRITTEN ANYTHING FOR YOU. / I CAN'T WAIT** [ ] [–]
(12"+=) *(12EMI 5574)* – No spoken word.

Apr 89. (7"/c-s) *(EM/TCEM 90)* <99216> **ROOMS ON FIRE. / ALICE** [16] [16]
(12"+=/12"w-poster+=)(3"cd-s+=) *(12EM/+P 90)(CDEM 90)* – Has anyone ever written anything for you.

Jun 89. (7"; STEVIE NICKS with BRUCE HORNSBY) **TWO KINDS OF LOVE. / REAL TEARS** [–] [ ]

Jun 89. (lp/c/cd) *(EMD/TCEMD/CDEMD 1008)* <91245> **THE OTHER SIDE OF THE MIRROR** [3] [10]
– Rooms on fire / Long way to go / Two kinds of love / Oh my love / Ghosts / Whole lotta trouble / Fire burning / Cry wolf / Alice / Juliet / Doing the best I can (escape from Berlin) / I still miss someone. *(re-iss. Mar94 cd/c; same) (lp re-iss. Sep00 on 'Simply Vinyl'; SVLP 236)*

Jul 89. (7") *(EM 97)* **LONG WAY TO GO. / REAL TEARS** [60] [ ]
(12"+=/12"g-f+=) *(12EM/+G 97)* – ('A'remix).
(c-s+=/3"cd-s+=) *(TC/CD EM 97)* – No spoken word.

Oct 89. (7") **WHOLE LOTTA TROUBLE. / GHOSTS** [–] [ ]

Oct 89. (7") *(EM 114)* **WHOLE LOTTA TROUBLE. / EDGE OF SEVENTEEN** [62] [–]
(12"+=/12"w-poster+=) *(12EM/+P 114)* – Beauty & the beast (live).
(c-s+=/cd-s+=) *(TC/CD EM 114)* – Rooms on fire.

Aug 91. (7"/7"s/c-s) *(EM/EMP/TCEM 203)* <98758> **SOMETIMES IT'S A BITCH. / DESERT ANGEL** [40] [56]
(12"+=/cd-s+=) *(12/CD EM 203)* – Battle of the dragons.

Aug 91. (cd)(c/lp) *(CDP 797623-2)(TC+/EMD 1024)* <91711> **TIMESPACE – THE BEST OF STEVIE NICKS** (compilation) [15] [30]
– Sometimes it's a bitch / Stop draggin' my heart / Whole lotta trouble / Talk to me / Stand back / Beauty and the beast / If anyone falls / Rooms on fire / Love's a hard game to play / Edge of seventeen / Leather and lace / I can't wait / Has anyone ever written anything for you. *(cd+=)* – Desert angel.

Nov 91. (7"/c-s) *(EM/TCEM 214)* **I CAN'T WAIT (remix). / EDGE OF SEVENTEEN (live)** [47] [–]
(cd-s+=) *(CDEM 214)* – ('A'version) / Sleeping angel.
(12") *(12EM 214)* – ('A'side) / ('A'dub version) / Sleeping angel.

— with **MICHAEL CAMPBELL** (co-writer) + **BERNIE LEADON** + **ANDY FAIRWEATHER LOW** + **WADDY WACHTEL** – guitars / **PETER MICHAEL** – percussion / **PAT DONALDSON** – bass / **BENMONT TENCH** – hammond organ / **ROY BITTAN** – piano / **KENNY ARONOFF** – drums

May 94. (cd/c) *(CD/TC EMC 3671)* <92246> **STREET ANGEL** [16] [45]
– Blue denim / Gretta / Street angel / Docklands / Listen to the rain / Destiny / Unconditional love / Love is like a river / Rose garden / Maybe love will change your mind / Just like a woman / Kick it / Jane.

Jun 94. (c-s) *(TCEM 328)* <98270> **MAYBE LOVE WILL CHANGE YOUR MIND / INSPIRATION** [42] [57]
(cd-s+=) *(CDEM 328)* – Has anyone ever written anything for you.
(cd-s) *(CDEMS 328)* – ('A'side) / Thousand days / I can't wait / Stand back.

Reprise / Reprise

May 01. (cd/c) <*(9362 47372-2/-4)*> **TROUBLE IN SHANGRI-LA** [43] [5]
– Trouble in Shangri-la / Candlebright / Sorcerer / Planets of the universe / Every day / Too far from Texas / That made me stronger / It's only love / Love changes / I miss you / Bombay sapphires / Fall from grace / Love is.

— STEVIE re-joined FLEETWOOD MAC

– compilations, etc. –

Jul 99. (3xcd-box) *EMI; (521085) / Modern-Atlantic;* <80393> **THE ENCHANTED WORKS OF STEVIE NICKS** [ ] May98 [85]

Feb 01. (cd) *EMI Plus; (576262-2)* **THE DIVINE STEVIE NICKS** [ ] [ ]

NICO

Born: CHRISTA PAFFGEN, 16 Oct'38, Cologne, Germany. Her father died in a concentration camp, and, as a girl, she travelled throughout Europe with her mother. Developing a fondness for opera, she learned to play classical piano and harmonium. In 1959, while vacationing in Italy, she was introduced by new friends to film director Federico Fellini and following a bit-part in 'La Dolce Vita', she became a top model, appearing in Vogue magazine. In the early 60's, while working in films, she became the girlfriend of French actor Alain Delon. She later give birth to his son, having already borne a daughter to actor/dancer Eric Emerson. In 1963, she fell in love with up and coming folk-star BOB DYLAN, who wrote a song for her, 'I'LL KEEP IT WITH MINE'. In 1965, at his suggestion, she moved to London and signed for Andrew Loog Oldham's new label, 'Immediate'. A single, 'I'M NOT SAYING' (written by GORDON LIGHTFOOT) was issued, although the record subsequently flopped, even after an appearance on 'Ready Steady Go'. She then moved to New York, where she met pop-artist ANDY WARHOL. He asked her to feature in an avant-garde film, 'Chelsea Girl', also asking her to join LOU REED, JOHN CALE, MO TUCKER, etc. in his managerial group, The VELVET UNDERGROUND. Together they made one glorious late 1966 album, 'THE VELVET UNDERGROUND AND NICO', NICO leaving soon after for a return to solo work. Decribed as 'The Edith Piaf of the Blank Generation', she was an avant-garde, moody songstress who was anti-pop music in every sense. After a liaison with BRIAN JONES of The ROLLING STONES, she became the opposite number of teenager and new pensmith JACKSON BROWNE who wrote songs for her debut 1968 album, 'CHELSEA GIRL' (notebly 'THESE DAYS'). Regarded as an artistic triumph, she nevertheless disagreed with producer Tom Wilson's string arrangements. Subsequently moving to Los Angeles, she started writing material for her follow-up 'Elektra' album, 'THE MARBLE INDEX'. She travelled constantly between America and Europe, starring in another underground film, 'La Cicatrice Interieupe' for Philippe Garrel. In 1971, she cut the JOHN CALE-produced 'DESERTSHORE', the track 'Le Petit Chevalier' featuring her son. Fleeing New York for France after she was involved in a bottle fight with a female Black Panther member, she later appeared at The Rainbow, London on 1st of June '74 alongside JOHN CALE, ENO and KEVIN AYERS. A track, 'THE END', was recorded, and 'Island' records promptly signed her for an album of the same name, with ENO and PHIL MANZANERA at the production helm. That year, she also contributed vocals to KEVIN AYERS' album, 'Confessions Of Dr. Dream', although she subsequently retired from music to live between Berlin, Los Angeles and Spain. In 1981, she made a comeback album, appropriately titled 'DRAMA OF EXILE', but after poor audience response on a SIOUXSIE & THE BANSHEES support slot, she again went AWOL, shacking up in Manchester, England with her live-in-boyfriend and poet JOHN COOPER CLARKE. After another dismissed vinyl return in 1985, she again retired, only to reappear at a 1987 ANDY WARHOL tribute. Tragically, on the 18th of July '88, on a holiday in Ibiza with CLARKE, she fell off her bike and died of a brain hemorrhage. • **Songwriters:** As said, and other covers; THE END (Doors) / DEUTSCHLAND UBER ALLES (German national anthem) / HEROES (David Bowie) / etc. Plus there are obviously a number of VELVET UNDERGROUND renditions littered about. • **Trivia:** In 1974, she joined LOU REED and JOHN CALE for a French filmed VELVET UNDERGROUND reunion.

Album rating: CHELSEA GIRL (*8) / THE MARBLE INDEX (*7) / DESERTSHORE (*7) / THE END (*5) / DRAMA OF EXILE (*4) / CAMERA OBSCURA (*4) / THE BLUE ANGEL collection (*6) / BEHIND THE IRON CURTAIN (*4) / LIVE IN TOKYO (*5) / posthumous:- HANGING GARDENS (*6) / HEROINE (*4) / INNOCENT & VAIN: AN INTRODUCTION TO NICO compilation (*7)

NICO – vocals (plus session people)

Immediate | not iss.

Aug 65. (7") *(IM 003)* **I'M NOT SAYIN'. / THE LAST MILE** [ ] [–]
(re-iss. May82; IMS 003) (re-iss. Apr03 on 'Munster'; 7173)
(above 'B'side featured JIMMY PAGE as guitarist/writer)

— In 1966, she teamed up with The VELVET UNDERGROUND on their eponymous lp. Breaking from them the following year, she returned to solo work, augmented by JOHN CALE + LOU REED. Her beau JACKSON BROWNE at the time also became her main songwriter.

not iss. | Verve

Feb 68. (lp) *<2353 025>* **CHELSEA GIRL** [–] [ ]
– The fairest of the seasons / These days / Little sister / Winter song / It was a pleasure then / Chelsea girls / I'll keep it with mine / Somewhere there's a father / Wrap your troubles in dreams / Eulogy to Lenny Bruce. *(UK-iss.Sep71 on 'MGM Select'; 2353 025) (re-iss. 1974 on 'Polydor'; same) (cd-iss. May88 & Apr94; 835 209-2)*

— Retained JOHN CALE as producer, etc.

Elektra | Elektra

Jul 69. (lp) *<(EKL 4029)>* **THE MARBLE INDEX** [ ] [ ]
– Prelude / Lawns of dawns / No one is there / Ari's song / Facing the wind / Julius Caesar (memento Hodie) / Frozen warnings / Evening of light. *(cd-iss. Apr91 on 'WEA'+=; 7559 61096-2)* – Roses in the snow / Nibelungen.

Reprise | Reprise

Jan 71. (lp) *<(RSLP 6424)>* **DESERTSHORE** [ ] [ ]
– Janitor of lunacy / Falconer / My only child / Le petit chevalier / Abschied / Afraid / Mutterlein / All that is my own. *(re-iss. 1974; K 44102) (cd-iss. Apr91 on 'WEA'; 7599 25870-2)*

— She retained **CALE** and brought in **ENO** – synthesizer / **PHIL MANZANERA** – guitar / **STERLING MORRISON** – guitar

Island | not iss.

Oct 74. (lp) *(ILPS 9311)* **THE END** [ ] [–]
– It has not taken long / Secret side / You forgot to answer / Innocent and vain / Valley of the kings / We've got the gold / The end / Das lied der Deutschen. *(cd-iss. Apr94; IMCD 174)*

— now with **ANDY CLARKE** – keyboards / **MUHAMMED HADI** – guitar / **DAVEY PAYNE** – sax / **STEVE CORDONA** – drums / **PHILIPPE QUILICHINI** – bass

Aura | not iss.

Jul 81. (lp) *(AUL 715)* **DRAMA OF EXILE** [ ] [–]
– Genghis Khan / Purple lips / One more chance / Henry Hudson / I'm waiting for the man / Sixty forty / The sphinx / Orly flight / Heroes. *(cdiss.Mar88 on 'Line'; LILP 400106) (cd re-iss. Jul92 on 'Great Expectations'; PIPCD 037) (cd re-iss. Aug96 on 'See For Miles'; SEECD 449)*

Flicknife | not iss.

Sep 81. (7") *(FLS 206)* **VEGAS. / SAETA** [ ] [–]

Half | not iss.

Jul 82. (7") *(1/2 1)* **PROCESSION. / ALL TOMORROW'S PARTIES** [ ] [–]
(12"+=) *(1/2 1-12)* – Secret side (live) / Femme fatale (live).

Aura | not iss.

Jun 83. (7") *(AUS 137)* **HEROES. / ONE MORE CHANCE** [ ] [–]

— with **JAMES YOUNG** – keyboards / **GRAHAM DIDS** – percussion

Beggars Banquet | not iss.

Jun 85. (7"/12"; as NICO & THE FACTION) **MY FUNNY VALENTINE. / MY HEART IS EMPTY** [ ] [–]

Jun 85. (lp/c/cd; as NICO & THE FACTION) *(BEG A/C/CD 63)* **CAMERA OBSCURA** [ ] [–]
– Camera obscura / Tananore / Win a few / My funny valentine / Das lied von einsamen Madchens / Fearfully in danger / My heart is empty / Into the arena / Konig. *(re-iss. Jan89 on 'Beggars Banquet-Lowdown' lp/c)(cd; BBL/+C 63)(BBL 63CD)*

— added **ERIC RANDOM** – percussion, etc / **TOBY TOMAN** – drums

Dojo not iss.

Apr 86. (d-lp/c/cd) *(DOJO LP/TC/CD 27)* **BEHIND THE IRON CURTAIN (live 1985)** [ ] [–]
– All saints night from a Polish motorway / One more chance / Frozen warnings / The song of the lonely girl / Win a few / Konig / Purple lips / All tomorrow's parties / Fearfully in danger / The end / My funny valentine / 60-40 / Tananoori / Janitor of lunacy / My heart is empty / Femme fatale.

1987. (lp) *(DOJOLP 50)* **LIVE IN TOKYO, JAPAN (live)** [ ] [–]
– My heart is empty / Purple lips / Tananore / Janitor of lunacy / You forgot to answer / 60-40 / My funny valentine / Sad lied von einsannen madchens / All tomorrow's parties / Femme fatale / The end. *(cd-iss. 1988 & Jun95; DOJOCD 50)*

—— NICO died 18th Jul'88 (see info above)

– compilations, others, etc. –

1983. (c) *R.O.I.R.; <A 117>* **DO OR DIE** [–] [ ]
(cd-iss. May93 & Nov94; RE 117CD) <(cd re-mast.Apr00; RUSCD 8261)>

Sep 85. (lp/c/cd) *Aura; (AU L/C/CD 731)* **THE BLUE ANGEL** (best of) [ ] [ ]
– Femme fatale / All tomorrow's parties / I'll keep it with mine / Chelsea girls / Janitor of lunacy / Heroes / One more chance / Sixty forty / Waiting for the man / The end.

Oct 85. (7") *Aura; (AUS 147)* **I'M WAITING FOR THE MAN. / PURPLE LIPS (live)** [ ] [–]

Feb 87. (12"ep) *Archive 4; (TOF 110)* **LIVE (live)** [ ] [–]

Mar 87. (pic-lp) *V.U.; (NICO 1)* **LIVE IN DENMARK (live)** [ ] [–]

May 88. (c) *Half; (1/2 CASS 2)* **EN PERSONNE EN EUROPE** [ ] [–]

Nov 88. (12"ep/cd-ep) *Strange Fruit; (SFPS/+CD 064) / Dutch East India; <DEI 8314>* **NICO / PEEL SESSIONS** (2/2/71) [ ] [ ]
– Secret side / No one is there / Janitor of lunacy / Frozen warnings.

Jun 89. (lp/cd) *Performance; (PERF 385/+CD)* **LIVE HEROES (live)** [ ] [–]

Nov 90. (cd/c/lp) *Emergo; (EM 9349-2/-4/-1)* **HANGING GARDENS** [ ] [–]

Jul 92. (cd) *Great Expectations; (PIPCD 039)* **CHELSEA GIRL LIVE (live)** [ ] [–]
(re-iss. Jun94 on 'Cleopatra'; CLEO 61062) (cd re-iss. Nov96 on 'See For Miles'; SEECD 461)

Sep 94. (cd) *Anagram; <(CDMGRAM 85)>* **HEROINE (live)** [ ] 1995 [ ]
(lp-iss.Oct00 on 'Get Back'; GET 68) (re-iss. Mar02; CDMGOTH 16)

Apr 96. (cd) *Cleopatra; <CLP 9709>* **ICON** [–] [ ]

Sep 96. (cd) *Visionary; (VICD 008)* **JANITOR OF LUNACY** [ ] [–]
(re-iss. Jun01 on 'Anagram'; CDGOTH 7)

Sep 96. (cd) *S.P.V.; (SPV 0849620-2)* **NICO'S LAST CONCERT (FATA MORGANA – DESERTSOUNDS IN THE PLANETARIUM) (live)** [ ] [–]
(<re-iss. Feb02; SPV 0769620-2>)

Sep 98. (cd) *Island; <565185>* **THE CLASSIC YEARS** [–] [ ]

Aug 99. (cd) *Koch World; <(34042-2)>* **COSMOS** [ ] [ ]

Feb 02. (cd) *Verve; (589421-2)* **INNOCENT & VAIN: AN INTRODUCTION TO NICO** [ ] [–]
– I'll keep it with mine / All tomorrow's parties / You forgot to answer / Wrap your troubles in dreams / Valley of the kings / Femme fatale / Eulogy to Lenny Bruce / Secret side / Little sister / It was a pleasure then / Innocent and vain / The end (live).

Apr 02. (cd) *Jungle; (FREUDCD 069)* **FEMME FATALE: THE AURA ANTHOLOGY** [ ] [–]

May 03. (d-cd) *Castle; (CMDDD 732)* **WAITING FOR THE MAN** (same as above) [ ] [–]

NILSSON

Born: HARRY EDWARD NELSON, 15 Jun'41, Brooklyn, New York, USA. Subsequently raised in California, he started a career as a supervisor at the Security First National Bank in Van Nuys. By day he was developing his songwriting and piano playing talents, eventually placing three of his tracks with PHIL SPECTOR (who duly recorded two with The RONETTES and one with the MODERN FOLK QUARTET). After a couple of early singles on the 'Tower' label, the budding singer/songwriter secured a contract with 'R.C.A.'. In the process of recording his debut album, 'PANDEMONIUM SHADOW SHOW' (1968), NILSSON's 'CUDDLY TOY' was covered by fellow 'R.C.A.' act, the MONKEES, finally persuading him to leave his job at the bank and concentrate on music full-time. There was a distinct BEATLES-esque feel to much of the debut, not merely down to a faithful cover of 'SHE'S LEAVING HOME' but in the orchestrated pop of 'WITHOUT HER' and 'IT'S BEEN SO LONG', NILSSON's rich voice and immaculate phrasing belying the fact he was American. Not much of a surprise then, that LENNON, McCARTNEY and Co. raved over the record, soon becoming good friends with the singer. The album also gained considerable praise from the critics, although NILSSON would have to wait until the summer of '69 before he gained any widespread commercial recognition. This came with his definitive reading of Fred Neil's 'EVERYBODY'S TALKIN', the wistful country-folk number used as the theme tune for the acclaimed 'Midnight Cowboy' movie and becoming a mainstay of the US Top 10 in 1969. The success of the single spurred on sales of 'ARIEL BALLET' (1968), while also creating interest for NILSSON's third album, 'HARRY' (1969). The same year, NILSSON's 'ONE' (from the debut) became a million seller for American rockers, THREE DOG NIGHT. Bizarrely enough, despite all this success, NILSSON never performed in front of a paying audience, while TV appearances were rare. The early 70's saw the singer record a critically acclaimed but poor selling album of RANDY NEWMAN covers, 'NILSSON SINGS NEWMAN' (1970) while the following year he wrote, narrated and sang the soundtrack for children's fantasy film, 'THE POINT' (1971). NILSSON really made his breakthrough in early '72 with a hauntingly intense version of PETE HAM and TOM EVANS' (of BADFINGER) 'WITHOUT YOU', the song latterly assuming an added poignancy following the suicides of both its writers. The accompanying album, 'NILSSON SCHMILSSON' (1972) subsequently went platinum, again showing the singer's penchant for diverse stylistic territory. 'SON OF SCHMILSSON' (1972) was a generally inferior version of its predecessor while 'A LITTLE TOUCH OF SCHMILSSON IN THE NIGHT' (1973) was a semi-successful attempt at pre-war schmaltz. NILSSON subsequently took another radical stylistic shift with 'PUSSY CATS' (1974), a darkly intense album of classic pop/rock covers recorded with, and produced by, drinking buddy JOHN LENNON. Recorded during the former BEATLES' 'lost' period (when he split from YOKO), the opus was a proverbial dark night of the soul for both artists. Following a further series of inconsistent albums throughout the late 70's including 'NILSSON . . . THAT'S THE WAY IT IS' (1976) and 'KNNILLSSONN' (1977), the singer virtually retired from the music business in the early 80's, raising a family and setting up an L.A.-based film distribution company. In the early 90's, NILSSON threw himself afresh into recording and writing following a heart attack. Tragically, he suffered a fatal attack on the 15th of January '94, just days after completing a new long player. The following year, the music business paid tribute with the album, 'FOR THE LOVE OF HARRY: EVERYBODY SINGS NILSSON', featuring contributions from the likes of BRIAN WILSON and RANDY NEWMAN. • **Covered:** YOU CAN'T DO THAT + MOTHER NATURE'S SON (Beatles) / RIVER DEEP, MOUNTAIN HIGH (Phil Spector) to name but a few. NILSSON's songs that have been hits for others:- ONE (Three Dog Night) / THE STORY OF ROCK AND ROLL (Turtles) / THE PUPPY SONG (David Cassidy) / etc. • **Trivia:** Early in 1969, he wrote first film score, 'Skidoo', and even had a bit part as a security guard. In 1974, he provided the score and starred alongside RINGO STARR for the film, 'Son Of Dracula'.

Album rating: PANDEMONIUM SHADOW SHOW (*6) / ARIEL BALLET (*6) / HARRY (*6) / NILSSON SINGS NEWMAN (*7) / THE POINT (*6) / NILSSON SCHMILSSON (*8) / SON SCHMILSSON (*6) / A LITTLE TOUCH OF SCHMILSSON IN THE NIGHT (*5) / SON OF DRACULA (*4) / PUSSY CATS (*6) / DUIT ON MON DEI (*4) / SANDMAN (*4) / . . .THAT'S THE WAY IT IS (*4) / KNNILLSSONN (*4) / GREATEST HITS compilation (*7) / FLASH HARRY (*4) / ALL THE BEST compilation (*7) / PERSONAL BEST: THE HARRY NILSSON ANTHOLOGY (*8)

NILSSON – vocals, piano with session people and orchestra

not iss. — Spindle Top

1963. (7"; as JOHNNY NILES) *<1929>* **DONNA I UNDERSTAND. / WIG JOB** [–] [ ]
<re-iss. 1963 on 'Mercury'; 72132>

not iss. — Crusader

1964. (7"; as BO-PETE) *<103>* **BAA BAA BLACKSHEEP. / (part 2)** [–] [ ]

not iss. — Try

1964. (7"; as BO-PETE) *<TRY 501>* **DO YOU WANNA (HAVE SOME FUN). / GROOVY LITTLE SUZIE** [–] [ ]

not iss. — Foto-Fi

1964. (7"; by FOTO-FI FOUR) *<107>* **STAND UP AND HOLLER (THE BEATLES ARRIVE IN AMERICA). / ISMAEL** [–] [ ]

not iss. — Tower

1964. (7") *<103>* **I'M GONNA LOSE MY MIND. / 16 TONS** [–] [ ]
1965. (7") *<136>* **YOU CAN'T TAKE YOUR LOVE AWAY FROM ME. / BORN IN GRENADA** [–] [ ]
1966. (7") **GROWING UP. / SHE'S YOURS** [–] [ ]
1966. (lp) *<ST 5095>* **SPOTLIGHT ON NILSSON** [–] [ ]
<re-iss. 1967; ST 5165>

R.C.A. — R.C.A.

Jun 67. (7") *<47-9206>* **WITHOUT HER. / FRECKLES** [–] [ ]
Sep 67. (7") *(RCA 1632) <47-9298>* **YOU CAN'T DO THAT. / TEN LITTLE INDIANS** [ ] [ ]
Dec 67. (7") *<47-9383>* **RIVER DEEP, MOUNTAIN HIGH. / SHE BANGS HYMNS OUT OF TUNE** [–] [ ]
Mar 68. (lp) *(RD/SF 7928) <LSP 3874>* **PANDEMONIUM SHADOW SHOW** [ ] [ ]
– Ten little Indians / 1941 / Cuddly toy / She sang hymns out of tune / You can't do that / Sleep late, my lady friend / She's leaving home / There will never be / Without her / Freckles / It's been so long / River deep, mountain high.
Mar 68. (7") *(RCA 1675) <47-9462>* **ONE. / SISTER MARIE** [ ] [ ]
Aug 68. (lp) *(RD/SF 7973) <LSP 3956>* **AERIAL BALLET** [ ] [ ]
– Good old desk / Don't leave me / Mr. Richland's favorite song / Little cowboy / Together / Everybody's talkin' / I said goodbye to me / Mr. Tinker / One / The wailing of the willow / Bath.
Apr 69. (lp) *(SF 8010)* **SKIDOO (soundtrack)** [ ] [–]

—— (Below 'A'side was now used in the film 'Midnight Cowboy')

Aug 69. (7") *(RCA 1707) <47-9544>* **EVERYBODY'S TALKIN'. / DON'T LEAVE ME** [ ] [6]
Sep 69. (lp) *(SF 8046) <4197>* **HARRY** [ ] Aug69 [ ]
– The puppy song / Nobody cares about the railroads anymore / Open your window / Mother nature's son / Fairfax rag / City life / Mournin' glory story / Marchin' down Broadway / I guess the Lord must be in New York City / Rainmaker / Mr. Bojangles / Simon Smith & his amazing dancing bear.
Sep 69. (7") *<9675>* **RAINMAKER. / I WILL TAKE YOU THERE** [–] [ ]
Oct 69. (7") *(RCA 1864)* **MAYBE. / THE PUPPY SONG** [ ] [–]
Oct 69. (7") *(RCA 1913) <74-0261>* **I GUESS THE LORD MUST BE IN NEW YORK CITY. / GOOD OLD DESK** [ ] Nov69 [34]
Feb 70. (7") *(RCA 1935) <74-0310>* **I'LL BE HOME. / WAITING** [ ] [ ]
Mar 70. (lp) *(SF 8166) <LSP 4289>* **NILSSON SINGS NEWMAN** [ ] [ ]
– Vine Street / Love story (you and me) / Yellow man / Caroline / Cowboy / The beehive state / I'll be home / Living without you / Dayton Ohio, 1903 / So long, dad. *(re-iss. Sep77; PL 42304) (cd-iss. Feb89; ND 90305)*
May 70. (7") *(RCA 1987) <74-0362>* **DOWN TO THE VALLEY. / BUY MY ALBUM** [ ] [ ]
Apr 71. (lp) *(SF 8166) <LSP 4417>* **THE POINT!** (animated TV film soundtrack) [46] Mar71 [25]
– Everything's got 'em / The town (narration) / Me and my arrow / The game (narration) / Poli high / The trial and banishment (narration) / Think about your troubles / Thursday (why I did not go to work today) / Blanket for a sail / Down to the valley / The pointed man (narration) / P.O.V. waltz / The clearing in the woods (narration) / Are you sleeping? / Oblio's return (narration). *(re-iss. Aug91 on 'Edsel' lp+=/cd+=; ED/+CD 340)* – (extended versions).
Mar 71. (7") *<74-0443>* **ME AND MY ARROW. / ARE YOU SLEEPING?** [–] [34]
Jun 71. (7") *<74-0524>* **WITHOUT HER. / GOOD OLD DESK** [–] [ ]
Jan 72. (7") *(RCA 2165) <74-0604>* **WITHOUT YOU. / GOTTA GET UP** [1] Dec71 [1]
(re-iss. Feb79 on 'RCA Gold')
Jan 72. (lp) *(SF 8242) <LSP 4515>* **NILSSON SCHMILSSON** [4] Nov71 [3]
– Gotta get up / Driving along / Early in the morning / Moonbeam / Down / Without you / Coconut / Let the good times roll / Jump into the fire / I'll never leave you. *(re-iss. Apr80; INTS 5002) (re-iss. Nov84 lp/c/cd; NL/NK/ND 83464) (re-iss. Sep86 on 'Fame' lp/c; FA/TCFA 3166) (cd re-iss. Oct87; ND 83464)*
Mar 72. (7") *<74-0673>* **JUMP INTO THE FIRE. / MOONBEAM** [–] [27]
May 72. (7") *(RCA 2214)* **COCONUT. / MOONBEAM** [42] [–]
Jun 72. (7") *<74-0718>* **COCONUT. / DOWN** [–] [8]
Jul 72. (lp) *(SF 8297) <LSP 4717>* **SON OF SCHMILSSON** [41] [12]
– Take 54 / Remember (Christmas) / Joy / Turn on your radio / You're breakin' my heart / Spaceman / The lottery song / At my front door / Ambush / I'd rather be dead / The most beautiful girl in the world.
Oct 72. (7") *(RCA 2266) <74-0788>* **SPACEMAN. / YOU'RE BREAKIN' MY HEART** [ ] Sep72 [23]
Dec 72. (7") *(RCA 2300) <74-0855>* **REMEMBER (CHRISTMAS). / THE LOTTERY SONG** [ ] [53]
<re-iss. Nov75; PB 10130>
Jul 73. (lp) *(SF 8371) <APL-1 0097>* **A LITTLE TOUCH OF SCHMILSSON IN THE NIGHT** [20] [46]
– Lazy Moon / For me and my gal / It had to be you / Always / Makin' whoopee / You made me love you (I didn't want to do it) / Lullaby in ragtime / I wonder who's kissing her now / What'll I do / Nevertheless (I'm in love with you) / This is all I ask / As time goes by. *(cd-iss. Aug91; ND 90582)*
Jul 73. (7") *(RCA 2395)* **AS TIME GOES BY. / MAKIN' WHOOPEE!** [ ] [–]
Aug 73. (7") *<APBO 0039>* **AS TIME GOES BY. / LULLABY IN RAGTIME** [–] [86]
Apr 74. (7") *(APBO 0238) <APBO 0246>* **DAYBREAK. / DOWN** [ ] [39]
May 74. (lp) *<(APL-1 0220)>* **SON OF DRACULA (Soundtrack)** [ ] [ ]
– It is he who will be King / Daybreak / At my front door / Count Down meets Merlin and Amber / Moonbeam / Perhaps this is all a dream / Remember (Christmas) / Intro: Without you / The Count's vulnerability / Down / Frankenstein, Merlin and the operation / Jump into the fire / The abdication of Count Down / The end (moonbeam).
(above was jointly issued on 'Rapple' & is a part compilation)
Sep 74. (7") *(RCA 2459) <PB 10001>* **MANY RIVERS TO CROSS. / DON'T FORGET ME** [ ] [ ]
Sep 74. (lp) *<(APL-1 0570)>* **PUSSY CATS** [ ] [60]
– Many rivers to cross / Subterranean homesick blues / Don't forget me / All my life / Old forgotten soldier / Save the last dance for me / Mucho Mungo – Mt. Elga / Loop de loop / Black sails / Rock around the clock. *(cd-iss. Jan92 on 'Edsel'; EDCD 337)*
Nov 74. (7") *<PB 10078>* **MUCHO MUNGO – MT. ELGA. / SUBTERRANEAN HOMESICK BLUES** [–] [ ]
Jan 75. (7") *(RCA 2504)* **SAVE THE LAST DANCE FOR ME. / ALL MY LIFE** [ ] [–]
Feb 76. (7") *<PB 10139>* **DON'T FORGET ME. / LOOP DE LOOP** [–] [ ]
Mar 75. (lp) *(RS 1008) <APL-1 0817>* **DUIT EN MON DEI** [ ] [ ]
– It's a jungle out there / Down by the sea / Kojak Columbo / Easier for me / Turn out the light / Salmon falls / Puget sound / What's your sign / Home / Good for God.
Jun 75. (7") *(RCA 2565) <PB 10183>* **KOJAK COLOMBO. / TURN OUT THE LIGHT** [ ] [ ]
Sep 75. (lp) *(RS 1015) <APL-1 1031>* **SANDMAN** [ ] [ ]
– I'll take a tango / Something true / Pretty soon there'll be nothing left for everybody / The ivy covered walls / Here's why I did not go to work today / How to write a song / The flying saucer song / Will she miss me / Jesus Christ you're tall.
Jan 76. (7") *(RCA 2649)* **SOMETHING TRUE. / PRETTY SOON THERE'LL BE NOTHING** [ ] [–]
May 76. (7") *(RCA 2687) <10634>* **SAIL AWAY. / MOONSHINE BANDIT** [ ] [ ]

Jul 76. (lp) *(RS 1062)* <1119> **NILSSON . . . THAT'S THE WAY IT IS** [ ] [ ]
– That is all / Just one look – Baby I'm yours / Moonshine bandit / I need you / A thousand miles away / Sail away / She sits down on me / Daylight has caught me / Zombie jambouree (back to back) / That is all (reprise).

Aug 76. (7"; as LYNDA LAWRENCE & NILSSON) *<10759>* **THAT IS ALL. / JUST ONE LOOK – BABY I'M YOURS** [–] [ ]

Jan 77. (7") *<11059>* **WHO DONE IT. / PERFECT DAY** [–] [ ]

Mar 77. (7") *(PB 9048)* **MOONSHINE BANDIT. / SHE SITS DOWN ON ME** [ ] [–]

Jun 77. (7") *<11144>* **ALL I THINK ABOUT IS YOU. / I NEVER THOUGHT I'D GET THIS LONELY** [–] [ ]

Jun 77. (7") *(PB 9104)* **ALL I THINK ABOUT IS YOU. / OLD BONES** [43] [–]

Jul 77. (lp/c) *(PL/PK 12276)* <2276> **KNNILLSSONN** [ ] [ ]
– All I think about is you / I never thought I'd get this lonely / Who done it / Lean on me / Goin' down / Old bones / Sweet surrender / Blanket for a sail / Laughin' man / Perfect day.

Nov 77. (7") *<11193>* **AIN'T IT KINDA WONDERFUL. / I'M BRINGING A RED RED ROSE** [–] [ ]

Nov 77. (7") *(PB 9177)* **LEAN ON ME. / WILL SHE MISS ME** [ ] [–]

HARRY NILSSON

Mercury / not iss.

Sep 80. (7") *(MER 40)* **I DON'T NEED YOU. / IT'S SO EASY** [ ] [–]

Sep 80. (lp) *(6302 022)* **FLASH HARRY** [ ] [–]
– Harry / Cheek to cheek / Best move / Old dirt road / I don't need you / Rain / I've got it / It's so easy / How long can disco go on / Bright side of life.

Nov 80. (7") *(MER 44)* **RAIN. / BRIGHT SIDE OF LIFE** [ ] [–]

Polydor / not iss.

Aug 84. (7") *(POSP 703)* **LONELINESS. / SILVER HORSE** [ ] [ ]

R.C.A. / not iss.

Dec 88. (lp/c) *(PL/PK 90251)* **A TOUCH MORE SCHMILSSON IN THE NIGHT** [ ] [–]
– Intro / I'm always chasing rainbows / Make believe / You made me love you (I didn't want to do it) / Trust in me / Lullaby in ragtime / All I think about is you / Perfect day / Always / It's only a paper moon / It had to be you / Thanks for the memory / Outro / Over the rainbow.

— HARRY virtually retired from the music business and was still a gun-control advocate after the death of his friend, JOHN LENNON. NILSSON died of a heart attack on the 15th January '94 at his home Agoura Hills, California.

– compilations, etc. –

on 'RCA' unless mentioned otherwise

1969. (7") *Tower; <518>* **GOOD TIME. / GROWING UP** [–] [ ]

Feb 73. (lp) *(SF 8326)* *<4543>* **AERIAL PANDEMONIUM BALLET** [ ] Jun71 [ ]

Sep 76. (7"m) *(RCA 2733)* **WITHOUT YOU. / EVERYBODY'S TALKIN' / KOJAK, COLOMBO** [22] [–]

Jan 77. (7") *<11318>* **ME AND MY ARROW. / SPACEMAN** [–] [ ]

Jan 77. (7") *(PB 9000)* **ME AND MY ARROW. / THURSDAY** [ ] [–]

Oct 77. (lp) *D.J.M.; (22075)* **EARLY TYMES** [ ] [–]

Jun 78. (lp/c) *(PL/PK 42728)* *<2798>* **GREATEST HITS** [ ] [ ]
(re-iss. Nov82; INTS 5233) (cd-iss. Jan84; PD 89081)

Oct 79. (lp) *K-Tel; (NE 1050)* **HARRY AND . . .** [ ] [–]

Jul 81. (7") *(RCA GOLD 9630)* **WITHOUT YOU. / EVERYBODY'S TALKIN'** [ ] [–]
(re-iss. Oct86 on 'Old Gold'; OG 9630)

Sep 81. (lp/c) *(RCA LP/K 3029)* **NILSSON'S GREATEST MUSIC** [ ] [–]

Feb 82. (c) *Orchid; (ORC 005)* **ALL FOR YOUR LOVE** [ ] [–]

Apr 88. (cd) *RCA Diamond;* **NILSSON** [ ] [–]

Oct 90. (cd) *(ND 90502)* **WITHOUT HER – WITHOUT YOU: THE VERY BEST OF NILSSON VOL.1** [ ] [–]

Jun 92. (cd) *(ND 90652)* **LULLABY IN RAGTIME: THE VERY BEST OF NILSSON** [ ] [ ]

Oct 92. (cd-ep) *Old Gold;* **WITHOUT YOU / EVERYBODY'S TALKIN' / COCONUT** [ ] [–]

Sep 93. (cd/c) *Music Club; (MCCD/MCMC 129)* **ALL THE BEST** [ ] [–]
– Without you / Everybody's talkin' / Mother nature's son / It's been so long / Good old desk / Without her / Mournin' glory story / Mr. Richland's favourite song / Mr.Bojangles / She's leaving home / Lulaby in ragtime / Makin' whoopee! / Cuddly toy / River deep, mountain high / Little cowboy / As time goes by.

Feb 94. (7"/c-s) *(74321 19309-7/-4)* **WITHOUT YOU. / EVERYBODY'S TALKIN'** [47] [ ]
(cd-s+=) *(74321 19309-2)* – Over the rainbow.

1994. (d-cd) *<66354-2>* **PERSONAL BEST: THE HARRY NILSSON ANTHOLOGY** [–] [ ]

Oct 94. (cd) *(74321 22315-2)* **THE BEST OF NILSSON** [ ] [–]

Oct 95. (cd) *R.P.M.; (RETRO 804)* **NILSSON '62 – THE DEBUT SESSIONS** [ ] [–]

NINE INCH NAILS

Formed: San Francisco, California, USA . . . 1989 by classically trained pianist, TRENT REZNOR. He turned his attention to the darker textures of 'PRETTY HATE MACHINE' in the late 80's following a stint working in a recording studio. A solo effort – the album was written and played wholly by REZNOR – its despair and bitter self-pity were set against walls of churning synths and industrial rhythms, the compelling 'HEAD LIKE A HOLE' subsequently becoming a minor hit thanks to heavy MTV rotation. Around the same time, REZNOR recruited a band and struck out on that year's Lollapolooza trek, previewing a harder hitting, guitar influenced sound. Although the debut album was equal parts DEPECHE MODE/MINISTRY, REZNOR's follow-up, the mini-album, 'BROKEN' (1992), followed the metal/industrial fusion of the live shows. REZNOR seemed more tormented than ever on the likes of 'HELP ME I AM IN HELL', an explicitly masochistic video for the 'HAPPINESS IN SLAVERY' single courting not inconsiderable controversy. A punishing album of remixes, 'FIXED' followed a couple of months later, featuring such good-time party favourites as 'FIST FUCK' and 'SCREAMING SLAVE'. Clearly, REZNOR was rather discontented with his lot, his scary reputation heightened when it was revealed that he'd rented the L.A. pad where Charles Manson and Family had murdered Sharon Tate and her friends back in 1969. While REZNOR was allegedly unaware of this spook factor when he rented the property, it nevertheless gave 'THE DOWNWARD SPIRAL' (1994) a grim new resonance (the album was recorded in said abode). The consummation of everything REZNOR had been working towards, the record was a masterful alternative metal/industrial landmark, exploring the depths of human despair and depravity in its multifarious forms. REZNOR's tormented musings obviously struck a chord with the American populace, the album making No.2 in the US charts while NIN were given a rapturous reception at that year's Woodstock anniversary festival. Another album of remixes, 'FURTHER DOWN THE SPIRAL', appeared the following year, while REZNOR set up his own 'Nothing' label, nurturing such famous talent as the equally scary MARILYN MANSON. It had been five long years since the emergence of any new NINE INCH NAILS material (apart from TRENT producing the soundtrack to Oliver Stone's movie, 'Natural Born Killers', however REZNOR and his nihilistic NIN completed their comeback set, 'THE FRAGILE' (1999). Packed with over twenty apocalyptic tracks it hit the top of the US charts (scraped Top 10 in the UK), doom, gloom and then boom, it was all here for America's forgotten youth of today. The subsequent tour was at least partly documented on live set 'AND ALL THAT COULD HAVE BEEN' (2002), an ironically appropriate title for a record which somehow failed to communicate the frenzy of NIN in full, furious flow. • **Songwriters:** 'The Terminator' REZNOR penned except PHYSICAL YOU'RE SO (Adam Ant). • **Trivia:** REZNOR appeared in the 1987 film 'LIGHT OF DAY'.

Album rating: PRETTY HATE MACHINE (*7) / BROKEN (*7) / THE DOWNWARD SPIRAL (*8) / FURTHER DOWN THE SPIRAL (*5) / THE FRAGILE (*6) / THINGS FALLING APART remix-set (*7) / AND ALL THAT COULD HAVE BEEN (*5)

TRENT REZNOR (b.17 May'65, Mercer, Pennsylvania, USA) – vocals, guitar, keyboards, bass, drums, programming / **JAMES WOOLEY** – keyboards / **RICHARD** – guitar / **CHRIS VRENNA** – drums

Island | Nothing-TVT

Nov 90. (12"ep/cd-ep) *(12IS/CID 482)* **DOWN IN IT (skin). / TERRIBLE LIE (mix) / DOWN IN IT (shred – demo)** [ ] [ ]
(cd-ep re-iss. Oct01 on 'TVT'; TVT 2611)

Sep 91. (7"/10") *(IS/10ISP 484)* **HEAD LIKE A HOLE. / ('A'-Copper mix)** [45] [ ]
(12"+=/cd-s+=) *(12IS/CID 484)* – ('A'-Opal mix).

Sep 91. (cd/c/lp) *(CID/ICT/ILPS 9973)* *<2610>* **PRETTY HATE MACHINE** [67] Nov90 [75]
– Head like a hole / Terrible lie / Down in it / Sanctified / Something I can never have / Kinda I want to / Sin / That's what I get / The only time / Ringfinger.

Nov 91. (c-s/7") *(C+/IS 508)* **SIN. / GET DOWN MAKE LOVE** [35] [ ]
(10"+=/cd-s+=) *(10IS/CID 508)* – Sin (dub).

Sep 92. (m-cd/m-c/m-lp) *(IMCD/ICM/ILPM 8004)* *<92246>* **BROKEN** [18] [7]
– Pinion / Wish / Last / Help me I am in Hell / Happiness is slavery / Gave up. *(free 7"+/cd+=)* – Physical (you're so) / Suck.

Nov 92. (m-cd/m-c/m-lp) *(IMCD/ICM/ILPM 8005)* **FIXED** (remixes) [ ] [–]
– Gave up / Wish / Happiness is slavery / Throw this away / Fist fuck / Screaming slave.

—— Below was controversally recorded at the house of the Charles Manson murders (some produced by /with FLOOD). Guests on 1 track each were **ADRIAN BELEW + DANNY LOHNER** – guitar / **CHRIS VRENNA + STEPHEN PERKINS + ANDY KUBISZEWSKI** + – drums (live:- **VRENNA, LOHNER, WOOLLEY + ROBIN FINCK**)

Mar 94. (cd/c/d-lp) *(CID/ICT/ILPSD 8012)* *<92346>* **THE DOWNWARD SPIRAL** [9] [2]
– Mr. Self destruct / Piggy / Heresy / March of the pigs / Closer / Ruiner / The becoming / I do not want this / Big man with a gun / A warm place / Eraser / Reptile / The downward spiral / Hurt.

Mar 94. (cd-ep) *<95938>* **MARCH OF THE PIGS / REPTILLIAN / ALL THE PIGS, ALL LINED UP / A VIOLET FLUID / UNDERNEATH THE SKIN** [–] [59]

Mar 94. (etched-7") *(IS 592)* **MARCH OF THE PIGS. / A VIOLENT FLUID** [45] [–]
(9"+=) *(9IS 592)* – All the pigs, all lined up / Underneath the skin.
(cd-s) *(CID 592)* – ('A'side) / Underneath the skin / Reptillian.
(cd-s+=) *(CIDX 592)* – All the pigs, all lined up / Big man with a gun.

Jun 94. (12"ep/cd-ep) *(12IS/CID 596)* **CLOSER / CLOSER TO GOD / MARCH OF THE FUCKHEADS / HERESY (BLIND) / MEMORABILIA** [25] [–]
(12"ep/cd-ep) *(12ISX/CIDX 596)* – ('A'side) – (deviation) – (further away) / ('A'original) / ('A'-Precursor) / ('A'-Internal).

Jun 94. (c-s) *<98263>* **CLOSER / MARCH OF THE PIGS (live)** [–] [41]

Jun 95. (cd/c) *(IMCD/IMA 8041)* *<INTDM-95811>* **FURTHER DOWN THE SPIRAL** (remixes) [ ] [23]
– Piggy (nothing can stop me now) / The art of self destruction, part one / Self destruction, part two / Heresy (version) / The downward spiral (the bottom) / Hurt (quiet) / Eraser (denial; realization) / At the heart of it all / Eraser (polite) / Self destruction, final / The beauty of being numb / Erased, over, out.

Sep 97. (cd-ep) *(IND 95542)* *<9554>* **THE PERFECT DRUG (mixes; original / Meat Beat Manifesto / Plug / Nine Inch Nails / Spacetime Continuum / The Orb)** [43] [46]
(above from the movie 'Lost Highway' on the 'Interscope' imprint)

Aug 99. (c-s/cd-s) *<97026>* **THE DAY THE WORLD WENT AWAY** [–] [17]

Sep 99. (d-cd/d-c/t-lp) *(CIDD/ICT/ILPST 8091)* *<490473>* **THE FRAGILE** [10] [1]
– Somewhat damaged / The day the world went away / Frail / Wretched / We're in this together / The fragile / Just like you imagined / Even deeper / Pilgrimage / No you don't / La mer / Great below / Way out i through / Into the void / Where is everybody / Mark has been made / Please / Starfuckers Inc. / Complication / I'm looking forward to joining you finally / Pilgrimage / Big come down / Underneath it all.

Nov 99. (cd-s) *(497140-2)* **WE'RE IN THIS TOGETHER / THE DAY THE WORLD WENT AWAY (quiet version) / THE DAY THE WORLD WENT AWAY (Porter Ricks mix)** [39] [ ]
(cd-s) *(497141-2)* – ('A'side) / 10 miles high / The new flesh.
(cd-s) *(497183-2)* – ('A'side) / Complication / The perfect drug.

Nov 00. (cd) *(CID 8102)* *<490744>* **THINGS FALLING APART** (mixes, etc.) [ ] [67]
– Slipping away / The great collapse / The wretched / Starfuckers Inc. / The frail / Where is everybody? / Metal.

Mar 02. (cd) *(CID 8113)* *<493185>* **AND ALL THAT COULD HAVE BEEN (live)** [54] Jan02 [26]
– Terrible lie / Sin / March of the pigs / Piggy / The frail / Wretched / Gave up / The great below / The mark has been made / Wish / Suck / Closer / Head like a hole / The day the world went away / Starfuckers, Inc. / Hurt. *(d-cd+=; CIDD 8113)* **STILL** – Something I can never have / Adrift and at peace / Fragile / Becoming / Gone still / The day the world went away / And all that could have been / Persistence of loss / Leaving hope.

□ NIPS / NIPPLE ERECTORS (see under ⇒ POGUES)

NIRVANA

Formed: Aberdeen, Washington, USA ... 1987 by singer/songwriter/guitarist KURT COBAIN and bassist KRIST NOVOSELIC. Recruiting drummer CHAD CHANNING, they soon became a talking point and pivotal band in nearby Seattle where the likes of SOUNDGARDEN and MUDHONEY were major players in the emerging grunge scene. Whereas those bands dealt in raw garage punk/metal, NIRVANA immediately stood out from the pack by dint of the subtle pop melodies which COBAIN craftily incorporated into his songs. They also fast gained a reputation for their ferocious live shows which drew comparisons with early WHO, if only for their sheer nihilistic energy, invariably ending in trashed equipment. Signing, of course, with the hub of the Seattle scene, 'Sub Pop', NIRVANA released their debut single, 'LOVE BUZZ' in October 1988, the album, 'BLEACH', following a year later. One of the seminal 'Sub Pop' releases alongside, MUDHONEY's 'SUPERFUZZ BIGMUFF' and TAD's 'GOD'S BALLS', this was a darkly brooding, often savagely angry collection, driven by bass and fuzz and interspersed with pockets of melody. The likes of 'SCHOOL' and the throbbing 'NEGATIVE CREEP' saw COBAIN lapse into his trademark howl, an enraged, blood curdling shriek, almost primal in its intensity. Conversely, 'ABOUT A GIRL' was an achingly melodic semi-acoustic shuffle, as steeped in hurt as the rest of the album but more resigned than angry. New guitarist JASON EVERMAN had contributed to the record's sonic bludgeon as well as paying for recording costs, although he soon parted ways (he went on to play with the much hyped MINDFUNK) with COBAIN and NOVOSELIC over the ever reliable, 'musical differences'. 'BLEACH' was heartily received by the indie/metal press, NIRVANA embarking on a heavy round of touring, first in the States, then Europe. Following the departure of CHANNING, MUDHONEY's DAN PETERS joined briefly and was involved with the 'SLIVER' single, a brilliant chunk of pop-noise which further enhanced NIRVANA's underground kudos and raised expectations for a follow-up album to fever pitch. 'NEVERMIND' (1991) let down no-one, except possibly the anally-retentive sad-kids who accused the band of selling out to a major label ('Geffen'). Released immediately after a blinding set at England's Reading festival (where NIRVANA, who probably drew the most frenetic crowd reaction of the day, had to make do with a paltry afternoon slot; the following year they'd be headlining), and with appetites whetted via import copies of 'SMELLS LIKE TEEN SPIRIT', the record was met with an ecstatic press reaction. While the album brought the grunge phenomenon into the mainstream, NIRVANA had already moved on to a blistering power pop/punk sound, best evidenced in the sardonic fury of the aforementioned 'SMELLS . . .'. Here was an anthem for the blank generation, for all the people who'd given up before even starting; COBAIN had condensed the collective frustration/despair/apathy into an incendiary slice of pop genius not witnessed since The SEX PISTOLS' heyday. 'COME AS YOU ARE' was another piece of semi-acoustic bruised beauty while 'TERRITORIAL PISSINGS' was as extreme as the record went, a rabid blast of hardcore punk introduced with a sarcastic send-up pilfered from The YOUNGBLOOD's 60's love 'n' peace classic, 'GET TOGETHER'. Most of the other tracks lay somewhere in between, COBAIN never letting up the intensity level for a minute, whether on the deceptively breezy 'IN BLOOM' or the stinging 'BREED'. For a three piece (the drum seat had now been filled by DAVE GROHL, ex-SCREAM), the group made one hell of a racket, but it was a racket which was never less than 100% focused, the GROHL/NOVOSELIC rhythmic powerhouse underpinning every track with diamond-edged precision. It's fair to say that 'NEVERMIND' literally changed the face of music, American indie bands coming to dominate the scene until the arrival of OASIS in the mid-90's. COBAIN was heralded as the spokesman of a generation, although it was a role he was both unwilling and unable to cope with. As the inevitable, punishing round of touring ensued, the singer's health began to suffer once more; never the healthiest of people, COBAIN suffered from a chronic stomach complaint as well as narcolepsy, a condition which causes the sufferer to sleep for excessive periods of time. What's more, he was concerned that the irony of his lyrics was lost on his growing legions of fans (which now included the macho 'jocks' whom COBAIN so despised) who now doted on his every word. Amid all this confusion, COBAIN was married to HOLE's COURTNEY LOVE on the 24th February '92, the couple almost losing custody of their newborn child, Frances, later that summer following revelations of drug abuse. The end of the year saw the release of a compilation of rare material, 'INCESTICIDE', including two storming VASELINES' (obscure but brilliant Scottish punk-popsters) covers, 'MOLLY'S LIPS' and 'SON OF A GUN'. Rumours of COBAIN's heroin abuse were rife, however, and the singer overdosed twice the following year. 'IN UTERO' (1993) reflected the turmoil, an uncompromising wall of noise (courtesy of STEVE ALBINI) characterising most of the album. The melodies were still there, you just had to dig deeper in the sludge to find them. Despite 'Geffen's misgivings, the record was a transatlantic No.1, its success engendering another round of live work. After a final American show in January, the group set off for Europe, taking a break at the beginning of March. COBAIN remained in Rome, where, on the 4th March, LOVE found him unconscious in their hotel room, the result of an attempted tranquilizer overdose. Although COBAIN eventually recovered, the tour was abandoned and the couple returned to their Seattle home. Though it didn't come as a complete surprise, the music world was stunned nonetheless when, on the 8th April, news broke that COBAIN had finally killed himself, blowing his own head off with a shotgun. The most widely mourned rock'n'roll death since JOHN LENNON, COBAIN's suicide even sparked off a series of 'copycat' incidents in America by obsessive fans. Posthumously released later that year, the acoustic 'UNPLUGGED IN NEW YORK' (1994) live set was heavy going, a tragic poignancy underpinning the spare beauty of tracks like 'DUMB' and 'PENNYROYAL TEA' (from 'IN UTERO') while the heart-rendingly resigned 'ALL APOLOGIES' sounds like COBAIN's final goodbye to a world that he could no longer bear to be a part of. Eventually picking up the pieces, GROHL formed The FOO FIGHTERS, turning his hand to guitar playing/songwriting and recruiting ex-GERM, PAT SMEAR. After time spent campaigning for his native, war torn Yugoslavia, NOVOSELIC returned with his own band, SWEET 75, a collaboration with diminutive Venezuelan lesbian folk-singer, YVA LAS VEGAS. They finally released one unstartling eponymous set in 1997, which just might be their only outing. The man can now be found in indie supergroup, EYES ADRIFT, alongside CURT KIRKWOOD (Meat Puppets) and BUD GAUGH (Sublime). • **Songwriters:** COBAIN wrote late 80's work. In the 90's, the group were credited with COBAIN lyrics. Covers; LOVE BUZZ (Shocking Blue) / HERE SHE COMES NOW (Velvet Underground) / DO YOU LOVE ME? (Kiss) / TURNAROUND (Devo) / JESUS WANTS ME FOR A SUNBEAM (Vaselines) / D7 (Wipers) / THE MAN WHO SOLD THE WORLD (David Bowie) / WHERE DID YOU SLEEP LAST NIGHT (Leadbelly).

Album rating: BLEACH (*8) / NEVERMIND (*10) / INCESTICIDE collection (*7) / IN UTERO (*10) / UNPLUGGED IN NEW YORK (*9) / FROM THE MUDDY BANKS OF THE WISHKAH (*8) / NIRVANA compilation (*10) / Sweet 75: SWEET 75 (*4)

KURT COBAIN (b.20 Feb'67, Hoquaim, Washington) – vocals, guitar / **KRIST NOVOSELIC** (b.16 May'65) – bass / **CHAD CHANNING** (b.31 Jan'67, Santa Rosa, Calif.) – drums

Tupelo | Sub Pop

Oct 88. (7") *<SP 23>* **LOVE BUZZ. / BIG CHEESE** | – |

—— Early '89, added **JASON EVERMAN** – guitar Also guest drummer on 2 tracks **DALE CROVER**

Aug 89. (lp,white or green-lp/cd) *(TUP LP/CD 6) <SP 34>* **BLEACH** | | Jun89
– Blew / Floyd the barber / About a girl / School / Paper cuts / Negative creep / Scoff / Swap meet / Mr.Moustache / Sifting / Big cheese. *(cd+=)* – Love buzz / Downer. *<US re-iss. Dec91 hit 89> (re-iss. Feb92 on 'Geffen'; GEFD 24433) (hit UK No.33) (c+=)* – Big cheese. *(re-iss. Oct95 on 'Geffen' cd/c; GFLD/GFLC 19291) (lp re-iss. Aug01 on 'Sub Pop';* **SP 34)** *(re-iss. Oct01 on 'Warners' cd/lp; 9878 40034-2/-1)*

Dec 89. (12"ep/cd-ep) *(TUP EP8/CD8)* **BLEW / LOVE BUZZ. / BEEN A SON / STAIN** | | –

—— **DAN PETERS** – drums (of MUDHONEY) repl. CHANNING (Apr90)

Jan 91. (7",7"green) *(TUP 25)* **SLIVER. / DIVE** | | Sep 90
(12"+=) *(TUP EP25)* – About a girl (live). *(US-iss.7"blue; SP 72)*
(cd-s++=) *(TUP CD25)* – Spank thru (live).

Feb 91. (7",7"green) *<SP 97>* **MOLLY'S LIPS. / ('Candy' by FLUID)** | – |

not iss. | Communion

Mar 91. (7"colrd) *<Communion 25>* **HERE SHE COMES NOW. / ('Venus In Furs' by MELVINS)** | – |

—— (Apr'91 trio) **DAVE GROHL** (b.14 Jan'69, Warren, Ohio) – drums, vocals (ex-SCREAM) repl. PETERS and EVERMAN, who joined MIND FUNK

Geffen | Geffen

Sep 91. (lp/c/cd) *<(DGC/+C/D 24425)>* **NEVERMIND** | 7 | 1
– Smells like teen spirit / In bloom / Come as you are / Breed / Lithium / Polly / Territorial pissings / Drain you / Lounge act / Stay away / On a plain / Something in the way. *(cd+=)* – Endless nameless. *(lp re-iss. Nov98 on 'Simply Vinyl'; SVLP 38)*

Oct 91. (c-s/cd-s) *<19050>* **SMELLS LIKE TEEN SPIRIT / EVEN IN HIS YOUTH** | – | 6

Nov 91. (7"/c-s) *(DGC/+C 5)* **SMELLS LIKE TEEN SPIRIT. / DRAIN YOU** | 7 | –
(12"pic-d+=) *(DGCTP 5)* – Aneurysm.
(cd-s++=) *(DGCCD 5)* – Even in his youth.
(12") *(DGCT 5)* – ('A'side) / Even in his youth / Aneurysm.

Mar 92. (c-s/cd-s) *<19120>* **COME AS YOU ARE. / DRAIN YOU (live)** | – | 32

Mar 92. (7"/c-s) *(DGC/+C 7)* **COME AS YOU ARE. / ENDLESS NAMELESS** | 9 | –
(12"+=/12"pic-d+=) *(DGCT/+P 7)* – School (live).
(cd-s++=) *(DGCTD 7)* – Drain you (live).

Jul 92. (7"/c-s) *(DGCS/+C 9)* **LITHIUM. / CURMUDGEON** | 11 | –
(12"pic-d+=) *(DGCTP 9)* – Been a son (live).
(cd-s++=) *(DGCSD 9)* – D7 (Peel session).

Jul 92. (c-s,cd-s) *<19134>* **LITHIUM / BEEN A SON (live)** – 64
Nov 92. (7"/c-s) *(GFS/+C 34)* **IN BLOOM. / POLLY** 28 –
(12"pic-d+=/cd-s+=) *(GFST P/D 34)* – Sliver (live).
Dec 92. (cd/c/lp) *<(GED/GEC/GEF 24504)>* **INCESTICIDE**
(rare material) 14 39
– Dive / Sliver / Stain / Been a son / Turnaround / Molly's lips / Son of a gun / (New wave) Polly / Beeswax / Downer / Mexican seafood / Hairspray queen / Aero zeppelin / Big long now / Aneurysm.

— In Feb'93, NIRVANA's 'OH, THE GUILT' appeared on double'A'side with JESUS LIZARD's 'Puss'. Issued on 'Touch & Go' 7"blue/cd-s; *(TG 83/+CD)*. It had UK No.12, and crashed out of the Top 60 the following week!.

— GOODBYE MR MACKENZIE's BIG JOHN played guitar for them in mid'93.

— In Aug'93, KURT COBAIN and WILLIAM S.BURROUGHS narrated 'The Priest, They Call Him By' on 10"lp/cd 'Tim Kerr'; *(92 10/CD 044)*

Aug 93. (7"/c-s) *(GFS/+C 54)* **HEART-SHAPED BOX. / MARIGOLD** 5 –
(12"+=/cd-s+=) *(GFST/+D 54)* – Milk it.
Sep 93. (cd/c/lp)<clear-lp> *<(GED/GEC/GEF 24536)><DGC 24607>* **IN UTERO** 1 1
– Serve the servants / Scentless apprentice / Heart-shaped box / Rape me / Frances Farmer will have her revenge on Seattle / Dumb / Very ape / Milk it / Penny royal tea / Radio friendly unit shifter / Tourette's / All apologies. *(cd+=)* – Gallons of rubbing alcohol flow through the strip. *(lp re-iss. Nov98 on 'Simply Vinyl'; SVLP 48)*
Dec 93. (7"/c-s) *(GFS/+C 66)* **ALL APOLOGIES. / RAPE ME** 32 –
(12"+=/cd-s+=) *(GFST/+D 66)* – MV.

— On the 4th March '94, KURT overdosed while on holiday in Italy and went into a coma. A month later, on the 8th April he committed suicide, by shooting himself through the mouth. He was only 27, and this was certainly the biggest rock star death since JOHN LENNON. For more details see HOLE and the COURTNEY LOVE story.

below album featured **LORI GOLDSTON** – cello + **MEAT PUPPETS' Curt & Cris Kirkwood** on 3rd, 4th & 5th last songs.

Nov 94. (cd/c/white-lp) *<(GED/GEC/GEF 24727)>*
UNPLUGGED IN NEW YORK (live acoustic) 1 1
– About a girl / Come as you are / Jesus doesn't want me for a sunbeam / Dumb / The man who sold the world / Pennyroyal tea / Polly / On a plain / Something in the way / Plateau / Oh me / Lake of fire / All apologies / Where did you sleep last night. *(lp re-iss. Nov98 on 'Simply Vinyl'; SVLP 53)*

— GROHL (now vox, guitar) formed The FOO FIGHTERS with ex-GERMS guitarist PAT SMEAR; meanwhile NOVOSELIC formed the trio SWEET 75

– compilations, etc. –

on 'Geffen' unless mentioned otherwise

Jul 95. (d-cd) *<(GES 00001)>* **BLEACH / INCESTICIDE**
Nov 95. (6xcd-s-box) *<(GED 24901)>* **6 CD SINGLE BOXED SET**
Oct 96. (cd/c/lp) *<(GED/GEC/GEF 25105)>* **FROM THE MUDDY BANKS OF THE WISHKAH (live)** 4 1
– Intro / School / Drain you / Aneurysm / Smells like teen spirit / Been a son / Lithium / Sliver / Spank thru / Scentless apprentice / Heart-shaped box / Milk it / Negative creep / Polly / Breed / Tourette's / Blew.
Oct 02. (cd) *Geffen; <(493507)>* **NIRVANA** 3 3
– You know you're right / About a girl / Been a son / Sliver / Smells like teen spirit / Come as you are / Lithium / In bloom / Heart-shaped box / Pennyroyal tea / Rape me / Dumb / All apologies (live) / The man who sold the world (live).

SWEET 75

KRIST NOVOSELIC – guitar (ex-NIRVANA) / **YVA LAS VEGAS** – vocals, bass / **ADAM WADE** – drums

Geffen Geffen

Aug 97. (cd/c) *<(GED/GEC 25140)>* **SWEET 75**
– Fetch / Lay me down / Bite my hand / Red dress / La vida / Six years / Take another stab / Poor Kitty / Ode to Dolly / Dogs / Cantos de Pilon / Nothing / Japan trees / Oral health.

— late in 2002, NOVOSELIC was part of EYES ADRIFT

NO DOUBT

Formed: Orange County, California, USA ... 1987 by JOHN SPENCE, TOM DUMONT, TONY KANAL and ADRIAN YOUNG (SPENCE rocking the band by committing suicide the following year). Having gone to ground for a while, they returned in the early 90's with new blonde-bombshell frontwoman, GWEN STEFANI. Her brother, ERIC STEFANI, was also a member at this stage, although he eventually departed, having landed a job working on 'The Simpsons' TV cartoon series. After two albums for 'Trauma', an eponymous debut and 'BEACON STREET COLLECTION' they were licensed to 'Interscope' in 1995. The following year, NO DOUBT finally cracked the American market with 'TRAGIC KINGDOM', a slow starter which eventually topped the charts. Produced by MATTHEW WILDER, the record was an 80'-esque amalgam of soft-metallic ska-pop/rock, fusing elements of The POLICE and MADNESS hand in hand with tasty MADONNA lookalike, GWEN STEFANI's cutesie-pie vocal pouting. The album boasted the MTV friendly hit singles, 'JUST A GIRL' and the massive selling ballad, 'DON'T SPEAK', which boosted long term UK sales of the album in 1997. Heavy-metal mag Kerrang!, also inconceivably took gorgeous GWEN to their leather-clad hearts (lending new weight to accusations of cock-rock inclinations). Having milked 'TRAGIC KINGDOM' dry of hits, NO DOUBT eventually returned in 1999, the 'NEW' singles UK Top 30 placing suggesting they hadn't been forgotten just yet. A year on they released the much anticipated long player, 'RETURN OF SATURN' (2000), lead track – and UK Top 40 hit – 'EX-GIRLFRIEND' setting the tone of the record as GWEN hits those twenty-something blues. Their defiant attempts at sparking a new wave revival remain undimmed and with 80's mania looming on the horizon like a particularly flint-eyed vulture, they may just pull it off. While structured with an underlying rock foundation, the aforementioned comeback set, 'RETURN TO SATURN' was an attempt to update the American New Wave sound so beloved of STEFANI and Co. While its lovingly crafted textures and 20-something restlessness of the lyrics conceivably appealed to an older audience, it's unclear exactly what market this record was aimed at. Its relatively short-lived residence in the charts prompted a link-up with all manner of name producers in an attempt to revitalise their approach. Thus the likes of SLY & ROBBIE, NELLEE HOOPER and even PRINCE were recruited to shape the reggae influenced, dancefloor pop of 'ROCK STEADY' (2001). 'THE SINGLES 1992-2003' (2003) meanwhile, deftly summed up the group's legacy over fifteen surprisingly consistent tracks, from 'TRAPPED IN A BOX' (taken from their eponymous debut) to the alluring 'UNDERNEATH IT ALL' (from their last studio set), their recent, 80's throwback cover of Talk Talk's 'IT'S MY LIFE' and all the exuberant, craftily contemporary hits in between. • **Songwriters:** STEFANI w/ TOM or TONY or ERIC (perm any three). • **Trivia:** GWEN was known to "hang out" with Scottish born GARBAGE singer SHIRLEY MANSON.

Album rating: NO DOUBT (*5) / THE BEACON STREET COLLECTION (*6) / TRAGIC KINGDOM (*7) / RETURN OF SATURN (*6) / ROCK STEADY (*6) / THE SINGLES 1992-2003 compilation (*8)

GWEN STEFANI (b. 3 Oct'69, Fullerton, Calif.) – vocals / **TOM DUMONT** – guitar / **TONY KANAL** – bass / **ADRIAN YOUNG** – drums / **ERIC STEFANI** – piano, keyboards

Interscope Interscope

Mar 92. (cd) *<IND 92109>* **NO DOUBT** –
– BND / Let's get back / Ache / Get on the ball / Move on / Sad for me / Doormat / Big city train / Trapped in a box / Sometimes / Sinking / A little something refreshing / Paulina / Brand new day. *(UK-iss.Jul96; same)*

Feb 95. (cd) *<BS 03>* **THE BEACON STREET COLLECTION** (out-takes) – [ ]
– Open the gate / Total hate 95 / Stricken / Greener pastures / By the way / Snakes / That's just me / Squeal / Doghouse / Blue in the face. *(UK-is.Apr97; same)*
(above album on 'Beacon Street')

— now without ERIC (see above)

Jun 96. (cd/c) *(IND/INC 90003) <92580>* **TRAGIC KINGDOM** [ ] Feb96 1
– Spiderwebs / Excuse me Mr. / Just a girl / Happy now? / Different people / Hey you / The climb / Sixteen / Sunday morning / Don't speak / You can do it / World go 'round / End it on this / Tragic kingdom. *(re-dist.Jan97 hit UK No.3)*

Jun 96. (c-s) *(INC 80034) <98116>* **JUST A GIRL / DIFFERENT PEOPLE** [ ] Dec95 23
(cd-s+=) *(IND 80034)* – Open the gate.
(re-iss. Oct96, hit UK 38)

Feb 97. (7"pic-d/c-s/cd-s) *(INSP/INC/IND 95515)* **DON'T SPEAK / DON'T SPEAK (alternate) / HEY YOU (acoustic) / GREENER PASTURES** 1 –

Jun 97. (c-s) *(INC 95539)* **JUST A GIRL / HEY YOU (live) / OB-LA-DI OB-LA-DA (live)** 3 –
(cd-s+=) *(INDX 95539)* – Different people.
(cd-s) *(IND 95539)* – ('A'side) / Open the gate / ('A'live) / End it on this (live).

Sep 97. (c-s) *(INC 95551)* **SPIDERWEBS / DJ'S (live)** 16 –
(cd-s+=) *(IND 95551)* – Let's get back / Excuse me sir (cd-rom version).
(cd-s) *(INDX 95551)* – ('A'side) / The climb (live) / Doghouse / Spiderwebs (cd-rom version).

Dec 97. (c-s) *(INC 95566)* **SUNDAY MORNING / SUNDAY MORNING (live)** 50 –
(cd-s+=) *(IND 95566)* – Oi to the world / By the way (live).
(cd-s) *(INDX 95566)* – (virtually the same tracks).

May 99. (7") *(HIGHS 22S)* **NEW. / NEW (new and approved remix)** 30 [ ]
(c-s) *(HIGHS 22)* – ('A'side) / (A'-New Doubt club mix)
(cd-s+=) *(HIGHS 22T)* – (all three above).
(above issued on 'Higher Ground')

Mar 00. (c-s) *(497298-4)* **EX-GIRLFRIEND / LEFTOVERS** 33 –
(cd-s+=) *(497298-2)* – ('A'-CD-Rom).
(cd-s) *(497299-2)* – ('A'side) / Big distraction / Full circle.

Apr 00. (cd/c) *(490638-2/-4) <490441>* **RETURN OF SATURN** 31 2
– Ex-girlfriend / Simple kind of life / Bathwater / Six feet under / Magic's in the make up / Artificial sweetener / Marry me / New / Too late / Comforting lie / Suspension without suspense / Staring problem / Home now / Dark blue. *(cd+=)* – Big distraction. *(UK cd re-iss. Oct00 +=; 490797-2)* – Ex-girlfriend (video) / Simple king of life (video).

Sep 00. (c-s) *(497416-4) <490365>* **SIMPLE KIND OF LIFE / BEAUTY CONTEST** 69 May00 38
(cd-s+=) *(497417-2)* – Under construction / ('A'-CD-ROM video).
(cd-s) *(497416-2)* – ('A'side) / Ex-girlfriend / Cellophane boy.

— in Jan'01, GWEN featured on MOBY's US-only hit, 'South Side'

— in Apr'01, she also featured on EVE's hit, 'Let Me Blow Ya Mind'

Dec 01. (cd/d-lp) *<(493158-2/-1)>* **ROCK STEADY** 43 9
– (intro) / Hella good / Hey baby (with BOUNTY KILLER) / Making out / Underneath it all (with LADY SAW) / Detective / Don't let me down / Start the fire / Running / In my head / Platinum blonde life / Waiting room / Rock steady.

Feb 02. (c-s; by NO DOUBT featuring BOUNTY KILLER) *(497668-4) <radio cut>* **HEY BABY / EX-GIRLFRIEND (Philip Steir remix)** 2 Nov01 5
(cd-s+=) *(497668-2)* – ('A'-Fabian mix) / ('A'-video).

Jun 02. (c-s) *(497736-4) <497720>* **HELLA GOOD / HELLA GOOD (Roger Sanchez release yourself mix)** 12 May02 13
(cd-s+=) *(497736-2)* – ('A'-skank remix with OUTKAST) / ('A'-video).
(12") *(497736-1)* – ('A'-skank remix with OUTKAST) / ('A'-Roger's release dub).

Sep 02. (c-s; by NO DOUBT featuring LADY SAW) *(497780-4) <497779>* **UNDERNEATH IT ALL / UNDERNEATH IT ALL (live acoustic)** 18 3
(cd-s+=) *(497779-2)* – Just a girl (live acoustic) / ('A'video).

Jul 03. (cd-s) *<980767>* **RUNNING / HELLA GOOD (live) / UNDERNEATH IT ALL (live) / HEY BABY (live)** – 62

Nov 03. (cd-s) *(9813724)* **IT'S MY LIFE / BATHWATER (invincible overlord remix) / IT'S MY LIFE (mixes + video)** 20 [ ]

Nov 03. (cd) *(986138-2) <014950-2>* **THE SINGLES 1992-2003** (compilation) 46 2
– Just a girl / It's my life / Hey baby (with BOUNTY KILLER) / Bathwater / Sunday morning / Hella good / New / Underneath it all (with LADY SAW) / Excuse me Mr. / Running / Spiderwebs / Simple kind of life / Don't speak / Ex-girlfriend / Trapped in a box. *(UK+=)* – Girls get the bass in the back (Hey baby remix with BOUNTY KILLER) / Underneath it all (live).
(above album will hit UK No.5 in Jan'04)

– compilations, etc. –

Jul 99. (cd-book) *Hallmark; (8081)* **STAR PROFILE** [ ] –

NOTORIOUS B.I.G.

Born: CHRISTOPHER WALLACE, 21 May'72, Brooklyn, New York, USA. Under the moniker BIGGY SMALLZ, WALLACE's talent as an NYC rapper caught the attention of east coast hip hop guru/owner of 'Bad Boy' records, Sean 'Puffy' Combs, who in turn brought the rising star to greater prominence through guest spots on records by the likes of MARY J. BLIGE. SMALLZ' own recording debut (as NOTORIOUS B.I.G.), the US Top 30 single, 'JUICY', found him marking out his own territory at the slicker R&B/swing end of the gangsta rap spectrum. Arrested many times for robbery, assault and weapon offenses, he at least knew what he was singing about, tackling the usual subjects of 'bitches', guns and money on the accompanying album, 'READY TO DIE' (1994). A string of Top 10 hits followed, inlcuding a collaboration with METHOD MAN and even a joint effort with west coast star TUPAC SHAKUR, soon to become a sworn enemy. What had started out as a simmering east/west rivalry between 'Bad boy' and L.A. label, 'Death Row', turned into a bitter feud with 2PAC and SMALLZ at its epicentre. Amid defiant threats exchanged both in the press and on vinyl, things spiralled out of control as 2PAC was gunned down by unknown assailants in Las Vegas on the 13th of September '96. The B.I.G. man's follow-up album, 'LIFE AFTER DEATH', dealt with the violence head on; the sense of fatalism running through many of the tracks was only compounded by the needless murder of BIGGIE himself, also gunned down (drive-by shooting in L.A.) on the 9th March 1997, only days before the album's release. Though the perpetrator of the crime remains unknown (a Crips gang member was said to be prime suspect), the incident only served to fan the flames of the dispute even higher. Every cynic knows that death sells; the massive transatlantic publicity surrounding this particular death ensured that the posthumously released record sold multi-millions. Two singles, 'HYPNOTIZE' and 'MO MONEY MO PROBLEMS', both topped the US charts, as did the tribute single, 'I"LL BE MISSING YOU', a joint effort of Puffy and SMALLS' wife, Faith Evans. In little more than six months, an already ailing rap scene had lost two of its most talented figureheads, a worrying sign of the genre's increasing inability to distinguish the boundary between art and reality.

Album rating: READY TO DIE (*8) / LIFE AFTER DEATH (*7) / BORN AGAIN (*6)

NOTORIOUS B.I.G. – vocals

not iss. Life

Oct 93. (c-s/cd-s; as BIGGY SMALLZ) *<79008>* **CRUISIN' (mixes)** – [ ]

Arista Arista

Oct 94. (c-s) *(74321 24010-4) <7-9004>* **JUICY / UNBELIEVABLE** 72 27
(12"+=/cd-s+=) *(74321 24010-1/-2)* – (2-'A'mixes).

Oct 94. (cd/c) *<(78612 73000-2/-4)>* **READY TO DIE** [ ] 15
– Intro / Things done changed / Gimme the loot / Machine gun funk /

Warning / Ready to die / One more chance / F*** me (interlude) / The what / Juicy / Everyday struggle / Me and my bitch / Big poppa / Respect / Friend of mine / Unbelievable / Suicidal thoughts. *(cd re-iss. May97; same)*

Mar 95. (12"/cd-s) *(74321 26341-1/-2)* <79015> **BIG POPPA. / WHO SHOT YA? / WARNING / BIG POPPA (mix)** 63 6

— In Apr'95, the man featured on the TOTAL single, 'Can't You See'.

Jun 95. (12",cd-s; The NOTORIOUS B.I.G. and METHOD MAN) *<79031>* **ONE MORE CHANCE – STAY WITH ME / THE WHAT** – 2

— In Jan'97, The NOTORIOUS B.I.G. collaborated with 2PAC, RADIO, DRAMACYDAL & STRETCH on Top 100 US single, 'RUNNIN''.

Mar 97. (d-cd/c/q-lp) *<(78612 73011-2/-4/-1)>* **LIFE AFTER DEATH** 23 1
– Life after death / Somebody's gotta die / Hypnotize / Mad rapper / Kick in the door / Lovin' you tonight / Last day / Dice / I love the dough / What's beef / B.I.G. / I'm coming out (more money) / Niggaz bleed / Story to tell / Notorious thugs / Interlude / Missing you / Another man / Cali (interlude) / Goin' back to Cali / 10 crack commandments / Playa later / Interlude / Nasty boy / Interlude / Sky's the limit / The world is filled / Interlude / My downfall / Long kiss goodnight / You're nobody. *(best bits re-iss. Nov97 cd/c; 78612 73019-22/-46) (re-iss. Feb98; same)*

— B.I.G. was shot dead on the 9th March, 1997

Apr 97. (c-s) *(74321 46641-4)* <79092> **HYPNOTIZE / I GOT A STORY TO TELL** 10 1
(12"+=/cd-s+=) *(74321 46641-1/-2)* – ('A'mixes).

Jul 97. (c-s) *(74321 49249-4)* <79100> **MO MONEY MO PROBLEMS / LOVIN' YOU TONIGHT** 6 1
(12"+=/cd-s+=) *(74321 49249-1/-2)* – ('A'mixes; instrumental / Razor-n-go).
(above credited in the States with PUFF DADDY & MASE)

Feb 98. (c-s; NOTORIOUS B.I.G. featuring 112) *(74321 56199-4)* <79131> **SKY'S THE LIMIT / GOIN' BACK TO CALI** 35 Nov97 26
(12"+=/cd-s+=) *(74321 56199-1/-2)* – Kick in the door.

— In Mar'98, the B.I.G. man featured with BUSTA RHYMES on PUFF DADDY & THE FAMILY's Top 20 (US) hit, 'Victory'.

Jan 00. (c-s/12"/cd-s; as The NOTORIOUS B.I.G. featuring PUFF DADDY & LIL' KIM) *(74321 73731-4/-1/-2)* *<radio cut>* **NOTORIOUS B.I.G. (mixes; radio / club / instrumental) / DEAD WRONG (main without Eminem) / ONE MORE CHANCE – STAY WITH ME (remix)** 16 Nov99 67

Dec 99. (cd/c/d-lp) *(74321 71718-2/-4/-1)* <73023> **BORN AGAIN** 70 1
– Born again intro / The Notorious B.I.G. (w/ LIL' KIM & PUFF DADDY) / Dead wrong (w/ EMINEM) / Hope you niggas sleep (w/ HOT BOYS & BIG TIMER) / Dangerous MC's (w/ MARK CURRY, SNOOP DOGG & BUSTA RHYMES) / Biggie (w/ JUNIOR M.A.F.I.A.) / Niggas / Big booty hoes (w/ TOO SHORT) / Would you die for me (w/ TOO SHORT) / Come on (w/ SADAT) / Rap phenomenom (w/ REDMAN & METHOD MAN) / Let me get down (w/ G-DEP, CRAIG MACK & MISSY ELLIOTT) / Tonight (w/ MOBB DEPP & JOE HOOKER) / If I should die before I wake (w/ BLACK ROB, ICE CUBE & BEANIE SIGEL) / Who shot ya / Can I get witcha (w/ LIL' CEASE) / I really want to show you (w/ K-CI, JOJO & NAS) / Ms. Wallace (outro).

□ NOTTING HILLBILLIES (see under ⇒ DIRE STRAITS)

Ted NUGENT

Born: 13 Dec'48, Detroit, Michigan, USA. After earlier moving to Chicago, he formed garage/psych-rock band, The AMBOY DUKES in 1966. They soon signed to 'Mainstream' US, releasing a debut single, 'BABY PLEASE DON'T GO' (a Big Joe Williams number, more famously covered by THEM), in 1967. Their eponymous 1968 debut album broke into the US Top 200, and by the summer, the classic psychedelic single, 'JOURNEY TO THE CENTER OF THE MIND', was in the US Top 20. Ironically enough, NUGENT was a vehement non-drug taker, sacking anyone in the band who dabbled with even the softest narcotics (TED preferred hunting animals instead, his love of blood sports was well-publicised). Although The AMBOY DUKES toured constantly in the States for the next couple of years, the band only managed minor chart placings. In 1971, they evolved into TED NUGENT & THE AMBOY DUKES, snapped up by FRANK ZAPPA's 'Discreet' label and subsequently unleashing two albums in the mid-70's before dissolving. In 1975, NUGENT secured a solo deal with 'Epic', shooting up the US Top 30 with an eponymous Tom Werman-produced debut in early '76. By this point, NUGENT had come a long way from his 60's roots, adopting a bare-chested stone-age axe-grinding image (a good few years before MANOWAR). His next album in 1976, 'FREE FOR ALL' (which featured MEAT LOAF) ventured further and was the first to earn him a Top 40 placing in the UK. Abrasive as ever, TED "The Deer Hunter" NUGENT took a break from boasting about his conquests (musical, animal or otherwise . . .) to record his third heavy-metal onslaught, 'CAT SCRATCH FEVER', another acclaimed album which featured such pussy-tickling gems as 'WANG DANG SWEET POONTANG' and the glorious title track. NUGE (who had recently demonstrated his affection for a fan by enscribing his name with a bowie knife on their arm!), reached his 70's climax with the ripping 1978 concert set, 'DOUBLE LIVE GONZO', and although he released two more sturdy studio albums that decade, 'WEEKEND WARRIORS' and 'STATE OF SHOCK', he would never quite attain such testosterone-fuelled heights again. After two middling early 80's albums (one of them being the live 'INTENSITIES IN 10 CITIES'), TED signed to 'Atlantic', delivering a rather poor, directionless affair thoughtfully titled, 'NUGENT' (1982). Taking a few years to recover, the loinclothed one returned in good old feminist-baiting style with 'PENETRATOR' (1984) and 'LITTLE MISS DANGEROUS' (1986), NUGENT rather unconvincingly claiming that the title track of the latter could cure the emerging AIDS virus. Even more unbelievable was the news that NUGE was forming a new AOR-orientated supergroup, The DAMN YANKEES alongside TOMMY SHAW (Styx), JACK BLADES (Night Ranger) and MICHAEL CARTELLONE (er, drums). This was all too horribly confirmed in 1990 with the release of their eponymous debut, the Top 20 album boasting a US Top 3 smash, 'HIGH ENOUGH'. This quartet released another set in 1992, 'DON'T TREAD', although the only thing The DAMN YANKESS were treading was water. Thankfully NUGE abandoned this project and returned to his familiar bloodthirsty neck of the woods with the 1995 solo album, 'SPIRIT OF THE WILD'. The 'NUGE was back in 2002 after an interminable layoff with 'CRAVEMAN', a great title and undoubtedly his meatiest collection of songs since the 70's. As reliably un-PC as ever but produced and executed with the kind of warped passion rarely witnessed in the man's latter day catalogue, the record found NUGENT spitting bile and oozing testosterone like a man possessed. • **Trivia:** In 1973, while working on a new record deal, he featured alongside other stars MIKE PINERA (Iron Butterfly), WAYNE KRAMER (MC5) and FRANK MARINO (Mahogany Rush), on the 'battle of the guitarists' stage shows. • **Note:** There was another group of the same name in the UK called The AMBOY DUKES, who released several singles on 'Polydor', around the mid-60's to '68.

Album rating: JOURNEYS & MIGRATIONS (*7) / TED NUGENT (*7) / FREE FOR ALL (*6) / CAT SCRATCH FEVER (*6) / DOUBLE LIVE GONZO! (*7) / WEEKEND WARRIORS (*5) / STATE OF SHOCK (*5) / SCREAM DREAM (*5) / INTENSITIES IN 10 CITIES (*6) / GREAT GONZOS! THE BEST OF TED NUGENT compilation (*6) / NUGENT (*2) / PENETRATOR (*5) / LITTLE MISS DANGEROUS (*4) / IF YOU CAN'T LICK 'EM, LICK 'EM (*4) / SPIRIT OF THE WILD (*4) / FULL BLUNTAL NUGITY (*5) / CRAVEMAN (*6)

AMBOY DUKES

TED NUGENT – guitar, vox / plus **JOHN DRAKE** – vocals / **STEVE FARMER** – rhythm guitar / **BILL WHITE** – bass / **RICK LOBER** – keyboards / **DAVID PALMER** – drums

Fontana Mainstream

1967. (7") *<676>* **BABY PLEASE DON'T GO. / PSALMS OF AFTERMATH** [–] [ ]

1967. (7") *(TF 971)* **LET'S GO GET STONED. / IT'S NOT TRUE** [ ] [–]

1968. (lp; stereo/mono) *(S+/TL 5468) <6104>* **THE AMBOY DUKES** [ ] Jan68 [ ]
– Baby please don't go / I feel free / Young love / Psalms of aftermath / Colors / Let's go get stoned / Down on Philips escalator / The lovely lady / Night time / It's not true / Gimme love. *(cd-iss. Dec92 on 'Repertoire'+=;)* – J.B. special.

—— **RUSTY DAY** – vocals repl. DRAKE + FARMER / **ANDY SOLOMAN** – keyboards repl. LOBER / **GREG ARAMA** – bass repl. WHITE
In the UK, they were now called The AMERICAN AMBOY DUKES

London Mainstream

Jul 68. (7") *<684>* **JOURNEY TO THE CENTER OF THE MIND. / MISSISSIPPI MURDERER** [–] [16]

Oct 68. (7") *<693>* **SCOTTISH TEA. / YOU TALK SUNSHINE, I BREATHE FIRE** [–] [ ]

Feb 69. (lp; stereo/mono) *(SH-T/HA-T 8378) <6112>* **JOURNEY TO THE CENTER OF THE MIND** [ ] Aug68 [74]
– Mississippi murderer / Surrender to your kings / Flight of the Byrd / Scottish tea / Dr. Slingshot / Journey to the center of the mind / Ivory castles / Why is a carrot more orange than an orange? / Missionary Mary / Death is life / Saint Philips friend / I'll prove I'm right / (Conclusion). *(cd-iss. Dec92 on 'Repertoire'+=; MDCD 0911)* – You talk sunshine, I breathe fire.

1969. (7") *<700>* **PRODIGAL MAN. / GOOD NATURED EMMA** [–] [ ]

1969. (lp; stereo/mono) *(SH-T/HA-T 8392) <6118>* **MIGRATION** [ ] [ ]
– Migration / Prodigal man / For his namesake / I'm not a juvenile delinquent / Good natured Emma / Inside the outside / Shades of green and grey / Curb your elephant / Loaded for bear. *(cd-iss. Dec92 on 'Repertoire'+=;)* – Sobbin' in my mug of bear.

1969. (7") *<704>* **FOR HIS NAMESAKE. / LOADED FOR BEAR** [–] [ ]

1969. (7") *<711>* **MIGRATION. / FLIGHT OF THE BIRDS** [–] [ ]

1969. (lp) *<6125>* **THE BEST OF THE ORIGINAL AMBOY DUKES** (compilation) [–] [ ]

Polydor Polydor

Mar 70. (lp) *<4012>* **MARRIAGE ON THE ROCKS – ROCK BOTTOM** [–] [ ]
– Marriage:- (a) Part 1 – Man / (b) Part 2 – Woman / (c) Part 3 – Music / Breast-fed 'gator (bait) / Get yer guns / Non-conformist wilderbeast man / Today's lesson / Children of the woods / Brain games of the yesteryear / The inexhaustable quest for the cosmic garbage (part 1 & 2) / (excerpt from Bartok).

—— **NUGENT** brought in new members **BOB GRANGE** – bass / **KJ KNIGHT** – drums retaining also **ANDY SOLOMAN** (RUSTY DAY joined CACTUS)

TED NUGENT & THE AMBOY DUKES

Mar 71. (lp) *<4035>* **SURVIVAL OF THE FITTEST** (live) [–] [ ]
– Survival of the fittest / Rattle my snake / Mr. Jones' hanging party / Papa's will / Slidin' on / Prodigal man. *(UK-iss.1974 on 'Polydor'; 2675 141)*

—— Disbanded in the early 70's, but re-formed with others **BOB GRANGE** – bass / **ANDY JEZOWSKI** – vocals / **GABRIEL MAGNO** – keyboards / **VIC MASTRIANNI** – drums

Discreet Discreet

Jun 74. (lp) *(K 59203) <2181>* **CALL OF THE WILD** [ ] [ ]
– Call of the wild / Sweet revenge / Pony express / Ain't it the truth / Renegade / Rot gut / Below the belt / Cannon balls. *(re-iss. Oct89 on 'Edsel' lp/cd; ED/+CD 278)*

Jun 74. (7") *(K 19200)* **SWEET REVENGE. / AIN'T IT THE TRUTH** [ ] [ ]

—— **Rev.ATROCIOUS THEODOLIUS** – guitar, vocals repl. MAGNO

1975. (lp) *(K 59203) <2203>* **TOOTH FANG & CLAW** [ ] [ ]
– Lady luck / Living in the woods / Hibernation / Free flight / Maybelline / The great white buffalo / Sasha / No holds barred. *(re-iss. Oct89 on 'Edsel'; lp/cd; ED/+CD 295)*

—— TED finally gave up AMBOY DUKES in 1975.

– compilations, etc. –

Apr 73. (d-lp) *Mainstream; <MRL 801>* **JOURNEYS & MIGRATIONS** [–] [ ]
<re-iss. Apr75 on 'Polydor'; 2801> (UK-iss.Feb83 on 'Audio Fidelity'; MRD 5008)

Jun 77. (d-lp) *Polydor; <2664 344)* **MARRIAGE ON THE ROCKS – ROCK BOTTOM / SURVIVAL OF THE FITTEST (AMBOY DUKES)** [ ] [–]

1977. (d-lp) *Warners; (K 69202)* **TWO ORIGINALS OF . . . (AMBOY DUKES)** [ ] [–]
– (CALL OF THE WILD & TOOTH, FANG & CLAW) albums

Jan 91. (cd/c) *Thunderbolt; (CDTB/THBC 097)* **ON THE EDGE** (early AMBOY DUKES material) [ ] [–]
(cd re-iss. Nov98; same)

May 91. (cd/c) *Thunderbolt; (CDTB/THBC 120)* **OVER THE TOP** (early AMBOY DUKES material) [ ] [–]
(cd re-iss. Nov98; same)

Aug 99. (cd; TED NUGENT & THE AMBOY DUKES) *Legacy; (494606-2)* **LOADED FOR BEAR** [ ] [ ]

Jun 00. (d-cd) *Thunderbolt; (CDTBD 010)* **ON THE EDGE / OVER THE TOP** [ ] [–]

TED NUGENT

(solo) with **ROB GRANGE** – bass / **DEREK ST.HOLMES** – vocals, guitar (ex-SCOTT) / **CLIFF DAVIS** – drums / plus guests

Epic Epic

Nov 75. (7") *<50172>* **MOTORCITY MADNESS. / WHERE HAVE YOU BEEN ALL MY LIFE** [–] [ ]

Mar 76. (lp/c) *(EPC/40 33692) <81196>* **TED NUGENT** [56] Nov75 [28]
– Stranglehold / Stormtroopin' / Hey baby / Just what the doctor ordered / Snakeskin cowboys / Motor city madhouse / Where have you been all my life / You make me feel right at home / Queen of the forest. *(cd-iss. Aug99 on 'Legacy'; 494605-2)*

Jun 76. (7") *(EPC 3900) <50197>* **HEY BABY. / STORMTROOPIN'** [ ] Mar76 [72]

Oct 76. (lp/c) *(EPC/40 81397) <34121>* **FREE-FOR-ALL** [33] Sep76 [24]
– Free for all / Dog eat dog / Writing on the wall / Turn it up / Together / Street rats / Hammer down / Light my way / Love you so much I told a lie. *(re-iss. Jan84; EPC 34121) (cd re-mast.Aug99 on 'Legacy'; 494604-2)*

Nov 76. (7") *<50301>* **DOG EAT DOG. / LIGHT MY WAY** [–] [91]

Nov 76. (7") *(EPC 4796)* **DOG EAT DOG. / LOVE YOU SO MUCH I TOLD A LIE** [ ] [–]

Jan 77. (7") *<50363>* **FREE-FOR-ALL. / STREET RAGS** [–] [ ]

Jun 77. (lp/c) *(EPC/40 82010) <34700>* **CAT SCRATCH FEVER** [28] [17]
– Cat scratch fever / Wang dang sweet poontang / Death by misadventure / Live it up / Home bound / Workin' hard, playin' hard / Sweet Sally / A thousand knives / Fist fightin' son of a gun / Out of control. *(cd-iss. Jun89; CD 32252) (cd re-iss. Aug93 on 'Columbia'; 468024-2) (cd re-mast.Aug99 on 'Legacy'; 494603-2)*

Jul 77. (7") *<50425>* **CAT SCRATCH FEVER. / WANG DANG SWEET POONTANG** [–] [ ]

Jul 77. (7") *(EPC 5482)* **CAT SCRATCH FEVER. / A THOUSAND NIGHTS** [ ] [–]

Feb 78. (7") *(EPC 5945) <50493>* **HOME BOUND. / DEATH BY MISADVENTURE** [ ] [70]

Feb 78. (d-lp) *(EPC 88282) <35069>* **DOUBLE LIVE GONZO! (live)** [47] [13]
– Just what the doctor ordered / Yank me, crank me / Gonzo / Baby please don't go / Great white buffalo / Hibernation / Stormtroopin' / Stranglehold / Wang dang sweet poontang / Cat scratch fever / Motor city madhouse.

Mar 78. (7") *<50533>* **YANK ME, CRANK ME (live). / CAT SCRATCH FEVER (live)** [–] [58]

—— **CHARLIE HUHN** – vocals, vocals repl. ST. HOLMES (to ST. PARADISE, etc) **DAVID HULL** – bass repl. BOB GRANGE (also to ST. PARADISE, who released one eponymous album for 'Warners' in '79)

Nov 78. (lp/c) *(EPC/40 83036) <35551>* **WEEKEND WARRIORS** [ ] [24]
– Need you bad / One woman / I got the feelin' / Tight spots / Venom soup / Smokescreen / Weekend warriors / Cruisin' / Good friends and a bottle of wine / Name your poison.

Dec 78. (7") *<50648>* **NEED YOU BAD. / I GOT THE FEELIN'** [–] [84]

—— **WALTER MONAHAN** – bass repl. HULL

Jun 79. (lp/c)<US-pic-lp> *(EPC/40 86092) <36000>* **STATE OF SHOCK** [ ] May79 [18]
– Paralyzed / Take it or leave it / Alone / It doesn't matter / State of shock / I want to tell you / It doesn't matter / Satisfied / Bite down hard / Snake charmer / Saddle sore. *(cd-iss. Aug93 on 'Columbia'; 471456-2)*

Jun 79. (7") *<50713>* **I WANT TO TELL YOU. / BITE DOWN HARD** [–] [ ]

Jul 79. (7"m) *(EPC 7723)* **I WANT TO TELL YOU. / PARALYSED / CAT SCRATCH FEVER** [ ] [–]

May 80. (7"/12") *(EPC/12 8640)* **FLESH AND BLOOD. / MOTOR CITY MADHOUSE** [ ] [–]

Jun 80. (lp/c) *(EPC/40 86111) <36404>* **SCREAM DREAM** [37] May80 [13]
– Wango tango / Scream dream / Hard as nails / I gotta move / Violent love / Flesh and blood / Spit it out / Come and get it / Terminus El Dorada / Don't cry, I'll be back before you know it baby. *(cd-iss. Aug93 on 'Columbia'; 471458-2)*

Jul 80. (7") *<50907>* **WANGO TANGO. / SCREAM DREAM** [–] [86]

Feb 81. (7") *<01046>* **LAND OF A THOUSAND DANCES. / THE TNT OVERTURE** [–] [ ]

Apr 81. (lp/c) *(EPC/40 84917) <37084>* **(INTENSITIES) IN 10 CITIES** [75] [51]
– Put up or shut up / Spontaneous combustion / My love is like a tire iron / Jailbait / I am a predator / Heads will roll / The flying lip lock / Land of a thousand dances / The TNT overture / I take no prisoners.

Dec 81. (lp/c) *(EPC/40 85408) <37667>* **GREAT GONZOS! THE BEST OF TED NUGENT** (compilation) [ ] [ ]
– Cat scratch fever / Just what the doctor ordered / Free-for-all / Dog eat dog / Motor city madness / Paralysed / Stranglehold / Baby please don't go / Wango tango / Wang dang sweet poontang. *(cd-iss. Feb97 on 'Columbia'; 471216-2)*

—— **DEREK ST. HOLMES** – vocals returned from WHITFORD / ST. HOLMES to repl. HUHN / **DAVE KISWINEY** – bass repl. MONAGHAN / **CARMINE APPICE** – drums (ex-VANILLA FUDGE, ex-CACTUS, etc.) repl. DAVIS

Atlantic Atlantic

Aug 82. (lp/c) *(K/K4 50898) <19365>* **NUGENT** [ ] Jul82 [51]
– No, no, no / Bound and gagged / Habitual offender / Fightin' words / Good and ready / Ebony / Don't push me / Can't stop me now / We're gonna rock tonight / Tailgunner.

Sep 82. (7") *<89998>* **BOUND AND GAGGED. / HABITUAL OFFENDER** [–] [ ]

Nov 82. (7") *<89978>* **NO, NO, NO. / HABITUAL OFFENDER** [–] [ ]

—— **NUGENT** recruited entire new band again! **BRIAN HOWE** – vocals / **ALAN ST. JOHN** – keyboards / **DOUG LABAHN** – bass / **BOBBY CHOUINARD** – drums

Feb 84. (lp/c) *(780 125-1/-4) <80125>* **PENETRATOR** [ ] [56]
– Tied up in love / (Where do you) Draw the line / Knockin' at your door / Don't you want my love / Go down fighting / Thunder thighs / No man's land / Blame it on the night / Lean mean R&R machine / Take me home.

Feb 84. (7") *(A 9705) <89705>* **TIED UP IN LOVE. / LEAN MEAN R&R MACHINE** [ ] [ ]

Apr 84. (7") *<89681>* **(WHERE DO YOU) DRAW THE LINE. / LEAN MEAN R&R MACHINE** [–] [ ]

—— Took time out to appear in 'Miami Vice' US TV programme. He also played on charity single 'Stars' by aggregation 'HEAR'N AID' circa Spring 1986.

—— **DAVE AMATO** – guitar, vocals repl. HOWE who joined BAD COMPANY / **RICKY PHILIPS** – bass (ex-BABYS) repl. LABAHN

Nov 86. (lp/c/cd) *(K 252388-1/-4/-2) <81632>* **LITTLE MISS DANGEROUS** [ ] Mar86 [76]
– High heels in motion / Strangers / Little Miss Dangerous / Savage dancer / Crazy ladies / When your body talks / My little red book / Take me away / Angry young man / Painkiller.

Apr 86. (7") *<89442>* **HIGH HEELS IN MOTION. / ANGRY YOUNG MAN** [–] [ ]

Jul 86. (7") *<89436>* **LITTLE MISS DANGEROUS. / ANGRY YOUNG MAN** [–] [ ]

—— **NUGENT** re-recruited **DEREK ST.HOLMES** – vocals, guitar / **DAVE KISWINEY** – bass / plus new drummer – **PAT MARCHINO**

Feb 88. (lp/c/cd) *(K 255385-1/-4/-2) <81812>* **IF YOU CAN'T LICK 'EM . . . LICK 'EM** [ ] [ ]
– Can't live with 'em / She drives me crazy / If you can't lick 'em . . . lick 'em / Skintight / Funlover / Spread your wings / The harder they come (the harder I get) / Separate the men from the boys, please / Bite the hand / That's the story of love.

DAMN YANKEES

TED NUGENT – guitar, vocals / **TOMMY SHAW** (b.11 Sep'53, Montgomery, Alabama) – vocals (ex-STYX) / **JACK BLADES** (b.24 Apr'54, Palm Beach, Calif.) – bass (ex-NIGHT RANGER) / **MICHAEL CARTELLONE** (b. 7 Jun'62, Cleveland, Ohio) – drums, non-s/writer

Warners Warners

Apr 90. (cd/c/lp) *<(7599 26159-2/-4/-1)>* **DAMN YANKEES** [26] Mar90 [13]
– Coming of age / Bad reputation / Runaway / High enough / Damn Yankees / Come again / Mystified / Rock city / Tell me how you want it / Piledriver.

Apr 90. (c-s,cd-s) *<19838>* **COMING OF AGE. / TELL ME HOW YOU WANT IT** [–] [60]

Jan 91. (7"/c-s) *(W 0006/+C) <19595>* **HIGH ENOUGH. / PILEDRIVER** [ ] Oct90 [3]
(12"+=/cd-s+=) *(W 0006 T/CD)* – Bonestripper.

Apr 91. (c-s,cd-s) *<19408>* **COME AGAIN. / ('A'radio version)** [–] [50]

Aug 92. (cd/c) *<(9362 45025-2/-4)>* **DON'T TREAD** [ ] [22]
– Don't tread on me / Fifteen minutes of fame / Where you goin' now / Dirty dog / Mister please / Silence is broken / Firefly / Someone to believe / This side of Hell / Double coyote / Uprising. *(re-iss. cd Feb95; same)*

Jan 93. (7"/c-s) *<18728>* **WHERE YOU GOIN' NOW. / THIS SIDE OF HELL** [ ] Sep92 [20]
(12"+=/cd-s+=) – ('A'version).

Apr 93. (c-s) *<18612>* **SILENCE IS BROKEN / DOUBLE COYOTE** [–] [62]
(12"+=/cd-s+=) – High enough (live) / ('A'live version).

—— **STEVE SMITH** – drums (ex-JOURNEY) repl. NUGENT, although the band became SHAW BLADES, releasing one 'Warners' album, 'HALLICINATION' (9362 45835-2/-4).

Ted NUGENT

—— returned w/ **DAVE AMATO** – guitar / **CHUCK WRIGHT** – bass / **PAT TORPEY** – drums / + co-writers ST. HOLMES + LUTZ

Atlantic Atlantic

Dec 95. (cd/c) *<(7567 82611)>* **SPIRIT OF THE WILD** [ ] May95 [86]
– Thighraceous / Wrong side of town / I shoot back / Toot, fang & claw / Lovejacker / Fred bear / Primitive man / Hot or cold / Kiss my ass / Heart & soul / Spirit of the wild / Just do it like this.

Spitfire Spitfire

Aug 01. (cd) *(SPITCD 175) <15175>* **FULL BLUNTAL NUGITY (live)** [ ] Jun01 [ ]
– KLSTRPHK / Paralyzed / Snakeskin cowboys / Wang dang sweet poontang / Free for all / Yank me, crank me / Hey baby / Fred bear (acoustic) / Cat scratch fever / Stranglehold / Great white buffalo / Motor city madhouse.

Sep 02. (cd) *(SPITCD 174) <15174>* **CRAVEMAN** [ ] [ ]
– KLSTRPHNKY / Crave / Rawdogs and warhogs / Damned if I do / At home there / Cum N gitya sum-o-this / Change my sex / I won't go away / Pussywhipped / Goin' down hard / Wang dang doodle / My baby likes my butter on her gritz / Sexpot / Earthtones.

– compilations, others, etc. –

Feb 83. (d-c) *Epic;* **TED NUGENT / FREE FOR ALL** [ ] [–]

Sep 86. (d-lp/d-c) *Raw Power; (RAWLP/TC 026)* **ANTHOLOGY** [ ] [–]
(re-iss. Feb91 on 'Castle' cd/c; CCS CD/MC 282)

Jun 93. (cd) *Sony;* **THE VERY BEST OF TED NUGENT** [ ] [ ]

May 94. (d-cd/d-c) *Epic-Legacy; (CD/40 47039)* **OUT OF CONTROL** [ ] [ ]

May 97. (cd) *Columbia; (471216-2) <64871>* **LIVE AT HAMMERSMITH '79 (live)** [ ] Mar97 [ ]

Gary NUMAN

Born: GARY WEBB, 8 Mar'58, Hammersmith, London, England. Inspired by 70's glam icons such as BOLAN and BOWIE as well as synthmeisters like KRAFTWERK, NUMAN formed punk outfit, MEAN STREET in 1977, subsequently appearing on the Various

Artists compilation, 'Live At The Vortex'. To end the year, he set up TUBEWAY ARMY, basically his solo project although he was accompanied on live work by PAUL GARDINER and his uncle, GERALD LIDYARD. The debut vinyl outing, 'THAT'S TOO BAD', was issued by indie punk label, 'Beggars Banquet' in early '78. An eponymous debut album passed virtually unnoticed, although things changed dramatically in June '79, when they/he had a first No.1 with the monotonic synth-noir of 'ARE FRIENDS ELECTRIC', spurred on by a compelling appearance on UK's 'Top Of The Pops'. Its parent album, 'REPLICAS', also shot to the top the same month. A busy year for NUMAN, in addition to collaborating with ROBERT PALMER, of all people (he was initially part of offshoot outfit, DRAMATIS), he found time to record a second No.1 album, 'THE PLEASURE PRINCIPLE'. This collection was previewed with the hypnotic, sweeping electronica of the 'CARS' single, by far his most well known track and one that enjoyed a rejuvenation in 1996 after it was used in a British TV advert. NUMAN scored yet another No.1 album with 'TELEKON' (1980) the following year, his futuristic synth-based pop/rock gracing the upper reaches of the singles chart in the form of 'WE ARE GLASS' and 'I DIE: YOU DIE'. By this point, however, NUMAN was well on his way to becoming perhaps one of most visible targets of critical derision in the whole of the music industry, his neo-futurist posturing, dalek vocals, pretentious lyrics and worst of all, his vocal support of Margaret Thatcher raising the not inconsiderable ire of the music press. Nevertheless, NUMAN had a fiercely loyal grassroots following of clone-like fans (second only to NUMAN himself as figures of fun among rock circles) who ensured most of his subsequent output made the Top 50 at least. Despite the presence of such luminaries as MICK KARN (JAPAN), ROGER TAYLOR (QUEEN) and erm, NASH THE SLASH (solo artist from Canada, apparently), 'DANCE' (1981) was a decidedly ungroovy set of steely electronica and his last to achieve mainstream success. NUMAN released two further, increasingly pompous albums, 'I, ASSASSIN' (1982) and 'WARRIORS' (1983) before forming his own label, 'Numa', in 1984 to issue his own product along with material by his brother JOHN's outfit, HOHOKAM. 80's albums like 'THE FURY' (1985), 'STRANGE CHARM' (1986), 'METAL RHYTHM' (1988) and 'AUTOMATIC' (1989) continued to appeal mainly to hardcore fans although 'OUTLAND' (1991) managed to nudge into the Top 40. However, since the awful 'MACHINE AND SOUL' (1992), NUMAN has fallen further into cult status, his releases failing to even break the Top 100. Come the new millennium, NUMAN was still churning out the albums, the harsh industrialised textures of 'PURE' (2000) suggesting that he could easily give the young pretenders of goth electronica a run for their money. It also suggested that after years in the musical wilderness, NUMAN may have found a creatively profitable niche for himself. • **Songwriters:** Wrote own material, with inspiration from psi-fi writers (i.e. WILLIAM S. BURROUGHS). Covered 1999 + U GOT THE LOOK (Prince). • **Trivia:** In the early 80's, he took up flying planes and bought his own aircraft (mainly warplanes).

Album rating: Tubeway Army: TUBEWAY ARMY (*4) / REPLICAS (*7) / Gary Numan: THE PLEASURE PRINCIPLE (*7) / TELEKON (*6) / LIVING ORNAMENTS 1979 (*4) / LIVING ORNAMENTS 1980 (*4) / DANCE (*4) / I, ASSASSIN (*5) / WARRIORS (*4) / BERSERKER (*4) / WHITE NOISE (*4) / THE FURY (*4) / STRANGE CHARM (*3) / EXHIBITION compilation (*7) / METAL RHYTHM (*4) / AUTOMATIC (*3; as Sharpe & Numan) / THE SKIN MECHANIC (*4) / OUTLAND (*4) / MACHINE AND SOUL (*4) / THE BEST OF . . . compilation (*7) / DREAM CORROSION (*4) / DARL LIGHT (*4) / DARK LIGHT (*4) / HUMAN (*4) / EXILE (*3) / PURE (*6)

TUBEWAY ARMY

GARY NUMAN – vocals, guitar, synthesizer, keyboards (ex-MEAN STREET) / **PAUL 'Scarlett' GARDINER** – bass / **GERALD 'Rael' LIDYARD** – drums

Beggars Banquet — Atco

Feb 78. (7") *(BEG 5)* **THAT'S TOO BAD. / OH! DIDN'T I SAY** [ ] [–]

— **BARRY BENN** – drums repl. BOB SIMMONDS who had repl. LIDYARD / added **SEAN BURKE** – guitar

Jul 78. (7"m) *(BEG 8)* **BOMBERS. / O.D. RECEIVER. / BLUE EYES** [ ] [–]

Aug 78. (lp,blue-lp) *(BEGA 4)* **TUBEWAY ARMY** [ ] [–]
– Listen to the sirens / My shadow in vain / The life machine / Friends / Something's in the house / Every day I die / Steal and you / My love is a liquid / Are you real / The dream police / Jo the waiter / Zero bass. *(re-iss. Aug79 lp/c; BEGA/BEGC 4); hit No.14) (re-iss. May83 on 'Fame' lp/c; FA/TC-FA 3060) (re-iss. Jul88 lp/c; BBL/+C 4)*

— **JESS LIDYARD** – drums returned to replace BARRY and SEAN

Mar 79. (7") *(BEG 17)* **DOWN IN THE PARK. / DO YOU NEED THE SERVICE?** [ ] [–]
(12"+=) *(BEG 17T)* – I nearly married a human 2.

May 79. (7"/7"pic-d) <US-7"/c-s> *(BEG 18/+P)* **ARE 'FRIENDS' ELECTRIC?. / WE ARE SO FRAGILE?** [1] [ ]

Jun 79. (lp/c) <credited as GARY NUMAN & TUBEWAY ARMY> *(BEGA/BEGC 7)* *<117>* **REPLICAS** [1] [ ]
– Me I disconnect from you / Are 'friends' electric? / The machman / Praying to the aliens / Down in the park / You are in my vision / Replicas / It must have been years / When the machines rock / I nearly married a human. *(re-iss. +cd.Sep88) (re-iss. cd/c Apr95 on 'Music Club')*

GARY NUMAN

— solo retaining **PAUL GARDINER** – bass / **CEDRIC SHARPLEY** – drums / **CHRIS PAYNE** – synth, viola / **BILLY CURRIE** – keyboards

Aug 79. (7") *(BEG 23)* **CARS. / ASYLUM** [1] [–]

Sep 79. (lp/c) *(BEGA/BEGC 10)* <38120> **THE PLEASURE PRINCIPLE** [1] Jan80 [16]
– Airplane / Metal / Complex / Films / M.E. / Tracks / Observer / Conversation / Cars / Engineers. *(re-iss. Sep88 lp/c; BBL/+C 10)*

Nov 79. (7") *(BEG 29)* **COMPLEX. / BOMBERS (live)** [6] [ ]
(12"+=) *(BEG 29T)* – Me I disconnect from you (live).

Jan 80. (7") *<7211>* **CARS. / METAL** [–] [9]

— **DENNIS HAINES** – keyboards repl. CURRIE who returned to ULTRAVOX and VISAGE; added **RUSSELL BELL** – guitar (on tour) .

May 80. (7") *(BEG 35)* **WE ARE GLASS. / TROIS GYMNPEDIES (1st MOVEMENT)** [5] [ ]

Aug 80. (7") *(BEG 46)* **I DIE: YOU DIE. / DOWN IN THE PARK (piano version)** [6] [–]

Sep 80. (lp/c) *(BEGA/BEGC 19)* <32103> **TELEKON** [1] [64]
– This wreckage / The aircrash bureau / Telekon / Remind me to smile / Sleep by windows / I'm an agent / I dream of wires / Remember I was a vapour / Please push no more / The joy circuit. *(free-7"w/ lp)* – REMEMBER I WAS A VAPOUR. / ON BROADWAY *(re-iss. Jul88 lp/c; BBL/+C 19)*

Sep 80. (7") **I DIE: YOU DIE. / SLEEP BY WINDOWS** [–] [ ]

Dec 80. (7") **REMIND ME TO SMILE. /** [–] [ ]

Dec 80. (7") *(BEG 50)* **THIS WRECKAGE. / PHOTOGRAPH** [20] [ ]

Apr 81. (d-lp/c) *(BOX/C 1)* **LIVING ORNAMENTS 1979-1980 (live)** [2] [–]

Apr 81. (lp) *(BEGA 24)* **LIVING ORNAMENTS 1979 (live)** [47] [–]
– Airplane / Cars / We are so fragile? / Films / Something's in the house / My shadow in vain / Conversation / The dream police / Metal.

Apr 81. (lp) *(BEGA 25)* **LIVING ORNAMENTS 1980 (live)** [39] [–]
– This wreckage / I die: you die / M.E. / Everyday I die / Down in the park / Remind me to smile / The joy circuit / Tracks / Are 'friends' electric? / We are glass.

— GARY now recruited famous stars to replace BELL, SHARPLEY, HAINES and PAYNE. They became DRAMATIS. Jul'81 he guested on PAUL GARDINER single 'STORMTROOPER IN DRAG' *(BEG 61/+T)*, which hit UK No.49. Next with stars **MICK KARN** – bass (of JAPAN) / **ROGER TAYLOR** – drums (of QUEEN) + **NASH THE SLASH** – violin (Canadian solo artist)

Aug 81. (7") *(BEG 62)* **SHE'S GOT CLAWS. / I SING RAIN** [6] [ ]
(12"+=) *(BEG 62T)* – Exhibition.

Sep 81. (lp/c) *(BEGA/BEGC 28)* <38-143> **DANCE** [3] [ ]
– Slowcar to China / Night talk / A subway called you / Cry the clock said /

She's got claws / Crash / Boys like me / Stories / My brother's time / You are you are / Moral. *(re-iss. Jan89 lp/c; BBL/+C 28)*

Nov 81. (7"; by GARY NUMAN and DRAMATIS) *(BEG 68)* **LOVE NEEDS NO DISGUISE. / TAKE ME HOME** 33 [ ]
(12"+=) *(BEG 68T)* – Face to face.

— GARY NUMAN now used session people.

Feb 82. (7") *(BEG 70)* **MUSIC FOR CHAMELEONS. / NOISE NOISE** 19 [ ]
(ext.12"+=) *(BEG 70T)* – Bridge? what bridge.

Jun 82. (7") *(BEG 77)* **WE TAKE MYSTERY (TO BED). / THE IMAGE IS** 9 [ ]
(ext.12"+=) *(BEG 77T)* – ('A'early version).

Aug 82. (7") *(BEG 81)* **WHITE BOYS AND HEROES. / WAR GAMES** 20 [ ]
(ext.12"+=) *(BEG 81T)* – Glitter and ash.

Sep 82. (lp/c) *(BEGA/BEGC 40)* *<900141>* **I, ASSASSIN** 8 [ ]
– White boys and heroes / War songs / A dream of Siam / Music for chameleons / This is my house / I, assassin / The 1930's rust / We take mystery (to bed). *(re-iss. Jan89 lp/c; BBL/+C 40)*

Aug 83. (7"/7"sha-pic-d) *(BEG 95/+P)* **WARRIORS. / MY CAR SLIDES (1)** 20 –
(ext.12"+=) *(BEG 95T)* – My car slides (2).

Sep 83. (lp/c) *(BEGA/BEGC 47)* **WARRIORS** 12 –
– Warriors / I am render / The iceman comes / This prison moon / My centurion / Sister surprise / The tick tock man / Love is like clock law / The rhythm of the evening. *(re-iss. Jan89 lp/c; BBL/+C 47)*

Oct 83. (7") *(BEG 101)* **SISTER SUPRISE. / POETRY AND POWER** 32 –
(ext.12"+=) *(BEG 101T)* – Letters.

Numa — not iss.

Oct 84. (7"/7"sha-pic-d) *(NU/+P 4)* **BERSERKER. / EMPTY BED, EMPTY HEART** 32 –
(12"+=) *(NUM 4)* – ('A'extended).

Nov 84. (lp/c) *(NUMA/+C 1001)* **BERSERKER** 45 –
– Berserker / This is new love / The secret / My dying machine / Cold warning / Pump it up / The God film / A child with the ghost / The hunter. *(c+=)* – (6 extra tracks). *(cd-iss. Dec95; NUMACD 1001)*

Dec 84. (7") *(NU 6)* **MY DYING MACHINE. / HERE I AM** 66 –
(ext.12"+=) *(NUM 6)* – She cries.

— next 45 with BILL SHARPE of SHAKATAK; and on 'Polydor' album 'Famous People'.

Feb 85. (7"/7"pic-d; by SHARPE & NUMAN) *(POSP/+P 722)* **CHANGE YOUR MIND. / REMIX, REMAKE, REMODEL** 17 –
(ext.12"pic-d+=) *(POSPX 722)* – Fools in a world of fire.

Apr 85. (d-lp/c) *(NUMA D/C 1002)* **WHITE NOISE (live)** 29 –
– (intro) / Berserker / Metal / Me, I disconnect from you / Remind me to smile / Sister surprise / Music for chameleons / The iceman comes / Cold warning / Down in the park / This prison moon / I die; you die / My dying machine / Cars / We take mystery (to bed) / We are glass / This is new love / My shadow in vain / Are 'friends' electric?. *(d-cd-iss. May93; NUMACD 1002)*

May 85. (7"ep/12"ep,12"blue-ep,12"white-ep) *(NU/+M 7)* **THE LIVE EP (live)** 27 –
– Are 'friends' electric? / Berserker / Cars / We are glass.

Jul 85. (7"/7"pic-d) *(NU/+P 9)* **YOUR FASCINATION. / WE NEED IT** 46 –
(ext.12"+=/ext.12"pic-d+=) *(NUM/+P 9)* – Anthem.

Sep 85. (7") *(NU 11)* **CALL OUT THE DOGS. / THIS SHIP COMES APART** 49 –
(ext.12"+=) *(NUM 11)* – No shelter.

Sep 85. (lp/pic-lp/c) *(NUMA/+P/K 1003)* **THE FURY** 24 –
– Call out the dogs / This disease / Your fascination / Miracles / The pleasure skin / Creatures / Tricks / God only knows / Creatures / I still remember. *(c+)* – (all tracks extended). *(cd-iss. 1986; CDNUMA 1003)* *(re-iss. cd Nov96; NUMACDX 1003)*

Nov 85. (7",7"red,7"white/ext-12",ext-12"red,ext-12"white) *(NU/+M 13)* **MIRACLES. / THE FEAR** 49 –

Apr 86. (7"/7"pic-d/ext-12"/ext-12"pic-d) *(NU/+P/M/MP 16)* **THIS IS LOVE. / SURVIVAL** 28 –
(all w/ free 7"flexi)
(d12"+=) *(NUMX 16)* – Call out the dogs (extended) / No shelter / This ship comes apart.

Jun 86. (7"/7"sha-pic-d/ext-12"/picture-12"pic-d/club-10") *(NU/+P/M/MP/DJ 17)* **I CAN'T STOP. / FACES** 27 –
(all w/ free 7"flexi)

Sep 86. (7"/7"pic-d/ext-12"/ext-12"pic-d; as SHARPE & NUMAN) *(NU/+P/M/MP 19)* **NEW THING FROM LONDON TOWN. / TIME TO DIE** 52 –

Oct 86. (lp/c)(cd) *(NUMA/+C 1005)(CDNUMA 1005)* **STRANGE CHARM** 59 –
– My breathing / Unknown and hostile / The sleep room / New thing from London Town / I can't stop / Strange charm / The need / This is love. *(re-iss. cd Nov96; NUMACDX 1005)*

Nov 86. (7"/7"pic-d/ext-12"/ext-12"pic-d) *(NU/+P/M/MP 21)* **I STILL REMEMBER. / PUPPETS** 74 –

— Early in 1987, he teamed up with RADIO HEART (see further below)

Polydor — not iss.

Jan 88. (7",7"white,7"blue,7"clear/ 7"pic-d/ext-12"/ext-12"pic-d; as SHARPE & NUMAN) *(POSP/+P/X/PX 894)* **NO MORE LIES. / VOICES** 34 –
(cd-s+=) *(POCD 894)* – ('A'extended) / Change your mind.

Illegal — I.R.S.

Sep 88. (7"/7"w-poster) *(ILS/+P 1003)* **NEW ANGER. / I DON'T BELIEVE** 46 –
(12"+=/12"g-f+=) *(ILST/ILSG 1003)* – Children.
(cd-s+=) *(ILSCD 1003)* – Creatures (live) / I can't stop (live).

Oct 88. (lp/c/cd) *(ILP/+C/CD 035)* *<IRS/+D 82005>* **METAL RHYTHM** 48 [ ]
– Respect / Don't call my name / New anger / America / Hunger / Voix / Young heart / Cold metal rhythm / This is emotion. *(pic-lp iss.Mar89; ILPX 035)*

Nov 88. (7"/7"pic-d) *(ILS/+PD 1004)* **AMERICA (remix). / RESPECT (live)** 49 –
(12"+=) *(ILST 1004)* – New anger (live).
(cd-s++=) *(ILSCD 1004)* – Call out the dogs (live).

— again with **ROGER ODELL** – drums / **TESSA MILES + LINDA TAYLOR** – backing vocals

SHARPE & NUMAN

Polydor — not iss.

May 89. (7"/7"pic-d) *(PO/+PD 43)* **I'M ON AUTOMATIC. / LOVE LIKE A GHOST** 44 –
(ext.12"+=/ext.12"pic-d+=) *(PZ/+PD 43)* – Voices ('89 remix).
(7"w-poster) *(POPB 43)* – ('A'side) / No more lies (new version).
(cd-s+=) *(POCD 43)* – (all 4 above).

Jun 89. (lp/c/cd) *(839520-1/-4/-2)* **AUTOMATIC** 59 –
– Change your mind / Turn off the world / No more lies / Breathe in emotion / Some new game / I'm on automatic / Rip it up / Welcome to love / Voices / Nightlife. *(cd+=)* – No more lies (12"version) / I'm on automatic (12"version).

GARY NUMAN

— solo with **RUSSELL BELL** – guitar / **CHRIS PAYNE** – keyboards, violin / **ADE ORANGE** – keyboards / **CEDRIC SHARPLY** – drums / **JOHN WEBB** – saxophone / **ANDY COUGHLAN** – bass / **VAL CHALMERS + EMMA CHALMER** – backing vocals

I.R.S. — Capitol

Oct 89. (lp/cd) *(EIRSA/+CD 1019)* **THE SKIN MECHANIC (live Sep88)** 55 –
– Survival / Respect / Call out the dogs / Cars / Hunger / Down in the park / New anger / Creatures / Are 'friends' electric / Young heart / We are glass / I die: you die.

Mar 91. (7",7"red/c-s) *(NUMAN 1/+C)* **HEART. / SHAME** 43 –
(12") – ('A'side) / Icehouse.
(cd-s) – ('A'side) / Tread careful.
(12") – ('A'side) / Are 'friends' electric?.

Mar 91. (lp/c/cd) *(EIRSA/+MC/CD 1039)* *<13077>* **OUTLAND** 39 [ ]
– Confession / My world storm / Interval 1 / From Russia infected / Interval 2 / They whisper you / Dark Sunday / Heart / Devotion / Outland / Interval 3 / 1999 / Dream killer.

Numa — not iss.

Sep 91. (7"/c-s) *(NUD/NUC 22)* **EMOTION. / IN A GLASSHOUSE** [ ] –
(12"+=) *(NUM 22)* – Hanoi.
(cd-s++=) *(NUCD 22)* – ('A'-different mix).

Mar 92. (7"/c-s) *(NU/+C 23)* **THE SKIN GAME. / DARK MOUNTAIN** 68 –
(12"+=/cd-s+=) *(NUM/NUCD 23)* – U got the look / ('A'-digi mix).

Jul 92. (7") *(NU 24)* **MACHINE + SOUL. / ('A'-promo mix)** 72 –
(cd-s+=) *(NUCD1 24)* – Cry baby / Wonder eye.

(cd-s+=) *(NUCD2 24)* – 1999 / The hauntings.
(12"+=) *(NUM1 24)* – Your fascination (live) / Outland (live) / Respect (live).
(12") *(NUM2 24)* – ('A'side) / Soul protection (live) / Confession (live) / From Russia infected (live).

Jul 92. (lp/c/cd) *(NUMA/+C/CD 1009)* **MACHINE + SOUL** [42] [–]
– Machine + soul / Generator / The skin game / Poison / I wonder / Emotion / Cry / U got the look / Love isolation. *(ext.cd re-iss. Sep93)*

—— Apr 94; He guested for GENERATOR on their version of 'ARE FRIENDS' ELECTRIC'.

—— NUMAN & DADAGANG; Apr 94 12"/cd-s LIKE A REFUGEE (I WON'T CRY) on 'Record Label', re-iss. Aug 94 as GARY NUMAN & FRIENDS

Aug 94. (12"ep/cd-ep) *(NU M/CD 25)* **DREAM CORROSION (THE LIVE EP)** [ ] [–]
– Noise, noise / It must have been years / I'm an agent / Jo the waiter.

Aug 94. (t-lp/d-c/d-cd) *(NUMA/+C/CD 1010)* **DREAM CORROSION (live)** [ ] [–]
– Mission / Machine and soul / Outland / Me, I disconnect from you / We are so fragile / Respect / Shame / Films / Dream killer / Down in the park / My world storm / Machman / Generator / Noise, noise / Cars / Voix / You are in my vision / It must have been years / That's too bad / Remind me to smile / I'm an agent / Are 'friends' electric / My breathing / I don't believe / Bombers / Jo the waiter / We are glass.

Oct 94. (12"ep/cd-ep) *(NU M/CD 26)* **A QUESTION OF FAITH** [ ] [–]
– A question of faith (agnostic edit) / Play like God / Whisper of truth / A question of faith (devout edit).

Mar 95. (cd/c/lp) *(NUMA/+C/CD 1011)* **SACRIFICE** [ ] [ ]
– Pray / Deadliner / A question of faith / Desire / Scar / Love and napalm / You walk in my soul / Magic / Bleed / The seed of life.

Mar 95. (12"/12"pic-d/cd-s/pic-cd-s) *(NU/+MP/CD/CDP 27)* **ABSOLUTION. / MAGIC (trick mix) / MAGIC (extended)** [ ] [–]

Jun 95. (12"ep/cd-ep) *(NUM/+CD 28)* **DARK LIGHT LIVE E.P. (live)** [ ] [–]
– Bleed / Everyday I die / The dream police / Listen to the sirens.

Jul 95. (d-cd/d-c) *(NUMA CD/C 1012)* **DARK LIGHT (live)** [ ] [ ]
– Pray / A question of faith / I dream of wires / Noise noise / Listen to the sirens / Everyday I die / Desire / Friens / Scar / Magic / Praying to the aliens / Replicas I / Mean street / Stormtrooper in drag / Dead liner / Bleed / The dream police / I die, you die / The hunter / Remind me to smile / Are friends "electric"? / Do you need the service? / Love and napalm / Jo the waiter / I'm an agent.

Nov 95. (d-c/d-cd; with MICHAEL R. SMITH) *(NUMA C/CD 1013)* **HUMAN** [ ] [–]
– Navigators / Bombay / We fold space / Cry in the dark / Manic / Empire / Little lost soul / Visitor / Magician / Undercover / Halloween / Embryo / Elm Street / Harmonos / Big alten / Blind faith / New life / Fairy tales / Disease / Tidal wave / Alone and afraid / Sahara / Cold / Do you wonder / Betrayal / Suspicion / Unborn / Lethal injection / Frantic / Mother / Black heart / Thunder road / Law and order / Needles / Climax / Inferno.

Eagle Spitfire

Oct 97. (cd/c) *(EAG CD/MC 008)* **EXILE** [48] [–]
– Dominion day / Prophecy / Dead heaven / Dark / Innocence bleeding / The angel wars / Absolution / An alien cure / Exile.

Apr 98. (c-s) *(EAGCS 008)* **DOMINION DAY / ANGEL WARS (extended)** [ ] [–]
(cd-s) *(EAGXS 008)* – ('A'side) / Voix (20th anniversary) / Dead heaven (extended) / Cars (live).
(cd-s) *(EAGXA 008)* – ('A'side) / Metal (20th anniversary) / Down in the park (20th anniversary) / Dominion day (live).

—— now with **STEVE HARRIS** – guitar / **ROB HOLIDAY** – guitar, keyboards / **MONTI** – drums, prog / **RICHARD BEASLEY** – drums

Oct 00. (cd) *(EAGCD 078)* <15088> **PURE** [58] Nov00 [ ]
– Pure / Walking with shadows / Rip / One perfect lie / My Jesus / Fallen / Listen to my voice / A prayer for the unborn / Torn / Little Invitro / I can't breathe. *(d-cd+=; EAGTE 078)* – (live):- Pure / My Jesus / Rip / Cars / Replicas / A prayer for the unborn (Greyed up remix) / Listen to my voice (Greyed up remix).

Jagged Halo Universal

May 02. (d-cd) *(JHCD 001)* <400008> **EXPOSURE – THE BEST OF GARY NUMAN 1977-2002** (compilation) [44] [ ]
– Films / I die: you die / Are 'friends' electric? / Pure / Dead Heaven / Down in the park / Me! I disconnect from you / Metal / She's got claws / Magic / We are glass / Music for chameleons / My shadow in vain (new version) / Everyday I die (new version) / My Jesus / Cars / Dominion day / Complex / We are so fragile / Rip / M.E. / We take mystery (to bed) / Dark / Remember I was a vapour / Listen to my voice / Deadliner / Exposure / Voix / A prayer for the unborn.

Jul 02. (cd-s) *(JHCDS 1)* **RIP / A PRAYER FOR THE UNBORN / M.E. (new version) / ('A'-video)** [29] [–]
(cd-s) *(JHCDSX 1)* – ('A'side) / This wreckage / Are 'friends' electric?

Jun 03. (cd-s; as GARY NUMAN Vs RICO) *(JHCDV 6)* *<40000>* **CRAZIER / LISTEN TO MY VOICE / ANCIENTS / CRAZIER (dub)** [13] Jul03 [ ]
(cd-s) *(JHCDX 6)* – ('A'side) / Big black sea / Garden man / ('A'dub).
(cd-s) *(JHCDS 6)* – ('A'side) / Ancients (version) / A prayer for the unborn / A prayer for the unborn (dub).

– compilations, etc. –

on 'Beggars Banquet' unless otherwise mentioned / * = TUBEWAY ARMY

Aug 79. (d7"*) *(BACK 2)* **THAT'S TOO BAD. / OH! I DIDN'T SAY/ / BOMBERS. / O.D. RECEIVER / BLUE EYES** [ ] [–]

Apr 81. (c-s*) *WEA; (SPC 4)* **ARE 'FRIENDS' ELECTRIC? / WE ARE SO FRAGILE? / DOWN IN THE PARK** [ ] [–]

Nov 82. (lp/c) *TV-Virgin; (TVA/TVC 7)* **NEW MAN NUMAN – THE BEST OF GARY NUMAN** [45] [–]

Apr 83. (12"ep,12"yellow-ep*) *(BEG 92E)* **TUBEWAY ARMY '78 VOL.1** [ ] [–]
– That's too bad (alternate mix) / Oh! didn't I say / Bombers / O.D. receiver / Blue eyes / Do you need the service.

Sep 84. (lp/pic-lp*) *(BEGA 55/+P)* **THE PLAN** [29] [–]
(re-iss. Jul88 lp/c; BBL/+C 55)

Dec 84. (12"ep,12"red-ep*) *(BEG 123E)* **TUBEWAY ARMY '78-'79 VOL.2** [ ] [–]
– Fade out / 1930 / The crazies / Only a downstate / We have a technical.

Dec 84. (12"ep,12"blue-ep*) *(BEG 124E)* **TUBEWAY ARMY '78-'79 VOL.3** [ ] [–]
– The Monday troup / Crime of assikon / The life machine / A game called Echo / Random / Oceans.

Aug 87. (12"ep/c-ep;*) *Strange Fruit; (SFPS/+C 032)* **THE PEEL SESSIONS** [ ] [–]
– Me I disconnect from you / Down in the park / I nearly married a human.

Aug 87. (7"/7"pic-d) *(BEG 199/+P)* **CARS (E-REG MODEL). / ARE FRIENDS ELECTRIC?** [16] [ ]
(c-s+=/ext-12"+=) *(BEG 199 C/T)* – We are glass / I die: you die.
(ext-12"+=) *(BEG 199TR)* – ('A'-Motorway mix).

Sep 87. (d-lp/d-cd) *(BEGA 88/+CD)(BEGC 88)* **EXHIBITION** [43] [–]
– Me, I disconnect from you / That's too bad / My love is a liquid / Music for chameleons / We are glass / Bombers / Sister Surprise / Are 'friends' electric / I dream of wires / Complex / Noise noise / Warriors / Everyday I die / Cars / We take mystery to bed / I'm an agent / My centurion / Metal / You are in my vision / I die: you die / She's got claws / This wreckage / My shadow in vain / Down in the park / The iceman comes. *(d-cd+=)* – (11 tracks)

Dec 87. (cd) *(BEGA 4CD)* **REPLICAS / THE PLAN** [ ] [–]
(re-iss. d-cd Dec93; BEGA 152CD)

Dec 87. (cd) *(BEGA 7CD)* **TUBEWAY ARMY / DANCE** [ ] [–]
(re-iss. d-cd Dec93; BEGA 151CD)

Dec 87. (cd) *(BEGA 10CD)* **THE PLEASURE PRINCIPLE / WARRIORS** [ ] [–]
(re-iss. d-cd Dec93; BEGA 153CD)

Dec 87. (cd) *(BEGA 19CD)* **TELEKON / I, ASSASSIN** [ ] [ ]
(re-iss. d-cd Dec93; BEGA 154CD)
(above series of cd's, omitted some tracks on each)

Oct 89. (d-lp/cd) *Castle; (CCS LP/CD 229)* **THE GARY NUMAN COLLECTION** [ ] [–]

Dec 89. (m-lp/cd) *Strange Fruit; (SFPMA/+CD 202)* **DOUBLE PEEL SESSIONS** [ ] [–]

1990. (pic-cd-ep) **THE SELECTION** [ ] [–]
– Cars ('E' reg.model) / Down in the park / I die: you die / Are 'friends' electric? / We are glass / Music for chameleons.

1990. (7") *Old Gold; (OG 9917)* **ARE FRIENDS ELECTRIC?. / I DID YOU** [ ] [–]

1990. (7") *Old Gold; (OG 9919)* **CARS. / WE ARE GLASS** [ ] [–]

Mar 92. (lp/c/cd) *Numa; (NUMA/+C/CD 1008)* **ISOLATE** [ ] [–]

Oct 92. (d-cd) *Numa; (NUMACD 1007)* **GHOST** [ ] [–]

Oct 92. (cd/lp) *Receiver; (RR CD/LP 170)* **THE OTHER SIDE OF GARY NUMAN** [ ] [–]

Dec 92. (cd) *Connoisseur; (CSAPCD 113)* **DOCUMENT SERIES PRESENTS . . .** [ ] [–]

Date	Release	UK	US
Aug 93.	(7"/c-s) *(BEG 264/+C)* **CARS. / ('A'mix)**	53	
	(12"sha-pic-d+=/cd-s+=) *(BEG 264 L/CD)* – Cars ('93 sprint mix) / Cars (Top Gear mix).		
Sep 93.	(d-cd)(c) *(BEGA 150CD)(BEGC 150)* **THE BEST OF GARY NUMAN 1978-1983**	70	-
Jul 94.	(cd) *Receiver; (RRCD 186)* **HERE I AM**		-
Mar 95.	(cd/c) *Polygram TV; (531 149-2/-4)* **GREATEST HITS**		-
Feb 96.	(cd) *When!; (WHENCD 006)* **TECHNO ARMY**		-
Mar 96.	(7"/c-s/cd-s) *Premier; (PRM/+MC/CD 1)* **CARS (premier mix) / ARE FRIENDS ELECTRIC (live) / DOWN IN THE PARK (live)**	17	
Mar 96.	(cd/c) *Premier;* **THE PREMIER HITS** (compilation)	21	-
Jul 96.	(3xcd) *Receiver; (RRXCD 505)* **THE STORY SO FAR**		-
Sep 96.	(cd/c) *Emporio; (EMPR CD/MC 666)* **THE BEST OF GARY NUMAN**		-
Oct 97.	(12") *Random; (RANDOM 2.1)* **METAL (remixes). / DANS LE PARC**		-
Nov 97.	(12"green) *Random; (RANDOM 2.2)* **I DIE YOU DIE (Greenhaus mix) / CARS (Mike Dearborn mix) / CARS (Dave Clarke mix)**		-
Jan 98.	(12"blue) *Random; (RANDOM 2.3)* **WARRIORS (Dave Angel mix). / ARE 'FRIENDS' ELECTRIC (Liberator DJ's mix) / REMEMBER I WAS VAPOUR (Steve Stoll mix)**		-
Feb 98.	(12") *Random; (RANDOM 2.4)* **WE ARE GLASS (Claude Young mix) / FILMS (Alex Hazzard remix) / THE ICEMAN COMES (Peter Lazonby mix)**		-
Feb 02.	(d-cd) *Snapper; (SMDCD 372)* **DARK WONDERS**		-
Apr 02.	(3xcd-box) *Castle; (CNETD 466) / Sanctuary; <81214>* **DISCONNECTION**	Oct02	

— GARY has also contributed to other DRAMATIS recordings as well as joining RADIO HEART for one eponymous set

N.W.A.

Formed: NIGGAZ WITH ATTITUDE, Compton, L.A., California, USA . . . mid-80's by EAZY-E (aka ERIC WRIGHT and son of 70's soulman/funk guru, CHARLES WRIGHT) who set up his own label, 'Ruthless Records', in 1985. Allegedly founded with illegal profits, the label was a pivotal player in the burgeoning West Coast rap scene along with 24-hour hip hop radio station, KDAY. Hooking up with WORLD CLASS WRECKING CRU members, DR. DRE (aka ANDRE YOUNG) and DJ YELLA (ANTOINE CARRABY) as well as ex-STEREO CREW rapper, ICE CUBE, EAZY-E formed the core of what would become NWA. Along with the likes of ARABIAN PRINCE and The DOC, this loose affiliation recorded a promising debut set, 'NWA AND THE POSSE' (1987). EAZY-E's brutally frank 'BOYZ 'N' THE HOOD' was a sobering taster of what was to come. With MC REN (aka LORENZO PATTERSON) on board, a more compact posse of DRE, YELLA, CUBE and EAZY crafted the epochal 'STRAIGHT OUTTA COMPTON' (1989). Opening with an ominous 'You are now about to witness the strength of street knowledge . . .', the record slammed into the savage bass crunch of the title track, expletives rattled off like bullets from the proverbial AK. Next up was the infamous 'F*** THA POLICE', the boys leering their way through a defiant two-fingured salute to L.A.'s finest. The F.B.I. were sufficiently worried about the track to send the group a written warning, although they should've been more concerned with 'GANGSTA GANGSTA', a track which engendered a generation of violent, crime-obsessed albums and 'Gangsta' artists. While the rest of the set failed to maintain the vicious intensity of the opening three tracks, the damage had been done; violence-obsessed mysogynists or documenters of social realism?, the debate is still raging almost a decade on. While the record was initially isssed as a low key domestic release, word soon got round and a distribution deal was signed with 'Priority' records, the album going on to to notch up sales of 750,000 before NWA had even toured. Like PUBLIC ENEMY before them, it was obvious that a fair portion of their audience were middle class white kids out for some vicarious thrills, a theory compounded when N.W.A.'s follow-up, 'EFIL4ZAGGIN' (1991) scaled the US charts. By this point, however, the posse were in dissaray; ICE CUBE had left after falling out with manager JERRY HELLER over royalty payments while DRE left soon after the record's release, accusing HELLER of turning EAZY-E against him. This in-fighting was set against a backdrop of UK obscenity charges aimed at 'EFIL..', copies of the album siezed by British customs officials. Among the tracks which raised the authorities ire were such inimitable ditties as 'TO KILL A HOOKER' and 'FINDUM, FUCKUM and FLEE'; although the group eventually won the case, the mindless nihilism of the bulk of the album indicated that NWA had crossed the line between commentary and hilarious, often dangerous self-parody. Which is a pity, as DRE turned in another fine production. No surprise then, that as NWA imploded, DRE's solo output towered over the likes of REN's 'KIZZ MY BLACK AZZ' (1992) and EAZY's 'REAL MUTHAPHUCKIN' G's' (1994), the latter an acerbic response to DRE's G-funk innovations. With 'THE CHRONIC' (1993), DRE traded in the ever popular JAMES BROWN for the more laid back GEORGE CLINTON, pioneering the use of FUNKADELIC/PARLIAMENT samples amid a haze of marijuana references. The record was released on his new 'Death Row' records, a joint project (you could say) with 'Interscope' and itself the subject of much recent controversy following the murder of rapper TUPAC SHAKUR and the much touted feud between the rival rap factions of east and west. While DRE's debut went triple platinum, influencing the likes of SNOOP DOGGY DOGG and his half-brother, WARREN G, the rapper was charged with battery (assault) in September '94 and sentenced to 8 months in prison. In March '95, EAZY-E succumbed to AIDS, his death finally seeing a reconciliation between DRE and ICE CUBE, the latter having gone on to even greater success. Yes, NWA sent shockwaves both through the rap scene and the white authorities and yes, 'STRAIGHT OUTTA COMPTON' remains one of the most visceral listening experiences of the 80's, but given the current bloodstained state of hip hop, the advent of 'gangsta' seems less and less like a bold step forward and more like a self-destructive blind alley. DR. DRE's album, '2001' (actually issued at the tail end of '99) was another commercial success, rumours abounded of a NWA reformation. While that never actually materialised, DRE's work on EMINEM's 'The Slim Shady' album ensured that both his production and recording career would continue to have relevance in the new millennium, something not to be sniffed at in the fast changing world of hip hop. • **Trivia:** Album 'EFIL4ZAGGIN' is actually NIGGAZ4LIFE spelt backwards (as seen on sleeve).

Album rating: N.W.A. AND THE POSSE (*6) / STRAIGHT OUTTA COMPTON (*9) / 100 MILES AND RUNNIN' mini (*6) / EFIL4ZAGGIN (*5) / GREATEST HITS compilation (*7) / Dr Dre: THE CHRONIC (*7) / 1ST ROUND KNOCKOUT (*6) / DR. DRE – 2001 (*6) / THE CHRONICLE: THE BEST OF THE WORKS . . . productions (*7) / Eazy-E: EAZY-DUZ-IT (*7) / 5150 HOME 4 THA SICK mini (*4) / IT'S ON (DR. DRE 187UM) KILLA mini (*5) / ETERNAL E compilation (*7) / STR8 OFF THA STREETZ OF MUTHAPHUKKIN COMPTON (*5) / MC Ren: KISS MY BLACK AZZ (*5) / SHOCK OF THE HOUR (*4) / THE VILLAIN IN BLACK (*4) / RUTHLESS FOR LIFE (*4) / THE N.W.A. LEGACY VOLUME 1 1988-1998 compilation (*7)

ICE CUBE (b. O'SHEA JACKSON, 15 Jun'69) – vocals (ex-C.I.A.) / **DR DRE** (b. ANDRE YOUNG, 18 Feb'65) – producer (also of WORLD CLASS WRECKIN' CREW) / **EAZY-E** (b. ERIC WRIGHT, 7 Sep'73) – vocals / **M.C. REN** (b. LORENZO PATTERSON, 16 Jun'??) – vocals / **DJ YELLA** (b. ANTOINE CARRABY, 11 Dec'??) – turntables

not iss. Macola

1987. (lp; Various Artists) **N.W.A. AND THE POSSE** [–] [ ]
(UK-iss.Oct89 on 'Rams Horn'; RHR 5134)

4th & Broad Ruthless

Aug 89. (7"/c-s) *(BRW/BRCA 144)* **EXPRESS YOURSELF. / STRAIGHT OUTTA COMPTON** [50] [ ]
(ext;12"+=/cd-s+=) *(12BRW/BRCD 144)* – ('A'-Bonus beats) / A bitch iz a bitch. *(re-iss. May90; same)* – hit UK No.26

Aug 89. (lp/c/cd) *(BR LP/CA/CD 534)* *<SL/4XL/CDL 57102>* **STRAIGHT OUTTA COMPTON** [41] [37]
– Straight outta Compton / Fu** the police / Gangsta gangsta / If it ain't ruff / Parental discretion iz advised / 8 ball (remix) / Something like that / Express yourself / Compton's in the house (remix) / I ain't tha 1 / Dopeman (remix) / Quiet on the set / Something to dance to. *(cd re-iss. Sep02 on 'E.M.I.'; 537936-2)* – (hit UK No.35 in Jul03)

Aug 90. (7"/c-s) *(BRW/BRCA 191)* **GANGSTA, GANGSTA / IF IT AIN'T RUFF** [70] [ ]
(12"+=/cd-s+=) *(12BRW/BRCD 191)* – Dopeman (remix).

— now without ICE CUBE who was now solo

Oct 90. (7"/c-s) *(BRW/BRCA 200)* *<7224>* **100 MILES AND RUNNIN'. / REAL NIGGAZ** [38] Aug90 [27]
(12"/cd-s) *(12BRW/BRCD 200)* – ('A'side) / Just don't bite it / Sa prize (pt.2) / Kamurshoi.

Apr 91. (12"/cd-s) **F*** THE POLICE. / ('A'mixes)** [–] [ ]
(above written for RODNEY KING, the black motorist beat up by police. The court case instigated the race riots all around America.

Jun 91. (cd/c/lp) *(BR CD/CA/LP 552)* *<57126>* **EFIL4ZAGGIN** [25] [1]
– Prelude / Real niggaz don't die / Real niggaz 4 life / Protest / Appetite for destruction / Don't drink that wine / Alwayz into somethin' / Message to B.A. / Real niggaz / To kill a hooker / One less bitch / Findum, f***um and flee / Automobile / She swallowed it / I'd rather f*** you / Approach to danger / 1-900-2 Compton / The dayz of wayback.

Nov 91. (7"/c-s) *(BRW/BRCA 238)* **ALWAYZ INTO SOMETHIN'. / EXPRESS YOURSELF** [60] [ ]
(12"+=/cd-s+=) *(12BRW/BRCD 238)* – Something 2 dance 2.

— disbanded and all went solo

– compilations, etc. –

Aug 96. (cd/c) *Priority; (CDPTY 126) / Ruthless; <50561>* **GREATEST HITS** [56] Jul96 [48]
– Live intro (1989) / Arrested / angsta gangsta / F*** tha police / Compton's in the house (live) / Break out / Straight outa Compton (extended mix) / If it ain't ruff / Real niggaz / I ain't tha 1 / Alwayz into something / Don't drink that wine / Just don't bite it / Cash money / Express yourself (remix) / 100 miles & runnin' / A bitch iz a bitch / Real niggaz don't die.

Mar 99. (d-cd/d-c; Various Artists) *Priority; <51111>* **THE N.W.A. LEGACY 1988-1998** [–] [77]

EAZY-E

4th & Broad Ruthless

Sep 89. (lp/c/cd) *(BR LP/CA/CD 535)* *<57100>* **EAZY-DUZ-IT** [ ] Dec88 [41]
– (Prelude) Still talkin' / Nobody move / 2 Hard muthas (featuring MC REN) / Boyz-n-the-hood (remix) / Eazy-duz-it / We want Eazy / Eazy-er said than dunn / Radio / No more ?'s / Imma break it down / Eazy – Chapter 8, verse 10. *(re-iss. Jun91 on 'Island' lp/c)(cd; ILPM/ICM 2070)(IMCD 124)*

Jan 93. (m-cd) *<53815>* **5150 HOME FOR THA SICK** [–] [70]
– Neighbourhood sniper / Niggaz my height don't fight / Merry mutha***** Xmas / Only if you want it.

Oct 93. (m-cd) *<5503>* **IT'S ON (DR.DRE) 187 UM KILLA** [ ] [5]
– Any last werdz / Real muthaphuckin G's / Still a nigga / Exxtra special thankz / Boyz-n-the-hood / Gimme that nutt / It's on.

Jan 94. (c-s,cd-s) *<5508>* **REAL MUTHAPHUCKIN' G'S / ANY LAST WERDZ** [–] [42]

— Early in 1995, EAZY-E featured on BONE THUGS N HARMONY's hit single, 'Foe Tha Love Of'.

— EAZY-E died of AIDS on the 26th March 1995 after only being diagnosed HIV a month earlier.

Dec 95. (c-s) *(662 816-4)* *<5532>* **JUST TAH LET U KNOW / THE MUTHAPHU**IN' REAL** [30] [45]
(12"+=/cd-s+=) *(662 816-6/-2)* – ('A'-Ruthless "G" mix) / ('A'-Ba-da-ba-do acappella mix).
(above issued on 'Epic')

Jan 96. (cd/c) *(CDPTY/PTYMC/PTYLP 122)* *<50544>* **ETERNAL E** (compilation) [ ] Dec95 [84]
– Automobile / Eazy-duz-it / Boyz-in-the-hood / Eazy-er said than dunn / Neighbourhood sniper / Radio / We want Eazy / Only if you want it / Nobody move / I'd rather funk you / 8 ball / Eazy street / Niggaz my height don't fight / No more ?'s.

Ruthless Ruthless

Feb 96. (cd/c) *(483 576-2/-4)* *<5504>* **STR8 OFF THA STREETZ OF MUTHAPH**IN – E.W. COMPTON** [66] [3]
– Just tah let u know / Lickin' smokin' phuckin' / What would you do / Sorry Louie / Nutz on ya chin / Ole school shit / Slippin on a 4 / My baby'z mama / Muthaphuckin' real / Hit the hoods / Gangsta beat 4 tha street / Eternal E / Creep n crawl.

MC REN

Ruthless Ruthless

Jul 92. (cd,c) *<53802>* **KIZZ MY BLACK AZZ** [–] [12]
– Check it out y'all / Behind the scenes / Hound dogz / Kiss my black azz / Right up my alley / Final frontier.

Nov 93. (cd,c) *<5505>* **SHOCK OF THE HOUR** [–] [22]
– Fuck what ya hear / All bullshit aside / Attack on Babylon / Shock of the hour / Still the same nigga / You wanna fuck her / Same ol' shit / Mr. Fuck up / One false move / Mayday on the front line / 11.55 / Do you believe.

Nov 93. (c-s,12") *<5510>* **SAME OL' SHIT. / (radio version)** [–] [90]

— Above sampled; LET'S GET IT ON (Marvin Gaye) / I GOT A GOOD THING (James Brown) / LAD DI DA DI (Doug E.Fresh).

Apr 96. (cd/c) *(483900-2/-4)* *<5544>* **THE VILLAIN IN BLACK** [ ] [31]
– Bitch made nigga killa / Bring it on / Mad scientist / Mind blown / Still the same nigga / Muhammed speaks / Live from Compton 'Saturday night' / It's like that / Keep it real / Great elephant.

Apr 98. (cd-s) *<78901>* **RUTHLESS FOR LIFE (mixes; LP / clean radio / instrumental)** [–] [ ]
(12"+=) *<78902>* – ('A'-A cappella).

Jun 98. (cd/c) *<69313>* **RUTHLESS FOR LIFE** [–] [100]
– Ruthless for life / Who in the f*** / N***a called Ren / Comin' after you / Voyage to Compton / Must be high / So whatcha want / Shot caller / All the same / Who got that street s*** / Pimpin' is free / CPT all day.

DR. DRE

Interscope Death Row

May 92. (cd-s) *<74547>* **DEEP COVER / (instrumental)** [–] [ ]
(above from the film of the same name on 'Epic')

Feb 93. (cd/c) *(7567 92233-2/-4)* *<57128>* **THE CHRONIC** [ ] [3]
– The chronic / Fuck wit Dre day (and everybody's celebrating) / Let me ride / The day the niggaz took over / Nuthin' but a "G" thang / Dreeez nuuuts / Bitches ain't shit / Lil' ghetto boy / A nigga witta gun / Rat-tat-tat-tat / The $20 sack pyramid / Lyrical gangbang / High powered / The doctor's office / Stranded on death row / The roach (the chronic outro). *(cd re-iss. Feb97; IND 57128) (re-iss. Aug00)* – hit UK No.52

Mar 93. (c-s) *<53819>* **NUTHIN' BUT A "G" THANG. / ('A'mix)** [ ] Jan93 [2]
(club-12"+=)(cd-s+=) – ('A'-freestyle mix).

May 93. (7"/c-s) *<53827>* **DRE DAY. / ('A'-flavour mix)** [ ] [8]
(cd-s+=) – ('A'extended club) / ('A'-UK Flavour mix) / ('A'instrumental) / ('A'again).
(12") – (A+B) / (above 2) / Puffin' on blunts and drinkin' tanqueray.

Aug 93. (c-s,cd-s,12") *<53839>* **LET ME RIDE / ('A'mixes)** [–] [34]

Jan 94. (c-s) *(A 8328C)* **NUTHIN' BUT A G THANG (club) / ('A'mix)** [31] [–]
(12") *(A 8328T) - ('A'-version) / Let me ride (extended club mix).*
(cd-s) *(A 8328CD)* – (their club mixes).

Aug 94. (7"/c-s) *(A 8292/+C)* **DRE DAY. / ('A'-UK radio mix)** [59] [–]
(12"+=) *(A 8292T)* – (4-'A'-Puffin' on blunts and drinkin' tanqueray mixes).
(cd-s+=) *(A 8292CD)* – ('A'-radio remix) / ('A'instrumental) / ('A'-2 other mixes).

— In Sep'94, DR.DRE was convicted of battery (assault) and sentenced to 8 months in prison

Interscope Hitman

Oct 94. (cd,c) *<51170>* **CONCRETE ROOTS – ANTHOLOGY** (compilation of various artists) [ ] [43]

— DR.DRE & ICE CUBE; below from the film 'Murder Was The Case'.

Mar 95. (7"/c-s) *(A 8197/+C)* **NATURAL BORN KILLAZ / THA DOGG POUND: What Would U Do?** [45] [ ]
(cd-s+=) *(A 8197CD)* – (2 'A'versions).

May 95. (c-s) *(PTYSC 103)* <53188> **KEEP THEIR HEADS RINGIN'. / TAKE A HIT (mix)** 25 Mar95 10
(12"+=/cd-s+=) *(PTY ST/CD 103)* – (other mixes).
above from the film 'Friday' on the label 'Priority')

Jun 98. (c-s/12"/cd-s; DR. DRE & LL COOL J) *(INC/INT/IND 95594)* **ZOOM / (instrumental)** 15 –

—— in Aug'99, DRE was credited on EMINEM's hit, 'Guilty Conscience'

Nov 99. (cd/d-lp) *<(4 90486-2/-1)>* **DR. DRE 2001** 4 2
– Lolo (w/ XZIBIT & TRAY-D) / The watcher / Fuck you (w/ THE DUDE & SNOOP DOGG) / Still D.R.E. (w/ SNOOP DOGG) / Big ego's (w/ HITTMAN) / Xplosive (w/ HITTMAN) / What's the difference (w/ EMINEM & XZIBIT) / Bar one (w/ TRACY NELSON, MS ROQ & EDDIE GRIFFIN) / Light speed (w/ EMINEM) / The next episode (w/ SNOOP DOGG) / Let's get high (w/ HITTMAN, KURUPT & MS ROQ) / Bitch niggaz (w/ SNOOP DOGG, HITTMAN & SIX-TWO) / Car bomb (w/ MEL-MAN & SHARI HENRY) / Education (w/ HITTMAN & MS ROQ) / Murderlink (w/ HITTMAN & MS ROQ) / Some L.A. niggaz (w/ DEFARI, XZIBIT, KNOCKTURNAL, TIMEBOMB, KING T, MC REN & KOKANE) / Pause 4 promo (w/ JAKE STEED) / Housewife (w/ KURUPT & HITTMAN) / Acrite (w/ HITTMAN) / Bang bang (w/ KNOCKTURNAL & HITTMAN) / The message (w/ MARY J. BLIGE & REIL). *(re-iss. Mar00; same)* – hit UK No.8 in Jan'01

Mar 00. (c-s/cd-s; as DR. DRE featuring SNOOP DOGG) *(497274-4/-2)* *<497192>* **STILL D.R.E. / THE MESSAGE (with MARY J. BLIGE & REIL)** 6 Nov99 93
(12")(cd-s) *(497274-1)(497286-2)* – ('A'side) / The next episode.

May 00. (c-s/cd-s; as DR. DRE featuring EMINEM) *(497341-4/-2)* **FORGET ABOUT DRE / STILL D.R.E. (mixes)** 7 Jan00 25
(12"/cd-s) *(497341-1/-2)* – ('A'side) / The next episode.

Jan 01. (c-s/12"; by DR. DRE featuring SNOOP DOGG) *(497476-4/-1)* *<497333>* **THE NEXT EPISODE. / BAD GUYS ALWAYS DIE (with EMINEM)** 3 May00 23
(cd-s+=) *(497476-2)* – ('A'instrumental) / ('A'-video).

—— late in 2001, DR. DRE was the mastermind behind a largely collective V/A set soundtrack, 'THE WASH', featuring SNOOP DOGG, etc.

Jan 02. (c-s/12"; by DR. DRE featuring KNOC-TURN'AL) *(497393-4/-1)* **BAD INTENTIONS. / THE WATCHER / THE NEXT EPISODE (with SNOOP DOGG)** 4 –
(cd-s+=) *(497393-2)* – ('A'-video).

– compilations, etc. –

Jun 96. (cd,c) *Triple X; <51226>* **1ST ROUND KNOCKOUT** (compilation) – 52
– Bridgette (D.O.C.) / It's not over (ROSE ROYCE) / Nicety / Sex is on / Turn off the lights / Nickel slick nigga / Juice / Funky flute / The fly / Deep cover / He's bionic.

—— In Oct'96, he featured on hit single by BLACKSTREET; 'No Diggity'.

—— In Dec'96, DR. DRE PRESENTS . . . THE AFTERMATH was the name of a Various Artists album for Interscope' <(IND/INC 90044)>

Nov 01. (cd) *Death Row; (DRE 1004)* **THE CHRONICLE: THE BEST OF THE WORKS . . .** –

Laura NYRO

Born: LAURA NIGRO, 18 Oct'47, Bronx, New York, USA, of Italian/Jewish parentage. The daughter of a jazz trumpeter, NYRO began songwriting at an early age, later attending Manhattan's High School of Music and Art (where she underwent a bad LSD trip). An aversion to hallucinogenics was not the only thing separating NYRO from the burgeoning hippie movement, the crowd at 1967's Monterey Festival booing her soul revue-style performance. Only her second ever experience in front a live audience, this unfortunate incident resulted in prolonged stage fright during the early part of her career. Nevertheless, the singer/songwriter's debut album, 'MORE THAN A NEW DISCOVERY' (1966), while doing little to trouble the charts, contained a wealth of material which would later be successfully interpreted by other artists; close harmony popsters, FIFTH DIMENSION, took 'WEDDING BELL BLUES' to No.1 (US) in 1969, while BLOOD, SWEAT & TEARS almost managed a similar feat with 'AND WHEN I DIE' and BARABRA STREISAND carried 'STONEY END' into the UK Top 30 in 1970. Among the cream of NYRO's work, these tracks managed to marry her wayward poetic flights of confessional fancy with killer hooks and a melodic verve in a way which she'd find hard to sustain over the course of her career. In the meantime, a young David Geffen was impressed enough to offer NYRO his services as manager, the future record mogul soon securing her a deal with 'Columbia'. The resulting follow-up set, 'ELI AND THE THIRTEENTH CONFESSION' (1968), found NYRO honing her unique take on white soul/gospel/R&B, the singer's lamenting/rapturous testimonials delivered with characteristically idiosyncratic phrasing atop unconventional arrangements and time changes. Despite her quirky style, there was enough hit potential in the material to provide yet more chart success for FIFTH DIMENSION ('STONED SOUL PICNIC' and 'SWEET BLINDNESS'), while THREE DOG NIGHT went Top 10 with a cover of 'ELI'S COMING'. NYRO herself eventually enjoyed a bit of belated chart action with 1970's 'NEW YORK TENDABERRY', an even more oblique set of unadorned piano/vocal expressionism. 'CHRISTMAS AND THE BEADS OF SWEAT' carried on in a similar vein later that year, while 'GONNA TAKE A MIRACLE' (1972) stands as perhaps NYRO's most enjoyable outing, a Gamble/Huff-produced tribute to the pop/soul sounds of the 60's which saw the singer hooking up with LaBELLE and covering such standards as 'JIMMY MACK' and 'NOWHERE TO RUN'. Taking time out to get married and enjoy a period of domestic simplicity, NYRO returned in 1976 with 'SMILE', the record meeting with largely favourable reviews but achieving only minor chart success. She seemed to have lost her momentum and subsequent albums such as 'NESTED' (1978) met with diminishing critical and commercial returns. Over the ensuing decade, the singer released only one further album, 'MOTHER'S SPIRITUAL' (1984), NYRO further embracing an eco-conscious, Earth-Mother philosophy as she entered middle age. Despite her low-profile approach, sporadic live performances are not unknown and a rare concert set, 'LIVE AT THE BOTTOM LINE', appeared in 1989. Modern day female singer/songwriter, SHAWN COLVIN, acknowledged the debt her generation owe to NYRO's innovations when she teamed up with the cult singer on a one-off US-only single, 'LET IT BE ME', in 1990. NYRO, meanwhile, proved that she was still actually capable of producing the goods when she felt like it, 1993's 'WALK THE DOG AND LIGHT THE LIGHT' garnering a fair amount of critical acclaim. Sadly, LAURA was to die of ovarian cancer on the 8th of April, 1997.

Album rating: MORE THAN A NEW DISCOVERY (*6) / ELI AND THE THIRTEENTH CONFESSION (*8) / NEW YORK TENDABERRY (*8) / CHRISTMAS AND THE BEADS OF SWEAT (*6) / GONNA TAKE A MIRACLE (*6) / SMILE (*6) / SEASON OF LIGHTS . . . LAURA NYRO IN CONCERT (*5) / NESTED (*4) / IMPRESSIONS compilation (*6) / MOTHER'S SPIRITUAL (*4) / LIVE AT THE BOTTOM LINE (*4) / WALK THE DOG AND LIGHT THE LIGHT (*5) / STONED SOUL PICNIC: THE BEST OF LAURA NYRO compilation (*7) / THE ESSENTIAL MASTERS collection (*7) / ANGEL IN THE DARK (*6) / LIVE: THE LOOM'S DESIRE (*5)

LAURA NYRO – vocals, piano

Verve | Verve Folkways

1966. (lp) *<FTS 3020>* **MORE THAN A NEW DISCOVERY** –
– Wedding bells blues / Goodbye Joe / Billy's blues / And when I die / Stoney end / Lazy Susan / Hands off the man / Buy and sell / He's a runner / Blowin' away / I never meant to hurt you / California shoeshine boys. *(UK-iss.1969 as 'THE FIRST SONGS'; SVLP 6022) <same for US; re-iss. Jan73 on 'Columbia'; CBS 31410>* – hit No.97.

Oct 66. (7") *(VS 1502)* <*5024*> **WEDDING BELL BLUES. / STONEY END**

May 67. (7") <*5038*> **GOODBYE JOE. / BILLY'S BLUES** –

Dec 67. (7") <*5051*> **AND WHEN I DIE. / FLIM FLAM MAN** –

C.B.S. Columbia

Jul 68. (7") *(CBS 3604)* <*44531*> **ELI'S COMIN'. / SWEET BLINDNESS**

Aug 68. (lp) *(CBS 63346)* <*9626*> **ELI AND THE THIRTEENTH CONFESSION**
– Luckie / Lu / Sweet blindness / Poverty train / Lonely women / Eli's comin' / Timer / Stoned good picnic / Emmie / Woman's blues / Once it was alright now (farmer Joe) / December's boudoir / The confession. *(re-iss. 1974) (cd-iss. Mar97 on 'Columbia'; 487240-2)*

Oct 68. (7") <*44592*> **SAVE THE COUNTRY. / TIMER** –

Jan 69. (7") <*44786*> **ONCE IT WAS ALRIGHT NOW (FARMER JOE). / LU** –

Feb 69. (7") *(CBS 4031)* **ONCE IT WAS ALRIGHT NOW (FARMER JOE). / WOMAN'S BLUES** –

Jan 70. (7") *(CBS 4719)* <*45041*> **TIME AND LOVE. / THE MAN WHO SENDS ME HOME**

Jan 70. (lp) *(CBS 63510)* <*9737*> **NEW YORK TENDABERRY** Oct69 32
– You don't love me when I cry / Captain for dark mornings / Tom cat good by / Mercy on Broadway / Save the country / Gibson Street / Time and love / The man who sends me home / Sweet lovin' baby / Captain Saint Lucifer / New york tendaberry. *(re-iss. 1974; same)*

Mar 70. (7") <*45089*> **SAVE THE COUNTRY. / NEW YORK TENDABERRY** –

— now with session people

Oct 70. (7") *(CBS 5218)* <*45230*> **UP ON THE ROOF. / CAPTAIN SAINT LUCIFER** 92

Dec 70. (lp) *(CBS 64157)* <*30259*> **CHRISTMAS AND THE BEADS OF SWEAT**
– Brown earth / When I was a freeport and you were the main drag / Blackpatch / Been on a train / Upon the roof / Upstairs by a Chinese lamp / Map to the treasure / Beads of sweat / Christmas in my soul. *(re-iss. 1974)*

Feb 71. (7") *(CBS 7028)* <*45298*> **WHEN I WAS A FREEPORT AND YOU WERE THE MAIN DRAG. / BEEN ON A TRAIN**

below was augmented by singing outfit, LaBELLE

Feb 72. (lp) *(CBS 64770)* <*30987*> **GONNA TAKE A MIRACLE** Dec71 46
– I met him on a Sunday / The bells / Monkey time – Dancing in the street / Desiree / You've really got a hold on me / Spanish harlem / Jimmy Mack / Wind / Nowhere to run / It's gonna take a miracle. *(re-iss. Feb89 on 'Beat Goes On'; BGOLP 27) (cd-iss. Nov91; BGOCD 27)*

Feb 72. (7") <*45537*> **IT'S GONNA TAKE A MIRACLE. / DESIREE**

— LAURA retired for 4 years after getting married.

Mar 76. (lp) *(CBS 81171)* <*33912*> **SMILE** 60
– Sexy mama / Children of the junks / Money / I am the blues / Stormy love / The cat-song / Midnite blue / Smile.

Aug 77. (lp) *(CBS 82183)* <*34786*> **SEASON OF LIGHTS . . . LAURA NYRO IN CONCERT (live)** Jun77
– The confession / And when I die / Upstairs by a Chinese lamp / Sweet blindness / Captain Saint Lucifer / Money / The cat-song / When I was a freeport and you were the main drag / Timer / Emmie.

Aug 78. (lp) *(CBS 82917)* <*35449*> **NESTED**
– Mr. Blue (the song of communications) / Rhythm and blues / My innocence / Crazy love / The nest / American dreamer / Spring blown / Sweet sky / Light pops principle / Child in a universe.

Mar 84. (lp) <*39215*> **MOTHER'S SPIRITUAL** –
– To a child / The right to vote / A wilderness / Melody in the sky / Late for love / A free thinker / Man in the Moon / Talk on a green tree / Trees of the ages / The brighter song / Roadnotes / Sophia / Mother's spiritual / Refrain. *(UK-iss.Oct90 on 'Line'; CLCD 9.00924)*

— She virtually retired from the music business around the mid-80's.

Cypress A&M

Oct 89. (lp/cd) *(YL/YD 0128)* <*6430*> **LIVE AT THE BOTTOM LINE (live)**
– Medley:- The confession – Hi heel sneakers / Roll of the ocean / Companion / Wild world / Medley:- My innocence – Sophia / To a child / And when I die / Park song / Broken rainbow / Women of the one world / Emmie / Wedding bell blues / The Japanese restaurant song / Stoned soul picnic / Medley:- La la means I love you – Trees of the ages – Up on the roof.

— In Nov'90, NYRO was credited on SHAWN COLVIN's single, 'LET IT BE ME' / 'CHRISTMAS SONG; CHESTNUTS ROASTING ON AN OPEN FIRE' on 'Columbia'.

Sony Sony

Jan 94. (cd/c) *(474296-2/-4)* <*52411*> **WALK THE DOG AND LIGHT THE LIGHT** Aug93
– Oh yeah maybe baby (the heebie jeebies) / A woman of the world / The descent of Luna Rose / Art of love / Like a flame (the animal rights song) / Louise's church / Broken rainbow / Walk the dog and light the light (song of the road) / To a child / I'm so proud – Dedicated to the one I love.

— on the 9th of April, 1997 LAURA died – she had just recorded . . .

Rounder Rounder

Apr 01. (cd) <*(ROUCD 3176)*> **ANGEL IN THE DARK** Mar01
– Angel in the dark / Triple goddess twilight / Will you still love me tomorrow / He was too good for me / Sweet dream fade / Serious playground / Be aware / Let it be me / Gardenia talk / Ooh baby baby / Embraceable you / La la means I love you / Walk on by / Animal grace / Don't hurt child / Coda.

– compilations, etc. –

on 'Verve Folkways' unless mentioned otherwise

1969. (7") <*5095*> **STONEY END. / FLIM FLAM MAN** –

1969. (7") <*5104*> **AND WHEN I DIE. / I NEVER MEANT TO HURT YOU** –

1969. (7") <*5112*> **GOODBYE JOE. / I NEVER MEANT TO HURT YOU** –

1971. (lp) *C.B.S.; (CBS 64400)* **HER SONGBOOK** –

Feb 73. (7") *C.B.S.; (1352)* **WEDDING BELL BLUES. / HANDS OFF THE MAN (FLIM FLAM MAN)** –

1975. (7") *C.B.S.; (13-33159)* **ELI'S COMING. / SAVE THE COUNTRY**

Dec 80. (lp) *CBS-Embassy; (31864)* **IMPRESSIONS** –

Jul 91. (cd/c) *Elite; (ELITE 015 CD/MC)* **CLASSICS** –
(re-iss. Sep93; same)

Feb 97. (d-cd) *Legacy; (485109-2)* <*4880*> **STONED SOUL PICNIC: THE BEST OF LAURA NYRO**
– Wedding bell blues / Blowing away / Billy's blues / Stoney end / And when I die / Lu / Eli's coming / Stone soul picnic / Timer / Emmie / Confession / Captain Saint Lucifer / Gibsome Street / New York tendaberry / Save the country / Blackpatch / Upstairs by a Chinese lamp / Beads of sweat / When I was a freeort and you were the main drag / I met him on a Sunday / Bells / Smile / Sweet blindness / Money / Mr. Blue / Wilderness / Mother's spiritual / Woman of the world / Louise's church / Broken rainbow / To a child / Lite a big flame (the animal rights song) / And when I die / Save the country.

Oct 00. (cd) *Columbia; (499942-2)* <*61567*> **THE ESSENTIAL MASTERS – THE BEST OF LAURA NYRO**

Oct 00. (cd) *Blue Plate;* <*403*> **LIVE FROM MOUNTAIN STAGE (live)** –

Jun 02. (d-cd) *Rounder;* <*(ROUCD 3186)*> **LIVE: THE LOOM'S DESIRE (live 1993 & 1994)** May02

OASIS

□ Phil OAKEY & Giorgio MORODER
(see under ⇒ HUMAN LEAGUE)

OASIS

Formed: Manchester, England ... summer 1992, by frontman LIAM GALLAGHER, rhythm guitarist PAUL 'BONEHEAD' ARTHURS, bassist PAUL McGUIGAN and drummer TONY McCARROLL. Initially called RAIN, they were soon joined by LIAM's older brother NOEL who had worked as a roadie for The INSPIRAL CARPETS. He was also a budding songwriter/guitarist with a concrete self-belief and after a year of rehearsals and occasional local gigs, they were signed by Creation's ALAN McGEE, after the eagle-eared Scotsman clocked them at a Glasgow gig in mid-1993. With a groundswell of interest not witnessed since the heady early days of The STONE ROSES, OASIS secured a near UK Top 30 placing with 'SUPERSONIC', a sneering, leering anthem with lyrics that SHAUN RYDER would've been proud to call his own. Later that summer the band released the follow-up, 'SHAKER MAKER', a rather tame effort in comparison which appeared to be modelled on the NEW SEEKERS' chestnut, 'I'd Like To Teach The World To Sing'. Nevertheless, what the single lacked in originality, it made up for in controversy and the stage was set for OASIS' first Top 10 hit, the classic 'LIVE FOREVER'. A life-affirming rush celebrating the strength of the human spirit, the song was lauded as single of the year, closely followed by the epochal debut album, 'DEFINITELY MAYBE' (1994). There were no maybes about it, this album defined an era in the same way that The SEX PISTOLS (an obvious influence) focused the frustrations of a generation with 'Never Mind The Bollocks', it's just a pity that the dubious 'Britpop' era spawned an interminable glut of production line indie chancers. The record opens on the same wave of freefall exhilaration as say, 'Exile On Main Street', (The ROLLING STONES were another oft cited influence), 'ROCK'N'ROLL STAR' alive with a palpable sense of what it actually means to want fame that badly. The feeling that this was "for real, man", never lets up until the last track fades, a visceral, exhaustive listen and one of the most consistent debut albums ever released. Another highlight from the album, the T.REX-esque nihilism of 'CIGARETTES AND ALCOHOL' was the next single, peaking at No.7 in late '94. Basically, OASIS were like all your favourite bands rolled into one, a kind of potted history of rock, NOEL having a unique talent for constructing classic songs that seemed somehow familiar yet annoyingly difficult to pin down. On top of this, LIAM was a natural, his piercing stare and cooly motionless stage presence coupled with his inimitably lethargic sneer a vital component of OASIS' rock'n'roll juggernaut. That Christmas the band narrowly missed No.1 with the string-laden, overtly BEATLES-esque 'WHATEVER', a poppier effort that hinted at the band's future direction. By this point, OASIS were a headline act, the scramble for tickets that accompanied any announcement of a gig becoming all too familiar over the next few years. As would the brothers' press profile, their loudmouth self-aggrandising and embarrassingly public fisticuffs becoming a regular feature of OASIS' increasingly cartoonish image. The first casualty of the well documented in-fighting was McCARROLL, his place in the drum seat subsequently filled by ALAN WHITE. The boasting was backed up by consistently strong material, however, and in the Spring of '95, OASIS deservedly scored their first No.1 with the soaring, yearning 'SOME MIGHT SAY'. The band's single releases had always been good value for money, the B-sides usually better than most indie bands' half-arsed lead tracks. This release was no exception, containing the affecting 'TALK TONIGHT' (NOEL on vocals) and the brilliant melodic noise of 'ACQUIESCE', arguably one of the group's finest tracks. Thus the stage was set for the media-created battle with the recently revitalised BLUR, both bands releasing a single simultaneously that August. In the event, despite the verbal jousting, BLUR took the top spot with 'Country House', OASIS forced to bite their tongue and, erm, 'ROLL WITH IT' at No.2. The Mancs had the last laugh, however, when their follow-up album '(WHAT'S THE STORY) MORNING GLORY' (1995) proceeded to sell multi-millions, catapulting OASIS into the musical stratosphere alongside U2 etc., something unheard of for a group who started out as, basically, another guitar band from Manchester. While the album lacked the serrated edge and amphetamine rush of the debut, the songwriting was once again faultless, tracks like 'WONDERWALL' (almost a Christmas No.1), 'DON'T LOOK BACK IN ANGER', and 'CHAMPAGNE SUPERNOVA' reflecting a newfound maturity and a more coffee-table friendly pop-rock sound. The rapid ascent of the GALLAGHER's continued the following year, with awards galore and a significant dent into the US market. The latter wasn't achieved without some cost to the band, however, as LIAM and NOEL had their most serious and most widely reported fracas to date, LIAM flying home midway through a US tour amid rumours that the band had split. It was merely a case of another day, another fight however, and the band went on to break British concert attendance records with two sell-out shows at Knebworth in August ('96). Early the following year, NOEL was the featured vocalist on The CHEMICAL BROTHERS' chart-topper, 'Setting Sun', effective psychedelia and right on. Return single in '97, 'D'YOU KNOW WHAT I MEAN?' hit No.1 and was reputed to have amassed UK sales of 162,000 copies on its first day of release (19th July). Shortly afterwards, their third album 'BE HERE NOW' was finally in the shops, the hype and media attention the record (and the brothers) received paying off big-time with a massive selling chart topper (No.2 in America). Probably its finest four minutes, 'STAND BY ME', surprisingly failed to make No.1, the album was also marked as a disappointment by some and was considered underwhelming to say the least. The posturing and epic feel of '(WHAT'S THE STORY) . . .' were still there but the record sounded like a parody of OASIS, if that's not a contradiction in terms. While the album broke records with its first day sales figures, it has hardly achieved the same momentum as its predecessor. A stop-gap collection of B-sides and rarities, 'THE MASTERPLAN' (1998), did little for any obsessed fan who already owned all the singles. In May '99, former drummer TONY McCARROLL won an out of court settlement of half a million – £18m for unpaid royalties was the figure he originally wanted. The old band took time out for the rest of the 90's (BONEHEAD and GUIGSY also bailed out), although the GALLAGHER brothers were never far away from controversy and the tabloids. 'STANDING ON THE SHOULDER OF GIANTS' (2000) proved that OASIS were in for the long haul, a studied, immaculately professional effort which indulged NOEL's passion for classic psychedelia while grafting on just enough contemporary flourishes to make it relevant. Hardly the rebellious ball of sonic phlegm we all knew and loved, then, but no doubt the first in a series of passable 30-something efforts designed to please their already ageing fanbase. Live set 'FAMILIAR TO MILLIONS' (2000) merely confirmed the fact, a Wembley Stadium gig which underlined the band's stodgy reliability. Even LIAM's wildcard rantings have become somewhat predictable if no less amusing. Previewed by the regal, spring-coiled riffing of 'THE HINDU TIMES', the much heralded 'HEATHEN CHEMISTRY' (2002) held few surprises save perhaps LIAM's charming, countrified 'SONGBIRD'. The rest was NOEL putting in a solid day at the office with reasonably efficient results; the requisite careworn ballad, 'LITTLE BY LITTLE' hit No.2, while the album itself hit No.1; yet big brother's insistence on a bombastic production did the band few favours. • **Songwriters:** NOEL, except I AM THE WALRUS + HELTER SKELTER (Beatles) / CUM ON FEEL THE NOIZE (Slade) / STREET FIGHTING MAN (Rolling Stones) / FEELIN' LONELY by Noel (Small Faces) / HEY HEY MY MY (INTO THE BLACK) (Neil Young). • **Trivia:** NOEL wrote 'SLIDE AWAY' on a Les Gibson guitar, which he bought from friend JOHNNY MARR (ex-Smiths) and which was once the property of PETE TOWNSHEND (The Who). After a long on-off relationship, LIAM married actress/singer, PATSY KENSIT. He has since divorced and is the beau of NICOLE APPLETON (of ALL SAINTS).

Album rating: DEFINITELY MAYBE (*10) / (WHAT'S THE STORY) MORNING GLORY? (*10) / BE HERE NOW (*7) / THE MASTERPLAN compilation (*7) / STANDING ON THE SHOULDER OF GIANTS (*6) / FAMILIAR TO MILLIONS (*5) / HEATHEN CHEMISTRY (*7)

LIAM GALLAGHER (b.21 Sep'72) – vocals / **NOEL GALLAGHER** (b.29 May'67) – guitar / **PAUL 'BONEHEAD' ARTHURS** (b.23 Jun'65) – guitar / **PAUL McGUIGAN** (b.19 May'71) – guitar / **TONY McCARROLL** – drums

Creation / Epic

Apr 94. (7") *(CRE 176) <55332>* **SUPERSONIC. / TAKE ME AWAY** [31] Jul94 [ ]
(12"+=) *(CRE 176T)* – I will believe (live).
(cd-s++=) *(CRECD 176)* – Columbia (demo).
(re-iss. Nov96 c-s repl.7" as so below; same); hit No.47)
(re-iss. Mar00 on 'Big Brother'; RKIDSCD 010)

Jun 94. (7"/c-s) *(CRE/+CS 182)* **SHAKERMAKER. / D'YER WANNA BE A SPACEMAN?** [11] [–]
(12"+=) *(CRE 182T)* – Alive (demo).
(cd-s++=) *(CRECD 182)* – Bring it on down (live).
(re-iss. Nov96; same); hit No.48)
(re-iss. Mar00 on 'Big Brother'; RKIDSCD 011)

Aug 94. (7"/c-s) *(CRE/+CD 185)* **LIVE FOREVER. / UP IN THE SKY (acoustic)** [10] [–]
(12"+=) *(CRE 185T)* – Cloudburst.
(cd-s++=) *(CRECD 185)* – Supersonic (live).
(re-iss. Nov96; same); hit No.42)
(re-iss. Mar00 on 'Big Brother'; RKIDSCD 012)

Aug 94. (cd/c/d-lp) *(CRE CD/MC/LP 169) <66431>* **DEFINITELY MAYBE** [1] Jan95 [58]
– Rock'n'roll star / Shakermaker / Live forever / Up in the sky / Columbia / Supersonic / Bring it down / Cigarettes and alcohol / Digsy's dinner / Slide away / Married with children. *(d-lp+=)* – Sad song. *(re-iss. Nov96 as '...SINGLES BOX – SILVER' cd/5xcd-s-box; CREDM 001/002); hit No.23) (cd re-iss. Feb00; same) (re-iss. Mar00 on 'Big Brother' cd/md/c/lp; RKID CD/MC/MC/LP 006)*

Oct 94. (7"/c-s) *(CRE/+CS 190)* **CIGARETTES AND ALCOHOL. / I AM THE WALRUS (live)** [7] [–]
(12"+=) *(CRE 190T)* – Fade away.
(cd-s++=) *(CRECD 190)* – Listen up.
(re-iss. Nov96; same); hit No.38)
(re-iss. Mar00 on 'Big Brother'; RKIDSCD 013)

Dec 94. (7"/c-s) *(CRE/+CS 195)* **WHATEVER. / (IT'S GOOD) TO BE FREE** [3] [–]
(12"+=) *(CRE 195T)* – Slide away.
(cd-s++=) *(CRECD 195)* – Half the world away.
(re-iss. Nov96; same); hit No.34)
(re-iss. Mar00 on 'Big Brother'; RKIDSCD 014)

— after a punch-up McCARROLL left and was replaced by drummer **ALAN WHITE** (b.26 May'72, London) (ex-IDHA) and brother of STEVE WHITE (long-time sticksman with PAUL WELLER)

Apr 95. (7"/c-s) *(CRE/+CS 204)* **SOME MIGHT SAY. / TALK TONIGHT** [1] [–]
(12"+=) *(CRE 204T)* – Acquiesce.
(cd-s++=) *(CRECD 204)* – Headshrinker.
(re-iss. Nov96; same); hit No.40)
(re-iss. Mar00 on 'Big Brother'; RKIDSCD 015)

— their first 5 singles also re-entered UK Top 60 in Jun'95

Aug 95. (7"/c-s) *(CRE/+CS 212)* **ROLL WITH IT. / IT'S BETTER, PEOPLE** [2] [–]
(12"+=) *(CRE 212T)* – Rockin' chair.
(cd-s+=) *(CRECD 212)* – Live forever (live).
(re-iss. Nov96; same)hit No.55)
(re-iss. Mar00 on 'Big Brother'; RKIDSCD 016)

Oct 95. (cd/c/d-lp) *(CRE CD/MC/LP 189) <67351>* **(WHAT'S THE STORY) MORNING GLORY?** [1] [4]
– Hello / Roll with it / Wonderwall / Don't look back in anger / Hey now! / Some might say / Cast no shadow / She's electric / Morning glory / Champagne supernova. *(d-lp+=)* – Bonehead's bank holiday. *(re-iss. Nov96 as '...SINGLES BOX – GOLD' cd/5xcd-s-box; CREMG 001/002); hit No.24) (re-iss. Mar00 on 'Big Brother' cd/md/c/lp; RKID CD/MD/MC/LP 007)*

Oct 95. (7"/c-s) *(CRE/+CS 215)* **WONDERWALL / ROUND ARE WAY** [2] [–]
(12"+=) *(CRE 215T)* – The swamp song.
(cd-s+=) *(CRECD 215)* – The masterplan.
(re-iss. Nov96; same); hit No.36)
(re-iss. Mar00 on 'Big Brother'; RKIDSCD 017)

Jan 96. (cd-s) *<49K 78216>* **WONDERWALL / ROUND ARE WAY / TALK TONIGHT / ROCKIN' CHAIR / I AM THE WALRUS (live)** [–] [8]

— NOEL also part of one-off supergroup The SMOKIN' MOJO FILTERS alongside PAUL WELLER and PAUL McCARTNEY. They had Top 20 hit with 'COME TOGETHER'.

Feb 96. (7"/c-s) *(CRE/+CS 221)* **DON'T LOOK BACK IN ANGER. / STEP OUT** [1] [–]
(12"+=) *(CRE 221T)* – Underneath the sky.
(cd-s++=) *(CRECD 221)* – Cum on feel the noize.
(re-iss. Nov96; same); hit No.53)
(re-iss. Mar00 on 'Big Brother'; RKIDSCD 018)

Jul 96. (cd-s) *<34K 78356>* **DON'T LOOK BACK IN ANGER / CUM ON FEEL THE NOIZE** [–] [55]

— NOEL met up with great pensmith and fan! BURT BACHARACH who wanted to do a collaboration. He also refused to accept his Ivor Novello award for best songwriter of the year, after he was told it would be shared with rivals BLUR. In Aug'96, NOEL objected to The SMURFS releasing 'WONDERWALL' on their album.

Jul 97. (7"/c-s) *(CRE/+CS 256)* **D'YOU KNOW WHAT I MEAN? / STAY YOUNG** [1] [–]
(12"+=) *(CRE 256T)* – Angel child (demo).
(cd-s++=) *(CRESCD 256)* – Heroes.
(re-iss. Mar00 on 'Big Brother'; RKIDSCD 019)

Aug 97. (cd/c/lp) *(CRECD/CCRE/CRELP 219) <68530>* **BE HERE NOW** [1] [2]
– D'you know what I mean? / My big mouth / Magic pie / Stand by me / I hope I think I know / Girl in the dirty shirt / Fade in-out / Don't go away / Be here now / All around the world / It's gettin' better (man) / All around the world (reprise). *(re-iss. Mar00 on 'Big Brother' cd/md/c/lp; RKID CD/MD/MC/LP 008)*

Sep 97. (7"/c-s) *(CRE/+CS 278)* **STAND BY ME. / (I GOT) THE FEVER** [2] [–]
(12"+=) *(CRE 278T)* – My sister lover.
(cd-s++=) *(CRESCD 278)* – Going nowhere.
(re-iss. Mar00 on 'Big Brother'; RKIDSCD 020)

Jan 98. (7"/c-s) *(CRE/+CS 282)* **ALL AROUND THE WORLD. / THE FAME** [1] [–]
(12"+=) *(CRE 282T)* – Flashbox.
(cd-s++=) *(CRESCD 282)* – Street fighting man.
(re-iss. Mar00 on 'Big Brother'; RKIDSCD 021)

Nov 98. (cd/d-lp)(c) *(CRE CD/LP 241)(C-CRE 241) <69647>* **THE MASTERPLAN** (compilation) [2] [51]
– Acquiesce / Underneath the sky / Talk tonight / Going nowhere / Fade away / The swamp song / I am the walrus / Listen up / Rockin' chair / Half the world away / (It's good) To be free / Stay young / Headshrinker / The masterplan. *(cd re-iss. Feb00; same) (re-iss. Mar00 on 'Big Brother' cd/md/c/lp; RKID CD/MD/MC/LP 009)*

— now without BONEHEAD who left after supplying his part to the forthcoming album (GUIGSY also bailed out, his replacement being **ANDY BELL** (ex-HURRICANE #1, ex-RIDE)

— In Oct'99, LIAM GALLAGHER was credited with STEVE CRADDOCK (of OCEAN COLOUR SCENE) on the UK Top 10 (JAM) tribute double-A side single, 'CARNATION' (flipped with BUFFALO TOM and 'Going Underground')

— added **GEM ARCHER** – guitar (ex-HEAVY STEREO)

Big Brother Epic

Feb 00. (7"/c-s) *(RKID/+CS 001)* **GO LET IT OUT. / LET'S ALL MAKE BELIEVE** [1] [–]
(12"+=)(cd-s+=) *(RKID 001T)(RKIDSCD 001)* – As long as they've got) Cigarettes in Hell.

Feb 00. (cd/c/lp) *(RKID CD/MC/LP 002) <63586>* **STANDING ON THE SHOULDER OF GIANTS** [1] Mar00 [24]
– Fuckin' in the bushes / Go let it out / Who feels love? / Put yer money where your mouth is / Little James / Gas panic! / Where did it all go wrong? / Sunday morning call / I can see a liar / Roll it over.

Apr 00. (7"/c-s) *(RKID/+CS 003)* **WHO FEELS LOVE? / ONE WAY ROAD** [4] [–]
(12"+=)(cd-s+=) *(RKID 003T)(RKIDSCD 003)* – Helter skelter (live).

Jul 00. (7"/c-s) *(RKID/+CS 004)* **SUNDAY MORNING CALL. / CARRY US ALL** [4] [–]
(12"+=)(cd-s+=) *(RKID 004T)(RKIDSCD 004)* – Full on.

Nov 00. (d-cd/c/t-lp) *(RKID CD/MC/LP 005) <85267>* **FAMILIAR TO MILLIONS (live)** [5] [ ]
– Fuckin' in the bushes / Go let it out / Who feels love? / Supersonic / Shakermaker / Acquiesce / Step out / Gas panic! / Roll with it / Stand by me / Wonderwall / Cigarettes and alcohol / Don't look back in anger / Live forever / Hey hey, my my (into the black) / Champagne supernova / Rock'n'roll star / Helter skelter. *(cd re-iss. Oct01; RKIDCD 005X)*

Apr 02. (7") *(RKID 23)* **THE HINDU TIMES. / JUST GETTING OLDER** [1] [–]
(12"+=)(cd-s+=) *(RKID 23T)(RKIDSCD 23)* – Idler's dream.

Jun 02. (7") *(RKID 24)* **STOP CRYING YOUR HEART OUT. / THANK YOU FOR THE GOOD TIMES** [2] [–]
(12"+=)(cd-s+=) *(RKID 24T)(RKIDSCD 24)* – Shout it out loud.

Jul 02. (cd/c/d-lp) *(RKID CD/MC/LP 25) <86586>* **HEATHEN CHEMISTRY** [1] [23]
– The Hindu times / Force of nature / Hung in a bad place / Stop crying your heart out / Songbird / Little by little / A quick peep / (Probably) All in the mind / She is love / Born on a different cloud / Better man.

Sep 02. (7") *(RKID 26)* **LITTLE BY LITTLE. / SHE IS LOVE** [2] [–]
(cd-s+=) *(RKIDSCD 26)* – My generation.

Feb 03. (7") *(RKID 27)* **SONGBIRD. / (YOU'VE GOT) A HEART OF A STAR** [3] [–]
(12"+=)(cd-s+=) *(RKID 27T)(RKIDSCD 27)* – Columbia (live).

– compilations, etc. –

Mar 00. (cd) *Chrome Dreams; (ABCD 047)* **MAXIMUM OASIS (AN AUDIO BIOGRAPHY)** [ ] [–]

OCEAN COLOUR SCENE

Formed: Moseley, Birmingham, England . . .mid-'89 out of The FANATICS, by SIMON FOWLER, DAMON MINCHELLA and OSCAR HARRISON, who released a one-off '45 for the 'Chapter 22' label before recruiting BOYS' guitarist STEVE CRADOCK. In the summer of 1990, OCS found manager JOHN MOSTYN, who signed them to his new '!Phffft' stable. A debut track, 'SWAY', helped secure a joint venture with 'Phonogram' for a follow-up, 'YESTERDAY TODAY'. The latter track breeched the Top 50 in March '91, and, just when it seemed as if a breakthrough was imminent, '!Phffft' was sold during the recording of their JIMMY MILLER-produced debut album. Now on 'Fontana', the momentum was lost as they re-recorded the whole project, a 1992 re-issue of 'SWAY' and the follow-up, 'GIVING IT ALL AWAY' sinking without trace. In April, the aforementioned eponymous album finally surfaced, although it brought criticism for its over-cooked production. After another 45, 'DO YOURSELF A FAVOUR' bombed, the group subsequently found themselves without a recording contract and up to their necks in debt. Aided by lawyer, Michael Thomas, they were successful in persuading Fontana's DAVE BATES to waive the million £'s they were still owing. OCS returned with a support slot to their newfound mate, PAUL WELLER, CRADOCK and FOWLER guested on his Autumn '93 classic 'Wildwood' album; CRADOCK subsequently became an integral part of WELLER's band over the course of the next year. Meanwhile in the summer of '94, OCEAN COLOUR SCENE supported OASIS and completed a 'Fontana' tour of the States supporting HOUSE OF LOVE and The CATHERINE WHEEL. A year later, all group members played for WELLER at some point, with CRADOCK and MINCHELLA guesting on his No.1 album, 'Stanley Road'. 1995 also saw the band recording their long-awaited follow-up album, having earlier signed to 'M.C.A.'. Early in '96 (with WELLER on organ), they scored their first of many Top 20 hits with 'THE RIVERBOAT SONG' (later chosen for Chris Evans' TFI Friday Show theme song). Dropping the indie-dance trappings of old, OCS adopted a heavier, funkier, white-soul/mod sound and a retro image to boot, dominating the charts in the wake of WELLER's massively successful return to a rootsier sound. 'YOU'VE GOT IT BAD' fared even better, followed by a BRENDAN LYNCH-produced album, 'MOSELEY SHOALS' (name of their own studio), which hit the UK Top 3. The record inevitably featured WELLER on a few other tracks and the man augmented the group on their 'Later With Jools Holland' spot. Two further Top 10 smashes, 'THE DAY WE CAUGHT THE TRAIN' (their classiest so far) and 'THE CIRCLE' were culled from the album, an odds'n'sods collection, 'B-SIDES, SEASIDES & FREERIDES' keeping their profile high prior to the release of new material. A couple of Top 5 hits, 'HUNDRED MILE HIGH CITY' and 'TRAVELLERS TUNE', preceded an Autumn '97 album, 'MARCHIN' ALREADY', a lesser work which nevertheless reached the top of the UK charts. An easy target for the critics, only time will tell whether OCS's retro-lite and almost wholly teenage audience can stay the course. 'ONE FROM THE MODERN' (1999), was the next Top 5 album on the retro production line, OCS defiantly standing by their Mod roots while opener and hit single, 'PROFITS IN PEACE', showed they were a caring type of band. 'SO LOW' was the next single. Enough said. Yet one suspects that while there is still an audience for OASIS there will still be an audience for OCEAN COLOUR SCENE, so indistinguishable are their respective markets. No surprise then that the admittedly fairly intoxicating 'UP ON THE DOWNSIDE' single made the UK Top 20, pushing the rather more workmanlike 'MECHANICAL WONDER' (2001) album into the Top 10. After ending the year on this relative high, the band released the obligatory festive period compilation which also reached the UK Top 20. While the release of a new OCS album is hardly the news that it once was, 'NORTH ATLANTIC DRIFT' (2003) demonstrated that they're at least consistent in their hard-graft, no-nonsense rock. While not exactly a departure, the album was a far less oppressive listen than its predecessor, perhaps signalling that they've grown content in their middle age. • **Songwriters:** FOWLER lyrics / group music; except DO YOURSELF A FAVOUR (Stevie Wonder & Syreeta) / DAYTRIPPER (Beatles) / ANYWAY ANYHOW ANYWHERE (Who) / ON THE WAY HOME (Neil Young) / etc.

Album rating: OCEAN COLOUR SCENE (*6) / MOSELEY SHOALS (*8) / B-SIDES, SEASIDES & FREERIDES collection (*5) / MARCHIN' ALREADY (*6) / ONE FROM THE MODERN (*5) / MECHANICAL WONDER (*5) / SONGS FROM THE FRONT ROW – THE BEST OF . . . (*7) / NORTH ATLANTIC DRIFT (*6) / ANTHOLOGY double compilation (*7)

FANATICS

SIMON FOWLER – vocals, acoustic guitar, harmonica / **DAMON MINCHELLA** – bass / **PAUL WILKES** – guitar / **OSCAR HARRISON** – drums, piano, vocals (ex- ECHO BASE) who repl. CAROLINE BULLOCK

Chapter 22 / not iss.

Mar 89. (12"ep) *(12CHAP 38)* **SUBURBAN LOVE SONGS** [ ] [–]
– Suburban love songs / 1.2.3.4. / My brother Sarah / Tight rope.

OCEAN COLOUR SCENE

STEVE CRADOCK – guitars, piano, vocals (ex-BOYS; late 80's mods) repl. WILKES

!Phffft / not iss.

Sep 90. (7") *(FIT 001)* **SWAY. / TALK ON** [ ] [–]
(ext-12"+=/ext-cd-s+=) (FITX/FITCD 001) – One of these days.

Mar 91. (7") *(FIT 002)* **YESTERDAY TODAY. / ANOTHER GIRL'S NAME / FLY ME** [49] [ ]
(12"+=/cd-s+=) *(FITX/FITCD 002)* – No one says.

Fontana / not iss.

Feb 92. (7") *(OCSS 1)* **SWAY. / MY BROTHER SARAH** [ ] [–]
(12"+=/cd-s+=) *(OCS 112/CD1)* – Mona Lisa eyes / Bellechoux.

Apr 92. (7") *(OCSS 2)* **GIVING IT ALL AWAY. / THIRD SHADE OF GREEN** [ ] [–]
(12"+=/cd-s+=) *(OCS 212/CD2)* – Flowers / Don't play.

Apr 92. (cd/c/lp) *(<512269-2/-4/-1>)* **OCEAN COLOUR SCENE** [ ] Sep92 [ ]
– Talk on / How about you / Giving it all away / Justine / Do yourself a favour / Third shade of green / Sway / Penny pinching rainy Heaven days / One of these days / Is she coming home / Blue deaf ocean / Reprise. *(re-iss. Sep96, hit UK 54)*

May 92. (7") *(OCSS 3)* **DO YOURSELF A FAVOUR. / THE SEVENTH FLOOR** [ ] [–]
(12"+=/cd-s+=) *(OCS 312/CD3)* – Patsy in green / Suspended motion.

M.C.A. / M.C.A.

Feb 96. (7"/c-s) *(MCS/+C 40021)* **THE RIVERBOAT SONG. / SO SAD** [15] [–]
(cd-s+=) *(MCSTD 40021)* – Charlie Brown says.

Apr 96. (c-s) *(MCSTD 40036)* *<55217>* **YOU'VE GOT IT BAD / I WANNA STAY ALIVE WITH YOU** [7] Jul96 [ ]
(cd-s+=) (MCSTD 40036) – Robin Hood / Huckleberry Grove.
(cd-s) (MCSXD 40036) – ('A'demo) / Here in my heart / Men of such opinion / Beautiful losers.

Apr 96. (cd/c/d-lp) *(<MCD/MCC/MCA 60008>)* **MOSELEY SHOALS** [2] [ ]
– The riverboat song / The day we caught the train / The circle / Lining your pockets / Fleeting mind / Forty past midnight / One for the road / It's my shadow / Policeman and pirates / Downstream / You've got it bad / Get away.

Jun 96. (c-s) *(MCSC 40046)* **THE DAY WE CAUGHT THE TRAIN / THE CLOCK STRUCK 15 HOURS AGO** [4] [–]
(cd-s+=) *(MCSTD 40046)* – I need a love song / Chicken bones and stones.
(cd-s) *(MCSXD 40046)* – ('A'acoustic) / Travellers tune / Justine.

Sep 96. (c-s) *(MCSC 40077)* **THE CIRCLE / MRS JONES** [6] [–]
(cd-s+=) *(MCSTD 40077)* – Cool cool water / Top of the world.
(cd-s) *(MCSXD 40077)* – ('A'acoustic) / Chelsea walk / Alibis / Daytripper (live).

Mar 97. (cd/c/d-lp) *(<MCD/MCC/MCA 60034>)* **B SIDES • SEASIDES & FREERIDES** (compilation) [4] [ ]
– Huckleberry grove / The day we caught the train (acoustic) / Mrs Jones / Top of the world / Here in my heart / I wanna stay alive with you / Robin Hood / Chelsea walk / Outside of a circle / The clock struck 15 hours ago / Alibis / Chicken bones and stones / Cool cool water / Charlie Brown says / Day tripper / Beautiful losers.

Jun 97. (7"/c-s) *(MCS/+C 40133)* **HUNDRED MILE HIGH CITY. / THE FACE SMILES BACK EASILY** [4] [–]
(cd-s+=) *(MCSTD 40133)* – Falling to the floor / Hello Monday.

Aug 97. (7"/c-s) *(MCS/+C 40144)* *<Alex 6055>* **TRAVELLERS TUNE / SONG FOR THE FRONT ROW** [5] Apr98 [ ]
(cd-s+=) *(MCSTD 40144)* – On the way home / All God's children need travelling shoes.

Sep 97. (cd/c/d-lp) *(<MCD/MCC/MCA 60048>)* **MARCHIN' ALREADY** [1] [ ]
– Hundred mile high city / Better day / Travellers tune / Big star / Debris road / Besides yourself / Get blown away / Tele he's not talking / Foxy's folk faced / All up / Spark and Cindy / Half a dream away / It's a beautiful thing. *(<also enhanced-cd; MCD 60053)>*

Nov 97. (7"/c-s) *(MCS/+C 40151)* **BETTER DAY. / THE BEST BET ON CHINASKI** [9] [–]
(cd-s+=) *(MCSTD 40151)* – On and on.

Feb 98. (7"/c-s) *(MCS/+C 40157)* **IT'S A BEAUTIFUL THING. / MARINERS WAY** [12] [ ]
(cd-s+=) *(MCSTD 40157)* – Going nowhere for a while / Expensive chair.
(above featured singer, P.P. ARNOLD)

Island / Ark 21

Aug 99. (c-s/7") *(C+/IS 757)* **PROFIT IN PEACE. / IF YOU GET YOUR WAY** [13] [–]
(cd-s+=) *(CID 757)* – Flood tide rising.

Sep 99. (cd/c/d-lp) *(CID/ICT/ILPS 8090)* **ONE FROM THE MODERN** [4] [–]
– Profit in peace / So low / I am the news / No one at all / Families / Step by step / July / Jane she got excavated / Emily Chambers / Soul driver / The waves / I won't get grazed.

—— In Oct'99, STEVE CRADDOCK was credited with LIAM GALLAGHER (of OASIS) on UK Top 10 (JAM) tribute double-A single, 'CARNATION' (flipped with 'Going Underground' by BUFFALO TOM)

Nov 99. (c-s/7") *(C+/IS 759)* **SO LOW. / HOPING YOU'RE MAKING IT TOO** [34] [–]
(cd-s+=) *(CID 759)* – The inheritors.
(cd-s+=) *(CIDX 759)* – Soul driver / Jane she got excavated.

Jun 00. (c-s/7") *(C+/IS 763)* **JULY. / I AM THE NEWS** [31] [–]
(cd-s+=) *(CID 763)* – ('A'-forza moderna mix).
(cd-s+=) *(CIDX 763)* – This understanding.

Mar 01. (c-s/7") *(C+/IS 774)* **UP ON THE DOWNSIDE. / THESE ARE THE ONES** [19] [–]
(cd-s+=) *(CID 774)* – Take you back.

Apr 01. (cd/lp) *(CID/ILPS 8104)* *<81007-2>* **MECHANICAL WONDER** [7] May01 [ ]
– Up on the downside / In my field / Sail on my boat / Biggest thing / We made it more / Give me a letter / Mechanical wonder / You are amazing / If I gave you my heart / Can't get back to the bassline. *(UK+=)* – Something for me.

Jul 01. (7") *(IS 779)* **MECHANICAL WONDER. / FIRE ON THE WIND** [49] [–]
(cd-s+=) *(CID 779)* – I was.

Nov 01. (cd/d-lp) *(CID/ILPS 8111)* *<810077>* **SONGS FOR THE FRONT ROW – THE BEST OF OCEAN COLOUR SCENE** (compilation) [16] [ ]
– The riverboat song / The day we caught the train / One for the road / Circle / You've got it bad / Hundred mile high city / Better day / Travellers tune / Get blown away / It's a beautiful thing / Profit in peace / So low / July / Up on the downside / Mechanical wonder / Huckleberry grove / Robin Hood (live) / Crazy lowdown ways. *(d-cd+=; CIDD 8111)* – LIVE AT STIRLING CASTLE

Dec 01. (7") *(IS 787)* **CRAZY LOWDOWN WAYS. / BEST FRIENDS AND LOVERS** [64] [–]
(cd-s+=) *(CID 787)* – Come home.

Sanctuary / Sanctuary

Jun 03. (7") *(SANXD 159E)* **I JUST NEED MYSELF. / I WANNA SEE THE BRIGHT LIGHTS TONIGHT** [13] [–]
(cd-s+=) *(SANXD 159X)* – Questions.
(cd-s) *(SANXD 159)* – ('A'side) / Will you take her love / Me I'm left unsure.

Jul 03. (cd/lp) *(SAN CD/LP 160)* <*84623*> **NORTH ATLANTIC DRIFT** [14] Aug03 [ ]
– I just need myself / Oh collector / North Atlantic drift / Golden Hate Bridge / Make the deal / For every corner / On my way / Second hand car / She's been writing / The song goes on / When evil comes. <*US cd+=*> – Will you take her love / Me, I'm left unsure / Questions / I want to see the bright lights.

Aug 03. (7") *(SANSE 219)* **MAKE THE DEAL. / I JUST NEED MYSELF (remix)** [35] [–]
(cd-s) *(SANXD 219)* – ('A'side) / Perfect strangers / I never believed it too.
(cd-s) *(SANXD 219X)* – ('A'side) / We rise / St. Cecelia.

– compilations, etc. –

Sep 03. (d-cd) *M.C.A.; (077360-2)* **ANTHOLOGY** [75] [–]
– One of those days / Sway / Yesterday today / Giving it all away / Do yourself a favour / The riverboat song / You've got it bad / The day we caught the train / The circle / Hundred mile high city / Traveller's tune / Better day / It's a beautiful thing / Profit in peace / So low / July (new version) / I am the new (new version) / Up on the down side / Mechanical wonder / Crazy lowdown ways // Another girls name / My brother SArah / Mona Lisa eyes / The seventh floor / Robin Hood / The face smiles back easily / Falling to the floor / Hello Monday / Song for the front row / On the way home / The best bet on Chinaski / On and on / Mariners way / Expensive chair / If you get your way / Flood tide rising / Free on the wind / I was / Come home / Best friends & lovers. *(t-cd+=; 980721-0)* – You've got it bad (demo) / Men of such opinion (demo) / Going nowhere for a while / The inheritors / July (Forenza Moderna mix) / These are the ones / Take you back / Anyway, anyhow, anywhere / Travellers tune (acoustic live) / Better day (acoustic live).

Phil OCHS

Born: 19 Dec'40, El Paso, Texas, USA. OCHS was raised by Scottish/Polish parents, his family finally settling in Perrysburg, Ohio where he was brought up. Having spent time following his family tradition in the military, OCHS subsequently studied journalism at the local state university. Together with his room-mate JIM GLOVER, (through whom he became more aware of economics and socialist politics), he formed country-folk duo, The SUNDOWNERS. The group's lifespan was brief, OCHS subsequently heading for the emerging folk scene in New York's Greenwich Village. Throwing himself headlong into radical politics, OCHS was soon making waves following his solo debut on 15th March '63 supporting JOHN HAMMOND. He soon built up a grassroots following, playing many benefit gigs as well as the prestigious Newport Folk Festival. In 1964, he was signed to 'Elektra' by owner Jac Holzman, making his vinyl debut early the following year with acoustic folk set 'ALL THE NEWS THAT'S FIT TO SING'. A strident set of protest songs, OCHS proved himself an intelligent, witty and inspring voice of dissent on such topical issues as the Cuban crisis and the spiralling Vietnam war, the record making the US Top 100 despite a TV ban. Later that summer, fellow folkie, JOAN BAEZ, took his more reflective 'THERE BUT FOR FORTUNE' into the UK Top 10, although such success would prove consistently elusive for OCHS himself. The title track of his next album, 'I AIN'T MARCHING ANYMORE' (1965) became an anthem for the 60's anti-war movement, although by 'PHIL OCHS IN CONCERT' (1966), the singer/songwriter was beginning to move away from direct political comment with tracks like the gentle 'CHANGES' and the aforementioned 'THERE BUT FOR FORTUNE'. Also including the mordant humour of 'LOVE ME, I'M A LIBERAL', the record went on to become one of OCHS' biggest sellers. However, with rival BOB DYLAN spearheading the newly electrified folk-rock explosion along with The BYRDS, OCHS decided to pursue a more ambitious direction. Relocating to L.A., the singer secured a new deal with 'A&M' through the help of brother/manager, MICHAEL, releasing 'PLEASURES OF THE HARBOR' in 1968. Something of a departure to say the least, the album saw OCHS' songs dressed up in sweeping orchestral arrangements. An eclectic collection, OCHS seemed to be lacking a musical focus, 'CROSS MY HEART' and 'FLOWER LADY' among the poppiest releases of his career while the title track and the epic 'CRUCIFIXION' were intensely introspective. There was also a nod to the satire of old with the jaunty 'OUTSIDE A SMALL CIRCLE OF FRIENDS'. While the album succeeded in raising the ire of the more traditional folkies, OCHS soldiered bravely on with 'TAPE FROM CALIFORNIA' (1968) a more consistent set combining the political and the personal. Among the highlights were 'WHITE BOOTS MARCHING IN A YELLOW LAND' (another Vietnam comment) and the seven minute plus 'JOE HILL', a compelling tale of a courageous but ultimately doomed union man. The same description could easily apply to OCHS himself. Severely troubled by the assassination of Bobby Kennedy and the ensuing riots at the 1968 democratic convention, OCHS became increasingly disillusioned. 'REHEARSALS FOR RETIREMENT' (1969) didn't make for easy listening, an angry, embittered record but all the more powerful for it. The sentiments of 'I KILL THEREFORE I AM' remain every bit as vital today as they were then while 'ANOTHER AGE' was almost pleading in tone. Like most of his 'A&M' releases, the record failed to take off and OCHS dreamed up the ill-advised idea of creating a persona which combined the rock'n'roll showmanship of ELVIS and the political fire of CHE GUEVARA. Nevertheless, the self-deprecatingly titled 'PHIL OCHS GREATEST HITS' (1970) remains arguably his most affecting release. Produced by Hollywood maverick, VAN DYKE PARKS, the record consisted of rollicking country-rock and more elaborate, PARKS-esque creations. The Spector-like, folk/gospel hybrid of 'ONE WAY TICKET HOME' was breathtaking, likewise the poignant, piano-led ballad, 'JIM DEAN OF INDIANA'. As for reclaiming his audience, however, the record was a non-starter. Touring the album, OCHS wore a gold lamé suit onstage in keeping with his new concept. The audience remained unimpressed however, booing the BUDDY HOLLY medleys which OCHS had bizarrely brought into his stage show. A live document of one particularly confrontational show was later released in 1975 as 'GUNFIGHT AT CARNEGIE HALL'. OCHS subsequently went into semi-retirement, losing his self-belief as an artist although he did travel to South America, playing a benefit gig in aid of the (then) recently overthrown Chilean leader. He also travelled to Africa where, in addition to cutting a couple of singles, 'NIKO MCHUMBA NGOBE' and 'BWATUE' (pre-empting PAUL SIMON by more than a decade) he was mysteriously attacked. His vocal chords were seriously damaged in the incident and this plunged OCHS further into depression and bouts of alcoholism. Finally, on the 9th of April, 1976, the singer hanged himself at his sister's home, tragically ending a career that had begun so buoyantly and full of hope. Music and politics, politics and life, were obviously inseparable to OCHS and his struggle for truth, for social justice was among the most courageous of the era.

Album rating: ALL THE NEWS THAT'S FIT TO SING (*7) / I AIN'T MARCHING ANYMORE (*7) / PHIL OCHS IN CONCERT (*7) / PLEASURES OF THE HARBOR (*7) / TAPE FROM CALIFORNIA (*6) / REHEARSALS FOR RETIREMENT (*6) / PHIL OCHS GREATEST HITS fresh recordings (*6) / GUNFIGHT AT CARNEGIE HALL (*5) / CHORDS OF FAME compilation (*7) / A TOAST TO THOSE WHO ARE GONE collection (*5)

PHIL OCHS – vocals, acoustic guitar / with **DANNY KALE** – acoustic guitar

Elektra Elektra

Mar 65. (lp) *(EKL 269)* <7269> **ALL THE NEWS THAT'S FIT TO SING** Nov64
– One more parade / The thresher / Talking Vietnam / Lou Marsh / Power and the glory / Celia / The bells / Automation song / Ballad of William Worthy / Knock on the door / Talking Cuban crisis / Bound for glory / Too many martyrs / What's that I hear. *(re-iss. Oct87 on 'Edsel'; ED 247) (re-iss. May89 on 'Carthage' lp/c; CG LP/C 4427) (cd-iss. May94 on 'Hannibal'+=; HNCD 4427)* – Bullets of Mexico.

Aug 65. (lp) *(EKL 287)* <7287> **I AIN'T MARCHING ANYMORE** May65
– I ain't marching anymore / In the heat of the summer / Draft dodger rag / That's what I want to hear / That was the president / Iron lady / The highway man / Links on the chain / Hills of West Virginia / The men behind the guns / Talking Birmingham jam / Ballad of the carpenter / Days of decision / Here's to the state of Mississippi. *(re-iss. May89 on 'Carthage' lp/c; CG LP/C 4422) (cd-iss. May94 on 'Hannibal'; HNCD 4422)*

Dec 65. (7") *(EKSN 45002)* **I AIN'T MARCHING ANYMORE. / THAT WAS THE PRESIDENT**

May 66. (lp) *(EKL 310)* <7310> **PHIL OCHS IN CONCERT (live)** Feb66
– I'm going to say it now / Bracero / Ringing of revolution / Is there anybody here? / Canons of Christianity / There but for fortune / Cops of the world / Santo Domingo / Changes / Love me, I'm a Liberal / When I'm gone.

A&M A&M

Nov 67. (7") **CROSS MY HEART. / FLOWER LADY** –

Jan 68. (lp; mono/stereo) *(AML/+S 913)* <4133> **PLEASURES OF THE HARBOR** Oct67
– Cross my heart / Flower lady / Outside of a small circle of friends / I've had her / Miranda / The party / Pleasures of the harbor / The crucifixion.

Jan 68. (7") *(AMS 716)* **OUTSIDE A SMALL CIRCLE OF FRIENDS. / MIRANDA**

Jul 69. (7") **THE WAR IS OVER. / THE HARDER THEY FALL** –

Oct 68. (lp) *(AMLS 919)* <4148> **TAPE FROM CALIFORNIA** Jul68
– Tape from California / White boots marching in a yellow land / Half a century high / Joe Hill / The war is over / The harder they fall / When in Rome / Floods of Florence.

May 69. (lp) *(AMLS 934)* <4181> **REHEARSALS FOR RETIREMENT**
– Pretty smart on my part / The doll house / I kill therefore I am / William Butler Yeats visits Lincoln Park and escapes unscathed / My life / The scorpion, departs but never returns / The world began in Eden and ended in Los Angeles / Doesn't Lenny live here anymore / Another age / Rehearsals for retirement.

Mar 70. (lp) *(AMLS 973)* <4253> **PHIL OCHS GREATEST HITS** (not a compilation)
– One way ticket home / Jim Dean of Indiana / My kingdom for a car / Boy in Ohio / Gas station women / Chords of fame / Ten cents a coup / Bach, Beethoven, Mozart and me / Basket in the pool / No more songs. *(re-iss. Jun86 on 'Edsel'; ED 201) (cd-iss. Jul90; EDCD 201)*

Mar 70. (7") **ONE WAY TICKET HOME. / MY KINGDOM FOR A CAR** –

—— PHIL semi-retired after recording Apr'70 live album 'GUNFIGHT AT CARNEGIE HALL'. It was only issued in Canada 1975.

Sep 72. (7") **KANSAS CITY BOMBER. / GAS STATION WOMEN** –

Feb 74. (7") **HERE'S TO THE STATE OF RICHARD NIXON. / POWER & THE GLORY** –

1974. (7") **BWATUE. / NIKO MCHUMBA NGOMBE** – Kenya –

1975. (lp) <9010> **GUNFIGHT AT CARNEGIE HALL (live)** –
– Mona Lisa / I ain't marchin' anymore / Oakie from Meskogee / Chords of fame / Buddy Holly medley:- Not fade away – I'm gonna love you too – Think it over – Oh boy – Everyday – It's so easy – Not fade away / Pleasures of the harbor / Tape from California / Elvis medley:- My baby left me – I'm ready – Heartbreak hotel – All shook up – Are you lonesome tonight – My baby left me (encore) / A fool such as I.

—— While visiting friend/singer/protester Victor Jaro in Chile, he was robbed and suffered throat damage which prevented him from singing. After bouts of heavy drinking and schizophrenia, he hanged himself on 9th Apr'76.

– compilations, others, etc. –

1976. (lp) *Folkways;* <5320> **SINGS FOR BROADSIDES** –

1976. (lp) *Folkways;* <5321> **BROADSIDE MAGAZINE INTERVIEWS** –

Jan 77. (d-lp) *A&M; (AMLM 64599)* <4599> **CHORDS OF FAME** 1974
– I ain't marchin' anymore / No more parades / Draft dodger rag / Here's to the state of Richard Nixon / The bells / Bound of glory / Too many martyrs / There but for fortune / I'm going to say it now / Santo Domingo / Changes / Is there anybody here? / Love me, I'm a Liberal / When I'm gone / Outside of a small circle of friends / Pleasures of the harbor / Tape from California / Chords of fame / Crucifixion / War is over / Jim Dean of Indiana / The power and the glory / Flower lady / No more songs.

1980. (lp) *Folkways;* <5362> **THE BROADSIDE TAPES** –
(UK-iss.Mar95 on 'Smithsonian Folkways' cd/c; SFW CD/MC 40008)

Mar 88. (lp)<cd/c> *Edsel; (ED 242) / Rhino;* <R2/R4 70080> **A TOAST TO THOSE WHO ARE GONE** (lost tapes) 1987
– Do what I have to do / Ballad of Billie Sol / Coloured town / A.M.A. song / William Moore / Paul Crump / Going down to Mississippi / I'll be there / Ballad of Oxford / No Christmas in Kentucky / A toast to those who are gone / I'm tired / City boy / Song of my returning. *(cd-iss. 1995 on 'Diablo'; DIAB 813)*

May 89. (d-lp/c/cd) *Elektra; (K 960832-1/-4/-2)* **THERE BUT FOR FORTUNE** (some live 1965-66)

Mar 91. (cd/c) *Rhino;* <R2/R4 70778> **THERE AND NOW: LIVE IN VANCOUVER 1968 (live)** –

Jun 97. (d-cd) *A&M; (540 728-2)* **THE LAST AMERICAN TROUBADOUR**

Jul 98. (cd) *Vanguard;* <(VCD 77017)> **LIVE AT NEWPORT**

Nov 00. (cd) *Vanguard;* <(VCD 79566)> **THE EARLY YEARS**

Oct 01. (d-cd) *Elektra;* <(8122 73564-2)> **ALL THE NEWS THAT'S FIT TO SING / I AIN'T MARCHING ANYMORE**

Jan 02. (cd) *Universal;* <(AA69493164-2)> **THE MILLENNIUM COLLECTION**

Sinead O'CONNOR

Born: 8 Dec'66, Glenageary, Ireland. Raised in Dublin, her parents divorced when she was 8, and she was later sent to a Dominican nun-run centre for girls with behavioural problems. In 1985, after attending Dublin's College of Music, she joined local band TON TON MACOUTE, where she met boyfriend and future manager, FACHTNA O'CEALLAIGH. In 1986, he arranged for her to guest on U2's The EDGE's soundtrack album, 'Captive'. She was soon spotted by Nigel Grainge and Chris Hill of 'Ensign' records, who signed her up later that year. In April the following year, she guested for stablemates WORLD PARTY (aka KARL WALLINGER) on album 'Private Revolution'. Finally at the end of '87, she issued her debut solo 45, 'TROY', while early the following year, SINEAD scored her first Top 20 hit with 'MANDINKA', reactivating sales of the previously debut album, 'THE LION AND THE COBRA'. The record presented O'CONNOR as a shaven-headed, angel-faced nightingale in wolf's clothing, her soul-wrenching vocals capable of conveying the rawest of emotions from visceral rage to heartfelt compassion. Self-produced, the record also revealed the Irish maverick to be adept at flitting between contrasting musical styles with surprising ease, from the hypnotic pop of the aforementioned 'MANDINKA' to the suggestive rhythmic pulse of 'I WANT YOUR (HANDS ON ME)'. But while she proved to be a fiercely independent, original pop star, O'CONNOR applied the same passion to fanning the flames of controversy, the first furore of many coming when she allegedly defended the IRA. At this point, O'CONNOR was perhaps more famous for her outspokeness than her music, although that changed with the massive worldwide (also transatlantic No.1) success of 'NOTHING COMPARES 2 U' in early 1990. A cover of an obscure PRINCE song with arrangements by NELLEE HOOPER, the track's languid atmospherics provided a perfect platform for O'CONNOR's tear-soaked vocals. The song catapulted her into the superstar bracket and the accompanying album, 'I DO NOT WANT WHAT I HAVEN'T GOT' (1990), sold by the million. Recorded amid the break-up of her first marriage, the album was a largely downbeat affair with the angry intensity of old strangely muted. O'CONNOR the fiesty firebrand was back with a vengeance in 1992, however, the singer infamously ripping up a photo of Pope John Paul II on American TV show, 'Saturday Night Live'. Hardly endearing her to the country's Catholic population, this incident, combined with her earlier refusal to play a show which began with a rendition of the American national anthem, undoubtedly contributed to the strength of the anti-SINEAD feelings running high at the Madison Square Garden BOB DYLAN tribute in October that year. Booed off stage, a tearful O'CONNOR was led away by KRIS KRISTOFFERSON in what must've been one of the most harrowing moments of her career. The attendant press overkill all but obscured the fact she actually had a new album on the shelves, a covers set of vintage torch ballads entitled 'AM I NOT YOUR GIRL'. While the record made the UK Top 10, it unsurprisingly failed to perform quite so well in the States. 1993 brought trauma of a more personal nature; O'CONNOR's allegations of abuse by her mother resulted in a family feud with her father and brother and a subsequent breakdown and suicide attempt. Facing her demons head-on, the singer recorded some of her most nakedly uncompromising material to date for 'UNIVERSAL MOTHER' (1994), the often bleak starkness of the lyrics contrasting with the warmth of the tranquil arrangements and melodies. Although critically acclaimed, the album failed to match the sales of her previous efforts and her subsequent refusal to give interviews led to a drop in profile over the ensuing few years. The first fruits of her new deal with 'Columbia', even the defiant 'THIS IS A REBEL SONG' failed to charge up the enthusiasm of the record buying public in late '97. While many may point out that O'CONNOR is her own worst enemy, there's no denying the potential of her talents and it'd be a tragedy if this survivor were to be confined to the musical margins. After yet more domestic controversy, she eventually re-emerged in 2000 with 'FAITH AND COURAGE', another testament to her continuing creativity and relevance as an artist against the (usually considerable) odds. The likes of 'NO MAN'S WOMAN' suggested that her fiercely independent fire had only been fanned by events of the last few years while the record's underlying spiritual bent confirmed her recent religious ordination. O'CONNOR once revealed in a magazine article that Van Morrison's 'VEEDON FLEECE' was one of her all-time favourite albums, a journey into the Irish mystic which perhaps informed the idea, if not the actual music of, 'SEAN-NOS NUA' (2002). Like VAN has done many times throughout his career, if never in such a concentrated burst, SINEAD cast her spell over the traditional music of her homeland in such a fashion as to reinvent it. Also in common with VAN, her interpretations were charged with a drifting, intoxicating spirituality, even when the subject matter – as so often in folk music – veered towards tragedy. Only a singer as determinedly singular in her approach as O'CONNOR could have gotten away with a title like 'SHE WHO DWELLS IN THE SECRET PLACE OF THE MOST HIGH SHALL ABIDE UNDER THE SHADOW OF THE ALMIGHTY' (2003), a collection of live, unreleased and B-side material. Despite stretching to more than thirty tracks, the material was never less than hypnotic: arguably no artist alive can bring quite so much of her own, wayward spirit to other peoples songs. • **The covers:** YOU DO SOMETHING TO ME + MY HEART BELONGS TO DADDY (Cole Porter) / SOMEONE TO WATCH OVER ME (Ira Gershwin) / DAMN YOUR EYES (Etta James) / SECRET LOVE (Doris Day) / ALL APOLOGIES (Nirvana). Her 1992 album was filled with covers originally sung by; WHY DONT YOU DO RIGHT? (Julie London; J.McCoy) / BEWITCHED, BOTHERED AND BEWILDERED (Ella Fitzgerald; L.Hart & R.Rodgers) / SECRET LOVE + BLACK COFFEE (Sarah Vaughan; F.Webster & S.Burke) / SUCCESS HAS MADE A FAILURE OF OUR HOME (Loretta Lynn; J.Mullins) / DON'T CRY FOR ME ARGENTINA (Elaine Page; Tim Rice & Andrew Lloyd Webber) / I WANT TO BE LOVED BY YOU (Marilyn Monroe; H.Stothart, H.Ruby & B.Kalmar) / GLOOMY SUNDAY (Billie Holiday; L.Javor, R.Seress & Lewis) / LOVE LETTERS (Alison Moyet; E.Heyman & V.Young) / HOW INSENSITIVE (Astrud Gilberto; V.de Morales, A.C.Jobim & Gimbel) / SCARLET RIBBONS (her mum & dad; J.Segal & E.Danzig). She co-writes w/COULTER or REYNOLDS and sample merchant TIM SIMENON for return 1994 album. Other covers; YOU MAKE ME FEEL SO REAL (Van Morrison).

Album rating: THE LION AND THE COBRA (*7) / I DO NOT WANT WHAT I HAVEN'T GOT (*9) / AM I NOT YOUR GIRL? (*5) / UNIVERSAL MOTHER (*6) / SO FAR . . . THE BEST OF SINEAD O'CONNOR compilation (*8) / FAITH AND COURAGE (*5) / SEAN-NOS NUA (*6) / SHE WHO DWELLS IN THE SECRET PLACE OF THE MOST HIGH SHALL ABIDE UNDER THE SHADOW OF THE ALMIGHTY (*7)

SINEAD O'CONNOR – vocals (ex-TON TON MACOUTE) / with **ENYA** + **MARCO PIRRONI**

Ensign Chrysalis

Oct 87. (7"/12") *(ENY/+X 610)* **TROY. / STILL LISTENING**

Nov 87. (lp/c)(cd) *(CHEN/ZCHEN 7)(CCD 1612) <41612>* **THE LION AND THE COBRA** 27 36
– Jackie / Mandinka / Jerusalem / Just like U said it would B / Never get old / Troy / I want your (hands on me) / Drink before the war / Just call me Joe. *(re-dist.Jan90 hit UK No.37; same)*

Dec 87. (7") *(ENY 611)* **MANDINKA. / DRINK BEFORE THE WAR** 17
(ext.12"+=) *(ENYX 611)* – ('A'dub mix).
(cd-s++=) *(ENYCD 611)* – Still listening.
(12"+=) *(ENYXR 611)* – ('A'-Jake's remix).

Apr 88. (7"; by SINEAD O'CONNOR with MC LYTE) *(ENY 613)* **I WANT YOUR (HANDS ON ME). / JUST CALL ME JOE**
(12"+=/cd-s+=) *(ENY X/CD 613)* – ('A'dance) / ('A'-Street mix).
(12"+=) *(ENYXR 613)* – ('A'-Knee-trembler mix) / ('A'-Hickey on the neck mix).

Oct 88. (7") *(ENY 618)* **JUMP IN THE RIVER. / NEVER GET OLD (live)**
(12"+=/cd-s+=) *(ENY X/CD 618)* – ('A'duet with KAREN FINLAY).

—— Early 1989, she appeared on THE THE's album 'Mind Bomb', singing on 'Kingdom Of Rain'.

Ensign Ensign

Jan 90. (7"/7"box) *(ENY/+B 630) <23488>* **NOTHING COMPARES 2 U. / JUMP IN THE RIVER** 1 Mar90 1
(12"+=/cd-s+=) *(ENY X/CD 630)* – Jump in the river (instrumental).

Mar 90. (cd)(c/lp) *(CCD 1759)(Z+/CHEN 14) <21759?* **I DO NOT WANT WHAT I HAVEN'T GOT** 1 1
– Feel so different / I an stretched on your grave / Three babies / The emperor's new clothes / Black boys in mopeds / Nothing compares 2 U / Jump in the river / You cause as much sorrow / The last day of our acquaintance / I do not want what I haven't got. *(re-iss. cd Mar94;)*

Jul 90. (7"/7"box) *(ENY/+B 633) <23528>* **THE EMPEROR'S NEW CLOTHES. / WHAT DO YOU WANT** 31 Jun90 60
(c-s+=) *(ENYMC 633)* – I am stretched on your grave.
(12"/cd-s) *(ENY X/CD 633)* – ('A'-Hank Shocklee remix) / I am stretched on your grave (Apple Brightness mix) / ('A'-Night until morning dub mix).

Oct 90. (7") *(ENY 635)* **THREE BABIES. / TROY (live)** 42
(c-s+=/12"+=/cd-s+=) *(ENY MC/X/CD 635)* – Damn your eyes / The value of ignorance.

May 91. (7") *(ENY 646)* **MY SPECIAL CHILD. / NOTHING COMPARES 2 U (live)** 42
(c-s+=/12"+=/cd-s+=) *(ENY MC/X/CD 646)* – ('A'instrumental) / The Emperor's new clothes (live).

Dec 91. (7"/cd-s) *(ENY/+CD 652)* **SILENT NIGHT. / IRISH WAYS & IRISH LAWS (live)** [60] [–]

— early in 1991, she was the first ever person to refuse her Grammy for alternative 1990 album. She protested about anti-legalizing Irish abortion on TV and press. After earlier ripping a photo of Pope John Paul II on US Saturday Night Live, she was booed off-stage (Oct92) at a Bob Dylan tribute concert at Madison Square Garden. Due to crowd noise which drowned out backing band, she eventually sang unaccompanied a Bob Marley! song 'War'. She announced that month she was to retire, although thankfully she retracted press statements by late '92.

— now with **CHRIS PARKER** – drums / **DAVID FINCK** – bass / **RICHARD TEE** – piano / **IRA SIEGAL** – guitar / **DAVE LEBOLT** – synthesizer / plus a host of saxists, flautists, violinists, trumpeters & backing singers

Sep 92. (7"/c-s) *(ENY/+MC 656)* **SUCCESS HAS MADE A FAILURE OF OUR HOME. / YOU DO SOMETHING TO ME** [18] [ ]
(cd-s+=) *(ENYCD 656)* – I want to be loved by you.
(cd-s) *(ENYSCD 656)* – ('A'side) / Someone to watch over me / My heart belongs to daddy.

Sep 92. (cd)(c/lp) *(CCD 1952)(Z+/CHEN 1952) <21952>* **AM I NOT YOUR GIRL?** [6] [27]
– Why don't you do right? / Bewitched, bothered and bewildered / Secret love / Black coffee / Success has made a failure of our lives / Don't cry for me Argentina / I want to be loved by you / Gloomy Sunday / Love letters / How insensitive / Scarlet ribbons / Don't cry for me Argentina (instrumental).

— In Oct'92, she collaborated on MARXMAN single 'Ship Ahoy'.

Dec 92. (7"/c-s) *(ENY/+MC 657)* **DON'T CRY FOR ME ARGENTINA. / AVE MARIA** [53] [ ]
(cd-s+=) *(CDENY 657)* – Scarlet ribbons.
(cd-s) *(CDENYS 657)* – ('A'side) / Love letters / Scarlet ribbons.

— In Jun'93, she was credited on WILLIE NELSON single 'Don't Give Up'.

Feb 94. (c-s/7") *(C+/IS 588)* **YOU MADE ME THE THIEF OF YOUR HEART. / THE FATHER AND HIS WIFE THE SPIRIT** [42] [ ]
(12"+=/cd-s+=) *(12IS/CID 588)* – ('A'mixes).
(above single from film 'In The Name Of The Father'; on 'Island')

— now with **JOHN REYNOLDS** – drums / **PHIL COULTER** – piano / **DAVE CLAYTON** – keyboards / **MARCO PIRRONI + VAN GILLIANO** – guitar / **TIM SIMENON**, etc.

Sep 94. (cd/c/lp) *(CD/TC+/CHEN 34) <30549>* **UNIVERSAL MOTHER** [19] [37]
– Fire on Babylon / John I love you / My darling child / Am I human? / Red football / All apologies / A perfect Indian / Scorn not his simplicity / All babies / In this heart / Tiny grief song / Famine / Thank you for hearing me.

Nov 94. (12"/c-s/cd-s) *(12/TC/CD ENY 662)* **THANK YOU FOR HEARING ME. / FIRE ON BABYLON (remix)** [13] [–]
(cd-s) *(CDENYS 662)* – ('A'side) / I believe in you / Streets of London / House of the rising sun.

— In Apr'95, she duetted with SHANE MacGOWAN on his 'HAUNTED' hit.

Aug 95. (c-s/cd-s) *(TC/CD ENY 663)* **FAMINE (extended) / FAMINE / ALL APOLOGIES** [51] [ ]
(12") *(12ENY 663)* – ('A'extended) / Fire on Babylon (M Beat remix).

Chrysalis Chrysalis

May 97. (c-ep/12"ep/cd-ep) *(TC/12/CD CHS 5051) <58651>* **GOSPEL OAK EP** [28] Jun97 [ ]
– This is to mother you / I am enough for myself / Petit poulet / 4 my love.

Nov 97. (cd/c) *(<821581-2/-4?>* **SO FAR . . . THE BEST OF SINEAD O'CONNOR** (compilation) [28] [ ]
– Herpone / Mandinka / Jackie / Troy / Nothing compares 2 U / I am stretched on your grave / Emperor's new clothes / Last day of our acquaintance / Success has made a failure of our home / Thank you for hearing me / Fire on Babylon / John I love you / Perfect Indian / You made me the thief of your heart / Empire / This is a rebel song.

Columbia Columbia

Nov 97. (c-s) *(665 299-4)* **THIS IS A REBEL SONG / REDEMPTION SONG (live)** [60] [–]
(cd-s+=) *(665 299-2)* – Fire on Babylon (live).
(cd-s) *(665 299-5)* – ('A'side) / Thank you for hearing me (live) / Last day of our acquaintance (live).

Atlantic Atlantic

Jun 00. (cd/c) *<(7567 83337-2/-4)>* **FAITH AND COURAGE** [61] [55]
– The healing room / No man's woman / Jealous / Dancing lessons / Daddy I'm fine / 'Til I whisper U something / Hold back the night / What doesn't belong to me / The state I'm in / The lamb's book of life / If U ever / Emma's song / Kyrie Eleison.

Jun 00. (cd-s) *(AT 0083CD)* **NO MAN'S WOMAN / THIS IS A REBEL SONG (remix) / HER MANTLE SO GREEN** [ ] [–]

Devolution not iss.

Aug 02. (12"/cd-s) *(DEVR 003 X/CDS)* **TROY (THE PHOENIX FROM THE FLAME) / (mixes)** [48] [–]
(cd-s) *(DEVR 003RX)* – ('A'-Creamer & K remix) / (('A'-Bob Searle remix).

Random Vanguard

Oct 02. (cd) *(RAMCD 001) <79724>* **SEAN-NOS NUA** [52] [ ]
– Peggy Gordon / Her mantle so green / Lord Franklin / The singing bird / Oro se do bheatha 'bhaile / Molly Malone / Paddy's lament / The Moorlough shire / The parting glass / Baidin fheilimi / My lagan love / Lord Baker (with CHRISTY MOORE) / I'll tell me ma.

Daisy Vanguard

Sep 03. (d-cd) *(IRL 003) <215/6>* **SHE WHO DWELLS IN THE SECRET PLACE OF THE MOST HIGH SHALL ABIDE UNDER THE SHADOW OF THE ALMIGHTY (live)** [ ] [ ]
– Regina caeh / O film et filiae / My love I bring / Do right woman, do right man / Love hurts / Ain't it a shame / Chiquitita / Brigidine Diana / It's all good / Love is ours / A hundred thousand angels / You put your arms around me (demo) / Emma's song / No matter how hard I try (demo) / Dense water, deeper down / This is a rebel song / 1000 mirrors (with ASIAN DUB FOUNDATION) / Big bunch of junkie lies / Song of Jerusalem / Molly Malone / Oro, se do bheatha 'bhaile / The singing bird / My lagan love / I am stretched on your grave / Nothing compares 2 U / John I love you / The Moorlough shore / You made me the thief of your heart / Paddy's lament / Thank you for hearing me / Fire on Babylon / The last day of our acquaintance.

– compilations, etc. –

Oct 02. (d-cd) *Ensign; (543153-2)* **THE LION AND THE COBRA / I DO NOT WANT WHAT I HAVEN'T GOT** [ ] [–]

OFFSPRING

Formed: Orange County, California, USA . . . 1984 out of MANIC SUBSIDAL and CLOWNS OF DEATH, by main songwriter DEXTER HOLLAND and GREG KRIESEL. With the addition of JAMES LILJA and KEVIN 'NOODLES' WASSERMAN they adopted THE OFFSPRING moniker, releasing a debut 45, 'I'LL BE WAITING' on the self-financed 'Black' label. With RON WELTY subsequently replacing LILJA, the band began working on demo material, eventually going into the studio with Thom Wilson. The results eventually surfaced in the form of the eponymous 'OFFSPRING' (1989), issued on the 'Nitro' label. An ambitious and experimental fusion of exotic hardcore, its schizoid ramblings not endearing the band to many outside the scene. The next few years were tough for the band as they struggled to find a steady record deal, even tougher for NOODLES who was stabbed at a benefit concert. They eventually found a sympathetic ear in the form of BRAD GUREWITZ (ex-BAD RELIGION) and his burgeoning 'Epitaph' operation, releasing a much improved follow-up album, 'IGNITION' in 1992. However, it wasn't until 1994 and their follow-up, 'SMASH', that OFFSPRING pogo'd into the US charts. Hard on the heels of GREEN DAY's phenomenal worldwide success, the 4-piece found a very successful niche in the larger than life, lads-together ska-core punk rock complete with dayglo choruses and brutally addictive hooklines. The album went on to sell over a million copies in the States and finally gained deserved recognition in Britain, especially after the 'SELF ESTEEM' track became a Top 40 smash early '95! Over the course of the ensuing two years, OFFSPRING almost became part of 'Columbia's roster, although in the end a follow-up, 'INXAY ON THE HOMBRE' appeared on 'Epitaph' in 1997. Building on the winning formula of its predecessor, the album scored another transatlantic Top 20. The dreadlocked DEXTER subsequently teamed up with JELLO BIAFRA (ex-DEAD KENNEDYS) to play some charity gigs under the banner of F.S.U. in aid of the homeless, human rights, etc. Album No.5 'AMERICANA' was delivered late in '98, nobody in their right minds prophecising it would unearth a UK chart-topper in the shape of fun novelty 45, 'PRETTY FLY (FOR A WHITE GUY)'. More of the same was to follow, British hits, 'THE KIDS AREN'T ALRIGHT' and 'SHE'S GOT ISSUES', boosting sales of an otherwise flagging album – a pretty fly move, indeed! Now in the major league of nu-punk heroes, OFFSPRING served up more metallic mania for the masses with 'CONSPIRACY OF ONE', a record which contained precious little in the way of sonic innovation but plenty of shoutalong riffage for longtime fans and the newly converted alike. Ditto 'SPLINTER' (2003), the veteran punks probably getting just a little bit too long in the tooth to care that much about making their music fit in with anyone's agenda but their own. • **Covered:** HEY JOE (hit; Jimi Hendrix) / SMASH IT UP (Damned) / KILLBOY POWERHEAD (Didjits).

Album rating: THE OFFSPRING (*4) / IGNITION (*6) / SMASH (*7) / IXNAY ON THE HOMBRE (*5) / AMERICANA (*5) / CONSPIRACY OF ONE (*5) / SPLINTER (*4)

DEXTER HOLLAND (b. BRYAN HOLLAND, 1966) – vocals, guitar / **NOODLES** (b. KEVIN WASSERMAN, 4 Feb'63, L.A.) – guitar / **GREG KRIESEL** (b.20 Jan'65, Glendale, Calif.) – bass / **JAMES LILJA** – drums

not iss. | Black

1987. (7") *<none>* **I'LL BE WAITING. / BLACKBALL** [–] [ ]

—— **RON WELTY** (b. 1 Feb'71) – drums (ex-FQX) repl. LILJA

not iss. | Nemesis

Aug 88. (7"ep) *<NEX 21>* **BAGHDAD EP** [–] [ ]
– Get it right / Hey Joe / Baghdad / The blurb.

1989. (cd) *<NECDX 44>* **THE OFFSPRING** [–] [ ]
– Jennifer lost the war / Elders / Out on patrol / Crossroads / Demons / Beheaded / Tehran / A thousand days / Black ball / I'll be waiting / Kill the president. *(UK-iss.Nov95 on 'Epitaph' cd/c; E 86460-2/-4) (cd re-iss. Jun00 on 'Nitro'; 15803-2)*

Epitaph | Epitaph

Oct 92. (cd/c/lp) *<(E 86424-2/-4/-1)>* **IGNITION** [ ] [ ]
– Session / We are one / Kick him when he's down / Take it like a man / Get it right / Dirty magic / Hypodermic / Burn it up / No hero / L.A.P.D. / Nothing from something / Forever and a day.

Sep 94. (cd/c/lp) *<(E 86432-2/-4/-1)>* **SMASH** [21] Apr94 [4]
– Time to relax / Nitro (youth energy) / Bad habit / Gotta get away / Genocide / Something to believe in / Come out and play / Self esteem / It'll be a long time / Killboy powerhead / What happened to you / So alone / Not the one / Smash.

Sep 94. (12"/c-s/cd-s) *(EPUK/+MC/CD 001)* **COME OUT AND PLAY. / SESSION / ('A'acoustic)** [ ] [–]

Oct 94. (7") *<IGN 3H)* *<65572>* **COME OUT AND PLAY. / COME OUT AND PLAY** [ ] [ ]
(above on 'Ignition'/<'Phantom'> (below ltd. on 'Flying')

Dec 94. (10"ep) *(GOD 008)* **COME OUT AND PLAY EP** [ ] [–]

Feb 95. (7"/c-s/12"/cd-s) *(7/MC/12/CD HOLE 001)* **SELF ESTEEM. / JENNIFER LOST THE WAR / BURN IT UP** [37] [–]

Aug 95. (7"/c-s/cd-s) *(WOOS 2/+CS/CDS)* **GOTTA GET AWAY. / SMASH** [43] [–]
(above single on 'Out Of Step' UK)

—— In the Spring of '96, they were fighting Epitaph and boss BRETT GUREWITZ for the right to sign with another label 'Columbia' in the US-only.

Jan 97. (7"m/cd-s) *(6495-7/-2)* **ALL I WANT. / WAY DOWN THE LINE** [31] [–]
(12"+=/cd-s+=) *(6491-1/-2)* – Smash it up.

Feb 97. (cd/lp) *(6487-2/-1)* *<67810>* **IXNAY ON THE HOMBRE** [17] [9]
– Disclaimer / Meaning of life / Mota / Me and my old lady / Cool to hate / Leave it behind / Gone away / I choose / Intermission / All I want / Way down the line / Don't pick it up / Amazed / Change the world.

Apr 97. (7"/cd-s) *(6504-7/-2)* **GONE AWAY. / D.U.I.** [42] [–]
(cd-s+=) *(6498-2)* – Cool to hate / Hey Joe.

Columbia | Columbia

Nov 98. (cd/c) *(491656-2/-4)* *<69661>* **AMERICANA** [10] [2]
– Welcome / Have you ever / Staring at the sun / Pretty fly (for a white guy) / The kids aren't alright / Feelings / She's got issues / Walla walla / End of the line / No brakes / Why don't you get a job? / Americana / Pay the man. *(pic-lp-iss.May99; 491656-0) (cd re-iss. Feb01; same)*

Jan 99. (7"/c-s) *(666880-7/-4)* *<41579>* **PRETTY FLY (FOR A WHITE GUY). / ('A'-The Geek mix)** [1] Nov98 [53]
(cd-s+=) *(666880-2)* – All I want (live).

Apr 99. (c-s) *(667354-4)* *<radio cut>* **WHY DON'T YOU GET A JOB? / BEHEADED 1999** [2] Mar99 [74]
(cd-s+=) *(667354-2)* – ('A'remix by Baka Boyz) / Pretty fly (for a white guy) (CD-ROM).
(cd-s) *(667354-5)* – ('A'remixes).

Aug 99. (c-s) *(667763-4)* **THE KIDS AREN'T ALRIGHT / PRETTY FLY (FOR A WHITE GUY) (live)** [11] [–]
(cd-s+=) *(667763-2)* – Why don't you get a job? (live).
(cd-s) *(667763-5)* – ('A'side) / Walla walla (live) / Pretty fly (for a white guy) (video).

Nov 99. (c-s) *(668377-4)* *<4274>* **SHE'S GOT ISSUES / PRETTY FLY (Baka Boyz Low Rider mix)** [41] [ ]
(cd-s+=) *(668377-2)* – ('A'side) / Kids aren't alright (Wise Guys mix) / Kids aren't alright (Wise Guys instrumental).
(cd-s) *(667377-5)* – ('A'side) / All I want (live in Vegas) / Kids aren't alright (CD-Rom video).

Nov 00. (c-s) *(669997-4)* *<radio cut>* **ORIGINAL PRANKSTER / DAMMIT, I CHANGED AGAIN** [6] [70]
(cd-s+=) *(669997-2)* – Gone away (live).
(cd-s) *(669997-5)* – ('A'side) / Come out swinging / Staring at the sun (live).

Nov 00. (cd/c/lp) *(498481-2/-4/-1)* *<61419>* **CONSPIRACY OF ONE** [12] [9]
– Intro / Come out swinging / Original prankster / Want you bad / Million miles away / Dammit, I change again / Living in chaos / Special delivery / One fine day / All along / Denial, revisited / Vultures / Conspiracy of one.

Mar 01. (c-s) *(670929-4)* **WANT YOU BAD / THE KIDS AREN'T ALRIGHT (live)** [15] [–]
(cd-s+=) *(670929-2)* – 80 times.
(cd-s) *(670929-5)* – ('A'side) / The kids aren't alright (live) / Autonomy.

Jun 01. (c-s) *(671408-4)* **MILLION MILES AWAY / STARING AT THE SUN (live)** [21] [–]
(cd-s+=) *(671408-2)* – Sin city / ('A'video).
(cd-s) *(671408-5)* – ('A'side) / Dammit, I changed again (live) / Bad habit (live).

Dec 01. (cd-s) *<672212>* **DEFY YOU / ONE HUNDRED PUNKS / SELF ESTEEM / WANT YOU BAD** [–] [77]

Dec 03. (cd) *(512201-2)* *<89026>* **SPLINTER** [74] [30]
– Neocon / The noose / Long way home / Hit that / Race against myself / (Can't get my) Head around you / The worst hangover ever / Never gonna find me / Lightning rod / Spare me the details / Da hui / When you're in prison.
(above set climbed to UK No.27 in Jan'04)

Mike OLDFIELD

Born: 15 May'53, Reading, England. He started playing guitar at the age of seven, and by 1968, had formed SALLYANGIE with sister SALLY. They signed to folk-orientated label, 'Transatlantic', who issued the lp, 'CHILDREN OF THE SUN'. After releasing a single, 'TWO SHIPS' / 'COLOURS OF THE WORLD', in September '69, they split their partnership to concentrate on other projects. Following a spell in the short-lived BAREFOOT, MIKE became the bassist for KEVIN AYERS' band, The WHOLE WORLD, in March 1970, subsequently appearing on two albums, 'SHOOTING AT THE MOON' and 'WHATEVERSHEBRINGSWESING', between 1971 and 1972. Around this time, MIKE started work on his own solo project, gaining financial support in 1972 from Richard Branson's newly formed 'Virgin' label (the same year, he also contributed session work for EDGAR BROUGHTON BAND and DAVID BEDFORD). 'TUBULAR BELLS' finally saw the light of day in May '73, immediately garnering critical acclaim from the music press. A near 50-minute concept piece, overdubbed many times by multi-instrumentalist, MIKE, it went into the Top 3 a year later. Aided by a surprise US Top 10 single (an album excerpt) used in the horror movie, 'The Exorcist', 'TUBULAR BELLS' repeated the feat Stateside. In September '74, his follow-up, 'HERGEST RIDGE', was completed, going straight in at No.1. Critically lambasted by some commentators as "Son of Tubular Bells", it only managed to hit No.87 in America, OLDFIELD coming in for further flak as an orchestral Tubular Bells (conducted by DAVID BEDFORD) was panned by the rock press. The period between 1975 and 1978 saw him branch into African and folk-type origins on the albums, 'OMMADAWN' and 'INCANTATIONS', although at the same time, he embarrassed his rock following by releasing mainly festive hit 45's. Nevertheless, his contribution to the 70's, in terms of both the classical and rock fields, was arguably only matched by PINK FLOYD. The early 80's brought OLDFIELD a succession of more mainstream pop/rock albums, culminating with 1983's Top 10 'CRISES' album, which spawned his biggest ever hit single, 'MOONLIGHT SHADOW' (it featured the celestial vocal chords of MAGGIE REILLY, a member of his band and new co-writing team). Surprisingly, his next single, 'SHADOW ON THE WALL', bombed, although it did succeed in raising the profile of ex-FAMILY frontman, ROGER CHAPMAN. OLDFIELD continued to achieve reasonable chart success throughout the remainder of the decade, even scoring the soundtrack to classic Vietnam movie, 'THE KILLING FIELDS'. Although he never quite regained the ground he had broken with his debut, he nevertheless returned in 1992 with a belated "follow-up" in the form of the almost identical, but still appealing, 'TUBULAR BELLS II'. This seemed to breathe more life into OLDFIELD's flagging career, 1996's 'VOYAGER' taking on the "space-race" theme. Another update of his most famous work, 'TUBULAR BELLS III' (1998), even returned him to the UK Top 5, Eastern-styled vocalist, AMAR, lending a soothing touch to a handful of tracks. Two further offerings in 1999, 'GUITARS' and 'THE MILLENNIUM BELL', were equally new age and thematic. The instrumental wizard attempted to wring yet more mileage out of his most famous work with 'TUBULAR BELLS 2003', a largely unnecessary revision of the original with endless, misguided thematic variations (from "Latin" to "Thrash" to "Jazz") on Part One. The variations on Part Two were admittedly more interesting, while John Cleese again added his dry, dulcit tones. • **Covered:** SAILOR'S HORNPIPE (trad.) / IN DULCE JUBILO (R.L. Pearsall) / WILLIAM TELL OVERTURE (Korsokov) / BLUE PETER (BBC copyright) / ARRIVAL (Abba) / WONDERFUL LAND (Shadows) / ETUDE (Franscisco Tarrega). • **Trivia:** In the mid-70's, MIKE also had time to session on albums by Virgin artists; DAVID BEDFORD (Star's End) / ROBERT WYATT (Rock Bottom) / TOM NEWMAN (Fine Old Tom). MIKE's sister, SALLY, also went on to have a UK Top 20 hit with, 'MIRRORS' (late '78).

Album rating: TUBULAR BELLS (*10) / HERGEST RIDGE (*7) / THE ORCHESTRAL TUBULAR BELLS (*6) / OMMADAWN (*8) / INCANTATIONS (*8) / EXPOSED (*4) / PLATINUM (*4) / QE2 (*4) / FIVE MILES OUT (*6) / CRISES (*6) / DISCOVERY (*4) / THE KILLING FIELDS soundtrack (*6) / THE COMPLETE MIKE OLDFIELD compilation (*7) / ISLANDS (*4) / EARTH MOVING (*4) / HEAVEN'S OPEN (*4) / TUBULAR BELLS II (*6) / ELEMENTS: THE BEST OF MIKE OLDFIELD compilation (*7) / THE SONGS OF DISTANT EARTH (*4) / VOYAGER (*4) / XXV: THE BEST OF MIKE OLDFIELD compilation (*6) / TUBULAR BELLS III (*5) / GUITARS (*4) / THE MILLENNIUM BELL (*3) / TUBULAR BELLS 2003 (*4)

MIKE OLDFIELD – guitar, bass, multi / except **TOM NEWMAN** – guitar / **JON FIELD** – flute / **STAN BROUGHTON** – drums / **LINDSAY COOPER** – wind; plus master of ceremonies, **VIVIAN STANSHALL** (ex-BONZO DOG BAND)

Virgin Virgin

May 73. (lp/c) *(T/TCV 2001)* *<105>* **TUBULAR BELLS** [1] Nov73 [3]
– Tubular bells (side 1) / Tubular bells (side 2). *(hit top Oct74) (iss.quad-lp.Jul74; QV 2001) (pic-lp Dec78; VP 2001) (cd-iss. Jun83; CDV 2001); hit UK No.28) (re-iss. Feb97 on 'E.M.I.'; LPCENT 18) (cd re-mast.May98; CDVX 2001)*

Feb 74. (7") *<55100>* **TUBULAR BELLS (edit). / TUBULAR BELLS (excerpt)** [–] [7]

Jun 74. (7") *(VS 101)* **MIKE OLDFIELD'S SINGLE (theme from Tubular Bells). / FROGGY WENT A-COURTIN'** [31] [–]

— now with **TERRY OLDFIELD** – wind / etc.

Sep 74. (lp/c) *(V/TCV 2013)* *<109>* **HERGEST RIDGE** [1] [87]
– Hergest ridge (side 1) / Hergest ridge (side 2). *(re-iss. Apr86 lp/c; OVED/+C 163) (cd-iss. Apr86; CDV 2013)*

Jan 75. (lp/c) *(V/TCV 2026)* **THE ORCHESTRAL TUBULAR BELLS (WITH THE ROYAL PHILHARMONIC ORCHESTRA)** (live & conducted by DAVID BEDFORD with guitar by OLDFIELD) [17] [–]
– The orchestral Tubular Bells part 1 / The orchestral Tubular Bells part 2. *(cd-iss. Jul87; CDV 2026) (re-iss. Sep89 on 'VIP-Virgin' lp/c/cd; VVIP/+C/D 101)*

Feb 75. (7") *(VS 112)* **DON ALFONSO. / IN DULCE JUBILO** [ ] [–]

— back-up were **JUBULA** (African musicians) / **PIERRE MOERLEN** (of GONG) / backing vocals by sister **SALLY OLDFIELD + CLODAGH SIMMONDS**

Nov 75. (lp/c) *(V/TCV 2043)* *<33913>* **OMMADAWN** [4] [ ]
– Ommadawn (side 1) / Ommadawn (side 2). *(quad-lp Feb76; QV 2043) (cd-iss. 1986; CDV 2043) (cd re-iss. Apr97 on 'Virgin-VIP'; CDVIP 185)*

Nov 75. (7") *(VS 131)* **IN DULCI JUBILO. / ON HORSEBACK** [4] [–]

Nov 75. (7") *<9508>* **OMMADAWN (excerpt). / ON HORSEBACK** [–] [ ]

Oct 76. (7") *(VS 163)* **PORTSMOUTH. / SPEAK (THO' YOU ONLY SAY FAREWELL)** [3] [–]

Nov 76. (7") *<9510>* **PORTSMOUTH. / ALGIERS** [–] [ ]

Feb 77. (7") *(VS 167)* **THE WILLIAM TELL OVERTURE. / ALGIERS** [ ] [–]

Dec 77. (7") *(VS 198)* **THE CUCKOO SONG. / PIPE TUNE** [ ] [–]

— added from last album; (see most musicians from following live album)

Nov 78. (d-lp/d-c) *(VDT/TCVDT 101)* **INCANTATIONS** [14] [–]
– Incantations (part 1) / Incantations (part 2) / Incantations (part 3) / Incantations (part 4). *(cd-iss. Feb87; CDVD 101); omits last of 4 minutes side 3) (re-iss. Apr92 cd/c; OVED CD/C 417)*

Apr 79. (7") *(VS 245)* **GUILTY. / INCANTATIONS (excerpt)** [22] [–]
(12"blue) *(VS 245-12)* – ('A'side) / Guilty (live).

— MIKE with **PIERRE MOERLEN** – drums, percussion / **RINGO McDONOUGH** – bodhran / **MIKE FRYE, BENOIT MOERLEN, DAVID BEDFORD** (also string arrangements) / **NICO RAMSDEN** – guitar / **PHIL BEER** – guitar, vocals / **PEKKA POHJOLA** – bass / **RAY GAY, RALPH IZEN, SIMO SALMINEN, COLIN MOORE** – trumpets / **SEBASTIAN BELL, CHRIS NICHOLLS** – flutes / **PETE LEMER, TIM CROSS** – keyboards / **MADDY PRIOR** – vocals / **JONATHAN KAHAN, DICK STUDT, BEN CRUFT, JANE PRYCE, LIZ EDWARDS, NICOLA HURTON** – violins / **VANESSA PARK, DAVID BUCKNALL, JESSICA FORD, NIGEL WARREN-GREEN** – cellos / **NICK WORTERS, JOE KIRBY** – bass / **DON McVAY, PAULINE MACK, DANNY DAGGERS, MELINDA DAGGERS, LIZ BUTLER, ROSS COHEN** – vocals, plus 11 piece choir.

Aug 79. (d-lp/d-c) *(VD/TCVD 2511)* **EXPOSED (live)** [16] [–]
– Incantations (parts 1 and 2) / Incantations (parts 3 and 4) / Tubular bells (part 1) / Tubular bells (part 2) / Guilty. *(d-cd-iss. Jul86; CDVD 2511)*

— trimmed backing group down.

Nov 79. (7") *(VS 317)* **BLUE PETER. / WOODHENGE** [19] [–]

Dec 79. (lp/c) *(V/TCV 2141)* **PLATINUM** [24] [–]
– Platinum:- Airborne – Platinum – Charleston North star – Platimun finale / Woodhenge / Sally / Punkadiddle / I got rhythm. *(cd-iss. 1986; CDV 2141) (re-iss. 1989 lp/c; OVED/C 233)*

— next featured **PHIL COLLINS** – drums

Virgin Epic

Sep 80. (7") *(VS 374)* **ARRIVAL. / POLKA** [ ] [–]

Oct 80. (lp/c) *(V/TCV 2181)* *<FE 37358>* **QE2** [27] [ ]
– Taurus I / Sheba / Conflict / Arrival / Wonderful land / Mirage / QE2 / Celt / Molly. *(cd-iss. 1986; CDV 2181) (re-iss. 1989 lp/c; OVED/+C 235)*

Nov 80. (7") *(VS 387)* **SHEBA. / WONDERFUL LAND** [ ] [–]

Dec 80. (d-lp/d-c) <13143> **AIRBORNE** [–] [ ]
– (see PLATINUM tracks, except 'Guilty' repl. – / / Tubular bells live part 1 / Incantations (segue of 20+ mins. studio and live recordings)

— MIKE brought in **MAGGIE REILLY** – vocals (ex-CADO BELLE) / **TIM CROSS** – keyboards / **MORRIS PERT** – percussion, drums (ex-BRAND X) / **RICK FENN** – bass, guitar / **PIERRE MOERLEN** – drums, percussion returned to repl. MIKE FRYE / added **TIM RENWICK** – bass, guitar

Mar 82. (7"/7"pic-d) *(VS/+Y 464)* **FIVE MILES OUT. / LIVE PUNKADIDDLE** [43] [ ]

Mar 82. (lp/c) *(V/TCV 2222)* *<FE 37983>* **FIVE MILES OUT** [7] [ ]
– Taurus II / Family man / Orabidoo / Mount Teidi / Five miles out. *(cd-iss. 1983; CDV 2222) (re-iss. Apr90 lp/c; OVED/+C 293) (re-iss. Oct94 on 'Virgin-VIP' cd/c;)*

Virgin Virgin

Jun 82. (7"/7"pic-d) *(VS/+Y 489)* *<02877>* **FAMILY MAN. / MOUNT TEIDI** [45] [ ]

Sep 82. (7"/7"pic-d) *(VS/+Y 541)* **MISTAKE. / WALDBERG (THE PEAK)** [ ] [–]

— MIKE retained REILLY + MOERLEN. New members were **SIMON PHILLIPS** – drums / **PHIL SPALDING** – bass / **GRAEME PLEETH** – keyboards / **SIMON HOUSE** – violin

May 83. (7"/7"pic-d)(12") *(VS/+Y 586)(VS 586-12)* **MOONLIGHT SHADOW. / RITE OF MAN** [4] [ ]

May 83. (cd/c/lp) *(CD/TC+/V 2262)* **CRISES** [6] [–]
– Crises / Moonlight shadow / In high places / Foreign affair / Taurus III / Shadow on the wall. *(re-iss. Mar91 cd/c; OVED CD/C 351) (re-iss. May94 on 'Virgin-VIP' cd/c; CD/TC VIP 118)*
(below vocals by ROGER CHAPMAN, ex-FAMILY)

Sep 83. (7"/ext.12") *(VS 625/+12)* **SHADOW ON THE WALL. / TAURUS III** [ ] [ ]

Jan 84. (7"/ext.12") *(VS 648/+12)* **CRIME OF PASSION. / JUNGLE GARDENIA** [61] [ ]

— retained **REILLY, PHILLIPS + SPALDING** – adding guitar / plus **BARRY PALMER** – vocals / **MICKEY SIMMONDS** – keyboards / **HAROLD ZUSCHRADER** – synth.

Jun 84. (7") *(VS 686)* **TO FRANCE. / IN THE POOL** [48] [ ]
(ext.12"+=) *(VS 686-12)* – Bones.

Jul 84. (cd/c/lp) *(CD/TC+/V 2308)* **DISCOVERY** [15] [–]
– To France / Poison arrows / Crystal gazing / Tricks of the light / Discovery / Talk about your life / Saved by a bell / The lake. *(re-iss. Apr92 cd/c; OVED CD/C 421)*

Sep 84. (7") *(VS 707)* **TRICKS OF THE LIGHT. / APEMAN** [ ] [ ]
(12"+=) *(VS 707-12)* – ('A'instrumental).

Nov 84. (7"/ext.12") *(VS 731/+12)* **ETUDE. / EVACUATION** [ ] [ ]

Dec 84. (cd/c/lp) *(CD/TC+/V 2328)* **THE KILLING FIELDS (Soundtrack)** [97] [ ]
– Pran's theme / Requiem for a city / Evacuation / Pran's theme 2 / Capture / Execution / Bad news / Pran's departure / Worksite / The year zero / Blood sucking / The year zero 2 / Pran's escape – The killing fields / The trek / The boy's burial – Pran sees the red cross / Good news / Etude. *(re-iss. Jun88 lp/c; OVED/+C 183)*

— **ANITA HEGERLAND + ALED JONES** – vocals repl. REILLY

Nov 85. (7") *(VS 836)* **PICTURES IN THE DARK. / LEGEND** [50] [ ]
(ext.12") *(VS 836-12)* – The trap.

Apr 86. (7"/7"sha-pic-d)(ext.12") *(VS/+S 863)(VS 863-12)* **SHINE. / THE PATH** [ ] [ ]

May 87. (7") *(VS 955)* **IN HIGH PLACES. / POISON ARROWS** [ ] [–]
(12"+=) *(VS 955-12)* – Jungle Gardenia.

— vocalists – **JON ANDERSON / KEVIN AYERS / BONNIE TYLER**

Sep 87. (7") *(VS 990)* **ISLANDS. / THE WIND CHIMES (part one)** [ ] [ ]
(c-s+=/ext.12"+=)(cd-s+=) *(VS/+C 990-12)(CDEP 6)* – When the night's on fire.

Oct 87. (cd/c/lp) *(CD/TC+/V 2466)* *<90645>* **ISLANDS** [29] [ ]
– The wind chimes (parts 1 & 2) / Islands / Flying start / North point / Magic touch / The time has come. *(cd+=)* – When the night's on fire. *(re-iss. Apr92 cd/c; OVED CD/C 418)*

Nov 87. (7") *(VS 1013)* **THE TIME HAS COME. / (final extract from) THE WIND CHIMES** [ ] [–]
(12"+=) *(VS 1013-12)* – ('A'original mix).

Nov 87. (7") **MAGIC TOUCH. / THE WIND CHIMES (part 1)** [–] [ ]

Feb 88. (7"/12") *(VS 1047/+12)* **FLYING START. / THE WIND CHIMES (part 2)** [ ] [ ]

Jul 89. (7") *(VS 1189)* **EARTHMOVING. / BRIDGE TO PARADISE** [ ] [ ]
(12"+=/cd-s+=) *(VS T/CD 1189)* – ('A'disco mix).

Jul 89. (cd/c/lp) *(CD/TC+/V 2610)* **EARTHMOVING** [30] [–]
– Holy / Hostage / Far country / Innocent / Runaway son / See the light / Earthmoving / Blue night / Nothing but – Bridge to Paradise. *(re-iss. Apr92 cd/c; OVED CD/C 420) (cd re-iss. Apr97 on 'Virgin-VIP'; CDVIP 169)*

Oct 89. (7") *(VS 1214)* **INNOCENT. / EARTHMOVING (club mix)** [ ] [ ]
(12"+=/cd-s+=) *(VS T/CD 1214)* – ('A'extended).

Jun 90. (cd/c/lp) *(CD/TC+/V 2640)* **AMAROK** [49] [–]
– Amarok (part 1) / Amarok (part 2). *(re-iss. Apr92 cd/c; OVED CD/C 422)*

— with **SIMON PHILLIPS** – drums / **DAVE LEVY** – bass / **MICKEY SIMMONDS** – keyboards / **ANDY LONGHURST** – keyboards / **COURTNEY PINE** – sax

Jan 91. (7"/12"/cd-s; as MICHAEL OLDFIELD) **HEAVEN'S OPEN. / EXCERPT FROM AMAROK** [ ] [–]

Feb 91. (cd/c/lp; as MICHAEL OLDFIELD) *(CD/TC+/V 2653)* **HEAVEN'S OPEN** [ ] [–]
– Make make / No dream / Mr. Shame / Gimme back / Heaven's open / Music from the balcony. *(re-iss. Apr92 cd/c; OVED CD/C 419)*

— solo playing most instruments, except some guests & a bagpipe band.

W.E.A. Reprise

Sep 92. (cd)(lp/c) *(4509 90618-2)(WX 2002/+C)* *<45041>* **TUBULAR BELLS II** [1] [ ]
– Sentinel / Dark star / Clear light / Blue saloon / Sunjammer / Red dawn / The bell / Weightless / The great pain / Sunset door / Tattoo / Altered state / Maya gold / Moonshine.

Sep 92. (7"/c-s/cd-s) *(YZ 698/+C/CD)* **SENTINEL (SINGLE RESTRUCTION). / EARLY STAGES** [10] [–]

Dec 92. (7"/c-s) *(YZ 708/+C)* **TATTOO. / SILENT NIGHT / SENTINEL (live)** [33] [–]
(cd-ep+=) *(YZ 708CD)* – Live At Edinburgh Castle:- Moonshine / Reprise / Maya gold.

Apr 93. (7"/c-s) *(YZ 737/+C)* **THE BELL. / SENTINEL** [50] [–]
(cd-s+=) *(YZ 737CD)* – ('A'-3 mixes).
(cd-s) *(YZ 737CDX)* – (5-'A'mixes).

Nov 94. (cd/c) *(<4509 98581-2/-4>)* **THE SONGS OF DISTANT EARTH** [24] Jan96 [ ]
– In the beginning / Let there be light / Supernova / Magellan / First landing / Oceania / Only time will tell / Prayer for the Earth / Lament for Atlantis / The chamber / Hibernaculum / Tubular world / The shining ones / Crystal clear / The sunken forest / Ascension / A new beginning. *(re-iss. Oct95; same)*

Dec 94. (c-s) *(YZ 871C)* **HIBERNACULUM / MOONSHINE** [47] [–]
(cd-s+=) *(YZ 871CDX)* – Solution hoedown / Jungle.
(cd-s) *(YZ 871CD)* – ('A'side) / The spectral army / The song of the boat men.

Aug 95. (c-s) *(YZ 880C)* **LET THERE BE LIGHT (Indian Lake mix) / LET THERE BE LIGHT (BT's entropic dub)** [51] [–]
(12") *(YZ 880T)* – ('A'-BT's pure luminescence remix) / ('A'-Hardfloor mix) / ('A'club mix).
(cd-s) *(YZ 880CD)* – (above club mix) repl.by – ('A'-Ultraviolet mix).

Sep 96. (cd/c) *(0630 15896-2/-4)* *<46487>* **VOYAGER** [12] [ ]
– The song of the sun / Celtic rain / The hero / Women of Ireland / The voyager / She moves through the fair / Dark island / Wild goose flaps its wings / Flowers of the forest / Mont St Michel.

Mar 97. (c-s) *(WEA 093C)* **WOMEN OF IRELAND / ('A'mix)** [ ] [–]
(12"+=/cd-s+=) *(WEA 093 T/CD)* – Mike's reel.
(re-iss. Nov97 hit No.70; same)

Nov 97. (cd/c) *(3984 21218-2/-4)* **XXV (THE BEST OF MIKE OLDFIELD)** (compilation) [ ] [–]
– Tubular bells / Hergest ridge / Ommadawn / Incantation / Moonlight shadow / Portsmouth / The killing fields / Sentinel (Tubular bells II) / The bell / Let there be light / Only time will tell / The voyager / Women of Ireland.

Aug 98. (cd/c) *(<3984 24349-2/-4>)* **TUBULAR BELLS III** [4] Sep98 [ ]
– The source of secrets / The watchful eye / Jewel in the crown / Outcast / Serpent dream / The inner child / Man in the rain / The top of the morning / Moonwatch / Secrets / Far above the clouds.

Oct 98. (c-s) *(WEA 194C)* **MAN IN THE RAIN / THE INNER CHILD (live)** [ ] [–]
(cd-s+=) *(WEA 194CD)* – Serpent's dream (live).

Apr 99. (12"/cd-s) *(WEA 206 T/CD1)* **FAR ABOVE THE CLOUDS / (mixes)** [53] [–]
(cd-s) *(WEA 206CD2)* – ('A'mixes).

May 99. (cd) *(<3984 27401-2>)* **GUITARS** [40] [ ]
– Muse / Cochise / Embers / Summit day / Out of sight / B blues / Four winds / Enigmatism / Out of mind / From the ashes.

Nov 99. (cd/c) *(<8573 80885-2/-4>)* **THE MILLENNIUM BELL** [ ] [ ]
– Peace on Earth / Pacha mama / Santa Maria / Sunlight shining through cloud / Doge's palace / Lake Constance / Mastermind / Broad sunlit uplands / Liberation / Amber light / The millennium bell.

May 03. (cd) <(2564 60204-2)> **TUBULAR BELLS 2003** [51] [ ]
– Part one: Introduction / Fast guitars / Basses / Latin / A minor tune / Blues / Thrash / Jazz / Ghost bells / Russian / Finale / Part two: Harmonics / Peace / Bagpipe guitars / Caveman / Ambient guitars / The sailor's hornpipe. *(ltd-cd w/dvd+=; 0927 49921-2)* – (mixes + video).

– compilations, etc. –

—— on 'Virgin' unless otherwise mentioned

Nov 76. (4xlp-box) *(VBOX 1)* **BOXED** [22] [–]
– (TUBULAR BELLS / HERGEST RIDGE / OMMADAWN / + COLLABORATIONS (singles, etc.) *(re-iss. 1985 4xlp/4xc; VBOX/TCVX 1) (4xcd-box Jul87; CDBOX 1)*

Dec 78. (7"ep/12"ep) *(VS/+T 238)* **TAKE 4** [72] [–]
– Portsmouth / In dulce jubilo / Wrekorder wrondo / Sailor's hornpipe.

Oct 85. (cd/c/d-lp) *(CD/C+/MOC 1)* **THE COMPLETE MIKE OLDFIELD** [36] [–]
– Arrival / In dulce jubilo / Portsmouth / Jungle gardenia / Guilty / Blue Peter / Waldberg (the peak) / Etude / Wonderful land / Moonlight shadow / Family man / Mistake / Five miles out / Crime of passion / To France / Shadow on the wall / Excerpt from Tubular Bells / Sheba / Mirage / Platinum / Mount Tiede / Excerpt from Ommadawn / Excerpt from Hergest Ridge / Excerpt from Incantations / Excerpt from Killing Fields.

Jun 88. (3"cd-ep) *(CDT 7)* **MOONLIGHT SHADOW (extended) / RITE OF MAN / TO FRANCE / JUNGLE GARDENIA** [ ] [–]

Jun 88. (cd-video) *(080446-1)* **THE WIND CHIMES (Soundtrack 1986)** [ ] [–]

Nov 90. (3xcd-box) *(TPAK 15)* **COLLECTORS' EDITION** [ ] [–]
– (THE ORCHESTRAL TUBULAR BELLS / OMMADAWN / HERGEST RIDGE)

Nov 90. (3xcd-box) *(TPAK 16)* **COLLECTORS' EDITION** [ ] [–]
– (QE2 / PLATINUM / FIVE MILES OUT)

Dec 90. (7"/c-s) **ETUDE. / GAKKAEN** [ ] [–]
(12"+=/cd-s+=) – ('A'extended) (with "ONO GAGUKU KAI").

—— (The above 'A'side was now used on TV ad for 'Nurofen'.)

Sep 93. (cd/c/d-lp) *(VT CD/MC/LP 18)* **ELEMENTS: THE BEST OF MIKE OLDFIELD** [5] [ ]
– Tubular bells – opening theme / Family man / Moonlight shadow / Heaven's open / Five miles out / To France / Foreign affair / In dulce jubilo / Shadow on the wall / Islands / Etude / Sentinel / Ommadawn – excerpt / Incantations part four – excerpt / Amarok – excerpt / Portsmouth.

Sep 93. (4xcd-box) *(CDBOX 2)* **ELEMENTS – MIKE OLDFIELD 1973-1991** [ ] [ ]
– (all TUBULAR BELLS & other album excerpts, plus singles to 1991)

Oct 93. (c-s) *(VSC 1477)* **MOONLIGHT SHADOW / MOONLIGHT SHADOW (extended version)** [52] [ ]
(cd-s+=) *(VSCDT 1477)* – In The Pool (Instrumental) / Bones (Instrumental).

Nov 93. (c-ep/cd-ep) **THE MIKE OLDFIELD CHRISTMAS EP** [ ] [–]
– In dulci jubilo / Portsmouth / etc.

Mar 99. (3xcd-box) *Disky; (HR 85458-2)* **MIKE OLDFIELD VOL.1** [ ] [ ]

Mar 99. (3xcd-box) *Disky; (HR 85459-2)* **MIKE OLDFIELD VOL.2** [ ] [ ]

Jun 01. (cd) *(CDV 2936)* **THE BEST OF TUBULAR BELLS** [60] [–]
– Tubular bells (part 1) / Sentinel / The bell / Far above the clouds / The millennium bell / Tubular bells (part 2).

Will OLDHAM

Born: Louisville, Kentucky, USA. OLDHAM was raised by a large family (later his brothers would join him in THE PALACE BROTHERS) and began his dark, revered career as an actor in John Sayles' 1987 mining vehicle 'Matewan'. After a few more made-for-TV movies, and a role in another bleedin' mining film, the repressed hillbilly for the 90's (at times compared to BECK!) photographed the front cover for SLINT's 'Spiderland', and for his troubles was awarded the assistance of McMAHAN and WALFORD on his debut album 'THERE IS NO ONE WHAT WILL TAKE CARE OF YOU' (1993). A deep crooner by nature, OLDHAM, eased his way (however unsteady he sounds on guitar), into insular tales of death, sex and er . . . death in a small town community. Several country/gospel/folk albums appeared around 1992/3; the return to basics, 'PALACE' (1994) and 'VIVA LAST BLUES' (1995), showed a marked improvement in song structure and production value. Having drifted between 'Drag City' in the US and 'Domino' in the UK, PALACE made one last attempt at sounding sadder and deeper than LEONARD COHEN ('ARISE THEREFORE'), before OLDHAM persevered under his own name, releasing the, at times, unlistenable 'JOYA' (1997) and the rarities collection 'LOST BLUES AND OTHER SONGS' (also '97). Perhaps his most remarkable contribution to the music scene, 'I SEE A DARKNESS' (1999), was issued under the alias BONNIE 'PRINCE' BILLY, and saw OLDHAM take comic twists and turns throughout the set (sending his image up on an alarming scale). The album, recorded in a nondescript house, played like a beautiful ode to the Greek tragedy, whilst managing to substain a 'live' feel throughout. 'DEATH TO EVERYONE', possibly the finest track, was so bleak and sombre that it could quite literally make one roll around the ground with laughter by its sheer piss-take alone. His humour was further in evidenced on the sharp and commercially viable 'EASE DOWN THE ROAD' (2001), under the aforementioned BONNIE 'PRINCE' BILLY nom de plume. The set, mainly comprised of melancholy love songs, boasting a tight collective of musicians (namely CATHERINE IRWIN, DAVID PAJO, JON THEODORE and arty film-maker HARMONY KORINE) to accompany an even brighter, if not mellower interpretation of OLDHAM's troubled persona. Stand-out tracks included the poetic 'A KING AT NIGHT', 'JUST TO SEE MY HOLLY HOME', which sounded suspiciously like a church choir jamboree and the fleeting title track, with its banjos et al. A new lyrical direction was also present; gone were the morbid Sunday afternoon trials and tribulations of OLDHAM's psyche, these being replaced with affectionate, if not downright rude stanzas heir to ARAB STRAP or the POGUES. No wonder JOHNNY CASH is a fan. The BONNIE PRINCE returned triumphant in 2003 with the stripped-bare 'MASTER AND EVERYONE', aguably his greatest achievement in music to date. Consisting of ten skeletal songs, OLDHAM's Kentucky neo-romantic alter-ego was beginning to make sense; it's rare to find an album of near perfection where every track is outstanding, and it was certainly true in this case. From the lush opener 'THE WAY' to the graceful backwoods haunt of 'WOLF AMONG WOLVES', musically and lyrically the album was in every way a finely-tuned masterpiece. Recruiting LAMBCHOP's guitarist and producer MARK NEVERS, plus roots singer MARY SLAYTON, it was equally about the subtle atmosphere created (especially NEVERS' weird spacy guitar effects) than it was about OLDHAM's beautifully poetic lyrics and flawless musical ark. We hear musicians creeping around in the background, OLDHAM tapping his foot on the floor to keep time, the deep wheezing of a pump organ – there's even a song dedicated to PJ HARVEY. All in all, a majestic and intrinsically sublime set, and, even though it may be foolish to compare BILLY to NICK DRAKE, this is the closest thing we'll get to the spare melodic greatness of 'Pink Moon' this side of the new century. OLDHAM is certainly a prince among paupers.

Album rating: Palace: THERE IS NO-ONE WHAT WILL TAKE CARE OF YOU (*8) / PALACE – DAYS IN THE WAKE (*6) / VIVA LAST BLUES (*7) / ARISE THEREFORE (*7) / LOST BLUES AND OTHER SONGS collection (*8) / Will Oldham: JOYA (*6) / ODE MUSIC mini (*4) / GUARAPERO: LOST BLUES 2 collection (*5) / Bonnie 'Prince' Billy: I SEE A DARKNESS (*8) / EASE DOWN THE ROAD (*8) / MORE REVERY mini (*6) / MASTER AND EVERYONE (*9)

PALACE BROTHERS

WILL OLDHAM – vocals, guitar / with **BRIAN McMAHAN** – guitar (of SQUIRREL BAIT and SLINT) / **BRITT WALFORD** – drums (of SLINT)

Big Cat — Drag City

May 93. (7") *(ABB 51S)* *<DC 25>* **OHIO RIVER BOAT SONG. / DRINKING WOMAN** [ ] [ ]

Jun 93. (lp/cd) *(ABB/+CD 050)* *<DC 34>* **THERE IS NO-ONE WHAT WILL TAKE CARE OF YOU** [ ] [ ]
– Idle hands are the Devil's playthings / Long before / I tried to stay healthy for you / The cellar song / Pulpit / There is no-one what will take care of you / O Lord are you in need / Merida / King me / I had a good mother and father / Riding / O Paul. *(UK-lp re-iss. Jun97; same as US) (cd re-iss. Jan01 on 'Domino'; REWIGCD 008)*

—— now OLDHAM completely solo

Domino — Drag City

Dec 93. (7") *<DC 37>* **COME IN. / TRUDY LIES** [–] [ ]

May 94. (7") *<DC 47>* **HORSES. / STABLE WILL** [–] [ ]

Jun 94. (cd-ep) *(RUG 21CD)* **COME IN / HORSES / STABLE WILL / TRUDY DIES** [ ] [–]

Sep 94. (cd/c/lp) *(WIG CD/MC/LP 14)* *<DC 50>* **PALACE** <aka 'DAYS IN THE WAKE'> [ ] Aug94 [ ]
– You will miss me when I burn / Pushkin / Come a little dog / I send my love to you / Meaulnes / No more workhouse blues / All is grace / Whither thou goest / (Thou without) Partner / I am a cinemagrapher. *<(re-iss. Dec97 as 'DAYS IN THE WAKE'; same)>*

Jan 95. (m-cd/m-lp; as PALACE SONGS) *(WIG CD/LP 18)* *<DC 57>* **HOPE** [ ] Nov94 [ ]
– Agnes, queen of sorrow / Untitled / Winter lady / Christmastime in the mountains / All gone, all gone / Werner's last blues to blokbuster.

—— with **PAUL OLDHAM** – guitar / **HAYDEN + JOHN STITH** – bass / **GORDON TOWNSEND** – drums

Mar 95. (7") *<DC 61>* **WEST PALM BEACH. / GULF SHORES** [–] [ ]

Jul 95. (7") *<DC 71>* **MOUNTAIN LOW. / (END OF) TRAVELING** [–] [ ]

Aug 95. (12"ep/cd-ep; as PALACE SONGS) *(RUG 35 T/CD)* **THE MOUNTAIN EP** [ ] [–]
– Mountain low / Gulf shores / (End of) Traveling / West Palm Beach.

—— now with **BRYAN RICH** – guitar / **LIAM HAYES** – organ / **JASON LOWENSTEIN** – bass

Aug 95. (cd/c/lp; as PALACE MUSIC) *(WIG CD/MC/LP 21)* *<DC 65 – PR 4>* **VIVA LAST BLUES** [ ] [ ]
– More brothers rides / Viva ultra / Brute choir / Mountain low / Tonight's decision (and thereafter) / Work hard – play hard / New partner / Cat's blues / We all, us three, will ride / Old Jerusalem.

Oct 95. (7") *<DC 64 – PR 1>* **O HOW I ENJOY THE LIGHT. / MARRIAGE** [–] [ ]

—— now simply as PALACE; with **NED OLDHAM** – bass / **DAVID GRUBBS** – piano / **MAYA TONE** – percussion, drums

Apr 96. (cd/c/lp) *(WIG CD/MC/LP 24)* *<DC 88>* **ARISE THEREFORE** [ ] [ ]
– Stablemate / Sucker's evening / Arise therefore / You have cum / Kid of Harith / Sun highlights / the lack in each / No gold digger / Disorder / Group of women / Give me children / Weaker soldier. *(also on ltd-cd; RUG 46CD)*

not iss. — Palace

Jun 96. (7") *<PR 13>* **FOR MEKONS ET AL. / STABLE WILL** [–] [ ]

Drag City — Drag City

Dec 96. (7"; as PALACE MUSIC) *<(DC 91)>* **LITTLE BLUE EYES. / THE SPIDER'S DUDE IS OFTEN THERE** [ ] [ ]

WILL OLDHAM

—— now under his own moniker

Jan 96. (7") *<DC 83>* **EVERY MOTHER'S SON. / NO MORE RIDERS** [–] [ ]

Mar 97. (7") *<(DC 118)>* **PATIENCE. / TAKE HOWEVER LONG YOU WANT** [ ] [ ]

Domino — Drag City

Nov 97. (cd/lp) *(WIG CD/LP 39)* *<DC 107>* **JOYA** [ ] Oct97 [ ]
– O let it be / Antagonism / New gypsy / Under what was oppression / The gator / Open your heart / Richer / Be still and know God (don't be shy) / Apocalypse, no! / I am still what I meant to be / Bolden boke boy / Idea and deed.

Palace — Acuarela

Oct 97. (cd-ep) *(WILL 1CD)* *<AFF 002>* **WESTERN MUSIC** [ ] Mar98 [ ]
– Always bathing in the evening / Western songs for J.L.L. / Three photographs / Jump in jump in, come in come in.

Drag City — Drag City

Jun 98. (12"/cd-s) *<(DC 100/+CD)>* **BLACK/RICH MUSIC** [ ] [ ]
– Do what you will do / Do what you will do / Risen Lord / Allowance / Allowance / Black/rich tune / Black/rich / Do what you will do.

Jun 98. (cd-ep) *<(DC 107X)>* **LITTLE JOYA** [ ] [ ]
– Prologue / Joya / Exit music for a dick.

Jan 00. (m-lp/m-cd) *<(DC 183/+CD)>* **ODE MUSIC** [ ] [ ]
– Ode #1 / Ode #2 / Ode #3 / Ode #4 / Ode #1a / Ode #1b / Ode #2a / Ode #5 / Ode #3a / Ode #4a.

Oct 02. (m-lp; as CONTINENTAL OP) *<(DC 195)>* **SLITCH MUSIC** (original soundtrack) [ ] [ ]

– compilations, etc. –

Apr 97. (cd/d-lp; as PALACE MUSIC) *Domino; (WIG CD/LP 33) / Drag City; <DC 110>* **LOST BLUES AND OTHER SONGS** [ ] [ ]
– Ohio river boat song / Riding / Valentine's day / Trudy dies / Come in / Little blue eyes / Horses / Stable will / Untitled / O how I enjoy the light / Marriage / West Palm Beach / Gulf shores / (End of) Travelling / Lost blues.

Oct 97. (7") *Skingraft; (GR 26)* **SIDES 5-6** [ ] [–]

Feb 00. (cd/lp) *Domino; (WIG CD/LP 74) / Drag City; <40111>* **GUARAPERO: LOST BLUES 2** [ ] [ ]
– Drinking woman / The spider's dude is often there / Gezundheit / Let the wires ring / Big balls / For the mekons et all / Stable Will / Every mother's son / No more rides / The risen Lord / Boy, have you cum / Patience / Take however long you want / Sugarcane juice drinker / Call me a liar / O Lord are you in need?

Jan 02. (one-sided-10"ep+book) *Konkurrent; (907538040-2)* **FOREST TIME** [ ] [–]

Oct 02. (7") *Isota; (SODY 005)* **WE ALL US THREE WILL RIDE. / BARCELONA** [ ] [–]

BONNIE 'PRINCE' BILLY

with **BOB ARELLANO, COLIN GAGON, PAUL OLDHAM + PETER TOWNSEND**

—— session people provided the backing for OLDHAM

not iss. — All City Nomad

Apr 98. (ltd-7"+purple) *<AC 7>* **BLACK DISSIMULATION. / NO SUCH AS WHAT I WANT** [–] [ ]
(UK-iss.Feb00; same as US)

Domino — Palace

May 98. (cd-s; tour) *(RUG 67CD)* **I AM DRINKING AGAIN / DREAMING MY DREAMS** [ ] [–]

Nov 98. (cd-ep) *(RUG 81CD)* **BLUE LOTUS FEET** [ ] [–]
– One with the birds / Southside of the world / When die song / I am the sky / Blue lotus feet / Pole star / Door of my heart.

Jan 99. (cd/lp) *(WIG CD/LP 59)* *<PR 22>* **I SEE A DARKNESS** [ ] [ ]
– A minor place / Nomadic revery (all around) / I see a darkness / Another day full of dread / Death to everyone / Knockturne / Madeleine- Mary / Song for the new breed / Today I was an evil one / Black / Raining in darling.

Jun 99. (7") *<PR 20>* **ONE WITH THE BIRDS. / SOUTHSIDE OF THE WORLD** [–] [ ]

1999. (7"blue) *<SP 462>* **LET'S START A FAMILY (BLACKS). / A WHOREHOUSE IN ANY HOUSE** [–] [ ]

1999. (7") *<LF 075>* **I CONFESS** [–] [ ]

—— <above 2 on 'Sub Pop' & 'Lowfly' – below on 'Western'>

Jul 00. (7"m; as BONNIE "BLUE" BILLY) *(West 009)* **LITTLE BOY BLUE** [ ] [–]
– Little boy blue I / Little boy blue II / Blue boy.

Sep 00. (cd-s; as BONNIE PRINCE BILLY & THE MARQUIS DE TREN) *(RUG 109CD)* *<PR 24>* **GET ON JOLLY** [ ] [ ]
– 2/15 / 25 / 81 / 86 / 64 / 66.

—— MARQUIS DE TREN included **MICK TURNER** (of DIRTY THREE)

Dec 00. (12"ep/cd-ep; as WILL OLDHAM & RYAN MURPHY) *(RUG 117)* *<DC 123>* **ALL MOST HEAVEN** [ ] [ ]
– Fall again / Fall and raise it on / Song of most / Song of all.

Mar 01. (cd) *(WIGCD 89)* *<PR 26>* **EASE DOWN THE ROAD** [ ] Apr01 [ ]
– May it always be / Careless love / A king at night / Just to see my holly

home / At break of day / After I made love to you / Ease down the road / the lion lair / Mrs William / Sheep / Grand dark feeling of emptiness / Rich wife full of happiness. *(w/ free cd-ep+=; WIGCD 89X)* **BONNIE 'PRINCE' BILLY WITH MIKE FELLOWS, JAMES LO, AND MATT SWEENEY** – What's wrong with a zoo / I send my love to you / Stablemate.

Temporary Residence Temporary Residence

Jun 01. (m-cd; as BONNY BILLY) <*(TRR 37)*> **MORE REVERY** ☐ 2000 ☐
– Someone's sleeping / Sweeter than anything / Same love that made me laugh / A dream of the sea / Strange things / Just to see you smile.

Domino Palace

2001. (cd-ep) <*MAP 001*> **GET THE FUCK ON JOLLY LIVE** [–] ☐
– XXV / II-XV / LXXXI / LXXXVI / LXIV / LXVI / XIII / CII.

Jan 03. (cd) *(wigcd 121)* <*pr 29cd*> **MASTER AND EVERYONE** [48] ☐
– The way / Ain't you wealthy, ain't you wise? / Master and everyone / Wolf among wolves / Joy and jubilee / Maundering / Lessons from what's poor / Even if love / Three questions / Hard life.

☐ OL' DIRTY BASTARD (see under ⇒ WU-TANG CLAN)

☐ OMD (see under ⇒ ORCHESTRAL MANOEUVRES IN THE DARK)

☐ 1-SPEED BIKE (see under ⇒ GODSPEED YOU BLACK EMPEROR!)

Yoko ONO

Born: 18 Feb'33, Japan. YOKO moved to New York City at the end of the 40's and was soon writing poems, joining the bohemian set. In the 60's, she branched into art/film making, meeting Beatle JOHN LENNON at one of her exhibitions. After/during his separation from wife Cynthia in 1968, LENNON invited YOKO to spend some time with him, subsequently recording an album together, 'TWO VIRGINS'. Deemed unlistenable by critics, the album's sound was compared to an experimental track on The BEATLES' "White Album", 'REVOLUTION #9' (the record was sold in a brown paper bag due to the cover shot which showed JOHN and YOKO naked), while a similarly uncompromising UNFINISHED MUSIC NO.2 set, 'LIFE WITH THE LIONS', was issued in 1969. She also married JOHN in Gibraltar on the 20th of March '69, subsequently forming The PLASTIC ONO BAND with her new husband and releasing a number of hit singles (e.g. 'GIVE PEACE A CHANCE', 'COLD TURKEY' and 'INSTANT KARMA!'). During this period, The BEATLES had another massive hit with the LENNON-penned 'The Ballad Of John And Yoko', detailing their constant harassment by the press. In a short space of time, the pair had become one of rock's most high profile couples, attracting the attention of the world's media (another dual lp, 'THE WEDDING ALBUM' was released late '69). Early in 1971, she debuted with her first solo album, 'YOKO ONO: PLASTIC ONO BAND', which was soon followed by the extremely weird 'FLY' album. The latter contained the ode to her son, 'DONT WORRY KYOKO', together with the poignant 'MRS. LENNON'. She combined solo activities with her PLASTIC ONO BAND work and an album, 'SOMETIME IN NEW YORK CITY', was trailed by her part in the success of the festive classic, 'HAPPY XMAS (WAR IS OVER)'. Early in 1973, YOKO released what has come to be regarded as her finest hour, 'APPROXIMATELY INFINITE UNIVERSE' (backed by the band, ELEPHANT'S MEMORY), an uncompromising but starkly beautiful piece of proto-feminist rock. With her previous solo albums only managing to scrape a US Top 200 placing, she delivered her fourth set, 'FEELING THE SPACE', a record that fared even worse. Her domestic life was equally rocky at this point, having split with JOHN early in 1974. They reconciled at the end of the year after she watched one of JOHN's famous last performances. She fell pregnant soon after, giving birth to their son, SEAN (coincidentally on JOHN's 35th birthday) on the 9th of October. After a 5-year hiatus from the music business, both were back with the collaborative single, '(JUST LIKE) STARTING OVER'. A JOHN & YOKO album, 'DOUBLE FANTASY', was issued soon after, featuring a welcome return to form on such tracks as LENNON's 'WOMAN', 'BEAUTIFUL BOY' and her own 'KISS KISS KISS'. Tragically, their comeback was short-lived following LENNON's death at the hands of crazed gunman, Mark Chapman on the 8th of December, 1980. Ironically enough, she had her first taste of success soon after, when she hit the singles chart with 'WALKING ON THIN ICE', a prelude to her cross-Atlantic Top 50 album, 'SEASON OF GLASS'. YOKO released two further albums in the 80's, signing to 'Capitol' in 1995 for her comeback, 'RISING', (O No!). She certainly hadn't mellowed with age but 'BLUEPRINT FOR A SUNRISE' (2001) did feature a handful of tracks which approached established rock music forms with influences ranging from funk to reggae.

Album rating: YOKO ONO – PLASTIC ONO BAND (*8) / FLY (*5) / APPROXIMATELY INFINITE UNIVERSE (*4) / FEELING THE SPACE (*4) / SEASONS OF GLASS (*6) / IT'S ALRIGHT (I SEE RAINBOWS) (*5) / STARPEACE (*4) / RISING (*5) / WALKING ON THIN ICE compilation (*7) / BLUEPRINT FOR A SUNRISE (*5)

YOKO ONO – vocals / **JOHN LENNON** – guitar / **KLAUS VOORMAN** – bass / **RINGO STARR** – drums

Apple Apple

Jan 71. (lp) *(SAPCOR 17)* <*3373*> **YOKO ONO – PLASTIC ONO BAND** ☐ ☐
– Why / Why not / Greenfield morning I pushed on empty baby carriage all over the city / AOS / Touch me / Paper shoes. *(cd-iss. Jun97 on 'Rykodisc'+=; RCD 10414)* – Open your box / Something more abstract / The south wind.

— added DEREK & THE DOMINOES musicians featuring ERIC CLAPTON

Oct 71. (7") *(APPLE 38)* <*1839*> **MRS. LENNON. / MIDSUMMER NEW YORK** ☐ ☐

Nov 71. (d-lp) *(SAPTU 101/2)* <*3380*> **FLY** ☐ ☐
– Midsummer New York / Mindtrain / Mind holes / Don't worry Kyoko / Mrs. Lennon / Hirake / Toilet piece – Unknown / O'wind (body is the scar of your mind) / Air male (tone deaf jam) / Don't count the waves / You / Fly / Telephone piece. *<(d-cd-iss. Apr99 on 'Rykodisc'; RCD 1041516)>*

Jan 72. (7") *(APPLE 41)* <*1846*> **MIND TRAIN. / LISTEN THE SNOW IS FALLING** ☐ ☐

— now backed by group ELEPHANT'S MEMORY

Nov 72. (7") <*1853*> **NOW OR NEVER. / MOVE ON FAST** [–] ☐

Feb 73. (d-lp) *(SAPD 01001)* <*3399*> **APPROXIMATELY INFINITE UNIVERSE** ☐ ☐
– Yang Yang / Death of Samantha / I want my love to rest tonight / What did I do! / Have you seen a horizon lately / Approximately infinite universe / Peter the dealer / Song for John / Cat man / What a bastard the world is / Waiting for the sunrise / I felt like smashing my face in a clear glass window / Winter song / Is winter here to stay? / Kite song / What a mess / Shiranakatta (I didn't know) / Air talk / I have a woman inside my soul / Move on fast / Now or never / Looking over from my hotel window. *<(d-cd-iss. Apr 99 on 'Rykodisc'; RCD 1041718)>*

Apr 73. (7") *(APPLE 47)* <*1859*> **DEATH OF SAMANTHA. / YANG YANG** ☐ Feb73 ☐

— now with numerous session people

Nov 73. (7") *(APPLE 48)* **RUN RUN RUN. / MEN MEN MEN** ☐ [–]

Nov 73. (lp) *(SAPCOR 26)* <*3412*> **FEELING THE SPACE** ☐ ☐
– Growing pain / Yellow girl / Coffin car / Woman of Salem / Run run run / If only / A thousand times yes / Straight talk / Angry young woman / She hits back / Woman power / Men men men. *<(cd-iss. Aug97 on 'Rykodisc'; RCD 10419)>*

Dec 73. (7") <*1867*> **WOMAN POWER. / MEN MEN MEN** [–] ☐

— She reunited in 1980 with JOHN LENNON on the album, 'DOUBLE FANTASY'. Sadly this was their last recording together (see above).

Geffen Geffen

Feb 81. (7") *(K 79202)* *<49638>* **WALKING ON THIN ICE. / IT HAPPENED** 35 58
(c-s+=) *(K 79202T)* – Hard times are over.

Jun 81. (lp/c) *(K/K4 99164)* *<2004>* **SEASON OF GLASS** 47 49
– Goodbye sadness / Mindweaver / Even when you're far away / Nobody sees me like you do / Turn of the wheel / Dogtown / Silver horse / I don't know why / Extension 33 / No, no, no / Will you touch me? / She gets down on her knees / Toyboat / Mother of the universe. *<(cd-iss. Aug97 on 'Rykodisc'; RCD 10421)>*

Aug 81. (7") *<2224>* **NO, NO, NO. / WILL YOU TOUCH ME?** –

Polydor Polydor

Feb 82. (7"/12") **NEVER SAY GOODBYE. / LONELINESS** –

Dec 82. (7") *(POSP 541)* **MY MAN. / LET THE TEARS DRY** Nov82

Dec 82. (lp/c) *(POLD/+C 5073)* *<6364>* **IT'S ALRIGHT (I SEE RAINBOWS)** 98
– My man / Never say goodbye / Spec of dust / Loneliness / Tomorrow may never come / It's alright / Wake up / Let the tears dry / Dream love / I see rainbows. *<(cd-iss. Aug97 on 'Rykodisc'+=; RCD 10422)>* – Dream love / Let the tears dry / Wake up.

— Early in 1984, another JOHN & YOKO posthumous album, 'MILK AND HONEY', was released, hitting UK No.3 + US No.11.

Nov 85. (7") **HELL IN PARADISE. / ('A'instrumental)**

Nov 85. (lp/c/cd) *<(827 530-1/-4/-2)>* **STAR PEACE**
– Hell in Paradise / I love all of me / Children power / Rainbow revolution / King of the zoo / Remember raven / Cape Clear / Sky people / You and I / It's gonna rain (living on tiptoe) / Star peace / I love you, Earth. *<(cd re-iss. Aug97 on 'Rykodisc'; RCD 10423)>*
below 2 credited as **YOKO ONO / IMA**

Capitol Capitol

Jan 96. (cd) *(CDEST 2276)* *<35817>* **RISING** Nov95
– Warzone / Wouldnit / Ask the dragon / New York woman / Talking to the universe / Turned the corner / I'm dying / Where do we go from here / Kurushi / Will I / Rising / Goodbye, my love / Revelations.

Jun 96. (cd) *<(CDP 8 37268-0)>* **RISING MIXES**

Oct 01. (cd) *<(5 36035-2)>* **BLUEPRINT FOR A SUNRISE**
– I want you to remember me "A" / I want you to remember me "B" / Is this what we do / Wouldnit "swing" / Soul got out of the box / Rising II / It's time for action! / I'm not getting enough / Mulberry / I remember everything / Are you looking for me?

Parlophone not iss.

Jun 03. (cd-s; as ONO) *(CDMIND 002)* **WALKING ON THIN ICE (the remixes; electro / Pet Shop Boys / Pet Shop Boys 12")** 35 –
(cd-s) *(CDMINDS 002)* – (remixes; Danny Tenaglia walked across the lake / Felix Da Housecat tribute / FKEK vocal).
(12") *(12MIND 002)* – (remixes; Pet Shop Boys / Danny Tenaglia).

– compilations, etc. –

on 'Rykodisc' unless mentioned otherwise

Mar 92. (6xcd-box) *<(RCD 102 24/29)>* **ONOBOX**

May 92. (cd/c) *<(RCD/RAC 20230)>* **WALKING ON THIN ICE** (best of above boxed set)
– Walking on thin ice / Even when you're far away / Kiss kiss kiss / Nobody sees me like you do / Yang yang / No no no / Death of Samantha / Mind weaver / You're the one / Spec of dust / Midsummer New York / Don't be scared / Sleepless nights / Kite song / She gets down on her knees / Give me something / Hell in Paradise / Woman power / O'oh. *(cd re-iss. Mar97; same)*

Aug 97. (cd) *Rykodisc; <(RCD 10420)>* **A STORY**

☐ OPERATION IVY (see under ⇒ RANCID)

☐ 'O'RANG (see under ⇒ TALK TALK)

☐ ORANGE JUICE (see under ⇒ COLLINS, Edwyn)

ORB

Formed: South London, England . . . 1989 by remix supremo and ex-KILLING JOKE roadie Dr. ALEX PATERSON. Working as an A&R bod for ambient label EG (home to he likes of BRIAN ENO), PATTERSON began recording similar ambient sounds in his spare time. He hooked up with the KLF's JIMMY CAUTY in 1988 and recorded an EP, 'KISS', using samples from NEW YORK's Kiss FM. The duo traded under the ORB moniker (which PATTERSON had taken from the WOODY ALLEN sci-fi film 'Sleepers') and released the record the following year on the 'WAU!Mr Modo' label, a joint venture between PATTERSON and ex-KILLING JOKE bassist YOUTH. Around this time the multi-talented PATTERSON was doing a spot of DJ'ing in the chill-out room of PAUL OAKENFOLD's Land of Oz club, where, in a well documented incident, he met STEVE HILLAGE (ex-GONG). The two struck up an immediate friendship (HILLAGE no doubt impressed by the fact that PATTERSON had been spinning one of his old tracks at the time) and a series of mutual collaborations ensued. Meanwhile, the ORB carved out a place in the cobwebbed corners of music history by making what was arguably the first ever ambient dance track, entitled, pause for breath, 'A HUGE EVER GROWING PULSATING BRAIN THAT RULES FROM THE CENTRE OF THE ULTRAWORLD'. The psychedelic/progressive rock influence was glaringly obvious, not only in the overblown title but in the slowly shifting rhythms and tripped-out dub effects. The ORB's heavy use of samples continued, this time running into trouble with MINNIE RIPPERTON's 'LOVING YOU'. Come 1990, the band found themselves in the enviable position of being in-demand remixers and amid their growing reputation released another single, the celestial 'LITTLE FLUFFY CLOUDS'. This time penned by PATTERSON/YOUTH, the single saw the ORB run into sample trauma again, with RICKIE LEE JONES reportedly none too happy that her, frankly, out-of-it sounding tones were used on the single. During the sessions for the single, PATTERSON met a young engineer, THRASH, who would go on to become a fully fledged ORB member in late '91 as a replacement for the recently departed CAUTY. The much anticipated debut album, 'ADVENTURES BEYOND THE ULTRAWORLD', released in April '91 on Big Life, was a sprawling double set of blissed-out almost-beats and shimmering ambience. It was also a catalyst for the burgeoning ambient scene that would spawn the likes of MIXMASTER MORRIS and the APHEX TWIN, the music spilling out of chill-out rooms across the country into fully paid-up ambient club nights. In June '92, the ORB stormed into the top 10 with the 'BLUE ROOM' single. At a record breaking 39 minutes long, it wasn't exactly radio-friendly although the band 'performed' it on Top Of The Pops, sitting nonchalantly playing chess and the act's cult popularity saw the subsequent album, 'UFORB', go straight in at No.1. Following a dispute with YOUTH, PATTERSON signed with Island, fighting a protracted battle for the ORB name which he eventually won. His first release for the label was a live album, imaginatively titled 'LIVE '93', and culled from the legendary ORB stage show at various locations around the globe. A collaboration with German techno exponent THOMAS FEHLMAN resulted in the harder sounding 'POMMEFRITZ' album which included such wonderfully titled tracks as 'MORE GILLS, LESS FISHCAKES'. Another two albums, 'ORBUS TERRARUM' (1995) and 'ORBLIVION' (1997) ploughed similarly obscure furrows and divided critical opinion, although both hit top 20. Along with the likes of PRIMAL SCREAM, the ORB helped define an era, bringing overt psychedelia back into the pop charts and updating the genre for the 90's. The ORB saw a welcome return to their usual spacy laid-back cosmic meanderings via the 2001 release 'CYDONIA' (named after a divison of Mars which astronauts believed was once inhabited by civilisation, mmmm). The only real difference between this and 'ORBLIVION' was the fact that PATERSON recruited two female vocalists; AKI OMORI and NINA WALSH. OMORI took the vocal duties on opener (and Top 40 single) 'ONCE MORE', while WALSH crooned over the spacy lullaby 'PLUM ISLAND'. The album was once again peppered with PATERSON's weirdness and THOMAS FEHLMANN and ANDY HUGHES' floating, almost mainstream production. • **Songwriters:** Most by WESTON and PATERSON. • **Trivia:** The ORB have remixed many including 'Mute' label stars; DEPECHE MODE / ERASURE & WIRE. In 1992, they caused upset in the Asian community by using their religious chants.

Album rating: ADVENTURES BEYOND THE ULTRAWORLD (*9) / U.F.ORB (*9) / LIVE 1993 (*6) / POMMEFRITZ (*6) / ORBUS TERRARUM (*5) / ORBLIVION (*7) / U.F.OFF – THE BEST OF THE ORB compilation (*7) / CYDONIA (*5) / F.F.W.D.: F.F.W.D. collaboration (*6)

ALEX PATERSON – synthesizer, keyboards / with **JIM CAUTY**

Wau! Mr Modo — not iss.

May 89. (ltd.12"ep; as ROCKMAN ROCK & LX DEE) *(MWS 010T)* **KISS EP** [ ] [–]
– Kiss your love / Suck my kiss mix / The roof is on fire / Ambiorix mix.

Oct 89. (12"ep) *(MWS 017T)* **A HUGE EVER GROWING PULSATING BRAIN THAT RULES FROM THE CENTRE OF THE ULTRAWORLD: LOVIN' YOU (Orbital mix). / ('A'bucket and spade mix) / WHY IS 6 SCARED OF 7?** [ ] [–]

Big Life — Mercury

Jun 90. (12"ep) *(BLR 270T)* **(above with new vocals)** [ ] [–]
(cd-ep) *(BLR 270CD)* – (above) / Loving you (ambient house).

Jul 90. (12"ep/cd-ep) *(BLR 27 T/CD)* **(above remixed) / ('A'-9 a.m. radio mix) / ('A'-Aubrey mix I)** [ ] [–]

Nov 90. (7") *(BLR 33)* **LITTLE FLUFFY CLOUDS. / ('A'-Ambient mix Mk.1)** [ ] [–]
(dance mix-12"ep+=/cd-ep+=) *(BLR 33 T/CD)* – Into the fourth dimension (Essenes beyond control).
(12"ep) *(BLR 33R)* – ('A'side) / ('A'-drum & vox version) / Into the fourth dimension.

— In Nov90, they collaborated on STEVE HILLAGE's SYSTEM 7 release 'Sunburst'.

— CAUTY was replaced by **STEVE HILLAGE** – guitar (ex-Solo artist, ex-GONG) / **MIQUETTE GIRAUDY** (ex-GONG) / **ANDY FALCONER**

Apr 91. (d-cd/d-c/d-lp) *(BLR CD/MC/LP 5)* *<511034>* **ADVENTURES BEYOND THE ULTRAWORLD** [29] Nov91 [ ]
– Little fluffy clouds / Earth (Gaia) / Supernova at the end of the universe / Back side of the Moon / Spanish castles in space / Perpetual dawn / Into the fourth dimension / Outlands / Star 6 & 7 8 9 / A huge ever growing pulsating brain that rules from the centre of the Ultraworld.

Jun 91. (7"/c-s) *(BLR 46/+C)* **PERPETUAL DAWN (SOLAR YOUTH). / STAR 6&789 (phase II)** [61] [–]
(cd-ep+=) *(BLR 46CD)* – Perpetual dawn: Solar flare.
(12"ep+=) *(BLRT 46)* – (above version) / ('B'side) / ('A'-Ultrabass 1 mix).
(12"ep) *(BLR 46R)* – ORB IN DUB: Towers of dub (ambient mix) / Perpetual dawn (ultrabass II). *(re-iss. Jan94; same)* – (hit No.18)

— In Nov91, SYSTEM 7 issued another release on '10-Virgin'; 'Miracle'.

Dec 91 (cd/c/lp) *(BLR CD/MC/LP 14) / Caroline; <CAROL 1717>* **THE AUBREY MIXES: THE ULTRAWORLD EXCURSIONS** (deleted after 1 day) [44] [ ]
– Little fluffy clouds / (Pal Joey mix) / Black side of the moon (Steve Hillage remix) / Spanish castles in Spain (Youth remix) / Outlands (Ready made remix) / A huge ever growing pulsating brain (Jim Caldy & Dr. Alex Patterson remix).

— **PATERSON** now with **THRASH (KRISTIAN WESTON)** – guitars, synthesizers, samplers, percussion, plus guests **YOUTH, STUART McMILLAN, GUY PRATT, JAH WOBBLE, STEVE HILLAGE, MIQUETTE GIRAUDY, THOMAS FEHLMANN, GREG HUNTER, ORDE MEIKLE, TOM GREEN, MARNEY PAX.**

Jun 92. (12"ep) *(BLRT 75)* **THE BLUE ROOM (part 1). / (part 2)** [8] [–]
(cd-ep) *(BLRDA 75)* – The blue room (40 minute version).
(cd-ep) *(BLRDB 75)* – The blue room (radio 7) / The blue room (excerpt 605) / Towers of dub (Mad Professor mix).

Jul 92. (d-cd/d-c/t-lp) *(BLR CD/MC/LP 18) <513749>* **UF ORB** [1] [ ]
– O.O.B.E. / U.F. Orb / Blue room / Towers of dub / Close encounters / Majestic / Sticky end. *(free live lp at some shops 'Soundtrack To The Film: ADVENTURES BEYOND THE ULTRAWORLD: PATTERNS & TEXTURES') (re-iss. Apr96 on 'Island; (cd)(c) IMCD 219)(ICM 8033)*

Oct 92. (c-s) **ASSASSIN (the oasis of rhythm mix)** [12] [ ]
(12"ep+=/cd-ep+=) *(BLR T/DA 81)* – U.F. ORB (Bandulu remix).
(cd-ep) *(BLRDB 81)* – ('A'-radio 7 mix) / ('A'-another live version) / ('A'-Chocolate hills of Bohol mix).

Nov 93. (c-ep/12"ep/cd-ep) *(BLR C/T/D 98)* **LITTLE FLUFFY CLOUDS. / ('A'mixes)** [10] [–]

Island — Island

Nov 93. (d-cd/d-c/q-lp) *(CIDD/ICTT/ILPSQ 8022) <535004>* **LIVE 93 (live)** [23] [ ]
– Plateau / The valley / Oobe / Little fluffy clouds / Star 6, 7, 8 & 9 / Towers of dub / Spanish castles in space / The blue room / Perpetual dawn / Assassin / Outlands / A huge ever pulsating brain that rules from the centre of the ultraworld. *(d-cd-iss. Mar97; IMCD 245)*

Jun 94. (cd/c/lp) *(ORB CD/MC/LP 1) <535007>* **POMMEFRITZ** [6] [ ]
– Pommefritz / More gills less fishcakes / We're paste to be grill you / Banger'n'chips / Allers ist schoen / His immortal logness.

— now w /out KRIS WESTON, who was repl. (after 1995 recording by) **ANDY HUGHES**

Mar 95. (cd/cd/c/d-lp) *(CID/CIDX/ICT/ILPSD 8037) <524099>* **ORBUS TERRARUM** [20] Apr95 [ ]
– Valley / Plateau / Oxbow lakes / Montagne d'or (der gute berg) / White river junction / Occidental / Slug dub.

May 95. (c-s) *(CIS 609)* **OXBOW LAKES / ('A'-Everglades mix)** [38] [–]
(12"+=) *(12IS/CID 609)* – ('A'-Sabres No.1 mix).
(12") *(12ISX 609)* – ('A'-Carl Craig psychic pals family wealth plan mix) / ('A'-Evensong string arrangement mix).
(cd-s) *(CIDX 609)* – (all 5 mixes above).

— In Jul'96, the label 'Deviant' released various artists compilation of their mixes 'AUNTIE AUBREY'S EXCURSIONS BEYOND THE CALL OF DUTY'.

— line-up **LX PATERSON / ANDY HUGHES / THOMAS FEHLMANN**

Jan 97. (12"/cd-s) *(12IS/CID 652) <854907>* **TOXYGENE. / DELTA Mk.II** [4] [ ]
(cd-s) *(CIDX 652)* – ('A'side) / Rose tinted.

Feb 97. (cd/c/d-lp) *(CID/ICT/ILPSD 8055) <524347>* **ORBLIVION** [19] [ ]
– Delta mk II / Ubiquity / Asylum / Bedouin / Molten love / Pi / S.A.L.T. / Toxygene / Log of deadwood / Secrets / Passing of time / 72.

May 97. (12"/cd-s) *(12IS/CID 657)* **ASYLUM. / ('A'-Blood Sugar's mix 1) / ('A'-Andrea Parker's Bezirkskrankenhaus mix)** [20] [ ]
(cd-s) *(CIDX 657)* –

Oct 98. (cd/d-lp) *(CID/ILPSD 8078) <524565>* **U.F.OFF – THE BEST OF** (compilation) [38] [ ]
– A huge ever growing pulsating brain rule from the centre of the world / Little fluffy clouds / Perpetual dawn / Blue room / Assassin / Pomme Fritz / Toxygene / Outlands / DJ Asylum / Mickey Mars / Towers of dub (part 1) / Oxbow lakes. *(d-cd+=; CIDD 8078)* – (other mixes).

Nov 98. (d12"ep) *(12ISD 729)* **LITTLE FLUFFY CLOUDS (mixes:- Danny Tenaglia's downtempo groove / Danny Tenaglia's detour mix / Adam Freeland Tsunami one mix / Cumulo nimbus mix / One True Parker mix)** [–] -non [–]

Feb 01. (12"/cd-s) *(12IS/CID 767)* **ONCE MORE . . . / ONCE MORE (Bedrock edit 2) / LITTLE FLUFFY CLOUDS (Danny Tenaglia's detour mix)** [38] [–]
(cd-s) *(CIDX 767)* – ('A'-Mark Pritchard mixes).

Feb 01. (cd/d-lp) *(CID/ILPSD 8100) <548206>* **CYDONIA** [ ] [ ]
– Once more . . . / Promise / Ghostdancing / Turn it down / Egnable / Firestar / A mile long lump of lard / Centuries / Plum island / Hamlet of kings / 1,1,1 / Thursday's keeper / Terminus.

– compilations, others, etc. –

Nov 91. (cd/c/lp) *Strange Fruit; (SFR CD/MC/LP 118)* **THE PEEL SESSIONS** [ ] [–]

– A huge ever growing brain that rules from the centre of the ultraworld. *(re-iss. Apr96; same)*

APOLLO XI

DR. ALEX PATERSON + guest **BEN WATKINS** (of SUNSONIC)

Wau! Mr Modo — not iss.

Feb 91. (12"/cd-s) *(APOLLO 11/+CD)* **PEACE (IN THE MIDDLE EAST) / ('A'-Sea Of Tranquility mix). / ('A'radio) / ('A'-Is This Really The Orb mix?)** [ ] [–]

F.F.W.D.

aka **ROBERT FRIPP** – guitar / **THOMAS FEHLMANN** – electronics / **KRIS WESTON** – electronics / **DR. ALEX PATERSON**

Intermodo — not iss.

Aug 94. (cd/c/d-lp) *(INTA 001 CD/TC/LP)* **F.F.W.D.** [48] [–]
– Hidden / Lucky saddle / Drone / Hempire / Collosus / What time is clock / Can of bliss / Elauses / Meteor storm / Buckwheat and grits / Klangtest / Suess wie eine nuss.

Roy ORBISON

Born: 23 Apr'36, Vernon, Texas, USA. After stints with local hillbilly groups The WINK WESTERNERS and The TEEN KINGS, he cut a solo single for the 'Jewel' label in 1955 before successfully auditioning for Sam Phillips' 'Sun' records. Written by two college friends, WADE MOORE and DICK PENNER, 'OOBY DOOBY' gave him his first Top 60 hit in 1956. Subsequent 50's rockabilly/pop singles for 'Sun' and 'R.C.A.' all failed, and after moving to Nashville with his wife, ORBISON focused his attentions on songwriting. 'CLAUDETTE' (written for his wife), was placed in the capable hands of The EVERLY BROTHERS who took the uptempo song into the US Top 30 (another, 'DISTANT DRUMS', was a massive hit for JIM REEVES, reaching No.1 after his untimely death in '66). In 1959, his solo career was re-activated when 'Monument' took the reins, ORBISON embracing a more ballad-esque approach which highlighted his lyrical genius, dramatic falsetto voice and trademark tearful crescendos. It was an approach which was to make the country boy a bonafide star; the following year, 'ONLY THE LONELY' was first of many million sellers throughout the early to mid sixties period. Classic after classic saw ROY O become a regular chart fixture, the likes of 'RUNNING SCARED', 'CRYING', 'DREAM BABY', 'IN DREAMS', 'BLUE BAYOU', 'IT'S OVER' and 'OH PRETTY WOMAN' transcending the era while his contemporaries sounded somewhat dated. His ubiquitous dark glasses were initially worn in 1963 after his regular spectacles were misplaced on a plane. In November '64, at the height of his success, ORBISON divorced Claudette due to her infidelity. Reconciled, they remarried in August '65, although tragedy struck ten months later when she was killed as her motorcycle hit a truck. Later that year, ROY O began a short-lived acting career, although his initial movie experience, 'The Fastest Guitar Alive', did poorly at the box-office. Nevertheless his solo career was still flourishing, especially in the UK, where his more countrified material was going down reasonably well. However, another tragedy befell him on the 14th September '68; while on tour, ORBISON's house caught fire, killing his two oldest sons, Roy Jr. and Tony. Understandably, perhaps, he subsequently semi-retired in 1970 to Bielefeld, Germany with his remaining son and new German-born wife, Barbara Wellhonen; together they reared another son, Roy Kelton. ORBISON's recording career went through a minor comeback (i.e. a cameo in the film 1980, 'Roadie', with Emmylou Harris duetting 'You've Lost That Lovin' Feelin') before he sued Wesley Rose (head of 'Monument') for $50m in backdated royalties. In 1987, his career finally got back on track as he signed to 'Virgin' and began making new inroads into world popularity. The following year, he joined the TRAVELING WILBURYS, alongside other superstars, BOB DYLAN, GEORGE HARRISON, JEFF LYNNE and TOM PETTY. Their 'VOLUME 1' album became a US Top 3 and UK Top 20 later in the year, although tragically ROY O was to die of a heart attack on the 6th of December. The legend had just completed a tremendous comeback album, 'MYSTERY GIRL', which posthumously peaked in the British and American Top 5 (would've anyway!). One of the record's highlights, 'YOU GOT IT', gave the man his first entry into the US Top 10 for nearly 25 years. His 1987 concert, 'A BLACK AND WHITE NIGHT', featured guest appearances by the cream of the roots-rock aristocracy including k.d. LANG (on a duet of 'CRYING' which became a UK Top 10 hit), BRUCE SPRINGSTEEN, TOM WAITS, BONNIE RAITT, JACKSON BROWNE and ELVIS COSTELLO among others . . . • **Songwriters:** A brilliant poet of our time, ROY wrote most of the songs himself, at times collaborating in the 60's with JOE MELSON (1960-1963 + 1967) and BILL DEES (1964-66). His final material in the late 80's, was co-written w / JEFF LYNNE & TOM PETTY. Covered CANDY MAN (Fred Neil) / MEAN WOMAN BLUES (Elvis Presley) / LET THE GOOD TIMES ROLL (Shirley & Lee) / THE COMEDIANS (Elvis Costello) / SHE'S A MYSTERY TO ME (U2) / I DROVE ALL NIGHT (Cyndi Lauper) / AFTER THE LOVE HAS GONE (Earth, Wind & Fire). His songs, 'BLUE BAYOU' and 'CRYING', were huge hits for LINDA RONSTADT and DON McLEAN respectively.

Best CD compilation: THE VERY BEST OF ROY ORBISON (*9)

ROY ORBISON – vocals with early **BOB MOORE** – bass / **BILLY PAT ELLIS** – drums

not iss. — Je-Wel

Jan 56. (7",78; by TEEN KINGS) *<101>* **OOBY DOOBY. / TRYING TO GET TO YOU** [–] [ ]

Sun — Sun

May 56. (7",78; ROY ORBISON & The TEEN KINGS) *<242>* **OOBY DOOBY. / GO! GO! GO!** [–] [59]

Sep 56. (7",78; ROY ORBISON & The TEEN KINGS) *<251>* **ROCK HOUSE. / YOU'RE MY BABY** [–] [ ]
(UK-iss.1964 on 'Ember'; EMBS 197)

Nov 56. (7",78; ROY ORBISON & The ROSES) *<265>* **SWEET AND EASY TO LOVE. / DEVIL DOLL** [–] [ ]

Dec 57. (7",78) *<284>* **CHICKEN HEARTED. / I LIKE LOVE** [–] [ ]

May 58. (7",78) *<353>* **SWEET AND EASY TO LOVE. / DEVIL DOLL** [–] [ ]

not iss. — RCA Victor

Sep 58. (7",78) *<7381>* **SWEET AND INNOCENT. / SEEMS TO ME** [–] [ ]

Dec 58. (7",78) *<7447>* **ALMOST 18. / JOLIE** [–] [ ]

London — Monument

Jul 59. (7",78) *<409>* **PAPER BOY. / WITH THE BUG** [–] [ ]

Dec 59. (7",78) *<412>* **UPTOWN. / PRETTY ONE** [–] [72]

Jun 60. (7",78) *(HLU 9149) <421>* **ONLY THE LONELY. / HERE COMES THAT SONG AGAIN** [1] May60 [2]

Oct 60. (7") *(HLU 9207) <425>* **BLUE ANGEL. / TODAY'S TEARDROPS** [11] Sep60 [9]

1961. (lp) *(HA-U 2342) <14002>* **LONELY AND BLUE** [ ] Dec60 [ ]
– Only the lonely / Bye bye love / Cry / Blue avanue / I can't stop loving you / Come back to me (my love) / Blue angel / Raindrops / (I'd be) A legend in my time / I'm hurtin' / Twenty-tow days / I'll say it's my fault. *(UK re-dist.May63, hit No.15)*

Mar 61. (7") *(HLU 9307) <433>* **I'M HURTIN'. / I CAN'T STOP LOVING YOU** [ ] Dec60 [27]

May 61. (7") *(HLU 9342) <438>* **RUNNING SCARED. / LOVE HURTS** [9] Apr61 [1]
(re-iss. 1975 on 'Monument')

Sep 61. (7") *(HLU 9405) <447>* **CRYING. / CANDY MAN** [25] [2] Aug61 [25]
(re-iss. 1975 on 'Monument')

Feb 62. (7") *(HLU 9511)* <456> **DREAM BABY. / THE ACTRESS** [2] [4]

May 62. (lp) *(HA-U 2437)* <4007> **CRYING** [ ] Apr62 [21]
– Crying / The great pretender / Love hurts / She wears my ring / Wedding day / Summersong / Dance / Lana / Loneliness / Let's make a memory / Nite life / Running scared. *(UK re-dist.Jun63, hit No.17)*

Jun 62. (7") *(HLU 9561)* <461> **THE CROWD. / MAMA** [40] [26]

Aug 62. (lp) <4009> **ROY ORBISON'S GREATEST HITS** (compilation) [–] [14]
– The crowd / Love star / Crying / Evergreen / Running scared / Mama / Candy man / Only the lonely / Dream baby / Blue angel / Uptown / I'm hurtin'. *(UK-iss.Sep67; 5007)* – hit No.40

Oct 62. (7") *(HLU 9607)* <467> **WORKIN' FOR THE MAN. / LEAH** [50] [33] [25]
(re-iss. 1975 on 'Monument')

Feb 63. (7") *(HLU 9676)* <806> **IN DREAMS. / SHAHDOROBA** [6] [7]

May 63. (7") *(HLU 9727)* <815> **FALLING. / DISTANT DRUMS** [9] [22]

Sep 63. (7") *(HLU 9777)* <824> **BLUE BAYOU. / MEAN WOMAN BLUES** [3] [29] [5]
(re-iss. 1975 on 'Monument')

Nov 63. (lp) *(HA-U/SH-U 8180)* <18003> **IN DREAMS** [6] Aug 63 [35]
– In dreams / Lonely wine / Shahdaroba / No one will ever know / Sunset / House without windows / Dream / Blue bayou / (They call you) Gigolette / All I have to do is dream / Beautiful dreamer / My prayer.

Dec 63. (7") <830> **PRETTY PAPER. / BEAUTIFUL DREAMER** [–] [15]
(UK-iss.1975 on 'Monument')

Feb 64. (7") *(HLU 9845)* **BORNE ON THE WIND. / WHAT'D I SAY** [15] [–]

Apr 64. (7") *(HLU 9882)* <837> **IT'S OVER. / INDIAN WEDDING** [1] [9]

Aug 64. (7") *(HLU 9919)* <851> **OH PRETTY WOMAN. / YO TE AMO MARIA** [1] [1]

—— (above featured/credited The CANDYMEN)

Sep 64. (lp) <18024> **MORE OF ROY ORBISON'S GREATEST HITS** (compilation) [–] [19]
(UK-iss.1968; SMO 5014)

Nov 64. (7") <HLU 9930> **PRETTY PAPER. / SUMMER SONG** [6] [–]

Nov 64. (lp) *(HA-U 8207)* **OH PRETTY WOMAN** (compilation) [4] [–]
– Oh pretty woman / It's over / Falling / Indian wedding / Borne on the wind / Distant drums / The crowd / Yo te amo / Maria / Candy man / Mama.

Feb 65. (7") *(HLU 9951)* <873> **GOODNIGHT. / ONLY WITH YOU** [14] [21]

Jul 65. (7") *(HLU 9978)* <891> **(SAY) YOU'RE MY GIRL. / SLEEPY HOLLOW** [23] [39]
London M.G.M.

Aug 65. (7") *(HLU 9986)* <13386> **RIDE AWAY. / WONDERIN'** [34] [25]

Sep 65. (lp) *(HA-U/SH-U 8252)* <4308> **THERE IS ONLY ONE ROY ORBISON** [10] [55]
– Ride away / You fool you / Two of a kind / This is your song / I'm in a blue, blue mood / If you can't say something nice / Claudette / Afraid to sleep / Sugar and honey / Summer love / Big as I can dream / Wondering.

Oct 65. (7") *(HLU 10000)* <13410> **CRAWLIN' BACK. / IF YOU CAN'T SAY SOMETHING NICE** [19] [46]

Jan 66. (7") *(HLU 10015)* <13446> **BREAKIN' UP IS BREAKIN' MY HEART. / WAIT** [22] [31]

Feb 66. (lp) *(HA-U/SH-U 8279)* <4322> **THE ORBISON WAY** [11] [ ]
– Crawling back / It ain't no big thing / Time changed everything / This is my land / The loner / Maybe / Breakin' up is breakin' my heart / Go away / A new star / Never / It wasn't very long ago / Why hurt the one who loves you.

Mar 66. (7") *(HLU 10034)* <13498> **TWINKLE TOES. / WHERE IS TOMORROW** [29] [39]

Jun 66. (7") *(HLU 10051)* **LANA. / HOUSE WITHOUT WINDOWS** [15] [–]
(above 45 an older 'Monument' recording)

Jul 66. (7") *(HLU 10067)* <13549> **TOO SOON TO KNOW. / YOU'LL NEVER BE SIXTEEN AGAIN** [–] [68]

Aug 66. (7") *(HLU 10067)* **TOO SOON TO KNOW. / YOU'LL NEVER BE SIXTEEN AGAIN** [3] [–]

Sep 66. (lp) *(HA-U/SH-U 8279)* <4379> **THE CLASSIC ROY ORBISON** [12] [ ]
– You'll never be sixteen again / Pantomine / Twinkle toes / Losing you / City life / Wait / Growing up / Where is tomorrow / I'll never get over you / Going back to Gloria / Never love again / Just another name for rock'n'roll. *(re-iss. +c+cd.Apr89 on 'Ocean'UK / 'Rhino'US)*

Nov 66. (7") *(HLU 10096)* **THERE WON'T BE MANY COMING HOME. / GOING BACK TO GLORIA** [18] [–]

Dec 66. (7") <13634> **COMMUNICATION BREAKDOWN. / GOING BACK TO GLORIA** [–] [60]

Feb 67. (7") *(HLU 10113)* <13685> **SO GOOD. / MEMORIES** [32] [ ]

1967. (lp) *(HA-U 8318)* <4424> **SINGS DON GIBSON** [ ] [ ]
– A legend in my time / I'm hurtin' / The same street / Far far away / Big hearted me / Sweet dreams / Oh, such a stranger / Blue blue day / What about me / Give myself a party / Too soon to know / Lonesome number one.

Aug 67. (7") *(HLU 10143)* <13764> **CRY SOFTLY, LONELY ONE. / PISTOLERO** [ ] [52]

Sep 67. (lp) *(HA-U/SH-U 8357)* <4514> **CRY SOFTLY, LONELY ONE** [ ] [ ]
– She / Communication breakdown / Cry softly, lonely one / Girl like me / It takes one to know one / That's a no-no / Just let me make believe / Here comes the rain baby / Memories / Time to cry / Only alive / Just one time.

Oct 67. (7") *(HLU 10159)* <13817> **SHE. / HERE COMES THAT SONG AGAIN** [ ] [ ]

Jan 68. (7") *(HLU 10176)* <13889> **BORN TO BE LOVED BY YOU. / SHY AWAY** [ ] [ ]

Jan 68. (lp) *(HA-U/SH-U 8358)* **FASTEST GUITAR ALIVE (1966 Soundtrack)** [ ] [–]
– Whirlwind / Medicine man / River / The fastest guitar alive / Rollin' on / Pistolero / Good time party / Heading south / Best friend / There won't be many coming home.

Jul 68. (7") *(HLU 10206)* <13950> **WALK ON. / FLOWERS** [39] [ ]

Sep 68. (7") *(HLU 10222)* <13991> **HEARTACHE. / SUGARMAN** [44] [ ]

1969. (lp) <4559> **GREAT SONGS** [–] [ ]

Apr 69. (7") *(HLU 10261)* <14039> **MY FRIEND. / SOUTHBOUND JERICO PATHWAY** [35] [ ]

May 69. (lp) <4636> **MANY MOODS** [–] [ ]
– Truly, truly, true / Unchained melody / I recommend her / More / Heartache / Amy / Good morning, dear / What now my love / Walk on / Yesterday's child / Try to remember.

Aug 69. (7") *(HLU 109285)* <14079> **PENNY ARCADE. / TENNESSEE OWNS MY SOUL** [27] [ ]

1969. (lp) <4683> **HANK WILLIAMS – THE ROY ORBISON WAY** [–] [ ]
– Kaw-liga / Jambalaya (on the bayou) / (Last night) I heard you crying in your sleep / You win again / Your cheatin' heart / Cold, cold heart / A mansion on the hill / I can't help it (if I'm still in love with you) / There'll be no teardrops tonight / I'm so lonesome I could cry.

Nov 69. (7") *(HLU 10294)* **BREAK MY MIND. / HOW DO YOU START OVER** [ ] [–]

Nov 69. (lp) *(HA-U/SH-U 8406)* **THE BIG 'O'** [ ] [–]
– Break my mind / Help me Rhonda / Money / Only you / Down the line / When I stop dreaming / Living touch / Land of 1000 dances / Scarlet ribbons / She won't head her love out / Casting spell / Penny arcade. *(UK iss.Oct75 & 1982 on 'Charly') (re-iss. +cd.May89 on 'Pickwick') (cd-iss. Feb93)*

—— (above credited The ART MOVEMENT)

1970. (7") <14105> **SHE CHEATS ON ME. / HOW DO YOU START OVER** [–] [ ]

Apr 70. (7") *(HLU 10310)* <14121> **SO YOUNG. / IF I HAD A WOMAN LIKE YOU** [ ] [ ]

Aug 71. (7") *(HLU 10339)* <14293> **(LOVE ME LIKE YOU DID IT) LAST NIGHT. / CLOSE AGAIN** [ ] [ ]

Feb 72. (7") *(HLU 10358)* <14358> **GOD LOVE YOU. / CHANGES** [ ] [ ]

1972. (7") <14413> **REMEMBER THE GOOD. / HARLEM WOMAN (or) IF ONLY FOR A WHILE** [–] [ ]

Sep 72. (7") *(HLU 10358)* <14441> **MEMPHIS TENNESSEE. / I CAN READ BETWEEN THE LINES** [ ] [ ]

1973. (lp) *(SH-U 8445)* <4867> **MEMPHIS** [ ] [ ]
– Memphis, Tennessee / Why a woman cries / Run baby run (back into my arms) / Take care of your woman / I'm the man on Susie's mind / I

can't stop loving you / Run the engines up high / It ain't no big thing / I fought the law / The three bells / Danny boy.

1973. (7") *<14552>* **BLUE RAIN (COMING DOWN). / SOONER OR LATER** [–] [ ]

1973. (7") *<14626>* **I WANNA LIVE. / YOU LAY EASY ON MY MIND** [–] [ ]

1974. (lp) *<4934>* **MILESTONES** [–] [ ]

Mercury Mercury

Sep 74. (7") *(6167014) 73610>* **SWEET MAMA BLUE. / HEARTACHE** [ ] [ ]

Apr 75. (7") *(6167067) <73652>* **HUNG UP ON YOU. / SPANISH NIGHTS** [ ] [ ]

1975. (7") *<73705>* **IT'S LONELY. / STILL** [–] [ ]

1976. (lp) *<SRMI 1045>* **I'M STILL IN LOVE WITH YOU** [–] [ ]
– Pledging my love / Rainbow love / Heartache / Still / Circle / All I need is time / Spanish nights / It's lonely / Crying time / Hung up on you / Sweet mama blue. *(cd-iss. Aug89)*

Monument Monument

May 76. (7") *(MNT 4247) <8690>* **BELINDA. / NO CHAIN AT ALL** [ ] [ ]

Nov 76. (7") *(MNT 4797) <200>* **(I'M A) SOUTHERN MAN. / BORN TO LOVE ME** [ ] [ ]

Feb 77. (lp) *(81809) <7600>* **REGENERATION** [ ] [ ]
– (I'm a) Southern man / N chain at all / Old love song / Can't wait / Born to love me / Blues in my mind / Something they can't take away / Under suspicion / I don't really want you / Belinda.

Apr 77. (7") *(MNT 5151) <215>* **DRIFTING AWAY. / UNDER SUSPICION** [ ] [ ]

—— In 1978, he underwent major heart surgery, but steadily recovered.

Asylum Asylum

May 79. (7") *(K 13153) <46048>* **EASY WAY OUT. / TEARS** [ ] [ ]

Jul 79. (lp/c) *(K/K4 53092) <6E 198>* **LAMINAR FLOW** [ ] [ ]
– Easy way out / Love is a cold wind / Lay it down / I care / We're into something good / Movin' / Poor baby / Warm spot hot / Tears / Friday night / Hound dog man. *(cd-iss. Feb93)*

Sep 79. (7") *<46541>* **LAY IT DOWN. / POOR BABY** [–] [ ]

Nov 79. (7") *(K 12391)* **LAY IT DOWN. / WARM SPOT HOT** [ ] [–]

—— (below duet with **EMMYLOU HARRIS** from the film 'Roadie')

Warners Warners

Jun 80. (7") *<49262>* **THAT LOVING YOU FEELING AGAIN. / (b-by Craig Hindley)** [–] [55]

Apr 81. (7") *(K 18432)* **UNTIL THE NIGHT IS OVER. / LONG WAY BACK TO LOVE** [ ] [–]

ZTT-Island Island

Aug 85. (7") *(ZTAS 9)* **WILD HEARTS (TIME). / WILD HEARTS (VOICELESS)** [ ] [ ]
(d7"+=) *(DZTAS 9)* – Ooby dooby (revive) / Crying (live).
(12"+=) *(12ZTAS 9)* – Ooby dooby / Wild hearts (and time again).

Virgin Virgin

Jun 87. (7") *(ROY 1) <99434>* **IN DREAMS. / LEAH** [ ] [ ]

Jul 87. (d-lp/c/cd) *(VGD/+C/CD 3524) <90604>* **IN DREAMS: THE GREATEST HITS** [86] Jan 89 [95]
– (new versions of old songs) Only the lonely / Leah / In dreams / Uptown / It's over / Crying / Dream baby / Blue angel / Working for the man / Candy man / Running scared / Falling / I'm hurtin' / Claudette / Oh pretty woman / Mean woman blues / Ooby dooby / Lana / Blue bayou.

—— In the fall of 1988, he teamed up with DYLAN, PETTY, HARRISON and LYNNE to form The TRAVELING WILBURYS. Tragedy struck on the 7th Dec'88, when ORBISON died of a heart attack. He had coincidentally just released comeback solo album.

Dec 88. (7") *(VS 1166) <99245>* **YOU GOT IT. / THE ONLY ONE** [3] [9]
(12"+=/3"cd-s+=) *(VS T/CD 1166)* – Crying (with k.d. LANG).

Jan 89. (cd/c/lp) *(CD/TC+/V 2576) <91058>* **MYSTERY GIRL** [2] [5]
– You got it / In the real world / (All I can do is) Dream you / A love so beautiful / California blue / She's a mystery to me / The comedians / The only one / Windsurfer / Careless heart.

Feb 89. (7") *(VS 1173)* **SHE'S A MYSTERY TO ME. / CRYING** [27] [ ]
(12"+=/cd-s+=) *(VS T/CD 1173)* – Dream baby (live).

Feb 89. (7") *<99227>* **SHE'S A MYSTERY TO ME. / DREAM BABY** [–] [ ]

Jul 89. (7") *(VS 1193) <99202>* **CALIFORNIA BLUE. / BLUE BAYOU (live with k.d.LANG)** [ ] [ ]
(12"+=) *(VST 1193)* – Leah (live).
(3"cd-s++=) *(VSCD 1193)* – In dreams (live).

Nov 89. (cd/c/lp) *(CD/TC+/V 2601) <91295>* **ROY ORBISON AND FRIENDS – A BLACK AND WHITE NIGHT (live Sep'87)** [51] [ ]
– Oh pretty woman / Only the lonely / In dreams / Dream baby (how long must I dream) / Leah / Move on down the line / Crying / Mean woman blues / Running scared / Blue bayou / Candy man / Uptown / Ooby dooby / The comedians / (All I can do is) Dream of you / It's over. *(re-iss. c+cd.Aug91; same) (cd re-iss. Mar03 on 'Orbison'; ROBW 7891)*

Nov 89. (7") *(VS 1224) <99159>* **OH PRETTY WOMAN ('87 version). / CLAUDETTE** [ ] [ ]
(12"+=/cd-s+=) *(VS T/CD 1224)* – ('A'-lp version).

– (selective) compilations, etc. –

Jul 64. (lp) *Ember; (NR 5013)* **THE EXCITING SOUNDS OF ROY ORBISON** [17] [–]

Oct 65. (7") *Monument; <906>* **LET THE GOOD TIMES ROLL. / DISTANT DRUMS** [–] [81]

Dec 65. (lp) *Monument; (SMO 5004)* **ORBISONGS** [ ] [ ]
(UK-iss.Jul67) – hit No.40 *(cd-iss. Dec95)*

Sep 66. (lp) *Monument; <6622>* **THE VERY BEST OF ROY ORBISON** [ ] [94]

Jan 73. (d-lp) *Monument; (MNT 67290)* **ALL-TIME GREATEST HITS** [39] [ ]
(cd-iss. Jan89) (re-iss. +cd.Dec88 on 'Skyline')

Nov 75. (lp) *Arcade; (ADEP 19)* **THE BEST OF ROY ORBISON** [1] [–]

Jul 81. (lp/c) *Monument-CBS; (MNT/40 10026)* **GOLDEN DAYS** [63] [ ]
(cd-iss. Jun92 & Jul98; 4715559)

Sep 84. (d-lp) *Charly; (CDX 4)* **THE SUN YEARS 1956-1958: THE DEFINITIVE COLLECTION** [ ] [–]
(cd-iss. Apr89 on 'Bear Family'; BCD 15461)

Oct 88. (lp/c/cd) *Telstar; (STA R/C/TCD 2330)* **THE LEGENDARY ROY ORBISON** [1] [–]
– It's over / Only the lonely / Goodnight / Lana / The crowd / All I have to do is dream / Dream baby / Mean woman blues / Oh pretty woman / Love hurts / My prayer / Falling / Blue angel / In dreams / Blue bayou / The great pretender / Pretty paper.

Oct 90. (cd/c/lp) *Telstar; (STA TCD/C/R 2441)* **BALLADS – 22 CLASSIC LOVE SONGS** [38] [–]

1991. (cd) *Magnum Force; (CDMF 079)* **LEGEND IN HIS TIME** [ ] [–]

Jun 92. (7"/c-s) *M.C.A.; (MCS/+MC 1652) <54287>* **I DROVE ALL NIGHT. / FOREVER FRIENDS (with SHEENA EASTON)** [7] [ ]
(cd-s+=) *(MCSCD 1652)* – Trickster:- Line of fire.

Aug 92. (7"/c-s; ROY ORBISON & k.d. LANG) *Virgin America; (VUS/+CS 63)* **CRYING. / FALLING** [13] [ ]
(cd-s+=) *(CDVUS 63)* – Oh pretty woman / She's a mystery to me.
(cd-s+=) *(CDXVUS 63)* – Only the lonely / It's over.

Oct 92. (7"/c-s) *Virgin America; (VUS/+CS 68)* **HEARTBREAK RADIO. / CRYING (with k.d. LANG)** [36] [ ]
(cd-s) *(CDVUS 68)* – ('A'side) / In dreams / You got it / Dream baby.
(cd-s) *(CDVUSX 68)* – ('A'side) / Blue angel / Claudette / Lana.

Nov 92. (lp/c/cd) *Virgin; (VUSLP/VUSMC/CDVUS 58)* **KING OF HEARTS** (1988 recordings) [23] [ ]
– You're the one / Heartbreak radio / We'll take the night / Crying (with k.d.LANG) / After the love has gone / Love in time / I drove all night / Wild hearts run out of time / Coming home / Careless heart (original demo).

Jun 93. (3xcd-box) *Sequel; (NXTCD 246)* **THE GOLDEN DECADE 1960-1969** [ ] [–]

Nov 93. (cd) *Monument; (4749562)* **LONELY AND BLUE / CRYING** [ ] [ ]

Nov 93. (cd) *Monument; (4749572)* **IN DREAMS / ORBISONGS** [ ] [ ]

Nov 93. (7"/c-s) *Virgin America; (VUS/+CS 79)* **I DROVE ALL NIGHT. / CRYING** [47] [ ]
(cd-s+=) *(CDVUS 79)* – Oh pretty woman / After the love has gone.

Oct 95. (3xcd-box) *K-Box; (KBOX 344)* **ROY ORBISON** [ ] [ ]

Jun 96. (cd) *Charly; (CPCD 8180)* **ROCKER: THE SUN YEARS** [ ] [ ]
(re-iss. Jun01 on 'Snapper'; SNAP 023CD)

Nov 96. (cd/c) *Virgin; (CDV/TCV 2804)* **THE VERY BEST OF ROY ORBISON** [18] [ ]

Dec 97. (cd) *Institute Of Art; (RTD 3970023CD)* **MY BOOK OF DREAMS** [ ] [ ]

Mar 98. (cd) *Eagle; (EABCD 095)* **THE MASTERS** [ ] [ ]

Jul 98. (cd/c) *Columbia; (463350-2/-4)* **THE BEST OF ROY ORBISON** [ ] [ ]

Jul 98. (cd) *Monument; (480570-2)* **THE DEFINITIVE COLLECTION** ☐ ☐
Oct 98. (cd/c) *Monument; (492743-2/-4)* **THE BIG O: THE ORIGINAL SINGLES COLLECTION** ☐ ☐
Aug 99. (d-cd) *Snapper; (SMDCD 181)* **THE ESSENTIAL SUN COLLECTION** ☐ ☐
Sep 99. (cd) *Platinum; (PLATCD 503)* **THE ROCK'N'ROLL BALLADS** ☐ ☐
Oct 99. (cd) *Castle Pie; (PIESD 147)* **DOMINO – ROY ROCKS** ☐ ☐
Jan 00. (cd/c) *Monument; (466712-2/-4)* **LOVE SONGS** ☐ ☐
May 00. (cd) *Music; (CD 41003)* **THE SUN YEARS: ORIGINAL SUN RECORDINGS** ☐ ☐
Jul 00. (3xcd-box) *Goldies; (GLD 3540-2)* **OH PRETTY WOMAN** ☐ ☐
Jul 00. (cd) *Members Edition; (UAE 31212)* **ROY ORBISON & FRIENDS** ☐ ☐
Sep 00. (cd/c) *Castle Pulse; (PLS CD/MC 373)* **ROCK'N'ROLL** ☐ ☐
Nov 00. (cd) *Disky; (SI 99892-2)* **GOLD** ☐ ☐
Jan 01. (cd/c) *Virgin TV; (VTD CD/MC 360)* **LOVE SONGS** 4 –
Aug 01. (7xcd-box) *Bear Family; (BCD 16423)* **ORBISON** ☐ ☐
Feb 02. (cd) *Mercury; (838433-2)* **I'M STILL IN LOVE WITH YOU** ☐ ☐
Feb 02. (cd) *Virgin; (CDV 2958)* **THE LOVE ALBUM** ☐ ☐
Mar 02. (cd) *Sony; (506214-2)* **SINGS THE TEARJERKERS** ☐ ☐
Oct 02. (cd/c) *Music Club; (MCCD/MCTC 507)* **BIG HITS FROM THE BIG O** ☐ ☐
Nov 02. (cd) *Planet Media; (PML 1087)* **HITS LIVE** ☐ ☐
Feb 03. (cd) *Metro; (METRCD 100)* **THE ESSENTIAL SUN YEARS** ☐ ☐
Mar 03. (cd) *Orbison; (HCC 19650)* **COMBO CONCERT** ☐ ☐
Jun 03. (cd) *Traditional Line; (TL 1316)* **BLUE BAYOU** ☐ ☐

William ORBIT

Born: London, England. The thinking man's techno purveyor, WILLIAM WAINWRIGHT's first foray's into electronica were with eighties act TORCH SONG. In 1987, after swapping WAINWRIGHT for the decidedly more exotic sounding ORBIT, he released an album of the same name. With the first release in the 'Strange Cargo' series, ORBIT began to make his mark in the burgeoning club scene. This success was consolidated when he formed BASS-O-MATIC as a vehicle for his more club orientated material, scoring a massive hit with 'FASCINATING RHYTHM' in 1990. With their PINK FLOYD references and hypnotic rhythms, the two albums released under the BASS-O-MATIC moniker pre-empted the subsequent trancey direction which dance music would follow after the decline of Rave. ORBIT returned to more familiar, moody territory with the second and third volumes of STRANGE CARGO. After the moderate success of BLUR's ORBIT produced '13' and the revival of MADONNA's entire career via the album 'Ray Of Light', ORBIT himself was working on something a tad more esoteric in the gap between these two sets. It was the modestly titled 'PIECES IN A MODERN STYLE' (2000), an album of exactly that; classical pieces that had been given a new twist by ORBIT. Featured on the album were such classics as 'ADAGIO FOR STRINGS' (which became a huge club hit when remixed by ATB), Satie's 'OGIVE NUMBER 1' and a retro formation of Beethoven's 'OPUS 132'. An interesting concept, if not let down by ORBIT's dedication to maintaining the original sound of the song, as some of the pieces were just bare-bones originals laced with a couple of clever beat tracks. • **Songwriters:** WAINWRIGHT – MAYER, except LOVE MY WAY (Psychedelic Furs) / FEEL LIKE JUMPING (Jackie Mitto) / SET THE CONTROLS FOR THE HEART OF THE SUN (Pink Floyd).

Album rating: Torch Song: WISH THING (*5) / William Orbit: ORBIT (*5) / STRANGE CARGO (*6) / STRANGE CARGO 2 (*4) / Bass-O-Matic: SET THE CONTROLS FOR THE HEART OF THE BASS (*7) / SCIENCE AND MELODY (*5) / William Orbit: STRANGE CARGO III (*5) / STRANGE CARGO 4 (HINTERLAND) (*4) / Torch Song: TOWARD THE UNKNOWN REGION (*5) / William Orbit: PIECES IN A MODERN STYLE (*6)

TORCH SONG

WILLIAM ORBIT – keyboards, electronics / **LAURIE MAYER** – vocals / **GRANT GILBERT** – saxophone

I.R.S. I.R.S.

1983. (7")(12") *(IR 9925)(PRSX 1027)* **PREPARE TO ENERGISE. / ('A'-Fong mix)** ☐ –
Jul 84. (lp/c) *(IRSA/IRSC 7046)* *<SP 70045>* **WISH THING** ☐ ☐
– Don't look now / Telepathy / Ode to Billy Joe / Another place / Prepare to energise / Tattered dress / Sweet thing / You said you were coming / Water clock secret.
Sep 84. (12") *(IRSX 110)* **DON'T LOOK NOW. / PREPARE TO ENERGISE** ☐ –
Dec 84. (12") *<SP 70978>* **TATTERED DRESS. / DON'T LOOK NOW** – ☐
Jan 85. (7") *(IRS 117)* **ODE TO BILLY JOE. / ZEBRA ROOM** ☐ –
(12"+=) *(IRSY 117)* – Mothdoom ecstasy.
1985. (lp) *<Y II-LP 001>* **ECSTASY** – ☐
– White night / Can't find my way home / Spear / Microdot daylight / The pentacle / Living out of time / Mothdoom ecstasy / Nails in the cross / The zebra room / Venus in furs / Dia del muerto.

Y 11 I.R.S.

May 86. (12") *(Y11 12-001)* **WHITE NIGHT. / MOTHDUB / MICRODOT DAYLIGHT** ☐ –
Nov 86. (7") *(Y11 002)* **CAN'T FIND MY WAY HOME. / LIVING OUT OF TIME** ☐ –
(12") *(Y11 12-002)* – ('A'-dance mix) / Spear / ('B'mix) / ('A'-acoustic instrumental) / Living out of time (Rico Conning remix).
1987. (lp/c) *<IRS-5862>* **EXHIBIT A** – ☐
– White night / Prepare to energize / Tattered dress / Living out of time / Can't find my way home / Sweet thing / Microdot daylight / Nails in the cross / Don't look now.

WILLIAM ORBIT

ORBIT with **MAYER** + **PETE NIKOLICH** – vocals

M.C.A. I.R.S.

Apr 87. (cd/c/lp) *(DMIRF/MIRFC/MIRF 1020)* *<42019>* **ORBIT** ☐ Jul87 ☐
– Love my way / Fool to myself / Heartbroken highway / Escape to Mexico / Rider in black / Swamp dog / Feel like jumping / Blue street / Cluny Ann / The night runs forever / Cry one more tear.
Aug 87. (7") *(WORB 1)* **LOVE MY WAY. / FEEL LIKE JUMPING** ☐ –
(12"+=) *(WORBT 1)* – ('A'-daytime mix) / ('A'-romantic mix).
Feb 88. (cd/c/lp) *(DMCF/MCFC/MCF 1030)* *<42098>* **STRANGE CARGO** ☐ ☐
– Via caliente / Jump jet / Secret garden / Scorpion / Jimmy's jag / Theme dream / Fire and mercy / Silent signals / Out of the ice / Riding to Rio / The mighty Limpopo.

I.R.S. Capitol

Nov 90. (lp/c/cd) *(EIRSA/+C/CD 1041)* *<13055>* **STRANGE CARGO 2** ☐ ☐
– Dark eyed kid / Atom dream / Ruby heart / El Santo / Dia del muerto / 777 / The thief and the serpent / The last lagoon / Millennium / Painted rock.

BASS-O-MATIC

WILLIAM ORBIT – instruments / with **SHARON MUSGRAVE** + **LAURIE MAYER** – vocals / **MATTHEW VAUGHAN** – keyboards, guitar / **RICK KENTON** – guitar, clavinet / **DEAN ROSS** – piano / **SUGAR J** – DJ / **STEVE ROBERTS** – harmonies / **SONIQUE** – loops / **LIZZIE TEAR** – guerilla war cry / **MC INNA ONE STEP** – MC / **MC MIDR ANGE** – scat / **MC A-SIDE** – rap

Virgin Atlantic

May 90. (7") *(VS 1265)* **IN THE REALM OF THE SENSES. / (fast and loose mix)** 66 –
(12") *(VST 1265)* – ('A'-mixes; fantasy / solaris / sensi).
(cd-s) *(VSCDT 1265)* – ('A'-side) / ('A'-mixes; fantasy / solaris / bassapella).
(12") *(VSTX 1265)* – ('A'-mixes; funky paradise / bonus paradise / u.f.o.od / burrito beat).

Aug 90. (7") *(VS 1274)* **FASCINATING RHYTHM. / (the loud edit)** 9
(cd-s+=) *(VSCDT 1274)* – ('A'side) / ('A'-soul odyssey mix) / ('A'-blue mix) / Set the controls (va va voom mix).
(12") *(VST 1274)* – ('A'-Lisa loud mix) / ('A'-soul odyssey mix) / ('A'-hook & swing mix pt.1) / Set the controls (va va voom mix).
(12") *(VSTX 1274)* – ('A'-Claudia Canniggia mix) / ('A'-blue mix) / ('A'-T-wah mix) / ('A'-hook & swing mix pt.2).
(12") *<0-96391>* – ('A'-side) / ('A'-mixes; Lisa loud / Claudia Canniggia / time tunnel / soul odyssey / hook & swing pt.1).

Oct 90. (cd/c/lp) *(CD/TC+/V 2641)* *<91616>* **SET THE CONTROLS FOR THE HEART OF THE BASS** 57 Feb91
– In the realm of the senses / Set the controls for the heart of the bass / Fascinating rhythm / Rat-cut-a-bottle / Love catalogue / Zombie mantra / Freaky angel / Wicked love / Ease on by / My tears have gone. *(cd+=/c+=)* – In the realm of the senses (funky paradise mix) / Fascinating rhythm (soul odyssey mix). *(re-iss. Apr92 cd/c; OVED CD/C 403) (cd re-iss. Apr97; CDVIP 1888)*

Dec 90. (7") *(VS 1295)* **EASE ON BY. / (ram factor ten mix)** 61 –
(12"+=) *(VST 1295)* – Rat cut a bottle / ('A'-strip down mix).
(cd-s+=) *(VSCDT 1295)* – Fascinating rhythm (Claudia Canniggia mix).
(12") *(VSTX 1295)* – ('A'-dub throb mix) / Rat cut a bottle (electro rat mix) / Zombie mantra / Soul surrender.

—— now with **SINDY** – vocals (ex-WELL RED) / **DIVINE + GLORY** – rap

Jul 91. (7") *(VS 1355)* **FUNKY LOVE VIBRATIONS. / ATTACK OF THE 50 FOOT DRUM DEMON (psycho biker)** 71 –
(12"+=) *(VST 1355)* – ('A'-concrete mix).
(cd-s++=) *(VSCDG 1355)* – ('A'-basso racer mix).

Sep 91. (7") *(VS 1372)* **GO GETTA NUTHA MAN. / (the whole shabang dub)** –
(cd-s) *(VSCDT 1372)* – ('A'side) / ('A'-the whole shabang mix) / Fascinating rhythm (live).
(12") *(VST 1372)* – ('A'-motor mix) / ('A'-the whole shabang mix) / ('A'-the whole shabang dub).

Oct 91. (cd/c/lp) *(CD/TC+/V 2670)* **SCIENCE AND MELODY** –
– Funky love vibrations / Science and melody / She's on the phone again / Attack of the 50 foot drum demon / Potentially fatal / Go getta nutha man / Raggafuzz / Mountain high.

Nov 91. (7") *(VS 1392)* **SCIENCE AND MELODY. / METAPHYSIK** –
(cd-s+=) *(VSCDG)* – ('A'-S&M mix) / Attack of the 50 foot drum demon (vaporub mix).
(12") *(VST 1392)* – ('A'-S&M mix) / ('A'-supersperm mix) / Attack of the 50 foot drum demon (vaporub mix).

WILLIAM ORBIT

Virgin I.R.S.

Mar 93. (cd/c) *(CDV/TCV 2707)* *<27703>* **STRANGE CARGO III**
– Water from a vine leaf / Into the paradise / Time to get wize / Harry flowers / Touch of the night / Story of light / Gringatcho demento / Hazy shade of random / Best friend paranoia / Monkey king / Deus ex machina / Water babies.

Jun 93. (c-s) *(VSC 1465)* **WATER FROM A VINE LEAF / ('A'-Acid Bath mix)** 59
(12"+=) *(VST 1465)* – ('A'mix).
(cd-s++=) *(VSCD 1465)* – (2-'A'mixes).

Warners Warners

Jan 95. (12") *(YZ 908T)* **MILLION TOWN (mixes; album / Dolores del amo / Kruder & Dorfmeister)** –
(cd-s+=) *(YZ 908CD)* – ('A'-No Dolores mix).

Feb 95. (cd/c/lp) *(<4509 99295-2/-4/-1>)* **STRANGE CARGO 4 (HINTERLAND)**
– Million town / She cries your name / Montok point / Hulaville / Kiss of the bee / El ninjo / Crimes of the future / The name of the wave / Say anything / Lost in blue / Hinterland / The last dream of Lucy Mariner.

TORCH SONG

Warners Discovery

Apr 95. (cd/c/lp) *(4509 98969-2 / 99102-4/-1)* *<77032>* **TOWARD THE UNKNOWN REGION** Jan96
– Raphael / Gumbo ya-ya / Shine on me / Blue night / TRuler of my heart / Ballad of Pearl and John / Toward the unknown region / Slip away / Kang kalika / Field of view. *(cd+=)* – Shine on me (aurora mix) / Shine on me (Emergen-c dub) / Gumbo ya ya (summon the bullroarer mix).

WILLIAM ORBIT

X.L. not iss.

Oct 97. (12") *(XSN 004)* **SCREAM (true grit). / SCREAM (miaow)** –

East West Maverick

Dec 99. (12") *(WEA 247T)* **BARBER'S ADAGIO FOR STRINGS / (Ferry Corsten mix)** 4 –
(cd-s+=) *(WEA 247CD)* – John Cage: In a landscape.

Jan 00. (d-cd) *(3984 28957-2)* *<47592>* **PIECES IN A MODERN STYLE** 2 Mar00
– Adagio for strings / In a landscape / Ogive number 1 / Cavalleria rusticana / Pavanne pour une infante defunte / L'inverno / Triple concerto / Xerxes / Piece in the old style 1 / Piece in the old style 3 / Opus 132.

Apr 00. (12") *(WEA 269T)* **RAVEL'S PAVANE POUR UNE INFANTE DEFUNTE / (Ferry Corsten mix)** 31 –
(cd-s+=) *(WEA 269CD)* – ('A'-single version).

– compilations, etc. –

Jun 96. (cd) *I.R.S.; (EIRSCD 1079)* *<36348>* **STRANGE CARGOS – THE BEST OF . . .**
– Water from a vine leaf / Dark eyed kid / Gringatcho demento / Fire and mercy / Via Calente / Time to get wize / Ruby heart (transmogrified) / Atom dream / Harry Flowers / Love my way / Riding to Rio / Story of light / Silent signals / Painted rock / Water babies.

Apr 00. (3xcd-box) *E.M.I.; (526099-2)* **STRANGE CARGO VOL.1-3** –

ORBITAL

Formed: Seven Oaks, London, England . . . late 80's by brothers PHIL and PAUL HARTNOLL. United by a shared love of electro and punk, they were inspired by the outdoor party scene of '89 and named themselves after the infamous circular motorway which ravers used in delirious pursuit of their next E'd-up shindig. A home produced 4-track demo, 'CHIME', brought the band almost instant fame and remains one of their best loved songs. Originally released on the small 'Oh-Zone' label, the track was given a full release in March 1990 on 'London' offshoot 'Ffrr', it's subtly euphoric charms elevating 'CHIME' into the top 20 and the brothers onto a memorable 'Top Of The Pops' appearance where they sported defiant 'No Poll Tax' t-shirts. Although dance culture has since become increasingly politiscized as a result of heavy handed legislation, it was unusual at the time for a techno act to be so passionately anti-establishment, an ethos the HARTNOLL brothers had carried over from their punk days and which would become a recurring theme throughout their career. Meanwhile, ORBITAL followed their debut with a trio of largely instrumental, synth-driven singles, the highlight being the pounding white noise of the BUTTHOLE SURFERS-sampling 'SATAN'. The track reached No.31 upon its release in August '91 although a subsequent live version stormed into the top 5 earlier this year. Their untitled debut album, released in September of the same year, showcased cerebral electronic soundscapes which nevertheless retained a melancholy, organic warmth while their live shows moved feet and minds en masse. Alongside events like the Shamen's Synergy, which attempted to mix the spectacle of rock 'n' roll with the communal energy of house, ORBITAL were pivotal in pioneering dance music in the live evironment. Rather than reproducing the songs live on stage, they improvised, restructuring tracks which had been pre-set into sequencers. This spontaneity was enhanced by an innovative light show utilising state of the art technology, a heady combination that saw ORBITAL headline the Glastonbury festival two years running

during the mid-90's. They were no less effective in the studio and their second untitled album was a finely tuned extension of the debut, encompassing such exotica as a sample from an Australian pedestrian crossing (!) With their third long player, 1994's cynically titled 'SNIVILISATION', the music took on an uneasy paranoia, seething with a bitter undercurrent that railed against the state of humanity in general, as well as issues closer to home such as the much hated Criminal Justice Bill. The record also introduced elements of drum 'n' bass, a dalliance that continued with their 'IN SIDES' album. Preceded by the near-half hour strangeness of 'THE BOX' single, the record marked the pinnacle of ORBITAL's sonic explorations, a luminous trip to the final frontiers of electronica. In spite of their experimentalism, a loyal following ensures that the duo are never short of chart success, the 'IN SIDES' album reaching No.5, while 1997 saw ORBITAL go top 3 in the singles chart twice (first with the aforementioned live version of 'SATAN' and then with their celebrated remake of 'THE SAINT'). After a slight delay, ORBITAL were back in circulation with a fifth set, 'THE MIDDLE OF NOWHERE' (1999), a happier affair that was premiered by hit single, 'STYLE'; the album also saw POOKA singers NATASHA JONES and SHARON LEWIS collaborate on the track, 'OTONO'. Not content with sticking to their staple, ORBITAL tried to cross the boundaries on their 2001 album 'THE ALTOGETHER', a strange mix of the group's previous six albums tempered by the arrival of guest vocalists et al. Prog rockers TOOL were sampled by the group on the swirling 'SURFIN' BIRD', while the duo tried desperately to jump on the indie bandwagon courtesy of the awful DAVID GRAY collaboration 'ILLUMINATE'. ORBITAL even attempted to pull off a remix of the DR. WHO theme, with hilarious consequences, whereas tracks 'OI!' and 'SHADOWS' saw a warm return to the group's previous works. 2002 saw the release of both the Top 40 'REST AND PLAY' EP, and the greatest hits set, 'WORK 1989-2002'. While the latter featured most of the essential tracks from the band's early period, the inclusion of the aforementioned 'ILLUMINATE' only served to highlight the glaring quality differential. The 'OCTANE' (2003) soundtrack was also slightly below par, suitably atmospheric in its TANGERINE DREAM-esque meandering but lacking the dark menace and rythmic celebration of their best work.
• **Songwriters:** The duo, except cover of THE SAINT (E. Astley) and noted samples; O EUCHARI (performed by Emily Van Evera).
• **Trivia:** Vox on tracks 'SAD BUT TRUE' & 'ARE WE HERE?' by ALISON GOLDFRAPP.

Album rating: UNTITLED (ORBITAL 1) (*7) / UNTITLED (ORBITAL II) (*7) / SNIVILIZATION (*8) / IN SIDES (*9) / THE MIDDLE OF NOWHERE (*8) / THE ALTOGETHER (*6) / WORK 1989-2002 compilation (*8) / OCTANE (*5)

PHIL HARTNOLL – keyboards / **PAUL HARTNOLL** – keyboards

Oh-Zone — not iss.

Jan 90. (12"ep) *(ZONE 001)* **CHIME. / DEEPER (full version)** [ ] [–]

Ffrr-London — Ffrr-London

Mar 90. (7"/c-s) *(F/+CS 135)* **CHIME. / DEEPER** [ ] [–]
(cd-ep+=) *(FCD 135)* – ('A'version).
(12"ep) *(FX 135)* – ('A'-JZM remix) / ('A'-Bacardi mix).

Jul 90. (7"ep) *(F 145)* **OMEN. / 2 DEEP / OPEN MIND** [ ] [–]
(cd-ep) *(FCD 145)* – (1st & 3rd track) / ('A'edit)
(12"ep) *(FX 145)* – Omen: The chariot / The tower / Wheel of fortune / The fool.
(12"ep) *(FXR 145)* – ('A'remixes).

Jan 91. (7") *(F 149)* **SATAN. / BELFAST** [31] [–]
(12"ep+=/cd-ep+=) *(FX/FCD 149)* – L.C.1. *(cd-ep re-iss. Aug95 on 'Internal'; LIECD 25)*
(12"ep) *(FXR 149)* – ('A'-rhyme & reason mix) / L.C.2 (outer limits mix) / Chime.

Aug 91. (12"/c-s) *(FX/FCS 163)* **MIDNIGHT. / CHOICE** [ ] [–]
(cd-s+=) *(FCD 163)* – Analogue test 90. *(re-iss. Aug95 on 'Internal'; LIECD 26)*
(12") *(FX 163)* – Midnight (Sasha mix) / Choice (Orbital & Eye & I mix).
(cd-s+=) *(FXCD 163)* – Analogue test 90 (remix).

Sep 91. (cd/c/lp) *(828248-2/-4/-1)* <351001> **UNTITLED (ORBITAL 1)** [71] [ ]
– The moebius / Speed freak / Oolaa / Desert storm / Fahrenheit 303 / Steel cube idolatry / High rise / Chime (live) / Midnight (live) / Belfast / Macrohead. *(cd w-out last track, repl. by)* – I think it's disgusting. *(c+=)* – Untitled. *(re-iss. Apr96 & Apr97 on 'Internal' cd/c; TRU CD/MC 9) (re-iss. Apr99 on 'London' cd/c; 828248-2/-4) (cd re-iss. Oct00 on 'Warners'; 3984 28230-2)*

Feb 92. (12"ep) *(FX 181)* **MUTATIONS (I): OOLAA (Joey Beltram remix) / OOLAA (Meat Beat Manifesto mix) / CHIME (Joey Beltram). / SPEED FREAK (Moby mix)** [24] [–]
(12"ep) *(FXR 181)* – MUTATIONS (II): Chime (Ray Keith mix) / Chime (Crime remix) / Steel cube idolatory / Farenheit 303.
(cd-ep) *(FCD 181)* – Oolaa (Joey Beltram mix) / Chime (Ray Keith mix) / Speed freak / Fahrenheit 303.

Internal — Ffrr-London

Sep 92. (12"ep/cd-ep) *(LIARX/LIECD 1)* **RADICCIO EP** [37] [–]
– Halycon / The naked and the dead.
(cd-ep) *(LIECD 2)* – The naked and the dead / Sunday.
(cd-ep re-iss. Aug95; LIECD 27)

Apr 93. (12"ep/c-ep) *(LIARX/LIEMC 7)* **LUSH 3-1. / LUSH 3-2 / LUSH 3-3 (Underworld mix)** [ ] [–]
(12"ep) *(LIAXR 7)* – LUSH 3-4 (Psychick Warriors Ov Gaia) / LUSH 3-5 (CJ Bollard).
(cd-ep) *(LIECD 7)* – (all 5 tracks).

Jun 93. (cd/c/lp) *(TRU CD/MC/LP 2)* <351026> **UNTITLED (ORBITAL II)** [28] [ ]
– Time becomes / Planet of the shapes / Lush 3-1 / Lush 3-2 / Impact (the Earth is burning) / Remind / Walk now . . . / Monday / Halycon + on + on / Input out. *(re-iss. Aug95; same) (re-iss. Apr99 on 'London' cd/c; 828386-2/-4) (cd re-iss. Oct00 on 'Warners'; 3942 28231-2)*

Mar 94. (cd-ep/12"ep) *(LIECD/LIARX 12)* **THE JOHN PEEL SESSIONS EP** [ ] [–]
– Lush (Euro-tunnel disaster '94) / Walk about / Semi detached / Attached.
(cd-ep) **DIVERSIONS EP** *(LIEDC 12)* – Impact USA / Lush 3 (Euro-Tunnel disaster '94) / Walkabout / Lush 3-5 (CJ Bolland) / Lush 3-4 (Warrior drift) / Lush 3-4 (Underworld).

Aug 94. (cd/c/d-lp) *(TRU CD/MC/LP 5)* <124027> **SNIVILIZATION** [4] [ ]
– Forever / I wish I had duck feet / Sad but true / Crash and carry / Science friction / Philosophy by numbers / Kein trink wasser / Quality seconds / Are we here? / Attached. *(re-iss. Aug95 & Apr97; same) (re-iss. Apr99 on 'London' cd/c; 828536-2/-4) (cd re-iss. Oct00 on 'Warners'; 3984 28233-2)*

Sep 94. (12"ep/c-ep) *(LIARX/LIEMC 15)* **ARE WE HERE? EP** [33] [–]
– Are we here?: Who are they? – Do they here? – They did it (mix).
(cd-ep+=/s-cd-ep+=) *(LIE CD/DC 15)* – Are we here?: What was that? – Criminal Justice bill? – Industry standard?.

— In May'95, they issued 'Belfast'/'Wasted (vocal mix)' on special cd-s which hit UK No.53. THERAPY? was on flip side with 'Innocent X'.

Aug 95. (d7"ep/12"ep/cd-ep/s-cd-ep) *(LIE/LIARX/LIECD/LIEDP 23)* **UNTITLED EP** [ ] [–]
– Times fly (slow) / Sad but new / Times fly (fast) / The tranquilizer.
(above was not eligible for UK chart position due to it's length)

Apr 96. (12"/cd-s) *(LIARX/LIECD 30)* **THE BOX. / THE BOX** [11] [–]
(cd-s+=) *(LICDP 30)* – (2 extra mixes).

Apr 96. (cd/cd/c/3x12"lp) *(TRU DC/CD/MC/LP 10)* <124087> **IN SIDES** [5] [ ]
– The girl with the sun in her head / P.E.T.R.O.L. / The box / Dwr budr / Adnan's / Out there somewhere? *(cd re-iss. Apr97 on 'Dutch East India'; 124129CD) (cd re-iss. Apr99 on 'London'; 828881-2) (cd re-iss. Oct00 on 'Warners'; 3984 28232-2)*

Jan 97. (cd-s) *(LIECD 37)* <850990> **SATAN (live at New York) / OUT THERE SOMEWHERE (live at New York)** [3] Sep97 [ ]
(cd-s) *(LICDP 37)* – ('A'-live at Chelmsford) / Lush 3 (live at Boston) / The girl with the sun in her head (live at Boston).
(cd-s) *(LICDD 37)* – ('A'-Industry standard edit) / Chime (live at Chelmsford) / Impact (live at Chelmsford).

— (due to length of above it also hit No.48 in the UK album charts)

FFRR-London — FFRR-London

Apr 97. (c-s/12"/cd-s) *(FCS/FX/FCD 296)* **THE SAINT / THE SINNER** [3] [ ]
(cd-s+=) *(FCDP 296)* – Belfast (live) / Petrol (live).

Aug 97. (cd/c; by MICHAEL KAMEN & ORBITAL) *(828939-2/-4)* **EVENT HORIZON (soundtrack)** [ ] [–]
– The forward decks / The main access corridor / Engineering / The event horizon.

Mar 99. (12") *(FX 358)* **STYLE. / OLD STYLE / BIG PIPE STYLE / NEW STYLE** [13] [–]
(cd-s) *(FCD 358)* – (first 2 tracks) / Mock Tudor.
(cd-s) *(FCDP 358)* – (third & fourth tracks) / An fhomhair.

Apr 99. (cd/c/d-lp) *(556076-2/-4/-1)* *<31065>* **THE MIDDLE OF NOWHERE** [4] [ ]
– Way out – > / Spare parts express / Know where to run / I don't know you people / Otono / Nothing left 1 / Nothing left 2 / Style. *(cd re-iss. Oct00 on 'Warners'; 3984 27194-2)*

Jul 99. (cd-s) *(FCDP 365)* **NOTHING LEFT / (mixes; Way Out West / Schizoid man)** [32] [–]
(cd-s) *(FCD 365)* – Much ado about nothing left / *Nothing* left out / Nothing left (Tsunami one remix).

Feb 00. (12"/cd-s; by ORBITAL & ANGELO BADALAMENTI) *(FX/FCD 377)* **BEACHED / BEACHED (long) / DOCTOR LOOK OUT** [36] [–]

Apr 01. (cd-s) *(FCD 395)* **FUNNY BREAK (ONE IS ENOUGH) / (mixes; weekend ravers / Up mix by Layo & Bushwacka)** [21] [–]
(cd-s) *(FCDP 395)* – Beelzebeat / ('A'mix by Plump DJ's) / ('A'-Down mix by Layo & Bushwacka).
(12") *(FX 395)* – ('A'-weekend ravers + Plump DJ mixes).
(12") *(FXX 395)* – ('A'-Layo & Bushwacka Up & Down mixes).

Apr 01. (cd) *(8573 87782-2)* *<31167>* **THE ALTOGETHER** [11] May01 [ ]
– Tension / Funny break (one is enough) / Oi! / Pay per view / Tootled / Last thing / Doctor? / Shadows / Waving not drowning / Illuminate / Meltdown.

May 02. (cd-ep) *(FCD 407)* **REST AND PLAY EP** [33] [–]
– Frenetic / Illuminate (with DAVID GRAY) / Chime (live style mix).
(cd-s) *(FCDP 407)* – (first 2 track/versions) / Monorail.
(12") *(FX 407)* – Frenetic (mix) / Chime (live style mix).

ffrr — Rhino

Jun 02. (cd/d-lp) *(0927 46190-2/-1)* *<74493>* **WORK 1989-2002** (compilation) [36] Aug02 [ ]
– Chime / Choice / Illuminate (with DAVID GRAY) / Satan / Nothing left / Halcyon and on and on / Impact / Are we here? / Style / The box / Frenetic (with LISA BILLSON) / Lush 3.1 / Funny break / Belfast.

E.M.I. — E.M.I.

Oct 03. (cd/lp) *(<593784-2/-1>)* **OCTANE** (soundtrack) [ ] [ ]
– Octane / Through the night / Strangeness in the night / Preacher / Moments of crisis / Frantic / Breaking and entering / Chasing the tanker / Total paranoia / Confrontation / Initiation / Meet the father / Blood is thicker / The road ahead.

ORCHESTRAL MANOEUVRES IN THE DARK

Formed: West Kirby, Liverpool, England . . . Autumn 1978, initially as The ID, by ANDREW McCLUSKEY and PAUL HUMPHREYS. After a one-off indie single, the coldly pulsing 'ELECTRICITY', for 'Factory', they signed to 'Virgin' subsidiary label, 'Dindisc'. Early in 1980, the group hit the UK Top 75 with 'RED FRAME – WHITE LIGHT', paving the way for an eponymous Top 30 parent album. Later that summer, they scored further chart successes with 'MESSAGES' and 'ENOLA GAY' (the name of the plane which dropped the Hiroshima bomb), the latter an infectiously melancholy swirl of electronica which belied its horrific subject matter. The song was also the highlight of the 'ORGANISATION' (1980) album, wherein the drum machines of previous recordings had been replaced with a live drummer, MALCOLM HOLMES. Heavily influenced by KRAFTWERK, OMD's cerebral electro-pop became progressively warmer and more commercial as the decade wore on. Beginning with the soporific lilt of 'SOUVENIR', McCLUSKEY and HUMPHREYS embarked upon the most successful period of their career, releasing a string of Top 5 hits and well-received albums, namely 'ARCHITECTURE & MORALITY' (1981), 'DAZZLE SHIPS' (1983), 'JUNK CULTURE' (1984) and 'CRUSH' (1985). O.M.D. were a constant feature in the singles chart through the early to mid 80's, like a more pretentious, less claustrophobic cousin to DEPECHE MODE, their biggest hit of the era being the breezy 'LOCOMOTION' (mercifully, not a cover of the LITTLE EVA number!), complete with horn stabs courtesy of the WEIR BROTHERS (NEIL & GRAHAM) who later joined the group as a permanent fixture. With the 'CRUSH' album, OMD enjoyed a brief flurry of Stateside success via the twee romanticism of the 'SO IN LOVE' and 'SECRET' singles, although by the release of the patchy 'PACIFIC AGE' (1986) the following year, the writing partnership of McCLUSKEY and HUMPHREYS was beginnning to falter. The latter eventually departed in 1989 to form The LISTENING POOL, while McCLUSKEY carried on with OMD as a solo project, resurfacing in early '91 with the annoying 'SAILING ON THE SEVEN SEAS', a Top 3 hit. The subsequent album, 'SUGAR TAX' (1991) also made the Top 3 although the revamped OMD was clearly an entirely different beast, airbrushed pop lacking the mystery and romance of the early material. A further album, 'LIBERATOR', carried on in a similar vein. • **Songwriters:** All material written by McCLUSKEY & HUMPHREYS, until the latter's exit. Covered; I'M WAITING FOR THE MAN (Velvet Underground) / NEON LIGHTS (Kraftwerk). • **Trivia:** An ID track 'JULIA'S SONG', appeared on an 'Open Eye' indie compilation album, 'Street To Street' in 1978.

Album rating: ORCHESTRAL MANOEUVRES IN THE DARK (*7) / ORGANISATION (*6) / ARCHITECTURE & MORALITY (*7) / DAZZLE SHIPS (*5) / JUNK CULTURE (*6) / CRUSH (*6) / THE PACIFIC AGE (*4) / IN THE DARK – THE BEST OF OMD compilation (*8) / SUGAR TAX (*5) / LIBERATOR (*5) / UNIVERSAL (*5) / THE OMD SINGLES compilation (*7)

ANDREW McCLUSKEY (b.24 Jun'59, Wirral, England) – vocals, bass, synthesizers (ex-DALEK I) / **PAUL HUMPHRIES** (b.27 Feb'60, London, England) – keyboards, synths. (ex-The ID) with backing from computer 'Winston'.

Factory — not iss.

May 79. (7") *(FAC 6)* **ELECTRICITY. / ALMOST** [ ] [–]

Dindisc — not iss.

Sep 79. (7") *(DIN 2)* **ELECTRICITY (re-recorded). / ALMOST** [ ] [–]

Feb 80. (7"/12") *(DIN 6/+12)* **RED FRAME – WHITE LIGHT. / I BETRAY MY FRIENDS** [67] [–]

— guests **DAVID FAIRBURN** – guitar / **MALCOLM HOLMES** – drums / **MARTIN COOPER** – sax

Feb 80. (2x12"lp/c) *(DID/+C 2)* **ORCHESTRAL MANOEUVRES IN THE DARK** [27] [–]
– Bunker soldiers / Almost / Mystereality / Electricity / The Messerschmit twins / Messages / Julia's song / Red frame – white light / Dancing / Pretending to see the future. *(re-iss. Aug84 on 'Virgin' lp/c; OVED/+C 96) (cd-iss. Jul87; DIDCD 2)*

May 80. (7") *(DIN 15)* **MESSAGES. / TAKING SIDES AGAIN** [13] [–]
(ext-10") *(DIN 15-10)* – Waiting for the man.

— added **DAVID HUGHES** – keyboards (ex-DALEK I LOVE YOU, ex-SECRETS) and now f/t member **MALCOLM HOLMES** – drums (ex-CLIVE LANGER & THE BOXES, ex-ID)

Sep 80. (7"/ext.12") *(DIN 22/+12)* **ENOLA GAY. / ANNEX** [8] [–]

Oct 80. (lp/c) *(DID/+C 6)* **ORGANISATION** [6] [–]
– Enola Gay / 2nd thought / VCL XI / Motion and heart / Statues / The misunderstanding / The more I see you / Promise / Stanlow. *(free 7"ep)* – INTRODUCING RADIOS / PROGRESS. / DISTANCE FADES BETWEEN US / WHEN I WAS SIX *(re-iss. Aug88 on 'Virgin' lp/c; OVED/+C 147) (cd-iss. Jul87; DIDCD 6)*

— **MALCOLM COOPER** – saxophone, keyboards (ex-DALEK I LOVE YOU) repl. HUGHES

Dindisc Epic

Aug 81. (7"/ext.10") *(DIN 24/+10)* **SOUVENIR. / MOTION AND HEART (Amazon version) / SACRED HEART** 3 –

Oct 81. (7"/ext.12") *(DIN 36/+12)* **JOAN OF ARC. / THE ROMANCE OF THE TELESCOPE (unfinished version)** 5

Nov 81. (lp/c) *(DID/+C 12) <37721>* **ARCHITECTURE & MORALITY** 3
– New stone age / She's leaving / Souvenir / Sealand / Joan Of Arc / Joan Of Arc (Maid of Orleans) / Architecture and morality / Georgia / The beginning and the end. *(cd-iss. 1988 on 'Virgin' lp/c; OVED/+C 276) (re-iss. Apr90; DIDCD 12) (cd re-iss. Jan95; CDIDX 12)*

Jan 82. (7") *(DIN 40)* **MAID OF ORLEANS (THE WALTZ JOAN OF ARC). / NAVIGATION** 4
(12"+=) *(DIN 40-12)* – Of all the things we've made.
(3"cd-s iss.Jun88; CDT 27)

Jan 82. (7") **SOUVENIR. / NEW STONE AGE** –

Virgin Epic-Virgin

Feb 83. (7"/7"pic-d)(12") *(VS/+Y 527)<VS 527-12)* **GENETIC ENGINEERING. / 4-NEU** 20 –

Mar 83. (lp/c) *(V/TCV 2261) <38543>* **DAZZLE SHIPS** 5
– Radio Prague / Genetic engineering / ABC auto-industry / Telegraph / This is Helena / International / Dazzle ships / The romance of the telescope / Silent running / Radio waves / Time zones / Of all the things we've made. *(cd-iss. 1985; CDV 2261) (re-iss. 1987 lp/c; OVED/+C 106) (cd re-iss. Apr97 on 'Virgin-VIP'; CDVIP 170)*

Apr 83. (7"/7"pic-d)(12") *(VS/+Y 580)(VS 580-12)* **TELEGRAPH. / 66 AND FADING** 42 –

May 83. (7") **TELEGRAPH. / THIS IS HELENA** –

Virgin A&M

Apr 84. (7"/7"sha-pic-d) *(VS/+Y 660)* **LOCOMOTION. / HER BODY IN MY SOUL** 5 Nov84
(ext.12") *(VS 660-12)* – The avenue. *(3"cd-s-iss.Jun88; CDT 12)*

May 84. (lp/c) *(V/TCV 2310) <5027>* **JUNK CULTURE** 9 Nov84
– Junk culture / Tesla girls / Locomotion / Apollo / Never turn away / Love and violence / Hard day / All wrapped up / White trash / Talking loud and clear. *(cd-iss. 1986; CDV 2310) (re-iss. Mar90 lp/c; OVED/+C 215) (cd re-iss. Aug98 on 'Virgin-VIP'; CDVIP 215)*

Jun 84. (7"/7"pic-d)(12") *(VS/+Y 685)(VS 685-12)***TALKING LOUD AND CLEAR. / JULIA'S SONG** 11 –

Aug 84. (7") *(VS 705)* **TESLA GIRLS. / TELEGRAPH (live)** 21 –
(12"+=)(c-s+=) *(VS 705-12)(TVS 705)* – Garden city.

Oct 84. (7"/7"pic-d) *(VS/+Y 727)* **NEVER TURN AWAY. / WRAP-UP** 70 –
(ext.12") *(VS 727-12)* – Waiting for the man (live).

May 85. (7") *(VS 766) <2746>* **SO IN LOVE. / CONCRETE HANDS** 27 Aug85 26
(ext;12")(ext.12"pic-d) *(VS 766-13)(VSY 766-14)* – Maria Gallante.
(d7"++=) *(VS 766)* – White trash (live).

Jun 85. (lp)(c) *(V/TCV 2349) <5077>* **CRUSH** 13 Jul85 38
– So in love / Secret / Bloc bloc bloc / Women III / Crush / 88 seconds in Greensboro / The native daughters of the west / La femme accident / Hold you / The lights are going out. *(cd-iss. Jan86; CDV 2349) (cd re-iss. Oct96 on 'Virgin-VIP'; CDVIP 155)*

Jul 85. (7") *(VS 796)* **SECRET. / DRIFT** 34 –
(ext-d12"+=) *(VS 796-12)* – Red frame – white light / I betray my friends.

Oct 85. (7"/7"sha-pic-d) *(VS/+S 811)* **LA FEMME ACCIDENT. / FIREGUN** 42
(ext.d12"+=) *(VSD 811-12)* – Locomotion (live) / Enola Gay (live).

Nov 85. (7") *<2794>* **SECRET. / FIREGUN** – 63

Feb 86. (7") *<2811>* **IF YOU LEAVE. / LA FEMME ACCIDENT** – 4

Apr 86. (7") *(VS 843)* **IF YOU LEAVE. / 88 SECONDS IN GREENSBORO** 48 –
(12") *(VS 843-12)* – ('A'extended) / Locomotion (live).

—— added The **WEIR BROTHERS** (NEIL & GRAHAM) (had guested on earlier songs)

Aug 86. (7"/7"pic-d) *(VS/+Y 888) <2872>* **(FOREVER) LIVE AND DIE. / THIS TOWN** 11 19
(12"+=) *(VS 888-13)* – ('A'extended).

Sep 86. (cd/c/lp) *(CD/TC+/V 2398) <5144>* **THE PACIFIC AGE** 15 Oct86 47
– Stay (the black rose and the universal wheel) / (Forever) Live and die / The Pacific age / The dead girls / Shame / Southern / Flame of hope / Goddess of love / We love you / Watch us fall.

Nov 86. (7") *(VS 911)* **WE LOVE YOU. / WE LOVE YOU (dub)** 54
(12"+=) *(VS 911-12)* – ('A'extended).
(d7"+=) *(VSD 911)* – If you leave / 88 seconds on Greensboro.
(free c-s w7"+=) *(VSC 911)* – Souvenir / Electricity / Enola Gay / Joan of Arc.

Apr 87. (7") *(VS 938)* **SHAME (re-recorded). / GODDESS OF LOVE** 52
(12"+=) *(VS 938-12)* – ('B're-recorded version).
(cd-s+=) *(MIKE 938-12)* – (Forever) Live and die / Messages.

Jan 88. (7") *(VSG 987) <3002>* **DREAMING. / SATELLITE** 50 Feb88 16
(ext.12"pic-d) *(VS 987-12)* – Gravity never failed.
(cd-s++=/3"cd-s++=) *(VDCD/+X 987)* – Dreaming.
(re-dist.Jun88, hit Uk No.60)
(10") *(VS 987-10)* – ('A'side) / ('A'William Orbit mix) / Messages / Secret.

Feb 88. (pic-cd/cd/c/lp) *(CDP/CD/TC+/OMD 1) <5186>* **IN THE DARK – THE BEST OF O.M.D.** (compilation) 2 46
– Electricity / Messages / Enola Gay / Souvenir / Joan of Arc / Maid of Orleans (Joan Of Arc waltz) / Talking loud and clear / Tesla girls / Locomotion / So in love / Secret / If you leave / (Forever) Live and die / Dreaming. *(cd+=)* – Telegraph / We love you (12"version) / La femme accident (12"version) / Genetic engineering. *(re-iss. Sep94; same)*

OMD

—— **ANDY McCLUSKEY** now sole survivor after others left 1989. HUMPHREYS formed The LISTENING POOL in the early 90's. / added **STUART BOYLE** – guitar / **NIGEL IPINSON** – keyboards / **PHIL COXON** – keyboards / **ABE JUCKS** – drums

Virgin Virgin

Mar 91. (7"/c-s) *(VS/+C 1310)* **SAILING ON THE SEVEN SEAS. / BURNING** 3
(12") *(VS 1310-12)* – ('A'extended) / Floating on the seven seas.
(cd-s) *(VSCDX 1310)* – ('A'extended) / Dancing on the seven seas / Big town.
(cd-s) *(VSCD 1310)* – ('A'side) / Floating on the seven seas / Dancing on the seaven seas (Larrabee mix) / Sugartax.

May 91. (cd/c/lp) *(CD/TC+/V 2648) <91715>* **SUGAR TAX** 3
– Sailing on the seven seas / Pandora's box / Then you turn away / Speed of light / Was it something I said / Big town / Call my name / Apollo XI / Walking on air / Walk tall / Neon lights / All that glitters.

Jun 91. (7"/c-s) *(VS/+C 1331)* **PANDORA'S BOX. / ALL SHE WANTS IS EVERYTHING** 7
(cd-s+=) *(VSCD 1331)* – ('A'-Constant pressure mix) / ('A'-Diesel fingers mix).
(12") *(VS 1331-12)* – (2-'A'mixes).
(cd-s) *(VSCDX 1331)* – (3-'A'mixes).

Sep 91. (7"/c-s) *(VS/+C 1368)* **THEN YOU TURN AWAY. / SUGAR TAX** 50
(cd-s+=) *(VSCD 1368)* – Area / ('A'-Inforce repeat mix).
(cd-s) *(VSCDG 1368)* – ('A'side) / ('A'-Repeat mix) / Sailing on the seven seas / Vox humana.

Nov 91. (7"/c-s) *(VS/+C 1380)* **CALL MY NAME. / WALK TALL** 50
(12") *(VS 1380-12)* – ('A'side) / Brides of Frankenstein.
(cd-s++=) *(VSCD 1380)* – ('A'side) / ('A'version) / Brides . . . (dub).

May 93. (7"/c-s) *(VS/+C 1444)* **STAND ABOVE ME. / CAN I BELIEVE YOU** 21
(cd-s+=) *(VSCDG 1444)* – ('A'-Transcendental mix) / ('A'-Hynofunk mix).
(12") *(VS 1444-12)* – ('A'side) / ('A'-Transcendental mix) / ('A'-10 minute version).

Jun 93. (cd/c/lp) *(CD/TC+/V 2715) <88225>* **LIBERATOR** 14
– Stand above me / Everyday / King of stone / Dollar girl / Dream of me (based on Love's theme) / Sunday morning / Agnus Dei / Love and hate you / Heaven is / Best years of our lives / Christine / Only tears. *(cd re-iss. Aug98 on 'VIP-Virgin'; CDVIP 217)*

Jul 93. (7"/c-s) *(VS/+C 1461)* **DREAM OF ME (BASED ON LOVE'S THEME). / ('A'mix)** 24
(cd-s+=) *(VSCDT 1461)* – Strange sensations / The place you fear the most.
(cd-s) *(VSCDX 1461)* – ('A'side) / Enola Gay / Dreaming / Call my name.

Sep 93. (7"/c-s) *(VS/+C 1471)* **EVERYDAY. / ELECTRICITY (live)** 59
(cd-s+=) *(VSCDT 1471)* – Walk tall (live) / Locomotion (live).

—— **STUART KERSHAW** – drums; repl. JUCKS

Aug 96. (c-s/cd-s) *(VSC/+DT 1599)* **WALKING ON THE MILKY WAY / MATTHEW STREET / NEW DARK AGE** 17 –
(cd-s) *(VSCDG 1599)* – ('A'side) / Joan of Arc (live) / Maid of Orleans (live) / Walking on air (live).

Sep 96. (cd/c) *(CDV/TCV 2807)* **UNIVERSAL** [24] [–]
– Universal / Walking on the Milky Way / The Moon & the Sun / The Black Sea / Very close to far away / The gospel of St Jude / That was then / Too late / The boy from the chemist is here to see you / If you're still in love with me / New head / Victory waltz.

Oct 96. (c-s) *(VSC 1606)* **UNIVERSAL / HEAVEN IS** [55] [–]
(cd-s+=) *(VSCDT 1606)* – Messages (live).
(cd-s) *(VSCDG 1606)* – ('A'side) / King of stone (live) / Talking loud & clear (live) / ('A'-album version).

Sep 98. (cd-s) *(VSCDT 1694)* **THE OMD REMIXES: ENOLA GAY (OMD vs SASH!) / ELECTRICITY (Micronauts mix) / SOUVENIR (Moby mix)** [35] [–]
(12") *(VST 1694)* – (first mix) / Souvenir (hard house) / Souvenir (7am version).
(12") *(VSTX 1694)* – (first two mixes) / Apollo XI (Northern electric soul remix).

Sep 98. (cd/c) *(CDV/TCV 2859)* <46520> **THE OMD SINGLES** (compilation) [16] Nov98 [ ]
– Electricity / Messages / Enola Gay / Souvenir / Joan of Arc / Maid of Orleans / Tesla girls / Locomotion / Talking loud and clear / So in love / If you leave / (Forever) Live and die / Dreaming / Sailing the seven seas / Pandora's box / Call my name / Dream of me (based on love's theme).

– compilations, etc. –

May 84. (lp) *Epic;* **ORCHESTRAL MANOEUVRES IN THE DARK** [–] [ ]
– (compilation of first 2 albums)

Feb 89. (12") *Old Gold; (OG 4099)* **ENOLA GAY. / ELECTRICITY** [ ] [–]

Mar 89. (12") *Old Gold; (OG 4109)* **SOUVENIR (extended). / TALKING LOUD AND CLEAR (extended)** [ ] [–]

Feb 89. (12") *Virgin; (SP12 285)* **BRIDES OF FRANKENSTEIN (OMD megaremixes: LOCOMOTION / SO IN LOVE / SECRET / IF YOU LEAVE / WE LOVE YOU)** [–] [ ]

Nov 90. (3xpic-cd-box) *Virgin; (TPAK 7)* **CD BOXED SET** [ ] [–]
– (first 3 albums)

☐ ORGANISATION (see under ⇒ KRAFTWERK)

Beth ORTON

Born: Dec'70, Norfolk, England. A one-time Buddhist nun (after her mother died of cancer), she was discovered in 1991/2 by WILLIAM ORBIT who saw her performing in a play. Her collaborative work with ORBIT (on the Japanese-only 'SUPERPINKYMANDY' CD) was subsequently heard by The CHEMICAL BROTHERS and RED SNAPPER, the former act employing her downbeat but poignant vocals on the 1995 'Exit Planet Dust' album track, 'Alive Alone'. The following year, she found herself on the books of 'Heavenly' records, delivering her debut album, 'TRAILER PARK' soon after. An affecting blend of fragile folk and subtle lo-fi trip-hop rhythms, it won praise from such diverse camps as Folk Roots magazine and Mixmag (it was even nominated for the 1997 Mercury Music Prize). The same year (1997), BETH's four singles scored successively higher chart placings, the re-released 'SHE CRIES YOUR NAME', revealing the melancholy depths of her NICK DRAKE/SANDY DENNY-esque muse. The lanky ORTON (she's 6 feet tall) ended the year on a high note, collaborating with her long-time hero, TERRY CALLIER on the Top 40 EP 'BEST BIT'. The princess of bedsitter music served up a second helping of rich, thought-provoking tunes in the shape of 1999's 'CENTRAL RESERVATION'. A deserved UK Top 20 success (with guest appearances from BEN WATT, BEN HARPER, DAVE ROBACK and DR. JOHN), BETH also made some headway in the States where she had befriended BECK (to namecheck but a few). Songs such as 'STOLEN CAR', the title track (both Top 40 hits) and 'STARS ALL SEEM TO WEEP' were emotionally and lyrically attuned like paintings set on the deepest canvas taking every colour imaginable from palettes of silver. • **Songwriters:** Most with rhythm section FRIEND and BARNES, except SHE CRIES YOUR NAME; she co-wrote this with WILLIAM ORBIT. Covered IT'S NOT THE SPOTLIGHT (Goffin – Goldberg) / I WISH I NEVER SAW THE SUNSHINE (Spector – Greenwich – Barry) / DON'T WANNA KNOW 'BOUT EVIL (John Martyn) / DOLPHINS (Fred Neil).

Album rating: SUPERPINKYMANDY (*5) / TRAILER PARK (*8) / CENTRAL RESERVATION (*8) / DAYBREAKER (*6) / PASS IN TIME compilation (*8)

BETH ORTON – vocals, acoustic guitar (ex-SPILL); with **TED BARNES** – guitar (of JUNCTIONS) / **ALI FRIEND** – double bass (of RED SNAPPER) / **WILL BLANCHARD** – drums (of SANDALS) / guest **DAVID BOULTER** – harmonium / + string section

not iss. Toshiba

1993. (cd) *(TOC 7984)* **SUPERPINKYMANDY** [–] Japan [–]
– Don't wanna know about evil / Faith will carry / Yesterday's gone / She cries your name / When you wake / Roll the dice / City blue / The prisoner / Where do you go / Release me.

Heavenly Dedicated

Jul 96. (7"one-sided) *(HVN 56)* **I WISH I NEVER SAW THE SUNSHINE** [ ] [–]

Sep 96. (10"ep/cd-ep) *(HVN 60 10/CD)* **SHE CRIES YOUR NAME / TANGENT. / SAFETY / IT'S NOT THE SPOTLIGHT** [ ] [–]

Oct 96. (cd/c/lp) *(HVNLP 17 CD/MC/LP)* <44007> **TRAILER PARK** [68] [ ]
– She cries your name / Tangent / Don't need a reason / Live as you dream / Sugar boy / Touch me with your love / Whenever / How far / Someone's daughter / I wish I never saw the sunshine / Galaxy of emptiness.

Jan 97. (10"ep/cd-ep) *(HVN 64 10/CD)* **TOUCH ME WITH YOUR LOVE. / PEDESTAL / GALAXY OF EMPTINESS** [60] [–]

Mar 97. (c-ep/10"ep/cd-ep) *(HVN 65 CS/10/CD)* **SOMEONE'S DAUGHTER. / I WISH I NEVER SAW THE SUNSHINE / IT'S THIS I AM I FIND** [49] [–]

Jun 97. (c-s) *(HVN 68CS)* **SHE CRIES YOUR NAME (1997 version) / IT'S NOT THE SPOTLIGHT** [40] [–]
(10"+=/cd-s+=) *(HVN 68-10/CD)* – Bullet / Best bit.

Heavenly Heavenly

Dec 97. (c-ep; BETH ORTON featuring TERRY CALLIER) *(<HVN 72CS>)* **BEST BIT EP** [36] [ ]
– Best bit / Skimming stone / Dolphins.
(12"ep+=/cd-ep+=) *(<HVN 72 12/CD>)* – Lean on me.

—— next with guitarist **BEN HARPER**

Mar 99. (c-s) *(HVN 89CS)* **STOLEN CAR / PRECIOUS MAYBE** [34] [ ]
(cd-s+=) *(HVN 89CD)* – I love how you love me.
(cd-s) *(HVN 89CD2)* – ('A'side) / Stars all seem to weep (shed version) / Touch me with your love (live).

Mar 99. (d-lp/c/cd) *(HVNLP 22/+MC/CD)* <19038> **CENTRAL RESERVATION** [17] [ ]
– Stolen car / Sweet decline / Couldn't cause me harm / So much more / Pass in time / Central reservation / Stars all seem to weep / Love like laughter / Blood red river / Devil song / Feel to believe / Central reservation.

Sep 99. (cd-s) *(HVN 92CD1)* **CENTRAL RESERVATION. / CENTRAL RESERVATION (Spiritual Life – Ibadan remix) / CENTRAL RESERVATION (William Orbit remix)** [37] [–]
(cd-s) *(HVN 92CD2)* – ('A'-Deep dish modern red rock mixes; remix edit / remix / 2000 dub).
(12") *(HVN 92-12)* – ('A'-Spiritual Life – Ibadan remix) / ('A'-Deep dish modern red rock 2000 dub).

Jul 02. (cd-ep) *(HVN 115CD)* **CONCRETE SKY EP** [ ] [–]
– Concrete sky / Ali's waltz / Bobby Gentry / Carmella (Four Tet remix).

Jul 02. (lp/cd) *(HVNLP 37/+CD)* <39918> **DAYBREAKER** [8] [ ]
– Paris train / Concrete sky / Mount Washington / Anywhere / Daybreaker / Carmella / God song / This one's gonna bruise / Ted's waltz / Thinking about tomorrow. *(ltd-cd-iss. Oct02; HVNLP 37CDX)*

Nov 02. (cd-s) *(HVN 125CDS)* **ANYWHERE / BEAUTIFUL WORLD / ANYWHERE (Two Lone Swordsmen remix) / ANYWHERE (video)** [55] [–]

Nov 02. (d12") <*ASW 77821*> **ANYWHERE (remixes)** [–] [ ]
– Anywhere (mixes; Two Lone Swordsmen / instrumental / Adrian Sherwood / instrumental) / Carmella (Four Tet remix) / Daybreaker / Daybreaker (instrumental).

Mar 03. (cd-s) *(HVN 129CD)* **THINKING ABOUT TPMORROW / DAYBREAKER (Roots Manuva mix) / DAYBREAKER (Four Tet mix)** [57] [–]

Sep 03. (cd) <*92266*> **THE OTHER SIDE OF DAYBREAK** (remixes) [–] [ ]

Sep 03. (d-cd) *(HVNLP 45CD)* <*56163*> **PASS IN TIME – THE DEFINITIVE COLLECTION** (compilation) [43] Oct03 [ ]
– She cries your name / Someone's daughter / Touch me with your love / Sugar boy / Galaxy of emptiness / I wish I never saw the sunshine / Best bit / The same day / Stolen car / Sweetest decline / Pass in time / Central reservation / Concrete sky / Thinking about tomorrow / Central reservation (Ibaden remix) / Where do I begin (with CHEMICAL BROTHERS) / Stars all seem to weep / Safety / Pedestal / Dolphins (with TERRY CALLIER) / It's not the spotlight / Don't wanna know 'bout evil / Where do you go / Water from a vine leaf (with WILLIAM ORBIT).

Ozzy OSBOURNE

Born: JOHN MICHAEL OSBOURNE, 3 Dec'48, Aston, Birmingham, England. After eleven years as frontman for BLACK SABBATH, OSBOURNE was given his marching orders, forming his own BLIZZARD OF OZZ in 1980 alongside LEE KERSLAKE (drums, ex-URIAH HEEP), BOB DAISLEY (bass, ex-RAINBOW, ex-CHICKEN SHACK), DON AVERY (keyboards) and guitar wizard, RANDY RHOADS (ex-QUIET RIOT). Signing to Don Arden's 'Jet' label, OZZY and the band released their self-titled debut in 1980, hitting the UK Top 10 and narrowly missing the US Top 20. Hailed as OZZY's best work since 'SABBATH's heyday, the unholy alliance of RHOADS's music and OSBOURNE's lyrics (which, if anything, looked even more to the 'dark side' than the 'SABBATH material) produced such wonderfully grim fare as 'CRAZY TRAIN', 'SUICIDE SOLUTION' (later the subject of much JUDAS PRIEST-style courtroom controversy) and the epic 'MR. CROWLEY', inspiring multitudes of schoolkids to raise their pinkie and forefinger in cod-satanic salutation. The record went double platinum in the States, as did the follow-up, 'DIARY OF A MADMAN' (1981) (credited to OZZY solo), a cross-Atlantic Top 20 hit. Proving once and for all that the music industry is peopled by hard-bitten control freaks, OZZY proceeded to chomp on a live dove at a record company meeting later that year. Another infamous incident occurred only a few months later when the singer gnashed the head off a bat thrown onstage by a fan at a concert in Des Moines, cementing his reputation as heavy metal monster extraordinaire and public enemy No.1. 1982 proved to be an eventful year for 'the Oz', tragedy striking when his close friend and right hand man, RHODES, died in a plane crash in March. Consolation and a modicum of much needed stability came with his subsequent marriage to Don Arden's daughter, Sharon, on the 4th of July '82, the brave lass subsequently becoming his manager. BRAD GILLIS replaced RHODES for the live album of BLACK SABBATH covers, 'TALK OF THE DEVIL' (1982), before JAKE E. LEE was brought in as a more permanent fixture prior to 'BARK AT THE MOON' (1983). The rhythm section had also undergone numerous personnel changes with a final line-up of TOMMY ALDRIDGE (drums, ex-BLACK OAK ARKANSAS,etc.) and BOB DAISLEY. Another double platinum smash, the release of the record saw OZZY undertaking a mammoth US tour during which he unwittingly relieved himself on a wall of the Alamo monument in San Antonio, consequently being charged and banned from playing there. OZZY had always been a hard drinker and drug user, Sharon finally forcing him to attend the first of many unsuccessful sessions at the Betty Ford Clinic in 1984. His albums continued to sell consistently, particularly in America, despite constant line-up changes. 1988 saw the arrival of guitarist ZAKK WYLDE, heralded as a true successor to the revered RHODES. The late 80's also saw OSBOURNE retiring to his Buckinghamshire mansion with Sharon and his three kids, eventually kicking the booze and re-emerging in 1991 after being cleared of causing the death of three fans. In three separate, well documented cases, parents claimed OZZY's 'SUICIDE SOLUTION' had driven their siblings to kill themselves. 'NO MORE TEARS' (1991) was a triumphant comeback, OSBOURNE claiming the album would be his last and subsequently embarking on a farewell tour. The last two shows of the jaunt were opened by a ROB HALFORD (of JUDAS PRIEST)-fronted BLACK SABBATH, RONNIE JAMES DIO refusing to perform. Talks of a 'SABBATH reunion came to nothing although OZZY couldn't resist another tour and eventually an album, OZZMOSIS (1995). The record made the Top 5 in America where he's still regarded as something of a Metal Godfather; maybe it's the Brummie accent. OZZY has since stunned the metal world by rejoining BLACK SABBATH for concerts and a reunion album in 1998. A true grandaddy of the metal scene and one of its most enduring celebrities, OZZY was nearing double figures with the release of 'DOWN TO EARTH' (2001). Backed up a by a band of sterling metal pedigree (ZAKK WYLDE, ROBERT TRUJILLO and MIKE BORDIN), OZZY barked out another helping of, well, OZZY, spiced up with a few contemporary production touches. How many other 70's metal gods can be assured of a Top 5 US chart placing with a new record (Top 20 UK). In fact, such an icon is our OZZ that, in a kind of Big Brother in leather keks kinda stylee, a fly on the wall TV documentary, 'The Osbournes', was about to give American viewers an often hilarious insight into the man's (and his family's) domestic life. • **Songwriters:** OZZY lyrics, RHOADS/band music. OZZY later collaborated with BOB DAISLEY. • **Trivia:** In 1987, he played a bible-punching preacher in the film 'Trick Or Treat'.

Album rating: OZZY OSBOURNE'S BLIZZARD OF OZZ (*7) / DIARY OF A MADMAN (*6) / TALK OF THE DEVIL (*6) / BARK AT THE MOON (*5) / THE ULTIMATE SIN (*5) / TRIBUTE (*8) / NO REST FOR THE WICKED (*5) / JUST SAY OZZY (*5) / NO MORE TEARS (*7) / LIVE & LOUD (*6) / OZZMOSIS (*6) / THE OZZMAN COMETH – THE BEST OF . . . compilation (*8) / DOWN TO EARTH (*6) / THE ESSENTIAL OZZY OSBOURNE compilation (*8)

OZZY OSBOURNE'S BLIZZARD OF OZZ

OZZY OSBOURNE – vocals / **RANDY RHOADS** – guitar (ex-QUIET RIOT) / **LEE KERSLAKE** – drums (ex-URIAH HEEP) / **BOB DAISLEY** – bass (ex-RAINBOW, ex-CHICKEN SHACK) / **DON AVERY** – keyboards

Jet Jet-CBS

Sep 80. (7") *(JET 197)* **CRAZY TRAIN. / YOU LOOKING AT ME LOOKING AT YOU** [49] [–]

Sep 80. (lp/c) *(JET LP/CA 234)* <*36812*> **OZZY OSBOURNE'S BLIZZARD OF OZZ** [7] Mar81 [21]
– I don't know / Crazy train / Goodbye to romance / Dee / Suicide solution / Mr. Crowley / No bone movies / Revelation (Mother Earth) / Steal away (the night). *(re-iss. Nov87 on 'Epic' lp/c; 450453-1/-4) (cd-iss. Nov87 on 'Jet'; CDJET 234) (re-iss. cd Nov95 on 'Epic'; 481674-2)*

Nov 80. (7") *(JET 7-003)* <*37640*> **MR. CROWLEY (live). / YOU SAID IT ALL (live)** [46] Apr82 [ ]
(12"+=/12"pic-d+=) *(JET/+P 12-003)* – Suicide solution (live).

Apr 81. (7") <*02079*> **CRAZY TRAIN. / STEAL AWAY (THE NIGHT)** [–] [ ]

OZZY OSBOURNE

(same line-up, except AVERY)

Oct 81. (lp/c) *(JET LP/CA 237) <37492>* **DIARY OF A MADMAN** [14] [16]
– Over the mountain / Flying high again / You can't kill rock and roll / Believer / Little dolls / Tonight / S.A.T.O. / Diary of a madman. *(cd-iss. May87; CDJET 237) (re-iss. Apr91 on 'Epic' cd/c; 463086-2/-4) (re-iss. cd Nov95 on 'Epic'; 481677-2)*

Nov 81. (7"/12") *(JET 7/12 017)* **OVER THE MOUNTAIN. / I DON'T KNOW** [ ] [–]

Nov 81. (7") *<02582>* **FLYING HIGH AGAIN. / I DON'T KNOW** [–] [ ]

Feb 82. (7") *<02707>* **LITTLE DOLLS. / TONIGHT** [–] [ ]

—— (Nov'81) **RUDY SARZO** – bass (ex-QUIET RIOT) repl. DAISLEY (to URIAH HEEP) **TOMMY ALDRIDGE** – drums (ex-BLACK OAK ARKANSAS, etc) repl. KERSLAKE

—— (Apr'82) **BRAD GILLIS** – guitar (of NIGHT RANGER) repl. RANDY RHOADS who was killed in a light aeroplane crash on 19th Mar'82.

Nov 82. (d-lp/d-c) *(JET DP/CD 401) <38350>* **TALK OF THE DEVIL** (live at Ritz Club, NY) <US-title 'SPEAK OF THE DEVIL'> [21] [14]
– Symptom of the universe / Snowblind / Black sabbath / Fairies wear boots / War pigs / The wizard / N.I.B. / Sweet leaf / Never say die / Sabbath bloody sabbath / Iron man – Children of the grave / Paranoid. *(re-iss. Sep87 on 'Epic' d-lp/d-c; 451124-1/-4) (cd-iss. Jun89; 451124-2)* – (omits dialogue). *(re-iss. cd/d-lp complete.Jul91 on 'Castle'; CCS CD/LP 296) (re-iss. cd Nov95 as 'SPEAK OF THE DEVIL' on 'Epic'; 481679-2)*

Dec 82. (7"/7"pic-d) *(JET/+P 7-030)* **SYMPTOM OF THE UNIVERSE (live). / N.I.B. (live)** [ ] [–]
(12"+=) *(JET 12-030)* – Children of the grave (live).

Feb 83. (7") *<03302>* **IRON MAN (live). / PARANOID (live)** [–] [ ]

—— (Dec'82) **JAKE E. LEE** (b.JAKEY LOU WILLIAMS, San Diego, California, USA) – guitar (ex-RATT) repl. GILLIS who returned to NIGHT RANGER / **DON COSTA** – bass repl. PETE WAY (ex-UFO) who had deputised for the departing RUDY SARZO who had returned to QUIET RIOT. (He later joined WHITESNAKE)

—— **OZZY, JAKE E + TOMMY** re-recruited **BOB DAISLEY** to repl. COSTA

Epic / CBS Assoc.

Nov 83. (7"/12",12"silver/12"pic-d) *(A/TA/WA 3915)* **BARK AT THE MOON. / ONE UP ON THE B-SIDE** [21] [ ]

Dec 83. (7") *<04318>* **BARK AT THE MOON. / SPIDERS** [–] [ ]

Dec 83. (lp/c) *(EPC/40 25739) <38987>* **BARK AT THE MOON** [24] [19]
– Rock'n'roll rebel / Bark at the Moon / You're no different / Now you see it (now you don't) / Forever / So tired / Waiting for darkness / Spiders. *(re-iss. Apr86 lp/c; EPC/40 32780) (cd-iss. Oct88; CD 32780) (re-iss. cd Nov95; 481678-2)*

Mar 84. (7") *(A 4260) <04383>* **SO TIRED. / FOREVER (live)** [ ] [ ]
(12"+=/d7"+=) *(TA/DA 4260)* – Waiting for darkness / Paranoid (live).

—— ALDRIDGE was briefly replaced (Mar-May84) on tour by CARMINE APPICE.

May 84. (7") *(A 4452)* **SO TIRED. / BARK AT THE MOON (live)** [20] [ ]
(12"+=,12"gold+=) *(WA 4452)* – Waiting for darkness / Suicide solution (live) / Paranoid (live).

—— **PHIL SOUSSAN** – bass repl. DAISLEY / **RANDY CASTILLO** – drums (ex-LITA FORD BAND) repl. ALDRIDGE

Jan 86. (7"/7"w-poster/12") *(A/QA/TA 6859)* **SHOT IN THE DARK. / ROCK'N'ROLL REBEL** [20] [–]

Feb 86. (lp/c) *(EPC/40 26404) <40026>* **THE ULTIMATE SIN** [8] [6]
– Lightning strikes / Killer of giants / Thank God for the bomb / Never / Shot in the dark / The ultimate sin / Secret loser / Never know why / Fool like you. *(cd-iss. Jul86; CD 26404) (pic-lp Aug86; EPC 11-26404) (re-iss. Feb89 on 'C.B.S.' lp/c/cd; 462496-1/-4/-2) (re-iss. Nov95; 481680-2)*

Mar 86. (7") *<05810>* **SHOT IN THE DARK. / YOU SAID IT ALL** [–] [68]

Jul 86. (7"/12") *(A/TA 7311)* **THE ULTIMATE SIN. / LIGHTNING STRIKES** [72] [–]

1988. (7") *<08463>* **SHOT IN THE DARK. / CRAZY TRAIN** [–] [ ]

—— (Aug'88) **ZAKK WILDE** (b.ZACH ADAMS, 14 Jan'66) – guitar repl. JAKE who formed BADLANDS. / **DAISLEY** returned to repl. SOUSSAN (to BILLY IDOL) / added **JOHN SINCLAIR** – keyboards

Oct 88. (lp/c/cd) *(46258-1/-4/-2) <44245>* **NO REST FOR THE WICKED** [23] [13]
– Miracle man / Devil's daughter / Crazy babies / Breaking all the rules / Bloodbath in Paradise / Fire in the sky / Tattooed dancer / The demon alcohol. *(cd+=)* – Hero. *(re-iss. Jun94 & Nov95; cd/c; 481681-2)*

Oct 88. (7"/7"sha-pic-d) *(653063-0/-9)* **MIRACLE MAN. / CRAZY BABIES** [ ] [–]
(12"+=/12"w-poster/cd-s+=) *(653063-6/-8/-2)* – The liar.

Dec 88. (7") *<08516>* **MIRACLE MAN. / MAN YOU SAID IT ALL** [–] [ ]

Feb 89. (7") *<68534>* **CRAZY BABIES. / THE DEMON ALCOHOL** [–] [ ]

—— Earlier in the year OZZY had accompanied LITA FORD on 45 'CLOSE MY EYES FOREVER'. In Apr'89, it was to reach UK/US Top50.

—— **TERRY 'GEEZER' BUTLER** – bass was used for tour work late 1988.

Feb 90. (cd/c/lp) *(465940-1/-4/-2) <45451>* **JUST SAY OZZY (live)** [69] [58]
– Miracle man / Bloodbath in Paradise / Shot in the dark / Tattooed dancer / Sweet leaf / War pigs. *(re-iss. cd Nov95; 481517-2)*

—— In the late 80's, OZZY retired to his Buckinghamshire mansion with his manager/wife Sharon Arden and 3 kids. He had also kicked his alcohol addiction. Returned 1991 after being cleared of causing death of fan. See last studio line-up. Augmented also by **MICHAEL INEZ** – bass, inspiration repl. BUTLER

Epic / Epic Assoc

Sep 91. (7") *(657440-7) <73973>* **NO MORE TEARS. / S.I.N.** [32] [71]
(c-s+=/12"+=/12"pic-d+=/cd-s+=) *(657440-8/-6/-?/-2)* – Party with the animals.

Oct 91. (cd/c/lp) *(467859-2/-4/-1) <46795>* **NO MORE TEARS** [17] [7]
– Mr. Tinkertrain / I don't want to change the world / Mama I'm coming home / Desire / No more tears / S.I.N. / Hellraiser / Time after time / Zombie stomp / A.V.H. / Road to nowhere. *(re-iss. cd Nov95; 481675-2)*

Nov 91. (7") *(657617-7) <74093>* **MAMA I'M COMING HOME. / DON'T BLAME ME** [46] Feb92 [28]
(12"+=) *(657617-8)* – I don't know / Crazy train.
(cd-s+=) *(657617-9)* – (Ozzy on the Steve Wright show)
(12"+=) *(657617-6)* – Time after time / Goodbye to romance.
<US-cd-ep+=> *<74265>* – Party with the animals.

Jun 93. (d-cd) *(473798-2) <46795>* **LIVE & LOUD (live)** [ ] [22]
– Intro / Paranoid / I don't want to change the world / Desire / Mr. Crowley / I don't know / Road to nowhere / Flying high again / Guitar solo / Suicide solution / Goodbye to romance / Shot in the dark / No more tears / Miracle man / Drum solo / War pigs / Bark at the Moon / Mama, I'm coming home / Crazy train / Black sabbath / Changes. *(re-iss. Nov95; 481676-2)*

Jun 93. (12"/cd-s) *(659340-6/-2)* **CHANGES (live). / CHANGES / NO MORE TEARS / DESIRE** [ ] [ ]

—— next featured **MIKE INEZ** – bass (of ALICE IN CHAINS)

Oct 95. (cd/c/lp) *(481022-2/-4/-1) <67091>* **OZZMOSIS** [22] [4]
– Perry Mason / I just want you / Ghost behind my eyes / Thunder underground / See you on the other side / Tomorrow / Denial / My little man / My Jekyll doesn't hide / Old LA tonight. *(re-iss. Apr99; same)*

Nov 95. (7"pic-d) *(662639-7)* **PERRY MASON. / LIVING WITH THE ENEMY** [23] [ ]
(cd-s+=) *(662639-2)* – The whole world's falling down.
(cd-s) *(662639-5)* – ('A'side) / No more tears / I don't want to change the world / Flying high again.

—— **ROBERT TRUJILLO** – bass (ex-SUICIDAL TENDENCIES) – bass repl. INEZ

Aug 96. (12") *(663570-6)* **I JUST WANT YOU. / AIMEE / VOODOO DANCER** [43] [ ]
(cd-s) *(663570-2)* – ('A'side) / Aimee / Mama, I'm coming home.
(cd-s) *(663570-5)* – ('A'side) / Voodoo dancer / Iron man (with THERAPY?).

Oct 01. (cd) *(498474-2) <63580>* **DOWN TO EARTH** [19] [4]
– Gets me through / Facing hell / Dreamer / No easy way out / That I never had / You know (part 1) / Junkie / Running out of time / Black illusion / Alive / Can you hear them?

May 02. (cd-s) *(672412-2)* **DREAMER / GETS ME THROUGH / BLACK SKIES / DREAMER (video)** [18] [–]

—— in Dec'03, OZZY and KELLY OSBOURNE hit UK No.1 with a version of 'CHANGES'

– compilations, others, etc. –

on 'Epic' UK / 'CBS Assoc.' unless otherwise stated

May 87. (d-lp/c/cd) *(450475-1/-4/-2) <40714>* **TRIBUTE (live 1981 with RANDY RHOADS)** [13] [6]
– I don't know / Crazy train / Revelation (Mother Earth) / Believer /

Mr. Crowley / Flying high again / No bone movies / Steal away (the night) / Suicide solution / Iron man – Children of the grave / Goodbye to romance / Paranoid / Dee *[not on cd]. (re-iss. Apr93 cd/c;) (re-iss. cd Nov95; 481516-2)*

Jun 87. (7"/12") *(650943-7/-6)* <07168> **CRAZY TRAIN (live 1981). / CRAZY TRAIN (live 1981)** [ ] [ ]

Jul 88. (12"ep/cd-ep) *(652 875-6/-2)* **BACK TO OZZ** [76] [–]
– The ultimate sin / Bark at the Moon / Mr. Crowley / Diary of a madman.

Aug 90. (cd) *Priority; <57129>* **TEN COMMANDMENTS** (rare) [–] [ ]

Mar 93. (d-cd) *(465211-2)* **BARK AT THE MOON / BLIZZARD OF OZZ** [ ] [ ]

Nov 97. (cd/c) *(487260-2/-4)* **THE OZZMAN COMETH – THE BEST OF** [68] [13]
– Black sabbath / War pigs / Goodbye to romance (live) / Crazy train (live) / Mr. Crowley (live) / Over the mountain (live) / Paranoid (live) / Bark at the moon / Shot in the dark / Crazy babies / No more tears / Mama, I'm coming home (live) / I just want you / I don't want to change the world / Back on earth. *(cd+=)* – Fairies wear boots / Beyond the wall of sleep.

Nov 98. (3xcd-box) *Epic; (492655-2)* **DIARY OF A MADMAN / BARK AT THE MOON / THE ULTIMATE SIN** [ ] [–]
(re-iss. Sep01; same)

May 03. (d-cd) *Sony TV; (510840-2) <86812>* **THE ESSENTIAL OZZY OSBOURNE** [21] Feb03 [81]
– Crazy train / Mr. Crowley / I don't know (live) / Suicide solution / Goodbye to romance / Over the mountain / Flying high again / Diary of a madman / Paranoid (live) / Bark at the Moon / You're no different / Rock'n'roll rebel / Crazy babies / Miracle man / Fire in the sky / Breakin' all the rules / Mama, I'm coming home / Desire / No more tears / Time after time / Road to nowhere / I don't want to change the world (live) / Perry Mason / I just want you / Thunder underground / See you on the other side / Gets me through / Dreamer / No easy way out.

□ OTHER ONES (see under ⇒ GRATEFUL DEAD)

□ OTHER TWO (see under ⇒ NEW ORDER)

OUTKAST

Born: Atlanta, Georgia, USA ... 1993 by ANDRE "DRE" BENJAMIN and ANTOINE "BIG BOI" PATTON, who came to realise their lyrical talents after a playground 'rap-battle' in high school. Things happened extremely fast for this pair of highly innovative rappers when they formed OUTKAST whilst still in education. They were subsequently signed by 'LaFace' when they were barely out of their teens. OUTKAST issued 'PLAYER'S BALL' in 1993 and watched their status, as little-known mavericks of the underground to hip-hop's brightest hopes as the song topped the singles chart and became gold in a matter of weeks. OUTKAST prepared for what was to become their debut album, the annoyingly titled 'SOUTHERNPLAYALISTICADILLIACMUZIK' (1994), which earned them a 'Best Newcomer' Gong at the 1995 Source awards. This was not hard to debate, as DRE and BIG BOI's lyrical panache had a certain ebb and flow that could not be imitated by anybody else. Like KOOL KEITH and DEL THA FUNKY HOMOSAPIEN, their rhymes weaved in and out of a spectacular production which boasted eclectic instruments and sharp beats, reminiscent of the UK's own House scene. 'ATLIENS' was delivered in 1996 to critical acclaim in the Hip-Hop world and spawned two massive singles 'ELEVATORS (ME AND YOU)' and 'ATLIENS' which both climbed to the top of the rap charts and demonstrated both artists' abilities to rap around each other in a sonic-style whilst never allowing time for a collision. 'AQUEMINI' (1998), which was voted one of the most essential Hip-Hop albums by Q magazine, was much the same thing, only tighter with a better production and a more left-field sound. If 'ATLIENS' was their 'Nevermind', then this was the collective's 'In Utero', with big, brash and inventive songs, the set was lyrically more important then a dozen other aggressive rappers. However, OUTKAST's best work was to arrive in 2000, in the form of 'STANKONIA'. A masterpiece from beginning to end, 'STANKONIA' was one of the freshest and dance-orientated hip-hop records ever released. The frightful pace of single 'B.O.B', with its tribal, DR JOHN-esque call of female backing vocalists in the chorus swept you off your feet with the sheer adrenaline of the track. While Top 3 single 'MISS JACKSON' had everybody singing "I'm sorry Miss Jackson, oooooooooooohhhhh!" and 'FRESH AND CLEAN' was the ultimate player's anthem for a Saturday night on the pull. Intricate, important, untouchable were three words to describe OUTKAST; a truly remarkable group who showed us there was so much more to Hip-hop than bouncing cars, blunts and bitches. While the cannily timed best of, 'BIG BOI AND DRE PRESENT . . . OUTKAST' (2001), sought to educate the new fans with classic oldies and tantalise both old and new afficionados with a handful of fiendishly funky new tracks, 'SPEAKERBOXXX / THE LOVE BELOW' (2003) defied convention for such a hotly anticipated follow-up. Recording and releasing two separate solo albums on one CD under the OUTKAST banner might have been dismissed as a gimmick had the music itself not been among the most spontaneous, charismatic and downright funky to be released under the aegis of hip hop – never mind pop – in the last few years. Endlessly inventive with an unfailing vision, BIG BOI's 'SPEAKERBOXXX' once again drew from the wealth of black music's heritage in order to create something new and take the music forward. 'THE LOVE BELOW' was an altogether different beast, jazzier but no less creative, mapping out ANDRE's diverse reference points with the same unfettered spirit. Considered individually, the albums surpassed the one-dimensional re-run of most of what passes for hip hop these days; taken together, this million selling US No.1 (featuring the catchy 'HEY YA' smash hit) threw down the gauntlet for the very future of the genre.

Album rating: SOUTHERNPLAYALISTICADILLACMUZIK (*8) / ATLIENS (*7) / AQUEMINI (*8) / STANKONIA (*9) / BIG BOI AND DRE PRESENT . . . compilation (*8) / SPEAKERBOXXX – THE LOVE BELOW (*8)

ANDRE "DRE" BENJAMIN (b.27 May'75) – vocals / **ANTOINE "BIG BOI" PATTON** (b. 1 Feb'75, Savannah, Georgia) – vocals

La Face-Arista La Face-Arista

May 94. (7"/c-s) *(74322 09422-7/-4) <2-4060>* **PLAYERS BALL. / (instrumental)** [ ] Nov93 [37]
(12"+=) *(74322 09422-1)* – (3-'A'mixes).
(cd-s++=) *(74322 09422-2)* – ('A'mix).

May 94. (cd/c) *<(73008 26010)>* **SOUTHERNPLAYALISTICADILLACMUZIK** [ ] [20]
– Peaches (intro) / Myintrotoletuknow / Ain't no thang / Welcome to Atlanta (interlude) / Southernplayalisticadillacmuzik / Call of da wild (featuring The GOODY MOB) / Player's ball (original) / Claimin' true / Club donkey ass (interlude) / Funky ride / Flim flam (interlude) / Git up, git out (featuring The GOODY MOB) / True dat (interlude) / Crumblin' erb / Hootie hoo / D.E.E.P. / Player's ball (reprise). *(cd re-iss. Sep98; same)*

Jul 94. (cd-s) *<2-4070>* **SOUTHERNPLAYALISTICADILLACMUZIK / (instrumental)** [–] [74]

Oct 94. (cd-s) *<2-4085>* **GIT UP, GIT OUT (mixes)** [–] [ ]

Jul 96. (cd-s) *<2-4177>* **ELEVATORS (ME & YOU) / (instrumental)** [–] [12]

Sep 96. (cd/c) *<(73008 26032-2/-4)>* **ATLIENS** [ ] [2]
– U may die / Two dope boyz in a Cadillac / Atliens / Wheelz of steel / Jazzy Belle / Elevators (me & you) / Ova da woods / Babylon / Wailin' / Mainstream / Decateur psalm / Millennium / E.T. / 13th floor – Growin' old / Elevators (reprise). *(cd re-iss. Jan01; same)*

Nov 96. (cd-s) *<2-4196>* **ATLIENS / WHEELZ OF STEEL** [–] [35]

Apr 97. (cd-s) *<2-4224>* **JAZZY BELLE / (Swift C's remix)** [–] [52]

— In Jun'98, OUTKAST were credited on US hit, 'Black Ice (Sky High)' with the GOODIE MOB

Sep 98. (cd/c/d-lp) *<(73008 26053-2/-4/-1)>* **AQUEMINI** [ ] [2]
– Chonkyfire / Rosa Parks / Aquemini / Da art of storytellin' (part 1 & 2) / Y'all scared / Synthesizer / Slump / Liberation / Skew it on the bar-b / Mamasita / West Savannah / Spottieottiedopalicious / Return of the G. *(cd re-iss. Jan01; same)*

Nov 98. (cd-s) *<64013>* **ROSA PARKS / (instrumental) / SKEW IT ON THE BAR-B** [–] [55]

— early '99, OUTKAST featured on COOL BREEZE's hit 'Watch For The Hook'

Apr 00. (cd-s) *<66478>* **DA ART OF STORYTELLIN' / (part 2)** [–] [ ]

Nov 00. (cd/d-lp) *<(73008 26072-2/-1)>* **STANKONIA** [10] [2]
– Intro / Gasoline dreams (with KHUJO GOODIE) / I'm cool (interlude) / So fresh so clean (with DUNGEON FAMILY) / Ms Jackson / Snappin' and trappin' / DF (interlude) / Spaghetti junction / Kim and Goodie (interlude) / I'll call B 4 I cum (with GANGSTA BOO & ECO) / B.O.B. / Xplosion / We love deez hoez / Humble mumble (with ERYKAH BADU) / Drinkin' again (interlude) / Horror / Red velvet / Gangsta shit (with SLIMM CALHOUN & C-BONE) / Cruisin' in the ATL (interlude) / Toilet tisha / Slum beautiful / Pre nump (interlude) / Stankonia (stanklove) / Good hair (interlude).

Dec 00. (12"/cd-s) *(74321 82294-1/-2)* *<2-4500>* **B.O.B. (BOMBS OVER BAGHDAD) / (instrumental) / ('A'video)** [61] Sep00 [ ]
(cd-s) *(74321 82174-2)* – ('A'mixes).

— the import of 'MS. JACKSON' originally hit UK No.48

Feb 01. (12"/c-s) *(74321 83682-1/-4)* *<24516>* **MS. JACKSON. / ('A'-Blacksmith club mix) / ('A'-Blacksmith instrumental)** [2] Jan01 [1]
(cd-s) *(74321 83682-2)* – ('A'-CD-Rom).

May 01. (c-s) *(74321 86340-4)* *<24537>* **SO FRESH SO CLEAN / SO FRESH SO CLEAN (Fatboy Slim remix)** [16] Feb01 [30]
(cd-s+=) *(74321 86340-2)* – Ms Jackson (Mr Drunk remix).
(12"+=) *(74321 86340-1)* – ('A'-instrumental).

Jan 02. (cd) *<(73008 26093-2)>* **BIG BOI AND DRE PRESENT . . . OUTKAST** [ ] Dec01 [18]
– Camp fire intro / Funkin' around / Ain't no thang / So fresh, so clean / Rosa Parks / The whole world (with KILLER MIKE) / Aquemini / B.O.B. / Southernplayalisticadillacmusik / Crumblin' erb / Ms. Jackson / Player's ball / Elevators (me and you) / Spottieottiedopaliscious / Git up, git out / Movin' cool (the after party).

Mar 02. (c-s; by OUTKAST featuring KILLER MIKE) *(74321 91759-4)* *<radio>* **THE WHOLE WORLD / ROSA PARKS** [19] Dec01 [19]
(cd-s+=) *(74321 91759-2)* – B.O.B. / ('A'video).
(12") *(74321 91759-1)* – ('A'side) / ('A'-instrumental).

Jul 02. (cd-s; by OUTKAST featuring KILLER MIKE & SLEEPY BROWN) *(AT 0134CD)* *<85355>* **LAND OF A MILLION DRUMS / (explicit version) / IT'S A MYSTERY** [46] [ ]
(12") *(AT 134T)* – ('A'side) / One track Mike / ('A'-instrumental).
(above issued on 'Atlantic')

— in May'03, BIG BOI featured on KILLER MIKE's hit, 'Adidas'

Sep 03. (12"/cd-s) *(82876 56723-1/-2)* **GHETTO MUSICK / (Benny Benassi club mix)** [55] [–]

Sep 03. (d-cd/d-lp) *<(82876 52905-2/50133-1)>* **SPEAKERBOXXX / THE LOVE BELOW** [44] [1]
– Intro / Ghetto musick / Unhappy / Bowtie (with SLEEPY BROWN & JAZZE PHA) / The way you move (with SLEEPY BROWN) / The rooster / Bust / War / Church / Bamboo (interlude) / Tomb of the boom (with KONKRETE, BIG GIPP & LUDACRIS) / E-Mac (interlude) / Knowing / Flip flop rock (with KILLER MIKE & JAY-Z) / Interlude / Reset (with KHUJO GOODIE & CEE LO) / D-Boi (interlude) / Last call (with SLIMM CALHOUN & LIL JON) / Bowtie (postlude) // The love below (intro) / Love hater / God (interlude) / Happy Valentine's day / Spread / Where are my panties? / Prototype / She lives in my lap (with ROSARIO DAWSON) / Hey ya! / Roses / Good day, good sir / Behold a lady / Pink & blue / Love in war / She's alive / Dracula's wedding (with KELIS) / My favorite things (with NORAH JONES) / Take off your cool / Vibrate / A day in the life of Benjamin Andre.
(above will hit UK No.8 early 2004 while below rose to No.4)

Nov 03. (cd-s) *(82876 57953-2)* *<radio>* **HEY YA! / GOOD DAY, GOOD SIR** [6] [1]
(12") *(82876 57953-1)* – ('A'side) / Ghetto musick / My favorite things.
(cd-s++=) *(82876 58010-2)* – ('A'video).

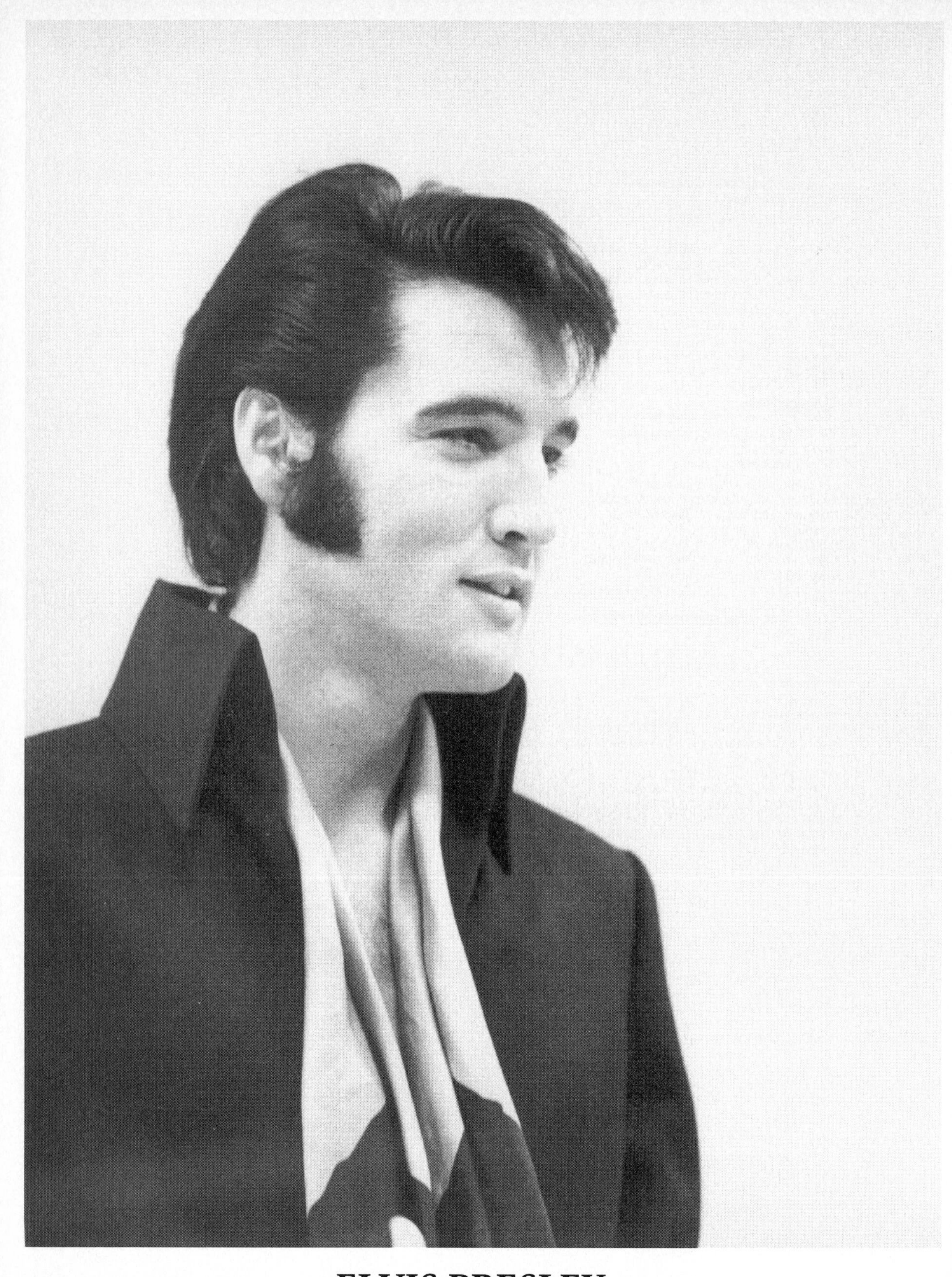

ELVIS PRESLEY

□ Jimmy PAGE (see under ⇒ LED ZEPPELIN)

□ PALACE (see under ⇒ OLDHAM, Will)

□ PALE FOUNTAINS (see under ⇒ SHACK)

Robert PALMER

Born: ALAN ROBERT PALMER, 19 Jan'49, Batley, Yorkshire, England. From the age of 3, PALMER lived with his family in Malta (his father being in the services), moving to London in 1969 after having his first musical experience in semi-pro group, MANDRAKE PADDLE STEAMER. Replacing the solo bound JESS RODEN, PALMER joined the ALAN BROWN SET, singing on the 'Deram' 45, 'GYPSY GIRL', later that year. The following year, he hooked up with jazz-rockers DADA, who boasted vocalist ELKIE BROOKS on their eponymous 'Atco' debut long player. Come 1971, the act had evolved into VINEGAR JOE, although after three poor selling albums for 'Island' (VINEGAR JOE / ROCK'N'ROLL GYPSIES / SIX-STAR GENERAL), they eventually split in March '74. After nearly replacing LOWELL GEORGE in LITTLE FEAT, PALMER was retained by 'Island' on a solo basis. His debut release, The LITTLE FEAT and METERS-enhanced 'SNEAKIN' SALLY THROUGH THE ALLEY' (1974), stiffed in the UK, although US sales almost resulted in a Top 100 placing. As well as a seamless cover of LITTLE FEAT's 'SAILIN' SHOES', the album's highlight was the ALLEN TOUSSAINT-penned title track although many of the collection's songs suffered from a characterlessness that coloured much of PALMER's subsequent output. The following year, he relocated to New York with his wife, subsequently flirting with reggae on his follow-up album, 'PRESSURE DROP'. Following a support slot on a LITTLE FEAT tour, the singer again relocated, this time to Nassau, Bahamas to consummate his love affair with the music of the Carribbean. The culmination of this period in PALMER's career was 1978's 'DOUBLE FUN', wherein the singer sauntered through a mellow, sun-bleached cover of ANDY FRASER's (ex-FREE) 'EVERY KINDA PEOPLE', subsequently PALMER's first US Top 20 hit. 'SECRETS' (1979) was a radical stylistic departure, anchored on balls-out rock and furnishing PALMER with a second Top 20 hit in MOON MARTIN's 'BAD CASE OF LOVING YOU (DOCTOR, DOCTOR)'. The immaculately attired crooner gained a deserved commercial leap in the early 80's with the 'CLUES' album, his polished-oak vocals combining surprisingly well with GARY NUMAN's synth-pop noodlings on the likes of 'JOHNNY AND MARY'. In 1982, the very ROD (STEWART)-ish 'SOME GUYS HAVE ALL THE LUCK' single gave PALMER some belated UK Top 20 success, the singer enjoying further British exposure three years later when he became frontman for the DURAN DURAN/CHIC offshoot, The POWER STATION. An often predictably derivative affair, they were also blatantly commercial, scoring with the likes of 'SOME LIKE IT HOT' and a cover of MARC BOLAN's 'GET IT ON'. Soon back on the solo trail, PALMER carried on in a hard rock stylee for his biggest album to date, 'RIPTIDE' (1985), a record which featured the Transatlantic Top 5 (US No.1) smash, 'ADDICTED TO LOVE'. An antiseptically raunchy piece of poppy-cock-rock, the single was accompanied by a semi-ironic video featuring PALMER surrounded by a troupe of blonde bombshells rocking in formation. Now an accomplished worldwide artist, PALMER emigrated to Lugano, Switzerland prior to releasing 'HEAVY NOVA' (1988). Another big seller, PALMER showed off his mastery of diverse styles, taking in everything from suave balladeering ('SHE MAKES MY DAY') to Swiss yodelling ('CHANGE HIS WAYS') as well as scoring another massive US hit with the cliched rock of 'SIMPLY IRRESISTIBLE'. A surprisingly endearing collaboration with UB40 on BOB DYLAN's 'I'LL BE YOUR BABY TONIGHT' powered the 'DON'T EXPLAIN' (1990) album into the UK Top 10 while 'RIDIN' HIGH' (1992) was a passable tribute to the Tin Pan Alley era. Though possessed of smoothly soulful, impressively adaptable vocal chords and an often faultless choice in material, PALMER's work invariably suffers from a lack of cohesion. That said, you can't go wrong with his greatest hits' set, 1989's 'ADDICTIONS VOl.1'. After an extended absence PALMER returned with 'RHYTHM AND BLUES' (1999), a limp set of coffee-table pop that yet again undersold his talent, or rather smothered it in a sterile production. Lone highlight was a cover of Lowell George's 'TWENTY MILLION THINGS' (a fitting tribute to the great man on the 20th anniversary of his death) which survived the worst of the studio excess. PALMER, sadly, too, passed away after suffering a heart attack in his Paris home on the 26th of September, 2003; a few months earlier he had released his final set, 'DRIVE'. • **Songwriters:** PALMER penned, except FROM A WHISPER TO A SCREAM (Allen Toussaint) / PRESSURE DROP (Lee Perry) / YOU REALLY GOT ME (Kinks) / JEALOUS + THE SILVER GUN (Alan Powell) / YOU ARE IN MY SYSTEM (System) / CAN WE STILL BE FRIENDS (Todd Rundgren) / SOME GUYS HAVE ALL THE LUCK (Persuaders) / I DIDN'T MEAN TO TURN YOU ON (hit; Cherrelle) / EARLY IN THE MORNING (Gap Band) / I'LL BE YOUR BABY TONIGHT (Bob Dylan) / MERCY MERCY ME (THE ECOLOGY) – I WANT YOU (Marvin Gaye) / WITCHCRAFT (hit; Frank Sinatra) / GIRL U WANT (Devo) / RESPECT YOURSELF (Staple Singers) / TV DINNERS (ZZ Top) / etc. • **Trivia:** PALMER produced many artists including The COMSAT ANGELS, DESMOND DEKKER and PETER BAUMANN.

Album rating: SNEAKIN' SALLY THROUGH THE ALLEY (*6) / PRESSURE DROP (*5) / SOME PEOPLE CAN DO WHAT THEY LIKE (*5) / DOUBLE FUN (*5) / SECRETS (*5) / CLUES (*5) / MAYBE IT'S LIVE (*4) / PRIDE (*4) / RIPTIDE (*7) / HEAVY NOVA (*5) / ADDICTIONS VOL.1 compilation (*7) / DON'T EXPLAIN (*4) / RIDIN' HIGH (*3) / ADDICTIONS 2 compilation (*5) / HONEY (*5) / THE VERY BEST OF ROBERT PALMER compilation (*8) / RHYTHM AND BLUES (*3) / LIVE AT THE APOLLO,

NEW YORK CITY (*5) / AT HIS VERY BEST compilation (*8) / DRIVE (*5)

ROBERT PALMER – vocals with various session people

Island Island

Sep 74. (lp) *(<ILPS 9294>)* **SNEAKIN' SALLY THROUGH THE ALLEY** [ ] May75 [ ]
– Sailing shoes / Hey Julia / Sneakin' Sally through the alley / Through it all there's you / Get outside / Blackmail / How much fun / From a whisper to a scream / Through it all there's you. *(re-iss. Jan87 lp/c/cd; ILPM/ICM/CID 9294) (cd-iss. Aug89; IMCD 20)*

Nov 74. (7") *<006>* **SNEAKIN' SALLY THROUGH THE ALLEY. / EPIDEMIC** [–] [ ]

Oct 75. (7") *(WIP 6250) <042> (WIP 6250)* **WHICH OF US IS THE FOOL. / GET OUTSIDE** [ ] [ ]

Feb 76. (7") *(WIP 6272) <049>* **GIMME AN INCH. / PRESSURE DROP** [ ] [ ]

Mar 76. (lp/c) *(<ILPS/ICT 9372>)* **PRESSURE DROP** [ ] Nov75 [ ]
– Give me an inch / Work to make it work / Back in my arms / Riverboat / Pressure drop / Here with you tonight / Trouble / Fine time / Which of us is the fool. *(re-iss. Jan87 lp/c/cd; ILPM/ICM/CID 9372) (cd-iss. Aug89; IMCD 24)*

Oct 76. (7") *(WIP 6345)* **MAN SMART, WOMAN SMARTER. / FROM A WHISPER TO A SCREAM** [ ] [–]

Oct 76. (lp/c) *(<ILPS/ICT 9420>)* **SOME PEOPLE CAN DO WHAT THEY LIKE** [46] [68]
– One lost look / Keep in touch / Man smart, woman smarter / Spanish moon / Have mercy / Gotta get a grip on you (part II) / What can you bring me / Hard head / Off the bone / Some people can do what they like. *(cd-iss. Nov89; IMCD 69)*

Oct 76. (7") *<075>* **MAN SMART, WOMAN SMARTER. / KEEP IN TOUCH** [–] [63]

Mar 77. (7") *<081>* **SOME PEOPLE CAN DO WHAT THEY LIKE. / ONE LOST LOOK** [–] [ ]

Jan 78. (lp/c) *(<ILPS/ICT 9476>)* **DOUBLE FUN** [ ] Mar78 [45]
– Every kinda people / Best of both worlds / Come over / Where can it go / Night people / Love can run faster / You overwhelm me / You really got me / You're gonna get what's coming. *(re-iss. Jan87 lp/c/cd; ILPM/ICM/CID 9476) (cd-iss. Aug89; IMCD 23)*

Mar 78. (7") *<100>* **EVERY KINDA PEOPLE. / HOW MUCH FUN** [–] [16]

Mar 78. (7") *(WIP 6425)* **EVERY KINDA PEOPLE. / KEEP IN TOUCH** [53] [–]

May 78. (7") *<105>* **COME OVER. / YOU OVERWHELM ME** [–] [ ]

Jun 78. (7") *(WIP 6445)* **BEST OF BOTH WORLDS. / ('A'dub version)** [ ] [ ]
(12"+=) *(WIP12 6445)* – Pressure drop.

May 79. (7") *(WIP 6481) <49016>* **BAD CASE OF LOVIN' YOU (DOCTOR, DOCTOR). / LOVE CAN RUN FASTER** [61] Jul79 [14]

Jun 79. (lp/c) *(<ILPS/ICT 9544>)* **SECRETS** [54] Jul79 [19]
– Bad case of loving you (doctor, doctor) / Too good to be true / Can we still be friends / In walks love again / Mean old world / Love stop / Jealous / Under suspicion / Woman you're wonderful / What's it take / Remember to remember. *(re-iss. Jan87 lp/c/cd; ILPM/ICM/CID 9544) (cd-iss. Aug89; IMCD 26)*

Jul 78. (7") *<8697>* **YOU'RE GONNA GET WHAT'S COMING. / WHERE CAN IT GO** [–] [ ]

Aug 79. (7") *(WIP 6515)* **JEALOUS. / WOMAN YOU'RE WONDERFUL** [ ] [–]

Sep 79. (7") *<49094>* **JEALOUS. / IN WALKS LOVE AGAIN** [–] [ ]

Nov 79. (7") *(WIP 6549)* **CAN WE STILL BE FRIENDS. / BACK IN MY ARMS** [ ] [–]

Dec 79. (7") *<49137>* **CAN WE STILL BE FRIENDS. / REMEMBER TO REMEMBER** [–] [52]

Aug 80. (7") *<49554>* **JOHNNY AND MARY. / STYLE KILLS** [–] [ ]

Aug 80. (7") *(WIP 6638)* **JOHNNY AND MARY. / WHAT'S IT TAKE** [44] [–]
(12"+=) *(WIP12 6638)* – Remember to remember.

Aug 80. (lp/c) *(<ILPS/ICT 9595>)* **CLUES** [31] Oct80 [59]
– Looking for clues / Sulky girl / Johnny and Mary / What do you care / I dream of wires / Woke up laughing / Not a second time / Found you now. *(re-iss. Jan87 lp/c/cd; ILPM/ICM/CID 9595) (cd-iss. Jan89; IMCD 21)*

Oct 80. (7") *<49620>* **LOOKING FOR CLUES. / WOKE UP LAUGHING** [–] [ ]

Nov 80. (7") *(WIP 6651)* **LOOKING FOR CLUES. / IN WALKS LOVE AGAIN** [33] [–]
(12") *(WIP12 6651)* – ('A'side) / Good care of you / Style kills.

Jun 81. (7") *(WIP 6678)* **NOT A SECOND TIME. / WOKE UP LAUGHING** [ ] [–]

Jan 82. (7"pic-d) *(WIP 6754) <50042>* **SOME GUYS HAVE ALL THE LUCK. / TOO GOOD TO BE TRUE** [16] [ ]
(12"pic-d) *(WIP12 6754)* – ('A'side) / Style kills / Si Chatouillieux / What do you care.

Mar 82. (lp/c) *(<ILPS/ICT 9665>)* **MAYBE IT'S LIVE (live)** [32] May82 [ ]
– Sneakin' Sally through the alley / What's it take / Best of both worlds / Every kinda people / Bad case of loving you (doctor, doctor) / Some guys have all the luck / Style kills / Si Chatouillieaux / Maybe it's you / What do you care. *(re-iss. Apr91 c; ICM 9665) (re-iss. May93 on 'Spectrum' cd/c; 550068-2/-4)*

Nov 82. (7"pic-d) *(WIP 6833)* **PRIDE. / PRIDE (instrumental)** [ ] [–]
(12") *(WIP 6833)* – ('A'side) / Parade of the obliterators.

Mar 83. (7"/12")*(IS/12IS 104) <99866>* **YOU ARE IN MY SYSTEM. / DEADLINE** [53] Jun83 [78]

Apr 83. (lp/c) *(ILPS/ICT 9720) <90065>* **PRIDE** [37] [ ]
– Pride / Deadline / Want you more / Dance for me / You are in my system / It's not difficult / Say you will / You can have it (take my heart) / What you waiting for / The silver gun. *(re-iss. Jan87 lp/c/cd; ILPM/ICM/CID 9720) (cd-iss. Jun89; IMCD 22)*

Jun 83. (7"pic-d) *(IS 121)* **YOU CAN HAVE IT (TAKE MY HEART). / THE SILVER GUN** [66] [–]

—— From early '85, PALMER became lead singer of DURAN DURAN off-shoot band The POWER STATION. Their eponymous lp, hit both UK + US Top 20's, and spawned a few hits 'SOME LIKE IT HOT', 'GET IT ON' & 'COMMUNICATION'. (see DURAN DURAN ⇒)

Oct 85. (7") *(IS 242) <99597>* **DISCIPLINE OF LOVE. / DANCE FOR ME** [ ] [82]
(12"+=) *(12IS 242)* – Woke up laughing.

Nov 85. (lp/c/cd) *(ILPS/ICT/CID 9801) <90471>* **RIPTIDE** [5] [8]
– Riptide / Hyperactive / Addicted to love / Trick bag / Get it through your heart / I didn't mean to turn you on / Flesh wound / Discipline of love / Riptide (reprise). *(cd-iss. 1988; CID 130) (re-iss. Apr91 lp/c; ILPM/ICM 9801)*

Dec 85. (7") *(IS 256)* **RIPTIDE. / BACK IN MY ARMS** [ ] [–]
(12") *(12IS 256)* – ('A'side) / No not much (live) / Trick bag (live)
(d7"++=) *(ISD 256)* – (12"tracks) / Johnny and Mary.

Feb 86. (7") *<99570>* **ADDICTED TO LOVE. / LET'S FALL IN LOVE TONIGHT** [–] [1]

Apr 86. (7"/12") *(IS/12IS 270)* **ADDICTED TO LOVE. / REMEMBER TO REMEMBER** [5] [–]
(7"sha-pic-d) *(ISP 270)* – ('A'side) / More.

May 86. (7") *<99545>* **HYPERACTIVE. / WOKE UP LAUGHING** [–] [33]

Jun 86. (7"/12") *(IS/12IS 283) <99537>* **I DIDN'T MEAN TO TURN YOU ON. / GET IT THROUGH YOUR HEART** [9] Aug86 [2]
(d7"+=) *(ISD 283)* – You are in my system / Johnny and Mary.

Oct 86. (7") *(IS 242)* **DISCIPLINE OF LOVE. / DANCE FOR ME** [68] [–]
(12"+=) *(12IS 242)* – Riptide (medley).
(d12"+=) *(12ISX 242)* – Remember to remember / Addicted to love.

Mar 88. (7") *(IS 352) <99377>* **SWEET LIES. / WANT YOU MORE** [ ] [94]
(12"+=) *(12IS 352)* – Riptide.
(cd-s++=) *(CID 352)* – ('A'extended).

E.M.I. Manhattan

Jun 88. (7"/7"pic-d) *(EM/+P 61) <50133>* **SIMPLY IRRESISTIBLE. / NOVA** [44] [2]
(12"+=/cd-s+=) *(12/CD EM 61)* – ('A'extended) / ('A'instrumental).

Jun 88. (cd/c/lp) *(CD/TC+/EMD 1007) <48057>* **HEAVY NOVA** [17] [13]
– Simply irresistible / More than ever / Change his ways / Disturbing behaviour / Early in the morning / It could happen to you / She makes my day / It could happen to you / Tell me I'm not dreaming / Between us / Casting a spell. *(re-iss. Mar94 cd/c; CD/TC EMD 1007)*

Oct 88. (7") *(EM 65)* **SHE MAKES MY DAY. / DISTURBING BEHAVIOUR** [6] [–]
(12"+=/cd-s+=) *(12/CD EM 65)* – Simply irresistible (extended).

Oct 88. (7") *<50157>* **EARLY IN THE MORNING. / DISTURBING BEHAVIOR** [–] [19]

May 89. (7"/7"pic-d) *(EM/+PD 85)* **CHANGE HIS WAYS. / MORE THAN EVER** [28] [ ]
(12") *(12EM 85)* – (2 different mixes).
(cd-s++=) *(CDEM 85)* – She makes my day.

Jun 89. (7") *<50206>* **TELL ME I'M NOT DREAMING (2 versions) / MORE THAN EVER** [–] [60]

Aug 89. (c-s/7") *(TC+/EM 99)* **IT COULD HAPPEN TO YOU. / CHANGE HIS WAYS** [71] [ ]
(12"+=) *(12EM 99)* – Early in the morning (get up mix).
(cd-s++=) *(CDEM 99)* – Casting a spell.

E.M.I. E.M.I.

Oct 90. (c-s/7"; ROBERT PALMER & UB40) *(TC+/EM 167)* **I'LL BE YOUR BABY TONIGHT. / DEEP END** [6] [ ]
(12"+=/cd-s+=) *(12/CD EM 167)* – ('A'version).

Nov 90. (cd/c/d-lp) *(CD/TC+/EMD 1018) <93935>* **DON'T EXPLAIN** [9] [88]
– Your mother should have told you / Light-years / You can't get enough of a good thing / Dreams to remember / You're amazing / Mess around / Happiness / History / I'll be your baby tonight / Housework / Mercy mercy me – I want you / Don't explain / Aeroplane / People will say we're in love / Not a word / Top 40 / You're so desirable / You're my thrill.

Nov 90. (c-s,cd-s) *<50338>* **YOU'RE AMAZING / SO EMBOLDENED** [–] [28]

Dec 90. (c-s/7") *(TC+/EM 173) <50344>* **MERCY MERCY ME (THE ECOLOGY) – I WANT YOU. / OH YEAH** [9] Feb91 [16]
(12"+=/cd-s+=) *(12/CD EM 173)* – (2-'A'&'B'versions).

Apr 91. (c-s/7") **HAPPINESS. / ALL SHOOK UP** [ ] [ ]
(12"+=/cd-s+=) – ('A'extended).

Jun 91. (c-s/7") *(TC+/EM 193)* **DREAMS TO REMEMBER. / MESS AROUND** [68] [–]
(12"+=) *(12EM 193)* – Happiness.
(cd-s+=) *(CDEM 193)* – Mercy mercy me (the ecology) – I want you.

Oct 92. (c-s/7") *(TC+/EM 251)* **WITCHCRAFT. / CHANCE** [50] [–]
(cd-s) *(CDEM 251)* – ('A'side) / She makes my day / Mercy mercy me – I want you.

Oct 92. (cd/c/d-lp) *(CD/MC+/EMD 1038) <98923>* **RIDIN' HIGH** [32] [ ]
– Love me or leave me / (Love is) The tender trap / You're my thrill / Want you more / Baby it's cold outside / Aeroplane / Witchcraft / What a little moonlight can do / Don't explain / Chance / Goody goody / Do nothin' till you hear from me / Honeysuckle rose / No not much / Ridin' high / Hard head.
(above featured many 40's + 50's covers)

Jul 94. (c-s/7") *(TC+/EM 331)* **GIRL U WANT. / NO FUSS** [57] [–]
(cd-s+=) *(CDEMS 331)* – ('A'mixes).

Aug 94. (c-s/7") *(TC+/EM 343)* **KNOW BY NOW. / MERCY MERCY ME – I WANT YOU** [25] [–]
(cd-s+=) *(CDEM 343)* – Simply irresistible.
(cd-s) *(CDEMS 343)* – ('A'side) / ('A'mixes) / In the stars / She makes my day.

Sep 94. (cd/c/lp) *(CD/TC+/EMD 1069) <30301>* **HONEY** [25] [ ]
– Honey A / Honey B / You're mine / Know by now / Nobody but you / Love takes time / Honeymoon / You blow me away / Close to the edge / Closer to the edge / Girl u want / Wham bam boogie / Big trouble / Dreams come true.

Dec 94. (c-s/7") *(TC+/EM 350)* **YOU BLOW ME AWAY. / SIMPLY IRRESISTIBLE** [38] [ ]
(cd-s) *(CDEM 350)* – ('A'side) / No control / ('A'mix) / Know by now.
(cd-s) *(CDEMS 350)* – ('A'side) / ('A'mixes) / Change his ways.

Sep 95. (c-s) *(TCEM 399)* **RESPECT YOURSELF / YOU BLOW ME AWAY** [45] [ ]
(cd-s+=) *(CDEM 399)* – Girl u want / Race to the end of the set medley:- Bad case of loving you (doctor, doctor) – Simply irrisistible – Some guys have all the luck – I didn't mean to turn you on – Looking for clues – Addicted to love – You are in my system – Know by now – Some like it hot – I want you – Every kinda people.
(cd-s) *(CDEMS 399)* – ('A'side) / Get it on (45 mix) / Some like it hot (7"mix) / Respect yourself (FX mix).

Oct 95. (cd/c) *(CD/TC EMD 1088) <55312>* **THE VERY BEST OF ROBERT PALMER** (compilation) [4] [ ]
– Addicted to love / Bad case of loving you (doctor, doctor) / Simply irresistible / Get it on (POWER STATION) / Some guys have all the luck / I didn't mean to turn you on / Looking for clues / You are in my system / Some like it hot (POWER STATION) / Respect yourself / I'll be your baby tonight (w/ UB40) / Johnny & Mary / She makes my day / Know by now / Every kinda people / Mercy mercy me – I want you (medley).

Eagle Pyramid

Apr 99. (cd/c) *(EAG CD/MC 063) <75865>* **RHYTHM AND BLUES** [ ] Jul99 [ ]
– True love / No problem / Let's get it on '99 / Stone cold / Sex appeal / Work to make it work '99 / All the will in the world / You're not the only one / Mr. Wise guy / I choose you / Dance for me / Twenty million things.

May 01. (cd) *(EAGCD 174) <20005>* **LIVE AT THE APOLLO, NEW YORK CITY (live 2000)** [ ] [ ]
– Some like it hot / Hyperactive / Discipline of love / Tell me I'm not dreaming / I didn't mean to turn you on / Looking for clues / Change his ways / Pride / Woke up laughing / Johnny & Mary / Riptide / Between us / Flesh wound / More than ever / Simply irresistible / Casting a spell / Addicted to love.

—— in Jan'03, SHAKE B4 USE vs ROBERT PALMER hit the UK Top 50 with a version of 'ADDICTED TO LOVE'

Universal Compendia

May 03. (cd) *(038098-2) <4886>* **DRIVE** [ ] [ ]
– Mama talk to your daughter / Why get up? / Who's fooling who? / Am I wrong? / TV dinners / Lucky / Stella / Dr. Zhivago's train / Ain't that just like a woman / Hound dog / Crazy cajun cake walk band / I need your love so bad.

—— on the 26th of September, 2003, PALMER died of a heart attack

– compilations, etc. –

on 'Island' unless mentioned otherwise

Jul 87. (lp/c) *C5; (C5/+K 501)* **THE EARLY YEARS** [ ] [–]
– (above featured before solo work with The ALAN BOWN SET)

Nov 89. (7") *(IS 438)* **BAD CASE OF LOVING YOU (DOCTOR, DOCTOR). / SWEET LIES** [ ] [ ]
(12"+=/cd-s+=) *(12IS/CID 438)* – What's it take.

Nov 89. (lp/c/cd) *(ILPS/ICT/CID 9944) <91318>* **ADDICTIONS VOL.1** [7] [79]
– Bad case of loving you (doctor, doctor) / Pride / Addicted to love / Sweet lies / Woke up laughing / Looking for clues / Some guys have all the luck / Some like it hot (POWER STATION) / What's it take? / Every kinda people / Johnny & Mary / Simply irresistible / Style kills.

Feb 92. (c-s/cd-s/7") *(CIS/CID/IS 498)* **EVERY KINDA PEOPLE. / ('A'radio mix)** [43] [–]

Mar 92. (cd/c) *(CID/ICT TV 4) <510345>* **ADDICTIONS VOL.2** [12] [ ]
– Remember to remember / Sneakin' Sally through the alley / Maybe it's you / You are in my system / I didn't mean to turn you on / Can we still be friends / Man smart, woman smarter / Too good to be true / Every kinda people / She makes my day / Best of both worlds / Give me an inch / You're gonna get what's coming / I dream of wires / The silver gun.

Jun 92. (c-s/cd-s/7") **YOU ARE IN MY SYSTEM. / YOU'RE GONNA GET WHAT'S COMING / TOO GOOD TO BE TRUE** [ ] [–]

Nov 95. (d-cd) *(ISDCD 2)* **ADDICTIONS VOL.1 & 2** [ ] [–]

May 99. (cd) *E.M.I.; (493575-2)* **WOKE UP LAUGHING (ADVENTURE IN TROPICAL MUSIC 1977-1997)** [ ] [–]

Sep 00. (cd) *EMI Gold; (CDGOLD 1054)* **THE ESSENTIAL COLLECTION** [ ] [–]

Jan 01. (cd) *Universal; (542267-2)* **THE UNIVERSAL MASTERS COLLECTION** [ ] [–]

Nov 02. (cd) *Universal TV; (069781-2) <069946>* **AT HIS VERY BEST** [40] [ ]
– Every kinda people / Bad case of loving you (doctor, doctor) / Johnny and Mary / Looking for clues / Some guys have all the luck / You are in my system / You can have it (take my heart) / Some like it hot (POWER STATION) / Addicted to love / I didn't mean to turn you on / Sweet lies / Simply irresistible / She makes my day / I'll be your baby tonight (with UB40) / Mercy mercy me (the ecology) – I want you (medley) / Sneakin' Sally through the alley / Riptide *[UK-only]* / I need your love so bad / TV dinners. *(re-dist.Oct03)* – hit UK No.38 *(re-iss. Nov03 +=dvd; 9814155)*

Mar 03. (cd) *Universal; (AA314 546556-2)* **20th CENTURY MASTERS** [ ] [–]

Aug 03. (t-cd) *Spectrum; (9808976)* **CLUES / DOUBLE FUN / SOME GUYS HAVE ALL THE LUCK** [ ] [–]

PANTERA

Formed: Texas, USA . . . 1981 by TERRY GLAZE, 'DIAMOND' DARRELL, VINCE ABBOTT and REX ROCKER, taking their name from the Spanish word for panther. Initially a vaguely glam-influenced hard-rock band in the packet-bulging tradition of KISS and AEROSMITH, PANTERA began their career with 'METAL MAGIC' (1983), issued on their own homegrown 'Metal Magic' label. The album was fairly well-received Stateside and saw the band gain a firm foothold on the lower rungs of the hair-rock ladder. With subsequent releases like 'PROJECTS IN THE JUNGLE' (1984) and 'I AM THE NIGHT' (1985), however, the group began to adopt a more muscular approach, consolidated with the arrival of PHIL ANSELMO (as a replacement for GLAZE) on 1988's 'POWER METAL'. With a growing reputation and the help of a recommendation from JUDAS PRIEST's ROB HALFORD, the band secured a major label deal with 'Atco'. The resulting album, 'COWBOYS FROM HELL' (1990) was a dramatic turnaround, gone was the 80's metal garb and cheesy choruses; check shirts, tattoos and a brutally uncompromising thrash-based groove had forcibly taken their place. Clearly, something had made these boys angry and 'A VULGAR DISPLAY OF POWER' (1992) was arguably the most articulate and succinct fix of metallic aggression to be had that year; the likes of 'F**KING HOSTILE' said it all. The record also gave PANTERA their first taste of chart success, the 'WALK' single making the UK Top 40. So it was, then, that the stage was set for PANTERA to both consolidate their position as one of the most unrelentingly intense groups in the nu-metal hierarchy and smash into the UK album chart at pole position with 'FAR BEYOND DRIVEN' (1994). Incredibly their seventh album, the group were now virtually unrecognisable from their rather tame origins, the record's grim vignettes (select 'I'M BROKEN' and 'THROES OF REJECTION' for that ultimate feel-bad factor) were accompanied by a suitably severe Black Sabbath cover, 'PLANET CARAVAN'. The set also saw PANTERA climb to the uppermost regions of the American charts, their services sought out for a contribution to 'The Crow' soundtrack (a cover of Poison Idea's 'THE BADGE'). Silent for most of 1995 (bar ANSELMO who moonlighted with DOWN; sole album, 'NOLA'), PANTERA returned with a vengeance the following year, releasing 'THE GREAT SOUTHERN TRENDKILLERS' (1996). Easing back a little on the speed pedal, the group achieved an even more savagely focused intensity, ANSELMO raging from the depths of his tortured soul. It may have lent his lyrics and delivery a stark harshness, but surviving on the very precipice of existence eventually caught up with ANSELMO when, later that summer (13th July), the singer narrowly escaped death from a heroin overdose, later admitting to being dead for five minutes. Shaken but hardly beaten, PANTERA returned the following year with a well-overdue concert set, 'OFFICIAL LIVE – 101 PROOF', proving that there are still few to match the sheer, unadulterated heaviness of their impact. 'REINVENTING THE STEEL' in 2000 kept them high in profile as it returned ANSELMO and Co to the US Top 5. • **Covered:** HOLE IN THE SKY (Black Sabbath) / CAT SCRATCH FEVER (Ted Nugent).

Album rating: METAL MAGIC (*5) / PROJECTS IN THE JUNGLE (*5) / I AM THE NIGHT (*5) / POWER METAL (*4) / COWBOYS FROM HELL (*6) / A VULGAR DISPLAY OF POWER (*8) / FAR BEYOND DRIVEN (*7) / THE GREAT SOUTHERN TRENDKILLERS (*6) / OFFICIAL LIVE 101 PROOF (*6) / REINVENTING THE STEEL (*6) / THE BEST OF PANTERA: FAR BEYOND THE GREAT SOUTHERN COWBOYS' VULGAR HITS compilation (*7) / Down: NOLA (*5)

TERRY GLAZE – vocals, guitar / **DARRELL ABBOTT** (b.20 Aug'66, Dallas, Texas) – guitar / **REX ROCKER** (b.REX BROWN, 27 Jul'64, Graham, Texas) – bass / **VINCENT PAUL ABBOTT** (b.11 Mar'64, Dallas) – drums

not iss. Metal Magic

1983. (lp) *<MMR 1983>* **METAL MAGIC** -
– Ride my rocket / I'll be alright / Tell me if you want it / Latest lover / Biggest part of me / Metal magic / Widowmaker / Nothin' on (but the radio) / Sad lover / Rock out!.

— GLAZE became TERRENCE LEE, DARRELL prefixed the word DIMEBAG and VINCE was now VINNIE PAUL

1984. (lp) *<MMR 1984>* **PROJECTS IN THE JUNGLE** -
– All over tonite / Out for blood / Blue lite turnin' red / Like fire / In over my head / Projects in the jungle / Heavy metal rules! / Only a heartbeat away / Killers / Takin' my life.

1985. (lp) *<MMR 1985>* **I AM THE NIGHT** -
– Hot and heavy / I am the night / Onward we rock! / D.S.G.S.T.S.T.S.M. / Daughters of the queen / Down below / Come-on eyes / Right on the edge / Valhalla / Forever tonight.

— **PHILIP ANSELMO** (b.30 Jun'68, New Orleans, Louisiana) – vocals repl. TERRY

May 88. (lp) *<MMR 1988>* **POWER METAL** -
– Rock the world / Power metal / We'll meet again / Over and out / Proud to be loud / Down below / Death trap / Hard ride / Burnnn! / P*S*T*88.

Atco Atco

Jul 90. (cd/c/lp) *<7567 91372-2/-4/-1>* **COWBOYS FROM HELL**
– Cowboys from Hell / Primal concrete sledge / Psycho holiday / Heresy / Cemetery gates / Domination / Shattered / Clash with reality / Medicine man / Message in blood / The sleep / The art of shredding.

Feb 92. (cd/c/lp) *<7567 91758-2/-4/-1>* **A VULGAR DISPLAY OF POWER** 64 44
– Mouth for war / A new level / Walk / F**king hostile / This love / Rise / No good (attack the radical) / Live in a hole / Regular people (conceit) / By demons be driven / Hollow.

Sep 92. (7"/c-s) *(A 5845/+C)* **MOUTH FOR WAR. / RISE** 73
(cd-s+=) *(A 5845CD)* – Cowboys from Hell / Heresy.
(12") *(A 5845T)* – ('A'side) / ('A'-superloud mix) / Domination / Primal concrete sledge.

Feb 93. (12"m) *(B 6076T)* **WALK. / COWBOYS FROM HELL / PSYCHO HOLIDAY (live)** 34
(cd-ep) *(B 6076CD)* – ('A'side) / Fucking hostile / By demons be driven.
(cd-ep) *(B 6076CDX)* – ('A'side) / No good (attack the radical)/ A new level / Walk (extended remixes by Jim 'Foetus' Thirlwell).

East West Atco

Mar 94. (12"/cd-s) *(B 5932 T/CD1)* **I'M BROKEN. / SLAUGHTERED** 19
(cd-s+=) *(B 5932CD2)* – Domination (live) / Primal concrete sledge.
(cd-s) *(B 5932CD3)* – ('A'side) / Cowboys from Hell (live) / Psycho holiday (live).
(12") *(B 5932X)* – ('A'side) / Walk (cervical edit) / Fuckin' hostile.

Mar 94. (cd/c/lp) *<7567 92302-2/-4/-1>* **FAR BEYOND DRIVEN** 3 1
– Strength beyond strength / Becoming / 5 minutes alone / I'm broken / Good friends and a bottle of pills / Hard lines, sunken cheeks / Slaughtered / 25 years / Shedding skin / Use my third arm / Throes of rejection / Planet Caravan.

May 94. (7"white) *(A 8293)* **5 MINUTES ALONE. / THE BADGE**

Oct 94. (7") *(A 5836)* **PLANET CARAVAN. / 5 MINUTES ALONE** 26
(12") *(A 5836T)* – ('A'side) / Cowboys from Hell / Heresay.
(cd-s) *(A 5836Cd1)* – ('A'side) / The badge / New level / Becoming.
(cd-s) *(A 5836CD2)* – ('A'side) / Domination / Hollow.

May 96. (cd/c/lp) *<7559 61908-2/-4/-1>* **THE GREAT SOUTHERN TRENDKILLERS** 17 4
– Drag the waters / War nerve / It can't destroy my body / 13 steps to nowhere / Sandblasted skin / Underground in America / Suicide note (part 1) / Suicide note (part 2).

— On 13th Jul'96, ANSELMO luckily survived a heroin overdose in which he was reported to be dead for five minutes.

Aug 97. (cd/c/lp) *<7559 62068-2/-4/-1>* **OFFICIAL LIVE – 101 PROOF (live)** 54 15
– New level / Walk / Becoming / 5 minutes alone / Sandblasted skin / Suicide note (part 2) / War nerve / This love / Dom – Hollow / Strength beyond strength / I'm broken / Cowboys from Hell / Cemetery gates / Fuckin' hostile / Where you come from / I can't hide.

Mar 00. (cd/c) *<7559 62451-2/-4>* **REINVENTING THE STEEL** 33 4
– Hellbound / Goddamn electric / Yesterday don't mean shit / You've got to belong to it / Revolution is my name / Death rattle / We'll grind that axe for a long time / Uplift / It makes them disappear / I'll cast a shadow.

Oct 01. (cd-ep) *<7261>* **REVOLUTION IS MY NAME EP** -
– Revolution is my name / Hole in the sky / Immortal insane / Cat scratch fever.

– compilations, etc. –

Sep 03. (cd+dvd) *Elektra; (8122 73729-2) <73932-2>* **THE BEST OF PANTERA: FAR BEYOND THE GREAT SOUTHERN COWBOYS' VULGAR HITS!** (UK title 'REINVENTING HELL') [ ] [38]

DOWN

PHIL ANSELMO – vocals / **PEPPER KEENAN** – guitar / **KIRK WINDSTEIN** – guitar / **TODD STRANGE** – bass / **JIMMY BOWER** – drums

East West East West

Sep 95. (cd/c/lp) *<(7559 61830-2/-4/-1)>* **NOLA** [68] [57]
– Pray for the locust / Stone the crow / Bury me in smoke / Eyes of the south / Pillars of eternity / Underneath everything / Swan song / Temptation's wings / Jail / Lifer / Rehab / Losing all / Hail the leaf.

☐ PAPA M (see under ⇒ SLINT)

PAPA ROACH

Formed: Vacaville, North California, USA . . . 1993 by schoolmates JACOBY SHADDIX aka COBY DICK, DAVE BUCKNER, JERRY HORTON and WILL JAMES, taking the inspiration for their moniker from the PONCHO SANCHEZ album, 'Papa Gato'. Influenced by Bay Area mavericks such as FAITH NO MORE and PRIMUS, the band set out playing a funk/hip-hop hybrid and rapidly built up a loyal local following while making a tentative start to their recording career with 'CACA BONITA' (1995). In 1996, WILL JAMES was replaced by the band's teenage roadie TOBIN ESPERANCE and the lads cut a sophomore album, 'OLD FRIENDS FROM YOUNG YEARS' (1997) on a miniscule budget. Playlisted by many local radio stations, the record – again released on their own 'Onion Hardcore Recordings' imprint – was instrumental in raising PAPA ROACH's profile and before long the Californian upstarts were playing on the same bill as SUICIDAL TENDENCIES, HUMAN WASTE PROJECT, WILL HAVEN etc. 1998's '5 TRACKS DEEP' EP sharpened their rap-metal chops and paved the way for a major label deal with 'Dreamworks'. The Hollywood-based label released the 'INFEST' album in 2000, a record that crept unannounced into the US Top 20 and finally established PAPA ROACH as major league contenders alongside KORN, LIMP BIZKIT, DEFTONES etc. Reliable if not exactly innovative exponents of the increasingly over subscribed nu-metal agenda, P-ROACH (as their fans know and love them) can safely regard themselves as fully paid up members of America's new rock establishment. 'LOVEHATETRAGEDY' (2002) found the 'ROACH crew largely laying off the more groove based elements of their sound in favour of a more straight up alt-metal approach although lyrically JACOBY SHADDIX was as reliably despondent as ever.

Album rating: OLD FRIENDS FROM YOUNG YEARS (*5) / INFEST (*6) / LOVEHATETRAGEDY (*6)

COBY DICK (b. JACOBY SHADDIX) – vocals / **JERRY HORTON** – guitar / **WILL JAMES** – bass / **DAVE BUCKNER** – drums

not iss. own label

Dec 94. (cd-ep) **POTATOES FOR CHRISTMAS** [–] [ ]
– Coffee thoughts / Mama's dress / Lenny's / Lulu Espidachi / Cheez-z-fux / I love babies / Dendrilopis.

1995. (cd-s) **CACA BONITA** [–] [ ]

—— **TOBIN ESPERANCE** – bass; repl. WILL

1997. (cd) **OLD FRIENDS FROM YOUNG YEARS** [–] [ ]
– Intro / Orange drive palms / Liquid diet / GrrBrr / iSEDuF**nDie / Dirty cut freak / Living room / 829 / Peewagon / Hedake / Shut up n die (reprise). *(hidden track+=)* – thanx.

1998. (cd-ep) **5 TRACKS DEEP** [–] [ ]
– Revenge in Japanese / My bad side / July / Tambienemy / Thrown away.

1999. (cd-ep) **LET 'EM KNOW** [–] [ ]
– Walking thru barbed wire / Legacy / Binge / Snakes / Tightrope.

Dreamworks Dreamworks

Aug 00. (cd) *<(450223-2)>* **INFEST** [9] Apr00 [5]
– Infest / Last resort / Broken home / Dead cell / Between angels and insects / Blood brothers *[on explicit version]* / Legacy *[on clean version]* / Revenge / Snakes / Never enough / Binge / Thrown away. *(hidden track+=)* – Tight rope. *(UK re-iss. Feb01 cd/cd+=; 45031 6-2/7-2)* – Dead cell (live) / Last resort (video).

Feb 01. (c-s) *(450920-4) <album cut>* **LAST RESORT / BROKEN HOME (session)** [3] May00 [57]
(cd-s+=) *(450920-2)* – Dead cell (session) / ('A'-CD-ROM).
(cd-s) *(450921-2)* – ('A'side) / ('A'session) / Between angels and insects (session).

Apr 01. (c-s) *(450908-4)* **BETWEEN ANGELS AND INSECTS / LAST RESORT (radio)** [17] [–]
(cd-s) *(450908-2)* – ('A'side) / Last resort (live) / Binge (live) / ('A'-CD-ROM).
(cd-s) *(450909-2)* – ('A'side) / Tight rope (live) / Barbed wire (live).

Jun 02. (c-s) *(450818-4) <450820>* **SHE LOVES ME NOT / NAKED IN FRONT OF THE COMPUTER** [14] [76]
(cd-s+=) *(450818-2)* – Blood brothers / ('A'-video).
(cd-s) *(450817-2)* – ('A'side) / Life is a bullet (live BBC1 version) / Lovehatetragedy (live BBC1 version).

Jun 02. (cd) *<(450389-2)>* **LOVEHATETRAGEDY** [4] [2]
– M-80 (explosive energy movement) / Life is a bullet (explicit) / Time and time again / Walking thru barbed wire / Decompression period / Born with nothing, die with everything (explicit) / She loves me not (explicit) / Singular indestructable droid / Black clouds / Code of energy (explicit) / Lovehatetragedy. *(UK+=)* – Gouge away / Never said it. *(special cd+=; 450367-2)* – Between angels and insects (video) / The last resort (video).

Oct 02. (7") *(450805-7) <450809>* **TIME AND TIME AGAIN. / SHE LOVES ME NOT (live)** [54] [ ]
(cd-s+=) *(450805-2)* – Code of energy (live) / ('A'-video).
(cd-s) *(450804-2)* – ('A'live) / Singular indestructable droid (live) / The last resort (live) / ('A'-video).

☐ PARAMOUNTS (see under ⇒ PROCOL HARUM)

☐ John PARISH & POLLY JEAN HARVEY (see under ⇒ HARVEY, PJ)

Graham PARKER

Born: 18 Nov'50, East London, England. Already something of a veteran (having played on the continent as well as fronting a succession of London outfits) when he placed an ad in Melody Maker for a backing band, singer/songwriter PARKER's emergence at the fag end of the pub-rock scene in the mid-70's was fortuitous in that he secured the services of The RUMOUR, a group formed from the remains of such scene stalwarts as BRINSLEY SCHWARZ and DUCKS DELUXE. With assistance from future 'Stiff' mainman, Dave Robinson (the brains behind The RUMOUR), he cut a demo tape and sent it to 'Phonogram', the label sufficiently impressed to sign him to their subsidiary label, 'Vertigo'. Featuring a line-up of PARKER, MARTIN BELMONT, BRINSLEY SCHWARZ, BOB ANDREWS, ANDREW BODNAR and STEVE GOULDING, the NICK LOWE-produced debut album, 'HOWLIN' WIND' (1976), remains one of the most enduring releases of PARKER's career. Mentioned in the same breath as classic American writers such as DYLAN and SPRINGSTEEN, his hungry, articulate approach had critics foaming at the mouth; while the sweaty fervour of tracks such as 'SOUL SHOES' and 'HEY LORD, DON'T ASK ME QUESTIONS' effectively demonstrated the combo's hard-nosed R&B approach, the gritty melancholy of 'BETWEEN YOU AND ME' left a deeper impression. A second set, 'HEAT TREATMENT', followed later that year, the fierce momentum holding out if not resonating with quite the same conviction. The record's minor chart success preceded a Top 30 hit with the 'PINK PARKER' EP in 1977 (featuring a cover of The Trammps' 'HOLD BACK THE NIGHT') and a Top 20 placing for the third album, 'STICK IT TO ME' (1977). While PARKER was now riding into the charts on the coat-tails of the punk/new wave explosion, critics laid into what they regarded as a poorly conceived rush job with constant comparisons to the emerging ELVIS COSTELLO not helping any. Unhappy with what he allegedly regarded as record company incompetence, PARKER reportedly cut the inferior live set, 'THE PARKERILLA' (1978) as a means of ending his tenure with 'Mercury'. Subsequently signing with 'Arista' in the States, the angry young man vented his pent-up frustration with the acclaimed 'SQUEEZING OUT SPARKS' (1979). An electrifying set more than living up to PARKER's early promise and widely held as his peak achievement, the album's simmering discontent was best sampled on the likes of 'LOCAL GIRLS' and 'DON'T GET EXCITED', while 'PASSION IS NO ORDINARY WORD' was testament to the man's cast-iron conviction. As well as making the Top 20 in Britain, the record broke PARKER, to a certain degree, in the States, where he was hailed by critics as one of the greatest songwriters of his generation. Yet he failed to build on all this, 'THE UP ESCALATOR' (1980) too often substituting lean invention for flabby formula; despite an all-time best chart placing in the UK, the album marked the beginning of a critical and commercial slump as well as the end of PARKER's musical partnership with his longtime backing band. 'ANOTHER GREY AREA' (1982) used an array of session players (including NICKY HOPKINS), carrying on in much the same vein as its predecessor with only the occasional inspired track to redeem it. Throughout the remainder of the 80's PARKER concentrated on the American market where he enjoyed minor success on a number of labels, enjoying something of a mini critical revival with 'THE MONA LISA'S SISTER' (1988) and 'HUMAN SOUL' (1989), which harnessed some of the wiry energy of old. While 'STRUCK BY LIGHTNING' (1991) and 'BURNING QUESTIONS' (1992) saw PARKER's new family man credentials take top billing, there was still enough firebrand R&B spark to keep longtime fans on their toes. Seemingly mellowing further with each passing year, 1995's '12 HAUNTED EPISODES' was a kind of PARKER equivalent to STING's 'Ten Summoner's Tales'. Much more rocking was the following year's concert set, 'LIVE FROM NEW YORK' (1996), the singer revamping the cream of his back catalogue with new backing crew, The EPISODES. Equally rocking was 'ACID BUBBLEGUM' (1996), an unlikely and only occasionally convincing attempt to recapture the raw and emotionally bleeding sound of old. Double set,'THE LAST ROCK'N'ROLL TOUR' (1997), meanwhile, added to the man's surfeit of live material, a fairly pointless concert document essential for only the most diehard fans. PARKER began the new decade on a similar to note to how he'd begun the previous one, detailing the small victories and daily defeats of domestic life with 'DEEPCUT TO NOWHERE' (2001). If there were more defeats than victories this time around then that only made for more compelling listening. • **Songwriters:** PARKER penned, except covers CUPID + A CHANGE IS GONNA COME (Sam Cooke) / SUBSTITUTE (Who) / IN BLOOM (Nirvana) / CREAM (Prince) / AROUND AND AROUND (Chuck Berry) / etc. • **Trivia:** In 1980, PARKER had book 'The Great Trouser Mystery' published.

Album rating: HOWLIN' WIND (*8) / HEAT TREATMENT (*7) / STICK TO ME (*6) / THE PARKERILLA (*3) / SQUEEZING OUT SPARKS (*8) / THE UP ESCALATOR (*6) / ANOTHER GREY AREA (*6) / THE REAL MACAW (*6) / STEADY NERVES (*4) / MONA LISA'S SISTER (*6) / HUMAN SOUL (*5) / LIVE! ALONE IN AMERICA (*5) / STRUCK BY LIGHTNING (*6) / BURNING QUESTIONS (*5) / THE BEST OF GRAHAM PARKER compilation (*8) / LIVE ALONE! DISCOVERING JAPAN (*5) / 12 HAUNTED EPISODES (*5) / LIVE FROM NEW YORK, NY (*4) / ACID BUBBLEGUM (*5) / THE LAST ROCK N ROLL TOUR (*4) / DEEPCUT TO NOWHERE (*5)

GRAHAM PARKER & THE RUMOUR

GRAHAM PARKER – vocals, guitar / **MARTIN BELMONT** – guitar (ex-DUCKS DELUXE) / **BRINSLEY SCHWARZ** – guitar (ex-BRINSLEY SCHWARZ) / **BOB ANDREWS** – keys, sax, guitar (ex-BRINSLEY SCHWARZ) / **ANDREW BODNAR** – bass / **STEVE GOULDING** – drums (both ex-BONTEMPS ROULEE)

		Vertigo	Mercury
Mar 76.	(7") *(6059 135)* **SILLY THING. / I'M GONNA USE IT NOW**		–
Apr 76.	(lp) *(6360 129) <SRM-1 1095>* **HOWLIN' WIND** – White honey / Nothin's gonna pull us apart / Silly thing / Gypsy blood / Between you and me / Back to schooldays / Soul shoes / Lady doctor / You've got to be kidding / Howlin' wind / Not if it pleases me / Hey Lord, don't ask me questions. *(free live 7"+=)* – KANSAS CITY. / SILLY THING *(re-iss. Apr89 on 'Beat Goes On'; BGO 48) (cd-iss. May90 on 'Polydor'; 826273-2) (cd re-iss. Jul01; 548667-2)*		
Jul 76.	(7") *(6059 147)* **SOUL SHOES. / WILD HONEY**		–
Sep 76.	(7") *<73834>* **SOUL SHOES. / YOU'VE GOT TO BE KIDDING**	–	
Oct 76.	(7") *(6059 158)* **HOTEL CHAMBERMAID. / DON'T ASK ME QUESTIONS**		–
Oct 76.	(lp) *(6360 137) <SRM-1 1117>* **HEAT TREATMENT** – Heat treatment / That's what they all say / Turned up too late / Black honey / Hotel chambermaid / Pourin' it all out / Back door love / Something you're goin' thru / Help me shake it / Fool's gold. *(re-iss. May89 on 'Beat Goes On'; BGO 45) (cd-iss. May90 on 'Polydor'; 826274-2) (cd re-iss. Jul01; 548682-2)*	52	
Dec 76.	(7") *<73876>* **HEAT TREATMENT. / BACK DOOR LOVE**	–	
Jan 77.	(7") *(6059 161)* **POURIN' IT ALL OUT. / HELP ME SHAKE IT**		–
Feb 77.	(7") *<73970>* **STICK TO ME. / HEAT IN HARLEM**	–	
Mar 77.	(7"pink-ep) *(PARK 001) <74000>* **THE PINK PARKER** – Hold back the night / (Let me get) Sweet on you / White honey / Soul shoes.	24	58
Oct 77.	(lp) *(9102 017) <SRM-1 3706>* **STICK TO ME** – Stick to me / I'm gonna tear your playhouse down / Problem child / Soul on ice / Clear head / The New York shuffle / Watch the Moon come down / Thunder and rain / The heat in Harlem / The raid. *(cd-iss. May90 on 'Polydor'; 824808-2) (cd re-iss. Jul01; 548680-2)*	19	
Nov 77.	(7") *(6059 185)* **THE NEW YORK SHUFFLE. / BLEEP**		–
Apr 78.	(7") *(PARK 2)* **HEY LORD, DON'T ASK ME QUESTIONS (live). / FOOL'S GOLD**	32	
May 78.	(d-lp) *(6641 797) <SRM 2100>* **THE PARKERILLA (live)** – Lady doctor / Fool's gold / I'm gonna tear your playhouse down / Hey Lord, don't ask me questions / Silly thing / The heat in Harlem / Gypsy blood / Back to schooldays / Heat treatment / Watch the Moon come down / The New York shuffle / Soul shoes / Hey Lord, don't ask me questions (studio 45 rpm). *(cd-iss. Jan94; 842263-2)*	14	

GRAHAM PARKER

—— solo but still augmented by The RUMOUR

		Vertigo	Arista
Feb 79.	(7") *(6059 219)* **PROTECTION. / I WANT YOU BACK (live)**		–
Mar 79.	(lp) *(9102 030) <4223>* **SQUEEZING OUT SPARKS** – Discovering Japan / Local girls / Nobody hurts you / You can't be too strong / Passion is no ordinary word / Saturday nite is dead / Love gets you twisted / Protection / Waiting for the UFO's / Don't get excited. *(cd-iss. Jul01; 548681-2)*	18	40
Mar 79.	(7") *<0439>* **I WANT YOU BACK (ALIVE). / MERCURY POISONING**	–	
May 79.	(7") *(6059 226)* **DISCOVERING JAPAN. / LOCAL GIRLS**		–

GRAHAM PARKER & THE RUMOUR

Stiff Arista

Apr 80. (7") *(BUY 72)* **STUPEFACTION. / WOMEN IN CHARGE** [ ] [–]

Apr 80. (lp/c) *(SEEZ/CSEEZ 23)* <9517> **THE UP ESCALATOR** [11] [40]
– No holding back / Devil's sidewalk / Stupefaction / Empty lives / The beating of another heart / Endless night / Paralyzed / Manoeuvres / Jolie Jolie / Love without greed. *(c+=)* – Women in charge. *(re-iss. Jun90 on 'Demon' lp/cd; FIEND/+CD 121) (cd re-iss. Jun96 on 'Razor & Tie'; RE 1980) (cd re-iss. Jan98 on 'Diablo'; DIAB 843) (cd re-iss. Oct03 on 'Lemon'++=; CDLEM 13)* – Hey Lord don't ask me questions.

Jun 80. (7") *(BUY 82)* **LOVE WITHOUT GREED. / MERCURY POISONING** [ ] [–]

GRAHAM PARKER

— solo, without The RUMOUR. PARKER now used **NICKY HOPKINS** – piano / **GEORGE SMALL** – keyboards / **HUGH McCRACKEN** – guitars, harmonica / **DAVID BROWN** – guitars / **DOUG STEGMEYER** – bass / **MICHAEL BRAUN** – drums / **KURT McKETTRICK** – sax, flute / **JIM CLOUSE** – sax / **PAUL PRESTINO** – banjo / **JACK DOUGLAS** – percussion / +backing vocalists

R.C.A. Arista

Feb 82. (7") *(PARK 100)* <0652> **TEMPORARY BEAUTY. / NO MORE EXCUSES** [50] [ ]

Mar 82. (lp/c) *(RCA LP/K 6029)* <9589> **ANOTHER GREY AREA** [40] [51]
– Temporary beauty / Another grey area / No more excuses / Dark side of the bright lights / Can't waste a minute / Big fat zero / You hit the spot / It's all worth nothing alone / Crying for attention / Thankless task / Fear not. *(re-iss. Jul91 on 'Great Expectations' lp/c/cd; PIP LP/MC/CD 026)*

Jul 82. (7") *(RCA 243)* <0687> **NO MORE EXCUSES. / YOU HIT THE SPOT** [ ] [ ]
(12"+=) *(RCAT 243)* – Another grey area.

— now with **SMALL** + **KEVIN JENKINS** – bass / **GILSON LAVIS** – drums (ex-SQUEEZE)

Jul 83. (7"/12") *(RCA/+T 346)* **LIFE GETS BETTER. / ANNIVERSARY** [ ] [–]

Sep 83. (lp/c) *(RCA LP/K 6086)* <8023> **THE REAL MACAW** [ ] [59]
– You can't take love for granted / Glass jaw / Just like a man / assive resistance / Sounds like chains / Life gets better / A miracle a minute / Beyond a joke / Last couple on the dance floor / Anniversary / (Too late) The smart bomb. *(re-iss. Jul91 on 'Great Expectations' lp/c/cd; PIP LP/MC/CD 027)*

Sep 83. (7") <9065> **LIFE GETS BETTER. / BEYOND A JOKE** [–] [94]

Oct 83. (7") *(RCA 361)* **YOU CAN'T TAKE LOVE FOR GRANTED. / GLASS JAW** [ ] [ ]

GRAHAM PARKER & THE SHOT

— with **SMALL, JENKINS** + **SCHWARTZ** plus **MICHAEL BRAUN** – drums repl. LAVIS

Elektra Elektra

Apr 85. (7"/12") *(EKR/+T 6)* **BREAK THEM DOWN. / EVERYONE'S HAND IS ON THE SWITCH** [ ] [–]
(d7"+=) *(EKR 6 – SAM 239)* – Bricks and mortar / Too much to think.

Apr 85. (lp/c)(cd) *(EKT 4/+C)(960388-2)* <60388> **STEADY NERVES** [ ] [57]
– Break them down / Mighty rivers / Lunatic fringe / Wake up (next to you) / When you do that to me / The weekend's too short / Take everything / Black Lincoln Continental / Canned laughter / Everyone's hand is on the switch / Locked into green. *(cd+=)* – Too much time to think.

Apr 85. (7") <69654> **WAKE UP (NEXT TO YOU). / BRICKS AND MORTAR** [–] [39]

Jun 85. (7") *(EKR 13)* **WAKE UP (NEXT TO YOU). / CANNED LAUGHTER** [ ] [–]
(12"+=) *(EKRT 13)* – Locked into green.

GRAHAM PARKER

— solo, with backers **BRINSLEY** / **ANDREW BODNAR** – bass / **JAMES HALLAWELL** – keyboards / **TERRY WILLIAMS** – drums

Demon R.C.A.

1988. (7") <8639> **(GET STARTED) START A FIRE. / ORDINARY GIRL** [–] [ ]

Jul 88. (7") *(D 1059)* **I'M JUST YOUR MAN. / I DON'T KNOW** [ ] [–]

Jul 88. (lp/c/cd) *(FIEND/+CASS/CD 122)* <8316> **THE MONA LISA'S SISTER** [ ] May88 [77]
– Don't let it break you down / Under the mask of happiness / Back in time / I'm just your man / OK Hieronymous / Get started, start a fire / The girl isn't ready / Blue highways / Success / I don't know / Cupid.

Nov 88. (7") *(D 1061)* **CUPID. / BLUE HIGHWAYS** [ ] [–]

Apr 89. (lp/c/cd) *(FIEND/+CASS/CD 141)* **LIVE! ALONE IN AMERICA (live)** [ ] [ ]
– White honey / Watch the moon come down / Black honey / Protection / Soul corruption / Gypsy blood / Back to schooldays / Durban poison / The 3 Martini lunch / Back in time / Hotel chambermaid / Don't let it break you down / You can't be too strong / A change is gonna come.

— retained **SCHWARZ, BODNAR, HALLIWELL. PETE THOMAS** – drums repl. TERRY Also incl.**STEVE NIEVE** – synth. / **BEIZEL SICKS** – percussion / **SONIA JONES MORGAN** + **CARMEN DAYE** – backing vox / **MOLLY DUNCAN** – tenor sax / **J. NEIL SIDWELL** – trombone / **MARTIN DROVER** – trumpet

Oct 89. (lp/c/cd) *(FIEND/+CASS/CD 163)* <9876> **HUMAN SOUL** [ ] Feb90 [ ]
– Little Miss understanding / My love's strong / Dancing for money / Call me your doctor / Big man on paper / Soultime / Everything goes / Sugar gives you energy / Daddy's a postman / Green monkeys / I was wrong / You got the world (rightwhere you want it) / Slash and burn. *(cd re-iss. Jan98 on 'Diablo'; DIAB 846)*

Demon B.M.G.

Jan 91. (12"ep/cd-ep) *(GP 12-1/CD1)* **THE KID WITH THE BUTTERFLY NET / STRONG WINDS. / GUARDIAN ANGELS / MUSEUM OF STUPIDITY / WRAPPING PAPER** [ ] [–]

Feb 91. (d-lp/c/cd) *(FIEND/+CASS/CD 201)* <3013> **STRUCK BY LIGHTNING** [ ] [ ]
– She wants so many things / They murdered the clown / Strong winds / The kid with the butterfly net / And it shook me / That's where she ends up / A brand new book / Weeping statues / Wrapping paper / Ten girls ago / I'm into something good / Over the border (to America) / The Sun is gonna shine again / Guardian angels / Children and dogs / When I was king / Museum piece / Museum of stupidity. *(cd re-iss. Jan98 on 'Diablo'; DIAB 847)*

Demon Capitol

Jul 92. (lp/c/cd) *(FIEND/+C/CD 721)* **BURNING QUESTIONS** [ ] [ ]
– Release me / Too many knots to untangle / Just like Joe Meek's blues / Love is a burning question / Platinum blonde / Long stem rose / Short memories / Here it comes again / Mr.Tender / Just like Herm & Hesse / Yesterdays cloud / Oasis / Worthy of your love / Substitute. *(cd re-iss. Jan98 on 'Diablo'; DIAB 848)*

Aug 92. (cd-ep) **BURNING QUESTIONS / RELEASE ME / PLATINUM BLONDE / SHORT MEMORIES** [ ] [–]

Oct 92. (cd-s) <15939> **HERE IT COMES AGAIN / SUBSTITUTE / CLASS ACT** [–] [ ]

Aug 93. (lp/c/cd) *(FIEND/+CASS/CD 735)* **LIVE ALONE! DISCOVERING JAPAN (live)** [ ] [–]
– That's what they all say / Platinum blonde / Mercury poisoning / Sweet 16 / No woman no cry / Lunatic fringe / Long stem rose / Discovering Japan / Hey Lord, don't ask me questions / Watch the Moon come down (revisited) / Just like Herman Hesse / Too many knots to untabgle / Chopsticks / Short memories. *(cd re-iss. Jan98 as 'ALONE IN JAPAN LIVE' on 'Diablo'; DIAB 849)*

Demon DakotaArts

Dec 94. (cd-ep) *(GPCD 3)* <1104 40001-2> **GRAHAM PARKER'S CHRISTMAS CRACKER** [ ] Nov94 [ ]
– Christmas is for mugs / New Year's revolution / Soul Christmas / (demo versions).

Grapevine Razor & Tie

Apr 95. (cd/c/lp) *(GRA CD/MC/LP 204)* <2817> **12 HAUNTED EPISODES** [ ] [ ]
– Partner for life / Pollinate / Force of nature / Disney's America / Haunted episodes / Next phase / Honest work / Cruel stage / See yourself / Loverman / Fly / First day of spring.

— line-up:- **PARKER** / + **MITCH MARGOLD** – keyboards / **KENNY AARONSON** – bass, steel guitar / **DENNIS McDERMOTT** – drums

Aug 96. (cd; as GP + THE EPISODES) <7000> **LIVE FROM NEW YORK, NY (live)** [–] [ ]
– Big man on paper / Fool's gold / Force of nature / Haunted episodes /

Fly / Here it comes again / Crawlin' from the wreckage / Partner for life / Disney's America / Stick to me / See yourself / Over the border / Love gets you twisted / Wake up (next to you) / Get started, start a fire / Protection / In bloom.

When! Razor & Tie

Mar 97. (cd) *(WENCD 015)* <2826> **ACID BUBBLEGUM** ☐ Sep96 ☐
– Turn it into hate / Sharpening axes / Get over it and move on / Bubblegum cancer / Impenetrable / She never let me down / Obsessed with Aretha / Beancounter / Girl at the end of the pier / Baggage / Milk train / Character assassination / They got it wrong as usual. *(re-iss. Jul97 on 'Essential'; ESSCD 583)*

Apr 97. (d-cd) *<2827>* **THE LAST ROCK'N'ROLL TOUR (live)** [-] ☐
– Turn it into hate / Don't let it break you down / Soul on ice / Weeping statues / Fool's gold / Local girls / Daddy's a postman / Impenetrable / Sharpening axes / Back door love / She never let me down / Obsessed with Aretha / Take everything / Stupefaction / Soul shoes / Saturday nite is dead / Get over it and move on / Cream / Glass jaw / Bubblegum cancer / Don't get excited / Around and around.

Evangeline Razor & Tie

Sep 01. (cd) *(GEL 4032)* <8287-2> **DEEPCUT TO NOWHERE** ☐ Aug01 ☐
– Dark days / I'll never play Jacksonville again / If it ever stops rainin' / Depend on me / High horse / Cheap chipped black nails / Blue horizon / Tough on clothes / Socks 'n' sandals / It takes a village idiot / Syphilis and religion / Last stop is nowhere.

– compilations, etc. –

May 80. (lp) *Vertigo; (9102 042)* **THE BEST OF GRAHAM PARKER & THE RUMOUR** ☐ ☐
– Soul shoes / Heat reatment / Howling wind / Hold back the night / Back to schooldays / You can't be too strong / Kansas City / Stick to me / The New York shuffle / Local girls / White honey / Hotel chambermaid / Between you and me / Hey Lord, don't ask me questions. *(re-iss. May82 lp/c; VERB/+C 001)*

May 84. (lp/c) *Philips; (PRICE/PRIMC 62)* **IT DON'T MEAN A THING IF IT AIN'T GOT THAT SWING** ☐ [-]

1991. (4xcd-box) *Demon; (GRAHAM 1)* **GRAHAM PARKER** ☐ [-]
– (MONA LISA'S SISTER / HUMAN SOUL / LIVE ALONE IN AMERICA / THE UP ESCALATOR)

Sep 93. (cd/c) *Vertigo; (512149-2/-4)* **THE BEST OF GRAHAM PARKER** ☐ ☐
– Silly thing / I'm gonna use it now / Between you and me / Back to schooldays / White honey / You can't hurry love / Pourin' it all out / That's what they all say / Hotel chambermaid / Fool's gold / Watch the Moon come down / I'm gonna tear your playhouse down / Thunder and rain / Hold back the night / New York shuffle / Soul shoes / Hey Lord, don't ask me questions / I want you back / Discovering Japan / Local girls / You can't be too strong / Mercury poisoning.

Jun 94. (cd) *Windsong; (WHISCD 002)* **LIVE ON THE TEST (live)** ☐ [-]

Aug 95. (d-cd) *Vertigo; (528603-2)* **HOWLING WIND / HEAT TREATMENT** ☐ [-]

May 96. (cd) *Nectar; (NTMCD 518)* **EPISODES** ☐ [-]

Jun 96. (cd) *Windsong; (WINCD 083)* **BBC LIVE IN CONCERT (live)** ☐ [-]

Oct 96. (d-cd) *Vertigo; (534100-2)* **VERTIGO** ☐ [-]

Feb 97. (3xcd-box) *Demon; (FBOOK 15)* **NO HOLDING BACK** ☐ [-]

May 97. (cd) *R.C.A.; (74321 48728-2)* **TEMPORARY BEAUTY** ☐ [-]

Mar 98. (cd) *Hux; (HUX 003)* **NOT IF IT PLEASES ME** ☐ [-]

May 99. (cd) *Music Club; (MCCD 390)* **STIFFS AND DEMONS 1980-1993** ☐ [-]

Jul 00. (cd) *Varese Sarabande; (302061006-2)* **BBC LIVE 1977-1991** ☐ [-]

Jul 01. (d-cd) *Vertigo; (548683-2)* **THAT'S WHEN YOU KNOW (THE ACOUSTIC DEMOS / LIVE AT MARBLE ARCH)** ☐ [-]

Sep 01. (cd) *Universal; (586357-2)* **INTRODUCTION TO GRAHAM PARKER & THE RUMOUR** ☐ [-]

Aug 03. (cd) *Lemon; (CDLEM 2)* **THE OFFICIAL ART VANDELAY TAPES** ☐ [-]

— In the US, 1976 a ltd 1,000 bootleg lp 'LIVE AT MARBLE ARCH' was issued. The **RUMOUR** also branched out with own releases includung several 45s and albums MAX (Jul 77, Vertigo) / FROGS, SPROUTS, CLOGS & KRAUTS (Apr 79, Stiff) / PURITY OF PRESENCE (Jul 80, Stiff).

☐ PARLIAMENT (see under ⇒ CLINTON, George)

Alan PARSONS PROJECT

Formed: London, England . . . 1975 by the man who engineered The BEATLES' 'Abbey Road' and PINK FLOYD's 'Dark Side Of The Moon'. While working at Abbey Road studios with the likes of STEVE HARLEY & COCKNEY REBEL and PILOT, he formed a working partnership/group with manager and lyricist, ERIC WOOLFSON. Intended as a one-off, the Edgar Allan-Poe 'TALES OF MYSTERY AND IMAGINATION' was released on 'Charisma' in 1976, the concept piece surprising critics and even hitting the US Top 40. The following year, PARSONS and Co signed a new contract with 'Arista', issuing the more conventionally accessible US Top 10 set, 'I ROBOT' (based on science fiction writer, Isaac Asimov's book of the same name. The group/project continued maintain US Top 30 status over the course of the late 70's/early 80's with albums such as 'PYRAMID' (1978), 'EVE' (1979), 'THE TURN OF A FRIENDLY CARD' (1980), 'EYE IN THE SKY' (1982) and 'AMMONIA AVENUE' (1984). These records spawned several major hit singles featuring an array of vocal talent including COLIN BLUNSTONE, CHRIS RAINBOW, LENNY ZAKATEK and DAVID TOWNSHEND. Later in the 80's, PARSONS employed the services of DAVID PATON on the 1985 project, 'VULTURE CULTURE' and JOHN MILES and GARY BROOKER on 'STEREOTOMY' in '86. However, the pop/rock appeal of PARSONS and his troupe of studio-bound sidemen waned after the relative commercial failure of 'GAUDI' (an album based on the works of Spanish architect, Antonio Gaudi). This seemed to be a major setback for PARSONS, who remained absent from the music scene for the ensuing six years, belatedly returning with a solo set, 'TRY ANYTHING ONCE', in 1993. The studio boffin followed this up with 1996's 'ON AIR', a concept set centering on man's preoccupation with flight, with vocal cameos by CHRISTOPHER CROSS, ERIC STEWART, NEIL LOCKWOOD and GRAHAM DYE. While never really hanging together with the cohesion of PARSONS' earlier efforts, it had its moments. A more illustrious array of guest singers graced 'THE TIME MACHINE' (1999), with the likes of TONY HADLEY and MAIRE BRENNAN adding lustre to the album's existentialist themes and abstract, electronically influenced textures.

Album rating: TALES OF MYSTERY AND IMAGINATION (*7) / I ROBOT (*6) / PYRAMID (*5) / EVE (*5) / THE TURN OF A FRIENDLY CARD (*6) / EYE IN THE SKY (*6) / THE BEST OF THE ALAN PARSONS PROJECT compilation (*6) / AMMONIA AVENUE (*6) / VULTURE CULTURE (*4) / STEREOTOMY (*4) / GAUDI (*4) / THE BEST OF THE ALAN PARSONS PROJECT VOL.2 compilation (*6) / THE INSTRUMENTAL WORKS collection (*4) / TRY ANYTHING ONCE (*4) / THE DEFINITIVE COLLECTION compilation (*6) / ON AIR (*5) / THE TIME MACHINE (*6)

ALAN PARSONS (b.1949) – guitar, keyboards, vocals, producer, engineer with **ERIC WOOLFSON** – keyboards, vocals / **IAN BAIRNSON** – guitars (ex-PILOT) / **DAVID PATON** – bass, vocals, guitar / **STUART TOSH** – drums

Charisma 20th Century

Jun 76. (lp) *(CDS/+MC 4003)* <508> **TALES OF MYSTERY AND IMAGINATION** [56] May76 [38]
– A dream within a dream / The raven / The tell-tale heart / The cask of Amontillado / (The system of) Doctor Tarr and Professor Feather / The fall of the House of Usher: Prelude – Arrival – Intermezzo – Pavane / Fall / To one in Paradise.

Jul 76. (7") *(CB 293)* <2297> **(THE SYSTEM OF) DOCTOR TARR AND PROFESSOR FEATHER. / A DREAM WITHIN A DREAM** ☐ [37]

Sep 76. (7") <2308> **THE RAVEN. / PRELUDE TO THE FALL OF THE HOUSE OF USHER** [-] [80]

Oct 76. (7") *(CB 298)* **TO ONE IN PARADISE. / THE CASK OF AMONTILLADO** ☐ [-]

— added **DUNCAN MACKAY** – keyboards

Arista Arista

Jun 77. (lp/c) *(SPARTY/TCARTY 1012)* *<7002>* **I ROBOT** 30 9
– I robot / I wouldn't want to be like you / Some other time / Breakdown / Don't let it show / The voice / Nucleus / Day after day / Total eclipse / Genesis Ch.1 V.32. *(re-iss. Mar89 lp/c/cd; 209/409/259 651)*

Aug 77. (7") *(ARIST 134)* *<0260>* **I WOULDN'T WANT TO BE LIKE YOU. / NUCLEUS** □ 36
(above featured **LENNY ZAKATEK** – vocals) / (below **DAVID TOWNSHEND** – vocals)

Dec 77. (7") *<0288>* **DON'T LET IT SHOW. / I ROBOT** – 92

Feb 78. (7") *(ARIST 158)* **I ROBOT. / SOME OTHER TIME** □ –

Feb 78. (7") *<0310>* **BREAKDOWN. / DAY AFTER DAY** – □

— added **STUART ELLIOTT** – drums (ex-10cc) repl. TOSH

May 78. (lp/c) *(SPART/TCART 1054)* *<4180>* **PYRAMID** 49 26
– Voyager / What goes up / The eagle will rise again / One more river / Can't take it with you / In the lap of the gods / Pyramania / Hyper-gamma-spaces / Shadow of a lonely man. *(re-iss. Apr88 lp/c/cd; 209/409/259 983)*

Jun 78. (7") *(ARIST 195)* **PYRAMANIA. / IN THE LAP OF THE GODS** □ –

Sep 78. (7") *<0352>* **WHAT GOES UP. / IN THE LAP OF THE GODS** – 87

Aug 79. (lp/c) *(SPARTY/TCARTY 1100)* *<9504>* **EVE** 74 13
– Lucifer / You lie down with dogs / I'd rather be a man / You won't be there / Winding me up / Damned if I do / Don't hold back / Secret garden / If I could change your mind. *(re-iss. Jul83 on 'Fame' lp/c; FA/TCFA 3071) (re-iss. May88 lp/c/cd; 208/408/258 981)*

Aug 79. (7") *(ARIST 294)* **LUCIFER. / I'D RATHER BE A MAN** □ –
(12") *(ARIST12 294)* – ('A'side) / Damned if I do / Secret garden.
(below featured **ZAKATEK – vocals** (also on Jan81, Dec83 singles)

Nov 79. (7") *(ARIST 312)* *<0454>* **DAMNED IF I DO. / IF I COULD CHANGE YOUR MIND** □ Sep79 27

Jan 80. (7") *<0491>* **SECRET GARDEN. / YOU WON'T BE THERE** – □

Mar 80. (7") *<0502>* **LUCIFER. / YOU LIE DOWN WITH DOGS** – □

— now w/out MACKAY

Nov 80. (lp/c) *(DL/TC ART 1)* *<9518>* **THE TURN OF A FRIENDLY CARD** 38 13
– May be a price to pay / Games people play / Time / I don't wanna go home / The gold bug / The turn of a friendly card: (part 1 – Snake eyes – The ace of swords; part 2 – Nothing left to lose). *(re-iss. May88 lp/c/cd; 208/408/258 982)*

Nov 80. (7") *(ARIST 374)* **THE TURN OF A FRIENDLY CARD. / MAY BE A PRICE TO PAY** □ –

Jan 81. (7") *(ARIST 386)* *<0573>* **GAMES PEOPLE PLAY. / THE ACE OF SWORDS** □ Nov80 16

Aug 81. (7") *(ARIST 423)* *<0598>* **TIME. / THE GOLD BUG** □ Apr81 15

Oct 81. (7") *<0635>* **SNAKE EYES. / I DON'T WANNA GO HOME** – 67
(above featured **CHRIS RAINBOW** – vocals) (also on May85 single)

May 82. (lp/c) *(204/404 666)* *<9599>* **EYE IN THE SKY** 28 7
– Sirius / Eye in the sky / Children of the Moon / Gemini / Silence and I / You're gonna get your finger burned / Psychobabble / Mammagamma / Step by step / Old and wise. *(re-iss. May87 lp/c/cd; 208/408/258 718)*

May 82. (7") *(ARIST 470)* *<0696>* **EYE IN THE SKY. / GEMINI** □ 3
(below featured **COLIN BLUNSTONE** – vocals (ex-ZOMBIES) (below **ELMER GANTRY**)

Nov 82. (7") *<1029>* **PSYCHOBABBLE. / CHILDREN OF THE MOON** – 57

Dec 82. (7") *(ARIST 494)* **OLD AND WISE. / CHILDREN OF THE MOON** 74 –

Feb 83. (7") *<1048>* **OLD AND WISE. / YOU'RE GONNA GET YOUR FINGERS BURNED** – □

Oct 83. (lp/c) *(APP/TCAPP 1)* *<8193>* **THE BEST OF THE ALAN PARSONS PROJECT** (compilation) 99 53
– I wouldn't want to be like you / Eye in the sky / Games people play / Time / Pyramania / You don't believe / Lucifer / Psychobabble / Damned if I do / Don't let it show / Can't take it with you / Old and wise. *(cd-iss. Feb87; 601050) (cd re-iss. Aug95; 610052)*

Feb 84. (7") *<9108>* **YOU DON'T BELIEVE. / LUCIFER** – 54

Feb 84. (lp/c/cd) *(206/406/256 100)* *<8204>* **AMMONIA AVENUE** 24 15
– Prime time / Let me go home / One good reason / Since the last goodbye / Don't answer me / Dancing on a high wire / You don't believe / Pipeline / Ammonia Avenue. *(re-iss. May88 lp/c/cd; 208/408/258 885)*

Feb 84. (7"/7"sha-pic-d) *(ARIS T/D 553)* **DON'T ANSWER ME. / YOU DON'T BELIEVE** 58 –
(12"+=) *(ARIST12 553)* – Games people play / Old and wise.

Feb 84. (7",12") *<9160>* **DON'T ANSWER ME. / DON'T LET IT SHOW** – 15

Jun 84. (7") *(ARIST 572)* *<9208>* **PRIME TIME. / THE GOLD BUG** □ May84 34
(12"+=) *(ARIST12 572)* – Pipeline (instrumental) / Sirius (instrumental).
(below featured **DAVID PATON** – vocals)

Jan 85. (7") *(ARIST 588)* *<9282>* **LET'S TALK ABOUT ME. / HAWKEYE** □ 56
(12+=) *(ARIST12 588)* – Pipeline.

Feb 85. (lp/c/cd) *(206/406/256 577)* *<8263>* **VULTURE CULTURE** 40 46
– Let's talk about me / Separate lives / Days are numbered (the traveller) / Sooner or later / Vulture culture / Hawkeye / Somebody out there / The same old sun. *(re-iss. May88 lp/c/cd; 208/408/258 884)*

Apr 85. (7") *<9349>* **DAYS ARE NUMBERED (THE TRAVELLER). / SOMEBODY OUT THERE** – 71

— next featured vocalists **JOHN MILES, CHRIS RAINBOW, GARY BROOKER**

Jan 86. (lp/c/cd) *(207/407/257 463)* *<8384>* **STEREOTOMY** □ 43
– Stereotomy / Beaujolais / Urbania / Limelight / In the real world / Where's the walrus? / Light of the world / Chinese whispers / Stereotomy two. *(re-iss. Jun88 lp/c/cd; 209/259/409 050)*

Mar 86. (7"/12") *(ARIST/+12 654)* *<9443>* **STEREOTOMY. / URBANIA (instrumental)** □ Feb86 82

— added **LAURIE COTTLE** – bass / **RICHARD COTTLE** – saxophone, synthesizers / **GEOFF BARRADALE** – vocals (with usual vocalists) repl. BROOKER

Jan 87. (7") *<9576><9548>* **STANDING ON HIGHER GROUND. / INSIDE LOOKING OUT** – □

Jan 87. (lp/c/cd) *(208/408/258 084)* *<8448>* **GAUDI** 66 57
– La Sagrada familia / Too late / Closer to Heaven / Standing on higher ground / Money talks / Inside looking out / Paseo de gracia (instrumental). *(re-iss. Feb90 cd/c/lp; 260/410/260 171)*

Jan 88. (lp/c/cd) *(208/408/258 634)* **LIMELIGHT: THE BEST OF THE ALAN PARSONS PROJECT VOL.2** (compilation) □ □
– Limelight / Same old sun / Ammonia avenue / Mammagamma / Since the last goodbye / I robot / Prime time / Hawkeye / Return of the friendly card / Silence and I. *(cd re-iss. Oct95)*

ALAN PARSONS

Oct 93. (cd/c/lp) *(74321 16730-2/-4/-1)* *<18741>* **TRY ANYTHING ONCE** □ □
– The three of me / Turn it up / Wine from the water / Breakaway / Jigue / Mr. Time / Siren song / Back against the wall / Re-jigue / Oh life (there must be more). *(cd+c+=)* – I'm talking to you / Dreamscape.

Total A&M

Mar 97. (cd) *(TOTCD 6)* *<161237>* **ON AIR** □ Sep96 □
– Blue blue sky / Too close to the sun / Blown by the wind / Cloudbreak (instrumental) / I can't look down / Brother up in Heaven / Fall free / Apollo (instrumental) / So far away / One day to fly / Blue blue sky. *(d-cd-iss. Aug99 on 'Artful'; ARTFULCD 26)*

— with **BAIRNSON, ELLIOTT, BLUNSTONE, RAINBOW**, etc.

Artful Miramar

Sep 99. (cd) *(ARTFULCD 28)* *<23146>* **THE TIME MACHINE** □ □
– The time machine (part 1) / Temporalia / Out of the blue / Call up / Ignorance is bliss / Rubber universe / The call of the wild / No future in the past / Press rewind / The very last time / Far ago and long away / The time machine (part 2).

– compilations, etc. –

Nov 87. (cd) *London; (832820-2)* **TALES OF MYSTERY AND IMAGINATION** □ □
– (remixed debut with new synth/guitar touches + narration by ORSON WELLS)

Nov 88. (lp/c/cd) *R.C.A.; (209/409/259 237)* **THE INSTRUMENTAL WORKS** □ –
– Pipeline / Where's the walrus? / I robot / Mammagamma / Hawkeye / Voyager / Paseo de Gracia / Urbania / The gold bug / Genesis Ch.1 V.32.

Dec 90. (cd-box/c-box) *Arista; (ND/NK 74374)* **ALAN PARSONS BOX SET** ☐ ☐
Nov 91. (cd/c) *Connoisseur; (VSOP CD/MC 170)* **ANTHOLOGY** ☐ -
Mar 95. (cd) *<5086>* **LIVE: THE BEST OF THE ALAN PARSONS PROJECT** - ☐
Sep 95. (d-cd) *R.C.A.; (74321 29208-2)* **BACK 2 BACK** ☐ -
Jan 96. (cd) *RCA Victor; (09026 68229-2)* **THE VERY BEST OF THE ALAN PARSONS PROJECT** ☐ -

Gram PARSONS

Born: CECIL INGRAM CONNOR, 5 Nov'46, Winter Haven, Florida, USA. Through a privileged but traumatic childhood in Waycross, Georgia, during which his father, Coon Dog, committed suicide and his mother died of alcohol-related illness (on the day he graduated from high school), GRAM diverted himself with music; although his first love was country, the traditional preserve of white Southerners, GRAM was inspired to get up on stage after witnessing the hip-swivelling suave of ELVIS PRESLEY. Developing his talents in high-school covers outfits such as The PACERS and The LEGENDS, he was also sidelining with solo gigs and, through manager, Buddy Freeman, secured an appearance on a Greenville, South Carolina, TV Station. This in turn led to GRAM forming The SHILOS (having previously sang as a duo with KENT LAVOIE – aka hitmaker, LOBO), a fairly staid folk outfit who recorded a session for a Greenville campus radio station (released in 1979 on 'Sundown' as 'GRAM PARSONS – THE EARLY YEARS 1963-65') and with whom PARSONS penned his most fully realised song to date, 'ZAH'S BLUES'. Inevitably, the band fell by the wayside following GRAM's enrolment at Harvard in 1965; bypassing classes for the lure of the local music scene, he barely lasted six months, hooking up with local musicians, IAN DUNLOP, JOHN NUESE and MICKEY GAUVIN to form The LIKE and pioneering a synthesis of R&B, rock'n'roll and country which would would inform the remainder of PARSON's relatively short career. Around this time, GRAM spoke of having a deal with 'R.C.A.' and although it's widely believed he never recorded for the label, two tracks, 'CAN'T TAKE IT ANYMORE' and 'REMEMBER', have recently been unearthed (thanks to eagle-eyed archives man, Ron Maharg) from the label's vaults. The former a BYRDS-esque jangle calling to mind 'Chimes Of Freedom' and the latter a version of 'NOVEMBER NIGHTS' (a staple of The LIKE's live set never recorded under its original title but subsequently covered by actor Peter Fonda), these tracks may well have been recorded at the same time as the legendary lost Brandon De Wilde session, which GRAM & Co. are rumoured to have played on (the actor was a close confidante of the band and a regular at their new communal home in The Bronx, New York); through the continuing efforts of GP obsessive and all-round top man, Keith Munro, the songs might just be given an official release – subject to legal complexities – in the near future through 'B.M.G.'. Whatever, they're certainly more representative of the direction PARSONS was headed than the lame film theme, 'THE RUSSIANS ARE COMING', which served as a debut single in Spring '67. By this point trading under The INTERNATIONAL SUBMARINE BAND moniker, GRAM & Co. were encouraged by the experimentation of renegade country artists like BUCK OWENS and the hard-driving B-side, 'TRUCK DRIVING MAN' was a truer taste of what was to come. After another flop single for 'Columbia', 'SUM UP BROKE', the group relocated to L.A., where the West Coast scene was sending out cultural shockwaves around the world. Hobnobbing with the likes of the aforementioned Peter Fonda, the group blagged a cameo role in hippy flick, 'The Trip', for which they also recorded a track, 'LAZY DAYS' (it belatedly turned up on the second FLYING BURRITO BROTHERS album). As country wasn't yet hip with the L.A. set, the song was rejected and the band ended up lip-synching to music by the more suitably psychedelic ELECTRIC FLAG. Bearing out such iniquities with their heads held high, the group eventually secured a contract with L.A. producer LEE HAZLEWOOD's 'L.H.I.' records. But the INTERNATIONAL SUBMARINE BAND that signed up wasn't the same beast that had moved to California only a matter of months earlier. DUNLOP and GAUVIN, tired of waiting around and eager to move in a more R&B/rock direction, hooked up with BARRY TASHIAN and BILLY BRIGGS for the first, short-lived incarnation of The FLYING BURRITO BROTHERS. PARSONS and NUESE, meanwhile, pursued their idea of a pure country sound; JON CORNEAL, BOB BUCHANAN (co-writer of PARSONS' classic 'HICKORY WIND') and CHRIS ETHRIDGE all played on the resulting album, 'SAFE AT HOME' (1968) alongside Nashville veteran, EARL 'LES' BALL and pedal steel player, J.D. MANESS. While half the album was out and out country (including covers of Johnny Cash's 'I STILL MISS SOMEONE' and Merle Haggard's 'SOMEBODY ELSE YOU'VE KNOWN'), PARSONS was already in the process of creating something fresh and exciting with his original material; the little-boy-lost charm of 'BLUE EYES' was irresistible while the chugging 'LUXURY LINER' became something of a country-rock standard covered by EMMYLOU HARRIS amongst others, the whole record characterised by GRAM's quavering, frail but emotional depth-charge singing. Retrospectively hailed as the first ever country-rock album, it was nevertheless ignored at the time and to all intents and purposes, The BYRDS' 'Sweetheart Of The Rodeo' (1968) was the record which really introduced the concept to a wider public and more significantly, the rock and country establishments. With sales of 'SAFE AT HOME' barely registering, GRAM wasn't slow in taking up an invitation to join the band (The BYRDS), and, along with CHRIS HILLMAN, formed the main thrust of their move away from folk-rock to stone country. An album consisting almost wholly of cover versions, 'Sweetheart..'s only two originals were penned by PARSONS, the poignant 'ONE HUNDRED YEARS FROM NOW' and the aforementioned autumnal beauty of 'HICKORY WIND'. Ironically, GRAM's distinctive vocals were erased (in favour of ROGER McGUINN) on all but the latter track prior to release, the controversial reason given that PARSONS was still contracted to HAZLEWOOD (note-the original versions were belatedly released as part of The BYRDS' 1990 'C.B.S.' box set). Despite shaking up the Grand Ole Opry, drawing critical acclaim and setting in motion a return to roots music that would reverbate well into the 70's, GRAM, in what was already becoming a familiar career pattern, was quickly tiring of life as a BYRD. Following a messy departure on the eve of a South African tour (newfound buddies The ROLLING STONES were instrumental in persuading GRAM that such a venture was really like, not a hip thing to do, man), PARSONS flew back to L.A. and mused upon his fabled vision of a "Cosmic American Music". HILLMAN soon joined him and along with pedal steel maestro, SNEAKY PETE KLEINOW and old cohorts CORNEAL and ETHRIDGE, realised that vision and then some, with The FLYING BURRITO BROTHERS. Taking the name from the brief project put together by DUNLOP, GAUVIN etc, the group blended country, soul, R&B and rock into a seamless strand of Americana that to this day has never been bettered. Yet after only two albums (see The FLYING BURRITO BROTHERS section for the full lowdown on the band's trailblazing, hellraising heyday), PARSONS again bailed out, spending more and more time with

KEITH RICHARDS; PARSONS influence on The 'STONES was obvious, from the reworked hoedown of 'Honky Tonk Woman' ('Country Honk') to the stoned backwoods bliss of their finest album, 'Exile On Main Street'. Although he was never credited, GRAM is rumoured to be floating around somewhere in the murk of the latter masterpiece, certainly spending enough time at RICHARDS' French villa/makeshift recording studio to lend the claims some weight. With his career in limbo, PARSONS eventually returned to L.A. in 1972 and began recording his first fully fledged solo album; unable to secure the production services of his hero, MERLE HAGGARD, GRAM did the next best thing and hired the man's recording engineer, Hugh Davies, leaving the lion's share of the knob-twiddling to another English friend, RIK GRECH (erstwhile FAMILY member and part of the short-lived BLIND FAITH). Employing ELVIS stalwarts such as JAMES BURTON and GLEN D. HARDIN, GRAM assembled a crack band with the angel-voiced EMMYLOU HARRIS at its epicentre; a struggling folk singer when PARSONS met her, HARRIS was the musical other half that he'd been searching for all his life and vice versa. PARSONS schooled her in the ways of cosmic country and her crystal pure soprano ringing against GRAM's flawed but impassioned holler remains one of the most sublime sounds ever laid down on vinyl. Grand claims perhaps, but the pairing's magic transformed well-worn standards like 'STREETS OF BALTIMORE' and 'WE'LL SWEEP OUT THE ASHES IN THE MORNING' into bittersweet soul food, highlights – along with the fragile 'A SONG FOR YOU' – of 'G.P.' (1973). Again the critics frothed (at least the ones who could recognise the talent, others were more sceptical of what PARSONS was trying to achieve) and again the public remained indifferent. Undeterred, GRAM, EMMYLOU and manager, Eddie Tickner, took advantage of Warner's (GRAM was now signed to 'Reprise') enthusiasm for a bonafide tour and set about forming a road band, The FALLEN ANGELS. Despite managing only eight shows in an incident-packed month which saw GRAM falling further into drug oblivion, the tour was by all accounts a freewheeling success if not exactly an effective promotional tool; fans still in their nappies when GRAM's ragged country roadshow came to town can get at least some idea of what the fuss was about via a live set recorded for broadcast over a Long Island, NY radio station; 'LIVE 1973 (live with The FALLEN ANGELS)' (1994). Back in L.A., his personal life continuing to unravel with each passing month, GRAM got it together one last time and, as he eagerly told his friends upon its completion, finally made the album he'd been hearing in his head for years. Although a hotch-potch of old and new, borrowed and blue, the songs on 'GRIEVOUS ANGEL' (1974) resonate as deeply as any in the history of country, or rock for that matter. GRAM's voice had taken on a new lease of life, his duets with HARRIS, 'HEARTS ON FIRE' and 'LOVE HURTS' blessed with the kind of spiritual intensity normally found in gospel music. Similarly, the PARSONS/HARRIS pairing transformed 'HICKORY WIND' from a wistful country ballad into a transcendant country ballad (despite its cheesy mock-live setting), while 'RETURN OF THE GRIEVOUS ANGEL' combined a Beat-cowboy narrative with soaring harmonies and a swooning chorus to mesmerising effect. If 'BRASS BUTTONS' and '$1000 WEDDING' were GRAM at his most intimately confessional, then closing track, 'IN MY HOUR OF DARKNESS', read like both a prayer of hope and an uncanny portent of GRAM's own death. Within a matter of weeks, road manager/professional nanny/best friend, Phil Kaufman, was driving out to the Joshua Tree monument, Arizona desert in a ramshackle hearse, GRAM's lifeless body in the back. GRAM PARSONS died on the 19th of September '73, officially from a drugs overdose although suspicion still surrounds the events that took place in the Joshua Tree Inn that night, where the singer was taking a break with friends prior to a scheduled tour. True to the pact they'd made (at the funeral of revered country picker, CLARENCE WHITE), Kaufman burned GRAM's body in the desert heat, a fitting end perhaps, for an artist who'd blazed his way through the musical consciousness like a comet. 'GRIEVOUS ANGEL' was finally issued posthumously in early '74, although seemingly (at least initially) not even GRAM's death could spark interest in his music. While EMMYLOU HARRIS went on to an impressive and successful career of her own, belatedly popularising some of GRAM's songs, the GRAM PARSONS legend has since taken on such mythical proportions that there's even an annual event held at Joshua Tree each year. Yet while the myth threatens to obscure the actual music, a cursory glance around the country/alt-country scene of today is proof enough that GRAM's vision has endured. The Brandon De Wilde tapes mentioned above have apparently just been discovered, although their exact content remains unclear at present.

Album rating: International Submarine Band: SAFE AT HOME (*5) / Gram Parsons: G.P. (*8) / GREVIOUS ANGEL (*8) / posthumous:- SLEEPLESS NIGHTS (*5) / GRAM PARSONS & THE FALLEN ANGELS (*6) / WARM EVENINGS, PALE MORNINGS, BOTTLED BLUES (*6) / COSMIC AMERICAN MUSIC demos (*4)

GRAM PARSONS – vocals, guitar / with **EMMYLOU HARRIS** – vocals / **JAMES BURTON** – guitar / **GLEN D.HARDIN** – piano / **RIK GRECH** – bass / etc.

Reprise Reprise

Jan 73. (7") *<1139>* **SHE. / THAT'S ALL IT TOOK** [–] [ ]

Mar 73. (lp) *(K 44228) <MS 2123>* **G.P.** [ ] [ ]
– Still feeling blue / We'll sweep out the ashes in the morning / A song for you / Streets of Baltimore / She / That's all it took / The new soft shoe / Kiss the children / Cry one more time / How much I've lied / Big mouth blues.

Mar 73. (7") *(K 14245)* **THE NEW SOFT SHOE. / SHE** [ ] [–]

Jan 74. (lp) *(K 54018) <MS 2171>* **GREVIOUS ANGEL** [ ] [ ]
– Return of the grevious angel / Hearts on fire / I can't dance / Brass buttons / $1000 wedding / Medley live from Northern Quebec:- (a) Cash on the barrelhead – (b) Hickory wind / Love hurts / Ooh Las Vegas / In my hour of darkness.

Jan 74. (7") *<1192>* **LOVE HURTS. / IN MY HOUR OF DARKNESS** [–] [ ]

— GRAM died on the 19th September '73 after recording 90% of above LP

– compilations, etc. –

May 76. (lp; GRAM PARSONS with The FLYING BURRITO BROTHERS) *A&M; (AMLH 64578) <4578>* **SLEEPLESS NIGHTS** [ ] [ ]

Mar 79. (lp) *Shiloh; <SLP 4088>* **GRAM PARSONS** (with The INTERNATIONAL SUBMARINE BAND) [–] [ ]

May 79. (lp) *Shiloh; <SRS 8702>* **GRAM PARSONS – THE EARLY YEARS 1963-65** [–] [ ]
(UK-iss.May84 on 'Sundown'; SDLP 1010)

Dec 81. (7") *Warners; <50013>* **THE RETURN OF THE GREVIOUS ANGEL (alt.take). / HEARTS ON FIRE** [–] [ ]

Jun 82. (lp) *Warners; (K 57008) <WS 5321>* **GRAM PARSONS** [ ] [ ]

Feb 83. (7"ep; GRAM PARSONS with EMMYLOU HARRIS & The FALLEN ANGELS) *Sundown; <GPEP 104>* **THE BIG FINISH** [–] [ ]

1983. (7") *Sierra; <GP 105>* **LOVE HURTS (live). / THE NEW SOFT SHOE (live)** [–] [ ]

Nov 83. (lp; GRAM PARSONS with The FALLEN ANGELS & EMMYLOU HARRIS) *Sundown; (SDLP 003) / Sierra; <GP 1973>* **LIVE 1973 (live)** [ ] Apr82 [ ]
(cd-iss. Jun94; CDSD 003) <(re-iss. Mar97 on 'Rhino'; 8122 72726-2)> <(cd re-iss. Jun99 on 'Sierra'; SXCD 6002)>

May 84. (lp/c) *Sundown; (SD LP/C 008)* **MELODIES** [ ] [–]

Nov 89. (cd) *Warners; (7599 26108-2)* **G.P. / GREVIOUS ANGEL** [ ] [ ]
(re-iss. Nov93; same)

Aug 92. (lp) *Raven;* **WARM EVENINGS, PALE MORNINGS, BOTTLED BLUES** [ ] [–]

Jun 95. (cd) *Sundown; (CDSD 077)* **COSMIC AMERICAN MUSIC: THE GRECH TAPES 1972** ☐ –

Nov 00. (cd/lp) *Sundazed; <(SC/+LP 11092)>* **ANOTHER SIDE OF THIS LIFEL THE LOST RECORDINGS OF GRAM PARSONS 1965-1966** ☐ ☐

INTERNATIONAL SUBMARINE BAND

PARSONS / + IAN DUNLOP – bass, sax / **MICKEY GAUVIN** – drums / **JOHN NUESE** – guitar

not iss. Ascot

1967. (7") *<2218>* **THE RUSSIANS ARE COMING. / TRUCK DRIVING MAN** – ☐

not iss. Columbia

1967. (7") *<43935>* **SUM UP BROKE. / ONE DAY WEEK** – ☐

not iss. L.H.I.

1967. (7") *<LHI 1205>* **LUXURY LINER. / BLUE EYES** – ☐

Apr 68. (lp) *<LHIS 12001>* **SAFE AT HOME** – ☐
– Blue eyes / I must be somebody else you've known / A satisfied mind / Polson Prison blues / That's all right / Miller's cave / I still someone / Luxury liner / Strong boy / Do you know how it feels to be lonesome. *(re-iss. 1985 on 'Statik'; STATLP 26) <re-iss. 1985 on 'Rhino'; RNLP 069> (cd-iss. Feb91 on 'Sundown'; CDSD 071)*

1968. (7") *<LHI 1217>* **MILLER'S CAVE. / SOMEBODY ELSE YOU'VE KNOWN** – ☐

☐ Andy PARTRIDGE (see under ⇒ XTC)

☐ PASSENGERS (see under ⇒ U2)

PAVEMENT

Formed: Stockton, California, USA ... 1989 by frontman STEPHEN MALKMUS and longtime friend/guitarist, SCOTT KANNBERG. They were soon joined by drummer GARY YOUNG (although this was initially a loose arrangement), the band recording their early US-only EP's at YOUNG's home studio, the first of which, 1989's 'SLAY TRACKS', was released on the self-financed 'Treble Kicker' label. A further two EP's, 'DEMOLITION PLOT J-7' and 'SUMMER BABE', together with a mini-lp, 'PERFECT SOUND FOREVER', were subsequently issued on the US indie, 'Drag City' over the course of the ensuing two years. The lo-fi, shambling charm of the likes of 'SUMMER BABE' eventually secured the band a UK deal with 'Big Cat' records, PAVEMENT consistently hitting the charts in Britain throughout their career. The debut album, 'SLANTED AND ENCHANTED' was finally released amid much anticipation in early 1992, its covertly melodic, avant-indie drawing inevitable but favourable comparisons with The PIXIES, The VELVET UNDERGROUND and even KING CRIMSON! Masterfully combining chaotic dischord and shards of crystalline harmony, the record's most compelling moments lay in the lazy melancholia of 'TRIGGER CUT' or 'ZURICH IS STAINED'. MALKMUS' brilliantly cryptic lyrics and offhand phrasing together with the twisted beauty of their music saw the band consistently dubbed as an American FALL. No bad thing, and besides, the band were carving out their own niche on the live circuit, by now augmented with extra sticksman, BOB NASTANOVICH and bassist MARK IBOLD, wildman YOUNG's infamous onstage antics an added attraction. The debut reached the lower reaches of the UK chart while a compilation of the early EP's, 'WESTING (BY MUSKET & SEXTANT)' (1993) made the Top 30. Prior to the release of the follow-up proper, 'CROOKED RAIN CROOKED RAIN' (1994), the band parted company on less than amicable terms with YOUNG, his replacement being STEVE WEST. This folk-ish record marked the band's most enticingly melodic affair to date, the keening 'CUT YOUR HAIR' single almost making the Top 40, the record itself reaching No.15 and cementing PAVEMENT's position as the crown kings of lo-fi. Although PAVEMENT failed to breach the Billboard chart, they built up a loyal following on the US underground scene on the back of constant touring, the defiantly experimental and diverse 'WOWEE ZOWEE!' (1995) proving that the band were making no concessions to radio programmers. There were still perfect PAVEMENT moments of stark beauty, as on the single, 'FATHER TO A SISTER OF THOUGHT'. While the album may have put off those after the immediate pop fix of 'CROOKED ...', PAVEMENT's next release, the meditative 'BRIGHTEN THE CORNERS' (1997) took a different tack again. It was clear that MALKMUS' songwriting was fast maturing, his work taking on a new depth and resonance that eschewed the stylistic grab-bag of old for a more straightforwardly direct approach. Feted by the likes of BLUR, who had previously pooh-pooh'd the American scene, PAVEMENT remain one of music's most resolutely individual bands. In 1999 and with drummer GARY YOUNG back into the fray, the band scored their first Top 30 single, 'CARROT ROPE', one of highlights on their Top 20 album, 'TERROR TWILIGHT'. Unfortunately, they bowed out towards the end of the decade. The break-up of PAVEMENT hadn't effected MALKMUS that much, as in 2001 he issued his solo set 'STEPHEN MALKMUS'. Like a lost PAVEMENT album, this is probably the direction the band would have headed in, considering the tone of the joyful 'TERROR TWILIGHT' compared with that of the stuffy, cynically serious 'BRIGHTEN THE CORNERS'. The songs were delightful, with MALKMUS' half-spoken soft vocals matching that of the jangling, uptempo songs such as 'JO JO'S JACKET' and the irresistible 'TROUBBBLE'. There were still dark overtones; 'BLACK BOOK' had the slightly singular twang of a PAVEMENT song circa 'WOWEE ZOWEE', whilst 'CHURCH ON WHITE' saw MALKMUS sing his first love song since 'MAJOR LEAGUES' with beautiful integrity. It certainly wasn't Swedish Reggae, but whatever ideas MALKMUS had up in that head of his were faithfully communicated onto this album. Credited to STEPHEN MALKMUS & THE JICKS, the man's sophomore solo effort, 'PIG LIB' (2003), wasn't quite so immediate, with less of the spontaneity and mishap of classic PAVEMENT and more of the musical bonhomie which characterises a more fruitful working relationship. It was certainly MALKMUS' most polished and rounded effort to date, although it could've done with a bit more edge and a bigger injection of the man's legendary wit. • **Covered:** THE CLASSICAL (Fall) / THE KILLING MOON (Echo & The Bunnymen). • **Trivia:** MALKMUS produced early 90's album 'Eyes Wide Smile' for FAITH OVER REASON. BOB and STEVEN played on SILVER JEW's (David Berman) album 'Starlite Walter'.

Album rating: PERFECT SOUND FOREVER mini (*5) / SLANTED AND ENCHANTED (*7) / WESTING (BY MUSKET & SEXTANT) compilation (*8) / CROOKED RAIN CROOKED RAIN (*7) / WOWEE ZOWEE (*8) / BRIGHTEN THE CORNERS (*7) / TERROR TWILIGHT (*8) / Stephen Malkmus: STEPHEN MALKMUS (*8) / PIG LIB (*6)

STEPHEN MALKMUS (b. 30 May'66, Santa Monica, California) – vocals, guitar / **SCOTT "SPIRAL STAIRS" KANNBERG** – guitar, vocals

not iss. Treble Kicker

1989. (7"ep) *<TK 001>* **SLAY TRACKS 1933-1969** – ☐
– You're killing me / Box elder / Maybe maybe / She believes / Price yeah!.

—— added **GARY YOUNG** (b.1953, Stockton) – drums

not iss. Drag City

1990. (7"ep) *<DC 2>* **DEMOLITION PLOT J-7** [–] [ ]
– Forklift / Spizzle trunk / Recorder grot / Internal K-dart / Perfect depth / Recorder grot (rally).

— (Aug90) added **BOB NASTANOVICH** – drums

1991. (10"m-lp) *<DC 4>* **PERFECT SOUND FOREVER** [–] [ ]
– Heckler spray / From now on / Angel carver blues – Mellow jazz docent / Drive by fader / Debris slide / Home / Krell vid-user.

— (mid '91) added **MARK IBOLD** (b. New York) – bass (ex-DUSTDEVILS)

Jan 92. (7"ep) *<DC 9>* **SUMMER BABE (Winter version) / MERCY: THE LAUNDROMAT. / BAPTISS BLACKTICK / MY FIRST MINE / MY RADIO** [–] [ ]

Big Cat Matador

Mar 92. (lp/c/cd) *(ABB 034/+C/CD) <OLE 038-2>* **SLANTED AND ENCHANTED** [72] [ ]
– Summer babe (winter version) / Trigger cut – Wounded – Kite at: 17 / No life singed her / In a mouth of a desert / Conduit for sale / Chesleys little wrists / Loretta's scars / Here / Two states / Perfume-V / Fame throwa / Jackals, false grails – The lonesome era / Our singer / Zurich is stained.

Jul 92. (7"/12"/cd-s) *(ABB 35 S/T/SCD) <OLE 042>* **TRIGGER CUT. / SUE ME JACK / SO STARK (YOU'RE A SKYSCRAPER)** [ ] [ ]

Nov 92. (12"ep/12"pic-d-ep/cd-ep) *(ABB 38 T/P/SCD) <OLE 044>* **WATERY, DOMESTIC EP** [58] [ ]
– Texas never whispers / Frontwards / Feed 'em to the (Linden) lions / Shoot the singer (1 sick verse).

Mar 93. (lp/c/cd) *(ABB 40/+C/CD) <Drag City; DC 14>* **WESTING (BY MUSKET & SEXTANT)** (first 4 US singles material) [30] [ ]
(cd/lp re-iss. Sep98/Jan99 on 'Drag City'; same as US)

— **STEVE WEST** (b. Richmond, Virginia) – drums; repl. GARY YOUNG – solo (single; 'PLANET MAN' 94)

Jan 94. (7"/12"/cd-s) *(ABB 55 S/T/CD) <OLE 082>* **CUT YOUR HAIR. / CAMERA / STARE** [52] [ ]

Feb 94. (lp/c/cd) *(ABB 56/+C/CD) <OLE 079>* **CROOKED RAIN CROOKED RAIN** [15] [ ]
– Silence kit / Elevate me later / Stop breathin / Cut your hair / Newark wilder / Unfair / Gold sound Z / 5-4 = unity / Range life / Heaven is a truck / Hit the plane down / Fillmore jive. *(s-lp w/free 7"; OLE 087)* – HAUNT YOU DOWN. / JAM KIDS *(cd re-iss. Feb02 on 'Domino';* **REWIGCD 010)**

Jul 94. (7") *(ABB 70S)* **GOLD SOUNDZ. / KNEELING BUS** [ ] [–]
(12"+=/cd-s+=) *(ABB 70 T/SCD)* – Strings of Nashville / The exit theory.

— line-up= **STEPHEN MALKMUS / MARK IBOLD / ROBERT NASTANOVICH / STEVE WEST / SPIRAL STAIRS (KANNEBERG) + FATAH RUARK**

Jan 95. (7") *(ABB 77S)* **RANGE LIFE. / COOLIN' BY SOUND** [ ] [–]
(12"+=/cd-s+=) *(ABB 77 T/SCD)* – Raft.

Mar 95. (7"/12") *(ABB 86 S/T) <OLE 134>* **RATTLED BY THE RUSH. / FALSE SKORPION / EASILY FOOLED** [ ] [ ]
(cd-s+=) *(ABB 86SCD)* – Brink of the clouds.

Apr 95. (3-sided d-lp/c/cd) *(ABB 84/+C/CD) <OLE 130>* **WOWEE ZOWEE!** [18] [ ]
– We dance / Rattled by the rush / Black out / Brinx job / Grounded / Serpentine pad / Motion suggests / Father to a sister of thought / Extradition / Best friends arm / Grave architecture / At & t / Flux = rad / Fight this generation / Kennel district / Pueblo / Half a canyon / Western homes.

Jun 95. (7"ep/12"ep/cd-ep) *(ABB 91 S/T/SCD) <OLE 169>* **FATHER TO A SISTER OF THOUGHT. / KRIS KRAFT / MUSSLE ROCK (IS A HORSE IN TRANSITION)** [ ] [ ]

Aug 95. (7") *<3G-08>* **DANCING WITH THE ELDERS. / (other artist)** [–] [ ]

— <above released on 'Third Gear'>

Jan 96. (cd-ep) *(ABB 110SCD) <OLE 188CD>* **PACIFIC TRIM EP:- GIVE IT A DAY / GANGSTERS & PRANKSTERS / SAGANAW** [ ] [ ]
(7"ep+=) *(ABB 110S) <OLE 188>* – I love Perth.

— now without FATAH

Domino Capitol

Jan 97. (7") *(RUG 51)* **STEREO. / BIRDS IN THE MAJIC INDUSTRY** [48] [–]
(cd-s) *(RUG 51CD)* – ('A'side) / Westie can drum / Winner of the . . .

Feb 97. (cd/c/lp) *(WIG CD/MC/LP 31) <55226>* **BRIGHTEN THE CORNERS** [27] [70]
– Stereo / Shady lane / Transport is arranged / Date with IKEA / Old to begin / Type slowly / Embassy row / Blue Hawaiian / We are underused / Passat dream / Starlings of the slipstream / Infinite spark.

Domino Matador

Apr 97. (7") *(RUG 53) <OLE 266>* **SHADY LANE (KROSSFADER). / UNSEEN POWER OF THE PICKET FENCE** [40] Jun97 [ ]
(cd-s) *(RUG 53CD)* – ('A'side) / Slowly typed / Cherry area.
(cd-s) *(RUG 53CDX)* – ('A'side) / Wanna mess you around / No tan lines.

— drummer **GARY YOUNG** returned

May 99. (7") *(RUG 90)* **CARROT ROPE. / AND THEN** [27] [–]
(cd-s) *(RUG 90CD1)* – ('A'side) / Harness your hopes / Roll with the wind.
(cd-s) *(RUG 90CD2)* – ('A'side) / Porpoise and the hand grenade / Rooftop rambler.

Jun 99. (cd/c/lp) *(WIG CD/MC/LP 66) <OLE 260>* **TERROR TWILIGHT** [19] [95]
– Spit on a stranger / Folk jam / You are a light / Cream of gold / Major leagues / Platform blues / Ann don't cry / Billie / Speak, see, remember / The hexx / Carrot rope.

Sep 99. (cd-s) *(RUG 96CD1)* **MAJOR LEAGUES / YOUR TIME TO CHANGE / STUB YOUR TOE / THE CLASSICAL** [ ] [–]
(cd-s) *(RUG 96CD2)* – ('A'side) / The killing moon / ('A'demo) / Decouvert de soleil.
(d7"set) *(RUG 96)* – (all above).

— KANNEBERG/STAIRS went on to form PRESTON SCHOOL OF INDUSTRY

STEPHEN MALKMUS

— solo with **JOHN MOEN** – percussion, drums

Domino Matador

Feb 01. (cd/lp) *(WIG CD/LP 090) <OLE 444>* **STEPHEN MALKMUS** [49] [ ]
– Black book / Phantasies / JoJo's jacket / Church on white / The hook / Discretion grove / Troubbble / Pink India / Trojan curfew / Vague space / Jenny & the ess-dog / Deado.

Apr 01. (7") *(RUG 123)* **DISCRETION GROVE. / SIN TAX** [60] [–]
(cd-s+=) *(RUG 123CD)* – Leisurely poison.

Jul 01. (7") *(RUG 128)* **JENNY & THE ESS-DOG. / ALIEN BOY** [ ] [–]
(cd-s+=) *(RUG 128CD)* – Keep the faith / That's what mama said.

Dec 01. (7") *(RUG 133)* **JO JO'S JACKET. / OPEN AND SHUT CASES** [ ] [–]
(cd-s) *(RUG 133CD)* – ('A'side) / Polish mule / The hook (live) / ('A'-CD-rom).

STEPHEN MALKMUS & THE JICKS

with **JOHN MOEN** – drums, vocals

Domino Matador

Mar 03. (cd/lp) *(WIG CD/LP 122) <OLE 572>* **PIG LIB** [?] [97]
– Water and a seat / Ramp of death / (Do not feed the) Oyster / Vanessa from Queens / Sheets / Animal midnight / Dark wave / Witch mountain bridge / Craw song / 1% of one / Us. *<US w/ free EP>* – Dynamic calories / Fractions and feelings / Old Jerry / The poet and the witch (live) / Shake it around (live).

May 03. (10"ep/cd-ep) *(RUG 158 T/CD)* **DARK WAVE** [?] [–]
– Dark wave / Dynamic calories / Fractions and feelings / Old Jerry / The poet and the witch (live) / Shake it around (live).

PEACHES

Born: MERRILL NISKER, Canada. Before becoming a savvy dildo-wearing temptress of the underground scene in 2000, Canadian artist and former music teacher flirted with the anti-folk scene (MERMAID CAFE) and also the avant jazz and electro-beat scene (FANCYPANTS HOODLUM, The SHITS) before issuing her debut album 'THE TEACHES OF PEACHES' for German underground label 'Kitty-Yo' in 2000. Relentlessly outspoken and deliberately rude, the set began with 'FUCK THE PAIN AWAY', a dance club hit due to its inclusion on the trendy Soulwax mix CD '2 Many DJS'; it also featured in a number of films (usually during sex scenes!). Mixing throbbing dirty synths, cold drum machines and PEACHES' half-sung lyrics, the set was reminscent of electro-punks, SUICIDE. Elsewhere, the album displayed her kinkiness even further, with memorable tracks 'LOVERTITS', 'SUCK AND LET GO' the brilliant single 'SET IT OFF'. Hairy, trans-European comedy rapper GONZALES popped up to duet on 'FELIX PART 2', while the set was lauded so much in the press that 'Beggars Banquet' re-issued it in 2002 with a bonus CD of remixes from the likes of KID 606 and TOBI NECMAN. In 2003, PEACHES returned with her excellent, wait for it, 'FATHERFUCKER' LP. Even lewder and sporting a Lincoln chin-beard, she rocked it up with IGGY POP on the sensational 'KICK IT' (a minor hit a year later) and got down and dirty in the gutter electronica of 'SHAKE YER DIX'. Not as underground, or nearly as good as her debut, this was still music that demanded the attention of every sleazebag on the planet. Quite simply – audio sexuality.

Album rating: THE TEACHES OF PEACHES (*7) / FATHERFUCKER (*6)

PEACHES – vocals / with **STEVE KEEPING** – drums

Kitty-Yo not iss.

Sep 00. (cd/2x12"lp) *(efa 55233-2/-1)* **THE TEACHES OF PEACHES** [ ] [–]
– Fuck the pain away / AA XXX / Rock show / Set it off / Cum undun / Diddle my skittle (with BITCH LAPLAP) / Hot rod / Lovertits / Suck and let go / Sucker / Felix partz. *(cd re-iss. Oct02 on 'X.L.'+=; XLCD 163)* – Keine melodien / Casanova (with MIGNON) / Sex (I'm a) / Felix partz (remake) / Fuck the pain away (a cappella) / Set it off (radio mix). *(5x12"iss.Nov02 ++=; XLLP 163X)* – AA XXX (a cappella) / Lovertits (a cappella) / Rock show (a cappella).

Oct 00. (12"/cd-s; by PEACHES & GONZALES) *(efa 55236-6/-2)* **RED LEATHER. / WE WANT IT / HOT PINK HOT SEX** [ ] [–]

Jan 01. (12"ep/cd-ep) *(efa 55231-6/-2)* **LOVERTITS EP** [ ] [–]
– Lovertits / Diddle my skittle (with BITCH LAPLAP) / AA XXX / Slap on.

Nov 01. (12"/cd-s) *(efa 55251-6/-2)* **SET IT OFF (Tobi Neumann radio mix) / SET IT OFF (DJ Assault accelerated funk mix) / FUCK THE PAIN AWAY (Kid 606 going back to Bali mix)** [ ] [–]

Columbia not iss.

Jun 02. (cd-s) *(672686-2)* **SET IT OFF (Tobi Neumann radio mix) / SET IT OFF (Punkers remix) / FUCK THE PAIN AWAY (Kid 606's going back to Bali mix) / SET IT OFF (video)** [36] [–]
(12") *(672686-6)* – ('A'mixes; Northern Lite / Tobi Neumann's GMF / DJ Assault's accelerated funk).

X.L. X.L.

Jun 03. (ltd-7") *(XLS 159)* **ROCKSHOW. / Electric Six: ROCKSHOW** [ ] [–]

Sep 03. (12") *(XLT 169)* **OPERATE. / SHAKE YER DIX** [ ] [–]

Sep 03. (cd/d-lp) *<(XLCD/XLLP 171) <40171>* **FATHERFUCKER** [ ] [ ]
– I don't give a . . . / I'm the kinda / I U she / Kick it (with IGGY POP) / Operate / Tombstone, baby / Shake yer dix (with MIGNON) / Rock'n'roll (with FREEDOM) / Stuff me up / Back it up, boys / The inch / Bag it.

PEARL JAM

Formed: Seattle, Washington, USA . . . 1991 by JEFF AMENT and STONE GOSSARD, who, together with MARK ARM, STEVE TURNER and ALEX VINCENT had previously played in pivotal Seattle band, GREEN RIVER (ARM and TURNER went on to form the noisier, and some still argue, superior MUDHONEY). Widely held to be the first ever "Grunge" act, GREEN RIVER's distortion-heavy mash-up of punk and metal is best sampled on the 'DRY AS A BONE' EP (1987), one of the first releases on the seminal 'Sub Pop' label. Following the band's demise, GOSSARD, AMENT and BRUCE FAIRWEATHER (who had replaced TURNER in GREEN RIVER) recruited vocalist ANDREW WOOD (ex-MALFUNKSHUN) and drummer GARY GILMOUR to form the short lived MOTHER LOVE BONE. After an EP and a cult debut album, 'APPLE' (1990), WOOD overdosed on heroin (March '90), effectively bringing the band to an untimely end. However, it was within these 70's influenced grooves that AMENT and GOSSARD laid the musical foundations for what would later become PEARL JAM. The group evolved from a tribute project for the dead WOOD put together by SOUNDGARDEN frontman, CHRIS CORNELL. Also featuring GOSSARD, AMENT, guitarist MIKE McCREADY, and SOUNDGARDEN sticksman MATT CAMERON, this loose aggregation released 'TEMPLE OF THE DOG' in 1991, a critically acclaimed opus that laid further groundwork for PEARL JAM's sound. With vocalist EDDIE VEDDER and drummer DAVE KRUSEN (subsequently superceded by DAVE ABBRUZZESE) replacing the SOUNDGARDEN boys, the outfit gradually evolved into PEARL JAM, the band still something of a cult act when their 'Epic' debut was released in America at the tail end of '91. 'TEN' eventually reached No.2 in the US chart and a hefty media buzz ensured a steady flow of UK imports, the record making the British Top 20 upon its February '92 release. With VEDDER penning the lyrics and GOSSARD and AMENT writing the music, 'TEN' was a powerfully assured debut, transforming the grunge monster into a sleekly melodic rock beast. VEDDER's soulful bellow was a key factor, the singer wringing emotion from every note of the anthemic 'ALIVE' and the affecting 'JEREMY'. Granted, comparisons to LED ZEPPELIN were a little unfair, but the band's lumbering sound seemed the antithesis of the cathartic rush with which NIRVANA had revolutionised a stale music scene and KURT COBAIN was spot on with his infamous criticisms, despite cries of sour grapes. While their intentions may have been honourable, PEARL JAM ushered in a tidal wave of dull as dishwater, sub-metal masquerading as grunge, most of it, funnily enough, released on major labels. Nevertheless, the kids loved it, especially the American ones, and the band embarked on a punishing touring schedule, finding time to make a cameo appearance as Matt Dillon's band in 'Singles', the Cameron Crowe film based on the Seattle music scene. As well as standing in for JIM MORRISON when The DOORS were eventually inducted into the Rock 'n' Roll Hall Of Fame, VEDDER performed a heart stopping version of BOB DYLAN's 'Masters Of War' (playing mandolin) at the veteran's anniversary concert in 1993. The same year also saw the release of a PEARL JAM follow-up, 'VS', the band's fiercely loyal fanbase propelling the album straight in at No.1 in the US charts. A more ragingly visceral affair, 'GO' gave VEDDER something to get his teeth into while the more reflective 'DAUGHTER' proved how affecting the band (and particularly VEDDER) could be when they dropped the derivative hard rock assault. Along with their mate NEIL YOUNG, PEARL JAM seemingly have an abiding love of vinyl, releasing 'VITALOGY' (1994) initially on record only, something which didn't prevent the band scaling the US chart once again. While not exactly vital, as the title might suggest, the record saw PEARL JAM going back to basics and injecting their behemoth-rock with a bit of stripped down energy. The following year saw PEARL JAM backing NEIL YOUNG on the so-so 'MIRROR BALL' (1995) album, the fruition of their musical partnership that had begun some years previous. In 1995, each member (except ABBRUZZESE), took time to carry out other projects, although the following year they returned to full force with 'NO CODE', an album that showed a lighter, acoustic side.

Unfortunately if not predictably, the fans were not best impressed by the album's more experimental turn and it quickly faded from view after a relatively brief stay at the US No.1 spot and the UK Top 3. More newsworthy was the band's feud with the Ticketmaster agency, a spat which precluded a full-scale tour. While the 'YIELD' (1998) album heralded a return to meatier fare, PEARL JAM records were beginning to follow the time-honoured heavy metal pattern of an initial high chart placing followed by a rapid descent into obscurity. All the signs were of a cult, diehard fanbase and one which lapped up both the mammoth US arena tour of summer '98 and its spin-off album, 'LIVE ON TWO LEGS' (1998). Bizarrely enough, the band then proceeded to score their biggest hit in years with a cover of the J.FRANK WILSON chestnut, 'LAST KISS'. Originally part of a fan-club only covers series, the single was given a full release due to popular demand and ended up narrowly missing the US No.1 slot in summer '99. The Tched Blake-produced 'BINAURAL' resumed normal service as PEARL JAM entered the new millennium seemingly oblivious to changing fads and fashions. A GRATEFUL DEAD for the post-grunge generation may be a comparison not too far off the mark although PEARL JAM adopted a slightly different attitude to bootlegging. While the late JERRY GARCIA and crew seemingly encouraged their fans to tape away to their hearts content, VEDDER's mob made a stubborn attempt to out-bootleg the bootleggers by recording every single date of their European and British tours and subsequently releasing them as a series of 72 double-CD sets. JERRY'll be turning in his grave and I was pulling the rest of my hair out updating this discography. VEDDER and Co were back in studio business come 2002, reading the 'RIOT ACT' to anyone who hadn't already had their fill with the interminable live sets. Musically, little had changed and it seemed PEARL JAM are determined to make as few concessions to contemporary musical mores as possible, probably a good thing, especially when it resulted in one of the more palatable albums of their stodgy oeuvre.
• **Songwriters:** VEDDER wrote lyrics / GOSSARD and AMENT the songs except F***IN' UP (Neil Young). GREEN RIVER covered AIN'T NOTHIN' TO DO (Dead Boys) / QUEEN BITCH (David Bowie). • **Trivia:** Backed actor MATT DILLON's band CITIZEN DICK in the 1992 film 'Singles'. VEDDER co-wrote and sang on 2 tracks; 'THE LONG ROAD' + 'THE FACE OF LOVE' on the 1996 movie 'Dead Man Walking'.

Album rating: Green River: REHAB DOLL – DRY AS A BONE (*7) / Mother Love Bone: STARDOG CHAMPION collection (*8) / Pearl Jam: TEN (*10) / VS (*8) / VITALOGY (*7) / NO CODE (*8) / YIELD (*7) / LIVE ON TWO LEGS (*6) / BINAURAL (*7) / RIOT ACT (*6) / LIVE bootleg series (*?) / LOST DOGS: B-SIDES & RARITIES collection (*6)
Three Fish: THREE FISH (*5) / THE QUIET TABLE (*5)

GREEN RIVER

MARK ARM (b.21 Feb'62, California) – vocals / **STEVE TURNER** (b.28 Mar'65, Houston, Texas) – guitar / **STONE GOSSARD** (b.20 Jul'66) – guitar / **JEFF AMENT** (b.10 Mar'63, Big Sandy, Montana) – bass / **ALEX VINCENT** – drums

not iss. Homestead

Sep 85. (12"ep) *<HMS 031>* **COME ON DOWN** –
– New god / Swallow my pride / Ride of your life / Corner of my eye / Tunnel of love. *(cd-ep-iss.May94; same)*

— **BRUCE FAIRWEATHER** – guitar repl. TURNER who later joined MUDHONEY

not iss. I.P.C.

Nov 86. (7"green) *<ICP 01>* **TOGETHER WE'LL NEVER. / AIN'T NOTHIN' TO DO** –

Glitterhouse Sup Pop

Jun 87. (12"ep) *<SP 11>* **DRY AS A BONE** –
– Unwind / Baby takes / This town / PCC / Ozzie. *(UK-iss.Mar91 on 'Tupelo'; TUPLP 17) (cd-iss. May94; same)*

Feb 89. (12"ep) *(GR 0031)* *<SP 15>* **REHAB DOLL** May88
– Searchin' / Ain't nothin' to do / Forever means / Rehab girl / Swallow my pride / Together we'll never / Smilin' and dyin' / Porkfist / Take a dive / One more stitch. (c-ep+=) *<SP 15A>* – Queen bitch. *(US re-iss. c+cd-lp Jul88 as 'DRY AS A BONE' / 'REHAB DOLL')*

— MARK ARM formed MUDHONEY

MOTHER LOVE BONE

formed by **AMENT, GOSSARD + FAIRWEATHER** plus **ANDREW WOOD** (b.1966) – vocals (ex-MALFUNKSHUN) / **GARY GILMOUR** – drums

Polydor Stardog

Mar 89. (m-lp) *<839011-2>* **SHINE** –
– Thru fade away / Midshaker meltdown / Halfass monkey boy / Medley:- Chloe dancer / Lady Godiva blues.

Jul 90. (cd/c/lp) *<(843191-2/-4/-1)>* **APPLE** Mar90
– This is Shangri-la / Stardog champion / Holy roller / Bone China / Come bite the apple / Stargazer / Heartshine / Captain hi-top / Man of golden words / Mr.Danny boy / Capricorn sister / Crown of thorns. *(above 2 re-iss. cd as 'STAR DOG CHAMPION' Sep92 on 'Polydor'; 514177-2 / <314512 884-2>) (hit US No.77)*

— ANDREW WOOD died on the 19th March '90 after a heroin overdose. AMENT and GOSSARD paid tribute to him by joining with SOUNDGARDEN ⇒ members in off-shoot outfit TEMPLE OF THE DOG. After this project was finished . . . PEARL JAM were formed

PEARL JAM

AMENT + GOSSARD with **EDDIE VEDDER** (b.23 Dec'66, Evanson, Illinois) – vocals / **MIKE McCREADY** (b. 5 Apr'65) – lead guitar / **DAVE ABBRUZZESE** (b.17 May'??) – drums repl. DAVE KRUZON

Epic Epic

Feb 92. (cd/c/lp/pic-lp) *(468884-2/-4/-1/-0)* *<47857>* **TEN** 18 Dec91 2
– Once / Even flow / Alive / Why go / Black / Jeremy / Oceans / Porch / Garden / Deep / Release. *(re-dist.Dec92 yellow-cd+=/m-d; 468884-5/-3)* – Alive (live) / Wash / Dirty Frank. *(lp re-iss. Feb99 on 'Simply Vinyl'; SVLP 68)*

Feb 92. (7"white/c-s) *(657572-7/-4)* **ALIVE. / WASH** 16
(12"+=/pic-cd-s+=) *(657572-6/-5)* – Once.

Apr 92. (7"/c-s) *(657857-7/-4)* **EVEN FLOW (remix). / OCEANS** 27
(12"white+=/cd-pic-s+=) *(657857-8/-2)* – Dirty Frank.

Sep 92. (7"white/c-s) *(658258-7/-4)* **JEREMY. / ALIVE (live)** 15
(12"pic-d+=) *(658258-6)* – Footsteps (live).
(pic-cd-s+=) *(658258-4)* – Yellow Ledbetter.

Oct 93. (cd/c/lp) *(474549-2/-4/-1)* *<53136>* **VS** 2 1
– Go / Animal / Daughter / Glorified G / Dissident / W.M.A. / Blood / Rearviewmirror / Rats / Elderly woman behind the counter in a small town / Leash / Indifference.

Oct 93. (12"ep/cd-ep) *(659795-6/-2)* **GO. / ALONE / ELDERLY WOMAN BEHIND THE COUNTER IN A SMALL TOWN (acoustic)**
(free c-s+=) *(659795-4)* – Animal (live).

Dec 93. (7"red/c-s) *(660020-7/-4)* **DAUGHTER. / BLOOD (live)** 18
(12"+=/cd-s+=) *(660020-6/-2)* – Yellow ledbetter (live).

May 94. (7"/c-s) *(660441-7/-4)* **DISSIDENT. / REARVIEWMIRROR (live)** 14
(cd-s+=) *(660441-2)* – Release / Even flow (versions).
(cd-s) *(660441-5)* – ('A'side) / Deep / Even flow / Why go (versions).

— ABBRUZZESE departed and was repl. after below album by **JACK IRONS** (ex-RED HOT CHILI PEPPERS)

Nov 94. (7"/c-s/cd-s) *(661036-7/-4/-2)* *<77771>* **SPIN THE BLACK CIRCLE. / TREMOR CHRIST** 10 58 18

Dec 94. (cd/c/d-lp) *(477861-2/-4/-1)* *<66900>* **VITALOGY** 6 1
– Last exit / Spin the black circle / Not for you / Tremor Christ / Nothingman / Whipping / Pry, to / Corduroy / Bugs / Satan's bed / Better man / Aye davanita / Immortality / Stupid mop.

— McCREADY now also moonlighted for MAD SEASON (see under ALICE IN CHAINS) – lead singer being LAYNE STALEY. Meanwhile, STONE GOSSARD set up own record label 'Loosegroove' and signed MALFUNKSHUN, DEVILHEAD, WEAPON OF CHOICE, BRAD and PROSE AND CONCEPTS.

Feb 95. (7"colrd/c-s/cd-s) *(661203-7/-4/-2)* **NOT FOR YOU. / OUT OF MY MIND (live)** [34] [–]

Dec 95. (7"/cd-s) *(662716-7/-2)* *<78199>* **MERKINBALL** [25] [7]
– I got I.D. / Long road.
(above both recorded w/ NEIL YOUNG)

—— Group had already featured on NEIL YOUNG's album 'MIRRORBALL'. GOSSARD featured on THERMIDOR's 1996 album 'Monkey On Rico'.

—— mid-96; JEFF AMENT featured for minor supergroup THREE FISH

Aug 96. (7"/c-s/cd-s) *(663539-7/-4/-2)* *<78389>* **WHO YOU ARE. / HABIT** [18] [31]

Sep 96. (cd/c/d-lp) *(484448-2/-4/-1)* *<67500>* **NO CODE** [3] [1]
– Sometimes / Habit / Who you are / In my tree / Smile / Hail hail / I'm open / Red mosquito / Lukin / Mankind / Black & red & yellow / Allnight. *(cd re-iss. Aug00; same)*

Jan 98. (7"/c-s) *(665394-7/-4)* *<78797>* **GIVEN TO FLY. / PILATE** [12] [21]
(cd-s+=) *(665394-2)* – Leatherman.

Feb 98. (cd/c/lp) *(489365-2/-4/-1)* *<68164>* **YIELD** [7] [2]
– Brain of J. / Faithfull / No way / Given to fly / Wishlist / Pilate / Do the evolution / • / MFC / Low light / In hiding / Push me, pull me / All those yesterdays.

May 98. (7"/c-s) *(665790-7/-4)* *<SNY 78896>* **WISHLIST. / U** [30] [47]
(cd-s+=) *(665790-2)* – Brain of J. (live).

—— **MATT CAMERON** – drums (ex-SOUNDGARDEN) repl. IRONS

Nov 98. (cd/c/d-lp) *(429859-2/-4/-1)* *<69752>* **LIVE ON TWO LEGS (live)** [68] [15]
– Corduroy / Given to fly / Hail hail / Daughter / Elderly woman behind the counter in a small town / Untitled / MFC / Go / Off he goes / Even flow / Red mosquito / Nothingman / Do the evolution / Better man / Black / F*ckin' up.

Aug 99. (7"red/cd-s) *(667479-7/-2)* *<79197>* **LAST KISS. / SOLDIER OF LOVE** [42] May99 [2]

May 00. (7"blue) *(669374-7)* *<79416>* **NOTHING AS IT SEEMS. / INSIGNIFICANCE** [22] Apr00 [49]
(cd-s+=) *(669374-2)* – ('A'side) / Better man (live) / Footsteps (live).

May 00. (cd/c/lp) *(494590-2/-4/-1)* *<63665>* **BINAURAL** [5] [2]
– Breakerfall / God's dice / Evacuation / Light years / Nothing as it seems / Thin air / Insignificance / Of the girl / Grievance / Rival / Sleight of hand / Soon forget / Parting ways.

Jul 00. (7"yellow) *(669628-7)* *<79452>* **LIGHT YEARS. / SOON FORGET (live)** [52] [ ]
(cd-s+=) *(669628-2)* – Grievance (live).

Oct 02. (7") *(673308-7)* *<SNY 79809>* **I AM MINE. / DOWN** [26] [43]
(cd-s) *(673308-2)* – ('A'side) / Bushleaguer / Undone.

Nov 02. (cd) *(510000-2)* *<86825>* **RIOT ACT** [34] [5]
– Can't keep / Save you / Love boat captain / Cropduster / Ghost / I am mine / Thumbing my way / You are / Get right / Green disease / Help help / Bushleaguer / 1/2 full / Arc / All or none.

– others, etc. –

on 'Epic' records unless mentioned otherwise

Jul 95. (cd-ep) *Epic; <77935>* **JEREMY / YELLOW LEDBETTER / FOOTSTEPS** [–] [79]

Jan 96. (cd-ep) *Epic; <77938>* **DAUGHTER / YELLOW LEDBETTER (live) / BLOOD (live)** [–] [97]

Sep 00. (d-cd) *(499623-2)* **LIVE: Palau Sant Jordi, Barcelona, Spain – May 25th, 2000** [ ] [–]

Sep 00. (d-cd) *(499624-2)* **LIVE: Parkbuhne, Wuhlheide, Berlin – June 25th, 2000** [ ] [–]

Sep 00. (d-cd) *(499626-2)* **LIVE: Spodek Arena, Katowice, Poland – June 16th, 2000** [ ] [–]

Sep 00. (d-cd) *(499628-2)* **LIVE: The Point Theater, Dublin, Ireland – June 1st, 2000** [ ] [–]

Sep 00. (d-cd) *(499629-2)* **LIVE: SECC Arena, Glasgow, Scotland – June 3rd, 2000** [ ] [–]

Sep 00. (d-cd) *(499630-2)* *<85073>* **LIVE: Sporthalle, Hamburg, Germany – June 26th, 2000** [ ] [ ]

Sep 00. (d-cd) *(499631-2)* *<85052>* **LIVE: Spodek Arena, Katowice, Poland – June 15th, 2000** [ ] [ ]

Sep 00. (d-cd) *(499632-2)* **LIVE: International Arena, Cardiff, Wales – June 6th, 2000** [ ] [–]

Sep 00. (d-cd) *(499633-2)* **LIVE: Rock Am Ring Eifel, Nurberg, Germany – June 9th, 2000** [ ] [–]

Sep 00. (d-cd) *(499634-2)* **LIVE: Estadio Do Restelo, Lisbon, Portugal – May 23rd, 2000** [ ] [–]

Sep 00. (d-cd) *(499635-2)* **LIVE: Hala Tivoli, Llubljana, Slovenia – June 19th, 2000** [ ] [–]

Sep 00. (d-cd) *(499636-2)* **LIVE: Wembley Arena, London, England – May 29th, 2000** [ ] [–]

Sep 00. (d-cd) *(499637-2)* *<85012>* **LIVE: Wembley Arena, London, England – May 30th, 2000** [ ] [ ]

Sep 00. (d-cd) *(499638-2)* **LIVE: Pinkpop, Heerden, Holland – June 12th, 2000** [ ] [–]

Sep 00. (d-cd) *(499639-2)* **LIVE: Evening News Arena, Manchester, England – June 4th, 2000** [ ] [–]

Sep 00. (d-cd) *(499640-2)* *<85064>* **LIVE: FILA Forum, Milan, Italy – June 22nd, 2000** [ ] [ ]

Sep 00. (d-cd) *(499641-2)* **LIVE: Rock In Park, Nurnberg, Germany – June 11th, 2000** [ ] [–]

Sep 00. (d-cd) *(499642-2)* **LIVE: Spectrum, Oslo, Norway – June 29th, 2000** [ ] [–]

Sep 00. (d-cd) *(499643-2)* **LIVE: Paegas Arena, Prague, Czechoslovakia – June 14th, 2000** [ ] [–]

Sep 00. (d-cd) *(499644-2)* **LIVE: Bercy, Paris, France – June 8th, 2000** [ ] [–]

Sep 00. (d-cd) *(499646-2)* **LIVE: City Square, Salzburg, Austria – June 18th, 2000** [ ] [–]

Sep 00. (d-cd) *(499647-2)* **LIVE: Velodromo Anaeta, San Sebastian, Spain – May 26th, 2000** [ ] [–]

Sep 00. (d-cd) *(499648-2)* **LIVE: Naval Museum, Stockholm, Sweden – June 28th, 2000** [ ] [–]

Sep 00. (d-cd) *(499649-2)* *<85061>* **LIVE: Arena, Verona, Italy – June 20th, 2000** [ ] [ ]

Sep 00. (d-cd) *(499650-2)* **LIVE: Hallenstadion, Zurich, Switzerland – June 23rd, 2000** [ ] [–]

Feb 01. (d-cd) *(501989-2) <E2K 85551> LIVE: Boston, Massachusetts Vol.1 – August 29th, 2000* [ ] [ ]

Feb 01. (d-cd) *(501990-2)* *<E2K 85545>* **LIVE: Jones Beach, New York, Vol.3 – August 25th, 2000** [ ] [ ]

Feb 01. (d-cd) *(501991-2)* *<E2K 85542>* **LIVE: Jones Beach, New York, Vol.2 – August 24th, 2000** [ ] [ ]

Feb 01. (d-cd) *(501992-2)* *<E2K 85536>* **LIVE: Columbus, Ohio – August 21st, 2000** [ ] [ ]

Feb 01. (d-cd) *(501993-2)* *<E2K 85518>* **LIVE: Tampa, Florida – August 12th, 2000** [ ] [ ]

Feb 01. (d-cd) *(501994-2)* *<E2K 85509>* **LIVE: Atlanta, Georgia – August 7th, 2000** [ ] [ ]

Mar 01. (d-cd) *<(E2K 85208)>* **LIVE: Virginia Beach, Virginia – August 3rd, 2000** [ ] [ ]

Mar 01. (d-cd) *<(E2K 85503)>* **LIVE: Charlotte, North Carolina – August 4th, 2000** [ ] [ ]

Mar 01. (d-cd) *<(E2K 85506)>* **LIVE: Greensboro, North Carolina – August 6th, 2000** [ ] [ ]

Mar 01. (d-cd) *<(E2K 85512)>* **LIVE: West Palm Beach, Florida. Vol.1 – August 9th, 2000** [ ] [ ]

Mar 01. (d-cd) *<(E2K 85515)>* **LIVE: West Palm Beach, Florida, Vol.2 – August 10th, 2000** [ ] [ ]

Mar 01. (d-cd) *<(E2K 85521)>* **LIVE: New Orleans, Louisiana – August 14th, 2000** [ ] [ ]

Mar 01. (d-cd) *<(E2K 85524)>* **LIVE: Memphis, Tennessee – August 15th, 2000** [ ] [ ]

Mar 01. (d-cd) *<(E2K 85527)>* **LIVE: Nashville, Tennessee – August 17th, 2000** [ ] [ ]

Mar 01. (d-cd) *<(E2K 85530)>* **LIVE: Indianapolis, Indiana – August 18th, 2000** [ ] [ ]

Mar 01. (d-cd) *<(E2K 85533)>* **LIVE: Cincinatti, Ohio – August 20th, 2000** [ ] [ ]

Mar 01. (d-cd) *<(E2K 85539)>* **LIVE: Jones Beach, New York, Vol.1 – August 23rd, 2000** [ ] [ ]

Mar 01. (d-cd) *<(E2K 85548)>* **LIVE: Saratoga, New York – August 27th, 2000** [ ] [ ]

Mar 01. (d-cd) *<(E2K 85554)>* **LIVE: Boston, Massachusetts Vol.2 – August 30th, 2000** [ ] [ ]

Mar 01. (d-cd) *<(E2K 85557)>* **LIVE: Philadelphia, Pennsylvania, Vol.1 – September 1st, 2000** [ ] [ ]

Mar 01. (d-cd) *<(E2K 85560)>* **LIVE: Philadelphia, Pennsylvania, Vol.2 – September 2nd, 2000** [ ] [ ]

Mar 01. (d-cd) *<(E2K 85563)>* **LIVE: Washington DC – September 4th, 2000** [ ] [ ]

Mar 01. (d-cd) *<(E2K 85566)>* **LIVE: Pittsburgh, Pennsylvania – September 5th, 2000** [ ] [ ]

Mar 01. (d-cd) *<(E2K 85572)>* **LIVE: Toronto, Canada – October 5th, 2000** [ ] [ ]

Mar 01. (d-cd) <*(E2K 85599)*> **LIVE: Dallas, Texas – October 17th, 2000**

Mar 01. (cd) *(502165-2)* <*E2K 85575*> **LIVE: Detroit, Michigan – October 7th, 2000**

Mar 01. (cd) *(502166-2)* <*E2K 85581*> **LIVE: Chicago, Illinois – October 9th, 2000**

Mar 01. (cd) *(502167-2)* <*E2K 85611*> **LIVE: Las Vegas, Nevada (10th Anniversary Show) – October 22nd, 2000**

Mar 01. (cd) *(502168-2)* <*E2K 85617*> **LIVE: San Diego, California – October 25th, 2000**

Mar 01. (cd) *(502169-2)* <*E2K 85635*> **LIVE: Boise, Idaho – November 3rd, 2000**

Mar 01. (t-cd) *(502170-2)* <*E2K 85641*> **Seattle, Washington – 6th November, 2000** 98

Apr 01. (cd) <*(E2K 85569)*> **LIVE: Montreal, Canada – October 4th, 2000**

Apr 01. (cd) <*(E2K 85578)*> **LIVE: East Troy, Wisconsin – October 8th, 2000**

Apr 01. (cd) <*(E2K 85584)*> **LIVE: St. Louis, Missouri – October 11th, 2000**

Apr 01. (cd) <*(E2K 85587)*> **LIVE: Kansas City, Missouri – October 12th, 2000**

Apr 01. (cd) <*(E2K 85590)*> **LIVE: Houston, Texas, Vol.1 – October 14th, 2000**

Apr 01. (cd) <*(E2K 85593)*> **LIVE: Houston, Texas, Vol.2 – October 15th, 2000**

Apr 01. (cd) <*(E2K 85602)*> **Lubbock, Texas – October 18th, 2000**

Apr 01. (cd) <*(E2K 85608)*> **LIVE: Phoenix, Arizona – October 21st, 2000**

Apr 01. (cd) <*(E2K 85614)*> **LIVE: Los Angeles, California – October 24th, 2000**

Apr 01. (cd) <*(E2K 85620)*> **LIVE: Fresno, California – October 27th, 2000**

Apr 01. (cd) <*(E2K 85623)*> **LIVE: San Bernadino, California – October 28th, 2000**

Apr 01. (cd) <*(E2K 85623)*> **LIVE: Sacramento, California – October 30th, 2000**

Apr 01. (cd) <*(E2K 85629)*> **LIVE: San Francisco, California – October 31st, 2000**

Apr 01. (cd) <*(E2K 85632)*> **LIVE: Portland, Oregon – November 2nd, 2000**

Apr 01. (cd) <*(E2K 85638)*> **LIVE: Seattle, Washington – November 5th, 2000**

Apr 01. (d-cd) <*(E2K 85805)*> **LIVE: Albuquerque, New Mexico – October 20th, 2000**

Jun 03. (d-cd) *(512222-2)* <*90128*> **RIOT ACT WORLD TOUR VOL.10: Perth, Australia – February 23rd 2003 (live)**

Jun 03. (d-cd) *(512223-2)* <*90336*> **RIOT ACT WORLD TOUR VOL.13: Tokyo, Japan – March 3rd 2003 (live)**

Jul 03. (t-cd) <*90500*> **RIOT ACT WORLD TOUR: State College, Pennsylvania – May 3rd 2003 (live)** -

Nov 03. (t-cd) *(510510-2)* <*90702*> **RIOT ACT WORLD TOUR No.66: New York, New York – July 8th 2003 (live)**

Nov 03. (d-cd) *(513638-2)* <*90662*> **RIOT ACT WORLD TOUR No.67: New York, New York – July 9th 2003 (live)**

Nov 03. (t-cd) *(513639-2)* <*90721*> **RIOT ACT WORLD TOUR No.68: Mansfield, Massachusetts – July 11th 2003 (live)**

Nov 03. (d-cd) *(513640-2)* <*85738*> **LOST DOGS: B-SIDES & RARITIES** 15
– All night / Sad / Down / Hitchhiker / Don't gimme no lip / Alone / In the moonlight / Education / Black, red, yellow / U / Leaving here / Gremmie out of control / Whale song / Undone / Hold on / Yellow Ledbetter / Fatal / Other side / Hard to imagine / Footsteps / Wash / Dead man walking / Strangest tribe / Drifting / Let me sleep / Last kiss / Street lew / Dirty Frank / Brother / Bee girl.

THREE FISH

JEFF AMENT – vocals, bass / **ROBBI ROBB** – vocals, guitar (of TRIBE AFTER TRIBE) / **RICHARD STUVERUD** – drums (of FASTBACKS)

Epic Epic

Jun 96. (cd/c/d-lp) *(484118-2/-4/-1)* <*67652*> **THREE FISH**
– Solitude / Song for a dead girl / Silence at the bottom / Intellgent fish / Zagreb / All messed up / Here in the darkness / Hall of intelligent fish / Strangers in my head / Lovely meander / Elusive ones / Build / Stupid fish / A secret place / Laced. *(d-lp+=)* – If miles were alive / Can I come along / Easy way.

Sep 96. (cd-s) **LACED / CAN I COME ALONG? / IF MILES WERE ALIVE . . .**

Jun 99. (cd/c) <*69964*> **THE QUIET TABLE** -
– Shiva and the astronaut / Tremor void / Myth of Abdou / Once in a day / Half long / Timeless / Hummingbird / My only foe / Transporting / Found a window / Resonate / Chaintreuse.

PENTANGLE

Formed: London, England . . . early '67, the original members forming the basis for the band's first three albums, arguably their only truly essential works. Comprising of the pure, jazz orientated vocals of JACQUI McSHEE with the immense talents of BERT JANSCH and JOHN RENBOURN on guitars and an innovative rhythm section of DANNY THOMPSON and TERRY COX on bass and drums respectively, PENTANGLE heralded the emergence of a fusion built around jazz and folk. Formed after RENBOURN and JANSCH had already had success with the sublime 'BERT AND JOHN' album, McSHEE joining after already having worked with RENBOURN on his first solo set, 'ANOTHER MONDAY'. The former ALEXIS KORNER rhythm section completed the band for 68's 'THE PENTANGLE', a brilliant and eclectic debut album produced by Shel Talmy and featuring folk standard, 'BRUNTON TOWN' as well as a blissful rendition of the Staple Singers' 'HEAR MY CALL'. The move into other genres continued on the next album, 69's 'SWEET CHILD', McSHEE's vocals shining on the enchanting 'SO EARLY IN THE SPRING' and the bluesy 'I'VE GOT A FEELING', while two Charles Mingus covers, 'GOODBYE PORK PIE HAT' and 'HAITIAN FLIGHT SONG' demonstrating the talents of COX and THOMPSON. 'BASKET OF LIGHT', released the following year, became a commercial hit, making the Top 5 in Britain and featuring 'LIGHT FLIGHT', which became a minor success in the singles chart and subsequently the theme tune to 60's TV series, 'Take Three Girls'. The overriding feature of this trilogy was the musicians' ability to complement each other in equal measure. After 'BASKET OF LIGHT', the material became progressively weaker as the band became less unified, while this in turn led to a break up in '73. While JANSCH and RENBOURN pursued their solo careers, the original line-up continued its interplay with McSHEE fronting the JOHN RENBOURN BAND between '74-'81. THOMPSON, meanwhile, worked with both JOHN MARTYN and NICK DRAKE, most notably on the former's 'Solid Air', and COX, after a stint as a session musician, backed French crooner, CHARLES AZNAVOUR. The original line-up re-formed in '82 for touring purposes as well as the reasonable long-player, 'OPEN THE DOOR', although commitments outwith the band meant that RENBOURN had been replaced by MIKE PIGGOTT. Although they released a few albums in the 80's and 90's, PENTANGLE never quite captured the spellbinding fusion sound of yesteryear. • **Songwriters:** JANSCH, RENBOURN and McSHEE, who also arranged traditional tunes. Amongst several covers, JANSCH did a fine version of HEARTBREAK HOTEL (hit; Elvis Presley).

Album rating: THE PENTANGLE (*6) / SWEET CHILD (*6) / BASKET OF LIGHT (*8) / CRUEL SISTER (*5) / SOLOMON'S SEAL (*5) / OPEN THE DOOR (*5) / IN THE ROUND (*5) / THE ESSENTIAL PENTANGLE VOL.1 & 2 compilations (*7's) / SO EARLY IN THE SPRING (*5) / ONE MORE ROAD (*5) / THINK OF TOMORROW (*4)
Bert Jansch: BERT JANSCH (*8) / IT DON'T BOTHER ME (*6) / JACK ORION (*8) / BERT & JOHN with John Renbourn (*6) / NICOLA (*6) / BIRTHDAY

BLUES (*6) / ROSEMARY LANE (*5) / MOONSHINE (*5) / L.A. TURNAROUND (*5) / SANTA BARBARA HONEYMOON (*5) / A RARE CONUNDRUM (*5) / AVOCET (*5) / 13 DOWN (*5) / HEARTBREAK (*5) / FROM THE OUTSIDE (*5) / LEATHER LAUDERETTE with Rod Clements (*5) / SKETCHES (*5) / THE ORNAMENT TREE (*5) / THE GARDENER: THE ESSENTIAL BERT JANSCH 1965-1971 compilation (*7) / WHEN THE CIRCUS COMES TO TOWN (*6) / TOY BALLOON (*4) / CRIMSON MOON (*4) / EDGE OF A DREAM (*5)

BERT JANSCH (b. 3 Nov'43, Glasgow, Scotland) – acoustic guitar, vocals / **JOHN RENBOURN** (b. 8 Aug'44, London, England) – guitars, sitar, vocals (ex-Solo artist) / **JACQUI McSHEE** (b.25 Dec'43) – vocals / **DANNY THOMPSON** (b. Apr'39, Devon, England) – double bass (ex-ALEXIS KORNER'S BLUES INC.) / **TERRY COX** (b. Buckinghamshire, England) – drums, percussion, glockenspiel, vocals (ex-ALEXIS KORNER'S BLUES INC.)

Transatla. Reprise

May 68. (7") *(BIG 109)* **TRAVELIN' SONG. / MIRAGE** [ ] [–]

Jun 68. (lp) *(TRA 162) <6315>* **THE PENTANGLE** [21] [ ]
– Let no man steal your thyme / Bells / Hear my call / Pentangling / Mirage / Way behind the Sun / Bruton Town / Waltz. *(cd-iss. 1988 on 'Transatlantic'/'Line'; 9.00549) (<cd-iss. Oct98 on 'Wooded Hill'+=; HILLCD 7>)* – Travelling song. *(cd re-iss. May01 on 'Castle'; CMRCD 131)* – Koan / The wheel / The casbah / Bruton town / Hear my call / Way behind the sun / Way behind the sun (instrumental).

Dec 68. (7") **LET NO MAN STEAL YOUR THYME. / WAY BEHIND THE SUN** [–] [ ]

Dec 68. (d-lp) *(TRA 178) <6334>* **SWEET CHILD** (half live / half studio) [ ] [ ]
– Market song / No more my Lord / Turn your money green / Haitian fight song / A woman like you / Goodbye pork pie hat / Three dances / Brentzal gay / La rotta / The Earl of Salisbury / Watch the stars / So early in the Spring / No exit / The time has come / Burton town / Sweet child / I loved a lass / Three part thing / Sovay / In time / In your mind / I've got a feeling / The trees they do grow high / Moon dog / Hole in my coal. *(cd-iss. 1988 on 'Transatantic'/'Line'; TACD 9.00552)* – (omits 3) *(<d-cd-iss. May01 on 'Castle'; CMRCD 132>)* – Haitian fight song (studio) / Way behind the sun / Hear my call / The bells / Traveling song / John Donne song (alt.) / Hole in the coal (alt.).

May 69. (7") *(BIG 124)* **ONCE I HAD A SWEETHEART. / I SAW AN ANGEL** [46] [ ]

Oct 69. (lp) *(TRA 205) <6372>* **BASKET OF LIGHT** [5] [ ]
– Light flight / Once I had a sweetheart / Springtime promises / Lyke-Wake dirge / Train song / Hunting song / Sally go round the roses / The cuckoo / House carpenter. *(cd-iss. Jul87 on 'Transatlantic'/'Line'; TACD 9.00555) (cd re-iss. 1989 on 'Transatlantic'/'Demon'; TRANDEMCD 7) (cd re-iss. Jun96 on 'Essential'; ESMCD 406) (cd re-iss. Jul01 on 'Castle'+=; CMRCD 207)* – Sally go round the roses (alt.) / Sally go round the roses (alt.) / Cold mountain / I saw an angel.

Feb 70. (7") *(BIG 128)* **LIGHT FLIGHT. / COLD MOUNTAIN** [43] [–]

Nov 70. (lp) *(TRA 228) <6430>* **CRUEL SISTER** [51] [ ]
– Cruel sister / A maid that's deep in love / When I was in my prime / Lord Franklin / Jack Orion. *(re-iss. Mar77 on 'Xtra'; XTRA 1172) (cd-iss. 1988 on 'Transatlantic'/'Line'; TACD 44.055) (cd re-iss. Jul01 on 'Castle'; CMRCD 206)*

Nov 71. (lp) *(TRA 240) <6463>* **REFLECTION** [ ] [ ]
– Wedding dress / Omie wise / Will the circle be unbroken / When I get home / Rain and snow / Helping hand / So clear / Reflection. *(cd-iss. 1988 on 'Transatlantic'/'Line';)*

Reprise Reprise

Sep 72. (lp) *(K 44197) <2100>* **SOLOMON'S SEAL** [ ] [ ]
– Sally free and easy / Cherry tree carol / The snows / High Germany / People on the highway / Willy O'Winsbury / No love is sorrow / Jump baby jump / Lady of Carlisle.

— Disbanded Mar'73. THOMPSON and COX returned to session work. THOMPSON also went solo and joined JOHN MARTYN's group, to mention just one. JANSCH and RENBOURN continued to work on solo albums, with the latter being augmented by McSHEE.

BERT JANSCH

Transatla. Vanguard

1965. (lp) *(TRA 125)* **BERT JANSCH** [ ] [–]
– Strolling down the highway / Smokey river / Oh how your love is strong / I have no time / Finches / Rambling's going to be the death of me / Veronica / Needle of death / Do you hear me now? / Alice's wonderland / Running from home / Courting blues / Casbah / Dreams of love / Angie. *(re-iss. 1980 + Jan88; TRS 117) (re-iss. Jun88 on 'Transatlantic'/'Demon'; TRANDEM 1) (cd-iss. Jun01 on 'Castle'; CMRCD 204)*

Dec 65. (lp) *(TRA 132)* **IT DON'T BOTHER ME** [ ] [–]
– Oh my babe / Ring-a-ding bird / Tinker's blues / Anti apartheid / The wheel / A man I'd rather be / My lover / It don't bother me / Harvest your thoughts of love / Lucky thirteen / As the day grows longer now / So long (been on the road so long) / Want my daddy now / 900 miles. *(re-iss. Jul76 as 'EARLY BERT' on 'Xtra'; XTRA 1163) (cd-iss. Oct93 on 'Transatlantic'/'Demon'+=; TDEMCD 16)* – The times has come / Soho / In this game / Dissatisfied blues. *(cd re-iss. Jun01 on 'Castle'; CMRCD 205)*

1966. (lp) *(TRA 143)* **JACK ORION** [ ] [–]
– The waggoner's lad / The first time ever I saw your face / Jack Orion / The gardener / Nottamun town / Henry Martin / Blackwaterside / Pretty Polly. *(re-iss. Jul76 as 'EARLY BERT VOL. 2' on 'Xtra'; XTRA 1164) (cd-iss. Aug01 on 'Castle'; CMRCD 304)*

1966. (lp; BERT JANSCH & JOHN RENBOURN) *(TRA 144)* **BERT AND JOHN** [ ] [–]
– Eastwind / Piano time / Goodbye pork pie hat / Soho / Tie tocative / Orlando / Red favourite / No exit / Along the way / The time has come / Stepping stones / After the dance. *(cd-iss. Aug01 on 'Castle'; CMRCD 203)*

1966. (7"ep) *(TRA EP 145)* **NEEDLE OF DEATH** [ ] [–]
– Running from home / Tinker's blues / Needle of death / The wheel.

Transatla. Reprise

Jun 67. (7") *(BIG 102)* **LIFE DEPENDS ON LOVE. / A LITTLE SWEET SUNSHINE** [ ] [–]

Jul 67. (lp) *(TRA 157)* **NICOLA** [ ] [–]
– Go your way my love / Woe is love my dear / Nicola / Come back baby / A little sweet sunshine / Love is teasing / Rabbit run / Life depends on love / Weeping willow blues / Box of love / Wish my baby was here / If the world isn't there. *(re-iss. Jul76 as 'EARLY BERT VOL. 3' on 'Xtra'+=; XTRA 1165)* – Come sing me a happy song to prove we can all get along the lumpy, bumpy road.

Dec 68. (lp) *(TRA 179) <6343>* **BIRTHDAY BLUES** [ ] [ ]
– Come and sing me a happy song / To prove / The bright new year / Tree song / Poison / Miss Heather / Rosemary Sewell / I've got a woman / A woman like you / I'm lonely / Promised land / Birthday blues / Wishing well blues.

Jun 71. (lp) *(TRA 235) <6455>* **ROSEMARY LANE** [ ] [ ]
– Tell me what is true love / Rosemary Lane / M'lady Nancy / A dream, a dream, a dream / Alman / Wayward child / Nobody's bar / Reynardine / Silly women / Peregrinations / Sylvie / Sarabanda / Bird song. *(re-iss. Jan77 as 'EARLY BERT VOL. 4' on 'Xtra'; XTRA 1170) (cd-iss. Sep94 on 'Transatlantic'/'Line'; TACD 9.007840) (cd re-iss. Oct98 on 'Wooded Hill'; HILLCD 2)*

Reprise Reprise

Feb 73. (lp) *(K 14234) <2129>* **MOONSHINE** [ ] [ ]
– Yarrow / Brought with the rain / January man / Night time blues / Moonshine / First time ever I saw your face / Rambleaway / Twa corbies / Oh my father. *(cd-iss. Sep95 on 'Jansch'; BJ 001CD) (cd re-iss. Jan01 on 'Castle'; CMRCD 112)*

Mar 73. (7") *(K 14234)* **OH MY FATHER. / THE FIRST TIME EVER I SAW YOUR FACE** [ ] [–]

Charisma Kicking Mule

Sep 74. (lp) *(CAS 1090)* **L.A. TURNAROUND** [ ] [ ]
– Fresh as a sweet Sunday morning / Chambertin / One for Jo / Travelling man / Open up the Watergate (let the sunshine in) / Stone monkey / Of love and lullaby / Needle of death / Lady nothing / There comes a time / Cluck old hen / The blacksmith.

Oct 74. (7") *(CB 240)* **IN THE BLEAK MIDWINTER. / ONE FOR JO** [ ] [ ]

Nov 75. (lp) *(CAS 1107)* **SANTA BARBARA HONEYMOON** [ ] [ ]
– Love a new / Mary and Joseph / Be my friend / Baby blue / Dance lady dance / You are my sunshine / Lost and gone / Blues run the game / Built another band / When the teardrops fell / Dynamite / Buckrabbit.

Nov 75. (7") *(CB 267)* **DANCE LADY DANCE. / BUILD ANOTHER BAND** [ ] [ ]

May 77. (lp) *(CAS 1127) <202>* **A RARE CONUNDRUM** [ ] [ ]
– Daybreak / One to a hundred / Pretty Saro / Doctor, doctor / 3 a.m. / The Curragh of Kildare / Instrumentally Irish / St.Flacre / If you see my love / Looking for a home / Poor mouth / Cat and mouse / Three chord trick / Lost love. *(cd-iss. Jun97; CASCD 1127)*

— In 1978 he appeared on CONUNDRUM & RICHARD HARVEY single, 'Black Birds of Brittany'.

Feb 79. (lp) *(CLASS 6)* **AVOCET** [ ] [ ]
– Avocet / Bittern / Kingfisher / Kittiwake / Lapwing / Osprey.

Sonet Kicking Mule

Apr 80. (7") *(SCK 44)* **TIME AND TIME. / UNA LINEA DI DOLCEZZA** [ ] [–]

Jul 80. (lp; by BERT JANSCH & CONUNDRUM) *(SNTF 162)* <309> **13 DOWN**
– Una linea di dolcezza / Let me sing / Down river / Nightfall / If I had a lover / Time and time / In my mind / Sovay / Where did my life go / Single Nose / Ask your daddy / Sweet mother Earth / Bridge. *(cd-iss. Sep98 on 'Kicking Mule'; KMCD 3909)*

Logo / Kicking Mule

Feb 82. (lp) *(GOL 1035)* **HEARTBREAK**
– Is it real? / Up to the stars / Give me the time / If I were a carpenter / Wild mountain thyme / Heartbreak hotel / Sit down beside me / No rhyme nor reason / Blackwater side / And not a word was said. *(re-iss. May89 on 'Hannibal'; HNBL 1312) (cd-iss. Jul93; HNCD 1312)*

Feb 82. (7") *(GO 409)* **HEARTBREAK HOTEL. / UP TO THE STARS**

Mausoleum / not iss.

Sep 85. (lp) *(KOMA 788006)* **FROM THE OUTSIDE** [–]
– Sweet rose in the garden / Black bird in the morning / Read all about it / Change the song / Shout / From the outside / If you're thinking 'bout me / Silver raindrops / Why me? / Get out of my life / Time is an old friend. *(cd-iss. Aug93 on 'Hypertension' +=; HYCD 200128)* – River running / High emotion / From the inside. *(cd re-iss. Mar01 on 'Castle'; CMRCD 170)*

Black Crow / not iss.

Mar 88. (lp/c/cd; BERT JANSCH & ROD CLEMENTS) *(CRO 218)* **LEATHER LAUNDERETTE** [–]
– Strolling down the highway / Sweet Rose / Brafferton / Ain't no more cane / Why me? / Sundown station / Knight's move / Brownsville / Bogie's bonny belle / Leather launderette / Been on the road so long.

— his backers now **PETER KIRTLEY** – guitar, b.vocals, percussion / **DANNY THOMPSON** – double bass, percussion, chimes / **STEVE BAKER** – blues harp / **STEFAN WULFF** – percussion / **FRANK WULFF** – percussion, alto-flute, etc.

Temple / Hypertension

Nov 90. (cd/c/lp) *(COMD2/CTP/TP 035)* **SKETCHES** [–]
– Ring-a-ding bird / One for Jo / Poison / The old routine / Needle of death / Oh my father / Running, running from home / Afterwards / Can't hide love / Moonshine / A woman like you / A windy day. *(cd+=)* – As the day grows longer now. *(cd/c re-iss. Feb94; same)*

Run River / Capitol

Nov 90. (lp/c/cd) *(RRA/+MC/CD 0012)* <71365> **THE ORNAMENT TREE** [1991]
– The ornament tree / Banks o' Sicily / Rambling boys of pleasure / Rock road to Dublin / Three dreamers / Mountain streams / Blackbird of Mullamore / Ladyfair / Road tae Dundee / Tramps and hawkers / January man / Dobbins flower vale. *(cd re-iss. Jan01 on 'Castle'; CMRCD 111)*

Cooking Vinyl / not iss.

Sep 95. (cd) *(COOKCD 092)* **WHEN THE CIRCUS COMES TO TOWN** [–]
– Walk quietly by / Open road / Back home / No-one around / Step back / When the circus comes to town / Summer heat / Just a dream / The lady doctor from Ashington / Stealing the night away / Honey don't you understand / Born with the blues / Morning brings peace of mind / Living in the shadows.

Cooking Vinyl / True North

Mar 98. (cd) *(COOKCD 138)* <TN 165> **TOY BALLOON** [Sep98]
– Carnival / She moves through the fair / All I got / Bett's dance / Toy balloon / Waitin' and wonderin' / Hey Doc / Sweet talking lady / Paper houses / Born and bred in old Ireland / How it all came down / Just a simple song.

When / Castle

Jun 00. (d-cd) *(WENCD 211)* <683> **CRIMSON MOON** [Aug00]
– Caledonia / Going home / Crimson moon / Down under / October song / Looking for love / Fool's mate / Riverbank / Omie wise / My Donald / Neptune's daughter / Singing the blues // Strolling down the highway / Needle of death / It don't bother me / Lucky thirteen / Blackwaterslide / The first time ever I saw your face / Rabbit run / Woe is love my dear / Nobody's bar / Rosemary lane. *(cd No.1 re-iss. Oct00; WENCD 211X)*

Sanctuary / Sanctuary

Oct 02. (cd) *(SANCD 136)* <84582> **EDGE OF A DREAM**
– On the edge of a dream / All this remains / What is on your mind / Sweet death / I cannot keep from crying / La luna / Gypsy Dave / Walking this road / The quiet joys of brotherhood / Black cat blues / Bright sunny morning.

– his compilations, etc. –

on 'Transatlantic' unless mentioned otherwise

1966. (lp) *Vanguard; (VSD 97212)* **LUCKY THIRTEEN** [–]
1969. (lp) *Vanguard; <VMD 6506>* **STEPPING STONES** [–]
Nov 69. (lp) *(TRANSAM 10)* **THE BERT JANSCH SAMPLER** [–]
Dec 72. (lp) *(TRANSAM 27)* **BOX OF LOVE – THE BERT JANSCH SAMPLER VOL. 2** [–]
– Oh how your love is strong / In this game / The gardener / Soho / I am lonely / Renegrinations / Casbah / Dissatisfied blues / As the day grows longer now / Box of love / Birthday blues / Nobody's bar.
Mar 78. (lp) *(MTRA 2007)* **ANTHOLOGY** [–]
1980. (lp) *(TRA 333)* **THE BEST OF BERT JANSCH** [–]
Jul 87. (cd) *(TRA 604/TRACD 604)* **THE ESSENTIAL COLLECTION VOL.1** [–]
Sep 87. (cd) *(TRA 607/TRACD 607)* **THE ESSENTIAL COLLECTION VOL.2** [–]
Jun 92. (cd) *Shanachie; <SHANCD 99004>* **THE BEST OF BERT JANSCH** [–]
Jul 92. (cd) *Transatlantic-Demon; (TDEMCD 9)* **THE GARDENER: THE ESSENTIAL BERT JANSCH 1965-1971** [–]
– The gardener / Alice's wonderland / Running from home / Tinker's blues / It don't bother me / The waggoner's lad / The first ever I saw your face / Go your way my love / My lover / Woe is love my dear / Black waterside / Rabbit run / A woman like you (studio) / Market song / A woman like you (live) / Wishing well / Rosemary Lane / Peregrinations / Poison / Miss Heather Rosemary Sewell / Reynardine / Bird song / When I get home / I am lonely.
Dec 92. (cd; as BERT JANSCH / JOHN RENBOURN) *Shanachie; <SHANCD 99006>* **AFTER THE DANCE** [–]
Jul 93. (cd) *Virgin; (CDVM 9024)* **THREE CHORD TRICK** (74-79 material) [–]
Jul 93. (cd) *(TDEMCD 16)* **BERT JANSCH / JACK ORION** [–]
Dec 93. (cd) *(TDEMCD 17)* **NICOLA / BIRTHDAY BLUES** [–]
Sep 93. (cd) *Windsong; (WINCD 039)* **BBC RADIO 1 LIVE IN CONCERT (live 1980-82 with CONUNDRUM)** [–]
Jul 96. (cd) *Essential; (ESMCD 407)* **BERT JANSCH / IT DON'T BOTHER ME** [–]
Aug 96. (cd) *Jansch; (BJ 002CD)* **LIVE AT 12 BAR** [–]
– Summer heat / Curragh of Kildare / Walk quietly by / Come back baby / Backwaterslide / Fresh as a sweet Sunday morning / Morning brings peace of mind / Lily of the west / Kingfisher / Trouble in mind / Just a dream / Blues run the game / Let me sing / Strolling down the highway / Woman like you / Instrumental. *(re-iss. Aug00 on 'Essential'; ESMCD 921)*
Jan 97. (cd) *Essential; (ESMCD 459)* **JACK ORION / NICOLA** [–]
Jul 97. (cd) *Essential; (ESMCD 519)* **BIRTHDAY BLUES / ROSEMARY LANE** [–]
Jun 98. (d-cd) *Recall; <153>* **BLACKWATER SIDE** [–]
Dec 98. (cd) *Big Beat; (CDWIKD 182)* **YOUNG MAN BLUES – LIVE IN GLASGOW – 1962-1964** [–]
Sep 00. (d-cd) *Essential; (CMEDD 009)* **DAZZLING STRANGER: ANTHOLOGY** [–]
– Caledonia / Going home / Crimson moon / Down under / October song / Looking for love / Fool's mate / Riverbank / Omie wise / My Donald / Neptune's daughter / Singing the blues // Strolling down the highway / Needle of death / It don't bother me / Lucky thirteen / Blackwaterslide / The first time ever I saw your face / Rabbit run / Woe is love my dear / Nobody's bar / Rosemary lane. *(cd No.1 re-iss. Oct00; WENCD 211X)*
Jan 01. (cd) *Castle; (<CMRCD 022>)* **DOWNUNDER: LIVE IN AUSTRALIA**
Apr 02. (cd) *Castle Pie; (PIESD 270)* **AN INTRODUCTION TO BERT JANSCH** [–]

PENTANGLE

— re-formed in the early 80's; **MIKE PIGGOTT** – guitar; repl. RENBOURN

Spindrift / Varrick

Jul 85. (lp) *(SPIN 111)* <VR 017> **OPEN THE DOOR**
– Open the door / Dragonfly / Mother Earth / Child of the winter / The dolphin / Lost love / Sad lady / Taste of love / Yarrow / Street song.
1985. (7") **DRAGON FLY. / THE DOLPHIN** [–]

— **NIGEL PORTMAN SMITH** (b. 7 Feb'50, Sheffield, England) – bass, keyboards, accordian, vocals repl. DANNY

Feb 86. (7") *(SURF 107)* **PLAY THE GAME. / SATURDAY MOVIE** [–]

1986. (d-lp) *(SPIN 120)* **IN THE ROUND** ☐ 1988 ☐
– Play the game / Open sea / She moved through the fair / Set me free / When the night is over come to me baby / Sunday morning blues / Chase that devil away / The Saturday movie / Suilagrar / Circle the Moon / Let me be. *(re-iss. Apr90 on 'Episode' d-lp/c/cd; TA LP/MC/CD 2001)*

1986. (7") *(SURF 121)* **SET ME FREE. / COME TO ME BABY** ☐ –

— **DANNY** returned to repl. SMITH

Shanachie Shanachie

Aug 89. (lp/c) *(<SHAN/+C 79066>)* **A MAID THAT'S DEEP IN LOVE** ☐ ☐
– Maid that's deep in love / Lord Franklin / Rain and snow / Cruel sister / Wedding dress / Omie wise / Will the circle be unbroken / When I was in my prime / When I get home.

— **ROD CLEMENTS** – guitar, mandolin (ex-LINDISFARNE) / **GERRY CONWAY** (b.11 Sep'47, Norfolk, England) – drums, percussion; repl. PIGGOTT + COX

Plane GreenLinnet

1990. (lp) *(PLANE 88648)* **SO EARLY IN THE SPRING** ☐ –
– Eminstra / So early in the spring / Blacksmith / Reynardine / Lucky black cat / Bramble briar / Lassie gathering nuts / Gaia / Baron of Brackley. *(re-iss. Jun96 on 'Park' cd/c; PRK CD/MC 35)*

— **PETER KIRTLEY** (b.26 Sep'45, Hebburn-on-Tyne, England) – vocals, guitars repl. CLEMENTS

Permanent Green Linnet

Oct 91. (cd/c/lp) *(PERM CD/MC/LP 3)* **THINK OF TOMORROW** ☐ –
– O'er the lonely mountain / Baby now it's over / Share a dream / he storyteller / Meat on the bone / Every yes ever no / Straight ahead / The toss of golden hair / The lark in the clear air / The bonny boy / Colour my paintbook. *(re-iss. Sep93 on 'Hypertension'; HY 200112LP) (cd re-iss. Mar95; HY 200112CD)*

Aug 92. (cd/c/lp) *(PERM CD/MC/LP 10)* **25TH YEAR ANNIVERSARY** ☐ –

May 93. (cd/c) *(PERM CD/MC 11)* **ONE MORE ROAD** ☐ ☐
– Travelling solo / Oxford City / Endless sky / The lily of the west / One more road / High Germany / Hey, hey soldier / Willy of Winsbury / Somali / Manuel / Are you going to Scarborough fair.

— (also some obvious trad. covers)

— **JANSCH, McSHEE, SMITH, KIRTLEY + CONWAY**

Hyperion not iss.

Jun 95. (cd) *(HYCD 20015-2)* **LIVE 1994 (live)** ☐ –
– Bramble briar / Sally free and easy / Kingfisher / Come back baby / When I was in my prime / Meet on the bone / Travelling solo / The bonny boy / Chasing love / Cruel sister / Yarrow / Reynardine.

– compilations, etc. –

on 'Transatlantic' unless mentioned otherwise

Jul 72. (lp) *(TRANSAM 23)* **HISTORY BOOK** ☐ –
Aug 73. (lp) *(TRANSAM 29)* **PENTANGLING** ☐ –
(re-iss. Aug 77 on 'Hallmark') (re-iss. May81)
1973. (7"m) *(BIG 567)* **LIGHT FLIGHT. / MARKET SONG / THE TIME HAS COME** ☐ –
1975. (d-lp) *(89503/4)* **THE PENTANGLE COLLECTION** ☐ –
(Europe only, re-iss. Apr88 on 'Castle' lp/c/cd; CCS/+MC/CD 184)
Jul 78. (lp) *(MTRA 2013)* **ANTHOLOGY** ☐ –
Mar 82. (d-lp) *Cambra; (CR 054)* **AT THEIR BEST** ☐ –
(c-iss.1985 on 'Autograph';)
Jul 87. (lp/cd) *(TRA LP/CD 602)* **THE ESSENTIAL PENTANGLE VOL.1** ☐ –
– Once I had a sweetheart / Hear my call / Hole in the coal / Omie Wise / Waltz / The trees they do grow / Sweet child / A woman like you / Reflection / Will the circle be unbroken / Watch the stars / Helping hand / Goodbye pork pie hat / When I was in my prime.
Sep 87. (lp/cd) *(TRA LP/CD 606)* **THE ESSENTIAL PENTANGLE VOL.2** ☐ –
– Pentangling / Bruton Town / Shake shake mama / Let no man steal your thyme / Soho / The cruel sister / Bells / Wedding dress / I've got a feeling / Three part thing / Rain and snow / Way behind the Sun / When I get home / The time has come.
Jul 90. (cd) *Shanachie; (SHANCD 79066)* **A MIND THAT'S DEEP DEEP IN LOVE** ☐ –
Aug 92. (cd) *Shanachie; (SHANCD 79078)* **EARLY CLASSICS** ☐ –
Mar 94. (cd) *Hyperion; (HY 20011-2)* **PEOPLE ON THE HIGHWAY 1968-1972** ☐ –
Apr 94. (c/cd) *Castle; (CCS/+CD 184)* **THE COLLECTION** ☐ –
Jan 95. (cd/c) *Ariola Express; (2/4 95942)* **IN YOUR MIND** ☐ –
Sep 95. (cd) *Band Of Joy; (BOJCD 013)* **LIVE AT THE BBC** ☐ –
DEc 97. (cd) *Strange Fruit; (SFRSCD 046)* **ON AIR** ☐ –
Feb 00. (cd) *Hypertension; (HYP 5156)* **ABOUT THYME** ☐ –
Mar 00. (d-cd) *Essential; (ESACD 857)* **ANTHOLOGY** ☐ –
Aug 00. (d-cd) *Essential; (ESACD 931)* **PENTANGLE FAMILY** ☐ –
Nov 00. (cd) *Park; (PRKCD 53)* **AT THE LITTLE THEATRE** ☐ –

PERE UBU

Formed: Cleveland, Ohio, USA . . . September '75 out of ROCKET FROM THE TOMBS, by DAVID THOMAS (aka CROCUS BEHEMOTH; his alter-ego) and PETER LAUGHNER. Along with CHARLIE WEINER (guitar), GLEN 'THUNDERHAND' HACH (guitar) and TOM 'FOOLERY' CLEMENTS (drums), they became residents at THOMAS's workplace, the Viking Saloon; he was apparently a bouncer! A revamped RFTT saw THOMAS and LAUGHNER being joined by CRAIG BELL (bass), GENE 'CHEETAH CHROME' O'CONNOR (guitar) and 'JOHNNY BLIZ' MADANSKY, and it was this line-up who recorded sessions for WMMS radio stations, later to surface as a posthumous 1990 cd, 'LIFE STINKS'. A few embryonic UBU tracks, 'FINAL SOLUTION' and '30 SECONDS OVER TOKYO', plus covers of 'SATISFACTION' (Rolling Stones) and 'SEARCH AND DESTROY' (Stooges), featured on these rare master tapes. Even 'SONIC REDUCER' was hijacked by The DEAD BOYS bound, CHEETAH and BLITZ, the pair being united with STIV BATORS, who replaced THOMAS before the ROCKETS split. Meanwhile, PERE UBU (THOMAS and LAUGHNER) recruited other musicians; TIM WRIGHT, ALLEN RAVENSTINE, TOM HERMAN plus SCOTT KRAUSS, and took their name from a play by French writer, Alfred Jarry. The large-framed THOMAS formed his own 'Hearthan' label, issuing a classic debut, '30 SECONDS OVER TOKYO', which led to gigs at (New York's) Max's Kansas City in early '76. Another gem, 'FINAL SOLUTION', was unleashed soon after, although LAUGHNER departed (at this stage the line-up numbered THOMAS, RAVENSTINE, HERMAN, KRAUSE and newcomer, TONY MAIMONE) prior to the release of their third and fourth rare 45's, 'STREET WAVES' and 'THE MODERN DANCE'. The latter subsequently became the name of their debut album which gained a release early in 1978 on the obscure US 'Blank' label (a few months later it surfaced in the UK on 'Mercury'). The sound was clearly a break from the "New Wave", echoing as it did a revival of the avant-garde (CAPTAIN BEEFHEART and ENO-era ROXY MUSIC). On the strength of this masterwork, they signed to the major 'Chrysalis' label and, six months later, wowed the music world with another abstract beauty, 'DUB HOUSING' (1978). After the disappointing 'NEW PICNIC TIME' (1979), however, they were unceremoniously dropped by their label, the band's wayward eccentricity floating right over the average pop picker's head. PERE UBU (who had replaced HERMAN with veteran, MAYO THOMPSON – formerly of RED CRAYOLA) subsequently found a home with UK indie, 'Rough Trade', although they split after two poorly-received studio sets, 'THE ART OF WALKING' (1980) and 'SONG OF THE BAILING MAN' (1982), the latter boasting the drumming talents of ANTON FIER. Over the course of the next five years, having released a debut album, 'THE SOUND OF THE SAND' early in '82, THOMAS embarked on an equally weird and anti-commercial solo career with albums, the live 'WINTER COMES HOME' (1983),

'VARIATIONS ON A THEME' (1983), 'MORE PLACES FOREVER; (1985), 'MONSTER WALKS THE WINTER LAKE' (1986) and 'BLAME THE MESSENGER' (1987). PERE UBU released a belated comeback album, 'THE TENEMENT YEARS', in 1988, a record which gathered together old UBU men, THOMAS, RAVENSTINE, MAIMONE and KRAUSE, while retaining CHRIS CUTLER and JIM JONES (previously part of THOMAS' solo band). For the 1989 set, 'CLOUDLAND', the group sought out former CAPTAIN BEEFHEART employee, ERIC DREW FELDMAN, who remained for a further two albums, 'WORLDS IN COLLISION' (1991) and 'STORY OF MY LIFE' (1993). Subsequently signing to 'Cooking Vinyl' (also now the rest home of BILLY BRAGG and The WEDDING PRESENT), PERE UBU cut one final effort, 'RAY GUN SUITCASE' (1995), before THOMAS once again opted for solo pastures with 'EREWHON' (1996). Sidestepping between solo and PERE UBU releases, THOMAS continued to create his own creative pop. UBU's 'PENNSYLVANIA' (1998) found him in a reflective mood – he had been living in England for some time now – while the solo DAVID THOMAS AND TWO PALE BOYS release 'MIRROR MAN' (1999) was pure rock-opera mixed with readings. To start the millennium, DAVID THOMAS AND FOREIGNERS (mainly Danish musicians!) got together for improv live set, 'BAY CITY' (2000); THOMAS AND TWO PALE BOYS (aka ANDY DIAGRAM and KEITH MOLINE) delivered a second batch of songs, 'SURF'S UP!', the following year. PERE UBU returned in the summer of 2002 via 'ST. ARKANSAS', their body of sound now over a quarter of a century old but still viable and conscious of today's discerning and fickle market. • **Songwriters:** All group compositions. THOMAS collaborated with others on solo work and covered SLOOP JOHN B. (Beach Boys).

Album rating: THE MODERN DANCE (*9) / DUB HOUSING (*7) / NEW PICNIC TIME (*7) / THE ART OF WALKING (*6) / 390 DEGREES OF SIMULATED STEREO (*4) / SONG OF THE BAILING MAN (*5) / TERMINAL TOWER: AN ARCHIVAL COLLECTION compilation (*9) / THE TENEMENT YEAR (*6) / ONE MAN DRIVES WHILE THE OTHER MAN SCREAMS early live (*5) / CLOUDLAND (*6) / WORLDS IN COLLISION (*6) / STORY OF MY LIFE (*6) / RAYGUN SUITCASE (*7) / DATAPANIK IN THE YEAR ZERO boxed collection (*8) / PENNSYLVANIA (*6) / APOCALYPSE NOW live (*6) / ST. ARKANSAS (*6) / David Thomas: THE SOUND OF THE SAND . . . (*6) / WINTER COMES HOME (*5) / VARIATIONS ON A THEME (*6) / MORE PLACES FOREVER (*5) / MONSTER WALKS THE WINTER LAKE (*4) / BLAME THE MESSENGER (*5) / MIRROR MAN (*7) / BAY CITY (*5) / SURF'S UP! (*6) / Rocket From The Tombs: THE DAY THE EARTH MET THE . . . (*6)

DAVID THOMAS (b.14 Jun'53) – vocals / **PETER LAUGHNER** (b.1953) – guitar / **TIM WRIGHT** – bass, guitar / **TOM HERMAN** (b.19 Apr'49) – guitar, bass / **SCOTT KRAUSE** (b.19 Nov'50) – drums / **ALLEN RAVENSTINE** (b. 9 May'50) – synthesizer

not iss. Hearthan

Dec 75. (7"ltd) *<HR 101>* **30 SECONDS OVER TOKYO. / HEART OF DARKNESS** [–] [ ]

— **DAVE TAYLOR** – synthesizer repl. RAVENSTINE

Mar 76. (7"ltd) *<HR 102>* **FINAL SOLUTION. / CLOUD 149** [–] [ ]

— **ALLEN RAVENSTINE** – synthesizer returned to repl. TAYLOR / **ALAN GREENBLATT** – guitar; repl. LAUGHNER who formed FRICTION (he died of drug & alcohol abuse 22nd June '77)

— **TONY MAIMONE** (b.27 Sep'52) – bass, piano repl. WRIGHT who joined DNA. (GREENBLATT left also) (were now a quintet with **THOMAS, HERMAN, KRAUSE, MAIMONE + RAVENSTINE**)

Nov 76. (7"ltd) *<HR 103>* **STREET WAVES. / MY DARK AGES** [–] [ ]

Aug 77. (7"ltd) *<HR 104>* **THE MODERN DANCE. / HEAVEN** [–] [ ]

Mercury Blank

Apr 78. (lp) *(9100 052) <001>* **THE MODERN DANCE** [ ] Jan78 [ ]
– Non-alignment pact / The modern dance / Laughing / Street waves / Chinese radiation / Life stinks / Real world / Over my head / Sentimental journey / Humor me. *(re-iss. Jan81 on 'Rough Trade'; ROUGH 22) (re-iss. Feb88 on 'Fontana' lp/cd; SF LP/CD 3) (cd re-iss. Jun98 on 'Cooking Vinyl'; COOKCD 141) <US cd-iss. Jun98 on 'Geffen'; 25206> (lp re-iss. May99 on 'Get Back'; GET 054)*

Radar not iss.

Apr 78. (12"ep) *(RDAR 1)* **DATAPANIK IN THE YEAR ZERO (remixes compilation)** [ ] [–]
– Heart of darkness / 30 seconds over Tokyo / Cloud 149 / Untitled / Heaven.

Chrysalis Rough Trade

Nov 78. (lp) *(CHR 1207) <ROUGH-US 14>* **DUB HOUSING** [ ] [ ]
– Navy / On the surface / Dub housing / Cagliari's mirror / Thriller / I will wait / Drinking wine Spodyody / Ubu dance party / Blow daddy-o / Codex. *(cd-iss. Mar89 on 'Rough Trade'; ROUGHCD 6002) (cd re-iss. Mar99 on 'Cooking Vinyl'; COOKCD 170) (lp re-iss. Feb00 on 'Get Back'; GET 58)*

Sep 79. (lp) *(CHR 1248) <ROUGH-US 20>* **NEW PICNIC TIME** [ ] [ ]
– One less worry / Make hay / Goodbye / The voice of the sand / Jehovah's kingdom comes / Have shoes will walk / 49 guitars and 1 girl / A small dark cloud / Small was fast / All the dogs are barking. *(cd-iss. Mar89 on 'Rough Trade'; ROUGHCD 6003) (cd re-iss. Mar99 on 'Cooking Vinyl'; COOKCD 171) (lp re-iss. Feb00 on 'Get Back'; GET 59)*

Oct 79. (7"m) *(CHS 2372)* **THE FABULOUS SEQUEL (HAVE SHOES WILL WALK). / HUMOR ME (live). / THE BOOK IS ON THE TABLE** [ ] [–]

— **MAYO THOMPSON** (b.26 Feb'44) – guitar, vocals (ex-RED CRAYOLA) repl. HERMAN who went solo

Rough Trade not iss.

Jun 80. (7") *(RT 049)* **FINAL SOLUTION. / MY DARK AGES** [ ] [–]

Sep 80. (lp) *(ROUGH 14)* **THE ART OF WALKING** [ ] [–]
– Go / Rhapsody in pink / Arabia * / Miles * / Misery goats / Loop / Rounder / Birdies / Lost in art / Horses / Crush this horn. *(re-iss. 1981; same)* – Arabian nights / Tribute to Miles; repl. *) *(cd-iss. Apr89 tracks as re-issue; ROUGHCD 14)<US = ROUGH-US-4CD> (cd re-iss. Nov99 on 'Cooking Vinyl'; COOKCD 157) <US cd re-iss. Nov99 on 'Thirsty Ear'; 57079> (lp re-iss. Sep01 on 'Get Back'; GET 81)*

Feb 81. (7") *(RT 066)* **NOT HAPPY. / LONESOME COWBOY DAVE** [ ] [–]

May 81. (lp) *(ROUGH 23)* **390° OF SIMULATED STEREO – UBU LIVE: VOLUME 1 (live 76-79)** [ ] [–]
– Can't believe it / Over my head / Sentimental journey / 30 seconds over Tokyo / Humor me / Real world / My dark ages / Street waves / Laughing / Non-alignment pact / Heart of darkness / The modern dance. *(cd-iss. Apr89; ROUGHCD 23)*

— added **ANTON FIER** (b.20 Jun'56) – drums, percussion (ex-FEELIES) / guest **EDDIE THORNTON** – trumpet

Jun 82. (lp) *(ROUGH 33)* **SONG OF THE BAILING MAN** [ ] [–]
– The long walk home / Use of a dog / Petrified / Stormy weather / West Side story / Thoughts that go by steam / Big Ed's used farms / A day such as this / The vulgar boatman bird / My hat / Horns are a dilemma. *(cd-iss. Apr89; ROUGHCD 33) (cd re-iss. Nov99 on 'Cooking Vinyl'; COOKCD 158) <US cd-iss. Nov99 on 'Thirsty Ear'; 57080> (lp re-iss. Jun02 on 'Get Back'; GET 90)*

— split mid 1982. MAYO returned to RED CRAYOLA (which also incl. most UBU's). KRAUSE + WRIGHT formed HOME & GARDEN, who released one album for 'Dead Man's Curve', 'HISTORY & GEOGRAPHY' (1986)

DAVID THOMAS & THE PEDESTRIANS

Rough Trade Recommended

Dec 81. (12"ep; by DAVID THOMAS) *(TRADE 5-12)* **VOCAL PERFORMANCES** [ ] [–]

— included **THOMPSON, KRAUSE, FIER & RAVENSTINE** plus **CHRIS CUTLER** (b. 4 Jan'47) – drums / **JOHN GREAVES** – bass (both ex-HENRY COW) / **PHILIP MOXHAM** – multi (ex-YOUNG MARBLE GIANTS) / **RICHARD THOMPSON** – guitar

Jan 82. (lp) *(ROUGH 30)* **THE SOUND OF THE SAND AND OTHER SONGS OF THE PEDESTRIANS** [ ] [ ]
– The birds are good ideas / Yiki Tiki / The crickets in the flats / Sound of the sand / The new atom mine / Big dreams / Happy to see you / Crush this horn – part 2 / Confuse did / Sloop John B. / Man's best friend.

Oct 82. (7") **PETRIFIED. /** [–] [ ]

— w/ **CHRIS CUTLER & LINDSAY COOPER** – bassoon (ex-MIKE OLDFIELD)

Feb 83. (lp; DAVID THOMAS & HIS LEGS) *(DTLP)* **WINTER COMES HOME (live Munich, 1982)** [ ] [–]
– A day such as this / Winter comes home / West side story / Sunset / Stormy weather / Poetic license / Rhapsody in pink / Dinosaurs like me / Petrified / Bones in action / Contrasted views of the archaeopterix.

— added **RICHARD THOMPSON** etc. (CUTLER, COOPER)

Dec 83. (lp) *(ROUGH 60)* **VARIATIONS ON A THEME**
– A day at the Botanical Gardens / Pedestrians walk / Bird town / The egg and I / Who is it / Song of hoe / Hurry back / The ram / Semaphore.

— **TONY MAIMONE** – bass repl. GREAVES who joined The FLYING LIZARDS

Rough Trade Twin/Tone

May 85. (lp) *(ROUGH 80)* *<TTR 8551>* **MORE PLACES FOREVER**
– Through the magnifying glass / Enthusiastic / Big breezy day / About true friends / Whale head king / Song of the bailing man / The farmer's wife / New broom.

DAVID THOMAS & THE WOODEN BIRDS

(**DAVID** retained **MAIMONE** and **CUTLER**) brought in **RAVENSTINE** again. (**DAVID HILD** – accordion of LOS LOBOS guested)

Apr 86. (lp/cd) *(ROUGH 90)* *<TTR/+CD 8667>* **MONSTER WALKS THE WINTER LAKE**
– My theory of similtanious similtude – Red tin bus / What happened to me / Monster walks the winter lake / Bicycle / Coffee train / My town / Monster Magge king of the seas / Monster thinks about the good days / What happened to us.

— **JIM JONES** (b.12 Mar'50) – guitar was added

Mar 87. (lp) *(ROUGH 120)* *<TTR 87105>* **BLAME THE MESSENGER**
– The long rain / My town / King Knut / A fact about trains / When love is uneven / Storm breaks / Having time / Velikovsky / The two-step.

PERE UBU

(**THOMAS, RAVENSTINE, MAIMONE, CUTLER, JONES** and **KRAUSE**)

Fontana Enigma

Mar 88. (lp/c)(cd) *(SF LP/MC 5)(834 537-2)* *<73343>* **THE TENEMENT YEAR**
– Something's gotta give / George had a hat / Talk to me / Busman's honeymoon / Say goodbye / Universal vibration / Miss you / Dream the Moon / Rhythm kind / The hollow Earth / We have the technology.

Jul 88. (7") *(UBU 1)* **WE HAVE THE TECHNOLOGY. / THE B-SIDE** –
(12"+=/cd-s+=) *(UBU 1-12/CD1)* – The postman drove a caddy / ('A'-different mix).

— **ERIC DREW FELDMAN** (b.16 Apr'55) – drums (ex-CAPTAIN BEEFHEART) repl. RAVENSTINE + CUTLER

Fontana not iss.

Mar 89. (7") *(UBU 2)* **WAITING FOR MARY (WHAT ARE WE DOING HERE?). / WINE DARK SPARKS** –
(12"+=/cd-s+=) *(UBU 2-12/CD2)* – Flat.

May 89. (lp/c/cd) *(838 237-1/-4/-2)* **CLOUDLAND** –
– Breath / Bus called happiness / Race the sun / Waiting for Mary / Cry / Flat * / Ice cream truck / Lost nation road / Monday night / Pushin' / The wire * / The waltz. *(cd+= *)*

Jun 89. (7") *(UBU 3)* **LOVE LOVE LOVE. / FEDORA SATELLITE** –
(cd-s+=) *(UBUCD 3)* – Say goodbye.
(12") *(UBU 3-12)* – ('A'-cajun house mix) / ('A'132 bpm mix) / ('A'side).

Oct 89. (7") *(UBU 4)* **BREATH. / BANG THE DRUM** –
(12"+=) *(UBU 4-12)* – Over my head (live) / Universal initiation (live).
(cd-s+=) *(UBUCD 4)* – Humor me (live).

Mar 91. (7") *(UBU 5)* **I HEAR THEY SMOKE THE BARBEQUE. / INVISIBLE MAN** –
(12"+=/cd-s+=) *(UBU 5-12/CD5)* – Around the fire.

May 91. (cd/c/lp) *(848 564-2/-4/-1)* **WORLDS IN COLLISION** –
– Oh Catherine / I hear they smoke the barbeque / Turpentine / Goodnight Irene / Mirror man / Cry cry / World's in collision / Life of Riley / Over the Moon / Don't look back / Playback / Nobody knows / Winter in the Netherlands.

May 91. (7") *(UBU 6)* **OH CATHERINE. / LIKE A ROLLING STONE** –
(12"+=/cd-s+=) *(UBU 6-12/CD6)* – Down by the river.

Fontana Imago

Jan 93. (cd/c) *(514159-2/-4)* *<21024>* **STORY OF MY LIFE**
– Wasted / Come home / Louisiana train wreck / Fedora satellite II / Heartbreak garage / Postcard / Kathleen / Honey Moon / Sleep walk / The story of my life / Last will and testament.

— **THOMAS / KRAUSS / JONES / TEMPLE / YELLIN**

Cooking Vinyl Tim/Kerr

Aug 95. (cd) *(COOKCD 089)* *<TK 100>* **RAY GUN SUITCASE**
– Folly of youth / Electricity / Beach Boys / Turquoise fins / Vacuum in my head / Memphis / Three things / Horse / Don't worry / Ray gun suitcase / Surfer girl / Red sky / Montana / My friend is a stooge for the media priests / Down by the river II.

Oct 95. (cd-ep) *(FRYCD 043)* *<TK 111-2>* **FOLLY OF YOUTH / BALL 'N' CHAIN (jam) / DOWN BY THE RIVER II (demo) / MEMPHIS (demo)** Feb96

Mar 96. (cd-ep) *<TK 830121>* **B EACH B OYS SEE DEE +** –
– Beach Boys / Down by the river / Louisiana train wreck / Montana.

DAVID THOMAS

— with **ANDY DIAGRAM** – trumpet (ex-PALE FOUNTAINS) / **PAUL HAMANN** – upright bass / **JIM JONES** – backing vocals

Cooking Vinyl Tim/Kerr

Sep 96. (cd; DAVID THOMAS & TWO PALE BOYS) *(COOKCD 105)* *<TK 145>* **EREWHON**
– Obsession / Planet of fools / Nowheresville / Fire / Lantern / Morbid sky / Weird cornfields / Kathlen / Highway 61 revisited.

PERE UBU

— **THOMAS** with **TOM HERMAN + JIM JONES** newcomer + **ROBERT WHEELER** – synthesizer / **MICHELE TEMPLE** – bass

Mar 98. (cd) *(COOKCD 139)* *<TK 155>* **PENNSYLVANIA**
– Woolie bullie / Highwaterville / Sad. TXT / Urban lifestyle / Drive / Indiangiver / Monday morning / Perfume / Silent spring / Mr. Wheeler / Muddy waters / Slow / Fly's eye / The duke's Saharan ambitions / Wheelhouse.

DAVID THOMAS

— with **ANDY DIAGRAM, LINDA THOMPSON, JACKIE LEVEN,** etc

Cooking Vinyl Thirsty Ear

Mar 99. (cd; by The PALE ORCHESTRA conducted by DAVID THOMAS) *(COOKCD 175)* *<57068>* **MIRROR MAN**
– Mirror man sees / Mirror man speaks – Lost nation road / The flying Dutchman of the interstate / Ballad of Florida – Montana / Ribbons on the road / Morbid sky / Nowheresville / Shadows on the face – Memphis / Over the moon – If the deer blinks / Bus called happiness / Weird cornfields.
next with **JORGEN TELLER** – guitar, organ / **PER BUHL ACS** – clarinet, bass / **P.O. JORGENS** – percussion

Hearpen Thirsty Ear

Aug 00. (cd; as DAVID THOMAS AND FOREIGNERS) *(HR 111)* *<57085>* **BAY CITY**
– Clouds of you / White room / Black coffee dawn / Salt / Nobody lives on the moon / Charlotte / The doorbell / 15 seconds / The radio talks to me / Shaky hands / Black rain / Turpentine / Untitled track.

— back with **DIAGRAM + KEITH MOLINE** – guitar

Glitterhouse Thirsty Ear

Mar 01. (cd; as DAVID THOMAS AND TWO PALE BOYS) *(GRCD 519)* *<57096>* **SURF'S UP!** Feb01
– Runaway / Man in the dark / Night driving / Surf's up / River / Ghosts / Spider in my stew / Come home – Green river.

– compilations, etc. –

Jun 97. (5xcd-box) *Hearpen; (HR 110)* **MONSTER** (compilation of all his solo work) –
(re-iss. Oct02; same)

PERE UBU

Glitterhouse SpinArt

May 02. (cd) *(GRCD 554)* *<SPART 108>* **ST. ARKANSAS** Jun02
– The fevered dream of Hernando DeSoto / Slow walking daddy / Michele / 333 / Hell / Lisbon / Steve / Phone home Jonah / Where's the truth / Dark.

– compilations, others, etc. –

Nov 85. (lp/cd) *Rough Trade; (ROUGH 83) / Twin/Tone; <TTR/+CD 8561>* **TERMINAL TOWER: AN ARCHIVAL COLLECTION** (early work)
– Heart of darkness / 30 seconds over Tokyo / Final solution / Cloud 149 /

Untitled / My dark ages / Heaven / Humor me / The book is on the table / Not happy / Lonesome cowboy Dave. *(cd re-iss. Jun98 on 'Cooking Vinyl'; COOKCD 142) <US cd re-iss. Jun98 on 'Geffen'; 25207> (lp re-iss. Feb01 on 'Get Back'; GET 73)*

Mar 89. (cd) *Rough Trade; (ROUGHCD 93)* **ONE MAN DRIVES WHILE THE OTHER MAN SCREAMS – LIVE VOL.2: PERE UBU ON TOUR** [ ] [-]

Nov 95. (4x7"box) *Cooking Vinyl; (FRY 045) / Tim/Kerr; <TK 107>* **THE HEARTHAN SINGLES** [ ] [ ]

Nov 95. (d-cd) *Movieplay Gold; (MPG 74178)* **THE MODERN DANCE / TERMINAL TOWER** [ ] [-]

Sep 96. (5xcd-box) *Cooking Vinyl; (COOKCD 098) / Geffen; <24969>* **DATAPANIK IN THE YEAR ZERO** [ ] [ ]
– (first 5 albums + 1 free rarities album)

Aug 99. (cd) *Cooking Vinyl; (COOKCD 185) / Thirsty Ear; <57074>* **APOCALYPSE NOW (live in Chicago 1991)** [ ] [ ]

Mar 03. (cd) *Hearthan; <(HR 113)>* **THE SHAPE OF THINGS** (live, April 7, 1976) [ ] Oct00 [ ]

ROCKET FROM THE TOMBS

CROCUS BEHEMOTH (aka DAVID THOMAS) – vocals, guitar / **PETER LAUGHNER** – guitar, vocals / **CHEETAH CHROME** (b. GENE O'CONNOR) – guitar, organ / **CRAIG "C.W." BELL** – bass / **JOHNNY BLITZ** (b. JOHNNY MADANSKY) – drums

they released no singles during their lifespan (Jan-Aug 1975); CHEETAH + BLITZ helped to form The DEAD BOYS

– compilations, etc. –

Mar 02. (cd) *Glitterhouse; (GRCD 549)* **THE DAY THE EARTH MET THE . . . ROCKET FROM THE TOMBS** [ ] [-]
– Raw power / So cold / What love is / Ain't it fun / Transfusion / Life stinks / Muckraker / 30 seconds over Tokyo / Satisfaction / Sonic reducer / Never gonna kill myself again / Final solution / Foggy notion / Amphetamine / Read it and weep / Seventeen / Frustration / Down in flames / Search and destroy.

—— (some tracks were initially from 1990 bootleg, 'LIFE STINKS')

Carl PERKINS

Born: CARL LEE PERKINGS, 9 Apr'32, Ridgely, Tennessee, USA. In the early 50's, CARL and his brothers JAY and CLAYTON formed their own honky tonk outfit The PERKINS BROTHERS; the G in their surname had been inexplicably dropped. After relocating to Jackson, Memphis with his wife and inspiration Valda Crider, he struck up a deal with Sam Phillips' legendary 'Sun' label (also home of ELVIS PRESLEY, ROY ORBISON, JOHNNY CASH and JERRY LEE LEWIS). Phillips initially marketed him as a hillbilly/C&W artist on the small subsidiary 'Flip', CARL's siblings (along with newcomer W.S. 'Fluke' HOLLAND) continuing to back him on his debut solo single, early 1955's 'MOVIE MAGG'. With the subsequent defection of ELVIS to 'R.C.A.', PERKINS was groomed as Sun's "Great White Hope", perfecting his trademark combination of black rhythm and white melody early the following year with third single, 'BLUE SUEDE SHOES'. The song narrowly missed the US No.1 spot (it hit No.10 in Britain), and became a future classic although ELVIS subsequently popularised it while PERKINS lay in hospital recovering from a serious car crash; his brothers also had a lucky escape although JAY (who suffered a broken neck) was to die a few years later. Unable to capitalise on his success, CARL found it hard to re-establish his name after his absence. Four more minor Hot 100 placings (the last two for 'Columbia' between '58-'59) was all PERKINS could manage although it was no reflection on his abundant talent. Disillusioned, he succumbed to alcoholism as his career slid into decline. Nevertheless, stars like The BEATLES and JOHNNY CASH (also now a fellow devout Christian!) ensured the PERKINS name would not be forgotten; the Fab Four covered his songs while the latter giant of Country took him on as guest guitarist/featured solo singer. The stuff of classic C&W lyrics indeed, CARL's rollercoaster life took another bitter twist in 1974 when, after signing a new deal with 'Mercury', he had to cope with both the suicide of his brother CLAYTON and the death of his father. A few years later, he put his musical partnership with CASH on hold and subsequently toured in his own right with his sons as backing. Although his records never reached the heady commercial heights of yore, PERKINS joined up with old 'Sun' pals CASH and LEWIS (later ORBISON too) in '85 to instigate the aptly-monikered 'SURVIVORS'. Having spent the rest of the 80's and most of the 90's taking er . . . 'One Day At A Time', CARL was to sadly die after a paralysing stroke on the 19th of January, 1998; but for bad timing and even worse luck, CARL would have made it as a major league star in his own right although his contribution to popular music was recognised in 1987 when he was inducted into the Rock'n'Roll Hall Of Fame.

Best CD compilation: THE BEST OF CARL PERKINS on 'Columbia'(*6)

CARL PERKINS – vocals, electric guitar / with brothers **JAY** – acoustic guitar / **CLAYTON** – bass / **W.S. 'FLUKE' HOLLAND** – drums

not iss. / Flip

Jan 55. (7") *<501>* **MOVIE MAGG. / TURN AROUND** [-] [ ]

London / Sun

Jul 55. (7") *<224>* **GONE, GONE, GONE. / LET THE JUKEBOX KEEP ON PLAYING** [-] [ ]

Apr 56. (7") *(HLU 8271) <234>* **BLUE SUEDE SHOES. / HONEY DON'T** [10] Feb56 [2]

Apr 56. (7") *<235>* **SURE TO FAIL. / TENNESSEE** [-] [ ]

Jun 56. (7") *<243>* **BOPPIN' THE BLUES. / ALL MAMA'S CHILDREN** [-] [70]

Nov 56. (7") *<249>* **DIXIE FRIED. / I'M SORRY, I'M NOT SORRY** [-] [ ]

Apr 57. (7") *(HLS 8408) <261>* **YOUR TRUE LOVE. / MATCHBOX** [ ] Feb 57 [67]

May 57. (7") *<274>* **THAT'S ALL RIGHT. / FOREVER YOURS** [-] [ ]

Dec 57. (7") *(HLS 8527)* **GLAD ALL OVER. / FOREVER YOURS** [ ] [-]

Dec 57. (7") *<287>* **GLAD ALL OVER. / LEND ME YOUR COMB** [-] [ ]

Apr 58. (7") *(HLS 8608)* **THAT'S ALL RIGHT. / LEND ME YOUR COMB** [ ] [-]

1958. (lp) *<LP 1225>* **CARL PERKINS** (US-title 'CARL PERKINS' DANCE ALBUM – TEENBEAT') [-] [ ]
– Blue suede shoes / Movie Magg / Sure to fall / Gone gone gone / Honey don't / Only you / All mama's children / Tennessee / Wrong yo-yo / Everybody's trying to be my baby / Matchbox / Your true love / Boppin' the blues. *(UK-iss.Nov59 on 'London') (UK-iss.'THE DANCE ALBUM' Jul81 on 'Charly', cd-iss. Apr87 on 'Topline')*

Philips / Columbia

Apr 58. (7") *<41131>* **PINK PEDAL PUSHERS. / JIVE AFTER JIVE** [-] [91]

Aug 58. (7") *<41207>* **LEVI JACKET. / POP, LET ME HAVE THE CAR** [-] [ ]

—— In Oct'58, brother JAY died of cancer, after a car accident 2 years prev.

Feb 59. (7") *<41269>* **Y-O-U. / THIS LIFE I LEAD** [-] [ ]

May 59. (7") *<41379>* **POINTED TOE SHOES. / HIGHWAY OF LOVE** [-] [93]

Jan 60. (7") *(PB 983) <41447>* **ONE TICKET TO LONELINESS. / I DON'T SEE ME IN YOUR ARMS ANYMORE** [ ] Oct 59 [ ]

1960. (7") *<41651>* **L-O-V-E-V-I-L-L-E. / TOO MUCH FOR A MAN TO UNDERSTAND** [-] [ ]

1960. (7") *<41825>* **HONEY, 'CAUSE I LOVE YOU. / JUST FOR YOU** [-] [ ]

Sep 61. (7") *<42061>* **ANYWAY THE WIND BLOWS. / THE UNHAPPY GIRLS** [-] Jul 61 [ ]

1961. (7") *<42405>* **HOLLYWOOD CITY. / THE FOOL I USED TO BE** [-] [ ]

1962. (7") *<42514>* **HAMBONE. / TWISTER SISTER** [-] [ ]

1962. (7") *<42753>* **FORGET ME NEXT TIME AROUND. / I JUST CAN'T GET BACK FROM THERE** [-] [ ]

— Next 45, featured The NASHVILE TEENS.

Brunswick Decca

1963. (7") *<31548>* **HELP ME FIND MY BABY. / FOR A LITTLE WHILE** [–] [ ]

1963. (7") *<31591>* **AFTER SUNDOWN. / I WOULDN'T HAVE YOU** [–] [ ]

Apr 64. (7") *(05905)* **HELP ME FIND MY BABY. / I WOULDN'T HAVE YOU** [ ] [–]

Jun 64. (7") *(5909)* **BIG BAD BLUES. / LONELY HEART** [ ] [ ]

Nov 64. (7") *(5923) <31709>* **THE MONKEY SHINE. / LET MY BABY BE** [ ] [ ]

1964. (7") *<31786>* **MAMA OF MY SONG. / ONE OF THESE DAYS** [–] [ ]

— CARL became live guitarist for friend and country singer JOHNNY CASH, as well as continuing solo, signing for . . .

Realm not iss.

1966. (lp) *(52305)* **WHOLE LOTTA CARL PERKINS** [ ] [–]
– Whole lotta shakin' goin' on / Tutti frutti / Shake, rattle and roll / Sittin' on top of the world / Ready Teddy / Long tall Sally / That's all right / Where the Rio Rosa flows / Good rockin' tonight / I got a woman / Hey, good lookin' / Jenny, Jenny.

Stateside Dollie

Mar 67. (7") *(SS 599) <505>* **A COUNTRY BOY'S DREAM. / IF I COULD COME BACK** [ ] [ ]

1967. (7") *<508>* **SHINE, SHINE, SHINE. / ALMOST LOVE** [–] [ ]

1967. (7") *<512>* **WITHOUT YOU. / YOU CAN TAKE THE BOY OUT OF THE COUNTRY** [–] [ ]

1968. (7") *<514>* **MY OLD HOMETOWN. / BACK TO TENNESSEE** [–] [ ]

Spark Dollie

May 68. (7") *(SRL 1009) <516>* **LAKE COUNTY COTTON COUNTRY. / IT'S YOU** [ ] [ ]

London Dollie

Sep 68. (lp) *(HAP/SHP 8366) <DLP 4001>* **COUNTRY BOY'S DREAMS** [ ] [ ]
– Country boys's dreams / If I could come back / Sweet misery / Stateside / Detroit City / Unmitigated gall / Shine, shine, shine / Dream on little dreamer / You can take the boy out of the door / The star of the show / Home (that's where the heart is) / Poor boy blues. *(cd-iss. May92 with extra tracks)*

C.B.S. Columbia

Feb 69. (7") *(CBS 3932) <44723>* **RESTLESS. / 1143** [ ] 1968 [ ]

1969. (7") *<44883>* **FOR YOUR LOVE. / FOUR LETTER WORD** [–] [ ]

1969. (7") *<44993>* **SOUL BEAT. / C.C.RIDER (YOU'RE SO BAD)** [–] [ ]

1969. (lp) *<CS 9931>* **ON TOP** [–] [ ]
– Superfool / I'm gonna set my foot down / A lion in the jungle / Baby, what you want me to do / Soul beat / Riverboat Annie / Champaign, Illinois / Power of my soul / Brown-eyed handsome man / C.C.rider *(UK-iss.1972 as 'BROWN-EYED HANDSOME MAN')*

— Next with country rock revival band **N.B.R.Q.; STEVE FERGUSON** – guitar / **JODY ST.NICHOLAS** – bass / **TOM STANLEY** – drums / **DON ADAMS** – trombone / **FRANK GADLER**

Mar 70. (lp) *(CBS 63826) <CS 9981>* **BOPPIN' THE BLUES** [ ] [ ]
– Blue suede shoes / I'm sorry, I'm not sorry / Let the juke box keep on playing / All mama's children / Honey don't / Dixie fried / Boppin' the blues / Your true love / That's alright / Matchbox / Lend me your comb / Gone, gone, gone. *(re-iss. Nov84 on 'Topline')*

May 70. (7")*(4991) <45107>* **ALL MAMA'S CHILDREN. / STEP ASIDE** [ ] [ ]

1970. (7") *<45132>* **STATE OF CONFUSION. / MY SON MY SUN** [–] [ ]

1970. (7") *<45253>* **JUST AS LONG. / WHAT EVERY BOY OUGHT TO KNOW** [–] [ ]

1971. (7") *<45347>* **ME WITHOUT YOU. / RED HEADED WOMAN** [–] [ ]

1971. (7") *<45466>* **COTTON TOP. / ABOUT ALL I CAN GIVE YOU IS LOVE** [–] [ ]

1971. (7") *<45582>* **HIGH ON LOVE. / TAKE ME BACK TO MEMPHIS** [–] [ ]

1971. (7") *<45694>* **SOMEDAY. / THE TRIP** [–] [ ]

Mercury Mercury

1974. (7") *<73393>* **HELP ME DREAM. / YOU TORE MY HEAVEN ALL TO HELL** [–] [ ]

Mar 74. (lp/c) *(6338 475) <SRM-1-691>* **MY KIND OF COUNTRY** [ ] [ ]
– (Let's get) Dixiefried / You tore my Heaven to hell / Love sweet love / One more loser going home / Just as long / Goin' to Memphis / Never look back / Honky tonk song / Lord, I sinned again last night / Help me dream / Ruby, don't take your love to town.

1974. (7") *<73425>* **(LET'S GET) DIXIE FRIED. / ONE MORE LOSER GOIN' HOME** [–] [ ]

1974. (7") *<73489>* **RUBY (DON'T TAKE YOUR LOVE TO TOWN). / SING MY SONG** [–] [ ]

— In Dec'74, his brother CLAYTON, takes his own life.

1975. (7") *<73653>* **YOU'LL ALWAYS BE A LADY TO ME. / LOW CLASS** [–] [ ]

Oct 77. (7") *(ELV 15) <73690>* **THE EP EXPRESS. / BIG BAD BLUES** [ ] [ ]

— (above was a tribute to the recently departed ELVIS PRESLEY)

— toured with sons **GREG** – bass / **STAN** – drums, plus **LEE McALPIN** – piano / **DAVID SEA** – saxophone

not iss. Suede

1976. (lp) *<NR 6778>* **CARL PERKINS SHOW (live)** [–] [ ]

not iss. Musichill

1970's. (7") *<MMI 1007>* **BORN TO BOOGIE. / TAKE ME BACK** [–] [ ]

Jet Jet

Mar 78. (7"m) *(UP 36365) <5054>* **BLUE SUEDE SHOES. / THAT'S ALL RIGHT / ROCK ON AROUND THE WORLD** [ ] [ ]

Mar 78. (lp/c) *(JETLP 208/) <KZ 56704>* **OL' BLUE SUEDES IS BACK** [38] [ ]
– Rock around the clock / That's alright mama / Kaw-liga / Tutti frutti / I'm in love again / Blue suede shoes / Be-bop-a-lula / Maybellene / Whole lotta shakin' goin' on / Hang up my rock'n'roll shoes / Shake, rattle and roll / Rock around the world.

Aug 78. (7") *(117)* **MUSTANG WINE. / THE WHOLE WORLD MISSES YOU** [ ] [–]

Nov 80. (7"ep) *(JET 182)* **TWENTY-FIVE** [ ] [–]
– Lovesick blues / Turn around / Miss misunderstood / Blue suede shoes.

— Next album 'THE SURVIVORS' in May '82 was shared with **JOHNNY CASH** and **JERRY LEE LEWIS** and issued on 'CBS'.

— The previous year, CARL guested on album 'Tug Of War' w / PAUL McCARTNEY. In 1985, he appeared in the John Landis film 'Into The Night'. Later that year, a British TV special 'BLUE SUEDE SHOES' is recorded with many rock celebrities incl. GEORGE HARRISON, RINGO STARR, ERIC CLAPTON, DAVE EDMUNDS, etc.

M.C.A. M.C.A.

Mar 86. (lp/c) *(MCF/+C 3315) <MCA 39035>* **CARL PERKINS** [ ] [ ]
– Matchbox / If I had a' known / Green green grass of home / Texas woman / Signs / Blue sued shoes / Honey don't / I'm walking / Matchbox / Susie Q / Memphis / Maybellene / Slippin' and slidin' / Be-bop-a-lula / Roll over Beethoven / Hound dog / Whole lotta shakin' goin' on / Lucille / Jailhouse rock / All shook up / That's alright mama / Bird dog / Rock Island line.

Universal Universal

Jun 89. (lp/c/cd) *(UVL 76001) <UVLC 76001>* **BORN TO ROCK** (with the JORDANAIRES) [ ] [ ]
– Born to rock / Charlene / The rain / Might wash your love away / Hambone / A lifetime last night / Cotton top / Baby, please answer the phone / Till I couldn't stand no more / Don't let go / Love makes dreams come true.

– (selective) compilations, etc. –

Jan 82. (3xlp-box) *Sun; (BOX 101)* **THE SUN YEARS** [ ] [–]
(cd-box iss.Feb90)

Sep 84. (lp) *Boplicity; (BOP 008)* **INTRODUCING CARL PERKINS** [ ] [–]
(cd-iss. Jul96; CDBOP 008)

Nov 86. (cd) *Bear Family; (BCD 15246)* **UP THROUGH THE YEARS 1954-1957** [ ] [–]

Jan 90. (cd-box) *Charly; (CDSUNBOX 2)* **THE CARL PERKINS CD BOX SET** [ ] [–]

Apr 90. (5xlp-box) *Bear Family; BCD 15494)* **THE CLASSIC CARL PERKINS** [ ] [–]

Apr 92. (cd) *Bear Family; (BCD 15593)* **COUNTRY BOY'S DREAM: THE DOLLIE MASTERS** [ ] [ ]

Jul 95. (cd) *Charly; (CPCD 8102)* **BOPPIN' BLUE SUEDE SHOES** ☐ ☐
Oct 96. (cd) *Summit; (SUMCD 4016)* **BLUE SUEDE SHOES** ☐ ☐
May 97. (cd) *Charly; (CPCD 8301)* **THE UNISSUED . . .** ☐ ☐
Jun 97. (cd) *Vampirella; (MCG 20014)* **RARE TRACKS** ☐ ☐
Aug 97. (cd) *Culture Press; (301282-2)* **TURN AROUND: RARE DEMO TRACKS 1963-1964** ☐ ☐
Mar 98. (d-cd) *Charly; (CPCD 8338-2)* **THE DEFINITIVE COLLECTION** ☐ ☐
Apr 98. (cd) *Magnum Force; (CDMF 84)* **FAMILY FRIENDS AND LEGENDS** ☐ ☐
Aug 98. (cd) *Columbia; (491451-2)* **THE BEST OF CARL PERKINS** ☐ ☐
Jul 99. (d-cd) *Snapper; (SMDCD 176)* **THE ESSENTIAL SUN COLLECTION** ☐ ☐
Feb 00. (cd) *Lifetime; (LT 5120)* **BLUE SUEDE SHOES** ☐ ☐
Feb 00. (cd) *Castle Pie; (PIESD 179)* **BLUE SUEDE SHOES** ☐ ☐
May 00. (cd) *Snapper; (SMMCD 584)* **A PORTRAIT OF . . .** ☐ ☐
Jun 00. (cd) *Connoisseur; (VSOPCD 304)* **LIVE AT GILLEY'S** ☐ ☐
Jun 00. (4xcd-box) *Bear Family; (BCD 1642-2)* **BACK ON TOP** ☐ ☐
Jul 00. (cd) *MagMid; (MM 055)* **THE MAN AND THE LEGEND: THE 1985 RECORDINGS** ☐ ☐
Feb 01. (cd) *EMI Plus; (5761570)* **THE STORY** ☐ ☐
May 01. (cd) *Music; (CD 6258)* **THE VERY BEST OF . . .** ☐ ☐
Dec 01. (cd) *Prestige; (CDSGP 0164)* **BLUE SUEDE SHOES** ☐ ☐
Feb 02. (cd/c) *Castle Pulse; (PLS CD/MC 565)* **THE BEST OF CARL PERKINS** ☐ ☐
Apr 02. (cd) *Castle Select; (SELCD 603)* **OL' BLUE SUEDE'S BACK: CARL PERKINS' TRIBUTE TO ROCK'N'ROLL** ☐ ☐
Jul 02. (d-cd) *Castle; (CMDDD 510)* **JET-PROPELLED – THE 1978 COMEBACK** ☐ ☐
Jul 03. (cd) *Rock'n'roll Heroes; (RR 004)* **ROCK'N'ROLL HERO** ☐ ☐

☐ Brendan PERRY (see under ⇒ DEAD CAN DANCE)

Lee PERRY

Born: RAINFORD HUGH PERRY, 20 Mar'36, Kendal, Parish of Hanover, Jamaica; although by some accounts he was born in St. Mary's, a different parish, in 1939. After leaving school in 1954 and briefly working as a bulldozer driver, he moved from the countryside to the capital, Kingston, in 1957, attracted by the soundsystems of DUKE REID. Rejected by REID because of the "look in PERRY's eye", he turned to the "downbeat" system of now legendary producer, 'SIR COXONE" DODD, who employed him to move equipment, select records and fight off rival soundsystem spies. Working with PERRY was ex-boxer and first Jamaican ska star, PRINCE BUSTER, whose success with the FOWLKES BROTHERS' 'Oh Carolina' encouraged COXONE to start up his own label and recording studio, 'Studio One'. PERRY acted as a right hand man throughout this embryonic time, learning the ropes and making a name for himself in ska circles. After Jamaica gained independence in '62, ska became encouraged as a homebred musical form and PERRY's career took off. The following year, along with organist JACKIE MILTON, he co-produced backing tracks for COXONE, as well as having sole control over DELROY WILSON's 'Spit In The Sky' and TOOTS & THE MAYTALS' 'Six And Seven Books'. By this point, relations between PERRY and COXONE were strained and after recording more than a dozen tracks (including his first collaboration with The WAILERS, who sang back-up on his song, 'MAN TO MAN' and his first hit, 'CHICKEN SCRATCH', from which he was to take his most famous nickname), he acrimoniously split from the label in '66. After recording his first attack on 'Coxone', 'RUN FOR COVER', Joe Gibbs signed up PERRY to run his 'Amalgamated' label with almost immediate results; in '67 he produced The PIONEER's groundbreaking 'Longshot' and his own tune, 'I AM THE UPSETTER' (a warning to COXONE and a term that was to become his second nickname) as well as 'KIMBLE', an ode to David Jansen's 'The Fugitive'. After falling out with Gibbs in '68, PERRY retaliated by releasing 'PEOPLE FUNNY BOY' which combined the melody of 'Longshot' and the sounds of a crying baby, just to emphasize his discontent. Selling 60,000 copies in Jamaica, the record helped to popularise the new 'reggae' beat, inspired, according to PERRY, by hearing the congregation of a 'Pocomania' revivalist church in full flow. PERRY's fame was to mushroom with the initiation of 'Upsetter Records' in '68 (originally with the help of Clive Chin and Errol Thompson), the man enjoyed instrumental hits with the studio's house band, The UPSETTERS aka GLADDY'S ALL STARS. PERRY's big break came in October '69 when 'RETURN OF DJANGO', an UPSETTER instrumental of FATS DOMINO's 'Sick And Tired' appeared in a British TV advertisement, capturing the No.5 spot on the charts and creating a UK fanbase of young white skinheads. Following this success, PERRY began to work exclusively with The WAILERS (featuring a young BOB MARLEY) in late '69; such classics as 'Mr Brown', 'Small Axe', 'My Cup', 'Try Me' and 'Duppy Conqueror' were recorded with PERRY a leading influence. A pivotal factor in the shaping of The WAILER's sound was PERRY's suggestion that MARLEY tighten up his voice and the band concentrate more on organ riffs (rather than the popular combination of horns and falsetto backing) while providing a more solid foundation of thunderous bass and drums for MARLEY's leads. These collaborations between SCRATCH and MARLEY remain some of the finest work PERRY ever produced and the following two years saw a plethora of now legandary and popularised songs including 'Kaya', 'Natural Mystic', PETER TOSH's '400 Years' and 'Beat Down Babylon' by JUNIOR BYLES. PERRY's relationship with MARLEY was never a smooth one and the honeymoon period of '69/'70 ended when The WAILERS took the BARRETT brothers from PERRY's original studio band and signed to 'Island' in '73. The early 70's also saw PERRY, in collaboration with OSBOURNE 'KING TUBBY' RUDDOCK, create a new sound by slowing down the beat and pioneering the new 'dub' style, in effect creating the concept of the 're-mix' in the process. He also cut the first hip-hop 'scratch' record with CHARLIE ACE, 'COW THIEF SKANK', rapping over the track that cuts between the beats of two different songs. In '74, the legendary 'Black Ark' studio was founded, having immediate success with 'Curly Locks' by JUNIOR BYLES and selling 100,000 copires worldwide. In the same year, PERRY worked on the dub masterpiece, 'BLACKBOARD JUNGLE', featuring one mix by PERRY and another by KING TUBBY, in opposing speakers. PERRY's production techniques at Black Ark are mythical; he used eccentric methods and basic equipment to make a four track sound like an eight track by dumping several cuts onto one and then repeating the process, whilst blowing marijuana smoke on the mastertapes as they rolled by and occasionally burying them in the garden after wiping them clean with his t-shirt(!). The magival aura that the studio acquired attracted the attentions of Chris Blackwell, who signed PERRY as a producer/writer for 'Island' in 1975. Over the course of the ensuing four years, the classic tracks became the studio's staple output; the death of Haile Selassie in August '75 led to the cutting of 'Jah Lives' by MARLEY, and in '76, 'Island' began to release a string of reverb-drenched, PERRY-produced classics, MAX ROMEO's 'War Inna Babylon', JAH LION's 'Columbia Colly', The UPSETTER's 'Super Ape', JUNIOR MURVIN's 'Police And Thieves' and CULTURE's anti-violence anthem, 'Two Sevens Clash', all reflecting the growing political tensions rife in Jamaica. As PERRY put the finishing touches to The CONGOES' 'Heart

Of The Congoes' album at the end of '77, the international fame that he was now acquiring meant that a growing number of white rockers were beating a path to his door, such as PAUL WELLLER, ROBERT PALMER, PAUL (and LINDA) McCARTNEY and The CLASH, who took their name from CULTURE's song and covered the aforementioned 'Police And Thieves'. As his reputation grew, so did his hours of production, fuelled by ganja, rum and dragon stout. Inevitably, the relationship with 'Island' deteriorated when they rejected three of his productions in a row, 'Heart Of The Congoes', PERRY's own debut vocal album, 'ROAST FISH, COLLIE WEED and CORN BREAD', and the jazzy 'RETURN OF THE SUPER APE'. Soon after, PERRY was fleeced by Dreadlock promoters who hustled him into funding a proposed Broadway musical about reggae, and PERRY turned his back on dreads, banning them from the premises. The beginning of '79, saw PERRY's final productions at Black Ark, including LINDA McCARTNEY and LEROY SIBBLE's 'GARDEN OF LIFE'. Soon after, his wife and business adviser, PAULINE, left, and PERRY set fire to his studio in an attempt to burn all the bridges of the past behind him. This episode led to ever increasing eccentric behaviour, people arriving at the defunct studio to find PERRY worshipping bananas, eating money and baptising visitors with a garden hose! It took the arrival of HANK TARGOWSKI from BLACK STAR LINER distributors to convince PERRY to clean up the master tapes, however, his mood swings continued. Now calling himself, PIPECOCK JACKXON in an apparent homage to MICHAEL JACKSON, he recorded albums of little musical significance. After with the aforemention man in '81, the early 80's saw PERRY working with The LITTLE TERRORISTS, a decidely dodgy outfit from all accounts, and The MAJESTICS, whilst finding time to record two below par lp's, the latter one, 'HISTORY, MYSTERY AND PROPHECY' for 'Island' records. It was to be his last output for the label after accusing CHRIS BLACKWELL of sabotaging his album by not releasing it in the UK, as well as being responsible for the death of BOB MARLEY and infamously calling BLACKWELL "a vampire" on the '85 cut, 'JUDGEMENT INNA BABYLON' after 'witnessed' him "drinking the blood of a chicken". After releasing 'ARMAGEDDON TIME' in '86, the mid-eighties saw PERRY working with ADRIAN SHERWOOD and his house band, The DUB SYNDICATE, to great effect on the album, 'TIME BOOM X DE DEVIL DEAD', hailed as his finest output since the heady days of the Black Ark, and many of the tracks from this session still remain unreleased in PERRY's private vaults. This partnership continued to produce the goods on the commercially successful 90's album, 'FROM THE SECRET LABORATORY', released on 'Island' despite PERRY's insistence that he would not work with the label again. The early 90's also saw the release by 'Heartbeat' of 'THE UPSETTER AND THE BEAT', recorded in the late 80's with his old mentor COXSONE DODD and released after a legal tangle between the two. Now residing in Switzerland, PERRY's international reputation has been boosted by a wave of interest in the completist Island anthology set, 'ARKOLOGY', with new fans delving into the mass of recording material available through recent re-issues and compilations. Dubmeister LEE 'SCRATCH' PERRY returned for a Meltdown gig in London in May 2003, promoting his newest batch of intergalactic tracks under the title 'ALIEN STARMAN', a record which featured a cover of the Temptations 'MY GIRL'. Influential throughout the entire history of Jamaican popular music, PERRY has been and continues to be an inspirational phenomenon. • **Trivia:** In 1980, PERRY cast a spell over MAGGIE THATCHER, prophesising that "the mirror God will chop off her head and kill the seven demons in her. As soon as this interview published, it happen".

Best CD compilation: ARKOLOGY boxed-set (*8)

LEE PERRY – vocals, etc

Year	Release	UK	US
		R&B	not iss.
1963.	(7") *(JB 102)* **PRINCE IN THE BLACK. / DON'T COPY**	– Jama	–
1963.	(7") *(JB 104)* **PRINCE AND DUKE. / OLD FOR NEW**	– Jama	–
1963.	(7") *(JB 106)* **MAD HEAD. / MAN AND WIFE**	– Jama	–
1964.	(7") *(JB 135)* **ROYALTY. / CAN'T BE WRONG**	– Jama	–
		Port-O-Jam	not iss.
1964.	(7") *(PJ 4003)* **BAD MINDED PEOPLE. / (other side by TOMMY McCOOK & HIS GROUP)**	– Jama	–
1964.	(7") *(PJ 4010)* **CHATTY CHATTY WOMAN. / (other side by TOMMY McCOOK & HIS GROUP)**	– Jama	–
		Island	not iss.
1965.	(7") *(WI 210)* **PLEASE DON'T GO. / BYE, ST. JOHNNY (with The SOULETTES)**		–
1965.	(7"; as UPSETTERS) *(WI 223)* **COUNTRY GIRL. / STRANGE COUNTRY**		–
	(above actually recorded by OSSIE & The UPSETTERS)		
		Rio	not iss.
1965.	(7"; by The UPSETTERS) *(R 70)* **WALK DOWN THE ISLE. / SO BAD**		–
		Ska Beat	not iss.
1965.	(7") *(JB 201)* **ROAST DUCK. / HAND TO HAND, MAN TO MAN**		–
1965.	(7") *(JB 203)* **TRAIL AND CROSSES. / JON TOM**		–
1965.	(7") *(JB 212)* **WISHES OF THE WICKED. / HOLD DOWN**		–
1965.	(7") *(JB 215)* **OPEN UP. / (other track by ROLAND ALPHONSO)**		–
1966.	(7") *(JB 251)* **THE WOODMAN. / GIVE ME JUSTICE**		–
		Island	not iss.
1966.	(7"; as KING PERRY) *(WI 292)* **DOCTOR DICK. / (other side by The SOUL BROTHERS)**		–
1966.	(7"; as KING PERRY & The SOULETTES) *(WI 298)* **RUB AND SQUEEZE. / (other side by SOUL BROTHERS)**		–
		Doctor Bird	not iss.
1966.	(7"; by OSSIE & The UPSETTERS) *(DB 1018)* **TURN ME ON. / TRUE LOVE**		–
—	(on above me thinks there's no PERRY connection)		
1966.	(7"; by The UPSETTERS) *(DB 1034)* **WILDCAT. / I LOVE YOU SO**		–
1967.	(7") *(DB 1073)* **RUN FOR COVER. / SOMETHING YOU'VE GOT (as LEE 'KING' PERRY & The SENSATIONS)**		–
1967.	(7") *(DB 1098)* **WHOP WHOP MAN. / WIND-UP DOLL (with The DYNAMITES)**		–
1968.	(7"; by The DEFENDERS – aka LEE PERRY & THE SENSATIONS) *(DB 1104)* **SET THEM FREE. / DON'T BLAME THE CHILDREN**		–
1968.	(7") *(DB 1146)* **PEOPLE FUNNY BOY. / (other side by BURT WALTERS)**		–
		Amalgamated	not iss.
1968.	(7") *(AMG 808)* **THE UPSETTER. / THANK YOU BABY**		–

UPSETTERS

— **LEE PERRY** + various UPSETTERS

Year	Release	UK	US
		Trojan	not iss.
1968.	(7"; by LEE 'SCRATCH' PERRY) *(TR 644)* **UNCLE DESMOND. / BRONCO**		–
		Duke	not iss.
1969.	(7") *(DU 11)* **EIGHT FOR EIGHT. / STAND BY ME (by The INSPIRATIONS)**		–
		Camel	not iss.
1969.	(7") *(CA 13)* **TASTE OF KILLING. / MY MOB**		–
		Punch	not iss.
1969.	(7") *(PH 18)* **RETURN OF THE UGLY. / I'VE CAUGHT YOU**		–
1969.	(7") *(PH 19)* **DRY ACID. / (other side by The REGGAE BOYS)**		–
1969.	(7") *(PH 21)* **CLINT EASTWOOD. / LENNOX MOOD**		–

Upsetter not iss.

1969. (7") *(US 300)* **EIGHT FOR EIGHT. / YOU KNOW WHAT I MEAN** [ ] [–]
Sep 69. (7") *(US 301)* **RETURN OF DJANGO. / DOLLAR IN THE TEETH** [5] [–]
Sep 69. (7") *(US 303)* **TEN TO TWELVE. / Lee Perry: PEOPLE FUNNY FI TRUE** [ ] [–]
Oct 69. (7") *(US 307)* **NIGHT DOCTOR. / (other track by The TERMITES)** [ ] [–]
Oct 69. (7") *(US 309)* **KIDDYO. / ENDLESSLY** [ ] [–]
(above actually by The SILVERTONES)
Vov 69. (7") *(US 310)* **A DANGEROUS MAN FROM M.I.5. / (other track by The WEST INDIANS)** [ ] [–]
Nov 69. (7") *(US 313)* **LIVE INJECTION. / (other track by The BLEECHERS)** [ ] [–]
Dec 69. (7") *(US 315)* **COLD SWEAT. / POUND GET A BLOW** [ ] [–]
Jan 70. (7") *(US 317)* **VAMPIRE. / (other track by The BLEECHERS)** [ ] [–]
1970. (7") *(US 318)* **SOULFUL I. / (other track by MILTON HENRY)** [ ] [–]
1970. (7") *(US 321)* **DRUGS AND POISON. / STRANGER ON THE SHORE** [ ] [–]
1970. (7"; by LEE 'SCRATCH' PERRY) *(US 324)* **YAKETY YAK. / TACKIO** [ ] [–]
1970. (7"; by LEE 'SCRATCH' PERRY) *(US 325)* **KILL THE ALL. / SOUL WALK** [ ] [–]
1970. (7") *(US 326)* **BRONCO. / ONE MORE** [ ] [–]
1970. (7") *(US 332)* **NA NA HEY HEY. / PICK FOLK KINKYEST** [ ] [–]
1970. (7") *(US 333)* **GRANNY SHOW. / (version)** [ ] [–]
1970. (7") *(US 334)* **FIRE FIRE. / JUMPER** [ ] [–]
1970. (7") *(US 335)* **THE PILLOW. / GROOVING** [ ] [–]
1970. (7") *(US 336)* **SELF CONTROL** [ ] [–]
1970. (7") *(US 338)* **FRESH UP. / TOOTHACHES** [ ] [–]
1970. (7") *(US 342)* **DREAMLAND. / (other track by BOB MARLEY)** [ ] [–]
1970. (7") *(US 343)* **SIPREANO. / FERRY BOAT** [ ] [–]
1970. (7") *(US 346)* **BIGGER JOKE. / RETURN OF THE VAMPIRE** [ ] [–]
1970. (7") *(US 352)* **HEART AND SOUL. / ZIG ZAG** [ ] [–]

Spinning Wheel not iss.

1970. (7") *(SW 100)* **HAUNTED HOUSE. / DOUBLE WHEEL** [ ] [–]
1970. (7") *(SW 101)* **THE MISER. / (other track by CHUCK JUNIOR)** [ ] [–]
1970. (7") *(SW 102)* **THE CHOKIN' KIND. / (other track by CHUCK JUNIOR)** [ ] [–]
1970. (7") *(SW 103)* **LAND OF KINKS. / (other track by O'NEIL HALL)** [ ] [–]

Trojan not iss.

1970. (7") *(TR 7748)* **FAMILY MAN. / MELLOW MOOD** [ ] [–]
1970. (7") *(TR 7749)* **CAPO. / MAMA LOOK** [ ] [–]

Punch not iss.

1970. (7") *(PH 27)* **THE RESULT. / FEEL THE SPIRIT** [ ] [–]

Bullet not iss.

1971. (7"; as LEE PERRY & The UPSETTERS) *(BU 461)* **ALL COMBINE. / (part 2)** [ ] [–]

Upsetter not iss.

1971. (7"; by The UPSETTERS & KING TEDDY) *(US 353)* **ILLUSION. / BIG JOHN WAYNE** [ ] [–]
1971. (7") *(US 361)* **CAPASETIC. / ALL AFRICANS** [ ] [–]
(above 'A' was actually by LORD COMIC, 'B' by LITTLE ROY)
1971. (7") *(US 365)* **EARTHQUAKE. / (other side by JUNIOR BYLES)** [ ] [–]
1971. (7") *(US 370)* **DARK MOON. / (other track by DAVID ISAACS)** [ ] [–]
1972. (7"; by LEE 'SCRATCH' PERRY) *(US 385)* **FRENCH CONNECTION. / (The UPSETTERS version)** [ ] [–]
1972. (7"; LEE PERRY & DENNIS ALCAPONE) *(US 389)* **BACK BITER. / (The UPSETTERS version)** [ ] [–]
1972. (7") *(US 393)* **CRUMMY PEOPLE. / (other track by BIG YOUTH)** [ ] [–]
1972. (7") *(US 394)* **WATER PUMP. / (part 2)** [ ] [–]
1972. (7") *(US 396)* **PUSS SEA HOLE. / (other track by WINSTON GROOVY)** [ ] [–]
1973. (7"; LEE PERRY solo) *(US 397)* **JUNGLE LION. / FREAKOUT SKANK** [ ] [–]
1973. (7"; by LEE PERRY & CHARLIE ACE) *(US 398)* **COW THE SKANK. / SEVEN AND THREE QUARTERS SKANK** [ ] [–]

Bread not iss.

1973. (7"; LEE PERRY solo) *(BR 1111)* **STATION UNDERGROUND. / (other track by CARLTON & SHOES)** [ ] [–]

Downtown not iss.

1973. (7") *(DT 499)* **BLACK IPA. / IPA SKANK** [ ] [–]
1973. (7") *(DT 506)* **SUNSHINE SHOWDOWN. / SUNSHINE VERSION** [ ] [–]
1973. (7"; LEE PERRY solo) *(DT 513)* **BUCKY SKANK. / MID EAST ROCK** [ ] [–]

Count Shelly

1974. (7") *(CS 502)* **SAN-SAN. / (other track by OSBOURNE GRAHAM)** [ ] [–]

Dip not iss.

1974. (7") *(DL 5031)* **ENTER THE DRAGON. / (other track by JOY WHITE)** [ ] [–]
1974. (7") *(DL 5032)* **REBELS TRAIN. / REBELS DUB** [ ] [–]
1974. (7"; LEE PERRY & The SILVERTONES) *(DL 5037)* **DUB A PUM PUM. / (version)** [ ] [–]
1974. (7") *(DL 5054)* **CANE RIVER ROCK. / RIVERSIDE ROCK** [ ] [–]
1974. (7"; LEE PERRY & JUNIOR BYLES) *(DL 5060)* **DREADER LOCKS. / MILITANT ROCK** [ ] [–]
1974. (7") *(DL 5073)* **KEY CARD. / DOMINO GAME** [ ] [–]

– (UPSETTERS) albums –

(on below label unless mentioned otherwise)

Trojan not iss.

1969. (lp) *Pama Special; (PSP 1014)* **CLINT EASTWOOD** [ ] [–]
1969. (lp) *(TTL 13)* **THE UPSETTER** [ ] [–]
(cd-iss. Apr96; CDTTL 13)
1969. (lp) *(TRL 19)* **THE RETURN OF DJANGO** [ ] [–]
(cd-iss. Apr96; CDTRL 19)
1970. (lp) *(TTL 28)* **SCRATCH THE UPSETTER AGAIN** [ ] [–]
(cd-iss. Apr95; CDTRL 352)
1970. (lp) *(TBL 119)* **THE GOOD, THE BAD AND THE UPSETTERS** [ ] [–]
(cd-iss. Aug93 on 'Lagoon'; LG 21083)
1970. (lp) *(TBL 125)* **EASTWOD RIDES AGAIN** [ ] [–]
(cd-iss. May96; CDTBL 125)
1970. (lp) *Pama; (SECO 24)* **THE MANY MOODS OF THE UPSETTERS** [ ] [–]
1971. (lp; LEE PERRY & Various Artists) *(TBL 166)* **AFRICA BLOOD** [ ] [–]
(re-iss. Jul80; same) (cd-iss. Jun96; CDTBL 166)
1971. (lp; UPSETTERS & Various) *(TBL 167)* **BATTLE AXE** [ ] [–]
(cd-iss. Sep96; CDTBL 167)
1974. (lp) *(TRLS 70)* **DOUBLE SEVEN** [ ] [–]
(cd-iss. Jul96; CDTRL 70)

LEE 'SCRATCH' PERRY & THE UPSETTERS

—— aka **EARL SMITH** – guitar / **BORIS GARDENER** – bass / **MICKEY + BENBOW** – drums / **E. STIRLING** – keyboards / etc

Island Island

Jul 76. (lp) *(ILPS 9417)* **SUPER APE** [ ] [ ]
– Zion's blood / Croaking lizard / Black vest / Underground / Curly dub / Dread lion / Three in one / Patience / Dub along / Super ape. *(re-iss. Sep90 on 'Reggae Refreshers' cd/c; RRCD/RRCT 13)*
Aug 76. (7") *(WIP 6326)* **ROAST FISH & CORN BREAD. / CORN FISH DUB** [ ] [–]
Aug 76. (7") *(WIP 6328)* **THREE IN ONE. / CURLY DUB** [ ] [–]
Nov 76. (7") *(WIP 6370)* **DREADLOCKS IN MOONLIGHT. / CUT THROAT** [ ] [–]
1979. (lp) **ON THE WIRE** [ ] [–]
– Lee 'Scratch' Perry on the wire / Exodus / For whom the bell tolls / The grim reaper / Yes my friends / Rock my soul / Seaside (mystic mirror) / I am the Upsetter / Keep on moving / Burn funky. *(cd-iss. Apr95 on 'Trojan'; CDTRL 348)*

LEE 'SCRATCH' PERRY

Cactus not iss.

1979. (lp) *(CTLP 112)* **REVOLUTION DUB** [ ] [–]
(re-iss. Nov90 on 'Greensleeves'; TSLP 9006) (cd-iss. Dec92 on 'Rhino'; RNCD 2120)

Black Ark — not iss.

1979. (lp) *(TSLP 9001)* **CLOAK AND DAGGER** — –
– Cloak and dagger / Sharp razor / Hail stone / Musical transplant / Liquid serenade / Side gate / Iron claw / Rude walking / Bad walking / Cave man skank / Pee Wee special. *(re-iss. May89; same)*

Seven Leaves — not iss.

Oct 82. (lp) *(SLLP 1)* **HEART OF THE ARK** — –
– I've never had it so good / What's the use / Don't be afraid / Forward with love / Rasta fari / 4 & 20 dreadlocks / Nuh fe run down / Ellaine. *(cd-iss. Jul94; SLCD 1)*

1983. (lp) *(SLLP 2)* **MEGATON DUB** — –
– Dem no know dub / Conscious man dub / Such is dub / Corn picker dub / Freedom dub / Megaton dub / Dreader dub / School girl dub. *(cd-iss. Sep94; SLCD 2)*

Sep 84. (lp) *(SLLP 5)* **MEGATON DUB 2** — –
(cd-iss. Sep94; SLCD 5)

LEE 'SCRATCH' PERRY & THE UPSETTERS

Trojan — Trojan

Dec 85. (7") *(TRO 9080)* **MERRY XMAS HAPPY NEW YEAR / RETURN OF DJANGO** — –
(12"+=) *(TROT 9080)* – All things are possible / Happy birthday.

May 86. (lp/c) *(TRLS/ZCTRL 227)* **MILLIONAIRE LIQUIDATOR** <US title 'BATTLE OF ARMAGIDEON'>
– Introducing myself / Drum song / Grooving / All things are possible / Show me that river / I am a madman / The joker / Happy birthday / Sexy lady / Time marches on. *(cd-iss. Oct88; CDTRL 227)*

Sep 86. (7") *(TRO 9082)* **ALL THINGS ARE POSSIBLE. / SEXY LADY** — –

Dec 86. (7"ep/12"ep) *(TRO/+T 9095)* **MERRY CHRISTMAS, HAPPY NEW YEAR** — –
– Merry Christmas (the dub mix) / I am a madman / Mad man dub wise.

On-U-Sound — not iss.

May 87. (lp/c) *(ONULP 43/+C)* **TIME BOOM Z DE DEVIL DEAD** — –
– S.D.I. / Blinkers / The jungle / De Devil dead / Music and science lovers / Kiss the champion / Allergic to lies / Time conquer. *(re-iss. Oct87 on 'Syncopate' lp/c; SYLP/TCSYLP 6000) (cd-iss. Oct87; CDP 748442-2)*

Syncopate — not iss.

Sep 87. (7"/10"; as LEE PERRY & The DUB SYNDICATE) *(SY/10SY 6)* **THE JUNGLE (radio plate). / THE JUNGLE (rhythm mix)** — –
(12"+=) *(12SY 6)* – Music and science.

Bullwackies — not iss.

Oct 88. (lp) *(WACKIES 2740)* **SATAN KICKED THE BUCKET** — –

Heartbeat — Rounder

May 89. (lp/c/cd) *(HB/+C/CD 53)* **CHICKEN SCRATCH**
– Please don't go / Chicken scratch / Feel like jumping / Solid as a rock / By Saint Peter / Tackoo / Roast duck / Man to man / Gruma / Jane Ann & the pumpkin / Just keep it up / Puss in bag.

Mango — Mango

Jan 90. (7") *(MNG 737)* **THE GROOVE. / PARTY TIME**
(12"+=) *(12MNG 737)* – ('A'mixes).

Jun 90. (lp) *(MLPS 1035)* **FROM THE SECRET LABORATORY**
– Secret laboratory / Inspector Gadget / Groove / Vibrate one / African hitchhiker / You tonight I was dead / Too much money / Push push / African headcharge in the Hackney Empire / Party time / Seven devils dead. *(cd-iss. Aug97 on 'Reggae Refreshers'; RRCD 55)*

Heartbeat — Network

Sep 91. (lp/cd) *(ZS/+CD 110)* <*NET LP/CD 018*> **LORD GOD MUSICK** — Jul91

May 92. (cd) *(CDHB 59)* **THE UPSETTER & THE BEAT** — –

Nov 92. (cd/c) *(HB CD/C 76)* **SOUNDZS FROM THE HOT LINE** — –

Rhino — Rhino

May 93. (cd) *(RNCD 2007)* **HOLD OF DEATH** — –

May 94. (cd) *(RNCD 2057)* **GUITAR BOOGIE DUB** — –

Apr 96. (cd) **(RNCD 2137) REGGAE EMPEROR** 7-

Sep 96. (cd; LEE 'SCRATCH' PERRY & THE SCIENTIST) (<*RN 7005*>) **AT THE BLACKHEART STUDIO**

Black Art — not iss.

Jul 97. (7"; UPSETTERS) *(ART 1)* **ENTER THE DRAGON. / BLACK BELT JONES** — –

Jul 97. (7"; LEE PERRY & JAH LLOYD) *(ART 2)* **WHITE BELLY RAT. / JUDAS DE WHITE BELLY RAT** — –

Secret — Secret

Jun 03. (cd) <*(SECCD 001)*> **ALIEN STARMAN**

– (selective) compilations, etc. –

1985. (lp/c) *Island; (IRG 13)* **REGGAE GREATS** — –
(re-iss. Sep90 on 'Reggae Refreshers' cd/c; RRCD/RRCT 10)

Feb 86. (lp/c) *Trojan; (TRLS/ZCTRL 195)* **THE UPSETTER COLLECTION** — –
(cd-iss. May89; CDTRL 195)

Jul 87. (lp/c/cd; LEE 'SCRATCH' PERRY & THE UPSETTERS) *Heartbeat; (HB/+C/CD 37)* **SOME OF THE BEST** — –

Feb 88. (lp/c/cd; LEE PERRY & FRIENDS) *Trojan; (TRLS/ZCTRL/CDTRL 254)* **GIVE ME POWER** — –

Jun 88. (d-cd; LEE 'SCRATCH' PERRY & FRIENDS) *Trojan; (CDPRY 1)* **THE UPSETTER COMPACT DISC** — –

Sep 92. (cd/lp) *Danceteria; (DAN CD/LP 066)* **LEE 'SCRATCH' PERRY MEETS BULLWACKIE IN SATAN'S DUB** — –
(re-iss. Nov94 on 'R.O.I.R.'; RE 178CD)

Apr 95. (cd; LEE 'SCRATCH' PERRY & KING TUBBY) *Lagoon; (LG 21107)* **DUB CONFRONTATION VOL.2** — –

Jun 95. (cd; LEE 'SCRATCH' PERRY & The UPSETTERS) *Justic League; (JLCD 5000)* **KUNG FU MEETS THE DRAGON** — –

Jun 95. (cd/lp; LEE 'SCRATCH' PERRY & THE MAD PROFESSOR) *Ariwa; (ARI CD/LP 114)* **BLACK ARK EXPERRYMENTS** — –

Sep 95. (cd; Various Artists) *Nectar; (NTMCD 511)* **LARKS FROM THE ARK** — –

Oct 95. (cd/lp; LEE 'SCRATCH' PERRY & THE MAD PROFESSOR) *Ariwa; (ARI CD/LP 115)* **EXPERRYMENTS AT THE GRASS ROOTS OF DUB** — –

Oct 95. (cd) *Reggae Best; (cd) (RB 3015)* **GLORY DUB** — –

Nov 95. (cd/lp; UPSETTERS) *Sprint; (SFCD 5)* **IN DUB AROUND THE WORLD** — –

Mar 96. (cd; LEE 'SCRATCH' PERRY & THE UPSETTERS) *Original Music; (OMCD 11)* **REMINAH DUB** — –

May 96. (cd) *Blue Silver; (CB 6007)* **INTRODUCING LEE PERRY** — –

Jun 96. (cd) *Graylan; (GRCD 008)* **MEET SCIENTIST AT BLACK ART STUDIO** — –

Sep 96. (cd/lp) *Ariwa; (ARI CD/LP 131)* **DUB TAKE THE VOODOO OUT OF REGGAE** — –

Jun 97. (cd) *Hit Squad; (HS 2CD)* **THE GREAT KING OF DUB** — –

Jul 97. (3xcd-box) *Island; (CRNCD 6)* **ARKOLOGY** 49

Jul 97. (cd/lp) *Upsetter; (UP CD/LP 002)* **THE BEST OF LEE 'SCRATCH' PERRY** — –

Jul 97. (cd) *ROIR; (RUSCD 8232)* **TECHNOMAJICAL** — –

☐ Mike PETERS (see under ⇒ ALARM)

PET SHOP BOYS

Formed: London, England ... August '81 by assistant editor of Smash Hits, NEIL TENNANT, together with architecture student CHRIS LOWE (ex-DUST). After two years spent plugging away at demos, they met disco producer Bobby 'O' Orlando, subsequently working together on the debut 1984 'Epic' single, 'WEST END GIRLS'. After the track flopped in Britain (it was a French & Belgian hit), they signed with manager Tom Watkins, who secured them a deal with 'Parlophone' early in 1985. Their first effort for the label, the sardonic 80's critique of 'OPPORTUNITIES (LET'S MAKE LOTS OF MONEY)' failed to make an impact, a Stephen Hague produced re-make of 'WEST END GIRLS' finally giving them a major breakthrough early the following year, hitting No.1 in many countries including Britain and the States. The debut album, 'PLEASE' (1986) was a Transatlantic Top 10 success, a classy collection of intelligent synth-pop, infectious melodies and wryly observant lyrics becoming the campy duo's trademark. 'OPPORTUNITIES' was hastily re-released in clanking, mechanically remixed form, almost making the Top 10, while a further single from the album, 'SUBURBIA', made No.8. Visually, the band were akin to a more stylish SPARKS or ERASURE, sharing the latter's sizeable gay following, while ironically also being idolised by thuggish football 'casuals' for their immaculate taste in designer wear. The 'BOYS even penned a song about the Italian strain of the expensively kitted out thug, 'PANINARO', featured on their mini remix album, 'DISCO' (1986). 'IT'S A SIN' gave the act their second No.1 later that summer while the duo teamed up with 60's songstress DUSTY SPRINGFIELD for 'WHAT HAVE I DONE TO DESERVE THIS', a Transatlantic No.2 hit. The fact that the Americans had taken so keenly to The PET SHOP BOYS was odd, given that nation's notorious inability to appreciate irony; it's arguably a testament to the group's finely honed melodic mastery and perfectionist production that they broke the US market where other quintessentially English pop bands have consistently failed. 'ACTUALLY' (1987) was another successful slice of sophisticated pop nous, containing the aforementioned two singles as well as the poignant 'RENT' and two further No.1 singles in 'HEART' and a flamboyant synth/strings remake of Elvis' 'ALWAYS ON MY MIND'. The group further indulged their penchant for remix albums with 'INTROSPECTIVE' (1988), which included a version of the track they'd produced for EIGHTH WONDER (featuring a pre-LIAM Patsy Kensit), 'I'M NOT SCARED'. The following year saw The PET SHOP BOYS working with such diverse artists as LIZA MINNELLI (who subsequently hit the charts with their melodramatic, collaborative cover of Stephen Sondheim's 'LOSING MY MIND') and ELECTRONIC, while the next group project, 'BEHAVIOUR' (1990), was uncharacteristically introspective, spawning a solitary hit single, the wistful 'BEING BORING'. Only the PET SHOP BOYS could get away with splicing U2's 'Where The Streets Have No Name' and FRANKIE VALLI's 'Can't Take My Eyes Off You', a masterstroke of tongue-in-cheek pop genius that reached No.4 in Spring '91. It would be another two years before 'VERY', a consummate distillation of the PET SHOP BOYS' unique grasp of pure pop, previewed by their celebratory cover of The Village People's 'GO WEST'. A limited edition dance CD, 'RELENTLESS', was included with initial copies of 'VERY', The PET SHOP BOYS proving they were hip to a music style they had helped to create. TENNANT and LOWE have maintained a fairly low profile of late, releasing a second volume of 'DISCO' remixes in 1994 and a B-sides collection in '95, 'ALTERNATIVE'. 'BILINGUAL' (1996) boasted the usual spread of UK hit singles, although The PET SHOP BOYS were getting old hat while wearing many of them in the process. Nearing the end of the millennium (aarrgghh!), credible pop music was now big fashion again, it was just that TENNANT and LOWE were losing themselves in the mire of mediocrity; the 1999 album 'NIGHTLIFE' (which featured the appallingly camp 'NEW YORK CITY BOY') the proof that they were losing the place. A few years on, the 'BOYS were back on the town with a collaborative effort, 'CLOSER TO HEAVEN'; all very high-brow but definitely low-key, outside the West End, that is. That the PET SHOP BOYS – a band so closely aligned with the 80's and, to a lesser extent, the 90's – should even choose to keep on recording into the millennium is a brave step although thankfully, 'RELEASE' (2002) made few concessions to musical fashion. Instead, it cast a knowing, wary eye over contemporary music without getting hung up on it. With JOHNNY MARR lending a seasoned hand and messrs TENNANT and LOWE freed from the role of uber-hip cultural commentators, the songs were given an unprecedented room to breathe. The result was an aethetic makeover of sorts, a record more befitting of their age. It seems incredible that such a modernist act have been recording for two decades yet that was the story which the highly entertaining 'POP ART' (2003) had to tell, a more complete anthology than 1991's 'DISCOGRAPHY' if no less playful. • **Covers:** SOMEWHERE (Leonard Bernstein & Stephen Sondheim) / etc.

Album rating: PLEASE (*6) / DISCO remixes (*5) / ACTUALLY (*7) / INTROSPECTIVE mixes (*5) / BEHAVIOUR (*7) / DISCOGRAPHY – THE COMPLETE SINGLES COLLECTION compilation (*8) / VERY (*7) / DISCO 2 remixes (*5) / ALTERNATIVE collection (*5) / BILINGUAL (*6) / NIGHTLIFE (*6) / RELEASE (*6) / DISCO 3 remixes (*4) / POPART: THE HITS compilation (*7)

NEIL TENNANT (b.10 Jul'54, Gosforth, Northumberland, England) – vocals / **CHRIS LOWE** (b. 4 Oct'59, Blackpool, England) – keyboards, synthesizers

Epic | Bobcat 12"

Apr 84. (7"/ext.12") *<A/TA 4292>* **WEST END GIRLS. / PET SHOP BOYS** [ ] [–]

Parlophone | EMI America

Jun 85. (7") *(R 6097) <8321>* **OPPORTUNITIES (LET'S MAKE LOTS OF MONEY). / IN THE NIGHT** [ ] Mar86 [ ]
(12") *(12R 6097)* – ('A'dance mix) / ('B'extended).
(12") *(12RA 6097)* – ('A' Latin version). / ('B'dub for money).

Nov 85. (7") *(R 6115) <8307>* **WEST END GIRLS. / A MAN COULD GET ARRESTED** [1] Jan86 [1]
(10") *(10R 6115)* – ('A'remixed) / ('B'extended).
(12"+=) *(12R 6115)* – ('A'dance mix).
(12") *(12EA 6115)* – ('A'-Shep Pettibone mix) / (A'dub mix) / ('B'extended).

Mar 86. (7") *(R 6116) <8338>* **LOVE COMES QUICKLY. / THAT'S MY IMPRESSION** [19] Aug86 [62]
(10"/12") *(10R/12R 6116)* – ('A'dance mix) / ('B'disco mix).

Mar 86. (lp/c)(cd) *(PSB/TCPSB 1)(CDP 7-46271-2) <17193>* **PLEASE** [3] [7]
– Two divide by zero / West End girls / Opportunities (let's make lots of money) / Love comes quickly / Suburbia / Tonight is forever / Violence / I want a lover / Later tonight / Why don't we live together / Opportunities (reprise).

May 86. (7") *(R 6129) <8330>* **OPPORTUNITIES (LET'S MAKE LOTS OF MONEY) (remix). / WAS THAT WHAT IT WAS** [11] [10]
(12") *(12R 6129)* – ('A'&'B'-Shep Pettibone mastermixes) / Opportunities (original dance mix) / Opportunities (reprise Shep Pettibone mix).

Sep 86. (7") *(R 6140) <8355>* **SUBURBIA. / PANINARO** [8] Nov86 [70]
('A'-Full horror mix-12") *(12R 6140)* – Jack the lad.
(c-s++=) *(TR 6140)* – Love comes quickly (Shep Pettibone remix).
(c-s) *(TCR 6140)* – ('A'-J.Mendelsohn remixed).
(d7"+=) *(RD 6140)* – Suburbia pt.2.

Nov 86. (lp/c)(cd) *(PRG/TCPRG 1001)(CDP 7-46450-2) <17246>* **DISCO** (The 12"mixes) [15] [95]
– In the night / Suburbia / Opportunities / Paninaro / Love comes quickly / West end girls.

Jun 87. (7") *(R 6158) <43027>* **IT'S A SIN. / YOU KNOW WHERE YOU WENT WRONG** [1] Aug87 [9]
(12"+=/c-s+=/cd-s+=) *(12R/TCR/CDR 6158)* – ('A'disco mix).
(12") *(12RX 6158)* – ('A'-Ian Levene remix) / ('B'-rough mix).

Aug 87. (7"; PET SHOP BOYS & DUSTY SPRINGFIELD) *(R 6163) <50107>* **WHAT HAVE I DONE TO DESERVE THIS? / A NEW LIFE** [2] Dec87 [2]
(ext;12"+=/c-s+=/cd-s+=) *(12R/TCR/CDR 6163)* – ('A'disco mix).

Sep 87. (cd/c/lp) *(CD/TC+/PCSD 104) <46972>* **ACTUALLY** [2] [25]
– One more chance / What have I done to deserve this? / Shopping / Rent / Hit music / It couldn't happen here / It's a sin / I want to wake up / Heart / King's Cross. *(re-iss. May88; PCSDX 104) (w/free US 12" or cd-s)* – Always on my mind.

Oct 87. (7") *(R 6168)* **RENT. / I WANT A DOG** [8] [ ]
(ext;12"+=/c-s+=/cd-s+=) *(12R/TCR/CDR 6168)* – Rent (dub).

Nov 87. (7") *(R 6171) <50123>* **ALWAYS ON MY MIND. / DO I HAVE TO?** [1] Mar88 [4]
(12"+=/c-s+=/cd-s+=) *(12R/TCR/CDR 6171)* – ('A'extended dance).
('A'-Phil Harding remix-12") *(12RX 6171)* – ('A'dub).

Mar 88. (7") *(R 6177)* **HEART. / I GET EXCITED (YOU GET EXCITED TOO)** [1] [ ]

('A'disco mix-12"+=/c-s+=/cd-s+=) *(12R/TCR/CDR 6177)* – ('A'dance mix).
('A'-J.Mendelsohn mix-12"+=) *(12RX 6177)* – ('A'dub).

Jun 88. (12"/cd-s) **ACTUALLY. / ALWAYS ON MY MIND** [–] [ ]

Sep 88. (7"/7"s) *(R/RS 6190) <50161>* **DOMINO DANCING. / DON JUAN** [7] [18]
(disco;12"+=/c-s+=/cd-s+=) *(12R/TCR/CDR 6190)* – ('A'alternative mix).
(demo-12"+=) *(12RX 6190)* – ('A'remix).

Oct 88. (cd/c/lp) *(CD/TC+/PCS 7325) <90868>* **INTROSPECTIVE** (12"mixes) [2] [34]
– Left to my own devices / I want a dog / Domino dancing / I'm not scared / Always on my mind – In my house / It's alright. *(re-iss. Mar89, 3x12"; PCSX 7325) (re-iss. Mar94)*

Nov 88. (7"/7"s) *(R/RS 6198) <50171>* **LEFT TO MY OWN DEVICES. / THE SOUND OF THE ATOM SPLITTING** [4] Jan89 [84]
(12"+=/c-s+=/cd-s+=) *(12R/TCR/CDR 6198)* – ('A'disco mixes).

Jun 89. (7"/c-s/ext.12"/ext.cd-s) *(R/TCR/12R/CDR 6220)* **IT'S ALRIGHT. / ONE OF THE CROWD / YOUR FUNNY UNCLE** [5] [ ]
(10") *(10R 6220)* – ('A'alternative mix) / ('A'extended dance).
(12") *(12RX 6220)* – ('A'-Tyree mix) / ('A'-Sterling Void mix).

— NEIL and CHRIS had guested late '89-91 for BERNARD SUMNER & JOHNNY MARR on their ELECTRONIC project. (see ⇒ NEW ORDER)

— On tour augmented by **COURTNEY PINE / PETE GLEADALAS / DANNY CUMMINGS**

— next featured **JOHNNY MARR** – guitar

Sep 90. (c-s/7") *(TC+/R 6269) <50329>* **SO HARD. / IT MUST BE OBVIOUS** [4] [62]
(12"+=) *(12R 6269)* – ('A'dub mix).
(cd-s++=) *(CDR 6269)* – ('A'dance mix).

Oct 90. (cd/c/lp) *(CD/TC+/PCSD 113) <94310>* **BEHAVIOUR** [2] [45]
– Being boring / This must be the place I waited years to leave / To face the truth / How can you expect to be taken seriously? / Only the wind / My October symphony / So hard / Nervously / The end of the world / Jealousy.

Nov 90. (c-s/7") *(TC+/R 6275)* **BEING BORING. / WE ALL FEEL BETTER IN THE DARK** [20] [ ]
(12"+=/cd-s+=) *(12R/CDR 6275)* – ('A'&'B'extended mixes).

Feb 91. (c-s,cd-s) *<50343>* **HOW CAN YOU EXPECT TO BE TAKEN SERIOUSLY? / WHAT HAVE I DONE TO DESERVE THIS?** [–] [93]

Mar 91. (c-s/7") *(TC+/R 6285)* **WHERE THE STREETS HAVE NO NAME (I CAN'T TAKE MY EYES OFF YOU). / HOW CAN YOU EXPECT TO BE TAKEN SERIOUSLY? (remix)** [4] [–]
(ext;12"+=/cd-s+=) *(12R/CDR 6285)* – But she's not your girlfriend.
(12"+=) *(12RX 6285)* – ('B'classical).

May 91. (c-s,cd-s) *<50351>* **WHERE THE STREETS HAVE NO NAME (I CAN'T TAKE MY EYES OFF YOU) / BET SHE'S NOT YOUR GIRLFRIEND** [–] [72]

May 91. (c-s/7") *(TC+/R 6283)* **JEALOUSY. / LOSING MY MIND** [12] [–]
(12"+=/cd-s+=) *(12R/CDR 6283)* – ('A'&'B'extended).
(cd-s+=) *(CDRS 6283)* – This must be the place / Waited for the years to leave (extended) / So hard (eclipsed mix).

Oct 91. (c-s/7") *(TC+/R 6301)* **DJ CULTURE. / MUSIC FOR BOYS** [13] [–]
(12"+=/cd-s+=) *(12R/CDR 6301)* – ('A'-II version).

Nov 91. (cd/c/lp) *(CD/TC+/PMTV 3) <97097>* **DISCOGRAPHY – THE COMPLETE SINGLES COLLECTION** (compilation) [3] [ ]
– West End girls / Love comes quickly / Opportunities (let's make lots of money) / Suburbia / It's a sin / What have I done to deserve this? / Rent / Always on my mind / Heart / Domino dancing / Left to my own devices / It's alright / So hard / Being boring / Where the streets have no name (I can't take my eyes off you)/ Jealousy / DJ culture / Was it worth it?

Dec 91. (c-s/7") *(TC+/R 6306)* **WAS IT WORTH IT? / MISERABLISM** [24] [ ]
(12"+=/cd-s+=) *(12R/CDR 6306)* – ('A'remixes).

Jun 93. (c-s/7") *(TC+/R 6348)* **CAN YOU FORGIVE HER? / HEY, HEADMASTER** [7] [ ]
(12"+=/cd-s+=) *(12R/CDR 6348)* – ('A'-Rollo remix) / ('A'-Rollo dub).
(cd-s) *(CDRS 6348)* – ('A'remix) / I want to wake up (Johnny Marr remix) / What keeps mankind alive? / ('A' MK dub).

Sep 93. (c-s/7") *(TC+/R 6356)* **GO WEST. / SHAMELESS** [2] [ ]
(12"+=/cd-s+=) *(12R/CDR 6356)* – ('A'mixes; movements).

Oct 93. (cd/c/lp) *(CD/TC+/PCSD 143) <89721>* **VERY** [1] [20]
– Can you forgive her? / I wouldn't normally do this kind of thing / Liberation / A different point of view / Dreaming of the Queen / Yesterday, when I was mad / The theatre / One and one make five / To speak is a sin / Young offender / One in a million / Go west. *(free-cd) (CDPSDX 143)* **VERY RELENTLESS** – My head is spinning / Forever is love / KDX 125 / We came from outer space / The man who has everything / One thing leads to another.

Dec 93. (c-s/7") *(TC+/R 6370)* **I WOULDN'T NORMALLY DO THIS KIND OF THING. / TOO MANY PEOPLE** [13] [ ]
(cd-s+=) *(CDR 6370)* – Violence (Hacienda mix) / West End girls (Sasha mix).
(cd-s) *(CDRS 6370)* – ('A'side) / ('A'mixes).

— re-issued all 14 singles from 1987-1992 on cd-ep's Nov93.

Apr 94. (c-s/7") *(TC+/R 6377)* **LIBERATION. / DECADENCE** [14] [ ]
(cd-s+=) *(CDR 6377)* – ('A'-E Smoove mix).
(cd-s/d12") *(CDRS/12RD 6377)* – ('A'-Murk mix) / ('B'unplugged mix) / Young offender (jam & spoon mix).

— Below a second Comic Relief charity single, featuring vox from the TV series of that name; JENNIFER 'Edina' SAUNDERS and JOANNA 'Patsy' LUMLEY.

May 94. (c-s/7"; as ABSOLUTELY FABULOUS) *(TC+/R 6382)* **ABSOLUTELY FABULOUS. / ('A'mix)** [6] [–]
(cd-s+=) *(CDR 6382)* – ('A'mixes).

Sep 94. (c-s) *(TCR 6386)* **YESTERDAY, WHEN I WAS MAD. / EUROBOY** [13] [ ]
(cd-s) *(CDR 6386)* – ('A'side) / If love were all / Can you forgive her? (swing version) / ('A'-Jam & Spoon mix).
(cd-s) *(CDRS 6386)* – ('A'-Coconut 1 remix) / ('A'-Junior Vasquez dub & RAF zone mix) / Some speculation.
(12") *(12R 6386)* – ('A'-Jam & Spoon mix) / ('A'-Junior Vasquez dub & RAF zone mix).

Sep 94. (cd/c/lp) *(CD/TC+/PCSD 159) <28105>* **DISCO 2** (remixes) [6] [75]

Jul 95. (c-s) *(TCR 6414)* **PANINARO '95 / IN THE NIGHT** [15] [ ]
(cd-s+=) *(CDR 6414)* – Girls and boys (live in Rio).
(12") *(12R 6414)* – ('A'-Tracy's mix) / ('A'-Sharon's Sexy Boyz dub) / ('A'-Tin Tin Out mix) / ('A'extended).
(12") *(12RS 6414)* – ('A'-Angel Morales deep dance mix) / ('A'-Girls Boys in dub mix) / ('A'-Hot'n'spicy dub mix).

Aug 95. (d-cd/d-c/t-lp) *(CD/TC+/PCSD 166) <34023>* **ALTERNATIVE** (B-sides) [2] [ ]
– In the night / A man could get arrested / That's my impression / Was that what it was? / Paninaro / Jack the lad / You know where you went wrong / A new life / I want a dog / Do I have to? / I get excited (you get excited too) / Don Juan / The sound of the atom splitting / One of the crowd / Your funny uncle / / It must be obvious / We all feel better in the dark / Bet she's not your girlfriend / Losing my mind / Music for boys / Miserablism / Hey, headmaster / What keeps mankind alive? / Shameless / Too many people / Violence (Hacienda version) / Decadence / If love were all / Euroboy / Some speculation.

Apr 96. (c-s) *(TCR 6431)* **BEFORE / THE TRUCK-DRIVER AND HIS MATE** [7] [ ]
(cd-s+=) *(CDR 6431)* – Hit and miss / In the night 1995 ('New Clothes Show').
(cd-s/3x12") *(12R/CDRS 6431)* – ('A'remixes by; Love To Infinity / Joey Negro / Danny Tenaglia).

— TENNANT now back with ELECTRONIC on hit single 'FORBIDDEN CITY'.

Aug 96. (c-s/12"pic-d) *(TCR/12RD 6443)* **SE A VIDA E (THAT'S THE WAY LIFE IS) / BETRAYED** [8] [ ]
(cd-s+=) *(CDR 6443)* – How I learned to hate rock'n'roll.
(cd-s) *(CDRS 6443)* – (mixes by; Mark Picchiotti / Deep Dish / Pink Noise).

Sep 96. (cd/c) *(CD/TC PCSD 113) <31088>* **BILINGUAL** [4] [39]
– Discoteca / Single / Metamorphosis / Electricity / Se a vida e (that's the way life is) / It always comes as a surprise / A red letter day / Up against it / The survivors / Before / To step aside / Saturday night forever.

Nov 96. (c-s) *(TCR 6452)* **SINGLE – BILINGUAL / DISCOTECA** [14] [ ]
(cd-s+=) *(CDR 6452)* – Confidential (demo) / ('A'mix).
(cd-s+=) *(CDRS 6452)* – ('A'mix) / The calm before the storm.

Mar 97. (12") *(12R 6460)* **A RED LETTER DAY. / THE BOY WHO COULDN'T KEEP HIS CLOTHES ON** [9] [ ]
(cd-s+=) *(CDR 6460)* – Delusions of grandeur.
(cd-s) *(CDRS 6460)* – ('A'mixes).

Jun 97. (c-s) *(TCR 6470)* **SOMEWHERE / THE VIEW FROM YOUR BALCONY** [9] [ ]
(cd-s+=) *(CDR 6470)* – To step aside (Ralphi's old school dub) / ('A'-Forthright vocal mix).
(cd-s) *(CDRS 6470)* – ('A'-orchestral) / Disco potential / ('A'-Trouser Enthusiasts mix) / ('A'-Forthright dub).

Jul 99. (c-s/cd-s) *(TCR/CDRS 6523)* **I DON'T KNOW WHAT YOU WANT BUT I CAN'T GIVE IT ANYMORE / SILVER AGE / SCREAMING** [15] [ ]
(cd-s) *(CDR 6523)* – ('A'-David Morales mix) / ('A'-Thee Maddkatt 80 Coutship Witness mix) / Je t'aime . . . moi non plus.

Oct 99. (c-s/cd-s) *(TCR/CDRS 6525)* **NEW YORK CITY BOY / THE GHOST OF MYSELF / NEW YORK CITY (almighty definite mix)** [14] [ ]
(cd-s) *(CDR 6525)* – ('A'side) / Casting a shadow / ('A'-Superchumbo's uptown mix).

Oct 99. (cd/c/lp) *(521847-2/-4/-1) <31086>* **NIGHTLIFE** [7] Nov99 [84]
– For your own good / Closer to Heaven / I don't know what you want but I can't give it any more / Happiness is an option / You only tell me you love me when you're drunk / Vampires / Radiophonic / The only one / Boy strange / In denial / New York city boy / Footsteps.

Jan 00. (12"/cd-s) *(12R/CDR 6533)* **YOU ONLY TELL ME YOU LOVE ME WHEN YOU'RE DRUNK (mixes)** [8] [–]
(cd-s) *(CDRS 6533)* – ('A'side) / Lies / Sail away.
(cd-s) *(CDRX 6533)* – ('A'mixes) / ('A'-CD-rom) / Always on my mind (live video) / Being boring (live video).

—— in Oct'01, The PET SHOP BOYS worked with the original cast of 'Closer To Heaven', a musical collaboration with playwright Jonathan Harvey

Mar 02. (cd-s) *(CDRS 6572)* **HOME AND DRY / SEXY NORTHERNER / ALWAYS** [14] [–]
(cd-s) *(CDR 6572)* – ('A'-ambient mix) / Break 4 love (with PETER RAUHOFER) / Break 4 love (Friburn & Urik hi pass remix with PATER RAUHOFER).

Apr 02. (cd) *(538150-2) <541486>* **RELEASE** [7] [73]
– Home and dry / I get along / Birthday boy / London / E mall / Samurai in autumn / Love is a catastrophe / Here / The night I fell in love / You choose. *(special cd+=; 538598-2)* – Home and dry (ambient mix) / Sexy northerner / Always / Closer to Heaven (slow version) / Nightlife / Friendly fire / Break 4 love (radio edit) / Home and dry / Home and dry (video).

Jul 02. (cd-s) *(CDRS 6581)* **I GET ALONG / SEARCHING FOR THE FACE OF JESUS / BETWEEN TWO ISLANDS** [18] [–]
(cd-s) *(CDR 6581)* – ('A'live) / Red letter day (live) / Love comes quickly (live).

Feb 03. (cd) *(582140-2) <84595>* **DISCO 3** (remixes) [36] [ ]
– Time on my hands / Positive role model / Try it (I'm in love with a married man) / London (Three Radikal Blaklite edit) / Somebody else's business / Here (PSB new extended mix) / If looks could kill / Sexy northerner (Superchumbo remix) / Home and dry (Blank & Jones remix) / London (Genuine piano mix). *(3xlp+=; 581458-1)* – (varied tracks).
(above issued on 'Sanctuary' US)

Nov 03. (cd-s) *(CDR 6620)* **MIRACLES / WE'RE THE PET SHOP BOYS / MIRACLES (Eric Prydz remix)** [10] [ ]
(12") *(12R 6620)* – ('A'-12" version) / ('A'-Lemon Jelly remix).
(cd-s+=) *(CDRS 6620)* – Transparent.

Nov 03. (d-cd/t-lp) *(593884-2/-1) <594837>* **POPART: THE HITS** (compilation) [30] [ ]
– Go west / Suburbia / Se a vida E (that's the way life is) / What have I done to deserve this? / Always on my mind / I wouldn't normally do this kind of thing / Home and dry / Heart / Miracles / Love comes quickly / It's a sin / Domino dancing / Before / New York City boy / It's alright / Where the streets have no name (I can't take my eyes off you) / A red letter day / Left to my own devices / I don't know what you want but I can't give it any more / Flamboyant / Being boring / Can you forgive her? / West End girls / I get along / So hard / Rent / Jealousy / DJ culture / You only tell me you love me when you're drunk / Liberation / Paninaro '95 / Opportunities (let's make lots of money) / Yesterday, when I was mad / Single – Bilingual / Somewhere. *(ltd-t-cd++; 595093-2)* – (bonus mixes).

Tom PETTY

Born: 20 Oct'52, Gainesville, Florida, USA. In 1968, he formed school band The SUNDOWNERS, who later became The EPICS. By 1971, this outfit had evolved into MUDCRUTCH which also comprised guitarists MIKE CAMPBELL, TOMMY LEADON (brother of EAGLES man BERNIE) and drummer RANDALL MARSH. Their demo tape eventually came to the attention of Denny Cordell (co-owner of 'Shelter' records with LEON RUSSELL), who was suitably impressed enough to sign the band in 1975. They released a solitary single, 'DEPOT STREET', an album's worth of material lurking in the vaults due to the band's subsequent demise. PETTY was retained by Shelter and in 1976 he instigated The HEARTBREAKERS together with CAMPBELL, keyboardist BENMONT TENCH, bassist RON BLAIR and drummer STAN LYNCH. Later that year, the band released the eponymous 'TOM PETTY & THE HEARTBREAKERS', a raw statement on the future of roots rock'n'roll (The BYRDS, BOB DYLAN and ROLLING STONES are the most frequently cited influences) which initially flopped in the States. Perversely, the album was relatively successful in the UK and Europe, PETTY and Co. capitalising on the interest with a European tour that eventually wound its way back to the US during the summer of '77. They had already hit the UK Top 40 with two classic singles, 'ANYTHING THAT'S ROCK'N'ROLL' and 'AMERICAN GIRL' and in May '78, their first US Top 40 hit, 'BREAKDOWN', was used on the movie, 'FM'. At last there was a Stateside buzz surrounding the band and two months later their second album, 'YOU'RE GONNA GET IT', hit both the US & UK Top 40. Despite the ensuing critical and commercial success, PETTY filed for bankruptcy the following year, owing more than half a million dollars after Shelter was sold to 'ABC' and then 'MCA', the latter company duly suing him for breach of contract. Fortunately, the warring parties came to an agreement when MCA decided to put his band on their Danny Bramson-run 'Backstreet' label. The late 1979 major label debut, 'DAMN THE TORPEDOES', sold only moderately in the UK, although it smashed into the US Top 3, sales of the album boosted by harder rocking tracks like 'REFUGEE' and 'DON'T DO ME LIKE THAT'. By this point PETTY was a major league star and he could afford to challenge his record company yet again, this time over the cover price of his forthcoming album, 'HARD PROMISES' (1981), which PETTY deemed too expensive. His persistence eventually won out and the album reached No.5 in the US, subsequently going platinum. The early 80's also saw PETTY hooking up with the delectable STEVIE NICKS on the 'STOP DRAGGIN' MY HEART AROUND' single (a US No.3) and producing DEL SHANNON's 'Drop Down And Get Me', with backing from The HEARTBREAKERS. Co-produced by PETTY, together with Jimmy Iovine and EURYTHMICS guitarist Dave Stewart, the acclaimed 'SOUTHERN ACCENTS' (1985) marked a newfound maturity, both lyrically and musically, the brooding 'DON'T COME AROUND HERE NO MORE' furnishing PETTY with his biggest UK hit single to date. Following a prolonged bout of touring and a further studio album, 'LET ME UP (I'VE HAD ENOUGH)', PETTY found himself in the company of rock's oldster hierarchy alongside BOB DYLAN, GEORGE HARRISON, JEFF LYNNE and ROY ORBISON in The TRAVELLING WILBURYS (who subsequently released two albums, rather confusingly titled 'TRAVELLING WILBURYS VOLUME 1' (1988) and 'TRAVELLING WILBURYS VOLUME 3' (1990). Around this time, PETTY also released his highly successful debut solo album, 'FULL MOON FEVER' (1989), with backing from a collection of HEARTBREAKERS and WILBURYS. One of his most overtly commercial outings, the record spawned the soaring 'FREE FALLIN' (a US Top 10) and contained what could be PETTY's signature tune, the defiant 'I WON'T BACK DOWN'. The album seemed to have breathed fresh life into PETTY's musical partnership with the HEARTBREAKERS and they teamed up once more for 1991's 'INTO THE GREAT WIDE OPEN', another highly melodic opus previewed by the impassioned 'LEARNING TO FLY' single. A follow-up PETTY solo set, 'WILDFLOWERS' (1994), was his first release for 'Warners', the singer having been back in the spotlight again after allegedly keeping the deal secret fom 'M.C.A.'. Much like NEIL YOUNG, PETTY remains a stubborn maverick, refusing to play record company games and staying true to his muse. Post-mid 90's PETTY once again gathered together The HEARTBREAKERS for the recording of 'SHE'S THE ONE' (1996), the soundtrack to the Ed Burns film of the same name. In the age of multi-artist, blockbusting soundtracks, PETTY's effort was something of a rarity as well as a pleasant, loose-limbed diversion from the craft and precision of his regular stuff. The record's chart placings (UK Top 40/US Top 20) confirmed that many fans simply regarded this as another – albeit slightly different – TOM PETTY album. Normal service was resumed on the harder rocking 'ECHO' (1999), Rick Rubin adding a bit of production muscle to another HEARTBREAKERS outing. Come the new millennium, PETTY and his HEARTBREAKERS sounded somewhat desperate on 'THE LAST DJ' (2002), clutching at rather bitter lyrical straws berating the worst aspects of the business which he's been an integral part of for so many years. While the record made the Top 10 in the US, it failed to register in the UK chart, the first such absence in many years. • **Covered:** SO YOU WANT TO BE A ROCK'N'ROLL STAR (Byrds) / NEEDLES AND PINS (Searchers) / FEEL A WHOLE LOT BETTER (Byrds) / SOMETHING IN THE AIR (Thunderclap Newman). • **Trivia:** PETTY made his major acting debut in 1997 via the Kevin Kostner epic, 'The Postman'; ten years earlier he made a brief appearance in 'Made In Heaven'.

Album rating: TOM PETTY & THE HEARTBREAKERS (*6) / YOU'RE GONNA GET IT (*7) / DAMN THE TORPEDOES (*8) / HARD PROMISES (*6) / LONG AFTER DARK (*5) / SOUTHERN ACCENTS (*6) / PACK UP THE PLANTATION – LIVE! (*4) / LET ME UP (I'VE HAD ENOUGH) (*5) / FULL MOON FEVER (*7) / INTO THE GREAT WIDE OPEN (*6) / GREATEST HITS compilation (*9) / WILDFLOWERS (*7) / SHE'S THE ONE (*5) / ECHO (*5) / ANTHOLOGY – THROUGH THE YEARS double compilation (*8) / THE LAST DJ (*4)

TOM PETTY AND THE HEARTBREAKERS

TOM PETTY – vocals, guitar (ex-MUDCRUTCH) / **MIKE CAMPBELL** (b. 1 Feb'54, Panama City, Florida) – guitar (ex-MUDCRUTCH) / **BELMONT TENCH** (b. 7 Sep'54, Gainesville) – keyboards (ex-MUDCRUTCH) / **RON BLAIR** (b.16 Sep'52, Macon, Georgia) – bass / **STAN LYNCH** (b.21 May'55, Gainsville) – drums

Island | Shelter

Jan 77. (7") <62006> **BREAKDOWN. / THE WILD ONE, FOREVER** [–] [ ]

Feb 77. (7") *(WIP 6377)* **AMERICAN GIRL. / THE WILD ONE, FOREVER** [ ] [–]

May 77. (lp/c) *(ILPS/ICT 5014)* <52006> **TOM PETTY AND THE HEARTBREAKERS** [24] [55]
– Rockin' around (with you) / Breakdown / Hometown blues / The wild one, forever / Anything that's rock'n'roll / Strangered in the night / Fooled again (I don't like it) / Mystery man / Luna / American girl. *(cd-iss. Jul87 on 'M.C.A.'; MCAD 37143) (re-iss. Nov90 cd/c; DMCL/MCLC 1715) (re-iss. 1991 cd/c; MCAD/MCA 10135) (re-iss. Apr92 cd/c; MCLD/MCLC 19012)*

May 77. (7") *(WIP 6377)* <62007> **AMERICAN GIRL. / FOOLED AGAIN (I DON'T LIKE IT)** [–] [ ]

Jun 77. (7"/12") *(WIP/+12 6369)* **ANYTHING THAT'S ROCK'N'ROLL. / FOOLED AGAIN (I DON'T LIKE IT)** [36] [ ]

Jul 77. (7"/12") *(WIP/+12 6403)* **AMERICAN GIRL. / LUNA** [40] [–]

Oct 77. (7") <62008> **BREAKDOWN. / FOOL AGAIN (I DON'T LIKE IT)** [–] [40]

May 78. (lp/c) *(ISA/ISC 5017)* <52029> **YOU'RE GONNA GET IT** [34] [23]
– When the time comes / You're gonna get it / Hurt / Magnolia / Too much ain't enough / I need to know / Listen to her heart / No second thoughts / Restless / Baby's a rock'n'roller. *(cd-iss. Jun88 on 'M.C.A.'; MCAD 31171) (re-iss. Apr92 cd/c; MCLD/MCLC 19013)*

Jun 78. (7"/12") *(WIP/+12 6426)* <62010> **I NEED TO KNOW. / NO SECOND THOUGHTS** [ ] [41]

Sep 78. (7"/12") *(WIP/+12 6455)* <62011> **LISTEN TO HER HEART. / I DON'T KNOW WHAT TO SAY TO YOU** [ ] [59]

M.C.A. | Backstreet

Nov 79. (lp/c) *(MCF/+C 3044)* <5105> **DAMN THE TORPEDOES** [57] [2]
– Refugee / Here comes my girl / Even the losers / Century city / Don't do me like that / Shadows of a doubt (a complex kind) / What are you doin' in my life? / Louisiana rain / You tell me. *(cd-iss. 1985; DMCA 108) (cd re-iss. Oct87; MCAD 5105) (cd re-iss. Jul88; DMCL 1872) (re-iss. Apr92 cd/c; MCLD/MCLC 19014)*

Nov 79. (7") *(MCA 539)* <41227> **HERE COMES MY GIRL. / DON'T BRING ME DOWN** [ ] Apr80 [59]
(12"+=) *(MCAT 539)* – Casa Dega.

Feb 80. (7"/7"pic-d) *(MCA/+P 559)* <41169> **REFUGEE. / IT'S RAINING AGAIN** [ ] Jan80 [15]

Jul 80. (7") *(MCA 596)* <41138> **DON'T DO ME LIKE THAT. / CENTURY CITY** [ ] Nov79 [10]
(d7"+=) *(MCAD 596)* – Somethin' else / Stories we can tell.

—— **DONALD DUNN** – bass; repl. RON BLAIR

Apr 81. (7") *(MCA 699)* <51100> **THE WAITING. / NIGHTWATCHMAN** [ ] [19]

May 81. (lp/c) *(MCF/+C 3098)* <5160> **HARD PROMISES** [32] [5]
– The waiting / A woman in love (it's not me) / Nightwatchman / Something big / King's road / Letting you go / A thing about you / Insider / The criminal kind / You can still change your mind. *(cd-iss. May86; CMCAD 31006) (cd re-iss. 1988; DIDX 344) (re-iss. Oct91 cd/c; MCLD/MCLC 19077)*

Jul 81. (7") *(MCA 730)* <51136> **A WOMAN IN LOVE (IT'S NOT ME). / GATOR ON THE LAWN** [ ] [79]

—— PETTY and his band then were credited with backing STEVIE NICKS of FLEETWOOD MAC on a single 'Stop Draggin' My Heart Around' Aug81 hit US No.3.

Jul 82. (7") *(MCA 788)* <41169> **REFUGEE. / THE INSIDER ("with STEVIE NICKS")** [ ] [ ]

—— **HOWARD EPSTEIN** (b.21 Jul'55) – bass repl. DUNN

Nov 82. (7") *(MCA 801)* <52144> **YOU GOT LUCKY. / BETWEEN TWO WORLDS** [ ] [20]

Nov 82. (lp/c) *(MCF/+C 3155)* <5360> **LONG AFTER DARK** [45] [9]
– A one story town / You got lucky / Deliver me / Change of heart / Finding out / We stand a chance / Straight into darkness / The same old you / Between two worlds / A wasted life. *(re-iss. May86; MCAD 5360) (cd re-iss. Oct87; CMCAD 31027) (re-iss. Oct90 cd/c; DMCL/MCLC 1818) (re-iss. Jun92 cd/c; MCLD/MCLC 19078)*

Dec 82. (7") *(MCA 805)* **STRAIGHT INTO DARKNESS. / HEARTBREAKERS BEACH PARTY** [ ] [–]

Apr 83. (7") *(MCA 814)* <52181> **CHANGE OF HEART. / HEARTBREAKERS BEACH PARTY** [ ] Feb83 [21]

Apr 85. (7"/12") *(MCA/+T 926)* <52496> **DON'T COME AROUND HERE NO MORE. / TRAILER** [50] Mar85 [13]

Apr 85. (lp/c) *(MCF/+C 3260)* <5486> **SOUTHERN ACCENTS** [23] [7]
– Rebels / It ain't nothin' to me / Don't come around here no more / Southern accents / Make it better (forget about me) / Spike / Dogs on the run / Mary's new car / The best of everything. *(cd-iss. 1986; MCAD 5486) (cd re-iss. Jan90; DMCL 1896) (re-iss. Nov90 cd/c; MCLD/MCLC 19079)*

Jun 85. (7") *(MCA 983)* <52605> **MAKE IT BETTER (FORGET ABOUT ME). / CRACKING UP** [ ] [54]
(12") *(MCAT 983)* – ('A'side) / ('A'instrumental).

Aug 85. (7") <52658> **REBELS. / SOUTHERN ACCENTS (live)** [–] [74]

Jan 86. (d-lp/d-c) *(MCMD/+C 7001)* *<8021>* **PACK UP THE PLANTATION (live)** [ ] Dec85 [22]
– So you want to be a rock'n'roll star / Needles and pins / The waiting / Breakdown / American girl / It ain't nothin' to me / Insider / Rockin' around (with you) / Refugee / I need to know * / Southern accents / Rebels / Don't bring me down / You got lucky * / Shout / The stories we can tell. *(cd-iss. Oct87; MCAD 8021)* – (omits *) *(re-iss. Nov91 cd/c; MCLD/MCLC 19142)*

Jan 86. (7") *<52772>* **NEEDLES AND PINS (live). / SPIKE (live)** [–] [37]

Feb 86. (7") *(MCA 1028)* **SO WANT TO BE A ROCK'N'ROLL STAR (live). / AMERICAN GIRL (live)** [ ] [–]
(12"+=) *(MCAT 1028)* – Spike (live).

Aug 86. (7"/12"; BOB DYLAN & THE HEARTBREAKERS) *(MCA/+T 1076)* **BAND OF THE HAND. / THEME FROM 'JOE'S DEATH'** [ ] [–]

Apr 87. (7") *(MCA 1148)* *<53065>* **JAMMIN' ME. / LET ME UP (I'VE HAD ENOUGH)** [ ] [18]
(12"+=) *(MCAT 1148)* – Make that connection.

Apr 87. (lp/c/cd) *(MCG/MCGC/DMCG 6014)* *<5836>* **LET ME UP (I'VE HAD ENOUGH)** [59] [20]
– Jammin' me / Runaway trains / The damage you've done / It'll all work out / My life – Your world / Think about me / All mixed up / A self made man / Ain't love strange / How many more days / Let me up (I've had enough). *(cd re-iss. Aug90; DMCL 1905) (re-iss. Nov92 cd/c; MCLD/MCLC 19141)*

Sep 87. (7") *(MCA 1190)* *<53153>* **ALL MIXED UP. / LET ME UP (I'VE HAD ENOUGH)** [ ] [ ]
(12"+=) *(MCAT 1190)* – Little bit of soul.

Nov 87. (7") *(MCA 1217)* **THINK ABOUT ME. / MY LIFE – YOUR WORLD** [ ] [–]
(12"+=) *(MCAT 1217)* – The damage you've done.

In 1988, before he went solo, TOM PETTY teamed up with BOB DYLAN, GEORGE HARRISON, JEFF LYNNE and ROY ORBISON in The TRAVELING WILBURYS

TOM PETTY

solo with **JEFF LYNNE** – guitar, bass keyboards, vocals, co-writer / **MIKE CAMPBELL** – guitar, bass mandolin, keyboards, co-writer / **PHIL JONES** – drums, percussion / +guests **GEORGE HARRISON, ROY ORBISON, BENMONT TENCH, JIM KELTNER, HOWIE EPSTIEN, KELSEY CAMPBELL.**

M.C.A. M.C.A.

Apr 89. (7") *(MCA 1334)* *<53369>* **I WON'T BACK DOWN. / THE APARTMENT SONG** [28] [12]
(12"+=/cd-s+=) *(MCAT/DMCAX 1334)* – Don't treat me like a stranger.

Jun 89. (lp/c/cd) *(MCG/MCG/DMCG 6034)* *<6253>* **FULL MOON FEVER** [8] May89 [3]
– Free fallin' / I won't back down / Love is a long road / A face in the crowd / Runnin' down a dream / Feel a whole lot better / Yer so bad / Depending on you / The apartment song / Alright for now / A mind with a heart of it's own / Zombie zoo. *(cd re-iss. Dec98 on 'Mobile Fidelity'; UDCD 735)*

Aug 89. (7"/c-s) *(MCA/+C 1359)* *<53682>* **RUNNIN' DOWN A DREAM. / ALRIGHT FOR NOW** [55] Jul89 [23]
(12"+=/cd-s+=) *(MCAT/DMCAX 1359)* – Down the line.

Nov 89. (7") *<53748>* **FREE FALLIN'. / DOWN THE LINE** [–] [7]

Nov 89. (7") *(MCA 1381)* **FREE FALLIN'. / LOVE IS A LONG ROAD** [64] [–]
(12"+=/cd-s+=) *(MCAT/DMCAX 1381)* – ('A'live version).

Feb 90. (7"/c-s) *<79030><53833>* **YER SO BAD. / LOVE IS A LONG ROAD** [–] [ ]

Feb 90. (7") *(MCA 1428)* **YER SO BAD. / A MIND WITH A HEART OF IT'S OWN** [ ] [–]
(12"+=/cd-s+=) *(MCAT/DMCAT 1428)* – Free fallin' (live).

Jul 90. (7") *(MCA 1449)* *<53781>* **A FACE IN THE CROWD. / A MIND WITH A HEART OF IT'S OWN** [ ] Feb90 [46]
(12"+=/cd-s+=) *(MCAT/DMCAT 1449)* – Refugee (live) / So you want to be a rock'n'roll star (live).

TOM PETTY AND THE HEARTBREAKERS

—— (originals reformed)

M.C.A. M.C.A.

Jun 91. (7"/c-s) *(MCS/+CS 1555)* *<54124>* **LEARNING TO FLY. / TOO GOOD TO BE TRUE** [46] [28]
(12"/cd-=) *(MCST/+D 1555)* – ('A'side) / Baby's a rock'n'roller / I need to know.

Jul 91. (lp/c/cd) *<(MCA/+C/D 10317)>* **INTO THE GREAT WIDE OPEN** [3] [13]
– Learning to fly / Into the great wide open / Two gunslingers / The dark of the Sun / All or nothin' / All the wrong reasons / Too good to be true / Out in the cold / You and I will meet again / Makin' some noise / Built to last.

Aug 91. (7"/c-s) *(MCS/+C 1570)* *<54131>* **INTO THE GREAT WIDE OPEN. / MAKIN' SOME NOISE** [ ] Oct91 [92]
(cd-s+=) *(MSCTD 1570)* – Strangered in the night / Listen to her heart.

Jan 92. (7"/c-s) *(MCS/+C 1610)* **KING'S HIGHWAY. / LEARNING TO FLY** [ ] [–]
(cd-s+=) *(MCSTD 1610)* – Into the great wide open / I won't back down.

Jan 92. (c-s) *<54357>* **KING'S HIGHWAY / ALL OR NOTHIN'** [–] [ ]

Mar 92. (7"/c-s) *(MCS/+CS 1616)* **TOO GOOD TO BE TRUE. / THE DARK SIDE OF THE SUN** [34] [–]
(cd-s+=) *(MCSTD 1616)* – Hurt / Don't come around here no more.
(cd-s+=) *(MCSXD 1616)* – Psychotic reaction / I'm tired / Lonely.

May 92. (cd-s) *<54436>* **PEACE IN L.A. / (peace mix)** [–] [ ]

Oct 93. (7"/c-s) *(MCS/+CS 1945)* **SOMETHING IN THE AIR. / THE WAITING** [53] [–]
(cd-s+=) *(MCSTD 1945)* – American girl.

Nov 93. (cd/c/lp) *(MCD/MCC/MCA 10964)* *<10813>* **GREATEST HITS** (compilation) [10] [8]
– American girl / Breakdown / Anything that's rock'n'roll / Listen to her heart / I need to know / Refugee / Don't do me like that / Even the losers / Here comes my girl / The waiting / You got lucky / Don't come around here no more / I won't back down / Runnin' down a dream / Free fallin' / Learning to fly / Into the great wide open / Mary Jane's last dance / Something in the air.

Dec 93. (c-s,cd-s) *<54732>* **MARY JANE'S LAST DANCE / THE WAITING** [–] [14]

Feb 94. (c-s) *(MCSCS 1966)* **MARY JANE'S LAST DANCE / KING'S HIGHWAY (live)** [52] [–]
(cd-s+=) *(MCSTD 1966)* – Make that connection (live) / Take out some insurance (live).
(cd-s) *(MCSXD 1966)* – ('A'side) / Casa dega / Gator on the lawn / Down the line.

TOM PETTY

—— with backing from HEARTBREAKERS, plus **STEVE FERRONE** – drums (ex-AVERAGE WHITE BAND, etc) repl. LYNCH

Warners Warners

Oct 94. (c-s) *(W 0272C)* *<18030>* **YOU DON'T KNOW HOW IT FEELS / GIRL ON L.S.D.** [ ] [ ]
(cd-s+=) *(W 0272CD)* – House in the woods.

Nov 94. (c-s,cd-s) *<18030>* **YOU DON'T KNOW HOW IT FEELS / GIRL ON L.S.D.** [–] [13]

Nov 94. (cd/c/lp) *<(9362 45792-2/-4/-1)>* **WILDFLOWERS** [36] [8]
– Wildflowers / You don't know how it feels / Time to move on / You wreck me / It's good to be king / Only a broken heart / Honey bee / Don't fade on me hard on me / Cabin down below / To find a friend / A higher place / House in the woods / Crawling back to you / Wake up time.

Feb 95. (c-s) *(W 0283C)* **YOU WRECK ME / CABIN DOWN BELOW (acoustic)** [ ] [–]
(cd-s+=) *(W 0283CD)* – Only a broken heart.

Apr 95. (c-s,cd-s) *<17925>* **IT'S GOOD TO BE KING / CABIN DOWN BELOW (acoustic)** [–] [68]

Aug 95. (c-s/cd-s) *<18026>* **A HIGHER PLACE / ONLY A BROKEN HEART (acoustic)** [–] [ ]

TOM PETTY AND THE HEARTBREAKERS

Aug 96. (cd/c) *<(9362 46285-2/-4)>* **SHE'S THE ONE (original soundtrack)** [37] [15]
– Walls (circus) / Grew up fast / Zero from outer space / Climb that hill / Change the locks / Angel dream (No.4) / Hope you never / Asshole / Supernatural radio / California / Hope on board / Walls (No.3) / Angel dream (No.2) / Hung up and overdue / Airport.

Sep 96. (c-s,cd-s) *<17593>* **WALLS / WALLS (No.3 version)** [–] [69]

Mar 97. (c-s) *(W 0371C)* **WALLS (CIRCUS) / HUNG UP AND OVERDUE** [ ] [–]
(cd-s+=) *(W 0371CD)* – Walls (No.3 version).

—— now a quartet

Apr 99. (cd/c) *<(9362 47294-2/-4)>* **ECHO** [43] [10]
– Room at the top / Swingin' / Counting on you / Free girl now / Lonesome sundown / Accused of love / Echo / Won't last long /

Billy the kid / I don't wanna fight / This one's for me / No more / About to give out / Rhino skin / One more day, one more night.

Nov 02. (cd) <(9362 47955-2)> **THE LAST DJ** [ ] Oct02 [9]
– The last DJ / Money becomes king / Dreamville / Joe / When a kid goes bad / Like a diamond / Lost children / Blue Sunday / You and me / The man who loves women / Have love will travel / Can't stop the sun.

– compilations, others, etc. –

on 'M.C.A.' unless mentioned otherwise

Sep 84. (d-c) *(MCA2 105)* **DAMN THE TORPEDOES. / HARD PROMISES** [ ] [–]

Apr 86. (12"ep) *(MCAT 1047)* **REFUGEE / DON'T DO ME LIKE THAT. / HERE COMES MY GIRL / THE WAITING** [ ] [–]

Nov 95. (6xcd-box) *(MCAD 611375)* **PLAYBACK** [ ] [ ]

Jun 01. (d-cd) <(170177-2)> **THROUGH THE YEARS – ANTHOLOGY** [14] Nov00 [ ]
– Breakdown / American girl / Hometown blues / The wild one, forever / I need to know / Listen to her heart / Too much ain't enough / Refugee / Here comes my girl / Don't do me like that / Even the losers / The waiting / Woman in love (it's not me) / Stop draggin' my heart around (with STEVIE NICKS) / You got lucky / Straight into darkness / Change of heart // Rebels / Don't come around here no more / The best of everything / So want to be a rock'n'roll star (live) / Jammin' me / It'll all work out / Love is a long road / Free fallin' / Yer so bad / I won't back down / Runnin' down a dream / Learning to fly / Into the great wide open / Two gunslingers / Mary Jane's last dance / Waiting on tonight / Surrender.

Apr 02. (cd) *TRaditional Line; <(TL 1338)>* **LIVE IN OAKLAND (live)** [ ] [ ]

Liz PHAIR

Born: 17 Apr'67, New Haven, Connecticut, USA. Chicago based, USA. After graduating in Art History, PHAIR concentrated full-time on her songwriting and, with the help of friend/COME guitarist, CHRIS BROKAW, eventually secured a contract with indie label, 'Matador' early in 1992. Hooking up with musicians BRAD WOOD, CASEY RICE and LEROY BACH, PHAIR translated her song sketches into a marathon double album, 'EXILE ON GUYVILLE', its title a typically PHAIR-esque play on the classic 'STONES album. An engagingly eclectic, often brazenly confessional affair, PHAIR had fashioned a folk-grunge mini-classic, fusing wry life-in-America / hard-hitting sexual lyrics with beautiful country harmonies in a similar vein to MAZZY STAR or THROWING MUSES. Critics loved it and in addition to the gushing reviews, PHAIR became the first woman since JONI MITCHELL (in 1974) to win the prestigious 'Village Voice' annual award. The sonic femme-thrust of 'SUPERNOVA' previewed follow-up, 'WHIP-SMART' (1994), a record that surprisingly received a less than enthusiastic response in comparison to its predecessor. While the album may have lacked a little of the debut's wayward charm, the songs were more focused and PHAIR's muse was as fertile, and occasionally as candid as ever (even if her much talked about stage-fright might've belied the bolshy, sexually liberated persona her music projected). While 1995 saw the release of a stop-gap odds'n'sods collection, 'JUVENILIA' (1995), it would be another three years before another studio set, 'WHITECHOCOLATESPACEEGG' (1998). Reaching the Top 40 in America, the album was once again the toast of the Rolling Stone readers, although her Lo-Fi ramblings sounded a tad similar to BELLY or even SLEATER-KINNEY for the more discerning Brits.

Album rating: EXILE IN GUYVILLE (*7) / WHIP-SMART (*8) / JUVENILIA compilation (*4) / WHITECHOCOLATESPACEEGG (*6)

LIZ PHAIR – vocals, guitar / **BRAD WOOD** – drums, percussion / **CASEY RICE** – guitar / **LEROY BACH** – bass

Minty Fresh / not iss.

Aug 93. (7") *(MF 4)* **CANARY. / CARNIVORE** [ ] [–]

Matador / Matador

Aug 93. (cd/c/lp) <(OLE 051-2/-4/-1)> **EXILE IN GUYVILLE** [ ] Jun93 [ ]
– 6'1" / Help me Mary / Glory / Dance of the seven veils / Never said / Soap star Joe / Explain it to me / Canary / Mesmerizing / Fuck and run / Girls! girls! girls! / Divorce song / Shatter / Flower / Johnny Sunshine / Gunshy / Stratford-On-Guy / Strange loop.

Sep 94. (7") <(OLE 103-7)> <98206> **SUPERNOVA. / COMBO PLATTER** [ ] Jul94 [78]

Atlantic / Atlantic

Sep 94. (cd/c/lp) <(7567 92429-2/-4/-1)><OLE 107> **WHIP-SMART** [ ] [27]
– Chopsticks / Supernova / Support system / X-ray man / Shane / Nashville / Go west / Cince de Mayo / Dogs of L.A. / Whip-smart / Jealousy / Crater lake / Alice Springs / May queen.

Oct 94. (7"/c-s) *(A 8224/+C)* **SUPERNOVA. / X-RAY MAN (remix)** [ ] [–]
(12"+=/cd-s+=) *(A 8224 T/CD)* – ('A'-clean version).

Matador – Capitol / Matador – Capitol

Aug 98. (cd/c/lp) <(OLE 191 – 7243 8 53554-2/-4/-1)> **WHITECHOCOLATESPACEEGG** [ ] [35]
– White chocolate space egg / Big tall man / Perfect world / Johnny Feelgood / Polyester bride / Love is nothing / Baby got going / Uncle Alvarez / Only son / Go on ahead / Headache / Ride / What makes you happy / Fantasize / Shitloads of money / Girls' room.

– compilations, etc. –

Aug 95. (d7"ep/cd-ep) *Matador; <(OLE 129-7/-2)>* **JUVENILIA** [ ] [ ]
– Jealousy / Turning Japanese / Animal girl / California / South Dakota / Batmobile / Dead shark / Easy.

PHISH

Formed: Burlington, Vermont, USA ... 1983 by TREY ANASTASIO, JON FISHMAN and GORDON while they were students at the local university. Following the addition of PAGE McCONNELL, the band began touring in earnest, playing gigs across the States and in the process building up a grassroots fanbase and a reputation gained largely by word of mouth. Not since the heady days of the 70's have a band become so huge by dint of sheer hard graft and a resolutely "authentic" sound, proving that even in these days of 99p single giveaways, record company marketing muscle isn't everything. An archetypal 'Great American Band', PHISH have undoubtedly tapped into the same constituency of MOR-friendly, liberal/hippy Americans who once followed (and probably still do) the GRATEFUL DEAD and now dig HOOTIE & THE BLOWFISH. It is for exactly this reason that despite being honoured with the obligatory Ben & Jerry's ice cream flavour in the States, PHISH will probably only ever attract a minority audience in Britain. Still, BLIND MELON proved at least a one-hit wonder was possible and with their first two independently released albums, 'JUNTA' (1988) and 'LAWN BOY' (1990), PHISH explored elements of blues, jazz, funk and rock in a similarly improvisational spirit to The SPIN DOCTORS , BLUES TRAVELER etc. In fact, PHISH actually toured with these bands under the banner of HORDE (Horizon Of Rock Developing Everywhere)(!?), some sharp-witted Stateside critic memorably dubbing this lot the "Living Dead" in honour of their interminable jam sessions. Packing out venues in almost every State, it was only a matter of time before the band were picked up by a major, 'Elektra' winning out and releasing 1992's 'A PICTURE OF NECTAR' set. 'RIFT' (1993) was PHISH's first major chart entry, the band reigning in their more wayward musical tendencies and even securing radio play for a couple of tracks from 1994's '(HOIST)' album. In the true spirit of JERRY GARCIA & Co, 1995 saw PHISH releasing that most reviled of rock artefacts, a double live album. The mellow, ALLMANS-esque 'FREE' incredibly remains the band's only bonafide single release, one of the stand-out tracks from 1997's 'BILLY BREATHES' album, a US Top 10 and their most successful to date. Now something of an American institution, PHISH seem to have effortlessly navigated the shark-infested waters of the US music business without compromising their original vision, 'SLIP STITCH AND PASS' (1997) and 'THE STORY OF THE GHOST' (1998) finding them swimming as freely as ever. Forget the double live album, PHISH went for nothing less than a live boxed set with 'HAMPTON COMES ALIVE' (1999), a sprawling multi-disc affair that conceivably went a long way to replicating the scope and intensity of their concert experience. Perhaps this was a ploy to placate diehard fans before the release of 'FARMHOUSE' (2000), a record that – as its title might've suggested – veered closer to the dusty paths of country rock than exploratory jams, with an engaging and very welcome focus on songwriting over instrumental flair. Amid a lengthy break, PHISH fans could content themselves with an extensive series of live releases, all of which, incredibly, cracked the US Top 200. The band returned in late 2002 with 'ROUND ROOM', back to noodling, perambulating business after the focused, easy grace of the preceding album. Not that they seemed much concerned about it, content to jam on song fragments rather than songs themselves. Much more interesting had been TREY ANASTASIO's eponymous solo debut (although he'd previously masterminded 1996's free jazz "supergroup" effort, 'SURRENDER TO THE AIR' alongside the likes of SUN RA alumni MARSHALL ALLEN and experimental guitarist MARC RIBOT) released earlier that year on 'Elektra'. With its complex, elastic grooves glued firmly in place by more discernible arrangements and a slick pop sheen, the record was an another giddy achievement in his extended PHISH layoff, ranking alongside his work with OYSTERHEAD (a trio of ANASTASIO, LES CLAYPOOL and STUART COPELAND) and generating the kind of kinetic momentum which made 2003's live 'PLASMA' so compelling. • **Covers:** BOOGIE ON REGGAE WOMAN (Stevie Wonder) / TUBTHUMPING (Chumbawamba) / SABOTAGE (Beastie Boys) / CRY BABY CRY (Beatles) / FUNKY BITCH (Son Seals) / QUINN THE ESKIMO (Bob Dylan) / WALK AWAY (James Gang) / CITIES + CROSSEYED AND PAINLESS (Talking Heads) / 2001 (Deodato) / POSSUM (. . . Holdsworth) / NELLIE KANE (. . . O'Brien) / BOLD AS LOVE + FIRE (Jimi Hendrix) / LOVING CUP (Rolling Stones) / FRANKENSTEIN (Edgar Winter Group) / ALBUQUERQUE (Neil Young) / DROWNED (Who) / TIMBER (Josh White) / HALLEY'S COMET (. . . Wright) / MY SOUL (. . . Chernier) / WIPEOUT (Ventures) / ROCK AND ROLL (Velvet Underground) / YA MAR (Mustangs) / MIRROR IN THE BATHROOM (Beat) / OLD HOME PLACE (Jayne / Webb) / WHEN THE CIRCUS COMES (Los Lobos) / BACK AT THE CHICKEN SHACK (Jimmy Smith) / LA GRANGE (ZZ Top) / DONNA LEE (Charlie Parker) / JOHNNY B. GOODE (Chuck Berry) / OVER THE RAINBOW (Arlen-Harberg) / "THE WHITE ALBUM" (Beatles) / etc.

Album rating: JUNTA (*6) / LAWN BOY (*6) / A PICTURE OF NECTAR (*6) / RIFT (*6) / (HOIST) (*6) / A LIVE ONE (*7) / STASH compilation (*7) / BILLY BREATHES (*8) / SLIP STITCH AND PASS (*7) / THE STORY OF THE GHOST (*7) / HAMPTON COMES ALIVE (*5) / FARMHOUSE (*6) / ROUND ROOM (*4) / Trey Anastasio: SURRENDER TO THE AIR (*5) / ONE MAN'S TRASH (*3) / TRAMPLED BY LAMBS AND PECKED BY THE DOVES (*3) / TREY ANASTASIO (*7) / PLASMA (*6)

TREY ANASTASIO (b. ERNEST GUISEPPE ANASTASIO III, 1964) – vocals, guitar / **JON FISHMAN** – drums, vocals / **MIKE GORDON** – bass, vocals / **PAGE McCONNELL** – keyboards, vocals

not iss. — own label

1988. (lp) **JUNTA** [–] [ ]
– Fee / You enjoy myself / Esther / Golgi apparatus / Foam / Dinner and a movie / Divided sky / David Bowie / Fluffhead / Fluff's travels / Contact. *<US d-cd-iss. Dec97 on 'Elektra'+=; 61413-2>* – Union federal / Sanity / Icculus.

Absolute A-Go-Go — Absolute A-Go-Go

Sep 90. (lp/c/cd) *<(AGO 1992/+MC/CD)>* **LAWN BOY** [ ] [ ]
– Squirming coil / Reba / My sweet one / Split open and melt / Oh kee pa ceremony / Bathtub gin / Run like an antelope / Lawn boy / Bouncing around the room. *<(cd re-iss. Jun97 on 'Elektra'; 7559 61273-2)>*

Elektra — Elektra

May 92. (cd/c) *<(7559 61274-2/-4)>* **A PICTURE OF NECTAR** [ ] [ ]
– Llama / Eliza / Cavern / Poor heart / Stash / Manteca / Guelah papyrus / Magilla / Landlady / Glide / Tweezer / The mango song / Chalk dust torture / Faht / Catapult / Tweezer (reprise). *(cd re-iss. Jun97; same)*

Feb 93. (cd/c) *<7559 61433-2>* **RIFT** [–] [51]
– All things reconsidered / It's ice / Silent in the morning / Sparkle / Horn, Weigh / The wedge / Mound / My friend, my friend / Rift / Maze / Lengthwise / The horse / Fast enough for you. *(UK cd-iss Jun97; same)*

Mar 94. (cd/c) *<7559 61628-2/-4>* **(HOIST)** [–] [34]
– Julius / Down with disease / If I could / Riker's mailbox / Axill (part 2) / Lifeboy / Sample in a jar / Wolfman's brother / Scent of a mule / Dog faced boy / Demand. *(UK cd-iss. Jun97; same)*

Jul 95. (d-cd) *<7559 61772-2>* **A LIVE ONE (live)** [–] [18]
– Bouncing around the room / Harry Hood / Chalk dust torture / You enjoy myself / Tweezer / Wilson / Stash / Squirming coil / Slave to the traffic light / Simple / Montana / Gumbo.

Jul 96. (cd) *<(7559 61933-2)>* **STASH** (compilation) [ ] [ ]
– Stash / Scent of a mule / Maze / Bouncing around the moon / Gumbo / Sample in a jar / Split open and melt / Fast enough for you / Down with disease / You enjoy myself / If I could.

Feb 97. (cd/c) *<(7559 61971-2/-4)>* **BILLY BREATHES** [ ] Oct96 [7]
– Free / Character zero / Waste / Taste / Cars trucks buses / Talk / Theme from the bottom / Train song / Bliss / Billy breathes / Swept away / Steep / Prince Caspian.

Mar 97. (c-s) *(A 4205C)* **FREE / STRANGE DESIGN** [ ] [ ]
(cd-s+=) *(A 4205CD)* – Theme from the bottom.

Oct 97. (cd/c) *<(7559 62121-2/-4)>* **SLIP STITCH AND PASS** [ ] [17]
– Cities / Wolfman's brother / Jesus just left Chicago / Weigh / Mike's song / Lawn boy / Weekapaug groove / Hello my baby / Taste.

Nov 98. (cd) *<(7559 62297-2)>* **THE STORY OF THE GHOST** [ ] [8]
– The ghost / Birds of a feather / Meat / Guyute / Fikus / Shafty / Limb by limb / Frankie says / Brian and Robert / Water in the sky / Roggae / Wading in the velvet sea / Moma dance / End of session.

Mar 00. (6xcd-box) *<(7559 62495-2)>* **HAMPTON COMES ALIVE (live 20th November, 1998)** [ ] Dec99 [ ]
– Rock and roll part 2 / Tube / Quinn the eskimo / Funky bitch / Guelah papyrus / Rift / Meat / Stash / Train song / Possum / Roggae / Driver / Split open and melt / Bathtub gin / Piper / Axilla / Roses are free / Farmhouse / Gettin' jiggy with it / Harry hood / Character zero / Cavern / Wilson / Big black furry creature from Mars / Lawn boy / Divided sky / Cry baby cry / Boogie on reggae woman / Nicu / Dogs stole things / Nellie Kane / Foam / Wading in the velvet sea / Guyute / Bold as love / Sabotage / Mike's song / Simple / The wedge / The mango song / Free / Ha ha ha / Free / Weekapaug groove / Tubthumping.

Jun 00. (cd/c) *<(7559 62521-2/-4)>* **FARMHOUSE** [ ] May00 [12]
– Farmhouse / Twist / Bug / Back on the train / Heavy things / Gotta jibboo / Dirt / Piper / Sleep / The inlaw Josie Wales / Sand / First tube.

Jan 03. (cd) *<(7559 62850-2)>* **ROUND ROOM** [ ] Dec02 [46]
– Pebbles and marbles / Anything but me / Round room / Mexican cousin / Friday / Seven below / Mock song / 46 days / All of these dreams / Walls of the cave / Thunderhead / Waves.

– compilations, etc. –

on 'Elektra' unless mentioned otherwise

Sep 01. (d-cd) *<EA 62702>* **LIVE PHISH 01** (Broome County Arena, Binghampton, New York – 12.14.94) [–] [97]

Sep 01. (d-cd) *<EA 62703>* **LIVE PHISH 02** (Sugarbush Summerstage, North Fayston, Vermont – 7.16.94) [–] [93]

Sep 01. (d-cd) *<EA 62704>* **LIVE PHISH 03** (Darien Lake Arts Center, Darien Center, New York – 9.14.00) [–] [ ]

Sep 01. (d-cd) *<EA 62705>* **LIVE PHISH 04** (Drum Logos, Fukuoka, Japan – 6.14.00) [–] [ ]

Sep 01. (d-cd) *<EA 62706>* **LIVE PHISH 05** (Alpine Valley Music Theater, East Troy, Wisconsin – 7.8.00) [–] [ ]

Oct 01. (d-cd) *<EA 62707>* **LIVE PHISH 06** (The Centrum, Worcester, Massachusetts – 11.27.98) [–] [ ]
Apr 02. (t-cd) *<EA 62751>* **LIVE PHISH 07** (World Music Theatre, Tinley Park, Illinois, 14.8.99) [–] [ ]
Apr 02. (d-cd) *<EA 62752>* **LIVE PHISH 08** (E Centre, Camden, New Jersey – 7.10.99) [–] [ ]
Apr 02. (t-cd) *<EA 62753>* **LIVE PHISH 09** (Townshend Family Park, Townshend, Vermont – 8.26.89) [–] [ ]
Apr 02. (t-cd) *<EA 62754>* **LIVE PHISH 10** (Veterans Memorial Auditorium, Columbus, Ohio – 6.22.94) [–] [ ]
Apr 02. (t-cd) *<EA 62755>* **LIVE PHISH 11** (McNichols Sports Arena, Denver, Colorado – 11.17.97) [–] [ ]
Apr 02. (t-cd) *<EA 62756>* **LIVE PHISH 12** (Deer Creek Music Center, Noblesville, Indiana – 8.13.96) [–] [ ]
Oct 02. (t-cd) *<EA 62806>* **LIVE PHISH 13** (Glen Falls Civic Center, Glens Fall, New York – 10.31.94) [–] [ ]
Oct 02. (t-cd) *<EA 62807>* **LIVE PHISH 14** (Rosemont Horizon, Rosemont, Illinois – 10.31.95) [–] [ ]
Oct 02. (t-cd) *<EA 62808>* **LIVE PHISH 15** (The Omni, Atlanta, Georgia – 10.31.98) [–] [ ]
Oct 02. (t-cd) *<EA 62809>* **LIVE PHISH 16** (Thomas & Mack Center, Las Vegas, Nevada – 10.31.98) [–] [ ]
May 03. (t-cd) *<EA 62868>* **LIVE PHISH 17** [–] [ ]
May 03. (t-cd) *<EA 62867>* **LIVE PHISH 18** [–] [ ]
May 03. (t-cd) *<EA 62868>* **LIVE PHISH 19** [–] [ ]
May 03. (t-cd) *<EA 62869>* **LIVE PHISH 20** [–] [ ]

TREY ANASTASIO

1996. (cd) *Elektra;* **SURRENDER TO THE AIR** [–] [ ]
1998. (cd) *P.D.; <1001>* **ONE MAN'S TRASH** [–] [ ]
2000. (cd; as TREY ANASTASIO & TOM MARSHALL) *P.D.; <1003>* **TRAMPLED BY LAMBS AND PECKED BY THE DOVES** [–] [ ]

not iss. Elektra

Apr 02. (cd) *<62749>* **TREY ANASTASIO** [–] [45]
– Alive again / Cayman review / Push on 'til the day / Night speaks to a woman / Flock of words / Money, love and change / Drifting / At the gazebo / Mr. Completely / Ray dawn balloon / Last tube / Ether Sunday.
Apr 03. (cd) *<62867>* **PLASMA (live)** [–] [ ]
– Curlew's call / Plasma / Magilla / When / Mozambique / Every story ends in stone / Small axe / First tube / Night speaks to a woman / Simple twist up Dave / Inner tube / Sand.

Wilson PICKETT

Born: 18 Mar'41, Prattville, Alabama, USA. Moving to Detroit with his family when still in his teens, PICKETT initially honed his vocal chops in a gospel act before joining The FALCONS. Comprising MACK RICE and EDDIE FLOYD amongst others, this R&B act were already famous for their US Top 20 hit, 'YOU'RE SO FINE'; with PICKETT on vocals, they scraped a further Top 75 in summer '62 with 'I FOUND A LOVE'. The singer subsequently went solo and after a one-off single on the 'Cub' label, signed to LLOYD PRICE's 'Double L' imprint. There, he scored a trio of respectable PRICE-penned R&B hits which also made their way into the lower regions of the pop chart, yet it took a deal with soul giant 'Atlantic' to see the 'wicked' PICKETT really earn his famous nickname. Although his first two singles for the company were unequivocal flops, producer JERRY WEXLER duly directed him to the 'Stax' studios in Memphis where he hooked up with house band BOOKER T & THE MG's. In summer '65, he emerged with 'IN THE MIDNIGHT HOUR' (written with ace MG's guitarist STEVE CROPPER), netting him his first major US chart hit (UK Top 20 a few months later). As well as unleashing his super-stud nails'n'whisky growl, this sweaty, shuffling, groin-grinding classic also assured PICKETT a place in soul history. The man's feral, dancefloor-rooted style was based on some of the MG's tightest ever playing, engendering a series of vital US (and to a lesser extent, UK) hits: '634-5789 (SOULSVILLE, U.S.A.)', 'LAND OF 1000 DANCES', 'MUSTANG SALLY', 'FUNKY BROADWAY' etc. In 1968, PICKETT found a kindred spirit in BOBBY WOMACK whose 'I'M A MIDNIGHT MOVER' he took into the Top 30 and who would continue to be a source of inspiration for him. He also worked with DUANE ALLMAN on an unlikely cover of The Beatles' 'HEY JUDE' (the album of the same name even saw him running through Steppenwolf's 'BORN TO BE WILD'!), one of the PICKETT's biggest UK hits (Top 20). An even more unlikely cover of The Archies' 'SUGAR SUGAR' suggested that he was running out of ideas; a temporary solution came in the form of rising Philly production prodigies, GAMBLE & HUFF, with whom he recorded 1970's 'WILSON PICKETT IN PHILADELPHIA' album. The record's 'ENGINE No.9' hit the Top 20 as did further early 70's G&H productions, 'DON'T KNOCK MY LOVE' and 'DON'T LET THE GREEN GRASS FOOL YOU'. These efforts marked his last stand as a major-league artist and amid the usual succession of label changes and personal problems (infamous for his volatile off-stage temperament and heavy drinking bouts, he was arrested on 21st November '74 for threatening behaviour with a gun), PICKETT made a living on the supper club cabaret circuit. He did, however, hit the charts one more time (in '87) with the obligatory remix of 'IN THE MIDNIGHT HOUR'. The 90's, meanwhile, saw him give up recording completely; the man's alcohol problem brought tragedy in 1993 when he was found guilty of knocking down and killing a pensioner while drink driving, receiving a one year jail sentence. PICKETT returned to the recording front in 1999 with the tellingly titled 'IT'S HARDER NOW'. • **Covered:** LAND OF A 1000 DANCES (c. Chris Kenner) / MUSTANG SALLY (Mack Rice; of The Falcons) / EVERYBODY NEEDS SOMEBODY TO LOVE (Solomon Burke) / FUNKY BROADWAY (Dyke & The Blazers) / STAG-O-LEE (Lloyd Price) / HEY JOE (Jimi Hendrix) / YOU KEEP ME HANGIN' ON (Supremes) / FIRE AND WATER (Free) / MAMA TOLD ME NOT TO COME (Randy Newman) / etc.

Best CD compilation: A MAN AND A HALF: THE BEST OF . . . (*8)

WILSON PICKETT – vocals (with session people)

not iss. Lupine

1962. (7") *<003>* **ANNA. / YOU'RE ON MY MIND** [–] [ ]

not iss. Cub

1963. (7") *<9113>* **MY HEART BELONGS TO YOU. / LET ME BE YOUR BOY** [–] [ ]
<re-iss. 1963 on 'Correctone'; 501>

Liberty Double L

May 63. (7") *<713>* **IF YOU NEED ME. / BABY CALL ON ME** [–] [64]
Aug 63. (7") *(LIB 10115) <717>* **IT'S TOO LATE. / I'M GONNA LOVE YOU** [ ] Jul63 [49]
Oct 63. (7") *<724>* **I'M DOWN TO MY LAST HEARTBREAK. / I CAN'T STOP** [–] [95]

Atlantic Atlantic

1964. (7") *<2233>* **I'M GONNA CRY. / FOR BETTER OR WORSE** [–] [ ]
1964. (7") *<2271>* **COME HOME BABY. / TAKE A LITTLE LOVE** [–] [ ]
Sep 65. (7") *(AT 4036) <2289>* **IN THE MIDNIGHT HOUR. / I'M NOT TIRED** [12] Jul65 [21]
Nov 65. (7") *(AT 4052) <2306>* **DON'T FIGHT IT. / IT'S ALL OVER** [29] [53]
Dec 65. (lp) *(ATL 5037) <SD 8114>* **IN THE MIDNIGHT HOUR** [ ] Oct65 [ ]
– In the midnight hour / Teardrops will fall / Take a little love / For better or worse / I found a love / That;s a man's way / I'm gonna cry / Don't fight it / Take this love I've got / Come home baby / I'm not tired / Let's kiss and make up. *(cd-iss Aug93 on 'Rhino'; 8122 71275-2)*

Feb 66. (7") *(AT 4072)* *<2320>* **634-5789 (SOULSVILLE, U.S.A.). / THAT'S A MAN'S WAY** [36] Jan66 [13]

Jun 66. (7") *(584 023)* *<2334>* **NINETY-NINE AND A HALF (WON'T DO). / DANGER ZONE** [ ] May66 [53]

Aug 66. (7") *(584 039)* *<2348>* **LAND OF A 1000 DANCES. / YOU'RE SO FINE** [22] Jul66 [6]

Sep 66. (lp) *(587/588 029)* *<SD 8129>* **THE EXCITING WILSON PICKETT** [ ] Aug66 [21]
– Land of 100 dances / Something you got / 634-5789 / Barefootin' / Mercy, mercy / You're so fine / In the midnight hour / 99 and a half (won't do) / Danger zone / I'm drifting / It's all over / She's so good to me. *(re-iss. Jun88) (cd-iss. Aug93 on 'Rhino')*

Nov 66. (7") *(584 066)* *<2365>* **MUSTANG SALLY. / THREE TIME LOSER** [28] [23]

Feb 67. (7") *(584 101)* *<2381>* **EVERYBODY NEEDS SOMEBODY TO LOVE. / NOTHING YOU CAN DO** [ ] [29]

Feb 67. (lp; mono/stereo) *(587/588 057)* *<SD 8138>* **THE WICKED PICKETT** [ ] Jan67 [42]
– Mustang Sally / New Orleans / Sunny / Everybody needs somebody to love / Ooh poo pah doo / She ain't gonna do right / Knock on wood / Time is on my side / Up tight good woman / You left the water running / Three time loser / Nothing you can do.

Mar 67. (7") *<2394>* **I FOUND A LOVE (pt.1). / (pt.2)** [–] [32]

May 67. (7") *(584 107)* **NEW ORLEANS. / SOUL DANCE NUMBER THREE** [ ] [–]

May 67. (7") *<2412>* **SOUL DANCE NUMBER THREE. / YOU CAN'T STAND ALONE** [–] [55] [70]

Aug 67. (lp; mono/stereo) *(587/588 057)* *<SD 8145>* **THE SOUND OF WILSON PICKETT** [ ] [54]
– Soul dance number three / Funky Broadway / I need a lot of loving every day / I found a love (part 1) / I found a love (part 2) / You can't stand alone / Mojo mamma / I found the one / Something within me / I'm sorry about that / Love is a beautiful thing.

Sep 67. (7") *(584 130)* *<2430>* **FUNKY BROADWAY. / I'M SORRY ABOUT THAT** [43] Aug67 [8]

Oct 67. (lp; mono/stereo) *(587/588 092)* *<SD 8151>* **THE BEST OF WILSON PICKETT** (compilation) [ ] [35]
– In the midnight hour / I found a love / 634-5789 / If you need me / Mustang Sally / Don't fight it / Everybody needs somebody to love / It's too late / Ninety-nine and a half (won't do) / Funky Broadway / Soul dance number three / Land of 1000 dances. *(re-iss. Apr82 lp/c; 780170-1/-4) (cd-iss. Jul87; 781737-2) (cd re-iss. Aug93; 7567 81737-2)*

Oct 67. (7") *(584 142)* *<2448>* **STAGGER-LEE. / I'M IN LOVE** [ ] [22] [45]

Feb 68. (7") *<2484>* **JEALOUS LOVE. / I'VE COME A LONG WAY** [–] [50]

Mar 68. (7") *(584 173)* **THAT KIND OF LOVE. / I'VE COME A LONG WAY** [ ] [–]

Apr 68. (lp; mono/stereo) *(587/588 107)* *<SD 8175>* **I'M IN LOVE** [ ] Feb68 [70]
– Jealous love / Stagger lee / That kind of love / I'm in love / Hello sunshine / Don't cry no more / We've got to have love / Bring it on home to me / She's looking good / I've come a long way. *(cd-iss. Jan96; 7567 80375-2)*

May 68. (7") *(584 183)* *<2504>* **SHE'S LOOKIN' GOOD. / WE'VE GOT TO HAVE LOVE** [ ] Apr68 [15]

Aug 68. (7") *(584 203)* *<2528>* **I'M A MIDNIGHT MOVER. / DEBORAH** [38] Jun68 [24]

Sep 68. (lp; mono/stereo) *(587/588 111)* *<SD 8183>* **THE MIDNIGHT MOVER** [ ] Jul68 [91]
– I'm a midnight mover / It's a groove / Remember, I been good to you / I'm gonna cry / Deborah / I found a true love / Down by the sea / Trust me / Let's get an understanding / For better or worse.

Nov 68. (7") *(584 221)* *<2558>* **I FOUND A TRUE LOVE. / FOR BETTER OR WORSE** [ ] Sep68 [42]

Nov 68. (7") *<2575>* **A MAN AND A HALF. / PEOPLE MAKE THE WORLD (WHAT IT IS)** [–] [42]

Dec 68. (7") *(584 236)* **HEY JUDE. / NIGHT OWL** [16] [–]

Jan 69. (7") *<2591>* **HEY JUDE. / SEARCH YOUR HEART** [–] [23]

Feb 69. (lp) *(588 170)* *<SD 8215>* **HEY JUDE** [ ] [97]
– Save me / Hey Jude / Back in your arms / Toe hold / Night owl / My own style of loving / A man and a half / Sit down and talk this over / Search your heart / Born to be wild / People make the world (what it is). *(cd-iss. Jan96; 7567 80375-2)*

Mar 69. (7") *(584 261)* *<2611>* **MINI SKIRT MINNIE. / BACK IN YOUR ARMS** [ ] [50]

Apr 69. (lp) *(2465 002)* *<SD 8250>* **RIGHT ON** [ ] [ ]
– Groovy little woman / Funky way / Sugar sugar / Sweet inspiration / This old town / You keep me hangin' on / Lord pity us all / It's still good / Woman likes to hear that / She said yes / Hey Joe / Steal away.

May 69. (7") *<2631>* **BORN TO BE WILD. / TOE HOLD** [–] [64]

Jul 69. (7") *<2648>* **HEY JOE. / NIGHT OWL** [–] [59]

Jan 70. (7") *(584 313)* *<2682>* **YOU KEEP ME HANGIN' ON. / NOW YOU SEE ME, NOW YOU DON'T** [ ] Nov69 [92]

May 70. (7") *(2091 005)* *<2722>* **SUGAR SUGAR. / COLE, COOKE AND REDDING** [ ] [25] [91]

Jul 70. (7") *(584 281)* **HEY JOE. / BORN TO BE WILD** [ ] [–]

Aug 70. (7") *<2753>* **SHE SAID YES. / IT'S STILL GOOD** [–] [68]

Oct 70. (7") *(2091 032)* *<2765>* **ENGINE No.9. / INTERNATIONAL PLAYBOY** [ ] [14]

Mar 71. (7") *<2781>* **DON'T LET THE GRASS FOOL YOU. / AIN'T NO DOUBT ABOUT IT** [–] [ ]

Apr 71. (7") *(2091 086)* **FIRE AND WATER. / DON'T LET THE GREEN GRASS FOOL YOU** [ ] [–]

Apr 71. (lp) *(2400 026)* *<SD 8270>* **ENGINE NO.9** <US title 'WILSON PICKETT IN PHILADELPHIA'> [ ] Sep70 [64]
– Run Joey run / Help the needy / Come right here / Bumble bee (sting me) / Don't let the green grass fool you / Get me back on time, engine number 9 (part 1) / Get me back on time, engine number 9 (part 2) / Days go by / International playboy / Ain't no doubt about it. *(cd-iss. US-title Jan96; 8122 72219-2)*

Jun 71. (lp) *(K 20078)* *<8290>* **THE BEST OF WILSON PICKETT, VOL.II** (compilation) [ ] May71 [73]
– Don't let the green grass fool you / Sugar sugar / Get me back on time, engine No.9 / I'm a midnight mover / A man and a half / Born to be wild / She's lookin' good / I'm in love / Hey Joe / Cole, Cooke & Redding / Hey Jude / You keep me hangin' on / I found a true love.

Oct 71. (7") *(2091 153)* *<2824>* **CALL MY NAME, I'LL BE THERE. / WOMAN LET ME BE DOWN HOME** [ ] Aug71 [52]

Dec 71. (7") *<2852>* **FIRE AND WATER. / PLEDGING MY LOVE** [–] [24]

Jan 72. (lp) *(K 40319)* *<8300>* **DON'T KNOCK MY LOVE** [ ] Dec71 [ ]
– Fire and water / (Your love has brought me) A mighty long way / Covering the same old ground / Don't knock my love (part 1) / Don't knock my love (part 2) / Call my name, I'll be there / Hot love / Not enough love to satisfy / You can't judge a book by its cover / Pledging my love / Mama told me not to come / Woman let me be down home.

Feb 72. (7") *(2091 124)* *<2797>* **DON'T KNOCK MY LOVE. / (part 2)** [ ] Apr71 [13]

Apr 72. (7") *(K 10166)* **DON'T LET THE GREEN GRASS FOOL YOU. / COVERING THE SAME OLD GROUND** [ ] Jan71 [17]

Jun 72. (7") *(K 10181)* *<2878>* **FUNK FACTORY. / ONE STEP AWAY** [ ] May72 [58]

Oct 72. (7") *<2909>* **MAMA TOLD ME NOT TO COME. / COVERING THE SAME OLD GROUND** [–] [99]

1973. (7") *<2961>* **INTERNATIONAL PLAYBOY. / COME RIGHT HERE** [ ] [–]

R.C.A. R.C.A.

Mar 73. (7") *<74 0898>* **MR. MAGIC MAN. / I SHO' LOVE YOU** [ ] [98]

Mar 73. (lp) *(SF 8390)* *<0312>* **MIZ LENA'S BOY** <US title 'MR. MAGIC MAN'> [ ] [ ]
– Take a closer look at the woman you're with / Memphis, Tennessee / Soft spoul boogie woogie / Help me make it through the night / Never my love / You lay'd it on me / Is your love life better / Two women and a wife / Why don't you make up your mind / Take the pollution out your throat.

Nov 73. (7") *(RCA 2430)* *<0049>* **TAKE A CLOSER LOOK AT THE WOMAN YOU'RE WITH. / TWO WOMEN AND A WIFE** [ ] Sep73 [90]

Feb 74. (7") *<(APB 0174)>* **SOFT SOUL BOOGIE WOOGIE. / TAKE THE POLLUTION OUT OF YOUR THROAT** [ ] [ ]

May 74. (lp) *(SF 8344)* *<4858>* **TONIGHT I'M MY BIGGEST AUDIENCE** [ ] [ ]
– Mr. Magic man / Only I can sing this love / Love is beautiful / I sure love you / Baby man / Sin was the blame / What it is / If you need me / I can't slip my true love away / I keep walking straight ahead.

Aug 74. (7") *(RCA 2450)* *<0309>* **TAKE YOUR PLEASURE WHERE YOU FIND IT. / WHAT GOOD IS A LIE** [ ] [ ]

Sep 74. (lp) *<APL1 0495>* **PICKETT IN THE POCKET** [–] [ ]
– Iron it out / Isn't that so / Take a look / I was too nice / Don't pass me by / What good is a lie / Young boy blues / Take your pleasure where you

find it / You're the one.

Nov 74. (7") <10067> **I WAS TOO NICE. / ISN'T THAT SO** [–] [ ]

Dec 74. (d-lp) <APL2 0669> **LIVE IN JAPAN (live)** [–] [ ]
– T.S.O.P. (The Sound Of Philadelphia) / Proud Mary / People make the world / Sugar sugar / Don't let the green grass fool you / I'm in love / In the midnight hour / Fire and water / I found a love / Never my love / Glory hallelujah / Mustang Sally / Land of a 1000 dances / Soft soul boogie / Mr.Magic man / Don't knock my love / Goodnight my love.

Jul 75. (lp) *(SF 8439)* <APL1 0856> **JOIN ME AND LET'S BE FREE** [ ] [ ]
– Join me and let's be free / Let's make love right / I've got a good friend / Smokin' in the United Nations / Gone / Good things / Higher consciousness / Bailin' hay on a rainy day / Mighty mouth.

D.J.M. Wicked

Nov 76. (7") <8101> **HOW WILL I EVER KNOW. / THE BEST PART OF A MAN** [–] [ ]

Nov 76. (lp) *(DJSL 064)* <26064> **PEACE BREAKER** [ ] [ ]

Feb 77. (7") <8107> **LOVE WILL KEEP US TOGETHER. / IT'S GONNA BE GOOD** [–] [ ]

Atlantic Big Tree

Aug 78. (7") <16121> **WHO TURNED YOU ON. / DANCE YOU DOWN** [ ] [ ]

Aug 78. (lp) *(K 50528)* <76011> **A FUNKY SITUATION** [ ] [ ]
– Dance with me / She's so tight / The night we called a day / Dance you down / Hold on to your hiney / Groovin' / Lay me like you hate me / Funky situation / Time to let the sunshine on me / Who turned you on.

Dec 78. (7") <16129> **GROOVIN'. / TIME TO LET THE SUNSHINE ON ME** [–] [ ]

EMI America EMI America

Nov 79. (7") <8027> **I WANT YOU. / LOVE OF MY LIFE** [–] [ ]

Nov 79. (lp) *(AML 3007)* <17019> **I WANT YOU** [ ] [ ]
– I want you / Love of my life / Shameless / Live with me / Groove city / Superstar / Granny.

Dec 79. (7"/12") *(EA/+12 104)* **GROOVE CITY. / YOU ARE THE LOVE OF MY LIFE** [ ] [–]

Jan 80. (7") <8034> **LIVE WITH ME. / GRANNY** [–] [ ]

Apr 80. (7") *(EA 107)* **SHAMELESS. / SUPERSTAR** [ ] [–]

Feb 81. (7") *(EA 120)* <8070> **DON'T UNDERESTIMATE THE POWER OF LOVE. / AIN'T GONNA GIVE YOU NO MORE** [ ] [ ]
(12"+=) *(EA12 120)* – I want you.

Mar 81. (lp) *(AML 3016)* <17043> **THE RIGHT TRACK** [ ] [ ]
– Back on the right track / If you can't beat 'em join 'em / Help me be without / I ain't gonna give you no more / Maybe this time / Don't underestimate the power of love / It's you.

May 81. (7") <8082> **BACK ON THE RIGHT TRACK. / IT'S YOU** [–] [ ]

not iss. Erva

1985. (7") <318> **LOVE DAGGER. / TIME TO LET THE SUNSHINE ON ME** [–] [ ]

not iss. Precision

1986. (7") <703> **MUSTANG SALLY (THE BOSS IS BACK). / ('A'instrumental)** [–] [ ]

Motown Motown

Jun 87. (7") <1898> **DON'T TURN AWAY. / CAN'T STOP NOW** [–] [ ]

Sep 87. (7") <1916> **IN THE MIDNIGHT HOUR (remix). / JUST LET HER KNOW** [–] [ ]

Oct 87. (7") *(ZB 41583)* **IN THE MIDNIGHT HOUR (remix). / ('A'original)** [62] [–]
(12"+=) *(ZT 41584)* – ('A'dub version).

Oct 87. (lp/c/cd) *(ZL/ZK/ZD 72615)* **AMERICAN SOUL MAN** [ ] [ ]
– A thing called love / When your heart speaks / Love never let me down / A man of value / (I wanna) Make love to you / In the midnight hour / Don't turn away / Just let her know / Can't stop now. *(re-iss. Mar94 on 'Spectrum' cd/c; 550178-2/-4)*

Dec 87. (7") <1938> **LOVE NEVER LET ME DOWN. / JUST LET HER KNOW** [–] [ ]
<re-iss. 1988 on 'M.C.A.'; 53407>

New York Catawba

Feb 88. (7"/12"; by WILSON PICKETT & JACKIE MOORE) *(NY/+T 101)* <100> **SECONDS. / SECONDS (instrumental)** [ ] [ ]

not iss. Montage

1988. (7"; by WILSON PICKETT & JACKIE MOORE) *<1218>* **PRECIOUS, PRECIOUS. /** [–] [ ]

— In October '93, PICKETT was given a 1-year jail sentence after being found guilty of drunk driving and killing a pensioner.

Bullseye Bullseye

Sep 99. (cd) *<(CDBB 9625)>* **IT'S HARDER NOW** [ ] [ ]
– Outskirts of town / Taxi love / What's under that dress / Soul survivor / It's harder now / It ain't easy / Bad people / All about sex / Better him than me / Stone crazy world.

– (selective) compilations, etc. –

Jun 93. (cd) *Rhino-Atlantic; <(8122 71212-2)>* **THE VERY BEST OF WILSON PICKETT** [ ] [ ]

Jul 93. (d-cd) *Rhino-Atlantic; <(8122 70287-2)>* **A MAN AND A HALF: THE BEST OF WILSON PICKETT** [ ] Apr92 [ ]
– I found a love (the FALCONS) / Let me be your boy / If you need me / It's too late / I'm gonna cry (cry baby) / Come home baby / In the midnight hour / Don't fight it / I'm not tired / That's a man's way / 634-5789 (Soulsville U.S.A.) / Ninety-nine and a half (won't do) / Land of 1000 dances / Mustang Sally / Three-time loser / Everybody needs somebody to love / Soul dance number three / You can't stand alone / Funky Broadway / I'm in love / Stagger Lee / Jealous love / I've come a long way / In the midnight hour (live & burnin') / I'm a midnight mover / I found a true love / She's looking good / A man and a half / Hey Jude / Mini-skirt Minnie / Toe hold / Hey Joe / You keep me hangin' on / She said yes / Cole, Cooke & Redding / Sugar sugar / Get me back on time engine number 9 / Don't let the green grass fool you / Don't knock my love (part 1) / Call my name, I'll be there / Fire and water / (Your love has brought me) A mighty long way / Funk factory / Funky Broadway. *(re-iss. Aug93; same)*

Jul 96. (cd) *Javelin; (CWNCD 2018)* **IF YOU NEED ME** [ ] [–]
(re-iss. Jul98 on 'Prestige'; CDSGP 0392)

Jun 98. (cd) *Camden; (74321 58814-2)* **TAKE YOUR PLEASURE WHERE YOU FIND IT (THE BEST OF THE R.C.A. YEARS)** [ ] [–]

Jul 01. (cd) *Cleopatra; (CLP 1010CD)* **THE BEST OF WILSON PICKETT** [ ] [ ]

☐ PiL (see under ⇒ PUBLIC IMAGE LTD.)

PINK

Born: ALECIA MOORE, 6 Sep'79, Doylestown, Philadelphia, Pennsylvania, USA. A main contributor to the late '90's/early 21st Century all-singing, all-dancing teen Pop movement, PINK soon received anti-pop credibility thanks to her more edgier album 'MISSUNDAZTOOD' and an on-going feud with BRITNEY SPEARS. PINK was raised on the local Philadelphia club scene and became a regular at Club Fever in her own town where she would sing self-penned songs every Friday night. She was quickly initiated into R&B/Hip-Hop combo SCHOOLS OF THOUGHT before auditioning for a manufactured, M.C.A.-funded R&B collective BASIC INSTINCT. This, however did not work out and a disgruntled PINK, along with a few other INSTINCT casualties formed CHOICE and signed to LA REID's 'Babyface' label, but, once again, imploded after failing to get along creatively. Producer DARYL SIMMONS asked her to co-write the song 'JUST TO BE LOVING YOU', and on the strength of her songwriting abilities she was signed by REID himself to record a solo album. It came in the form of 'CAN'T TAKE ME HOME' (2000) and was worked on by a number of songwriters, collaborators and musicians. On the back of smash hit singles 'THERE YOU GO' and the fun 'YOU MAKE ME SICK', PINK's debut album ended up going triple platinum, a feat which earned her a support slot with teeny-bopper boy band 'N SYNC. But this was only the beginning of the petit, pink-haired lady's success as her collaborative efforts with MISSY ELLIOTT, CHRISTINA AGUILERIA, LIL' KIM and MYA on a rendition of 'LADY MARMALADE' soon made her a household name. 'GET THE PARTY STARTED' was issued the following year and became one of the most anthemic party records ever, with an oh-so catchy chorus, cheeky video and a back-beat laden with Hip-Hop style ornamentations, PINK was fast becoming a superstar – a sort of BRITNEY SPEARS' bright and sexual wicked twin, if you will. On subject of Miss SPEARS, PINK apparently sent the pop diva a bunch of lilies to apologise after she blasted her in an American interview. Of course, SPEARS was allergic to the vibrant perfume of the plant, a practical joke that was wittingly executed. 'M!SSUNDAZTOOD' appeared in 2001, with guest appearances from Aerosmith's STEVEN TYLER and 4-Non Blondes' LINDA PERRY, who also contributed immensely to the rockier production that could be heard throughout the album. All in all the set failed to live up to its expectations, with most of the songs coming over as a half-assed shot at something that vaguely represented the rap/rock/R&B/Hip-hop/soul and pop genres; a melting pot of candy floss. That said, it was the kind of proverbial candy floss that sticks to your teeth, fingers, face – in other words, it got everywhere. PINK returned late in 2003, this time displaying a rather more raunchy, sexed-up rockier image. LINDA PERRY was still on board, but with only three songs credited to her name. The big surprise, however was the recruitment of songwriter and frontman for underground punk band RANCID, TIM ARMSTRONG, who seemed to push PINK into a scuzzed-out direction without having her commit total commercial suicide. Massive hit 'TROUBLE', with its punky power chords and snotty chrous was evidence of PINK's new found transformation, and like KYLIE, we even saw her dabble in a little bit of electronica with rude girl of the moment PEACHES (on 'OH MY GOD'). To some, it all seemed a tad moot, especially 'GOD IS A DJ' which was destined to become a dancefloor smash and contained the lines "If god is a DJ, then life is a dancefloor" – obvious to the point of almost wretching. But in the age of BRITNEY and BEYONCe, PINK was somewhat of a revelation, keeping the punk spirit alive with her revealing choice of wardrobe and her outspoken, shut-up-and-listen public image. And, of course, the pink hair-do.

Album rating: CAN'T TAKE ME HOME (*7) / M!SSUNDAZTOOD (*7) / TRY THIS (*8)

PINK – vocals / with producers, etc.

LaFace – Arista LaFace – Arista

May 00. (cd/c) *<(73008 26062-2/-4)>* **CAN'T TAKE ME HOME** [13] Apr00 [26]
– Split personality / Hell wit ya / Most girls / There you go / You make me sick / Let me let you know / Love is such a crazy thing / Private show / Can't take me home / Stop falling / Do what U do / Hiccup / Is it love. *(cd+=)* – There you go (mix) / Most girls (mix).

May 00. (c-s) *(74321 75760-4) <24456>* **THERE YOU GO / (instrumental)** [6] Feb00 [7]
(cd-s) *(74321 75760-2)* – ('A'side) / ('A'-Hani radio) / ('A'-CD-Rom).

Sep 00. (c-s) *(74321 79201-4) <24490>* **MOST GIRLS / HICCUP** [5] Aug00 [4]
(12"/cd-s) *(74321 79201-1/-2)* – ('A'side) / ('A'-X-Men vocal mix) / There you go (sovereign mix) / ('A'CD-Rom).

Jan 01. (c-s) *(74321 82870-4) <radio cut>* **YOU MAKE ME SICK / YOU MAKE ME SICK (dub)** [9] [33]
(cd-s+=) *(74321 82870-2)* – ('A'-El B remix).
(12"++=) *(74321 82870-1)* – ('A'-version).

—— in Apr'01, PINK featured alongside CHRISTINA AGUILERA, LIL' KIM & MYA on the transatlantic No.1 single, 'LADY MARMALADE'

Jan 02. (c-s/cd-s) *(74321 91337-4/-2) <15074>* **GET THE PARTY STARTED / (Redman remix) / (instrumental)** [2] Oct01 [4]
(cd-s) *(74321 91338-2)* – (mixes; K5 Wek Kraft / Pink noise disco / video).

Jan 02. (cd/c) *(74321 91324-2/-4) <14718-2>* **M!SSUNDAZTOOD** [2] Nov01 [6]
– Missundaztood / Don't let me get me / Just like a pill / Get the party started / Respect (with SCRATCH) / 18 wheeler / Family portrait / Misery (with STEVEN TYLER) / Dear diary / Eventually / Lonely girl (with LINDA PERRY) / Numb / Gone to California / My Vietnam. *(special cd+=; 74321 96251-2)*

May 02. (c-s) *(74321 93921-4)* **DON'T LET ME GET ME / (John Shanks remix)** [6] Apr02 [8]
(cd-s+=) *(74321 93921-2) <15117>* – ('A'-Maurice's Nu Soul mix) / ('A'-video).

Sep 02. (c-s) *(74321 95921-4)* **JUST LIKE A PILL / JUST LIKE A PILL (Jacknife Lee mix)** [1] [8]
(cd-s+=) *(74321 95921-2) <radio>* – Get the party started (live).

Dec 02. (c-s) *(74321 98205-4)* **FAMILY PORTRAIT / JUST LIKE A PILL** [11] [20]
(cd-s+=/12"+=) *(74321 98205-2/-1) <98210>* – Just like a pill (version).

Jul 03. (c-s; as PINK featuring WILLIAM ORBIT) *(674106-4) <radio>* **FEEL GOOD TIME / FEEL GOOD TIME (Borris & Beck's feel good dub)** [3] [60]
(cd-s) *(674106-2)* – ('A'side) / ('A'-D-Bop full throttle mix) / ('A'-Borris & Beck's massive vocal).

—— (from the movie, 'Charlie's Angels Full Throttle' iss. on 'Columbia')

Oct 03. (7"clear/c-s) *(82876 57175-7/-4)* **TROUBLE. / DELERIUM** [7] Dec03 [68]
(cd-s+=) *(74321 57217-2) <58646>* – Free / ('A'-video).

Nov 03. (cd/d-lp) *(82876 57185-2/-1) <52139>* **TRY THIS** [3] [9]
– Trouble / God is a DJ / Last to know / Tonight's the night / Oh my god (with PEACHES) / Catch me while I'm sleeping / Waiting for love / Save my life / Try too hard / Humble neighbourhoods / Walk away / Unwind / Feel good time *[UK-only]* / Love song.

PINK FLOYD

Formed: London, England ... 1965 initially as The ABDABS by ROGER WATERS, RICHARD WRIGHT and NICK MASON, (with others; CLIVE METCALFE – bass, KEITH NOBLE and JULIETTE GALE on vocals). The latter three were dismissed, when the band enlisted SYD BARRETT and adopted the moniker PINK FLOYD (the name taken from bluesmen PINK ANDERSON and FLOYD COUNCIL). In March '66, they secured a residency at the Marquee Club, where their Sunday afternoon gigs were described as "spontaneous underground". Having played the UFO club late in 1966, they were subsequently signed to EMI's 'Columbia' records by their new management team of Peter Jenner and Andrew King. PINK FLOYD's March '67 debut outing, 'ARNOLD LAYNE' (about a transvestite washing-line thief), surprisingly escaped a BBC ban. One of the first missives from the psychedelic underground to reach the Top 20, it was characterised by SYD's whimsically affected vocals. On the 29th of April, they were top of the bill at Alexandria Palace's 14-hour Technicolour Dream, one of the psychedelic era's most infamous events. Their follow-up, 'SEE EMILY PLAY' (originally titled 'GAMES FOR MAY'), hit the Top 10, preceding their classic debut album, 'THE PIPER AT THE GATES OF DAWN' (a pioneering work in the sense that it contained no singles). The collection dominated by BARRETT's eccentric songwriting, it featured the cosmic 'ASTRONOMY DOMINE' alongside the acid-fuelled space-rock of 'INTERSTELLAR OVERDRIVE'. These were contrasted with idiosyncratic ramblings like 'BIKE', 'MATILDA MOTHER' and 'SCARECROW'. Their third 45, 'APPLES AND ORANGES', suprisingly flopped late in 1967, BARRETT's mental condition deteriorating rapidly due to his excessive use of LSD. He increasingly missed shows and studio sessions, PINK FLOYD bringing in DAVE GILMOUR (an old school-friend of SYD's) to compensate. In the April '68, BARRETT was asked to leave the group, retreating to a life of reclusiveness in his mother's Cambridge home. It was widely speculated that PINK FLOYD would be creatively bankrupt without SYD, especially after a further single, 'IT WOULD BE SO NICE', flopped. However, WATERS and

WRIGHT took up the reins on the bulk of the songwriting duties, the band soon unleashing their second, more percussive effort, 'A SAUCERFUL OF SECRETS'. Released to ecstatic reviews, the album repeated the debut's success. The tracks, 'SET THE CONTROLS FOR THE HEART OF THE SUN', 'LET THERE BE MORE LIGHT' and SYD's harrowing farewell, 'JUGBAND BLUES' being the undisputed highlights. On the 29th of June, they played their first free concert at London's Hyde Park, alongside JETHRO TULL and ROY HARPER. They finished the year with another flop single, 'POINT ME AT THE SKY', their last in the UK for 11 years. They now concentrated on albums, releasing the under par soundtrack to the Barbet Schroeder- directed 'MORE'. It was basically an instrumental set, 'CIRRUS MINOR' being the standout track of the Top 10 album. Later in '69, they moved to EMI's new 'Harvest' label, issuing the part live, part solo, double album, 'UMMA GUMMA'. Each member contributed a piece of individually credited material, the best being WATERS' bizarre creation, 'SEVERAL SPECIES OF SMALL FURRY ANIMALS GATHERED TOGETHER IN A CAVE AND GROOVING WITH A PICT'. The live disc combined the cream of their sprawling stage improvisations, 'CAREFUL WITH THAT AXE, EUGENE' making its first album appearance. In the autumn of 1970, they released their fifth album, 'ATOM HEART MOTHER' (their first No.1), a record consisting of one patchy, experimental, side of more conventionally structured songs, while the other was a side-long collage with RON GEESIN playing on the title track. The trumpeter was to collaborate with ROGER WATERS the same year, on a soundtrack for the Roy Battersby documentary film, 'THE BODY'. On the 15th of May '71, PINK FLOYD played at the Crystal Palace Garden Party, introducing a new piece of music, 'RETURN TO THE SUN OF NOTHING', which, in six months time, became 'ECHOES'. This composition subsequently took up a whole side of their Top 3 album, 'MEDDLE', which also featured 'ONE OF THESE DAYS', 'A PILLOW OF WINDS' and 'FEARLESS' (the latter notable for its sample of the Anfield Kop). The following year, their most recent recordings were used on another Schroeder film, 'La Vallee', the album being released as 'OBSCURED BY CLOUDS', and although disappointing many die hard FLOYD fans, it cracked the Top 50 in the States. The same year, the group premiered their own music film, 'LIVE AT POMPEII', in Edinburgh. In March 1973, after its spectacular January showing at the Planetarium, the masterpiece, 'DARK SIDE OF THE MOON', was unveiled. A meticulous concept set which the band had worked on for over a year, it dealt with such taboo themes as lunacy, depression and death. These subjects were dealt with on such compelling tracks as 'US AND THEM', 'BREATHE', 'TIME' and the Top 20 US hit 'MONEY'. Scaling both the UK and US charts, the album went on to amass sales of over 10 million, incredibly residing in the chart for nearly 300 consecutive weeks. It has subsequently become regarded by many as the greatest album of all time, breathing new life into stereo headphones. They returned to London's Earl's Court for a spectacular laser show, featuring the albums' all-girl backing singers, The BLACKBERRIES. In 1974, they did a benefit gig, raising £10,000 for their recently disabled friend, ROBERT WYATT (NICK MASON also producing his 'Rock Bottom' album). In the summer of '75, their majestic Knebworth Festival performance previewed another best selling album and subsequent chart-topper, 'WISH YOU WERE HERE'. The record featured some of PINK FLOYD's most enduring songs including the space-jazz ode to SYD BARRETT, 'SHINE ON YOU CRAZY DIAMOND', the oppressive futurism of 'WELCOME TO THE MACHINE', the ROY HARPER-sung 'HAVE A CIGAR' and the wistful melancholy of the title track. It was rounded off by a reprised version of 'SHINE ON', the recording sessions blessed with a rare visit by the song's subject, SYD. Late in 1976, they let loose their 40-foot inflatable pig after a promotional session for their forthcoming 'ANIMALS' album sleeve shot. The Civil Aviation Authority was alerted to warn pilots of the danger, but it was never found. However, the Top 3 album was sighted in shops early the following year. While MASON had produced albums for The DAMNED ('Music For Pleasure') and STEVE HILLAGE ('Green'), GILMOUR and WRIGHT released their own solo albums in 1978, 'DAVID GILMOUR' and 'WET DREAM' respectively. FLOYD returned in late 1979 with a new ROGER WATERS-penned concept double, 'THE WALL', which spawned a decidedly unfestive Christmas chart topper in the lugubrious 'ANOTHER BRICK IN THE WALL (PART II)'. This was another unrelentingly cynical concept piece, centering on the life of PINK, a disillusioned pop star. The next few years were spent making it into a film, directed by Alan Parker and issued in 1982 (BOB GELDOF played the main character). By the time of its release, WRIGHT had already left the band after quarrelling with WATERS. In Spring 1983, they/WATERS issued a comeback album of sorts, 'THE FINAL CUT', which again hit UK No.1. However, it was found overbearingly depressing, derided by critics as a poor "son of The Wall". The year ended with WATERS recording a solo album, 'THE PROS AND CONS OF HITCH HIKING', subsequently fighting GILMOUR and MASON in court for the use of the PINK FLOYD name. In 1984, GILMOUR released his second solo album, 'ABOUT FACE', followed a year later by a NICK MASON / RICK FENN set, 'PROFILES'. With WATERS finally leaving in 1986, WRIGHT returned a year later to boost their ever-impressive live shows (which helped them win the court battle with WATERS). PINK FLOYD returned with an extended GILMOUR-led line-up in 1987 on the Top 3 album, 'A MOMENTARY LAPSE OF REASON', which produced a couple of minor hit singles, 'ON THE TURNING AWAY' and 'ONE SLIP'. A live double album, 'THE DELICATE SOUND OF THUNDER' (which, ironically enough, sounded more PINK FLOYD than ever before). A seven year studio hiatus was broken in 1994 with the release of chart-topper 'THE DIVISION BELL', regarded by long-time fans as a return to form. Following this one-off, PINK FLOYD have continued to keep their name alive purely on the back of concert and compilation sets. The huge transatlantic success of 1995's 'PULSE' was followed five years later by 'IS THERE ANYBODY OUT THERE? THE WALL: LIVE 1980-1981' (2000), a belated document of the band's live performances inspired by their famous 1979 album. 'ECHOES: THE BEST OF PINK FLOYD' (2001), meanwhile, attempted a more broad overview of the band's long and complex career. • **Trivia:** MASON also made a 30-minute autobiographical film, 'Life Could Be A Dream' with his other outlet, racing driving, the main feature. In 1995, GILMOUR featured on JOHN 'RABBIT' BUNDRICK's ambient album, 'Dream Jungle'.

Album rating: THE PIPER AT THE GATES OF DAWN (*9) / A SAUCERFUL OF SECRETS (*8) / MORE soundtrack (*4) / UMMA GUMMA (*7) / ATOM HEART MOTHER (*7) / RELICS collection (*7) / MEDDLE (*8) / OBSCURED BY CLOUDS (*6) / THE DARK SIDE OF THE MOON (*10) / WISH YOU WERE HERE (*10) / ANIMALS (*8) / THE WALL (*9) / A COLLECTION OF GREAT DANCE SONGS collection (*4) / THE FINAL CUT (*5) / WORKS collection (*5) / A MOMENTARY LAPSE OF REASON (*5) / THE DELICATE SOUND OF THUNDER (*7) / THE DIVISION BELL (*6) / PULSE (*4) / IS THERE ANYBODY OUT THERE? THE WALL LIVE 1980-1981 live (*5) / ECHOES: THE BEST OF PINK FLOYD compilation (*8) / David Gilmour: DAVID GILMOUR (*5) / ABOUT FACE (*5) / Richard Wight: WET DREAM (*4) / Nick Mason: FICTITIOUS SPORTS (*4) / PROFILES with Rick Fenn (*4)

SYD BARRETT (b. ROGER KEITH BARRETT, 6 Jan'46) – vocals, guitar / **RICHARD WRIGHT** (b.28 Jul'45, London) – keyboards / **ROGER WATERS** (b. GEORGE WATERS, 9 Sep'44, Surrey, England) – bass, vocals, percussion / **NICK MASON** (b.27 Jan'45, Birmingham, England) – drums, percussion

Columbia Tower

Mar 67. (7") *(DB 8156)* <333> **ARNOLD LAYNE. / CANDY AND THE CURRANT BUN** [20] [ ]

Jun 67. (7") *(DB 8214)* <356> **SEE EMILY PLAY. / SCARECROW** [6] [ ]

Aug 67. (lp; mono/stereo) *(SX/SCX 6157)* **THE PIPER AT THE GATES OF DAWN** [6] [–]
– Astronomy domine / Lucifer Sam / Matilda mother / Flaming / Pow R. Toc H. / Take up thy stethoscope and walk / Interstellar overdrive / The gnome / Chapter 24 / Scarecrow / Bike. *(re-iss. May83 on 'Fame' lp/c; FA/TCFA 3065) (cd-iss. Feb87; CDP 746384-2) (re-iss. Oct94 on 'E.M.I.' cd/c; CD/TC EMD 1073) (re-iss. Aug97 on 'E.M.I.' cd/lp hit UK No.44; CD+/EMD 1110)*

Nov 67. (lp) <ST 5093> **PINK FLOYD** (nearly as above) [–] [ ]

Nov 67. (7") *(DB 8310)* **APPLES AND ORANGES. / PAINTBOX** [ ] [–]

Jan 68. (7") <378> **FLAMING. / THE GNOME** [–] [ ]

—— added **DAVID GILMOUR** (b. 6 Mar'44, Cambridge, England) – guitar; who soon repl. BARRETT who later went solo

Apr 68. (7") *(DB 8401)* <426> **IT WOULD BE SO NICE. / JULIA DREAM** [ ] [ ]

Jun 68. (lp; mono/stereo) *(SX/SCX 6258)* <ST 5131> **A SAUCERFUL OF SECRETS** [9] [ ]
– Let there be more light / Remember a day / Set the controls for the heart of the sun / Corporal Clegg / A saucerful of secrets / See saw / Jugband blues. *(re-iss. Aug86 on 'Fame' lp/c; FA/TCFA 3163) (cd-iss. Feb87; CDP 746383-2) (re-iss. Jul94 on 'E.M.I.' cd/c; CD/TC EMD 1063)*

Jul 68. (7") <440> **LET THERE BE MORE LIGHT. / REMEMBER A DAY** [–] [ ]

Dec 68. (7") *(DB 8511)* **POINT ME AT THE SKY. / CAREFUL WITH THAT AXE, EUGENE** [ ] [–]

Jul 69. (lp/c) *(SCX/TCSCX 6346)* <ST 5169> **MORE (soundtrack)** [9] [ ]
– Cirrus minor / The Nile song / Crying song / Up the Khyber / Green is the colour / Cymbaline / Party sequence / Main theme / Ibiza bar / More blues / Quicksilver / A Spanish piece / Dramatic theme. *(cd-iss. Apr87; CDP 746386-2) (re-iss. Sep95 on 'E.M.I.' cd/c; CD/TC EMD 1084)*

Harvest Harvest

Nov 69. (d-lp)(d-c) *(SHDW 1-2)(TC2SHWD 4501)* <388> **UMMA GUMMA** (live */ others solo) [5] [74]
– Astronomy domine * / Careful with that axe, Eugene * / Set the control for the heart of the sun * / A saucerful of secrets * / RICHARD WRIGHT:- Sysyphus (parts 1-4) / ROGER WATERS:- Grantchester Meadows / Several species of small furry animals gathered together in a cave and grooving with a pict / DAVID GILMOUR: – The narrow way (parts 1-3) / NICK MASON:- The Grand Vizier's garden party – part 1; Entrance – part 2; Entertainment / part 3; Exit. *(d-cd-iss. Mar87; CDS 746404-2) (re-iss. Oct94 on 'E.M.I.' d-cd/d-c; CD/TC EMD 1074)*

Oct 70. (lp/c) *(SHVL/TCSHVL 781)* <382> **ATOM HEART MOTHER** [1] [55]
– Atom heart mother; (a) Father's shout – (b) Breast milky – (c) Mother fore – (d) Funky dung – (e) Mind your throats please – (f) Remergence / If / Summer '68 / Fat old Sun / Alan's psychedlic breakfast / Rise and shine / Sunny side up / Morning glory. *(cd-iss. Mar87; CDP 746381-2) (re-iss. Oct94 on 'E.M.I.' cd/c; CD/TC EMD 1072)*
(above featured **RON GEESIN** – horns, co-writer)

Nov 71. (lp/c) *(SHVL/TCSHVL 795)* <832> **MEDDLE** [3] [70]
– One of these days / A pillow of winds / Fearless (interpolating 'You'll never walk alone') / San Tropez / Seamus / Echoes. *(re-iss. Nov83 on 'Fame' lp/c; ATAK/TCATAK 35) (cd-iss. Aug84; CDP 746034-2) (re-iss. cd Apr89 on 'Mobile Fidelity'; UDCD 518) (re-iss. Aug94 on 'E.M.I.' cd/c; CD/TC EMD 1061)*

Dec 71. (7") <3240> **ONE OF THESE DAYS. / FEARLESS** [–] [ ]

Jun 72. (lp/c) *(SHVL/TCSHVL 4020)* <11078> **OBSCURED BY CLOUDS** [6] [46]
– Obscured by clouds / When you're in / Burning bridges / The gold it's in the . . . / Wots . . . uh the deal / Mudmen / Childhood's end / Free four / Stay / Absolute curtains. *(cd-iss. Apr87; CDP 746385-2) (re-iss. Sep95 on 'E.M.I.' cd/c; CD/TC EMD 1083)*

Jul 72. (7") <3391> **FREE FOUR. / STAY** [–] [ ]

Mar 73. (lp/c) *(SHVL/TCSHVL 804)* <11163> **THE DARK SIDE OF THE MOON** [2] [1]
– Speak to me / Breathe / On the run / Time / The great gig in the sky / Money / Us and them / Any colour you like / Brain damage / Eclipse. *(cd-iss. Aug84; CDP 746001-2) (re-iss. cd.Mar93; same); hit UK No.4) (re-iss. Jul94 on 'E.M.I.' cd/c; CD/TC EMD 1064) (re-iss. Feb97 on 'E.M.I.'; LPCENT 11)*

May 73. (7") <3609> **MONEY. / ANY COLOUR YOU LIKE** [–] [13]

Oct 73. (7") <3832> **US AND THEM. / TIME** [–] [ ]

Harvest Columbia

Sep 75. (lp/c) *(SHVL/TCSHVL 814)* <33453> **WISH YOU WERE HERE** [1] [1]
– Shine on you crazy diamond (parts 1-5) / Welcome to the machine / Have a cigar / Wish you were here / Shine on you crazy diamond (parts 6-9). *(cd-iss. Aug84; CDP 746035-2) (re-iss. Jul94 on 'E.M.I.' cd/c; CD/TC EMD 1062)*

Oct 75. (7") <10248> **HAVE A CIGAR. / SHINE ON YOU CRAZY DIAMOND (excerpt)** [–] [ ]

Jan 77. (lp/quad-lp/c) *(SHVL/Q4SHVL/TCSHVL 815)* <34474> **ANIMALS** [2] Feb77 [3]
– Pigs on the wing (part 1) / Dogs / Pigs (three different ones) / Sheep / Pigs on the wing (part 2). *(cd-iss. Jul86; CDP 746128-2) (re-iss. Jul94 on 'E.M.I.' cd/c; CD/TC EMD 1060)*

Nov 79. (7") *(HAR 5194)* <11187> **ANOTHER BRICK IN THE WALL (PART 2). / ONE OF MY TURNS** [1] Jan80 [1]

Dec 79. (d-lp/d-c) *(SHWD/TC2SHWD 411)* <36183> **THE WALL** [3] [1]
– In the flesh / The thin ice / The happiest days of our lives / Another brick in the wall (part 2) / Mother / Goodbye blue sky / Empty spaces / Young lust / One of my turns / Don't leave me now / Another brick in the wall (part 3) / Goodbye cruel world / Hey you / Is there anybody out there? / Nobody home / Vera / Comfortably numb / The show must go on / Run like hell / Waiting for the worms / Stop / The trial / Outside the wall. *(d-cd-iss. Sep84; CDS 746036-2) (re-iss. UK & US Jul90;) (re-iss. Oct94 on 'E.M.I.' cd/c; CD/TC EMD 1071)*

Apr 80. (7") <11265> **RUN LIKE HELL. / DON'T LEAVE ME NOW** [–] [53]

Jun 80. (7") <11311> **COMFORTABLY NUMB. / HEY YOU** [–] [ ]

Jun 82. (7") <03118> **ONE OF MY TURNS. / ANOTHER BRICK IN THE WALL (part 2)** [–] [ ]

Jul 82. (video) **THE WALL (soundtrack)** [–] [–]
– (tracks from above + new singles)

Aug 82. (7") *(HAR 5222)* <01342> **WHEN THE TIGERS BROKE FREE. / BRING THE BOYS BACK HOME** [39] [ ]

—— now just main trio **WATERS, GILMOUR, MASON.**(WRIGHT left to form ZEE) guests on lp were **ANDY BROWN** – organ, **RAY COOPER** – perc., **MICHAEL KAMEN** – piano, **RALPH RAVENSCROFT** – saxophone.

Mar 83. (lp/c) *(SHPF/TCSHPF 1983)* <38243> **THE FINAL CUT** [1] [6]
– The post war dream / Your possible pasts / One of the few / The hero's return / The gunners dream / Paranoid eyes / Get your filthy hands off my desert / The Fletcher memorial home / Southampton dock / The final cut / Not now John / Two suns in the sunset. *(cd-iss. Jul86; CDP 746129-2) (re-iss. Oct94 on 'E.M.I.' cd/c; CD/TC EMD 1070)*

May 83. (7") *(HAR 5224)* <03905> **NOT NOW JOHN. / THE HERO'S RETURN (pts.1 & 2)** [30] [ ]
(12"+=) *(12HAR 5224)* – ('A'version).

—— **MASON** and **GILMOUR** recruited new members below to replace WATERS who went solo. **TIM RENWICK** – guitar (ex-SUTHERLAND BROTHERS & QUIVER, ex-TV SMITH) / **GUY PRATT** – bass (ex-KILLING JOKE, ex-ICEHOUSE) / **SCOTT PAGE** – saxophone / **RICK WRIGHT** – keyboards also returned p/t.

E.M.I. Columbia

Sep 87. (lp/c/cd) *(EMD/TCEMD/CDEMD 1003)* <40599> **A MOMENTARY LAPSE OF REASON** [3] [3]
– Signs of life / Learning to fly / The dogs of war / One slip / On the turning away / Yet another movie / Round and around / A new machine (part 1) / Terminal frost / A new machine (part 2) / Sorrow.

Sep 87. (12"pink-ep) *(EMP 26)* <07363> **LEARNING TO FLY (edit) / ONE SLIP (edit). / TERMINAL FROST (lp version)** [ ] [70]
(cd-ep+=) *(CDEM 26)* – Terminal frost (DYOL version).

Dec 87. (7"/7"pink) *(EM/+P 34)* <07660> **ON THE TURNING AWAY. / RUN LIKE HELL (live)** [55] [ ]
(12"+=/cd-s+=) *(12/CD EM 34)* – ('A'live).

Jun 88. (7"/7"pink) *(EM/+G 52)* **ONE SLIP. / TERMINAL FROST** [50] [ ]
(12"+=/12"w-poster+=)(cd-s+=) *(12EM/+P 52)(CDEM 52)* – Dogs of war (live).

Nov 88. (d-lp/d-c/d-cd) *(EQ/TCEQ/CDEQ 5009)* <44484> **THE DELICATE SOUND OF THUNDER (live)** [11] [11]
– Shine on you crazy diamond / Learning to fly / Yet another movie / Round and around / Sorrow / The dogs of war / On the turning away / One of these days / Time / Wish you were here / Us and them * / Money / Another brick in the wall (part 2) / Comfortably numb / Run like hell. *(d-cd+= *)*

—— with **GILMOUR, MASON + WRIGHT** plus **GUY PRATT / TIM RENWICK / BOB EZRIN** – keyboards, percussion / **DICK PARRY** – tenor sax / **GARY WALLIS** – percussion / **JON CARIN** – programming + add.keyboards / + backing vocalists

Apr 94. (cd/c/lp) *(CD/TC+/EMD 1055)* <64200> **THE DIVISION BELL** [1] [1]
– Cluster one / What do you want from me / Poles apart / Marooned / A great day for freedom / Wearing the inside out / Take it back / Coming back to life / Keep talking / Lost for words / High hopes.

May 94. (c-s/7"colrd) *(TC+/EMS 309)* <77493> **TAKE IT BACK. / ASTRONOMY DOMINE (live)** [23] [73]
(cd-s+=) *(CDEMS 309)* – ('A'mix).

Oct 94. (c-s/7") *(TC+/EMS 342)* **HIGH HOPES. / KEEP TALKING** [26] [ ]
(12"+=/cd-s+=) *(12/CD EMS 342)* – One of these days.

Jun 95. (d-cd/d-c/q-lp)(video) *(CD/TC+EMD 1078)(MVD 4914363)* <67065> **PULSE (live)** [1] [1]
– Shine on you crazy diamond / Astronomy domine / What do you want from me / Learning to fly / Keep talking / Coming back to life / Hey you / A great day for freedom / Sorrow / High hopes / Another brick in the wall (part 2) / One of these days *[not on cd]* / Speak to me / Breathe / On the run / Time / The great gig in the sky / Money / Us and them / Any colour you like / Brain damage / Eclipse / Wish you were here / Comfortably numb / Run like hell.

– compilations, etc. –

May 71. (lp) *Starline; (SRS 5071) / Harvest; <759>* **RELICS** [32] [ ]
– Arnold Layne / Interstellar overdrive / See Emily play / Remember a day / Paintbox / Julia dream / Careful with that axe, Eugene / Cirrus minor / The Nile song / Biding my time / Bike. *(re-iss. Oct78 on 'Music For Pleasure' lp/c; MFP/TCMFP 50397) (re-iss. Feb96 on 'E.M.I.' cd/c; CD/TC EMD 1082) (lp re-iss. Aug97 on 'E.M.I.'; EMD 1113)*

Jan 74. (d-lp)(d-c) *Harvest; (SHDW 403)(TC2EXE 1013)* <11257> **A NICE PAIR** [21] Dec73 [36]
– (THE PIPER AT THE GATES OF DAWN / A SAUCERFUL OF SECRETS)

Dec 79. (11xlp-box) *Harvest; (PF 11)* **THE FIRST XI (67-77)** [ ] [ ]

Nov 81. (lp/c) *Harvest; (SHVL/TCSHVL 822)* <37680> **A COLLECTION OF GREAT DANCE SONGS** (remixes) [37] [31]
– One of these days / Money / Another brick in the wall (part 2) / Wish you were here / Shine on you crazy diamond / Sheep. *(re-iss. 1985 on 'Fame' lp/c; ATAK/TCATAK 31) (cd-iss. Nov88; CDP 790732-2)*

Nov 81. (7"w-drawn) *Harvest; (HAR 5217)* **MONEY. / LET THERE BE MORE LIGHT** [–] [–]

Jun 83. (lp) *Capitol; <12276>* **WORKS (68-73)** [–] [68]

Nov 91. (12"/cd-s) *See For Miles; (SEA/+CD 4)* **TONITE LET'S ALL MAKE LOVE IN LONDON** [ ] [–]

Nov 92. (9xcd-box) *E.M.I.; (PFBOX 1)* <53180> **SHINE ON** [ ] [ ]
– (A SAUCERFUL OF SECRETS – MOMENTARY LAPSE . . . + rare singles) *(re-iss. Sep98; CDS 780557-2)*

Nov 93. (cd) *See For Miles; (SFM 2)* **TONITE LET'S ALL MAKE LOVE IN LONDON . . . PLUS** [ ] [–]
– Interstellar overdrive / Nick's boogie / (interviews with David Hockney & Lee Marvin).

Nov 95. (cd) *See For Miles; (SFMCD 3)* **LONDON '66-'67** [ ] [–]
– Interstellar overdrive / Nick's boogie.

Mar 00. (d-cd/d-c) *E.M.I.; (523562-2/-4)* <62055> **IS THERE ANYBODY OUT THERE? – THE WALL LIVE 1980-1981 (live)** [15] May00 [19]
– (master of ceremonies) / In the flesh / The thin ice / Another brick in the wall (part 1) / The happiest days of our lives / Another brick in the wall (part 2) / Mother / Goodbye blue sky / Empty spaces / What shall we do now? / Young lust / One of my turns / Don't leave me now / Another brick in the wall (part 3) / The last few bricks / Goodbye cruel world / Hey you / Is there anybody out there? / Nobody home / Vera / Bring the boys back home / Comfortably numb / The show must go on / (master of ceremonies) / In the flesh / Run like hell / Waiting for the worms / (stop) / The trial / Outside the wall.

Nov 01. (d-cd/d-c/q-lp) *(<5 36111-2/-4/-1>)* **ECHOES: THE BEST OF PINK FLOYD** [2] [2]
– Astronomy domine / See Emily play / The happiest days of our lives / Another brick in the wall (part 2) / Echoes / Hey you / Marooned / The great gig in the sky / Set the controls for the heart of the sun / Money / Keep talking / Sheep / Sorrow / Shine on you crazy diamond (parts 1-7) / Time / The Fletcher memorial home / Comfortably numb / When the tigers broke free / One of these days / Us and them / Learning to fly / Arnold Layne / Wish you were here / Jugband blues / High hopes / Bike.

DAVID GILMOUR

solo with **MICK WEAVER** – keyboards / **RICK WILLIS** – bass / **JOHN WILLIE WILSON** – drums

Harvest Columbia

Jun 78. (lp/c) *(SHVL/TCSHVL 817)* <35388> **DAVID GILMOUR** [17] [29]
– Mihalis / There's no way out of it / Cry from the street / So far away / Short and sweet / Raise my rent / No way / Deafinitely / I can't breathe anymore. *(re-iss. 1983 on 'Fame' lp/c; FA/TCFA 4130791)*

Jun 78. (7") *(HAR 5167)* <10803> **THERE'S NO WAY OUT OF IT. / DEAFINITELY** [ ] [ ]

—— with various on session incl. STEVE WINWOOD, JEFF PORCARO & JON LORD

Feb 84. (7"/ext.12") *(HAR/12HAR 5226)* <04378> **BLUE LIGHT. / CRUISE** [ ] [62]

Mar 84. (lp/c)(cd) *(SHSP 24-0079-1/-4)(CDP 746031-2)* <39296> **ABOUT FACE** [21] [32]
– Until we sleep / Murder / Love on the air / Blue light / Out of the blue / All lovers are deranged / You know I'm right / Cruise / Let's get metaphysical / Near the end. *(re-iss. Mar87 on 'Fame' lp/c; FA/TCFA 3171)*

May 84. (7"/7"pic-d) *(HAR/+P 5229)* **LOVE ON THE AIR. / LET'S GET METAPHYSICAL** [ ] [ ]

RICHARD WRIGHT

solo with **SNOWY WHITE** – guitar / **MEL COLLINS** – saxophone / **LARRY STEELE** – bass / **REG ISADORE** – drums

Harvest Columbia

Sep 78. (lp/c) *(SHVL/TCSHVL 818)* <35559> **WET DREAM** [ ] [ ]
– Medterranean c / Against the odds / Cat cruise / Summer elegy / Waves / Holiday / Mad Yannis dance / Drop in from the top / Pink's song / Funky deux.

—— In 1984, he formed ZEE duo, and returned to FLOYD later in the 80's.

—— with **DAVE HARRIS** – guitar, vocals, keyboards, synth (ex-FASHION)

Apr 84. (7"/ext.12"; by ZEE) *(HAR/12HAR 5227)* **CONFUSION. / EYES OF A GYPSY** [ ] [–]

Apr 84. (lp/c; by ZEE) *(SHSP 240101/-1/-4)* **IDENTITY** [ ] [–]
– Confusion / Voices / Private person / Strange rhythm / Cuts like a diamond / By touching / How do you do it / Seems we are dreaming.

E.M.I. Capitol

Oct 96. (cd/c) *(CD/TC+/EMD 1098)* <53645> **BROKEN CHINA** [61] Nov96 [ ]
– Breaking water / Night of a thousand furry toys / Hidden fear / Runaway / Underground / Satellite / Woman of custom / Interlude / Black cloud / Far from the harbour wall / Drowning / Reaching for the rail / Blue room in Venice / Sweet July / Along the shoreline / Breakthrough.

NICK MASON

solo with **CARLA BLEY** and **ROBERT WYATT**

Harvest Columbia

May 81. (lp/c) *(SHSP/TCSHSP 4116)* <37307> **FICTITIOUS SPORTS** [ ] [ ]
– Can't get my motor to start / I was wrong / Siam / Hot river / Boo to you too / Do ya / Wervin' / I'm a mineralist.

Aug 85. (lp; by NICK MASON & RICK FENN) *(MAF 1)* <40142> **PROFILES** [ ] [ ]
– Malta / Lie for a lie / Rhoda / Profiles (part 1 & 2) / Israel / And the address / Mumbo jumbo / Zip code / Black ice / At the end of the day / Profiles (part 3).

Sep 85. (7"; by NICK MASON & RICK FENN) *(HAR 5238)* **LIE FOR A LIE. / AND THE ADDRESS** [ ] [–]
(12"+=) *(12HAR 5238)* – Mumbo jumbo.

PIXIES

Formed: Boston, Massachusetts, USA . . . 1986 by L.A. born frontman and self-confessed UFO freak, BLACK FRANCIS (real name, deep breath . . . CHARLES MICHAEL KITRIDGE THOMPSON IV) along with guitarist JOEY SANTIAGO. Famously placing a newspaper ad requesting musicians with a penchant for PETER, PAUL AND MARY and HUSKER DU, the only taker was KIM DEAL who subsequently brought in drummer DAVID LOVERING. Originally trading under the moniker PIXIES IN PANOPLY, the band soon trimmed this down to the punchier PIXIES and began kicking up a storm on the Boston music scene with their spiky, angular noise-pop (that's two thirds noise, one third pop) and wilfully cryptic lyrics. Along with fellow Bostonians THROWING MUSES, the band were signed to '4 a.d.' by a suitably impressed Ivo Watts-Russell, the label releasing The PIXIES' debut 'COME ON PILGRIM' in late '87. Stunningly different, the record galvanised the early PIXIES sound, a bizarre hybrid of manic, strangulated vocals (often sung in Spanish), searing melodic noise and schizophrenic, neo-latin rhythms. The album drew an early core of believers but it wasn't until the release of 'SURFER ROSA' (1988) that the band were hailed as the saviours of indie rock. Taking the formula of the debut to its brain splintering conclusion, the likes of 'BONE MACHINE', the incendiary 'SOMETHING AGAINST YOU' and careering 'BROKEN FACE' were utterly compelling in their blistering intensity. The sheer unhinged abandon with which BLACK FRANCIS threw himself into these songs has to be heard to be believed. You begin to fear that the man really has lost it when he asks 'WHERE IS MY MIND' in his inimitable melancholy howl. DEAL was equally affecting on the gorgeous 'GIGANTIC', the track building from a metaphorical whisper to a scream. Truly essential, 'SURFER ROSA' remains one of the most pivotal alternative rock records of the last fifteen years. Following their first headline UK tour, the band hooked up with producer Gil Norton for the 'DOOLITTLE' (1989) album. Previewed by the haunting 'MONKEY GONE TO HEAVEN', the record showcased a cleaner, more pop-friendly sound, most notably on (then) upcoming single, 'HERE COMES YOUR MAN'. Swoonfully poptastic, this song was guaranteed to have even the most miserable SMITHS fan grinning ear to ear, putting the toss that passes for modern 'indie-pop' to eternal shame. The demented 'DEBASER' was another highlight, becoming a dependable fixture at indie discos for oh, aeons. As well as a mammoth world tour, DEAL found time for her side project, The BREEDERS. A collaboration with the delectable TANYA DONELLY (ex-THROWING MUSES), the pair released the acclaimed 'POD' album in 1990. Later that year came 'BOSSANOVA', another breathtaking collection that had the music press in rapture. Lyrically, BLACK was in his element, losing himself in science fiction fantasy while the band raged and charmed in equal measure. The album reached No.3 in the UK charts and The PIXIES could apparently do no wrong, consolidating their position as one of the biggest American acts in Europe. Yet the critics turned on them with the release of 'TROMPE LE MONDE' (1991), in keeping with the times a decidedly grungier affair. Accusations of "Heavy Metal" were way off the mark. In reality, the record was still chokka with stellar tunes, you just had to dig deeper to find them. 'PLANET OF SOUND', 'SPACE (I BELIEVE IN)' and 'MOTORWAY TO ROSWELL' were all quintessential PIXIES, FRANCIS as endearingly fascinated as ever with the mysteries of the universe. Sadly, the singer was soon to turn his obsession into a solo venture, The PIXIES gone almost as quickly as they had arrived, leaving behind a brief but rich sonic legacy. With FRANCIS changing his name to the rather dull FRANK BLACK, he went on to release a moderately successful eponymous solo debut in 1993 and a wryly titled follow-up, 'TEENAGER OF THE YEAR' (1994), DEAL going on to make a further album with The BREEDERS. Inevitably, none of these projects approached the deranged genius of The PIXIES (Rock will never see their like again). The frontman continued to surface periodically and three albums, 'THE CULT OF RAY' (1996), 'FRANK BLACK AND THE CATHOLICS' (1998) and 'PISTOLERO' (1999), have all met with diminishing fanbase response. 'DOG IN THE SAND' followed in 2001, a more down home effort which featured some of his best songwriting for years. The fact that SANTIAGO was back on board was hardly a hindrance while occasional glimpses of FRANK's legendary lyrical genius suggested there was life in the old (black) dog yet. The man's feverish creativity continued apace with the simultaneous release, in 2002, of both 'DEVIL'S WORKSHOP' and 'BLACK LETTER DAYS'. Rarely, if ever, can an artist sustain quality over such a protracted format, especially bearing in mind that the latter disc stretches to almost 20 tracks. While this, at least, might conceivably have been more focused had it been edited down to size, there's a ramshackle continuity about the record that makes for strangely addictive listening. While ' . . .WORKSHOP' was the more sonically adrenalised of the two, both albums found BLACK's inimitable, impenetrable muse travelling America's stranger side roads. Reportedly inspired by a stint in therapy, 'SHOW ME YOUR TEARS' (2003) was perhaps the singer's most honest and uninhibitedly emotional set of songs. While these aren't adjectives one would normally associate with BLACK's oblique musical charms, and while there was still enough lyrical weirdness to placate longtime fans, the self-analysis seemed to have done his creative juices no end of good. • **Songwriters:** BLACK FRANCIS penned except; WINTERLONG + I'VE BEEN WAITING FOR YOU (Neil Young) / EVIL HEARTED YOU (Yardbirds) / HEAD ON (Jesus & Mary Chain) / CECILIA ANN (Surftones) / BORN IN CHICAGO (Paul Butterfield's Blues Band) / I CAN'T FORGET (Leonard Cohen). FRANK BLACK solo:- JUST A LITTLE (Beau Brummels) / RE-MAKE, RE-MODEL (Roxy Music) / HANG ON TO YOUR EGO (Beach Boys).

Album rating: COME ON PILGRIM mini (*7) / SURFER ROSA (*10) / DOOLITTLE (*9) / BOSSANOVA (*8) / TROMPE LE MONDE (*7) / DEATH TO THE PIXIES compilation (*8) / Frank Black: FRANK BLACK (*8) / TEENAGER OF THE YEAR (*8) / THE CULT OF RAY (*5) / FRANK BLACK & THE CATHOLICS (*5) / PISTOLERO (*5) / DOG IN THE SAND (*6) / DEVIL'S WORKSHOP (*5) / BLACK LETTER DAYS (*5) / SHOW ME YOUR TEARS (*6)

BLACK FRANCIS (b. CHARLES MICHAEL KITRIDGE THOMPSON IV, 1965, Long Beach, Calif.) – vocals, guitar / **JOEY SANTIAGO** (b.10 Jun'65, Manila, Philippines) – lead guitar / **KIM DEAL** (Mrs.JOHN MURPHY) (b.10 Jun'61, Dayton, Ohio) – bass, vocals / **DAVE LOVERING** (b. 6 Dec'61) – drums

		4.a.d.	Elektra
Oct 87.	(m-lp) *(MAD 709) <61296>* **COME ON PILGRIM** – Caribou / Vamos / Islade encounter / Ed is dead / The holiday song / Nimrod's son / I've been tried / Levitate me.		
Mar 88.	(lp/c)(cd) *(CAD/+C 803)(CAD 803CD) <61295>* **SURFER ROSA** – Bone machine / Break my body / Something against you / Broken face / Gigantic / River Euphrates / Where is my mind? / Cactus / Tony's theme / Oh my golly! / Vamos / I'm amazed / Brick is red. *(cd+=)* – COME ON PILGRIM (m-lp)		
Aug 88.	(12"ep/cd-ep) *(BAD 805/+CD)* **GIGANTIC. / RIVER EUPHRATES. / VAMOS. / IN HEAVEN (LADY IN THE RADIATOR SONG)**		–
Mar 89.	(7") *(AD 904)* **MONKEY GONE TO HEAVEN. / MANTA RAY**	60	

(12"+=/cd-s+=) *(BAD 904/+CD)* – Weird at my school / Dancing the manta ray.

Apr 89. (lp/c)(cd) *(CAD/+C 905)(CAD 905CD) <60856>*
DOOLITTLE [8] [98]
– Debaser / Tame / Wave of mutilation / I bleed / There goes my gun / Here comes your man / Dead / Monkey gone to Heaven / La la love you / Mr. Grieves / Crackity Jones / #13 baby / Silver / Hey / Gouge away.

Jun 89. (7") *(AD 909) <66694>* **HERE COMES YOUR MAN. / INTO THE WHITE** [54] [ ]
(12"+=/cd-s+=) *(BAD 909/+CD)* – Wave of mutilation (UK surf) / Bailey's walk.

—— KIM DEAL was also part of amalgamation The BREEDERS

Jul 90. (7"/c-s) *(AD/+C 0009) <66616>* **VELOURIA. / I'VE BEEN WAITING FOR YOU** [28] [ ]
(12"+=/cd-s+=) *(BAD 0009/+CD)* – Make believe / The thing.

Aug 90. (cd)(lp/c) *(CAD 0010CD)(CAD/+C 0010) <60963>*
BOSSANOVA [3] [70]
– Cecilia Ann / Rock music / Velouria / Allison / Is she weird / Ana / All over the world / Dig for fire / Down to the wall / The happening / Blown away / Hang wire / Stormy weather / Havalina.

Oct 90. (7"/c-s) *(AD/+C 0014) <66596>* **DIG FOR FIRE. / VELVETY (instrumental)** [62] [ ]
(12"+=/cd-s+=) *(BAD 0014/+CD)* – Winterlong / Santo.

May 91. (7") *(AD 1008)* **PLANET OF SOUND. / BUILD HIGH** [27] [ ]
(c-s+=)(12"+=/cd-s+=) *(BADC 1008)(BAD 1008/+CD)* – Evil hearted you / Theme from Narc.

Sep 91. (cd)(lp/c) *(CAD 1014CD)(CAD/+C 1014) <61118>*
TROMPE LE MONDE [7] [92]
– Trompe de Monde / Planet of sound / Alec Eiffel / The sad punk / Head on / U-mass / Palace of the brine / Letter to Memphis / Bird dream Of the Olympus mons / Space (I believe in) / Subbacultcha / Distance equals rate times time / Lovely day / Motorway to Roswell / The Navajo know.

Nov 91. (7") *(AD 1999)* **ALEC EIFFEL. / MOTORWAY TO ROSWELL** [ ] [–]
(12"+=)(cd-s+=) *(BAD 1999)(PIX 1999CD)* – Planet of sound (live) / Tame (live).

Feb 92. (12"ep) *<66444>* **ALEC EIFFEL / LETTER TO MEMPHIS (instrumental). / BUILD LIFE / EVIL HEARTED YOU** [–] [ ]

—— disbanded late in '92, with BLACK FRANCIS going solo as FRANK BLACK.

– compilations, etc. –

on '4 a.d.' / 'Elektra' unless otherwise mentioned

Sep 97. (7") *(AD 7010)* **DEBASER (demo). / #13 BABY** [23] [ ]
(cd-s) *(BAD 7010CD)* – ('A'studio) / Bone machine / Gigantic / Isla de Encanta.
(cd-s) *(BADD 7010CD)* – ('A'live) / Holiday song (live) / Cactus (live) / Nimrod's son (live).

Oct 97. (d-cd/d-c) *(DAD/+C 7011) / <62118>* **DEATH TO THE PIXIES** [28] [ ]
– Cecilia Ann / Planet of sound / Tame / Here comes your man / Debaser / Wave of mutilation / Dig for fire / Caribou / Holiday song / Nimrod's son / U mass / Bone machine / Gigantic / Where is my mind / Velouria / Gouge away / Monkey gone to Heaven / Debaser / Rock music / Broken face / Isla De Encanta / Hangfire / Dead / Into the white / Monkey gone to Heaven / Gouge away / Gouge away / Here comes your man / Alidon / Hey / Gigantic / Crackity Jones / Something against you / Tame / Wave of mutilation / Where is my mind / Ed is dead / Vamos / Tony's theme. *(de-luxe version hit No.20 q-lp/d-cd; DADD 7011/+CD)*

Jul 98. (cd) *(GAD 8013) <62185>* **PIXIES AT THE BBC (live)** [45] [ ]
– Wild honey pie / There goes my gun / Dead / Subbacultcha / Manta Ray / Is she weird? / Ana / Down to the well / Wave of mutilation / Letter to Memphis / Levitate me / Caribou / Monkey gone to Heaven / Hey / In Heaven (lady in the radiator song).

FRANK BLACK

—— with **ERIC DREW FELDMAN** – bass, keyboards, synthetics (ex-CAPTAIN BEEFHEART) / **NICK VINCENT** – drums, percussion / + extra guitars **SANTIAGO, MORRIS TEPPER + DAVID SARDY**

4 a.d. | Elektra

Mar 93. (lp/cd)(c) *(CAD 3004/+CD)(CADC 3004) <61467>*
FRANK BLACK [9] [ ]
– Los Angeles / I heard Ramona sing / Hang on to your ego / Fu Manchu / Places named after numbers / Czar / Old black dawning / Ten percenter / Brackish boy / Two spaces / Tossed (instrumental version) / Parry the wind high, low / Adda Lee / Every time I go around here / Don't ya rile 'em. *(cd re-iss. Jul98; GAD 3004CD)*

Apr 93. (7") *(AD 3005) <8782-2>* **HANG ON TO YOUR EGO. / THE BALLAD OF JOHNNY HORTON** [ ] [ ]
(cd-s+=) *(BAD 3005CD)* – Surf epic.

—— same trio augmented by **SANTIAGO, TEPPER + LYLE WORKMAN** – guitar

May 94. (7") *(AD 4007)* **HEADACHE. / ('A'mix)** [53] [–]
(10"/cd-s) *(BADD 4007/+CD)* – ('A'side) / Men in black / At the end of the world / Oddball.
(cd-s) *(BAD 4007CD)* – ('A'side) / Hate me / This is where I belong / Amnesia.

May 94. (d-lp/cd)(c) *(DAD 4009/+CD)(DADC 4009) <61618>*
TEENAGER OF THE YEAR [21] [ ]
– Whatever happened to Pong? / Thalassocracy / (I want to live on an) Abstract plain / Calistan / The vanishing spies / Speedy Marie / Headache / Sir Rockaby / Freedom rock / Two reelers / Fiddle riddle / Ole Mulholland / Fazer eyes / I could stay here forever / The hostess with the mostest / Superabound / Big red / Space is gonna do me good / White noise maker / Pure denizen of the citizens band / Bad, wicked world / Pie in the sky. *(re-iss. Jul98; GAD 4009CD)*

—— FRANK BLACK had earlier in the year teamed up with ex-SEX PISTOL; GLEN MATLOCK to form tribute band FRANK BLACK & THE STAX PISTOLS

Noise Annoys | not iss.

Dec 95. (cd/d-lp) *(ANAN CD/V 7)* **THE BLACK SESSIONS (live in Paris)** [ ] [–]
– Two spaces / (I want to live on an) Abstact plain / Headache / Old black dawning / Superabound / Calistan / The vanishing spies / Sir Rockaby / Big red / The Jacques Tati / Oddball / Men in black / Czar / Freedom rock / (Whatever happened to) Pong / Thalasocracy / White noise maker / Los Angeles / Handyman / Modern age / Jumping beans / (I want to live on an) Abstact plain (acoustic). *(re-iss. Oct97; same)*

—— now w/ **LYLE WORKMAN** – lead guitar / **DAVID McCAFFREY** – bass / **SCOTT BOUTIER** – drums

Epic | Warners

Dec 95. (ltd-7") *(662 671-7)* **THE MARXIST. / BETTER THINGS** [ ] [–]

Jan 96. (7") *(662 786-7)* **MEN IN BLACK. / JUST A LITTLE** [37] [–]
(cd-s+=) *(662 786-2)* – Re-make, re-model.
(cd-s) *(662 786-5)* – ('A'side) / You never heard of me / Pray a little faster / Announcement.

Jan 96. (cd/c/lp) *(481 647-2/-4/-1) <43070>* **THE CULT OF RAY** [39] [ ]
– The Marxist / Men in black / Punk rock city / You ain't me / Jesus was right / I don't want to hurt you (every single time) / Mosh, don't pass the guy / Kicked in the taco / Creature crawling / Adventure and the resolution / Dance war / The cult of Ray / Last stand of Shazeb Andleeb. *(cd re-iss. Oct01 on 'Cooking Vinyl'; COOKCD 221)*

Jul 96. (7") *(663 463-7)* **I DON'T WANT TO HURT YOU (EVERY SINGLE TIME). / YOU AIN'T ME (live)** [63] [–]
(cd-s+=) *(663 463-2)* – The Marxist / Better things.
(cd-s) *(663 463-5)* – ('A'live) / Men in black (live) / Village of the sun (live) / The last stand of Shazeb Andleeb (live).

FRANK BLACK AND THE CATHOLICS

with **LYLE WORKMAN, DAVE McCAFFREY + SCOTT BOUTIER**

Play It Again Sam | SpinArt

Apr 98. (7"ep/cd-ep) *(BIAS 347 7/CD)* **ALL MY GHOSTS / LIVING ON SOUL / HUMBOULDT COUNTY MASSACRE / CHANGING OF THE GUARDS** [ ] [–]

May 98. (cd/c/lp) *(BIAS 370 CD/MC/LP) <SPART 067CD>*
FRANK BLACK AND THE CATHOLICS [61] [ ]
– All my ghosts / Back to Rome / Do you feel bad about it / Dog gone / I gotta move / I need peace / King and Queen of Siam / Six sixty six / Solid gold / Steak 'n' sabre / Suffering / The man who was too loud. *(ltd-cd+=; BIAS 370CDX)* – All my ghosts / Living on soul / Humboldt county massacre / Changing of the guards. *(cd re-iss. Jul00 on 'SpinArt'; same as US)*

—— **RICK GILBERT** – guitar; repl. WORKMAN

Mar 99. (cd) *(CDBIAS 390CD) <SPART 070CD>* **PISTOLERO** [ ] [ ]
– Bad harmony / I switched you / Western star / Tiny heart / You're such a wire / I loved your brain / Smoke up / Billy Radcliffe / So hard to make things out / Eighty five weeks / I think I'm starting to lose it / I want to rock and roll / Skeleton man / So bay. *(lp-iss.Nov99 on 'SpinArt'; SPART 70)*

— added **ERIC DREW FELDMAN** – keyboards + **JOEY SANTIAGO** – guitar / **DAVE PHILIPS** – guitar / **MORRIS TEPPER** – guitar

Cooking Vinyl What Are?

Jan 01. (cd) *(FRYCD 098)* **ROBERT ONION / PAN AMERICAN HIGHWAY / ANGST** –

Jan 01. (cd) *(COOKCD 200)* *<4833>* **DOG IN THE SAND**
– Blast off / I've seen your picture / St. Francis dam disaster / Robert Onion / Stupid me / Bullet / The swimmer / Hermaphroditos / I'll be blue / Llano del Rio / If it takes all night / Dog in the sand.

Feb 01. (cd-s) *(FRYCD 099)* **ST. FRANCIS DAM DISASTER / CONSTANT SORROW MAN / SLEEP** –

Aug 02. (cd) *(COOKCD 243)* *<SPART 112>* **DEVIL'S WORKSHOP**
– Velvety / Out of state / His kingly cave / San Antonio, TX / Bartholomew / Modern age / Are you headed my way? / Heloise / The scene / Whiskey in your shoes / Fields of marigold.

Aug 02. (cd) *(COOKCD 240)* *<SPART 113>* **BLACK LETTER DAYS**
– The black rider / California bound / Chip away boy / Cold heart of stone / Black letter day / Valentine and Garuda / How you went so far / End of miles / 1826 / The farewell bend / Southbound bevy / I will run after you / True blue / Jane the queen of love / Jet black river / 21 reasons / Whispering weeds / The black rider.

Aug 03. (cd-s) *(FRYCD 161)* **EVERYTHING IS NEW / TAKE WHAT YOU WANT / DOWN IN THE HOLE** –

Sep 03. (cd) *(COOKCD 262)* *<SPART 129>* **SHOW ME YOUR TEARS**
– Nadine / Everything is new / My favorite kiss / Jaina blues / New house of the Pope / Horrible day / Massif centrale / When will happiness find me again? / Goodbye Lorraine / This old heartache / The snake / Coastline / Manitoba.

– compilations, etc. –

Jul 95. (12"ep/cd-ep) *Strange Fruit; (SFPS/+CD 091)* **PEEL SESSION** –
– Handyman / The man who was too loud / The Jacques Tati / Sister Isabel.

Nov 97. (cd-ep; with TEENAGE FANCLUB) *Strange Fruit; (SFRSCD 042)* **THE JOHN PEEL SESSION** –

Mar 01. (cd) *4 a.d.; (GAD 2103CD)* **THE COMPLETE B-SIDES** 53 –

☐ PIZZAMAN (see under ⇒ COOK, Norman)

PLACEBO

Formed: South London, England . . . October '94 by the cosmopolitan pair of BRIAN MOLKO (son of American and Scottish – Dundee – parents) and STEFAN OLSDAL, who had attended the same school in Luxembourg. They met up again in a London tube having spent time in the States and Sweden respectively. Early the following year, they recruited Swedish drummer, ROBERT SCHULTZBERG, the trio subsequently becoming joint winners of the 'In The City' Battle Of The Bands competition. Late in '95, PLACEBO shared a one-off single, 'BRUISE PRISTINE', with the band, SOUP, on 'Fierce Panda' records. After only a handful of gigs, they signed for 'Deceptive' (home of ELASTICA), leading to tours with ASH, BUSH and WHALE. A solitary single later ('COME HOME'), MOLKO and Co., hit the proverbial jackpot via a deal with Virgin/Hut subsidiary, 'Elevator'. The openly bisexual, cross-dressing MOLKO, drew comparisons with 70's glam idols like BOLAN and BOWIE, the music, however, traded in the glitter for a darker listening experience. Taking the fast lane out of the post-grunge pile-up, they fused elements of avant-garde rock and cerebral metal, MOLKO's paint-stripping shrill drawing comparisons with Rush's GEDDY LEE and DAVID SURKAMP of the more obscure Pavlov's Dog. Their eponymous debut album was released in mid-'96 to a fawning music press, metal-mag Kerrang's strong support helping the record dent the UK Top 40. Hit singles 'TEENAGE ANGST' and the Top 5 'NANCY BOY', helped regenerate sales of a collection which many hailed as one of the years' best. In addition to the more incendiary tracks, the album also contained such hauntingly reflective songs as 'LADY OF THE FLOWERS' and 'HANG ON TO YOUR IQ'. PLACEBO – with STEVE HEWITT replacing SCHULTZBERG – were back with a bang (so to speak!) in the Autumn of '98, two blistering UK Top 5 singles in quick succession, 'PURE MORNING' and 'YOU DON'T CARE ABOUT US', premiering their equally superb sophomore set, 'WITHOUT YOU I'M NOTHING' – 'EVERY YOU EVERY ME' and collaborative title track with MOLKO's idol BOWIE, kept the band in high profile the following year. With 'BLACK MARKET MUSIC' (2000), MOLKO took his brooding sexual vision to its twisted climax on an album which ranks as one of PLACEBO's most darkly satisfying to date. Longtime fans will be glad to know that the ever androgynous frontman is still wrestling with his soiled demons, content to provide a mascara-smeared foil to the bloke-rock clogging up the music biz. Still going strong after three albums, PLACEBO issued their fourth, the hauntingly titled 'SLEEPING WITH GHOSTS' (2003). It saw a more mature MOLKO letting down his glam-rock snottiness, in favour of dark rock in the vein of MUSE and The COOPER TEMPLE CLAUSE. As always, his high-pitched whine was ever present as were the complex guitar rhythms and the off-kilter backbeat by the ever reliable OLSDAL and HEWITT. Add to the mix some dark electronica and the occasional ballad ('ENGLISH SUMMER RAIN') and what emerged was a deliciously brash and delicately dark pop-rock record that would be hard not to impress the rock fraternity. • **Songwriters:** Group, except BIGMOUTH STRIKES AGAIN (Smiths) / 20TH CENTURY BOY (T.Rex) / JOHNNY & MARY (Robert Palmer).

Album rating: PLACEBO (*9) / WITHOUT YOU I'M NOTHING (*8) / BLACK MARKET MUSIC (*6) / SLEEPING WITH GHOSTS (*6)

BRIAN MOLKO (b. 1972) – vocals, guitars, bass / **STEFAN OLSDAL** (b. Sweden) – bass, guitars, keyboards / **ROBERT SCHULTZBERG** – drums, percussion, didgeridoo

Fierce Panda not iss.

Nov 95. (7") *(NING 13)* **BRUISE PRISTINE. / (Soup: 'Meltdown')** –

Deceptive not iss.

Feb 96. (7") *(BLUFF 024)* **COME HOME. / DROWNING BY NUMBERS** –
(cd-s+=) *(BLUFF 024CD)* – Oxygen thief.

Elevator Caroline

Jun 96. (7") *(FLOOR 001)* **36 DEGREES. / DARK GLOBE** –
(cd-s+=) *(FLOORCD 001)* – Hare Krishna.

Jun 96. (cd/c/lp) *(CD/MC/LP FLOOR 002)* *<7575>* **PLACEBO** 40 Jul96
– Come home / Teenage angst / Bionic / 36 degrees / Hang on to you IQ / Nancy boy / I know / Bruise pristine / Lady of the flowers / Swallow. *(re-dist.Jan97 hit UK No.5; same)*

Sep 96. (7"/cd-s) *(FLOOR/+CD 003)* **TEENAGE ANGST. / BEEN SMOKING TOO LONG / HUG BUBBLE** 30 –
(7"m) *(FLOORX 003)* – ('A'-V.P.R.O. radio session) / Flesh mechanic (demo) / HK farewell.

Jan 97. (7") *(FLOOR 004)* **NANCY BOY. / SLACKERBITCH** 4
(cd-s+=) *(FLOORCD 004)* – Bigmouth strikes again / Hug bubble.
(cd-s) *(FLOORCDX 004)* – ('A'side) / Eyesight to the blind / Swallow (Brad Wood mix) / Miss Moneypenny.

May 97. (c-s/cd-s) *(FLOOR MC/CD 005)* **BRUISE PRISTINE / THEN THE CLOUDS WILL OPEN FOR ME / BRUISE PRISTINE (One Inch Punch remix)** 14 –
(cd-s) *(FLOORCDX 005)* – ('A'side) / Waiting for the sun of man / Serenity (Lionrock remix).

— **STEVE HEWITT** (b. Northwich, England) – drums; repl. SCHULTZBERG

Elevator Hut

Aug 98. (cd-ep) *(FLOORCD 6)* **PURE MORNING / MARS LANDING PARTY / LEELOO** 4 –
(cd-ep) *(FLOORCDX 6)* – ('A'-lp version) / Needledick / The innocence of sleep.

Sep 98. (c-s/cd-s) *(FLOOR C/CD 7)* <95363> **YOU DON'T CARE ABOUT US / 20TH CENTURY BOY / ION** [5] [ ]
(cd-s) *(FLOORDX 7)* – ('A'side) / ('A'-Les Rhythmes Digitales remix) / ('A'-Howie B remix).

Oct 98. (cd/c/lp) *(CDFLOOR/FLOORMC/FLOORLP 8)* <46531> **WITHOUT YOU I'M NOTHING** [7] Nov98 [ ]
– Pure morning / Brick shithouse / You don't care about us / Ask for answers / Without you I'm nothing / Allergic (to thoughts of Mother Earth) / The crawl / Every you every me / My sweet prince / Summer's gone / Scared of girls / Burger queen.

Jan 99. (7") *(FLOORLH 9)* **EVERY YOU EVERY ME. / NANCY BOY (Blue Amazon remix)** [11] [–]
(c-s+=/cd-s+=) *(FLOORCD 9)* – ('A'-Jimmy Cauty remix).
(cd-s) *(FLOORDX 9)* – ('A'side) / ('A'-Sneaker Pimps version) / ('A'-Brothers In Rhythm remix).

Aug 99. (cd-ep; featuring DAVID BOWIE) *(FLOORCD 10)* **WITHOUT YOU I'M NOTHING / ('A'-Unkle remix) / ('A'-Americruiser remix) / ('A'-Brothers In Rhythm remix)** [–] nochart [–]

Jul 00. (c-s/cd-s) *(FLOOR C/CD 11)* **TASTE IN MEN / THEME FROM FUNKY REVEREND / TASTE IN MEN (Alpinestars Kamikaze skimix)** [16] [–]
(cd-s) *(FLOORDX 11)* – ('A'side) / Johnny & Mary / Taste in men (Adrian Sherwood Go Go dub mix).
(12"++=) *(FLOORT 11)* – (all above).

Sep 00. (c-s/cd-s) *(FLOOR C/CD 12)* **SLAVE TO THE WAGE / LENI / BUBBLEGUM** [19] [–]
(cd-s/12"+=) *(FLOOR DX/X 12)* – ('A'-album version) / Holocaust / ('A'-Les Rythmes Digitales new wave mix).

Oct 00. (cd/c/lp) *(CDFLOOR/FLOORMCX/FLOORLP 13)* *<10316>* **BLACK MARKET MUSIC** [6] [ ]
– Taste in men / Days before you came / Special K / Spite & malice / Passive aggressive / Black-eyed / Blue American / Slave to the wage / Commercial for Levi / Haemoglobin / Narcoleptic / Peeping Tom.

Mar 01. (cd-s) *(CDFLOOR 14)* **SPECIAL K / DUB PSYCHOSIS / PASSIVE AGGRESSIVE (Brothers In Rhythm remix)** [ ] [–]
(12"+=) *(TFLOOR 14)* – Little Mo / Slave to the wage (I can't believe it's a remix).
(cd-s) *(CDFLOORX 14)* – ('A'-Timo Maas remix) / (above 2).

Elevator AstralWerks

Mar 03. (7") *(FLOOR 16)* **THE BITTER END. / DADDY COOL** [12] [–]
(cd-s+=) *(FLOORCD 16)* – Teenage angst (piano version) / ('A'-video).
(cd-s) *(FLOORDX 16)* – ('A'side) / Evalia / Drink you pretty.

Mar 03. (cd/lp) *(CDFLOOR/FLOORLP 17)* <81936> **SLEEPING WITH GHOSTS** [11] Apr03 [ ]
– Bulletproof Cupid / English summer rain / This picture / Sleeping with ghosts / The bitter end / Something rotten / Plasticine / Special needs / I'll be yours / Second sight / Protect me from what I want / Centrefolds.

Jun 03. (7") *(FLOOR 18)* **THIS PICTURE. / WHERE IS MY MIND (XFM live)** [23] [–]
(cd-s+=) *(FLOORCD 18)* – Soulmates.

Sep 03. (7") *(FLOOR 19)* **SPECIAL NEEDS. / ENGLISH SUMMER RAIN (freelance hellraiser remix)** [27] [–]
(cd-s+=) *(FLOORCD 19)* – Plasticine (lounge version).

– compilations, etc. –

Sep 03. (d-cd) *Elevator; (591967-2)* **PLACEBO / BLACK MARKET MUSIC** [ ] [–]

☐ Robert PLANT (see under ⇒ LED ZEPPELIN)

☐ PLASTIC ONO BAND (see under ⇒ LENNON, John)

☐ P.M. (see under ⇒ EMERSON, LAKE & PALMER)

POCO

Formed: Los Angeles, California, USA . . . August '68 as POGO, by ex-BUFFALO SPRINGFIELD members RICHIE FURAY and JIM MESSINA, plus ex-BOENZEE CRYQUE pardners, RUSTY YOUNG and GEORGE GRANTHAM. RANDY MEISNER (formerly a member of The POOR) was also a brief member, subsequently departing to join RICK NELSON's STONE CANYON BAND and later The EAGLES. Early in '69, POGO signed to 'Epic', soon altering their name due to legal threats from a comic strip of the same name. Their debut album 'PICKIN' UP THE PIECES' managed a US Top 75 placing, its hippy harmonising and folk/country embellished, mellow-rock stylings laying the foundations for The EAGLES' subsequent multi-platinum flight. An eventual replacement for MEISNER was found in TIMOTHY B. SCHMIT, who, ironically, had previously lost out to the former at an earlier audition. The eponymous second set followed in summer 1970, its laidback hooks again ensnaring critics and newly converted country-rock fans alike. Something of a one-off for a genre that wasn't exactly renowned for uncompromising experimentation, the whole of the album's second side was devoted to a latin-country workout catchily titled 'EL TONTO DE NADIE REGRASA'. But it was in the free flowing, dope smoking climes of the live arena where the likes of POCO excelled and, with Heads turning to country in droves (even The GRATEFUL DEAD were mellowing out on pedal steel), the band made the US Top 30 in early '71 with the concert set, 'DELIVERIN''. Fed up with touring, MESSINA quit for a life of MOR pop mush in (KENNY) LOGGINS & MESSINA, a new guitarist found in PAUL COTTON. This line-up remained steady for a further two years, during which time the band recorded a handful of albums including the acclaimed 'A GOOD FEELIN' TO KNOW' (1973). The exhilarating title track remains one of their best-loved and most enduring moments; at their best, POCO were certainly a match for high flying contemporaries, The EAGLES, FURAY becoming increasingly frustrated by his band's middling commercial returns. When he departed to form the short-lived supergroup, SOUTHER-HILLMAN-FURY, pedal steel maestro, RUSTY YOUNG, steered POCO through the remainder of the 70's with a succession of competent, if workmanlike efforts. One of the standout tracks from this period was undoubtedly 'ROSE OF CIMARRON', a UK radio staple which surprisingly failed to make much of an impression in the US Top 100. Ironically, it was only after yet another member, SCHMIT, had defected to the rival EAGLES camp that POCO scored a bonafide US chart hit with 'CRAZY LOVE', the attendant 'LEGEND' (1979) album also making the Top 20. This marked a last stand of sorts, however, as country-rock was relegated to a fairly lowly placing on the agenda of America's changing musical climate at the dawn of the 80's. The bedraggled troupe soldiered on before finally hanging up their saddles after the lacklustre 'INAMORATA' (1984). The inevitable reunion of original members, FURAY, MESSINA, GRANTHAM, MEISNER and YOUNG came together in 1989, the revamped POCO scoring a syrupy Top 40 hit with the RICHARD MARX-penned 'CALL IT LOVE'. The single was accompanied, of course, by a comeback album, 'LEGACY' (1989) and the obligatory tour; with FURAY now a man of the cloth, he was hardly suited to the rock'n'roll lifestyle and amid increasing tension with his bandmates, departed in the early 90's. POCO, meanwhile, sauntered on down the trail, YOUNG, as ever, leading the way. 2002's 'RUNNING HORSE' also added little to the band's legacy with MARX again bringing his AOR chops to the table in a production capacity. Unsurprisingly then, there was little of the ragged country glory of old, or the rich harmony work with which they made their name. • **Songwriters:** Group penned together and individually, with FURAY and COTTON contributing the most. Covered BRASS BUTTONS (Gram Parsons) / etc. • **Trivia:** STEELY DAN's DONALD FAGEN provided them with synthesized sound on their 'INDIAN SUMMER' album.

Album rating: PICKIN' UP THE PIECES (*7) / POCO (*6) / DELIVERIN' (*6) / FROM THE INSIDE (*5) / A GOOD FEELIN' TO KNOW (*7) / CRAZY EYES (*6) / SEVEN (*6) / CANTAMOS (*5) / HEAD OVER HEELS (*7) / THE VERY BEST OF POCO compilation (*7) / LIVE (*4) / ROSE OF CIMMARON (*7) / INDIAN SUMMER (*7) / LEGEND (*6) / UNDER THE GUN (*5) / BLUE AND GRAY (*4) / COWBOYS & ENGLISHMEN (*3) / GHOST TOWN (*4) / INAMORATA (*4) / LEGACY (*5) / POCO: THE FORGOTTEN TRAIL 1969-1974 compilation (*6) / RUNNING HORSE (*3)

RICHIE FURAY (b. 9 May'44, Yellow Springs, Ohio) – guitar, vocals / **JIM MESSINA** (b. 5 Dec'47, Maywood, Calif.) – guitar, vocals / **RUSTY YOUNG** (b.23 Feb'46, Long Beach, Calif.) – pedal steel guitar / **GEORGE GRANTHAM** (b.20 Nov'47, Cordell, Oklahoma) – drums, vocals / **RANDY MEISNER** (b. 8 Mar'46, Scottsbluff, Nebraska) – bass, vocals (RANDY left before debut recording)

Epic Epic

Jun 69. (7") *<10501>* **PICKIN' UP THE PIECES. / FIRST LOVE** –

Jun 69. (lp) *<26460>* **PICKIN' UP THE PIECES** – 63
– Foreward – What a day / Nobody's fool / Calico lady / First love / Make me smile – Short changed / Pickin' up the pieces / Grand junction / Oh yeah / Just in case it happens / Tomorrow / Consequently so long. *(UK-iss.1974; EPC 65327) (re-iss. Mar86 on 'Edsel'; XED 161) (cd-iss. Jul95; EK 66227)*

Nov 69. (7") *<10543>* **MY KIND OF LOVE. / HARD LUCK** –

—— added **TIMOTHY B. SCHMIT** (b.30 Oct'47, Sacramento, Calif.) – bass, vocals (ex-NEW BREED)

Jul 70. (lp) *(EPC 64082) <26522>* **POCO** Jun90 58
– Hurry up / You better think twice / Honky tonk downstairs / Keep on believin' / Anyway bye bye / Don't let it pass by / Nobody's fool / El Tonto de Nadie Regrasa.

Aug 70. (7") *(EPC 5141) <10636>* **YOU BETTER THINK TWICE. / ANYWAY BYE BYE** 72

Feb 71. (lp) *(EPC 64204) <30209>* **DELIVERIN' (live)** 26
– I guess you made it / C'mon / Hear that music / Kind woman / Hard luck – Child's claim to fame / Pickin' up the pieces / You'd better think twice / A man like me / Just in case it happens, yes indeed / Grand junction / Consequently so long.

Apr 71. (7") *(EPC 7138) <10714>* **C'MON. / I GUESS YOU MADE IT** Mar71 69

—— **PAUL COTTON** (b.26 Feb'43) – guitar, vocals (ex-ILLINOIS SPEED PRESS) repl. MESSINA. (He joined LOGGINS & MESSINA)

Nov 71. (7") *(EPC 7631) <10804>* **JUST FOR ME AND YOU. / OL' FORGIVER**

Dec 71. (lp) *(EPC 64543) <30753>* **FROM THE INSIDE** Sep71 52
– Bad weather / Ol' forgiver / Railroad days / From the inside / Hoe down / Just for me and you / What am I gonna do / You are the one / Do you feel it too / What if I should say I love you.

Jan 72. (7") *<10816>* **RAILROAD DAYS. / YOU ARE THE ONE** –

Jan 73. (7") *(EPC 8240) <10890>* **A GOOD FEELIN' TO KNOW. / EARLY TIMES**

Jan 73. (lp) *(EPC 65126) <31601>* **A GOOD FEELIN' TO KNOW** Nov72 69
– And settling down / Ride the country / I can see everything / Go and say goodbye / Keeper of the fire / Early times / A good feelin' to know / Restrain / Sweet lovin'.

Jan 73. (7") *<10958>* **I CAN SEE EVERYTHING. / GO AND SAY GOODBYE** –

Mar 73. (7") *(EPC 1344)* **AND SETTLING DOWN. / I CAN SEE EVERYTHING** –

Nov 73. (lp) *(EPC 65631) <32354>* **CRAZY EYES** Sep73 38
– Blue water / Fool's gold / Here we go again / Brass buttons / A right along / Crazy eyes / Magnolia / Let's dance tonight. *(cd-iss. Jul95; EK 66968)*

Nov 73. (7") *<11055>* **FOOL'S GOLD. / HERE WE GO AGAIN** –

Feb 74. (7") *<11092>* **BLUE WATER. / MAGNOLIA** –

—— Trimmed to a quartet when RICHIE formed SOUTHER-HILLMAN-FURAY

Jun 74. (lp) *(EPC 80082) <32895>* **SEVEN** May74 68
– Skatin' / Drivin' wheel / You've got your reasons / Just call my name / Faith in the families / Krikkit's song (passing through) / Rocky mountain breakdown / Angel. *(cd-iss. Jul95; EK 66985)*

Jun 74. (7") *<11141>* **ROCKY MOUNTAIN BREAKDOWN. / FAITH IN THE FAMILIES** –

Nov 74. (7") *<50076>* **BITTER BLUE. / HIGH AND DRY** –

Dec 74. (lp) *(EPC 80596) <33192>* **CANTAMOS** Nov74 76
– Sagebush serenade / Susannah / High and dry / Western Waterloo / One horse blue / Bitter blue / Another time around / Whatever happened to your smile / All the ways. *<(cd-iss. Apr03 on 'Wounded Bird'; WOU 3192)>*

A.B.C. A.B.C.

Jul 75. (lp) *(ABCL 5137) <890>* **HEAD OVER HEELS** 43
– Keep on tryin' / Lovin' arms / Let me turn back to you / Makin' love / Down in the quarter / Sittin' on a fence / Georgia, bind my ties / Us / Flyin' solo / Dallas / I'll be back again.

Sep 75. (7") *(EPC 7631) <12126>* **KEEP ON TRYIN'. / GEORGIA, BIND MY TIES** 50

Feb 76. (7") *(ABC 4096) <12159>* **MAKIN' LOVE. / FLYIN' SOLO**

—— added **AL GARTH** – fiddle, saxophone (to **YOUNG, GRANTHAM, SCHMIT & COTTON**)

May 76. (lp) *(ABCL 5166) <946>* **ROSE OF CIMARRON** 89
– Rose of cimarron / Stealaway / Just like me / Company's comin' / Slow poke / Too many nights too long / P.N.S. (when you come around) / Starin' at the sky / All alone together / Tulsa turnaround. *(re-iss. Feb82 on 'M.C.A.'; MCL 1638) (re-iss. Apr92 cd/c; MCLD/MCLC 19015) (cd re-iss. Apr94 on 'One Way'; MCAD 22076)*

Jul 76. (7") *<12204>* **ROSE OF CIMARRON. / TULSA TURNAROUND** – 94

Oct 76. (7") *(ABC 4149)* **STARIN' AT THE SKY. / P.N.S. (WHEN YOU COME AROUND)** –

—— returned to a quartet when AL GARTH departed

Apr 77. (7") *<12295>* **INDIAN SUMMER. / ME AND YOU** – 50

Apr 77. (lp) *(ABCL 5220) <989>* **INDIAN SUMMER** 57
– Indian summer / Twenty years / Me and you / Downfall / Win or lose / Living in the band / Stay (night until noon) / Find out in time / The dance medley:- When the dance is over – Never gonna stop – When the dance is over (reprise).

May 77. (7") *(ABC 4178)* **INDIAN SUMMER. / FIND OUT IN TIME** –

—— **CHARLIE HARRISON** (b. England) – bass, vocals (ex-AL STEWART) repl. TIM to EAGLES / **STEVE CHAPMAN** (b. England) – drums, vocals (ex-AL STEWART) repl. GEORGE to The SECRETS / added **KIM BULLARD** (b. Atlanta, Georgia) – keyboards (ex-CROSBY, STILLS & NASH) (US tour)

Jan 79. (lp) *(ABCL 5264) <1099>* **LEGEND** Nov78 14
– Boomerang / Spellbound / Barbados / Little darlin' / Love comes love goes / Heart of the night / Crazy love / The last goodbye / Legend. *(re-iss. Jun88 on 'M.C.A.'; DMCL 1879) (re-iss. Jan93 cd/c; MCLD/MCLC 19143)*

Jan 79. (7") *(ABC 4240) <12439>* **CRAZY LOVE. / BARBADOS** 17

M.C.A. M.C.A.

Jun 79. (7") *(MCA 509) <41023>* **HEART OF THE NIGHT. / THE LAST GOODBYE** May79 20

Sep 79. (7") *<41103>* **LEGEND. / INDIAN SUMMER** –

May 80. (7") *(MCA 589)* **LEGEND. / ROSE OF CIMARRON** –

Jul 80. (7") *(MCA 635) <41269>* **UNDER THE GUN. / REPUTATION** 48

Aug 80. (lp) *(MCF 3076) <5132>* **UNDER THE GUN** Jul80 46
– Under the gun / While we're still young / The everlasting kind / Down to the wire / Footsteps of a fool / Reputation / Midnight rain / A fool's Paradise / Friends in the distance / Made of stone.

Oct 80. (7") *<41326>* **MIDNIGHT RAIN. / FOOL'S PARADISE** – 74

Jan 81. (7") *<51034>* **FRIENDS IN THE DISTANCE. / EVERLASTING KIND** –

Jul 81. (7") *<51172>* **WIDOWMAKER. / DOWN ON THE RIVER AGAIN** –

Jul 81. (lp) *<5227>* **BLUE AND GRAY** – 76
– Glorybound / Blue and gray / Streets of Paradise / The writing on the wall / Down the river again / Please wait for me / Widowmaker / Here comes that girl again / Sometime / The land of glory. *(UK cd-iss. Apr94 on 'One Way'; MCAD 22068)*

Feb 82. (lp) *<5288>* **COWBOYS AND ENGLISHMEN** –
– Sea of heartbreak / No relief in sight / There goes my heart / Ashes / Feudin' / Cajun Moon / Ribbon of darkness / If you could read my mind / While you're on your way / The price of love. *(UK cd-iss. Apr94 on 'One Way'; MCAD 22067)*

Mar 82. (7") *<52001>* **SEA OF HEARTBREAK. / FEUDIN'** [–] [ ]

Atlantic Atlantic

Oct 82. (7") *<89970>* **GHOST TOWN. / HIGH SIERRA** [–] [ ]

Oct 82. (lp) *(K 50902) <80008>* **GHOST TOWN** [ ] [ ]
– Ghost town / How will you feel tonight / Shoot for the moon / The midnight rodeo / Cry no more / Break of hearts / Love's so cruel / Special care / When hearts collide / High Sierra.

Dec 82. (7") *<89919>* **SHOOT FOR THE MOON. / THE MIDNIGHT RODEO (IN THE LEAD TONIGHT)** [–] [50]

Jun 83. (7") *<89851>* **BREAK OF HEARTS. /** [–] [ ]

—— **FURAY** returned reforming early line-up with **GRANTHAM, COTTON, SCHMIT + YOUNG**

May 84. (lp) *<80184>* **INAMORATA** [–] [ ]
– Days gone by / This old flame / Daylight / Odd man out / How many moons / When you love someone / Brenda X / Standing in the fire / Save a corner of your heart / The storm.

Apr 84. (7") *<89674>* **DAYS GONE BY. / DAYLIGHT** [–] [80]

Jun 84. (7") *<89650>* **THIS OLD FLAME. / SAVE A CORNER OF YOUR HEART** [–] [ ]

Aug 84. (7") *<89629>* **THE STORM. / SAVE A CORNER OF YOUR HEART** [–] [ ]

—— They split 1984 but reformed 5 years later. **FURAY, MESSINA, GRANTHAM, MEISNER + RUSTY YOUNG.**

R.C.A. R.C.A.

Oct 89. (7") *(PB 49339) <9038>* **CALL IT LOVE. / LOVIN' YOU EVERY MINUTE** [ ] Aug89 [18]
(12"+=/cd-s+=) *(PT/PD 49340)* – Who else?.

Nov 89. (lp/c/cd) *(PL/PK/PD 90395) <9694>* **LEGACY** [ ] Sep89 [40]
– When it all began / Call it love / The nature of love / What do people know / Nothin' to hide / Look within * / Rough edges / Who else? / Lovin' you every minute / If it wasn't for you / Follow your dreams. *(cd+= *)*

Nov 89. (7") *<9131>* **NOTHIN' TO HIDE. / IF IT WASN'T FOR YOU** [–] [39]

—— **YOUNG + COTTON + GRANTHAM** reunited; added guest **CRAIG FULLER**

not iss. Drifter's Church

2002. (cd) *<3>* **RUNNING HORSE** [–] [ ]
– One tear at a time / Every time I hear that train / If your heart needs a hand / Never loved . . . never hurt like this / Forever / Never get enough / If you can't stand to lose / I can only imagine / Shake it / That's what love is all about / Running horse.

– compilations, etc. –

Aug 75. (d-lp) *Epic; (EPC 88135) <33537>* **THE VERY BEST OF POCO** [ ] Jul75 [90]
<cd-iss. 1989; > – (omits 2 tracks). *<(cd re-iss. Feb03; 495241-2)>*

Mar 76. (lp) *Epic; (EPC 80705) <33336>* **POCO LIVE (live late '74)** [ ] [ ]
– Blue water / Fools gold / Rocky mountain breakdown / Bad weather / Ride the country / Angel / High and dry / Restrain / A good feelin' to know.

Nov 77. (12"ep) *A.B.C.; (4130)* **ROSE OF CIMARRON / INDIAN SUMMER. / KEEP ON TRYIN' / STARIN' AT THE SKY** [ ] [–]

Mar 80. (lp) *Epic; <36210>* **POCO: THE SONGS OF PAUL COTTON** (his POCO compositions) [–] [ ]

Mar 80. (lp/c) *C.B.S.; (CBS/40 31781) / Epic; <36211>* **POCO: THE SONGS OF RICHIE FURAY**(his POCO compositions) [ ] [ ]

Aug 89. (cd) *M.C.A.; <MCAD 42323>* **CRAZY LOVING: THE BEST OF POCO 1975-1982** [–] [ ]
– Heart of the night / Keep on tryin' / Midnight rain / Widowmaker / Crazy love / The price of love / Too many nights too long / Ashes – Feudin' (instrumental) / Sometimes (we are all we got) / Legend / Indian summer / Under the gun / Rose of cimarron.

Jan 90. (cd) *CBS-Legacy; <487483-2>* **POCO: THE FORGOTTEN TRAIL (1969-74)** [–] [ ]
(UK-iss.Jun97; same)

Jun 97. (cd) *Beat Goes On; (BGOCD 359)* **FROM THE INSIDE / A GOOD FEELIN' TO KNOW** [ ] [–]

Jun 97. (cd) *Half Moon; (HMNCD 008)* **THE ESSENTIAL COLLECTION** [ ] [–]

Mar 98. (cd) *Beat Goes On; (BGOCD 370)* **THE VERY BEST OF POCO** [ ] [–]

P.O.D.

Formed: San Ysidro, San Diego, California, USA . . . 1992 by guitarist MARCOS and drummer WUV. A year later, the full line-up comprised vocalist SONNY (WUV's cousin) and bass player TRAA. Marked out a Christian metal/hard-rock act in the mould of RAGE AGAINST THE MACHINE (with dub, reggae, hip-hop and hardcore punk all thrown in), P.O.D. – PAYABLE ON DEATH were soon supporting the likes of The VANDALS, PENNYWISE and GREEN DAY, which helped them shift over 40,000 copies of four independent CD's ('BROWN', 'SNUFF THE PUNK', 'LIVE' and the EP 'WARRIORS'). These were mainly released on their own 'Rescue' records before they were snapped up by 'Atlantic' in 1998. Their first official release, 'THE FUNDAMENTAL ELEMENTS OF SOUTHTOWN' went platinum in 1999 and at that year's San Diego Music Awards, P.O.D. earned top honors for Best Hard Rock or Metal Group. The following year, they toured with Ozzfest and also played alongside STAIND and CRAZY TOWN for the MTV Campus Invasion Tour. The band released a follow-up, 'SATELLITE' in the autumn of 2001, a record that sold even better than their previous effort. The band were subsequently dealt a serious blow with the departure of founder member MARCOS, and it was initially unclear whether his replacement by former LIVING SACRIFICE man JASON TRUBY would result in a radically different sound. If the eponymous title perhaps suggested a new beginning, in reality 'PAYABLE ON DEATH' (2003) was a departure only in the sense that it was more coherent and streamlined than the band's previous efforts.

Album rating: THE FUNDAMENTAL ELEMENTS OF SOUTHTOWN (*6) / SATELLITE (*7) / PAYABLE ON DEATH (*5)

P.O.D. PAYABLE ON DEATH

SONNY – vocals / **MARCOS** – guitar / **TRAA** – bass / **WUV** – drums

not iss. Rescue

1996. (cd) **BROWN** [–] [ ]
– Intro / Know me / Selah / Visions / Brown / One day / Punks rock / Breathe Babylon / Funk jam / Preach / Reggae jam / Full color / Seeking the wise / Live and die / Outro. *<re-iss. Aug00 on 'Diamante'; 5628> (UK-iss.Jun03 on 'Butterfly'; 885120)*

1997. (m-cd) *<8887>* **SNUFF THE PUNK** [–] [ ]
– Coming back / Let the music do the talking / Draw the line / Who is right? / Get it straight / Run / Snuff the punk / Can you feel it? / Three in the power of one / Every knee. *<re-iss. Apr00 on 'Diamante'+=; 5621>* – (bonus track).

1998. (m-cd) **PAYABLE ON DEATH LIVE (live)** [–] [ ]
– One day / Draw the line / Selah / Know me / Punk-reggae jam / Breath Babylon / Preach / Full color. *<re-iss. Jun01 on 'Diamante'; 5636>*

not iss. Tooth & Nail

May 99. (cd-ep) *<71148>* **THE WARRIORS EP** [–] [ ]
– Intro / Southtown / Breathe Babylon / Rosa Linda / Draw the line / Full color / Sabbath.

P.O.D.

Atlantic Atlantic

Mar 00. (cd) *<(7567 83216-2)>* **THE FUNDAMENTAL ELEMENTS OF SOUTHTOWN** [ ] Aug99 [51]
– Greetings / Hollywood / Checkin' levels / Rock the party / Lie down / Set your eyes to Zion / Lo siento / Bullet the blue sky / Psalm 150 / Image / Shouts / Tribal / Freestyle / Follow me / Outkast.

Jan 02. (cd) *<(7567 83475-2)>* **SATELLITE** [16] Sep01 [6]
– Set it off / Alive / Boom / Youth of the nation / Celestial / Satellite / Ridiculous (with EEK-A-MOUSE) / The messenjah / Guitarras de amor / Anything right (with CHRISTIAN LINDSKOG of BLINDSIDE) / Ghetto / Masterpiece conspiracy / Without jah, nothin' (with HR) / Thinking about forever / Portrait. *(UK+=)* – Whatever it takes. *(cd re-iss. Sep02 w/dvd+=; 7567 83597-2)*

Jan 02. (c-s) *(AT 0119C)* **ALIVE / CALL-OUT HOOK #1** 19 Nov01 41
(cd-s+=) *(AT 0119CD)* <85165> – Call-out hook #2.
May 02. (c-s) *(AT 0127C)* **YOUTH OF THE NATION / ALIVE (semi-acoustic)** 36 –
(cd-s+=) *(AT 0127CD)* <85249> – Sabbath.
Aug 02. (7"pic-d)<cd-s> *(AT 0135)* <85340> **BOOM. / SET IT OFF (Tweaker remix) / HOLLYWOOD (live)** – Jul02 –
Oct 02. (cd-s) *(AT 0139CD)* <85363> **SATELLITE / CRITIC / YOUTH OF THE NATION** – –

—— **JASON TRUBY** – guitar (ex-LIVING SACRIFICE) repl. MARCOS

May 03. (7") *(W 608)* **SLEEPING AWAKE. / BRUISE** 42 –
(cd-s+=) *(W 608CD)* <101094> – The passportal.
(above issued on 'Warners')
Nov 03. (cd) *(7567 96220-2)* <83661> **PAYABLE ON DEATH** – 9
– Wildfire / Will you / Change the world / Execute the sounds / Find my way / Revolution / The reasons / Freedom fighters / Waiting on today / I and identify / Asthma / Eternal.

□ POET & THE ROOTS

(see under ⇒ JOHNSON, Linton Kwesi)

POGUES

Formed: North London, England ... late 1983 by Tipperary-raised SHANE MacGOWAN, SPIDER STACEY and JEM FINER. MacGOWAN had earlier been part of punk outfit, The NIPPLE ERECTORS through 1978-1981; this motley crew released a solitary single, 'KING OF THE BOP' before shortening their name to The NIPS. A further few singles appeared and even an album, 'ONLY AT THE END OF THE BEGINNING', recommended for diehard POGUES fiends only. POGUE MAHONE (Gaelic for "kiss my arse") was subsequently formed by MacGOWAN and JAMES FEARNLEY (also a NIP), adding drinking buddies, ANDREW RANKEN, plus female singer/bassist CAIT O'RIORDAN. By Spring '84, they'd formed their own self-titled label, issuing a classic debut single, 'DARK STREETS OF LONDON'. Boasting all the Celtic melancholy, romance and gritted-teeth attitude which marked the best of the band's work, the track rather unfairly but predictably received an official BBC radio ban (apparently after the beeb managed to translate their name). A month later they secured a deal with 'Stiff', opting instead for The POGUES. Their Stan Brennan-produced debut album, 'RED ROSES FOR ME', broke into the UK Top 100 as they acquired growing support from live audiences the length and breadth of the country. Whether interpreting trad Irish folk songs or reeling off brilliant originals, the POGUES were apt to turn from high-spirited revelry ('STREAMS OF WHISKEY') to menacing threat ('BOYS FROM THE COUNTY HELL') in the time it took to neck a pint of guinness (in MacGOWAN's case, not very long at all). April '85 saw the release of perhaps their finest single (and first Top 20 hit), the misty-eyed, ELVIS COSTELLO-produced 'A PAIR OF BROWN EYES'. COSTELLO also oversaw the accompanying album, 'RUM, SODOMY & THE LASH' (1985), a debauched, bruisingly beautiful classic which elevated The POGUES to the position of modern day folk heroes. MacGOWAN's gift for conjuring up a feeling of time and place was never more vivid than on the likes of the aforementioned 'A PAIR..', the rousing 'SALLY MacLENNANE' and the cursing malice of 'THE SICK BED OF CUCHULAINN', while O'RIORDAN put in a spine-tingling performance as a Scottish laird on the traditional 'I'M A MAN YOU DON'T MEET EVERY DAY'. On the 16th of May '86, the latter married COSTELLO and when she subsequently left that November (after writing the Top 50 hit 'HAUNTED' for the Alex Cox film, 'Sid & Nancy'), a vital component of POGUES chemistry went with her. Around the same time, the group played 'The McMahon Gang' in Cox's movie 'Straight To Hell', meeting ex-CLASH singer JOE STRUMMER on the set: the veteran punk would subsequently deputise for the absent MacGOWAN on an early 1988 US tour. This period also saw them peak at No.3 in the album charts with 'IF I SHOULD FALL FROM GRACE WITH GOD', an album which spawned an unlikely No.2 Christmas 1987 hit in 'FAIRY TALE OF NEW YORK'. A drunken duet with KIRSTY MacCOLL, the track was certainly more subversive than the usual Yuletide fodder and for a brief period, The POGUES were bonafide pop stars, their rampant collaboration with The DUBLINERS on 'IRISH ROVER' earlier that year having already breached the Top 10. Live, the band were untouchable, MacGOWAN's errant, tin-tray wielding genius the stuff of legend, particularly for many who witnessed their storming Glasgow Barrowlands performances (needless to say, Rangers fans were mercifully thin on the ground at these celebratory Celtic shindigs). Inevitably, MacGOWAN's hard-drinking ways were beginning to affect his writing and 'PEACE AND LOVE' (1989) signalled a slow slide into mediocrity. 1990's 'HELL'S DITCH' carried on in much the same vein, although this was to be MacGOWAN's final album under The POGUES banner, his failing health incompatible with the demands of a successful major label band. While the gap-toothed frontman eventually got a solo career together, The POGUES bravely soldiered on with a surprisingly impressive hit single, 'TUESDAY MORNING', lifted from their 1993 UK Top 20 "comeback" album, 'WAITING FOR HERB'. Two years on, a nostalgically titled follow-up set, 'POGUE MAHONE', failed to rekindle their former glory, while MacGOWAN continued to dominate the limelight. In 1999, some of the POGUES (SPIDER, HUNT + RANKIN) got together as The WISEMEN, while FINER has emerged with the band LONGPLAYER. • **Songwriters:** Group compositions, except; THE BAND PLAYED WALTZING MATILDA (Eric Bogle) / DIRTY OLD TOWN (Ewan MacColl) / WILD ROVER + MADRA RUM (trad.) / MAGGIE MAY (Rod Stewart) / HONKY TONK WOMAN (Rolling Stones) / WHISKEY IN THE JAR (Thin Lizzy) / MISS OTIS REGRETS (Cole Porter) / GOT A LOT O' LIVIN' TO DO (Elvis Presley) / HOW COME (Ronnie Lane) / WHEN THE SHIP COMES IN (Bob Dylan). FINER became main writer in the mid-90's with others contributed some material. • **Trivia:** In the early '90s, they supplied the soundtrack for TV play 'A Man You Don't Meet Every Day'. The song 'Fiesta' was subsequently used on Vauxhall-Tigra TV ad after the rights were sold from their 1988 album.

Album rating: RED ROSES FOR ME (*8) / RUM, SODOMY & THE LASH (*9) / IF I SHOULD FALL FROM GRACE WITH GOD (*8) / PEACE AND LOVE (*6) / HELL'S DITCH (*6) / THE BEST OF THE POGUES compilation (*9) / THE BEST OF THE REST OF THE POGUES compilation (*7) / WAITING FOR HERB (*6) / POGUE MAHONE (*5) / THE VERY BEST OF THE POGUES compilation (*8)

NIPS

SHANE MacGOWAN (b.25 Dec'57, Kent, England) – vocals, guitar / **ADRIAN THRILLS** – guitar (NME journalist) / **SHANE 'HASLER' BRADLEY** – bass / **ARCANE** – drums / + others

Soho | not iss.

Jun 78. (7"; as NIPPLE ERECTORS) *(SH 1/2)* **KING OF THE BOP. / NERVOUS WRECK** – [–]

—— **LARRY HINDRICKS** – guitar; repl. THRILLS

—— **MARK HARRIS** – drums repl. ARCANE

Aug 79. (7") *(SH 4)* **ALL THE TIME IN THE WORLD. / PRIVATE EYES** – [–]

—— **GAVIN DOUGLAS** – drums repl. LARRY

—— **JAMES FEARNLEY** (b.10 Oct'54, Manchester, England) – accordion (appeared on album)

Feb 80. (7") *(SH 9)* **GABRIELLE. / VENGEANCE** □ –
(re-iss. 1980 on 'Chiswick'; CHIS 119)

Oct 80. (lp) *(HOHO 1)* **ONLY AT THE END OF THE BEGINNING** □ –
– Love to make you cry / Vengeance / Gabrielle / King of the bop / Ghost town / Fuss 'n' bother / Venus in bovver boots / Happy song / Stupid cow / I don't want nobody to love / Infatuation / Maida Ada / Hit parade / Can't say no.

Test Press — not iss.

Oct 81. (7") *(TP 5)* **HAPPY SONG. / NOBODY TO LOVE** □ –

— split in 1982. HASLER was soon to join MEN THEY COULDN'T HANG.

– compilation –

Nov 87. (m-lp) *Big Beat; (WIKM 66)* **BOPS, BABES, BOOZE & BOVVER** □ –
– King of the bop / Nervous wreck / So pissed off / Stavordale Rd. N5 / All the time in the world / Private eye / Gabrielle / Vengeance.

POGUES

MacGOWAN + FEARNLEY plus **SPIDER STACEY** (b.PETER, 14 Dec'58, Eastbourne, England) – tin whistle (ex-NIPS) / **JEM FINER** (b.JEREMY, 29 Jul'55, Stoke, England) – banjo, guitar / **CAIT O'RIORDAN** – bass, vocals / **ANDREW RANKEN** (b.13 Nov'53, London) – drums

Pogue Mahone — not iss.

May 84. (7"; as POGUE MAHONE) *(PM 1)* **DARK STREETS OF LONDON. / THE BAND PLAYED WALTZING MATHILDA** □ –
(re-iss. Jun84 as The POGUES on 'Stiff'; BUY 207)

Stiff — not iss.

Sep 84. (lp) *(SEEZ 55)* **RED ROSES FOR ME** 89 –
– Transmetropolitan / The battle of Brisbane / The auld triangle / Waxie's dargle / Boys from the county Hell / Sea shanty / Dark streets of London / Streams of whiskey / Poor daddy / Dingle regatta / Greenland whale fisheries / Down in the ground where the dead men go / Kitty. *(cd-iss. May87; CDSEEZ 55) (re-iss. Jan89 on 'WEA' lp/c; WX 240/+C)* (cd re-iss. Jan89; *244494-2)*

Oct 84. (7") *(BUY 212)* **BOYS FROM THE COUNTY HELL. / REPEALING OF THE LICENSING LAWS** □ –
(d7"+=) *(BUY 212 – 207)* – (see debut 45).

Mar 85. (7"/7"pic-d) *(BUY/DBUY 220)* **A PAIR OF BROWN EYES. / WHISKEY YOU'RE THE DEVIL** 72 –
(12"+=) *(BUYIT 22)* – Muirshin Durkin.

— added p/t **PHIL CHEVRON** (b. RYAN, 17 Jun'57, Dublin, Ireland) – guitar, producer (ex-RADIATORS FROM SPACE)

Jun 85. (7",7"green/7"sha-pic-d) *(BUY/PBUY 224)* **SALLY MacLENNANE. / WILD ROVER** 51 –
(12"+=) *(BUYIT 224)* – The leaving of Liverpool.
(c-s++=) *(BUYC 224)* – Wild cats of Kilkenny.

Aug 85. (lp/c/cd) *(SEEZ/CSEEZ/CDSEEZ 58)* **RUM, SODOMY & THE LASH** 13 –
– The sick bed of Cuchulainn / The old main drag / Wild cats of Kilkenny / I'm a man you don't meet every day / A pair of brown eyes / Sally MacLennane / Dirty old town / Jesse James / Navigator / Billy's bones / The gentleman soldier / And the band played waltzing Matilda. *(cd+=)* – A pistol for Paddy Garcia. *(re-iss. Jan89 on 'WEA' lp/c; WX 241/+C) (cd-iss. Jan89; 244495-2)*

Aug 85. (7"/7"pic-d) *(BUY/PBUY 229)* **DIRTY OLD TOWN. / A PISTOL FOR PADDY GARCIA** 62 –
(12"+=) *(BUYIT 229)* – The parting glass.

Feb 86. (7"ep/12"ep/c-ep/7"pic-ep) *(BUY/BUYIT/BUYC/PBUY 243)* **POGUETRY IN MOTION** 29 –
– A rainy night in Soho / The body of an American / London girl / Planxty Noel Hill.

Aug 86. (7") *(MCA 1084)* **HAUNTED. / JUNK THEME** 42 –
(12"+=) *(MCAT 1084)* – Hot dogs with everything.
(above single from the motion picture, 'Sid & Nancy' on 'MCA')

— **DARRYL HUNT** (b. 4 May'50, Bournemouth, England) – bass (ex-PRIDE O' THE CROSS) repl. CAIT

Mar 87. (7"; by The POGUES & The DUBLINERS) *(BUY 258)* **THE IRISH ROVER. / THE RARE OLD MOUNTAIN DEW** 8 –
(12"+=) *(BUYIT 258)* – The Dubliners fancy.

— added **TERRY WOODS** (b. 4 Dec'47, Dublin) – banjo (now 8-piece)

Pogue Mahone-EMI — Island

Nov 87. (7"; The POGUES featuring KIRSTY MacCOLL) *(NY 7)* **FAIRYTALE OF NEW YORK. / BATTLE MARCH MEDLEY** 2 □
(12"+=)(cd-s+=) *(NY 12)(CDNY 1)* – Shanne Bradley.

Jan 88. (cd/c/lp) *(CD/TC+/NYR 1) <90872>* **IF I SHOULD FALL FROM GRACE WITH GOD** 3 88
– If I should fall from grace with God / Turkish song of the damned / Bottle of smoke / Fairytale of New York (featuring KIRSTY MacCOLL) / Metropolis / Thousands are sailing / Fiesta / Medley:- The recruiting sergeant – The rocky road to Dublin – Galway races / Streets of Sorrow – Birmingham Six / Lullaby of London / Sit down by the fire / The broad majestic Shannon / Worms. *(cd+=)* – South Australia / The battle march medley. *(re-iss. Jan89 on 'WEA' lp/c; WX 243/+C) (cd-iss. Jan89; 244494-2)*

Feb 88. (7") *(FG 1)* **IF I SHOULD FALL FROM GRACE WITH GOD. / SALLY MacLENNANE (live)** 58 □
(12"red-ep)(cd-ep+=) **ST. PATRICK'S NIGHT** *(SGG 1-12)(CDFG 1)* – A pair of brown eyes (live) / Dirty old town (live).

Jul 88. (7") *(FG 2)* **FIESTA. / SKETCHES OF SPAIN** 24 –
(12"+=)(cd-s+=) *(FG 2-12)(CDFG 2)* – South Australia.

WEA — Island

Dec 88. (7") *(YZ 355)* **YEAH, YEAH, YEAH, YEAH, YEAH. / THE LIMERICK RAKE** 43 –
(12"+=/cd-s+=) *(YZ 355 T/CD)* – ('A'extended) / Honky tonk woman.

Jun 89. (7"/c-s) *(YZ 407/+C)* **MISTY MORNING, ALBERT BRIDGE. / COTTON FIELDS** 41 –
(12"+=) *(YZ 407T)* – Young ned of the hill.
(3"cd-s++=) *(YZ 407CD)* – Train of love.

Jul 89. (lp/c)(cd) *(WX 247/+C)(246086-2) <91225>* **PEACE AND LOVE** 5 □
– White City / Young ned of the hill / Misty morning, Albert Bridge / Cotton fields / Blue heaven / Down all the days / U.S.A. / Lorelei / Gartloney rats / Boat train / Tombstone / Night train to Lorca / London you're a lady / Gridlock.

Aug 89. (7"/c-s) *(YZ 409/+C)* **WHITE CITY. / EVERY MAN IS A KING** □ –
(12"+=) *(YZ 409TX)* – Maggie May (live).
(cd-s+=) *(YZ 409CD)* – The star of the County Down.

May 90. (7"/c-s; The POGUES & The DUBLINERS) *(YZ 500/+C)* **JACK'S HEROES. / WHISKEY IN THE JAR** 63 –
(12"+=/cd-s+=) *(YZ 500 T/CD)* – ('B'extended).

— (theme song used by Eire in World Cup; manager Jack Charlton)

Aug 90. (7") *(YZ 519)* **SUMMER IN SIAM. / BASTARD LANDLORD** 64 –
(12"+=/cd-s+=) *(YZ 519 T/CD)* – Hell's ditch (instrumental) / The Irish rover.

Sep 90. (cd)(lp/c) *(9031 72554-2)(WX 366/+C) <422846>* **HELL'S DITCH** 12 □
– The sunnyside of the street / Sayonara / The ghost of a smile / Hell's ditch / Lorca's novena / Summer in Siam / Rain street / Rainbow man / The wake of the Medusa / House of the gods / Five green onions and Jean / Maidria Rua / Six to go.

Apr 91. (cd-s) **SAYONARA / CURSE OF LOVE / INFINITY** – □

Sep 91. (7") *(YZ 603)* **A RAINY NIGHT IN SOHO (remix). / SQUID OUT OF WATER** 67 –
(12"+=) *(YZ 603)* – Infinity.
(cd-s+=) *(YZ 603CD)* – POGUETRY IN MOTION (ep).

Sep 91. (cd)(lp/c) *(9031 75405-2)(WX 430/+C)* **THE BEST OF THE POGUES** (compilation) <US-title 'ESSENTIAL POGUES'> 11 □
– Fairytale of New York / Sally MacLennane / Dirty old town / The Irish rover / A pair of brown eyes / Streams of whiskey / A rainy night in Soho / Fiesta / Rain street / Misty morning, Albert Bridge / White City / Thousand are sailing / The broad majestic Shannon / The body of an American.

Dec 91. (7") *(YZ 628)* **FAIRYTALE OF NEW YORK. / FIESTA** 36 –
(12"+=/cd-s+=) *(YZ 628 T/CD)* – A pair of brown eyes / Sick bed of Cuchulainn / Maggie May.

— p/t JOE STRUMMER is deposed by member SPIDER who takes over vox.

May 92. (7"/c-s) *(YZ 673/+C)* **HONKY TONK WOMAN. / CURSE OF LOVE** 56 –
(12"+=) *(YZ 673T)* – Infinity.
(cd-s+=) *(YZ 673CD)* – The parting glass.

Jun 92. (cd)(lp/c) *(9031 77341-2)(WX 471/+C)* **THE BEST OF THE REST OF THE POGUES** (compilation out-takes) □ –
– If I should fall from grace with God / The sick bed of Cuchulainn / The

old main drag / Boys from the County Hell / Young Ned of the hill / Dark streets of London / The auld triangle / Repeal of the licensing laws / Yeah yeah yeah yeah yeah / London girl / Honky tonk women / Summer in Siam / Turkish song of the damned / Lullaby of London / The sunnyside of the street / Hell's ditch.

— (Sep'91) MacGOWAN left when his health deteriorated (JOE STRUMMER deputised for him on tour)

— added 8th member & producer **MICHAEL BROOK** – infinite guitar

WEA Chameleon

Aug 93. (7"/c-s) *(YZ 758/+C)* **TUESDAY MORNING. / FIRST DAY OF FOREVER** [18] [ ]
(cd-s+=) *(YZ 758CD)* – Turkish song of the damned (live).
(cd-s) *(YZ 758CDX)* – ('A'side) / London calling / I fought the law (both live with JOE STRUMMER).

Sep 93. (cd/c/lp) *(4509 93463-2/-4/-1)* <61598> **WAITING FOR HERB** [20] Oct98 [ ]
– Tuesday morning / Smell of petroleum / Haunting / Once upon a time / Sitting on top of the world / Drunken boat / Big city / Girl from the Wadi Hammamat / Modern world / Pachinko / My baby's gone / Small hours.

Jan 94. (7"/c-s) *(YZ 771/+C)* **ONCE UPON A TIME. / TRAIN KEPT ROLLING ON** [66] [–]
(12"+=/cd-s+=) *(YZ 771 T/CD)* – Tuesday morning / Paris St. Germain.

— FEARNEY and WOODS departed, apparently due to the brief Christmas comeback of SHANE MacGOWAN

— **SPIDER / JEM / DARRYL + RANKEN** added **JAMIE CLARKE** – banjo / **JAMES McNALLY** – accordion, uilleann pipes / **DAVID COULTER** – mandolin, tambourine

Sep 95. (7"colrd/c-s) *(WEA 011 X/C)* **HOW COME. / EYES OF AN ANGEL** [ ] [–]
(cd-s+=) *(WX 011CD)* – Tuesday morning (live) / Big city (live).

Oct 95. (cd/c/lp) *(0630 11210-2/-4/-1)* **POGUE MAHONE** [ ] [–]
– How come / Living in a world without her / When the ship comes in / Anniversary / Amadie / Love you 'till the end / Bright lights / Oretown / Pont Mirabeau / Tosspint / Four o'clock in the morning / Where that love's been gone / The sun and the moon.

— note:- The POGUES also appeared on the flip side to KIRSTY MacCOLL's Cole Porter tribute single, 'Miss Otis Regrets' on the track 'JUST ONE OF THOSE THINGS'.

– compilations, etc. –

Mar 01. (cd/c) *Warners ESP; (8573 87459-2/-4)* **THE VERY BEST OF THE POGUES** [18] [–]

Jan 02. (cd) *Castle; (CMRCD 388)* **STREAMS OF WHISKEY** [ ] [–]

POISON

Formed: Harrisburg, Pennsylvania, USA . . . March '84 by former SPECTRES members BRET MICHAELS and RIKKI ROCKETT, the line-up completed by BOBBY DALL and C.C. DEVILLE. Like a cartoon bubblegum version of FASTER PUSSYCAT or HANOI ROCKS, this super-glam metal outfit exploded onto the US rock scene in a sea of peroxide bleach circa late '86, their aptly titled debut album, 'LOOK WHAT THE CAT DRAGGED IN' (1986) reaching No.3 in the US charts, aided and abetted by the singalong sleaze anthem, 'TALK DIRTY TO ME'. Needless to say, the rest of the album was painfully amateurish at best, hilarious at worst. Still, the Americans lapped it up and made sure the follow-up, 'OPEN UP AND SAY . . . AAH!' (1988) climbed to No.2. The obligatory "sensitive" ballad, in this case 'EVERY ROSE HAS ITS THORN' was a massive hit on both sides of the Atlantic (US No.1), a lonesome strumathon that EXTREME would've been proud to call their own. The album spawned a further three Stateside singles, including a cover of the old LOGGINS & MESSINA chestnut, 'YOUR MAMA DON'T DANCE'. 'FLESH AND BLOOD' (1990) was the band's most successful album to date, going Top 5 in both the British and American charts, POISON making a conscious effort to distance themselves from their mascara'd days of old. Nevertheless, they retained the ability to release annoyingly pointless pop-metal nonsense like 'UNSKINNY BOP'. By the release of 1993's 'NATIVE TONGUE' opus, the MICHAELS and Co. were trying so painfully hard to create a credible image, they employed the TOWER OF POWER horn section! If they were under the illusion that this would give them instant soul power then POISON were clearly even more clueless than their music gave them credit for. The ploy didn't work and the album failed to sell as much as its predecessor, MICHAELS more newsworthy for his shortlived affair with PAMELA ANDERSON than his music. The POISON posse finally emerged into a radically altered rock landscape in the new millennium with a couple of half-baked albums which will undoubtedly be of interest to hardcore fans only. The bulk of 'CRACK A SMILE . . . AND MORE' (2000) was composed of material from aborted 1994 sessions cobbled together with a few outtakes and MTV Unplugged material. The godawful cover probably tells you all you need to know, although the ageing Glam rockers at least have the grace to poke fun at their increasingly archaic image on the likes of 'TRAGICALLY UNHIP' while a rendition of the Dr. Hook nugget, 'COVER OF THE ROLLING STONE' is worth a laugh. 'POWER TO THE PEOPLE' (2000), meanwhile, featured a mixture of new studio tracks and live cuts from their 1999 comeback tour. The big news for fans is that lead guitar hearthrob C.C. DEVILLE was back in action and even had a shot at lead vocals. 'HOLLYWEIRD' (2002), then, was the "comeback" album from the original line-up, a harder-rocking affair than candyfloss glam of old with some brave attempts at tackling more complex lyrical fare and a wholly unnecessary cover of Pete Townshend's 'SQUEEZE BOX'. • **Trivia:** Late in 1990, BRET co-wrote and produced girlfriend SUSIE HATTON's debut album. He landed the lead role in the 1996 movie 'A Letter From Death Row'.

Album rating: LOOK WHAT THE CAT DRAGGED IN (*6) / OPEN UP AND SAY . . . AAH! (*7) / FLESH & BLOOD (*7) / SWALLOW THIS LIVE (*5) / NATIVE TONGUE (*5) / GREATEST HITS 1986-1996 compilation (*7) / CRACK A SMILE . . . AND MORE collection (*5) / POWER TO THE PEOPLE (*4) / HOLLYWEIRD (*5)

BRET MICHAELS (b. BRET MICHAEL SYCHAK, 15 Mar'63) – vocals / **C.C. DEVILLE** (b. BRUCE ANTHONY JOHANNESSON, 14 May'62, Brooklyn, N.Y.) – lead guitar (ex-SCREAMING MIMI) repl. MATT SMITH / **BOBBY DALL** (b. ROBERT KUY KENDALL, 2 Nov'63, Miami, Florida) – bass / **RIKKI ROCKETT** (b. RICHARD REAM, 8 Aug'61, Mechanicsburg, Pennsylvania) – drums

Music For Nations Capitol

Oct 86. (lp/pic-lp/c) *(MFN 69/+P/C)* <12523> **LOOK WHAT THE CAT DRAGGED IN** [ ] Jul86 [3]
– Cry tough / I want action / I won't forget you / Play dirty / Look what the cat dragged in / Talk dirty to me / Want some, need some / Blame it on you / #1 bad boy / Let me go to the show. *(re-iss. Apr89 lp,pic-lp,c/cd.Apr89; same/MFN 69CD) (re-iss. Jul94 cd/c; same) (re-iss. May96 on 'EMI Gold' cd/c; CD/TC GOLD 1027)*

May 87. (7") *(KUT 125)* <5686> **TALK DIRTY TO ME. / WANT SOME, NEED SOME** [67] Mar87 [9]
(12"pic-d+=/12"+=) *(P+/12KUT 125)* – (interview).

Jun 87. (7") <44004> **I WANT ACTION. / PLAY DIRTY** [–] [50]

Aug 87. (7") *(KUT 127)* **CRY TOUGH. / LOOK WHAT THE CAT DRAGGED IN** [ ] [–]
(12"pic-d+=/12"+=) *(P+/12KUT 127)* – ('A'-U.S. remix). *(re-iss. Apr89; same)*

Capitol Capitol

Sep 87. (7") <44038> **I WON'T FORGET YOU. / BLAME IT ON YOU** [–] [13]

Apr 88. (7"/7"w-poster/ 7"s) *(CL/+P/Z 486)* <44145> **NOTHIN' BUT A GOOD TIME. / LOOK BUT YOU CAN'T TOUCH** [35] [6]
(12"+=/12"g-f+=) *(12CL/+G 486)* – Livin' for a minute.

May 88. (lp/pic-lp)(c/cd)(pic-cd) *(EST/+P 2059)(TC/CD+/EST 2059) (CDP 748493L) <48493>* **OPEN UP AND SAY . . .AAH!** [23] [2]
– Love on the rocks / Nothin' but a good time / Back to the rocking horse / Good love / Tearin' down the walls / Look but you can't touch / Fallen angel / Every rose has its thorn / Your mama can't dance / Bad to be good. *(re-iss. Mar94 cd/c; same) (cd re-iss. Nov99 on 'Axe Killer'; AXE 305333-2)*

Oct 88. (7"/7"s) *(CL/+S 500) <44191>* **FALLEN ANGEL. / BAD TO BE GOOD** [59] Jul88 [12]
(12"+=/12"pic-d+=) *(12CL/+P 500)* – (interview).

Oct 88. (7") *<44203>* **EVERY ROSE HAS ITS THORN. / LIVING FOR THE MINUTE** [–] [1]

Jan 89. (7"/7"s/7"sha-pic-d) *(CL/+S/P 520)* **EVERY ROSE HAS ITS THORN. / BACK TO THE ROCKING HORSE** [13] [–]
(12"+=/12"g-f+=)(cd-s+=) *(12CL/+G 520)(CDCL 520)* – Gotta face the hangman.

Apr 89. (7"/7"green) *(CL/+S 523) <44203>* **YOUR MAMA DON'T DANCE. / TEARIN' DOWN THE WALLS** [13] Feb89 [10]
(12"+=/12"green+=)(cd-s+=) *(12CL/+B 523)(CDCL 523)* – Love on the rocks.

Jul 89. (7"/7"s)(c-s) *(CL/+X 539)(TCCL 539)* **NOTHIN' BUT A GOOD TIME. / LIVIN' FOR THE MINUTE** [48] [–]
(12"+=/12"pic-d+=)(cd-s+=) *(12CL/+P 539)(CDCL 539)* – Look what the cat dragged in (live).

Jun 90. (c-s/7") *(TC+/CL 582) <44584>* **UNSKINNY BOP. / SWAMP JUICE (SOUL-O)** [15] [3]
(12"+=/12"pic-d+=)(cd-s+=) *(12CL/+P 582)(CDCL 582)* – Valley of lost souls / Poor boy blues.

Jul 90. (cd/c/lp) *(CD/TC+/EST 2126) <918132>* **FLESH & BLOOD** [3] [2]
– Strange days of Uncle Jack / Valley of lost souls / Unskinny bop / (Flesh and blood) Sacrifice / Swamp juice (soul-o) / Let it play / Life goes on / Come Hell or high water / Ride the wind / Don't give up an inch / Something to believe in / Ball and chain / Life loves a tragedy / Poor boy blues. *(re-iss. cd Sep94;)*

Oct 90. (c-s/7") *(TC+/CL 594) <44617>* **SOMETHING TO BELIEVE IN. / BALL AND CHAIN** [35] [4]
(12"+=) *(12CL 594)* – Look what the cat dragged in / Your mama don't dance / Every rose has its thorn.
(10"yellow+=/cd-s+=) *(10/CD CL 594)* – (Bret Michaels interview).

Jan 91. (c-s,12") *<44616>* **RIDE THE WIND. / COME HELL OR HIGH WATER** [–] [38]

Apr 91. (c-s,12") *<44705>* **LIFE GOES ON. / SOMETHING TO BELIEVE IN (acoustic)** [–] [35]

Nov 91. (7"/7"clear) *(CL/+P 640)* **SO TELL ME WHY. / GUITAR SOLO** [25] [ ]
(12"+=/cd-s+=) *(12/CD CL 640)* – Unskinny bop (live) / Ride the wind (live).
(12"pic-d+=/pic-cd-s+=) *(12/CD CLP)* – Only time will tell / No more Lookin' back (poison jazz).

Dec 91. (cd/c/d-lp) *(CD/TC+/ESTU 2159) <98046>* **SWALLOW THIS LIVE** (live / studio tracks *) [52] [51]
– Intro / Look what the dragged in / Look but you can't touch / Good love / I want action / Something to believe in / Poor boy blues / Unskinny bop / Every rose has its thorn / Fallen angel / Your mama don't dance / Nothin' but a good time / Talk dirty to me / So tell me why* / Souls on fire* / Only time will tell* / No more lookin' back (poison jazz).

—— (Nov'91) DeVILLE left, and was replaced (Jun'92) by **RICHIE KOTZEN** (b. 3 Feb'70, Reading, Pennsylvania) – guitar

Feb 93. (c-s/7") *(TC+/CL 679) <44905>* **STAND. / STAND (CHR edit)** [25] Jan93 [50]
(cd-s) *(CDCL 679)* – ('A'side) / Native tongue / The scream / Whip comes down / ('A'-lp version).

Feb 93. (cd/c/lp) *(CD/TC+/ESTU 2190) <98961>* **NATIVE TONGUE** [20] [16]
– Native tongue / The scream / Stand / Stay alive / Until you suffer some (Fire and ice) / Body talk / Bring it home / 7 days over you / Richie's acoustic thang / Ain't that the truth / Theatre of the soul / Strike up the band / Ride child ride / Blind faith / Bastard son of a thousand blues.

Apr 93. (7"pic-d/c-s) *(CLP/TCCL 685)* **UNTIL YOU SUFFER SOME (FIRE AND ICE). / STAND (acoustic)** [32] [ ]
(cd-s+=) *(CDCL 685)* – Bastard son of a thousand blues / ('A'mix).
(12"colrd+=) *(12CL 685)* – Strike up the band / ('A'mix).

—— **BLUES SARACENO** (b.17 Oct'71) – guitar; repl. KOTZEN

Feb 97. (cd) *(<CTMCD 312)>* **GREATEST HITS 1986-1996** (compilation + two new) [ ] [ ]
– Nothin' but a good time / Talk dirty to me / Unskinny bop / Every rose has its thorn / Fallen angel / I won't forget you / Stand / Ride the wind / Look what the cat dragged in / I want action / Life goes on / (Flesh and blood) Sacrifice / Cry tough / Your mama don't dance / So tell me why / Something to believe in / Sexual thing / Lay your body down.

—— **C.C. DEVILLE** – guitar; returned to repl. SARACENO

Cyanide Cyanide

Jun 00. (cd) *<CYND 6969>* **POWER TO THE PEOPLE** [–] [ ]
– Power to the people / Can't bring me down / The last song / Strange / I hate every bone in your body but mine / live:- Intro / Look what the cat dragged in / I want action / Something to believe in / Love on the rocks / C.C. solo / Fallen angel / Let it play / Riki solo / Every rose has its thorn / Unskinny bop / Nothin' but a good time / Talk dirty to me.

May 02. (cd) *<(CYND 6975)>* **HOLLYWEIRD** [ ] [ ]
– Hollyweird / Squeeze box / Shooting star / Wishful thinkin' / Get 'ya some / Emperor's new clothes / Devil woman / Wasteland / Livin' in the now / Stupid, stoned and dumb / Home (Bret's story) / Home (C.C.'s story). *(UK+=)* – Rockstar.

– compilations, etc. –

May 00. (cd) *Capitol; <(524781-2)>* **CRACK A SMILE . . . AND MORE** (rec. 1994 . . .) [ ] Mar00 [ ]
– Best thing you ever had / Stand up, make love / Baby gets around a bit / Cover of the Rolling Stone / Be the one / Mr. Smiley / Sexual thang / Lay your body down / No ring, no gets / That's the way (I like it) / Tragically unhip / Doin' as I seen on my TV / One more for the bone / Face the hangman / Your mama don't dance (live unplugged).

Mar 03. (cd) *Disky; (76273-2)* **ROCK CHAMPIONS** [ ] [–]

POLICE

Formed: London, England . . .early 1977 by drummer STEWART COPELAND, vocalist/bassist STING (b. GORDON SUMNER) and guitarist HENRY PADOVANI. In May '77, this line-up released a debut punk single, 'FALL OUT', for Miles Copeland's (brother of STEWART) indie label, 'Illegal'. Immediately after the record's release, they were invited by GONG member MIKE HOWLETT to join veteran guitarist ANDY SUMMERS in live band, STRONTIUM 90. Following PADOVANI's departure in August of the same year (to form the brilliantly monikered FLYING PADOVANI BROTHERS), SUMMERS took his place in The POLICE, this modified line-up initially sessioning on EBERHARD SCHOENER's 'Video Flashback' album. Like all the best 'punk' bands of the time, The POLICE weren't actually punk at all, the members all coming from some kind of 'muso' background, SUMMERS having noodled for the likes of KEVIN AYERS and KEVIN COYNE while COPELAND had drummed for prog-rock merchants, CURVED AIR and STING had plucked his bass for the jazzy LAST EXIT. Not exactly the best credentials for the 'anyone can play' ethos of punk but The POLICE succeeded by infusing their complex reggae-tinged pop/rock with insidiously catchy hooks and radio friendly melodies while keeping most of their songs down to an acceptable post-hippy playing time. They also cultivated a trendy bleached haired image, sporting their new blonde barnets on a Wrigley's Spearmint Gum TV ad. After supporting SPIRIT of all people, the group signed to 'A&M', releasing their debut single, 'ROXANNE', soon after. Initially, this paeon to a lady of the night failed to score a chart position, although it was subsequently released a year later, reaching No.12 in the UK charts. The follow-up, 'CAN'T STAND LOSING YOU', was a minor chart hit as was the debut album, 'OUTLANDOS D'AMOUR' (1978). An impressive collection with a strong rhythmic thrust and a few token nods to punk, the album was finally given its due when it was resurrected the following year, reaching the Top 10 in the Spring of '79. Later that summer The POLICE captured their first No.1 single with the power pop of the 'MESSAGE IN A BOTTLE' single, swiftly followed by a No.1 album in 'REGATTA DE BLANC' (aka WHITE REGGAE; 1979). Again the record illustrated the band's masterful grasp of dynamics, using time changes to enhance rather than detract from the pop appeal of their songs. From the space reggae of 'WALKING ON THE MOON' to the melodic lament of 'THE BED'S TOO BIG WITHOUT YOU', The POLICE were continually charting new musical territory. It was only a matter of time before the group broke through worldwide, including the lucrative American market. That break came with the 'ZENYATTA MONDATTA' (1980) album and its attendant hits, 'DON'T STAND SO CLOSE TO ME' and the lyrically rhythmic genius of 'DE DO DO DO, DE DA DA DA'. By the release of 'GHOSTS IN THE MACHINE' (1981), The POLICE were now a world beating act, once more delivering the goods with a more instrumentally diverse opus best sampled on the exotically effervescent 'EVERY LITTLE THING SHE DOES IS MAGIC'. STING's lyrics were also taking on a new depth, notably on 'INVISIBLE SUN', wherein the singer commented on the strife-torn Northern Ireland. Bearing in mind that STING's songs formed the bulk of the band's output – leading to simmering discontentment in the ranks – it's surprising how well the trio gel on their final release and undisputed masterpiece, 'SYNCHRONICITY' (1983). The brooding atmospherics of 'EVERY BREATH YOU TAKE' (a massive worldwide No.1) formed the album's centrepiece while the melancholy 'WRAPPED AROUND YOUR FINGER' and the pummelling 'SYNCHRONICITY 2' illustrated the band's ability to craft a consistently satisfying but varied musical palate. The aforementioned tensions ultimately led to the band's demise, although an official announcement wasn't made until 1986, the trio working on solo projects in the meantime. Predictably, STING was the only member who went on to any commercial success – massive success in the event – while COPELAND and SUMMERS lingered in relative obscurity. The former had already released a string of 7"s under the KLARK KENT moniker at the turn of the decade as well as scoring the soundtrack for cult film 'Rumblefish' (featuring vocals of ex-WALL OF VOODOO man, STAN RIDGWAY). During the mid-80's, he went on to make an album of African music, 'THE RHYTHMATIST' (1985) for 'A&M' and a one-off 7" with ADAM ANT, 'OUT OF BOUNDS'. More recently, COPELAND has scored various films including 'Talk Radio', 'Wall Street' and 'First Power', going on to form ANIMAL LOGIC with bassist STANLEY CLARKE and vocalist DEBORAH HOLLAND. SUMMERS, meanwhile, continued his collaboration with ROBERT FRIPP (they'd released the 'I ADVANCE MASKED' album in 1982) on 'BEWITCHED' (1984) before going on to release a series of eclectic solo albums.

Album rating: OUTLANDOS D'AMOUR (*8) / REGATTA DE BLANC (*7) / ZENYATTA MONDATTA (*7) / GHOST IN THE MACHINE (*7) / SYNCHRONICITY (*8) / EVERY BREATH YOU TAKE – THE SINGLES compilation (*9) / GREATEST HITS compilation (*9) / LIVE! collection (*4)

STING (b. GORDON SUMNER, 2 Oct'51, Wallsend, England) – vocals, bass (ex-LAST EXIT) / **HENRY PADOVANI** (b. Corsica) – guitar, vocals / **STEWART COPELAND** (b.19 Jul'52, Alexandria, Egypt) – drums, vocals (ex-CURVED AIR)

Illegal — not iss.

May 77. (7") *(IL 1)* **FALL OUT. / NOTHING ACHIEVING** [ ] [–]
(re-act.Dec79 reached UK No.47)

— **ANDY SUMMERS** (b. ANDREW SOMERS, 31 Dec'42, Blackpool, England) – guitar (ex-KEVIN AYERS, ex-KEVIN COYNE, ex-ERIC BURDON, ex-SOFT MACHINE) soon repl. HENRY (after brief spell as 4-piece) left to form his FLYING PADOVANI BROTHERS

A&M — A&M

Apr 78. (7",12") *(AMS 7348)* **ROXANNE. / PEANUTS** [ ] [–]
(re-iss. Apr79; same) – hit UK No.12

Aug 78. (7",7"sha-pic-d,7"in most colours) *(AMS 7381)* **CAN'T STAND LOSING YOU. / DEAD END JOB** [42] [–]
(re-iss. Jun79; same) – hit UK No.2

Oct 78. (lp/blue-lp/c) *(AMLH/AMLN/CAM 68502)* <4753> **OUTLANDOS D'AMOUR** [ ] Feb79 [23]
– Next to you / So lonely / Roxanne / Hole in my life / Peanuts / Can't stand losing you / Truth hits everybody / Born in the 50's / Be my girl – Sally / Masoko tanga. *(resurrected Apr79 made No.6) (cd-iss. Mar89; CDA 68502) (re-iss. Oct92 cd/c; CD/C MID 126)*

Oct 78. (7") *(AMS 7402)* **SO LONELY. / NO TIME THIS TIME** [ ] [ ]
(re-dist.Feb80; same) – hit UK No.6

Jan 79. (7") <2096> **ROXANNE. / DEAD END JOB** [–] [32]

Apr 79. (7") <2147> **CAN'T STAND LOSING YOU. / NO TIME THIS TIME** [–] [ ]

Sep 79. (7",7"green,7"sha-pic-d) *(AMS 7474)* <2190> **MESSAGE IN A BOTTLE. / LANDLORD** [1] Nov79 [74]

Oct 79. (lp/c) *(AMLH/CAM 64792)* <4792> **REGGATTA DE BLANC** [1] [25]
– Message in a bottle / Reggata de blanc / It's alright for you / Bring on the night / Deathwish / Walking on the Moon / On any other day / The bed's too big without you / Contact / Does everyone stare / No time this time. *(cd-iss. Mar89; CDA 64792) (re-iss. Oct92 cd/c; CD/C MID 127)*

Nov 79. (7"/12") *(AMS/+P 7494)* **WALKING ON THE MOON. / VISIONS OF THE NIGHT** [1] [–]

Jan 80. (7") **BRING ON THE NIGHT. / VISIONS OF THE NIGHT** [–] [ ]

Sep 80. (7"/7"sha-pic-d) *(AMS/+P 7564)* **DON'T STAND SO CLOSE TO ME. / FRIENDS** [1] [–]

Oct 80. (lp/c) *(AMLH/CAM 64831)* <4831> **ZENYATTA MONDATTA** [1] [5]
– Don't stand so close to me / Driven to tears / When the world is running down, you make the best of what's still around / Canary in a coalmine / Voices in my head / Bombs away / De do do do, de da da da / Behind my camel / Man in a suitcase / Shadows in the rain / The other way of stopping. *(cd-iss. Sep86; CDA 64831)*

Oct 80. (7") <2275> **DE DO DO DO, DE DA DA DA. / FRIENDS** [–] [10]

Dec 80. (7"/7"pic-d) *(AMS/+P 7578)* **DE DO DO DO, DE DA DA DA. / A SERMON** [5] [–]

Feb 81. (7") <2301> **DON'T STAND SO CLOSE TO ME. / A SERMON** [–] [10]

Sep 81. (7") *(AMS 8164)* **INVISIBLE SUN. / SHAMELLE** [2] [–]

Sep 81. (7") <2371> **EVERY LITTLE THING SHE DOES IS MAGIC. / SHAMBELLE** [–] [3]

Oct 81. (lp/c) *(AMLK/CKM 63730)* <3730> **GHOST IN THE MACHINE** [1] [2]
– Spirits in the material world / Every little thing she does is magic / Invisible sun / Hungry for love / emolition man / Too much information / Rehumanize yourself / One world (not three) / Omega man / Darkness / Omega man / Secret journey / Darkness. *(cd-iss. 1983; CDA 63730)*

Oct 81. (7"/7"pic-d) *(AMS/+P 8174)* **EVERY LITTLE THING SHE DOES IS MAGIC. / FLEXIBLE STRATEGIES** [1] [–]

Dec 81. (7") *(AMS 8194)* **SPIRITS IN THE MATERIAL WORLD. / LOW LIFE** [12] [–]

Jan 82. (7") <2390> **SPIRITS IN THE MATERIAL WORLD. / FLEXIBLE STRATEGIES** [–] [11]

Apr 82. (7") <2408> **SECRET JOURNEY. / DARKNESS** [–] [46]

May 83. (7"/7"pic-d) *(AM/+SP 117)* <2542> **EVERY BREATH YOU TAKE. / MURDER BY NUMBERS** [1] [1]
(d7"+=) *(AM 117)* – Truth hits everybody / Man in a suitcase.

Jun 83. (lp/c/cd) *(AMLX/CXM/CDA 63735)* <3735> **SYNCHRONICITY** [1] [1]
– Synchronicity / alking in your footsteps / O my God / Mother / Miss Gradenko / Synchronicity II / Every breath you take / King of pain / Wrapped around your finger / Tea in the sahara. *(c+=/cd+=)* – Murder by numbers. *(re-iss. Mar93 cd/c; CD/C MID 186)*

Jul 83. (7"/7"pic-d-x3) *(AM/+P 127)* **WRAPPED AROUND YOUR FINGER. / SOMEONE TO TALK TO** [7] [–]
(12"+=/12"pic-d+=) *(AMX/+P 127)* – Message in a bottle (live) / I burn for you.

Aug 83. (7") <2569> **KING OF PAIN. / SOMEONE TO TALK TO** [–] [3]

Oct 83. (7") *(AM 153)* <2571> **SYNCHRONICITY II. / ONCE UPON A DAYDREAM** [17] [16]

Jan 84. (7"/12") *(AM/+X 176)* **KING OF PAIN. / TEA IN THE SAHARA (live)** [17] [–]
Jan 84. (7") *<2614>* **WRAPPED AROUND YOUR FINGER. / TEA IN THE SAHARA (live)** [–] [8]

— Split up although not officially, until 1986. STING, ANDY SUMMERS and STEWART COPELAND

– compilations, etc. –

on 'A&M' unless otherwise mentioned

Jun 80. (6x7"box) *(AMPP 6001)* **SIX PACK** [17] [ ]
– (first 5 – A&M singles re-issued in blue vinyl, plus added 45 below) **THE BED'S TOO BIG WITHOUT YOU. / TRUTH HITS EVERYBODY**

Sep 86. (7"/12") *(AM/+Y 354) <2879>* **DON'T STAND SO CLOSE TO ME '86. / (live version)** [24] [46]

Nov 86. (lp/c/cd) *(EVERY/EVERC/EVECD 1) <3902>* **EVERY BREATH YOU TAKE – THE SINGLES** [1] [7]
– Roxanne / Can't stand losing you / Message in a bottle / Walking on the Moon / Don't stand so close to me '86 / De do do do, de da da da / Every little thing she does is magic / Invisible Sun / Spirits in the material world / Every breath you take / King of pain / Wrapped around your finger. *(c+=/cd+=)* – So lonely. *(re-iss. UK Mar92 hit No.31)*

Nov 86. (7"/12") *(AM/+Y 363)* **ROXANNE '86. / SYNCHRONICITY II** [ ] [–]

Jan 87. (7") **WALKING ON THE MOON. / MESSAGE IN A BOTTLE** [–] [ ]

Apr 88. (3"cd-ep) *(AMCD 905)* **COMPACT HITS** [ ] [–]
– Roxanne / Can't stand losing you / Canary in a coalmine / Bed's too big without you.

Jun 89. (d-c) *(AMC 24103)* **REGATTA DE BLANC / SYNCHRONICITY** [ ] [–]

Oct 92. (cd/c/lp) *(540030-2/-4/-1)* **THE POLICE: GREATEST HITS** (like above) [10] [–]

Oct 93 (4xcd-box) *<0150>* **MESSAGE IN A BOX: THE COMPLETE RECORDINGS** [–] [79]

May 95. (7"sha-pic-d/12") *(581037-7/-1)* **CAN'T STAND LOSING YOU (live). / VOICES IN MY HEAD (mix)** [27] [ ]
(cd-s+=) (581037-2) – Roxanne live).
(d12") *(581061-1)* – Voices in my head (8 remixes).

May 95. (d-cd/d-c) *(540222-2/-4) <0222>* **THE POLICE LIVE! (live)** [25] [86]
– Next to you / So lonely / Truth hits everybody / Walking on the Moon / Hole in my life / Fall out / Bring on the night / Message in a bottle / The bed's too big without you / Peanuts / Roxanne / Can't stand losing you / Landlord / Born in the 50's / Be my girl – Sally / Synchronicity I / Synchronicity II / Walking in your footsteps / Message in a bottle / O my God / De do do do, de da da da / Wrapped around your finger / Tea in the Sahara / Spirits in the material world / King of pain / Don't stand so close to me / Every breathe you take / Roxanne / Can't stand losing you / So lonely.

— see also STING (GRD-only) for combined STING & THE POLICE releases

POLYPHONIC SPREE

Formed: Dallas, Texas, USA ... 2000 by frontman/lyricist TIM DeLAUGHTER in a bizarre postscript to the ill-fated TRIPPING DAISY outfit after the death of his bandmate WES BERGGREN. The aforementioned TRIPPING DAISY began in 1991 by DeLAUGHTER, BERGGREN, MARK PIRRO and BRYAN WAKELAND and signing to 'Island', the band debuted with the 'BILL' album in 1994. Sporting a psychedelic punk/hard-rock sound similar to JANE'S ADDICTION (DeLAUGHTER's whining vocals a bizarre cross between PERRY FARRELL and LIAM GALLAGHER!), the group soon attracted a growing following on the American alternative scene. With media coverage also gathering strength, the band released a follow-up set, 'i am an ELASTIC FIRECRACKER' (complete with sleevework by deceased artist, Gugliemo Achille Cavellini) in early '96. The record was their most successful to date, scraping into the lower regions of the US Top 100, while the swaggering 'PIRANHA' single made the Top 75. A third album, 'JESUS HITS US LIKE AN ATOM BOMB' (1998), was a slightly disappointing set and sadder still was the untimely death of BERGGREN who o.d'd in 1999. With its twenty or so members (including PIRRO) and DeLAUGHTER's loose open-door policy, the Dallas congregation were established when they issued a cassette-only mini-LP 'THE BEGINING STAGES OF . . .' (2000), before playing countless live shows around Texas. The independent label 'Good' issued the set, and, with their white sinuous robes, uplifting dreamy psychedelic gospel and quasi-religious overtones ("Jesus is love", and all that), the collective were soon becoming uber cult. It wasn't long before the British music press got their grubby little hands on the band – after all, they were still filthy with the overt favouritism and lazy handling of certain garage rock groups, it was refreshing to see around 23 robe-wearing happy Texans don the cover of a publication. The group added new material to their already existing mini-album and re-issued it as their debut LP 'THE BEGINNING STAGES OF . . .' (2002). The music it contained – all in sections – was that of strange, breezy psychedelic pop in the vein of MERCURY REV or The FLAMING LIPS, but with the general communal ethos applied by the likes of LAMBCHOP (who'd also boasted quite a line-up). After the clever pop/rock of TRIPPING DAISY, DeLAUGHTER obviously had strong intentions of creatiing joyful Americana; a sometimes ecstatic blend of gospel, pop and lo-fi with warm instrumentation and DeLAUGHTER's cracked vocals floating over the whole thing, The POLYPHONIC SPREE were a ray of sunshine that blasted into the often bleak world of American alt-rock.

Album rating: BILL (*5) / i am an ELASTIC FIRECRACKER (*8) / JESUS HITS US LIKE AN ATOM BOMB (*5) / Polyphonic Spree: THE BEGINNING STAGES OF . . . (*8)

TRIPPING DAISY

TIM DeLAUGHTER – vocals, guitar / **WES BERGGREN** – guitar / **MARK PIRRO** – bass / **BRYAN WAKELAND** – drums, percussion

Island Red / Dragon St.

Jul 94. (cd/c/lp) *(CIRD/IRCT/IRLP 1001) <70392>* **BILL** [ ] Nov92 [ ]
– My umbrella / One through four / Lost and found / Change of mind / On the ground / The morning / Blown away / Brown-eyed pickle boy / Miles and miles of pain / Triangle. *<cd re-iss. 1997 on 'Polygram'; 555002>*

Jul 94. (12"ep/cd-ep) *(12IR/CIRD 102)* **MY UMBRELLA / IT'S SAFE, IT'S SOCIAL (live). / GET IT ON (live) / WE'RE ONLY GONNA DIE (live)** [ ] [–]

Island / Island

Feb 96. (c-s/7") *(C+/IS 636)* **I GOT A GIRL. / MARGARITA TROPENZANDO** [ ] [–]
(12"+=/cd-s+=) *(12IS/CID 636)* – Cause tomb shop / Noose.

Feb 96. (cd/lp) *(CIRD/IRLP 1004) <314-524 112-2>* **i am an ELASTIC FIRECRACKER** [ ] Aug95 [95]
– Rocket pop / Bang / I got a girl / Piranha / Motivation / Same dress new day / Trip along / Raindrop / Step behind / Noose / Prick / High.

Mar 96. (7") *(IS 638)* **PIRANHA. / CREATURE** [72] [–]
(12"+=/cd-s+=) *(12IS/CID 638)* – High.

1997. (m-cd) *<531095>* **TIME CAPSULE** [–] [ ]
– Rise / Cause tomb shop / Creature / Boobie the clown / I'm a fish / Blue train.

— added **ERIC DREW FELDMAN** – producer, multi (ex-CAPTAIN BEEFHEART, ex-FRANK BLACK)

Jul 98. (cd) *<(524518-2)>* **JESUS HITS US LIKE AN ATOM BOMB** [ ] [ ]
– Field day jitters / Waited a light year / Sonic bloom / Bandaids for Mire / Mechanical breakdown / Your socks have no name / Geeareohdoubleyou / New plains medicine / Our drive to the sun – Can a man mark / Human contact / Pillar / 8 ladies / About the movies / Tiny men / Indian poker (pt.2 & 3).

not iss. / Good

1999. (cd-s) *<GR 002>* **BEDHEAD. / (other by Centro-Matic)** [–] [ ]

— when WES died of a drug o.d. in 1999, TIM, MARK and BRYAN formed . . .

POLYPHONIC SPREE

TIM DeLAUGHTER – vocals / **MARK PIRRO** – bass / **BRYAN WAKELAND** – drums / **RYAN FITZGERALD** – guitar / **EVAN HISEY** – organ / **TOBY HALBROOKS** – theremin, electronics, whistle / **MARK McKEEVER** – keyboards, trumpet / **JEFF BOUCK** – percussion / **MIKE MELENDI** – percussion / **ANDREW TINKER** – french horn / **AUDREY EASLEY** – flute, piccolo / **JAMES REIMER** – trombone / **RICK RASURA** – classic harp / **LOGAN REESE** – trumpet / **RICK NELSON** – violin / **JENNIFER JOBE** – vocals / **MICHAEL TURNER** + **ROY IVY** + **JOHN VINEYARD** + **CHRISTY STEWART** + **JENNIE KELLY** + **KELLY REPKA** + **JESSICA JORDAN** + **JULIE DOYLE** – backing vocals

Good / Good

Jul 02. (cd) *<(GR 004CD)>* **THE BEGINNING STAGES OF . . .** [ ] Jun02 [ ]
– Section 1 (Have a day – Celebratory) / Section 2 (It's the sun) / Section 3 (Days like this keep me warm) / Section 4 (La la) / / Section 5 (Middle of the day) / Section 6 (Hanging around the day – part one) / Section 7 (Hanging around the day – part two) / Section 8 (Soldier girl) / Section 9 (Light and day – Reach for the sun) / Section 10 (A long day). *(re-iss. Sep02 on '679 Recordings' cd/lp; 5046 60918-2/-1) (cd w/dvd-iss.Jun03 +=; 2564 60352-5)* – (videos). *(hit UK No.70)*

Fierce Panda / not iss.

Aug 02. (cd-s) *(NING 123CD)* **SOLDIER GIRL / SUN (section 2) / SOLDIER GIRL (string version) / SOLDIER GIRL (radio) / SOLDIER GIRL (section 8)** [ ] [–]

679 Recordings / not iss.

Oct 02. (7") *(679L 012)* **HANGING AROUND. / FIVE YEARS** [39] [–]
(cd-s+=) *(679L 012CD1)* – ('A'version) / ('A'-Video).
(cd-s) *(679L 012CD2)* – ('A'live) / What will be will be (live) / Soldier girl (live).

— now with **JOE BUTCHER** – sho-bud pedal steel, synths

Feb 03. (12") *(679L 015T2)* **LIGHT AND DAY. / SOLDIER GIRL (instrumental) / THE MARCH (symphonic version)** [40] [–]
(cd-s+=) *(679L 015CD1)* – ('A'-video).
(cd-s) *(679L 015CD2)* – ('A'side) / Have a day / Days like this keep me warm / ('A'-video).

Jul 03. (12"/cd-s) *(679L 014 X/CD)* **SOLDIER GIRL. / IT'S THE SUN (new version) / SOLDIER GIRL (Death In Vegas remix)** [26] [–]

Iggy POP

Born: JAMES JEWEL OSTERBERG, 21 Apr'47, Ypsilanti, Michigan, USA. The son of an English father and American mother, he joined The IGUANAS as a drummer in 1964. They issued a cover of Bo Diddley's 'MONA', which was limited to 1,000 copies sold at gigs. The following year, he became IGGY POP and joined The PRIME MOVERS with bassist RON ASHETON, although they folded, IGGY subsequently moving to Chicago. In 1967, he returned to Michigan and formed The (PSYCHEDELIC) STOOGES with RON and his drummer brother SCOTT. They were soon joined by DAVE ALEXANDER, IGGY making his celluloid debut in the avant-garde film, 'Francois De Moniere' with girlfriend NICO. In 1968, the band gigged constantly, on one occasion IGGY being charged with indecent exposure. The following year, A&R man Danny Fields, while looking to sign MC5, instead signed The STOOGES to 'Elektra', furnishing them with a $25,000 advance. Their eponymous debut (produced by JOHN CALE – another VELVET UNDERGROUND connection), later proved to be way ahead of its time. Tracks such as 'NO FUN', '1969' and 'I WANNA BE YOUR DOG', were howling proto-punk, garage classics, later covered by The SEX PISTOLS, SISTERS OF MERCY and SID VICIOUS! respectively. The album just failed to secure a Top 100 placing, the second album faring even worse commercially, although it was hailed by the more discerning critics of the day as a seminal work. From the primal nihilism of 'DIRT', to the psychedelic kiss-off, 'I FEEL ALRIGHT (1970)', it seemed, to The STOOGES at least, as if flower-power had never happened. They were subsequently dropped by their label, following drug-related problems and dissension in the ranks. IGGY moved to Florida, becoming a greenkeeper while taking up golf more seriously, a healthier pastime than his penchant for self-mutilation. In 1972, he had a chance meeting with DAVID BOWIE and manager TONY DeFRIES, who persuaded IGGY to reform his STOOGES and sign a MainMan management deal, this in turn leading to a 'C.B.S.' contract. After his/their flawed classic, 'RAW POWER' (not one of BOWIE's best productions), they folded again, citing drugs as the cause. It was, however, even more of an embryonic punk record, the amphetamine rush of 'SEARCH AND DESTROY' highly influential on the "blank generation" that would trade-in their STEELY DAN albums for anything with two chords and a sneering vocal. In 1975, IGGY checked in to a psychiatric institute, weaning himself off heroin. His only true friend, BOWIE, who regularly visited him in hospital, invited him to appear on his 'LOW' album. He signed to 'R.C.A.' (home of BOWIE) in 1977, issuing the BOWIE-produced debut solo album, 'THE IDIOT', which, due to the recent "new wave" explosion, broke him into the UK Top 30 and US Top 75. It contained the first BOWIE/POP collaboration, 'CHINA GIRL', later a smash hit for BOWIE. His second solo release, 'LUST FOR LIFE' (also produced by BOWIE in '77), was another gem, again deservedly reaching the UK Top 30 (the title track was later resurrected in 1996 after appearing on the soundtrack to the cult Scottish movie, 'Trainspotting'). In 1979, IGGY moved to 'Arista' records, shifting through various infamous personnel, although his commercial appeal was on the wane. The first half of the 80's saw IGGY desperately trying to carve out a successful solo career while combating his continuing drug problems. Albums such as, 'SOLDIER' (1980), 'PARTY' (1981) and 'ZOMBIE BIRDHOUSE' (1982) marking the nadir of POP's chequered career. Finally teaming up again with BOWIE for 1986's 'BLAH BLAH BLAH', the proclaimed "Godfather Of Punk" at last gained some belated recognition, his revival of a 1957 Johnny O'Keefe hit, 'REAL WILD CHILD', giving IGGY his first Top 10 hit (UK). Still with 'A&M' records and adding ex-SEX PISTOLS guitarist STEVE JONES, he consolidated his recovery with 'INSTINCT' (1988). His new lease of life prompted 'Virgin America' to give IGGY (who had recently taking up acting) a new contract, the 1990 set, 'BRICK BY BRICK' featuring the GN'R talents of SLASH and DUFF McKAGAN. To end the year, IGGY showed his caring side by duetting with former punkette, DEBORAH HARRY, on AIDS benefit single, 'WELL DID YOU EVAH!' (a bigger hit for NANCY Sinatra & LEE Hazlewood in 1971). He resurfaced once again in 1993 with 'AMERICAN CAESAR', a full-length set which contained some of his raunchiest tracks for some time, including 'WILD AMERICA', 'F*****' ALONE' and Richard Berry's 'LOUIE LOUIE'. Busying himself with more film work, he eventually broke his recording silence with an umpteenth album, 'NAUGHTY LITTLE DOGGIE' (1996). Mr. POP was back on song in the Autumn of '99, the album 'AVENUE B' delivering his usual raw power with all the finesse of a man taking a motorcycle ride to Hell. 'NAZI GIRLFRIEND', 'LONG DISTANCE' and even a cover of Johnny Kidd's 'SHAKIN' ALL OVER', all testament to a guy not yet ready to get out his pipe and slippers. Seeing as he's only ever enjoyed fleeting run-ins with the pop charts, it probably didn't bother the IG one iota that 'BEAT 'EM UP' (2001) didn't come within sniffing distance of the Top 40. Still, he's always got plenty of other subjects to rail against and his latest record is no exception. Apart from anything else, 'BEAT

'EM UP' should surely scoop the most gratuitously tasteless sleeve of the year award. In 2003, IGGY brought out yet another dose of high-octane retro-punk via 'SKULL RING', backing courtesy of The TROLLS, The STOOGES, GREEN DAY, SUM 41 and PEACHES. • **IGGY covered;** SOMETHING WILD (John Hiatt) / LIVIN' ON THE EDGE OF THE NIGHT (Rifkin / Rackin) / SEX MACHINE (James Brown). • **Trivia:** In 1987, IGGY made a cameo appearance in the film, 'The Color Of Money'. In 1990, his film & TV work included, 'Cry Baby', 'Shannon's Deal', Tales From The Crypt' & 'Miami Vice'. In 1991, he starred in the opera! 'The Manson Family' and five years later, 'The Crow'.

Album rating: Stooges: THE STOOGES (*8) / FUN HOUSE (*10) / RAW POWER as Iggy & the Stooges (*7) / METALLIC K.O. (*5) / Iggy Pop: THE IDIOT (*9) / LUST FOR LIFE (*9) / TV EYE (*3) / NEW VALUES (*5) / SOLDIER (*5) / PARTY (*4) / ZOMBIE BIRDHOUSE (*4) / BLAH-BLAH-BLAH (*6) / INSTINCT (*5) / BRICK BY BRICK (*7) / AMERICAN CAESAR (*6) / NAUGHTY LITTLE DOGGIE (*5) / NUDE & RUDE: THE BEST OF IGGY POP compilation (*8) / AVENUE B (*7) / BEAT 'EM UP (*5) / SKULL RING (*6)

STOOGES

IGGY POP – vocals / **RON ASHETON** (b. RONALD RANKLIN ASHETON JR., 17 Jul'48, Washington, D.C.) – guitar / **DAVE ALEXANDER** (b. DAVID MICHAEL ALEXANDER, 3 Jun'47, Ann Arbor) – bass / **SCOTT ASHETON** (b. SCOTT RANDOLPH ASHETON, 16 Aug'49, Washington) – drums

Elektra Elektra

Sep 69. (lp) *<(EKS 74051)>* **THE STOOGES** Aug69
– 1969 / I wanna be your dog / We will fall / No fun / Real cool time / Ann / Not right / Little doll. *(re-iss. Mar77; K 42032) <US cd-iss. 1988; 74051-2> (cd-iss. Nov93; 7559 60667-2)*

Oct 69. (7") *<EK 45664>* **I WANNA BE YOUR DOG. / 1969** –

— added guests **STEVE MACKAY** – saxophone / **BILL CHEATHAM** – 2nd guitar

Dec 70. (lp) *<(EKS 74071)>* **FUN HOUSE**
– Down on the street / Loose / T.V. eye / Dirt / I feel alright (1970) / Fun house / L.A. blues. *(re-iss. Mar77; K 42051) <US cd-iss. 1988; 74071-2> (cd-iss. Nov93; 7559 60669-2)*

Dec 70. (7") *<EKM 45695>* **I FEEL ALRIGHT (1970). / DOWN ON THE STREET** –

— broke-up in 1972. **IGGY** re-formed the group with **SCOTT** and **RON** (now bass)

IGGY AND THE STOOGES

JAMES WILLIAMSON – guitar repl. DAVE (died 10 Feb'75)

C.B.S. Columbia

Jun 73. (lp) *(CBS 65586) <KC 32111>* **RAW POWER** May73
– Search and destroy / Gimme danger / Hard to beat * / Penetration / Raw power / I need somebody / Shake appeal / Death trip. *(re-iss. May77 on 'CBS-Embassy'; 31464)*, hit UK No.44, *track repl. by – Your pretty face is going to Hell. *(re-iss. Nov81; CBS 32081) <US cd-iss. 1988 on 'Columbia'; > (UK re-iss. May89 on 'Essential' cd/c/lp; ESS CD/MC/LP 005) (cd-iss. all tracks) (re-iss. May94 & Apr97 on 'Columbia' cd/c; 485176-2/-4) (lp re-iss. Jul98 on 'Simply Vinyl'; SVLP 33)*

Jun 73. (7") *<45877>* **SEARCH AND DESTROY. / PENETRATION** –

— added **SCOTT THURSTON** – keyboards (on last 1974 tour, before disbanding) The ASHETONS formed The NEW ORDER (US version), with RON moving on to DESTROY ALL MONSTERS who had three 45's for UK label 'Cherry Red' in the late 70's.

– compilations, others, etc. –

1977. (white-d-lp) *Visa; <IMP 1015>* **METALLIC K.O.** –
– Raw power / Head on / Gimme danger / Rich bitch / Cock in my pocket / Louie Louie. *(originally issued 1976 on French 'Skydog'; SGIS 008) (re-iss. May88 as 'METALLIC KO x 2' on 'Skydog' lp/cd; 62232-1/2) (cd-iss. Sep94; same) (re-iss. Sep96 & May98 on 'Dressed To Kill'; DTKLP 001)*

1977. (7"ep) *Bomp; <EP 113>* **I'M SICK OF YOU** –
– I'm sick of you / Tight pants / Scene of the crime.

1977. (7"ep; by IGGY POP & JAMES WILLIAMSON) *Bomp; <EP 114>* **JESUS LOVES THE STOOGES** –
– Jesus loves the Stooges / Consolation prizes / Johanna. *(re-iss. 10"ep.Nov94;)*

1977. (7") *Siamese; <PM 001>* **I GOT A RIGHT. / GIMME SOME SKIN** –
(UK-iss.Dec95 on 'Bomp'; REVENGE 2)

Feb 78. (lp,green-lp; as IGGY POP with JAMES WILLIAMSON) *Radar; (RAD 2) / Bomp; <BLP 4001>* **KILL CITY** Nov77
– Sell your love / Kill city / I got nothin' / Beyond the law / Johanna / Night theme / Night theme reprise / Master charge / No sense of crime / Lucky monkeys / Consolation prizes. *(re-iss. ! on 'Elektra';) (cd-iss. Feb89 on 'Line'; LICD 9.00131) (cd-iss. Jan93;) (re-iss. 10"lp Feb95 on 'Bomp'; BLP 4042-10) (cd-iss. ; BCD 4042)*

Apr 78. (7") *Radar; (ADA 4)* **KILL CITY. / I GOT NOTHIN'** –

1978. (7"ep) *Skydog; (SGIS 12)* **(I GOT) NOTHING** – France –
– I got nothing / Gimme danger / Heavy liquid.

Aug 80. (lp/c) *Elektra; (K/K4 52234) <EF 7095>* **NO FUN**
(1969-70 best of THE STOOGES)

1983. (lp) *Invasion; <E 1019>* **I GOT A RIGHT** –

1987. (lp) *Revenge; (MIG 2)* **I GOT A RIGHT** – France –

1987. (7") *Revenge; (SS 1)* **I GOT A RIGHT. / NO SENSE OF CRIME** – France –

1987. (7") *Revenge; (BF 50) KILL CITY. / I'M SICK OF YOU* – France –

Dec 87. (lp) *Fan Club; (FC 037)* **RUBBER LEGS** – France –
– Rubber legs / Open up and bleed / Johanna / Cock in my pocket / Head on the curb / Cry for me. *(free 7")* – GIMME DANGER (live). / I NEED SOMEBODY (live) *(cd-iss. Apr97 on 'Last Call'; 422248)*

1988. (cd-ep) *Revenge; (CAX 1)* **PURE LUST** – France –
– I got a right / Johanna / Gimme some skin / I got nothing.

1988. (cd-ep) *Revenge; (CAX 2)* **RAW POWER** – France –
– Raw power / Head on the curb / Purple haze / Waiting for the man.

1988. (12"pink-ep,cd-ep) *Revenge; (CAX 3)* **GIMME DANGER** – France –
– Gimme danger / Open up and bleed / Heavy liquid / I got nothing / Dynamite boogie.

1988. (7") *Revenge; (SS 6)* **JOHANNA. / PURPLE HAZE** – France –

Sep 88. (pic-lp; as IGGY & THE STOOGES) *Revenge; (LPMIG 6)* **DEATH TRIP** – France –

May 88. (cd; as IGGY & THE STOOGES) *Revenge; (HTM 16)* **OPEN UP AND BLEED** – France –
(re-iss. Feb96 on 'Bomp' cd/lp; BCD/BLP 4051) (cd re-iss. Jul96; 890016)

Dec 88. (lp; as IGGY & THE STOOGES) *Revenge; (MIG 7)* **LIVE AT THE WHISKEY A GO-GO** –
(cd-iss. Nov94 & Feb97; 895104F)

Dec 88. (lp; as IGGY & THE STOOGES) *Electric; (190069)* **RAW STOOGES VOL.1** – German –

Dec 88. (lp; as IGGY & THE STOOGES) *Electric; (190070)* **RAW STOOGES VOL.2** – German –

May 92. (cd) *Line; (LICD 921175)* **I'M SICK OF YOU / KILL CITY** –

Jun 94. (cd; IGGY & THE STOOGES) *New Rose; (890028)* **MY GIRL HATES MY HEROIN** –
(re-iss. Feb97 on 'Wrote Music'; 7890028) (re-iss. Sep97 on 'Revenge'; MIG 28)

Jul 94. (cd; IGGY & THE STOOGES) *New Rose; (642100)* **NIGHT OF DESTRUCTION** –
(re-iss. as 6xcd-s-box on 'Wind'; WM 375)

Jul 94. (cd; IGGY & THE STOOGES) *New Rose; (642042)* **TILL THE END OF THE NIGHT** –
(re-iss. Apr97; same) (re-iss. Sep97 on 'Revenge'; MIG 42)

Sep 94. (cd; IGGY & THE STOOGES) *New Rose; (642011)* **LIVE 1971 & EARLY LIVE RARITIES (live)** –
(re-iss. Apr97; same)

Sep 94. (cd; IGGY & THE STOOGES) *New Rose; (895002)* **RAW MIXES VOL.1** –

Sep 94. (cd; IGGY & THE STOOGES) *New Rose; (895003)* **RAW MIXES VOL.2** –

Sep 94. (cd; IGGY & THE STOOGES) *New Rose; (895004)* **RAW MIXES VOL.3** –

Feb 95. (10"lp/cd) *Bomp; (BLP/BCD 4049)* **ROUGH POWER** –

— Also in France; **THE STOOGES**(12"ep) / **SHE CREATURES OF HOLLYWOOD HILLS**

Jul 96. (cd) *Revenge; (642050)* **WILD ANIMAL (live 1977)** –

Jul 96. (cd) *Revenge; (893334)* **PARIS HIPPODROME 1977 (live)** –

Jul 96. (cd; as IGGY & THE STOOGES) *Trident; (PILOT 008)* **YOUR PRETTY FACE IS GOING TO HELL** –

Mar 97. (cd; IGGY & THE STOOGES) *Bomp; (BCD 4063)* **YEAR OF THE IGUANA** –

Apr 97. (cd; STOOGES) *Arcade; (301563-2)* **THE COMPLETE RAW MIXES** [ ] [–]

Sep 97. (cd/lp; IGGY & THE STOOGES) *Bomp; (BCD/BLP 4069)* **CALIFORNIA BLEEDING** [ ] [–]

Nov 97. (cd) *King Biscuit; (88003)* **KING BISCUIT FLOWER HOUR** [ ] [–]

Mar 98. (cd) *Snapper; (SMMCD 528)* **LIVE IN L.A. 1973 (live)** [ ] [–]

Apr 98. (cd) *King Biscuit; (KBFHCD 001)* **KING BISCUIT PRESENTS . . .** [ ] [–]

May 88. (12"ep; IGGY & THE STOOGES) *Revenge; (CAX 8MAXI)* **I GOT NOTHING. / SEARCH AND DESTROY / COCK IN MY POCKET** [ ] [–]

Jun 98. (lp; IGGY & THE STOOGES) *Get Back; (GET 33LP)* **RUBBER** [ ] [–]

Nov 99. (7"pic-d; as IGGY & THE STOOGES) *Munster; (MR 7125)* **I GOT NOTHING. /** [ ] [ ]

IGGY POP

— had already gone solo, augmented by **DAVID BOWIE** – producer, keyboards / **RICKY GARDINER** – guitar / **TONY SALES** – bass / **HUNT SALES** – drums (latter 2; ex-TODD RUNDGREN) / guest **CARLOS ALOMAR** – guitar

R.C.A. R.C.A.

Feb 77. (7") *<10989>* **SISTER MIDNIGHT. / BABY** [–] [ ]

Mar 77. (lp/c) *(PL/PK 12275) <2275>* **THE IDIOT** [30] [72]

– Sister midnight / Nightclubbing / Fun time / Baby / China girl / Dum dum boys / Tiny girls / Mass production. *(re-iss. Apr90 on 'Virgin' lp/c/cd; OVED/OVEDC/CDOVD 277)*

May 77. (7") *(PB 9093)* **CHINA GIRL. / BABY** [ ] [ ]

— **STACEY HEYDON** – guitar / **SCOTT THURSTON** – keyboards repl. BOWIE + ALOMAR

Sep 77. (lp/c) *(PL/PK 12488) <2488>* **LUST FOR LIFE** [28] [ ]

– Lust for life / Sixteen / Some weird sin / The passenger / Tonight / Success / Turn blue / Neighbourhood threat / Fall in love with me. *(re-iss. 1984 lp/c; NL/NK 82488) (re-iss. Apr90 on 'Virgin' lp/c/cd; OVED/OVEDC/CDOVD 278) (lp re-iss. Nov97 on 'Virgin'; LPCENT 40)*

Oct 77. (7") *(PB 9160)* **SUCCESS. / THE PASSENGER** [ ] [ ]

— **IGGY** retained **THURSTON**, and recruited **SCOTT ASHETON** – drums / **FRED 'SONIC' SMITH** – guitar (ex-MC5) / **GARY RAMUSSEN** – bass (The SALES brothers later to BOWIE's TIN MACHINE)

Apr 78. (7") *(PB 9213)* **I GOT A RIGHT (live). / SIXTEEN (live)** [ ] [ ]

May 78. (lp/c) *(PL/PK 12796)* **TV EYE (live 1977)** [ ] [ ]

– T.V. eye / Funtime / Sixteen / I got a right / Lust for life / Dirt / Nightclubbing / I wanna be your dog. *(cd-iss. Jul94 on 'Virgin'; CDOVD 448)*

— **IGGY / THURSTON** now with **JAMES WILLIAMSON** – guitar, producer / **JACKIE CLARKE** – bass (ex-IKE & TINA TURNER) / **KLAUS KREUGER** – drums (ex-TANGERINE DREAM) / **JOHN HORDEN** – saxophone

Arista Arista

Apr 79. (lp/c) *(SPART/TC-SPART 1092) <4237>* **NEW VALUES** [60] [ ]

– Tell me a story / New values / Girls / I'm bored / Don't look down / The endless sea / Five foot one / How do ya fix a broken part / Angel / Curiosity / African man / Billy is a runaway. *(re-iss. Mar87; 1201144) (re-iss. Oct90 cd/lp; 260/210 997)*

May 79. (7") *(ARIST 255) <0438>* **I'M BORED. / AFRICAN MAN** [ ] [ ]

Jul 79. (7"/7"pic-d) *(ARIP/+D 274)* **FIVE FOOT ONE. / PRETTY FLAMINGO** [ ] [–]

— **IGGY / KREUGER** recruited **IVAN KRAL** – guitar (ex-PATTI SMITH) / **PAT MORAN** – guitar / **GLEN MATLOCK** – bass (ex-SEX PISTOLS, ex-RICH KIDS) / **BARRY ANDREWS** – keyboards (ex-XTC, ex-LEAGUE OF GENTLEMEN) (THURSTON formed The MOTELS)

Jan 80. (lp/c) *(SPART/TC-SPART 1117) <4259>* **SOLDIER** [62] [ ]

– Knockin' 'em down (in the city) / I'm a conservative / I snub you / Get up and get out / Ambition / Take care of me / I need more / Loco mosquito / Mr. Dynamite / Play it safe / Dog food. *<US re-iss. Oct87; 201160> (cd-iss. Apr91; 251 160)*

Jan 80. (7") *(ARIST 327)* **LOCO MOSQUITO. / TAKE CARE OF ME** [ ] [–]

— **IGGY / KRAL** now with **ROB DuPREY** – guitar / **MICHAEL PAGE** – bass / **DOUGLAS BROWNE** – drums (BARRY ANDREWS formed SHRIEKBACK)

May 81. (7") *(ARIST 407)* **BANG BANG. / SEA OF LOVE** [ ] [–]

Jun 81. (lp/c) *(SPART/TC-SPART 1158) <9572>* **PARTY** [ ] [ ]

– Pleasure / Rock and roll party / Eggs on plate / Sincerity / Houston is hot tonight / Pumpin' for Jill / Happy man / Bang bang / Sea of love / Time won't let me. *(re-iss. Jan87 lp/c; 203/403 806) (cd-iss. Sep89 on 'R.C.A.'; 253 806)*

— **IGGY / DuPREY** found new people **CHRIS STEIN** – guitar, producer (ex-BLONDIE) / **CLEM BURKE** – drums (ex-BLONDIE)

Animal-Chrysalis Animal

Aug 82. (7") *(CHFLY 2634)* **RUN LIKE A VILLAIN. / PLATONIC** [ ] [ ]

Sep 82. (lp/c) *(CHR/ZCHR 1399) <APE 6000>* **ZOMBIE BIRDHOUSE** [ ] [ ]

– Run like a villain / The villagers / Angry hills / Life of work / The ballad of Cookie McBride / Ordinary bummer / Eat to be eaten / Bulldozer / Platonic / The horse song / Watching the news / Street crazies.

— In 1984, he sang the title song on Alex Cox's movie 'REPO MAN'. For the same director, he appeared in the 1985 film 'SID & NANCY' about SID VICIOUS.

— **IGGY** now with **ERDAL KIZILCAY** – drums, bass, synthesizers / **KEVIN ARMSTRONG** – guitar / **BOWIE + STEVE JONES** (guest writers)

A&M A&M

Sep 86. (7"/12") *(AM/+Y 358) <2874>* **CRY FOR LOVE. / WINNERS & LOSERS** [ ] [ ]

Oct 86. (lp/c/cd) *<(AMA/AMC/CDA 5145)>* **BLAH-BLAH-BLAH** [43] [75]

– Real wild child (wild one) / Baby, it can't fail / Shades / Fire girl / Isolation / Cry for love / Blah-blah-blah / Hideaway / Winners and losers. *(cd+=)* – Little Miss Emperor. *(cd re-iss. 1989; 395 145-2) (re-iss. Jun91 cd/c; CD/C+/MID 159)*

Nov 86. (7"/12") *(AM/+Y 368) <2909>* **REAL WILD CHILD (WILD ONE). / LITTLE MISS EMPEROR** [10] [ ]

Feb 87. (7") *(AM 374)* **SHADES. / BABY IT CAN'T FAIL** [ ] [ ]

(12"+=) *(AMY 374)* – Cry for love.

Apr 87. (7"/12") *(AM/+Y 392)* **FIRE GIRL. / BLAH-BLAH-BLAH (live)** [ ] [ ]

Jun 87. (7") *(AM 397)* **ISOLATION. / HIDEAWAY** [ ] [ ]

(12"+=) *(AMY 397)* – Fire girl (remix).

— IGGY now with **STEVE JONES** – guitar / **PAUL GARRISTO** – drums (ex-PSYCHEDELIC FURS) / **SEAMUS BEAGHEN** – keyboards / **LEIGH FOXX** – bass

Jul 88. (lp/c/cd) *<(AMA/AMC/ADA 5198)>* **INSTINCT** [61] [ ]

– Cold metal / High on you / Strong girl / Tom tom / Easy rider / Power & freedom / Lowdown / Tuff baby / Squarehead.

Aug 88. (7") *(AM 452)* **COLD METAL. / INSTINCT** [ ] [ ]

(12"+=/12"pic-d+=) *(AM Y/P 452)* – Tuff baby.

Nov 88. (7") *(AM 475)* **HIGH ON YOU. / SQUAREHEAD** [ ] [ ]

(12"+=) *(AMY 475)* – Tuff baby (remix).

— **ALVIN GIBBS** – guitar (ex-UK SUBS) repl. STEVE JONES (continued solo) / **ANDY McCOY** – bass (ex-HANOI ROCKS) repl. FOXX (to DEBORAH HARRY)

Nov 88. (lp/c/cd) **LIVE AT THE CHANNEL (live 17.9.88)** [–] [ ]

– Instinct / Kill city / 1969 / Penetration / Power & freedom / Your pretty face / High on you / 5 foot 1 / Johanna / Easy rider / Tuff baby / 1970 / Search & destroy / Squarehead / No fun / I wanna be your dog. *(UK-iss.May94 on 'New Rose'; 642005) (re-iss. cd Sep97 on 'Revenge'; MIG 40-41)*

— now with **SLASH** – guitar / **DUFF McKAGAN** – bass (both of GUNS N' ROSES) / **KENNY ARONOFF** – drums

Virgin America Virgin America

Jan 90. (7"/c-s) *(VUS/+C 18) <VSC 1228>* **LIVIN' ON THE EDGE OF THE NIGHT. / THE PASSENGER** [51] [ ]

(12"+=/12"pic-d+=/cd-s+=) *(VUS T/TE/CD 18)* – Nightclubbing / China girl.

Jun 90. (7"/c-s) *(VUS/+C 22)* **HOME. / LUST FOR LIFE** [ ] [ ]

(12"+=/cd-s+=) *(VUS T/CD 22)* – Pussy power / Funtime.

Jul 90. (cd/c/lp) *(CDVUS/VUSMC/VUSLP 19) <91381>* **BRICK BY BRICK** [50] [90]

– Home / Main street eyes / I won't crap out / Candy / Butt town / The undefeated / Moonlight lady / Something wild / Neon forest / Stormy night / Pussy power / My baby wants to rock & roll / Brick by brick / Livin' on the edge of the night. *(c re-iss. Apr92; OVEDC 426)*

(below 'A'side featured **KATE PIERSON** – vox (of B-52's)

Oct 90. (7"/c-s) *(VUS/+C 29) <98900>* **CANDY. / PUSSY POWER (acoustic demo)** [67] [28]

(10"+=/cd-s+=) *(VUS 29)* – My baby wants to rock'n'roll (acoustic demos).

(12"/cd-s) *(VUS T/CD 29)* – ('A'side) / The undefeated / Butt town (acoustic demo).

— Oct 90, IGGY dueted with DEBORAH HARRY on UK Top 50 single 'DID YOU EVAH'; *Chrysalis; CHS 3646)*

— with **LARRY MULLEN** (U2) – drums, percussion / **HAL CRAGIN** – bass / **ERIC SCHERMERHORN** – guitar plus guests **MALCOLM BURN** – guitars, etc

Aug 93. (7"ep/c-ep/12"ep/cd-ep) *(VUS/+C/T/CD 74)* **THE WILD AMERICA EP** 63
– Wild America / Credit card / Come back tomorrow / My angel.

Sep 93. (cd/c/d-lp) *(CDVUS/VUSMC/VUSLP 64) <39002>* **AMERICAN CAESAR** 43
– Character / Wild America / Mixin' the colors / Jealousy / Hate / It's our love / Plastic & concrete / F***in' alone / Highway song / Beside you / Sickness / Boogie boy / Perforation / Problems / Social life / Louie Louie / Caesar / Girls of N.Y

May 94. (10"ep) *(VUS A/C 77)* **BESIDE YOU / EVIL CALIFORNIA. / HOME (live) / FUCKIN' ALONE** 47 –
(cd-ep) *(VUSCD 77)* – ('A'side) / Les amants / Louie Louie (live) / ('A'acoustic).

Feb 96. (cd/c/lp) *(CDVUS/VUSMC/VUSLP 102) <41327>* **NAUGHTY LITTLE DOGGIE**
– I wanna live / Pussy walk / Innocent world / Knucklehead / To belong / Keep on believing / Outta my head / Shoeshine girl / Heart is saved / Look away.

Sep 99. (cd) *(CDVUS 163) <48216>* **AVENUE B**
– No shit / Nazi girlfriend / Avenue B / Miss Argentina / Afraid to get close / Shakin' all over / Long distance / Corruption / She called me daddy / I felt the luxury / Espanol / Motorcycle / Facade.

Oct 99. (7") *(VUS 155)* **CORRUPTION. / ROCK STAR GRAVE** –
(cd-s+=) *(VUSCD 155)* – Hollywood affair.

Jun 01. (cd) *(CDVUS 200) <10574>* **BEAT 'EM UP** Jul01
– Mask / L.O.S.T. / Howl / Football / Saviour / Beat 'em up / Talking snake / The jerk / Death is certain / Go for the throat / Weasels / Drink new blood / It's all shit / Ugliness / V.I.P.

— backed by **The TROLLS, The STOOGES, SUM 41, GREEN DAY, PEACHES**

Sep 03. (cd) *(CDVUS 246) <80774>* **SKULL RING** Nov03
– Little electric chair / Perverts in the sun / Skull ring / Superbabe / Loser / Private hell / Little know it all / Whatever / Dead rock star / Rock show / Here comes the summer / Motor Inn / Inferiority complex / Supermarket / Til wrong feels right / Blood on your cool.

– compilations, etc. –

May 82. (7") *RCA Gold; (GOLD 549)* **THE PASSENGER. / NIGHTCLUBBING** –

Sep 84. (lp/c) *R.C.A.; (PL/PK 84597)* **CHOICE CUTS**

Apr 88. (cd-ep) *A&M; (AMCD 909)* **COMPACT HITS** –
– Real wild child (the wild one) / Isolation / Cry for love / Shades.

Jan 92. (cd) *Arista; (262 178)* **POP SONGS** –

Jan 93. (3xcd-box) *Virgin; (TPAK 21)* **LUST FOR LIFE / THE IDIOT / BRICK BY BRICK**

Jun 93. (cd) *Revenge; (642044)* **LIVE NYC RITZ '86 (live)** –

Aug 93. (cd/c) *Revenge; (642/644 050)* **SUCK ON THIS!** –

Aug 95. (cd) *Skydog;* **WE ARE NOT TALKING ABOUT COMMERCIAL SHIT** –

Aug 95. (cd) *Skydog;* **WAKE UP SUCKERS** –

Aug 96. (cd) *M.C.A.; (MCD 84021)* **THE BEST OF IGGY POP LIVE (live)**

Sep 96. (cd) *Camden RCA; (74321 41503-2)* **POP MUSIC** –

Oct 96. (cd/c/d-lp) *Virgin; (CDVUS/VUSMC/VUSLP 115) <42351>* **NUDE & RUDE: THE BEST OF IGGY POP**
– I wanna be your dog / No fun / Search & destroy / Gimme danger / I'm sick of you / Funtime / Nightclubbing / China girl / Lust for life / The passenger / Kill city / Real wild child / Cry for love / Cold metal / Candy / Home / Wild America.

Nov 96. (7"colrd/c-s) *Virgin; (VUS/+C 116)* **LUST FOR LIFE / (GET UP I FEEL LIKE BEING A) SEX MACHINE** 26 –
(cd-s+=) *(VUSCD 116)* – ('A'live) / I wanna be your dog (live).

Dec 96. (cd) *The Network; (3D 013)* **IGGY POP** –

Apr 97. (cd) *Wotre; (642007)* **LIVE IN BERLIN '91** –

Sep 97. (d-cd) *Snapper; (SMDCD 142)* **HEAD ON** –

Nov 97. (cd) *Other People's Music; (OPM 2116CD)* **HEROIN HATES YOU** –

Nov 97. (cd) *Eagle; (EABCD 011)* **THE MASTERS** –

Feb 98. (c-s) *Virgin; (VSC 1689)* **THE PASSENGER / LUST FOR LIFE** 22 –
(12"+=/cd-s+=) *(VS T/CDT 1689)* – Nightclubbing.

Aug 98. (cd) *A&M; (540943-2)* **BLAH BLAH BLAH / INSTINCT** –

POP GROUP

Formed: Bristol, England ... 1978 by MARK STEWART, JON WADDINGTON, DAVID WRIGHT, SEAN OLIVER and BRUCE SMITH. Inspired by punk's nihilistic energy and influenced by everyone from ROLAND KIRK to CAN and LEE PERRY, The POP GROUP harnessed their competing forces into a funky but defiant howl of rage at newly elected Prime Minister, Margaret Thatcher, with 1979's debut single, 'SHE IS BEYOND GOOD AND EVIL'. Issued on Jake Riviera's newly established 'Radar' label, the track was hailed as one of the most innovative releases of the post-punk era. With OLIVER and WRIGHT subsequently replaced by SIMON UNDERWOOD and GARETH SAGER – the latter introducing screeching free-jazz sax into the equation – The POP GROUP recorded a landmark debut album, 'Y' (1979). Produced by reggae veteran DENNIS BOVELL, the record presaged the primal intensity of The BIRTHDAY PARTY with spontaneous layers of visceral noise, militant lyrics and tortured vocals underpinned by CHIC-style basslines and dub dynamics. NICK CAVE, for one, was irrevocably changed after witnessing The POP GROUP in full flight, confessing (early 1999) on Channel 4 that the seminal 'WE ARE ALL PROSTITUTES' was among the most "violent, paranoid" music he'd ever heard. Essential ingredients for decent rock'n'roll of course, the band's first single for 'Rough Trade' offering it up in spades. A second album, 'FOR HOW MUCH LONGER DO WE TOLERATE MASS MURDER' (1980), was, if anything, even more intense but hardly helped widen the band's limited appeal. Something had to give and inevitably it all ended in tears, the band subsequently embroiled in legal wrangles with their label and signing off after a split single with The SLITS. STEWART went on to work with The ON-U SOUND posse, issuing records as MARK STEWART & THE MAFFIA (and later solo in his own right), while SAGER went on to form RIP, RIG + PANIC. UNDERWOOD achieved brief but enduring acclaim as founder of PIGBAG while WADDINGTON formed MAXIMUM JOY. OLIVER, sadly, was to die of heart failure in 1990, having recently co-written TERENCE TRENT D'ARBY's massive 'Wishing Well'. As cult as they come, The POP GROUP are widely acknowledged as laying the foundations for a fertile Bristol music scene which would subsequently spawn such revered artists as MASSIVE ATTACK, NENEH CHERRY, NELLEE HOOPER, PORTISHEAD, TRICKY etc. • **Songwriters:** STEWART lyricist / group compositions.

Album rating: Y (*7) / FOR HOW MUCH LONGER ... (*8) / WE ARE TIME (*5) / WE ARE ALL PROSTITUTES compilation (*7) / Mark Stewart: LEARNING TO COPE WITH COWARDICE (*6) / AS THE VENEER OF DEMOCRACY BEGINS TO FADE (*6) / MARK STEWART (*5) / METATRON (*5) / CONTROL DATA (*5)

MARK STEWART – vocals / **JOHN WADDINGTON** – guitar / **DAVID WRIGHT** – saxophone / **SEAN OLIVER** – bass / **BRUCE SMITH** – drums, percussion

Radar not iss.

Mar 79. (7"/12") *(ADA 29/1229)* **SHE IS BEYOND GOOD AND EVIL. / 3:38** –

— **SIMON UNDERWOOD** – bass; repl. OLIVER who joined ESSENTIAL LOGIC / **GARETH SAGER** – guitar, saxophone; repl. WRIGHT who joined ESSENTIAL LOGIC

Apr 79. (lp) *(RAD 20)* **Y** [ ] [-]
– Thief of fire / Snowgirl / Blood money / Savage sea / We are time / Words disobey me / Don't call me Pain / The boys from Brazil / Don't sell your dreams. *(re-iss. May96 on 'Radarscope' cd+=/lp; SCAN CD/LP 14)* – She is beyond good and evil.

—— **DAN KATSIS** – bass (also of GLAXO BABIES) repl. SIMON who joined PIGBAG / added **TRISTAN HONSINGER** – cello

Rough Trade – Y / not iss.

Oct 79. (7") *(RT 023)* **WE ARE ALL PROSTITUTES. / OUR CHILDREN SHALL RISE UP AGAINST** [ ] [ ]

—— **PAUL STUART** – drums; repl. SMITH who joined SLITS

Mar 80. (7") *(RT 039 – Y1)* **(In The Beginning – by SLITS). / WHERE THERE'S A WILL THERE'S A WAY** [ ] [-]

Mar 80. (lp) *(ROUGH 9 – Y2)* **FOR HOW MUCH LONGER DO WE TOLERATE MASS MURDER?** [ ] [-]
– Forces of oppression / Feed the hungry / One out of many / Blind faith / How much longer . . . / Justice / There are no spectators / Communicate / Rob a bank.

Dec 80. (lp) *(ROUGH 12 – Y5)* **WE ARE TIME (live)** [ ] [-]
– Kiss the book / Amnesty report / Springer / Sense of purpose / We are time / Trap / Thief of fire / Genius or lunatic / Colour blind / Spanish inquisition. *(re-iss. Aug84; same)*

—— split 1980, when GARETH formed RIP, RIG & PANIC with other ex-POP GROUP members, SEAN and BRUCE. WADDINGTON and CATSIS formed MAXIMUM JOY

– compilations, etc. –

Jun 98. (cd/lp) *Radarscope; (SCAN CD/LP 31)* **WE ARE ALL PROSTITUTES** [ ] [-]
– We are all prostitutes / Blind faith / Justice / Amnesty report / Feed the hungry / Where there's a will / Forces of oppression / Spanish inquisition / No spectators / Amnesty report II.

POP WILL EAT ITSELF

Formed: Stourbridge, Midlands, England . . . early 1985 initially as WILD AND WANDERING by vocalist/guitarist CLINT MANSELL, guitarist/keyboardist ADAM MOLE, bassist RICHARD MARCH and drummer GRAHAM CRABB. After the wittily titled '2000 LIGHT ALES FROM HOME' EP, the band adopted the POP WILL EAT ITSELF moniker in early '86. Their debut release, 'POPPIES SAY GRRR . . . EP' was originally sold at a Dudley gig, although after this DIY effort was made more widely available, it subsequently became an NME single of the week and was playlisted on night time Radio One. Later that summer, the band signed to Craig Jennings' indie label, 'Chapter 22', Jennings becoming their manager after a few more singles (including a cover of SIGUE SIGUE SPUTNIK's brilliantly vacant 'LOVE MISSILE F1-11'). By the release of the impressive debut album, 'BOX FRENZY' (1987) these self-styled 'GREBO GURU's were in the process of progressing from their early guitar pop to a sample-driven hybrid of heavy punk (a la KILLING JOKE) and psyche-pop. While songs like 'BEAVER PATROL' were criticised for their schoolboy sexism, indie chart hits like the driven genius of 'THERE IS NO LOVE BETWEEN US ANYMORE' and the anthemic 'DEF CON ONE' proved they were major contenders. Fittingly then, they were duly signed up by 'R.C.A.' and scored further minor chart successes with 'CAN U DIG IT' and 'WISE UP! SUCKER', while a follow-up album, 'THIS IS THE DAY, THIS IS THE HOUR, THIS IS THIS' (1989) made the Top 30. By this point the band had long since abandoned a conventional drum kit for an electronic model and in the Spring of 1990, PWEI turned out their most dance-friendly track to date in 'TOUCHED BY THE HAND OF CICCIOLINA'. A collaboration with the infamous Italian porn star-turned MP (only in Italy!) of the same name, the record was released just in time for the World Cup, complete with crowd noises and chanting. That year's album, 'THE POP WILL EAT ITSELF CURE FOR SANITY', confirmed the trend with 'DANCE OF THE MAD BASTARDS' and 'X, Y AND ZEE'. Nevertheless, by the release of 'THE LOOKS OR THE LIFESTYLE' (1992), the band had reverted back to a living, breathing human drummer in the form of FUZZ. Although the record spawned their biggest hit to date, the Top 10 'GET THE GIRL! KILL THE BADDIES', PWEI were subsequently dropped by RCA after the live 'WEIRD'S BAR & GRILL' (1993), the band also largely dismissed by a music press that had new fish to fry. Down but not out, the grebo troopers signed a new deal with the indie label, 'Infectious', hooking up with 'FUN-DA-MENTAL' in 1994 for the anti-nazi effort, 'ICH BIN EIN AUSLANDER'. The record was a minor hit, although their fifth studio effort, the harder-edged 'DOS DEDOS MIS AMIGOS' became their highest charting album to date, almost reaching the Top 10 and proving that they could get along just fine without a major label. If any more proof was needed, the defiantly titled remix album, 'TWO FINGERS MY FRIENDS', showed that PWEI were nothing if not resilient. • **Songwriters:** Group compositions except; LIKE AN ANGEL (Mighty Lemon Drops) / ORGONE ACCUMULATOR (Hawkwind) / EVERYTHING THAT RISES (Eno) / ROCK-A-HULA BABY (Elvis Presley).

Album rating: BOX FRENZY (*8) / NOW FOR A FEAST compilation (*7) / THIS IS THE DAY, THIS IS THE HOUR, THIS IS THIS (*7) / . . . CURE FOR SANITY (*5) / THE LOOKS OF THE LIFESTYLE (*6) / WEIRD'S BAR & GRILL (*4) / 16 DIFFERENT FLAVOURS OF HELL compilation (*7) / DOS DEDOS MIS AMIGOS (*5) / TWO FINGERS MY FRIENDS remixes (*5)

CLINT MANSELL (b. 7 Jan'63, Coventry, England) – vocals, guitar / **ADAM MOLE** (b. 8 Apr'62) – guitar, keyboards / **GRAHAM CRABB** (b.10 Oct'64, Sutton Coldfield, England) – drums / **RICHARD MARCH** (b. 4 Mar'65, York, England) – bass

Iguana / not iss.

Feb 86. (12"ep; as WILD & WANDERING) *(VYK 14)* **2000 LIGHT ALES FROM HOME** [ ] [-]
– Dust me down / Stand by me / Real cool time / Interlong / Apple tree (pt.1 & 2).

Desperate / not iss.

May 86. (7"ep) *(SRT 1)* **THE POPPIES SAY GRRRR . . . EP** [ ] [-]
– I'm sticking with you hoo / Sick little girl / Mesmerized / There's a psychopath in my soup / Candydiosis. *(re-iss. Jun86; DAN 1)*

Chapter 22 / Rough Trade

Oct 86. (7"ep) *(CHAP 9)* **POPPIECOCK** [ ] [-]
– The Black country chainsaw massacreee / Monogamy / Oh Grebo I think I love you / Titanic clown / B-B-B-Breakdown.
(12"ep+=) *(12CHAP 9)* – THE POPPIES SAY GRRRR . . . EP.

Jan 87. (12"/7") *(12+/CHAP 11)* **SWEET SWEET PIE. / DEVIL INSIDE / RUNAROUND** [ ] [-]

May 87. (7") *(CHAP 13)* **LOVE MISSILE F1-11. / ORGONE ACCUMULATOR** [ ] [ ]
(12"ep+=) **THE COVERS EP** *(12CHAP 13)* – Everything that rises / Like an angel.
(12"ep+=) *(L12CHAP 13)* – ('A'-Designer Grebo mix) / Everything that rises (new version).

Sep 87. (7"pink,7"clear/7") *(L+/CHAP 16)* **BEAVER PATROL. / BUBBLES** [ ] [-]
(12"+=) *(12CHAP 16)* – Oh Grebo I think I love you (new version).

Oct 87. (lp/c/cd) *(CHAP LP/MC/CD 18) <ROUGHUS 33/+C/CD>* **BOX FRENZY** [ ] [ ]
– Grebo guru / Beaver patrol / Let's get ugly / U.B.L.U.D. / Inside you / Evelyn / There is no love between us anymore / She's surreal / Intergalactic love mission / Love missile F1-11 / Hit the hi-tech groove / Razorblade kisses. *(cd re-mast.Feb03 on 'Castle'+=; CMRCD 651)* – Bubbles / Ugly / Picnic in the sky / On the razor's edge / Kiss that girl / Def con one / Hi tech groove (live) / She's surreal (live) / Pop Will Eat Itself at DEf Con One.

Jan 88. (7"pic-d/7") *(L+/CHAP 20)* **THERE IS NO LOVE BETWEEN US ANYMORE. / PICNIC IN THE SKY** [66] [-]
(12"+=) *(12CHAP 20)* – On the razor's edge / Kiss that girl.
(ext.12"+=) *(L12CHAP 20)* – ('A'extended high mix) / Hit the hi-tech groove (the M&K mix).
(12") *(CLUBCHAP 20)* – (above 2 tracks).

Jul 88. (7") *(PWEI 001)* **DEF CON ONE. / INSIDE YOU (live)** [63] [–]
(12"+=) *(PWEI 12-001)* – She's surreal (live) / Hit the hi-tech groove (live).
(12"+=) *(PWEIL 12-001)* – ('A'-Doomsday power mix) / She's surreal (live).

Dec 88. (lp/c/cd) *(CHAP LP/MC/CD 33)* **NOW FOR A FEAST** (compilation) [ ] [–]
– The Black country chainstore massacreee / Monogamy / Oh Grebo I think I love you / Titanic clown / B-B-B-Breakdown / Sweet sweet pie / Like an angel / I'm sniffin' with you hoo / Sick little girl / Mesmerized / There's a psychopath in my soup / Candydiosis / The devil inside / Orgone accumulator. *(cd re-mast.Feb03 on 'Castle'++; CNRCD 650)* – Everything that rises / Like an angel / Beaver patrol / Bubbles / There is no love between us anymore / Picnic in the sky / Def cone one / Inside you (live).

R.C.A. R.C.A.

Feb 89. (7"/7"orange,7"green/7"s) *(PB 42621/42619/42729)* **CAN U DIG IT. / POISON TO THE MIND** [38] [–]
(cd-s+=) *(PD 42620)* – Radio PWEI (acapella) / ('A'-12"version).
(12"++=) *(PT 42620)* – The fuses have been lit.

Apr 89. (7"/7"pic-d) *(PB PB 42761/42793)* **WISE UP! SUCKER. / ORGYONE STIMULATOR** [41] [–]
(c-s+=)(12"+=/cd-s+=) *(PK 42761)(PT/PD 42762)* – ('A'extended) / Can u dig it (riffs mix).
(10") *(PJ 42762)* – ('A'side) / ('A'extended) / ('A'version).

May 89. (lp/c/cd) *(PL/PK/PD 74106)* <9742> **THIS IS THE DAY, THIS IS THE HOUR, THIS IS THIS** [24] [ ]
– PWEI is a four letter word / Preaching to the perverted / Wise up! sucker / Sixteen different flavours of Hell / Inject me / Can u dig it? / The fuses have been lit / Poison to the mind / Def con one / Radio PWEI / Shortwave transmission on up to the minuteman / Satellite ecstatica / Now now James, we're busy / Wake up! time to die . . . *(cd+=)* – Wise up sucker (mix). *(re-iss. cd Nov93; 74321 15792-2)*

Aug 89. (7"ep)(7"g-f-ep)(7"sha-pic-ep)(c-ep)(12"ep)(cd-ep) *(PB 42883)(PA 43021)(PA 43022)(PK 43023)(PT 42884)(PD 42894)* **VERY METAL NOISE POLLUTION EP** [45] [–]
– Very metal noise pollution / P.W.E.I.-zation / 92° F / Def con one 1989 A.D.
(12") *(PT 43068)* – Def con 1989 AD including:- Twilight zone / Preaching to the perverted / P.W.E.I.-zation / 92° F.

May 90. (7"/c-s) *(PB/PK 43735)* **TOUCHED BY THE HAND OF CICCIOLINA. / THE INCREDI-BULL MIX** [28] [–]
(12"+=) *(PT 43736)* – ('A'-Extra time mix).
(cd-s) *(PD 43736)* – ('A'-Extra time mix) / ('A'-Diva Futura mix) / ('A'-Renegade Soundwave mix – Smoothneck).
(12") *(PT 43738)* – ('A'-Diva Futura mix) / ('A'-Renegade Soundwave mix – Smoothneck).

Oct 90. (7"/c-s) *(PB/PK 44023)* **DANCE OF THE MAD. / PREACHING TO THE PERVERTED** [32] [–]
(12"ep+=/cd-ep+=) **PWEI VS. THE MORAL MAJORITY EP** *(PT/PD 44023)* – ('A'other mix).

Oct 90. (cd/c/lp) *(PD/PK/PL 74828)* **CURE FOR SANITY** [33] [–]
– Incredible PWEI vs. The Moral Majority / Dance of the mad bastards / 88 seconds . . . and still counting / X Y & Zee / City Zen radio 1990-2000 FM / Dr. Nightmares medication time / Touched by the hand of Cicciolina / 1000 x no! / Psycho sexual / Axe of men / Another man's rhubarb / Medicine man speaks with forked tongue / Nightmare at 20,000 feet / Very metal noise pollution / 92 degrees (the 3rd degree) / Lived in splendour, died in chaos / The beat that refused to die. *(re-iss. May91 pic-lp; PL 75041) (re-iss. cd Nov93; 74321 15791-2)*

Jan 91. (7"/c-s) *(PB/PK 44243)* **X Y & ZEE. / AXE OF MEN** [15] [–]
(12"box+=) *(PT 44243)* – Psychosexual.
(12"+=/cd-s+=) *(PT/PD 44243)* – ('A'-Intergalactic mix) / ('A'-Sensory amp mix).

May 91. (7"/c-s) *(PB/PK 44555)* **92 DEGREES. / INCREDIBLE PWEI VS. DIRTY HARRY** [23] [–]
(10"+=/12"+=/cd-s+=) *(PX/PT/PD 44555)* – Another man's rhubarb.

May 92. (7"/c-s) *(PB/PK 45467)* **KARMADROME. / EAT ME DRINK ME LOVE ME** [17] [–]
(12"+=) *(PT 45467)* – Dread alert in the karmadrome / ('A'version).
(cd-s) *(PD 45467)* – ('A'side) / PWEI-zation (original metal noise pollution).
(12"pic-d+=) *(PTP 45467)* – PWEI-zation (original . . .) / Eat me drink me dub . . .

Aug 92. (7"/c-s) *(74321 11013-7/-4)* **BULLETPROOF! / ('A'-On-U-Sound mix)** [24] [–]
(12"pic-d+=/cd-s+=) *(74321 11013-6/-2)* – Good from far, far from good.
(12") *(74321 11013-8)* – ('A'-Mile high mix) / ('A'-No half measures mix).

Sep 92. (cd/c/lp) *(74321 10265-2/-4/-1)* **THE LOOKS OR THE LIFESTYLE** [15] [–]
– England's finest / Eat me, drink me, love me, kill me / Mother / Get the girl, kill the baddies! / I've always been a coward baby / Spoken drug song / Karmadrome / Urban futuristic (son of South Central) / Pretty pretty / I was a teenage grandad / Harry Dean Stanton / Bulletproof!. *(re-iss. cd Nov93; 74321 15790-2)*

—— added 5th member **FUZZ TOWNSHEND** (b. JOHN TOWNSHEND, 31 Jul'64, Birmingham, England) – drums

Jan 93. (7"/c-s) *(74321 12880-7/-4)* **GET THE GIRL! KILL THE BADDIES!. / ('A'-Adrian Sherwood mix)** [9] [–]
(12"+=/cd-s+=) *(74321 12880-6/-2)* – ('A'-Black country & western mix) or ('A'boilerhouse mix).
(cd-s) *(74321 12880-5)* – ('A'side) / Urban futuristic (live) / Can u dig it? (live) / Wise up! sucker! (live).

Feb 93. (cd/c/lp) *(74321 13343-2/-4/-1)* **WEIRD'S BAR AND GRILL (live)** [44] [–]
– England's finest / Eat me drink me love me kill me / Get the girl, kill the baddies!! / Wise up! sucker / 88 seconds and counting / Karmadrome / Token drug song mother / Preaching to the perverted / Axe of men / Nightmare at 20,000 feet / Always been a coward / Can U dig it / Bullet proof / Urban futuristic / There is no love between us anymore / Def con one. *(cd+=/c+=)* – Harry Dean Stanton teenage grandad.

Oct 93. (cd/c/lp) *(74321 15317-2/-4/-1)* **16 DIFFERENT FLAVOURS OF HELL** (compilation) [73] [–]
– Def con one / Wise up! sucker / Can U dig it / Touched by the hand of Cicciolina (extra time mix) / Dance of the mad / X Y & Zee (sunshine mix) / 92 degrees (Boilerhouse The Birth mix) / Karmadrome / Bullet proof / Get the girl! kill the baddies! / Another man's rhubarb / Rockahula baby / Wise up sucker / Cicciolina (Renegade Soundwave mix). *(cd+=)* – Preaching to the perverted (remix) / Eat me drink me love me kill me / PWEI-zatin.

Infectious Nothing-Interscope

Oct 93. (c-s) *(INFECT 1MC)* <95887> **R.S.V.P. / FAMILUS HORRIBILUS** [27] Feb94 [ ]
(cd-ep+=) *(INFECT 1CD)* – ('B'remixes) / ('B'live).
(12"ep+=/cd-ep+=) *(INFECT 1/+CDX)* – ('A'side) / ('B'-Higher later space mix agency vocal).

Feb 94. (7"/7"pic-d) *(INFECT 4 G/P)* **ICH BIN EIN AUSLANDER. / CP1 #2** [28] [–]
(12"+=/cd-s+=) *(INFECT 4/+CD)* – ('A'-Fun-Da-Mental instrumental) / ('A'-Fun-Da-Mental extra).
(12"+=) *(INFECT 4TX)* – ('A'-Drone ranger mix) / Intense.

Sep 94. (7"colrd) *(INFECT 9GG)* **EVERYTHING'S COOL. / LET IT FLOW** [23] [–]
(7"colrd) *(INFECT 9SO)* – ('A'side) / Wild west.
(cd-s) *(INFECT 9CD)* – ('A'side) / ('A'-Youth remix) / R.S.V.P. (Fluke mix).
(cd-s) *(INFECT 9CDX)* – ('A'side) / Ich bin ein Auslander (live) / Familus horribilus (live) / R.S.V.P. (live).

Sep 94. (cd/c) *(INFECT 10 CD/MC)* <92393> **DOS DEDOS MIS AMIGOS** [11] [ ]
– Ich bin ein Auslander / Kick to kill / Familus horribilus / Underbelly / Fatman / Home / Cape connection / Menofearthereaper / Everything's cool / R.S.V.P. / Babylon. *(also d-lp/d-c/d-cd; INFECT 10 LPX/MCX/CDX)*

Mar 95. (d-cd/d-c) *(INFECT 10 CDR/MCR)* <22> **TWO FINGERS MY FRIENDS!** (remixes) [25] [ ]
– Ich bin ein Auslander (Fun-Da-Mental) / Kick to kill (Jim Foetus seersucker mix) / Familus horribilus (mega web 2) / Underbelly (Renegade Soundwave blackout mix) / Fatman (Hoodlum Priest Fatboy mix) / Home (Orb sweet sin and salvation mix) / Cape Connection (Transglobal Underground Cossack in UFO encounter mix) / Menofearthereaper (concrete no fee, no fear mix) / Everything's cool (safe as milk mix) / R.S.V.P. (made in Japan, live at the Budokan double live Gonzo F mix) / Babylon (Loop Guru Babylon a dub fire mix) // Ich bin ein Auslander (Die Krupps mix) / Familus horribilus (Hia Nyg vocal mix) / Cape Connection (golden claw versus clock and dagger mix) / Intense / C.P.I. #2 / Cape Connection (TGV aliens, bodacious aliens mix) / Everything's cool (Dragonfly mix) / RSVP (Fluke lunch mix) / Cape Connection (Secret Knowledge transfered up mix) / Underbelly (The Drum Club bugsong mix). *(cd re-iss. Jan01; INFECT 10CDRX)*

—— CRABB left to pursue own career; he formed The BUZZARD and other project The Golden Claw Music, while MARCH formed BENTLEY RHYTHM ACE

– compilations, etc. –

Jun 96. (cd) *Camden; (74321 39339-2)* **WISE UP SUCKERS** [ ] [-]
Apr 97. (cd) *Strange Fruit; (<SFRSCD 005>)* **THE BBC RADIO 1 SESSIONS 1986-1987** [ ] [ ]
Oct 02. (cd) *Castle; (CMEDD 589)* **POP WILL EAT ITSELF 1986-1994** [ ] [-]

☐ PORNO FOR PYROS (see under ⇒ JANE'S ADDICTION)

PORTISHEAD

Formed: Bristol, England . . . 1993 by duo GEOFF BARROW and BETH GIBBONS, who took their name from a local coastal town. After working as MASSIVE ATTACK's studio runner and writing one of the better songs on NENEH CHERRY's 'HOMEBREW' album, BARROWS recruited covers band stalwart GIBBONS and the band signed to 'Go! Discs' off-shoot 'Go! Beat'. Named after BARROW's faded seaside resort hometown of Portishead near Bristol, the group debuted with a short film, 'TO KILL A DEAD MAN'. A retro spy movie pastiche, the film (which starred PORTISHEAD in an acting capacity) and its accompanying soundtrack were indicative of the cinematic melodrama which would characterise the band's groundbreaking debut. Released in August '94 amid much anticipation, and preceeded by the singles 'NUMB' and 'SOUR TIMES', 'DUMMY' was a wracked, claustrophobic melange of painfully slow hip hop rhythms, droning hammond, knife-edge guitar and rumbling bass. Spiced with a sprinkling of obscure samples and topped off by the sublime lament of GIBBONS' vocals, the sound PORTISHEAD had created was one of the most striking definitions of the phenomena that would come to be known as 'Trip Hop'. Along with MASSIVE ATTACK, TRICKY et all, the band insisted the label was a lazy attempt at pigeonholing but what really set PORTISHEAD apart was simply the otherness of their sound, a strange grace that made the unrelenting lyrical bleakness and despair bearable. Who knows, winning the Mercury Music Prize in 1995 may have cheered them up a bit, although it would be a long before they would resurface (meanwhile, BARROW guested on EARTHLING's 'Radar' set). During the summer of '97, PORTISHEAD delivered their first product in over two years, albeit a limited-edition 12"-only single, 'COWBOYS'. Nevertheless, the track was indeed a modern day classic, subsequently appearing on the flip of their Top 10 single, 'ALL MINE' – BETH was never better. As for their sophomore parent album, 'PORTISHEAD' (1997) – which made No.2 and nearly the Top 20 in America! – people would have been better not to compare it with their debut. Just when the fans thought it would take until the year 2000 for a third set, a live stop-gap, 'PNYC', came out the following year. BETH GIBBONS eventually returned with 'OUT OF SEASON' (2002), backed up by RUSTIN MAN (the nom de plume of PAUL WEBB, ex-TALK TALK) and shorn of the cinematic production which framed her vocals in PORTISHEAD. The result was as disarming as it was natural, the sorrowful songstress finally having her voice accompanied (by sympathetic, restrained, jazz-folksy instrumentation) rather than providing the final layer in an aural collage. • **Songwriters:** BARROW-GIBBONS, but most with UTLEY. Sample; MORE MISSION IMPOSSIBLE (Lalo Schifrin) / SPIN IT JIG (Smokey Brooks) / ELEGANT PEOPLE (Weather Report) / MAGIC MOUNTAIN (War) / I'LL NEVER FALL IN LOVE AGAIN (Johnnie Ray; at slow speed!) / ISAAC MOODS (Isaac Hayes). • **Trivia:** Have remixed for the likes of DEPECHE MODE (In Your Room) / RIDE (I Don't Know Where It Comes From) / GRAVEDIGGAZ (Nowhere To Run).

Album rating: DUMMY (*10) / PORTISHEAD (*8) / PNYC (*6) / Beth Gibbons & Rustic Man: OUT OF SEASON (*8)

BETH GIBBONS – vocals / **GEOFF BARROW** (b.1971) – programming, synthesizer with **ADRIAN UTLEY** – guitar, bass / **CLIVE DEAMER** – drums / **DAVE McDONALD** – nose flute / **RICHARD NEWELL** – drum programme / **NEIL SOLMAN** – synthesizers, organ / **ANDY HAGUE** – trumpet

Go Beat Polygram

Jun 94. (c-s) *(GODMC 114) <857561>* **NUMB / NUMBED IN MOSCOW** [ ] [ ]
(12"+=/cd-s+=) *(GOD X/CD 114)* – Revenge of the numbed / Numb: Earth – Linger / Extra numb
(cd-s++=) *(GOLCD 114)* – A tribute to Monk and Cantella.
Aug 94. (c-s) *(GODMC 116)* **SOUR TIMES / SOUR SOUR TIMES** [57] [-]
(12"+=) *(GODX 116)* – Lot more / Sheared times.
(re-iss. Apr95, hit UK No.13)
(cd-s++=) *(GODCD 116)* – Airbus reconstruction.
(cd-s) *(GOLCD 116)* – ('A'side) / It's a fire / Pedestal / Theme from 'To Kill A Dead Man'.
Aug 94. (cd/c/lp) *(<828552-2/-4/-1>)* **DUMMY** [2] Jan95 [79]
– Mysterons / Sour times / Strangers / It could be sweet / Wandering star / Numb / Roads / Pedestal / Biscuit / Glory box.
Oct 94. (c-s) *(GODMC 120)* **GLORY BOX / TOY BOX** [13] [ ]
(12"+=/cd-s+=) *(GOD X/CD 120)* – Scorn / Sheared box.
Jan 95. (cd-s) *<857816>* **SOUR TIMES (NOBODY LOVES ME) / AIRBUS RECONSTRUCTION** [-] [53]
Jun 97. (12"ltd) *(571277-1)* **COWBOYS. / COWBOYS (instrumental)** [ ] [-]
Sep 97. (c-s) *(571597-4) <871881>* **ALL MINE / COWBOYS** [8] [ ]
(12"+=/cd-s+=) *(571597-1-2)* – Cowboys (instrumental).
Oct 97. (cd/c) *(<539189-2/-4>)* **PORTISHEAD** [2] [21]
– Cowboys / All mine / Undenied / Half day closing / Over / Humming / Mourning air / Seven months / Only you / Elysium / Western eyes.
Nov 97. (12"/cd-s) *(571993-1/-2)* **OVER. / OVER (remix) / OVER (instrumental)** [25] [ ]
(cd-s) *(571995-2)* – ('A'side) / Half day closing (live) / Humming (live).
Mar 98. (c-s) *(569474-4)* **ONLY YOU / ELYSIUM (Parlour Talk remix)** [35] [ ]
(12"+=/cd-s+=) *(569475-1/-2)* – Only you (NYC) / Only you.
Nov 98. (cd/c/d-lp) *(<559424-2/-4/-1>)* **PNYC (live)** [40] [ ]
– Humming / Cowboys / All mine / Mysterons / Only you / Half day closing / Over / Glory box / Sour times / Roads / Strangers.

—— UTLEY moonlighted with the MOUNT VERNON ARTS LAB via a collaborative mini-set, 'WARMINSTER' (1999).

BETH GIBBONS & RUSTIN MAN

BETH – vocals / with **PAUL WEBB** (RUSTIN MAN) – multi (ex-TALK TALK) / plus **ADRIAN UTLEY** – multi / + ex-TALK TALK members

Go Beat Sanctuary

Oct 02. (cd/lp) *(066574-2/-1) <94648>* **OUT OF SEASON** [28] [ ]
– Mysteries / Tom the model / Show / Romance / Sand river / Spider monkey / Resolve / Drake / Funny time of year / Rustin man. *<US+=>* – Candy says (live) / (hidden track).
Mar 03. (7") *(GOB 55)* **TOM THE MODEL. / SPIDER MONKEY (live)** [70] [-]
(cd-s+=) *(GOBCD 55)* – ('A'-live) / ('A'video).

☐ John POWER (see under ⇒ CAST)

☐ POWER STATION (see under ⇒ DURAN DURAN)

☐ PRAS (see under ⇒ FUGEES)

PREFAB SPROUT

Formed: Consett, Durham, England ... 1982 by budding singer/songwriter and Newcastle University student, PADDY McALOON, along with his brother MARTIN on bass and drummer, MICK SALMON. A debut single, 'LIONS IN MY OWN GARDEN (EXIT SOMEONE)' was rejected by many major labels although its 1,000 copies (released on the self-financed 'Candle' label) shifted quickly enough for local man Keith Armstrong to sign them to the new independent label, 'Kitchenware'. After a respectable showing in the indie charts with the follow-up, 'THE DEVIL HAS ALL THE BEST TUNES', the label struck a deal with 'C.B.S.' who released the band's first Top 75 entry, 'DON'T SING' in early '84. The debut album, 'SWOON', was released the following month to sporadic critical fervour, an impressive collection of clever, jazz-tinged pop with eloquent, carefully crafted lyrics. Preceded by two unsuccessful issues of the wistful 'WHEN LOVE BREAKS DOWN', 'STEVE McQUEEN' (1985; re-titled 'TWO WHEELS GOOD' in America after an objection from McQUEEN's family) had the music press in rapture. Their first album to be produced by 80's guru THOMAS DOLBY, the songs were more directly melodic than the debut, enhancing the dreamy romance of much of the material while the country-inflected 'FARON YOUNG' was the first of McALOON's fond tributes to his musical heroes. 'WHEN LOVE BREAKS DOWN' was eventually a hit third time round when it was issued later that year although it would be 1988 before a new PREFAB SPROUT album was on the shelves, the masterful 'FROM LANGLEY PARK TO MEMPHIS'. The writing and arranging were more ambitious than ever, McALOON effortlessly updating the extravagance of an earlier golden era on the likes of 'HEY MANHATTAN' and 'VENUS OF THE SOUP KITCHEN', the latter featuring gospel act The ANDRAE CROUCH SINGERS. STEVIE WONDER made an appearance with his inimitable harmonica playing on 'NIGHTINGALES', with PETE TOWNSHEND also guesting on the album, such was the ever burgeoning reputation of the PREFAB SPROUT frontman. The intoxicating 'CARS AND GIRLS' was aimed at BRUCE SPRINGSTEEN's alleged narrow song repertoire, although McALOON had obviously forgotten the boss's 'Nebraska'. 'THE KING OF ROCK'N'ROLL's irresistible hook saw the group score their first, and only, Top 10 hit single to date. While 'PROTEST SONGS' (1989) was a collection initially pencilled in for four years previous, 'JORDAN: THE COMEBACK' (1990) was the next PREFAB SPROUT album proper, a lengthy quasi-concept album partly dedicated to ELVIS PRESLEY, while also paying tribute to such unlikely figures as Jesse James and Fred Astaire, over a bewitching musical backdrop. 1992's compilation, 'A LIFE OF SURPRISES', filled in a large gap between their next set, 'ANDROMEDA HEIGHTS', which, finally released in '97 hit the UK Top 10 for a week. A kind of updated, sanitised version of SLIM WHITMAN's 'Gunfighter Ballads', at least in spirit, 'THE GUNMAN AND OTHER STORIES' (2001) found the ever unpredictable PADDY McALOON indulging his love of the Western myth. While this Tony Visconti-produced affair at least reclaimed 'Cowboy Dreams' from JIMMY NAIL, critics were divided over the merits of such a polished production and the relative absence of McALOON's trademark wit and eccentricity, a state of affairs perhaps reflected in the record's lowly Top 60 (UK) chart position. Even before McALOON made his solo debut, the chances were it wasn't going to be your average collection of songs he'd been collecting for just such an occasion. In the event, 'I TRAWL THE MEGAHERTZ' (2003) was as striking and as singular as its title, the ever unpredictable songwriter coming to grips with his mortality in cathartic and soul-scouring fashion. The twenty-minute plus title track was almost an album in itself, strung out on swells of plaintive strings and brass.

Album rating: SWOON (*6) / STEVE McQUEEN (*8) / FROM LANGLEY PARK TO MEMPHIS (*7) / PROTEST SONGS (*6) / JORDAN: THE COMEBACK (*7) / A LIFE OF SURPRISES – THE BEST OF PREFAB SPROUT compilation (*9) / ANDROMEDA HEIGHTS (*5) / THE GUNMAN AND OTHER STORIES (*5) / Paddy McAloon: I TRAWL THE MEGAHERTZ (*6)

PADDY McALOON (b. 7 Jun'57) – vocals, guitar / **WENDY SMITH** (b.31 May'63) – some guitar, vocals / **MARTIN McALOON** (b. 4 Jan'62) – bass / **MICK SALMON** – drums

Candle — not iss.

Aug 82. (7") *(CANDLE 1)* **LIONS IN MY OWN GARDEN (EXIT SOMEONE). / RADIO LOVE** [ ] [–]
(re-iss. May83 on 'Kitchenware'; SK 4) (re-iss. May83 on 'Kitchenware-Rough Trade'; SK 4 – RT 141)

Kitchenware — Epic

Oct 83. (7") *(SK 7)* **THE DEVIL HAS ALL THE BEST TUNES. / WALK ON** [ ] [–]
(Dec83:- 12"+=) *(SK 8)* – Lions in my own garden / Radio love.

Jan 84. (7") *(SK 9)* **DON'T SING. / GREEN ISAAC II** [64] [–]
(12"+=) *(SK 9-12)* – He'll have to go.

— **GRAHAM LANT** – drums; repl. SALMON

Feb 84. (lp/c) *(KW LP/C 1) <39872>* **SWOON** [22] [ ]
– Don't sing / Cue fanfare / Green Isaac I / Here on the eerie / Cruel / Couldn't bear to be special / I never play basketball now / Ghost town blues / Elegance / Technique / Green Isaac II. *(re-iss. Mar88 on 'C.B.S.' lp/c/cd; 460908-1/-4/-2) (re-iss. Mar93 & Feb97 cd/c; 460908-2/-4)*

Mar 84. (7") *(SK 10)* **COULDN'T BEAR TO BE SPECIAL. / SPINNING BELINDA** [ ] [–]
(12"+=) *(SK 10-12)* – Donna Summer.

— **NEIL CONTI** (b.12 Feb'59, London, England) – drums; repl. GRAHAM

Oct 84. (7") *(SK 19)* **WHEN LOVE BREAKS DOWN. / DIANA** [ ] [–]
(d7"+=) *(SKDP 19)* – The yearning loins / Donna Summer.
(12"++=) *(SKK 19)* – Cruel.

Mar 85. (7") *(SK 21)* **WHEN LOVE BREAKS DOWN (remix). / THE YEARNING LOINS** [ ] [–]
(d7"+=) *(SK 21-12)* – The Devil has all the best tunes / Walk on.
(d7"+=) *(SKDQ 21)* – Lions in my own garden (exit someone). / Radio love.

Jun 85. (7") *(SK 22)* **FARON YOUNG. / SILHOUETTES** [74] [–]
(d7"+=) *(SKDP 22)* – When love breaks down / The yearning loins.
(12") *(SKX 22)* – ('A'-Truckin' mix) / ('B'-full version).

Jun 85. (lp/c)(cd) *(KW LP/C 3)(CD 26522) <40100>* **STEVE McQUEEN** <US-title 'TWO WHEELS GOOD'> [21] [ ]
– Faron Young / Bonny / Appetite / When love breaks down / Goodbye Lucille (Johnny Johnny) / Hallelujah / Moving the river / Horsin' around / Desire as / Blueberry pies / When the angels. *<US+=>* – The yearning loins / He'll have to go / Faron (truckin' mix). *(re-iss. Mar90 & May97 on 'C.B.S.' cd/c/lp; 466336-2/-4/-1)*

Aug 85. (7") *(SK 23)* **APPETITE. / HEAVEN CAN WAIT** [ ] [–]
(d12"+=) *(SKXDP 23)* – Oh, the Swiss / Faron Young (truckin' mix) / Silhouettes.

Oct 85. (7") *(SK 21)* **WHEN LOVE BREAKS DOWN. / THE YEARNING LOINS** [25] [–]
(12"+=) *(SK 21-12)* – Spinning Belinda / Donna Summer.
(d7"++=) *(SKD 21)* – He'll have to go.

Feb 86. (7"/7"sha-pic-d) *(SK/+X 24)* **JOHNNY JOHNNY. / WIGS** [64] [–]
(12"+=) *(SKK 24)* – The guest who stayed forever.

Feb 88. (7") *(SK 35)* **CARS AND GIRLS. / VENDETTA** [44] [–]
(10"+=) *(SKQ 35)* – Real life (just around the corner).
(12"++=/pic-cd-s++=) *(SKK/CDDSK 35)* – Faron Young (truckin' mix).

Mar 88. (lp/c/cd) *(KW LP/C/CD 9) <44208>* **FROM LANGLEY PARK TO MEMPHIS** [5] [ ]
– The king of rock'n'roll / Cars and girls / I remember that / Enchanted / Nightingales / Hey Manhattan! / Knock on wood / The golden calf / Nancy (let your hair down for me) / The Venus of the soup kitchen. *(cd re-iss. May97 on 'Columbia'; 460124-2)*

Apr 88. (7"/7"box) *(SKQ/SKB 37)* **THE KING OF ROCK'N'ROLL. / MOVING RIVER** [7] [–]
(12"+=) *(SKX 35)* – Dandy of the blue river / Tin can pot.
(cd-s+=) *(CDDSK 35)* – Dandy of the blue river / He'll have to go.

Jul 88. (7"/7"box) *(SK/+B 38)* **HEY MANHATTAN! / TORNADO** [72] [–]
(12"+=/12"g-f+=/cd-s+=) *(SKX/SKGT/CDSK 38)* – ('A'-JFK version) / Donna Summer.

Nov 88. (7") *(SK 39)* **NIGHTINGALES. / LIONS IN MY OWN GARDEN** [ ] [–]
(d7"ep+=) *(SKEP 39)* – The Devil has all the best tunes.
(12"+=/cd-s+=) *(SKX/CDSK 39)* – Life of suprises / Bearpark.
(12") *(SKK 39)* – ('A'extended) / The king of rock'n'roll (live).

Feb 89. (7"/7"pic-d) *(SK/+P 41)* **THE GOLDEN CALF. / THE VENUS OF THE SOUP KITCHEN** [ ] [–]
(12"+=/cd-s+=) *(SKX/CDSK 41)* – ('A'long version) / Bonny (live).
(below album was to have been released in 1985, thus its low cat.no.)

Jun 89. (lp/c/cd) *(KW LP/C/CD 4)* **THE PROTEST SONGS** [18] [–]
– The world awake / Life of suprise / Horse chimes / Wicked things / Dublin / Tiffany's / Diana / Talkin' Scarlet / 'Till the cows come home / Pearly gates. *(cd re-iss. May91 & Mar93 & Feb97 on 'Columbia'; 465118-2)*

Aug 90. (7"/c-s) *(SK/+C 47)* **LOOKING FOR ATLANTIS. / MICHAEL** [51] [–]
(12"+=) *(SKK 47)* – King of rock'n'roll / Cars and girls.
(cd-s++=) *(CDSK 47)* – When love breaks down.

Aug 90. (cd/c/lp) *(KW CD/C/LP 14) <46132>* **JORDAN: THE COMEBACK** [7] Sep90 [ ]
– Looking for Atlantis / Wild horses / Machine gun Ibiza / We let the stars go / Carnival 2000 / Jordan: the comeback / Jesse James symphony / Jesse James bolero / Moon dog / All the world loves lovers / All boys believe anything / The ice maiden / Paris Smith / The wedding march / One of the broken / Michael / Mercy / Scarlet nights / Doo wop in Harlem. *(re-iss. May94 & May97 & Feb01 cd/c; 467161-2)*

Oct 90. (7"/c-s) *(SK/+C 48)* **LET THE STARS GO. / CRUEL** [50] [–]
(12"+=) *(SKK 48)* – Don't sing / Couldn't bear to be special.
(cd-s+=) *(CDSK 48)* – Faron Young / Hey Manhattan (JFK version).

Dec 90. (7"ep/12"ep/cd-ep) *(SK/SKK/CDSK 49)* **JORDAN: THE EP** [35] [–]
– Carnival 2000 / One of the broken / The ice maiden / Jordan: The comeback.

Kitchenware-Columbia / Columbia

Jun 92. (7"/c-s) *(SK/+C 58)* **THE SOUND OF CRYING. / ONE OF THE BROKEN** [23] [–]
(cd-s+=) *(CDSK 58)* – Nightingales / Faron Young.
(cd-s) *(CDSKX 58)* – ('A'full version) / The golden calf / Looking for Atlantis.

Jul 92. (cd/c/lp) *(471886-2/-4/-1) <52847>* **A LIFE OF SURPRISES – THE BEST OF PREFAB SPROUT** (compilation) [3] Oct92 [ ]
– The king of rock'n'roll / When love breaks down / The sound of crying / Faron Young / Carnival 2000 / Goodbye Lucille 1 (Johnny Johnny) / I remember that / Cruel / Cars and girls / We let the stars go / Life of surprises / Appetite / If you don't love me / Wild horses / Hey Manhattan! / All the world loves lovers.

Jul 92. (7"/c-s) *(SK/+C 60)* **IF YOU DON'T LOVE ME. / ('A'mix)** [33] [–]
(cd-s) *(CDSK 60)* – ('A'side) / ('A'-String driven thing mix) / Nero the zero / Real life (just around the corner).
(cd-s) *(CDSKX 60)* – ('A'side) / ('A'-No strings attached mix) / Lions in my own garden (exit someone) / Hey Manhattan (JFK mix).

Sep 92. (7"/c-s) *(SK/+C 62)* **ALL THE WORLD LOVES LOVERS. / MACHINE GUN IBIZA** [61] [–]
(cd-s) *(CDSK 62)* – ('A'side) / Knock on wood / Desire as / Moondog.
(cd-s+=) *(CDSKX 62)* – Till the cows come home / Enchanted.

Jan 93. (7"/c-s) *(SK/+C 63)* **LIFE OF SURPRISES. / THE KING OF ROCK'N'ROLL** [24] [–]
(cd-s+=) *(CDSK 63)* – If you don't love me.
(12") *(SKK 63)* – ('A'side) / If you don't love me (2 mixes).

Mar 93. (cd-s) *(SKCD 64)* **I REMEMBER THAT / THE WORLD AWAKE** [ ] [–]

Apr 97. (c-s) *(SKC 70)* **A PRISONER OF THE PAST / WHERE THE HEART IS** [30] [–]
(cd-s+=) *(SKCD 70)* – Just because I can.
(cd-s) *(SKZD 70)* – ('A'side) / The king of rock'n'roll / Cars and girls.

May 97. (cd/c) *(KW CD/MC 30) <87297>* **ANDROMEDA HEIGHTS** [7] [ ]
– Electric guitars / A prisoner of the past / The mystery of love / Life's a miracle / Anne Marie / Whoever you are / Steal your thunder / Avenue of stars / Swans / The fifth horseman / Weightless / Andromeda heights.

Jul 97. (c-s) *(SKC 71)* **ELECTRIC GUITARS / DRAGONS** [53] [–]
(cd-s+=) *(SKCD 71)* – End of the affair.
(cd-s) *(SKZD 71)* – ('A'side) / Girl I'm here / Never trust a spell.

—— virtually the **McALOON's** + **RICHIE MORALES** – drums / **CARLOS ALOMAR** – guitar / **JEFF PEVAR** – guitar / **TONY VISCONTI** etc.

Liberty / Liberty

Jun 01. (cd-s) *(CDPREFAB 001)* **COWBOY DREAMS / BLUE ROSES / COWBOY DREAMS (version)** [ ] [–]

Jun 01. (cd/c) *(<5 32613-2/-4>)* **THE GUNMAN AND OTHER STORIES** [60] [ ]
– Cowboy dreams / Wild card in the pack / I'm a troubled man / The streets of Laredo – Not long for this world / Love will find someone for you / Cornfield ablaze / When you get to know me better / The gunman / Blue roses / Farmyard cat.

– compilations, etc. –

1988. (cd) *C.B.S.; (CDPS 241)* **SWOON / STEVE McQUEEN** [ ] [–]
(re-iss. May97 on 'Columbia'; PS 21CD)

Feb 93. (d-cd) *Columbia; (471886-2)* **A LIFE OF SURPRISES / STEVE McQUEEN** [ ] [–]

Feb 95. (d-cd) *Columbia; (478482-2)* **STEVE McQUEEN / FROM LANGLEY PARK TO MEMPHIS** [ ] [–]
(re-iss. Sep00; 499925-2)

May 97. (d-cd) *Columbia; (PS 22CD)* **FROM LANGLEY PARK TO MEMPHIS / JORDAN: THE COMEBACK** [ ] [–]

—— PADDY McALOON also nearly issued a solo 7", 'HORSIN' AROUND' along with the help of LOUISE and DEIRDRE RUTKOWSKI of SUNSET GUN

Oct 99. (cd) *Epic; (496285-2)* **38 CARAT COLLECTION** [ ] [–]

PADDY McALOON

with session band

Liberty / Liberty

Jun 03. (cd) *(<583910-2>)* **I TRAWL THE MEGAHERTZ** [ ] [ ]
– I trawl the megahertz / Esprit de corps / Fall from grace / We were poor . . . / Orchid 7 / I'm 49 / Sleeping rough / Ineffable / . . .But we were happy.

Elvis PRESLEY

Born: ELVIS AARON PRESLEY, 8 Jan'35, Tupelo, Mississippi, USA. One of twin sons (the other Jesse was stillborn), he was raised in Memphis, Tennessee. Between the summer of '53 and '54, he spent time in Sam Phillips' 'Sun' studios, cutting demos. With the arrival of back-up session players, SCOTTY MOORE and BILL BLACK, his first single, a rousing cover of Arthur Crudup's 'THAT'S ALL RIGHT MAMA', gained local airplay even before its release on the 'Sun' label. After a brief flirtation with country, he opted for R&B after his young audiences lapped up his pelvic action. Although Sam Phillips initially thought ELVIS was a black blues singer, he still chose to feature ELVIS's country recordings on the flip sides. Colonel Tom Parker became his manager in 1955, soon securing a large 5-figure deal with 'R.C.A.', who also bought out his contract with 'Sun' records; the attention ELVIS's riotous stage shows had received prompted an intense bidding war. His major debut, 'HEARTBREAK HOTEL', sparked off a new phenomenom at the start of 1956 which soon gave him a massive selling No.1. PRESLEY appeared on many TV shows around this time, the newfound star going on to appear in his first feature film, 'Love Me Tender' (named after his song, see also further film discography). The constant demand for ELVIS's records saw many simultaneous releases clogging the charts; he scored a further nine US No.1's in the States (namely 'I WANT YOU, I NEED YOU, I LOVE YOU', 'DON'T BE CRUEL', 'HOUND DOG', 'LOVE ME TENDER', 'TOO MUCH', 'ALL SHOOK UP', 'LET ME BE YOUR TEDDY BEAR', 'JAILHOUSE ROCK' and 'DON'T'), before being controversially

drafted into the army on the 24th of March '58. While serving his country over a two-year period, ELVIS suffered the death of his mother, Gladys, something which was to deeply affect him in the years to come. During this period, several singles were issued, the records (including chart-topping 'HARD HEADED WOMAN' and 'A BIG HUNK O LOVE') recorded just prior to his draft. After being promoted to Sergeant, his army time expired in March 1960, another US No.1, 'STUCK ON YOU', celebrating his return to "civvie" street. ELVIS returned to the Nashville studios and began working on a new ballad-esque style backed with an uptempo beat, a sound that was only vaguely reminiscent of his pre-army days. His films too, (around three a year in the 60's), contained a sort of manufactured pop, guided no doubt by the vast sums of money it stimulated. However, in spells between 1960 and 1965, ELVIS did create some truly wonderful pop records including 'IT'S NOW OR NEVER', 'ARE YOU LONESOME TONIGHT?', 'WOODEN HEART', 'RETURN TO SENDER', 'DEVIL IN DISGUISE', 'VIVA LAS VEGAS' and 'CRYING IN THE CHAPEL' to name but a few. In 1965, he also released the first of a series of gospel albums, 'HIS HAND IN MINE', while on the 1st of May '67, he married long-time girlfriend, Priscilla Beaulieu. After she bore him a child, Lisa Marie, in 1968, they separated in 1972 and divorced a year later (she subsequently became an actress, most notably on the 'Dallas' soap). In the late '60's, ELVIS revived a somewhat commercially declining singles career when 'IN THE GHETTO' then 'SUSPICIOUS MINDS' hit the Top 3. His work in the 70's showed him moving into the money-spinning cabaret circuit as his live appearances were mainly in Las Vegas and Hawaii. While "The King" was still a top performer, as loyal fans old and new flocked to see his larger frame (squeezing out of a white glitzy suit) churn out another exhaustive show, he was barely a shadow of the rock'n'roll hero he once was. A combination of a special diet, prescribed drugs, junk food (binges) and alcohol eventually proved too much for ailing heart and tragically on the 16th of August 1977, he was found dead in his Graceland home by girlfriend, Ginger Alden. His funeral saw over 75,000 fans/mourners flocking to the gates of his home in Gracelands. The King Of Rock was dead. Following the death of ELVIS, many tabloids reported sightings of a living Elvis and speculation about his doomed life has been catapulted into the ridiculous. The King should've been laid to rest in peace, his music the only thing to live on. In fact, ELVIS went on to have numerous hit compilations and the odd hit single, none more so than when JUNKIE XL sent his updated remixed version of 'A LITTLE LESS CONVERSATION' to the top of the UK charts in 2002. The PAUL OAKENFOLD twist on ELVIS's 'RUBBERNECKIN' nearly followed suit in '03, both giving the King crossover dance hits a quarter of a century after his death!
• **Songwriters:** Covered (singles only mentioned):- THAT'S ALL RIGHT MAMA + MY BABY LEFT ME (Arthur 'Big Boy' Crudup) / BLUE MOON OF KENTUCKY (Bill Monroe) / BABY LET'S PLAY HOUSE (Arthur Gunter) / BLUE SUEDE SHOES (Carl Perkins) / TUTTI FRUTTI + RIP IT UP (Little Richard) / HOUND DOG (Freddie Bell . . . & Big Mama Thornton) / ALL SHOOK UP (Otis Blackwell) / ONE BROKEN HEART FOR SALE (Blackwell-Scott) / ONE NIGHT (Smiley Lewis) / A FOOL SUCH AS I (Hank Snow) / MY WISH CAME TRUE (Ivory Joe White) / IT'S NOW OR NEVER + SURRENDER + ASK ME (Italian trad.) / ARE YOU LONESOME TONIGHT? (Vaughn Deleath) / I FEEL SO BAD (Chuck Willis) / WITCHCRAFT (Spiders) / WHAT'D I SAY (Ray Charles) / BOSSA NOVA BABY (Lieber-Stoller) / SUCH A NIGHT (Johnnie Ray) / FRANKIE & JOHNNY (?) / LOVE LETTERS (Dick Haymes) / BIG BOSS MAN (Jimmy Reed) / U.S. MALE (Jerry Reed) / YOU'LL NEVER WALK ALONE (hit. Gerry & The Pacemakers) / IN THE GHETTO (Mac Davis) / SUSPICIOUS MINDS (Mark James) / THE WONDER OF YOU (Ray Peterson) / KENTUCKY RAIN (Eddie Rabbit) / YOU DON'T HAVE TO SAY YOU LOVE ME (Dusty Springfield) / THERE GOES MY EVERYTHING (Engelbert Humperdink) / I REALLY WANT TO KNOW (Les Paul & Mary Ford) / RAGS TO RICHES (Tony Bennett) / I JUST CAN'T HELP BELIEVIN' (B.J.Thomas) / UNTIL IT'S TIME FOR YOU TO GO (Buffy Sainte-Marie) / AN AMERICAN TRILOGY (Mickey Newbury) / BURNING LOVE (Arthur Alexander) / STEAMROLLER BLUES (James Taylor) / POLK SALAD ANNIE (Tony Joe White) / I'VE GOT A THING ABOUT YOU BABY (Billy Lee Riley) / PROMISED LAND (Chuck Berry) / MY BOY (hit. Richard Harris) / HURT (Timi Yuro) / GREEN, GREEN GRASS OF HOME (Tom Jones) / MY WAY (Paul Anka) / TOMORROW'S A LONG TIME (Bob Dylan) / etc. • **Filmography:** LOVE ME TENDER (1956) / LOVING YOU (1957) / JAILHOUSE ROCK (1957) / KING CREOLE (1958) / G.I.BLUES (1960) / WILD IN THE COUNTRY (1961) / FLAMING STAR (1961) / BLUE HAWAII (1961) / FOLLOW THAT DREAM (1962) / KID GALAHAD (1962) / GIRLS! GIRLS! GIRLS! (1962) / IT HAPPENED AT THE WORLD'S FAIR (1963) / FUN IN ACAPULCO (1963) / KISSIN' COUSINS (1964) / VIVA LAS VEGAS (1964) / ROUSTABOUT (1964) / GIRL HAPPY (1965) / TICKLE ME (1965) / HAREM HOLIDAY (1965, 'HARUM SCARUM'-US title) / FRANKIE AND JOHNNY (1966) / PARADISE, HAWAIIAN STYLE (1966) / CALIFORNIA HOLIDAY (1966, 'SPINOUT'-US title) / DOUBLE TROUBLE (1967) / CLAMBAKE (1968) / STAY AWAY JOE (1968) / SPEEDWAY (1968) / LIVE A LITTLE, LOVE A LITTLE (1968) / CHARRO (1969) / THE TROUBLE WITH GIRLS (1969) / CHANGE OF HABIT (1970) / (This was his last feature film, but many concerts were recorded)

Best CD compilation: PRESLEY – THE ALL-TIME GREATEST HITS (*10)

with **SCOTTY MOORE** – guitar / **BILL BLACK** – bass / + session drummers

		not iss.	Sun
Aug 54.	(7") *<209>* **THAT'S ALL RIGHT MAMA. / BLUE MOON OF KENTUCKY** *<re-iss. Nov55 on 'R.C.A.'; 6380>*	–	
Oct 54.	(7") *<210>* **GOOD ROCKIN' TONIGHT. / I DON'T CARE IF THE SUN DON'T SHINE** *<re-iss. Nov55 on 'R.C.A.'; 6381>*	–	
Jan 55.	(7") *<215>* **MILK COW BLUES BOOGIE. / YOU'RE A HEARTBREAKER** *<re-iss. Nov55 on 'R.C.A.'; 6382>*	–	
May 55.	(7") *<217>* **I'M LEFT, YOU'RE RIGHT, SHE'S GONE. / BABY LET'S PLAY HOUSE** *<re-iss. Nov55 on 'R.C.A.'; 6383>*	–	
Aug 55.	(7") *<223>* **MYSTERY TRAIN. / I FORGOT TO REMEMBER TO FORGET** *<re-iss. Nov55 on 'R.C.A.'; 6357>* *(all UK rel.Feb59 & Mar64 on 'RCA')*	–	

— added **D.J. FONTANA** – drums (on tour and then on session)

— now adding on session **FLOYD CRAMER** – piano / **CHET ATKINS** – guitar / **HANK GARLAND** – guitar / **'BOOTS' RANDOLPH** – saxophone

— He was also backed and at times credited with **The JORDANAIRES; GORDON STOKER, HOYT HAWKINS, NEAL MATTHEWS** and **HUGH JARRETT.**

		H.M.V.	R.C.A.
Mar 56.	(7")(78) *(7M 385)(POP 182)* *<47-6420>* **HEARTBREAK HOTEL. / I WAS THE ONE**	2	1
		Feb56	19
Mar 56.	(lp) *<LPM 1254>* **ELVIS PRESLEY**	–	1

– Blue suede shoes* / I'm counting on you* / Money honey* / I got a sweetie (I got a woman)* / One sided love affair* / I'm gonna sit right down and cry over you* / Tryin' to get to you* / I love you because / Just because / Blue moon / I'll never let you go / Tutti frutti. (tracks * =on next album too) *(UK-iss.Oct56;) (re-iss. Mar85 on 'R.C.A.' lp/c/cd; (NL/NK/ND 89046) (pic-lp.Oct88 on 'R.C.A.'; PD 81254)*

May 56. (7")(78) *(7M 405)(POP 213)* **BLUE SUEDE SHOES. / TUTTI FRUTTI** 9 –

Jul 56. (7")(78) *(7M 424)(POP 235) <47-6540>* **I WANT YOU, I NEED YOU, I LOVE YOU. / MY BABY LEFT ME** 14 1 May56 31

Sep 56. (7",78) *(POP 249) <47-6604>* **HOUND DOG. / DON'T BE CRUEL** 2 Jul56 1
(re-iss. Jun78 on 'R.C.A.'; PB 9265) – (hit UK No.24)

Sep 56. (7",78) *(POP 253) <476643>* **LOVE ME TENDER. / ANYWAY YOU WANT ME (THAT'S HOW I WILL BE)** 11 1 Oct56 20

Nov 56. (lp) *(CLP 1093) <LPM 1382>* **ROCK'N'ROLL NO.1** <US title 'ELVIS'> * 1
– That's all right / Lawdy Miss Clawdy / Mystery train / Playing fpr keeps / Poor boy / Money honey / I'm counting on you / My baby left me / I was the one / Shake rattle and roll / I'm left, you're right, she's gone / You're a heartbreaker / Tryin' to get to you / Blue suede shoes. *(re-iss. Mar59 as 'ELVIS'; CLP 1093)* – (hit No.4) *(re-iss. May72 as 'ROCK'N'ROLL' on 'R.C.A.'; SF 8233)* – (hit No.34) *(re-iss. Sep81 on 'R.C.A.' lp/c; NL/NK 89125)*

Nov 56. (7",78) *(POP 272)* **BLUE MOON. / I DON'T CARE IF THE SUN DON'T SHINE** 9 –

Feb 57. (7",78) *(POP 295)* **MYSTERY TRAIN. / LOVE ME** 25 –

Mar 57. (7",78) *(POP 305)* **RIP IT UP. / BABY LET'S PLAY HOUSE** 27 –

Apr 57. (lp) *(CLP 1105)* **ROCK'N'ROLL NO.2** * –
– Rip it up / When my blue moon turns to gold again / Love me / Long tall Sally / First in line / Old Shep / So glad you're mine / How's the world treating you / Any place is Paradise / Paralysed / Ready Teddy / How do think I feel. *(re-iss. 1962 on 'R.C.A.' mono/stereo; RD/SF 7528) (re-iss. Jan84 on 'R.C.A.' lp/c; NL/NK 81382) (cd-iss. May90; ND 81382)*

May 57. (7",78) *(POP 330) <47-6800>* **TOO MUCH. / PLAYING FOR KEEPS** 6 1 Jan57 21

Jun 57. (7",78) *(POP 359) <47-6870>* **ALL SHOOK UP. / THAT'S WHEN YOUR HEARTACHES BEGIN** 1 1 Mar57 58

—— ELVIS was now backed by a variety of session men. SCOTTY and BILL left. In Jun'58, **BOB MOORE** – bass / **HANK GARLAND** – guitar repl. them

R.C.A. R.C.A.

Jul 57. (7",78) *(RCA 1013) <47-7000>* **(LET ME BE YOUR) TEDDY BEAR. / LOVING YOU** 3 1 Jun57 20

Aug 57. (10"lp) *(RC 24001) <LPM 1515>* **LOVING YOU (film soundtrack)** * Jul57 1
– Mean woman blues / (Let me be your) Teddy bear / Loving you / Got a lot o' livin' to do / Lonesome cowboy / I need you so / Have I told you lately that I love you / True love / Party / Blueberry hill / Hot dog / Don't leave me now. *(re-iss. Sep77 lp/c +=; PK/PL 42358)* – (hit UK No.24) *(re-iss. Aug81 on 'RCA International' INTS 5109) (re-iss. Jan84 lp/c; NL/NK 81515) (cd-iss. Oct87; ND 81515)*

Oct 57. (7",78) *(RCA 1020)* **PARTY. / GOT A LOT OF LIVIN' TO DO** 2 –

Nov 57. (7",78) *(RCA 1025)* **SANTA BRING MY BABY BACK TO ME. / SANTA CLAUS IS COMING TO TOWN** 7 –

Nov 57. (lp) *(RD 27052) <LOC 1035>* **ELVIS' CHRISTMAS ALBUM** * 1
– Santa Claus is coming to town / White Christmas / Precious Lord it is no secret (what God can do) / Blue Christmas / Santa bring my baby back to me / I'll be home for Christmas / Here comes Santa Claus (right down Santa Claus lane) / O little town of Bethlehem / Silent night / Take my hand / I believe / (There'll be) Peace in the valley (for me). *(re-iss. Nov58; same) (re-iss. Nov71 on 'RCA International; INTS 1126)* – (hit No.7) *(re-iss. Jan84 lp/c; NL/NK 89116) (re-iss. Nov85; PL 85486) (re-iss. Oct79 on 'RCA-Camden' lp/c; CDS/CAM 1155) (re-iss. Nov75 on 'Pickwick' diff; CAM 462)*

Jan 58. (7",78) *(RCA 1028) <47-7035>* **JAILHOUSE ROCK. / TREAT ME NICE** 1 1 Oct57 18
(re-iss. May77; PB 2695) – (hit UK No.44 Aug77) *(re-iss. Jan83, hit No.27, also on 7"pic-d diff B-side THE ELVIS MEDLEY)*

Feb 58. (7",78) *(RCA 1043) <47-7150>* **DON'T. / I BEG OF YOU** 2 1 Jan58 8

—— ELVIS was served US army draft notice in Dec'57. He finally – after much fan/film producer protest – joined army on 24 Mar'58. He has had enough time to record many songs and appeared on celluloid once again (aka KING CREOLE film).

Apr 58. (7",78) *(RCA 1058) <47-7240>* **WEAR MY RING ROUND YOUR NECK. / DON'T CHA THINK IT'S TIME** 3 2 Jun58 15

Jul 58. (7",78) *(RCA 1070) <47-7280>* **HARD HEADED WOMAN. / DON'T ASK ME WHY** 2 1 Jun58 25

Sep 58. (7",78) *(RCA 1081)* **KING CREOLE. / DIXIELAND ROCK** 2 –

Oct 58. (lp) *(RD 27088) <LPM 1884>* **KING CREOLE (film soundtrack)** 4 Sep58 2
– King Creole / As long as I have you / Crawfish / Lover doll / Hard headed woman / Don't ask me why / Trouble / New Orleans / Dixieland rock / Steadfast, loyal and true / Young dreams. *(re-iss. 1963 & Feb69; same) (re-iss. Aug81 on 'RCA International'; INTS 5013) (re-iss. Jan84 lp/c; NL/NK 83733) (cd-iss. Oct87; ND 83733)*

Jan 59. (7",78) *(RCA 1100) <47-7410>* **ONE NIGHT. / I GOT STUNG** 1 4 Oct58 8
(re-iss. May77; PB 2696)

Apr 59. (7",78) *(RCA 1113) <47-7506>* **(NOW AND THEN THERE'S) A FOOL SUCH AS I. / I NEED YOUR LOVE TONIGHT** 1 2 Mar59 4
(re-iss. May77; PB 2697)

Jul 59. (7",78) *(RCA 1136) <47-7600>* **A BIG HUNK O' LOVE. / MY WISH CAME TRUE** 4 1 Jun59 12
(all singles from Jul'57 were re-iss. Mar60)

—— ELVIS was now demobbed from the army 5 Mar'60. His session men now are **FLOYD CRAMER** – piano / **SCOTTY MOORE** – guitar

Mar 60. (7",78) *(RCA 1187) <47-7740>* **STUCK ON YOU. / FAME AND FORTUNE** 3 1 17

Jun 60. (mono-lp)(stereo-lp) *(RD 27171)(SF 5060) <LSP 2231>* **ELVIS IS BACK!** 1 May60 2
– Make me no it / The girl of my best friend / Dirty dirty / I will be home again / The thrill of your love / Feeling / Soldier boy / Such a night / It feels so right / Like a baby / Fever / Reconsider baby / The girl next door. *(re-iss. Apr84 lp/c; NL/NK 89013) (cd-iss. Jul89; ND 89013)*

Jul 60. (7") *(RCA 1194)* **A MESS OF BLUES. / THE GIRL OF MY BEST FRIEND** 2 –

Jul 60. (7") *<47-7777>* **IT'S NOW OR NEVER. / A MESS OF BLUES** – 1 32

Oct 60. (7") *(RCA 1207)* **IT'S NOW OR NEVER. / MAKE ME KNOW IT** 1 –
(re-iss. May77; PB 2698) – (hit UK No.39 in Aug77)

Dec 60. (mono-lp)(stereo-lp) *(RD 27192)(SF 5078) <LSP 2256>* **G.I. BLUES (Film soundtrack)** 1 Oct60 1
– Tonight is so right for love / What's she really like / Big boots / Frankfurt special / Wooden heart / Shoppin' around / Pocketful of rainbows / G.I. blues / Doin' the best I can / Didja ever / Blue suede shoes. *(re-iss. Sep77; same)* – (hit UK No.14) *(re-iss. Aug81 on 'RCA International'; INTS 5104) (re-iss. Jan84 lp/c; NL/NK 83735) (cd-iss. Oct87; ND 83735)*

Jan 61. (7") *(RCA 1216) <47-7810>* **ARE YOU LONESOME TONIGHT? / I GOTTA KNOW** 1 1 Nov60 20
(re-iss. May77; PB 2699) – (hit UK No.46 Aug77)

Mar 61. (7") *(RCA 1226)* **WOODEN HEART. / TONIGHT IS SO RIGHT FOR LOVE** 1 –
(re-iss. May77; PB 2700) – (hit UK No.49 Aug77)

May 61. (mono-lp)(stereo-lp) *(RD 27211)(SF 5094) <LSP 2328>* **HIS HAND IN MINE** 3 Jan61 13
– His hand in mine / I'm gonna walk dem golden stairs / Milky white way / My father's house / Known only to him / Mansions over the hilltop / I believe in the sky / If we never meet again / Working on the building / Jesus knows what I need / Joshua fit the battle / Swing low sweet chariot. *(re-iss. Aug81 on 'RCA International'; INTS 5105) (re-iss. Jan84 lp/c; NL/NK 83935) (cd-iss. Oct88; ND 83935)*

May 61. (7") *(RCA 1227) <47-7850>* **SURRENDER (TORNA A SURRIENTO). / LONELY MAN** 4 1 Feb61 32
(re-iss. May77; PB 2701)

Aug 61. (7") *(RCA 1244) <47-7880>* **WILD IN THE COUNTRY. / I FEEL SO BAD** [1] [26]
May61 [5]

Oct 61. (7") *(RCA 1258) <47-7908>* **(MARIE'S THE NAME) HIS LATEST FLAME. / LITTLE SISTER** [4] [26]
Aug61 [5]
(re-iss. May77; PB 2702)

Oct 61. (mono-lp)(stereo-lp) *(RD 27224)(SF 5106) <LSP 2370>* **SOMETHING FOR EVERYBODY** [2] Jul61 [1]
– There's always me / Give me the right / Gently / It's a sin / Sentimental me / Starting today / I'm coming home / I slipped I stumbled I fell / Put the blame on me / I want you with me / Judy / In your arms. *(re-iss. Jan84 lp/c; NL/NK 84116) (cd-iss. Dec90;)*

Dec 61. (mono-lp)(stereo-lp) *(RD 27238)(SF 5115) <LSP 2426>* **BLUE HAWAII (Soundtrack)** [1] Oct61 [1]
– Blue Hawaii / Almost always true / Moonlight swim / No more / Can't help falling in love / Rock a hula baby / Island of love / Hawaiin sunset / Hawaiin wedding song / Alohaoe / Beach boy blues / Slicin' sands / Ku ui Po / Ito eats. *(re-iss. Sep77; SF 8145)* – (hit UK No.26) *(re-iss. Aug84 lp/c; NL/NK 83683) (cd-iss. Oct87; ND 83683)*

Jan 62. (7") *(RCA 1270) <47-7968>* **ROCK-A-HULA-BABY. / CAN'T HELP FALLING IN LOVE** [1] [23]
Dec61 [2]
(re-iss. May77; PB 2703)

May 62. (7") *(RCA 1280) <47-7992>* **GOOD LUCK CHARM. / ANYTHING THAT'S PART OF YOU** [1] [1]
Mar62 [31]
(re-iss. May77; PB 2704)

Jun 62. (mono-lp)(stereo-lp) *(RD 27265)(SF 5135) <LSP 2523>* **POT LUCK** [1] [4]
– Kiss me quick / Just for old times sake / Fountain of love / Gonna get back home somehow / Such an easy question / Night rider / Suspicion / Stepping out of line / I fell I've known you forever / That's someone you never forget / Something blue / I'm yours. *(re-iss. Apr81 on 'RCA International'; INTS 5074) (re-iss. Jul84 lp/c; NL/NK 89098) (cd-iss. Apr88; ND 89098)*

Aug 62. (7") *(RCA 1303) <47-8041>* **SHE'S NOT YOU. / JUST TELL HER JIM SAID HELLO** [1] [5]
Jul62 [55]
(re-iss. May77; PB 2705)

Nov 62. (7") *(RCA 1320) <47-8100>* **RETURN TO SENDER. / WHERE DO YOU COME FROM** [1] [2]
Oct62 [99]
(re-iss. May77; PB 2706) – (hit UK No.42 Aug77)

Jan 63. (lp; mono/stereo) *(RD/SF 7534) <LSP 2621>* **GIRLS! GIRLS! GIRLS! (Film soundtrack)** [2] Dec62 [3]
– Girls! girls! girls! / I don't wanna be tired / Because of love / Return to sender / Where do you come from / I don't want to / We'll be together / A boy like me a girl like you / Song of the shrimp / The walls have ears / Earth boy / Thanks to the rolling sea / We're coming in loaded. *(re-iss. Oct79; lp/c; PL/PK 42354) (re-iss. Aug81 on 'RCA International'; INTS 5107) (re-iss. Jun84 lp/c; NL/NK 89048) (re-iss. Sep86 on 'RCA-Camden' lp/c; CDS/CAM 1221)*

Feb 63. (7") *(RCA 1337) <47-8134>* **ONE BROKEN HEART FOR SALE. / THEY REMIND ME TOT MUCH OF YOU** [12] [11]
[53]

May 63. (lp; mono/stereo) *(RD/SF 7565) <LSP 2697>* **IT HAPPENED AT THE WORLD'S FAIR (Film Soundtrack)** [4] Apr63 [4]
– Beyond the bend / Relax / Take me to the fair / Happy ending / They remind to much of you / One broken heart for sale / I'm falling in love tonight / Cotton candy land / A world of our own / How would you like to be. *(re-iss. Aug81 on 'RCA International'; INTS 5033) (re-iss. Jan84 lp/c; NL/NK 82568)*

Jun 63. (7") *(RCA 1355) <47-8188>* **(YOU'RE THE) DEVIL IN DISGUISE. / PLEASE DON'T DRAG THAT STRING AROUND** [1] [3]
(re-iss. May77; PB 2707)

Oct 63. (7") *(RCA 1374) <47-8243>* **BOSSA NOVA. / WITCHCRAFT** [13] [8]
[32]

Dec 63. (7") *(RCA 1375) <447-0639>* **KISS ME QUICK. / SOMETHING BLUE** [14] Apr64 [34]

Dec 63. (lp; mono/stereo) *(RD/SF 7609) <LSP 2756>* **FUN IN ACAPULCO (Film Soundtrack)** [9] Mar64 [3]
– Fun in Acapulco / The bullfighter was a lady / Margueritta / There's no room to rhumba in a sports car / Dinero y amor / Mexico / I think I'm gonna like it here / Bossa nova baby / Vino / El Toro / You can'y say no to acapulco / Guadalajara / Love me tonight / Slowly but surely. *(re-iss. Oct79 lp/c; PL/PKM 42357) (re-iss. Aug81 on 'RCA International'; INTS 5106)*

Mar 64. (7") *(RCA 1390) <47-8360>* **VIVA LAS VEGAS. / WHAT'D I SAY** [17] [29]
May64 [21]

Jun 64. (7") *(RCA 1404) <47-8307>* **KISSIN' COUSINS. / IT HURTS ME** [10] [12]
Feb64 [29]

Jun 64. (lp; mono/stereo) *(RD/SF 7645) <LSP 2894>* **KISSIN' COUSINS (Film Soundtrack)** [5] Apr64 [6]
– Kissin' cousins / Smokey mountain boy / Anyone could fall in love with you / Catchin' on fast / Tender feeling / Once is enough / (It's a) Long lonely highway / Barefoot ballet / Echoes of love / Kissin' cousins (reprise). *(re-iss. Oct79 lp/c; PL/PK 42355) (re-iss. Aug81 on 'RCA International'; INTS 5108) (re-iss. Nov84 lp/c; NL/NK 84115) (re-iss. Sep86 on 'RCA Camden' lp/c; CDS/CAM 1222)*

Aug 64. (7") *(RCA 1411) <47-8400>* **SUCH A NIGHT. / NEVER ENDING** [13] Jul64 [16]

Oct 64. (7") *(RCA 1422) <47-8440>* **AIN'T THAT LOVIN' YOU BABY. / ASK ME** [15] [16]
[12]

Nov 64. (7") *(RCA 1430) <HO-0808>* **BLUE CHRISTMAS. / WHITE CHRISTMAS** [11]

Jan 65. (lp; mono/stereo) *(RD/SF 7678) <LSP 2999>* **ROUSTABOUT (Film Soundtrack)** [12] Nov64 [1]
– Roustabout / Little Egypt / Poison Ivy league / Hard knocks / It's a wonderful world / Big love big heartache / There's a brand new day on the horizon / Wheels of my heels / Carny town / One track heart / It's carnival time. *(re-iss. Oct79 lp/c; PL/PK 42356) (re-iss. Aug81 on 'RCA International'; INTS 5110) (re-iss. Nov84 lp/c; NL/NK 89049)*

Mar 65. (7") *(RCA 1443) <47-8500>* **DO THE CLAM. / YOU'LL BE GONE** [19] Feb64 [21]

Apr 65. (lp; mono/stereo) *(RD/SF 7714) <LSP 3338>* **GIRL HAPPY (Film Soundtrack)** [8] [8]
– Girl happy / Spring fever / Fort Lauderdale / You'll be gone / Chamber of commerce / Startin' tonight / Puppet on a string / Do not disturb / Cross my heart and hope to die / Wolf call / The meanest girl in town / I've got to find my baby / Do the clam. *(re-iss. Aug81 on 'RCA International'; INTS 5034) (re-iss. Nov84 lp/c; NL/NK 83338)*

May 65. (7") *(RCA 1455) <447-0643>* **CRYING IN THE CHAPEL. / I BELIEVE IN THE MAN IN THE SKY** [1] [3]
(re-iss. May77; PB 2708) – (hit UK No.43 Aug77)

Jun 65. (7") *<47-8585>* **(SUCH AN) EASY QUESTION. / IT FEELS SO RIGHT** [–] [11]
[55]

Sep 65. (7") *<47-8657>* **I'M YOURS. / (IT'S A) LONG LONELY HIGHWAY** [–] [11]

Sep 65. (mono-lp) *(RD 7723)* **FLAMING STAR AND SUMMER KISSES** [11] [–]
– (compilation of 'FLAMING STAR' Film soundtrack EP + 'LOVING YOU' lp) *(re-iss. Jun69 as 'FLAMING STAR' on 'RCA INternational'; INTS 1012)* – (hit UK No.2) *(re-iss. Apr79 on 'RCA Camden' lp/c; CDS/CAM 1185)*

Nov 65. (7") *<447-0650>* **PUPPET ON A STRING. / WOODEN HEART** [–] [14]

Nov 65. (7") *(RCA 1489)* **TELL ME WHY. / PUPPET ON A STRING** [15] [–]

Nov 65. (lp; mono/stereo) *(RD/SF 7752) <LSP 3450>* **ELVIS FOR EVERYONE!** [8] Sep65 [10]
– You're cheatin' heart / Summer kisses / Winter tears / For the millionth and the last time / Finders keepers losers weepers / In my way / Tomorrow night / Forget me never / Met her tonight / Memphis Tennessee / Sound advice / Santa Lucia / When it rains it really pours. *(re-iss. 1972; SF 8232) (re-iss. Apr84 lp/c; NL/NK 84232) (cd-iss. Apr95;)*

Jan 66. (7") *<47-8740>* **TELL ME WHY. / BLUE RIVER** [–] [33]
[95]

Jan 66. (lp; mono/stereo) *(RD/SF 7767) <LSP 3468>* **HAREM HOLIDAY (Film Soundtrack)** <US title 'HARUM SCARUM'> [11] Nov65 [8]
– Harem holiday / My desert serenade / Go west young man / Hey little girl / Mirage / Shake that tambourine / Golden coins / So close yet so far (from Paradise) / Animal instinct / Wisdom of ages. *(re-iss. Aug80 on 'RCA International'; INTS 5035) (re-iss. Apr84 lp/c; NL/NK 82558)*

Feb 66. (7") *(RCA 1504)* **BLUE RIVER. / DO NOT DISTURB** [22] [–]

Mar 66. (7") *(RCA 1509) <47-8780>* **FRANKIE AND JOHNNY. / PLEASE DON'T STOP LOVING ME** [21] [25]

Apr 66. (lp; mono/stereo) *(RD/SF 7793) <LSP 3553>* **FRANKIE AND JOHNNY (Film Soundtrack)** [11] [20]
– Frankie and Johnny / Come along / What every woman lives for / Petunia

the gardeners daughter / Beginners luck / Chesay / Down by the riverside / When the saints go marching in / Please don't stop loving me / Look out / Everybody come aboard / Shout it out / Hard luck. *(re-iss. Aug80 on 'RCA International'; INTS 5036) (re-iss. Apr84 lp/c; NL/NK 82559)*

Jun 66. (7") *(RCA 1526) <47-8870>* **LOVE LETTERS. / COME WHAT MAY** 6 19

Jul 66. (lp; mono/stereo) *(RD/SF 7810) <LSP 3643>* **PARADISE, HAWAIIAN STYLE (Film Soundtrack)** 7 15
– Paradise Hawaiian style / Queenie Wamine's papaya / Scratch my back (then I'll scratch yours) / House of sand / Datin' / Drums of the islands / Stop where you are / A dogs life / Sand castles / This is my heaven. *(re-iss. Aug80 on 'RCA International'; INTS 5037) (re-iss. Apr84 lp/c; NL/NK 89010)*

Oct 66. (7") *(RCA 1545) <47-8941>* **ALL THAT I AM. / SPINOUT** 17 B-side 40

Nov 66. (lp; mono/stereo) *(RD/SF 7820) <LSP 3702>* **CALIFORNIA HOLIDAY (Film Soundtrack)** <US-title 'SPINOUT'> 17 18
– Stop look and listen / Adam and evil / All that I am / Am I ready / Never say yes / Beach shack / Spinout / Smorgasbord / Tomorrow is a long time / Down in the alley / I'll be back / I'll remember you. *(re-iss. Aug80 on 'RCA International' lp/c; INT S/K 5038)*

Nov 66. (7") *(RCA 1557) <47-8950>* **IF EVERY DAY WAS LIKE CHRISTMAS. / HOW WOULD YOU LIKE TO BE** 13

Feb 67. (7") *(RCA 1565) <47-9056>* **INDESCRIBABLY BLUE. / FOOLS FALL IN LOVE** 21 33

Apr 67. (lp; mono/stereo) *(RD/SF 7867) <LSP 3758>* **HOW GREAT THOU ART** 11 18
– How great thou art / In the garden / Without him / By and by / Somebody bigger than you and I / Stand by me / Farther along / Where could I go to but the Lord / Crying in the chapel / If the Lord wasn't by my side / So high / Run on / Where no one stands alone. *(re-iss. Jul84 lp/c; NL/NK 83758) (cd-iss. Apr88; ND 83758)*

May 67. (7") *(RCA 1593)* **YOU GOTTA STOP. / LOVE MACHINE** 38 –

Aug 67. (7") *(RCA 1616) <47-9115>* **LONG-LEGGED GIRL (WITH THE SHORT DRESS ON). / THAT'S SOMEONE YOU NEVER FORGET** 49 63 92

Aug 67. (lp; mono/stereo) *(RD/SF 7892) <LSP 3787>* **DOUBLE TROUBLE (Film Soundtrack)** 34
– Double trouble / Baby if you'll give me all your love / City by night / Could I fall in love / Old McDonald / I love only one girl / Long legged girl (with the short dress on) / It won't be long / There is so much world to see / Blue river / Never ending / What now what next where to. *(re-iss. Aug80 on 'RCA International'; INTS 5039)*

Sep 67. (7") *(RCA 1628) <47-9287>* **THERE'S ALWAYS ME. / JUDY** 56 78

Nov 67. (7") *(RCA 1642) <47-9341>* **BIG BOSS MAN. / YOU DON'T ME** Oct67 38

Feb 68. (7") *(RCA 1663) <47-9425>* **GUITAR MAN. / HI-HEEL SNEAKERS** 19 43

Apr 68. (lp; mono/stereo) *(RD/SF 7917) <LSP 3893>* **CLAMBAKE (Film Soundtrack)** 19 Feb68 40
– Clambake / Who needs money / A house that has everything / Confidence / Hey hey hey / You don't know me / Guitar man / The girl I never loved / How can you lose what you never had / Big boss man / Singing trees / Just call me lonesome. *(re-iss. Aug80 on 'RCA International'; INTS 5040) (re-iss. Jan84 lp/c; NL/NK 82565)*

May 68. (7") *(RCA 1688) <47-9465>* **U.S. MALE. / STAY AWAY** 15 28 Mar68 67

Jul 68. (7") *(RCA 1714) <47-9547>* **YOUR TIME HASN'T COME YET BABY. / LET YOURSELF GO** 22 72 Jun68 71

Aug 68. (lp; mono/stereo) *(RD/SF 7957) <LSP 3989>* **SPEEDWAY (Film Soundtrack)** 82
– Speedway / There ain't nothing like a song / Your time hasn't come yet baby / Who are you (who am I) / He's your uncle not your dad / Let yourself go / Your groovy self (by NANCY SINATRA) / Western union / Five sleepy heads / Mine / Goin' home / Suppose. *(re-iss. Aug81 on 'RCA International'; INTS 5041) (re-iss. Jan84 lp/c; NL/NK 85012)*

Oct 68. (7") *(RCA 1747) <47-9600>* **YOU'LL NEVER WALK ALONE. / WE CALL ON HIM** 44 Apr68 90

Nov 68. (7") *<47-9670>* **IF I CAN DREAM. / EDGE OF REALITY** – 12

Dec 68. (7") *(RCA 1768) <47-9610>* **A LITTLE LESS CONVERSATION. / ALMOST IN LOVE** 69 Sep68 95

Feb 69. (7") *(RCA 1795)* **IF I CAN DREAM. / MEMORIES** 11 –

Mar 69. (7") *<47-9731>* **MEMORIES. / CHARRO** – 35

Jun 69. (7") *(RCA 1831) <47-9741>* **IN THE GHETTO. / ANY DAY NOW** 2 May69 3

Aug 69. (lp; mono/stereo) *(RD/SF 8029) <LSP 4155>* **FROM ELVIS IN MEMPHIS** 1 Jun69 13
– Wearin that loved-in look / Only the strong survive / I'll hold you in my heart / Long black limousine / It keeps right on a-turnin' / I'm moving on / Power of my love / Gentle on my mind / After loving you / True love travels on a gravel road / Any day now / In the ghetto. *(cd-iss. Mar91;) (re-iss. Mar94 cd/c;)*

Aug 69. (7") *(RCA 1869) <47-9747>* **CLEAN UP YOUR OWN BACK YARD. / THE FAIR'S MOVING ON** 21 Jul69 35

Nov 69. (7") *(RCA 1900) <47-9764>* **SUSPICIOUS MINDS. / YOU'LL THINK OF ME** 2 Sep69 1

Feb 70. (7") *(RCA 1916) <47-9768>* **DON'T CRY DADDY. / RUBBERNECKIN'** 8 Nov69 6

—— His live band mid '69 for album **JAMES BURTON** – lead guitar / **JOHN WILKINSON** – guitar / **CHARLIE HODGE** – guitar / **JERRY SCHEFF** – bass / **LARRY MUHOBERAC** – keyboards / **RONNIE TUTT** – drums back up groups were The IMPERIALS and also The SWEET INSPIRATIONS

Mar 70. (d-lp) *(SF 8080-1) <LSP 6020>* **FROM MEMPHIS TO VEGAS – FROM VEGAS TO MEMPHIS** 3 Nov69 12
– FROM MEMPHIS TO VEGAS (live at the International, Vegas) – Blue suede shoes / Johnny B. Goode / All shook up / Hound dog / Are you lonesome tonight / I can't stop loving you / Me babe / Medley; Mystery train – Tiger man / Words / In the ghetto / Suspicious minds / Can't help falling in love. FROM VEGAS TO MEMPHIS (studio sessions) – Elvis back in Memphis / Inherit the wind / This is the story / Stranger in my hometown / A little bit of green / The fair's moving on / And the grass don't pay no mind / From a jack to a king / You'll think of me / Without love (there's nothing). *(re-iss. Jun84; NL 89068) (cd-iss. Dec91;)* – (first lp only)

—— **GLEN D. HARDIN** – piano (ex-CRICKETS) repl. TOTT

May 70. (7") *(RCA 1949) <47-9701>* **KENTUCKY RAIN. / MY LITTLE FRIEND** 21 Feb70 16

Jul 70. (7") *(RCA 1974) <47-9835>* **THE WONDER OF YOU. / MAMA LIKED THE ROSES** 1 May70 9
(re-iss. May77; PB 2709) – (hit UK No.48)

Jul 70. (lp) *(SF 8128) <LSP 4362>* **ON STAGE – FEBRUARY 1970 (live)** 2 Jun70 13
– See see rider blues / Release me (and let me live again) / Sweet Caroline / Runaway / The wonder of you / Polka salad Annie / Yesterday / Proud Mary / Walk a mile in my shoes / Let it be me (je't appartiens). *(re-iss. Mar91 cd/c/lp;)*

Nov 70. (7") *(RCA 1999) <47-9873>* **I'VE LOST YOU. / THE STEP IS LOVE** 9 Aug70 32

Jan 71. (7") *(RCA 2046) <47-9916>* **YOU DON'T HAVE TO SAY YOU LOVE ME. / PATCH IT UP** 9 Oct70 11

Jan 71. (lp) *(SF 8162) <LSP 4445>* **THAT'S THE WAY IT IS (live Las Vegas)** 12 Dec70 21
– I just can't help believin' / Twenty days and twenty nights / How the web was woven / Patch it up / Mary in the morning / You don't have to say you love me / You've lost that lovin' feeling / I've lost you / Just pretend / Stranger in the crowd / The next step is love / Bridge over troubled water. *(re-iss. Jan84 lp/c; NL/NK 84114) (re-iss. Jul93 cd/c;)*

Mar 71. (7") *(RCA 2060) <47-9960>* **THERE GOES MY EVERYTHING. / I REALLY DON'T WANT TO KNOW** 6 Dec70 21

Mar 71. (lp) *(SF 8172) <LSP 4460>* **ELVIS COUNTRY (I'M 10,000 YEARS OLD)** 6 Jan71 12
– Snowbird / Tomorrow never comes / Little cabin on the hill / Whole lotta shakin' goin' on / Funny how time slips away / I really don't want to know / There goes my everything / It's your baby / You rock it / Fool / Faded love / I washed my hands in muddy water / Make the world go away / I was born about 10,000 years ago *(re-iss. Aug84)(re-iss. cd+c Jul93)*

May 71. (7") *(RCA 2084) <47-9980>* **RAGS TO RICHES. / WHERE DID THEY GO, LORD** 9 Mar71 33

May 71. (7") *<47-9985>* **LIFE. / ONLY BELIEVE** – 53

Jul 71. (lp) *(SF 8202) <LSP 4530>* **LOVE LETTERS FROM ELVIS** 7 Jun71 33
– Love letters / When I'm over you / I'll never know / Got my mojo working / Heart of Rome / It ain't no big thing (but it's growing) / Only believe / This is our dance / Cindy Cindy / Life. *(re-iss. Aug81 on 'RCA International'; INTS 5081) (re-iss. Nov84 lp/c; NL/NK 89011) (cd-iss. Jun88; ND 89011)*

Sep 71. (7") *(RCA 2125) <47-9998>* **I'M LEAVIN'. / HEART OF ROME** 23 Aug71 36

Oct 71. (7") *<48-1017>* **IT'S ONLY LOVE. / THE SOUND OF YOUR CRY** – 51

Nov 71. (7") *(RCA 2158)* **I JUST CAN'T HELP BELIEVIN'. / HOW THE WEB WAS WOVEN** 6 –

Nov 71. (7") *<74-0572>* **MERRY CHRISTMAS BABY. / O COME, ALL YE FAITHFUL** –

Mar 72. (7") *(RCA 2188) <74-0619>* **UNTIL IT'S TIME FOR YOU TO GO. / WE CAN MAKE THE MORNING** 5 Feb72 40

May 72. (lp) *(SF 8266) <LSP 4671>* **ELVIS NOW** 12 Jan72 43
– Help me make it through the night / Miracle of the rosary / Hey Jude / Put your hand in the hand / Until it's time for you to go / We can make the morning / Early mornin' rain / Sylvia / Fools rush in (where angels feared to tread) / I was born about ten thousand years ago. *(re-iss. Jul93 cd/c;)*

Jun 72. (7") *(RCA 2229) <74-0672>* **AN AMERICAN TRILOGY. / THE FIRST TIME EVER I SAW YOUR FACE** 8 Apr72 66

Jul 72. (lp) *(SF 8296) <LSP 4776>* **ELVIS AS RECORDED AT MADISON SQUARE GARDEN (live)** 3 11
– Introduction; / Theme from 2001 – a space odyssey / That's all right / Proud Mary / Never been to Spain / You don't have to say you love me / You've lost that lovin' feelin' / Polk salad Annie / Love me / All shook up / Heartbreak hotel / Medley; / (Let me your) Teddy bear – Don't be cruel – Love me tender – The impossible dream / Hound dog / Suspicious minds / For the good times / An American trilogy / Funny how time slips away / I can't stop loving you / Can't help falling in love.

Aug 72. (lp/c) *(SF 8275) <LSP 4690>* **HE TOUCHED ME** (gospel) 38 Apr72 79
– He touched me / I've got confidence / Amazing Grace / Seeing is believing / He is my everything / Bosom of Abraham / An evening prayer / Lead me, guide me / There is no god but God / Thing called love / I, John / Reach out to Jesus.

Sep 72. (7") *(RCA 2267) <74-0769>* **BURNING LOVE. / IT'S A MATTER OF TIME** 7 Aug72 2

Dec 72. (7") *(RCA 2304) <74-0815>* **ALWAYS ON MY MIND. / SEPARATE WAYS** 9 B-side 20

Feb 73. (d-lp) *(DPS 2040) <VPSX 6089>* **ALOHA FROM HAWAII VIA SATELLITE** (TV special rec. 14th Jan '73) 11 1
– Theme from 2001 (a space odyssey) / See see rider / Burning love / Something / You gave me a mountain / Steamroller blues / My way / Love me Johnny B. Goode / It's over / I can't stop loving you / Blue suede shoes / I'm so lonesome I could cry / Hound dog / What now my love / Fever / Welcome to my world / Suspicious minds / I'll remember you / Medley; Long tall Sally – Whole lotta shakin goin' on – An American trilogy – A big hunk o' love – I can't help falling in love. *(re-iss. Aug84 lp/c; PL/PK 82642) (cd-iss. Sep86; PD 82642)* (cd re-iss. Oct95;)

May 73. (7") *(RCA 2359)* **POLK SALAD ANNIE. / SEE SEE RIDER** 23 –

Jul 73. (7") *(RCA 2393) <74-0910>* **FOOL. / STEAMROLLER BLUES** 16 17

Sep 73. (lp) *(SF 8378) <APL 0283>* **ELVIS** 16 52
– Fool / Where do I go from here / Love me, love the life I lead / I'm still here / It's impossible / (That's what you get) For lovin' me / Padre / I'll take you home again Kathleen / I will be true / Don't think twice, it's alright. *(re-iss. Mar94;)*

Nov 73. (7") *(RCA 2435) <APBO 0088>* **RAISED ON ROCK. / FOR OL' TIMES SAKE** 36

Nov 73. (lp) *<(APL1 0388)>* **RAISED ON ROCK** 50
– Raised on rock / Are you sincere / Find out what's happening / I miss you / Girl of mine / For 'ol times sake / If you don't come back / Just a little bit / Sweet Angeline / Three corn patches. *(re-iss. Mar94 cd/c;)*

Mar 74. (7") *<(APBO 0196)>* **TAKE GOOD CARE OF HER. / I'VE GOT A THING ABOUT YOU BABY** 33 Mar74 39

May 74. (lp) *<(APL1 0475)>* **GOOD TIMES** 42 90
– Take good care of her / Loving arms / I got a feeling in my body / If that isn't love / She wears my ring / I've got a thing about you baby / My boy / Spanish eyes / Talk about the good times / Good time Charlie got the blues. *(re-iss. Mar94 cd/c;)*

Jun 74. (7") *<(APBO 0280)>* **IF YOU TALK IN YOUR SLEEP. / HELP ME** 40 17

Aug 74. (lp) *<(APL1 0606)>* **ELVIS AS RECORDED LIVE ON STAGE (live in Memphis)** 44 33
– See see rider / I got a woman / Love me / Trying to get to you / Medley; Long tall Sally – Whole lotta shakin' goin on / Mama don't dance / Flip flop and fly / Jailhouse rock / Hound dog / Why me Lord / How great thou art / Blueberry hill / Can't stop loving you / Help me / An American trilogy / Let there be me / My baby left me / Lawdy Miss Clawdy / Can't help falling in love / Closing vamp.

Oct 74. (7") *(RCA 2458)* **MY BOY. / LOVING ARMS** 5 –

Dec 74. (7") *<(PB 10074)>* **PROMISED LAND. / IT'S MIDNIGHT** 9 Oct74 14

Jan 75. (7") *<PB 10191>* **MY BOY. / THINKING ABOUT YOU** – 20

Feb 75. (lp) *<(APL1 0873)>* **PROMISED LAND** 21 47
– Promised land / There's a honky tonk angel (who will take me back in) / Help me / Mr. Songman / Love song of the year / It's midnight / Your love's been a long time comin' / If you talk in your sleep / Thinking about you / You ask me to. *(cd-iss. Dec91;)*

May 75. (7") *(RCA 2562) <PB 10278>* **T-R-O-U-B-L-E. / MR. SONGMAN** 31 35

Jun 75. (lp) *(RS 1011) <APL1 1039>* **TODAY** 48 57
– T.R.O.U.B.L.E. / And I love you so / Susan when she tried / Woman without love / Shake a hand / Pieces of my life / Fairy tale / I can help / Bringin' it back / Green green grass of home.

Oct 75. (7") *<PB 10401>* **BRINGING IT BACK. / PIECES OF MY LIFE** – 65

Nov 75. (7") *(RCA 2635)* **GREEN GREEN GRASS OF HOME. / THINKING ABOUT YOU** 29 –

Apr 76. (7") *(RCA 2674) <PB 10601>* **HURT. / FOR THE HEART** 37 28

Jun 76. (lp) *(RS 1060) <APL1 1506>* **FROM ELVIS PRESLEY BOULEVARD, MEMPHIS, TENNESSEE** 29 41
– Hurt / Never again / Blue eyes crying in the rain / Danny boy / The last farewell / For the heart / Bitter they are, harder they fall / Solitaire / Love coming down / I'll never fall in love again. *(re-iss. Jan85 lp/c; PL/PK 89266) (re-iss. Jul93 cd/c;)*

Feb 77. (7") *(PB 857) <PB 10857>* **MOODY BLUE. / SHE THINKS I STILL CARE** 6 31

Jul 77. (7") *(PB 998) <PB 10998>* **WAY DOWN. / PLEDGING MY LOVE** 1 18

—— On the 16th August 1977, ELVIS died of heart failure. Below are songs he recorded just prior to death.

Aug 77. (lp/c) *(PL/PK 12428) <AFL 2428>* **MOODY BLUE** (some live) 3 3
– Unchained melody / If you love me (let me know) / Little darlin' / He'll have to go / Let me be there / Way down / Pledging my love / Moody blue / She thinks I still care. *(re-iss. Sep81 lp/c; RCA LP/K 3021) (re-iss. Jan85 lp/c; NL/NK 90252) (cd-iss. Oct88; ND 90252)*

– (selective) posthumous comps, etc. –

all below releases were issued on 'R.C.A.' unless stated otherwise

Aug 77. (lp/c) *(PL/PK 12274) <APL 2274>* **WELCOME TO MY WORLD** 7 44
– Welcome to my world / Help me make it through the night / Release me (and let me love again) / I really don't know what to know / For the good times / Make the world go away / Gentle on my mind / I'm so lonesome I could cry / Your cheatin' heart / I can't stop loving you. *(re-iss. Sep81 lp/c; RCA LP/K 3020)*

Sep 77. (lp/c) *RCA Starcall; (HY/+C 1023)* **PICTURES OF ELVIS** 52 –

Oct 77. (lp) *Charly;* **THE SUN YEARS** 31 –

Nov 77. (d-lp/d-c) *(PL/PK 02587) <APL1 2587>* **ELVIS IN CONCERT (live)** 13 Oct77 5
– (Elvis' fans comment, and opening riff to 2001) / See see rider / That's alright / Are you lonesome tonight? / You gave me a mountain / Jailhouse rock / How great thou art / I really don't want to know / (Elvis introduces his father) / Hurt. *(re-iss. Jul93 cd/c;)*

Nov 77. (7") *(PB 1165) <11165>* **MY WAY (live). / AMERICA, THE BEAUTIFUL (live)** 9 22

Apr 78. (lp/c) *(PL/PK 12772) <AFL 2772>* **HE WALKS BESIDE ME** (gospel) 37
– He is my everything / Miracle of the rosary / Where did they go Lord / Somebody bigger than you and I / An evening prayer / The impossible dream / If I can dream / Padre / Known only to him / Who am I / How great thou art.

May 78. (lp/c) *(PL/PK 42101)* **THE '56 SESSIONS VOL.1** 47 –
(re-iss. Sep81 lp/c; RCA LP/K 3025)

Nov 78. (lp) *<KKL 7065>* **ELVIS – A CANADIAN TRIBUTE** – 86

Jan 79. (lp/c) *(PL/PK 13082) <CPL 3082>* **A LEGENDARY PERFORMER VOL.3** 43

Apr 79. (lp/c) *(PL/PK 13279) <AQL 3279>* **OUR MEMORIES OF ELVIS** 72

Sep 79. (lp/c) *(PL/PK 13448) <AQL 3448>* **OUR MEMORIES OF ELVIS VOL.2** [ ] [ ]

Nov 79. (d-lp/d-c) *K-Tel; (NE 1062)* **LOVE SONGS** [4] [–]

Dec 79. (7"/12") *(PB/PC 9464)* **IT WON'T SEEM LIKE CHRISTMAS (WITHOUT YOU). / MERRY CHRISTMAS BABY** [13] [–]

Jun 80. (lp/c) *(INTS/INTK 5031)* **ELVIS PRESLEY SINGS LEIBER AND STOLLER** [32] [–]
(re-iss. Apr84 lp/c; NL/NK 89099)

Aug 80. (8xlp-box) *(ELVIS 25) <CPL 3699>* **ELVIS AARON PRESLEY** [21] [27]
– (AN EARLY LIVE PERFORMANCE / AN EARLY BENEFIT PERFORMANCE / COLLECTOR'S GOLD FROM THE MOVIE YEARS / THE TV SPECIALS / THE LAS VEGAS YEARS / LOST SINGLES / ELVIS AT THE PIANO – THE CONCERT YEARS (PART 1) / THE CONCERT YEARS (concluded).

Aug 80. (7") *(RCA 4)* **IT'S ONLY LOVE. / BEYOND THE REEF** [3] [–]

Nov 80. (lp/c) *K-Tel; (NE 1101/CE 2101)* **INSPIRATION** (gospel) [6] [–]

Nov 80. (7") *(RCA 16)* **SANTA CLAUS IS BACK IN TOWN. / I BELIEVE** [41] [–]

Feb 81. (7") *(RCA 43) <PB 12158>* **GUITAR MAN (remix). / FADED LOVE** [43] [28]

Mar 81. (lp/c) *(RCA LP/K 5010) <AAL 3917>* **GUITAR MAN** [33] [49]
– Guitar man / After loving you / Too much monkey business / Just call me lonesome / Lovin' arms / You asked me to / Clean up your own backyard / She thinks I still care / Faded love / I'm movin' on.

Apr 81. (7") *(RCA 48)* **LOVING ARMS. / YOU ASKED ME TO** [47] [–]

May 81. (d-lp/d-c) *(RCA LP/K 5029) <CPL 4031>* **THIS IS ELVIS** (soundtrack) [47] [ ]
(re-iss. May84 d-lp/d-c; BL/BK 84031)

Nov 81. (lp/c) *K-Tel; (NE 1141)* **THE ULTIMATE PERFORMANCE** [45] [–]

Feb 82. (lp/c) *(RCA LP/K 3060)* **THE SOUND OF YOUR CRY** [31] [–]

Feb 82. (7") *(RCA 196)* **ARE YOU LONESOME TONIGHT? (live version). / FROM A JACK TO A KING (live)** [25] [–]

Mar 82. (11x7"ep-box) *(EP 1)* **THE EP COLLECTION** [97] [–]

Jun 82. (7"/7"pic-d) *(RCA/+P 232)* **THE SOUND OF YOUR CRY. / I'LL NEVER KNOW** [59] [–]

Aug 82. (d-lp/d-c) *(RCA LP/K 1000)* **ROMANTIC ELVIS 20 LOVE SONGS – ROCKIN' ELVIS 60's** [62] [–]
(re-iss. May84 lp/c; PL/PK 89124)

Nov 82. (7",7"pic-d) *<PB 13351>* **THE ELVIS MEDLEY: Jailhouse Rock-Teddy Bear-Hound Dog-Don't Be Cruel-Burning Love-Suspicious Minds. / JAILHOUSE ROCK** [–] [71]

Dec 82. (lp/c) *(NL/NK 89025)* **IT WON'T SEEM LIKE CHRISTMAS WITHOUT YOU** [80] [–]
(re-dist.Nov84; same)

Apr 83. (pic-lp) *(RCALP 9020)* **JAILHOUSE ROCK / LOVE IN LAS VEGAS** [40] [–]
– (compilation of music from the 2 films)

Apr 83. (7") *(RCA 332)* **(YOU'RE SO SQUARE) BABY, I DON'T CARE. / TRUE LOVE** [61] [–]
(12"pic-d) *(RCAP 332)* – ('A'side) / One-sided love affair / Tutti frutti.

Aug 83. (lp/c) *(RCA LP/K 3105) <AHL 4678>* **I WAS THE ONE** [83] May83 [ ]

Nov 83. (7") *(RCA 369)* **I CAN HELP. / THE LADY LOVES ME (w/ ANN-MARGARET)** [30] [–]
(10"pic-d+=) *(RCAP 369)* – If every day was like Christmas.

Nov 83. (lp/c) *(PL/PK 84848)* **A LEGENDARY PERFORMER VOL.4** [91] [–]

Mar 84. (lp/c) *(PL/PK 89287)* **I CAN HELP** [71] [–]

Apr 84. (lp/c) *(PG/PH 89387) <3601>* **ELVIS – THE FIRST LIVE RECORDINGS** [69] Mar84 [ ]

Oct 84. (7") *(RCA 459)* **THE LAST FAREWELL. / IT'S EASY FOR YOU** [48] [–]
(12"+=) *(RCAT 459)* – Shake, rattle and roll / Flip, flop and fly / That's all right (mama) / My heart cries for you.

Nov 84. (6xlp-box/6xc-box) *(PL/PK 85172) <5172>* **ELVIS – A GOLDEN CELEBRATION** [ ] [80]

Jan 85. (7") *(RCA 476)* **THE ELVIS MEDLEY. / BLUE SUEDE SHOES** [51] [–]

May 85. (lp/c/cd) *(PL/PK/PD 85418)* **RECONSIDER BABY** [92] [–]

Jul 85. (7") *(PB 49943)* **ALWAYS ON MY MIND. / TOMORROW NIGHT** [59] [–]
(12"+=) *(PT 49943)* – Ain't that loving you baby / Dark moon.

Oct 85. (lp/c/cd) *Telstar; (STA R/C/TCD 2264)* **BALLADS** [23] [–]

Mar 87. (7") *(ARON 1)* **BOSSA NOVA BABY (remix). / AIN'T THAT LOVIN' YOU BABY** [47] [–]
(12"+=) *(ARONT 1)* – I'm coming home / Rock-a-hula baby.
(12") *(PT 49745)* – ('A'side) / ('A'-Stretch mix) / I'm coming home.

Aug 87. (d-lp/d-c/d-cd) *(PL/PK/PD 90100) <6382>* **PRESLEY – THE ALL TIME GREATEST HITS** <US title 'THE TOP TEN HITS'> [4] [ ]
– Heartbreak Hotel / Blue suede shoes / Hound dog / Love me tender / Too much / All shook up / Teddy bear / Paralysed / Party / Jailhouse rock / Don't / Wear my ring around your neck / Hard headed woman / King Creole / One night / A fool such as I / Big hunk o' love / Stuck on you / Girl of my best friend / It's now or never / Are you lonesome tonight? / Wooden heart / Surrender / His latest flame / Can't help falling in love / Good luck charm / She's not you / Return to sender / Devil in disguise / Crying in the chapel / Love letters / If I can dream / In the ghetto / Suspicious minds / Don't cry daddy / The wonder of you / I just can't help believing / American trilogy / Burning love / Always on my mind / My boy / Suspicion / Moody blue / Way down / It's only love.

Aug 87. (d-lp/d-c/cd) *(PL/PK/PD 86414)* **THE COMPLETE SUN SESSIONS** [ ] [–]

Aug 87. (7") *(ARON 2)* **LOVE ME TENDER. / TEDDY BEAR** [56] [–]
(12"+=) *(ARONT 2)* – If I can dream / Bossa nova baby (extended).

Jan 88. (7"/12"/cd-s) *(PB 49595)* **STUCK ON YOU. / ANYWAY YOU WANT ME** [58] [–]

Jan 89. (lp/c/cd) *(PL/PK/PD 90250)* **ESSENTIAL ELVIS VOLUME 2: STEREO '57** [60] [–]

Jul 90. (cd/c/lp) *(PD/PK/PL 90486)* **ESSENTIAL ELVIS – VOLUME 3: HITS LIKE NEVER BEFORE** [71] [–]

Aug 90. (cd/c/lp) *(PD/PK/PL 82227)* **THE GREAT PERFORMANCES** [62] [ ]

Jul 91. (7") *(PB 49177)* **ARE YOU LONESOME TONIGHT? (live '69). / RUNAWAY (live)** [68] [–]
(12"+=/cd-s+=) *(PT/PD 49177)* – Baby, What You Want Me To Do (Live) / Reconsider Baby (Live)

Aug 91. (3xcd/3xc/3xlp) *(PD/PK/PL 90574)* **COLLECTOR'S GOLD** [57] [ ]

Feb 92. (cd/c/d-lp) *(PD/PK/PL 90642)* **FROM THE HEART – HIS GREATEST LOVE SONGS** [4] [ ]

Aug 92. (7"/c-s) *(74321 11077-7/-4)* **DON'T BE CRUEL. / ALL SHOOK UP** [42] [–]
(cd-s+=) *(74321 11077-2)* – Jailhouse rock / I need your love tonight.

Mar 93. (cd) *(74321 13430-2)* **KID GALAHAD / GIRLS! GIRLS! GIRLS!** [ ] [ ]

Mar 93. (cd) *(74321 13431-2)* **IT HAPPENED AT THE WORLD'S FAIR / FUN IN ACAPULCO** [ ] [ ]

Mar 93. (cd) *(74321 13432-2)* **VIVA LAS VEGAS / ROUSTABOUT** [ ] [ ]

Mar 93. (cd) *(74321 13433-2)* **HARUM SCARUM / GIRL HAPPY** [ ] [ ]

Jun 94. (cd/c) *(07863 66360-2/-4)* **FRANKIE & JOHNNY / PARADISE, HAWAIIAN STYLE** [ ] [ ]

Jun 94. (cd/c) *(07863 66361-2/-4)* **SPINOUT / DOUBLE TROUBLE** [ ] [ ]

Jun 94. (cd/c) *(07863 66362-2/-4)* **KISSIN' COUSINS / CLAMBAKE / STAY AWAY, JOE** [ ] [ ]

Sep 94. (cd/c/d-lp) *(74321 22871-2/-4/-1)* **THE ESSENTIAL COLLECTION** [6] [ ]

Oct 95. (cd-ep) *(74321 32012-2)* **TWELTH OF NEVER / BURNING LOVE / WALK A MILE IN MY SHOES** [21] [–]

May 96. (cd-ep) *(74321 33686-2)* **HEARTBREAK HOTEL / I WAS THE ONE** [45] [–]

May 97. (c-s) *(74321 48541-4)* **ALWAYS ON MY MIND / SEPARATE WAYS** [13] [ ]
(cd-s) *(74321 48541-2)* – ('A'side) / Are you lonesome tonight? / Moody blue / Way down.

Jun 97. (cd/c) *(74321 48984-2/-4)* **ALWAYS ON MY MIND – ULTIMATE LOVE SONGS** [3] [ ]

Jul 97. (4xcd-box) *<(07863 67469-2)>* **PLATINUM: A LIFE IN MUSIC** [ ] [80]

Feb 98. (cd/c) *(74321 55628-2/-4)* **BLUE SUEDE SHOES (The Ultimate Rock'n'roll Collection)** [39] [ ]

Jul 99. (3xcd-box/3xc-box) *<(07863 67732-2/-4)>* **ARTIST OF THE CENTURY** [ ] [ ]

Nov 00. (d-cd/c) *(74321 81102-2/-4)* **THE 50 GREATEST HITS** [8] [–]

Mar 01. (cd) *(74321 84708-2)* **THE LIVE GREATEST HITS (live)** [50] [–]

Apr 01. (cd-s) *(74321 84844-2)* **SUSPICIOUS MINDS (live) / SUSPICIOUS MINDS (studio)** [15] [–]
(cd-s) *(74321 85582-2)* – ('A'side) / The wonder of you.
Oct 01. (cd-s) *(74321 90402-2)* **AMERICA THE BEAUTIFUL / IF I CAN DREAM / AMAZING GRACE / IF I CAN DREAM (video)** [69] [ ]
Nov 01. (d-cd) *(74321 90075-2)* **THE 50 GREATEST LOVE SONGS** [21] [–]
Jun 02. (c-s; as ELVIS VS. JXL) *(74321 94357-4) <060575>* **A LITTLE LESS CONVERSATION. / (original)** [1] [50]
(12"+=/cd-s+=) *(74321 94357-1/-2)* – ('A'-version).
(above featured JUNKIE XL)
Sep 02. (cd/c/d-lp) *(07863 68079-2/-4/-1)* **ELV1S – 30 NO.1 HITS** [1] [1]
– Heartbreak hotel / Don't be cruel / Hound dog / Love me tender / Too much / All shook up / Teddy bear / Jailhouse rock / Don't / Hard headed woman / One night / Now and then there's a fool such as I / Big hunk o' love / Stuck on you / It's now or never / Are you lonesome tonight / Wooden heart / Surrender / (Marie's the name) His latest flame / Can't help falling in love / Good luck charm / She's not you / Return to sender / You're the Devil in disguise / Crying in the chapel / In the ghetto / Suspicious minds / The wonder of you / Burning love / Way down / A little less conversation (JXL remix).
Sep 03. (12") *(82876 54218-1)* **RUBBERNECKIN' (remix with Paul Oakenfold) / (extended)** [5] [94]
(cd-s+=) *(82876 54341-2) <54218>* – (original).
Oct 03. (cd/c/d-lp) *(82876 57008-2/-4/-1) <51108>* **ELVIS – 2ND TO NONE** [4] [3]
– That's all right / I forgot to remember to forget / Blue suede shoes / I want you, I need you, I love you / Love me / Mean woman blues / Loving you / Treat me nice / Wear my ring around your neck / King Creole / Trouble / I got stung / I need your love tonight / A mess of blues / I feel so bad / Little sister / Rock-a-hula baby / Bossa nova baby / Viva Las Vegas / If I can dream / Memories / Don't cry daddy / Kentucky rain / You don't have to say you love me / An American trilogy / Always on my mind / Promised land / Moody blue / I'm a roustabout / Rubberneckin' (with PAUL OAKENFOLD).
Nov 03. (cd) *(82876 57489-2) <52393>* **CHRISTMAS PEACE** (festive) [41] [ ]

– (selective) pre-death compilations, etc. –

on 'R.C.A.' unless mentioned otherwise

Mar 56. (7"ep) *<EPA 747>* **ELVIS PRESLEY** [–] [20]
Jun 57. (7"ep) *(RCX 101) <EPA 4054>* **PEACE IN THE VALLEY** [ ] Apr57 [25]
– (There'll be) Peace in the valley (for me) / It is no secret / I believe / Take my hand precious Lord. *(UK re-iss. Mar60)*
Jun 57. (7"ep) *<EPA2 1515>* **LOVING YOU, VOLUME 2** [–] lp-cht [18]
Aug 57. (7"ep) *<EPA 4041>* **JUST FOR YOU** [–] lp-cht [18]
Jan 58. (7"ep) *(RCX 106)* **JAILHOUSE ROCK** [18] Nov57 [ ]
– Jailhouse rock / Young and beautiful / Don't leave me now / Baby I don't care / I want to be free. *(re-iss. Mar60 + Feb82)*
Oct 58. (lp) *(RB 16069) <LPM 1707>* **ELVIS' GOLDEN RECORDS** [ ] Apr58 [3]
(re-iss. 1970; (SF 8129) (re-iss. Sep81 as 'VOL.1' on 'RCA International' lp/c; INTS/INTK 5143) (re-iss. Nov84 lp/c; NL/NK 81707) (cd-iss. 1988; PD 85196)
Mar 59. (lp) *<LPM 1990>* **FOR LP FANS ONLY** [–] [19]
(UK cd-iss. Nov89; ND 90359)
Jul 59. (lp) *(RD 27128) <LPM 2011>* **A DATE WITH ELVIS (early Sun recordings)** [4] Sep59 [32]
– Blue Moon of Kentucky / Young and beautiful / Baby I don't care / Milk cow blues boogie / Baby let's play house / Good rockin' tonight / Is it so strange / I forgot to remember to forget. *(re-iss. Aug80 + Apr84) (cd-iss. Nov89; ND 90360)*
Feb 60. (7"ep) *(RCX 175)* **STRICTLY ELVIS** [26] Jan57 [ ]
– Old Shep / Any place is Paradise / Paralysed / Is it so strange.
Jun 60. (lp) *(RD 27159) <LPM 2075>* **50,000,000 ELVIS FANS CAN'T BE WRONG – ELVIS' GOLDEN RECORDS VOLUME 2** [4] Feb60 [31]
(re-iss. Sep81 as 'ELVIS GOLDEN VOL.2' on 'RCA International' lp/c; INTS/INTK 5144) (cd-iss. Nov84;)
Jun 62. (7"ep) *(RCX 211)* **FOLLOW THAT DREAM** [34] [ ]
– Follow that dream No.15 / Angel / What a wonderful world / I'm not the marrying kind.
Jan 63. (7"ep) *(RCX 7109)* **KID GALAHAD** [16] Sep62 [ ]
– King of the whole wide world No.30 / This is living / Riding the rainbow / Home is where the heart is / I got lucky / Whistling tune.
Apr 64. (lp) *(RD 7630) <LSP 2765>* **ELVIS' GOLDEN RECORDS, VOLUME 3** [6] Sep63 [3]
(re-iss. Sep81 on 'RCA International' lp/c; INTS/INTK 5145) (re-iss. Nov84 lp/c; NL/NK 82765) (cd-iss. Dec90;)
Apr 64. (7"ep) *(RCX 7141)* **LOVE IN LAS VEGAS** [ ] [92]
– If you think I don't need you / I need somebody to lean on / C'mon everybody / Today tomorrow and forever.
Jul 65. (7"ep) *(RCX 7173)* **TICKLE ME VOLUME 1** [ ] [70]
– I feel that I've known you forever / Night rider / Slowly but surely / Dirty dirty feeling / Put the blame on me.
Sep 65. (lp) *(RD 7762) <LPS 3450>* **ELVIS FOR EVERYONE!** (UK title 'ELVIS FOR EVERYBODY') [8] [10]
(UK re-iss. +c.May72, hit No.48)
Apr 68. (lp) *(RD/SF 7924) <LSP 3921>* **ELVIS' GOLD RECORDS, VOLUME 4** [ ] [33]
(re-iss. Sep81 on 'RCA International' lp/c; (NL/NK 83921) (re-iss. Apr84 lp/c; (NL/NK 83921) (cd-iss. Dec90;)
Apr 69. (lp) *(RD 8011)* **ELVIS – N.B.C. TV SPECIAL** [2] Jan69 [8]
(re-iss. UK Aug78 hit No.50) (re-iss. Aug81 & Nov84) (cd-iss. Mar91)
Feb 70. (lp) *(RCA 555)* **PORTRAIT IN MUSIC** [36] [ ]
Nov 70. (4xlp) *(LPM 6401)* **WORLD WIDE 50 GOLD AWARD HITS** [49] [45]
(c-iss.May72 – 2 Volumes 25 hits in each)
Jul 71. (7"m) *(2104)* **HEARTBREAK HOTEL. / HOUND DOG / DON'T BE CRUEL** [10] [–]
Jul 71. (lp/c) *(INTS 1286)* **C'MON EVERYBODY** [5] [ ]
—— (above & below album were budget, below on 'RCA Camden').
Jul 71. (lp)(c) *(CDM 1088)(CAM 415)* **YOU'LL NEVER WALK ALONE** (gospel) [20] Apr71 [ ]
Sep 71. (lp/c) *(INTS 1026)* **ALMOST IN LOVE** [38] [ ]
Nov 71. (7"m) *(2153)* **JAILHOUSE ROCK. / ARE YOU LONESOME TONIGHT?. / (LET ME BE YOUR) TEDDY BEAR / STEADFAST, LOYAL AND TRUE** [42] [–]
Nov 71. (lp/c) *(PL/PK 42371)* **ELVIS SINGS THE WONDERFUL WORLD OF CHRISTMAS** [7] [ ]
(cd-iss. Nov89)
Dec 71. (lp)(c) *(CDM 1154)(CAM 496)* **I GOT LUCKY** [26] [ ]
(re-iss. Nov75 on 'RCA Camden')
Nov 72. (lp/c) *RCA Camden; <2595>* **BURNING LOVE AND HITS FROM HIS MOVIES, VOL.2** [ ] [22]
Jan 73. (lp/c) *RCA Camden; (CDS 1118/CAM 428) <2611>* **SEPARATE WAYS** [ ] [46]
Feb 74. (lp/c) *(APK1 1349)* **A LEGENDARY PERFORMER VOL.1** [20] [ ]
Dec 74. (lp/c) *(PL/PK 17527)* **HITS OF THE 70'S** [ ] [ ]
(re-iss. Sep77, hit No.30)
Jun 75. (d-lp/d-c) *Arcade; (ADEP 12)* **40 GREATEST HITS** [1] [–]
(re-iss. Nov78 on 'RCA', hit No.40)
Aug 75. (lp/c) *RCA Starcall; (NL/NK 42757)* **THE ELVIS PRESLEY SUN COLLECTION** [16] [ ]
(re-iss. Mar79) (re-iss. Oct83, cd-iss. Aug88 on 'RCA')
Sep 76. (7") *(RCA 2729)* **THE GIRL OF MY BEST FRIEND. / A MESS OF BLUES** [9] [–]
Nov 76. (7") *(RCA 2768)* **SUSPICION. / (IT'S A) LONG LONELY HIGHWAY** [9] [–]
Feb 77. (lp/c) *(PL/PK 42003)* **ELVIS IN DEMAND** [12] [ ]
(re-iss. Sep81)
May 77. (7") *(RCA 2694)* **ALL SHOOK UP. / HEARTBREAK HOTEL** [41] [ ]

PRETENDERS

Formed: London, England ... March '78 by American singer/songwriter CHRISSIE HYNDE together with Hereford based musicians, guitarist JAMES HONEYMAN-SCOTT, bassist PETE FARNDON and drummer GERRY MACKLEDUFF. Prior to forming the band, HYNDE had spent the early 70's at Kent State University before moving to London in 1973 and securing work as an NME journalist. The following year, she relocated to Paris, to join the cringingly titled FRENCHIES, meeting CHRIS SPEDDING who invited her to contribute backing vocals on his 1977 album, 'Hurt'. Prior to this, HYNDE had returned to her home in Ohio in 1975 to join R&B group, JACK RABBIT. On the move again, she returned to London the following year to form The BERK BROTHERS (DAVE & FRED), before they replaced her with JOHNNY MOPED. Her self-penned songs were strong enough, however, to attract the attention of DAVE HILL, (then in the process of setting up his own label, 'Real') for whom she cut a demo tape in August '77. HILL subsequently asked HYNDE to form a band, and voila, The PRETENDERS were born. Their first single was a cover of The Kinks' 'STOP YOUR SOBBING', produced by NICK LOWE (ex-BRINSLEY SCHWARZ) and garnering much critical acclaim for its fresh faced new wave/ power-pop in the wake of punk overload. Another minor hit followed in the emotionally fragile 'KID' before the group hit big at the tail end of '79 with 'BRASS IN POCKET'. A simmering, swaggering slice of white pop-funk, the record became a UK No.1 and HYNDE was fast gaining a reputation as one of the finest songwriters around with an evocatively sultry voice to match. If there were any doubters then 'PRETENDERS' (1980) silenced them, a brilliant debut with a consistently engaging stylistic diversity. In addition to the singles, the album boasted the reggae-esque 'PRIVATE LIFE' and the gorgeous 'LOVERS OF TODAY', the individual musicians acquitting themselves with impressive conviction, notably the talented HONEYMAN-SCOTT. The album made The PRETENDERS a household name, the band subsequently undertaking an US stadium tour. While in America, HYNDE met her hero, RAY DAVIES (ex-KINKS), the pair duly becoming lovers (while DAVIES would eventually become her common-law husband and father of her first child, Natalie, the pair were allegedly refused a marriage certificate when the registrar became annoyed by their constant arguing!). The much anticipated follow-up, 'PRETENDERS II' (1981), was eventually released in August '81 to mixed reviews. The singles, 'MESSAGE OF LOVE' and the pop jangle of 'TALK OF THE TOWN' along with the steamy 'THE ADULTRESS' were highlights, although overall the album lacked the energy and verve of the debut. Later that summer, FARNDON was kicked out due to his spiralling drug use, narcotics also to blame for the death of HONEYMAN-SCOTT, found dead in his London flat two days later. Picking up the pieces, HYNDE went back into the studio with temporary replacements, guitarist BILLY BREMNER (ex-DAVE EDMUNDS' ROCKPILE) and bassist TONY BUTLER (future BIG COUNTRY) to record the driving melancholy of 'BACK ON THE CHAIN GANG' (written for HONEYMAN-SCOTT). With semi-permanent members ROBBIE McINTOSH and MALCOLM FOSTER brought in on guitar and bass respectively, the band began a new chapter in early '83. Incredibly, tragedy struck again almost immediately with PETE FARNDON becoming another fatal drugs casualty. A single eventually surfaced towards the end of the year, the undulating '2,000 MILES', while a third album, 'LEARNING TO CRAWL', appeared in early '84. Though the album contained some stellar PRETENDERS moments, it once more met with mixed reviews and performed better in America than Britain. The following year was to be an eventful one for HYNDE, meeting and subsequently marrying JIM KERR (SIMPLE MINDS) as well as playing Live Aid and topping the UK charts via her UB40 collaboration, a remake of the old SONNY & CHER chestnut, 'I GOT YOU BABE'. HYNDE eventually re-emerged with a slightly modified PRETENDERS line-up and a new deal with 'WEA' in late '86, the group scoring their first Top 10 hut in years with the infectiously chugging 'DON'T GET ME WRONG'. This was swiftly followed by the 'GET CLOSE' (1986) album, a warmer sounding affair with HYNDE singing to her new daughter (born to KERR) on the lovely 'HYMN TO HER', while revealing an increasing political awareness with 'HOW MUCH DID YOU GET FOR YOUR SOUL'. Indeed, 1988 saw her billed on the Nelson Mandela concert alongside UB40 at Wembley Stadium (she also scored another Top 10 collaboration with the band that summer, 'BREAKFAST IN BED'), while also becoming involved in various animal rights activities. HYNDE eventually turned her hand to The PRETENDERS once more at the turn of the decade, now virtually solo with a revolving cast of musicians backing her on 'PACKED' (1990) and 'LAST OF THE INDEPENDENTS' (1994). While not scaling the giddy heights of old, these releases proved HYNDE was still capable of writing affectingly melodic pop/rock. The unplugged set was inevitable really, HYNDE releasing 'THE ISLE OF VIEW' in 1995, a collection of spartan reworkings of old classics. The PRETENDERS return album proper, 'VIVA EL AMOR!' (1999), saw CHRISSIE and her band find old favour with her 80's fanbase (it reached the UK Top 40), the opening track 'POPSTAR' truly a single that deserved better airplay. With 'GREATEST HITS' (2000) marking the end of the band's lengthy tenure with Warners, 'LOOSE SCREW' (2002) became The PRETENDERS' first release for 'Eagle' records ('Artemis' in the States). Not that this downscaling had any kind of marked effect on their approach, except perhaps that HYNDE's lyrics were more coruscating than ever, whether the target was errant lovers or her own shortcomings. • **Songwriters:** Group compositions, except as said plus; MAY THIS BE LOVE (Jimi Hendrix) / IF THERE WAS A MAN (co-w/ John Barry) / NOT A SECOND TIME (Beatles) / CREEP (Radiohead). • **Trivia:** CHRISSIE caused controversy in June '89, when she attended a Greenpeace Rainbow Warriors press conference, telling how she (a staunch vegetarian) once firebombed McDonalds burger shop. The day after, one of their shops in Milton Keynes was firebombed and CHRISSIE was asked/told to sign a retracting statement, or be taken to court.

Album rating: PRETENDERS (*8) / PRETENDERS II (*7) / LEARNING TO CRAWL (*8) / GET CLOSE (*5) / THE SINGLES compilation (*8) / PACKED! (*4) / LAST OF THE INDEPENDENTS (*6) / THE ISLE OF VIEW (*5) / VIVA EL AMOR (*6) / GREATEST HITS compilation (*8) / LOOSE SCREW (*5)

CHRISSIE HYNDE (b. 7 Sep'51, Akron, Ohio) – vocals, guitar / **JAMES HONEYMAN-SCOTT** (b. 4 Nov'57, Hereford, England) – guitar, keyboards (ex-CHEEKS) / **PETE FARNDON** (b.1953, Hereford) – bass / **GERRY MACKLEDUFF** – drums

		Real	Sire
Jan 79.	(7") *(ARE 6)* **STOP YOUR SOBBING. / THE WAIT**	34	–
——	**MARTIN CHAMBERS** (b. 4 Sep'51, Hereford) – drums repl. GERRY		
Jun 79.	(7") *(ARE 9)* **KID. / TATTOOED LOVE BOYS**	33	Jul 80
Nov 79.	(7") *(ARE 11)* **BRASS IN POCKET. / SWINGING LONDON**	1	–
	(12"+=) *(ARET 11)* – Nervous but shy. *(c-ep-iss.Apr81; SPC 5)*		
Jan 80.	(lp/c) *(RAL/+C 3)* *<6083>* **PRETENDERS**	1	9
	– Precious / The phone call / Up the neck / Tattooed love boys / Space invader / The wait / Stop your sobbing / Kid / Private life / Brass in pocket / Lovers of today / Mystery achievement. *(cd-iss. 1983 on 'WEA'; 256774-2)*		
Feb 80.	(7") *<49181>* **BRASS IN POCKET. / SPACE INVADER**	–	14
Apr 80.	(7") *(ARE 12)* **TALK OF THE TOWN. / CUBAN SLIDE AND SLIDE**	8	
May 80.	(7") *<49506>* **STOP YOUR SOBBING. / PHONE CALL**	–	65
Feb 81.	(7") *(ARE 15)* **MESSAGE OF LOVE. / PORCELAIN**	11	Apr81
Aug 81.	(lp/c) *(RAL/+C 3)* *<3572>* **PRETENDERS II**	7	10
	– The adultress / Bad boys get spanked / Message of love / I go to sleep / Birds of Paradise / Talk of the town / Pack it up / Waste not, want not / Day after day / Jealous dogs / Waste not want not / English rose / Louie Louie. *(cd-iss. Nov86 & Jul93 on 'WEA'; 256774-2)*		
Aug 81.	(7") *<49819>* **LOUIE LOUIE. / IN THE STICKS**	–	
Aug 81.	(7") *(ARE 17)* **DAY AFTER DAY. / IN THE STICKS**	45	–
	(12"+=) *(ARE 17a)* – The adultress.		
Nov 81.	(7") *(ARE 18)* **I GO TO SLEEP. / THE ENGLISH ROSE**	7	–
	(12"+=) *(ARE 18T)* – Waste not, want not.		

Jan 82. (7") **I GO TO SLEEP. / WASTE NOT, WANT NOT** [–] [ ]

— (Sep'82) **BILLY BREMNER** – guitar (ex-NICK LOWE, ex-DAVE EDMUNDS' ROCKPILE) repl. HONEYMAN-SCOTT who died of drug overdose 16 Jun'82 / **TONY BUTLER** – bass (of BIG COUNTRY) repl. FARNDON (died o.d. 14 Apr'83)

Sep 82. (7") *(ARE 19) <29840>* **BACK ON THE CHAIN GANG. / MY CITY HAS GONE** [17] Dec82 [5]
(12"+=) *(ARE 19T)* – ('A'-part 2).

— (Feb83) **HYNDE** and **CHAMBERS** brought in new members **ROBBIE McINTOSH** (25 Oct'57) – guitar (ex-MANFRED MANN'S EARTH BAND, ex-NIGHT) repl. BREMNER who rejoined NICK LOWE etc. / **MALCOLM FOSTER** (b.13 Jan'56) – bass repl. BUTLER who rejoined BIG COUNTRY

Nov 83. (7") *(ARE 20)* **2000 MILES. / THE LAW IS THE LAW** [15] [–]
('A'fast or slow versioned 12"+=) *(ARE 20T)* – Money (live).

Nov 83. (7") *<29444>* **MIDDLE OF THE ROAD. / 2,000 MILES** [–] [19]

Jan 84. (lp/c)(cd) *(WX 2/+C)(923980-2) <23980>* **LEARNING TO CRAWL** [11] [5]
– Middle of the road / Back on the chain gang / Time the avenger / Watching the clothes / Show me / Thumbelina / My city was gone / Thin line between love and hate / I hurt you / 2000 miles.

Feb 84. (7"/12") *(ARE 21/+T)* **MIDDLE OF THE ROAD. / WATCHING THE CLOTHES** [ ] [–]

— added **PAUL CARRACK** – keyboards (ex-ACE, ex-ROXY MUSIC, ex-solo artist)

Mar 84. (7") *<29317>* **SHOW ME. / FAST OR SLOW (THE LAW IS THE LAW)** [–] [28]

Apr 84. (7") *(ARE 22) <29249>* **THIN LINE BETWEEN LOVE AND HATE. / TIME THE AVENGER** [49] Jun84 [83]
(12"+=) *(ARE 22T)* – Bad boys get spanked.

— Sep 85, CHRISSIE HYNDE guests on UB40's 'I Got You Babe' which hits No.1. Three years later the same team hit no.6 with 'Breakfast In Bed'. PRETENDERS regroup with **HYNDE, McINTOSH** and **TIM STEVENS** – bass / **BLAIR CUNNINGHAM** – drums (ex-HAIRCUT 100) repl. CHAMBERS (on some) and **BERNIE WORRELL** – keyboards

W.E.A. Warners

Sep 86. (7") *(YZ 85) <28630>* **DON'T GET ME WRONG. / DANCE** [10] [10]
(12"+=) *(YZ 85T)* – ('A'extended).

Oct 86. (lp/c)(cd) *(WX 34/+C)(240976-2) <25488>* **GET CLOSE** [6] [25]
– My baby / When I change my life / Light of the Moon / Dance * / Tradition of love / Don't get me wrong / I remember you / How much did you get for your soul / Chill factor / Hymn to her / Room full of mirrors. *(c+=/cd+= *)*

Nov 86. (7") *(YZ 93)* **HYMN TO HER. / ROOM FULL OF MIRRORS** [8] [–]
(12"+=) *(YZ 93T)* – Stop your sobbing (demo).

Feb 87. (7") *<28496>* **MY BABY. / ROOM FULL OF MIRRORS** [–] [64]

Mar 87. (7") *(YZ 110)* **MY BABY. / TRADITION OF LOVE (remix)** [ ] [–]
(12"+=) *(YZ 110T)* – Thumbelina.
(7"ep+=) *(YZEP 110)* – Private life / Middle of the road.

Apr 87. (7") **HYMN TO HER. / TRADITION OF LOVE** [–] [ ]

Aug 87. (7"; as PRETENDERS 007) *(YZ 149) <28259>* **IF THERE WAS A MAN. / INTO VIENNA** [49] [ ]
(12"+=) *(YZ 149T)* – Where has everybody gone.

Oct 87. (lp/c)(cd) *(WX 135/+C)(242229-2) <25664>* **THE SINGLES** (compilation) [6] [69]
– Stop your sobbing / Kid / Brass in pocket / Talk of the town / I go to sleep / Day after day / Message of love / Back on the chain gang / Middle of the road / 2000 miles / Show me / Thin line between love and hate / Don't get me wrong / Hymn to her / My baby / I got you babe (w/ UB40) / What you gonna do about it.

Oct 87. (7") *(YZ 156)* **KID (remix). / STOP YOUR SOBBING (original)** [ ] [–]
(12"+=/cd-s+=) *(YZ 156 T/CD)* – ('B' 1978 demo) / What you gonna do about it ('87 remix).
Jun'88, she guested again with UB40 on hit single 'BREAKFAST IN BED'.

— added guest **JOHNNY MARR** – guitar (ex-SMITHS) repl. McINTOSH

Apr 89. (7"/12"/3"cd-s) *(PRE/+T/CD 69)* **WINDOWS OF THE WORLD. / 1969** [ ] [–]

— (above from the film '1969', a one-off on label 'Polydor')

— now virtually **CHRISSIE** solo, augmented by **BLAIR CUNNINGHAM** – drums / **BILLY BREMNER + DOMINIC MILLER** – guitar / **JOHN McKENZIE** – bass / plus others

May 90. (7"/c-s) *(YZ 469/+C) <19820>* **NEVER DO THAT. / NOT A SECOND TIME** [ ] [ ]
(12"+=) *(YZ 469T)* – The wait.
(cd-s++=) *(YZ 469CD)* – Spirit of life.

May 90. (cd)(lp/c) *(9031 71403-2)(WX 346/+C) <26219>* **PACKED!** [19] [48]
– Never do that / Let's make a pact / Millionaires / May this be love / No guarentee / When will I see you / Sense of purpose / Downtown (Akron) / How do I miss you / Hold a candle to this / Criminal. *(cd re-iss. Nov94; 9031 71403-2)*

Oct 90. (7") *(YZ 507)* **SENSE OF PURPOSE. / SPIRIT OF LIFE** [ ] [–]
(12"+=) *(YZ 507T)* – Brass in pocket.
(cd-s++=/c-s++=) *(YZ 507 CD/C)* – Not a second time.

— Oct 91, CHRISSIE's vox was credited on single 'SPIRITUAL HIGH', by MOOD SWINGS. It finally hit UK no. 47 early '93.

— She wrote most with B. STEINBERG + T.KELLY. Covered; FOREVER YOUNG (Bob Dylan).

— **CHRISSIE** + main band **MARTIN CHAMBERS** – drums / **ADAM SEYMOUR** – guitar / **ANDY HOBSON** – bass

Apr 94. (7"/c-s) *(YZ 815/+C) <18160>* **I'LL STAND BY YOU. / REBEL ROCK ME** [10] Aug94 [16]
(cd-s+=) *(YZ 815CD1)* – Bold as love.
(cd-s) *(YZ 815CD2)* – ('A'side) / Message of love / Brass in pocket / Don't get me wrong.

May 94. (cd/c) *(4509 95822-2/-4/-1) <45572>* **LAST OF THE INDEPENDENTS** [8] [41]
– Hollywood perfume / Night in my veins / Money talk / 977 / Revolution / All my dreams / I'll stand by you / I'm a mother / Tequila / Every mother's son / Rebel rock me / Love colours / Forever young.

May 94. (c-s,cd-s) *<18163>* **NIGHT IN MY VEINS / ANGEL OF THE MORNING** [–] [71]

Jun 94. (7"/c-s) *(YZ 825/+C)* **NIGHT IN MY VEINS. / BAD BOYS GET SPANKED** [25] [–]
(cd-s+=) *(YZ 825CD)* – My city was gone / Tattooed love boys.

Oct 94. (7"/c-s) *(YZ 848/+C)* **977. / I'LL STAND BY YOU (live)** [66] [–]
(cd-s+=) *(YZ 848CD1)* – Hollywood perfume (live) / Kid (live).
(cd-s) *(YZ 848CD2)* – ('A'side) / Back on the chain gang (live) / Night in my veins (live) / Precious (live).

Sep 95. (c-s) *(WEA 014C)* **KID (acoustic) / THE ISLE OF VIEW (acoustic)** [73] [–]
(cd-s+=) *(WEA 014CD)* – Creep (acoustic).

Oct 95. (cd/c) *(0630 12059-2/-4) <46085>* **THE ISLE OF VIEW (live acoustic)** [23] [100]
– Sense of purpose / Chill factor / Private life / Back on the chain gang / Kid / I hurt you / Criminal / Brass in pocket / 2000 miles / Hymn to her / Lovers of today / The phone call / I go to sleep / Revolution. *(cd+=)* – The Isle of View.

Nov 95. (c-s/cd-s) *(WEA 024 C/CD)* **2000 MILES (acoustic) / TEQUILA** [ ] [–]
(cd-s+=) *(WEA 024CDX)* – Happy Christmas / Night in my veins.

Apr 97. (c-s/12"/cd-s) *(NEG 104 C/T/CD)* **GOIN' BACK. / (other track by The LA'S)** [ ] [–]
(above issued on 'Blanco Y Negro')

May 99. (c-s) *(WEA 207C)* **HUMAN / THE HOMECOMING (Street version)** [33] [–]
(cd-s+=) *(WEA 207CD)* – ('A'-Glass mix).

May 99. (cd/c) *(<3984 27152-2/-4>)* **VIVA EL AMOR!** [32] [ ]
– Popstar / Nails in the road / Human / From the heart down / Who's who / Dragway 42 / Baby's breath / One more time / Legalise me / Biker / Samurai / Rabo de nube.

Aug 99. (c-s) *(WEA 219C)* **POPSTAR / THE NEEDLE AND THE DAMAGE DONE** [ ] [–]
(cd-s+=) *(WEA 219CD)* – Samurai.

— in Jun'00, CHRISSIE HYNDE featured on HYBRID's No.32 hit version of 'KID 2000'

Sep 00. (cd/c) *(<8573 84607-2/-4>)* **GREATEST HITS** (compilation) [21] Nov00 [ ]
– Brass in pocket / Message of love / Don't get me wrong / Kid / Human (Tin Tin Out remix) / I go to sleep / Forever young / I got you babe (UB40 & CHRISSIE HYNDE) / Night in my veins / Spiritual high (state of independence) (MOODSWINGS & CHRISSIE HYNDE) / Talk of the town / Stop your sobbing / Hymn to her / 2000 miles / Breakfast in

bed (UB40 & CHRISSIE HYNDE) / Popstar / Middle of the road / Thin line between love and hate / Back on the chain gang / I'll stand by you. *(re-dist.Apr02)* – hit No.29

Eagle — Artemis

May 03. (cd-s) *(EAGXS 257)* **YOU KNOW WHO YOUR FRIENDS ARE / COMPLICADA (complex person Spanish version)** [ ] [–]

May 03. (cd) *(EAGCD 256) <751153>* **LOOSE SCREW** [55] Nov02 [ ]
– Lie to me / Time / You know who you're friends are / Complex person / Fools must die / Kinda nice, I like it / Nothing breaks like a heart / I should of / Clean up woman / The losing / Saving grace / Walk like a panther.

Aug 03. (cd-s; promo) *(EAGXS 261)* **SAVING GRACE** [ ] [–]

Oct 03. (cd-s) *(EAGXS 268)* **THE LOSING / DON'T GET ME WRONG (live)** [ ] [–]

– compilations, etc. –

Jul 94. (cd/c) *Carlton; (4509 91885-2/-4)* **DON'T GET ME WRONG** [ ] [–]

PRETTY THINGS

Formed: Dartford, Kent, England . . . 1963 by DICK TAYLOR and PHIL MAY. The former had once been a member of LITTLE BOY BLUE & THE BLUE BOYS, an embryonic version of The ROLLING STONES. The pair added BRIAN PENDLETON, JOHN STAX and PETE KITLEY, the latter being replaced by drummer VIV PRINCE. Taking their name from a BO DIDDLEY song, they soon signed to 'Fontana', employing the management team of Bryan Morrison and James Duncan, the latter of whom wrote their summer '64 debut Top 50 hit, 'ROSALYN'. Their pure roots/R&B follow-up, 'DON'T BRING ME DOWN' (which drew inspiration from black American blues artists of the 50's) dented the UK Top 10, preceding their eponymous Top 10 album in early '65. Unlike the STONES (of whom they were dubbed by the press as uglier cousins), their hits had dried up by 1967, due to a misguided foray into psychedelia. Later that year, they moved to 'Columbia' records, releasing two flop 45's, before they embarked on their most ambitious project so far, 'S.F. SORROW'. It was the first ever "rock opera", inspiring PETE TOWNSHEND (The Who) to write his legendary 'Tommy'. The album was a commercial flop and critically lambasted by the press, although it has since become regarded as an innovative piece of work that was essential to the development of "rock" music. During its recording, TAYLOR left to become a producer, the band folding but regrouping for a heavier 'Harvest' set, 'PARACHUTE' (1970). They struggled on regardless, subsequently signing for LED ZEPPELIN's heavyweight 'Swan Song' label in '74. Two mediocre albums followed before they the band split in '76 after their remaining founder member, MAY, departed. They re-formed many times and still tread the boards on the blues circuit alongside members of The YARDBIRDS. A more or less original line-up of the band inevitably came together for a late 90's reunion although few might've predicted that they'd attempt a recording of the classic 'S.F. SORROW' in its entirety live in the studio. The result was 'RESURRECTION' (1999), which hardly improved upon the original although was notable for the inimitable narration of ARTHUR BROWN. Presumably buoyed up by the project, they proceeded to record a bonafide new album, 'RAGE . . . BEFORE BEAUTY' (1999), albeit with a raft of covers including Jagger/Richard's 'PLAY WITH FIRE' and P.F. Sloan's 'EVE OF DESTRUCTION'. • **Songwriters:** Most by PHIL MAY, except covers; PRETTY THING + ROADRUNNER + MONA (Bo Diddley) / CRY TO ME (Bert Berns) / A HOUSE IN THE COUNTRY (Ray Davies; Kinks) / REELIN' AND ROCKIN' (Chuck Berry) / I'M A KING BEE (Muddy Waters) / SHAKIN' ALL OVER (Johnny Kidd & The Pirates) / etc. • **Trivia:** The group made cameo appearances in the films, 'What's Good For The Goose' (1969 w /Norman Wisdom) and 'The Monster Squad' (1980 w /Vincent Price). They were given a tribute by BOWIE in 1973, when he covered their first two hits on his 'PIN-UPS' album.

Album rating: THE PRETTY THINGS (*7) / GET THE PICTURE (*6) / EMOTIONS (*6) / S.F. SORROW (*7) / PARACHUTE (*6) / FREEWAY MADNESS (*6) / SILK TORPEDO (*5) / SAVAGE EYE (*5) / CROSSTALK (*4) / LIVE AT THE HEARTBREAK HOTEL (*4) / OUT OF THE ISLAND (*4) / THE PRETTY THINGS 1967-1971 compilation (*7) / . . .RAGE BEFORE BEAUTY (*4) / RESURRECTION (*5)

PHIL MAY (b. 9 Nov'44, Kent, England) – vocals / **DICK TAYLOR** (28 Jan'43) – lead guitar / **BRIAN PENDLETON** (b.13 Apr'44, Wolverhampton, England) – rhythm guitar / **JOHN STAX** (b.JOHN FULLEGAR, 6 Apr'44) – bass / **VIV PRINCE** (b. 9 Aug'44, Loughborough, Leicestershire, England) – drums (PETE KITLEY, then VIV ANDREWS sessioned on 1st-two 45's)

Fontana — Fontana

Jun 64. (7") *(TF 469) <1916>* **ROSALYN. / BIG BOSS MAN** [41] Oct64 [ ]

Oct 64. (7") *(TF 503) <1941>* **DON'T BRING ME DOWN. / WE'LL BE TOGETHER** [10] Jan65 [ ]

Feb 65. (7") *(TF 537) <1508>* **HONEY I NEED. / I CAN NEVER SAY** [13] [ ]

Mar 65. (lp) *(TL 5239) <67544>* **THE PRETTY THINGS** [6] [ ]
– Roadrunner / Judgement day / 13 Chester street / Honey I need / Big city / Unkown blues / Mama, keep your big mouth shut / Oh baby doll / She's fine she's mine / Don't you lie to me / The Moon is rising / Pretty thing. *(re-iss. Jul90 lp/c/cd; 646054-1/-4/-2) (lp re-iss. Nov01 on 'Norton'; ED 282) (cd re-iss. Jul02 on 'Repertoire'+=; REP 4927)* – Rosalyn / Big boss man / Don't bring me down / We'll be together / I can never say / Get yourself home. *(cd re-iss. Feb03 on 'Snapper'; SDPCD 115)*

Jul 65. (7") *(TF 585) <1518>* **CRY TO ME. / JUDGEMENT DAY** [28] [ ]

Dec 65. (7") *(TF 647) <1540>* **MIDNIGHT TO SIX MAN. / CAN'T STAND THE PAIN** [46] [ ]

Dec 65. (lp) *(TL 5280) <5280>* **GET THE PICTURE** [ ] [ ]
– You don't believe me / Buzz the jerk / Get the picture? / Can't stand the pain / Rainin' in my heart / We'll play house / You'll never do it baby / I had a dream / I want your love / London town / Cry to me / Gonna find me a substitute. *(re-iss. Mar84; 6438 214) (cd-iss. Jul90; 846459-2) (cd re-iss. Apr98 on 'Snapper'+=; SMMCD 549)* – Get a buzz / Sittin' all alone / Midnight to six man / Come see me / L.S.D. / Me needing you. *(lp re-iss. Nov01 on 'Norton'; ED 283) (cd re-mast.Sep02 on 'Repertoire'+=; REP 4928) (cd re-iss. Jan03 on 'Snapper'+=; SDPCD 114)*

— **SKIP ALAN** (b. ALAN ERNEST SKIPPER, 11 Jun'44) – drums repl. PRINCE on some

Fontana — Blue Thumb

Apr 66. (7") *(TF 688)* **COME SEE ME. / l.s.d.** [43] [ ]

Jul 66. (7") *(TF 722)* **A HOUSE IN THE COUNTRY. / ME NEEDING YOU** [50] [ ]

Dec 66. (7") *(TF 773)* **PROGRESS. / BUZZ IN THE JERK** [ ] [ ]

Apr 67. (7") *(TF 829)* **CHILDREN. / MY TIME** [ ] [ ]

May 67. (lp; stereo/mono) *(S+/TL 5425)* **EMOTIONS** [ ] [–]
– Death of a socialite / Children / The sun / There will never be another day / House of ten / Out in the night / One long glance / Growing in my mind / Photographer / Bright lights of the city / Tripping / My time. *(re-iss. Apr91 +=; 846705-2) (cd re-iss. Apr98 on 'Snapper'+=; SMMCD 550)* – A house in the country / Me needing you / Progress. *(cd re-iss. Jan03 on 'Snapper'++=; SDPCD 111)* – Photographer / There will never be another day / My time / The sun / Progress. *(cd re-mast.Sep02 on 'Repertoire'+++=; REP 4929)* – Death of a socialite (single version) / Photographer (undubbed).

— **PHIL + DICK** were left to recruit new members **JOHN POVEY** (b.20 Aug'44) – keyboards, vocals (ex-FENMEN) repl. PENDLETON / **WALLY ALLEN** – bass, vocals (ex-FENMEN) repl. SKIP / **MITCH MITCHELL** – (session) drums repl. SKIP

Columbia — Rare Earth

Nov 67. (7") *(DB 8300)* **DEFLECTING GREY. / MR. EVASION** [ ] [–]

— **BOBBIE GRAHAM** – drums (also on session) repl. MITCHELL

Feb 68. (7") *(DB 8353)* **TALKIN' ABOUT THE GOOD TIMES. / WALKING THROUGH MY DREAMS** [ ] [–]

— **JOHN 'TWINK' ADLER** – percussion, vocals (ex-TOMORROW, etc) repl. GRAHAM

Nov 68. (7") *(DB 8494) <5005>* **PRIVATE SORROW. / BALLOON BURNING**

Dec 68. (lp; mono/stereo) *(SX/SCX 6306) <506>* **S.F. SORROW** Feb70
– S.F. sorrow / Bracelets of fingers / She says good morning / Private sorrow / Balloon burning / Death / Baron Saturday / I see you / The journey / Well of destiny / Trust / Old man going / Loneliest person. *(re-press.1970; same) (re-iss. Oct87 on 'Edsel'; XED 236) (cd-iss. Oct90; EDCD 236) (lp re-iss. Jun00 on 'Snapper'; SMMLP 565) (cd re-iss. Feb03 on 'Snapper'+=; SDPCD 109)* – Defecting grey / Mr. Evasion / Talkin' about the good times / Walking through my dreams. *(cd re-mast.Sep02 on 'Repertoire'++=; REP 4930)* – Private sorrow / Balloon burning / Defecting grey (acetate).

— **SKIP ALAN** – drums, vocals (returned from SUNSHINE) repl. TWINK who joined PINK FAIRIES (new one joining MAY, POVEY and ALLEN plus below) **VICTOR UNITT** – guitar, vocals (ex-EDGAR BROUGHTON) repl. TAYLOR (⇒ producer)

Harvest Rare Earth

Apr 70. (7") *(HAR 5016)* **THE GOOD MR. SQUARE. / BLUE SERGE BLUES**

Jun 70. (lp) *(SHVL 774) <515>* **PARACHUTE** 43
– Scene one / The good Mr. Square / She was tall, she was high / In the square / The letter / Rain / Miss Fay regrets / Cries from the midnight circus / Grass / Sickle clowns / She's a lover / What's the use / Parachute. *(re-iss. Sep88 on 'Edsel' lp/cd; ED/+CD 289) (cd re-iss. Jun99 on 'Snapper'+=; SMDCD 566)* – Blue Serge blues / October 26 / Cold stone / Stone-hearted mama / Summer time / Circus mind. *(lp re-iss. DEc01 on 'Rare Earth'; same as US) (cd re-mast.Sep02 on 'Repertoire'+=; REP 4931) (cd re-iss. Jan03 on 'Snapper'+=; SDPCD 110)*

— **PETER TOLSON** (b.10 Sep'51, Bishops Stortford, England) – guitar, vocals (ex-EIRE APPARANT) repl. UNITT (who returned to EDGAR BROUGHTON BAND)

Oct 70. (7") *(HAR 5031)* **OCTOBER 26. / COLD STONE**

May 71. (7"m) *(HAR 5037)* **STONE-HEARTED MAMA. / SUMMERTIME / CIRCUS MIND**

— **STUART BROOKS** – bass, vocals repl. WALLY who went into producing

Warners Warners

Dec 72. (lp) *(K 46190) <2680>* **FREEWAY MADNESS**
– Love is good / Havana bound / Peter / Rip off train / Over the moon / Religion's dead / Country road / All night sailor / Onion soup / Another bowl? *(cd-iss. Sep00 on 'Snapper'+=; SMMCD 603)* – Religion's dead (live) / Havana bound (live) / Love is good (live) / Onion soup (live). *(cd re-mast.Sep02 on 'Repertoire'++=; REP 4932)* – Over the moon (single version) / Havana bound (single version). *(cd re-iss. Jan03 on 'Snapper'+=; SDPCD 117)*

Jan 73. (7") **OVER THE MOON. / HAVANA BOUND** –

— added **GORDON EDWARDS** (b.26 Dec'46, Southport, England) – keyboards (to **MAY, ALAN, POVEY, TOLSON and BROOKS**)

Swan Song Swan Song

Oct 74. (lp) *(SSK 59400) <8411>* **SILK TORPEDO**
– Dream – Joey / Maybe you tried / Atlanta / L.A.N.T.A. / Is it only love / Come home momma / Bridge of God / Singapore silk torpedo / Belfast cowboys / Bruise in the sky. *(cd-iss. Nov98 on 'Snapper'+=; SMMCD 559)* – Singapore silk torpedo (live) / Dream – Joey (live). *(cd re-mast.Sep02 on 'Repertoire'++=; REP 4933)* – Joey (single version) / I'm keeping (single version). *(cd re-iss. Jan03 on 'Snapper'+=; SDPCD 112)*

Dec 74. (7") *(K 19401)* **JOEY. / IS IT ONLY LOVE**

Jun 75. (7") *(K 19403)* **I'M KEEPING. / ATLANTA**

— **JACK GREEN** (b.12 Mar'51, Glasgow, Scotland) – bass, vocals (also as EDWARDS, ex-SUNSHINE) repl. BROOKS

Aug 75. (7") *(K 19404) <70107>* **JOEY. / COME HOME MOMMA**

Feb 76. (7") *(K 19405)* **SAD EYE. / REMEMBER THAT BOY** –

Apr 76. (7") **REMEMBER THAT BOY. / IT ISN'T ROCK'N'ROLL** –

May 76. (lp) *(SSL 59401) <8414>* **SAVAGE EYE** Feb 76
– Under the volcano / My song / Sad eye / Remember that boy / It isn't rock'n'roll / I'm keeping / It's been so long / Drowned man / Theme for Michelle. *(cd-iss. Sep98 on 'Snapper'+=; SMMCD 560)* – Tonight (single version) / Love me a little (demo) / Dance all night (demo). *(cd re-mast.Sep02 on 'Repertoire'+=; REP 4934) (cd re-iss. Jan03 on 'Snapper'+=; SDPCD 113)*

May 76. (7") *(K 19406)* **TONIGHT. / IT ISN'T ROCK'N'ROLL** –

— Last original PHIL MAY went solo augmented by the FALLEN ANGELS (see below). POVEY also departed leaving only 4 (SKIP, PETER, JACK and GORDON) calling themselves METROPOLIS between mid '76-late'77. JACK also joined T.REX and GORDON went to The KINKS.

PHIL MAY & THE FALLEN ANGELS

with **MICKEY FINN** – guitar (ex-T.REX) / **BILL LOVELADY** – guitar / **BRIAN JOHNSTON** – keyboards (ex-STREETWALKERS) / **WALL ALLEN** – bass / **CHICO GREENWOOD** – drums / etc.

Philips not iss.

1978. (lp) *(6410 969)* **PHIL MAY & THE FALLEN ANGELS** – Dutch –
– Fallen angels / California / 13 floor suicide / Dance again / Shine on baby / My good friend / Cold wind / I keep on / Dogs of war / Girl like you. *(UK-iss.1982;) (re-iss. Feb85;)*

PRETTY THINGS

re-formed ex-members in 1980. (**PHIL MAY, DICK TAYLOR, JOHN POVEY, PETER TOLSON, WALLY ALLEN** and **SKIP ALAN**)

Warners Warners

Aug 80. (lp) *(K 56842) <3466>* **CROSS TALK**
– I'm calling / Edge of the night / Sea of blue / Office love / Lost that girl / Bitter end / Falling again / It's so hard / She don't / No future. *(cd-iss. Sep00 on 'Snapper'+=; SMMCD 602)* – Wish fulfillment / Sea about me / The young pretenders. *(cd re-mast.Sep02 on 'Repertoire'+=; REP 4935) (cd re-iss. Jan03 on 'Snapper'+=; SDPCD 116)*

Aug 80. (7") *(K 17670)* **I'M CALLING. / SEA OF BLUE**

— Disbanded 1981, but re-formed briefly as . . .

ZAC ZOLAR AND ELECTRIC BANANA

Butt not iss.

1984. (7") **TAKE ME HOME. / JAMES MARSHALL** –

— (above appeared on 'Minder' TV series) *(re-iss. Aug86 on 'Shanghai'; MGLS 2)*

PRETTY THINGS

re-formed by **MAY + TAYLOR** in 1984. Now with **JOE SHAW** – guitar / **DAVE WINTOUR** – bass / **KEVIN FLANAGAN** – saxophone / **JOHN CLARKE** – drums

Big Beat not iss.

Aug 84. (lp) *(WIK 24)* **LIVE AT THE HEARTBREAK HOTEL (live)** –
– Big boss man / Midnight to six man / I'm a king bee / Honey I need / Shakin' all over / Rosalyn / Roadrunner / Mama keep your big mouth shut / Raining in my heart / Reelin' and rockin' / Don't bring me down / Mona.

— **ROLF TER VELD** – bass + **BERTRAM ENGEL** – drums (ex-UDO LINDENBERG, ex-PANIKORCHESTER) repl.WINTOUR, FLANAGAN + CLARKE

In-Akustik not iss.

Jun 88. (cd) *(INAK 8708)* **OUT OF THE ISLAND** –
– Cry to me / Baby doll / She's fine, she's mine / Get the picture / Havana bound / Can't stop / Loneliest person / £.s.d. / Private sorrow / The moon is rising / Big city / Cause and effect / Well known blues / You don't believe me / Judement day. *(re-iss. May95; same)*

— **MAY + TAYLOR** again re-formed them again in 1989, with new **GLEN MATLOCK** – bass, vocals (ex-SEX PISTOLS, ex-RICH KIDS) / **FRANK HOLLAND** – guitar, keyboards / **BOBBY WEBB** – keyboards, vocals / **MARK ST. JOHN** – drums, bass, vocals

Trax not iss.

Sep 89. (7") *(7TX 12)* **EVE OF DESTRUCTION. / GOIN' DOWNHILL** –
(12"+=) *(12TX 12)* – Can't stop.

— (on tour) **STEVE BROWNING** – bass repl. MATLOCK

— Re-formed again in 1991, with **PHIL MAY / DICK TAYLOR** (ex-MEKONS) / **JIMMY McCARTY** (ex-YARDBIRDS) / **RICHARD HITE** (ex-CANNED HEAT)

PRETTY THINGS & THE YARDBIRD BLUES BAND

Super-blues-group / collab with ex-YARDBIRDS and plenty covers

Demon not iss.

Oct 91. (cd) *(FIENDCD 708)* **CHICAGO BLUES JAM 1991** –
– Can't judge the book / Down in the bottom / Hush hush / Can't hold

out / Spoonful / She fooled me / Time is on my side / Scratch my back / Long tall Shorty / Diddley daddy / Ain't got you / Caress my baby / Here's my picture / Chain of fools / Don't start crying now.

Feb 94. (cd) *(FIENDCD 748)* **WINE, WOMEN & WHISKEY** ☐ ☐
– Wine, women and whiskey / Sure look good to me / No questions / The amble / It's all over now / Bad boy / Spoonful (bare bones remix) / French champagne / My back scratcher / Can't hold out (big city remix) / Diddley daddy (street corner remix) / I'm cryin' / Gettin' all wet.

PRETTY THINGS 'N MATES (WITH MATTHEW FISHER)

featuring a plethora of famous cover versions

Kingdom not iss.

May 94. (cd) *(CDKVL 9031)* **A WHITER SHADE OF DIRTY WATER** ☐ ☐
– He's waitin' / Strychnine / Pushing too hard / Kicks / Candy / Louie, Louie / 96 tears / Let's talk about girls / Sometimes good guys don't wear black / I'm a man / Red river rock / Midnight to 6 man '93.

PRETTY THINGS

— re-formed again 1995, **MAY, TAYLOR, POVEY, ALLEN, ALAN + HOLLAND**

Jun 96. (7"pic-d) *(FRPS 006)* **EVE OF DESTRUCTION. / ROSALYN / PASSION OF LOVE** ☐ ☐

Snapper Madfish

Mar 99. (cd) *(SMACD 814) <128142>* **. . .RAGE BEFORE BEAUTY** ☐ ☐
– Passion of love / Vivian Prince / Everlasting flame / Love keeps hanging on / Eve of destruction / Not givin' in / Pure cold stone / Blue turns to red / Goodbye, goodbye / Goin' downhill / Play with fire / Fly away / Mony mony / God give me the strength (to carry on). *(re-iss. Apr01; SMDCD 626) (cd re-mast.Sep02 on 'Repertoire'; REP 4936)*

Snapper Snapper

Apr 01. (cd) *(<SMMCD 624>)* **RESURRECTION** (S.F. SORROW live in the studio 6th September, 1998) ☐ ☐

– (selective) compilations, etc. –

Mar 82. (lp/c) *See For Miles; (CM/+K 103)* **THE PRETTY THINGS 1967-1971** ☐ ☐ *(cd-iss. Oct89; SEECD 103)*

Jun 84. (lp) *Edsel; (ED 139)* **LET ME HEAR THE CHOIR SING** ☐ ☐

Feb 86. (lp) *Bam Caruso; (KIRI 032)* **CLOSED RESTAURANT BLUES** ☐ ☐

May 86. (lp/c) *Harvest; (EMS/TCEMS 1119)* **CRIES FROM THE MIDNIGHT CIRCUS** (1968-1971) ☐ ☐

Nov 88. (cd) *Radioactive; (HORN 004)* **THE PRETTY THINGS** ☐ ☐

Aug 91. (cd) *Repertoire; (REP 4089WZ)* **MORE ELECTRIC BANANA** ☐ ☐

Apr 92. (cd) *Band Of Joy; (BOJCD 3)* **ON AIR** ☐ ☐

Oct 95. (d-cd) *Fragile; (FRA 005D)* **UNREPENTANT – BLOODY BUT UNBOWED** ☐ ☐ *(re-iss. Mar98 on 'Snapper'; SSDCD 002)*

Jun 97. (cd) *See For Miles; (SEECD 476)* **THE EP COLLECTION** ☐ ☐

May 01. (cd) *Snapper; (<SMMCD 625>)* **LATEST WRITS GREATEST HITS** ☐ ☐

Jul 01. (d-cd) *Snapper; (<SMDCD 343>)* **THE RHYTHM & BLUES YEARS** ☐ ☐

Oct 01. (d-cd) *Snapper; (<SMDCD 344>)* **THE PSYCHEDELIC YEARS 1966-1970** ☐ ☐

Mar 02. (d-cd) *Snapper; (<SMDCD 390>)* **CROSSTALK / FREEWAY MADNESS** ☐ ☐

Sep 02. (t-cd) *Repertoire; (<REP 4937>)* **SINGLES A's & B's** ☐ ☐

Nov 02. (10"m-lp) *Norton; (TED 1001)* **DEFECTING GREY** ☐ ☐

Apr 03. (d-cd) *Snapper; (<SMDCD 415>)* **S.F. SORROW / RESURRECTION** ☐ ☐

Jun 03. (cd) *Repertoire; (<REP 4990>)* **THE VERY BEST OF THE PRETTY THINGS** ☐ ☐

Aug 03. (d-cd) *Repertoire; (<REP 4938>)* **THE BBC SESSIONS** ☐ ☐

PRIMAL SCREAM

Formed: Glasgow, Scotland . . . summer 1984 by JESUS & MARY CHAIN drummer BOBBY GILLESPIE. Signing to JAMC's label, 'Creation', in 1985, they cut two singles, GILLESPIE leaving The 'MARY CHAIN after the debut, 'ALL FALL DOWN' (1985). The first album, 'SONIC FLOWER GROOVE' (1987), was recorded by the current band line-up core of ANDREW INNES, ROBERT 'THROB' YOUNG and MARTIN DUFFY (save MANI, ex-STONE ROSES, who joined up in 1996) along with an ever-changing array of additional musicians. Released on 'Creation' boss ALAN McGEE's 'WEA' subsidiary label, 'Elevation', the album saw the band pretty much live up to their name, a primitive take on raw ROLLING STONES, STOOGES etc. with a bit of BYRDS jingle jangle thrown in. This sound served the band well through their second album, PRIMAL SCREAM (1989) until the release of 'LOADED' in early 1990. Back at 'Creation' and enamoured with the Acid House explosion, the band had enlisted the esteemed ANDREW WEATHERALL to remix 'I'M LOSING MORE THAN I'LL EVER HAVE' from the second lp. More a revolution than a remix, WEATHERALL created the stoned funk shuffle of 'LOADED', in the process bringing indie and rave kids together on the same dancefloor for the first time. PRIMAL SCREAM were now set on pushing the parameters of rock, releasing a trio of singles that defined an era, 'COME TOGETHER' (1990) was 90's style hedonist gospel that converted even the most cynical of rock bores while 'HIGHER THAN THE SUN' (1991) was perhaps the 'SCREAM's stellar moment, a narcotic lullaby beamed from another galaxy. Combining all the aforementioned tracks with a trippy 13TH FLOOR ELEVATORS cover, a heavyweight dub workout and a clutch of STONES-like beauties, 'SCREAMADELICA' (1991) was flawless. Opening with the euphoric 'MOVIN' ON UP' (the best song the 'STONES never wrote), the album effortlessly proved that dance and rock were essentially carved out of the same soulful root source, a seam that's been mined by any artist that's ever mattered. A landmark album, 'SCREAMADELICA' was awarded the Mercury Music prize in 1992 and for sheer breadth of vision the record has yet to meet its match. Inevitably, then, the GEORGE DRAKOULIAS-produced follow-up, 'GIVE OUT BUT DON'T GIVE UP' (1994) was a disappointment in comparison. Recorded in MEMPHIS, the record saw PRIMAL SCREAM trying far too hard to achieve a roughshod R&B grit. Where before they had made The STONES' sound their own, now they came across as mere plagiarists, and over-produced plagiarists at that. Granted, the likes of 'JAILBIRD' and 'ROCKS' were funkier than any of the insipid indie competition around at the time and GILLESPIE's epileptic handclap routine was always more endearing than the run-of-the-mill rock posturing. Rumours of severe drug abuse abounded at this point and few were shocked when, in January 1994, it emerged that DUFFY had survived a near fatal stabbing in America. For the next couple of years, the band kept a fairly low profile, only a contribution to the 'Trainspotting' soundtrack and an unofficial Scottish 'Euro '96' single confirmed the 'SCREAM were still in existence. But while Scotland stumbled to defeat (again!!), PRIMAL SCREAM cleaned up their act and recorded the wonderful 'VANISHING POINT' (1997). Apparently cut as an alternative soundtrack to cult 70's road movie 'Kowalski', this album was the true follow-up/comedown to the psychedelic high of 'SCREAMADELICA'. 'OUT OF THE VOID' was the band's darkest moment to date while the title track and 'STUKA' were fractured, paranoid psych-outs. Only the vintage screenshow of

'GET DUFFY' and the mellow 'STAR' offered any respite. Big on dub and low on derivation, the album was a spirited return to form for one of Scotland's most enduring and groundbreaking bands. The year of 2000 saw the 'SCREAM return with all guns blazing for the destructive release of 'EXTERMINATOR'. An aptly titled album, this was worrying music for the post Millennium tensions of anti-capitalist marches and technology protests. It shaped its own poisonous force as the listener ventured further into the set: 'KILL ALL HIPPIES' was certainly a phrase derived from the punk movement, while 'SWASTIKA EYES' had a morbid, self-asserting ring to it. GILLESPIE mixed in exuberant styles such as hip-hop ('PILLS'), trance ('ACCELERATOR') and a bit of old MY BLOODY VALENTINE tones into the devilish bru. One could only describe 'EXTERMINATOR' as a very squealing, scary disjointed affair, sort of like the soundtrack to a Jean Luc Godard horror pic, if he, er, did a horror that is. All in all, PRIMAL SCREAM were wise to return to wigged-out psychedelia – a style they were criticised for getting out of – with the self-indulgent 'VANISHING POINT'. 'EXTERMINATOR' is a valuable lesson in the art of punk: it's loud, it has balls, it's offensive, it's not all tuneful, and most importantly, it makes sense. This method was also applied to The 'SCREAM's seventh album proper, 'EVIL HEAT' (2002) which delved even deeper into GILLESPIE's obsession with dark, throbbing soundscapes. Possibly the musical equivalent to being repeatedly run over by a tank and then turned into a metal blob, the set curiously explored the avant-metal punk scene a little bit closer, with single 'MISS LUCIFER' spitting and bubbling like an unsteady jar of boiling acid. Basslines thrashed (especially on 'SKULL X'), keyboards sounding like they were being set on fire and GILLESPIE pumped up his frontman image by turning a piece of deadpan vocal into a plethora of screams. Apart from the SUICIDE connections, and the screeching, industrial electro-clash of it all, 'EVIL HEAT' (complete with sinister homemade, cut'n'paste album jacket) included some cringe-worthy moments: the lazy, drugged-up slur of nu-blues number 'THE LORD IS MY SHOTGUN', supermodel KATE MOSS' dreary rendition of the Lee Hazlewood song 'SOME VELVET MORNING' and the re-working of 'RISE' (originally entitled 'BOMB THE PENTAGON', but shamelessly re-titled for fears of American distribution). Former MY BLOODY VALENTINE casualty KEVIN SHIELDS took on the recording duty, doing his damndest to make it sound as dirty and as translucent as possible. PRIMAL SCREAM exist to be one of the globe's truest punk-rawk bands – a rare thing in these money spinning, 3-chord, pop-producing times. Like the BBC, they educate, entertain and inform . . . they also make one hell'uva racket too. • **Songwriters:** GILLESPIE, YOUNG and BEATTIE, until the latter's replacement by INNES. Covered CARRY ME HOME (Dennis Wilson) / UNDERSTANDING (Small Faces) / 96 TEARS (? & The Mysterians) / KNOW YOUR RIGHTS (Clash) / MOTORHEAD (Motorhead).

Album rating: SONIC FLOWER GROOVE (*5) / PRIMAL SCREAM (*6) / SCREAMADELICA (*10) / GIVE OUT BUT DON'T GIVE UP (*7) / VANISHING POINT (*8) / ECHO DEK (*6) / EXTERMINATOR (*8) / EVIL HEAT (*6) / DIRTY HITS compilation (*9)

BOBBY GILLESPIE (b.22 Jun'64) – vocals (ex-WAKE, also drummer of JESUS & MARY CHAIN) / **JIM BEATTIE** – guitar / **ROBERT YOUNG** – bass / **TOM McGURK** – drums / **MARTIN ST. JOHN** – tambourine

Creation | not iss.

May 85. (7") *(CRE 017)* **ALL FALL DOWN. / IT HAPPENS** [ ] [–]

— added **PAUL HARTE** – rhythm guitar (GILLESPIE left JESUS & MARY)

Apr 86. (7") *(CRE 026)* **CRYSTAL CRESCENT. / VELOCITY GIRL** [ ] [–]
(12"+=) *(CRE 026T)* – Spirea X.

— **STUART MAY** – rhythm guitar (ex-SUBMARINES) repl. HARTE (Dec'86) / **ANDREW INNES** – rhythm guitar (of REVOLVING PAINT DREAM) repl. MAY / Guest drummers **PHIL KING** (studio) + **DAVE MORGAN** (tour) repl. McGURK

Elevation | not iss.

Jun 87. (7") *(ACID 5)* **GENTLE TUESDAY. / BLACK STAR CARNIVAL** [ ] [–]
(12"+=) *(ACID 5T)* – I'm gonna make you mine.

Sep 87. (7") *(ACID 5)* **IMPERIAL. / STAR FRUIT SURF RIDER** [ ] [–]
(12"+=/s12"+=) *(ACID 5T/+W)* – So sad about us / Imperial (demo).

Oct 87. (lp/c)(cd) *(ELV 2/+C)(242-182-2)* **SONIC FLOWER GROOVE** [62] [ ]
– Gentle Tuesday / Treasure trip / May the sun shine bright for you / Sonic sister love / Silent spring / Imperial / Love you / Leaves / Aftermath / We go down slowly. *(re-iss. Jul91; same)*

— (Jun'87) **GAVIN SKINNER** – drums; repl. ST. JOHN

— (Feb'88) Now a trio **GILLESPIE, YOUNG + INNES** augmented by **JIM NAVAJO** – guitar (BEATTIE formed SPIREA X; SKINNER also left)

— (Feb'89) added **HENRY OLSEN** – bass (ex-NICO) / **PHILIP 'TOBY' TOMANOV** – drums (ex-NICO, ex-DURUTTI COLUMN, ex-BLUE ORCHIDS)

Creation | Mercenary

Jul 89. (7") *(CRE 067)* **IVY IVY IVY. / YOU'RE JUST TOO DARK TO CARE** [ ] [–]
(12"+=)(cd-s+=) *(CRE 067T)(CRESCD 067)* – I got you split wide open over me.

Sep 89. (lp/c/cd) *(CRE LP/C/CD 054)* *<2100>* **PRIMAL SCREAM** [ ] [ ]
– Ivy Ivy Ivy / You're just dead skin to me / She power / You're just too dark to care / I'm losing more than I'll ever have / Gimme gimme teenage head / Lone star girl / Kill the king / Sweet pretty thing / Jesus can't save me. *(free 7"ltd.)* – SPLIT WIDE OPEN (demo). / LONE STAR GIRL (demo) *(cd re-iss. Jan01; same)*

— trimmed to a trio again (**GILLESPIE, YOUNG + INNES**)

Creation | Sire

Feb 90. (7") *(CRE 070)* **LOADED. / I'M LOSING MORE THAN I'LL EVER HAVE** [16] [–]
(ext.12"+=/'A'Terry Farley remix-12"+=)(ext.cd-s+=) *(CRE 070 T/X)(CRESCD 070)* – Ramblin' Rose (live).

Jul 90. (7"/c-s)(ext.12")(ext.cd-s) *(CRE/+CS 078)(CRE 078T(CRESCD 078)* *<26384>* **COME TOGETHER (Terry Farley mix). / COME TOGETHER (Andrew Weatherall mix)** [26] Aug90 [ ]
(12") *(CRE 078X)* – ('A'-HypnotoneBrainMachine mix) / ('A'-BBG mix).

Jun 91. (7"/ext.12") *(CRE 096/+T)* **HIGHER THAN THE SUN. / ('A' American Spring mix)** [40] [–]
(cd-s+=) *(CRESCD 096)* – Higher than the Orb.

— guest spot on above from **JAH WOBBLE** – bass

Aug 91. (7"/ext.12")(c-s) *(CRE 110/+T)(CRECS 110)* **DON'T FIGHT IT, FEEL IT. / ('A'scat mix featuring Denise Johnson)** [41] [–]
(cd-s+=) *(CRESCD 110)* – ('A'extended version).

Sep 91. (cd/c/d-lp) *(CRE CD/C/LP 076)* *<26714>* **SCREAMADELICA** [8] [ ]
– Movin' on up / Slip inside this house / Don't fight it, feel it / Higher than the Sun / Inner flight / Come together / Loaded / Damaged / I'm comin' down / Higher than the Sun (a dub symphony in two parts) / Shine like stars. *(cd re-iss. Jan01; same) (lp-iss.Jun01 on 'Simply Vinyl'; SVLP 344)*

Jan 92. (7"ep/c-ep) *(CRE/+CS 117)* *<40193>* **DIXIE-NARCO EP** [11] [ ]
– Movin' on up / Carry me home / Screamadelica.
(12"ep+=)(cd-ep+=) *(CRE 117T)(CRESCD 117)* – Stone my soul.

— In Jan'94, MARTIN DUFFY was stabbed in Memphis, although he recovered soon after.

— Line-up:- **GILLESPIE, YOUNG, INNES, DUFFY + DAVID HOOD + DENISE JOHNSON** + guest **GEORGE CLINTON** – vocals

Mar 94. (7"/c-s) *(CRE/+CS 129)* *<18189>* **ROCKS. / FUNKY JAM** [7] Apr94 [ ]
(12")(cd-s) *(CRE 129T)(CRESCD 129)* – ('A'side) / Funky jam (hot ass mix) / Funky jam (club mix).

Apr 94. (cd/c/lp) *(CRE CD/C/LP 146)* *<45538>* **GIVE OUT, BUT DON'T GIVE UP** 2 ☐
– Jailbird / Rocks / (I'm gonna) Cry myself blind / Funky jam / Big jet plane / Free / Call on me / Struttin' / Sad and blue / Give out but don't give up / I'll be there for you. *(cd re-iss. Feb00 & Jan01; same)*

Jun 94. (7"/c-s) *(CRE/+CS 145)* **JAILBIRD. / ('A'-Dust Brothers mix)** 29 –
(12"+=) *(CRE 145T)* – ('A'-Toxic Trio stay free mix) / ('A'-Weatherall dub chapter 3 mix).
(cd-s++=) *(CRESCD 145)* – ('A'-Sweeney 2 mix).

Nov 94. (7"/c-s) *(CRE/+CS 183)* **(I'M GONNA) CRY MYSELF BLIND (George Drakoulias mix). / ROCKS (live)** 51 –
(cd-s+=) *(CRESCD 183)* – I'm losing more than I'll ever have (live) / Struttin' (back in our minds) (Brendan Lynch remix).
(10") *(CRE 183X)* – ('A'side) / Struttin' (back in our minds) (Brendan Lynch remix) / Give out, but don't give up (Portishead remix) / Rockers dub (Kris Needs mix).

Jun 96. (c-s/cd-s; PRIMAL SCREAM, IRVINE WELSH AND ON-U SOUND PRESENT . . .) *(CRECS-CRESCD 194)* **THE BIG MAN AND THE SCREAM TEAM MEET THE BARMY ARMY UPTOWN (mixes:- full strength fortified dub / electric soup dub / a jake supreme)** 17 –

—— In Oct'96, GILLESPIE, INNES, YOUNG & DUFFY were joined by **MANI MOUNFIELD** – bass (ex-STONE ROSES)

Creation Reprise

May 97. (c-s) *(<CRECS 245>)* **KOWALSKI / 96 TEARS** 8 ☐
(cd-s+=) *(<CRESCD 245>)* – Know your rights / ('A'-Automator mix).

Jun 97. (c-s) *CRECS 263)* **STAR / JESUS** 16 –
(cd-s+=) *(CRESCD 263)* – Rebel dub / How does it feel to belong.
(12"+=) *(CRE 263T)* – ('A'mixes).

Jul 97. (cd/d-lp)(c) *(CRE CD/LP 178)(CCRE 178)* *<46559>* **VANISHING POINT** 2 ☐
– Burning wheel / Get Duffy / Kowalski / Star / If they move, kill 'em / Out of the void / Stuka / Medication / Motorhead / Trainspotting / Long life. *(cd re-iss. Jan01; same)*

Oct 97. (7") *(CRE 272)* **BURNING WHEEL. / HAMMOND CONNECTION** 17 –
(12"+=)(cd-s+=) *(CRE 272T)(CRESCD 272)* – ('A'-Chemical Brothers remix) / Higher than the sun (original).

Oct 97. (cd/7"box) *(CRE CD/L7 224)* **ECHO DEK** (remixes) 43 –
– Duffed up / Revolutionary / Ju-87 / First name unknown / Vanishing dub / Last train / Wise blood / Dub in vain. *(cd re-iss. Feb00 & Jan01; same)*

Feb 98. (7") *(CRE 284)* **IF THEY MOVE, KILL 'EM. / BADLANDS** ☐ –
(12"+=)(cd-s+=) *(CRE 284T)(CRESCD 284)* – ('A'-My Bloody Valentine Arkestra mix) / ('A'-Darklands 12"disco mix).

—— added on 1998 tour **JIM HUNT** – saxophone / **DUNCAN MACKAY** – trumpet / **DARREN MOONEY** – drums

Creation Astralwerks

Nov 99. (c-s) *(CRECS 326)* **SWASTIKA EYES / ('A'mix)** 22 –
(12"/cd-s) *(CRE 326T)(CRESCD 326)* – ('A'-Chemical Brothers mix) / ('A'-Spectre mix) / ('A'side).

Jan 00. (cd/md/c/d-lp) *(CRECD/CREMD/CCRE/CRELP 239)* *<49260>* **EXTERMINATOR** 3 May00 ☐
– Kill all hippies / Accelerator / Exterminator / Swastika eyes / Pills / Blood money / Keep your dreams / Insect royalty / MBV Arkestra (if they move kill 'em) / Swastika eyes / Shoot speed – Kill light / I'm 5 years ahead of my time. *(cd re-iss. Jan01; same)*

Mar 00. (7") *(CRE 332)* *<8169>* **KILL ALL HIPPIES. / EXTERMINATOR (Massive Attack remix)** 24 Nov00 ☐
(cd-s+=) *(CRESCD 332)* – The revenge of the Hammond connection.
(12"+=) *(CRE 332T)* – ('A'mixes).

Sep 00. (12")(cd-s) *(CRE 333T)(CRESCD 333)* **ACCELERATOR / I'M 5 YEARS AHEAD OF MY TIME / WHEN THE KINGDOM COMES** 34 –

Columbia Astralwerks

Jul 02. (12"/cd-s) *(672825-6/-2)* **MISS LUCIFER / (mixes: panther / hip to hip / bone to bone)** 23 –

Aug 02. (cd/lp) *(508923-2/-1)* *<87027>* **EVIL HEAT** 9 ☐
– Deep hit of morning sun / Miss Lucifer / Autobahn 66 / Detroit / Rise / The Lord is my shotgun / City / Some velvet morning / Skull X / A scanner darkly / Space blues number 2.

Oct 02. (cd-s) *(673312-2)* **AUTOBAHN 66 / AUTOBAHN 66 (alter ego remix) / SUBSTANCE D** 44 –
(12") *(673312-6)* – (first & third tracks + alter ego instr).
(cd-s) *(673312-5)* – ('A'side) / ('A'live) / Shoot speed kill light.

Nov 03. (cd/lp) *(513603-2/-1)* *<594300>* **DIRTY HITS** (compilation) 25 Dec03 ☐
– Loaded / Movin' on up / Come together / Higher than the sun (Orb remix) / Rocks / Jailbird / I'm gonna cry myself blind / Burning wheel / Kowalski / Long life / Swastika eyes / Kill all hippes / Accelerator / Shoot speed – Kill light / Miss Lucifer / Deep hit of morning sun / Some velvet morning (with KATE MOSS) / Autobahn 66. *(ltd d-cd+=; 5136039)* – (remixes of all tracks).

Nov 03. (12"; by PRIMAL SCREAM & KATE MOSS) *(674402-6)* **SOME VELVET MORNING. / COUNTRY BLUES 1 / ('A'-disco hater dub)** 44 –
(cd-s+=) *(674402-2)* – ('A'-video).

– others, etc. –

Nov 97. (12") *Creation; (PSTLS 1)* **STUKA (Two Lone Swordsmen mixes)** ☐ –

PRINCE

Born: PRINCE ROGERS NELSON, 7 Jun'58, Minneapolis, Minnesota, USA. Named after his father JOHN's jazz band, The PRINCE ROGER TRIO (which featured his mother Mattie on vocals), one of the young PRINCE's earliest musical experiences was witnessing JAMES BROWN in concert at the age of ten, a performer whose approach to music would heavily influence PRINCE's future career. By the time (1972) he was invited to play in his cousin CHARLES SMITH'S high school band, GRAND CENTRAL, alongside ANDRE ANDERSON (by whose family PRINCE had been adopted), the musical prodigy had already mastered guitar and piano, in addition to writing his own material. The following year, the band evolved into CHAMPAGNE as PRINCE became the leader following the replacement of SMITH by MORRIS DAY. Being in control was something PRINCE would make central to his steep career trajectory as he grew older, although he was wise enough to learn the ropes first. His initial studio experience came when he played session guitar for Sound 80 Studios' PEPE WILLIE, subsequently cutting a demo with the help of CHRIS MOON who guided him in the ways of recording. MOON also introduced him to OWEN HUSNEY whose hustling skills eventually secured PRINCE a groundbreaking solo deal with 'Warners' in 1978, allowing him complete control over every step of the creative process. His debut effort, 'FOR YOU' was released in October, a fairly conventional collection of slinky soul that spawned an American R&B hit in 'SOFT AND WET', the lewdness of the lyrics fairly tame in light of what was to come. While PRINCE played all the instruments and produced the record himself, for the eponymous 'PRINCE' (1980), the diminutive one brought in a cast of musicians for a more rock-based approach, namely guitarist DEZ DICKERSON, keyboardist GAYLE CHAPMAN, bassist ANDRE CYMONE (the same ANDRE of PRINCE's childhood who had by now changed his name), drummer BOBBY Z and MATT FINK on more keyboards. The result was a US Top 20 single with the playful funk-pop of 'I WANNA BE YOUR LOVER', a song addressed to singer Patrice Rushen. Following the album's relative success, PRINCE took his new band out on the road for the first time, meeting with consistently positive reviews. CHAPMAN was soon ousted in favour of LISA COLEMAN as the band previewed songs from the new album, 'DIRTY MIND' (1980), the first PRINCE release in which he gave free reign to his frequently sexually explicit lyrical muse. 'HEAD' was self-explanatory while 'SISTER' rather dodgily put forward the case for incest, the music moving ever further from the R&B of the debut and flirting with synth-heavy new wave.

The album's lyrical frankness precluded any mainstream coverage although The ROLLING STONES were impressed enough to invite PRINCE to support them the following year. In the event, the shows were calamitous, The 'STONES infamously partisan crowd not taking too kindly to PRINCE's soulful androgyny. November of the same year saw the release of 'CONTROVERSY', an aptly titled album which divided the critics. While PRINCE once again dabbled with different styles and explored human desire on the likes of 'JACK U OFF', the record lacked the melodic immediacy of its predecessor. On a more positive note, PRINCE embarked on his most successful tour to date, building up a grassroots fanbase that would help make '1999' (1983) the biggest album of his career thus far. By the time of the record's release, PRINCE's backing band had evolved in to The REVOLUTION with a couple of personnel changes along the way; the questionably named BROWN MARK replaced ANDRE who had departed for a solo career while WENDY MELVOIN was recruited in place of DICKERSON. '1999's synth- throb of a title track gave PRINCE his first real UK success while the infectiously commercial 'LITTLE RED CORVETTE' (his first Top 10 hit, boosted by heavy MTV rotation) proved PRINCE could write top pop material to rival any stars of the day. While the album's best moments could've probably been squeezed onto a single record, there was a marked maturity in the songwriting which reached fruition with 'PURPLE RAIN' (1984), arguably the most fully realised record of PRINCE's career. The album was actually the soundtrack to the near-autobiographical film of the same name, the first single to be lifted from it, 'WHEN DOVES CRY', giving PRINCE his first No.1 in May '84. This poignant portrayal of family strife also gave PRINCE his biggest UK hit to date, reaching No.4 later that summer. Other highlights of the album included the epic title track and the loose-limbed soul-rock of 'LET'S GO CRAZY', the latter complete with a searing HENDRIX-style guitar climax. The purple-clad genius' career subsequently went stratospheric, a Purple Rain tour breaking box office records with sales of the album running into the millions worldwide. As well as furnishing CHAKA KHAN with her first hit in years ('I FEEL FOR YOU), PRINCE also wrote the controversial 'Sugar Walls' for Scottish-born SHEENA EASTON, a US Top 10 hit which further incensed the moral minority. Never the most communicative of stars, the mystique surrounding PRINCE grew deeper with the release of 'AROUND THE WORLD IN A DAY' (1985), a largely esoteric collection of psychedelic pop interspersed with the melodic brilliance of 'RASPBERRY BERET', possibly the finest song PRINCE has yet penned. This was also the album upon which PRINCE began attempting to reconcile the carnal with the spiritual, a preoccupation which would dominate his music in the years to come. 'AROUND THE WORLD . . .' was released on PRINCE's newly formed, Minneapolis-based record company (and lavish recording complex), 'Paisley Park', also home to friends like The FAMILY, SHEILA E. (who had also become part of PRINCE's touring band), GEORGE CLINTON etc. Concentrating on his new baby, PRINCE announced, BEATLES-style, that he was retiring from live work, only to later backtrack on his decision and undertake a tour in support of the 'PARADE' (1986) album. Another soundtrack, this time for PRINCE's derided 'Under The Cherry Moon', the music stood apart from the movie, taking the blueprint of its predecessor as a starting point and embroidering it with pop nous (notably on the sensuous 'GIRLS AND BOYS'). The record also provided PRINCE with his third No.1 single in the shape of 'KISS', a supple, teasing funk workout later famously covered by TOM JONES. At the end of the tour, PRINCE disbanded The REVOLUTION, going solo for the next few albums while recruiting a new band for live work. 'SIGN O' THE TIMES' (1987) was PRINCE's most thorough exploration of sex and religion, a satisfyingly diverse double set that marked the maturation of everything the artist had been working toward up to that point. While the gloriously dirty funk of the title track incorporated a comment on the degradation of the social fabric, the muted musical foreplay of 'IF I WAS YOUR GIRLFRIEND', and indeed the vast majority of tracks found PRINCE back on familiar lyrical territory. 'The BLACK ALBUM' concentrated almost solely on the mechanics of sex via some visceral uncut funk yet allegedly, PRINCE considered the album was 'immoral' (!) and recalled it from 'Warners' German pressing plant at the last minute. Officially released late in 1994, the album remained a favourite talking point for years among PRINCE obsessives and casual observers alike, bootleggers no doubt making a fortune. Presumably his white album, then, 'LOVESEXY' (1988) was the flipside to its predecessor's libidinous funk, the insistent pop of the title track a UK No.1. Though the album sold relatively poorly in the States, PRINCE's commercial fortunes were revived with the 'BATMAN' soundtrack, a multi-million seller which topped the charts on both sides of the Atlantic. If not exactly the most profound of his albums, it was certainly more listenable than the weak 'MUSIC FROM GRAFFITI BRIDGE' (1990). Thankfully, PRINCE seems to have let up on his film aspirations in recent years, though his musical output doesn't seem to have benefited that much. Nevertheless, the 90's started on a high note with the massive 'DIAMONDS AND PEARLS' (1991) album, credited to PRINCE & THE NEW POWER GENERATION. This band had already backed PRINCE on the 'GRAFFITI BRIDGE' project, this time around their playing injecting a more spontaneous live feel to proceedings. The sexy strut of 'CREAM' and the more intense funk lewdness of 'GET OFF' dominated the set (a remixed import single of the former hit the UK Top 40!), while 'MONEY DON'T MATTER 2 NIGHT' was deeply affecting, soul baring stuff. Following the release of the '(SYMBOL)' (1992) album – a patchy collection partly redeemed by the jazzy leer of 'SEXY M.F.' – PRINCE bizzarely announced he was changing his name to 'symbol' (I can't get that damn sign on my computer!), followed by yet more rumours that he wished to be known as VICTOR, then finally T.A.F.K.A.P. (The Artist Formerly Known As PRINCE). More controversy followed with revelations that PRINCE wanted out of his contract with 'Warners', unhappy that he was restricted to one album a year. In protest, he took to wearing a mask onstage and painting the word 'Slave' on his face, subsequently releasing the lush charm of 'THE MOST BEAUTIFUL GIRL IN THE WORLD' on independent labels worldwide. Fulfilling his contract, T.A.F.K.A.P. released a further couple of largely uninspired albums, 'THE GOLD EXPERIENCE' (1995) and 'CHAOS AND DISORDER' (1996), before disbanding the N.P.G. and retreating into silence. Now regarded as something of a joke by the music press, it remains to be seen whether this eminently capable genius can regain the giddy heights of his early 80's domination. His last ("THE ARTIST") set, 'RAVE UN2 THE JOY FANTASTIC', did little to regain his diminishing audience (he covered Sheryl Crow's(!) 'EVERYDAY IS A WINDING ROAD'; sexfunk is dead.
• **Songwriters:** A prolific pensmith, he also wrote songs under pseudonyms CAMILLE, JAMIE STARR, CHRISTOPHER, etc., and has written hits especially for SHEENA EASTON (Sugar Walls) and BANGLES (Manic Monday). Note: WENDY AND LISA wrote 'MOUNTAINS' before departing for own duo. In 1996, he covered; BETCHA BY GOLLY WOW! (Stylistics) / I CAN'T MAKE YOU LOVE ME (Bonnie Raitt) / LA LA MEANS I LOVE YOU (Delfonics) / ONE OF US (hit; Joan Osborne). • **Trivia:** In 1988, his sister TYKA NELSON signed for 'Chrysalis', although her album failed to take off.

Album rating: FOR YOU (*5) / PRINCE (*6) / DIRTY MIND (*7) / CONTROVERSY (*6) / 1999 (*8) / PURPLE RAIN (*8) / AROUND THE WORLD IN A DAY (*6) / PARADE (*7) / SIGN 'O' THE TIMES (*9) / LOVESEXY (*8) / BATMAN (*6) / GRAFITTI BRIDGE (*8) / DIAMONDS AND PEARLS (*8) / SYMBOL (UNTITLED) (*8) / THE HITS 1 compilation (*9) / THE HITS 2 compilation (*9) / EXODUS (*5; as New Power Generation) / THE BEAUTIFUL EXPERIENCE mini (*5) / COME (*4) / THE GOLD EXPERIENCE (*6) / CHAOS AND DISORDER (*5) / EMANCIPATION (*4) / NEW POWER SOUL (*5; as New Power Generation) / CRYSTAL BALL boxed-set (*5) / THE VAULT – OLD FRIENDS 4 SALE collection (*4) / RAVE UN2 THE JOY FANTASTIC (*5) / THE VERY BEST OF . . . compilation (*8)

PRINCE – vocals, multi-instrumentalist, synthesizers, producer, everything

Warners Warners

Oct 78. (lp,c) *<3150>* **FOR YOU** [-] [ ]
– For you / In love / Soft and wet / Crazy you / Just as long as we're together / Baby / My love is forever / So blue / I'm yours. *(UK-iss.Sep86 lp/c; K/K4 56989) (cd-iss. Oct87; K2 56989)*

Nov 78. (7") *<8619>* **SOFT AND WET. / SO BLUE** [-] [92]

Jan 79. (7") *<8713>* **JUST AS LONG AS WE'RE TOGETHER. / IN LOVE** [-] [ ]

—— **PRINCE** – vocals, guitar live back-ups **DEZ DICKERSON** – guitar / **GAYLE CHAPMAN** – keyboards / **ANDRE CYMONE** – bass / **MATT FINK** – keyboards / **BOBBY Z** – drums

Nov 79. (7") *<49050>* **I WANNA BE YOUR LOVER. / MY LOVE IS FOREVER** [-] [11]

Dec 79. (7") *(K 17537)* **I WANNA BE YOUR LOVER. / JUST AS LONG AS WE'RE TOGETHER** [41] [-]

Jan 80. (lp/c) *(K/K4 56772) <3366>* **PRINCE** [ ] Oct79 [22]
– I wanna be your lover / Why you wanna treat me so bad? / Sexy dancer / When we're dancing close and slow / With you / Bambi / Still waiting / I feel for you / It's gonna be lonely. *(cd-iss. 1986; K2 56772)*

Feb 80. (7") *<49178>* **WHY YOU WANNA TREAT ME SO BAD?. / BAD** [-] [ ]

—— (Feb80) live **LISA COLEMAN** – keyboards repl. GAYLE

Apr 80. (7"/12") *(K 17590/+T)* **SEXY DANCER. / BAMBI** [ ] [-]

May 80. (7") *<49226>* **STILL WAITING. / BAMBI** [-] [ ]

Sep 80. (7") *<49559>* **UPTOWN. / CRAZY YOU** [-] [ ]

Oct 80. (lp/c) *(K/K4 56862) <3478>* **DIRTY MIND** [ ] [45]
– Dirty mind / When you were mine / Do it all night / Gotta broken heart again / Uptown / Head / Sister / Party up. *((re-iss. 1989) (cd-iss. Dec85; K2 56862)*

Nov 80. (7") *<49638>* **DIRTY MIND. / WHEN WE'RE DANCING CLOSE AND SLOW** [-] [ ]

Mar 81. (7"/12") *(K 17768/+T)* **DO IT ALL NIGHT. / HEAD** [ ] [-]

Jun 81. (7") *(K 17819)* **GOTTA STOP (MESSIN' ABOUT). / UPTOWN (live)** [ ] [-]
(12"+=) *(K 17819T)* – Head (live).
(12") *(K 17819TX)* – ('A'side) / I wanna be your lover (live).

—— (mid'81) live **BROWN MARK** – bass repl. ANDRE who ventured solo

Oct 81. (7"/12") *(K 17866/+T) <49808>* **CONTROVERSY. / WHEN YOU WERE MINE** [ ] [70]

Nov 81. (lp/c) *(K/K4 56950) <3601>* **CONTROVERSY** [ ] [21]
– Controversy / Sexuality / Do me, baby / Private joy / Ronnie talk to Russia / Let's work / Annie Christian / Jack u off. *(cd-iss. 1984; K2 56950)*

Apr 82. (7"/12") *(K 17922/+T) <50002>* **LET'S WORK. / RONNIE TALK TO RUSSIA** [ ] [ ]
(12") *<50028>* – ('A'side) / Gotta stop.

Jun 82. (7") *<29942>* **DO ME, BABY. / PRIVATE JOY** [-] [ ]

PRINCE & THE REVOLUTION

—— live **WENDY MELVOIN** – guitar repl. DEE

Jan 83. (7") *(W 9896) <29896>* **1999. / HOW COME U DON'T CALL ME ANYMORE** [25] Oct82 [44]
(free c-s w/7") *(W 9896C)* – 1999 / Controversy / Dirty mind / Sexuality.
(12"+=) *(W 9896T)* – D.M.S.R. *<US re-dist.Jun83 hit No.12>*

Feb 83. (lp/c) *(W 3809/+C) <23720>* **1999** [ ] [26]
– 1999 / Little red Corvette / Delirious / Let's pretend we're married / D.M.S.R. * / Delirious / Automatic / Something in the water / Free / Lady cab driver / All the critics love u in New York / International lover. *(re-iss. Nov83 as d-lp/d-c; 923720-1/-4)* – hit UK No.30. *(cd-iss. Sep84; 923720-2)* – (omits *)

Feb 83. (7") *<29746>* **LITTLE RED CORVETTE. / ALL THE CRITICS LOVE U IN NEW YORK** [-] [6]

Apr 83. (7") *<29548>* **LET'S PRETEND WE'RE MARRIED. / IRRESISTIBLE BITCH** [-] [52]

Apr 83. (7") *(W 9688)* **LITTLE RED CORVETTE. / LADY CAB DRIVER** [54] [-]
(12") – ('A'extended) / Automatic lover / International lover.

Sep 83. (7") *<29503>* **DELIRIUS. / HORNY TOAD** [-] [8]

Nov 83. (7") *(W 9436)* **LITTLE RED CORVETTE. / HORNY TOAD** [66] [-]
(ext.12"+=) *(W 9436)* – D.M.S.R.

Jun 84. (7"/12") *(W 9296/+T) <29286>* **WHEN DOVES CRY. / 17 DAYS** [4] May84 [1]
(d12"+=/c-s+=) *(W 9296 T/C)* – 1999 / D.M.S.R.

Jul 84. (lp,purple-lp/c/cd) *(925110-1/-4/-2) <25110>* **PURPLE RAIN** (Music From The Motion Picture) [7] [1]
– Let's go crazy / Take me with u / The beautiful ones / Computer blue / Darling Nikki / When doves cry / I would die 4 U / Baby I'm a star / Purple rain. *<US-iss.as d-lp, w/ += tracks by The TIME + APOLLONIA 6> (re-iss. Jan92 hit UK No.59) (re-iss. cd/c Feb95) (lp re-iss. Jun99; ame)*

Jul 84. (7") *<29216>* **LET'S GO CRAZY. / EROTIC CITY** [-] [1]

Sep 84. (7"/7"sha-pic-d) *(W 9174/+P) <29174>* **PURPLE RAIN. / GOD** [8] [2]
(12") *(W 9174T)* – ('A'side) / ('A'vocal + instrumental).

Nov 84. (7") *(W 9121) <29121>* **I WOULD DIE 4 U. / ANOTHER LONELY CHRISTMAS** [58] [8]
(12"+=) *(W 9121T)* – Free.
(12") *(W 9121TE)* – ('A'&'B' US remixes).

Jan 85. (7"/12") *(K 1999/+T)* **1999. / LITTLE RED CORVETTE** [2] [-]
(free c-s w/7"+=) *(W 1999C)* – 1999 / Uptown / Controversy / D.M.S.R. / Sexy dancer.

Feb 85. (7") *(K 2000)* **LET'S GO CRAZY. / TAKE ME WITH U** [7] [-]
(ext.12"+=) *(K 2000T)* – Erotic city.

Feb 85. (7") *<29079>* **TAKE ME WITH U. / BABY I'M A STAR** [-] [25]

—— added live **SHEILA E.** (b.ESCOVEDO) – percussion, vocals / **ERIC LEEDS** – saxophone

Paisley Park Paisley Park

Apr 85. (lp/c/cd) *(925286-1/-4/-2) <25286>* **AROUND THE WORLD IN A DAY** [5] [1]
– Around the world in a day / Paisley Park / Condition of the heart / Raspberry beret / Tambourine / America / Pop life / The ladder / Temptation.

May 85. (7"/7"sha-pic-d) *(W 9052/+P)* **PAISLEY PARK. / SHE'S ALWAYS IN MY HAIR** [18] [-]
(12"+=) *(W 9052T)* – ('A'extended).

May 85. (7") *<28972>* **RASPBERRY BERET. / SHE'S ALWAYS IN MY HAIR** [-] [2]

Jul 85. (7"/12") *(W 8929/+T)* **RASPBERRY BERET. / HELLO** [25] [-]

Jul 85. (7") *<28998>* **POP LIFE. / HELLO** [-] [7]

Oct 85. (7") *<28999>* **AMERICA. / GIRL** [-] [46]

Oct 85. (7"/ext-12") *(W 8858/+T)* **POP LIFE. / GIRL** [60] [-]

Feb 86. (7"/7"pic-d/ext-12") *(W 8751/+P/T) <28751>* **KISS. / LOVE OR MONEY** [6] [1]

Apr 86. (lp,pic-lp/c/cd) *(925395-1/-4/-2) <25395>* **PARADE (Music from the film 'Under The Cherry Moon')** [4] [3]
– Christopher Tracey's parade / New position / I wonder u / Under the cherry moon / Girls and boys / Life can be so nice / Venus de Milo / Mountains / Do u lie / Kiss / Anotherloverholdenyohead / Sometimes it snows in April.

May 86. (7") *(W 8711) <28711>* **MOUNTAINS. / ALEXA DE PARIS** [45] [23]
(10"white/12") *(W 8711 TW/T)* – ('A'&'B'extended).

Aug 86. (7"/7"sha-pic-d) *(W 8586/+P)* **GIRLS AND BOYS. / UNDER THE CHERRY MOON** [11] [-]
(12"+=) *(W 8586T)* – Erotic city.
(d7"+=) *(W 8586F)* – She's always in my hair / 17 days.

Oct 86. (7") *<28620>* **ANOTHERLOVERHOLDENYOHEAD. / GIRLS AND BOYS** [-] [63]

Oct 86. (7"/ext-12"/ext-12"pic-d) *(W 8521/+T/TP)* **ANOTHERLOVERHOLDENYOHEAD. / I WANNA BE YOUR LOVER** [36] [-]
(d7"+=) *(W 8521F)* – Mountains / Alexa de Paris.

PRINCE

—— solo, without WENDY & LISA who formed own duo. He retained live **FINK, LEEDS & SHEILA E.** adding **MICO WEAVER** – guitar / **BONI BOYER** – keyboards / **LEVI STEACER JR.** – bass / **CAT GLOVER** – dancer, vocals

Mar 87. (7") *(W 8399) <28399>* **SIGN 'O' THE TIMES. / LA LA LA HE HE HE HE** 10 3
(12"/12"pic-d) *(W 8399/+T/TP)* – ('A'&'B'extended).

Mar 87. (d-lp/c)(cd) *(WX 88/+C)(925577-2) <25577>* **SIGN 'O' THE TIMES** 4 6
– Sign 'o' the times / Play in the sunshine / Housequake / Ballad of Dorothy Parker / It / Starfish and coffee / Slow love / Hot thing / Forever in my life / U got the look / If I was your girlfriend / Strange relationship / I could never take the place of your man / The cross / It's gonna be a beautiful night / Adore.

Jun 87. (7"/7"peach/c-s/ext-12"/ext-12"pic-d) *(W 8334/+E/C/T/TP) <28334>* **IF I WAS YOUR GIRLFRIEND. / SHOCKADELICA** 20 May87 –

— (next 'A'side featured backing vocals by solo artist SHEENA EASTON now living in California with all her well-invested millions!)

Aug 87. (7"/c-s) *(W 8289/+C) <28289>* **U GOT THE LOOK. / HOUSEQUAKE** 11 Jul87 2
('B'ext-12"+=/12"pic-d+=) *(W 8289 T/TP)* – ('A'long version).

Nov 87. (7"/c-s) *(W 8288/+C) <28288>* **I COULD NEVER TAKE THE PLACE OF YOUR MAN. / HOT THING** 29 10 63
(12"+=/12"pic-d+=) *(W 8288 T/TP)* – ('B'extended).

Apr 88. (7"/c-s) *(W 7900/+C) <27900>* **ALPHABET ST. / THIS IS NOT MUSIC, THIS IS A TRIP** 9 8
(12"/cd-s) *(W 7900 T/CD)* – ('A'&'B'extended).

May 88. (lp/c)(cd) *(WX 164/+C)(925720-2) <25720>* **LOVESEXY** 1 11
– I no / Alphabet St. / Glam slam / Anna Stesia / Dance on / Lovesexy / When 2 r in love / I wish U Heaven / Positivity. *(re-iss. cd/c Feb95)*

Jul 88. (7"/12") *(W 7806/+T)* **GLAM SLAM. / ESCAPE** 29 –
(cd-s+=) *(W 7806CD)* – Escape (free yo mind from this rat race).

Oct 88. (7") *(W 7745)* **I WISH U HEAVEN. / SCARLET PUSSY (by 'Camille')** 24 –
(12"+=/cd-s+=) *(W 7745 T/CD)* – ('A' pts.2 & 3).

Jun 89. (7"/c-s/ext-12"/ext-12"pic-dcd-s/3"cd-s) *(W 2924/+C/T/TP/CD/CDX) <22924>* **BATDANCE. / 200 BALLOONS** 2 1
('A'-Batmix-12"+=) *(W 2924TX)* – ('A'-Vicki Vale mix).

Jun 89. (lp/c)(cd/pic-cd) *(WX 281/+C)(925 936-2/489-2) <25936>* **BATMAN** 1 1
– The future / Electric chair / The arms of Orion / Partyman / Vicki waiting / Trust / Lemon crush / Scandalous / Batdance. *(re-iss. cd/c Feb95; same)*

Aug 89. (7"/c-s/remix-12"/ext-12") *(W 2814/+C/T/TX) <22814>* **PARTYMAN. / FEEL U UP** 14 18
(12"pic-d/cd-s) *(W 2814 TP/CD)* – ('A'video mix). / ('B'long stroke mix).

Oct 89. (7"/c-s; PRINCE with SHEENA EASTON) *(W 2757/+C) <22757>* **THE ARMS OF ORION. / I LUV U IN ME** 27 36
(12"+=/cd-s+=/12"pic-d+=) *(W 2757 T/CD/TP)* – ('A'extended).

— live **PATRICE RUSHDEN** – keyboards (solo artist) repl. BOYER + GLOVER / **MICHAEL BLAND** – drums repl. SHEILA E. / **CANDY DULFER** – saxophone repl. LEEDS

Jul 90. (7"/c-s) *(W 9751/+C) <19751>* **THIEVES IN THE TEMPLE. / (Part 2)** 7 6
('A'remix; 12"+=/cd-s+=/12"pic-d+=) *(W 9751 T/CD/TP)* – ('A'dub).

Aug 90. (cd)(d-lp/c) *(927493-2)(WX 361/+C) <27493>* **MUSIC FROM GRAFFITI BRIDGE (soundtrack)** 1 6
– Can't stop this feeling I got / New power generation / The question of U / Elephants and flowers / Joy in repetition / Tick, tock, bang / Thieves in the temple. *(also other tracks by 'The TIMES' etc.)*

Oct 90. (7"/c-s) *(W 9525/+C) <19525>* **NEW POWER GENERATION. / (Part 2)** 26 64
(12"+=/cd-s+=/12"pic-d+=) *(W 9525 T/CD/TP)* – Melody cool (extended remix).

PRINCE & THE NEW POWER GENERATION

— with **LEVI SEACER JR.** – guitar, vox / **TOMMY BARBARELLA** – keys, synths / **SONNY T.** – bass, vox / **ROSIE GAINES** – co-vocals, organ, synths / **MICHAEL B.** – drums / **TONY M.** – rap/vox / **KIRKY JOHNSON** – perc., vox / **DAMON DICKSON** – perc., vox

Aug 91. (7"/c-s) *(W 0056/+C) <19225>* **GETT OFF (remix). / HORNY PONY** 4 21
(12"+=) *(W 0056T)* – ('A'-Thrust mix).
(cd-s+=) *(W 0056CD)* – ('A'-Purple pump mix).
(above: as a m-lp, its US import hit UK chart! at No.33)

Sep 91. (7"/c-s) *(W 0061/+C) <19175>* **CREAM. / HORNY PONY** 15 1
(12"+=/cd-s+=) *(W 0061 T/CD)* – Gangster glam.

Sep 91. (cd)(d-lp/c) *(925379-2)(WX 432/+C) <25379>* **DIAMONDS AND PEARLS** 2 3
– Thunder / Daddy pop / Diamonds and pearls / Cream / Strollin' / Willing and able / Gett off / Walk don't walk / Jughead / Money don't matter 2 night / Push / Insatiable / Live 4 love. *(re-iss. cd/c Feb95)*

Nov 91. (7"/c-s) *(W 0075/+C) <19083>* **DIAMONDS AND PEARLS. / LAST DANCE** 25 4
(cd-s+=) *(W 0075CD)* – 2 the wire (Grammy instrumental) / Do you dance (remix).

Dec 91. (c-s,cd-s) *<19090>* **INSATIABLE / I LOVE U IN ME** – 77

Mar 92. (7"/c-s/cd-s) *(W 0091/+C/CD) <19020>* **MONEY DON'T MATTER 2 NIGHT. / CALL THE LAW** 19 23
(12"+=) *(W 0091T)* – Push.

Jun 92. (7"/c-s) *(W 0113/+C)* **THUNDER. / VIOLET THE ORGAN DRIVER** 28 –
(12"+=/cd-s+=/12"pic-d+=) *(W 0113 T/CD/TP)* – Gett off (thrust dub).

— **MAYTE** – vocals; repl. ROSIE

Jul 92. (7"/c-s) *(W 0123/+C) <18817>* **SEXY M.F. / STROLLIN'** 4 66
(12"+=/cd-s+=) *(W 0123 T/CD)* – Daddy Pop.

Sep 92. (7"/c-s) *(W 0132/+C)* **MY NAME IS PRINCE. / 2 WHOM IT MAY CONCERN** 7 –
(12"+=) *(W 0132T)* – Sexy mutha.
(cd-s++=) *(W 0132CD)* – ('A'extra mix).

Sep 92. (c-s,cd-s) *<18707>* **MY NAME IS PRINCE / SEXY MUTHA** – 36

Nov 92. (12"/cd-s) *(W 0142 T/CD)* **MY NAME IS PRINCE (remixes). / (other mixes)** 51 –

Oct 92. (cd)(d-lp/c) *(9362 45037-2)(WX 490/+C) <45037>* **(SYMBOL)** 1 5
– My name is Prince / Sexy MF / Love 2 the 9's / The morning papers / The Max / Segue / Blue light / I wanna melt with U / Sweet baby / The continental / Dawn U / Arrogance / The flow / 7 / And God created woman / 3 chains o' gold / Segue / The sacrifice of Victor.

Nov 92. (7"/c-s) *(W 0147/+C) <18824>* **7. / 7 (acoustic)** 27 7
(cd-s+=) *(W 0147CD)* – ('A'other mixes).

Mar 93. (7"/c-s) *(W 0162/+C) <18583>* **THE MORNING PAPERS. / LIVE 4 LOVE** 52 44
(cd-s+=) *(W 0162CD)* – Love 2 the 9's.

Sep 93. (cd/c/d-lp) *<(9362 45431-2/-4/-1)>* **THE HITS 1** (compilation) 5 46
– When doves cry / Pop life / Soft and wet / I feel for you / Why you wanna treat me so bad? / When you were mine / Uptown / Let's go crazy / 1999 / I could never take the place of your man / Nothing compares 2 U / Adore / Pink cashmere / Alphabet St. / Sign 'o' the times / Thieves in the temple / Diamonds and pearls / 7.

Sep 93. (cd/c/d-lp) *<(9362 45435-2/-4/-1)>* **THE HITS 2** (compilation) 5 54
– Controversy / Dirty mind / I wanna be your lover / Head / Do me, baby / Delirious / Little red Corvette / I would die 4 U / Raspberry beret / If I was your girlfriend / Kiss / Peach / U got the look / Sexy M.F. / Gett off / Cream / Pope / Purple rain.

Sep 93. (3xcd/3xc) *<(9362 45440-2/-4)>* **THE HITS / THE B-SIDES** 4 19
– (all of above plus corresponding 'B'sides)
+ Hello / 200 ballooons / Escape / Gotta stop (messin' about) / Horny toad / Feel U up / Girl / I love U in me / Erotic city / Shockadelica / Irresistable bitch / Scarlet pussy / La, la, la, he, he, hee / She's always in my hair / 17 days / How come U don't call me anymore / Another lonely Christmas / God / Tears in your eyes / Power fantastic.

Sep 93. (c-s,cd-s) *<18371>* **PINK CASHMERE / SOFT AND WET (remix)** – 50

Oct 93. (7"/c-s) *(W 0210/+C)* **PEACH. / WISH U HEAVEN** 14 –
(cd-s+=) *(W 0210CD)* – Girls & boys / My name is Prince.
(cd-s) *(W 0210CD2)* – ('A'side) / Money don't matter 2 nite / Partyman / Mountains.

Dec 93. (7"pic-d/c-s) *(W 0215 P/C)* **CONTROVERSY. / THE FUTURE** 5 –
(cd-s) *(W 0215CD1)* – ('A'side) / The future (remix) / Glam slam / D.M.S.R.
(cd-s) *(W 0215CD2)* – ('A'side) / Paisley Park / Anotherloverholenyohead / New power generation.

Warners Bellmark

Mar 94. (7"/c-s) *(NPG 60155/+C) <72514>* **THE MOST BEAUTIFUL GIRL IN THE WORLD. / BEAUTIFUL** 1 3
(12"+=/cd-s+=) *(NPG 60155 T/CD)* – ('A'mixes).

May 94. (12"ep/c-ep/cd-ep) *(NPG 60212 T/C/CD)* <71003> **THE BEAUTIFUL EXPERIENCE** [18] [92]
– (7 versions of last single)

—— Musicians: **PRINCE / MICHAEL B. / SONNY T. / TOMMY BARBARELLA / MR.HAYES / MAYLE**

Warners Warners

Aug 94. (cd/c/lp) *<(9362 45700-2/-4/-1)>* **COME** [1] [15]
– Come / Space / Pheromone / Loose! / Papa / Race / Dark / Solo / Letitgo / Orgasm.

Aug 94. (7"pic-d/c-s) *(W 0260/+C)* *<18074>* **LETITGO. / SOLO** [30] [31]
(cd-s+=) *(W 0260CD)* – Alexa de Paris / Pope.

Mar 95. (cd-ep) *(W 0289CD)* *<17903>* **PURPLE MEDLEY / PURPLE MEDLEY (extended) / PURPLE MEDLEY (Kirk J's B-side remix)** [33] [84]

NEW POWER GENERATION

N.P.G. N.P.G.

Mar 95. (7"ep/c-ep/12"ep/cd-ep) *(NPG 0061045/+C/T/CD)* **GET WILD / BEAUTIFUL GIRL (sax version) / HALLUCINATION RAIN** [19] [–]

Apr 95. (cd/c/lp) *(NPG 6103-2/-4/-1)* **EXODUS** [11] [–]
– N.P.G. operator intro / Get wild / Segue / DJ gets jumped / New power soul / DJ seduces Sonny / Segue / Count the days / The good life / Cherry, Cherry / Segue / Return of the bump squad / Mashed potato girl intro / Segue / Big fun / New power day / Segue / Hallucination rain / N.P.G. bum rush the ship / The exodus has begun / Outro.

Aug 95. (cd-s) *<17859>* **THE GOOD LIFE / GET WILD** [–] [ ]

Aug 95. (c-s) *(NPG 0061515C)* **THE GOOD LIFE / FACE THE MUSIC** [29] [–]
(cd-s+=/12") *(NPG 0065151 CD/T)* – ('A'-mixes; Bullets go bang / Big city / etc). *(re-iss. Jun97; hit UK No.15; 006151 9/5/0 NPG)*

Oct 95. (c-s) *(NPG 6133-9)* **COUNT THE DAYS / (album)** [ ] [–]
(cd-s+=) *(NPG 6133-5)* – New power soul.

PRINCE (symbol)

or T.A.F.K.A.P. (The Artist Formerly Known As PRINCE)

Warner-NPG Warner-NPG

Sep 95. (c-s) *(W 0315C)* *<17811>* **EYE HATE U / ('A'mix)** [20] [12]
(cd-s) *(W 0315CD)* – ('A'mixes).

Sep 95. (cd/c/lp) *<(9362 45999-2/-4/-1)>* **THE GOLD EXPERIENCE** [4] [6]
– P control / npq operator / Endorphinmachine / Shhh / We march / npq operator / The most beautiful girl in the world / Dolphin / npq operator / Now / npq operator / 319 / npq operator / Shy / Billy Jack bitch / Eye hate u / npq operator / Gold.

Nov 95. (c-s) *(W 0325C)* *<17715>* **GOLD / ROCK AND ROLL IS ALIVE! (AND IT LIVES IN MINNEAPOLIS)** [10] [58]
(cd-s+=) *(W 0325CD)* – Eye hate U (extended remix).

—— In Apr 96, he wrote music for the film soundtrack 'GIRL 6' hit US 75

—— performed by New Power Generation; **MR. HAYES, TONY BARBARELLA, SONNY T, MICHAEL B** plus **KIRK JOHNSON, ROSIE GAINES + NPG HORNS**

Jul 96. (cd/c) *<(9362 46317-2/-4)>* **CHAOS AND DISORDER** [14] [26]
– Chaos and disorder / Dinner with Dolores / The same December / Right the wrong / Zannalee / I rock, therefore I am / Into the light / I will / Dig u better dead / Had u.

Jul 96. (c-s) *(9362 43742-4)* **DINNER WITH DOLORES / HAD U** [36] [–]
(cd-s+=) *(9362 43742-2)* – Right the wrong.

The ARTIST with The NEW POWER GENERATION

E.M.I. NPG-Warner

Nov 96. (t-cd/t-c) *(CD/TC EMD 1102)* *<NPG 54982>* **EMANCIPATION** [18] [11]
– Jam of the year / Right back here in my arms / Somebody's somebody's / Get yo groove on / Courtin' time / Betcha by golly wow / We gets up / White mansion / Darned if I do / I can't make U love me / Mr. Happy / In this bed I scream / Sex in the summer / Soul sanctuary / Emale / Curious child / Dreamin' about U / Joint 2 joint / The holy river / Let's have a baby / Saviour / The plan / Friend lover sister mother-wife / Slave / New world / The human body / Face down / La la la means I love you / Style / Sleep around / Da da da / My computer / One of us / The love we make / Emancipation.

Dec 96. (c-s/cd-s) *(TC/CD EM 463)* **BETCHA BY GOLLY WOW! / RIGHT BACK HERE IN MY ARMS** [11] [–]
(cd-s) *(CDEMS 463)* – ('A'mix).

Mar 97. (c-s/cd-s) *(TC/CD EM 467)* **THE HOLY RIVER / SOMEBODY'S SOMEBODY / THE MOST BEAUTIFUL GIRL IN THE WORLD** [19] [ ]
(cd-s) *(CDEMS 467)* – ('A'side) / The most beautiful girl in the world (Mustang mix) / Somebody's somebody / On sale now!

NPG NPG

Mar 98. (4xcd-box) *<(BCT 9871CD)>* **CRYSTAL BALL** (out-takes & 4th cd new) [ ] [62]
– Crystal ball / Dream factory / Acknowledge me / Ripopgodazippa / Lovesign (Shock G remix) / Hide the bone / 2morrow / So dark / Movie star / Tell me how u wanna be done // Interactive / Da bang / Calhoun Square / What's my name / Crucial / An honest man / Sexual suicide / Cloreen bacon skin / Good love / Strays of the world // Days of wild / Last heart / Poom poom / She gave her angels / 18 & over / The ride / Get loose (remix) / P. control (club mix) / Make your mama hapy / Goodbye // The truth / Don't play me / Circle of amour / 3rd eye / Dionne / Man in a uniform / Animal kingdom / The other side of the pillow / Fascination / One of your tears / Comeback / Welcome 2 the dawn (acoustic). *<US mail-order cont.5th cd+=>* – KAMASUTRA (instrumental ballet score).

(SYMBOL) THE NEW POWER GENERATION

—— now with **CHAKA KHAN, LARRY GRAHAM + DOUG E FRESH**

NPG-RCA NPG

Jul 98. (cd/c) *(74321 60598-2/-4)* *<9872>* **NEWPOWER SOUL** [38] [22]
– New power soul / Mad sex / Until u're in my arms again / When U love somebody / Shoo-bed-ooh / Push it up / Freaks on this side / Come on / The one / (I like) Funky music.

Nov 98. (c-s) *(74321 63472-4)* **COME ON / COME ON (late night mix)** [65] [ ]
(cd-s+=) *(74321 63472-2)* – Come on (The Artist remix).

The ARTIST

Arista Arista

Nov 99. (cd) *(74321 72574-2)* *<14624>* **RAVE UN2 THE JOY FANTASTIC** [ ] [18]
– Rave un2 the joy fantastic / Undisputed / The greatest romance ever sold / Segue / Hot wit U / Tangerine / So far so pleased / The sun and the moon and the stars / Everyday is a winding road / Segue / Man o war / Baby knows / I love you but I don't trust you anymore / Silly game / Strange but true / Wherever U go whatever U do / 1800 new funk ad.

Feb 00. (cd-s) *(74321 74500-2)* *<13749>* **THE GREATEST ROMANCE EVER SOLD (mixes)** [65] Oct99 [63]

– compilations, others, etc. –

on 'WEA/Warners' unless mentioned otherwise

Oct 88. (cd-s) *(921186-2)* **WHEN DOVES CRY / PURPLE RAIN** [ ] [ ]

Oct 88. (cd-s) *(921787-2)* **LET'S GO CRAZY (extended) / TAKE ME WITH U** [ ] [ ]

Oct 88. (cd-s) *(921842-2)* **LITTLE RED CORVETTE (dance mix) / 1999 (extended)** [ ] [ ]

Oct 88. (cd-s) *(921188-2)* **KISS / GIRLS AND BOYS / UNDER THE CHERRY MOON** [ ] [ ]

Nov 94. (cd/c) *<(45793)>* **THE BLACK ALBUM** (finally released!) [36] [47]
– Le grind / Cindy C. / Dead on it / When 2 R in love / Bob George / Superfunkycalifragisexy / 2 nigs united for West Compton / Rockhard in a funky place.

Dec 98. (c-s) *(W 467C)* **1999 / HOW COME U DON'T CALL ME ANYMORE** [10] [ ]
(12"+=/cd-s+=) *(W 467 T/CD)* – DMSR.
(re-iss. Dec99; same) – hit No.51

Feb 99. (m-cd) *<1999>* **1999: THE NEW MASTERS EP** [–] [ ]

Aug 99. (cd/c) *<(9362 47522-2/-4)>* **THE VAULT . . . OLD FRIENDS 4 SALE** (out-takes 1985-1994) [47] [85]
– The rest of my life / It's about that walk / She spoke 2 me / 5 women /

When the lights go down / My little pill / There is lonely / Old friends 4 sale / Sarah / Extraordinary.

Nov 99. (d-cd) *Charly; (CDVAL 1112)* **THE EARLY YEARS ('94 EAST)** [ ] [–]

Jul 01. (cd/c) *Warners-ESP; <(8122 74272-2/-4)>* **THE VERY BEST OF . . .** [2] [66]

John PRINE

Born: 10 Oct'46, Maywood, Illinois, USA. The young JP learned guitar from his elder brother and started to both write and play in his early teens. Graduating from High School in 1964, he spent two years working as a postman before being drafted into the army. Although the Vietnam war was beginning to take its toll on America's young men, PRINE was lucky enough to be posted to Germany, where he whiled away his time in the motor pool and entertained his barrack-room buddies with his strikingly original and obliquely observed compositions. After his discharge from the army, he returned to work for the US mail and continued his songwriting although still on an amateur basis. He made his professional debut in a Chicago folk club ("the 5th Peg") in 1970 and was persuaded by the club's owner that his talents lay in the direction of music rather than mail delivery. Soon after, he was introduced to KRIS KRISTOFFERSON and 50's crooner, PAUL ANKA, to whom he played a few of his (now classic) compositions. Both were astounded by his mature writing style and the diverse range of emotions running through his subject matter. (Let's face it, songs on masturbation:- 'DONALD AND LYDIA', were not exactly thick on the ground in early 70's America). The pair arranged for him to make some demos and thereafter KRISTOFFERSON invited him to play a few songs on his show. In the audience that particular night was Jerry Wexler of Atlantic Records who was bowled over and immediately offered him a recording deal. The singer's eponymous debut album was immediately hailed as a groundbreaking record and met with great critical and grass-roots popular success although it performed poorly by way of sales. This was quickly followed by 'DIAMONDS IN THE ROUGH' (1972) which again showcased his wry observations of life's trials and tribulations. Once again, critical plaudits were huge, while commercial success was moderate. At the time, PRINE was being promoted – complete with denim jacket – as the "new Dylan", a term he felt less than happy about. However, he was beginning to acquire a solid groundbase of loyal fans. More importantly, leading artists were beginning to listen to – and include his songs on – their albums; everybody who was anybody in the US folk/country world wanted to cover a PRINE composition. Third album, 'SWEET REVENGE' (1973), disappointed both fans and critics with a flawed attempt at exploring new horizons. However, this session did produce one popular song, 'DEAR ABBIE', demonstrating that his muse hadn't completely deserted him. 'COMMON SENSE' was released in 1975 and again it was generally agreed that PRINE had produced a "bummer!". Moreover, Atlantic Records had by now decided that he was definitely not the new Dylan. They almost immediately ended their 5-year association by mutual agreement. Three years passed while he took stock, subsequently composing and polishing enough material to impress the 'Asylum' label. The fruits of his labour finally emerged in the shape of 'BRUISED ORANGE' (1978), another PRINE classic regarded by many as a return to the promise he showed earlier in the decade. JP took a more lighthearted approach to his sixth album, 'PINK CADILLAC' (1979), an uncharacteristically electrified set which lacked the spark of its acoustic predecessor. This was followed by the more sedate 'STORM WINDOWS' (1979), which contained some remixed material from the previous sessions. This was to be JOHN's last effort for four years, although he continued to work on material and collaborations with other writers and artists. Around this time the man took the decision to start his own label, 'Oh Boy', an exercise that dug deep into his finances and time, resulting in his temporary, although somewhat lengthy absence from the spotlight. Fans were thrown a crumb of comfort in 1982 with the release of that rare PRINE curiosity, a Christmas single, 'I SAW MUMMY KISSING SANTA CLAUS' – backed unceremoniously by 'SILVER BELLS' (yuk!). The aptly titled 'AIMLESS LOVE' (1984) album was another lacklustre effort yet despite ignoring recording and concert work, PRINE's standing among his peers had never been higher and he continued to write, play and guest on various projects while still trying to kickstart his label. This he partly achieved with his ninth album, 'GERMAN AFTERNOONS', which received a nomination for Best Contemporary Folk Album of 1987; this was probably due to the NANCI GRIFFITHS cover of one of its better tracks, 'THE SPEED OF THE SOUND OF LONELINESS'. PRINE was back to something approaching his old style, although all was not going well in his personal life. A second marriage had failed (check the lyrics of the aforementioned!) and the recent death from cancer of his close friend, singer/songwriter and erstwhile collaborator, Steve Goodman, had left its mark. Once more, he disappeared into the shadows of depression with the only output being a double live album of old favourites, 'JOHN PRINE LIVE' (1987). It was rumoured in some camps that, following the death of his close friend that PRINE had given up the business completely and it was to take three years coaxing and cajoling by his long-time musical buddies (including BONNIE RAITT, BRUCE SPRINGSTEEN, TOM PETTY, JOHN MELLENCAMP and DAVID LINDLEY), before he resurfaced with the well received 'THE MISSING YEARS' (1991). Agents were once more beating a path to his door and his back catalogue was being rediscovered by new legions of fans. A resulting Grammy Award finally gave PRINE the recognition he undeniably deserved and vindicated both his fans and co-artists' loyalty over those "missing years". More importantly, that elusive element, commercial success, had finally come within JOHN's grasp; he found himself very much in demand again for concerts, tours and other ventures. His soundtrack contribution to the movie, 'Falling from Grace', further enhanced his reputation; he even released a Christmas album (!). 'LOST DOGS AND MIXED BLESSINGS' (1995) took off in yet another direction, while he even hosted a TV series, 'Town and Country' for Channel 4. JOHN also re-married and relocated to the Irish Republic. After surviving a throat cancer operation, he returned in 1999 with 'IN SPITE OF OURSELVES', a covers album of duets with everyone from IRIS DeMENT to EMMYLOU HARRIS. 'SOUVENIRS' (2000), meanwhile, was a collection of PRINE's most treasured compositions initially re-recorded for the German market but subsequently given a full release, among them the still wonderful 'ANGEL FROM MONTGOMERY'.

Album rating: JOHN PRINE (*9) / DIAMONDS IN THE ROUGH (*8) / SWEET REVENGE (*5) / COMMON SENSE (*3) / PRIME PRINE – THE BEST OF JOHN PRINE compilation (*9) / BRUISED ORANGE (*8) / PINK CADILLAC (*5) / STORM WINDOWS (*3) / AIMLESS LOVE (*5) / GERMAN AFTERNOONS (*6) / JOHN PRINE LIVE (*6) / THE MISSING YEARS (*8) / GREAT DAYS: THE JOHN PRINE ANTHOLOGY compilation (*9) / A JOHN PRINE CHRISTMAS mini (*3) / LOST DOGS AND MIXED BLESSINGS (*5) / LIVE ON TOUR (*6) / IN SPITE OF OURSELVES (*6) / SOUVENIRS (*4)

JOHN PRINE – vocals, guitar

Atlantic Atlantic

Sep 71. (7") *<2815>* **SAM STONE. / BLUE UMBRELLA** –

Apr 72. (lp) *(K 40357) <SD 8296>* **JOHN PRINE** Dec71
– Illegal smile / Spanish pipedream / Hello in there / Sam Stone / Paradise / Pretty good / Your flag Decal won't get you into Heaven anymore / Far from me / Angel from Montgomery / Quiet man / Donald and Lydia / Six o'clock news / Flashback blues. *<US cd-iss. 1990; 19156-2> (UK cd-iss. Jul96 on 'Warners'; 7567 81541-2)*

Apr 72. (7") *<2857>* **ILLEGAL SMILE. / QUIET MAN** –

Nov 72. (lp) *(K 40427) <SD 7240>* **DIAMONDS IN THE ROUGH** Oct72
– Everybody / The torch singer / Souvenirs / The late John Garfield blues / Sour grapes / Billy the bum / The frying pan / Yes I guess they oughta name a drink after you / Take the star out of the window / The great compromise / Clocks and spoons / Rocky mountain time / Diamonds in the rough. *<cd-iss. 1990; 7240-2>*

Jan 73. (7") *(K 10271) <2925>* **EVERYBODY. / CLOCKS AND SPOONS** Oct72

Jun 73. (7") *(K 10350)* **SPANISH PIPEDREAM. / ILLEGAL SMILE** –

Feb 74. (7") *<3013>* **GRANDPA WAS A CARPENTER. / ONOMATOPOEIA** –

May 74. (lp) *(K 40524) <SD 7274>* **SWEET REVENGE** Oct73
– Sweet revenge / Please don't bury me / Christmas in prison / Dear Abby / Blue umbrella / Often is a word I seldom use / Onomatopoeia / Grandpa was a carpenter / The accident (things could be worse) / Mexican home / A good time / Nine pound hammer. *<cd-iss. 1990;7274-2>*

1974. (7") *<3218>* **QUIET MAN. / ILLEGAL SMILE** –

1975. (lp) *(K 50137) <SD 18127>* **COMMON SENSE** Apr75 66
– Middle man / Common sense / Come back to us Barbara Lewis Hare Krishna Beauregard / Wedding day in Funeralville / Way down / My own best friend / Forbidden Jimmy / Saddle in the rain / That close to you / He was in Heaven before he died / You never can tell. *<cd-iss. 1990; 18127-2>*

Jun 75. (7") *<3276>* **MIDDLE MAN. / SADDLE IN THE RAIN** –

Nov 75. (7") *<3297>* **COMMON SENSE. / COME BACK TO US BARBARA LEWIS HARE KRISHNA BEAUREGARD** –

Jan 77. (lp) *<SD 18202>* **PRIME PRINE – THE BEST OF JOHN PRINE** (compilation)
– Sam Stone / Saddle in the rain / Please don't bury me / The great compromise / Grandpa was a carpenter / Donald and Lydia / Illegal revenge / Dear Abby / Souvenirs / Come back to us Barbara Lewis Hare Krishna Beauregard / Hello in there. *(cd-iss. Feb95 on 'WEA'; 7567 81504-2)*

— now with a plethora of session people

Asylum Asylum

Aug 78. (lp) *(K 53084) <6E 139>* **BRUISED ORANGE** Jul78
– Fish and whistle / There she goes / If you don't want my love / That's the way the world goes 'round / Bruised orange (chain of sorrow) / Sabu visits the twin cities alone / Aw heck / Crooked piece of time / Iron ore Betty / The hobo song. *<cd-iss. 1989 (UK-iss.Mar99) on 'Oh Boy'; OBRCD 6>*

Oct 78. (7") *(K 13136)* **THERE SHE GOES. / BRUISED ORANGE**

Oct 79. (lp) *(K 52164) <6E 222>* **PINK CADILLAC** Sep79
– Chinatown / Automobile / Killing the blues / No name girl / Saigon / Cold war (this cold war with you) / Baby let's play house / Down by the side of the road / How lucky / Ubangi stomp. *<cd-iss. 1989 (UK Mar99) on 'Oh Boy'; OBRC 7>*

Aug 80. (lp) *<6E 286>* **STORM WINDOWS**
– Shop talk / Living in the future / It's happening to you / Sleepy eyed boy / All night blue / Just wanna be with you / Storm windows / Baby Ruth / One red rose / I had a dream. *<cd-iss. 1989 (UK Mar99) on 'Oh Boy'; OBRCD 8>*

Demon Oh Boy

Nov 84. (7"red) *<OBR 001>* **I SAW MOMMY KISSING SANTA CLAUS. / SILVER BELLS** –

Feb 85. (lp/c/cd) *(FIEND 84) <OBR 002/+C/CD>* **AIMLESS LOVE** Nov84
– Be my friend tonight / Aimless love / Me, myself and I / The oldest baby in the world / Slow boat to China / The bottomless lake / Maureen, Maureen / Somewhere someone's falling in love / People puttin' people down / Unwed fathers / Only love. *<cd-iss. 1987 on 'Mobile Fidelity'; MFCD 856> (cd re-iss. Mar99; same as US)*

Aug 87. (lp/cd) *(FIEND/+CD 103) <OBR 003/+CD>* **GERMAN AFTERNOONS** 1986
– Lulu walls / Speed of the sound of loneliness / Sailin' around / If she were you / Linda goes to Mars / I just want you to dance with me / Love love love / Bad boys / They'll never take her love from me / Paradise.

Sep 87. (7"green) *<OBR 004>* **LET'S TALK DIRTY IN HAWAIIN. / KOKOMO** –

Jan 88. (d-lp/c/cd) *<OBR/+C/CD 005>* **JOHN PRINE LIVE (live)**
– Come back to us Barbara Lewis Hare Krishna Beauregard / Six o'clock news / The oldest baby in the world / Angel from Montgomery / Grandpa was a carpenter / Blue umbrella / Fish and whistle / Sabu visits the twin cities alone / Living in the future / Illegal smile / Mexican home / Speed of the sound of loneliness / The accident (things could be worse) / Sam Stone / Souvenirs / Aw heck / Donald and Lydia / That's the way that the world goes round / Hello in there. *(UK-iss.Mar99; same as US)*

This Way Up Oh Boy

Jul 92. (cd/c) *(512774-2/-4)<OBR 009>* **THE MISSING YEARS** Sep91
– Picture show / All the best / The sins of Mephisto / Everybody wants to feel like you / It's a big old goofy world / I want to be with you always / Daddy's little pumpkin / Take a look at my heart / The great run / Way back then / Unlonely / You got cold / Everything is cool / Jesus: the missing years. *(cd re-iss. Mar99; same as US)*

Nov 94. (m-cd) *<OBR 011>* **A JOHN PRINE CHRISTMAS** –
– Everything is cool / All the best (live) / Silent night all day long / If you were the woman and I was the man / Silver bells / I saw mommy kissing Santa Claus / Christmas in prison / A John Prine Christmas.

Rykodisc Oh Boy

Sep 95. (cd) *(RCD 10333) <OBR 013>* **LOST DOGS & MIXED BLESSINGS** Apr95
– New train / Ain't hurtin' nobody / All the way with you / Lake Marie / We are the lonely / Humidity built the snowman / Day is done / Quit hollerin' at me / Big fat love / Same thing happened to me / This love is real / Leave the lights on / He forgot it was Sunday / I love you so much it hurts.

Oh Boy Oh Boy

May 97. (cd) *<(OBR 015)>* **LIVE ON TOUR (live)** Apr97
– Picture show / Quit hollerin' at me / You got gold / Unwed fathers / Space monkey / The late John Garfield blues / Storm windows / Jesus: the missing years / Humidity built the snowman / Illegal smile / Daddy's little pumpkin / Lake Marie / If I could / Stick a needle in my eye / You mean so much to me.

— In Nov'98, PRINE's label released V/A set, 'Lucky 13', which included 3 tracks by himself, namely 'Let's talk dirty in Hawaiian', 'Beautiful World' and 'Kokomo'.

Sep 99. (cd) *<(OBR 019)>* **IN SPITE OF OURSELVES**
– We're not the jet set (w/ IRIS DeMENT) / So sad (to watch good love go bad) (w/ CONNIE SMITH) / Wedding bells – Let's turn back the years (w/ LUCINDA WILLIAMS) / When two worlds collide (w/ TRISHA YEARWOOD) / Milwaukee here I come (w/ MELBA MONTGOMERY) / I know one (w/ EMMYLOU HARRIS) / It's a cheating situation (w/ DOLORES KEANE) / Back street affair (w/ PATTY LOVELESS) / Loose talk (w/ CONNIE SMITH) / Let's invite them over (w/ IRIS DeMENT) / Til a tear becomes a rose (w/ FIONA PRINE) / In a town this size (w/ DOLORES KEANE) / We could (w/ IRIS DeMENT) / We must have been out of our minds (w/ MELBA MONTGOMERY) / In spite of ourselves (w/ IRIS DeMENT) / Dear John (I sent your saddle home).

Ulftone Oh Boy

Sep 00. (cd) *(UTCD 023) <OBR 021CD>* **SOUVENIRS** Oct00
– Souvenirs / Fish and whistle / Far from me / Angel from Montgomery / Donald and Lydia / Christmas in prison / Storm windows / Grandpa was a carpenter / The late John Garfield blues / Blue umbrella / Six o'clock news / People puttin' people down / Sam Stone / Please don't bury me / Hello in there.

– compilations, etc. –

Feb 94. (d-cd) *Rhino; (8122 71400-2)* **GREAT DAYS: THE JOHN PRINE ANTHOLOGY** Aug93
– Illegal smile / Spanish pipedream / Hello in there / Sam Stone / Paradise / Donald and Lydia / The late John Garfield blues / Yes I guess they ought to name a drink after you / The great compromise / Sweet revenge / Please don't bury me / Christmas in prison / Dear Abby (live) / Blue umbrella / Common sense / Come back to us Barbara Lewis Hare Krishna Beauregard / Saddle in the rain / He was in Heaven before he died / Fish and whistle / That's the way the world goes 'round / Bruised orange (chain of sorrow) / Sabu visits the twin cities alone / Automobile / Killing the blues / Down by the side of the road / Living in the future / It's happening to you / Storm windows / One red rose / Souvenirs / Aimless love / The oldest baby in the world / People puttin' people down / Unwed fathers / Angel from Montgomery (live with BONNIE RAITT) / Linda goes to Mars / Bad boy / Speed of the sound of loneliness (live) / It's a big old goofy world (live) / The sins of Mephisto / All the best.

PROCOL HARUM

Formed: Southend, Essex, England ... 1959 as The PARAMOUNTS, by five schoolboys; BOB SCOTT, GARY BROOKER, ROBIN TROWER, CHRIS COPPING and MICK BROWNLEE. They played a number of local gigs, BROOKER soon taking over vocal chores when SCOTT failed to show. In 1962, they left school and acquired manager Peter Martin. The following year, with a few personnel changes, the band signed to EMI's 'Parlophone' label, soon hitting the UK Top 40 with an R&B cover of The COASTERS' 'POISON IVY'. Their follow-up, a re-working of THURSTON HARRIS's 'LITTLE BITTY PRETTY ONE', failed to emulate their minor earlier success, and, after a few more covers, they folded in late summer '66. • **Note other covers:** I FEEL GOOD ALL OVER (Drifters) / I'M THE ONE WHO LOVES YOU (Major Lance) / BAD BLOOD (Coasters) / BLUE RIBBONS (Jackie DeShannon) / CUTTIN' IN (Johnny Guitar Watson) / YOU'VE NEVER HAD IT SO GOOD (P.F.Sloan). In 1967, BROOKER and lyricist KEITH REID advertised in the Melody Maker for musicians, soon settling with MATTHEW FISHER, RAY ROYER, DAVE KNIGHTS and BOBBY HARRISON. They became PROCOL HARUM (taking the name from the Latin "procul", meaning "far from these things"), and with help from producer Denny Cordell, they unleashed their mesmeric debut 45, 'A WHITER SHADE OF PALE', for 'Deram'. Adapted from a classical suite by BACH (No.3 in d major; 'Air On A G String'), its neo-gothic/baroque organ refrain combined with REID's extremely surreal lyrics to create a quasi-psychedelic million seller (stayed at No.1 for 6 weeks in the UK charts). With record company pressures to tour, ROYER and HARRISON departed from the group, replaced by former PARAMOUNTS; TROWER and WILSON. Later that year, they moved with producer CORDELL to 'Regal Zonophone', having another major stab at the Top 10 with 'HOMBURG'. The increasingly enjoyed greater success Stateside and by 1970, the band's line-up was identical to the earlier PARAMOUNTS of '63 (see above). In 1972, with their live album riding high in the charts, they resurrected their old 1967 number, 'CONQUISTADOR', subsequently a major hit on both sides of the Atlantic. PROCOL HARUM continued to gain respect from US and Canadian audiences, although the single, 'PANDORA'S BOX', in 1975, gave them a renewed UK chart thrust. Its parent album, 'PROCOL'S NINTH', also returned them to The Top 50, including a cover of The BEATLES' 'EIGHT DAYS A WEEK'. After another patchy album, BROOKER split the band, joining the ERIC CLAPTON BAND before going solo. Like many other rock dinosaurs, the band reformed for a one-off album in the early 90's, surprising many with its inclusion of ROBIN TROWER (he had already established himself as a guitar hero in the 70's & 80's). The band returned once more in 2003 with 'THE WELL'S ON FIRE', a back to basics effort which, while not graced by TROWER's timeless class, managed to recreate the spirit of their best work while simultaneously flourishing selective contemporary influences.

Album rating: PROCOL HARUM (*6) / SHINE ON BRIGHTLY (*6) / A SALTY DOG (*6) / HOME (*6) / BROKEN BARRICADES (*7) / PROCOL HARUM LIVE IN CONCERT WITH THE EDMUNTON SYMPHONY ORCHESTRA (*6) / GRAND HOTEL (*6) / EXOTIC BIRDS AND FRUIT (*6) / PROCOL'S NINTH (*6) / SOMETHING MAGIC (*4) / THE PRODIGAL STRANGER (*3) / GREATEST HITS compilation (*7) / THE WELL'S ON FIRE (*6)

PARAMOUNTS

GARY BROOKER (b.29 May'45) – vocals, keyboards / **ROBIN TROWER** (b. 9 Mar'45) – guitar / **DIZ DERRICK** – bass repl. CHRIS COPPING who went to Leicester University (Sep63) / **B.J. WILSON** (b.18 Mar'47) – drums repl. MICK BROWNLEE (Jan63).

		Parlophone	not iss.
Dec 63.	(7") *(R 5093)* **POISON IVY. / I FEEL GOOD ALL OVER**	35	–
Feb 64.	(7") *(R 5107)* **LITTLE BIT PRETTY ONE. / A CERTAIN GIRL**		–
Jun 64.	(7") *(R 5155)* **I'M THE ONE WHO LOVES YOU. / IT WON'T BE LONG**		–
Nov 64.	(7") *(R 5187)* **BAD BLOOD. / DO I**		–
Mar 65.	(7") *(R 5272)* **BLUE RIBBONS. / CUTTIN' IN**		–
Oct 65.	(7") *(R 5351)* **YOU'VE NEVER HAD IT SO GOOD. / DON'T YA LIKE MA LOVE**		–

PROCOL HARUM

BROOKER with also **MATTHEW FISHER** (b. 7 Mar'46) – organ (ex-SCREAMING LORD SUTCH) / **RAY ROYER** (b. 8 Oct'45) – guitar / **DAVE KNIGHTS** (b.28 Jun'45) – bass / **BOBBY HARRISON** (b.28 Jun'43) – drums / **KEITH REID** (b.10 Oct'46) – lyrics

		Deram	Deram
May 67.	(7") *(DM 126) <7507>* **A WHITER SHADE OF PALE. / LIME STREET BLUES** *<US re-iss. Jan73 on 'A&M'; 1389>*	1	5

— **ROBIN TROWER** – guitar (ex-PARAMOUNTS) repl. ROYER who formed FREEDOM / **B.J. WILSON** – drums (ex-PARAMOUNTS) repl. HARRISON who also formed FREEDOM

		Regal Zonophone	A&M
Sep 67.	(7") *(RZ 3002) <885>* **HOMBURG. / GOOD CAPTAIN CLACK** *(re-iss. Oct75 on 'Fly'; BUG 2)*	6	34
Dec 67.	(lp) *(LRZ 1001) <18008>* **PROCOL HARUM** – Conquistador / She wandered through the garden fence / Something following me / Mabel / Cerdes (outside the gate of) / Homburg / Christmas camel / Kaleidoscope / Salad days / Good Captain Clack / Repent Walpurgis / A whiter shade of pale. *(re-iss. May85 as 'A WHITER SHADE OF PALE' on 'Sierra' lp/c; FEDB/CFEDB 5008) (cd-iss. Jun97 as 'A WHITER SHADE OF PALE' on 'Repertoire'; RR 4666) (cd re-mast.May01 on 'Westside'+=; WESM 527)* – Lime Street blues / Homburg / Salad days (are here again) / Mabel / Cerdes (outside the gates of) / Something following me / Magdalene (my regal zonophone) / Quite rightly so / Shine on brightly.		Sep67 47
Apr 68.	(7") *(RZ 3007) <927>* **QUITE RIGHTLY SO. / IN THE WEE SMALL HOURS OF SIXPENCE**	50	
Dec 68.	(lp; stereo/mono) *(S+/LRZ 1004) <SP 4151>* **SHINE ON BRIGHTLY** – Quite rightly so / Shine on brightly / Skip softly (my moonbeams) / Wish me well / Rambling on / Magdalene (my regal zonophone) / In held twas I:- a) Glimpses of Nirvana – (b) Twas tea-time at the circus – (c) In the Autumn of my madness – (d) Look to your soul – (e) Grand finale. *(re-iss. Sep85 on 'Sierra' lp/c; FEDB/CFEDB 5026) (cd-iss. Nov92 on 'Castle'; CLACD 321) (<cd re-iss. Jun97 on 'Repertoire'+=; RR 4667>)* – In the wee small hours of sixpence / In the wee small hours of sixpence (alt.) / Quite rightly so (take 4) / Quite rightly so (extended mono) / Il tuo diamante. *(cd re-mast.May01 on 'Westside'+=; WESM 533)*		Oct68 24
May 69.	(lp) *(SLRZ 1009) <SP 4179>* **A SALTY DOG** – A salty dog / The milk of human kindness / Too much between us / The Devil came from Arkansas / Boredom / Juicy John Pink / Wreck of the Hesperus / All this and more / Crucifiction Lane / Pilgrim's progress. *(re-iss. 1971 on 'Music For Pleasure'; MFP 5275) (re-iss. May85 on 'Sierra' lp/c; FEDB/CFEDB 5012) (cd-iss. 1986 on 'Mobile Fidelity'; MFCD 823) (cd re-iss. Jul92 on 'Castle'; CLACD 289) (<cd re-iss. Sep97 on 'Repertoire'+=; REP 4668>)* – Long gone geek. *(cd re-mast.May01 on 'Westside'; WESM 534)*	27	32
Jun 69.	(7") *(RZ 3019)* **A SALTY DOG. / LONG GONE CREEK**	44	–
Jul 69.	(7") *<1111>* **THE DEVIL CAME FROM KANSAS. / BOREDOM**	–	

— **CHRIS COPPING** – organ, bass (ex-PARAMOUNTS) repl. FISHER + KNIGHTS

Jun 70.	(7") *<1218>* **WHISKEY TRAIN. / ABOUT TO DIE**	–	
Jun 70.	(lp) *(SLRZ 1014) <SP 4261>* **HOME** – Whiskey train / Dead man's dream / Still there'll be more / Nothing that I didn't know / About to die / Barnyard story / Piggy pig pig / Whaling	49	34

stories / Your own choice. *(re-iss. Apr89 on 'Castle' lp/c/cd; CLA LP/MC/CD 142) (<cd re-iss. Sep97 on 'Repertoire'; REP 4669>) (cd re-mast.May01 on 'Westside'+=; WESM 535)* – Rockin' warm-up – Go go go / The dead man's dream (take 7) / Still there'll be more (instrumental take 3) / About to die / Barnyard story / Piggy pig pig / Your own choice / Whaling stories (take 2).

Chrysalis A&M

Jun 71. (lp) *(ILPS 9158)* <*SP 4294*> **BROKEN BARRICADES** [42] May71 [32]
– Simple sister / Broken barricades / Memorial drive / Luskus Delph / Power failure / Song for a dreamer / Playmate of the mouth / Poor Mohammed. *(re-iss. 1974 lp/c; CHS/ZCHS 1057) (<cd re-mast.Sep02 on 'Repertoire'+=; REP 4980>)* – Broken barricades (single version) / Power failure (single version) / Simple sister (mono).

Jun 71. (7") <*1264*> **BROKEN BARRICADES. / POWER FAILURE** [–] [ ]

Oct 71. (7") <*1287*> **SIMPLE SISTER. / SONG FOR A DREAMER** [–] [ ]

—— **DAVE BALL** (b.30 Mar'50) – guitar repl. ROBIN TROWER (later solo) / added **ALAN CARTWRIGHT** (b.10 Oct'45) – bass (to **BROOKER, COPPING, WILSON, REID + BALL)**

Apr 72. (lp) *(CHR 1004)* <*SP 4335*> **PROCOL HARUM IN CONCERT WITH THE EDMUNTON SYMPHONY ORCHESTRA (live)** [48] [5]
– Conquistador / Whaling stories / A salty dog / All this and more / In held 'twas I; a) Glimpses of Nirvana – (b) 'Twas teatime at the circus – (c) In the Autumn of my madness – (d) I know if I'd been wiser – (e) Grand finales. *(<cd re-mast.Sep02 on 'Repertoire'; REP 4981>)*

May 72. (7") <*1347*> **CONQUISTADOR (live). / A SALTY DOG (live)** [–] [16]

Jul 72. (7") *(CHR 2003)* **CONQUISTADOR (live). / LUSKUS DELPH** [22] [–]

Chrysalis Chrysalis

Mar 73. (lp/c) *(<CHR/ZCHR 1037>)* **GRAND HOTEL** [ ] [21]
– Grand hotel / Toujours l'amour / A rum tale / T.V. Ceaser / A souvenir of London / Bringing home the bacon / Robert's box / For licorice John / Fires (which burnt brightly) / Robert's box. *(cd-iss. Oct95 on 'Essential'; ESMCD 290) (<cd re-mast.Apr01 on 'Repertoire'+=; REP 4916>)* – Grand hotel (single version) / Robert's box (single version).

Apr 73. (7") *(CHS 2010)* **ROBERT'S BOX. / A RUM TALE** [ ] [–]

Apr 73. (7") <*2011*> **BRINGING HOME THE BACON. / TOUJOURS L'AMOUR** [–] [ ]

Aug 73. (7") <*2013*> **GRAND HOTEL. / FIRE'S (WHICH BURNT BRIGHTLY)** [–] [ ]

Aug 73. (7") *(CHS 2015)* **A SOUVENIR OF LONDON. / TOUJOURS L'AMOUR** [ ] [–]

—— **MICK GRABHAM** – guitar (ex-PLASTIC PENNY, ex-COCHISE) repl. BALL to BEDLAM

Apr 74. (lp/c) *(<CHR/ZCHR 1058>)* **EXOTIC BIRDS AND FRUIT** [ ] [86]
– Nothing but the truth / Beyond the pale / As strong as Samson / The idol / The thin edge of the wedge / Monsieur R. Monde / Fresh fruit / Butterfly boys / New lamps for old. *(cd-iss. Oct95 on 'Essential'; ESMCD 291) (<cd re-mast.Mar01 on 'Repertoire'+=; REP 4791>)* – Drunk again / As strong as Samson (single version).

Apr 74. (7") *(CHS <2032>)* **NOTHING BUT THE TRUTH. / DRUNK AGAIN** [ ] [ ]

Jul 75. (7") *(CHS <2073>)* **PANDORA'S BOX. / THE PIPER'S TUNE** [16] [ ]

Aug 75. (lp/c) *(<CHR/ZCHR 1080>)* **PROCOL'S NINTH** [41] [52]
– Pandora's box / Fools gold / Taking the time / The unquiet zone / The final thrust / I keep forgetting / Without a doubt / The piper's tune / Typewriter torment / Eight days a week. *(cd-iss. Oct95 on 'Essential'; ESMCD 292) (<cd re-mast.Mar01 on 'Repertoire'; REP 4919>)*

Oct 75. (7") *(CHS 2079)* **THE FINAL THRUST. / TAKING THE TIME** [ ] [–]

Jan 76. (7") *(CHS 2084)* **AS STRONG AS SAMSON. / THE UNQUIET ZONE** [ ] [–]

—— **PETE SOLLEY** – keyboards (ex-ARTHUR BROWN, ex-SNAFU, ex-CHRIS FARLOWE) repl. CARTWRIGHT (COPPING now bass only)

Jan 77. (7") <*2115*> **WIZARD MAN. / SOMETHING MAGIC** [–] [ ]

Feb 77. (7") *(CHS 2138)* **WIZARD MAN. / BACKGAMMON** [ ] [–]

Mar 77. (lp/c) *(<CHR/ZCHR 1130>)* **SOMETHING MAGIC** [ ] [ ]
– Something magic / Skating on thin ice / Wizard man / The mark of the claw / Strangers in space / The worm and the tree (part 1 – Introduction – Menace – Occupation / part 2 – Enervation – Expectancy – Battle / part 3 – Regeneration – Epilogue). *(cd-iss. Oct95 on 'Essential'; ESMCD 293) (<cd re-mast.Mar01 on 'Repertoire'+=; REP 4918>)* – Wizard man (single version) / Backgammon (single version).

—— Disbanded mid-77. WILSON joined JOE COCKER. GRABHAM to MICKEY JUPP. GARY BROOKER joined ERIC CLAPTON band and went solo. PROCOL HARUM re-formed Oct'91, TIM RENWICK instead of TROWER.

—— re-formed in 1991. **BROOKER** – vocals, piano / **KEITH REID** – words / **ROBIN TROWER** – lead guitar / **MATTHEW FISHER** – hammond organ / with guests **DAVE BRONZE** – bass / **MARK BRZEZICKI** – drums (of BIG COUNTRY) / **JERRY STEVENSON** – mandolin, guitar

Zoo-B.M.G. Zoo

Feb 92. (cd/c/lp) *(HH CD/MC/LP 90589)* **THE PRODIGAL STRANGER** [ ] [ ]
– The truth won't fade away / Holding on / Man with a mission / (You can't) Turn back the page / One more time / A dream in ev'ry home / The hand that rocks the cradle / The king of hearts / All our dreams are sold / Perpetual motion / Learn to fly / The pursuit of happiness.

—— in Jul'95, PROCOL HARUM members guested on a classical album, 'THE LONG GOODBYE' with The London Philharmonic Orchestra

—— re-formed with **BROOKER, REID, FISHER + GEOFF WHITEHORN** plus rhythm **MATT PEGG + MARK BRZEZICKI**

Eagle Red

Mar 03. (cd) *(EAGCD 209)* <*20006*> **THE WELL'S ON FIRE** [ ] [ ]
– An old English dream / Shadow boxed / A robe of silk / The blink of an eye / The VIP room / The question / The world is rich / Fellow travellers / Wall Street blues / The emperor's new clothes / So far behind / Every dog will have his day / Weisselklenzenacht (the signature).

– compilations, others, etc. –

Mar 64. (7"ep) *Parlophone; (GEP 8908)* **THE PARAMOUNTS** [ ] [–]
– Little bitty pretty one / A certain girl / Poison Ivy / I feel good all over.

1971. (lp) *Fly; (TON 4)* **THE BEST OF PROCOL HARUM** [ ] [–]
<US-iss.Oct73 on 'A&M'; 4401>

Apr 72. (7"m) *MagniFly; (ECHO 101)* **A WHITER SHADE OF PALE. / HOMBURG / A SALTY DOG** [13] [–]

Apr 72. (d-lp/d-c) *Cube; (TOOFA 7)* **PROCOL HARUM – A WHITER SHADE OF PALE / A SALTY DOG** [26] [–]
(re-iss. Jan75, Mar78, Oct81; same)

Mar 76. (lp) *Decca; (ROOTS 4)* **ROCK ROOTS** [ ] [–]

Mar 78. (7") *Fly; (BUG 77)* **A WHITER SHADE OF PALE. / CONQUISTADOR** [ ] [ ]
(re-iss. Mar79; HBUG 77) (re-iss. Aug82 on 'Dakota'; BAK 1)

Mar 78. (d-lp/d-c) *Cube; (TOOFA/ZCTOF 10)* **SHINE ON BRIGHTLY / HOME** [ ] [–]

May 78. (lp) *Hallmark; (SHM 956)* **PROCOL HARUM'S GREATEST HITS** [ ] [–]

Aug 78. (7") *Chrysalis; (CHS 2244)* **CONQUISTADOR. / A SALTY DOG** [ ] [–]

Aug 78. (7"ep) *E.M.I.; (NUT 2834)* **THE PARAMOUNTS** [ ] [–]
– Poison Ivy / I feel glad all over / Blue ribbons / Cuttin' in.

Oct 81. (d-lp/c) *Cube; (PLAT/ZCPLT 1003)* **THE PLATINUM COLLECTION** [ ] [–]

Apr 82. (lp) *Ace; (6886555)* **PROCOL HARUM** (67-69) [ ] [–]
(re-iss. Apr82 on 'Impact'; 7486 552) (re-iss. Oct82 on 'Dakota'; COUNT/ZCCNT 13)

Aug 82. (7") *Dakota; (BAK 2)* **HOMBURG. / A SALTY DOG** [ ] [–]

Apr 83. (lp; by PARAMOUNTS) *Edsel; (ED 112)* **WHITER SHADES OF R'N'B** [ ] [–]
(cd-iss. Aug87 + Sep91; EDCD 112)

Oct 84. (d-lp/c) *Sierra; (FEDD/CFEDD 1004)* **OFF THE RECORD WITH PROCOL HARUM** [ ] [–]

Apr 86. (d-lp/d-c/cd) *Castle; (CCS LP/MC/CD 120)* **THE COLLECTION** [ ] [–]
– A whiter shade of pale / Homburg / Too much between us / A salty dog / The Devil came back from Kansas / Whaling stories / Good Captain Clack / All this and more / Quite rightly so / Shine on brightly / Grand hotel / Bringing home the bacon / Toujours l'armour / Broken barricades / Power failure / Conquistador (live) / Nothing but the truth / Butterfly boys / Pandora's box / Simple sister.

Feb 87. (7") *Old Gold; (OG 9692)* **CONQUISTADOR. / PANDORA'S BOX** [ ] [–]

Mar 88. (d-lp/c/cd) *That's Original; (TFO LP/MC/CD 5)* **SHINE ON BRIGHTLY. / A SALTY DOG** [ ] [–]

Mar 88. (cd-ep) *Special Edition; (CD 3-14)* **A WHITER SHADE OF PALE / HOMBURG / CONQUISTADOR / A SALTY DOG** [ ] [–]

Jun 88. (7") *Old Gold; (OG 9225)* **A WHITER SHADE OF PALE. / HOMBURG**
Jun 88. (cd) *A&M; (CD 2515)* **CLASSICS**
Jul 88. (lp/c/cd) *Knight; (KN LP/MC/CD 10005)* **NIGHTRIDING: PROCOL HARUM**
Dec 88. (lp/c/cd) *Fun; (FUN/+C/CD 9028)* **20 GREATEST HITS**
1991. (cd)(c/lp) *Chrysalis; (MPCD 1638)(Z+/CNW 4)* **PORTFOLIO**
Feb 92. (cd-box) *Castle; (CLABX 910)* **3 ORIGINALS**
– (HOME / A SALTY DOG / A WHITER SHADE OF PALE).
Jun 92. (cd) *Dojo; (EARLD 6)* **THE EARLY YEARS**
Oct 94. (cd) *Disky; (CUCD 05)* **PROCOL HARUM**
Jan 95. (cd) *B.R.Music; (BRCD 106)* **BEST OF PROCOL HARUM**
Jul 95. (cd-ep) *Essential;* **A WHITER SHADE OF PALE / A SALTY DOG / REPENT WALPURGIS**
Sep 95. (cd/c) *Essential; (ESS CD/MC 295)* **HOMBURG & OTHER HITS – THE BEST OF PROCOL HARUM**
Jun 97. (3xcd-box) *Westside; (<WESX 301>)* **30th ANNIVERSARY COLLECTION**
Jul 99. (cd) *Strange Fruit; (SFRSCD 089)* **LIVE IN CONCERT**
Nov 99. (cd) *Westside; (WESA 821)* **PANDORA'S BOX: THE PROCOL HARUM STEREO VERSIONS**
Oct 00. (cd) *Metro; (METRCD 038)* **GREATEST HITS**
Feb 02. (d-cd) *Metro; (<METRDCD 502>)* **CLASSIC TRACKS AND RARITIES: AN ANTHOLOGY**
Jul 02. (cd) *Beat Goes On; (<BGOCD 556>)* **PROCOL HARUM / SHINE ON BRIGHTLY**
Jul 02. (d-cd) *Repertoire; (<REP 4680>)* **THE BEST OF PROCOL HARUM: 22 CLASSIC TRACKS**
Sep 02. (3xcd-box) *Repertoire; (REP 4971)* **SINGLES A'S & B'S**
Sep 02. (cd) *Repertoire; (<REP 4982)* **LIQUORICE JOHN DEATH** Nov03
Mar 03. (cd) *Beat Goes On; (<BGOCD 558>)* **A SALTY DOG / HOME**
Jun 03. (d-cd) *Metro; (<METRDCD 521>)* **THE FIRST FOUR ALBUMS**
Aug 03. (cd) *Repertoire; (<REP 4791>)* **THE ESSENTIAL COLLECTION (1967-1991)**

PRODIGY

Formed: Braintree, Essex, England … early 90's by LIAM HOWLETT together with MC MAXIM REALITY, LEEROY THORNHILL and KEITH FLINT. With their roots in hip hop, this irrepressible quartet of techno terrorists spread their first waves of discontent through the harder end of the rave scene, releasing the 'WHAT EVIL LURKS' EP in March '91 on the (then) fledgling 'XL' label. One track, the rave call to arms of 'EVERYBODY IN THE PLACE' would rocket to No.2 the following Christmas, hot on the heels of the PRODIGY's seminal debut hit (No.3), 'CHARLY'. A masterstroke of genius, HOWLETT sampled a veteran Government TV ad warning children off playing with fire (a recurring lyrical obsession) and welded it to fuck-off, hoover synths and a juggernaut breakbeat. The mixed result: proof that ravers had a sense of humour/irony and a string of low-rent imitations sampling everything from 'Sesame Street' to 'Rhubarb and Custard'. Borrowing from ARTHUR BROWN's hoary old chestnut of the same name, 'FIRE' gave the PRODIGY their third Top 20 hit in a row, closely followed by 'THE PRODIGY EXPERIENCE' (1992). More assured and inventive than most of the weak cash-in albums to come out of the 12" dominated rave scene, the record proffered alternate versions of the hits and killer new tracks like the brilliant breakbeat-skank, 'OUT OF SPACE'. By this point the group were also making waves with their formidable live show, still largely gracing raves yet a far cry from your average P.A. featuring a scantily clad diva miming to a 15-minute set. By 1993, HOWLETT was extending his horizons; a much in demand remixer, he worked on material for such diverse acts as DREAM FREQUENCY and FRONT 242 as well as poring over new PRODIGY tracks. The first of these, the wailing 'ONE LOVE' was initially realeased as a white label, apparently to keep in touch with their underground roots. The record still charted of course, going Top 10 in late '93 after a full release. 'NO GOOD START THE DANCE' was the sound of a group in transition, a speeded-up female vocal alternating with a thundering techno assault. The single made the Top 5 in Spring '94, but it was hardly representative of what lay in store on 'MUSIC FOR THE JILTED GENERATION' later that summer. Opening with a sinister tap-tapping typewriter and spoken word intro, then slamming into a dark, twisting techno groove, it was clear HOWLETT was no longer "luvved up". The album was breathtaking in its sweep, mapping out the future of techno, PRODIGY style, incorporating heavy riffing (on the two fingered salute to the Criminal Justice Bill, 'THEIR LAW', a collaboration with POP WILL EAT ITSELF), 70's style funky flute (the evocative '3 KILOS') and even a trio of tracks, 'THE NARCOTIC SUITE', climaxing the album in blistering form. Obvious highlights were the utterly compelling 'VOODOO PEOPLE' (riffs AND funky flute!; arguably The PRODIGY's finest moment to boot) and the military stomp of 'POISON' (complete with techno-gothic video; a must-see). The album was a UK No.1, establishing the band as major contenders who had far outstripped the narrow confines of 'dance', as was evidenced at their shows over the ensuing two years. White-gloved ravers blew their whistles hopefully, waiting in vain for 'CHARLY' or 'NO GOOD START THE DANCE', while more recent converts contorted and thrashed wildly to the new material (when, that is, they weren't threatening to shove the raver's eardrum-rupturing whistles where the sun doesn't shine!). By late '95/early '96, The PRODIGY were also showcasing new material at live gigs, including an incendiary little ditty entitled 'FIRESTARTER'. Primarily KEITH's baby, the 'song' was released as a single in Spring '96, giving The PRODIGY their first No.1. FLINT had, by now, fashioned his once flowing locks into a formidable luminous green mohican and had also developed a stage act that made IGGY POP (circa The STOOGES) look like a librarian. The fine, upstanding British public were subsequently treated to the new improved KEITH via the brilliant video (claustrophobically shot in the London Underground) on Top Of The Pops, resulting in an avalanche of complaints. Of course, the kids loved it, even toddlers were heard to garble 'I'm a twisted firestarter' while dragging their hapless mums into Woolies to bag a copy. As for the song itself, FLINT took a starring role, spitting out his demented cockney threats over depth charge beats. The next single, 'BREATHE', was even better, an ominous JOY DIVISION-esque guitar riff segueing into the hardest funkiest breakbeats this side of The CHEMICAL BROTHERS. Arguably the single of the year, the track raised expectations for the forthcoming PRODIGY opus to fever pitch. Almost inevitably, then, 'THE FAT OF THE LAND' (1997) was something of a letdown. There was nothing to match the dark majesty of 'BREATHE' (included on the album along with 'FIRESTARTER'), but there were plenty of other tracks to 'melt some brains' as HOWLETT put it. The insistent techno-hop of 'DIESEL POWER' (with KOOL KEITH guesting) attested to the group's love of hardcore rap, while the BEASTIE BOYS-sampling 'FUNKY SHIT' and MC MAXIM-led 'MINDFIELDS' were high-octane PRODIGY crowd pleasers. Minus points, however, for the dull collaboration with CRISPIAN MILLS (KULA SHAKER), 'NARAYAN' and the pointless cover of L7's 'FUEL MY FIRE'. Far more compelling was the insidiously funky 'CLIMBATIZE'. But it was the album's opener which had the nation's moral guardians and pro-women groups in a tizzy;

whatever the inspiration for 'SMACK MY BITCH UP', The PRODIGY were as defiant and unapologetic as ever. Politics aside, the album may not have fully met expectations but it still trampled on the competition. Live, The PRODIGY remain a revelation, an electric maelstrom of colour and sound (and grimacing!), with an ability to mobilise a crowd unmatched in the musical spectrum. In saying that, if they rely on punk cliches without pushing the boundaries of dance music – which is what they do best – they risk becoming a caricature of themselves. • **Songwriters:** HOWLETT except samples of BABY D ('Casanova') on 'BREAK & ENTER', and KELLY CHARLES on 'YOU'RE NO GOOD FOR ME'. 'FULL THROTTLE' is also reminiscent of JOAN ARMATRADING's 'Me Myself I'.

Album rating: EXPERIENCE (*8) / MUSIC FOR THE JILTED GENERATION (*10) / THE FAT OF THE LAND (*7)

KEITH FLINT (b.17 Sep'69) – vocals, dancer / **LIAM HOWLETT** (b.21 Aug'71) – keyboards / **MC MAXIM REALITY** (b.KEITH PALMER, 21 Mar'67) – rapper-vox, dancer / **LEEROY THORNHILL** (b.7 Oct'69) – dancer, vocals

X.L. Elektra

Mar 91. (12"ep) *(XLT 17)* **WHAT EVIL LURKS / WE GONNA ROCK. / ANDROID / EVERYBODY IN THE PLACE** [ ] [–]

Aug 91. (7"/c-s) *(XLS/XLC 21) <66411>* **CHARLY. / CHARLY (original mix)** [3] [ ]
(12"+=/cd-s+=) *(XLT/CDXLS 21)* – Pandemonium / Your love.

Dec 91. (7"/c-s) *(XLS/XLC 26)* **EVERYBODY IN THE PLACE. / G-FORCE (ENERGY FLOW)** [2] [–]
(12"+=) *(XLT 26)* – Crazy man / Rip up the sound system.
(cd-s++=) *(XLS 26CD)* – ('A'remix).

Sep 92. (7"/c-s) *(XLS/XLC 30) <66370>* **FIRE. / JERICHO (original mix)** [11] [ ]
(12"+=/cd-s+=) *(XLT/XLS 30CD)* – Fire (sunrise version) / Jericho (genaside II remix).

Oct 92. (cd/c/lp) *(XLCD/XLMC/XLLP 110) <61365>* **EXPERIENCE** [12] [ ]
– Jericho / Music reach (1/2/3/4) / Wind it up / Your love (remix) / Hyperspeed (G-Force part 2) / Charly (trip into drum and bass version) / Out of space / Everybody in the place (155 and rising) / Weather experience / Fire (sunrise version) / Ruff in the jungle bizness / Death of the Prodigy dancers (live).

Nov 92. (7"/c-s) *(XLS/XLC 35) <66346>* **OUT OF SPACE (remix). / RUFF IN THE JUNGLE BIZNESS (uplifting vibes remix)** [5] Dec92 [ ]
(12"+=)(cd-s+=) *(XLT/XLS 35CD)* – ('A'techno underworld remix) / Music reach (1,2,3,4) (live).

Apr 93. (7"/c-s) *(XLS/XLC 39) <66319>* **WIND IT UP (REWOUND). / WE ARE THE RUFFEST** [7] [ ]
(12"+=) *(XLT 39)* – Weather experience (remix).
(cd-s++=) *(XLS 39CD)* – ('A'edit).

Oct 93. (c-ep/12"ep/cd-ep) *(XLC/XLT/XLS 47CD)* **ONE LOVE / RHYTHM OF LIFE (original mix). / FULL THROTTLE (original mix) / ONE LOVE (Jonny L remix)** [8] [–]

May 94. (12"/c-s) *(XLT/XLC 51)* **NO GOOD (START THE DANCE) / NO GOOD (bad for you mix) / NO GOOD (CJ Bolland's museum mix)** [4] [–]
(cd-s+=) *(XLS 51CD)* – No Good (original mix).

below album with **PHIL BENT** – flute / **LANCE RIDDLER** – guitar

X.L. Mute

Jul 94. (cd/c/d-lp) *(XLCD/XLMC/XLLP 114) <55642>* **MUSIC FOR THE JILTED GENERATION** [1] Mar95 [ ]
– Intro / Break & enter / Their law (featuring POP WILL EAT ITSELF) / Full throttle / Voodoo people / Speedway (theme from 'Fastlane') / The heat (the energy) / Poison / No good (start the dance) / One love (edit) – The narcotic suite / 3 kilos / Skylined / Claustrophobic sting.

Sep 94. (12"ep) *(XLT 54) <67007>* **VOODOO PEOPLE (original mix) / VOODOO PEOPLE (Dust Brothers remix). / VOODOO PEOPLE (Haiti Island mix) / GOA (THE HEAT, THE ENERGY PART 2)** [13] [ ]
(cd-ep) *(XLS 54CD)* – (3rd track repl.by) ('A'edit).

Mar 95. (c-s) *(XLC 58)* **POISON ('95) / ('A'-Rat Poison mix) / SCIENIDE** [15] [ ]
(12"+=/cd-s+=) *(XLT/XLS 58CD)* – ('A'-Environmental science dub mix).

X.L. Geffen

Mar 96. (c-s) *(XLC 70) <17387>* **FIRESTARTER / MOLOTIV BITCH** [1] Jan97 [30]
(12"+=/cd-s+=) *(XLT/XLS 70CD)* – ('A'-Empiron mix) / ('A'instrumental).

— All singles re-issued Apr96 hitting UK Top 75.

Nov 96. (c-ep/12"ep) *(XLC/XLT 80)* **BREATHE / THEIR LAW featuring PWEI (live at Phoenix fesival '96). / POISON (live at the Tourhout & Werchter festival '96)** [1] [ ]
(cd-ep+=) *(XLS 80CD)* – The trick.

Jul 97. (cd/c/lp) *(XL CD/MC/LP 121) <46606>* **THE FAT OF THE LAND** [1] [1]
– Smack my bitch up / Breathe / Diesel power / Funky shit / Serial thrilla / Mindfields / Narayan / Firestarter / Climbatize / Fuel my fire.

Nov 97. (12"/c-s) *(XLT/XLC 90) <43946>* **SMACK MY BITCH UP. / NO MAN ARMY** [8] [89]
(cd-s+=) *(XLS 90CD)* – Minefields (heavy rock dub) / ('A'-DJ Hype remix).

— now without LEEROY

X.L. Warners

Jul 02. (12")(cd-s) *(XLT 145)(XLS 145CD) <42456>* **BABY'S GOT A TEMPER. / (dub) / (instrumental) (acappella)** [5] [ ]

MAXIM

— solo with various personnel

X.L. X.L.

May 00. (c-s; by MAXIM featuring SKIN) *(XLC 119)* **CARMEN QUESAY / CARMEN QUEASY (digital dubz digi dub)** [33] [ ]
(12"+=)(cd-s+=) *(XLT 119)(XLS 119CD)* – ('A'instrumental).

Sep 00. (cd-s) *(XLS 121CD)* **SCHEMING / SCHEMING (Blood of Abraham mix) / PRISM** [53] [–]
(12") *(XLS 121)* – ('A'-original) / (2nd track above) / ('A'-Zed bias mix).
(cd-s) *(XLS 121CD2)* – ('A'-Zed Bias) / ('A'-instrumental) / ('A'-King cheetah more saliva mix).

Oct 00. (cd/c/lp) *(XL CD/MC/LP 134) <342>* **HELL'S KITCHEN** [ ] [ ]
– Hatriao's wall / Killing evhture / Carmen queasy / Spectral wars / Hell's kitchen / Scheming / Worldwind syndicates / Soul yeller / Voiversal scientist / My web / Dominant genes / Backward bullet.

PSYCHEDELIC FURS

Formed: London, England ... 1977 by RICHARD and TIM BUTLER, JOHN ASHTON, ROGER MORRIS and DUNCAN KILBURN, who eventually completed the line-up with drummer VINCE ELY. Gaining a bit of much needed credibility via a Radio One John Peel session, the band signed to 'Epic-C.B.S.' in 1978 and released a debut single, 'WE LOVE YOU', late the following year. This was followed in early 1980 by a classic second single, 'SISTER EUROPE' and a Top 20 eponymous debut album. A vintage slice of post-punk miserabilism tracing the classic linage of VELVET UNDERGROUND, ROXY MUSIC, 'BOWIE etc., the record's discordant mesh of jagged melody, inwardly spiralling guitar and BUTLER's cracked monotone placed The PSYCHEDELIC FURS firmly at the forefront of the alternative rock scene. Subsequently relocating to New York, they worked on an even better follow-up, 'TALK TALK TALK' (1981), a record which might've made more concessions to pop/rock convention but made up for it with gloriously subversive songwriting; 'INTO YOU LIKE A TRAIN' was leeringly self explanatory, 'DUMB WAITERS' tripped out on a mangled STOOGES vibe while the lugubrious 'PRETTY IN PINK' provided the 'FURS with a near-Top 40 hit and remains their best known track. With ex-BIRTHDAY PARTY man, PHIL CALVERT, replacing ELY (who teamed up with ROBYN HITCHCOCK), the band hooked up with TODD RUNDGREN for the disappointing 'FOREVER NOW' (1982), a combination that looked interesting on paper but somehow failed to translate onto vinyl. The record nevertheless made the UK Top 20, as did 1984's 'MIRROR MOVES', by which time line-up changes had seen KEITH FORSEY and MARS WILLIAMS replace CALVERT and founding members KILBURN and MORRIS. Despite flashes of darkly melodic inspiration, a suffocatingly slick production erased any traces of mystery or danger, further testing the patience of many longtime fans. A re-released 'PRETTY IN PINK' (issued to coincide with the film of the same name, inspired by the song itself) illustrated just how lifeless the newer material was, while the terminally dull 'MIDNIGHT TO MIDNIGHT' (1987) showed no signs of an imminent return to form. With ELY back on the drum stool, a further late 80's effort, 'BOOK OF DAYS' (1989), attempted a more credible approach to diminishing commercial returns and minimal critical reaction. Finally, after 1991's 'WORLD OUTSIDE', the band hung up their 'FURS for good, BUTLER going on to form LOVE SPIT LOVE with RICHARD FORTUS and FRANK FERRER, releasing a one-off eponymous album for 'Imago-R.C.A.' in 1994. • **Songwriters:** RICHARD BUTLER + FURS, except MACK THE KNIFE (Bobby Darin).

Album rating: THE PSYCHEDELIC FURS (*8) / TALK TALK TALK (*7) / FOREVER NOW (*7) / MIRROR MOVES (*6) / MIDNIGHT TO MIDNIGHT (*5) / ALL OF THIS AND NOTHING compilation (*7) / BOOK OF DAYS (*4) / WORLD OUTSIDE (*4) / B-SIDES AND LOST GROOVES collection (*5) / SHOULD GOD FORGET: A RETROSPECTIVE double compilation (*8)

RICHARD BUTLER (b. 5 Jun'56, Kingston-Upon-Thames, England) – vocals / **JOHN ASHTON** (b.30 Nov'57) – lead guitar / **ROGER MORRIS** – guitar / **TIM BUTLER** (b. 7 Dec'58) – bass / **DUNCAN KILBURN** – saxophone, keyboards / **VINCE ELY** – drums (ex-UNWANTED)

Epic — not iss.

Oct 79. (7") *(EPC 8005)* **WE LOVE YOU. / PULSE** [ ] [–]

C.B.S. — Columbia

Feb 80. (7") *(CBS 8179)* **SISTER EUROPE. / ****** [ ] [–]

Mar 80. (lp/c) *(CBS/40 84084)* <36791> **THE PSYCHEDELIC FURS** [18] [ ]
– India / Sister Europe / Imitation of Christ / Fall / Pulse / We love you / Wedding song / Blacks / Radio / Flowers. *(re-iss. Mar83) (cd-iss. Apr89 & Feb99; 493343-2) (<cd re-iss. Mar02 on 'Columbia'+=; UK-506362-2 / US-85918>)* – Susan's strange / Soap commercial / Mack the knife / Flowers (demo).

Oct 80. (7") *(CBS 9059)* **MR. JONES. / SUSAN'S STRANGE** [ ] [ ]

Apr 81. (7") *(A 1166)* **DUMB WAITERS. / DASH** [59] [ ]

May 81. (lp/c) *(CBS/40 84892)* <37339> **TALK TALK TALK** [30] [89]
– Dumb waiters / Pretty in pink / I wanna sleep with you / No tears / Mr. Jones / Into you like a train / It goes on / So run down / All of this and nothing / She is mine. *(re-iss. Nov84 lp/c; CBS/40 32539) (cd-iss. Apr89; CD 32539) (cd re-iss. Mar96 on 'Columbia'; 483663-2) (<cd re-iss. Mar02 on 'Columbia'+=; UK-506363-2 / US-85917)>* – Mr. Jones / So run down / All this and nothing (demo).

Jun 81. (7"/7"pic-d) *(A/WA 1327)* **PRETTY IN PINK. / MACK THE KNIFE** [43] [ ]
(12"+=) *(A13 1327)* – Soap commercial.

—— **PHIL CALVERT** – drums (ex-BIRTHDAY PARTY) repl. ELY (to ROBYN HITCHCOCK)

Jul 82. (7") *(A 2549)* <03197> **LOVE MY WAY. / AEROPLANE (dance mix)** [42] [ ]

Sep 82. (lp/c) *(CBS/40 85909)* <38261> **FOREVER NOW** [20] [61]
– Forever now / Love my way / Goodbye / Only you and I / Sleep comes down / President Gas / Run and run / Danger / No easy street / Yes I do (merry-go-round). *(c+=)* – Shadow. *(re-iss. Apr86 lp/c; CBS/40 85909) (<cd re-iss. Mar02 on 'Columbia'+=; UK 506364-2 / US- 85916>)* – Alice's house / Aeroplane / I don't want to be your shadow / Mary go round / President gas (live) / No easy street (live).

Oct 82. (7") *(A 2665)* <03340> **DANGER. / (I DON'T WANT TO BE YOUR) SHADOW** [ ] [ ]
(12"+=) *(TA 2665)* – Goodbye (mix).

Feb 83. (7") <03340> **LOVE MY WAY. / SHADOW** [–] [44]

May 83. (7") <03930> **PRESIDENT GAS. / RUN AND RUN** [–] [ ]

—— **KEITH FORSEY** – drums repl. CALVERT who joined CRIME & THE CITY SOLUTION / **MARS WILLIAMS** – saxophone (ex-WAITRESSES) repl. KILBURN + MORRIS

Mar 84. (7"/12") *(A/TA 4300)* **HEAVEN. / HEARTBEAT (remix)** [29] [–]

May 84. (lp/c) *(CBS/40 25950)* <39278> **MIRROR MOVES** [15] [43]
– The ghost in you / Here come cowboys / Heaven / Heartbeat / My time / Like a stranger / Alice's house / Only a game / Highwire days. *(re-iss. Jan87 lp/c; 450356-1/-4) (cd-iss. May87; CD 25950) (re-iss. Jun94 on 'Columbia' cd/c; 450356-2/-4)*

May 84. (7"/7"pic-d) *(A/WA 4470)* <04416> **THE GHOST IN YOU. / CALYPSO DUB** [68] [59]
(12"+=) *(TA 4470)* – President Gas (live).

Jul 84. (7") <04577> **HERE COME COWBOYS. / ANOTHER EDGE** [–] [ ]

Sep 84. (7") <04627> **HEAVEN. / ALICE'S HOUSE** [–] [ ]

Oct 84. (7"/12") *(A/TA 4654)* **HEARTBEAT (Mendelssohn mix). / MY TIME** [ ] [–]
(d7"+=) *(DA 4654)* – Here comes cowboys / Heaven.

—— **PAUL GARISTO** – drums repl. DORSEY. <below 45 on 'A&M' US>

Apr 86. (7") <2826> **PRETTY IN PINK. / (dub)** [–] [41]

Aug 86. (7"/7"pic-d) *(A/WA 7242)* **PRETTY IN PINK (film version). / LOVE MY WAY** [18] [–]
(12"+=) *(TA 7242)* – ('A'version).
(d7"+=) *(DA 7242)* – Heaven / Heartbeat.

Oct 86. (7") *(650183-7)* <06420> **HEARTBREAK BEAT. / NEW DREAM** [ ] Mar87 [26]
(12"+=) *(650186-6)* – ('A'version).
(free c-s w/7"+=) *(650183-0)* – Sister Europe / Into you like a train / President Gas.

Jan 87. (7") *(FURS 3)* **ANGELS DON'T CRY. / NO RELEASE** [ ] [ ]
(free c-s w/7"+=) *(FURSD 3)* – We love you / Pretty in pink / Love my way.

Feb 87. (lp/c/cd) *(450256-1/-4/-2)* <40466> **MIDNIGHT TO MIDNIGHT** [12] [29]
– Heartbreak beat / Shock / Shadow in my heart / Angels don't cry / Midnight to midnight / One more word / Torture / All of the law / No release * / Petty in pink. *(cd+= *) (re-iss. Feb89 lp/c/cd; 463399-1/-4/-2)*

Apr 87. (7") <07224> **SHOCK. / PRESIDENT GAS (live)** [–] [ ]

Jun 87. (7") **ANGEL'S DON'T CRY. / MACK THE KNIFE** [–] [ ]

—— **VINCE ELY** – drums returned to repl. GARISTO (to CURE) + WILLIAMS

Jul 88. (7") *(FURS 4)* <07974> **ALL THAT MONEY WANTS. / BIRDLAND** [75] [ ]
(12"+=) *(FURST 4)* – No easy street (live).
(d7"++=) *(FURSEP 4)* – Heaven (live).
(cd-s++=) *(CDFURS 4)* – No tears (live).

Aug 88. (lp/c/cd) *(461110-1/-4/-2)* <44377> **ALL OF THIS AND NOTHING** (compilation) [67] [ ]
– President Gas / All that money wants / Imitation of Christ / Sister Europe / Love my way / Highwire days / Dumb waiters / Pretty in pink / Ghost in you / Heaven / Heartbreak beat / All of this and nothing. *(cd+=)* – No easy street / She is mine. *(re-iss. Apr91 & Oct00 cd/c; 461110-2)*

Nov 88. (7") <38-08499> **HEAVEN. / INDIA** [–] [ ]

Nov 89. (lp/c/cd) *(465982-1/-4/-2)* <45412> **BOOK OF DAYS** [74] [ ]
– Entertain me / Book of days / Should God forget / Torch / Parade / Mother-son / House / Wedding / I don't mine.

Jan 90. (7"/7"pic-d) *(FURS/+P 5)* **HOUSE. / WATCHTOWER** [ ] [–]
(10") *(FURSQT 5)* – ('A'side) / ('A'-Flashback mix) / Badman / Totch (electric).
(cd-s+=) *(CDFURS 5)* – Badman / Torch (electric).

—— **BUTLER, ASHTON + BUTLER** recruited **DON YALLITCH** – drums repl. ELY

East West — Epic

Jun 91. (7"/c-s) *(73855)* **UNTIL SHE COMES. / MAKE IT MINE** [ ] [–]
(12"+=/cd-s+=) *(73855)* – Sometimes / ('A'remix).

Jul 91. (c-s,cd-s) <74055> **UNTIL SHE COMES / SOMETIMES** [–] [ ]

Jul 91. (cd)(lp/c) *(9031 74669-2)(WX 422/+C)* <74669> **WORLD OUTSIDE** [68] [ ]
– Valentine / In my head / Until she comes / Don't be a girl / Sometimes / Tearing down / There's a world / Get a room / Better days / All about you. *(re-iss. cd Feb95; same)*

Sep 91. (7"/c-s) **DON'T BE A GIRL. / GET A ROOM (acoustic)** [ ] [ ]
(12"+=/cd-s+=) – (2 'A'versions).

—— disbanded after above

– compilations, etc. –

on 'C.B.S.' or 'Columbia' unless mentioned otherwise

Nov 82. (c-ep) *(A 2909)* **GREATEST ORIGINAL HITS** [ ] [–]
– Sister Europe / Pretty in pink / Dumb waiters / Love my way. *(re-iss. Mar83.as 7"ep.)*

Sep 86. (c-ep) *(450130-4)* **THE 12" TAPE** [ ] [–]
– Pretty in pink / Love my way / Heaven / Heartbeat / Ghost in you.

Jan 92. (7") **PRETTY IN PINK. / (B-side by the Only Ones)** [ ] [–]
(cd-s+=) – (other track by Only Ones).

Oct 91. (cd) *Castle; (CCSCD 308)* **THE COLLECTION** [ ] [–]

May 95. (cd) *Columbia; (480363-2) <57889>* **B SIDES AND LOST GROOVES** [ ] Oct94 [ ]

Feb 97. (cd) *Strange Fruit; (SFRSCD 003)* **RADIO ONE SESSIONS** [ ] [–]

Oct 97. (d-cd) *(487389-2)* **SHOULD GOD FORGET: A RETROSPECTIVE** [ ] [ ]
– India / Sister Europe / Pulse / Mack the knife / Blacks / We love you / Imitation of Christ / Soap commercial / Pretty in pink / Mr. Jones / Into you like a train / I wanna sleep with you / Merry go round / President Gas / LOve my way / Sleep comes down / I don't want to be your shadow / Alice's house / The ghost in you / Here come cowboys / Heaven / Highwire days / Heartbeat / All of the law / Heartbreak beat / All that money wants / Entertain me / Should God forget / Torch / Get a room / Until she comes / All about you / There's a world outside.

Mar 02. (cd) *Sony; (506035-2) <86191>* **BEAUTIFUL CHAOS (GREATEST HITS LIVE)** [ ] Nov01 [ ]

Oct 02. (3xcd-box) *(509506-2)* **THE PSYCHEDELIC FURS / TALK TALK TALK / FOREVER NOW** [ ] [–]

Sep 03. (cd) *Sony; (512232-2)* **SUPER HITS** [ ] [ ]

LOVE SPIT LOVE

RICHARD BUTLER – vocals / **RICHARD FORTUS** – guitar / **TIM BUTLER** – bass / **FRANK FERRER** – drums

Imago-RCA Imago-RCA

Oct 94. (cd/c) *(72787 21055-2/-4) <21030>* **LOVE SPIT LOVE** [ ] [ ]
– Seventeen / Superman / Half a life / Jigsaw / Change in the weather / Wake up / Am I wrong / Green / Please / Codeine / St. Mary's gate / More. *(<d-cd-iss. Feb01 on 'Burning Airlines'+=; PILOT 41>)* – All she wants / Codeine (acoustic) / More than money (alt. take) / Song (acoustic) / Wake up (acoustic) / Wake up (live) / I am wrong (video) / Change in the weather (video).

Oct 94. (c-s,cd-s) *<25073>* **AM I WRONG / CODEINE** [–] [83]

PUBLIC ENEMY

Formed: New York, USA . . . early 80's by CHUCK D (b. CARLTON RIDENHOUR), a student at Adelphi University in Long Island. MC'ing for a local DJ crew, Spectrum City, CHUCK met the outfit's mainman, HANK SHOCKLEE (who would subsequently become PUBLIC ENEMY's co-producer), the pair subsequently teaming up for BILL STEPHNEY's rap show on WBAU. Producing rough mixes and co-hosting the show, CHUCK developed his hard hitting lyrical style while SHOCKLEE undertook his earliest experiments in creating funky noise collages. The inimitable FLAVOR FLAV (b. WILLIAM DRAYTON) was an avid listener, eventually joining the show as a co-host; the stage was set for the formation of PUBLIC ENEMY. Mulling over the offer of a record deal from 'Def Jam' via Rick Rubin, CHUCK eventually formulated the concept of the group alongside co-conspirators SHOCKLEE and STEPHNEY. With a brief to combine the caustic hip hop of RUN-D.M.C. and the radical attitude of The CLASH, they appointed DJ Terminator X (b. NORMAN RODGERS), PROFESSOR GRIFF (b. RICHARD GRIFFIN) as 'Minister Of Information' and a militaristic back-up troupe named the S1W's (Security Of The First World). They also set up a formidable production team, the aptly monikered BOMB SQUAD, consisting of CHUCK, ERIC 'VIETNAM' SADLER, HANK and his brother KEITH. Taking their name from an early demo track (included in reworked form on the debut album), 'PUBLIC ENEMY No.1', the group unleashed their debut album, 'YO! BUM RUSH THE SHOW' (1987). The intent was clear from the start; the sleeve depicted the crew standing menacingly over a turntable in a darkened basement, their faces semi-submerged in shadows while the PE logo featured a sniper surrounded by a mock rifle sight. The music inside was equally uncompromising, by 1987 standards anyway. Opening with the pre-driveby fury of 'YOU'RE GONNA GET YOURS' (still arguably PE's finest moment), the record combined 70's funk samples (METERS, FRED WESLEY etc.), punishing beats, noise collages and even a guitar solo by LIVING COLOR's VERNON REID ('SOPHISTICATED BITCH'). The political campaign was kickstarted with 'RIGHTSTARTER (MESSAGE TO A BLACK MAN)', CHUCK D possessing one of the most loudest, most portentous voices in rap. This was clearly a man who meant business, not another mealy-mouthed hip hop boaster. 'IT TAKES A NATION OF MILLIONS TO HOLD US BACK' (1988) was PE's tour de force, hip hop's tour de force, even. With the BOMB SQUAD creating a multi-layered blanket of noise (a hybrid of their trademark, screeching JAMES BROWN horn stabs, incendiary political samples and dextrous scratching), CHUCK D raged through what amounted to a whole new black manifesto. In terms of emotional directness and righteous anger, this record makes even the most vicious "Gangsta" album sound like a cash-in thrown together during a lunch break. Among the highlights were 'BRING THE NOISE' (later the subject of a collaborative re-vamp with ANTHRAX), 'DON'T BELIEVE THE HYPE' and the pulsing paranoia of 'BLACK STEEL IN THE HOUR OF CHAOS'. PE even managed to make a SLAYER riff sound groovy, mangling it up on 'SHE WATCH CHANNEL ZERO' while The BOMB SQUAD seemingly provided the base material for MADONNA's 'JUSTIFY MY LOVE' with 'SECURITY OF THE FIRST WORLD'. The album went Top 10 in the UK, propelling PUBLIC ENEMY into the media spotlight. The group were already the subject of much controversy and following anti-semitic remarks made by PROFESSOR GRIFF in a newspaper interview, the media circus went into overdrive. Although GRIFF and PUBLIC ENEMY soon parted ways, these events informed much of the group's new material. CHUCK D's initial response was the inflammatory 'FIGHT THE POWER', the rapper railing against what he perceived to be a white, European conspiracy to wipe out the black race. The song was given added resonance after appearing in Spike Lee's 'Do The Right Thing' over scenes of race rioting'. 'WELCOME TO THE TERRORDOME' was the next single, an awesome, intimidating narrative. Much of 'FEAR OF A BLACK PLANET' (1990) portrayed PE as victims, hounded by a predominantly white media and while there were accusations of racism, CHUCK had previously clearly stated that the group's agenda was not anti-white. Musically, the album wasn't quite as resourcefully ambitious as its predecessor, although tracks such as '911 IS A JOKE' and 'BURN, HOLLYWOOD, BURN' were classic PUBLIC ENEMY, the record becoming PE's biggest seller to date (Top 5 UK, Top 10 US). Later that year, it came to light that the group had been mentioned in an FBI report to congress, underlining the scale of PE's influence. With SISTER SOULJAH now on board, 'APOCALYPSE '91 . . .THE ENEMY STRIKES BLACK' was as militant as ever, at least lyrically. Expressing outrage at the American state's refusal to celebrate Martin Luther King's birthday, 'BY THE TIME I GET TO ARIZONA' set swathes of towering funk against SOULJAH's almost gospel tones and CHUCK's irate rapping. Elsewhere, tracks like 'NIGHTTRAIN' and '1 MILLION BOTTLEBAGS' saw the rapper railing against the self-destructiveness of his own community. More commercial and with a cleaner production than PE's previous releases, the album reached the US Top 5. In the three years prior to the next album, FLAV (who had been arrested on a domestic charge) again found himself on the wrong side of the law in late '93, following an incident with his neighbour. After a spell in rehab for drug addiction, FLAV was back in action for 'MUSE SICK-N-HOUR MESS AGE' (1994), scoring with the funky 'GIVE IT UP' and 'SO WHATCHA GONNA DO NOW' wherein CHUCK berated the pointless negativity of gangsta rap. Although the record was a relative success, PUBLIC ENEMY felt they had taken the concept to its limit, calling it a day the following year (one of their last shows was an emotional affair at England's 'Phoenix Festival'). CHUCK D had always been peerless both as an entertainer and an educator, but it was the latter route that he subsequently chose for his post-PUBLIC ENEMY activites, lecturing on the college circuit as well as writing a book and hosting a news show on America's CNN. While this one-man think tank is not on the ball 100% of time (some controversial comments on the Northern Ireland situation at a Glasgow Barrowlands gig spring to mind), he remains a fiercely articulate voice for the disenfranchised among the black community. PUBLIC ENEMY's legacy meanwhile, transcends all boundaries of race and culture, no hip hop artists have yet come close. Of late (after a final set, 'HE GOT GAME' for their old label), PUBLIC ENEMY have emerged on the independent, 'Play It Again Sam', although 1999's 'THERE'S A POISON GOIN' ON', was poorly received; CHUCK D's latest project CONFRONTATION CAMP looked the more promising for the future. While hip hop had long since abandoned politics for vanity and violence, PUBLIC ENEMY are still one of the sanest voices in their field, even if not as many people – especially younger people – are taking as much notice as they once did. 'REVOLVERLUTION' (2002) was at least a partial attempt to reach out to that audience with a more contemporary, user friendly batch of new tracks, remixes, interview clips, live cuts and the like.

Album rating: YO! BUMRUSH THE SHOW (*8) / IT TAKES A NATION OF MILLIONS TO HOLD US BACK (*9) / FEAR OF A BLACK PLANET (*9) / APOCALYPSE 91 . . . THE ENEMY STRIKES BACK (*8) / GREATEST MISSES part compilation (*4) / MUSE SICK-N-HOUR MESS AGE (*5) / HE GOT GAME (*5) / THERE'S A POISON GOIN' ON (*4) / REVOLVERLUTION (*5)

CHUCK D (b. CARLTON RIDENHOUR, 1 Aug'60) – vocals / **FLAVOR FLAV** (b. WILLIAM DRAYTON, 16 Mar'59) – multi-instrumentalist, classically trained pianist / **TERMINATOR X** (b. NORMAN LEE RODGERS, 25 Aug'66) – DJ / **PROFESSOR GRIFF** (b. RICHARD GRIFFIN) – information-vocals / plus part-time **JAMES ALLEN + JAMES NORMAN**

<Please note they never released a 7" in US>

Def Jam / Def Jam

Mar 87. (7") *(650497-7)* **PUBLIC ENEMY No.1. / TIMEBOMB** [ ] [ ]
(12"+=) *(650497-6) <440671-9>* – Son of Public Enemy No.1 (Flavor Whop version).

Apr 87. (lp/c/cd) *(450482-1/-4/-2) <40658>* **YO! BUMRUSH THE SHOW** [ ] [ ]
– You're gonna get yours / Sophisticated bitch / Miuzi weighs a ton / Timebomb / Too much posse / Rightstarter (message to a black man) / Public enemy No.1 / M.P.E. / Yo! bumrush the show / Raise the roof / Megablast / Terminator X speaks with his hands. *(cd re-iss. Sep93 & Jul95; 527441-2)*

Jun 87. (7") *(650975-7)* **YOU'RE GONNA GET YOURS. / MIUZI WEIGHS A TON** [ ] [ ]
(12"+=) *(650975-6) <440686-1>* – ('A'dub mix) / ('A'-Terminator X getaway mix) / Rebel without a pause.

Nov 87. (7"/7"pic-d) *(651245-7/-0)* **REBEL WITHOUT A PAUSE (vocal). / ('A'instrumental)** [37] [–]
(12"+=) *(651245-6)* – Terminator X speaks with his hands / Sophisticated bitch.
(12"+=) *(651245-8)* – Bring the noise (noise version) / Sophisticated bitch.

Dec 87. (12"; by The BLACK FLAMES) *<440749-1>* **ARE YOU MY WOMAN? / BRING THE NOISE** [–] [ ]
(12"+=) *(440754-5>* – ('A'-Noise version) / ('A'-acappella mix).

Jan 88. (7") *(651335-7)* **BRING THE NOISE. / SOPHISTICATED BITCH** [32] [–]
(12"+=/s12"+=) *(651335-6/-8)* – ('A'noise versions) / ('A'acappella version) / ('A'-instrumental).

Jun 88. (7"/s7") *(652833-7/-0)* **DON'T BELIEVE THE HYPE. / PROPHETS OF RAGE** [18] [ ]
(12"+=) *(652833-6) <4407934>* – The rhythm, the rebel (acappella) / ('B'-power version).
(cd-s+=) *(652833-2)* – Bring the noise / ('B'-power version).

Jul 88. (lp/c/cd) *(462415-1/-4/-2) <4303>* **IT TAKES A NATION OF MILLIONS TO HOLD US BACK** [8] [42]
– Countdown to armageddon / Bring the noise / Don't believe the hype / Cold lampin' with Flavor / Terminator X to the edge of panic / Mind terrorist / Louder than a bomb / Caught, can we get a witness / Show 'em whatcha got / She watch Channel Zero?! / Night of the living baseheads / Black steel in the hour of chaos / Security of the first world / Rebel without a pause / Prophets of rage / Party for your right to fight. *(re-iss. cd Jul95; 527358-2)*

Oct 88. (7"/s7") *(653046-7/-0)* **NIGHT OF THE LIVING BASEHEADS. / TERMINATOR X TO THE EDGE OF PANIC** [63] [ ]
(12"+=/cd-s+=) *(653046-8/-2)* – ('A'-Anti high blood pressure mix) / ('A'-Terminator X meets DST and Chuck Chillout instrumental mix).
(s7") *(653046-9) - ('A'side) / ('A'-Terminator X meets DST . . .).*
(US-12"+=) *<4408121>* – Cold lampin' with Flavor.

1989. (12"ep) *<4468216>* **BLACK STEEL IN THE HOUR OF CHAOS (radio version) / ('A'instrumental). / TOO MUCH POSSE / CAUGHT, CAN I GET A WITNESS (dub mix) / B-SIDE WINS AGAIN** [–] [ ]

Jun 89. (7") *(ZB 42877)* **FIGHT THE POWER. / ('A'version)** [29] [ ]
(ext.12"+=/ext.cd-s+=) *(ZT/ZD 42878) <MOT 4647>* – ('A'-Flavor meets Spike Lee mix).
(above was issued on a one-off 'Motown' deal).

Jan 90. (7"/c-s) *(655476-0/-4)* **WELCOME TO THE TERRORDOME. / ('A'-Terromental version)** [18] [ ]
(12"+=/cd-s+=) *(655476-8/-2) <4473135>* – Terrorbeat / Black steel in the hour of chaos.

—— Trimmed when PROFESSOR GRIFF left permanently to go solo. He soon released debut 'PAWNS IN THE GAME' with his LAST ASIATIC DISCIPLES. A year later he followed this with second album 'KAD'S II WIZ *7* DOME'.

Apr 90. (7"/c-s) *(655837-7/-4)* **911 IS A JOKE. / REVOLUTIONARY GENERATION** [41] [ ]
(12"+=/cd-s+=) *(655837-8/-2) <4473179>* – ('A'&'B'-instrumentals).
(12") *(655837-5)* – ('A'side) / Son of Public Enemy (Flavor Whop version) / Bring the noise (no noise version) / Rebel without a pause.

Apr 90. (cd/c/lp) *(466281-2/-4/-1) <45413>* **FEAR OF A BLACK PLANET** [4] [10]
– Contract on the world love jam / Brothers gonna work it out / 911 is a joke / Incident at 66.6 FM / Welcome to the terrordome / Meet the G that killed me / Pollywanacraka / Anti-nigger machine / Burn Hollywood burn / Power to the people / Who stole the soul / Fear of a black planet / Revolutionary generation / Can't do nuttin' for ya man / Reggae Jax / Leave this off your fuckin' charts / B side wins again / War at 33 1/3 / Final count of the collision between us and the damned. *(re-iss. cd Jul95; 523446-2)*

Jun 90. (7"/c-s) *(656018-0/-4)* **BROTHERS GONNA WORK IT OUT (remix). / WAR AT 33 1/3** [46] [ ]
(12"+=/12"w-poster+=) *(656018-6/-8) <4473391-1>* – Bring the noise (no noise instrumental) / ('B'instrumental).
(cd-s+=) *(656018-2) <44K73391>* – Anti-nigger machine / Don't believe the hype.

Oct 90. (7"/c-s) *(656385-7/-4)* **CAN'T DO NUTTIN' FOR YA MAN. / ('A'-Bass in your face mix)** [53] [–]
(12"+=/cd-s+=) *(656385-6/-2)* – ('A'-dub in your face mix).
(12") *(656385-8)* – ('A'-full rub mix) / Get the f . . . out of Dodge (uncensored) / Powersave / Burn Hollywood burn.

—— added **SISTER SOULIJAH** – vocals

—— (May'91) FLAVOR FLAV served 30 days in jail for an earlier incident in which he was said to have hit the mother of his 3 children Karen Ross.

—— Jun'91, teamed up with ANTHRAX on a hit single version of 'BRING THE NOISE'.

Sep 91. (7"/c-s) *(657530-7/-4)* **CAN'T TRUSS IT (Goree Island Conga radio mix). / ('A'-Almighty raw 125th street bootleg mix** [22] [50]
(cd-s+=) *(657530-7)* *<44K73869>* – Move! (censored radio mix).
(12"++=) *(657530-6)* – ('A'-instrumental).

Oct 91. (cd/c/d-lp) *(468751-2/-4/-1)* *<47374>* **APOCALYPSE 91 . . .THE ENEMY STRIKES BACK** [8] [4]
– Lost at birth / Rebirth / Night train / Can't truss it / I don't wanna be called yo niga / How to kill a radio consultant / By the time I get to Arizona / Move! / 1 million bottlebags / More news at 11 / Shut 'em down / A letter to the New York post / Get the f . . . outta Dodge / Bring the noise (w/ ANTHRAX). *(re-iss. cd Jul95; 523479-2)*

Jan 92. (7"/c-s) *(657761-7/-4)* **SHUT 'EM DOWN (Pe-Te rock mixx). / BY THE TIME I GET TO ARIZONA** [21] [ ]
(12"+=/12"pic-d+=/cd-s+=) *(657761-6/-8/-2)* *<44K74165>* – ('A'rock mixx instrumental) / ('A'bald beat acappella) / ('B'side dubbed).

Mar 92. (7"/c-s) *(657864-7/-4)* **NIGHT TRAIN (Pe-Te rock . . .mixx). / MORE NEWS AT 11 (Funk minister . . .mixx)** [55] [ ]
(12"+=/12"pic-d+=) *(657864-6/-8)* – ('A'-Pete Rock LIRR Strong island mixx).
(cd-s++=) *(657864-2)* *<44K74254>* – ('A'instrumental mixx).

Sep 92. (cd/c/lp) *(472031-2/-4/-1)* *<53014>* **GREATEST MISSES** (part compilation) [14] [13]
– Tie goes to the runner / Hitt da road Jack / Get off my back / Air hoodlum got ta do what I gotta do / Hazy shade of criminal megablast (remix) / Louder than a bomb (telephone groove) / How to kill a radio consultant (DJ check chillout..) / Who stole the soul (mixx) / Party for your right to fight (metromix) / You're gonna get yours (version). *(cd+=)* – Shut 'em down (live in the UK). *(re-iss. cd Jul95; 523487-2)*

Mar 93. (cd/c) *(473052-2/-4)* **THE 12" MIXES** [ ] [–]

—— PROFESSOR GRIFF, TERMINATOR X, and newcomer SISTER SOULJAH all had own releases for various labels from 1990 onwards.
FLAVOR FLAV was charged late '93, for drunkenly attempting to shoot his neighbour, after he allegedly thought his wife was committing adultery.

Jul 94. (c-s,cd-s) *<853316>* **GIVE IT UP / BEDLAM** [–] [33]

Aug 94. (c-ep/12"ep/cd-ep) *(DEFMC/12DEF/DEFCD 1)* **GIVE IT UP. / ('A'-main version) / Bedlam (instrumental)** [18] [–]
(cd-s+=) *(DEFDX 1)* – Live and undrugged (part 2) / Harry Allen interactive highway / Bedlam (instrumental).

Aug 94. (cd/c/lp) *<(523362-2/-4/-1)>* **MUSE SICK-N-HOUR MESS AGE** [12] [14]
– Whole lotta love / Theatrical / Give it up / What side you on? / Body count / Stop in the name / What kind of power we got? / So watcha gone do now? / White Heaven – black Hell / Race against time / Used to call it dope / Aintnuthin' buttersong / Live & undrugged parts I & II / I ain't madd at all / Death of carjacka / I stand accused / Gold complexx / Hitler day / Harry Allen superhighway.

Dec 94. (12"ep/cd-ep) *(12DEF/DEFCD 2)* **I STAND ACCUSED / WHAT KIND OF POWER WE GOT** [ ] [ ]
(cd-s+=) *(DEFCDX 2)* – I stand accused (Sleek'sschool of self-defence mix) / Mao Tse Tung.

—— On 26th May'95, FLAVOR was jailed for drug possession. He was sent to a rehab centre and given three years probation. While in Italy in July, he broke his leg in a motorcycle accident.

Jul 95. (c-s) *(DEFMC 5)* **SO WHATCHA GONNA DO NOW? / BLACK STEEL IN THE HOUR OF CHAOS** [50] [ ]
(12"+=/cd-s+=) *(12DEF/DEFCD 5)* – ('A'-Drive by s**t mix) / ('A'-Drive by instrumental).

May 98. (cd/c/d-lp) *<(558130-2/-4/-1)>* **HE GOT GAME** [50] [26]
– Resurrection / He got game / Unstoppable / Shake your booty / Is your god a dog / House of the rising sun / Revelation 33 1/3 revolutions / Game face / Politics of the Sneaker Pimps / What you need is Jesus / Super agent / Go cat go / Sudden death (interlude).

May 98. (c-s) *(568985-4)* **HE GOT GAME / ('A'mix)** [16] [ ]
(12"+=/cd-s+=) *(568985-1/-2)* – Resurrection (mixes).

Play It Again Sam | Play It again Sam

Jul 99. (cd/c/d-lp) *<(PIASX CD/MC/LP 004)>* **THERE'S A POISON GOIN' ON** [55] [ ]
– Dark side of the wall: 2000 / Do you wanna go our way / LSD / Here I go / 41.19 / Crash / Crayola / First the sheep then the shepherd? / World tour sessions / Last mass of the caballeros / I / What what / Kervorkian / Swindlers list.

Sep 99. (12") *(PIASX 005T)* **DO YOU WANNA GO OUR WAY?? (extended). / (instrumental) / CRAYOLA** [66] [–]
(cd-s) *(PIASX 005CD)* – ('A'clean version) / I / ('A'video).

Def Jam | Koch

Oct 02. (cd) *(238388-2)* *<8388>* **REVOLVERLUTION** [ ] Jul02 [ ]
– Gotta give the peeps what they need / Revolverlution / Miuzi weighs a ton / Put it up / Can a woman make a man lose his mind? / (Public Enemy service announcement #1) / Fight the power / By the time I get to Arizona / Post concert Arizona / Son of a Bush / 54321 . . . boom / Welcome to the terrordome / B side wins again / Get your shit together / (Public Enemy service announcement #2) / Shut em down / Now a' daze / Public Enemy No.1. *(bonus cd+=)* – The making of Burn Hollywood Burn (with BIG DADDY KANE & FLAVOR FLAV) / Gotta give the peeps what they need / What good is a bomb (with PROFESSOR GRIFF & 7th OCTAVE).

TERMINATOR X

P.R.O. Div. | P.R.O. Div

Dec 90. (12"ep) *(RAL 6564456)* **WANNA BE DANCIN'. / GROOVE WITH THE X-MAN / BUCK-WHYLIN / ('A'instrumental)** [ ] [ ]

May 91. (cd/c/lp) *(RAL 468421-2/-4/-1)* *<RAL 46896>* **TERMINATOR X AND THE VALLEY OF THE JEEP BEATS** (with various help credited to that particular group or artist) [ ] [97]

May 91. (12"ep) *<RAL 4473737>* **HONEY DON'T PLAY DAT (vocal & instrumental). / JUVENILE DELINQUINTZ (vocal & instrumental)** [–] [ ]

Aug 91. (12"ep) *<RAL 4473903>* **JUVENILE DELINQUINTZ (two radio versions & instrumental). / BACK TO THE SCENE OF THE BASS (two versions & instrumental)** [–] [ ]

Jun 94. (cd/c) *<(523343)* **TERMINATOR X AND THE GODFATHERS OF THREATT: SUPER BAD** [ ] [ ]
– (various artists like above)

—— SISTER SOULJAH also had US releases on 'Epic'; the singles 'THE FINAL SOULTION; SLAVERY'S BACK IN EFFECT' *<497407-1>* and 'THE HATE THAT HATE PRODUCED' *<497421-0>*. These just preceded April '92 album 'DEGREES OF POWER' *<EK 48713360>*.

CHUCK D

Mercury | Mercury

Oct 96. (c-s) *(MERMC 476)* **NO / (LP version)** [55] [–]
(12"+=/cd-s+=) *(MER X/CD 476)* – (mixes; clean no holds barred / clean Mr Elite / instrumental).

Oct 96. (cd/c) *<(532944-2/-4)>* **AUTOBIOGRAPHY OF MISTACHUCK** [ ] [ ]
– Mistachuck / Free big Willie / No / Generation wrekked / Niggativity . . . do I dare disturb the universe / Talk show created the fool / But you can kill the nigger in you / Underdog / Paid / Endonesia / Pride / Horizontal heron.

—— in Jun'01, CHUCK D would guest on PUBLIC DOMAIN's UK hit, 'Rock Da Funky Beats'

PUBLIC IMAGE LTD.

Formed: London, England . . . July '78 by ex-SEX PISTOLS frontman, JOHNNY ROTTEN, who reverted to his real name, JOHN LYDON. He recruited local friends, guitarist KEITH LEVENE (ex-CLASH), bassist JAH WOBBLE and Canadian drummmer JIM WALKER, re-signing to 'Virgin' in the process. 'PUBLIC IMAGE', both the debut single and the title track of the debut album, was a raucous slice of post-PISTOLS sonic energy, the record coming wrapped in a mock-newspaper sleeve and reaching the UK Top 10 late in 1978. The album followed it into the Top 30 at the end of the year, hardly a departure from punk but a convincing statement of intent nevertheless; tracks such as 'RELIGION', 'ANNA LISA' and 'ATTACK' formed the basis for LYDON's subsequent experiments. Preceded by the bizarre 'DEATH DISCO' single, 'METAL BOX 1' (1979) was a strikingly differerent beast, its pristine packaging (three 12" 45's inside a metal film can, something much copied by record company marketing departments in the years to come) rather deceptively encasing a dark, often disturbing set of experimental, Eastern-influenced material. As far from punk as LYDON has ever ventured, the record utilised monotonic repetition, LEVENE's shards of splintered guitar dissecting the vague structures of WOBBLE's rubbery basslines while LYDON wailed and ranted like a damned soul. John Peel was a particular champion of the record, playlisting virtually all its disturbing but accessible tracks, 'CAREERING', 'POPTONES' and 'GRAVEYARD' highlighting what came to be regarded as one of the last classic "punk/alternative" albums of the 70's. Surely one of the most avant-garde releases to ever grace the Top 20, the album even hit the charts a second time (Top 50) when it was re-issued in double-album format as 'SECOND EDITION' two months later. Following a patchy live album, 'PARIS AU PRINTEMPS' (1980), WOBBLE departed on a sour note, leaving LYDON and LEVENE to mastermind 'FLOWERS OF ROMANCE' (1981). A comparatively weaker effort, the record nevertheless almost made the Top 10 and the more contrived moments were interspersed with a few gems, notably the Burundi-esque title track, a Top 30 hit single. LEVENE was also soon to leave in less than pleasant circumstances following the success of 'P.I.L.'s biggest hit single to date, the compelling 'THIS IS NOT A LOVE SONG'. LYDON subsequently completed the lacklustre 'THIS IS WHAT YOU WANT . . . THIS IS WHAT YOU GET' opus with the help of session musicians, disbanding the group around the time of the album's release in the summer of '84. By this point, LYDON had moved to Los Angeles and his career slowed up somewhat, although he subsequently reformed 'P.I.L.' in late '85. Using such respected (and glaringly un-punk) musos as STEVE VAI, RYUICHI SAKAMOTO, GINGER BAKER and RAVI SHANKAR, LYDON recorded the minimally titled 'ALBUM' (also released as 'CASSETTE' and 'COMPACT DISC', of course). The BILL LASWELL-produced effort remains his last consistent collection, the 'SINGLE', 'RISE', almost making the Top 10, a driving, resonating, infectiously commercial example of LYDON doing what he does best (although I could be wrong . . .). For the remainder of the 80's, LYDON was content to churn out formula 'JOHNNY ROTTEN'-to-order type material that often incorporated bland Americanised rock backing. This only served to further entrench him in the mire of self-parody. Albums like 'HAPPY?' (1987) and '9' (1989) achieved only minimal commercial success although LYDON was back in the Top 20 in 1990 with 'DON'T ASK ME', the punk veteran's comment on the topical subject of the environment. The single was cannily included by 'Virgin' on a best of set, the hopefully titled 'GREATEST HITS – SO FAR' (1990). Then again, LYDON proved he could still cut the mustard with his late '93 LEFTFIELD collaboration, 'OPEN UP'. When LYDON lets rip, as he does here (a blood curdling wail of 'Burn, Hollywood, burn'), he is still the most frightening man in rock, no contest. Just to prove it, he hooked up once more with the original SEX PISTOLS line-up for the aptly titled 'Filthy Lucre' tour, appearing on 'Top Of The Pops' and scaring young children all over again with his gravity-defying hairdo.

Album rating: PUBLIC IMAGE (*9) / METAL BOX 1 (*10) / FLOWERS OF ROMANCE (*5) / LIVE IN TOKYO (*5) / THIS IS WHAT YOU WANT . . . THIS IS WHAT YOU GET (*4) / ALBUM (*7) / HAPPY? (*6) / 9 (*5) / GREATEST HITS – SO FAR compilation (*8) / THAT WHAT IS NOT (*4) / PLASTIC BOX boxed set (*8) / John Lydon: PSYCHO'S PATH (*4)

JOHN LYDON (b.31 Jan'56, Finsbury Park, London, England) – vocals (ex-SEX PISTOLS) / **KEITH LEVENE** (b. London, England) – guitar (ex-CLASH) / **JAH WOBBLE** (b. JOHN WORDLE) – bass / **JIM WALKER** (b. Canada) – drums (ex-FURIES)

—— (most singles just credit "PiL")

Virgin Warners

Oct 78. (7") *(VS 228)* **PUBLIC IMAGE. / THE COWBOY SONG** [9] [–]

Dec 78. (lp/c) *(V/TCV 2114)* <3288> **PUBLIC IMAGE** [22] [ ]
– Theme / Religion I / Religion II / Annalisa / Public image / Low life / Attack / Fodderstompf. *(re-iss. Apr86 lp/c; OVED/+C 160) (cd-iss. Jun88; CDV 2114)*

—— **DAVE CROWE** – drums repl. WALKER who joined The PACK (with KIRK BRANDON) added **JEANNETTE LEE** – keyboards, synthesizer

Jun 79. (7") *(VS 274)* **DEATH DISCO. / NO BIRDS DO SING** [20] [–]
(12"+=) *(VS 274-12)* – Death disco megamix.

Sep 79. (7"/ext.12") *(VS 299/+12)* **MEMORIES. / ANOTHER** [60] [–]

Dec 79. (3x12"box)<lp> *(METAL 1)* <3288> **METAL BOX 1**
<US-title 'SECOND EDITION'> [18] Jul80 [ ]
– Albatross / Memories / Swan lake/ / Poptones / Careering / No birds / Graveyard / / The suit / Bad baby / Socialist – Chant – Radio 4. *(re-iss. Feb80 as 'SECOND EDITION' d-lp/c; VD/TCVD 2512); hit UK No.46) (cd-iss. Jun86; CDVD 2512) (original; cd-iss. Jun90; MTLLCD 1) (d-cd-iss. Mar03 on 'E.M.I.'; 581749-2)*

—— **RICHARD DUDANSKI** – drums (ex-101'ERS, ex-BASEMENT 5) repl. CROWE

—— (he had joined during Apr-Sep'79) (below French titles of above songs)

Nov 80. (lp/c) *(V/TCV 2183)* **PARIS AU PRINTEMPS (live 'PARIS IN THE SPRING')** [61] [–]
– Theme / Psalmodie (Chant) / Precipitamment (Careering) / Sale bebe (Bad baby) / La vie ignoble (Low life) / Attaque (Attack) / Timbres de pop (Poptones). *(re-iss. Mar84 lp/c; OVED/+C 50)*

—— (Jul'80) trimmed to a quartet when JAH WOBBLE went solo. / **MARTIN ATKINS** (b. 3 Aug'59, Coventry, England) (aka BRIAN BRAIN) – drums repl. DUDANSKI who joined RAINCOATS. (ATKINS was sacked Jul80, most of drums by LYDON and LEVENE)

Mar 81. (7") *(VS 397)* **FLOWERS OF ROMANCE. / HOME IS WHERE THE HEART IS** [24] [–]
(12"+=) *(VS 397-12)* – ('A'instrumental).

Apr 81. (lp/c) *(V/TCV 2189)* <3536> **FLOWERS OF ROMANCE** [11] [ ]
– Four enclosed walls / Track 8 / Phenagen / Flowers of romance / Under the house / Hymie's him / Banging the door / Go back / Francis massacre. *(re-iss. Mar84 lp/c; OVED/+C 51) (cd-iss. Apr90 & Mar94; CDV 2189) (cd re-iss. Jun01 on 'Disky'; VI 64642-2)*

—— **KEN LOCKIE** – keyboards (ex-COWBOYS INTERNATIONAL, ex-Solo) repl. LEE / added (May82) **MARTIN ATKINS** – drums / **PETE JONES** – bass

Aug 83. (7") *(VS 529)* **THIS IS NOT A LOVE SONG. / PUBLIC IMAGE** [5] [–]
(12"+=) *(VS 529-12)* – Blue water / ('A'remix).
(re-iss. Jun88 cd-ep; CDT 14)

—— LYDON + ATKINS were joined by US session people from New Jersey; **JOSEPH GUIDA** – guitar / **TOM ZVONCHECK** – keyboards / **LOUIE BERNARDI** – bass

Virgin Elektra

Sep 83. (2x12"/c) *(VGD/+C 3508)* **LIVE IN TOKYO (live)** [28] [–]
– Annalisa / Religion / Low life / Solitaire / Flowers of romance / This is not a love song / Death disco / Bad life / Banging the door / Under the house. *(cd-iss. 1986; VGDCD 3508)*

May 84. (7"/ext.12") *(VS 675/+12)* **BAD LIFE. / QUESTION MARK** [71] [–]

Jul 84. (lp/c) *(V/TCV 2309)* <60365> **THIS IS WHAT YOU WANT . . . THIS IS WHAT YOU GET** [56] [ ]
– Bad life / This is not a love song / Solitaire / Tie me to the length of that / The pardon / Where are you? / 1981 / The order of death. *(re-iss. 1986 lp/c; OVED/+C 176) (cd-iss. Apr90; CDV 2309)*

Aug 84. (lp; as KEITH LEVENE & PiL) *<XYZ 007>* **THE COMMERCIAL ZONE** [–] [ ]
– (as last album, with LEVENE's guitar parts more obvious)

—— Disbanded mid'84, but reformed by LYDON late '85 with on session **STEVE VAI** – guitar (ex-ALCATRAZZ) / **RYUICHI SAKAMOTO** – keys (ex-YELLOW MAGIC ORCHESTRA) / **GINGER BAKER** (ex-CREAM, etc) / **TONY WILLIAMS** (ex-MILES DAVIES, etc) / **RAVI SHANKER** – violin

Jan 86. (7"/12") *(VS 841/+12)* **RISE. / ('A'instrumental)** [11] [–]

Feb 86. (cd/c/lp) *(CD/TC+/V 2366)* <60438> **ALBUM** [14] [ ]
– FFF / Rise / Fishing / Round / Bags / Home / Ease. *(re-iss. 1989 lp/c; OVED/+C 245)*

Apr 86. (7") *(VS 855)* **HOME. / ROUND** [75] [–]
(12"+=) *(VS 855-12)* – ('A'-lp version).
(d7"+=) *(VSD 855)* – Rise / ('A'instrumental).

— (Feb86) **LYDON** recruited **LU EDMUNDS** – guitar, keys (ex-DAMNED, ex-MEKONS) / **JOHN McGEOGH** – guitar (of ARMOURY SHOW, ex-SIOUXSIE & THE BANSHEES) / **ALAN DIAS** – bass / **BRUCE SMITH** – drums (ex-RIP, RIG & PANIC, ex-SLITS, ex-POP GROUP)

Virgin | Virgin

Aug 87. (7") *(VS 988)* **SEATTLE. / SELFISH RUBBISH** [47] [–]
(12"+=/c-s+=) *(VS/+C 988-12)* – The suit.

Sep 87. (cd/c/lp) *(CD/TC+/V 2455)* *<90642>* **HAPPY?** [40] [ ]
– Seattle / Rules and regulations / The body / Save me / Hard times / Open and revolving / Angry / Fat chance hotel. *(re-iss. Apr90 lp/c; OVED/+C 299)*

Oct 87. (7") *(VS 1010)* **THE BODY. / RELIGION (new version)** [100] [–]
(12"+=) *(VST 1010)* – Angry.
(12") *(VSR 1010)* – ('A'extended remix) / ('A'-U.S. remix) / Angry.

— trimmed to a quartet when EDMUNDS dispersed.

Apr 89. (7") *(VS 1181)* **DISAPPOINTED. / SAME OLD STORY** [38] [–]
(ext.12"+=/12"pic-d+=/3"cd-s+=) *(VS T/TY/CD 181)* – ('A'version).

Jun 89. (cd/c/lp) *(CD/TC+/V 2588)* *<91062>* **9** [36] [ ]
– Happy / Disappointed / Warrior / U.S.L.S. 1 / Sand castles in the snow / Worry / Brave new world / Like that / Same old story / Armada.

Jul 89. (7"/7"g-f) *(VS 1195)* **WARRIOR. / U.S.L.S. 1** [ ] [–]
(ext.12"+=) *(VST 1195)* – ('A'instrumental).
(3"cd-s+=) *(VSCD 1195)* – ('A'extended).
(12") *(VSTX 1195)* – ('A'-Dave Dorrell remix) / ('A'instrumental).

Oct 90. (7"/c-s) *(VS/+C 1231)* **DON'T ASK ME. / RULES AND REGULATIONS** [22] [–]
(cd-s+=) *(VSCD 1231)* – Warrior (original).
(12") *(VST 1231)* – ('A'extended) / Warrior (remix).

Oct 90. (cd/c/lp) *(CD/TC+/V 2644)* *<86196>* **GREATEST HITS – SO FAR** (compilation) [20] [ ]
– Public image / Death disco / Memories / Careering / Flowers of romance / This is not a love song / Rise / Home / The body / Rules and regulations / Disappointed / Warrior / Don't ask me / Seattle.

— **MIKE JOYCE** – drums (ex-SMITHS, ex-BUZZCOCKS) repl. BRUCE

Feb 92. (7") *(VS 1390)* **CRUEL. / LOVE HOPE** [49] [–]
(cd-s+=) *(VSCD 1390)* – Rise (live) / Home (live).
(10"+=) *(VST 1390)* – Happy (live).

Feb 92. (cd/c/lp) *(CD/TC+/V 2681)* *<86263>* **THAT WHAT IS NOT** [46] [ ]
– Acid drops / Lucks up / Cruel / God / Covered / Love hope / Unfairground / Think tank / Emperor / Good things.

— In Nov'93, LYDON was credited on acclaimed dance hit & UK No.19 'Open Up' by LEFTFIELD / LYDON on 'Hard Hands' records.

— Early '96, JOHN LYDON (ROTTEN) re-grouped with The SEX PISTOLS for summer tours in Britain, Europe and America.

– compilations, etc. –

Mar 99. (4xcd-box) *Virgin; PILBOX 1)* **PLASTIC BOX** [ ] [–]

JOHN LYDON

Virgin America | Virgin America

Jun 97. (cd/c) *(CDVUS/VUSMC 130)* *<44209>* **PSYCHO'S PATH** [ ] [ ]
– Grave ride / Dog / Psychopath / Sun / Another way / Dis-ho / Take me / No and a yes / Stump / Armies / Open up.

Jul 97. (12"/cd-s) *(VUS T/CD 122)* **SUN. / GRAVE RIDE / PSYCHOPATH** [42] [–]

PUDDLE OF MUDD

Formed: Kansas City, Missouri, USA ... 1998 by WESLEY SCANTLIN, PAUL PHILLIPS, DOUG ARDITO and GREG UPCHURCH. PUDDLE OF MUDD's rise from obscurity to post-grunge kings is an intriguing story and virtually begins with a LIMP BIZKIT gig in 1999. POM's frontman and songwriter SCANTLIN apparently snuck backstage at the said gig and handed one of FRED DURST's security men a demo tape of his band. One year down the line and the struggling ensemble found themselves shellshocked when DURST himself contacted them and offered to sign SCANTLIN and his cohorts to the newly established 'Flawless' label. Now based in L.A. and augmented by JOSH FREESE (of The VANDALS), their major label debut set 'COME CLEAN' was issued in 2001. A fairly average rock record to most observers outside the mainstream metallic world, the soon-to-be US Top 10'er was helped along by singles 'BLURRY' and 'CONTROL', which displayed the usual hard-rock/grunge formula of many NIRVANA copyists. The main problem with PUDDLE OF MUDD is that they followed the same verse/chorus/verse triad (go to STAIND, NICKELBACK and TOOL for more examples). It's sometimes hard to believe that bands like PUDDLE OF MUDD even attempt to extract creative capital from such a thoroughly exhausted genre as grunge. It's even harder to believe that there are people willing to shell out money for it (it hit US Top 20!). 'LIFE ON DISPLAY' (2003) wasn't the sound of a band flogging a dead horse, it was the sound of a band flogging the skeleton of a dead horse.

Album rating: ABRASIVE (*5) / COME CLEAN (*7) / LIFE ON DISPLAY (*4)

WES SCANTLIN – vocals / **PAUL PHILLIPS** – guitar / **DOUG ARDITO** – bass / **GREG UPCHURCH** – drums

not iss. | Phatt Phunk

Jul 01. (cd) *<13180>* **ABRASIVE** [–] [ ]
– Abrasive / Nobody told me / Streesed out / Hour glass man / Migrain / Said / All I ask for / Purple heart / Locket / Time / Piss it all away.

Interscope | Interscope

Sep 01. (cd) *<(493074-2)>* **COME CLEAN** [12] [9]
– Control / Drift & die / Out of my head / Nobody told me / Blurry / She hates me (explicit) / Bring me down / Never change / Basement / Said / Piss it all away. *(cd re-iss. Jan02; 493335-2) (special cd-iss. May02 +=; 493247-2)* – Abrasive / Control (acoustic) / Control (video).

Feb 02. (7"/c-s) *(497658-7/-4)* *<497397>* **CONTROL. / ABRASIVE** [15] Oct01 [68]
(cd-s+=) *(497658-2)* – ('A'-acoustic) / ('A'-video).

Jun 02. (c-s) *(497735-4)* *<radio>* **BLURRY / ALL ASK FOR (demo)** [8] Dec01 [5]
(cd-s+=) *(497734-2)* – Out of my head (live) / ('A'-video).
(cd-s) *(497735-2)* – ('A'side) / Control (live) / Bring me down (live).

Sep 02. (c-s) *(497798-4)* *<radio>* **SHE HATES ME / SHE HATES ME (clean) / NOBODY TOLD ME (live)** [14] Oct02 [13]
(cd-s+=) *(497798-2)* – Blurry (live).
(cd-s) *(497805-2)* – ('A'-live acoustic) / Blurry (live acoustic) / ('A'-video).

Polydor | Flawless

Nov 03. (cd) *(986148-3)* *<10800-2>* **LIFE ON DISPLAY** [ ] [20]
– Away from me / Heel over head / Nothing left to lose / Change my mind / Spin you around / Already gone / Think / Cloud 9 / Bottom / Freak of the world / Sydney / Time flies.

Dec 03. (7") *(981481-1)* *<radio>* **AWAY FROM ME. / LIFE AIN'T FAIR** [55] [72]
(cd-s+=) *(981481-0)* – Blurry (live) / ('A'video).

PUFF DADDY

Born: SEAN COMBS, 4 Nov'70, Harlem, New York, USA. Growing up near Mt. Vernon, the up and coming millionaire MC inforced his humble quest in becoming a businessman by applying to Howard University (in Washington) and persuading his childhood chum-cum-rapper HEAVY D to employ him at 'Uptown Records'. As the months passed by, COMBS had worked his way up from dogsbody to A&R man to executive producer on FATHER MC's hit album 'FATHER'S DAY' (1990). However, his time with the company was short-lived when in 1992 (at Uptown's peak, following the success of MARY J BLIGE and HEAVY D AND THE BOYZ), COMBS was fired, shattering all images of the bigtime. He reluctantly founded a new imprint 'Bad Boy' in 1993. Working from his apartment with little more than a workforce of five, remixing the odd track here and there for various artists in the small hours of the morning. By the end of 1993 he had signed two of the record company's main artists: CRAIG MACK and old friend the NOTORIOUS B.I.G. The following year, MACK's single 'FLAVA IN YA EAR' had become a huge hit in the states, boasting guest appearances from LL COOL J, BUSTA RYMES and NOTORIOUS. The single went platinum and went on to be Bad Boy's first major success. The words of NOTORIOUS B.I.G. were spreading like wildfire through America, and, in 1995 he achieved a Top 10 spot with his single 'Big Poppa', and a double Platinum certificate for his debut album 'Ready To Die'. COMBS signed two R&B acts, FAITH EVANS (who was the B.I.G. man's wife) and TOTAL (who was also connected to the aforementioned rapper), the pair both going on to sell double platinum. After COMBS had remixed tracks for BOYZ II MEN and MARIAH CAREY, a feud between Death Row's 2PAC SHAKUR and infamous label manager SUGE KNIGHT erupted when SHAKUR was rumoured to be sleeping with FAITH EVANS. Verbal abuse was constantly spat from America's two coasts, and in September 1996, SHAKUR was shot dead. Six months later, NOTORIOUS B.I.G. was also killed, his assailants unknown. After the death of NOTORIOUS, COMBS abandoned his PUFF DADDY solo project to mourn the once great seminal rapper. However, he subsequently exploded onto the hip hop scene early '97 with the brash 'CAN'T NOBODY HOLD ME DOWN'; the worldwide No.1, 'I'LL BE MISSING YOU' (a revamp of The Police's 'EVERY BREATH YOU TAKE') was attributed to B.I.G. and featured his widow FAITH EVANS. 'NO WAY OUT' the debut album, followed in 1998 and won the Grammy award for best rap album and best performance for the aforementioned 'I'LL BE MISSING YOU'. Along with a contribution to the 'Godzilla' soundtrack, 'COME WITH ME', which hit Top 5 for him and its maker, JIMMY PAGE (of LED ZEPPELIN), PUFF DADDY issued his sophomore set 'FOREVER' in 1999. Its sharp melodies and sublime, chilled out temperament, helped it climb up the American Billboard charts, the DADDY had now come of age. The self-proclaimed 'Bad Boy' of rap returned after hiding out in his studio for two years, stepping out occasionally with his then girlfriend – Latino lovely JENNIFER LOPEZ – to go to court on charges of assault. But things all changed for Mr. COMBS when LOPEZ dumped him, forcing him back into the rap game, even changing his name to P. DIDDY (what did it mean? And what exactly did the name PUFF DADDY seriously suggest?). 'THE SAGA CONTINUES' (2001), issued by P. DIDDY and THE BAD BOY FAMILY, was just another showcase for BAD BOY rappers BLACK ROB and G. DEP, who weren't that notorious before the release of the album, and weren't that notorious after. In fact, the only thing that saved the set from near disaster was the anthemic 'BAD BOY FOR LIFE', and even in that the MCs couldn't manage to spell the word DIDDY correctly. 'THE SAGA . . .' was just another way for COMBS to remind everyone that he was still a player and not a pauper, instead of trying to convince people that his rhymes were tight and his 'family' even tighter. But like J-LO herself sang; "Try to impress me with your Bling-Bling / thought I told you love don't cost a thing". The DIDDY man launched himself back into the fray with 'WE INVENTED THE REMIX' (2002), a rather preposterous title even if the P.'s remixes were admittedly fairly radical, offering up a couple of sterling versions of 'I NEED A GIRL' and yet another remake of 'BAD BOY . . .'. Guests and hired hands included everyone from GINUWINE, USHER and IRV GOTTI to BUSTA RHYMES and KEITH MURRAY.

Album rating: NO WAY OUT (*6) / FOREVER (*6) / P. Diddy & The Bad Boy Family: THE SAGA CONTINUES . . . (*5) / WE INVENTED THE REMIX (*6)

PUFF DADDY – vocals, etc + guests

Arista Arista

Mar 97. (c-s; PUFF DADDY featuring MASE) *(74321 46455-4) <79083>* **CAN'T NOBODY HOLD ME DOWN / ('A'-instrumental club mix)** 19 Jan97 1
(12"+=/cd-s+=) *(74321 46455-2/-1)* – ('A'-Bad Boy mixes; clean / instrumental / extended club).

Jun 97. (c-s; PUFF DADDY & FAITH EVANS featuring 112 & THE LOX) *(74321 49910-4)* **I'LL BE MISSING YOU / ('A'instrumental)** 1 1
(12"+=/cd-s+=) *(74321 49910-1/-2)* – ('A'mixes).
(above was a tribute to the recently deceased NOTORIOUS B.I.G.)

Jul 97. (cd/c/d-lp; PUFF DADDY & THE FAMILY) *<(8612 73012-2/-4/-1)>* **NO WAY OUT** 10 1
– No way out / Victory / Been around the world / What you gonna do? / Don't stop what you're doing / If I should die tonight / Do you know? / Young G's / I love you baby / It's all about the Benjamins / Pain / Is this the end? / I got the power / Friend / Senorita / I'll be missing you / Can't nobody hold me down.

— In Jul'97, PUFF featured on SWV's cross-Atlantic hit, 'Someone'

Oct 97. (c-s; PUFF DADDY & THE FAMILY) *(74321 53944-4) <79130>* **BEEN AROUND THE WORLD / IT'S ALL ABOUT THE BENJAMINS (instrumental)** 20 2
(cd-s+=) *(74321 53944-2)* – ('A'mixes; gangsta mental / ain't armand).
(cd-s) *(74321 53946-2)* – ('A'side) / It's all about the Benjamins (mixes; rock remix I & II).
(12") *(74321 53944-1)* – ('A'mixes).

Jan 98. (c-s; PUFF DADDY & THE FAMILY) *(74321 56197-4)* **IT'S ALL ABOUT THE BENJAMINS / IT'S ALL ABOUT THE BENJAMINS (DJ Ming & FS Drum & Bass mix)** 18 Nov97 2
(cd-s+=) *(74321 56197-2)* – ('A'-original) / ('A'-Dave Grohl mix 2).

Mar 98. (c-s,cd-s; PUFF DADDY & The FAMILY featuring THE NOTORIOUS B.I.G. & BUSTA RHYMES) *<79155>* **VICTORY / (mixes; Nine Inch Nails / drama) / BEEN AROUND THE WORLD** – 19

Jul 98. (cd-s; PUFF DADDY featuring JIMMY PAGE) *(666079-2) <78954>* **COME WITH ME / (extended)** 2 Jun98 4
(cd-s+=) *(666284-5)* – ('A'mixes; Morello / live).
(cd-s) *(666284-2)* – (4-'A'mixes) / Out there.
(above taken from the film, 'Godzilla', issued on 'Epic' records)

— In Jul'98, he featured on MASE's US Top 10 hit, 'Lookin' At Me'.

— early '99, he featured on FAITH EVANS' Top 10 hit, 'All Night Long'.

Aug 99. (c-s; by PUFF DADDY featuring HURRICANE G) *(74321 69479-4)* **PE 2000 / (radio instrumental)** 13
(12"+=/cd-s+=) *(74321 69447-1/69479-2)* – (mixes; club / radio Spanish / club Spanish).
(cd-s) *(74321 69498-2)* – ('A'side) / Victory / Missing you / Gangsta shit.

Aug 99. (cd/c) *(74321 68906-2/-4) <73033>* **FOREVER** 9 2
– Forever (intro) / What you want / I'll do this for you / Do you like it . . . do you want it . . . (with JAY-Z) / Satisfy you (with R KELLY) / Is this the end, pt.2 (with TWISTA) / I hear voices (with CARL THOMAS) / Fake thugs dedication (with REDMAN) / Daddy speaks! (interlude) / Angels with dirty faces (with BIZZY BONE) / Gangsta SH*T / P.S. 112 / Pain (with G-DEP) / Reverse / Real niggas (with NOTORIOUS B.I.G. & LIL' KIM) / Journey through the life (with NAS & BEANIE SEAGAL) / Best friend (with MARIO WINANS) / Mad rapper / P.E. 2000 (with HURRICANE G). *(explicit version; 74321 68905-2/-4)*

Oct 99. (c-s; PUFF DADDY feat. MARIO WINIANS & MAD RAPPER) *(74321 71231-4) <79318>* **BEST FRIEND / (instrumental)** 24 59
(cd-s) *(74321 71232-2)* – ('A'side) / Satisfy you / Do you like it . . . do you want it.
(cd-s) *(74321 71231-2)* – ('A'mixes).

Feb 00. (cd-s; as PUFF DADDY featuring R. KELLY) *(74321 74559-4/-1/-2) <79283>* **SATISFY YOU / (instrumental) / PE 2000 (instrumental) / PE 2000 (rock)** 8 Sep99 6

P. DIDDY & THE BAD BOY FAMILY

— a slight name change!; with **BLACK ROB, MARK CURRY, G-DEP, LOON, HOODFELLAZ, FAITH EVANS, MARIO WINANS, KAIN, MARSHA**, etc

Aug 01. (c-s/cd-s) *<73013>* **THANK YOU** [–] [ ]

Sep 01. (c-s; as P. DIDDY, BLACK ROB & MARK CURRY) *(74321 88998-4) <79400>* **BAD BOY FOR LIFE / LET'S GET IT (remix)** [13] Jul01 [33]
(12"+=) *(74321 88998-1)* – ('A'-instrumental).
(cd-s++=) *(74321 88998-2)* – ('A'video).

Aug 01. (cd) *<(78612 73045-2)>* **THE SAGA CONTINUES . . .** [ ] [2]
– The saga continues / Bad boy for life / Toe game (interlude) / That's crazy / Let's get it / Shiny suit man / Diddy / Blast off / Airport (interlude) / Roll with me / On top / Where's Sean? / Child of the ghetto / Incomplete (interlude) / So complete / Smoke / Lonely / I need a girl (to Bella) / Nothing's gonna stop me now (interlude) / If you want this money / I don't like that (interlude) / Back for good now / Can't believe / The last song / Thank you.

— in Nov'01, P. DIDDY guested on JANET JACKSON's hit, 'Son Of A Gun'

Jan 02. (c-s; as P. DIDDY featuring The NEPTUNES) *(74321 91165-4) <79408>* **DIDDY / BAD BOY FOR LIFE (remix)** [19] Oct01 [66]
(12"+=) *(74321 91165-1)* – ('A'-instrumental) / Special delivery (G. Dep radio mix).
(cd-s++=) *(74321 91165-2)* – ('A'video).

May 02. (cd) *(74321 94540-2) <78612 73062-2>* **WE INVENTED THE REMIX** [17] [1]
– Intro / Special delivery (mix with G. DEP, GHOSTFACE KILLAH & KEITH MURRAY) / I need a girl – part 2 (remix with GINUWINE, LOON & MARIO WINANS) / Bad boy for life (mix with BUSTA RHYMES & M.O.P) / I need a girl – part 1 (with USHER & LOON) / The remix phenomenon (interlude) / Unfoolish (remix with ASHANTI & NOTORIOUS B.I.G.) / Dance with me – Peaches and cream (remix with 112, LUDACRIS & BEANIE SIGEL) / No more drama (remix with MARY J. BLIGE) / So complete (remix with CHERI DENNIS) / Notorious B.I.G. (remix with NOTORIOUS B.I.G. & LIL' KIM) / That's crazy (remix with BLACK ROB & MISSY ELLIOTT) / Woke up in the morning (remix with CARL THOMAS & NOTORIOUS B.I.G.) / You gets no love (remix with FAITH EVANS & G. DEP).

Jul 02. (c-s; by P. DIDDY featuring USHER & LOON) *(74321 94724-4) <79436>* **I NEED A GIRL (part 1) / (part 2)** [4] [2] Apr02 [4]
(12"+=/cd-s+=) *(74321 94724-1/-2)* – ('A'-To Bella mix).

— in Mar'03, P. DIDDY featured on B2K's hit, 'Bump Bump Bump'

Aug 03. (12"; by P. DIDDY & KELIS) *(MCST 40331)* **LET'S GET ILL. / LET'S GET ILL (Darren Emerson remix)** [25] [–]
(cd-s) *(MCSTD 40331)* – ('A'-version) / ('A'-Deep Dish mixes).

PULP

Formed: Sheffield, England . . . 1981 originally as ARABACUS PULP by JARVIS COCKER while still at school. Following on in the tradition of geek heart-throbs like BUDDY HOLLY, JARVIS COCKER achieved the knicker-wetting adulation he'd always aspired to through sheer hard graft and the determination of the downtrodden. His long road to stardom began in the mid-80's with the release of the 'IT' mini-lp and a prestigious JOHN PEEL session. Further releases like the 'LITTLE GIRL AND OTHER PIECES' (1985) and 'DOGS ARE EVERYWHERE' (1986) EP's saw COCKER developing as a wry and sharply observant chronicler of working class drudgery and sexual frustration, his inimitable brand of camped-up showmanship unhampered by a spell in a wheel chair (his injuries allegedly sustained after falling from a window when trying to show off to a woman!). By the release of 'FREAKS' (1987), the core of the latter day PULP was in place, violinist/guitarist RUSSELL SENIOR and keyboardist CANDIDA DOYLE beginning to move away from the band's early LEONARD COHEN/FALL hybrid to a more arty MONOCHROME SET/ULTRAVOX (John Foxx era!) type vibe. Most of the band moved to London in the late 80's, with bassist STEVE MACKAY and drummer NICHOLAS BANKS stabilising the line-up. In this incarnation, the sleek, new-look PULP recorded the 'SEPARATIONS' (1991) album, a more ambitious affair which spawned the enduringly glitter-tastic 'MY LEGENDARY GIRLFRIEND' single. The track's success encouraged PULP to set up their own label, 'Gift', through which they released a string of early 90's EP's, becoming critical darlings with some sections of the music press alongside fellow pop sculptors like SAINT ETIENNE. It wasn't long before the enigmatic JARVIS and crew were on the roster of 'Island', releasing their breakthrough 'HIS 'N' HERS' album in 1994. Previewed by the driving, tongue-in-cheek query of the 'DO YOU REMEMBER THE FIRST TIME?' single (a short film was released to tie in with the track, featuring various biz figureheads candidly talking about their "first time"), the album expertly dissected the sexual undertow of working class Britain with an incisive accuracy, mordant humour and lashings of glam posturing. The album made the UK Top 10, becoming a consistent seller and setting COCKER up as a fashion icon (Bri-Nylon, national health specs etc.). The singer was to become a star on the same scale as BRETT ANDERSON (Suede) following the success of the landmark 'COMMON PEOPLE' single. A classic pop song that almost made No.2 on the back of the Britpop zeitgeist, the single was a brilliant portrayal of the British class divide set to an almost 80's style synth-led backdrop. After the headlining act dropped out, PULP stepped in to put in one of the most acclaimed performances of their career at the 1995 Glastonbury festival, releasing the 'DIFFERENT CLASS' album in October to round off the most successful year to date in the band's career. With the social commentary as cutting as ever (the controversial 'SORTED FOR E'S AND WHIZZ') and their gift for effortlessly poignant pop intact ('DISCO 2000'), PULP consolidated their position as Britain's leading exponents of home-grown pop genius. A more downbeat COCKER returned late in '97 with the Top 10 hit, 'HELP THE AGED' (all monies going to that particular charity), while Britain awaited with much anticipation the porn-inspired 'THIS IS HARDCORE' set in '98. Another to hit the UK Top 10 (nowhere in America!), the record dabbled with the darker side of fame, set to a lounge-feel, sweaty background of a claustrophic Britain. Following up the difficult ' . . . HARDCORE' set wasn't going to be easy, but with the aid of the legendary SCOTT WALKER as producer, PULP managed to issue a new album in the form of 'WE LOVE LIFE' (2001). Nearly three years in the making, the set reverted back to early PULP material such as songs found on 'HIS 'N' HERS' or the group's commercially brilliant 'DIFFERENT CLASS'. 'WICKERMAN' and 'THE TREES' were both fine examples of a band that had withstood the wintry climate of the music industry and still maintained an ounce of dignity and professionalism. WALKER, who had never produced before, made PULP sound as intriguing and as heart-felt as anything he has ever done. The missing JARVIS (or er, DARREN SPOONER) was back again for 2003 via the mysterious RELAXED MUSCLE side-project, albeit with heavy gothic make-up et al. The 'MUSCLE featured RICHARD HAWLEY (ex-LONGPIGS) and JASON BUCKLE, while the music on one-off set, 'A HEAVY NITE WITH . . .', was decidedly on the SUICIDE-meets-CABARET VOLTAIRE front. • **Songwriters:** COCKER + SIMON HINKLER collaborated on debut. COCKER, SENIOR, C. DOYLE, MANSELL penned, until 90's when COCKER was main contributor. • **Trivia:** COCKER and MACKAY directed videos for TINDERSTICKS and The APHEX TWIN. • **Note:** Not to be confused with other band fronted by ANDY BEAN +

PAUL BURNELL, who released in 1979; LOW FLYING AIRCRAFT single.

Album rating: IT (*4) / FREAKS (*4) / SEPARATIONS (*5) / PULPINTRO – THE GIFT RECORDINGS compilation (*7) / HIS 'N' HERS (*9) / MASTERS OF THE UNIVERSE collecttion (*5) / DIFFERENT CLASS (*9) / THIS IS HARDCORE (*8) / WE LOVE LIFE (*7) / HITS compilation (*8) / Relaxed Muscle: A HEAVY NITE WITH . . . (*7)

JARVIS COCKER (b. Sep'62) – vocals, guitar, piano / **SIMON HINKLER** – keyboards, vocals repl. PETER DALTON / **PETER BOAM** – bass repl. JAMIE PINCHBECK who had repl. DAVID LOCKWOOD / **DAVID HINKLER** – keyboards, trombone / **GARY WILSON** – drums (of ARTERY) repl. WAYNE FURNISS who had repl. JIMMY SELLERS who had repl. MARK SWIFT

— plus guests **SASKIA COCKER** + **GILL TAYLOR** – b.vox / **TIMM ALLCARD** – keyboards

Red Rhino | not iss.

Apr 83. (m-lp) *(REDLP 29)* **IT** [ ] [–]
– My lighthouse / Wishful thinking / Joking aside / Boats and trains / Blue girls / Love love / In many ways. *(cd-iss. Mar94 on 'Cherry Red'; CDMRED 112 w/drawn)* (cd+=) – Looking for life / Everybody's problem / There was. *(re-iss. cd Dec94 on 'Fire'; REFIRE CD15)* (cd+=) – Looking for life. *<US cd-iss. 1997 on 'Velvel'; 79750> (cd re-iss. Nov02 on 'Fire'+=; SFIRE 004CD)*

May 83. (7") *(RED 32)* **MY LIGHTHOUSE (remix). / LOOKING FOR LIFE** [ ] [–]

Sep 83. (7") *(RED 37)* **EVERYBODY'S PROBLEM. / THERE WAS** [ ] [–]

— **RUSSELL SENIOR** – guitar, violin, vocals; repl. DAVID

— **CANDIDA DOYLE** – keyboards, vocals; repl. SIMON who joined ARTERY then the MISSION)

— **MAGNUS DOYLE** – drums repl. GARY, SASKIA, GILL + TIMM

— **PETER MANSELL** – bass repl. BOAM

Fire | not iss.

Nov 85. (12"ep) *(FIRE 5)* **LITTLE GIRL AND OTHER PIECES** [ ] [–]
– Little girl (with blue eyes) / Simultaneous / Blue glow / The will to power. *(re-iss. Oct91)*

Jun 86. (12"ep) *(BLAZE 10)* **DOGS ARE EVERYWHERE / THE MARK OF THE DEVIL. / 97 LOVERS / ABORIGINE / GOODNIGHT** [ ] [–]
(re-iss. Oct91)

Jan 87. (7"/ext.12") *(BLAZE 17/+T)* **THEY SUFFOCATE AT NIGHT. / TUNNEL** [ ] [–]

Mar 87. (7"/12") *(BLAZE 21/+T)* **MASTER OF THE UNIVERSE (sanitised version). / MANON / SILENCE** [ ] [–]
(re-iss. Oct91)

May 87. (lp) *(FIRE LP5)* **FREAKS** [ ] [–]
– Fairground / I want you / Being followed home / Master of the universe / Life must be so wonderful / There's no emotion / Anorexic beauty / The never-ending story / Don't you know / They suffocate at night. *(cd-iss. Apr93; FIRE CD5) <US cd-iss. 1997 on 'Velvel'; 79752> (cd re-iss. Jul02; SFIRE 013CD)*

— **STEPHEN MACKAY** – bass repl. STEPHEN HAVENLAND who had repl. PETER

— **NICHOLAS BANKS** – drums, percussion repl. MAGNUS

Sep 90. (12"ep) *(BLAZE 44T)* **MY LEGENDARY GIRLFRIEND. / IS THIS HOUSE? / THIS HOUSE IS CONDEMNED** [ ] [–]
(re-iss. Oct91)

Aug 91. (12"ep/cd-ep) *(BLAZE 51 T/CD)* **COUNTDOWN. / DEATH GOES TO THE DISCO / COUNTDOWN (edit)** [ ] [–]
(re-iss. Oct91)

Oct 91. (cd/c/lp) *(FIRE 33/22/11 026)* **SEPARATIONS** [ ] [–]
– Love is blind / Don't you want me anymore / She's dead / Separations / Down by the river / Countdown / My legendary girlfriend / Death II / This house is condemned. *(re-iss. Jun92; same) <US cd-iss. 1995 on 'Razor & Tie'; 2090-2> (cd re-iss. Apr02; SFIRE 025CD)*

Gift | not iss.

May 92. (12"ep/cd-ep) *(GIF 1/+CD)* **O.U. (GONE GONE) / SPACE / O.U. (GONE GONE) (radio edit)** [ ] [–]

Oct 92. (12"ep/cd-ep) *(GIF 3/+CD)* **BABIES. / STYLOROC (NIGHTS OF SUBURBIA) / SHEFFIELD** – SEX CITY [ ] [–]

Feb 93. (7") *(7GIF 6)* **RAZZAMATAZZ. / INSIDE SUSAN (abridged; Stacks – 59 Lynhurst Grove)** [ ] [–]
(12"ep+/cd-ep+=) *(GIF 6/+CD)* – (B-side; A STORY IN 3 PARTS).

Island | Polygram

Oct 93. (cd/c)(lp) *(IMCD/IMCT 159)(ILPM 2076) <2076-518451>* **PULPINTRO – THE GIFT RECORDINGS** (compilation) [ ] [ ]
– Space / O.U. (gone gone) / Babies / Styloroc (nights of suburbia) / Razzamatazz / Sheffield – Sex city / Medley of stacks: Inside Susan (a story in 3 songs) Stacks – Inside Susan – 59 Lyndhurst Grove.

Nov 93. (7") *(IS 567)* **LIPGLOSS. / YOU'RE A NIGHTMARE** [50] [ ]
(12"+=)(cd-s+=) *(12IS/CID 567)* – Deep fried in Kelvin. *(re-iss. Aug96) (re-iss. Oct96 on 7"red)*

Mar 94. (7"/c-s) *(IS/CIS 574)* **DO YOU REMEMBER THE FIRST TIME?. / STREET LITES** [33] [ ]
(12"+=)(cd-s+=) *(12IS/CID 574)* - **The babysitter.** *(re-iss. Aug96, hit 73) (re-iss. Oct96 7"biege)*

Apr 94. (cd/c/lp) *(CID/ICT/ILPS 8025) <524006>* **HIS 'N' HERS** [9] Jun94 [ ]
– Joyriders / Lipgloss / Acrylic afternoons / Have you seen her lately? / She's a lady / Happy endings / Do you remember the first time? / Pink glove / Someone like the Moon / David's last summer.(cd,c+=) – Babies (remix).

May 94. (7"ep/c-ep/12"ep/cd-ep) *(IS/CIS/12IS/CID 595)* **THE SISTERS EP** [19] [–]
– Babies / Your sister's clothes / Seconds / His'n'hers. *(re-iss. Aug96) (re-iss. Oct96 on white 7"ep)*

May 95. (c-s) *(CIS 613)* **COMMON PEOPLE. / UNDERWEAR** [2] [–]
(cd-s+=) *(CID 613)* – ('A'-Motiv8 mix) / ('A'-Vocoda mix). *(re-iss. Aug96) (re-iss. Oct96 7"yellow/12")*
(cd-s) *(CIDX 613)* – ('A'side) / Razzmatazz (acoustic) / Dogs are everywhere (acoustic) / Joyriders (acoustic).

— Below second side (double A) caused controversy with tabloids and parents, due to its mis-use of drugs in JARVIS's lyrics. JARVIS was to become the hero to most and villain to the few early in 1996 at a certain awards ceremony (skinny J.C. vs. St.MICHAEL & the bouncers; who won? – you decide).

Sep 95. (c-s) *(CIS 620)* **MIS-SHAPES / SORTED FOR E'S AND WIZZ** [2] [–]
(cd-s+=) *(CID 620)* – P.T.A. (Parent Teacher Association) / Common people (live at Glastonbury). *(re-iss. Oct96 7"blue/12")*
(cd-s+=) *(CIDX 620)* – Common people (Motiv8 mix). *(re-iss. Aug96)*

Oct 95. (cd/c/lp) *(CID/ICT/ILPS 8041) <524165>* **DIFFERENT CLASS** [1] [ ]
– Mis-shapes / Pencil skirt / Common people / I spy / Disco 2000 / Live bed show / Something changed / Sorted out for E's and wizz / F.E.E.L.I.N.G.C.A.L.L.E.D.L.O.V.E. / Underwear / Monday morning / Bar Italia.

Nov 95. (c-s) *(CIS 623)* **DISCO 2000 / ANSAPHONE** [7] [–]
(cd-s+=) *(CID 623)* – ('A'-Motiv8 Gimp dub & Discoid mixes). *(re-iss. Aug96) (re-iss. Oct96 7"orange/12")*
(cd-s+=) *(CIDX 623)* – Live bed show (extended).

Mar 96. (c-s) *(CIS 632)* **SOMETHING CHANGED / MILE END** [10] [–]
(cd-s+=) *(CID 632)* – F.E.E.L.I.N.G.C.A.L.L.E.D.L.O.V.E (The Moloko mix) / F.E.E.L.I.N.G.C.A.L.L.E.D.L.O.V.E. (live from Brixton Academy). *(re-iss. Aug96) (re-iss. Oct96 7"pink/12")*

— now without SENIOR, who wanted to pursue new projects

Nov 97. (c-s/7") *(C+/IS 679)* **HELP THE AGED. / LAUGHING BOY** [8] [–]
(cd-s+=) *(CID 679)* – Tomorrow never lies.

Mar 98. (c-s) *(CIS 695)* **THIS IS HARDCORE / LADIES MAN** [12] [–]
(cd-s+=) *(CID 695)* – Professional.
(cd-s) *(CIDX 695)* – ('A'mixes).

Mar 98. (cd/c/d-lp) *(ILPSD/ICT/CID 8066) <524492>* **THIS IS HARDCORE** [1] [ ]
– The fear / Dishes / Party hard / Help the aged / This is hardcore / TV movie / A little soul / I'm a man / Seductive Barry / Sylvia / Glory days / Day after the revolution.

Jun 98. (c-s) *(CIS 708)* **A LITTLE SOUL / COCAINE SOCIALISM** [22] [–]
(cd-s+=) *(CID 708)* – Like a friend.
(cd-s) *(CIDX 708)* – ('A'alternative mix) / ('A'-Lafayette Velvet revisited mix) / That boy's evil.

Sep 98. (c-s/cd-s) *(CIS/CID 719) <572418>* **PARTY HARD / WE ARE THE BOYZ / THE FEAR** [29] [ ]
(cd-s) *(CIDX 719)* – ('A'mixes by Stretch'n'Vern & All Seeing I).

Oct 01. (cd-s) *(CID 786)* **SUNRISE / THE TREES / SUNRISE (fat truckers scott free mix)** 28 –
(cd-s) *(CIDX 786)* – (first 2) / The trees (felled by I Monster).
(12") *(12IS 786)* – ('A'side) / The trees (felled by I Monster) / Sunrise (All Seeing I remix) / The trees (Lovejoy mix).

Oct 01. (cd/d-lp) *(CID/ILPSD 8109)* *<586540>* **WE LOVE LIFE** 6
– Weeds / Weeds II (the origin of the species) / The night that Minnie Temperley died / The trees / Wickerman / I love life / The birds in your garden / Bob Lind / Bad cover version / Roadkill / Sunrise.

Apr 02. (cd-s) *(CID 794)* **BAD COVER VERSION / YESTERDAY / FOREVER IN MY DREAMS** 27 –
(cd-s) *(CIDX 794)* – ('A'-video mix) / Disco 2000 (by NICK CAVE) / Sorted? (by ROISON MURPHY).

Nov 02. (cd) *(CID 8126)* **HITS** (compilation) 71 –
– Babies / Razzmatazz / Lipgloss / Do you remember the first time? / Common people / Underwear / Sorted for E's & wizz / Disco 2000 / Something changed / Help the aged / This is hardcore / A little soul / Party hard / The trees / Bad cover version / Sunrise / Last day of the miner's strike.

– compilations, etc. –

Jun 94. (cd/c/lp) *Fire; (FIRE CD/MC/LP 36)* **MASTERS OF THE UNIVERSE – PULP ON FIRE 1985-86** –
– Little girl (with blue eyes) / Simultaneous / Blue glow / The will to power / Dogs are everywhere / The mark of the Devil / 97 lovers / Aborigine / Goodnight / They suffocate at night / Tunnel / Master of the universe (sanitised version) / Manon.

Mar 96. (d-cd/c/d-lp) *Nectar; (NTM CDD/C/LP 521)* **COUNTDOWN 1992-1983** 10 –
– Countdown / Death goes to the disco / My legendary girlfriend / Don't you want me anymore / She's dead / Down by the river / I want you / Being followed home / Master of the universe / Don't you know / They suffocate at night / Dogs are everywhere / Mark of the Devil / 97 lovers / Little girl (with blue eyes) / Blue glow / My lighthouse / Wishful thinking / Blue girls / Countdown (extended).

Jul 98. (cd) *Connoisseur; (VSOPCD 256)* **DEATH GOES TO THE DISCO** –

Sep 98. (cd) *E.M.I.; <79737>* **FRESHLY SQUEEZED (EARLY YEARS)** –

RELAXED MUSCLE

DARREN SPOONER (JARVIS) + **WAYNE MARSDEN** (RICHARD HAWLEY) + **JASON BUCKLE**

Rough Trade not iss.

Apr 03. (7"/cd-s) *(RTRADES/+CD 073)* **THE HEAVY. / ROD OF IRON / BRANDED!** –

Jul 03. (7") *(RTRADES 106)* **BILLY JACK. / SEXUALIZED** –
(cd-s+=) *(RTRADESCD 106)* – The year of the dog.

Oct 03. (cd/lp) *(RTRADE CD/LP 131)* **A HEAVY NITE WITH . . .** –
– The heavy / 3 way accumulator / Beastmaster / Billy Jack / Rod of iron / Tuff it out / Sexualized / Muscle music / B-real / Previous / Battered / Mary. *(cd bonus +=)* – Sexualized (video) / Billy Jack n(video).

QUEEN

Finley QUAYE

Born: 25 Mar'74, Leith, Edinburgh, Scotland . . . to a native Scots mother who died of a heroin overdose when he was still at primary school; his Ghanian jazz-playing father was absent for most of FINLEY's troubled upbringing. Subsequently living between grandparents in Edinburgh and auntie/uncle in Manchester, he also spent a lot of his youth in London. With many notable industry connections stemming from his father's side of the family (i.e. uncle ERIC QUAYE, percussionist with OSIBISA and half-brother CALEB QUAYE, a session man for the likes of ELTON JOHN), FINLEY naturally gravitated towards a career in music. Probably his most famous relative TRICKY, is rather confusingly, actually QUAYE's nephew (his sister, MAXIN QUAYE is Tricky's mother!), the pair subsequently collaborating on a couple of tracks, one of which, 'DUPPY UMBRELLA' was a lengthy ode to magic mushrooms featuring a guest spot from IGGY POP (no relation!). One of his earliest musical endeavours was playing drums with the Rainbow Tribe hippy community in London, the reggae loving QUAYE eventually securing a deal with major 'Epic' records. In 1997, the fruits of his labour were revealed, the sun-kissed pop/reggae/hip-hop charm of his 'MAVERICK A STRIKE' album gaining him a wide cross-section of fans and a Top 3 UK chart placing. This acclaimed opus also spawned three major Top 30 hits, the biggest selling being, 'EVEN AFTER ALL'. Afterwards, QUAYE was reluctant to issue an album until three years later when 'VANGUARD' (2000) finally surfaced. Disappointing in every aspect, the album's helmsman failed to capture the essence and soul previously heard on QUAYE's earlier albums. That is not to say all the blame should've been pinned on him; QUAYE himself tried to get away with some appalling lyrics, while the spiritual direction of the set veered off the proverbial road and came crashing to an almighty halt. • **Songwriters:** Self-penned except; CROSSTOWN TRAFFIC (Jimi Hendrix).

Album rating: MAVERICK A STRIKE (*7) / VANGUARD (*6) / MUCH MORE THAN MUCH LOVE (*4)

FINLEY QUAYE – vocals; with session men

Epic Sony

Jun 97. (c-s) *(664455-4)* **SUNDAY SHINING / MASHING UP LUCIFER: STONE THE DEVIL** 16 –
(12"/cd-s) *(664455-6/-2)* – ('A'side) / Sunday best / I need a lover / Singing from the same hymn sheet.

Sep 97. (c-s/cd-s) *(664971-4/-2)* **EVEN AFTER ALL / BURNING** 10 –
(cd-s+=) *(664971-5)* – ('A'mixes).

Sep 97. (cd/c/lp) *(488758-2/-4/-1)* <68506> **MAVERICK A STRIKE** 3 Oct97
– Ultra stimulation / It's great when you're together / Sunday shining / Even after all / Ride on and turn the people on / The way of the explosive / Your love gets sweeter / Supreme I preme / Sweet and loving man / Red rolled and seen / Failing / I need a lover / Maverick a strike. *(cd re-iss. Jul98; same)*

Nov 97. (c-s) *(665338-4)* **IT'S GREAT WHEN WE'RE TOGETHER / MORNING PRACTICE** 29 –
(cd-s+=) *(665338-5)* – ('A'mix) / Even after all (live).
(cd-s) *(665338-2)* – ('A'side) / ('A'mix) / Birds of one feather / Crosstown traffic.

Feb 98. (c-s) *(665606-4)* **YOUR LOVE GETS SWEETER / EVERYBODY KNOWS** 16 –
(cd-s+=) *(665606-5)* – ('A'-The Abbey Road version) / Le saint des delinquents.
(cd-s) *(665606-2)* – ('A'side) / ('A'-The Abbey Road version) / Can't be left alone / Maverick a dub.

Aug 98. (cd-s) *(666079-2)* **ULTRA STIMULATION / WHITE PAPER** 51 –
(c-s+=) *(666079-4)* – ('A'-Ultra vibration).
(cd-s) *(666079-5)* – ('A'side) / ('A'-Ultra vibration) / Too many guns.

Sep 00. (c-s) *(669803-4)* **SPIRITUALIZED / THINK FOR YOURSELF / TRIBAL WAR** 26 –
(cd-s) *(669803-5)* – (first two tracks) / ('A'-A Guy Called Gerald remix) / ('A'-CD-rom).
(cd-s) *(669803-2)* – ('A'side) / ('A'-Francois Kervorkian 12" vocal mix) / The wizard.

Oct 00. (cd/c/lp) *(499710-2/-4/-1)* <85143> **VANGUARD** 35 Jan01
– Broadcast / Spiritualized / Emperor / Burning / Everybody knows / Feeling blue / When I burn off into the distance / Chad Valley / Calendar / British air rage / White paper / Hey now.

Dec 00. (12") *(670566-6)* **WHEN I BURN OFF INTO THE DISTANCE. / ('A'-Primal Scream mix) / SPIRITUALIZED (Francois K vibin' vocal mix)** –
(cd-s) *(670566-5)* – (first 2 tracks) / First.
(cd-s) *(670566-2)* – ('A'side) / Spiritualized (acoustic version) / Sunday shining (acoustic version).

Sep 03. (cd) *(512549-2)* <90741> **MUCH MORE THAN MUCH LOVE** 56 Mar04
– Something to say / Beautiful nature / Dice (with WILLIAM ORBIT) / Waiting for you / Lovers return / Face to face / Overriding volunteer / Living without you / Now and forever / This is how I feel / Pearls of wisdom / Adorable / Overcome. *<US+=>* – Your love gets sweeter.

Oct 03. (12"/cd-s) *(674306-6/-2)* <49K-76894> **DICE (mixes; radio / Layo & Bushwacka! missing you / Ilya / Finley's)** –

QUEEN

Formed: London, England . . . early 1971 by guitarist BRIAN MAY, drummer ROGER TAYLOR and vocalist par excellence FREDDIE MERCURY, bassist JOHN DEACON completing the line-up. MAY had left school in 1963 (with a whopping ten O-levels), joining teen group The OTHERS who issued one single for 'Fontana' in 1965, 'OH YEAH'. Together with TAYLOR, he then went on to form SMILE in 1969, a project that met with little success although they did release one 45 for 'Mercury US', 'EARTH' / 'STEP ON ME'. The pair then hooked up with the Zanzibar-born MERCURY and formed QUEEN in 1971, JOHN DEACON subsequently recruited on bass. After spending most of 1972 in the studio, QUEEN were picked up by 'E.M.I.' when engineer John Anthony sent the company a demo tape. The group made their live debut in April '73 at London's famed Marquee club, but prior to any QUEEN release, FREDDIE MERCURY (as LARRY LUREX!) issued a one-off 'EMI' solo single that summer, 'I CAN HEAR MUSIC' / 'GOIN' BACK' (the former an old BEACH BOYS number). A month later, QUEEN simultaneously unleashed their eponymous Roy Thomas-Baker produced debut album, and single, 'KEEP YOURSELF ALIVE'. Influenced by LED ZEPPELIN and the more garish elements of glam-rock, the group had fashioned a unique, densely layered sound around MERCURY's impressive vocal acrobatics and MAY's fluid, coin-pick guitar style. Though the album didn't exactly set the charts alight, the band subsequently set out on a heavy touring schedule, supporting friends to be, MOTT THE HOOPLE, in late '73. Success eventually came with the piano-led bombast of the 'SEVEN SEAS OF RHYE' single, the track making the Top 10 in February '74 and paving the way for 'QUEEN II' the following month. The album reached No.5, consolidating QUEEN's new position as a headline act; while MERCURY was allegedly known to be fairly shy in real life, onstage he embodied everything that the word QUEEN implied with a passionate theatricality unmatched in rock music. The group really came into their own with the 'KILLER QUEEN' single, an infectious slice of jaunty high camp that reached No.2 in late '74. The following month, QUEEN released their strongest album to date, 'SHEER HEART ATTACK', an eminently listenable collage of killer hooks, neo-metal riffs, O.T.T. choruses and satin-clad dynamics that contained the likes of 'STONE COLD CRAZY' and the next single, 'NOW I'M HERE'. But QUEEN, to use a particularly crap pun, were finally crowned, commercially at least with the 'BOHEMIAN RHAPSODY' single in late 1975. Surely one of the most annoyingly overplayed singles of all time next to 'Stairway To Heaven', the song was nevertheless something of an innovation at the time, a grandiose epic that gave new meaning to the term 'rock opera'; forget concept albums, QUEEN could condense such lofty conceits into a meagre 6 minutes! The song was accompanied by what is widely regarded as the first promotional video, a quintessentially 70's affair that, in retrospect, resembles the title sequence of 'Doctor Who'. Nevertheless, the single gave QUEEN an astonishing nine week run at the top of the charts over the Christmas period, ensuring similar success for the highly ambitious 'NIGHT AT THE OPERA' (1975) album. Apparently the most expensive project recorded up to that point, the record took QUEEN's bombastic pretensions to new limits, MERCURY's multi tracked vocals setting new standards in studio mastery. While most of QUEEN's work was penned by MERCURY and MAY, TAYLOR and DEACON were also talented songsmiths, the latter contributing one of the group's loveliest songs, 'YOU'RE MY BEST FRIEND', its heartfelt simplicity counterbalancing some of the album's more excessive moments. 'NIGHT AT THE OPERA' also went Top 5 in the States, QUEEN having broken America with their irrepressible stage show earlier that year. Their ascent into world beater status continued with 'A DAY AT THE RACES' (1976), another No.1 album which spawned a further massive hit in 'SOMEBODY TO LOVE' and contained the classic camp of 'GOOD OLD FASHIONED LOVER BOY'. The anthemic double header of the 'WE ARE THE CHAMPIONS' / 'WE WILL ROCK YOU' single reached No.2 the following year, presaging QUEEN's move away from operatic artifice to more straightahead stadium rock. 'NEWS OF THE WORLD' (1977) and 'JAZZ' (1978) confirmed this, both albums selling well despite their lack of inventiveness. The riff-heavy 'FAT BOTTOMED GIRLS' could only have been recorded in the 70's, a gloriously unreconstructed paeon to shapely women that just wouldn't do in todays PC-controlled climate. While other rock monsters of the 70's were washed away on the tide of dour aggression that was punk, QUEEN looked to other musical forms to keep their sound fresh, namely 50's style rockabilly on the classic 'CRAZY LITTLE THING CALLED LOVE', MERCURY coming on like a camp ELVIS in the video, decked out in biker gear with a leather cap, of course, de rigueur. The group also flirted with disco on the bass-heavy 'ANOTHER ONE BITES THE DUST", a US No.1 that was later sampled by GRANDMASTER FLASH. Both tracks were featured on 'THE GAME' (1980), QUEEN'S most consistent album since the mid-70's and a transatlantic chart topper. After a partially successful sidestep into soundtrack work with 'FLASH GORDON' (1980), QUEEN rounded up the highlights of the preceding decade with a multi platinum greatest hits set. While the band had been selling more records of late in the States than the UK, this trend was reversed with 'UNDER PRESSURE', a collaboration with DAVID BOWIE which topped the British charts. 'HOT SPACE' (1982) ranks as one of QUEEN's dodgiest albums but with 'THE WORKS' (1984), QUEEN once again enjoyed a run of Top 10 singles with the likes of 'RADIO GA-GA' and 'I WANT TO BREAK FREE'. While these were listenable enough they lacked the pop brilliance of QUEEN's best 70's work. Live, QUEEN were still a massive draw, MERCURY's peerless ability to work a crowd evidenced on his famous Live Aid appearance in 1985. While the group's back catalogue subsequently clogged up the album charts, QUEEN returned with new material in the shape of 'A KIND OF MAGIC' (1986). Maybe Live Aid went to QUEEN's collective head, the album suffering from a kind of plodding stadium-friendly malaise that saw the group descending into self-parody. Nevertheless, the record made No.1, as QUEEN continued to tour the world and play to record breaking audiences. The band returned to the fray with 'THE MIRACLE' in 1989, another No.1 album that contained few surprises. Nor did 'INNUENDO' (1991), although bearing in mind MERCURY's rumoured failing health, it'd be churlish to criticise what must have been a very difficult album for the singer to finish. On the 23rd of November, 1991, a matter of months after the album's release, MERCURY succumbed to AIDS. The following month, 'BOHEMIAN RHAPSODY' was re-released and once again topped the UK charts, raising money for research into the killer disease. A tribute concert was held the following Spring at Wembley Stadium, the cream of the music world's top drawer stars paying their respects including ELTON JOHN, GUNS N' ROSES, GEORGE MICHAEL and DEF LEPPARD. Inevitably, QUEEN split although a posthumous album was released in 1995, featuring material that MERCURY had been working on prior to his death. While it didn't exactly add anything significant to QUEEN's stunning legacy, it tied up the loose ends, bringing the saga of one of music's most flamboyantly colourful bands to a dignified close. • **MERCURY covered:** THE GREAT PRETENDER (Platters). The CROSS covered FOXY LADY (Jimi Hendrix), BRIAN MAY covered ROLLIN' OVER (Small Faces).

Album rating: QUEEN (*7) / QUEEN II (*6) / SHEER HEART ATTACK (*8) / A NIGHT AT THE OPERA (*7) / A DAY AT THE RACES (*5) / NEWS OF THE WORLD (*6) / JAZZ (*5) / LIVE KILLERS (*7) / THE GAME (*6) / HOT SPACE (*4) / FLASH (*3) / THE WORKS (*4) / A KIND OF MAGIC (*5) / LIVE MAGIC (*6) / THE MIRACLE (*6) / INNUENDO (*6) / QUEEN'S GREATEST HITS compilation (*9) / GREATEST HITS II compilation (*8)

FREDDIE MERCURY (b. FREDERICK BULSARA, 5 Sep'46, Zanzibar, Africa. In 1959, he moved with family to Feltham, Middlesex, England) – vocals, piano / **BRIAN MAY** (b.19 Jul'47, London, England) – guitar, vocals, keyboards / **ROGER MEDDOWS-TAYLOR** (b.26 Jul'49, King's Lynn, Norfolk, England) – drums, vocals / **JOHN DEACON** (b.19 Aug'51, Leicester, England) – bass, vocals

		E.M.I.	Elektra
Jul 73.	(7") *(EMI 2036)* <45863> **KEEP YOURSELF ALIVE. / SON AND DAUGHTER**		

Jul 73. (lp/c) *(EMC/TCEMC 3006)* <75064> **QUEEN** [ ] Oct73 [83]
– Keep yourself alive / Doing all right / Great King Rat / My fairy king / Liar / The night comes down / Modern times rock'n'roll / Son and daughter / Jesus / Seven seas of rhye *[US only] (hit UK No.24 Mar74) (re-iss. Aug82 on 'Fame' lp/c; FA/TCFA 3040) (cd-iss. Nov86; CDP 746204-2) (cd-iss. May88; CDFA 3040) <US cd-iss. Jun91 on 'Hollywood'+=; 61064-2>* – Mad the swine, keep yourself alive (long lost retake) / Liar (1991 remix) *(re-iss. Apr94 on 'Parlophone' cd/c; CD/TC PCSD 139)*

Nov 73. (7") *<45884>* **LIAR. / DOING ALL RIGHT** [–] [ ]

Feb 74. (7") *(EMI 2121) <45891>* **SEVEN SEAS OF RHYE. / SEE WHAT A FOOL I'VE BEEN** [10] [ ]

Mar 74. (lp/c) *(EMA/TCEMA 767) <75082>* **QUEEN II** [5] May74 [49]
– Procession / Father to son / White queen (as it began) / Some day one day / The loser in the end / Ogre battle / The fairy feller's master-stroke / Nevermore / The march of the black queen / Funny how love is / Seven seas of rhye. *(re-iss. Apr84 on 'Fame' lp/c; FA/TCFA 3099) (cd-iss. Nov86; CDP 746205-2) (re-iss. May88; CDFA 3099) <US cd-iss. Oct91 on 'Hollywood'+=; 61232-2>* – See what a fool I've been / Ogre battle – 1991 remix / Seven seas of rhye – 1991 remix. *(re-iss. Apr94 on 'Parlophone' cd/c; CD/TC PCSD 140)*

Oct 74. (7") *(EMI 2229) <45226>* **KILLER QUEEN. / FLICK OF THE WRIST** [2] Jan75 [12]

Nov 74. (lp,red-lp/c-s) *(EMC/TCEMC 3061) <1026>* **SHEER HEART ATTACK** [2] Dec74 [12]
– Brighton rock / Killer Queen / Tenement funster / Flick of the wrist / Lily of the valley / Now I'm here / In the lap of the gods / Stone cold crazy / Dear friends / Misfire / Bring back that Leroy Brown / She makes me (stormtrooper in stilettoes) / In the lap of the gods . . . revisited. *(re-iss. 1984 lp/c; ATAK/TCATAK 22) (cd-iss. 1984; CDP 746052-2) (cd-iss. Jun88; CDP 746206-2) <US cd-iss. Nov88 on 'Hollywood'+=; 61036-2>* – Stone cold sober – 1991 remix) *(re-iss. Aug93 on 'Parlophone' cd/c; CD/TC PCSD 129)*

Jan 75. (7") *(EMI 2256)* **NOW I'M HERE. / LILY OF THE VALLEY** [11] [–]

Apr 75. (7") *<45268>* **LILY OF THE VALLEY. / KEEP YOURSELF ALIVE** [–] [ ]

Nov 75. (7") *(EMI 2375) <45297>* **BOHEMIAN RHAPSODY. / I'M IN LOVE WITH MY CAR** [1] Dec75 [9]

Dec 75. (lp/c) *(EMTC/TCEMTC 103) <1053>* **A NIGHT AT THE OPERA** [1] [4]
– Death on two legs (dedicated to . . .) / Lazing on a Sunday afternoon / I'm in love with my car / You're my best friend / '39 / Sweet lady / Seaside rendezvous / The prophet's song / Love of my life / Good company / Bohemian rhapsody / God save the Queen. *(re-iss. 1984 lp/c; ATAK/TCATAK 27) (cd-iss. 1984; CDP 746050-2) (cd-iss. Jun88; CDP 746207-2) <US cd-iss. Aug91 on 'Hollywood'+=; 61065-2>* – I'm in love with my car – 1991 remix / You're my best friend – 1991 remix. *(re-iss. Aug93 on 'Parlophone' cd/c; CD/TC PCSD 130)*

Jun 76. (7") *(EMI 2494) <45318>* **YOU'RE MY BEST FRIEND. / '39** [7] May76 [16]

Nov 76. (7") *(EMI 2565) <45362>* **SOMEBODY TO LOVE. / WHITE MAN** [2] [13]

Dec 76. (lp/c) *(EMTC/TCEMTC 104) <101>* **A DAY AT THE RACES** [1] Jan77 [5]
– Tie your mother down / You take my breath away / Long away / The millionaire waltz / You and I / Somebody to love / White man / Good old fashioned lover boy / Drowse / Teo Torriate (let us cling together). *(re-iss. 1984 lp/c; ATAK/TCATAK 28) (cd-iss. 1984; CDP 746051-2) (cd-iss. Jun88; CDP 746208-2) <US cd-iss. Mar91 on 'Hollywood'+=; 61035-2>* – Tie your mother down – remix / Somebody to love – remix. *(re-iss. Aug93 on 'Parlophone' cd/c; CD/TC PCSD 131) (lp re-iss. Nov97; LPCENT 29)*

Mar 77. (7") *(EMI 2593)* **TIE YOUR MOTHER DOWN. / YOU AND I** [31] [–]

Mar 77. (7") *<45385>* **TIE YOUR MOTHER DOWN. / DROWSE** [–] [49]

May 77. (7"ep) *(EMI 2623)* **QUEEN'S FIRST EP** [17] [–]
– Good old fashioned lover boy / Death on two legs (dedicated to . . .) / Tenement funster / White Queen (as it began).

Jun 77. (7") *<45412>* **LONG AWAY. / YOU AND I** [–] [ ]

Oct 77. (7") *(EMI 2708) <45441>* **WE ARE THE CHAMPIONS. / WE WILL ROCK YOU** [2] [4]

Nov 77. (lp/c) *(EMA/TCEMA 784) <112>* **NEWS OF THE WORLD** [4] [3]
– We will rock you / We are the champions / Sheer heart attack / All dead, all dead / Spread your wings / Fight from the inside / Get down make love / Sleeping on the sidewalk / Who needs you / It's late / My melancholy blues. *(re-iss. 1984 lp/c; ATAK/TCATAK 20) (cd-iss. Jun88; CDP 746209-2) <US cd-iss. Mar91 on 'Hollywood'+=; 61037-2>* – We will rock you – 1991 remix. *(re-iss. Aug93 on 'Parlophone' cd/c; CD/TC PCSD 132)*

Feb 78. (7") *(EMI 2575)* **SPREAD YOUR WINGS. / SHEER HEART ATTACK** [34] [–]

Apr 78. (7") *<45478>* **IT'S LATE. / SHEER HEART ATTACK** [–] [74]

Oct 78. (7") *(EMI 2870) <45541>* **BICYCLE RACE. / FAT BOTTOMED GIRLS** [11] Nov78 [24]

Nov 78. (lp/c) *(EMA/TCEAM 788) <166>* **JAZZ** [2] [6]
– Mustapha / Fat bottomed girls / Jealousy / Bicycle race / If you can't beat them / Let me entertain you / Dead on time / In only seven days / Dreamer's ball / Fun it / Leaving home ain't easy / Don't stop me now / More of that jazz. *(re-iss. 1984 lp/c; ATAK/TCATAK 24) (cd-iss. Jun88; CDP 746210-2) <US cd-iss. Jun91 on 'Hollywood'+=; 61062-2>* – Fat bottomed girls – 1991 remix / Bicycle race – 1991 remix. *(re-iss. Feb94 on 'Parlophone' cd/c; CD/TC PCSD 133)*

Feb 79. (7") *(EMI 2910)* **DON'T STOP ME NOW. / IN ONLY SEVEN DAYS** [9] [–]

Feb 79. (7") *<46008>* **DON'T STOP ME NOW. / MORE OF THAT JAZZ** [–] [86]

Apr 79. (7") *<46039>* **JEALOUSY. / FUN IT** [–] [ ]

Jun 79. (d-lp/d-c) *(EMSP/TC2EMSP 330) <702>* **LIVE KILLERS (live)** [3] [16]
– We will rock you / Let me entertain you / Death on two legs / Killer Queen / Bicycle race / I'm in love with my car / Get down, make love / You're my best friend / Now I'm here / Dreamer's ball / '39 / Keep yourself alive / Don't stop me now / Spread your wings / Brighton rock / Bohemian rhapsody / Tie your mother down / Sheer heart attack / We will rock you / We are the champions / God save the Queen. *(re-iss. 1984 lp/c; ATAK/TCATAK 23) (cd-iss. Jun88; CDP 746211-2) <US cd-iss. Nov88 on 'Hollywood'; 61066-2> (re-iss. Apr94 on 'Parlophone' cd/c; CD/TC PCSD 138)*

Jul 79. (7") *(EMI 2959)* **LOVE OF MY LIFE (live). / NOW I'M HERE (live)** [63] [–]

Aug 79. (7") *<46532>* **WE WILL ROCK YOU (live). / LET ME ENTERTAIN YOU (live)** [–] [ ]

Oct 79. (7") *(EMI 5001)* **CRAZY LITTLE THING CALLED LOVE. / WE WILL ROCK YOU (live)** [2] [–]

Dec 79. (7") *<46579>* **CRAZY LTTLE THING CALLED LOVE. / SPREAD YOUR WINGS** [–] [1]

Feb 80. (7") *(EMI 5022)* **SAVE ME. / LET ME ENTERTAIN YOU (live)** [11] [–]

Jun 80. (7") *(EMI 5076) <46652>* **PLAY THE GAME. / HUMAN BODY** [14] [42]

Jul 80. (lp/c) *(EMA/TCEMA 795) <513>* **THE GAME** [1] [1]
– Play the game / Dragon attack / Another one bites the dust / Need your loving tonight / Crazy little thing called love / Rock it (prime jive) / Don't try suicide / Sail away sweet sister / Coming soon / Save me. *(re-iss. 1984 lp/c; ATAK/TCATAK 21) (cd-iss. Jun88; CDP 746213-2) <US cd-iss. Jun91 on 'Hollywood'+=; 61063-2>* – Dragon attack – 1991 remix. *(re-iss. Feb94 on 'Parlophone' cd/c; CD/TC PCSD 134)*

Aug 80. (7") *(EMI 5102)* **ANOTHER ONE BITES THE DUST. / DRAGON ATTACK** [7] [–]

Aug 80. (7") *<47031>* **ANOTHER ONE BITES THE DUST. / DON'T TRY SUICIDE** [–] [1]

Oct 80. (7") *<47086>* **NEED YOUR LOVING TONIGHT. / ROCK IT (PRIME JIVE)** [–] [44]

Nov 80. (7") *(EMI 5126) <47092>* **FLASH. / FOOTBALL FIGHT** [10] Jan81 [42]

Dec 80. (lp/c) *(EMC/TCEMC 795) <518>* **FLASH GORDON (Soundtrack)** [10] [23]
– Flash's theme / In the space capsule (the love theme) / Ming's theme (in the court of Ming the merciless) / The ring (hypnotic seduction of Dale) / Football fight / In the death cell (love theme reprise) / Execution of Flash / The kiss (Aura resurrects Flash) / Arboria (planet of the tree men) / Escape from the swamp / Flash to the rescue / Vultan's theme (attack of the hawk men) / Battle theme / The wedding march / The marriage of Dale and Ming (and Flash approaching) / Flash's theme reprise (victory celebrations) / The hero. *(re-iss. 1984 lp/c; ATAK/TCATAK 26) (cd-iss. Jun88; CDP 746214-2) <US cd-iss. Aug91 on 'Hollywood'+=; 61203-2>* – Flash – 1991 remix. *(re-iss. Apr94 on 'Parlophone' cd/c; CD/TC PCSD 137)*

Nov 81. (lp/c) *(EMTV/TCEMTC 30) <564>* **QUEEN'S GREATEST HITS** (compilation) [1] [14]
– Bohemian rhapsody / Another one bites the dust / Killer queen / Fat bottomed girls / Bicycle race / You're my best friend / Don't stop me now / Save me *[or US= Keep yourself alive / Under pressure]* / Crazy little thing called love / Somebody to love / Now I'm here / Good old-fashioned lover boy / Play the game / Flash / Seven seas of Rhye / We will rock you / We are the champions. *(cd-iss. Aug84; CDP 746033-2) (re-*

hit at No.7 – Dec91) (re-iss. Jun94 on 'Parlophone' cd/c; CD/TC PCSD 141)

Nov 81. (7"; by QUEEN and DAVID BOWIE) *(EMI 5250)* *<47235>* **UNDER PRESSURE. / SOUL BROTHER** [1] [29]

Apr 82. (7") *(EMI 5293) <47452>* **BODY LANGUAGE. / LIFE IS REAL (SONG FOR LENNON)** [25] [11]

May 82. (lp/c) *(EMA/TCEMA 797) <60128>* **HOT SPACE** [4] [22]
– Staying power / Dancer / Back chat / Body language / Action this day / Put out the fire / Life is real (song for Lennon) / Calling all girls / Las Palabras de amor / Cool cat / Under pressure. *(cd-iss. Jun88; CDP 746215-2) (re-iss. Aug89 on 'Fame' cd/c/lp; CD/TC+/FA 3228) <US cd-iss. Mar91 on 'Hollywood'+=; 61038-2>* – Body language – 1991 remix. *(re-iss. Feb94 on 'Parlophone' cd/c; CD/TC PCSD 135)*

Jun 82. (7") *(EMI 5316)* **LAS PALABRAS DE AMOR. / COOL CAT** [17] [–]

Jul 82. (7") *<69981>* **CALLING ALL GIRLS. / PUT OUT THE FIRE** [–] [60]

Aug 82. (7"/ext.12") *(EMI/12EMI 5325) <69941>* **BACKCHAT. / STAYING POWER** [40] [ ]

E.M.I. Capitol

Jan 84. (7") *(QUEEN 1) <5317>* **RADIO GA GA. / I GO CRAZY** [2] [16]
(ext.12") *(12QUEEN 1)* – ('A'dub version).

Mar 84. (lp/c)(cd) *(WORK/TCWORK 1)(CDP 7460160-2) <12322>* **THE WORKS** [2] [23]
– Radio ga ga / Tear it up / It's a hard life / Man on the prowl / Machines (or back to humans) / I want to break free / Keep passing the open windows / Hammer to fall / Is his he world we created?. *<US cd-iss. Dec91 on 'Hollywood'+=; 61233-2>* – Radio Ga Ga (12"mix) / I want to break free (12"mix) / I go crazy. *(re-iss. Feb94 on 'Parlophone' cd/c; CD/TC PCSD 136)*

Apr 84. (7"/ext.12") *(QUEEN/12QUEEN 2) <5350>* **I WANT TO BREAK FREE (remix). / MACHINES (OR BACK TO HUMANS)** [3] [45]

Jul 84. (7"/12"pic-d) *(QUEEN/12QUEENP 3) <5372>* **IT'S A HARD LIFE. / IS THIS THE WORLD WE CREATED?** [6] [72]
(12"+=) *(12QUEEN 3)* – ('A'extended remix).

Sep 84. (7"/'A'-Headbangers-12") *(QUEEN/12QUEEN 4) <5424>* **HAMMER TO FALL. / TEAR IT UP** [13] [ ]

Dec 84. (7"/ext.12") *(QUEEN/12QUEEN 5)* **THANK GOD IT'S CHRISTMAS. / MAN ON THE PROWL / KEEP PASSING OPEN WINDOWS** [21] [–]

— In the mid 80's & before, each individual had also launched solo

Nov 85. (7"/ext-12") *(QUEEN/12QUEEN 6) <5530>* **ONE VISION. / BLURRED VISION** [7] [61]

Feb 86. (7") *<5568>* **PRINCES OF THE UNIVERSE. / A DOZEN RED ROSES FOR MY DARLING** [–] [ ]

Mar 86. (7"/ext.12"/ext.12"pic-d) *(QUEEN/12QUEEN/12QUEENP 7) <5590>* **A KIND OF MAGIC. / A DOZEN RED ROSES FOR MY DARLING** [3] Jun86 [42]

May 86. (lp/c)(cd) *(EU/TCEU 3509)(CDP 746267-2) <12476>* **A KIND OF MAGIC** [1] [46]
– One vision / A kind of magic / One year of love / Pain is so close to pleasure / Friends will be friends / Who wants to live forever / Gimme the prize / Don't lose your head / Princes of the universe. *(cd+=)* – A kind of 'A kind of magic – Friends will be friends – Who wants to live forever. *<US cd-iss. Jun91 on 'Hollywood'+=; 61152>* – Forever, One vision.

Jun 86. (7"/7"pic-d) *(QUEEN/+P 8)* **FRIENDS WILL BE FRIENDS. / SEVEN SEAS OF RHYE** [14] [–]
(12"+=) *(12QUEEN 8)* – ('A'extended mix).

Jul 86. (7") *<5633>* **DON'T LOSE YOUR HEAD. / PAIN IS SO CLOSE TO PLEASURE** [–] [ ]

Sep 86. (7") *(QUEEN 9)* **WHO WANTS TO LIVE FOREVER. / KILLER QUEEN** [24] [–]
(12"+=) *(12QUEEN 9)* – ('A'-lp version) / Forever.

Dec 86. (d-lp/c)(cd) *(EMC/TCEMC 3519)(CDP 746413-2)* **LIVE MAGIC (live)** [3] [–]
– One vision / Tie your mother down / I want to break free / Hammer to fall / Seven seas of rhye / We are the champions / Another one bites the dust / Is this the world we created? / Bohemian rhasody / Radio Ga Ga / Friends will be friends / We will rock you / Under pressure / A kind of music / God save the Queen. *(re-iss. Dec91 on 'Parlophone')*

— During this lull in QUEEN activity, FREDDIE MERCURY had released some solo singles and collaborated with MONTSERRAT CABALLE. TAYLOR had formed The CROSS

Parlophone Capitol

Apr 89. (c-s/7") *(TC+/QUEEN 10) <44372>* **I WANT IT ALL. / HANG ON IN THERE** [3] [50]
(12"+=/cd-s+=) *(12/CD QUEEN 10)* – ('A'album version).

May 89. (lp/c/cd) *(PCSD/TCPCSD/CDPCSD 107) <92357>* **THE MIRACLE** [1] [24]
– Party / Khashoggis ship / The miracle / I want it all / The invisible man / Breakthru / Rain must fall / Scandal / Was it all worth it / My baby does me. *(cd+=)* – Hang on in there / Chinese torture / The invisible man (ext). *<US cd-iss. Oct91 on 'Hollywood' ++=; 61134-2>* – Scandal (12"mix).

Jun 89. (c-s/7"/7"sha-pic-d) *(TC+/QUEEN/+PD 11)* **BREAKTHRU. / STEALIN'** [7] [–]
(12"+=/cd-s+=) *(12/CD QUEEN 11)* – ('A'extended).

Aug 89. (c-s/7"/7"clear) *(TC+/QUEEN/+X 12)* **INVISIBLE MAN. / HIJACK MY HEART** [12] [–]
(cd-s+=/12"+=/12"clear+=) *(CD/12 QUEEN/+X 12)* – ('A'extended).

Oct 89. (c-s/7") *(TC+/QUEEN 14) <44457>* **SCANDAL. / MY LIFE HAS BEEN SAVED** [25] [ ]
(12"+=/cd-s+=) *(12/CD QUEEN 14)* – ('A'extended).

Dec 89. (c-s/7") *(TC+/QUEEN 15)* **THE MIRACLE. / STONE COLD CRAZY (live)** [21] [ ]
(12"+=/cd-s+=) *(12/CD QUEEN 15)* – My melancholy blues (live).

Parlophone Hollywood

Jan 91. (c-s/7") *(TC+/QUEEN 16)* **INNUENDO. / BIJOU** [1] [ ]
('A'-Explosion mix; cd-s+=12"+=/12"pic-d+=) *(CD/12 QUEEN/+P 16)* – Under pressure (extended).

Feb 91. (cd/c/lp) *(CD/TC+/PCSD 115) <61020>* **INNUENDO** [1] [30]
– Innuendo / I'm going slightly mad / Headlong / I can't live with you / Don't try so hard / Ride the wild wind / All God's people / These are the days of our lives / Delilah / Hit man / Bijou / The show must go on.

Mar 91. (c-s/7"/7"sha-pic-d) *(TC+/QUEEN/+P 17)* **I'M GOING SLIGHTLY MAD. / HIT MAN** [22] [ ]
(12"+=/cd-s+=) *(12/CD QUEEN 17)* – Lost opportunity.

May 91. (c-s/7") *(TC+/QUEEN 18)* **HEADLONG. / ALL GOD'S PEOPLE** [14] [ ]
(cd-s+=/12"+=/12"pic-d+=) *(CD/12 QUEEN/+P 18)* – Mad the swine.

Oct 91. (c-s/7") *(TC+/QUEEN 19)* **THE SHOW MUST GO ON. / KEEP YOURSELF ALIVE** [16] [ ]
(12"+=) *(12QUEEN 19)* – (Queen talks – interview).
(cd-s++=) *(CDQUEEN 19)* – Body language.
(cd-s) – ('A'side) / Now I'm here / Fat bottomed girls / Los Palabras de amor.

Oct 91. (cd/c/d-lp) *(CD/TC+/PMTV 2) <61311>* **GREATEST HITS II** (compilation) (US title 'CLASSIC QUEEN') [1] [4]
– A kind of magic / Under pressure / Radio Ga Ga / I want it all / I want to break free / Innuendo / It's a hard life / Breakthru / Who wants to live forever / Headlong / The miracle / I'm going slightly mad / The invisible man / Hammer to fall / Friends will be friends / The show must go on / One vision. *(hit UK No.29 in May93)* (US-version +=)– Bohemian rhapsody / Stone cold crazy / One year of love / Tie your mother down / These are the days of our lives / Keep yourself alive.

— On the 23rd November 1991, FREDDIE lost his silent 2-year battle against AIDS.

Dec 91. (c-s/12"/cd-s/7") *(TC/12/CD+/QUEEN 20) <64794>* **BOHEMIAN RHAPSODY. / THESE ARE THE DAYS OF OUR LIVES** [1] [2]

Jun 92. (12")(c-s) *<64725>* **WE WILL ROCK YOU. / WE ARE THE CHAMPIONS** [–] [52]

Sep 92. (cd) *<61265>* **GREATEST HITS** [–] [11]

Apr 93. (c-ep/cd-ep/7"ep; by GEORGE MICHAEL & QUEEN) *(TC/CD+/R 6340) <61479>* **FIVE LIVE EP** [1] album [46]
– Somebody to love / Medley: Killer – Papa was a rollin' stone / These are the days of our lives (with LISA STANSFIELD) / Calling you.
(cd-ep) *(CDRS 6340)* – ('A'side) / Medley: Killer / Papa was a rollin' stone (with PM DAWN).
(12"+=) *(12RS 6340)* – Medley: Killer / Papa was a rollin' stone – instrumental.

— <In the US, the EP's main track 'SOMEBODY TO LOVE', hit No.30; *<64647>*>

— In Feb'95, FREDDIE and BRIAN featured on EDDIE HOWELL's re-issued 1977 single 'THE MAN FROM MANHATTAN'.

Oct 95. (c-s) *(TCQUEEN 21)* **HEAVEN FOR EVERYONE / IT'S A BEAUTIFUL DAY** [2] [ ]
(cd-s+=) *(CDQUEEN 21)* – ('A'-lp version).
(cd-s) *(CDQUEENS 21)* – ('A'side) / Keep yourself alive / Seven seas of rhye / Killer queen.

Nov 95. (cd/c/lp) *(CD/TC+/PCSD 167) <62017>* **MADE IN HEAVEN** [1] [58]
– It's a beautiful day / Made in Heaven / Let me live / Mother love / My life has been saved / I was born to love you / Heaven for everyone / Too much love will kill you / You don't fool me / A winter's tale / It's a beautiful day (reprise) / Yeh / Track 13.

Dec 95. (c-s/7") *(TC+/QUEEN 22)* **A WINTER'S TALE. / THANK GOD IT'S CHRISTMAS** [6] [ ]
(cd-s+=) *(CDQUEEN 22)* – Rock in Rio blues.
(cd-s) *(CDQUEENS 22)* – ('A'side) / Now I'm here / You're my best friend / Somebody to love.

Feb 96. (c-s/7") *(TC+/QUEEN 23)* **TOO MUCH LOVE WILL KILL YOU. / WE WILL ROCK YOU / WE ARE THE CHAMPIONS** [15] [ ]
(cd-s+=) *(CDQUEEN 23)* – Spread your wings.

Jun 96. (c-s/7"pic-d) *(TCQUEEN/QUEENP 24)* **LET ME LIVE. / MY FAIRY KING / DOIN' ALRIGHT / LIAR** [9] [ ]
(cd-s) *(CDQUEEN 24)* – ('A'side) / Fat bottomed girls / Bicycle race / Don't stop me now.

Nov 96. (c-s) *(TCQUEEN 25)* **YOU DON'T FOOL ME / ('A'remix)** [17] [–]
(12") *(12QUEEN 25)* – ('A'-Freddie's club + revenge mixes).
(cd-s+=) *(CDQUEEN 25)* – ('A'-Dancing Divas mix) / ('A'-sexy club mix).

Nov 97. (cd/c/d-lp) *(823091-2/-4/-1)* **QUEEN ROCKS** [7] [ ]
– No-one but you / We will rock you / Tie your mother down / Seven seas of rhye / I can't live with you / Hammer to fall / Stone cold crazy / Fat bottomed girls / Keep yourself alive / Tear it up / One vision / Killer queen / Sheer heart attack / I'm in love with my car / Put out the fire / Headlong / It's late / I want it all. *<US-title 'ROCKS VOL.1' diff tracks; 162132>*

Jan 98. (c-s) *(TCQUEEN 27)* **NO-ONE BUT YOU / TIE YOUR MOTHER DOWN** [13] [ ]
(12"+=/cd-s+=) *(QUEENPD/CDQUEEN 27)* – We will rock you (mix) / Gimme the prize (mix).

Nov 98. (c-s; by QUEEN / WYCLEF JEAN featuring PRAS MICHEL & FREE) *(DRMC 22364)* **ANOTHER ONE BITES THE DUST / (mix)** [5] [ ]
(12"+=/cd-s+=) *(DRM T/CD 22364)* – (Wyclef Jean remix) / (Black Rock Star remix).
(above from the movie, 'Small Soldiers', released on 'Dreamworks')

Nov 99. (cd/c/d-lp) *(523452-2/-4/-1)* **GREATEST HITS III** (hits/collaborations & solo material) [5] [ ]
– The show must go on / Under pressure / Barcelona / Too much love / Somebody to love / You don't fool me / Heaven for everyone / Las palabras / Driven by you / Living on my own / Let me live / The great pretender / Princess of the universe / Another one bites the dust / No one but you / These are the days of our lives / Thank God it's Christmas.

Dec 99. (7"pic-d; QUEEN & DAVID BOWIE) *(QUEENPD 28)* **UNDER PRESSURE. / BOHEMIAN RHAPSODY** [14] [ ]
(c-s+=/cd-s+=) *(TC/CD QUEEN 28)* – Thank God it's Christmas.
(cd-s) *(CDQUEENS 28)* – ('A'mixes).

—— In Jul'00, QUEEN were back at No.1 collaborating with pop group FIVE on a rendition of 'WE WILL ROCK YOU'

– compilations, etc. –

on 'EMI'UK / 'Capitol'US, unless otherwise mentioned.

Dec 85. (14xlp-box) *(QB 1)* **THE COMPLETE WORKS** [ ] [ ]

Nov 88. (3"cd-ep) *(QUECD 1)* **SEVEN SEAS OF RHYE / SEE WHAT A FOOL I'VE BEEN / FUNNY HOW LOVE IS** [ ] [–]

Nov 88. (3"cd-ep) *(QUECD 2)* **KILLER QUEEN / FLICK OF THE WRIST / BRIGHTON ROCK** [ ] [–]

Nov 88. (3"cd-ep) *(QUECD 3)* **BOHEMIAN RHAPSODY / I'M IN LOVE WITH MY CAR / YOU'RE MY BEST FRIEND** [ ] [–]

Nov 88. (3"cd-ep) *(QUECD 4)* **SOMEBODY TO LOVE / WHITE MAN / TIE YOUR MOTHER DOWN** [ ] [–]

Nov 88. (3"cd-ep) *(QUECD 5)* **GOOD OLD FASHIONED LOVER BOY / DEATH ON TWO LEGS (DEDICATED TO . . .) / TENEMENT FUNSTER / WHITE QUEEN (AS IT BEGAN)** [ ] [–]

Nov 88. (3"cd-ep) *(QUECD 6)* **WE ARE THE CHAMPIONS / WE WILL ROCK YOU / FAT BOTTOMED GIRLS** [ ] [–]

Nov 88. (3"cd-ep) *(QUECD 7)* **CRAZY LITTLE THING CALLED LOVE / SPREAD YOUR WINGS / FLASH** [ ] [–]

Nov 88. (3"cd-ep) *(QUECD 8)* **ANOTHER ONE BITES THE DUST / DRAGON ATTACK / LAS PALABRAS DE AMOR** [ ] [–]

Nov 88. (3"cd-ep) *(QUECD 9)* **UNDER PRESSURE / SOUL BROTHER / BODY LANGUAGE** [ ] [–]

Nov 88. (3"cd-ep) *(QUECD 10)* **RADIO GA GA / I GO CRAZY / HAMMER TO FALL** [ ] [–]

Nov 88. (3"cd-ep) *(QUECD 11)* **I WANT TO BREAK FREE / MACHINES (OR BACK TO HUMANS) / IT'S A HARD LIFE** [ ] [–]

Nov 88. (3"cd-ep) *(QUECD 12)* **A KIND OF MAGIC / A DOZEN RED ROSES FOR MY DARLING / ONE VISION** [ ] [–]

Dec 89. (lp/c/cd) *Band Of Joy; (BOJ LP/MC/CD 001)* **QUEEN AT THE BEEB (live)** [67] [–]

Jun 92. (d-cd) *Parlophone; <CDPCSD 725) / Hollywood; <61104>* **QUEEN: LIVE AT WEMBLEY 1986 (live; ex-video)** [2] [53]
– One vision / Tie your mother down / In the lap of the gods / Seven seas of Rhye / Tear it up / A kind of magic / Under pressure / Another one bites the dust / Who wants to live forever / I want to break free / Impromptu / Brighton rock solo / Now I'm here / Love of my life / Is this the world we created / Baby I don't care / Hello Mary Lou / Tutti frutti / Gimme some lovin' / Bohemian rhapsody / Hammer to fall / Crazy little thing called love / Big spender / Radio ga ga / We will rock you / Friends will be friends / We are the champions / God save the Queen. *(re-iss. Jun03; 591092-2)* (hit UK No.38)

Oct 94. (d-cd/d-c) *Parlophone; (CD/TC PCSD 161)* **GREATEST HITS 1 & 2** [37] [ ]

Dec 95. (20xcd-box) *E.M.I.; (QUEENBOX 20)* **ULTIMATE QUEEN** [ ] [ ]

Nov 00. (3xcd-box) *Parlophone; (529883-2)* **GREATEST HITS VOL.I, II & III** [63] [ ]

Mar 03. (12"/cd-s; as QUEEN & VANGUARD) *Nebula; (NEB T/CD 041)* **FLASH (mixes)** [15] [–]

FREDDIE MERCURY

C.B.S. Columbia

Sep 84. (7"/7"pic-d/ext.12") *(A/WA/TA 4375) <04606>* **LOVE KILLS. / ROT WANG'S PARTY (by Giorgio Moroder)** [10] [69]
(above from film 'Metropolis' & co-written w / Georgio Moroder)

Apr 85. (7"/ext.12") *(A/TA 6019) <04869>* **I WAS BORN TO LOVE YOU. / STOP ALL THE FIGHTING** [11] [76]
(d7"+=) *(DA 6019)* – Love kills (extended) / Stop all the fighting (extended).

May 85. (lp/c/cd) *(CBS/+40/CD 86312) <40071>* **MR. BAD GUY** [6] [ ]
– Let's turn it on * / Made in Heaven / I was born to love you * / Foolin' around / Mr. Bad guy / Man made Paradise / There must be more to life than this / Living on my own * / Your kind of lover / My love is dangerous / Love me like there's no tomorrow. *(c+cd+=)* – (* extended tracks).

Jul 85. (7"/7"sha-pic-d) *(A/WA 6413)* **MADE IN HEAVEN (remix). / SHE BLOWS HOT AND COLD** [57] [–]
(ext.12"+=) *(TA 6413)* – ('A'extended).

Sep 85. (7"/12"/12"g-f) *(A/TA/GA 6555) <05455>* **LIVING ON MY OWN. / MY LOVE IS DANGEROUS** [50] [–]

Oct 85. (7") **LIVING ON MY OWN. / SHE BLOWS HOT AND COLD** [–] [ ]

Nov 85. (7"/ext.12") *(A/TA 6725)* **LOVE ME LIKE THERE IS NO TOMORROW. / LET'S TURN IT ON** [ ] [–]
(below from Dave Clark musical 'Time')

E.M.I. not iss.

May 86. (7"/ext.12") *(EMI/+12 5559)* **TIME. / TIME (instrumental)** [ ] [–]

Parlophone Capitol

Feb 87. (7"/7"sha-pic-d) *(R/RP 6151) <5696>* **THE GREAT PRETENDER. / EXERCISES IN FREE LOVE** [4] [ ]
(12"+=) *(12R 6151)* – ('A'extended).

FREDDIE MERCURY with MONTSERRAT CABALLE

—— (with female Spanish opera star)

Polydor Hollywood

Oct 87. (7") *(POSP 887)* **BARCELONA. / EXERCISES IN FREE LOVE** (her version) [8] [ ]
(c-s+=/12"+=/12"pic-d+=/cd-s+=) *(POSP C/X/P/CD 887)* – ('A'extended).

Oct 88. (lp/c)(cd) *(POLH/+C 44)(<837277-2>)* **BARCELONA** [25] [ ]
– Barcelona / La Japonaise / The fallen priest / Ensueno / The golden boy / Guide me home / How can I go on / Overture piccante. *(re-iss. Aug92, hit UK No.15)*

Oct 88. (7") *(POSP 23)* **THE GOLDEN BOY. / THE FALLEN PRIEST** [ ] [ ]
(12"+=)(cd-s+=) *(POSPX 23)(PZ 23CD)* – ('A'instrumental).

Jan 89. (7"/7"pic-d) *(POSP/POSX 29)* **HOW CAN I GO ON. / OVERTURE PICCANTE** [ ] [ ]
(12"+=)(cd-s+=) *(POSPX 29)(PZ 29CD)* – Guide me home.
(below were posthumous releases)

Jul 92. (7"/c-s/cd-s) *(PO/+CS/CD 221)* **BARCELONA. / EXCERCISES IN FREE LOVE** [2] [ ]
(12"+=) *(P 221)* – ('A'extended).

Oct 92. (7"/c-s) **HOW CAN I GO ON. / THE GOLDEN BOY** [ ] [ ]
(cd-s+=) – The fallen priest.
(12"+=/cd-s+=) – Guide me home / Overture piccante.

Parlophone not iss.

Nov 92. (cd/c/lp) *(CD/TC+/PCSD 124)* **THE FREDDIE MERCURY ALBUM** (compilation) [4] [–]
– The great pretender / Foolin' around / Time / Your kind of love / Exercises in free love / In my defence / Mr. Bad guy / Let's turn it on / Living on my own / Love kills / Barcelona (w / MONSERRAT CABALLE).

Dec 92. (c-s/7") *(TC+/R 6331)* **IN MY DEFENCE. / LOVE KILLS (original)** [8] [–]
(cd-s+=) *(CDR 6331)* – Mr. Bad guy / Living on my own (mix).

Jan 93. (c-s/7") *(TC+/R 6336)* **THE GREAT PRETENDER. / STOP ALL THE FIGHTING** [29] [–]
(cd-s+=) *(CDR 6336)* – Exercises in free love / ('A'-Malouf mix).

Jul 93. (c-s/7") *(TC+/R 6355)* **LIVING ON MY OWN. / ('A'mix)** [1] [–]
(12"+=/cd-s+=) *(12R/CDR 6355)* – ('A'mixes).

– compilations, etc. –

Oct 00. (3xcd-box) *Parlophone; (528047-2)* **SOLO** [13] [–]
– (MR. BAD GUY / BARCELONA / bonus)

Oct 00. (9xcd-box) *Parlophone; (527964-0)* **THE SOLO COLLECTION** [ ] [–]

— **JOHN DEACON** played bass on The IMMORTALS May'86 'M.C.A.' single 'NO TURNING BACK', from the film 'Biggles'.

BRIAN MAY

— with **EDDIE VAN HALEN** – guitar / **PHIL CHEN** – bass / **FRED MANDEL** – keyboards / **ALAN GRATZER** – drums etc.

E.M.I. Capitol

Oct 83. (7"; as BRIAN MAY & FRIENDS) *(EMI 5436)* **STARFLEET. / SON OF STARFLEET** [65] [–]

Oct 83. (7"; as BRIAN MAY & FRIENDS) *<B-5278>* **STARFLEET. / STARFLEET (extended)** [–] [ ]

Oct 83. (m-lp/c; as BRIAN MAY & FRIENDS) *(SFLT 107806-1/-4) <15014>* **STARFLEET PROJECT** [35] [ ]
– Starfleet / Let me out / Bluesbreakers.

— In the Autumn of '89, BRIAN MAY wrote the song 'WHO WANTS TO LIVE FOREVER' and gave it to charity for single by youngsters IAN MEESON & BELINDA GHILETT; 'EMI' 7"/12" *(ODO/12ODO 112)*

Parlophone Hollywood

Nov 91. (7"/c-s) *(R/TCR 6304)* **DRIVEN BY YOU. / JUST ONE LIFE (dedicated to the memory of Philip Sayer)** [6] [–]
(b-guitar version; 12"+=/cd-s+=) *(12R/CDR 6034)* – Driven by you (Ford Ad version).

Sep 92. (7"/c-s) *(R/TCR 6320)* **TOO MUCH LOVE WILL KILL YOU. / I'M SCARED** [5] [–]
(cd-s+=/s-cd-s+=) *(CDR/+S 6320)* – Driven by you (feat. COZY POWELL + NEIL MURRAY).

Oct 92. (cd/c/lp) *(CD/C+/PCSD 123) <61404>* **BACK TO THE LIGHT** [6] [ ]
– The dark / Back to the light / Love token / Resurrection / Too much love will kill you / Driven by you / Nothin' but blue / I'm scared / Last horizon / Let your heart rule your head / Just one life / Rollin' over. *(re-iss. Jun93 in gold-cd; CDPCSDX 123)*

— In Oct'92, BRIAN featured on HANK MARVIN's (Shadows) version of QUEEN's song 'WE ARE THE CHAMPIONS'.

Nov 92. (7"/c-s) *(R/TCR 6329)* **BACK TO THE LIGHT. / NOTHING BUT BLUE (guitar version)** [19] [–]
(B-guitar cd-s+=) *(CDR 6329)* – Blues breaker.
(cd-s) *(CDRX 6329)* – ('A'side) / Star fleet / Let me out.

Parlophone Elektra

Apr 93. (c-s) *<64642>* **DRIVEN BY YOU** [–] [ ]

Jun 93. (c-s; by BRIAN MAY with COZY POWELL) *(TCR 6351)* **RESURRECTION / LOVE TOKEN** [23] [–]
(12"pic-d+=/cd-s+=) *(12RPF/CDRS 6351)* – Too much love will kill you (live).
(cd-s) *(CDR 6351)* – ('A'side) / Driven by you (two) / Back to the light (live) / Tie your mother down (live).

Dec 93. (7"/c-s) *(R/TCR 6371)* **LAST HORIZON. / LET YOUR HEART RULE YOUR HEAD** [51] [–]
(cd-s/s-cd-s) *(CDR/+S 6371)* – ('A'side) / ('A'live) / We will rock you (live) / ('A'album mix).

— **MAY** – vox, guitar with **COZY POWELL** – drums / **NEIL MURRAY** – bass / **SPIKE EDNEY** – keyboards / **JAMIE MOSES** – guitar, vocals / **CATHY PORTER + SHELLEY PRESTON** – vox

Feb 94. (cd/c/d-lp; by BRIAN MAY BAND) *(CD/C+/PCSD 150)* **LIVE AT THE BRIXTON ACADEMY (live London, 15th June 1993)** [20] [–]
– Back to the light / Driven by you / Tie your mother down / Love token / Headlong / Love of my life / '39 – Let your heart rule your head / Too much love will kill you / Since you've been gone / Now I'm here / Guitar extravagance / Resurrection / Last horizon / We will rock you / Hammer to fall.

May 98. (7") *(R 6498)* **THE BUSINESS (Rock On Cozy mix). / MAYBE BABY** [51] [–]
(cd-s+=) *(CDR 6498)* – (Brian talks) / ('A'-CD-Rom video).

Jun 98. (cd/c/lp) *(494973-2/-4/-1) <162103>* **ANOTHER WORLD** [23] [ ]
– Space / The business / China belle / Why don't we try again / On my way up / Cyborg / Guv'nor / Wilderness / Slow down / One rainy wish / All the way from Memphis / Another world.

Aug 98. (c-s/cd-s) *(TCR/CDR 6504)* **WHY DON'T WE TRY AGAIN / ONLY MAKE BELIEVE / F.B.I.** [44] [–]

– (MAY) compilations, etc. –

Nov 95. (cd) *Javelin; (HADCD 190)* **THEMES AND DREAMS** [ ] [–]

Dec 95. (cd-s) *Koch; (34337-2)* **BLACK WHITE HOUSE** [ ] [–]

— with APPICE (veteran drummer) + SLASH (of Guns N' Roses)

Feb 96. (cd-s; by BRIAN MAY with CARMINE APPICE'S GUITAR ZEUS) **NOBODY KNEW (BLACK WHITE HOUSE) / NOBODY KNEW (BLACK WHITE HOUSE) (long version)** [ ] [–]

ROGER TAYLOR

E.M.I. Elektra

Aug 77. (7") *(EMI 2679)* **I WANNA TESTIFY. / TURN ON THE T.V.** [ ] [–]

Apr 81. (7") *(EMI 5157)* **FUTURE MANAGEMENT. / LAUGH OR CRY** [49] [–]

Apr 81. (lp/c) *(EMC/TCEMC 3369) <5E-522>* **FUN IN SPACE** [18] [ ]
– No violins / Laugh or cry / Future management / Let's get crazy / My country I & II / Good times are now / Magic is loose / Interlude in Constantinople / Airheads / Fun in space. *(cd-iss. May96 on 'Parlophone'; CDPCS 7380)*

Apr 81. (7") *<E-47151>* **LET'S GET CRAZY. / LAUGH OR CRY** [–] [ ]

Jun 81. (7") *(EMI 5200)* **MY COUNTRY. / FUN IN SPACE** [ ] [–]

E.M.I. Capitol

Jun 84. (7"/ext.12") *(EMI/+12 5478)* **MAN ON FIRE. / KILLING TIME** [66] [–]

Jul 84. (lp/c) *(RTA/TCRTA 1) <EJ-240137-1>* **STRANGE FRONTIER** [30] [ ]
– Strange frontier / Beautiful dreams / Man on fire / Racing in the street / Masters of war / Killing time / Abandon fire / Young love / It's an illusion / I cry for you (love, hope & confusion). *(cd-iss. May96 on 'Parlophone'; CDPCS 7381)*

Aug 84. (7") *(EMI 5490)* **STRANGE FRONTIER. / I CRY FOR YOU (remix)** [ ] [–]
(ext.12"+=) *(EMI12 5490)* – Two sharp pencils.

The CROSS

ROGER with **PETER NOONE** – bass / **CLAYTON MOSS** – guitar / **SPIKE EDNEY** – keyboards / **JOSH MacRAE** – drums

Virgin Virgin

Sep 87. (7"/ext.12")(cd-s) *(VS/+T 1007)(CDEP 10)* **COWBOYS AND INDIANS. / LOVE LIES BLEEDING** [74] [ ]
(c-s+=) *(VSTC 1007)* – ('A'extended).

Jan 88. (7") *(VS 1026)* **SHOVE IT. / ROUGH JUSTICE** [ ] [ ]
(ext.12"+=) *(VS 1026-12)* – ('A'-Metropolix mix).
(cd-s+=) *(CDEP 20)* – Cowboys and Indians / ('A'extended).

Jan 88. (lp/c/cd) *(V/TCV/CDV 2477) <90857>* **SHOVE IT** [58] Apr88 [ ]
– Shove it / Heaven for everyone / Love on a tightrope (like an animal) / Cowboys and Indians / Stand up for love / Love lies bleeding (she was a wicked, wily waitress) / Contact. *(cd+=)* – Rough justice – 2nd shelf mix.

Mar 88. (7") *(VS 1062)* **HEAVEN FOR EVERYONE. / LOVE ON A TIGHTROPE (LIKE AN ANIMAL)** [ ] [ ]
(12"+=) *(VST 1062)* – Contact.

Jul 88. (7") *(VS 1100)* **MANIPULATOR. / STAND UP FOR LOVE** [ ] [ ]
(12"+=) *(VS 1100-12)* – ('A'extended).

Parlophone not iss.

Apr 90. (7") *(R 6251)* **POWER TO LOVE. / PASSION FOR TRASH** [ ] [-]
(12"+=/cd-s+=) *(12R/CDR 6251)* – ('A'extended).

May 90. (cd/c/lp) *(CD/TC+/PCS 7342)* **MAD, BAD AND DANGEROUS TO KNOW** [ ] [-]
– On top of the world ma / Liar / Closer to you / Breakdown / Penetration guru / Power to love / Sister blue / Better things / Old men (lay down) / Final destination. *(cd+=)* – Foxy lady.

ROGER TAYLOR

— with **JASON FALLOON** – guitars / **PHIL SPALDING** – bass / **MIKE CROSSLEY** – piano, keyboards / **CATHERINE PORTER** – backing vocals / **JOSHUA J. MacRAE** – programming

Parlophone not iss.

Apr 94. (c-s/7") *(TC+/R 6379)* **NAZIS 1994. / ('A'radio mix)** [22] [-]
(12"red+=) *(12R 6379)* – ('A'extended) / ('A'-Big science mix).
(cd-s++=) *(CDR 6379)* – ('A'kick mix) / ('A'-Schindler's extended mix).

Sep 94. (cd/c) *(CD/TC PCSD 157)* **HAPPINESS?** [22] [-]
– Nazis 1994 / Happiness / Revelations / Touch the sky / Foreign sand / Freedom train / You had to be there / The key / Everybody hurts sometime / Loneliness . . . / Dear Mr. Murdoch / Old friends.

— Below featured a Japanese classically trained drummer, pianist & co-composer **YOSHIKI** plus **JIM CREGAN** – guitars / **PHIL CHEN** – bass / **DICK MARX** – strings arrangement

Sep 94. (c-s/7"colrd; by ROGER TAYLOR & YOSHIKI) *(TC+/R 6389)* **FOREIGN SAND. / ('A'mix)** [26] [-]
(12"pic-d+=/cd-s+=) *(12R/CDR 6389)* – You had to be there / Final destination.

Nov 94. (7") *(R 6399)* **HAPPINESS. / RIDE THE WILD WIND (live)** [32] [-]
(12") *(12R 6399)* – ('A'side) / Dear Mr.Murdoch / Everybody hurts sometime (live) / Old friends (live).
(cd-s) *(CDR 6399)* – ('A'side) / Loneliness / Dear Mr. Murdoch / I want to break free (live).

Sep 98. (7"/cd-s) *(R/CDR 6507)* **PRESSURE ON. / PEOPLE ON STREETS (mashed) / TONIGHT (dub sangria)** [45] [-]

Sep 98. (cd/c/lp) *(496724-2/-4/-1)* **ELECTRIC FIRE** [53] [-]
– Pressure on / Nation of haircuts / Believe in yourself / Surrender / People on the streets / Whispers / No more fun / Tonight / Where are you now / Working class hero / London town c'mon down.

Mar 99. (7") *(R 6517)* **SURRENDER. / LONDON TOWN, C'MON DOWN** [38] [-]
(cd-s+=) *(CDR 6517)* – A nation of haircuts (club cut).
(cd-s) *(CDRS 6517)* – ('A'live) / No more fun (live) / Tonight (live) / ('A'-CD-Rom video).

QUEENS OF THE STONE AGE

Formed: Palm Springs, California, USA . . . 1991 as KYUSS by JOHN GARCIA, JOSH HOMME, SCOTT REEDER and ALFREDO HERNANDEZ. Initially playing bluesy punk, the group's rather lacklustre debut, 'WRETCH', was followed up by the blinding intensity of 'BLUES FOR THE RED SUN' (1992). Seemingly coming from out of nowhere, it had taken MASTERS OF REALITY retro guru CHRIS GOSS to develop the band's latent genius. A smouldering slab of frazzled flare-rock, the band had dragged garage-psych stoned and stumbling into the 90's, carving a new benchmark for would-be sonic archivists. Live, most commentators were in agreement that KYUSS were peerless, the group soon finding themsleves playing on the same bill as the likes of DANZIG and METALLICA. 'Elektra' were sufficiently impressed to offer the band a deal when their label went belly-up, KYUSS once again working with GOSS on the fuzzed-up bludgeon of 'WELCOME TO SKY VALLEY' (1994). Despite the critical raving, the group's label were unsure how to market their hippy-rock sound with the result that KYUSS' record sales were less than impressive. So it was then, that after a final masterpiece, 'AND THE CIRCUS LEAVES TOWN' (1995), the group decided to call it a day. The fact that KYUSS were just obviously beginning to reach their full potential was illustrated with the 'QUEENS OF THE STONE AGE' (1997) set. A combination of unreleased KYUSS material and a clutch of new, even more mind-altering tracks from HOMME's similarly titled new outfit (also numbering GOSS, VAN CONNER and VIC THE STICK), the album was a disorientatingly heavy testament (including a suitably trippy cover of Black Sabbath's 'INTO THE VOID') to one of the most criminally ignored bands of the 90's. Meanwhile, KYUSS' former frontman, GARCIA, was making his name with a new outfit, UNIDA. QUEENS OF THE STONE AGE carried the KYUSS flag into the new millennium courtesy of a new major label deal with 'Interscope' and the highly acclaimed 'RATED R' (2000) album. A record that featured highly in many end of year polls and finally saw HOMME, OLIVERI and Co gain the popular rock god homages that their music had always begged, 'RATED R' started as it meant to go on with 'FEEL GOOD HIT OF THE SUMMER' gratuitously reeling off a list of narcotics ad nauseam. While markedly more hallucinogenically swinging than its predecessor with more elaborate instrumentation and arrangements, the California stoners proved their desert-grunge could still scorch at a hundred paces on the likes of the demented 'TENSION HEAD'. 'LEG OF LAMB', meanwhile, recalled MASTERS OF REALITY at their trippy best. QOTSA returned in the summer of 2002 to issue their much anticipated follow-up to 'RATED R', but this time with MARK LANEGAN on full-time guitar duties and ex-NIRVANA and FOO FIGHTERS frontman DAVE GROHL on drumming duties. 'SONGS FOR THE DEAF' was all the better for it, and although the band weren't necessarily moving in new circles, their music was still punctuated with the same jaded desert rock vibe that had made those early KYUSS albums so enjoyable. GROHL, hammering away like a madman, reminded people of how good he still was on the drums and DEAN WEEN cranked up the tension even higher with his impeccable guitar playing. Meanwhile HOMME and OLIVERI began working on the soundtrack to the film 'Dangerous Lives Of Altar Boys' and dabbled in a brand new project – HEADBAND – with ex-MARILYN MANSON bassist TWIGGY RAMIREZ and CASEY CHAOS from heavy rockers AMEN. To add to HOMME's vast and varied canon was The DESERT SESSIONS, a side project born from the ashes of KYUSS' "generator parties". Including all that was cool in the LA rock scene, The DESERT SESSIONS played out like the Robert Altman of rock, enlisting everybody from PJ HARVEY to TWIGGY RAMIREZ. Their first releases were issued in an approximate one year period (1998-99) via whopping six volumes on the alternative label 'Man's Ruin'. However, the best of the bunch was collected by the 'Southern Lord' imprint who delivered 'VOL. 7-8' in 2001, featuring the insane desert-stomp 'UP IN HELL', not to mention collaborations by BEN SHEPARD (of SOUNDGARDEN), JOHN McBAIN (MONSTER MAGNET), BRANT BJORK (KYUSS), CHRIS GOSS (MASTERS OF REALITY) and QUEENS regular MARK LANEGAN to name but a few. 'VOL. 9 & 10' were released in 2003 and featured guests DEAN WEEN (WEEN), JOEY CASTILLO (DANZIG) and NATASHA SCHNIEDER (ELEVEN) as well a ballad with PJ HARVEY 'CRAWL HOME' (which hit the Top 40 in the UK). As confusing as the KYUSS and QOTSA output may be (see below for further and more rigorous inspection), it is hard to ignore their diverse and varied musical ambitions especially with tracks as brilliant as 'HANGING TREE' and 'AVON'; they also made it on to the 'SONGS FOR THE DEAF' set. • **Covered:** EVERYBODY'S GONNA BE HAPPY + WHO'LL BE THE NEXT IN LINE (Kinks) / NEVER SAY NEVER (Romeo Void) / THE MOST EXALTED POTENTATE OF LOVE (Cramps). Desert Sessions covered: ECCENTRIC MAN (Groundhogs).

Album rating: Kyuss: WRETCH (*7) / BLUES FOR THE RED SUN (*9) / WELCOME TO SKY VALLEY (*8) / . . .AND THE CIRCUS LEAVES TOWN (*8) / QUEENS OF THE STONE AGE (*8) / MUCHAS GRACIAS compilation (*8) / Queens Of The Stone Age: QUEENS OF THE STONE AGE (*8) / RATED R (*9) / SONGS FOR THE DEAF (*8) / Desrt Sessions: VOL.I/II (*7) / VOL.III/IV (*6) / VOL.V/VI (*6) / 7 & 8 (*7) / 9 & 10 (*7)

KYUSS

JOHN GARCIA – vocals / **JOSH HOMME** (b. 1973) – guitar / **SCOTT REEDER** – bass; repl. NICK OLIVERI (b. 1971) who joined the DWARVES / **ALFREDO HERNANDEZ** (b. 1966) – drums

Dali-Chameleon Dali-Chameleon

Nov 91. (cd) *<61256-2>* **WRETCH** [-] [ ]
– HWY 74 (beginning of what's about to happen) / Love has passed me by / Son of a bitch / Black widow / Katzenjammer / Deadly kiss / The law / Isolation / I'm not / Big bikes / Stage III. *(UK-iss.Feb98; same as US)*

Feb 93. (cd/c) *<(3705 61340-2/-4)>* **BLUES FOR THE RED SUN** [ ] [ ]
– Thumb / Green machine / Molten universe / 50 million years trip / (Downside up) / Thong song / Apothecaries' weight / Catepillar march / Freedom run / 800 / Writhe / Capsized. *(cd+=)* – Allen's wrench / Mondo generator / Yeah.

Elektra Warners

Jun 94. (cd/c/lp) *<(7559 61571-2/-4/-1)>* **WELCOME TO SKY VALLEY** [ ] [ ]
– I / Gardenia / Asteroid / Supa scoopa and mighty scoop / II / 100 degrees / Space cadet / Demon cleaner / III / Odyssey / Conan troutman / N.O. / Whitewater. *(lp-iss.Nov99 on 'White & Black'; WB 7524)*

Sep 94. (7"blue) *(EKR 192)* **DEMON CLEANER. / FREEDOM RUN (live)** [ ] [ ]
(cd-s) *(EKR 192CD1)* – ('A'side) / Day one (to Dave & Chris) / El rodeo / Hurricane.
(cd-s) *(EKR 192CD2)* – ('A'side) / Gardenia (live) / Thumb (live) / Conan trout man (live).

Feb 95. (cd-s) *(EKR 197CD)* **GARDENIA / U.N. SANDPIPER / CONAN TROUT MAN (live)** [ ] [ ]

Jun 95. (cd/c) *<(7559 61811-2/-4)>* **. . .AND THE CIRCUS LEAVES TOWN** [ ] [ ]
– Hurricane / One inch man / Thee of boozeroony / Gloria Lewis / Phototropic / El rodeo / Jumbo blimp jumbo / Tango zizzle / Size queen / Catamarran / Spaceship landing.

—— split in 1995 leaving some recordings below. HOMME formed QUEENS OF THE STONE AGE, which was released by below label as KYUSS' epitaph album. He was joined by **VAN CONNER** – bass (SCREAMING TREES) / **CHRIS GOSS** (MASTER OF REALITY) / **VIC THE STICK** – drums

Mans Ruin Mans Ruin

Jul 97. (10") *(MR 015)* **INTO THE VOID. / FATSO FORGETSO** [ ] [ ]

Dec 97. (cd) *<(MR 063)>* **QUEENS OF THE STONE AGE** [ ] [ ]
– KYUSS: Into the void / Fatso forgotso / Fatso Forgotso phase II / QUEENS OF THE STONE AGE: If only everything / Born to hula / Spiders and vinegaroons. *(re-iss. Aug00; same)*

QUEENS OF THE STONE AGE

—— **JOSH HOMME** – vocals, guitar / **NICK OLIVERI** – bass / **ALFREDO HERNANDEZ** – drums

Mans Ruin Mans Ruin

Jan 96. (7"; as GAMMA RAY) *<MR 036>* **GAMMA RAY. / IF ONLY EVERYTHING / BORN TO HULA** [-] [ ]

Sep 98. (10"ep/cd-ep) *<(MR 141/+CD)>* **QUEENS OF THE STONE AGE / BEAVER EP** [ ] [ ]
– The bronze / These aren't the droids you're looking for / BEAVER: Absence without leave / Morocco.

Roadrunner Mans Ruin

Oct 98. (cd) *(RR 8674-2) <MR 151CD>* **QUEENS OF THE STONE AGE** [ ] [ ]
– Regular John / Avon / If only / Walkin' on the sidewalks / You would know / How to handle a rope / Mexicola / Hispanic impressions / You can't quit me baby / Give the mule what he wants / I was a teenage hand model.

—— added **DAVE CATCHING** – guitar, steel guitar, piano / **NICKY LUCERO** – drums

Interscope Interscope

Jun 00. (cd) *<(490683-2)>* **RATED R** [54] [ ]
– Feel good hit of the summer / The lost art of keeping a secret / Leg of lamb / Auto pilot / Better living through chemistry / Monsters in the parasol / Quick and to the pointless / In the fade / Tension head / Lightning song / I think I lost my headache. *(lp-iss.Nov00+=; 490864-1)* – Ode to Clarissa. *(cd re-iss. Nov00 w/ free cd+=; same)* – FEEL GOOD HIT OF THE SUMMER EP

Aug 00. (7") *<(497387-7)>* **THE LOST ART OF KEEPING A SECRET. / ODE TO CLARISSA** [31] [ ]
(cd-s+=) *<(497392-2)>* – Monsters in the parasol (live).
(cd-s) *<(497391-2)>* – ('A'side) / Born to hula / ('A'-CD-Rom).

Nov 00. (cd-ep) *(497455-2) <497443-2>* **FEEL GOOD HIT OF THE SUMMER EP** [ ] [-]
– Feel good hit of the summer / Never say never / You're so vague / Who'll be the next in line / Feel good hit of the summer (CD-ROM video).

—— **OLIVERI** + **HOMME** recruited **DAVE GROHL** – drums (of FOO FIGHTER) / **MARK LANEGAN** – vocals (ex-SCREAMING TREES) / **DEAN WEEN** – guitar (of WEEN)

Aug 02. (cd) *<(493435-2)>* **SONGS FOR THE DEAF** [4] [17]
– You think I ain't worth a dollar, but I feel like a millionaire / No one knows / First it giveth / A song for the deaf / The sky is fallin' / Six shooter / Hangin' tree / Go with the flow / Gonna leave you / Do it again / God is on the radio / Another love song / A song for the deaf. *(UK+=)* – Mosquito song *[hidden US]* / The lost art of keeping a secret (live) / Everybody's gonna be happy. *(cd w/dvd+=; 493444-0) (d-lp-iss.Sep02; 439435-1)*

Nov 02. (7"colrd) *(497812-7) <radio>* **NO ONE KNOWS. / TENSION HEAD (live)** [15] [51]
(cd-s+=) *(497812-2)* – Gonna leave you (Spanish version).
(cd-s) *(497808-2)* – ('A'side) / A song for the deaf (live) / Avon (live) / ('A'video).

Apr 03. (12"clear) *(497869-0)* **GO WITH THE FLOW. / NO ONE KNOWS (Unkle reconstruction)** [21] [-]
(cd-s+=) *(497869-2)* – Hanging tree (live) / ('A'-video).
(cd-s) *(497870-2)* – ('A'side) / Regular John (live) / Do it again (live).

Aug 03. (7"red) *(9810506)* **FIRST IT GIVETH. / THE MOST EXALTED POTENTATE OF LOVE** [33] [-]
(cd-s+=) *(9810505)* – A song for the deaf (the blind can goes get fucked remix) / ('A'-video).
(cd-s) *(9810507)* – ('A'side) / Wake up screaming / You think I ain't worth a dollar, but I feel like a millionaire (Troy mix).

– KYUSS compilation –

Oct 00. (cd) *Elektra; <(7559 62571-2)>* **MUCHAS GRACIAS – THE BEST OF KYUSS** [ ] [ ]
– U.N. sandpiper / Shine / 50 million year trip (downside up) / Mudfly / Demon cleaner / A day early and a dollar extra / I'm not / Hurricane / Flip

the phrase / Fatso forgotso / El rodeo / Gardenia (live) / Thumb (live) / Conan Troutman (live) / Freedom run (live).

DESERT SESSIONS

JOSH HOMME with **PETER STAHL** – vocals (ex-WOOL, of EARTHLINGS) / **FRED DRAKE** – guitar (of EARTHLINGS) / **DAVE CATCHINGS** – bass (of EARTHLINGS) / **BEN SHEPHERD** – bass (ex-SOUNDGARDEN, of WELLWATER CONSPIRACY) / **ALFREDO HERNANDEZ** – drums

not iss. Man's Ruin

Nov 97. (d10"lp) *<MR 81>* **VOL.1: INSTRUMENTAL DRIVING MUSIC FOR FELONS** [–] [ ]
– Girl boy Tom / Monkey in the middle / Cowards way out / Robotic lunch.

— added **BRANT BJORK** – percussion, drums (of FU MANCHU) / **JOHN McBAIN** (WELLWATER CONSPIRACY)

Feb 98. (d10"lp/cd) *<MR 82>* **VOL.II: STATUS, SHIPS COMMANDER BUTCHERED** [–] [ ]
– Johnny the boy / Screamin' eagle / Cake (who shit on the?). *<cd+=>* – VOL.1

May 98. (d10"lp) *<MR 111>* **VOL.III: SET CO-ORDINATES FOR THE WHITE DWARF!!!** [–] [ ]
– Nova / At the helm of Hell's ships / Avon / Sugar rush.

— **HOMME + HERNANDEZ + NICK OLIVERI** recruited **CHRIS GOSS** – vocals (of MASTERS OF REALITY) / **MARIO LALLI** – guitar (of FATSO JETSON) / **TONY TONRAY** – drums (of FATSO JETSON) / **LARRY LALLI** – bass / **T. FRESH** – turntables / etc.

Sep 98. (lp/cd) *<MR 112>* **VOL.IV: HARD WALLS AND LITTLE TRIPS** [–] [ ]
– The gosso king of Crater Lake / Monster in the parasol / Jr. high love / Eccentric man / Hohleg. *<cd+=>* – VOL.III

Sep 99. (lp) *<MR 121>* **VOL.V: POETRY FOR THE MASSES** [–] [ ]
– You think I ain't worth a dollar, but I . . .. / Punk rock caveman living in a prehistoric . . .. / Going to a hanging / Letters to mommy / The day I die.

Sep 99. (lp/cd) *<MR 122/123>* **VOL.VI: POETRY FOR THE MASSES** [–] [ ]
– A #1 / Like a drug / Take me to your leader / Teens of Thailand / Rickshaw / Like a drug (instrumental). *<cd+=>* – VOL.V

— **HOMME** with **MARK LANEGAN, CHRIS GOSS, ALAIN JOHANNES, BRENDON McNICHOL, FRED DRAKE + SAMANTHA MALONEY**

not iss. Southern Lord

Oct 01. (cd; as JOSH HOMME & FRIENDS) *<12>* **DESERT SESSIONS 7 & 8** [–] [ ]
– Don't drink poison / Hanging tree / Winners / Polly wants a crack rock / Up in Hell / Nenada / The idiots guide / Interpretive reading / Covousier / Cold sore super stars / Making a cross. *<hidden tracks+=>* – Ending / Piano bench breaks.

— with **PJ HARVEY, JOSH FREESE, TWIGGY RAMIREZ, TROY VAN LEEUWEN, JOEY CASTILLO, DEAN WEEN, DAVE CATCHING, ALAIN JOHANNES**, etc

Island Ipecac

Oct 03. (cd) *(9865704) <44>* **DESERT SESSIONS 9: I SEE YOU HEARIN ME / DESERT SESSIONS 10: I HEART DISCO** [ ] [ ]
– Dead in love / I wanna make it wit chu / Covered in punks blood / There will never be a better time / Crawl home / I'm here for your daughter / Powered wig machine / In my head . . . or something / Holey dime / A girl like me / Creosote / Subcutaneous phat. *(d-lp iss.Nov03 +=; 9865812)* – Bring it back gentle / Shepherd's pie.

Nov 03. (7"; as JOSH HOMME & PJ HARVEY) *(IS 835)* **CRAWL HOME. / WHORES HUSTLE AND HUSTLERS WHORE** [41] [–]
(cd-s+=) *(CID 835)* – It / ('A'-video).

QUEENSRYCHE

Formed: Bellevue, Seattle, Washington, USA . . . 1980 initially as The MOB by high school friends, CHRIS DE GARMO, MICHAEL WILTON, EDDIE JACKSON and SCOTT ROCKENFIELD. With the addition of classically trained vocalist GEOFF TATE, the act assumed the QUEENSRYCHE moniker after an enduring track on their eponymous debut EP. The 12" was released by record shop owners Kim and Diana Harris who had set up the independent '206' label expressly for this purpose. Following the record's underground success, 'EMI America' snapped the band up for a seven album deal and promptly re-issued the record before setting them to work on a debut album with producer James Guthrie. The result was 'THE WARNING' (1984), a rather underwhelming affair handicapped by an unsympathetic final mix. 'RAGE FOR ORDER' (1986) was the first QUEENSRYCHE release to hint at the band's future cerebro-metal direction, TATE's impressive vocal muscle flexing a taster of what was in store with 'OPERATION MINDCRIME' (1988). One of the landmark metal releases of that year, the record was a 1984-style concept affair dealing with media brainwashing and social turmoil, conjuring up a convincingly chilling vision of a future gone wrong. Interspersed with snippets of dialogue, broadcasts etc., the songs effortlessly created an atmosphere of tension and portent, TATE veering between prophetic threat and despairing menace while the band's twin guitar attack raged and insinuated in equal measure. ' . . .MINDCRIME' subsequently went gold in America while selling over a million copies worldwide with nary a hit single to support it. Firmly established as the foremost thinking man's metal band, they could afford to be a bit more instinctive with their next release, the acclaimed 'EMPIRE' (1990). More a collection of set pieces, the record's highlight was the hypnotic 'SILENT LUCIDITY', a US Top 10 hit with heavy MTV rotation, the album itself reaching No.7. Other highlights included the brawny 'JET CITY WOMAN', the final single (save a re-release of 'SILENT LUCIDITY' which made the UK Top 20) before a period of relative inactivity. QUEENSRYCHE finally re-emerged in 1994 with 'PROMISED LAND', a more introspective and meditative effort which nevertheless made the US Top 3, cementing the band's position as prime purveyors of intelligent hard rock/metal. Taking a little too much experimentation on board with their next long-playing effort in '97 ('HEAR IN THE NOW FRONTIER'), QUEENSRYCHE for once failed to get the right response from the buying public. Shifting to 'Atlantic' for 'Q2K' (1999), the band – now without DeGARMO – were treading water when the set only managed to squeeze into the US Top 50 for one week. The double concert set, 'LIVE EVOLUTION' (2001), compressed the band's considerable legacy into four seamlessly executed suites, all the more impressive in its majesty given the absence of DeGARMO, who had, by this point, departed the ranks, although he did contribute to their next studio set. The record's encouraging critical reception may just have spurred them on to make 'TRIBE' (2003) one of their most cohesive and ambitious albums in over a decade, with the scope and reach of both the lyrics and music surpassing any of their contemporaries. • **Trivia:** PAMELA MOORE was a guest singer on 'SUITE SISTER MARY'. • **Songwriters:** DeGARMO or TATE / WILSON except; SCARBOROUGH FAIR – CANTICLE (Simon & Garfunkel) / GONNA GET CLOSE TO YOU (Lisa Diabello).

Album rating: THE WARNING (*5) / RAGE FOR ORDER (*7) / OPERATION: MINDCRIME (*8) / EMPIRE (*7) / PROMISED LAND (*6) / HEAR IN THE NOW FRONTIER (*6) / Q2K (*5) / GREATEST HITS compilation (*7) / LIVE EVOLUTION (*6) / TRIBE (*5)

GEOFF TATE (b.14 Jan'59, Stuttgart, Germany) – vocals / **CHRIS DeGARMO** (b.14 Jun'63, Wenatchee, Washington) – guitar / **MICHAEL WILTON** (b.23 Feb'62, San Francisco, Calif.) – guitar / **EDDIE JACKSON** (b.29 Jan'61, Robstown, Texas) – bass / **SCOTT ROCKENFIELD** (b.15 Jun'63, Seattle, Washington) – drums

EMI America EMI America

Sep 83. (12"ep) *(12EA 162) <19006>* **QUEENSRYCHE** [ ] m-lp [81]
– Queen of the Reich / Nightrider / Blinded / The lady wore black. *<first issued 1982 on '206' records; R 101>*

Sep 84. (7") *(EA 183)* **TAKE HOLD OF THE FLAME. / NIGHTRIDER** [ ] [ ]

Sep 84. (lp/c) *(EJ 240220-1/-4)* *<E2 46557>* **THE WARNING** [ ] [61]
– The warning / En force / Deliverance / No sanctuary / NM 156 / Take hold of the flame / Before the storm / Child of fire / Roads to madness. *(cd-iss. Mar87; CDP 746 557-2) (re-iss. Aug91 cd/c; QY 1) (re-iss. cd Oct94 & Apr00; CDP 746557-2)*

Jul 86. (lp/c) *(AML/TCAML 3105)* *<E2 46330>* **RAGE FOR ORDER** [66] [47]
– Walk in the shadows / I dream in infrared / The whisper / Gonna get close to you / The killing words / Surgical strike / Neue regel / Chemical youth (we are rebellion) / London / Screaming in digital / I will remember. *(cd-iss. Feb87; CDP 746330-2) (re-iss. Aug91 cd/c; CD/TC AML 3105) (re-iss. cd Oct94; same)*

Aug 86. (7") *(EA 22)* **GONNA GET CLOSE TO YOU. / PROPHECY** [ ] [ ]
(d7"+=) *(EAD 22)* – Queen of the Reich / Deliverance.

Manhattan Manhattan

May 88. (lp/c/cd) *(MTL/TCMTL/CDMTL 1023)* *<48640>* **OPERATION: MINDCRIME** [58] [50]
– I remember now / Anarchy-X / Revolution calling / Operation: Mindcrime / Speak / Spreading the disease / The mission / Suite Sister Mary / The needle lies / Electric requiem / Breaking the silence / I don't believe in love / Waiting for 22 / My empty room / Eyes of a stranger. *(re-iss. cd Oct94; CDP 748640-2) <(cd re-iss. Sep01 +=; 534499-2)* – Lady wore black / Road to madness.

Oct 88. (10"ep) *(10QP 1)* **OVERSEEING THE OPERATION. / EXCERPTS FROM OPERATION MINDCRIME** [ ] [ ]
– Suite sister Mary / I Remember Now / Revolution Calling / Operation: Mindcrime / Breaking The Silence / Eyes Of A Stranger.

Apr 89. (7") *(MT 65)* **EYES OF A STRANGER. / QUEEN OF THE REICH** [59] [ ]
(12"+=/12"g-f+=) *(12MT/+G 65)* – Walk in the shadows / Take hold of the flame.
(cd-s+=) *(CDMT 65)* – Take hold of the flame / Prophecy.

E.M.I. USA E.M.I.

Sep 90. (7"/7"sha-pic-d) *(MT/+PD 90)* **EMPIRE. / SCARBOROUGH FAIR – CANTICLE** [61] [ ]
(12"+=/cd-s+=) *(12/CD MT 90)* – Prophecy.

Sep 90. (cd/c/d-lp) *(CD/TC+/1058)* *<E2 92806>* **EMPIRE** [13] [7]
– Best I can do / The thin line / Jet city woman / Della Brown / Another rainy night (without you) / Empire / Resistance / Silent lucidity / Hand on heart / One and only / Anybody listening?

Apr 91. (7"/7"box/c-s) *(MT/MTS/TCMTP 94)* *<50345>* **SILENT LUCIDITY. / THE MISSION (live)** [34] Mar91 [9]
(12"+=) *(12MTP 94)* – Eyes of a stranger.
(cd-s+=) *(CDMT 94)* – Della Brown.

Jun 91. (7"/c-s) *(MT/CTMT 97)* **BEST I CAN. / I DREAM IN INFRARED (acoustic remix)** [36] [ ]
(10"+=) *(10MT 97)* – Prophecy.
(cd-s++=) *(CDMT 97)* – ('A'radio edit).

Aug 91. (7"/7"sha-pic-d) *(MT/+PD 98)* **JET CITY WOMAN. / EMPIRE (live)** [39] [ ]
(12"+=) *(12MTS 98)* – Walk in the shadows (live).
(cd-s) *(CDMT 98)* – ('A'side) / Walk in the shadows (live) / Queen of The Reich.

Nov 91. (cd+video) *<97048>* **OPERATION: LIVECRIME (live)** [–] [38]

Aug 92. (7"/c-s) *(MT/CTMT 104)* **SILENT LUCIDITY. / I DON'T BELIEVE IN LOVE** (live) [18] [–]
(12"pic-d) *(12MTPD 104)* – ('A'side) / Last time in Paris / Take hold of the fame.
(cd-s) *(CDMT 104)* – ('A'side) / Suite Sister Mary (live) / Last time in Paris.
(cd-s) *(CDMTS 104)* – ('A'side) / Eyes of a stranger (live) / Operation: Mindcrime.

Oct 94. (cd/c/clear-lp) *(CD/TC+/MTL 1081)* *<30711>* **PROMISED LAND** [13] [3]
– 9:28 a.m. / I am I / Damaged / Out of mind / Bridge / Promised land / Disconnected / Lady Jane / My global mind / One more time / Someone else?.

Jan 95. (12"gold) *(12MT 109)* **I AM I. / REAL WORLD / SOMEONE ELSE?** [40] [ ]
(cd-s+=/s-cd-s+=) *(CDMT/+S 109)* – Dirty li'l secret.

Mar 95. (7"pic-d/c-s) *(MTPD/TCMT 111)* **BRIDGE. / THE KILLING WORDS (live)** [40] [ ]
(cd-s+=) *(CDMTS 111)* – The lady wore black (live) / Damaged (live).
(cd-s) *(CDMTSX 111)* – ('A'side) / Silent lucidity (live) / My empty room (live) / Real world (live).

Mar 97. (cd/c) *(CD/TC EMC 3764)* *<56141>* **HEAR IN THE NOW FRONTIER** [46] [19]
– Sign of the times / Cuckoo's nest / Get a life / Voice inside / Some people fly / Saved / You / Miles away / Reach / All I want / Hit the black / Anytime – anywhere / Spool.

—— **MICHAEL WILTON** – guitar; repl. DeGARMO

Atlantic Atlantic

Nov 99. (cd) *<(7567 83225-2)>* **Q2K** [ ] Sep99 [46]
– Falling down / Sacred ground / One life / When the rain comes . . . / How could I? / Beside you / Liquid sky / Breakdown / Burning man / Wot kinda man / The right side of my mind.

Metal-Is Sanctuary

Oct 01. (d-cd) *(MISDD 016)* *<84523>* **LIVE EVOLUTION (live at The Moore Theatre, Seattle – 27th & 28th July 2001)** [ ] Sep01 [ ]
– NM 156 / Walk in the shadows / Roads to madness / The lady wore black / London / Screaming in digital / Take hold of the flame / Queen of the Reich / I remember now / Revolution calling / Spreading the disease / Requiem / Spreading the disease / The mission / Suite Sister Mary / I don't believe in / Eyes of a stranger / I am I / Damaged / Empire / Silent lucidity / Another rainy night / Jet city woman / Liquid sky / Sacred ground / Falling down / Hit the black / Breakdown / The right side of my mind.

—— **CHRIS DeGARMO** – guitar returned to repl. WILTON

Jul 03. (cd) *(MISCD 018)* *<84578>* **TRIBE** [ ] [56]
– Open / Losing myself / Desert dance / Falling behind / The great divide / Rhythm of hope / Tribe / Blood / The art of life / Doin' fine.

– compilations, etc. –

1988. (cd) *E.M.I. USA; <CDP7 90615-2>* **QUEENSRYCHE** [–] [ ]

Oct 99. (d-cd) *Axe Killer; (AXE 3052182CD)* **OPERATION: MINDCRIME / QUEEN OF THE RYCHE** [ ] [–]

Jul 00. (cd) *E.M.I.; <(8 49422-2)>* **GREATEST HITS** [ ] [ ]
– Queen of the Reich / The lady wore black / The warning / Take hold of the flame / Walk in the shadows / I dream in infrared / I don't believe in love / Eyes of a stranger / Jet city woman / Empire / Silent lucidity / I am I / The bridge / Sign of the times. *(cd-extra+=)* – Chasing blue skies / Someone else.

QUICKSILVER MESSENGER SERVICE

Formed: San Francisco, California, USA . . . late 1964 by JIM MURRAY, JOHN CIPOLLINA, DAVID FREIBERG and CASEY SONOBAN. Also present at their early rehearsals were SKIP SPENCE and DINO VALENTI, who was later jailed for possession of drugs. In June '65, CIPOLLINA, MURRAY and FREIBERG were joined by GREG ELMORE and GARY DUNCAN (both from The BROGUES, who released a few US 45's in 1965). Two years later, they received a great reception at The Monterey International Pop Festival, although MURRAY left when the group signed to 'Capitol'. They had previously recorded two tracks, 'CODINE' and 'BABE, I'M GONNA LEAVE YOU', for the (late '67) Various Artists soundtrack album, 'REVOLUTION' on 'United Artists'. In the summer of '68, they finally released their eponymous debut, which, amid much anticipation, reached the US Top 75. Their 1969 follow-up, 'HAPPY TRAILS', featuring a 25-minute improvised version of BO DIDDLEY's 'WHO DO YOU LOVE', crashed into the US Top 30. Apparently as close an appropriation of what it was actually like to have your ears massaged/assaulted in the San Francisco ballrooms as you're likely to hear, the part-live album nevertheless sounds dated. Although NICKY HOPKINS impressed with THE ROLLING STONES, his addition to the QUICKSILVER line-up for 1969's 'SHADY GROVE' didn't create the musical spark the band needed and with VALENTE back in the fold after his stint in prison, things went downhill. He came to dominate the band's output over the remainder of their career, his average material dulling the spontaneity that had characterised QUICKSILVER's earlier work and effecting a transformation in their sound from psychedelic rock to workmanlike rock'n'roll. While the band had their sole top 50 hit with 'FRESH AIR' in 1970, the album it was taken from and the rest of their 70's output was bog standard stuff which suffered from the aforementioned lack of honed songwriting and a constantly changing line-up. THE QUICKSILVER MESSENGER SERVICE finally delivered its last lacklustre communication in 1975 after a 3-year hiatus, CIPOLLINA going off to join MAN, FREIBERG joining STARSHIP. • **Songwriters:** CIPOLLINA + FREIBERG, until VALENTI's virtual take-over in 1970 as alter-ego JESSE ORIS FARROW (although others still individually contributed). • **Trivia:** Debut album was produced by NICK GRAVENITES and HARVEY BROOKS of ELECTRIC FLAG.

Album rating: QUICKSILVER MESSENGER SERVICE (*7) / HAPPY TRAILS (*8) / SHADY GROVE (*5) / JUST FOR LOVE (*5) / WHAT ABOUT ME (*6) / QUICKSILVER (*4) / COMIN' THRU (*4) / ANTHOLOGY compilation (*6) / SOLID SILVER (*4) / MAIDEN OF THE CANCER MOON collection (*5) / THE ULTIMATE JOURNEY compilation (*7) / PIECE BY PIECE (*1) / SONS OF MERCURY (1968-1975) compilation (*8)

JOHN CIPOLLINA (b.24 Aug'43, Berkeley, Calif.) – guitar, vocals (ex-DEACONS) / **GARY DUNCAN** (b. GARY GRUBB, 4 Sep'46) – guitar, vocals repl. SKIP SPENCE / **DAVID FREIBERG** (b.24 Aug'38, Boston, Mass.) – bass, vocals / **GREG ELMORE** (b. 4 Sep'46, San Diego, Calif.) – drums repl. CASEY SONOBAN

Capitol Capitol

May 68. (lp) *<(ST 2904)>* **QUICKSILVER MESSENGER SERVICE** [ ] [63]
– Pride of man / Light your windows / Dino's song / Gold and silver / It's been too long / The fool. *(re-iss. Jul86 on 'Edsel'; ED 200) (cd-iss. Mar89; CDP 791146-2) (cd-iss. Jul92 on 'Edsel'; EDCD 200)*

Jun 68. (7") *<2194>* **PRIDE OF MAN. / DINO'S SONG** [–] [ ]

Nov 68. (7") *<2320>* **BEARS. / STAND BY ME** [–] [ ]

Mar 69. (lp) *<(EST 120)>* **HAPPY TRAILS** [ ] [27]
– Who do you love suite:- Who do you love (pt.1) – Who do you love – Where do you love – How do you love – Which do you love – Who do you love (pt.2) / Mona / Maiden of the Cancer Moon / Calvary / Happy trails. *(re-iss. Jun81 on 'Greenlight' lp/c; GO/TC-GO 2012) (cd-iss. Mar89; CDP 791215-2) (cd re-iss. Dec92 on 'Beat Goes On'; BGOCD 151)*

Jul 69. (7") *<2557>* **WHO DO YOU LOVE (edit). / WHICH DO YOU LOVE** [–] [91]

— **NICKY HOPKINS** (b.24 Feb'44, London, England) – keyboards (ex-STEVE MILLER BAND) repl. DUNCAN

Nov 69. (7") *<2670>* **HOLY MOLY. / WORDS CAN'T SAY** [–] [ ]

Dec 69. (lp) *<(EST 391)>* **SHADY GROVE** [ ] [25]
– Shady Grove / Flute song / Three or feet from home / Too far / Holy Moly / Joseph's coat / Flashing lonesome / Words can't say / Edward, the mad shirt grinder. *(re-iss. Feb87 on 'Edsel'; XED 208) (cd-iss. Sep90; EDCD 208)*

Feb 70. (7") *<2800>* **SHADY GROVE. / THREE OR FOUR FEET FROM HOME** [–] [ ]

— added now officially ex-part time member **DINO VALENTI** (b. CHESTER POWERS, 7 Nov'43, Danbury, Connecticut) – guitar, vocals / **GARY DUNCAN** – guitar, vocals returned to 6-piece w / **JOHN, NICKY, DAVID + GREG**

Aug 70. (lp) *<(EA-ST 498)>* **JUST FOR LOVE** [ ] [27]
– Wolf run (part 1) / Just for love (part 1) / Cobra / The hat / Freeway flyer / Gone again / Fresh air / Just for love (part 2) / Wolf run (part 2). *(cd-iss. Dec92 on 'Beat Goes On'; BGOCD 141)*

Sep 70. (7") *<2920>* **FRESH AIR. / FREEWAY FLYER** [–] [49]

— **MARK NATALFIN** – keyboards (ex-PAUL BUTTERFIELD) repl. (on 3 tracks) HOPKINS. Also on below lp: **JOSE RICO REYES** – percussion / **MARTINE FIERRO** – wind / **RON TAORMINA** – saxes / **FRANK MORIN** – sax / **PAT O'HARA** – trombone / **KEN BALZELL** – trumpet

Feb 71. (lp) *<(EA-ST 630)>* **WHAT ABOUT ME** [ ] Jan71 [26]
– What about me / Local color / Baby baby / Won't kill me / Long haired lady / Subway / Spindrifter / Good old rock and roll / All in my mind / Call on me. *(re-iss. Jul89 on 'Beat Goes On'; BGOLP 58) (cd-iss. Oct90; BGOCD 58)*

Mar 71. (7") *<3046>* **WHAT ABOUT ME. / GOOD OLD ROCK AND ROLL** [–] [100]

— Now a quintet when CIPOLLINA left to form COPPERHEAD / **MARK RYAN** – bass (ex-COUNTRY JOE & THE FISH) repl. DAVID to JEFFERSON STARSHIP

Nov 71. (lp) *<(SW 819)>* **QUICKSILVER** [ ] [ ]
– Hope / I found love / Song for Frisco / Play my guitar / Rebel / Fire Brothers / Out of my mind / Don't cry my lady love / The truth. *(cd-iss. Jan94 on 'Beat Goes On'; BGOCD 217)*

Nov 71. (7") *<3233>* **HOPE. / I FOUND LOVE** [–] [ ]

— **CHUCK STEAKS** – organ repl. NATAFLIN

May 72. (lp) *<(ST 11002)>* **COMIN' THRU** [ ] [ ]
– Doin' time in the U.S.A. / Chicken / Changes / California state correctional facility blues / Forty days / Mojo / Don't lose it. *(cd-iss. Jul91 on 'Beat Goes On' lp/cd; BGO/+CD 88)*

May 72. (7") *<3349>* **DOIN' TIME IN THE U.S.A. / CHANGES** [–] [ ]

— Mid'72, contributed 2 tracks for live lp 'The Last Days Of Fillmore'.

— (May73) **JOHN NICHOLAS** – bass (ex-IT'S A BEAUTIFUL DAY) repl. RYAN / added **HAROLD ACEVES** – 2nd drummer (6-piece DINO, GARY, GREG + CHUCKS)

— (Feb74) **BOB HOGAN** – keyboards (ex-MILES DAVIS) repl. STEAKS / **SKIP OLSEN** – bass repl. BOB FLURIE who had repl. JOHN NICHOLAS

— (Mar75) **DINO, GARY, GREG, SKIP** plus the returning **JOHN CIP . . . + DAVID** on tour / added **MICHAEL LEWIS** – piano

Oct 75. (lp) *<(ST 11462)>* **SOLID SILVER** [ ] [89]
– Gypsy lights / Heebie jeebies / Cowboy on the run / I heard you singing / Worryin' shoes / The letter / They don't know / Flames / Witches' moon / Bittersweet Moon. *(cd-iss. Sep93 on 'Edsel'; EDCD 376)*

Nov 75. (7") *(CL 15859) <4206>* **GYPSY LIGHTS. / WITCHES MOON** [ ] [ ]

— Had already broken up, after brief re-union. CIPOLLINA joined MAN but was to die on 29th May '89 of emphysema lung disease. FREIBERG returned to STARSHIP. In 1987, GARY DUNCAN resurrected QUICKSILVER MESSENGER SERVICE with FREIBERG and others

Jul 86. (lp) *<12498>* **PEACE BY PIECE** [–] [ ]
– Good thang / 24 hour deja vu / Midnight sun / Swamp girl / Wild in the city / Pool hall chili / Pistolero / Peace by piece. *(cd-iss. Sep99 on 'Captain Trip'; CTCD 094)*

— some original members, included others from The GRATEFUL DEAD, JEFFERSON AIRPLANE and (HUEY LEWIS &) THE NEWS, played a benefit in San Francisco; they subsequently issued 'SHAPESHIFTER' in 1996/97

– compilations, others, etc. –

Oct 73. (lp) *Capitol; (STSP 13) <ST 11165>* **ANTHOLOGY** [ ] May73 [ ]
– Pride of man / Dino's song / Fool / Bears / Mona / Edward, the mad shirt grinder / Three or four feet from home / Fresh air / Just for love / Spindrifter / Local color / What about me / Don't cry my lady love / Hope / Fire brothers / I found love. *(cd-iss. Jun95 on 'Beat Goes On'; BGOCD 270)*

Sep 83. (d-lp) *Psycho; (PSYCHO 10)* **MAIDEN OF THE CANCER MOON** (live Fillmore, Jun'68) [ ] [–]
<(d-cd-iss. Sep98 on 'U.R.'; UR 006)

Apr 86. (lp) *See For Miles; (SEE 61)* **THE ULTIMATE JOURNEY** [ ] [–]
– Who do you love / Pride of man / Codine / Dino's song / Gold and silver / Joseph's coat / Shady grove / Fresh air / Too far / Stand by me / What about me / Mona. *(cd-iss. Aug93 & Jan99; SEECD 61)*

Aug 91. (d-cd/d-c) *Rhino; <R2AS/R2AP 70747>* **SONS OF MERCURY (THE BEST OF QUICKSILVER MESSENGER SERVICE 1968-1975)** [–] [ ]
– Babe I'm gonna leave you / Codine / I hear you knockin' (it's too late) / Pride of man / Light your windows / Dino's song / The fool / Gold and silver / Bears / Who do you love? / Mona / Maiden of the cancer moon / Calvary / Happy trails / Shady grove / Flute song / Joseph's coat / Edward, the mad shirt grinder / Fresh air / Cobra / Subway / What about me? / Local color / Hope / Fire brothers / Don't cry my lady love / I found love / Doin' time in the U.S.A. / Gypsy lights / Cowboy on the run.

Sep 97. (d-cd) *Pymander; (P 007)* **SHAPE SHIFTER** [ ] [–]

Aug 00. (cd) *Captain Trip; (CTCD 071)* **LIVE AT FIELD STONE (live)** [ ] [–]

Mar 01. (d-cd) *Collector's Choice; <(CCM 1092)>* **LOST GOLD AND SILVER: THE UNRELEASED . . .** [ ] Mar00 [ ]

Aug 01. (cd) *E.M.I.; (534697-2)* **MASTERS OF ROCK: THE VERY BEST OF . . .** [ ] [–]

Nov 02. (cd) *Disky; (SI 905117)* **WHO DO YOU LOVE** [ ] [–]

May 03. (cd) *Capitol; <(536156-2)>* **CLASSIC MASTERS** [ ] Jan02 [ ]

The ROLLING STONES

RADIOHEAD

Formed: Oxford, England . . . 1988 by frontman THOM YORKE, guitarist ED O'BRIEN and bassist COLIN GREENWOOD with drummer PHIL SELWAY completing the line-up. Dubbing themselves ON A FRIDAY, the band began gigging around Oxford, subsequently boasting a triple guitar attack following the addition of COLIN's brother, JONNY. Initially, the group also fleshed out their sound with a couple of saxaphone players (though it's now difficult to imagine what that must have sounded like). With the various members trooping off to complete their respective educations, the RADIOHEAD story really began in the summer of '91 when the band got back together and adopted the aforesaid moniker (after a TALKING HEADS song). Signed to the ever vigilant 'Parlophone', the band enjoyed some airplay with their first release, a Spring '92 EP with 'PROVE YOURSELF' as the lead track. Next up was the seminal 'CREEP', an incendiary anthem for anyone who'd ever felt rejected/alienated (and let's face it, that's most of the population), the song stiffing first time round but subsequently kickstarting RADIOHEAD's career. The track also used the group's trademark soft bit/quiet bit dynamics to stunning effect, a method which would come to form the basis for some of the band's best tracks. In the meantime, RADIOHEAD eventually scraped in to the lower regions of the Top 40 with the abrasive 'ANYONE CAN PLAY GUITAR', the debut album, 'PABLO HONEY' making the UK Top 30 around the same time in early '93. Though it had its moments, the album lacked consistency with YORKE seemingly searching for some kind of vocal identity. While the record found enthusiastic champions in some sections of the music press, by and large, RADIOHEAD were passed over. All that changed, however, when 'CREEP' exploded in the States, the record obviously striking a deep chord with the multitudes who weren't part of the 'American Dream'. Taking the first flight over there, RADIOHEAD capitalised on this surprise success, the band treated like homecoming heroes and selling out concerts night after night. In a bizarre reversal of the standard process, this US success laid the groundwork for the re-release of 'CREEP' in the UK, where it became a Top 10 hit, sales of the album also enjoying a healthy re-invigoration. With such a universal theme, it was no surprise that the track was also a massive hit all over the world, RADIOHEAD finding themselves in the strange position of being international pop stars yet at the same time, regarded merely as a competent indie band in their home country. 'THE BENDS' (1995) convincingly silenced the doubters once and for all, a groundbreaking album with a spectral musical vision which rarely failed to take the breath away. Opening with the searing, reverbating 'PLANET TELEX' the record proceeded to juxtapose howling guitar menace against bleakly beautiful melodies, echoing synth and acoustic strumming, YORKE painting piercingly vivid images with his tortured musings on the nature of the human psyche. The fragile majesty of 'FAKE PLASTIC TREES' was RADIOHEAD at their most sublime, YORKE's ability to hit those high notes pivotal to the resigned melancholy of his vocals. The churning claustrophobia of 'BLACK STAR' sounded like the final fling of a condemned man, positively revelling in its own pain and misery, while the funereal 'STREET SPIRIT' was a ghostly coda, its award-winning video perfectly evoking the track's haunting feeling of time standing still. Basically, the album wiped the floor with the competition, laying waste to the snot-nosed chaff of Brit-pop and confirming that there was indeed a thinking man's alternative to OASIS. R.E.M. felt the same way, inviting the band to support them on tour later that year, something of a dream come true for RADIOHEAD who had long been massive fans of STIPE & Co. The summer of '95 also saw the release of the 'HELP' album, a project involving the cream of the British music scene with proceeds from album sales donated to the War Child charity (which raised money for war torn Bosnia). RADIOHEAD contributed 'LUCKY', a song apparently written about the band's newfound position as one of the most highly regarded group's in the world. Stunning though the track is, it sounds more like a dirge than a celebration, the searing guitar line evoking a feeling of utter desolation and emptiness. Probably the best example of YORKE's self-acknowledged struggle to sound anything other than melancholy, the track was one of many highlights on 'OK COMPUTER' (1997), RADIOHEAD's feverishly anticipated follow-up to the poll-topping 'THE BENDS'. A densely complex, almost initially impenetrable album, 'OK..' was a demanding beast, previewed by the wildly ambitious 'PARANOID ANDROID', a kind of post-prog symphony in three parts. The oscillating guitar vibration of 'AIRBAG' kicked off proceedings in much the same fashion as 'PLANET TELEX', but then things started getting weird. 'SUBTERRANEAN HOMESICK ALIEN' was truly adrift in space, the guitars twinkling and shimmering like tiny constellations, while with 'EXIT MUSIC (FOR A FILM)' (written for closing sequence of the revamped 'Romeo And Juliet' movie), YORKE's vocal was so eerily intimate, it sounded as if he was in the same room, the song building to a majestic climax via unearthly choral parts and swooning synths. 'LET DOWN' was an almost BYRDS-esque follow-up to 'CREEP', its pealing guitar and infectious melody framing a similar theme and creating what was conceivably the nearest the record came to conventional rock. Much of the album was vaguely reminiscent of the more cerebral moments on U2's 'Unforgettable Fire', although YORKE has never come so close to sounding like BONO as on 'CLIMBING THE WALLS', for once managing to avoid the bruised resignation that normally colours his voice. With 'NO SURPRISES', RADIOHEAD cleverly contrasted an almost child-like musical lullaby with lyrics expressing a hopeless world weariness. Of their contemporaries, only SPIRITUALIZED and MOGWAI were making music this far out, RADIOHEAD once again almost sweeping the board at the end of year polls and bravely taking rock music into the future rather than fawning over a Union Jack-clad past. With 'KID A' (2000) they took the music into the future with a vengeance; whether this was a brave new sonic world or a sterile wasteland of short-circuit experimentation remains a moot point. Maybe it should've been titled 'All That You CAN Leave Behind', YORKE and Co putting to bed the bruised beauty of their best work with brutal determination. The oblique, serrated electronica and disjointed dirgescapes offered up nothing in the way of redemptive miserabilism never mind a hook or a melody. Perseverance dragged brief snatches of genius screaming petulantly from the broodingly dense mix yet the effort was hardly relative to the meagre rewards on offer. More, YORKE's vocal, previously a thing of exotic desolation, begins to grate against the unremitingly bleak backdrop, reduced to one of the dismal whole's gratuitously mechanical constituent parts – in other words a classic! 'AMNESIAC' (2001) was an equally daunting if not quite so wilfully oppressive listen, its material drawn from the same sessions as its predecessor. Despite featuring the studio debut of established live favourites 'KNIVES OUT' and 'YOU AND WHOSE ARMY?', the album merely confirmed that RADIOHEAD had absolutely no intention of resuming normal service anytime soon. On the contrary, they kept up their new adrenaline-paced release schedule with 'I MIGHT BE WRONG: LIVE RECORDINGS' (2001), a clipped concert set again inspired by the template of 'KID A'. Whether they'd taken the not inconsiderable criticism to heart or whether they really were making a conscious effort to put some kind of discernable structure back into the music, 'HAIL TO THE THIEF' (2003) did at least make some concessions to convention. The likes of opener '2 + 2 = 5' possessed some familiar reference points, while the sinister 'SAIL TO THE MOON' ranked as perhaps the most discomfortingly effective piece of music they've written in years.

Album rating: PABLO HONEY (*7) / THE BENDS (*10) / OK COMPUTER (*10) / KID A (*9) / AMNESIAC (*7) / I MIGHT BE WRONG: LIVE RECORDINGS mini (*5) / HAIL TO THE THIEF (*7)

THOM YORKE (b. 7 Oct'68) – vocals, guitar / **ED O'BRIEN** (b.15 Apr'68) – guitar, vocals / **JON GREENWOOD** (b. 5 Nov'71) – guitar / **COLIN GREENWOOD** (b.26 Jun'69) – bass / **PHIL SELWAY** (b.23 May'67) – drums

Parlophone Capitol

May 92. (c-ep/12"ep/cd-ep) *(TCR/12R/CDR 6312)* **DRILL EP** [ ] [ ]
– Prove yourself / Stupid car / You / Thinking about you.

Sep 92. (c-ep/12"ep/cd-ep) *(TCR/12R/CDR 6078)* **CREEP / LURCEE. / INSIDE MY HEAD / MILLION $ QUESTION** [ ] [–]

Feb 93. (c-ep/12"ep/cd-ep) *(TCR/12R/CDR 6333)* **ANYONE CAN PLAY GUITAR. / FAITHLESS, THE WONDER BOY / COKE BABIES** [32] [–]

Feb 93. (cd/c/lp) *(CD/TC+/PCS 7360)* *<81409>* **PABLO HONEY** [25] Jun93 [32]
– You / Creep / How do you? / Stop whispering / Thinking about you / Anyone can play guitar / Ripcord / Vegetable / Prove yourself / I can't / Lurgee / Blow out.

Apr 93. (c-s,cd-s) *<44932>* **CREEP / FAITHLESS, THE WONDER BOY** [–] [34]

May 93. (c-ep/12"ep/cd-ep) *(TCR/12R/CDR 6345)* **POP IS DEAD / BANANA CO. (acoustic). / CREEP (live) / RIPCORD (live)** [42] [–]

Sep 93. (7") *(RS 6359)* **CREEP. / YES I AM** [7] [–]
(cd-s+=) *(CDR 6359)* – Blow out (remix) / Inside my head (live).
(12"clear) *(12RG 6359)* – ('A'-acoustic KROQ) / You (live) / Vegetable (live) / Killer cars (live).

Oct 94. (c-ep/12"ep) *(TCR/12R 6984)* *<58274>* **MY IRON LUNG / THE TRICKSTER / LEWIS (mistreated) / PUNCHDRUNK LOVESICK SINGALONG** [24] [ ]
(cd-s) *(CDRS 6394)* – (1st & 4th track) / Lozenge of love.
(cd-s) *(CDR 6394)* – (1st & 2nd track) / Permanent daylight / You never wash up after yourself.

Mar 95. (c-s) *(TCR 6405)* *<58537>* **HIGH & DRY / PLANET TELEX** [17] Feb96 [ ]
(cd-s+=) *(CDR 6405)* – Killer cars / Planet Telex (LFO JD mix).
(cd-s+=) *(CDRS 6405)* – Maquiladora / Planet Telex (hexadecimal mix).
(12") *(12R 6405)* – Planet Telex (hexadecimal mix) / Planet Telex (LFO JD mix) / Planet Telex (hexadecimal dub) / High & dry.

Mar 95. (cd/c/lp) *(CD/TC+/PCS 7372)* *<29626>* **THE BENDS** [6] [88]
– Planet Telex / The bends / High & dry / Fake plastic trees / Bones (nice dream) / Just / My iron lung / Bulletproof . . .I wish I was / Black star / Sulk / Street spirit (fade out).

May 95. (c-ep/cd-ep) *(TCR/CDRS 6411)* *<58424>* **FAKE PLASTIC TREES / INDIA RUBBER / HOW CAN YOU BE SURE?** [20] Jul95 [ ]
(cd-s) *(CDR 6411)* – ('A'side) / ('A'acoustic) / Bulletproof..I wish I was (acoustic) / Street spirit (fade out) (acoustic).

Aug 95. (c-ep/12"ep) *(TCR/12R 6415)* **JUST / PLANET TELEX (Karma Sun Ra mix) / KILLER CARS (mogadon mix)** [19] [–]
(cd-s) *(CDR 6415)* – ('A'side) / Bones (live) / Planet Telex (live) / Anyone can play guitar (live).

Jan 96. (7"white) *(R 6419)* *<82523>* **STREET SPIRIT (FADE OUT). / BISHOP'S ROBES** [5] [ ]
(cd-s+=) *(CDRS 6419)* – Talk show host.
(cd-s) *(CDR 6419)* – ('A'side) / Banana co. / Molasses.

Feb 96. (c-s,cd-s) *<58537>* **HIGH AND DRY / FAKE PLASTIC TREES** [–] [78]

Jun 97. (7") *(NODATA 01)* **PARANOID ANDROID. / POLYETHYLENE (PARTS 1 & 2)** [3] [–]
(cd-s+=) *(CDNODATAS 01)* – Pearly.
(cd-s) *(CDNODATA 01)* – ('A'side) / A reminder / Melatonin.

Jun 97. (cd/c/d-lp) *(CD/TC+/NODATA 02)* *<55229>* **OK COMPUTER** [1] [21]
– Airbag / Paranoid android / Subterranean homesick alien / Exit music (for a film) / Karma police / Electioneering / Climbing up the walls / No surprises / Lucky / The tourist.

Aug 97. (cd-s) *(CDNODATA 03)* **KARMA POLICE / CLIMBING UP THE WALLS (Fila Brazillia & Zero 7 mixes)** [8] [ ]
(12"+=) *(12NODATA 03)* – Meeting in the aisle.
(cd-s) *(CDNODATAS 03)* – ('A'side) / Meeting in the aisle / Lull.

Jan 98. (12") *(12NODATA 04)* **NO SURPRISES. / PALO ALTO** [4] [ ]
(c-s+=/cd-s+=) *(TC/CD NODATA 04)* – How I made my millions.
(cd-s) *(CDNODATAS 04)* – ('A'side) / Airbag (live) / Lucky (live).

Apr 98. (m-cd) *(858701-2)* **AIRBAG / PEARLY (remix) / MEETING IN THE AISLE / A REMINDER / POLYTHENE (parts 1 & 2) / MELATONIN / PALO ALTO** [ ] [–]
(above wasn't legitimate to chart in Britain)

Apr 98. (m-cd) *<58071>* **AIRBAG / HOW AM I DRIVING (EP)** [–] [56]

Oct 00. (cd/c) *(<2435 27753-2/-4>)* **KID A** [1] [1]
– Everything in its right place / Kid A / The national anthem / How to disappear completely / Treefingers / Optimistic / In limbo / Idioteque / Morning bell / Motion picture soundtrack.

May 01. (12") *(12FHEIT 45102)* **PYRAMID SONG. / THE AMAZING SOUNDS OF ORGY / FAST TRACK** [5] [–]
(cd-s) *(CDSHEIT 45102)* – (first 2 tracks) / Trans Atlantic drawl.
(cd-s) *(CDFHEIT 45102)* – (first & third tracks) / Kinetic.

Jun 01. (cd/c/d-lp) *(CD/TC/LP FHEIT 45101)* *<32764>* **AMNESIAC** [1] [2]
– Packt like sardines in a crushd tin box / Pyramid song / Pulk-pull revolving doors / You and whose army? / I might be wrong / Knives out / Morning bell / Amnesiac / Dollars & cents / Hunting bears / Like spinning plates / Life in a glasshouse.

Aug 01. (12"/cd-s) *(12/CD FHEIT 45103)* **KNIVES OUT / CUTTOTH. / LIFE IN A GLASSHOUSE (extended)** [13] [–]
(cd-s) *(CDSFHEIT 45103)* – ('A'side) / Worrywort / Fog.

Nov 01. (m-cd/m-lp) *(CD/12 FHEIT 45104)* *<36616>* **I MIGHT BE WRONG: LIVE RECORDINGS (live)** [23] [44]
– The national anthem / I might be wrong / Morning bell / Like spinning plates / Idioteque / Everything in its right place / Dollars and cents / True love waits.

May 03. (12"/cd-s) *(12R/CDR 6608)* **THERE THERE. / PAPERBAG WRITER / WHERE BLUEBIRDS FLY** [4] [–]

Jun 03. (cd/d-lp) *(584543-2/-1)* *<84543>* **HAIL TO THE THIEF** [1] [3]
– 2 + 2 = 5 / Sit down. stand up / Sail to the Moon / Backdrifts / Go to sleep / Where I end and you begin / We suck young blood / The gloaming / There

there / I will / A punchup at a wedding / Myxomatosis / Scatterbrain / A wolf at the door.

Aug 03. (cd-s) *(CDRS 6613)* **GO TO SLEEP / I AM CITIZEN INSANE / FOG** [12] [–]
(12") *(12R 6613)* – (first 2 tracks) / I am a wicked child.
(cd-s) *(CDR 6613)* – ('A'side) / I am a wicked child / Gagging order.

Nov 03. (cd-s) *(CDR 6623)* **2 + 2 = 5 / MYXOMATOSIS (Christian Vogel remix) / THERE THERE (demo)** [15] [–]
(cd-s) *(CDRS 6623)* – ('A'side) / Scatterbrain (Four Tet remix) / I will (1st mix).
(12") *(12R 6623)* – ('A'side) / Myxomatosis (Christian Vogel remix) / Scatterbrain (Four Tet remix).

☐ RAEKWON (see under ⇒ WU-TANG CLAN)

Gerry RAFFERTY

Born: 16 Apr'47, Paisley, Scotland. In 1968, he joined The HUMBLEBUMS, alongside TAM HARVEY and future comedian, BILLY CONNOLLY. The trio signed up to folk label, 'Transatlantic', recording two albums, 'HUMBLEBUMS' (1969) & 'OPEN UP THE DOOR' (1970), together before parting ways. RAFFERTY subsequently released a debut solo album, 'CAN I HAVE MY MONEY BACK', in 1971 before moving to London and forming STEALER'S WHEEL with RAB NOAKES and JOE EGAN. Signed to 'A&M', the band went through some major personnel upheaval prior to the release of their eponymous album in late '72, PAUL PILNICK, TONY WILLIAMS and ROB COOMBES replacing RAB NOAKES, IAN CAMPBELL and ROGER BROWN respectively. Overseen by veteran production duo, LEIBER & STOLLER, the album was characterised by gentle, folky harmonies and an unerring ear for pop melody, the haunting 'NEXT TO ME' resonating long after the first listen. Then of course, there was the 'Dylanesque' shuffle of 'STUCK IN THE MIDDLE OF YOU', a transatlantic Top 10 upon its original 1973 release and later an integral, ingeniously effective part of Quentin Tarantino's infamous 'Reservoir Dogs' movie. There was almost as much confusion surrounding the identity of the STEALER'S WHEEL line-up as there was among Tarantino's panicked criminal pros, RAFFERTY leaving for a couple of months before returning in time for a follow-up. By this point, all the original members (who themselves had been temporarily replaced!) were gone and the core duo of EGAN and RAFFERTY roped in a crew of session players to complete 'FERGUSLIE PARK' (1973). Another set of consummate folk-pop, the record was nevertheless a commercial disappointment save for a minor Top 30 hit, 'STAR'. Disillusioned, the pair completed one further set, the equally impressive 'RIGHT OR WRONG' (1975), before permanently parting company and embarking on respective solo careers. After a number of years grappling with business problems, RAFFERTY emerged in early '78 with the 'CITY TO CITY' album. Changing tack to a more contemporary, MOR style, RAFFERTY scored a massive international hit (and a US No.1) with the 'BAKER STREET' single, RAPHAEL RAVENSCROFT's famous sax riff forming the basis of this world-weary classic. The track's success saw album sales go through the roof, RAFFERTY becoming something of a reluctant overnight superstar. Shunning the limelight and choosing not to promote the album in America (where it went platinum), RAFFERTY instead began work on a follow-up, 'NIGHT OWL' (1979). While failing to scale the commercial heights of its predecessor, the record was a sizeable success nonetheless, RAFFERTY's inimitably understated approach again delighting fans who put it into the UK Top 10. Subsequent albums such as 'SLEEPWALKING' (1982) and 'NORTH AND SOUTH' (1988) weren't quite as inspired, RAFFERTY taking a sabbatical during the mid-80's (although he did contribute to MARK KNOPFLER's 'Local Hero' soundtrack and produce The PROCLAIMERS' 1987 single, 'Letter From America'). He continued to record in the 90's, if sporadically, such seasoned hands as pedal steel player, B.J. COLE, lending their expertise to 1993's 'ON A WING AND A PRAYER', the record also featuring the backing vocal and co-writing talents of brother JIM. • **Songwriters:** STEALER'S WHEEL was virtually a writing partnership for RAFFERTY and EGAN. GET OUT OF MY LIFE WOMAN (Allen Toussaint).

Album rating: CAN I HAVE MY MONEY BACK? (*6) / Stealer's Wheel: STEALER'S WHEEL (*7) / FERGUSLIE PARK (**7**) / RIGHT OR WRONG (*6) / Gerry Rafferty: CITY TO CITY (**8**) / NIGHT OWL (*7) / SNAKES AND LADDERS (*6) / SLEEPWALKING (*4) / NORTH AND SOUTH (*4) / RIGHT DOWN THE LINE – THE BEST OF GERRY RAFFERTY compilation (*6) / ON A WING & A PRAYER (*4) / OVER MY HEAD (*4) / ONE MORE DREAM – THE VERY BEST OF GERRY RAFFERTY compilation (**8**)

GERRY RAFFERTY – vocals, guitar (with session people including future STEALER'S WHEEL members)

Transatla. Blue Thumb

1971. (lp) *(TRA 241)* *<BTS 58>* **CAN I HAVE MY MONEY BACK** [ ] [ ]
– New street blues / Didn't I / Mr. Universe / Mary Skeffington / Long way round / Can I have my money back / Sign on the dotted line / Make you break you / To each and everyone / One drink down / Don't count me out / Half a chance / Where I belong. *<US re-iss. 1978; 6031> (re-iss. Sep81 lp/c; TRS/KTRS 112) (re-iss. Apr85 on 'Autograph' c; ASK 769) (re-iss. cd+c Apr93 on 'Ariola Express') (cd re-iss. Oct98 on 'Wooded Hill'; HILLCD 3)*

Oct 71. (7") *(BIG 139)* **CAN I HAVE MY MONEY BACK. / SO SAD THINKING** [ ] [–]

Jan 72. (7") **CAN I HAVE MY MONEY BACK. / SIGN ON THE DOTTED LINE** [–] [ ]

STEALER'S WHEEL

GERRY with **JOE EGAN** – vocals, keyboards / **PAUL PILNICK** – guitar (ex-BIG THREE) repl. RAB NOAKES who went solo / **TONY WILLIAMS** – bass repl. IAN CAMPBELL / **ROD COOMBES** – drums repl. ROGER BROWN

A&M A&M

Oct 72. (7") *(AMS 7033)* **LATE AGAIN. / I GET BY** [ ] [–]

Nov 72. (7") *(AMS 7036)* *<1416>* **STUCK IN THE MIDDLE WITH YOU. / JOSE** [ ] Feb73 [6]
(re-dist.May73, hit UK No.8)

Dec 72. (lp) *(AMLH 68121)* *<4377>* **STEALER'S WHEEL** [ ] [50]
– Late again / Stuck in the middle with you / Another meaning / I get by / Outside looking in / Johnny's song / Next to me / Jose / Gets so lonely / You put something better inside of me.

Feb 73. (7") *(AMS 7046)* **YOU PUT SOMETHING BETTER INSIDE OF ME. / NEXT TO ME** [ ] [–]

— Group had disbanded when RAFFERTY had been replaced by **LUTHER GROSVENOR** (ex-SPOOKY TOOTH) for 2 months. **DELISLE HARPER** – bass repl. others

— By mid'73, they were a basic duo (**RAFFERTY & EGAN**) augmented by **BERNIE HOLLAND** – guitar / **CHRIS MERCER** – saxophone / **ANDREW STEELE** – drums / **CHRIS NEILL** – harmonica and loads more sessioners.

Aug 73. (7") *(AMS 7079)* **EVERYTHING'L TURN OUT FINE. / JOHNNY'S SONG** [33] [–]

Aug 73. (7") *<1450>* **EVERYONE'S AGREED THAT EVERYTHING WILL TURN OUT FINE. / NEXT TO ME** [–] [49]

Nov 73. (lp) *(AMLH 68209)* *<4419>* **FERGUSLIE PARK** [ ] [ ]
– Good businessman / Star / Wheelin' / Waltz (you know it makes sense!) / What more could you want / Over my head / Blind faith / Nothing's gonna change my mind / Steamboat row / Back on my feet again / Who cares / (Everyone's agreed that) Everything will turn out fine.

Dec 73. (7") *(AMS 7094)* *<1483>* **STAR. / WHAT MORE COULD I WANT** [25] [29]

Apr 74. (7") *<1529>* **WHEELIN'. / YOU PUT SOMETHING BETTER INSIDE OF ME** [–] [ ]

Feb 75. (7") *(AMS 7152)* **RIGHT OR WRONG. / THIS MORNING** [ ] [–]

Feb 75. (lp) *(AMLH 68293)* <4517> **RIGHT OR WRONG** [ ] [ ]
– Benediction / Found my way to you / This morning / Let yourself go / Home from home / Go as you please / Wishbone / Don't get me wrong / Monday morning / Right or wrong.

May 75. (7") *(AMS 7170)* **FOUND MY WAY TO YOU. / WISHBONE** [ ] [–]

May 75. (7") <1675> **FOUND MY WAY TO YOU. / THIS MORNING** [–] [ ]

—— Broke up again later in the year. JOE EGAN went solo, as did GERRY.

– compilations, etc. –

Sep 78. (lp) *A&M; (AMLH 64708)* <4708> **THE BEST OF STEALER'S WHEEL** [ ] [ ]
– Stuck in the middle with you / Nothing's gonna change my mind / Star / This morning / Steamboat row / Next to me / Right or wrong / Go as you please / Benediction / Waltz (you know it makes sense!) / Blind faith / Late again / Wheelin' / Jose. *(re-iss. 1981 on 'Music For Pleasure'; MFP 50501) (cd/c-iss.Jun90 on 'Connoisseur'; CSAP CD/MC 106)*

Sep 78. (7") *A&M;* <2075> **(EVERYONE AGREED THAT) EVERYTHING'L TURN OUT FINE. / WHO CARES** [–] [ ]

Mar 82. (7") *Old Gold; (OG 9148)* **STUCK IN THE MIDDLE WITH YOU. / STAR** [ ] [–]

Sep 98. (cd) *Spectrum; (552496-2)* **STUCK IN THE MIDDLE** [ ] [–]

GERRY RAFFERTY

with many session people.

U.A. U.A.

Oct 77. (7") *(UP 36278)* **CITY TO CITY. / MATTIE'S RAG** [ ] [ ]

Jan 78. (lp/c) *(UAS/TCK 30104)* <840> **CITY TO CITY** [6] [1]
– he ark / Baker Street / Right down the line / City to city / Stealin' time / Mattie's rag / Whatever's written in your heart / Home and dry / Island / Waiting for the day. *(re-iss. Mar85 on 'Fame' lp/c; FA/TC-FA 3119) (cd-iss. Jul89; CDFA 3119) (cd re-iss. Apr99 on 'D.C.C.'; GZS 1075)*

Feb 78. (7") *(UP 36346)* <1192> **BAKER STREET. / BIG CHANGE IN THE WEATHER** [3] Apr78 [2]
above featured **RAPHAEL RAVENSCROFT** – saxophone

May 78. (7") *(UP 36403)* **WHATEVER'S WRITTEN IN YOUR HEART. / WAITING FOR THE DAY** [ ] [–]

Aug 78. (7") <1233> **RIGHT DOWN THE LINE. / WAITING FOR THE DAY** [–] [12]

Sep 78. (7") *(UP 36445)* **RIGHT DOWN THE LINE. / ISLAND** [ ] [–]

Nov 78. (7") <1266> **HOME AND DRY. / MATTIE'S RAG** [–] [28]

May 79. (7") *(UP 36512)* **NIGHT OWL. / WHY DON'T YOU TALK TO ME** [5] [–]

May 79. (lp/c) *(UAK/TCK 30238)* <958> **NIGHT OWL** [9] [29]
– Days gone down (still got the light in your eyes) / Night owl / The way that you do it / Why won't you talk to me / Get it right next time / Take the money and run / Family tree / Already gone / The tourist / It's gonna be a long night. *(re-iss. 1985 on 'Liberty' lp/c; ATAK/TC-ATAK 37) (re-iss. Jul86 on 'Fame' lp/c; FA/TC-FA 3147) (cd-iss. Jul89; CDFA 3147)*

May 79. (7") <1298> **DAYS GONE DOWN (STILL GOT THE LIGHT IN YOUR EYES). / WHY WON'T YOU TALK TO ME?** [–] [17]

Aug 79. (7") *(BP 301)* <1316> **GET IT RIGHT NEXT TIME. / IT'S GONNA BE A LONG NIGHT** [30] [21]

Mar 80. (7") *(BP 340)* **BRING IT ALL HOME. / IN TRANSIT** [54] [ ]

Mar 80. (lp/c) *(UAK/TCK 30298)* <1039> **SNAKES AND LADDERS** [15] [61]
– The Royal Mile / I was a boy scout / Welcome to Hollywood / Wastin' away / Look at the Moon / Bring it all home / The garden of England / Johnny's song / Didn't I / Syncopatin' Sandy / Cafe le Cabotin / Don't close the door. *(cd-iss. Mar89 on 'Liberty'; CZ 162)*

Oct 80. (7") *(BP 354)* <1366> **THE ROYAL MILE (SWEET DARLIN'). / WASTIN' AWAY** [67] Jul80 [54]

Liberty Liberty

Aug 82. (7") *(BP 413)* **SLEEPWALKING. / WHEN I REST** [ ] [ ]

Sep 82. (lp/c) *(LEG/TCG 30352)* <51132> **SLEEPWALKING** [39] [ ]
– Standing at the gates / Good intentions / A change of heart / On the way / Sleepwalking / Cat and mouse / The right moment / As wise as a serpent. *(re-iss. Sep84 on 'Fame' lp/c; FA/TC-FA 3113) (re-iss. Aug86 on 'E.M.I.' lp/c; ATAK/TC-ATAK 84) (cd-iss. Mar89; CZ 163) (cd re-iss. Feb01 on 'EMI Plus'; 576089-2)*

Nov 82. (7") *(BP 415)* **A CHANGE OF HEART. / GOOD INTENTIONS** [ ] [–]

Nov 82. (7") **STANDING AT THE GATES. / GOOD INTENTIONS** [–] [ ]

—— he took some time off, although he did appear on MARK KNOPFLER's 'Local Hero' 1983 soundtrack and in 1987 produced 'Letter From America' by The PROCLAIMERS.

London Polydor

Apr 88. (7") *(LON 170)* **SHIPYARD TOWN. / HEARTS DESIRE** [ ] [–]
(12"+=/cd-s+=) *(LON X/CD 170)* – ('A'lp version).

May 88. (lp/c)(cd) *(LON LP/C 55)(828089-2)* <835449> **NORTH AND SOUTH** [43] Jun88 [ ]
– North and south / Moonlight and gold / Tired of talking / Hearts run dry / A dangerous age / Shipyard town / Winter's come / Nothing ever happens down here / On a night like this / Unselfish love. *(re-iss. Apr91; same)*

—— now with **PAVEL ROSAK** – keyboards, drums, bass, percussion, programming / **HUGH BURNS** – electric guitars, co-producer / **MEL COLLINS** – sax / **B.J. COLE** – pedal steel / **ARRAN AHMUN** – percussion / **MO FOSTER** – bass / **BRYN HAWORTH** – bottleneck guitar / etc. Note: Brother **JIM RAFFERTY** also provided backing vocals & co-songwriting.

A&M Avalanche

Nov 92. (7"/c-s/cd-s) **I COULD BE WRONG. / BAKER STREET / LIFE GOES ON** [ ] [–]

Feb 93. (cd/c) *(517495-2/-4)* <0016> **ON A WING & A PRAYER** [73] [ ]
– Time's caught up on you / I see red / It's easy to talk / I could be wrong / Don't speak of my heart / Get out of my life woman / Don't give up on me / Hang on / Love and affection / Does he know what he's taken on / The light of love / Life goes on. *(cd re-iss. Jul02 on 'Spectrum'; 517238-2)*

Polydor Avalanche

Jun 95. (cd) *(523599-2)* <0017> **OVER MY HEAD** [ ] [ ]
– Bajan moon / The waters of forgetfulness / Down and out / Over my head / The girl's got no confidence / Wrong thinking / Lonesome polecat / Right or wrong / Late again / Clear day / Out the blue / A new beginning / Her father didn't like me anyway.

– (his) compilations, others, etc. –

Apr 74. (lp) *Transatlantic; (TRA 270)* **GERRY RAFFERTY REVISITED** [ ] [–]

Jul 87. (cd) *Transatlantic; (TRACD 601)* **THE COLLECTION** [ ] [–]

Apr 78. (7") *Logo; (GO 314)* **MARY SKEFFINGTON. / SHOESHINE BOY** [ ] [–]

Sep 78. (lp) *Logo; (VISA 7006)* **GERRY RAFFERTY** [ ] [–]

Apr 84. (lp/c) *Cambra; (CR/+T 132)* **THE FIRST CHAPTER** [ ] [–]

Jun 88. (lp) *Demon; (TRANDEM 3)* **BLOOD AND GLORY** [ ] [–]

Nov 89. (cd/c/lp) *E.M.I.; (CD/TC+/UAG 30333)* **RIGHT DOWN THE LINE – THE BEST OF GERRY RAFFERTY** [ ] [–]
– Baker Street / Whatever's written in your heart / Bring it all home / Right down the line / Get it right next time / Night owl / A dangerous age / Family tree / Shipyard town / The right moment / Look at the Moon. *(cd+=)* – The way that you do it / Tired of talking / The garden of England / Sleepwalking / As wise as a serpent.

Feb 90. (7") *E.M.I.; (EM 132)* **BAKER STREET (remix). / NIGHT OWL (remix)** [53] [–]
(12"+=) *(12EM 132)* – ('A'extended).
(cd-s++=) *(CDEM 132)* – Bring it all home (remix).

Apr 95. (cd) *Castle; (CCSCD 428)* **THE TRANSATLANTIC YEARS** [ ] [–]

Oct 95. (cd/c) *Polygram TV; (529279-2/-4)* **ONE MORE DREAM – THE VERY BEST OF . . .** [17] [–]
– Get it right next time / The garden of England / Baker street / Moonlight and gold / Stuck in the middle with you / Night owl / Waiting for the day / Right down the line / Tired of talkin' / Bring it all home / The girl's got no confidence / Days gone down / Everyone's agreed that everything will turn out fine / Over my head / Shipyard town / Whatever's written in your heart.

Feb 96. (cd/c) *True Trax; (TRT CD/MC 196)* **THE EARLY YEARS** [ ] [–]

Mar 97. (d-cd) *Raven;* <63> **CLOWNS TO THE LEFT, JOKERS TO THE RIGHT: 1970-1982** [–] [ ]

Jun 98. (cd) *EMI Gold; (494941-2)* **BAKER STREET** [ ] [–]

Oct 98. (cd) *Castle Select; (SELCD 547) / Phantom;* <21864-2> **DON'T COUNT ME OUT: THE VERY BEST OF THE TRANSATLANTIC YEARS** [–] [ ]

Dec 99. (cd) *Disky;* <85442> **BAKER STREET** [–] [ ]

May 00. (cd) *Essential; (ESMCD 879)* **CAN I HAVE MY MONEY BACK – THE BEST OF GERRY RAFFERTY** [ ] [–]

RAGE AGAINST THE MACHINE

Formed: Los Angeles, California, USA . . . 1992 by rapper/vocalist ZACK DE LA ROCHA and guitarist TOM MORELLO along with bassist TIMMY C and drummer BRAD WILK. Signed to 'Epic' partly on the strength of their infamous live reputation, the band divebombed their way into the UK charts after performing the incendiary 'KILLING IN THE NAME OF' on cult 'yoof' TV show (now sadly missed), 'The Word'. One of the most visceral, angry and overtly political records of the 90's, the song formed the centrepiece of their pivotal 1993 eponymous debut album. A revelatory hybrid of monster riffing and knotty hip hop rhythms, the album was venom-spewing and utterly defiant. While detractors argued that the band's position on the roster of a major corporation was untenable, RATM countered that they had to get their message across to as wide an audience as possible. The vital point was that this was one SERIOUSLY angry young man, raging against all kinds of injustice, mainly the ruling white American capitalist system. Most of the tracks (highlights being 'BOMBTRACK', BULLET IN THE HEAD' and 'KNOW YOUR ENEMY') were positively seething with anger but crucially, they were also funky as hell and this is where RATM scored over their square-jawed copyists. Music aside, how many bands in the 90's have had the balls to be openly political?, or rather, how many bands even know the meaning of protest? In a music world of drug-inspired vacancy, RATM provided a vital injection of reality. Putting their money where their mouth was, or rather putting their modesty thereabouts, the band walked on stage naked at a show in Philadelphia, the initials PMRC (Parent Music Resource Centre) scrawled across their respective chests in defiance of the risible censorship organisation. Political dissent was nothing new to either TOM or ZACK, MORELLO's father being a member of the Mau Mau's (Kenyan Guerrillas) who fought for an end to British colonialism while his uncle JOMO KENYATTA was imprisoned, later becoming the Kenyan president. LA ROCHA's father, meanwhile, was a noted L.A. muralist and political activist. While the band continued to stir up controversy with their live work (including a sold out 1993 UK tour and blinding set at the 1994 Glastonbury Festival), a follow-up album wasn't released until 1996. When it eventually surfaced, 'EVIL EMPIRE' was something of a disappointment, lacking the focus and some of the funkiness of the debut, although it did hit US No.1. The cover art too, lacked the impact of the first album (a powerful photo of a buddhist monk setting himself on fire in protest at the Vietnam war). Nevertheless, the group put in a brilliant performance at that year's Reading Festival, whipping the crowd into a frenzy and almost upstaging headliners, The PRODIGY. The impressively talented and ever inventive MORELLO subsequently hooked up with the Essex electro-punks on the acclaimed 'NO MAN ARMY' track. Three years in the making (as per usual), the third album, 'THE BATTLE OF LOS ANGELES' (1999), once again pulled no punches and deservedly topped the US chart (only Top 30 in Britain!). Tracks such as the single, 'GUERRILLA RADIO', 'MIC CHECK' and 'NEW MILLENNIUM HOMES', were certainly the highlights as the band undertook an extensive world tour. After the 'RENEGADES' covers set late in 2000, DE LA ROCHA departed – rumours were subsequently rife that CYPRESS HILL's frontman B-REAL would take his place. In the event no-one took his place. Or at least someone took his place – that someone being former SOUNDGARDEN frontman CHRIS CORNELL – but the group morphed into an altogether different entity, AUDIOSLAVE. Like most so-called supergroup amalgamations, this much heralded project failed to fully live up to the hype: pitting CORNELL's 70's sludge predelictions against the militant sonic efficiency of RAGE was never going to result in fireworks although admittedly it didn't end in tears. The group's eponymous debut, released in late 2002, was a curious beast, coming together definitively on the single 'COCHISE' but otherwise sounding only partly realised, lacking either the sting of RATM or the grand designs of CORNELL.

Album rating: RAGE AGAINST THE MACHINE (*9) / EVIL EMPIRE (*7) / THE BATTLE OF LOS ANGELES (*7) / RENEGADES (*8) / Audioslave: AUDIOSLAVE (*6)

ZACK DE LA ROCHA (b.1970, Long Beach, Calif.) – vocals / **TOM MORELLO** (b.1964, New York City, NY) – guitars / **TIMMY C.** (b. TIM COMMERFORD) – bass / **BRAD WILK** (b.1968, Portland, Oregon) – drums

Epic Epic

Feb 93. (7"/12"white/cd-s) *(658492-7/-6/-2)* **KILLING IN THE NAME. / CLEAR THE LANE / DARKNESS OF GREED** [25] [–]

Feb 93. (cd/c/lp) *(472224-2/-4/-1) <52959>* **RAGE AGAINST THE MACHINE** [17] Nov92 [45]
– Bombtrack / Killing in the name / Take the power back / Settle for nothing / Bullet in the head / Know your enemy / Wake up / Fistful of steel / Township rebellion / Freedom. *(lp re-iss. Feb99 on 'Simply Vinyl'; SVLP 69)*

Apr 93. (7") *(659258-7)* **BULLET IN THE HEAD. / BULLET IN THE HEAD (remix)** [16] [–]
(12"/cd-s) *(659258-6/-2)* – Bullet in the head / Settle for nothing.

Sep 93. (7") *(659471-7)* **BOMBTRACK. / ('A'mix)** [37] [–]
(12"+=/cd-s+=) *(659471-6/-2)* – ('A'version).

Feb 94. (cd-s; w-drawn) *(659821-2)* **FREEDOM** [–] [–]

Apr 96. (7"colrd/cd-s) *(663152-7/-2)* **BULLS ON PARADE. / HADDA BE PLAYING ON THE JUKEBOX** [8] [–]

Apr 96. (cd/c/lp) *(481026-2/-4/-1) <57523>* **EVIL EMPIRE** [4] [1]
– People of the sun / Bulls on parade / Vietnow / Revolver / Snakecharmer / Tire me / Down rodeo / Without a face / Wind below / Roll right / Year of tha boomerang.

Aug 96. (7"orange) *(663628-7)* **PEOPLE OF THE SUN. / ZAPATA'S BLOOD (live)** [26] [–]
(cd-s+=) *(663628-2)* – Without a face (live).
(cd-s) *(663628-5)* – ('A'side) / Killing in the name (live) / Bullet in the head (live).

—— TIMMY C. now as **Y.tim.K**

Oct 99. (7") *(668314-7) <79720>* **GUERRILLA RADIO. / THE GHOST OF TOM JOAD** [32] [69]
(cd-s+=) *(668314-2)* – No shelter.
(cd-s) *(668314-5)* – ('A'side) / F*** tha police (live) / Freedom (live).

Nov 99. (cd/c) *(491993-2/-4) <69630>* **THE BATTLE OF LOS ANGELES** [23] [1]
– Testify / Guerrilla radio / Calm like a bomb / Mic check / Sleep now in the fire / Born of a broken man / Born as ghosts / Maria / Voice of the voiceless / New millennium homes / Ashes in the fall / War within a breath.

Apr 00. (7"colrd) *(669136-7)* **SLEEP NOW IN THE FIRE. / ('A'live)** [43] [ ]
(cd-s) *(669136-2)* – ('A'side) / Bulls on parade (live) / ('A'-CD-Rom).
(cd-s) *(669136-5)* – ('A'side) / Guerilla radio (live) / Freedom (live).

Nov 00. (cd/c/lp) *(499921-2/-4/-1) <85289>* **RENEGADES** (covers) [71] [14]
– Microphone fiend / Pistol grip pump / Kick out the jams / Renegades of funk / Beautiful world / I'm housin' / In my eyes / How could I just kill a man / The ghost of Tom Joad / Down on the street / Street fighting man / Maggie's farm. *(other cd+=; 499921-0/-9/-8/-7)* – Kick out the jams (live) / How could I just kill a man.

—— RATM split in October 2000

– compilations, etc. –

Apr 97. (10"ep) *Revelation; (REV 056)* **PEOPLE OF THE SUN (live) / WITHOUT A FACE (live) / INTRO BLACK STEEL IN THE HOUR OF CHAOS (live). / ZAPATA'S BLOOD (live) / BULLS ON PARADE / HADDA BE PLAYING ON THE JUKEBOX (live)** [ ] [–]

AUDIOSLAVE

CHRIS CORNELL – vocals (ex-SOUNDGARDEN) / **TOM MORELLO, TIM COMMERFORD + BRAD WILK**

Epic Sony

Nov 02. (cd) *(510130-2) <86968>* **AUDIOSLAVE** 19 7
– Cochise / Show me how to live / Gasoline / What you are / Like a stone / Set it off / Shadow on the sun / I am the highway / Exploder / Hypnotize / Bring em back alive / Light my way / Getaway car / The last remaining light. *<lp-iss.Feb03; E 286968>*

Jan 03. (cd-s) *(673276-2)* **COCHISE / WE GOT THE WHIP / GASOLINE (live on Letterman) / ('A'-video)** 24 69

Apr 03. (7") *(673788-7)* **LIKE A STONE. / SET IT OFF (live on Letterman)** 31 –
(cd-s+=) *(673788-5)* – ('A'-live Radio 1 session).
(cd-s) *(673788-2)* – ('A'side) / Super stupid (live Radio 1 session) / Gasoline (live Radio 1 session) / ('A'-video).

Dec 03. (7"red) *<674148>* **SHOW ME HOW TO LIVE. / SUPER STUPID (live at the BBC)** – 67

RAINBOW

Formed: 1975 ... by former DEEP PURPLE guitar guru, RITCHIE BLACKMORE. Recruiting New York band ELF wholesale, including the esteemed metal warbler RONNIE JAMES DIO, BLACKMORE recorded the eponymous debut album ('RITCHIE BLACKMORE'S RAINBOW') in the summer of '75. While 'PURPLE lumbered towards imminent implosion, BLACKMORE took the Brontosaurus-rock blueprint to mystical new heights, the classic 'MAN ON THE SILVER MOUNTAIN' being the prime example. By the release of the seminal 'RAINBOW RISING' (1976), the ubiquitous COZY POWELL was on the drum stool. The record (released under the slightly clipped moniker of BLACKMORE'S RAINBOW) featured such enduring BLACKMORE stage favourites as 'TAROT WOMAN', 'STARGAZER' and 'A LIGHT IN THE BLACK', arguably the most cohesive set of the guitarist's career. After a live album, more line-up changes ensued, BOB DAISLEY finally stepping in for MARK CLARKE, who had temporarily replaced BAIN (DAVID STONE was now the new keyboard man in place of TONY CAREY). Although 'LONG LIVE ROCK'N'ROLL' (1978) was another hard-rock classic, it wasn't until DIO had departed for BLACK SABBATH that the band enjoyed their greatest success. Recruiting ex-MARBLES vocalist, GRAHAM BONNET, as a replacement, and surprisingly enlisting old 'PURPLE mucker ROGER GLOVER on bass, the band hit the UK Top 10 twice in a row at the turn of the decade with 'SINCE YOU BEEN GONE' and 'ALL NIGHT LONG'. Watertight, marvellously crafted melodic rock, both songs featured on the 'DOWN TO EARTH' (1979) album. POWELL left the following year, as did BONNET, BLACKMORE recruiting JOE LYNN TURNER as frontman. Their next single, 'I SURRENDER', was their biggest hit to date, an epic slice of American-influenced rock that stands among metal's greatest moments. The album, 'DIFFICULT TO CURE' (1981) made the UK Top 5 although it was clear RAINBOW had adopted a more commercial approach in an attempt to break America, subsequent efforts failing to make much impact, however. With no pot of gold at the end of this particular rainbow, BLACKMORE eventually folded the band in 1984, with plans to resurrect the classic Mk.II DEEP PURPLE line-up. Ten years on, BLACKMORE (again leaving 'PURPLE) resurrected another version of RAINBOW, a 1995 album, 'STRANGER IN US ALL', purely for BLACKMORE diehards. The veteran guitarist took a radically different tack on 'SHADOW OF THE MOON' (1998), the first recorded fruits of his collaboration with musical partner/fiancee, CANDICE NIGHT. Released under the moniker of BLACKMORE'S NIGHT (apparently not an awful pun on the old DP chestnut but a reference to the happy couple . . .), the album found RITCHIE and his young vocalist exploring Renaissance-era music via elements of new age, world, rock and folk. Such distinctly un-rock'n'roll instrumentation as pennywhistle, hurdy gurdy and mandolin contributed to the ambience while IAN ANDERSON even made an appearance with a blast of his trademark flute. Written with the anticipation of a full stage tour, 'UNDER A VIOLET MOON' (1999) was similar if less restrained, BLACKMORE again demonstrating his mastery of the acoustic guitar. In a hitherto unprecedented burst of creativity, the man continued his immersion in archaic motifs with 2001's 'FIRES AT MIDNIGHT' (although how Bob Dylan's 'THE TIMES THEY ARE A-CHANGIN' fit into the latter's medieval tapestry is anyone's guess), 2003's live (for a select, olde English-attired audience) 'PAST TIME WITH GOOD COMPANY' (within which Rainbow's '16th CENTURY GREENSLEEVES' was an admittedly better fit) and yet another studio set, 'GHOST OF A ROSE' (2003).

Album rating: RITCHIE BLACKMORE'S RAINBOW (*6) / RAINBOW RISING (*8) / LIVE ON STAGE (*4) / LONG LIVE ROCK'N'ROLL (*6) / DOWN TO EARTH (*6) / DIFFICULT TO CURE (*5) / THE BEST OF RAINBOW compilation (*7) / STRAIGHT BETWEEN THE EYES (*5) / BENT OUT OF SHAPE (*4) / FINAL VINYL (*4) / STRANGER IN US ALL (*4) / THE VERY BEST OF RAINBOW compilation (*6) / Blackmore's Night: SHADOW OF THE MOON (*4) / UNDER A VIOLET MOON (*4) / FIRES AT MIDNIGHT (*6) / PAST TIMES WITH GOOD COMPANY (*5) / GHOST OF A ROSE (*4)

RITCHIE BLACKMORE'S RAINBOW

RITCHIE BLACKMORE (b.14 Apr'45, Weston-Super-Mare, England) – guitar with (ex-ELF) men **RONNIE JAMES DIO** – vocals / **MICKEY LEE SOULE** – keyboards / **CRAIG GRUBER** – bass / **GARY DRISCOLL** – drums

Oyster Oyster

Aug 75. (lp/c) *(OYA 2001) <6049>* **RITCHIE BLACKMORE'S RAINBOW** 11 30
– Man on the silver mountain / Self portrait / Black sheep of the family / Catch the rainbow / Snake charmer / Temple of the king / If you don't like rock'n'roll / Sixteenth century Greensleeves / Still I'm sad. *(re-iss. Aug81 on 'Polydor; 2490 141) (re-iss. Aug83 on 'Polydor' lp/c; SPE LP/MC 7) (cd-iss. 1988 & Jan93 on 'Polydor'; 825089-2) (cd re-iss. Jun99; 547360-2)*

Oct 75. (7") *(OYR 103) <14290>* **MAN ON THE SILVER MOUNTAIN. / SNAKE CHARMER**

— RITCHIE only retained **DIO,** recruiting new members **TONY CAREY** – keyboards / **JIMMY BAIN** – bass / **COZY POWELL** – drums

Polydor Oyster

May 76. (lp/c; as BLACKMORE'S RAINBOW) *(2490 137) <1601>* **RAINBOW RISING** 11 48
– Tarot woman / Run with the wolf / Starstruck / Do you close your eyes / Stargazer / A light in the black. *(re-iss. Aug83 lp/c; SPE LP/MC 35) (cd-iss. Nov86; 823089-2) (cd re-iss. Jun99; 547361-2)*

RAINBOW

Jul 77. (d-lp) *(2657 016) <1801>* **RAINBOW ON STAGE (live)** 7 65
– Kill the king: (a) Man on a silver mountain, (b) Blues, (c) Starstruck / Catch the rainbow / Mistreated / Sixteenth century Greensleeves / Still I'm sad. *(re-iss. Jan84; SPDLP 6) (cd-iss. Nov86; 823656-2)*

Aug 77. (7") *(2066 845)* **KILL THE KING: MAN ON THE SILVER MOUNTAIN. / MISTREATED** 44 –
(re-iss. Jul81; same) ; reached UK No.41

— **MARK CLARKE** – bass (ex-COLOSSEUM, ex-URIAH HEEP) repl. BAIN who joined WILD HORSES / **BOB DAISLEY** – bass (ex-WIDOWMAKER, ex-CHICKEN SHACK) repl. CLARKE / **DAVID STONE** – keyboards (ex-SYMPHONIC SLAM) repl. CAREY

Polydor Polydor

Mar 78. (7") *(2066 913) <14481>* **LONG LIVE ROCK'N'ROLL. / SENSITIVE TO LIGHT** 33
(re-iss. Jul81; same)

Apr 78. (lp/c) *(POLD/+C 5002) <6143>* **LONG LIVE ROCK'N'ROLL** 7 89
– Long live rock'n'roll / Lady of the lake / L.A. connection / Gates of Babylon / Kill the king / The shed (subtle) / Sensitive to light / Rainbow eyes. *(re-iss. Aug83 lp/c; SPE LP/MC 34) (cd-iss. Jan93; 825090-2) (cd re-iss. Jun99; 547363-2)*

Sep 78. (7"red) *(2066 968)* **L.A. CONNECTION. / LADY OF THE LAKE** 40 –
(re-iss. 7"black Jul81; same)

— **BLACKMORE** retained only **COZY POWELL / GRAHAM BONNET** – vocals (ex-Solo artist, ex-MARBLES) repl. DIO who went solo / **ROGER GLOVER** – bass, vocals (ex-DEEP PURPLE) repl. DAISLEY / **DON AIREY** – keyboards repl. STONE

Aug 79. (clear-lp/c) *(POLD/+C 5023) <6221>* **DOWN TO EARTH** 6 66
– All night long / Eyes of the world / No time to lose / Makin' love / Since you been gone / Love's no friend / Danger zone / Lost in Hollywood. *(re-iss. Apr84 lp/c; SPE LP/MC 69) (cd-iss. Dec86; 823705-2) (cd re-iss. Jun99; 547364-2)*

Aug 79. (7") *(POSP 70) <2014>* **SINCE YOU BEEN GONE. / BAD GIRLS** 6 Oct79 57
(re-iss. Jul81; same)

Feb 80. (7") *(POSP 104) <2060>* **ALL NIGHT LONG. / WEISS HEIM** 5
(re-iss. Jul81; same)

— **JOE LYNN TURNER** – vocals, repl. BONNET who continued solo career. / **BOBBY RONDINELLI** – drums repl. POWELL who later joined E.L.P.

Jan 81. (7") *(POSP 221)* **I SURRENDER. / MAYBE NEXT TIME** 3 –
(re-iss. Jul81; same)

Feb 81. (lp/c) *(POLD/+C 5036) <6316>* **DIFFICULT TO CURE** 3 50
– I surrender / Spotlight kid / No release / Vielleicht das nachster zeit (Maybe next time) / Can't happen here / Freedom fighter / Midtown tunnel vision / Difficult to cure. *(re-iss. Aug84 lp/c)(cd; SPE LP/MC 76)(800-018-2) (cd re-iss. Jun99; 547365-2)*

Jun 81. (7") *(POSP 251)* **CAN'T HAPPEN HERE. / JEALOUS LOVER** 20 –

Nov 81. (m-lp) *<502>* **JEALOUS LOVER** –
– Jealous lover / Can't happen here / I surrender / Weiss Helm.

— **DAVE ROSENTHAL** – keyboards; repl. AIREY who joined OZZY OSBOURNE

Polydor Mercury

Mar 82. (7"blue/ext-12"blue) *(POSP/+X 421) <76146>* **STONE COLD. / ROCK FEVER** 34 40

Apr 82. (lp/c) *(POLD/+C 5056) <4041>* **STRAIGHT BETWEEN THE EYES** 5 30
– Death alley driver / Stone cold / Bring on the night (dream chaser) / Tite squeeze / Tearin' out my heart / Power / Miss Mistreated / Rock fever / Eyes of fire. *(cd-iss. Nov83; 800-028-2) (cd re-iss. Apr94; 521709-2) (cd re-iss. Jun99; 547366-2)*

— **BLACKMORE** still had in his ranks **GLOVER, TURNER, ROSENTHAL, /** and **CHUCK BURGI** – drums (ex-BRAND X) repl. RONDINELLI

Aug 83. (7"/7"pic-d) *(POSP/+P 631) <815660>* **STREET OF DREAMS. / IS ANYBODY THERE** 52 60
(12"+=) *(POSPX 631)* – Power (live).

Sep 83. (lp/c)(cd) *(POLD/+C 5116)(<815-305-2>)* **BENT OUT OF SHAPE** 11 34
– Stranded / Can't let you go / Fool for the night / Fire dance / Anybody there / Desperate heart / Street of dreams / Drinking with the devil / Snowman / Make your move. *(cd re-iss. Jun99; 547367-2)*

Oct 83. (7"/7"sha-pic-d) *(POSP/+P 654)* **CAN'T LET YOU GO. / ALL NIGHT LONG (live)** 43
(12"+=) *(POSPX 654)* – Stranded (live).

— Split late '83 . . . BLACKMORE and GLOVER reformed DEEP PURPLE

RITCHIE BLACKMORE'S RAINBOW

— re-formed for comeback concerts & an album. His new band:- **DOOGIE WHITE** – vocals / **PAUL MORRIS** – keyboards / **GREG SMITH** – bass / **JOHN O'REILLY** – drums

Arista Beacon

Sep 95. (cd/c) *(74321 30337-2/-4) <51565>* **STRANGER IN US ALL** 1996
– Wolf to the Moon / Cold hearted woman / Hunting humans (insatiable) / Stand and fight / Ariel / Too late for tears / Black masquerade / Silence / Hall of the mountain king / Still I'm sad.

– compilations, etc. –

Sep 78. (d-lp) *Polydor; (268 3078)* **RITCHIE BLACKMORE'S RAINBOW / RAINBOW RISING** –

Nov 81. (d-lp/d-c) *Polydor; (POLDV/PODVC 2)* **THE BEST OF RAINBOW** 14
– All night long / Man on the silver mountain / Can't happen here / Lost in Hollywood / Since you been gone / Stargazer / Catch the rainbow / Kill the king / 16th century Greensleeves / I surrender / Long live rock'n'roll / Eyes of the world / Starstruck / A light in the black / Mistreated. *(cd-iss. 1983; 800-074-2)*

Feb 83. (d-c) *Polydor; (3574 141)* **DOWN TO EARTH / DIFFICULT TO CURE** –

Feb 86. (d-lp/d-c)(d-cd) *Polydor; (PODV/+C 8)(<827-987-2>)* **FINYL VINYL** (live 80's material) 87
– Spotlight kid / I surrender / Miss mistreated / Jealous lover / Can't happen here / Tearin' out my heart / Since you been gone / Bad girl / Difficult to cure / Stone cold / Power / Man on the silver mountain / Long live rock'n'roll / Weiss heim. *(d-cd re-iss. Jun99; 547368-2)*

Feb 88. (7") *Old Gold; (OG 9772)* **SINCE YOU BEEN GONE. / ALL NIGHT LONG** –

Oct 89. (d-lp/c/cd) *Connoisseur; (RPVSOP LP/MC/CD 143)* **ROCK PROFILE VOL.1** –
(above credited to RITCHIE BLACKMORE contains early sessions and PURPLE work) (cd.omits interview tracks + 1 song)

Dec 90. (d-cd/c/d-lp) *Connoisseur; (DPVSOP CD/MC/LP 155)* **LIVE IN GERMANY 1976 (live)** –

Jul 91. (cd/d-lp) *Connoisseur; (RPVSOP CD/LP 157)* **ROCK PROFILE VOLUME 2** –
(above also credited to RITCHIE BLACKMORE cont. RAINBOW material, etc.)

Jun 93. (cd-s) *Old Gold; (OG)* **I SURRENDER / SINCE YOU BEEN GONE / ALL NIGHT LONG** –

Jan 94. (cd) *R.P.M.; (RPM 120)* **SESSION MAN** –

Jun 94. (cd) *R.P.M.; (PRM)* **TAKE IT! – SESSIONS 63-68** –

Aug 97. (cd) *Polydor; (537687-2)* **THE VERY BEST OF RAINBOW**

Feb 02. (cd) *Spectrum; (544651-2)* **POT OF GOLD** –

May 02. (cd) *Polydor; (589652-2)* **ALL NIGHT LONG: AN INTRODUCTION TO RAINBOW**

May 03. (d-cd) *Polydor; (065538-2)* **CATCH THE RAINBOW: THE ANTHOLOGY**

BLACKMORE'S NIGHT

RITCHIE with **CANDICE NIGHT** (b. 8 May'71, Hauppauge, Long Island, New York) – vocals / **LADY GREEN** – violin / etc

Edel Edeltone

Oct 97. (cd) *(0099022WHE) <3755>* **SHADOW OF THE MOON** Feb98
– Shadow of the Moon / The clock ticks on / Be mine tonight / Play minstrel play / Ocean gypsy / Minstrel hall / Magical world / Writing on the wall / Renaissance faire / Memmingen / No second chance / Mond tanz / Spirit of the sea / Greensleeves / Wish you were here. *(re-iss. May98 on 'H.T.D.'; HTDCD 84) (cd re-iss. May00 on 'Candlelight'; LIGHTCD 1)*

— added **JOHN FORD** – bass / **KEVIN DUNNE** – drums / **JENS JOHANSSON** – keyboards / etc.

Pony Canyon Intersound

Jun 99. (cd) *(PCCY 01377) <3741>* **UNDER A VIOLET MOON** Jul99
– Under a violet moon / Castles and dreams / Past time with good company / Morning star / Avalon / Possum goes to Prague / Wind in the willows / Gone with the wind / Beyond the sunset / March the heroes home / Spanish nights (I remember it well) / Catherine Howard's fate / Durch den wald zum balch haus / Fool's gold / Now and then / Self portrait.

S.P.V. S.P.V.

Aug 01. (cd) *(<085-7243-2>)* **FIRES AT MIDNIGHT** Jul01
– Written in the stars / The times they are a-changin' / I still remember / Home again / Crowning of the king / Fayre thee well / Fires at midnight / Hanging tree / The storm / Mid winter's night / All because of you / Waiting just for you / Praetorius (courante) / Benzai-ten / Village on the sand / Again someday.

Oct 02. (d-cd) *(<092-7449-2>)* **PAST TIMES WITH GOOD COMPANY (live)** Feb03
– Shadow of the Moon / Play minstrel play / Minstrel hall / Past times with good company / Fires at midnight / Under a violet moon / Soldier of fortune / 16th Century Greensleeves / Beyond the sunset / Morning star /

Home again / Renaissance faire / I still remember / Durch den wald zum bachhaus / Writing on the wall. *(ltd-cd+=; 095-7449-0)* – Fires at midnight / Mid winter's night.

Jun 03. (cd) *(<085-7499-2>)* **GHOST OF A ROSE**
– Way to Mandalay / 3 black crows / Diamonds and rust / Cartouche / Queen for a day (part 1) / Queen for a day (part 2) / Ivory tower / Nur eine minute / Ghost of a rose / Mr. Peagram's Morris and sword / Loreley / Where are we going from here / Rainbow blues / All for one / Dandelion wine. *(ltd-cd+=; 085-7499-0)* – Just one minute.

RAIN PARADE

Formed: Los Angeles, California, USA . . . 1981 as The SIDEWALKS by Minneapolis college mates DAVID ROBACK and MATT PIUCCI. They also numbered DAVID's younger brother STEVEN and WILL GLENN, before they opted for a name change. Their vinyl debut came with the BYRDS-like 'WHAT'S SHE DONE TO YOUR MIND' in 1982 while they found a permanent drummer in EDDIE KALWA. DAVID moonlighted with another project, RAINY DAY, but a disappointing covers album was soon forgotten when 'EMERGENCY THIRD RAIL POWER TRIP' hit the shops. Purveyors of the burgeoning "Paisley Underground" scene, the set was a throwback to the psychedelic sound of PINK FLOYD/KALEIDOSCOPE, while the guitar plucking was reminiscent of TELEVISION. The record gained a UK release on Demon's off-shoot 'Zippo' label, as did their 1984 mini-lp 'EXPLOSIONS IN THE GLASS PALACE'. The record was recorded without co-leader DAVID, however, who had left earlier in the year. 'Island' records gave them their break in '85 but surely damaged their growing reputation when they rush-released a live-set recorded in Japan, 'BEYOND THE SUNSET'. With MATT and STEVEN the sole remaining members, they recruited JOHN THOMAN and MARK MARCUM although the 1986 album, 'CRASHING DREAM', was appropriately titled, Island soon ditching them. They took a two-year hiatus before going back into the studio to finish off a double album. It never found its way to the shops, as PIUCCI joined a re-formed CRAZY HORSE, while the rest became VIVA SATURN. Relocating to San Francisco, STEVEN ROBACK and Co delivered a handful of worthy releases, none more so than 1995's 'Restless' set, 'BRIGHTSIDE'. • **Songwriters:** All written by the ROBACK's and group, except AIN'T THAT NOTHIN' (Television) / LIKE A HURRICANE (Neil Young) / WHAT GOES ON (Velvet Underground).

Album rating: EMERGENCY THIRD RAIL POWER TRIP (*7) / EXPLOSIONS IN THE GLASS PALACE mini (*6) / BEYOND THE SUNSET (*6) / CRASHING DREAM (*6) / Viva Saturn: VIVA SATURN mini (*5) / SOUNDMIND (*6) / BRIGHTSIDE (*7)

DAVID ROBACK – vocals, guitar, percussion / **MATT PIUCCI** – guitar, vocals, sitar / **WILL GLENN** – keyboards / **STEVEN ROBACK** – bass, vocals / **EDDIE KALWA** – drums

not iss. Llama

1982. (7") *<DK 002>* **WHAT'S SHE DONE TO YOUR MIND. / KALEIDOSCOPE** –

Zippo Enigma

Aug 84. (lp) *(ZING 001) <ENIGMA 19>* **EMERGENCY THIRD RAIL POWER TRIP** 1983
– Talking in my sleep / This can't be today / I look around / 1 hr. half ago / Carolyn's song / What she's done to your mind / Look at Merri / Saturday's asylum / Kaleidoscope / Look both ways.

— trimmed to a quartet when DAVE left to form RAINY DAY (later OPAL). He is now part of duo MAZZY STAR

1984. (m-lp) *(ZANE 003) <71081>* **EXPLOSIONS IN THE GLASS PALACE**
– You are my friend / Prisoners / Blue / Broken horse / No easy way down.

Feb 85. (7") *(ZIPPO 45-1)* **YOU ARE MY FRIEND. / THIS CAN'T BE TODAY** 1984

— **MARK MARCUM** – drums repl. KALWA

— added **JOHN THOMAN** – guitar, vocals

Island Restless

Jun 85. (lp/c) *(IMA/IMC 17) <72086>* **BEYOND THE SUNSET** 78
(live in Tokyo 1984)
– Night shade / Prisoners / This can't be today / Blue / Eyes closed / Ain't that nothin' / Don't feel bad / 1 hr. 1/2 ago / Blue / No easy way down / Cheap wine.

Island Island

Oct 85. (lp/c) *(ILPS/ICT 9805) <90499-1/-4>* **CRASHING DREAM**
– Depending on you / My secret country / Don't feel bad / Mystic green / Sad eyes kill / Shoot down the railroad man / Fertile crescent / Invisible people / Gone west / Only business.

— disbanded when PIUCCI formed GONE FISHIN' then joined CRAZY HORSE

– compilations, etc. –

Feb 92. (cd) *Mau Mau; (MAUCD 610)* **EMERGENCY THIRD RAIL POWER TRIP / EXPLOSIONS IN THE GLASS PALACE** –

Sep 02. (cd) *Cloud; (CLOUD 6)* **PERFUME RIVER (live)** –
– Kaleidoscope / This can't be today / Prisoners / Crashing dream / Blue / You are my friend / Sad eyes kill / No easy way down / Broken horse / Ain't that nothin' / What she's done to your mind / Saturday's asylum / Like a hurricane / What goes on.

VIVA SATURN

STEVEN ROBACK – guitar, piano, vocals / **JOHN THOMAN** – guitar / **MARK MARCUM**

World Service Heyday

Jun 89. (m-lp) *(SERVS 003)* **VIVA SATURN**
– So glad / Brought it on yourself / Remember I'm dead / Old world / Wild town.

— **MATT PIUCCI** – guitar, vocals; repl. MARK

— added **ROSS INDEN** – bass / **CARLO NUCCIO** – drums

Normal Heyday

May 94. (cd) *(NORMAL 139CD) <ADE 009CD>* **SOUNDMIND** 1992
– Still she waits / Love the sugar / Believe / Haven't felt like / Soundmind / Suicidal lamb / Raised / Better get your nerve Paradise / Mermaid / Waiting for the train.

Restless Restless

Jul 95. (cd) *<(72909-2)>* **BRIGHTSIDE**
– Send a message / Black cloud / Brightside / Here comes April / Abondoned car string me out a line / Mourn the light / Distracted / Nothing helps / Heart of you / One for my baby.

— after one shelved set, STEVEN ROBACK contemplated a solo career

□ RAIN TREE CROW (see under ⇒ JAPAN)

Bonnie RAITT

Born: 8 Nov'49, Burbank, California, USA. Brought up in a Quaker family (her dad John was also an actor!), she learned guitar as a young child, receiving the instrument as a Christmas present and subsequently catching the blues bug at college in Cambridge, Massachusetts (reading African studies). Branching out from her love of folk music (JOAN BAEZ was a favourite) to records by JOHN LEE HOOKER, SON HOUSE and MISSISSIPPI FRED McDOWELL, the young RAITT became a well known blues performer on the Northeastern circuit alongside bassist, DAN 'FREEBO' FRIEDBERG (sometimes sharing a stage with her idols, MISSISSIPPI JOHN HURT, HOWLIN' WOLF and SIPPIE

WALLACE). Her boyfriend, Dick Waterman, became her manager and, influenced by BOB DYLAN, MUDDY WATERS and JOHN HAMMOND, RAITT began recording for 'Warner Brothers' in 1971. Establishing her own individual blend of country blues and LA-style soft rock, her eponymous debut album set the tone for her later work with a combination of self penned songs and carefully selected covers (by the likes of JACKSON BROWNE, ROBERT JOHNSON and RANDY NEWMAN). Her second set, 'GIVE IT UP', followed in 1972 and featured the lusty Chris Smithers' cover, 'LOVE ME LIKE A MAN', Jackson Browne's 'UNDER THE FALLING SKY' and Eric Katz's 'LOVE HAS NO PRIDE'. Recorded after RAITT's relocation to LA, 1973's 'TAKIN' MY TIME' (with contributions from TAJ MAHAL, JIM KELTNER, BILL PAYNE and LOWELL GEORGE) featured such outstanding tracks as 'KOKOMO BLUES'. Over the ensuing decade, RAITT moved towards an out and out rock direction, exemplified in 1977's 'SWEET FORGIVENESS' (her most successful 'Warner Brothers' album, peaking at US 25), recorded with her regular touring band of WILL McFARLANE (guitar), JEFF LABES (keyboards), DENNIS WHITTED (drums), FREEBO (bass) and vocalists MICHAEL McDONALD and JOHN DAVID SOUTHER. The record provided RAITT with her first US Top 60 hit single, a rocking version of Del Shannon's 'RUNAWAY'. 1982's 'GREEN LIGHT' (a US Top 40 album) featured a new backing outfit, The BUMP BAND, which numbered ex-FACES keyboard man, IAN McLAGAN, drummer RICKY FATAAR (ex-BEACH BOYS), bassist RAY OHARA and guitarist JOHNNY LEE SCHELL. RAITT subsequently disappeared from the scene to undergo drugs and alcohol rehabilitation, resurfacing in 1985 when she took part in the ARTISTS AGAINST APARTHEID project. Her last album for 'Warners' was 'NINE LIVES', a modest selling record which included songs by KARLA BONOFF, TOM SNOW, BRYAN ADAMS, WILL JENNINGS, RICHARD KERR and ERIC KATZ. It also featured her old friend and blues mentor, SIPPIE WALLACE, singing on their version of Toots & The Maytals' 'TRUE LOVE IS HARD TO FIND'. In 1987, RAITT joined a programme for recovering alcoholics and after recovering, spent two days recording with PRINCE in Minneapolis. Her benefit work also increased in 1987 when she took part in The July Fourth Disarmament Festival in the Soviet Union, Stop Contra Aid, Amnesty International, Farm Aid and a film about homeless awareness. Real success had been a long time coming, although she bounced back with 'BABY OF MINE' (a duet recorded with DON WAS) from the Disney covers album, 'Stay Awake' (1988); the single's release led to a new recording deal with 'Capitol'. Her first album for her new company, 1989's DON WAS-produced 'NICK OF TIME', (highlights being the self-penned title track, 'THE ROAD'S MY MIDDLE NAME' and JOHN HIATT's 'THING CALLED LOVE') was aimed at the AOR market, subsequently netting her three Grammy's and gave her a UK chart debut at number No.51 (a chart topper in America). This elevated her into the superstar bracket, leading to guest spots on projects by the likes of DAVID CROSBY, EMMYLOU HARRIS and B.B. KING to name but a few. RAITT's next album, 'LUCK OF THE DRAW' (1991), was an even bigger seller (US Top 3 and UK Top 40), although the songs (from the likes of JOHN HIATT, PAUL BRADY and herself) weren't quite as strong. RAITT's personal life became stable following her marriage to actor, MICHAEL O'KEEFE, in 1991 after years of singing about broken hearts and no-good men. 1994 saw a return to previous highs with 'LONGING IN THEIR HEARTS', an album that reaped more Grammy's and went deservedly multi-platinum. A concert set, 'ROAD TESTED' (1995), was incredibly her first such outing despite her legendary live status. Featuring duets with JACKSON BROWNE and BRUCE HORSNBY, it also contained a disappointing collaboration with BRYAN ADAMS, although excellent versions of Talking Heads' 'BURNING DOWN THE HOUSE' and John Prine's 'ANGEL FROM MONTGOMERY' were enough to save the album. Having started out in her long career using an acoustic, thumb-picking style of playing and progressing to slide guitar, she has become perhaps the only woman in the "rock" world to be recognised as a guitar virtuoso (RAITT was initially tutored by the late, great LOWELL GEORGE of LITTLE FEAT). For 1998's 'FUNDAMENTAL', RAITT ditched Don Was and brought in producers of the moment Mitchell Froom and Tchad Blake. Unfortunately, the latter pair's more adventurous studio techniques sat particularly uncomfortably with RAITT's earthy style, experiments with cajun, reggae and caribbean music falling particularly flat. Production duties back within her own remit on 'SILVER LINING' (2002), RAITT turned in one of her most engaging albums in years, guest spots from the likes of STEVE CROPPER and ROY ROGERS adding texture and colour. While her guitar playing was never less than dazzling, the spotlight fell squarely on RAITT's ever maturing vocals, showcased to particularly heart-rending effect on 'WOUNDED HEART'. Her increasingly high profile as a quality adult contemporary artist was reflected in another US Top 20 placing. • **Covered:** WALKING BLUES (Robert Johnson) / UNDER THE FALLING SKY (Jackson Browne) / LOVE HAS NO PRIDE (Eric Kaz) / GUILTY (Randy Newman) / WHAT IS SUCCESS (Allen Toussaint) / WOMEN BE WISE (Wallace-Beach) / MY FIRST NIGHT ALONE WITH YOU (. . . Vassey) / SUGAR MAMA (McClinton-Clark) / LOUISE (Paul Siebel) / NO WAY TO TREAT A LADY (Bryan Adams) / THE GLOW (. . . Hildebrand) / BUILT TO MAKE ME LEAVE HOME (. . . Randle) / WITH YA, WON'T CHAS (. . . Schell) / YOUR GOOD THING (Hayes-Porter) / YOUR GONNA GET WHAT'S COMING (Robert Palmer) / GOIN' WILD FOR YOU BABY (Snow-Batteau) / etc. In 1989 most were written by JOHN HIATT and others including SOMETHING TO TALK ABOUT (S.Eikhardt) / I CAN'T MAKE YOU LOVE ME (Reid / Shamblin).

Album rating: BONNIE RAITT (*5) / GIVE IT UP (*6) / TAKIN' MY TIME (*7) / STREETLIGHTS (*6) / HOME PLATE (*4) / SWEET FORGIVENESS (*5) / THE GLOW (*6) / GREEN LIGHT (*6) / NINE LIVES (*5) / NICK OF TIME (*8) / THE BONNIE RAITT COLLECTION compilation (*7) / LUCK OF THE DRAW (*8) / LONGING IN THEIR HEARTS (*7) / ROAD TESTED (*5) / FUNDAMENTAL (*5) / SILVER LINING (*5) / THE BEST OF BONNIE RAITT compilation (*7)

BONNIE RAITT – vocals, guitar, steel guitar / **FREEBO** – bass / **A.C.REID** – tenor sax / etc.

Warners Warners

Nov 71. (lp) <*(WS 1953)*> **BONNIE RAITT** [ ] [ ]
– Bluebird revisited / I'm a mighty tight woman / Thank you / Finest lovin' man / Any day woman / Big road / Walking blues / Danger heartbreak dead ahead / Since I fell for you / I ain't blue / Woman be wise. *(re-iss. Jun76; K 56255) <(cd-iss. Oct01 on 'Warner-ESP'; 8122 78377-2)>*

Dec 71. (7") *<7554>* **BLUEBIRD. / WOMAN BE WISE** [–] [ ]

Nov 72. (lp) *(K 46189) <BS 2643>* **GIVE IT UP** [ ] Oct72 [ ]
– Give it up or let me go / Nothing seems to matter / I know / If you gotta make a fool of somebody / Love me like a man / Stayed too long at the fair / Under the falling sky / You got to know how / You told me baby / Love has no pride. *(<cd-iss. Mar02 on 'Warners-ESP'; 8122 78378-2)>*

Dec 72. (7") *(K 16226) <7645>* **STAYED TOO LONG AT THE FAIR. / UNDER THE FALLING SKY** [ ] [ ]

— now on session **LOWELL GEORGE / BILL PAYNE / JIM KELTNER + TAJ MAHAL**

Oct 73. (7") *<7758>* **YOU'VE BEEN IN LOVE TOO LONG. / EVERYBODY'S CRYIN' MERCY** [–] [ ]

Nov 73. (lp) *(K 46261) <BS 2729>* **TAKIN' MY TIME** [ ] Oct73 [87]
– You've been in love too long / I gave my love a candle / Let me in / Everybody's cryin' mercy / Cry like a rainstorm / Wah she go do / I feel the same / I thought I was a child / Write me a few of your lines – Kokomo

blues / Guilty. *(re-iss. Jun76; K 56254) (cd-iss. Feb93; 7599 27275-2) <(cd re-iss. Mar02 on 'Warners-ESP'; 8122 78379-2)>*

Oct 74. (7") *<8044>* **I GOT PLENTY. / YOU GOTTA BE READY FOR LOVE (IF YOU WANNA BE MINE)** –

Nov 74. (lp) *(K 56075) <BS 2818>* **STREETLIGHTS** Oct74 80
– That song about the Midway / Rainy day man / Angel from Montgomery / I got plenty / Streetlights / What is success / Ain't nobody home / Everything that touches you / Got you on my mind / You gotta be ready for love (if you wanna be mine). *(cd-iss. 1989; 927286-2) <(cd re-iss. Oct01 on 'Warners-ESP'; 8122 78380-2)>*

Nov 75. (7") *<8166>* **MY FIRST NIGHT ALONE WITH YOU. / GOOD ENOUGH** –

Dec 75. (lp/c) *(K/K4 56160) <BS 2864>* **HOME PLATE** Oct75 43
– What do you want the boy to do / Good enough / Run like a thief / Fool yourself / My first night alone with you / Walk out the front door / Sugar mama / Pleasin' each other / I'm blowin' away / Your sweet and shiny eyes. *(cd-iss. Feb93; 7599 27292-2) <(cd re-iss. Mar02 on 'Warners-ESP'; 8122 78381-2)>*

May 76. (7") *<8189>* **WALK OUT THE FRONT DOOR. / RUN LIKE A THIEF** –

Jun 76. (7") *(K 16728)* **I'M BLOWIN' AWAY. / RUN LIKE A THIEF** –

—— In 1976, she duetted w/**GEOFF MULDAUR** on single 'WHEN YOU TOUCH ME THIS WAY' / SINCE I'VE BEEN WITH YOU BABE'.

—— Her touring band were **WILL McFARLANE** – guitar / **JEFF LABES** – keyboards / **DENNIS WHITTED** – drums / **FREEBO** – bass (as always) + guests **MICHAEL McDONALD + J.D. SOUTHER** on guest backing vocals

Apr 77. (lp/c) *(K/K4 56323) <BS 2990>* **SWEET FORGIVENESS** 25
– Sweet forgiveness / Gamblin' man / Two lives / Runaway / About to make me leave home / Three time loser / My opening farewell / Takin' my time / Home / Louise. *<(cd-iss. Oct01 on 'Warners-ESP'; 8122 78382-2)>*

May 77. (7") *<8382>* **RUNAWAY. / LOUISE** – 57

May 77. (7") *(K 16953)* **RUNAWAY. / HOME** –

Aug 77. (7") *<8430>* **THREE TIME LOSER. / TWO LIVES** –

Aug 77. (7") *(K 17003)* **THREE TIME LOSER. / LOUISE** –

Nov 77. (7") *<8485>* **GAMBLIN' MAN. / ABOUT TO MAKE ME LEAVE HOME** –

Oct 79. (lp/c) *(K 56706) <3369>* **THE GLOW** 30
– I thank you / Your good thing (is about to end) / Sleep's dark and silent gate / The glow / Bye bye baby / The boy can't help it / (I could have been your) Best old friend / You're gonna get what's coming / (Goin') Wild for you baby. *(cd-iss. Feb93; 7559 27403-2) <(cd re-iss. Mar02 on 'Warners-ESP'; 8122 78383-2)>*

Nov 79. (7") *<49116>* **YOU'RE GONNA GET WHAT'S COMING. / THE GLOW** – 73

Mar 80. (7") *<49185>* **(I COULD HAVE BEEN YOUR) BEST OLD FRIEND. / (GOIN') WILD FOR YOU BABY** –

—— In mid-80's, she released 'Asylum' 45; 'DON'T IT MAKE YOU WANNA DANCE'. At the same time she and J.D. SOUTHER issued 'ONCE IN A LIFETIME' / 'YOU'RE ONLY LONELY'.

—— next feat. **The BUMP BAND** incl. **IAN McLAGAN** – keyboards (ex-SMALL FACES) / **JOHNNY LEE SCHELL** – guitar / **RAY O'HARA** – bass / **RICKY FATAAR** – drums

Feb 82. (7") *<50022>* **CAN'T GET ENOUGH. / KEEP THIS HEART IN MIND** –

Feb 82. (lp/c) *(K/K4 56980) <BSK 3630>* **GREEN LIGHT** 38
– Keep this heart in mind / River of tears / Can't get enough / Me and the boys / I can't help myself / Willya wontcha / Let's keep it between us / Baby come back / Talk to me / Green light. *<(cd-iss. Mar02 on 'Warners-ESP'; 8122 78384-2)>*

Apr 82. (7") *<29992>* **ME AND THE BOYS. / RIVER OF TEARS** –

Apr 82. (7") *(K 17943)* **ME AND THE BOYS. / KEEP THIS HEART IN MIND** –

—— BONNIE semi-retired in 1982 to go through a period of drug rehabilitation and attend a form of alcoholics anonymous.

Sep 86. (lp/c/cd) *(925486-1/-4/-2) <25486>* **NINE LIVES** Aug 86
– No way to treat a lady / Runnin' back to me / Who but a fool / Crime of passion / All day, all night / Stand up to the night / Excited / Freezin' (for a little human love) / True love is hard to find / Angel. *<(cd re-iss. Oct01 on 'Warners-ESP'; 8122 78385-2)>*

Sep 86. (7") *<28615>* **NO WAY TO TREAT A LADY. / STAND UP TO THE NIGHT** –

Feb 87. (7") *<28450>* **CRIMES OF PASSION. / STAND UP TO THE NIGHT** –

—— In Oct '88, she teamed up with DON WAS of WAS (NOT WAS) on 'A&M' single 'BABY MINE'. Their vocalists **SWEAT PEA ATKINSON + SIR HARRY BOWENS** plus guests **DAVID CROSBY & GRAHAM NASH, FATAAR & SCHELL, KIM WILSON,** etc.

Capitol Capitol

Apr 89. (cd/c/lp) *(CD/TC+EST 2095) <91268>* **NICK OF TIME** 51 1
– Nick of time / A thing called love / Love letter / Cry on my shoulder / Real man / Nobody's girl / Have a heart / Too soon to tell / I will not be denied / I ain't gonna let you break my heart again / The road's my middle name. *(re-dist.Apr90)*

May 89. (c-s/7") *(TC+/CL 530) <44364>* **NICK OF TIME. / THE ROAD'S MY MIDDLE NAME** Aug89
(12"+=/cd-s+=) *(12/CD CL 530)* – I ain't gonna let you break my heart again. *(re-dist.Mar90) <re-iss. May90; hit US No.92>*

Mar 90. (7") *<44501>* **HAVE A HEART. / THE ROAD'S MY MIDDLE NAME** – 49

May 90. (7") *(CL 576)* **A THING CALLED LOVE. / NOBODY'S GIRL** –
(12"+=/cd-s+=) *(12/CD CL 576)* – The road's my middle name.

—— next featured **HIATT** plus **BRUCE HORNSBY + RICHARD THOMPSON**

Jul 91. (cd/c/lp) *(CD/TC+/EST 2145) <96111>* **LUCK OF THE DRAW** 38 2
– Something to talk about / Good man, good woman / I can't make you love me / Tangled and dark / Come to me / No business / One part of my lover / Not the only one / Papa come quick (Jody and Chico) / Slow ride / Luck of the draw / All at once.

Jul 91. (c-s/7") *(TC+/CL 619) <44724>* **SOMETHING TO TALK ABOUT. / ONE PART OF MY LOVER** 5
(12"+=) *(12CL 619)* – I ain't gonna let you break my heart again.
(cd-s++=) *(CDCL 619)* – Nick of time. *(re-iss. Feb92; same)*

Aug 91. (c-s/7") *(TC/+CL 627) <44764>* **NOT THE ONLY ONE. / COME TO ME** Mar92 34
(12"+=/cd-s+=) *(12/CD CL 627)* – Papa come quick (Jody and Chico).

Dec 91. (c-s/7") *(TC+/CL 639) <44729>* **I CAN'T MAKE YOU LOVE ME. / COME TO ME** 50 Nov91 18
(cd-s+=) *(CDCL 639)* – Tangled and dark.

Jun 92. (c-s/7") *(TC+/CL 666)* **GOOD MAN, GOOD WOMAN. / NICK OF TIME** –
(cd-s+=) *(CDCL 666)* – Thing called love / One part be my lover.

Apr 94. (c-s) *(TCCL 713) <58125>* **LOVE SNEAKIN' UP ON YOU / HELL TO PAY** 69 Mar94 19
(cd-s+=) *(CDCL 713)* – Nick of time / Baby be mine.

Apr 94. (cd/c) *(CD/TC EST 2227) <81427>* **LONGING IN THEIR HEARTS** 26 Mar94 1
– Love sneakin' up on you / Longing in their hearts / You / Cool, clear water / Circle dance / I sho do / Dimming of the day / Feeling of falling / Steal your heart away / Storm warning / Hell to pay / Shadow of doubt.

Jun 94. (c-s) *(TCCL 718)* **YOU / I CAN'T MAKE YOU LOVE ME** 31 –
(cd-s+=) *(CDCL 718)* – I ain't gonna let you break my heart again / All at once.
(cd-s) *(CDCLS 718)* – ('A'side) / This thing called love / Longing in their hearts / Good man, good woman.

Jul 94. (c-s) *<58195>* **YOU / FEELING OF FALLING** – 92

May 95. (c-s) *(74321 26624-4) <12795>* **YOU GOT IT / FEELING OF FALLING** Feb95 33
(cd-s+=) *(74321 26624-2)* – Circle dance.
(above single issued on 'Arista' & from movie 'Boys On The Side')

Nov 95. (c-s; BONNIE RAITT & BRYAN ADAMS) *(TCCL 763) <58500>* **ROCK STEADY (live) / COME TO ME (live)** 50 73
(cd-s+=) *(CDCL 763)* – Thing called love (live with BRUCE HORNSBY).

Nov 95. (cd/c) *(CD/TC EST 2274) <33702>* **ROAD TESTED (live)** 69 44
– Thing called love / Something to talk about / Never make your move too soon / Shake a little / Matters of the heart / Love me like a man / The Kokomo medley: Write me a few of your lines – Kokomo blues / My opening farewell / Dimming of the day / Longing in their hearts / Love sneakin' up on you / Burning down the house / I can't make you love me / I believe I'm in love / Rock steady / Angel from Montgomery.

Apr 96. (c-s) *(TCCL 771)* **BURNING DOWN THE HOUSE (live) / SHAKE A LITTLE (live)** –
(cd-s+=) *(CDCL 771)* – I can't make you love me (live) / Rock steady (live).

Apr 98. (cd) *<(8 56397-2)>* **FUNDAMENTAL** 17
– The fundamental things / Cure for love / Round & round / Spit of love /

Lover's will / Blue for no reason / Meet me half way / I'm on your side / Fearless love / I need love / One belief away.

Apr 02. (cd) <(5 31816-2)> **SILVER LINING** ☐ 13
– Fool's game / I can't help you now / Silver lining / Time of our lives / Gnawin' on it / Monkey business / Wherever you may be / Valley of pain / Hear me Lord / No gettin' over you / Back around / Wounded heart.

May 03. (cd) <(5 82113-2)> **THE BEST OF BONNIE RAITT** (compilation) 37 Sep03 47
– A thing called love / Nick of time / Nobody's girl *[UK-only]* / Love letter *[US-only]* / Have a heart *[US-only]* / Something to talk about / Not the only one / I can't make you love me / Love sneakin' up on you / You / Dimming of the day / Love me like a man (live) / Rock steady (live) *[UK-only]* / I believe I'm in love with you (live) *[UK-only]* / Spit of love / One belief away *[US-only]* / I can't help you now / Gnawing on it *[US-only]* / Silver lining / Time of our lives *[UK-only]* / Hear me Lord.

Jun 03. (cd-s) *(CDCL 846)* **SILVER LINING / BLUE FOR NO REASON / BURNING DOWN THE HOUSE (live)** ☐ ☐

– compilations, etc. –

Aug 90. (cd/c) *Warners; <(2-/4-26242)>* **THE BONNIE RAITT COLLECTION** ☐ Jun90 61
– Finest lovin' man / Give it up or let me go / Women be wise (live with SIPPIE WALLACE) / Under the falling sky / Love me like a man / Love has no pride / I feel the same / Guilty / Angel from Montgomery / What is success / My first night alone without you / Sugar mama / Louise / About to make me leave home / Runaway / The glow / (Goin') Wild for you baby / Willya wontcha / True love is hard to find / No way to treat a lady.

☐ RAKIM (see under ⇒ B, Eric & RAKIM)

RAMMSTEIN

Formed: Germany ... 1994 by former East German Olympic swimmer, TILL LINDEMANN, plus his 30-something long-time companions, OLIVER RIEDEL, RICHARD Z. KRUSPE, FLAKE LORENZ, PAUL LANDERS and CHRISTOPH SCHEIDER. Naming themselves after the German airbase at Ramstein (originally went by the name of ORGASM DEATH GIMMICK), the industrial shock metallers, like a fusion of LAIBACH, MINISTRY and fellow countrymen, EINSTURZENDE NEUBAUTEN, RAMMSTEIN had five hit singles in their home country. This was due to their OTT stage extravaganzas which featured TILL singing (in his native tongue) covered in a metallic coat of fire before he unveiled to show off his muscular, naked body complete with very large dildo strapped upside his leather belt!. Meanwhile, the naked OLIVER (bar his white socks), RICHARD (wearing a white wedding dress) and the rest of the bare-cheeked crew played their aggro-rock to a backdrop of Leni Riefenstahl's (Hitler's fave!) controversial film, 'Olympiad'. A German-only released debut album was finally upstaged by a second, 'SEHNSUCHT' (1997), which went on to surprisingly sell over half a million copies in the States. In the Autumn of '98, RAMMSTEIN were at the centre of some accusations of neo Nazi-ism when English tabloids branded them with that unfortunate tag. Around the same time, the single 'DU HAST' (actually a cover of Depeche Mode's 'STRIPPED') was given a British release and it looked as if these brassnecked technoid show-offs were going to eventually invade our shores. RAMMSTEIN's long-awaited studio follow-up album, 'MUTTER', was unleashed to the public in spring 2001, the broody ensemble were now on their way to becoming Germany's best export since SCHENKER and The SCORPIONS.

Album rating: HERZELEID (*5) / SEHNSUCHT (*7) / LIVE AUS BERLIN (*5) / MUTTER (*8)

TILL LINDEMANN (b. 4 Jan'63) – vocals / **RICHARD Z. KRUSPE** (b.24 Jun'67) – guitar / **PAUL LANDERS** (b. 9 Dec'64) – guitar / **OLIVER RIEDEL** (b.11 Apr'71) – bass / **FLAKE LORENZ** (b. 6 Nov'66) – keyboards / **CHRISTOPH DOOM SCHNEIDER** (b.11 May'66) – drums

Ils Inter. not iss.

Jul 95. (cd-s) **DU RIECHST SO GUT / WOLLT IHR DAS BETT IN FLAMEN SEHEN? / DU RIECHST SO GUT (scal remix)** – German –

Sep 95. (c) *(529160)* **HERZELEID** – German –
– Wollt ihr das bett in flamen sehen? / Der meister / Weisses fleisch / Asche zu asche / Seeman / Du riechst so gut / Das alte leid / Heirate mich / Herzeleid / Laichzeit / Rammstein. *<US cd-iss. Dec96 on 'Slash'; 529160-2>*

Jan 96. (cd-s) **SEEMAN / DER MEISTER / RAMMSTEIN IN THE HOUSE (timewriter remix)** – German –

London Slash

Apr 97. (cd-s) *(573665)* **ENGEL / SEHNSUCHT / RAMMSTEIN (Eskimos & Egypt radio mixes x3)** – German –

Jul 97. (cd-s) **DU HAST / BUCK DICH / DU HAST (Jacob Hellner remix) / DU HAST (Clawfinger remix)** – German –
(UK-iss.Nov98; LONCD 422)

Nov 97. (cd) *(537304-2) <539901>* **SEHNSUCHT** ☐ Jan98 45
– Sehnsucht / Engel / Tier / Bestrafe mich / Du hast / Buck dich / Spiel mit mir / Klavier / Alter Mann / Eifersucht / Kuss mich (fellfrosch) / Engel / Du hast. *(re-iss. Mar99 on 'XIII Bis'; 18795-2)*

Nov 97. (cd-s) **DAS MODELL / KOKAIN / ALTER MANN (special version) / (CD-Rom)** – German –

May 98. (cd-s) **DU RIECHST SO GUT '98** – German –
– Du riechst so gut (remixes; Faith No More / Gunter Schulz & Hiwatt Mashall / Sascha Knoietzko / Olaf Bruhn / Sascha Moser / Jacob Hellner & Marc Stagg / Gunter Schulz / video.

Aug 99. (c)<cd> *(<547590-2>)* **LIVE AUS BERLIN (live)** – ☐
– Spiel / mit mir / Bestrafe mich / Weisses fleisch / Sehnsucht / Asche zu asche / Wilder wein / Heirate mich / Du riechst so gut / Du hast / Buck dich / Engel / Rammstein / Laichzeit / Wollt ihr das bett in flammen sehen? / Seeman.

Universal Universal

Feb 01. (cd-s) *(587940)* **SONNE / ADIOS / SONNE (Clawfinger k.o. remix) / SONNE (Clawfinger t.k.o. remix)** – German –

Apr 01. (cd) <(549639-2)> **MUTTER** ☐ 77
– Mein herz brennt / Links 2 3 4 / Sonne / Ich will / Feuer frei! / Mutter / Spielurhr / Zwitter / Rein raus / Adios / Nebel. *(special cd May02 +=; 589367-2)* – Ich will (live) / Links 2 3 4 in arbelt (live) / Sonne (live) / Spleluhr (live).

May 01. (cd-s) *(587095)* **LINKS 2 3 4 / HALLELUJA / LINKS 2 3 4 (Clawfinger geradeaus remix) / LINKS 2 3 4 (Westbam technoelectro mix) / LINKS 2 3 4 (Westbam hard rock cafe mix)** – German –

Sep 01. (cd-s) *(563271)* **ICH WILL / ICH WILL (live: Berlin) / ICH WILL (Westbam mix) / ICH WILL (Paul Van Dyk mix) / PET SEMATARY (live) / ICH WILL (CD-Rom)** – German –

M.C.A. M.C.A.

May 02. (cd-s) *(MCSTD 40280)* **ICH WILL / LINKS 2 3 4 (Clawfinger Geradeaus remix) / DU HAST (remix by Jacob Hellner)** 30 –
(cd-s) *(MCSXD 40280)* – ('A'side) / Halleluja / Stripped (heavy mental mix by Charlie Clouser).

Nov 02. (cd-s) *(MCSTD 40302)* **FEUER FREI! (video) / (interview & history) / Buck dich / Du hast / (photo gallery 9 shots)** 35 –
(cd-s) *(MCSXD 40302)* – ('A'-Rammstein vs. Junkie XL remix) / Mutter / ('A'-remix 95) / (photo gallery & interview).

– compilations, etc. –

Mar 99. (6xcd-box) *Polygram; (569815)* **ORIGINAL SINGLES KOLEKTION** – German –
– Du riechst so gut / Seeman / Engel / Engel (fan edition) / Du hast / Das modell.

RAMONES

Formed: Forest Hills, New York, USA . . . August '74 as a trio by JOHNNY, JOEY and DEE DEE, who all took the working surname RAMONE (although they were brothers only in the loosest sense of the term). One of the prime movers (many would subsequently cite them as the first) in the emergent US punk scene, the band began a residency at the legendary NY club, CBGB's, TOMMY coming in on the drum stool in order to free JOEY up for suitably deranged vocal duties. In June '75, the band were dealt a slight setback when they failed an audition for RICK DERRINGER's 'Blue Sky' label in front of 20,000 fans at a JOHNNY WINTER concert, although later that year manager, Danny Fields, found up and coming new wave label, 'Sire' (run by Seymour Stein) considerably more receptive. Released around the same time as their pivotal (and highly influential) London Roundhouse gig, the band's eponymous summer '76 debut album presented a sound every bit as exhilaratingly juvenile and humorously warped as their leering, mop-topped scruffiness might suggest. Ripping out gloriusly dumb, two-minute buzz-saw classics on such perennial punk subjects as solvent abuse ('I WANNA SNIFF SOME GLUE'), girls (most of the album) and erm, chainsaws ('CHAIN SAW'), The RAMONES had invented themselves as larger than life, cartoon yob no-wavers well ahead of their time, their attitude alone copied by countless two-bit punk bands (and a few great ones) the length and breadth of the British Isles. Barely pausing for breath (or whatever it was these guys inhaled), the new yoik brudders followed up with 'LEAVE HOME' (1977), another strychnine-fuelled session of primitive but tuneful terrace chant anthems, RAMONES style; from this point onwards, the words 'Gabba Gabba Hey' would be forever carved in the stone of the punk lexicon. The album even managed a minor dent in the UK charts, a full scale assault led later that year with the brilliantly throwaway 'SHEENA IS A PUNK ROCKER'. The climax of the early RAMONES blitzkrieg came with 'ROCKET TO RUSSIA' (1977), the lads easing ever so slightly off the gas pedal and taking the credo of mangled, two minute surf-pop to its dayglo conclusion; the hilarious 'CRETIN HOP', 'ROCKAWAY BEACH' and 'TEENAGE LOBOTOMY' remain among the most definitive moments in the RAMONES' dog-eared catalogue. A rather disappointing Top 60 placing failed to do the record justice, although by this stage the band were beginning to make some inroads into the home market. Further evidence, if any was needed, that The RAMONES' chief writer was at the peak of his powers came with the blistering 'Chinese Rocks', a HEARTBREAKERS track co-penned by DEE DEE. With the departure of TOMMY (into production work) the following year, ex-VOID-OID MARC BELL was recruited in his place, rechristened, of course, MARKY RAMONE. Incredibly, the tried and tested formula (with a few notable exceptions, a guitar solo (!) on 'GO MENTAL' and a ballad, 'QUESTIONINGLY') continued to excite with 'ROAD TO RUIN' (1978), their first album to break into the UK Top 40 and the resting place of the legendary 'I WANNA BE SEDATED'. The riotous 'IT'S ALIVE' (1979) captured the RAMONES concert experience head-on, neatly wrapping up the first stage of the boys' career and providing a handy overview of their career to date. Every punk band coped with the scene's fragmentation in their own way, The RAMONES not so wisely choosing to indulge their love of classic 60's pop via the genre's guru, Phil Spector. The results were predictably confused, many longtime RAMONES headbangers balking at their UK Top 10 cover of The Ronettes' 'BABY I LOVE YOU'. Subsequent 80's efforts such as 'PLEASANT DREAMS' (1981) and 'SUBTERRANEAN JUNGLE' (1983) lacked the ragged glory of their earlier work although with the replacement of MARKY with RICHIE (aka RICHARD REINHARDT) in 1984, 'TOO TOUGH TO DIE' (1985) found the band sharpening their attack and presenting a united front against the hardcore pretenders of the day. They couldn't keep it up though, and the limitations of their art really began to bite deep on the bedraggled 'ANIMAL BOY' (1986) and 'HALFWAY TO SANITY' (1987). DEE DEE bailed out after 'BRAIN DRAIN' (1989), replacement C.J. effecting something of a rejuvenation on 'MONDO BIZARRO' (1992). The following year's 'ACID EATERS' saw the band pay tribute to the 60's sounds which had inspired them, while in turn, many of the younger bands who had actually been inspired by The RAMONES would soon be calling the shots at America's major labels. Yet despite this punk revival and the success of such acts as GREEN DAY and OFFSPRING, The RAMONES finally decided to call it a day in early 1996 following the release of the 'ADIOS AMIGOS' set and the accompanying tour. Fans of all ages were shocked to hear the news of JOEY's death (of lymphoma) in NY on the 15th of April, 2001. Barely a year later (5th June 2002), DEE DEE also passed away. • **Songwriters:** DEE DEE and group, except; DO YOU WANNA DANCE (Bobby Freeman) / SURFIN' BIRD (Trashmen) / BABY I LOVE YOU (Ronettes; Phil Spector) / NEEDLES AND PINS (Searchers) / STREET FIGHTIN' MAN (Rolling Stones) / TAKE IT AS IT COMES (Doors) / R.A.M.O.N.E.S. (Motorhead) / ANY WAY YOU WANT IT (Dave Clark) / SPIDER-MAN (Harris-Webster) / etc. In '77, DEE DEE co-wrote 'CHINESE ROCKS' for The HEARTBREAKERS. • **Trivia:** The RAMONES featured in the films 'Blank Generation' (1976) & 'Rock'n'roll High School' (Roger Corman 1979).

Album rating: RAMONES (*9) / LEAVE HOME (*8) / ROCKET TO RUSSIA (*8) / ROAD TO RUIN (*7) / IT'S ALIVE (*6) / END OF THE CENTURY (*7) / PLEASANT DREAMS (*6) / SUBTERRANEAN JUNGLE (*6) / TOO TOUGH TO DIE (*7) / ANIMAL BOY (*6) / HALFWAY TO SANITY (*4) / RAMONES MANIA compilation (*9) / BRAIN DRAIN (*4) / LOCO LIVE (*3) / MONDO BIZARRO (*3) / ACID EATERS (*3) / ADIOS AMIGOS (*5) / WE'RE OUTTA HERE (*5)

JOEY RAMONE (b. JEFFREY HYMAN, 19 May'51) – vocals (was drummer) / **JOHNNY RAMONE** (b. JOHN CUMMINGS, 8 Oct'51, Long Island, N.Y.) – guitar, vocals / **DEE DEE RAMONE** (b. DOUGLAS COLVIN, 18 Sep'52, Fort Lee, Virginia) – bass, vocals / **TOMMY RAMONE** (b. TOM ERDELYI, 29 Jan'49, Budapest, Hungary) – drums

Sire Sire

Jul 76. (lp) *(9103 253)* *<7520>* **RAMONES** [ ] May76 [ ]
– Blitzkrieg bop / Beat on the brat / Judy is a punk / I wanna be your boyfriend / Chain saw / Now I wanna sniff some glue / I don't wanna go down to the basement / Loudmouth / Havana affair / Listen to my heart / 53rd & 3rd / Let's dance / I don't wanna walk around with you / Today your love, tomorrow the world. *(re-iss. Sep78; SRK 6020) <(cd-iss. Oct99 on 'Rhino'; 7559 27421-2)> <(cd re-mast.Jun01 on 'Rhino'+=; 8122 74306-2)>* – (extra tracks).

Jul 76. (7") *(6078 601)* *<725>* **BLITZKRIEG BOP. / HAVANA AFFAIR** [ ] May76 [ ]

Oct 76. (7"m) *<734>* **I WANNA BE YOUR BOYFRIEND. / CALIFORNIA SUN (live) / I DON'T WANNA WALK AROUND WITH YOU (live)** [-] [ ]

Feb 77. (7"m) *(6078 603)* **I REMEMBER YOU. / CALIFORNIA SUN (live) / I DON'T WANNA WALK AROUND WITH YOU (live)** [ ] [-]

Mar 77. (lp) *(9103 254)* *<7528>* **LEAVE HOME** [45] Feb77 [ ]
– Glad to see you go / Gimme gimme shock treatment / I remember you / Oh oh I love her so / Babysitter * / Suzy is a headbanger / Pinhead / Now I wanna be a good boy / Swallow my pride / What's your game / California sun / Commando / You're gonna kill that girl / You should never have opened that door / California sun. *(re-iss. Jun77 'Carbona Not Glue' replaced *; other re-iss's same) (re-iss. Sep78; SRK 6031) (re-iss. Nov87 on 'Mau Mau'; MAU 602) <(cd re-iss. Oct99 on 'Rhino'; 7599 27422-2)> <(cd re-mast.Jun01 on 'Rhino'+=; 8122 74307-2)>* – (extra tracks).

May 77. (7"m,12"m) *(6078 606)* *<746>* **SHEENA IS A PUNK ROCKER. / COMMANDO / I DON'T CARE** [22] [81]

Jul 77. (7"m) *(6078 607)* *<738>* **SWALLOW MY PRIDE. / PINHEAD / LET'S DANCE (live)** [36] Mar77 [ ]

Nov 77. (7"m,12"m) *(6078 611)* **ROCKAWAY BEACH. / TEENAGE LOBOTOMY / BEAT ON THE BRAT** [ ] [–]

Nov 77. (7") *<1008>* **ROCKAWAY BEACH. / LOCKET LOVE** [–] [66]

Dec 77. (lp) *(9103 255)* *<6042>* **ROCKET TO RUSSIA** [60] Nov77 [49]
– Cretin hop / Rockaway beach / Here today, gone tomorrow / Locket love / I don't care / Sheena is a punk rocker / We're a happy family / Teenage lobotomy / Do you wanna dance? / I wanna be well / I can't give you anything / Ramona / Surfin' bird / Why is it always this way. *(re-iss. Sep78; SRK 6042) <(cd-iss. Oct99 on 'Rhino'; 7559 27424-2)> <(cd re-mast.Jun01 on 'Rhino'+=; 8122 74309-2)>* – (extra tracks).

Feb 78. (7") *<1017>* **DO YOU WANNA DANCE?. / BABYSITTER** [–] [86]

Mar 78. (7"m) *(6078 615)* **DO YOU WANNA DANCE? / IT'S A LONG WAY BACK TO GERMANY / CRETIN HOP** [ ] [–]

—— **MARKY RAMONE** (b. MARC BELL, 15 Jul'56) – drums (ex-RICHARD HELL & THE VOID-OIDS, ex-DUST) repl. TOMMY who continued producing others.

Sep 78. (7",7"yellow,12"yellow,12"red) *(SRE 1031)* *<1025>* **DON'T COME CLOSE. / I DON'T WANT YOU** [38] [ ]

Oct 78. (yellow-lp) *<(SRK 6063)>* **ROAD TO RUIN** [32] [ ]
– I just want to have something to do / I wanted everything / Don't come close / I don't want you / Needles and pins / I'm against it / I wanna be sedated / Go mental / Questioningly / She's the one / Bad brain / It's a long way back. *(cd-iss. Oct99; 7559 27426-2) <(cd re-mast.Jun01 on 'Rhino'+=; 8122 74308-2)>* – (extra tracks).

Nov 78. (7") *<1045>* **NEEDLES AND PINS. / I WANTED EVERYTHING** [–] [ ]

Jan 79. (7") *(SIR 4009)* **SHE'S THE ONE. / I WANNA BE SEDATED** [ ] [–]

May 79. (d-lp/c) *(SRK/SRC 26074)* **IT'S ALIVE (live)** [27] [–]
– Rockaway beach / Teenage lobotomy / Blitzkrieg bop / I wanna be well / Glad to see you go / Gimme gimme shock treatment / You're gonna kill that girl / I don't care / Sheena is a punk rocker / Havana affair / Commando / Here today, gone tomorrow / Surfin' bird / Cretin hop / Listen to my heart / California sun / I don't wanna walk around with you / Pinhead / Do you wanna dance? / Chain saw / Today your love, tomorrow the world / Now I wanna be a good boy / Judy is a punk / Suzy is a headbanger / Let's dance / Oh oh I love her so / Now I wanna sniff some glue / We're a happy family. *(cd-iss. Nov93 on 'Warners'; 7599 26069-2) (cd re-iss. Jan96; 9362 46045-2)*
(above album features TOMMY on drums)

Sep 79. (7") *<1051>* **DO YOU WANNA DANCE? / ROCK'N'ROLL HIGH SCHOOL** [–] [ ]

Sep 79. (7") *(SIR 4021)* **ROCK'N'ROLL HIGH SCHOOL. / SHEENA IS A PUNK ROCKER (live) / ROCKAWAY BEACH (live)** [67] [–]

Jan 80. (lp/c) *<(SRK/SRC 6077)>* **END OF THE CENTURY** [14] [44]
– Do you remember rock'n'roll radio? / I'm affected / Danny says / Chinese rock / The return of Jackie and Judy / Let's go / Baby I love you / I can't make it on time / This ain't Havana / Rock'n'roll high school / All the way / High risk insurance. *(re-iss. cd Mar94; 7599 27429-2) <(cd re-mast.Aug02 on 'Rhino'+=; 8122 78155-2)>* – (bonus tracks).

Jan 80. (7") *(SIR 4031)* *<49182>* **BABY, I LOVE YOU. / HIGH RISK INSURANCE** [8] [ ]

Apr 80. (7") *<49261>* **DO YOU REMEMBER ROCK'N'ROLL RADIO?. / LET'S GO** [–] [ ]

Apr 80. (7") *(SIR 4037)* **DO YOU REMEMBER ROCK'N'ROLL RADIO?. / I WANT YOU AROUND** [54] [–]

Jul 81. (7") *(SIR 4051)* *<49812>* **WE WANT THE AIRWAVES. / ALL'S QUIET ON THE EASTERN FRONT** [ ] [ ]

Jul 81. (lp/c) *<(SRK/SRC 3571)>* **PLEASANT DREAMS** [ ] [58]
– We want the airwaves / All's quiet on the Eastern front / The KKK took my baby away / Don't go / You sound like you're sick / It's not my place / She's a sensation / 7-11 / You didn't mean anything to me / Come on now / This business is killing me / Sitting in my room. *(re-iss. cd Mar94 & Jun00; 7599 23571-2) <(cd re-mast.Aug02 on 'Rhino'+=; 8122 78156-2)>* – (bonus tracks).

Oct 81. (7") *(SIR 4052)* **SHE'S A SENSATION. / ALL'S QUIET ON THE EASTERN FRONT** [ ] [–]

May 83. (lp/c) *(WX/+C 3800)* *<23800>* **SUBTERRANEAN JUNGLE** [ ] [83]
– Little bit o' soul / I need your love / Outsider / What'd ya do / Highest trails above / Somebody like me / Psycho therapy / Time has come today / My-my kind of girl / In the park / Time bomb / Everytime I eat vegetables It makes me think of you. *(re-iss. cd Mar94 & Jun00; 7599 23800-2) <(cd re-mast.Aug02 on 'Rhino'+=; 8122 78157-2)>* – (bonus tracks).

Jun 83. (7") *(W 9606)* **TIME HAS COME TODAY. / PSYCHO THERAPY** [ ] [–]
(12"+=) *(W 9606T)* – Baby I love you / Don't come close.

—— **RICHIE RAMONE** (b. RICHARD REINHARDT, aka BEAU) – drums (ex-VELVETEENS) repl. MARC

Beggars Banquet / Sire

Nov 84. (7") *<29107>* **HOWLING AT THE MOON (SHA LA LA). / WART HOG** [–] [ ]

Jan 85. (lp/c) *(BEGA/BEGC 59)* *<25187>* **TOO TOUGH TO DIE** [63] Oct84 [ ]
– Mama's boy / I'm not afraid of life / Too young to die / Durango 95 / Wart hog / Danger zone / Chasing the night / Howling at the Moon (sha-la-la) / Daytime dilemma (dangers of love) / Planet Earth 1988 / Human kind / Endless vacation / No go. *<(cd re-mast.Aug02 on 'Rhino'+=; 8122 78158-2)>* – (bonus tracks).

Jan 85. (7") *(BEG 128)* **HOWLING AT THE MOON (SHA-LA-LA). / CHASING THE NIGHT** [ ] [–]
(d7"+=)(12"pic-d+=) *(BEG 128D)(BEGTP 128)* – Smash you / Street fighting man.

Jun 85. (7") *(BEG 140)* **BONZO GOES TO BITBURG. / DAYTIME DILEMMA (DANGERS OF LOVE)** [ ] [–]
(12"+=) *(BEG 140T)* – Go home Annie.

Apr 86. (7") *(BEG 157)* **SOMETHING TO BELIEVE IN. / SOMEBODY PUT SOMETHING IN MY DRINK** [69] [–]
(12"+=) *(BEG 157T)* – (You) Can't say anything nice.

May 86. (lp/c) *(BEGA/BEGC 70)* *<25433>* **ANIMAL BOY** [38] [ ]
– Somebody put something in my drink / Animal boy / Love kills / Apeman hop / She belongs to me / Crummy stuff / My brain is hanging upside down (Bonzo goes to Bitburg) / She belongs to me / Mental hell / Eat that rat / Freak of nature / Hair of the dog / Something to believe in.

Jun 86. (7") *<28599>* **SOMETHING TO BELIEVE IN. / ANIMAL BOY** [–] [ ]

Jul 86. (7") *(BEG 167)* **CRUMMY STUFF. / SHE BELONGS TO ME** [ ] [–]
(12"+=,12"red+=) *(BEG 167 T)* – I don't want to live this life.

—— **MARKY RAMONE** – drums returned to repl. CLEM BURKE (ex-BLONDIE) who had repl. RICKY (above now with originals JOEY, DEE DEE and JOHNNY)

Sep 87. (7") *(BEG 198)* **A REAL COOL TIME. / INDIAN GIVER** [ ] [–]
(12"+=) *(BEG 198T)* – Life goes on.

Sep 87. (lp/c) *(BEGA/BEGC 89)* *<25641>* **HALFWAY TO SANITY** [78] [ ]
– I wanna live / Bop 'til you drop / Garden of serenity / Weasel face / Go lil' Camaro go / I know better now / Death of me / I lost my mind / A real cool time / I'm not Jesus / Bye bye baby / Worm man. *(cd-iss. Dec87 +=; BEGA 89CD)* – Indian giver / Life goes on.

Nov 87. (7"/12") *(BEG 201/+T)* **I WANNA LIVE. / MERRY CHRISTMAS (I DON'T WANT TO FIGHT TONIGHT)** [ ] [ ]

Chrysalis / Sire

Aug 89. (lp/c/cd) *(CHR/ZCHR/CCD 1725)* *<25905>* **BRAIN DRAIN** [75] Jun89 [ ]
– I believe in miracles / Zero zero UFO / Don't bust my chops / Punishment fits the crime / All screwed up / Palisades Park / Pet sematary / Learn to listen / Can't get you outta my mind / Ignorance is bliss / Come back, baby / Merry Christmas (I don't want to fight tonight).

Sep 89. (7") *(CHS 3423)* **PET SEMATARY. / ALL SCREWED UP** [ ] [–]
(12"+=) *(CHS12 3423)* – Zero zero UFO.

Sep 89. (7") *<22911>* **PET SEMATARY. / SHEENA IS A PUNK ROCKER** [–] [ ]

—— **C.J. RAMONE** (b. CHRISTOPHER JOSEPH WARD, 8 Oct'65, Long Island, N.Y.) – bass repl. DEE DEE who became rap artist DEE DEE KING

Oct 91. (cd/c/d-lp) *(CCD/ZCHR/CHR 1901)* **LIVE LOCO (live)** [ ] [ ]
– The good, the bad and the ugly / Django 95 / Teenage lobotomy / Psycho therapy / Blitzkrieg bop / Rock'n'roll radio / I believe in miracles / Gimme gimme shock treatment / Rock'n'roll high school / I wanna be sedated / The KKK took my baby away / I wanna live / Bonzo goes to Bitzburg / Too tough to die / Sheena is a punk rocker / Rockaway beach / Pet semetary / Don't bust my shape / Palisades park / Mama's boy / Animal

boy / Wart hog / Surfin' bird / Cretin hop / I don't wanna walk around with you / Today your love, tomorrow the world / Pinhead / Somebody put something in my drink / Beat on the brat / Judy is a punk / Chinese rocks / Love kills / Ignorance is bliss.

Radioactive Radioactive

Sep 92. (cd/c/lp) *<(RAR D/C 10615)>* **MONDO BIZARRO** [ ] [ ]
– Censorshit / The job that ate my brain / Poison heart / Anxiety / Strength to endure / It's gonna be alright / Take it as it comes / Main man / Tomorrow she goes away / I won't let it happen again / Cabbies on crack / Heidi is a heartache / Touring.

Chrysalis Radioactive

Nov 92. (c-s/7"yellow) *(TC+/CHS 3917)* **POISON HEART. / CENSORSHIT (live)** [69] [–]
(12"+=) *(12CHS 3917)* – Chinese rocks (live) / Sheena is a punk rocker (live).
(cd-s+=) *(CDCHS 3917)* – Rock and roll radio (live).

Dec 93. (cd/c/lp) *(CD/TC+/CHR 6052) <10913>* **ACID EATERS** [ ] [ ]
– Journey to the center of the mind / Substitute / Out of time / The shape of things to come / Somebody to love / When I was young / 7 and 7 is / My back pages / Can't seem to make you mine / Have you ever seen the rain / I can't control myself / Surf city.

— Album of covers; SUBSTITUTE (Who) / I CAN'T CONTROL MYSELF (Troggs) / SURF CITY (Jan & Dean) / OUT OF TIME (Rolling Stones) / THE SHAPE OF THINGS TO COME (Headboys) / etc.

Jun 95. (cd/c/lp) *(CD/TC+/CHR 6104) <11273>* **ADIOS AMIGOS** [62] [ ]
– I don't want to grow up / I'm makin' monsters for my friends / It's not for me to know / The crusher / Life's a gas / Take the pain away / I love you / Cretin family / Have a nice day / Scattergun / Got a lot to say / She talks to rainbows / Born to die in Berlin.

— split after tour early the following year, although they had a brief reunion on the 6th August, 1996 at The Palace, Los Angeles

Eagle Radioactive

Nov 97. (cd) *(EAGCD 010) <11555>* **WE'RE OUTTA HERE!** (their last show) [ ] [ ]
– Durango 95 / Teenage lobotomy / Psycho therapy / Blitzkrieg bop / Do you remember rock and roll radio / I believe in miracles / Gimme gimme shock treatment / Rock'n'roll high school / I wanna be sedated / Spider-man / The K.K.K. took my baby away / I just want to have something to do / Commando / Sheena is a punk rocker / Rockaway beach / Pet sematary / The crusher / Love kills / Do you wanna dance / Someone put something in my drink / I don't want you / Wart hog / Cretin hop / R.A.M.O.N.E.S. / Today your love, tomorrow the world / Pinhead / 53rd & 3rd / Listen to your heart / We're a happy family / Chinese rock / Beat on the brat / Any way you want it.

— after what we think is their final release, MARKY RAMONE went solo

– compilations, etc. –

Aug 80. (7") *R.S.O.; (RSO 70) / Sire; <2090 512>* **I WANNA BE SEDATED. / THE RETURN OF JACKIE AND JUDY** [ ] [ ]

— (above from Various Artists Film Soundtrack 'Rock'n'roll High School' also incl. 'Medley: Blitzkrieg bop – Teenage lobotomy – California sun – Pinhead – She's the one')

Nov 80. (7"ep) *Sire; (SREP 1)* **MELTDOWN WITH THE RAMONES** [ ] [ ]
– I just wanna have something to do / Questioningly / I wanna be your boyfriend / Here today, gone tomorrow.

Jun 88. (7") *Sire; <27663>* **I WANNA BE SEDATED. / (part 2)** [–] [ ]

Jun 88. (d-lp/c/cd) *Sire; (925709-1/-4/-2) <25709>* **RAMONES MANIA** [ ] [–]
– I wanna be sedated / Teenage lobotomy / Do you remember rock'n'roll radio? / Gimme gimme shock treatment / Beat on the brat / Sheena is a punk rocker / I wanna live / Pinhead / Blitzkrieg bop / Cretin hop / Rockaway beach / Commando / I wanna be your boyfriend / Mama's boy / Bop 'til you drop / We're a happy family / Bonzo goes to Bitburg / The outsider / Psycho therapy / Wart hog / Animal boy / Needles and pins / Howlin' at the Moon / Somebody put something in my drink / We want the airwaves / Chinese rocks / I just want to have something to do / The KKK took my baby away / Indian giver / Rock'n'roll high school.

Sep 90. (cd/c/d-lp) *Sire; (7599 26220-2/-4/-1)* **ALL THE STUFF (AND MORE)** (demos 1976-77, etc) [ ] [–]

May 99. (d-cd+book) *Megaworld; (MEGBK 02)* **BLITZKREIG BOP** [ ] [–]

Aug 99. (d-cd) *Sire; <(8122 7581-2)>* **HEY HO LET'S GO – THE RAMONES ANTHOLOGY** [ ] [ ]

Aug 00. (cd) *Burning Airlines; <(PILOT 79)>* **YOU DON'T COME CLOSE** [ ] [ ]

May 01. (d-cd) *Sire; <(8122 73557-2)>* **HEY HO LET'S GO! (THE RAMONES ANTHOLOGY)** [74] [ ]

Aug 01. (cd) *E.M.I.; (534696-2)* **MASTERS OF ROCK – THE VERY BEST OF THE RAMONES** [ ] [–]

Sep 01. (7"/cd-s) *Musical Tragedies; (EFA 12615-7/-2)* **JUDY IS A PUNK. / (other track by New York Dolls)** [ ] [–]

Apr 02. (cd) *EMI Gold; (538472-2)* **THE BEST OF THE CHRYSALIS YEARS** [ ] [–]

Aug 02. (3xcd-box) *E.M.I.; (541080-2)* **THE CHRYSALIS YEARS** [ ] [–]

Nov 02. (cd) *W.S.M.; (8122 76101-2)* **LOUD FAST RAMONES – THEIR TOUGHEST HITS** [ ] [–]

— JOEY also on "HOLLY & JOEY" 7" – 1982 'I Got You Babe' on 'Virgin'.

— In August '88, JOHNNY teamed up with DEBBIE HARRY for 7" – 'Go Lil Camara Go'. In 1994, JOEY RAMONE featured (+ on cover sleeve) of SIBLING RIVALRY's 'In A Family Way' EP for 'Alternative Tentacles'.

JOEY RAMONE

with a plethora of session players

Sanctuary Sanctuary

Dec 01. (cd-s) *<84541>* **MERRY CHRISTMAS (I DON'T WANT TO FIGHT TONIGHT)** [–] [ ]

Feb 02. (cd) *(SANC 108CD) <84542>* **DON'T WORRY ABOUT ME** [ ] [ ]
– What a wonderful world / Stop thinking about it / Mr. Punchy / Maria Bartiromo / Spirit in my house / Venting (it's a different world today) / Like a drug I never did before / Searching for something / I got knocked down (but I'll get up) / 1969 / Don't worry about me.

Dec 02. (cd-ep) *<84589>* **CHRISTMAS SPIRIT . . . IN MY HOUSE** [–] [ ]
– Christmas (baby please come home) / Merry Christmas (I don't want to fight tonight) / Spirit in my house / Don't worry about me / What a wonderful world.

DEE DEE RAMONE

writes with **REY**

World Dom. World Dom.

Jun 94. (cd/lp) *<(1571757-2/-1)>* **I HATE FREAKS LIKE YOU** [ ] [ ]
– I'm making monsters for my friends / Don't look in my window / Chinese bitch / It's not for me to know / Runaway / All's quiet on the Eastern Front / I hate it / Life is like a little smart Alleck / I hate creeps like you / Trust me / Curse on me / I'm seeing strawberry's again / Lass mich in Fuhe / I'm making monsters for my friends.

Other People's Music Other People's Music

Sep 97. (cd) *<(OPM 2118CD)>* **ZONKED** [ ] [ ]
– I'm zonked, los hombres / Fix yourself up / I am seeing UFO's / Get off of the scene / Never never again / Bad horoscope / It's so bizarre / Get out of my room / Someone who don't fit in / Victim of society / My Chico / Disguises / Why is everybody always against Germany.

Blackout Blackout

Oct 97. (7") *(BLK 5008E7)* **I AM SEEING UFO'S. / BAD HOROSCOPE** [ ] [–]

Nov 97. (cd) *(BLK 5008ECD)* **AIN'T IT FUN** [ ] [ ]
– I'm zonked los hombres / Fix yourself up / I am seeing UFO's / Get off the scene / Never again / Bad horoscope / It's so bizarre / Get out of the room / Someone who doesn't fit in / Victim of society / My Chico / Disguises / Why is everyone always against Germany / Please kill me.

Corazong not iss.

Mar 00. (cd) *(2000 006)* **HOP AROUND** [ ] [–]
– I don't wanna die in the basement / Mental patient / Now I wanna be sedated / Rock & roll vacation in L.A. / Get out of this house / 38th & 8th / Nothin' / Hop around / What about me? / I saw a skull instead of my head / I wanna you / Master plan / Born to lose / Hurtin' kind / I'm horrible. *(re-iss. Jul02; same)*

Eagle Conspiracy

Sep 00. (cd) *(EAGCD 156) <10>* **GREATEST AND LATEST** [ ] [ ]
– Blitzkrieg bop / Timebomb / Sheena is a punk rocker / Shaking all over / I wanna be sedated / Cretin hop / Teenage lobotomy / Gimme gimme shock treatment / Motorbikin' / Come on now / Cathy's clown / Pinhead / Rockaway beach / Fix yourself up / Sidewalk surfin' / Beat on the brat. *(re-iss. Mar02; same)*

RANCID

Formed: Albany, California, USA . . . 1987 as tattooed ska-punk act, OPERATION IVY, by TIM 'LINT' ARMSTRONG and MATT FREEMAN (alias MATT McCALL), who also numbered JESSE MICHAELS and DAVE MELLO in their ranks. This quartet would become a cult act of the late 80's, although they only managed to squeeze out one album, 'ENERGY', in 1989. ARMSTRONG and FREEMAN continued to work with various outfits, including MDC, a band that they often supported at the infamous Gilman Street Club in Berkeley. In 1990, the pair were joined by BRETT REED and thus RANCID were spawned. After the release of a self-financed EP, 'I'M NOT THE ONLY ONE' in '92, the trio inked a deal with BRETT GUREWITZ's 'Epitaph' records. They subsequently added second guitarist LARS FREDERIKSON, who was to swell the ranks following the release of their well-received eponymous debut in 1993. With the early 90's resurgence of punk and youthful peers such as OFFSPRING and GREEN DAY making commercial headway, RANCID were well placed to capitalise on their particular brand of gut-level hardcore. Following the release of a 1994 EP, 'RADIO RADIO RADIO' on FAT MIKE's (NOFX) independent 'Fat Wreck Chords' label, the band cracked the elusive US Top 100 with their second album, 'LET'S GO' (1994). The following year, RANCID scored with an even higher placed album, ' . . . AND OUT COME THE WOLVES', a Top 60 success. In 1998, like The CLASH over 20 years before them, RANCID adopted some roots reggae and ska into their umpteenth set, 'LIFE WON'T WAIT' (Jamaican, BUJU BANTON and MIGHTY MIGHTY BOSSTONES' mainman DICKY BARRETT guested). The results surprisingly worked as the album went Top 40 in America and Britain. In summer 2000, the mighty RANCID delivered another eponymous album which hit the UK Top 75. • **Trivia:** ARMSTRONG also set up his own label, 'Hellcat', his best signings being DROPKICK MURPHYS, The PIETASTERS, GADJITS, HEPCAT and US BOMBS.

Album rating: Operation Ivy: ENERGY (*6) / Rancid: RANCID (*7) / LET'S GO (*6) / . . .AND OUT COME THE WOLVES (*8) / LIFE WON'T WAIT (*7) / RANCID (*6) / INDESTRUCTIBLE (*7)

OPERATION IVY

TIM ARMSTRONG – vocals, guitar / **MATT FREEMAN** (as MATT McCALL) – bass / **JESSE MICHAELS** – vocals / **DAVE MELLO** – drums

not iss. — Lookout!

Jan 88. (7"ep) *<LOOKOUT 3>* **HECTIC EP** [–] [ ]
– Junkies running dry / Here we go again / Hoboken / Yellin' in my ear / Sleep long / Healthy body.

May 89. (lp) *<LOOKOUT 10>* **ENERGY** [–] [ ]
– Knowledge / Sound system / Jaded / Take warning / The crowd / Bombshell / Unity / Vulnerability / Bankshot / One of these days / Gonna find you / Bad town / Smiling / Caution / Freeze up / Artificial life / Room without a window / Big city / Missionary. *(UK-iss.Oct94 lp/c/cd+=; LOOKOUT 10/+MC/CD)* – HECTIC EP + / Officer / I got no.

— they split in May '89, DAVE joined SCHLONG while JESSE became a Buddhist monk! but ten years later formed COMMON RIDER with members from SQUIRTGUN. ARMSTRONG and FREEMAN worked with the DANCE HALL CRASHERS and DOWNFALL, while both joined MDC, FREEMAN more so; he featured on the group's 1990 set, 'Hey Cop, If I Had A face Like Yours'.

RANCID

ARMSTRONG + FREEMAN added **BRETT REED** – drums (ex-SMOG)

not iss. — Lookout!

Jan 02. (7"ep) *<LOOK 059>* **RANCID** [–] [ ]
– I'm not the only one / Battering ram / The sentence / Media controller / Idle hands. *(UK-iss.Dec94 & Nov00; same as US)*

Epitaph — Epitaph

May 93. (cd/c/lp) *<(E 86428-2/-4/-1)>* **RANCID** [ ] [ ]
– Adina / Hyena / Detroit / Rats in the hallway / Another night / Animosity / Otta my mind / Whirlwind / Rejected / Injury / The bottle / Trenches / Holiday sunrise / Unwritten rules / Get out of my way / (untitled).

— added **LARS FREDERIKSON** – guitar (ex-UK SUBS)

Apr 94. (7"ep) *<FAT 509>* **RADIO, RADIO, RADIO EP** [ ] [ ]
– Radio / Dope sick girl / Just a feeling / Someone gunna die.
(above on 'Fat Wreck Chords'

Jan 95. (cd/c/d-10"lp) *<(E 86434-2/-4/-1)>* **LET'S GO** [ ] Jun94 [97]
– Nihilism / Radio / Sidekick / Salvation / Tenderloin / Let's go / As one / Burn / Ballad of Jimmy & Johnny / Gunshot / I am the one / Gave it away / Ghetto box / Harry Bridges / Black and blue / St. Mary / Dope sick girl / International cover-up / Solidarity / Midnight / Motorcycle ride / Name / 7 years down.

Feb 95. (cd-s) *<8645-2>* **ROOTS RADICALS / I WANNA RIOT** [–] [ ]

Aug 95. (cd/c/lp) *<(E 86444-2/-4/-1)>* **. . .AND OUT COME THE WOLVES** [55] [45]
– Maxwell murder / 11th hour / Roots radicals / Time bomb / Olympia Wa. / Lock, step and gone / Junkie man / Listed M.I.A. / Ruby Soho / Daly city train / The way I feel / Avenues and alleyways / As wicked / You don't care nothin' / Wars end / Disorder and disarray / Old friend / She's automatic / Journey to the end of the East Bay.

Oct 95. (7"ep/cd-ep) *(WOOS 8 S/CDS)* **TIME BOMB / THE WAR'S END / BLAST 'EM** [56] [–]
(above issued on 'Out Of Step')

May 96. (7"ep/cd-ep) *(86464-7/-2)* **RUBY SOHO. / THAT'S ENTERTAINMENT / DISORDER AND DISARRAY** [ ] [–]

Jun 98. (d-cd/d-c/d-lp) *(6497-2/-4/-1) <86497>* **LIFE WON'T WAIT** [32] [35]
– Intro / Bloodclot / Black lung / Life won't wait / New dress / Warsaw / Hooligan / Crane fist / Leicester Square / Backslide / Who would've thought / Cas culture and violence / Wolf / 1998 / Lady Liberty / Wrongful suspicion / Turntable / Something in the world today / Corazon de oro / Coppers.

Aug 98. (7"ep/cd-ep) *(1005-7/-2)* **BLOODCLOT. / ENDRINE / STOP** [ ] [ ]

Dec 98. (7"ep/cd-ep) *(1009-7/-2)* **HOOLIGANS / CASH, CULTURE AND VIOLENCE (bass drop mix) / THINGS TO COME (dance hall mix)** [ ] [ ]

Jul 00. (cd/c/lp) *(0427-2/-4/-1) <80427>* **RANCID** [68] [68]
– Don Giovanni / Disgruntled / It's quite alright / Let me go / I am forever / Poison / Loki / Blackhawk down / Rwanda / Corruption / Antennas / Rattlesnake / Not to regret / Radio Havana / Axiom / Black derby jacket / Meteor of war / Dead bodies / Fuck you / Young Al Capone / Golden gate fields / Churchill Downs.

Nov 00. (7"/cd-s) *(1040-7/-2)* **LET ME GO. / BEN ZANOTTO / DEAD AND GONE** [ ] [–]

Warners — Warners

Aug 03. (cd) *<(9362 48529-2)>* **INDESTRUCTIBLE** [29] [15]
– Indestructible / Fall back down / Red hot moon / David Courtney / Start now / Out of control / Django / Arrested in Shanghai / Travis Bickle / Memphis / Spirit of '87 / Ghost band / Tropical London / Roadblock / Born frustrated / Back up against the wall / Ivory Coast / Stand your ground / Otherside. *(red-d-lp+=; 9362 48529-1)* – Killing zone.

Sep 03. (7") *(W 618)* **FALL BACK DOWN. / KILLING ZONE** [42] [–]
(cd-s+=) *(W 618CD)* – Stranded.

– compilations, others, etc. –

Mar 02. (lp/cd; split w/ NOFX) *B.Y.O.; <(BYO 079/+CD)>* **BYO SPLIT SERIES VOL.3** [75] [ ]
– (tracks by NOFX) / (covers of NOFX by RANCID)

☐ RAPEMAN (see under ⇒ BIG BLACK)

☐ RAPHAELS (see under ⇒ BIG COUNTRY)

RAPTURE

Formed: New York City, New York, USA . . . early 1998 by VITO ROCCOFORTE and LUKE JENNER. This experimental punk group released their debut album, 'MIRROR', in 1999 – think TELEVION, TALKING HEADS and PiL. The band's blistering three-minute sonic assaults may not have been to everyone's taste but they could not fail to grab your attention. In 2001 the group recruited bass player MATT SAFER and released the mini-set, 'OUT OF THE RACES AND ONTO THE TRACKS' (for 'Sub Pop'), which had critics championing them as leaders of the post-New Wave revival. The following year the band became a four-piece with the inclusion of multi-instrumentalist, GABRIEL ANDRUZZI, and released their finest collection of songs on the 'HOUSE OF JEALOUS LOVERS' EP. The RAPTURE finally delivered the album 'ECHOES' in 2003, which displayed their funk-punk rock minimalism even further. Not as brilliant as the hype suggested, the group still managed to maintain a spiritual GANG OF FOUR appeal and tracks such as 'OPEN UP YOUR HEART' and 'THE COMING OF SPRING' drew those TALKING HEADS comparisons in even closer. Although the album was spiky and often relentlessly abrasive, final track 'INFATUATION' was a little bit of a disappointment, and on some of the album's weaker moments you could almost hear them try too hard, sometimes lost in the syncopation. This said, 'ECHOES' was a great reminder that the post-punk vehicle had still got enough fuel in it to keep running for a good decade yet. • **Covered:** DUMB WAITERS (Psychedelic Furs).

Album rating: MIRROR mini (*5) / OUT OF THE RACES AND ONTO THE TRACKS mini (*5) / ECHOES (*6)

LUKE JENNER – vocals, guitar / **VITO ROCCOFORTE** – drums / + bassist

not iss. | Gold Standard

1998. (7") *<GSL 36>* **THE CHAIR THAT SQUEAKS. / DUMB WAITERS** [–] [ ]
(UK-iss.Jul01 & Jul02; same as US)

Gravity | Gravity

Jan 99. (m-lp/m-cd) *<(GRAVITY 36/+CD)>* **MIRROR** [ ] [ ]
– In finite clock! / Notes . . . / Olio / Frames frames frames / Mirror / Alienation / Dusk at Maureen's / Kid 606 in love with the underground.

—— **MATT SAFER** – bass; repl. original

Sub Pop | Sub Pop

Jun 01. (10"white-m-lp/m-cd) *<(SP/+CD 505)>* **OUT OF THE RACES AND ONTO THE TRACKS** [ ] May01 [ ]
– Out of the races and onto the tracks / Modern romance / Caravan / The jam / The pop song / Confrontation. *(re-iss. Oct02; same)*

Output | not iss.

Apr 02. (12") *(OPRDFA 001)* **HOUSE OF JEALOUS LOVERS. / HOUSE OF JEALOUS LOVERS (Morgan Geist remix) / SILENT MORNING** [ ] [–]
(re-iss. Mar03; same)

Jul 02. (12") *(OPRDFA 003)* **OLIO. / (mixes)** [ ] [–]

—— added **GABRIEL ANDRUZZI** – multi

Aug 03. (12") *(OPRDFA 005)* **HOUSE OF JEALOUS LOVERS (Maurice Fulton remix). / KILLING (original)** [ ] [–]

Mercury | Universal

Aug 03. (7") *(9811125)* **HOUSE OF JEALOUS LOVERS. / ALABAMA SUNSHINE** [27] [ ]
(cd-s+=) *(9810767)* – ('A'-Maurice Fulton mix).
(cd-s) *(9810768)* – ('A'side) / ('A'-Tom Middleton remix) / Killing (ends remix). *(re-iss. Sep03 on 'Output'+=; OPRDFA 006)*

Sep 03. (cd) *(9865447)* *<128302>* **ECHOES** [32] [ ]
– Olio / Heaven / Open up your heart / I need your love / The coming of spring / House of jealous lovers / Echoes / Killing / Sister savior / Love is all / Infatuation. *(lp-iss.on 'Output'; OPRDFA 007)*

Dec 03. (7") *(9814183)* **SISTER SAVIOUR. / ECHOES (DFA remix)** [51] [ ]
(cd-s) *(9814181)* – ('A'-Blackstrobe remix) / ('A'-DFA vocal remix).
(12"/12") *(OPRDFA 008/+X)* – ('A'mixes).

☐ RATS (see under ⇒ RONSON, Mick)

Chris REA

Born: 4 Mar'51, Middlesbrough, England . . . from Irish/Italian parentage. Picking up the guitar in the early 70's, by 1973 REA had joined MAGDALENE, taking the place of DAVID COVERDALE who had departed for WHITESNAKE. The following year, the singer released a debut one-off solo single for 'Magnet', 'SO MUCH LOVE'. MAGDALENE, meanwhile, changed their name to The BEAUTIFUL LOSERS in 1975 and although they won a Melody Maker 'Best Newcomer Award', they subsequently split in '77. As well as guesting on HANK MARVIN's 'Guitar Syndicate' album, REA struck out on a long and fairly fruitful solo career, signing a new long-term deal with 'Magnet'. Almost instant success came the following year with 'FOOL IF YOU THINK IT'S OVER', REA's gravel voiced AOR appeal sitting well within the American market where the single almost went Top 10. Later that Autumn, the track was re-promoted in the UK and REA scored his first domestic hit, narrowly scraping into the Top 30. Amid this early excitement, GUS DUDGEON produced the singer/songwriter's debut album, 'WHATEVER HAPPENED TO BENNY SANTINI?' (1978), the record's title referring to the, frankly ridiculous name his label wanted him to adopt. This bluff northerner was assuredly his own man, however, soon building up a cult following and consistently nudging into the lower regions of the chart with early 80's albums like 'TENNIS' (1980), 'CHRIS REA' (1982) and 'WATER SIGN' (1983). Comparisons were often made with MARK KNOPFLER and indeed, they shared a certain slow buring charm as well as similar audiences. By the release of 'SHAMROCK DIARIES' (1985), word was out, and REA finally began reaping significant commercial rewards with a Top 20 album (by this point, the singer had already achieved superstar status in Germany). Released in Spring '86, 'ON THE BEACH' was a great summer album, the sun-kissed jazzy noodling of the title track perfect driving music. The brassy 'LET'S DANCE' gave REA his biggest hit UK hit single to date late the following year (No.12), while the accompanying 'DANCING WITH STRANGERS' (1987) opus made No.2 in the album charts, REA further warming the cockles of many a housewife's heart with his perennial yuletide chestnut, 'DRIVING HOME FOR CHRISTMAS' (originally released the previous year). 1988 brought the first chapter of REA's career to some kind of conclusion, the singer signing a new deal with 'W.E.A.' and releasing a summation of the cream of his work to date, 'NEW LIGHT THROUGH OLD WINDOWS'. With 'THE ROAD TO HELL' (1989), REA's muse took him down to the proverbial crossroads where he presumably signed his musical soul away for a darkly intoxicating No.1 album of AOR spook-blues. His biggest selling album to date, REA was now in the major league alongside ERIC CLAPTON, PHIL COLLINS etc., 'AUBERGE' (1991) giving REA his second chart topping set. In the 90's the singer has continued to be a regular chart fixture with the likes of 'GOD'S GREAT BANANA SKIN' (1992) and 'ESPRESSO LOGIC' (1993). REA evoked some of his latin heritage with 1996's 'LA PASSIONE' soundtrack while 'THE BLUE CAFE' (1998) was a thoughtful set of blues-based, slide inflected ruminations anchored to contemporary rhythms. The fact that his classic 'ON THE BEACH' had been (surprisingly successfully) transformed into a superclub anthem no doubt at least partly inspired 'KING OF THE BEACH' (2000). This found REA in suitably mellow mood, sunning his muse in the caribbean to create a work of breezy escapism. Again, the dance world picked up on the vibe, remixing 'ALL SUMMER LONG' into an Ibiza classic. Around this time, he truly took the road to (comedy) hell, lining up with the other masochistic hopefuls to be abused by Vic & Bob on BBC 2's brilliant 'Shooting Stars'. The beach was probably the subject furthest from REA's mind when he was recording 'DANCING DOWN THE STONY ROAD' (2002), as cathartic an album as he's ever made. After a battle with cancer, the singer returned to his first love with a passionate vengeance, singing or rather, undergoing, the blues like a man possessed, shouting down his demons and emerging emotionally victorious on the other side. • **Trivia:** He guested on CATHERINE HOWE's 1978 album, 'Truth Of The Matter'. In 1982, ELKIE BROOKS scored a UK Top 20 hit with her interpretation of 'FOOL'.

Album rating: WHATEVER HAPPENED TO BENNY SANTINI? (*6) / DELTICS (*5) / TENNIS (*4) / CHRIS REA (*4) / WATER SIGN (*4) / WIRED TO THE MOON (*5) / SHAMROCK DIARIES (*5) / ON THE BEACH (*7) / DANCING WITH STRANGERS (*7) / NEW LIGHT THROUGH OLD WINDOWS compilation (*7) / THE ROAD TO HELL (*8) / AUBERGE (*6) / GOD'S GREAT BANANA SKIN (*5) / ESPRESSO LOGIC (*5) / THE VERY BEST OF CHRIS REA compilation (*7) / LA PASSIONE soundtrack (*3) / THE BLUE CAFE (*4) / KING OF THE BEACH (*6) / THE ROAD TO HELL VOL.2 (*5) / THE VERY BEST OF CHRIS REA compilation (*7) / DANCING DOWN THE STONY ROAD (*6)

CHRIS REA – vocals, guitar (with various session people)

Magnet — U.A.

May 74. (7") *(MAG 10)* **SO MUCH LOVE. / BORN TO LOSE** — [ ] [–]

— Returned to MAGDALENE who changed their name to The BEAUTIFUL LOSERS in 1975. They won 'Melody Maker's Best Newcomers award', but in 1977, they disbanded. REA returned to solo work, re-signing longer term contract for 'Magnet'.

Apr 78. (7") *(MAG 111) <1198>* **FOOL (IF YOU THINK IT'S OVER). / MIDNIGHT LOVE** — [ ] Jun78 [12]
(re-dist.UK Sep78, hit No.30)

Jun 78. (lp/c) *(MAG/TC-MAG 5021) <879>* **WHATEVER HAPPENED TO BENNY SANTINI?** — [ ] [49]
– Whatever happened to Benny Santini? / he closer you get / Because of you / Dancing with Charlie / Bows and bangles / Fool (if you think it's over) / Three angels / Just one of these days / Standing in your doorway / Fires of Spring. *(re-iss. Jun83; MAGL 5021) (cd-iss. 1983; CDMAG 5021) (re-iss. Feb88 on 'WEA' lp/c; WX 184/+C) (cd re-iss. Feb88 on 'WEA'; 242368-2) (re-iss. Mar93 on 'Pickwick';) (re-iss. Sep95 on 'Warners')*

Jun 78. (7",7"red) *(MAG 121) <1252>* **WHATEVER HAPPENED TO BENNY SANTINI? / THREE ANGELS** — [ ] Nov78 [71]

Feb 79. (lp/c) *(MG/TC-MAGL 5028) <UA 959>* **DELTICS** — [54] [ ]
– Twisted wheel / The things lovers should do / Dance (don't think) / Raincoat and a rose / Cenotaph – Letter from Amsterdam / Deltics / Diamonds / She gave it away / Don't want your best friend / Diamonds / No qualifications / Seabird. *(re-iss. +cd. Feb88 on 'WEA')*

Mar 79. (7"/12") *(MAG/+12 144) <1285>* **DIAMONDS. / CLEVELAND CALLING** — [44] [44]

Jun 79. (7") *(MAG 151)* **RAINCOAT AND A ROSE. / NO QUALIFICATIONS** — [ ] [ ]

Magnet — Columbia

Feb 80. (7") *(MAG 163)* **TENNIS. / IF YOU REALLY LOVE ME** — [ ] [ ]

Feb 80. (lp/c) *(MAGL/TC-MAG 5032) <36435>* **TENNIS** — [60] [ ]
– Tennis / Since I don't see you anymore / Dancing girls / No work today / Everytime I see you smile / For ever and ever / Good news / Friends across the water / Only with you / Stick it / Tennis.

May 80. (7") *(MAG 176)* **DANCING GIRLS. / FRIENDS ACROSS THE WATER** — [ ] [ ]

Jan 82. (7") *(MAG 215) <02727>* **LOVING YOU. / LET ME BE THE ONE** — [65] Mar88 [88]

Mar 82. (lp/c) *(MAGL/ZC-MAGL 5040) <37664>* **CHRIS REA** — [52] [ ]
– Loving you / If you choose to go / Guitar Street / Do you still dream / Every beat of my heart / Goodbye little Colombus / One sweet tender touch / Do it for love / Just want to be with you / Runaway / When you know your love has died. *(re-iss. Sep87 on 'WEA' lp/c; WX 187/+C) (cd-iss. Feb88; 242371-2)*

May 82. (7") *(MAG 225)* **EVERY BEAT OF MY HEART. / DON'T LOOK BACK** — [ ] [ ]

Jul 82. (7") *(MAG 233)* **LET IT LOOSE. / SIERRA SIERRA** — [ ] [ ]
(12"+=) *(MAG12 233)* – Urban Samurai.
(free-7"ep+=) *(MAGD 233)* – Fool (if you think it's over) / The closer you get / Diamonds / Guitar Street.

Apr 83. (7") *(MAG 244)* **I CAN HEAR YOUR HEARTBEAT. / FROM LOVE TO LOVE** — [60] [ ]

Jun 83. (lp/c) *(MAGL/ZCMAGL 5084)* **WATER SIGN** — [64] [ ]
– Nothing's happening by the sea / Deep water / Candles / Love's strange ways / Texas / Let it loose / I can hear your heartbeat / Midnight blue / Hey you / Out of the darkness. *(re-iss. Sep87 on 'WEA' lp/c; WX 188/+C) (cd-iss. Feb88; 242372-2)*

Jul 83. (7") *(MAG 245)* **LOVE'S STRANGE WAYS. / SMILE** — [ ] [ ]

Feb 84. (7"/12") *(MAG 255)* **I DON'T KNOW WHAT IT IS BUT I LOVE IT. / MYSTERY MAN** — [65] [–]

Apr 84. (lp/c) *(MAGL/ZCMAGL 5057)* **WIRED TO THE MOON** — [35] [ ]
– Bombollini / Touche d'amour / Shine, shine, shine / Wired to the Moon / easons / I don't know what it is but I love you / Ace of hearts / Holding out / Winning. *(re-iss. Sep87 on 'WEA' lp/c; WX 189/+C) (cd-iss. Feb88; 242 373-2) (re-iss. +cd.Jul91 on 'East West')*

May 84. (7") *(MAG 259)* **BOMBOLLINI. / TRUE LOVE** — [ ] [ ]
(12"+=) *(MAGT 259)* – Excerpts from Bombollini.

Jun 84. (7") *(MAG 260)* **TOUCHE D'AMOUR. / ('A'instrumental)** — [ ] [ ]
(ext.12"+=) *(MAGT 260)* – Let it loose – I can hear your heartbeat – I don't know what it is but I love it (medley).

Sep 84. (7") *(MAG 269)* **ACE OF HEARTS. / I CAN HEAR YOUR HEARTBEAT** — [ ] [ ]
(12"+=/c-s+=) *(MAGT/ZCMAG 269)* – From love to love / True love / Smile.

Mar 85. (7") *(MAG 276)* **STAINSBY GIRLS. / AND WHEN SHE SMILES** — [27] [ ]
(12"+=/c-s+=) *(MAGT/ZCMAG 276)* – Sunrise / Dancing shoes / September blue.
(d7"+=) *(MAGD 276)* – Bittersweet / Auf Immer und Ewig.

May 85. (lp/c/cd) *(MAGL/ZCMAG/CDMAG 5062)* **SHAMROCK DIARIES** — [15] [ ]
– Steel river / Stainsby girls / Chisel Hill / Josephine / One golden rule / All summer long / Stone / Shamrock diaries / Love turns to lies / Hired gun. *(re-iss. Sep87 on 'WEA' lp/c; WX 190/+C)* i(cd-iss. Feb88' *242374-2) (re-iss. Jul91 on 'East West')*

Jun 85. (7") *(MAG 280)* **JOSEPHINE (remix). / DANCING SHOES** — [67] [–]
(12"+=) *(MAGT 280)* – Every time it rains.

Nov 85. (7") *(MAG 269)* **ACE OF HEARTS (remix). / I CAN HEAR YOUR HEARTBEAT (live)** — [ ] [ ]
(12"+=) *(MAGT 269)* – From love to love / True love / Smile.

Mar 86. (7") *(MAG 283)* **IT'S ALL GONE. / BLESS THEM ALL** — [69] [–]
(12"+=/c-s+=) *(MAGT/ZCMAG 283)* – Crack that mould / Look out for me / Let's dance.

Apr 86. (lp/c/cd) *(MAGL/ZCMAG/CDMAG 5069)* **ON THE BEACH** — [11] [ ]
– On the beach / Little blonde plaits / Giverny / Lucky day / Just passing through / It's all gone / Hello friend / Two roads / Light of hope / Auf immer und ewig. *(c+=/cd+=)* – Bless them all / Freeway / Crack that mould. *(re-iss. Feb88 on 'WEA' lp/c; WX 191/+C) (re-iss. Jun91 on 'East West')*

Jun 86. (7") *(YZ 195)* **ON THE BEACH. / IF ANYBODY ASKS YOU** — [57] [ ]
(12"+=) *(YZ 195T)* – ('A'extended remix).
(d7"+=) *(YZ 195CD)* – One golden rule (live) / Midnight blue (live).

Dec 86. (7") *(MAG 298)* **DRIVING HOME FOR CHRISTMAS. / HELLO FRIEND** — [ ] [–]
(d7"+=) *(MAGD 298)* – It's all gone (live) / Steel river (live).

Magnet — Motown

May 87. (7"/c-s) *(MAG 299) <1900>* **LET'S DANCE. / I DON'T CARE ANYMORE** — [12] [81]
(12"+=) *(MAGT 299)* – ('A'extended).
(cd-s+=) *(CDMAG 29)* – Josephine (French version).

Aug 87. (7") *(MAG 300)* **LOVING YOU AGAIN. / DONAHUE'S BROKEN WHEEL** — [47] [ ]
(12"+=) *(MAGT 300)* – ('A'extended).

Sep 87. (lp/c/cd) *(MAGL/ZCMAG/CDMAG 5071)* **DANCING WITH STRANGERS** — [2] [ ]

– Joys of Christmas / I can't dance to that / Windy Town / Gonna buy a hat / Curse of the traveller / Let's dance / Que sera / Josie's tune / Loving you again / That girl of mine / September blue. *(cd+=)* – I don't care anymore / Donahue's broken wheel / Danielle's breakfast. *(re-iss. +cd.Jul91 on 'East West')*

Nov 87. (7") *(MAG 314)* **JOYS OF CHRISTMAS. / DRIVING HOME FOR CHRISTMAS** [67] [–]
(12"+=) *(MAGT 314)* – Hello friend (remix).
(cd-s+=) *(CDMAG 314)* – Yes I do.

Jan 88. (7") *(MAG 318)* **QUE SERA. / SE SEQUI (instrumental)** [73] [ ]
(12"+=) (MAGT 318) – ('A'extended).
(cd-s+=) *(CDMAG 318)* – One sweet tender touch.

W.E.A. Motown

Jul 88. (7") *(YZ 195)* **ON THE BEACH (SUMMER '88). / I'M TAKING THE DAY OUT** [12] [ ]
(12"+=/cd-s+=) *(YZ 195 T/CD)* – It's all gone (live).

Oct 88. (7") *(YZ 320)* **I CAN HEAR YOUR HEARTBEAT. / LOVING YOU AGAIN (live)** [74] [ ]
(12"+=/cd-s+=) *(YZ 320 T/CD)* – Giverny.

W.E.A. Geffen

Oct 88. (lp/c)(cd) *(WX 200/+C)(243841-2) <24232>* **NEW LIGHT THROUGH OLD WINDOWS – THE BEST OF CHRIS REA** (new mixes) [5] [92]
– Let's dance / Working on it / Ace of hearts / Josephine / Candles / On the beach / Fool (if you think it's over) / I can hear your heartbeat / Shamrock diaries / Stainsby girls / Windy town / Driving home for Christmas / Steel river.

Dec 88. (d7"/12"ep/3"cd-ep) *(YZ 325 T/CD)* **DRIVING HOME FOR CHRISTMAS. / FOOTSTEPS IN THE SNOW // JOYS OF CHRISTMAS. / SMILE** [53] [ ]

Jan 89. (7") *(YZ 350)* **WORKING ON IT. / ONE GOLDEN RULE** [53] [–]
(12"+=) *(YZ 350T)* – ('A'extended).
(cd-s+=) *(YZ 350CD)* – Stainsby girls.

Mar 89. (7") *<27535>* **WORKING ON IT. / LOVING YOU AGAIN** [–] [73]

Sep 89. (7") *(YZ 431)* **THE ROAD TO HELL. / HE SHOULD KNOW BETTER** [10] [ ]
(12") *(YZ 431T)* – ('A'side) / The road to Hell (pt.2) / Josephine (French re-recorded).
(cd-s) *(YZ 431CD)* – (all 4 tracks).

Oct 89. (lp/c)(cd) *(WZ 317/+C)(246285-2) <24276>* **THE ROAD TO HELL** [1] [ ]
– The road to Hell (part 1 & 2) / You must be evil / Texas / Looking for a rainbow / Your warm and tender love / Daytona / That's what they all say / I just wanna be with you / Tell me there's a Heaven. *(re-iss. cd/c Feb95)*

Nov 89. (7"/c-s) *(YZ 448/+C)* **THAT'S WHAT THEY ALL SAY. / 1975** [ ] [–]
(12"+=) *(YZ 448T)* – ('A'extended rainbow mix).
(cd-s++=) *(YZ 448CD)* – Driving home for Christmas.

Feb 90. (7"/c-s) *(YZ 455/+C)* **TELL ME THERE'S A HEAVEN. / AND WHEN SHE SMILES** [24] [–]
(12"+=) *(YZ 455T)* – Curse of the traveller.
(cd-s++=) *(YZ 455CD)* – Little blonde plaits.

Apr 90. (7"/c-s) *(YZ 468/+C)* **TEXAS. / LET'S DANCE** [69] [–]
(12") *(YZ 468T)* – ('A'side) / ('B'live) / The road to Hell (part 1 & 2).
(cd-s+=) *(YZ 468CD)* – Working on it.

East West East West

Feb 91. (c-s) *(YZ 555C)* **AUBERGE / HUDSON'S DREAMS** [16] [–]
(12"+=/cd-s+=) *(YZ 555 T/CDX)* – Every second counts.
(cd-s) *(YZ 555CD)* – ('A'side) / Let's dance / On the beach summer '88 / The road to Hell (pt.2).

Feb 91. (cd)(lp/c) *(9031 75693-2) (WZ 407/+C) <91662>* **AUBERGE** [1] [ ]
– Auberge / Gone fishing / You're not a number / Heaven / Set me free / Red shoes / Sing a song of love to me / Every second counts / Looking for the summer / And you my love / The mention of your name.

Apr 91. (7"/c-s) *(YZ 566/+C)* **HEAVEN. / THEME FROM THE PANTILE JOURNALS** [57] [–]
(12"+=) *(YZ 566T)* – Teach me to dance.
(cd-s) *(YZ 566CD)* – ('A'side) / Stainsby girls / Josephine / Tell me there's a Heaven.

Jun 91. (7"/c-s) *(YZ 584/+C)* **LOOKING FOR THE SUMMER. / SIX UP** [49] [–]
(12"+=) *(YZ 584T)* – Urban Samurai.
(cd-s++=) *(EW 584CD)* – Theme from the Pantile / Teach me to dance.

Nov 91. (7"/c-s) *(YZ 629/+C)* **WINTER SONG. / FOOTPRINTS IN THE SNOW / TELL ME THERE'S A HEAVEN** [27] [–]
(cd-s+=) *(YZ 629CD)* – True to you.

Oct 92. (7"/c-s) *(YZ 699/+C)* **NOTHING TO FEAR. / NOTHING TO FEAR (edit) / STRANGE DANCE** [16] [–]
(cd-s) *(YZ 699CD)* – ('A'side) / Daytona (live) / On the beach (live).
(cd-s) *(YZ 699CDX)* – ('A'side) / The road to Hell (live) / Working on it (live).

Nov 92. (cd)(lp/c) *(4509 90995-2)(WX 496/+C) <92228>* **GOD'S GREAT BANANA SKIN** [4] Jan93 [ ]
– Nothing to fear / Miles is a cigarette / God's great banana skin / Nineties blues / Too much pride / Boom boom / I ain't the fool / There she goes / I'm ready / Black dog / Soft top hard shoulder.

Nov 92. (7"/c-s) *(YZ 706/+C)* **GOD'S GREAT BANANA SKIN. / I SAW YOU COMING** [31] [–]
(cd-s+=) *(YZ 706CDX)* – She's gonna change everything / You must be evil.
(cd-s) *(YZ 706CD)* – ('A'side) / Just passing through (live) / Footprints in the snow (live) / Winter song (live).

—— his band: **ROBERT AHWAI** – guitar / **MAX MIDDLETON** – piano, keyboards / **SYLVIN MARC** – bass / **MARTIN DITCHAM** – drums, percussion

Jan 93. (7"/c-s) *(YZ 710/+C)* **SOFT TOP HARD SHOULDER. / (half-time version)** [53] [–]
(cd-s+=) *(YZ 710CD)* – Melancholy / The van stomp – Glasgow horizon.
(cd-s) *(YZ 710CDX)* – ('A'side) / One fine day / One sweet & tender touch / Sierra, Sierra.

Jul 93. (7"/c-s) *(YZ 732/+C)* **TOO MUCH PRIDE (new version). / GONE FISHIN' (live)** [ ] [–]
(cd-s+=) *(YZ 732CD2)* – Munich 1993 improvised intro (live) / On the beach (live).
(cd-s) *(YZ 732CD1)* – ('A'side) / Gone fishing (live) / Nothing to fear (live) / Soft top, hard shoulder (live).

Oct 93. (7"/c-s) *(YZ 772/+C)* **JULIA. / I THOUGHT I WAS GOING TO LOSE YOU** [18] [–]
(cd-s+=) *(YZ 772CD)* – Jordan 191.

Nov 93. (cd/c/lp) *(4509 94311-2/-4/-1) <92316>* **ESPRESSO LOGIC** [8] Feb94 [ ]
– Espresso logic / Red / Soup of the day / Johnny needs a fast guitar / Between the Devil and the deep blue sea / Julia /Summer love / New way / Stop / She closed her eyes.

Dec 93. (7"/c-s) *(YZ 783/+C)* **ESPRESSO LOGIC. / WE DON'T HAVE A PROBLEM** [ ] [–]
(cd-s+=) *(YZ 783CD)* – That's the way it goes.

Oct 94. (cd/c) *(<4509 98040-2/-4>)* **THE VERY BEST OF CHRIS REA** (compilation) [3] [ ]
– The road to Hell / Josephine / Let's dance / Fool (if you think it's over) / Auberge / Julia / Stainsby girls / If you were me (with ELTON JOHN) / On the beach / Looking for the summer / I can hear your heartbeat / Go your own way / God's great banana skin / Winter song / Gone fishing / Tell me there's a Heaven.

Nov 94. (c-s) *(YZ 835C)* **YOU CAN GO YOUR OWN WAY / RUBY BLUE** [28] [–]
(12"+=/cd-s+=) *(YZ 835 T/CD)* – Three little green candles.

Dec 94. (7"/c-s) *(YZ 885/+C)* **TELL ME THERE'S A HEAVEN. / STAINSBY GIRLS** [70] [–]
(cd-s) *(YZ 885CD)* – ('A'side) / And when she smiles / Curse of the traveller / Little blonde plaits.
(below from the film written by CHRIS REA himself)

Nov 96. (c-s; CHRIS REA & SHIRLEY BASSEY) *(EW 072C)* **'DISCO' LA PASSIONE / (Adams & Gielen mix)** [41] [–]
(12"/cd-s) *(EW 072 T/CD)* – Horses.

Nov 96. (cd/c) *(0630-16695-2/-4)* **LA PASSIONE (soundtrack)** [43] [–]
– La passione (film theme) / Dov'e il signore? / Shirley do you own a Ferrari? / Girl in a sports car / When the grey skies turn to blue / Horses / Olive oil / Only to fly / You must follow / 'Disco' La passione / Dov'e il signore? part two / Le Mans.

May 97. (c-s) *(EW 103C)* **GIRL IN A SPORTS CAR / DINO** [ ] [–]
(cd-s+=) *(EW 103CD)* – Olive Oil.

Jan 98. (cd/c) *(3984 21688-2/-4)* **THE BLUE CAFE** [10] [–]
– Square peg, round hole / Since I found you / Miss your kiss / Shadows of the big man / Where do we go from here? / Thinking of you / As long as I have your love / Anyone quite like you / Sweet summer day / Stick by you / I'm still holding on / The blue cafe.

Feb 98. (c-s) *(EW 152C)* **SQUARE PEG, ROUND HOLE / THE MAN'S SO COOL** [ ] [–]
(cd-s+=) *(EW 152CD)* – ('A'-Front Room mix) / ('A'drum'n'bass).

Nov 99. (cd-s) *(EW 209CD)* **NEW TIMES SQUARE (mixes; Joe's radio / extended / Manhattan / trance / Hamburg St)** [ ] [–]

Nov 99. (cd/c) *(8573 80399-2/-4)* **THE ROAD TO HELL VOL.2** [ ] [–]
– Can't get through / Good morning / E / Last open road / Coming off the ropes / Evil No.2 / Keep on dancing / Marvin / Firefly / I'm in my car / New Times square.

Sep 00. (cd-s) *(EW 220CD1)* **ALL SUMMER LONG / ALL SUMMER LONG (Jose Padilla & DJ Pippa mix) / (Katcha remix)** [ ] [–]
(cd-s) *(EW220CD2)*– ('A'-Jose Padilla . . . mix) / On the beach / Josephine.

Oct 00. (cd/c) *(8573 85017-2/84596-4)* **KING OF THE BEACH** [26] [–]
– King of the beach / All summer long / Sail away / Still beautiful / The bones of angels / Guitar street / Who do you love / The memory of a good friend / Sandwriting / Tamatave / God gave me an angel / Waiting for a blue sky. *(cd+=)* – Mississippi.

Jan 01. (cd-s) *(EW 223CD)* **WHO DO YOU LOVE / THERE'S ONLY YOU / MISSISSIPPI** [ ] [–]

Nov 01. (cd/c) *(0927 42128-2/-4)* **THE VERY BEST OF CHRIS REA** (compilation) [69] [–]
– The road to hell (part 2) / Fool (if you think it's over) / Let's dance / You can go your own way / Julia / Stainsby girls / Tell me there's a heaven / Josephine / Steel river / On the beach / I can hear your heartbeat / All summer long / Blue cafe / Auberge / Driving home for Christmas / Nothing to fear / Saudade (parts 1 & 2 – tribute to Ayrton Senna).

Jazzy Blue WEA

Sep 02. (d-cd) *(JBLUECD 01X)* <25481> **DANCING DOWN THE STONY ROAD** (US title 'STONY ROAD') [14] Dec02 [ ]
– Easy rider / Heading for the city / Stony road / Dancing the blues away / Catfish girl / Burning feet / Slow dance / Segway / Mississippi / So lonely // Ride on / Give that girl a diamond / When the good Lord talked to Jesus / Qualified / Sun is rising / Someday my peace will come / Got to be moving on / Ain't going down this way / Changing times / The hustler.

Otis REDDING

Born: 9 Sep'41, Dawson, Georgia, USA. Singing in a gospel choir as a child and later winning a succession of talent contests with LITTLE RICHARD covers, REDDING's prescient abilities were noted by PHIL WALDEN who, at the time, was managing local R&B outfit, JOHNNY JENKINS & THE PINETOPPERS. OTIS soon became a driver/occasional singer with the act, his/their first release being the 'SHOUT BAMALAMA' single released on the 'Confederate' label in 1960. The following year, after OTIS' marriage to ZELDA, they issued 'GETTIN' HIP' on 'Alshire', while 1962 saw the release of a further single, 'LOVE TWIST' on 'Gerald' records. During this time, OTIS was only given the odd vocal spot, although this changed following the group's 'Atlantic'-sponsored recording session at the burgeoning 'Stax' studios. REDDING was allotted the time left over from JENKINS' session, putting it to good use and cutting two tracks, a soul shouter, 'HEY HEY BABY' and a ballad, 'THESE ARMS OF MINE'. Impressed, 'Stax' released the two tracks as a single on their subsidiary, 'Volt', the latter song becoming a minor US hit in mid '63. By mutual agreement and a special contract, 'Atlantic (aka Atco)' decided to allow the label to continue releasing REDDING material. Backed by 'Stax' house band, BOOKER T & THE MG's, the singer scored another minor hit with the lovesick ballad, 'PAIN IN MY HEART', releasing a similarly titled album the following year. REDDING led the way in 'Stax's back to basics soul crusade, the singer being widely credited with altering the sound of black music with his radically inventive horn parts. Though he wasn't an accomplished musician, he had an intuitive feel for rhythm and melody which he'd translate to his backing band, most of his material recorded spontaneously with a minimal number of takes. Co-written with MG, STEVE CROPPER, 'MR PITIFUL' was a slightly self-mocking caricature of REDDING as the king of soul heartbreak, its driving, emotive delivery overshadowing the baleful 'THAT'S HOW STRONG MY LOVE IS' when it was released as the B-side of the latter in the Spring of '65. REDDING's first real breakthrough, however, came with another poignant ballad, 'I'VE BEEN LOVING YOU TOO LONG', a near-Top 20 hit later that summer. After a follow-up album, 'THE GREAT OTIS REDDING SINGS SOUL BALLADS' (1965) failed to chart, REDDING had a surprise UK Top 20 hit towards the end of the year with a cover of The Temptations' 'MY GIRL', paving the way for the success of his seminal third album, 'OTIS BLUE (OTIS REDDING SINGS SOUL)', one of the most revered records in the soul canon. As well as featuring the enduring, much covered classic, 'RESPECT', the album boasted three SAM COOKE covers, including the uplifting 'CHANGE GONNA COME', as well as his famous cover of The Rolling Stones' 'I CAN'T GET NO SATISFACTION'. Though REDDING continued to sell respectably in the States, he was a massive crossover success in the UK, his profile heightened by an ecstatically received performance on hip 60's TV Show, 'Ready Steady Go'. By all accounts, REDDING was an inspirational live performer, his frenetic delivery and magnetic enthusiasm drawing rave reviews and striking fear into the heart of any act unlucky enough to have to follow him. REDDING returned to the UK in 1967, following the release of 'OTIS REDDING'S DICTIONARY OF SOUL' (which included the soul sophistication of 'TRY A LITTLE TENDERNESS and a follow-up of sorts to 'MR. PITIFUL', the rhythmic punch of 'FA-FA-FA-FA-FA (SAD SONG)'), he and his band given a rapturous reception with many stars of the day present in the audience. In June, REDDING was the first black soul singer to perform at a predominantly white rock event, namely the Monterey Pop Festival. His acclaimed performance finally saw the singer gaining the Stateside respect that had long been his due. Later that summer, an album of duets with fellow 'Stax' artist, CARLA THOMAS, 'KING AND QUEEN' dented the US Top 40. Lifted from the record, the brilliant 'TRAMP', in which OTIS' backwoods country hick was pitted against the worldly wise THOMAS, gave REDDING another American Top 30 single. Following an operation for throat problems, REDDING went back into the studio late in '67 and cut a final series of tracks, one song in particular, (SITTIN' ON) THE DOCK OF THE BAY', becoming his epitaph; on the 10th of December, 1967, REDDING's private plane crashed into Lake Monona, Madison, the singer and four members of his backing band, The BAR-KAYS subsequently drowning. As a stunned music world tried to come to terms with the tragedy, thousands attended REDDING's funeral in his hometown of Macon, the aforementioned 'SITTIN'..' subsequently scaling the American charts upon its posthumous release early in '68. REDDING's voice honey-sweet and fragile in contrast to the earthiness of old, the song was a heart-rendingly wistful acoustic folk/soul hybrid, the singer's death adding to its poignancy. The song reflected a new found maturity (also evident in the subsequent album of the same name) which indicated that REDDING was only beginning to realise his full potential, his contribution incalculable to not only black soul but music in general. • **Covered:** DOCK OF THE BAY (c. Steve Cropper) / MY GIRL (Temptations) / PAIN IN MY HEART (Irma Thomas) / DAY TRIPPER (Beatles) / SHAKE! (Sam Cooke) / KNOCK ON WOOD (Eddie Floyd) / PAPA'S GOT A BRAND NEW BAG (James Brown) / A LOVER'S QUESTION (Clyde McPhatter) / AMEN (Impressions) / etc. • **Trivia:** Late in 1973, his son DEXTER issued single GOD BLESS. In the early 80's, he was joined by other son OTIS and their cousin MARK LOCKET who transpired as The REDDINGS. All on vocals and instruments, they released 2 albums THE AWAKENING and CLASS on the 'Believe' label.

Album rating: PAIN IN MY HEART (*7) / THE GREAT OTIS REDDING SINGS SOUL BALLADS (*7) / OTIS BLUE – OTIS REDDING SINGS SOUL (*9) / THE SOUL ALBUM (*6) / COMPLETE & UNBELIEVABLE . . . THE OTIS REDDING DICTIONARY OF SOUL (*8) / KING AND QUEEN with Carla Thomas (*7) / OTIS REDDING LIVE IN EUROPE (*7) / HISTORY OF OTIS REDDING compilation (*8) / posthumous:- THE DOCK OF THE BAY (*6) / THE IMMORTAL OTIS REDDING (*5) / . . .IN PERSON AT THE WHISKY A GO GO (*6) / LOVE MAN compilation (*5) / THE BEST OF OTIS REDDING compilation (*7) / PURE OTIS (*5) / THE VERY BEST OF OTIS REDDING compilation (*7) / OTIS! THE DEFINITIVE OTIS REDDING compilation (*9)

OTIS REDDING – vocals (solo with session people)

London / Volt

Oct 62. (7") <103> **THESE ARMS OF MINE. / HEY HEY BABY** [–] [85]
Jul 63. (7") <109> **THAT'S WHAT MY HEART NEEDS. / MARY'S LITTLE LAMB** [–] [ ]
Nov 63. (7") *(HLK 9833)* <112> **PAIN IN MY HEART. / SOMETHING IS WORRYING ME** [ ] [61]

— His backing included BOOKER T. & THE MG'S plus JOHNNY JENKINS.

Mar 64. (7") *(HLK 9876)* <116> **COME TO ME. / DON'T LEAVE ME THIS WAY** [ ] [69]
Apr 64. (lp) <161> **PAIN IN MY HEART** [–] [ ]
– Pain in my heart / The dog / Stand by me / Hey hey baby / You send me / I need your lovin' / Louie Louie / These arms of mine / Something is worrying me / Security / That's what my heart needs / Lucille. *(UK-iss.Apr67 on 'Atlantic', hit No.28) (cd-iss. Aug93)*
May 64. (7") *(2091020)* **SECURITY. / WONDERFUL WORLD** [ ] [–]
Jun 64. (7") <117> **SECURITY. / I WANT TO THANK YOU** [–] [97]
Oct 64. (7") <121> **CHAINED AND BOUND. / YOUR ONE AND ONLY MAN** [–] [70]

Atlantic / Volt

Apr 65. (7") *(4024)* <124> **MR.PITIFUL. / THAT'S HOW STRONG MY LOVE IS** [ ] [41] Feb65 [74]
May 65. (7") <126> **I'VE BEEN LOVING YOU TOO LONG (TO STOP NOW). / I'M DEPENDING ON YOU** [–] [21]
Aug 65. (7") *(2091062)* **I'VE BEEN LOVING YOU TOO LONG. / RESPECT** [ ] [–]
Sep 65. (lp) *(SD 33248)* <411> **THE GREAT OTIS REDDING SINGS SOUL BALLADS** [ ] Mar65 [ ]
– That's how strong my love is / Chained and bound / A woman, a lover, a friend / Your one and only man / Nothing can change this love / It's too late / For your precious love / I want to thank you / Come to me / Home in your heart / Keep your arms around me / Mr. Pitiful. *(hit UK chart No.30, Apr66) (re-iss. Jun88 on 'Atco', cd-iss. Jul91) (cd-iss. May93)*
Sep 65. (7") <128> **RESPECT. / OLE MAN TROUBLE** [–] [35]
Nov 65. (7") *(4050)* **MY GIRL. / DOWN IN THE VALLEY** [11] [–]
Nov 65. (7") <130> **JUST ONE MORE DAY. / I CAN'T TURN YOU LOOSE** [–] [85]
Feb 66. (lp) *(ATL 5041)* <412> **OTIS BLUE (OTIS REDDING SINGS SOUL)** [6] Oct 65 [75]
– My girl / (I can't get no) Satisfaction / Respect / Shake! / I've been loving you too long / You don't miss your water / Rock me baby / Wonderful world / Down in the valley / Change gonna come / Ole man trouble. *(UK re-iss. Jan67, hit No.7) (re-iss. 1974 + Dec83 +c) (cd-iss. Jun91 on 'Atco')*
Mar 66. (7") *(4080)* <132> **(I CAN'T GET NO) SATISFACTION. / ANY OLE WAY** [33] [31]
Jul 66. (7") *(584019)* <136> **MY LOVER'S PRAYER. / DON'T MESS WITH CUPID** [37] Jun66 [61]
Jul 66. (lp) *(587-011)* <413> **THE SOUL ALBUM** [22] Apr66 [54]
– Just one more day / It's growing / Cigarettes and coffee / Chain gang / Nobody knows you (when you're down and out) / Good to me / Scratch my back / Treat her right / Everybody makes a mistake / Any ole way / 634-5789. *(cd-iss. Jul91 on 'Atco') (cd-iss. Jun93)*
Aug 66. (7") *(584030)* **I CAN'T TURN YOU LOOSE. / JUST ONE MORE DAY** [29] [–]
Nov 66. (7") *(584049)* <138> **FA FA FA FA FA (SAD SONG). / GOOD TO ME** [23] Sep66 [29]
Jan 67. (lp) *(588-050)* <415> **OTIS REDDING'S DICTIONARY OF SOUL** [23] Nov 66 [73]
– Fa-fa-fa-fa-fa (sad song) / I'm sick y'all / Tennessee waltz / Sweet Lorene / Try a little tenderness / Day tripper / My lover's prayer / She put the hurt on me / Ton of joy / You're still my baby / Hawg for you / Love have mercy. *(re-iss. Jun88, cd-iss. Jul91 on 'Atco') (cd-iss. Jun93)* (US-title 'COMPLETE AND UNBELIEVABLE . . . THE OTIS REDDING DICTIONARY OF SOUL')
Jan 67. (7") *(584070)* <141> **TRY A LITTLE TENDERNESS. / I'M SICK Y'ALL** [46] Dec 66 [25]
Mar 67. (7") *(K 10051)* **RESPECT. / THESE ARMS OF MINE** [ ] [–]
(re-iss. Feb72)

Stax / Volt

Mar 67. (7") *(601005)* **DAY TRIPPER. / SHAKE!** [43] [–]
Apr 67. (7") *(601007)* <146> **LET ME COME ON HOME. / I LOVE YOU MORE THAN WORDS CAN SAY** [48] B-side [78]
May 67. (7"; by OTIS REDDING & CARLA THOMAS) *<216>* **TRAMP. / TELL IT LIKE IT IS** [–] [26]
Jun 67. (7") *(601011)* **SHAKE (live). / 634-5789 (live)** [28] [–]
Jun 67. (7") <149> **SHAKE. / YOU DON'T MISS YOUR WATER** [–] [ ]

— Some releases on 'Stax' now with CARLA THOMAS, daughter of singer RUFUS.

Jun 67. (lp; as OTIS REDDING & CARLA THOMAS) *(589-007)* <716> **KING AND QUEEN** [18] Apr67 [36]
– Knock on wood / Let me be good to you / Tramp / Tell it like it is / When something is wrong with my baby / Lovey dovey / New Year's resolution / It takes two / Are you lonely for me baby / Bring it on home to me / Ooh Carla, Ooh Otis. *(re-iss. Jun88) (cd-iss. Jul91; 7567 82256-2)*
Jul 67. (7"; by OTIS REDDING & CARLA THOMAS) *(601 012)* **TRAMP. / OOH CARLA OOH OTIS** [18] [–]
Aug 67. (7") *(601 017)* <152> **GLORY OF LOVE. / I'M COMING HOME** [ ] Jul67 [60]
Sep 67. (lp) <416> **LIVE IN EUROPE (live)** [–] Aug67 [32]
– Respect / Can't turn you loose / I've been loving you too long / My girl / Shame / Satisfaction / Fa-fa-fa-fa-fa (sad song) / These arms of mine / Day tripper / Try a little tenderness. *(UK-iss.Mar68; 589 016)* – hit No.2 *(re-iss. Aug69 on 'Atco'; 228 017) (cd-iss. Aug93) (cd-iss. Feb95 & Sep95 on 'Warners')*
Oct 67. (7"; as OTIS REDDING & CARLA THOMAS) *(601 021)* <228> **KNOCK ON WOOD. / LET ME BE GOOD TO YOU** [35] Aug67 [30]
Nov 67. (7") *(601027)* **SATISFACTION. / I'VE BEEN LOVING YOU TOO LONG** [ ] [–]

— on the 10th of December '67, OTIS was killed in a plane crash

– (selective) compilations, etc. –

Dec 67. (lp/c) *Volt; <(418)>* **THE HISTORY OF OTIS REDDING** [2] [9]
(re-iss. 1969 on 'Atco'; 228 001)
below released on 'Volt'/ 'Stax' unless mentioned otherwise
Feb 68. (7") *(601 031)* <157> **(SITTIN' ON) THE DOCK OF THE BAY. / MY SWEET LORENE** [3] Jan68 [1]
Mar 68. (7"; by OTIS REDDING & CARLA THOMAS) *(601 033)* <244> **LOVEY DOVEY. / NEW YEAR'S RESOLUTION** [ ] Feb68 [68]
May 68. (lp) *(230 001)* <419> **DOCK OF THE BAY** (late 1967 sessions) [1] Mar68 [4]
– The dock of the bay / Home in your heart / I want to thank you / Your one and only man / Nothing can change this love / It's too late / For your precious love / Keep your arms around me / Come to me / A woman, a lover, a friend / Chained and bound / That's how strong my love is. *(re-iss. Jul69 on 'Atco'; 228 022) (re-iss. Nov71)*
May 68. (7") *(601 040)* <163> **THE HAPPY SONG (DUM DUM). / OPEN THE DOOR** [24] Apr68 [25]
below released on 'Atlantic' UK/ 'Atco' US unless mentioned
Feb 68. (7") *(K 10111)* **MY GIRL. / MR. PITIFUL** [36] [ ]
(re-iss. 1972, 1980 & Mar84)
Jul 68. (7") *(584199)* <6592> **HARD TO HANDLE. / AMEN** [15] B-side [36]
Aug 68. (lp) <252> **THE IMMORTAL OTIS REDDING** [19] Jul68 [58]
(re-iss. Jan72 on 'Atco') (cd-iss. Aug93; 7567 80270-2)
Sep 68. (7") <6612> **I'VE GOT DREAMS TO REMEMBER. / NOBODY'S FAULT BUT MINE** [–] [41]
Oct 68. (7") *(584220)* **I'VE GOT DREAMS TO REMEMBER. / CHAMPAGNE AND WINE** [ ] [–]
Nov 68. (lp) *(587148)* <265> **OTIS REDDING IN PERSON AT THE WHISKEY A GO-GO (live 1966)** [ ] [82]
– I can't turn you loose / Pain in my heart / Just one more day / Mr.Pitiful / (I can't get no) Satisfaction / I'm depending on you / Any ole way / These arms of mine / Papa's got a brand new bag / Respect. *(cd-iss. Dec94 & Sep95 on 'Warners')*
Dec 68. (7") *(584234)* <6636> **PAPA'S GOT A BRAND NEW BAG (live). / DIRECT ME** [ ] Nov68 [21]
Below released on 'Atco' unless mentioned.

Date	Release	UK	US
Mar 69.	(7") *(584249)* <6654> **A LOVER'S QUESTION. / YOU MADE A MAN OUT OF ME**		Feb69 48
May 69.	(7") <6677> **LOVE MAN. / CAN'T TURN YOU LOOSE**	–	72
Jun 69.	(7") *(226001)* **LOVE MAN. / THAT'S HOW STRONG MY LOVE IS**	43	–
Jun 69.	(lp) *(228 025)* <289> **LOVE MAN** *(re-iss. Nov71 on 'Atlantic') (cd-iss. Jul92 on 'Rhino')*		46
Jan 71.	(lp) *(2400 018)* <333> **TELL THE TRUTH** (rec.1967) – Demonstration / Tell the truth / Out of sight / Give away none of my love / Wholesale love / I got the will / Johnny's heartbreak / Snatch a little piece / Slippin' and slidin' / The match game / A little time / Swingin' on a string. *(cd-iss. Jul92 on 'Rhino'; 8122 70295-2)*		Aug70
Jul 73.	(lp/c) *(K/K4 60016)* <801> **THE BEST OF OTIS REDDING** *(cd-iss. Mar87)*		Sep72 76
Jul 87.	(lp/c/cd) *(241118-1/-4/-2)* **DOCK OF THE BAY – THE DEFINITIVE COLLECTION**		
Jul 92.	(cd/c) *Castle; (CCS CD/MC 339)* **THE COLLECTION** – My girl / Stand by me / Higher and higher / The happy song / I love you more than words can say / Amen / Fa-fa-fa-fa-fa (sad song) / I've been losing you too long / The glory of love / I've got dreams to remember / Love man / Free me / Papa's got a brand new bag / (Sittin' on) The dock of the bay.		–
Mar 93.	(3xcd-box) <*(7567 81762-2)*> **THE OTIS REDDING STORY**		
Oct 93.	(4xcd-box) <*(8122 71439-2)*> **OTIS: THE DEFINITIVE OTIS REDDING**		
May 98.	(cd) *Rhino;* <*(8122 72955-2)*> **LOVE SONGS**		
Oct 98.	(d-cd) *Rhino;* <*(8122 75471-2)*> **THE OTIS REDDING ANTHOLOGY: DREAMS TO REMEMBER**		
Oct 00.	(d-cd/d-c) *Atlantic;* <*(9548 38087-2/-4)*> **THE VERY BEST OF OTIS REDDING**	26	

RED HOT CHILI PEPPERS

Formed: Hollywood, California, USA . . . 1983 after four years as ANTHEM, by schoolfriends ANTHONY KIEDIS (aka ANTWAN THE SWAN), Israeli-born HILLEL SLOVAK, MICHAEL 'FLEA' BALZARY and JACK IRONS. This motley bunch of funky funsters then proceeded to sign with 'E.M.I.' stark naked as part of a now famous publicity stunt. The exhibitionist streak was to be a mainstay of their early career, most famously on the cover for the ABBEY ROAD EP (1988), the lads wearing nought but one sock, strategically placed (no prizes for guessing where!) in a send-up of the classic Beatles' album of the same name. With IRONS and SLOVAK under contractual obligations to their own group, WHAT IS THIS?, drummer JACK SHERMAN (ex-CAPTAIN BEEFHEART) and guitarist CLIFF MARTINEZ (ex-WEIRDOS, ex-TEENAGE JESUS & THE JERKS) filled in on the 1984 eponymous debut album, a promising start which introduced the band's mutant funk-punk hybrid. Taking their cue from the cream of 70's funk (obvious reference points were SLY STONE, JAMES BROWN, The METERS, etc.) and injecting it with a bit of L.A. hardcore mayhem, the CHILI PEPPERS came up with such gonzoid grooves as 'GET UP AND JUMP' and 'POLICE HELICOPTER', although the most interesting track was the haunting 'GRAND PAPPY DU PLENTY', a kind of pre-'Twin Peaks' slice of instrumental noir. The GEORGE CLINTON-produced follow-up, FREAKY STYLEY (1985) sounded more cohesive, most impressively on the galvanising defiance of the hypnotic title track. Alongside fairly faithful covers of Sly Stone's 'IF YOU WANT ME TO STAY' and The Meters' 'HOLLYWOOD (AFRICA)', the group "got down" with their own groove thang on the likes of 'JUNGLE MAN' and 'AMERICAN GHOST DANCE'. 'CATHOLIC SCHOOL GIRLS RULE' and 'SEX RAP', meanwhile, left no doubt as to the CHILI PEPPERS' feminist-baiting agenda. While these records were American-only affairs, the band's manic reputation was beginning to reach across the Atlantic, 'UPLIFT MOFO PARTY PLAN' (1988) intoducing the band to a receptive UK audience. Tougher than their earlier releases, the record consolidated the group's place at the forefront of the burgeoning funk-metal explosion, their brash, kaleidoscopic sound injecting a bit of colour and excitement to Blighty's rather dour rock scene. The party was cut somewhat short, however, with the death of SLOVAK in June, yet another victim of a heroin overdose. With KEIDIS also a heroin addict, IRONS (who subsequently formed the band, ELEVEN) obviously didn't like the way things were going and decided to bail out. Eventual replacements were found in guitarist JOHN FRUSCIANTE and drummer CHAD SMITH, the group throwing themselves into the recording of 'MOTHER'S MILK' (1989). Unfairly criticised in some quarters, the album contained some of the CHILI PEPPERS' finest moments to date. 'KNOCK ME DOWN' was an impassioned plea for sanity in the face of drugs hell, the group enjoying MTV exposure for the first time with the video. A brilliant, celebratory cover of Stevie Wonder's 'HIGHER GROUND' also scored with MTV, easing the band slowly out of cultdom. 'TASTE THE PAIN' was an uncharacteristically introspective (by the CHILI's standards anyhow) song, no doubt also borne of the band's recent troubles and showing a newfound maturity in songwriting. More trouble was to follow in April '90, when that young scamp, KIEDIS, was given a 60-day jail sentence for sexual battery and indecent exposure to a female student (the following year, FLEA and SMITH were both charged with offences of a similar nature). As well as clearly possessing red hot libidos, by the early 90's the band had become red hot property following the release of the RICK RUBIN-produced 'BLOOD SUGAR SEX MAGIK' (1991). Their first release for new label, 'Warners', at last the band had fulfilled their potential over the course of a whole album (a US Top 3). With another series of striking videos, the CHILI PEPPERS almost scored a US No.1 with the aching ballad, 'UNDER THE BRIDGE' while the body-jerk funk-rock of 'GIVE IT AWAY' made the UK Top 10. A multi million seller, the album catapulted The RED HOT CHILI PEPPERS into the big league, the band subsequently securing a prestigious headlining slot on the 1992 Lollapalooza tour. Always an utterly compelling live proposition, the group's hyperactive stage show is the stuff of legend, what with KEIDIS' manic athletics and FLEA's (possibly) JIMI HENDRIX-inspired upside down bass playing, hanging feet-up by a rope!!!. By the release of 'ONE HOT MINUTE' (1995), a transatlantic Top 5, FRUSCIANTE had been replaced with DAVE NAVARRO (ex-JANE'S ADDICTION), adding a new dimension to the band's sound. For many, the album was the 'CHILI PEPPERS' peak achievement, from the dreamy 'WALKABOUT' to the japery of 'AEROPLANE', the latter becoming a UK hit single. While many of the group's funk-rock contemporaries folded or fell by the wayside when that scene went out of fashion, the RED HOT CHILI PEPPERS developed into one of America's most entertaining, and biggest selling 'alternative' acts through a combination of sheer hard work, talent and concrete self belief (and no doubt a hefty dose of shagging!). Never the most stable of bands, rumours of a 'PEPPERS split were rife in 1997, although they still managed to hit the UK Top 10 with their fantastic cover of The Ohio Players' 'LOVE ROLLERCOASTER' (straight from the Beavis & Butt-Head film). With the returning FRUSCANTE out from the bench to replace NAVARRO, the band were back with a bang on 1999's 'CALIFORNICATION'. Meanwhile, another stab at the singles chart paid off with a transatlantic Top 20 hit, 'SCAR TISSUE'. With the release of 2002's 'BY THE WAY', the RED HOT CHILI PEPPERS proved themselves to be one of the few acts in popular music to carry off almost twenty years' worth of consistently wonderful music. Incredibly, the band still look great, still sound fresh and still have that edge of danger that almost all rock artists lose along with their figures as middle age looms. Granted, their hooks and melodies may be sounding that bit more wistful, and their words that bit more wiser these days, but if that translates into songs as gorgeous as single 'BY THE WAY', growing old can only be a good thing. Two decades of keeping the funk flame alive was marked with the release of 2003's 'GREATEST HITS', largely covering the post-'MOTHERS MILK' era. • **Songwriters:** Group compositions except other covers; SUBTERRANEAN HOMESICK BLUES (Bob Dylan) / FIRE + CASTLES MADE OF SAND (Jimi Hendrix) / MOMMY WHERE'S DADDY (Frank Zappa) / THEY'RE RED HOT (Robert Johnson) / SEARCH AND DESTROY (Iggy Pop) / SUFFRAGETTE CITY (David Bowie) / WHY DON'T YOU LOVE ME (Hank Williams) / TINY DANCER (Elton John) / TEENAGER IN LOVE (Dion & The Belmonts).

Album rating: RED HOT CHILI PEPPERS (*5) / FREAKY STYLEY (*5) / THE UPLIFT MOFO PARTY PLAN (*6) / MOTHER'S MILK (*7) / BLOOD SUGAR SEX MAGIK (*8) / WHAT HITS!? compilation (*7) / PLASMA SHAFT collection (*4) / OUT IN L.A. collection (*3) / ONE HOT MINUTE (*6) / CALIFORNICATION (*6) / BY THE WAY (*8) / GREATEST HITS compilation (*8)

ANTHONY KIEDIS (ANTWAN THE SWAN) (b. 1 Nov'62, Grand Rapids, Michigan) – vocals / **HILLEL SLOVAK** (b.13 Apr'62, Haifa, Israel) – guitar / **MICHAEL 'FLEA' BALZARY** (b.16 Oct'62, Melbourne, Australia) – bass / **JACK IRONS** (b.18 Jul'62, Los Angeles, California) – drums

EMI America — EMI America

1984. (lp/c/cd) *<790616-1/-4/-2>* **THE RED HOT CHILI PEPPERS** [–] [ ]
– True men don't kill coyotes / Baby appeal / Buckle down / Get up and jump / Why don't you love me / Green heaven / Mommy where's daddy? / Out in L.A. / Police helicopter / You always sing / Grand pappy du plenty. *(UK-iss.Aug90 on 'EMI Manhattan' cd/c/lp; CD/TC+/MTL 1056) (re-iss. Jun93 on 'Fame' cd/c; CD/TC FA 3297) (lp re-iss. Dec99 on 'Simply Vinyl'; SVLP 156)*

— (Due to contractual reasons, SLOVAK and IRONS couldn't play on debut. They were deputised by session men **JACK SHERMAN** – guitar (ex-CAPTAIN BEEFHEART) / & **CLIFF MARTINEZ** – drums (ex-WEIRDOS, ex-TEENAGE JESUS & THE JERKS)

— **HILLEL SLOVAK** returned from WHAT IS THIS? to repl. SHERMAN guests included **MACEO PARKER + FRED WESLEY** (of FUNKADELIC / PARLIAMENT)

1985. (lp/c/cd) *<790617-1/-4/-2>* **FREAKY STYLIE** [–] [ ]
– Jungle man / Hollywood (Africa) / American ghost dance / If you want me to stay / Never mind / Freaky stylie / Blackeyed blonde / The brothers cup / Battle ship / Lovin' and touchin' / Catholic school girls rule / Sex rap / Thirty dirty birds / Yertle the turtle. *(UK-iss.Aug90 on 'EMI Manhattan' cd/c/lp; CD/TC+/MTL 1057) (re-iss. Dec94 on 'Fame' cd/c; CD/TC FA 3309)*

Aug 85. (7") *(EA 205)* **HOLLYWOOD (AFRICA). / NEVER MIND** [ ] [ ]
(remixed-12"+=) *(12EA 205)* – ('A'dub version).

— **JACK IRONS** returned from WHAT IS THIS? to repl. MARTINEZ

Jan 88. (7") *(EA 241)* **FIGHT LIKE A BRAVE. / FIRE** [ ] [ ]
(12"+=/12"pic-d+=) *(12EA/+P 241)* – ('A'-Mofo mix) / ('A'-Knucklehead mix).

EMI Manhattan — EMI Manhattan

Mar 88. (cd/c/lp) *(CD/TC+/AML 3125) <48036>* **THE UPLIFT MOFO PARTY PLAN** [ ] Nov87 [ ]
– Fight like a brave / Funky crime / Me and my friends / Backwoods / Skinny sweaty man / Behind the sun / Subterranean homesick blues / Special secret song inside / No chump love sucker / Walkin' on down the road / Love trilogy / Organic anti-beat box band. *(lp re-iss. Aug00 on 'Simply Vinyl'; SVLP 242)*

May 88. (7"ep) *(MT 41)* **THE ABBEY ROAD EP** [ ] [–]
– Backwoods / Hollywood (Africa) / True men don't kill coyotes.
(12"ep+=) *(12MT 41)* – Catholic school girls rule.

— **ANTWAN & FLEA** (now adding trumpet) brought in new lads **JOHN FRUSCIANTE** (b. 5 Mar'70, New York City) – guitar repl. HILLEL who died (of heroin OD) 25 Jun'88. **CHAD SMITH** (b.25 Oct'62, St. Paul, Minnesota) – drums repl. IRONS who later formed ELEVEN and joined PEARL JAM

E.M.I. USA — E.M.I.

Aug 89. (7"/7"sha-pic-d/12"pic-d) *(MT/MTPD/12MTPD 70)* **KNOCK ME DOWN. / PUNK ROCK CLASSIC / PRETTY LITTLE DITTY** [ ] [ ]
(12") *(12MT 70)* – (first 2 tracks) / Special secret song inside / Magic Johnson.
(cd-s) *(CDMT 70)* – (first 2 tracks) / Jungle man / Magic Johnson.

Aug 89. (cd/c/lp) *(CD/TC+/MTL 3125) <92152>* **MOTHER'S MILK** [ ] [52]
– Good time boys / Higher ground / Subway to Venus / Magic Johnson / Nobody weird like me / Knock me down / Taste the pain / Stone cold bush / Fire / Pretty little ditty / Punk rock classic / Sexy Mexican maid / Johnny kick a hole in the sky. *(lp-iss.Apr01 on 'Simply Vinyl'; SVLP 328)*

Dec 89. (7") *(MT 75)* **HIGHER GROUND. / MILLIONAIRES AGAINST HUNGER** [55] [ ]
('A'-Munchkin mix-cd-s+=) *(CDMT 75)* – Mommy where's daddy / Politician (mini rap).
(12") *(12MT 75)* – ('A'-Munchkin mix) / ('A'dub mix) / Politician (mini rap) / Mommy where's daddy.
(12") *(12MTX 75)* – ('A'side) / ('A'-Munchkin mix) / ('A'dub mix) / Politician (mini rap).

Jun 90. (c-s/7") *(TC+/MT 85)* **TASTE THE PAIN. / SHOW ME YOUR SOUL** [29] [ ]
(12"+=/9"square-pic-d+=) *(12/10 MT 85)* – Castles made of sand (live).
(cd-s++=) *(CDMT 85)* – Never mind.
(remixed-12"+=) *(12MTX 85)* – If you want me to stay / Never mind.

Aug 90. (c-s/7") *(TC+/MT 88)* **HIGHER GROUND. / FIGHT LIKE A BRAVE** [54] [ ]
(12"+=/12"pic-d+=) *(12MT/+PD 88)* – ('A'-Daddy-O mix).
(cd-s+=) *(CDMT 88)* – Behind the sun / Out in L.A.

Warners — Warners

Sep 91. (cd)(d-lp/c) *(7599 26681-2)(WX 441/+C) <26681>* **BLOOD SUGAR SEX MAGIK** [25] [3]
– The power of equality / If you have to ask / Breaking the girl / Funky monks / Suck my kiss / I could have lied / Mellowship slinky in B major / The righteous & the wicked / Give it away / Blood sugar sex magik / Under the bridge / Naked in the rain / Apache Rose peacock / The greeting song / My lovely man / Sir psycho sexy / They're red hot. *(re-iss. Mar92 cd/c; same)*

Dec 91. (c-s,cd-s) *<19147>* **GIVE IT AWAY / SEARCH AND DESTROY** [–] [73]

Mar 92. (c-s,cd-s) *<18978>* **UNDER THE BRIDGE / THE RIGHTEOUS AND THE WICKED** [–] [2]

Mar 92. (7"/s7"/c-s) *(W 0084/+W/C)* **UNDER THE BRIDGE. / GIVE IT AWAY** [26] [–]
(12"/cd-s) *(W 0084 T/CD)* – ('A'side) / Search and destroy / Soul to squeeze / Sikamikanico.

— (the last track also featured on 'Wayne's World' film/single)

— **ZANDER SCHLOSS** (THELONIUS MONSTER) – guitar; repl. FRUSCANTE who went solo 'TO CLARA' in 1994 on 'American'

Aug 92. (7"/c-s) *(W 0126/+C)* **BREAKING THE GIRL. / FELA'S COOK** [41] [ ]
(12"+=/cd-s+=) *(W 0126 T/CD)* – Suck my kiss (live) / I could have lied (live).

— (Aug'92) **ARIK MARSHALL** (b.13 Feb'67, Los Angeles) – guitar (ex-MARSHALL LAW) repl. SCHLOSS

Jun 93. (c-s) *(W 188C)* **GIVE IT AWAY / IF YOU HAVE TO ASK (Friday night fever blister mix)** [ ] [–]
(12"+=/cd-s+=) *(W 188 TP/CD1)* – ('A'-extended + Rasta mixes).
(cd-s) *(W 188CD2)* – ('A'side) / ('A'-Disco Krisco mix) / ('A'-Scott & Garth mix).

Aug 93. (c-s,cd-s) *<18401>* **SOUL TO SQUEEZE / NOBODY WEIRD LIKE ME** [–] [22]

— **DAVE NAVARRO** (b. 7 Jun'67, Santa Monica, Calif.) – guitar (ex-JANE'S ADDICTION) repl. MARSHALL

Jan 94. (c-s) *(W 0225C)* **GIVE IT AWAY / SOUL TO SQUEEZE** [9] [–]
(cd-s+=) *(W 0225CD1)* – ('A'-extended & Rasta mixes).
(cd-s) *(W 0225CD2)* – ('A'side) / If you have to ask (Friday night fever blister mix) / ('A'-Scott & Garth mix) / Nobody weird like me (live).

(12") *(W 0225T)* – ('A'extended) / ('A'-Rasta mix) / If you have to ask (disco krisco mix).

Apr 94. (7"blue/c-s) *(W 0237/+C)* **UNDER THE BREDGE. / SUCK MY KISS (live)** [13] [–]
(cd-s+=) *(W 0237CD)* – Sikamikanico / Search and destroy (live).
(cd-s) *(W 0237CDX)* – ('A'side) / I could have lied (live) / Fela's cock / Give it away (in progress; demo).

Aug 95. (c-s) *(W 0316C)* **WARPED / PEA** [31] [–]
(cd-s+=) *(W 0316CD)* – Melancholy mechanics.

Sep 95. (cd/c/lp) *<(9362 45733-2/-4/-1)>* **ONE HOT MINUTE** [2] [4]
– Warped / Aeroplane / Deep kick / My friends / Coffee shop / Pea / One big mob / Walkabout / Tearjerker / One hot minute / Falling into grace / Shallow be thy name / Transcending.

Oct 95. (c-s) *(W 0317C)* **MY FRIENDS / LET'S MAKE EVIL** [29] [–]
(12"+=/cd-s+=) *(W 0317 TX/CD)* – Coffee shop / Stretch.

Feb 96. (c-s) *(W 0331C)* **AEROPLANE / SUFFRAGETTE CITY (live)** [11] [–]
(cd-s+=) *(W 0331CD)* – Suck my kiss (live).
(cd-s) *(W 0331CDX)* – ('A'side) / Backwoods (live) / Transcending (live) / Me and my friends (live).

— FLEA + CHAD splintered with THERMIDOR, which was formed by ROBBIE ALLEN and DAVID KING. An album 'MONKEY ON RICO' was released in the Spring.

Jun 97. (7"/c-s/cd-s) *(GFS/+C/TD 22188)* **LOVE ROLLERCOASTER. / Engelbert Humperdinck: Lesbian Seagull** [7] [–]
(above from the 'Beavis & Butt-Head Do America' film; on 'Geffen')

— (Apr'98) **JOHN FRUSCANTE** returned to repl. NAVARRO (who formed SPREAD)

May 99. (c-s) *(W 490C) <16913>* **SCAR TISSUE / GONG LI** [15] [9]
(cd-s+=) *(W 490CD2)* – Instrumental No.1.

Jun 99. (cd/c) *<(9362 47386-2/-4)>* **CALIFORNICATION** [5] [3]
– Around the world / Parallel universe / Scar tissue / Otherside / Get on top / Californication / Easily / Porcelain / Emit remmus / Velvet glove / Savoir / Purple stain / Right on time / Road trippin'.

Aug 99. (c-s) *(W 500C)* **AROUND THE WORLD / YERTLE TRILOGY** [35] [ ]
(cd-s+=) *(W 500CD2)* – Me and my friends.
(cd-s) *(W 500CD1)* – ('A'side) / Parallel universe / Teatro jam.

Jan 00. (cd-s) *(W 510CD1) <album cut>* **OTHERSIDE / HOW STRONG / ROAD TRIPPIN' (without strings) / OTHERSIDE (CD-Rom)** [33] [14]
(cd-s) *(W 510CD2)* – ('A'side) / My lovely man / Around the world (CD-Rom).

Aug 00. (c-s/cd-s) *(W 534 C/CD) <album cut>* **CALIFORNICATION / END OF THE SHOW (live) / I COULD HAVE LIED (live) / END OF SHOW (live)** [16] May00 [69]

Jan 01. (c-s) *(W 546C)* **ROAD TRIPPIN' / CALIFORNICATION (live)** [30] [–]
(cd-s+=) *(W 546CD1)* – BloodSugarSexMagick (live) / ('A'-CD-ROM).
(cd-s) *(W 546CD2)* – ('A'side) / Under the bridge (live) / If you have to ask (live).

Jul 02. (7") *(W 580)* **BY THE WAY. / TIME** [2] [34]
(cd-s+=) *(W 580CD1) <42459>* – Teenager in love.
(cd-s) *(W 580CD2)* – Search and destroy (live).

Jul 02. (cd/c/lp) *<(9362 48140-2/-4/-1)>* **BY THE WAY** [1] [2]
– By the way / Universally speaking / This is the place / Dosed / Don't forget me / The zephyr song / Can't stop / I could die for you / Midnight / Throw away your television / Cabron / Tear / On Mercury / Minor thing / Warm tape / Venice queen.

Oct 02. (7") *(W 592)* **THE ZEPHYR SONG. / OUT OF RANGE** [11] [49]
(cd-s+=) *(W 592CD2) <radio>* – Rivers of Avalon.
(cd-s) *(W 592CD1)* – ('A'side) / Body of water / Someone.

Feb 03. (7"red) *(W 599)* **CAN'T STOP. / CHRISTCHURCH FIREWORKS MUSIC (live)** [22] [57]
(cd-s+=) *(W 599CD1)* – If you have to ask (live).
(cd-s) *(W 599CD2)* – ('A'mix) / Right on time (live) / Nothing to lose (live).

Jun 03. (cd-s) *(W 609CD1)* **UNIVERSALLY SPEAKING / SLOWLY DEEPLY** [27] [–]
(cd-s) *(W 609CD2)* – ('A'side) / By the way (live acoustic) / Don't forget me (live).

Nov 03. (cd-s) *(W 630CD)* **FORTUNE FADED / ESKIMO / BUNKER HILL** [11] [–]

Nov 03. (cd) *<(9362 48545-2)>* **GREATEST HITS** (compilation) [4] [18]
– Under the bridge / Give it away / Californication / Scar tissue / Soul to squeeze / Otherside / Suck my kiss / By the way / Parallel universe / Breaking the girl / My friends / Higher ground / Universally speaking / Road trippin' / Fortune faded / Save the population. *(cd w/dvd+=; 9362 48956-2)*

– compilations, others, etc. –

Oct 92. (cd/c/d-lp) *EMI USA; (CD/TC+/MTL 1071) <94762>* **WHAT HITS!?** [23] [22]
– Higher ground / Fight like a brave / Behind the Sun / Me & my friends / Backwoods / True men don't kill coyotes / Fire / Get up and jump / Knock me down / Under the bridge / Show me your soul / If you want me to stay / Hollywood / Jungle man / The brothers cup / Taste the pain / Catholic school girls rule / Johnny kick a hole in the sky. *(cd re-dist.Mar03)* – hit UK No.44

Oct 94. (d-cd) *Warners; (9362 45649-2)* **PLASMA SHAFT** (rare mixes/live) [ ] [ ]

Nov 94. (cd/c/lp) *E.M.I.; (CD/TC+/MTL 1062)* **OUT IN L.A.** (rare remixes, demos & live) [61] [82]

Nov 95. (3xcd-box) *E.M.I.; (CDOMB 004)* **THE RED HOT CHILI PEPPERS / FREAKY STYLIE / THE UPLIFT MOFO PARTY PLAN** [ ] [ ]

Apr 98. (cd/c) *EMI-USA; <72434-94139-2/-4>* **ESSENTIAL RED HOT CHILI PEPPERS: UNDER THE COVERS** [–] [ ]

Jun 00. (cd) *E.M.I.; (527294-2)* **MOTHER'S MILK / THE UPLIFT MOFO PARTY PLAN / FREAKY STYLEY** [ ] [–]

REDMAN

Born: REGGIE NOBLE, 17 Apr'69, Newark, New Jersey, USA. Discovering hip hop in his late teens, REDMAN started out as a DJ before being discovered by EPMD's ERICK SERMON at a club night in Newark. SERMON subsequently took REDMAN under his wing after the budding rapper was thrown out of the family home by his mother, encouraging his rhyming skills and enrolling him as a fully fledged member of The Hit Squad (see EPMD). Making his vinyl debut via a couple of tracks on EPMD's 'Business As Usual' opus, REDMAN's roughshod rapping was given free rein on a debut solo album for the 'R.A.L.' label, the acclaimed 'WHUT?, THEE ALBUM' (1992). With REDMAN enjoying widespread exposure on the victorious Hit Squad 1992 US tour, sales of the record were impressive enough to warrant a UK release later that year through 'Sony'. Though EPMD split up soon after, REDMAN went on to a highly successful solo career, scoring Top 20 US hits with DARE IZ A DARKSIDE (1994) and 'MUDDY WATERS' (1996), the latter his first album for 'Def Jam'. REDMAN returned after a three year gap, to issued the average 'MALPRACTICE' (2001), a basic rehash of his previous albums. Including guests such as MISSY ELLIOTT and GEORGE CLINTON and featuring the hit single 'LET'S GET DIRTY (I CAN'T GET INTO THE CLUB)', the album was comprised of REDMAN's usual variation of comedy skits and phat bass-driven songs. The end result was something tepid and boring, a weak comeback after such a long break from the scene.

Album rating: WHUT? THEE ALBUM (*6) / DARE IZ A DARKSIDE (*6) / MUDDY WATERS (*6) / DOC'S DA NAME 2000 (*6) / MALPRACTICE (*5)

REDMAN – vocals; with various personnel

Sony R.A.L.

Dec 92. (cd/c) *(472259-2/-4) <52967>* **WHUT? THEE ALBUM** [ ] Oct92 [49]
– Psycho ward / Time 4 sum aksion / Da funk / (news break) / So ruff / Rated "R" / Watch yo nuggets / Psycho dub / Jam 4 U / Blow your mind / Hardcore / Funky uncles / Redman meets Reggie Noble / Tonight's da night / Blow your mind (remix) / I'm a bad / (sessed one night) / How to roll a blunt / (sooper lover interview) / Day of sooperman lover / Encore. *(re-iss. May00; 542424-2)*

R.A.L. R.A.L.

Dec 94. (cd/c) *<(523846-2/-4)>* **DARE IZ A DARKSIDE** [ ] Nov94 [13]
– Tonight's da nite / Slide and rock on / Wuditlooklike / Winicumhround / Rockafella / Journey throo da darkside / Million a 1 buddah spots / We run

N.Y. / Noorotic / Green island / Can't wait / Vasically / Bobyahad2drs / Sooperman luva II / Cosmic slop / Rockafella (R.I.P.).

Dec 94. (c-s,cd-s) *<851466>* **CAN'T WAIT / ('A'instrumental)** – 94
Def Jam Def Jam

Aug 95. (12",c-s; REDMAN & METHOD MAN) *<579924>* **HOW HIGH / ('A'remix)** – 13

Mar 96. (12",c-s) *<98084>* **FUNKORAMA / (track by The Wixtons)** – 81

Dec 96. (cd/lp) *<(533470-2/-1)>* **MUDDY WATERS** 12
– (intro) / Iz he 4 real / Rock da spot / Welcome (interlude) / Case closed / Pick it up / Smoke Buddah / Whateva man / On fire / What do ya feel / Skit / Creepin' / It's like that (my big brother) / Da bump / Sheshall / What U lookin' 4 / Rollin' / Sopperman luva III.

Dec 96. (12") *<573201>* **IT'S LIKE THAT (MY BIG BROTHER) (4 versions) / THAT'S HOW IT IS (IT'S LIKE THAT)** – 95

Jul 97. (12"/cd-s; REDMAN & METHOD MAN) *(574685-1/-2)* **WHATEVA MAN. / ('A'remixes)** Jan97 42

— in Oct'98, REDMAN featured on DRU HILL's US Top 3 hit, 'How Deep Is Your Love'

Dec 98. (cd/d-lp) *<(558945-2/-1)>* **DOC'S DA NAME 2000** 11
– Welcome 2 da bricks / Monkee out / I'll bee dat / Get it live / Who took the satellite van / Jersey yo / Cloze ya doorz / I don't care / Boodah break / Million chickenhead march / Keep on 99 / Well allritecall / Pain in da ass stewardess / Da goodness / My zone / Da da dahhh / GPN / Down south funk / Dog / Beat drop / We got the satellite van / Brick city mashin' / Soopa man love IV / I gotta secret.

May 99. (12"/cd-s) *(870 773-1/923-2)* **DA GOODNESS. / I'LL BE DAT / I'VE GOT A SECRET** 52

— along with METHOD MAN, REDMAN featured on the minor US hit by D'ANGELO, 'Left & Right'

May 01. (cd-s; by REDMAN featuring DJ KOOL) *<572917>* **LET'S GET DIRTY (I CAN'T GET IN THE CLUB)** – 97

May 01. (cd) *<(548381-2)>* **MALPRACTICE** 57 4
– Roller coaster malpractice intro (with ADAM F & G FORBES) / Diggy doc / Lick a shot / Let's get dirty (I can't get in da club) (with DJ KOOL) / WKYA / 2-way madness (skit) / Real niggaz (with SCARFACE, TREACH, MALLY G & ICARUS) / Uh-huh / Da bullshit (with ICARUS) / Who wants to fuck a millionaire (skit) / Enjoy da ride (with METHOD MAN & SAUKRATES) / Jerry swinger stickup (skit) / JUMP (with GEORGE CLINTON) / Muh fuck / Bricks two (with DOUBLE-O, d-Don, ROZ & SHOOGA BEAR) / Wrong 4 dat (with KEITH MURRAY) / Judge Juniqua (skit) / Dat bitch (with MISSY 'MISDEMEANOR' ELLIOTT) / What I'ma do now / Soopaman luva 5 (part 1) / Soopaman luva 5 (part 2). *(bonus+=)* – Smash sumthin' (with ADAM F) / U don't know how to ack.

Sep 01. (c-s/12"; by REDMAN featuring ADAM F) *(588693-4/-4)* **SMASH SUMTHIN' / LET'S GET DIRTY (I CAN'T GET IN THE CLUB) (mixes w/ Gorillaz extended)** 11
(cd-s+=) *(588693-2)* – ('A'-video).

□ RED NOISE (see under ⇒ NELSON, Bill)

Lou REED

Born: LOUIS FIRBANK, 2 Mar'42, Freeport, Long Island, New York, USA. In 1958, he formed The JADES, who released two REED-penned singles, 'LEAVE HER FOR ME' / 'SO BLUE' and 'LEAVE HER FOR ME' / 'BELINDA' for 'Time' and 'Dot' respectively. Late in '64, he joined the 'Pickwick' stable of writers, achieving a local minor hit when The PRIMITIVES issued his 'The Ostrich' / 'Sneaky Pete' 45. Later in the year, he helped for the seminal VELVET UNDERGROUND. An integral part of the group's songwriting prowess, he departed in September 1970, going solo and signing to 'R.C.A.'. His eponymous 1972 debut (with Richard Robinson on production), scraped into the US Top 200, gaining nothing in renewed respect. Later that year, helped by stablemates DAVID BOWIE and MICK RONSON, he unleashed 'TRANSFORMER', gaving him his first major triumph when it reached the Top 30 on both sides of the Atlantic. It was boosted by 'WALK ON THE WILD SIDE' (a superb Top 20 single), the piano-led melancholy of 'PERFECT DAY', the raw glam of 'VICIOUS' and one-that-got-away 'SATELLITE OF LOVE'. His next album, 'BERLIN' (1973), although unfairly panned by US critics, still managed a Top 10 placing in Britain. On reflection, its subject matter of suicide and child neglect ('THE BED' and 'THE KIDS') didn't help win any new friends and it still stands as one of the most unrelentingly bleak listens in the history of rock. After the claustrophobic confessions of 'BERLIN', the live 'ROCK 'N' ROLL ANIMAL' (1974) album must have come as something of a relief to R.C.A. A technically faultless back-up band roared through a selection of old VELVETS numbers with REED hollering over the top, and while the set represented something of a concession to commercial credibility (by REED's standards anyway) it captured little of the VELVET UNDERGROUND's subtlety. It also saw REED sinking further into self-parody, hamming up his studied image of sleazy decadence to the max. 'SALLY CAN'T DANCE', released later the same year, was REED in full emotionless flight, an icy collection of biting cynicism that included the infamous 'ANIMAL LANGUAGE' track. But laughing LOU hadn't played his ace card yet, that musical two fingered salute fell to 1975's 'METAL MACHINE MUSIC', the one everyone talks about but have never had the will or mental endurance to listen to the whole way through. A double album of impenetrable feedback noise interspersed with inhuman screams, hums etc., the record successfully alienated most of REED's long suffering fans amid critical meltdown. In true contrary style, he sashayed sweetly back with the mellow 'CONEY ISLAND BABY' (1976), although the lyrics remained as brutally frank as ever. His first record for 'Arista', 'ROCK 'N' ROLL HEART' (1976) was indeed as vacantly awful as the title suggests, though the punk-inspired 'STREET HASSLE' (1978) showcased a re-energised REED, most impressively on the malicious guitar workout of 'DIRT' and the swaggering title track. After a tedious live album, REED started to show uncharacteristic signs of maturity in both his music and lyrics with 'THE BELLS' (1979) and 'GROWING UP IN PUBLIC' (1980). At the turn of the 80's, he hooked up with former Void-Oid, ROBERT QUINE, a partnership that resulted in one of the most consistent and accomplished sets in REED's solo career, 'THE BLUE MASK'. Newly married and back at his original stable, 'R.C.A.', REED proffered more domestic lyrical fare alongside darker musings. QUINE remained for one more studio album, the similarly focused 'LEGENDARY HEARTS', before breaking ranks. 1984's 'NEW SENSATIONS' was fairly low-key while 'MISTRIAL' (1986) saw REED introduce a few drum machine tracks in typical 80's style. These were competent albums but hardly essential and only the most devout REED believer could've predicted the creative, commercial and critical renaissance that would ensue with 1989's 'NEW YORK' album. A skeletal strum-athon, this was LOU REED in the raw with the sparsest of musical accompaniment. Back on familiar territory, his sardonic tales of the Big Apple's seedier side made for compelling listening. 'SONGS FOR DRELLA' (1990), a collaboration with JOHN CALE, was a heartfelt tribute to ANDY WARHOL, while 'MAGIC AND LOSS' (1992) was a sincere series of stark meditations on life and death. Despite an ill-advised VELVET UNDERGROUND reunion, REED retained critical favour, going on to release another well-received album in 1996, 'SET THE TWILIGHT REELING'. Rather than relying on the cosy reflections of an ageing iconic life, REED entered his fourth decade as a solo artist with more contrary perversity than most young bucks can muster these days. The aptly titled 'ECSTASY' (2000) found the cantankerous ex-VELVET fearlessly analysing the more uncomfortable dimensions of man's primal urges. He may be reaching pensionable age but his visceral guitar work still throbbed with the energy of misspent youth, REED aided and abetted by the rhythm section of FERNANDO SAUNDERS and TONY 'THUNDER' SMITH. 'THE RAVEN' (2003), meanwhile, has to rank as one of the more unconventional projects REED has undertaken in recent years. In setting the works of Edgar Allan Poe to music at the request of theatre director Robert Wilson, REED exorcised some of his own demons in line with Poe's dark imaginings. The resulting album – the double-set version of which came complete with the production's spoken word performances from the likes of Willem Dafoe and Steve Buscemi – ran the gamut of REED's stylistic arsenal, while musical guests included everyone from DAVID BOWIE and ORNETTE COLEMAN to the FIVE BLIND BOYS OF ALABAMA. • **Songwriters:** REED compositions except, SEPTEMBER SONG (Kurt Weill) / SOUL MAN (Sam & Dave). In 1979 and 1980, he co-wrote with MICHAEL FORFARA plus other group members. The single, 'CITY LIGHTS', was co-written with NILS LOFGREN. • **Trivia:** Surprisingly in 1973, WALK ON THE WILD SIDE was not banned from airplay. It contained lyrics "giving head", which had been overlooked by unstreet-wise cred. radio producers. LOU has been married twice, first to cocktail waitress, Betty on the 9th of January '73, then to Sylvia Morales on the 14th of February '80. He played guitar and composed four tracks on NICO's 'Chelsea Girl' lp in 1967. Nine years later he produced NELSON SLATER's 'Wild Angel' album, also contributing guitar, piano and vocals. In 1979 and 1981 he co-composed with NILS LOFGREN and KISS on their 'NILS' and 'THE ELDER' albums respectively. In the late 80's, he guested for RUBEN BLADES and his old friend MAUREEN TUCKER. He was also backing vocalist on SIMPLE MINDS' 'This is Your Land' / DION's 'King of The New York Streets' and TOM TOM CLUB's version of 'Femme Fatale'.

Album rating: LOU REED (*5) / TRANSFORMER (*9) / BERLIN (*7) / ROCK'N'ROLL ANIMAL (*6) / SALLY CAN'T DANCE (*5) / LOU REED LIVE (*5) / METAL MACHINE MUSIC (*1) / CONEY ISLAND BABY (*7) / ROCK AND ROLL HEART (*4) / WALK ON THE WILD SIDE – THE BEST OF LOU REED compilation (*7) / STREET HASSLE (*7) / LIVE – TAKE NO PRISONERS (*3) / THE BELLS (*5) / GROWING UP IN PUBLIC (*4) / ROCK AND ROLL DIARY 1967-1980 compilation (*6) / THE BLUE MASK (*6) / LEGENDARY HEARTS (*6) / LIVE IN ITALY (*4) / NEW SENSATIONS (*7) / MISTRIAL (*5) / NEW YORK (*8) / RETRO compilation (*7) / SONGS FOR DRELLA with John Cale (*7) / MAGIC AND LOSS (*7) / BETWEEN THOUGHT AND EXPRESSION: THE LOU REED ANTHOLOGY boxed-compilation (*7) / SET THE TWILIGHT REELING (*6) / PERFECT NIGHT LIVE IN LONDON (*6) / ECSTASY (*8) / NYC MAN compilation (*8) / THE RAVEN (*7)

LOU REED – vocals, guitar (ex-VELVET UNDERGROUND) / with **STEVE HOWE** – guitar / **RICK WAKEMAN** – keyboards (both of YES) / **CLEM CATTINI** – drums (ex-TORNADOES)

R.C.A. R.C.A.

Jun 72. (7") *<0727>* **GOING DOWN. / I CAN'T STAND IT** [-] [ ]

Jul 72. (lp) *(SF 8281) <4701>* **LOU REED** [ ] Jun72 [ ]
– I can't stand it / Going down / Walk and talk it / Lisa says / Berlin / I love you / Wild child / Love makes you feel / Ride into the Sun / Ocean. *(cd-iss. Feb00 on 'RCA-Camden'; 74321 72712-2)*

Aug 72. (7") *(RCA 2240) <0784>* **WALK AND TALK IT. / WILD CHILD** [ ] [ ]

— now with **MICK RONSON** – guitar / **HERBIE FLOWERS + KLAUS VOORMANN** – bass / **JOHN HALSEY + RITCHIE DHARMA + BARRY DE SOUZA** – drums / **RONNIE ROSS** – saxophone / **DAVID BOWIE** – backing vocals, producer

Nov 72. (lp) *(LSP 4807) <4807>* **TRANSFORMER** [13] [29]
– Vicious / Andy's chest / Perfect day / Hangin' round / Walk on the wild side / Make up / Satellite of love / Wagon wheel / New York telephone conversation / I'm so free / Goodnight ladies. *(re-iss. Feb81 lp/c; INT S/K 5061); hit UK No.91) (re-iss. 1984 lp/c; NL/NK 83806) (cd-iss. 1985 & Oct87 & Aug95; PD 83806) (re-iss. Sep98 cd/c; 74321 60181-2/-4) (lp re-iss. Nov98 on 'Simply Vinyl'; SVLP 58) (lp re-iss. Mar99; NL 83806) (re-dist.Sep01)* – hit UK No.16

Nov 72. (7") *(RCA 2303) <0887>* **WALK ON THE WILD SIDE. / PERFECT DAY** [10] [16]
(re-iss. May79 on 'RCA Gold'; GOLD 5)

Feb 73. (7") *<0964>* **SATELLITE OF LOVE. / WALK AND TALK IT** [-] [ ]

Mar 73. (7") *(RCA 2318)* **SATELLITE OF LOVE. / VICIOUS** [ ] [-]

Apr 73. (7") *<0054>* **VICIOUS. / GOODNIGHT LADIES** [-] [ ]

— all new band **DICK WAGNER + STEVE HUNTER** – guitar (both ex-ALICE COOPER) / **STEVE WINWOOD** – keyboards / **JACK BRUCE** – bass / **AYNSLEY DUNBAR** – drums / etc.

Oct 73. (7") *<0172>* **HOW DO YOU THINK IT FEELS. / LADY DAY** [-] [ ]

Oct 73. (lp) *(RS 1002) <0207>* **BERLIN** [7] [98]
– Berlin / Lady day / Men of good fortune / Caroline says I / How do you think it feels / Oh Jim / Caroline says II / The kids / The bed / Sad song. *(re-iss. Oct81 lp/c; INT S/K 5150) (re-iss. 1984 lp/c; NL/NK 84388) (cd-iss. Jun86; PD 84388) (cd re-iss. Mat98; 7863 67489-2) (lp re-iss. Feb99 on 'Simply Vinyl'; SVLP 66) (lp re-iss. Mar99; 7863 67489-1)*

Feb 74. (7") *(APBO 0221)* **CAROLINE SAYS I. / CAROLINE SAYS II** [ ] [-]

— **PRAKASH JOHN** – bass (ex-ALICE COOPER) repl. TONY LEVIN / **JOSEF CHIROWSKY** – keyboards / **WHITNEY GLEN** – drums (ex-ALICE COOPER)

Feb 74. (lp/c) *(APL 1/4 0472) <0472>* **ROCK'N'ROLL ANIMAL (live)** [26] [45]
– (intro) – Sweet Jane / Heroin / White light – white heat / Lady day / Rock and roll. *(re-iss. May81 lp/c; INT S/K 5086) (re-iss. 1984 lp/c; NL/NK 83664) (cd-iss. Jun86; PD 83664)*

Apr 74. (7") *<(APBO 0238)>* **SWEET JANE (live). / LADY DAY (live)** [ ] [ ]

— **MICHAEL FORFARA** – keyboards repl. JOSEF

Aug 74. (7") *<10053>* **SALLY CAN'T DANCE. / VICIOUS** [-] [ ]

Sep 74. (lp/c) *(APL 1/4 <0611)>* **SALLY CAN'T DANCE** [ ] [10]
– Ride Sally ride / Animal language / Baby face / N.Y. stars / Kill your sons / Billy / Sally can't dance / Ennui. *(cd-iss. Mar87; PD 80611) (re-iss. cd Feb89; ND 90308)*

Oct 74. (7") *(RCA 2467) <10081>* **SALLY CAN'T DANCE. / ENNUI** [ ] [ ]

Mar 75. (lp) *(RS 1007) <0959>* **LOU REED LIVE (live)** [ ] [62]
– Walk on the wild side / I'm waiting for the man / Vicious / Oh Jim / Satellite of love / Sad song. *(re-iss. Feb81 lp/c; INT S/K 5071) (cd-iss. Mar87 + Feb90; ND 83752)*

— LOU now used synthesizer only.

Jul 75. (d-lp) *<(CPL2 1101)>* **METAL MACHINE MUSIC – (THE AMINE B RING)** [ ] [ ]
– Metal machine music A1 / A2 / A3 / A4. *(re-iss. Mar91 on 'Great Expectations' cd/d-c/d-lp; PIPD C/M/L 023) (cd re-iss. Jan01; 74465 99752-2)*

— Band now featured **MICHAEL SUCHORSKY** – percussion / **BOB KULICK** – guitar / **BRUCE YAW** – bass

Jan 76. (lp) *(RS 1035) <0915>* **CONEY ISLAND BABY** [52] [41]
– Crazy feeling / Charley's girl / She's my best friend / Kicks / A gift / Oooh baby / Nobody's business / Coney Island baby. *(re-iss. Mar81 lp/c; INT S/K 5082) (re-iss. 1984 lp/c; NL/NK 83807) (cd-iss. Dec86 & Sep89; PD 83807)*

Mar 76. (7") *(RCA 2666) <10573>* **CHARLEY'S GIRL. / NOWHERE AT ALL** [ ] [ ]

May 76. (7") *<10648>* **CRAZY FEELING. / NOWHERE AT ALL** [-] [ ]

Arista Arista

Nov 76. (lp/c) *(ARTY/TC-ARTY 142) <4100>* **ROCK AND ROLL HEART** [ ] [64]
– I believe in love / Banging on my drum / Follow the leader / You wear it so well / Ladies pay / Rock and roll heart / Temporary thing. *(cd-iss. Feb93; 262271)*

Nov 76. (7") *<0215>* **I BELIEVE IN LOVE. / SENSELESSLY CRUEL** [-] [ ]

Apr 77. (7") *(105)* **ROCK AND ROLL HEART. / SENSELESSLY CRUEL** [ ] [-]

— **STUART HEINRICH** – guitar, vocals repl. KULICK / **MARTY FOGEL** – saxophone repl. YAW

Apr 78. (lp/c) *(SPART/TC-SPART 1045) <4169>* **STREET HASSLE** [ ] [89]
– Gimme some good times / Dirt / Street hassle / I wanna be black / Real good time together / Shooting star / Leave me alone / Wait. *(cd-iss. Feb93; 262270)*

Apr 78. (12") **STREET HASSLE. / (same track)** –
Jul 78. (12"ep) *(ARIST12 198)* **STREET HASSLE. / Waiting For The Man + Venus In Furs (by "The VELVET UNDERGROUND")** –

— **ELLARD BOLES** – bass, guitar repl. HEINRICH. (Below released 'RCA' UK)

Mar 79. (d-lp)<red,blue-lp> *(XL 03066)* *<8502>* **LIVE – TAKE NO PRISONERS (live)** Nov78
– Sweet Jane / I wanna be black / Satellite of love / Pale blue eyes / Berlin / I'm waiting for the man / Coney Island baby / Street hassle / Walk on the wild side / Leave me alone.

— **REED** now with **FORFARA, BOLES, SUCHORSKY, FOGEL** and **DON CHERRY** – trumpet

Oct 79. (lp/c) *(SPART/TC-SPART 1093)* *<4229>* **THE BELLS** May 79
– Stupid man / Disco mystic / I want to boogie with you / With you / Looking for love / City lights / All through the night / Families / The bells. *(cd-iss. Aug92; 262 918)*
Jun 79. (7") *<0431>* **CITY LIGHTS. / I WANT TO BOOGIE WITH YOU** –
Oct 79. (7") *(ARIST 308)* **CITY LIGHTS. / SENSELESSLY CRUEL** –

— **CHUCK HAMMER** – synthesizer, guitar repl. FOGEL & CHERRY

May 80. (lp/c) *(SPART/TC-SPART 1131)* *<9522>* **GROWING UP IN PUBLIC**
– How do you speak to an angel / My old man / Keep away / Growing up in public / Standing on ceremony / So alone / Love is here to stay / The power of positive drinking / Smiles / Think it over / Teach the gifted children. *(cd-iss. Aug92; 262 917)*
Jun 80. (7") *<0535>* **THE POWER OF POSITIVE DRINKING. / GROWING UP IN PUBLIC** –

— now with **ROBERT QUINE** – guitar / **FERNANDO SAUNDERS** – bass, vocals / **DOANE PERRY** – drums

R.C.A. R.C.A.

Mar 82. (lp/c) *(RCA LP/K 6028)* *<4221>* **THE BLUE MASK** Feb82
– My house / Women / Underneath the bottle / The gun / The blue mask / Average guy / The heroine / Waves of fear / The day John Kennedy died / Heavenly arms. *(cd-iss. Feb98; ND 84780)*
Mar 83. (lp/c) *(RCA LP/K 6071)* *<4568>* **LEGENDARY HEARTS**
– Legendary hearts / Don't talk to me about work / Make up mind / Martial law / The last shot / Turn out the light / ow wow / Betrayed / Bottoming out / Home of the brave / Rooftop garden. *(re-iss. Oct86 lp/c; NL/NK 89843) (re-iss. Apr91 cd/c; ND/NK 89843)*
Apr 83. (7") *<13558>* **MARTIAL LAW. / DON'T TALK TO ME ABOUT WORK** –
Jan 84. (d-lp/c) *(PL/PK 89156)* **LIVE IN ITALY (live)** –
– Sweet Jane / I'm waiting for the man / Martial law / Satellite of love / Kill your sons / Betrayed / Sally can't dance / Waves of fear / Average guy / White light – white heat / Some kinda love / Sister Ray / Walk on the wild side / Heroin / Rock and roll.

— line-up now **SAUNDERS** plus **FRED MAHER** – drums / **PETER WOOD** – piano, synthesizer, accordion / **L. SHANKER** – electric violin

Mar 84. (7") *<13841>* **I LOVE YOU SUZANNE. / MY FRIEND GEORGE** –
May 84. (12") *<13849>* **MY RED JOY STICK. / ('A' remix)** –
May 84. (lp/c) *(PL/PK 84998)* *<4998>* **NEW SENSATIONS** 92 56
– I love you, Suzanne / Endlessly jealous / My red joystick / Turn to me / New sensations / Doin' the things that we want to / What becomes a legend most / Fly into the Sun / High in the city / My friend George / Down at the arcade. *(cd-iss. Jul86; PD 84998)*
May 84. (7") *(RCA 417)* **I LOVE YOU, SUZANNE. / VICIOUS** –
(12"+=) *(RCAT 417)* – Walk on the wild side.
1985. (7") *<7-89468>* **MY LOVE IS CHEMICAL. / PEOPLE HAVE TO MOVE** –
(above issued on 'Atlantic' and taken from 'White Nights' movie)
Apr 86. (12") *<14427>* **THE ORIGINAL WRAPPER. / (2 'A' versions)** –
Apr 86. (lp/c/cd) *(PL/PK/PD 87190)* *<7190>* **MISTRIAL** 69 47
– Mistrial / No money down / Outside / Don't hurt a woman / Video violence / Spit it out / The original wrapper / Mama's got a lover / I remember you / Tell it to your heart. *(re-iss. Oct88 lp/c/cd; NL/NK/ND 90253)*
Jun 86. (7") *(RCA 501)* *<14368>* **NO MONEY DOWN. / DON'T HURT A WOMAN**
(12"+=) *(RCAT 501)* *<14388>* – ('A'dub version).

— Next from the film 'Soul Man'.

A&M A&M

Jan 87. (7"; LOU REED & SAM MOORE) *(AM 364)* **SOUL MAN. / Sweet Sarah (by 'Tom Scott')** 30 Nov86
<US-12"+=> *<364>* – My love is chemical.

— new band **MIKE RATHKE** – guitar / **ROB WASSERMAN** – bass / **FRED MAHER** – drums / **MAUREEN TUCKER** – drums on 2 (ex-VELVET UNDERGROUND)

Sire Sire

Jan 89. (lp/c)(cd) *(WX 246/+C)(925 829-2)* *<25829>* **NEW YORK** 14 40
– Romeo had Juliette / Halloween parade / Dirty Blvd. / Endless cycle / There is no time / The last great American whale / Beginning of a great adventure / Busload of faith / Sick of you / Hold on / Good evening Mr. Waldheim / Xmas in February / Strawman / Dime store mystery. *(re-iss. Feb95 cd/c;)*
Feb 89. (7") *<9 22875-7>* **ROMEO HAD JULIETTE. / BUSLOAD OF FAITH (live)** –
Feb 89. (7") *(W 7547)* **DIRTY BLVD. / THE LAST GREAT AMERICAN WHALE** –
(12"+=) *(W 7547T)* – The room.
Apr 90. (cd)(lp/c; by LOU REED / JOHN CALE) *(7599 <26140-2>)(WX 345/+C)* **SONGS FOR DRELLA** 22
– Smalltown / Open house / Style it takes / Work / Trouble with classicists / Starlight / Faces and names / Images / Slip away (a warning) / It wasn't me / I believe / Nobody but you / A dream / Forever changed / Hello it's me. *(re-iss. Feb91 & Jan97; same)*
(above re-united the two VELVET UNDERGROUND members, tributing the recently deceased ANDY WARHOL)

— **MICHAEL BLAIR** – percussion, drums, vocals repl. MAHER

Jan 92. (cd/lp/c) *(7599 <26662-2>)(WX 435/+C)* **MAGIC AND LOSS** 6 80
– Dorita – the spirit / What's good – the thesis / Power and glory – the situation / Magician – internally / Sword of Damocles – eternally / Goodby mass – in a chapel bodily termination / Cremation – ashes to ashes / Dreamin' – escape / No chance – regret / Warrior king – revenge / Harry's circumcision – reverie gone astray / Gassed and stoked – loss / Power and glory part II – magic transformation / Magic and loss – the summation. *(cd re-iss. Jan97; same)*
Mar 92. (c-s) *(W 0090C)* **WHAT'S GOOD. / THE ROOM** –
(12"+=/cd-s+=) *(W 0090 T/CD)* – Harry's circumcision / A dream.

— now with just **FERNANDO SAUNDERS** – basses / **TONY 'Thunder' SMITH** – drums / **MIKE RATHKE** – guitars / + guest **LAURIE ANDERSON** – backing vocals

Reprise Reprise

Feb 96. (cd/c) *<(9362 46159-2/-4)>* **SET THE TWILIGHT REELING** 26
– Egg cream / NYC man / Finish line / Trade in / Hang on to your emotions / Sex with your parents (motherfucker) part II (live) / Hooky wooky / The proposition / Adventurer / Riptide / Set the twilight reeling.
May 96. (c-s) *(W 0351C)* **HOOKY WOOKY / ON THE RUN**
(cd-s) *(W 0351CD)* – ('A'side) / This magic moment / You'll never know you loved.
Apr 98. (cd/c) *<(9362 46917-2/-4)>* **PERFECT NIGHT LIVE IN LONDON (live)**
– I'll be your mirror / Perfect day / The kids / Vicious / Busload of faith / Kicks / Talking book / Into the divine / Coney Island baby / New sensations / Why do you talk / Riptide / Original wrapper / Sex with your parents / Dirty Blvd.
Apr 00. (cd/c) *<(9362 47425-2/-4)>* **ECSTASY** 54
– Paranoia key of E / Mystic child / Mad / Ecstasy / Modern dance / Tatters / Future farmers of America / Turning time around / White prism / Rock minuet / Baton rouge / Like a possum / Rouge / Big sky.
Feb 03. (cd) *<(9362 48372-2)>* **THE RAVEN** Jan03
– The conqueror worm * / Overture / Old Poe * / Prologue (Ligiea) * / Edgar Allan Poe / The valley of unrest * / Call on me (with LAURIE ANDERSON) / The city in the sea – Shadow * / A thousand departed friends / Change / The fall of the House of Usher * / The bed / Perfect day / The raven (with WILLEM DaFOE) / Balloon / Broadway song (with STEVE BUSCEMI) / The tell-tale heart part 1 * / Blind rage / The tell-tale heart part 2 * / Burning embers / Imp of the perverse * / Vanishing act / The cask * / Guilty * / Guilty (with ORNETTE COLEMAN) / A wild being from birth * / I wanna know (the pit and the pendulum) (with BLIND BOYS OF ALABAMA) / Science of the mind / Annabel Lee – The bells * / Hop frog (with DAVID BOWIE) / Every frog has his day * / Tripitena's speech / Who am I? (Tripitena's song) / Courtly orangutans * / Fire music * / Guardian angel. *<(ltd d-cd+= *; 9362 48373-2)>*

– compilations, others, etc. –

—— Below releases issued on 'RCA' unless mentioned otherwise

Apr 77. (lp/c) *(PL/PK 12001)* <2001> **WALK ON THE WILD SIDE – THE BEST OF LOU REED** [ ] [ ]
(cd-iss. Mar87 & Oct91; PD 83753)

Jan 79. (lp/c) *(NL/NK 42731)* **VICIOUS** [ ] [ ]

Dec 80. (d-lp) *Arista; (DARTY 8)* **ROCK AND ROLL DIARY 1967-1980** [ ] [ ]
– (above featured 8 tracks by Velvet Underground)

Aug 81. (7") *RCA Gold; (GOLD 523)* **WALK ON THE WILD SIDE. / VICIOUS** [ ] [–]
(re-iss. Oct86 & Mar89 on 'Old Gold'; OG 9635)

Sep 82. (lp) *(SF 8281)* **I CAN'T STAND IT** [ ] [ ]

Oct 85. (7") *A&M; (AM 283)* **SEPTEMBER SONG. / Oh Heavenly Action (by 'Mark Bingham with Johnny Adams & Aaron Neville')** [ ] [ ]

May 86. (c) *(NK 89895)* **MAGIC MOMENTS** [ ] [–]

Sep 86. (lp/c) *Fame; (FA/TC-FA 3164)* **NEW YORK SUPERSTAR** [ ] [–]

Feb 89. (3"cd-ep) *(PD 49453)* **WALK ON THE WILD SIDE / PERFECT DAY / SATELLITE OF LOVE / VICIOUS** [ ] [ ]

Sep 89. (lp/c/cd) *(PL/PK/PD 90389)* **RETRO** [29] [ ]
– Walk on the wild side / Satellite of love / I love you Suzanne / Wild child / How do you think it feels / Lady day / Coney Island baby / Sweet Jane (live) / Vicious / Sally can't dance / Berlin / Caroline says II / Kill your sons / White light – white heat (live). *(cd+=)* – I'm waiting for the man (VELVET UNDERGROUND) / Heroin (VELVET UNDERGROUND).

Mar 92. (3xcd-box/3xc-box) *(PD/PK 90621)* **BETWEEN THOUGHT AND EXPRESSION: THE LOU REED ANTHOLOGY** [ ] Apr92 [ ]

Jan 95. (d-cd) *(74321 29209-2)* **STREET HASSLE / THE BELLS** [ ] [ ]

Jan 95. (d-cd) *(74321 29210-2)* **TRANSFORMER / BERLIN** [ ] [ ]

Oct 95. (cd/c; by LOU REED & VELVET UNDERGROUND) *Global TV; (RAD CD/MC 21)* **LOU REED & VELVET UNDERGROUND** [ ] [–]

Aug 96. (cd) *(07863 66864-2)* **DIFFERENT TIMES – LOU REED IN THE 70'S** [ ] [–]

Oct 96. (cd) *Camden-RCA; (74321 43157-2)* **LOU REED LIVE IN CONCERT (live)** [ ] [–]

Sep 97. (cd/c) *Camden-RCA; (74321 52375-2/-4)* **PERFECT DAY** [ ] [ ]

Nov 97. (cd) *Eagle; (EABCD 012)* **THE MASTERS** [ ] [–]

Apr 99. (cd/c) *RCA-Camden; (74321 66046-2/-4)* **THE VERY BEST OF LOU REED** [ ] [–]

May 01. (cd) *Burning Airlines; (PILOT 083)* **HAMPSTEAD NEW YORK 26.12.72 (live)** [ ] [ ]

Aug 02. (cd) *Superior; (SU 29025)* **AMERICAN POET** [ ] [–]

May 03. (d-cd) *(82876 50131-2)* <50564> **NYC MAN** [31] Jun03 [ ]
– Who am I (Tripitena's song) / Sweet Jane (VELVET UNDERGROUND) / Rock and roll (VELVET UNDERGROUND) / I'm waiting for the man (VELVET UNDERGROUND) / White light – white heat (VELVET UNDERGROUND) / Street hassle / Berlin / Caroline says II / The kids / Walk on the wild side / Kill your sons / Vicious / Blue mask / I'll be your mirror / Magic and loss / Ecstasy / I wanna be black / Temporary thing / Shooting star / Legendary hearts / Heroin / Coney Island baby / Last shot / The bells / Perfect day / Sally can't dance / NYC man / Dirty Blvd. / Rocket minuet / Pale blue eyes (VELVET UNDERGROUND).

REEF

Formed: London-based from Bath, England ... 1994 by GARY STRINGER, KENWYN HOUSE, JACK BESSANT and DOMINIC GREENSMITH. Following a PAUL WELLER support slot, REEF were snapped up by corporate giants, 'Sony', hitting the ears of the nation in 1995, when a Minidisc TV commercial featured one of their tracks, 'NAKED'. This became their second! Top 30 hit, although they shunned STILTSKIN-like now-made-it-through-TV-ad comparisons. Their debut album, 'REPLENISH' followed later that summer, a decidedly un-Brit-poppy hybrid of loudmouthed funky, heavy country/blues fusing the rootsy sounds of BLACK CROWES or LENNY KRAVITZ with LED ZEPPELIN. The record crashed into the UK Top 10, REEF wowing festival audiences as well as playing a riotous gig on Newquay beach. The year ended with further controversy when the band made an in-store appearance at Tower records in Birmingham, STRINGER allegedly inciting the crowd to loot CD's from the racks and the show breaking down in confusion as the electricity cut out. After a relatively quiet start to '96, the group returned with the anthemic 'PLACE YOUR HANDS ON' which stormed into the charts at No.6 in October, the track becoming the band's signature tune as well as one of Chris Evans' themes on his 'TFI Friday' show. A follow-up album, the GEORGE DRAKOULIAS-produced 'GLOW', topped the charts in early '97, another rootsy, Glastonbury via American Deep South melange of raunchy, soulful pop with the odd mellow moment like 'CONSIDERATION'. Consolidating their position as Britain's foremost purveyors of unreconstructed 70's via 90's rock, the band undertook another round of festival appearances, including a homecoming gig at rain-drenched Glastonbury. With growing confidence and a two-year lay-off, REEF coasted back in '99 with their third and most critically acclaimed set to date, 'RIDES' (notable for the guest appearance by BECK (HANSEN)'s dad, DAVID CAMPBELL on string arrangements!). A year and a bit later, REEF only managed to make the UK Top 20 with the slightly less adventurous 'GETAWAY' (2000). • **Covers:** WAR PIGS (Black Sabbath).

Album rating: REPLENISH (*6) / GLOW (*7) / RIDES (*8) / GETAWAY (*6) / TOGETHER – THE BEST OF REEF compilation (*7) / REEF LIVE (*5)

GARY STRINGER – vocals / **KENWYN HOUSE** – guitar / **JACK BESSANT** – bass / **DOMINIC GREENSMITH** – drums

Sony-S2 Sony

Apr 95. (c-s) *(661360-4)* **GOOD FEELING / WAKE** [24] [–]
(cd-s+=) *(661360-2)* – End.
(12"pic-d++=) *(661360-6)* – Water over stone.

May 95. (7"colrd/c-s) *(662062-7/-4)* **NAKED. / CHOOSE TO LIVE** [11] [–]
(cd-s+=) *(662062-2)* – Fade.

Jun 95. (cd/c/lp) *(480698-2/-4/-1)* <67281> **REPLENISH** [9] [ ]
– Feed me / Naked / Good feeling / Repulsive / Mellow / Together / Replenish / Choose to live / Comfort / Loose / End / Reprise.

Jul 95. (7"colrd/c-s) *(662277-7/-4)* **WEIRD. / ACOUSTIC ONE** [19] [–]
(cd-s) *(662277-2)* – ('A'side) / Sunrise shakers / Together / End (live).

—— Sep'96, STRINGER sustained a gash in his hand when attacked by a gang in a pub.

Oct 96. (c-s) *(663571-4)* **PLACE YOUR HANDS / UNCOMFORTABLE** [6] [–]
(cd-s+=) *(663571-2)* – The snob / Weird (Australian edit).
(cd-s) *(663571-5)* – ('A'side) / Repulsive (live) / Speak lark (live) / Naked (live).

Jan 97. (c-s) *(664097-4)* **COME BACK BRIGHTER / RESIGNATION** [8] [–]
(cd-s+=) *(664097-2)* – It's not what I need / Hawaiian tooth.
(cd-s) *(664097-5)* – ('A'side) / Back into line / Dom and Gary / Robot part.

Feb 97. (cd/c/lp) *(486940-2/-4/-1)* <67971> **GLOW** [1] [ ]
– Place your hands / I would have left you / Summer's in bloom / Lately stomping / Consideration / Don't you like it? / Come back brighter / Higher vibration / I'm not scared / Robot riff / Yer old / Lullaby. *(cd re-iss. Jan01; same)*

Mar 97. (7"red/c-s) *(664312-7/-4)* **CONSIDERATION / ALLOTMENT** [13] [–]
(cd-s+=) *(664312-2)* – New thinking / ('A'radio mix).
(cd-s) *(664312-5)* – ('A'side) / Claypits / Higher vibration (live) / Come back brighter (live).

Jul 97. (c-s) *(664703-4)* **YER OLD / SUMMER'S IN BLOOM (live)** [21] [–]
(cd-s+=) *(664703-2)* – Place your hands (live) / Yer old (Young version).
(cd-s) *(664703-5)* – ('A'side) / Higher vibration (live) / Lately stomping (live) / ('A'live).

Mar 99. (c-s) *(666954-4)* **I'VE GOT SOMETHING TO SAY / FOOT ONE** [15] [–]
(cd-s+=) *(666954-2)* – Buried.
(cd-s) *(666954-5)* – ('A'side) / Who are you / Choose to live (live).

Apr 99. (cd/c) *(492882-2/-4)* **RIDES** [3] [–]
– New bird / I've got something to say / Wandering / Metro / Hiding / Sweety / Locked inside / Back in my place / Undone & sober / Who are you / Love feeder / Moaner snap / Funny feeling / Electric Sunday.

May 99. (c-s) *(667373-4)* **SWEETY / TRIUMPHANT ANTHEM** [46] [–]
(cd-s+=) *(667373-2)* – Bullitt.
(cd-s) *(667373-5)* – ('A'side) / New bird (version) / This day.

Aug 99. (7") *(667851-7)* **NEW BIRD. / BACK IN MY PLACE** [73] [–]
(cd-s+=) *(667851-2)* – Sweety (video).

Jul 00. (c-s) *(669595-4)* **SET THE RECORD STRAIGHT / GENTLE MORNING** [19] [–]
(cd-s+=) *(669595-2)* – Haze.
(cd-s) *(669595-5)* – ('A'side) / Life seems so clean / Nothing town.

Aug 00. (cd/c) *(498891-2/-4)* **GETAWAY** [15] [–]
– Set the record straight / Superhero / Getaway / Solid / All I want / Hold on / Saturday / Won't you listen / Levels / Pretenders / I do not know what they will do.

Dec 00. (cd-s) *(669938-2)* **SUPERHERO / INSIDE OUT / BLOODY MARY / SUPERHERO (secret gig video)** [ ] [–]
(cd-s) *(669938-5)* – ('A'side) / Nothing can change / Whistledown / ('A'-CD-ROM).

May 01. (c-s) *(670822-4)* **ALL I WANT / NAKED (live)** [51] [–]
(cd-s+=) *(670822-2)* – Come back brighter (live) / ('A'-CD-ROM).

Jan 03. (7"red) *(673164-7)* **GIVE ME YOUR LOVE. / SAY WHAT YOU WANT / THANK YOU BABY** [44] [–]
(cd-s+=) *(673164-2)* – ('A'-video).
(cd-s) *(673164-5)* – ('A'side) / Steal away / Place your hands (Rob Orton mix) / ('A'-remix video).

Jan 03. (cd/lp) *(509435-2/-1)* *<700104>* **TOGETHER: THE BEST OF . . .** (compilation) [52] Feb03 [ ]
– Give me your love / Good feeling / Naked / Weird / Place your hands / Come back brighter / Consideration / Yer old / I've got something to say / Set the record straight / Lucky number / Stone for your love / Talk to me / Just dropped in (to see what condition my condition was in).

Snapper — not iss.

Jun 03. (cd-s) *(SMASCD 051)* **WASTER / WAR PIGS / TALK TO ME (live)** [56] [–]
(cd-s) *(SMASCD 051X)* – ('A'side) / War pigs (live) / Saturday (live).

Jun 03. (cd) *(SMACD 869)* **REEF LIVE (live)** [ ] [–]
– Good feeling / I would have left you / Come back brighter / Lucky number / Place your hands / Set the record / Straight / Talk to me / Saturday / Stone for your love / Don't you like it? / Summers in bloom / Who are you? / Lately stomping / Yer old / End / Give me your love / Waster / Naked.

☐ Vernon REID (see under ⇒ LIVING COLOUR)

☐ RELAXED MUSCLE (see under ⇒ PULP)

R.E.M.

Formed: Athens, Georgia, USA . . . spring 1980 by MICHAEL STIPE and PETER BUCK, MIKE MILLS and BILL BERRY, who soon played at a local party under the name TWISTED KITES. In 1981, through manager Jefferson Holt, they released their debut MITCH EASTER-produced 45, 'RADIO FREE EUROPE'. With its soaring melody and jangly guitar playing off STIPE's low-key vocals, the sound was unique and caught the ears of 'I.R.S.' label boss, MILES COPELAND. The latter duly signed them up and retained EASTER for the mini-lp 'CHRONIC TOWN' (1982). The five-song set was received with gushing enthusiasm and set the scene for R.E.M.'s first album proper, 'MURMUR' (1983). Co-produced by EASTER and DON DIXON, the album was a stunning debut which sharpened the hooks, honed the pealing guitar sound and generally engendered a compelling air of mystique. Much of this was down to STIPE's impenetrable lyrics and vague execution which enhanced rather than detracted from the melodic melancholy of songs like 'TALK ABOUT THE PASSION'. While this inventiveness wasn't quite consolidated with 'RECKONING' (1984), the album was slightly more accessible, leading to a Top 30 placing in the American charts. Boasting the ambling country poignancy of '(DON'T GO BACK TO) ROCKVILLE', what the record lacked in innovation it made up for in songwriting skill. Never content to tread water, the band recorded 'FABLES OF THE RECONSTRUCTION' (1985) in London with veteran folk producer JOE BOYD, an interesting pairing which made for a trippy, heavily atmospheric sound. Even the poppier 'DRIVER 8' wasn't free of the edginess which characterised the record. Dextrously combining sonic exploration and heart-melting melodies, 'LIFE'S RICH PAGEANT' (1986) was a bold step forward. Tracks like 'FALL ON ME', 'I BELIEVE' and 'CUYAHOGA' showed an assured poise which the band were undoubtedly developing through their ceaseless touring and snowballing critical acclaim. 'DOCUMENT' (1987) was even more focused, STIPE actually beginning to sound comprehensible. The sardonic, brooding 'THE ONE I LOVE' single gave R.E.M. their first US Top 10 hit, while the band's 'Warners' debut, 'GREEN' (1988), finally saw the band become a mainstream act, in terms of commercial success at least. The unashamed jaunty pop of 'STAND' (1989) gave the band their biggest hit to date while 'ORANGE CRUSH' (1989) echoed the muted moodiness of 'THE ONE I LOVE'. Elsewhere, gems like 'WORLD LEADER PRETEND' were artful examples of that rare ability to create subtle, intelligent songs that were still annoyingly hummable. After 'GREEN's release, R.E.M. undertook a mammoth world tour with the result that the next album, 'OUT OF TIME', didn't hit the shelves until 1991. For most people it was well worth the wait. Preceded by the starkly melancholy 'LOSING MY RELIGION' with its mournful mandolin refrain, 'OUT OF TIME' was a multi-million seller, hitting the top spot on both sides of the Atlantic. While 'SHINY HAPPY PEOPLE' was a mite sickly sweet after 10,000 listens, and 'RADIO' was an ill-advised foray into rap, acoustic flavoured diamonds like 'HALF A WORLD AWAY', 'COUNTRY FEEDBACK' and 'ME IN HONEY' rendered the album a classic. Equally successful but much harder going, 1992's 'AUTOMATIC FOR THE PEOPLE' was a moody masterpiece. Focusing on the more painful aspects of human existence, the album wasn't as immediate as its predecessor but the lucid beauty of tracks like 'NIGHTSWIMMING' and 'MAN ON THE MOON' (written about their tragic comic-hero, Andy Kaufman and later made into a film starring Jim Carrey, c.1999) soon slipped insidiously into your subconscious. Silencing rumours that MICHAEL STIPE was suffering from Aids, R.E.M. bounced back with the grungy 'MONSTER' (1994) album. Despite confident hits like 'WHAT'S THE FREQUENCY KENNETH' and 'CRUSH WITH EYELINER', R.E.M. were capable of more imaginative fare. The subsequent tour (the first since the late 80's) came to a premature halt when BILL BERRY suffered a brain haemorrhage. After a successful recovery, the band reconvened to record 1996's 'NEW ADVENTURES IN HI-FI' (sadly, the last with BERRY). Written mainly on the road, the album was a return to more familiar R.E.M. territory, rich in imagery and possessed of all the qualities that make R.E.M. one of rock's most respected bands. Between ' . . .HI-FI' and 98's slightly disappointing Top 3 set 'UP', BUCK took up posts in MINUS 5 (with YOUNG FRESH FELLOWS' SCOTT McCAUGHEY) and lounge-pop/jazz supergroup, TUATARA. The aforementioned 'UP' was certainly their most pensive and melancholy record to date, UK Top 30 singles such as 'DAYSLEEPER', 'LOTUS' and 'AT

MY MOST BEAUTIFUL', sitting alongside their use of LEONARD COHEN lyrics on 'HOPE'. Come the new millennium, R.E.M. were looking back as well as forward on the shiny, happy but ultimately unfulfilled 'REVEAL' (2001), attempting a marriage of their classic songcraft with the more recent experimentalism. Despite moments of lush, summery abandon, it doesn't quite come off, STIPE and Co sounding like they're still grappling with that sonic mid-life crisis. Another crisis was on hand in April 2001 when PETER BUCK allegedly got into some serious mischief while on a BA flight; his case would take until early the following year to settle. • **Songwriters:** Group compositions except 'B'side covers; THERE SHE GOES AGAIN + PALE BLUE EYES + FEMME FATALE (Velvet Underground) / TOYS IN THE ATTIC (Aerosmith) / KING OF THE ROAD (Roger Miller) / CRAZY (Pylon) / AFTER HOURS (Lou Reed) / LOVE IS ALL AROUND (Troggs) / FIRST WE TAKE MANHATTAN (Leonard Cohen) / LAST DATE (Floyd Cramer) / TIGHTEN UP (Booker T. & The MG's) / SEE NO EVIL (Television) / ACADEMY EIGHT SONG (Mission of Burma) / WALL OF DEATH (Richard Thompson) / FUNTIME (Iggy Pop) / SUMMERTIME (Gershwin) / BABY BABY (Vibrators) / WHERE'S CAPTAIN KIRK? (Spizz) / PARADE OF WOODEN SOLDIERS (Tchaikovsky) / TOM'S DINER (Suzanne Vega) / MOON RIVER (Henry Mancini) / THE ARMS OF YOU (Robyn Hitchcock) / THE LION SLEEPS TONIGHT (Tokens) / DARK GLOBE (Syd Barrett) / SPONGE (Vic Chesnutt) / FAVORITE WRITER (Magnapop) / OUT IN THE COUNTRY (Nichols-Williams). • **Trivia:** R.E.M. stands for Rapid Eye Movement.

Album rating: CHRONIC TOWN mini (*6) / MURMUR (*9) / RECKONING (*9) / FABLES OF THE RECONSTRUCTION (*8) / LIFE'S RICH PAGEANT (*8) / DEAD LETTER OFFICE compilation (*7) / DOCUMENT (*8) / EPONYMOUS compilation (*7) / GREEN (*8) / THE BEST OF R.E.M. compilation (*9) / OUT OF TIME (*9) / AUTOMATIC FOR THE PEOPLE (*10) / MONSTER (*7) / NEW ADVENTURES IN HI-FI (*8) / UP (*7) / REVEAL (*7) / IN TIME: THE BEST OF R.E.M. 1988-2003 compilation (*8) / Hindu Love Gods: HINDU LOVE GODS (*5)

MICHAEL STIPE (b. JOHN MICHAEL STIPE, 4 Jan'60, Decatur, Atlanta) – vocals / **PETER BUCK** (b. 6 Dec'56, Oakland, Calif.) – guitar / **MIKE MILLS** (b.17 Dec'58, Orange County, Calif.) – bass, keyboards, vocals / **BILL BERRY** (b.31 Jul'58, Duluth, Minnesota) – drums, vocals

not iss. — Hib-Tone

Jul 81. (7") *(HT-0001)* **RADIO FREE EUROPE. / SITTING STILL** [-] [ ]

I.R.S. — I.R.S.

Aug 82. (m-lp) *<SP 70502>* **CHRONIC TOWN** [-] [ ]
– Wolves, lower / 1,000,000 / Gardening at night / Stumble / Carnival of sorts (box cars). *(re-iss. Feb85; IRS 70502)*

Aug 83. (7") *(PFP 1017) <9916>* **RADIO FREE EUROPE. / THERE SHE GOES AGAIN** [ ] Jul83 [78]

Aug 83. (lp/c) *(SP/CS 70604) <70604>* **MURMUR** [ ] May83 [36]
– Radio free Europe / Pilgrimage / Laughing / Talk about the passion / Moral kiosk / Perfect circle / Catapult / Sitting still / 9-9 / Shaking through / We walk / West of the fields. *(cd-iss. 1988; CDA 7014) (cd re-iss. Mar91 ++; CDMID 129)* – There she goes again / 9-9 (live) / Gardening at night (live) / Catapult (live).

Nov 83. (7") *(PFP 1026)* **TALK ABOUT THE PASSION. / SHAKING THROUGH** [ ] [-]
(12"+=) *(PFSX 1026)* – Carnival of sorts (box cars) / 1,000,000.

Mar 84. (7") *(IRS 105) <9927>* **S). CENTRAL RAIN (I'M SORRY). / KING OF THE ROAD** [ ] Jun84 [85]
(12") *(PFSX 105)* – ('A'side) / Voice of Harold / Pale blue eyes.

Apr 84. (lp/c) *(IRS A/C 7045) <70044>* **RECKONING** [91] [27]
– Harborcoat / 7 Chinese Bros. / So. central rain (I'm sorry) / Pretty persuasion / Time after time (Annelise) / Second guessing / Letter never sent / Camera / (Don't go back to) Rockville / Little America. *(cd-iss. 1988 on 'A&M'; CDA 7045) (re-iss. Oct94 on 'A&M' cd/c;)*

Jun 84. (7") *(IRS 107)* **(DON'T GO BACK TO) ROCKVILLE. / WOLVES** [ ] [-]
(12"+=) *(IRSX 107)* – 9 minus 9 (live) / Gardening at night (live).

Jun 84. (7") *<IR 9931>* **(DON'T GO BACK TO) ROCKVILLE. / CATAPULT (live)** [-] [ ]

Jul 85. (7") *(IRM 102)* **CAN'T GET THERE FROM HERE. / BANDWAGON** [ ] [-]
(12"+=) *(IRT 102)* – Burning Hell.

Jul 85. (lp/c) *(MIR F/C 1003) <5592>* **FABLES OF THE RECONSTRUCTION – RECONSTRUCTION OF THE FABLES** [35] Jun85 [28]
– Feeling gravitys pull / Maps and legends / Driver 8 / Life and how to live it / Old Man Kensey / Can't get there from here / Green grow the rushes / Kokoutek / Auctioneer (another engine) / Good advices / Wendell Gee. *(cd-iss. Apr87; DMIRF 1003) (re-iss. cd Jan90; DMIRL 1503) (lp re-iss. Dec99 on 'Simply Vinyl'; SVLP 151)*

Oct 85. (7") *<52678>* **DRIVER 8. / CRAZY** [-] [ ]

Oct 85. (7") *(IRM 105)* **WENDELL GEE. / CRAZY** [ ] [-]
(d7"+=) *(IRMD 105)* – Ages of you / Burning down.
(12"+=) *(IRT 105)* – Driver 8.

Aug 86. (7") *(IRM 121) <52883>* **FALL ON ME. / ROTARY TEN** [ ] [94]
(12"+=) *(IRMT 121)* – Toys in the attic.

Aug 86. (lp/c) *(MIRG/+C 1014) <5783>* **LIFE'S RICH PAGEANT** [43] [21]
– Begin the begin / These days / Fall on me / Cuyahoga / Hyena / Underneath the bunker / The flowers of Guatemala / I believe / What if we give it away? / Just a touch / Swan swan H / Superman. *(cd-iss. Dec86; DMIRG 1014) (re-iss. cd Sep91; DMIRL 1507)*

Mar 87. (7") *(IRM 128)* **SUPERMAN. / WHITE TORNADO** [ ] [-]
(12"+=) *(IRMT 128)* – Femme fatale.

Aug 87. (7") *(IRM 145)* **IT'S THE END OF THE WORLD AS WE KNOW IT (AND I FEEL FINE). / THIS ONE GOES OUT (live)** [ ] [-]
(12"+=) *(IRMT 145)* – Maps and legends (live).

Sep 87. (7") *<53171>* **THE ONE I LOVE. / MAPS AND LEGENDS (live)** [-] [9]

Oct 87. (lp/c/cd) *(MIRG/MIRGC/DMIRG 1025) <42059>* **DOCUMENT** [28] Sep87 [10]
– Finest worksong / Welcome to the occupation / Exhuming McCarthy / Disturbance at Heron House / Strange / It's the end of the world as we know it (and I feel fine) / The one I love / Fireplace / Lightnin' Hopkins / King of birds / Oddfellows local 151. *(cd re-iss. Sep91 +=; DMIRL 1508)* – Finest worksong (other mix) / Last date / The one I love (live) / Time after time etc. (live) / Disturbance at the Heron house (live) / Finest worksong (lengthy club mix). *(lp re-iss. Apr99; 499466-1)*

Nov 87. (7") *(IRM 146)* **THE ONE I LOVE. / LAST DATE** [51] [-]
(12"+=/cd-s+=) *(IRMT/DIRM 146)* – Disturbance at the Heron House (live).

Jan 88. (7") *(IRM 161)* **FINEST WORKSONG. / TIME AFTER TIME, ETC.** [50] [-]
(12"+=) *(IRMT 161) <23850>* – ('A'-lengthy club mix).
(cd-s+=) *(DIRM 161)* – It's the end of the world and we know it (and I feel fine).

Jan 88. (7") *<53220>* **IT'S THE END OF THE WORLD AS WE KNOW IT (AND I FEEL FINE). / LAST DATE** [-] [69]

Warners — Warners

Nov 88. (lp/c)(cd) *(WX 234/+C)<(7599-25795-2)>* **GREEN** [27] [12]
– Pop song '89 / Get up / You are the everything / Stand / World leader pretend / The wrong child / Orange crush / Turn you inside-out / Hairshirt / I remember California / Untitled song. *(lp re-iss. Jul99; same)*

Jan 89. (7"/s7") *(W 7577/+X) <27688>* **STAND. / MEMPHIS TRAIN BLUES** [51] [6]
(12"+=/3"cd-s+=/3"s-cd-s+=) *(W 7577 T/CD/CDX)* – (The eleventh untitled song).

Mar 89. (7"/s7"/7"box/c-s) *(W 2960/+X/B/C)* **ORANGE CRUSH. / GHOST RIDERS** [28] [-]
(12"+=/3"cd-s+=) *(W 2960 T/CD)* – Dark globe.

Jun 89. (7") *<27640>* **POP SONG '89 / ('A'acoustic)** [-] [86]

Jul 89. (7"/s7") *(W 2833/+W)* **STAND. / POP SONG '89 (acoustic)** [48] [-]
(12"+=/3"cd-s+=/3"s-cd-s+=) *(W 2833 T/CD/CDX)* – Skin tight (live).

— (all above 7"singles were re-iss. in 4xbox Dec89)

Sep 89. (7") *(7-22791>* **GET UP. / FUNTIME** [-] [ ]

— R.E.M. toured early '91 as BINGO HAND JOB.

Feb 91. (7"/c-s) *(W 0015/+C) <19392>* **LOSING MY RELIGION. / ROTARY ELEVEN** [19] Mar91 [4]
(12"+=/cd-s+=) *(W 0015 T/CD)* – After hours (live).
(cd-s) *(W 0015CDX)* – ('A'side) / Stand (live) / Turn you inside-out (live) / World leader pretend (live).

Mar 91. (cd/c/lp) *<(7599 26496-2/-4/-1)>* **OUT OF TIME** [1] [1]
– Radio song / Losing my religion / Low / Near wild Heaven / Endgame /

Shiny happy people / Belong / Half a world away / Texarkana / Country feedback / Me in honey. *(lp re-iss. Jul99; same)*

— (the album feat. PETER HOLSAPPLE – guitar (ex-DB'S) / KRS-1 – rapper) MICHAEL STIPE released album with KRS-1 'CIVILIZATION VS.TECHNOLOGY' Oct91.

May 91. (7"/c-s) *(W 0027/+C)* <19242> **SHINY HAPPY PEOPLE. / FORTY SECOND SONG** 6 Jul91 10
(12"+=/cd-s+=) *(W 0027 T/CD)* – Losing my religion (live acoustic).
(cd-s) *(W 0027CDX)* – ('A'side) / I remember California (live) / Get up (live) / Pop song '89 (live).
(above 'A'side feat. KATE PIERSON of The B-52'S)

Aug 91. (7"/c-s) *(W 0055/+C)* **NEAR WILD HEAVEN. / POP SONG '89** 27 –
(12"+=) *(W 0055T)* – Half a world away (live).
(cd-s) *(W 0055CDX)* – ('A'side) / Tom's diner (live) / Low (live) / Endgame (live).

Nov 91. (7"/c-s) *(W 0072/+C)* **RADIO SONG. / LOVE IS ALL AROUND (live)** 28 –
(12"+=) *(W 0072T)* – Shiny happy people (music mix).
(cd-s) *(W 0072CDX)* – ('A'side) / You are my everything (live) / Orange crush (live) / Belong (live).

Oct 92. (7"/c-s) *(W 0136/+C)* **DRIVE. / WORLD LEADER PRETEND** 11 –
(cd-s+=) *(W 0136CD)* – First we take Manhattan /
(cd-s) *(W 0136CDX)* – ('A'side) / It's a free world, baby / Winged mammal theme / First we take Manhattan.

Oct 92. (c-s,cd-s) <18729> **DRIVE / WINGED MAMMAL THEME** – 28

Oct 92. (cd)(lp/c) <(9362 45055)>*(WX 488/+C)* **AUTOMATIC FOR THE PEOPLE** 1 2
– Drive / Try not to breathe / The sidewinder sleeps tonight / Everybody hurts / New Orleans instrumental No.1 / Sweetness follows / Monty got a raw deal / Ignoreland / Star me kitten / Man on the Moon / Nightswimming / Find the river.

Nov 92. (7"/c-s) *(W 0143/+C)* **MAN ON THE MOON. / TURN YOU INSIDE-OUT** 18 –
(cd-s+=) *(W 0143CD)* – Arms of love.
(cd-s) *(W 0143CDX)* – ('A'side) / Fruity organ / New Orleans instrumental /2 / Arms of love.

Jan 93. (c-s,cd-s) <18642> **MAN ON THE MOON / NEW ORLEANS INSTRUMENTAL #2** – 30

Feb 93. (7"/c-s) *(W 0152/+C)* **THE SIDEWINDER SLEEPS TONIGHT. / GET UP** 17 –
(cd-s) *(W 0152CD1)* – ('A'side) / The lion sleeps tonight (live) / Fretless.
(cd-s) *(W 0152CD2)* – ('A'side) / Organ song / Star me kitten (demo).

Apr 93. (7"/c-s) *(W 0169/+C)* **EVERYBODY HURTS. / POP SONG '89** 7 –
(cd-s) *(W 0169CD1)* – ('A'side) / Mandolin strum / New Orleans instrumental No.1 (long version).
(cd-s) *(W 0169CD2)* – ('A'side) / Dark globe / Chance (dub).

Jul 93. (7"/c-s) *(W 0184/+C)* **NIGHTSWIMMING. / LOSING MY RELIGION (live)** 27 –
(one-sided-12"pic-d/cd-s) *(W 0184 TP/CD)* – ('A'side) / World leader pretend (live) / Low (live) / Belong (live).

Aug 93. (c-s) <18638> **EVERYBODY HURTS / MANDOLIN STRUM** – 29
(12"orange+=) <9362 40989-04> – Belong / Orange crush (live).
(12"white or blue)(cd-ep) <9362 40992-08> – ('A'side) / Star me kitten (demo) / Losing my religion (live) / Organ song.

Dec 93. (7"/c-s) *(W 0211/+C)* **FIND THE RIVER. / EVERYBODY HURTS (live)** 54 –
(cd-s+=) *(W 0211CD1)* – World leader pretend (live).
(cd-s+=) *(W 0211CD2)* – Orange crush (instrumental).

Sep 94. (7"/c-s) *(W 0265/+C)* <18050> **WHAT'S THE FREQUENCY, KENNETH? / ('A'instrumental)** 9 21
(cd-s) *(W 0265CD)* – ('A'side) / Monty got a raw deal (live) / Everybody hurts (live) / Man on the Moon (live).

Oct 94. (cd/c/lp) <(9362 45740-2/-4/-1)> **MONSTER** 1 1
– What's the frequency, Kenneth? / Crush with eyeliner / King of comedy / I don't sleep I dream / Star 69 / Strange currencies / Tongue / Bang and blame / I took your name / Let me in / Circus envy / You.

Nov 94. (7"/c-s) *(W 0275/+C)* <17994> **BANG AND BLAME / ('A'instrumental)** 15 19
(cd-s) *(W 0275CD)* – ('A'side) / Losing my religion (live) / Country feedback (live) / Begin the begin (live).

Jan 95. (7"/c-s) *(W 0281 X/C)* **CRUSH WITH EYELINER. / ('A'instrumental)** 23 –
(cd-s) *(W 0281CD)* – ('A'side) / Calendar bag / Fall on me (live) / Me in honey (live) / Finest worksong (live).

— On 1st March, 1995, BILL BERRY suffered a brain haemorrhage, after collapsing during a concert in Switzerland. Thankfully, he steadily recovered during the following few months.

Apr 95. (7"/c-s) *(W 0290 X/C)* <17900> **STRANGE CURRENCIES. / ('A'instrumental)** 9 47
(cd-s) *(W 0290CD)* – ('A'side) / Drive (live) / Funtime (live) / Radio free Europe (live).

Jul 95. (c-s) *(W 0308 X/C)* **TONGUE / ('A'instrumental)** 13 –
(cd-s) *(W 0308CD)* – ('A'side) / Bang and blame (live) / What's the frequency, Kenneth? (live) / I don't sleep, I dream (live).

Aug 96. (c-s) *(W 0369C)* <17529> **E-BOW THE LETTER / TRICYCLE** 4 49
(cd-s+=) *(W 0369CD)* – Wall of death / Departure.

Sep 96. (cd/c/d-lp) <(9362 46320-2/-4/-1)> **NEW ADVENTURES IN HI-FI** 1 2
– How the west was won and where it got us / The wake-up bomb / New test leper / Undertow / E-bow the letter / Leave / Departure / Bittersweet me / Be mine / Binky the doormat / Zither / So fast, so numb / Low desert / Electrolite.

Oct 96. (c-s) *(W 0377C)* <17490> **BITTERSWEET ME / UNDERTOW (live)** 19 46
(cd-s+=) *(W 0377CD)* – Wichita lineman (live) / New test leper (acoustic).

Dec 96. (c-s) *(W 0383C)* <43810> **ELECTROLITE / THE WAKE-UP BOMB (live)** 29 96
(cd-s+=) *(W 0383CD)* – King of comedy (808 State mix) / Binky the doormat (live).

— now without BERRY whose place was taken up by guests

Oct 98. (c-s) *(W 0455C)* <17129> **DAYSLEEPER / EMPHYSEMA** 6 57
(cd-s+=) *(W 0455CD)* – Why not smile (Oxford American version).
(3"cd-s) *(W 0466CDX)* – Daysleeper / Sad professor (live in the studio).

Oct 98. (cd/c/lp) *(9362 47151-2/-4/-1)* <47112> **UP** 2 3
– Airportman / Lotus / Suspicion / Hope / At my most beautiful / The apologist / Sad professor / You're in the air / Walk unafraid / Why not smile / Daysleeper / Diminished / Parakeet / Falls to climb.

Dec 98. (c-s) *(W 466C)* **LOTUS / SURFING THE GANGES** 26 –
(cd-s+=) *(W 466CD)* – Lotus (weird mix).
(3"cd-s) *(W 466CDX)* – Lotus / Suspicion (live in the studio).

Mar 99. (cd-s) *(W 477CD)* **AT MY MOST BEAUTIFUL / THE PASSENGER (live at 'Later With Jools Holland') / COUNTRY FEEDBACK (live at 'Later With Jools Holland')** 10 –
(3"cd-s) *(W 477CDX)* – ('A'live) / So. central rain (live at 'Later With Jools Holland').

Jun 99. (cd-s) *(W 488CD)* **SUSPICION / ELECTROLITE ('Later With Jools Holland' version) / MAN ON THE MOON ('Later With Jools Holland' version)** – tour –
(3"cd-s+=) *(W 488CDX)* – ('A'live) / Perfect circle ('Later With Jools Holland' version).

Jan 00. (c-s) *(W 516C)* <radio cut> **THE GREAT BEYOND / MAN ON THE MOON (live)** 3 Dec99 57
(cd-s) *(W 516CD)* – ('A'side) / Everybody hurts (live) / The one I love (live).
(above was taken from the movie/soundtrack, 'Man On The Moon', in which they contributed several other tracks)

Apr 01. (c-s) *(W 559C)* <42365> **IMITATION OF LIFE / THE LIFTING** 6 May01 83
(cd-s+=) *(W 559CD)* – Beat a drum (Dalkey demo) / 2JN.

May 01. (cd/c/lp) <(9362 47946-2/-4/-1)> **REVEAL** 1 6
– Lifting / I've been high / All the way to Reno (you're gonna be a star) / She just wants to be / Disappear / Saturn return / Beat a drum / Imitation of life / Summer turns to high / The chorus and the ring / I'll take the rain / Beachball.

Jul 01. (c-s) *(W 568C)* **ALL THE WAY TO RENO (YOU'RE GONNA BE A STAR) / 165 HILLCREST (instrumental)** 24 –
(cd-s) *(W 568CDX)* – ('A'side) / Yellow river / Imitation of life (live) / Imitation of life (live – video).

Nov 01. (c-s) *(W 573C)* **I'LL TAKE THE RAIN / 32 CHORD SONG** 44 –
(cd-s+=) *(W 573CD1)* – I've been high (CD-Rom video).
(cd-s++=) *(W 573CD2)* – She just want to be (live).

Oct 03. (7") *(W 624)* **BAD DAY. / FAVORITE WRITER** 9
(cd-s+=) *(W 624CD1)* – ('A'video).
(cd-s)<cd-s+=> *(W 624CD2)* <42668> – ('A'side) / Out in the country / Adagio.

Oct 03. (cd) <(9362 48381-2)> **IN TIME: THE BEST OF R.E.M. 1988-2003** (compilation) [1] [8]
– Man on the moon / The great beyond / Bad day / What's the frequency, Kenneth? / All the way to Reno (you're gonna be a star) / Losing my religion / E-bow the letter / Orange crush / Imitation of life / Daysleeper / Animal / The sidewinder sleeps tonite / Stand / Electrolite / All the right friends / Everybody hurts / At my most beautiful / Nightswimming. *<(ltd d-cd+=; 9362 48602-2)>* – Pop song '89 (acoustic) / Turn you inside out (live) / Fretless / Chance (dub) / It's a free world baby / Drive (live) / Star me kitten / Revolution / Leave / Why not smile / The lifting (demo) / Beat a drum (demo) / 2JN / The one I love (live) / Country feedback (live). *(hit UK No.36 + US No.16)*

– compilations, others, etc. –

—— on 'I.R.S.' unless mentioned otherwise

May 87. (lp/c/cd) *<(SP/CS/CDA 70054)>* **DEAD LETTER OFFICE** (b-sides, rarities, etc.) [60] [52]
– Crazy / There she goes again / Burning down / Voice of Harold / Burning Hell / White tornado / Toys in the attic / Windout / Ages of you / Pale blue eyes / Rotary ten / Bandwagon / Femme fatale / Walters theme / King of the road. *(cd+=)* – CHRONIC TOWN *(re-iss. Oct94 on 'A&M' cd/c; CD/C MID 195)*

Oct 88. (lp/c/cd) *(MIRG/MIRGC/DMIRG 1038)* *<6262>* **EPONYMOUS** [69] [44]
– Radio free Europe / Gardening at night / Talk about the passion / So. central rain / (Don't go back to) Rockville / Can't get there from here / Driver 8 / Romance / Fall on me / The one I love / Finest worksong / It's the end of the world as we know it (and I feel fine).

Oct 88. (7") *(IRM 173)* **THE ONE I LOVE. / FALL ON ME** [ ] [–]
(12"+=/cd-s+=) *(IRMT/DIRM 173)* – So. central rain (I'm sorry).

May 90. (c) *A&M; (AMC 24109)* **MURMUR / RECKONING** [ ] [ ]

Sep 91. (cd/c/lp) *(DMIRH/MIRHC/MIRH 1)* **THE BEST OF R.E.M.** [7] [–]
– Carnival of sorts / Radio free Europe / Perfect circle / Talk about the passion / So. central rain / (Don't go back to) Rockville / Pretty persuasion / Green grow the rushes / Can't get there from here / Driver 8 / Fall on me / I believe / Cuyahoga / The one I love / Finest worksong / It's the end of the world as we know it (and I feel fine).

Sep 91. (7"/c-s) *(IRM/+C 178)* **THE ONE I LOVE. / CRAZY** [16] [ ]
(cd-s) *(DIRMT 178)* – ('A'side) / This one goes out (live) / Maps and legends (live).
(cd-s) *(DIRMX 178)* – ('A'side) / Driver 8 (live) / Disturbance at the Heron House (live).

Dec 91. (7"/c-s) *(IRM/+C 180)* **IT'S THE END OF THE WORLD (AS WE KNOW IT). / RADIO FREE EUROPE** [39] [ ]
(cd-s+=) *(DIRMT 180)* – Time after time, etc. (live).

—— When MICHAEL STIPE went off guesting for groups incl. GOLDEN PALOMINOS; others splintered off into . . .

HINDU LOVE GODS

not iss. I.R.S.

Sep 85. (7") *<IRS-52867>* **NARRATOR. / GONNA HAVE A GOOD TIME TONIGHT** [–] [ ]

—— with **WARREN ZEVON** – vocals (they guested on his late '89 album, 'Sentimental Hygene')

Reprise Giant

Nov 90. (7") *(W 9502)* **RASPBERRY BERET. / WANG DANG DOODLE** [ ] [–]
(12"+=/cd-s+=) *(W 9502 T/CD)* – Mannish boy.

Nov 90. (cd/c/lp) *<(7599 24406-2/-4/-1)>* **HINDU LOVE GODS** [ ] [ ]
– Walkin' blues / Travelin' riverside blues / Raspberry beret / Crosscut saw / Junco pardner / Mannish boy / Wang dang doodle / Battleship chains / I'm a one woman man / Vigilante man.

☐ RENTALS (see under ⇒ WEEZER)

REO SPEEDWAGON

Formed: Champaign, Illinois, USA . . . 1968 by NEAL DOUGHTY and ALAN GRATZER, who soon recruited GARY RICHRATH, TERRY LUTTRELL and GREG PHILBIN. With help from manager Irving Azoff, they signed to 'Epic' records in 1971, releasing their eponymous debut album soon after. Through constant touring and a highly productive recording schedule, the band built up a hefty national following, although early albums like 'LOST IN A DREAM' (1975) and 'THIS TIME WE MEAN IT' (featuring contributions from SLY STONE, of all people; 1975) only managed minor US chart placings. However, by the release of 'R.E.O.' in 1976, frontman CRONIN had returned following a brief period as a solo artist, his co-writing skills (along with RICHRATH) contributing to the band's subsequent breakthrough. The live 'YOU GET WHAT YOU PLAY FOR' (1977) was the group's first multi million seller while the appallingly titled 'YOU CAN TUNE A PIANO, BUT YOU CAN'T TUNA FISH' (1978) followed suit, their first US Top 30 placing. The group were also moving away from the rather faceless snooze-rock of old to a more poppy, hook-laden style, the shift paying off in 1981 when the 'SPEEDWAGON scored dual US No.1's with the melancholic balladry of single, 'KEEP ON LOVING YOU' and accompanying album, 'HI INFIDELITY'. An AOR classic in the mould of JOURNEY, STYX, BOB SEGER or KANSAS, 'HI . . .' was highly melodic, infectious and endearing despite the rather sappy vocal delivery and the group's chronic unfashionability. Tunes like 'TOUGH GUYS' and 'TAKE IT ON THE RUN' made great driving material, though you'd never admit as much to your mates. The follow-up, 'GOOD TROUBLE' (1982) was by all accounts a disappointment although the band were back on track by the mid-80's with the 'WHEELS ARE TURNIN' (1984) album and its attendant No.1 single, 'CAN'T FIGHT THIS FEELING'. REO SPEEDWAGON continued to enjoy fair to middling US success throughout the remainder of the decade although since the departure of RICHRATH in 1990, the band have struggled to make an impact on the charts. • **Songwriters:** RICHRATH until 1976 when CRONIN returned to co-write most. • **Trivia:** Took their name from a 1911 fire truck.

Album rating: REO SPEEDWAGON (*6) / R.E.O. T.W.O. (*7) / RIDIN' THE STORM OUT (*6) / LOST IN A DREAM (*5) / THIS TIME WE MEAN IT (*5) / R.E.O. (*4) / REO SPEEDWAGON LIVE – YOU GET WHAT YOU PAY FOR (*5) / YOU CAN TUNE A PIANO, BUT YOU CAN'T TUNA FISH (*6) / NINE LIVES (*5) / A DECADE OF ROCK AND ROLL 1970 TO 1980 compilation (*6) / HI INFIDELITY (*6) / GOOD TROUBLE (*4) / WHEELS ARE TURNIN' (*5) / LIFE AS WE KNOW IT (*4) / THE HITS compilation (*6) / THE EARTH, A SMALL MAN, HIS DOG AND A CHICKEN (*3) / A SECOND DECADE OF ROCK AND ROLL 1981-1991 compilation (*5) / BUILDING THE BRIDGE (*3)

GARY RICHRATH (b.18 Oct'49, Peoria, Illinois) – lead guitar / **NEAL DOUGHTY** (b.29 Jul'46, Evanston, Illinois) – keyboards, organ / **ALAN GRATZER** (b. 9 Nov'48, Syracuse, N.Y.) – drums / **TERRY LUTTRELL** – vocals / **GREG PHILBIN** – bass

Epic Epic

Jan 72. (7") *<10827>* **PRISON WOMEN. / SOPHISTICATED LADY** [–] [ ]

Jun 72. (7") *<10847>* **157 RIVERSIDE AVENUE. / FIVE MEN WERE KILLED TODAY** [ ] [ ]

Jul 72. (lp) *(EPC 64813)* *<31089>* **REO SPEEDWAGON** [ ] Dec71 [ ]
– Gypsy woman's passion / 157 Riverside Avenue / Anti-establishment man / Lay me down / Sophisticated lady / Five men were killed today / Prison women / Dead at last. *(re-iss. Nov81 on 'C.B.S.'; CBS 32096) (re-iss. Jun93 on 'Sony Collectors' cd/c; 982967-2/-4)*

Aug 72. (7") *<10892>* **GYPSY WOMAN'S PASSION. / LAY ME DOWN** [–] [ ]

—— **KEVIN CRONIN** (b. 6 Oct'51, Evanston) – vocals, guitar repl. LUTTRELL

Dec 72. (lp) *<31745>* **R.E.O. T.W.O.** [–] [ ]

– Let me ride / How the story goes / Little Queenie / Being kind / Music man / Like you do / Flash tan queen / Golden country.

Apr 73. (7") *<10975>* **GOLDEN COUNTRY. / LITTLE QUEENIE** –

— **MIKE MURPHY** – vocals repl. CRONIN who became unrecorded solo artist

Jan 74. (lp) *<32378>* **RIDIN' THE STORM OUT** –
– Ridin' the storm out / Whiskey night / Oh woman / Find my fortune / Open up / Movin' / Son of a poor man / Start a new life / It's everywhere / Without expression.

Feb 74. (7") *<11078>* **RIDIN' THE NIGHT STORM. / WHISKEY NIGHT** –

Jun 74. (7") *<11132>* **OPEN UP. / START A NEW LIFE** –

Nov 74. (lp) *<32948>* **LOST IN A DREAM** – 98
– Give me a ride / Throw the chains away / Sky blues / You can fly / Lost in a dream / Down by the dam / Do your best / Wild as the western wind / They're on the road / I'm feeling good.

Apr 75. (7") *<50059>* **THROW THE CHAINS AWAY. / SKY BLUES** –

— **KEVIN CRONIN** returned to repl. MURPHY

Aug 75. (7") *<50120>* **OUT OF CONTROL. / RUNNING BLIND** –

Jul 75. (lp) *<33338>* **THIS TIME WE MEAN IT** – 74
– Reelin' / Headed for a fall / River of life / Out of control / You better realise / Gambler / Candalera / Lies / Dance / Dream weaver.

Nov 75. (7") *<50180>* **HEADED FOR A FALL. / REELIN'** –

Jun 76. (7") *<50254>* **KEEP PUSHIN' / TONIGHT** –

Jun 76. (lp) *<34143>* **R.E.O.** –
– Keep pushin' / Any kind of love / Summer love / Our time is gonna come / Breakaway / Flying turkey trot / Tonight / Lightning.

Nov 76. (7") *<50288>* **FLYING TURKEY TROT. / KEEP PUSHIN'** –

May 77. (7") *<50367>* **RIDIN' THE STORM OUT (live). / BEING KIND (live)** – 94

Aug 77. (d-lp) *(EPC 88265) <34494>* **REO SPEEDWAGON LIVE / YOU GET WHAT YOU PLAY FOR (live)** Mar77 72
– Like you do / Lay me down / Any kind of love / Being kind (can hurt someone sometimes) / Keep pushin' / (Only) A summer love / Son of a poor man / (I believe) Our time is gonna come / Flying turkey trot / Gary's guitar solo / 157 Riverside Avenue / Ridin' the storm out / Music man / Little Queenie / Golden country.

Aug 77. (7") *<50459>* **FLYING TURKEY TROT (live). / KEEP PUSHIN' (live)** –

— **BRUCE HALL** (b. 3 May'53) – bass repl. PHILBIN

Jul 78. (lp) *(EPC 82554) <35082>* **YOU CAN TUNE A PIANO, BUT YOU CAN'T TUNA FISH** Apr78 29
– Roll with the changes / Time for me to fly / Runnin' blind / Blazin' your own trail again / Sing to me / Lucky for you / Do you know where your woman is tonight / The unidentified flying tuna trot / Say you love me or say goodnight. *(re-iss. Sep82; EPC 32115)*

Jun 78. (7") *(EPC 6415) <50545>* **ROLL WITH THE CHANGES. / THE UNIDENTIFIED FLYING TUNA TROT** May78 58

Jul 78. (7") *<50582>* **TIME FOR ME TO FLY. / RUNNIN' BLIND** – 56

Jul 79. (7") *<50764>* **EASY MONEY. / I NEED YOU TONIGHT** –

Aug 79. (lp/c) *(EPC/40 83647) <35988>* **NINE LIVES** 33
– Heavy on your love / Drop it (an old disguise) / Only the strong survive / Easy money / Rock'n 'roll music / Take me / I need you tonight / Meet me on the mountain / Back on the road again.

Oct 79. (7") *(EPC 7918) <50790>* **ONLY THE STRONG SURVIVE. / DROP IT (AN OLD DISGUISE)**

Aug 80. (7") *(EPC 8903)* **ONLY THE STRONG SURVIVE. / MEET ME ON THE MOUNTAIN** –

Nov 80. (7") *<50953>* **KEEP ON LOVING YOU. / TIME FOR ME TO FLY** – 1

Feb 81. (7") *(EPC 9544)* **KEEP ON LOVING YOU. / FOLLOW MY HEART** 7 –

Apr 81. (lp/c) *(EPC/40 84700) <36844>* **HI INFIDELITY** 6 Dec80 1
– Don't let him go / Keep on loving you / Follow my heart / In your letter / Take it on the run / Tough guys / Out of season / Shakin' it loose / Someone tonight / I wish you were there. *(re-iss. Nov84 lp/c; EPC/40 32538) (cd-iss. 1988 on 'C.B.S.'; CD 84700) (lp re-iss. Nov98 on 'Simply Vinyl'; SVLP 42)*

Jun 81. (7") *(EPC 1207) <01054>* **TAKE IT ON THE RUN. / SOMEONE TONIGHT** 19 Mar81 5

Jun 81. (7") *<02127>* **DON'T LET HIM GO. / I WISH YOU WERE THERE** – 24

Sep 81. (7") *(EPC 1562) <02457>* **IN YOUR LETTER. / SHAKIN' IT LOOSE** Aug81 20

Jul 82. (7") *(EPC 2495) <02967>* **KEEP THE FIRE BURNIN'. / I'LL FOLLOW YOU** Jun82 7

Jul 82. (lp/c) *(EPC/40 85789) <38100>* **GOOD TROUBLE** 29 7
– Keep the fire burnin' / Sweet time / Girl with the heart of gold / Every now and then / I'll follow you / The key / Back in my heart again / Let's bebop / Stillness of the night / Good trouble. *(re-iss. 1986; EPC 32789)*

Sep 82. (7") *(EPC 2715) <03175>* **SWEET TIME. / STILLNESS OF THE NIGHT** Aug82 26

Oct 82. (7") *(EPC 2889) <03400>* **THE KEY. / LET'S BEBOP**

Oct 84. (7") *<04659>* **I DO'WANNA KNOW. / ROCK AND ROLL STAR** – 29

Nov 84. (lp/c/cd) *(EPC/40/CD 26137) <39593>* **WHEELS ARE TURNIN'** 7
– I do'wanna know / One lonely night / Thru the window / Rock and roll star / Live every moment / Can't fight this feeling / Gotta feel more / Break his spell / Wheels are turnin'.

Jan 85. (7") *<04713>* **CAN'T FIGHT THIS FEELING. / BREAK HIS SPELL** – 1

Feb 85. (7") *(A 4880)* **CAN'T FIGHT THIS FEELING. / ROCK AND ROLL STAR** 16 –
(12"+=) *(TA 4880)* – Keep on loving you.

May 85. (7") *(A 6248) <04848>* **ONE LONELY NIGHT. / WHEELS ARE TURNIN'** Mar85 19
(12"+=) *(TA 6225)* – Take it on the run.

Jul 85. (7") *(A 6466) <05412>* **LIVE EVERY MOMENT. / GOTTA FEEL MORE** 34

Nov 85. (7") *(A 6673)* **WHEREVER YOU'RE GOING. / SHAKIN' IT LOOSE** –

Mar 87. (7") *(650390-7) <06656>* **THAT AIN'T LOVE. / ACCIDENTS CAN HAPPEN** Jan87 16

Apr 87. (lp/c/cd) *(450380-1/-4/-2) <40444>* **LIFE AS WE KNOW IT** Feb87 28
– New way to love / That ain't love / In my dreams / One too many girlfriends / Variety tonight / Screams and whispers / Can't get you out of my heart / Over the edge / Accidents can happen / Tired of getting nowhere.

May 87. (7") *<07055>* **VARIETY TONIGHT. / TIRED OF GETTING NOWHERE** – 60

Oct 87. (7") *(651040-7) <07255>* **IN MY DREAMS. / OVER THE EDGE** Jul87 19

— **GRAHAM LEAR** – drums (ex-SANTANA) repl. GRATZER

Sep 88. (7") *(651646-7) <07901>* **HERE WITH ME. / WHEREVER YOU'RE GOIN' (IT'S ALRIGHT)** Jun88 20
(12"+=/cd-s+=) *(651646-6/-2)* – Keep on loving you / Take it on the run.

Nov 88. (7") *<08030>* **I DON'T WANT TO LOSE YOU. / ON THE ROAD AGAIN** –

— (Apr'89) **MILES JOSEPH** – guitar (ex-PLAYER) repl. RICHRATH

— (1990) **CRONIN, DOUGHTY & HALL** brought in new members **DAVE AMATO** – lead guitar, vocals (ex-TED NUGENT) repl. MILES JOSEPH / **BRYAN HITT** – drums (ex-WANG CHUNG) repl. LEAR / added **JESSE HARMS** – keyboards, vocals (ex-JOHN HIATT, ex-RY COODER)

Aug 90. (7") *<73499>* **LIVE IT UP. / ALL HEAVEN BROKE LOOSE** –

Sep 90. (cd/c/lp) *(467013-1/-4/-2) <45246>* **THE EARTH, A SMALL MAN, HIS DOG AND A CHICKEN** Aug90
– Love is a rock / The heart survives / Live it up / All Heaven broke loose / Love in the future / Half way / Love to hate / You won't see me / Can't lie to my heart / L.I.A.R. / Go for broke.

Oct 90. (c-s,cd-s) *<73540>* **LOVE IS A ROCK. / GO FOR BROKE** – 65

Jan 91. (c-s,cd-s) *<73659>* **L.I.A.R. / HALF WAY** –

— split some time in 1991 before re-forming later

not iss. Essential

Jul 96. (cd) *<119>* **BUILDING A BRIDGE** –
– Can't stop rockin' / I still love you / Building the bridge / When I get home / Then I met you / Look the other way / After tonight / Hey wait a minute / One true man / She's gonna love me / Ballad of the Illinois Opry.

– compilations, etc. –

Below releases on 'Epic' unless mentioned.

May 80. (7") *<50858>* **TIME FOR ME TO FLY. / LIGHTNING** – 77

Jul 80. (d-lp/d-c) *(EPC/40 22131) <36444>* **A DECADE OF ROCK'N'ROLL 1970 TO 1980** Apr80 55
– Sophisticated lady / Music man / Golden country / Son of a poor man /

Lost in a dream / Reelin' / Keep pushin' / Our time is gonna come / Breakaway / Lightning / Like you do / Flying turkey trot / 157 Riverside Avenue / Ridin' the storm out / Roll with the changes / Time for me to fly / Say you love me or say goodnight / Only the strong survive / Back on the road again. *(re-iss. Jul82; same)*

Apr 83. (7") *<03846>* **KEEP THE FIRE BURNIN'. / TAKE IT ON THE RUN** – [ ]

Apr 83. (7") *<03847>* **IN YOUR LETTER. / DON'T LET HIM GO** – [ ]

Aug 84. (7"ep/c-ep) *Scoop; (7SR/7SC 5049)* **6 TRACK HITS** [ ] –
– Only the strong survive / Meet me on the mountain / Shakin' it loose / In your letter / I need you tonight / Roll with the changes.

Nov 85. (lp/c) *(EPC/40 26640)* **BEST FOOT FORWARD – THE BEST OF REO SPEEDWAGON** [ ] –
(re-iss. Jan92 cd/c; 468603-2/-4) (cd re-iss. Oct94; 477510-2)

Feb 86. (7"ep) *Old Gold; (OG 4010)* **KEEP ON LOVIN' YOU. / (2 other tracks by 'Journey' & 'Meat Loaf')** [ ] –

Jun 88. (lp/c/cd) *(460856-1/-4/-2) <44202>* **THE HITS** [ ] 56
(cd/c re-iss. Jul98; 465595-2/-4)

Aug 88. (3"cd-s) <> **KEEP ON LOVIN' YOU. / TIME FOR ME TO FLY** – [ ]

Oct 91. (cd/c/lp) *(468958-2/-4/-1)* **A SECOND DECADE OF ROCK'N'ROLL 1981-1991** [ ] [ ]
– Don't let him go / Tough guys / Take it on the run / Shakin' it loose / Keep the fire burnin' / Roll with the changes / I do wanna know / Can't fight this feeling / Live every moment / That ain't love / One too many girlfriends / Variety tonight / Back on the road again / Keep on loving you '89 / Love is a rock / All Heavens broke loose / L.I.A.R. / Live it up.

Jan 00. (cd) *(495324-2)* **THE BALLADS** [ ] [ ]

REPLACEMENTS

Formed: Minneapolis, Minnesota, USA . . . 1980 originally as The IMPEDIMENTS by the STINSON brothers – TOMMY and BOB – along with CHRIS MARS and chief songwriter/frontman, PAUL WESTERBERG. Legendary purveyors of ramshackle three-chord punk rock, The REPLACEMENTS' early efforts were so lo-fi they were off the end of the scale. Signed to Minneapolis indie stalwart, 'Twin Tone', the band debuted with 'SORRY MA, FORGOT TO TAKE OUT THE TRASH' (1981), the record's raw-nerve attitude, cathartic melodies and twisted humour shining through the garden shed (and a particularly dilapidated one at that) production. The following year's 'STINK' stepped on the gas and upped the nihilism ('GIMME NOISE', 'FUCK SCHOOL') although 'HOOTENANNY' (1983) and 'LET IT BE' (1984) used the hormonal energy to more satisfying and constructive ends. The latter set, especially, saw WESTERBERG's breathtakingly intuitive way with a melody reach fruition; granted, the likes of 'GARY'S GOT A BONER' didn't suggest another ELVIS COSTELLO in the ascendant but the bruised beauty of 'SIXTEEN BLUE' put WESTERBERG head and shoulders above most of his contemporaries (with the honourable exception of, perhaps, HUSKER DU). The record's charms were powerful enough to attract the major label attentions of 'Sire' and in late '85, The REPLACEMENTS released the Tommy Erdelyi (formerly TOMMY RAMONE)-produced 'TIM'. Furnished with a bigger budget, the group tempered their ragged sound while retaining much of the threadbare authenticity, the hooks as razor sharp as ever. It was to be the last album to feature the departing BOB, the band's notoriously shambolic live appearances robbed of the man's more erm, eccentric tendencies (playing in a dress – radical for the time! – or indeed in the nude, was not uncommon). With ROBERT 'SLIM' DUNLAP brought in as a replacement (ha!), the band recorded what many fans and critics alike regard as their finest hour, 'PLEASED TO MEET ME' (1987). More musically adventurous in line with their growing eclecticism, the album also found WESTERBERG's songwriting prowess at its unprecedented best, 'SKYWAY' soaring heavenward while 'CAN'T HARDLY WAIT' was the killer pop song he'd been threatening to pen since the band's inception. Criminally, the rave reviews and positive momentum surrounding the album's release failed to translate into sales, The REPLACEMENTS sounding strangely muted on 1989's 'DON'T TELL A SOUL'. While the minor concessions to commerciality resulted in a Top 60 US chart entry, the band were on their last legs and 1990's 'ALL SHOOK DOWN' was a WESTERBERG solo effort in all but name. The split eventually came in 1992, TOMMY forming BASH & POP (who released an album, 'FRIDAY NIGHT IS KILLING ME' the following year), while WESTERBERG worked on his solo debut proper, '14 SONGS' (1993). Although the writing was faultless, the record lacked the unkempt charm of old, any chance of a full REPLACEMENTS reunion suffering a serious setback as BOB succumbed to a drugs overdose the following year. In the latter half of the 90's (while MARS was also delivering the odd album), WESTERBERG found acceptance – in the way of US chart fame – via two further sets, 'EVENTUALLY' (1996) and 'SUICAINE GRATIFACTION' (1999). You couldn't disguise the fact (well, you could for a while!) that his next project, GRANDPABOY, was just what WESTERBERG needed – a return to basic, anthemic rock with a twist of punk. Early in 2002, the mysterious (until now) GRANDPABOY unleashed his 'MONO' album (recorded in er, mono), most fans however opted for his simultaneous release 'STEREO', although this set was billed under his proper PAUL WESTERBERG name. While 'MONO' was obviously raw and retrofied harking back to say, The Stones' "Exile . . ." days, 'STEREO' was the complete article and returned him into the US Top 100. The following year saw a similar, simultaneous release of a solo set, 'COME FEEL ME TREMBLE' and a blues set, 'DEAD MAN SHAKE', credited to WESTERBERG's alter-ego GRANDPABOY. Both were pretty much in line with his recent studio tinkerings, the former reeling out a patchy collection of heads-down guitar mangling (its best moment coming with a singular cover of Jackson Browne's 'THESE DAYS') and the latter consisting of an equally lo-fi clutch of bluesy songwriting experiments and engaging covers, among them Jimmy Reed's 'TAKE OUT SOME INSURANCE', John Prine's 'SOUVENIRS' and Hank Williams' 'I'M SO LONESOME I COULD CRY'. • **Songwriters:** Penned by WESTERBERG, except; I WILL DARE (Kiss) / ROUTE 66 (Bobby Troupe) / 20TH CENTURY BOY (T-Rex) / HEY GOOD LOOKING (Hank Williams) / CRUELLA DE VILLE (from '101 Dalmations'). • **Trivia:** Were quoted after a tour as saying 'Better hours, 9 to 5; 9 at night to 5 in the morning, that is'. Their '87 single 'ALEX CHILTON', was dedicated to legendary BOX TOPS leader.

Album rating: SORRY MA, FORGOT TO TAKE OUT THE TRASH (*6) / STINK mini (*5) / HOOTENANNY (*6) / LET IT BE (*9) / TIM (*7) / BOINK!! compilation (*8) / PLEASED TO MEET ME (*8) / DON'T TELL A SOUL (*7) / ALL SHOOK DOWN (*6) / ALL FOR NOTHING – NOTHING FOR ALL compilation (*8) / Paul Westerberg: 14 SONGS (*7) / EVENTUALLY (*6) / SUICAINE GRATIFACTION (*5) / STEREO (*7) / COME FEEL ME TREMBLE (*5) / Grandpaboy: MONO (*6) / DEAD MAN SHAKE (*6) / Chris Mars: HORSESHOES AND HAND GRENADES (*6) / 75% LESS FAT (*5) / TENTERHOOKS (*6) / ANONYMOUS BOTCH (*4)

PAUL WESTERBERG (b.31 Dec'60) – vocals, rhythm guitar / **BOB STINSON** (b.17 Dec'59) – lead guitar / **TOMMY STINSON** (b. 6 Oct'66, San Diego, Calif.) – bass / **CHRIS MARS** (b.26 Apr'61) – drums

not iss. Twin Tone

Aug 81. (7") *<TTR 8120>* **I'M IN TROUBLE. / IF ONLY YOU WERE LONELY** – [ ]

Aug 81. (lp) *<TTR 8123>* **SORRY MA, FORGOT TO TAKE OUT THE TRASH** – [ ]
– Takin' a ride / Careless / Customer / Hanging downtown / Kick your door down / Otto / I bought a headache / Rattlesnake / I hate music / Johnny's gonna die / Shiftless when idle / More cigarettes / Don't ask

why / Something to do / I'm in trouble / Love you till Friday / Shut up / Raised in the city. *(UK-iss.Mar88 on 'What Goes On'; GOES ON 017) (cd-iss. Apr93 on 'Roadrunner'; RR 9089-2) (cd re-iss. Mar95; TTR 8123-2) <(cd re-mast.Aug02 on 'Restless'; REST 7376-2)>*

Jun 82. m-(lp) *<TTR 8228>* **STINK** [-] [ ]
– Kids don't follow / Fuck school / Stuck in the middle / God damn job / White and lazy / Dope smokin' moron / Go / Gimme noise. *(UK-iss.Mar88 on 'What Goes On'; GOES ON 020) (cd-iss. Apr93 on 'Roadrunner'; RR 9090-2) (cd re-iss. Mar95; 8228-2) <(cd re-iss. Aug02 on 'Restless'; REST 73763)>*

Apr 83. (lp) *<TTR 8332>* **HOOTENANNY** [-] [ ]
– Hootenanny / Run it / Color me impressed / Will power / Take me down to the hospital / Mr. Whirly / Within your reach / Buck hill / Lovelines / You lose / Hayday / Treatment bound. *(UK-iss.Mar88 on 'What Goes On'; GOES ON 021) (cd-iss. Apr93 on 'Roadrunner'; RR 9091-2) (cd re-iss. Feb95; TTR 8332-2) <(cd re-mast.Aug02 on 'Restless'; REST 73760)>*

Aug 84. (12") *<TTR 8440>* **I WILL DARE. / 20TH CENTURY BOY / HEY GOOD LOOKING (live)** [-] [ ]

Zippo / Twin Tone

Oct 84. (lp) *(ZONG 002) <TTR 8441>* **LET IT BE** [ ] [ ]
– I will dare / We're comin' out / Tommy gets his tonsels out / Black diamond / Androgynous / Unsatisfied / Seen your video / Gary's got a boner / Sixteen blue / Answering machine. *(cd-iss. Apr93 on 'Roadrunner'; RR 9092-2) (cd-iss. Mar95 & Sep98 on 'R.C.A.'; 74321 60574-2) <(cd re-mast.Aug02 on 'Restless'; REST 73761)>*

1985. (c) **THE SHIT HITS THE FAN (live bootleg)** [-] [ ]

Sire / Sire

Nov 85. (lp/c) *(K 925330-1/-4) <25330>* **TIM** [ ] [ ]
– Hold my life / I'll buy / Kiss me on the bus / Dose of thunder / Waitress in the sky / Swingin' party / Bastards of young / Lay it down clown / Left of the dial / Litle mascara / Here comes a regular. *(cd-iss. Jul93; 7599 25330-2)*

Mar 86. (7") *(W 8727)* **SWINGIN' PARTY. / LEFT OF THE DIAL** [ ] [-]

May 86. (7") *(W 8679)* **KISS ME ON THE BUS. / LITTLE MASCARA** [ ] [-]

— **ROBERT 'SLIM' DUNLAP** (b.14 Aug'51, Plainview, Minnesota) – guitar; repl. BOB (he was to die on the 18th of February 1995 o.d.)

Apr 87. (lp/c/cd) *(K 925557-1/-4/-2) <25557>* **PLEASED TO MEET ME** [ ] [ ]
– I.O.U. / Alex Chilton / I don't know / Nightclub jitters / The ledge / Never mind / Valentine / Shooting dirty pool / Red red wine / Skyway / Can't hardly wait. *(cd re-iss. Jul93; 7599 25557-2)*

Jun 87. (7") *(W 8297)* **ALEX CHILTON. / ELECTION DAY** [ ] [-]
(12"+=) *(W 8297T)* – Nightclub jitters / Route 66.

Jul 87. (7") *<28151>* **CAN'T HARDLY WAIT. / COOL WATER** [-] [ ]

Jan 89. (lp/c/cd) *(K 925721-1/-4/-2) <25721>* **DON'T TELL A SOUL** [ ] [57]
– Talent show / Back to back / We'll inherit the Earth / Achin' to be / They're blind / Anywhere's better than here / Asking me lies / I won't / Rock'n'roll ghost / Darlin' one. *(cd re-iss. Jul93; 7559 25831-2)*

Apr 89. (7") *<22992>* **I'LL BE YOU. / DATE TO CHURCH (with TOM WAITS)** [-] [51]

(below w/ guests **STEVE BERLIN / MICHAEL BLAIR / BELMONT TENCH / JOHN CALE** / etc.

Sep 90. (cd/c/lp) *<(7599 26298-2/-4/-1)>* **ALL SHOOK DOWN** [ ] [69]
– Merry go round / One wink at a time / Nobody / Bent out of shape / Sadly beautiful / Someone takes the wheel / When it began / All shook down / Attitude / Happy town / Torture / My little problem / The lost. *(cd re-iss. Jul93 & Feb95; same)*

— (Mar'91) **STEVE FOLEY** – drums; repl. MARS who went solo

— disbanded late in 1991, TOMMY formed BASH & POP, while WESTERBERG and MARS went solo

– compilations, others, etc. –

Apr 86. (m-lp/m-c) *Glass; (MGA LP/MC 016)* **BOINK!!** [ ] [-]
– Color me impressed / White and lazy / Within your reach / If only you were lonely / Kids don't follow / Nowhere is my home / Take me down to the hospital / Go.

Nov 97. (d-cd) *Reprise; <(9362 46807-2)>* **ALL FOR NOTHING / NOTHING FOR ALL** [ ] [ ]
– Left of the dial / Kiss me on the bus / Bastards of young / Here comes a regular / Skyway / Alex Chilton / The ledge / Can't hardly wait / I'll be you / Achin' to be / Talent show / Anywhere's better than here / Merry-go-round / Sadly beautiful / Nobody / Someone take the wheel / Can't hardly wait (the TIM version) / Birthday gal / Beer for breakfast / Till we're nude / Election day / Jungle rock / All he wants to do is fish / Date to church / Cruella De Ville / We know the night / Portland / Wake up / Satellite / Like a rolling pin / Another girl, another planet / Who knows / All shook down.

PAUL WESTERBERG

Sire / Warners

Jun 93. (cd/c) *<(9362 45255-2/-4)>* **14 SONGS** [ ] [44]
– Knockin' on mine / First glimmer / World class fad / Runaway wind / Dice behind your shades / Even here we are / Silver naked ladies / A few minutes of silence / Someone I once knew / Black eyed Susan / things / Something is me / Mannequin shop / Down love.

Jul 93. (7"/c-s) *(W 0183/+C)* **WORLD CLASS FAD. / SEEING HER** [ ] [ ]
(12"/cd-s) *(W 0183 T/CD)* – ('A'side) / Men without ties / Down love.

Oct 93. (7"/c-s) *(W 0209/+C)* **WORLD CLASS FAD. / CAN'T HARDLY WAIT (live)** [ ] [ ]
(cd-s+=) *(W 0209CD1)* – Left of the dial (live) / Another girl another planet (live).
(cd-s) *(W 0209CD2)* – ('A'side) / Waiting for somebody / Dyslexic heart / Answering machine (live).

Apr 96. (cd/c) *(9362 46251-2/-4) <46176>* **EVENTUALLY** [ ] [50]
– These are the days / Century / Love untold / Ain't got me / You've had it with you / Mamadaddydid / Hide n seekin' / Once around the weekend / Trumpet clip / Angels walk / Good day / Time flies tomorrow.

Capitol / Capitol

Apr 99. (cd/c) *(499145-2/-4) <59004>* **SUICAINE GRATIFACTION** [ ] Mar99 [ ]
– It's a wonderful lie / Self defence / The best thing that ever happened / Lookin' out forever / Born for me / The final hurrah / Tears rolling up our sleeves / The fugitive kind / Sunrise always listens / Whatever makes you happy / Actor in the street / Bookmark.

GRANDPABOY

— aka **PAUL WESTERBERG**

not iss. / Monolyth

1997. (7") *<7 1313>* **I WANT MY MONEY BACK. / UNDONE** [-] [ ]

1997. (cd-ep) *<1315>* **GRANDPABOY** [-] [ ]
– Hot un / Ain't done much / Psychopharmacology / Lush and green / Homelessexual.

Vagrant / Vagrant

Apr 02. (cd) *<(VR 368CD)>* **MONO** [ ] Feb02 [ ]
– High time / Anything but that / Let's not belong together / Silent film star / Knock it right out / 2 days 'til tomorrow / Eyes like sparks / Footsteps / Kickin' the stall / Between love and like / AAA.

PAUL WESTERBERG

Vagrant / Vagrant

Apr 02. (cd) *<(VAG 369CD)>* **STEREO** [ ] [81]
– Baby learns to crawl / Dirt to mud / Only lie worth telling / Got you down / No place for you / Boring enormous / Nothing to no one / We may be the one / Don't want never / Mr. Rabbit / Let the bad times roll / Call that gone? / (untitled). *(re-iss. Jun02 on 'B-Unique'+=; BUN 025)* – MONO

Oct 03. (cd) *<VAG 387CD>* **COME FEEL ME TREMBLE** [-] [ ]
– Dirty diesel / Making me go / Hillbilly junk / Soldier of misfortune / My daydream / What a day (for a night) / Wild & lethal / Crackle & drag (original take) / Crackle & drag (alt. version) / Never felt like this before / Knockin' em back / Pine box / Meet me down in the alley / These days.

GRANDPABOY

Fat Possum / Fat Possum

Oct 03. (cd/lp) *<(0377-2/-1)>* **DEAD MAN SHAKE** [ ] [ ]
– MPLS / Do right in your eyes / Vampires & failures / No matter what you say / Take out some insurance / Cleaning house / Natural mean lover / Get a move on / Bad boy blues / Souvenirs / I'm so lonesome I could cry / O.D. blues / Dead man shake / What kind of fool am I?

RESIDENTS

Formed: Shreveport, North Louisiana, USA . . . 1966 by mysterious line-up. Soon relocating to San Mateo, California in the early 70's, they made a few untitled homemade recordings. They subsequently sent these to Hal Haverstadt of 'Warners' who promptly returned them, the address marked; 'for the attention of the residents'. Adopting the latter as their moniker, they later issued the two newly named tapes in the early 70's, 'RUSTY COAT HANGER FOR THE DOCTOR' and 'THE BALLAD OF STUFFED TRIGGER' respectively. In 1972, they shifted base to San Francisco, founding the independently distributed 'Ralph' records. Their "real" debut lp, 'MEET THE RESIDENTS' was issued in 1974, its title and cover art a tongue-in cheek take-off of The BEATLES. They then released a series of very limited edition lp's, 'THIRD REICH AND ROLL' in 1976, a collection of mangled 50's and 60's covers, carrying on where FRANK ZAPPA left off (albeit in a much weirder fashion). Later in the year, The RESIDENTS and DEVO competed for the best re-constructed version of The STONES' 'SATISFACTION', however, the latter won out in the end. After more comical parodying of The BEATLES and others, they unleashed the 'ESKIMO' set in 1979. This seminal meisterwork was recorded over a lengthy period of time, weird in the extreme, it featured tribal rhythms behind sub-lingual voices (VIC REEVES in "club style" must have taken inspiration). In 1980, the 'COMMERCIAL ALBUM' was released, containing forty tracks of exactly one minute in length, it was another to explore the barren frontiers of possibilities in music. They continued throughout the 80's with even more obscurity than their earlier 70's work. This included highlights 'MARK OF THE MOLE' (1981), 'THE TUNE OF TWO CITIES' (1982) and the biblical opera 'GOD IN THREE PERSONS' (1988). The following decade, 'FREAK SHOW' (1991), was first to emerge from the pack, its fake-theatrical doodlings too much for new fans to take on. With the advent of the CD-ROM, The RESIDENTS produced the interactive 'GINGERBREAD MAN' (1995), its play-at-will approach making it never the same twice. The safer 'HAVE A BAD DAY' soundtrack in 1996 was accompanied by yet another interactive CD, 'BAD DAY ON THE MIDWAY'; it was getting beyond a joke, so to speak. In October, 1998, the one-eyeball'd legends set out their religious stall via, 'WORMWOOD: CURIOUS STORIES FROM THE BIBLE', a post-modernist look into the teaching and doctrine of the great book, although with their usual bizarre rhythms. 'ROADWORMS: THE BERLIN SESSIONS' (2000) and the 30th anniversary 'DEMONS DANCE ALONE' (2002) – post-9/11-penned – showed The RESIDENTS were no-one's fools when it comes to uncompromising individualism. • **Songwriters:** Group penned, except tribute/covers lp's of ELVIS PRESLEY, HANK WILLIAMS, GEORGE GERSHWIN and JAMES BROWN material.

Album rating: MEET THE RESIDENTS (*7) / THE THIRD REICH AND ROLL (*6) / FINGERPRINCE (*6) / NOT AVAILABLE (*6) / DUCK STAB – BUSTER AND GLEN (*7) / ESKIMO (*8) / NIBBLES compilation (*6) / THE COMMERCIAL ALBUM (*8) / MARK OF THE MOLE (*6) / THE TUNES OF TWO CITIES (*4) / INTERMISSION mini (*4) / RESIDUE OF THE RESIDENTS (*4) / TITLE IN LIMBO with Renaldo & The Loaf (*4) / GEORGE AND JAMES (*4) / RALPH BEFORE '84 – VOLUME 1 compilation (*6) / WHATEVER HAPPENED TO VILENESS FATS (*4) / RALPH BEFORE '84 – VOLUME 2 compilation (*6) / THE BIG BUBBLE – PART 4 OF THE MOLE TRILOGY (*4) / THE PAL TV LP (*4) / HEAVEN? collection (*6) / HELL? collection (*6) / 13th ANNIVERSARY SHOW (*5) / STARS AND HANK FOREVER – THE AMERICAN COMPOSERS SERIES VOL.2 (*4) / GOD IN THREE PERSONS (*4) / THE MOLE SHOW earlier recording (*4) / THE KING AND EYE (*4) / FREAKSHOW (*4) / PRESENT OUR FINEST FLOWERS (*4) / GINGERBREAD MAN (*4) / RESIDUE DEUX (*4) / HAVE A BAD DAY (*7) / WORMWOOD: CURIOUS STORIES FROM THE BIBLE (*7) / ROADWORMS: THE BERLIN SESSIONS (*) / DEMONS DANCE ALONE (*6)

The RESIDENTS (4) – instruments, vocals, noises / assisted by **SNAKEFINGER** (b. PHILIP LITHMAN) (ex-CHILLI WILLI & THE RED HOT PEPPERS)

not iss. Ralph

Dec 72. (d-7"ltd) *<RR 1272>* **SANTA DOG** (under false psedonyms) –
– Fire (IVORY & THE BRAINEATERS) / Lightning (DELTA NUDES) / Explosion (COLLEGE WALKERS) / Aircraft damage (credited to ARF + OMEGA).

Feb 74. (lp-ltd) *<RR 0274>* **MEET THE RESIDENTS** –
– Boots / Numb erone / Guylum Bardot / Breath and length / Consuelo's departure / Smelly tongues / Rest aria / Skratz / Spotted pinto bean / Infant tango / Seasoned greetings / N-ER-GEE (crisis blues). *(re-iss. re-mixed Aug77; RR 0677)* – (lost 7 minutes). *(re-iss. Dec88 on 'Torso' cd/lp; CD/40 416) (cd re-iss. Mar98 on 'Euro Ralph'; CD 018)*

— In Oct'75, they issued 500 copies US of lp 'BLORP ESETTE' for 'LAFMS'; *005>*

Feb 76. (lp-ltd) *<RR 1075>* **THE THIRD REICH AND ROLL** –
– Swastikas on parade / Hitler was a vegetarian. *<re-iss. 1978; same>*

Sep 76. (7"ltd) *<RR 0776>* **SATISFACTION. / LOSER = WEED** –
<re-iss. Aug78 as 7"yellow; RR 7803>

Jan 77. (7"ep-ltd) *<RR 0377>* **BABYFINGERS** –
– Monstrous intro / Death in Barstow / Melon collie lassie / Flight of the bumble roach / Walter Westinghouse. *<re-iss. 1979 on 'W.E.I.R.D.' 7"pink; 1>*

Feb 77. (lp-ltd) *<RR 1276>* **FINGERPRINCE** –
– You yesyesyes / Home age conversation / Godsong / March de la winni / Bos sy / Boo who / Tourniquet of roses / You yesyesyes again / Six things to a cycle. *(re-iss. twice 1978; same) (cd-iss. Dec87 on 'Torso'; TORSOCD 047)*

Aug 77. (7") *<RR 0577>* **(THE BEATLES PLAY THE RESIDENTS AND THE RESIDENTS PLAY THE BEATLES)** –
– Beyond the valley of a day in the life / Flying.

Feb 78. (7"ep) *<RR 1177>* **DUCK STAB EP** –
– Constantinople / Sinister exaggerator / The Booker tease / Blue rosebuds / Laughing song / Bach is dead / Elvis and his boss.

Oct 78. (lp) *<RR 1174>* **NOT AVAILABLE** –
– Edweena / The making of a soul / Ships a going down / Never known questions epilogue. *(UK-iss.cd Sep94 on 'Indigo'; 7539-2)*

Nov 78. (lp) *<RR 0278>* **DUCK STAB / BUSTER AND GLEN** –
– DUCK STAB + / Lizard lady / Semolina / Birthday boy / Weight-lifting Lulu / Krafty cheese / Hello skinny / The electrocutioner. *(cd-iss. Jul87 on 'Torso'; TORSOCD 406>*

Dec 78. (7") *<RR 7812>* **SANTA DOG 78. / SANTA DOG** –

Aug 79. (lp) *<SM 7908>* **SUBTERRANEAN MODERN** –

— more guests **CHRIS CUTLER** – percussion / **DON PRESTON** – synth

Sep 79. (lp,white-lp) *<ESK 7906>* **ESKIMO** –
– The walrus hunt / Birth / Arctic hysteria / The angry Angakok / A spirit steals a child / The festival of death. *(cd-iss. Jul87 on 'Torso'; TORSOCD 404) (cd re-iss. 1996 on 'Ralph Euro'; CD 016)*

Virgin Ralph

Sep 79. (lp; with SNAKEFINGER) *(VR 3)* *<DJ 7901>* **NIBBLES** <US title 'PLEASE DO NOT STEAL IT' – DJ compilation> Mar79
– Yesyesyesyes / Santa dog '78 / Gloria / Rest aria / Semolina / The spot / Never known questions / Constantinople / Laughing song / The mocking of a soul / Skratz / Good lovin' / Blue rosebuds / Six things to a cycle / The electrocutioner.

Pre Ralph

Oct 80. (lp) *(PREX 2)* *<6559>* **THE RESIDENTS COMMERCIAL ALBUM**
– Easter woman / Perfect love / Picnic boy / End of home / Amber / Japanes watercolour / Red rider / My second wife / Suburban bathers / Floyd / Dimples and toes / The nameless souls / Die in terror / Love leaks out / Act of being polite / Medicine man / Tragic bells / Loss of innocence / The simple song / Ups and downs / Possessions / Give it someone else / Phantom / Less not more / My work is so behind / Birds in the trees / Handful of desire / Moisture / Love is . . . / Troubled man / La la loneliness / Nice old man / The talk of creatures / Fingertips / In between dreams / Margaret Freeman / The coming of the crow / When we were young.

Oct 80. (7"ep) *(PRE 009)* **THE RESIDENTS COMMERCIAL SINGLE**
– Amber / Red rider / Picnic boy / When we were young / Phantom / Moisture.

1980. (12"ep) *<RZ 8006-D>* **DISKOMO** –
– Diskomo / Goosebump: Disasterplants – Farmers – Twinkle.

1981. (lp) *<8152>* **MARK OF THE MOLE** –
– Hole-worker at the mercies of nature / Voices of the air / The ultimate disaster / Won't you keep us working / First warning / Back to normality / The sky falls / Why are we crying / The tunnels are filling / It never stops / Migration / March to the sea / The observer / Hole-worker's new hymn / Hole-worker's vs Man and machine / Another land / Rumors / Arrival / Deployment / Saturation / The new machine / Idea / Construction / Failure / Reconstruction / Success / Final confrontation / Success / Final confrontation / Driving the moles away / Don't tread on me / The short war / Resolution. *(UK cd-iss. Sep94 on 'Indigo'; 7540-2)*

Ralph Recommended

May 82. (lp) *(RZ 8202)* **THE TUNES OF TWO CITIES** Mar82
– Serenade for Missy / Mousetrap / Smack your lips clap your teeth / A maze of jigsaws / God of darkness / Smokebams / Mourning the undead / Song of the wild / Happy home / The secret seed / The evil disposer.

Jul 83. (12"ep) *(RALPH 1) <RZ 8252>* **INTERMISSION**
– Lights out / Shorty's lament / Moles are coming / Would we be alive / New hymn. *(lp-iss.1989 on 'Torso'; TORSO 33-055)*

1983. (lp) *<RZ 8302>* **RESIDUE OF THE RESIDENTS** –
– The sleeper / Whoopy snorp / Kamakazi lady / Boy in love / Shut up! shut up! / Anvil forest / Diskomo / Jailhouse rock / Up & down / Walter Westinghouse / Saint Nix / Open up.

New Ralph New Ralph

Jan 84. (lp; with RENALDO & THE LOAF) *(RR 8351)* **TITLE IN LIMBO**

Korova Recommended

Jul 84. (7") *(KOW 36)* **IT'S A MAN'S MAN'S MAN'S WORLD. / I'LL GO CRAZY**

Aug 84. (lp/c) *(KODE/CODE 9) <RZ 8402>* **GEORGE & JAMES** (some live)
– Rhapsody in blue / I got rhythm / Summertime / Live at the Apollo: I'll go crazy / Try me / Think / I don't mind / Lost someone / Please please please / Night train. *(c+=)* – (extra track). *(cd-iss. Sep94 & Oct00 on 'Indigo'; 2122-2)*

DoubleVision Ralph

Dec 84. (lp) *(DV 9) <RZ 8452>* **WHATEVER HAPPENED TO VILENESS FATS**
– Whatever happened to Vileness Fats / Atomic shopping carts / Adventures of a troubled heart / Search for the short man / The importance of evergreen / Broccoli and saxophone / Disguised as meat / Thoughts busily betraying / Lord, it's lonely / The knife fight. *(UK cd-iss. Sep94 on 'Indigo'; 7537-2)*

1985. (lp) *<RZ 8552>* **THE BIG BUBBLE – PART 4 OF THE MOLE TRILOGY** –
– Sorry / Hop a little / Go where ya wanna go / Gotta gotta get / Cry for the fire / Die stay-go / Vinegar / Fire fly / The big bubble / Fear for the future / Kula bocca says so. *(cd-iss. Sep94 on 'Indigo'; 7541-2)*

Sep 85. (red-lp) *(DVR 17)* **THE PAL TV LP** –

Torso Torso

Oct 86. (d-lp) *(TORSO 33-018) <2614220>* **13TH ANNIVERSARY SHOW (live in Japan & Holland)**
– Jailhouse rock / Where is she? / Picnic in the jungle / I got rhythm / Passing in the bottle / Monkey and Bunny / This is a man's man's man's world / Walter Westinghouse / Easter woman guitar solo / Diskomo / Hello skinny / Constantinople / Hop a little / Cry for the fire / Kamikaze. *(cd-iss. Sep94 on 'Indigo'; 7534-2)*

Nov 86. (lp) *(TORSO33 022) <2614202>* **STARS & HANK FOREVER! – THE AMERICAN COMPOSER'S SERIES VOL.II (THE MUSIC OF HANK WILLIAMS AND JOHN PHILIP SOUSA)**
– Hank Williams:- Hey good lookin' / Six more miles (to the graveyard) / Kaw-liga / Ramblin' man / Jambalaya / John Philip Sousa:- Sousaside: a) Nobles of the mystic shrine, b) The stars & stripes forever, c) El capitan, d) The liberty bell, e) Semper fidelis, f) The Washington post. *(re-iss. Sep94 on 'Indigo'; 7530-1)*

Dec 86. (7"pic-d) *(TORSO7 022)* **KAW-LIGA. / THE STARS AND STRIPES FOREVER**
(12"pic-d) *(TORSO12 022)* – (mixes; prairie / single / original / horror).

Jun 87. (7") *(TORSO7 032)* **HIT THE ROAD JACK. / ELSIE**
(12") *(TORSO12 032)* – ('A'side) / Jambalaya / Firefly (live) / The big bubble (live) / Cry for the fire (live).

Aug 88. (d-lp/cd/dat) *(TORSO 33/CD/DAT 055) <2614226>* **GOD IN THREE PERSONS**
– Hard and tenderly / Devotion / The thing about them / Their early yearsx / Loss of a loved one / The touch / The service / Confused / Fine fat flies / Time / Silver sharp / Kiss of flesh / Pain and pleasure. *(re-iss. lp Sep94 & Oct00 on 'Indigo'; 7531-1)*

Mar 89. (cd-s) *(TORSOCD 322)* **KAW-LIGA (the housey mix / the stripped mix / Nightmare mix II)**

1989. (lp/cd) *<2614262>* **THE MOLE SHOW LIVE (live)** –
– Voices of the air / The secret seed / Narration / The ultimate disaster / God of darkness / Migration / Smack your lips clap your feet / Another land / The new machine / Call of the wild / Final confrontation / Satisfaction / Happy home. *(UK cd-iss. Sep94 on 'Indigo'; 7542-2)*

1989. (3"pic-cd-ep) *(TORSOCD 355)* **DOUBLE SHOT / LOSS OF LOVED ONE (extended) / KISS OF FLESH (instrumental)** –

1989. (lp/cd) *<14263-26>* **THE KING AND EYE** –
– Blue suede shoes / Don't be cruel / Heartbreak hotel / All shook up / Return to sender / Teddy bear / Devil in disguise / Stuck on you / Big hunk o' love / A fool such as I / Little sister / His latest flame / Burning love / Viva Las Vegas / Love me tender / Hound dog. *(UK cd-iss. Sep94 on 'Indigo'; 7535-2)*

1989. (cd-ep) *(TORSOCD 421)* **DISKOMO / WHOOPY SNORP / SAINT NIX / DISKOMO LIVE** –

May 90. (7") *(70166)* **DON'T BE CRUEL. / DON'T / SUPPOSING**
(cd-s+=) *(CD166)* – The toy factory / Ghost music.

Indigo East Side Digital

1991. (cd/lp) *<8060-2/-1>* **FREAKSHOW** –
– Everyone comes to the freak show / Harry the head / Herman the human mole / Wanda the worm woman / Jack the boneless boy / Benny the bouncing bum / Mickey the mumbling midget / Lillie / Nobody laughs when they leave. *(re-iss. Sep94 on 'Indigo' cd)(lp; 2125-2)(7532-1)*

1992. (7") *<SP 02>* **BLOWOFF** –
(above issued on 'Cryptic')

1995. (cd) *(INDIGO 2129-2) <8107-2>* **GINGERBREAD MAN**
– The weaver / The dying oilman / The confused transsexual The sold-out artist / The ascetic / The old soldier / The aging musician / The butcher / The old woman / Ginger's lament.

Aug 96. (cd) *(INDIGO 2133-2) <8120-2>* **HAVE A BAD DAY**
– Bad day on the midway / Dagmar, the dog woman / I ain't seen no rats / Tears of the taxman / God's teardrops / The seven tattoos / The marvels of mayhem / Lottie the human log / Ugly liberation / Daddy's poems / The red head of death / Timmy.

— returned in 1998

Sep 98. (cd) *(8535-2) <81332>* **WORMWOOD: CURIOUS STORIES FROM THE BIBLE** Oct98
– In the beginning / Fire fall / They are the meat / Melncholy clumps / How to get a head / Cain and Abel / Mr. Misery / Tent peg in the temple / God's magic finger / Spilling the seed / Dinah and the unclean skin / Bathsheba bathes / Bridegroom of blood / Hanging by his hair / Seven ugly cows / Burn baby burn / Kill him / I hate Heaven / Judas slaves / Revelation.

Jul 00. (cd/d-lp) *(9431-2/-1) <8153>* **ROADWORMS: THE BERLIN SESSIONS** (on the road)
– Un-American band / How to get a head / Hanging by his hair / God's magic finger / Tent pig in the temple / Fire fall / Cain and Abel / Dinah and the unclean skin / Abraham / Burn baby burn / Judas saves.

Ralph Euro East Side Digital

Nov 02. (cd) *(2048-2) <8167-2>* **DEMONS DANCE ALONE** Sep02
– Tongue / Loss: Life would be wonderful – The weatherman – Ghost child – Caring – Honey bear – The car thief – Neediness / Denial:- Thundering skies – Mickey Macaroni – Betty's body – My brother Paul – Baja / Three metaphors:- Beekeeper's daughter – Wolverines – Make me moo / Demons dance alone. *(d-cd-iss. ; 2079-2)*

– others, etc. –

Sep 94. (lp)(cd) *Torso; (TORSO 33-199)(7536-2)* **CUBE E**
Sep 94. (cd) *Indigo; (2124-2)* **POOR KAW LIGA'S PAIN**
Sep 94. (cd/lp) *Indigo; (7543-2/-6)* **POOR KAW LIGA (housey mix)**
Oct 94. (cd) *Cargo; (2129-2)* **THE RESIDENTS** –

– compilations, etc.

Oct 84. (lp/c) *Korova; (KODE/CODE 10)* **RALPH BEFORE '84 – VOLUME 1** [ ] [–]
– It's a man's man's man's world / Diskomo / Hello skinny / (I left my heart in) San Francisco / Happy home / Smack your lips / Yesyesyesyes / Jailhouse rock / Monkey and Bunny / Festival of death.

Jan 85. (lp) *Korova; (KODE 12)* **RALPH BEFORE '84 – VOLUME 2** [ ] [–]
– Eva's warning / Halloween / Evolution / What use / Mahogany wood / Same ole me / Tritone / Melvyn's repose / Yeti: what are you / Nelda danced at day break / Norrgarden nyvia.

Jan 86. (cd) *Rykodisc; <RCD 20012>* **HEAVEN?** [–] [ ]
– The importance of evergreen / It's a man's man's man's world / H.E.L.L. no! / Japenese watercolours / I got rhythm / Ups and downs / Serenade for Missy / Eastern woman / Amber / The census taker / Happy home / Crashing / Redrider / Floyd / The moles are coming / Resolution / Mahogany wood / Simple song / Kula bocca says no / Love leaks out / New hymn / Whater happened to Vileness Fats / Twinkle / Festival of death (excerpt).

Jan 86. (cd) *Rykodisc; <RCD 20013>* **HELL?** [–] [ ]
– The ultimate disaster (excerpt) / Lights out / Where is she? / The coming of the crow / Lizard lady / Die interior / Shut up! shut up! / Shorty's lament / Hello skinny / Kamikaze lady / Secret seed / Sonny / Smelly tongues / Monkey and Bunny / Farmers / Satisfaction / Sinister exaggerator / Loss of innocence / The sleeper / Final confrontation (excerpt).

Nov 92. (cd/c/lp) *Euro Ralph; (80782)* **PRESENT OUR FINEST FLOWERS** [ ] [ ]
– Gone again / Sour song / Six amber things / Mr. Lonely / Perfect goat / Blue tongues / Jungle bunny / I'm dreaming of a white sailor / Or maybe a marine / Kick a picnic / Dead wood / Baby sister / Forty-four no more / He also serves / Ship of fools / Be kind to U-web footed friends. *(re-iss. cd Sep94 & Oct00 on 'Indigo'; 2121-2)*

May 97. (4xcd-box) *Cargo; (RESBOX 1)* **25th ANNIVERSARY BOX SET** [ ] [–]

Jul 97. (4xcd-box) *Euro Ralph; (INDIGO 2137-2)* **OUR TIRED, OUR POOR, OUR HUDDLED MASSES** [ ] [ ]

Apr 98. (cd) *East Side Digital; <8132-2>* **RESIDUE DEUX** [–] [ ]
– Sleeper / Whoopy snorp / Kamikazi lady / A boy in love / Shut up! shut up! / Anvil forest / Diskomo / Jailhouse rock / Ups and downs / Scent of mint / Saint Nix / Open up / From the plains of Mexico / In San Francisco / Dumbo the clown / Is he really bringing roses? / Time's up / Daydream believer / Prelude for a toddler / Toddler's lullaby / Sagety is cootie wootie / Daydream in space.

Mar 01. (cd) *Euro Ralph; (9846-2) <8157-2>* **ICKY FLIX** [ ] [ ]

Apr 02. (cd) *East Side Digital; <8166-2>* **PETTING ZOO** [–] [ ]

☐ Martin REV (see under ⇒ SUICIDE)

☐ REVENGE (see under ⇒ NEW ORDER)

☐ REVOLTING COCKS (see under ⇒ MINISTRY)

Damien RICE

Born: 7 Dec'73, Celbridge, County Kildare, Ireland. Spending his childhood growing up near the River Liffey, DAMIEN formed the indie-rock outfit JUNIPER in the mid-90's and was signed to 'Polygram' records in 1997, however contractual disagreements eventually split the band. RICE subsequently moved to Tuscany before travelling across Europe, busking his own songs before returning to Ireland in 1999. He had written a handful of tracks which he demo'd to movie composer and uber-producer DAVID ARNOLD (the man responsible for the new James Bond movies). ARNOLD encouraged RICE to record an album and donated enough money so that he could set up his own studio. He issued the single 'THE BLOWER'S DAUGHTER' which became a moderate hit in his native country, before releasing the critically lauded debut album 'O' in 2002. Much more rewarding and interesting than the troubadour winge of DAVID GRAY, RICE fell somewhere between 'Tea For The Tillerman'-era CAT STEVENS, LEONARD COHEN and even MERCURY REV during their 'See You On The Other Side' period. Hushed vocals, wind-swept pianos and floating melodies were all present on what was perhaps the most gentle acoustic release of the year. Missed by many first time around, it received a second life in 2003 via massive radio play and a more aggressive advertising campaign which led to a UK Top 40 placing for the album and classy single, 'CANNONBALL'.

Album rating: O (*8)

DAMIEN RICE – vocals, multi / with session band

Damien Rice Music — not iss.

Sep 01. (cd-s) *(drm 001cd)* **THE BLOWER'S DAUGHTER / THE PROFESSOR & LA FILLE DANSE / MOODY MOODAY – THE BLOWER'S DAUGHTER (original demo)** [–] Irish [–]

Feb 02. (cd) *(drm 002cd)* **O** [–] Irish [–]
– Delicate / Volcano / The blower's daughter / Cannonball / Older chests / Amie / Cheers darlin' / Cold water / I remember / Eskimo. *(hidden tracks+=)* – Prague / Silent night. *(UK-iss.Jul02; same) (re-iss. Jul03 on '14th Floor'; 5046 64788-2)* – (hit UK No.23) *<US-iss.Jun03 on 'Vector'; 48507>*

May 02. (cd-s) *(drm 003cd)* **CANNONBALL / LONELILY (original demo) / WOMAN LIKE A MAN (live unplugged) / CANNONBALL (instrumental)** [–] Irish [–]

Oct 02. (cd-s) *(drm 004cd)* **VOLCANO / DELICATE (live acoustic) / VOLCANO (instrumental) / (hidden demo & CD-ROM track)** [–] Irish [–]

Mar 03. (cd-ep) *(dr 01)* **WOMAN LIKE A MAN EP** [ ] [–]
– Woman like a man / Delicate / Lonelily / The professor.

Aug 03. (7") *(dr 02)* **CANNONBALL** [ ] [–]

Oct 03. (cd-s) *(dr 03cd1)* **CANNONBALL / MOODY MOODAY / ('A'video)** [32] [–]
(cd-s) *(dr 03cd2)* – ('A'live) / Amie (live) / The blower's daughter (live).

☐ Keith RICHARDS (see under ⇒ ROLLING STONES)

Jonathan RICHMAN

Born: 16 May'51, Boston, Massachusetts, USA. After a period in the late 60's working as a contributor for local music papers, 'Vibrations' & 'Fusion', he formed his first real band, MODERN LOVERS, in 1971. With the help of producer KIM FOWLEY, they recorded a successful demo for 'Warners' in 1972, although the label subsequently shelved their JOHN CALE-produced debut album and soon dropped the group. RICHMAN & Co. finally split in late '74, only to re-form again six months later and record a debut single, 'ROADRUNNER', for 'United Artists'. They then moved to West Coast label 'Beserkley', who bought the unreleased Warners tapes and finally packaged the songs as an eponymous album in 1976. Featuring the classic MODERN LOVERS line-up of JERRY HARRISON, ERNIE BROOKS and DAVID ROBINSON, the album was one of the more genuine efforts to lay claim to the vastly oversubscribed 'first punk album' tag. Carrying on where his heroes The VELVET UNDERGROUND left off, RICHMAN fashioned an idiosyncratic update of late 60's garage-rock, his REED-y vocals carrying epistles of adolescent angst over a simplistic but effective musical backing. While UK Top 20 hit, 'ROADRUNNER', may have whetted fans appetites for more of the same, a belated follow-up album, 'JONATHAN RICHMAN & THE MODERN LOVERS' (1977) was a different beast altogether. While HARRISON and BROOKS were now tending greener new wave pastures with The TALKING HEADS and The CARS respectively, the revamped MODERN LOVERS line-up of ROBINSON, LEROY

RADCLIFFE and GREG KERANEN were following RICHMAN's more whimsically eccentric path, cutting retro pop, acoustic-based tracks about aliens, insects and erm, abominable snowmen. A second album that year, 'ROCK'N'ROLL WITH THE MODERN LOVERS', confirmed RICHMAN's new strategy, hitting the British Top 50 despite itself and spawning a second hit (Top 5) in the bizarre instrumental, 'EGYPTIAN REGGAE'. Critics were divided, some hailing the man as a wayward genius, some confounded at what they perceived as a waste of good talent. Whatever, after a late 70's lay-off, RICHMAN continued to plow his singular furrow throughout the following decade with an ever changing cast of musicians and different labels. Amid the grating childishness, the man was still capable of a wistful charm and the occasional sting of biting poignancy, fans and critics alike generally agreed that 'JONATHAN SINGS!' (1984) remains his finest release from this period. Towards the end of the decade, he recruited BRENDAN TOTTEN and JOHNNY AVILA for the leaner 'MODERN LOVERS '88' before abandoning the backup for good and going it alone. His 1989 eponymous solo debut was followed up with a misguided attempt at C&W, 'JONATHAN GOES COUNTRY' (1990), while a Spanish-language set, '!JONATHAN, TE VAS A EMOCIONAR!' (1994) surely tested the patience of even his most loyal fans. Much more promising were 1995's 'YOU MUST ASK THE HEART' and the following year's 'SURRENDER TO JONATHAN', the latter his first for a major label ('WEA') after years in the commercial wilderness. During the latter half of the 90's, RICHMAN stuck to his task of coming up with the odd album, 1999's 'I'M SO CONFUSED', a slight return to the old fun JONNO of yore. Fans however were disappointed with RICHMAN's US-only issued 'HER MYSTERY NOT OF HIGH HEELS AND EYE SHADOW' (2001), which showcased two instrumentals and four songs sung in Spanish. However, live, the old Modern Lover still packed a retro punch. • **Trivia:** JOHN CALE (ex-Velvet Underground), went on to record his brilliant 'PABLO PICASSO'.

Album rating: THE MODERN LOVERS (*8) / JONATHAN RICHMAN & THE MODERN LOVERS (*7) / ROCK'N'ROLL WITH THE MODERN LOVERS (*6) / THE MODERN LOVERS LIVE (*5) / BACK IN YOUR LIFE (*6) / THE JONATHAN RICHMAN SONGBOOK compilation (*7) / JONATHAN SINGS! (*6) / ROCKIN' AND ROMANCE (*5) / IT'S TIME FOR JONATHAN RICHMAN & THE MODERN LOVERS (*5) / MODERN LOVERS '88 (*5) / JONATHAN RICHMAN (*4) / JOHNATHAN GOES COUNTRY (*4) / 23 GREAT RECORDINGS BY JONATHAN RICHMAN & THE MODERN LOVERS compilation (*8) / HAVING A PARTY WITH JONATHAN RICHMAN collection (*4) / I, JONATHAN (*6) / JONATHAN, TE VAS A EMOCIONAR! (*5) / YOU MUST ASK THE HEART (*5) / SURRENDER TO JONATHAN (*6) / I MUST BE KING: THE BEST OF JONATHAN RICHMAN compilation (*6) / I'M SO CONFUSED (*6) / HER MYSTERY NOT OF HIGH HEELS AND EYE SHADOW (*5)

MODERN LOVERS

were formed by **RICHMAN** – vocals, guitar / with **JERRY HARRISON** – keyboards, vocals / **ERNIE BROOKS** – bass, vocals / **DAVID ROBINSON** – drums (left Nov73 to DMZ, after recording debut)

U.A. U.A.

Jun 75. (7") *(UP 36006)* **ROADRUNNER. / IT WILL STAND** [ ] [ ]

Beserkley Beserkley

Oct 76. (7") *<5701>* **ROADRUNNER. / Friday On My Mind (by Earthquake)** [–] [ ]

Oct 77. (lp/c) *(BSERK/BSERC 1) <BZ/+CA 0050>* **THE MODERN LOVERS** (1972 demos) [ ] Oct76 [ ]
– Roadrunner / Astral plane / Old world / Pablo Picasso / I'm straight / She cracked / Hospital / Someone I care about / Girlfriend / Modern world. *(re-iss. Nov87; same> <re-iss. Nov89 on 'Rhino'; RNLP 70091> (cd-iss. Feb93 on 'Rev-Ola'+=; CREV 007CD)* – (3 extra tracks). *(lp re-iss. Jun00 on 'Get Back'; GET 66)*

— HARRISON (also to TALKING HEADS) and BROOKS joined ELLIOTT MURPHY

JONATHAN RICHMAN & THE MODERN LOVERS

with also **LEROY RADCLIFFE** – guitar, vox / **GREG KERANEN** – bass, vox / **DAVID ROBINSON** – drums

Feb 77. (7") *<5743>* **NEW ENGLAND. / HERE COME THE MARTIAN MARTIANS** [–] [ ]

Jun 77. (7") *(BZZ 1)* **ROADRUNNER (once). / ROADRUNNER (twice)** [11] [–]
(re-iss. Jul82 on 'Old Gold'; OG 9113)

Oct 77. (lp/c) *(BSERK/BSERC 2) <BZ/+CA 0048>* **JONATHAN RICHMAN & THE MODERN LOVERS** [ ] Jan77 [ ]
– Rockin' shopping center / Back in the U.S.A. / Important in your life / New England / Lonely financial zone / Hi dear / Abominable snowman in the market / Hey there little insect / Here comes the Martian Martians / Springtime / Amazing Grace. *<re-iss. Nov87; same> (cd-iss. Feb93 on 'Rev-Ola'; CREV 008CD)*

Aug 77. (lp/c) *(BSERK 9) <BZ/+CA 0053>* **ROCK'N'ROLL WITH THE MODERN LOVERS** [50] Feb77 [ ]
– The sweeping wind (kwa ti feng) / Ice cream man / Rockin' rockin' leprechauns / Summer morning / Afternoon / Fly into the mystery / South American folk song / Roller coaster by the sea / Dodge veg-o-matic / Egyptian reggae / Coomyah / The wheels on the bus / Angels watching over you. *<re-iss. Nov87; same> (cd-iss. Feb93 on 'Rev-Ola'; CREV 009CD)*

Sep 77. (7") *(BZZ 2)* **EGYPTIAN REGGAE. / ROLLER COASTER BY THE SEA** [5] [ ]

— **D.SHARPE** – drums repl. ROBINSON / **ASA BREMNER** – bass repl. KERANEN

Dec 77. (lp/c) *(BSERK/BSERC 12) <BZ/+CA 055>* **THE MODERN LOVERS LIVE (live)** [ ] [ ]
– I'm a little airplane / Hey there little insect / Egyptian reggae / Ice cream man / I'm a little dinosaur / My little kookenhaken / South American folk song / New England / Morning of our lives. *<re-iss. Nov87; same> (cd-iss. Feb93 on 'Rev-Ola'; CREV 010CD) (cd re-iss. Apr97 on 'Wooded Hill'; HILLCD 15)*

Jan 78. (7"; as MODERN LOVERS) *(BZZ 7)* **MORNING OF OUR LIVES (live). / ROADRUNNER (thrice) (live)** [28] [ ]

Apr 78. (7"; as MODERN LOVERS) *(BZZ 14)* **NEW ENGLAND. / ASTRAL PLANE (live)** [ ] [–]

Jul 78. (7") *(BZZ 19)* **ABDUL & CLEOPATRA. / OH CAROL** [ ] [ ]

Dec 78. (7") *(BZZ 25)* **BUZZ BUZZ BUZZ. / HOSPITAL (live)** [ ] [ ]

Feb 79. (lp/c) *(BSERK/BSERC 17) <BZ/+CA 0060>* **BACK IN YOUR LIFE** [ ] [ ]
– Abdul and Cleopatra / (She's gonna) Respect me / Lover please / Affection / Buzz buzz buzz / Back in your life / Party in the woods tonight / My love is a flower (just beginning to bloom) / I'm nature's mosquito / Emaline / Lydia / I hear you calling me. *<re-iss. Nov86; same> (cd-iss. Feb93 on 'Rev-Ola'; CREV 011CD) (cd re-iss. Apr97 on 'Wooded Hill'; HILLCD 14)*

Mar 79. (7") *(BZZ 28)* **LYDIA. / IMPORTANT IN YOUR LIFE** [ ] [ ]

JONATHAN RICHMAN

Jan 80. (lp) *(DSERK 19)* **JONATHAN RICHMAN SONGBOOK – THE BEST OF . . .** (compilation) [ ] [ ]

— JONATHAN retired in the late 70's, until 1982. Joining him were **KEN FORFIA** – keyboards / **BETH HARRINGTON** – guitar / **GREG KERANEN** – bass, vocals / **MICHAEL GUARDABASCIO** – drums, vocals / **ELLIE MARSHALL** – backing vocals

Rough Trade Sire

Aug 84. (lp/c) *(ROUGH/+C 52)* **JONATHAN SINGS!** [ ] [ ]
– That summer feeling / This kind of music / The neighbors / Somebody to hold me / These conga drums / Stop this car / Not yet three / Give Paris one more chance / You're the one for me / When I'm walking.

May 85. (7") *(RT 152)* **THAT SUMMER FEELING. / THIS KIND OF MUSIC** [ ] [ ]
(12"+=) *(RTT 152)* – The tag game.

— re-formed again with **JONATHAN, ELLIE, MICHAEL** and newcomer **ANDY PALEY** – toy piano

Jun 85. (lp/c) *(ROUGH/+C 72)* **ROCKIN' AND ROMANCE** [ ] [ ]
– The beach / My jeans / Bermuda / The U.F.O. man / Down in Bermuda / V. Van Gogh / Walter Johnson / I'm just beginning to live / The fenway / Chewing gum wrapper / The Baltimores / Up in the sky sometime / Now is better than before.

Aug 85. (7") *(RT 154)* **I'M JUST BEGINNING TO LIVE. / CIRCLE I** [ ] [ ]
(12"+=) *(RTT 154)* – Shirin & Fahrad.

JONATHAN RICHMAN & THE MODERN LOVERS

Feb 86. (lp/c) *(ROUGH/+C 92)* **IT'S TIME FOR JONATHAN RICHMAN & THE MODERN LOVERS** [ ] [ ]
– It's you / Let's take a trip / This love of mine / Neon sign / Double chocolate malted / Just about seventeen / Corner store / The desert / Yo Jo Jo / When I dance / Shirin & Fahrad / Ancient and long ago.

— **JONATHAN** recruited complete new line-up **BRENDAN TOTTEN** – guitar / **JOHNNY AVILA** – drums

Demon Rounder

Feb 88. (lp/cd) *(FIEND/+CD 106) <ROUNDER/+CD 9014>* **MODERN LOVERS '88** [ ] [ ]
– Dancin' late at night / When Harpo played his harp / Gail loves me / New kind of neighborhood / African lady / I love hot nights / California desert party / Everything's gotta be right / Circle 1 / I have come out to play / The theme from 'Moulin Rouge'!.

JONATHAN RICHMAN

Special Delivery Rounder

Aug 89. (lp/c/cd) *<(SPD/+C/CD 1024)>* **JONATHAN RICHMAN** [ ] [ ]
– Malagueno de Jojo / Action packed / Everyday clothes / Fender Stratocaster / Blue Moon / Closer / I eat with Gusto / Damn!! you bet / Miracles will start to happen / Sleepwalk / Que reste t'll de nos amours / A mistake today for me / Cerca.

— now with **TOM BRUMLEY** – guitar

Aug 90. (lp/c/cd) *<(SPD/+C/CD 1037)>* **JONATHAN GOES COUNTRY** [ ] [ ]
– Since she started to ride / Reno / You're the one for me / Your good girl's gonna go bad / I must be king / You're crazy for takin' the blues / Rodeo wind / Corner store / The neighbours / Men walks among us / I can't stay mad at you / Satisfied mind.

Rounder Rounder

Dec 92. (cd/c) *<(ROU CD/C 9036)>* **I, JONATHAN** [ ] [ ]
– Parties in the U.S.A. / Tandem jump / You can't talk to the dude / Velvet underground / I was dancing in the lesbian bar / Rooming house on Venice beach / That summer feeling / Grunion run / A higher power / Twilight in Boston.

May 94. (cd) *<(ROUCD 9040)>* **JONATHAN, TE VAS A EMOCIONAR!** [ ] [ ]
– Pantomima de el amor Brujo / Harpo en su Harpa / No te oye / No mas por fun / Papel de chicle / Los vecinos / Compadrito corazon / Melodia tradicional Ecuadoriana / Shirin y Farad / Reno / Cerca / El U.F.O. man / Ahora es Mejor / Sabor A.Mi / Una Fuerza alla.

May 95. (cd/c) *<(ROU CD/C 9047)>* **YOU MUST ASK THE HEART** [ ] [ ]
– To hide a little thought / The heart of Saturday night / Vampire girl / Just because I'm Irish / That's how I feel / Let her go into darkness / The rose / You must ask the heart / Nothing can change this love / Amorcito corazon / City vs. country / Walter Johnson / Nishi.

Vapor – Warners Vapor – Warners

Sep 96. (cd/c) *<(9362 46296-2/-4)>* **SURRENDER TO JONATHAN** [ ] [ ]
– Just look at me / That little sleeper car / Not just a plus list on the guest list anymore / My little girl's got a full time daddy now / Rock'n'roll drummer straight from the hospy-tel / atisfy / When she kisses me / Egyptian reggae / To hide a little thought / I was dancing in the lesbian bar / Surrender / Floatin' / French style.

— next with **DARRYL JENIFER** – bass / **TOMMY LARKINS** – drums

Feb 99. (cd) *<(9362 47086-2/-4)>* **I'M SO CONFUSED** [ ] [ ]
– When I dance / Nineteen in Naples / I'm so confused / True love is not nice / Love me like I love / Hello from Cupid / If she don't love me / The lonely little thrift store / Affection / I can hear her fighting with herself / The night is still young / I can't find my best friend.

not iss. Vapor

Oct 01. (cd) *<48216>* **HER MYSTERY NOT OF HIGH HEELS AND EYE SHADOW** [–] [ ]
– Her mystery not of high heels and eye shadow / Springtime in New York / Me and her got a good thing goin' baby / Couples must fight / I took a chance on her / Maybe a walk home from Natick High School / Give Paris one more chance / My love for her ain't sad / Leaves on the sidewalk after the rain / Tonight / Yo tengo una novia / El joven se estremece / Con el merengue / Vampiresa mujer (Vampire girl).

– compilations, etc. –

Oct 81. (lp) *Bomp; <LBOM 1>* **THE ORIGINAL MODERN LOVERS** [–] [ ]
(UK-iss.Jun87 on 'Link'; 400.310) <re-iss. 1991 on 'Ubik'; BAKTUN 004> <(UK-iss.Feb97 & Nov00 on 'Bomp'; BLP 4021)>

Jul 82. (7") *Old Gold; (OG 9112)* **EGYPTIAN REGGAE. / MORNING OF OUR LIVES (live)** [ ] [–]

1987. (cd) *Rhino; <RNCD 75889>* **THE BEST OF JONATHAN RICHMAN AND THE MODERN LOVERS** [–] [ ]

1988. (cd) *Rounder; (CDS1)* **JONATHAN RICHMAN & BARRENCE WHITFIELD** [–] [ ]

Feb 91. (cd/c/lp) *Essential; (ESS CD/MC/LP 128)* **23 GREAT RECORDINGS BY JONATHAN RICHMAN AND THE MODERN LOVERS** [ ] [–]
– Roadrunner / Dignified & old / Pablo Picasso / I'm straight / Astral plane / Girl friend / Government centre / New teller / It will stand / Morning of our lives / Abominable snowman in the market / Important in your life / My little kookenhaken / Dodge veg-o-matic / Lonely financial zone / Roller coaster by the sea / New England / Egyptian reggae / Ice cream man / Buzz buzz buzz / Abdul & Cleopatra / Roadrunner (twice). *(c+=)* – She cracked / Hospital. *(re-iss. cd Sep93 on 'Castle'; CSCD 397)*

Nov 91. (cd) *Cheree; (CHEREE 22)* **HAVING A PARTY WITH JONATHAN RICHMAN (live US tour in '83)** [ ] [–]
– The girl stands up to me now / Cappuccino bar / my career as a homewrecker / She doesn't laugh at my jokes / When she kisses me / They're not tryin' on the dance floor / At night / When I say wife / 1963 / Monologue about bermuda / Our swingin' pad / Just for fun.

Apr 94. (cd) *Castle; (CCSCD 397)* **THE COLLECTION** [ ] [–]

May 94. (cd) *New Rose; (422439)* **LIVE AT THE LONGBRANCH SALOON (live)** [ ] [–]
<(US+re-iss. Aug98 on 'Last Call'; 303821)>

Apr 95. (cd; by MODERN LOVERS) *Rounder; (ROUCD 9042)* **PRECISE MODERN LOVERS ORDER** [ ] [–]
(originally issued in 1992 on French 'Fan Club'; 422439)

Jun 95. (cd) *Nectar; (NPMCD 506)* **A PLEA FOR TENDERNESS** [ ] [–]

Jul 97. (cd) *Snapper; (SMDCD 115)* **RADIO ON / STOP AND SHOP** [ ] [–]

Aug 98. (cd) *Castle; (SELCD 521)* **ROADRUNNER** [ ] [–]

Nov 98. (cd) *Cooking Vinyl; (COOKCD 166)* **I MUST BE KING: THE BEST OF JONATHAN RICHMAN** [ ] [–]
– That summer feeling / Fender stratocaster / Foggy notion / No mas po fun (Just for fun) / You're the one for me / Girls stand up to me now / Satisfied mind / Velvet underground / Pablo Picasso / A plea for tenderness / Corner stone / Neighbours / Dignified and old / Parties in the USA / I must be king / El UFO man / Action packed / Roadrunner.

Sep 00. (cd) *Target; (47038)* **BUZZ BUZZ BUZZ: AN INTROSPECTIVE** [ ] [–]

Feb 02. (cd) *Rounder; <(ROUCD 11596)>* **ACTION PACKED: THE BEST OF JONATHAN RICHMAN** [ ] [ ]

RIDE

Formed: Oxford, England . . . 1988 by local art college students MARK GARDENER, ANDY BELL and LAURENCE COLBERT. They drafted in STEVE QUERALT and journalist/manager Dave Newton who subsequently secured them some London gigs. These led to a deal with 'Creation' records and they released their eponymous debut EP early in 1990, the record quickly selling out of its limited number and squeezing into the UK Top 75. The disc showcased the band's spiralling guitar-scapes and contained an early classic in the cathartic 'DRIVE BLIND'. It was hotly pursued by two further Top 40 EP's, 'PLAY' and 'FALL', the latter containing their best track to date (at that point) in 'TASTE'. Come October, with the "shoegazing" scene in full flow, they nearly secured a Top 10 place with their stunning debut album, 'NOWHERE'. 1991 was spent in the studio (excluding Reading Festival), and the fruits were heard early in '92 on their superb 8-minute single 'LEAVE THEM ALL

BEHIND'. This slow burning psychedelic epic gave them their first Top 10 entry and was a prelude to their second, more BYRDS-esque album, 'GOING BLANK AGAIN'. The record went Top 5, despite being derided by certain music critics. Frictions began to appear and it was thought a two-year sabbatical would solve the problem. BELL took time off to help out his Swedish wife and stablemate IDHA (OVELIUS) on her debut album. In 1994, RIDE were back with 'CARNIVAL OF LIGHT', but again they received lukewarm reviews. Early the next year, GARDENER took off to the States, leaving them all behind (ouch!). Their swansong, 'TARANTULA' was annoyingly deleted after one week, as BELL and GARDENER considered separate solo ventures. • **Songwriters:** Lyrics MARK or ANDY / group compositions except covers EIGHT MILES HIGH (Byrds) / THE MODEL (Kraftwerk) / HOW DOES IT FEEL TO FEEL (Creation) / THAT MAN (Small Faces) / UNION CITY BLUE + ATOMIC (Blondie). • **Trivia:** In 1991, they headlined the Slough Music Festival in front of over 8,000 fans.

Album rating: SMILE (*7) / NOWHERE (*8) / GOING BLANK AGAIN (*7) / CARNIVAL OF LIGHT (*6) / LIVE LIGHT (*4) / TARANTULA (*6) / OX4: THE BEST OF RIDE compilation (*7)

MARK GARDENER – vocals, guitar / **ANDY BELL** (b.11 Aug'70, Cardiff, Wales) – guitar, vocals / **STEPHAN QUERALT** – bass / **LAURENCE COLBERT** – drums

Creation Sire

Jan 90. (12"ep)(cd-ep) *(CRE 072T)(CRESCD 072)* **RIDE** [71] [–]
– Chelsea girl / Drive blind / Close my eyes / All I can see. *(re-iss. Oct90; same)*

Apr 90. (12"ep)(cd-ep) *(CRE 075T)(CRESCD 075)* **PLAY** [32] [–]
– Like a daydream / Silver / Furthest sense / Perfect time.

Jun 90. (m-cd,m-c) *<26390>* **SMILE** (first two EP's) [–] [ ]
– Chelsea girl / Drive blind / All I can see / Close my eyes / Like a daydream / Silver / Furthest sense / Perfect time. *(UK-iss.Nov92; CRECD 126) (cd re-iss. Sep01 on 'Ignition'; IGNCD 8)*

Oct 90. (12"ep)(cd-ep) *(CRE 087T)(CRESCD 087)* **FALL** [34] [–]
– Dreams burn down / Taste / Here and now / Nowhere.

Oct 90. (cd/lp)(c) *(CRE CD/LP 74)(CREC 74) <26462>*
NOWHERE [11] Dec90 [ ]
– Seagull / Kaleidoscope / Polar bear / Dreams burn down / In a different place / Decay / Paralysed / Vapour trail. *(cd+=)* – Taste / Here and now / Nowhere. *(cd re-iss. Sep01 on 'Ignition'; IGNCD 9)*

Jan 91. (cd-ep) *<40055>* **VAPOUR TRAIL** [–] [ ]

Mar 91. (c-ep)(12"ep)(cd-ep) *(CRECS 100)(CRE 100T)(CRESCD 100)* **TODAY FOREVER** [14] [–]
– Unfamiliar / Sennen / Beneath / Today.

Feb 92. (c-ep)(12"ep)(cd-ep) *(CRECS 123)(CRE 123T)(CRESCD 123) <40332>* **LEAVE THEM ALL BEHIND. / CHROME WAVES / GRASSHOPPER** [9] [ ]

Mar 92. (cd/2x12"lp)(c) *(CRE CD/LP 124)(CCRE 124) <26836>*
GOING BLANK AGAIN [5] [ ]
– Leave them all behind / Twisterella / Not fazed / Chrome waves / Mouse trap / Time of her life / Cool your boots / Making Jusy smile / Time machine / OX4. *(cd re-iss. Sep01 on 'Ignition'; IGNCD 10)*

Apr 92. (c-ep)(12"ep)(cd-ep) *(CRECS 150)(CRE 150T)(CRESCD 150) <40448>* **TWISTERELLA / GOING BLANK AGAIN. / HOWARD HUGHES / STAMPEDE** [36] [ ]

—— In Oct'93, 'Fright' records issued 'UNION CITY BLUE' *(FRIGHT 060) (re-iss. Apr97; same)*

Apr 94. (12"ep/12"clear-ep)(cd-ep) *(CRE 155T/+C)(CRESCD 155)* **BIRDMAN / ROLLING THUNDER 2. / LET'S GET LOST / DON'T LET IT DIE** [38] [–]

Jun 94. (7"/c-s) *(CRE/+MC 184)* **HOW DOES IT FEEL TO FEEL? / CHELSEA GIRL** [58] [–]
(12")(cd-s) *(CRES 184T)(CRESCD 184)* – ('A'side) / Walkabout / At the end of the universe.

Jun 94. (pic-cd/d-lp)(c) *(CRE CD/LP 147)(C-CRE 147) <45610>*
CARNIVAL OF LIGHT [5] [ ]
– Moonlight medicine / 1000 miles / From time to time / Natural grace / Only now / Birdman / Crown of creation / How does it feel to feel? / Endless road / Magical spring / Rolling thunder / I don't know where it comes from. *(cd re-iss. Sep01 on 'Ignition'; IGNCD 11)*

Sep 94. (c-s) *(CRECS 189)* **I DON'T KNOW WHERE IT COMES FROM. / TWISTERELLA** [46] [–]
(12")(cd-s) *(CRE 189T)(CRESCD 189)* – ('A'side) / Drive blind / From time to time / How does it feel to feel (live w / The CREATION).
(cd-s) *(CRESCD 189R)* – ('A'-Apollo 11 mix) / Moonlight medicine (ride on the wire mix by Portishead) / A journey to the end of the universe (version).

—— split officially early '96. MARK citing ANDY's near takeover of vocal duties.

Feb 96. (12"ep/cd-ep) *(CRE 199T)(CRESCD 199)* **BLACK NITE CRASH** [67] [–]

Mar 96. (cd/lp)(c) *(CRE CD/LP 180)(CCRE 180) <61893>*
TARANTULA [21] [ ]
– Black nite crash / Sunshine – Nowhere to run / Dead man / Walk on water / Deep inside my pocket / Mary Anne / Castle on the hill / Gonna be alright / Dawn patrol / Ride the wind / Burnin' / Starlight motel. *(cd re-iss. Sep01 on 'Ignition'; IGNCD 12)*
above was only available for 1 week only

—— On the 30th of June '96, MARK GARDENER released his limited solo cd-single 'MAGDALEN SKY / CAN'T LET IT DIE (demo)' for Oxford-based 'Shifty Disco' *(DISCO 9706)*. *(re-iss. Jun97; same)*

—— split around the same time; ANDY BELL formed HURRICANE #1

– compilations, etc. –

Oct 95. (cd,c) *Elektra; <61884>* **LIVE LIGHT (live)** [–] [ ]
– Seagull / Magical Spring / From time to time / Chelsea girl / Birdman / Only now / Leave them all behind / Let's get lost. *(UK-iss.Jul97 on 'Mutiny' cd/lp; 80002-2/-1)*

Sep 01. (3xcd-box) *Ignition; (IGNCD 13)* **BOXED SET** [ ] [–]

Sep 01. (cd) *Ignition; (<IGNCD 14>)* **OX4: THE BEST OF RIDE** [ ] [ ]
– Chelsea girl / Drive blind / Like a daydream / Taste / Dreams burn down / Vapour trail / Unfamiliar / Leave them all behind / Twisterella / OX4 / Birdman / From time to time / How does it feel to feel? / I don't know where it comes from / Black nite crash.

Aug 03. (cd) *Ignition; (IGNCD 15)* **WAVES: THE RADIO 1 SESSIONS 1990-1994** [ ] [–]

□ RIFF RAFF (see under ⇒ BRAGG, Billy)

□ RIGOR MORTIS (see under ⇒ WHO)

Minnie RIPERTON

Born: 8 Nov'47, Chicago, Illinois, USA. Having studied music in her teens, RIPERTON subsequently secured a job as receptionist for legendary blues/soul label, 'Chess', with whom she also recorded as a member of girl group The GEMS. Formed in 1961, the latter outfit released a few singles as well as providing backing vocals for such luminaries as FONTELLA BASS and ETTA JAMES. Following a one-off solo single, 'LONELY GIRL' (under the nom de plume, ANDREA DAVIS), RIPERTON became lead singer of psychedelic soul outfit, The ROTARY CONNECTION. Beginning with an eponymous 1968 debut album on the 'Cadet Concept' label, the group proceeded to release a total of six albums over the ensuing four years. Although a few of their songs – most notably 'AMEN' – enjoyed heavy rotation on FM radio, they never crossed over to the mainstream in the same way as contemporaries like SLY STONE. By the time the 'CONNECTION had delivered their final album, 'HEY LOVE' (1971), RIPERTON had already initiated her solo career via the 'Janus' label with 'COME TO MY GARDEN' (1970); her spine-tingling 5-octave singing voice was especially dazzling on the sublime 'LES FLEUR'. RIPERTON susbsequently attracted the attention of STEVIE WONDER, for whom she sang backing vocals on his 1974 album, 'Fulfillingness' First Finale'. She also toured with WONDER as a member of his WONDERLOVE backing band and the soul superstar co-produced (under the pseudonym, EL TORO NEGRO) a couple of tracks on her 'Epic' sophomore effort, 'PERFECT ANGEL' (1974). Alongside the orgasmic 'EVERY TIME HE COMES AROUND', the album featured pop-soul classic, 'LOVIN' YOU', furnishing MINNIE with a US chart topper (UK No.2) and finally giving her the exposure she deserved. It wasn't to last though and inexplicably, neither 'ADVENTURES IN PARADISE' (1975) nor 'STAY IN LOVE' (1977) made much commercial headway outside America. Tragically, RIPERTON was revealed to be suffering from breast cancer (undergoing a mastectomy in 1976), the singer devoting much of her time throughout her final years to the American Cancer Society. Although her illness became progressively worse, she continued to perform and record during this time, a final album, entitled simply 'MINNIE', released by 'Capitol' in 1979. With her death on July 12th the same year, soul music had lost one of its most talented, beautiful and original singers. Like former SUPREME, FLORENCE BALLARD, she'd been cut down in her prime, aged only 31. A posthumous collection of previously unreleased vocals with newly recorded instrumental backing, 'LOVE LIVES FOREVER', was released by 'Capitol' and hit the Top 40 in 1980.

Album rating: COME TO MY GARDEN (*6) / PERFECT ANGEL (*7) / ADVENTURES IN PARADISE (*5) / STAY IN LOVE (*5) / MINNIE (*5) / LOVE LIVES FOREVER (*5) / THE BEST OF MINNIE RIPERTON compilation (*7)

MINNIE RIPERTON – vocals (with various sessioners)

not iss. G.R.T.

1970's. (lp) *<30001>* **COME TO MY GARDEN** (rec.1969) –
– Les fleur / Completeness / Come to my garden / Memory band / Rainy day in Centerville / Close your eyes and remember / Oh, by the way / Expecting / Only when I'm dreaming. *<re-iss. Nov74 on 'Janus'; 7011> (UK cd-iss. May95 on 'Blue Moon'; CDBM 080) (UK cd re-iss. May97 on 'Aim'; AIM 1060) <(cd re-iss. Aug02 on 'Castle'+=; CMRCD 550)>* – Whenever whenever.

Epic Epic

Jun 74. (7") *<11139>* **EVERY TIME HE COMES AROUND. / REASONS** –
Sep 74. (7") *(EPC 2660) <50020>* **SEEING YOU THIS WAY. / THE EDGE OF A DREAM** Aug74
(re-iss. Jan75; same)
Oct 74. (lp/c) *(EPC/40 80426) <32561>* **PERFECT ANGEL** (hit UK chart May75) 33 Aug74 4
– Perfect angel / Every time he comes around / Lovin' you / Our lives / Reasons / It's so nice / Take a little trip / Seeing you this way / The edge of a dream.
Mar 75. (7") *(EPC 3121) <50057>* **LOVIN' YOU. / THE EDGE OF A DREAM** 2 Jan75 1
Jun 75. (7") *(EPC 3360)* **SEEING YOU THIS WAY. / IT'S SO NICE TO SEE OLD FRIENDS** –
Jun 75. (lp/c) *(EPC/40 69142) <33454>* **ADVENTURES IN PARADISE** May75 18
– Baby, this love I have / Feelin' that your feelin's right / When it comes down to it / Minnie's lament / Love and its glory / Adventures in Paradise / Inside my love / Alone in Brewster Bay / Simple things / Don't let anyone bring you down.
Sep 75. (7") *(EPC 3574) <50128>* **INSIDE MY LOVE. / DON'T LET ANYONE BRING YOU DOWN** Jul75 76
Oct 75. (7") *<50155>* **WHEN IT COMES DOWN TO IT. / MINNIE'S LAMENT** –
Jan 76. (7") *<50166>* **SIMPLE THINGS. / MINNIE'S LAMENT** –
Jan 76. (7") *(EPC 3796)* **WHEN IT COMES DOWN TO IT. / LOVE AND IT'S GLORY** –
Apr 76. (7") *<50190>* **ADVENTURES IN PARADISE. / WHEN IT COMES DOWN TO IT** –
Mar 77. (7") *(EPC 5032) <50337>* **STICK TOGETHER. / (part 2)**
Mar 77. (lp/c) *(EPC/40 81457) <34191>* **STAY IN LOVE** 71
– Young, willing and able / Could it be I'm in love / Oh darlin' . . . life goes on / Can you feel what I'm saying? / Gettin' ready for your love / Stick together / Wouldn't matter where you are / How could I love you more / Stay in love.
Jun 77. (7") *<50394>* **WOULDN'T MATTER WHERE YOU ARE. /** –
Sep 77. (7") *<50427>* **YOUNG, WILLING AND ABLE. / HOW COULD I LOVE YOU MORE** –

Capitol Capitol

May 79. (7") *(CL 16082) <4706>* **MEMORY LANE. / I'M A WOMAN**
—— on the 12th of July '79 (aged 30) MINNIE died of cancer
Aug 79. (lp/c) *<(EST/TCEST 11936)>* **MINNIE** May79 29
– Memory lane / Lover and friend / Return to forever / Love hurts / Dancin' & acting crazy / Never existed before / I'm a woman / Light my fire. *(re-iss. May82 on 'Fame' lp/c; FA/TCFA 3027)*
Sep 79. (7") *(CL 16102) <4761>* **LOVER AND FRIEND. / RETURN TO FOREVER**
Nov 79. (7") *<4902>* **HERE WE GO. / RETURN TO FOREVER** –
(below album recorded 1978 with new accompaniment)
Oct 80. (lp/c) *<(EST/TCEST 12097)>* **LOVE LIVES FOREVER** Aug80 35
– Here we go / I'm in love again / Strange affair / Island in the Sun / Give me time / You take my breath away / Song of life (la-la-la).
Jan 81. (7") *<4955>* **ISLAND IN THE SUN. / GIVE ME TIME** –
Apr 81. (7") *(CL 16165)* **ISLAND IN THE SUN. / LIGHT MY FIRE** –
(12"+=) *(12CL 16165)* – Lover and friend.

– compilations, etc. –

Nov 81. (lp/c) *Capitol; (EST/TC-EST 12189)* **THE BEST OF MINNIE RIPERTON**
– Perfect angel / Memory lane / Loving you / Can you feel what I'm saying / Here we go / Inside my love / Lover and friend / Woman of heart and mind / Young, willing and able / You take my breath away / Adventures in Paradise.
Nov 87. (7") *Old Gold; (OG 9725)* **LOVING YOU. / INSIDE MY LOVE** –
Aug 93. (cd) *Capitol; <(CDP 780516-2)>* **CAPITOL GOLD: THE BEST OF MINNIE RIPERTON**
– Perfect angel / Lover and friend / Memory lane / Woman of heart and mind / Loving you / Young, willing and able / Can you feel what I'm saying / Stick together / Wouldn't matter where you are / Stay in love / Inside my love / Here we go / Give me time / You take my breath away / Adventures in Paradise / Simple things / Light my fire.
Feb 98. (cd) *Chess-M.C.A.; <(MCD 0939-2)>* **HER CHESS YEARS**
Sep 01. (cd) *Stateside; (535127-2)* **LES FLEURS: THE MINNIE RIPERTON ANTHOLOGY**

Robbie ROBERTSON

Born: JAIME ROBBIE ROBERTSON, 5 Jul'43, Toronto, Canada. An integral part of The BAND (as guitarist and songwriter), one of America's most revered rock groups, ROBERTSON diversified into acting and production (he'd already overseen NEIL DIAMOND's 'Beautiful Noise' album in 1976) following the group's demise in the late 70's. His most high profile project during this period was 'Carny', a film about American freak shows for which he wrote the score as well as starring in. Passing up the opportunity to become part of a reformed BAND in the mid-80's, ROBERTSON instead concentrated on developing a belated solo career. Co-produced by mood master, Daniel Lanois and boasting the likes of U2, PETER GABRIEL, NEIL YOUNG and even the GIL EVANS horn formation, the album steered clear of the rich roots-rock of The BAND, opting instead for a highly original blend of atmospheric sophistication best sampled on the sultry 'SOMEWHERE DOWN THE CRAZY RIVER'. The latter track was an unexpected UK Top 20 hit, while the album itself sold respectably, making the lower regions of the British Top 50 and the American Top 40. Hardly the most prolific of artists, it would be another four years before the release of a follow-up, 'STORYVILLE' (1991). This time around mining the rich seam of New Orleans music in tandem with assorted METERS and NEVILLE BROTHERS, he moved seamlessly through a variety of Crescent City styles incorporating blues, gospel and R&B via his trademark half-spoken vocal style. Despite widespread critical acclaim and a Top 30

UK chart position, the record failed to launch ROBERTSON into the major league of adult rock. Moving back into film, the singer hooked up with The RED ROAD ENSEMBLE for the soundtrack to US TV documentary, 'THE NATIVE AMERICANS', released on disc in 1994. American Indians also informed much of the lyrical subject matter on 1998's 'CONTACT FROM THE UNDERWORLD OF RED BOY' wherein ROBERTSON – with the help of Scots DJ/Producer HOWIE B – experimented more openly than ever before with electronic soundscapes. • **Trivia:** Other film parts; 'The Coal Miner's Daughter' (1980) + 'The Right Stuff' (1983).

Album rating: ROBBIE ROBERTSON (*7) / STORYVILLE (*6) / MUSIC FOR THE NORTH AMERICANS (*5) / CONTACT FROM THE UNDERWORLD OF RED BOY (*5)

ROBBIE ROBERTSON – vocals, guitar, keyboards / with **BILL DILLON** – guitar / **TONY LEVIN** – bass / **MANU KATCHE** – drums, percussion / **DANIAL LANOIS** – percussion, guitar, bass, co-producer / **PETER GABRIEL** – vocals / **U2** / **GARTH HUDSON + RICK DANKO**, etc

Geffen Geffen

Oct 87. (7") *<28175>* **SHOWDOWN AT THE BIG SKY. / HELL'S HALF ACRE** [–] [ ]

Oct 87. (lp/c)(cd) *(WX 133/+C)(924160-2) <24160>* **ROBBIE ROBERTSON** [47] [38]
– Fallen angel / Showdown at the big sky / Broken arow / Sweet fire of love / American roulette / Somewhere down the crazy river / Hell's half acre / Sonny get caught in the moonlight / Testimony. *(re-iss. Jan91 lp/c/cd; GEF/+C/D 24160) (re-iss. cd Oct95; GFLD 19294)*

Oct 87. (7") *(GEF 32)* **FALLEN ANGEL. / HELL'S HALF ACRE** [ ] [–]
(12"+=) *(GEF 32T)* – Tailgate.

Nov 87. (7") *<28111>* **SOMEWHERE DOWN THE CRAZY RIVER. / HELL'S HALD ACRE** [–] [ ]

Jun 88. (7") *(GEF 40)* **SOMEWHERE DOWN THE CRAZY RIVER. / BROKEN ARROW** [15] [–]
(12"+=) *(GEF 40T)* – Tailgate.

Sep 88. (7") *(GEF 46)* **FALLEN ANGEL. / HELL'S HALF ACRE** [ ] [–]
(12"+=/cd-s+=) *(GEF 46 T/CD)* – Tailgate.

Sep 91. (lp/c/cd) *<(GEF/+C/D 24303)>* **STORYVILLE** [30] [69]
– Night parade / Hold back the dawn / Go back to your woods / Soap box preacher / Day of reckoning (burnin' for you) / What about now / Shake this town / Break in the rules / Resurrection / Sign of the rainbow. *(re-iss. cd Oct95; GFLD 19295)*

Capitol Capitol

Oct 94. (cd/c; ROBBIE ROBERTSON & The RED ROAD ENSEMBLE) *(CD/TC EST 2238) <28295>* **(MUSIC FOR) THE NATIVE AMERICANS** [ ] [ ]
– Coyote dance / Mahk tchi (heart of the people) / Ghost dance / The vanishing breed / It's a good day to die / Golden feather / Akua Tutu / Words of fire, deeds of blood / Cherokee morning song / Skinwalker / Ancestor song / Twisted hair.

Mar 98. (cd) *<(8 54243-2)>* **CONTACT FROM THE UNDERWORLD OF RED BOY** [ ] [ ]
– The sound is fading / The code of Handsome Lake / Making a noise / Unbound / Sacrifice / Rattlebone / Peyote healing / In the blood / Stomp dance (unity) / The lights / Take your partner by the hand.

– compilations, etc. –

May 03. (cd) *E.M.I.; <(5 39858-2)>* **CLASSIC MASTERS** [ ] Jul02 [ ]

Smokey ROBINSON

Born: WILLIAM ROBINSON, 19 Feb'40, Detroit, Michigan, USA. In 1954, he formed The MATADORS who subsequently became The MIRACLES. After a suitably miraculous period at 'Motown' (where BERRY GORDY had made him vice-president) during which he not only scored an incredible number of hits with his own group but wrote and produced classics for other artists, ROBINSON initiated a solo career in 1973 with the 'SMOKEY' album. Given an encouraging critical response, he continued to wrap his silken falsetto around a far more laid back, sophisticated sound, becoming an expert romantic balladeer in the process but appealing largely to an older audience. Albums such as 'A QUIET STORM' (1975) sold moderately but SMOKEY wasn't back in the chart spotlight until 1979's 'WHERE THERE'S SMOKE' and its steamy accompanying (US Top 5) single, 'CRUISIN'. 'WARM THOUGHTS' (1980) and 'BEING WITH YOU' (1981) continued the creative renaissance, the latter's title track furnishing him with a (very!) rare UK No.1 (US No.2). Yet the 80's proved a difficult period both personally and commercially, only 1987's 'ONE HEARTBEAT' album breaching the Top 30 while its single, 'JUST TO SEE HER', made the Top 10. An addiction to crack certainly didn't help while SMOKEY's romantic infidelities continued to trouble him. Having resigned his vice-presidency in 1988, ROBINSON finally left 'Motown' in 1990 and signed to the 'S.B.K.' label for 1992's 'DOUBLE GOOD EVERYTHING'. Seven years on, SMOKEY decided to have one more crack under the spotlight, the album 'INTIMATE' (1999) was certainly not his best work by a long way.

Album rating: SMOKEY (*6) / PURE SMOKEY (*5) / A QUIET STORM (*6) / SMOKEY'S FAMILY ROBINSON (*5) / DEEP IN MY SOUL (*5) / LOVE BREEZE (*5) / SMOKIN' (*4) / WHERE THERE'S SMOKE (*6) / WARM THOUGHTS (*8) / BEING WITH YOU (*7) / YES IT'S YOU LADY (*5) / TOUCH THE SKY (*5) / BLAME IT ON LOVE & ALL THE GREAT HITS compilation (*7) / ESSAR (*4) / SMOKE SIGNALS (*5) / ONE HEARTBEAT (*6) / LOVE, SMOKEY (*5) / DOUBLE GOOD EVERYTHING (*4) / INTIMATE (*4)

SMOKEY ROBINSON – vocals (with session people)

Motown Tamla

Jun 73. (7") *<54233>* **SWEET HARMONY. / WANT TO KNOW MY MIND** [–] [48]

Oct 73. (lp/c) *(STG/CSTG 8012) <328>* **SMOKEY** [ ] Jul73 [70]
– Holly / Medley: Never my love – Never can say goodbye / A silent partner in a three-way love affair / Just my soul responding / Sweet harmony / Will you love me tomorrow / Wanna know my mind / The family song / Baby come close. *(re-iss. Oct81 lp/c; STMS/CSTMS 5011)*

Jan 74. (7") *(TMG 883)* **JUST MY SOUL RESPONDING. / SWEET HARMONY** [35] [–]

May 74. (7") *(TMG 898) <54239>* **BABY COME CLOSE. / A SILENT PARTNER IN A THREE-WAY LOVE AFFAIR** [ ] Nov73 [27]

May 74. (7") *<54246>* **IT'S HER TURN TO LIVE. / JUST MY SOUL RESPONDING** [–] [82]

Jun 74. (lp/c) *(STML/CSTML 11265) <331>* **PURE SMOKEY** [ ] Apr74 [99]
– It's her turn to live / The love between me and the kids / Asleep on my love / I am I am / Just passing through / Virgin man / She's only a baby herself / Fulfill your need / A tattoo. *(re-iss. Feb82 lp/c; STMS/CSTMS 5043)*

Sep 74. (7") *<54250>* **VIRGIN MAN. / FULFILL YOUR NEED** [–] [56]

Dec 74. (7") *<54251>* **I AM I AM. / THE FAMILY SONG** [–] [56]

May 75. (7") *(TMG 949) <54258>* **BABY THAT'S BACKATCHA. / JUST PASSING THROUGH** [ ] Apr75 [26]

Jun 75. (lp/c) *(STML/CSTML 11268) <337>* **A QUIET STORM** [ ] Apr75 [36]
– Quiet storm / The agony and the ecstasy / Baby that's backatcha / Wedding song / Happy (love theme from the film 'Lady Sings The Blues') / Love letters / Coincidentally. *(re-iss. Feb82 lp/c; STMS/CSTMS 5044)*

Sep 75. (7") *<54261>* **THE AGONY AND THE ECSTASY. / WEDDING SONG** [–] [36]

Jan 76. (7") *(TMG 1019) <54265>* **QUIET STORM. / ASLEEP ON MY LOVE** [ ] [61]

Apr 76. (lp/c) *(STML/CSTML 12021) <341>* **SMOKEY'S FAMILY ROBINSON** [ ] [57]
– When you came / Get out of town / Do like I do / Open / So in love / Like nobody can / Castles made of sand.

May 76. (7") *<54267>* **OPEN. / COINCIDENTALLY** [–] [81]

Mar 77. (7") *(TMG 1065)* **THERE WILL COME A DAY (I'M GONNA TO HAPPEN TO YOU). / AN OLD-FASHIONED MAN** [ ] [–]

Apr 77. (lp/c) *(STMP/CSTMP 12055) <350>* **DEEP IN MY SOUL** [ ] Feb77 [47]
– Vitamin U / There will come a day (I'm gonna happen to you) / It's been a long time (since I been in love) / Let's do the dance of life together / If you want my love / You cannot laugh alone / In my corner / The humming song (lost for words).

Jun 77. (7") *(TMG 1076) <54284>* **VITAMIN U. / HOLLY** [ ] [ ]

Sep 77. (7") *(TMG 1085) <54288>* **THEME FROM BIG TIME. / (part 2)**

Sep 77. (lp/c) *(STML/CSTML 12068) <355>* **BIG TIME** (soundtrack)
– Theme from Big Time / J.J.'s theme / Hip trip / He is the light of the world / So nice to be with you / Shona's theme (with dialogue) / If we're gonna act like lovers / The agony and the ecstasy / Theme from Big Time (reprise).

Feb 78. (lp/c) *(STML/CSTML 12076)* **SMOKEY'S WORLD** (compilation) –
– Big time / Baby that's backatcha / Quiet storm / There will come a day / Sweet harmony / It's her turn to live / I am I am / An old-fashioned man / Vitamin U / Just my soul responding / A silent partner in a 3-way love affair / Virgin man / The agony and the ecstasy / Baby come close / Open.

Apr 78. (7") *(TMG 11086)* **MADAM X. / THE AGONY AND THE ECSTASY** –

May 78. (lp/c) *(STML/CSTML 12081) <359>* **LOVE BREEZE** Apr78 75
– Why you wanna see my bad side / Love so fine / Feeling you feeling me / Madam X / Shoe soul / Trying it again / Daylight and darkness / I'm loving you softly.

Jul 78. (7") *(TMG 1114) <54293>* **DAYLIGHT AND DARKNESS. / WHY YOU WANNA SEE MY BAD SIDE** Jun78 75

Nov 78. (7") *(TMG 1129) <54296>* **SHOE SOUL. / I'M LOVING YOU SOFTLY**

Jan 79. (d-lp) *<363>* **SMOKIN' (live)** –

—— early '79, SMOKEY featured with STEVIE WONDER, DIANA ROSS and MARVIN GAYE on minor hit single, 'POPS WE LOVE YOU'.

Jul 79. (7") *(TMG 1152) <54301>* **GET READY. / EVER HAD A DREAM**

Aug 79. (lp/c) *(STML/CSTML 12115) <366>* **WHERE THERE'S SMOKE** Jun79 17
– Smoke / It's a good night / I love the nearness of you / The hurt on you / Ever had a dream / Fire get ready / Share it / Cruisin'. *(re-iss. Oct81; same)*

Sep 79. (7") *<54306>* **CRUISIN'. / EVER HAD A DREAM** – 4

Sep 79. (7") *(TMG 1164)* **CRUISIN'. / THE HUMMING SONG (LOST FOR WORDS)** –

Apr 80. (7") *(TMG 1182) <54311>* **LET ME BE THE CLOCK. / TRAVELLIN' THROUGH** Mar80 31

Apr 80. (lp/c) *(STML/CSTML 12134) <375>* **WARM THOUGHTS** Mar80 14
– Let me be the clock / Heaven on pride (light on love) / Into each rain some life must fall / Wine, women and song / Melody man / What's in your life for me / I want to be your love / Travellin' through. *(re-iss. Oct81; same)*

Jun 80. (7") *(TMG 1191) <54313>* **HEAVY ON PRIDE (LIGHT ON LOVE). / I LOVE THE NEARNESS OF LOVE**

Nov 80. (7") *<54318>* **I WANT TO BE YOUR LOVE. / WINE, WOMEN AND SONG** –

Feb 81. (7") *(TMG 1223) <54321>* **BEING WITH YOU. / WHAT'S IN YOUR LIFE FOR ME** 1 2

Apr 81. (lp/c) *(STML/CSTML 12151) <375>* **BEING WITH YOU** 17 Mar81 10
– Being with you / Food for thought / If you wanna make love (come round here) / Who's sad / Can't fight love / You are forever / As you do / I hear the children singing. *(re-iss. Apr85 lp/c; WL/WK 72256) (cd-iss. Sep93; 530219-2)*

Jun 81. (7") *<54325>* **BEING WITH YOU – AQUI CON TIGO. / AQUI CON TIGO** –

Oct 81. (7") *(TMG 1237) <54327>* **YOU ARE FOREVER. / I HEAR THE CHILDREN SINGING** Jun81 59

Nov 81. (7") *<54332>* **WHO'S SAD. / FOOD FOR THOUGHT** –

Feb 82. (7") *(TMG 1255) <1601>* **TELL ME TOMORROW. / (part 2)** 51 Jan82 33
(12"+=) *(TMGT 1255)* – Being with you / Aqui con tigo.

Feb 82. (lp/c) *(STML/CSTML 12165) <6001>* **YES IT'S YOU LADY** 33
– Tell me tomorrow / Yes it's you lady / An old fashioned love / Are you still here / The only game in town / International baby / Merry go ride / I'll try something new / Destiny.

May 82. (7"/12") *(TMG/+T 1262) <1615>* **AN OLD FASHIONED LOVE. / DESTINY** Apr82 60

Sep 82. (7") *<1630>* **YES IT'S YOU LADY. / ARE YOU STILL HERE** –

Feb 83. (7") *(TMG 1295) <1655>* **I'VE MADE LOVE TO YOU A THOUSAND TIMES. / INTO EACH RAIN SOME LIFE MUST FALL**
(12"+=) *(TMGT 1295)* – (Greatest hits medley).

Mar 83. (lp/c) *(STML/CSTML 12175) <6030>* **TOUCH THE SKY** Jan83 50
– Touch the sky / Gimme what you want / Even tho' / Gone again / All my life's a lie / Sad time / Dynamite / I've made love to you a thousand times.

May 83. (7") *(TMG 1307) <1678>* **TOUCH THE SKY. / ALL MY LIFE'S A LIE**

Aug 83. (7"; by SMOKEY ROBINSON & BARBARA MITCHELL) *(TMG 1313) <1684>* **BLAME IT ON LOVE. / EVEN THO'** Jun83 48

Sep 83. (lp/c) *(STML/CSTML 12193) <6064>* **BLAME IT ON LOVE & ALL THE GREAT HITS** (compilation) Aug83
(cd/c-iss.Feb91; WK/WD 72542)

Oct 83. (7") *<1700>* **WOULDN'T YOU LIKE TO KNOW. / DON'T PLAY ANOTHER LOVE SONG** –

—— in Dec'83, SMOKEY featured on RICK JAMES' US Top 50 hit 'Ebony Eyes'.

Jun 84. (7"/12") *(TMG/+T 1344) <1735>* **AND I DON'T LOVE YOU. / DYNAMITE**

Jul 84. (lp/c) *(ZL/ZK 72152) <6098>* **ESSAR** Jun84
– And I don't love you / Train of thought / I can't find / Why are you running from my love / Gone forever / Close encounters of the first kind / Little girl, little girl / Girl I'm standing there / Driving thru life in the fast lane.

Nov 84. (7") *<1756>* **I CAN'T FIND. / GIMME WHAT YOU WANT** –

—— early '85, he featured on the 'WE ARE THE WORLD' charity No.1 single

Mar 85. (7") *<1786>* **TRAIN OF THOUGHT. / FIRST TIME ON A FERRIS WHEEL** –

Jan 86. (7"/12") *(ZB 40553) <1828>* **HOLD ON TO YOUR LOVE. / TRAIN OF THOUGHT** Nov85

Mar 86. (lp/c/cd) *(ZL/ZK/ZD 72394) <6156>* **SMOKE SIGNALS** Feb86
– Some people (will do anything for love) / Sleepless nights / Because of you (it's the best it's ever been) / Be kind to the growing mind / Te quiero como si no hubicra un manama / Hold on to your love / Photograph in my mind / No time to stop believing / Wishful thinking / Hanging on by a thread.

May 86. (7") *(ZB 40717) <1839>* **SLEEPLESS NIGHTS. / CLOSE ENCOUNTERS OF THE FIRST KIND**
(12"+=) *(ZT 40718)* – Mickey's monkey / I gotta dance to keep me from crying / Some people (will do anything for love).

Sep 86. (7") *<1855>* **BECAUSE OF YOU (IT'S THE BEST IT'S EVER BEEN). / GIRL I'M STANDING THERE** –

Jan 87. (7") *<1868>* **LOVE WILL SET YOU FREE (theme from 'Solar Babies'). / (part 2)** –

Mar 87. (7") *(ZB 41147) <1877>* **JUST TO SEE HER. / I'M GONNA LOVE YOU LIKE THERE'S NO TOMORROW** 52 8
(12"+=) *(ZT 41148)* – SMOKEY ROBINSON & THE MIRACLES:- You really got a hold on me / That's what love is made of / Ooh baby baby.

May 87. (lp/c/cd) *(ZL/ZK/ZD 72580) <6226>* **ONE HEARTBEAT** Mar87 26
– Just to see her / One heartbeat / It's time to stop shoppin' around / Why do happy memories hurt so bad / You don't know what it's like / What's too much / Love brought us here tonight / Love don't give no reason / Keep me.

Jun 87. (7") *<1897>* **ONE HEARTBEAT. / LOVE WILL SET YOU FREE** – 10

Jul 87. (7"/12") *(ZB/ZD 41526)* **ONE HEARTBEAT. / JUST TO SEE HER** –

Nov 87. (7") *<1911>* **WHAT'S TOO MUCH. / I'VE MADE LOVE TO YOU A THOUSAND TIMES** – 79

—— early in '88, SMOKEY feat on DOLLY PARTON single I KNOW YOU BY HEART.

Mar 88. (7") *<1925>* **LOVE DON'T GIVE NO REASON. / HANGING ON BY A THREAD** –

Mar 88. (7") *(ZB 41783)* **LOVE DON'T GIVE NO REASON. / ('A'instrumental)** –
(12"+=) *(ZT 41784)* – ('A'dance mix) / ('A'dub mix).
(cd-s+=) *(ZD 41784)* – Going to a go-go / You've really got a hold on me.

Feb 90. (7") *<2031>* **EVERYTHING YOU TOUCH. / IT'S THE SAME GOOD FEELING**

Mar 90. (cd/c/lp) *<(6268)>* **LOVE, SMOKEY**
– Love is the light / Love 'n life / Same old love / I can't find / Take me through the night / Everything you touch / Don't wanna be just physical / Come to me soon / You made me feel love / Jasmin / Easy / Just another kiss / Unless you do it again.

May 90. (7") *<903>* **(IT'S THE) SAME OLD LOVE. / (instrumental)** –
Jul 90. (7") *<927>* **TAKE ME THROUGH THE NIGHT. / UNLESS YOU DO IT AGAIN** –

S.B.K. S.B.K.

Jan 92. (7") *<07370>* **DOUBLE GOOD EVERYTHING. / GUESS WHAT I GOT FOR YOU** Oct91 91
(12"+=/c-s+=/cd-s+=) – Skid row.
Feb 92. (cd/c/lp) *(SBK CD/TC/LP 17) <97968>* **DOUBLE GOOD EVERYTHING** Nov91
– Why / Double good everything / Be who you are / I love your face / Can't get enough / Rack me back / When a woman cries / You take me away / Skid row.

Universal Universal

Oct 99. (cd) *<(E1 53741-2)>* **INTIMATE**
– Sleeping in / Easy to love / Love love again / Intimate / I'm the one / Just let me love you / All of mine / The bottom line / Feelings flowing / Ready to roll / Tu me besas muy rico / Intimate (reprise).

– compilations, etc. –

on 'Tamla Motown' unless mentioned
Jul 82. (lp/c) *(TMS/TMC 3510)* **HOT SMOKEY** –
Aug 82. (7"/12") *(TMG 1274)* **CRUISIN'. / THE ONLY GAME IN TOWN** –
Jun 83. (lp/c) *K-Tel; (NE1/CE2 175)* **THE SMOKEY ROBINSON STORY** –
Nov 88. (lp/c/cd; shared with MARVIN GAYE) *Telstar;* **LOVE SONGS** 69 –
Nov 92. (cd/c) *K-Tel; (530121-2/-4)* **THE GREATEST HITS** 65
Jun 94. (4xcd-box) **35th ANNIVERSARY COLLECTION**

— see the MIRACLES for SMOKEY ROBINSON & THE MIRACLES releases

Tom ROBINSON

Born: 1 Jun'50, Cambridge, England. Sent to reform school as a lad, the young ROBINSON met guitarist DANNY KUSTOW and subsequently formed DAVANQ in the early 70's. Duly relocating to London, ROBINSON put together cabaret-folk outfit, CAFE SOCIETY, releasing an eponymous solo album on RAY DAVIES' (KINKS) 'Konk' label in 1974. Relations between the band and DAVIES soon soured, the project falling by the wayside as ROBINSON formed his own outfit, The TOM ROBINSON BAND. With a stable line-up cementing around KUSTOW, MARK AMBLER and DOLPHIN TAYLOR, the group were signed up by 'E.M.I.', immediately hitching a ride on the emerging punk juggernaut with stompalong classic, '2-4-6-8 MOTORWAY'. The track's UK Top 5 success was followed with the live EP, 'RISING FREE', ROBINSON's radical political manifesto introduced with the celebratory 'SING IF YOU'RE GLAD TO BE GAY' and the defiant 'DON'T TAKE NO FOR AN ANSWER'. Adopted by the music press as something of a new wave cause celebre, TRB, along with the likes of The CLASH, espoused a more positive strand of protest than the bleak nihilism of many punk acts, their anti-racist, pro-individual freedom stance represented by the clenched fist logo on debut album, 'POWER IN THE DARKNESS' (1978). Brimming with anthemic rallying cries for the disaffected yet rarely lapsing into laboured preaching, the album confirmed ROBINSON's credentials as an articulate spokesman for the punk generation. And it wasn't just empty rhetoric, ROBINSON putting his politics where his mouth was and playing a host of benefit gigs (chiefly anti-racism and gay/lesbian rights events) both at home and in the States where he was something of a minor hero on the college circuit. Following the departure of AMBLER and TAYLOR, however, ROBINSON struggled through a TODD RUNDGREN-produced follow-up set, 'TRB 2' (1979). Preceded by the flop PETER GABRIEL collaboration, 'BULLY FOR YOU', the album's bland sloganeering was met with a frosty critical reception and relatively poor sales (despite a UK Top 20 placing); the TOM ROBINSON BAND fell apart, its mainman subsequently suffering a nervous breakdown. Upon his recovery, the singer formed a new outfit, SECTOR 27, initiating his own label, 'Panic' and releasing an eponymous album in 1980. A more experimental post-punk affair, the album was well received but failed to sell and again, ROBINSON changed his plans. Moving to Hamburg, Germany in early '82, he cut his first solo album proper, 'NORTH BY NORTHWEST', another strong effort which found him developing a more conventional singer/songwriter style. This paid dividends the following year when 'WAR BABY' made the UK Top 10, its laidback, swinging sophistication contrasting with the three-chord assault of old. An equally classy follow-up, 'LISTEN TO THE RADIO: ATMOSPHERICS', just nudged into the Top 40 later that year, another collaboration with PETER GABRIEL. Together with a further minor hit in Steely Dan's 'RIKKI DON'T LOSE THAT NUMBER', the singles were included on the fine 1984 set, 'HOPE AND GLORY', ROBINSON's most successful album since the late 70's. 'STILL LOVING YOU' (1986) saw the man's muse become increasingly mellow as he entered fatherhood (it emerged that he was actually bi-sexual, not homosexual) although the album failed to match even its predecessor's limited success. Throughout the remainder of the 80's and on into the 90's, ROBINSON regularly performed with original members of TRB as well as touring, writing and recording as a solo artist. Featuring such disparate guests as CHRIS REA and T.V. SMITH, 1994's 'LOVE OVER RAGE' album boasted ROBINSON's most confident set of songs in almost a decade, proving that he didn't have to rely on mere nostalgia to make a living.

Album rating: POWER IN THE DARKNESS (*8) / TRB TWO (*5) / SECTOR 27 (*4; by SECTOR 27) / TOM ROBINSON BAND compilation (*7) / NORTH BY NORTHWEST (*7) / HOPE AND GLORY (*6) / STILL LOVING YOU (*5) / WE NEVER HAD IT SO GOOD with Jakko M. Jakszuk (*4) / LIVING IN A BOOM TIME (*5) / LOVE OVER RAGE (*5) / HAVING IT BOTH WAYS (*5) / RISING FREE – THE BEST OF TOM ROBINSON compilation (*7)

TOM ROBINSON BAND

TOM ROBINSON – vocals, bass (ex-CAFE SOCIETY, ex-DAVANQ) / **DANNY KUSTOW** – guitar (ex-DAVANQ) / **MARK AMBLER** – keyboards repl. ANTON MAUVE, BRET SINCLAIR & MARK GRIFFITHS / **DOLPHIN TAYLOR** – drums, vocals repl. NICK TREVISICK (ex-CAFE SOCIETY)

E.M.I. Harvest

Oct 77. (7") *(EMI 2715) <4533>* **2-4-6-8 MOTORWAY. / I SHALL BE RELEASED** 5
Feb 78. (7"ep) *(EMI 2749)* **RISING FREE (live)** 18 –
– Don't take no for an answer / Right on sister / Sing if you're glad to be gay / Martin.
May 78. (7") *(EMI EMI 2787)* **UP AGAINST THE WALL. / I'M ALRIGHT JACK** 33 –
May 78. (lp/c) *(EMC/TC-EMC 3226) <11778>* **POWER IN THE DARKNESS** 4
– Up against the wall / Grey Cortina / Too good to be true / Ain't gonna take it / Long hot summer / Winter of 79 / Man you never saw / Better decide which side you're on / You gotta survive / Power in the darkness / 2-4-6-8 Motorway. *(re-iss. Aug83 lp/c; EMS/TC-EMS 106668-1/-4) (re-iss. Oct94 on 'Cooking Vinyl' cd/c; COOK C/CD 076) (cd re-iss. Aug96 on 'Razor & Tie'; RE 2018)*
Aug 78. (7") *(EMI 2847)* **TOO GOOD TO BE TRUE. / POWER IN THE DARKNESS** –
Sep 78. (7") *<4568>* **RIGHT ON SISTER. / GLAD TO BE GAY** –

— (mid'78) **IAN PARKER** – keyboards repl. NICK PLYTAS (ex-ROOGALATOR) who had repl. AMBLER (Apr'78).

— (Dec78) **PRESTON HEYMAN** – drums (ex-BRAND X) repl. DOLPHIN who joined STIFF LITTLE FINGERS.

Mar 79. (7") *(EMI 2916) <4726>* **BULLY FOR YOU. / OUR PEOPLE** 68
Mar 79. (lp/c) *(EMC/TC-EMC 3296) <11930>* **TRB TWO** 18
– All right all night / Why should I mind / Black angel / Let my people be / Blue murder / Bully for you / Crossing over the road / Sorry Mr. Harris / Law and order / Days of rage / Hold out. *(re-iss. Aug83 lp/c; EMS/TC-EMS 165215-1/-4) (re-iss. Oct94 on 'Cooking Vinyl' cd/c; COOK CD/C 077) (cd re-iss. Aug96 on 'Razor & Tie'; RE 2019)*
May 79. (7"; w-drawn) *(EMI 2946)* **ALRIGHT ALL NIGHT. / BLACK ANGEL** –

— **CHARLIE MORGAN** – drums repl. the returning TREVISICK who had repl. HEYMAN. The latter joined KATE BUSH. **GEOFF SHARKEY** – guitar repl. KUSTOW / added **GRAHAM COLLIER** – double bass / **GEOFF DALY** – saxophone

Aug 79. (7"; TOM ROBINSON & THE VOICE SQUAD) *(EMI 2967)* **NEVER GONNA FALL IN LOVE (AGAIN). / GETTING TIGHTER** –

— Disbanded late summer '79. **TOM ROBINSON** now vocals, guitar went solo with back-up from SECTOR 27. **STEVE BLANCHARD** – guitar / **DEREK QUINTON** – drums / **JO BURT** – bass (recorded one withdrawn lp, 'SECTOR 27', on 'Regal Zonophone')

SECTOR 27

— were now given full billing.

Panic not iss.

Jul 80. (7") *(SEC 27)* **NOT READY. / CAN'T KEEP AWAY** –
Oct 80. (7") *(SEC 28)* **INVITATION, WHAT HAVE WE GOT TO LOSE? / DUNGANNON** –

Fontana I.R.S.

Nov 80. (lp) *(6359 039) <70013>* **SECTOR 27**
– Invitation / Not ready / Mary Lynne / Looking at you / 523 / Total recall / Where can we go tonight / Take it or leave it / Bitterly disappointed / One fine day. *(cd-iss. Jun96 +=; 532642-2)* – (extra tracks).

Panic not iss.

Jan 81. (7") *(SEC 29)* **TOTAL RECALL. / STORNOWAY** –
May 81. (7") *(SEC 30)* **MARTIN'S GONE. / CHRISTOPHER CALLING** –

TOM ROBINSON

— went solo again. (SECTOR 27 as a trio branched out on own). **TOM** added **STEVE LAURIE** – drums / **RICHARD MAZDA** – guitar, producer / etc

Panic Geffen

Jun 82. (lp) *(ROBBO 1)* **NORTH BY NORTHWEST** –
– Now Martin's gone / Atmospherics / Can't keep away (part 2) / Looking for a bonfire / Merrily up on high / Those days / In the cold / The night tide / Dungannon / Love comes. *(re-iss. 1986 on 'Castle' lp/c/cd; CLA LP/MC/CD 128) (cd-iss. Jun97 & Apr02 on 'Castaway Northwest'+=; CNWVP 003CD)* – Tango an der wand / Now Richard's gone / Airtraum tango dob / Any favours / Out to lunch.
Jul 82. (7") *(NIC 1)* **NOW MARTIN'S GONE. / ATMOSPHERICS** –
(re-iss. Feb83 as 5-track-12"ep; NIC 1-12) – ATMOSPHERICS
Jun 83. (7") *(NIC 2)* **WAR BABY. / HELL YES** 6 Sep84
(12"+=) *(NIC 2-12)* – Martin's gone (original).
Nov 83. (7") *(NIC 3)* **LISTEN TO THE RADIO: ATMOSPHERICS. / DON'T DO ME ANY FAVOURS** 39 –
(12"+=) *(NIC 3-12)* – Out to lunch.

Castaway-RCA Geffen

Jun 84. (7") *(TR 1)* **BACK IN THE OLD COUNTRY. / BEGGIN'**
(12"+=) *(TRT 1)* – ('A'live version).
Sep 84. (7"/12") *(TR/+T 2)* **RIKKI DON'T LOSE THAT NUMBER. / CABIN BOY (live)** 58 –
Sep 84. (lp/c) *(ZL/ZK 70484)* **HOPE AND GLORY** 21
– War baby / Atmospherics: Listen to the radio / Cabin boy / Blond and blue / Hope and glory / Murder at the end of the day / Prison / Rikki don't lose that number / Old friend / Looking for a bonfire.
May 85. (7"/12") *(ZB/ZT 400 19/20)* **PRISON. / MORE LIVES THAN ONE** –

— TOM brought back **BLANCHARD + BURT** plus **RED** – drums

Jul 86. (7") *(TR 3)* **(IT AIN'T NOTHIN' LIKE) THE REAL THING. / THE WEDDING** –
(12"+=) *(TRT 3)* – ('A'extended).
Sep 86. (lp/c/cd) *(ZL/ZK/ZD 71129)* **STILL LOVING YOU**
– Feels so good – Hurt so bad / (It ain't nothin' like) The real thing / Still loving you / Take me home again / You tattooed me / Drive all night / Living in a love town / Spain / This little romance / The wedding. *(cd re-iss. Sep00 on 'Castaway Northwest'; CNWVP 006CD)*
Sep 86. (7"/12") *(TR/+T 4)* **STILL LOVING YOU. / THE SATURDAY DISCO** –
Jan 87. (7"; TOM ROBINSON & KIKI DEE) *(TR 5)* **FEELS SO GOOD. / NORTHERN RAIN** –
(12"+=) *(TRT 5)* – You tattooed me / Change.
Jun 87. (7") *(ZB 41333)* **SPAIN. / DRIVE ALL NIGHT** –
(12"+=) *(ZT 41333)* – (It ain't nothin' like) The real thing.

Musidisc not iss.

Oct 90. (cd/c/lp; TOM ROBINSON & JAKKO M. JAKSZUK) *(10666-2/-4/-1)* **WE NEVER HAD IT SO GOOD** –
– We never had it so good / Drinking through the desert / Blood brother / What have I ever done to you / The baby rages on / Tomboy / Kiss and roll over / Hard cases / Can't stop: Peter's theme / My own sweet way.
Nov 90. (7"; as TOM ROBINSON & JAKKO M. JAKSZUK) *(10666-7)* **BLOOD BROTHER. / ('A'version)** –
(12"+=) *(10666-6)* – What have I ever done to you / Rigging.

Cooking Vinyl Scarface

Sep 92. (lp/c/cd) *(COOK/+C/CD 052)* **LIVING IN A BOOM TIME** –
– Folk song (intro) / Living in a boom time / More lives than one / Yuppie scum / My own sweet way / Castle island / Digging it up / The Brits / War baby / Back in the old country. *(re-iss. Mar94 cd/c; same)*
Jan 93. (c-ep/cd-ep) *(FRY C/CD 022)* **WAR BABY (live). / BLOOD BROTHER / WE DIDN'T KNOW (WHAT WAS GOING ON)** –

— now w / **ROBIN MILLAR** – rhythm guitar / **CHRIS REA** – slide guitar / **MARK AMBLER** – keyboards / **WINSTON BLISSETT** – bass / **MARTIN DITCHAM** – drums / **MARK RAMSDEN** – saxophone / **T.V.SMITH + ANDY MITCHELL** – backing vocals

May 94. (lp/c/cd) *(COOK/+C/CD 066) <53913>* **LOVE OVER RAGE**
– Roaring / Hard / Loved / Days / Driving / Green / DDR / Fifty / Silence / Chance.
Jun 94. (cd-ep) *(FRYCD 028)* **HARD / GREEN / LIVING IN A BOOM TIME / PORTOBELLO TERRACE** –
Jul 94. (cd-ep) *(FRYCD 029)* **LOVED / FIFTY / YUPPY SCUM / GLAD TO BE GAY '94** –
Sep 94. (cd-ep) *(FRYCD 031)* **DAYS (THAT CHANGED THE WORLD) / ROARING / THE BRITS COME ROLLING BACK** –
May 96. (cd/c) *(COOK CD/C 097)* **HAVING IT BOTH WAYS** –
– Disrespect / One / Rum thunderbird / Cold cold ground / Fool to myself / Hot dog / Sorry / Raining in Connecticut / Congo blue / Castaway / The last word.
Jul 96. (cd-ep) *(FRYCD 050)* **RAINING IN CONNECTICUT / DISRESPECT / RUM THUNDERBIRD / RAINING IN CONNECTICUT (mix)** –

– compilations, etc. –

Dec 81. (lp) *E.M.I.; (EMS 1005)* **TOM ROBINSON BAND** –
(re-iss. May82 on 'Fame'; FA 3028)
Nov 82. (lp) *Panic; (ROBBO 2)* **CABARET '79 (live)** –
Oct 83. (7") *Old Gold; (OG 9379)* **2-4-6-8 MOTORWAY. / DON'T TAKE NO FOR AN ANSWER** –
Apr 87. (lp/c; TOM ROBINSON & THE CREW) *Dojo; (DOJO LP/CD 51)* **MIDNIGHT AT THE FRINGE (live)** –
Sep 87. (7") *E.M.I.; (EM 28)* **2-4-6-8 MOTORWAY (live). / ('A'original)** –
(12"+=) *(12EM 28)* – Sing if you're glad to be gay.
Sep 87. (cd/c/lp) *E.M.I.; (CD/TC+/EMC 3540)* **COLLECTION 77-87** –
Mar 89. (lp/cd) *Line; (MS LP4/CD9.00695)* **GLAD TO BE GAY CABARET** –
Jun 89. (cd) *Line; (LICD 9.005888)* **LAST TANGO** –
Oct 89. (d-lp/c/cd) *Connoisseur; (VSOP LP/MC/CD 138)* **BACK IN THE OLD COUNTRY** –
– Listen to the radio: Atmospherics / Too good to be true / Up against the wall / Northern rain / I shall be released / 2-4-6-8 motorway / Drive all night / Don't take no for an answer / Where can we go tonight / Back in the old country / Alright all night / War baby / Power in the darkness / Crossing over the road / Rikki don't lose that number / Looking for a

bonfire / Hard cases / Still loving you / Not ready / Bully for you / Long hot summer. *(d-lp/c+=)* – Mary Lynne / Bitterly disappointed.

Jun 92. (d-cd) *Line; (LICD 921215)* **GLAD TO BE GAY / LAST TANGO** –
(re-iss. Aug95; same)

Aug 92. (cd) *Pop Almanac; (PACD 7005)* **WINTER OF '89** –

Jun 93. (cd/c) *Optima; (OPTM CD/C 012)* **TOM ROBINSON** –

Jul 94. (cd) *Music De-Luxe; (MSCD 6)* **MOTORWAY** –

Mar 96. (cd/c) *EMI Gold; (CD/TC GOLD 1015)* **THE GOLD COLLECTION** –

Jun 96. (cd) *Fontana; (532642-2)* **SECTOR 27 COMPLETE** –
(re-iss. Apr02 on 'Castaway Northwest'; CNWVP 012CD)

Jun 97. (cd) *EMI Gold; (CDGOLD 1098)* **RISING FREE – THE BEST OF TOM ROBINSON** –

Jun 97. (cd; with JAKKO M. JAKSZUK) *Castaway Northwest; (CNWVP 001CD)* **BLOOD BROTHER** –
(above was virtually 'WE NEVER HAD IT SO GOOD' & extra tracks)

Jul 97. (cd) *Castaway Northwest; (CNWVP 002CD)* **LAST TANGO / MIDNIGHT AT THE FRINGE** –

Aug 97. (cd) *Castaway Northwest; (CNWVP 003CD)* **GLAD TO BE GAY (CABARET '79)** –

Apr 98. (d-cd) *Snapper; (<SMDCD 118>)* **THE UNDISCOVERED: MODERN CLASSICS** Sep98

Sep 00. (cd) *Castaway Northwest; (CNWVP 007CD)* **WAR BABY** –

Nov 00. (cd) *Secret; (SECRET 001CD)* **THE CAFE SOCIETY ARCHIVES** –

Mar 01. (cd) *Castaway Northwest; (CNWVP 011CD)* **RARE** –

May 01. (cd) *Castaway Northwest; (CNWVP 013CD)* **SMELLING DOGS** (some BBC archives) –

□ ROCKET FROM THE TOMBS
(see under ⇒ PERE UBU)

□ ROCKETS (see under ⇒ CRAZY HORSE)

□ ROCKPILE (see under ⇒ EDMUNDS, Dave)

□ Nile RODGERS (see under ⇒ CHIC)

ROLLING STONES

Formed: London, England ... mid-1962 by JONES, JAGGER and RICHARDS. After a residence at Richmond blues club, 'The Crawdaddy', the band were signed by A&R man DICK ROWE to 'Decca', who had just rejected The BEATLES. Their debut single, a cover of Chuck Berry's 'COME ON ', almost hit top 20, and the band were well on the way to crystallising their image as the original bad boys of rock. Hairier, uglier and more rebellious (publicly anyway) than The BEATLES, manager/hustler extrordinaire, ANDREW LOOG OLDHAM, wasted no time in playing the outlaw card for all it was worth. Working the press like a true pro, he elicited a string of publicity grabbing headlines, culminating with the infamous "Would you let your daughter marry a ROLLING STONE?" Which, of course, made the band even more desirable in the eyes of those self same teenage daughters and as The 'STONES snaked their way across the country the following year on a joint headlining tour with The RONETTES, what had begun as hysteria and isolated fisticuffs had escalated into full-on rioting with promoters quaking in their boots. That summer, they scored their first No.1 single with a cover of Buddy Holly's 'NOT FADE AWAY', now beginning to usurp The BEATLES as the UK's premier knicker-wetting phenomenon. As for the music, the early 'STONES' sound was a fairly derivative take on black America yet it possessed a primal, sexual intensity that made their Merseyside rivals sound like choirboys. Rhythm was everything and in full flight WATT's fluid, unswerving backbeat locked in perfect unholy union with WYMAN's bass and RICHARDS' demonic guitar grooves. JONES, meanwhile, casually lashed out searing slide guitar and JAGGER, the blueprint for decades of wannabe's to come, pouted, preened and snarled in equal measure. The first three albums, 'THE ROLLING STONES' (1964), '12 x 5' (1964) and 'THE ROLLING STONES NOW' (1965) were made up largely of R&B and blues covers, the latter marginally topping the other two with the most focused number JAGGERS/RICHARDS had come up with by that point, 'HEART OF STONE' and an electrifying reading of Willie Dixon's 'LITTLE RED ROOSTER'. Apparently revealed to KEITH RICHARDS in a dream, one of the most recognisable and famous riffs in rock history formed the core of The 'STONES' breakthrough hit, '(I CAN'T GET NO) SATISFACTION'. Despite the controversial lyrics which earned a boycott from US radio and further enhanced their reputation as leering malcontents, the record hit the top of the charts on both sides of the Atlantic during the summer of '65. This opened the floodgates for a wave of No.1 singles: 'GET OFF MY CLOUD' (1965), '19TH NERVOUS BREAKDOWN' (1966) and 'PAINT IT BLACK' (1966), the latter a brooding psychedelic-tinged stampede that featured some nifty sitar playing by a cross-legged BRIAN JONES. 'AFTERMATH' (1966) was a huge step forward with JONES adding exotic touches in line with his growing admiration for the JouJouka musicians of Morocco. Meanwhile, the JAGGER/RICHARDS songwriting partnership was blossoming, tackling social issues with trenchant ease; 'MOTHER'S LITTLE HELPER' as well as the usual sexual politics; 'UNDER MY THUMB'. It was around this time that JAGGER began assuming the multitude of different masks he would use onstage and off, as one journalist aptly pointed out; "MICK JAGGER was an interesting bunch of guys". His cocky, chameleon-like affectations stood in stark contrast to KEITH RICHARDS' sullen, slightly aloof distance but it was exactly this homo-erotic chemistry that fuelled The STONES and fashioned the decadent legend of 'The Glimmer Twins' as they'd come to be known in the 70's. 'BETWEEN THE BUTTONS' (1967) contained another salacious rebel anthem in 'LET'S SPEND THE NIGHT TOGETHER' alongside the ebb and flow wistfulness of 'RUBY TUESDAY'. By this time, though, the powers that be had had just about enough of these unkempt subversives and their dubious morals. The infamous Redlands drug bust in February '67 was probably the most famous of all The 'STONES' run-in's with the law, although by no means the most serious and in the end, RICHARDS' conviction was quashed on appeal while JAGGER was given a year's probation. Yet only a few days later, MICK talked defiantly to the press about revolution and The 'STONES recorded their acerbic reply to The BEATLES' 'All You Need Is Love'. With LENNON and McCARTNEY collaborating, the band cut 'WE LOVE YOU'. Allegedly written by JAGGER in jail as a tribute to the fans who had stood by him, it came out sounding like a deliciously snide riposte to the authorities, complete with the sounds of heavy footsteps and a cell door clanging shut. While they were successful with occasional ventures into warped psychedelia, The 'STONES remained first and foremost a rock'n'roll band and their attempt at a psychedelic concept album, 'THEIR SATANIC MAJESTIES REQUEST' (1967) was always destined to sound half-baked at best. The stellar '2000 LIGHT YEARS FROM HOME' and 'SHE'S A RAINBOW' saved the album from being a complete failure although it didn't even come close to rivalling 'Sgt. Pepper'. A more honest response to The BEATLES' magnum opus, 'BEGGARS BANQUET' (1968) was the first album in a staggering burst of creativity that would see The ROLLING STONES release four of the best albums in the history of rock over a five year period.

Preceded by the much needed No.1 hit, 'JUMPIN' JACK FLASH', (which marked the beginning of a fruitful partnership with JIMMY MILLER), the album saw the band realign themselves with roots music to startling effect. At this point The 'STONES' were not simply imitating their heroes of the American South, they had made the music truly their own. Inspired by Mikhail Bulgakov's novel, 'The Master And Margarita', 'SYMPATHY FOR THE DEVIL' was pure malevolent genius, MICK casting himself gleefully in the role of Beelzebub over an irresistible voodoo funk. Similarly controversial were the topical 'STREET FIGHTIN' MAN' and the leering 'STRAY CAT BLUES' which centred on a rock star and an obliging 15 year old groupie, the grinding rhythm oozing illicit sex. These subversive broadsides were alternated with threadbare country blues numbers that, save for JAGGER's barrow boy via Louisiana vocals, sounded so authentic you could almost smell the corn bread. During sessions for the follow-up, 'LET IT BLEED' (1969), BRIAN JONES had left the band and was found dead in controversial circumstances a month later on the 3rd of July, 1969, at his Pooh Corner home. He had never really recovered from having control of the band wrestled from him and his unstable personality buckled under a frightening drug intake. Preceded by The 'STONES' last No.1 single, 'HONKY TONK WOMAN', 'LET IT BLEED' was eventually released the same fateful month as the Altamont disaster and possessed a vivid essence of brooding portent, most obvious on the opening track 'GIMME SHELTER', with its thundering rhythm and near-hysterical urging. 'MIDNIGHT RAMBLER' was equally chilling while RICHARDS made his vocal debut on 'YOU GOT THE SILVER', his voice a ragged sliver of emotive simplicity that stood in direct contrast to MICK's affectations. Closing with the aching desolation of 'YOU CAN'T ALWAYS GET WHAT YOU WANT', the album was another example, if one was needed at all, that The 'STONES' preferred harsh realism to dopey idealism and had never really embraced the hippy philosophy. Perhaps it was fitting then, that The 'STONES' were, quite literally, centre stage when that hopeful euphoria of the 60's finally came to an end during the last bitterly cold days of 1969. As the band played a free gig at a barren speedway track in Altamont, Northern California, poor organisation and delays contributed to bad vibes which were exacerbated by brutal, acid-crazed Hell's Angels. Supposedly acting in a security capacity, one of their number ended up stabbing an innocent fan to death while many others were beaten up, The 'STONES' ferried out by helicopter in fear of their lives. By the release of 'STICKY FINGERS' (1971), the dark potency of the previous albums had gone, save for a few tracks, notably MARIANNE FAITHFUL's bleakly beautiful 'SISTER MORPHINE'. The band had pushed things to the limit and from here on in they retreated. Nevertheless, the best was yet to come, and 'STICKY FINGERS' kept 'up the momentum. 'DEAD FLOWERS' was a rollicking country hoedown shot through with typically twisted humour while JAGGER assumed his inimitable Delta Bluesman mantle for the inspired cover of Mississippi Fred McDowell's 'YOU GOT TO MOVE'. Elsewhere, tracks like 'BROWN SUGAR' and 'BITCH' were quintessential 'STONES, revelling in their own mythology. This was also the first stuio material to feature ex-BLUESBREAKER, MICK TAYLOR, who'd joined in '69 as a replacement for BRIAN JONES. Athough his distinctive style was an integral part of the band's early 70's sound, he'd later leave amid growing disatisfaction with the JAGGER/RICHARDS domination of the band. 'EXILE ON MAIN STREET' (1972) remains one of the best double album ever released and quite possibly staking a claim for the best album, bar none, ever released. Big claims, yet this was the pure, unadulterated essence of that cliched thing called rock'n'roll, no cobwebbed history lecture, but a living, breathing, sweating justification for white boys playing the blues. Recorded in a dank, humid basement in RICHARDS' villa in the South of France, the production is so murky that JAGGER's vocals verge on the indecipherable at points and the whole thing seems continually on the brink of collapse. Yet this only serves to enhance the unerringly strong material and elegantly wasted mood of the record. From the aural massage of 'TUMBLING DICE' to the raggedy-assed beauty of 'LOVING CUP', the down home gospel of 'SHINE A LIGHT' to KEITH RICHARDS' off-the-cuff anthem 'HAPPY', The 'STONES, or rock music, for that matter, would never sound so spiritually debauched again. In comparison, 'GOAT'S HEAD SOUP' (1973) was inevitably a let down, the band sounding tired and listless, although JAGGER at least sounded half-convincing on his tender ballad, 'ANGIE'. MICK TAYLOR's last album, 'IT'S ONLY ROCK'N'ROLL' (1974) was 'STONES by numbers and didn't bode well for the coming decade. 'BLACK AND BLUE' (1976) saw ex-FACE, RON WOOD brought into the fold and a half hearted attempt at reggae stylings. By this point, the band were a massive live draw but often sloppy on stage due in no small part to the band's collosal drug intake. It came as little surprise to even the most casual 'STONES observer when, in February 1977, RICHARDS was busted in Toronto holding serious amounts of Class A. Amid alleged rumours of a huge pay-off, KEITH was eventually let off fairly leniently and yet again, the 'STONES lived to fight another day, another 20 years in fact, and counting. Too long some might say, as 'SOME GIRLS' (1978) was the last 'STONES album that actually sounded like they meant it. Although the disco experimentalism of 'MISS YOU' was rather lukewarm, the album contained the last great JAGGER/RICHARDS song, 'BEAST OF BURDEN'. 'EMOTIONAL RESCUE' (1980) was dull and formulaic while 1981's 'TATTOO YOU' redeemed itself slightly with a rawer sound and the sprightly, if cliched hit 'START ME UP'. THE ROLLING STONES were, by now, one of the biggest acts on the stadium rock circuit, particularly in the U.S.A. and although their studio output was stagnating, the band's live show was still worth the admission price, especially now that KEITH had cleaned up his act and could get through a whole set without falling asleep on stage. 'UNDERCOVER' (1984) was a typically ill-advised 80's attempt at experimentation and as such, an unmitigated disaster, while 'DIRTY WORK' (1986) was only marginally less tedious. After a brief lull, the band returned with 1989's 'STEEL WHEELS' and while the single 'MIXED EMOTIONS' was their best in a decade, the album favoured glossy production and slick professionalism over content. With a move to 'Virgin' amid million pound deals, 'VOODOO LOUNGE' (1994) was touted as a dangerous return to form, although it was their first as a quartet as WYMAN departed. In the event, it was as flaccid and cliched as anything the band had done. The pared down, semi-acoustic 'STRIPPED' (1995) was listenable although as the prospect of a creative rebirth grows ever more remote, maybe one more album would suffice. This came in the shape of 1997's 'BRIDGES TO BABYLON', another commercial success that spawned a few minor hits, the near 60 year olds still drawing the crowds (not in Britain though as the taxman became their enemy once again). JAGGER was back in the new millennium with another instalment in his intermittent solo career although 'GODDESS IN THE DOORWAY' (2001) was hardly anything to write home about. It nevertheless cracked the US and UK Top 50, helped no doubt by a UK TV documentary about its making. After rolling for a staggering forty years, it was inevitable some kind of compilation would be unveiled to celebrate such an admittedly impressive landmark. 'FORTY LICKS' (2002), found the 'STONES bring their catalogue up to date, creaming off choice cuts from each of the four decades without even beginning to exhaust the wealth and depth of that incredible legacy. • **Trivia:** JAGGER's relationship with singer MARIANNE FAITHFULL ended in 1970, when he met Nicaraguan model, Bianca Rosa Perez-Mora and later married her on the 12th of May '71. They split in 1978, probably over Marsha Hunt's allegations that MICK was the father of her child. After a long relationship with Jerry Hall (formerly Bryan Ferry's girlfriend), he later married her on the 21st November '90. JAGGER's film work included:- NED KELLY (1969) / PERFORMANCE (1970) / FITZCARALDO (1981). WYMAN's marriage (since 1959) ended abruptly in the mid-80's, after his 2-year relationship with 16 year-old, Mandy Smith, was revealed in The News Of The World. They married relatively quietly on the 2nd of June '89, but controversially divorced in 1992, with the now famous Mandy allegedly sueing for half a million. • **Songwriters:** JAGGER-RICHARDS mostly except covers; NOT FADE AWAY (Buddy Holly) / ROUTE 66 (Nelson Riddle Orchestra) / I JUST WANT TO MAKE LOVE TO YOU (Willie Dixon) / HONEST I DO (Jimmy Reed) / I NEED YOU BABY (Bo Diddley) / POISON IVY (Coasters) / NOW I'VE GOT A WITNESS ... (Gene Pitney) / LITTLE BY LITTLE (Pitney / Spector) / COME ON + CAROL + YOU CAN'T CATCH ME + TALKIN' 'BOUT YOU + LITTLE QUEENIE + AROUND AND AROUND + BYE BYE JOHNNY (Chuck Berry) / CAN I GET A WITNESS (Holland-Dozier-Holland) / MONEY (Barrett Strong) / I WANNA BE YOUR MAN (Beatles) / LITTLE BY LITTLE (w/Spector) / YOU CAN MAKE IT IF YOU TRY (Gene Allison; hit) / WALKING THE DOG (Rufus Thomas) / SUSIE Q (Dale Hawkins) / UNDER THE BOARDWALK (Drifters) / I CAN'T BE SATISFIED + MANNISH BOY (Muddy Waters) / DOWN HOME GIRL (Jerry Butler) / IT'S ALL OVER NOW (Valentinos) / LITTLE RED ROOSTER (Willie Dixon) / PAIN IN MY HEART + MY GIRL (Otis Redding) / EVERYBODY NEEDS SOMEBODY TO LOVE (Solomon Burke) / DOWN THE ROAD APIECE (Will Bradley) / TIME IS ON MY SIDE (Irma Thomas) / SHE SAID YEAH (Jackson/Christy) / I DON'T KNOW WHY (Stevie Wonder) / MERCY, MERCY (Don Covay) / GOOD TIMES (Sam Cooke) / CRY TO ME (Betty Harris; hit) / HITCH HIKE (Marvin Gaye) / THAT'S HOW STRONG MY LOVE IS (Otis Redding) / OH BABY (WE GOT A GOOD THING GOIN') (Gonzales Ozen) / PRODIGAL SON (Robert Wilkins) / YOU BETTER MOVE ON (Arthur Alexander) / LOVE IN VAIN (Robert Johnson; trad.) / AIN'T TOO PROUD TO BEG + JUST MY IMAGINATION (Temptations) / I'M A KING BEE + SHAKE YOUR HIPS (Slim Harpo) / CHERRY OH BABY (? reggae) / GOING TO A GO-GO (Smokey Robinson / Miracles) / HARLEM SHUFFLE (Bob & Earl) / TWENTY FLIGHT ROCK (Eddie Cochran) / CORRINA (Taj Mahal) / etc. KEITH RICHARDS solo wrote with JORDAN. RONNIE WOOD covered TESTIFY (Parliaments) / AM I GROOVIN' YOU (Bert Berns) / SEVEN DAYS (Bob Dylan) / SHOW ME (J. Williams).

Album rating (UK): THE ROLLING STONES (*8) / THE ROLLING STONES NO.2 (*8) / OUT OF OUR HEADS (*7) / AFTERMATH (*7) / BIG HITS (HIGH TIDE AND GREEN GRASS) compilation (*8) / GOT LIVE IF YOU WANT IT (*5) / BETWEEN THE BUTTONS (*7) / THEIR SATANIC MAJESTIES REQUEST (*5) / BEGGARS BANQUET (*10) / THROUGH THE PAST, DARKLY (BIG HITS VOL.2) compilation (*8) / LET IT BLEED (*9) / GET YER YA-YA'S OUT! (*7) / STONE AGE exploitation (*7) / STICKY FINGERS (*8) / GIMME SHELTER exploitation (*6) / HOT ROCKS 1964-1971 compilation US (*10) / MILESTONES exploitation (*6) / EXILE ON MAIN ST. (*10) / ROCK 'N' ROLLING STONES exploitation (*5) / GOATS HEAD SOUP (*6) / IT'S ONLY ROCK'N'ROLL (*6) / MADE IN THE SHADE compilation (*6) / METAMORPHOSIS exploitation (*5) / ROLLED GOLD – THE VERY BEST OF THE ROLLING STONES compilation (*10) / BLACK AND BLUE (*6) / LOVE YOU LIVE (*5) / GET STONED exploitation (*7) / SOME GIRLS (*7) / EMOTIONAL RESCUE (*5) / TATTOO YOU (*6) / STILL LIFE (AMERICAN CONCERTS 1981) (*3) / STORY OF THE STONES exploitation (*6) / UNDERCOVER (*5) / REWIND 1971-1984 (THE BEST OF THE ROLLING STONES) compilation (*7) / DIRTY WORK (*6) / STEEL WHEELS (*6) / FLASHPOINT (*4) / JUMP BACK – THE BEST OF THE ROLLING STONES 1971-1993 compilation (*8) / VOODOO LOUNGE (*8) / STRIPPED (*6) / BRIDGES TO BABYLON (*6) / NO SECURITY (*5) / FORTY LICKS compilation (*10) / Mick Jagger: SHE'S THE BOSS (*5) / PRIMITIVE COOL (*4) / WANDERING SPIRIT (*6) / GODDESS IN THE DOORWAY (*5) / Keith Richards: TALK IS CHEAP (*8) / . . .LIVE AT THE HOLLYWOOD PALLADIUM (*5) / MAIN OFFENDER (*5)

MICK JAGGER (b.26 Jul'43, Dartford, Kent, England) – vocals, harmonica / **KEITH RICHARDS** (b.18 Dec'43, Dartford) – rhythm guitar / **BRIAN JONES** (b.28 Feb'43, Cheltenham, England) – lead guitar / **CHARLIE WATTS** (b. 2 Jun'41, Islington, London) – drums (ex-BLUES INC.) / **BILL WYMAN** (b.WILLIAM PERKS, 24 Oct'36, Lewisham, London) – bass repl. DICK TAYLOR who later joined PRETTY THINGS / **IAN STEWART** – piano (was 6th member, pushed to the background by manager)

		Decca	London
Jun 63.	(7") _(F 11675)_ **COME ON. / I WANT TO BE LOVED**	21	–
Nov 63.	(7") _(F 11764) <9641>_ **I WANNA BE YOUR MAN. / STONED**	12	Jan64
Feb 64.	(7") _(F 11845)_ **NOT FADE AWAY. / LITTLE BY LITTLE**	3	–
Mar 64.	(7") _<9657>_ **NOT FADE AWAY. / I WANNA BE YOUR MAN**	–	48
Apr 64.	(lp) _(LK 4605) <375>_ **THE ROLLING STONES** (US-title 'ENGLAND'S NEWEST HITMAKERS – THE ROLLING STONES)	1	Jun64 11
	– (Get your kicks on) Route 66 / I just want to make love to you / Honest I do / I need you baby (Mona) / Now I've got a witness (like uncle Phil and uncle Gene) / Little by little / I'm a king bee / Carol / Tell me (you're coming back) / Can I get a witness / You can make it if you try / Walking the dog. _(US)_ – Not fade away. / – Mona _(re-iss. Jul84 lp/c; LKD/KSDC 4605) (cd-ss.1985 on 'London'; 820 047-2) (re-iss. Jun95 on 'London' cd/c/lp; 844460-2/-4/-1)_		
Jun 64.	(7") _(F 11934) <9687>_ **IT'S ALL OVER NOW. / GOOD TIMES, BAD TIMES**	1	Aug64 26
Jul 64.	(7") _<9682>_ **TELL ME (YOU'RE COMING BACK). / I JUST WANT TO MAKE LOVE TO YOU**	–	24
Oct 64.	(7") _<9708>_ **TIME IS ON MY SIDE. / CONGRATULATIONS**	–	6
Nov 64.	(7") _(F 12014)_ **LITTLE RED ROOSTER. / OFF THE HOOK**	1	–
Nov 64.	(lp) _<402>_ **12 x 5**	–	3
	– Around and around / Confessin' the blues / Empty heart / Time is on my side / Good times bad times / It's all over now / 2120 South Michigan Avenue / Under the boardwalk / Congratulations / Grown up wrong / If you need me / Susie Q. _(UK-iss.Aug84 lp/c; LKD/KDKHAC 5335) (cd-iss. Nov84 on 'London'; 820 048-2) (re-iss. Jun95; 844461-2/-4/-1)_		
Jan 65.	(lp) _(LK 4661)_ **THE ROLLING STONES No.2**	1	–
	– Everybody needs somebody to love / Down home girl / You can't catch me / Time is on my side / What a shame / Grown up wrong / Down the road apiece / Under the boardwalk / I can't be satisfied / Pain in my heart / Off the hook / Susie Q. _(re-iss. 1986;)_		
Jan 65.	(7") _<9725>_ **HEART OF STONE. / WHAT A SHAME**	–	19
Feb 65.	(7") _(F 12104) <9741>_ **THE LAST TIME. / PLAY WITH FIRE**	1	9
			Mar65 96
Mar 65.	(lp) _<420>_ **THE ROLLING STONES NOW!**	–	5
	– Everybody needs somebody to love / Down home girl / You can't catch me / Heart of stone / I need you baby (Mona) / Down the road apiece / Off the hook / Pain in my heart / Oh baby (we got a good thing goin') / Little red rooster / Surprise surprise. _(UK-iss.Aug88 cd; 820133-2) (re-iss. Jun95 on 'London' cd/c/lp; 844462-2/-4/-1)_		
May 65.	(7") _(F 12220)_ **(I CAN'T GET NO) SATISFACTION. / THE SPIDER AND THE FLY**	1	–
Jun 65.	(7") _<9766>_ **(I CAN'T GET NO) SATISFACTION. / THE UNDER ASSISTANT WEST COAST MAN**	–	1
Sep 65.	(lp; mono/stereo) _(LK/SKL 473) <429>_ **OUT OF OUR HEADS**	2	Aug 65 1
	– She said yeah * / Mercy, mercy / Hitch hike / That's how strong my love is / Good times / Gotta get away * / Talkin' 'bout you * / Cry to me / Oh baby (we got a good thing going) * / Heart of stone / The under assistant west coast man / I'm free. _<UK tracks above * were repl. by in US>_ – I'm		

alright (live) / (I can't get no) Satisfaction / Play with fire / The spider and the fly / One more try. *(re-iss. Jul84 lp/c)(cd; LKD/LSLSC 5336)(820 049-2) (re-iss. Jun95 on 'London' cd/c/lp; 844463-2/-4/-1)*

Sep 65. (7") *<9792>* **GET OFF OF MY CLOUD. / I'M FREE** – 1

Oct 65. (7") *(F 12263)* **GET OFF OF MY CLOUD. / THE SINGER NOT THE SONG** 1 –

Nov 65. (lp) *<451>* **DECEMBER'S CHILDREN (AND EVERYBODY'S)** – 4
– She said yeah / Talkin' 'bout you / You better move on / Look what you've done / The singer not the song / Route 66 (live) / Get off of my cloud / I'm free / As tears go by / Gotta get away / Blue turns to grey / I'm movin' on (live). *(UK-iss.Aug88 cd; 820 135-2) (re-iss. Jun95 on 'London' cd/c/lp; 844464-2/-4/-1)*

Dec 65. (7") *<9808>* **AS TEARS GO BY. / GOTTA GET AWAY** – 6

Feb 66. (7") *(F 12331)* **19th NERVOUS BREAKDOWN. / AS TEARS GO BY** 1 –

Feb 66. (7") *<9823>* **19th NERVOUS BREAKDOWN. / SAD DAY** – 2

Apr 66. (lp; mono/stereo)(c) *(LK/SKL 4786)(KSKC 4786) <451>* **AFTERMATH** 1 Jul66 2
– Mother's little helper / Stupid girl / Lady Jane / Under my thumb / Doncha bother me / Goin' home / Flight 505 / High and dry / Out of time / It's not easy / I am waiting / Take it or leave it / Think / What to do. *(US version+=)* – Paint it black. *(re-iss. May85 lp/c)(cd; SKLD/ 4786)(820 050-2) (re-iss. Jun95 on 'London' cd/c/lp; 844466-2/-4/-1)*

May 66. (7") *<901>* **PAINT IT BLACK. / STUPID GIRL** – 1

May 66. (7") *(F 12395)* **PAINT IT BLACK. / LONG LONG WHILE** 1 –

Jul 66. (7") *<902>* **MOTHER'S LITTLE HELPER. / LADY JANE** – 8 / 24

Sep 66. (7") *(F 12497) <903>* **HAVE YOU SEEN YOUR MOTHER BABY, STANDING IN THE SHADOW?. / WHO'S DRIVING YOUR PLANE?** 5 9

Nov 66. (lp; mono/stereo)(c) *(TXL/TXS 101)(KSKC 101) <1>* **BIG HITS (HIGH TIDE AND GREEN GRASS)** (compilation) 4 Apr 66 3
– Have you seen your mother baby, standing in the shadows? / Paint it black / It's all over now / The last time / Heart of stone / Not fade away / Come on / (I can't get no) Satisfaction / Get off my cloud / As tears go by / 19th nervous breakdown / Lady Jane / Time is on my side / Little red rooster. *(re-iss. Jun95 on 'London' cd/c/lp; 844465-2/-4/-1)*

Dec 66. (lp) *<493>* **GOT LIVE IF YOU WANT IT (live, Royal Albert Hall)** – 6
– Under my thumb / Get off of my cloud / Lady Jane / Not fade away / I've been loving you too long (to stop now) (studio) / Fortune teller (studio) / The last time / 19th nervous breakdown / Time is on my side / I'm alright / Have you seen your mother baby, standing in the shadow? / (I can't get no) Satisfaction. *(UK-iss.Aug88 cd; 820 137-2) (re-iss. Jun95 on 'London' cd/c/lp; 844467-2/-4/-1)*

Jan 67. (7") *(F 12546) <904>* **LET'S SPEND THE NIGHT TOGETHER. / RUBY TUESDAY** 3 55 / 1

Jan 67. (lp; mono/stereo)(c) *(LK/SKL 4852)(KSKC 4852) <499>* **BETWEEN THE BUTTONS** 3 Feb67 2
– Yesterday's papers / My obsession / Back street girl* / Connection / She smiled sweetly / Cool, calm and collected / All sold out / Please go home* / Who's been sleeping here? / Complicated / Miss Amanda Jones / Something happened to me yesterday. *(US version*; = tracks repl. by)* – Let's spend the night together / Ruby Tuesday. *(cd-iss. Jul85; 820 138-2) (re-iss. lp/cd. Dec91 on 'UFO' with free booklet) (re-iss. Jun95 on 'London' cd/c/lp; 844468-2/-4/-1)*

Jul 67. (lp) *<509>* **FLOWERS** (compilation) – 3
(UK cd-iss. Aug88; 820 139-2) (re-iss. cd Jun95 on 'London')

Aug 67. (7") *(F 12654) <905>* **WE LOVE YOU. / DANDELION** 8 50 / 14

Nov 67. (7") *<906>* **SHE'S A RAINBOW. / 2,000 LIGHT YEARS FROM HOME** – 25

Dec 67. (lp; mono/stereo)(c) *(TXL/TXS 103)(KTXC 103) <2>* **THEIR SATANIC MAJESTIES REQUEST** 3 2
– Sing this all together / Citadel / In another land / 2,000 man / Sing this all together (see what happens) / She's a rainbow / The lantern / Gomper / 2,000 light years from home / On with the show. *(re-iss. Feb86 lp/c/cd; 820 129-1/-4/-2) (re-iss. Jun95 on 'London' cd/c/lp; 844469-2/-4/-1)*

Dec 67. (7"; by BILL WYMAN) *<907>* **IN ANOTHER LAND. / THE LANTERN** – 87

May 68. (7") *(F 12782) <908>* **JUMPIN' JACK FLASH. / CHILD OF THE MOON** 1 3

Aug 68. (7") *<909>* **STREET FIGHTING MAN. / NO EXPECTATIONS** – 48

Dec 68. (lp; mono/stereo)(c) *(LK/SKL 4955)(KSKC 4955) <539>* **BEGGARS BANQUET** 3 5
– Sympathy for the Devil / No expectations / Dear doctor / Parachute woman / Jigsaw puzzle / Street fighting man / Prodigal son / Stray cat blues / Factory girl / Salt of the Earth. *(cd-iss. Jan83; 800 084-2) (re-iss. Jul84 lp/c; SKDL/KSKC 4955) (re-iss. Jun95 on 'London' cd/c/lp; 844471-2/-4/-1)*

— (Jun'69) **MICK TAYLOR** (b.17 Jan'48, Hertfordshire, England) – lead guitar (ex-JOHN MAYALL's BLUESBREAKERS) repl. BRIAN JONES who was found dead by his girlfriend on 3 Jul'69, after a heavy drink/drugs binge.

Jul 69. (7") *(F 12952) <910>* **HONKY TONK WOMEN. / YOU CAN'T ALWAYS GET WHAT YOU WANT** 1 1

Sep 69. (lp; mono/stereo)(c) *(LK/SKL 5019)(KSKC 5019) <3>* **THROUGH THE PAST DARKLY (BIG HITS VOL.2)** (compilation) 2 2
– Jumping Jack Flash / Mother's little helper / 2,000 light years from home / Let's spend the night together / You'd better move on / Street fighting man / She's a rainbow / Ruby Tuesday / Dandelion / Sittin' on the fence / Honky tonk women. *(re-iss. Jun95 on 'London' cd/c/lp; 844472-2/-4/-1)*

— (all UK singles so far were re-iss. Mar82)

Dec 69. (lp/c) *(SLK/KSKC 5025) <4>* **LET IT BLEED** 1 3
– Gimme shelter / Love in vain / Country honk / Live with me / Let it bleed / Midnight rambler / You got the silver / Monkey man / You can't always get what you want. *(cd-iss. Feb86; 820 052-2) (re-iss. Jun95 UK+US on 'London' cd/c/lp; 844473-2/-4/-1)*

Sep 70. (lp/c) *(SKL/KSKC 5065) <5>* **GET YER YA YA'S OUT** (live, New York, Nov'69) 1 Oct69 6
– Jumpin' Jack Flash / Carol / Stray cat blues / Love in vain / Midnight rambler / Sympathy for the Devil / Live with me / Little Queenie / Honky tonk women. *(cd-iss. Aug88; 820 131-2) (re-iss. Jun95 on 'London' cd/c/lp; 844474-2/-4/-1)*

— In 1970, MICK JAGGER starred in his second feature film 'Performance'. Below single was his first solo 45 from the film.

Nov 70. (7"; by MICK JAGGER) *(F 13067)* **MEMO FROM TURNER. / ('B'side by 'Jack Nitzsche')** 32

Apr 71. (lp/c) *(SKL/KSKC 5084)* **STONE AGE** (compilation) 4 –
– Look what you've done / It's all over now / Confessin' the blues / One more try / As tears go by / The spider and the fly / My girl / Paint it black / If you need me / The last time / Blue turns to grey / Around and around.

Rolling Stones Rolling Stones

Apr 71. (7"m) *(RS 19100)* **BROWN SUGAR. / BITCH / LET IT ROCK** 2 –

Apr 71. (lp/c) *(<COC/KCOC 59100>)* **STICKY FINGERS** 1 1
– Brown sugar / Sway / Wild horses / Can't you hear me knocking? / You gotta move / Bitch / I got the blues / Sister Morphine / Dead flowers / Moonlight mile. *(re-iss. Nov79 on 'E.M.I.'; CUN 59100) <US re-iss. 1980; MFSL 1-060> (cd-iss. Nov86 on 'C.B.S.'; CK 40488) (re-iss. Nov89 on 'CBS' UK/US lp/c/cd; 450 195-1/-4/-2) (re-iss. cd Jun94 on 'Virgin' UK+US; 7243-8-39504-2-3) (re-iss. Aug94 on 'Virgin' cd/c; CDV/TCV 2730) (lp re-iss. Nov97 on 'Virgin'; LPCENT 38)*

Apr 71. (7") *<19100>* **BROWN SUGAR. / BITCH** – 1

Jun 71. (7") *<RS 19101>* **WILD HORSES. / SWAY** – 28

Apr 72. (7") *(<RS 19103>)* **TUMBLING DICE. / SWEET BLACK ANGEL** 5 7

Jun 72. (d-lp/c) *(COC/KCOC 69100) <2900>* **EXILE ON MAIN ST.** 1 1
– Rocks off / Rip this joint / Shake your hips / Casino boogie / Tumbling dice / Sweet Virginia / Torn and frayed / Sweet black angel / Loving cup / Happy / Turd on the run / Ventilator blues / I just want to see his face / Let it loose / All down the line / Stop breaking down / Shine a light / Soul survivor. *(re-iss. Nov79 on 'E.M.I.'; CUNSP 69100) (re-iss. Nov89 on 'CBS' lp/c/cd UK/US; 450 196-1/-4/-2) (re-iss. Aug94 on 'Virgin' cd/c; CDV/TCV 2731)*

Jun 72. (7") *<19104>* **HAPPY. / ALL DOWN THE LINE** – 22

Aug 73. (7") *(RS <19105>)* **ANGIE. / SILVER TRAIN** 5 1

Sep 73. (lp/c) *(<COC/KCOC 59101>)* **GOATS HEAD SOUP** 1 1
– Dancing with Mr.D / 100 years ago / Coming down again / Doo doo doo doo doo (heartbreaker) / Angie / Silver train / Hide your love / Winter / Can you hear the music / Star star. *(re-iss. Nov79 on 'E.M.I.'; CUN 59101) (re-iss. Nov89 on 'CBS' UK/US; 450 207-1/-4/-2) (re-iss. Aug94 on 'Virgin' cd/c; CDV/TCV 2735)*

Jan 74. (7") *<19109>* **DOO DOO DOO DOO DOO (HEARTBREAKER). / DANCING WITH MR.D** – 15

Jul 74. (7") *(RS 19114) <19304>* **IT'S ONLY ROCK'N'ROLL. / THROUGH THE LONELY NIGHTS** 10 16

Oct 74. (lp/c) *(COC/KCOC 59103) <79101>* **IT'S ONLY ROCK'N'ROLL** 2 1
– If you can't rock me / Ain't too proud to beg / It's only rock'n'roll / Till the next goodbye / Time waits for no one / Luxury / Dance little sister / If you really want to be my friend / Short and curlies / Fingerprint file. *(re-iss. Nov79 on 'E.M.I.'; CUN 59103) (re-iss. Nov89 on 'CBS' UK/US lp/c/cd; 450 202-1/-4/-2) (re-iss. Aug94 on 'Virgin' cd/c; CDV/TCV 2733)*

Oct 74. (7") *(19302)* **AIN'T TOO PROUD TO BEG. / DANCE LITTLE SISTER** – 17

Jun 75. (lp/c) *(COC/KCOC 59104) <79102>* **MADE IN THE SHADE** (compilation) 14 6
– Brown sugar / Tumbling dice / Happy / Dance little sister / Wild horses / Angie / Bitch / It's only rock'n'roll (but I like it) / Doo doo doo doo doo (heartbreaker) / Rip this joint. *(re-iss. Nov89 on 'CBS' UK/US lp/c/cd; 450 201-1/-4/-2)*

—— (Apr-Dec75) **RON WOOD** – lead guitar (ex-FACES, ex-CREATION, etc) repl. MICK TAYLOR who left Dec74 and later joined JACK BRUCE BAND

Apr 76. (7") *(RS 19121)* **FOOL TO CRY. / CRAZY MAMA** 6 –

Apr 76. (7") *<19304>* **FOOL TO CRY. / HOT STUFF** – 10 49

May 76. (lp/c) *(COC/KCOC 59106) <79104>* **BLACK AND BLUE** 2 1
– Hot stuff / The hand of fate / Cherry oh baby / Memory motel / Hey Negrita / Melody / Fool to cry / Crazy mama. *(re-iss. Nov79 on 'E.M.I.; CUN 59106) (re-iss. Nov89 on 'C.B.S.' UK/US; 450 203-1/-4/-2) (re-iss. Aug94 on 'Virgin' cd/c; CDV/TCV 2736)*

Sep 77. (d-lp/d-c) *(COC/KCOC 89101) <9001>* **LOVE YOU LIVE (live)** 3 5
– Fanfare for the common man / Honky tonk woman / If you can't rock me / Get off of my cloud / Happy / Hot stuff / Star star / Tumbling dice / Fingerprint file / You gotta me / You can't always get what you want / Mannish boy / Crackin' up / Little red rooster / Around and around / It's only rock'n'roll / Brown sugar / Jumpin' Jack Flash / Sympathy for the Devil. *(re-iss. Nov79 on 'E.M.I.'; CUNSP 69101) (re-iss. Nov89 on 'C.B.S.' UK/US d-lp/c/cd; 450 208-1/-4/-2) (cd re-iss. Apr98 on 'Virgin'; CDV 2857)*

May 78. (7"/ext.12"pink) *(EMI/12EMI 2802) <19307>* **MISS YOU. / FARAWAY EYES** 3 1

Jun 78. (lp/c) *(<CUN/TCCUN 39108>)* **SOME GIRLS** 2 1
– Miss you / When the whip comes down / Just my imagination / Some girls / Lies / Far away etes / Respectable / Before they make me run / Beast of burden / Shattered. *(re-iss. Nov89 on 'C.B.S' UK/US lp/c/cd; 450 197-1/-4/-2) (re-iss. Aug94 on 'Virgin' cd/c;)*

Sep 78. (7") *<19309>* **BEAST OF BURDEN. / WHEN THE WHIP COMES DOWN** – 8

Sep 78. (7") *(EMI 2861)* **RESPECTABLE. / WHEN THE WHIP COMES DOWN** 23 –

Dec 78. (7") *<19310>* **SHATTERED. / EVERYTHING IS TURNING TO GOLD** – 31

Jun 80. (7") *(RSR 105) <20001>* **EMOTIONAL RESCUE. / DOWN IN THE HOLE** 9 3

Jul 80. (lp/c) *(CUN/TCCUN 39111) <16015>* **EMOTIONAL RESCUE** 1 1
– Dance (pt.1) / Summer romance / Send it to me / Let me go / Indian girl / Where the boys go / Down in the hole / Emotional rescue / She's so cold / All about you. *(re-iss. Nov89 on 'C.B.S.' UK/US; 450 206-1/-4/-2) (re-iss. Aug94 on 'Virgin' cd/c; CDV/TCV 2737)*

Sep 80. (7") *(RSR 106) <21001>* **SHE'S SO COLD. / SEND IT TO ME** 33 26

Mar 81. (lp/c) *(CUN/TCCUN 39112) <16028>* **SUCKING IN THE 70'S** (compilation + new) 15
– Shattered / Everything is turning to gold / Hot stuff / Time waits for no one / Fool to cry / Mannish boy / When the whip comes down (live) / I was a dancer (part 2) / Crazy mama / Beast of burden. *(re-iss. Nov89 on 'C.B.S.' UK/US; 450 205-1/-4/-2)*

Aug 81. (7") *(RSR 108) <21003>* **START ME UP. / NO USE IN CRYING** 7 2

Sep 81. (lp/c) *(CUN/TCCUN 39114) <16052>* **TATTOO YOU** 2 1
– Start me up / Hang fire / Slave / Little T & A / Black limousine / Neighbours / Worried about you / Tops / Heaven / No use in crying / Waiting on a friend. *(re-iss. Nov89 on 'C.B.S.' UK/US; 450 198-1/-4/-2) (re-iss. Aug94 on 'Virgin' cd/c; CDV/TCV 2732)*

Nov 81. (7") *(RSR 109) <21004>* **WAITING ON A FRIEND. / LITTLE T & A** 50 13

Mar 82. (7") *<21300>* **HANG FIRE. / NEIGHBORS** – 20

Jun 82. (7") *(RSR 110) <21301>* **GOING TO A GO-GO (live). / BEAST OF BURDEN (live)** 26 25

Jun 82. (lp/pic-lp/c) *(CUN/CUNP/TCCUN 39115) <39113>* **STILL LIFE (AMERICAN CONCERTS 1981)** 4 5
– Under my thumb / Let's spend the night together / Shattered / Twenty flight rock / Going to a go-go / Let me go / Time is on my side / Just my imagination / Start me up / (I can't get no) Satisfaction / Take the A train / Star-spangled banner. *(re-iss. Nov89 on 'C.B.S.' UK/US lp/c/cd; 450 204-1/-4/-2) (cd re-iss. Apr98 on 'Virgin'; CDV 2856)*

Sep 82. (7") *(RSR 111) <99978>* **TIME IS ON MY SIDE (live). / TWENTY FLIGHT ROCK (live)** 62
(12"+=) *(12RSR 111)* – Under my thumb (live).

Nov 83. (7") *(RSR 113) <99813>* **UNDERCOVER OF THE NIGHT. / ALL THE WAY DOWN** 11 9
(ext.12"+=) *(12RSR 113)* – Feel on baby (instrumental dub).

Nov 83. (lp/c/cd) *(CUN 165436-1/-4/-2) <90120>* **UNDERCOVER** 3 4
– Undercover of the night / She was hot / Tie you up / Wanna hold you / Feel on baby / Too much blood / Pretty beat up / Too tough / All the way down / It must be hell. *(re-iss. Nov89 on 'C.B.S.' UK/US; 450 200-1/-4/-2) (re-iss. Aug94 on 'Virgin' cd/c; CDV/TCV 2741)*

Jan 84. (7"/12"sha-pic-d) *(RSR/+P 114) <99788>* **SHE WAS HOT. / I THINK I'M GOING MAD** 42 44

Apr 84. (7") *<99724>* **TOO TOUGH. / MISS YOU** –

Jul 84. (lp/c/cd) *(CUN 1) <90176>* **REWIND 1971-1984 (THE BEST OF THE ROLLING STONES)** (compilation) 23 86
– Brown sugar / Undercover of the night / Start me up / Tumbling dice / It's only rock'n'roll (but I like it) / She's so cold / Hang fire / Miss you / Beast of burden / Fool to cry / Waiting on a friend / Angie / Emotional rescue. *(cd+= 2 extra) (re-iss. Nov89 on 'C.B.S.' UK/US; 450 199-1/-4/-2)*

—— In 1984, JAGGER guested dual vocals w / MICHAEL JACKSON on The JACKSONS' 'State Of Shock'. He also recorded debut solo album 'She's The Boss', which was released 1985. Later mid'85, he appeared at LIVE AID with DAVID BOWIE duetting on (Martha & The Vandellas) song 'DANCING IN THE STREET'. When issued as a charity single, it made UK No.1 / US No.7 (see BOWIE ⇒).

—— 12th Dec'85, IAN STEWART their long-serving 6th member died of a heart attack.

C.B.S. Rolling Stones

Mar 86. (7"/7"w-poster) *(A/QA 6864) <05802>* **HARLEM SHUFFLE. / HAD IT WITH YOU** 13 5
('A'-New York mix; 12"+=/12"w-poster+=) *(TA/QTA 6864)* – ('A'-London mix).

Mar 86. (lp/c/cd) *(CUN/40/CD 86321) <40250>* **DIRTY WORK** 4 4
– One hit (to the body) / Fight / Harlem shuffle / Hold back / Too rude / Winning ugly / Back to zero / Dirty work / Had it with you / Sleep tonight. *(re-iss. Nov89 on 'C.B.S.' UK/US; 465 953-1/-4/-2) (re-iss. Aug94 on 'Virgin' cd/c; CDV/TCV 2743)*

May 86. (7"/'A'-London mix-12") *(A/TA 7160) <05906>* **ONE HIT (TO THE BODY). / FIGHT** 28

—— During this lull in group activity, JAGGER and RICHARDS ventured solo amidst rumours of disbandment. In 1989, they re-surfaced.

Aug 89. (7"/c-s) *(655 193-7/-4) <69008>* **MIXED EMOTIONS. / FANCY MAN BLUES** 36 5
(cd-s+=) *(655 193-2)* – Tumbling dice / Miss you.
(cd-s+=) *(655 214-2)* – Shattered / Waiting on a friend.
(12"+=) *(655 193-8)* – ('A'-Chris Kimsey's mix).

Sep 89. (lp/c/cd) *(465 752-1/-4/-2) <45333>* **STEEL WHEELS** 2 3
– Sad sad sad / Mixed emotions / Terrifying / Hold on to your hat / Hearts for sale / Blinded by love / Rock and a hard place / Can't be seen / Almost hear you sigh / Continental drift / Break the spell / Slipping away. *(cd re-iss. Dec92;) (re-iss. Aug94 on 'Virgin' cd/c; CDV/TCV 2742)*

Nov 89. (7"/c-s) *(655 422-7/-4) <73057>* **ROCK AND A HARD PLACE. / COOK COOK BLUES** 63 23
('A'dance-12"+=) *(655 422-8)* – ('A'-Oh-oh hard dub mix).
(cd-s+=) *(655 448-2)* – It's only rock'n'roll / Rocks off.
(cd-s+=) *(655 448-5)* – Emotional rescue / Some girls.
(12") *(655 422-5)* – ('A'-Michael Brauer mix) / ('A'side) / ('A'-bonus beats mix).

Jun 90. (7") *<73093>* **ALMOST HEAR YOU SIGH. / BREAK THE SPELL** – 50

Jun 90. (7"/c-s) *(656 065-7/-4)* **ALMOST HEAR YOU SIGH. / WISH I'D NEVER MET YOU** 31 –
(c-s+=) *(656 065-2)* – Mixed emotions.
(cd-s+=) *(656 065-5)* – Miss you / Waiting on a friend.
(12")(cd-s) – ('A'side) / Beast of burden / Angie / Fool to cry.

Aug 90. (7"/c-s) *(656 122-7/-4)* **TERRIFYING (remix). / ROCK AND A HARD PLACE (remix)** [ ] [ ]
('A'-dance-12"+=) *(656 122-6)* – Harlem shuffle (London mix).
(cd-s) *(655 122-5)* – ('A'side) / Start me up / Shattered / If you can't rock me.

Sony Sony

Mar 91. (7"/c-s) *(656 756-7/-4) <73742>* **HIGHWIRE. / 2000 LIGHT YEARS FROM HOME (live)** [29] [57]
(12"+=/cd-s+=) *(656 756-6/-2)* – Sympathy for the Devil (live) / I just want to make love to you (live).
(cd-s+=) *(656 756-5)* – Play with fire (live) / Factory girl (live).

Apr 91. (d-cd/cd/c/lp) *(468 135-9/-2/-4/-1) <47456>* **FLASHPOINT (live)** [6] [16]
– Start me up / Sad sad girl / Miss you / Ruby Tuesday / Tou can't always get what you want / Factory girl / Little red rooster / Paint it black / Sympathy for the Devil / Brown sugar / Jumpin' Jack Flash / (I can't get no) Satisfaction / Sexdrive (studio) / High wire (studio). *(cd+=)* – Rock and a hard place / Can't be seen. *(cd re-iss. Apr98 on 'Virgin'; CDV 2855)*

May 91. (7"/c-s) *(656 892-7/-4)* **RUBY TUESDAY (live). / PLAY WITH FIRE (live)** [59] [–]
(12"+=) *(656 892-6)* – You can't always get what you want (live) / Rock and a hard place (live).
(3"cd-s+=) *(656 892-1)* – You can't always get what you want (live) / Undercover of the night (live).
(cd-s) *(656 892-5)* – ('A'side) / Harlem shuffle / Winning ugly London mix).

— In Nov'91, The STONES signed to 'Virgin', and BILL WYMAN soon quit.

Virgin Virgin

Nov 93. (d-lp/c/cd) *(V/TCV/CDV 2726)* **JUMP BACK: THE BEST OF THE ROLLING STONES 1971-1993** (compilation) [16] [–]
– Start me up / Brown sugar / Harlem shuffle / It's only rock'n'roll (but I like it) / Mixed emotions / Angie / Tumbling dice / Fool to cry / Rock and a hard place / Miss you / Hot stuff / Emotional rescue / Respectable / Beast of burden / Waiting on a friend / Wild horses / Bitch / Undercover of the night. *(re-iss. Oct94 & Jun95;)*

— WYMAN replaced by sessioners **DARRYL JONES** – bass / **CHUCK LEAVELL** – piano

Jul 94. (7"/c-s) *(VS/+C 1503) <38446>* **LOVE IS STRONG. / THE STORM** [14] [91]
(cd-s+=) *(VSCDT 1503)* – So young / ('A'-Bob Clearmountain mix).
(cd-s) *(VSCDX 1503)* – ('A'-Teddy Riley mixes; 5 mixes + other).

Jul 94. (cd/c/d-lp) *(8397821-2/-4/1) <39782>* **VOODOO LOUNGE** [1] [2]
– Love is strong / You got me rocking / Sparks will fly / The worst / New faces / Moon is up / Out of tears / I go wild / Brand new car / Sweethearts together / Suck on the jugular / Blinded by rainbows / Baby break it down / Thru and thru. *(cd-rom-iss.Jun95; VMED 2)*

Oct 94. (7"/c-s) *(VS/+C 1518)* **YOU GOT ME ROCKING. / JUMP ON TOP OF ME** [23] [ ]
(cd-s+=) *(VSCDG 1518)* – ('A'-Perfecto mix) / ('A'-sexy dub mix).
(12") *(VST 1518)* – ('A'-Perfecto mix) / ('A'-sexy dub) / ('A'-trance).

Dec 94. (7"/c-s) *(VS/+C 1524) <38459>* **OUT OF TEARS. / I'M GONNA DRIVE** [38] Oct94 [60]
(cd-s+=/s-cd-s+=) *(VSCD T/X 1524)* – Sparks will fly / ('A'-Bob Clearmountain remix).

Jul 95. (7"/c-s) *(VSP/VSC 1539)* **I GO WILD. / ('A'-Scott Litt remix)** [29] [–]
(cd-s+=) *(VSCDX 1539)* – ('A'version) / ('A'-Luis Resto straight vocal mix).

Nov 95. (c-s) *(VSC 1562)* **LIKE A ROLLING STONE / BLACK LIMOUSINE / ALL DOWN THE LINE** [12] [–]
(cd-s+=) *(VSCDT 1562)* – ('A'edit).

Nov 95. (cd/c/d-lp) *(CD/TC+/V 2801) <41040>* **STRIPPED (live)** [9] [9]
– Street fighting man / Like a rolling stone / Not fade away / Shine a light / The spider and the fly / I'm free / Wild horses / Let it bleed / Dead flowers / Slipping away / Angie / Love in vain / Sweet Virginia / Little baby.

Sep 97. (7"pic-d/c-s) *(VS/+C 1653)* **ANYONE SEEN MY BABY? / ('A'-Soul Solution remix)** [22] [ ]
(12"+=/cd-s+=) *(VSCDT 1653)* – ('A'-Armand's Rolling Steelo).

Oct 97. (cd/c) *(CD/TC+/V 2840) <44712>* **BRIDGES TO BABYLON** [6] [3]
– Flip the switch / Anybody seen my baby? / Low down / Already over me / Gunface / You don't have to mean it / Out of control / Saint of me / Might as well get juiced / Always suffering / Too tight / Thief in the night / How can I stop.

Jan 98. (7"pic-d) *(VSY 1667) <38626>* **SAINT OF ME. / ANYWAY YOU LOOK AT IT** [26] Feb98 [94]
(cd-s+=) *(VSCDX 1667)* – ('A'-Deep Dish grunge garage remix).
(cd-s) *(VSCDT 1667)* – Gimme shelter (live) / Anybody seen my baby? (Phil Jones remix) / ('A'-Deep Dish grunge garage remix).
(d12"+=) *(VSTX 1667)* – ('A'mixes incl. Armand's Rolling Steelo mix of 'B'side).
(d12"+=) *(VSTDT 1667)* – ('A'mixes; Deep Dish & Garage).

Aug 98. (7"pic-d) *(VSY 1700)* **OUT OF CONTROL. / ('A'-In Hand With Fluke mix)** [51] [–]
(cd-s+=) *(VSCDT 1700)* – ('A'-In hand with Fluke instrumental).
(pic-cd-s) *(VSCDX 1700)* – ('A'-Saber final mix) / ('A'-Bi-Polar At The Controls mix) / ('A'-Bi-Polar's Fat Controller mix).

— next featured guests, DAVE MATTHEWS and TAJ MAHAL

Nov 98. (cd/c/lp) *(CD/TC+/V 2880) <46740>* **NO SECURITY (live 1997)** [67] [34]
– (intro) / You got me rocking / Gimme shelter / Flip the switch / Memory hotel / Corinna / Saint of me / Waiting on a friend / Sister morphine / Live with me / Respectable / Thief in the night / The last time / Out of control.

— In Dec'99, a VARIOUS ARTISTS version of 'IT'S ONLY ROCK'N'ROLL' made the UK Top 20

Oct 02. (d-cd/d-c) *(CDVD/TCVD 2964) <13378>* **FORTY LICKS** (compilation) [2] [2]
– Street fighting man / Gimme shelter / (I can't get no) Satisfaction / The last time / Jumpin' Jack Flash / You can't always get what you want / 19th nervous breakdown / Under my thumb / Not fade away / Have you seen your mother, baby (standing in the shadows) / Sympathy for the Devil / Mother's little helper / She's a rainbow / Get off my cloud / Wild horses / Ruby Tuesday / Paint it black / Honky tonk women / It's all over now / Let's spend the night together / Start me up / Brown sugar / Miss you / Beast of burden / Don't stop / Happy / Angie / You got me rocking / Shattered / Fool to cry / Love is strong / Mixed emotions / Keys to your love / Anybody seen my baby? / Stealing my heart / Tumbling dice / Undercover of the night / Emotional rescue / It's only rock'n'roll (but I like it) / Losing my touch.

Dec 02. (7") *(VS 1838) <546821>* **DON'T STOP. / DON'T STOP (new rock remix)** [36] [ ]
(cd-s+=) *(VSCDT 1838)* – Miss you (remix).

Mercury Mercury

Sep 03. (7") *(981061-3)* **SYMPATHY FOR THE DEVIL (2003 remix by The Neptunes). / (Full Phatt remix)** [14] [ ]
(12"+=) *(981061-5)* – (Fatboy Slim remix).
(cd-s++=) *(981059-9)* – (Neptunes full mix) / (original).

– (selective) compilations, etc. –

below releases issued on 'Decca' UK/ 'Abkco' US unless mentioned

Jul 71. (7"m) *(F 13195)* **STREET FIGHTING MAN. / SURPRISE SURPRISE / EVERYBODY NEEDS SOMEBODY TO LOVE** [21] [–]

Aug 71. (lp/c) *(SLK/KSKC 5101)* **GIMME SHELTER** [19] [–]

Jan 72. (d-lp/c) *<606-7>* **HOT ROCKS 1964-1971** [–] [4]
(UK cd-iss. 1983 on 'Decca'; 800 083-2) (re-iss. Jul90 cd/c/lp; 820 140-2/-4/-1) <US cd-iss. 1989 on 'Abko'> (re-iss. Jun95 on 'London' cd/c/d-lp; 844475-2/-4/-1)

Feb 72. (lp/c) *(SKL/KSKC 5098)* **MILESTONES** [14] [–]

Nov 72. (lp/c) *(SKL/KSKC 5149)* **ROCK'N'ROLLING STONES** [41] [–]

Dec 72. (lp/c) *<626-7>* **MORE HOT ROCKS (BIG HITS & FAZED COOKIES)** [–] [9]
(UK cd-iss. Aug88; 820 515-2) (re-iss. cd Nov90;) (re-iss. Jun95 on 'London' cd/c; 844478-2/-4)

Apr 73. (7") *(F 13404)* **YOU CAN'T ALWAYS GET WHAT YOU WANT. / SAD DAY** [ ] [42]

May 75. (7") *(F 13584)* **I DON'T KNOW WHY. / TRY A LITTLE HARDER** [ ] [42]

Jun 75. (lp/c) *(SKL/KSKC 5212)* **METAMORPHISIS** (early demos) [45] [8]

Sep 75. (7") *(F 13597)* **OUT OF TIME. / JIVING SISTER FANNY** [45] [81]

Nov 75. (d-lp)(d-c) *(ROST 1-2)(K2R 26)* **ROLLED GOLD – (THE VERY BEST OF THE ROLLING STONES)** [7] [–]
– Come on / I wanna be your man / Not fade away / Carol / It's all over now / Little red rooster / Time is on my side / The last time / (I can't get no) Satisfaction / Get off my cloud / 19th nervous breakdown / As tears go by / Under my thumb / Lady Jane / Out of time / Paint it black / Have you seen your mother baby, standing in the shadows? / Let's spend the

night together / Ruby Tuesday / Yesterday's papers / We love you / She's a rainbow / Jumpin' Jack Flash / Honky tonk women / Sympathy for the Devil / Street fighting man / Midnight rambler / Gimme shelter.

Oct 77. (lp/c) *Arcade; (ADE P/C 32)* **GET STONED** [13] [–]

Oct 82. (d-lp/d-c) *K-Tel; (NE2/CE2 201)* **THE STORY OF THE STONES** [24] [–]

Sep 89. (d-lp/d-c/d-cd) *(820 900-1/-4/-2) / Abkco; <1218>* **SINGLES COLLECTION: THE LONDON YEARS** [ ] [91]
(re-iss. Jun95)

Jun 90. (7") *(LON/+CS 264)* **PAINT IT BLACK. / HONKY TONK WOMAN** [61] [–]
(12"+=/remix-12"+=) *(LONX/+R 264)* – Sympathy for the Devil.

Jul 90. (3xcd-box) *Columbia; (466918-2)* **COLLECTOR'S EDITION** [ ] [ ]

– solo releases –

MICK JAGGER

(see also other single late 1970)

C.B.S. / Columbia

Feb 85. (7") *(A 4722) <04743>* **JUST ANOTHER NIGHT. / TURN THE GIRL LOOSE** [32] [12]
('A'extended-12"+=) *(TA 4722)* – ('A'dub version).

Mar 85. (lp/c/cd) *(CBS/40/CD 86310)* **SHE'S THE BOSS** [6] [13]
– Lonely at the top / Half a loaf / Hard woman / Lucky in love / Secrets / Just another night / She's the boss / Running out of luck / Turn the girl loose. *(re-iss. cd Aug95 on 'East West'; 7567 82553-2)*

Apr 85. (7"/12") *(A/TA 6213) <04893>* **LUCKY IN LOVE. / RUNNING OUT OF LUCK** [ ] [38]

Jul 86. (7") *<34-06211>* **RUTHLESS PEOPLE. / I'M RINGING** [–] [51]
(above from the film 'Ruthless People', issued on 'Epic' records)

Aug 87. (7"/s7") *(651028-7/-0) <07306>* **LET'S WORK. / CATCH US CATCH CAN** [31] [39]
(12"+=) *(651028-6)* – ('A'dance mix).

Sep 87. (lp/c/cd) *(460 123-1/-4/-2)* **PRIMITIVE COOL** [26] [41]
– Throwaway / Let's work / Radio control / Say you will / Primitive cool / Kow Tow / Shoot off your mouth / Party doll / War baby. *(re-iss. cd Aug95 on 'East West'; 7567 82554-2)*

Nov 87. (7"/7"pic-d) *(THROW/+P 1) <07653>* **THROWAWAY. / PEACE FOR THE WICKED** [ ] [67]
('A'remixed; 12"+=/cd-s+=) *(THROW T/C 1)* – ('A'vocal dub mix).

Feb 88. (7") *<07703>* **SAY YOU WILL. / SHOOT OFF YOUR MOUTH** [–] [ ]

Atlantic / Atlantic

Jan 93. (7"/c-s) *(A 7401/+C) <87410>* **SWEET THING. / WANDERING SPIRIT** [24] [84]
(12"+=/cd-s+=) *(A 7410 T/CD)* – ('A'dub mix).

Feb 93. (cd/c/lp) *(<7567 82436-2/-4/-1>)* **WANDERING SPIRIT** [12] [11]
– Wired all night / Sweet thing / Out of focus / Don't tear me up / Put me in the trash / Use me / Evening gown / Mother of a man / think / Wandering spirit / Hang on to me tonight / I've been lonely for so long / Angel in my heart / Handsome Molly. *(re-iss. cd Aug95 on 'East West'; same)*

Apr 93. (7"/c-s) *(A 7368/+C)* **DON'T TEAR ME UP. / EVERYBODY KNOWS ABOUT MY GOOD THING** [ ] [–]
(12"+=/cd-s+=) *(A 7368 T/CD)* – Sweet thing (funky guitar edit).

Jul 93. (7"/c-s) *(A 7332/+C)* **OUT OF FOCUS. / HIPGRASS** [ ] [ ]
(12"+=/cd-s+=) *(A 7332 T/CD)* – ('A'mix).

Virgin / Virgin

Nov 01. (cd/d-lp) *(CDVUS/VUSLP 214) <11288>* **GODDESS IN THE DOORWAY** [44] [39]
– Visions of paradise / Joy / Dancing in the starlight / God gave me everything / Hide away / Don't call me up / Goddess in the doorway / Lucky day / Everybody getting high / Gun / Too far gone / Brand new set of rules.

Mar 02. (7") *(VUSP 240)* **VISIONS OF PARADISE. / GOD GAVE ME EVERYTHING (Dan The Automator remix)** [43] [ ]
(cd-s) *(VUSCD 240)* – ('A'side) / If things could be different / Blue.

KEITH RICHARDS

(covers 'A'side= Chuck Berry / 'B'= Jimmy Cliff)

Rolling Stones / Rolling S.

Nov 78. (7") *(RSR 102) <19311>* **RUN RUDOLPH RUN. / THE HARDER THEY COME** [ ] [ ]

Virgin / Virgin

Oct 88. (lp/c/cd) *(V/TCV/CDV 2554) <90973>* **TALK IS CHEAP** [37] [24]
– Talk is cheap / Take it so hard / Struggle / I could have stood you up / Make no mistake / You don't move me / It means a lot / Whip it up / How I wish / Rock awhile / Locked away. *(re-iss. Sep90 on 'Virgin' lp/c/cd; OVED/+C/CD 338)*

Oct 88. (7") *(VS 1125) <99297>* **TAKE IT SO HARD. / I COULD HAVE STOOD YOU UP** [ ] [ ]
(12"+=/3"cd-s+=) *(VST/VSCD 1125)* – It means a lot.

Apr 89. (7") *(VS 1179) <99240>* **MAKE NO MISTAKE. / IT MEANS A LOT** [ ] [ ]
(12"+=/cd-s+=) *(VST/VSCD 1179)* – ('A'extended).

Virgin / Virgin

Nov 91. (cd/c/lp) *(CDVUS/VUSMC/VUSLP 45) <91808>* **KEITH RICHARDS AND THE X-PENSIVE WINOS LIVE AT THE HOLLYWOOD, PALLADIUM, DECEMBER 15, 1988 (live)** [ ] Dec91 [ ]
– Take it so hard / How I wish / I could have stood you up / Too rude / Make no mistake / Time is on my side / Big enough / Whip it up / Locked away / Struggle / Happy / Connection / Rockawhile.

Oct 92. (cd/c/lp) *(CDVUS/VUSMC/VUSLP 59) <86499>* **MAIN OFFENDER** [45] [99]
– 999 / Wicked as it seems / Eileen / Words of wonder / Yap yap / Bodytalks / Hate it when you leave / Runnin' too deep / Will but you don't / Demon.

— RICHARDS writes with JORDAN and some with WACHTEL.

Henry ROLLINS

Born: HENRY GARFIELD, 13 Feb'61, Washington DC, USA. After cutting his teeth in the 'straight edge' (militantly clean living) hardcore punk scene of the late 70's, ROLLINS made his name with the seminal BLACK FLAG. Recruited in time for their 'DAMAGED' (1981) opus, ROLLINS added a manic intensity to the brilliant 'SIX PACK' as well as new numbers like 'LIFE OF PAIN' and the title track. So extreme was the record that MCA's top man, Al Bergamo, tried to block the record's release even though thousands of copies had already been pressed. ROLLINS honed his writing and performing talents over a further series of albums, eventually going solo after the release of 'LOOSE NUT' (1985). 'HOT ANIMAL MACHINE' (1987) was a crudely visceral debut, ROLLINS indicating that, if anything, his solo career was going to be even more uncompromising than his work with BLACK FLAG. Later the same year, the singer released the mini album, 'DRIVE BY SHOOTING' under the pseudonym, HENRIETTA COLLINS AND THE WIFE-BEATING CHILD HATERS, a taste of ROLLINS' particularly tart brand of black humour. By 1988, The ROLLINS BAND line-up had solidified around guitarist CHRIS HASKETT (who'd played on the earlier releases), bassist ANDREW WEISS and drummer SIMON CAIN, releasing the IAN MACKAYE (of hardcore gurus, FUGAZI)-produced 'LIFE TIME' (1988) album later that year. An incendiary opus, the record was The ROLLINS BAND blueprint, setting the agenda for future releases with a lyrical incisiveness and musical ferocity that would be hard to equal. Following a slot on the hugely successful 1991 Lollapalooza tour, The ROLLINS BAND moved from cult status to a major label deal with 'Imago/RCA', releasing 'THE END OF SILENCE' in early '92. Fiercely self-analytic, ROLLINS had always used the stage and the rock medium, to a certain extent, as a kind of therapy, dredging up his childhood demons and tackling them head on. With '. . ..SILENCE', ROLLINS had penned his most introspective work to date, leaving no stone unturned. The fact that he'd had seen his best friend, Joe Cole, gunned down in cold blood had obviously deeply affected the singer and subsequently the material on the album. This intensely personal exorcism is what made ROLLINS' shows so damn compelling; for

ROLLINS, this was far and beyond mere entertainment, for the most part at least, and this was no doubt a major contributing factor in the band's constant live work. As well as a punishing regime of physical exercise, ROLLINS found time to run his own publishing company, 2.13.61 (showcasing work of underground authors as well as ROLLINS' own material, including his acclaimed collection of short stories, 'Black Coffee Blues') and tour his darkly observant, often hilarious and ultimately inspiring spoken word sets. A choice selection of the latter were included on the double-set, 'BOXED LIFE' (1993). The ROLLINS BAND, meanwhile, returned in 1994 with 'WEIGHT', their most commercially successful set to date, and a record which finally made inroads into the UK market, almost making the Top 20. Musically, the album was more accessible than its predecessor, firmly establishing ROLLINS & Co as 'alternative rock' heavyweights. More recently, ROLLINS has expanded his jack-of-all-trades CV with another burst of acting (he'd made his onscreen debut alongside LYDIA LUNCH in 1991's 'Kiss Napoleon Goodbye'), appearing in 'The Chase' and 'Johnny Mnemonic' as well as scoring a cameo in the much heralded De Niro/Pacino face-off, 'Heat'. In mid '96, ROLLINS was the subject of a lawsuit (an 8-figure sum) by Imago for allegedly signing with 'Dreamworks' while under contract, the singer claiming he was let go by the major distributors of the label, 'B.M.G.'. Despite all this, the singer returned to the fray in 1997 with a new album, 'COME IN AND BURN', the record actually appearing on 'Dreamworks'. Come the new millennium, ROLLINS had parted company with his longtime backing musicians and teamed up with MOTHER SUPERIOR, a three-piece unit who had already been making waves in their own right. The resulting 'GET SOME GO AGAIN' (2000) was an impressively back to basics effort from a man who just seems to get angrier with age. With ROLLINS becoming something of an all-round celebrity, it remains to be seen whether he can retain the outsider intensity of old (though it wouldn't be an idea to argue with the man!). The aforementioned album was matched by 2001's much stronger 'NICE'. On this record, ROLLINS stormed his way through the rock-steady beats and wailing heavy guitars, occasionally backed by horns or a female backing singer to great lighthearted effect. • **Covers:** GHOST RIDER (Suicide) / EX-LION TAMER (Wire) / DO IT (Pink Fairies) / LET THERE BE ROCK (Ac-Dc) / FRANKLIN'S TOWER (Grateful Dead).

Album rating (music only): HOT ANIMAL MACHINE (*6) / LIFE TIME (*5) / DO IT! (*6) / HARD VOLUME (*6) / TURNED ON (*6) / THE END OF SILENCE (*8) / WEIGHT (*7) / BLACK COFFEE BLUES mini (*5) / COME IN AND BURN (*5) / GET SOME – GO AGAIN (*5) / NICE (*6)

HENRY ROLLINS – vocals (ex-BLACK FLAG, ex-SOA) / with **CHRIS HASKETT** (b. Leeds, England) – guitar (ex-SURFIN' DAVE) / **BERNIE WANDEL** – bass / **MICK GREEN** – drums

Fundam. Texas Hotel

Jul 87. (lp) *(SAVE 024)* *<TXH 001>* **HOT ANIMAL MACHINE** ☐ ☐
– Black and white / Followed around / Lost and found / There's a man outside / Crazy lover / A man and a woman / Hot animal machine I / Ghost rider / Move right in / Hot animal machine 2 / No one. *(cd-iss. Oct88 +=; SAVE 024CD)* – DRIVE BY SHOOTING ep. *(cd re-iss. Mar94 on 'Intercord'; 986976)*

— In Oct'87, he shared 'LIVE' lp with GORE, released on Dutch 'Eksakt' label; *EKSAKT 034*

Dec 87. (lp; solo) *<TXH 005>* **BIG UGLY MOUTH** (spoken word live early '87) – ☐
(UK cd-iss. Mar93 on '1/4 Stick'; QS 9CD)
(below saw him do a reverse MICHAEL JACKSON and black-up)

Jan 88. (12"ep; as HENRIETTA COLLINS and THE WIFEBEATING CHILDHATERS featuring HENRY ROLLINS) *(HOLY 5)* *<TXH 03>* **DRIVE BY SHOOTING** ☐ Aug87 ☐
– Drive by shooting (watch out for that pig) / Ex-lion tamer / Hey Henriezza / Can you speak this? / I have come to kill you / Men are pigs.

ROLLINS BAND

retained **HASKETT** and recruited **ANDREW WEISS** – bass / **SIMEON CAIN** – drums

Sep 88. (lp/cd) *(SAVE 065/+CD)* *<TXH 008>* **LIFE TIME** ☐ ☐
– Burned beyond recognition / What am I doing here? / 1000 times blind / Lonely / Wreck-age / Gun in mouth blues / You look at you / If you're alive / Turned out. *(cd+=)* – Do it / Move right in / Next time. *(cd re-iss. Mar94 on 'Intercord'; 986977)*

World Service Texas Hotel

Jan 89. (lp) *(SERVM 004)* *<TXH 013CD>* **DO IT! (live/studio)** ☐ Apr89 ☐
– Do it / Move light in / Next time / Joe is everything, everything is Joe / Black and white / Lost and found / Followed around / Wreck age / Lonely / Hot animal machine #1 / You look at you / Gun in mouth blues / Turned out / Thousand times blind / No one. *(re-iss. cd Mar94 on 'Intercord'; 986978)*

Apr 89. (d-lp; solo) *<TXH 015>* **SWEATBOX** (spoken word live) – ☐
(UK d-cd-iss. Mar93 on '1/4 Stick'; QS 10CD)

Nov 89. (m-lp/cd) *(SERV 010 LP/CD)* *<TXH 018>* **HARD VOLUME** ☐ ☐
– Hard / What have I got / I feel like this / Planet Joe / Love song / Turned inside out / Down and away. *(cd+=)* – Joyriding with Frank. *(cd-iss. Mar94 on 'Intercord'; 986979)*

— In 1989, a Swiss cassette found its way into UK; 'READINGS: SWITZERLAND' on 'Action' *ACTIONK 001*

— In 1990, WARTIME was an extra-curricular activity headed by ROLLINS and ANDREW WEISS. An cd-ep surfaced 'FAST FOOD FOR THOUGHT' on 'Chrysalis'; *MPCD 1753*

1990. (lp; solo) *<TXH >* **LIVE AT McCABE'S (spoken word live)** – ☐
– Exhaustion / Misunderstanding / I wish someone had told me / Travel tips. *(UK cd-iss. Mar93 on '1/4 Stick'; QS 11CD)*

not iss. Sub Pop

1990. (7",7"red,7"pink) *<SP 72>* **I KNOW YOU. / EARACHE MY EYE** – ☐

1/4 Stick 1/4 Stick

Nov 90. (lp/cd) *<(QS 02/+CD)>* **TURNED ON (live '89)** ☐ ☐
– Lonely / Do it / What have I got / Tearing / Out there / You didn't need / Hard / Followed around / Mask / Down & away / Turned inside out / The Dietmar song / Black & white / What do you do / Crazy lover.

— in July '91, HENRY ROLLINS & The HARD-ONS released their collaboration 'LET THERE BE ROCK' issued on 'Vinyl Solution' (VS 30/+CD)

Imago-RCA Imago-RCA

Feb 92. (12") *(PT 49113)* **LOW SELF OPINION. / LIE, LIE, LIE** ☐ ☐

Feb 92. (cd/c/d-lp) *(PD/PK/PL 90641)* *<21006>* **THE END OF SILENCE** ☐ ☐
– Low self opinion / The end of silence / Grip / Tearing / You didn't need / Almost real / Obscene / What do you do? / Blues jam / Another life / Just like you.

Aug 92. (7") *(72787 87250-18-7)* **TEARING. / EARACHE IN MY EYE (live)** 54 ☐
(12"+=/cd-s+=) *(72787 87250-18-1/-2)* – (There'll be no) Next time / Ghost rider.

Jan 93. (2xcd-box/2xc-box) *(72787 21009-2/-4)* **THE BOXED LIFE** (compilation of alter-ego workings) ☐ ☐

— In early '94, he acted in the film 'The Chase', and was about to be seen in 'Johnny Mnemonic'.

— **MELVIN GIBBS** – bass repl. HASKINS who left in 1993.

Apr 94. (cd/c/clear d-lp) *<(72787 21034-2/-4/-1)>* **WEIGHT** 22 33
– Disconnect / Fool / Icon / Civilized / Divine object of hatred / Liar / Step back / Wrong man / Volume 4 / Tired / Alien blueprint / Shine.

Aug 94. (7"/c-s) *(74321 213057-7/-4)* **LIAR. / DISCONNECT** 27 ☐
(cd-s+=) *(74321 213057-2)* – Right here too much / Nightsweat.

not iss. Thirsty Ear

Apr 97. (m-cd) *<21321>* **BLACK COFFEE BLUES** – ☐
– Black coffee blues / Invisible woman blues / Monster / Exhaustion blues / I know you.

Dreamworks Dreamworks

Apr 97. (cd/c) *<(DRD/DRC 50011)>* **COME IN AND BURN** ☐ Mar97 89
– Shame / Starve / All I want / The end of something / On my way to the cage / Thursday afternoon / During a city / Neon / Spilling over the side / Inhale exhale / Saying goodbye again / Rejection / Disappearing act.

Jul 97. (7") *(DRMS 22271)* **THE END OF SOMETHING. / ALSO RAN** – –
(cd-s) *(DRMCD 22271)* – ('A'side) / ('A'-We Change remix) / Threshold.
(cd-s) *(DRMXD 22271)* – ('A'side) / ('A'-Grooverider remix) / Stray.

—— **ROLLINS** introduced new band MOTHER SUPERIOR:- **JIM WILSON** – guitar / **MARCUS BLAKE** – bass / **JASON MacKENROTH** – drums, saxophone

Feb 00. (cd) <*(4 50216-2)*> **GET SOME – GO AGAIN**
– Illumination / Get some go again / Monster / Love's so heavy / Thinking cap / Action / I go day glo / Are you ready? / On the day / You let yourself down / Brother interior / Hotter and hotter / Illuminator. *(d-cd+=; 450971-2)* – Side by side / 100 miles / Fuck yo mama / What have I got / Get some go again (video) / Action (live) / E.P.K.

S.P.V. — Sanctuary

Aug 01. (cd/d-lp) *(SPV 0857250-2/-1)* <*84512*> **NICE**
– One shot / Up for it / Gone inside the zero / Hello / What's the matter man / Your number is one / Stop look and listen / I want so much more / Hangin' around / Going out strange / We walk alone / Let that devil out.

– compilations, etc. –

Mar 93. (d-cd) *1/4 Stick; (QS 12CD)* **HUMAN BUTT** (book readings) — 1991
Mar 93. (cd-box) *1/4 Stick; (QS 13CD)* **DEEP THROAT**
– (all 4 spoken word releases).
Nov 94. (d-cd) *Imago;* <*(74321 24238-2)*> **GET IN THE VAN** (book readings; life on the road with BLACK FLAG)
Nov 94. (book) *Imago;* **HENRY: PORTRAIT OF A SINGER SINGER** (spoken word)
Jul 96. (cd) *Thirsty Ear;* <*2.13.61*> **EVERYTHING** (spoken word) –
Oct 98. (cd) *Dreamworks;* <*(DRD 50054)*> **THINK TANK** (spoken word)

Mick RONSON

Born: 1946, Hull, England. In 1964, he formed his first band, The RATS, although after a couple of singles over the next few years, they laid low. RONSON re-surfaced the band for a one-off psychedelic track, 'THE RISE AND FALL OF BERNIE GRIPPLESTONE', which, recorded in late '67, only made it to the demo stage. Guitarist RONSON subsequently went into session work, notably for MICHAEL CHAPMAN on his 'Fully Qualified Survivor' album, before his initial association with BOWIE under the group name, HYPE. Around the same time (1971), RONNO made a prog-rock attempt, although the single '4TH HOUR OF MY SLEEP', failed miserably. Alongside drummer WOODY WOODMANSEY on BOWIE's 'Man Who Sold The World', they soon became known as The SPIDERS FROM MARS, named after BOWIE's 1972 album, 'Ziggy Stardust & The Spiders From Mars'. RONSON left for a solo career in 1974 after featuring on late 1973 album, 'Bowie Pin-Ups'. Retained by MainMan productions & 'RCA' records, he issued a solo debut, 'SLAUGHTER ON 10th AVENUE', which featured a version of ELVIS' 'LOVE ME TENDER' and RONSON's most famous track, 'ONLY AFTER DARK'. In between this and his 1975 follow-up, 'PLAY DON'T WORRY', he had a short spell with MOTT THE HOOPLE, who were shortly to disband soon after. Their frontman, IAN HUNTER, who MICK had also toured alongside, formed a partnership with him as The HUNTER-RONSON BAND. For the next decade and a half, RONSON was his guitarist, a dual album, 'YUI ORTA', finally being issued in 1990. MICK's work during this period had included stints with BOB DYLAN on his ROLLING THUNDER REVUE of '75-'76, where he met ROGER McGUINN of The BYRDS. MICK subsequently produced his 'Cardiff Rose' album. He also went on to work in the late 70's for JOHN COUGAR (Chestnut Street Incident), RICH KIDS (Ghosts Of Princes In Towers) and DAVID JOHANSEN (In Style). After a lean spell in the 80's, RONSON returned in 1992, producing MORRISSEY's 'Your Arsenal', and guesting alongside old mates BOWIE and HUNTER at FREDDIE MERCURY's Wembley Tribute, that April. It was rumoured at the time, that MICK was suffering from cancer and he was to die on the 30th of April, 1993, prior to completing most of his long-awaited third album, 'FROM HEAVEN TO HULL', released in 1994. The latter set – from which a portion of the sales revenue was donated to the T.J. Martell cancer foundation – was finished off by RONSON's friends, including DAVID BOWIE (who handled the cover of Bob Dylan's 'LIKE A ROLLING STONE'), CHRISSIE HYNDE, DEF LEPPARD's JOE ELLIOT and of course IAN HUNTER. The former MOTT THE HOOPLE frontman took lead vocals on a closing rendition of 'ALL THE YOUNG DUDES', taken from the aforementioned Wembley date. All in all the record was a fitting tribute to one of rock music's best loved and most missed musicians. • **Songwriters:** Self-penned except; SLAUGHTER ON 10th AVENUE (Rodgers) / SEVEN DAYS + I'M THE ONE (... Peacock) / WOMAN (... Taylor) / THE GIRL CAN'T HELP IT (Little Richard) / WHITE LIGHT WHITE HEAT (Velvet Underground) / GROWING UP AND I'M FINE + MOONAGE DAYDREAM + LIFE ON MARS? (Bowie). The RATS covered; PARCHMAN FARM (Mose Allison) / EVERY DAY I HAVE THE BLUES (Arthur Alexander) / SPOONFUL (Willie Dixon) / I'VE GOTTA SEE MY BABY EVERYDAY (Chris Andrews). • **Trivia:** His sister, MARGARET RONSON, provided backing vocals for his debut album. MICK's 80's production work was for the obscure outfits, The PAYOLAS and LOS ILLEGALS.

Album rating: SLAUGHTER ON 10th AVENUE (*7) / PLAY DON'T WORRY (*5) / posthumous: HEAVEN AND HULL (*4) / ONLY AFTER DARK (*6) / MAIN MAN (*6) / SHOWTIME (*5) / INDIAN SUMMER soundtrack (*5) / JUST LIKE THIS (*6)

RATS

MICK RONSON – guitar / + unknown

Oriole — not iss.

Nov 64. (7") *(CB 1967)* **PARCHMAN FARM. / EVERY DAY I HAVE THE BLUES** — –

—— **WOODY WOODMANSEY** – drums repl. ? / (entire new members with RONSON) / included JOHN CAMBRIDGE

Columbia — not iss.

Mar 65. (7") *(DB 7483)* **SPOONFUL. / I'VE GOT MY EYES ON YOU BABY** — –
Jun 65. (7") *(DB 7607)* **I GOTTA SEE MY BABY EVERYDAY. / HEADIN' BACK (TO NEW ORLEANS)** — –

—— Disbanded. (see biography for BOWIE details, etc.)

RONNO

MICK RONSON – guitar / **BENNY MARSHALL** / etc.

Vertigo — Vertigo

Jul 71. (7") *(6059 029)* <*100*> **4th HOUR OF MY SLEEP. / POWERS OF DARKNESS**

—— He then played on BOWIE albums 'ZIGGY STARDUST', 'ALADDIN SANE' & 'PIN-UPS'.

MICK RONSON

solo with **AYNSLEY DUNBAR** – drums / **TREVOR BOLDER** – bass / **MIKE GARSON** – piano

R.C.A. — R.C.A.

Jan 74. (7") *(APBO 212)* <*0212*> **LOVE ME TENDER. / ONLY AFTER DARK**
Mar 74. (lp/c) (<*APL/APK 1-0353*>) **SLAUGHTER ON 10th AVENUE** — 9
– Love me tender / Growing up and I'm fine / Only after dark / Music is

lethal / I'm the one / Medley: Pleasure man – Hey ma get papa / Slaughter on 10th Avenue. *(cd-iss. Sep97 on 'Snapper'+=; SMMCD 503)* – Leave my heart alone / Love me tender / Slaughter on 10th Avenue (live).

Apr 74. (7") *(APBO 5022)* <0291> **SLAUGHTER ON 10th AVENUE. / LEAVE MY HEART ALONE**

— From Sep-Dec'74, RONSON joined MOTT THE HOOPLE, and featured on only one single 'SATURDAY GIGS'. He continued on already recorded 2nd solo album.

Feb 75. (7") *(RCA 2482)* <10237> **BILLY PORTER. / HAZY DAYS**

Feb 75. (lp/c) *(<APL/APK 1-0681>)* **PLAY DON'T WORRY** 29
– Billy Porter / Angel No.9 / This is for you / White light – white heat / Play don't worry / Hazy days / The girl can't help it / Empty bed (lo me ne andrail) / Woman. *(cd-iss. Sep97 on 'Snapper'+=; SMMCD 504)* – Seven days / Stone love / I'd rather be me / Life on Mars / Pain in the city / Dogs (French girl) / 28 days jam / Woman (acoustic).

— MICK went off to play for BOB DYLAN, IAN HUNTER, and produce many (see biography). In 1990 he was on record again with IAN HUNTER on album 'YUI ORTA'. (see Ian HUNTER)

— Sadly, MICK was to die of cancer on the 30th of April, 1993

Epic Epic

Apr 94. (c-s) *(660358-4)* **DON'T LOOK DOWN. / SLAUGHTER ON 10th AVENUE** 55 -
(12"+=/cd-s+=) *(660358-6/-2)* – Billy Porter / Love me tender.
(above with JOE ELLIOTT of DEF LEPPARD on vocals).

May 94. (cd/c/lp) *(474742-2/-4/-1)* <53796> **HEAVEN AND HULL**
– Don't look down / Like a rolling stone / When the world falls down / Trouble with me / Life's a river / You and me / Colour me / Takes a long line / Midnight love / All the young dudes.

– compilations, etc. –

May 82. (7") *RCA Gold; (GOLD 546)* **BILLY PORTER. / SLAUGHTER ON 10th AVENUE** -

Sep 94. (d-cd) *Trident; (GY 003) / Griffin'* <344> **ONLY AFTER DARK** 1995

Mar 98. (cd) *Strange Fruit; (SFRSCD 057)* **BBC LIVE IN CONCERT (with the HUNTER-RONSON GROUP)** -

Apr 98. (d-cd) *Snapper; (SMDCD 119) / Recall;* <119> **MAIN MAN**
– Billy Porter / Angel No.9 / Woman / Seven days / Stone love / Pain in the city / Dogs / 28 days jam / Slaughter on 10th Avenue / Only after dark / Please man'hey ma get papa / Music is lethal / Empty (io me ne Andrei) / White light – white heat / Hazy days / Woman (alt.) / The girl can't help it / Life on Mars? / I'm the one / Pain in the city / Play don't worry / Love me tender (live).

Jun 98. (cd; by the RATS) *Angel Air; (SJPCD 022)* **THE RISE AND FALL OF BERNIE GRIPPLESTONE AND THE RAT FROM HULL** -

Oct 00. (cd) *Burning Airlines; (<PILOT 057>)* **INDIAN SUMMER** (soundtrack) Jan01
– Indian summer / Tinker Street / Satellite 1 / (interlude) Get on with it / Ballad of Jack Daniels / Blue velvet skirt / Midnight love / Satellite 1 / Blue velvet skirt (reprise) / Plane to England / China / I'd give anything to see you (closing theme).

Feb 01. (cd) *Burning Airlines; (<PILOT 016>)* **SHOWTIME (live)** May00
– Crazy love / Hey grandma / Takin' a train / Junkie / I'd give anything to see you / Hard life / Just like this / Sweet dreamer / F.B.I. / White light – white heat / Darling let's have another baby / Slaughter on 10th Avenue.

Feb 01. (cd) *Burning Airlines; (<PILOT 050>)* **JUST LIKE THIS** (rec.1976-77) Apr99
– Just like this / I'd give anything / Takin' a train / Hard life / (I'm just a) Junkie for your love / Crazy love / Hey grandma / Is that any way / I've got no secrets / Hard headed woman / Roll like the river / Angel No.9.

May 03. (cd) *Alchemy; (STRTR 167)* **HARD LIFE** -

Linda RONSTADT

Born: 15 Jul'46, Tucson, Arizona, USA. Raised by Mexican/German parents, the young RONSTADT grew up singing a combination of country/rock'n'roll covers and Mexican folk songs. After hearing The BYRDS, she was inspired to relocate to L.A. in the mid-60's where she hooked up with guitarist, BOB KIMMEL, in folk-rock band, The STONE PONEYS. Through manager, Herb Cohen, the group eventually secured a deal with 'Capitol', releasing three flop albums, though they're probably best remembered for their one-off, MIKE NESMITH-penned hit,'DIFFERENT DRUM', the single making the US Top 20 in late '67. The group's final effort was completed by RONSTADT after KIMMEL and third member, KENNY EDWARDS both bailed out. Thrown into the solo deep end, RONSTADT subsequently struggled through a turbulent, commercially barren period in the early 70's, struggling to find a niche. Setting up home in L.A.'s Topanga Canyon alongside the countrified, singer/songwriter elite (NEIL YOUNG, JONI MITCHELL etc.), RONSTADT went through a series of producers, managers and backing musicians, hiring the (future) EAGLES for her 1972 eponymous solo debut. Along with those aforementioned purveyors of chart-smooth country-rock, RONSTADT signed to 'Asylum' in 1973, a new label set up by biz maestro, David Geffen. Her debut for the label, 'DON'T CRY NOW', was largely produced by fellow Topangan-ite and EAGLES collaborator, J.D. SOUTHER, with whom RONSTADT subsequently became romantically entwined. With the album failing to be completed on schedule, Englishman PETER ASHER (previously of 60's pop duo, PETER & GORDON) was brought in to finish the project. Eventually released in late '73, the album kickstarted RONSTADT's career, ASHER subsequently becoming her manager and guiding her towards superstardom. In ASHER, she'd finally found a mentor who could package her crystal pure voice and dusky looks for a mainstream market, RONDSTADT finally covering material that was sympathetic to her vocal style. A version of Betty Everett's 'YOU'RE NO GOOD' became a Christmas US No.1 the following year, the 'HEART LIKE A WHEEL' (1975) album following suit and finally establishing RONSTADT among the rock hierarchy. The album was a considered mix of rootsy oldies and similarly accented current material (affecting readings of James Taylor's 'YOU CAN CLOSE YOUR EYES' and Little Feat's 'WILLIN'), a winning combination which would serve her well over the latter 70's period. On subsequent albums, however, she increasingly moved away from the country/folk bias of her earlier work, incorporating motown soul/R&B into 'PRISONER IN DISGUISE' (1976) and covering a trio of songs by the (then) unknown KARLA BONOFF on 'HASTEN DOWN THE WIND'. With 'SIMPLE DREAMS' (1977), RONSTADT was back at No.1, covering a couple of songs by cult L.A. gunslinger, WARREN ZEVON, the sardonic 'POOR, POOR, PITIFUL ME' and the raw beauty of 'CARMELITA'. With the punk wars raging in an attempt to break the stranglehold of a perceived decadent rock aristocracy (the back slapping L.A. mob were particularly reviled), RONSTADT bravely attempted a cover of Elvis Costello's 'ALISON' on 1978's 'LIVING IN THE USA'. While COSTELLO was reportedly none too impressed with the result, RONSTADT made a rather ill-advised attempt to get hip with the new breed on 'MAD LOVE' (1980), covering a further three COSTELLO songs on a set which met with critical derision. The fact that RONSTADT's backing band were called The CRETONES (!) says it all really. 'GET CLOSER' received an even rougher ride from the press and it was clear RONSTADT needed a speedy rethink as to where her career was going. In a shrewd move, the singer made a stylistic U-turn, subsequently recording three albums of orchestrated, easy listening standards. Predictably, 'WHAT'S NEW' (1983), 'LUSH LIFE' (1984) and 'FOR SENTIMENTAL REASONS' (1986) were all big sellers, resurrecting her ailing career. Equally successful was the 'TRIO' (1987) album, a country set recorded with friends EMMYLOU HARRIS and DOLLY PARTON, RONSTADT scoring a Transatlantic Top 10 hit later that summer via a syrupy duet with JAMES INGRAM, 'SOMEWHERE OUT THERE'. RONSTADT made another stylistic volte-face in the late 80's/early 90's, going back to her roots and recording a couple of albums of Mexican/Spanish folk, 'CANCIONES DE MI PADRE (MY FATHER'S SONG) (1987) and 'MAS CANCIONES' (1991). These releases were interspersed with a more conventional pop set, 'CRY LIKE A RAINSTORM – HOWL LIKE THE WIND' (1989), the drippy duet with AARON NEVILLE, 'DON'T KNOW MUCH' giving RONSTADT her biggest UK hit to date. In the 90's, RONSTADT once again found herself in the commercial fringes, 'WINTER LIGHT' (1993) and 'FEELS LIKE HOME' (1995) barely making the (US) Top 100. Nevertheless, she remains a consistent live draw and a widely respected vocalist with the ability to effortlessly slide between genres. • **Songwriters:** Owes much to other artists' material; I'LL BE YOU BABY TONIGHT (Bob Dylan) / SILVER THREADS AND GOLDEN NEEDLES (Springfields) / DESPERADO (Eagles) / WHEN WILL I BE LOVED (Everly Brothers) / IT DOESN'T MATTER ANYMORE + THAT'LL BE THE DAY + IT'S SO EASY (Buddy Holly) / THE TRACKS OF MY TEARS (Miracles) / HEATWAVE (Martha & The Vandellas) / CRAZY (Patsy Cline) / SOMEONE TO LAY DOWN BESIDE ME (Karla Bonoff) / TUMBLING DICE (Rolling Stones) / BLUE BAYOU (Roy Orbison) / BACK IN THE USA (Chuck Berry) / LOVE ME TENDER (Elvis Presley) / OOH BABY BABY (Smokey Robinson) / JUST ONE LOOK (Doris Troy) / GIRLS TALK (Elvis Costello) / HURT SO BAD (Little Anthony & The Imperials) / I KNEW YOU WHEN (Billy Joe Royal) / EASY FOR YOU TO SAY + SHATTERED (Jimmy Webb) / DON'T KNOW MUCH (Bill Medley) / WHEN SOMETHING IS WRONG WITH MY BABY (Sam & Dave) / FEELS LIKE HOME (Randy Newman) / AFTER THE GOLDRUSH (Neil Young) / THE WAITING (Tom Petty) / etc. • **Trivia:** In 1980, she made her acting debut on stage production of 'The Pirates Of Penzance'. In 1983, she starred in the film version.

Album rating: HAND SOWN HOME GROWN (*4) / SILK PURSE (*5) / LINDA RONSTADT (*4) / DON'T CRY NOW (*6) / DIFFERENT DRUM compilation (*6) / HEART LIKE A WHEEL (*8) / PRISONER IN DISGUISE (*6) / HASTEN DOWN THE WIND (*6) / GREATEST HITS compilation (*7) / A RETROSPECTIVE exploitation (*6) / SIMPLE DREAMS (*7) / LIVING IN THE USA (*5) / MAD LOVE (*5) / GREATEST HITS, VOLUME 2 compilation (*6) / GET CLOSER (*4) / WHAT'S NEW (*6) / LUSH LIFE (*5) / FOR SENTIMENTAL REASONS (*5) / TRIO with Dolly Parton & Emmylou Harris (*7) / CANCIONES DE MI PADRE (*5) / CRY LIKE A RAINSTORM – HOWL LIKE THE WIND (*5) / MAS CANCIONES (*5) / FRENESI (*4) / WINTER LIGHT (*6) / FEELS LIKE HOME (*5) / DEDICATED TO THE ONE I LOVE (*5) / WE RAN (*5) / WESTERN WALL – THE TUCSON SESSIONS with Emmylou Harris (*5) / THE VERY BEST OF . . . compilation (*8 Rhino / *7 Elektra)

STONE PONEYS

featured **LINDA** – vocals / plus **BOB KIMMEL** – guitar / + **KENNY EDWARDS** with sessioners / **BILLY MUNDI** – drums

not iss. Sidewalk

1966. (7") <937> **SO FINE. / EVERYBODY HAS THEIR OWN IDEAS** –

Capitol Capitol

Mar 67. (lp) *<ST 2666>* **THE STONE PONEYS** –
– Sweet summer blue and gold / If I were you / Just a little bit of rain / Bicycle song (soon now) / Orion / Wild about my lovin' / Back home / Meredith (on my mind) / Train and the river / All the beautiful things / 2:10 train.

Mar 67. (7") *<5838>* **ALL THE BEAUTIFUL THINGS. / SWEET SUMMER BLUE AND GOLD** –

Jun 67. (7") *<5910>* **EVERGREEN. / ONE FOR ALL** –

— She was now credited/billed with The STONE PONEYS.

Dec 67. (7") *(CL 15523) <2004>* **DIFFERENT DRUM. / I'VE GOT TO KNOW** Nov67 13

Jun 67. (lp) *<ST 2763>* **EVERGREEN – THE STONE PONEYS VOLUME 2** – 100
– December dream / Song about the rain / Autumn afternoon / I've got to know / Evergreen (parts 1 & 2) / Different drum / Driftin' / One for one / Back on the street again / Toys in time / New hard times.

Feb 68. (7") *<2110>* **UP TO MY NECK IN MUDDY WATER. / CARNIVAL BEAR** – 93

Apr 68. (lp) *<ST 2863>* **LINDA RONSTADT, STONE PONEYS & FRIENDS: VOL.3** –
– Golden song / Merry-go-round / Love is a child / By the fruits of their labors / Hobo (morning glory) / Star and a stone / Let's stick together / Up to my neck in muddy water / Aren't you the one / Wings / Some of Shelly's blues / Stoney end.

May 68. (7") *<2195>* **SOME OF SHELLY'S BLUES / HOBO (MORNING GLORY)** –

— When EDWARDS left, the group folded

LINDA RONSTADT

went solo, after she made a US Christmas 45 with the TURTLES.

Capitol Capitol

Apr 69. (lp) *(E-ST 208)* **HAND SOWN – HOME GROWN**
– Baby you've been on my mind / Silver threads and golden needles / Bet no one ever hurt this bad / A number and a name / The only mamma that'll walk the line / Break my mind / I'll be your baby tonight / It's about time / We need a lot more of Jesus (and a lot less of rock and roll) / The dolphins. *(US re-iss. 1975)*

Apr 69. (7") *(CL 15590) <2438>* **THE DOLPHINS. / THE WRONG WAY AROUND**

Oct 69. (7") *(CL 15612)* **BABY YOU'VE BEEN ON MY MIND. / I'LL BE YOUR BABY TONIGHT**

Sep 70. (lp) *(E-ST 407) <407>* **SILK PURSE**
– Lovesick blues / Are my thoughts with you? / Will you love me tomorrow? / Nobody's / Louise / Long long time / Mental revenge / I'm leaving it all up to you / He darkens the Sun / Life is like a mountain railway.

Sep 70. (7") *(CL 15657) <2846>* **LONG LONG TIME. / NOBODY'S** Aug70 25

Dec 70. (7") *<2767>* **WILL YOU LOVE ME TOMORROW?. / LOVESICK BLUES** –

Jan 71. (7") *<3021>* **(SHE'S A) VERY LOVELY WOMAN. / THE LONG WAY AROUND** 70

— She recruited tour/studio band of future EAGLES / **BERNIE LEADON** – guitar / **GLEN FREY** – guitar / **RANDY MEISNER** – bass / **DON HENLEY** – drums

Feb 72. (lp) *(EA-ST 635) <635>* **LINDA RONSTADT**
– Rock me on the water / Crazy arms / I won't be hangin' around / I still miss someone / In my reply / I fall to pieces / Ramblin' round / Birds / Rescue me. *(re-iss. May82 on 'Fame')*

Apr 72. (7") *(CL 15717) <3273>* **ROCK ME ON THE WATER. / CRAZY ARMS** Feb 72 85

Apr 72. (7") *<3210>* **I FALL TO PIECES. / CAN IT BE TRUE?** –
(She now used numerous sessioners)

Asylum Asylum

Nov 73. (lp) *(SYL 9012) <5064>* **DON'T CRY NOW** 45
– I can almost see it / Love has no pride / Silver threads and golden needles / Desperado / Don't cry now / Sail away / Colorado / The fast one / Everybody loves a winner / I believe in you. *(re-iss. Jun76)*

Dec 73. (7") *<11026>* **LOVE HAS NO PRIDE. / I CAN ALMOST SEE IT** – 51

Apr 74. (7") *<11032>* **SILVER THREADS AND GOLDEN NEEDLES. / DON'T CRY FOR NOW** – 67

— With PETE ASHER for the second time producing, she had to make contractual album for 'Capitol'. Augmented by **ANDREW GOLD** – guitar, keyboards, etc.

Dec 74. (7") *<3990>* **YOU'RE NO GOOD. / WHEN WILL I BE LOVED** – 1

Jan 75. (lp) *(E-ST 11358)* <11358> **HEART LIKE A WHEEL** [ ] Nov 74 [1]
– You're no good / It doesn't matter anymore / Faithless love / The dark end of the street / Heart like a wheel / When will I be loved / Willin' / I can't help it (if I'm still in love with you) / Keep me blowing away / You can close your eyes. *(re-iss. Dec86)*

Jan 75. (7") *(CL 15804)* **YOU'RE NO GOOD. / I CAN'T HELP IT** [ ] [–]

Apr 75. (7") *(CL 15820)* <4050> **WHEN WILL I BE LOVED. / IT DOESN'T MATTER ANYMORE** [ ] [2] [47]

Asylum Asylum

Oct 75. (7") *(AYM 550)* <45282> **HEAT WAVE. / LOVE IS A ROSE** [ ] [5] [63]

Nov 75. (7") <45271> **SILVER BLUE. / LOVE IS A ROSE** [–] [ ]

Jan 76. (lp) *(SYL 8761)* <1045> **PRISONER IN DISGUISE** [ ] Sep 75 [4]
– Love is a rose / Hey mister, that's me up on the jukebox / Roll um easy / The tracks of my tears / Prisoner in disguise / Herat wave / Many rivers to cross / The sweetest gift / You tell me that I'm falling down / I will always love you / Silver blue.

Jan 76. (7") <45295> **THE TRACKS OF MY TEARS. / THE SWEETEST GIFT** [–] [25]

Mar 76. (7") *(K 13034)* **THE TRACKS OF MY TEARS. / PRISONER IN DISGUISE** [42] [–]

Aug 76. (lp) *(K 53045)* <1072> **HASTEN DOWN THE WIND** [32] [3]
– Lose again / The tattler / If he's ever near / That'll be the day / Lo siento mi vida / Hasten down the wind / Rivers of Babylon / Give one heart / Try me again / Crazy / Down so low / Someone to lay down beside me. *(cd-iss. Sep89)*

Sep 76. (7") *(K 13053)* <45340> **THAT'LL BE THE DAY. / TRY ME AGAIN** [ ] Aug 76 [11]

Oct 76. (7") *(K 13065)* <45402> **LOSE AGAIN. / LO SIENTO MI VIDA** [ ] May77 [76]

Dec 76. (lp) *(K 53055)* <1092> **GREATEST HITS** (compilation) [37] [6]
– You're no good / Silver threads and golden needles / Desperado / Love is a rose / That'll be the day / Long long time / Different drum / When will I be loved? / Love has no pride / Heat wave / It doesn't matter anymore / Tracks of my tears. *(cd-iss. 1984)*

Feb 77. (7") *(K 13071)* <45361> **SOMEONE TO LAY DOWN BESIDE ME. / CRAZY** [ ] Dec 76 [42]

Sep 77. (7") <45431> **BLUE BAYOU. / OLD PAINT** [–] [3]

Sep 77. (7") *(K 13094)* **POOR POOR PITIFUL ME. / OLD PAINT** [ ] [–]

Oct 77. (7") <45438> **IT'S SO EASY. / LO SIENTO MI VIDA** [–] [5]

Nov 77. (lp) *(K 53065)* <104> **SIMPLE DREAMS** [15] Sep77 [1]
– It's so easy / Carmelita / Simple man, simple dream / Sorrow lives here / I will never marry / Blue bayou / Poor poor pitiful me / Maybe I'm right / Tumbling dice / Old paint. *(cd-iss. Jan87)*

Nov 77. (7") *(K 13100)* **IT'S SO EASY. / SORROW LIVES HERE** [ ] [–]

Jan 78. (7") *(K 13106)* **BLUE BAYOU. / MAYBE I'M RIGHT** [35] [–]

Feb 78. (7") <45462> **POOR POOR PITIFUL ME. / SIMPLE MAN, SIMPLE DREAM** [–] [31]

Mar 78. (7") *(K 13120)* **TUMBLING DICE. / CARMELITA** [ ] [–]

May 78. (7") <45479> **TUMBLING DICE. / I WILL NEVER MARRY** [–] [32]

Sep 78. (7") *(K 13133)* <45519> **BACK IN THE U.S.A. / WHITE RHYTHM & BLUES** [ ] Aug 78 [16]

Oct 78. (lp) *(K 53085)* <155> **LIVING IN THE U.S.A.** [39] Sep 78 [1]
– Back in the U.S.A. / When I grow too old to dream / Just one look / Alison / White rhythm & blues / All that you dream / Ooh baby baby / Mohammed's radio / Blowing away / Love me tender.

Oct 78. (7") <45546> **OOH BABY BABY. / BLOWIN' AWAY** [–] [7]

Nov 78. (7") *(K 13139)* **OOH BABY BABY. / BLACK ROSES** [ ] [–]

Feb 79. (7") <46011> **JUST ONE LOOK. / LOVE ME TENDER** [–] [44]

Apr 79. (7",7"pic-d) *(K 13149)* **ALISON. / ALL THAT YOU DREAM** [66] [–]

Apr 79. (7") <46034> **ALISON. / MOHAMMED'S RADIO** [–] [ ]

Feb 80. (7") *(K 12419)* <46602> **HOW DO I MAKE YOU. / RAMBLER GAMBLER** [ ] Jan 80 [10]

Feb 80. (lp) *(K 52210)* <510> **MAD LOVE** [65] [3]
– Mad love / Party girl / How do I make you / I can't let go / Hurt so bad / Look out for my love / Cost of love / Justine / Girls talk / Talking in the dark.
(above has backing from The CRETONES)

Jun 80. (7") *(K 12444)* <46624> **HURT SO BAD. / JUSTINE** [ ] Apr 80 [8]

Jul 80. (7") <46654> **I CAN'T LET GO. / LOOK OUT FOR MY LOVE** [–] [31]

Nov 80. (lp) *(K 52255)* <516> **GREATEST HITS, VOLUME 2** (compilation) [ ] [26]
– It's so easy / I can't let go / Hurt so bad / Blue bayou / How do I make you / Back in the U.S.A. / Ooh baby baby / Poor poor pitiful me / Tumbling dice / Just one look / Someone to lay down beside me. *(cd-iss. 1983)*

— (next featured **J.D. SOUTHER** – vocals)

Elektra Elektra

Oct 82. (7") *(9969948)* <69948> **GET CLOSER. / SOMETIMES YOU JUST CAN'T WIN** [ ] [29]

Oct 82. (lp) *(E 0185)* <60185> **GET CLOSER** [ ] [31]
– Get closer / The Moon is a harsh mistreess / I knew you when / Easy for you to say / People gonna talk / Talk to me of Mendocino / I think it's gonna work out fine / Mr. Radio / Lies / Tell him / Sometimes you just can't win / My blue tears. *(cd-iss. Jan84)*

Jan 83. (7"/12") *(E 9853/+T)* <69853> **I KNEW YOU WHEN. / TALK TO ME OF MENDOCINO** [ ] [37]

Mar 83. (7"/12") *(E 9877/+T)* **TELL HIM. / MR. RADIO** [ ] [ ]

Apr 83. (7") <69838> **EASY FOR YOU TO SAY. / MR. RADIO** [–] [54]

— next 2 albums credit The NELSON RIDDLE ORCHESTRA.

Nov 83. (lp/c/cd) *(960 260-1/-4/-2)* <60260> **WHAT'S NEW** [31] [3]
– What's new / I've got a crush on you / Guess I'll hang my tears out to dry / Crazy he calls me / Someone to watch over me / I don't stand a ghost of a chance with you / What'll I do / Lover man (oh where can you be) / Good-bye. *(re-iss. Nov 86)*

Mar 84. (7") *(E 9780)* <69780> **WHAT'S NEW. / CRAZY HE CALLS ME** [ ] Nov83 [53]

Dec 84. (lp/c) *(960 387-1/-4)* <60387> **LUSH LIFE** [100] Nov84 [13]
– When I fall in love / Skylark / It never entered my mind / Mean to me / When your lover has gone / I'm a fool to want you / You took advantage of me / Sophisticated lady / Can't we be friends / My old flame / Falling in love again / Lush life. *(cd-iss. Jun87)*

Jan 85. (7") *(E 9667)* **FALLING IN LOVE AGAIN. / SOPHISTICATED LADY** [ ] [ ]

— next credited NELSON RIDDLE & HIS ORCHESTRA (NELSON died mid-80's)

Sep 86. (lp/c/cd) *(960 474-1/-4/-2)* <60474> **FOR SENTIMENTAL REASONS** [ ] [ ]
– When you wish upon a star / Bewitched, bothered & bewildered / You go to my head / But not for me / My funny valentine / I get along without you very well / Am I blue / I love you for sentimental reasons / Straighten up and fly right / Little girl blue / 'Round midnight.

Jun 87. (7"; as LINDA RONSTADY & JAMES INGRAM) *(MCA 1132)* <52973> **SOMEWHERE OUT THERE. / ('A'instrumental)** [8] Dec86 [2]
(12"+=) *(MCAT 1132)* – ('A'version).
(above 45 on 'MCA' and lifted from the film 'An American Tail')

— in Mar'87, she teamed up with DOLLY PARTON & EMMYLOU HARRIS (⇒) on album TRIO. It hits No.6 in the States, and a number of 45's are lifted from it by Warners.

Nov 87. (lp/c/cd) *(960 765-1/-4/-2)* <60765> **CANCIONES DE MI PADRE (MY FATHER'S SONG)** [ ] [42]
– Por un amor / Los Laureles / Hay unos ojos / La cigarra / Tu solo tu / Y andale / Rogaciano el huapanguero / La charreada / Dos arbolitos / Corrido de cananea / La barca de guaymas / La calandria / El sol que tu eres. *(re-iss. cd Nov93)*

Elektra Elektra

Oct 89. (lp/c)(cd) *(EKT 76/+C)(960872-2)* <60872> **CRY LIKE A RAINSTORM – HOWL LIKE THE WIND** [43] [7]
– Still within the sound of my voice / Cry like a rainstorm / All my life / I need you / Don't know much / Adios / Trouble again / I keep it hid / So right, so wrong / Shattered / When something is wrong with my baby / Goodbye my friend.
(below with AARON NEVILLE)

Nov 89. (7"/c-s) *(EKR 101/+C)* <69261> **DON'T KNOW MUCH. / HURT SO BAD** [2] Sep89 [2]
(12"+=/cd-s+=) *(EKR 101 T/CD)* – I can't let go.

Jan 90. (7") *(EKR 105)* <64987> **ALL MY LIFE. / SHATTERED** [ ] [11]
(12"+=/cd-s+=) *(EKR 105 T/CD)* – Love has no pride.

May 90. (7"; LINDA RONSTADT featuring AARON NEVILLE) <64968> **WHEN SOMETHING IS WRONG WITH MY BABY. / TRY ME AGAIN** [–] [78]

— Oct 91, she again duetted with AARON NEVILLE on his 'A&M' 45, 'CLOSE YOUR EYES'

Nov 91. (cd/c) *(7559 61239-2/-4)* <61239> **MAS CANCIONES** [ ] [88]
– Tata dios / El Toro Relajo / Mi ranchito / La Mariquita / Gritenme

Piedras del Campo / Siempre hace Frio / El Curcifijo de Piedra / Palomita de ojos negros / Pena de los amores / El Camino / El Gustito / El Sueno.

Aug 92. (cd/c) <81383> **FRENESI** [–] [ ]
– Frenesi / Mentira Salome / Alma adentro / Entre abismos / Cuando me querias tu / Piel canela / Verdad amarga / Despojos / En mi soledad / Piensa en mi / Quireme mucho / Perfidia / Te quiero dijiste.

Nov 93. (7"/c-s) *(EKR 177/+C)* **WINTER LIGHT. / DON'T KNOW MUCH** [ ] [ ]
(cd-s+=) *(EKR 177CD)* – Blue bayou / Alison.

Dec 93. (cd/c) <(7559 61545-2/-4)> **WINTER LIGHT** [ ] [92]
– Heartbeats accelerating / Do what you gotta do / Anyone who had a heart / Don't talk (put your head on my shoulder) / Oh no, not my baby / It's too soon to know / I just don't know what to do with myself / A river for him / Adonde voy / You cant treat the wrong man right / Winter light.

Feb 94. (c-s) *(EKR 179C)* **HEARTBEATS ACCELERATING / THE SECRET GARDEN** [ ] [ ]
(cd-s) *(EKR 179CD)* – ('A'side) / Don't know much / Desperado / A river for him.

Mar 95. (cd/c) <(7559 61703-2/-4)> **FEELS LIKE HOME** [ ] [75]
– The waiting / Walk on / High Sierra / After the gold rush / The blue train / Feels like home / Teardrops will fall / Morning blues / Women 'cross the river / Lover's return.

Mar 95. (c-s) **THE WAITING / DESPERADO** [ ] [ ]
(cd-s+=) – Poor poor pitiful me / Cry like a rainstorm.

Jul 96. (cd/c) <(7599 61916-2/-4)> **DEDICATED TO THE ONE I LOVE** [ ] [78]
– Dedicated to the one I love / Be my baby / In my room / Devoted to you / Baby, I love you / Angel baby / We will rock you / Winter light / Brahms' lullaby / Good night.

Jun 98. (cd) <7599 62206-2> **WE RAN** [–] [ ]
– When we ran / If I should fall behind / Give me a reason / Ruler of my heart / Just like Tom Thumb's blues / Cry 'til my tears run dry / I go to pieces / Heartbreak kid / Damage / Icy blue heart / Dreams of San Joaquin.

Sep 99. (cd/c; as LINDA RONSTADT & EMMYLOU HARRIS) <(7559 62408-2/-4)> **WESTERN WALL – THE TUCSON SESSIONS** [ ] [73]
– Loving the highwayman / Raise the dead / For a dancer / Western wall / 1917 / He was mine / Sweet spot / Sisters of mercy / Fallin' down / Valerie / This is to mother you / All I left behind / Across the border.

Oct 00. (cd) <62572> **A MERRY LITTLE CHRISTMAS** (festive) [–] [ ]

– compilations, etc. –

(STONE PONEYS =*)

1972. (lp/c) *Pickwick; (SPC 3298)* **STONEY END** * [ ] [–]

Jun 75. (lp) *Capitol;* <ST 11383> **THE STONE PONEYS FEATURING LINDA RONSTADT** * [–] [ ]

Apr 77. (lp/c) *Capitol;* <11269> **DIFFERENT DRUM** * [–] Feb74 [92]

Jul 77. (7") *Capitol; (CL 15933)* **DIFFERENT DRUM. / IT DOESN'T MATTER ANYMORE** [ ] [–]

Jul 77. (d-lp) *Capitol; (CAPSP 102)* <11629> **A RETROSPECTIVE** [ ] May77 [ ]

Sep 76. (7") *Asylum; (K 13049)* **DESPERADO. / SILVER THREADS AND GOLDEN NEEDLES** [ ] [–]

Nov 86. (cd-box) *Asylum;* <(60489-2)> **'ROUND MIDNIGHT WITH NELSON RIDDLE AND HIS ORCHESTRA** [ ] [ ]
– (WHAT'S NEW / LUSH LIFE / FOR SENTIMENTAL REASONS)

Dec 99. (4xcd-box) *Elektra;* <(7559 62472-2)> **THE LINDA RONSTADT BOX SET** [ ] [ ]

Sep 02. (cd) *Rhino;* <RCD 76109> **THE VERY BEST OF LINDA RONSTADT** [–] [ ]

Sep 03. (cd) *Elektra; (8122 73605-2)* **THE VERY BEST OF LINDA RONSTADT** [46] [–]
– (tracks different to same title above)

ROOTS

Formed: Philadelphia, Pennsylvania, USA … 1989 originally as the SQUARE ROOTS by rappers TARIQ TROTTER (aka BLACK THOUGHT) and AHMIR-KHALIB THOMPSON (aka ?UESTLOVE), who subsequently recruited a live band around LEON HUBBARD (aka HUB) and MALIK B. Taking the form back to basics, these dedicated hip-hop purists proceeded to build up a sizeable grassroots following through constant live work. In 1993, The ROOTS unearthed their debut set, 'ORGANIX', a record that boasted the lengthy, 12-minute+ 'THE SESSION (LONGEST POSSE CUT IN HISTORY)'. Word soon spread and the group were subsequently signed to 'Geffen', releasing their follow-up full length album, the well-received 'DO YOU WANT MORE', in late '94. Feted by such rap luminaries as CHUCK D and GENIUS/GZA, The ROOTS were finally afforded their due commercial success when their third release, 'ILLADELPH HALFLIFE' (1996) almost made the US Top 20. They achieved further Stateside success in spring of the following year when the 'WHAT THEY DO' single was a Top 40 hit. Long overdue critical and commercial (US Top 5) success finally arrived with 'THINGS FALL APART' (1999), a rich, mellow, unrelentingly creative hip hop odyssey featuring the likes of MOS DEF and COMMON. While equally inventive, 'PHRENOLOGY' (2002) was much more freewheeling in its approach, cutting and weaving through a smorgasbord of different contemporary flavours and textures. Hit single, 'BREAK YOU OFF', was a case in point, a MUSIQ collaboration which careened from nu-soul to string-drenched drum'n'bass in a dizzying crescendo. Elsewhere, the hip hop activists casually reeled off everything from frenetic hardcore to blissed out R&B, with hi-calibre guests like TALIB KWELI, JILL SCOTT and NELLY FURTADO keeping things sweet. • **Note:** not to be confused with the similarly named reggae group.

Album rating: ORGANIX (*5) / FROM THE GROUND UP mini (*5) / DO YOU WANT MORE?!!!??! (*6) / ILLADELPH HALFLIFE (*6) / THINGS FALL APART (*8) / ROOTS COME ALIVE (*6) / PHRENOLOGY (*7)

TARIQ TROTTER (aka BLACK THOUGHT) – rapper / **AHMIR-KHALIB THOMPSON** (aka ?UESTLOVE) – drums / **LEON 'HUB' HUBBARD** – bass / **MALIK ABDUL-BASIT** – rapper

not iss. Remedy

1993. (cd) <001> **ORGANIX** [–] [ ]
– The roots is comin' / Pass the popcorn / The anti-circle / Writers block / Good music (prelude) / Good music / Grits / Leonard I-V / I'm out deah / Essaywhuman?!!??! (live) / There's a riot goin' on (part 2) / Popcorn revisited / Peace / Common dust / The session (longest posse cut in history) / Syreeta's having a baby / Carryin' on.

Talkin' Loud Geffen

Jun 94. (m-cd/m-lp) *(518941-2/-1)* **FROM THE GROUND UP** [ ] [ ]
– Worldwide / Do you want more / It's comin' / Distortion to static / Mellow my man / Dat scat. *(cd+=)* – Do you want more (Beat mix).

—— guests included RAHZEL THE GODFATHER OF NOYZE + SCOTT STORCH

Geffen Geffen

Jul 94. (12") <21934> **DISTORTION TO STATIC** [–] [ ]

Nov 94. (cd/c/lp) <(GED/GEC/GEF 24708)> **DO YOU WANT MORE?!!!??!** [ ] Jan95 [ ]
– (intro) – There's somethin' goin' on / Proceed / Distortion to static / Mellow my man / I remain calm / Datskat / Lazy afternoon / ? vs Rahzel / Do you want more?!!!??! / What goes on (part 7) / Essaywhuman / Swept away / You ain't fly / Silent treatment / Lesson (part 1) / Unlocking. *(cd re-iss. Sep97; same)*

Feb 95. (12") <22004> **PROCEED I** [–] [ ]

Apr 95. (12"ep) <22050> **SILENT TREATMENT (mixes; radio / Kelo's clean / Da beatminerz / Black Thought's '87 you and yours / Question's)** [–] [ ]

Jul 95. (c-s; by the ROOTS & ROY AYERS) <5176> **PROCEED II** [–] [ ]

Jul 96. (cd-s) <22216> **CLONES / SECTION** [–] [ ]

Nov 96. (cd) <(GED 24972)> **ILLADELPH HALFLIFE** [ ] Sep96 [21]
– Intro / Respond – React / Section / Panic!!!!!!! / It just don't stop / Episodes / Push up ya lighter / What they do / ? vs. Scratch (the token D.J. cut) / Concerto of the desperado / Clones / Universe at war / No alibi / Dave vs. us / No great pretender / The hypnotic / Ital (the universal side) / One shine / The adventures in Wonderland / (outro).

Apr 97. (12"/cd-s) *(GFST/+D 22240)* **WHAT THEY DO. /** [ ] Dec96 [34]

M.C.A. M.C.A.

Feb 99. (12"/cd-s; The ROOTS featuring ERYKAH BADU) *(MCST/+D 48110)* <55539> **YOU GOT ME. / ADRENALINE** [31] [39]

Mar 99. (cd)(d-lp) *(MCD 11830)<(MCA 2-11948)>* **THINGS FALL APART** [ ] [4]
– Act won (things fall apart) / Table of contents (parts 1 & 2) / The next movement / Step into the realm / The spark / Dynamite / Without a doubt / Ain't sayin' nothin' new / Double trouble / Act too (love of my life) / 100% Dundee / Diedre vs. Dice / Adrenaline / 3rd acts: ? vs. Scratch 2 . . . electric boogaloo / You got me / Don't see us / Return to innocence lost.

Oct 99. (cd-s) *<79288>* **WHAT YOU WANT (mixes; radio / album / instrumental / acappella)** [–] [ ]

Nov 99. (d-cd/d-c) *<112059>* **THE ROOTS COME ALIVE (live)** [–] [50]
– Live at the T-Connection / Next movement / Step into the realm / Proceed / Mellow my man – Jusufckwithis / Love of my life / Ultimate / Don't see us / 100% Dundee / Adrenaline! / Essaywhuman?!!!! / Silent treatment / Notice / You got me / Encore / What you want / We got you / Lesson – part III (it's over now) / All I know / Ya'll know who / For the love of money.

Jan 03. (cd)(d-lp) *(113158-2)<(112996-1)>* **PHRENOLOGY** [ ] Nov02 [28]
– Phrentrow / Rock you / !!!!!! / Sacrifice (with NELLY FURTADO) / Rolling with heat / Waok (ay) rollcall / Thought @ work / The seed (2.0) (with CODY CHESNUTT) / Break you off (with MUSIQ) / Water / Quills / Pussy galore / Complexity (with JILL SCOTT) / Something in the way of things (in town) (with JILL SCOTT).

Mar 03. (12"/cd-s) *(MCST/+D 40316)* **THE SEED (2.0) versions** [33] [–]

Aug 03. (12") *(MCST 40330)* **BREAK YOU OFF / (instrumental) / ROCK YOU** [59] [99]
(cd-s) *(MCSTD 40330)* – (first 2 tracks) / Ultimate (live) / ('A'video).

□ Ricky ROSS (see under ⇒ DEACON BLUE)

□ Francis ROSSI (see under ⇒ STATUS QUO)

□ ROSSINGTON-COLLINS BAND (see under ⇒ LYNYRD SKYNYRD)

David Lee ROTH

Born: 10 Oct'55, Bloomington, Indiana, USA. Suffering from hyperactivity from an early age, he attended a child clinic at the age of eight. His family subsequently moved to Pasadena, where he later joined the group, MAMMOTH, in 1973. Two years later, this outfit had evolved into VAN HALEN, ROTH taking centre stage as their inimitably OTT frontman over a period of ten years. During this time, the group became one of the biggest hard rock/metal acts in the world as well as regularly hitting the pop charts. By the mid-80's, however, ROTH was getting restless, recording a mini solo album, 'CRAZY FROM THE HEAT', as a side project in early '85. Scoring a US Top 3 hit with one of its singles, a memorable cover of The Beach Boys' 'CALIFORNIA GIRLS', 'Diamond' DAVE finally decided to take the plunge and leave VAN HALEN later that summer. Enlisting a cast of crack rock troopers including guitarist STEVE VAI (ex-FRANK ZAPPA) and much touted bassist, BILLY SHEEHAN (ex-TALAS, future MR. BIG), ROTH cut a fully fledged solo album, 'EAT 'EM AND SMILE'. Released in the summer of '86, the album was roundly praised in the rock press, making the US Top 5. Alive with the singer's infectious enthusiasm and natural talent for showmanship, the record was a consistently entertaining listen, the brilliant 'YANKEE ROSE' making the US Top 20. Its follow-up, 'SKYSCRAPER', duly appeared a couple of years later, the sleeve depicting DAVE in the throes of his latest obsession, rock climbing. Fittingly then, there was a lofty, widescreen sound to much of the album, the soaring 'JUST LIKE PARADISE' giving ROTH his first solo UK Top 10 hit. By the release of 'A LITTLE AIN'T ENOUGH' (1991), both VAI and SHEEHAN had departed, the album missing their instrumental spark and underlining ROTH's increasingly formulaic approach. Though the album made the US Top 5, it failed to spawn any hit singles, ROTH subsequently sacking his band and heading for New York. Not that he fared much better in the Big Apple, the singer running into personal problems and failing to kickstart his ailing career with the poor 'YOUR FILTHY LITTLE MOUTH' (1994). Not a man to be held down for long, motormouth DAVE subsequently re-united with VAN HALEN. Or at least, he almost reunited with VAN HALEN, departing unamicably once more after recording just a handful of new songs with them. Instead he gathered together The DLR BAND for the 1998 album of the same name. More gonzoid than any of his 90's releases put together, it went some way toward recapturing that restless spirit he possessed after the first time he left VAN HALEN. After a lengthy absence, the blonde-maned legend returned with 'DIAMOND DAVE' (2003), a thoroughly entertaining covers set which ocassionally fell flat but in its best moments (a big band treatment of the classic 'ICE CREAM MAN', originally covered on VH's debut) proved that ROTH always had as much taste as he had ego. • **Songwriters:** ROTH written (most with STEVE VAI '86-88), except JUST A GIGOLO (Ted Lewis) / I AIN'T GOT NOBODY (Marian Harris) / THAT'S LIFE (hit; Frank Sinatra) / TOBACCO ROAD (Nashville Teens).

Album rating: CRAZY FROM THE HEAT mini (*5) / EAT 'EM AND SMILE (*7) / SKYSCRAPER (*5) / A LITTLE AIN'T ENOUGH (*4) / YOUR FILTHY LITTLE MOUTH (*3) / THE BEST OF . . . compilation (*7) / DLR BAND (*5) / DIAMOND DAVE (*5)

DAVID LEE ROTH – vocals (ex-VAN HALEN) with **DEAN PARKS + EDDIE MARTINEZ + SID McGINNIS** – guitar / **EDGAR WINTER** – keyboards, sax, synthesizers, vocals / **JAMES NEWTON HOWARD** -synthesizers / **WILLIE WEEKS** -bass / **JOHN ROBINSOB** – drums / **SAMMY FIGUEROA** – percussion / **BRIAN MANN** -synthesizers

Warners Warners

Feb 85. (7") *(W 9102) <29102>* **CALIFORNIA GIRLS. / ('A'remix)** [68] Jan85 [3]
(above featured CARL WILSON of The BEACH BOYS on backing vocals)

Feb 85. (m-lp/m-c) *(925222-1/-4) <25222>* **CRAZY FROM THE HEAT** [91] [15]
– Easy street / Just a gigolo – I ain't got nobody / Coconut Grove / California girls.

Apr 85. (7") *(W 9040) <29040>* **JUST A GIGOLO – I AIN'T GOT NOBODY. / ('A'remix)** [ ] Mar85 [12]

— **STEVE VAI** – guitar (ex-FRANK ZAPPA) / **BILLY SHEEHAN** – bass (ex-TALAS) / **BRETT TUGGLE** – keyboards / **GREGG BISSONETTE** (b. 9 Jun'59) – drums

Jul 86. (7"/7"sha-pic-d) *(W 8656/+P) <28656>* **YANKEE ROSE. / SHYBOY** [ ] [16]
(12"+=) *(W 8656T)* – Easy street.

Jul 86. (lp/c)(cd) *(WX 56/+C)(925470-2) <25470>* **EAT 'EM AND SMILE** [28] [4]
– Yankee Rose / Shyboy / I'm easy / Ladies' nite in Buffalo? / Goin' crazy! / Tobacco Road / Elephant gun / Big trouble / Bump and grind / That's life.

Sep 86. (7") *<28584>* **GOIN' CRAZY! / OOCO DEO CALOR (Spanish version)** [–] [66]

Nov 86. (7") *<28511>* **THAT'S LIFE. / BUMP AND GRIND** [–] [85]

— **MATT BISSONETTE** – bass repl. SHEEHAN who joined OZZY OSBOURNE

Jan 88. (lp/c)(cd) *(WX 140/+C)(925671-2) <25671>* **SKYSCRAPER** [11] [6]
– Knucklebones / Just like paradise / The bottom line / Skyscraper / Damn good / Hot dog and a shake / Stand up / Hina / Perfect timing / Two fools a minute. *(cd+=)* – California girls / Just a gigolo – I ain't got nobody. *(re-iss. Jan89 lp/c)(cd; WX 236/+C)(925824-2)*

Feb 88. (7") *(W 8119) <28119>* **JUST LIKE PARADISE. / THE BOTTOM LINE** [27] Jan88 [6]
(12"pic-d+=/3"cd-s+=) *(W 8119 TP/CD)* – Yankee Rose.

Apr 88. (7") *<28108>* **STAND UP. / KNUCKLEBONES** [–] [64]

Jul 88. (7") *<27825>* **DAMN GOOD. / SKYSCRAPER** [–] [ ]

Jul 88. (7"/12") *(W 7753/+T)* **DAMN GOOD. / STAND UP** [72] [–]

Nov 88. (7") *(W 7650)* **CALIFORNIA GIRLS. / JUST A GIGOLO** ☐ [-]
(12"+=) *(W 7650T)* – I ain't got nobody.
(cd-s++=) *(W 7650CD)* – Yankee Rose.

— (Apr'89-Jan'90) **ROCKY RICHETTE** – guitar (ex-STEPPENWOLF, ex-BLACK ROSE) repl. STEVE VAI who went solo and joined WHITESNAKE

— (Oct'90) **TODD JENSEN** – bass (ex-HARLOW) repl. MATT / **DEZZI REXX** + **JOE HOLMES** – guitar repl. JASON BECKER + ROCKY RICHETTE

W.E.A. Warners

Dec 90. (7"/c-s) *(W 0002/+C)* **A LITTLE AIN'T ENOUGH. / BABY'S ON FIRE** [32] ☐
(12"+=/cd-s+=) *(W 0002 T/CD)* – Tell the truth.

Jan 91. (cd)(lp/c) *<(7599 26477-2)>(WX 403/+C)* **A LITTLE AIN'T ENOUGH** [4] [18]
– A little ain't enough / Shoot it / Lady Luck / Hammerhead shark / Tell the truth / Baby's on fire / 40 below / Sensible shoes / Last call / The dogtown shuffle / It's showtime! / Drop in the bucket.

Mar 91. (7"/5"sha-pic-d) *(W 0016/+P/C)* **SENSIBLE SHOES. / A LIL AIN'T ENOUGH** ☐ ☐
(12"/cd-s) *(W 0016 T/CD)* – ('A'side) / California girls / Just a gigolo / I ain't got nobody.

Feb 94. (7"/c-s) *(W 0229/+C)* **SHE'S MY MACHINE. / MISSISSIPPI POWER** [64] ☐
(cd-s+=) *(W 0229CD1)* – Land's edge / Yo breathin' it.
(cd-s+=) *(W 0229CD2)* – ('A'mixes).

Mar 94. (cd/c/lp) *<(9362 45391-2/-4/-1)>* **YOUR FILTHY LITTLE MOUTH** [28] [78]
– She's my machine / Everybody's got the monkey / Big train / Experience / A little luck / Cheatin' heart cafe / Hey, you never know / No big 'ting / Yo breathin' it / Your filthy little mouth / Land's edge / Night life / Sunburn / You're breathin' it (urban NYC mix).

May 94. (7"/c-s) *(W 0249/+C)* **NIGHT LIFE. / JUMP (live)** [72] ☐
(cd-s+=) *(W 0249CD1)* – She's my machine (live).
(cd-s) *(W 0249CD2)* – ('A'side) / Panama (live) / Big train (live) / Experience (live).

— returned to VAN HALEN briefly in 1996 – then ROTH formed DLR BAND

not iss. Wawazat

Jun 98. (cd) *<1217>* **DLR BAND** [-] ☐
– Slam dunk! / Blacklight / Counter-blast / Lose the red dress (keep the shoes) / Little Texas / King of the hill / Going places . . . / Wa wa zat!! / RElentless / Indeedido / Right tool for the job / Tight / Weekend with the babysitter / Black sand.

Magna Carta Magna Carta

Jul 03. (cd) *<(MA 9069-2)>* **DIAMOND DAVE** ☐ ☐
– You got the blues, not me . . . / Made up my mind / Stay while the night is still young / Shoo bop / She's looking good / Soul kitchen / If 6 was 9 / Tomorrow never knows / Medicine man / Let it all hang out Thug pop / Act one / Ice cream man / Bad habits.

– compilations, etc. –

Nov 97. (cd/c) *Warners; <(8122 72941-2/-4)>* **THE BEST OF DAVID LEE ROTH** ☐ ☐
– Don't piss me off / Yankee rose / A lil' ain't enough / Just like Paradise / Big train / Big trouble / It's showtime / Hot dog and a shake / Skyscraper / Shyboy / She's my machine / Stand up / Tobacco road / Easy street / California girls / Just a gigolo / I ain't got nobody / Sensible shoes / Goin' crazy / Ladies nite in Buffalo / Land's edge.

☐ Kelly ROWLAND (see under ⇒ DESTINY'S CHILD)

☐ Kevin ROWLAND (see under ⇒ DEXYS MIDNIGHT RUNNERS)

ROXY MUSIC

Formed: Newcastle, England . . . 1970 by art school graduate and teacher, BRYAN FERRY alongside GRAHAM SIMPSON. Early in 1971, they invited ANDY MACKAY and electronic wizard BRIAN ENO to join, finally settling with the debut album line-up a year later, when they added PHIL MANZANERA and PAUL THOMPSON. The concept of ROXY MUSIC was the brainchild of FERRY, who attempted to realise his vision of a musical equivalent to the pop art he'd become fascinated with at college. Fashioning the band in an outlandish hybrid of decadent glamour and future shock experimentalism, FERRY made sure ROXY MUSIC would be hot property after only a handful of gigs. At this point, the other prime mover behind ROXY MUSIC was BRIAN ENO, who shaped the band's pioneering sound by wrenching all manner of bizarre electronic noises from his mini-moog, feeding the rest of the instruments through an EMS modular synth and masterminding pre-recorded special effects. Signed to 'Island', the band released their self-titled debut in the summer of 1972. Produced by PETE SINFIELD (the KING CRIMSON lyricist), the album effortlessly fused FERRY's suave crooning, a pulsing rhythm section and ENO's inspired electronic experimentation, garnering rave reviews and defying any attempts to pigeonhole the band's sound. But it was the follow-up single, 'VIRGINIA PLAIN' (1972), which launched the band into pop stardom. A careering blast of avant-pop that managed to incorporate a lyric focusing on one of FERRY's surrealist paintings, the single breached the upper echelons of the charts. By this juncture, SIMPSON had been given his marching orders and the band went through a bewildering succession of personnel changes, FERRY retaining strict control throughout. After another top ten hit with 'PJAMARAMA' in 1973, ROXY MUSIC released their second album, 'FOR YOUR PLEASURE' later the same year. Juxtaposing the ironic wig-out of tracks like 'DO THE STRAND' and 'BEAUTY QUEEN' with the vivid desolation of 'IN EVERY DREAM HOME A HEARTACHE', the album distilled the essence of FERRY's original vision. ENO left soon after, his more extreme experimental leanings at odds with the direction in which FERRY wanted to take the band. FERRY also began a solo career around this time which he ran in tandem with the band, releasing an album of covers, 'THESE FOOLISH THINGS', in 1973. ROXY MUSIC, meanwhile, released their third masterpiece, 'STRANDED', a month later. The first album to feature new recruit EDDIE JOBSON (ex-CURVED AIR), the record was less confrontational but more assured in terms of songwriting, FERRY excelling himself with the haunted romanticism of 'MOTHER OF PEARL' and the sweeping grandeur of 'A SONG FOR EUROPE'. A typically ROXY slice of ambiguous, discordant pop, the single, 'STREET LIFE', gave the band yet another Top 10 hit. By the following summer, FERRY had another solo album on the shelves; 'ANOTHER TIME, ANOTHER PLACE' saw him revelling in the role of slicked-back sophisticate, while ROXY's 'COUNTRY LIFE' saw the band in rock-out mode on tracks like 'THE THRILL OF IT ALL', while still buffing the sound with an ironic sheen. Despite a promising single, 'LOVE IS THE DRUG', 'SIREN' (1975) found FERRY's studied musings sounding jaded. Less then a year later, the band split, with McKAY and MANZANERA off to work on solo projects while JOBSON joined FRANK ZAPPPA. FERRY, meanwhile, concentrated on his burgeoning solo career, hitting Top 5 with the funky 'LET'S STICK TOGETHER', following it up with the good-time album of the same name, for once going a bit easier on the irony.

'IN YOUR MIND' (1977) kept up the momentum, spawning the hit, 'TOKYO JOE', and seeing FERRY branch out into original material. Recorded in L.A. with aging session musicians, the sober tones of 'THE BRIDE STRIPPED BARE' (1978) was never going to gain much headway during the height of the punk explosion, yet it remains one the more accessible of FERRY's solo albums. The same year, he cannily reformed ROXY MUSIC, 'MANIFESTO' (1979) heralding a smoother, cleaner sound with the emphasis on FERRY's wistful crooning. The singles 'ANGEL EYES' and 'DANCE AWAY' were the first in a string of tortured pop nuggets that breached the upper reaches of the charts at the turn of the decade, the band finally reaching No.1 with their sublime cover of JOHN LENNON's 'JEALOUS GUY' in 1981. 'FLESH AND BLOOD' (1980) and 'AVALON' (1982) were commercial but finely honed and exquisitely melodic, the latter a quintessentially 80's piece of synthesizer sophistication which inspired many 'New wave-futurist' bands of the 80's. On this high note, FERRY disbanded ROXY MUSIC finally in 1982 and resumed his solo career, carving out a niche as a purveyor of refined, complex adult orientated pop on albums 'BOYS AND GIRLS' (1985) and 'BETE NOIR' (1987). TAXI (1993) saw him return to covers material while 'MAMOUNA' (1994) was an accomplished, mature set of original material. FERRY's first solo album of the new millennium was the ROBIN TROWER-produced 'FRANTIC' (2002), featuring a satisfying combination of choice covers (including a Bob Dylan double header, 'DON'T THINK TWICE IT'S ALRIGHT' and 'IT'S ALL OVER NOW, BABY BLUE') and originals co-written with both DAVE STEWART and BRIAN ENO. • **Songwriters:** FERRY / MANZANERA with contributions from MACKAY and ENO, until the latter bailed out. They covered; IN THE MIDNIGHT HOUR (Wilson Pickett) / EIGHT MILES HIGH (Byrds) / JEALOUS GUY (John Lennon) / LIKE A HURRICANE (Neil Young). • **FERRY's solo covers:-** A HARD RAIN'S A-GONNA FALL (Bob Dylan) / SYMPATHY FOR THE DEVIL (Rolling Stones) / DON'T EVER CHANGE (Crickets) / THESE FOOLISH THINGS (Col Porter?) / PIECE OF MY HEART (hit; Janis Joplin) / I LOVE HOW YOU LOVE ME (Paris Sisters) / DON'T WORRY BABY (Beach Boys) / TRACKS OF MY TEARS (Miracles) / IT'S MY PARTY (Leslie Gore) / BABY I DON'T CARE (Leiber-Stoller) / WALK A MILE IN MY SHOES (Joe South) / THE IN-CROWD (Dobie Gray) / WHAT A WONDERFUL WORLD (Sam Cooke) / YOU ARE MY SUNSHINE (Ray Charles) / SMOKE GETS IN YOUR EYES (Platters) / HELP ME MAKE IT THROUGH THE NIGHT (Kris Kristofferson) / FINGERPOPPIN' (Hank Ballard) / FUNNY HOW TIME SLIPS AWAY (Jimmy Ellidge) / LET'S STICK TOGETHER (Wilbert Harrison) / THE PRICE OF LOVE (Everly Brothers) / IT'S ONLY LOVE (Barry White) / SHAME SHAME SHAME (Shirley & Company) / HEART ON MY SLEEVE (Gallagher & Lyle) / SHE'S LEAVING HOME + YOU WON'T SEE ME (Beatles) / WHEN SHE WALKS IN THE ROOM (Searchers) / TAKE ME TO THE RIVER (Al Green) / YOU DON'T KNOW (Sam & Dave) / PARTY DOLL (Buddy Knox) / FEEL THE NEED (Detroit Emeralds). Note:- JOHNNY MARR (ex-Smiths) co-wrote THE RIGHT STUFF with him. FERRY returned in 1993 with a covers album 'TAXI'. • **Trivia:** FERRY married model, Lucy Helmore, on the 26th of June '82 after a 70's relationship with Jerry Hall had finished. He was said to have turned down the Keith Forsey-penned song, 'DON'T YOU FORGET ABOUT ME', a No.1 for SIMPLE MINDS.

Album rating: ROXY MUSIC (*8) / FOR YOUR PLEASURE (*9) / STRANDED (*8) / COUNTRY LIFE (*7) / SIREN (*6) / VIVA! ROXY MUSIC (*5) / GREATEST HITS compilation (*8) / MANIFESTO (*6) / FLESH + BLOOD (*5) / AVALON (*7) / THE HIGH ROAD mini (*4) / THE ATLANTIC YEARS 1973-1980 compilation (*8) / Bryan Ferry: THESE FOOLISH THINGS (*7) / ANOTHER TIME, ANOTHER PLACE (*5) / LET'S STICK TOGETHER (*6) / IN YOUR MIND (*5) / THE BRIDE STRIPPED BARE (*6) / BOYS AND GIRLS (*7) / BETE NOIRE (*5) / TAXI (*4) / MAMOUNA (*5) / AS TIME GOES BY (*3) / FRANTIC (*6) / Bryan Ferry & Roxy Music compilations:- STREET LIFE: 20 GREAT HITS (*9) / THE ULTIMATE COLLECTION (*8) / MORE THAN THIS – THE BEST OF . . . (*8)

BRYAN FERRY (b.26 Sep'45, Washington, Durham, England) – vocals, piano / **ANDY MACKAY** (b.23 Jul'46, London, England) – saxophone, oboe, wind inst. / (BRIAN) **ENO** (b.15 May'48, Woodbridge, Suffolk, England) – synthesizers-keyboards / **GRAHAM SIMPSON** – bass, vocals / **PHIL MANZANERA** (b. PHILIP TARGETT-ADAMS, 31 Jan'51, London) – guitar (ex-QUIET SUN) repl. DAVID O'LIST (ex-NICE) who had repl. original ROGER BUNN (Jul'71). / **PAUL THOMPSON** (b.13 May'51, Jarrow, Northumberland, England) – drums repl. original DEXTER LLOYD (Jul'71).

Island Reprise

Jun 72. (lp/c) *(ILPS/ICT 9200)* <RS 2114> **ROXY MUSIC** 10
– Re-make/re-model / Ladytron / If there is something / 2 H.B. / The bob (medley) / Chance meeting / Would you believe? / Sea breezes / Bitters end. *(re-iss. Feb77 on 'Polydor' lp)(c; 2302 048)(3100 348) (re-iss. Jan87 & Sep91 on 'EG' lp/c/cd+=; EG LP/MC/CD 6)* – Virginia plain.

— (May'72) **RIK KENTON** (b.31 Oct'45) – bass; repl. SIMPSON

Aug 72. (7") *(WIP 6144)* <1124> **VIRGINIA PLAIN. / THE NUMBERER** 4

— (Jan'73) **JOHN PORTER** – bass; repl. KENTON who went solo

Island Warners

Mar 73. (7") *(WIP 6159)* **PJAMARAMA. / THE PRIDE AND THE PAIN** 10

Mar 73. (lp/c) *(ILPS/ICT 9232)* <2696> **FOR YOUR PLEASURE** 4
– Do the strand / Beauty queen / Strictly confidential / Editions of you / In every dream home a heartache / The bogus man / Grey lagoons / For your pleasure. *(re-iss. Feb77 on 'Polydor' lp)(c; 2302 049)(3100 349) (re-iss. Jan87 on 'E.G.' lp/c/cd; EG LP/MC/CD 8) (cd+c.Sep91 on 'EG') (re-iss. Feb97 on 'E.M.I.'; LPCENT 19)*

Jul 73. (7") <7719> **DO THE STRAND. / EDITIONS OF YOU** –

— (Jul'73) **EDDIE JOBSON** (b.28 Apr'55, Billingham, Teeside, England) – keyboards, violin (ex-CURVED AIR) repl. ENO who went solo

— session bassmen incl. **JOHN GUSTAFSON** (studio) / **SAL MAIDA** (tour) repl. PORTER (other 5= **FERRY, MANZANERA, MACKAY, JOBSON & THOMPSON)**

Island Atco

Nov 73. (7") *(WIP 6173)* **STREET LIFE. / HULA KULA** 9 –

Nov 73. (lp/c) *(ILPS/ICT 9252)* <7045> **STRANDED** 1
– Street life / Just like you / Amazona / Psalm / Serenade / A song for Europe / Mother of pearl / Sunset. *(re-iss. Feb77 on 'Polydor' lp)(c; 2302 050)(3100 350) (re-iss. Jan87 on 'E.G.' lp/c/cd; EG LP/MC/CD 10) (cd+c. Sep91 on 'EG')*

— brought in **JOHN WETTON** (b.1949, Derby, England) – tour bass (ex-FAMILY, ex-KING CRIMSON, etc.) repl. MAIDA

Oct 74. (7") *(WIP 6208)* **ALL I WANT IS YOU. / YOUR APPLICATIONS FAILED** 12 –

Nov 74. (lp/c) *(ILPS/ICT 9303)* <106> **COUNTRY LIFE** 3 Jan75 37
– The thrill of it all / Three and nine / All I want is you / Out of the blue / If it takes all night / Bitter-sweet / Triptych / Casanova / A really good time / Prairie rose. *(re-iss. Feb77 on 'Polydor' lp)(c; 2302 051)(3100 351) (re-iss. Jan87 on 'E.G.' lp/c/cd; EG LP/MC/CD 16) (cd+c.Sep91 on 'EG')*

Nov 74. (7") <7018> **THE THRILL OF IT ALL. / YOUR APPLICATIONS FAILED** –

Sep 75. (7") *(WIP 6248)* **LOVE IS THE DRUG. / SULTANESQUE** 2 –

Oct 75. (lp/c) *(ILPS/ICT 9344)* <127> **SIREN** 4 50
– Love is the drug / End of the line / Sentimental fool / Whirlwind / She sells / Could it hapen to me / Both ends burning / Nightingale / Just another high. *(re-iss. Feb77 on 'Polydor' lp)(c; 2302 052)(3100 352) (re-iss. Jan87 on 'E.G.' lp/c/cd; EG LP/MC/CD 20) (cd+c.Sep91 on 'EG')*

Dec 75. (7") *(WIP 6262)* **BOTH ENDS BURNING. / FOR YOUR PLEASURE** 25

Dec 75. (7") <7042> **LOVE IS THE DRUG. / BOTH ENDS BURNING** – 30

— **RICK WILLS** – tour bass repl. WETTON who stayed on with FERRY

— Disbanded officially mid'76, leaving behind one more album

Jul 76. (lp/c) *(ILPS/ICT 9400)* <139> **VIVA! ROXY MUSIC (live 1973-1975)** [6] [81]
– Out of the blue / Pjamarama / The bogus man / Chance meeting / Both ends burning / If there is something / In every dream home a heartache / Do the strand. *(re-iss. Feb77 on 'Polydor' lp)(c; 2302 053)(3100 353) (re-iss. Jan87 on 'E.G.' lp/c/cd; EG LP/MC/CD 25) (cd+c.Sep91 on 'EG')*

— After split ANDY MACKAY continued solo work, as did PHIL MANZANERA. EDDIE JOBSON joined FRANK ZAPPA.

BRYAN FERRY

also had simultaneous solo career. (same labels). He used various session people, including many members of ROXY MUSIC.

Sep 73. (7") *(WIP 6170)* **A HARD RAIN'S GONNA FALL. / 2 HB** [4] [ ]
Oct 73. (lp/c) *(ILPS/ICT 9249)* <7304> **THESE FOOLISH THINGS** [5] [ ]
– A hard rain's a-gonna fall / River of salt / Don't ever change / Piece of my heart / Baby I don't care / It's my party / Don't worry baby / Sympathy for the Devil / Tracks of my tears / You won't see me / I love how you love me / Loving you is sweeter than ever / These foolish things. *(re-iss. Aug84 on 'Polydor' lp/c;) (re-iss. Jan87 on 'E.G.' lp/c/cd; EG LP/MC/CD 9)*
May 74. (7") *(WIP 6196)* **THE IN-CROWD. / CHANCE MEETING** [13] [–]
Jul 74. (lp/c) *(ILPS/ICT 9284)* <18113> **ANOTHER TIME, ANOTHER PLACE** [4] [ ]
– The in-crowd / Smoke gets in your eyes / Walk a mile in my shoes / Funny how time slips away / You are my sunshine / (What a) Wonderful world / It ain't me babe / Fingerpoppin' / Help me make it through the night. *(re-iss. Aug84 on 'Polydor' lp/c;) (re-iss. Jan87 on 'E.G.' lp/c/cd; EG LP/MC/CD 14)*
Aug 74. (7") *(WIP 6205)* **SMOKE GETS IN YOUR EYES. / ANOTHER TIME, ANOTHER PLACE** [17] [–]
Jun 75. (7") *(WIP 6234)* **YOU GO TO MY HEAD. / RE-MAKE RE-MODEL** [ ] [–]

— Solo again, with ex-ROXY MUSIC men **PAUL THOMPSON + JOHN WETTON**. Added **CHRIS SPEDDING** – guitar (ex-SHARKS)

Island Atlantic

Jun 76. (7") *(WIP 6307)* **LET'S STICK TOGETHER. / SEA BREEZES** [4] [ ]
Aug 76. (7"ep) *(IEP 1)* **EXTENDED PLAY** [7] [–]
– The price of love / Shame shame shame / Heart on my sleeve / It's only love.
Sep 76. (lp/c) *(ILPS/ICT 9367)* <18187> **LET'S STICK TOGETHER** [19] [ ]
– Let's stick together / Casanova / Sea breeze / Shame shame shame / 2HB / The price of love / Chance meeting / It's only love / You go to my head / Re-make/re-model / Heart on my sleeve. *(re-iss. Aug84 on 'Polydor' lp/c/cd;) (re-iss. Jan87 on 'E.G.' lp/c/cd; EG LP/MC/CD 24)*
Nov 76. (7") <3364> **HEART ON MY SLEEVE. / RE-MAKE/RE-MODEL** [–] [86]

— added **PHIL MANZANERA** – guitar / **ANN ODELL** – keyboards / **MEL COLLINS** – sax / plus many backing singers.

Polydor Atlantic

Jan 77. (7") *(2001 704)* **THIS IS TOMORROW. / AS THE WORLD TURNS** [9] [ ]
Feb 77. (lp/c) *(2302/3100 055)* <18216> **IN YOUR MIND** [5] [ ]
– This is tomorrow / All night operator / One kiss / Love me madly again / Tokyo Joe / Party doll / Rock of ages / In your mind. *(re-iss. Jan87 on 'E.G.' lp/c/cd; EG LP/MC/CD 27)*
Apr 77. (7") *(2001 711)* **TOKYO JOE. / SHE'S LEAVING HOME** [15] [–]
Jun 77. (7") **TOKYO JOE. / AS THE WORLD TURNS** [–] [ ]

— FERRY continued to use many different musicians, too many to mention.

Apr 78. (7") *(POSP 3)* **WHAT GOES ON. / CASANOVA** [67] [ ]
Apr 78. (lp/c) *(POLD/+C 5003)* **THE BRIDE STRIPPED BARE** [13] [ ]
– Sign of the times / Can't let go / Hold on (I'm coming) / The same old blues / When she walks in the room / Take me to the river / What goes on / Carrickfergus / That's how strong my love is / This island Earth. *(re-iss. Jan87 on 'E.G.' lp/c/cd; EG LP/MC/CD 36)*
Jul 78. (7") *(2001 798)* **SIGN OF THE TIMES. / FOUR LETTER LOVE** [37] [–]
Nov 78. (7") **SIGN OF THE TIMES. / CAN'T LET GO** [–] [ ]
Nov 78. (7") *(2001 834)* **CARRICKFERGUS. / WHEN SHE WALKS IN THE ROOM** [ ] [ ]

ROXY MUSIC

re-formed with **FERRY, MANZANERA, MACKAY, THOMPSON,** plus **PAUL CARRACK** – studio keyboards (ex-ACE) / **DAVID SKINNER** – tour keyboards / **GARY TIBBS** – bass (ex-VIBRATORS)

Polydor-EG Atco

Feb 79. (7") *(POSP 32)* **TRASH. / TRASH 2** [40] [–]
Mar 79. (lp/c)(pic-lp) *(POLH/+C 001)(EGPD 001)* <114> **MANIFESTO** [7] [23]
– Manifesto / Trash / Angel eyes / Still falls the rain / Stronger through the years / Ain't that so / My little girl / ance away / Cry cry cry / Spin me round. *(re-iss. Jan87 on 'E.G.' lp/c/cd+=; EG LP/MC/CD 38)* – Angel eyes (12"disco version).
Apr 79. (7") *(POSP 44)* **DANCE AWAY. / CRY CRY CRY** [2] [–]
Apr 79. (7") <7100> **DANCE AWAY. / TRASH 2** [–] [44]
Aug 79. (7"/ext.12") *(POSP/+X 67)* **ANGEL EYES. / MY LITTLE GIRL** [4] [ ]
May 80. (7") *(POSP 93)* **OVER YOU. / MANIFESTO** [5] [–]
May 80. (lp/c) *(POLH/+C 002)* <102> **FLESH + BLOOD** [1] [35]
– In the midnight hour / Oh yeah (on the radio) / Same old scene / Flesh and blood / My only love / Over you / Eight miles high / Rain rain rain / No strange delight / Running wild. *(re-iss. Jan87 on 'E.G.' lp/c/cd; EG LP/MC/CD 46)*
May 80. (7") <7301> **OVER YOU. / MY ONLY LOVE** [–] [80]
Jul 80. (7") *(2001 972)* **OH YEAH (ON THE RADIO). / SOUTH DOWNS** [5] [ ]
Nov 80. (7") *(ROXY 1)* **SAME OLD SCENE. / LOVER** [12] [–]
Dec 80. (7") **IN THE MIDNIGHT HOUR. /** [–] [ ]

— Earlier 1980, CARRACK joined SQUEEZE, and TIBBS joined ADAM & THE ANTS. Session men used at the time **NEIL HUBBARD** – guitar / **ALAN SPENNER** – bass / **ANDY NEWMARK** – drums repl. THOMPSON

E.G. Warners

Feb 81. (7") *(ROXY 2)* <7329> **JEALOUS GUY. / TO TURN YOU ON** [1] [ ]
Apr 82. (7"/12") *(ROXY/+X 3)* **MORE THAN THIS. / INDIA** [6] [–]
May 82. (lp/c) *(EGHP/+C 50)* <23686> **AVALON** [1] [53]
– More than this / The space between / India / While my heart is still beating / Main thing / Take a chance with me / Avalon / To turn you on / True to life / Tara. *(re-iss. Jan87 on 'E.G.' lp/c/cd; EG LP/MC/CD 50) (re-iss. Apr92 on 'Virgin' lp/c; OVED/+C 397)*
Jun 82. (7") *(ROXY 4)* **AVALON. / ALWAYS UNKNOWING** [13] [ ]
Sep 82. (7"/12") *(ROXY/+X 5)* **TAKE A CHANCE WITH ME. / THE MAIN THING** [26] [–]
Sep 82. (7") <29978> **TAKE A CHANCE ON ME. / INDIA** [–] [ ]
Nov 82. (7") <29912> **MORE THAN THIS. / ALWAYS UNKNOWING** [–] [ ]

— added **GUY FLETCHER + JIMMY MAELEN** – keyboards / **MICHELLE COBBS + TAWATHA AGEE**

Mar 83. (m-lp/c) *(EGM LP/MC 1)* <23808> **THE HIGH ROAD (live)** [26] [67]
– Can't let go / My only love / Like a hurricane / Jealous guy.

— Had already disbanded again late 1982. MANZANERA and MACKAY became The EXPLORERS, and FERRY went solo again.

BRYAN FERRY

E.G. Warners

May 85. (7") *(FERRY 1)* **SLAVE TO LOVE. / VALENTINE (instrumental)** [10] [ ]
(12"+=) *(FERRYX 1)* – ('A'instrumental).
Jun 85. (lp/c/cd) *(EG LP/MC/CD 62)* <25082> **BOYS AND GIRLS** [1] [63]
– Sensation / Slave to love / Don't stop the dance / A wasteland / Windswept / The chosen one / Valentine / Stone woman / Boys and girls. *(re-iss. Jan87; same) (re-iss. cd+c.Sep91)*
Aug 85. (7") *(FERRY 2)* **DON'T STOP THE DANCE. / NOCTURNE** [21] [ ]
(12"+=) *(FERRYX 2)* – Windswept (instrumental).
Nov 85. (7"/7"pic-d) *(FERRY/FEREP 3)* **WINDSWEPT. / CRAZY LOVE** [46] [ ]
(12"+=) *(FERRYX 3)* – Feel the need / Broken wings.
Mar 86. (7") *(FERRY 4)* **IS YOUR LOVE STRONG ENOUGH. / WINDSWEPT (instrumental)** [22] [ ]
(12"+=) *(FERRYX 4)* – ('A'mix).
Jul 86. (7") **HELP ME. / BROKEN WINGS** [–] [ ]

Virgin Reprise

Sep 87. (7"/12") *(VS 940/+12)* **THE RIGHT STUFF. / ('A'instrumental)** [37] [ ]
(c-s+=) *(VSC 940)* – ('A'extended) / ('A'dub version).

Nov 87. (cd/c/lp) *(CD/TC+/V 2474)* <25598> **BETE NOIRE** [9] [63]
– Limbo / Kiss and tell / New town / Day for night / Zamba / The right stuff / Seven deadly sins / The name of the game / Bete noire. *(cd re-iss. Dec88; CDVP 2474)*

Feb 88. (7") *(VS 1034)* <28117> **KISS AND TELL. / ZAMBA** [41] [31]
(12"+=)(cd-s+=) *(VST 1034)(CDEP 19)* – ('A'&'B'remixes).

Jun 88. (7") *(VS 1066)* **LIMBO (Latin mix). / BETE NOIRE (instrumental)** [ ] [ ]
(12"+=/cd-s+=) *(VS T/CD 1066)* – ('A'mix).

Feb 93. (7"/c-s) *(VS/+C 1400)* **I PUT A SPELL ON YOU. / THESE FOOLISH THINGS** [18] [ ]
(cd-s+=) *(VSCDX 1400)* – Ladytron (live) / While my heart is still beating (live).
(cd-s) *(VSCDG 1400)* – ('A'-5 mixes).

Mar 93. (cd/c/lp) *(CD/TC+/V 2700)* <45246> **TAXI** [2] [79]
– I put a spell on you / Will you love me tomorrow / Answer me / Just one look / Rescue me / All tomorrow's parties / Girl of my best friend / Amazing Grace / Taxi / Because you're mine.

May 93. (7"/c-s) *(VS/+C 1455)* **WILL YOU LOVE ME TOMMOROW. / A HARD RAIN'S A-GONNA FALL** [23] [ ]
(cd-s+=) *(VSCDT 1455)* – A wasteland (live) / Windswept (live).
(cd-s) *(VSCDG 1455)* – ('A'side) / Crazy love / Feel the need / When she walks in the room.

Aug 93. (c-s) *(VSC 1468)* **GIRL OF MY BEST FRIEND / NOCTURNE** [57] [ ]
(cd-s+=) *(VSCDT 1468)* – Are you lonesome tonight? / Valentine.
(cd-s) *(VSCDG 1468)* – Let's stick together / Boys and girls (live) / The bogus man (live).

—— now with a plethora of musicians

Virgin Virgin

Sep 94. (cd/c/lp) *(CD/TC+/V 2751)* <39838> **MAMOUNA** [11] [94]
– Don't want to know / N.Y.C. / Your painted smile / Mamouna / The only face / The 39 steps / Which way to turn / Wildcat days / Gemini Moon / Chain reaction.

Oct 94. (7"/c-s) *(VS/+C 1508)* **YOUR PAINTED SMILE. / DON'T STOP THE DANCE** [ ] [ ]
(cd-s+=) *(VSCDG 1508)* – In every dream home a heartache (live) / Bete noire (live).

Feb 95. (c-s) *(VSC 1528)* **MAMOUNA / THE 39 STEPS (Brian Eno mix)** [57] [ ]
(cd-s+=) *(VSCDG 1528)* – Jealous guy (live) / Slave to love (live).

Oct 99. (cd/c) *(CD/TC VIR 89)* <48270> **AS TIME GOES BY** [16] [ ]
– As time goes by / The way you look tonight / Easy living / I'm in the mood for love / Where or when / When somebody thinks you're wonderful / Sweet and lovely / Miss Otis regrets / Time on my hands / Lover, come back to me / Falling in love again / Love me or leave me / You do something to me / Just one of those things / September song.

Apr 02. (cd) *(CDVIR 167)* <812138> **FRANTIC** [6] [ ]
– It's all over now, baby blue / Cruel / Goin' down / Goddess of love / Don't think twice, it's alright / Nobody loves me / Ja nun hons pris / A fool for love / Goodnight Irene / Hiroshima (Ash Howes mix) / San Simeon / One way love / I thought.

May 02. (cd-s) *(DINSCD 238)* **GODDESS OF LOVE / WHICH WAY TO TURN / SMOKE DREAMS OF YOU** [ ] [–]

– (FERRY) compilations, others, etc. –

Jun 88. (3"cd-ep) *E.G.; (CDT 10)* **LET'S STICK TOGETHER / SHAME SHAME SHAME / CHANCE MEETING / SEA BREEZES** [ ] [–]

Oct 88. (7") *E.G.; (EGO 44)* **LET'S STICK TOGETHER ('88 remix). / TRASH** [12] [ ]
(12"+=) *(EGOX 44)* – Shame shame shame / Angel eyes.
(cd-s+=) *(EGOCD 44)* – Casanova / Sign of the times.

Nov 88. (lp/c/cd/pic-cd; BRYAN FERRY & ROXY MUSIC) *E.G.; (EG TV/MTV/CTV/CPTV 2)* **THE ULTIMATE COLLECTION** [6] [ ]
– Let's stick together ('88 remix) / The in-crowd / Angel eyes (ROXY MUSIC) / He'll have to go / Tokyo Joe / All I want is you (ROXY MUSIC) / Jealous guy (ROXY MUSIC) / The price of love / Don't stop the dance / Love is the drug (ROXY MUSIC) / This is tomorrow / Slave to love / Help me / Avalon (ROXY MUSIC) / Dance away (ROXY MUSIC).

Feb 89. (7") *E.G.; (EGO 46)* **THE PRICE OF LOVE (R&B mix). / LOVER** [49] [ ]
(12"+=) *(EGOX 46)* – Don't stop the dance (remix) / Nocturne.
(cd-s+=) *(EGOCD 46)* – Don't stop the dance (remix) / Slave to love (remix).

Apr 89. (7") *E.G.; (EGO 48)* **HE'LL HAVE TO GO. / CARRICKFERGUS** [63] [ ]
(cd-s+=) *(EGOCD 48)* – Take me to the river / Broken wings.
(12") *(EGOX 48)* – ('A'side) / Windswept / Is your love strong enough.

Dec 89. (3xc-box/3xcd-box) *E.G.; (EGBM/EGBC 5)* **THESE FOOLISH THINGS / LET'S STICK TOGETHER / BOYS AND GIRLS** (free w / Island Various Artists compilations) [ ] [–]

Oct 95. (cd/c/d-lp) *Virgin; (CD/TC+/V 2791)* **MORE THAN THIS – THE BEST OF BRYAN FERRY & ROXY MUSIC** [15] [ ]

Jul 00. (cd/c) *Virgin; (CDV/TCV 2921)* **SLAVE TO LOVE** [11] [–]
– (with also ROXY MUSIC tracks).

– (ROXY MUSIC) compilations, etc. –

—— on 'E.G.' unless mentioned otherwise

Oct 77. (7") *Polydor; (2001 739)* **VIRGINIA PLAIN. / PJAMARAMA** [11] [ ]

Nov 77. (lp)(c) *Polydor; (2303 073)(3100 407)* **GREATEST HITS** [20] [ ]
– Virginia Plain / Do the strand / All I want is you / Out of the blue / Pjamarama / Editions of you / Love is the drug / Mother of pearl / Song for Europe / Thrill of it all / Street life. *(re-iss. Jan87 on 'E.G.' lp/cd; EG LP/CD 31)*

Jan 78. (7") *Polydor; (2001 756)* **DO THE STRAND. / EDITIONS OF YOU** [ ] [–]

Dec 81. (7xlp-box/ 7xc-box) *(EG BS/BC 1)* **THE FIRST SEVEN ALBUMS** [ ] [–]
– (ROXY MUSIC / FOR YOUR PLEASURE / STRANDED / COUNTRY LIFE / SIREN / MANIFESTO / FLESH AND BLOOD).

Nov 83. (lp/c)(cd) *(EG LP/MC 54)(815 849-2) / Atco; <90122>* **THE ATLANTIC YEARS 1973-1980** [23] [ ]

Apr 86. (d-lp/c)(cd) (BRYAN FERRY & ROXY MUSIC) *(EGTV/EGMTV/EGCTV 1)* <25857> **STREET LIFE: 20 GREAT HITS** [1] Aug89 [100]
– Virginia plain / A hard rain's a-gonna fall (BRYAN FERRY) / Pjamarama / Do the strand / These foolish things (BRYAN FERRY) / Street life / Let's stick together (BRYAN FERRY) / Smoke gets in your eyes (BRYAN FERRY) / Love is the drug / Sign of the times (BRYAN FERRY) / Dance away / Angel eyes / Oh yeah / Over you / Same old scene / The midnight hour / More than this / Avalon / Slave to love (BRYAN FERRY) / Jealous guy.

Jun 88. (3"cd-ep) *(CDT 8)* **JEALOUS GUY / LOVER / SOUTHDOWN** [ ] [ ]

Dec 89. (3xc-box/3xcd-box) *(EGBM/EGBC 3)* **ROXY MUSIC – THE EARLY YEARS** [ ] [ ]
– (ROXY MUSIC / FOR YOUR PLEASURE / STRANDED)

Dec 89. (3xc-box/3xcd-box) *(EGBM/EGBC 4)* **ROXY MUSIC – THE LATER YEARS** [ ] [ ]
– (MANIFESTO / FLESH AND BLOOD / AVALON)

Oct 90. (cd/c/d-lp) *(EG CD/MC/LP 77)* **HEART STILL BEATIN' (live in France '82)** [ ] [ ]

Oct 90. (7") **LOVE IS THE DRUG (live). / EDITIONS OF YOU (live)** [ ] [–]
(12"+=/cd-s+=) – Do the strand (live).

Oct 94. (3xcd-box) **THE COMPACT COLLECTION** [ ] [ ]

Nov 95. (4xcd-box) *Virgin; (CDBOX 5)* **THE THRILL OF IT ALL – ROXY MUSIC 1972-1982** [ ] [ ]

Apr 96. (c-ep/12"ep/cd-ep) *Virgin; (VS C/T/CDT 1580)* **LOVE IS THE DRUG (Rollo & Sister Bliss Monster mixes; 3) / ('A'-original version)** [33] [ ]

Jun 01. (cd) *Virgin; (CDV 2939)* **THE BEST OF ROXY MUSIC** [12] [–]

ROYKSOPP

Formed: Tromso, Norway ... early 90's by TORBJORN BRUNDTLAND and his collegue SVIEN BERGE. The pair, who met in college and began recording in the twilight years of the millennium, were signed to R&S offshoot label 'Appolo' (where they issued the 'TRAVELLER'S DREAM' LP under the moniker AEDENA CYCLE), but as their partnership collapsed, so did the deal. They spent years apart, finally re-emerging in 1998 for a few low-key singles, until influential dance label 'Wall Of Sound' snapped them up and released the sublime 'EPLE' EP (2001). Also featuring the track 'POOR LENO', the downbeat, breezy chillout electronica gave many an excuse to dig up their old ENO records (and buy a few rip-off "chill-out" compilation albums while they were at it). The same year ROYKSOPP delivered their debut album 'MELODY A.M.', a multi-textured album full of swirling musical landscapes and stoned sublimeness akin to the likes of FOUR TET, but less experimental than, say, BOARDS OF CANADA. The album, in all its technicoloured glory went on to be nominated for many awards including MTV's "best dance album", although there wasn't really much dancing to be done. Ultimately, ROYKSOPP appealed to those exhausted clubbers, detoxing themselves on a beach somewhere after a night/morning out, or the hard-house freak who thought it was avant garde to listen to something this mellow and strange. As popularity beckoned and the group's music was used in a (shudder) car advert, much was in doubt about the individuality of their music. However, it will take a genius to recreate and reproduce an album that matches the emotional intensity of 'MELODY A.M.'.

Album rating: MELODY A.M. (*8)

TORBJORN BRUNDTLAND + SVEIN BERGE – electronics

		Wall Of Sound	Wall Of Sound
Jul 01.	(12"/cd-s) *(WALL T/D 071) <5071>* **EPLE / EPLE (Bjorn Torske mix) / ROYKSOPP'S NIGHT OUT**		
Oct 01.	(cd/lp) *(WALL CD/LP 027) <90148>* **MELODY A.M.**		
	– So easy / Eple / Sparks / In space / Poor Leno / A higher place / Royksopp's night out / Remind me / She's so / 40 years back / Come. *(re-iss. Aug02; same)* – hit UK No.9. *<US re-iss. Oct02 on 'Astralwerks'+=; 13352>* – mixes:- Remind me (2 mixes + dub) / Poor Leno (2 mixes + dub) / Eple (dub).		
Dec 01.	(12"/cd-s) *(WALL T/D 073)* **POOR LENO (mixes; edit / Sander Kleinenberg northern beach / Istanbul forever)**	59	
	(12") *(WALLT 073Y)* – ('A'album) / ('A'-Silicone Soul hypno house mix).		
Aug 02.	(cd-s) *(WALLD 074X)* **REMIND ME (mixes; radio / James Zabela / SO EASY**	21	–
	(12") *(WALLT 074X)* – ('A'mixes; Tom Middleton cosmos / Ernest St. Laurent moonfish / someone else's).		
	(cd-s/12") *(WALL D/T 074R)* – ('A'mixes).		
Nov 02.	(cd-s) *(WALLD 079)* **POOR LENO / POOR LENO (Jakatta mix) / POOR LENO (Royksopp's Istanbul forever mix)**	38	–
	(cd-s) *(WALLD 079V)* – ('A'side) / ('A'-Silicone Soul's hypno beat mix) / So easy / ('A'-video).		
	(12") *(WALLT 079)* – ('A'-Jakatta mix) / ('A'-Silicone Soul's hypno beat mix) / ('A'album version).		
Feb 03.	(cd-s/12") *(WALL D/T 080)* **EPLE / EPLE (Fatboy Slim remix) / EPLE (shakedown remix)**	16	–
	(cd-s/12") *(WALL D/T 080 V/X)* – (mises; edit / Boris & Michi's eplistic-scratch-attack / Black strobe).		
Jun 03.	(cd-s) *(WALLD 084)* **SPARKS / DON'T GO / SO EASY (Derrick Carter so BHQ remix)**	41	–
	(12") *(WALLT 084)* – (Roni Size remixes).		
	(12") *(WALLT 084Y)* – ('A'side) / So easy (Derrick Carter so BHQ remix) / ('A'-Murk downtown Miami mix).		
	(cd-s) *(WALLD 084V)* – ('A'-Murk downtown Miami mix) / REmind me (someone else's mix) / ('A'-video).		

□ RTZ (see under ⇒ BOSTON)

Todd RUNDGREN

Born: 22 Jun'48, Upper Darby, Pennsylvania, USA. In 1967, he and another ex-WOODY'S TRUCK STOP member, CARSTEN VAN OSTEN, formed The NAZZ (taking the name from a YARDBIRDS b-side). In 1968, after supporting The DOORS a year previously, they signed to 'Screen Gems/Columbia'. An eponymous debut album sold moderately, RUNDGREN leaving the band in the middle of '69, after the completion of two further albums of psychedelic metal. In 1970, he became an in-house producer for Albert Grossman's 'Bearsville', his first job being for The AMERICAN DREAM. Later in the year, he formed his own band, RUNT (his nickname), releasing an album of the same name which spawned his first Top 20 hit, 'WE GOTTA GET YOU A WOMAN'. Following a further RUNT album, he decided to use his own name for future releases. In 1972, after taking over the production duties from GEORGE HARRISON on BADFINGER's 'Straight Up' set, he unleashed a truly wonderful solo debut, 'SOMETHING / ANYTHING?'. The double album reached the Top 30, a cut from it, 'I SAW THE LIGHT", making the US Top 20 (a year later Top 40 in the UK). Playing every instrument himself, it encompassed almost every style in the pop/rock pantheon. Among the many highlights were; the aforementioned single, 'HELLO IT'S ME', 'MARLENE', COULDN'T I JUST TELL YOU' and 'COLD MORNING LIGHT'. His next effort, 'A WIZARD, A TRUE STAR' was a wildly ambitious concept piece that attempted to reconstruct psychedelia. Although the record overreached itself, failing commercially as a result, it nevertheless contained a smattering of RUNDGREN gems including 'JUST ONE VICTORY'. Prolific in his songwriting, he returned after only nine months with yet another double set, 'TODD', an unrelentingly snooze-worthy affair. To complement his wide ranging solo work under many styles, TODD formed a band, UTOPIA, who were a much more free flowing, progressive rock/jazz outfit. Their first self-titled outing was released at the end of '74, while RUNDGREN himself worked on his monumental 'INITIATION'. Released in '75, it was largely lambasted by the press, although inside the hour-long lp was the minor classic hit, 'REAL MAN' and the 30-odd minute 'A TREATISE ON COSMIC FIRE' (which was split into three parts). RUNDGREN increasingly seemed to lose his penchant for experimentalism, although UTOPIA's 'RA' album was the exception. The album, 'OOPS! WRONG PLANET' (also 1977), took a more commercial direction, while at the same time, TODD was painstakingly producing MEAT LOAF's grandiose 'Bat Out Of Hell'. For the remainder of the 70's and throughout the first half of the 80's, TODD combined his solo output with UTOPIA releases. Most of these were well-received commercially, although critically, he was often unfairly savaged by the music press. Following UTOPIA's ultimate demise in 1986, RUNDGREN spent a few years studio-bound working on other people's projects before recruiting ex-JOURNEY bassist ROSS VALORY and former TUBES drummer PRAIRIE PRINCE for the impressive, soul-centric live-in-the-studio set, 'NEARLY HUMAN' (1989), featuring an unlikely cover of Elvis Costello's 'TWO LITTLE HITLERS'. While 90's sets like 'NO WORLD ORDER' (1994) and the quasi-lounge revisionism of 1997's 'WITH A TWIST' (which featured makeovers of 'I SAW THE LIGHT' and 'THE DREAM GOES ON FOREVER' amongst others) kept him busy, he increasingly channelled his creative energies into the musical possibilities of the internet. 'ONE LONG YEAR' (2000) gathered together bits and pieces he'd already previewed online, although on the evidence of 'I HATE

MY FRICKIN' I.S.P.', RUNDGREN's cyberspace adventures weren't without mishap. • **Songwriters:** Phenomenal pensmith, although he did fit in a number of near perfect covers; DO YA (Move) / GOOD VIBRATIONS (Beach Boys) / LOVE OF THE COMMON MAN (from West Side Story?) / MOST LIKELY TO GO YOUR WAY (Bob Dylan) / TIN SOLDIER (Small Faces) / STRAWBERRY FIELDS FOREVER + RAIN (Beatles) / IF SIX WAS NINE (Jimi Hendrix) / HAPPENINGS TEN YEARS TIME AGO (Yardbirds) / etc? • **Trivia:** In 1983, TODD co-wrote the Top 20 hit 'KISSING WITH CONFIDENCE' for WILL POWERS (see under Carly SIMON). TODD's others major productions have included GRAND FUNK (1973) / HALL & OATES (1974) / TOM ROBINSON (1978) / TUBES (1979) / PSYCHEDELIC FURS (1982) / etc. Note:- TODD has just released in 1992 a compilation album of his production work.

Album rating: Nazz: NAZZ (*6) / NAZZ NAZZ (*5) / NAZZ III (*5) / compilation:- THE BEST OF NAZZ (*7) / Todd Rundgren: RUNT (*6; as Runt) / THE BALLAD OF TODD RUNDGREN (*7; as Runt) / SOMETHING – ANYTHING? (*9) / A WIZARD, A TRUE STAR (*6) / TODD (*4) / TODD RUNDGREN'S UTOPIA (*4; as Todd Rundgren's Utopia) / INITIATION (*8) / ANOTHER LIVE (*4; as Todd Rundgren's Utopia) / FAITHFUL (*6) / RA (*7; as Utopia) / OOPS! WRONG PLANET (*6; as Utopia) / HERMIT OF MINK HOLLOW (*8) / BACK TO THE BARS (*5) / ADVENTURES IN UTOPIA (*6; as Utopia) / DEFACE THE MUSIC (*6; as Utopia) / HEALING (*5) / SWING TO THE RIGHT (*4; as Utopia) / UTOPIA (*4; as Utopia) / THE EVER POPULAR TORTURED ARTIST EFFECT (*7) / OBLIVION (*4; as Utopia) / POV (*4; as Utopia) / A CAPPELLA (*4) / NEARLY HUMAN (*6) / SECOND WIND (*4) / REDUX '92: LIVE IN JAPAN (*4; as Utopia) / NO WORLD ORDER – LITE (*3) / THE INDIVIDUALIST (*5) / WITH A TWIST (*4) / ONE LONG YEAR (*5) / greatest compilation:- THE BEST OF TODD RUNDGREN "GO AHEAD, IGNORE ME." (*9)

NAZZ

TODD RUNDGREN – lead guitar, vocals, composer / **ROBERT 'Stewkey' ANTONI** (b.17 Nov'47, Rhode Island, N.Y.) – vocals, piano / **CARSTEN VAN OSTEN** (b.24 Sep'46, New Jersey) – bass, vocals / **THOM MOONEY** (b. 5 Jan'48, Pennsylvania) – drums

Screen Gems / Screen Gems

Sep 68. (7") *(SGC 219 001) <001>* **HELLO IT'S ME. / OPEN MY EYES** — 66

Apr 69. (lp) *(SGC 221 001) <SD 5001>* **NAZZ** — Oct68

– Open my eyes / See what you can be / Back of your mind / Hello it's me / Wildwood blues / If that's the way you feel / When I get my plane / The lemming song / Crowded / She's goin' down. *<US re-iss. Oct83 on 'Rhino'; 109> <Cd-iss.1990's; R2 70109>*

Apr 69. (7") *(SGC 219 002) <002>* **HELLO IT'S ME. / CROWDED** — –

May 69. (lp,red-lp) *<SD 5002>* **NAZZ NAZZ** — – 80

– Forget all about it / Not wrong long / Rain rider / Gonna cry today / Meridian Leeward / Under the ice / Hang on Paul / Kiddie boy / Featherbedding lover / Letters don't count / A beautiful song. *<US re-iss. Oct83 on 'Rhino'; RNLP 110> <cd-iss. 1990's; R2 70110>*

May 69. (7") *(SGC 219 003) <006>* **NOT WRONG LONG. / UNDER THE ICE**

Nov 70. (7") *<009>* **SOME PEOPLE. / MAGIC ME** — –

Dec 70. (lp,green-lp) *<SD 5003>* **NAZZ III** — –

– Some people / Only one winner / Kicks / It's not that easy / Old time lovemaking / Magic me / Loosen up / Take the hand / How can you call that beautiful / Plenty of lovin' / Christopher Colombus / You are my window. *<US re-iss. Nov83 on 'Rhino'; RNLP 111> <cd-iss. 1990's; 70111>*

— Had already disbanded early 1970, after completion of III'rd album.

RUNT

— was formed by **RUNDGREN** now on – lead vocals, guitar / **TONY SALES** – bass / **HUNT SALES** – drums

not iss. / Ampex

Nov 70. (7") *<31001>* **WE GOTTA GET YOU A WOMAN. / BABY LET'S SWING** — – 20

Dec 70. (lp) *<10105>* **RUNT** — –

– Broke down and busted / Believe in me / We gotta get you a woman / Who's that man / Once burned / Devil's bite / I'm in the cliche / There are no words / Baby let's swing / The last thing you said / Don't tie my hands / Birthday carol. *(UK-iss.Apr72 on 'Bearsville'; K 44505) <US re-iss. Oct87 on 'Rhino'; 70686> (cd-iss. May93 on 'Rhino-Bearsville'; 812270686-2)*

— **N.D.SMART** – drums repl. HUNT who later joined IGGY POP then TIN MACHINE

May 71. (7") *<31002>* **BE NICE TO ME. / BROKE DOWN AND BUSTED** — – 71

May 71. (lp) *<10116>* **THE BALLAD OF TODD RUNDGREN** — –

– Long flowing robe / The ballad / Bleeding / Wailing wall / The range war / Chain letter / A long time, a long way to go / Boat on the Charles / Be nice to me / Hope I'm around / Parole / Remember me. *(UK-iss.Apr72 on 'Bearsville'; K 45506) <US re-iss. Oct87 on 'Rhino'; 71109> (cd-iss. May93 on 'Rhino-Bearsville'; 812271109-2)*

Aug 71. (7") *<31004>* **A LONG TIME, A LONG WAY TO GO. / PAROLE** — – 92

TODD RUNDGREN

— now completely solo except for one side of the d-lp which was frequented by session people.

Bearsville / Bearsville

Mar 72. (d-lp) *(K 65501) <2066>* **SOMETHING / ANYTHING?** — 29

– I saw the light / It wouldn't have made any difference / Wolfman Jack / Cold morning light / It takes two to tango (this is for the girls) / Sweeter memories / (intro) Breathless / The night the carousel burned down / Saving grace / Marlene / Song of the Viking / I went to the mirror / Black Maria / One more day (one word) / Couldn't I just tell you / Torch song / Little red lights / Dust in the wind / Piss Aaron / Hello it's me / Some folks is even whiter than me / You left me sore / Slut. *<US re-iss. Nov87 on 'Rhino'; > (re-iss. Jul89 on 'Essential' d-lp/c/cd; ESD LP/MC/CD 007) (re-iss. Jun93 on 'Rhino-Bearsville'; 812271107-2)*

Mar 72. (7") *<0003>* **I SAW THE LIGHT. / BLACK MARIA** — – 16

Mar 72. (7") *(K 15502)* **I SAW THE LIGHT. / MARLENE** — –

Jul 72. (7") *<0007>* **COULDN'T I JUST TELL YOU. / WOLFMAN JACK** — – 93

May 73. (7"m) *(K 15506)* **I SAW THE LIGHT. / BLACK MARIA / LONG FLOWING ROBE** — 36 –

(re-iss. Nov76)

Jun 73. (lp) *(K 45513) <213>* **A WIZARD, A TRUE STAR** — 86

– International feel / Never never land / Tic tic tic it wear off / You need your head / Rock and roll pussy / Dogfight giggle / You don't have to camp around / Flamingo / Zen archer / Just another onionhead – Da da Dali / When the shit hits the fan – Sunset Blvd. / Le feel internacionale / Sometimes I don't know what to feel / Does anybody love you? / I'm so proud – Ooh ooh baby – La la means I love you – Cool jerk / Is it my name? / Just one victory. *(re-iss. Nov80 on 'Island'; IRSP 10) (re-iss. Apr89 on 'Castle' lp/c/cd; CLA LP/MC/CD 134) (re-iss. May93 on 'Rhino-Bearsville' cd; 812270864-2)*

Oct 73. (7") *(K 15509)* **WE GOTTA GET YOU A WOMAN. / COULDN'T I JUST TELL YOU** — –

Dec 73. (7") *(K 15513) <0009>* **HELLO IT'S ME. / COLD MORNING LIGHT** — Sep73 5

Dec 73. (7") *<0015>* **SOMETIMES I DON'T KNOW WHAT TO FEEL. / DOES ANYONE LOVE YOU?** — –

— He now used many musicians that were to appear as first UTOPIA incarnation

Mar 74. (d-lp) *(K 85501) <6952>* **TODD** — 54

– How about a little fanfare? / I think you know / The spark of life / An elpee's worth of toons / A dream goes on forever / Lord Chancelor's nightmare song / Drunken blue rooster / The last ride / Everybody's going to Heaven / King Kong reggae / Number one lowest common denominator / Useless begging / Sidewalk cafe / Izzat love / Heavy metal kids / In and out of Chakras we go / Don't you ever learn / Sons of 1984. *(re-iss. Dec89 on 'Castle' d-lp/c/cd; CLD LP/MC/CD 177) (re-iss. May93 on 'Rhino-Bearsville' cd; 812271108-2)*

May 74. (7") *(K 15515) <0020>* **A DREAM GOES ON FOREVER. / HEAVY METAL KIDS** — 69

— **TODD** formed UTOPIA with **MOODY KLINGMAN** – keyboards / **RALPH SHUCKETT** – bass / **JOHN SIEGLER** – bass, cello / **M.FROG LABAT** – synthesizers (TODD also released solo material)

Nov 74. (lp; by TODD RUNDGREN'S UTOPIA) *(K 55501) <6954>* **TODD RUNDGREN'S UTOPIA** — 34

– Utopia (theme) / Freak parade / Freedom fighter / The ikon. *(re-iss. cd May93 on 'Rhino-Bearsville'; 812270865-2)*

Feb 75. (7") *(K 15519) <0301>* **WOLFMAN JACK. / BREATHLESS** — 1974

Jun 75. (lp) *(K 55504) <6981>* **INITIATION** [ ] [86]
– Real man / Born to synthesize / The death of rock and roll / Eastern intrigue / Initiation / Fair warning / A treatise on cosmic fire: Intro-Prana, (ii) The fire of mind – or solar fire, (iii) The fire of spirit – or electric fire, (i) The internal fire – or fire by friction (Muladhara – The dance of Kundalini / Svadhishthana – Bam, bham, mam, yam, ram, lam, thank you mahm / Manipura – seat of fire / Anahata – the hals of air / Vishudda – sounds beyond ears / Anja – sights beyond eyes / Brahmarandhra – nirvana shakti) / Outro-Prana. *(cd-iss. May93 on 'Rhino-Bearsville'; 812270866-2)*

Sep 75. (7") *(K 15521) <0304>* **REAL MAN. / PRANA** [ ] [83]

—— trimmed slightly when LABAT departed.

Oct 75. (lp; as TODD RUNDGREN'S UTOPIA) *(K 55508) <6961>* **ANOTHER LIVE (live)** [ ] [66]
– Another life / The wheel / The seven rays / (intro) – Mister Triscuts / West Side Story theme / Something's coming / Just one victory / Heavy metal kids / Do ya / Just one victory. *(cd-iss. Aug93 on 'Rhino-Bearsville'; 812270867-2)*

Apr 76. (lp) *(K 55510) <6963>* **FAITHFUL** [ ] [54]
– Happenings ten years time ago / Good vibrations / Rain / Most likely you go your way and I'll go mine / If six was nine / Strawberry fields forever / Black and white / Love of the common man / When I pray / Cliche / The verb "to love" / Boogies (hamburger hell). *(cd-iss. Jun93 on 'Rhino-Bearsville'; 812270868-2)*

Jun 76. (7") *<0309>* **GOOD VIBRATIONS. / WHEN I PRAY** [–] [34]

Jun 76. (7") *(K 15524)* **LOVE OF THE COMMON MAN. / GOOD VIBRATIONS** [ ] [–]

Nov 76. (7") *<0310>* **LOVE OF THE COMMON MAN. / BLACK AND WHITE** [–] [ ]

UTOPIA

with **TODD** now completely changed line-up into **ROGER POWELL** – keyboards (from late '75) / **JOHN 'Willie' WILCOX** – drums / **KASIM SULTON** – bass

Jan 77. (lp) *(K 55514) <6965>* **RA** [27] [79]
– (overture) / Communion with the sun / Magic dragon theatre / Jealousy / Eternal love / Sunburst finish / Hiroshima / Singing and the glass guitar. *(cd-iss. May93 on 'Rhino-Bearsville'; 812270869-2)*

Feb 77. (7") *(K 15531) <0317>* **COMMUNION WITH THE SUN. / SUNBURST FINISH** [ ] [ ]

—— TODD played/produced 'BAT OUT OF HELL' album for MEAT LOAF, which included some UTOPIANS and was massive seller from 1978 onwards.

Sep 77. (lp) *(K 55517) <6970>* **OOPS! WRONG PLANET** [59] [73]
– Trapped / Windows / Love in action / Crazy lady blue / Back on the street / Marriage of Heaven and Hell / The martyr / Abandon city / Gangrene / My angel / Rape of the young / Love is the answer. *(cd-iss. Jun93 on 'Rhino-Bearsville'; 812270870-2)*

Oct 77. (7") *(K 15536) <0321>* **LOVE IS THE ANSWER. / THE MARRIAGE OF HEAVEN AND HELL** [ ] [ ]

TODD RUNDGREN

Apr 78. (lp) *(K 55521) <6981>* **HERMIT OF MINK HOLLOW** [42] [36]
– All the children sing / Can we still be friends / Hurting for you / Too far gone / Onomatopoeia / Determination / Bread / Bag lady / You cried wolf / Lucky guy / Out of control / Fade away. *(cd-iss. May93 on 'Rhino-Bearsville'; 812270784-2)*

May 78. (7") *(K 15539) <0324>* **CAN WE STILL BE FRIENDS. / DETERMINATION** [ ] [29]
<some US copies had 'OUT OF CONTROL' on B-side>

Jul 78. (7") *<0330>* **YOU CRIED WOLF. / ONOMATOPOEIA** [–] [ ]

Nov 78. (7") *(K 15543)* **ALL THE CHILDREN SING. / BAG LADY** [ ] [–]

Dec 78. (d-lp) *(K 65511) <6986>* **BACK TO THE BARS (live)** [ ] [75]
– Real man / Love of the common man / The verb "to love" / Love in action / A dream goes on forever / Sometimes I just don't know what to think / The range war / Black and white / The last ride / Cliche / Don't you ever learn / Never never land / Black Maria / Zen archer / Medley: I'm so proud – Ooh ooh baby – La la means I love you / I saw the light / It wouldn't have made any difference / Eastern intrigue / Initiation / Couldn't I just tell you / Hello it's me. *(cd-iss. Jun93 on 'Rhino-Bearsville'; 812271109-2)*

Feb 79. (7") *<0335>* **IT WOULDN'T HAVE MADE ANY DIFFERENCE. / DON'T YOU EVER LEARN** [–] [ ]

UTOPIA

Island Bearsville

Jan 80. (lp/c) *(ILPS/ZCI 9602) <6991>* **ADVENTURES IN UTOPIA** [57] [32]
– The road to Utopia / You make me crazy / Second nature / Set me free / Caravan / Last of the new wave riders / Shot in the dark / The very last time / Love alone / Rock love. *<(cd-iss. May93 on 'Rhino'; 8122 70872-2)>*

Mar 80. (7") *(WIP 6581) <49180>* **SET ME FREE. / UMBRELLA MAN** [ ] [27]

May 80. (7") *<49247>* **THE VERY LAST TIME. / LOVE ALONE** [–] [76]

Oct 80. (lp) *(ILPS 9642) <3487>* **DEFACE THE MUSIC** [ ] [65]
– I just want to touch you / Crystal ball / Where does the world go to hide / Silly boy / Alone / That's not right / Take it home / Hoi poloi / Life goes on / Feel too good / Always late / All smiles / Everybody else is wrong. *(cd-iss. May93 on 'Rhino-Bearsville'; 812270873-2)*

Oct 80. (7") *<49545>* **SECOND NATURE. / YOU MAKE ME CRAZY** [–] [ ]

Nov 80. (7"ep) *(IEP 12)* **I JUST WANT TO TOUCH YOU EP** [ ] [–]
– I just want to touch you / Silly boy / Life goes on / All smiles.

Dec 80. (7") *<49579>* **I JUST WANT TO TOUCH YOU. / ALWAYS LATE** [–] [ ]

TODD RUNDGREN

Feb 81. (7") *<49696>* **TIME HEALS. / TINY DEMONS** [–] [ ]

Feb 81. (lp) *(ILPS 9567) <3522>* **HEALING** [ ] [48]
– Healer / Pulse / Flesh / Golden goose / Compassion / Shine / Healing (part 1, 2 & 3). *(free-7"ltd.w.a.)* – TIME HEALS. / TINY DEMONS *(re-iss. Dec81 on 'Avatar' lp/c; AALP/BHS 3522) (cd-iss. May93 on 'Rhino-Bearsville'; 812270874-2)*

Jan 82. (7") *<49771>* **COMPASSION. / HEALING** [–] [ ]

UTOPIA

Avatar Bearsville

Mar 82. (lp) *(BRK <3666>)* **SWING TO THE RIGHT** [ ] [ ]
– Swing to the right / Lysistrata / The up / Junk rock (million monkeys) / Shinola / For the love of money / Last dollar on Earth / Fahrenheit 451 / Only human / One world. *(cd-iss. Mar93 on 'Rhino-Bearsville'; 812270785-2)*

Apr 82. (7") *<50062>* **ONE WORLD. / SPECIAL INTEREST** [–] [ ]

May 82. (7") *(AAA 126)* **ONE WORLD. / JUNK ROCK (MILLION MONKEYS)** [ ] [–]

Jun 82. (7") *<29947>* **LYSISTRATA / JUNK ROCK (MILLION MONKEYS)** [–] [ ]

Nov 82. (7"ep) *(AVAB 1)* **TIME HEALS / TINY DEMONS / I SAW THE LIGHT / CAN WE STILL BE FRIENDS** [ ] [–]

Epic Network

Nov 82. (7") *(EPCA 2972) <69859>* **FEET DON'T FAIL ME NOW. / FORGOTTEN BUT NOT GONE** [ ] [82]

Nov 82. (lp/c) *(EPC/40 25207) <60183>* **UTOPIA** [ ] [84]
– Libertine / Bad little actress / Feet don't fail me now / Neck on up / Say yeah / Call it what you will / I'm looking at you but I'm talking to myself / Hammer in the heart / Burn three times / There goes my inspiration. *(w/ free UK+US m-lp)* – Princess of the universe / Infrared and ultraviolet / Forgotten but not gone / Private Heaven / Chapter and verse. *(cd-iss. Aug93 on 'Rhino-Bearsville'; 812270713-2)*

Jan 83. (7") *<69859>* **HAMMER IN MY HEART. / I'M LOOKING AT YOU BUT I'M TALKING TO MYSELF** [–] [ ]

TODD RUNDGREN

Lambourghini Bearsville

Mar 83. (7") *<29686>* **BANG THE DRUM ALL DAY. / CHANT** [–] [63]

Aug 83. (lp/c) *(LMGLP/ZCLMG 2000) <23732>* **THE EVER POPULAR TORTURED ARTIST EFFECT** [ ] Feb83 [66]
– Hideaway / Influenza / Don't hurt yourself / There goes my baybay / Tin soldier / Emperor of the highway / Bang the drum all day / Drive / Chant. *(cd-iss. Jun93 on 'Rhino-Bearsville'; 812270876-2)*

Aug 83. (7") *(LMG 1)* **BANG THE DRUM ALL DAY. / DRIVE** [ ] [–]

Sep 83. (7") *<29759>* **HIDEAWAY. / EMPEROR OF THE HIGHWAY** [–] [ ]

UTOPIA

W.E.A. Passport

Apr 84. (lp/c) *(WX 4/+C) <6029>* **OBLIVION** [ ] [74]
– Itch in my brain / Love with a thinker / Bring me my longbow / If I didn't try / Too much water / Maybe I could change / Crybaby / Welcome to my revolution / Winston Smith takes it on the jaw / I will wait.

May 84. (7") *(YZ 5) <7923>* **CRYBABY. / WINSTON SMITH TAKES IT ON THE JAW** [ ] [ ]

Jul 84. (7") *(YZ 11)* **LOVE WITH A THINKER. / WELCOME TO MY REVOLUTION** [ ] [–]

Food For Thought Passport

Jun 85. (lp/c) *(GRUB 5) <6044>* **POV** [ ] May 85 [ ]
– Play this game / Style / Stand for something / Secret society / Zen machine / Mated / Wildlife / Mimi gets mad / Mystified / More light.

Jun 85. (7") *(YUM 107)* **MATED. / MAN OF ACTION** [ ] [–]

Jun 85. (7") *<7927>* **MATED. / STAND FOR SOMETHING** [–] [ ]

—— (Oct85) TODD is credited on duet with BONNIE TYLER on single 'LOVING YOU IS A DIRTY JOB'.

TODD RUNDGREN

Warners Warners

Oct 85. (7") *(W 8852) <28821>* **SOMETHING TO FALL BACK ON. / LOCKJAW** [ ] [ ]
(12"+=) *(WT 8862)* – ('A'dance mix).

Nov 85. (lp/c) *(925128-1/-4) <25128>* **A CAPPELLA** [ ] [ ]
– Blue Orpheus / Johnee Jingo / Pretending to care / Hodja / Lost horizon / Something to fall back on / Miracle in the bazaar / Lockjaw / Honest work / Mighty love.

—— Early in 1986, UTOPIA split and ROGER POWELL went solo. TODD returned to solo work in 1988 augmented by **ROSS VALORY** – bass (ex-JOURNEY) / **PRAIRIE PRINCE** – drums (ex-TUBES) (same label)

May 89. (lp/c/cd) *(K 92588-1/-4/-2) <25881>* **NEARLY HUMAN** [ ] [ ]
– The want of a nail / The waiting game / Parallel lines / Can't stop running / Unloved children / Fidelity / Feel it / Hawking / I love my life. *(cd+=)* – Two little Hitlers.

May 89. (7") *<22868>* **PARALLEL LINES. / I LOVE MY LIFE** [–] [ ]

Feb 91. (cd/c/lp) *(7599-26478-2/-4/-1) <26478>* **SECOND WIND** [ ] [ ]
– Change myself / Love science / Who's sorry now / The smell of money / If I have to be alone / Love in disguise / Kindness / Public servant / Goya's eyes / Second wind.

Jun 93. (cd/c) *<(8122-71185-2/-4)>* **REDUX '92: LIVE IN JAPAN (Utopia live)** [ ] [ ]
– Fix your gaze / Zen machine / Trapped / Princess of the universe / Abandon city / Hammer in my heart / Swing to the right / Ikon / Hiroshima / Back on the street / Only human / Love in action / Caravan / Last of the new wave riders / One world / Love is the answer.

Food For Thought Rhino

Sep 94. (d-cd/d-c) *(CD/C+/GRUB 30) <R2/R4 71266>* **NO WORLD ORDER / LITE** [ ] Jul93 [ ]
– Worldwide epiphany / No world order / Worldwide epiphany / Day job / Property / Fascist Christ / Love thing / Time stood still / Proactivity / No world order / World epiphany / Time stood still / Love thing / Time stood still / World made flesh / Fever broke. *(d-cd+=)* – (10 different versions of above).

not iss. Pony Canyon

1995. (cd; as TR-i) *<00720>* **THE INDIVIDUALIST** [–] [ ]
– Tables will turn / If not now, when? / Family values / The ultimate crime / Espresso (all jacked up) / The individualist / Cast the first stone / Beloved infidel / Temporary sanity / Woman's world.

E.M.I. E.M.I.

Oct 97. (cd) *<(859866-2)>* **WITH A TWIST** (re-workings in acoustic/lounge style) [ ] [ ]
– I saw the light / Influenza / Can we still be friends / Mated / It wouldn't have made any difference / Love is the answer / Fidelity / Never neverland / Hello it's me / I want you / The dream goes on forever.

Artemis Artemis

Jun 00. (cd) *<(69967 75104-2)>* **ONE LONG YEAR** [ ] [ ]
– I hate frickin I.S.P. / Buffalo grass / Jerk / Bang on the ukulele daily / Where does the time go? / Love of the common man / Mary and the holy ghost (instrumental) / Yer fast (and I like it) / Hit me like a train / The surf talks.

– compilations, etc. –

1984. (lp; by NAZZ) *Rhino; <RNLP 116>* **THE BEST OF NAZZ** [–] [ ]

Nov 87. (lp/c/cd; UTOPIA) *Passport; <PB/+C/CD 6053>* **TRIVIA** [–] [ ]

Feb 88. (d-lp/c/cd; by TODD RUNDGREN) *Raw Power; (RAW LP/TC/CD 035)* **ANTHOLOGY** [ ] 1989 [ ]
– Can we still be friends / All the children sing / Too far gone / Sweet memories / It wouldn't have made any difference / Hello it's me / I saw the light / Just one victory / Love of the common man / The verb 'to love' / Sometimes I don't know what to feel / Couldn't I just tell you / Tiny demons / Initiation / Real man / A long time a long way to go / Long flowing robe / Compassion / We gotta get you a woman / A dream goes on forever / The last ride / Don't you ever learn / Bang the drum all day / Zen archer.

Mar 88. (d-lp/d-c/d-cd; by RUNT /+/ TODD RUNDGREN) *That's Original; (TFO LP/MC/CD 3)* **RUNT / HERMIT OF MINK HOLLOW** [ ] [–]

Mar 88. (d-lp/d-c/d-cd; by UTOPIA) *That's Original; (TFO LP/MC/CD 9)* **OOPS! SORRY WRONG PLANET / ADVENTURES IN UTOPIA** [ ] [–]

Jun 88. (d-lp/d-c/d-cd; by UTOPIA) *Castle; (CCS LP/MC/CD 181)* **THE UTOPIA COLLECTION** [ ] [–]
– Where does the world go to hide / Freedom fighters / All smiles / Lysistrata / Always late / Love in action / Rock love / Set me free / The seven rays / Traped / Swing to the right / One world / Heavy metal kids / The very last time / Crazy lady blue / Feel too good / Love alone / Love is the answer.

Sep 88. (cd-ep) *Special Edition; (CD 3-6)* **BANG THE DRUM ALL DAY / I SAW THE LIGHT / CAN WE STILL BE FRIENDS / ALL THE CHILDREN SING** [ ] [–]

Oct 88. (7") *Old Gold; (OG)* **I SAW THE LIGHT. / (other artist)** [ ] [–]

1989. (d-lp; by TODD RUNDGREN) *Rhino; <R1 71491>* **ANTHOLOGY (1968-1985)** [–] [ ]
(UK-iss.d-cd Aug93 on 'Rhino-Bearsville';)

Apr 92. (cd) *Rhino; <R2>* **AN ELPEE'S WORTH OF PRODUCTIONS** (various) [ ] [–]

May 95. (cd; by UTOPIA) *Rhino; (8122 70892-2)* **ANTHOLOGY** [ ] [ ]

Jul 96. (cd; as UTOPIA) *Rhino; (8122 72287-2)* **THE PASSPORT COLLECTION** [ ] [ ]

Apr 98. (cd) *Canyon; (PCCY 01121)* **UP AGAINST IT** [ ] [ ]

RUN-D.M.C.

Formed: Hollis, New York, USA . . . 1982 by JOE SIMMONS (aka RUN) and MC D. (aka DARRYL McDANIELS) along with DJ JAM-MASTER JAY (aka JASON MIZEL) These schoolboy friends had persuaded JOE's brother, RUSSELL (owner of 'Rush' productions and future co-chairman of the seminal 'Def Jam' label) to let them make a record, the result being the seminal 1983 single, 'IT'S LIKE THAT' / 'SUCKER M.C.'S'. Oft quoted as the record which kickstarted modern hip-hop, 'SUCKER M.C.'S' substituted the conventional live backing band of the day for stripped down, pulverising drum machine beats. RUN-D.M.C. also had attitude aplenty, their leather-clad, sneaker-obsessed B-Boy image more accurately reflecting street culture and what was going down in the underground clubs. With the help of RUSSELL, they signed to 'Profile', releasing their eponymous debut the following year. Underscoring their uncompromising vision, the record introduced the group's pioneering marriage of metal and rap on the stinging 'ROCK BOX', subsequently going gold. 1985 saw the group make an appearance in the film, 'Krush Groove' (based on the life of RUSSELL) alongside the likes of KURTIS BLOW and The BEASTIE BOYS as well as releasing a follow-up album, 'KING OF ROCK' (1985), taking their rock/rap hybrid to new extremes. But it was 'RAISING HELL' (1986) which really put RUN-D.M.C. on the map, their genius collaborative effort with AEROSMITH (then in a career trough) on the latter's 'WALK THIS WAY' making them chart stars (Top 5 UK, Top 10 US). From the style frenzy of 'MY ADIDAS' to the vocal wordplay of 'PETER PIPER' and 'IT'S TRICKY' the record led the mid-80's hip hop zeitgeist, becoming the first rap album to go platinum. The BEASTIE BOYS' 1986 debut, 'License To Ill' followed suit, a multi-million seller which topped the US chart and an anarchic joint tour with the BEASTIE's further consolidated RUN-D.M.C.'s reputation as the kings of rap. A year is a long time in hip hop, and by the release of 'TOUGHER THAN LEATHER' (1988), hard hitting young upstarts like PUBLIC ENEMY were crossing over to the lucrative white audience with a vengeance. Although tracks like 'RUN'S HOUSE' and 'BEATS TO THE RHYME' stood up among the best of their earlier work, the record lacked the fire of old, while a film of the same name failed miserably at the box office. 'BACK FROM HELL' (1990) barely scraped into the US charts and though the record had its moments, it failed to remedy the group's critical and commercial decline. A difficult period for them, SIMMONS and McDANIELS had undergone various personal problems, the latter suffering from alcoholism while SIMMONS was accused of rape. They eventually re-emerged three years later on 'DOWN WITH THE KING' (1993), its title a reference to their recent religious conversion. With contributions from the cream of the rap fraternity, the album was a reasonable success, their first foray into the US Top 10 in five years. However, along with the likes of the once mighty JUNGLE BROTHERS, RAKIM etc., RUN-D.M.C. have failed to re-invent themselves (like old buddies The BEASTIE BOYS), their sound now somewhat dated in a hip hop scene which thrives on constant flux. Although they did finally re-emerge in the new millennium, 'CROWN ROYAL' (2001; although it was scheduled for '99) sounded as tired as their image looked. One time grandmasters of the rock crossover track, RUN-DMC did that legacy few favours on the featured collaborations with LIMP BIZKIT ('THEM GIRLS') and KID ROCK ('THE SCHOOL OF OLD') while even the contributions of NAS and METHOD MAN failed to inject any passion.

Album rating: RUN-D.M.C. (*8) / KING OF ROCK (*7) / RAISING HELL (*8) / TOUGHER THAN LEATHER (*6) / BACK FROM HELL (*6) / RUN-D.M.C.'S GREATEST HITS TOGETHER FOREVER 1983-1991 compilation (*8) / DOWN WITH THE KING (*6) / CROWN ROYAL (*4) / GREATEST HITS compilation (*8)

RUN (b. JOSEPH SIMMONS, 14 Nov'64) – vocals / **D.M.C.** (b. DARRYL McDANIELS, 31 May'64) – vocals / **JAM-MASTER JAY** (b. JASON MIZELL, 21 Jan'65) – turntables, programming

4th & Broad — Profile

1983. (7") **IT'S LIKE THAT. / SUCKER M.C.'s** [–] [ ]

Jun 84. (lp) *(1202>* **RUN-D.M.C.** [–] [53]
– Hard times / Rock box / Jam-master Jay / Hollis Crew (krush-groove 2) / Sucker M.C.'s (krush-groove 1) / It's like that / Wake up / 30 days / Jay's game. *(UK-iss.May85 lp/c; BR LP/CA 506) (cd-iss. 1990 on 'London'; 846 561-2) (re-iss. Apr91 on 'Profile' cd/c/lp; FILE CD/CT/R 202) (cd re-iss. Sep99 on 'Arista'; 07822 16406-2)*

Jun 84. (7") *(BRW 8)* **ROCK BOX. / ('A'vocal dub)** [ ] [ ]
(12"+=) *(12BRW 8)* – ('A'dub version).

Sep 84. (7") **30 DAYS. / (instrumental)** [–] [ ]

Jan 85. (7") **HOLLIS CREW. / (instrumental)** [–] [ ]

Feb 85. (lp/c)(pic-lp) *(BR LP/CA 504)(PBRLP 504) <1205>*
KING OF ROCK [ ] [52]
– Rock the house / King of rock / You talk too much / Jam-master jammin' / Roots, rap, reggae / Can you rock it like this / You're blind / It's not funny / Daryll and Joe (krush-groove 3). *(cd-iss. May88; BRCD 504) (re-iss. Apr91 on 'Profile' cd/c; FILE CD/CT 205) (cd re-iss. Sep99 on 'Arista'; 07822 16407-2)*

Mar 85. (7") *(BRW 21)* **KING OF ROCK. / JAM MASTER JAMMIN'** [ ] [ ]
(12"+=) *(12BRW 21)* – You talk too much.

Mar 86. (7") *(BRW 25)* **YOU TALK TOO MUCH. / DARRYL AND JOE (KRUSH-GROOVE 3)** [ ] [ ]
(12"+=) *(12BRW 25)* – ('A'instrumental) / Sucker M.C.'s (krush-groove 1).

Apr 86. (7") **JAM-MASTER JAMMIN'. / (part 2)** [–] [ ]

May 86. (7") **CAN YOU ROCK IT LIKE THIS. / TOGETHER FOREVER** [–] [ ]

London — Profile

Jun 86. (7") *(LON 101)* **MY ADIDAS. / PETER PIPER** [62] [ ]
(12"+=) *(LONX 101)* – ('A'instrumental).

Jul 86. (lp/c)(cd) *(LON LP/C 21)(828018-2) <1217>* **RAISING HELL** [41] Jun86 [3]
– Peter Piper / It's tricky / My Adidas / Walk this way / Is it live / Perfection / Hit it run / Raising hell / You be illin' / Dumb girl / Son of Byford / Proud to be black. *(cd re-iss. Sep99 on 'Arista'; 07822 16408-2) (lp re-iss. Jun01 on 'Simply Vinyl'; SVLP 347)*

Jul 86. (7") *<5112>* **WALK THIS WAY. / KING OF ROCK** [–] [4]

Aug 86. (7"; RUN-D.M.C. featuring AEROSMITH) *(LON 104)*
WALK THIS WAY. / ('A'instrumental) [8] [–]
(12"+=) *(LONX 104)* – My Adidas.

Feb 87. (7") *(LON 118) <5119>* **YOU BE ILLIN'. / HIT IT RUN** [42] Oct86 [29]
(12"+=) *(LONX 118)* – ('A'instrumental).

May 87. (7") *(LON 130) <5131>* **IT'S TRICKY. / PROUD TO BE BLACK** [16] Feb87 [57]
(12"+=) *(LONX 130)* – ('A'club tempo mix) / ('A'-Scratchappella) / ('A'reprise).

Sep 87. (7") *(LON 154)* **PETER PIPER. / MY ADIDAS** [ ] [–]
(12"+=) *(LONX 154)* – Walk this way / King of rock.

Nov 87. (7"/7"g-f) *(LON/+G 163)* **XMAS IN HOLLIS. / PETER PIPER** [56] [–]
(12"+=) *(LONX 163)* – My Adidas / Walk this way / King of rock.

Apr 88. (7"/7"pic-d) *(LON/+P 177)* **RUN'S HOUSE. / BEATS TO THE RHYME** [37] [ ]
(12"+=/cd-s+=) *(LON X/CD 177)* – ('A'&'B'instrumental).

Jun 88. (lp/c)(cd) *(LON LP/C 38)(828070-2) <1265>*
TOUGHER THAN LEATHER [13] May88 [9]
– Run's house / Mary, Mary / They call us Run DMC / Beats to the rhyme / Radio station / Papa crazy / Tougher than leather / I'm not going out like that / How d'ya do it Dee? / Miss Elaine / Soul to rock and roll / Ragtime. *(re-iss. Nov92 on 'Profile' cd/c; PCD/PCT 1265) (cd re-iss. Sep99 on 'Arista'; 07822 16409-2)*

Jul 88. (7") *<5211>* **MARY, MARY. / ROCK BOX** [–] [75]

Aug 88. (7"/7"s) *(LON/+S 191)* **MARY, MARY. / RAISING HELL** [ ] [–]
(12"+=) *(LONX 191)* – ('A'instrumental).

M.C.A. — Profile

Aug 89. (7"/c-s) *(MCA/+C 1360) <PROF 262>*
GHOSTBUSTERS THEME II. / ('A'instrumental) [65] [ ]
(12"+=/cd-s+=) *(MCA T/CD 1360) <PRO FT/CD 262>* – Pause.

Profile — Profile

Nov 90. (7"/c-s) *<(PROF/+C 315)>* **WHAT'S IT ALL ABOUT. / THE AVE** [48] [ ]
(12"+=) *<(PROFT 315)>* – ('A'&'B'instrumentals).
(cd-s+=) *<(PROCD 315)>* – ('A'instrumental) / ('A'version).

Nov 90. (cd/c/lp) *<(FILE CD/CT/R 1401)>* **BACK FROM HELL** [ ] [81]
– Back from hell / Bob your head / Livin' in the city / Sucker DJs / What's it all about / Word is born / Pause / Not just another groove / P upon a tree / Party time / Naughty / Kick the frama lama lama / Groove to the sound / Don't stop. *(cd re-iss. Sep99 on 'Arista'; 07822 16410-2)*

Mar 91. (7"/c-s) **FACES. / BACK FROM HELL (remix)** [ ] [ ]
(12"+=) – ('A'radio mix) / ('A'instrumental).
(cd-s) – (2 'A'versions see above) / (2 'B'versions).
(12") – (4 'A'mixes – 3 above).

Nov 91. (cd/c/lp) *<(FILE CD/CT/R 1419)>* **RUN DMC GREATEST HITS TOGETHER FOREVER 1983-1991** (compilation) [ ] [ ]
– Sucker M.C.'s (krush groove 1) / Walk this way / Together forever (krush groove 4) (live at Hollis Park '84) / King of rock / Run's house / It's tricky / Pause / You be illin' / My Adidas / Here we go (live at The Funhouse) / Rock box / What's it all about / Hard times / Beats to the rhyme / Jam-master Jay / Peter Piper / It's like that / Christmas in Hollis.

Mar 93. (12"/cd-s) *(PROF T/CD 39) <5391>* **DOWN WITH THE KING. / ('A'instrumental)** [69] [21]
(re-iss. Nov93 UK; same)

May 93. (cd/c/lp) *<(FILE CD/CT/R 1440)>* **DOWN WITH THE KING** [44] [7]
– Down with the king / C'mon everybody / Can I get it to yo / Hit 'em hard / To the maker / In the head / Ooh, what ya gonna do / Big Willie / Three little Indians / In the house / Kick it (can I get a witness) / Get open / What's next / Wreck shop / For ten years. *(cd re-iss. Sep99 on 'Arista'; 07822 16412-2)*

Jul 93. (c-s)(12") *(5400)(7400)* **OOH, WHATCHA GONNA DO. / ('A'mixes)** [ ] [–]

Apr 94. (12")(cd-s) *(5405)(7405)* **WHAT'S NEXT. / CAN I GET IT, YO / PIED PIPER** [ ] [–]

Sep 97. (cd-s; RUN-DMC VS JASON NEVINS) *Smile; (SM 9065-2)* **IT'S LIKE THAT (mixes)** [ ] [ ]

Feb 98. (12"/cd-s; RUN-DMC VS JASON NEVINS) *Columbia; <665293-6/-2>* **IT'S LIKE THAT (mixes)** [63] [ ]

(yes! the above version actually hit the UK charts! before it gained another official release)

Mar 98. (10"/c-s/12"/cd-s; RUN-DMC VS JASON NEVINS) *Smile (SM 9065/+4/1/2)* **IT'S LIKE THAT (mixes)** [1] [ ]

May 98. (cd) *(FILECD 474)* **TOGETHER FOREVER – GREATEST HITS 1983-1998** (compilation) [31] [–]

– (same as earlier compilation + add recent hit remixes).

Arista Arista

Mar 01. (7") *(74321 84805-7)* **ROCK SHOW. / WALK THIS WAY (with AEROSMITH)** [ ] [–]

(cd-s+=) *(74321 84805-2)* – Peter Piper.

Apr 01. (cd/c/d-lp) *(74321 84063-2/-4/-1) <16400>* **CROWN ROYAL** [ ] [37]

– It's over (with JERMAINE DUPREE) / Queens day (with NAS & The PRODIGY) / Crown royal / Them girls (with FRED DURST) / The school of old (with KID ROCK) / Take the money and run (with EVERLAST) / Rock show (with STEPHAN JENKINS) / Here we go 2001 (with SUGAR RAY) / Ahhh (with CHRIS DAVIS) / Let's stay together (together forever) (with JAGGED EDGE) / Ay papi (with FAT JOE) / Simmons incorporated (with METHOD MAN).

—— disbanded November 2002

Apr 03. (12"/cd-s; as RUN DMC featuring JACKNIFE LEE) *(82876 51371-1/-2)* **IT'S TRICKY 2003 (mixes)** [20] [–]

Apr 03. (cd) *(74321 98060-2)* **GREATEST HITS** (compilation) [15] [–]

– It's like that (feat. JASON NEVINS) / Walk this way (feat. AEROSMITH) / Sucker MC's / My Adidas / King of rock / It's tricky / Can you rock it like this / You be illin' / Rock box / Run's house / Peter Piper / Bounce / Beats to the rhyme / Jam Master Jay / Hard times / Down with the king / Mary Mary / What's it all about / It's tricky 2003 (feat. JACKNIFE LEE).

– others, etc. –

Sep 86. (7") *4th & Broadway; (BRW 56)* **KING OF ROCK. / ROCK BOX (vocal)** [ ] [–]

(12"+=) *(12BRW 56)* – Jam master Jay.

(12"+=) *(12BRWX 56)* – ('A'-Cut-up version) / Jay's game / Rock box.

Nov 95. (10x12"box) *Profile; (1004)* **12" SINGLES BOX SET** [ ] [–]

Mar 98. (12"; RUN-DMC VS JASON NEVINS) *Time; (TIME 094)* **IT'S LIKE THAT (mixes)** [ ] [–]

May 98. (12"; RUN-DMC VS JASON NEVINS) *Epidrome; (EPD 66665698)* **IT'S TRICKY (mixes)** [ ] [ ]

Sep 02. (cd) *Arista; <10607>* **GREATEST HITS** (diff. to UK) [–] [ ]

RUSH

Formed: Toronto, Canada . . . 1969 by ALEX LIFESON, GEDDY LEE and JOHN RUTSEY. Initially a hard-rock power outfit in the classic British mould of CREAM and LED ZEPPELIN, they toured local bars and clubs, culminating in a hometown support slot with The NEW YORK DOLLS. Immediately prior to this (1973), RUSH formed their own label, 'Moon', issuing a cover of Buddy Holly's 'NOT FADE AWAY' as their debut 45. An eponymous debut followed in early '74 and was soon picked up by DJ, Donna Halper, who sent a copy to Cliff Burnstein at 'Mercury' records. The company signed RUSH for a 6-figure sum, re-mixing (courtesy of Terry 'Broon' Brown) and re-releasing the record to minor US success (bubbled under the Top 100). Although a tentative start, GEDDY's helium-laced shrill was employed to stunning effect on tracks such as 'WORKING MAN', 'FINDING MY WAY' and 'WHAT YOU'RE DOING'. However, with drummer NEIL PEART replacing RUTSEY, RUSH began to develop the unique style which would characterise their classic 70's work. As well as being a consummate sticksman, PEART masterminded the band's lyrical flights of fantasy, beginning with 'FLY BY NIGHT' (1975). With the conceptually similar YES still world-beating favourites, RUSH found it difficult to progress commercially. Creatively however, the trio attempted to wrestle the symphonic-rock crown from their transatlantic neighbours with such mystical, grandiose fare as 'BY-TOR AND THE SNOW DOG'. Later the same year, they released the under par 'CARESS OF STEEL', which featured the self-indulgently lengthy 'FOUNTAIN OF LAMNETH'. This stage of RUSH's career reached its zenith in 1976 with the concept album, '2112', based on the work of novelist and philosopher Ayn Rand. Boasting a spectacular side-long 20-minute title track/overture, this feted prog-rock/sci-fi classic gave RUSH their long-awaited breakthrough, the record almost achieving a US Top 60 placing. In the course of the previous three years, the band's fanbase had swelled considerably, enabling them to get away with releasing a live double set, 'ALL THE WORLD'S A STAGE'. Featuring electrifying renditions of RUSH's most exquisite material to date, the album was hailed as an instant classic, its Top 40 success in the States leading to massive import sales in Europe. This persuaded the band to bring their live show to Britain/Europe, their wildly enthusiastic reception encouraging them to stay on in Wales and record 'A FAREWELL TO KINGS'. Not surprisingly, the album made the UK (& US) Top 40, its success boosted by a UK Top 40 hit/EP, 'CLOSER TO THE HEART' early the following year. 1978's 'HEMISPHERES' set was the last to feature PEART's trademark epics, the album consolidating the band's growing UK support, while their native Canada lavished upon them the title, 'Ambassadors Of Music'. While many bands of their ilk floundered critically, RUSH began the 80's on a high note, scoring a rare UK Top 20 hit single with 'SPIRIT OF RADIO'. Taken from their million-selling 'PERMANENT WAVES' opus, the track was characteristic of the shorter, leaner sound that RUSH would pursue throughout the coming decade. Not escaping the increasing technological influence of 80's music, the band adopted a more keyboard-orientated approach on albums such as 'MOVING PICTURES' (1981), 'SIGNALS' (1982), 'GRACE UNDER PRESSURE' (1984) and 'POWER WINDOWS' (1985). Finally parting company with their longstanding producer, TERRY BROWN, they further refined their sound on the 1987 album, 'HOLD YOUR FIRE', which spawned a near UK Top 40 single, 'TIME STAND STILL' (credited AIMEE MANN of 'TIL TUESDAY). After the compulsory live set, 'A SHOW OF HANDS', the band opted for a fresh start with 'Atlantic', 'PRESTO' (1989) being the first fruits of this new alliance. Incredibly, despite regular critical derision from the trendier sections of the music press, RUSH went on to even greater success in the 90's, both 'ROLL THE BONES' (1991) and 'COUNTERPARTS' (1993) making the US Top 5 (now only Top 30 in Britain!). Certainly, PRIMUS' well-documented admiration has done the band no harm, LIFESON even bringing in the latter band's LES CLAYPOOL for a guest spot on his ill-advised VICTOR project. The same year (1996), RUSH released their umpteenth set, 'TEST FOR ECHO', the band looking good for their 30th anniversary just prior to the millennium. Of late (November 2000 to be exact), GEDDY LEE has become a solo artist, releasing his debut solo album 'MY FAVOURITE HEADACHE' to lukewarm reviews. Despite a traumatic time for PEART in his personal life, losing both his wife and daughter within a year of each other, RUSH re-emerged in 2002 with 'VAPOR TRAILS'. Solid and thoughtful, it proved the Canadians were still relevant in the new millennium even if they were long past their 30th anniversary. With 'RUSH IN RIO' (2003), moreover, they not only proved they could still push boundaries on stage, they also proved that there's still a huge, wildly appreciative audience for their work. PEART especially, can be heard going for broke here, both feeding on, and thriving off, the kind of energy that perhaps can only be generated by the exuberance of a Latin audience. • **Trivia:** Early in 1982, GEDDY guested for BOB & DOUG McKENZIE (aka Rick Moranis & Dave Thomas) on their US Top 20 single 'Take Off'.

Album rating: RUSH (*6) / FLY BY NIGHT (*6) / CARESS OF STEEL (*5) / 2112 (*8) / ALL THE WORLD'S A STAGE (*8) / A FAREWELL TO KINGS (*7) / HEMISPHERES (*6) / PERMANENT WAVES (*6) / MOVING PICTURES (*7) / EXIT . . . STAGE LEFT (*5) / SIGNALS (*6) / GRACE UNDER PRESSURE (*5) / POWER WINDOWS (*5) / HOLD YOUR FIRE (*5) / A SHOW OF HANDS (*5) / PRESTO (*5) / CHRONICLES compilation (*7) / ROLL THE BONES (*5) / COUNTERPARTS (*4) / TEST FOR ECHO (*5) / DIFFERENT STAGES live compilation (*5) / VAPOR TRAILS (*5) / RUSH IN RIO (*7) / Alex Lifeson: VICTOR (*3) / Geddy Lee: MY FAVOURITE HEADACHE (*5)

GEDDY LEE (b. GARY LEE WEINRIB, 29 Jul'53, Willowdale, Toronto, Canada) – vocals, bass, keyboards / **ALEX LIFESON** (b. ALEX ZIVOJINOVICH, 27 Aug'53, Surnie, British Columbia, Canada) – lead guitar / **JOHN RUTSEY** – drums

not iss. Moon

1973. (7") **NOT FADE AWAY. / YOU CAN'T FIGHT IT** [–] [ ]

Mercury Mercury

Aug 74. (7") *<73623>* **FINDING MY WAY. /** [–] [ ]

Feb 75. (lp) *(9100 011) <1011>* **RUSH** [ ] Jul74 [ ]
– Finding my way / Need some love / Take a friend / Here again / What you're doing / In the mood / Before and after / Working man. *(c-iss.Apr82; 7142 365) (re-iss. Jun83 lp/c; PRICE/PRIMC 18) (cd-iss. Apr87; 822 541-2)*

Feb 75. (7") *<73647>* **WHAT YOU'RE DOING. / IN THE MOOD** [–] [ ]

—— (Autumn '74) **NEIL PEART** (b.12 Sep'52, Hamilton, Ontario, Canada) – drums, vocals, lyrics repl. RUTSEY

Apr 75. (lp) *(9100 013) <1023>* **FLY BY NIGHT** [ ] Feb75 [ ]
– Anthem / Best I can / Beneath, between and behind / By-Tor & the snowdog: (i) At the tobes of Hades – (ii) Across the Styx – (iii) Of the battle – (iv) Epilogue / Fly by night / Making memories / Rivendell / In the end. *(c-iss.Apr82; 7142 389) (re-iss. Jun83 lp/c; PRICE/PRIMC 19) (cd-iss. Apr87; 822 542-2)*

May 75. (7") *<73681>* **FLY BY NIGHT. / ANTHEM** [–] [ ]
<re-iss. Dec77; 73990>

Nov 75. (7") *<73737>* **BASTILLE DAY. / LAKESIDE PARK** [–] [ ]

Mar 76. (lp) *(9100 018) <1046>* **CARESS OF STEEL** [ ] Oct75 [ ]
– Bastille day / I think I'm going bald / Lakeside Park / The necromancer: (I) Unto darkness – (II) Under the shadow – (III) REturn of the prince / In the valley / Didacts and narpets / No one at the bridge / Panacea / Bacchus plateau / The fountain. *(c-iss.Apr82; 7142 421) (re-iss. Jun83 lp/c; PRICE/PRIMC 20) (cd-iss. Apr87; 822 543-2)*

Jun 76. (lp) *(9100 039) <1079>* **2112** [ ] Apr76 [61]
– Overture / The temples of Syrinx / Discovery / Presentation / Oracle. The dream / Soliliquy / Grand finale / A passage to Bangkok / The twilight zone / Lessons / Tears / Something for nothing. *(re-iss. Jan85 lp/c; PRICE/PRIMC 79) (cd-iss. Apr87; 822 545-2)*

Jun 76. (7") *<73803>* **LESSONS. / THE TWILIGHT ZONE** [–] [ ]

Mar 77. (d-lp) *(6672 015) <7508>* **ALL THE WORLD'S A STAGE (live)** [ ] Sep76 [40]
– Bastille day / Anthem / Fly by night / In the mood / Something for nothing / Lakeside park / Overture / The temple of Syrinx / Presentation / Soliloquy / Grand finale / By-Tor and the snowdog / In the end / Working man / Finding my way / What you're doing. *(c-iss.Apr78; 7553 047) (re-iss. Sep84 d-lp/d-c; PRID/+C 1) (cd-iss. Apr87 – = a few tracks; 822 552-2)*

Dec 76. (7") *<73873>* **FLY BY NIGHT (live). / IN THE MOOD (live) / SOMETHING FOR NOTHING (live)** [–] [88]

Feb 77. (7") *<73912>* **THE TEMPLES OF SYRINX. / MAKING MEMORIES** [–] [ ]

Sep 77. (lp) *(9100 042) <1184>* **A FAREWELL TO KINGS** [22] [33]
– A farewell to kings / Xanadu / Closer to the heart / Cinderella man / Madrigal / Cygnus X-1. *(re-iss. Apr86 lp/c; PRICE/PRIMC 92) (cd-iss. Apr87; 822 546-2)*

Nov 77. (7") *<73958>* **CLOSER TO THE HEART. / MADRIGAL** [–] [76]

Jan 78. (7"ep) *(RUSH 7)* **CLOSER TO THE HEART. / BASTILLE DAY / THE TEMPLES OF SYRINX** [36] [–]
(12"ep+=) *(RUSH 12)* – Anthem.

Nov 78. (lp)(c)<US-pic-lp> *(9100 059)(7142 647) <3743>* **HEMISPHERES** [14] [47]
– Prelude / Apollo (bringer of wisdom) Hemispheres / Dionysus (bringer of love) / Armageddon (the battle of heart and mind) / Cygnus (bringer of balance) / The sphere (a kind of dream) / Circumstances / The trees / La villa Strangiato. *(cd-iss. Apr87; 822 547-2) (re-iss. Mar88 lp/c; PRICE/PRIMC 118)*

Jan 79. (7") *<74051>* **CIRCUMSTANCES. / THE TREES** [–] [ ]

Jan 80. (lp)(c) *(9100 071)(7142 720) <4001>* **PERMANENT WAVES** [3] [4]
– Spirit of radio / Freewill / Jacob's ladder / Entre nous / Different strings / Natural science. *(cd-iss. Apr87; 822 548-2)*

Feb 80. (7") *<76044>* **SPIRIT OF RADIO. / CIRCUMSTANCES** [–] [51]

Feb 80. (7") *(RADIO 7)* **SPIRIT OF RADIO. / THE TREES** [13] [–]
(12"+=) *(RADIO 12)* – Working man.

Apr 80. (7") *<76060>* **DIFFERENT STRINGS. / ENTRE NOUS** [–] [ ]

Feb 81. (7") *<76095>* **LIMELIGHT. / XYZ** [–] [55]

Feb 81. (lp/c) *(6337/7141 160) <4013>* **MOVING PICTURES** [3] [3]
– Tom Sawyer / Red Barchetta / XYZ / Limelight / The camera eye / Witch hunt (part III of fear) / Vital signs. *(cd-iss. 1983; 800 048-2)*

Mar 81. (7") *(VITAL 7)* **VITAL SIGNS. / IN THE MOOD** [41] [–]
(12"+=) *(VITAL 12)* – A passage to Bangkok / Circumstances.

May 81. (7") *<76109>* **TOM SAWYER. / WITCH HUNT** [–] [44]

Oct 81. (7") *<76124>* **FREEWILL (live). / CLOSER TO THE HEART (live)** [–] [ ]

Oct 81. (d-lp/d-c) *(6619/7558 053) <7001>* **EXIT . . . STAGE LEFT (live)** [6] [10]
– The spirit of radio / Red Barchetta / YYZ / A passage to Bangkok *[not on cd]* / Closer to the heart / Beneath, between and behind / Jacob's ladder / Broon's bane / The trees / Xanadu / Freewill / Tom Sawyer / La villa Strangiato. *(cd-iss. Apr87; 822 551-2)*

Oct 81. (7") *(EXIT 7)* **TOM SAWYER (live). / A PASSAGE TO BANGKOK (live)** [25] [–]
(12"+=) *(EXIT 12)* – Red Barchetta (live).

Dec 81. (7") *(RUSH 1) <76124>* **CLOSER TO THE HEART (live). / THE TREES (live)** [ ] [69]

Aug 82. (7") *(RUSH 8) <76179>* **NEW WORLD MAN. / VITAL SIGNS (live)** [42] [21]
(12"+=) *(RUSH 8-12)* – Freewill (live).

Sep 82. (lp/c) *(6337/7141 243) <403>* **SIGNALS** [3] [10]
– Subdivisions / The analog kid / Chemistry / Digital man / The weapon / New world man / Losing it / Countdown. *(cd-iss. 1983; 810 002-2)*

Oct 82. (7") *<76196>* **SUBDIVISIONS. / COUNTDOWN** [–] [ ]

Oct 82. (7"/7"pic-d) *(RUSH/+P 9)* **SUBDIVISIONS. / RED BARCHETTA (live)** [53] [–]
(12"+=) *(RUSH 9-12)* – Jacob's ladder (live).

Apr 83. (7"/7"sha-pic-d) *(RUSH 10/+PD)* **COUNTDOWN. / NEW WORLD MAN** [36] [ ]
(12"+=) *(RUSH 10-12)* – Spirit of radio (live) / (interview excerpts).

Apr 84. (lp/c)(cd) *(VERH/+C 12)(818 476-2) <818476>* **GRACE UNDER PRESSURE** [5] [10]
– Distant early warning / After image / Red sector A / The enemy within / The body electric / Kid gloves / Red lenses / Between the wheels.

May 84. (7") *(RUSH 11)* **THE BODY ELECTRIC. / THE ANALOG KID** [56] [ ]
(10"red+=/12"+=) *(RUSH 11 10/12)* – Distant early warning.

Oct 85. (7") *(RUSH 12) <884191>* **THE BIG MONEY. / TERRITORIES** [ ] [45]
(12"+=) *(RUSH 12-12)* – Red sector A (live).
(d7"+=) *(RUSHD 12)* – Closer to the heart / Spirit of radio.
(7"g-f) *(RUSHG 12)* – ('A'side) / Middletown dreams.

Nov 85. (lp/pic-lp/c)(cd) *(VERH/+P/C 31)(826 098-2) <826098>* **POWER WINDOWS** [9] Oct85 [10]
– The big money / Grand designs / Manhattan project / Marathon / Territories / Middletown dreams / Emotion detector / Mystic rhythms.

Oct 87. (7") *(RUSH 13)* **TIME STAND STILL. / FORCE TEN** [41] [ ]
(12"pic-d+=) *(RUSHP 13-12)* – The enemy within (live).
(12"++=) *(RUSH 13-12)* – Witch hunt (live).

Nov 87. (lp/c)(cd) *(VERH/+C 47)(832 464-2) <832464>* **HOLD YOUR FIRE** [10] Sep87 [13]
– Force ten / Time stand still / Open secrets / Second nature / Prime mover / Lock and key / Mission / Turn the page / Tai Shan / High water.

Mar 88. (7") *(RUSH 14)* **PRIME MOVER. / TAI SHAN** [ ] [ ]
(12"+=) *(RUSH 14-12)* – Open secrets.
(12"++=) *(RUSHR 14-12)* – New world man (live).
(cd-s+=) *RUSHCD 14)* – Distant early warning (live) / New world man (live).

(7"white) *(RUSHR 14)* – ('A'side) / Distant early warning (live).

Jan 89. (d-lp/c/cd) *(836 346-1/-4/-2)* <836346> **A SHOW OF HANDS (live)** 12 21
– (intro) / The big money / Subdivisions / Marathon / Turn the page / Manhattan project / Mission / Distant early warning / Mystic rhythms / Witch hunt (part III of fear) / The rhythm method / Force ten / Time stand still / Red sector A / Closer to the heart.

Atlantic Atlantic

Dec 89. (lp/c)(cd) *(WX 327/+C)(782 040-2)* <82040-1/-4/-2> **PRESTO** 27 Nov89 16
– Show don't tell / Chain lightning / The pass / War paint / Scars / Presto / Superconductor / Anagram (for Mongo) / Red tide / Hand over fist / Available light.

Jan 90. (7") **SHOW DON'T TELL. /** –

Sep 91. (cd)(lp/c) <*(7567 82293-2)*>*(WX 436/+C)* **ROLL THE BONES** 10 3
– Dreamline / Bravado / Roll the bones / Face up / Where's my thing? (part IV 'Gangster Of Boats' trilogy) / The big wheel / Heresy / Ghost of a chance / Neurotica / You bet your life.

Feb 92. (7") *(A 7524)* **ROLL THE BONES. / SHOW DON'T TELL** 49
(cd-s+=) *(A 7524CD)* – (interviews) / Anagram.
(7"sha-pic-d) *(A 7524TE)* – ('A'side) / The pass / It's a rap part 1.

Apr 92. (7") *(A 7491)* **GHOST OF A CHANCE. / DREAMLINE**
(cd-s+=) *(A 7491CD)* – Chain lightning / Red tide.

Oct 93. (cd/c/lp) <*(7567 82528-2/-4/-1)*> **COUNTERPARTS** 14 2
– Animate / Stick it out / Cut to the chase / Nobody's hero / Between sun & moon / Alien shore / The speed of love / Double agent / Leave that thing alone / Cold fire / Everyday glory.

Sep 96. (cd/c) <*(7567 82925-2/-4)*> **TEST FOR ECHO** 25 5
– Test for echo / Driven / Half the world / The color of right / Time and motion / Totem / Dog years / Virtuality / Resist / Limbo / Carve away the stone.

Nov 98. (t-cd/d-c) *(7567 80921-2/-4)* <*83122*> **DIFFERENT STAGES (live history)** 35
– Dreamline / Limelight / Driven / Bravado / Animate / Show don't tell / The trees / Nobody's hero / Closer to the heart / 2112: i) Overture, ii) Temples in Syrinx, iii) Discovery, iv) Presentation, v) Oracle: the dream, vi) Soliloquy, vii) Grand finale // Test for echo / Analog kid / Freewill / Roll the bones / Stick it out / Resist / Leave that thing alone / The rhythm method / Natural science / The spirit of radio / Tom Sawyer / XYZ // Bastille day / By Tor and the snow dog / Xanadu / A farewell to kings / Something for nothing / Cygnus X-1 / Anthem / Working man / Fly by night / In the mood / Cinderella man.

May 02. (cd) <*(7567 83531-2)*> **VAPOR TRAILS** 38 6
– One little victory / Ceiling unlimited / Ghost rider / Peaceable kingdom / The stars look down / How it is / Vapor trail / Secret touch / Earthshine / Sweet miracle / Nocturne / Freeze (Fear part 4) / Out of the cradle.

Nov 03. (t-cd) <*(7567 83672-2)*> **RUSH IN RIO (live)** Oct03 33
– Tom Sawyer / Distant early warning / New world man / Roll the bones / Earthshine / YYZ / The pass / Bravado / The big money / The trees / Freewill / Closer to the heart / Natural science / One little victory / Driven / Ghost rider / Secret touch / Dreamline / Red sector 'A' / Leave that thing alone / O baterista / Resist / 2112 / Limelight / La villa strangiato / The spirit of radio / By-Tor and the snow dog / Cygnus X-1 / Working man / Between sun & moon / Vital signs.

– compilations, others, etc. –

on 'Mercury' unless otherwise mentioned

May 78. (t-lp)(d-c) *(6641 779)(7649 103)* <*9200*> **ARCHIVES** Apr78
– (RUSH / FLY BY NIGHT / CARESS OF STEEL)

Sep 81. (lp/c) <*6337/7141 171*> **RUSH THROUGH TIME** –

Feb 88. (7") *Old Gold; (OG 9767)* **SPIRIT OF RADIO. / CLOSER TO THE HEART** –

Oct 90. (d-cd/d-c/t-lp) *Vertigo; (838 936-2/-4/-1) / Mercury;* <*838936*> **CHRONICLES** 42 Sep90 51
– Finding my way / Working man / Fly by night / Anthem / Bastille day / Lakeside park / 2112: a) Overture, b) The temples of Syrinx / What you're doing (live) / A farewell to kings / Closer to the heart / The trees / La villa Strangiato / Freewill / Spirit of radio/ / Tom Sawyer / Red barchetta / Limelight / A passage to Bangkok (live) / Subdivisions / New world man / Distant early warning / Red sector A / The big money / Manhattan project / Force ten / Time stand still / Mystic rhythms (live) / Show don't tell.

VICTOR

ALEX LIFESON – guitar, bass, keyboards / **BILL BELL** – wobble & slide guitar, co-writer / **PETER CARDINALI** – bass / **BLAKE MANNING** – drums / + guests EDWIN – vocals (of I MOTHER EARTH) + LES CLAYPOOL – bass (of PRIMUS)

Atlantic Atlantic

Feb 96. (cd/c) <*(7567-82852-2/-4)*> **VICTOR** Jan96 99
– Don't care / Promise / Start today / Mr. X / At the end / Sending a warning / Shut up shuttin' up / Strip and go naked / The big dance / Victor / I am the spirit.

GEDDY LEE

with **BEN MONK** – guitar, violin (ex-FM) / **MATT CAMERON** – drums (ex-SOUNDGARDEN)

Atlantic Atlantic

Nov 00. (cd) <*(7567 83384-2)*> **MY FAVOURITE HEADACHE**
– My favourite headache / The present tense / Window to the world / Working at perfekt / Runaway train / The angels' share / Moving to Bohemia / Home on the strange / Slipping / Still / Grace to grace.

Leon RUSSELL

Born: HANK WILSON, 2 Apr'41, Lawton, Oklahoma, USA. Having learned to play the piano at an early age, he soon mastered a string of other instruments and by the late 50's – still in his teens – had progressed to nightclubs, augmenting RONNIE HAWKINS and JERRY LEE LEWIS. By the early 60's, RUSSELL had relocated to California where he secured session work under the name of RUSSELL BRIDGES. He became a regular contributor to PHIL SPECTOR's "wall of sound", other sessions including HERB ALPERT's 'Taste Of Honey' & The BYRDS 'Mr. Tambourine Man'. In the mid-60's, he arranged a hit for GARY LEWIS & THE PLAYBOYS; 'This Diamond Ring', while also also signing a solo deal with 'A&M' records. His work for others continued, including sessions for GENE CLARK (ex-Byrds) and arranging a hit single, 'Feelin' Groovy', for HARPER'S BIZARRE. In 1968 he formed ASYLUM CHOIR with MARC BENNO, releasing an eponymous album which found a cult audience but little critical acclaim. Subsequently befriending rootsy soul duo, DELANEY & BONNIE, RUSSELL produced their 'Accept No Substitute' (1969) album as well as augmenting them on their 'Friends' tour (later 'friends' would include such luminaries as ERIC CLAPTON and GEORGE HARRISON). That year also saw JOE COCKER taking RUSSELL's 'DELTA LADY' into the UK Top 10, the workaholic jack-of-all-musical trades the brains behind COCKER's celebrated 'Mad Dogs and Englishmen' tour the following year. Incredibly, he also found time to start up his own label, 'Shelter', along with A&M producer, Denny Cordell, the first releases being a follow-up ASYLUM CHOIR effort and RUSSELL's own eponymous 1970 debut. Performed in his own inimitable blues/gospel drenched, backwoods bayou style, RUSSELL's chunky piano chords graced a clutch of covers (including Screamin' Jay Hawkins' 'I PUT A SPELL ON YOU' and a rather more unlikely 'GIVE PEACE A CHANCE') alongside enjoyable originals. As well as launching RUSSELL's own career, 'Shelter' was instrumental in setting out J.J.CALE, amongst others, on a long and illustrious (if low key) career. With exposure from the 'Mad Dogs..' tour doing him no harm, RUSSELL's debut made a minor dent in the US charts, although the superior follow-up, 'LEON RUSSELL AND THE SHELTER PEOPLE' (1971) broke the American Top 20 and the British Top 30, another mix of hard hitting interpretations (this time a handful of scorching DYLAN covers; 'HARD RAIN'S A-GONNA FALL', 'IT TAKES A LOT TO LAUGH, IT TAKES A TRAIN TO CRY' and 'IT'S ALL

OVER NOW, BABY BLUE') and idiosyncratic self-penned material. August '71 saw him joining the fray for GEORGE HARRISON's 'Concert For Bangladesh', while the following year's 'CARNEY' was an even bigger success, a near US-No.1 which saw the impressively bearded singer/songwriter using his chequered history in the music business as inspiration. Despite the clown symbolism which he used on the record, RUSSELL's services were in demand constantly, the pianist even writing and producing two tracks with DYLAN, 'Watching The River Flow' and 'When I Paint My Masterpiece'. He also lent a hand to his wife, MARY MCREARY, releasing her solo debut, 'Butterflies In Heaven', in 1973, as well as working with her on 1976's 'THE WEDDING ALBUM'. 'HANK WILSON'S BACK' (1973) introduced RUSSELL's country alter ego, a direction he would subsequently pursue with WILLIE NELSON as well as forming his own bluegrass combo at the turn of the decade. While the bulk of RUSSELL's latter 70's output met with minimal critical and commercial success, the 'WILLIE AND LEON' (1979) set made the US Top 30 and spawned a massive country hit with the cover of Elvis Presley's 'HEARTBREAK HOTEL'. The 80's saw RUSSELL's solo recording activities take a back seat, 'HANK WILSON VOL.II' (1984) his last album for almost a decade. He eventually returned in 1992 with the BRUCE HORNSBY-produced 'ANYTHING CAN HAPPEN', an aptly titled effort which saw RUSSELL's experimental excursions receive a frosty reception from critics. Nevertheless, he remains something of a backroom legend in the music industry, his place in the annals of rock history assured. The man made a more solid comeback in 1999 with 'FACE IN THE CROWD', a partial revisiting of the deep south piano plonking with which he originally made his name, son TEDDY JACK aiding and abetting him on production duties. **Covers:** BEWARE OF DARKNESS (George Harrison) / THE BATTLE OF NEW ORLEANS (Jimmy Driftwood) / MASTERS OF WAR + THE MIGHTY QUINN (Bob Dylan) / ROLL IN MY SWEET ARMS BABY (Lester Flatt) / IF I WERE A CARPENTER (Tim Hardin) / JAMBALAYA + I'M SO LONESOME I COULD CRY (Hank Williams) / and other covers from 'HANK WILSON'S BACK'.JUMPING JACK FLASH (Rolling Stones) / YOUNG BLOOD + IDOL WITH THE GOLDEN HEAD (Leiber-Stoller) / SWEEPING THROUGH THE CITY (. . . Casal) / I SERVE A LIVING SAVIOR (. . . Watson) / SOME DAY (. . . Henderson) / TOO MUCH MONKEY BUSINESS (Chuck Berry) / JEZEBEL (. . . Shanklin) / etc. • **Trivia:** In 1977, his song 'THIS MASQUERADE', won a Grammy award for GEORGE BENSON.

Album rating: LEON RUSSELL (*7) / LEON RUSSELL & THE SHELTER PEOPLE (*7) / CARNEY (*7) / LEON LIVE (*6) / HANK WILSON'S BACK, VOL.1 (*6; as Hank Wilson) / STOP ALL THAT JAZZ (*4) / WILL O' THE WISP (*5) / WEDDING ALBUM with Mary Russell (*5) / BEST OF LEON compilation (*7) / MAKE LOVE TO THE MUSIC with Mary Russell (*4) / AMERICANA (*4) / ONE FOR THE ROAD with Willie Nelson (*5) / LIFE & LOVE (*5) / THE LIVE ALBUM with the New Grass Revival (*4) / HANK WILSON VOL.II (*3; as Hank Wilson) / ANYTHING CAN HAPPEN (*5) / GIMME SHELTER compilation (*8)

LEON RUSSELL – vocals, piano, trumpet, guitar, etc.

not iss. A&M

1964. (7") *<734>* **MISTY. / CINDY** [–] [ ]

Dot Dot

Nov 65. (7") *(DS 16771)* **EVERYBODY'S TALKIN' 'BOUT THE YOUNG. / IT'S ALRIGHT WITH ME** [ ] [ ]

—— LEON joined ASYLUM CHOIR with MARC BENNO. They made two albums in the late 60's. Early in 1970, RUSSELL augmented both DELANEY & BONNIE plus JOE COCKER before returning to solo work.

A&M Shelter

May 70. (7") *<301>* **ROLL AWAY THE STONE. / HUMMINGBIRD** [–] [ ]

Jun 70. (lp) *(AMLS 982) <8901>* **LEON RUSSELL** [ ] Dec69 [60]
– A song for you / Dixie lullaby / I put a spell on you / Shoot out on the plantation / Hummingbird / Delta lady / Prince of peace / Old masters / Give peace a chance / Hurt somebody / Pisces apple lady / Roll away the stone. *(re-iss. Apr76 on 'Island'; ISA 5005) (cd-iss. Nov90 on 'Sequel'; NEXCD 146)*

May 71. (7") **THE BALLAD OF MAD DOGS AND ENGLISHMEN. / LET IT BE** [–] [ ]

A&M Shelter

May 71. (lp) *(AMLS 65003) <8903>* **LEON RUSSELL AND THE SHELTER PEOPLE** [29] [17]
– Stranger in a strange land / Of thee I sing / Hard rain's a-gonna fall / Crystal closet queen / Home sweet Oklahoma / Alcatraz / The ballad of mad dogs and Englishmen / It takes a lot to laugh, it takes a train to cry / She smokes like a river / Sweet Emily / Beware of darkness. *(re-iss. Apr76 on 'Island'; ISA 5006) (cd-iss. 1991 on 'Sequel'+=; NEXCD 137)* – It's all over now, baby blue / Love minus zero – No limit / She belongs to me.

May 71. (7") *<7302>* **HOME SWEET OKLAHOMA. / IT TAKES A LOT TO LAUGH, IT TAKES A TRAIN TO CRY** [–] [ ]

Apr 72. (7") *<7305>* **ME AND BABY JANE. / A HARD RAIN'S A-GONNA FALL** [–] [ ]

Jun 72. (7") *<7316>* **A SONG FOR YOU. / A HARD RAIN'S A-GONNA FALL** [–] [ ]

Aug 72. (lp) *(AMLH 68911) <8911>* **CARNEY** [ ] Jul72 [2]
– Tight rope / Out in the woods / Me and baby Jane / Manhattan island serenade / Cajun love song / Roller derby / Carney / Acid Annapolis / If the shoe fits / My cricket / This masquerade / Magic mirror. *(cd-iss. Nov90 on 'Sequel'; NEXCD 147)*

Aug 72. (7") *<7325>* **TIGHT ROPE. / THIS MASQUERADE** [–] [11]

Sep 72. (7") *(AMS 7026)* **TIGHT ROPE. / DELTA LADY** [ ] [–]

Dec 72. (7") *(AMS 7045) <7328>* **SLIPPING INTO CHRISTMAS. / CHRISTMAS IN CHICAGO** [ ] Xmas [ ]
(re-iss. Dec76 on 'Island'; WIP 6365)

Aug 73. (t-lp) *<8917>* **LEON LIVE (live Long Beach Arena)** [–] Jul73 [9]
– Medley:- I'll take you there – Idol with the golden head – The mighty Quinn – I serve a living savior – The mighty Quinn / Shoot out on the plantation / Dixie lullaby / Queen of the roller derby / Roll away the stone / It's been a long time baby / Great day / Alcatraz / Crystal closet queen / Prince of peace / Sweet Emily / Stranger in a strange land / Out in the woods / Some day / Sweeping through the city / Medley:- Jumping Jack Flash – Young blood / Medley:- Of thee I sing – Yes I am – Delta lady / It's all over now, baby blue. *(UK-iss.Jan92 on 'Sequel' d-cd; NEDCD 172)*

Aug 73. (7") *<7337>* **QUEEN OF THE ROLLER DERBY (live). / ROLL AWAY THE STONE** [–] [89]

Sep 73. (lp; as HANK WILSON) *(AMLS 68923) <8923>* **HANK WILSON'S BACK** [ ] [28]
– Roll in my sweet baby's arms (part 1 & 2) / She thinks I still care / I'm so lonesome I could cry / I'll sail my ship alone / Jambalaya / A six pack to go / Battle of New Orleans / Uncle Pen / Am I that easy to forget / Truck drivin' man / The window up above / Lost highway / Goodnight Irene. *(cd-iss. Oct90 on 'Sequel'; REXCD139)*

Sep 73. (7"; as HANK WILSON) *<7336>* **ROLL IN MY SWEET BABY'S ARMS. / I'M SO LONESOME I COULD CRY** [–] [78]

Nov 73. (7"; as HANK WILSON) *<7338>* **UNCLE PEN. / SIX PACK TO GO** [–] [ ]

Apr 74. (7") *(AMS 7107) <40210>* **IF I WERE A CARPENTER. / WILD HORSES** [ ] [73]

Jul 74. (lp) *(AMLS 68262) <2108>* **STOP ALL THAT JAZZ** [ ] [34]
– If I were a carpenter / Smashed / Leaving Whipporwhill / Spanish Harlem / Streaker's ball / Working girl / Time for love / The ballad of Hollis Brown / Mona Lisa please / Stop all that jazz. *(re-iss. Apr76 on 'Island'; ISA 5009) (cd-iss. Apr91 on 'Sequel'; NEXCD 151)*

Jul 74. (7") *<40277>* **TIME FOR LOVE. / LEAVING WHIPPORWHILL** [–] [ ]

Jun 75. (lp) *(AMLS 68309) <2138>* **WILL O' THE WISP** [ ] [30]
– Will o' the wisp / Little hideaway / Make you feel good / Can't get over losing you / My father's shoes / Stay away from sad songs / Back to the island / Down on deep river / Bluebird / Laying right here in Heaven / Lady blue. *(re-iss. Apr76 on 'Island'; ISA 5008) (cd-iss. Apr91 on 'Sequel'; NEXCD 157)*

Aug 75. (7") *(AMS 7199) <40378>* **LADY BLUE. / LAYING RIGHT HERE IN HEAVEN** [ ] [14]

Dec 75. (7") *<40483>* **BACK TO THE ISLAND. / LITTLE HIDEAWAY** – 53

Feb 76. (7") *<62004>* **BLUEBIRD. / BACK TO THE ISLAND** –

LEON & MARY RUSSELL

Mary was his wife. **MARY McCREARY** – vocalist with LITTLE SISTER (ex-SLY & THE FAMILY STONE).

Paradise Paradise

Jun 76. (lp) *(K 56244) <2943>* **THE WEDDING ALBUM** Apr76 34
– Rainbow in your eyes / Like a dream come true / Love's supposed to be that way / Fantasy / Satisfy you / You are on my mind / Lavender blue / Quiet nights / Windsong / Daylight.

Jun 76. (7") *<8208>* **RAINBOW IN YOUR EYES. / LOVE'S SUPPOSED TO BE THAT WAY** – 52

Sep 76. (7") *<8274>* **SATISFY YOU. / WINDSONG** –

Jun 77. (lp) *<3066>* **MAKE LOVE TO THE MUSIC** –
– Easy love / Joyful noise / Now now boogie / Say you will / Make love to the music / Love crazy / Love is in your eyes / Hold on to this feeling / Island in the sun.

Jun 77. (7") *<8369>* **SAY YOU WILL. / LOVE CRAZY** –

Oct 77. (7") *<8438>* **EASY LOVE. / HOLD ON TO THIS FEELING** –

LEON RUSSELL

—— solo again on same label

Aug 78. (lp) *(K 56534) <3172>* **AMERICANA**
– Let's get started / Elvis and Marilyn / From Maine to Mexico / When a man loves a woman / It's only me / Midnight lover / Housewife / Ladies of the night / Shadow and me / Jesus on my side.

Oct 78. (7") *(K 17244) <8667>* **ELVIS AND MARILYN. / ANITA BRYANT**

Jan 79. (7") *<8719>* **FROM MAINE TO MEXICO. / MIDNIGHT LOVER** –

—— Mid'79, he partners WILLIE NELSON for d-lp 'WILLIE AND LEON', see further.

1979. (lp) *(K 56891) <3341>* **LIFE & LOVE**
– One more love song / You girl / Struck by lightning / Strange love / Life and love / On the first day / High horse / Sweet mystery / On the borderline.

Warners Paradise

Jan 81. (7") *<49662>* **OVER THE RAINBOW. / I'VE JUST SEEN A FACE** –

Mar 81. (lp; as LEON RUSSELL & THE NEW GRASS REVIVAL) *(K 56891) <3532>* **THE LIVE ALBUM (live)**
– Over the rainbow / I've just seen a face / One more love song / I believe to my soul / Pilgrim land / Georgia blues / Prince of peace / Rollin' in my sweet baby's arms / Stranger in a strange land / I want to be at the meeting / Wild horses / Jambalaya / Caribbean / Jumpin' Jack Flash.

1984. (lp; as HANK WILSON) *<0002>* **HANK WILSON VOL.II** –
– Wabash cannonball / Oh lonesome me / Tennessee waltz / Heartaches by the number / If you've got the money honey (I've got the time) / Tumbling tumbleweeds / I'm movin' on / Waltz across Texas / Don't let the stars get in your eyes / On the wings of a dove / I'll be there if you ever want me / I saw the light.

—— retired from solo music biz, until 1992, when he co-wrote songs with BRUCE HORNSBY.

Virgin Am. Virgin

May 92. (cd/c) *(CDVUS/VUSMC 50)* **ANYTHING CAN HAPPEN**
– Anything can happen / Black halos / No man's land / Too much monkey business / Angel ways / Life of the party / Stranded on Easy Street / Jezebel / Love slave / Faces of the children.

Eldorado ARKK

May 98. (cd) *(ELDCD 004) <ARK 1002-2>* **LEGEND IN MY TIME: HANK WILSON VOL.3**
– Sixteen tons / Night life / Act naturally / Sweet dreams / Daddy sang bass / He stopped loving her today / Mama don't let your babies grow up to be / Funny how time slips away / Okie from Muskogee / Crazy / Love's gonna live here / He'll have to go / Legend in my time.

not iss. Saga

Jan 99. (cd) *<5003>* **FACE IN THE CROWD** –
– Love is a battlefield / Dr. Love / Down in the flood / So hard to say goodbye / Betty Ann / This heart of mine / Message from my baby / Blue eyes and a black heart / What will I do without you / Mean and evil / The Devil started talking / Don't bring the blues to bed. *<re-iss. Sep01 on 'Leon Russell'; 30011>*

not iss. Leon Russell

2000. (cd) *<30008>* **SIGNATURE SONGS** –
– A song for you / One more love song / Tightrope / Stranger in a strange land / Hummingbird / Back to the island / Out in the woods / Lady blue / Delta lady / Magic mirror / This masquerade.

Aug 01. (cd) *<30010>* **GUITAR BLUES** –
– Ways of a woman / House of blues / Rip Van Winkle / This love I have for you / Lost inside the blues / Dark carousel / It's impossible / My hard times / Strange power of love / Make everything alright / The same old song / End of the road.

Oct 01. (cd; with The NEWGRASS REVIVAL) *<30012>* **RHYTHM & BLUEGRASS: HANK WILSON VOL.4** –
– I've just seen a face / Footprints in the snow / Columbus stockade blues / I believe to my soul / Rough and rocky road / Mystery train / When my blue moon turns to gold / In the pines / Open up the door / Bluebirds are singing for me / Rhythm & bluegrass / Pilgrim land.

Apr 02. (cd) *<30013>* **MOONLIGHT & LOVE SONGS** –
– Orchestra tuning / The very thought of you / That's all / My funny valentine / Smoke gets in your eyes / Stormy weather / Once in awhile / That lucky old sun / 'Round midnight / The shadow of your smile / As time goes by / Angel eyes.

– compilations, others, etc. –

Jan 72. (7" by 'ASYLUM CHOIR') *Shelter;* **STRAIGHT BROTHER. / TRYIN' TO STAY ALIVE** –

1974. (lp) *Olympic; <7112>* **LOOKING BACK** –

Jan 77. (lp) *Island; (ISA 5013) / Shelter; <52004>* **THE BEST OF LEON** Oct76 40

Jan 77. (7") *Island; (WIP 6290)* **TIGHT ROPE. / THIS MASQUERADE** –

Jan 92. (cd/c) *Castle; (CCS CD/MC 313)* **THE COLLECTION** –
– A song for you / Lady blue / Tight rope / Blue bird / This masquerade / Roll away the stone / Beware of darkness / Crystal closet queen / Delta lady / Back to the island / Stranger in a strange land / Hummingbird / Queen of the roller derby / Of thee I sing / Streaker's ball / Roll in my sweet baby's arms / Magic mirror / If I were a carpenter / Out in the woods / The battle of New Orleans.

Nov 96. (d-cd) *E.M.I.; <52644>* **GIMME SHELTER: THE BEST OF LEON RUSSELL** –
– Hello little friend / Sweet home Chicago / Tryin' to stay 'live / Ballad for a soldier / Song for you / Dixie lullaby / Hummingbird / Delta lady / Pisces apple lady / Old masters (masters of war) / Home, sweet Oklahoma / She smiles like a river / Beware of darkness / Tight rope / Me and baby Jane / Manhattan island serenade / Magic mirror / This masquerade / Roll away the stone / Prince of peace / Sweet Emily / Roll in my sweet baby's arms / She thinks I still care / In the jailhouse now / If I were a carpenter . . . / Leaving Whiporwhill / Time for love / Will o' the wisp / Little hideaway / Back to the island / Bluebird / Lady blue / She belongs to me / Wild horses / Anything can happen / Faces of the children / Everybody's talkin' 'bout the young / It's alright with me.

Dec 99. (cd) *Paradise Island; <1001>* **BLUES: SAME OLD SONG** –

☐ Mike RUTHERFORD (see under ⇒ GENESIS)

The SEX PISTOLS

SADE

Born: HELEN FOLASADE ADU, 16 Jan'59, Ibadan, Nigeria. Raised by her mother in Clacton, Essex, England, she moved to Camden Town, London in '84. The previous year, after spells with ARRIVA and funk outfit, PRIDE, she launched her solo career, having signed to 'Epic' records for a large advance. Helped by an appearance on Channel 4's 'The Tube', her first 45, 'YOUR LOVE IS KING', broke her into the UK Top 10, while the debut album, 'DIAMOND LIFE', made UK No.2 and steadily found an audience in the States, where it hit Top 5. A fashion model from the early 80's, she turned her head to sophisticated, romantic pop/soul music, ideal for the new compact disc era, the velvety lounge-sophistication of 'SMOOTH OPERATOR' making the US Top 10. A coffee table jazz-lite landmark, the album went on to sell millions and transform SADE into a sultry 80's superstar. Previewed by her appearance at Live Aid and another slice of teasing sensuality in 'THE SWEETEST TABOO', a follow-up set, 'PROMISE' (1985), provided the singer with a transatlantic No.1. The following year saw her working on the soundtrack to the 'Absolute Beginners' movie, in which she would also play a cameo role. While sticking fairly rigidly to the tried and tested formula, subsequent albums, 'STRONGER THAN PRIDE' (1988) and 'LOVE DELUXE' (1992) were quality releases despite their lack of strong singles, SADE continuing to enjoy greater success in the States. With only a 'BEST OF' compilation in '94 to quell the fans' thirst, SADE returned after the millennium with a fresh batch of songs, 'LOVERS ROCK' (2000). Boosted by the hit single, 'BY YOUR SIDE', it climbed into the UK Top 20 and US Top 3. The subsequent tour was documented on 'LOVERS LIVE' (2002), a consummate concert set displaying SADE's natural onstage ease and effortless rapport with her devoted longtime fans.

Album rating: DIAMOND LIFE (*7) / PROMISE (*6) / STRONGER THAN PRIDE (*6) / LOVE DELUXE (*5) / THE BEST OF SADE compilation (*7) / LOVERS ROCK (*6) / LOVERS LIVE (*5)

SADE ADU – vocals / with **STUART MATTHEWMAN** (b.1961) – guitar, sax / **PAUL DENHAM** (b.1958) – bass / **ANDREW HALE** (b.1963) – keyboards / **PAUL COOK** – drums

Epic | Portrait

Jan 84. (7") *(A 4137) <05408>* **YOUR LOVE IS KING. / LOVE AFFAIR WITH LIFE** | 6 | Jun85 | 54
(12"+=) *(TA 4137)* – Smooth operator / Snake bite.

May 84. (7") *(A 4437)* **WHEN AM I GONNA MAKE A LIVING. / SHOULD I LOVE YOU** | 36 | – |
(12"+=) *(TA 4437)* – Why can't we live together.

Jul 84. (lp/c/cd) *(EPC/40/CD 26044) <39581>* **DIAMOND LIFE** | 2 | Feb85 | 5
– Smooth operator / Your love is king / Hang on to your love / Frankie's first affair / When am I going to make a living / Cherry pie / Sally / I will be your friend / Why can't we live together. *(cd re-iss. May95 & Dec98; 481178-2) (cd re-iss. Oct99; MILLEN 12) (lp re-iss. Oct99 on 'Scorpio'; FR 35981)*

Sep 84. (7") *(A 4655) <04807>* **SMOOTH OPERATOR. / SPIRIT** | 19 | Feb85 | 5
(12"+=) *(TA 4655)* – Red eyes.

Sep 84. (7") **HANG ON TO YOUR LOVE. / CHERRY PIE** | – | |

Oct 85. (7"/12") *(A/TA 6609) <05713>* **THE SWEETEST TABOO. / YOU'RE NOT THE MAN** | 31 | Nov85 | 5

Nov 85. (lp/c/cd) *(EPC/40/CD 86318) <40263>* **PROMISE** | 1 | Dec85 | 1
– Is it a crime / The sweetest taboo / War of the hearts / Jezebel / Mr. Wrong / Never as good as the first time / Fear / Tar baby / Maureen. *(c+=)* – Punch drunk / You're not the man. *(re-iss. Mar90 cd/c/lp; 465575-2/-4/-1)*

Dec 85. (7"/12") *(A/TA 6742)* **IS IT A CRIME. / PUNCH DRUNK** | 49 | | –

Mar 86. (7"/12") *(A/TA 7061) <05846>* **NEVER AS GOOD AS THE FIRST TIME. / KEEP HANGIN' ON (live instrumental)** | | | 20

Jul 86. (7") **IS IT A CRIME. / (long version)** | – | |

Epic | Epic

Mar 88. (7"/s7") *(SADE/+P 1)* **LOVE IS STRONGER THAN PRIDE. / SUPER BIEN TOTAL** | 44 | | –
(12"+=/cd-s+=) *(SADET/CDSADE 1)* – ('B'extended).

May 88. (lp/c/cd) *(460497-1/-4/-2) <44210>* **STRONGER THAN PRIDE** | 3 | | 7
– Love is stronger than pride / Paradise / Nothing can come between us / Haunt me / Turn my back on you / Keep looking / Clean heart / Give it up / I never thought I'd see the day / Siempre hay esperanza.

May 88. (7") *(SADE 2)* **PARADISE (remix). / ('A'instrumental)** | 29 | | –
(12"+=) *(SADET 2)* – ('A'extended).
(cd-s+=) *(CDSADE 2)* – Hang on to your love (US remix) / Keep hanging on (live).

May 88. (7") *<07904>* **PARADISE. / SUPER BIEN TOTAL** | – | | 16

Aug 88. (7") *(SADE 3)* **NOTHING CAN COME BETWEEN US. / MAKE SOME ROOM** | | |
(12"+=/cd-s+=) *(SADET/CDSADE 3)* – You're not the man.

Nov 88. (7") *(SADE 4)* **TURN MY BACK ON YOU. / KEEP LOOKING** | | |
(12"+=/cd-s+=) *(SADET/CDSADE 4)* – ('A'extended) / ('A'mix).

Jan 89. (7") **LOVE IS STRONGER THAN PRIDE. / MAKE SOME ROOM** | – | |

Oct 92. (7"/c-s) *(658356-7/-4) <74734>* **NO ORDINARY LOVE. / PARADISE (remix)** | 26 | | 28
(cd-s+=) *(658356-2)* – ('A'version).
(12"+=) *(658356-6)* – ('B'-drums and Sade mix).
(returned to UK chart in Jun'93 and hit No.14)

Nov 92. (cd/c/lp) *(472626-2/-4/-1) <53178>* **LOVE DELUXE** | 10 | | 3
– No ordinary love / Feel no pain / I couldn't love you more / Like a tattoo / Kiss of life / Cherish the day / Pearls / Bullet proof soul / Mermaid. *(cd re-iss. Aug98; same)*

Nov 92. (7"/c-s) *(658829-7/-4)* **FEEL NO PAIN. / LOVE IS STRANGER THAN PRIDE (Mad Professor remix)** | 56 | | –
(cd-s+=) *(658829-2)* – ('A'version).

May 93. (7"/c-s) *(659116-7/-4) <74848>* **KISS OF LIFE. / ROOM 55** | 44 | Mar93 | 78
(12"+=/cd-s+=) *(659116-6/-2)* – ('A'version).

Jul 93. (c-s) *(659481-4)* **CHERISH THE DAY / CHERISH THE DAY (Ronin remix)** | 53 | | –
(12"+=/cd-s+=) *(659481-6/-2)* – ('A'-Pal Joey remix).

Nov 94. (cd/c/lp) *(477793-2/-4/-1) <66686>* **THE BEST OF SADE** (compilation) | 6 | | 9
– Your love is king / Hang on to your love / Smooth operator / Jezebel / The sweetest taboo / Is it a crime / Never as good as the first time / Love is stronger than pride / Paradise / Nothing can come between us / No ordinary love / Like a tattoo / Kiss of life / Please send me someone to love /

Cherish the day / Pearls. *(re-iss. Nov00 cd/c; 500594-2/-4) (lp re-iss. Mar01 on 'Simply Vinyl'; SVLP 285)*

—— her band became SWEETBACK and released one eponymous set in 1997 – SADE has since went into a hiatus, until . . .

Nov 00. (c-s) *(669999-4) <radio cut>* **BY YOUR SIDE / BY YOUR SIDE (Neptune's remix)** [17] Jan01 [75]
(12"+=) *(669999-6)* – ('A'-Yard mix) / ('A'-Reggae mix).
(cd-s++=) *(669999-2)* – ('A'-video).

Nov 00. (cd/c/lp) *(500766-2/-4/-1) <85185>* **LOVERS ROCK** [18] [3]
– By your side / Flow / King of sorrow / Somebody already broke my heart / All about our love / Slave song / The sweetest gift / Every word / Immigrant / Lovers rock / It's only love that gets you through.

Mar 01. (c-s) *(670867-4)* **KING OF SORROW / (Guru remix)** [59] [ ]
(12"+=/cd-s+=) *(670867-6/-2)* – ('A'-Fun Lovin' Criminals remix) / ('A'-Cottonbelly remix).

Feb 02. (cd) *(506125-2) <86373>* **LOVERS LIVE (live)** [51] [10]
– Cherish the day / Somebody already broke my heart / Smooth operator / Jezebel / Kiss of life / Slave song / The sweet gift / The sweetest taboo / Paradise / No ordinary love / By your side / Flow / Is it a crime.

– compilations, etc. –

Dec 88. (d-cd) *C.B.S.; (CDSD 241)* **DIAMOND LIFE / PROMISE** [ ] [–]

1992. (7") *Old Gold;* **YOUR LOVE IS KING. / SMOOTH OPERATOR** [ ] [–]

Nov 98. (3xcd-box) *Epic; (485328-2)* **DIAMOND LIFE / PROMISE / STRONGER THAN PRIDE** [ ] [ ]

SAINT ETIENNE

Formed: North London, England . . . early 90's by music journo, BOB STANLEY and PETE WIGGS. Naming themselves after French football team, St. Etienne, after originally toying with the name, REARDON (the snooker player!), they signed to up-and-coming indie label 'Heavenly'. With MOIRA LAMBERT on vocals (borrowed from FAITH OVER REASON), the outfit's first vinyl foray was a sublime dub/indie-dance cover of Neil Young's 'ONLY LOVE CAN BREAK YOUR HEART'. Re-released after securing their first minor hit, 'NOTHING CAN STOP US', the track brought ST. ETIENNE to the attention of both the dance and indie scene. By this point however, a full-time vocalist (guest DONNA SAVAGE of the DEAD FAMOUS PEOPLE featured on their version of the Field Mice's 'KISS AND MAKE UP') had been recruited in the shape of SARAH CRACKNELL, whose sensuous, playful voice graced the bulk of 'FOXBASE ALPHA' (1991). A stunning debut album mixing and matching disco samples, trippy bass-lines and airy atmospherics into a pot-pourri of kitschy pop genius, the record was released to rave reviews and its relatively lowly chart position barely reflected its importance. With word now out, the group narrowly missed the UK Top 20 with their next single, 'JOIN OUR CLUB', although by early 1993 they found themselves bonafide pop stars when 'YOU'RE IN A BAD WAY' became their biggest hit to date. The accompanying album, 'SO TOUGH', cemented SAINT ETIENNE's position as top swoon-pop ironists, a masterfully sampledelic set featuring such classy compositions as 'HOBART PAVING', 'AVENUE' (also a Top 40 hit) and 'CALICO'. Following CRACKNELL's high profile collaboration with TIM BURGESS (Charlatans) for the Xmas hit, 'I WAS BORN ON CHRISTMAS DAY', the oufit completed their fourth set, 'TIGER BAY', a record which slightly disappointed their fan/fox base with its more experimental approach. Although the future of the group seemed in doubt with CRACKNELL working on solo material, a brilliant return to form with the 'HE'S ON THE PHONE' single boded well for the future. 1996 brought collaborations ('RESERECTION' with Frenchman ETIENNE DAHO), a club remix set ('CASINO CLASSICS') and a Top 40 solo single from SARAH CRACKNELL ('ANYMORE'). Her full length debut, 'LIPSLIDE' was released the following year to chart oblivion although SAINT ETIENNE were back within sniffing distance of the Top 10 with 1998's 'SYLVIE' single. As the track promised, 'GOOD HUMOUR' (1998) was a return to the song-based stucture of their debut, as knowingly and lovingly crafted as ever. In contrast, 'SOUND OF WATER' (2000) was more expansive, charting the depths of oceanic electronica while occasionally coming up for air, their pop instincts never far from the shimmering surface. In contrast, 'FINISTERRE' (2002) revisited, in part, the mix'n'match policy of old, succeeding in proving that they've still got that magpie eye for pop glitter if not exactly capturing the spirit of the early 90's. • **Songwriters:** STANLEY-WIGGS except a few with CRACKNELL plus outside covers WHO DO YOU THINK YOU ARE (Scott-Dyer) / MY CHRISTMAS PRAYER (Billy Fury) / WESTERN WIND (trad.) / STRANGER IN PARADISE (hit; Tony Bennett) / IS IT TRUE (Marc Bolan) / HOW I LEARNED TO LOVE THE BOMB (TV Personalities). • **Trivia:** Sang a version of RIGHT SAID FRED's 'I'M TOO SEXY' on a 1992 'Heavenly' compilation ep.

Album rating: FOXBASE ALPHA (*8) / SO TOUGH (*7) / YOU NEED A MESS OF HELP TO STAND ALONE compilation (*6) / TIGER BAY (*6) / TOO YOUNG TO DIE – THE SINGLES compilation (*7) / CASINO CLASSICS (*6) / GOOD HUMOUR (*6) / SOUND OF WATER (*6) / SMASH THE SYSTEM: THE SINGLES AND MORE 1990-1999 compilation (*7) / FINISTERRE (*5) / Sarah Cracknell: LIPSLIDE (*5)

BOB STANLEY (b.25 Dec'64, Horsham, Sussex) – keyboards / **PETE WIGGS** (b.15 May'66, Reigate, Surrey) – keyboards, synthesizers / **MOIRA LAMBERT** – vocals (of FAITH OVER REASON)

white label | not iss.

1988. (12"; as the NEXT PROJECTED SOUND) *<none>* **BRUTAL GENERATION** [–] [–]

Heavenly | Warners

Jul 90. (7"/12") *(HVN 2/212)* **ONLY LOVE CAN BREAK YOUR HEART. / ('A'version)** [ ] [–]
(12") *(HVN 212R)* – ('A'-A mix of two halves mix by Andy Weatherall) / The Official Saint Etienne world cup theme.

—— **DONNA SAVAGE** – vocals (of DEAD FAMOUS PEOPLE) repl. MOIRA

Sep 90. (7"/12") *(HVN 4/412)* **KISS AND MAKE UP. / SKY'S DEAD** [ ] [–]
(cd-s+=) *(HVN 412R)* – ('A'extended).
(12") *(HVN 4CD)* – ('A'mixes by Pete Helber incl. dub version).

—— **SARAH CRACKNELL** – vocals (ex-solo artist) repl. DONNA

May 91. (7"/12") *(HVN 9/912)* **NOTHING CAN STOP US. / SPEEDWELL** [54] [ ]
(cd-s+=) *(HVN 9CD)* – ('A'instrumental).
(12"++=) *(HVN 912R)* – ('B'-Flying mix) / ('B'-Project mix) / 3-D tiger.
below A-side featured MOIRA LAMBERT / B-side featured Q-TEE

Aug 91. (7"/12"/c-s) *(HVN 12/+12/+CS)* **ONLY LOVE CAN BREAK YOUR HEART. / FILTHY** [39] [–]
(cd-s+=) *(HVN 12CD)* – ('A'-A mix of two halves).

Oct 91. (cd/c/lp) *(HVN CD/MC/LP 1) <26793>* **FOXBASE ALPHA** [34] Jan92 [ ]
– This is Radio Etienne / Only love can break your heart / Wilson / Carnt sleep / Girl VII / Spring / She's the one / Stoned to say the least / Nothing can stop us / Etienne gonna die / London belongs to me / Like the swallow / Dilworth's theme. *(cd re-iss. Dec01; same)*

Jan 92. (12"ep) *<0-40395>* **NOTHING CAN STOP US (mixes) / SPEEDWELL** [–] [ ]

Feb 92. (c-s) *<19078>* **ONLY LOVE CAN BREAK YOUR HEART / STONED TO SAY THE LEAST** [–] [97]
(12"+=) *<0-40196>* – ('A'mixes).

May 92. (7"/c-s) *(HVN 15/+CS)* **JOIN OUR CLUB. / PEOPLE GET REAL** [21] [–]
(12"+=/cd-s+=) *(HVN 15 12/CD)* – ('A'-Chemically friendly zoom mix) / Scene '93.

Sep 92. (c-ep/12"ep/cd-ep) *(HVN 23 CS/12/CD)* **AVENUE / SOME PLACE ELSE. / PAPER / JOHNNY IN THE ECHO CAFE** [40] [–]

(cd-s) *(HVN 23CDR)* – ('A'club mix) / ('A'-Marshall mix) / ('A'-Venusian mix) (all remixed by A.R. KANE or GORDON KING).

— added **IAN CATT** – guitar, programmer

Feb 93. (7"/c-s) *(HVN 25/+CS)* **YOU'RE IN A BAD WAY. / CALIFORNIA SNOW STORY** [12] [–]
(12"+=/cd-s+=) *(HVN 25 12/CD)* – Archway people / Duke Duvet.

Mar 93. (cd/c/lp) *(HVN CD/MC/LP 6)* <45166> **SO TOUGH** [7] [ ]
– Mario's cafe / Railway jam / Date with Spelman / Calico / Avenue / You're in a bad way / Memo to Pricey / Hobart paving / Leafhound / Clock milk / Conchita Martinez / No rainbows for me / Here come clown feet / Junk the morgue / Chicken soup. *(re-iss. Jun93 with free ltd.cd 'YOU NEED A MESS OF HELP TO STAND ALONE' compilation; HVN CDX 6)* – Who do you think you are / Archway people / California snow storm / Kiss and make up / Duke duvet / Filthy / Join our club / Paper / Some place else / Speedwell.

May 93. (7"/c-s) *(HVN 29/+CS)* **HOBART PAVING. / WHO DO YOU THINK YOU ARE** [23] [–]
(12"+=/cd-s+=) *(HVN 29 12/CD)* – Your head my voice (voix revirement) / Who do you think you are (Quex-Rd) (Aphex Twin remixes).

Jun 93. (12"/cd-s) <40910> **WHO DO YOU THINK YOU ARE (mixes)** [–] [ ]

Dec 93. (7"/c-s) *(HVN 36/+CS)* **I WAS BORN ON CHRISTMAS DAY. / MY CHRISTMAS PRAYER** [37] [–]
(12"+=/cd-s+=) *(HVN 36 12/CD)* – Snowplough / Peterloo.
(above 'A' featured dual vocals with TIM BURGESS of The CHARLATANS)

Dec 93. (cd/c/lp) *(HVN CD/MC/LP 7)* **YOU NEED A MESS OF HELP TO STAND ALONE** [ ] [–]
– (see last album)

Feb 94. (7"/c-s) *(HVN 37/+CS)* **PALE MOVIE. / HIGHGATE ROAD INCIDENT** [28] [–]
(12"/cd-s) *(HVN 37 12/CD)* – ('A'side) / ('A'-Stentorian dub) / ('A'-Secret Knowledge trouse assassin mix) / ('A'-Lemonentry mix).

Feb 94. (cd/c/lp) *(HVN CD/MC/LP 8)* <45634> **TIGER BAY** [8] Jun94 [ ]
– Urban clearway / Former lover / Hug my soul / Like a motorway / On the shore / Marble lions / Pale movie / Cool kids of death / Western wind / Tankerville / Western wind / Boy scouts of America.

May 94. (7"/c-s) *(HVN 40/+CS)* **LIKE A MOTORWAY. / YOU KNOW I'LL MISS YOU WHEN YOU'RE GONE / SUSHI RIDER** [47] [–]
(12"/cd-s) *(HVN 40 12/CD)* – ('A'side) / ('A'-Chekhov warp mix) / ('A'-David Holmes mix) / (Skin up, you're already dead) (Dust Brothers mix).

Sep 94. (c-ep/cd-ep) *(HVN 42 CS/CD)* <41591> **HUG MY SOUL / I BUY AMERICAN RECORDS / HATE YOUR DRUG / LA POUPEE QUI FAIT NON (NO, NO, NO) (live)** [32] [ ]
(12"ep) *(HVN 4012)* – ('A'side) / ('A'-Sure Is Pure) / ('A'-Motiv8) / ('A'-Secret Knowledge).
(cd-ep+=) *(HVN 42CDR)* – (above tracks) / ('A'-Juan "Kinky" Hernandez mix).

Feb 95. (fan club-cd) *(HVNCD 9)* **I LOVE TO PAINT** [–] [–]

Heavenly M.C.A.

Oct 95. (c-s) *(HVN 50CS)* <55268> **HE'S ON THE PHONE / ('A'-Motiv8 mix)** [11] Jan96 [ ]
(cd-s+=) *(HVN 50CDR)* – Cool kids of death (Underworld mix) / How I learned to love the bomb.
(cd-s) *(HVN 50CD)* – ('A'side) / Groveley Road / Is it true / The process.

Nov 95. (cd/c/d-lp) *(HVN CD/MC/LP 10)* **TOO YOUNG TO DIE – THE SINGLES** (compilation) [17] [–]
– Only love can break your heart / Kiss and make up / Nothing can stop us / Join our club / People get real / Avenue / You're in a bad way / Who do you think you are / Hobart paving / I was born on Christmas day / Pale movie / Like a motorway / Hug my soul / He's on the phone. *(cd w/cd 'THE REMIX ALBUM'; HVN LP 10CDR)(+=)* – (9 remixes).

— next with French dance artist ETIENNE DAHO and on 'Dindisc'/'Alex'US.

Jan 96. (m-cd; as ST. ETIENNE DAHO) *(DINSD 150)* <5567> **RESERECTION** [50] Feb96 [ ]
– Reserection / Jungle pulse / A amours / Accident / Le baiser francais / Jungle pulse.

Oct 96. (d-cd/d-c/t-lp) *(HVNLP 16 CD/MC/LP)* **CASINO CLASSICS** [34] [–]
– remixes by Chemical Brothers / PFM / Underworld / Way out West / Andrew Weatherall / Lionrock / David Holmes / Monkey Mafia / Death In Vegas / Sure Is Pure / Billy Nasty / Gordon King / Secret Knowledge / The Aloof / Broadcast / Aphex Twin / Primax / Psychonauts / Balearico. *(d-cd re-iss. Apr02; same)*

— SARAH had already tried out a solo career

SARAH CRACKNELL

Gut not iss.

Jul 96. (cd-s) *(CDGUT 3)* **ANYMORE / OH BOY, THE FEELING WHEN YOU HELD MY HAND / FIFTH FLOOR / ANYMORE** [39] [–]
(cd-s) *(CXGUT 3)* – ('A'mixes; radio / 4anymore / Nino's liquid steel / Faster pussycat, kill kill).

Apr 97. (c-s/cd-s) *(CA/CD GUT 7)* **GOLDIE / EMPIRE STATE HIGH / AUSSIE SOAP GIRL / GOLDIE** [ ] [–]

May 97. (cd/c) *(GUT CD/MC 2)* **LIPSLIDE** [ ] [–]
– Ready or not / Desert baby / Coastal town / Home / Anymore / How far / Goldie / Taxi / Taking off for France / If you leave me / Penthouse girl, basement boy / Can't stop now.

— SARAH also released, 'KELLY'S LOCKER' mini-cd in Japan Sep'00

SAINT ETIENNE

— **SARAH** returned to the fold in 1997

Creation not iss.

Jan 98. (7") *(CRE 279)* **SYLVIE. / ZIPCODE** [12] [–]
(cd-s+=) *(CRESCD 279)* – Afriad to go home / Hill street connection.
(cd-s) *(CRESCD 279X)* – ('A'mixes; trouser enthusiasts tintinnabulation x2 / Stretch'n'Vern / Faze action Friday night boiler).

Apr 98. (c-s) *(CRECS 290)* **THE BAD PHOTOGRAPHER / HIT THE . . .** [27] [–]
(cd-s+=) *(CRESCD 290)* – Swim swan swim / Madelaine.
(cd-s) *(CRESCD 290X)* – ('A'side) / 4.35 in the morning (Kid Loco remix) / Foto (Bronx Dogs mix) / Uri Geller bent my boyfriend (Add N To X mix).

May 98. (cd/lp) *(CRE CD/LP 225)* **GOOD HUMOUR** [18] [–]
– Woodcabin / Sylvie / Split screen / Mr Donut / Goodnight Jack / Lose that girl / The bad photographer / Been so long / Postman / Erica America / Dutch TV. *(also ltd-cd; CRECD 225L)*

Kung Fu Fighting not iss.

Feb 99. (ltd-7") *(CHANME 02)* **LOVER PLAY THE BASS. / CATNAP** [ ] [–]

Mantra Sub Pop

May 99. (cd-ep) <SP 466> **PLACES TO VISIT** [–] [ ]
– Ivy house / 52 pilot / We're in the city / Artieripp / Sadie's anniversary / Half timbered / Garage for Gunther.

Sep 99. (ltd-7") *(AMY 009)* **SATURDAY. / (split w/ Fugu)** [–] French [–]
(above issued on 'Amberley')

Mar 00. (12") *(MNT 053T)* **HOW WE USED TO LIVE. / ROSE NECK / RED SETTER** [ ] [–]
(cd-s+=) *(MNT 053CD)* – ('A'mixes; aim / aim instrumental / Dot Allison mix / Dot Allison instrumental).

— In May'00, SAINT ETIENNE were credited on PAUL VAN DYK's UK Top 10 hit, 'Tell Me Why (The Riddle)'

May 00. (cd/c/lp) *(MNT CD/MC/LP 1018)* *<SP 509>* **SOUND OF WATER** [33] [ ]
– Late morning / Heart failed (in the back of a taxi) / Sycamore / Don't back down / Just a little overcome / Boy is crying / Aspects of Lambert / Downey, CA / How we used to live / The place at dawn.

Jun 00. (12"/cd-s) *(MNT 054 T/CD1)* **HEART FAILED (IN THE BACK OF A TAXI) (mixes; futureshock vocal / Two Lone Swordsmen / Bridge & tunnel all not too well for Otto and Ulli)** [50] [–]
(cd-s) *(MNT 054CD2)* – ('A'side) / Thank you / Bar conscience.

Jan 01. (12") *(MNT 60T)* **BOY IS CRYING. / HOW WE USED TO LIVE (Paul Van Dyk mix)** [34] [–]
(cd-s+=) *(MNT 60CD2)* – Northwestern (si.cut.db mix).
(cd-s) *(MNT 60CD1)* – ('A'side) / Northwestern / Shoot out the lights.

Mantra Mantra

Aug 02. (cd-s) *(MNT 73CD)* **ACTION / ANDERSON / 7 SUMMERS** [41] [–]
(cd-s/12") *(MNT 73 CD2/T)* – ('A'-Mr. Joshua edit/club) / ('A'-DJ Tiesto mix) / ('A'-Laub mix).

Oct 02. (cd/lp) *(<MNT CD/LP 1033>)* **FINISTERRE** [55] [ ]
– Action / Amateur / Language lab / Soft like me / Summerisle / Stop and think it over / Shower scene / The way we live now / New thing / B92 / The more you know / Finisterre.

– compilations, etc. –

Sep 01. (d-cd) *Columbia; (503427-2)* **SMASH THE SYSTEM (THE SINGLES AND MORE 1990-1999)** [ ] [–]
– Only love can break your heart / Kiss and make up / Nothing can stop us / Spring / Can't sleep / Filthy / Join our club / People get real / *(t-lp-iss.Sep02 on 'Simply Vinyl'; 512504-2)*

Oct 02. (12") *Heavenly; (VJAY 24)* **ONLY LOVE CAN BREAK YOUR HEART. / THE SEA** [ ] [–]

☐ Richie SAMBORA (see under ⇒ BON JOVI)

SANTANA

Formed: San Francisco, California, USA ... October '66 as The SANTANA BLUES BAND, by Mexican-born/Tijuana-raised CARLOS SANTANA. The guitarist's distinctly pure, fluid sound was backed by a constantly changing personnel over the years, though the best work was driven by the powerhouse rhythm section of drummer, MICHAEL SHRIEVE, and percussionist JOSE 'CHEPITO' AREAS. A compelling fusion of Latin stylings and psychedelic-tinged blues jamming, the band's early work has often been copied but rarely equalled. In 1968, the BLUES BAND part of the name was jettisoned and under the more effective moniker of SANTANA they played San Francisco's Fillmore West. Later the same year, CARLOS guested on the album, 'THE LIVE ADVENTURES OF AL KOOPER AND MIKE BLOOMFIELD' which brought him to the attention of 'Columbia' records. Following a show-stopping performance at The Woodstock Festival, their long-awaited eponymous debut album cracked the US Top 5 in late '69. The record, together with their next two follow-up albums, 'ABRAXAS' (1970) and 'SANTANA III' (1971), secured SANTANA's position as one of US rock's leading lights, the latter two sets hitting No.1 in America as well as spawning the hits 'BLACK MAGIC WOMAN', 'EVERYBODY'S EVERYTHING' and a dazzling, frenetic cover of TITO PUENTE's 'OYE COMO VA'. Following an indulgent live set featuring BUDDY MILES, SANTANA released 'CARAVANSERAI' in 1972, a transitional piece that signalled a tentative move away from blues towards the jazz-fusion that would come to characterise most of the band's later 70's output. Around this time CARLOS became a devotee of Indian guru, SRI CHIMNOY, recording the 'LOVE DEVOTION SURRENDER' (1973) album with the similarly converted JOHN McLAUGHLIN. A contemplative piece of ethereal jazz, it had a spiritual partner in the following year's 'ILLUMINATIONS', recorded with fellow CHIMNOY disciple and jazz composer ALICE COLTRANE. Meanwhile, the SANTANA band released 'WELCOME' (1973) and 'BORBOLETTA' (1974), which further explored complex jazz textures, although 1976's 'AMIGOS' returned to a more grounded Latin-rock sound. It was short-lived though, and late 70's albums such as 'MOONFLOWER' (1977) and 'INNER SECRETS' (1978) bordered on the snooze-worthy with their directionless experimentation. 'ZEBOP' (1981) began the new decade on a high note, a masterful set that spawned the US hit single, 'WINNING'. The 80's also saw a solo effort, 'HAVANA MOON' (1983) and the grammy-award winning 'BLUES FOR SALVADOR' (1987) as well as a film score for 'La Bamba'. Following a deal with 'Island', SANTANA has continued his prolific output, releasing the 'BROTHERS' album in 1994 – a collaboration with sibling JORGE. When the phrase "re-inventing yourself" was thought up, they must have had CARLOS SANTANA in mind because what happened by the end of the decade transformed the SANTANA we once knew into Latino Blues stars of the new millennium. The record in question, 'SUPERNATURAL' (1999), was a record inspired by the gods and only CARLOS could hand-pick a team of guest singers/musicians (DAVE MATTHEWS, EVERLAST, LAURYN HILL, WYCLEF JEAN, EAGLE EYE CHERRY and ERIC CLAPTON) to complement this "tight" masterwork. However, it would be matchbox20's ROB THOMAS who stole some of the spotlight, providing cooler than cool vocal chords on multi-million selling single, 'SMOOTH'; it would be no surprise when SANTANA cleaned up most of the top awards in next years' Grammys. From the cover art to the minimalist title to the range of tasteful guest stars, 'SHAMAN' (2002) was basically an attempt to repeat the phenomenal success of its predecessor. While THOMAS was still on board, he concentrated on writing this time around, tailoring songs to both MUSIQ and SEAL, although the pick of the collaborations was arguably 'THE GAME OF LOVE', fronted by MICHELLE BRANCH. • **Songwriters:** CARLOS penned with group, except covers:- JIN-GO-LA-BA (Michael Babatunde Olatunji) / BLACK MAGIC WOMAN (Fleetwood Mac) / GYPSY WOMAN (Curtis Mayfield) / PEACE ON EARTH (Alice Coltrane) / STORMY (Classics IV) / SHE'S NOT THERE (Zombies) / WELL ALL RIGHT (Buddy Holly) / ONE CHAIN (Four Tops) / WINNING (Russ Ballard) / THIRD STONE FROM THE SUN (Jimi Hendrix) / WHO'S THAT LADY (Isley Brothers) / FULL MOON (Paola Rustichelli) / RIGHT ON (Marvin Gaye) / I'VE BEEN TO THE MOUNTAIN TOP (... King) / etc. • **Trivia:** In 1973, CARLOS married Urmila, a Sri Chimnoy devotee. He also became highly religious, changing his name to DEVADIP, which means 'The Light Of The Lamp Supreme'. In the mid-70's, Bill Graham took over the management of SANTANA. For lovers of anything SANTANA, his brother JORGE (in Latin-rock band MALO) had success in April '72 with an eponymous album, which hit US No.14. A single lifted from it, 'SALI VECITO', made No.18. MALO went on to release three more 'Warner Bros.' albums; DOS (1972) / EVOLUTION (1973) + ASCENSION (1974).

Album rating: SANTANA (*7) / ABRAXAS (*8) / SANTANA III (*7) / CARLOS SANTANA & BUDDY MILES! LIVE! solo/collaboration with Buddy Miles (*4) / CARAVANSERAI (*8) / LOVE DEVOTION SURRENDER solo/collaboration with Mahavishnu John McLaughlin (*6) / WELCOME (*6) / ILLUMINATIONS solo/collaboration with Turiya Alice Coltrane (*4) / SANTANA'S GREATEST HITS compilation (*8) / BORBOLETTA (*6) / LOTUS (*6) / AMIGOS (*7) / FESTIVAL (*6) / MOONFLOWER (*6) / INNER SECRETS (*4) / ONENESS: SILVER DREAMS – GOLDEN REALITY solo as Devadip (*5) / MARATHON (*5) / THE SWING OF DELIGHT solo (*4) / ZEBOP! (*6) / SHANGO (*5) / HAVANA MOON solo (*5) / BEYOND APPEARANCES (*4) / FREEDOM (*6) / BLUES FOR SALVADOR solo (*6) / VIVA! SANTANA boxed-compilation (*8) / SPIRITS DANCING IN THE FLESH (*5) / MILAGRO (*5) / SACRED FIRE – LIVE IN SOUTH AMERICA (*4) / BROTHERS as Santana Brothers (*4) / DANCE OF THE RAINBOW SERPENT boxed-set (*7) / SUPERNATURAL (*7) / SHAMAN (*5)

CARLOS SANTANA (b.20 Jul'47, Autlan de Navarro, Mexico) – lead guitar / **GREGG ROLIE** (b.17 Jun'47, Seattle, Washington) – keyboards, vocals / **DAVID BROWN** (b.15 Feb'47, New York) – bass repl. GUS RODRIGUES (in 1967) / **MIKE SHRIEVE** (b. 6 Jul'49, San Francisco) – drums repl. BOB LIVINGSTONE (in '67). He had repl. ROD HARPER / **JOSE CHEPITO AREAS** (b.25 Jul'46, Leon, Nicaragua) – percussion / **MIKE CARABELLO** (b.18 Nov'47, San Francisco) – congas repl. TOM FRAZER – guitar

C.B.S. Columbia

Oct 69. (7") *(CBS 4593)* **PERSUASION. / SAVOR** [ ] [–]

Oct 69. (7") *<45010>* **JIN-GO-LA-BA. / PERSUASION** [–] [56]

Nov 69. (lp) *(CBS 63015) <9781>* **SANTANA** [26] Sep69 [4]
– Waiting / Evil ways / Shades of time / Savor / Jin-go-la-ba / Persuasion / Treat / You just don't care / Soul sacrifice. *(re-iss. Mar70; CBS 63815) (re-iss. Mar81 lp/c; CBS/40 32003) (cd-iss. May87; CD 63815) (cd re-iss. May92 & Apr98 on 'Columbia'; 489542-2)*

Jan 70. (7") *<45069>* **EVIL WAYS. / WAITING** [–] [9]

Apr 70. (7") *(CBS 4940)* **EVIL WAYS. / JIN-GO-LA-BA** [ ] [–]

Nov 70. (lp) *(CBS 64087) <30130>* **ABRAXAS** [7] Sep 70 [1]

– Singing winds, crying beasts / Black magic woman – Gypsy queen / Oyo como va / Incident at Neshabur / Se a cabo / Mother's daughter / Samba pa ti / Hope you're feeling better / El Nicoya. *(re-iss. Mar81 lp/c; CBS/40 32032) (cd-iss. Mar86; CD 64087) (cd re-iss. Mar91; CD 32032) (cd re-iss. Apr98 on 'Columbia'; 489543-2)*

Dec 70. (7") *(CBS 5325)* <45270> **BLACK MAGIC WOMAN. / HOPE YOU'RE FEELING BETTER** [ ] Nov70 [4]

Mar 71. (7") *(CBS 7046)* <45330> **OYE COMO VA. / SAMBA PA TI** [ ] Feb71 [13]

— added **NEAL SCHON** (b.27 Feb'54) – guitar / **COKE ESCOVEDO** (b. THOMAS ESCOVEDO, 30 Apr'41, Calif.) – percussion

Oct 71. (lp) *(CBS 69015)* <30595> **SANTANA III** [6] [1]
– Batuka / No one to depend on / Taboo / Toussaint l'overture / Everybody's everything / Guajira / Everything's coming our way / Jungle strut / Para los rumberos. *(re-iss. Mar82 lp/c; CBS/40 32058) (cd-iss. Mar87; CD 69015) (re-iss. Jun94 on 'Columbia' cd/c; 476830-2) (cd re-iss. Apr98; 489554-2)*

Nov 71. (7") *(CBS 7546)* <45472> **EVERYBODY'S EVERYTHING. / GUAJIRA** [ ] Oct71 [12]

Mar 72. (7") *(CBS 7842)* <45552> **NO ONE TO DEPEND ON. / TABOO** [ ] Feb72 [36]

Jul 72. (lp; by CARLOS SANTANA & BUDDY MILES) *(CBS 65142)* <31308> **CARLOS SANTANA & BUDDY MILES! LIVE! (live)** [29] [8]
– Marbles / Lava / Evil ways / Faith interlude / Them changes / Free form funkafide filth. *(re-iss. Sep84 lp/c; CBS/40 32271)*

Oct 72. (7"; by CARLOS SANTANA & BUDDY MILES) *(CBS 8338)* <45666> **EVIL WAYS (live). / THEM CHANGES (live)** [ ] Aug72 [84]

— **ARMANDO PERAZA** – percussion repl. CARABELLO and ESCOVEDO (latter died 30 Apr'85) / **TOM RUTLEY** – bass repl. BROWN

Nov 72. (lp) *(CBS 65299)* <31610> **CARAVANSERAI** [6] [8]
– Eternal caravan of reincarnation / Waves within / Look up (to see what's coming down) / Just in time to see the sun / Song of the wind / All the love of the universe / Future primitive / Stone flower / La fuente del ritmo / Every step of the way. *(re-iss. Nov81 lp/c; CBS/40 32060) (cd-iss. 1988; CD 65299)*

Jan 73. (7") <45753> **LOOK UP (TO SEE WHAT'S COMING DOWN). / ALL THE LOVE OF THE UNIVERSE** [–] [ ]

Jul 73. (lp; by CARLOS DEVADIP SANTANA AND MAHAVISHNU JOHN McLAUGHLIN) *(CBS 69073)* <32034> **LOVE DEVOTION SURRENDER** [7] [14]
– A love supreme / Naima / The lie divine / Let us go into the house of the Lord / Meditation. *(re-iss. Oct92 & Jun94 on 'Columbia' cd/c; 982830-2/-4)*
(above album featured below newcomers (**RAUCH + LEWIS**) + **PERAZA, JAN HAMMER** – keyboards / **BILLY COBHAM** – drums / **LARRY YOUNG** – keyboards)

— **CARLOS** retained **AREAS, PERAZA + SHRIEVE** and brought in newcomers **TOM COSTER** – keyboards, vocals repl. ROLIE who formed JOURNEY / **RICHARD KERMODE** – keyboards repl. SCHON who also formed JOURNEY / **DOUG RAUCH** – bass repl. RUTLEY / added **LEON THOMAS** – vocals / **JAMES MINGO LEWIS** – congas

Nov 73. (lp) *(CBS 69040)* <32445> **WELCOME** [8] [25]
– Going home / Love, devotion and surrender / Samba de sausalito / When I look into your eyes / Yours is the light / Mother Africa / Light of life / Flame-sky / Welcome. *(re-iss. 1984 lp/c; CBS/40 32194)*

Nov 73. (7") *(CBS 1925)* <45999> **WHEN I LOOK INTO YOUR EYES. / SAMBA DE SAUSALITO** [ ] [ ]

Sep 74. (lp; by TURIYA ALICE COLTRANE & DEVADIP CARLOS SANTANA) *(CBS 69063)* <32900> **ILLUMINATIONS** [40] [79]
– Guru Sri Chimnoy aphorism / Angel of air – Angel of water / Bliss: The eternal now / Angel of sunlight / Illuminations. *(cd-iss. Mar96 on 'Columbia; 483810-2)*
above w/ **ALICE** – keyboards, etc.

— **GREG WALKER** – vocals + sessioners repl. KERMODE, LEWIS and THOMAS

Nov 74. (lp/c) *(CBS/40 69084)* <33135> **BORBOLETTA** [18] Oct74 [20]
– Spring manifestations / Canto de los flores / Life is anew / Give and take / One with the Sun / Aspirations / Practice what you preach / Mirage / Here and now / Flor de canela / Promise of a fisherman / Borboletta. *(re-iss. Nov83 lp/c; CBS/40 32157) (re-iss. cd Nov93 on 'Sony Collectors';)*

Nov 74. (7") *(CBS 2829)* **PRACTICE WHAT YOU PREACH. / CANTO DE LOS FLORES** [ ] [–]

Jan 75. (7") *(CBS 3005)* <10073> **MIRAGE. / FLOR DE CANELA** [ ] [ ]

Mar 75. (7") <10088> **GIVE AND TAKE. / LIFE IS ANEW** [–] [ ]

— (Below triple album was issued initially in Japan 1973)

Dec 75. (t-lp) *(CBS 66325)* **LOTUS (live)** [ ] [–]
– Meditation / Going home / A-1 funk / Every step of the way / Black magic woman – Gypsy queen / Oye como va / Yours is the light / Batuka / Xibaba (she-ba-ba) / Savor / Stone flower / (introduction) / Castillos de arena (pt.1) / Waiting / Se a cabo / Samba pa ti / Toussaint l'overture / Incident at Neshabur. *(re-iss. Dec90 d-cd/d-c; 467943-2/-4)*

— **LEON NDUGU CHANCLER** – drums repl. SHRIEVE and AREAS / **IVORY STONE** – bass repl. RAUCH

Mar 76. (7") *(CBS 4143)* <10421> **EUROPA. / TAKE ME WITH YOU** [ ] Nov76 [ ]

Apr 76. (lp/c) *(CBS/40 86005)* <33576> **AMIGOS** [21] [10]
– Dance sister dance (baila mi Hermana) / Take me with you / Let me / Gitano / Tell me are you tired / Europa (Earth's cry, Heaven's smile) / Let it shine. *(re-iss. Jun84 lp/c; CBS/40 32476) (cd-iss. Mar87; CD 86005) (re-iss. cd Jun92)*

May 76. (7") *(CBS 4335)* <10336> **LET IT SHINE. / TELL ME ARE YOU TIRED** [ ] [77]

Aug 76. (7") *(CBS 4512)* <10353> **DANCE SISTER DANCE (BAILA MI HERMANA). / LET ME** [ ] [ ]

— **JOSE AREAS** returned to repl. PERAZA / **PABLO TELEZ** – bass repl. STONE

Dec 76. (lp/c) *(CBS/40 86020)* <34423> **FESTIVAL** [27] [27]
– Carnaval / Let the children play / Jugando / Carnival / Give me love / Verao Vermelho / Let the music set you free / Revelations / Reach up / The river / Try a little harder / Maria Caracoles.

Jan 77. (7") *(CBS 4927)* **REVELATIONS. / REACH UP** [ ] [–]

Jan 77. (7") <10524> **REVELATIONS. / GIVE ME LOVE** [–] [ ]

Mar 77. (7") *(CBS 5102)* <10481> **LET THE CHILDREN PLAY. / CARNAVAL** [ ] [ ]

— Trimmed slightly when CHANCLER vacated

Sep 77. (7") *(CBS 5671)* <10616> **SHE'S NOT THERE. / ZULU** [11] [27]

Oct 77. (d-lp/c) *(CBS/40 88272)* <34914> **MOONFLOWER (live + studio)** [7] [10]
– Dawn – Go within / Carnaval / Let the children play / Jugando / I'll be waiting / Zulu / Bahia / Black magic woman – Gypsy queen / Dance sister dance (baila mi Hermana) / Europa (Earth's cry, Heaven's smile) / She's not there / Flor de Luna (Moonflower) / Soul sacrifice / Heads, hands & feet / El Morocco / Transcendance / Savor / Toussaint l'overture. *(re-iss. Apr85 d-lp/c; CBS/40 86098) (cd-iss. Apr89; CD 33280) (re-iss. cd Jun96; 463370-2)*

Jan 78. (7") *(CBS 6055)* **BLACK MAGIC WOMAN (live). / TRANSCENDANCE** [ ] [–]

Jan 78. (7") <10677> **BLACK MAGIC WOMAN (live). / I'LL BE WAITING (live)** [–] [ ]

Aug 78. (7"; by CARLOS SANTANA) *(CBS 6520)* **I'LL BE WAITING. / FLOR DE LUNA (MOONFLOWER)** [ ] [–]

— **CARLOS** retained only **WALKER + COSTER** and introduced **ARMANDO PERAZA** returned to repl. AREAS / **DAVID MARGEN** – bass repl. TELLEZ / added **GRAHAM LEER** – drums / **CHRIS RHYME** – keyboards / **RAUL REKOW** – percussion / **CHRIS SOLBERG** – guitar, keyboards, vocals

Oct 78. (7") <10839> **WELL ALL RIGHT. / JERICHO** [–] [69]

Oct 78. (7") *(CBS 6755)* **WELL ALL RIGHT. / WHAM!** [53] [–]
(12"+=) *(CBS12-6755)* – Life is a lady – Holiday.

Nov 78. (lp/c) *(CBS/40 86075)* <35600> **INNER SECRETS** [17] [27]
– Dealer / Spanish rose / Well all right / One chain (don't make no prison) / Stormy / Open invitation / Wham! / The facts of love / Life is a lady – Holiday / Move on. *(cd-iss. 1986 & Jun92; CD 86075)*

Jan 79. (7") *(CBS 6998)* **ONE CHAIN (DON'T MAKE NO PRISON). / MOVE ON** [ ] [–]

Jan 79. (7") <10873> **STORMY. / MOVE ON** [–] [32]

Mar 79. (lp/c; as DEVADIP) *(CBS/40 86037)* <35686> **ONENESS: SILVER DREAMS, GOLDEN REALITY** [55] [87]
– The chosen hour / Arise awake / Light versus darkness / Jim Jeannie / Transformation day / Victory / Silver dreams golden smiles / Cry of the wilderness / Guru's song / Oneness / Life is just a passing parade / Golden dawn / Free as the morning sun / Song for Devadip. *(cd-iss. Mar97 on 'Columbia'; 487238-2)*

Apr 79. (7") <10938> **ONE CHAIN (DON'T MAKE NO PRISON). / LIFE IS A HOLIDAY** [–] [59]

— **ALEX LIGERTWOOD** (b.18 Dec'46, Glasgow, Scotland) – vocals (ex-BRIAN AUGER) repl. WALKER / **ALAN PASQUE** – keyboards, vocals repl. COSTER + RHYME

Oct 79. (7") *(CBS 7971)* <11144> **YOU KNOW THAT I LOVE YOU. / AQUA MARINE** [ ] [35]

Oct 79. (lp/c) *(CBS/40 86098)* <36154> **MARATHON** [28] [25]
– Marathon / Lightning in the sky / Aqua marine / You know that I love you / All I ever wanted / Stand up – Runnin' / Summer lady / Love / Stay / Hard times. *(cd-iss. May87; CD 86098)*

Feb 80. (7") *(CBS 8160)* **ALL I EVER WANTED. / LOVE** [57] [–]

Feb 80. (7") <11218> **ALL I EVER WANTED. / LIGHTNING IN THE SKY** [–] [ ]

Jun 80. (7") *(CBS 8649)* **AQUA MARINE. / STAND UP – RUNNIN'** [ ] [–]

Sep 80. (d-lp/d-c; by CARLOS SANTANA) *(CBS/40 84514)* <36590> **THE SWING OF DELIGHT** [65] [65]
– Swapan tari / Love theme from 'Sparticus' / Phuler Matan / Song for my brother / Jharna kala / Gardenia / La Llave / Golden hours / Shere Khan, the tiger.
(above featured The MILES DAVIS QUINTET of the 60's)

— added **ORESTES VILATO** – percussion / **RICHARD BAKER** – keyboards

Apr 81. (7") *(A-1139)* <01050> **WINNING. / BRIGHTEST STAR** [ ] [17]

Apr 81. (lp/c) *(CBS/40 84946)* <37158> **ZEBOP!** [33] [9]
– Changes / E papa re / Primera invasion / Searchin' / Over and over / Winning / Tales of Kilimanjaro / The sensitive kind / American gypsy / I love you much too much / Brightest star / Hannibal. *(cd-iss. Dec85; CD 84946)*

Jun 81. (7") *(A-1388)* **CHANGES. / AMERICAN GYPSY** [ ] [–]

Sep 81. (7") *(A-1556)* <02178> **THE SENSITIVE KIND. / AMERICAN GYPSY** [ ] Jul81 [56]

Jan 82. (7") <02519> **SEARCHIN'. / TALES OF KILIMANJARO** [–] [ ]

— **CARLOS** retained only **LEAR, MARGEN, BAKER + VILATO**

Aug 82. (lp/c) *(CBS/40 85915)* <38122> **SHANGO** [35] [22]
– The Nile / Hold on / Night hunting time / Nowhere to run / Nueva York / Oxun / Body surfing / What does it take / Let me inside / Warrior / Shango. *(cd-iss. 1983; CD 85914)*

Aug 82. (7") <03160> **HOLD ON. / OXUN** [–] [15]

Nov 82. (7") <03376> **NOWHERE TO RUN. / NUEVA YORK** [–] [66]

CARLOS SANTANA

solo, featuring **WILLIE NELSON, BOOKER T.JONES & The FABULOUS THUNDERBIRDS**

Apr 83. (7") <03925> **WATCH YOUR STEP. / TALES OF KILIMANJARO** [–] [ ]

Apr 83. (7") *(A-3330>* **WATCH YOUR STEP. / LIGHTNIN'** [ ] [–]

Apr 83. (lp/c) *(CBS/40 25350)* <38642> **HAVANA MOON** [84] [31]
– Watch your step / Lightnin' / Who do you love / Mudbone / One with you / Ecuador / Tales of Kilimanjaro / Havana Moon / Daughter of the night / They all went to Mexico / Vereda tropical. *(cd-iss. May87' CD 25350)*

May 83. (7") *(A-3359)* **THEY ALL WENT TO MEXICO. / MUDBONE** [ ] [–]

Jun 83. (7") <04034> **HAVANA MOON. / LIGHTNIN'** [–] [ ]

SANTANA

CARLOS only retained **VILATO** plus sessioners

Mar 85. (7") *(A-4514)* <04758> **SAY IT AGAIN. / TOUCHDOWN RAIDERS** [ ] Feb85 [46]
(12"+=) *(TA-4514)* – She's not there / ('A'instrumental).

Mar 85. (lp/c) *(CBS/40 86307)* <39527> **BEYOND APPEARANCES** [58] [50]
– Breaking out / Written in sand / How long / Brotherhood / Spirit / Say it again / Who loves you / I'm the one who loves you / Touchdown raiders / Right now. *(cd-iss. Mar86; CD 86307)*

May 85. (7") *(A-6284)* **HOW LONG. / RIGHT NOW** [ ] [–]
(12"+=) *(TA-6284)* – She's not there.

May 85. (7") <04912> **I'M THE ONE WHO LOVES YOU. / RIGHT NOW** [–] [ ]

— **CARLOS** re-united **GREGG ROLIE, MIKE SHRIEVE, JOSE AREAS** +sessioners

Feb 87. (lp/c/cd) *(450 500-1/-4/-2)* <40272> **FREEDOM** [ ] [95]
– Vera Cruz / She can't let go / Once it's gotcha / Love is you / Songs of freedom / Deeper, dig deeper / Praise / Mandela / Before we go / Victim of circumstance.

May 87. (7"/12") *(650417-7/-6)* <06654> **VERA CRUZ. / MANDELA** [ ] Mar87 [ ]

May 87. (7") <07038> **VERA CRUZ (remix). / MANDELA** [–] [ ]

Jul 87. (7") <07140> **PRAISE. / LOVE IS YOU** [–] [ ]

— SANTANA touring band **ROLIE, CHESTER THOMPSON** – keyboards / **TOM COSTER** – synthesizers / **ALFONSO JOHNSON** – bass / **GRAHAM LEER** – drums / **BUDDY MILES** – vocals / **ARMANDO PERAZA, PAUL REKOW + ORESTES VILATO** – percussion

Nov 87. (lp/c/cd; by CARLOS SANTANA) *(460 258-1/-4/-2)* <40875> **BLUES FOR SALVADOR** [ ] [ ]
– Bailando / Aquatic park / Bella / I'm gone / 'Trane / Deeper, dig deeper / Mingus / Now that you know / Hannibal / Blues for Salvador.
(above featured mainly session people)

— **CARLOS** retained **THOMPSON + PERAZA,** plus recruited **BENNY RIETVELD** – bass / **ALEX LIGERTWOOD** – vocals, guitar / **WALFREDO REYES** – drums, timbales, perc with host of guests (over 15).

Jun 90. (cd/c/lp) *(466913-2/-4/-1)* <46065> **SPIRITS DANCING IN THE FLESH** [68] [85]
– Let there be light – Spirits dancing in the flesh / Gypsy woman / It's a jungle out there / Soweto (African libre) / Choose / Peace on Earth . . . Mother Earth . . . Third stone from the Sun / Full Moon / Who's that lady / Jin-go-la-ba / Goodness and mercy.

Jun 90. (7") *(656027-7)* **GYPSY WOMAN. / GOODNESS AND MERCY** [ ] [ ]
(12"+=/cd-s+=) *(656027-6/-2)* – Black magic woman (live) / Oye como va (live) / She's not there (live).

— Next with samples from MILES DAVIS and JOHN COLTRANE.

Polydor Polydor

Apr 92. (cd/c/d-lp) *(513197-2/-4/-1)* <513197> **MILAGRO** [ ] [ ]
– Medley:- Introduction by BILL GRAHAM – Milagro / Medley:- I've been to the mountain top – Somewhere in Heaven / Medley:- Saja – Right on / Your touch / Life is for living / Red prophet / Aqua que va ceer / Make somebody happy / Free all the people (South Africa) / Medley:- Gypsy – Grajoonca / We don't have to wait / Adios.

Nov 93. (cd/c) <(521082-2/-4)> **SACRED FIRE** (live in South America) [ ] [ ]
– Angels all around us / Vive le Vada (life is for living) / Esperando / No one to depend on / Black magic woman – Gypsy queen / Oye como va / Samba pa ti / Guajira / Make somebody happy / Toussaint l'overture / Soul sacrifice / Don't try this at home / Europa / Jingo-la-ba.

— with brother **JORGE** – guitar (ex-MALO) + **CARLOS HERNANDEZ**

Island Island

Sep 94. (cd/c; by SANTANA BROTHERS) *(CID/ICT 8034)* <523677> **BROTHERS** [ ] [ ]
– Transmutation industrial / Thoughts / Luz amor y vida / En aranjouz con tu amour / Contigo / Blues Latino / La olaza / Brujo / The trip / Reflections / Morning in Marin.

Arista Arista

Aug 99. (cd/c) <(07822 19080-2/-4)> **SUPERNATURAL** [1] Jun99 [1]
– (Da le) Yaleo / Love of my life (w/ DAVE MATTHEWS) / Put your lights on (w/ EVERLAST) / Africa bamba / Smooth (w/ ROB THOMAS) / Do you like the way (w/ LAURYN HILL) / Maria Maria (w/ WYCLEF JEAN) / Migra / Corazon Espinado / Wishing it was (w/ EAGLE EYE CHERRY) / El farol / Primavera / The calling (w/ ERIC CLAPTON).

Oct 99. (c-s/cd-s; SANTANA featuring ROB THOMAS) *(74321 70949-4/-2)* <13718> **SMOOTH / EL FAROL** [75] Jul99 [1]
(re-iss. Mar00 c-s/cd-s; 74321 74876-4/-2) – hit No.3

Jul 00. (c-s/cd-s; as SANTANA featuring the PRODUCT G&B) *(74321 76937-4/-2)* <13773> **MARIA MARIA / (mixes; Wyclef + Pumpin' Dolls)** [6] Jan00 [1]

Oct 02. (cd/c) *(74321 95938-2/-4)* <14737> **SHAMAN** [15] [1]
– Adouma / Nothing at all (with MUSIQ) / The game of love (with MICHELLE BRANCH) / You are my kind (with SEAL) / Amore (sexo) (with MACY GRAY) / Foo foo / Victory is won / Since Supernatural (with GOVERNOR WASHINGTON & MELKIE JEAN) / America (with P.O.D.) / Sideways (with CITIZEN COPE) / Why don't you & I (with CHAD KROEGER) / Feels like fire (with DIDO) / Aye aye aye / Hoy es adios (with ALEJANDRO LERNER) / One of these days (with OZOMATLI) / Novus (with PLACIDO DOMINGO).

Nov 02. (c-s; by SANTANA & MICHELLE BRANCH) *(74321 95944-4)* **THE GAME OF LOVE / COME TO MY WORLD** [16] [5]
(cd-s+=) *(74321 95944-2)* <radio> – Curacion / ('A'video).

– compilations, others, etc. –

on 'CBS/ Columbia' until mentioned otherwise.

Mar 73. (7") *(CBS 1155)* **OYE COMO VA. / BLACK MAGIC WOMAN** [ ] [–]
(re-iss. Feb76; CBS 3950)

Aug 74. (lp/c) *(CBS/40 69081) <3050>* **SANTANA'S GREATEST HITS** 14 Jul74 17
– Evil ways / Jin-go-la-ba / Hope you're feeling better / Samba pa ti / Persuasion / Black magic woman / Oye como va / Everything's coming up roses / Se a cabo / Everybody's everything. *(cd-iss. Jun87; CD 69081) (re-iss. Feb88 lp/c; CBS/40 32386) (cd re-iss. Jul99 on 'Columbia'; CDZ 32386)*

Sep 74. (7") *(CBS 2561) <46067>* **SAMBA PA TI. / INCIDENT AT NESHABUR** 27
(re-iss. Feb79; CBS 7063)

Oct 80. (t-lp) *(CBS 66354)* **BOX SET** (first 3 albums)

Jul 84. (7") *(A-4587)* **SHE'S NOT THERE. / SAMBA PA TI** –

Feb 86. (12"ep) *Old Gold; (OG 4005)* **SAMBA PA TI / JIN-GO-LA-BA. / SHE'S NOT THERE / EVIL WAYS** –

Oct 86. (lp/c/cd) *K-Tel; (NE1/CE2/NCD3 338)* **VIVA! SANTANA – THE VERY BEST OF SANTANA** 50 –

Jan 88. (7") *Old Gold; (OG 9753)* **SAMBA PA TI. / SHE'S NOT THERE** –

May 88. (cd) *Arcade; (ADEHCD 828-0)* **THE VERY BEST OF SANTANA – VOLUME ONE** –

May 88. (cd) *Arcade; (ADEHCD 828-1)* **THE VERY BEST OF SANTANA – VOLUME TWO** –

Jun 88. (d-lp/c/d-cd) *That's Original; (TFO LP/MC/CD 14)* **WELCOME / CARLOS SANTANA & BUDDY MILES LIVE** –

Oct 88. (t-lp/d-c/d-cd) *(462500-1/-4/-2) <44344>* **VIVA! SANTANA** (best + live)
– Everybody's everything / Black magic woman – Gypsy queen / Guajira / Jungle strut / Jingo / Ballin' / Bambara / Angel Negro / Incident at Neshabur / Just let the music speak / Super boogie – Hong Kong blues / Song of the wind / Abi cama / Vitalo / Paris finale / Brotherhood / Open invitation / Aqua marine / Dance, sisters, dance / Europa / Peraza 1 / She's not there / Bambele / Evil ways / Daughter of the night / Peraza II / Black magic woman – Gypsy woman (live) / Oyo como va / Persuasion / Soul sacrifice. *(d-cd re-iss. Jun97; same)*

May 89. (3"cd-ep) **BLACK MAGIC WOMAN / SAMBA PA TI / OYE COMO VA / JIN-GO-LA-BA** –

Jun 89. (lp/cd) *Thunderbolt; (THBVL/CDTB 071)* **PERSUASION** –
(cd re-iss. Apr98 on 'MagMid'; MM 003)

Jan 90. (lp/cd) *Thunderbolt; (THBVL/CDTB 079)* **LATIN TROPICAL** –
(cd re-iss. Jun98 on 'MagMid'; MM 007)

Oct 90. (cd) *Thunderbolt; (CDTB 087)* **ACAPULCO SUNRISE** –
(re-iss. May97 on 'C.M.C.'; 100182) (re-iss. Mar99 on 'MagMid'; MM 024)

May 92. (cd) *Traditional Line; (TL 1315)* **LIVE IN MONTREUX 1971 (live)** –

Jun 92. (cd/c) *(468267-2/-4)* **THE BEST OF SANTANA**
(re-iss. Oct94; same)

Mar 93. (d-cd) *(465221-2)* **SANTANA / ABRAXAS**

May 93. (cd) *F.N.A.C.;* **NINETEEN SIXTY EIGHT** –

Sep 93. (cd/c) *Sony Collectors; (983259-2/-4)* **SALSA, SAMBA & SANTANA** –

Nov 93. (d-cd) *Sound Wings; (ACD 23057-2)* **SAMBA PA TI** –

Feb 94. (cd) *Thunderbolt; (CDTB 502)* **EVOLUTION** –

Mar 94. (cd) *Charly; (CDCD 1168)* **SOUL SACRIFICE** –

Apr 94. (3xcd) *Pulsar; (PULS 302)* **THE SUPER COLLECTION** –

Nov 96. (cd/c) *Tring; (QED 056)* **AS YEARS GO BY** –

Jul 94. (cd/c) *Success; (1348)* **SANTANA JAM** –

Jul 94. (cd/c) *Success;* **EVERY DAY I HAVE THE BLUES** –

Jul 94. (cd/c) *Success;* **WITH A LITTLE HELP FROM MY FRIENDS** –

Oct 94. (cd) *Charly; (CDCD 1187)* **LATIN ROCK FUSIONS** –

Feb 95. (cd/c) *B.A.M.;* **PEARLS OF THE PAST** –

Apr 95. (cd/c) *Muskateer; (MU 5/4 025)* **THE EARLY YEARS** –

Sep 95. (3xcd-box) *Legacy-Columbia; (C3K 64605)* **DANCE OF THE RAINBOW SERPENT**

Oct 95. (cd/c) *Collectors Choice; (462563-2/-4)* **SAMBA PA TI** –

Nov 95. (3xcd-box) *The Collection; (KBOX 346)* **THE COLLECTION** –

Mar 97. (d-cd) *Legacy; (485106-2)* **LIVE ROCK . . . AT FILLMORE (live)** –

Apr 97. (cd) *(CDX 32386)* **THE VERY BEST**

May 97. (cd) *C.M.C.; (101182)* **LIVE** –

May 97. (d-cd) *Laserlight; (24359)* **SANTANA** –

May 97. (cd) *Experience; (EXP 027)* **SANTANA VOL.1** –

May 97. (cd) *Experience; (EXP 028)* **SANTANA VOL.2** –

Mar 98. (d-cd) *Charly; (CPCD 83312)* **AWAKENING** –

Apr 98. (cd) *<65561>* **THE BEST OF SANTANA** – 82

Aug 98. (d-cd/d-c) *Sony TV; (SONYTV 47 CD/MC)* **THE ULTIMATE COLLECTION** 23 –
(re-dist.Mar00) – hit No.12

Jun 99. (cd) *Columbia: (494678-2)* **BLACK MAGIC WOMAN – THE BEST OF SANTANA**

Jul 99. (cd) *Akarma; (AK 068CD)* **SF MISSION DISTRICT LIVE (live)** –

Jul 99. (d-cd) *Yeaah; (YEAAH 4)* **FRIED NECKBONES AND HOME FRIES** –

— Note: Most albums up to 1974 were also issued on quad-lp. SUCH IS LIFE album late '93, must have been by other band of same name.

Joe SATRIANI

Born: 15 Jul'57, Bay Area, San Francisco, California, USA, although he was raised in Carle Place, Long Island. In addition to working as a guitar teacher (STEVE VAI and METALLICA's KIRK HAMMETT are among his more famous ex-pupils), six-string maestro SATRIANI played in various rock outfits (i.e. The SQUARES), before eventually making his vinyl debut in 1985 with an eponymous EP. A debut album, 'NOT OF THIS EARTH' (1987) followed soon after, introducing SATRIANI as more then yet another fretboard acrobat; conventional song structures and strong melodies were given just as much emphasis as the (admittedly impressive) soloing and flying-fingered technicality. So it was then, that SATRIANI attracted conventional rock fans and guitar freaks alike, a follow-up effort, 'SURFING WITH THE ALIEN' (1987), hitting the US Top 30, a remarkable feat for an instrumental opus. A master of mood, SATRIANI's forte was the ability to segue smoothly from grinding jazz-tinged raunch rock like 'SATCH BOOGIE' into the beautiful lilt of 'ALWAYS WITH YOU, ALWAYS WITH ME'. 'FLYING IN A BLUE DREAM' (1989) developed this approach, a flawless album which took in everything from dirty boogie ('BIG BAD MOON') to PRINCE-esque white funk ('STRANGE') as well as the obligatory ballad (the corny yet heartfelt 'I BELIEVE'), careering guitar juggernauts ('BACK TO SHALLA-BAL') and even a back-porch banjo hoedown (!), 'THE PHONE CALL'. The album also introduced SATRIANI the singer, and as might be expected, his vocal talents didn't quite match his celebrated axe skills. Nevertheless, it was a brave attempt to advance even further down the song-centric route and his voice did have a certain sly charm although the most affecting tracks on the album remained the new-agey efforts where SATRIANI was talking through his instrument (so to speak!); just listen to the likes of 'THE FORGOTTEN', lie back and melt! A third effort followed in 1992, 'THE EXTREMIST' almost making the UK Top 10 and consolidating SATRIANI's reputation as one of the foremost players of his era. A double set, 'TIME MACHINE' (1993) collected rare and previously released material with a smattering of new tracks while a fourth album proper was eventually released in the form of the eponymous 'JOE SATRIANI' (1995), following the guitarist's brief stint in DEEP PURPLE. In 1997, a live set appeared although this was shared alongside fellow guitar troopers STEVE VAI and ERIC JOHNSON. Veteran collaborators HAMM and CAMPITELLI were back in place for 1998's 'CRYSTAL PLANET', a welcome return to the all-instrumental inventiveness of his late 80's work. While this further explored the parameters of his own unique sonic territory, 'ENGINES OF CREATION' (2000) found SATRIANI gamely attempting to translate his six-string alchemy into an electronic framework. As with JEFF BECK's recent plunge into the digital age, the album worked best when the guitar components went with the electronic flow rather than trying to stem it. 'LIVE IN SAN

FRANCISCO' (2001) was recorded at that city's legendary Fillmore Auditorium, and while SATRIANI may be just the latest in a long line of artists to have cut albums there, he proved that his talent is one of the more unique to have graced that stage. As good a primer as any for the uninitiated, it drew liberally from the cream if his studio work, although there were no sneak previews of 2002's 'STRANGE BEAUTFUL MUSIC', wherein the fretmaster dabbled in ethnic sounds and elements of electronica to middling success. • **Trivia:** JOE also guested on ALICE COOPER's 'Hey Stoopid' and SPINAL TAP's 'Break Like The Wind'.

Album rating: NOT OF THIS EARTH (*6) / SURFING WITH THE ALIEN (*7) / FLYING IN A BLUE DREAM (*8) / THE EXTREMIST (*5) / TIME MACHINE part compilation (*6) / JOE SATRIANI (*6) / G3 LIVE IN CONCERT with Eric Johnson & Steve Vai (*7) / CRYSTAL PLANET (*6) / ENGINES OF CREATION (*5) / LIVE IN SAN FRANCISCO (*6) / STRANGE BEAUTIFUL MUSIC (*5)

JOE SATRIANI – guitar, bass, keyboards, percussion, etc. / with band **JEFF CAMPITELLI** – drums, percussion, DX / **JOHN CUNIBERTI** – percussion, vocals / **BONGO BOB SMITH** – electronics, drums / **JEFF KREEGER** – synthesizer

not iss. Rubina

1985. (12"ep) <1> **JOE SATRIANI** [–] [ ]
– Banana mango / Dreaming #11 / I am become death / Saying goodbye.

Food For Thought Combat

Feb 87. (lp) *(GRUB 7) <88561-8110-2>* **NOT OF THIS EARTH** [ ] Nov86 [ ]
– Not of this Earth / The snake / Rubina / Memories / Brother John / The enigmatic / Driving at night / Hordes of locusts / New day / The headless horseman. *(re-iss. Sep88 cd/c; CD/T GRUB 7) (re-iss. Feb93 cd/c/lp; CD/T+/GRUB 7X) (re-iss. May93 on 'Relativity' cd/c; 462972-2/-4)*

—— he was now joined by **STU HAMM** – bass / **JONATHAN MOVER** – drums

Food For Thought Relativity

Nov 87. (lp) *(GRUB 8) <8195>* **SURFING WITH THE ALIEN** [ ] [29]
– Surfing with the alien / Ice 9 / Crushing day / Always with you, always with me / Satch boogie / Hill of the skull / Circles / Lords of Karma / Midnight / Echo. *(re-iss. Sep88 cd/c; CD/T GRUB 8) (re-iss. Feb93 cd/c/lp; CD/T+/GRUB 8X) (re-iss. May93 on 'Relativity' cd/c; 462973-2/-4)*

Jun 88. (7") *(YUM 112)* **ALWAYS WITH YOU, ALWAYS WITH ME. / SURFING WITH THE ALIEN** [ ] [ ]

Dec 88. (12"ep) *(YUMT 114) <8265>* **DREAMING #11** [ ] m-lp [42]
– The crush of love / Ice 9 / Memories (live) / Hordes of locusts (live). *(re-iss. May93 on 'Relativity' cd-ep/c-ep; 473604-2/-4)*

—— SATRIANI now on vocals for 6 tracks & returned to original line-up:- **HAMM + CAMPITELLI**

Nov 89. (cd/c/lp) *(CD/T+/GRUB 14) <1015>* **FLYING IN A BLUE DREAM** [ ] [23]
– Flying in a blue dream / The mystical potato head groove thing / Can't slow down / Headless / Strange / I believe / One big rush / Big bad moon / The feeling / The phone call / Day at the beach (new rays from an ancient Sun) / Back to Shalla-bal / Ride / The forgotten (part one) / The forgotten (part two) / The bells of Lal (part one) ? The bells of Lal (part two) / Into the light. *(re-iss. Feb93 cd/c/lp; CD/T+/GRUB 14X) (re-iss. May93 on 'Relativity' cd/c; 465995-2/-4)*

Mar 90. (7") *(YUM 118)* **BIG BAD MOON. / DAY AT THE BEACH (NEW RAYS FROM AN ANCIENT SUN)** [ ] Nov89 [ ]
(12"+=/cd-s+=) *(YUMT 118)* – ('A'extended).

Mar 91. (7") **I BELIEVE. / FLYING IN A BLUE DREAM** [ ] [ ]
(12"+=/cd-s+=) – ('A'remix).

—— now with **ANDY JOHNS** on production, etc.

Epic Relativity

Aug 92. (cd/c/lp) *(471672-2/-4/-1) <1053>* **THE EXTREMIST** [13] [22]
– Friends / The extremist / War / Cryin' / Rubina's blue sky happiness / Summer song / Tears in the rain / Why / Motorcycle driver / New blues.

Feb 93. (12"ep/cd-ep) *(658953-2/-4)* **THE SATCH EP** [53] [ ]
– The extremist / Cryin' / Banana mango / Crazy.

Nov 93. (2xcd/2xc/3xlp) *(474515-2/-4/-1) <1177>* **TIME MACHINE** (out-takes & new) [32] [95]
– Time machine / The mighty turtle head / All alone (a.k.a. left alone) / Banana mango 11 / Thinking of you / Crazy / Speed of light / Baroque / Dweller of the threshold / Banana mango / Dreaming #11 / I am become death / Saying goodbye / Woodstock jam / Satch boogie / Summer song / Flying in a blue dream / Cryin' / The crush of love / Tears in the rain / Always with me, always with you / Big bad Moon / Surfing with the alien / Rubina / Circles / Drum solo / Lords of Karma / Echo.

Oct 95. (cd/c) *(481102-2/-4) <1500>* **JOE SATRIANI** [21] [51]
– Cool #9 / If / Down down down / Luminous flesh giants / SMF / Look my way / Home / Moroccan sunset / Killer bee bop / Slow down blues / (You're) My world / Sittin' 'round. *(re-iss. Aug00; same)*

May 97. (cd/c; shared with ERIC JOHNSON & STEVE VAI) *(487539-2/-4)* **G3 LIVE IN CONCERT (live 2nd November, 1996 at Northrop Auditorium, Minneapolis)** [ ] [ ]
– Cool No.9 / Flying in a blue dream / Summer song / (tracks by ERIC JOHNSON) / (tracks by STEVE VAI) / The jam songs (featuring all 3 G's):- Going down. *(video+=)* – My guitar wants to kill your mama / Red house. *(cd re-iss. Aug00; same)*

Mar 98. (cd/c) *(489473-2/-4) <68018>* **CRYSTAL PLANET** [32] [50]
– Up in the sky / House full of bullets / Crystal planet / Love thing / Trundrumbalind / Lights of Heaven / Raspberry jam delta-V / Ceremony / With Jupiter in mind / Secret player / A train of angels / A piece of liquid / Psycho monkey / Time / Z.Z.'s song.

Mar 00. (cd) *(497665-2) <67860>* **ENGINES OF CREATION** [ ] [ ]
– Devil's side / Flavor crystal / Borg sex / Until we say goodbye / Attack / Champagne / Clouds race across the sky / The power cosmic 2000 (part 1) / The power cosmic 2000 (part 2) / Slow and easy / Engines of creation.

Jul 01. (d-cd) *(503314-2) <85737>* **LIVE IN SAN FRANCISCO (live)** [ ] Jun01 [ ]
– Time / Devil's slide / The crush of love / Satch boogie / Borg sex / Flying in a blue dream / Ice 9 / Cool #9 / Circles / Until we say goodbye / Ceremony / The extremist / Summer song / House full of bullets / One big rush / Raspberry jam delta-V / Crystal planet / Love things / Bass solo / The mystical potato head groove thing / Always with me, always with you / Big bad moon / Friends / Surfing with the alien / Rubina.

—— **MATT BISSONETTE** – bass; repl. HAMM

Sep 02. (cd) *(508076-2) <86294>* **STRANGE BEAUTIFUL MUSIC** [ ] Jun02 [ ]
– Oriental melody / Belly dancer / Starry night / Chords of life / Mind storm / Sleep walk / New last jam / Mountain song / What breaks a heart / Seven strings / Hill groove / The journey / The traveler / You saved my life.

– compilations, etc. –

Oct 94. (3xcd-box) *Relativity; (477519-2)* **NOT OF THIS EARTH / SURFING WITH THE ALIEN / FLYING IN A BLUE DREAM** [ ] [ ]

☐ SCARFACE (see under ⇒ GETO BOYS)

Michael SCHENKER (GROUP)

Born: 10 Jan'55, Savstedt, Germany. Famous for forming teutonic rockers The SCORPIONS with his brother RUDOLF in 1971, he went on to join English band, UFO, with whom he cut four albums (PHENOMENON / FORCE IT / NO HEAVY PETTIN' / LIGHTS OUT). SCHENKER subsequently returned to Germany in 1978 where he briefly rejoined The SCORPIONS for the 1979 album, 'LOVEDRIVE', augmenting them live before striking out on his own and forming the MICHAEL SCHENKER GROUP. Recruiting GARY BARDEN, MO FOSTER, SIMON PHILIPS and ex-COLOSSEUM II keyboard whizz, DON AIREY, the guitarist released an eponymous debut in 1980. Dominated by SCHENKER's sizzling axework, the album smashed into the UK Top 10, the guitarist's impressive pedigree ensuring healthy sales. For the subsequent tour, however, SCHENKER made the first personnel changes (PAUL RAYMOND, CHRIS GLEN and COZY POWELL replacing AIREY, FOSTER and PHILIPS respectively) in what would become a familiar pattern and no doubt contribute to the group's eventual spiral into mediocrity. This was the line-up which played on 'MSG' (1981), SCHENKER ripping out what

could be his theme tune in 'ATTACK OF THE MAD AXEMAN'. Like The SCORPIONS, MSG enjoyed obsessive adulation in Japan, as witnessed on 1982's barnstorming double live set, 'ONE NIGHT AT BUDOKAN'. More line-up changes ensued, chief among them being ex-RAINBOW vocalist, GRAHAM BONNET replacing BARDEN, while former RORY GALLAGHER sticksman, TED McKENNA, was recruited in place of POWELL (who joined WHITESNAKE). With BONNET's earthier tones and significant songwriting input, the resulting album, 'ASSAULT ATTACK' (1982) was a bluesier affair albeit with SCHENKER's stinging guitar still vying for attention. Following BONNET's resumption of his solo career, BARDEN was welcomed back into the fold for 'BUILT TO DESTROY' (1983) and 'ROCK WILL NEVER DIE' (1984), two lacklustre albums which didn't exactly do much for SCHENKER's reputation. Inevitably, the group splintered, with the guitarist going back to Germany to reconsider his battle plan. When he resurfaced in late '87 with 'PERFECT TIMING', the 'M' in MSG now stood for McAULEY, SCHENKER having teamed up with former FAR CORPORATION / GRAND PRIX vocalist ROBIN McAULEY for a more accessible melodic rock approach. The group enjoyed moderate success although by the release of 1992's 'M.S.G.', they seemed bankrupt of ideas and the record was roundly slated by critics. Marginally more inspired was the 'CONTRABAND' (1991) project, a collaboration with the likes of TRACII GUNS and BOBBY BLOTZER. The days of the guitar hero may well be over, however, and SCHENKER was conspicuous by his absence from the metal scene for most of the 90's. After an extended absence the ageing teutonic axeman returned to the fray in the late 90's with a flurry of releases beginning with 1997's comeback set, 'WRITTEN IN THE SAND'. 1999 saw the release of both the 'UNFORGIVEN' studio set and a concert double set from the subsequent tour, 'THE UNFORGIVEN WORLD TOUR: LIVE'. Another live set, 'FLYING GOD' was released the same year. Come the new millennium, his guitar playing was as surprisingly virile as it had ever been with 'ADVENTURES OF THE IMAGINATION' (2000), an all-instrumental affair featuring veteran skins pounder AYNSLEY DUNBAR. More of the same was on offer with 'MS 2000: DREAMS & EXPRESSIONS' (2001), with over twenty, largely short, sharp shocks of SCHENKER fret acrobatics, rather pretentiously given single letter titles. 'ARACHNOPHOBIAC' followed in 2003.
• **Trivia:** CONTRABAND covered Mott The Hoople's 'ALL THE WAY FROM MEMPHIS'.

Album rating: MICHAEL SCHENKER GROUP (*5) / MSG (*4) / ONE NIGHT AT BUDOKAN (*6) / ASSAULT ATTACK (*4) / BUILT TO DESTROY (*4) / ROCK WILL NEVER DIE (*4) / PORTFOLIO compilation (*6) / McAuley-Schenker Group: PERFECT TIMING (*5) / SAVE YOURSELF (*4) / MSG (*4) / Michael Schenker (Group): WRITTEN IN THE SAND (*4) / FLYING GOD (*4) / THE UNFORGIVEN (*5) / THE UNFORGIVEN WORLD TOUR (*4) / ADVENTURES OF THE IMAGINATION (*6) / MS2000: DREAMS AND EXPRESSIONS (*5) / ARACHNOPHOBIAC (*4)

MICHAEL SCHENKER – lead guitar (ex-SCORPIONS, ex-UFO) / **GARY BARDEN** – vocals / **DON AIREY** – keyboards (ex-COLOSSEUM II) / **MO FOSTER** – bass / **SIMON PHILLIPS** – drums

Chrysalis Chrysalis

Aug 80. (lp/c) *(<CHR/ZCHR 1302>)* **MICHAEL SCHENKER GROUP** 8 100
– Armed and ready / Cry for the nations / Victim of illusion / Bijou pleasurette / Feels like a good thing / Into the arena / Looking out from nowhere / Tales of mystery / Lost horizons. *(re-iss. Jun84 on 'Fame' lp/c; FA41 3105-1/-4) (<cd-iss. Feb00 on 'Liberty'; 524630-2>)*

Aug 80. (7"colrd) *(CHS 2455)* **ARMED AND READY. / BIJOU PLEASURETTE** 53

Oct 80. (7"clear) *(CHS 2471)* **CRY FOR THE NATIONS. / INTO THE ARENA (live)** 56
(12"+=) *(CHS12 2471)* – Armed and ready (live).

— **PAUL RAYMOND** – keyboards (ex-UFO, etc.) repl. AIREY / **CHRIS GLEN** – bass (ex-SENSATIONAL ALEX HARVEY BAND) repl. FOSTER / **COZY POWELL** – drums (ex-RAINBOW, ex-Solo artist) repl. PHILLIPS

Aug 81. (7"clear) *(CHS 2541)* **READY TO ROCK. / ATTACK OF THE MAD AXEMAN**

Sep 81. (lp/c) *(<CHR/ZCHR 1336>)* **MSG** 14 81
– Ready to rock / Attack of the mad axeman / On and on / Let sleeping dogs lie / But I want more / Never trust a stranger / Looking for love / Secondary motion. *(cd-iss. May86; CCD 1336)*

Feb 82. (d-lp/d-c) *(<CTY/ZCTY 1375>)* **ONE NIGHT AT BUDOKAN (live)** 5
– Armed and ready / Cry for the nations / Attack of the mad axeman / But I want more / Victim of illusion / Into the arena / On and on / Never trust a stranger / Let sleeping dogs lie / Courvoisier concert / Lost horizons / Doctor doctor / Are you ready to rock. *(d-cd-iss. Sep91; CCD 1375) (cd re-iss. Jun96 on 'Beat Goes On'; BGOCD 312)*

— **GRAHAM BONNET** – vocals (ex-RAINBOW, ex-Solo, ex-MARBLES) repl. BARDEN + RAYMOND / **TED McKENNA** – drums (ex-SENSATIONAL ALEX HARVEY BAND, ex-RORY GALLAGHER) repl. COZY who joined WHITESNAKE

Sep 82. (7"clear,7"pic-d) *(CHS 2636)* **DANCER. / GIRL FROM UPTOWN** 52
(12"+=) *(CHS12 2636)* – ('A'extended).

Oct 82. (lp/c/pic-lp) *(<CHR/ZCHR/PCHR 1393>)* **ASSAULT ATTACK** 19
– Assault attack / Rock you to the ground / Dancer / Samurai / Desert song / Broken promises / Searching for a reason / Ulcer. *(cd-iss. Aug96 on 'Beat Goes On'; BGOCD 321)*

— **GARY BARDEN** – vocals returned to repl. BONNET who went solo / added **DEREK ST. HOLMES** – keyboards (ex-TED NUGENT) (on tour **ANDY NYE** – keyboards)

Sep 83. (lp/c/pic-lp) *(<CHR/ZCHR/PCHR 1441>)* **BUILT TO DESTROY** 23
– Rock my nights away / I'm gonna make you mine / The dogs of war / Systems failing / Captain Nemo / Still love that little devil / Red sky / Time waits (for no one) / Walk the stage. *(cd-iss. Jan97 on 'Beat Goes On'; BGOCD 344)*

Jun 84. (lp/c) *(<CUX/ZCUX 1470>)* **ROCK WILL NEVER DIE (live)** 24
– Captain Nemo / Rock my nights away / Are you ready to rock / Attack of the mad axeman / Into the arena / Rock will never die / Desert song / I'm gonna make you mine / Doctor, doctor.

— When CHRIS GLEN departed, most of others also departed

McAULEY-SCHENKER GROUP

— added **ROBIN McAULEY** (b.20 Jan'53, County Meath, Eire) – vox (ex-FAR CORPORATION) / **MITCH PERRY** – guitar / **ROCKY NEWTON** – bass / **BOBO SCHOPF** – drums

E.M.I. Capitol

Oct 87. (7") *(EM 30) <44079>* **GIMME YOUR LOVE. / ROCK TILL YOU'RE CRAZY**
(12"+=/12"remix+=) *(12EM/+S 30)* – ('A'extended).

Oct 87. (cd/c/lp) *(CD/TC+/EMC 3539) <46985>* **PERFECT TIMING** 65 95
– Gimme your love / Here today, gone tomorrow / Don't stop me now / No time for losers / Follow the night / Get out / Love is not a game / Time / I don't wanna lose / Rock 'til you're crazy.

Jan 88. (7"/12"/12"remix) *(EM/12EM/12EMS 40) <44113>* **LOVE IS NOT A GAME. / GET OUT**

Apr 88. (7") *<44156>* **FOLLOW THE NIGHT. / DON'T STOP ME NOW** –

— **McAULEY & SCHENKER** now with **BOBO SCHOPF** – drums / **STEVE MANN** (b.9 Aug'56) – rhythm guitar / **ROCKY NEWMAN** (b.11 Sep'57) – bass (ex-LIONHEART)

Oct 89. (cd/c/lp) *(CD/TC+/EMC 3567) <92752>* **SAVE YOURSELF** 92
– Save yourself / Bad boys / Anytime / Get down to bizness / Shadow of the night / What we need / I am your radio / There has to be another way / This is my heart / Destiny. *(cd+=)* – Take me back.

Apr 90. (c-s/7") *(TC+/EM 127) <44471>* **ANYTIME. / WHAT WE NEED**
(12"+=/12"pic-d+=/cd-s+=) *(12EM/12EMPD/CDEM 127)* – ('A'version).

— **SCHENKER** with **ROBIN McAULEY** – vocals / **JEFF PILSON** – bass (ex-DOKKEN) / **JAMES KOTTAK** – drums (ex-KINGDOM COME)

E.M.I. Impact

Feb 92. (12"ep/cd-ep) **NEVER ENDING NIGHTMARE**
– Nightmare / Bad boys (acoustic) / What happens to me (acoustic) / We believe in love (acoustic) / Nightmare (album version).

Feb 92. (cd)(c/lp; as SCHENKER – McAULEY) *(CDP 798487-2)(EUS MC/LP 3) <10385>* **M.S.G.**
– Eve / Paradise / When I'm gone / The broken heart / We believe in love / Crazy / Invincible / What happens to me / Lonely nights / This night is gonna last forever / Never ending nightmare. *(cd re-iss. Jul96 on 'Beat Goes On'; BGOCD 316)*

MICHAEL SCHENKER GROUP

Zero Michael Schenker

Dec 97. (cd) *(XRCN 1283) <109>* **WRITTEN IN THE SAND**
– Brave new world / Cry no more / I believe / Back to life / Written in the sand / Essenz / Love never dies / I will be there / Take me through the night / Down the drain / Into the arena / Cry for nations. *(re-iss. Nov01 on 'S.P.V.'; 085-7625-2)*

Feb 99. (cd) *(XRCN 10009)* **FLYING GOD** –
– A self made man / Venus / Pushed to the limit / Stopped by a bullet (of love) / Dreaming of summer / Doctor doctor '95 / Lights out '95 / Brave new world / Essenz / Written in the sand / Back to life / I believe / Into the arena / Cry for the nations.

S.P.V. Shrapnel

Feb 99. (cd) *(085-1868-2) <SH 1126>* **THE UNFORGIVEN**
– Rude awakening / The mess I've made / In and out of time / Hello angel / Fat city N.O. / Tower / Pilot of your soul / Forever and more / Turning off the emotion / Live for today / Illusion / The storm.

Oct 99. (d-cd) *(085-2153-2) <SH 1131>* **THE UNFORGIVEN WORLD TOUR LIVE (live)**
– Armed and ready / Only you can rock me / Natural thing / Pushed to the limit / Written in the sand / Captain Nemo / Into the arena / Essence / Pilot of your soul / The mess I've made / Fat city / On and on / Attack of the mad axeman / Assault attack / Another piece of meat / Love to love / Too hot to handle / Lights out / Bijou pleasurette – Positive forward / Doctor doctor / Rock bottom.

Mar 00. (cd) *(085-2172-2) <SH 1140>* **ADVENTURES OF THE IMAGINATION**
– Achtung fertig, los / Open gate / Three fish dancing / Michael Schenker, Junior / Aardvark in a VW smoking a cigar / I want to be with you / Old man with sheep on Mars / At the end of the day / Hand in hand.

— with **SHANE GAALASS** – drums + **BARRY SPARKS** – bass

Feb 01. (cd) *(085-7217-2) <SH 1144>* **MS 2000: DREAMS AND EXPRESSIONS**
– D / R / E / A / M / S / A / N / D / E / X / P / R / E / S / S / I / O / N / S.

— next with **STU HAMM** – bass + **JEREMY COLSOPN** – drums

Mascot Shrapnel

Jun 03. (cd) *(M 7081CD) <SH 1163>* **ARACHNOPHOBIAC**
– Evermore / Illusion / Arachnophobiac / Rock and roll believer / Sands of time / Weathervane / Over now / One world / Break the cycle / Alive / Fatal strike.

– compilations, etc. –

Jun 87. (lp/c)(cd) *Chrysalis; (CNW/ZCNW 1)(MPCD 1598)* **PORTFOLIO** –
– Doctor doctor (UFO) / Rock bottom (UFO) / Rock will never die / Armed and ready / Ready to rock / Assault attack / Ulcer / Attack of the mad axeman / I'm a loser / Reasons to love / Too hot to handle / Only you can rock me (UFO) / Lights out (UFO) / Arbory hill / Love drive (SCORPIONS) / Searching for a reason / Rock my nights away / Captain Nemo.

Jul 91. (cd/c) *Castle; (CCS CD/MC 294)* **THE COLLECTION** –

Oct 92. (cd/c) *Chrysalis; (CD/TC CHR 1949)* **THE ESSENTIAL MICHAEL SCHENKER GROUP** –

Apr 93. (cd) *Connoisseur; (VSOPCD 185)* **ANTHOLOGY** –
– (with UFO tracks) *(re-iss. Aug95 on 'Griffin';)*

Nov 93. (cd) *Windsong; (WINCD 043)* **BBC RADIO 1 LIVE IN CONCERT (live)** –

Apr 94. (cd) *Chrysalis; (CDCHR 6071)* **THE STORY OF MICHAEL SCHENKER GROUP** –

Jun 94. (cd/c) *Music Club; (MC CD/TC 160)* **ARMED AND READY – THE BEST OF MICHAEL SCHENKER GROUP** –

Mar 97. (cd; SCHENKER & McAULEY GROUP) *Disky; (CR 86993-2)* **CHAMPIONS OF ROCK** –

Aug 01. (cd) *E.M.I.; 534698-2)* **MASTERS OF ROCK** –

Nov 01. (cd) *S.P.V.; (<085-7266-2>)* **THANK YOU**

Apr 02. (cd) *S.P.V.; (<085-7282-2>)* **THANK YOU 2**

Oct 02. (cd) *Mascot; (M 7076CD) / Shrapnel; <SH 1158>* **THANK YOU 3** Sep02

Nov 02. (4xcd-box) *Zoom Club; (ZCRCD 87BOX)* **REACTIVATE – LIVE**

□ Fred SCHNEIDER (see under ⇒ B-52's)

□ Neal SCHON & Jan HAMMER (see under ⇒ JOURNEY)

SCORPIONS

Formed: Hanover, Germany . . . 1971 by the SCHENKER brothers (MICHAEL and RUDOLPH) together with KLAUS MEINE, LOTHAR HEINBERG and WOLFGANG ZIONY. After a well-received debut, 'LONESOME CROW' (1973), on the domestic 'Brain' records, the band underwent a turbulent series of personnel changes which resulted in ULRICH ROTH replacing MICHAEL (who went on to join U.F.O.), JURGEN ROSENTHAL replacing ZIONY and FRANCIS BUCHHOLZ coming in for the departing LOTHAR. Signing worldwide to 'R.C.A.', the new-look SCORPIONS released a follow-up, 'FLY TO THE RAINBOW' in 1974. Archetypal German hard-rock, The SCORPIONS' sound consisted of initially jazz-inflected, lumbering riffs punctuated with piercing solos and topped off with MEINE's strangely accessible nasal whine. They developed this approach over a number of 70's albums, 'IN TRANCE' (1976), erm.. 'VIRGIN KILLERS' (1977), etc. The live 'TOKYO TAPES' (1979) brought the first half of the group's career to a neat close, ROTH subsequently departing to form ELECTRIC SUN, disillusioned at the band's increasingly commercial direction. His replacement was MATHIAS JABS although MICHAEL SCHENKER returned briefly, guesting on three tracks for the 'LOVEDRIVE' (1979) set. Now signed to 'Harvest' ('Mercury' in the States), the group had produced their most radio-friendly collection to date, the album taking them into the UK (Top 40) and US (Top 60) charts for the first time. 'ANIMAL MAGNETISM' (1980) fared even better, almost breaking the UK Top 20 with the NWOBHM in full swing, the record also featuring the anthemic live favourite, 'THE ZOO'. 'BLACKOUT' (1982) finally broke the group in America, achieving double platinum status. 1984's 'LOVE AT FIRST STING' fared even better, selling twice as much as its predecessor and spawning a Top 30 hit single with the stop-start riffing of 'ROCK YOU LIKE A HURRICANE'. The SCORPIONS were now seemingly tailoring their music for the US market, concentrating more on melody and hooklines with each successive release. Save for the massive selling concert set,'WORLD WIDE LIVE' (1985), it was to be a further four years before the group released a new album as they became the first Western rock group to play in the Soviet Union, 'SAVAGE AMUSEMENT' finally surfacing in 1988. The SCORPIONS' anthemic rock continued to attract a bigger audience Stateside than in Britain, the group scoring a Top 5 US hit single (and a worldwide No.1) in 1991 with the lighter-waving ballad, 'WIND OF CHANGE'. Sadly not referring to MEINE finally having that awful mullet cut off, the song instead dealt with the sweeping changes in the communist bloc (a version was actually recorded in Russian!). They continued to eschew tales of loose women and 'crazy' nights for more serious political matters on 'FACE THE HEAT' (1993), exploring the social effect of their country's reunification. Four albums have since emerged from the German dinosaurs, 'LIVE BITES' (1995), 'PURE INSTINCT' (1995), 'EYE TO EYE' (1999) and the year 2000's METALLICA-meets-orchestra type effort 'MOMENT OF GLORY', a record that featured The Berlin Philharmonic!

Album rating: ACTION (or) LONESOME CROW (*4) / FLY TO THE RAINBOW (*4) / IN TRANCE (*6) / VIRGIN KILLERS (*6) / TAKEN BY FORCE (*4) / TOKYO TAPES (*5) / LOVEDRIVE (*6) / ANIMAL MAGNETISM (*5) / BLACKOUT (*6) / LOVE AT FIRST STING (*6) / WORLD WIDE LIVE (*6) / SAVAGE AMUSEMENT (*5) / CRAZY WORLD (*4) / FACE THE HEAT (*4) / LIVE BITES (*3) / DEADLY STING compilation (*6) / PURE INSTINCTS (*4) / EYE TO EYE (*3) / MOMENT OF GLORY with the Berliner Philharmonica (*4) / ACOUSTICA (*4)

KLAUS MEINE (b.25 May'52) – vocals / **MICHEL SCHENKER** (b.10 Jan'55, Savstedt, Germany) – lead guitar / **RUDOLF SCHENKER** (b.31 Aug'52, Hildesheim, Germany) – guitar (ex-COPERNICUS) / **LOTHAR HEIMBERG** – bass / **WOLFGANG DZIONY** – drums

Brain | not iss.

1973. (lp) *<1001>* **LONESOME CROW** [–] German [–]
– It all depends / Action / Lonesome crow / I'm goin' mad / Leave me / In search of the peace of mind / Inheritance. *(re-iss. Aug74 as 'I'M GOIN' MAD & OTHERS' on 'Billingsgate'; 1004) (re-iss. Nov77 as 'GOLD ROCK' on 'Brain'; 004 0016) (re-iss. May80 as 'ACTION' on 'Brain'; 0040 150) (UK-iss.Nov82 on 'Heavy Metal' lp/c/pic-lp; HMI LP/MC/PD 2) (cd-iss. 1988 on 'Brain'; 825 739-2) (re-iss. Jul91 on 'Metal Masters' cd/c/lp; METAL MCD/K/PS 114)*

—— (Jun'73) **ULRICH ROTH** – lead guitar repl. MICHAEL who joined UFO / **JURGEN ROSENTHAL** – drums repl. WOLFGANG / **FRANCIS BUCHHOLZ** (b.19 Feb'50) – bass repl. LOTHAR

R.C.A. | R.C.A.

Nov 74. (lp) *(RS 1023) <APL-1 4025>* **FLY TO THE RAINBOW** [ ] [ ]
– Speedy's coming / They need a million / Drifting Sun / Fly people fly / This is my song / Fly away / Fly to the rainbow. *(re-iss. Oct85 lp/c; NL/NK 70084) (cd-iss. Apr88; ND 70084)*

Apr 75. (7") *<10574>* **SPEEDY'S COMING. / THEY NEED A MILLION** [–] [ ]

—— (1975) **RUDY LENNERS** – drums repl. JURGENS

Mar 76. (lp) *(RS 1039) <PPL-1 4028>* **IN TRANCE** [ ] [ ]
– Dark lady / In trance / Life's like a river / Top of the bill / Living and dying / Robot man / Evening wind / Sun in my hand / Longing for fire / Night lights. *(re-iss. Jun83; INTS 5251) (re-iss. 1984 lp/c; NL/NK 70028) (cd-iss. Feb90; ND 70028)*

Nov 76. (7") *<10691>* **IN TRANCE. / NIGHT LIGHTS** [–] [ ]

Feb 77. (lp) *(PPL1 4225) <APL-1 4225>* **VIRGIN KILLERS** [ ] [ ]
– Pictured life / Catch your train / In your park / Backstage queen / Virgin killer / Hell cat / Crying days / Polar nights / Yellow raven. *(re-iss. Apr88 lp/cd; NL/ND 70031)*

—— **HERMAN RAREBELL** (b.18 Nov'53, Lubeck, Germany) – drums (ex-STEPPENWOLF) repl. RUDY

Apr 78. (lp/c) *(PL/PK 28309) <APL-1 2628>* **TAKEN BY FORCE** [ ] [ ]
– Steamrock fever / We'll burn the sky / I've got to be free / The riot of your time / The sails of Charon / Your light / He's a woman she's a man / Born to touch your feelings. *(re-iss. Sep81 lp/c; RCA LP/K 3024) (re-iss. Oct88 lp/c/cd; NL/NK/ND 70081)*

Feb 79. (d-lp) *(NL 28331)* **THE TOKYO TAPES (live)** [ ] [ ]
– All night long / Pictured life / Backstage queen / Polar nights / In trance / We'll burn the sky / Suspender love / In search of the peace of mind / Fly to the rainbow / He's a man, she's a man / Speedy's coming / Top of the bill / Hound dog / Long tall Sally / Steamrock fever / Dark lady / Kojo no tsuki / Robot man. *(re-iss. 1984 lp/c; NL/NK 70008) (d-cd-iss. Nov88; PD 70008)*

—— (Dec'78) **MATHIAS JABS** (b.25 Oct'56) – lead guitar repl. ULRICH who formed ELECTRIC SUN. **MICHAEL SCHENKER** also guested on 3 tracks on next album, joining **KLAUS, RUDOLF, HERMAN, FRANCIS + MATHIAS**

Harvest | Mercury

Mar 79. (7") *<76008>* **LOVING YOU SUNDAY MORNING. / COAST TO COAST** [–] [ ]

Apr 79. (lp/c) *(SHSP/TC-SHSP 4097) <3795>* **LOVEDRIVE** [36] [55]
– Loving you Sunday morning / Another piece of meat / Always somewhere / Coast to coast / Can't get enough / Is there anybody there? / Lovedrive / Holiday. *(re-iss. Nov83 on 'Fame' lp/c; FA41 3080-1/-4) (cd-iss. Nov88; CDFA 3080)*

May 79. (7") *(HAR 5185)* **IS THERE ANYBODY THERE? / ANOTHER PIECE OF MEAT** [39] [–]

Aug 79. (7"/12") *(HAR/12HAR 5188)* **LOVEDRIVE. / COAST TO COAST** [69] [–]

Apr 80. (lp/c) *(SHSP/TC-SHSP 4113) <3825>* **ANIMAL MAGNETISM** [23] [52]
– Make it real / Don't make no promises (your body can't keep) / Hold me tight / Twentieth century man / Lady starlight / Fallin' in love / Only a man / The zoo / Animal magnetism. *(re-iss. Aug85 on 'E.M.I.'; ATAK/TC-ATAK 48) (re-iss. May89 on 'Fame' cd/c/lp; CD/TC+/FA 3217)*

May 80. (7") *(HAR 5206) <76070>* **MAKE IT REAL. / DON'T MAKE NO PROMISES (YOUR BODY CAN'T KEEP)** [72] [ ]

Jul 80. (7") *<76084>* **LADY STARLIGHT. /** [–] [ ]

Aug 80. (7") *(HAR 5212)* **THE ZOO. / HOLIDAY** [75] [–]

—— In 1981, MICHAEL SCHENKER briefly returned to repl. JABS while MEINE had throat surgery. Everything resumed as 1980 line-up re-appeared in 1982.

Mar 82. (lp/c) *(SHVL/TC-SHVL 823) <4039>* **BLACKOUT** [11] [10]
– Blackout / Can't live without you / No one like you / You give me all I need / Now! / Dynamite / Arizona / China white / When the smoke is going down. *(re-iss. May85 on 'Fame' lp/c; FA/TCFA 3126) (re-iss. Nov88; CDFA 3126)*

Mar 82. (7"/7"pic-d) *(HAR/+P 5219) <76153>* **NO ONE LIKE YOU. / NOW!** [64] Jun82 [65]

Jul 82. (7") *(HAR 5221)* **CAN'T LIVE WITHOUT YOU. / ALWAYS SOMEWHERE** [63] [–]

Feb 84. (7") *(HAR 5225) <818440>* **ROCK YOU LIKE A HURRICANE. / COMING HOME** [ ] [25]

Mar 84. (lp/c) *(SHSP 24-0007-1/-4) <814981>* **LOVE AT FIRST STING** [17] [6]
– Bad boys running wild / Rock you like a hurricane / I'm leaving you / Coming home / The same thrill / Big city nights / As soon as the good times roll / Crossfire / Still loving you. *(re-iss. Nov87 on 'E.M.I.' lp/c; ATAK/TC-ATAK 69) (re-iss. Aug89 on 'Fame' cd/c/lp; CD/TC+/FA 3224)*

Aug 84. (7"/12"/12"pic-d) *(HAR/12HAR/12HARP 5231)* **BIG CITY NIGHTS. / BAD BOYS RUNNING WILD** [ ] [–]

Mar 85. (7") *(HAR 5232) <880082>* **STILL LOVING YOU. / HOLIDAY** [ ] Jun84 [64]
(12"+=) *(12HAR 5232)* – Big city nights.

Jun 85. (d-lp/d-c) *(SCORP/TC-SCORP 1) <824344>* **WORLD WIDE LIVE (live)** [18] [14]
– Countdown / Coming home / Blackout / Bad boys running wild / Loving you Sunday morning / Make it real / Big city nights / Coast to coast / Holiday / Still loving you / Rock you like a hurricane / Can't live without you / Another piece of meast / Dynamite / The zoo / No one like you / Can't get enough (part 1) / Six string sting / Can't get enough (part 2). *(d-cd-iss. Feb86; CDP 746155-2)*

Jun 85. (7") *(HAR 5237)* **NO ONE LIKE YOU (live). / THE ZOO (live)** [ ] [–]

Apr 88. (cd/c/lp)(pic-lp) *(CD/TC+/SHSP 4125) <832963>* **SAVAGE AMUSEMENT** [18] [5]
– Don't stop at the top / Rhythm of love / Passion rules the game / Media overkill / Walking on the edge / We let it rock . . . you let it roll / Every minute every day / Love on the run / Believe in love. *(pic-lp-iss.May88; SHSPP 4125)*

May 88. (7"/7"box/7"pic-d) *(HAR/+X/P 5240) <870323>* **RHYTHM OF LOVE. / WE LET IT ROCK . . . YOU LET IT ROLL** [59] [75]
(12"+=) *(12HAR 5240)* – Love on the run (mix).

Aug 88. (7"/7"pic-d) *(HAR 5241)* **BELIEVE IN LOVE. / LOVE ON THE RUN** [ ] [–]
(12"+=) *(12HAR 5241)* – ('A'version).

Feb 89. (7") *(HAR 5242)* **PASSION RULES THE GAME. / EVERY MINUTE EVERY DAY** [74] [–]
(12"+=/12"pic-d+=) *(12HAR/+P 5242)* – Is there anybody there?
(cd-s++=) *(CDHAR 5242)* – ('A'extended).

Vertigo | Mercury

Nov 90. (cd/c/lp) *(846908-2/-4/-1) <846908>* **CRAZY WORLD** [ ] [21]
– Tease me please me / Don't believe her / To be with you in Heaven / Wind of change / Restless nights / Lust or love / Kicks after six / Hit between the eyes / Money and fame / Crazy world / Send me an angel. *(re-dist.Oct91; hit UK No.27)*

Dec 90. (7"/c-s) *(VER/+MC 52)* **DON'T BELIEVE HER. / KICKS AFTER SIX** [ ] [–]
(12"+=/12"g-f+=/cd-s+=) *(VER X/XG/CD 52)* – Big city nights / Holiday (live).

Mar 91. (7"red/c-s) *(VER/+MC 54)* **WIND OF CHANGE. / RESTLESS NIGHTS** [53] [–]
(12"red+=) *(VERXP 54)* – The zoo (live)

(cd-s+=) *(VERCD 54)* – To be with you in Heaven / Blackout (live).
(12"red+=) *(VERPX 54)* – Zoo (live).

May 91. (c-s,cd-s) *<868180>* **WIND OF CHANGE / MONEY AND FAME** [–] [4]

Sep 91. (7"/c-s) *(VER/+MC 58)* **WIND OF CHANGE. / RESTLESS NIGHTS** [2] [–]
(12"pic-d+=) *VERX 58)* – Hit between the eyes / Blackout (live).
(cd-s+=) *(VERCD 58)* – Blackout (live) / To be with you in Heaven.

Nov 91. (c-s,cd-s) *<868956>* **SEND ME AN ANGEL / RESTLESS NIGHTS** [–] [44]

Nov 91. (7"/c-s) *(VER/+MC 60)* **SEND ME AN ANGEL. / WIND OF CHANGE (Russian)** [27] [–]
(12"+=/cd-s+=) *(VER X/CD 60)* – Tease me, please me (live) / Lust or love (live).

— (May'92) BUCHHOLZ departed repl. by **RALPH RIECKERMANN** (b. 8 Aug'??, Lubeck) – bass

Mercury Mercury

Sep 93. (cd/c/lp) *(<518280-2/-4/-1>)* **FACE THE HEAT** [51] [24]
– Alien nation / No pain, no gain / Someone to touch / Under the same sun / Unholy alliance / Woman / Hate to be nice / Taxman woman / Ship of fools / Nightmare Avenue / Lonely nights / Destin / Daddy's girl

Nov 93. (c-s) *(MERMC 395)* **UNDER THE SAME SUN / SHIP OF FOOLS** [ ] [ ]
(12"+=) *(12MER 395)* – Alien nation / Rubber fucker.
(cd-s++=) *(MERCD 395)* – Partners in crime.

Apr 95. (cd) *(<526903-2>)* **LIVE BITES (live 1988-95)** [ ] [ ]
– Tease me, please me / Is anybody / Rhythm of love / In trance / No pain no gain / When the smoke is going down / Ave Maria no morro / Living for tomorrow / Concerto in V / Alien nation / Hit between the eyes / Crazy world / Wind of change / Heroes don't cry / White dove.

— line-up **KLAUS, RUDOLF, MATTHIAS + RALPH** were joined by **CURT CRESS + PITTI HECHT** – drums / **LUKE HERZOG + KOEN VAN BAEL** – keyboards

East West Atlantic

May 96. (cd/c/lp) *(0630 14524-2) <82913>* **PURE INSTINCT** [ ] [99]
– Wild child / But the best for you / Does anyone know / Stone in my shoe / Soul behind the face / Oh girl (I wanna be with you) / When you came into my life / Where the river flows / Time will call your name / You and I / Are you the one?

Jun 96. (c-s/cd-s) *(W 0042 C/CD)* **YOU AND I / SHE'S KNOCKING AT MY DOOR / YOU AND I (extended)** [ ] [–]

Coalition – eastwest Coalition – eastwest

Mar 99. (7"pic-d) *(COLA 074)* **TO BE NO.1. / MIND LIKE A TREE** [ ] [–]
(cd-s+=) *(COLA 074CD)* – ('A'-CD-Rom version).

Mar 99. (cd) *<(3984 26830-2)>* **EYE TO EYE** [ ] [ ]
– Mysterious / To be No.1 / Obsession / 10 light years away / Mind like a tree / Eye to eye / What you give you get back / Skywriter / Yellow butterfly / Freshly squeezed / Priscilla / Du bist so schmutzig / Aleyah / Moment is a million years.

EMI Classics EMI Classics

Jul 00. (cd; with The Berliner Philharmonica) *(<CDC 557019-2>)* **MOMENT OF GLORY** [ ] [ ]
– Hurricane 2000 (rock you like a hurricane) / Moment of glory / Send me an angel (with ZUCCHERO) / Wind of change / Medley: Crossfire – Dynamite – He's a woman she's a man / Deadly sting suite / Here in my heart (with LYNN LIECHTY) / Still loving you / Big city nights / Lady Starlight (with LYNN LIECHTY).

Sep 00. (cd-ep; with The Berliner Philharmonica) *(8891410)* **HERE IN MY HEART / WIND OF CHANGE / MOMENT OF GLORY (video)** [ ] [–]

WEA WEA

Jun 01. (dvd/cd) *(88167) <88246>* **ACOUSTICA** [ ] [ ]
– The zoo / Always somewhere / Life is too short / Holiday / You and I / When love kills love / Dust in the wind / Send me an angel / Catch your train / I wanted to cry (but the tears wouldn't let me) / Wind of change / Love of my life / Drive / Still loving you / Hurricane 2001.

– compilations, etc. –

on 'R.C.A.' unless mentioned otherwise

Nov 79. (12"ep) *(PC 9402)* **ALL NIGHT LONG / FLYING TO THE RAINBOW. / SPEEDY'S COMING / IN TRANCE** [ ] [–]

Sep 81. (lp/c) *(RCA LP/K 3035) <3516>* **THE BEST OF THE SCORPIONS** [ ] Nov79 [ ]
– Steamrock fever / Pictured life / Robot man / Backstage queen / Speedy's coming / Hell-cat / He's a woman, she's a man / In trance / Dark lady / The sails of Charon / Virgin killer. *(re-iss. Feb89 lp/c/cd; NL/NK/ND 74006)*

Nov 89. (cd/c/lp) *E.M.I.; (CD/TC+/EMD 1014) / Mercury; <842002>* **BEST OF ROCKERS 'N' BALLADS** [ ] [43]
(re-iss. Sep91 on 'Fame'; CD/TC FA 3262)

Feb 90. (lp/c/cd) *(NL/NK/ND 74517) <5085>* **THE BEST OF THE SCORPIONS, VOL.2** [ ] Jul84 [ ]

Feb 90. (cd) *(ND 70672)* **HOT AND HEAVY** [ ] [ ]

Nov 90. (cd/c/lp) *E.M.I.; (CD/TC+/EMC 3586)* **STILL LOVING YOU** [ ] [ ]
(re-iss. Feb92 cd/c/lp; CD/TC+/EMD 1031)

Dec 90. (cd/c/lp) *Connoisseur; (VSOP CD/MC/LP 156)* **HURRICANE ROCK** [ ] [–]

Oct 91. (3xcd-box) *E.M.I.; (CDS 797963-2)* **SCORPIONS 3 CD SET** [ ] [–]
– (WORLDWIDE LIVE / SAVAGE AMUSEMENT / ROCKERS 'N' BALLADS)

Dec 91. (cd/c) *(ND/NK 75029)* **HOT AND SLOW (THE BEST OF THE BALLADS)** [ ] [–]

Sep 93. (cd) *(74321 15119-2)* **HOT AND HARD** [ ] [ ]

Feb 95. (cd) *E.M.I.; (CDEMC 3698)* **DEADLY STING** [ ] [ ]

Sep 99. (cd) *E.M.I.; (497013-2)* **THE BEST OF THE SCORPIONS** [ ] [–]

Mar 00. (d-cd) *Axe Killer; (<AXE 305646CD>)* **IN TRANCE / VIRGIN KILLER** [ ] [ ]

□ Mike SCOTT (see under ⇒ WATERBOYS)

Gil SCOTT-HERON

Born: 1 Apr'49, Chicago, Illinois, USA. The son of a footballer father (who enjoyed a spell with Glasgow Celtic) and a librarian mother, SCOTT-HERON spent the bulk of his childhood in Jackson, Tennessee, raised by his grandmother following his parents' separation. By the time GIL was back living with his mother in New York and attending high school, he had already began to master piano, his precocious talent for writing subsequently recognised by one of his teachers and leading to SCOTT-HERON completing his studies at noted private school, Fieldston. From there he moved on to Lincoln University, following in the footsteps of his literary hero, Langston Hughes, and subsequently taking a year out to write his first novel, 'The Vulture' (recently republished by the illustrious Canongate Books imprint, Payback Press!). Musically, SCOTT-HERON cited influences as diverse as RICHIE HAVENS, BILLIE HOLIDAY, OTIS REDDING and JOSE FELICIANO; more obvious was the radical style of THE LAST POETS (whom after witnessing at a show in Ohio, allegedly inspired SCOTT-HERON to take up performing) as well as the melting pot of African and Latin sounds that echoed through the Chelsea district of New York where he lived. GIL made his recording debut with 'SMALL TALK AT 125th AND LENOX' (1972), a set largely comprised of poems set to a sparse percussive backing, released on Bob Thiele's 'Flying Dutchman' label. Updating the tradition of the African griot, SCOTT-HERON laid out an uncompromising manifesto for the black man, executed with mordant humour and sly wit and railing against consumerism, drug addled hippies, false prophets and white oppression. The record's worth hearing for the brilliant 'WHITEY ON THE MOON' alone, that's if you can stomach the rampant homophobia of 'THE SUBJECT WAS FAGGOTS'; clearly, SCOTT-HERON's vision of a brighter tomorrow had no place for gay men. Nevertheless, 'PIECES OF A MAN' (1973) was a stunning, often tenderly poignant follow-up, benefitting from a fuller sound courtesy of keys player/co-writer, BRIAN JACKSON along with such notable players as BERNARD

PURDIE, RON CARTER and flautist HUBERT LAWS. 'LADY DAY AND JOHN COLTRANE' remains one of GIL's most uplifting songs, the singer stepping off the soapbox for once and celebrating the power of music. In stark contrast, 'THE REVOLUTION WILL NOT BE TELEVISED' was SCOTT-HERON at his most glaringly effective, ominously intoning the death knell for white, middle class inertia over a hypnotic, stinging bassline. Often cited as one of the earliest prototype rap tracks, its most readily identifiable antecedant was 'Television, Drug Of The Nation' by THE DISPOSABLE HEROES OF HIP HOPRISY, a group closer in spirit to SCOTT-HERON's work than many rap acts. But the man was most affecting when he addressed the everyday tragedies of human experience; any listener not moved by the likes of 'PIECES OF A MAN' and 'HOME IS WHERE THE HATRED IS' must have a heart of steel. Following his departure from 'Flying Dutchman', SCOTT-HERON recorded 'WINTER IN AMERICA' (1974) on the US independent, 'Strata East'. As well as the atmospheric lament of the title track, the album featured one of the singer's most famous tracks, 'THE BOTTLE' a much covered, funky, flute-driven testament to the dangers of alcohol. The following year, he signed to the newly formed 'Arista', scoring a Top 30 album with 'THE FIRST MINUTE OF A NEW DAY' (1975). Co-credited to BRIAN JACKSON, the album was the first to feature The MIDNIGHT BAND, a backing troupe which the pair led right through into the 80's with varying line-ups. The record also provided a minor US R&B hit with the disco influenced 'JOHANNESBURG', once again conclusively proving that dancefloor didn't necessarily mean braindead. Throughout the latter part of the 70's and on into the early 80's, SCOTT-HERON maintained an impressively consistent, unusually prolific recording schedule, his coffee-rich vocals and enduring blend of jazz, blues and soul providing an often lone voice of sanity in the decadent, coke-fuelled music scene of the time. As well as documenting the very real threat of nuclear power ('WE ALMOST LOST DETROIT', 'SHUT 'EM DOWN'), he continued to address the concerns of working class blacks ('INNER CITY BLUES', 'BLUE COLLAR') and the contentious issue of drugs ('ANGEL DUST'). His scathing political commentary also continued apace, 'B-MOVIE', from the acclaimed 'REFLECTIONS' (1981) set, nailing the newly elected REAGAN with pinpoint accuracy. It's all the more ironic, then, that SCOTT-HERON releases petered out after the early 80's, the singer falling prey to the drug and alcohol abuse he'd spoken out so militantly against throughout his career. Maybe the state of politics (US and British) was just too much for him to take, after all, if SCOTT-HERON's articulate defense of humanist principles was ever needed at all, it was in the moral wasteland of that vilified decade. Though a belated comeback album, 'SPIRITS' (1994) failed to impress many fans, SCOTT-HERON continues to tour ceaselessly, his live show still impressive if you're lucky enough to catch him on a good night. Though his golden period may be over, arguably, GIL has nothing left to prove, his back catalogue standing up amongst the cream of black music history. • **Covered:** INNER CITY BLUES (Marvin Gaye) / GRANDMA'S HANDS (Bill Withers). GIL was the original voice-over for the "You know you've been Tangoed" TV ad. LaBELLE covered his song 'THE REVOLUTION WILL NOT BE TELEVISED' in 1974.

Album rating: SMALL TALK AT 125th AND LENOX (*6) / FREE WILL (*7) / PIECES OF A MAN (*7) / WINTER IN AMERICA (*7) / THE REVOLUTION WILL NOT BE TELEVISED compilation (*8) / THE FIRST MINUTE OF A NEW DAY with Brian Jackson (*7) / FROM SOUTH AFRICA TO SOUTH CAROLINA with Brian Jackson (*6) / IT'S YOUR WORLD with Brian Jackson (*7) / BRIDGES with Brian Jackson (*6) / SECRETS with Brian Jackson (*6) / 1980 with Brian Jackson (*6) / REAL EYES (*6) / REFLECTIONS (*7) / MOVING TARGET (*5) / THE BEST OF GIL SCOTT-HERON compilation (*7) / THE TALES OF GIL SCOTT-HERON AND THE AMNESIA EXPRESS (*6) / SPIRITS (*8) / GHETTO STYLE compilation (*8)

GIL SCOTT-HERON – vocals, piano, guitar

Philips | Flying Dutchman

1970. (lp) *<10131>* **SMALL TALK AT 125th AND LENOX** (rap poems) [–] [ ]
– Introduction – The revolution will not be televised / Omen / Brother / Comment #1 / Small talk at 125th & Lenox / The subject was faggots / Evolution (and flashback) / Plastic pattern people / Whitey on the moon / The vulture / Enough / Paint it black / Who'll pay reparations on my soul? / Everyday. *(cd-iss. Jun97 on 'RCA Victor'; 07863 66611-2)*

1972. (lp) *<10153>* **FREE WILL** [–] [ ]
– Free will / The middle of your day / The get out of the ghetto blues / Speed kills / Did you hear what they said? / The King Alfred plan / No knock / Wiggy / Ain't no new thing / Billy Green is dead / Sex education: ghetto style / . . .And then he wrote "meditations". *<cd-iss. Nov01 on 'B.M.G.'+=; 74321 85161-2>* – Free will (alt.) / Speed kills (alt.) / The King Alfred plan (alt.) / No knock (alt.) / Wiggy (alt.) / Ain't no new thing / Billy Green is dead / Free will.

— added **BRIAN JACKSON** – keyboards / **DANNY BOWENS** – bass / **BOB ADAMS** – drums

Apr 73. (lp) *(6369 415) <10143>* **PIECES OF A MAN** [ ] [ ]
– Lady Day and John Coltrane / When you are who you are / The revolution will not be televised / Home is where the hatred is / I think I'll call it morning / Save the children / The needle's eye / Pieces of a man / A sign of the ages / Or down you fall / The prisoner.

Apr 73. (7") *(6073 705)* **WHEN YOU ARE WHO YOU ARE. / LADY DAY AND JOHN COLTRANE** [ ] [ ]

R.C.A. | Flying Dutchman

Jul 75. (lp) *(SF 8428) <BXL1-0613>* **THE REVOLUTION WILL NOT BE TELEVISED** [ ] Mar74 [ ]
– The revolution will not be televised / Sex education: ghetto style / The get out of the ghetto blues / No knock / Lady Day and John Coltrane / Pieces of a man / Home is where the hatred is / Brother / Save the children / Did you hear what they said? *(cd-iss. May89 on 'Bluebird-RCA' lp/c/cd+=; NL/NK/ND 86994)* – (extra track).

not iss. | Stata East

1974. (lp) *<19742>* **WINTER IN AMERICA** [–] [ ]
– Peace go with you brother / Rivers of my father / A very precious time / Back home / The bottle / Song for Bobby Smith / Your daddy loves you / H2o gate blues / Peace go with you brother. *(cd-iss. Sep92; 66051015) (cd re-iss. Mar99 on 'Charly'; CDGR 225)*

GIL SCOTT-HERON & BRIAN JACKSON

— next featured The MIDNIGHT BAND

— **JOSEF BLOCKER + REGGIE BRISBANE** – drums repl. ADAMS

Arista | Arista

Jul 75. (lp) *(ARTY 106) <4030>* **THE FIRST MINUTE OF A NEW DAY** [ ] Jun75 [30]
– Offering / The liberation song (red, black and green) / Must be something / Ain't no such thing as Superman / Pardon our analysis (we beg your pardon America) / Winter in America / Guerilla / Western sunrise / Alluswe. *(cd-iss. Feb99 on 'TVT'; 4350)*

Jul 75. (7") *<0117>* **AIN'T NO SUCH THING AS SUPERMAN. / WE BEG YOUR PARDON AMERICA** [–] [ ]

Oct 75. (7") *(ARIST 23) <0152>* **(WHAT'S THE WORD) JOHANNESBURG. / FELL TOGETHER** [ ] [ ]

Jan 76. (lp) *(ARTY 121) <4044>* **FROM SOUTH AFRICA TO SOUTH CAROLINA** [ ] Oct75 [ ]
– (What's the word) Johannesburg / A toast to the people / The summer of '42 / Beinnings (first minute of a new day) / South Carolina (Barnwell) / Essex / Fell together / A lovely day.

Nov 76. (7") *<0225>* **THE BOTTLE. /** [–] [ ]

Nov 76. (lp) *(DARTY 1) <5001>* **IT'S YOUR WORLD (live)** [ ] [ ]
– Seventeenth street / Tomorrow's trane (gospel trane) / Must be something / It's your world / New York City / The bottle / Possum Slim / Home is where the hatred is / Bicentennial blues / Sharing.

— **JOSEF BLOCKER + REGGIE BRISBANE** – drums repl. ADAMS

Dec 77. (lp) *(SPARTY 1031) <4147>* **BRIDGES** [ ] Oct77 [ ]
– Hello Sunday! hello road! / Song of the wind / Racetrack in France / Vildgolia (deaf, dumb and blind) / Under the hammer / We almost lost Detroit / Tuskeegee No.626 / Delta man (where I'm coming from) / 95 South (all of the places we've been).

Dec 77. (7") *(ARIST 169)* **HELLO SUNDAY, HELLO ROAD. / THE BOTTLE (live)**
Dec 77. (7") *<0285>* **HELLO SUNDAY, HELLO ROAD. / SONG OF THE WIND**
Mar 78. (7") *<0317>* **UNDER THE HAMMER. / RACETRACK IN FRANCE**

—— **GREG PHILLINGANES** – keyboards repl. BOWENS

Jul 78. (7") *<0366>* **ANGEL DUST. / THIRD WORLD REVOLUTION**
Sep 78. (lp) *(SPARTY 1073) <4189>* **SECRETS** 61
– Angel dust / Madison Avenue / Cane / Third world revolution / Better days ahead / Three miles down / Angola, Louisiana / Show bizness / A prayer for everybody / To be free.
Oct 78. (7") *(ARIST 215) <0390>* **SHOW BIZNESS. / BETTER DAYS AHEAD**

—— retained only **JACKSON** + recruited **ED GRADY** – guitar / **KENNY POWELL** – drums / **GLEN TURNER** – keyboards / **CARL CORNWALL** + **VERNON JAMES** – tenor sax, flute / **KENNY SHEFFIELD** – trumpet

Feb 80. (lp) *<9514>* **1980** 82
– Shut 'um down / Alien / Willing / Corners / 1980 / Push comes to shove / Shah mot / Late last night. *(UK-iss.Jul85; 201733)*
Mar 80. (7"/ext-12") *<0488>* **SHUT 'UM DOWN. / BALTIMORE**
May 80. (7") *<0505>* **WILLING. /**

GIL SCOTT-HERON

Dec 80. (lp) *<9540>* **REAL EYES**
– The train from Washington / Not needed / Waiting for the axe to fall / Combinations / A legend in his own mind / You could be my brother / The Klan / Your daddy loves you.
Dec 80. (7") *<0583>* **LEGEND IN HIS OWN MIND. /**
Aug 81. (7") *<0634>* **STORM MUSIC. /**
Oct 81. (7") *<0647>* **B-MOVIE. /**
Dec 81. (lp) *(SPARTY 1180) <9566>* **REFLECTIONS**
– Storm music / Grandma's hands / Is that jazz? / Morning thoughts / Inner city blues (poem – The siege of New Orleans) / Gun / B-movie. *(cd-iss. Feb97; 254094)*
Feb 82. (7") *(ARIST 452)* **STORM MUSIC. / B-MOVIE**
(12"+=) *(ARIST12 452)* – Gun.
Sep 82. (7") **FAST LANE. / BLUE COLLAR**
Sep 82. (lp) *(204921) <9606>* **MOVING TARGET**
– Fast lane / Washington D.C. / No exit / Blue collar / Ready or not / Explanations / Black history – The word. *(cd-iss. Feb97; 254921)*
May 83. (7") *(ARIST 527)* **(WHAT'S THE WORD) JOHANNESBURG. / WAITING FOR THE AXE TO FALL**
(12"+=) *(ARIST12 527)* – B-Movie (intro, poem, song).
Aug 84. (7") *(ARIST 573)* **RE-RON. / B-MOVIE**
(12") *(ARIST12 573)* – Re-Ron (the missing brain mix). / B-Movie (intro, poem, song).
Sep 84. (lp/c) *(206/406 618)* **THE BEST OF GIL SCOTT-HERON** (compilation)
– The revolution will not be televised / The bottle / Winter in America / Ain't no such thing as Superman / Re-Ron / Shut 'em down / Angel dust / B-movie. *(cd-iss. Apr88; 256 618)*
Nov 85. (7"/10") *(ARIST/+10 643)* **WINTER IN AMERICA. / JOHANNESBURG**

—— now with **ROBBIE GORDON** – bass, percussion / **RON HOLLOWAY** – saxophone

Essential Rykodisc

Mar 90. (7") *(GILL 003)* **SPACE SHUTTLE (vocal). / ('A'original mix)**
(12"+=) *(GILT 003)* – ('A'deep club mix) / Pieces of gold – medley.
(12"+=) *(GILTY 003)* – ('A'deep club dub) / War is very ugly.
(cd-s+=) *(GILTX 003)* – The bottle / Pieces of gold – medley.
Mar 90. (cd/c/d-lp) *(ESD CD/MC/LP 201)* **THE TALES OF GIL SCOTT-HERON AND HIS AMNESIA EXPRESS (live)**
– Washington DC / Save the children / Angel dust / Gun / Blue collar / Amen (hold on to your dream) / Three miles down / The bottle.

Mother T.V.T.

Jul 94. (cd/c) *(MUM CD/C 9415) <TVT 43102>* **SPIRITS**
– Message to the messengers / Spirits / Give her a call / Laly's song / Spirits past / The other side (parts 1-3) / Work for peace / Don't give up. *(lp-iss.Mar99 on 'TVT'; same as US)*
Oct 94. (12"/cd-s) **DON'T GIVE UP. / MESSAGE TO THE MESSENGERS / THE BOTTLE (live)**

– others, etc. –

Jul 80. (7"/12"; GIL SCOTT-HERON & BRIAN JACKSON) *Inferno; (HEAT 23/+12)* **THE BOTTLE (drunken mix). / THE BOTTLE (sober mix)**
(re-iss. Jan81 on 'Champagne' 7"/12"; VAT/+S 302)
1981. (lp) *Audio Fidelity; (1017)* **THE BOTTLE** (1973)
Mar 88. (12"m) *Old Gold; (OG 4054)* **THE BOTTLE. / JOHANNESBURG / WINTER IN AMERICA**
Nov 90. (d-cd) *Arista; (353913)* **GLORY (THE GIL SCOTT-HERON COLLECTION)**
Apr 94. (cd/c) *Castle; (CCS CD/MC 403)* **MINISTRY OF INFORMATION (live)**
– Winter in America / Alien / The bottle / Is that jazz / Washington DC / Gun / B-movie.
Nov 98. (cd) *Camden-BMG; (74321 628062)* **GHETTO STYLE**
– The revolution will not be televised / Or down you fall / The needle's eye / I think I'll call it morning / When you are who you are / Save the children / Did you hear what they said? / Free will / Speed kills / Middle of your day / Pieces of a man / A sign of the ages / The get out of the ghetto blues / Lady day & John Coltrane / Home is where the hatred is / No knock / The revolution will not be televised (early version) / Sex education ghetto style / Small talk at 125th & Lenox / King Alfred plan / Billy Green is dead.
Feb 99. (cd) *R.C.A.; <63141>* **EVOLUTION: THE VERY BEST OF GIL SCOTT-HERON**
Oct 99. (12")(cd-s) *Joeboy; (JBV 008)(JBCD 017)* **THE BOTTLE**

SCREAMING TREES

Formed: Ellensburg, Washington, USA ... 1985 by girthsome brothers VAN and GARY LEE CONNER along with frontman MARK LANEGAN and drummer MARK PICKEREL. Following early effort, 'CLAIRVOYANCE' (1986) for the tiny 'Velvetone' label, the group signed to respected US indie, 'S.S.T.', making their debut with the convincing 'EVEN IF AND ESPECIALLY WHEN' (1987). Fuelled by raging punk, The SCREAMING TREES were nevertheless characterised by the spectral hue of 60's psychedelia running through much of their music, LANEGAN's exotic, JIM MORRISON-esque vocals adding an air of brooding mystery on the likes of fans' favourite, 'TRANSFIGURATION'. Another couple of stirring sets, 'INVISIBLE LANTERN' (1988) and 'BUZZ FACTORY' (1989), followed before the group released a one-off EP for 'Sub Pop'. With the emerging grunge phenomenon in nearby Seattle on the cusp of world domination, The SCREAMING TREES were obviously a promising prospect for major label A&R and it came as little surprise when they signed for 'Epic'. That same year, prior to their debut for the label, the various 'TREES occupied themselves with solo projects, GARY LEE forming PURPLE OUTSIDE and releasing 'MYSTERY LANE', while brother VAN issued the eponymous 'SOLOMON GRUNDY' set the same year, both appearing on 'New Alliance'. Best of the lot, however, was LANEGAN's windswept 'WINDING SHEET', an intense, largely acoustic collection featuring a cover of Leadbelly's 'WHERE DID YOU SLEEP LAST NIGHT' (as later covered in frightening style by KURT COBAIN). Co-produced by CHRIS CORNELL, the subsequent SCREAMING TREES effort, 'UNCLE ANAESTHESIA' (1991), saw the group moving towards a more overt 70's rock sound, while 'SWEET OBLIVION' (1992) saw PICKEREL replaced with BARRETT MARTIN on a more low-key set which stood at odds with the grunge tag unwillingly forced on the band. Augmented by such Seattle "luminaries" as TAD and DAN PETERS (MUDHONEY) along with DINOSAUR JR.'s J. MASCIS,

LANEGAN cut an acclaimed solo follow-up, 'WHISKEY FOR THE HOLY GHOST' (1993), before beginning the long and arduous work on the material which would eventually come to make up 'DUST' (1996). Widely held up as the group's most affecting work to date, the George Drakoulias-produced album perfectly captured their threadbare grit and world-weary mysticism, the disparate elements of their sound finally fusing in harmony and exorcising the lingering spirit of grunge. During the latter part of the 90's, LANEGAN was again a solo artist, two albums for 'Sub Pop' ('Beggars Banquet' in Britain), 'SCRAPS AT MIDNIGHT' (1998) and 'I'LL TAKE CARE OF YOU' (1999), being released to mixed response and sliding out of the hard/grunge-rock circle. Meanwhile, VAN CONNOR was back in action via GARDENER, a collaborative duo that also featured Seaweed's AARON STAUFFER. In mid '99, this supergroup of sorts delivered their Lo-Fi psychedelic album for 'Sub Pop', 'NEW DAWNING TIME'. LANEGAN continued to nurse his alt-country blues on his fifth solo effort, 'FIELD SONGS' (2001), his grainy narratives given added muscle by such alt-rock notables as BEN SHEPHERD, BILL RIEFLIN, DUFF McKAGEN and MIKE JOHNSON. Mini-set, 'HERE COMES THAT WEIRD CHILL' (2003), meanwhile, featured guest spots from various MASTERS OF REALITY and AFGHAN WHIGS personnel, the perfect company for LANEGAN's brooding, coruscating narratives and an appropriately twisted cover of Captain Beefheart's 'CLEAR SPOT'. • **Covered:** SLIDE MACHINE (13th Floor Elevators). • **Note:** Not to be confused with the English band on 'Native' records.

Album rating: OTHER WORLDS mini (*4) / EVEN IF AND ESPECIALLY WHEN (*7) / INVISIBLE LANTERN (*5) / BUZZ FACTORY mini (*5) / UNCLE ANAESTHESIA (*6) / ANTHOLOGY – THE S.S.T. YEARS 1985-1989 compilation (*7) / SWEET OBLIVION (*7) / DUST (*9) / Mark Lanegan: THE WINDING SHEET (*6) / WHISKEY FOR THE HOLY GHOST (*7) / SCRAPS AT MIDNIGHT (*6) / I'LL TAKE CARE OF YOU (*8) / FIELD SONGS (*6) / Mark Lanegan Band: HERE COMES THAT WEIRD CHILL mini (*6)

MARK LANEGAN (b.25 Nov'64) – vocals / **GARY LEE CONNER** (b.22 Aug'62, Fort Irwin, Calif.) – guitar, vocals / **VAN CONNER** (b.17 Mar'67, Apple Valley, Calif.) – bass, vocals / **MARK PICKEREL** – drums, percussion

not iss. Velvetone

1986. (m-lp) <none> **CLAIRVOYANCE** [–] [ ]
– Orange airplane / You tell me all these things / Standing on the edge / Forever / Seeing and believing / I see stars / Lonely girl / Strange out here / The turning / Clairvoyance.

S.S.T. S.S.T.

Feb 87. (m-lp/m-cd) <SST/+C/CD 105> **OTHER WORLDS** [–] [ ]
– Like I said / Pictures in my mind / Turning / Other worlds / Barriers / Now your mind is next to mine. *(UK-iss.May93; same as US)*

Sep 87. (lp/cd) <(SST 132/+CD)> **EVEN IF AND ESPECIALLY WHEN** [ ] [ ]
– Transfiguration / Straight out to any place / World painted / Don't look down / Girl behind the mask / Flying / Cold rain / Other days and different planets / The pathway / You know where it's at / Back together / In the forest. *(cd re-iss. May93; same)*

Jul 88. (12"ep; shared w/ BEAT HAPPENING) *(AGARR 020)* <110> **POLLY PEREGUIN E.P.** [ ] [–]
(above issued on UK '53rd & 3rd') <US-iss.on 'Positive'>

Sep 88. (lp/c/cd) <(SST 188/+C/CD)> **INVISIBLE LANTERN** [ ] [ ]
– Ivy / Walk through to the other side / Line & circles / Shadow song / Grey diamond desert / Smokerings / The second I awake / Invisible lantern / Even if / Direction of the sun / Night comes creeping / She knows.

Mar 89. (m-lp/m-cd) <(SST 248/+CD)> **BUZZ FACTORY** [ ] [ ]
– Where the twain shall meet / Windows / Black sun morning / Too far away / Subtle poison / Yard trip / Flower web / Wish bringer / Revelation revolution / The looking glass cracked / End of the universe.

Glitterhouse Sub Pop

Dec 89. (d7"w /1-white) *(GR 80)* <SP 48B> **CHANGE HAS COME. / DAYS / / FLASHES. / TIME SPEAKS HER GOLDEN TONGUE** [ ] [ ]
(re-iss. Dec90 cd-ep+=; GRCD 80) – I've seen you before. *(re-iss. May93; same)*

— LEE CONNER also formed PURPLE OUTSIDE in 1990, releasing 'MYSTERY LANE'. Brother VAN with SOLOMON GRUNDY issued eponymous same year also for 'New Alliance'.

Epic Epic

Oct 90. (12"ep) *<73539>* **UNCLE ANAESTHESIA / WHO LIES IN DARKNESS. / OCEAN OF CONFUSION / SOMETHING ABOUT TODAY (numb inversion version)** [–] [ ]

Jun 91. (cd/c/lp) *(467 307-2/-4/-1)* *<EK 46800>* **UNCLE ANAESTHESIA** [ ] Mar91 [ ]
– Beyond this horizon / Bed of roses / Uncle anaesthesia / Story of her fate / Caught between / Lay your head down / Before we arise / Something about today / Alice said / Time for light / Disappearing / Ocean of confusion / Closer.

— **BARRETT MARTIN** (b.14 Apr'67, Olympia, Washington) – drums repl. PICKEREL who later joined TRULY

Oct 92. (cd/c/lp) *(471 724-2/-4/-1)* *<48996>* **SWEET OBLIVION** [ ] [ ]
– Shadow of the season / Nearly lost you / Dollar bill / More or less / Butterfly / For celebrations past / The secret kind / Winter song / Troubled times / No one knows / Julie Paradise.

Feb 93. (12"ep/pic-cd-ep) *(658 237-6/-2)* **NEARLY LOST YOU. / E.S.K. / SONG OF A BAKER / WINTER SONG (acoustic)** [50] [–]

Apr 93. (7"pic-d) *(659 179-7)* **DOLLAR BILL. / (THERE'LL BE) PEACE IN THE VALLEY FOR ME (acoustic)** [52] [–]
(12"colrd+=/cd-s+=) *(659 179-6/-2)* – Tomorrow's dream.

Jul 96. (cd/c/lp) *(483 980-2/-4/-1)* *<64178>* **DUST** [32] [ ]
– Halo of ashes / All I know / Look at you / Dying days / Make my mind / Sworn and broken / Witness / Traveler / Dime western / Gospel plow.

Sep 96. (7") *(663 351-7)* **ALL I KNOW. / WASTED TIME** [ ] [ ]
(cd-s+=) *(663 351-2)* – Silver tongue.
(cd-s) *(663 351-5)* – ('A'side) / Dollar bill / Nearly lost you / Winter song (acoustic).

Nov 96. (7"white) *(663 870-7)* **SWORN AND BROKEN. / BUTTERFLY** [ ] [–]
(cd-s+=) *(663 870-2)* – Dollar bill (U.S. radio session) / Caught between – The secret kind (U.S. radio session).

— on a long holiday from each other, maybe for ever, VAN CONNER now moonlighting in VALIS with DAN PETERS of MUDHONEY, while BARRETT plays on tour with R.E.M., while joining PETER BUCK's supergroup, TUATARA. LANEGAN continued solo (see below)

– compilations, others, etc. –

Nov 91. (d-lp/d-cd) *<(SST 260/+CD)>* **ANTHOLOGY . . . THE S.S.T. YEARS 1985-1989** [ ] [ ]

MARK LANEGAN

— with on first **MIKE JOHNSON** – guitar / **JACK ENDINO** – bass, guitar / **KURT COBAIN** – guitar, vocals / **CHRIS NOVOSELIC** – bass / **MARK PICKEREL** – drums / **STEVE FISK** – keyboards

Glitterhouse Sub Pop

May 90. (red-lp/cd) *(GR 085/+CD)* *<SP 61>* **THE WINDING SHEET** [ ] [ ]
– Mockingbirds / Museum / Undertow / Ugly Sunday / Down in the dark / Wild flowers / Eyes of a child / The winding sheet / Woe / Ten feet tall / Where did you sleep last night? / Juarez / I love you little girl. *(c+cd+=)* – I love you little girl. *(re-iss. Apr94 & Oct99; same) (cd re-iss. Jun01; SP 618)*

Sep 90. (7") *(GR 0101)* **DOWN IN THE DARK. / LOVE YOU LITTLE GIRL** [ ] [–]

— next w / **J.MASCIS + MARK JOHNSON** (Dinosaur Jr.) / **TAD DOYLE** (Tad) / **DAN PETERS** (Mudhoney) / **KURT FEDORA** (Gobblehoof)

Sub Pop Sub Pop

Jan 94. (lp/cd) <(SP/+CD 78249)> **WHISKEY FOR THE HOLY GHOST** [ ] [ ]
– The river rise / Borracho / House a home / Kingdoms of rain / Carnival / Riding the nightingale / El Sol / Dead on you / Shooting gallery / Sunrise / Pendulum / Jesus touch / Beggar's blues. *(cd re-iss. Oct99 & Jun01; SPCD 132)*

May 94. (cd-ep) <(SPCD 131-327)> **HOUSE A HOME / SHOOTING GALLERY / UGLY SUNDAY / SUNRISE** [ ] [ ]

Beggars Banquet Sub Pop

Jul 98. (cd) *(BBQCD 204)* <SP 419> **SCRAPS AT MIDNIGHT** [ ] [ ]
– Hospital roll call / Hotel / Stay / Black bell ocean / Last one in the world /

Wheels / Waiting on a train / Day and night / Praying ground / Because of this.

Sep 98. (7"colrd) *(BBQ 328)* **STAY. / SLIDE MACHINE** [ ] [-]
(cd-s+=) *(BBQ 328CD)* – Death don't have no mercy.

Sep 99. (cd/lp) *(BBQ CD/LP 215)* *<SP 445>* **I'LL TAKE CARE OF YOU** [ ] [ ]
– Carry home / I'll take care of you / Shiloh town / Creeping coastline of lights / Ba dee da / Consider me / On Jesus program / Little Sadie / Together again / Shanty man's life / Boogie boogie.

Jun 01. (cd) *(BBQCD 224)* *<SP 502>* **FIELD SONGS** [ ] May01 [ ]
– One way street / No easy action / Miracle / Pill hill serenade / Don't forget me / Kimiko's dream house / Resurrection song / Field song / Love / Blues for D / She done too much / Fix.

— now with **DEAN WEEN** – guitar (of WEEN) / **JOSH HOMME** – bass, guitar, drums (of QUEENS OF THE STONE AGE) / **NICK OLIVERI** – organ, synthesizer (of QUEENS OF THE STONE AGE) / **DAVE CATCHING** – guitar / **CHRIS GOSS** – bass, guitar, vocals (ex-MASTERS OF REALITY) GREG DULLI – drums (ex-AFGHAN WHIGS)

Nov 03. (10"m-lp/m-cd; by MARK LANEGAN BAND) *(BBQ 373 TT/CD)* *<81373>* **HERE COMES THAT WEIRD CHILL** [ ] [ ]
– Methamphetamine blues / On the steps of the cathedral / Clear spot / Message to mine / Lexington slow down / Skeletal history / Wish you well / Sleep with me (version).

SCRITTI POLITTI

Formed: London, England . . . late '77 by Leeds art student (and former Young Communist), 'GREEN' GARTSIDE, along with NIAL JINKS and TOM MORLEY. Politically motivated punks, their first release, 'SKANK BLOC BOLOGNA' (issued on their own 'St. Pancras' label) created enough interest for a John Peel session, the tracks subsequently released on 'Rough Trade' in 1979. By the release of the classic 'SWEETEST GIRL' single in summer '81, only MORLEY remained from the original line-up, GREEN now steering the band in an altogether more endearing new-wave art-pop/white reggae vein. The track (which featured the piano talents of ROBERT WYATT) was a minor chart hit, likewise the follow-up singles, 'FAITHLESS' and 'JERUSALEM'. All three were included on the much anticipated debut set, 'SONGS TO REMEMBER' (1982), GREEN's dreamy falsetto, musical eclecticism and unerring way with an insidious pop hook (not to mention clever-clever lyric) making him – by this juncture SCRITTI POLITTI were basically a studio vehicle for GREEN – a critical darling and one of 'Rough Trade's most unlikely success stories; the album almost made the UK Top 10, becoming the label's biggest selling release to date. Subsequently relocating to New York and moving up to 'Virgin', GREEN sought out such accomplished US musicians as MARCUS MILLER (former bassist for MILES DAVIS), who accompanied him on his first (UK) Top 10 hit, 'WOOD BEEZ (PLAY LIKE ARETHA FRANKLIN)' in 1984. A succession of different sessioners played on subsequent singles, 'ABSOLUTE', 'HYPNOTISE' and 'THE WORD GIRL', although FRED MAHER and DAVID GAMSON went on to augment GREEN on the follow-up album, 'CUPID AND PSYCHE '85' (1985). Again including all the singles, this slick set of Arif Mardin-produced dancefloor pop-soul also included 'PERFECT WAY', the track which broke SCRITTI POLITTI (albeit briefly) in the States and was later given the honour of a cover by aforementioned jazz legend, MILES DAVIS. The trumpeter also contributed to 'OH PATTI (DON'T FEEL SORRY FOR LOVERBOY)', GREEN's first single after three years of beavering away in the studio. The accompanying album, 'PROVISION' (1988), further refined the man's luxuriant pop vision with an altogether more straightforward approach, GAMSON again providing the lush synth textures. Despite the quality, further singles, 'FIRST BOY IN TOWN (LOVESICK)' and 'BOOM! THERE SHE WAS' lingered in the lower regions of the singles chart. After another interminable lay-off, GREEN returned in 1991 for a Top 20 collaborative cover of The Beatles' 'SHE'S A WOMAN' with ragga loveman, SHABBA RANKS, a further duet with SWEETIE IRIE (a version of Gladys Knight's hit, 'TAKE ME IN YOUR ARMS') not quite so successful. With no album forthcoming in the 90's so far, it does seem as if GREEN had finally abandoned SCRITTI POLITTI as a front for his musical activities although it's likely that this pop maverick will emerge at one point in one form or another. Ah, to see a prophecy come true. Re-inventing himself as a bearded rapper type (well his backing group were anyhow), GREEN and SCRITTI POLITTI came storming back from oblivion on the long-awaited fourth set, 'ANOMIE AND BONHOMIE' (1999). • **Trivia:** SCRITTI POLITTI is nearly Italian for political writing. MADNESS had a 1986 hit with 'THE SWEETEST GIRL'. That year also saw GREEN and GAMSON write the title track for AL JARREAU's album, 'L Is For Lover'.

Album rating: SONGS TO REMEMBER (*8) / CUPID & PSYCHE (*7) / PROVISION (*4) / ANOMIE AND BONHOMIE (*6)

GREEN (b. GREEN STROHMEYER-GARTSIDE, 22 Jun'56, Cardiff, Wales) – vocals, guitar / **TOM MORLEY** – linn drum / **MATTHEW 'K'** – programme organiser / **NIAL JINKS** – bass

St.Pancras / not iss.

Nov 78. (7") *(SCRIT 1)* **SKANC BLOG BOLOGNA. / IS AND OUGHT OF THE WESTERN WORLD** [ ] [-]

Rough Trade / not iss.

Sep 79. (12"ep) *(RT 027T)* **4 A SIDES** [ ] [-]
– Doubt beat / Confidences / Bibbly O'tek / P.A.'s.

Nov 79. (7"ep) *(SCRIT 2 – RT 034)* **WORK IN PROGRESS** (PEEL SESSIONS) [ ] [-]
– Hegamony / Scritlocks door / Opec-Immac / Messthetics.

— added **MIKE MacEVOY** – synthesizers, vocoder / **MGOTSE** – d.bass / guest **ROBERT WYATT** – piano

Aug 81. (7"/12") *(RT 091/+T)* **THE SWEETEST GIRL. / LIONS AFTER SLUMBER** [64] [-]

— **JOE CANG** – bass repl. NIAL / **STEVE SIDWELL** – trumpet / **JAMIE TALBOT** – saxophone repl. MGOTSE

Apr 82. (7"/12") *(RT 107/+T)* **FAITHLESS. / FAITHLESS PART II (instrumental)** [56] [-]

Jul 82. (7"/7"pic-d) *(RT 111/+P)* **ASYLUMS IN JERUSALEM. / JAQUES DERRIDA** [43] [-]
(12"+=) *(RT 111T)* – ('A'extended).

Aug 82. (lp) *(ROUCH/+C 20)* **SONGS TO REMEMBER** [12] [-]
– Asylums in Jerusalem / A slow soul / Jacques Derrida / Lions after slumber / Faithless / Sex / Rock-a-boy blue / Gettin' havin' & holdin' / The sweetest girl. *(cd-iss. May87; ROUGH/+CD 20) (cd re-iss. Oct01 on 'Virgin'; CDV 2944)*

— **GREEN** recruited US musicians **MARCUS MILLER** – bass (ex-MILES DAVIS) / **STEVE FERRONE** – drums (ex-BRIAN AUGER) / **PAUL JACKSON Jnr.** – guitar / (MORLEY went solo and released one 1985 single for 'Zarjazz', 'WHO BROKE THE LOVE?')

Virgin / Warners

Mar 84. (7"/7"pic-d) *(VS 657/+P)* *<28811>* **WOOD BEEZ (PLAY LIKE ARETHA FRANKLIN). / ('A'dub)** [10] Jan86 [91]
(12"+=) *(VS 657T)* – ('A'extended).

— **GREEN** with **ROBBIE BUCHANAN** + **DAVID FRANK** – keyboards / **FRED MAHER** – drums

Jun 84. (7"/7"pic-d) *(VS 680/+P)* **ABSOLUTE. / ('A'version)** [17] [ ]
(12"+=) *(VS 680T)* – ('A'extended).

— **GREEN** now with **DAVID GAMSON** – keyboards / **ALLAN MURPHY** – guitar

Nov 84. (7"/7"pic-d) *(VS 725/+P)* **HYPNOTISE. / ('A'version)** [68] [ ]
(12"+=) *(VS 725T)* – ('A'extended).

— **NICK MOROCH** – guitar was added to above guests for album below.

May 85. (7"/7"sha-pic-d) *(VS 747/+P)* **THE WORD GIRL. / FLESH AND BLOOD** [6] [ ]
(12"+=) *(VS 747-12)* – ('A'&'B'versions).

Jun 85. (lp/c/cd) *(V/TCV/CDV 2350) <25302>* **CUPID AND PSYCHE '85** | 5 | 50
– The word girl / Small talk / Absolute / A liitle knowledge / Don't work that way / Perfect way / Lover to fall / Wood beez (pray like Aretha Franklin) / Hypnotize. *(cd+=)*– (other versions). *(re-iss. Apr90 lp/c; OVED/C 294)*

Aug 85. (7") *(VS 780) <28949>* **PERFECT WAY. / ('A'version)** | 48 | 11
(12"+=) *(VS 780-12)* – ('A'extended).

— **GREEN** with numerous session people, + guest MILES DAVIS

Apr 88. (7") *(VS 1006)* **OH PATTI (DON'T FEEL SORRY FOR LOVERBOY). / ('A'instrumental)** | 13 |
(12"+=/12"pic-d+=) *(VST/+P 1006)* – ('A'extended).
(cd-s+=) *(VSCD 1006)* – Best thing ever.
(c-s++=) *(VSTC 1006)* – ('A'-Drumless mix).

Jun 88. (lp/c/cd) *(V/TCV/CDV 2515) <25686>* **PROVISION** | 8 |
– Boom! there she was / Overnite / First boy in this town / All that we are / Best thing ever / Oh Patti (don't feel sorry for loverboy) / Bam salute / Sugar and spice / Philosophy now. *(cd+=)* – Oh Patti (extended) / Boom! . . . (dub). *(re-iss. Aug91 cd/c;)*

Jul 88. (7") *(VS 1082)* **FIRST BOY IN TOWN (LOVESICK). / WORLD COME BACK TO LIFE** | 63 | –
(12"+=) *(VST 1082)* – ('A'instrumental).
(cd-s+=) *(VSCD 1082)* – ('A'extended remix).

Oct 88. (7") *(VS 1143) <27973>* **BOOM! THERE SHE WAS. / PHILOSOPHY NOW** | 55 | Jun88 53
(12"+=/3"cd-s+=) *(VS T/CD 1143)* – ('A'mix) / ('A'dub version).

Mar 91. (7"/c-s; SCRITTI POLITTI & SHABBA RANKS) *(VS/+C 1333)* **SHE'S A WOMAN. / LITTLE WAY (different)** | 20 | –
(12"+=) *(VST 1333)* – ('A'-Apollo 440 remix).
(cd-s+=) *(VSCD 1333)* – Wood beez (pray like Aretha Franklin).
(12") *(VSTX 1333)* – ('A'-William Orbit remix) / ('A'-Tutology business mix).

Jul 91. (7"/c-s) *(VS/+C 1346)* **TAKE ME IN YOUR ARMS. / ('A'instrumental) / ('A'mix)** | 47 | –
(12"+=/cd-s+=) *(VS T/CD 1346)* – She's a woman.
above single credited SWEETIE IRIE on the sleeve. GREEN abandoned SCRITTI although he still writes for and with others until . . .

Jul 99. (cd-s) *(VSCDT 1731)* **TINSEL TOWN TO THE BOOGIEDOWN / DEAD CERTAINTY** | 46 | –
(12"/cd-s) *(VST/VSCDX 1731)* – ('A'mixes).

Jul 99. (cd/c) *(CDV/TCV 2884) <8 47488>* **ANOMIE AND BONHOMIE** | 33 |
– Umm / Tinsel town to the boogiedown / First goodbye / Die alone / Mystic handyman / Smith n' slappy / Born to be / World you understand is over and over / Here come July / Prince among men / Brushed with oil dusted with powder.

– compilations, others, etc. –

on 'Virgin' unless mentioned otherwise

Jun 88. (3"cd-ep) *(CDT 13)* **THE WORD GIRL / FLESH AND BLOOD / ('A'-Turntable mix)** | | –

Nov 88. (3"cd-ep) *(CDT 34)* **WOOD BEEZ (PRAY LIKE ARETHA FRANKLIN) / ('A'dub) / SMALL TALK** | | –

Apr 90. (3"cd-ep) *(VVCS 1)* **ABSOLUTE / (3 tracks by other artists)** | | –

SEAHORSES

Formed: based London, England . . . 1996 by ex-STONES ROSES guitarist JOHN SQUIRE who allegedly 'discovered' frontman CHRIS HELME busking in his native Yorkshire. With STUART FLETCHER and ANDY WATTS completing the line-up, the band hooked up with producer Tony Visconti and quickly entered a studio in L.A. to begin work on their debut set, 'DO IT YOURSELF'. In stark contrast to the infamously drawn out sessions for the final 'ROSES album, all the tracks were laid down inside a month and the record was in the shops by Spring '97. Inevitably, the hype surrounding the whole thing tended to obscure the question of whether the record was actually any good or not; the bulk of critics (perhaps only too eager to get the boot in to SQUIRE, a previously unassailable indie guitar god) thought not, or at least panned the set for its inoffensive blandness. Certainly, there was nothing to match the quality of any track from the STONE ROSES sublime debut, although on its own terms, the record's vaguely enjoyable, bluesy indie-rock would've counted as a decent debut by a new band. Somewhat akin to a folk-ish cross between IAN BROWN and LIAM GALLAGHER (who, incidentally, co-penned 'LOVE ME AND LEAVE ME'), HELME's singing, as with SQUIRE's guitar flash, was as competent yet ultimately forgettable as any second division Brit-rock outfit. With the album lacking any real songwriting magic (bar say 'LOVE IS THE LAW' and 'BLINDED BY THE SUN'), some fans began to wonder just who was the mysterious X factor into the STONE ROSES, although enough people thought differently to take the album to No.2 in the UK chart. With a string of successful singles and festival appearances also now under their belt, British sales of the debut are approaching the half million mark; SQUIRE may at last be achieving the success that has long seemed his due, ironically, with the most underwhelming material of his career. However, the SEAHORSES were treading water (so to speak!) during the latter half of '98, HELME expressing to mainman SQUIRE he wanted more of a say in the music/lyrics he was to sing. Inevitably, with more of a whimper than a bang, the band were no more, speculating tabloid rumours of yet another STONES ROSES reformation; HELME was meanwhile plotting his own solo career. After the end of The SEAHORSES, SQUIRE himself disappeared for a few years before delivering his solo effort in 2002, 'TIME CHANGES EVERYTHING'. A rather mediocore album from the outset, here was a songwriter with nothing to prove, unlike RICHARD ASHCROFT (who didn't do so well). Centered around jangly guitar parts, plus the wishful-thinking folk of DYLAN and NILSSON (not to mention the impending presence of the bloody ROLLING STONES), SQUIRE had managed to uphold his brilliant and taut lyricism, adding in a few hammond organs and token slide guitars. Would impress fans of PAUL WELLER, OCEAN COLOUR SCENE, et al.

Album rating: DO IT YOURSELF (*7) / John Squire: TIME CHANGES EVERYTHING (*6)

JOHN SQUIRE (b.24 Nov'62, Broadheath, Lancashire, England) – guitar / **CHRIS HELME** – vocals, acoustic guitar / **STUART FLETCHER** – bass / **ANDY WATTS** – drums, vocals

Geffen | Geffen

May 97. (7"/c-s/cd-s) *(GFS/+C/TD 22243)* **LOVE IS THE LAW. / DREAMER / SALE OF THE CENTURY** | 3 | –

May 97. (cd/c/lp) *(<GED/GEC/GEF 25134>)* **DO IT YOURSELF** | 2 |
– I want you to know / Blinded by the sun / Suicide drive / The boy in the picture / Love is the law / Happiness is eggshaped / Love me and leave me / Round the universe / 1999 / Standing on your head / Hello.

Jul 97. (7"/c-s/cd-s) *(GFS/+C/TD 22266)* **BLINDED BY THE SUN. / KILL PUSSYCAT KILL / MOVING ON** | 7 | –

Sep 97. (7"/c-s/cd-s) *(GFS/+C/TD 22282)* **LOVE ME AND LEAVE ME. / SHINE / FALLING IS EASY** | 16 | –

Dec 97. (7"/c-s/cd-s) *(GFS/+C/TD 22297)* **YOU CAN TALK TO ME. / DON'T TRY / 3 WIDE** | 15 | –

— **MARK HEANEY** – drums; repl. WATTS

— in Feb'99, the SEAHORSES announced they had split

JOHN SQUIRE

SQUIRE – vocals, guitar + **ANDY TREACEY** – drums (of FAITHLESS) / **JONATHAN WHITE** – bass (of GROOVE ARMADA) / **JOHN ELLIS** – keyboards

North Country | not iss.

Sep 02. (cd/d-lp) *(NCCD/NCLP 001)* **TIME CHANGES EVERYTHING** | 17 | –
– Joe Louis / I miss you / Shine a little light / Time changes everything /

Welcome to the valley / 15 days / Transatlantic near death experience / All I really want / Strange feeling / Sophia.

Oct 02. (7") *(NC 001)* **JOE LOUIS. / HOME SWEET HOME** 43 –
(cd-s+=) *(NCCDA 001)* – 15 days (home demo).
(cd-s) *(NCCDB 001)* – ('A'side) / See you on the other side / I miss you (home demo).

SEAL

Born: SEALHENRY SAMUEL, 13 Feb'63, Paddington, London, England – of Nigerian/Brazilian parentage. After beginning his performing career singing in the Capital's pubs, SEAL took off for the Far East and Asia. Upon his return to the Britain, SEAL hooked up with techno boffin, ADAMSKI, the pair penning the seminal 'KILLER' track, an evocative house/soul epic which topped the UK chart in 1990. With SEAL on vocal duties, his rich, mahogany tones gained widespread exposure, laying the groundwork for a highly successful solo career. Swiftly netted by 'Z.T.T.', SEAL began work on his eponymous debut with veteran producer, Trevor Horn. Previewed by the massive worldwide hit, 'CRAZY', 'SEAL' (1991) established the soul/rock/pop giant (six and a half foot!) as a household name, deftly turning his hand to a variety of styles with a voice that could probably turn lead into gold. Later that year the singer scored a further UK Top 10 with a revamped, rockier 'KILLER', complete with a B-side cover of 'HEY JOE', a track made famous by JIMI HENDRIX amongst others. The HENDRIX connection continued with SEAL reworking 'MANIC DEPRESSION' alongside JEFF BECK for the 1993 tribute album, 'STONE FREE'. Laden with awards, including an Ivor Novello, SEAL subsequently went to ground, again working with Trevor Horn on a follow-up album. Incredibly, again titled 'SEAL' (1994), the record's contents nevertheless belied its unimaginative title, the singer working with a plethora of respected musicians including WENDY & LISA, JONI MITCHELL, WILLIAM ORBIT and the aforementioned JEFF BECK. Another UK No.1, the record finally broke SEAL in America after 'KISS FROM A ROSE' was included on the 'Batman Forever' soundtrack. Following on from 1998's 'HUMAN BEING', an album which once again sold more in the States than his homeland, SEAL went through at least one false start before releasing 'SEAL IV' (2003). A competent if not quite so memorable collection, the record found the ivory-voiced singer relying on his peerless tonsils rather than the variable quality of the songwriting. • **Covered:** THE WIND CRIES MARY (Jimi Hendrix).

Album rating: SEAL (*7) / SEAL (2) (*7) / HUMAN BEING (*5) / SEAL IV (*5)

SEAL – vocals, acoustic guitar (ex-ADAMSKI) with many session people

Z.T.T. Sire

Nov 90. (7"/c-s) *(ZANG 8/+C) <19298>* **CRAZY. / SPARKLE** 2 May91 7
(12"+=/cd-s+=) *(ZANG 8 T/CD)* – ('A'extended).

Apr 91. (7"ep/c-ep) *(ZANG 11/+C)* **THE FUTURE LOVE EP** 12
– Future love paradise / A minor groove / Violet.
(12"+=/cd-s+=) *(ZANG 11 T/CD)* – ('A'extended).

May 91. (cd/c/lp) *(ZTT 9 CD/C/LP) <26627>* **SEAL** 1 Jun91 24
– The beginning / Deep water / Crazy / Killer / Whirlpool / Future love Paradise / Wild / Show me / Violet.

Jul 91. (7"/c-s) *(ZANG 21/+C)* **THE BEGINNING. / DEEP WATER (acoustic)** 24
(cd-s+=) *(ZANG 21CD)* – ('A'-Giro mix) / ('A'remix).
(12") *(ZANG 21T)* – ('A'remix) / ('A'-Giro mix) / ('A'dub mix).

Nov 91. (7"ep/c-ep) *(ZANG 12/+C) <19119>* **KILLER EP** 8 Mar92 100
– Killer / Hey Joe / Come see what love has done.
(12"+=/cd-s+=) *(ZANG 23 T/CD)* – ('A'-Killer . . . on the loose remixes).

Feb 92. (7"/7"sha-pic-d/c-s) *(ZANG 27/+PD/C)* **VIOLET. / WILD** 39
(cd-s+=) *(ZANG 27CD)* – Show me / Whirlpool.

— with a plethora of musicians, the principals being; **GUS ISIDORE, WENDY MELVOIN, LISA COLEMAN & JAMIE MUHOBERAC** (the first 3 co-writers). Guests incl. **JEFF BECK, JONI MITCHELL, LUIS JARDIM, ANNE DUDLEY, ANDY NEWMARK, WILLIAM ORBIT, PINO PALLADINO, GAVIN WRIGHT, BETSY COOK** + producer **TREVOR HORN**

May 94. (7"/c-s) *(ZANG 51/+C) <18138>* **PRAYER FOR THE DYING. / DREAMING IN METAPHORS** 14 21
(cd-s+=) *(ZANG 51CD)* – Crazy (acoustic) / ('A'acoustic).

May 94. (cd/c/lp) *(4509 96256-2/-4/-1) <45415>* **SEAL** 1 Jun94 16
– Bring it on / Prayer for the dying / Dreaming in metaphors / Don't cry / Fast changes / Kiss from a rose / People asking why / Newborn friend / If I could / I'm alive / Bring it on (reprise).

Jul 94. (c-s) *(ZANG 52C)* **KISS FROM A ROSE. / I'M ALIVE (SON OF BONTEMPI)** 20 –
(7"+=/12"+=/cd-s+=) *(ZANG 52/+T/CD2)* – (2 'A'mixes).
(cd-s) *(ZANG 52CD1)* – ('A'side) / The wind cries Mary / Blues in E.

Oct 94. (c-s) *(ZANG 58C)* **NEWBORN FRIEND / ('A'mix)** 45
(12"+=) *(ZANG 58T)* – ('A'mix).
(cd-s++=) *(ZANG 58CD)* – ('A'mix).

Jul 95. (c-s) *(ZANG 70C) <17896>* **KISS FROM A ROSE / I'M ALIVE (SON OF BONTEMPI)** 5 Jun95 1
(12"+=/cd-s+=) *(ZANG 70 T/CD)* – I'm alive (Sasha & BT remix).

Nov 95. (c-s) *(ZANG 75C)* **DON'T CRY / PRAYER FOR THE DYING / DON'T CRY (YOU'RE NOT ALONE)** 51 –
(cd-s+=) *(ZANG 75CD)* – ('B'extended).

Feb 96. (c-s,cd-s) *<17708>* **DON'T CRY / FAST CHANGES** – 33
(below from the movie 'Space Jam' on 'Warner Sunset' US)

Mar 97. (c-s) *(ZEAL 1C) <87046>* **FLY LIKE AN EAGLE / ('A'instrumental)** 13 Nov96 10
(12") *(ZEAL 1T)* – ('A'mixes).
(cd-s) *(ZEAL 1CD)* – ('A'mixes).

Warners Warners

Nov 98. (c-s) *(W 464C)* **HUMAN BEINGS / PRINCESS** 50 –
(cd-s+=) *(W 464CD)* – Human beings (reprise).

Nov 98. (cd/c/lp) *<9362 46828-2/-4>)* **HUMAN BEING** 44 22
– Human beings / State of grace / Latest craze / Just like you said / Princess / Lost my faith / Excerpt from / When a man is wrong / Colour / Still love remains / No easy way / Human beings (reprise).

Sep 03. (cd-s) *(W 620CD1)* **GET IT TOGETHER** 25 –
– (mixes; Peter Rauhofer's classic / Superchumbo's guiding light).
(cd-s/12") *(W 620 CD2/T)* – (Bill Hamel vocal mix) / (wide horizon remix) / (Roy's soldiers of universal love remix).

Sep 03. (12"/cd-s) *<16574>* **WAITING FOR YOU. / LONELIEST STAR** – 89

Sep 03. (cd) *(9362 48541-2) <48566>* **SEAL IV** 4 3
– Get it together / Love's divine / Waiting for you / My vision / Don't make me wait / Let me roll / Touch / Where there's gold / Loneliest star / Heavenly (ggod feeling) / Tinsel town / Get it together (reprise).

Nov 03. (cd-s) *(W 629CD) <42685>* **LOVE'S DIVINE** 68 Jan04 87
– (mixes; Deepsky club / The Passengerz sanctuary / radio / Light-n-lovely / Murk dark-n-dirty dub).

SEARCHERS

Formed: Kirkdale, Liverpool, England . . . 1961 by MIKE PENDER and JOHN McNALLY, who soon found TONY JACKSON and NORMAN McGARRY (the latter being replaced by CHRIS CURTIS). Naming themselves after the famous film starring John Wayne, they became the backing band of club singer, JOHNNY SANDON. Like The BEATLES, they played The Cavern and recorded at The Star-Club in Germany in 1962/63, soon signed to 'Pye' by A&R man, TONY HATCH. Their first 45, 'SWEETS FOR MY SWEET' (written by DOC POMUS & MORT SHUMAN; for The DRIFTERS), hit the UK top spot, the first of a string of hits over the next three years, many of which competed for chart space with the aforementioned BEATLES. These included such classy harmony-laden pop ditties as 'SUGAR AND SPICE' (another written by HATCH) and their second No.1 smash, 'NEEDLES AND PINS' (written by JACK NITZSCHE and SONNY BONO). Their third chart topper, 'DON'T THROW YOUR LOVE AWAY' was issued in Spring '64, this time around penned by The ORLONS. However, JACKSON subsequently departed to form his own outfit, taking his characteristic falsetto voice with him. His replacement, FRANK ALLEN, made sure that the hits kept flowing however, a version of Jackie DeShannon's 'WHEN YOU WALK IN THE ROOM' hitting No.3. The SEARCHERS had already found an audience in the States, scoring their biggest hit to date (Top 3) with the US-only 'LOVE POTION NUMBER NINE'. The times they were a-changin' however, The SEARCHERS' star beginning to fade with their attempt at protest folk-pop, 'WHAT HAVE THEY DONE TO THE RAIN' (written by MALVINA REYNOLDS) only hitting No.13 in the UK (Top 30 US). Although CURTIS and PENDER were still writing some hits, the group had their last stand late in 1966 with 'HAVE YOU EVER LOVED SOMEBODY'. After three flops the following year (an injustice for the first of them, 'POPCORN DOUBLE FEATURE' – later re-hashed by The FALL), they were dropped by 'Pye'. The band subsequently fell by the wayside and into the cabaret scene during the 70's, although they returned with an ill-advised attempt at "new wave" in 1979. A few years later, they played a Royal Variety Show performance alongside the likes/dislikes (delete according to taste) of CLIFF RICHARD, LONNIE DONEGAN and ADAM & THE ANTS. MIKE PENDER continues to tour on the golden oldies circuit, refusing to let go of the jingly-jangly 60's. • **Other cover versions:** SOME DAY WE'RE GONNA LOVE AGAIN (Barbara Lewis) / LOVE POTION NUMBER NINE (Clovers) / BUMBLE BEE (LaVern Baker) / TAKE ME FOR WHAT I'M WORTH (P.F. Sloan) / TAKE IT OR LEAVE IT (Rolling Stones) / and loads of lp tracks.

Best CD compilation: THE ULTIMATE COLLECTION (*7)

MIKE PENDER (b. MICHAEL JOHN PRENDERGAST, 3 Mar'42) – vocals, lead guitar / **JOHN McNALLY** (b.30 Aug'41) – vocals, rhythm guitar / **TONY JACKSON** (b.16 Jul'40) – vocals, bass / **CHRIS CURTIS** (b. CHRISTOPHER CRUMMEY, 26 Aug'41, Oldham, England) – vocals, drums; repl. NORMAN McGARRY who joined RORY STORME & THE HURRICANES replacing RINGO STARR

Pye — Mercury

Jun 63. (7") *(7N 15533) <72172>* **SWEETS FOR MY SWEET. / IT'S ALL BEEN A DREAM** — [1] Mar64 [ ]

Aug 63. (lp; mono) *(NPL 18086)* **MEET THE SEARCHERS** — [2] [–]
– Sweets for my sweet / Alright / Love potion No.9 / Farmer John / Stand by me / Money / Da doo ron ron / Ain't gonna love ya / Since you broke my heart / Tricky Dickey / Where have all the flowers gone / Twist and shout. *(re-iss. 1966 on 'Golden Guinea'; GGL 0349) (re-iss. Feb81 on 'P.R.T.'; same) (re-iss. Oct87 on 'P.R.T.' lp/c/cd; PYL/PYM/PYC 6014) (cd re-iss. Dec89 on 'Castle'; CLACD 165) (cd re-iss. Mar01 on 'Castle'+=; CMRCD 155)* – It's all been a dream / Liebe / Farmer John / Mais c'etait un reve / (stereo versions of LP). *(lp re-iss. Apr03 on 'Get Back'; GET 625)*

Pye — Liberty

Oct 63. (7") *(7N 15566) <55646>* **SUGAR AND SPICE. / SAINTS AND SEARCHERS** — [2] Dec63 [ ]
<US re-iss. Apr64; 55689> hit No.44>

Nov 63. (lp; mono) *(NPL 18089)* **SUGAR AND SPICE** — [5] [–]
– Sugar and spice / Don't cha know? / Some other guy / One of these days / Listen to me / Unhappy girls / (Ain't that) Just like me / Oh my lover / Saints and searchers / Cherry stones / All my sorrows / Hungry for love. *(re-iss. 1967 on 'Marble Arch'; MAL 704) (re-iss. Feb81 on 'P.R.T.'; same) (re-iss. Oct87 on 'P.R.T.' lp/c/cd; PYL/PYM/PYC 6015) (cd re-iss. Dec89 on 'Castle'; CLACD 166) (cd re-iss. Mar01 on 'Castle'+=; CMRCD 156)* – C'est de notre age / Suss ist sie / Ils la chantaient il y a langtemps / Saturday night out / Bye bye Johnny / I don't want to go on without you / (stereo versions of LP).

Pye — Kapp

Jan 64. (7") *(7N 15594) <577>* **NEEDLES AND PINS. / SATURDAY NIGHT OUT** — [1] Feb64 [13]

Mar 64. (lp) *<3363>* **MEET THE SEARCHERS – NEEDLES AND PINS** — [–] [22]
– (tracks from last 2 albums plus title track)

Mar 64. (7") *<584>* **AIN'T THAT JUST LIKE ME. / AIN'T GONNA KISS YA** — [–] [61]

Apr 64. (7") *(7N 15630) <593>* **DON'T THROW YOUR LOVE AWAY. / I PRETEND I'M WITH YOU** — [1] May64 [16]

May 64. (lp; mono) *(NPL 18092)* **IT'S FAB! IT'S GEAR! IT'S THE SEARCHERS** — [4] [–]
– Sea of heartbreak / Glad all over / It's in her kiss / Livin' lovin' wreck / Where have you been / Shimmy shimmy / Needles and pins / This empty place / Gonna send you back to Georgia / I count the tears / High heel sneakers / Can't help forgiving you / Sho' know a lot about love / Don't throw your love away. *(re-iss. 1968 on 'Marble Arch'; MAL 798) (re-iss. Feb81 on 'P.R.T.'; same) (re-iss. Oct87 on 'P.R.T.' lp/c/cd; PYL/PYM/PYC 6016) (cd re-iss. Dec89 on 'Castle'; CLACD 167) (cd re-iss. Mar01 on 'Castle'+=; CMRCD 157)* – I pretend I'm with you / Someday we're gonna love again / No one else could love you / Tausend nadelstiche (Needles & pins) / C'est arrive comme ca / I (who have nothing) / Shame, shame, shame / (stereo versions of LP).

Jul 64. (7") *(7N 15670) <609>* **SOMEDAY WE'RE GONNA LOVE AGAIN. / NO ONE ELSE COULD LOVE YOU** — [11] Aug64 [34]

— **FRANK ALLEN** (b. FRANCIS RENAUD McNEICE, 14 Jul'43, Hayes, England) – vocals, bass (ex-CLIFF BENNETT & THE REBEL ROUSERS) repl. JACKSON, who formed TONY JACKSON & VIBRATIONS

Sep 64. (7") *(7N 15694) <618>* **WHEN YOU WALK IN THE ROOM. / I'LL BE MISSING YOU** — [3] Oct64 [35]

Oct 64. (lp) *<3409>* **THIS IS US** — [–] [97]
– (near same track listing as above album)

Nov 64. (7") *(7N 15739) <644>* **WHAT HAVE THEY DONE TO THE RAIN. / THIS FEELING INSIDE** — [13] Jan65 [29]

Dec 64. (7") *<Winners Circle; 27>* **LOVE POTION NO.9. / HI HEEL SNEAKERS** — [–] [3]

Feb 65. (7") *(7N 15794) <658>* **GOODBYE MY LOVE. / TILL I MET YOU** — [4] Mar65 [52]

— <US-title of above 'GOODBYE MY LOVER GOODBYE'>

Mar 65. (lp; mono) *(NPL 18111) <3412>* **SOUNDS LIKE SEARCHERS** <US-title 'THE NEW SEARCHERS'> — [8] [ ]
– Everybody come and clap your hands / If I could fine someone / Magic potion / I don't want to go on without you / Bumble bee / Something you got baby / Let the good times roll / A tear fell / Till you say you'll be mine / You wanna make her happy / Everything you do / Goodnight baby. *(re-iss. Feb81 on 'P.R.T.'; same) (re-iss. Oct87 on 'P.R.T.' lp/c/cd; PYL/PYM/PYC 6017) (cd re-iss. Mar01 on 'Castle'+=; CMRCD 158)* – When you walk in the room / I'll be missing you / What have they done to the rain / This feeling inside / The system / Goodbye my love / Till I met you / Wenn ich dich seh / (stereo versions of LP).

Mar 65. (7") *<Winners Circle; 49>* **BUMBLE BEE. / A TEAR FELL** — [–] [21]

Jul 65. (7") *(7N 15878) <686>* **HE'S GOT NO LOVE. / SO FAR AWAY** — [12] [79]

Oct 65. (lp) *<3449>* **THE SEARCHERS No.4** — [–] [ ]
– (virtually the same as next album)

Oct 65. (7") *(7N 15950)* **WHEN I GET HOME. / I'M NEVER COMING BACK** — [35] [–]

Oct 65. (7") *<706>* **DON'T YOU KNOW WHY. / YOU CAN'T LIE TO A LIAR** — [–] [ ]

Nov 65. (7") *(7N 15992) <729>* **TAKE ME FOR WHAT I'M WORTH. / TOO MANY MILES** — [20] Jan66 [76]

Nov 65. (lp; mono) *(NPL 18120) <3477>* **TAKE ME FOR WHAT I'M WORTH** — [ ] 1966 [ ]
– I'm ready / I'll be doggone / Does she really care for me / It's time / Too many miles / You can't lie to a liar / Don't you know why / I'm your loving man / Each time / Be my baby / Four strong winds / Take me for what I'm worth. *(re-iss. Feb81 on 'P.R.T.'; same) (cd-iss. Mar01 on 'Castle'+=; CMRCD 159)* – He's got no love / So far away / When I get home / I'm never coming back / I'll be doggone (alt.) / Once upon a time / (stereo versions of LP).

— **JOHN BLUNT** (b.28 Mar'47, London, England) – drums repl. CURTIS

Apr 66. (7") *(7N 17094)* **TAKE IT OR LEAVE IT. / DON'T HIDE IT AWAY** — [31] [–]

Oct 66. (7") *(7N 17170) <783>* **HAVE YOU EVER LOVED SOMEBODY. / IT'S JUST THE WAY LOVE WILL COME AND GO** — [48] [94]

Jan 67. (7") *(7N 17225) <811>* **POPCORN DOUBLE FEATURE. / LOVERS** — [ ] [ ]

Apr 67. (7") *(7N 17308)* **WESTERN UNION. / I'LL CRY TOMORROW** — [ ] [–]

Nov 67. (7") *(7N 17424)* **SECONDHAND DEALER. / CRAZY DREAMS** — [ ] [–]

Liberty | World Pacific

Nov 68. (7") *(LBF 15159) <77908>* **UMBRELLA MAN. / OVER THE WEEKEND** □ □
Jul 69. (7") *(LBF 15340)* **KINKY KATHY ABERNATHY. / SUZANNA** □ –

— (late 1969) **BILLY ADAMSON** – drums, vocals; repl. BLUNT

R.C.A. | R.C.A.

Aug 71. (7") *(RCA 2057) <74-0484>* **DESDEMONA. / THE WORLD IS WAITING FOR TOMORROW** □ 94
Oct 71. (7") *(RCA 2139) <0652>* **LOVE IS EVERYWHERE. / AND A BUTTON** □ □
Apr 72. (7") *(RCA 2231)* **SING SINGER SING. / COME ON BACK TO ME** □ –
Aug 72. (7"m) *(RCA 2248)* **NEEDLES AND PINS. / WHEN YOU WALK IN THE ROOM / COME ON BACK TO ME** □ –
Oct 72. (7") *(RCA 2288)* **VAHEVALA. / MADMAN** □ –
Nov 72. (lp) *(SF 8289)* **SECOND TAKE** □ –
– Sugar and spice / Don't throw your love away / Farmer John / Come on back to me / When you walk in the room / Needles and pins / Desdemona / Goodbye my love / Love potion No.9 / Sweets for my sweet / Take me for what I'm worth / What have they done to the rain. *(<cd-iss. Dec00 on 'Beat Goes On'+=; BGOCD 512>)* – The world is waiting for tomorrow / Love is everywhere / And a button / Sing singer sing / Vahevala / Madman / Solitaire / Spicks and specks / I really don't have the time / Indigo spring.
Feb 73. (7") *(RCA 2330)* **SOLITAIRE. / SPICKS AND SPECKS** □ –

— Resigned themselves to oldies circuit in the US.

Sire | Sire

Oct 79. (7") *(SIR 4029)* **HEARTS IN HER EYES. / DON'T HANG ON** □ –
Feb 80. (7") *(SIR 4036)* **IT'S TOO LATE. / THIS KIND OF LOVE AFFAIR** □ –
Feb 80. (7") **IT'S TOO LATE. / DON'T HANG ON** – □
Mar 80. (lp) *(SRK <6082>)* **THE SEARCHERS** □ □
– Hearts in her eyes / Switchboard Susan / Feeling fine / Back to the war / This kind of love affair / Lost in your eyes / It's too late / Love's melody / No dancing / Love's gonna be strong / Don't hang on. *<US tracks differed>*
Jul 80. (7") *(SIR 4046)* **LOVE'S MELODY. / CHANGING** □ –
Mar 81. (7") *(SIR 4049)* **ANOTHER NIGHT. / BACK TO THE WAR** □ –
May 81. (lp) *(<SRK 3523>)* **PLAY FOR TODAY** <US title 'LOVE'S MELODIES'> □ □
– Another night / September girls / Murder in my heart / She made a fool of you / Silver / Sick and tired / Radio romance / Infatuation / Almost Saturday night / Everything but a heartbeat / Little bit of Heaven / New day.
May 81. (7") *<49665>* **LOVE'S MELODY. / LITTLE BIT OF HEAVEN** – □

— Around mid-80's, group dispersed into 2 sections (aka MIKE PENDER'S SEARCHERS and other SEARCHERS). The others took MIKE to court in 1988. **SPENCER JAMES** – guitar, vocals; repl. PENDER

Arista | not iss.

Apr 90. (cd/c/lp) *(259/409/209 459)* **HUNGRY HEARTS** □ –
– Forever in love (near to Heaven) / Love lies bleeding / Lonely weekend / Somebody told me / Every little tear / Sweets for my sweet (new 1988 version) / No other love / This boy's in love / Fooled myself once again / Baby, I do / Push, push / Needles and pins.

– (selective) compilations, etc. –

on 'Pye' unless stated otherwise

Sep 63. (7") *Philips; (BF 1274)* **SWEET NUTHINS (live in Hamburg). / WHAT'D I SAY** 48 –
Oct 63. (7"ep) *(NEP 24177)* **AIN'T GONNA KISS YA** 12 –
Dec 88. (d-lp/c/cd) *Castle; (CCS LP/MC/CD 208)* **THE COMPLETE COLLECTION** □ –
– Sweets for my sweet / Listen to me / When you walk in the room / Goodbye my love / Don't want to go on without you / What have they done to the rain / Don't throw your love away / Ain't gonna kiss ya / Since you broke my heart / Goodnight baby / Hungry for love / When I get home / Needles and pins / (Ain't that) Just like me / Take it or leave it / Bumble bee / Someday we're gonna love again / Farmer John / Sugar and spice / Have you ever loved somebody / Take me for what I'm worth / Western Union / He's got no love / Love potion No.9. *(re-iss. Nov91 cd/c; CCS CD/MC 303)*
Jul 89. (lp/c/cd) *See For Miles; (SEE/+K/CD 275)* **THE EP COLLECTION** □ –
May 90. (lp/c/cd) *Castle; (CTV CD/MC/LP 003)* **THE ULTIMATE COLLECTION** □ –
Feb 92. (3xcd-box) *Sequel; (NEXCD 170)* **30th ANNIVERSARY COLLECTION** □ –
Feb 92. (3xcd-box) *Castle; (CLABX 913)* **THE SEARCHERS CD BOX SET** □ –
Nov 92. (cd) *See For Miles; (SEECD 359)* **THE EP COLLECTION VOL.2** □ –
May 97. (cd) *Music Club; (MCCD 291)* **THE BEST OF THE SEARCHERS** □ –
May 98. (cd) *Raven; (<RVCD 64>)* **THE SIRE SESSIONS (ROCKFIELD 1979-1980)** □ □
Apr 00. (d-cd) *Sequel; (NEECD 381)* **THE PYE ANTHOLOGY 1963-1967** □ □
Sep 00. (cd) *Castle Pie; (PIESCD 232)* **WHEN YOU WALK IN THE ROOM** □ –
Apr 01. (cd/c) *Castle Select; (SEL CD/MC 509)* **GREATEST HITS COLLECTION** □ □
Nov 01. (cd) *Castle; (CMRCD 394)* **THE SWEDISH RADIO SESSIONS** □ –
Nov 01. (cd) *Disky; (SI 64934-2)* **SWEETS FOR MY SWEET** □ –
Apr 02. (cd) *Castle; (<CMBCD 485>)* **LIVE AT THE IRON DOOR CLUB** □ □
May 02. (cd) *Bear Family; (BCD 1660-2)* **AT THE STAR CLUB** □ –
Sep 02. (cd) *Castle Select; (SELCD 611)* **THE R&B SOUND** □ –
Jun 03. (cd) *Castle; (<CMEDD 726>)* **40th ANNIVERSARY COLLECTION 1963-2003** □ □

Bob SEGER

Born: 6 May'45, Dearborn, Michigan, USA. Coming from an impoverished working class background, SEGER began developing his hard hitting brand of rock'n'roll in the early 60's, eventually joining (DOUG BROWN &) THE OMENS as a keyboard player. Tha material was co-written by SEGER and BROWN, the pair even managing a spoof of BARRY SADLER's 'The Ballad Of The Green Berets' under the pseudonym of The BEACH BUMS in early '66. The OMENS subsequently became BOB SEGER & THE LAST HEARD, the hard gigging troupe garnering a hardcore local following and releasing a handful of singles on the small 'Hideout' and 'Cameo' labels. Early in '68, Eddie 'Punch' Andrews became their manager as the band were now billed as The BOB SEGER SYSTEM; with a 'Capitol' contract in hand, a line-up of SEGER, DAN HONAKER, TONY NEME, BOB SCHULTZ and PEP PERRINE scored a US Top 20 hit with the blistering white R&B of 'RAMBLIN' GAMBLIN' MAN', a fitting title track for the freewheeling 1969 debut album. The group's Motor City following helped place the record in the lower reaches of the American chart although subsequent singles failed to build on this initial success. Disbanding The SYSTEM, SEGER replaced the departing SCHULTZ and NEME with DON WATSON, recording his solo debut set, 'MONGREL' (1970). The musical chairs continued as the singer hooked up with musicians DAVE TEEGARDEN, SKIP VANWINKLE KNAPE and MICHAEL BRUCE for 72's 'SMOKIN' O.P.'s', a set of eclectic covers with the added bluster of a revamped 'HEAVY MUSIC' and the distinction of being SEGER's first album issued on his own label, 'Palladium'. The rootsy 'BACK IN '72' (1973), despite boasting the backing talents of JJ CALE and one MARCY LEVY (later reborn as MARCELLA DETROIT of SHAKESPEAR'S SISTER fame), failed to raise SEGER above cult acclaim. Likewise 'SEVEN' (1974), although it did spawn a minor hit in the brawny 'GET OUT OF DENVER'. SEGER's hard-bitten determination finally began to pay off in the mid-70's as he formed his finest backing unit to date in The SILVER BULLET BAND (namely DREW ABBOTT, ROBIN

ROBBINS, CHRIS CAMPBELL, ALTO REED and CHARLIE ALLEN MARTIN) and returned to 'Capitol' for the 'BEAUTIFUL LOSER' album. Combining his trademark JOHN FOGERTY-esque grit with a newfound maturity and precision, SEGER was hailed in some quarters as the new BRUCE SPRINGSTEEN; certainly, in America at least, the singer's hard driving, pretension-free nuggets of everyday wisdom went down a storm and with the superior 'NIGHT MOVES' (1977), SEGER at last found himself in the Top 10. Proving that he was now as equally adept at delivering more sensitive material as high-octane rock'n'roll, the singer breached the US Top 5 with the album's moving title track. 'STRANGER IN TOWN' (1978) kept up the momentum, again, like its predecessor, utilising The MUSCLE SHOALS' rhythm section for added authenticity. Brushing aside the new wave pretenders, SEGER was now something of an American institution, finally topping the charts in 1980 with the ballad-heavy 'AGAINST THE WIND' album. The record also saw him making the UK Top 30 for the first time, although his British sales would never match the multi-platinum success afforded him in the States. Though hardly prolific in the 80's, his two studio albums, 'THE DISTANCE' (1982) and 'LIKE A ROCK' (1986) both made the US Top 5, dependable million sellers which satisfied his loyal fans if not exactly breaking any new ground. SEGER was naturally in his element in the live environment, a scathing in-concert cover of Creedence Clearwater Revival's 'FORTUNATE SON' making the latter set an essential purchase. With The SILVER BULLET BAND whittled away to its barest bones throughout the 80's, SEGER's work may lack the intensity of old, though his two most recent albums, 'THE FIRE INSIDE' (1991) and 'IT'S A MYSTERY' (1995) illustrated that SEGER himself was far from a spent force. • **Songwriters:** SEGER wrote most except, RIVER DEEP MOUNTAIN HIGH + NUTBUSH CITY LIMITS (Ike & Tina Turner) / BO DIDDLEY (Bo Diddley) / IF I WERE A CARPENTER (Tim Hardin) / LOVE THE ONE YOU'RE WITH (Stephen Stills) / BLIND LOVE + 16 SHELLS FROM A 30.6 (Tom Waits) / SHE CAN'T DO ANYTHING WRONG (C. Davis-Richmond) / C'EST LA VIE (Chuck Berry) / etc. • **Trivia:** SEGER's songs have been covered by many including ROSALIE (Thin Lizzy) / GET OUT OF DENVER (Eddie & The Hot Rods) / WE'VE GOT TONITE (Kenny Rogers & Sheena Easton).

Album rating: RAMBLIN' GAMBLIN' MAN (*6) / NOAH (*6) / MONGREL (*5) / BRAND NEW MORNING (*5) / BACK IN '72 (*5) / SMOKIN' O.P.'s (*6) / SEVEN (*6) / BEAUTIFUL LOSER (*7) / 'LIVE' BULLET (*7) / NIGHT MOVES (*8) / STRANGER IN TOWN (*7) / AGAINST THE WIND (*6) / NINE TONIGHT (*6) / THE DISTANCE (*6) / LIKE A ROCK (*6) / THE FIRE INSIDE (*6) / THE FIRE INSIDE (*5) / GREATEST HITS compilation (*8) / IT'S A MYSTERY (*5) / GREATEST HITS 2 compilation (*7)

BOB SEGER & The LAST HEARD

BOB SEGER – vocas, guitar with **DAN HONAKER** – bass, guitar, vocals / **PEP PERRINE** – drums, vocals / **DOUG BROWN** – keyboards

not iss. | Hideout

May 66. (7") *<1013>* **EAST SIDE STORY. / EAST SIDE SOUND** [–] [ ]

— <above & below 45's, were soon distributed by 'Cameo' 438 + 465>

Jul 66. (7") *<1014>* **PERSECUTION SMITH. / CHAIN SMOKIN'** [–] [ ]

not iss. | Cameo

Dec 66. (7") *<444>* **SOCK IT TO ME, SANTA. / FLORIDA TIME** [–] [ ]

1967. (7") *<473>* **VAGRANT WINTER. / VERY FEW** [–] [ ]

1967. (7") *<494>* **HEAVY MUSIC (part 1). / HEAVY MUSIC (part 2)** [–] [ ]

BOB SEGER SYSTEM

— repl. BROWN with **BOB SCHULTZ** – keyboards, saxophone / **TONY NEME** – guitar, keyboards

Capitol | Capitol

Jan 68. (7") *<2145>* **2 + 2 = WHAT?. / DEATH ROW** [–] [ ]

Dec 68. (7") *(CL 15574) <2297>* **RAMBLIN' GAMBLIN' MAN. / TALES OF LUCY BLUE** [ ] [17]

Jan 69. (lp) *<172>* **RAMBLIN' GAMBLIN' MAN** [–] [62]
– Ramblin' gamblin' man / Tales of Lucy Blue / Ivory / Gone / Down home / Train man / White wall / Black eyed girl / 2 + 2 = what? / Doctor Fine / The lost song (love needs to be loved). *(UK-iss.Nov77; CAPS 1013) (re-iss. Jun81 on 'Greenlight'; GO 2018)*

May 69. (7") *<2480>* **IVORY. / LOST SONG (LOVE NEEDS TO BE LOVED)** [–] [97]

Jan 70. (7") *<2576>* **LENNIE JOHNSON. / NOAH (or) OUT LOUD** [–] [ ]

Mar 70. (7") *<2640>* **INNERVENUS EYES. / LONELY MAN** [–] [ ]

Apr 70. (lp) *<236>* **NOAH** [–] [ ]
– Noah / Innervenus eyes / Lonely man / Loneliness is a feeling / Cat / Jumpin' humpin' hip hypocrite / Follow the children / Lennie Johnson / Paint them a picture Jane / Death row.

May 70. (7") *(CL 15642) <2748>* **LUCIFER. / BIG RIVER** [ ] Mar70 [84]

Oct 70. (lp) *<499>* **MONGREL** [–] [ ]
– Song to Rufus / Evil Edna / Highway child / Big river / Mongrel / Lucifer / Teachin' blues / Leavin' on my dream / Mongrel too / River deep mountain high. *(UK-iss.Nov77; CAPS 1010) (re-iss. Jun81 on 'Greenlight'; GO 2022) (re-iss. Jul83 on 'Fame' lp/c; FA/TC-FA 3072)*

BOB SEGER

— added **DON WATSON** – keyboards to repl SCHULTZ + NEME

— now with **DAVE TEEGARDEN** – drums / **SKIP VANWINKLE KNAPE** – keyboards, bass / **MICHAEL BRUCE** – guitar

Nov 71. (lp) *<731>* **BRAND NEW MORNING** [–] [ ]
– Brand new morning / Maybe today / Sometimes / You know who you are / Railroad days / Louise / Song for him / Something like.

Nov 71. (7") *<3187>* **LOOKIN' BACK. / HIGHWAY CHILD** [–] [96]

Reprise | Palladium

Jul 72. (7") *<1079>* **IF I WERE A CARPENTER. / JESSE JAMES** [–] [76]

Aug 72. (lp) *(K 44214) <2109>* **SMOKIN' O.P.'s** [ ] Jul72 [ ]
– Bo Diddley / Love the one you're with / If I were a carpenter / Hummingbird / Let it rock / Turn on your love light / Jesse James / Someday / Heavy music. *(re-iss. Apr80; 11746)*

Nov 72. (7") *<1117>* **TURN ON YOUR LOVE LIGHT. / Bo Diddley: BO DIDDLEY** [–] [ ]

— SEGER's back-up back included **DICK SIMS** – keyboards / **TOM CARTMELL** – sax / **JAMIE OLDAKER** – drums / **SERGIO PASTORA** – percussion / **MARCY LEVY** – backing vocals

Mar 73. (lp) *(K 44227) <2126>* **BACK IN '72** [ ] [ ]
– Midnight rider / So I wrote you a song / Stealer / Rosalie / Turn the page / Back in '72 / Neon sky / I've been working / I've got time.

Apr 73. (7") *<1143>* **ROSALIE. / NEON SKY** [–] [ ]

Nov 73. (7") *(K 14243)* **ROSALIE. / BACK IN '72** [ ] [–]

— His band all left to join ERIC CLAPTON. Newcomers **KENNY BUTTREY** – drums / **RANDY MEYERS** – drums / **RICK MANSKA** – keyboards / **TOMMY COGBILL** – bass / + guitars.

Jun 74. (7") *<1171>* **NEED YA. / SEEN A LOT OF FLOORS** [–] [ ]

Jul 74. (lp) *(K 44262) <2184>* **SEVEN / CONTRASTS** [ ] [ ]
– Get out of Denver / Long song comin' / Need ya / School teacher / Cross of gold / U.M.C. (Upper Middle Class) / Seen a lot of floors / 20 years from now / All your love. *(re-iss. Apr80; 11748) (re-iss. Jun81 on 'Greenlight'; GO 2006)*

Aug 74. (7") *(K 14364) <1205>* **GET OUT OF DENVER. / LONG SONG COMIN'** [ ] [80]

Nov 74. (7") *<1316>* **U.M.C. (UPPER MIDDLE CLASS). / THIS OLD HOUSE** [–] [ ]

— new line-up consisted of **DREW ABBOTT** – guitar / **ROBIN ROBBINS** – keyboards / **CHRIS CAMPBELL** – bass / **ALTO REED** – saxophone / **CHARLIE ALLEN MARTIN** – drums

Capitol | Capitol

May 75. (7") *<4062>* **BEAUTIFUL LOSER. / FINE MEMORY** [–] [ ]

Aug 75. (lp/c) *<(EST/TC-EST 11378)>* **BEAUTIFUL LOSER** [ ] Apr75 [ ]
– Beautiful loser / Black night / Katmandu / Jody girl / Travellin' man /

Momma / Nutbush city limits / Sailing nights / Fine memory. *(re-iss. Jun85 on 'Fame'; FA41 3117-1)*

Aug 75. (7") *(CL 15831) <4116>* **KATMANDU. / BLACK NIGHT** [ ] [43]

Nov 75. (7") *<4183>* **NUTBUSH CITY LIMITS. / TRAVELIN' MAN** [–] [ ]

BOB SEGER & THE SILVER BULLET BAND

Aug 76. (d-lp/d-c) *(ESTSP/TC-ESTSP 16) <11523>* **LIVE BULLET (live Detroit)** [ ] Apr76 [34]
– Nutbush city limits / Travellin' man / Beautiful loser / Jody girl / Lookin' back / Get out of Denver / Let it rock / I've been workin' / Turn the page / U.M.C. (Upper Middle Class) / Bo Diddley / Ramblin' gamblin' man / Heavy music / Katmandu. *(cd-iss. Oct88; CDP 746085-2) (cd re-iss. Feb95; CDP 746085-2)*

Jun 76. (7") *<4269>* **NUTBUSH CITY LIMITS (live). / LOOKIN' BACK** [–] May76 [69]

Aug 76. (7") *CL 15884) <4300>* **TRAVELLIN' MAN (live). / BEAUTIFUL LOSER (live)** [ ] [ ]

—— Next 2 albums also credited The MUSCLE SHOALS RHYTHM SECTION on one side apiece. They were **DAVID HOOD** – bass / **ROGER HAWKINS** – drums / **BARRY BECKETT + JIMMY JOHNSON** – horns / **DOUG RILEY** – keyboards / **PETE CARR** – guitar / + **GLENN FREY**

Nov 76. (7") *(CL 15895)* **MAINSTREET. / COME TO POPPA** [ ] [–]

Mar 77. (lp/c) *<(EST/TC-EST 11557)>* **NIGHT MOVES** [ ] Nov76 [8]
– Rock and roll never forgets / Night moves / The fire down below / Sunburst / Sunspot baby / Mainstreet / Come to poppa / Ship of fools / Mary Lou. *(re-iss. May82 on 'Fame' lp/c; FA/TC-FA 3022) (cd-iss. Oct88 & Feb95; CDP 746075-2)*

Mar 77. (7") *(CL 15904) <4369>* **NIGHT MOVES. / SHIP OF FOOLS** [ ] Dec76 [4]

Apr 77. (7") *<4422>* **MAINSTREET. / JODY GIRL** [–] [24]

Jul 77. (7") *<4449>* **ROCK AND ROLL NEVER FORGETS. / THE FIRE DOWN BELOW** [–] [41]

Sep 77. (7") *(CL 15938)* **ROCK AND ROLL NEVER FORGETS. / SHIP OF FOOLS** [ ] [–]

—— **DAVE TEEGARDEN** – drums (ex-STK) repl. CHARLIE (was paralysed from car crash)

May 78. (silver-lp/c) *<(EST/TC-EST 11698)>* **STRANGER IN TOWN** [31] [4]
– Hollywood nights / Still the same / Old time rock & roll / Till it shines / Feel like a number / Ain't got no money / We've got tonite / Brave strangers / The famous final scene. *(cd-iss. Oct88 & Feb95; CDP 746074-2)*

May 78. (7") *(CL 15990) <4581>* **STILL THE SAME. / FEEL LIKE A NUMBER** [ ] [4]

Jul 78. (7") *<4618>* **HOLLYWOOD NIGHTS. / BRAVE STRANGERS** [–] [ ]

Aug 78. (7"silver) *(CL 16004)* **HOLLYWOOD NIGHTS. / OLD TIME ROCK & ROLL** [42] [–]

Jan 79. (7") *(CL 16028) <4653>* **WE'VE GOT TONITE. / AIN'T GOT NO MONEY** [41] Oct78 [13]

Mar 79. (7") *(CL 16073)* **TILL IT SHINES. / BEAUTIFUL LOSER** [ ] [–]
(12"+=) *(12CL 16073)* – Get out of Denver.

Apr 79. (7") *<4702>* **OLD TIME ROCK & ROLL. / SUNSPOT BABY** [–] [28]

Mar 80. (7") *(CL 16130) <4836>* **FIRE LAKE. / LONG TWIN SILVER LINE** [ ] Feb80 [6]

Mar 80. (lp/c) *<(EST/TC-EST 12041)>* **AGAINST THE WIND** [26] [1]
– The horizontal bop / You'll accomp'ny me / Her strut / No man's land / Long twin silver line / Against the wind / Good for me / Betty Lou's getting out tonight / Fire Lake / Shinin' brightly. *(cd-iss. 1986 & Feb95; CDP 746060-2) <cd re-mast.Jun03; CAP 84316>*

May 80. (7") *(CL 16143) <4863>* **AGAINST THE WIND. / NO MAN'S LAND** [ ] Apr80 [5]

Aug 80. (7") *(CL 16163) <4904>* **YOU'LL ACCOMP'NY ME. / BETTY LOU'S GETTING OUT TONIGHT** [ ] Jul80 [14]

Oct 80. (7"m) *(CL 16174)* **AGAINST THE WIND. / GET OUT OF DENVER / NUTBUSH CITY LIMITS** [ ] [–]

Nov 80. (7") *<4951>* **THE HORIZONTAL BOP. / HER STRUT** [–] [42]

Sep 81. (d-lp/d-c) *(ESTSP/TC2-ESTSP 23) <12182>* **NINE TONIGHT (live)** [24] [3]
– Nine tonight / Tryin' to live my life without you / You'll accomp'ny me / Hollywood nights / Old time rock & roll / Mainstreet / Against the wind / The fire down below / Her strut / Feel like a number / Fire Lake / Betty Lou's gettin' out tonight / We've got tonight / Night moves / Rock and roll never forgets / Let it rock. *(cd-iss. Feb95; CDP 746086-2)*

Sep 81. (7") *<5042>* **TRYIN' TO LIVE MY LIFE WITHOUT YOU (live). / BRAVE STRANGERS (live)** [–] [5]

Oct 81. (7"/12") *(CL/12CL 223)* **HOLLYWOOD NIGHTS (live). / BRAVE STRANGERS (live)** [49] [–]

Dec 81. (7") *(CL 235)* **WE'VE GOT TONIGHT (live). / FEEL LIKE A NUMBER (live)** [60] [–]
(12"+=,12"red+=) *(12CL 235)* – Brave strangers (live).

Dec 81. (7") *<5077>* **FEEL LIKE A NUMBER (live). / HOLLYWOOD NIGHTS (live)** [–] [48]

—— **SEGER** retained **CHRIS CAMPBELL + ALTO REED,** and recruited **ROY BITTAN** – keyboards (of BRUCE SPRINGSTEEN's E-STREET BAND) / **RUSS KUNKEL** – drums / **WADDY WACHTEL** – guitar / **CRAIG FROST** – keyboards (ex-GRAND FUNK RAILROAD)

Dec 82. (7") *(CL 275) <5187>* **SHAME ON THE MOON. / HOUSE BEHIND A HOUSE** [ ] [2]

Dec 82. (lp/c) *<(EST/TC-EST 12254)>* **THE DISTANCE** [45] [5]
– Even now / Makin' Thunderbirds / Boomtown blues / Shame on the Moon / Love's the last to know / Roll me away / House behind a house / Comin' home / Little victories. *(cd-iss. Oct88; CDP 746 005-2)*

Mar 83. (7") *(CL 284) <5213>* **EVEN NOW. / LITTLE VICTORIES** [73] [12]
(d7"+=/c-s+=) *(CLD/TCCL 284)* – We've got tonight / Brave strangers.

Jun 83. (7") *(CL 297) <5235>* **ROLL ME AWAY. / BOOMTOWN BLUES** [ ] May83 [27]
(below 'A'side was used on the film 'Teachers')

Jan 85. (7") *(CL 350) <5413>* **UNDERSTANDING. / EAST L.A.** [ ] Nov84 [11]
(12"+=) *(12CL 350)* – We've got tonite.

—— **DON BREWER** – drums (ex-GRAND FUNK RAILROAD) repl. KUNKEL

Mar 86. (7") *(CL 396) <5532>* **AMERICAN STORM. / FORTUNATE SON (live)** [ ] [13]
(12"+=) *(12CL 396)* – Hollywood nights (live).
(d7"++=) *(CLD 396)* – Hollywood nights.

Apr 86. (lp/c) *(EST/TC-EST 2011) <12398>* **LIKE A ROCK** [35] [3]
– American storm / Like a rock / Miami / The ring / Tightrope / The aftermath / Sometimes / It's you / Somewhere tonight. *(cd-iss. Oct88 +=; CDP 746195-2)* – Living inside my heart / Like a rock (edit) / Fortunate son (live).

Jul 86. (7") *(CL 408) <5592>* **LIKE A ROCK. / LIVING INSIDE MY HEART** [ ] May86 [12]
(12"+=) *(12CL 408)* – Katmandu.

Aug 86. (7") *<5623>* **IT'S YOU. / THE AFTERMATH** [–] [52]

Nov 86. (7") *<5658>* **MIAMI. / SOMEWHERE TONIGHT** [–] [70]
(below solo 45 from the 'Beverley Hills Cop II' film on 'M.C.A.')

Aug 87. (7"/12") *(MCA/T 1172) <53094>* **SHAKEDOWN. / THE AFTERMATH** [ ] May87 [1]

Sep 91. (cd/c/lp) *(CD/TC+/EST 2149) <91134>* **THE FIRE INSIDE** [54] [7]
– Take a chance / The real love / Sightseeing / Real at the time / Always in my heart / The fire inside / Which way / New coat of paint / The mountain / The long way home / Blind love / She can't do anything wrong.

Aug 91. (c-s,cd-s) *<44743>* **THE REAL LOVE / THE MOUNTAIN** [–] [24]

Sep 91. (7") **THE REAL LOVE. / WHICH WAY** [ ] [–]
(12"+=) – The mountain.
(cd-s++=) – Hollywood nights.

Mar 92. (c-s/cd-s/7") *(TC/CD+/648)* **THE FIRE INSIDE. / THE REAL LOVE** [ ] [ ]

Jan 95. (7") *(CL 734)* **WE'VE GOT TONIGHT. / HOLLYWOOD NIGHTS** [22] [–]
(c-s+=/cd-s+=) *(TC/CD+/CL 734)* – C'est la vie.
(cd-s) *(CDCLS 734)* – ('A'side) / Night moves (live) / Nutbush city limits (live).

Feb 95. (cd/c/lp) *(CD/TC+/EST 2241) <30334>* **GREATEST HITS** (compilation) [6] Nov94 [8]
– Roll me away / Night moves / Turn the page / You'll accomp'ny me / Hollywood nights / Still the same / Old time rock & roll / We've got tonight / Against the wind / Main street / The fire inside / Like a rock / C'est la vie / In your time.

Apr 95. (c-s) *(TCCL 741)* **NIGHT MOVES / EVEN NOW / WE'VE GOT TONIGHT (live)** [50] [–]
(cd-s+=) *(CDCL 741)* – American storm.
(cd-s) *(CDCLS 741)* – ('A'side) / Katmandu (live) / The fire down below / The famous final scene.

Jul 95. (c-s/cd-s) *(TC/CD CL 749)* **HOLLYWOOD NIGHTS / ROCK AND ROLL NEVER FORGETS / HOLLYWOOD NIGHTS (live)** [52] [–]
(cd-s) *(CDCLS 749)* – ('A'side) / Come to poppa / Fire lake.
Nov 95. (cd/c) *(CD/TC EST 2271)* <99774> **IT'S A MYSTERY** [ ] [27]
– Rite of passage / Lock and load / By the river / Manhattan / I wonder / It's a mystery / Revisionism street / Golden boy / I can't save you, Angelene / 16 shells from a 30.6 / West of the Moon / Hands in the air.
Feb 96. (c-ep/cd-ep) *(TC/CD CL 765)* **LOCK AND LOAD / THE FIRE INSIDE / LIKE A ROCK / MANHATTAN** [57] [ ]
(cd-ep) *(CDCLS 765)* – ('A'side) / It's a mystery / Roll me away / Mainstreet.

– compilations, etc. –

on 'Capitol' unless mentioned otherwise
Jun 77. (7"ep) *Reprise; (K 14476)* **EXTENDED PLAY** [ ] [–]
– Get out of Denver / Back in '72 / Midnight rider / Rosalie.
Nov 77. (7"m) *(CL CL 15956)* **TURN THE PAGE. / GET OUT OF DENVER (live) / HEAVY MUSIC (live)** [ ] [–]
Sep 83. (7") *<5276>* **OLD TIME ROCK & ROLL. / TILL IT SHINES** [–] [48]
Mar 84. (7") *(CL 326)* **OLD TIME ROCK & ROLL. / ROLL ME AWAY** [ ] [–]
(12"+=) *(12CL 326)* – Makin' Thunderbirds.
Nov 03. (cd) **GREATEST HITS 2** [–] [23]
– Understanding (from 'Teachers' soundtrack) / The fire down below / Her strut / Beautiful loser / Sunspot baby / Katmandu / Shame on the moon / Fire lake / Tryin' to live my life without you (live) / Shakedown (from 'Beverly Hills Cop II' soundtrack) / Manhattan / New coat of paint / Chances are (with MARTINA McBRIDE from 'Hope Floats' soundtrack) / Rock and roll never forgets. *<bonus +=>* – Satisfied / Tomorrow / Turn the page (video).

□ SENSATIONAL ALEX HARVEY BAND
(see under ⇒ HARVEY, Alex)

SEPULTURA

Formed: Belo Horizonte, Brazil . . . 1983 by brothers MAX and schoolboy IGOR CAVALERA alongside JAIRO T. and PAOLO JR., taking the name SEPULTURA from the MOTORHEAD song, 'Dancing On Your Grave' (Sepultura meaning 'grave' in Portuguese). Influenced largely by black metal bands such as VENOM, as well as British punk, SEPULTURA's earliest release was a split album with fellow Brazilian death metallers, OVERDOSE, entitled 'BESTIAL DEVASTATION' (1984). Another rudimentary thrash effort followed in 'MORBID VISIONS' (1985), again released on the small 'Cogumelo' label. It was nevertheless enough to see the band snapped up by 'Roadrunner', who released the 'SCHIZOPHRENIA' set in early '87. With ANDREAS KISSER replacing JAIRO T, SEPULTURA at last began to focus some of their unbridled sonic savagery, MAX's trademark growl assuming the bowel quaking chill it had always threatened as the ubiquitous Scott Burns worked his magic at the mixing desk. With BURNS in a production capacity, the masterful 'BENEATH THE REMAINS' (1989) finally signalled the arrival of a major force on the international metal scene. Breathtakingly dynamic, the album twisted and turned like a joyrider on speed, switching from breakneck thrash to pummeling sludge-riffing with untrammelled ferocity. Though you still couldn't actually make out what CAVALERA was saying, the unearthly roar of his voice was a revelation, almost an instrument in itself with its own rhythmic thrust. And while many thrash acts gave the impression of playing aggressively purely because that's what was expected of them, the likes of 'INNER SELF' and 'STRONGER THAN HATE' reeked of the genuine frustration, despair and disillusionment of growing up in an impoverished third world country. One of the last great thrash albums of the 80's, the record marked the end of the first stage in SEPULTURA's development; the next album, 'ARISE' (1991), was released as the scene was in its death throes and on this showing it was clear they weren't going to be left behind. On many tracks, the pace was slowed to a seismic turbo-Sabbath grind, gut-wrenchingly heavy and immensely powerful; SEPULTURA were redefining the boundaries of metal with each successive release. Already massive in Brazil (SEPULTURA had played the huge 'Rock In Rio' festival in 1990), the group narrowly missed the UK Top 10 with 'CHAOS A.D.' (1993). Taking the more basic approach of its predecessor even further, the record adopted a markedly more political lyrical stance than anything they'd released to date, the anger ferociously focused into bitter diatribes like 'SLAVE NEW WORLD'. Having previously injected a malignant power into MOTORHEAD's 'Orgasmatron' (which even LEMMY couldn't muster) a couple of years back, here SEPULTURA steamrollered NEW MODEL ARMY's 'The Hunt', proving that punk was as close as metal, if not more so, to the group's charred heart. But SEPULTURA really guaranteed their place in the rock hall of fame with 'ROOTS' (1996), voted by Kerrang! magazine as one of the best metal albums ever released. Stunning in both its stylistic breadth and unrelenting intensity, this was the masterpiece SEPULTURA had been working towards from the beginning of their career. Leaving most of their peers banging their heads on the starting post, the record embraced the cultural heritage of their native Brazil (with the help of rainforest tribe, the Xavantes) to concoct a haunting fusion of ethno-metal and hypnotic tribal spiritualism. The rock world was stunned when SEPULTURA disbanded early in 1997, one of the few metal acts to quit while they were on top (MAX has since formed SOULFLY, taking up where 'ROOTS' more rhythmic sound left off). However, that was certainly not the end, as SEPULTURA regrouped the following year complete with new frontman, DERRICK GREEN. An excellent comeback set, 'AGAINST', astonished most hardcore fans, GREEN's earthy vocal chords giving the group another dimension. While its lack of commercial chart success might've suggested otherwise, 'NATION' (2001) – the band's first album recorded in Brazil for over a decade – was the sound of a band finally rediscovering itself after the upheavals of the late 90's. A quasi concept set with cold war-style cover art, the record found GREEN, CAVALERA and Co wielding a focused anger that many modern metal acts either can't muster or fail to articulate, the presence of JELLO BIAFRA on 'POLITRICKS' heightening the sense of seething injustice. With concert set 'UNDER A PALE GREY SKY' (2002), SEPULTURA fans were transported back to the turbulent period immediately prior to MAX's departure. Deeply emotionally wounded from the death of his stepson, the singer poured every ounce of his battered soul into this blistering tour de force of live performance. The brutal, electrifying charge of SEPULTURA Mk.1 in full flight was a tall order to follow, even for the band CAVALERA left behind. Yet with 'ROORBACK' (2003), they again proved themselves committed to giving it their best shot. Ugly, hostile and uncompromising are some the best compliments anyone can give in relation to the kind of metal SEPULTURA continue to deal in, and their latest set merited all three. Best of all though, was a murderous makeover of U2's 'BULLET THE BLUE SKY', DERRICK GREEN extracting the lyric's true horror like a demented dentist. • **Songwriters:** Group penned, except DRUG ME (Dead Kennedys) / SYMPTOM OF THE UNIVERSE (Black Sabbath) / CLENCHED FIST (Ratos De Porao) / INTO THE CRYPT OF RAYS + PROCREATION (OF THE WICKED) (Celtic Frost) / GENE MACHINE – DON'T BOTHER ME (Bad Brains) / BELA LUGOSI'S

DEAD (Bauhaus) / ANNIHILATION (Crucifix) / RISE ABOVE (Black Flag) / MESSIAH (Hellhammer) / ANGEL (Massive Attack) / BLACK STEEL IN THE HOUR OF CHAOS (Public Enemy) / MONGOLOID (DEvo) / MOUNTAIN SONG (Jane's Addiction) / PIRANHA (Exodus).

Album rating: MORBID VISIONS (*4) / SCHIZOPHRENIA (*7) / BENEATH THE REMAINS (*9) / ARISE (*6) / CHAOS A.D. (*7) / ROOTS (*9) / BLOOD-ROOTED compilation (*7) / AGAINST (*8) / NATION (*6) / UNDER A PALE GREY SKY (*7) / ROORBACK (*7)

MAX CAVALERA (b. MASSIMILANO A. CAVALERA, 4 Aug'69) – vocals, guitar / **JAIRO T** -guitar/ **PAULO JR.** (b.PAULO XISTO PINTO JR., 30 Apr'69) – bass / **IGOR CAVALERA** (b.4 Sep'70) – drums

Cogumelo | not iss.

Nov 84. (m-lp; shared with OVERDOSE) *(803248)* **BESTIAL DEVASTATION** [–] Brazil [–]
– Bestial devastation / Antichrist / Necromancer / Warriors of death. *(cd-iss. Mar97 on 'Bestial'; SBD 001)*

Nov 85. (lp) **MORBID VISIONS** [–] [–]
– Morbid visions / Mayhem / Troops of doom / War / Crucifixion / Show me the wrath / Funeral rites / Empire of the damned / The curse. *(UK-iss.Apr89 on 'Shark' German; SHARK 004) (UK-iss.Nov91 on 'Roadracer' w/ 'BESTIAL DEVASTATION' cd/c/lp; RO 9276-2/-4/-1) (re-iss. Apr94 + Aug95 on 'Roadrunner'; same)*

— **ANDREAS KISSER** (b.24 Aug'68, Sao Bernado Do Campo, Brazil) – lead guitar; repl. JAIRO T

Shark | New Renaissance

Feb 88. (lp/cd) *(SHARK/+CD 006)* **SCHIZOPHRENIA** [–] German [ ]
– Intro / From the past comes the storms / To the wall / Escape to the void / Inquisition symphony / Screams behind the shadows / Septic schizo / The abyss / R.I.P. (Rest In Pain). *(c+=/cd+=)* – Troops of doom. *(re-iss. cd/c/lp Apr94 & Aug95 & May00 on 'Roadrunner'; RR 8764-2)*

Roadracer | Roadracer

Apr 89. (lp/c/cd) <*(RO 9511-1/-4/-2)*> **BENEATH THE REMAINS** [ ] [ ]
– Beneath the remains / Inner self / Stronger than hate / Mass hypnosis / Sarcastic existence / Slaves of pain / Lobotomy / Hungry / Primitive future. *(re-iss. Apr94 & Aug95 on 'Roadrunner'; same)*

Mar 91. (cd/c/lp/pic-lp) <*(RO 9328-2/-4/-1/-8)*> **ARISE** [40] [ ]
– Arise / Dead embryonic cells / Desperate cry / Murder / Subtraction / Altered state / Under siege (regnum Irae) / Meaningless movements / Infected voice. (pic-lp+=) – Orgasmatron. *(re-iss. Apr94 & Aug95 on 'Roadrunner'; same)*

Mar 91. (c-ep/12"ep/cd-ep) *(RO 2424-4/-6/-3)* **UNDER SIEGE (REGNUM IRAE). / TROOPS OF DOOM (re-recorded) / ORGASMATRON** [ ] [ ]

Feb 92. (c-ep/12"ep/cd-ep) *(RO 2406-4/-6/-3)* **ARISE. / INNER SELF (live) / TROOPS OF DOOM (live)** [ ] [ ]

Roadrunner | Epic

Sep 93. (7"pic-d-ep/c-ep/12"ep/cd-ep) *(RR 2382-7/-4/-6/-3)* **TERRITORY. / POLICIA / BIOTECH IS GODZILLA** [66] [ ]

Oct 93. (cd/c/lp) *(RR 9000-2/-4/-1)* *<57458>* **CHAOS A.D.** [11] [32]
– Refuse-Resist / Territory / Slave new world / Amen / Kaiowas / Propaganda / Biotech is Godzilla / Nomad / We who are not as others / Manifest / The Hunt / Clenched fist *(cd-tin-box.Mar94; 9000-0)* *(+=)* – Policia / Inhuman nature. *(re-iss. Aug95+=; same)* – Chaos B.C. / Kaiowas (tribal jam) / Territory (live) / Amen – Inner self (live). *(re-iss. Oct96; same)*

— Early in '94, MAX was arrested and fined for stamping on the Brazilian flag. He is said to have done it accidentally.

Feb 94. (7"ep/c-ep/12"ep/12"purple-ep/cd-ep/s-cd-ep) *(RR 2377-7/-4/-6/-8/-3/-5)* **REFUSE – RESIST. / INHUMAN NATURE / PROPAGANDA** [51] [ ]

May 94. (cd-s) *(RR 2374-3)* **SLAVE NEW WORLD / DESPERATE CRY** [46] [ ]
(c-ep/etched-12"ep/cd-ep) *(RR 2374-4/-8/-5)* – ('A'side) / Crucificados Pelo systema / Drug me / Orgasmatron (live).

Feb 96. (7"colrd) *(RR 2320-7)* **ROOTS BLOODY ROOTS. / SYMPTOM OF THE UNIVERSE** [19] [ ]
(cd-s) *(RR 2320-2)* – ('A'side) / Procreation (of the wicked) / Refuse – resist (live) / Territory (live).
(cd-s) *(RR 2320-5)* – ('A'side) / Propaganda (live) / Beneath the remains (live) / Escape to the void (live).

Feb 96. (cd/c/lp) <*(RR 8900-2/-4/-1)*> **ROOTS** [4] [27]
– Roots bloody roots / Attitude / Cut-throat / Ratamahatta / Breed apart / Straighthate / Spit / Lookaway / Dusted / Born stubborn / Jasco / Itsari / Ambush / Endangered species / Dictatorshit. *(cd+=)* – Chaos B.C. / Symptom of the universe / Kaiowas (live). *(re-iss. Oct96 as 'THE ROOTS OF SEPULTURA' cd w/ bonus cd of 20 unreleased + rare tracks; RR 8900-8)*

Aug 96. (7") *(RR 2314-7)* **RATAMAHATTA. / MASS HYPNOSIS (live)** [23] [ ]
(cd-s) *(RR 2314-2)* – ('A'side) / War / Slave new world (live) / Amen – Inner self (live).
(cd-s) *(RR 2314-5)* – ('A'side) / War / Roots bloody roots (demo) / Dusted (demo).

Dec 96. (7") *(RR 2299-7)* **ATTITUDE. / DEAD EMBRYONIC CELLS (live)** [46] [ ]
(cd-s) *(RR 2299-2)* – ('A'side) / Lookaway (master vibe mix) / Mine.
(cd-s) *(RR 2299-5)* – ('A'side) / Kaiowas (tribal jam) / Clenched fist (live) / Biotech is Godzilla (live).

— split late '96, when MAX was told he was no longer wanted. He subsequently formed SOULFLY, while SEPULTURA went to ground for a year. They returned with a new singer **DERRICK GREEN** (ex-ALPHA JERK)

Oct 98. (cd/c/lp) *(<RR 8700-2/-4/-1>)* **AGAINST** [40] [82]
– Against / Choke / Rumors / Old earth / Floaters in mud / Boycott / Tribus / Common bonds / F.O.E. / Reza / Unconscious / Kamaitachi / Drowned out / Hatred aside / T3rcermillennium.

Nov 98. (cd-s) *(RR 2219-3)* **CHOKE / GENE MACHINE (demo) / DON'T BOTHER ME (demo) / AGAINST (demo)** [ ] [ ]

Jul 99. (cd-s) *(RR 2169-3)* **AGAINST / THE WASTE / TRIBUS / COMMON BONDS (alternate mix)** [ ] [ ]

Mar 01. (cd) *(<RR 8560-2>)* **NATION** [ ] [ ]
– Sepulnation / Revolt / Border wars / One man army / Vox populi / The ways of faith / Uma cura / Who must die? / Saga / Tribe to a nation / Politricks / Human cause / Reject / Water / Valtio. *(special-cd+=; RR 8560-5)* – Bela Lugosi's dead / Annihilation / Rise above / Revolt (demo) / Roots bloody roots (live).

S.P.V. | S.P.V.

May 03. (cd) <*(SPV 085-7483-2)*> **ROORBACK** [ ] Aug03 [ ]
– Come back alive / Godless / Apes of God / More of the same / Urge / Corrupted / As it is / Mind war / Leech / The rift / Bottomed out / Activist / Outro. *(UK bonus+=)* – Bullet the blue sky / Bullet the blue sky (video). *(ltd-d-cd+=; SPV 092 7483-0)* – REVOLUSONGS EP:- Messiah / Angel / Black steel in the hour of chaos / Mongloid / Mountain song / Bullet the blue sky / Piranha.

– compilations, etc. –

Nov 89. (cd) *Shark; (CDSHARK 012)* **MORBID VISIONS / CEASE TO EXIST** [–] German [–]

May 90. (c) *Shark; (SHARKMC 017)* **SCHIZOPHRENIA / MORBID VISIONS** [–] German [–]

Aug 97. (cd) *Roadrunner; (<RR 8821-2>)* **BLOOD ROOTED** [ ] [ ]
– Procreation (of the wicked) / Inhuman nature / Policia / War / Criucificados pelo sistema / Symptom of the universe / Mine / Lobotomy / Dusted / Roots bloody roots / Drug me / Refuse – resist / Slave new world / Propaganda / Beneath the remains / Escape to the void / Kaiowas / Clenched fist / Biotech is Godzilla. *(re-iss. May00; same)*

May 00. (cd) *Roadrunner; <(RR 8765-2)>* **MORBID VISIONS / BESTIAL DEVASTATION** [ ] [ ]

Sep 02. (d-cd) *Roadrunner; <(RR 8436-2)>* **UNDER A PALE GREY SKY** [ ] [ ]
– Itsari (intro) / Roots bloody roots / Spit / Territory / Monologo ao pe do ouvido / Breed apart / Attitude / Cut-throat / Troops of doom / Beneath the remains – Mass hypnosis / Born stubborn / Desperate cry / Necromancer / Dusted / Endangered species / We who are not as others / Straighthate / Dictatorshit / Refuse – Resist / Arise – Dead embryonic cells / Slave new world / Biotech is Godzilla / Inner self / Policia / We gotta know / Kaiowas / Ratamahatta / Orgasmatron.

☐ Will SERGEANT

(see under ⇒ ECHO & THE BUNNYMEN)

☐ SET FIRE TO FLAMES

(see under ⇒ GODSPEED YOU BLACK EMPEROR!)

SEVENDUST

Formed: Atlanta, Georgia, USA . . . 1994 initially as CRAWLSPACE by MORGAN ROSE, VINCE HORNSBY, CLINT LOWERY, JOHN CONNOLLY and LAJON WITHERSPOON, the latter a black funk singer poached from his brother COREY's band (now a STUCK MOJO member). One single, 'MY RUIN' was independently issued under this moniker (also appeared on V/A set 'Mortal Kombat: More Kombat') and was to subsequently surface on the SEVENDUST debut album. Under the wing of manager, JAY JAY FRENCH (ex-TWISTED SISTER), the band signed to 'TVT', although it was by sheer chance as the label's A&R men were detoured by a hard-of-hearing cab driver who took them to one of their gigs, not a strip club as requested. Their bruising, aggro-rock sound (with similarities between LIVING COLOUR and/or MINISTRY) was soon being given radio airplay in the States via an excellent eponymous set in '97. A second set, 'HOME' (1999) repeated the riff-laden formula, only this time it payed off with a US Top 20 placing. MORGAN, meanwhile (who'd married COAL CHAMBERS' RAYNA FOSS), was possibly up for a bit of paternity leave following the subsequent birth of their new baby. Third set, 'ANIMOSITY' (2001) offered up little in the way of artistic progression, following their standard electro-enhanced piledriving formula with dogged determination and winning a US Top 30 chart placing. 2003's 'SEASONS' earned an even better chart placing despite its coruscatingly brutal grooves and bleak subject matter. The Butch Walker-masterminded set benefitted from the latter's proven pop production chops, bringing an accessibility to proceedings without diluting the album's dark power.

Album rating: SEVENDUST (*6) / HOME (*7) / ANIMOSITY (*6) / SEASONS (*7)

LAJON WITHERSPOON – vocals / **CLINT LOWERY** – guitar / **JOHN CONNOLLY** – guitar / **VINCE HORNSBY** – bass / **MORGAN ROSE** – drums

TVT TVT

Sep 98. (cd/c) *<(TVT 5730-2/-4)>* **SEVENDUST** [ ] Apr97 [ ]
– Black / Bitch / Terminator / Too close to hate / Wired / Prayer / Face / Speak / Will it bleed / My ruin / Born to die.

Loud-Epic TVT

Oct 99. (cd/c) *(4961579) <5820>* **HOME** [ ] [19]
– Home / Denial / Headtrip / Insecure / Reconnect / Waffle / Rumble fish / Licking cream / Grasp / Crumble / Feel so / Grasshopper / Bender. *(cd re-iss. Sep00 on 'TVT'; same as US)*

Mar 00. (cd-s) *<668536>* **LICKING CREAM / (other by SKUNK ANANSIE)** [–] [ ]

Nov 01. (cd) *<5870>* **ANIMOSITY** [–] [28]
– Tits on a boar / Praise / Trust / Crucified / Xmas day / Dead set / Shine / Follow / Damaged / Live again / Beautiful / Redefine / Angel's son. *(UK-iss.May03 on 'Island'+=; CID 8132)* – Angel's son (live) / Black (live).

Island TVT

May 03. (cd-s) *(CID 822)* **ANGEL'S SON / LIVE AGAIN (acoustic) / ANGEL'S SON (acoustic)** [ ] [–]

Oct 03. (cd) *(CID 8140) <5993>* **SEASONS** [ ] [14]
– Disease / Enemy / Seasons / Broken down / Separate / Honesty / Skeleton song / Disgrace / Burned out / Suffocate / Gone / Face to face. *(UK+=)* – Rain / Coward.

SEX PISTOLS

Formed: London, England ... summer 1975 out of The SWANKERS by PAUL COOK, STEVE JONES and GLEN MATLOCK, the latter two regular faces at MALCOLM McLAREN's 'Sex' boutique on the capital's King's Road. With the NEW YORK DOLLS already on his CV, McLAREN was well qualified to mastermind the rise and fall of The SEX PISTOLS as he dubbed his new plaything, the entrepreneur/svengali installing another 'Sex' customer, the green-haired JOHN LYDON, as a suitably sneering frontman. JONES soon renamed the latter JOHNNY ROTTEN, informing his farting rear-end, "You're rotten, you are"; the tone of the SEX PISTOLS was set. After a few local gigs, the group supported JOE STRUMMER's 101'ers in April '76, their bedraggled, low-rent bondage chic troupe of followers including the likes of SIOUXSIE SIOUX (later of BANSHEES fame) and one SID VICIOUS, allegedly the perpetrator behind the infamous glass-throwing incident at the 100 Club punk all-dayer in which a girl was partially blinded. Controversy, intentional or otherwise, hung around the group like a bad smell and made The SEX PISTOLS into minor legends with barely one single under their belts. Signed to 'E.M.I.' for £40,000, their debut release, 'ANARCHY IN THE U.K.' (having already shocked those of a sensitive disposition after being aired on the 'So It Goes' TV pop show) was finally released in November '76. An inflammatory slice of primal nihilism which surpassed even The STOOGES' finest efforts, the track initially climbed into the Top 40 before being unceremoniously withdrawn following the band's riotous appearance on a local chat/news programme, 'Today'. With JONES swearing copiously at presenter Bill Grundy, the tabloids had a field day, stirring up the moral majority and prompting more "must we subject our pop kids to this filth" editorials than you could shake a snotty stick at. 'E.M.I.' of course, bailed out (writing off the advance as a particularly bad debt) early the following year, while MATLOCK was fired around the same time for being, well, er . . . too nice. His replacement was the aforementioned VICIOUS, a suitably violent and abusive character who duly became more of a punk anti-hero/caricature than McLAREN could ever have dreamed. After a short period in label limbo, The 'PISTOLS signed to 'A&M' in March '77 for another six figure sum; the honeymoon period was probably the shortest in recording history as the band's infamous antics at the post-signing party, together with protests from other artists on the label saw the UK's foremost punk band once again minus a recording contract. Once again, the band retained the loot from the advance and once again, a single, 'GOD SAVE THE QUEEN', was withdrawn (some copies did find their way into circulation and now fetch considerably more than the original 50p price tag). Arguably The SEX PISTOLS' defining moment, this jaw-clenching two-fingured salute to the monarchy and everything it represented was to truly make the band public enemy No.1, its release coinciding sweetly with her highness' silver jubilee year. Re-released by new label 'Virgin' (virtually the only company willing to take the band on for a meagre £15,000 advance), the single was predictably banned by the BBC, though that didn't prevent it from outselling the official No.1 at the time, Rod Stewart's 'I Don't Want To Talk About It'. That long, hot summer also saw the band hiring a boat and sailing up and down the Thames in a publicity stunt which ended in chaos; cue yet more controversy and howls of derision from the nation's moral guardians. Knuckle-headed English royalists decided to take matters into their own hands, both COOK and ROTTEN attacked in separate incidents as another blankly brilliant single, 'PRETTY VACANT', gatecrashed the Top 10. Previewed by the seething, squalling outrage of 'HOLIDAYS IN THE SUN', the legendary debut album, 'NEVER MIND THE BOLLOCKS, HERE'S THE SEX PISTOLS' was finally released at the end of the year. While the record undeniably contained some filler, it remains the classic punk statement, the blistering 'BODIES' and the gleeful kiss-off to their former employers, 'E.M.I.', almost standing up against the intensity of the singles (included in their entirety). As ever, controversy clouded its release, the album reaching No.1

in spite of the word 'Bollocks' – a near contravention of the 1889 Indecent Advertisements Act(!) – resulting in boycotts from many major outlets. Constantly on the verge of falling apart, the band subsequently flew to America for a string of chaotic dates, the final round of blanks in The SEX PISTOLS' depleted armoury. Amid sporadic showdowns with Deep South cowboys and SID's ever worsening heroin problem, ROTTEN (bowing out on stage in San Francisco with the immortal phrase "Ever get the feeling you've been cheated") effectively ended the whole sorry affair with his departure after the final gig. While LYDON (the name he now reverted back to) went on to form PUBLIC IMAGE LTD., McLAREN had other ideas for the splintered remains of the band, namely jetting off to Rio De Janeiro to record a single with exiled trainrobber, RONNIE BIGGS. The result, 'NO ONE IS INNOCENT (A PUNK PRAYER BY RONNIE BIGGS)', made the Top 10 in summer '78, although VICIOUS was absent from the recording, holed up in New York with his similarly addicted girlfriend, Nancy Spungeon. He did find time to record a peerless rendition of Paul Anka's 'MY WAY', the single taking on an added poignancy following his untimely but hardly surprising death early the following year; out on bail after being charged with the murder of Spungeon in October, VICIOUS succumbed to a fatal heroin overdose on the 2nd of February '79. The following month saw the belated release of McLAREN's pet project, an artistically licensed celluloid account of The SEX PISTOLS' history entitled 'THE GREAT ROCK'N'ROLL SWINDLE'. Widely criticised for its blatant exclusion of GLEN MATLOCK, the glaring absence of ROTTEN as an active participant and its paper-thin storyline, the movie was nevertheless an occasionally exhilarating, often hilarious trip through the misspent youth of Britain's best-loved punk band. While a perfunctory cover of Eddie Cochran's 'C'MON EVERYBODY' (a posthumous VICIOUS recording) made the Top 10 later that summer and 'Virgin' continued to flog The SEX PISTOLS' dead corpse with a variety of exploitation jobs, COOK and JONES formed the short-lived PROFESSIONALS. Although they didn't invent punk, The SEX PISTOLS certainly helped popularise it and while they were at least partly responsible for an avalanche of unlistenably amateurish shit, the band's uncompromising approach permanently altered the machinations of the music industry and took three-chord rock'n'roll to its ultimate conclusion. Despite the fact original fans had long since given up on the UK ever descending into anarchy, the original 'PISTOLS line-up of LYDON, MATLOCK, JONES and COOK reformed in summer '96 for a handful of outdoor gigs and an accompanying live album. Opinion was divided as to whether this blatantly commercial venture (billed as "The Filthy Lucre Tour") was in keeping with the original punk spirit; probably not, although few paying punters complained about what was subsequently hailed as one of the events of the summer and it was certainly a safer bet than the new GREEN DAY album . . . • **Songwriters:** Group compositions, until COOK & JONES took over in 1978. They also covered; NO FUN (Stooges) / ROCK AROUND THE CLOCK (Bill Haley) / JOHNNY B. GOODE (Chuck Berry) / STEPPING STONE (Boyce-Hart) / etc. • **Trivia:** In 1979, they took McLAREN to court for unpaid royalties. In 1986, the official receiver, through McLAREN paid a 7-figure out of court settlement to LYDON, JONES, COOK and SID's mother.

Album rating (selective): NEVER MIND THE BOLLOCKS, HERE'S THE SEX PISTOLS (*10) / THE GREAT ROCK'N'ROLL SWINDLE soundtrack (*8) / FLOGGING A DEAD HORSE compilation (*8) / KISS THIS compilation (*8) / FILTHY LUCRE LIVE (*6) / JUBILEE compilation (*8)

JOHNNY ROTTEN (b. JOHN LYDON, 31 Jan'56) – vocals / **STEVE JONES** (b. 3 Sep'55) – guitar / **GLEN MATLOCK** (b.27 Aug'56) – bass / **PAUL COOK** (b.20 Jul'56) – drums

E.M.I. — not iss.

Nov 76. (7") *(EMI 2566)* **ANARCHY IN THE U.K. / I WANNA BE ME** — 38 — –

—— (Feb'77) **SID VICIOUS** (b.JOHN RITCHIE, 10 May'57) – bass, vocals (ex-SIOUXSIE & THE BANSHEES) repl. MATLOCK who soon formed RICH KIDS

A&M — not iss.

Mar 77. (7"w-drawn) *(AMS 7284)* **GOD SAVE THE QUEEN. / NO FEELINGS** — – — –

—— Were soon paid off yet again. Above copies filtered through and soon became a collectors item).

Virgin — Warners

May 77. (7") *(VS 181)* **GOD SAVE THE QUEEN. / DID YOU NO WRONG** — 2 — –

—— (above was banned by the BBC, and outsold the official No.1 at the time; Rod Stewart's 'I Don't Want To Talk About It'.)

Jul 77. (7") *(VS 184)* **PRETTY VACANT. / NO FUN** — 6 — –

Oct 77. (7") *(VS 191)* **HOLIDAYS IN THE SUN. / SATELLITE** — 8 — –

Nov 77. (7") **PRETTY VACANT. / SUBMISSION** — – —

Nov 77. (lp/c) *(V/TCV 2086)* *<3147>* **NEVER MIND THE BOLLOCKS, HERE'S THE SEX PISTOLS** — 1 — 106

– Holidays in the sun / Bodies / No feelings / Liar / God save the Queen / Problems / Seventeen / Anarchy in the UK / Submission / Pretty vacant / New York / E.M.I. *(7" free w/some copies of 'Submission'; SPOTS 001)* – **SUBMISSION** (one-sided). *(pic-lp Jan78; VP 2086) (re-iss. Oct86 lp/c; OVED/+C 136) (cd-iss. Oct86; CDV 2086) (re-iss. cd May93; CDVX 2086) (re-iss. 1996 on cd w/ free 'SPUNK' bootleg tracks) <cd-iss. Jul96 on 'Alex; 5695>*

—— ROTTEN left, reverted to JOHN LYDON and created new band PUBLIC IMAGE LTD. His place was temporarily taken by **RONNIE BIGGS** (the Great Train Robber escapee now exiled in Brazil) 'A'-side vocals / **SID VICIOUS** – 'B'side vocals

Jun 78. (7") *(VS 220)* **NO ONE IS INNOCENT (A PUNK PRAYER BY RONNIE BIGGS). / MY WAY** — 7 — –

(12") *(VS 220-12 A1/2)* – The biggest blow (a punk prayer by Ronnie Biggs) / My way.

(12"+=) *(VS 220-12 A3)* – (above listing) / (interview).

—— On 11 Oct'78, SID was charged with the murder of girlfriend NANCY SPUNGEON. MALCOLM McLAREN/'Virgin' bailed him out, but he died 2 Feb'79 of drug overdose. The 1979/80 singles were all taken from THE GREAT ROCK'N'ROLL SWINDLE film.

Feb 79. (7") *(VS 240)* **SOMETHING ELSE. / FRIGGIN' IN THE RIGGIN'** — 3 — –

Mar 79. (d-lp/d-c) *(VD/TCV 2510)* *<45083>* **THE GREAT ROCK'N'ROLL SWINDLE (Film Soundtrack)** — 7 —

– God save the Queen symphony / Rock around the clock / Johnny B. Goode / Roadrunner / Black Arabs / Watcha gonna do about it (* on some) / Who killed Bambi? / Silly thing / Substitute / No lip / (I'm not your) Stepping stone / Lonely boy / Somethin' else / Anarchie pour le UK / Einmal war Belsen vortrefflich / No one is innocent / My way / C'mon everybody / E.M.I. / The great rock'n'roll swindle / You need hands / Friggin' in the riggin'. *(re-iss. 1-lp May80; V 2168) (re-iss. Apr89 lp/c; OVED/+C 234) (d-cd iss.Jul86; CDVD 2510) (re-iss. cd May93; CDVDX 2510)*

Apr 79. (7") *(VS 256)* **SILLY THING. / WHO KILLED BAMBI?** — 6 —

—— (above 'A'vocals – **STEVE JONES**, 'B'vocals – **EDDIE TENPOLE TUDOR**) (below 'A'vocals – **SID VICIOUS**)

Jun 79. (7") *(VS 272)* **C'MON EVERYBODY. / GOD SAVE THE QUEEN SYMPHONY / WATCHA GONNA DO ABOUT IT** — 3 —

Aug 79. (lp/c) *(VR/ 2)* **SOME PRODUCT: CARRI ON SEX PISTOLS** — 6 — –

– The very name (the Sex Pistols) / From beyond the grave / Big tits across America / The complex world of Johnny Rotten / Sex Pistols will play / Is the Queen a moron / The fuckin' rotter. *(cd-iss. May93; CDVR 2)*

Oct 79. (7") *(VS 290)* **THE GREAT ROCK'N'ROLL SWINDLE. / ROCK AROUND THE CLOCK** — 21 —

Dec 79. (lp/c; by SID VICIOUS) *(V/TCV 2144)* **SID SINGS** — 30 — –

– Born to lose / I wanna be your dog / Take a chance on me / (I'm not your) Stepping stone / My way / Belsen was a gas / Somethin' else / Chatterbox / Search and destroy / Chinese rocks / My way. *(re-iss. Aug88 lp/c; OVED/+C 85)* (cd-iss. Feb89; *CDV 2144)*

— There were other SID VICIOUS exploitation releases later.

Feb 80. (lp/c) *(V/TCV 2142)* **FLOGGING A DEAD HORSE** 23 –
– (singles compilation) *(re-iss. Apr86 lp/c; OVED/+C 165) (cd-iss. Oct86; CDV 2142)*

Jun 80. (7") *(VS 339)* **(I'M NOT YOUR) STEPPING STONE. / PISTOLS PROPAGANDA** 21 –

— COOK and JONES were now The PROFESSIONALS

– compilations, exploitation releases –

Note; on 'Virgin' until mentioned otherwise.

Jan 80. (lp) *Flyover; (YX 7247)* **THE BEST OF . . . AND WE DON'T CARE** –

Dec 80. (6x7"box) *(SEX 1)* **PISTOLS PACK** –
– GOD SAVE THE QUEEN. / PRETTY VACANT / / HOLIDAYS IN THE SUN. / MY WAY / / SOMETHING ELSE. / SILLY THING / / C'MON EVERYBODY. / THE GREAT ROCK'N'ROLL SWINDLE / / STEPPING STONE. / ANARCHY IN THE U.K. / / BLACK LEATHER. / HERE WE GO AGAIN
(below 45 credited EDDIE TENPOLE TUDOR)

Sep 81. (7") *(VS 443)* **WHO KILLED BAMBI?. / ROCK AROUND THE CLOCK** –

1983. (7") *(VS 609)* **ANARCHY IN THE UK. / NO FUN** –
(12"+=) *(VS 609-12)* – E.M.I.

Jan 85. (7"/7"pic-d)(12") *Cherry Red; (PISTOL 76P)(12PISTOL 76)* **LAND OF HOPE AND GLORY. ("EX-PISTOLS") / FLOWERS OF ROMANSK** 69 –

Jan 85. (m-lp) *Chaos; (MINI 1)* **THE MINI-ALBUM** –
(pic-m-lp.Jan86; AMPL 37) (cd-iss. Mar89; APOCA 3)

Mar 87. (7",7"yellow,7"pink) *Chaos; (DICK 1)* **SUBMISSION. / NO FEELINGS** –
(12",12"colrd) *(EXPORT 1)* – ('A'side) / Anarchy in the U.K.

Feb 85. (lp) *Receiver; (RRLP 101)* **THE ORIGINAL PISTOLS LIVE (live)** –
(pic-lp Jun86 on 'American Phono.'; APKPD 13) (re-iss. Jan89 on 'Dojo'; DOJOLP 45) (re-iss. May86 on 'Fame' lp/c; FA 41-3149-1/-4) (cd-iss. Jul89; CDFA 3149)

1985. (lp) *Receiver; (RRLP 102)* **AFTER THE STORM** –
(above with tracks by NEW YORK DOLLS) (cd-iss. Jul91; RRCD 102)

Aug 85. (lp) *Konnexion;* **LIVE WORLDWIDE (live)** –

Nov 85. (lp) *Receiver;* **WHERE WERE YOU IN '77** –

Nov 85. (lp/pic-lp) *Bondage;* **BEST OF SEX PISTOLS LIVE (live)** –

Nov 85. (lp) *Hippy;* **NEVER TRUST A HIPPY** –

Nov 85. (lp) *'77 Records;* **POWER OF THE PISTOLS** –

Feb 86. (lp) *McDonald-Lydon; (JOCK 1)* **THE LAST SHOW ON EARTH (live)** –

Apr 86. (12") *McDonald-Lydon; (JOCK 1201)* **ANARCHY IN THE U.K. (live). / FLOGGING A DEAD HORSE** –

Aug 86. (lp) *McDonald-Lydon; (JOCKLP 3)* **THE SEX PISTOLS 10th ANNIVERSARY ALBUM** –

Aug 86. (12"ep) *Archive 4; (TOF 104)* **ANARCHY IN THE UK / I'M A LAZY SOD. / PRETTY VACANT / SUBSTITUTE** –

Jan 87. (6xlp-box) *McDonald-Lydon; (JOCK BOX1)* **THE FILTH AND THE FURY** –
– FILTH & THE FURY / LAST SHOW ON EARTH / 10th ANNIVERSARY ALBUM / ITALIAN DEMOS / NO FUTURE USA / THE REAL SID & NANCY

May 88. (lp/cd) *Restless; <72255-1/-2>* **BETTER LIVE THAN DEAD (live)** –

Jun 88. (cd/lp) *M.B.C.; (JOCK/+LP 12)* **IT SEEMED TO BE THE END UNTIL THE NEXT BEGINNING** –

Jun 88. (3"cd-s) *(CDT 3)* **ANARCHY IN THE U.K. / E.M.I. / NO FUN** –

Oct 88. (m-lp) *Specific; (SPAW 101)* **ANARCHY WORLDWIDE** –

Oct 88. (cd-ep) *Specific; (SPCFC 102)* **CASH FOR CHAOS** –
– Submission (live) / God save the Quen / Liar.

Oct 88. (cd-ep) *Classic Tracks; (CDEP 13C)* **THE ORIGINAL PISTOLS (live)** –
– Anarchy in the U.K. / Pretty vacant / No fun / Substitute.

Dec 88. (3"cd-s) *(CDT 37)* **GOD SAVE THE QUEEN / DID YOU NO WRONG / DON'T GIVE ME NO LIP CHILD** –

Jun 89. (lp,pink-lp,green-lp/c) *Link; (LINK LP/MC 063)* **LIVE AND LOUD (live)** –
(cd-iss. Oct92; LINKCD 063)

Dec 89. (lp/c/cd,pic-cd) *Receiver; (RR LP/MC/CD 117)* **NO FUTURE U.K.?** –

Feb 90. (cd/c) *Action Replay; (CDAR/ARLC 1008)* **THE BEST OF AND THE REST OF THE SEX PISTOLS** –

1990. (12"blue-ep) *Receiver; (REPLAY 3012)* **THE EARLY YEARS LIVE** –
– Anarchy in the U.K. / Pretty vacant / Liar / Dolls (aka 'New York').

Jan 91. (d-lp) *Receiver; (RRLD 004)* **PRETTY VACANT** –
(d-cd-iss. Jul93; RRDCD 004)

Sep 92. (7"/c-s) *(VS/+C 1431)* **ANARCHY IN THE U.K. / I WANNA BE ME** 33
(cd-s+=/s-cd-s+=) *(VSCD T/X 1431)* – ('A'demo).

Oct 92. (cd) *Streetlink; (STRCD 019)* **EARLY DAZE – THE STUDIO COLLECTION** –
(re-iss. May93 on 'Dojo'; DOJOCD 119)

Oct 92. (cd/c/d-lp) *(V/TC/CDV 2702) / Alex; <2931>* **KISS THIS** 10
– Anarchy in the UK / God save the Queen / Pretty vacant / Holidays in ther Sun / I wanna be me / Did you no wrong / No fun / Satellite / Don't give me no lip child / (I'm not your) Stepping stone / Bodies / No feelings / Liar / Problems / Seventeen / Submission / New York / E.M.I. / My way / Silly thing. // *(cd w/bonus cd+=)* **LIVE IN TRONDHEIM 21st JULY 1977** :- Anarchy in the UK / I wanna be me / Seventeen / New York / E.M.I. / No fun / No feelings / Problems / God save the Queen.

Nov 92. (7") *(VS 1448)* **PRETTY VACANT. / NO FEELINGS (demo)** 56 –
(12"+=) *(VST 1448)* – Satellite (demo) / Submission (demo).
(cd-s+=) *(VSCDG 1448)* – E.M.I. (demo) / Satellite (demo).
(cd-s) *(VSCDT 1448)* – ('A'side) / Seventeen (demo) / Submission (demo) / Watcha gonna do about it?

Mar 93. (cd) *Dojo; (DOJOCD 66)* **LIVE AT CHELMSFORD PRISON** –

Nov 93. (cd) *Dojo; (DOJOCD 73)* **BETTER LIVE THAN DEAD** –

Jul 95. (cd) *Dojo; (DOJOCD 216)* **WANTED – THE GOODMAN TAPES** –

Oct 95. (d-cd) *Essential; (ESDCD 321)* **ALIVE** –

Jan 96. (cd) *Dojo; (DOJOCD 222)* **PIRATES OF DESTINY** –

Jan 97. (7") *Man's Ruin; (MR 053)* **split with the UGLYS** –

Mar 97. (7") *Man's Ruin; (MR 056)* **split with the SOPHISTICATES** –

Jun 97. (cd) *Emporio; (EMPRCD 716)* **RAW** –

May 02. (7") *(VS 1832)* **GOD SAVE THE QUEEN. / GOD SAVE THE QUEEN (Neil Barnes & Sex Pistols extended mix)** 15 –
(12"+=/cd-s+=) *(VST/VSCDT 1832)* – ('A'-Neil Barnes dance mix).

Jun 02. (cd) *(CDV 2961) <812566>* **JUBILEE** 29
– God save the Queen / Anarchy in the UK / Pretty vacant / Holidays in the sun / No one is innocent / My way / Somethin' else / Friggin' in the riggin' / Silly thing / C'mon everybody / The great rock'n'roll swindle / (I'm not your) Steppin' stone / Pretty vacant (live) / E.M.I. (unlimited edition) / God save the Queen (video) / Anarchy in the UK (video) / Pretty vacant (video).

— The original SEX PISTOLS re-formed at the back end of '95. Messrs LYDON, JONES, COOK + MATLOCK finally returned live on 24th June 1996, with packed out Finsbury Park concert. Embarked on their 'Filthy Lucre' tour soon after.

Virgin America / Caroline

Jul 96. (7"silver) *(VUS 113)* **PRETTY VACANT – LIVE. / BODIES – LIVE** 18 –
(cd-s+=) *(VUSCD 113)* – No fun (live) / Problems (live).

Aug 96. (cd/c/lp) *(41926) <7541>* **FILTHY LUCRE LIVE (live)** 26
– Seventeen / New York / Did you no wrong / God save the Queen / Liar / Satellite / (I'm not your) Stepping stone / Holidays in the sun / Submission / No feelings / Pretty vacant / E.M.I. / Problems / Anarchy in the UK / No fun.

— JONES was also part-member of transatlantic supergroup, NEUROTIC OUTSIDERS, alongside DUFF McKAGAN and MATT SORUM (Guns N' Roses) and JOHN TAYLOR (Duran Duran). They released an eponymous album for 'Maverick' in August '96 and from it they lifted the single, 'JERK'.

Ron SEXSMITH

Born: RONALD ELDON SEXSMITH, 1964, St. Catherine's, nr. Niagara Falls, Canada. Subsequently relocating to Toronto, the babyfaced 30-something singer/songwriter held down a day job as a courier while amassing the material he hoped would secure him a record deal. Word got out with the release of a cassette-only affair (as RON SEXSMITH AND THE UNCOOL) in 1991, 'GRAND OPERA LANE'. A refreshingly unpretentious troubadour with a crystal vocal style reminiscent of AARON NEVILLE (with perhaps the hesitant fragility of TIM HARDIN and the bite of ELVIS COSTELLO), SEXSMITH hooked up with noted producer, MITCHELL FROOM for his eponymous solo debut proper. Released on 'Interscope' at the tail end of '95 (Spring '96 in Britain), the record received almost unanimous praise from the press, especially from the more adult-muso end of the media spectrum. Dedicated to the late HARRY NILSSON, the record revealed SEXSMITH to be a songwriter in the truly classic sense of the term, maintaining the sparsest of acoustic backing and relying on subtlety and mood rather than vulgar confessionals. A writer's writer (ELVIS COSTELLO, JOHN HIATT and RICHARD THOMPSON number among his biggest fans), the man continued along the same unassuming path for 1997's 'OTHER SONGS', a largely downbeat, monochromatic collection of snapshots from the humble lens of one of rock's most unlikely heroes. People were asking of his 'WHEREABOUTS' (1999) long before the set's release date. Puns aside, the Canadian's overtly DYLAN-esque fourth album was much of the same as his last recordings. It would seem he was getting stuck in a kind of 60's/70's time warp, although it was popular with the bedsitter brigade. The boyish troubadour made a few significant changes with 'BLUE BOY' (2001), not least the substitution of the ubiquitous Mitchell Froom/Tchad Blake production axis for STEVE EARLE (and his partner RAY KENNEDY). Unsurprsingly then, the record displayed traces of EARLE's survivor's grit, firming up SEXSMITH's sound and adding greater depth and gravitas to the songs rather than fluffing up the arrangements. Stylistically varied, the material was his strongest and most forthright to date, even taking a detour into West Coast jazz on standout track 'FOOLPROOF'. RON subjected himself to another stylistic shake-up on 'COBBLESTONE RUNWAY' (2002), gamely laying his delicate craft open to the vagaries of technology. Never straying into full-blown electronica, but rather letting the genre's subtle, ebbing textures work for him, he arrived at an engaging compromise which thankfully failed to impose upon the gentle humanity of his lyrics.

Album rating: GRAND OPERA LANE (*5) / RON SEXSMITH (*7) / OTHER SONGS (*6) / WHEREABOUTS (*6) / BLUE BOY (*7) / COBBLESTONE RUNWAY (*7)

RON SEXSMITH – vocals, guitars; with MITCHELL FROOM, JERRY MARETTA, BRAD JONES (2nd lp guest SHERYL CROW)

not iss. / own label

1991. (c; as RON SEXSMITH AND THE UNCOOL) <none> **GRAND OPERA LANE** [–] [ ]
– In this love / Spending money / Don't mind losing / Tell you / Gonna get what's mine / Speaking with the angel / Every word of it / Some people / Trains / Savin' her love / The laughing crowd.

Interscope / Interscope

May 96. (cd/c) *<(IND/INC 92485)>* **RON SEXSMITH** [ ] Nov95 [ ]
– Secret heart / There's a rhythm / Words we never use / Summer blowin' town / Lebanon, Tennessee / Speaking with the angel / In place of you / Heart with no companion / Several miles / From a few streets over / First chance I get / Wastin' time / Galbraith Street.

Aug 96. (cd-s; promo) *(IND 95507)* **SECRET HEART** [–] [–]

Jun 97. (cd/c) *<(IND/INC 90123)>* **OTHER SONGS** [ ] [ ]
– Thinking out loud / Strawberry blonde / Average Joe / Thinly veiled disguise / Nothing good / Pretty little cemetery / It never fails / Clown in broad daylight / At different times / Child star / Honest mistake / So young / While you're waiting / April after all.

Jun 98. (cd-ep) *(IND 95564)* **STRAWBERRY BLONDE / SAME OLD EYES / YOU WERE THERE / REAQUAINTED** [ ] [–]

Jun 99. (cd) *<INTD 90299)>* **WHEREABOUTS** [ ] May99 [ ]
– Still time / Right about now / Must have heard it wrong / Riverbed / Feel for you / In a flash / Idiot boy / Beautiful view / One grey morning / Doomed / Every passing day / Seem to recall.

Cooking Vinyl / Cooking Vinyl

Jun 01. (cd) *(COOKCD 214) <614>* **BLUE BOY** [ ] [ ]
– This song / Cheap hotel / Don't ask why / Foolproof / Tell me again / Just my heart talkin' / Not too big / Miracle in itself / Thirsty love / Never been done / Thumbelina farewell / Parable / Keep it in mind / Fallen.

Parlophone / Nettwerk

Nov 02. (cd) *(542998-2) <30284>* **COBBLESTONE RUNWAY** [ ] Oct02 [ ]
– Former glory / These days / Least that I can do / God loves everyone / Disappearing act / For a moment / Gold in them hills / Heart's desire / Dragonfly on Bay Street / The less I know / Up the road / Best friends. *<(bonus+=)>* – Gold in them hills (remix).

Feb 03. (cd-s; by RON SEXSMITH & CHRIS MARTIN) *(CDR 6605)* **GOLD IN THEM HILLS (remix) / GOLD IN THEM HILLS (album version) / YOU CROSS MY MIND** [ ] [–]

SHACK

Formed: Liverpool, England ... mid-80's out of semi-successful indie-pop outfit The PALE FOUNTAINS. MICK HEAD, his brother JOHN HEAD and CHRIS McCAFFREY, almost immediately recruited THOMAS 'JOCK' WHELAN and ANDY DIAGRAM (the latter from DISLOCATION DANCE and The DIAGRAM BROS) to form the seminal, tragedy struck PALE FOUNTAINS. Their debut single, '(THERE'S ALWAYS) SOMETHING ON MY MIND', set the tone for their melancholy, melodic, 60's-inspired alt-pop, like a cross between The BEATLES and LOVE. 'Virgin' were quick off the mark to sign them, their contract off to a promising start when follow-up single, 'THANK YOU', hit the Top 50 late in '82. However, sales of subsequent 45's and debut album, 'PACIFIC STREET' (1984), didn't quite meet expectations, its brassy tropical feel (with colourful image to match) a touch exotic for the average indie fan. A second album, the IAN BROUDIE-produced '...FROM ACROSS THE KITCHEN TABLE', emerged early the following year, the pleasant but hardly inspiring 'JEAN'S NOT HAPPENING' summing up PALE FOUNTAINS appeal. With their chart potential having almost completely dried up, The PALE FOUNTAINS split as the brothers HEAD re-emerged as SHACK. Along with new boys, DAVE BUTCHER, JUSTIN SMITH and MICHAEL CURTIS, they were the first act to sign for the 'Ghetto Recording Company', the first fruits of their efforts being the 1988 set, 'ZILCH'. Displaying an even stronger BEATLES influence, the album was a sterling slab of subtle, intelligent indie-pop. However, it took all of two years for the band to return, the single 'I KNOW YOU WELL' calling to mind The BEATLES' 'Taxman' with its knotty stop-start rhythms. A solitary single, 'AL'S VACATION', arrived in Spring '91 and although an album was completed, a studio fire destroyed what was thought to be the only existing master tape. Fortunately, producer Chris Allison unearthed a DAT master, although he subsequently lost it again after leaving it in a hired car. Incredibly, the fabled tape later turned up in Germany (!), the belated album finally issued in '95 (prior to that, the HEAD brothers kept themselves busy by supporting ARTHUR LEE in 1992 at Liverpool) as 'WATERPISTOL' by 'Marina' records. MICHAEL HEAD was back in a solo capacity in 1998, members of SHACK backing him up on his inaugural release, 'THE MAGICAL WORLD OF THE STRANDS'. A year later, acclaim had finally reached SHACK, with the release of the poignant 'HMS FABLE'. Described as a cross between MERCURY REV's 'Deserter's Songs' and the BEATLES' 'Abbey Road', the set documented the highs and lows in the last few years of the HEAD brothers. From heroin addiction to musical misfortune, it was all there; of course, a SHACK album wouldn't have been complete without any of these things! In turn, the music press went crazy at this stunning comeback, the result being that the album entered the British charts at No.25. Singles such as 'NATALIE'S PARTY' and 'COMEDY' furthered the band's reputation, even if the general public didn't pay much attention to this wonderful discovery. 'HMS FABLE' also topped many magazines' 'Album Of the Year' polls – a well deserved reward for a hard working but unlucky outfit.

Album rating: Pale Fountains: PACIFIC STREET (*6) / . . .FROM ACROSS THE KITCHEN TABLE (*4) / LONGSHOT FOR YOUR LOVE compilation (*6) / Shack: ZILCH (*7) / WATERPISTOL (*6) / Michael Head: THE MAGICAL WORLD OF THE STRANDS (*6) / Shack: H.M.S. FABLE (*9) / HERE'S TOM WITH THE WEATHER (*8)

PALE FOUNTAINS

MICK HEAD (b.28 Nov'61) – vocals, guitar / **JOHN HEAD** (b. 4 Oct'65) – lead guitar / **CHRIS McCAFFREY** – bass / **ANDY DIAGRAM** – trumpet (ex-DISLOCATION DANCE, ex-DIAGRAM BROS) / **THOMAS 'JOCK' WHELAN** – drums, percussion / + 6th member **M. BARRADAS** – oil drums, percussion

Operation Twilight — not iss.

Jul 82. (7") *(OPT 09)* **(THERE'S ALWAYS) SOMETHING ON MY MIND. / JUST A GIRL** ☐ ☐–

Virgin — not iss.

Oct 82. (7") *(VS 557)* **THANK YOU. / MEADOW OF LOVE** 48 ☐–

May 83. (7"/12") *(VS 568/+12)* **PALM OF MY HAND. / LOVE'S A BEAUTIFUL PLACE** ☐ ☐–

Jan 84. (7"/12") *(VS 614/+12)* **UNLESS. / NATURAL** ☐ ☐–

Feb 84. (lp/c) *(V/TCV 2274)* **PACIFIC STREET** ☐ ☐–
– Reach / Something on my mind / Unless / Southbound excursion / Natural / Faithful pillow (part 1) / (Don't let your love) Start a war / Beyond Friday's field / Abergele next time / Crazier / Faithful pillow (part 2). *(re-iss. Aug87 lp/c; OVED/+C 143) (cd-iss. Nov89; CDV 2274)*

Mar 84. (7"/12") *(VS 668/+12)* **(DON'T LET YOUR LOVE) START A WAR. / LOVE SITUATION** ☐ ☐–

—— now without BARRADAS

Jan 85. (7"/12") *(VS 735/+12)* **JEAN'S NOT HAPPENING. / BICYCLE THIEVES** ☐ ☐–

Feb 85. (lp/c) *(V/TCV 2333)* **. . .FROM ACROSS THE KITCHEN TABLE** ☐ ☐–
– Shelter / Stole the love / Jean's not happening / Bicycle thieves / Limit / 27 ways to get back home / Bruised arcade / These are the things / It's only hard / . . .From across the kitchen table / Hey / September sting. *(re-iss. Apr86 lp/c; OVED/+C 164) (cd-iss. Jul89; CDV 2333)*

Jun 85. (7") *(VS 750)* **. . .FROM ACROSS THE KITCHEN TABLE. / BICYCLE THIEVES** ☐ ☐–
(12"+=) *(VS 750-12)* – Thank you.
(d7"++=) *(VS 750)* – Just a girl.

—— disbanded when DIAGRAM returned to DISLOCATION DANCE (sadly, McCAFFREY was to die in August '89)

– compilations, etc. –

Jul 99. (cd/lp) *(MA 37)* **LONGSHOT FOR YOUR LOVE** ☐ ☐–
– Just a girl / (There's always) Something on my mind / Lavinia's dream / Longshot for your love / Thank you / The Norfolk broads / Benoit's Christmas / Hey there Fred / Palm of my hand / Free / We have all the time in the world / Just a girl / Love situation.

SHACK

—— **MICK HEAD** + **JOHN HEAD** with **DAVE BUTCHER** – keyboards / **JUSTIN SMITH** – bass / **MICHAEL KURTIS** – drums

Ghetto — not iss.

Mar 88. (7") *(GTG 1)* **EMERGENCY. / LIBERATION** ☐ ☐–
(12"+=) *(GTGT 1)* – Faith.
(cd-s+=) *(CDGTG 1)* – What's it like . . .

Mar 88. (lp/c/cd) *(GHETT/+C/D 1)* **ZILCH** ☐ ☐–
– Emergency / Someone's knocking / John Kline / Realization / I need you / High rise, low life / Who killed Clayton Square? / Who'd believe it? / What's it like . . . / The believers. *(cd+=)* – Liberation / Faith / High rise low life (the Bert Hardy mix).

Jun 88. (7") *(GTG 2)* **HIGH RISE LOW LIFE. / WHO KILLED CLAYTON SQUARE?** ☐ ☐–
(12"+=/cd-s+=) *(GTGT/CDGTG 2)* – ('A'-Bert Hardy mix).

Jul 90. (7") *(GTG 11)* **I KNOW YOU WELL. / FEEL NO WAY** ☐ ☐–
(ext.12") *(GTG 11T)* – ('A'-If you want it mix).
(cd-s++=) *(CDGTG 11)* – ('A'extended).

Apr 91. (7") *(GTG 14)* **AL'S VACATION. / IRISH** ☐ ☐–
(12"+=) *(GTGT 14)* – Feel no way.

—— an album was recorded but destroyed after a studio fire (see above).

Marina — not iss.

Nov 95. (cd/lp) *(MA 16 – MACD 44632)* **WATERPISTOL** ☐ ☐–
– Sgt. Major / Neighbours / Stranger / Dragonfly / Mood of the morning / Walter's song / Time machine / Mr. Appointment / Undecided / Hazy / Hey mama / London town. *(re-iss. Feb98 & Jul99 cd/lp; MAR 16)*

MICHAEL HEAD

—— with other members of SHACK as backing

Megaphone — not iss.

Feb 98. (cd/lp) *(CD/LP MEGA 01)* **THE MAGICAL WORLD OF THE STRANDS** ☐ ☐–
– Queen Matilda / Something like you / And luna / X hits the spot / The prize / Undecided (reprise) / Glynys and Jaqui / It's harvest time / Loaded man / Hocken's hey / Fontilan.

Apr 98. (7") *(7MEGA 02)* **SOMETHING LIKE YOU. / GREEN VELVET JACKET** ☐ ☐–
(cd-s+=) *(CDMEGA 02)* – Queen Matilda (demo). *(re-iss. Oct98; same)*

SHACK

London — Sire

Jun 99. (c-s) *(LONCS 427)* **COMEDY / UNCLE DELANEY / COMEDY (No Strings)** 44 ☐–
(cd-s) *(LONCD 427)* – (first two tracks) / Petroleum.
(cd-s) *(LONCDP 427)* – ('A'side) / 24 hours / Solid gold.

Jun 99. (cd/c) *(556113-2/-4) <31071>* **H.M.S. FABLE** 25 Aug99 ☐
– Natalie's party / Comedy / Pull together / Beautiful / Lend's some dough / Captain's table / Streets of Kenny / Re-instated / I want you / Cornish town / Since I met you / Daniella.

Aug 99. (c-s) *(LONCS 436)* **NATALIE'S PARTY / FLANNERY** 63 ☐–
('A'-Youth mix; cd-s+=) *(LONCD 436)* – Extra extra.
(cd-s) *(LONCDP 436)* – ('A'side) / Too late for me now / Miss Christine.

Feb 00. (cd-s) *(LONCD 445)* **OSCAR / STREETS OF KENNY (acoustic) / QUEEN MATILDA (acoustic)** 67 ☐–
(cd-s) *(LOCDP 445)* – ('A'side) / Captain's table (acoustic) / Daniella (acoustic).

North Country — North Country

Aug 03. (cd/lp) *(NCCD/NCLP 002) <41480>* **HERE'S TOM WITH THE WEATHER** 55 Sep03 ☐
– As long as I've got you / Soldier man / Byrds turn to stone / The girl with the long brown hair / On the terrace / Miles apart / Meant to be / Carousel / On the streets tonight / Chinatown / Kilburn High Road / Happy ever after.

Sep 03. (7") *(NC 002)* **BYRDS TURN TO STONE. / NOT AFRAID OF LOVING YOU** 63 ☐–
(cd-s+=) *(NCCDA 002)* – As long as I've got you (alt.take).
(cd-s) *(NCCDB 002)* – ('A'side) / Streets of Kenny (live at V2003) / Pull together (live at V2003).

– compilations, etc. –

Oct 03. (cd) *B-Unique; (<BUN 057>)* **THE FABLE SESSIONS** ☐ ☐

SHADOWS

Formed: London, England . . . 1958 as THE FIVE CHESTERNUTS by HANK MARVIN, BRUCE WELCH and PETE CHESTER (son of comedian Charlie Chester) along with GERALD HURST and NEIL JOHNSON. Following a one-off flop single, 'TEENAGE LOVE', for 'Columbia' in Autumn of that year, they were spotted by CLIFF RICHARD manager, John Foster, who needed a replacement for guitarist KEN PAVEY. Six-string wizard MARVIN agreed to join on the condition that WELCH was also hired, the susbsequent addition of IAN SAMWELL and TERRY SMART fleshing out a unit which was now trading under The DRIFTERS moniker. In November '58, CLIFF replaced SAMWELL (who became their manager in 1959) with JET HARRIS and the new-look beat combo backed up RICHARD on his famous 'LIVIN' LOVIN' DOLL' single. More upheaval followed at the tail end of the year as TONY MEEHAN replaced SMART (who went off to join the merchant navy!). By this point, the quartet had managed a further couple of singles in their own right, 'FEELIN' FINE' and 'JET BLACK'. Neither was successful and to compound their problems, the band had an injuction slapped on them by the US soul/R&B outfit of the same name. After a final flop 45 at the tail end of the year (featuring a rare vocal) things took a serious turn for the better the following summer as the rumbling Wild West-style guitar atmospherics of 'APACHE' saw them topping the UK chart. A benchmark track that saw the bespectacled MARVIN embraced by many young wannabe guitar heros as a role model, the song was subsequently turned into a 70's funk/breakbeat classic by MICHAEL VINER'S INCREDIBLE BONGO BAND. It also signalled the beginning of an incredible (largely instrumental) chart run that lasted right through until the hippy revolution of the mid-late 60's. 'MAN OF MYSTERY', 'F.B.I.', 'FRIGHTENED CITY', 'THE SAVAGE' and 'KON TIKI' all went Top 10 over 1960/'61, the latter track giving them their second No.1 while their eponymous album also topped the charts. A more laid-back, quintessentially English counterpoint to the surf instrumentals sweeping the American West Coast, the SHADOWS sound was hugely influential on many young guitarists who snapped up their records in droves; 1962 saw the band score three No.1's in a row with 'WONDERFUL LAND', the 'OUT OF THE SHADOWS' album and 'DANCE ON', topping it with another No.1 in '63, 'FOOT TAPPER'. By this point JET HARRIS and TONY MEEHAN had both been replaced (by BRIANs, BENNETT and LOCKING respectively), the pair going on to score three 1963 UK Top 5 singles in their own right (i.e. 'DIAMONDS', 'SCARLETT O'HARA' and 'APPLEJACK'). While still a regular fixture on the chart, The SHADOWS' began losing their identity as they added more vocals to their repertoire towards the middle of the decade. By 1967, their (lone) star was really beginning to fade and after the October '68 release of joint CLIFF RICHARD set, 'ESTABLISHED 1958', the band split to concentrate on solo projects. While BENNETT's material failed to spark much interest, MARVIN's eponymous 1969 solo set made the UK Top 20. 1969 also saw MARVIN duetting with CLIFF on Top 10 hit, 'THROW DOWN A LINE', following it up in 1970 with 'JOY OF LIVING'. The SHADOWS also returned that year on 'Parlophone' with a flop album of pop/rock standards, 'SHADES OF ROCK', only to disband the same year. MARVIN and WELCH then got together with Aussie guitarist, JOHN FARRAR to form a vocal trio although the project again proved relatively short-lived and commercially unsuccessful. The SHADOWS re-formed for a second time in 1973 with a line-up of MARVIN, WELCH, FARRAR and BENNETT, WELCH undertaking vocal duties for their 1975 Eurovision entry (!), 'LET ME BE THE ONE'. Although the song was runner-up it did furnish them with a much needed Top 20 hit. This pushed the brilliantly titled 'SPECS APPEAL' (1975) album into the Top 30. The late 70's brought another mini-revival with a Top 5 cover of 'DON'T CRY FOR ME ARGENTINA' (from the musical, 'Evita'), a Top 10 reading of 'THEME FROM THE DEER HUNTER (CAVATINA)', a Top 5 CLIFF collaboration, 'THANK YOU VERY MUCH' and a No.1 album of covers from all walks of musical life (everything from Blondie's 'HEART OF GLASS' to Art Garfunkel's 'BRIGHT EYES'). Though they wouldn't hit the singles chart again, The SHADOWS stepped into middle-age with a winning formula of fine but not specy-tacular (sorry) renditions of classics from every genre and era of music history, making regular appearances in the Top 10 album chart throughout the 80's. MARVIN also carried his solo career into the 80's/90's to occasional success, working with the likes of BRIAN MAY and MARK KNOPFLER. • **Songwriters:** First songs written by/with PETE CHESTER or IAN SAMWELL. The group, mainly MARVIN and WELCH pen some, but mainly use other worldly sources; JERRY LORDAN wrote APACHE / WONDERFUL LAND / etc. His wife PETRINA penned A PLACE IN THE SUN. Their producer NORRIE PARAMOUR wrote THE FRIGHTENED CITY + THE SAVAGE. MAN OF MYSTERY + KON-TIKI (Michael Carr). They also covered ('A'singles only, their were loads more); DANCE ON (Avons) / DON'T MAKE MY BABY BLUE (hit; Frankie Laine) / THE WARLORD (Jerome Moross) / MAROC 7 + LET ME BE THE ONE (Paul Ferris; a friend) / SLAUGHTER ON 10th AVENUE (Richard Rodgers) / DON'T CRY FOR ME ARGENTINA (Tim Rice-Andrew Lloyd Webber) / DEER HUNTER (John Williams) / RODRIGO'S GUITAR CONCERTO (Manuel; Geoff Love) / RIDERS IN THE SKY (Stan Jones; hit, Ramrods) / EQUINOXE V (Jean-Michel Jarre) / MOZART FORTE (Mozart; hit, Waldo De La Rios) / TELSTAR (Tornados) / TREAT ME NICE (Elvis Presley) / MISSING (Vangelis) / GOIN' HOME (Mark Knopfler) / MOONLIGHT SHADOW (Mike Oldfield) / DANCING IN THE DARK (Bruce Springsteen) / EASTENDERS-HOWARD'S WAY + PULASKI (TV themes) / SNOWMAN (hit; Aled Jones) / etc, etc, etc. • **Trivia:** WELCH was married in 1959, although he left his wife eight years later for singer OLIVIA NEWTON JOHN. The group appeared in CLIFF's films; THE YOUNG ONES / SUMMER HOLIDAY (title track penned by MARVIN & BENNETT) / WONDERFUL LIFE / ALADDIN . . . + CINDERELLA (wrote and performed the pantomines).

Best CD compilation: 20 GOLDEN GREATS (*8)

HANK MARVIN (b. BRIAN RANKIN, 28 Nov'41, Newcastle, England) – lead guitar / **BRUCE WELCH** (b.CRIPPS, 2 Nov'41, Bognor Regis, England) – rhythm guitar / **GERALD HURST** – vocals / **PETER CHESTER** – drums / **NEIL JOHNSON** – bass

		Columbia	not iss.
Aug 58.	(7",78; as FIVE CHESTERNUTS) *(DB 4165)* **TEENAGE LOVE. / JEAN DOROTHY**		–
——	(Oct'58) they were also the backing for CLIFF RICHARD		
——	**IAN SAMWELL** – bass + **TERRY SMART** – drums; repl. all bar **MARVIN** + **WELCH** (Oct-Dec'58) / **JET HARRIS** (b.TERRENCE, 6 Jul'39, London) – bass (ex-VIPERS) repl. IAN SAMWELL who became their manager in 1959) / **TONY MEEHAN** (b. DANIEL, 2 Mar'43, London) – drums (ex-VIPERS) repl. TERRY SMART who joined the merchant navy		
Feb 59.	(7",78; as DRIFTERS) *(DB 4263)* **FEELIN' FINE. / DON'T BE A FOOL WITH LOVE**		–
Jul 59.	(7"; as DRIFTERS) *(DB 4325)* **JET BLACK. / DRIFTIN'** (above single released in the US as "The FOUR JETS")		
——	the SHADOWS name was taken to avoid confusion with American soul/R&B group, they also remained as CLIFF RICHARD's backers		

Columbia Atlantic

Dec 59. (7",78) *(DB 4387)* **SATURDAY DANCE. / LONESOME FELLA** [ ] [–]
(above 'A'side featured vocals by BRUCE)

Jul 60. (7") *(DB 4484)* **APACHE. / QUARTERMASTER'S STORES** [1] [–]

Oct 60. (7") *(DB 4530)* **MAN OF MYSTERY. / THE STRANGER** [5] [ ]

Jan 61. (7") *(DB 4580)* **F.B.I. / MIDNIGHT** [6] [–]

May 61. (7") *(DB 4637)* **FRIGHTENED CITY. / BACK HOME** [3] [–]

Jun 61. (7") **FRIGHTENED CITY. / F.B.I.** [–] [ ]

Aug 61. (7") *(DB 4698)* **KON TIKI. / 36-24-36** [1] [ ]

Sep 61. (lp; mono/stereo) *(33SX 1374/SCX 3414)* **THE SHADOWS** [1] [–]
– Shadoogie / Nivram / Blue star / Theme from a filletted plaice / Sleepwalk / See you in my dreams / Stand up and say that / All my sorrows / That's my desire / Find me a golden street / Big boy / Gonzales / My resistance is low / Baby my heart. *(re-iss. +c.May83 on 'Fame')*

— **BRIAN BENNETT** (b. 9 Feb'40, London) – drums; repl. MEEHAN

Nov 61. (7") *(DB 4726)* **THE SAVAGE. / PEACE PIPE** [10] [–]

Feb 62. (7") *(DB 4790)* **WONDERFUL LAND. / STARS FELL ON STOCKTON** [1] [ ]

— **BRIAN 'Licorice' LOCKING** – bass; repl. JET HARRIS (who still featured on next LP's tracks) to own duo with MEEHAN

Jul 62. (7") *(DB 4870)* **GUITAR TANGO. / WHAT A LOVELY TUNE** [4] [ ]

Oct 62. (lp; mono/stereo) *(33SX 1458/SCX 3449)* **OUT OF THE SHADOWS** [1] [–]
– The rumble / The bandit / Perfidia / Cosy / Some are lonely / Little B / Spring is nearly here / Bo Diddley / Kinda cool / 1861 / South of the border / Are they all like you / Tales of a raggy tramline. *(re-iss. +c.Aug86 on 'Awareness')*

Dec 62. (7") *(DB 4948)* **DANCE ON. / ALL DAY** [1] [–]

Dec 62. (7") **DANCE ON. / RUMBLE** [–] [ ]

Mar 63. (7") *(DB 4984)* **FOOT TAPPER. / THE BREEZE AND I** [1] [–]

May 63. (7") *(DB 7047)* **ATLANTIS. / I WANT YOU TO BUY ME** [2] [–]

Jun 63. (lp) *(33SX 1522)* **GREATEST HITS** (compilation) [2] [–]
– Apache / Man of mystery / F.B.I. / Midnight / Frightened city / Kon-tiki / 36-24-36 / The savage / Peace pipe / Wonderful land / Stars fell on Stockton / Guitar tango / The boys / Dance on / The stranger. *(re-iss. Aug71 / re-iss. May74, hit No.48) (cd-iss. May89 on 'E.M.I.')*

Sep 63. (7") *(DB 7106)* **SHINDIG. / IT'S BEEN A BLUE DAY** [6] [–]

— **JOHN ROSTILL** (b.16 Jun'42, Birmingham, England) – bass (ex-INTERNS) repl. LOCKING; they shared duties on below album

Nov 63. (7") *(DB 7163)* **GERONIMO. / SHAZAM** [11] [–]

Feb 64. (7") *(DB 7231)* **THEME FOR YOUNG LOVERS. / THIS HAMMER** [12] [–]

May 64. (7") *(DB 7261)* **THE RISE & FALL OF FLINGEL BUNT. / IT'S A MAN'S WORLD** [5] [–]

May 64. (lp; mono/stereo) *(33SX 1619/SCX 3511)* **DANCE WITH THE SHADOWS** [2] [–]
– Chattanooga choo choo / Blue shadows / Fandango / Tonight / That's the way it goes / Don't it make you feel good / Big 'B' / Dakota / In the mood / The lonely bull / French dressing / The high and the mighty / Zambesi / Temptation.

Jun 64. (7") **THE RISE AND FALL OF FLINGEL BUNT. / THEME FOR YOUNG LOVERS** [–] [ ]

Aug 64. (7") *(DB 7342)* **RHYTHM AND GREENS. / THE MIRACLE** [22] [ ]

Nov 64. (7") *(DB 7416)* **GENIE WITH THE LIGHT BROWN LAMP. / PRINCESS** [17] [–]

— Next with vocals as was alternate singles until MAROC 7 instrumental

— **HANK + BRIAN** also added keyboards to repertoire

Feb 65. (7") *(DB 7476)* **MARY ANNE. / CHU-CHI** [17] [–]

May 65. (7") *(DB 7588)* **STINGRAY. / ALICE IN SUNDERLAND** [19] [–]

Jul 65. (lp; mono/stereo) *(33SX 1736/SCX 3554)* **SOUND OF THE SHADOWS** [4] [–]
– A little bitty tear / Five hundred miles / Let it be me / Brazil / Lost city / Blue sky, blue sea, blue me / Bossa roo / Cotton pickin' / Santa Ana / The windjammer / Deep purple / Dean's theme / Breakthru / National provincial samba.

Jul 65. (7") *(DB 7650)* **DON'T MAKE MY BABY BLUE. / MY GRANDFATHER** [10] [–]

Nov 65. (7") *(DB 7769)* **WARLORD. / WISH I COULD SHIMMY** [18] [–]

Dec 65. (lp; mono/stereo) *(33SX 1791/SCX 3578)* **MORE HITS!** (compilation) [ ] [–]
– Foot tapper / Atlantis / Shindig / Theme for young lovers / Geronimo / Shazam / The rise and fall of Flingel Bunt / Genie with the light brown lamp / Mary-Anne / Stingray / Rhythms and greens / Don't make my baby blue / Lute number / Drum number. *(re-iss. Aug85) (cd-iss. May89 on 'E.M.I.')*

Mar 66. (7") *(DB 7853)* **I MET A GIRL. / LATE LAST NIGHT** [22] [–]

May 66. (lp; mono/stereo) *(33SX/SCX 6041)* **SHADOW MUSIC** [5] [–]
– Razzamatazz / I only want to be with you / Babes in the wood / Only one way to love / Stay around / In the past / Bento-San / Fly me to the Moon / 4th street / A sigh (un sospero) / Don't stop now / March to Drina / The magic doll / Now that you're gone / Maid Marion's theme.

Jun 66. (7") *(DB 7952)* **A PLACE IN THE SUN. / WILL YOU BE THERE** [24] [–]

Oct 66. (7") *(DB 8034)* **THE DREAMS I DREAM. / SCOTCH ON THE SOCKS** [42] [–]

Mar 67. (7") *(DB 8170)* **MAROC 7. / BOMBAY DUCK** [24] [–]

Jul 67. (lp) *(SCX 6148)* **JIGSAW** [8] [–]
– Prelude in E major / Jigsaw / Waiting for Rosie / With a hym hym on my knee / Chelsea boot / Winchester cathedral / Green eyes / Stardust / Marie Elena / Tennessee waltz / Trains and boats and planes / Cathy's clown / Semi-detached Mr.James / Friday on my mind. *(re-iss. Apr90 on 'Beat Goes On';)*

Sep 67. (7") *(DB 8264)* **TOMORROW'S CANCELLED. / SOMEWHERE** [ ] [–]

Dec 67. (lp) *(SCX 6199)* **FROM HANK, BRUCE, BRIAN AND JOHN** [ ] [–]
– Snap, crackle and how's your dad / Evening glow / A thing of beauty / Naughty Nippon nights / The wild roses / The letter / San Francisco / The day I met Marie / Holy cow / I'm a believer. *(re-iss. Apr90 on 'Beat Goes On';)*

Jan 68. (7"; as HANK MARVIN & THE SHADOWS) *(DB 8326)* **LONDON'S NOT TOO FAR. / RUNNING OUT OF THE WORLD** [ ] [–]

Mar 68. (7") *(DB 8372)* **DEAR OLD MRS. BELL. / TRYING TO FORGET THE ONE YOU LOVE** [ ] [–]

— The SHADOWS split late '68, after release in October of shared lp 'ESTABLISHED 1958' with CLIFF RICHARD.

SHADOWS

— re-formed in mid'69. **ALAN HAWKSHAW** – guitar, keyboards repl. WELCH (see further below)

Parlophone not iss.

Oct 69. (7"; by HANK MARVIN) **SLAUGHTER ON 10th AVENUE. / MIDNIGHT COWBOY** [ ] [–]

— augmented by bassmen; **HERBIE FLOWERS, DAVE RICHMOND + BRIAN HODGES**

Oct 70. (lp) *(SCX 6420)* **SHADES OF ROCK** [ ] [–]
– Proud Mary / My babe / Lucille / Johnny B.Goode / Paperback writer / (I can't get no) Satisfaction / Bony Moronie / Get back / Something / River deep, mountain high / Memphis / What'd I say.

— they disbanded again in 1970; ROSTILL rejoined the TOM JONES band but was tragically electrocuted on the 26th November '73 when playing guitar in his home

MARVIN, WELCH & FARRAR

— formed trio (**FARRAR** – b. Australia), augmented by **HAWKSHAW, RICHMOND / CLEM CATTINI** – drums / **PETER VINCE** – organ

Regal Zonophone not iss.

Jan 71. (7") *(RZ 3030)* **FAITHFUL. / MR. SUN** [ ] [–]

Feb 71. (lp) *(SRZA 8502)* **MARVIN, WELCH & FARRAR** [30] [–]
– You're burning bridges / A thousand conversations / Brownie Kentucky / My home town / Silvery rain / Throw down a line / Baby I'm calling you / Faithful / Mistress Fate & Father Time / Take her away / Wish you were here / Mr. Sun / Strike a light. *(cd-iss. Aug91 on 'See For Miles';) – (extra tracks).*

— the trio now augmented by **BENNETT, HAWKSHAW + RICHMOND**

May 71. (7") *(RZ 3035)* **LADY OF THE MORNING. / TINY ROBIN** [ ] [–]

Nov 71. (lp) *(SRZA 8504)* **SECOND OPINION** [ ] [–]
– Black eyes / Tiny Robin / Ronnie / Far away falling / Lady of the morning / Let's say goodbye / Lonesome mole / The time to come / Thank Heaven's I've got you / Come back to natre / All day, all night blues. *(cd-iss. Aug91 on 'See For Miles';)* – (extra tracks)

Apr 72. (7") *(RZ 3048)* **MARMADUKE. / STRIKE A LIGHT** [ ] [–]

—— early in 1972, when WELCH's girlfriend (OLIVIA NEWTON-JOHN) broke off engagement, he attempted suicide. The remaining 5 members became part of

MARVIN & FARRAR

E.M.I. not iss.

Aug 73. (7") *(EMI 2044)* **MUSIC MAKES MY DAY. / SKIN DEEP** [ ] [–]

Aug 73. (lp) *(EMA 755)* **HANK MARVIN AND JOHN FARRAR** [ ] [–]
– So hard to live with / Music makes my day / Skin deep / If I rewrote yesterdays / Galadrie / Love oh love / Help me into your wagon / Small and lonely night / You never can tell / Nobody cares / Lord how it's hurting. *(cd-iss. Aug91 on 'See For Miles' with extra tracks)*

SHADOWS

—— re-formed (**MARVIN, WELCH, FARRAR + BENNETT**)

E.M.I. not iss.

Nov 73. (7") *(EMI 2081)* **TURN AROUND AND TOUCH ME. / JUNGLE JAM** [ ] [–]

—— added **ALAN TARNEY** – bass

Dec 73. (lp/c) *(EMA/TCEMA 762)* **ROCKIN' WITH CURLY LEADS** [45] [–]
– Pinball wizard – See me, feel me / Years away / Deep roots / Humbucker / Jungle jam / Gracie / Good vibrations / Rockin' with curly leads / Turn around and touch me / Wide mouthed frog / Gutbucket / Jumpin' Jack input.

Apr 74. (7"; by BRUCE WELCH) *(EMI 2141)* **PLEASE MR. PLEASE. / SONG OF YESTERDAY** [ ] [–]

—— same 5-piece, but **WELCH** now vocals, **TARNEY** – piano

Mar 75. (7") *(EMI 2269)* **LET ME BE THE ONE. / STAND UP LIKE A MAN** [12] [–]

Apr 75. (lp/c) *(EMC/TCEMC 3066)* **SPECS APPEAL** [30] [–]
– God only knows / Cool clear air / Rose, Rose / This house runs on sunshine / Colarado songbird / No no Nina / Don't throw it all away / Honourable puff-puff / Spider juice / Let me be the one / Like strangers / Stand up like a man.

Jun 75. (7") *(EMI 2310)* **RUN BILLY RUN. / HONOURABLE PUFF-PUFF** [ ] [–]

Oct 75. (7"; as MARVIN & FARRAR) **SMALL AND LONELY NIGHT. / GALADRIEL (SPIRIT OF STARLIGHT)** [ ] [–]

Nov 75. (lp) *(EMC 3095)* **LIVE AT THE PARIS OLYMPIA (live April'75)** [ ] [–]
– The rise and fall of Flingel Bunt / Man of mystery / Lady of the morning / Nivram / Tiny Robin / Sleepwalk / Guitar tango / Honourable puff-puff / Apache / Shadoogie / Marmaduke / Somewhere / Little 'B' / Medley (Lucille – Rip it up – Blue suede shoes). *(re-iss. Apr81 on 'M.F.P.', w/free other live at Sankei Hall) (cd-iss. Feb92)*

Jun 76. (7") *(EMI 2461)* **IT'LL BE ME BABE. / LIKE STRANGERS** [ ] [–]

—— In Jan'77, the TV advertised compilation '20 GOLDEN GREATS' hit No.1

—— **FRANCIS MONKMAN** – keyboards repl. FARRAR who went to solo & Australia. / **ALAN JONES** – bass repl. TARNEY

Jul 77. (7") *(EMI 2660)* **ANOTHER NIGHT. / CRICKET BAT BOOGIE** [ ] [–]

Aug 77. (lp/c) *(EMC/TCEMC 3195)* **TASTY** [ ] [–]
– Cricket bat boogie / Return to the Alamo / Another night / Goodbye yellow brick road / Honky tonk woman / Montezuma's revenge / Walk don't run / Superstar / Bermuda triangle / The most beautiful girl in the world / Creole nights.

Aug 78. (7") *(EMI 2838)* **LOVE DE LUXE. / SWEET SATURDAY NIGHT** [ ] [–]

—— **CLIFF HALL** – keyboards (ex-CLIFF RICHARD Band) repl. MONKMAN to SKY They were now virtually a trio of **MARVIN, WELCH & BENNETT**

Nov 78. (7") *(EMI 2890)* **DON'T CRY FOR ME ARGENTINA. / MONTEZUMA'S REVENGE** [5] [–]

—— In Feb79, their album with CLIFF 'THANK YOU VERY MUCH' hit No.5.

Apr 79. (7") *(EMI 2939)* **THEME FROM 'THE DEER HUNTER'. / BERMUDA TRIANGLE** [9] [–]

Sep 79. (lp/c) *(EMC/TCEMC 3310)* **STRING OF HITS** [1] [–]
– Riders in the sky / Parisienne walkways / Heart of glass / Classical gas / You're the one that I want / Theme from 'The Deer Hunter' / Bridge over troubled water / Don't cry for me Argentina / Song for Duke / Bright eyes / Rodrigo's guitar de Aranjuez / Baker street. *(re-iss. Sep85 on 'M.F.P.', cd-iss. Sep88) (cd-iss. Oct87)*

Oct 79. (7") *(EMI 5004)* **RODRIGO'S GUITAR CONCERTO. / SONG FOR DUKE** [ ] [–]

Jan 80. (7") *(EMI 5027)* **RIDERS IN THE SKY. / RUSK** [12] [–]

Jul 80. (7") *(EMI 5083)* **HEART OF GLASS. / RETURN OF THE ALAMO** [ ] [–]

Polydor not iss.

Aug 80. (7") *(POSP 148)* **EQUINOXE V. / FENDER BENDER** [50] [–]

Sep 80. (lp)(c) *(2442 179)(3184 147)* **CHANGE OF ADDRESS** [17] [–]
– Mozart forte / Midnight creeping / Change of address / Just the way you are / Indigo-Outdigo / Arty's party / Albatross / Hello Mr. W.A.M. / Temptation / If you leave me now / Equinoxe V. *(re-iss. Aug83)*

Nov 80. (7") *(POSP 187)* **MOZART FORTE. / MIDNIGHT CREEPING** [ ] [–]

Apr 81. (7") *(POSP 255)* **THE THIRD MAN. / THE FOURTH MAN** [44] [–]

Sep 81. (7") *(POSP 316)* **TELSTAR. / SUMMER LOVE '59** [ ] [–]

Sep 81. (lp/c) *(POLD/+C 5046)* **HITS RIGHT UP YOUR STREET** [15] [–]
– Telstar / Chi Mai (theme from 'The Life & Times Of David Lloyd George') / We don't talk anymore / Imagine; Woman / Hats off to Wally / One day I'll fly away / Summer love '59 / Misty / This ole house / The winner takes all / Sailing / Nut rocker / Thing-me-jig / More than I can say / Cowboy cafe / The third man.

Nov 81. (7") *(POSP 376)* **IMAGINE; WOMAN. / HATS OFF TO WALY** [ ] [–]

May 82. (7") *(POSP 439)* **TREAT ME NICE. / SPOT THE BALL** [ ] [–]

Jul 82. (7") *(POSP 485)* **THE THEME FROM 'MISSING'. / THE SHADY LADY** [ ] [–]

Sep 82. (2xlp/d-c) *(SHAD S/C 1)* **LIFE IN THE JUNGLE** [24] [–]
– Life in the jungle / High noon / The theme from 'Missing' / Treat me nice / Cat'n'mouse / Chariots of fire / No dancing / Riders of the range / The old romantics / You rescue me / Lili Marlene / Raunchy. *(re-iss. as lp Jan85) (cd-iss. May89)* **LIVE AT ABBEY ROAD (live)** – The third man / Thing-me-jig / Runaway / All I have to do is dream / It doesn't matter anymore / Johnny B.Goode / Over in a flash / Summer love '59 / Oh! boy / Crying in the rain / Arty's party. *(cd-iss. May89)*

Aug 83. (7") *(POSP 629)* **DIAMONDS. / ELEVEN IS** [ ] [–]

Oct 83. (lp/c) *(POLD/+C 5120)* **XXV** [34] [–]
– Africa / Goin' home (theme from 'Local Hero') / Up where we belong / You don't have to say you love me / The modern way / Diamonds / Time is tight / Memory / Liverpool days / Queen of hearts / A whiter shade of pale. *(cd-iss. 1988)*

Oct 83. (7") *(POSP 647)* **GOIN' HOME. / CAT'N'MOUSE** [ ] [–]

Aug 84. (7") *(POSP 694)* **ON A NIGHT LIKE THIS. / THING-ME-JIG** [ ] [–]

Nov 84. (lp/c) *(POLD/+C 5169)* **GUARDIAN ANGEL** [98] [–]
– How do I love thee / Hammerhead / The Saturday western / On a night like this / Look back on love / Johnny Staccato / I will return / (I'm gonna be your) Guardian angel / Can't play your game / Turning point / Our Albert. *(cd-iss. Nov86; 823797-2)*

May 86. (7") *(POSP 792)* **MOONLIGHT SHADOW. / JOHNNY STACCATO** [ ] [–]

May 86. (lp/c)(cd) *(PRO LP/MC 8)(829358-2)* **MOONLIGHT SHADOWS** [6] [–]
– Moonlight shadow / Walk of life / I just called to say I love you / Hello / Every breath you take / Nights in white satin / The power of love / Three times a lady / Against all odds / Hey Jude / Dancing in the dark / Imagine / I know him so well / Memory / Sailing / A whiter shade of pale. *(re-iss. cd/c Apr95)*

Aug 86. (7") *(POSP 808)* **DANCING IN THE DARK. / TURNING POINT** [ ] [–]
(12"+=) *(POSPX 808)* – ('A'version).

Nov 86. (7") *(POSP 847)* **EASTENDERS; HOWARD'S WAY. / NO DANCING!** [ ] [–]

Oct 87. (7") *(POSP 886)* **PULASKI. / CHANGE OF ADDRESS** [ ] [–]

Oct 87. (lp/c)(cd) *(SHAD/+C 1)(833682-2)* **SIMPLY SHADOWS** [11] [–]
– I knew you were waiting (for me) / We don't need another hero / Theme from 'The Snowman' / Careless whisper / Don't give up / I guess that's why they call it the blues / A heart will break tonight / The lady in red / Pulaski / Take my breath away / Eastenders / I want to know what love is / Skye boat song / Jealous guy / Chain reaction / Howard's way.

Nov 87. (7") *(POSP 898)* **THEME FROM THE SNOWMAN. / OUTDIGO** ☐ -

Apr 89. (7") *(PO 47)* **MOUNTAINS OF THE MOON. / STACK-IT** ☐ -
(cd-s+=) *(PZCD 47)* – Turning point.

May 89. (lp/c)(cd) *(SHAD/+C 30)(839357-2)* **STEPPIN' TO THE SHADOWS** 11 -
– You win again / I wanna dance with somebody (who loves me) / He ain't heavy, he's my brother / Candle in the wind / Farewell my lovely / Mountains of the Moon / Nothing's gonna change my love for you / Heaven is a place on Earth / When the going gets tough / Alone / All I ask of you / Stack-it / Shoba / You keep me hangin' on / Some people / One moment in time. *(re-iss. cd+c May93 on 'Spectrum')*

Oct 90. (cd/c/lp) *(847120-2/-4/-1)* **REFLECTION** 6 -
– Eye of the tiger / Crockett's theme / Right here waiting / Every little thing she does is magic / Sealed with a kiss / Uptown girl / Strawberry fields forever / Riders in the sky '90 / Flashdance / Something's gotten hold of my heart / Love changes everything / Nothing's gonna stop us now / Bilitis / You'll never walk alone / Always on my mind / Megamix.

Oct 91. (cd/c/lp) *(511374-2/-4/-1)* **THEMES AND DREAMS** 21 -
– Crockett's theme / Up where we belong / Take my breath away / Theme from The Deerhunter / Walking in the air / If you leave me now / One day I'll fly away / Africa / Every breath you take / Memory / Nights in white satin / Candle in the wind / You win again / Sailing / Just the way you are / Moonlight shadow.

– (selective) compilations, etc. –

Jan 77. (lp/c) *E.M.I.; (EMTV/TCEMTV 3)* **20 GOLDEN GREATS** 1 -
– Apache / Frightened city / Guitar tango / Kon-tiki / Genie with the light brown lamp / The warlord / A place in the Sun / Atlantis / Wonderful land / F.B.I. / The savage / Geronimo / Shindig / Stingray / Theme for young lovers / The rise and fall of Flingel Bunt / Maroc 7 / Dance on / Man of mystery / Foot tapper. *(cd-iss. Aug87; CDP 746243-2)*

Nov 86. (cd; as MARVIN, WELCH & FARRAR) *See For Miles; (SEE 78)* **STEP FROM THE SHADOWS** ☐ -
(cd-iss. Nov89; SEECD 78) (re-iss. cd/lp Apr93)

Jan 89. (lp/c/cd) *See For Miles; (SEE/+K/CD 246)* **THE EP COLLECTION** ☐ -

Dec 89. (lp/c/cd) *Polydor; (841520-1/-4/-2)* **AT THEIR VERY BEST** ☐ -

Dec 89. (7"ep/cd-ep) *Polydor; (PD/PZCD 61)* **SHADOWMIX** ☐ -
– Apache – Wonderful land – Rise and fall of Flingel Bunt – Kon Tiki – F.B.I. – Man of mystery – Apache.

Feb 90. (d-cd/d-c/d-lp) *E.M.I.; CD/TC+/EM 1354)* **THE ORIGINAL CHART HITS 1960-1980** ☐ -
(d-cd+=) – (11 tracks).

Sep 90. (lp/c/cd) *See For Miles; (SEE/+K/CD 296)* **THE EP COLLECTION VOL.2** ☐ -

Mar 91. (cd) *E.M.I.; (CZ 378)* **THE SHADOWS / OUT OF THE SHADOWS** ☐ -

Sep 91. (6xcd-box) *E.M.I.; (CDSHAD 1)* **THE EARLY YEARS** ☐ -

Feb 92. (cd) *E.M.I.; (CZ 477)* **SHADOW MUSIC / SHADES OF ROCK** ☐ -

May 93. (cd/c) *Polygram TV; (843798-2/-4)* **SHADOWS IN THE NIGHT – 16 CLASSIC TRACKS** 22 -

Oct 93. (cd) *See For Miles; (SEECD 375)* **THE EP COLLECTION VOLUME 3** ☐ -

Oct 94. (cd/c) *Polygram TV; (523821-2/-4)* **THE BEST OF HANK MARVIN & THE SHADOWS** 19 -

May 95. (3xcd-box) *E.M.I.; (CDSHAD 2)* **THE FIRST 20 YEARS AT THE TOP – 75 ORIGINALS 1959-1979** ☐ -

Oct 97. (cd) *E.M.I.; (CDABBEY 104)* **AY ABBEY ROAD** ☐ ☐

Nov 98. (cd; as HANK MARVIN & THE SHADOWS) *Polygram TV; (559211-2/-4)* **THE FIRST 40 YEARS** 56 -

Dec 98. (3xcd-box) *Disky; (HR 85328-2)* **GOOD VIBRATIONS** ☐ ☐

Jul 00. (cd/c) *E.M.I.; (527586-2/-4)* **50 GOLDEN GREATS** 35 -

May 03. (cd) *E.M.I.; (583110-2)* **A'S, B'S & EP'S** ☐ ☐

SHAMEN

Formed: Aberdeen, Scotland ... 1984 as ALONE AGAIN OR (named after a LOVE track from '67) by COLIN ANGUS and McKENZIE brothers DEREK and KEITH. After two singles (one for 'Polydor'; DREAM COME TRUE), they became The SHAMEN, releasing the singles 'YOUNG TILL YESTERDAY' (1986) and 'SOMETHING ABOUT YOU' (1987) on their own 'Moksha' label. The debut album, 'DROP' (1987), followed soon after and at this point the band were touting a fairly derivative indie take on classic West coast psychedelia combined with overtly political/drug orientated lyrics. As Angus became increasingly preoccupied with the nascent dance scene, however, DEREK McKENZIE split ranks and was replaced by WILL SINOTT. After the controversial single, 'JESUS LOVES AMERIKA' (1988), ANGUS and SINOTT relocated to London, immersing themselves in the burgeoning acid house scene. The 'SHAMEN VS BAM BAM' (1988) moved the duo ever further into electronic territory and though the 'IN GORBACHEV WE TRUST' (1989) album fitted with the indie/dance crossover zeitgeist, The SHAMEN were one of the only acts to take the phenomenon to its ultimate conclusion. After a last outing for 'Moksha', the band signed to the 'One Little Indian' label in 1989. Their second single for the label, 'PROGEN' (1990), finally saw The SHAMEN make their mark on the dance scene. Although it barely scraped into the charts, the track was huge on the club scene and climbed to No.4 upon its re-release (in remixed form) the following year. In addition to this pivotal track, the album 'EN-TACT' (1990), contained the liquid psychedelia of 'HYPERREAL' (featuring the velvet tones of Polish singer PLAVKA) and the dancefloor manifesto of 'MAKE IT MINE', both minor hit singles. Having initially had DJ EDDIE RICHARDS play acid house at their gigs, The SHAMEN had now developed the 'Synergy' live experience, a pioneering integration of live electronica and top flight DJ's (including the likes of MIXMASTER MORRIS and PAUL OKENFOLD) that attempted to create a cultural fusion between the excitement of live performance and the communal vibe of the party scene. Just as the band were beginning to realise their dreams, WILL SINOTT drowned while swimming off the coast of The Canary Islands in May '91. ANGUS eventually decided to carry on and recruited RICHARD WEST aka Mr C, a veteran of the house scene, having DJ'd at the seminal RIP club. He was a natural choice, having rapped on the revamped 'PROGEN' single and collaborated on the 'Synergy' gigs, his inimitable cockney patois possessing a ragamuffin charm. He was also visually striking and along with SOUL FAMILY SENSATION singer JHELISSA ANDERSON, would become the public face of the The SHAMEN, ANGUS cannily content to communicate with the media via E-mail. The 'L.S.I. (LOVE, SEX, INTELLIGENCE)' (1992) single introduced a more commercial sound to the new look SHAMEN, as did the unashamed pop/dance of controversial hit, 'EBENEEZER GOODE' (1992) (the question of whether Mr C did actually sing 'E's are good' was endlessly debated by those tireless moral guardians of the nation's wellbeing). Many longtime fans couldn't stomach the new sound although the band gained a whole new following of pop kids enamoured with cheeky chappy Mr C. The million selling 'BOSS DRUM' (1992) album combined the aforementioned chart fodder with typically SHAMEN-esque communiques on 'Archaic Revivals' and the like (i.e.'RE-EVOLUTION', the title track etc.). 1995 saw ex-SOUL II SOUL chanteuse VICTORIA WILSON JAMES replace ANDERSON and a new album in the shops, 'AXIS MUTATIS'.

Although the record included the celebratory dance pop of single 'DESTINATION ESCHATON', overall it was more cerebral with a companion ambient album, 'ARBOR BONA/ARBOR MALA', released at the same time. 'HEMPTON MANOR' (1996) carried on The SHAMEN's overriding theme of transformation through mind altering substances and although the media profile of the band has shrunk considerably over the last couple of years, The SHAMEN have kept fans abreast of their activities with a rather fabby self-produced internet web-site, 'Nemeton'. • **Songwriters:** All written by COLIN and DEREK, until latter's departure and replacement by the late WILL SINOTT. ANGUS & WEST took over in '91. Covered; GRIM REAPER OF LOVE (Turtles) / FIRE ENGINE + SLIP INSIDE THIS HOUSE (13th Floor Elevators) / LONG GONE (Syd Barrett) / SWEET YOUNG THING (Monkees) / PURPLE HAZE (Jimi Hendrix). • **Trivia:** In Apr'88, they were dropped from a McEwans lager TV ad, because of their then anti-commercial approach.

Album rating: DROP (*5) / IN GORBACHEV WE TRUST (*7) / PHORWARD mini (*6) / EN-TACT (*9) / BOSS DRUM (*8) / AXIS MUTATIS (*7) / ARBOR BONA – ARBOR MALA (*7) / HEMPTON MANOR (*6) / THE SINGLES COLLECTION compilation (*8)

ALONE AGAIN OR

COLIN ANGUS (b.24 Aug'61) – keyboards / **DEREK McKENZIE** (b.27 Feb'64) – vocals, guitar / **KEITH McKENZIE** (b.30 Aug'61) – drums

All One — not iss.

Dec 84. (7") *(ALG 1)* **DRUM THE BEAT (IN MY SOUL). / SMARTIE EDIT** [–]

All One – Polydor — not iss.

Mar 85. (7") *(ALG 2)* **DREAM COME TRUE. / SMARTER THAN THE AVERAGE BEAR** [–]
(12") *(ALGX 2)* – ('A'-Splintered version) / ('B'-Ursa Major) / Drum the beat (shall we dance?).

SHAMEN

— added **ALISON MORRISON** – bass, keyboards

One Big Guitar — not iss.

Apr 86. (12"ep) *(OBG 003T)* **THEY MAY BE RIGHT . . . BUT THEY'RE CERTAINLY WRONG** [–]
– Happy days / Velvet box / I don't like the way the world is turning.

— **PETER STEPHENSON** (b. 1 Mar,62, Ayrshire) – keyboards repl. ALISON

Moksha — not iss.

Nov 86. (7"m) *(SOMA 1)* **YOUNG TILL YESTERDAY. / WORLD THEATRE / GOLDEN HAIR** [–]
(12"m) *(SOMA 1T)* – (first 2 tracks) / It's all around / Strange days dream.

May 87. (7") *(SOMA 2)* **SOMETHING ABOUT YOU. / DO WHAT YOU WILL** [–]
(12"+=) *(SOMA 2T)* – Grim reaper of love.

Jun 87. (lp/c) *(SOMA LP/C 1)* **DROP** [–]
– Through with you / Something about you / Four letter girl / The other side / Passing away / Young till yesterday / Happy days / Where do you go / Through my window / I don't like the way the world is turning / World theatre / Velvet box. *(c+=)* – Do what you will. *(cd-iss. Nov88 ++=; SOMACD 1)* – Strange days dream. *(re-iss. Jan92 on 'Mau Mau' lp/c/cd; MAU/+MC/CD 613)*

Sep 87. (7") *(SOMA 3)* **CHRISTOPHER MAYHEW SAYS. / SHITTING ON BRITAIN** [–]
(12"+=) *(SOMA 3T)* – Fire engine / Christopher Mayhew says a lot.

— **WILL SINOTT** (b.23 Dec'60, Glasgow, Scotland) – bass repl. DEREK (COLIN now vocals, guitar)

Feb 88. (7") *(SOMA 4)* **KNATURE OF A GIRL. / HAPPY DAYS** [–]
(12"+=) *(SOMA 4T)* – What's going down / Sub knature of a girl.

Ediesta — not iss.

Jun 88. (7") *(CALC 069)* **JESUS LOVES AMERIKA. / DARKNESS IN ZION** [–]
(12"+=) *(CALCT 069)* – Do what you will.
(cd-s++=) *(CALCCD 069)* – Sub knatural dub.

— now a duo of **COLIN** + **WILL**

Desire — not iss.

Nov 88. (12"; as SHAMEN VS BAM BAM) *(WANTX 10)* **TRANSCENDENTAL. / ('A'-housee mix)** [–]

Demon — Demon

Jan 89. (lp/c/cd) *(<FIEND/+C/CD 666>)* **IN GORBACHEV WE TRUST**
– Synergy / Sweet young thing / Raspberry infundibulum / War prayer / Adam Strange / Jesus loves Amerika / Transcendental / Misinformation / Raptyouare / In Gorbachev we trust / (Fundamental). *(c+=)* – Resistance (once again). *(cd+=)* – Yellow cellaphane day / Mayhew speaks out.

— added **SANDRA** – percussion

Moksha — not iss.

Apr 89. (7") *(SOMA 6)* **YOU, ME & EVERYTHING. / RERAPTYOUARE** [–]
('A'-Evil edits; 12"+=/cd-s+=) *(SOMA 6 T/CD)* – Ed's bonus beats.

May 89. (10"m-lp/c/cd) *(SOMA LP/C/CD 3)* **PHORWARD** [–]
– You, me & everything (else) / Splash 2 / Negation state / Reraptyouare / SDD 89 / Phorward. *(free 7")* – (The S&N Sessions) *(c+=/cd+=)* – Happy days / Knature of a girl.

— **JOHN DELAFONS** – percussion repl. SANDRA

One Little Indian — Epic

Nov 89. (12"ep/cd-ep) *(30TP 12/7CD)* **OMEGA AMIGO / OMEGA A. / OMEGA PRE-MIX / PH 1** [–]

Mar 90. (7") *(36 TP7)* **PRO>GEN (Beatmasters mix). / ('A'dub version)** [55] [–]
(12") *(36 TP12L)* – ('A'-C-mix F+) / ('B'side) / Lightspan (Ben Chapman mix).
(c-s++=) *(36 TP7C)* – ('A'-Paul Oakenfold 'Land Of Oz' mix).
(12") *(36 TP12)* – (above mix) / Lightspan (Ben Chapman mix).
(cd-s) *(36 TP7CD)* – (above 2 mixes) / ('A'-Steve Osborne mix).

Sep 90. (7"/c-s) *(46 TP7/+C)* **MAKE IT MINE (Lenny D vox). / ('A'-Evil Ed mix)** [42] Feb92
(12"/cd-s) *(46TP 12/7CD) <742 36/41>* – ('A'-Lenny D mix) / ('A'-Progress mix) / ('A'-Lenny D vox) / Something wonderful.
(12") *(46 TP12L)* – ('A'-Evil Ed mix) / ('A'-Outer Limits mix) / Pro>gen (Land of Oz mix) / ('A'-Micro minimal mix).

Oct 90. (cd)(c)(2x12"lp) *(TPLP 22 CD/MC/SP) <48722>* **EN-TACT** [31]
– Human N.R.G. / Pro>gen (land of Oz) / Possible worlds / Omega amigo / Evil is even / Hypereal / Lightspan / Make it mine V 2.5 / Oxygen restriction / Here are my people (orbital delays expected). *(cd+=)* – (Oxygen reprise (V 2.0 mix) / Human NRG (Massey mix) / Make it mine (pirate radio mix) / (etc.) *(re-iss. Nov90 lp; TPLP 22)*

Mar 91. (7"/c-s) *(48 TP7/+C)* **HYPERREAL (William Orbit mix). / ('A'-lp version)** [29] [–]
(12") *(48 TP12)* – ('A'versions incl. Maguire + dub) / In the bag.
(cd-s) *(48 TP7CD)* – ('A'versions incl. Meatbeat Manifesto mix) / In the bag.
(12") *(48 TP12L)* – ('A'-Meatbeat Manifesto mixes) / ('A'-Maguire + Dirty dubbing mixes).
(above featured **PLAVKA** (b. Poland) – vocals)

— on the 23rd May '91, WILL drowned while on holiday abroad

Jul 91. (7"/c-s) *(52 TP7/+C) <74044>* **MOVE ANY MOUNTAIN – PROGEN '91 (Beatmasters edit). / ('A'-The Goat From The Well Hung Parliament mix)** [4] Nov91 [38]
(12") *(52 TP12) <74043>* – ('A'-mixes; Landslide / Devil / Rude / R.I.P. in the Land Of Oz).
(cd-s) *(52 TP7CD) <74044>* – ('A'mixes; Beatmasters / Landslide / F2 Mello / Mountains in the sky).

Sep 91. (3xlp/c/cd) *(TPLP 32/+MC/CD)* **PROGENCY 2(8 versions)** [23] [–]

— New line-up **COLIN** plus **MR.C** – vocals, rhythm / + **JHELSA ANDERSON** – backing vox (ex-SOUL FAMILY SENSATION) / **BOB BREEKS** – live keyboards / **GAVIN KNIGHT** – live drums / **RICHARD SHARPE** – occasional analogue

Jun 92. (7"/12") *(68 TP 7/12) <74437>* **L.S.I. (LOVE SEX INTELLIGENCE). / POSSIBLE WORLDS** [6]
(c-s+=/cd-s+=) *(68 TP 7 C/CD)* – Make it mine (Moby mix).

Aug 92. (7"/c-s) *(78 TP7/+C)* **EBENEEZER GOODE. / ('A'dub)** [1]
(12"+=/cd-s+=) *(78 TP 12/7CD)* – ('A'mix) / L.S.I. (mix).

Oct 92. (lp/c/cd) *(TPLP 42/+C/CD) <52925>* **BOSS DRUM** [3]
– Boss drum / L.S.I.: Love Sex Intelligence / Space time / Librae solidi denari / Ebeneezer Goode (Beatmasters mix) / Comin' on / Phorever people / Fatman / Scientas / Re: evolution.

Oct 92. (7"/c-s) *(88 TP 7/+C) <74953>* **BOSS DRUM. / OMEGA AMIGO** 4 Apr93
(cd-s+=) *(88 TP7CD)* – (3 'A'mixes).
(12"-2 diff.) *(88 TP12)* – (5 'A'mixes either J.Robertson or Beatmasters).
(cd-s++=) *(88 TP7CDL)* – ('A'-Steve Osbourne mixes & Youth).

Dec 92. (7"ep/c-ep/12"ep/cd-ep) *(98 TP 7/7C/12/CD) <74898>* **PHOREVER PEOPLE. / ('A'dub + 'A'-Hyperreal orbit mix)** 5
(cd-s++=) *(98 TP7CDL)* – ('A'mixes).

Feb 93. (c-s; as SHAMEN with TERENCE McKENNA) *(118 TP7C)* **RE:EVOLUTION / ('A'mix)** 18
(12"+=/cd-s+=) *(118 TP 12/7CD)* – ('A'mixes).

Oct 93. (c-ep/12"ep/cd-ep) *(108 TP 7C/12/7CD)* **THE S.O.S. EP** 14
– Comin' on / Make it mine / Possible worlds.
(cd-ep) *(108 TP7CDL)* – ('A'mixes).

—— now with vocalist **VICTORIA WILSON-JAMES**

Aug 95. (c-s) *(128 TP7C) <78038>* **DESTINATION ESCHATON (Beatmasters mix) / ('A'-Deep melodic mix)** 15
(cd-s) *(128 TP7CD)* – ('A'-Shamen acid: Escacid) / (2 'A'-Hardfloor mixes).
(cd-s) *(128 TP7CDL)* – (2 'A'-Basement Boys mixes) / (3 'A'-Beatmasters mixes).

Oct 95. (c-s) *(138 TP7C)* **TRANSAMAZONIA (Beatmasters mix) / ('A'-Visnadi mix) / ('A'-Watershed instrumental) / ('A'-LTJ Bukin mix)** 28
(12"+=) *(138 TP12)* – ('A'-Deep dish mix).
(cd-s) *(138 TP7CD)* – (6 'A'mixes including; Alex Party Aguirre / Zion Train).
(cd-s+=) *(138 TP7CDL)* – ('A'-Nuv Idol mix).

Oct 95. (d-lp/c/cd) *(TPLP 52/+C/CD) <57796>* **AXIS MUTATIS** 27
– Destination Eschaton / Transamazonia / Conquistador / Mauna Kea to Andromeda / Neptune / Prince of Popacatapertl / Heal the separation / Persephone's quest / Moment / Axis mundi / Eschaton omega (deep melodic techno). *(cd/c/d-lp with other cd/c/d-lp) (TPLP 52 CDL/CL/L)* **ARBOR BONA / ARBOR MALA** – Asynptotic Escaton / Sefirotic axis (a)(b)(c) Formation (d) Action / Extraterrestrial / Deneter / Beneath the underworld / Xochipilis return / Rio Negro / Above the underworld / A moment in dub / Pizarro in Paradiso / West of the underworld / Anticipation Escaton (be ready for the storm) / Out in the styx.

Feb 96. (c-s) *(158 TP7C)* **HEAL (THE SEPARATION) / ('A'mix)** 31
(cd-s) *(158 TP7CD)* – ('A'mixes; organ / science park / PM Dawn / Steve Osborne ambient – H.E.L.P. breakfast / Beatmasters / foul play vocal).
(cd-s) *(158 TP7CDL)* – ('A'mixes; mighty organ / live '95) / Boss drum (Lionrock dub) / Phorever people (Todd Terry).

Oct 96. (3x12"lp/c/cd) *(TPLP62/+C/CD)* **HEMPTON MANOR** –
– Freya / Urpflanze / Cannabeo / Khat / Bememe / Indica / Rausch / Kava / El-fin / Monoriff.

Dec 96. (c-s) *(169 TP7C)* **MOVE ANY MOUNTAIN '96 / ('A'mix)** 35
(12"/cd-s) *(169 TP 12P/7CD)* – (mixes; Beatmasters radio / Tony De Vit edit) / Indica / L.S.I. (Beat edit).
(cd-s) *(169 TP7CDL)* – (mixes:- Tomka / Tony De Vit / Sneaker Pimps / Beatmasters 12").

Jan 97. (cd/c) *(TPLP 72 CD/C)* **THE SHAMEN COLLECTION** (compilation)

Jan 97. (cd/c) *(TPLP 72 CDR/CR)* **THE SHAMEN REMIX COLLECTION – STARS ON 45** (compilation)
(both above re-iss. Apr98 d-cd/d-c; TPLP 72 CDE/CE) – hit UK No.26

Moksha Moksha

Oct 98. (cd-ep) *(<MOKSHA 3CD>)* **UNIVERSAL (mixes:- 1999 vocal / 187 B.P. metamix (major) / 1999 dance vocal / Sharp trade life dub / Mr.C tech house mix / 187 Lockdown dark dub)** Nov98

– compilations, others, etc. –

Aug 88. (lp/c)(cd) *Materiali Sonori; (MASO 33041/+C)(MASOCD 9008)* **STRANGE DAY DREAMS** – Italy –
(re-iss. cd Oct91 imported) (re-iss. Jan93; same)

Dec 89. (m-lp/cd) *Communion; (COMM 4 LP/CD)* **WHAT'S GOING DOWN** –

Nov 93. (cd/c/lp) *Band Of Joy; (BOJ CD/MC/LP 006)* **ON AIR (live BBC sessions)** 61 –
(cd re-iss. Mar98 on 'Strange Fruit'; SFRSCD 055)

Mar 98. (12") *Moksha; (AGC 002)* **U-NATIONS** –

Mar 02. (cd) *Music Club; (MCCD 484)* **HYSTERICOOL – THE BEST OF THE ALTERNATIVE MIXES** –

SHANGRI-LA'S

Formed: Andrew Jackson High, Queens, New York, USA . . . as The BON BONS by sisters BETTY & MARY WEISS along with twins MARY-ANN and MARGIE GANSER. The girls were handed their big music biz break after being discovered by producer GEORGE 'SHADOW' MORTON who changed their name and signed them to 'Red Bird', the label owned by NY songwriters Jerry Leiber and Mike Stoller. MORTON himself penned 'REMEMBER (WALKING IN THE SAND)', an eerily melodramatic ballad with an ambitious production that cast SHADOW as an East Coast version of PHIL SPECTOR. The single hit the US Top 5 (UK Top 20) in September '64 and primed The SHANGRI-LA'S for their entrance into pop legend with 'LEADER OF THE PACK'. A half-spoken/half-sung (in MARY's trademark emotionally loaded, cheerleader-style NY accent) tale of tearful teen love, rebellion and death complete with revving motorbike/smashing glass sound effects, the track topped the US chart in late '64 and established a new benchmark in pop artistry. Further brilliantly overwrought creations followed over the next two years although only the more customary girly 'GIVE HIM A GREAT BIG KISS' and the runaway anguish of 'I CAN NEVER GO HOME ANYMORE' were significant hits. Following summer 66's unsettling spoken monologue, 'PAST, PRESENT AND FUTURE', the girls moved to 'Mercury' for a greatest hits package and a final couple of singles, 'THE SWEET SOUND OF SUMMER' and 'TAKE YOUR TIME'. The SHANGRI-LA'S split in 1967 amid legal problems with both the GANSER twins subsequently meeting unpleasant deaths (MARY ANN from encephalitis and MARGE from a drugs overdose). MORTON, meanwhile, went on to work with the likes of MOTT THE HOOPLE and The NEW YORK DOLLS.

Best CD compilation: THE BEST OF THE SHANGRI-LA'S (*8)

MARY WEISS – lead vocals / **BETTY WEISS** – vocals / **MARY-ANN GANSER** – vocals / **MARGE GANSER** – vocals

Red Bird Red Bird

Sep 64. (7") *<RB10 008>* **REMEMBER (WALKING IN THE SAND). / IT'S EASIER TO CRY** 14 Aug64 5

Dec 64. (7") *<RB10 014>* **LEADER OF THE PACK. / WHAT IS LOVE?** 11 Oct64 1

Jan 65. (7") *<RB10 018>* **GIVE HIM A GREAT BIG KISS. / TWIST AND SHOUT** Dec64 18

Jan 65. (7") *<RB10 019>* **MAYBE. / SHOUT** Dec64 91

1965. (lp) *<RB20 101>* **THE SHANGRI-LAS – LEADER OF THE PACK** Mar65
– Give him a great big kiss / Leader of the pack / Bull dog / It's easier to cry / What is love? / Remember (walking in the sand) / Twist and shout / Maybe / So much in love / Shout / Good night, my love / Pleasant dreams / You can't sit down. *(re-iss. 1983 on 'Charly'; CRM 2028)*

1965. (7") *<RB10 025>* **OUT IN THE STREETS. / THE BOY** Mar65 53

1965. (7") *<RB10 030>* **GIVE US YOUR BLESSINGS. / HEAVEN ONLY KNOWS** May65 29

1965. (7") *<RB10 036>* **RIGHT NOW AND NOT LATER. / TRAIN FROM KANSAS CITY** Sep65 99

1965. (lp) *<RB20 014>* **SHANGRI-LAS '65** –
– Right now and not later / Never again / Give us your blessings / Sophisticated boom boom / I'm blue / Heaven only knows / The train from Kansas City / Out in the streets / What's a girl supposed to do / The dum dum ditty / You cheated, you lied / The boy. *(UK-iss.Mar84 on 'Charly'; CRM 2029)*

Jan 66.	(7") <*(RB10 043)*> **I CAN NEVER GO HOME ANYMORE. / BULLDOG**		Nov65	6
Mar 66.	(7") <*(RB10 048)*> **LONG LIVE OUR LOVE. / SOPHISTICATED BOOM BOOM**		Jan66	33
—	now without MARGE			
May 66.	(7") <*(RB10 053)*> **HE CRIED. / DRESSED IN BLACK**		Apr66	65
Aug 66.	(7") <*(RB10 068)*> **PAST, PRESENT AND FUTURE. / PARADISE**		Jun66	59
		Mercury		Mercury
1966.	(lp) *(MCL 20096)* <61099> **GOLDEN HITS** (compilation) – Leader of the pack / The train from Kansas City / Heaven only knows / Remember (walking in the sand) / I can never go home anymore / What is love? / Past, present and future / Out in the streets / Give him a great big kiss / Long live our love / Give us your blessings / Sophisticated boom boom. *(re-iss. 1973 on 'Philips' lp)(c; 6336 215)(7175 031)*			
1967.	(7") *(MF 962)* **THE SWEET SOUND OF SUMMER. / I'LL NEVER LEARN**			
1967.	(7") *(MF 979)* **TAKE YOUR TIME. / FOOTSTEPS ON THE ROOF**			

— split in 1967. In 1971 MARY ANN died of encephalitis, MARGE died of a drug overdose

– (selective) compilations, etc. –

Oct 72.	(7") *Kama Sutra; (2013 024)* **LEADER OF THE PACK. / REMEMBER (WALKING IN THE SAND)** *(re-iss. Jul82 & Jun88 on 'Old Gold'; OG 9085)*	3	–
May 76.	(7") *Charly; (CYS 1009)* **LEADER OF THE PACK. / GIVE HIM A GREAT BIG KISS**	7	–
May 76.	(7") *Contempo; (CS 9032)* **LEADER OF THE PACK. / REMEMBER (WALKING IN THE SAND)**	7	–
Feb 90.	(cd/c/lp) *Instant; (CD/TC+/INS 5021)* **REMEMBER** *(re-iss. Apr96 on 'Hallmark' cd/c; 30412-2/-4)*		–
Apr 95.	(cd) *R.P.M.; (RPM 136)* **MYRMIDONS OF MELODRAMA**		–
Feb 97.	(cd) *Spectrum; (552764-2)* **THE BEST OF THE SHANGRI-LAS**		–
Oct 99.	(cd) *Castle Pie; (PIESCD 149)* **LEADER OF THE PACK**		–
Apr 02.	(cd) *R.P.M.; (RPM 506)* **MYRMIDONS OF MELODRAMA: THE DEFINITIVE COLLECTION**		
Nov 02.	(cd) *Repertoire; (REP 4908)* **THE VERY BEST OF THE SHANGRI-LAS**		

Del SHANNON

Born: CHARLES WEEDON WESTOVER, 30 Dec'34, Coopersville, Michegan, USA. Although he'd learned the guitar while still in his teens, his break didn't come until 1960 when he met keyboard player, MAX CROOK. The pair formed CHARLIE JOHNSON & HIS LITTLE BIG SHOW BAND, in turn attracting the attention of DJ Ollie McLaughlin who introduced them to 'Big Top' label owners Harry Balk and Irving Micahnik. CHARLES was signed solo as DEL SHANNON with CROOK remaining as his co-writer sidekick, the duo hitting paydirt almost immediately with 1961's classic 'RUNAWAY'. A transatlantic No.1, the single segued from SHANNON's brooding, bitter verses into a rollercoaster falsetto-vocal chorus, the whole thing driven along on minor chords and underpinned by CROOK's trademark 'Musitron' organ. It was a striking musical formula that saw follow-up single, 'HATS OFF TO LARRY', make the Top 10 in both Britain and America. Yet as his Stateside profile waned, so he became more popular in Britain where his tough yet melodic sound and uncompromising self-penned material found a more appreciative audience. Over his golden period of '62-'63, both 'HEY! LITTLE BABY' and 'THE SWISS MAID' narrowly missed the UK No.1 spot while 'LITTLE TOWN FLIRT' and 'TWO KINDS OF TEARDROPS' went Top 5. SHANNON subsequently met and played alongside The BEATLES on a 1963 tour and became the first American artist to cover a Fab Four track, releasing 'FROM ME TO YOU' in summer '63. That year also saw him sever ties with Balk and Micahnik, the singer briefly setting up his own label ('Berlee') amid the ensuing legal battle. He then relocated to New York and signed to the 'Amy' imprint where he scored his last significant hit with the blistering 'KEEP SEARCHIN''. 1965 found British duo PETER & GORDON covering SHANNON's 'I GO TO PIECES' while DEL himself was breaking the mould by cutting a whole album of HANK WILLIAMS tunes. The following year he signed to L.A.'s 'Liberty' where producer Snuff Garrett and arranger LEON RUSSELL were fresh from turning twee teensters GARY LEWIS & THE PLAYBOYS into lucrative chart material. An attempt to groom SHANNON for teen idol status was doomed to failure, the label subsequently shelving an ambitious album of orchestrated ('AND THE MUSIC PLAYS ON') pop/rock which the singer had recorded alongside JIMMY PAGE, JOHN PAUL JONES and NICKY HOPKINS. With his chart days clearly behind him, SHANNON moved into production work towards the end of the decade, taking the helm for The SHIRELLES and BRIAN HYLAND. The early 70's found him label-hopping with various comeback single attempts, even releasing an Australian-only single in 1975. Throughout the latter half of the decade the singer struggled with alcoholism although by the early 80's he'd recovered sufficiently to have a final crack at the US Top 40 with the country-style, TOM PETTY-produced 'SEA OF LOVE' single. Further sporadic singles emerged before SHANNON began work on a new album with JEFF LYNNE in 1990. Tragically, by the time 'ROCK ON' (1991) was released, SHANNON was dead; he'd committed suicide (by shooting himself) on 8th February 1990 after reportedly suffering severe depression. His death was made all the more poignant with the revelation that he'd been mooted as a replacement for ROY ORBISON in The TRAVELING WILBURYS.

• **Covered:** THE SWISS MAID (Roger Miller) / HANDY MAN (Jimmy Jones) / DO YOU WANT TO DANCE? (Bobby Freeman) / MEMPHIS (Chuck Berry) / TWIST AND SHOUT (Isley Brothers) / CRYING + RUNNING SCARED + PRETTY WOMAN (Roy Orbison) / NEEDLES AND PINS + WHEN YOU WALK IN THE ROOM (Searchers) / RAG DOLL (Four Seasons) / A WORLD WITHOUT LOVE (hit; Peter & Gordon) / THE BIG HURT (Toni Fisher) / UNDER MY THUMB (Rolling Stones) / KICKS (Paul Revere) / RED RUBBER BALL (Cyrkle) / PIED PIPER (Crispian St. Peters) / SUMMER IN THE CITY (Lovin' Spoonful) / SUNNY (Bobby Hebb) / TELL HER NO (Zombies).

Best CD compilation: GREATEST HITS (*7)

DEL SHANNON – vocals (with session people incl. MAX CROOK – keyboards)

		London		Big Top
Apr 61.	(7") *(HLX 9317)* <3067> **RUNAWAY. / JODY**	1	Feb61	1
Sep 61.	(7") *(HLX 9402)* <3075> **HATS OFF TO LARRY. / DON'T GILD THE LILY, LILY**	6	May61	5
Nov 61.	(7") *(HLX 9462)* <3083> **SO LONG BABY. / THE ANSWER TO EVERYTHING**	10	Sep61	28
Nov 61.	(lp) *(HA-X 2402)* <1303> **RUNAWAY WITH ...** – Misery / Daydreams / His latest flame / The prom / The search / Runaway / I wake up crying / Wide wide world / I'll always love you / Lies / He doesn't care / Jody.			
Nov 61.	(7") <3091> **HEY! LITTLE GIRL. / I DON'T CARE ANYMORE**	–		38
Mar 62.	(7") *(HLX 9515)* **HEY! LITTLE BABY. / YOU NEVER TALKED ABOUT ME**	2		–
Mar 62.	(7") <3098> **GINNY IN THE MIRROR. / I WON'T BE THERE**	–		
Aug 62.	(7") *(HLX 9587)* <3112> **CRY MYSELF TO SLEEP. / I'M GONNA MOVE ON**	29	Jun62	99
Sep 62.	(7") <3117> **THE SWISS MAID. / YOU NEVER TALKED ABOUT ME**	–		64

Oct 62. (7") *(HLX 9609)* **THE SWISS MAID. / GINNY IN THE MIRROR** [2] [–]

Jan 63. (7") *(HLX 9653) <3131>* **LITTLE TOWN FLIRT. / THE WAMBOO** [4] Dec62 [12]

Apr 63. (7") *(HLX 9710) <3143>* **TWO KIND OF TEARDROPS. / KELLY** [5] [50]

May 63. (lp) *(8071)* **HATS OFF TO LARRY** (compilation) [ ] [–]
– The Swiss maid / Cry myself to sleep / Ginny in the mirror / You never talked about me / Don't gild the lily, Lily / I won't be there / Hats off to Larry / The answer to everything / Hey little girl / I'm gonna move on / I don't care anymore / So long baby.

Jun 63. (7") *<3152>* **FROM ME TO YOU. / TWO SILHOUETTES** [–] [77]

Aug 63. (7") *(HLX 9761)* **TWO SILHOUETTES. / MY WILD ONE** [23] [–]

Oct 63. (lp) *(HA-X 8091) <1308>* **LITTLE TOWN FLIRT** [15] Jun63 [12]
– Two kind of teardrops / Dream baby / Happiness / Two silhouettes / She thinks I still care / My wild one / Runaround Sue / From me to you / Kelly / Hey baby / Go away little girl / Little town flirt.

London Berlee

Oct 63. (7") *(HLU 9800) <501>* **SUE'S GONNA BE MINE. / SINCE SHE'S GONE** [21] [71]

Mar 64. (7") *(HLU 9858) <502>* **THAT'S THE WAY LOVE IS. / TIME OF THE DAY** [ ] [ ]

Stateside Amy

Mar 64. (7") *(SS 269) <897>* **MARY JANE. / STAINS ON MY LETTER** [35] [ ]

Jul 64. (7") *(SS 317) <905>* **HANDY MAN. / GIVE HER LOTS OF LOVIN'** [36] [22]

Oct 64. (7") *(SS 349) <911>* **DO YOU WANT TO DANCE? / THIS IS ALL I HAVE TO GIVE** [ ] Sep64 [43]

Jan 65. (lp) *(SL 10115) <8003>* **HANDY MAN** [ ] Nov64 [ ]
– Memphis / That's the way love is / Ruby baby / I'll be lonely tomorrow / I can't fool around anymore / Handy man / Crying / Mary Jane / A world without love / I ran all the way home / Give her lots of lovin' / Twist and shout.

Jan 65. (7") *(SS 368) <915>* **KEEP SEARCHIN' (WE'LL FOLLOW THE SUN). / BROKEN PROMISES** [3] Nov64 [9]

Mar 65. (7") *(SS 395) <919>* **STRANGER IN TOWN. / OVER YOU** [40] Feb65 [30]

May 65. (lp) *(SL 10130) <8004>* **DEL SHANNON SINGS HANK WILLIAMS** [ ] [ ]
– Your cheatin' heart / Kaw-liga / I can't help it / Honky tonk blues / (See I hear) That lonesome whistle / You win again / Ramblin' man / Hey good looking / Long gone lonesome blues / Weary blues / I'm so lonesome, I could cry / Cold cold heart.

Jun 65. (7") *(SS 430) <925>* **BREAK UP. / WHY DON'T YOU TELL HIM** [ ] May65 [95]

Sep 65. (7") *(SS 452) <937>* **MOVE IT ON OVER. / SHE STILL REMEMBERS TONY** [ ] [ ]

Sep 65. (lp) *(SL 10140) <8006>* **1,661 SECONDS WITH DEL SHANNON** [ ] [ ]
– Stranger in town / She cried / Needles and pins / Broken promises / Why don't you tell him / Do you wanna dance / I go to pieces / I'm gonna be strong / Rag doll / Over you / Running scared / Keep searchin'.

Mar 66. (7") *(SS 494) <947>* **I CAN'T BELIEVE MY EARS. / I WISH IT WASN'T ME TONIGHT** [ ] [ ]

Liberty Liberty

Apr 66. (7") *(LIB 55866) <55866>* **THE BIG HURT. / I GOT IT BAD** [ ] [94]

Jun 66. (7") *(LIB 55889) <55889>* **FOR A LITTLE WHILE. / HEY LITTLE STAR** [ ] [ ]

Sep 66. (7") *<55894>* **SHOW ME. / NEVER THOUGHT I COULD** [–] [ ]

Nov 66. (7") *<55904>* **UNDER MY THUMB. / SHE WAS MINE** [–] [ ]

Nov 66. (lp; stereo/mono) *(S+/LBY 1320) <LST 7452>* **THIS IS MY BAG** [ ] [ ]
– Lightnin' strikes / The cheater / Kicks / Action / It's too late / Never thought I could / The big hurt / Everybody loves a clown / Hey! little star / When you walk in the room / For a little while / Oh pretty woman.

Jan 67. (7") *(LIB 55939) <55939>* **SHE. / WHAT MAKES YOU RUN** [ ] [ ]

Feb 67. (lp; stereo/mono) *(S+/LBY 1335) <LST 4779>* **TOTAL COMMITMENT** [ ] [ ]
– Under my thumb / Red rubber ball / She was mine / Where were you when I needed you / The joker went wild / The Pied Piper / Sunny / Show me / Time won't let me / What makes you run / I can't be true / Summer in the city.

Jun 67. (7") *(LIB 10277)* **MIND OVER MATTER. / LED ALONG** [ ] [–]

Jun 67. (7") *<55961>* **LED ALONG. / I CAN'T BE TRUE** [–] [ ]

Oct 67. (7") *<55993>* **RUNAWAY (live '67). / HE CHEATED** [–] [ ]

Oct 67. (7") *(LBF 15020)* **RUNAWAY '67. / SHOW ME** [ ] [–]

—— early in '68, 'Liberty' shelved the album 'AND THE MUSIC PLAYS ON'. It featured session men JIMMY PAGE, JOHN PAUL JONES + NICKY HOPKINS.

Mar 68. (7") *(LBF 15061) <56018>* **THINKIN' IT OVER. / RUNNING ON BACK** [ ] [ ]

May 68. (7") *(LBF 15079) <56036>* **GEMINI. / MAGICAL MUSICAL BOX** [ ] [ ]

Jul 68. (lp) *(LBL/LBS 83114E) <LST 7539>* **THE FURTHER ADVENTURES OF CHARLES WESTOVER** [ ] [ ]
– Thinkin' it over / Be my friend / Silver birch / I think I love you / River cool / Colour flashing hair / Gemini / Runnin' on back / Conquer / Been so long / Magical music box / New Orleans (Mardi Gras). *(cd-iss. Aug98 on 'Beat Goes On'+=; BGOCD 402)* – She / Runaway / What's the matter baby / Early in the morning / In my arms again.

Feb 69. (7") *<56070>* **RAINDROPS. / YOU DON'T LOVE ME** [–] [ ]

Stateside Dunhill

Sep 69. (7") *(SS 8025) <4193>* **COMIN' BACK TO ME. / SWEET MARY LOU** [ ] [ ]

Mar 70. (7") *(SS 8040) <4224>* **SISTER ISABELLE. / COLORADO RAIN** [ ] [ ]

U.A. U.A.

Oct 72. (7") *(UP 35460)* **WHAT'S A MATTER, BABY. / EARLY IN THE MORNING** [ ] [–]

May 73. (7") *(UP 35535)* **KELLY. / COOPERSVILLE YODEL** [ ] [–]

Jun 73. (lp) *(UAS 29474) <LA 151>* **LIVE IN ENGLAND (live)** [ ] [ ]
– Hats off to Larry / Handy man / The Swiss maid / Hey! little girl / Little town flirt / Kelly / Crying / Two kinds of teardrops / Coopersville yodel / The answer to everything / Keep searchin' (We'll follow the sun) / What's a matter, baby / So long baby / Runaway. *(re-iss. May82 on 'Fame' lp/c; FA/TCFA 3020)*

Oct 74. (7") *(UP 35740)* **AND THE MUSIC PLAYS ON. / IN MY ARMS AGAIN** [ ] [–]

not iss. Island

1975. (7") *<021>* **TELL HER NO. / RESTLESS** [–] [ ]

1975. (7") *<038>* **CRY BABY CRY. / IN MY ARMS AGAIN** [–] [ ]

—— between 1975-76, he issued Australian 45; OH HOW HAPPY. / THE GHOST. Retired for the rest of the 70's, but returned in the early 80's after a bout of alcoholism. First batch of releases co-produced with TOM PETTY.

Demon Network

Dec 81. (7") *<47951>* **SEA OF LOVE. / MIDNIGHT TRAIN** [–] [33]

Apr 82. (7") *<48006>* **TO LOVE SOMEONE. / LIAR** [–] [ ]

May 83. (lp) *(FIEND 8) <568>* **DROP DOWN AND GET ME** [ ] Dec81 [ ]
– Sea of love / Life without you / Out of time / Sucker for your love / To love someone / Drop down and get me / Maybe tomorrow / Liar / Never stop tryin' / Midnight train. *(UK-version +=)* – Cheap love. *(cd-iss. Jun98 on 'Varese Sarabande'; VAR 5927) (cd re-iss. Nov98 on 'See For Miles'++=; SEECD 6878)* – Help me.

May 83. (7") *(D 1017)* **CHEAP LOVE. / DISTANT GHOST** [ ] [–]

Nov 83. (7") *(D 1019)* **SEA OF LOVE. / HELP ME** [ ] [–]

not iss. Warners

1985. (7") *<29098>* **IN MY ARMS AGAIN. / YOU CAN'T FORGIVE ME** [–] [ ]

1985. (7") *<28853>* **STRANGER ON THE RUN. / WHAT YOU GONNA DO WITH THAT BEAUTIFUL MODY OF YOURS** [–] [ ]

—— after another Australian-only single (WALK AWAY) in 1987, he signed to 'Silvertone' in the UK 1989. Tragically, after more fits of depression, he committed suicide on 8th of February 1990.

Silvertone M.C.A.

Mar 91. (7") *(ORE 24)* **WALK AWAY. / NOBODY'S BUSINESS** [ ] [–]
(cd-s+=) *(ORE 24T)* – Let's dance.

Apr 91. (cd/c/lp) *(ORE CD/MC/LP 514) <10296>* **ROCK ON!** [ ] [ ]
– Walk away / Who left who / Are you lovin' me too / Callin' out my name / I go to pieces / Lost in a memory / I got you / What kind of fool do you think I am? / When I had you / Let's dance. *(re-iss. cd/c Apr94; same)*

Jun 91. (7") *(ORE 26)* **ARE YOU LOVIN' ME TOO. / ONE WOMAN MAN** ☐ –
(cd-s+=) *(ORE 26CDS)* – Who left who.

– (selective) compilations, etc. –

Apr 71. (lp) *Sunset; (SLS 50211)* **TENTH ANNIVERSARY ALBUM** ☐ –
Mar 78. (lp) *Sunset; (SLS 50412)* **AND THE MUSIC PLAYS ON** (unissued lp from 1968) ☐ –
– It's the feeling / Mind over matter / Silently / Cut and come again / My love has gone / Led along / Life is but nothing / And the music plays on / Easy to say, easy to do / Friendly with you / Raindrops / He cheated / Leaving you behind / Runaway '67.
Mar 84. (lp) *Edsel; (XED 121)* **RUNAWAY HITS** ☐ –
(cd-iss. Nov86; EDCD 121)
Apr 86. (lp) *Edsel; (ED 174)* **I GO TO PIECES** ☐ –
(cd-iss. 1990; EDCD 174)
Jul 91. (cd/c) *Connoisseur; (VSOP CD/MC 161)* **LOOKING BACK: HIS BIGGEST HITS** ☐ –
– Runaway / Hats off to Larry / Don't gild the lily / So long baby / The answer to everything / Hey little girl / I don't care anymore / You never talked about me / I won't be there / Ginny in the mirror / cry myself to sleep / Swiss maid / Little town flirt / Two kinds of teardrops / Kelly / Two silhouettes / From me to you / Sue's gonna be mine / That's the way love is / Mary Jane / Handy man / World without love / Do you wanna dance / Keep searchin' / Broken promises / I go to pieces / Stranger in town / Break up / Why don't you tell him / Move it on over.
Aug 91. (cd) *E.M.I.; (CZ 427)* **THE LIBERTY YEARS** ☐ –
Oct 93. (cd) *Charly; (CPCD 8001)* **DEL SHANNON'S GREATEST HITS** ☐ –
(re-iss. Apr02 on 'Snapper'; SNAP 074CD)
Jun 95. (cd) *Beat Goes On; (BGOCD 280)* **LIVE IN ENGLAND / . . .AND THE MUSIC PLAYS ON** ☐ –
Mar 96. (cd) *Beat Goes On; (BGOCD 307)* **THIS IS MY BAG / TOTAL COMMITMENT** ☐ –
Sep 97. (cd) *Beat Goes On; (BGOCD 367)* **RUNAWAY WITH DEL SHANNON / HATS OFF TO DEL SHANNON** ☐ –
Oct 97. (d-cd) *Charly; (COCD 8315-2)* **THE DEFINITIVE COLLECTION** ☐ –
Nov 97. (d) *Music Club; (MCCD 326)* **THIS IS DEL SHANNON** ☐ –
Feb 98. (d-cd) *Raven; (RVCD 51)* **DEL SHANNON 1961-1990 (A COMPLETE ANTHOLOGY)** ☐ –
Feb 98. (cd) *Disky; <(WB 88551-2)>* **THE VERY BEST OF DEL SHANNON** ☐ ☐
Mar 98. (cd) *Beat Goes On; (BGOCD 388)* **LITTLE TOWN FLIRT / HANDY MAN** ☐ –
Aug 98. (cd) *Beat Goes On; (BGOD 404)* **SINGS HANK WILLIAMS / 1,661 SECONDS OF . . .** ☐ –
Nov 98. (d-cd) *Snapper; (SMDCD 197)* **THE DEFINITIVE COLLECTION** (different) ☐ ☐
Jul 01. (cd) *Castle Select; (SELCD 535)* **KEEP SEARCHIN'** ☐ ☐

☐ SHARPE & NUMAN (see under ⇒ NUMAN, Gary)

☐ SHELLAC (see under ⇒ BIG BLACK)

☐ Pete SHELLEY (see under ⇒ BUZZCOCKS)

SIGUR ROS

Formed: Reykjavik, Iceland . . . early 1994 by guitarist and squeaky vocalist JON POR BIRGISSON and GEORG HOLM, later recruiting ORRI PALL DYRASON and keyboardist KJARTAN SVEINSSON. The original 3-piece line-up (consisting of BIRGISSON, HOLM and then drummer AGUST) entered a downtrodden studio and managed to record one track before their shoestring budget expired. The song was sent to 'Smekkleyse' records and was subsequently included on a compilation featuring various other artists signed to the label. The first set 'VON' (1997) was quickly delivered, pointing the road to success for these experimental debutants. At their peak, keyboard and piano player SVEINSSON was added, who arguably became a vehicle for the group's stark, uplifting and eerie sound. From 'VON BRIGOI' (the group's second set, translated: Recycle Bin), 'LEIT AF LIFI' was released as a single in summer 1998. The band had underestimated their widespread acclaim when the single rocketed to the Icelandic No.1 and stayed a further 8 weeks at the top spot! But with the good came the bad: the departure of lifelong friend and original drummer AGUST. This major setback almost put the band's future into jeopardy when they returned to the studio and came to near collapse during the recording sessions of 'AGAETIS BYRJUN' (1999). DYRASON was added to the line-up following a spectacular radio broadcasted show in the Icelandic Opera House. At the same time, SIGUR ROS had struck a deal with London based 'Fat Cat', who issued the 'SVEFN-G-ENGLAR' EP in 1999. In Iceland 'AGAETIS BYRJUN' was doing the same thing to crowds as RADIOHEAD's 'Ok Computer' did when it was released on these shores. Which, in all circumstances, is not hard to see why, since SR had (practically) the same ideals as RADIOHEAD did. Cresendos of earth quaking guitars (that didn't really sound like guitars at all), soft piano and BIRGISSON's uniquely high falsetto vocals that reminisced of the COCTEAU TWINS' 'Baby talk'. Not surprising then that multi-instrumentalists GODSPEED YOU BLACK EMPEROR! invited the 'ROS to join them on tour. The result: The greatest show on earth, quite possibly! After selling more albums in their native Iceland than a certain Ms. SPEARS (this is true!) and regretfully donating 'SVEFN-G-ENGLAR' to Tom Cruise's 'Vanilla Sky' OST, SIGUR ROS engrossed themselves in the mimbars of northern Iceland and recorded the wistful '()' in 2002. Yes, that's right – '()'. Just as The Beatles' eponymous album was christened 'The White Album' by fans, SIGUR ROS's effort became known as 'THE UNTITLED ALBUM', as no information was provided in the album sleeve and all tracks were, well, untitled. If it all sounded a bit pretentious, that's because it was, with BIRGISSON bordering on the line of childishness and pure musical poetry; '()' was an album that could not be ignored. From its grandiose opening, through to the set's middle section and coda, this was really music you could eat. Some of it sounded like GODSPEED, although slowed down to 25rpm, and BIRGISSON's promise of singing in English was missing. However, musically the LP was an elegant and mysterious journey heavily featuring the quartet's scrawled signature of falsetto vocals, eerie organ drones, sparse arrangements, plus a newly added string section to boot. Marvellous!

Album rating: VON (*6) / VON BRIGOI remixes (*5) / AGAETIS BYRJUN (*8) / () (*7)

JON POR BIRGISSON – vocals, guitar / **GEORG HOLM** – bass / **AGUST** – drums

Smekkleysa | not iss.

1997. (cd) *(SM 67CD)* **VON (HOPE)** – Iceland –
– Sigur Ros / Dogun / Hun joro . . . / Leit ao lifi / Myrkur / 18 sekundur fyrir solaruppras / Hafsol / Verold ny og oo / Von / Mistur / Syndir Guos (opinberun frelsarans) / Rukrym.

—— added **KJARTAN SVEINSSON** – keyboards

1998. (cd) *(SM 67CDR)* **VON BRIGOI (RECYCLE BIN)** (remixes/recycled) – Iceland –
– Syndir Guos (by BIOGEN) / Syndir Guos (by MUM) / Leit af lifi (by PLASTMIC) / Myrkur (by ILA) / Myrkur (by DIRTY-BIX) / 180 sekundur fyrir solaruppras (by CURVER) / Hun Joro (by HASSEBRAEOUR) / Von (by GUS GUS) / Leit af lifi (by SIGUR ROS).

—— **ORRI PALL DYRASON** – drums; repl. AGUST

Fat Cat | Play It Again Sam

Oct 99. (12"ep) *(12FAT 036)* **SVEFN-G-ENGLAR EP** ☐ –
– Sven-g-englar / Vioar vel til loftarasa / Verold ny og oo.
(cd-ep) *(CDFAT 036)* – (first two tracks) / Nyjalagio (live) / Syndir Guos (live). *(re-iss. Feb00 & Apr01; same)*

Mar 00. (12"ep/cd-ep) *(12/CD FAT 039)* **NY BATTERI** [ ] [–]
– Rafmagnio buio / Ny battery / Bium bium bambalo / Danarfregnir og Jaroafarir.

Aug 00. (cd/lp) *(FAT CD/LP 11) <1>* **AGAETIS BYRJUN** [52] [ ]
– Into / Svefn-g-englar / Staralfur / Flugufrelsarinn / Ny batteri / Hjartao hamast (bamm bamm bamm) / Vioar vel til lofttarasa / Olsen Olsen / Agaetis byrjun / Avalon. *(issued 1999 in Iceland; SM 79CD)*

— in early 2001, SIGUR ROS collaborated with HILMAR ORN HILMARSSON on the soundtrack of 'ANGELS OF THE UNIVERSE' for 'Krunk' records

Fat Cat M.C.A.

Oct 02. (cd/lp) *(FAT CD/LP 22) <AA88 113091-2>* **()** [49] [ ]
– () (part I) / () (part II) / () (part III) / () (part IV) / () (part V) / () (part VI) / () (part VII) / () (part VIII).

May 03. (10"ep/3"cd-ep) *(10/CD FAT 02)* **()** [72] [–]

SILVERCHAIR

Formed: Newcastle, Australia ... 1992 by schoolmates DANIEL JOHNS, his songwriting partner BEN GILLIES and CHRIS JOANNOU. After winning a national talent contest, SILVERCHAIR were lucky enough to have one of their tracks, 'TOMORROW', playlisted by Australia's foremost "alternative" radio stations. Released as a single in summer 1994, the song scaled the domestic charts, the pubescent schoolboys becoming overnight sensations. A follow-up, 'PURE MASSACRE' repeated the feat, as did their debut album, 'FROGSTOMP', its enjoyable, if cliched grunge/rock stylings proving a massive (Top 10) hit in the States. Finally given a British release in late summer '95, the album squeezed into the Top 50, although it didn't have quite the same impact. Early the following year, their track 'ISRAEL'S SON' was cited by the lawyer of two teenage Americans who were charged with murdering one of their own relatives. The SILVERCHAIR rollercoaster continued early in 1997 with the 'FREAKSHOW' album, a set that once again took its cue from the cream of American alt-rock (i.e. PEARL JAM, STONE TEMPLE PILOTS, etc.) and predictably performed well in the US charts. The lads even began to progress a little further in Britain, the Top 40 album spawning two similarly successful singles, 'FREAK' and 'ABUSE ME'. Returning with a third album, 'NEON BALLROOM' (1999), SILVERCHAIR sold out to the mainstream and bypassed their metallic roots for a more tuneful, string-laden style. However, the record still coined in enough sales for it to dent the US Top 50 (UK Top 30), although the boyz to men development had certainly not worked critically. 2002's 'DIORAMA', on the other hand, suggested they'd used the lengthy break between albums wisely, refining their previously clumsy sound into something altogether more classy and melodic. At least part of that was down to producer Daniel Bottril of course, who created sympathetic space for JOHNS' significantly improved singing and guitar playing, creating a whole that was closer in feel to experimental pop than post-grunge rock. • **Trivia:** Concert pianist, DAVID HELFGOTT (the movie 'Shine' was made about him!), guested on the track, 'EMOTION SICKNESS'.

Album rating: FROGSTOMP (*7) / FREAKSHOW (*5) / NEON BALLROOM (*4) / THE BEST OF SILVERCHAIR, VOL.1 compilation (*6) / DIORAMA (*6)

DANIEL JOHNS – vocals, guitar / **CHRIS JOANNOU** – bass / **BEN GILLIES** – drums

Columbia Columbia

Jul 95. (12") *(662264-6)* **PURE MASSACRE. / STONED** [71] [ ]
(cd-s+=) *(662264-2)* – Acid rain / Blind.

Sep 95. (7"/c-s) *(662395-7/-4)* **TOMORROW. / BLIND (live)** [59] [ ]
(cd-s) *(662395-2)* – ('A'side) / Leave me out (live) / Undecided (live).

Sep 95. (cd/c) *(480340-2/-4) <67247>* **FROGSTOMP** [49] Aug95 [9]
– Israel's son / Tomorrow / Faultline / Pure massacre / Shade / Blind / Leave me out / Suicidal dream / Madman / Undecided / Cicada / Findaway. *(cd re-iss. Aug01; same)*

Feb 97. (cd/c/pic-lp) *(487103-2/-4/-1) <67905>* **FREAKSHOW** [38] [12]
– Slave / Freak / Abuse me / Lie to me / No association / Cemetry / Pop song for us rejects / Door / Learn to hate / Petrol and chlorine / Roses / Nobody came. *(cd re-iss. May02; same)*

Mar 97. (10"/cd-s) *(664076-0/-5)* **FREAK. / SLAVE / (interview)** [34] [ ]
(cd-s) *(664076-2)* – ('A'side) / New race / Punk song #2 / (interview with Daniel, Ben & Chris).

Jul 97. (c-s/cd-s) *(664790-4/-2)* **ABUSE ME / FREAK (Remix for us rejects) / BLIND** [40] [ ]
(cd-s) *(664790-5)* – ('A'side) / Surfin' bird / Slab (Nick Laurnoise mix).

Feb 99. (7") *(667088-7)* **ANTHEM FOR THE YEAR 2000. / MILLENNIUM BUG** [ ] [–]
(cd-s+=) *(667088-2)* – London's burning / (untitled).

Mar 99. (cd/c) *(493309-2/-4) <69816>* **NEON BALLROOM** [29] [50]
– Emotion sickness / Anthem for the year 2000 / Ana's song (open fire) / Spawn again / Miss you love / Dearest helpless / Do you feel the same / Black tangled heart / Point of view / Satin sheets / Paint pastel princess / Steam will rise.

May 99. (7") *(667345-7)* **ANA'S SONG (OPEN FIRE). / ('A'-acoustic)** [45] [–]
(cd-s+=) *(667345-5)* – Trash.
(cd-s) *(667345-2)* – ('A'side) / Anthem for the year 2000 (Paul Mac remix) / London's burning.

Aug 99. (cd-ep) **MISS YOU LOVE / WASTED / FIX ME / MINOR THREAT** [ ] [–]

Nov 00. (d-cd) *(501300-2)* **THE BEST OF SILVERCHAIR, VOL.1** (compilation) [ ] [ ]
– Anthem for the year 2000 / Freak / Ana's song (open fire) / Emotion sickness / Israel's son / Tomorrow / Cemetary / The door / Miss you love / Abuse me / Pure massacre / Untitled / New race / Trash / Ana's song (open fire) (acoustic mix) / Madman (vocal) / Blind / Punk song No.2 / Wasted – Fix me / Minor threat / Freak (remix) / Spawn.

Atlantic Atlantic

Jul 02. (cd) *<(7567 83559-2)>* **DIORAMA** [ ] [91]
– Across the night / The greatest view / Without you / World upon your shoulders / One way mule / Tuna in the brine / Too much of not enough / Luv your life / Lever / My favourite thing / After all these years.

☐ SILVER MT. ZION
(see under ⇒ GODSPEED YOU BLACK EMPEROR!)

☐ Gene SIMMONS (see under ⇒ KISS)

Carly SIMON

Born: 25 Jun'45, New York, New York City, USA. In 1963, CARLY formed folk duo, The SIMON SISTERS along with older sister, LUCY. The pair recorded a few 45's and a children's album on the 'Kapp' label, before branching out on her own in 1966. CARLY subseqently went solo in the early 70's after signing to 'Elektra', an eponymous debut album (in which she worked with film critic, Jacob Brackman) hitting the shops the following year. A Top 30 success as was the follow-up, 'ANTICIPATION' (1971), she went on to work with producer, Richard Perry, beefing up her sound and inspiring both her singing ability and songwriting skills; one of her greatest songs (to this day!) 'YOU'RE SO VAIN' topped the American charts and was apparently about Warren Beaty. This classic transatlantic hit previewed the accompanying chart-topping 'NO SECRETS' album, generally regarded as her finest hour. The striking singer/songwriter married her male counterpart, JAMES TAYLOR, at the height of her fame and the couple were to subsequently hook up on a version of Charlie & Inez Foxx's 'MOCKINGBIRD'; released in 1974 it featured on yet another top selling album, 'HOTCAKES'. Her mid 70's work was much in the mould of the typically slick L.A. sound, although she did excel herself on the classy 'NOBODY DOES IT BETTER' (written by Marvin Hamlisch & Carole Bayer Sager for the Bond film, 'The Spy Who Loved Me') in 1977. More US Top 50 albums were to follow, although only the single, 'JESSE' gave her any notable chart success. It was around this time that her showcase marriage began to hit the rocks. Having separated in '82, she and TAYLOR were divorced the following year, CARLY, like most artists of her generation, losing her way in the unforgiving 80's. Nevertheless, early '87 saw her 'COMING AROUND AGAIN' (from the movie, 'Heartburn' starring Meryl Streep) with her Top 20 hit of the same name, a short-lived revival seeing the similarly-titled album making the US Top 30. Over the ensuing decade, CARLY continued to release the odd album, each selling moderately well and seeing her move further into the adult/contemporary bracket. While 1997's 'FILM NOIR' was, unsurprisingly, inspired by celluloid legends, SIMON took a broader sweep for the 'BEDROOM TAPES' (2000), drawing on not only Gershwin show tunes but the full range of classic American music which presumably inspired her to pick up a pen and a microphone in the first place. • **Covered:** IT KEEPS YOU RUNNING (Doobie Brothers) / DEVOTED TO YOU (Everly Brothers) / WHY (Chic) / etc. She recorded 2 standards/covers albums TORCH and MY ROMANCE. CARLY also collaborated on several numbers.

Album rating: CARLY SIMON (*5) / ANTICIPATION (*6) / NO SECRETS (*7) / HOTCAKES (*6) / PLAYING POSSUM (*5) / THE BEST OF CARLY SIMON compilation (*7) / ANOTHER PASSENGER (*5) / BOYS IN THE TREES (*6) / SPY (*5) / COME UPSTAIRS (*5) / TORCH (*4) / HELLO BIG MAN (*5) / SPOILED GIRL (*4) / COMING AROUND AGAIN (*6) / GREATEST HITS LIVE (*5) / MY ROMANCE (*4) / HAVE YOU SEEN ME LATELY? (*4) / LETTERS NEVER SENT (*5) / CLOUDS IN MY COFFEE boxed-set (*6) / FILM NOIR (*5) / THE VERY BEST OF CARLY SIMON compilation (*7) / THE BEDROOM TAPES (*5) / ANTHOLOGY compilation (*8)

SIMON SISTERS

CARLY & LUCY – dual vocals

London / Kapp

Apr 64. (7") *(HLR 9893) <586>* **WINKIN', BLINKIN' AND NOD. / SO GLAD I'M HERE** [ ] [73]

Aug 65. (7") *(HLR 9984)* **CUDDLEBUG. / NO ONE TO TALK MY TROUBLES TO** [ ] [ ]

— Split in 1966, when LUCY went off to get married. The following year, CARLY moved to France but returned to sign for Albert Grossman management. After dispute with him, she met producer JAC HOLZMAN who signed her to 'Elektra' in 1969.

CARLY SIMON

CARLY – vocals, piano, guitar was augmented by session musicians.

Elektra / Elektra

Apr 71. (lp) *(K 42077) <74082>* **CARLY SIMON** [ ] [30]
– That's the way I've always heard it should be / Alone / One more time / The best thing / Just a sinner / Dan, my fling / Another door / Reunions / Rolling down the hills / The love's still growing. *(quad-lp iss.Apr77) (cd-iss. Jan96; 7559 60672-2)*

May 71. (7") *(K 12232) <45724>* **THAT'S THE WAY I'VE ALWAYS HEARD IT SHOULD BE. / ALONE** [ ] Apr71 [10]

Dec 71. (lp) *(K 42101) <75016>* **ANTICIPATION** [ ] Nov71 [30]
– Anticipation / Legend in your own time / Our first day together / The girl you think you see / Summer's coming around again / Share the end / The garden / Three days / Julie through the glass / I've got to have you. *(cd-iss. Oct89; 960 679-2)*

Dec 71. (7") *<45759>* **ANTICIPATION. / THE GARDEN** [–] [13]

Mar 72. (7") *(K 12043) <45774>* **LEGEND IN YOUR OWN TIME. / JULIE THROUGH THE GLASS** [ ] [50]

Sep 72. (7") **SHARE THE END. / THE GIRL YOU THINK YOU SEE** [–] [ ]

Nov 72. (7") *(K 12077) <45824>* **YOU'RE SO VAIN. / HIS FRIENDS ARE MORE THAN FOND OF ROBIN** [3] [1]

Jan 73. (lp/c) *(K/K4 42127) <75049>* **NO SECRETS** [3] Dec72 [1]
– The right thing to do / The Carter family / You're so vain / His friends are more than fond of Robin / We have no secrets / Embrace me you child / Waited so long / It was so easy / Night owl / When you close your eyes. *(quad-lp Apr77) (cd-iss. Jul93; 7559 60684-2)*

Mar 73. (7") *<45843>* **THE RIGHT THING TO DO. / WE HAVE NO SECRETS** [–] [17]

Mar 73. (7") *(K 12232)* **THE RIGHT THING TO DO. / THE WAY I'VE ALWAYS HEARD IT SHOULD BE** [17] [–]

Jan 74. (7") *(K 12145) <45887>* **HAVEN'T GOT TIME FOR THE PAIN. / MIND ON MY MAN** [ ] May74 [14]

Mar 74. (lp/c) *(K/K4 52005) <1002>* **HOTCAKES** [19] Jan74 [3]
– Just not true / Hotcakes / Misfit / Forever my love / Mockingbird / Grown up / Haven't got time for the pain / Safe and sound / Mind on my man / Think I'm gonna have a baby / Older sister. *(quad-lp iss.Apr77)*

Mar 74. (7"; CARLY SIMON & JAMES TAYLOR) *(K 12134) <45880>* **MOCKINGBIRD. / GROWN UP** [34] Jan74 [5]

May 75. (lp/c) *(K/K4 52020) <1033>* **PLAYING POSSUM** [ ] [10]
– After the storm / Love out on the street / Look me in the eyes / More and more / Slave / Attitude dancing / Waterfall / Sons of summer / Are you ticklish / Playing possum. *(quad-lp iss.Apr77)*

Jun 75. (7") *(K 12178) <45246>* **ATTITUDE DANCING. / ARE YOU TICKLISH** [ ] May75 [21]

Jun 75. (7") *<45248>* **LOOK ME IN THE EYES. / SLAVE** [–] [ ]

Aug 75. (7") *(K 12187) <45263>* **WATERFALL. / AFTER THE STORM** [ ] Jul75 [78]

Oct 75. (7") *<45278>* **MORE AND MORE. / LOVE OUT IN THE STREET** [–] [94]

Dec 75. (lp/c) *(K/K4 52025) <1048>* **THE BEST OF CARLY SIMON** (compilation) [ ] [17]
– That's the way I've always heard it / Should be / The right thing to do / Mockingbird / Legend in our own time / Haven't you got time for the pain / You're so vain / No secrets / Night owl / Anticipation / Attitude dancing. *(cd-iss. 1983; K2 52025) (re-iss. +cd.May91)*

Jun 76. (7") *<45323>* **IT KEEPS YOU RUNNIN'. / LOOK ME IN THE EYES** [–] [46]

Jun 76. (7") *(K 12217)* **IT KEEPS YOU RUNNIN'. / BE WITH ME** [ ] [–]

Jun 76. (lp/c) *(K/K4 52036) <1064>* **ANOTHER PASSENGER** [ ] [29]
– Half a chance / It keeps you runnin' / Fairweather father / Cowtown / He likes to roll / In times when my head / One love stand / Riverboat gambler / Darkness 'til dawn / Dishonesty modesty / Libby / Be with me.

Aug 76. (7") *(K 12237) <45341>* **HALF A CHANCE. / LIBBY** [ ] [ ]

Jul 77. (7") *(K 12261) <45413>* **NOBODY DOES IT BETTER. / AFTER THE STORM** [7] [2]
(above single from the James Bond film 'The Spy Who Loved Me')

Apr 78. (7") *(K 12289) <45477>* **YOU BELONG TO ME. / IN A SMALL MOMENT** [ ] [6]

Apr 78. (lp/c) *(K/K4 52066) <128>* **BOYS IN THE TREES** [ ] [10]
– You belong to me / Boys in the trees / Back down to Earth / Devoted to you / De bat (fly in me face) / Haunting / Tranquillo (melt my heart) / You're the one / In a small moment / One man woman / For old times sake.

Aug 78. (7") *(K 12315)* **TRANQUILLO (MELT MY HEART). / FOR OLD TIMES SAKE** [ ] [–]

Nov 78. (7"; CARLY SIMON & JAMES TAYLOR) *(K 12313) <45506>* **DEVOTED TO YOU. / BOYS IN THE TREES** [ ] Aug78 [36]

Feb 79. (7") *<45544>* **TRANQUILO (MELT MY HEART). / BACK DOWN TO EARTH** [–] [ ]

Jun 79. (lp/c) *(K/K4 52147) <506>* **SPY** [ ] [45]
– Vengeance / We're so close / Just like you do / Coming to get you / Never been gone / Pure sin / Love you by heart / Spy / Memorial day.

Jun 79. (7") *(K 12362) <46051>* **VENGEANCE. / I LOVE YOU BY HEART** [ ] [48]

Aug 79. (7") *(K 12380) <46514>* **SPY. / PURE SIN** [ ] [ ]

Warners / Warners

Jun 80. (7") *(K 17644)* **COME UPSTAIRS. / JAMES** [ ] [–]

Jul 80. (lp/c) *(K/K4 56828) <3443>* **COME UPSTAIRS** [ ] [36]
– Come upstairs / Stardust / Them / Jesse / James / In pain / The three of us in the dark / Take me as I am / The desert.

Nov 80. (7") *(K 17689) <49518>* **JESSE. / STARDUST** [ ] Jul80 [11]

Sep 81. (lp/c) *(K/K4 56935) <3592>* **TORCH** [ ] [50]
– Blue of blue / I'll be around / I got it bad and that ain't good / I get along without you very well / Body and soul / Hurt / Spring is here / Pretty strange / What shall we do with the child / Not a day goes by.

Jan 82. (7") *(K 17898) <49880>* **HURT. / FROM THE HEART** [ ] [ ]

Jul 82. (7") *(K 79300) <4051>* **WHY. / WHY (instrumental)** [10] [74]
(12"+=) *(K 79300T)* – ('A'extended).
(re-iss. Jun89; U 7501/+T) – (hit UK 56)
(above single from the film 'Soup For One' on 'Mirage' records). In Aug'83, she provided the singing part on UK No.17 hit single 'Kissing

With Confidence' by WILL POWERS.

Sep 83. (lp/c) *(923886-1/-4)* *<23886>* **HELLO BIG MAN** [ ] [69]
– You know what to do / Menemsha / Damn you get to me / Is this love / Orpheus / It happens everyday / Such a goody boy / Hello big man / You don't feel the same / Floundering. *(cd-iss. Jul86; 923886-2)*

Sep 83. (7") *<29484>* **YOU KNOW WHAT TO DO. / ORPHEUS** [–] [83]

Feb 84. (7") *<29428>* **HELLO BIG MAN. / DAMN YOU GET TO ME** [–] [ ]

not iss. Planet

1984. (7") **SOMEONE WAITS FOR YOU. / ('A'version)** [–] [ ]

Epic Epic

Jun 85. (7"/12") *(A/TA 6388)* *<05419>* **TIRED OF BEING BLONDE. / BLACK HONEYMOON** [ ] [70]

Aug 85. (lp/c/cd) *(CBS/40/CD 26376)* *<39970>* **SPOILED GIRL** [ ] Jul85 [88]
– My new boyfriend / Come back home / Tonight and forever / Spoiled girl / Tired of being blonde / The wives are in Connecticut / Anyone but me / Interview / Make me feel something / Can't give it up. *(c+=/cd+=)* – Black honeymoon. *(cd re-iss. Jun91)*

Aug 85. (7"/12") *(A/TA 6654)* *<05596>* **MY NEW BOYFRIEND. / THE WIVES ARE IN CONNECTICUT** [ ] [ ]

next 45 was from film 'Heartburn'.

Arista Arista

Jan 87. (7") *(ARIST 687)* *<9525>* **COMING AROUND AGAIN. / ITSY BITSY SPIDER** [12] Oct86 [18]
(12"+=) *(ARIST12 687)* – If it wasn't love.

Apr 87. (7") *(RIS 8)* *<9587>* **GIVE ME ALL NIGHT. / TWO HOT GIRLS (ON A HOT SUMMER'S NIGHT)** [ ] [61]
(12"+=) *(RIST 8)* – Hold what you've got.

Jun 87. (lp/c/cd) *(208/408/258 140)* *<8443>* **COMING AROUND AGAIN** [25] Apr87 [25]
– Coming around again / Give me all night / As time goes by / Do the walls come down / It should have been me / The stuff that dreams are made of / Two hot girls (on a hot summer's night) / You have to hurt / All I want is you / Hold what you've got / Itst bitsy spider. *(re-iss. Nov90 cd/c; 261/411 038)*

Aug 87. (7") *(RIS 33)* *<9619>* **THE STUFF THAT DREAMS ARE MADE OF. / AS TIME GOES BY** [ ] [ ]
(12"+=) *(RIST 33)* – Sleight of hand.

Oct 87. (7") *<9653>* **ALL I WANT IS YOU. / TWO HOT GIRLS (ON A HOT SUMMER NIGHT)** [–] [54]

Nov 87. (7") *(RIS 47)* **ALL I WANT IS YOU. / YOU HAVE TO HURT** [ ] [–]

Sep 88. (lp/c/cd) *(209/409/259 196)* *<8526>* **GREATEST HITS LIVE (live)** [49] [87]
– You're so vain / Nobody does it better / Coming around again / It happen every day / Anticipation / Right thing to do / Do the walls come down / You belong to me / Two hot girls (on a hot summer night) / All I want is you / Never been gone. *(re-iss. cd Oct95)*

Sep 88. (7")<US-c-s> *(111 701)* **YOU'RE SO VAIN (live). / DO THE WALLS COME DOWN (live)** [ ] [ ]
(12"+=/cd-s+=) *(611/661 701)* – Coming around again (live) / Itsy bitsy spider (live).

Nov 88. (7") *(111 807)* **NOBODY DOES IT BETTER (live). / ALL I WANT IS YOU (live)** [ ] [ ]
(12"+=/cd-s+=) *(611/661 807)* – Never been gone (live).

— Below 45 was from the movie, 'Working Girl'.

Feb 89. (7") *<9793>* **LET THE RIVER RUN. / THE TURN OF THE TIDE** [–] [49]

Mar 89. (7"/c-s) *(112 124)* **LET THE RIVER RUN. / CARLOTTA'S HEART** [ ] [–]
(12"+=/cd-s+=) *(612/662 124)* – Medley: Coming around again – Itsy bitsy spider.

Mar 90. (cd/c/lp) *(210/410/260 602)* *<8582>* **MY ROMANCE** [ ] [46]
– My romance / By myself / I see your face / When your lover is gone / In the wee small hours / My funny valentine / Something wonderful / Little girl blue / He was good to me / What has she got / Bewitched / Danny boy / Time after time. *(re-iss. May92 cd/c; 262/412 019)*

Oct 90. (cd/c/lp) *(261/411/211 044)* *<8650>* **HAVE YOU SEEN ME LATELY?** [ ] [60]
– Better not tell her / Didn't I? / Have you seen me lately? / Life is eternal / Waiting at the gate / Happy birthday / Holding me tonight / It's not like him / Don't wrap it up / Fisherman's song / We just got here.

Oct 90. (c-s,cd-s) *<2083>* **BETTER NOT TELL HER. / HAPPY BIRTHDAY** [–] [ ]

Jan 91. (c-s,cd-s) *<2164>* **LIFE IS ETERNAL / WE JUST GOT HERE** [–] [ ]

Nov 94. (cd/c) *<(07822 18752-2/-4)>* **LETTERS NEVER SENT** [ ] [ ]
– (intro) / Letters never sent / Lost in your love / Like a river / Time works on all the wild young men / Touched by the Sun / Davy / Halfway 'round the world / What about a holiday / The reason / Private / Catch it like a fever / Born to break my heart / I'd rather it was you.

Dec 95. (3xcd-box/3xc-boxc) *<(07822 18798-2/-4)>* **CLOUDS IN MY COFFEE** (compilation) [ ] [ ]

Oct 97. (cd/c) *<(07822 18984-2/-4)>* **FILM NOIR** [ ] [84]
– You won't forget me / Ev'rytime we say goodbye / Lili Marlene / Last night when we were young (with JIMMY WEBB) / Spring will be a little late this year / Film noir / Laura / I'm a fool to want you / Fools coda / Two sleepy people (with JOHN TRAVOLTA) / Don't smoke in bed / Somewhere in the night.

Jun 00. (cd) *<(07822 14627-2)>* **THE BEDROOM TAPES** [ ] [90]
– Our affair / So many stars / Big dumb guy / Scar / Cross the river / I forget / Actress / I'm really the kind / We you dearest friends / Whatever became of her / In honor of you (George).

— late in 2001, CARLY was found on JANET JACKSON's hit, 'Son Of A Gun (I Betcha Think This Song Is About You)'

Rhino Rhino

Nov 02. (cd) *<(8122 78166-2)>* **CHRISTMAS IS ALMOST HERE** (festive) [ ] [ ]

– compilations, etc. –

On 'Elektra' unless otherwise mentioned.

Sep 76. (7") *(K 12233)* **YOU'RE SO VAIN. / ANTICIPATION** [ ] [–]
(re-iss. Sep85 on 'Old Gold'; OG 9521)

Sep 76. (7") **MOCKINGBIRD. / LEGEND IN** [ ] [–]

Apr 81. (lp/c) *Hallmark; (SHM/HSC 3062)* **YOU'RE SO VAIN** [ ] [–]

Oct 82. (d-c) **ANTICIPATION / NO SECRETS** [ ] [–]

Dec 82. (7") *Mirage; (CARLY 1)* **COME UPSTAIRS. / JESSE** [ ] [–]
(12"+=) *(CARLY 1T)* – ('A'version).

Apr 91. (7"/c-s) *(EKR 123/+C)* **YOU'RE SO VAIN. / DO THE WALLS COME DOWN** [41] [–]
(12"+=) *(EKR 123T)* – Coming around again / Itsy bitsy spider.
(cd-s) *(EKR 123CD)* – ('A'side) / The girl you think you see / Anticipation.

May 91. (lp/c/cd) *(EKT 86/+C/CD)* **THE BEST OF CARLY SIMON** [ ] [ ]

Mar 99. (cd/c) *Global TV; <(RAD CD/MC 103)>* **THE VERY BEST OF CARLY SIMON** [22] Oct98 [ ]
– You're so vain / Nobody does it better / Why / Coming around again / The right thing to do / We have no secrets / You belong to me / That's the way I've always heard it should be / Mockingbird / Anticipation / Legend in your own time / The street that dreams are made of / All I want is you / Give me all night / Like a river / Better not tell her / Angel from Montgomery / Let the river run.

Jan 03. (d-cd) *Rhino; <(8122 78167-2)>* **ANTHOLOGY** [ ] Nov02 [ ]

□ Paul SIMON (see under ⇒ SIMON & GARFUNKEL)

SIMON AND GARFUNKEL

Formed: New York, USA ... 1957 as TOM & JERRY by ART GARFUNKEL (b. ARTHUR GARFUNKEL, 5 Nov'41, Queens, New York) and PAUL SIMON (b.13 Oct'41, Newark, New Jersey). Though the pair scored their first hit in 1957 with the lightweight rock'n'roll of 'HEY SCHOOLGIRL', it would be almost a decade later before they met with any real success. In the meantime, SIMON released a series of obscure singles under various pseudonyms including TRUE TAYLOR (!) and JERRY LANDIS, wisely opting for a plain and simple PAUL SIMON as his songs began to take on a more folky hue. GARFUNKEL, meanwhile, had gone back to college, although by 1964 the duo had reunited, subsequently signing with 'C.B.S.' and recording a tentative debut album, 'WEDNESDAY MORNING 3 A.M.' The record's dismal sales figures prompted SIMON to return to Europe, where he'd been living the previous year. He duly recorded an eponymous solo album in London, the set featuring many SIMON compositions (including the evocative 'HOMEWARD BOUND', the railway station weighing so heavily on SIMON's homesick heart actually being Widnes in England) which he'd later re-record with GARFUNKEL and which would become mainstays of the S&G repertoire. Back in New York, producer Tom Wilson had taken it upon himself to revamp the acoustic 'SOUND OF SILENCE' (from 'WEDNESDAY . . .') in an electric folk-rock style, de rigeur in 1965. The result was stunning, as powerful and revelatory as the BYRDS' re-working of 'Mr. Tambourine Man', the track storming to the top of the US charts (The BACHELORS subsequently took the track to No.3 in Britain). SIMON returned from Blighty poste-haste, hooking up with GARFUNKEL once again for what would become the most commercially successful period of his career. 'SOUND OF SILENCE' the album was hurriedly released to consolidate the duo's new found fame, a set largely comprising folk-rock reworkings of SIMON's back catalogue and spawning two further US Top 5 hits in the shape of bedsit classic, 'I AM A ROCK' and the aforementioned 'HOMEWARD BOUND', a worldwide smash. 'PARSLEY, SAGE, ROSEMARY & THYME' (1966) polished up the clean-cut harmonies and witnessed SIMON's songwriting develop apace; 'SCARBOROUGH FAIR / CANTICLE' was an inventive attempt to splice two traditional songs, while '7 O'CLOCK NEWS / SILENT NIGHT' fairly effectively overlaid the traditional Christmas carol with bad tidings in the form of a grim newscast. 'FOR EMILY, WHEREVER I MAY FIND HER', meanwhile, arguably ranks as one of SIMON's most emotive and personal performances. The following summer saw SIMON play a major hand in organising the Monterey Pop Festival, SIMON & GARFUNKEL subsequently headlining the first day of the event. The summer of '68, meanwhile, finally saw S&G break big-time in Britain, both with the evergreen pop fizz of 'MRS. ROBINSON' (written as part of the soundtrack which S&G penned for 'The Graduate', a cult flick turned blockbuster starring Dustin Hoffman and Anne Bancroft) and their biggest album to date, 'BOOKENDS'. A transatlantic No.1, the record is still regarded by many as representing the peak of S&G's career, an even more ambitious set then its predecessor, encompassing everything from the autumnal melancholy of 'HAZY SHADE OF WINTER' to the BEATLES-esque 'OLD FRIENDS'. Even greater success was to come though, the duo making rock/pop history in 1970 when 'BRIDGE OVER TROUBLED WATER' simultaneously made the UK and US Top spot in both its single and album format, the latter staying in the UK chart for an incredible 300 weeks. Its title track was the album's main selling point, an epic, exquisitely arranged ballad sung by GARFUNKEL, the song becoming the group's signature tune, even more so than say, 'MRS ROBINSON'. Other highlights included the celebratory 'CECILIA', 'THE BOXER' and the adapted Peruvian folk tune, 'EL CONDOR PASA'. GARFUNKEL was dissatisfied, however, both with the direction in which SIMON was steering the group and the fact that the latter dominated the songwriting front. At the peak of their fame, then, S&G disbanded, creating a legend in their wake. While GARFUNKEL concentrated on acting, SIMON continued with the solo career he'd begun in 1965, scoring almost immediately with the buoyant pop-reggae of 'MOTHER AND CHILD REUNION', a transatlantic Top 5 hit single in early 1972. The track was released the same month as the album, his second effort to bear an eponymous title and a UK No.1 to boot. Widely acclaimed, the record proved conclusively that SIMON could fashion his own distinct musical identity, experimenting with an array of musical styles on the likes of 'ME AND JULIO DOWN BY THE SCHOOLYARD' and 'DUNCAN'. 'THERE GOES RHYMIN' SIMON' (1973) and the Grammy Award-winning 'STILL CRAZY AFTER ALL THESE YEARS' (1975) were even more successful, if more overtly commercial, the latter featuring a rare duet with GARFUNKEL, 'MY LITTLE TOWN'. SIMON suffered a critical roasting, however, with 'ONE TRICK PONY' (1980), the ambitious soundtrack to his flop film of the same name. Reuniting briefly with GARFUNKEL in 1981, the pair gave a hugely popular free concert in New York's Central Park (released as a double album the following year), although a mooted studio project was abandoned. Left to his own devices, SIMON came up 'HEARTS AND BONES' (1983), a patchy effort which nevertheless included some of SIMON's most affecting material. With 'GRACELAND' (1986), the singer/songwriter changed tack again, looking to African rhythms and musicians for inspiration. The result was a highly infectious, exotic fusion of SIMON's innate feel for pop melody and traditional African sounds, recorded in collaboration with the likes of LADYSMITH BLACK MAMBAZO. Despite the initial fuss over SIMON's supposed breach of the anti-apartheid cultural boycott (through recording and touring the album in South Africa), the groundbreaking charm of tracks like 'THE BOY IN THE BUBBLE', 'DIAMONDS ON THE SOLES OF HER SHOES' and 'YOU CAN CALL ME AL' was eventually recognised when the album won a Grammy. The record also resurrected SIMON's UK career, making No.1, as did the follow-up, 'THE RHYTHM OF THE SAINTS' (1990), a similar project, constructed around compelling Brazilian percussion. More recently, SIMON has been working on 'SONGS FROM THE CAPEMAN', a concept project based on the life of Salvador Agron, a Puerto Rican criminal turned writer. Working with Nobel-prize winning poet/playwright, Derek Walcott, the album was one of SIMON's most ambitious recordings to date. Unfortunately for SIMON, the effort he put into 'SONGS FROM THE CAPEMAN' went largely unrewarded and come the new millennium he went back to basics with his first studio set in ten years, 'YOU'RE THE ONE' (2000). Together with veteran but youthful sounding musical accomplices BAKITHI KUMALO, VINCENT NGUINI and STEVE GADD, SIMON crafted a cerebral yet spontaneous album which inherited the rich rhythmic grace of his past work while simultaneously showcasing his insight, intelligence and lightness of touch as a singer/songwriter. On the other end of the musical scale, ART GARFUNKEL balanced his acting work with a recording career, releasing a string of albums throughout the 70's and 80's, 'ANGEL CLARE' (1973) and 'BREAKAWAY' (1975) being the most successful, the latter featuring a fine cover of Stevie Wonder's 'I BELIEVE (WHEN I FALL IN LOVE IT WILL BE FOREVER)'. The angelic voiced singer was at his best performing other people's material, his most famous hit coming in early '79 with the poignant 'BRIGHT EYES' (penned by none other than Wombling free MIKE BATT), the theme tune from animated film, 'Watership Down'. Chart success eluded GARFUNKEL in the 80's although he continued to record for 'Columbia', releasing an album, 'UP UNTIL NOW' (1993), duetting on one track with JAMES TAYLOR. Following the live 'ACROSS AMERICA' (1996), GARFUNKEL hooked up with Nashville singer/songwriter BUDDY MONDLOCK for 2002's 'EVERYTHING WAITS TO BE NOTICED'. If it was a nifty title, then the writing (a fair part of it by ART himself) and performing within was none too shabby either, SIMON's former foil showcasing some of his most engaging work for many a year.

• **Covered:** THE TIMES THEY ARE A-CHANGIN' (Bob Dylan) / BYE BYE LOVE (Everly Brothers). PAUL SIMON covered GO TELL IT TO THE MOUNTAIN (trad). GARFUNKEL covered loads including ALL I KNOW (Jimmy Webb) / SECOND AVENUE (Tim Moore) / BREAKAWAY (Gallagher & Lyle) / I ONLY HAVE EYES FOR YOU (Flamingos) / WONDERFUL WORLD (Sam Cooke) / SINCE I DON'T HAVE YOU (Skyliners) / SO MUCH IN LOVE (Tymes) / MISS YOU NIGHTS (Cliff Richard) / WHEN A MAN LOVES A WOMAN (Percy Sledge) / RAG DOLL (Four Seasons) / etc. • **ART's filmography:** CATCH 22 (1970 with Alan Arkin) / CARNAL KNOWLEDGE (1971 w/ Ann-Margret, Candice Bergen & Jack Nicholson) / BAD TIMING (1979 w/ Teresa Russell) / ILLUSIONS (1980) / GOOD TO GO (1986) / MOTHER GOOSE ROCK'N'RHYME (1989 TV Disney musical with PAUL). Note PAUL cameod in the 1977 Woody Allen film 'Annie Hall'. • **Trivia:** PAUL's video for the 1986 single, 'YOU CAN CALL ME AL', featured comic actor Chevy Chase.

Album rating: WEDNESDAY MORNING 3 A.M. (*6) / SOUNDS OF SILENCE (*7) / PARSLEY, SAGE, ROSEMARY & THYME (*7) / THE GRADUATE soundtrack (*5) / BOOKENDS (*8) / BRIDGE OVER TROUBLED WATER (*9) / SIMON AND GARFUNKEL'S GREATEST HITS compilation (*10) / THE CONCERT IN CENTRAL PARK (*7) / THE DEFINITIVE SIMON AND GARFUNKEL compilation (*10) / THE ESSENTIAL . . . compilation (*8) / Paul Simon:- THE PAUL SIMON SONGBOOK (*6) / PAUL SIMON (*8) / THERE GOES RHYMIN' SIMON (*7) / LIVE RHYMIN' (*5) / STILL CRAZY AFTER ALL THESE YEARS (*8) / GREATEST HITS, ETC compilation (*7) / ONE-TRICK PONY (*5) / HEARTS AND BONES (*4) / GRACELAND (*8) / NEGOTIATIONS AND LOVE SONGS 1971-1986 compilation (*8) / THE RHYTHM OF THE SAINTS (*7) / PAUL SIMON'S CONCERT IN THE PARK (*7) / 1964-1993 boxed set (*6) / SONGS FROM THE CAPEMAN (*4) / YOU'RE THE ONE (*5) / Art Garfunkel: ANGEL CLARE (*7) / BREAKAWAY (*6) / WATERMARK (*5) / FATE FOR BREAKFAST (*4) / SCISSORS CUT (*4) / LEFTY (*4) / THE ART GARFUNKEL ALBUM compilation (*6) / UP 'TIL NOW (*4) / THE VERY BEST OF – ACROSS AMERICA (*4) / SONGS FROM A PARENT TO A CHILD (*5)

TOM AND JERRY

TOM = ART GARFUNKEL / JERRY = PAUL SIMON

Gala / Big

Dec 57. (7") *<613>* **HEY! SCHOOLGIRL. / DANCIN' WILD** [–] [49]
<US re-iss. 1960 on 'King'; 5167>

1958. (7") *<616>* **OUR SONG. / TWO TEENAGERS** [–] [ ]

1958. (7") *<618>* **DON'T SAY GOODBYE. / THAT'S MY STORY** [–] [ ]
<US re-iss. 1959 on 'Hunt' & flipped over; 319>

1959. (7") *<621>* **BABY TALK. / TWO TEENAGERS** [–] [ ]
<US re-iss. 1971 on 'Bell' w/ diff.B-side by RONNIE LAWRENCE; 120>

1959. (7") *(GSP 806) BABY TALK. / (b-side by PAUL SHELDON)* [ ] [–]

Pye Int. / Ember

May 63. (7") *(7N 25202) <1094>* **I'M LONESOME. / LOOKING AT YOU** [ ] 1962 [ ]

not iss. / ABC Para..

1962. (7") *<10363>* **SURRENDER, PLEASE SURRENDER. / FIGHTING MAD** [–] [ ]

1966. (7") *<10788>* **THAT'S MY STORY. / TIA-JUANA BLUES** [–] [ ]

– PAUL SIMON under pseudonyms –

TRUE TAYLOR

not iss. / Big

1958. (7") *<614>* **TRUE OR FALSE. / TEENAGE FOOL** [–] [ ]

JERRY LANDIS

not iss. / M.G.M.

1959. (7") *<12822>* **ANNA BELLE. / LONELINESS** [–] [ ]

not iss. / Warwick

1959. (7") *<522>* **SWANEE. / TOOT, TOOT TOOTSIE GOODBYE** [–] [ ]

1960. (7") *<552>* **SHY. / JUST A BOY** [–] [ ]

1960. (7") *<588>* **ID LIKE TO BE THE LIPSTICK ON YOUR COLLAR. / JUST A BOY** [–] [ ]

1961. (7") *<619>* **PLAY ME A SAD SONG. / IT MEANS A LOT TO THEM** [–] [ ]

not iss. / Canadian A

1961. (7") *<130>* **I'M LONELY. / I WISH I WEREN'T IN LOVE** [–] [ ]

not iss. / Amy

Dec 62. (7") *<875>* **THE LONE TEEN RANGER. / LISA** [–] [97]
<re-iss. 1963 on 'Jason Scott'; 2>

Oriole / Tribute

May 64. (7"; in US- by PAUL KANE) *(CB 1930 <128>* **CARLOS DOMINGUEZ. / HE WAS MY BROTHER** [ ] [ ]

TICO & THE TRIUMPHS

not iss. / Madison

Dec 61. (7") *<169>* **MOTORCYCLE. / I DON'T BELIEVE THEM** [–] [ ]
<re-iss. Dec61 on 'Amy'; 835> <hit US No.99>

not iss. / Amy

1962. (7") *<845>* **EXPRESS TRAIN. / WILDFLOWER** [–] [ ]

1962. (7") *<860>* **CRY, LITTLE BOY, CRY. / GET UP & DO THE WONDER** [–] [ ]

Feb 63. (7"; by TICO) *<876>* **CARDS OF LOVE. / NOISE** [–] [ ]

ARTIE GARR

pseudonym of ART GARFUNKEL

not iss. / Warwick

1959. (7") *<515>* **DREAM ALONE. / BEAT LOVE** [–] [ ]

not iss. / Octavia

1960. (7") *<8002>* **PRIVATE WORLD. / FORGIVE ME** [–] [ ]

PAUL SIMON

released solo below.

C.B.S. / Columbia

May 65. (lp) *<62579>* **THE PAUL SIMON SONGBOOK** [ ] [ ]
– I am a rock / Leaves that are green / A church is burning / April come she will / The sound of silence / Patterns / A most peculiar man / He was my brother / Kathy's song / The side of a hill / A simple desultory Philippic / Flowers never bend with the rainfall. *(cd-iss. Jan88)*

Jul 65. (7") *(201797)* **I AM A ROCK. / LEAVES THAT ARE GREEN** [ ] [ ]

SIMON AND GARFUNKEL

both vocals, acoustic guitar

C.B.S. / Columbia

Oct 64. (lp) *<9049>* **WEDNESDAY MORNING 3 A.M.** [–] [ ]
– You can tell the world / Last night I had the strangest dream / Bleecker Street / Sparrow / Benedictus / The sound of silence / He was my brother / Peggy-O / Go tell it to the mountain / The sun is burning / The times they are a-changin' / Wednesday morning 3 a.m. *(US re-dist.Jan66, hit No.30) (UK-iss.Nov68; 63370)* – hit No.24. *(re-iss. Nov85 lp/c; CBS/40 32575) (cd-iss. Dec85; CD 63370)*

Jul 65. (7"ep) *(EP 6053)* **SIMON AND GARFUNKEL** [ ] [ ]
– Bleecker Street / Sparrow / Wednesday morning 3 a.m. / The sound of
silence.

Dec 65. (7") *(201977) <43396>* **THE SOUND OF SILENCE. / WE'VE GOT A GROOVY THING GOIN'** [ ] Nov65 [1]

Mar 66. (lp) *(BPG 62690) <9269>* **SOUND OF SILENCE** [13] Feb66 [21]
– The sound of silence / Leaves that are green / Blessed / Kathy's song / Somewhere they can't find me / Anji / Homeward bound / Richard Cory / A most peculiar man / April come she will / We've got a groovy thing goin' / I am a rock. *(re-iss. Mar81 lp/c; CBS/40 32020) (cd-iss. Dec85; CD 62690)*

Mar 66. (7") *(202045) <43511>* **HOMEWARD BOUND. / LEAVES THAT ARE GREEN** [9] Feb66 [5]

Jun 66. (7") *(202303) <43617>* **I AM A ROCK. / FLOWERS NEVER BEND WITH THE RAINFALL** [17] May66 [3]
(7"ep+=) *(EP 6074)* – The sound of silence / Blessed.

Sep 66. (7") *(202285) <43728>* **THE DANGLING CONVERSATION. / THE BIG BRIGHT GREEN PLEASURE MACHINE** — Aug66 25

Oct 66. (lp) *(BPG 62860) <9363>* **PARSLEY, SAGE, ROSEMARY & THYME** — 4
– Dangling conversation / Scarborough fair – Canticle / Patterns / For Emily, whenever I may find her / The big bright green pleasure machine / A poem on the underground all / Cloudy / A simple desultory Philippic (or how I was Robert McNamara'd into submission) / The 59th Street Bridge song (feelin' groovy) / Flowers never bend with the rainfall / 7 o'clock news – Silent night / Parsley, sage, Rosemary and thyme. *(UK re-dist.Aug68, hit No.13) (re-iss. Mar81 lp/c; CBS/40 32031) (cd-iss. Jul87; CD 62825) (cd re-iss. Apr89; CD 32031)*

Nov 66. (7") *(202378) <43873>* **A HAZY SHADE OF WINTER. / FOR EMILY, WHENEVER I MAY FIND HER** — 13

Mar 67. (7") *(202608) <44046>* **AT THE ZOO. / THE 59th STREET BRIDGE SONG (FEELIN' GROOVY)** — 16

Jun 67. (7"ep) *(EP 6360)* **FEELIN' GROOVY** — –
– The 59th Street bridge song (feelin' groovy) / The big bright green pleasure machine / A hazy shade of winter / Homeward bound.

Aug 67. (7") *(2911) <44232>* **FAKIN' IT. / YOU DON'T KNOW WHERE YOUR INTEREST LIES** — Jul67 23

Mar 68. (7") *(3317) <44465>* **SCARBOROUGH FAIR; CANTICLE. / APRIL COME SHE WILL** — Feb68 11

Jul 68. (7") *(3443) <44511>* **MRS. ROBINSON. / OLD FRIENDS; BOOKENDS** 4 Apr68 1

Jul 68. (lp) *(BPG 63101) <9529>* **BOOKENDS** 1 May 68 1
– Bookends theme / Save the life of my child / America / Overs / (voices of old people) – Old friends / Bookends / Fakin' it / Punky's dilemma / Mrs. Robinson / A hazy shade of winter / At the zoo. *(re-iss. Nov82 lp/c; CBS/40 32073) (cd-iss. Dec85; CD 63101)*

Oct 68. (lp) *(BPG 70042)<3180>* **THE GRADUATE (Film Soundtrack; with tracks by DAVE GRUISIN *)** 3 Mar68 1
– The sound of silence / The singleman party foxtrot * / On the strip * / Sunporch cha-cha-cha * / Mrs.Robinson / A great effect * / Scarborough fair – Canticle / April come she will / Whew * / The folks * / The big bright green pleasure machine. *(re-iss. Feb84 lp/c; CBS/40 32359) (cd-iss. Dec85; CD 70042) (cd re-iss. Apr89; CD 32359) (cd-iss. Apr91 on 'Sequel';) (re-iss. Feb94 on 'Columbia' cd/c; CD/40 32359)*

Dec 68. (7"ep) *(EP 6400)* **MRS. ROBINSON** 9 –
– Mrs.Robinson / April come she will / Scarborough fair – Canticle / The sound of silence.

Apr 69. (7") *(4162) <44785>* **THE BOXER. / BABY DRIVER** 6 7

Feb 70. (7") *(4790) <45079>* **BRIDGE OVER TROUBLED WATER. / KEEP THE CUSTOMER SATISFIED** 1 1
(re-iss. Feb78 + Jul84; CBS 4596)

Feb 70. (lp) *(63699) <9914>* **BRIDGE OVER TROUBLED WATER** 1 1
– Bridge over troubled water / El Condor Pasa / Cecilia / Keep the customer satisfied / So long, Frank Lloyd Wright / The boxer / Baby driver / The only living boy in New York / Why don't you write me / Bye bye love / Song for the asking. *(re-iss. on quad 1974; CQ 30995) (cd-iss. Dec82; CD 63699) (re-iss. Sep93 cd/c; 462488-2/-4) (cd re-iss. Dec95 on 'Columbia'; 480418-2)*

Apr 70. (7") *(4916) <45133>* **CECILIA. / THE ONLY LIVING BOY IN NEW YORK** — 4

Sep 70. (7") *<45237>* **EL CONDOR PASA. / WHY DON'T YOU WRITE ME** – 18

—— Both went solo, after ART wanted to concentrate on acting career.

– (selective) compilations, etc. –

Note; Released on 'CBS/ Columbia' unless otherwise mentioned

Jul 72. (lp/c) *(CBS/40 69003) <31350>* **SIMON AND GARFUNKEL'S GREATEST HITS** 2 Jun72 5
– Mrs.Robinson / For Emily, wherever I may find her / The boxer / Feelin' groovy / The sound of silence / I am a rock / Scarborough fair (Canticle) / Homeward bound / Bridge over troubled water / America / Kathy's song / If I could / Bookends / Cecilia. *(cd-iss. Mar87; CD 69003)*

Sep 72. (7") *(8336) <45663>* **AMERICA. / FOR EMILY, WHENEVER I MAY FIND HER** 25 97 / 53

Nov 81. (lp/c) *(CBS/40 24005)* **THE SIMON AND GARFUNKEL COLLECTION** 4 –
– I am a rock / Homeward bound / America / 59th Street Bridge song / Wednesday morning 3 a.m. / El condor pasa / At the Zoo / Scarborough fair (Canticle) / The boxer / The sound of silence / Mrs.Robinson / Keep the customer satisfied / Song for the asking / Hazy shade of winter / Cecilia / Old friends / Bookends / Bridge over troubled water. *(cd-iss. Apr85 + 1988; CD 24005)*

—— SIMON AND GARFUNKEL re-united for one-off concert 20 Dec'81.

Geffen Warners

Mar 82. (d-lp/d-c) *(GEF/40 96008) <3654>* **THE CONCERT IN CENTRAL PARK (live)** 6 6
– Mrs. Robinson / Homeward bound / America / Scarborough fair / Me and Julio down by the schoolyard / Wake up little Susie / April come she will / Slip slidin' away / Still crazy after all these years / American tune / 50 ways to leave your lover / Late in the evening / Bridge over troubled water / A heart in New York / The 59th Street bridge song (feelin' groovy) / The sound of silence / Kodachrome / Old friends: bookends / Maybellene / The boxer. *(re-iss. May88 lp/c/cd; GEF/40/CD 96008)*

Mar 82. (7") *(GEF 2287)* **WAKE UP LITTLE SUSIE (live). / THE BOXER (live)** — –

Mar 82. (7") *<50053>* **WAKE UP LITTLE SUSIE (live). / ME AND JULIO DOWN BY THE SCHOOLYARD (live)** – 27

1988. (cd) *(CDSG 241)* **BRIDGE OVER TROUBLED WATER / PARSLEY, SAGE, ROSEMARY & THYME**

Nov 91. (7"/c-s/cd-s) *(657 653-7/-4/-2)* **A HAZY SHADE OF WINTER. / SILENT NIGHT – SEVEN O'CLOCK NEWS (Medley)** 30

Nov 91. (lp/c/cd) *Sony-Columbia; (MOOD/+C/D 21)* **THE DEFINITIVE SIMON & GARFUNKEL** 8
– Wednesday morning 3 a.m. / The sound of silence / Homeward bound / Cathy's song / I am a rock / For Emily wherever I may find her / Scarborough fair (canticle) / The 59th Street bridge song (feelin' groovy) / Seven o'clock news – Silent night / A hazy shade of winter / El Condor pasa (If I could) / Mrs.Robinson / America / At the zoo / Old friends / Bookends theme / Cecilia / The boxer / Bridge over troubled water / Song for the asking. *(hit UK No.12 in Aug'97)*

Feb 92. (7") *Sony-Columbia; (657 806-7)* **THE BOXER. / CECILIA** 75 –
(cd-ep+=/cd-ep+=) *(657 806-2/-5)* – The only living boy in New York.

Aug 92. (2xcd-box) *(465212-2)* **PARSLEY, SAGE, ROSEMARY & THYME / BOOKENDS**

Oct 96. (3xcd-box) *(485324-2)* **BRIDGE OVER TROUBLED WATER / SOUNDS OF SILENCE / THE GRADUATE** — –

Jan 00. (d-cd/d-c) *Sony TV; (SONYTV 81 CD/MC)* **TALES FROM NEW YORK – THE VERY BEST OF SIMON & GARFUNKEL** 9 –

Nov 03. (d-cd) *Sony TV; (513470-2) / Columbia; <90716>* **THE ESSENTIAL SIMON AND GARFUNKEL** <US track listing> 25 Oct03 27
– Wednesday morning, 3 a.m. (live) / Bleecker Street / The sound of silence / Leaves that are green (live) / A most peculiar man (live) / I am a rock / Richard Cory / Kathy's song / Scarborough fair – Canticle / Homeward bound / Sparrow (live) / The 59th Street Bridge song (feelin' groovy) / The dangling conversation / A poem on the underground wall (live) / A hazy shade of winter / At the zoo / Mrs. Robinson / Fakin' it / Old friends / Bookends theme / America / Overs (live) / El condor pasa (If I could) / Bridge over troubled water / Cecilia / Keep the customer satisfied / So long, Frank Lloyd Wright / The boxer / Baby driver / The only living boy in New York / Song for the asking / For Emily, whenever I may find her / My little town.

PAUL SIMON

(solo with session people)

C.B.S. Columbia

Feb 72. (7") *(7793) <45547>* **MOTHER AND CHILD REUNION. / PARANOIA BLUES** 5 4

Feb 72. (lp/c) *(CBS/40 69007) <30750>* **PAUL SIMON** 1 4
– Mother and child reunion / Duncan / Everything put together falls apart / Run that body down / Armistice day / Me and Julio down by the schoolyard / Peace like a river / Papa hobo / Hobo's blues / Paranoia blues / Congratulations. *(re-iss. 1974 on quad; CQ 30750) (re-iss. Dec87 on 'WEA' lp/c/cd; 925588-1/-4/-2)*

Apr 72. (7") *(7264) <45585>* **ME AND JULIO DOWN BY THE SCHOOLYARD. / CONGRATULATIONS** 15 22

Jul 72. (7") *<45638>* **DUNCAN. / RUN THAT BODY DOWN** – 52

May 73. (lp/c) *(CBS/40 69035) <32280>* **THERE GOES RHYMIN' SIMON** 4 2
– Kodachrome / Tenderness / Take me to the Mardi Gras / Something so right / One man's ceiling is another man's floor / American tune / Was a sunny day / Learn how to fall / St. Judy's comet / Loves me like

a rock. *(re-iss. 1974 on quad; CQ 32280) (re-iss. Dec87 on 'WEA' lp/c/cd; 925589-1/-4/-2)*

May 73. (7") *<45859>* **KODACHROME. / TENDERNESS** [–] [2]

May 73. (7") *(1578)* **TAKE ME TO THE MARDI GRAS. / KODACHROME** [7] [–]

Sep 73. (7") *(1700) <45907>* **LOVES ME LIKE A ROCK. / LEARN HOW TO FALL** [39] Aug73 [2]

Feb 74. (7") *(1979) <45900>* **AMERICAN TUNE. / ONE MAN'S CEILING IS ANOTHER MAN'S FLOOR** [ ] Nov73 [35]

— Below in concert with URUBOMBA and The JESE DIXON SINGERS.

Mar 74. (lp/c) *(CBS/40 69059) <32855>* **PAUL SIMON IN CONCERT / LIVE RHYMIN' (live)** [ ] [33]
– Jesus is the answer / The boxer / Duncan / El Condor pasa (if I could) / Me and Julio down by the schoolyard / American tune / Homeward bound / America / Mother and child reunion / Loves me like a rock / Bridge over troubled water / The sound of silence. *(re-iss. Dec87 on 'WEA' lp/c/cd; 925590-1/-4/-2)*

May 74. (7") *(2349) <46038>* **THE SOUND OF SILENCE (live). / MOTHER AND CHILD REUNION (live)** [ ] [ ]

Nov 74. (7") *(2822)* **SOMETHING SO RIGHT. / TENDERNESS** [ ] [ ]

Aug 75. (7") *<10197>* **GONE AT LAST (w/ PHOEBE SNOW). / TAKE ME TO THE MARDI GRAS** [–] [23]

Oct 75. (7"; PAUL SIMON & PHOEBE SNOW with The JESSE DIXON SINGERS) *(3594)* **GONE AT LAST. / TENDERNESS** [ ] [–]

Oct 75. (lp/c) *(CBS/40 86001) <33540>* **STILL CRAZY AFTER ALL THESE YEARS** [6] [1]
– Still crazy after all these years / My little town / I do it all for love / 50 ways to leave your lover / Night game / Gone at last / Some folks lives roll easy / Have a good time / You're kind / Silent eyes. *(re-iss. 1976 on quad; Q 86001) (cd-iss. Dec85; CD 86001) (re-iss. Dec87 on 'WEA' lp/c/cd; 925591-1/-4/-2)*

Oct 75. (7"; SIMON & GARFUNKEL) *<10230>* **MY LITTLE TOWN. / Art Garfunkel: RAG DOLL** [–] [9]

Nov 75. (7"m; SIMON & GARFUNKEL) *(3712)* **MY LITTLE TOWN. / Art Garfunkel: RAG DOLL / YOU'RE KIND** [ ] [–]

Dec 75. (7") *(3887) <10270>* **50 WAYS TO LEAVE YOUR LOVER. / SOME FOLKS LIVES ROLL EASY** [23] [1]

Apr 76. (7") *<10332>* **STILL CRAZY AFTER ALL THESE YEARS. / I DO IT FOR YOUR LOVE** [–] [40]

Apr 76. (7") *(4188)* **STILL CRAZY AFTER ALL THESE YEARS. / SILENT EYES** [ ] [–]

Nov 77. (7") *(5770) <10630>* **SLIP SLIDIN' AWAY. / SOMETHING SO RIGHT** [36] Oct77 [5]

Nov 77. (lp/c) *(CBS/40 10007) <35032>* **GREATEST HITS, ETC.** (part compilation) [6] [18]
– Slip slidin' away / Stranded in a limousine / Still crazy after all these years / Have a good time / Duncan / Me and Julio down by the schoolyard / Something so right / Kodachrome / I do it for your love / 50 ways to leave your lover / American tune / Mother and child reunion / Loves me like a rock / Take me to the Mardi Gras. *(re-iss. Nov86 lp/c; 450166-1/-4) (cd-iss. Mar87; CD 69003)*

— See ART GARFUNKEL discography further on for other single

May 78. (7") *(6290) <10711>* **STRANDED IN A LIMOSINE. / HAVE A GOOD TIME** [ ] [ ]

Warners Warners

Aug 80. (lp/c) *(K/K4 56846) <3472>* **ONE-TRICK PONY** [17] [12]
– Late in the evening / That's why God made the movies / One-trick pony / How the heart approaches what it yearns / Oh, Marion / Ace in the hole / Nobody / God bless the absentee / Jonah / Long, long day. *(cd-iss. 1987; K2 56846)*

Aug 80. (7") *(K 17666) <49511>* **LATE IN THE EVENING. / HOW THE HEART APPROACHES WHAT IT YEARNS** [58] [6]

Nov 80. (7") *(K 17715) <49601>* **ONE TRICK PONY. / LONG, LONG DAY** [ ] Oct80 [40]

Jan 81. (7") *(K 17745) <49675>* **OH, MARION. / GOD BLESS THE ABSENTEE** [ ] [ ]

— See ART GARFUNKEL discography again for duet A HEART IN NEW YORK single

— Early '83, PAUL collaborated with RANDY NEWMAN on US No.51 single THE BLUES

Nov 83. (lp/c/cd) *(923942-1/-4/-2) <23942>* **HEARTS AND BONES** [34] [35]
– Allergies / Hearts and bones / When numbers get serious / Think too much (part 1) / Song about the Moon / Think too much (part 2) / Train in the distance / Renee and Georgette Margritte with the dog after the war / Cars are cars / The late great Johnny Ace.

Nov 83. (7") *(W 9453) <29453>* **ALLERGIES. / THINK TOO MUCH** [ ] [44]

Feb 84. (7") *<29333>* **SONG ABOUT THE MOON. / THINK TOO MUCH** [–] [ ]

Aug 86. (7")(12") *(W 8667) <28667>* **YOU CAN CALL ME AL. / GUMBOOTS** [4] [44]
<re-iss. Mar87 US, hit No.23>

Sep 86. (lp/c)(cd) *(WX 52/+C)(925477-2) <25447>* **GRACELAND** [1] [3]
– The boy in the bubble / Graceland / I know what I know / Gumboots / Diamonds on the sole of her shoes / You can call me Al / Under African skies / Homeless / Crazy love Vol.2 / That was your mother / All around the world of the myth of fingerprints.

Nov 86. (7") *(W 8509)* **THE BOY IN THE BUBBLE. / ('A'remix)** [33] [–]
(12"+=) *(W 8509T)* – Hearts and bones.

Dec 86. (7") *<28522>* **GRACELAND. / HEARTS AND BONES** [–] [81]
(re-iss. US 1988)

Feb 87. (7") *<28460>* **THE BOY IN THE BUBBLE. / CRAZY LOVE VOL. 2** [–] [86]

Apr 87. (7"/12") *() <28389>* **DIAMONDS ON THE SOLES OF HER SHOES. / ALL AROUND THE WORLD OF THE MYTH OF FINGERPRINTS** [–] [ ]

Apr 87. (7") *(W 8349)* **GRACELAND. / CRAZY LOVE VOL.2** [ ] [–]
(12"+=) *(W 8349T)* – The late great Johny Ace.

Aug 87. (7") *(W 8221) <28221>* **UNDER AFRICAN SKIES. / I KNOW WHAT I KNOW** [ ] [ ]
(12"+=) *(W 8221T)* – Homeless. (above w/LINDA RONSTADT)

Oct 90. (7") *(W 9549) <19549>* **THE OBVIOUS CHILD. / THE RHYTHM OF THE SAINTS** [15] [92]
(12"+=) *(W 9549T)* – You can call me Al.
(cd-s++=) *(W 9549CD)* – The boy in the bubble.

Oct 90. (cd)(lp/c) *<(9 26098-2)>(WX 340/+C)* **THE RHYTHM OF THE SAINTS** [1] [4]
– The obvious child / Can't run but / The coast / Proof / Further to fly / She moves on / Born at the right time / The cool cool river / Spirit voices / The rhythm of the saints.

Feb 91. (7") *(W 0003)* **PROOF. / THE OBVIOUS CHILD** [ ] [–]
(12"/cd-s) *(W 0003 T/CD)* – ('A'side) / The cool cool river / American tune.

Apr 91. (7") *(W 0026)* **BORN AT THE RIGHT TIME. / FURTHER TO FLY** [ ] [–]
(12"+=) *(W 0026T)* – You can call me Al.
(cd-s++=) *(W 0026CD)* – Me and Julio down by the schoolyard / 50 ways to leave your lover.

Nov 91. (cd)(d-lp/c) *<(9 26737-2)>(WX 448/+C)* **THE CONCERT IN THE PARK – AUGUST 15th 1991 (live)** [60] [–]
– The obvious child / The boy in the bubble / She moves on / Kodachrome / Born at the right time / Train in the distance / Me and Julio down by the schoolyard / I know what I know / Cool cool river / Bridge over troubled water / Proof / Coast / Graceland / You can call me Al / Still crazy after all these years / Loves me like a rock / Diamonds on the sole of her shoes / Hearts and bones / Later in the evening / America / The boxer / Cecelia / Sound of silence.

Nov 97. (cd/c) *<(9362 46814-2/-4)>* **SONGS FROM THE CAPEMAN** (The Broadway Musical) [ ] [42]
– Adios Hermanos / Born in Puerto Rico / Satin summer nights / Bernadette / The vampires / Quality / Can I forgive him / Sunday afternoon / Killer wants to go to college / Time is an ocean / Virgil / Killer wants to go to college II / Trailways bus.

Oct 00. (cd/c) *<(9362 47844-2/-4)>* **YOU'RE THE ONE** [20] [19]
– That's where I belong / Darling Lorraine / Old / You're the one / The teacher / Look at that / Senorita with a necklace of tears / Pigs, sheep and wolves / Hurricane eye / Quiet.

– (PAUL SIMON) compilations, others, etc. –

on 'C.B.S.' / 'Columbia' unless mentioned otherwise

Nov 88. (d-lp/c/cd) *(WX 223/+C)(925789-2) <25789>* **NEGOTIATIONS AND LOVE SONGS** [17] [ ]
– Mother and child reunion / Me and Julio down by the schoolyard / Something so right / St.Judy's comet / Loves me like a rock / Have a good time / 50 ways to leave your lover / Still crazy after all these years / Late in the evening / Slip slidin' away / Hearts and bones / Train in the distance /

Rene and Georgette Magritte with their dog after the war / Diamonds on the soles on her shoes / You can call me Al / Kodachrome. *(d-lp+=)* – Graceland.

Nov 88. (7") *(W 7655)* **MOTHER AND CHILD REUNION. / TRAIN IN THE DISTANCE** [ ] [ ]
(12"+=/cd-s+=) *(W 7655 T/CD)* – The boy in the bubble.

Feb 89. (c) *Venus; (VENUMC 5)* **THE MAGIC OF PAUL SIMON** [ ] [–]

May 93. (cd) *Royal; (RC 82112)* **PAUL SIMON & FRIENDS** [ ] [–]

Sep 93. (3xcd-box) *Warners; (9362 45474-2)* **1964-1993** [ ] [ ]

Sep 93. (cd/c) *Warners; (9362 45408-2/-4)* **ANTHOLOGY** [ ] [ ]

May 00. (cd/c) *Warner ESP; (9362 47721-2/-4)* **GREATEST HITS – SHINING LIKE A GUITAR** [6] [–]

ART GARFUNKEL

(solo with session people)

C.B.S. Columbia

Sep 73. (7") *(1777) <45926>* **ALL I KNOW. / MARY WAS AN ONLY CHILD** [ ] [9]

Oct 73. (lp/c) *(CBS/40 89021) <31472>* **ANGEL CLARE** [14] Sep73 [5]
– Travelling boy / Down in the willow garden / I shall sing / Old man / Feuilles oh! – Do spacemen pass dead souls on their way to the Moon? / All I know / Woyaya / Mary was an only child / Barbara Allen / Another lullaby. *(also on quad-lp; CQ 31474) (cd-iss. 1988; CD 69021) (re-iss. Jul89 on 'Pickwick'; 982185)*

Feb 74. (7") *(2013) <45983>* **I SHALL SING. / FEUILLES OH! – DO SPACEMEN PASS DEAD SOULS ON THEIR WAY TO THE MOON?** [ ] Dec 73 [38]

Sep 74. (7") *(2672) <10020>* **SECOND AVENUE. / WOYAYA** [ ] [34]

—— (above 1973/74 releases as "GARFUNKEL")

Sep 75. (7") *(3575) <10190>* **I ONLY HAVE EYES FOR YOU. / LOOKING FOR THE RIGHT ONE** [1] Aug75 [18]

Oct 75. (lp/c) *(CBS/40 86002) <33700>* **BREAKAWAY** [7] [7]
– I believe (when I fall in love it will be forever) / Rag doll / Breakaway / Disney girls / Waters of March / My little town / I only have eyes for you / Looking for the right one / 99 miles from L.A. / The same old tears on a new background. *(re-iss. Nov85 lp/c; CBS/40 32574) (cd-iss. Apr86; CD 86002) (re-iss. Sep89 on 'Pickwick' lp/c/cd; 902199-1/-4/-2) (cd re-iss. Sep93 on 'Sony Collectors';) (cd re-iss. Feb87; 468873-2)*

—— See PAUL SIMON section, for their hit duet MY LITTLE TOWN.

Dec 75. (7") *<10273>* **BREAKAWAY. / DISNEY GIRLS** [–] [ ]

Jan 76. (7") *(3888)* **BREAKAWAY. / THE SAME OLD TEARS ON A NEW BACKGROUND** [ ] [–]

May 76. (7") *(4348)* **I BELIEVE (WHEN I FALL IN LOVE IT WILL BE FOREVER). / WATERS OF MARCH** [ ] [–]

Nov 77. (7") *(5683) <10608>* **CRYING IN MY SLEEP. / MR.SHUCK'N'JIVE** [ ] [ ]

Jan 78. (7"; ART GARFUNKEL, PAUL SIMON & JAMES TAYLOR) *(6061) 19676>* **(WHAT A) WONDERFUL WORLD. / WOODEN PLANES** [ ] [17]

Feb 78. (lp/c) *(CBS/40 86054) <34975>* **WATERMARK** [25] [19]
– Crying in my sleep / Marionette / Shine it on me / Watermark / Saturday suit / All my love's laughter / (What a) Wonderful world / Mr. Shuck 'n' jive / Paper chase / She moved through the fair / Someone else (1958) / Wooden planes. *(re-iss. Jan87 lp/c; 450378-1/-4) (cd-iss. Apr94 on 'Sony')*

Apr 78. (7") *(6325)* **MARIONETTE. / ALL MY LOVE'S LAUGHTER** [ ] [–]

Feb 79. (7") *(6847)* **BRIGHT EYES. / KEHAAR'S THEME** [1] [–]
(above from animated film 'Watership Down') *(re-iss. Jul84)*

Mar 79. (7") *<10933>* **AND I KNOW. / IN A LITTLE WHILE (I'LL BE ON MY WAY)** [–] [ ]

Apr 79. (lp/c) *(CBS/40 86090) <35780>* **FATE FOR BREAKFAST** [2] [67]
– In a little while (I'll be on my way) / Since I don't have you / And I know / Sail on a rainbow / Miss you nights / Bright eyes / Finally a reason / Beyond the tears / Oh how happy / When someone doesn't want you / Take me away. *Cd-iss.Jul97 on 'Columbia'; 487946-2)*

May 79. (7") *<10999>* **SINCE I DON'T HAVE YOU. / WHEN SOMEONE DOESN'T WANT YOU** [–] [53]

Jun 79. (7") *(7371)* **SINCE I DON'T HAVE YOU. / AND I KNOW** [38] [–]

Aug 79. (7") **BRIGHT EYES. / SAIL ON A RAINBOW** [–] [ ]

Aug 81. (7"; ART GARFUNKEL & PAUL SIMON) *(A 1495) <02307>* **A HEART IN NEW YORK. / IS THIS LOVE** [ ] [66]

Sep 81. (lp/c) *(CBS/40 85259) <37392>* **SCISSORS CUT** [51] [ ]
– Scissors cut / A heart in New York / Up in the world / Hang on in / So easy to begin / Can't turn my heart away / The French waltz / The romance / In cars / That's all I've got to say.

Oct 81. (7") *(A 1708)* **SCISSORS CUT. / SO EASY TO BEGIN** [ ] [–]

—— Late 1981, he had re-united with PAUL SIMON for live one-off album.

Oct 84. (7") *(A 4674)* **SOMETIME WHEN I'M DREAMING. / SCISSORS CUT** [ ] [–]

Nov 84. (lp/c/cd) *(CBS/40/CD 10046)* **THE ART GARFUNKEL ALBUM** (compilation) [12] [–]
– Bright eyes / Break away / A heart in New York / I shall sing / 99 miles from L.A. / All I know / I only have eyes for you / Watermark / Sometimes when I'm dreaming / Travelin' boy / The same old tears on a new background / (What a) Wonderful world / I believe (when I fall in love it will be forever) / Scissors cut. *(cd re-iss. Oct90; 466333-2)*

Nov 86. (7"; with AMY GRANT) **CAROL OF THE BIRDS. / THE DECREE** [–] [ ]

Dec 86. (lp/c) *(CBS/40 26704) <40212>* **THE ANIMALS' CHRISTMAS** [ ] [ ]
– The annunciation / The creatures of the field / Just a simple little tune / The decree / Incredible phat / The friendly beasts / The song of the camel / Words from an old Spanish carol / Carol of the birds / The frog / Herod / Wild geese.

Jan 88. (7") *<07711>* **SO MUCH IN LOVE. / KING OF TONGA** [–] [ ]

Feb 88. (7") *(651 450-7)* **SO MUCH IN LOVE. / SLOW BREAKUP** [ ] [–]
(12"+=/cd-s+=) *(651 450-6/-2)* – (What a) Wonderful world / I only have eyes for you.

Mar 88. (7") *<07949>* **THIS IS THE MOMENT. / SLOW BREAKUP** [–] [ ]

Mar 88. (lp/c/cd) *(460694-1/-4/-2) <40942>* **LEFTY** [ ] [ ]
– This is the moment / I have a love / So much in love / Slow breakup / Love is the only chain / When a man loves a woman / I wonder why / King of Tonga / If love takes you away / The promise.

May 88. (7") *(651 632-7)* **WHEN A MAN LOVES A WOMAN. / KING OF TONGA** [ ] [–]

May 88. (7") *<08511>* **WHEN A MAN LOVES A WOMAN. / I HAVE A LOVE** [–] [ ]

Columbia Columbia

Nov 93. (cd/c/lp) *(474853-2/-4) <47113>* **UP 'TIL NOW** [ ] Oct93 [ ]
– Crying in the rain (w/ JAMES TAYLOR) / All I know / Just over the Brooklyn Bridge / The sound of silence / The breakup / Skywriter / The decree / It's all in the game / One less holiday / Since I don't have you / Two sleepy people / Why worry / All my love's daughter.

Virgin Virgin

Dec 96. (cd/c) *(VT CD/MC 113) <20001>* **ACROSS AMERICA (live)** [59] May97 [ ]
– Heart in New York / Crying in the rain / Scarborough fair / Poem on the underground wall / Homeward bound / All I know / Bright eyes / El condor pasa (If i could) / Bridge over troubled water / Mrs. Robinson / 59th Street Bridge song (feelin' groovy) / I will / April come she will / Sound of silence / Grateful / Goodnight my love.

Liberty Blue Note

Feb 03. (cd; as ART GARFUNKEL with MAIA SHARP & BUDDY MONDLOCK) *<(5 40990-2)>* **EVERYTHING WAITS TO BE NOTICED** [ ] Oct02 [ ]
– Bounce / The thread / The kid / Crossing lines / Everything waits to be noticed / Young and free / Perfect moment / Turn, don't turn away / Wishbone / How did you know? / What I love about rain / Every now and then / Another only one.

– (ART GARFUNKEL) compilations, etc. –

Oct 79. (3xlp-box) *C.B.S.;* **ART GARFUNKEL** [ ] [ ]
(first 3 albums)

1984. (7") *Columbia;* **BRIGHT EYES. / THE ROMANCE** [–] [ ]

Jun 97. (cd) *<67674>* **SONGS FROM A PARENT TO A CHILD** (covers) [–] [ ]

Aug 98. (cd) *Columbia; (491473-2)* **THE BEST OF ART GARFUNKEL** [ ] [–]

Nina SIMONE

Born: EUNICE WAYMON, 21 Feb'33, Tryon, North Carolina, USA. NINA SIMONE is that rare thing in popular music, a true original, perhaps the last of the true originals. Her recorded output – which runs the gamut from Broadway show tunes, Weill-Brecht interpretations, smoky jazz, joyous gospel, blues and soul-pop to African-rooted chants, funereal folk and fierce protest song – is certainly not easy listening but it is infinitely rewarding. Perhaps the most frustrating thing about SIMONE and her rich body of work is that it is still, to a certain extent, overlooked. Always an enigmatic and mysterious figure, the singer seems to have been relegated to a relatively marginal role in pop/rock history judging by the dearth of retrospective coverage and analysis of her work. While the likes of say ARETHA FRANKLIN or even BILLIE HOLIDAY are constantly celebrated and re-evaluated in the media, SIMONE is rarely afforded so much attention. Similarly, the fact that many younger music fans identify her with one song, 'MY BABY JUST CARES FOR ME', is a crying shame. It seems she's always been struggling against the grain, from her earliest days as one child among seven in a poor family. She began playing piano as a toddler and, with a methodist minister as a mother, Eunice unsurprisingly received her early vocal training in church. Her prodigious talent persuaded her music teacher to raise money to send her to boarding school and from there, on to New York's prestigious Juilliard School of Music. Despite being a brilliant student, her dreams of being the first black concert pianist were frustrated amid bitter disappointment, something which may well have shaped her contradictory and often caustic style. She began working as a music teacher and piano accompanist before taking a summer job at an Atlantic City club which entailed singing as well as playing piano. Adopting a nom de plume inspired by French actress Simone Signoret, Eunice christened herself NINA SIMONE and, for the first time in her professional career, took centre stage. In the summer of '59, NINA scored her first (million selling) hit (US Top 20) with 'I LOVES YOU PORGY', from Gershwin's 'PORGY & BESS'. Incredibly, it would also prove to be her last hit, at least in the States. Not that this proved a barrier to success, the singer carving herself a successful career outwith the pop mainstream as an albums artist. The success of the single had boosted her profile to the extent of playing New York's Carnegie Hall and the Newport Blues and Jazz Festival, live work documented on 'NINA AT NEWPORT' (1960) and 'NINA SIMONE AT CARNEGIE HALL' (1963) respectively. Through the first half of the 60's she recorded for the 'Colpix' label, patenting her trademark across-the-board approach and fine tuning the unique interpretive skills which marked her out as such a burning talent. Never more in her element than when seated at a piano with a baying crowd in thrall to her muse, SIMONE continually pushed the boundaries in terms of the art of live performance. In keeping with her fiery temperament, her shows were (and still are) infamously and unpredictably erratic. Yet on a good night, the High Priestess of Soul (an inaccurate tag which she apparently detested) could put a spell on her audience stronger than any voodoo SCREAMIN' JAY HAWKINS might've unearthed. It may be a cliche but NINA's voice was (and is) an instrument in itself, a strange, exotic instrument at that. At once sensual, sexy, sour, androgynous, playful and tender, often with a wonderful contrary undertow, SIMONE could butter the listener up in one sentence and swoop on him/her like an Alfred Hitchcock-approved flock of birds in the next. Her innovative and unorthodox use of dramatic silence, phrasing, timing and tone made her a master of mood while her ability to combine the white, European tradition of classical composition with the black, African tradition of earthy spirituality made her piano playing a thing of wonder. Despite the avalanche of concert material released during the 60's, many of NINA's live albums remain among her best. 1964's 'NINA SIMONE IN CONCERT' was just such a record, marking her debut for 'Philips' and showcasing the classic 'MISSISSIPPI GODDAM'. A raging yet heartfelt harangue which NINA had penned after the death of four black children in a Birmingham, Alabama church bombing, the song was indicative of the singer's increasing involvement in the civil rights and black power movements. It mightn't have endeared her to the more staid elements of her supper club audience but it undoubtedly won her a whole new set of admirers. The slowly seething 'BACKLASH BLUES' – from 1967's 'SINGS THE BLUES' album, her first for 'R.C.A.' – was recorded in a similar vein with a lyric penned by fellow activist and friend Langston Hughes. Other notable politically themed songs from this period included 'OLD JIM CROW' and the Martin Luther King tribute 'WHY? (THE KING OF LOVE IS DEAD)'. Yet throughout her career SIMONE has sung about the reality of female existence, in the general sense and also more narrowly from the point of view of a black female. If she attempted to articulate the fury of black america in the face of State-sanctioned prejudice, then her attempts at articulating the situation of black women cut twice as deep. The self-penned 'FOUR WOMEN' cleverly portrayed a quartet of African American women with varied but equally hard-bitten experience. Ironically, NINA was rewarded for her efforts with a radio ban. While the song made its debut on 1966's 'WILD IS THE WIND' album, SIMONE's stand-out long player from the mid-60's is generally held to be 'HIGH PRIESTESS OF SOUL' (1966), ranging from bittersweet, orchestrated ballads like 'DON'T YOU PAY THEM NO MIND' to the percussive grace of 'COME YE'. The latter had a distant cousin in the hypnotic, call and response chant of 'SEE LINE WOMAN', as starkly different to other early period classics like Jacques Brel's 'NE ME QUITTE PAS' as it was possible to be. Yet this was a singer who thrived on diversity and contrariness, a tactic she continued to use during her later 'R.C.A.' years. Although it's certainly not the orthodox view, these years (1967-1974) were arguably her most creatively fruitful. Following on from the aforementioned blues set, NINA tackled soul on 1967's 'SILK & SOUL' although hardly in a conventional sense. While many people would recognise it as the toe-tapping instrumental theme tune to Barry Norman's glory years as the BBC's ace film critic, NINA's version of 'I WISH I KNEW HOW IT WOULD FEEL TO BE FREE' is a revelation, a plea from the collective unconscious to envisage life as it could be. The live 'NUFF SAID' (1968) opened with a dizzying cover of The Bee Gees' 'IN THE MORNING'. SIMONE's ability to turn from starry-eyed affirmation to the lowdown, gutter-scraping groove of 'GIN HOUSE BLUES' in more or less the same breath was just another element of her multi-faceted genius; when she sings about being "in her sin" you can almost feel the liquor searing her throat. 'AIN'T GOT NO – I GOT LIFE', a medley from flower power musical hair which narrowly missed the UK No.1 – was pure NINA, subverting and transforming the hippy sentiment into something more raw and ineffably human. 1969's live 'BLACK GOLD', meanwhile, featured a tantalising cover of Sandy Denny's 'WHO KNOWS WHERE THE TIME GOES' but was notable primarily for the vintage performance of 'YOUNG, GIFTED AND BLACK'. Although popularised in its rocksteady incarnation by BOB & MARCIA, the track was penned by SIMONE and WELDON IRVINE Jr. as a graceful tribute to Lorraine Hansberry, the first black writer to score a hit play on Broadway. NINA's spoken intro displayed all the acerbic wit, humour and tenderness so obvious in her music, still promoting the cause of her people yet doing it without the militancy of her earlier work. She mightn't have been so young in the late 60's/early 70's but in 'TO LOVE SOMEBODY' (1969) she proved she was gifted enough to interpret a whole album's worth of white singer-songwriter material and make it her own. Although the touching title track made the UK Top 5 and confirmed her identification with the GIBB brothers' muse, pick of the bunch was Leonard Cohen's 'SUZANNE', alchemised from melancholy meditation to pure, uninhibited joy. 'NINA SIMONE AND PIANO' (1969) was a different beast altogether, just NINA and her little old piano exploring themes of love, life, religion, death and the universe. A great lost classic, the album was roundly ignored at the time but has since been given its due by modern critics. Blues as confessional, 'NOBODY'S FAULT BUT MINE' was almost painful in its cathartic intimacy while the likes of 'THE HUMAN TOUCH' and 'THE DESPERATE ONES' unflinchingly addressed humanity's perilous position. The times they were certainly a-changin'. By the turn of the decade, the black power movement was on the back foot, the hippy dream had been slain at Altamont and the Vietnam war had intensified. As ever, NINA reflected the times by connecting up the personal, the political and the religious. With its newsprint collage sleeve suggesting impending doom, 1973's 'EMERGENCY WARD' signalled both a national crisis and perhaps a personal one. The record's document of a performance for black GI's at a New Jersey military base hinged around an ingenious medley of George Harrison's 'MY SWEET LORD' and an apocalyptic poem, 'TODAY IS A KILLER'. Backed by a baptist choir, NINA combined devotion and blasphemy in one fell swoop by identifying God himself as the killer. A hard act to follow although NINA was already winding down her career. The wonderful 'IT IS FINISHED' (1974) was her goodbye to the mainstream music industry and her American homeland. Unsurprising then that the likes of 'DAMBALA' sounded a note of final farewell while 'OBEAH WOMAN' suggested the pull of her African roots. The album also featured her sneering, coruscating cover of Tina Turner's 'FUNKIER THAN A MOSQUITO'S TWEETER', proof that SIMONE could've ruled the dance floor had she taken that direction. Yet the high priestess had renounced her crown, going off to live, at various times, in Barbados, Liberia, Switzerland and, her current home, the south of France. She recorded only sporadically, releasing 1978's 'BALTIMORE' album on Chip Taylor's 'C.T.I.' label and cutting 'FODDER ON MY WINGS' in Paris in 1982, an album inspired by her exile and featuring NINA on harpsichord. Stranger still, NINA made a comeback in the British singles chart after 'MY BABY JUST CARES FOR ME' was used in a TV perfume ad. The song topped the UK chart, becoming the biggest hit of her career and introducing her to a whole new generation of listeners. NINA's profile remained fairly high in the early 90's what with the publication of her autobiography, 'I Put A Spell On You' and link-ups with MARIA BETHANIA and MIRIAM MAKEBA. The belated British chart success was repeated in 1994 when 'FEELING GOOD' (another from a sexy TV ad, this time Galaxy milk chocolate) scraped into the Top 40. She's received countless awards for her contribution to popular music, including an honorary Doctorate in Music and Humanities. While NINA the performer remains as reliably volatile as ever (as evidenced by her show at the 2001 Bishopstock Festival in England) there are few, if any, living artists who can boast a body of work as rich, as all-encompassing and as emblematic of the human condition as this legendary Griot. Sadly, one of popular music's last real icons died at her French home on the 21st of April 2003.

Album rating: AT THE TOWN HALL (*6) / NINA AT NEWPORT (*8) / FORBIDDEN FRUIT (*5) / NINA AT THE VILLAGE GATE (*6) / NINA SIMONE IN CONCERT (*8) / FOLKSY NINA (*6) / BROADWAY – BLUES – BALLADS (*5) / I PUT A SPELL ON YOU (*7) / PASTEL BLUES (*5) / LET IT ALL OUT (*5) / WILD IS THE WIND (*8) / HIGH PRIESTESS OF SOUL (*8) / . . .SINGS THE BLUES (*6) / SILK & SOUL (*8) / 'NUFF SAID (*7) / THE BEST OF . . . compilation on Philips (*7) / THE BEST OF . . . compilation on RCA (*6) / NINA SIMONE AND PIANO (*5) / BLACK GOLD (*6) / HERE COMES THE SUN (*5) / EMERGENCY WARD (*5) / BALTIMORE (*5) / FODDER ON MY WINGS (*4) / LET IT BE ME (*5) / NINA'S BACK! (*5) / THE BLUES (*6) / A SINGLE WOMAN (*5) / FEELING GOOD – THE VERY BEST OF NINA SIMONE compilation (*9) / GOLD compilation (*8)

NINA SIMONE – vocals / with session backing & orchestra

Parlophone Bethlehem

Jul 59. (7") *(R 4583)* *<11021>* **I LOVES YOU, PORGY. / LOVE ME OR LEAVE ME** □ 18

Pye Int. Colpix

Sep 59. (7"/78) *(7N/N 25029)* **SOLITAIRE. / CHILLY WINDS DON'T BLOW** □ □

1960. (lp) *(NPL 28014)* **AT THE TOWN HALL (live)** □ –
– Black is the colour of my true love's hair / Exactly like you / The other woman / Under the lowest / You can have him / Summertime / Cotton eyed Joe / Return home / Wild is the wind / Fine and mellow. *(re-iss. May88 on 'Official' lp/c; OFF/+4 6012)*

Aug 60. (7") *<PX 158>* **NOBODY KNOWS WHEN YOU'RE DOWN AND OUT. / BLACK IS THE COLOR OF MY TRUE LOVE'S HAIR** – 93

Jan 61. (7") *<PX 175>* **TROUBLE IN MIND. / COTTON EYED JOE** – 92

Feb 61. (lp) *<412>* **NINA AT NEWPORT (live 30th June 1960)** – 23
– Trouble in mind / Porgy / Little Liza Jane / You'd be so nice to come home to / Flo me la / Nina's blues / In the evening by the moonlight. *(re-iss. Oct69 on 'Marble Arch';) (re-iss. Dec88 on 'Official' lp/c/cd; OFF/+4/8 6014)*

Pye Jazz Colpix

1962. (lp) *(NJL 36)* **FORBIDDEN FRUIT** □ –
– Rags and old iron / No good man / Gin house blues / I'll look around / I love to love / Work song / Where can I go without you / Just say I love him / Memphis June / Forbidden fruit. *(re-iss. 1964 on 'Colpix'; PXL 419)*

Colpix Colpix

1963. (7") *(PX 200)* **YOU CAN HAVE HIM. / RETURN HOME** □ □

1964. (lp) *(PXL 421)* **NINA AT THE VILLAGE GATE (live)** □ –
– Just in time / He was too good to me / House of the rising sun / Bye, bye, blackbird / Brown baby / Zungo / If he changed my name / Children, go where I send you. *<(cd-iss. Sep90 on 'Blue Note'; CDP 795058-2)> (cd e-iss.Mar91 on 'Roulette'; CDROU 1030)*

1964. (7") *(PX 799)* **EXACTLY LIKE YOU. / THE OTHER WOMAN** □ □
(re-iss. Jun68 on 'Pye International'; 7N 25466)

1965. (lp) *(PXL 465)* **FOLKSY NINA** □ –
– Silver city bound / When I was a young girl / Erets zavat chalav / Lass from the low country / The young knight / The twelfth of never / Vanctihu / You can sing a rainbow / Hush, little baby.

Philips Philips

Sep 64. (lp) *<135>* **NINA SIMONE IN CONCERT (live)** – □
– I loves you Porgy / Plain gold ring / Pirate Jenny / Old Jim Crow / Don't smoke in bed / Go limp / Mississippi goddam. *(UK-iss.1965; BL 7678) (cd/c-iss.Nov93 on 'Remember'; RMB 7/4 5011)*

Jan 65. (7") *(BF 1388)* **DON'T LET ME BE MISUNDERSTOOD. / MONSTER** □ □

Apr 65. (lp) *(BL 7671)* **BROADWAY – BLUES – BALLADS** □ –
– Don't let me be misunderstood / Night song / The laziest gal in town / Something wonderful / Don't take all night / Nobody / I am blessed / Of this I'm sure / Seeline woman / Our love (will see us through) / How can I / The last rose of summer. *<(cd-iss. Feb94 on 'Verve'; 518 190-2)>*

Jul 65. (7") *(BF 1415)* **I PUT A SPELL ON YOU. / GIMME SOME** 49 □

Jul 65. (lp) *(BL 7671)* *<172>* **I PUT A SPELL ON YOU** 18 Jun65 99
– I put a spell on you / Tomorrow is my turn / Ne me quitte pas / Marriage is for old folks / July tree / Gimme some / Feeling good / One September day / Blues on purpose / Beautiful land / You've got to learn / Take care of business. *(re-iss. Jul93 on 'Ce De International' cd/c; CD/MC 62067)*

Dec 65. (lp) *(BL 7683)* <187> **PASTEL BLUES** [ ] Oct65 [ ]
– Be my husband / Nobody knows when you're down and out / The end of the line / Trouble in mind / Tell me more and more and then some / Chilly winds don't blow / Ain't no use / Strange fruit / Sinnerman.

Jan 66. (7") *(BF 1465)* **EITHER WAY I LOSE. / BREAK DOWN AND LET IT OUT** [ ] [ ]

Jul 66. (lp; stereo/mono) *(S+/BL 7722)* **LET IT ALL OUT** [ ] [–]
– Mood indigo / The other woman / Love me or leave me / Don't explain / Little girl blue / Chauffeur for myself / Ballad of Hollis Brown / This year's kisses / Images / Nearer blessed Lord.

Sep 66. (lp; stereo/mono) *(S+/BL 7726)* <207> **WILD IS THE WIND** [ ] [ ]
– I love your lovin' ways / Four women / What more can I say / Lilac wine / That's all I ask / Break down and let it all out / Why keep on breaking my heart / Wild is the wind / Black is the colour of my true love's hair / If I should lose you / Either way I lose.

RCA Victor RCA Victor

Aug 67. (7") *(RCA 1583)* **DO I MOVE YOU? / DAY AND NIGHT** [ ] [ ]

Sep 67. (lp; stereo/mono) *(SF/RD 7883)* **. . .SINGS THE BLUES** [ ] [–]
– Do I move you? / Day and night / Romance in the dark / Real real / My man's gone now / Backlash blues / I want a little sugar in my bowl / Buck / Since I fell for you / House of the rising sun / Blues for mama. *(re-iss. Aug85 lp/c; NL/NK 89265) (re-iss. Dec98 on 'Alto'; AA 002)*

Jan 68. (lp; stereo/mono) *(SF/RD 7967)* <3837> **SILK & SOUL** [ ] Nov67 [ ]
– It be's that way sometime / The look of love / Go to hell / Love o' love / Cherish / I wish I knew how it would feel to be free / Turn me on / Turning point / Some say / Consummation.

May 68. (7") *(RCA 1697)* **WHY? (THE KING OF LOVE IS DEAD). / (part 2)** [ ] [ ]

Oct 68. (7") <9602> **DO WHAT YOU GOTTA DO. / PEACE OF MIND** [–] [83]

Oct 68. (7") *(RCA 1743)* **AIN'T GOT NO – I GOT LIFE. / DO WHAT YOU GOTTA DO** [2] [7]

Dec 68. (7") <9686> **AIN'T GOT NO; I GOT LIFE. / REAL REAL** [–] [94]

Jan 69. (7") *(RCA 1779)* **TO LOVE SOMEBODY. / I CAN'T SEE NOBODY** [5] [–]

Feb 69. (lp; stereo/mono) *(SF/RD 7979)* <LSP 4065> **'NUFF SAID (live)** [11] [ ]
– In the morning / Sunday in Savannah / Backlash blues / Please read me / Gin house blues / Why? (the king of love is dead) / Peace of mind / Ain't got no – I got life / I loves you, Porgy / Take my hand precious Lord / Do what you gotta do.

Mar 69. (7") *(RCA 1805)* **REVOLUTION. / LOVE O' LOVE** [ ] [ ]

Aug 69. (7") *(RCA 1879)* **IN THE MORNING. / CHERISH** [ ] [ ]

Nov 69. (7") *(RCA 1903)* <0269> **TO BE YOUNG, GIFTED AND BLACK. / SAVE ME** [ ] [76]

Dec 69. (lp) *R.C.A.; (SF 8074)* **NINA SIMONE AND PIANO** [ ] [–]
– Seems I'm never tired lovin' you / Nobody's fault but mine / I think it's going to rain today / Everyone's gone to the moon / Compensation / Who am I / Another pring / Human touch / I get along without you very well / Desperate ones.

Jun 70. (7") *(RCA 1961)* **DO WHAT YOU GOTTA DO. / TURN ME ON** [ ] [ ]

Sep 70. (7") *(RCA 1968)* **WHY MUST YOUR LOVE WELL BE SO DRY. / WHATEVER I AM** [ ] [ ]

Feb 71. (lp) *(SF 8142)* <4248> **BLACK GOLD (live)** [ ] [ ]
– (introduction) / Black is the colour of my true love's hair / Ain't got no – I got life / Westwind / Who knows where the time goes / Assignment sequence / To be young, gifted and black.

Sep 71. (lp) *(SF 8192)* <4536> **HERE COMES THE SUN** [ ] Aug71 [ ]
– Here comes the sun / Just like a woman / O-o-h child / Mr. Bojangles / New world coming / Angel of the morning / How long must I wander / My way. *(re-iss. Jul80 lp/c; INT S/K 5025)*

Jan 73. (lp) *(SF 8304)* **EMERGENCY WARD** [ ] [–]
– My sweet Lord / Today is a killer / Poppies / Isn't it a pity.

C.T.I. C.T.I.

May 78. (7") *(CTSP 14)* **BALTIMORE. / FORGET** [ ] [ ]

Aug 78. (lp) *(CTI 7084)* **BALTIMORE** [ ] [ ]
– Everything must change / Family / My father always promised / Music for lovers / Rich girl / That's all I want from you / Baltimore / Forget / Balm in Gilead / If you pray right. *(re-iss. Feb84; CTI 9010) (re-iss. Mar88 on 'C.B.S.' lp/c; 460730-1/-4)* <*cd-iss. Jan95 on 'Sony Jazz'; 476906-2*>

Polygram Polygram

Mar 84. (lp) <*(1067 885)*> **FODDER ON MY WINGS (live in Paris 1982)** [ ] [ ]
– I sing just to know that I'm alive / Fodder in my wings / Vous etes seul mais je desire etre avec vous / Ily'a un Baume a Gilead / Heaven belongs to you / Liberian calypso / Thandewye / I was just a stupid dog to them / Colour is a beautiful thing / There is no returning.

not iss. Verve

May 87. (lp/c) <*831 437-1/-4*> **LET IT BE ME (live at Vine Street)** [ ] [ ]
– My baby just cares for me / Sugar in my bowl / Fodder in my wings / Be my husband / Just like a woman / Balm in Gilead / Stars / If you pray right (Heaven belongs to you) / If you knew – Let it be me / Baltimore.

Jungle V.P.I.

Apr 89. (lp/c/cd) *(FREUD/+C/CD 28)* <*VPI/+C/CD 1007*> **NINA'S BACK!** [ ] Feb86 [ ]
– It's cold out here / Porgy / I sing just to know that I'm alive / For a while / Fodder in my wings / Touching and caring / Saratoga / You must have another year. *(cd re-iss. Mar99 on 'Charly'; CDGR 288) (cd re-iss. Aug00 on 'MagMid'; MM 059)*

May 89. (7"/c-s) *(JUNG 51/+C)* **IT'S COLD OUT HERE. / I SING JUST TO KNOW THAT I'M ALIVE** [ ] [–]
(12"+=/cd-s+=) *(JUNG 51 T/CD)* – Mississippi goddam (live) / My baby.

Nov 89. (lp/c/cd) *(FREUD/+C/CD 32)* **LIVE AND KICKIN' (live)** [ ] [–]
– I loves you, Porgy / Four women / The other woman / Pirate Jenny / For a while / You took my teeth / Sugar in my bowl / Blacklash blues / Do what you gotta do / Mississippi goddam / Seeline woman / I sing just to know that I'm alive / My baby just cares for me. <*US-iss.1998 on 'Overall'; 1002*>

Elektra Elektra

Aug 93. (cd/c) <*(7559 61503-2/-4)*> **A SINGLE WOMAN** [ ] [ ]
– A single woman / Lonesome cities / If I should lose you / Folks who live on the hill / Love's been good to me / Papa, can you hear me / Il n'y a pas d'amour / Just say I love him / The more I see you / Marry me.

— 21st April, 2003, NINA died at her home in Carry-le-Rouet, France

– (selective) compilations, etc. –

Dec 68. (7") *Philips; (BF 1736)* **I PUT A SPELL ON YOU. / DON'T LET ME BE MISUNDERSTOOD** [28] [–]

Dec 68. (lp; stereo/mono) *Philips; (S+/BL 7764)* **HIGH PRIESTESS OF SOUL** [ ] [–]

Jul 70. (lp) *R.C.A.; <4374>* **THE BEST OF NINA SIMONE** [–] [ ]
– In the morning / I shall be released / Day and night / It be's that way sometime / I want a little sugar in my bowl / My man's gone now / Why? (the king of love is dead) / Compensation / I wish I knew how it would feel to be free / Go to hell / Do what you gotta do / Suzanne. *(UK-iss.Sep89 lp/c/cd; PL/PK/PD 90376)*

Apr 85. (7") *Charly; (CYZ7 112)* **MY BABY JUST CARES FOR ME. / LOVE ME OR LEAVE ME** [ ] [–]
(12")(cd-s re-iss. Oct87+=; (CYZ12 112)(CD1) – Little girl blue. – hit No.5

May 85. (lp/c) *Charly; (CR/TCCR 30217)* **MY BABY JUST CARES FOR ME** [ ] [–]
(cd-iss. Mar86; CDCHARLY 6) (re-dist.Nov87) – hit No.56

Feb 92. (cd/c) *Edsel; (EDCD/CED 347)* **SONGS OF THE POETS** [ ] [–]

Jun 94. (c-s/cd-s) *Mercury; (MER MC/CD 403)* **FEELING GOOD** [40] [–]

Jul 94. (cd/c) *Verve-Polygram TV; <(522 669-2/-4)>* **FEELING GOOD – THE VERY BEST OF NINA SIMONE** [9] [ ]
– Feeling good / My baby just cares for me / Don't let me be misunderstood / Ne me quitte pas / Take me to the water / I put a spell on you / Don't explain / Mississippi goddam / Don't smoke in bed / I loves you Porgy / Work song / Love me or leave me / Strange fruit / Nobody knows when you're down and out / I'm going back home / The other woman / Sinnerman / Mood indigo / I'm gonna leave you / See-line woman.

Feb 97. (cd) *Mercury; <(846 543-2)>* **NINA SIMONE IN CONCERT / I PUT A SPELL ON YOU** [ ] [ ]

Sep 97. (cd) *R.C.A.; (07863 66997-2)* **SAGA OF GOOD LIFE AND HARD TIMES** [ ] [ ]

Sep 97. (cd) *Music Club; (MCCD 312)* **THE GREAT NINA SIMONE** [ ] [–]

Nov 97. (d-cd) *Eagle; (EABCD 017)* **THE MASTERS** [ ] [–]

Nov 97. (cd) *Verve; <(539 050-2)>* **ULTIMATE DIVAS** [ ] [ ]

Jan 98. (d-cd/d-c) *Global TV; (RAD CD/MC 84)* **THE BEST OF NINA SIMONE** [ ] [–]

May 98.	(cd) *Verve;* <(529 867-2)> **NINA SIMONE SINGS NINA SIMONE**		
Aug 98.	(cd) *Collectables; (CCLCD 62072)* **FORBIDDEN FRUIT / NINA AT NEWPORT**		
Aug 98.	(cd) *Collectables; (CCLCD 62082)* **FOLKSY NINA / WITH STRINGS**		
Sep 98.	(cd) *Verve;* <(526702-2)> **AFTER HOURS**		
Sep 98.	(d-cd) *R.C.A,; (07863 67635-2)* **SUGAR IN MY BOWL – THE VERY BEST OF NINA SIMONE 1967-1972**		
Nov 98.	(cd) *Raven; (RVCD 71)* **TO LOVE SOMEBODY / HERE COMES THE SUN**		
Jun 99.	(cd) *Collectables; (COLCD 63062)* **THE AMAZING NINA SIMONE / NINA SIMONE AT THE TOWN HALL**		
Jun 99.	(cd) *Collectables; (COLCD 63082)* **NINA'S CHOICE**		–
Aug 99.	(d-cd) *Westside; (WESD 210)* **NINA AT NEWPORT / AT THE VILLAGE GATE . . . AND ELSEWHERE**		
Aug 99.	(d-cd) *Collection; (KBOX 242)* **NINA SIMONE**		
Sep 99.	(cd) *Camden-RCA; (74321 69881-2)* **NINA SIMONE AND PIANO / SILK & SOUL**		–
Sep 99.	(cd) *Delta; (47018)* **LOVE ME OR LEAVE ME**		–
Nov 99.	(cd) *Charly; (CDGR 295)* **NINA SIMONE**		–
Nov 99.	(d-cd) *Westside; (WESD 225)* **FORBIDDEN FRUIT / NINA SINGS ELLINGTON / FOLKSY NINA**		
Dec 99.	(cd) *Castle; (PIESD 182)* **NINA SIMONE**		–
Mar 00.	(cd) *Metro; (METRCD 010)* **NINA: THE ESSENTIAL NINA SIMONE**		–
May 00.	(cd) *Metrodome; (METRO 329)* **MY BABY JUST CARES FOR ME**		–
Jun 00.	(d-cd) *Snapper; (SMDCD 278)* **MISUNDERSTOOD**		
Jul 00.	(cd) *Verve;* <(543 604-2)> **FINEST HOUR**		
Oct 00.	(cd) *Castle Pie; (PIESD 182)* **GIN HOUSE BLUES – NINA SIMONE IN CONCERT**		
Mar 01.	(cd) *Music DeLuxe; (MDCD 008)* **PRIVATE COLLECTION**		–
Jun 03.	(d-cd) *Universal Jazz;* <(98080 87)> **GOLD**	33 Jul03	

SIMPLE MINDS

Formed: Gorbals, Glasgow, Scotland . . . early 1978 after four members (frontman JIM KERR, guitarists CHARLIE BURCHILL and DUNCAN BARNWELL and drummer BRIAN McGEE) had left punk band, JOHNNY & THE SELF ABUSERS. Taking the group name from a line in a BOWIE song, the band gigged constantly at Glasgow's Mars Bar, finally being signed on the strength of a demo tape by local Edinburgh music guru and record store owner, Bruce Findlay. Also becoming the band's manager, Findlay released their debut album, 'LIFE IN A DAY' (1979) on his own 'Zoom' label, the record scoring a Top 30 placing. Its minor success led to a deal with 'Arista' who released the follow-up, 'REEL TO REEL CACOPHONY' (1979), a set of post-punk, electronic experimentation best sampled on the evocative synth spirals of 'FILM THEME'. SIMPLE MINDS took another about turn with 'EMPIRES AND DANCE' (1980), an album heavily influenced by the harder end of the Euro-disco movement, the abrasive electro pulse of the 'I TRAVEL' single becoming a cult dancefloor hit. Initially released as a double set, 'SONS AND FASCINATION' / 'SISTER FEELINGS CALL' (1981), marked the first fruits of a new deal with 'Virgin' and gave the group their first major success, peaking at No.11 in the UK chart on the back of the Top 50 single, 'LOVE SONG'. SIMPLE MINDS were beginning to find their niche, incorporating their artier tendencies into more conventional and melodic song structures. This was fully realised with 'NEW GOLD DREAM (81-82-83-84)' (1982), a record which marked the pinnacle of their early career and one which arguably, they've since failed to better. Constructed with multiple layers of synth, the band crafted a wonderfully evocative and atmospheric series of undulating electronic soundscapes, often married to pop hooks, as with 'GLITTERING PRIZE' and 'PROMISED YOU A MIRACLE' (the group's first Top 20 hits), but more effectively allowed to veer off into dreamier territory on the likes of 'SOMEONE SOMEWHERE IN SUMMERTIME'. While SIMPLE MINDS and U2 were often compared in terms of their anthemic tendencies, a closer comparison could be made, in spirit at least, between 'NEW GOLD..' and U2's mid-80's experimental classic, 'The Unforgettable Fire'. The album reached No.3 in the UK charts, a catalyst for SIMPLE MINDS' gradual transformation from an obscure cult act to stadium candidates, this process helped along nicely by the success of 'SPARKLE IN THE RAIN' (1984), the band's first No.1 album. Though it lacked the compelling mystery of its predecessor, the record featured such memorable SIMPLE MINDS' moments as 'UP ON THE CATWALK', 'SPEED YOUR LOVE TO ME' and an inventive cover of Lou Reed's 'STREET HASSLE'. For better or worse, the album also boasted SIMPLE MINDS' first truly BIG anthem, the sonic bombast of 'WATERFRONT'. But the track that no doubt finally alienated the old faithful was 'DON'T YOU (FORGET ABOUT ME)', the theme tune for quintessentially 80's movie, 'The Breakfast Club' and surely one of the most overplayed records of that decade. The song had stadium-friendly written all over it, subsequently scaling the US charts and paving the way for the transatlantic success of 'ONCE UPON A TIME' (1985). Unashamedly going for the commmercial pop/rock jugular, the album was heady, radio orientated stuff, the likes of 'ALIVE AND KICKING', 'SANCTIFY YOURSELF' and 'OH JUNGLELAND' among the most definitive anthems of the stadium rock genre. Predictably, the critics were unimpressed, although they didn't really stick the knife in until the release of the overblown 'BELFAST CHILD', a UK No.1 despite its snoozeworthy meandering and vague political agenda. The accompanying album, 'STREET FIGHTING YEARS' (1989) brought more of the same, although it cemented SIMPLE MINDS' position among the coffee table elite. Down to a trio of KERR, BURCHILL and and drummer, MEL GAYNOR, the group hired a team of session players for their next album, 'REAL LIFE' (1991), the record almost spawning a Top 5 hit in the celebratory 'LET THERE BE LOVE'. Although the album narrowly missed the UK top spot, it held nothing new, nor did their next release, 'GOOD NEWS FROM THE NEXT WORLD' (1995). Although KERR and BURCHILL brought back DEREK FORBES and signed a new deal with 'Chrysalis' for 1998's 'NEAPOLIS' set, the band only managed to scrape into the UK Top 20. You couldn't help feeling a little sorry for JIM KERR (one-time spouse of CHRISSIE HYNDE), not only does a young pretender like LIAM GALLAGHER hook up with his then wife (PATSY KENSIT), but his band became something of an anachronism in the ever changing world of 90's music. This was realized come their 2002 release 'CRY', a leap backwards into the world of old SIMPLE MINDS. Granted, the group had started using loops and adding a little guitar playing here and there, but what remained was a keyboard-driven album that gave us little in the way of musical vision. While U2 have at least made an attempt to move with the times, SIMPLE MINDS' sound is so deeply rooted in the 80's that it seems inconceivable they could ever make any kind of relevant departure. Those words may well have to be eaten judging by the unheralded and unanticipated acclaim generated by 'OUR SECRETS ARE THE SAME' (2003), the much talked of but hitherto unheard set shelved in the mid to late 90's. The album's savvy pop smarts harked back to their early 80's purple period, only underlining the shortcomings of 'NEAPOLIS', while the sassy momentum of 'JEWELLER TO THE STARS' could've easily regenerated KERR and Co's contemporary credibility. • **Songwriters:** All group compositions or KERR-BURCHILL. Covered BIKO (Peter Gabriel) / SIGN O' THE TIMES (Prince) / DON'T YOU FORGET ABOUT ME (Keith Forsey-Steve Chiff) / GLORIA (Them) / THE MAN WHO SOLD THE WORLD (David Bowie) / HOMOSAPIEN (Pete Shelley) / DANCING BAREFOOT (Patti Smith) / NEON LIGHTS (Kraftwerk) / HELLO I LOVE YOU (Doors) / BRING ON THE DANCING HORSES (Echo & The Bunnymen) / THE NEEDLE & THE DAMAGE DONE (Neil Young) / FOR YOUR PLEASURE (Roxy Music) / ALL TOMORROW'S PARTIES (Velvet Underground). • **Trivia:** SIMPLE MINDS played LIVE AID and MANDELA DAY concerts in 1985 and 1988 respectively.

Album rating: LIFE IN A DAY (*7) / REAL TO REAL CACOPHONY (*5) / EMPIRES AND DANCE (*8) / SONS AND FASCINATION – SISTER FEELING CALL (*8) / CELEBRATION compilation (*7) / NEW GOLD DREAM (81-82-83-84) (*8) / SPARKLE IN THE RAIN (*8) / ONCE UPON A TIME (*8) / LIVE IN THE CITY OF LIGHT (*6) / STREET FIGHTING YEARS (*5) / REAL LIFE (*5) / GLITTERING PRIZE – SIMPLE MINDS 81-92 compilation (*9) / GOOD NEWS FROM THE NEXT WORLD (*4) / NEAPOLIS (*3) / NEON LIGHTS (*4) / THE BEST OF SIMPLE MINDS compilation (*8) / CRY (*4) / OUR SECRETS ARE THE SAME "lost album" (*6)

JOHNNY & THE SELF ABUSERS

JIM KERR (b. 9 Jul'59) – vocals / **CHARLIE BURCHILL** (b.27 Nov'59) – guitar / **BRIAN McGEE** – drums / **TONY DONALD** – bass / **JOHN MILARKY** – guitar / **ALAN McNEIL** also

Chiswick / not iss.

Nov 77. (7") *(NS 22)* **SAINTS AND SINNERS. / DEAD VANDALS** [ ] [–]

SIMPLE MINDS

— (KERR, BURCHILL + McGEE) recruited **MICK McNEILL** (b.20 Jul'58) – keyboards / **DEREK FORBES** (b.22 Jun'56) – bass (ex-SUBS) + **DUNCAN BARNWELL** – guitar (left before recording)

Zoom / not iss.

Apr 79. (7") *(ZUM 10)* **LIFE IN A DAY. / SPECIAL VIEW** [62] [–]

Apr 79. (lp) *(ZULP 1)* **LIFE IN A DAY** [30] [–]
– Someone / Life in a day / Sad affair / All for you / Pleasantly disurbed / No cure / Chelsea girl / Wasteland / Destiny / Murder story. *(re-iss. Oct82 on 'Virgin' lp/c; VM/+C 6) (re-iss. 1985 on 'Virgin' lp/c; OVED/+C 95) (cd-iss. Jul86; VMCD 6)*

Jun 79. (7") *(ZUM 11)* **CHELSEA GIRL. / GARDEN OF HATE** [ ] [–]

Arista / Arista

Nov 79. (lp/c) *(SPART/TC-SPART 1109)* **REAL TO REAL CACOPHONY** [ ] [ ]
– Real to real / Naked eye / Citizen (dance of youth) / Carnival (shelter in a suitcase) / Factory / Cacophony / Veldt / Premonition / Changeling / Film theme / Calling your name / Scar. *(re-iss. Oct82 on 'Virgin' lp/c; V/TCV 2246) (re-iss. 1985 on 'Virgin' lp/c; OVED/+C 124) (cd-iss. May88; CDV 2246)*

Jan 80. (7") *(ARIST 325)* **CHANGELING. / PREMONITION (live)** [ ] [–]

Sep 80. (lp/c) *(SPART/TC-SPART 1140)* **EMPIRES AND DANCE** [41] [ ]
– I travel / Today I died again / Celebrate / This fear of gods / Capital city / Constantinople line / Twist-run-repulsion / Thirty frames a seconds / Kant-kino / Room. *(re-iss. Oct82 on 'Virgin' lp/c; V/TCV 2247) (cd-iss. May88; CDV 2247)*

Oct 80. (7") *(ARIST 372)* **I TRAVEL. / NEW WARM SKIN** [ ] [ ]
(w/ free 7"blue flexi) – KALEIDOSCOPE. / FILM DUB THEME
(12") *(ARIST 12-372)* – ('A'side) / Film dub theme.

Feb 81. (7") *(ARIST 394)* **CELEBRATE. / CHANGELING (live)** [ ] [ ]
(12"+=) *(ARIST 12-394)* – I travel (live).

Virgin / A&M

May 81. (7"/remix.12") *(VS 410/+12)* **THE AMERICAN. / LEAGUE OF NATIONS** [59] [–]

— **KENNY HYSLOP** (b.14 Feb'51, Helensburgh, Scotland) – drums (ex-SKIDS, ex-ZONES, ex-SLIK) repl. McGEE who joined ENDGAMES; in 1994 he became a songwriter for LES McKEOWN (ex-BAY CITY ROLLERS)

Aug 81. (7"/12") *(VS 434/+12)* **LOVE SONG. / THE EARTH THAT YOU WALK UPON (instrumental)** [47] [–]

Sep 81. (2xlp/d-c) *(V/TCV 2207)* **SONS AND FASCINATION / SISTER FEELINGS CALL** [11] [ ]
– SONS AND FASCINATION – In trance as mission / Sweat in bullet / 70 cities as love brings the fall / Boys from Brazil / Love song / This Earth that you walk upon / Sons and fascination / Seeing out the angels. SISTER FEELINGS CALL – Theme for great cities * / The American / 20th Century promised land / Wonderful in young life / League of nations / Careful in career / Sound in 70 cities. *(issued separately Oct81; V 2207 / OVED 2) (cd-iss. Apr86 + Apr90; CDV 2207)* – (omits tracks *)

Oct 81. (7") *(VS 451)* **SWEAT IN BULLET. / 20th CENTURY PROMISED LAND** [52] [–]
(d7"+=) *(VSD 451)* – League of nations (live) / Premonition (live).
(12"+=) *(VS 451-12)* – League of nations (live) / In trance as mission (live).

Apr 82. (7") *(VS 488)* **PROMISED YOU A MIRACLE. / THEME FOR GREAT CITIES** [13] [–]
(12"+=) *(VS 488-12)* – Seeing out the angel (instrumental mix).

— **MIKE OGLETREE** – drums (ex-CAFE JAQUES) repl. HYSLOP who formed SET THE TONE

Aug 82. (7"/12") *(VS 511/+12)* **GLITTERING PRIZE. / GLITTERING THEME** [16] [ ]

— **MEL GAYNOR** (b.29 May'59) – drums (ex-sessions) repl. MIKE who joined FICTION FACTORY

Sep 82. (lp/c)<gold-lp> *(V/TCV 2230) <4928>* **NEW GOLD DREAM (81-82-83-84)** [3] Jan83 [69]
– Someone, somewhere in summertime / Colours fly and the Catherine wheel / Promised you a miracle / Big sleep / Somebody up there likes you / New gold dream (81-82-83-84) / Glittering prize / Hunter and the hunted / King is white and in the crowd. *(cd-iss. Jul83 & Apr92; CDV 2230) (re-iss. Apr92 lp/c; OVED/+C 393)*

Nov 82. (7"/7"pic-d) *(VS/+Y 538)* **SOMEONE, SOMEWHERE IN SUMMERTIME. / KING IS WHITE AND IN THE CROWD** [36] [ ]
(12"+=) *(VS 538-12)* – Soundtrack for every Heaven.

Nov 82. (7") **PROMISED YOU A MIRACLE. / THE AMERICAN** [–] [ ]

Nov 83. (7"/12") *(VS 636/+12)* **WATERFRONT. / HUNTER AND THE HUNTED (live)** [13] [ ]

Jan 84. (7"/7"pic-d) *(VS/+Y 649)* **SPEED YOUR LOVE TO ME. / BASS LINE** [20] [ ]
(12"+=) *(VS 649-12)* – ('A'extended).

Feb 84. (cd/c/lp,white-lp) *(CD/TC+/V 2300) <4981>* **SPARKLE IN THE RAIN** [1] [64]
– Up on the catwalk / Book of brilliant things / Speed your love to me / Waterfront / East at Easter / White hot day / Street hassle / "C" Moon cry like a baby / The kick inside of me / Shake off the ghosts. *(re-iss. cd Mar91; same)*

Mar 84. (7"/7"pic-d)(12") *(VS/+Y 661)(VS 661-12)* **UP ON THE CATWALK. / A BRASS BAND IN AFRICA** [27] [ ]

Apr 85. (7"/7"sha-pic-d)(12") *(VS/+S 749)(VS 749-12) <2703>* **DON'T YOU (FORGET ABOUT ME). / A BRASS BAND IN AFRICA** [7] Feb85 [1]
(re-iss. Jun88 cd-s; CDT 2)

— **KERR, BURCHILL, McNEILL + GAYNOR** brought in new member **JOHN GIBLING** – bass (ex-PETER GABRIEL sessions) to repl. FORBES

Oct 85. (7"/12") *(VS 817/+12)* **ALIVE AND KICKING. / ('A'instrumental)** [7] [–]
(12"+=) *(VS 817-13)* – Up on the catwalk (live).

Oct 85. (cd/c/lp,pic-lp) *(CD/TC+/V 2364) <5092>* **ONCE UPON A TIME** [1] [10]
– Once upon a time / All the things she said / Ghost dancing / Alive and kicking / Oh jungleland / I wish you were here / Sanctify yourself / Come a long way. *(lp re-iss. Mar01 on 'Simple Vinyl'; SVLP 312)*

Oct 85. (7") *<2783>* **ALIVE AND KICKING. / UP ON THE CATWALK (live)** [–] [3]

Jan 86. (7") *(SM 1) <2810>* **SANCTIFY YOURSELF. / ('A'instrumental)** [10] [14]
(d7"+=) *(SMP 1)* – Love song (live) / Street hassle (live).
(12") *(SM 1-12)* – ('A'mix). / ('A'dub instrumental).

Apr 86. (7") *(VS 860) <2828>* **ALL THE THINGS SHE SAID. / DON'T YOU (FORGET ABOUT ME)** [9] [28]
(12"+=) *(VS 860-12)* – Promised you a miracle (US mix).

Nov 86. (7") *(VS 907)* **GHOSTDANCING. / JUNGLELAND (instrumental)** [13] [ ]
(12"+=/cd-s+=) *(VS/MIKE 907-12)* – ('A'instrumental) / ('B'instrumental).

May 87. (d-cd/d-c/d-lp) *(CDVSM/SMDCX/SMDLX 1)* <6850> **LIVE IN THE CITY OF LIGHT (live)** [1] Jul87 [96]
– Ghostdancing / Big sleep / Waterfront / Promised you a miracle / Someone somewhere in summertime / Oh jungleland / Alive and kicking / Don't you (forget about me) / Once upon a time / Book of brilliant things / East at Easter / Sanctify yourself / Love song / Sun City – Dance to the music / New gold dream (81-82-83-84).

Jun 87. (7"/10") *(SM 2/+10)* **PROMISED YOU A MIRACLE (live). / BOOK OF BRILLIANT THINGS (live)** [19] [ ]
(12"+=/c-s+=) *(SM/+C 2-12)* – Glittering prize (live) / Celebrate (live).

—— **KERR, BURCHILL + McNEILL** were basic trio, w/other 2 still sessioning.

Feb 89. (7") *(SMX 3)* **BELFAST CHILD. / MANDELA DAY** [1] [ ]
(c-s+=/12"ep+=/12"box-ep+=/cd-ep+=) **BALLAD OF THE STREETS** *(SMX C/T/C/CD 3)* – Biko.

Apr 89. (7") *(SMX 4)* **THIS IS YOUR LAND. / SATURDAY GIRL** [13] [ ]
(c-s+=/12"+=/12"g-f+=/3"cd-s+=) *(SMX C/T/TG/CD 4)* – Year of the dragon.

May 89. (cd/c/lp) *(MIND D/C/S 1)* <3927> **STREET FIGHTING YEARS** [1] [70]
– Soul crying out / Wall of love / This is your land / Take a step back / Kick it in / Let it all come down / Biko / Mandela day / Belfast child / Street fighting years. *(re-iss. Dec89 box-cd/c +=; SMBX D/C 1)* – (interview cassettes).

Jul 89. (7"/c-s) *(SMX/+C 5)* **KICK IT IN. / WATERFRONT ('89 mix)** [15] [ ]
(12"+=/cd-s+=) *(SMX T/CD 5)* – Big sleep (live).
(12"g-f+=) *(SMXTG 5)* – ('A'mix).

Dec 89. (7"ep/c-ep/12"ep/cd-ep) *(SMX/+C/T/CD 6)* **THE AMSTERDAM EP** [18] [ ]
– Let it all come down / Sign o' the times / Jerusalem.
(12"ep+=/cd-ep+=) *(SMX TR/X 6)* – Sign o' the times (mix).

—— **KERR, BURCHILL + GAYNOR** brought in sessioners **MALCOLM FOSTER** – bass / **PETER JOHN VITESSE** – keyboards / **STEPHEN LIPSON** – bass, keyboards / **ANDY DUNCAN** – percussion / **GAVIN WRIGHT** – string leader / **LISA GERMANO** – violin

Mar 91. (7"/c-s) *(VS/+C 1332)* **LET THERE BE LOVE. / GOODNIGHT** [6] [ ]
(12"+=) *(VST 1332)* – Alive and kicking (live).
(cd-s++=) *(VSCD 1332)* – East at Easter (live).

Apr 91. (cd/c/lp) *(CD/TC+/V 2660)* <5352> **REAL LIFE** [2] [74]
– Real life / See the lights / Let there be love / Woman / Stand by love / African skies / Let the children speak / Ghostrider / Banging on the door / Travelling man / Rivers of ice / When two worlds collide.

May 91. (7"/c-s) *(VS/+C 1343)* **SEE THE LIGHTS. / THEME FOR GREAT CITIES ('91 edit)** [20] [–]
(12"+=/cd-s+=) *(VS T/CD 1343)* – Soul crying out (live).

May 91. (c-s,cd-s) <1553> **SEE THE LIGHTS / GOODNIGHT** [–] [40]

Aug 91. (7"/c-s) *(VS/+C 1358)* **STAND BY LOVE. / KING IS WHITE AND IN THE CROWD (live)** [13] [ ]
(12"+=/cd-s+=) *(VS T/CD 1358)* – Let there be love (live).

Oct 91. (7"/c-s) *(VS/+C 1382)* **REAL LIFE. / SEE THE LIGHTS** [34] [ ]
(ext.12"+=) *(VST 1382)* – Belfast child (extended).
(cd-s++=) *(VSCD 1382)* – Ghostrider.

Oct 92. (7"/c-s) *(VS/+C 1440)* **LOVE SONG. / ALIVE AND KICKING** [6] [ ]
(ext.cd-s+=) *(VSCDG 1440)* – ('B'instrumental).
(cd-s+=) *(VSCDX 1440)* – Travelling man / Oh jungleland.

Oct 92. (cd/c/lp) *(SMTV D/C/S 1)* **GLITTERING PRIZE – SIMPLE MINDS 81-92** (compilation) [1] [–]
– Waterfront / Don't you (forget about me) / Alive and kicking / Sanctify yourself / Love song / Someone somewhere in summertime / See the lights / Belfast child / The American / All the things she said / Promised you a miracle / Ghostdancing / Speed your love to me / Glittering prize / Let there be love / Mandela Day. *(lp re-iss. Oct00 on 'Simply Vinyl'; SVLP 258)*

—— **KERR + BURCHILL** with guests MARK BROWNE, MALCOLM FOSTER, MARCUS MILLER + LANCE MORRISON – bass / MARK SCHULMAN, TAL BERGMAN + VINNIE COLAIUTA – drums

Virgin Virgin

Jan 95. (7"/c-s/cd-s) *(VS/+C/+DG 1509)* <38467> **SHE'S A RIVER. / E55 / ('A'mix)** [9] [52]
(cd-s) *(VSCDX 1509)* – ('A'side) / Celtic strings / ('A'mix).

Jan 95. (cd/c/lp) *(CD/TC+/V 2760)* <39922> **GOOD NEWS FROM THE NEXT WORLD** [2] [87]
– She's a river / Night music / Hypnotised / Great leap forward / 7 deadly sins / And the band played on / My life / Criminal world / This time.

Mar 95. (7"/c-s) *(VS/+C 1534)* **HYPNOTISED. / #4** [18] [–]
(cd-s+=) *(VSCDX 1534)* – ('A'-Tim Simenon extended remixes) / ('A'-Malfunction mix).
(cd-s) *(VSCDT 1534)* – ('A'side) / Up on the catwalk (live) / And the band played on (live) / She's a river (live).

—— **KERR + BURCHILL** brought back **DEREK FORBES** – bass / **MEL GAYNOR** – drums / also **HAMI LEE** – additional programming

Chrysalis not iss.

Mar 98. (c-s) *(TCCHS 5078)* **GLITTERBALL / WATERFRONT (Union Jack mix)** [18] [–]
(cd-s+=) *(CDCHSS 5078)* – Love song (Philadelphia Bluntz mix).
(cd-s) *(CDCHS 5078)* – ('A'side) / Don't you forget about me (Jam & Spoon mix) / Theme for great cities (Fila Brazillia mix).

Mar 98. (cd/c) *(493712-2/-4)* **NEAPOLIS** [19] [–]
– Song for the tribes / Glitterball / War babies / Tears of a guy / Superman v supersoul / Lightning / If I had wings / Killing Andy Warhol / Androgyny.

May 98. (ext;c-s/7") *(TC+/CHS 5088)* **WAR BABIES. / I TRAVEL (Utah Saints mix)** [43] [–]
('A'-Bascombe mix;cd-s+=) *(CDCHS 5088)* – Theme for great cities '98 (Fluke's Atlantis mix) / ('A'-Johnson Somerset extended mix).

Eagle Red Ink

Sep 01. (cd-ep) *(EAGEP 198)* **DANCING BAREFOOT EP** [ ] [–]
– Dancing barefoot / Gloria / Being boiled / Love will tear us apart.

Sep 01. (cd) *(EAGCD 194)* <55944> **NEON LIGHTS** [ ] Oct01 [ ]
– Gloria / The man who sold the world / Homosapien / Dancing barefoot / Neon lights / Hello I love you / Bring on the dancing horses / The needle & the damage done / For your pleasure / All tomorrow's parties.

Dec 01. (12") *(REMOTE 016)* **HOMOSAPIEN (Malcolm Duffy mix). / HOMOSAPIEN (Malcolm Duffy dub mix)** [ ] [–]
(cd-s+=) *(REMOTE 016CD)* – ('A'-Malcolm Duffy edit).
(above issued on 'Remote')

—— in Feb'02, SIMPLE MINDS featured/vs on JOHN '00' FLEMING's single 'Belfast Trance' (i.e. 'Belfast Child')

Mar 02. (cd-s) *(EAGXA 218)* **CRY / LEAD THE BLIND / HOMOSAPIEN (Vince Clarke remix)** [47] [–]
(cd-s) *(EAGXS 218)* – ('A'side) / For what it's worth / The garden.

Apr 02. (cd) *(EAGCD 196)* <59145> **CRY** [ ] [ ]
– Cry / Spaceface / New sunshine morning / One step closer / Face in the sun / Disconnected / Lazy lately / Sugar / Sleeping girl / Cry again / Slave nation / The floating world.

Jun 02. (cd-s) *(EAGXS 232)* **SPACEFACE / NEW SUNRISE** [ ] [–]

—— in Jun'02, LIQUID PEOPLE vs. SIMPLE MINDS had a hit with 'Monster' which sampled 'CHANGELING'

Absolute not iss.

Sep 02. (12") *(ABR 014)* **CRY (phunk investigation club mix). / CRY (dub mix) / CRY (radio)** [ ] [–]
(cd-s) *(ABR 015)* – ('A'-Tazz Glasgoal vocal + tech-house dub).

Dec 02. (12") *(ABR 027)* **SPACEFACE (remixes)** [ ] [–]

Feb 03. (12") *(ABR 036)* **SPACEFACE (remixes)** [ ] [–]

Mar 03. (12") *(ABR 041)* **DON'T YOU (FORGET ABOUT ME) (remixes)** [ ] [–]

– compilations, others, etc. –

on 'Virgin' unless otherwise mentioned

Jan 82. (7") *Arista; (ARIST 448)* **I TRAVEL. / THIRTY FRAMES A SECOND (live)** [ ] [–]
(12"+=) *(ARIST12 448)* – ('A'live).

Feb 82. (lp/c) *Arista; (SPART/TCSPART 1183)* **CELEBRATION** [45] [ ]
(re-iss. Oct82 on 'Virgin' lp/c; V/TCV 2248) (re-iss. Apr89 on 'Virgin' lp/c; OVED/+C 275) (cd-iss. Aug89; CDV 2248)

Apr 83. (12") *(VS 578-12)* **I TRAVEL (mix). / FILM THEME** [ ] [–]

Aug 90. (5xcd-box-ep) *(SMTCD 1)* **THEMES – VOLUME ONE** [ ] [–]
– (Apr79 – LIFE IN A DAY – Apr82 – PROMISED YOU A MIRACLE singles)

Sep 90. (5xcd-box-ep) *(SMTCD 2)* **THEMES – VOLUME TWO** [ ] [–]
– (Aug82 – GLITTERING PRIZE – Apr85 – DON'T YOU (FORGET ABOUT ME) singles)

Oct 90. (5xcd-box-ep) *(SMTCD 3)* **THEMES – VOLUME THREE** [ ] [–]
– (Oct85 – ALIVE AND KICKING – Jun87 – PROMISED YOU A MIRACLE (live) singles)

Nov 90. (5xcd-box-ep) *(SMTCD 4)* **THEMES – VOLUME FOUR** | | – |
– (Feb89 – BELFAST CHILD, Dec89 – THE AMSTERDAM EP)

Nov 90. (3xcd-box) *(TPAK 2)* **COLLECTOR'S EDITION** | | – |
– (LIFE IN A DAY / REEL TO REAL CACOPHONY / EMPIRES AND DANCE)

Nov 01. (d-cd) *(CDVD 2953)* **THE BEST OF SIMPLE MINDS** | 34 | – |

Jun 03. (cd) *(SIMCD 13)* **OUR SECRETS ARE THE SAME** | | – |
– Swimming towards the sun / Jeweller to the stars / Space / Death by chocolate / Waiting for the end of the world / Neon city cowboys / She knows / Hello / Happy is the man / Sleeping.

SIMPLY RED

Formed: Manchester, England . . . 1984 by the flame-haired MICK HUCKNALL, who had cut his teeth in power-punk outfit, The FRANTIC ELEVATORS. The band released four independent singles in all, the last of which, 'HOLDING BACK THE YEARS' would go on to become a massive SIMPLY RED hit. Hooking up with manager Elliot Rashman, HUCKNELL formed an early incarnation of SIMPLY RED with EDDIE SHERWOOD, OJO and MOG, these musicians soon replaced with former DURUTTI COLUMN men, TONY BOWERS, CHRIS JOYCE and TIM KELLET. Subsequently signing with 'Elektra', the band scored immediately with a biting pop/funk cover of The VALENTINE BROTHERS' 'MONEY'S TOO TIGHT (TO MENTION)', political sentiments many people could identify with in Thatcher's brutal economic regime of the 80's. The single deservedly made the Top 20 in the summer of '85, introducing HUCKNALL's dynamic vocal acrobatics and paving the way for a Top 40 album, 'PICTURE BOOK' (1985). Though a second single, the uptempo 'COME TO MY AID' stiffed in the lower regions of the chart, a ponderous remake of the aforementioned 'HOLDING . . .' became a US No.1 the following Spring, giving the debut album a whole new lease of life. The ballad also narrowly missed the top of the UK charts, establishing HUCKNALL as a distinctive fixture in pop's rich tapestry as well as an unlikely sex symbol. In early '87, SIMPLY RED were back in the Top 20 with 'THE RIGHT THING', preceding a follow-up album, 'MEN AND WOMEN'. Partly co-penned with seasoned Motown writer, LAMONT DOZIER, the album was a more ambitious attempt at updating classic soul for the 80's. Though the rather dull cover of COLE PORTER's 'EV'RY TIME WE SAY GOODBYE' was another big hit, another couple of singles flopped and SIMPLY RED's position in the major league wasn't yet assured. That honour came with 'A NEW FLAME' (1989), an unashamed effort to capture the coffee table middle ground between pop, soul, rock and jazz which furnished SIMPLY RED with their first UK No.1 placing. The album's centrepiece was a tepid reading of the old HAROLD MELVIN chestnut, 'IF YOU DON'T KNOW ME BY NOW', a huge worldwide hit. In between dating models and fending off the tabloids, HUCKNALL subsequently took time out from his new found fame to pen the best selling and most consistent album of his career, 'STARS' (1991). Previewed by the sassy 'SOMETHING GOT ME STARTED', the record found HUCKNALL revelling in his role of dreadlocked love god, his voice swooning and keening over a set of impressive originals. Though SIMPLY RED were constantly harangued by the more cynical factions of the music press, the group had amassed legions of devoted fans, their support making 'STARS' one of the most popular albums of the 90's. Following a couple of years of heavy touring and some time out, SIMPLY RED returned in 1995 with 'FAIRGROUND', something of a departure with its dancefloor backing track nicked from The GOODMEN's club smash, 'GIVE IT UP'. The single gave SIMPLY RED their first No.1, closely followed by yet another No.1 album, 'LIFE' (1995), consolidating the group's position as one of the UK's most popular musical exports. The following year, HUCKNALL illustrated his love of reggae, hooking up with SLY & ROBBIE for a smoking dub-friendly version of the Gregory Isaacs standard, 'NIGHT NURSE'. The track was also part of his next set, simply-entitled 'BLUE' (1998), a record which saw him cover at least four more including 'Neil Young's 'MELLOW MY MIND', The Hollies hit 'THE AIR THAT I BREATHE' and Dennis Brown's 'GHETTO GIRL'. Towards the end of '99, HUCKNALL and his SIMPLY RED crew delivered the uncool seventh studio set, 'LOVE AND THE RUSSIAN WINTER', another to hit the UK Top 10. It was all getting a little stagnant when another compilation, 'IT'S ONLY LOVE' (containing all the recent hits) hit the shops for Xmas 2000. Three years in waiting, 'HOME' (2003) was hardly likely to win over any of the band's detractors although there were definitely moments to savour. On the likes of 'HOME LOAN BLUES', and the spot-on cover of Dennis Brown's 'MONEY IN MY POCKET', there were hints of the bruised agit-soul of years gone by although HUCKNALL did himself few favours with ham-fisted versions of the Stylistics' 'YOU MAKE ME FEEL BRAND NEW' and HALL & OATES-sampling fluff like 'SUNRISE'.
• **Songwriters:** HUCKNALL compositions, some with LAMONT DOZIER. Covered:- LET ME HAVE IT ALL (Sly Stone) / EV'RY TIME WE SAY GOODBYE (Cole Porter) / LOVE FIRE (Bunny Wailer) / IT'S ONLY LOVE (Barry White; c. J & V Cameron).

Album rating: PICTURE BOOK (*7) / MEN AND WOMEN (*8) / A NEW FLAME (*9) / STARS (*9) / LIFE (*7) / GREATEST HITS (HOLDING BACK THE YEARS 1985-96) compilation (*9) / BLUE (*5) / LOVE AND THE RUSSIAN WINTER (*4) / IT'S ONLY LOVE compilation (*6) / HOME (*4)

FRANTIC ELEVATORS

MICK HUCKNALL – vocals, guitar / **NEIL MOSS** – guitar, piano / **BRIAN TURNER** – piano, bass / **KEVIN WILLIAMS** – drums

		T.J.M.	not iss.
Jun 79.	(7"m) *(TJM 5)* **VOICE IN THE DARK. / PASSION / EVERY DAY I DIE**		–
Jan 80.	(7"demo) *(TJM 6)* **HUNCHBACK OF NOTRE DAME. / SEE NOTHING AND EVERYTHING / DON'T JUDGE ME**		–
		Eric's	not iss.
Nov 80.	(7") *(ERICS 006)* **YOU KNOW WHAT YOU TOLD ME. / PRODUCTION PREVENTION**		–
		Crackin'Up	not iss.
Apr 81.	(7") *(CRACK 1)* **SEARCHING FOR THE ONLY ONE. / HUNCHBACK OF NOTRE DAME**		–
		No Waiting	not iss.
Oct 82.	(7") *(WAIT 1)* **HOLDING BACK THE YEARS. / PISTOLS IN MY BRAIN**		–

— HUCKNALL formed SIMPLY RED

– compilations, etc. –

Sep 87. (m-lp) *T.J.M.; (TJM 101)* **THE EARLY YEARS** | | – |
(re-iss. Jul88 by "MICK HUCKNALL & FRANTIC ELEVATORS" on 'Receiver' cd/lp; CD+/KNOB 2)

1992. (cd) *Classic Artists; (MER 004)* **SIMPLY MICK HUCKNALL** | | – |

SIMPLY RED

MICK HUCKNALL (b. 8 Jun'60) – vocals (ex-FRANTIC ELEVATORS) / **DAVID FRYMAN** – guitar (originals EDDIE SHERWOOD – ex-BITING TONGUES, OJO & MOG repl. by below) / **TONY BOWERS** – bass (ex-DURUTTI COLUMN, ex-MOTHMEN) / **CHRIS JOYCE** – drums (ex-DURUTTI COLUMN, ex-MOTHMEN, ex-PINK MILITARY) / **FRITZ McINTYRE** – guitar / **TIM KELLETT** – brass (ex-DURUTTI COLUMN)

Elektra Elektra

Jun 85. (7"/7"pic-d) *(EKR 9/+P)* **MONEY$ TOO TIGHT (TO MENTION). / OPEN UP THE RED BOX** [13] [ ]
(ext.12"+=) *(EKR 9T)* – Every bit of me.
(12") *(EKR 9TX)* – ('A'-Cutback mix) / ('A'dub) / ('B'side).

Aug 85. (7") *(EKR 19)* **COME TO MY AID. / VALENTINE** [66] [ ]
(ext.12"+=) *(EKR 19T)* – Granma's hand.
('A'-Survival mix-12"++=) *(EKR 19TX)* – ('A'heavy dub mix).

— **SYLVAN RICHARDSON** – guitar repl. FRYMAN (but on below lp)

Oct 85. (lp/c)(cd) *(EKT 27/+C)(960 452-2) <60452>* **PICTURE BOOK** [34] Apr86 [16]
– Come to my aid / Sad old Red / Look at you now / Heaven / Jericho / Money$ too tight (to mention) / Holding back the years / Open up the red box / No direction / Picture book. *(pic-lp iss.May86; EKT 27P) (hit UK No.2 in May87) (re-mast.cd Feb92 on 'East West'; 9031-76993-2,* hit UK No.39)

Nov 85. (7"/7"sha-pic-d/7"gf) *(EKR 29/+P/F) <69564>* **HOLDING BACK THE YEARS. / I WON'T FEEL BAD** [51] Mar86 [1]
(ext.12"+=) *(EKR 29T)* – Drowning in my own tears.

WEA Elektra

Feb 86. (7"/7"red) *(YZ 63/+R)* **JERICHO. / JERICHO THE MUSICAL** [53] [ ]
(ext.12"+=) *(YZ 63T)* – Money$ too tight (to mention) (live) / Heaven (live).

May 86. (7") *(YZ 70)* **HOLDING BACK THE YEARS. / DROWNING IN MY OWN TEARS** [2] [–]
(ext.12"+=) *(YZ 70T)* – Picture book in dub.

Jul 86. (7") *<69528>* **MONEY$ TOO TIGHT (TO MENTION). / PICTURE BOOK (dub)** [–] [28]

Jul 86. (7"/7"box) *(YZ 75/+B)* **OPEN UP THE RED BOX (remix). / LOOK AT YOU NOW (live)** [61] [ ]
(d7"+=) *(YZ 75F)* – Holding back the years / Drowning in my own tears.
(ext.12"+=) *(YZ 75T)* – Heaven the movie (live).
(d12"+++=) *(YZ 75TF)* – (all above) / Picture book in dub.

— **AZIZ IBRAHIM** – guitar repl. SYLVAN / added **IAN KIRKHAM** – saxophone / **JANETTE SEWELL** – b.vocals

Feb 87. (7"/7"s) *(YZ 103/+V) <69487>* **THE RIGHT THING. / THERE'S A LIGHT** [11] [27]
(d7"+=) *(YZ 103F)* – Holding back the years / Drowning in my own tears.
(ext.12"+=/ext.12"clear-pic-d+=) *(YZ 103 T/TP)* – Ev'ry time we say goodbye.

Mar 87. (lp/c)(cd) *(WX 85/+C)(242-071-2) <60727>* **MEN AND WOMEN** [2] [31]
– The right thing / Infielity / Suffer / I won't feel bad / Ev'ry time we say goodbye / Let me have it all / Love fire / Move on out / Shine / Maybe someday . . . *(re-mast.Feb95;)*

May 87. (7") *(YZ 114)* **INFIDELITY. / LADY GODIVA'S ROOM** [31] [ ]
(12"/12"pic-d) *(YZ 114 T/TP)* – ('A'-Stretch mix) / Love fire (Massive Red mix) / ('B'side).

Jul 87. (7") *(YZ 141)* **MAYBE SOMEDAY . . . / LET ME HAVE IT ALL (remix)** [ ] [ ]
(12"+=) *(YZ 141T)* – Broken man. *(US; b-side)*

Nov 87. (7") *(YZ 161)* **EV'RY TIME WE SAY GOODBYE. / LOVE FOR SALE (live in studio)** [11] [–]
(10"+=) *(YZ 161TE)* – Sad old Red / Broken man.
(12"+=/12"s+=) *(YZ 161 T/TW)* – ('A'live in studio).
(cd-s++=) *(YZ 161CD)* – Sad old Red.

Mar 88. (7") *(YZ 172)* **I WON'T FEEL BAD. / LADY GODIVA'S ROOM** [68] [ ]
(12"+=) *(YZ 172T)* – ('A'-Arthur Baker remix).
(cd-s++=) *(YZ 172CD)* – The right thing.

Jul 88. (7") **LET ME HAVE IT ALL. / SUFFER** [–] [ ]

— **HEITOR T.P.** – guitar repl. IBRAHIM and SEWELL

Jan 89. (7") *(YZ 349) <69317>* **IT'S ONLY LOVE. / TURN IT UP** [13] [57]
('A'-Valentine mix-10"+=) *(YZ 349TE)* – I'm gonna lose you.
(12") *(YZ 349T)* – ('A'-Valentine mix) / ('B'side) / X.
(Valentine-3"cd-s+=/3"cd-s+=) *(YZ 349CD/+X)* – The right thing.

Feb 89. (lp/c)(cd) *(WX 242/+C)(244 689-2) <60828>* **A NEW FLAME** [1] [22]
– It's only love / A new flame / You've got it / To be with you / More / Turn it up / Love lays its tune / She'll have to go / If you don't know me by now / Enough. *(re-mast.Feb92; ,* hit UK No.44)

Apr 89. (7") *(YZ 377) <69297>* **IF YOU DON'T KNOW ME BY NOW. / MOVE ON OUT (live)** [2] [1]
(12"+=) *(YZ 377T)* – Shine (live).
(3"cd-s++=/cd-s++=) *(YZ 377CD/+X)* – Sugar daddy.
(10"+=) *(377TE)* – The great divide (S.H.T.G.).

Jul 89. (7"/c-s) *(YZ 404/+C)* **A NEW FLAME. / MORE** [17] [ ]
(10"+=) *(YZ 404TE)* – I asked her for water (live) / Funk on out (live).
(12"+=/3"cd-s+=) *(YZ 404 T/CD) – I asked her for water (live) / Resume (live).*

Oct 89. (7"/c-s) *(YZ 424/+C)* **YOU'VE GOT IT. / HOLDING BACK THE YEARS (live acoustic)** [46] [–]
(12"+=/cd-s+=) *(YZ 424 T/CD)* – I wish.
(10"++=) *(YZ 424TE)* – I know you got soul.

Oct 89. (7") **YOU'VE GOT IT. / SHE'LL HAVE TO GO** [–] [ ]

— **HUCKNALL, McINTYRE, KELLETT, HEITOR + KIRKHAM** recruit newcomers **GOTA** – drums, percussion, programs repl. JOYCE / **SHAUN WARD** – bass repl. BOWERS / added guest **JESS BAILEY** – programmer

East West East West

Sep 91. (7"/c-s) *(YZ 614/+C) <98711>* **SOMETHING GOT ME STARTED. / A NEW FLAME** [11] [27]
('A'-Perfecto mix-12"+=) *(YZ 614T)* – ('A'instrumental).
(cd-s++=) *(YZ 614CD)* – Come on in my kitchen.

Oct 91. (cd)(lp/c) *(9031-75284-2)(WX427/+C) <91773>* **STARS** [1] [76]
– Something got me started / Stars / Thrill me / Your mirror / She's got it bad / For your babies / Model / How could it fall / Freedom / Wonderland.

Nov 91. (7"/c-s) *(YZ 626/+C) <98636>* **STARS. / STARS (PM-Ized mix)** [8] Jan92 [44]
('A'-Comprende mix-12"+=) *(YZ 626T)* – Ramblin' on my mind / Something got me started (Hurley's House mix).
(cd-s++=) *(YZ 626CD)* – (all above except 'B'side).

Feb 92. (7")(c-s) *(YZ 642)(9031-76339-4)* **FOR YOUR BABIES. / ('A'-French version)** [9] [ ]
(12"+=) *(YZ 642T)* – Freedom (Perfecto mix).
(cd-s+=) *(YZ 642CDX)* – Me & the Devil blues / Freedom (how long mix).

Apr 92. (7"/c-s) *(YZ 671/+C)* **THRILL ME. / ('A'-Nellie Hooper mix)** [33] [ ]
(cd-s+=) *(YZ 671CD)* – ('A'live) / When you've got a good friend.
(12") *(YZ 671T)* – ('A'-Connoisseur mix) / ('A'-Stewart Levine's club mix) / ('A'-Nellie Hooper dub).

Jul 92. (7") *(YZ 689)* **YOUR MIRROR. / ('A'live)** [17] [ ]
(c-s) *(YZ 689C)* – ('A'side) / More live) / Something got me started.
(cd-s) *(YZ 689CD)* – ('A'side) / Same old Red (live) / She's got it bad (live).

Nov 92. (7"ep/c-ep/cd-ep/s-cd-ep) *(YZ 716/+C/CD/CDX)* **MONTREAUX EP (live)** [11] [ ]
– Love for sale / Drowning in my own tears / Granma's hand / Lady Godiva's room.

— **DEE JOHNSON** – backing vocals; repl.TIM

Sep 95. (c-s) *(EW 001C)* **FAIRGROUND / ('A'extended)** [1] [ ]
(cd-s+=) *(EW 001CD1)* – Stars (live) / The right thing (live).
(cd-s+=) *(EW 001CD2)* – ('A'-In the Garden mix) / ('A'-Too precious mix) / ('A'-Rollo and Sister Bliss remix).

Oct 95. (cd/c/lp) *(0630-12069-2/-4/-1) <61853>* **LIFE** [1] [75]
– You make me believe / So many people / Lives and loves / Fairground / Never never love / So beautiful / Hillside avenue / Remembering the first time / Out on the range / We're in this together.

Dec 95. (c-s) *(EW 015C)* **REMEMBERING THE FIRST TIME / (Too precious mix)** [22] [–]
(cd-s+=) *(EW 015CD1)* – Enough (live) / A new flame (live).
(cd-s) *(EW 015CD2)* – ('A'-mixes; extended cool disco / SPS mambo / Too precious dub / Satoshi Tomiie classic / Remembering the ambient times).

Feb 96. (c-s) *(EW 029C)* **NEVER NEVER LOVE / (too precious mix)** [18] [–]
(cd-s) *(EW 029CD1)* – ('A'side) / Fairground (live) / You make me believe (Merv's Amazon mix) / Groovy situation (live).
(cd-s) *(EW 029CD2)* – ('A'mixes; Too precious / Grooving with the angels / DJ Muggs master / DJ Muggs instrumental / US R&B).

— In Apr'96 as SIMPLY RED & WHITE, they released football version of 'DAYDREAM BELIEVER (CHEER UP PETER REID)', which hit No.41.

Jun 96. (c-s) *(EW 046C)* **WE'RE IN THIS TOGETHER / YOU MAKE ME BELIEVE (live) / HILLSIDE AVENUE (live)** [11] [–]
(cd-s) *(EW 046CDX)* – (first two tracks) / ('A'-Universal feeling (mix).
(cd-s) *(EW 046CD)* – ('A'side) / Money's too tight (live) / ('A'-Universal feeling mix).

Oct 96. (cd/c) *(0630 16552-2/-4) <61993>* **GREATEST HITS (HOLDING BACK THE YEARS 1985-1996)** (compilation) 1
– Holding back the years / Money's too tight to mention / The right thing / It's only love / A new flame / You've got it / If you don't know me by now / Stars / Something got me started / Thrill me / Your mirror / For your babies / So beautiful / Angel / Fairground.

Oct 96. (c-s) *(EW 074C)* **ANGEL / (Mousse T soul mix)** 4 –
(cd-s+=) *(EW 074CD1)* – ('A'-mixes; rubbadubb / soundtrack / wondrous angel dub).
(cd-s+=) *(EW 074CD2)* – ('A'-live from Montreux Jazz Festival / Money's too tight (edited disco vocal).

— In Sep'97, they teamed up with SLY & ROBBIE on the No.13 hit 'NIGHT NURSE' *(East West EW 129 C/CD1/CD2)*

May 98. (c-s) *(EW 164C)* **SAY YOU LOVE ME / SO JUNGIFUL** 7 –
(cd-s+=) *(EW 164CD)* – So many people (live) / Never never never (live).

May 98. (cd/c/lp) *(3984 23097-2/-4/-1) <62222>* **BLUE** 1
– Mellow my mind / Blue / Say you love me / To be free / The air that I breathe / Someday in my life / The air that I breathe reprise / Night nurse / Broken man / Come get me angel / Ghetto girl / Love has said goodbye again / High fives.

Aug 98. (c-s/cd-s) *(EW 181 C/CD1)* **THE AIR THAT I BREATHE / LIVES AND LOVES (live) / TU SEI DENTRO DI ME (SOMEDAY IN MY LIFE)** 6 –
(cd-s) *(EW 181CD2)* – ('A'-reprise) / ('A'side) / Love has said goodbye again (Rae & Christian mix).

Nov 98. (c-s/cd-s) *(EW 191 C/CD1)* **GHETTO GIRL (mixes; remix / dub / blood & fire sound system)** 34 –
(cd-s) *(EW 191CD2)* – So beautiful (live) / Ghetto girl (live) / Say you love me (live) / So beautiful (live Cd-Rom).

Oct 99. (c-s) *(EW 208C)* **AIN'T THAT A LOT OF LOVE / (Phats & Small mutant disco vocal)** 14 –
(cd-s+=) *(EW 208CD1)* – ('A'-Johnny Vicious filter factory dub).
(cd-s) *(EW 208CD2)* – ('A'side) / ('A'-video) / Come on in my kitchen.
(12") *(EW 208T)* – ('A'side) / Come on in my kitchen.

Nov 99. (cd/c/lp) *(3984 29942-2/-4/-1) <62481>* **LOVE AND THE RUSSIAN WINTER** 6
– The spirit of love / Ain't that a lot of love / Your eyes / The sky is a gypsy / Back into the universe / Words for girlfriends / Thank you / Man made the gun / Close to you / More than a dream / Wave the old world goodbye.

Feb 00. (c-s) *(EW 212C)* **YOUR EYES / (Mousse T super funk mix)** 26 –
(cd-s+=) *(EW 212CD1)* – ('A'-Mousse T acoustic string end mix).
(cd-s/12") *(EW 212 CD2/T)* – ('A'mixes; Mousse T super funk / ignorants / Jimmy Gomez funky).

Nov 00. (cd/c) *(8573 85537-2/-4)* **IT'S ONLY LOVE** (compilation) 27 –
– If you don't love me by now / Holding back the years / Say you love me / The air that I breathe / It's only love / You've got it / Ev'ry time we say goodbye / For your babies / Lady Godiva's room / Your eyes (Mousse T acoustic) / Thank you / Remembering the first time / Angel / Night nurse / Never never love / More / Mellow my mind / Stars / Ain't that a lot of love.

simplyred.com simplyred.com

Mar 03. (c-s) *(SRS 001 MC/CD1)* **SUNRISE (mixes; radio / love to infinity classic / love to infinity club / video)** 7 –
(cd-s) *(SRS 001CD2)* – ('A'-mixes).

Mar 03. (cd) *(SRA 001CD) <70004>* **HOME** 2 Jun03
– Home / Fake / Sunrise / You make me feel brand new / Home loan blues / Positively 4th street / Lost weekend / Money in my pocket / Something for you / It's you / Home (reprise). *(ltd-cd-iss. Nov03 w/dvd+=; SRA 001CDX)*

Jul 03. (c-s/cd-s) *(SRS 002 MC/CD1)* **FAKE (remixes; radio / album / love to infinity / phunk investigation radio)** 21 –
(cd-s) *(SRS 002CD2)* – ('A'live) / Lost weekend (live) / Money in my pocket (live).

Dec 03. (c-s) *(SRS 003MC)* **YOU MAKE ME FEEL BRAND NEW / (Antillas vocal edit) / (love to infinity radio mix)** 7 –
(cd-s+=) *(SRS 003CD1)* – ('A'-video).
(cd-s) *(SRS 003CD2)* – ('A'-live) / Home (live) / Something for you (live).

SIOUXSIE & THE BANSHEES

Formed: London, England . . . September '76 by SIOUXSIE SIOUX and STEVE SEVERIN, both members of the infamous 'Bromley Contingent' punk troupe who religiously followed The SEX PISTOLS during the turbulent early years of their career; an early incarnation of The BANSHEES even featured future PISTOL, SID VICIOUS on drums, the outfit mangling the Lord's Prayer at the legendary 100 Club punk all-dayer in summer '76. SIOUX gained further notoriety following her appearance (as a fan) on the fateful edition of Bill Grundy's 'Today' programme wherein his tete-a-tete with the 'PISTOLS outraged the country's more upstanding citizens. Cutting a striking dash through the punk scene with her Nazi chic and proto-goth garb, SIOUXSIE and her BANSHEES (who, after much to-ing and fro-ing, were eventually completed by JOHN McKAY amd KENNY MORRIS) toured constantly throughout 1977, eventually signing to 'Polydor' the following year after their original label, 'Track', went bust. A debut single, 'HONG KONG GARDEN' was a sprightly slice of oriental flavoured post-punk which hit the Top 10 with ease and introduced the band outwith the confines of the London scene. 'THE SCREAM' (1978) was instantly hailed as a classic upon its release a few months later, the record's queasy, churning goth-psychedelia breaking new ground and spearheading a new direction for many bands inspired by a movement already dying on its feet. For many recent converts, then, 'JOIN HANDS' (1979) was a disappointment, a turgid affair which lacked the bite of its predecessor and presaged a band breakdown; McKAY and MORRIS upped sticks and left mid-tour, ROBERT SMITH (The CURE) briefly deputising before a new guitarist was eventually found in erstwhile MAGAZINE man, JOHN McGEOGH. The drum seat, meanwhile, was taken by ex-SLITS man, BUDGIE, who would subsequently become SIOUXSIE's beau and eventual husband. The revamped line-up bounced back in 1980 with the enchanting 'HAPPY HOUSE' (a Top 20 hit that Spring) and an accompanying Top 5 album, 'KALEIDOSCOPE', investing their sound with a newly acquired accessibility and ensuring a degree of crossover success for SIOUXSIE's icy sensuality. 'JU JU' (1981) further refined the group's subtle gothic tapestries, again taking the band into the UK Top 10 and spawning a clutch of minor hits while 'ONCE UPON A TIME – THE SINGLES' neatly rounded up the first instalment in The BANSHEES' career. More overtly experimental was the following year's 'A KISS IN THE DREAMHOUSE', utilising strings and flirting with club sounds. 1983 saw a flurry of side project activity as SIOUXSIE and BUDGIE formed The CREATURES, releasing 'FEAST', the first of two albums together (they also had a major hit with Mel Torme's 'RIGHT NOW'). SEVERIN, meanwhile, formed The GLOVE with SMITH (who had also rejoined the BANSHEES ranks as a part-time, temporary replacement for the departing McGEOGH), releasing the 'BLUE SUNSHINE' album the same year. No new BANSHEES material surfaced, although an atmospheric cover of The Beatles' 'DEAR PRUDENCE' hit No.3 and gave them their biggest selling single to date. The track featured on 1983's live set, 'NOCTURNE', while the following year's 'HYAENA', saw SMITH making his presence felt over the course of a haunting set that was unfairly panned by the critics. With SMITH subsequently finding the demands of a dual lifestyle too tiring, ex-CLOCKDVA man, JOHN CARRUTHERS was drafted in for 'TINDERBOX' (1986), an album which carried on in much the same vein, spawning a sizeable hit with the infectious

'CITIES IN DUST'. Perhaps the band really were running out of ideas as their detractors suggested, a suitably gothic Top 20 rendition of Bob Dylan's 'THIS WHEEL'S ON FIRE' trailing a whole album's worth of competent but hardly inspiring cover versions. Featuring yet another guitarist, JON KLEIN, 1988's 'PEEPSHOW' was a much more compelling proposition, a perversely eclectic selection best sampled on the mutant dancefloor hit, 'PEEK-A-BOO'. Now something of an alternative institution, SIOUXSIE & THE BANSHEES cruised into the 90's with their most chart-friendly original material to date, the swooning 'KISS THEM FOR ME' (the band's first – and to date only – major US hit) single and attendant 'SUPERSTITION' (1991) album. Despite the latter set's commercial and critical success, the group reached the end of its natural lifespan in the mid-90's, bowing out on a high with the majestic 'THE RAPTURE'. Officially splitting in April '96, SIOUXSIE was working on new CREATURES material with spouse BUDGIE, while SEVERIN scored the soundtrack for the movie, 'Visions Of Ecstasy'. The aforementioned CREATURES finally resurfaced via 'ANIMA ANIMUS' (1999), an album that boasted a few minor hits; SIOUXSIE was now looking rather Elizabeth Taylor-ish although when she wailed and her BUDGIE drummed it was safe there was no lasting comparison. • **Songwriters:** All written by SIOUXSIE / SEVERIN except; HELTER SKELTER (Beatles) / 20th CENTURY BOY (T.Rex) / IL EST NE LE DIVIN ENFANT (French festive song) / ALL TOMORROW'S PARTIES (Velvet Underground). THROUGH THE LOOKING GLASS was a covers album containing THE PASSENGER (Iggy Pop) / YOU'RE LOST LITTLE GIRL (Doors) / GUN (John Cale) / THIS TOWN AIN'T BIG ENOUGH FOR THE BOTH OF US (Sparks) / SEA BREEZES (Roxy Music) / STRANGE FRUIT (Billie Holiday) / WALL OF MIRRORS (Kraftwerk) / LITTLE JOHNNY JEWEL (Television) / TRUST IN ME ('Jungle Book' animated film). • **Trivia:** SEVERIN produced ALTERED IMAGES debut 45 'Dead Pop Stars'.

Album rating: THE SCREAM (*9) / JOIN HANDS (*7) / KALEIDOSCOPE (*7) / JU JU (*7) / ONCE UPON A TIME – THE SINGLES compilation (*9) / A KISS IN THE DREAMHOUSE (*7) / NOCTURNE (*5) / HYAENA (*7) / TINDERBOX (*7) / THROUGH THE LOOKING GLASS (*5) / PEEP SHOW (*5) / SUPERSTITION (*5) / TWICE UPON A TIME compilation (*7) / THE RAPTURE (*5) / THE BEST OF SIOUXSIE & THE BANSHEES compilation (*6) / Creatures: FEAST (*5) / BOOMERANG (*4) / ANIMA ANIMUS (*6) / Glove: BLUE SUNSHINE (*5)

SIOUXSIE SIOUX (b. SUSAN DALLION, 27 May'57) – vocals / **STEVEN SEVERIN** (b. STEVEN BAILEY, 25 Sep'55) – bass / **JOHN McKAY** – guitar; repl. PT FENTON; who had repl. MARCO PIRRONI (he joined The MODELS and later ADAM & THE ANTS) / **KENNY MORRIS** – drums repl. SID VICIOUS who later became bassman for SEX PISTOLS

Polydor Polydor

Aug 78. (7") *(2059 052)* **HONG KONG GARDEN. / VOICES** [7] [–]

Oct 78. (7") **HONG KONG GARDEN. / OVERGROUND** [–] [ ]

Nov 78. (lp/c) *(POLD/+C 5009)* <6207> **THE SCREAM** [12] [ ]
– Pure / Jigsaw feeling / Overground / Carcass / Helter skelter / Mirage / Metal postcard / Nicotine stain / Suburban relapse / Switch. *(cd-iss. Mar89 & Mar95 on 'Wonderland'; 839 008-2) (cd re-iss. Mar95)*

Mar 79. (7") *(POSP 9)* **THE STAIRCASE (MYSTERY). / 20th CENTURY BOY** [24] [–]

Jun 79. (7") *(POSP 59)* **PLAYGROUND TWIST. / PULLED TO BITS** [28] [–]

Sep 79. (lp/c) *(POLD/+C 5024)* **JOIN HANDS** [13] [–]
– Poppy day / Regal zone / Placebo effect / Icon / Premature burial / Playground twist / Mother / Oh mein papa / The Lord's prayer. *(cd-iss. Mar89 & Mar95 on 'Wonderland'; 839004-2)*

Sep 79. (7") *(2059 151)* **MITTAGEISEN (METAL POSTCARD). / LOVE IN A VOID** [47] [–]

— **BUDGIE** (b.PETER CLARK, 21 Aug'57, St.Helens, England) – drums (ex-SLITS, ex-PLANETS, ex-BIG IN JAPAN, etc.) repl. MORRIS who bailed out (he subsequently released a solo 12", 'LA MAIN MORTE', for 'Temple' records in '86) / **JOHN McGEOGH** (b. 1955, Greenock, Scotland) – guitar (of MAGAZINE) finally repl. ROBERT SMITH (of The CURE) + JOHN CARRUTHERS who repl. McKAY (he finally formed ZOR GABOR in 1986 – with vocalist LINDA CLARK – and released one single, 'TIGHTROPE', for 'In-Tape' early '87)

Mar 80. (7") *(POSP 117)* **HAPPY HOUSE. / DROP DEAD** [17] [–]

May 80. (7") *(2059 249)* **CHRISTINE. / EVE WHITE EVE BLACK** [24] [–]

Aug 80. (lp)(c) *(2442 177)(3184 146)* **KALEIDOSCOPE** [5] [–]
– Happy house / Tenant / Trophy / Hybrid / Lunar camel / Christine / Desert kisses / Red light / Paradise place / Skin. *(cd-iss. Mar89 & Mar95 on 'Wonderland'; 839006-2)*

Nov 80. (7"/dance-12") *(POSP/+X 205)* **ISRAEL. / RED OVER WHITE** [41] [–]

May 81. (7") *(POSP 273)* **SPELLBOUND. / FOLLOW THE SUN** [22] [–]
(12"+=) *(POSPX 273)* – Slap dash snap.

Jun 81. (lp/c) *(POLS/+C 1034)* **JU JU** [7] [–]
– Spellbound / Into the light / Arabian knights / Halloween / Monitor / Night shift / Sin in my heart / Head cut / Voodoo dolly. *(cd-iss. Mar89 & Mar95 on 'Wonderland'; 839005-2)*

Jul 81. (7") *(POSP 309)* **ARABIAN KNIGHTS. / SUPERNATURAL THING** [32] [–]
(12"+=) *(POSPX 309)* – Congo conga.

— SIOUXSIE & BUDGIE as The CREATURES hit Top 30 with WILD THINGS EP.

Dec 81. (lp/c) *(POLS/+C 1056)* **ONCE UPON A TIME – THE SINGLES** [21] [–]
– Hong Kong garden / Mirage / The staircase (mystery) / Playground twist / Happy house / Christine / Israel / Spellbound / Arabian knights / Fireworks. *(cd-iss. Mar89 on 'Wonderland'; 831542-2)*

May 82. (7") *(POSPG 450)* **FIREWORKS. / COAL MIND** [22] [–]
(12"+=) *(POSPX 450)* – We fall.

Sep 82. (7") *(POSP 510)* **SLOWDIVE. / CANNIBAL ROSES** [41] [–]
(12"+=) *(POSPX 510)* – Obsession II.

Nov 82. (lp/c) *(POLD/+C 5064)* **A KISS IN THE DREAMHOUSE** [11] [–]
– Cascade / Green fingers / Obsession / She's a carnival / Circle / Melt! / Painted bird / Cocoon / Slowdive. *(cd-iss. Apr89 & Mar 95 on 'Wonderland'; 839007-2)*

Nov 82. (7") *(POSP 539)* **MELT! / IL EST NE LE DIVIN ENFANT** [49] [ ]
(12"+=) *(POSPX 539)* – A sleeping rain.

— **ROBERT SMITH** – guitar (of The CURE) returned part-time to repl. McGEOGH who later joined The ARMOURY SHOW.

— In 1983, SMITH and SEVERIN had also splintered into The GLOVE, with SIOUXSIE and BUDGIE re-uniting as The CREATURES (see further on).

Wonderland – Polydor Geffen

Sep 83. (7") *(SHEG 4)* **DEAR PRUDENCE. / TATTOO** [3] [–]
(12"+=) *(SHEX 4)* – There's a planet in my kitchen.

Nov 83. (d-lp/c) *(SHAH/+C 1)* **NOCTURNE (live)** [29] [–]
– Intro – The rite of Spring / Israel / Dear Prudence / Paradise place / Melt! / Cascade / Pulled to bits / Night shift / Sin in my heart / Slowdive / Painted bird / Happy house / Switch / Spellbound / Helter skelter / Eve white eve black / Voodoo dolly. *(cd-iss. Apr89 & Mar95; 839009-2)*

Mar 84. (7") *(SHE 6)* **SWIMMING HORSES. / LET GO** [28] [–]
(12"+=) *(SHEX 6)* – The humming wires.

May 84. (7") *(SHE 7)* **DAZZLE. / I PROMISE** [33] [–]
(12"+=) *(SHEX 7)* – Throw them to the lions / ('A'mix).

Jun 84. (lp/c)(cd) *(SHEH P/C 1)(821510-2)* <24030> **HYAENA** [15] [ ]
– Dazzle / We hunger / Take me back / Belladonna / Swimming horses / Bring me the head of the preacher man / Running town / Pointing bone / Blow the house down. *(re-iss. cd Mar95; same)*

— **JOHN CARRUTHERS** – guitar (ex-CLOCKDVA, ex-JEFFREY LEE PIERCE) returned to repl. SMITH who had CURE commitments.

Oct 84. (12"ep) *(SHEEP 8)* **THE THORN (live)** [47] [–]
– Voices / Placebo effect / Red over white / Overground.

Oct 85. (7") *(SHE 9)* **CITIES IN DUST. / AN EXECUTION** [21] [–]
(12"+=) *(SHEX 9)* – Quarter drawing of the dog.

Feb 86. (7") *(SHE 10)* **CANDYMAN. / LULLABY** [34] [–]
(12"+=) *(SHEX 10)* – Umbrella.

Apr 86. (lp/c)(cd) *(SHE LP/MC 3)(829145-2)* <24092> **TINDERBOX** [13] [88]
– Candyman / The sweetest chill / This unrest / Cities in dust / Cannons / Partys fall / 92° / Lands End. *(cd+=)* – An execution / Quarter drawing of the dog / Lullaby / Umbrella / Candyman (extended). *(re-iss. cd Mar95; same)*

Jan 87. (7") *(SHE 11)* **THIS WHEEL'S ON FIRE. / SHOOTING SUN** [14] [–]
(12"+=) *(SHEX 11)* – Sleepwalking (on the high wire).

Feb 87. (lp/c)(cd) *(SHE LP/MC 3)(831474-2) <24134>* **THROUGH THE LOOKING GLASS** [15] [ ]
– Hall of mirrors / Trust in me / This wheel's on fire / Strange fruit / This town ain't big enough for the both of us / You're lost little girl / The passenger / Gun / Sea breezes / Little Johnny Jewel. *(re-iss. cd Mar95; same)*

Mar 87. (7") *(SHE 12)* **THE PASSENGER. / SHE'S CUCKOO** [41] [–]
(12"+=) *(SHEX 12)* – Something blue.

— **JON KLEIN** (b. 9 May'??, Bristol, England) – guitar (ex-SPECIMEN) repl. CARRUTHERS / added **MARTIN McCARRICK** (b.29 Jul'??) – cello, keyboards (ex-MARC ALMOND, ex-The GLOVE) (to SIOUXSIE, SEVERIN, BUDGIE + KLEIN)

Jul 87. (7"/7"pic-d/c-s) *(SHE/+P/+PC 13)* **SONG FROM THE EDGE OF THE WORLD. / THE WHOLE PRICE OF BLOOD** [59] [–]
(12"+=) *(SHEX 13)* – Mechanical eyes.

Jul 88. (7"/7"g-f) *(SHE/+G 14) <27760>* **PEEK-A-BOO. / FALSE FACE** [16] [53]
(c-s+=/cd-s+=) *(SHE CS/CD 14)* – Catwalk / ('A'-Big suspender mix).
(12"+=) *(SHEXR 14)* – ('A'-2 other mixes).

Sep 88. (lp/c)(cd) *(SHE LP/MC 5)(837240-2) <24205>* **PEEPSHOW** [20] [68]
– Peek-a-boo / Killing jar / Scarecrow / Carousel / Burn-up / Ornaments of gold / Turn to stone / Rawhead and bloodybones / The last beat of my heart / Rhapsody. *(re-iss. cd Mar95; same)*

Sep 88. (7"/7"g-f/7"pic-d) *(SHE/+G/P 15)* **KILLING JAR. / SOMETHING WICKED (THIS WAY COMES)** [41] [–]
(12"+=/cd-s+=) *(SHE X/CD 15)* – Are you still dying, darling.

Nov 88. (7"/7"g-f) *(SHE/+G 16)* **THE LAST BEAT OF MY HEART. / EL DIABLO LOS MUERTOS** [44] [ ]
(12"+=) *(SHEX 16)* – Sunless.
(cd-s++=) *(SHECD 16)* – ('B'mix).

— In Autumn'89, The CREATURES issued singles and 'BOOMERANG' album.

May 91. (7"/c-s) *(SHE/+CS 19) <19031>* **KISS THEM FOR ME. / RETURN** [32] [23]
(ext-12"+=/12"pic-d+=) *(SHE X/XD 19)* – Staring back.
(cd-s++=) *(SHECD 19)* – ('A'side).

Jun 91. (cd/c/lp) *(847731-2/-4/-1)) <24387>* **SUPERSTITION** [25] [65]
– Kiss them for me / Fear (of the unknown) / Cry / Drifter / Little sister / Shadowtime / Silly thing / Got to get up / Silver waterfalls / Softly / The ghost in you. *(re-iss. cd Mar95; same)*

Jul 91. (7"/c-s) *(SHE/+CS 20)* **SHADOWTIME. / SPIRAL TWIST** [57] [ ]
(12"+=/cd-s+=) *(SHE X/CD 20)* – Sea of light. / ('A'-Eclipse mix).

— Below single from the film 'Batman Returns'.

Jul 92. (7"/c-s) *(SHE/+CS 21)* **FACE TO FACE. / I COULD BE AGAIN** [21] [ ]
(cd-s+=) *(SHECD 21)* – ('A'-catatonic mix) / Hothead.
(12") *(SHEX 21)* – ('A'side) / ('A'-catatonic mix) / Hothead.

Oct 92. (cd/c/lp) *(517160-2/-4/-1)* **TWICE UPON A TIME – THE THING** [26] [ ]
– Fireworks / Slowdive / Melt / Dear Prudence / Swimming horses / Dazzle / Overground (from The Thorn) / Cities in dust / Candyman / This wheel's on fire / The passenger / Peek-a-boo / The killing jar / The last beat of my heart / Kiss them for me / Shadowtime / Fear (of the unknown) / Face to face. *(re-iss. cd Mar95; same)*

— In Aug 94, SIOUXSIE partnered MORRISSEY on his single, 'INTERLUDE'.

Dec 94. (c-s) *(SHECS 22)* **O BABY. / OURSELVES** [34] [–]
(cd-s+=) *(SHECD 22)* – ('A'-Manhattan mix).
(cd-s) *(SHECDX 22)* – ('A'side) / Swimming horses (live) / All tomorrow's parties (live).

Jan 95. (cd/c/lp) *(523725-2/-4/-1) <24630>* **THE RAPTURE** [33] [ ]
– O baby / Tearing apart / Stargazer / Fall from grace / Not forgotten / Sick child / The lonely one / Falling down / Forever / The rapture / The double life / Love out me.

Feb 95. (7"/c-s) *(SHE/+CS 23)* **STARGAZER. / HANG ME HIGH** [64] [ ]
(cd-s+=) *(SHECD 23)* – Black Sun.
(cd-s) *(SHECDX 23)* – ('A'-Mambo sun) / ('A'-Planet queen mix) / ('A'-Mark Saunders mix).

— Split Apr'96 although SIOUXSIE and BUDGIE recorded a third album as The CREATURES. SEVERIN has written for the film 'Visions Of Ecstacy'.

– compilations, etc. –

Feb 87. (12"ep) *Strange Fruit; (SFPS 012)* **THE PEEL SESSIONS (29.11.77)** [ ] [–]
– Love in a void / Mirage / Suburban relapse / Metal postcard. *(c-ep-iss.Jun87; SFPSC 012) (cd-ep-iss.Mar88; SFPSCD 012)*

Feb 89. (12"ep/cd-ep) *Strange Fruit; (SPPS/+CD 066)* **THE PEEL SESSIONS** (Feb'78) [ ] [–]
– Hong Kong garden / Carcass / Helter skelter / Overground.

Sep 02. (cd) *Universal; (<065152-2>)* **THE BEST OF SIOUXSIE & THE BANSHEES** [ ] Nov02 [ ]
– Dear Prudence / Hong Kong garden / Cities in dust / Peek-a-boo / Happy house / KIss them for me / Face to face / Dizzy / Israel / Christine / Spellbound / Stargazer / Arabian knights / The killing jar / This wheel's on fire. *(<d-cd+=; 065150-2>)* – (bonus mixes).

CREATURES

(SIOUXSIE & BUDGIE)

Polydor — not iss.

Sep 81. (d7"ep/d7"gf-ep) *(POSP D/G 354)* **WILD THINGS** [24] [–]
– Mad-eyed screamer / So unreal / But not them / Wild thing / Thumb.

Wonderland — Geffen

May 83. (7") *(SHE 1)* **MISS THE GIRL. / HOT SPRING IN THE SNOW** [21] [–]

May 83. (lp/c) *(SHE LP/MC 1)* **FEAST** [17] [–]
– Morning dawning / Inoa 'ole / Ice house / Dancing on glass / Gecko / Sky train / Festival of colours / Miss the girl / A strutting rooster / Flesh.

Jul 83. (7") *(SHE 2)* **RIGHT NOW. / WEATHERCADE** [14] [–]
(12"+=) *(SHEX 2)* – Festival of colours.

Oct 89. (7") *(SHEP 17)* **STANDING THERE. / DIVIDED** [53] [–]
(12"+=/cd-s+=) *(SH X/CD 17)* – Solar choir / ('A'-Andalucian mix).
('A'-La Frontera mix-10"+=) *(SHET 17)* – Solar choir.

Nov 89. (lp/c/cd) *(841463-1/-4/-2) <24275>* **BOOMERANG** [ ] [ ]
– Standing there / Manchild / You! / Pity / Killing time / Willow / Pluto drive / Solar choir * / Speeding * / Fury eyes / Fruitman / Untiedundone * / Simoom * / Strolling wolf / Venus sands / Morriha. *(extra tracks on cd= *)*

Feb 90. (7"/7"box) *(SHE/+B 18)* **FURY EYES. / ABSTINENCE** [ ] [–]
(12"/cd-s) *(SHE P/CD 18)* – ('A'-20/20 mix) / ('A'dub) / ('A'-Fever mix).

Sioux — Record Of Substance

Jun 98. (7") *(SIOUX 1)* **SAD CUNT. / SAD CUNT (chix'n'dix mix)** [ ] [–]

Aug 98. (10"ep/cd-ep) *(SIOUX 2 V/CD) <1>* **ERASER CUTS** [ ] [ ]
– Pinned down / Guillotine / Thank you / Slipping away.

Oct 98. (7"green) *(SIOUX 3V)* **2ND FLOOR. / TURN IT ON** [ ] [–]
(12"on 'Hydrogen Jukebox'+=)(cd-s+=) *(DUKE 044DJV)(SIOUX 3CD)* – ('A'-Girl eats boy mix) / ('A'-Emperor Sly mix).

Dec 98. (cd-ep) *(SIOUX 5CD)* **EXTERMINATING ANGEL** [–] mail-o [–]
– Exordium (one night in France) / Interim (NYC & Paris) / Remake (the James Hardway) / Remodel (album mix).

Sioux — Instinct

Feb 99. (cd/c/2x10"lp) *(SIOUX 4 CD/C/V) <413>* **ANIMA ANIMUS** [ ] [ ]
– 2nd floor / Disconnected / Turn it on / Take mine / Say / I was me / Prettiest thing / Exterminating angel / Another planet / Don't go to sleep without me.

Mar 99. (7"clear) *(SIOUX 6V)* **SAY. / ALL SHE COULD ASK FOR** [72] [–]
(cd-s) *(SIOUX 6CD)* – ('A'side) / Broken.
(cd-s) *(SIOUX 6CDX)* – ('A'-Witchman remix) / ('A'-Justice & Endemic void remix).

Mar 99. (12"ltd) *(DUKE 055DJV)* **SAY (Witchman 4x4 mix). / THANK YOU (Dub Pistols brings you joy mix)** [ ] [–]

Jul 99. (12"ltd) *(DUKE 064DJV)* **DISCONNECTING (Beloved's mix). / PRETTIEST THING (Super Chumbo's mix)** [ ] [–]
(above singles on 'Hydrogen Dukebox')

Sep 99. (10"blue/cd-s) *(SIOUX 9 V/CD)* **PRETTIEST THING (Super Chumbo's waking dream mix) / TURN IT ON (Emperor Sly's elemental mix) / GUILLOTINE (bitten by the black dog)** [ ] [–]
(cd-s) *(SIOUX 9CDX)* – ('A'-mixes; Howie B hormonal / album / subsonic legacy).

Nov 99. (cd/d-lp) *(DUKE 066 CD/DJV) <433>* **HYBRIDS** (remixes) [ ] [ ]
(re-iss. Aug01; same)

Dec 00. (m-cd) <*516*> **U.S. RETRACE** (compilation) [–] [ ]
– Pinned down / Guillotine / Turn it on (bound 'n' gagged mix) / All she could ask for / Broken / Turn it on (Emperor Sly's elemental mix) / Thank you / Slipping away.

Sioux Sioux

Jun 01. (cd) <*79611*> **SEQUINS IN THE SUN** (compilation) [–] [ ]
– All she could ask for / Disconnected / Turn it on / Take mine / Pinned down / Guillotine / 2nd floor / Pluto drive – Nightclubbing / Prettiest thing / Exterminating angel.

Oct 03. (cd-s) *(SIOUX 14)* **GODZILLA! / (instrumental) / (video)** [53] [–]

The GLOVE

(SEVERIN & ROBERT SMITH) also incl. **MARTIN McCARRICK** – cello / **ANNE STEPHENSON + GINNY HEWES** – strings / **ANDY ANDERSON** – drums / (JEANETTE) **LANDRAY** – dual vocals w/**SMITH**

Wonderland RoughTrade

Aug 83. (7") *(SHE 3)* **LIKE AN ANIMAL. / MOUTH TO MOUTH** [52] [–]
(12"+=) *(SHEX 3)* – Animal (club mix).

Aug 83. (lp/c) *(SHE LP/MC 2)* <*ROUGHUS 85*> **BLUE SUNSHINE** [35] [ ]
– Like an animal / Looking glass girl / Sex-eye-make-up / Mr. Alphabet says / A blues in drag / Punish me with kisses / This green city / Orgy / Perfect murder / Relax. *(re-iss. Sep90 lp/c/cd+=; 815019-1/-4/-2)* – Mouth to mouth / The tightrope / Like an animal (club mix).

Nov 83. (7") *(SHE 5)* **PUNISH ME WITH KISSES. / THE TIGHTROPE** [ ] [–]

SISTERS OF MERCY

Formed: Leeds, England ... 1980 by frontman/lyricist extraordinaire, ANDREW ELDRITCH along with guitarist, GARY MARX. The original "goth" combo, ELDRITCH and Co. were among the first acts to define the genre in its lasting image of black-clad, po-faced rockers meditating on dark, impenetrable lyrics, decipherable only for those willing to substitute make-up for flour or wear pointy boots (and, more importantly, never to emerge in daylight!). For their early releases, the group employed a drum machine, christened Doktor Avalanche, issuing material on their self-financed label, 'Merciful Release'. Following the debut single, 'DAMAGE DONE', ELDRITCH and MARX recruited guitarist BENN GUNN and bassist CRAIG ADAMS, fleshing out the sound on a further series of 7 and 12 inchers, the 'ALICE' EP drawing widespread interest with its goth/alternative/dance fusion. GUNN was then replaced with ex-DEAD OR ALIVE guitarist, WAYNE HUSSEY, for the piledriving theatrics of 'TEMPLE OF LOVE'. During this time, the group had also built up a live reputation, supporting the likes of The BIRTHDAY PARTY and The PSYCHEDELIC FURS as well as appearing at the Leeds Futurama festival. Word was spreading, and in 1984, The SISTERS OF MERCY and their label were signed to a worldwide deal with 'WEA'. A debut album, 'FIRST AND LAST AND ALWAYS', appeared the following year, a worthwhile effort which saw the group almost break into the UK Top 10. Yet only a month after the record's release, the band announced they were to split, tension between ELDRITCH and MARX resulting in the latter leaving the group first. After a final concert at London's Royal Albert Hall, a bitter legal battle ensued between ELDRITCH and ADAMS/HUSSEY. At stake was the SISTERS OF MERCY moniker, ELDRITCH eventually winning out, though not before he'd hastily released a single and album, 'GIFT' (1986), under The SISTERHOOD, primarily to prevent ADAMS and HUSSEY using the title. The latter two subsequently formed The MISSION while ELDRITCH relocated to Berlin/Hamburg, retaining ex-GUN CLUB bassist, PATRICIA MORRISON (who'd played on 'GIFT') and recording 'FLOODLAND' (1987) with the help of his ever-faithful drum machine. The preceding single, 'THIS CORROSION' was suitably grandiose, all ominous vocals and OTT production courtesy of JIM STEINMAN, the single giving ELDRITCH his first UK Top 10 hit. The album achieved a similar feat, incorporating a more overtly rhythmic feel to create a kind of doom-disco sound (perfect for goths who couldn't dance anyway!). MORRISON subsequently left, ELDRITCH recruiting an array of diverse musicians including TIM BREICHENO, ANDREAS BRUHN and punk veteran, TONY JAMES (ex-SIGUE SIGUE SPUTNIK, ex-GENERATION X) to record 'VISION THING' (1990). Employing a more commercial hard rock sound, 'MORE' was one of The SISTERS' most effective singles to date while again the album was a Top 20 success. Further acclaim came in 1992 with the surprisingly consistent retrospective, 'SOME GIRLS WANDER BY MISTAKE' (1992), and its attendant single, a brilliant re-vamp of 'TEMPLE OF LOVE', Israeli warbler, OFRA HAZA, adding that extra mystical touch. After a 1991 joint tour with PUBLIC ENEMY (nice idea, but probably taking the Lollapollooza ethic a bit too far) was abandoned after poor ticket sales, not much has been heard from The SISTERS OF MERCY. ELDRITCH remains an enigmatic figure, any significant activity normally resulting in intense interest from the music press. The odds are that he'll return, though whether in the guise of The SISTERS OF MERCY remains to be seen. • **Covered:** EMMA (Hot Chocolate) / 1969 (Stooges) / GIMME SHELTER (Rolling Stones) / KNOCKIN' ON HEAVEN'S DOOR (Bob Dylan).

Album rating: FIRST AND LAST AND ALWAYS (*8) / GIFT (*7; as Sisterhood) / FLOODLAND (*8) / VISION THING (*7) / SOME GIRLS WANDER BY MISTAKE compilation (*8) / GREATEST HITS VOLUME 1 – A SLIGHT CASE OF OVERBOMBING compilation (*7)

ANDREW ELDRITCH (b. ANDREW TAYLOR, 15 May'59, East Anglia, England) – vocals / **GARRY MARX** (b. MARK PEARMAN) – guitar / + drum machine DOKTOR AVALANCHE

Merciful Release not iss.

1980. (7"m) *(MR 7)* **THE DAMAGE DONE. / WATCH / HOME OF THE HITMAN** [ ] [–]

— added **BEN GUNN** (b. BENJAMIN MATTHEWS) – guitar / **CRAIG ADAMS** (b. 4 Apr'62) – bass (ex-EXPELAIRES)

C.N.T. not iss.

Feb 82. (7") *(CNT 002)* **BODY ELECTRIC. / ADRENOCHROME** [ ] [–]

Merciful BrainEater

Nov 82. (7") *(MR 015)* **ALICE. / FLOORSHOW** [ ] [–]

Mar 83. (7") *(MR 019)* **ANACONDA. / PHANTOM** [ ] [–]

Apr 83. (12"ep) *(MR 021)* **ALICE. / FLOORSHOW / 1969 / PHANTOM** [ ] [ ]

May 83. (12"ep) *(MR 023)* **THE REPTILE HOUSE** [ ] [ ]
– Kiss the carpet / Lights / Valentine / Burn / Fix. *(re-iss. Apr94)*

— **WAYNE HUSSEY** (b. JERRY LOVELOCK, 26 May'58, Bristol, England) – guitar (ex-DEAD OR ALIVE, ex-HAMBI & THE DANCE) repl. BEN

Oct 83. (7") *(MR 027)* **TEMPLE OF LOVE. / HEARTLAND** [ ] [–]
(ext.12"+=) *(MRX 027)* – Gimme shelter.

Jun 84. (7"; as The SISTERS) *(MR 029)* **BODY AND SOUL. / TRAIN** [46] [–]
(12"+=) *(MR 029T)* – After hours / Body electric.

Merciful Release Elektra

Oct 84. (7") *(MR 033)* **WALK AWAY. / POISON DOOR** [45] [–]
(above w/free 7"flexi) *(MR 033 – SAM 218)* – Long Train.
(12"+=) *(MR 033T)* – On the wire.

Feb 85. (7") *(MR 035)* **NO TIME TO CRY. / BLOOD MONEY** [63] [–]
(12"+=) *(MR 035T)* – Bury me deep.

Mar 85. (lp/c) *(MR 337 L/C)* <*60405*> **FIRST AND LAST AND ALWAYS** [14] [ ]
– Black planet / Walk away / No time to cry / A rock and a hard place / Marian / First and last and always / Possession / Nine while nine /

Amphetamine logic / Some kind of stranger. *(cd-iss. Jul88; 240616-2) (re-iss. re-mastered.Jul92 on 'East West' lp/c; MR 571 L/C) (cd re-mast.Jun92; 9031 77379-2)*

— disbanded mid-'85 ... GARRY MARX helped form GHOST DANCE. HUSSEY and ADAMS formed The MISSION after squabbles with ANDREW over use of group name.

— **ELDRITCH** with ever faithful drum machine adopted

The SISTERHOOD

— recruited **PATRICIA MORRISON** (b.14 Jan'62) – bass, vocals (ex-FUR BIBLE, ex-GUN CLUB) / **JAMES RAY** – guitar / **ALAN VEGA** – synthesizers (ex-SUICIDE) / **LUCAS FOX** – drums (ELDRITCH moved to Berlin, Germany)

Merciful — not iss.

Feb 86. (7") *(SIS 001)* **GIVING GROUND (remix). / GIVING GROUND (album version)** [ ] [–]

Jul 86. (lp/c) *(SIS 020/+C)* **GIFT** [90] [–]
– Jihad / Colours / Giving ground / Finland red, Egypt white / Rain from Heaven. *(cd-iss. Sep89; SIS 020CD) (re-iss. Jul94 cd/c; 1131684-2/-4)*

— JAMES RAY went solo (backed with The PERFORMANCE), subsequently issuing a couple of 45's, 'MEXICO SUNDOWN BLUES' and 'TEXAS', for 'Merciful Release'. At the turn of the decade, he and his new outfit, JAMES RAY'S GANGWAR, issued a few more, 'DUSTBOAT' and 'WITHOUT CONSCIENCE', the former from a part compilation set, 'A NEW KIND OF ASSASSIN' (1989). In 1992 and '93, the band delivered two more, 'DIOS ESTA DE NUESTRO LADO' and 'THIRD GENERATION'.

The SISTERS OF MERCY

— were once again **ELDRITCH + MORRISON** obtaining rights to name

Merciful-WEA — Elektra

Sep 87. (7") *(MR 39)* **THIS CORROSION. / TORCH** [7] [ ]
(c-s+=/12"+=/cd-s+=) *(MR 39 C/T/CD)* – Colours.

Nov 87. (lp/c)(cd) *(MR 441 L/C)(242246-2) <60762>*
FLOODLAND [9] [ ]
– Dominion / Mother Russia / Flood I / Lucretia my reflection / 1959 / This corrosion / Flood II / Driven like the snow / Neverlan. *(c+=)*– Torch. *(cd-s++=)* – Colours.

Feb 88. (7") *(MR 43)* **DOMINION. / SANDSTORM / UNTITLED** [13] [–]
(d12"+=) *(MR 43TB)* – Emma.
(c-s+=/3"cd-s+=) *(MR 43 C/CD)* – Ozy-Mandias.

May 88. (7"/ext.12"/ext.3"cd-s) *(MR 44/+T/CD)* **LUCRETIA MY REFLECTION. / LONG TRAIN** [20] [ ]

— (Feb'90) **ELDRITCH** w/drum machine, recruited complete new line-up / **TONY JAMES** (b.1956) – bass, vocals (ex-SIGUE SIGUE SPUTNIK, ex-GENERATION X) / **ANDREAS BRUHN** (b. 5 Nov'67, Hamburg, Germany) – guitar / **TIM BRICHENO** (b. 6 Jul'63, Huddersfield, England) – guitar (ex-ALL ABOUT EVE) / guests were **MAGGIE REILLY** – b.vocals (ex-MIKE OLDFIELD) / **JOHN PERRY** – guitar (ex-ONLY ONES)

Oct 90. (7"/c-s) *(MR 47/+C)* <66595> **MORE. / YOU COULD BE THE ONE** [21] [ ]
(cd-s+=/cd-s+=) *(MR 47CD/+X)* – ('A'extended).

Oct 90. (cd)(c/lp) *(9031 72663-2)(MR 449 C/L) <61017>*
VISION THING [11] [ ]
– Vision thing / Ribons / Destination Boulevard / Something fast / When you don't see me / Doctor Jeep / More / I was wrong. *(cd re-iss. Jul00; same)*

Dec 90. (7") *(MR 51)* **DOCTOR JEEP. / KNOCKIN' ON HEAVEN'S DOOR (live)** [37] [ ]
(12"+=/cd-s+=) *(MR 51 T/CD)* – ('A'extended).
(ext.12") *(MR 51TX)* – Burn (live) / Amphetamine logic (live).

— (Oct91) **TONY JAMES** split from ELDRITCH amicably.

— Next featured vocals by **OFRA HAZA**

East West — Elektra

Apr 92. (7") *(MR 53)* **TEMPLE OF LOVE (1992). / I WAS WRONG (American fade)** [3] [ ]
(ext.12"+=) *(MR 53T)* – Vision thing (Canadian club mix).
(cd-s+=) *(MR 53CD)* – When you don't see me (German release).

Apr 92. (cd)(c/d-lp) *(9031 76476-2)(MR 449 C/L) <61306>*
SOME GIRLS WANDER BY MISTAKE (1980-1983 material) [5] [ ]
– Alice / Floorshow / Phantom / 1969 / Kiss the carpet / Lights / Valentine / Fix / Burn / Kiss the carpet (reprise) / Temple of love / Heartland / Gimme shelter / Damage done / Watch / Home of the hitmen / Body electric / Adrenochrome / Anaconda.

— now just **ANDREW ELDRITCH** on own with guests

Aug 93. (7"/c-s) *(MR 59/+C)* **UNDER THE GUN. / ALICE (1993)** [19] [–]
(12"+=/cd-s+=) *(MR 59 T/CD)* – ('A'-Jutland mix).

Aug 93. (cd/c/d-lp) *(4509 93579-2/-4/-1) <61399-2/-4>*
GREATEST HITS VOLUME 1 – A SLIGHT CASE OF OVERBOMBING (compilation) [14] [ ]
– Under the gun / Temple of love (1992) / Vision thing / Detonation boulevard / Doctor Jeep / More / Lucretia my reflection / Dominion – Mother / This corrosion / No time to cry / Walk away / Body and soul.

— ELDRITCH and his gang seem to have split from the music scene

– compilations, etc. –

Jan 94. (cd) *Cleopatra; <(CLEO 6642CD)>* **FIRST, LAST FOREVER** [ ] [ ]

Roni SIZE (REPRAZENT)

Born: RYAN WILLIAMS, 29 Oct'69, St. Andrews, Bristol, England. Kicked out of school at the age of 16, SIZE became a DJ on the thriving late 80's Bristol club/music scene as well as running a music workshop at the 'Basement Project', a local youth centre. Familiarising himself with the complexities of samplers and drum machines, the budding producer progressed to cutting his own dub plates and after releasing his debut on the label ('V' records) run by fellow Bristolian drum'n'bass purveyor, DJ KRUST, SIZE subsequently initiated his own imprint, 'Full Cycle'. Developing his style over a string of 12" vinyl releases, both on 'V' (notably the sabre rattling snares and chunky basslines of '94's 'TIMESTRETCH') and 'Full Cycle', this dreadlocked pioneer (of Jamaican descent) eventually arrived at the tough but soulful drum'n'bass sophistication of the massively acclaimed 'NEW FORMS' (1997) album. Though mastermided by SIZE, the record was recorded via an eclectic posse of stalwarts known as REPRAZENT i.e. silky voiced chanteuse, ONALLEE, MC DYNAMITE, longtime musical collaborators DJ's KRUST, DIE and SUV along with a trio of conventional musicians; bassist SI JOHN (of groundbreaking Bristolian acid-jazzers, The FEDERATION), guitarist STEVE GRAHAM and PORTISHEAD sticksman, CLIVE DEAMER. Released on the ever hip 'Talkin' Loud' label and surprise winner of the prestigious 'Mercury' music award, the aptly titled 'NEW FORMS' took the genre into uncharted territory, as equally innovative as the work of GOLDIE and LTJ BUKEM yet more readily accessible. Clocking in at over two hours, the album was perhaps too much to take in one sitting although given time, its charms soon revealed themselves; a self-acknowledged fan of funk and soul (QUINCY JONES was a much cited influence), SIZE had managed to craft a record that was synapse shatteringly futuristic yet retained an organic warmth missing in much modern dance music. The Top 20 charting single, 'BROWN PAPER BAG' was as fine a taster as any, its seismic bass depth charges and free flowing rapping more than justifying the not inconsiderable hype (its now a backing recording used by the BBC on some of their TV programmes – listen out!). With a plethora of side projects in the pipeline and artists queuing up for remix work, it seems that for once, SIZE really does matter. BREAKBEAT ERA was RONI and DJ DIE's next musical operation, jazzy drum'n'bass were obviously still the concept although singer-songwriter LEONIE LAWS had joined the posse. Having delivered a one-off set, 'ULTRA OBSCENE' (1999), RONI RIZE was scheming yet another futuristic assault. RONI SIZE & REPRAZENT returned in 2000 with 'IN THE MODE', an album which almost lived up to the calibre of its predecessor. This time around SIZE had halved the running time of most tracks, condensing and concentrating the rhythmic payload for maximum effect. MC DYNAMITE started as he meant to go on with the breakbeat blitzkrieg of opener 'RAILING PT.2' while everyone's favourite guest METHOD MAN and RAHZEL (of The ROOTS) kept up the quality on 'GHETTO CELEBRITY' and 'IN TUNE WITH THE SOUND' respectively. SIZE returned in 2002 with his first bonafide solo album, 'TOUCHING DOWN', a lone wolf effort in stark contrast with the multi-voiced, collective creations he's presided over in the past. While there was a sense of the stripped-down drum'n'bass presented here being hermetically sealed, SIZE had clearly lost none of the dark intensity of his musical vision even if made for occasionally claustrophobic listening.

Album rating: NEW FORMS (*9) / IN THE MODE (*7) / Breakbeat Era: ULTRA-OBSCENE (*7) / Roni Size: TOUCHING DOWN (*5)

RONI SIZE – vocals (with various technicians)

V | not iss.

1992. (12") *(V 005)* **IT'S A JAZZ THING. / THE CALLING** [ ] [–]
(re-iss. Dec94; same) (re-iss. Apr97; V 022)

1993. (12") *(V 006)* **MUSIC BOX (mixes)** [ ] [–]

Nov 94. (12") *(V 007)* **TIMESTRETCH (mixes)** [ ] [–]
(re-iss. Sep00; same)

May 95. (12") *(V 008R)* **ALL THE CREW (Big Up remix)** [ ] [–]

Jun 95. (12") *(V 010)* **FASHION** [ ] [–]
(12") *(V 010R)* – (mixes)
(re-iss. Sep00; same)

Full Cycle | not iss.

Jun 95. (12"; RONI SIZE & D.J. KRUST) *(FCY 2)* **DAYLIGHT. / TOUCH** [ ] [–]

Jun 96. (12") *(FCY 9)* **BRUTE FORCE (mixes)** [ ] [–]
(re-iss. Apr97; same)

RONI SIZE REPRAZENT

RONI SIZE – vocals / **ONALLEE** (TRACIE) – vocals (ex-BLUE AEROPLANES, ex-SOURMASH) / **DYNAMITE MC** (DOMINIC) – rap / **FI JOHNS** – bass (of The FEDERATION) / **CLIVE DEEMER** – drums (of PORTISHEAD, ex-HAWKWIND) / **STEVE GRAHAM** – acoustic guitar / **DJ DIE** – turntables / **DJ KRUST** – turntables / **DJ SUV** – turntables

Talkin' Loud | Mercury

1996. (cd-ep) *(TLCD 15)* *<INT 578 619>* **REASONS FOR SHARING EP** [ ] [ ]
– Share the fall / Down / Sounds fresh / Trust me.

—— early in '97, a SKYLAB vs RONI SIZE 12"/cd-s/12"remix 'THE TRIP' was issued by the 'Eye Q' imprint; (EYEUK 011/+CD/R)

Jun 97. (12"/cd-s) *(TLX/TLCD 21)* **SHARE THE FALL / NEW FORMS (featuring BAHAMADIA)** [37] [ ]
(12") *(TLXX 21)* – ('A'mixes by; Grooverider / Krust / Way Out West).

Jun 97. (cd/c/d-lp) *(<534 933-2/-4/-1>)* **NEW FORMS** [8] Oct97 [ ]
– Railing / Brown paper bag / New forms / Let's get it on / Digital / Matter of fact / Mad cat / Heroes / Share the fall / Watching windows / Beatbox / Morse code / Destination. *(some w/free cd/c/d-lp+=)* – Intro / Hi potent / Trust me / Change my life / Share the fall / Down / Jazz / Ballet dance. *(cd re-iss. Aug00; same)*

Aug 97. (12") *(TLX 25)* **HEROES. / ELECTRIKS** [31] [–]
(cd-s+=) *(TLCD 25)* – ('A'-original unknown) / ('A'-Basement Jaxx mix).
(12") *(TLXX 25)* – ('A'mixes).

Oct 97. (12") *(TLX 28)* *<568.203-2>* **BROWN PAPER BAG. / WESTERN** [20] [–]
(cd-s+=) *(TLCC 28)* – Hi potent.
(12") *(TLXX 28)* – ('A'mixes; Photek / Nobukzzu Takemeom, etc).

Mar 98. (12"/cd-s) *(TLX/TLCD 31)* **WATCHING WINDOWS (vocal mix) / (Ed Rush & Optical mixes) / (DJ Die mix) / (Nuyorican mix)** [28] [ ]
(12"/cd-s) *(TLDD/TLXX 31)* – ('A'remixes).

Dec 98. (ltd-12") *(566589-1)* **WATCHING WINDOWS (DJ Die mixes)** [ ] [–]

BREAKBEAT ERA

RONI SIZE / DJ DIE / + LEONIE LAWS – vocals / with **ADRIAN UTLEY + JEFF ROSE + ROB CHANT** – guitar / **TOBY PASCOE** – drums

X.L. | Interscope

Jul 98. (c-s)(12")(cd-s) *(XLC 95)(XLT 95)(XLS 95CD)* **BREAKBEAT ERA. / BREAKBEAT ERA** [38] [–]

Aug 99. (12") *(XLT 107)* *<97124>* **ULTRA-OBSCENE. / OUR DISEASE** [48] [ ]
(cd-s+=) *(XLS 107CD2)* – Rancid (Rinse revamp).
(cd-s) *(XLS 107CD)* – ('A'side) / Life is my friend / Love to be loved.

Aug 99. (cd/lp) *(XLDCD/XLLP 130)* *<90428>* **ULTRA-OBSCENE** [31] Sep99 [ ]
– Past life / Rancid / Ultra-obscene / Bullitproof / Breakbeat era / Time 4 breaks / Late morning / Anti-everything / Animal machine / Our disease / Max / Control freak / Terrible funk / Sex change / Life is my friend. *(also 7x12"box+=; XLDX 130)* – Rancid (rinse revamp) / Our disease (remix) / Control freak (instrumental).

Nov 99. (12") *(<FH 719-12>)* **BULLITPROOF (remixes)** [ ] [ ]
(above issued on 'Under One Sun')

Feb 00. (12") *(XLT 115)* **BULLITPROOF. / TERRIBLE FUNK** [65] [–]
(cd-s+=) *(XLS 115CD)* – ('A'mixes).
(cd-s) *(XLS 115CD2)* – ('A'mixes).

RONI SIZE & REPRAZENT

Talkin' Loud | Talkin' Loud

Sep 00. (c-s) *(TLMC 61)* **WHO TOLD YOU / OUT OF THE GAME** [17] [–]
(12"+=) *(TLX 61)* – ('A'-Roni Size & Die Quicksand mix).
(cd-s++=) *(TLCD 61)* – ('A'-video).

Oct 00. (cd/c)(q-lp) *(548176-2/-4)(548180-1)* *<548201>* **IN THE MODE** [15] [ ]
– Railing (part 2) / In + out / System check / Ghetto celebrity (with METHOD MAN) / Lucky pressure / Balanced chaos / Switchblade / In tune with the sound (with RAHZEL) / Who told you / Heavy rotation / Staircase / Mexican / Dirty beats / Out of the game *[not q-lp]* / Centre of the storm (with ZACK DE LA ROCHA) / Idi banashapan / Snapshot / Play the game. *(re-iss. Mar01; same)*

Mar 01. (12"/cd-s) *(TLX/+CD 63)* **DIRTY BEATS / DIRTY BEATS (D-Product mix) / SATISFIED FRIENDS** [32] [–]
(cd-s) *(TLXDD 63)* – ('A'mixes).
(12") *(TLXX 63)* – ('A'mixes).
(12") *(TLXXX 63)* – ('A'mixes).

Jun 01. (12"/cd-s) *(TLX/+CD 64)* **LUCKY PRESSURE (mixes; radio / MJ Cole / Roni Size hit)** [58] [–]
(12") *(TLXX 64)* – ('A'-mixes).

RONI SIZE

with **RICHIE GLOVER** – bass / **STEVE GRAHAM** – guitar / **DAMIAN LeGASSICK** – keyboards

Full Cycle | Full Cycle

Oct 02. (12") *(FYC 044)* **SOUND ADVICE. / KEEP STRONG** [69] [–]

Oct 02. (cd) *(<FCYCDLP 010>)* **TOUCHING DOWN** [72] [ ]
– Sound advice / Forget me knots / Playtime / Scrambled eggs / Uncensored / At the movies / Vocoda funk / Sorry for you / Feel the heat / Siren sounds / Keep strong / Find myself / Reel dark one / Swings and roundabouts / Zak attak / Snapshot 3.

Oct 02. (12") *(FYC 045)* **PLAYTIME. / EAT MY SHORTS** [53] [–]

Nov 02. (12") *(FYC 046)* **SCRAMBLED EGGS. / SWINGS AND ROUNDABOUTS** [57] [–]

Jan 03. (12") *(FYC 048)* **FEEL THE HEAT. / MOVE UP** [55] [–]

Feb 03. (12") *(FYC 053)* **SNAPSHOT 3. / SORRY FOR YOU** [61] [–]

Jun 03. (12") *(FYC 054)* **SIREN SOUNDS (Ray Keith remix). / AT THE MOVIES (Simon 'Bassline' Smith remix)** [67] [–]

Aug 03. (12") *(FYC 056)* **SOUND ADVICE (EZ Rollers remix). / FORGET ME NOTS (DJ Bailey remix)** [61] [–]

– others, etc. –

May 98. (12") *Ultra; (UL 020)* **IT'S A JAZZ THING. / PLAY IT FOR ME: DJ Die** [ ] [–]

Nov 99. (12") *Full Cycle; (FCY 020)* **26 BASS. / SNAPSHOT** [ ] [–]
(re-iss. Jan01; same)

Sep 00. (12") *V; (V 014)* **BOX OF TRICKS. / DAZE** [ ] [–]

Sep 00. (12") *V; (V 019)* **SOUL POWER. / SILENT PARTNER** [ ] [–]

□ SKIN (see under ⇒ SKUNK ANANSIE)

SKUNK ANANSIE

Formed: London, England . . . early 1994 by striking, shaven-headed black lesbian frontwoman, SKIN and bassist CASS LEWIS. With ACE and ROBBIE FRANCE completing the line-up, SKUNK ANANSIE kicked up enough of a stink to get themselves signed after only a handful of gigs. Their first single, however, was an unofficial limited edition mail order affair lifted from a BBC Radio One Evening Session, 'LITTLE BABY SWASTIKKKA'. A debut single proper, 'SELLING JESUS' hit the shops and the Top 50 in March '95, its controversial content attracting even more interest than the band's burgeoning live reputation. A further couple of furious indie-metallic missives followed in the shape of 'I CAN DREAM' and 'CHARITY', while the band hooked up with labelmate BJORK on her 'Army Of Me' single. Surely one of the most radical acts to ever be associated with the metal scene, the intense interest surrounding scary SKIN and her uncompromising musical vision/political agenda guaranteed a Top 10 placing for the debut album, 'PARANOID & SUNBURNT' (1995). One of the record's most soul-wrenching tracks, 'WEAK', became their biggest hit to date (Top 20) the following January, SKIN's cathartic howl akin to a more soulful PATTI SMITH. Temporary replacement LOUIS was succeeded in turn by MARK RICHARDSON prior to their next Top 20 hit, 'ALL I WANT', one of the many highlights on their second set, 'STOOSH' (1996). Even more scathing than their debut, this angst-ridden collection saw SKUNK ANANSIE championed by Kerrang!, the lead track, 'YES IT'S FUCKING POLITICAL' summing things up perfectly. Riding high in the end of year polls, the Top 10 album contained a further three hit singles, 'TWISTED (EVERYDAY HURTS)', 'HEDONISM (JUST BECAUSE YOU FEEL GOOD)' and 'BRAZEN (WEEP)'. Subsequently signing to 'Virgin' records, SKIN and her band previewed their excellent third album, 'POST ORGANIC CHILL' (1999), with yet another Top 20 single, 'CHARLIE BIG POTATO'; sonic ballads 'SECRETLY' and 'LATELY' followed it into the UK charts shortly afterwards. With falling sales of their last set, it was inevitable that the the group would finally split in April 2001. It was a less confrontational but no less intense SKIN who re-emerged in 2003 with her debut solo album, 'FLESHWOUNDS' (2003). Starkly personal in its lyrical content with romantic oblivion eating away at its core, the record accompanied SKIN's heartbroken catharsis with self-consciously post-modern rock arrangements, flirting with electronica but never consummating an occasionally uneasy relationship. A tender but rather out of context rendition of Electronic's 'GETTING AWAY WITH IT' was added to later pressings of the album. • **Songwriters:** SKIN – ARRAN, some with other two.

Album rating: PARANOID & SUNBURNT (*7) / STOOSH (*9) / POST ORGANIC CHILL (*8) / Skin: FLESHWOUNDS (*6)

SKIN (b. DEBORAH DYER, 3 Aug'67, Brixton, London) – vocals / **ACE** (b. MARTIN KENT, 30 Mar'67, Cheltenham, England) – guitar / **CASS LEWIS** (b. RICHARD LEWIS, 1 Sep'60) – bass / **ROBBIE FRANCE** – drums

		One Little Indian	Sony
Mar 95.	(10"white/c-s) *(101 TP10/TP7C)* **SELLING JESUS. / THROUGH RAGE / YOU WANT IT ALL**	46	–
	(cd-s+=) *(101 TP7CD)* – Skunk song. *(re-iss. Mar99; same)*		
Jun 95.	(10"lime/c-s) *(121 TP10/TP7C)* **I CAN DREAM. / AESTHETIC ANARCHIST / BLACK SKIN SEXUALITY**	41	–
	(cd-s+=) *(121 TPCD)* – Little baby Swastikkka. *(re-iss. Mar99; same)*		

— **LOUIS** – drums; repl. ROBBIE

Aug 95.	(c-s) *(131 TP7C)* **CHARITY / I CAN DREAM (version)**	40	–
	(cd-s+=) *(131 TP7CD)* – Punk by numbers.		
	(cd-s+=) *(131 TP7CDL)* – Kept my mouth shut.		
	(10"colrd) *(131 TP10)* – ('A'side) / Used / Killer's war. *(re-iss. Mar99; same)*		
Sep 95.	(lp/c/cd) *(TPLP 55/+C/CD) <67216>* **PARANOID & SUNBURNT**	8	
	– Selling Jesus / Intellectualise my blackness / I can dream / Little baby swastikkka / All in the name of pity / Charity / It takes blood & guts to be this cool but I'm still just a cliche / Weak / And here I stand / 100 ways to be a good girl / Rise up. *(cd re-iss. Mar99; same)*		
Jan 96.	(c-s) *(141 TP7C)* **WEAK / TOUR HYMN**	20	–
	(cd-s+=) *(141 TP7CD)* – Selling Jesus ('Strange Days' film version).		
	(cd-s) *(141 TP7CDL)* – ('A'side) / Charity (clit pop mix) / 100 ways to be a good girl (anti matter mix) / Rise up (Banhamoon mix). *(re-iss. Mar99; same)*		
Apr 96.	(c-s) *(151 TP7C)* **CHARITY / I CAN DREAM (live)**	20	–
	(cd-s+=) *(151 TP7CD)* – Punk by numbers (live).		
	(cd-s) *(151 TP7CDL)* – ('A'side) / And here I stand (live) / It takes blood & guts to be this cool but I'm still just a cliche (live) / Intellectualise my blackness (live). *(re-iss. Mar99; same)*		

— **MARK RICHARDSON** (b.28 May'70, Leeds, England) – drums; repl. LOUIS

Sep 96.	(7") *(161 TP7)* **ALL I WANT. / FRAGILE**	14	–
	(cd-s+=) *(161 TP7CD)* – Punk by numbers / Your fight.		
	(cd-s) *(161 TP7CDL)* – ('A'side) / But the sex was good / Every bitch but me / Black skinhead coconut dogfight. *(re-iss. Mar99; same)*		
Oct 96.	(lp/c/cd) *(TPLP 85/+C/CD) <67555>* **STOOSH**	9	
	– Yes it's fucking political / All I want / She's my heroine / Infidelity (only you) / Hedonism (just because you feel good) / Twisted (everyday hurts) / We love your apathy / Brazen (weep) / Pickin on me / Milk is my sugar / Glorious pop song.		
Nov 96.	(c-s) *(171 TP7C)* **TWISTED (EVERYDAY HURTS) / SHE'S MY HEROINE (polyester & cotton mix)**	26	–
	(cd-s+=) *(171 TP7CD1)* – Milk in my sugar (cement mix) / Pickin on me (instrumental pick'n'mix).		
	(cd-s) *(171 TP7CD2)* – ('A'-Cake mix) / Pickin on me (pick'n'mix) / Milk in my sugar (instrumental cement mix) / Yes it's fucking political (comix). *(re-iss. Mar99; same)*		
Jan 97.	(c-ep/cd-ep) *(181 TP7C/+D)* **HEDONISM (JUST BECAUSE YOU FEEL GOOD) / SO SUBLIME / LET IT GO / STRONG**	13	–
	(cd-ep) *(181 TP7CDL)* – ('A'side) / Song recovery / Contraband / I don't believe. *(re-iss. Mar99; same)*		
Jun 97.	(cd-ep) *(191 TP7CD1)* **BRAZEN (WEEP) / TWISTED (EVERYDAY HURTS) (radio 1 session) / ALL I WANT (radio 1 session) / IT TAKES BLOOD & GUTS TO BE THIS COOL BUT I'M STILL JUST A CLICHE (radio 1 session)**	11	–
	(cd-ep) *(191 TP7CD2)* – ('A'-Dreadzone remix) / ('A'-Hani's Weeping club mix) / ('A'-Ventura's Underworld mix) / ('A'-Stealth Sonic Orchestra remix) / ('A'-Cutfather & Joe electro mix).		
	(cd-ep) *(191 TP7CD3)* – ('A'-Junior Vasquez's Arena anthem) / ('A'-Paul Oakenfold & Steve Osborne mix) / ('A'-Dreadzone's instrumental mix) / ('A'-Junior Vasquez's riff dub) / ('A'-Hani's Hydro instrumental mix). *(re-iss. Mar99; same)*		

		Virgin	Virgin
Mar 99.	(c-s) *(VSC 1725)* **CHARLIE BIG POTATO / FEEL / 80'S MELLOW DRONE**	17	–
	(cd-s+=) *(VSCDT 1725)* – ('A'-CD-Rom video).		
	(cd-s) *(VSCDX 1725)* – ('A'side) / Sane / Jack knife ginal.		
Mar 99.	(cd/c/lp) *(CD/TC+/V 2881) <47764>* **POST ORGANIC CHILL**	16	
	– Charlie big potato / On my hotel T.V. / We don't need who you think you are / Tracey's flaw / The skank heads / Lately / Secretly / Good things don't always come to you / Cheap honesty / You'll follow me down / And this is nothing that I thought I had / I'm not afraid.		
May 99.	(c-s/cd-s) *(VSC/+DT 1733)* **SECRETLY / KING PSYCHEDELIC SIZE / PAINKILLERS**	16	–
	(cd-s) *(VSCDX 1733)* – ('A'side) / Breathing / ('A'-Optical vocal mix).		
Jul 99.	(c-s/cd-s) *(VSC/+DT 1738)* **LATELY / THE DECADENCE OF YOUR STARVATION / CHARLIE BIG POTATO (Smokin' Jo skin up mix)**	33	–

(cd-s) *(VSCDX 1738)* – ('A'side) / This pill's too painful / Secretly (Armand Van Helden's mix).

Oct 99. (c-s/cd-s) *(VSC/+DT 1754)* **YOU'LL FOLLOW ME DOWN / YOU'LL FOLLOW ME DOWN (The Rollo & Sister Bliss mix) / YOU'LL FOLLOW ME DOWN (Golden Ashes mix)** [ ] [–]

(cd-s) *(VSCDX 1754)* – ('A'side) / Hedonism (just because you make me feel good) (live) / The skank heads (live).

— In June 2000, SKIN was featured on MAXIM (of the PRODIGY's) debut single, 'Carmen Queasy'

— SKUNK ANANSIE disbanded in April 2001

SKIN

with **CASS LEWIS** – bass + a plethora of session people

E.M.I. not iss.

May 03. (7") *(EM 622)* **TRASHED. / THE GIRL WHO NEVER CRIES** [30] [–]

(cd-s+=) *(CDEM 622)* – On and on / (interview).

Jun 03. (cd) *(584159-2)* **FLESHWOUNDS** [43] [–]

– Faithfulness / Trashed / Don't let me down / Listen to yourself / Lost / The trouble with me / Getting away with it / You've made your bed / I'll try / Burnt like you / 'Til morning comes / Faithfulness (radio mix).

Sep 03. (12"/cd-s) *(12/CD EM 624)* **FAITHFULNESS (Scumfrog mix). / FAITHFULNESS (Kinky Boy rock goth mix)** [64] [–]

SLADE

Formed: Wolverhampton, Midlands, England ... 1964 as The VENDORS, by DAVE HILL and DON POWELL, becoming The IN-BE-TWEENS the following year and recording a demo EP for French label, 'Barclay'. Their official debut 45, 'YOU BETTER RUN' (with newcomers NODDY HOLDER and JIMMY LEA), flopped late in '66, the group retiring from studio activity until 1969 when they became AMBROSE SLADE at the suggestion of Fontana's Jack Baverstock. A belated debut album, 'BEGINNINGS', sold poorly although ex-ANIMALS bass player, CHAS CHANDLER, recognised the band's potential after spotting them performing in a London night club (the band now residing in the capital) and subsequently became their manager/producer. Kitted out in bovver boots, jeans, shirt and braces, SLADE topped their newly adopted 'ard look with skinheads all round, CHANDLER moulding the band's image and sound in an attempt to distance them from the fading hippy scene. Although they attracted a sizable grassroots following, SLADE's appropriately titled first album, 'PLAY IT LOUD' (on 'Polydor') failed to translate into sales. However, they finally cracked the UK Top 20 in May 1971 via a rousing cover of Bobby Marchan's 'GET DOWN AND GET WITH IT', the track bringing SLADE into the living rooms of the nation through a Top Of The Pops appearance. By this point, HOLDER and Co. had grown some hair, painted their boots sci-fi silver and initiated the roots of "Slademania" (foot-stomping now all the rage). The noisy, gravel-throated HOLDER (complete with tartan trousers, top hat and mutton-chop sideburns), the bare-chested, glitter-flecked HILL and the not so flamboyant LEA and POWELL, became part of the glam-metal brigade later in the year, 'COZ I LUV YOU' hitting the top of the charts for 4 weeks. Competing with the likes of GARY GLITTER, T. REX and SWEET, the lads amassed a string of anthemic UK chart toppers over the ensuing two years, namely 'TAKE ME BACK 'OME', 'MAMA WEER ALL CRAZEE NOW', 'CUM ON FEEL THE NOIZE', 'SKWEEZE ME PLEEZE ME' and the perennial festive fave 'MERRY XMAS EVERYBODY'. The noize level was markedly lower on the pop-ballad, 'EVERYDAY' (1974), a song that only hit No.3, glam-rock/pop shuddering to a halt around the same time. Their chart-topping albums, 'SLAYED?' (1972), 'SLADEST' (1973) and 'OLD NEW BORROWED AND BLUE' (1974) were now shoved to the back of people's record collections, PINK FLOYD, MIKE OLDFIELD and GENESIS now vying for the attention of the more discerning rock fan. Late '74 saw the release of a film/rockumentary 'SLADE IN FLAME'; issued as an album, it only managed a Top 10 placing. SLADE found it even harder to compete with the burgeoning punk/new wave scene, only re-emerging into the Top 10 in 1981 with 'WE'LL BRING THE HOUSE DOWN', released on their own 'Cheapskate' records. Three years later, the loveable rogues with the 'Bermingim' accent scored yet again, 'MY OH MY' just narrowly missing the No.1 spot, while the follow-up, 'RUN RUNAWAY' made the Top 10. Both records surprised observers by cracking the elusive US charts, the former hitting No.37, the latter No.20; a year previously, metal act, QUIET RIOT had taken Slade's 'CUM ON FEEL THE NOIZE' into the US Top 5 and subsequently charted with another, 'MAMA WEER ALL CRAZEE NOW'. SLADE continued on their merry way, untroubled by the fashion crimes of the 80's. The following decade saw the band chart once more, 'RADIO WALL OF SOUND' blasting out HOLDER's frantic yell to an appreciative Kerrang!- friendly audience. The jovial HOLDER has regained his footing as a celebrity in the 90's, VIC REEVES and BOB MORTIMER giving him and SLADE the highest accolade by inventing a whole series of irreverent sketches based around the band. OASIS, too, have contributed to the cult of NODDY, regularly performing 'CUM ON FEEL THE NOIZE' on stage. • **Songwriters:** HOLDER-LEA or LEA-POWELL penned except IN-BETWEENS:- TAKE A HEART (Sorrows) / CAN YOUR MONKEY DO THE DOG (Rufus Thomas) / YOU BETTER RUN (Rascals). AMBROSE SLADE:- BORN TO BE WILD (Steppenwolf) / AIN'T GOT NO HEAT (Frank Zappa) / IF THIS WORLD WERE MINE (Marvin Gaye) / FLY ME HIGH (Justin Hayward) / MARTHA MY DEAR (Beatles) / JOURNEY TO THE CENTER OF MY MIND (Ted Nugent). SLADE:- THE SHAPE OF THINGS TO COME (Max Frost & The Troopers; Mann-weill) / ANGELINA (Neil Innes) / COULD I (Griffin-Royer) / JUST A LITTLE BIT (?) / DARLING BE HOME SOON (Lovin' Spoonful) / LET THE GOOD TIMES ROLL (Shirley & Lee) / MY BABY LEFT ME – THAT'S ALL RIGHT (Elvis Presley) / PISTOL PACKIN' MAMA (Gene Vincent) / SOMETHIN' ELSE (Eddie Cochran) / OKEY COKEY (seasonal; trad) / HI HO SILVER LINING (Jeff Beck) / STILL THE SAME (Bob Seger) / YOU'LL NEVER WALK ALONE (Rogers-Hammerstein) / AULD LANG SYNE (trad.) / SANTA CLAUS IS COMING TO TOWN (festive) / LET'S DANCE (Chris Montez) / etc.

Album rating: Ambrose Slade: BEGINNINGS (*4) / Slade: PLAY IT LOUD (*4) / SLADE ALIVE! (*5) / SLAYED? (*6) / SLADEST compilation (*7) / OLD, NEW, BORROWED AND BLUE (*5) / SLADE IN FLAME (*6) / NOBODY'S FOOLS (*5) / WHATEVER HAPPENED TO SLADE (*4) / SLADE ALIVE VOL.2 (*5) / RETURN TO BASE (*4) / WE'LL BRING THE HOUSE DOWN (*5) / TILL DEAF US DO PART (*4) / ON STAGE (*5) / THE AMAZING KAMIKAZE SYNDROME (*4) / ROGUES GALLERY (*4) / YOU BOYZ MAKE BIG NOIZE (*4) / WALL OF HITS compilation (*6) / FEEL THE NOIZE: THE VERY BEST OF SLADE compilation (*8)

The IN-BE-TWEENS

JOHNNY HOWELLS – vocals / **MICKEY MARSTON** – guitar / **DAVE HILL** (b. 4 Apr'52, Fleet Castle, Devon, England) – guitar / **DAVE JONES** – bass / **DON POWELL** (10 Sep'50, Bilston, Staffordshire) – drums

Barclay not iss.

1965. (7"ep) **TAKE A HEART / LITTLE NIGHTINGALE. / (2 tracks by 'The Hills')** [–] France [–]

1965. (7"ep) **TAKE A HEART. / CAN YOUR MONKEY DO THE DOG / OOP OOP I DO** [–] France [–]

— **NODDY HOLDER** (b. NEVILLE HOLDER, 15 Jun'50, Walsall, England) – vox, guitar repl. HOWELLS / **JIM LEA** (b.14 Jun'52, Wolverhampton) – bass, piano repl. MARSTON + JONES

Columbia / not iss.

Nov 66. (7"; as N' BETWEENS) *(DB 8080)* **YOU BETTER RUN. / EVIL WITCHMAN** [ ] [–]

AMBROSE SLADE

(**HOLDER, HILL, LEA + POWELL**)

Fontana / Fontana

Apr 69. (lp) *(STL 5492)* *<67592>* **BEGINNINGS** [ ] [ ]
– Genesis / Everybody's next one / Knocking nails into my house / Roach daddy / Ain't got no heat / Pity the mother / Mad dog Cole / Fly me high / If this world were mine / Martha my dear / Born to be wild / Journey to the centre of my mind. *(re-iss. Jun91 & Jun99 on 'Polydor' cd/c; 849 185-2/-4)*

May 69. (7") *(TF 1015)* **GENESIS. / ROACH DADDY** [ ] [–]

SLADE

(same line-up + label)

Oct 69. (7") *(TF 1056)* **WILD WINDS ARE BLOWING. / ONE WAY HOTEL** [ ] [–]

Mar 70. (7") *(TF 1079)* **SHAPE OF THINGS TO COME. / C'MON C'MON** [ ] [–]

Polydor / Cotillion

Sep 70. (7") *(2058 054)* **KNOW WHO YOU ARE. / DAPPLE ROSE** [ ] [–]

Nov 70. (lp) *(2383 026)* *<9035>* **PLAY IT LOUD** [ ] [ ]
– Raven / See us here / Dapple rose / Could I / One way hotel / The shape of things to come / Know who you are / I remember / Pouk Hill / Angelina / Dirty joker / Sweet box. *(re-iss. Jun91 cd/c; 849 178-2/-4)*

May 71. (7"m) *(2058 112)* *<44128>* **GET DOWN AND GET WITH IT. / DO YOU WANT ME / THE GOSPEL ACCORDING TO RASPUTIN** [16] [ ]

Polydor / Polydor

Oct 71. (7") *(2058 155)* **COZ I LUV YOU. / LIFE IS NATURAL** [1] [–]

Jan 72. (7") *(2058 195)* *<15041>* **LOOK WOT YOU DUN. / CANDIDATE** [4] [ ]

Jan 72. (7") *<15044>* **COZ I LOVE YOU. / GOTTA KEEP A-ROCKIN' (live)** [–] [ ]

Mar 72. (lp) *(2383 101)* *<5508>* **SLADE ALIVE! (live)** [2] [ ]
– Hear me calling / In like a shot from my gun / Darling be home soon / Know who you are / Gotta keep on rockin' / Get down and get with it / Born to be wild. *(re-iss. Nov84 lp/c; SPE LP/MC 84) (re-iss. Jun91 cd/c; 841 114-2/-4)*

May 72. (7") *(2058 231)* *<15046>* **TAKE ME BAK 'OME. / WONDERIN'** [1] Sep72 [97]

Aug 72. (7") *(2058 274)* *<15053>* **MAMA WEER ALL CRAZEE NOW. / MAN WHO SPEAKS EVIL** [1] Nov72 [76]

Nov 72. (7") *(2058 312)* *<15060>* **GUDBUY T'JANE. / I WON'T LET IT 'APPEN AGAIN** [2] Mar73 [68]

Dec 72. (lp)(c) *(2383 163)* *<5524>* **SLAYED?** [1] [69]
– How d'you ride / The whole world's goin' craze / Look at last nite / I won't let it 'appen again / Move over / Gudbuy t'Jane / Gudbuy gudbuy / Mama weer all crazee now / I don't mind / Let the good times roll. *(cd-iss. May91; 849 180-2)*

Feb 73. (7") *(2058 339)* *<15069>* **CUM ON FEEL THE NOIZE. / I'M MEE, I'M NOW AN' THAT'S ORL** [1] May73 [98]

Jun 73. (7") *(2058 377)* **SKWEEZE ME PLEEZE ME. / KILL 'EM AT THE HOT CLUB TONITE** [1] [–]

Jul 73. (7") *<15080>* **LET THE GOOD TIMES ROLL. / FEEL SO FINE – I DON' MINE** [–] [ ]

Polydor / Reprise

Sep 73. (7") *(2058 407)* **MY FRIEND STAN. / MY TOWN** [2] [–]

Sep 73. (lp) *(2442 119)* *<2173>* **SLADEST** (compilation) [1] [ ]
– Wild things are blowing / Shape of things to come / Know who you are / Pounk Hill / One way hotel / Get down and get with it / Coz I luv you / Look wot you dun / Tak me bak ome / Mama weer all crazee now / Gudbuy t'Jane / Look at last night / Cum on feel the noize / Skweeze me pleeze me. *(cd-iss. Mar93; 837 103-2)*

Sep 73. (7") *<1182>* **SKWEEZE ME PLEEZE ME. / MY TOWN** [–] [ ]

Polydor / Warners

Dec 73. (7") *(2058 422)* *<7759>* **MERRY XMAS EVERYBODY. / DON'T BLAME ME** [1] [ ]
(re-iss. Dec80, Dec81 (No.32), Dec82 (No.67), Dec83 (No.20), Dec84 (No.47).

Feb 74. (lp) *(2383 261)* *<2770>* **OLD NEW BORROWED AND BLUE** <US title 'STOMP YOUR HANDS, CLAP YOUR FEET'> [1] [ ]
– Just want a little bit / When the lights are out / My town / Find yourself a rainbow / Miles out to sea / We're really gonna raise the roof / Do we still do it / How can it be / Don't blame me / My friend Stan / Everyday / Good time gals. *(cd-iss. May91; 849 181-2)*

Mar 74. (7") *(2058 453)* *<7777>* **EVERYDAY. / GOOD TIME GALS** [3] [ ]

Jun 74. (7") *(2058 492)* **THE BANGIN' MAN. / SHE DID IT TO ME** [3] [–]

Jul 74. (7") *<7808>* **WHEN THE LIGHTS ARE OUT. / HOW CAN IT BE** [–] [ ]

Oct 74. (7") *(2058 522)* **FAR FAR AWAY. / OK YESTERDAY WAS YESTERDAY** [2] [–]

Nov 74. (lp) *(2442 126)* *<2865>* **SLADE IN FLAME (Film Soundtrack)** [6] [93]
– How does it feel? / Them kinda monkeys can't swing / So far so good / Summer song (wishing you were here) / O.K. yesterday was yesterday / Far far away / This girl / Lay it down / Standin' on the corner. *(re-iss. Nov82 on 'Action Replay'; REPLAY 1000) (cd-iss. May91; 849 182-2)*

Feb 75. (7") *(2058 547)* **HOW DOES IT FEEL. / SO FAR SO GOOD** [15] [–]

Apr 75. (7") *<8134>* **HOW DOES IT FEEL. / O.K. YESTERDAY WAS YESTERDAY** [–] [ ]

May 75. (7") *(2058 585)* **THANKS FOR THE MEMORY (WHAM BAM THANK YOU MAM). / RAINING IN MY CHAMPAGNE** [7] [–]

Nov 75. (7") *(2058 663)* **IN FOR A PENNY. / CAN YOU JUST IMAGINE** [11] [–]

Jan 76. (7") *(2058 690)* **LET'S CALL IT QUITS. / WHEN THE CHIPS ARE DOWN** [11] [–]

Mar 76. (lp) *(2383 377)* *<2936>* **NOBODY'S FOOLS** [14] [ ]
– Nobody's fools / Do the dirty / Let's call it quits / Pack up your troubles / In for a penny / Get on up / L.A. jinx / Did your mama ever tell ya / Scratch my back / I'm a talker / All the world is a stage. *(cd-iss. May91; 849 183-2)*

Apr 76. (7") *(2058 716)* **NOBODY'S FOOL. / L.A. JINX** [ ] [–]

Apr 76. (7") *<8185>* **NOBODY'S FOOL. / WHEN THE CHIPS ARE DOWN** [–] [ ]

Barn-Polydor / not iss.

Feb 77. (7") *(2014 105)* **GYPSY ROADHOG. / FOREST FULL OF NEEDLES** [48] [–]

Mar 77. (lp) *(2314 103)* **WHATEVER HAPPENED TO SLADE** [ ] [–]
– Be / Lightning never strikes twice / Gypsy roadhog / Dogs of vengeance / When fantasy calls / One eyed Jacks with moustaches / Big apple blues / Dead men tell no tales / She's got the lot / It ain't love but it ain't bad / The soul, the fall and the motion. *(cd-iss. May93; 849 184-2)*

Apr 77. (7") *(2014 106)* **BURNING IN THE HEAT OF LOVE. / READY STEADY KIDS** [ ] [–]

Oct 77. (7") *(2014 114)* **MY BABY LEFT ME – THAT'S ALL RIGHT (Medley). / O.H.M.S.** [32] [–]

Mar 78. (7") *(2014 121)* **GIVE US A GOAL. / DADDIO** [ ] [–]

Oct 78. (7") *(2014 127)* **ROCK'N'ROLL BOLERO. / MY BABY'S GOT IT** [ ] [–]

Nov 78. (lp) *(2314 106)* **SLADE ALIVE VOL.2** [ ] [–]
– Get on up / Take me bak 'ome / Medley: My baby left me – That's all right / Be / Mama weer all crazee now / Burning in the heat of love / Everyday / Gudbuy t' Jane / One-eyed Jacks with moustaches / C'mon feel the noize. *(cd-iss. May93; 849 179-2)*

Barn / not iss.

Mar 79. (7"yellow) *(BARN 002)* **GINNY GINNY. / DIZZY MAMA** [ ] [–]

Oct 79. (7") *(BARN 010)* **SIGN OF THE TIMES. / NOT TONIGHT JOSEPHINE** [ ] [–]

Oct 79. (lp) *(NARB 003)* **RETURN TO BASE** [ ] [–]
– Wheels ain't coming down / Hold on to your hats / Chakeeta / Don't waste your time / Sign of the times / I'm a rocker / Nuts, bolts and screws / My baby's got it / I'm mad / Lemme love into ya / Ginny, Ginny.

Dec 79. (7") *(BARN 011)* **OKEY COKEY. / MY BABY'S GOT IT** [ ] [–]

Cheapskate / not iss.

Sep 80. (7"ep) *(CHEAP 5)* **SLADE ALIVE AT READING '80 (live)** [44] [–]
– When I'm dancing I ain't fightin' / Born to be wild / Somethin' else / Pistol packin' mama / Keep a rollin'.

Nov 80. (7") *(CHEAP 11)* **MERRY XMAS EVERYBODY. / OKEY COKEY / GET DOWN AND GET WITH IT** [70] [–]

Jan 81. (7") *(CHEAP 16)* **WE'LL BRING THE HOUSE DOWN. / HOLD ON TO YOUR HATS** [10] [–]

Mar 81. (lp/c) *(SKATE/KAT 1)* **WE'LL BRING THE HOUSE DOWN** [25] [–]
– Night starvation / Wheels ain't coming down / I'm a rocker / Nuts, bolts and screws / We'll bring the house down / Dizzy mama / Hold on to your hats / Lemme love into ya / My baby's got it / When I'm dancing I ain't fightin'. *(cd-iss. Nov96 on 'Castle'; CLACD 418) (cd re-iss. Sep99; 547412-2)*

Mar 81. (7") *(CHEAP 21)* **WHEELS AIN'T COMING DOWN. / NOT TONIGHT JOSEPHINE** [60] [–]

May 81. (7") *(CHEAP 24)* **KNUCKLE SANDWICH NANCY. / I'M MAD** [ ] [–]

R.C.A. CBS-Assoc.

Sep 81. (7") *(RCA 124)* **LOCK UP YOUR DAUGHTERS. / SIGN OF THE TIMES** [29] [–]

Nov 81. (lp/c) *(RCA LP/K 6021)* **TILL DEAF US DO PART** [ ] [–]
– Rock and roll preacher (hallelujah I'm on fire) / Ruby red / Lock up your daughters / Till deaf us do part / That was no lady that was my wife / She brings out the devil in me / A night to remember / M'hat m'coat / It's your body not your mind / Let the rock and roll out of control / Knuckle sandwich Nancy / Till deaf resurrected. *(cd-iss. Apr93 & Nov96 on 'Castle'; CLACD 377 & 415) (cd re-iss. Sep99; 547407-2)*

Mar 82. (7") *(RCA 191)* **RUBY RED. / FUNK PUNK AND JUNK** [51] [–]
(d7"+=) *(RCAD 191)* – Rock'n'roll preacher (live) / Take me back 'ome (live).

Nov 82. (7") *(RCA 291)* **(AND NOW – THE WALTZ) C'EST LA VIE. / MERRY XMAS EVERYBODY (ALIVE & KICKIN')** [50] [–]

Dec 82. (lp/c) *(RCA LP/K 3107)* **ON STAGE (live)** [ ] [–]
– Rock and roll preacher / When I'm dancing I ain't fightin' / Tak me bak 'ome / Everyday / Lock up your daughters / We'll bring the house down / A night to remember / Mama weer all crazee now / Gudbuy t'Jane / You'll never walk alone. *(cd-iss. Jul93 & Nov96 on 'Castle'; CLACD 380 & 420) (cd re-iss. Sep99; 547413-2)*

Nov 83. (7"m) *(RCA 373)* **MY OH MY. / MERRY XMAS EVERYBODY (live) / KEEP YOUR HANDS OFF MY POWER SUPPLY** [2] [–]

Dec 83. (lp/c) *(PL/PK 70116)* **THE AMAZING KAMIKAZE SYNDROME** [49] [–]
– Slam the hammer down / In the doghouse / Run runaway / High and dry / My oh my / Cocky rock boys / Ready to explode / (And now – The waltz) C'est la vie / Cheap 'n' nasty love / Razzle dazzle man. *(cd-iss. Apr93 & Nov96 on 'Castle'; CLACD 381 & 419) (cd re-iss. Sep99; 547411-2)*

Jan 84. (7"/12") *(RCA/+T 385)* **RUN RUNAWAY. / TWO TRACK STEREO, ONE TRACK MIND** [7] [–]

Apr 84. (lp) *<39336>* **KEEP YOUR HANDS OFF MY POWER SUPPLY** [–] [33]
<cd-iss. 1988; ZK 3936>

Apr 84. (7") *<04398>* **RUN RUNAWAY. / DON'T TAME A HURRICANE** [–] [20]

Jul 84. (7") *<04528>* **MY OH MY. / HIGH AND DRY** [–] [37]

Nov 84. (7") *(RCA 455)* **ALL JOIN HANDS. / HERE'S TO . . . (THE NEW YEAR)** [15] [–]
(12"+=) *(RCAT 455)* – Merry xmas everybody (live & kickin').

Jan 85. (7") *(RCA 475)* **7 YEAR (B)ITCH. / LEAVE THEM GIRLS ALONE** [60] [–]
(12"+=) *(RCAT 475)* – We'll bring the house down (live).

Mar 85. (lp/c) *(PL/PK 70604) <39976>* **ROGUES GALLERY** [ ] [ ]
– Hey ho wish you well / Little Sheila / Harmony / Myzsterious Mizster Jones / Walking on water, running on alcohol / 7 year (b)itch / I'll be there / I win, you lose / Time to rock / All join hands. *(cd-iss. Sep99; 547406-2)*

Mar 85. (7",7"pic-d) *(PB 40027)* **MYZSTERIOUS MIZSTER JONES. / MAMA NATURE IS A ROCKER** [50] [–]
(ext.12"+=) *(PT 40028)* – My oh my (piano and vocal version).

Apr 85. (7") *<04865>* **LITTLE SHEILA. / LOCK UP YOUR DAUGHTERS** [–] [86]

Nov 85. (7") *(PB 40449)* **DO YOU BELIEVE IN MIRACLES. / MY OH MY (swing version)** [54] [–]
(d7"+=) *(PB 40549)* – (see below d12" for extra tracks)
(12"+=) *(PT 40450)* – Time to rock.
(12"++=) *(PT 40550)* – Santa Claus is coming to town / Auld lang syne / You'll never walk alone.

Feb 87. (7"/12") *(PB 4113 7/8)* **STILL THE SAME. / GOTTA GO HOME** [73] [–]
(d7"+=) *(PB 41147D)* – The roaring silence / Don't talk to me about love.

Apr 87. (7") *(PB 41271)* **THAT'S WHAT FRIENDS ARE FOR. / WILD WILD PARTY** [ ] [–]
(12"+=) *(PT 41272)* – Hi ho silver lining / Lock up your daughters (live).

Apr 87. (lp/c/cd) *(PL/PK/PD 71260)* **YOU BOYZ MAKE BIG NOIZE** [ ] [–]
– Love is like a rock / That's what friends are for / Still the same / Fools go crazy / She's heavy / We won't give in / Won't you rock with me / Ooh la la in L.A. / Me and the boys / Sing shout (knock yourself out) / The roaring silence / It's hard having fun nowadays / You boyz make big noize / Boyz (instrumental). *(cd re-iss. Apr93 & Nov96 on 'Castle'; CLACD 379 & 417) (cd re-iss. Sep99; 547408-2)*

Cheapskate-RCA not iss.

Jun 87. (7") *(BOYZ 1)* **YOU BOYZ MAKE BIG NOIZE. / ('A'instrumental)** [ ] [–]
(12"+=) *(TBOYZ 1)* – ('A'-USA mix).

Nov 87. (7") *(BOYZ 2)* **WE WON'T GIVE IN. / LA LA IN L.A.** [ ] [–]

Nov 88. (7") *(BOYZ 3)* **LET'S DANCE (1988 remix). / STANDING ON THE CORNER** [ ] [–]
(cd-s+=) *(BOYZCD 3)* – Far far away / How does it feel.

Polydor not iss.

Oct 91. (7"/c-s) *(PO/+CS 180)* **RADIO WALL OF SOUND. / LAY YOUR LOVE ON THE LINE** [21] [–]
(cd-s+=) *(PZCD 180)* – Cum on feel the noize.

Nov 91. (cd/c/lp) *(511 612-2/-4/-1)* **WALL OF HITS** (compilation & new hits) [34] [ ]
– Get down and get with it / Coz I luv you / Look wot you dun / Take me bak 'ome / Gudbuy t'Jane / Cum on feel the noize / Skweeze me pleeze me / My friend Stan / Everyday / Bangin' man / Far far away / Let's call it quits / My oh my / Run run away / Radio wall of sound / Universe / Merry Xmas everybody. *(cd/c+=)* – How does it feel / Thanks for the memory (wham bam thank you mam).

Nov 91. (7"/c-s) **UNIVERSE. / MERRY CHRISTMAS EVERYBODY** [ ] [–]
(12"+=/cd-s+=) – Gypsy roadhog.

—— SLADE continued to do the odd gig/concert

– compilations, etc. –

on 'Polydor' unless stated otherwise

Jun 80. (12"ep) *Six Of The Best; (SUPER45 3)* **SIX OF THE BEST** [ ] [–]
– Night starvation / When I'm dancing I ain't fightin' / I'm a rocker / Don't waste your time / Wheels ain't coming down / Nine to five.

Nov 80. (lp) *(POLTV 13)* **SLADE SMASHES** [21] [–]

Apr 81. (d-lp/d-c) *(2689/3539 101)* **THE STORY OF SLADE** [ ] [–]
(cd-iss. VOL.1 & VOL.2 Nov90 on 'Bear Tracks'; BTCD 97941-1/-2)

Dec 81. (7"ep) *(POSP 399)* **CUM ON FEEL THE NOIZE / COZ I LUV YOU. / TAKE ME BAK 'OME / GUDBUY T'JANE** [ ] [–]
(12"ep+=) *(POSPX 399)* – Coz I luv you.

Dec 82. (7"/7"pic-d) *Speed; (SPEED/+P 201)* **THE HOKEY COKEY. / GET DOWN AND GET WITH IT** [ ] [–]

May 84. (lp/c) *(SLAD/+C 1)* **SLADE'S GREATS** [ ] [–]

Nov 85. (7"/12") *(POSP/+X 780)* **MERRY CHRISTMAS EVERYBODY (remix). / DON'T BLAME ME** [48] [–]
(re-iss. Dec86, hit No.71)

Nov 85. (lp/c) *Telstar; (STAR/STAC 2271)* **CRACKERS – THE SLADE CHRISTMAS PARTY ALBUM** [34] [–]

1988. (cd-ep) *Counterpoint; (CDEP 12C)* **HOW DOES IT FEEL / FAR FAR AWAY / (2 tracks by Wizzard)** [ ] [–]

Mar 89. (3"cd-ep) *R.C.A.; (PD 42637)* **MY OH MY / KEEP YOUR HANDS OFF MY POWER SUPPLY / RUNAWAY / ONE TRACK STEREO, ONE TRACK MIND** [ ] [–]

Apr 91. (cd/c/lp) *R.C.A.; (ND/NK/NL 74926)* **COLLECTION 81-87** [ ] [–]
(re-iss. Apr93 on 'Castle' cd/c; CCS CD/MC 372) (cd re-iss. Sep99 on 'Polydor'; 547410-2)

Dec 95. (c) *Prestige; (CASSGP 0253)* **KEEP ON ROCKIN'** [ ] [–]

Jan 97. (cd/c) *(537 105-2/-4)* **GREATEST HITS – FEEL THE NOIZE** [19] [–]
– Get down and get with it / Coz I luv you / Look wot you dun / Take me bak 'ome / Mama weer all crazee now / Gudbuy t'Jane / Cum on feel the noize / Skweeze me pleaze me / My friend Stan / Everyday / Bangin' man / Far far away / How does it feel to feel / In for a penny / We'll bring the house down / Lock up your daughters / Oh my my / Run run away / All

join hands / Radio wall of sound / Merry Xmas everybody. *(re-iss. Dec99 as 'GREATEST HITS – FEEL THE NOIZE'; same)*

Mar 97. (cd) *Music Corp; (TMC 9606)* **THE GENESIS OF SLADE** [ ] [–]

Dec 98. (c-s; SLADE VS FLUSH) *Polydor; (563352-4)* **MERRY XMAS EVERYBODY '98 REMIX / ('A'remix)** [30] [–]
(12"+=) *(563353-1)* – ('A'mix).
(cd-s+=) *(563353-2)* – Cum on feel the noize.

SLAYER

Formed: Los Angeles, California, USA . . . late 1981 by TOM ARAYA, JEFF HANNEMAN, KERRY KING and former jazz drummer, DAVE LOMBARDO. One of the heaviest, fastest and generally more extreme outfits to emerge from the initial wave of thrash-metal, SLAYER recorded their first couple of releases, 'SHOW NO MERCY' (1984) and the 'HAUNTING THE CHAPEL' EP (1984) for the 'Metal Blade' label. A largely unfocused blur of manic drumming and powerdrill guitar shredding, these early efforts also showcased a lyrical excess to match the 'music', heralding a new era in which initially thrash outfits, then death-metal merchants, trawled new depths of goriness (the PMRC would probably use the term depravity). 'HELL AWAITS' (1985) followed in much the same fashion and it wasn't until the epochal 'REIGN IN BLOOD' (1987) that SLAYER began to assume the status of metal demi-gods. Cannily signed up by RICK RUBIN to the ultra-hip 'Def Jam' (home to such groundbreaking rap outfits as The BEASTIE BOYS and PUBLIC ENEMY), SLAYER not only benefitted from the added kudos of a 'street' label but were touted by the rock press as having produced the ultimate speed-metal album. From its trademark black-period Goya-esque artwork to the breakneck precision of the playing and the wildly controversial lyrical fare ('NECROPHOBIC', 'RAINING BLOOD' etc.), 'REIGN IN BLOOD' was a landmark metal release, which in many respects has never been bettered in its respective field. The biggest fuss, however, was reserved for 'ANGEL OF DEATH', a track detailing the horrific atrocities of Nazi butcher, Joseph Mengele. 'Def Jam's distributor, 'Columbia' refused to handle the album, with 'Geffen' stepping in to facilitate the group's first Top 100 (US) entry. While SLAYER allegedly hold right-wing political views, the disturbingly soft-spoken ARAYA maintains that his lyrics do not promote war or violence but merely reflect the darker aspects of humanity. Whatever, there was no denying the power of SLAYER's music, especially on the more composed 'SOUTH OF HEAVEN' (1988). No doubt finally realising that only too often they sacrificed effectiveness for speed, SLAYER took their proverbial foot off the accelerator. Sure, there were still outbursts of amphetamine overkill, but with the likes of the apocalyptic title track, the chugging fury of 'MANDATORY SUICIDE' (complete with chilling spoken word outro) and a raging cover of Judas Priest's 'DISSIDENT AGGRESSOR', SLAYER had at last harnessed the malign potential which they had always promised. The record brought the band an unprecedented UK Top 30 chart placing, proof that the group were now being taken seriously as major thrash contenders alongside METALLICA, MEGADETH and ANTHRAX. The acclaimed 'SEASONS IN THE ABYSS' (1990) confirmed that SLAYER were not merely contenders but challengers for the thrash throne. With 'SEASONS..', the group succeeded in combining their instinct for speed with a newfound maturity, resulting in one of the most intense yet accessible metal records ever released. The doom-obsessed, bass-crunching likes of 'EXPENDABLE YOUTH', 'SKELETONS OF SOCIETY' and the brooding title track recalled the intensity of prime 70's BLACK SABBATH while even the harder tracks like 'WAR ENSEMBLE' and 'BLOOD RED' displayed traces of melody. The obligatory lyrical shock tactics came with 'DEAD SKIN MASK' an eery meditation reportedly inspired by serial killer, Ed Gein. Again produced by RUBIN and released on his fledgling 'Def American' label, the album made the UK Top 20 and finally broke the group into the US Top 40. Promoting the record with the legendary 'Clash Of The Titans' tour (also featuring MEGADETH, SUICIDAL TENDENCIES and TESTAMENT), SLAYER had finally made it into the metal big league and summing up the first blood-soaked chapter of their career, the group duly released the live double set, 'DECADE OF AGGRESSION' (1991). Amid much rumour and counter-rumour, LOMBARDO finally left the band for good in Spring '92, ex-FORBIDDEN sticksman, PAUL BOSTOPH, drafted in as a replacement. A long-awaited sixth set, 'DIVINE INTERVENTION', finally arrived in 1994, a consolidation of SLAYER's hallowed position in the metal hierarchy and the group's first assault on the US Top 10. The heaviest band ever (as Kerrang! readers acclaimed them!) spewed back with 'UNDISPUTED ATTITUTE' (1996), although it was 1998's 'DIABOLUS IN MUSICA' (apparently a "devilish" musical scale banned by churches in the 15th century!) which brought their brutal gore back to the fore. Surely a contender for album title of the year 'GOD HATES US ALL' (2001) nailed SLAYER's brutal musical colours to their upside down mast once and for all. As unrelenting, savage, nihilsitic and downright nasty as you could possibly ask a metal album to be, SLAYER went back to their roots with a maniacal vengeance that showed the young pretenders up as the lightweights they are. • **Songwriters:** ARAYA words / HANNEMAN music, also covered IN-A-GADDA-DA-VIDA (Iron Butterfly) / DISORDER + WAR + UK 82 (as 'US 92'; 3 from 1993 film 'Judgment Night') (Exploited). 'UNDISPUTED ATTITUDE' album all covers; ABOLISH GOVERNMENT (TSOL) / I WANNA BE YOUR DOG (Iggy Pop) / (GBH) / GUILTY OF BEING WHITE (Minor Threat) / other covers from (Verbal Abuse), (D.I.), (Dr Know) and (DRI).

Album rating: SHOW NO MERCY (*5) / HELL AWAITS (*7) / REIGN IN BLOOD (*9) / SOUTH OF HEAVEN (*9) / SEASONS IN THE ABYSS (*8) / DECADE OF AGGRESSION (*8) / DIVINE INTERVENTION (*7) / UNDISPUTED ATTITUDE (*6) / DIABOLUS IN MUSICA (*5) / GOD HATES US ALL (*7) / SOUNDTRACK TO THE APOCALYPSE boxed compilation (*7)

TOM ARAYA (b. 6 Jun'61, Chile) – vocals, bass / **JEFF HANNEMAN** (b.31 Jan'64) – lead guitar / **KERRY KING** (b. 3 Jun'64, Huntington Park, Calif.) – lead guitar / **DAVE LOMBARDO** (b.16 Feb'65) – drums

Roadrunner Metal Blade

Jun 84. (lp) *(RR 9868) <MBR 1013>* **SHOW NO MERCY** [ ] Feb84 [ ]
– Evil has no boundaries / The antichrist / Die by the sword / Fight till death / Metalstorm – Face the slayer / Black magic / Tormentor / The final command / Crionics / Show no mercy. *<US re-iss. pic-lp Dec88; 72214-1> (re-iss. Aug90 on 'Metal Blade' cd/c/lp; CD/T+/ZORRO 7) (cd re-iss. Feb96 on 'Metal Blade'; 3984 14032CD)*

Oct 84. (12"ep) *(RR12 55087)* **HAUNTING THE CHAPEL. / CHEMICAL WARFARE / CAPTOR OF SIN** [ ] [ ]
(re-iss. Oct89 as cd-ep; RR 2444-2)

Roadrunner Enigma

May 85. (lp/c) *(RR 9795-1/-4) <72297>* **HELL AWAITS** [ ] [ ]
– Hell awaits / Kill again / At dawn they sleep / Praise of death / Necrophiliac / Crypts of eternity / Hardening of the arteries. *(cd-iss. Feb89; RR34 9795) (re-iss. Aug90 on 'Metal Blade' cd/c/lp; CD/T+/ZORRO 8) (cd re-iss. Feb96 on 'Metal Blade'; 3984 14031CD)*

London Def Jam

Apr 87. (lp/c/pic-lp) *(LON LP/C/PP 34) <24131>* **REIGN IN BLOOD** [47] Oct86 [94]
– Angel of death / Piece by piece / Necrophobic / Alter of sacrifice / Jesus saves / Criminally insane / Reborn / Epidemic / Post mortem / Raining blood. *(cd-iss. Dec94 on 'American'; 74321 24848-2)*

May 87. (7"red) *(LON 133)* **CRIMINALLY INSANE (remix). / AGGRESSIVE PERFECTER** [64] [ ]
(12"+=) *(LONX 133)* – Post mortem.

Jun 88. (lp/c)(cd) *(LON LP/C 63)(828 820-2)* <24203> **SOUTH OF HEAVEN** [25] [57]
– South of Heaven / Silent scream / Live undead / Behind the crooked cross / Mandatory suicide / Ghosts of war / Read between the lies / Cleanse the soul / Dissident aggressor / Spill the blood. *(cd re-iss. Dec94 on 'American'; 74321 24849-2)*

Sep 88. (12") *(LONX 201)* **MANDATORY SUICIDE. / IN-A-GADDA-DA-VIDA** [ ] [–]

American | Def American

Oct 90. (cd/c/lp) *(849 6871-2/-4/-1)* <24307> **SEASONS IN THE ABYSS** [18] [40]
– War ensemble / Blood red / Spirit in black / Expendable youth / Dead skin mask / Hallowed point / Skeletons of society / Temptation / Born of fire / Seasons in the abyss. *(cd re-iss. Dec94 on 'American'; 74321 24850-2)*

Oct 91. (d-cd/d-c/d-lp) *(510 605-2/-4/-1)* <26748> **DECADE OF AGGRESSION (live)** [29] [ ]
– Hell awaits / The anti-Christ / War ensemble / South of Heaven / Raining blood / Altar of sacrifice / Jesus saves / Dead skin mask / Seasons in the abyss / Mandatory suicide / Angel of death / Hallowed paint / Blood red / Die by the sword / Black magic / Captor of sin / Born of fire / Post mortem / Spirit in black / Expendable youth / Chemical warfare. *(cd re-iss. Dec94; 74321 24851-2)*

Oct 91. (7") *(DEFA 9)* **SEASONS IN THE ABYSS (live). / AGGRESSIVE PERFECTOR (live)** [51] [ ]
(12"+=) *(DEFA 9-12)* – Chemical warfare.
(12"pic-d+=)(cd-s+=) *(DEFAP 9-12)(DEFAC 9)* – ('A'-experimental).

—— (May'92) **PAUL BOSTAPH** (b. 4 Mar'65, Hayward, Calif.) – drums repl. LOMBARDO

Oct 94. (cd/c/lp) *(74321 23677-2/-4/-1)* <26748> **DIVINE INTERVENTION** [15] [8]
– Killing fields / Sex. murder. art / Fictional reality / Dittohead / Divine intervention / Circle of beliefs / SS-3 / Serenity in murder / 213 / Mind control.

Sep 95. (7"ep) *(74321 26234-7)* **SERENITY IN MURDER / RAINING BLOOD. / DITTOHEAD / SOUTH OF HEAVEN** [ ] [–]
(cd-s) *(74321 26234-2)* – ('A'side) / At dawn they sleep (live) / Dead skin mask (live) / Divine intervention (live).
(cd-s) *(74321 31248-2)* – ('A'side) / Angel of death / Mandatory suicide / War ensemble.

—— (after below) **JOHN DETTE** – drums (ex-TESTAMENT) repl. BOSTOPH who joined lightweight TRUTH ABOUT SEAFOOD

May 96. (cd/c/10"d-lp) *(74321 35759-2/-4/-1)* <43072> **UNDISPUTED ATTITUDE** [31] [34]
– Disintigration – Free money / Verbal abuse – Leeches / Abolish government – Superficial love / Can't stand you / Ddamm / Guilty of being white / I hate you / Filler – I don't want to hear it / Spiritual law / Sick boy / Mr. Freeze / Violent pacification / Richard hung himself / I wanna be your god / Gemini. *(cd w/ free cd+=)(74321 38325-2)* – Witching hour / Dittohead / Divine intervention.

Sub Pop | Sub Pop

Aug 96. (7") <*(SP 368)*> **ABOLISH GOVERNMENT. / T.S.O.L.: Abolish Government** [ ] [ ]
(re-iss. Oct01; *same*)

—— there was also a SLAYER tribute album released Nov95; 'SLATANIC SLAUGHTER' on 'Black Sun' cd/lp; *BS 003 CD/LP)*

Columbia | Columbia

Jun 98. (cd/c/lp) *(491302-2/-4/-1)* <69192> **DIABOLUS IN MUSICA** [27] [31]
– Bitter peace / Death's head / Stain of mind / Overt enemy / Perversions of pain / Love to hate / Desire / In the name of God / Scrum / Screaming from the sky / Point. *(cd re-iss. Aug00; same)*

Sep 01. (cd)(lp) <*(586331-2)*>*(486394-1)* **GOD HATES US ALL** [31] [28]
– Darkness of Christ / Disciple / God send death / New faith / Cast down / Threshold / Exile / Seven faces / Bloodline / Deviance / Warzone / Here comes the pain / Payback.

– compilations, etc. –

Dec 88. (lp/c) *Roadrunner; (RR/+34 9574) / Enigma; <72015-1>* **LIVE UNDEAD (live 1984)** [ ] Oct87 [ ]
– Black magic / Die by the sword / Captor of sin / The antichrist / Evil has no boundaries / Show no mercy / Aggressive perfector / Chemical warfare. *(re-iss. Sep91 on 'Metal Blade' cd/c/lp; CD/T+/ZORRO 29) (cd re-iss. Feb96 on 'Metal Blade'+=; 3984 14011CD)* – HAUNTING THE CHAPEL

Dec 03. (3xcd-box+dvd) *American; <(00016370-2)>* **SOUNDTRACK TO THE APOCALYPSE** [ ] Nov03 [ ]

Percy SLEDGE

Born: 25 Nov'41, Leighton, Alabama, USA. Another soul legend to begin his singing career in the church, SLEDGE subsequently moved into the secular music world in the early-mid 60's as part of The ESQUIRES COMBO. His break came in 1966 when local DJ Quin Ivy helped produce SLEDGE's landmark classic, 'WHEN A MAN LOVES A WOMAN'. With its ardent, intense vocals and proclamation of love's eternal endurance, the song quickly became a hallowed soul standard and a new benchmark for aspiring balladeers. As well as hiring SPOONER OLDHAM for the sombre farfisa organ part, Ivy released the record independently before licensing it to budding Southern Soul sponsors, 'Atlantic'. Unsurprisingly, it topped the US chart and broke the UK Top 5, announcing the arrival of yet another rich talent from the ever fertile American south. Follow-up, 'WARM AND TENDER LOVE', proved it was no mercurial one-off, making the US Top 20 and preceding a whole album of heartfelt romantic testament named after his debut hit. Working with the cream of country-soul writers such as OLDHAM, DAN PENN and CHIPS MOMAN, SLEDGE scored a further US Top 20 hit, 'IT TEARS ME UP', later that year. Increasingly, however, the man's chart placings failed to reflect the quality of his work. While his superior version of the OLDHAM/MOMAN classic, 'DARK END OF THE STREET' (from 1967's 'THE PERCY SLEDGE WAY' album) somehow never made it onto 7" vinyl, SLEDGE did score one further Top 20 hit in Spring '68 with the sublime 'TAKE TIME TO KNOW HER'. While not attempting as daring a marriage as say, RAY CHARLES, SLEDGE was one of the era's most subtle interpretors of the link between country and soul; having already covered Charlie Rich's 'BEHIND CLOSED DOORS' on his debut album, SLEDGE went on to perform Kris Kristofferson's 'HELP ME MAKE IT THROUGH THE NIGHT', released as a single in 1970. By this point, however, his career was in commercial decline and although he subsequently signed to Phil Walden's Southern Rock bastion, 'Capricorn', he could only manage one last minor hit with 1974's 'I'LL BE YOUR EVERYTHING'. Although he was dogged by ill health, SLEDGE made a successful living on the golden oldies circuit over the forthcoming decades, his famous debut single resurrected in 1987 when it hit the UK Top 5 all over again after being used in a Levi's jeans ad. In 1994 he released his first new material in over a decade in the shape of the 'BLUE NIGHT' album, featuring guest spots by the likes of STEVE CROPPER and BOBBY WOMACK. • **Trivia:** In 1991, poodle-haired howler, MICHAEL BOLTON, also took 'WHEN A MAN . . .' into the UK Top 10.

Best CD compilation: THE ULTIMATE COLLECTION – THE BEST OF . . . (*7)

PERCY SLEDGE – vocals (with session people)

Atlantic | Atlantic

May 66. (7") *(584 001)* **WHEN A MAN LOVES A WOMAN. / LOVE ME LIKE YOU MEAN IT** [4] Mar66 [1]
(re-iss. 1974) (12"iss.Apr80)

Jul 66. (7") *(584 034)* <2342> **WARM AND TENDER LOVE. / SUGAR PUDDIN'** [34] [17]

Jul 66. (lp; mono/stereo) *(587/588 105)* <8125> **WHEN A MAN LOVES A WOMAN** [ ] May66 [37]
– When a man loves a woman / You're pouring water on a drowning man /

Love makes the world go round / Love me like you meant it / My adorable one / Put a little lovin' on me / Love me all the way / When she touches me / Thief in the night / You fooled me / Success. *(re-iss. 1970)*

Oct 66. (7") *<2358>* **IT TEARS ME UP. / HEART OF A CHILD** [–] [20]

Nov 66. (7") *(584 055)* **HEART OF A CHILD. / MY ADORABLE ONE** [ ] [–]

Jan 67. (7") *(584 071)* **IT TEARS ME UP. / OH HOW HAPPY** [ ] [–]

Feb 67. (lp; mono/stereo) *(587/588 048) <8132>* **WARM AND TENDER SOUL** [ ] Nov66 [ ]
– Make it good and make it last / When a man loves a woman / Walkin' in the Sun / Warm and tender love / The God love / Out of left field / Behind closed doors / Just out of reach / I believe in you / I believe in you / Take time to know her. *(re-iss. +c.Aug86 on 'Blue Moon')*

Feb 67. (7") *(584 080) <2383>* **BABY, HELP ME. / YOU'VE LOST THAT SOMETHING WONDERFUL** [ ] [87]

Apr 67. (7") *(584 108) <2396>* **OUT OF LEFT FIELD. / IT CAN'T BE STOPPED** [ ] [59]

Jun 67. (7") *<2414>* **LOVE ME TENDER. / WHAT AM I LIVING FOR** [–] [40] [91]

Aug 67. (7") *<2434>* **JUST OUT OF REACH (OF MY TWO EMPTY ARMS). / HARD TO BELIEVE** [–] [66]

Oct 67. (7") *(584 140)* **PLEDGING MY LOVE. / YOU DON'T MISS YOUR WATER** [ ] [ ]

Nov 67. (lp; mono/stereo) *(587/588 081) <8146>* **THE PERCY SLEDGE WAY** [ ] Aug67 [ ]
– Dark end of the street / You send me / I had a talk with my woman / What am I living for / I've been loving you too long / Drown in my own tears / My special prayer / Just out of reach / Pledging my love / You don't miss your water . . .

Nov 67. (7") *<2453>* **COVER ME. / BEHIND EVERY GREAT MAN THERE IS A WOMAN** [–] [42]

Apr 68. (7") *(584 177) <2490>* **TAKE TIME TO KNOW HER. / IT'S ALL WRONG BUT IT'S ALRIGHT** [ ] Mar68 [11]

May 68. (lp) *<8180>* **TAKE TIME TO KNOW HER** [–] [ ]
– Take time to know her / Feed the flame / Out of left field / Cover me / Come softly to me / Sudden stop / Spooky / Baby help me / It's all wrong but it's alright / High cost of leaving / Between these arms / I love everything about you. *(cd-iss. Jan03; 7567 80800-2)*

Jul 68. (7") *<2539>* **SUDDEN STOP. / BETWEEN THESE ARMS** [–] [63]

Sep 68. (7") *<2563>* **YOU'RE ALL AROUND ME. / SELF PRESERVATION** [–] [ ]

Nov 68. (7") *(584 225)* **COME SOFTLY TO ME. / YOU'RE ALL AROUND ME** [ ] [–]

Jan 69. (7") *<2594>* **MY SPECIAL PRAYER. / BLESS YOUR SWEET LITTLE SOUL** [–] [93]

May 69. (7") *(584 264) <2616>* **ANY DAY NOW. / THE ANGELS LISTENED IN** [ ] Apr69 [86]

Aug 69. (7") *(584 286) <2646>* **KIND WOMAN. / WOMAN OF THE NIGHT** [ ] [ ]

Nov 69. (7") *(584 300) <2679>* **TRUE LOVE TRAVELS ON A GRAVEL ROAD. / FAITHFUL AND TRUE** [ ] [ ]

Nov 69. (lp; mono/stereo) *(587/588 153) <8210>* **THE BEST OF PERCY SLEDGE** (compilation) [ ] Feb69 [ ]
– When a man loves a woman / Out of left field / Take time to know her / Warm and tender / Just out of reach (of my two empty arms) / Dark end of the street / Cover me / Sudden stop / Baby help me / It tears me up / My special prayer / You're all around me. *(re-iss. 1972 & 1980)*

Feb 70. (7") *<2719>* **TOO MANY RIVERS TO CROSS. / PUSHING MY PRIDE AGAIN** [–] [ ]

May 70. (7") *<2754>* **HELP ME MAKE IT THROUGH THE NIGHT. / THIEF IN THE NIGHT** [–] [ ]

Aug 70. (7") *<2826>* **THAT'S THE WAY I WANT TO LIVE MY LIFE. / STOP THE WORLD TONIGHT** [–] [ ]

1970. (lp) *<9257>* **IN SOUTH AFRICA (live)** [–] [ ]
– My special prayer / Cover me / Heart of a child / Take time to know her / Warm and tender love / I gotta get a message to you / Silent night / Come softly to me / What am I living for / When a man loves a woman.

1971. (7") *<2886>* **SUNDAY BROTHER. / EVERYTHING YOU'LL EVER NEED** [–] [ ]

Mar 72. (7") *(K 10144)* **RAINBOW ROAD. / STANDING ON THE MOUNTAIN** [ ] [–]

Jun 72. (7"m) **BABY HELP ME. / WARM AND TENDER LOVE / TAKE TIME TO KNOW HER** [ ] [–]

Aug 73. (7") *(K 10358) <2963>* **SUNSHINE. / UNCHANGING LOVE** [ ] [ ]

Capricorn Capricorn

Oct 74. (7") *<0209>* **I'LL BE YOUR EVERYTHING. / BLUE WATER** [–] [62]

Nov 74. (7") *(2089 009)* **I'LL BE YOUR EVERYTHING. / WALKIN' IN THE SUN** [ ] [–]

Nov 74. (lp) *<0147>* **I'LL BE YOUR EVERYTHING** [–] [ ]
– Walkin' in the sun / Behind closed doors / Make it good and make it last / The good love I believe in you / I'll be your everything / If this is the last time / Hard to be friends / Blue water / Love among people.

Feb 75. (7") *<0220>* **BEHIND CLOSED DOORS. / IF THIS IS THE LAST TIME** [–] [ ]

1977. (7") *<0273>* **WHEN A BOY BECOMES A MAN. / WHEN SHE TOUCHES ME** [–] [ ]

— PERCY retired for a while after being dogged by ill health

Monument Monument

1983. (7") **SHE'S TOO PRETTY TO CRY. / ?** [–] [ ]

1983. (lp) *<(MNT 25369)>* **PERCY** [ ] [ ]
– Bring your lovin' to me / You had to be there / All night rain / She's too pretty to cry / I still miss someone / The faithful kind / Home type thing / Personality / I'd put angels around you / Hard lovin' woman. *(re-iss. Jul87 on 'Charly' lp/c; CRB/TCCRB 1152) (cd-iss. Jul87; CDCHARLY 95)*

Demon not iss.

Jul 89. (lp/cd) *(FIEND/+CD 140)* **WANTED AGAIN** (rec.1986-87) [ ] [–]
– Keep the fire burning / Wanted again / Kiss an angel good morning / Hey good lookin' / If you've got the money honey / He'll have tp go / Today I started lovin' you again / She thinks I still care / Wabash cannonball / For the good times. *(cd re-iss. Jun98 on 'Diablo'; DIAB 859)*

Virgin – Pointblank Virgin – Pointblank

Nov 94. (cd/c) *<(VPB CD/TC 21)>* **BLUE NIGHT** [ ] [ ]
– You got away with love / Love come knockin' / Why did you stop / I wish it would rain / Blue night / These ain't teardrops / Your love will save the world / First you cry / Going home tomorrow / The grand blvd. / I've got dreams to remember.

– (selective) compilations, etc. –

Jan 87. (7"/12") *Atlantic; (YZ 96/+T)* **WHEN A MAN LOVES A WOMAN. / WARM AND TENDER LOVE** [2] [–]
(cd-s+=) *(500 068)* –

Feb 87. (lp/c)(cd) *Atlantic; (WX 89/+C)(780212-2)* **WHEN A MAN LOVES A WOMAN (THE ULTIMATE COLLECTION)** [36] [ ]
– When a man loves a woman / It tears me up / Take time to know her / My special prayer / Baby help me / It's all wrong but it's right / You're all around me / Dark end of the street / Warm and tender love / Love me tender / Out of left field / Come softly to me / What am I living for? / You're pouring water on a drowning man / Just out of reach / Cover me / Sudden stop / You really got a hold on me / That's how strong my love is / Put a little lovin' in me.

Mar 93. (cd) *Rhino-WEA; <(8122 70285-2)>* **IT TEARS ME UP: THE BEST OF PERCY SLEDGE** [ ] Mar92 [ ]

Jan 95. (cd/c) *K-Tel; (ECD3/EMC2 087)* **WHEN A MAN LOVES A WOMAN** [ ] [–]

Jun 95. (cd) *Collection; (COL 048)* **THE COLLECTION** [ ] [–]

Feb 96. (cd) *Music De-Luxe; MSCD 026)* **BEHIND CLOSED DOORS** [ ] [–]

Nov 96. (cd) *Summit; (SUMCD 4009)* **A LITTLE TENDERNESS** [ ] [–]

May 97. (cd) *A-Play; (10058-2)* **WHEN A MAN LOVES A WOMAN** [ ] [–]

Jul 97. (cd) *Koch Int.; (322698)* **WHEN A MAN LOVES A WOMAN** [ ] [–]

Jan 98. (cd; shared with JOHNNY OTIS) *Members Edition; (UAE 3009-2)* **PERCY SLEDGE & JOHNNY OTIS** [ ] [–]

Jul 01. (cd) *Cleopatra; (CLP 1013CD)* **ALL-TIME GREATEST HITS** [ ] [–]

Oct 01. (cd) *Platinum; (PLATCD 691)* **THE SOULFUL SOUND OF PERCY SLEDGE** [ ] [–]

Jul 03. (cd) *Forever Gold; (FG 263)* **THE BEST OF PERCY SLEDGE** [ ] [–]

SLINT

Formed: Louisville, Kentucky, USA . . . 1988 by former SQUIRREL BAIT partners, BRIAN McMAHAN and BRITT WALFORD, who had already teamed up with DAVID PAJO and ETHAN BUCKLER prior to the latter band's division into BASTRO and SLINT. The influential noiseniks made their debut the following year with the self-financed, STEVE ALBINI-produced album, 'TWEEZ', a willfully weird clutch of mainly instrumental guitar/bass-led creations named after their family members (including a dog!). While WALFORD (aka SHANNON DOUGHTY) moonlighted on The BREEDERS first album, 'Pod', BUCKLER would subsequently leave to form KING KONG, replacement TODD BRASHER installed as work commenced on a BRIAN PAULSON-produced follow-up set, 'SPIDERLAND'. Upon its release (on 'Touch & Go') in '91, the album generated a healthy amount of column inches praising its uncategorisable guitar-scapes, Scotland's own MOGWAI later citing the record as a pivotal reference point. While rumours circulated that the album's recording had almost sent SLINT over the edge, the individual members were obviously sane enough to work on various projects including WILL OLDHAM's PALACE BROTHERS (WALFORD, McMAHAN and BRASHER) and TORTOISE (PAJO). A final postscript to the SLINT story came in 1993 with the release of double-A side ("untitled") single, 'GLENN' / 'RHODA' (the latter a cut from '89), with McMAHAN, however, embarking on his own adventure, The FOR CARNATION with SLINT buddy PAJO; other members DOUGLAS McCOMBS, GRANT BARGER and JOHN HERNDON. This quintet released the EP, 'FLIGHT SONGS' (1995), while the mini-set 'MARSHMALLOWS' (1996) was without the much in-demand PAJO. Not released in Britian, it finally surfaced in 1997 as 'PROMISED WORKS', containing the debut EP tracks. Like in SLINT, McMAHAN enforced the dizzy guitars and whispering sung/spoken vocals that made the aforementioned group sound so interesting, GALAXIE 500 and GASTR DEL SOL were also names that were thrown in as noteworthy comparisons. Adding LEONARD COHEN-esque incoherence to the mix, a slightly surreal view of life encouraged McMAHAN's lyrics and influence to reach higher dynamic points within his sound and vision. With his brother MICHAEL on guitar, BOB BRUNO, TODD COOK and moonlighting RADAR BROS drummer STEVE GOODFRIEND, The FOR CARNATION were reborn for an album which was scheduled for release early 2000. Meanwhile, following PAJO's stint with avant-jazz combo, TORTOISE, the musical Jack-of-all trades followed a similar dusty path to the aforementioned WILL OLDHAM, on his eponymous 1997 debut solo set (released under the AERIAL-M moniker), foregoing vocals in favour of backporch strumming. Licensed from 'Drag City' to 'Domino' in the UK, the rootsy homegrown affair showed a mellower side to the normally uncompromising guitarist and paved the way for two further releases over the course of the following year, EP's 'M IS . . .' and 'OCTOBER'. PAJO's increasingly interesting full-time project AERIAL M reached a peak with the release of his remix album 'POST-GLOBAL MUSIC' (1999), a record which saw single 'WEDDING SONG NO.3' get the mixing treatment from DJ YOUR FOOD, FLACCO and BUNDY K. BROWN. A back-to-roots move, and a transformation had PAJO change what was once M, AERIAL M and M IS THE THIRTEENTH LETTER to the new post-rock infused PAPA M. He issued his best to date under this moniker, the sweeping, placid and intimately creepy 'LIVE FROM A SHARK CAGE' at the end of 1999. A slow-burning blend of echoing guitars, badly recorded keyboards and lo-fi stoned beats, the album began with the sweet chamber drone of 'ARUNDAL' moving into the xylophone driven, wintery 'ROADRUNNER'. Elsewhere on the set, PAJO advanced into the quiet eerie proportions of songwriting; the brooding atmosphere on 'CROWD OF ONE' (in which PAJO's recently deceased grandfather's answering machine messages are played over a floating ambient guitar) matches that of some of TORTOISE's more experimental works, where 'KNOCKING THE CASKET' was a banjo-laden lament, PAJO himself knocking on his acoustic guitar, to keep a beat while stomping his foot on a wooden floor. This was to ultimately lead the way for his next outing, the EP 'PAPA M SINGS', in which he put his voice to the test by singing songs in a country style, similar to friend and PALACE man WILL OLDHAM. PAJO recorded the EP on a four-track and passed it around friends. Luckily they liked it. The EP was issued on MOGWAI's 'Rock Action' in Febuary 2001 and boasted the hugely satisfying bitter-sweet/drunk love song 'JADED LOVER'. 'PISSING IN THE WIND', a donkey-paced front porch banjo track had him singing sarcastically about the 'Drag City' imprint, while the slide-guitar rambling in ode-to-a-lover 'TRUE LOVE' reminded listeners of how talented a guitarist PAJO actually was. Sure, his voice was a bit flat, but that all added to the folksy, Kentucky image honed by OLDHAM et al. Later that year, PAJO began work on his follow-up to ' . . .SHARK CAGE' and appeared as a guest on MOGWAI's 'Rock Action' album. PAJO sang again on the 2002 release 'SONGS FOR MAC' where this time PAPA M took two songs by unknowns, MAC FINLEY and AUBREY ROZIER, and covered them knowing most of his audience hadn't heard the originals. A brief and well laid-out EP, the two songs that featured were competent and displayed PAJO's trademark Louisville drawl. The set also saw a switch to the little known label 'Western Vinyl'. Meanwhile PAJO was said to be switching to the mainstream; an unlikely pairing with BILLY CORGAN and his new supergroup ZWAN.

Album rating: TWEEZ (*7) / SPIDERLAND (*8) / For Carnation: PROMISED WORKS collection of US EP's (*6) / THE FOR CARNATION (*8) / Aerial-M: AS PERFORMED BY . . . (*7) / POST-GLOBAL MUSIC (*7) / Papa M: LIVE FROM A SHARK CAGE (*8) / WHATEVER, MORTAL (*7)

BRIAN McMAHAN – vocals, guitar (ex-SQUIRREL BAIT) / **DAVID PAJO** – guitar / **ETHAN BUCKLER** – bass / **BRITT WALFORD** – drums (ex-SQUIRREL BAIT)

Jennifer Hartman | Jennifer Hartman

Sep 89. (lp) <*(JHR 136)*> **TWEEZ**
– Ron / Nan ding / Carol / Kent / Charlotte / Darlene / Warren / Pat / Rhoda. <*(re-iss. May93 on 'Touch & Go' lp/cd; TG 138/+D)*>

— **TODD BRASHER** – bass; BUCKLER who formed KING KONG

Touch & Go | Touch & Go

Mar 91. (lp/cd) <*(TGLP 64/+cd)*> **SPIDERLAND**
– Breadcrumb trail / Nosferatu man / Don, Aman / Washer / For dinner . . . / Good morning, captain. *(re-iss. Sep98; same)*

Sep 94. (10"/cd-s) <*(TG 132/+cd)*> **SLINT**
– Glenn / Rhoda.

— had already disbanded in 1992, WALFORD + McMAHAN later joined the PALACE BROTHERS; the latter also formed The FOR CARNATION. PAJO (a part-timer with TFC) subsequently joined TORTOISE before forming AERIAL-M.

The FOR CARNATION

BRIAN McMAHAN with **DAVID PAJO** – guitar / **DOUGLAS McCOMBS** – bass / **JOHN HERNDON** – drums / **GRANT BARGER** – engineer, co-writer

Matador | Matador

Jun 95. (cd-ep) <*(OLE 131-2)*> **FIGHT SONGS EP** Apr95
– Grace beneath the pines / How I beat the Devil / Get and stay get March.

— **BRAD WOOD, JOHN WEISS + TIM RUTH**; repl. PAJO

Mar 96. (m-cd/m-lp) <*OLE 172-2/-1*> **MARSHMALLOWS** [–] [ ]
– On the swing / I wear the gold / Imyr, marshmallow / Winter lair / Salo / Preparing to receive you.

Runt / not iss.

Jun 97. (cd) *(RUNT 30)* **PROMISED WORKS** (compilation of the EP and mini-set) [ ] [–]

— **McMAHAN** recruited his brother **MICHAEL McMAHAN** – guitar / **BOBB BRUNO** – guitar, sampler, keyboards / **TODD COOK** – bass / **STEVE GOODFRIEND** – drums / forthcoming set in March 2000 also incl. **KIM DEAL** – vocals (ex-PIXIES) / **RACHEL HAYDEN** – vocals (of that dog.) + **JOHN McENTIRE** – (who else?, on production)

Domino / Touch & Go

Mar 00. (cd/lp) *(WIG CD/LP 77)* <*TG 214*> **THE FOR CARNATION** [ ] [ ]
– Empowered man's blues / A tribute to / Being held / Smoother / Tales (live from the crypt) / Moonbeams.

AERIAL-M

DAVID PAJO – guitars (with **LATETIA SADIER** on first)

not iss. / Palace

Dec 95. (7"; as M IS THE THIRTEENTH LETTER) <*PR 11*> **SAFELESS. / NAPOLEON** [–] [ ]

not iss. / All City

Dec 96. (7") **VOL DE NUIT. / (other track by MONADE)** [–] [ ]

Domino / Drag City

Sep 97. (cd/lp) *(WIG CD/LP 037)* <*DC 114*> **AS PERFORMED BY . . . AERIAL-M** [ ] Aug97 [ ]
– Dazed and awake / Aass / Wedding song No.2 / Rachmaninoff / Skrak theme / Compassion for M / Always farewell.

Feb 98. (7"m)<cd-ep> *(RUG 062)*<*DC 144CD*> **M IS . . . / WEDDING THEME NO.3 / MOUNTAINS HAVE EARS** [ ] Dec97 [ ]

Jun 98. (7") *(RUG 070)* <*DC 155*> **OCTOBER** [ ] Feb99 [ ]
– Vivea / Last caress.

Feb 99. (cd/lp) *(WIG CD/LP 63)* <*DC 170*> **POST-GLOBAL MUSIC** [ ] Jan99 [ ]
– Wedding song No.3 (FLACCO mix) / Wedding song (TIED + TICKLED TRIO remix) / Wedding song No.3 (BUNDY K. BROWN mix) / Attention span deficit disorder disruption a journey wherein (. . . seeks the gateway out of the world of red dust and learns that running between the raindrops won't save you from the chocolate thunder) (DJ YOUR FOOD mix).

PAPA M

— aka **DAVID PAJO**

Nov 99. (cd/d-lp) *(WIG CD/LP 71)* <*DC 170*> **LIVE FROM A SHARK CAGE** [ ] Oct99 [ ]
– Arundel / Roadrunner / Pink holler / Plastic energy man / Drunken spree / Bups / Crowd of one / I am not lonely with cricket / Knocking the casket / Up north kids / Arundel.

Jul 00. (cd-ep) <*MTOURCD 1*> **1999 TOUR EP** [–] [ ]
– Up north kids No.2 / She said yes.

Rock Action / Sea Note

Apr 01. (cd-ep)<12"ep> *(ROCKACTCD 7)* <*SN 8*> **PAPA M SINGS** [ ] Jan01 [ ]
– Jaded lover / Pissing in the wind / I of mine / Who am I / True love / London homesick blues.

Awkward / Awkward

Nov 01. (7") <*(AWKWARD 10)*> **MAMA YOU BEEN ON MY MIND. / (other by UNHOME)** [ ] [ ]

— now augmented by **BRITT WALFORD** – drums (ex-SLINT) **WILL OLDHAM** – guitars, etc / + TARA JANE O'NEIL – guitar (ex-RODAN)

Domino / Drag City

Nov 01. (cd/d-lp) *(WIG CD/LP 103)* <*DC 194*> **WHATEVER, MORTAL** [ ] [ ]
– Over Jordan / Beloved woman / Roses in the snow / Sorrow reigns / Krusty / The lass of Roch Royal / Many splendored thing / Glad you're here with me / Tamu / Sabotage / Purple eyelid / The unquiet grave / Northwest passage.

Western Vinyl / Western Vinyl

Mar 02. (cd-ep) <*(WV 014)*> **SONGS OF MAC** [ ] [ ]
– So warped / The person and the skeleton.

— PAJO subsequently joined ZWAN (yes, BILLY CORGAN's outfit)

Tiger Style / Tiger Style

Mar 03. (7") <*(TS 041)*> **ORANGE WORLD. / (other by ENTRANCE)** [ ] [ ]

Drag City / Drag City

Mar 03. (cd-ep) <*DC 241*> **ONE** [–] [ ]
– Flashlight tornado / Beloved woman / I am the light of this world.

Apr 03. (cd-ep) <*(DC 242)*> **TWO** [ ] [ ]
– (untitled) / (untitled) / (untitled).

Jul 03. (cd-ep) <*(DC 243)*> **THREE** [ ] [ ]
– Wild mountain thyme / Truckstop girl / Who knows.

Nov 03. (cd-ep) <*(DC 247)*> **FOUR** [ ] [ ]
– Long may you burn / Red curtains / Local boy makes good.

SLIPKNOT

Formed: Des Moines, Iowa, USA . . . 1995 by members 0, 1, 2, 3, 4, 5, 6, 7 and 8 – aka DJ SID WILSON, JOEY JORDISON, PAUL GRAY, CHRIS FEHN, JAMES ROOT, CRAIG JONES, SHAWN CRAHAN, MIC THOMPSON and singer (or screamer) COREY TAYLOR. The menacing 9-piece recorded and released the now rare album 'MATE. FEED. KILL. REPEAT' in 1996, receiving mass attention from record labels in the process. The ensemble signed with 'Roadrunner' in 1997 and released their self-titled debut album in 1999. The album (predictably) gained a huge cult following from the widespread majority of dysfunctional teens all over the globe. In a way, it's not hard to describe SLIPKNOT's music: fast, heavy, vicious, ferocious, venomous and crude – in fact a few journos made them out to be Rock's answer to 'The Texas Chainsaw Massacre'. The mask-clad spooksters have found their niche within the flow of sports metal in the US; bands such as KORN and white chumps LIMP BIZKIT thrive off the money made from these double-bass drum pedallers. But as a band, the angsty punk-metallers are not bad, mixing in a blend of tricky, thumping and downright blastferic lyrics along with the pounding guitars and drums. It's what grandmothers have nightmares about. During the months touring to promote their self-titled debut album, the group of intensely intense metallers – for some obscure reason – became hugely popular with the amount of 'KNOT followers exceeding that of a huge, sinister American cult. Soon the troupe of rubber monsters were featured on every T-shirt worn by every prepubescent kid who, just two weeks ago, thought the Kylie Minogue album was a classic (hence the alleged statement by TAYLOR that all SLIPKNOT fans were "maggots"). Sick of this worrying sight and worried themselves over the musical direction in which the record company wanted the follow-up album to go, the group cut and issued the dark, theatrical and utterly insane sophomore set 'IOWA' (2001). More Black Metal than early BLACK SABBATH, the group were slightly in danger of turning into G.G. ALLIN's backing band. 'LEFT BEHIND' tore the speakers apart with its emotional apathy accumulating in thrash guitar noise that was the musical equivalent of being fisted by a robot. The end result was the creeping 15-minute epitaph to their home town, 'IOWA', in which TAYLOR was said to be (whilst recording the track) "puking, bleeding, trampling on glass and being burnt by hot wax" . . . Hot wax?! You have been warned. For those still not satiated after such sonic torture, there was the re-emergence of STONE SOUR, the band with which TAYLOR and ROOT had first began to terrorize the metal scene. After seeking out fellow conspirators SEAN ECONOMAKI and JOSH RAND, together with new faces JOEL EKMAN and SID WILSON, the band contributed 'BOTHER' for the soundtrack to the 2002 'Spiderman' remake. As a taster for their eponymous album, released the same year, it heralded a promise that was pretty much fulfilled. Leaving behind the theatrics of SLIPKNOT and actually vocalising to the best of his not inconsiderable abilities, TAYLOR pretty much stole the show on a set of songs all the better for taking their foot off the gas. MURDERDOLLS, the side project of JORDISON and his compadre TRIPP EISEN (of STATIC-X), was a different matter altogether, a self-indulgent, splattercore shamble through various strands of moribund metal going by the tongue-in-cheek title 'BEYOND THE VALLEY OF THE MURDER DOLLS' (2002).

Album rating: MATE. FEED. KILL. REPEAT (*5) / SLIPKNOT (*8) / IOWA (*8) / Stone Sour: STONE SOUR (*7) / Murderdolls: BEYOND THE VALLEY OF THE MURDERDOLLS (*6)

COREY TAYLOR – vocals / **MIC THOMPSON** – guitar / **JIM ROOT** – guitar / **PAUL GRAY** – bass / **JOEY JORDISON** – drums / **CHRIS FEHN** – percussion / **SHAWN CRAHAN** – percussion / **CRAIG JONES** – samples, programmes / **SID WILSON** – DJ

not iss. ismist

Jul 97. (cd) *<ismCD 0032>* **MATE. FEED. KILL. REPEAT** [–] [ ]
– Slipknot / Gently / Do nothing – Bitchslap / Only one / Tattered and torn / Confessions / Some feel / Killers are quite.

Roadrunner Roadrunner

Jun 99. (cd) *<(RR 8655-2)>* **SLIPKNOT** [37] [51]
– 74261000027 / Eyel ESS / Wait and bleed / Surfacing / Spit it out / Tattered and torn / Frail limb nursery / Purity / Liberate / Prosthetics / No life / Diluted / The only one. *(other cd+=; RR 8655-5)* – Me inside / Get this / Interloper (demo) / Despise (demo). *(pic-lp iss.Aug00; RR 8655-6)*

Feb 00. (cd-s) *(RR 2112-5)* **WAIT AND BLEED / SPIT IT OUT (overcaffeinated hyper-molt mix) / SIC (Spaceship Console mix) / WAIT AND SEE (live promo video)** [27] [–]

Sep 00. (7") *(RR 2090-7)* **SPIT IT OUT. / SURFACING (live)** [28] [–]
(cd-s+=) *(RR 2090-3)* – Wait and bleed (live) / ('A'-video).

Aug 01. (cd/d-lp) *(1208564-2/-1) <618564>* **IOWA** [1] [3]
– (515) / People = shit / Disasterpiece / My plague / Everything ends / The heretic anthem / Gently / Left behind / The shape / I am hated / Skin ticket / New abortion / Metabolic / Iowa.

Oct 01. (7"pic-d) *(2320335-7)* **LEFT BEHIND. / LIBERATE (live)** [24] [–]
(cd-s+=) *(2320335-5)* – Surfacing (live) / ('A'-video).

Jul 02. (cd-s) *(RR 2045-3)* **MY PLAGUE (new abuse mix) / SIC (live) / HERETIC ANTHEM (live) / MY PLAGUE (explicit video)** [43] [–]

STONE SOUR

COREY TAYLOR – vocals / **JIM ROOT** – guitar / **JOSH RAND** – guitar / **SEAN ACONOMAKI** – bass / **JOEL EKMAN** – drums / **SID WILSON** – DJ

Roadrunner Roadrunner

Aug 02. (cd) *<(RR 8425-2)>* **STONE SOUR** [41] [46]
– Get inside / Orchids / Cold reader / Blotter / Choose / Monolith / Inhale / Bother (by COREY TAYLOR) / Blue study / Take a number / Idle hands / Tumult / Omega.

Mar 03. (cd-s) *<(RR 2024-3)>* **BOTHER / RULES OF EVIDENCE / WICKED / BOTHER (video)** [28] Jan04 [56]

Jul 03. (cd-s) *(RR 2009-3)* **INHALE / INSIDE THE CYNIC / INHALE (rough mix) / INHALE (video)** [63] [–]

MURDERDOLLS

JOEY JORDISON – guitar / **TRIPP EISEN** – guitar, vocals (of STATIC-X) / **WEDNESDAY 13** – vocals, guitar / **ERIC GRIFFIN** – bass / **BEN GRAVES** – drums

Roadrunner Roadrunner

Aug 02. (cd) *<(RR 8426-2)>* **BEYOND THE VALLEY OF THE MURDERDOLLS** [40] [ ]
– Slit my wrist / Twist my sister / Dead in Hollywood / Love at first fright / People hate me / She was a teenage zombie / Die my bride / Grave robbing U.S.A. / 197666 / Dawn of the dead / Let's go to war / Dressed to depress / Kill Miss America / B-movie scream queen / Motherfucker, I don't care. *(re-iss. Jul03 +=; RR 8426-8)* – Crash crash / Hit and . . . / Let's fuck / I take drugs / White wedding / I love to say fuck / Dead in Hollywood (video) / White wedding (video) / Love at first fright (video).

Jul 03. (cd-s) *(RR 2015-3)* **WHITE WEDDING / I LOVE TO SAY FUCK / I TAKE DRUGS / WHITE WEDDING (video)** [24] [–]

Nov 03. (cd-s) *(RR 2022-3)* **DEAD IN HOLLYWOOD / CRASH CRASH / LET'S FUCK / DEAD IN HOLLYWOOD (director's cut video)** [54] [–]

SLITS

Formed: London, England . . . early 1977 as the foremost all-girl outfit on the punk scene (until BUDGIE joined that is) and initially comprising ARI UP (aka ARIANNA FOSTER), KATE KORUS, SUZI GUTSY and PALMOLIVE. By the time the group had secured a support slot on The CLASH's Spring 1977 tour, KORUS and GUTSY had been replaced by VIV ALBERTINE and TESSA POLLITT respectively, the band's infamously amateurish approach compensated by their bolshy hardline feminist attitude. Although they had two John Peel sessions under their belts, The SLITS didn't actually sign a deal until 1979, having turned down the 'Real' label (home to The HEARTBREAKERS and PRETENDERS) the previous year. In the event the not-so "TYPICAL GIRLS" signed with 'Island' and set to work on a debut album with reggae producer, Dennis Bovell, the aforementioned BUDGIE (PETER CLARK) coming in as a replacement for PALMOLIVE who departed midway through the recording sessions. A Top 30 hit upon its release in late '79, the seminal 'CUT' showcased ARI's distinctive vocal phrasing against a compelling backdrop of unorthodox tribal rhythms and raw guitar abrasion, the sleeve's cover shot of the lasses getting butt naked and muddy generating almost as much interest as the music. With BUDGIE decamping to SIOUXSIE & THE BANSHEES, BRUCE SMITH was recruited in his place and despite the presence of respected jazz trumpeter, DON CHERRY (father of NENEH), a dreadful untitled bootleg/jam affair did the band no favours. Much more enjoyable was the subsequent cover of John Holt's 'MAN NEXT DOOR', released as a single a couple of months later in the summer of 1980. A further single followed on the 'Human' label before The SLITS signed to 'C.B.S.' for a final disappointing patchy album, 'RETURN OF THE GIANT SLITS' (1981), the group disbanding in early '82. While SMITH joined Bristolian avant-funk collective RIP, RIG & PANIC, the remaining members (minus POLLITT) went on to be part of colossus ensemble, The NEW AGE STEPPERS. • **Songwriters:** Group compositions, except I HEARD IT THROUGH THE GRAPEVINE (Marvin Gaye). • **Trivia:** Early in 1978, they were sighted in the punk film, 'Jubilee'.

Album rating: CUT (*9) / UNTITLED (*1) / RETURN OF THE GIANT SLITS (*6) / IN THE BEGINNING collection (*4) / THE PEEL SESSIONS collection (*7)

ARI UP (b. ARIANNA FOSTER) – vocals / **VIVIEN ALBERTINE** – guitar (ex-FLOWERS OF ROMANCE) repl. KATE KORUS to KLEENEX (Feb77) / **TESSA POLLITT** – bass repl. SUZI GUTSY who formed The FLICKS. / **PALMOLIVE** – drums (ex-FLOWERS OF ROMANCE) was repl. (Oct78) by **BUDGIE** (b. PETER CLARK, 21 Aug'??, St.Helens, England) – percussion, drums (ex-BIG IN JAPAN, ex-SECRETS,etc)

Island Antilles

Sep 79. (lp/c) *(ILPS/ZCI 9573) <7072>* **CUT** [30] [ ]
– Instant hit / So tough / Spend spend spend / Shoplifting / FM / Newtown / Ping pong affair / Love and romance / Typical girls / Adventures close to home. *(cd-iss. Apr90; IMCD 89) (cd re-mast.Oct00 +=; IMCD 275)* – I heard it through the grapevine / Liebe and romanza (slow version).

Sep 79. (7") *(WIP 6505)* **TYPICAL GIRLS. / I HEARD IT THROUGH THE GRAPEVINE** [60] [ ]
(12"+=) *(12WIP 6505)* – Typical girls (brink style) / Liebe and romanze.

— **BRUCE SMITH** – drums (of POP GROUP) repl. BUDGIE to SIOUXSIE & BANSHEES jazz-trumpeter **DON CHERRY** guested

		Y – Rough Trade	not iss.
Mar 80.	(7") *(Y1 – RT 039)* **IN THE BEGINNING THERE WAS RHYTHM. / (B-side by the Pop Group)**		–
May 80.	(lp) *(Y3LP)* **UNTITLED (Y3LP)** (bootleg demo jam) – A boring life / Slime / Or what it is / No.1 enemy / Once upon a time in a living room / Bongos on the lawn / Face place / Let's do the split / Mosquitos / Vaseline / No more rock and roll for you.		–
Jun 80.	(7") *(Y4 – RT 044)* **MAN NEXT DOOR. / MAN NEXT DOOR (dub version)**		–

—— added guest **STEVE BERESFORD** – keyboards, guitar (of FLYING LIZARDS)

		Human	not iss.
Nov 80.	(7") *(HUM 4)* **ANIMAL SPACE. / ANIMAL SPACIER**		–
		C.B.S.	Epic
1981.	(12"m) **ANIMAL SPACE. / ANIMAL SPACIER / IN THE BEGINNING THERE WAS RHYTHM**	–	
Aug 81.	(7") *(A 1498)* **EARTHBEAT. / BEGIN AGAIN RHYTHM**		–
	(12"+=) *(A13 1498)* – Earthdub.		
Oct 81.	(lp/c) *(CBS/40 85269)* **RETURN OF THE GIANT SLITS** – Earthbeat / Or what it is? / Face place / Walkabout / Difficult fun / Animal space – Spacier / Improperly dressed / Life on Earth. *(free-7"w/ lp) (XPS 125)* – AMERICAN RADIO INTERVIEW (Winter 1980). / FACE DUB		
Dec 81.	(7") *(49-02567>* **EARTHBEAT. / OR WHAT IT IS?**	–	

—— Parted ways early 1982. BRUCE joined RIP, RIG & PANIC. All except TESSA were part of colossus band NEW AGE STEPPERS.

– compilations, others, etc. –

on 'Strange Fruit' unless otherwise mentioned

Feb 87.	(12"ep) *(SFPS 021)* **THE PEEL SESSION** (27.9.77) – Love and romance / Vindictive / Newtown / Shoplifting.		–
Nov 88.	(m-lp/m-cd) *(SFPMA/+CD 207)* **THE DOUBLE PEEL SESSIONS** (27.9.77 + 22.5.78) – (THE PEEL SESSION) + So tough / Instant hit / FM.		–
Aug 97.	(cd) *Jungle; (FREUDCD 057) / Cleopatra; <65>* **IN THE BEGINNING (live)** – Vindictive / A boring life / Slime / New town / Love and romance / Shoplifting / Number one enemy / Number one enemy (acoustic) / In the beginning / New town / Man next door / I heard it through the grapevine / Typical girls / Fade away / In the beginning.		
Feb 98.	(cd) *(SFRCD 052) <8304>* **THE PEEL SESSIONS** – (THE DOUBLE PEEL SESSIONS) + Difficult fun / In the beginning / Earthbeat – Wedding song.		

SLY & THE FAMILY STONE

Formed: San Francisco, California, USA . . . 1966, initially as The STONERS by former DJ/Producer, SLY STONE (born SYLVESTER STEWART) with brother FREDDIE, sister ROSEMARY and cousin LARRY GRAHAM. They adopted the name SLY & THE FAMILY STONE after gigging around local bars/clubs in Oakland and in 1967 they signed to 'Epic', releasing their debut album, 'A WHOLE NEW THING'. The record introduced the superfly new sound created by one of the first inter-racial, inter-gender and inta-drugs outfits to emerge between the rock/soul divide. With SLY casting himself HENDRIX-like in the role of Afro-American uber-hippie, he and his family were pioneers of the "Psychedelic Soul" movement, re-influencing old hands like The TEMPTATIONS and The ISLEY BROTHERS. Their breakthrough came with the 1968 single, 'DANCE TO THE MUSIC', a skilfully honed melange of doo-wop, soul and acid-funk that shook even the most stoned of hippy asses. The album of the same name followed later that year, crystallising the bands distinctive cross-over sound. Possibly their finest moment, the irresistible swing of 'EVERYDAY PEOPLE' was almost gospel-like in its passionate intensity. The single's B-side, 'SING A SIMPLE SONG', was similarly evangelical and illustrated that musically, at least, in The FAMILY STONE all the soul brothers and sisters were born equal. Each family member was given a fair deal in the mix, both instrumentally and vocally, and along with the band's unique hyrid of styles, this musical equanimity defined their sound. The classic 'STAND' (1969) album fully captured this collective, celebratory fanfare, including the aforementioned tracks as well as the 15-minute bass-heavy pulse of 'SEX MACHINE'. It also introduced SLY's penchant for mordant humour with 'DON'T CALL ME NIGGER, WHITEY'. As the 60's dream turned sour, this penchant would become ever more pronounced, 'HOT FUN IN THE SUMMERTIME' (1969) a wry observation on America's summer of discontent. Come 1970, SLY had moved to L.A. where he immersed himself in cocaine and the vacuum of the back-slapping Hollywood elite. 'THANK YOU (FALLETTINME BE MICE ELF AGIN)' (1970) was an edgy piece of taut funk that indicated the way SLY was headed. Partly composed in SLY's infamous drug den of a motorhome, where he lived gypsy-style around L.A., 'THERE'S A RIOT GOIN' ON' finally appeared in 1971. Reflecting the drug-induced paranoia and detachment of the recording sessions, most of the tracks were blurred snatches of dirty, slow burning funk, topped off by SLY's ravaged vocal chords. The deceptively laid-back groove of 'FAMILY AFFAIR' belied a grim lyrical content which extended to the whole album. From his embalming cocoon of Grade-A narcotics, SLY gave a hazily cynical commentary on the decline of American civilisation and the album remains a darkly brooding classic. With drug busts, financial pressures and hassles from militant black nationalists who didn't care for SLY's racially mixed philosophy, it was two years before 'FRESH' (1973) was released. While the sound recalled the band's effervescent charisma of old, a distinct edginess remained in the watertight grooves. The cool pop-funk of 'IF YOU WANT ME TO STAY' (1973) was the 'FAMILY STONE's last top 20 single. 'SMALL TALK' (1974) was almost overwhelmingly bland save for the title track and from there on in, SLY lost it big time. A drug casualty of the saddest order, SLY's latter 70's output was unremarkable at best. • **Songwriters:** All by SLY and group except; I CAN'T TURN YOU LOOSE (Otis Redding) / YOU REALLY GOT ME (Kinks). • **Trivia:** On the 5th of June '74, SLY married Kathy Silva on stage at Madison Square Garden. Two months earlier, she had borne him his first child, Bubb Ali (all three pictured on the album cover of 'SMALL TALK'). She divorced SLY in '75, and he filed for bankruptcy early '76.

Album rating: A WHOLE NEW THING (*5) / DANCE TO THE MUSIC (*6) / LIFE (*6) / STAND! (*9) / GREATEST HITS compilation (*8) / THERE'S A RIOT GOIN' ON (*9) / FRESH (*7) / SMALL TALK (*6) / HIGH ON YOU (*5; by Sly Stone) / HEARD YA MISSED ME, WELL I'M BACK (*4) / BACK ON THE RIGHT TRACK (*4) / AIN'T BUT THE ONE WAY (*4) / TAKIN' YOU HIGHER – THE BEST OF SLY & THE FAMILY STONE compilation (*8)

SLY STONE

SLY STONE's early US recordings under various pseudonyms

—— first 2 with brother FREDDIE and sister ROSE? (most doo-wop sound)

1959.	(7"; by STEWART BROTHERS) *<Ensign; 4032>* **THE RAT. / RA RA ROO**	–	
1960.	(7"; by STEWART BROTHERS) *<Keen; 2113>* **SLEEP ON THE PORCH. / YUM YUM YUM**	–	
1961.	(7"; by DANNY STEWART) *<Luke 1008>* **A LONG TIME ALONE. / I'M JUST A FOOL**	–	
1961.	(7"; by SYLVESTER STEWART) *<G&P; 901>* **A LONG TIME ALONE. / HELP ME WITH MY BROKEN HEART**	–	
1961.	(7"; by the VISCANES) *<Tropo; 101>* **STOP WHAT YOU ARE DOING. / I GUESS I'LL BE**	–	
1961.	(7"; by the VISCANES) *<VPM; 1006>* **YELLOW MOON. / UNCLE SAM NEEDS YOU**	–	

1961. (7"; by SLY STEWART) **YELLOW MOON. / HEAVENLY ANGEL** –

1964. (7"; by SLY STEWART) *<Autumn; 3>* **I JUST LEARNED HOW TO SWIM. / SCAT SWIM** –

1965. (7"; by SLY) *<Autumn; 14>* **BUTTERMILK. / (part 2)** –

1965. (7"; by SLY) *<Autumn; 26>* **TEMPTATION WALK. / (part 2)** –

— SLY at this time was producing Autumn acts The BEAU BRUMMELS, BOBBY FREEMAN and The MOJO MEN. He also became well-known local DJ for K-DIA.

SLY & THE FAMILY STONE

SLY STONE (b. SYLVESTER STEWART, 15 Mar'44, Dallas, Texas) – vox, guitar, keyboards (ex-SLY & THE MOJO MEN) / **FREDDIE STONE** (b. FRED STEWART, 5 Jun'46, Dallas) – guitar / **CYNTHIA ROBINSON** (b.12 Jan'46, Sacramento, Calif.) – trumpet / **ROSEMARY STONE** (b. ROSEMARY STEWART, 21 Mar'45, Vallejo, Calif.) – vocals, piano / **LARRY GRAHAM** (b.14 Aug'46, Beaumont, Texas) – bass / **JERRY MARTINI** (b. 1 Oct'43, Colorado) – saxophone / **GREG ERRICO** (b. 1 Sep'46) – drums

not iss. Loadstone

1966. (7") *<3951>* **I AIN'T GOT NOBODY. / I CAN'T TURN YOU LOOSE** –

Columbia Epic

1967. (lp) *<30333>* **A WHOLE NEW THING** –
– Underdog / If this room could talk / Run run run / Turn me loose / Let me hear it from you / Advice / I cannot make it / Trip to your heart / I hate to love her / Bad risk / That kind of person / Day. *(cd-iss. Jul95 on 'Epic'; EK 66424)*

1967. (7") *<10229>* **(I WANT TO TAKE YOU) HIGHER. / UNDERDOG** –

Mar 68. (7") *(DB 8369) <10256>* **DANCE TO THE MUSIC. / LET ME HEAR IT FROM YOU** Jan68 8

Direction Epic

Jun 68. (7") *(58-3568)* **DANCE TO THE MUSIC. / LET ME HEAR IT FROM YOU** 7 –

Sep 68. (lp) *(8-63412) <26371>* **DANCE TO THE MUSIC** Apr68
– Dance to the music / (I want to take you) Higher / I ain't got nobody (for real) / Dance to the medley: Music is alive – Dance in – Music lover / Ride the rhythm / Color me true / Are you ready / Don't burn baby / I'll never fall in love again. *(re-iss. Oct73 on 'Embassy'; EMB 31030) (cd-iss. Jul94 on 'Epic'; 480906-2)*

Sep 68. (7") *(58-3707) <10353>* **M'LADY. / LIFE** 32 93 Jun68 93

Jan 69. (lp) *(8-63461) <26397>* **M'LADY** (US-title 'LIFE') Nov68
– Dynamite! / Chicken / Plastic Jim / Fun / Into my own thing / Harmony / Life / Love city / I'm an animal / M'lady / Jane is a groupie.

Mar 69. (7") *(58-3938) <10407>* **EVERYDAY PEOPLE. / SING A SIMPLE SONG** 36 1 Nov68 89

May 69. (7") *(58-4279) <10450>* **STAND!. / I WANT TO TAKE YOU HIGHER** 22 Apr69 60
<re-prom.May70 but flipped over, hit US No.38>

Jul 69. (lp) *(8-63655) <26456>* **STAND!** Apr69 13
– Stand! / Don't call me nigger, Whitey / I want to take you higher / Somebody's watching you / Sing a simple song / Everyday people / Sex machine / You can make it if you try. *(cd-iss. Feb95 on 'Epic'; EK 64422)*

Aug 69. (7") *(58-4471) <10497>* **HOT FUN IN THE SUMMERTIME. / FUN** 2

Feb 70. (7") *(58-4782) <10555>* **THANK YOU (FALLETTINME BE MICE ELF AGIN). / EVERYBODY IS A STAR** Dec69 1

C.B.S. Epic

May 70. (7") *(5054)* **I WANT TO TAKE YOU HIGHER. / YOU CAN MAKE IT IF YOU TRY** –

Jan 71. (lp) *(EPC 69002) <30325>* **GREATEST HITS** (compilation) Oct70 2
– I want to take you higher / Everybody is a star / Stand / Life / Fun / You can make it if you try / Dance to the music / Everyday people / Hot fun in the summertime / M'lady / Sing a simple song / Thank you (falletinme be mice elf agin). *(<quad-lp 1975; EQ 30325>) (re-iss. Mar81 on 'Epic'; EPC 32029) (re-iss. Jun90 on 'Epic' cd/c/lp; EPC 462524-2/-4/-1)*

Epic Epic

Nov 71. (7") *(EPC 7632) <10805>* **FAMILY AFFAIR. / LUV 'N' HAIGHT** 15 Oct71 1

Jan 72. (lp/c) *(EPC/40 64613) <30986>* **THERE'S A RIOT GOIN' ON** 31 Nov71 1
– Luv 'n' haight / Just like a baby / Poet / Family affair / Africa talks to you 'The Asphalt Jungle' / Brave & strong / Smilin' / Time / Spaced cowboy / Runnin' away / Thank you for talkin' to me Africa. *(UK-iss.w/free ltd.7"ep & newspaper) (re-iss. Feb86 on 'Edsel' lp/c; XED/CED 165) (cd-iss. Jan91; EDCD 165) (re-iss. May94 cd/c; 467063-2/-4)*

Mar 72. (7") *(EPC 7810) <10829>* **RUNNIN' AWAY. / BRAVE & STRONG** 17 Jan72 23

Apr 72. (7") *<10850>* **SMILIN'. / LUV 'N' HAIGHT** – 42

— (Jan73) **RUSTEE ALLEN** – bass repl. LARRY (formed GRAHAM CENTRAL STATION) **ANDY NEWMARK** – drums repl. ERRICO. / added **PAT RICCO** – saxophone

Jun 73. (lp/c) *(EPC/40 69039) <32134>* **FRESH** 7
– In time / If you want me to stay / Let me have it all / Frisky / Thankful 'n' thoughtful / The skin I'm in / I don't know (satisfaction) / Keep on dancin' / Que sera sera / If it were left up to me / Babies makin' babies. *(re-iss. May87 on 'Edsel' lp/c/cd; XED/CED/EDCD 232) (cd re-iss. Sep96 on 'Columbia'; 485170-2)*

Aug 73. (7") *(EPC 1655) <11017>* **IF YOU WANT ME TO STAY. / THANKFUL 'N' THOUGHTFUL** Jun73 12

Oct 73. (7") *<11060>* **FRISKY. / IF IT WERE LEFT UP TO ME** – 79

Jan 74. (7") *(EPC 1981)* **QUE SERA SERA. / IF IT WERE LEFT UP TO ME** –

— **BILL LORDAN** – drums repl. NEWMARK who became session man

Jul 74. (lp/c) *(EPC/40 69070) <32930>* **SMALL TALK** 15
– Small talk / Say you will / Mother beautiful / Time for livin' / Can't strain my brain / Loose booty / Holdin' on / Wishful thinking / Better thee than me / Livin' while I'm livin' / This is love.

Jul 74. (7") *(EPC 2530) <11140>* **TIME FOR LIVIN'. / SMALL TALK** 32

Jan 75. (7") *(EPC 1882) <50033>* **LOOSE BOOTY. / CAN'T STRAIN MY BRAIN** Oct84 84

SLY STONE

Oct 75. (lp/c) *<EPC/40 69165) <33835>* **HIGH ON YOU** 45
– I get high on you / Crossword puzzle / That's lovin' you / Who do you love / Green-eyed monster girl / Organize / Le lo li / My world / So good to me / Greed.

Oct 75. (7") *(EPC 3596) <50135>* **I GET HIGH ON YOU. / THAT'S LOVIN' YOU** Sep75 52

Dec 75. (7") *<50175>* **LE LO LI. / WHO DO YOU LOVE** –

Mar 76. (7") *<50201>* **CROSSWORD PUZZLE. / GREED** –

SLY & THE FAMILY STONE

— reformed with last line-up

Dec 76. (lp/c) *(EPC/40 81641) <33698>* **HEARD YA MISSED ME, WELL I'M BACK**
– Heard ya missed me, well I'm back / What was I thinkin' / In my head / Sexy situation / Blessing in disguise / Everything in you / Mother is a hippie / Let's be together / The thing / Family again.

Feb 77. (7") *<50331>* **FAMILY AGAIN. / NOTHING LESS THAN HAPPINESS** –

Warners Warners

Sep 79. (7") *(K 17474) <49062>* **REMEMBER WHO YOU ARE. / SHEER ENERGY**

Oct 79. (lp/c) *(K/K4 56640) <3303>* **BACK ON THE RIGHT TRACK**
– Remember who you are / Back on the right track / If it's not addin' up . . . / The same thing (makes you laugh, makes you cry) / Shine it on / It takes all kinds / Who's to say / Sheer energy. *(cd-iss. Jan96; 7599 26858-2)*

Dec 79. (7") *<49132>* **THE SAME THING (MAKES YOU LAUGH, MAKES YOU CRY). / WHO'S TO SAY** –

— In 1981, SLY guested on album 'THE ELECTRIC SPANKING OF WAR BABIES' by George Clinton's FUNKADELIC.

– compilations, etc. –

— on 'Epic' unless stated otherwise

1972. (lp; by SLY STONE) *Sculpture; <SCP 2001>* **RECORDED IN SAN FRANCISCO: 1964-67** –

Mar 73. (7") *(EPC 1148)* **FAMILY AFFAIR. / DANCE TO THE MUSIC** –

Feb 75. (7"ep) *(EPC 3048)* **DANCE TO THE MUSIC / COLOUR ME TRUE. / STAND! / RIDE THE RHYTHM** □ [–]

May 75. (d-lp) *(EPC 22004)* <33462> **HIGH ENERGY** □ □
– (A WHOLE NEW THING / LIFE)

1975. (7") *<50119>* **HOT FUN IN THE SUMMERTIME. / FUN** [–] □

1975. (7") *(152282)* **DANCE TO THE MUSIC. / LIFE** □ [–]

1975. (7") *(152302)* **HOT FUN IN THE SUMMERTIME. / M'LADY** □ [–]

1975. (7") *(152317)* **FAMILY AFFAIR. / RUNNIN' AWAY** □ [–]

1975. (7") *(152331)* **IF YOU WANT ME TO STAY. / FRISKY** □ [–]

Jan 77. (7") *(EPC 4879)* **DANCE TO THE MUSIC. / I WANT TO TAKE YOU HIGHER** □ [–]

Mar 79. (7") *(EPC 7070)* **DANCE TO THE MUSIC. / STAND!** □ [–]

Nov 79. (7") *(EPC 8017)* *<50795>* **DANCE TO THE MUSIC. / SING A SIMPLE SONG** □ □

Jan 80. (lp) *(EPC 83640)* *<35974>* **TEN YEARS TOO SOON** (disco remixes) □ □

Aug 80. (7") *(EPC 8853)* **DANCE TO THE MUSIC. / EVERYDAY PEOPLE** □ [–]
(re-iss. Jul82 on 'Old Gold'; OG 9188)

May 82. (d-lp) *(EPC 22119)* *<37071>* **ANTHOLOGY** □ Dec81 □
(re-iss. Sep87 lp/c; 460175-1/-4)

Sep 87. (7") Portrait; *(SLY 1)* **DANCE TO THE MUSIC. / FAMILY AFFAIR** □ □
(12"+=) *(SLYT 1)* – Everyday people / Runnin' away.

Apr 91. (cd/c) *Thunderbolt; (CDTB/THBC 119)* **FAMILY AFFAIR** □ [–]

Nov 91. (cd/c) *Castle; (CCS CD/MC 307)* **THE COLLECTION** □ [–]

Dec 91. (cd) *Thunderbolt; (CDTB 129)* **IN THE STILL OF THE NIGHT** □ [–]

Jul 92. (cd/c) *Sony; (471758-2/-4)* **TAKIN' YOU HIGHER – THE BEST OF SLY & THE FAMILY STONE** □ □
– Dance to the music / I want to take you higher / Family affair / Thank you (falletinme be mice elf agin) / I get high on you / Stand / M'lady / Skin I'm in / Everyday people / Sing a simple song / Hot fun in the summertime / Don't call me nigger, Whitey / Brave & strong / Life / Everybody is a star / If you want me to stay / (You caught me) Smilin' / Que sera sera / Running away / Family affair (remix). *(cd re-iss. Oct94 on 'Epic'; 477506-2)*

Feb 94. (cd/c) *Javelin; (HAD CD/MC 119)* **SPOTLIGHT ON SLY & THE FAMILY STONE** □ [–]

Mar 94. (cd) *Charly;* **REMEMBER WHO YOU ARE** □ [–]

Sep 94. (cd) *Ace; (CDCHD 539)* **PRECIOUS STONE: IN THE STUDIO WITH SLY STONE** (rec.1963-65) □ [–]

Dec 94. (cd/c) *Prestige; (CD/CAS SGP 0125)* **EVERY DOG HAS IT'S DAY** □ [–]

Feb 95. (cd; by SLY STONE & THE MOJO MEN) *(KLMCD 005)* **PEARLS FROM THE PAST** □ [–]

— Thunderbolt records issued 2 albums of SLY STONE productions in Apr87 + Oct87 respectively, named 'DANCE TO THE MUSIC' & 'FAMILY AFFAIR'.

SLY STONE

Warners Warners

Mar 83. (lp) *(923700-1)* *<23700-1>* **AIN'T BUT THE ONE WAY** □ □
– L.O.V.I.N.U. / One way / Ha ha, hee hee / Hobo Ken / Who in the funk do you think we are / You really got me / Sylvester / We can do it / High, y'all. *(cd-iss. Jan96; 7599 23700-2)*

— In 1984, SLY joined BOBBY WOMACK on tour. He later guested on JESSE JOHNSON's 'A&M' US No.53 hit single 'Crazay' (Oct86) *AM 360 /<2878>.*

not iss. A&M

Oct 86. (7") *<2890>* **EEK-A-BO-STATIK. / BLACK GIRLS (RAE DAWN CHONG)** [–] □

Dec 86. (7"w/ MARTHA DAVIS) **STONE LOVE AND AFFECTION. / BLACK GIRLS (RAE DAWN CHONG)** [–] □

SMALL FACES

Formed: East London, England … mid '65 by RONNIE LANE, KENNY JONES and JIMMY WINSTON, who subsequently found lead singer and ex-child actor, STEVE MARRIOTT. After a successful residency at Leicester Square's Cavern Club, the band were snapped up by 'Decca' records as potential usurpers to The WHO's mod crown. Their debut single, 'WHATCHA GONNA DO ABOUT IT' (1965) graced the Top 20 with its roughshod R&B and amid the ensuing attention the band received, WINSTON was kicked out after shamelessly trying to promote himself as the lynchpin of the group. With IAN McLAGAN drafted in as a replacement, the band hit Top 3 with the 'SHA LA LA LA LEE' (1966) single. Despite the cliched boy-meets-girl lyric, the record was a wildly exhilarating rush of amphetamine pop and suddenly The SMALL FACES were big news. After another Top 10 single and a critically acclaimed eponymous debut album, the band were being mentioned in the same breath as The BEATLES and The ROLLING STONES. Indeed, in August '66 they deposed The Fab Four's 'ELEANOR RIGBY' at the top of the charts with 'ALL OR NOTHING'. Come 1967, the band had left 'Decca' and signed with ANDREW LOOG-OLDHAM's 'Immediate' label, releasing 'HERE COMES THE NICE'. The single marked a change in direction and in keeping with the times, was vaguely psychedelic. After a similarly adventurous second album that bore a decidedly unadventurous title ('SMALL FACES' yet again), the band released their most well-known track, the slightly twee, deeply dippy 'ITCHYCOO PARK' (later reduced to dross by M-PEOPLE). Next came the abrasive 'TIN SOLDIER' (1967) single after which the band began working on their psychedelic masterpiece, 'OGDEN'S NUT GONE FLAKE' (1968). An engaging blend of trippy R&B and cockney charm, the album's influence was far reaching and it gets re-issued with the same tireless regularity as 'OCEAN WELLER SCENE' namedrop the band. Timeless as it was, the record proved to be the group's swansong and after a few singles, including the gorgeous 'AFTERGLOW (OF YOUR LOVE)' (1969), the band split with MARRIOTT flouncing off to form HUMBLE PIE. Meanwhile JONES, LANE and McLAGAN ditched the psychedelic overtones, recruited RON WOOD and ROD STEWART, renaming the band The FACES; lad-rock was born! The FACES peddled a distinctive strain of ramshackle, boozy, bluesy rock that was apparently best heard in a live setting surrounded by sweaty males. Their debut, 'FIRST STEP' (1970), was a boisterous statement of intent which included the ragged charm of 'THREE BUTTON HAND ME DOWN' and a raw cover of DYLAN's 'WICKED MESSENGER'. 'LONG PLAYER' (1971) was equally ballsy, while 'A NOD IS AS GOOD AS A WINK …TO A BLIND HORSE' (1971) saw the band in full flight, WOOD going hell for leather on 'MISS JUDY'S FARM' and the gloriously un-PC raunch of 'STAY WITH ME'. The McLAGAN/LANE penned 'YOU'RE SO RUDE' was a leering gem and LANE excelled himself with the lovely 'DEBRIS'. As STEWART's solo career skyrocketed, the band began to splinter, unbalanced by ROD's high profile. After the slightly disappointing 'OOH LA LA' (1973) album, LANE left to go solo, The FACES basically becoming STEWART's backing band and after a final below par live album, RON WOOD left for The ROLLING STONES. There was a brief SMALL FACES reunion (minus LANE) in the late 70's and although the band had a deal with 'Atlantic', no commercial success was forthcoming. JONES went on to join The WHO, while MARRIOTT re-formed HUMBLE PIE but any chances of a further reunion were dealt a fatal blow in 1991 when MARRIOTT tragically died in a fire at his Essex home. After a respectable, if hardly commercial solo career, RONNIE LANE finally succumbed to Multiple Sclerosis in 1997. A sad end for two pioneering musicians who, through both The FACES and The SMALL FACES, heavily influenced the course of popular music; stand up BLUR, PULP, OASIS, PRIMAL SCREAM, The BLACK CROWES etc. • **Songwriters:** MARRIOTT and LANE except; WHATCHA GONNA DO ABOUT IT (Ian Samwell-Smith; their early producer) / SHA-LA-LA-LA-LEE (c.Kenny Lynch & Mort Schuman) / EVERY LITTLE BIT HURTS (Brenda Holloway) / TAKE THIS HURT OFF ME (Don Covay) / YOU'VE REALLY GOT A HOLD ON ME (Miracles) / etc. The FACES covered MAYBE I'M AMAZED (Paul McCartney) / I WISH IT WOULD RAIN (Temptations) / etc. • **Trivia:** The FACES had come together initially as the supergroup, QUIET MELON, which included ART WOOD, LONG JOHN BALDRY and JIMMY HOROWITZ.

Album rating: THE SMALL FACES (*6) / FROM THE BEGINNING out-takes (*6) / SMALL FACES (*5) / THERE ARE BUT FOUR SMALL FACES (*7) / OGDENS' NUT GONE FLAKE (*8) / THE AUTUMN STONE collection (*5) / Faces: FIRST STEP (*6) / LONG PLAYER (*7) / A NOD'S AS GOOD AS A WINK (TO A BLIND HORSE) (*7) / OOH LA LA (*6) / COAST TO COAST – OVERTURE FOR BEGINNERS (*5; as Rod Stewart & The Faces) / SNAKES AND LADDERS: THE BEST OF THE FACES compilation (*7) / Small Faces: PLAYMATES (*3) / 78 IN THE SHADE (*4) / ULTIMATE COLLECTION compilation (*8)

STEVE MARRIOTT (b.30 Jan'47, Bow, London) – vocals, guitar (ex-solo artist) / **JIMMY WINSTON** (b. JAMES LANGWITH, 20 Apr'45, Stratford, London) – organ / **RONNIE LANE** (b. 1 Apr'45, Plaistow, London) – bass, vocals / **KENNY JONES** (b.16 Sep'48, Stepney, London) – drums

Decca / Press

Aug 65. (7") *(F 12208) <45-9794>* **WHATCHA GONNA DO ABOUT IT?. / WHAT'S A MATTER, BABY** [14] Jan66 [ ]

— **IAN McLAGAN** (b.12 May'45, Hounslow, England) – keyboards repl. WINSTON who went solo

Nov 65. (7") *(F 12276)* **I'VE GOT MINE. / IT'S TOO LATE** [ ] [–]

Jan 66. (7") *(F 12317) <45-9826>* **SHA-LA-LA-LA-LEE. / GROW YOUR OWN** [3] Apr66 [ ]

May 66. (7") *(F 12393) <45-5007>* **HEY GIRL. / ALMOST GROWN** [10] Jul66 [ ]

May 66. (lp) *(LK 4790)* **SMALL FACES** [3] [–]
– Shake / Come on children / You better believe it / It's too late / One night stand / Whatcha gonna do about it? / Sorry she's mine / E to D / You need loving / Don't stop what you're doing / Own up / Sha-la-la-la-lee. *(cd-iss. Jul88 on 'London'+= 820 572-2)* – What's a matter baby / I've got mine / Grow your own / Almost grown.

Decca / RCA Victor

Aug 66. (7") *(F 12470) <47-8949>* **ALL OR NOTHING. / UNDERSTANDING** [1] Sep66 [ ]

Nov 66. (7") *(F 12500) <47-9055>* **MY MIND'S EYE. / I CAN'T DANCE WITH YOU** [4] Dec66 [ ]

Feb 67. (7") *(F 12565)* **I CAN'T MAKE IT. / JUST PASSING** [26] [–]

Apr 67. (7") *(F 12619)* **PATTERNS. / E TO D** [ ] [–]

May 67. (lp) *(LK 4879)* **FROM THE BEGINNING** (out-takes, demos, etc) [17] [–]
– Runaway / My mind's eye / Yesterday, today and tomorrow / That man / My way of giving / Hey girl / Tell me have you ever seen me? / Come back and take this hurt off me / All or nothing / Baby don't do it / Plum Nellie / Sha-la-la-la-lee / You really got a hold on me / What'cha gonna do about it? *(re-iss. Aug84; DOA 2) (cd-iss. Jan89 on 'London'+=; 820 766-2) (cd re-iss. Jun03 on 'Deram'+=; 844633-2)* – My mind's eye (French EP version) / Hey girl (French EP version) / Take this hurt off me (version) / Baby don't you do it (version) / What'cha gonna do about it (BBC session).

Immediate / Immediate

Jun 67. (7") *(IM 050) <1902>* **HERE COMES THE NICE. / TALK TO YOU** [12] [ ]

Jun 67. (lp; mono/stereo) *(IMLP/IMSP 008)* **SMALL FACES** [12] [–]
– Green circles / Become like you / Get yourself together / All our yesterdays / Talk to you / Show me the way / Up the wooden hills to Bedfordshire / Eddie's dreaming / (Tell me) Have you ever seen me / Something I want to tell you / Feeling lonely / Happy boys happy / Things are going to get better / My way of giving. *(cd-iss. May91 as 'GREEN CIRCLES (FIRST IMMEDIATE ALBUM)' on 'Sequel'; NEXCD 163) (+=)* – Green circles (take 2) / Donkey rides, a penny, a glass / Have you ever seen me (take 2). *(cd re-iss. Apr97 on 'Essential'; ESMCD 476)*

Aug 67. (7") *(IM 052) <501>* **ITCHYCOO PARK. / I'M ONLY DREAMING** [3] Nov67 [16]

Nov 67. (7") *(IM 062) <5003>* **TIN SOLDIER. / I FEEL MUCH BETTER** [9] Mar68 [73]
(re-iss. May75; IMS 100)

Feb 68. (lp) *<Z12-52-002>* **THERE ARE BUT FOUR SMALL FACES** [–] [ ]
– Here comes the nice / All or nothing / Lazy Sunday / Sha-la-la-la-lee / Collibosher / The Autumn stone / Whatcha gonna do about it? / My mind's eye / Itchycoo Park / Hey girl / The universal / Runaway / Call it something nice / I can't make it / Afterglow (of your love) / Tin soldier. (

Apr 68. (7") *(IM 064) <5007>* **LAZY SUNDAY. / ROLLIN' OVER** [2] [ ]
(re-iss. Oct82; same)

Jun 68. (lp; mono/stereo) *(IMLP/IMSP 012) <Z12-52-008>* **OGDENS' NUT GONE FLAKE** [1] [ ]
– Ogden's nut gone flake / Afterglow (of your love) / Long agos and worlds apart / Rene / Son of a baker / Lazy Sunday / Happiness Stan / Rollin' over / The hungry intruder / The journey / Mad John / Happy days / Toy town. *<US re-iss. Mar73 on 'Abkco'; 4225> (re-iss. Dec75; IML 1001) (re-iss. Jun77; IML 2001) (re-iss. export Aug78 on 'Charly'; CR 300015) (re-iss. Mar80 on 'Virgin'; V 2159) (re-iss. Oct86 on 'Castle' lp/cd+=; CLA LP/CD 116)* – Tin soldier (live). *(re-cd-iss. in box Feb91 on 'Castle'; CLACT 016) (cd re-iss. Feb97 on 'Original Recordings'; ORRLP 001) (cd re-iss. Apr97 on 'Essential'; ESMCD 477)*

Jul 68. (7") *(IM 069) <5009>* **THE UNIVERSAL. / DONKEY RIDES, A PENNY, A GLASS** [16] [ ]

Nov 68. (7") *<5012>* **THE JOURNEY. / MAD JOHN** [–] [ ]

Mar 69. (7") *(IM 077) <5014>* **AFTERGLOW (OF YOUR LOVE). / WHAM BAM, THANK YOU MAM** [36] [ ]

Mar 69. (d-lp) *(IMAL 01/02)* **THE AUTUMN STONE** (rarities, live, etc) [ ] [ ]
– Here comes the nice / The Autumn stone / Collibosher / All or nothing / Red balloon / Lazy Sunday / Rollin' over / If I were a carpenter / Every little bit hurts / My mind's eye / Tin soldier / Just asking / Call it something nice / I can't make it / Afterglow (of your love) / Sha-la-la-la-lee / The universal / Itchycoo Park / Hey girl / Wide eyed girl / On the wall / What'cha gonna do about it / Wham bam thank you mam. *(re-iss. Jul84; IMLD 1) (re-iss. May86 on 'Castle' lp/c/cd; CLA LP/MC/CD 114) (re-iss. 1991) (cd re-mast.Apr97 on 'Essential'+=; ESMCD 478)* – Donkey rides a peeny a glass / All or nothing (live) / Tin soldier (live) / Rollin' over (live). *(cd re-iss. Mar03 on 'Snapper'; SNIP 404CD) (cd re-iss. May03 on 'Sunspot'; SPOT 536)*

— disbanded Mar'69 when STEVE MARRIOTT formed HUMBLE PIE. The remaining members became The FACES

The FACES

alongside **ROD STEWART** (b.10 Jan'45, London) – vocals (also Solo artist, ex-JEFF BECK) / **RON WOOD** (b. 1 Jun'47, Hillingdon, England) – guitar (ex-JEFF BECK GROUP, ex-CREATION)

(note: in the US, debut lp still credited to The SMALL FACES)

Warners / Warners

Feb 70. (7") *(WB 8005)* **FLYING. / THREE-BUTTON HAND-ME-DOWN** [ ] [–]

Mar 70. (lp) *(WS 3000)* **FIRST STEP** [45] [–]
– Wicked messenger / Devotion / Shake, shudder, shiver / Stone / Around the plynth / Flying / Pineapple and the monkey / Nobody knows / Looking out the window / Three-button hand-me-down. *(re-iss. Dec71 lp/c; K/K4 46053) (re-iss. Jul87 on 'Edsel'; ED 240) (cd-iss. Sep91; EDCD 240) (cd re-iss. Sep93; 7599 26376-2)*

Mar 71. (7") *(WB 8018)* **HAD ME A REAL GOOD TIME. / REAR WHEEL SKID** [ ] [–]

Mar 71. (lp) *(WS 3011) <1892>* **LONG PLAYER** [31] [29]
– Bad 'n' ruin / Tell everyone / Sweet lady Mary / Richmond / Maybe I'm amazed / Had a real good time / On the beach / I feel so good / Jerusalem. *(re-iss. Dec71 lp/c; K/K4 46064) (cd-iss. Sep93; 7599 26191-2)*

Apr 71. (7") **MAYBE I'M AMAZED. / OH LORD I'M BROWNED OFF** [–] [ ]

Nov 71. (7") *(K 16136)* **STAY WITH ME. / DEBRIS** [6] [–]

Nov 71. (lp/c) *(K/K4 56006) <2574>* **A NOD IS AS GOD AS A WINK . . . TO A BLIND HORSE** [2] [6]
– Miss Judy's farm / You're so rude / Love lives here / Last orders please /

Stay with me / Debris / Memphis / Too bad / That's all I need. *(cd-iss. Sep93; 7599 25929-2)*

Dec 71. (7") *<7545>* **STAY WITH ME. / YOU'RE SO RUDE** [–] [17]

Feb 73. (7") *(K 16247) <7681>* **CINDY INCIDENTALLY. / SKEWIFF** [2] [48]

Apr 73. (lp/c) *(K/K4 56011) <2665>* **OOH LA LA** [1] [21]
– Silicone grown / Cindy incidentally / Flags and banners / My fault / Borstal boys / Fly in the ointment / If I'm on the late side / Glad and sorry / Just another monkey / Ooh la la. *(cd-iss. Sep93; 7599 26368-2)*

May 73. (7") **OOH LA LA. / BORSTAL BOYS** [–] [ ]

—— **TETSU YAMAUCHI** (b.21 Oct'47, Fukuoka, Japan) – bass (ex-FREE) repl. RONNIE LANE who went solo

Nov 73. (7") *(K 16341)* **POOL HALL RICHARD. / I WISH IT WOULD RAIN** [8] [ ]

ROD STEWART & THE FACES

due to ROD's solo successes

Mercury Mercury

Jan 74. (lp) *(9100 011) <1-697>* **COAST TO COAST – OVERTURE FOR BEGINNERS (live)** [3] [63]
– It's all over now / Cut across Shorty / Too bad / Every picture tells a story / Angel / Stay with me / I wish it would rain / I'd rather go blind / Borstal boys / Amazing Grace / Jealous guy. *(cd-iss. Nov87; 832 128-2)*
(above also featured ROD's songs from solo career)

Warners Warners

Nov 74. (7") *(K 16494)* **YOU CAN MAKE ME DANCE SING OR ANYTHING. / AS LONG AS YOU TELL HIM** [12] [ ]

—— Late '75, crumbled again, as ROD STEWART enjoyed overwhelming solo stardom. RON WOOD went off to join The ROLLING STONES.

– (FACES) compilations, etc. –

Oct 75. (d-lp) *Warners; (K 66027)* **TWO ORIGINALS OF THE FACES** [ ] [–]
– (FIRST STEP / LONG PLAYER)

Apr 77. (lp/c) *Riva; (K/K4 56172) <2897>* **SNAKES AND LADDERS – THE BEST OF THE FACES** [24] [ ]
– Pool hall Richard / Cindy incidentally / Ooh la la / Sweet Lady Mary / Flying / Pineapple and the monkey / You can make me dance, sing or anything / Had me a real good time / Stay with me / Miss Judy's farm / Silicone grown / That's all you need.

May 77. (7"ep) *Riva; (RIVA 8)* **THE FACES** [41] [ ]
– Cindy incidentally / Stay with me / Memphis / You can make me dance, sing or anything.

Sep 80. (lp/c) *Pickwick; (SSP/SSC 3074)* **THE FACES FEATURING ROD STEWART** [ ] [–]

Nov 92. (cd/c) *Mercury; (514 180-2/-4)* **THE BEST OF ROD STEWART & THE FACES** [58] [–]

May 93. (cd/c; ROD STEWART & THE FACES) *Spectrum; (550026-2/-4)* **AMAZING GRACE** [ ] [–]

SMALL FACES

SMALL FACES re-formed by **JONES, McLAGAN** + reinstated **MARRIOTT** incomer **RICKY WILLS** – bass (ex-Peter FRAMPTON'S CAMEL, ex-ROXY MUSIC, etc)

Atlantic Atlantic

Jul 77. (7") *(K 10983)* **LOOKIN' FOR A LOVE. / KO'D (BY LUV)** [ ] [ ]

Aug 77. (lp/c) *(K/K4 50375) <SD 19113>* **PLAYMATES** [ ] [ ]
– High and happy / Never too late / Tonight / Say larvee / Find it / Lookin' for a love / Playmates / Drive in romance / This song's just for you / Smilin' in tune. *(cd-iss. Jun92 on 'Repertoire';)*

Nov 77. (7") *(K 11043)* **STAND BY ME (STAND BY YOU). / HUNGRY AND LOOKING** [ ] [ ]

—— added on tour **JIMMY McCULLOCH** (b.1953, Glasgow, Scotland) – guitar (of WINGS)

Jun 78. (7") *(K 11173)* **FILTHY RICH. / OVER TOO SOON** [ ] [ ]

Sep 78. (lp/c) *(K/K4 50468) <SD 19171>* **78 IN THE SHADE** [ ] [ ]
– Over too soon / Too many crossroads / Let me down gently / Thinkin' about love / Stand by me (stand by you) / Brown man do / Soldier / Reel sour / You ain"t seen nothin' yet / Filthy rich. *(cd-iss. Nov93 on 'Repertoire';)*

—— Disbanded again mid'78. KENNY JONES joined The WHO. McCULLOCH died 27th Sep'79. MARRIOTT re-formed HUMBLE PIE. He was to tragically die in his Essex home after it went on fire 20 Apr'91. Founder member RONNIE LANE finally died in June '97 after 18 years suffering from multiple sclerosis.

– (selective) compilations, etc. –

Nov 75. (7") *Immediate; (IMS 102)* **ITCHYCOO PARK. / MY MIND'S EYE** [9] [–]

Mar 76. (7") *Immediate; (IMS 106)* **LAZY SUNDAY. / (TELL ME) HAVE YOU EVER SEEN ME** [36] [–]

May 90. (cd/c/d-lp) *Castle TV; (CTV CD/MC/LP 004)* **THE ULTIMATE COLLECTION** [ ] [–]
(cd re-iss. Dec91 as 'THE COMPLETE COLLECTION'; CCSCD 302)

Jun 90. (cd/c/lp) *See For Miles; (SEE 293/+C/CD)* **THE SINGLES A's & B's** [ ] [–]

Nov 95. (4xcd-box) *Charly; (IMMBOX 1)* **THE IMMEDIATE YEARS** [ ] [–]

May 96. (d-cd/d-c/d-lp) *Deram; (844583-2/-4/-1)* **THE DECCA ANTHOLOGY 1965-1967** [66] [–]

Nov 96. (d-cd) *Charly; (CPCD 82602)* **THE VERY BEST OF THE SMALL FACES** [ ] [–]

Oct 98. (3xcd-box) *Essential; (ESMBX 302)* **SMALL FACES / OGDEN'S NUT GONE FLAKE / THE AUTUMN STONE** [ ] [ ]

Apr 99. (d-cd) *Sequel; (NEECD 311)* **THE DARLINGS OF THE WAPPING WHARF** [ ] [ ]

Nov 99. (cd/lp) *Strange Fruit; (SFRS CD/LP 087)* **THE BBC SESSIONS** [ ] [ ]

Jan 00. (cd) *Universal; (E 844942-2)* **UNIVERSAL MASTERS COLLECTION** [ ] [–]

Feb 00. (d-cd) *Charly; (CDVAL 1152)* **THE ULTIMATE COLLECTION** [ ] [–]

Apr 00. (cd) *Disky; <(SI 99078-2)>* **THE BEST OF THE 60'S** [ ] [ ]

Sep 01. (cd) *Decca; (882973-2)* **THE BEST OF THE SMALL FACES** [ ] [ ]

May 03. (d-cd) *Sanctuary; (TDSAN 004) <27977>* **ULTIMATE COLLECTION** [24] [ ]
– What'cha gonna do about it? / I've got mine / It's too late / Sha-la-la-la-lee / Grow your own / Hey girl / Shake / Come on children / You better believe it / One night stand / Sorry she's mine / Own up time / You need loving / Don't stop what you are doing / E too D / All or nothing / Understanding / My mind's eye / I can't dance with you / I can't make it / Just passing / Patterns / Yeasterday today and tomorrow / That man / Baby don't do it / Here comes the nice / Talk to you / Tell me have you ever seen me / Things are going to get better / My way of giving / Green circles / Get yourself together / Up the wooden hills to Bedfordshire / Eddie's dreaming / Itchycoo Park / I'm only dreaming / Tin soldier / I feel much better / Ogden's nut gone flake / Afterglow of your love / Song of a baker / Lazy Sunday / Rollin' over / Mad John / Happy days toy town / The universal / Donkey rides a penny a glass / Wham bam thank you mam / Don't burst my bubble / The autumn stone.

SMASHING PUMPKINS

Formed: Chicago, Illinois, USA . . . late 80's by BILLY CORGAN, JAMES IHA, D'ARCY WRETZKY. The son of a jazz guitarist and former member of local goth band, The MARKED, CORGAN initiated The SMASHING PUMPKINS as a three piece using a drum machine, before the band recruited sticksman, JIMMY CHAMBERLAIN. After a debut single for a local label, 'I AM ONE', and the inclusion of two tracks on a local compilation album, the group came to the attention of influential Seattle label, 'Sub Pop'. After only one single, 'TRISTESSA', The SMASHING PUMPKINS moved once more, signing to Virgin subsidiary, 'Hut', in the UK, 'Caroline' in America. Produced by BUTCH VIG, a debut album, 'GISH', was released in early '92, its grunge pretensions belying a meandering 70's/psychedelic undercurrent which distanced the band from most of their contemporaries. Nevertheless, the group amassed a sizable student/grassroots following which eventually saw the debut go gold in the States, a re-released 'I AM ONE' sneaking into the UK Top 75 later that year. With the masterful 'SIAMESE DREAM' (1993), the band went from underground hopefuls to alternative rock frontrunners, the album fully realising the complex 'PUMPKINS sound in a delicious wash of noise and gentle melody. Influenced by acoustic LED ZEPPELIN fused with slices of 70's PINK FLOYD, CORGAN's croaky but effective voice was at its best on the pastel, NIRVANA-esque classics, 'TODAY' and 'DISARM', while the 'PUMPKINS went for the jugular on the likes of 'CHERUB ROCK', 'ROCKET' and 'GEEK U.S.A.'. The album made the Top 5 in Britain, Top 10 in the States, selling multi-millions and turning the band into a 'grunge' sensation almost overnight, despite the fact that their mellotron stylings and complex arrangements marked them out as closer in spirit to prog-rock than punk. Amidst frantic touring, the band released the outtakes/B-sides compilation, 'PISCES ISCARIOT' (1994), the next album proper surfacing in late '95 as the sprawling double set, 'MELLON COLLIE AND THE INFINITE SADNESS'. Dense and stylistically breathtaking, the album veered from all-out grunge/thrash to acoustic meandering and avant-rock doodlings, a less cohesive whole than its predecessor but much more to get your teeth into. Inevitably, there were criticisms of self-indulgence, though for a two-hour set, there was a surprising, compelling consistency to proceedings; among the highlights were 'BULLET WITH BUTTERFLY WINGS', 'TONIGHT, TONIGHT' and the visceral rage of '1979'. The record scaled the US charts, where The SMASHING PUMPKINS were almost reaching the commercial and critical heights of NIRVANA, the group also taking Britain by storm, headlining the 1995 Reading Festival. Never the most stable of bands, disaster struck the following year when new boy (keyboard player) JONATHAN MELVOIN died of a drugs overdose and heroin addict CHAMBERLAIN was finally kicked out. More recently (early 1998), IHA released an acclaimed solo album of acoustic strumming ('LET IT COME DOWN') while the others recorded fresh songs with a drum machine, taking things full circle. That summer, the 'PUMPKINS showed a softer side to their character when the mournful but still effective album, 'ADORE', hit the Top 5. 1999 saw two major personnel changes via the return of CHAMBERLAIN and the departure of D'ARCY (who was replaced by ex-HOLE bassist MELISSA AUF DER MAUR); one last set would appear in 2000, 'MACHINA – THE MACHINES OF GOD'. In a postscript to the messy break-up of The SMASHING PUMPKINS, BILLY CORGAN began putting together a supergroup, hand-picking musicians such as DAVID PAJO (ex-SLINT and currently PAPA M), MATT SWEENEY (of post-rockers CHAVEZ) and A PERFECT CIRCLE bassist PAZ LENCHANTIN. Along with PUMPKINS drummer JIMMY CHAMBERLAIN the group emerged as ZWAN, playing a handful of gigs in America during 2001. Buzz was now circling CORGAN's new mantle, with some critics dismissing it purely as a vanity project. They were pleasantly surprised then, when the quintet issued 'MARY STAR OF THE SEA' in 2003 to rave reviews and massive sales. Like a lost PUMPKINS record, with PAJO firmly replacing IHA on guitar duties and CHAMBERLAIN's thunderous backbone still intact, it was ultimately CORGAN's record and solid proof of his majestic songwriting skills. ZWAN was however shortlived, as CORGAN disbanded the project shortly after the album's release. • **Songwriters:** CORGAN, except several with IHA. Covered; A GIRL NAMED SANDOZ (Eric Burdon & The Animals) / LANDSLIDE (Fleetwood Mac) / DANCING IN THE MOONLIGHT (Thin Lizzy) / NEVER LET ME DOWN (Depeche Mode) / YOU'RE ALL I'VE GOT TONIGHT (Cars) / CLONES (WE'RE ALL) (Alice Cooper) / DREAMING (Blondie) / A NIGHT LIKE THIS (Cure) / DESTINATION UNKNOWN (Missing Persons) / SAD PETER PAN with Red Red Meat (Vic Chesnutt). • **Miscellaneous:** IHA and D'ARCY set up their own label, 'Scratchie', for whom the outfit, FULFLEJ recorded an album ('Wack-Ass Tuba Riff') in 1996 with the pair making guest appearances.

Album rating: GISH (*6) / SIAMESE DREAM (*9) / MELLON COLLIE AND THE INFINITE SADNESS (*9) / PISCES ISCARIOT compilation (*5) / THE AEROPLANE FLIES HIGH boxed set (*6) / ADORE (*5) / MACHINA – THE MACHINES OF GOD (*5) / (ROTTEN APPLES) GREATEST HITS compilation (*7) / EARPHORIA (*6) / Zwan: MARY STAR OF THE SEA (*7) / James Iha: LET IT COME DOWN (*5)

BILLY CORGAN (b.17 Mar'67) – vocals, guitar / **JAMES IHA** (b.26 Mar'68, Elk Grove, Illinois) – guitar / **D'ARCY (WRETZKY)** (b. 1 May'68, South Haven, Michigan) – bass, vocals / **JIMMY CHAMBERLIN** (b.10 Jun'64, Joliet, Illinois) – drums

not iss. | Limited Potential

Apr 90. (7") *<Limp 006>* **I AM ONE. / NOT WORTH ASKING** [–] [ ]

Glitterhouse | Sub Pop

Dec 90. (7",7"pink) *<SP 90>* **TRISTESSA. / LA DOLLY VITA** [–] [ ]
(UK-12"+=; May93) *(SP 10-137)* – Honeyspider.

Hut | Caroline

Aug 91. (12") *(HUTT 6)* **SIVA. / WINDOW PAINE** [ ] [–]
Feb 92. (12"ep/cd-ep) *(HUTT/CDHUT 10)* **LULL EP** [ ] [–]
– Rhinoceros / Blue / Slunk / Bye June (demo).
Feb 92. (cd/c/lp) *(HUT CD/MC/LP 002) <1705>* **GISH** [ ] Aug91 [ ]
– I am one / Siva / Rhinoceros / Bury me / Crush / Suffer / Snail / Tristessa / Window paine / Daydream. *(re-iss. May94; diff.versions cd/lp; HUT CDX/LPX 002)*
Jun 92. (c-ep/12"ep/cd-ep) *(HUT C/T/CD 17)* **PEEL SESSIONS** [ ] [–]
– Siva / A girl named Sandoz / Smiley.
Aug 92. (12"ep/cd-ep) *(HUTT/CDHUT 18)* **I AM ONE. / PLUME / STARLA** [73] [–]
(10"ep) *(HUTTEN 18)* – ('A'side) / Terrapin (live) / Bullet train to Osaka.
Jun 93. (7"clear) *(HUT 31)* **CHERUB ROCK. / PURR SNICKETY** [31] [–]
(12"/cd-s) *(HUTT/CDHUT 31)* – ('A'side) / Pissant / French movie theme / (Star spangled banner).
Jul 93. (cd/c/d-lp) *(HUT CD/MC/LP 011) <88267>* **SIAMESE DREAM** [4] [10]
– Cherub rock / Quiet / Today / Hummer / Rocket / Disarm / Soma / Geek U.S.A. / Mayonaise / Spaceboy / Silverfuck / Sweet sweet / Luna. *(d-lp re-iss. Dec99 on 'Caroline'; CAROL 17401)*
Sep 93. (7"red) *(HUT 37)* **TODAY. / APATHY'S LAST KISS** [44] [–]
(c-s/12"/cd-s) *(HUTC/HUTT/CDHUT 37)* – ('A'side) / Hello kitty kat / Obscured.
Feb 94. (7"purple) *(HUT 43)* **DISARM. / SIAMESE DREAM** [11] [–]
(12"/cd-s) *(HUT T/CD 43)* – ('A'side) / Soothe (demo) / Blew away.
(cd-s) *(HUTDX 43)* – ('A'side) / Dancing in the moonlight / Landslide.
Oct 94. (cd/c/gold-lp) *<39834>* **PISCES ISCARIOT** (compilation of B-sides & rarities) [–] [4]
– Soothe / Frail and bedazzled / Plume / Whir / Blew away / Pissant / Hello Kitty Kat / Obscured / Landslide / Starla / Blue / A girl named Sandoz / La dolly vita / Spaced. *<w/ free gold-7"; CAR 1767-7>* **NOT WORTH ASKING. / HONEY SPIDER II** *(UK-iss.Oct96 cd/c/lp; HUT CD/MC/LP 41)*

Hut | Virgin

Dec 94. (7"peach) *(HUTL 48)* **ROCKET. / NEVER LET ME DOWN** [ ] [–]
(4x7"box-set) *(SPBOX 1)* **SIAMESE SINGLES** – (last 3 singles 1993-94 + above)
Oct 95. (c-s/cd-s) *(HUT C/CD 63) <38522>* **BULLET WITH BUTTERFLY WINGS / . . .SAID SADLY** [20] [25]
Oct 95. (d-cd/d-c) *(CD/TC HUTD 30) <40861>* **MELLON COLLIE AND THE INFINITE SADNESS** [4] [1]
– DAWN TO DUSK:- Mellon Collie and the infinite sadness / Tonight, tonight / Jellybelly / Zero / Here is no why / Bullet with butterfly wings / To forgive / An ode to no one / Love / Cupid de Locke / Galapogos / Muzzle / Porcelina of the vast oceans / Take me down. // TWILIGHT TO STARLIGHT:- Where boys fear to tread / Bodies / Thirty-three / In the arms of sleep / 1979 / Tales of a scorched Earth / Thru the eyes of Ruby / Stumbleine / X.Y.U. / We only come out at night / Beautiful / Lily (my one and only) / By starlight / Farewell and goodnight. *(re-iss. Apr96 as t-lp+=; HUTTLP 30)* – Tonight reprise / Infinite sadness.

— added on tour **JONATHAN MELVOIN** – keyboards (ex-DICKIES) (brother of WENDY; ex-WENDY & LISA, ex-PRINCE)

Jan 96. (c-ep/12"ep/cd-ep) *(HUT C/T/CD 67) <38547>* **1979 / UGLY. / BELIEVE / CHERRY** [16] [12]
(12"ep/cd-ep; Mar96) *(HUT TX/CDX 67)* – 1979 REMIXES: Vocal / Instrumental / Moby / Cement.

May 96. (c-ep) *(HUTC 69) <38547>* **TONIGHT, TONIGHT / MELADORI MAGPIE / ROTTEN APPLES** [7] Jun96 [36]
(cd-ep+=) *(HUTCD 69)* – Medellia of the gray skies.
(cd-ep) *(HUTDX 69)* – ('A'side) / Jupiter's lament / Blank / Tonite (reprise).

— On 12th Jul'96, MELVOIN died of a heroin overdose. CHAMBERLIN, who found him dead, was charged with drug offences and sacked by the remaining trio who were said to sick of his long-lasting drug addiction. In August, they were replaced for tour by **DENNIS FLEMION** – keyboards (ex-FROGS) + **MATT WALKER** – drums (of FILTER)

Sep 96. (m-cd) *(HUTCD 73) <38545>* **ZERO EP** [ ] May96 [46]
– Zero / God / Mouths of babes / Tribute to Johnny / Marquis in spades / Pennies / Pastichio medley: (excerpts).

Nov 96. (cd-ep) *(HUTCD 78) <38574>* **THIRTY THREE / THE LAST SONG / THE AEROPLANE FLIES HIGH (TURNS LEFT, LOOKS RIGHT) / TRANSFORMER** [21] [39]
(cd-ep) *(HUTDX 78)* – ('A'side) / The bells / My blue Heaven.

Nov 96. (5xcd-ep;box) *<SPBOX 2>* **THE AEROPLANE FLIES HIGH** [–] [42]
– (BULLET WITH BUTTERFLY WINGS / 1979 / TONIGHT, TONIGHT / THIRTY THREE / ZERO)

— early in '97, CORGAN provided six songs for 'RANSOM' film soundtrack credited to conductor JAMES HORNER (Hollywood HR 62086-2)

Jun 97. (c-s) *(W 0404C)* **THE END IS THE BEGINNING IS THE END / THE BEGINNING IS THE END IS THE BEGINNING** [10] [–]
(cd-s+=) *(W 0404CD)* – The ethers tragic / The guns of love disastrous.
(12"/cd-s) *(W 0410 T/CD)* – ('A'mixes; 2 Fluke mixes / 2 Rabbit in The Moons mixes / Hallucination Gotham mix).
(above from the film 'Batman & Robin' on 'Warners')

May 98. (7") *(HUT 101) <38647>* **AVA ADORE. / CZARINA** [11] Jun98 [42]
(c-s+=/cd-s+=) *(HUT C/CD 101)* – Once in a while.

Jun 98. (cd/c/d-lp) *(CDHUT/TCHUT/HUTDLP 51) <45879>* **ADORE** [5] [2]
– To Sheila / Ava adore / Perfect / Daphne decends / Once upon a time / Tear / Crestfallen / Appels + oranjes / Pug / The tale of Dusty and Pistol Pete / Annie-dog / Shame / Behold! the night mare / For Martha / Blank page / 17.

Sep 98. (c-s/cd-s) *(HUT C/CD 106) <38650>* **PERFECT / SUMMER / PERFECT (Nellee Hooper mix)** [24] [54]
(cd-s) *(HUTDX 106)* – ('A'side) / Daphne descends (Oakenfold Perfecto mix) / Daphne descends (Kerry B mix).

— **CHAMBERLAIN** was now back in the fold

— **MELISSA AUF DER MAUR** – bass (ex-HOLE) repl. D'ARCY

Feb 00. (c-s/cd-s) *(HUT C/CD 127)* **STAND INSIDE YOUR LOVE / SPEED KILLS** [23] [–]

Feb 00. (cd/c/d-lp) *(CDHUT/HUTMC/HUTDLP 59) <48936>* **MACHINA / THE MACHINES OF GOD** [7] [3]
– The everlasting gaze / Rain drops & sun showers / Stand inside your love / I of the mourning / The sacred and profane / Try, try, try / Heavy metal machine / This time / The imploding voice / Glass and the ghost children / Wound / The crying tree of Mercury / With every light / Blue skies bring tears / Age of innocence.

Sep 00. (cd-s) *(HUTCD 140)* **TRY, TRY, TRY / HERE'S TO THE ATOM BOMB** [73] [–]

— the band split in November 2000; CORGAN was back with ZWAN in '03

– compilations, etc. –

on 'Hut' UK / 'Virgin' America unless stated otherwise

Nov 01. (cd) *(CDHUT 70) <11316>* **(ROTTEN APPLES) GREATEST HITS** [28] [31]
– Siva / Rhinoceros / Drown / Cherub rock / Today / Disarm / Bullet with butterfly wings / 1979 / Zero / Tonight, tonight / Eye / Ava adore / Perfect / The everlasting gaze / Stand inside your love / Try, try, try / Real love / Untitled. *(d-cd+=; CDHUTD 70)* – Lucky 13 / Aeroplane flies high (turns left looks right) / Because you are / Slow down / Believe / My mistake / Marquis in spades / Here's to the atom bomb / Sparrow / Waiting / Saturnine / Rock on / Set the ray to Jerry / Winterlong / Soot and stars / Blissed and gone.

Nov 02. (cd) *(CDHUT 79) <42706>* **EARPHORIA (live)** [ ] [ ]
– Sinfony / Quiet / Disarm / Cherub rock / Today / Bugg superstar / I am one / Pulseczar / Soma / Slunk / French movie theme / Geek U.S.A. / Mayonnaise / Silverfuck / Why am I so tired.

ZWAN

BILLY CORGAN – vocals, guitar / **JIMMY CHAMBERLIN** – drums / **MATT SWEENEY** – guitar (ex-CHAVEZ, ex-SKUNK) / **DAVID PAJO** – guitar, bass (ex-SLINT, ex-TORTOISE) / **PAZ LENCHANTIN** – bass (of A PERFECT CIRCLE)

Reprise Reprise

Feb 03. (cd/d-lp) *<(9362 48436-2/-1)>* **MARY STAR OF THE SEA** [33] Jan03 [3]
– Lyric / Settle down / Declarations of faith / Honestly / El sol / Of a broken heart / Ride a black swan / Heartsong / Endless summer / Baby let's rock! / Ywah! / Desire / Jesus, I – Mary star of the sea / Come with me. *(ltd cd w/dvd+=; 9362 48425-2)* – My life and times / Rivers we can't cross / Mary star of the sea / Love lies in ruin / For your love / Down down down / New poetry / W.P. / Jesus, I / God's gonna set this world on fire / To love you / Consumed / My life and times / Danger boy / Spilled milk.

Feb 03. (7") *(W 600)* **HONESTLY. / NUMBER OF THE BEAST** [28] [–]
(cd-s+=) *(W 600CD)* – Freedom ain't what it used to be.

Jun 03. (7") *(W 607)* **LYRIC. / NOBODY 'CEPT YOU (live)** [44] [–]
(cd-s+=) *(W 607CD)* – Autumn leaves.

— split mid September 2003

JAMES IHA

JAMES IHA – vocals, guitar / **NEAL CASAL** – guitar / **ADAM SCHLESINGER** – piano (of FOUNTAINS OF WAYNE) / **GREG LEISZ** – steel guitar / **JOHN GINTY** – hammond organ / **SOLOMON SNYDER** – bass / **MATT WALKER** – drums / **NINA GORDON** (of VERUCA SALT) also a part of initial basement set-up

Feb 98. (cd/c/lp) *(CDHUT/HUTMC/HUTLP 47) <45411>* **LET IT COME DOWN** [ ] [ ]
– Be strong now / Sound of love / Beauty / See the sun / Country girl / Jealousy / Lover, lover / Silver string / Winter / One and two / No one's gonna hurt you.

Feb 98. (12"ep/cd-ep) *(HUT T/CD 99)* **BE STRONG NOW / MY ADVICE. / TAKE CARE / FALLING** [ ] [–]

Elliott SMITH

Born: 1969, Dallas, Texas, USA, although raised from a young age by his father in Portland, Oregon, after his parents divorced. The singer/songwriter relocated to university digs in Brooklyn, New York, playing in mid-90's noisy alternative rock band, HEATMISER. They released four rare albums, 'DEAD AIR' (1993), 'YELLOW NO.5' (1994; a mini-set), 'COP AND SPEEDER' (1995) and 'MIC CITY SONS' (1996), while ELLIOTT, meantime had opted for a more sedate solo career. He delivered three very well received albums for the 'Kill Rock City' imprint', namely 'ROMAN CANDLE' (1994), 'ELLIOTT SMITH' (1995) and 'EITHER/OR' (1997) – all licensed in 1998 to the UK arm of 'Domino' – before he inked a deal with 'DreamWorks'. This was due to the plaudits heaped upon him after appearing on stage alongside CELINE DION and TRISHA YEARWOOD at the "Oscars" ceremony! An unlikely story you may think, although the truth is, he provided part of the soundtrack to one of the best films of the year, 'Good Will Hunting'. His unfashionable (especially his taste in clothing and headgear – sometimes a tammy) approach was slightly reminiscent of SIMON & GARFUNKEL, BIG STAR or the lo-fi RICHARD DAVIES (of CARDINAL). His fourth album, 'XO', hit the shops later in 1998 and ELLIOTT looked certain to make his impact on the music scene. Sounding very much at home in his new big budget environment, 'FIGURE 8' (2000) found SMITH taking the opportunity to imbue his songcraft with the luxurious feel of classic BEATLES-meets-CS&N-meets-ERIC MATTHEWS while never relinquishing the skid row wisdom of his lyrical genius. ELLIOT was still in the process of recording his next album, 'FROM A BASEMENT ON A HILL', when he unexpectedly commited suicide on 21st October 2003.

Album rating: Heatmiser: DEAD AIR (*6) / COP AND SPEEDER (*7) / MIC CITY SONS (*6) / Elliott Smith: ROMAN CANDLE (*7) / ELLIOTT SMITH (*7) / EITHER/OR (*8) / XO (*7) / FIGURE 8 (*7)

HEATMISER

ELLIOTT SMITH – vocals / **NEIL GUST** – guitar, vocals / **SAM COOMES** – bass / **TONY LASH** – drums

not iss. — own label

1992. (c) **THE MUSIC OF HEATMISER** –
– Lowlife / Bottle rocket / Buick / Just a little prick / Dirt / Mightier than you.

not iss. — Wake

1993. (7") **STRAY. / CAN'T BE TOUCHED** –
<re-iss. 1995 on 'Cavity Search'; CSR 02>

Frontier — Frontier

Jul 93. (cd/c) *<(31057-2/-4)>* **DEAD AIR** Jun93
– Still / Candyland / Mock up / Dirt / Bottle rocket / Blackout / Stray / Can't be touched / Cannibal / Don't look down / Sands hotel / Low life / Buick / Dead air.

Jul 94. (m-cd) *<(31062-2)>* **YELLOW NO.5**
– Wake / Fortune 500 / The corner seat / Idler / Junior mint / Yellow No.5.

Apr 95. (cd) *<(31063-2)>* **COP AND SPEEDER**
– Disappearing ink / Bastard John / Flamel / Temper / Why did I decide to stay? / Collect to NYC / Hitting on the waiter / Busted lip / Antonio Carlos Jobim / It's not a prop / Something to lose / Sleeping pill / Trap door / Nightcap.

Caroline — Cavity Search

Jun 95. (7") *<CSR 7>* **SLEEPING PILL. / TEMPER** –
Apr 96. (7") *<CSR 25>* **EVERYBODY HAS IT. / DIRTY DREAM** –
Oct 96. (cd) *(CAR 75402) <CSR 35-2>* **MIC CITY SONS**
– Get lucky / Plainclothes man / Low flying jets / Rest my head against the wall / Fix is in / Eagle eye / Cruel reminder / You gotta move / Pop in G / Blue highway / See you later.

— split after SMITH was already making a name for himself as a solo act, while COOMES was in a duo with JANET WEISS called QUASI.

ELLIOTT SMITH

- vocals, drums, bass, saxophones, etc.

not iss. — Cavity Search

Dec 94. (cd) *<CSR 13-2>* **ROMAN CANDLE** –
– Roman candle / Condor avenue / No name #I / No name #II / No name #III / Drive all over town / No name #IV / The last call / Kiwi mad-dog 20-20. *(UK-iss.Mar98 on 'Cavity Search'; same as US) (re-iss. Aug98 on 'Domino' cd/lp; REWIG CD/LP 002)*

Kill Rock Stars — Kill Rock Stars

Feb 95. (7"m) *<KRS 239>* **NEEDLE IN THE HAY. / ALPHABET TOWN / SOME SONG**
Jul 95. (lp/cd) *<KRS 246/+CD>* **ELLIOTT SMITH** –
– Needle in the hay / Christian brother / Clementine / Southern belle / Single file / Coming up roses / Satellite / Alphabet town / St.Ides heaven / Good to go / White lady loves you more / Biggest lie. *(UK-iss.Mar98; same) (re-iss. Aug98 on 'Domino' cd/lp; REWIG CD/LP 001)*

Oct 96. (7"m) *<KRS 266>* **SPEED TRIALS. / ANGELES / I DON'T THINK I'M EVER GONNA FIGURE IT OUT**
Mar 97. (lp/cd) *<KRS 269/+CD>* **EITHER/OR**
– Speed trials / Alameda / Ballad of big nothing / Between the bars / Pictures of me / No name No.5 / Rose parade / Punch and Judy / Angeles / Cupid's trick / 2:45 am / Say yes. *(UK-iss.Jun98 on 'Domino' cd/lp; WIG CD/LP 51)*

1997. (7"; by ELLIOTT SMITH & PETE KREBS) **NO CONFIDENCE MAN. / SHIPTOWN** –
(below issued on 'Suicide Queen')
1997. (cd-s) *<S 005CD>* **DIVISION DAY. / NO NAME #6** –
(UK-iss.May00; same as US; re-Feb00)

Jun 98. (7") *(RUG 74)* **BALLAD OF BIG NOTHING. / SOME SONG / DIVISION DAY**
(cd-s+=) *(RUG 74CD)* – Angeles.

— now with a plethora of session people + strings

DreamWorks — DreamWorks

Aug 98. (cd/c) *<(DRD/DRC 50048)>* **XO**
– Sweet Adeline / Tomorrow tomorrow / Waltz #2 (XO) / Baby Britain / Pitseleh / Independence day / Bled white / Waltz #1 / Amity / Oh well, okay / Bottle up and explode! / A question mark / Everybody cares, everybody understands / I didn't understand. *<(lp-iss.on 'Bongload'; BL 35)>*

Dec 98. (c-s) *<(DRMS 22347)>* **WALTZ #2 (XO) / OUR THING** 52 Feb99
(cd-s+=) *(DRMCD 22347)* – How to take a fall.

Apr 99. (7") *(DRMS7 50953)* **BABY BRITAIN. / WALTZ No.1** 55 –
(cd-s+=) *(DRMDM 50950)* – The enemy is you.
(cd-s) *(DRMDM 50951)* – ('A'side) / Some song / Bottle up and explode.

Jan 00. (7"/cd-s) *<459037>* **HAPPINESS. / SON OF SAM** –
Apr 00. (cd) *<(4 50225-2)>* **FIGURE 8** 37 99
– Son of Sam / Somebody that I used to know / Junk bond trader / Everything reminds me of her / Everything means nothing to me / LA / In the lost and found (honky Bach) – The roost / Stupidity tries / Easy way out / Wouldn't mama be proud? / Color bars / Happiness – The gondola man / Pretty Mary K / I better be quiet now / Can't make a sound / Bye. *<(lp-iss.Jul00 on 'Bongload'; BL 48)>*

Jun 00. (7") *(450949-7)* **SON OF SAM. / A LIVING WILL** 55 –
(cd-s+=) *(450949-2)* – Figure 8.

— ELLIOTT died on 21st October, 2003

Patti SMITH

Born: 31 Dec'46, Chicago, Illinois, USA. She started to write for New York magazine 'Rock' in 1969, having earlier being shipped around by her family between Paris and London. In the early 70's, PATTI began writing poetry full-time and met fellow rock-scribe, LENNY KAYE, who provided guitar accompaniment for her beat-poet monologues at readings/gigs. By 1971 she was writing for 'Creem' magazine and soon developed a professional musical partnership with playwright, SAM SHEPHERD. A prolific time for SMITH, come Christmas '72 she had two books of poetry, 'Witt' and '7th Heaven' in the stores and, after contributing to TODD RUNDGREN's 'A WIZARD, A TRUE STAR' album, he credited her for nicknaming him 'Runt'. RICHARD SOHL was recruited alongside SMITH and KAYE for a one-off single in 1974, 'HEY JOE / PISS FACTORY' on the small 'MER' label. A suitably caustic slice of proto-punk, it later gained airplay after being picked up by 'Sire' records. Meanwhile, SMITH completed the line-up of what would become The PATTI SMITH GROUP with IVAN KRAAL and JAY DEE DAUGHERTY, signing to 'Arista' and starting work on the 'HORSES' (1975) album with JOHN CALE producing. From the monochrome androgyny of the cover shot to the DIY three chord thrash which formed the bulk of the musical backing, the album was a blueprint for a generation of both American and British punk/new wave artists. Although SMITH's vocals were something of an acquired taste, her distinctive intonation was a perfect vehicle for the image rich symbolism of her free flowing lyrics. 'GLORIA' and 'LAND OF 1,000 DANCES' were transformed into wired, beat-inspired flashes of nervous energy, while quieter moments like the intro to 'REDONDO BEACH' and 'FREE MONEY' possessed a stark beauty. After this alternative tour de force, the follow-up, 'RADIO ETHIOPIA' (1976), came as something of a departure. Possessing a more straightforward hard-rock approach save for the chaotic feedback-drenched exploration of the title track, the album received mixed reviews. After SMITH survived breaking her neck after falling from the stage at a gig, it was to be another two years before the release of her next album. 'EASTER' (1978) was a confident comeback which moved even further into commercial rock territory without extinguishing the livewire spark that had made 'HORSES' so compelling. The record contained an unlikely collaboration with BRUCE SPRINGSTEEN, 'BECAUSE THE NIGHT', which saw SMITH breach the upper reaches of the singles charts on both sides of the Atlantic and propelled the album to similar success. 'WAVE' (1979) sounded slightly unfocused although it attained a higher chart placing Stateside than its predecessor. After a final tour in 1979, SMITH bowed out of the music business for domestic bliss with her new husband FRED 'SONIC' SMITH (ex-MC5). Together with her spouse, SOHL and DOUGHERTY, she recorded a low-key comeback album in 1988, 'DREAM OF LIFE', although tragedy struck in the 90's when both SOHL and her husband died from heart failure. With many artists namechecking her as an influence, SMITH recorded 'GONE AGAIN' (1996) amid a mini-renaissance. A tribute to FRED, it was filled with a sense of loss and yearning, echoing the intensity of her earlier work. 'PEACE AND NOISE' (1997), was surprisingly released only a year later than its predecessor and showed signs she could easily get back to her poetic past. Three years later, 'GUNG HO' (2000), delivered all sorts of emotions, from its opener, 'ONE VOICE' (a tribute to the work of Mother Teresa) to the heartbreaking 'LO AND BEHOLDEN', all marked a fine return to form for the former goddess of punk. • **Songwriters:** Lyrics PATTI, some music KAYE. Covered HEY JOE (Jimi Hendrix) / LAND OF A THOUSAND DANCES (Cannibal & The Headhunters) / MY GENERATION (The Who) / GLORIA (Them) / SO YOU WANNA BE A ROCK'N'ROLL STAR (Byrds) / 5-4-3-2-1 (Manfred Mann) / DOWNTOWN TRAIN (Tom Waits) / WICKED MESSENGER (Bob Dylan) / WHEN DOVES CRY (Prince). • **Trivia:** In 1974, she co-wrote with ex-boyfriend ALLEN LANIER, his groups' (BLUE OYSTER CULT) 'Career Of Evil'. Her albums were produced by JOHN CALE (1st) / JACK DOUGLAS (2nd) / JIMMY IOVINE (3rd) / TODD RUNDGREN (4th) / FRED SMITH and JIMMY IOVINE (1988).

Album rating: HORSES (*9) / RADIO ETHIOPIA (*7) / EASTER (*7) / WAVE (*6) / DREAM OF LIFE (*5) / GONE AGAIN (*6) / PEACE AND NOISE (*6) / GUNG HO (*6) / LAND (1975-2002) compilation (*8)

PATTI SMITH – vocals, poetry / with **LENNY KAYE** – guitar / **RICHARD SOHL** – piano

not iss. | M.E.R.

Aug 74. (7") *<601>* **HEY JOE. / PISS FACTORY** [–] [ ]
(UK-iss.Mar78 on 'Sire'; SRE 1009)

— added **IVAN KRAL** – bass, guitar, piano / **JAY DEE DAUGHERTY** – drums

Arista | Arista

Dec 75. (lp) *(ARTY 122) <4066>* **HORSES** [ ] [47]
– Gloria / Redondo Beach / Birdland / Free money / Kimberly / Break it up / Land: Horses – Land of a thousand dances – La mer (de) / Elegie. *(re-iss. Aug88 lp/c/cd; 201/401/252-112) (cd re-iss. Jul96+=; 18827-2)* – My generation (live).

Apr 76. (7") *(ARIST 47)<AS 0171>* **GLORIA. / MY GENERATION (live)** [ ] [ ]
(re-iss. 12"-Sep77; ARIST 12135)

Oct 76. (lp/c) *(SPARTY/TCSPARTY 1001) <4097>* **RADIO ETHIOPIA** [ ] [ ]
– Ask the angels / Ain't it strange / Poppies / Pissing in the river / Pumping (my heart) / Distant fingers / Radio Ethiopia / Abyssinia. *(re-iss. Aug88 lp/c/cd; 201/401/251-117) (re-iss. cd Jul96; 18825-2)*

— Her tour featured **LEIGH FOXX** – bass repl. SOHL. Others augmenting at the time **ANDY PALEY** (ex-ELLIOT MURPHY) + **BRUCE BRODY** – keyboards (ex-JOHN CALE)

PATTI SMITH GROUP

with **KAYE, KRAAL, DAUGHERTY, BRODY + SOHL**

Mar 78. (7") *(ARIST 181) <AS 0318>* **BECAUSE THE NIGHT. / GOD SPEED** [5] [13]

Mar 78. (lp/c) *(SPARTY/TCSPARTY 1043) <4171>* **EASTER** [16] [20]
– Till victory / Space monkey / Because the night / Ghost dance / Babelogue / Rock'n'roll nigger / Privilege (set me free) / We three / 25th floor / High on rebellion / Easter. *(re-iss. Jan83 on 'Fame' lp/c; FA/TCFA 3058) (re-iss. Aug88 lp/c/cd; 201/401/251-128) (re-iss. cd Jul96; 18826-2)*

Jun 78. (7") *(ARIST 191)* **PRIVILEGE (SET ME FREE). / ASK THE ANGELS** [72] [–]
(12"+=) *(ARIST 12191)* – 25th floor (live) / Bablefield (live).

— **FRED 'Sonic' SMITH** – drums (ex-MC5) repl. DAUGHERTY to TOM VERLAINE

May 79. (7") *(ARIST 264)* **FREDERICK. / FIRE OF UNKNOWN ORIGIN** [63] [–]

May 79. (lp/c) *(SPART/TCART 1086) <4221>* **WAVE** [41] [18]
– Frederick / Dancing barefoot / Citizen ship / Hymn / Revenge / So you want to be a rock'n'roll star / Seven ways of going / Broken flag / Wave. *(re-iss. Aug88 lp/c/cd; 201/401/251-139) (re-iss. cd Jul96; 18829-2)*

Jun 79. (7") *<AS 0427>* **FREDERICK. / FREDERICK (live)** [–] [90]

Jul 79. (7") *(ARIST 281)* **DANCING BAREFOOT. / 5-4-3-2-1 (live)** [ ] [–]

Aug 79. (7"m) *<AS 0453>* **SO YOU WANT TO BE A ROCK'N'ROLL STAR. / 5-4-3-2-1 / FIRE OF UNKNOWN ORIGIN** [–] [ ]

Sep 79. (7") *(ARIST 291)* **SO YOU WANT TO BE A ROCK'N'ROLL STAR. / FREDERICK (live)** [ ] [–]

— PATTI retired Mar'80 with her new husband FRED SMITH to bring up children. BRUCE BRODY was another to join ex-TELEVISION singer TOM VERLAINE's band.

PATTI SMITH

re-appeared in 1988 with still **SOHL, DAUGHERTY & SONIC**

Fierce | Fierce

Feb 88. (7"m) *(white label)* **BRIAN JONES. / STOCKINGED FEET / JESUS CHRIST** [ ] [–]

Arista | Arista

Jul 88. (7")<US-c-s> *(109877) <AS1/CAS 9689>* **PEOPLE HAVE THE POWER. / WILD LEAVES** [ ] [ ]
(12"+=) *(609877)<AD1 9688>* – Where duty calls.
(cd-s++=) *(659877)* – ('A'-album version).

Jul 88. (lp/c/cd) *(209/409/259-172) <8453>* **DREAM OF LIFE** [70] [65]
– People have the power / Going under / Up there, down there / Paths that cross / Dream of life / Where duty calls / (I was) Looking for you / The Jackson song. *(re-iss. cd.Apr92;) (cd re-iss. Jul96; 18828-2)*

— RICHARD SOHL was to die from a cardiac arrest on 3 Jun'90. PATTI returned to reciting and recording her poetry in 1995. Now with some of her original group (**DAUGHERTY + KAYE**), **TONY SHANAHAN** – bass / **LUIS RESTO** – keyboards and on some **TOM VERLAINE** – guitar (ex-TELEVISION) / **OLIVER RAY** – guitars. Album featured guest spots from JOHN CALE, JEFF BUCKLEY and JANE SCARPANTONI – cello

Jul 96. (cd/c) *(74321 38474-2/-4) <18747>* **GONE AGAIN** [44] [55]
– Gone again / Beneath the Southern Cross / About a boy / My madrigal / Summer cannibals / Dead to the world / Wing / Ravens / Wicked messenger / Fireflies / Farewell reel.

Aug 96. (cd-ep) *(74321 40168-2)* **SUMMER CANNIBALS / COME BACK LITTLE SHEEBA / GONE AGAIN (live) / PEOPLE HAVE THE POWER** [ ] [–]
(cd-ep) *(74321 40299-2)* – ('A'side) / People have the power (live) / Beneath the Southern cross / Come in my kitchen.

— **OLIVER RAY** ; repl. RESTO

Nov 97. (cd/c) *<(07822 18986-2/-4)>* **PEACE AND NOISE** [ ] Sep97 [ ]
– Waiting underground / Whirl away / 1959 / Spell / Don't say nothing / Dead city / Blue poles / Death singing / Memento Mori / Last call.

Mar 00. (cd) *<(07822 14618-2)>* **GUNG HO** [ ] [ ]
– One voice / Lo and beholden / Boy cried wolf / Persuasion / Gone pie / China bird / Glitter in their eyes / Strange messengers / Grateful / Upright come / New party / Libbie's song / Gung ho.

– compilations, others, etc. –

Apr 83. (7") *Arista; (ARIST 513)* **BECAUSE THE NIGHT. / GLORIA** [ ] [–]
(12") *(ARIST 12513)* – ('A'side) / Redondo beach / Dancing barefoot / Free money.

Jul 84. (7") *Old Gold; (OG 9458)* **BECAUSE THE NIGHT. / GLORIA** [ ] [–]

Sep 91. (3xcd-box) *R.C.A.; (354.226)* **BOX SET** [ ] [ ]
– (RADIO ETHIOPIA / HORSES / WAVE albums)

Apr 02. (cd) *Arista; <(07822 14708-2)>* **LAND (1975-2002)** [ ] Mar02 [ ]
– Dancing barefoot / Babelogue / Rock'n'roll nigger / Gloria / Pissing in a

river / Free money / People have the power / Because the night / Frederick / Summer cannibals / Ghost dance / Ain't it strange / 1959 / Beneath the southern cross / Glitter in their eyes / Paths that cross / When doves cry. *(free cd+=)* – Piss factory (version) / Redondo beach (demo) / Distant fingers (demo) / 25th floor (live) / Come back little Sheba (version) / Wander I go (version) / Dead city (live) / Spell (live) / Wing (live) / Boy cried wolf (live) / Birdland (live) / Higher learning (live) / Notes to the future (live).

SMITHS

Formed: Manchester, England ... late '82 by (STEPHEN PATRICK) MORRISSEY and JOHNNY MARR. An intellectually intense, budding pop scholar and music journalist, MORRISSEY had previously had a book, 'James Dean Isn't Dead', published by 'Babylon' and had served a stint as UK president of The NEW YORK DOLLS fan club. MARR, meanwhile, had cut his six-string teeth in a variety of Manc beat combos, the pair initially forming a songwriting partnership and subsequently bringing in drummer MIKE JOYCE and bassist ANDY ROURKE to realise their vision of The SMITHS. Kicking off at The Ritz in Manchester, the group played a series of debut gigs around the country, earning rave reviews and attracting the interest of indie label, 'Rough Trade'. Turning down a deal with the local 'Factory', The SMITHS recorded a one-off single for 'Rough Trade', 'HAND IN GLOVE', the track championed by John Peel and subsequently topping the indie charts. Wooed by the majors, MORRISSEY and Co. stuck to their principals and inked a long-term contract with 'Rough Trade'. Later that year saw the release of the Top 30 hit, 'THIS CHARMING MAN', the first real glimpse of the The SMITHS' strange allure, MARR's rhythmic exuberance buoying MORRISSEY's morose verbal complexities. This was also the first time the Great British public were treated to the legendary sight of MORRISSEY sashaying and shimmying across the Top Of The Pops stage sporting a hearing aid and a back pocketfull of gladioli. Defiantly original, The SMITHS rapidly amassed a large, fiercely partisan fanbase with MORRISSEY as chief deity, MARR running a close second. A follow-up single, 'WHAT DIFFERENCE DOES IT MAKE', narrowly missed the Top 10 in early '84 with the breathlessly anticipated debut, 'THE SMITHS', hitting the shelves the following month. It didn't disappoint, a darkly ruminating kick in the eye for the tosspot music scene of the mid-80's and a compelling showcase for the unbounded potential of the MORRISSEY/MARR writing partnership. While the album missed the No.1 slot by a whisker, a high profile scrape with the tabloids followed soon after, the press hounds rounding on what they supposed to be ambiguous references to child abuse. The highly articulate MORRISSEY vocally put matters to right, the singer finally vindicated when a mother of one of the Moors murder victims openly supported the 'SUFFER THE LITTLE CHILDREN' track, another target of press speculation. The SMITHS were nothing if not controversial, MORRISSEY's pro-miserablist, anti-royalist and openly celibate stance making him the first real 'bedsit' non-pop star and drawing more and more attention to the group. No bad thing of course, when the music was as good as 'HEAVEN KNOWS I'M MISERABLE NOW' and 'WILLIAM, IT WAS REALLY NOTHING', another couple of fine Top 20 singles released later that summer. Both were included on the brilliant 'HATFUL OF HOLLOW' (1984) set along with a number of BBC session recordings and a few new tracks, notably the haunting 'PLEASE PLEASE PLEASE LET ME GET WHAT I WANT' and one of The SMITHS' trump cards, 'HOW SOON IS NOW' (previously released as a B-side to 'WILLIAM ...' and subsequently as a single in its own right in early '85), a churning mantra presumably laying bare the depths of MORRISSEY's tortured soul with its bitter lyrical plea; that pop/dance outfit SOHO later managed to incorporate its ominous guitar reverb into a club hit is surely one of the great wonders of modern music. The following month saw the release of the acclaimed 'MEAT IS MURDER', MORRISSEY partly substituting the navel gazing of old for a more socially-pointed stance; slap happy headmasters, teenage thugs, child abusers and of course, those partial to a bit of steak, being the prime targets of the frontman's razor-sharp lyrical barbs. MORRISSEY wasn't hogging all the limelight, however, MARR's nimble fingered genius on the likes of 'THAT JOKE ISN'T FUNNY ANYMORE' seeing him touted as the greatest British guitarist since ERIC CLAPTON. The album gave the group their first No.1, solidifying their position as the biggest "indie" band of the decade, The SMITHS now at the peak of their powers. Next up was the irrepressible 'THE BOY WITH THE THORN IN HIS SIDE' and the scathing wit of 'BIGMOUTH STRIKES AGAIN', both featured on, and acting as preludes to 'THE QUEEN IS DEAD' (1986). Though the album was delayed due to record company hassles, with personnel difficulties (ROURKE briefly kicked out for heroin abuse, the addition of CRAIG GANNON) also arising, it remains The SMITHS' magnum opus and, for many, the album of the decade. Effortlessly segueing from the darkly claustrophobic (the stinging social commentary of the title track and to a lesser extent, the lugubrious 'NEVER HAD NO ONE EVER') to the whimsically witty ('VICAR IN A TUTU') and on to the heartbreakingly poignant ('THERE IS A LIGHT THAT NEVER GOES OUT'), the album was breathtaking in its emotional sweep and musical focus. Though they would never quite reach those heights again, The SMITHS' highly prolific recording schedule continued apace with the anthemic 'PANIC' (indie kids delighting in its clarion call of 'Hang the DJ') and the breezy 'ASK', probably The SMITHS most commercial moment. The fact that, like most of their singles, it failed to break the Top 10, led to the group announcing a split with 'Rough Trade' and a new deal with 'E.M.I.'. Further controversy followed around this time as CRAIG GANNON was sacked, the guitarist duly sueing the group. Early '87 saw the release of another semi-compilation of old and new material, 'THE WORLD WON'T LISTEN', essential if only for the classic MORRISSEY angst of 'HALF A PERSON' and the sublime 'OSCILLATE WILDLY'. Though the wellspring of the MORRISSEY/MARR muse was seemingly bottomless, relations between the pair were reaching breaking point and by the release of the 'STRANGEWAYS HERE WE COME' (1987) opus, The SMITHS had already split. The album's morbid, fractured sound apparently confirmed the growing musical differences between the group's main protaganists, an inevitability perhaps, for such a consistently intense and perfectionist band. A posthumous live album, 'RANK' (1988) appeared the following year, documenting the London stop on The SMITHS' final frenzied tour of 1986. Various compilations were released in successive years, especially after 'Warners' secured the rights to The SMITHS' back catalogue in 1992, heralding a period when, ironically, most of the material was only available on US import! While MARR sessioned for the likes of The PRETENDERS and BRYAN FERRY before working with THE THE and forming ELECTRONIC with NEW ORDER's BERNARD SUMNER, MORRISSEY went on to a relatively successful, if comparitively drab solo career. As is so often the case, the sum of The SMITHS parts was always less than the whole, the group's influence on modern rock music incalculable, their unique sound echoing through the strains of countless indie success stories and untold hopefuls alike. • **Songwriters:** Lyrics – MORRISSEY / music –

MARR, except HIS LATEST FLAME (Elvis Presley) / GOLDEN LIGHTS (Twinkle).

Album rating: THE SMITHS (*10) / HATFUL OF HOLLOW part compilation (*9) / MEAT IS MURDER (*10) / THE QUEEN IS DEAD (*10) / THE WORLD WON'T LISTEN part compilation (*8) / STRANGEWAYS HERE WE COME (*8) / LOUDER THAN BOMBS import (*8) / RANK (*7) / BEST . . . I compilation (*10) / BEST II compilation (*9) / THE VERY BEST OF THE SMITHS compilation (*8)

MORRISSEY (b. STEPHEN PATRICK MORRISSEY, 22 May'59) – vocals (ex-NOSEBLEEDS) / **JOHNNY MARR** (b. JOHN MAHER, 31 Oct'63) – guitar, harmonica, mandolins, piano / **ANDY ROURKE** (b.1963) – bass / **MIKE JOYCE** (b. 1 Jun'63) – drums

Rough Trade | Sire

May 83. (7") *(RT 131)* **HAND IN GLOVE. / HANDSOME DEVIL** [ ] [–]

Nov 83. (7") *(RT 136)* **THIS CHARMING MAN. / JEANE** [25] [–]
(12") *(RTT 136)* – ('A'side) / Accept yourself / Wonderful woman.

Jan 84. (7") *(RT 146)* **WHAT DIFFERENCE DOES IT MAKE?. / BACK TO THE OLD HOUSE** [12] [–]
(12"+=) *(RTT 146)* – These things take time.

Feb 84. (lp/c) *(ROUGH/+C 61)* <25065> **THE SMITHS** [2] [ ]
– Reel around the fountain / You've got everything now / Miserable lie / Pretty girls make graves / The hand that rocks the cradle / Still ill / Hand in glove / What difference does it make? / I don't owe you anything / Suffer little children. *(cd-iss. May87; ROUGHCD 61) (cd re-iss. 1989 on 'Line'; LICD 9.00308) (re-iss. cd/c)(ltd-10"lp Nov93 on 'WEA'; 4509 91892-2/-4)(SMITHS 1)*

May 84. (7") *(RT 156)* **HEAVEN KNOWS I'M MISERABLE NOW. / SUFFER LITTLE CHILDREN** [10] [ ]
(12"+=) *(RTT 156)* – Girl afraid.

Aug 84. (7") *(RT 166)* **WILLIAM, IT WAS REALLY NOTHING. / PLEASE PLEASE PLEASE LET ME GET WHAT I WANT** [17] [ ]
(12"+=) *(RTT 166)* – How soon is now?

Nov 84. (lp/c) *(ROUGH/+C 76)* **HATFUL OF HOLLOW** (with BBC sessions *) [7] [–]
– William, it was really nothing / What difference does it make? * / These things take time * / This charming man * / How soon is now? / Handsome devil * / Hand in glove / Still ill * / Heaven knows I'm miserable now / This night has opened my eyes * / You've got everything now * / Accept yourself * / Girl afraid / Back to the old house * / Reel around the fountain * / Please please please let me get what I want. *(cd-iss. May87; ROUGHCD 76) (re-iss. cd/c)(ltd-d10"lp Nov93 on 'WEA'; 4509 91893-2/-4)(SMITHS 2)*

Jan 85. (7") *(RT 176)* **HOW SOON IS NOW?. / WELL I WONDER** [24] [–]
(12"+=) *(RTT 176)* – Oscillate wildly.

Feb 85. (7") **HOW SOON IS NOW?. / THE HEADMASTER RITUAL** [–] [ ]

Feb 85. (lp/c) *(ROUGH/+C 81)* <25269> **MEAT IS MURDER** [1] [ ]
– The headmaster ritual / Barbarism begins at home / Rusholme ruffians / I want the one I can't have / What she said / Nowhere fast / That joke isn't funny anymore / Nowhere fast / Well I wonder / Meat is murder. *(cd-iss. May87; ROUGHCD 81) (re-iss. cd/c)(ltd-d10"lp Nov93 on 'WEA'; 4509 91895-2/-4)(SMITHS 3)*

Mar 85. (7") *(RT 181)* **SHAKESPEARE'S SISTER. / WHAT SHE SAID** [26] [ ]
(12"+=) *(RTT 181)* – Stretch out and wait.

Jul 85. (7") *(RT 186)* **THAT JOKE ISN'T FUNNY ANYMORE. / MEAT IS MURDER (live)** [49] [ ]
(12"+=) *(RTT 186)* – Nowhere fast / Shakespeare's siste / Stretch out and wait (all live).

Sep 85. (7") *(RT 191)* **THE BOY WITH THE THORN IN HIS SIDE. / ASLEEP** [23] [ ]
(12"+=) *(RTT 191)* – Rubber ring.

— added **CRAIG GANNON** – guitar, bass (ex-AZTEC CAMERA, ex-BLUEBELLS)

May 86. (7") *(RT 192)* **BIGMOUTH STRIKES AGAIN. / MONEY CHANGES EVERYTHING** [26] [ ]
(12"+=) *(RTT 192)* – Unloveable.

Jun 86. (lp/c) *(ROUGH/+C 96)* <25426> **THE QUEEN IS DEAD** [2] [70]
– Frankly Mr. Shankly / I know it's over / Never had no one ever / Cemetery gates / Big mouth strikes again / Vicar in a tutu / There is a light that never goes out / Some girls are bigger than others / The queen is dead / The boy with the thorn in his side. *(cd-iss. May87; ROUGHCD 96) (re-iss. cd/c)(ltd-d10"lp Nov93 on 'WEA'; 4509 91896-2/-4)(SMITHS 4)*

Jul 86. (7") *(RT 193)* **PANIC. / VICAR IN A TUTU** [11] [ ]
(12"+=) *(RTT 193)* – The draize train.

Oct 86. (7") *(RT 194)* **ASK. / CEMETRY GATES** [14] [ ]
(12"+=/c-s+=) *(RTT 194/+C)* – Golden lights.

— Reverted to a quartet, when GANNON left to join The CRADLE.

Feb 87. (7") *(RT 195)* **SHOPLIFTERS OF THE WORLD UNITE. / HALF A PERSON** [12] [ ]
(12"+=) *(RTT 195)* – London.

Feb 87. (lp/c/cd) *(ROUGH/+C/CD 101)* **THE WORLD WON'T LISTEN** (part compilation) [7] [–]
– Panic / Ask / London / Big mouth strikes again / Shakespeare's sister / There is a light that never goes out / Shoplifters of the world unite / The boy with the thorn in his side / Asleep / Unloveable / Half a person / Stretch out and wait / That joke isn't funny anymore / Oscillate wildly / You just haven't earned it yet baby / Rubber ring. *(c+=)* – Money changes everything. *(re-iss. cd/c)(ltd-d10"lp Nov93 on 'WEA'; 4509 91898-2/-4)(SMITHS 5)*

Apr 87. (7") *(RT 196)* **SHEILA TAKE A BOW. / IS IT REALLY SO STRANGE?** [10] [ ]
(12"+=) *(RTT 196)* – Sweet and tender hooligan.

Jun 87. (d-lp/d-c/d-cd) *(ROUGH/+C/CD 255)* <25569> **LOUDER THAN BOMBS** (compilation) [38] Apr87 [62]
– Is it really so strange? / Sheila take a bow / Sweet and tender hooligan / Shoplifters of the world unite / Half a person / London / Panic / Girl afraid / Shakespeare's sister / William, it was really nothing / You just haven't earned it yet, baby / Golden lights / Ask / Heaven knows I'm miserable now / Unloveable / Asleep / Oscillate wildly / These things take time / Rubber ring / Back to the old house / Hand in glove / Stretch out and wait / This night has opened my eyes / Please, please, please, let me get what I want. *(cd re-iss. Feb95 on 'WEA'; 4509 93833-2)*

Aug 87. (7") *(RT 197)* **GIRLFRIEND IN A COMA. / WORK IS A FOUR-LETTER WORD** [13] [ ]
(12"+=/c-s+=) *(RTT 197/+C)* – I keep mine hidden.

Sep 87. (lp/c/cd) *(ROUGH/+C/CDR 106)* <25649> **STRANGEWAYS HERE WE COME** [2] [55]
– A rush and a push and the land is ours / I started something I couldn't finish / Death of a disco dancer / Girlfriend in a coma / Stop me if you think you've heard this one before / Last night I dreamt that somebody loved me / Unhappy birthday / Paint a vulgar picture / Death at one's elbow / I won't share you. *(re-iss. cd/c)(ltd-d10"lp Nov93 on 'WEA'; 4509 91899-2/-4)(SMITHS 6)*

Oct 87. (7") **STOP ME IF YOU THINK YOU'VE HEARD THIS ONE BEFORE. / I KEEP MINE HIDDEN** [–] [ ]

Nov 87. (7") *(RT 198)* **I STARTED SOMETHING I COULDN'T FINISH. / PRETTY GIRLS MAKE GRAVES** [23] [ ]
(12"+=) *(RTT 198)* – Some girls are bigger than others (live).
(c-s++=) *(RTT 198C)* – What's the world (live).

Dec 87. (7") *(RT 200)* **LAST NIGHT I DREAMT THAT SOMEBODY LOVED ME. / NOWHERE FAST (BBC version)** [30] [ ]
(12"+=) *(RTT 200)* – Rusholme Russians (BBC version).
(cd-s++=) *(RTT 200CD)* – William, it was really nothing (BBC version).

— they broke-up in August '87, ROURKE and JOYCE splintered with ADULT NET before joining MORRISSEY when he went solo.

– compilations, etc. –

Note; on 'Rough Trade' UK / 'Sire' US, unless otherwise mentioned.

Aug 88. (lp/c/cd/dat) *(ROUGH/+C/CD 126)* <25786> **RANK (live October '86)** [2] [77]
– The queen is dead / Panic / Vicar in a tutu / Ask / Rusholme ruffians / The boy with the thorn in his side / What she said / Is it really so strange? / Cemetry gates / London / I know it's over / The draize train / Still ill / Bigmouth strikes again / (Marie's the name) His latest flame – Take me back to dear old blighty. *(re-iss. cd/c)(ltd-d10"lp Nov93 on 'WEA'; 450991900-2/-4)(SMITHS 7)*

Nov 88. (3"cd-ep) *(RTT 215CD)* **THE HEADMASTER RITUAL / NOWHERE FAST (live) / MEAT IS MURDER (live) / STRETCH OUT AND WAIT (live)** [ ] [–]

Nov 88. (3"cd-ep) *(RTT 171CD)* **BARBARISM BEGINS AT HOME / SHAKESPEARE'S SISTER / STRETCH OUT AND WAIT** [ ] [–]

— (Note:- 12"singles from Jan84 / May84 / Sep85 / Jul86 / Oct86 were issued on 3"cd-ep Nov88 – add suffix of CD to cat no.).

Oct 88. (12"ep/cd-ep) *Strange Fruit; (SFPS/+CD 055)* **THE PEEL SESSIONS** (18.5.83) [ ] [-]
– What difference does it make? / Reel around the fountain / Miserable lie / Handsome devil.

—— Note; Below on 'WEA' UK/ 'Sire' US unless otherwise mentioned.

Jul 92. (7"/c-s) *(YZ 0001/+C)* **THIS CHARMING MAN. / WONDERFUL WOMAN / ACCEPT YOURSELF** [8] [-]
(cd-s+=) *(YZ 0001CD)* – Jeane.

Aug 92. (cd)(lp/c) *(4509 90044-2)(SMITHS 8/+C) <45042>* **BEST . . . 1** [1] [ ]
– This charming man / William, it was really nothing / What difference does it make / Stop me if you think you've heard it before / Girlfriend in a coma / Half a person / Rubber ring / How soon is now? / Hand in glove / Shoplifters of the world unite / Sheila take a bow / Some girls are bigger than others / Panic / Please please please let me get what I want.

Sep 92. (7"/c-s) *(YZ 0002/+C)* **HOW SOON IS NOW. / HAND IN GLOVE** [16] [-]
(cd-s+=) *(YZ 0002CD1)* – The queen is dead / Handsome devil / I started something I couldn't finish.
(cd-s+=) *(YZ 0002CD2)* – I know it's over / Suffer little children / Back to the old house.

Oct 92. (7"/c-s) *(YZ 0003/+C)* **THERE IS A LIGHT THAT NEVER GOES OUT. / HANDSOME DEVIL (live)** [25] [ ]
(cd-s+=) *(YZ 0003CD1)* – I don't owe you anything / Hand in glove / Jeane.
(cd-s+=) *(YZ 0003CD2)* – Money changes everything (live) / Some girls are bigger than others (live) / Hand in glove (live).

Nov 92. (cd)(lp/c) *(4509 90406-2)(SMITHS 9/+C)* **BEST II** [29] [ ]
– The boy with a thorn in his side / The headmaster ritual / Heaven knows I'm miserable now / Ask / Osciliate wildly / Nowhere fast / Still ill / That joke isn't funny anymore / Shakespeare's sister / Girl afraid / Reel around the fountain / Last night I dreamt somebody loved me / There is a light that never goes out.

Feb 95. (7"/c-s) *(YZ 0004/+C)* **ASK. / CEMETARY GATES** [62] [-]
(cd-s+=) *(YZ 0004CD)* – Golden lights.

Mar 95. (cd/c) *(4509 99090-2/-4)* **"SINGLES"** [5] [ ]
– Hand in glove / This charming man / What difference does it make? / Heaven knows I'm miserable now / William, it was really nothing / How soon is now? / Shakespeare's sister / That joke isn't funny anymore / The boy with the thorn in his side / Bigmouth strikes again / Panic / Ask / Shoplifters of the world unite / Sheila take a bow / Girlfriend in a coma / I started something I couldn't finish / Last night I dreamt that somebody loved me / There is a light that never goes out.

Jun 01. (cd) *(8573 88948-2)* **THE VERY BEST OF THE SMITHS** [30] [-]

SMOG

Formed: Silver Springs, Maryland, USA . . . 1988 by sole member, BILL CALLAHAN. The painfully introverted grandaddy of the American lo-fi scene (although he professes to loathe that particular term), CALLAHAN began releasing his bedroom creations in the late 80's as a series of mainly instrumental cassette-only affairs. All issued on his own 'Disaster' imprint, 'MACRAME GUNPLAY' (1988), 'COW' (1989), 'A TABLE SETTING' (1990) and 'TIRED MACHINE' (1990) set the tone for a debut album proper, 'SEWN TO THE SKY' (1991). This was originally released only in the States on the 'Drag City' label and carried on in the same vein as its skeletal predecessors; CALLAHAN only really began taking SMOG in a more conventionally song-structured direction with the 'FORGOTTEN FOUNDATION' (1992) album and only really started whetting critical appetites with 1993's acclaimed 'JULIUS CAESAR'. The latter set was recorded with sometime collaborator CYNTHIA 'CINDY' DALL, boasting sharper, more robust songwriting embellished with string flourishes and synth tinkling although the lyrical misery continued unabated. The mood blackened further on 1994's mini-album, 'BURNING KINGDOM', the reclusive pessimeister making WILL OLDHAM sound like a circus clown. Yet while CALLAHAN's sad-eyed music could be overbearingly claustrophobic, it was more often genuinely moving, the painstakingly recounted tales of everday heartbreak/failure featured on 'WILD LOVE' (1995) and the 'KICKING A COUPLE AROUND' EP offering up an almost voyeuristic view into the man's insular world. The bitter fruit of 'THE DOCTOR CAME AT DAWN' (1996) and 'RED APPLE FALLS' (1997) further confirmed BILL as the crown prince of sad-core, a label he'd no doubt detest even more than lo-fi. 'KNOCK KNOCK' (1999) was described as an album for teenagers and definitely one of his best, SMOG were now becoming the most popular one-man band in America. The man's ironic humour and love of wordplay were all too evident in the title of his umpteenth opus 'DONGS OF SEVOTION' (2000), wherein CALLAHAN knelt once more at the alter of his melancholy, minimalistic muse. Worshippers found much to praise in the likes of 'NINETEEN' and 'PERMANENT SMILE', the high priest of pathos wringing as much emotion from his own faltering experience as the third person character sketches. In a (undoubtedly ironic) PRINCE-like move, BILL altered the SMOG moniker to (SMOG) for 'RAIN ON LENS' (2001), a continuation of 'DONGS..' hypnotic studies of the human condition. The unrelentingly prolific Mr. CALLAHAN was back in 2003 with 'SUPPER', his most immediate, amiable and candid work in many a year. Longtime SMOG observers will be comforted to know that he's lost none of his morose genius although there were hints of contentment here, not least the really rather sweet 'OUR ANNIVERSARY'.

Album rating: SEWN TO THE SKY (*6) / FORGOTTEN FOUNDATION (*7) / JULIUS CAESAR (*8) / BURNING KINGDOM mini (*5) / WILD LOVE (*7) / THE DOCTOR CAME AT DAWN (*8) / RED APPLE FALLS (*7) / KNOCK KNOCK (*8) / DONGS OF SEVOTION (*7) / RAIN ON LENS (*7) / ACCUMULATION: NONE collection (*6)

BILL CALLAHAN (b. 1966) – vocals, guitar, etc

not iss. — Disaster

1988. (c) *<none>* **MACRAME GUNPLAY** [-] [ ]

1989. (m-c) *<none>* **COW** [-] [ ]
– Cow / Frozen at sea / Fusilage / On a scale of fish to fish / Stash / Souped up / Black olive / Hoover penny.

1990. (c) *<none>* **A TABLE SETTING** [-] [ ]

1990. (c) *<none>* **TIRED TAPE MACHINE** [-] [ ]

1990. (lp) *<none>* **SEWN TO THE SKY** [-] [ ]
– Souped up II / Kings tongue / Garb / Hollow out cakes / Confederate bills and pinball slugs / Coconut cataract / Fruit bats / Peach pit / Disgust / Russian winter / Polio shimmy / Smog / Lost my key / Fried piper / Fables / Puritan work ethic / A jar of sand / I want to tell you about a man / Olive drab spectre / The weightlifter. *<(re+UK-iss.Nov95 on 'Drag City'; DC 74)>*

not iss. — #1 hits

1991. (7"ep) *<none>* **MY SHELL / ASTRONAUT. / (tracks by SUCKDOG)** [-] [ ]

Matador — Drag City

Aug 91. (7"ep) *<DC 6>* **FLOATING EP** [-] [ ]
– Mice / Turb / Floating / Red apples / Hole in the heart / Cursed.

May 92. (lp/cd) *<DC 13>* **FORGOTTEN FOUNDATION** [-] [ ]
– Burning kingdom / Filament / High school freak / Your dress / Barometric pressure / Guitar innovator / Evil tyrant / Head of stone I / Head of stone II / Long gray hair / Kiss your lips (with LISA CARVER) / Bad ideas for country songs I / Bad ideas for country songs II / Dead river / Bad investment / Brown bag / Let me have that jar back / This insane cop / 97th street / Do the bed / I'm smiling / With a green complexion. *<cd re-iss. Jan96 & Jan01; same>*

—— now with **CINDY DALL** – vocals, etc

Jul 94. (cd/lp) *(OLE 097-2/-1) <DC 31>* **JULIUS CAESAR** [ ] Nov93 [ ]
– Strawberry rash / Your wedding / 37 push ups / Stalled on the tracks / One less star / Golden / When you talk / I am star wars / Connections / When the power goes out / Chosen one / What kind of angel / Stick in the mud. *(cd re-iss. Jan01 on 'Domino'; REWIGCD 005)*

City Slang — Drag City

Nov 94. (m-cd/m-lp) *(EFA 04946-2/-1) <DC 41>* **BURNING KINGDOM** [ ] Jul94 [ ]
– My shell / Renee died 1:45 / My family / Drunk on the stars / Not lonely anymore / Desert.

Mar 95. (7"yellow) *(EFA 04951-7) <DC 38>* **A HIT. / WINE STAINED LIPS** Mar94

Apr 95. (cd/lp) *(EFA 04952-2/-1) <DC 60>* **WILD LOVE** Mar95
– Bathysphere / Wild love / Sweet Smog children / Bathroom floor / Emperor / Limited capacity / It's rough / Sleepy Joe / Candle / Be hit / Prince alone in the studio / Goldfish bowl. *(cd re-iss. Jan01 on 'Domino'; REWIGCD 007)*

Domino Drag City

May 96. (12"ep/cd-ep) *(RUG 45 T/CD) <DC 81>* **KICKING A COUPLE AROUND EP** Apr96
– Your new friend / Back in school / I break horses / The orange glow of a stranger's living room.

Sep 96. (cd/lp) *(WIG CD/LP 27) <DC 95>* **THE DOCTOR CAME AT DAWN**
– You moved in / Somewhere in the night / Lize / Spread your bloody wings / Carmelite light / Everything you touch becomes a crutch / All your women things / Whistling teapot (rag) / Four hearts in a can / Hangman blues.

Nov 96. (7") *(HM 19)* **CAME BLUE. / SPANISH MOSS** – German –
(above issued on 'Hausmusik') <below on 'Shrimper'>

1997. (d7") *<SHR7 04>* **SWING SET** –

May 97. (cd/lp) *(WIG CD/LP 35) <DC 116>* **RED APPLE FALLS**
– Morning papers / Blood red bird / Red apples / I was a stranger / To be of use / Red apple falls / Ex-con / Inspirational / Finer days.

Oct 97. (7") *(RUG 58)* **EX-CON. / JUST LIKE NAPOLEON** –
(cd-s+=) *(RUG 58CD)* – Little girl shoes / Duckpond blues.

Dec 98. (7") *<DC 161>* **HELD. / COLD-BLOODED OLD TIMES** –

Jan 99. (7") *<DC 167>* **LOOK NOW. / THE ONLY MOTHER** –

Feb 99. (cd/lp) *(WIG CD/LP 60) <DC 161>* **KNOCK KNOCK** Jan99
– Let's move to the country / Held / River guard / No dancing / Teenage spaceship / Cold-blooded old times / Sweet treat / Hit the ground running / I could drive forever / Left only with love.

May 99. (7") *(RUG 83)* **HELD. / LOOK NOW / THE ONLY MOTHER** –
(cd-s+=) *(RUG 83CD)* – Held (acoustic).

Oct 99. (7") *(RUG 98)* **COLD-BLOODED OLD TIMES. / ('A'acoustic)** –
(cd-s+=) *(RUG 98CD)* – I break horses / Chosen one.

Apr 00. (cd/d-lp) *(WIG CD/LP 76) <DC 169>* **DONGS OF SEVOTION**
– Justice aversion / Dress sexy at my funeral / Strayed / The hard road / Easily led / Bloodflow / Nineteen / Distance / Devotion / Cold discovery / Permanent smile.

Jul 00. (7") *(RUG 111) <DC 192>* **STRAYED. / BLOODFLOW (acoustic)**
(cd-s) *(RUG 111CD)* – COW (cassette tracks).

2000. (cd-ep) **THE MANTA RAYS OF TIME** –

—— <above iss. on 'Spunk' records>

Dec 00. (12"ep/cd-ep) *(RUG 118 T/CD) <196>* **'NEATH THE PUKE TREE**
– I was a stranger / Your sweet entrance / A jar of sound / Orion obscured by stars / Coacheecayoo.

Sep 01. (cd/lp) *(WIG CD/LP 99) <DC 187>* **RAIN ON LENS**
– Rain on lens 1 / Song / Natural decline / Keep some steady friends around / Dirty pants / Lazy rain / Short drive / Live as if someone is always watching you / Rain on lens 2 / Revanchism.

Apr 03. (cd/lp) *(WIG CD/LP 127) <DC 235>* **SUPPER** Mar03
– Feather by feather / Butterflies drowned in wine / Morality / Ambition / Vessel in vain / Truth serum / Our anniversary / Driving / A guiding light.

– compilations, etc. –

Nov 02. (cd/lp) *Domino; (WIG CD/LP 116) / Drag City; <DC 200CD>* **ACCUMULATION: NONE** (B-sides)
– Astronaut / A hit / Spanish moss / Chosen one / Floating / Real live dress / Came blue / Little girl shoes / Cold blooded old times / White ribbon / I break horses / Hole in the heart.

SNOOP DOGGY DOGG

Born: CALVIN BROADUS, 20 Oct'72, Long Beach, California, USA; he was given his nickname by his mother(!). Unleashed in 1993 when his debut DR. DRE (ex-N.W.A.) produced album 'DOGGYSTYLE' created furore amongst the moral majority in America, SNOOP swaggered his way to the forefront of the new G-funk strain of Gangsta-rap like a doberman on heat. Signed to DRE's 'Death Row' label (he also guested on the man's 'Nuthin' But A G Thang'), the canine sensation sniffed out a Top 10 position for the 'WHAT'S MY NAME' single before notching up record-breaking sales of his chart-topping debut album. Before the record's release (August '93), however, SNOOP (a convicted teenage drug dealer) was arrested when a local hood was killed; shots were allegedly fired by his bodyguard MALIK out of SNOOP's car. The rapper was released after being bailed for a $1m and early in 1994, he hit London under a storm of protest, not least from tabloid press; The Daily Star's memorable front page headline ran; 'KICK THIS EVIL BASTARD OUT!'. Of course, this only spurred on Brit youngsters' enthusiasm, especially after he was premiered on C4's 'The Word', complete with interview; a film 'Murder Was The Case' (based around a track SNOOP was famous for) hit Stateside No.1 in November '94. Never out of the headlines on drug charges, etc, SNOOP was finally acquitted of murder and manslaughter early '96 (a mistrial was the judge's verdict). Later that year, the rapper delivered his sophomore set, 'THA DOGGFATHER', another chart-topper (Top 20 in the UK). SNOOP DOGG was indeed back on the prowl, the man even delighting his pop fans with a hit cover of the Gap Band's 'Snoop's UPSIDE YOUR HEAD'. From 1997-1999, SNOOP was never far from some sort of controversial headlines (either drug busts, shootings or whatever) and it was amazing he found the time to deliver two further long-players, 'DA GAME IS TO BE TOLD, NOT TO BE SOLD' (1998) and 'TOP DOGG' (1999). 'THA LAST MEAL' (2000) featured a whole host of up-and-coming producers such as JELLY ROLL, MEECH WELLS and SOOPAFLY. Although sounding as if it was entirely produced by DR. DRE (who actually produced three tracks), "tha set" failed because of SNOOP alone, who's half-baked half rhymes sounded more and more like a stoned old man with each release. Add this to the fact that SNOOP had nothing left to rap about (he did bitches, blunts and bouncy cars about three albums ago) and that he basically regurgitated his old material said something about the mainstream West Coast scene. SNOOP subsequently went into making a soft-core porn video available through tha intanet. The canine one redeemed himself to a certain degree with 'PAID THA COST TO BE DA BO$$' (2002), the JAMES BROWN reference of the title not the only nod to the past with a stodgy update of Parliament classic 'Flashlight', imaginatively entitled 'STOPLIGHT'. A rehash of Robert Palmer's 'I DIDN'T MEAN TO TURN YOU ON' was equally uninspired although SNOOP was in his element on the sleaze-hop of 'LOLLIPOP' and the two NEPTUNES productions, 'FROM THA CHUUUCH TO DA PALACE' and 'BEAUTIFUL' were probably the strongest tracks he's put his name to in many a year.

Album rating: DOGGYSTYLE (*7) / THA DOGGFATHER (*7) / DA GAME IS TO BE TOLD, NOT TO BE SOLD (*6) / TOP DOGG (*8) / THA LAST MEAL (*5) / DEATH ROW'S SNOOP DOGGY DOGG GREATEST HITS compilation (*7) / PAID THA COST TO BE THA BO$$ (*7)

SNOOP DOGGY DOGG – vocals / with The DOGG POUND & The DRAMATICS plus **WARREN G / KURUPT / NANCY FLETCHER / DAT NIGGA DAZ / D.O.C. RBX / THE LADY OF RAGE / LIL HERSHEY LOC (MALIK) / NATE DOGG**

Death Row- East West | Death Row- Interscope

Dec 93. (7"/c-s) *(A 8337/+C)* *<98340>* **WHAT'S MY NAME? / ('A'club mix)** [20] Nov93 [8]
(12"+=/cd-s+=) *(A 8337 T/CD)* – ('A'-Explicit mix) / ('A'instrumental) / Who am I (what's my name?).

Dec 93. (cd/c) *<(IND/INC 92279)>* **DOGGYSTYLE** [38] Nov93 [1]
– Bathtub / G funk intro / Gin and juice / Tha shiznit / Lodi dodi / Murder was the case / Seria killa / Who am I (what's my name)? / For all my niggaz & bitches / Aint no fun (if the homies cant have none) / Doggy Dogg world / GZ and hustlas / Pump pump. *(cd re-iss. Apr01 on 'Death Row'; DROW 116) (d-lp iss.Jul01; DROW 116LP)*

Feb 94. (7"/c-s) *(A 8316/+C)* *<98318>* **GIN AND JUICE / ('A'-Laid back mix)** [39] [8]
(12"+=/cd-s+=) *(A 8316 T/CD)* – (2-'A'mixes).

Aug 94. (c-s) *(A 8289C)* **DOGGY DOGG WORLD / ('A'-Perfecto mix)** [32] [–]
(12"+=/s12"+=/cd-s+=) *(A 8289 T/TX/CD)* – ('A'-Dr.Dre mix) / ('A'-Perfecto x-rated mix).

—— He stood trial for murder on the 13th of January '95. At the end of '94, he and 3 band members (RICHARD BROWN, DARRYL DANIEL + DELMAR ARNAUDE) were arrested and charged with possession of drugs. In Oct'95, SNOOP'S trial finally got underway, due to his attorney Johnnie Cochran being slightly busy with the O.J. Simpson case!. THA DOGG POUND album hit US No.1 in November '95. He was cleared of murder and attempted manslaughter early '96. While on bail, he had guested on 2 PAC's 'All Eyez on Me' album. Other credits were with NATE DOGG on his late 1996 US Top 40 single, 'Never Leave Me Alone'.

Nov 96. (cd/c/lp) *<(IND/INC/INTLP 90038)>* **THA DOGGFATHER** [15] [1]
– Intro / Tha Doggfather / Ride 4 me / Up jump tha boogie / Freestyle conversation / When I grow up / Snoop bounce / Gold rush / (Tear 'em off) Me & my doggz / You thought / Vapors / Groupie / 2001 / Sixx minutes / (O.J.) Wake up / Snoops upside ya head / Blueberry / Traffic jam / Doggyland / Downtown assassins / Outro. *(cd re-iss. Apr01 on 'Death Row'; DROW 117)*

Dec 96. (c-s) *(INC 95520)* **SNOOPS UPSIDE YA HEAD / ('A'mix)** [12] [–]
(cd-s+=) *(IND 95520)* – ('A'mixes).
(12"+=) *(INT 95520)* – ('A'mixes).

—— In Apr'97, SNOOP partnered the late 2PAC on a UK Top 20 single, 'WANTED DEAD OR ALIVE'.

Apr 97. (c-s/12"/cd-s) *(INC/INT/IND 95530)* **VAPORS. / ('A'live) / SNOOPS UPSIDE YA HEAD** [18] [ ]

Sep 97. (c-s/cd-s) *(664990-4/-5)* **WE JUST WANNA PARTY WITH YOU (mixes with JD NAS) / ESCOBAR 97** [21] [ ]
(cd-s+=) *(664990-2)* – Some cow fonque (more tea vicar).
(above on 'Columbia')

Jan 98. (c-s) *(INC 95550)* **THA DOGGFATHER / ('A'mix)** [36] [ ]
(cd-s) *(IND 95550)* – ('A'mixes).
(cd-s) *(INT 95550)* – ('A'mixes).

—— shortened his moniker to SNOOP DOGG

Priority | No Limit

Aug 98. (cd/d-lp) *(CDPTY/PTYLP 153)* *<50000>* **DA GAME IS TO BE SOLD, NOT TO BE TOLD** [28] [1]
– Snoop worls / Slow down / Woof! / Gin & juice II / Show me love / Hustle & ball / Don't let go / Tru tank dogs / Whatcha gon do? / Still a G thang / 20 dollars to my name / D.O.G.'s get lonely 2 / Ain't nut'in personal / DP gangsta / Game of life / See ya when I get there / Pay for P / Picture this / Doggz gonna get ya / Hoes, money & clout / Get 'bout it & rowdy.

Aug 98. (c-s/cd-s) *<53450>* **STILL A G THANG / FULL FLEDGED PIMPIN** [–] [19]

—— In Oct'98, SNOOP was credited on the massive US hit (minor UK one in November) for KEITH SWEAT, 'Come And Get With Me'.

Dec 98. (c-s/cd-s; as SNOOP DOGG featuring MYSTIKAL & FIEND) *<53462>* **WOOF / WOOF (instrumental) / IT'S ALL A T*T** [–] [62]

May 99. (cd) *(CDPTY 171)* *<50052>* **TOP DOGG** [48] [2]
– Dolomite (intro) / Buck 'em (with STICKY FINGERS) / Trust me (with SYLK E. FINE & SUGA FREE) / My heart goes boom / Dolomite / Snoopafella / In love with a thug / 6 bedtime stories / Down 4 my N's (with C-MURDER & MAGIC) / Betta days / Somethin bout yo bidness (with RAPHAEL) / B- please (with XZIBIT & NATE DOGG) / Doin' too much / Gangsta ride (with SILKK THE SHOCKER) / Ghetto symphony (with MIA X & FIEND) / Party with a D.P.G. / Buss 'n rocks / Just dippin' (with DR. DRE & JEWELL) / Don't tell (with WARREN G & MAUSEBURG) / 20 minutes (with GOLDIE LOC) / I love my momma.

Sep 99. (-; as SNOOP DOGG featuring XZIBIT & NATE DOGG) *<radio cut>* **B-PLEASE** [–] [77]

—— In Jun'00, SNOOP featured on MARIAH CAREY's US Top 30 hit, 'Crybaby'

—— SNOOP DOGG was also part of the team augmenting DR. DRE (i.e. on the hit single, 'The Next Episode')

Dec 00. (cd) *(CDPTY 199)* *<23225>* **THA LAST MEAL** [ ] [4]
– (intro) / Hennesey n Buddah / Snoop Dogg (what's my name part 2) / True lies / Wrong idea / Go away / Set it off / Stacey Adams / Lay low / Bring it on / Game court (skit) / Issues / Brake fluid (biiitch pump yo brakes) / Ready 2 ryde / Loosen' control / I can't swim / Leave me alone / Back up off me / Y'all gone miss me. *(re-iss. Mar01 cd/d-lp; CDPTYX/ PTYLP 199)* – hit No.62

Apr 01. (cd-s) *(PTYCD 134)* *<radio cut>* **SNOOP DOGG / Y'ALL GONE MISS ME** [13] Jan01 [77]
(12") *(PTYST 134)* – ('A'side) / ('A'-instrumental).
(c-s) *(PTYC 134)* – ('A'-clean) / Y'all gone miss me (clean) / Back up ho (clean).

Jul 01. (cd-s; by SNOOP DOGG featuring TYRESE & MR. TAN) *<158986>* **JUST A BABY BOY** [–] [90]

Aug 01. (12"/cd-s; by SNOOP DOGG featuring MASTER P, NATE DOGG, BUTCH CASSIDY & THA EASTSIDAZ) *(PTY T/CD 133)* *<radio cut>* **LAY LOW. / BRING IT ON / TRUE LIES** [ ] Mar01 [50]
(c-s) *(PTYC 133)* – ('A'-clean) / Bring it on (clean).

—— in Oct'01, SNOOP featured with R.L. & LIL' KIM on the hit single, 'Do U Wanna Roll (Dolittle Them)'

Nov 01. (cd) *(CDPTY 218)* *<50030>* **DEATH ROW'S SNOOP DOGGY DOGG GREATEST HITS** (compilation) [ ] [28]
– Nuthin' but a "G" thang (with DR. DRE) / Head doctor (with SWOOP G) / Gin and juice / Eastside party (with NATE DOGG) / Murder was the case (remix) / Ain't no fun (if the homies can't have none) (with WARREN G, KURUPT & NATT DOGG) / Doggfather (remix) / Midnight love (with RAPHAEL SAADIQ & DAZ DILLINGER) / Eastside / Who am I (what's my name)? / Doggy Dogg world (with THA DOGG POUND & DRAMATICS) / Too high (poly high) (with DAZ DILLINGER & BIG PIMPIN') / Vapors / Usual suspects (with THREAT) / Keep it real (with MACK 10, BAD AZZ & TECHNIEC) / Snoop bounce (with TIM COMMERFORD & TOM MORELLO).

Capitol | Capitol

Nov 02. (12"/cd-s) *(12CL/CDCL 841)* **FROM THA CHUUUCH TO DA PALACE. / (instrumental) / PAPER'D UP (clean)** [27] [77]

Nov 02. (cd/d-lp) *<(5 39157-0/-1)>* **PAID THA COST TO BE DA BO$$** [ ] [12]
– Don Doggy / Da bo$$ would like to see you / Stoplight / From tha chuuuch to da palace (with PHARRELL) / I believe in you (with LATOIYA WILLIAMS) / Lollipop (with JAY-Z, SOOPAFLY & NATE DOGG) / Ballin' (with DRAMATICS & LIL' HALF DEAD) / Beautiful (with PHARRELL & UNCLE CHARLIE WILSON) / Paper'd up (with MR. KANE & TRACI NELSON) / Wasn't your fault / Bo$$ playa (with ARCH BISHOP DON MAGIC JUAN) / Hourglass (with MR. KANE & GOLDIE LOC) / The one and only / I miss that bitch (with E-WHITE) / From Long Beach 2 Brick City (with REDMAN, NATE DOGG & WARREN G) / Suited n booted / You got what I want (with LUDACRIS & GOLDIE LOC) / Batman & Robin (with LADY OF RAGE & RBX) / A message 2 Fat Cuzz / Pimp slapp'd. *(re-dist.Apr03)* – hit UK No.64

—— in Feb'03, SNOOP & NATE DOGG featured on WC's hit, 'The Streets'

Mar 03. (12"; by SNOOP DOGG featuring PHARRELL & UNCLE CHARLIE WILSON) *(12CL 842)* **BEAUTIFUL. / (instrumental) / BALLIN' (clean version)** [23] [6]
(cd-s+=) *(CDCL 842)* – ('A'-video).

– compilations, others, etc. –

Aug 99. (cd-book) *Star Profile; (8246)* **STAR PROFILE** [ ] [–]

Dec 00. (cd) *Death Row; <(33349-2)>* **DEAD MAN WALKING** [ ] Nov00 [24]
(re-iss. Apr01; DROW 115)

Apr 01. (12"; by SNOOP DOGGY DOGG & 2PAC) *ZYX; (JIG 50201-2)* **FATHA FIGGA. /** [ ] [–]

Oct 02. (d-cd) *Virgin; (812882-2)* **THA LAST MEAL / TOPP DOGG** [ ] [ ]

Tha EASTSIDAZ

SNOOP DOGG, TRAY DEEE + GOLDIE LOC

		not iss.	Dogg House – TVT
Jan 00.	(cd-s) *<2041>* **G'D UP (mixes)**	–	47
Feb 00.	(cd) *<2040>* **SNOOP DOGG PRESENTS THA EASTSIDAZ**	–	8
Jun 00.	(cd-s; by SNOOP DOGG presents THA EASTSIDAZ featuring JAYE FELONY & BLAQTHOVEN) *<2004>* **GOT BEEF**	–	99
Aug 01.	(cd) *<2230>* **SNOOP DOGG PRESENTS THA EASTSIDAZ**	–	4

SNOW PATROL

Formed: Glasgow, Scotland . . . 1996 as POLARBEAR by Belfast-born Dundee University students GARY LIGHTBODY and MARK McCLELLAND; RICHARD COLBURN (with the assistance of BELLE & SEBASTIAN's STUART MURDOCH) augmented early on. Unfortunately, after only one single, 'STARFIGHTER PILOT' (for Glasgow's Stow College label, 'Electric Honey'), and due to the already established US outfit POLAR BEAR (note the space!) getting the dry hump – so to speak, they changed their moniker. Subsequently inking a deal with 'Jeepster' (home to BELLE . . .), SNOW PATROL gently breezed into the ears and minds of their audience via two singles, 'LITTLE HIDE' and ONE HUNDRED THINGS YOU SHOULD HAVE DONE IN BED', both highlights from the brittle guitar-pop band's debut long-player, 'SONGS FOR POLAR BEARS' (1998). Still located somewhere around Glasgow (with some sidelining with Scotland's indie conglomorate, REINDEER SECTION), the dreamy SNOW PATROL collected themselves together for a second set, 'WHEN IT'S ALL OVER WE STILL HAVE TO CLEAR UP' (2001). Bedsitter music, indeed. Another brilliant addition to GARY LIGHTBODY's already impressive CV came in the form of 'FINAL STRAW' issued in 2003. A strange mixture of rocky power ballads (in a good way!), PINK FLOYD-infused psychedelia and soft, melodic folk, the set pleased indie fan-boy types and rock/pop lovers alike. As diverse as it comes, switching from one musical genre to the next, LIGHTBODY maintained the casual instrumentation of the likes of his other project The REINDEER SECTION and even gave COLDPLAY a run for their money with the excellent rock-out of 'SOMEWHERE A CLOCK IS TICKING'. While other bands strive to be emo – emotional harcore – GARY LIGHTBODY proved that real emotions could be equally as subtle on soft, unwinding tracks such as 'SAME' as they could be on audacious guitar-led wig-outs. In short, a triumph in the ever confusing world of indie rock.

Album rating: SONGS FOR POLAR BEARS (*6) / WHEN IT'S ALL OVER WE STILL HAVE TO CLEAR UP (*6) / FINAL STRAW (*9)

GARY LIGHTBODY – guitar, vocals / **MARK McCLELLAND** – bass, keyboards / **RICHARD COLBURN** – drums, keyboards / with **STUART MURDOCH** – piano (of BELLE & SEBASTIAN)

		Electric Honey	not iss.
Jun 97.	(cd-s; as POLARBEAR) *(EHRCD 007)* **STARFIGHTER PILOT / HOLY COW / SAFETY**		–

—— **JOHN QUINN** – drums; repl. COLBURN

—— added live contributor: **TOM SIMPSON** – turntables

		Jeepster	Imprint
Feb 98.	(7") *(JPR7 004)* **LITTLE HIDE. / STICKY TEENAGE TWIN** (cd-s+=) *(JPRCDS 004)* – Limited edition / JJ.		–
May 98.	(7") *(JPR7 005)* **ONE HUNDRED THINGS YOU SHOULD HAVE DONE IN BED. / MY LAST GIRLFRIEND** (cd-s+=) *(JPRCDS 005)* – T.M.T. / I could stay away forever.		–
Aug 98.	(cd/lp) *(JPR CD/LP 004) <113141>* **SONGS FOR POLAR BEARS** – Downhill from here / Starfighter pilot / The last shot ringing in my ears / Absolute gravity / Get balsamic vinegar . . . quick you fool / Mahogany / NYC / Little hide / Make up / Velocity girl / Days without paracetamol / Fifteen minutes old / Favourite friend / One hundred things you should have done in bed. *<US cd re-iss. 1999 on 'Never'; 4039>*		
Nov 98.	(7") *(JPR7 007)* **VELOCITY GIRL. / ABSOLUTE GRAVITY** (cd-s+=) *(JPRCDS 007)* – When you're right, you're right.		–
Jun 99.	(cd-s) *(JPRCDS 013)* **STARFIGHTER PILOT (the Spynci new radio edit) / RAZE THE CITY / RIOT, PLEASE** (cd-s) *(JPRCDS 013R)* – (remixes; Cut La Roc and Belle & Sebastian).		–

		Jeepster	Jeepster
Nov 00.	(cd-s) *(JPRCDS 020)* **ASK ME HOW I AM / IN COMMAND OF CARS / TALK TO THE TREES**		–
Mar 01.	(cd-s) *(JPRCDS 021)* **ONE NIGHT IS NOT ENOUGH / MONKEY MOBE / WORKWEAR SHOP**		–
Mar 01.	(cd/lp) *(JPR CD/LP 012) <4052>* **WHEN IT'S ALL OVER WE STILL HAVE TO CLEAR UP** – Never gonna fall in love again / Ask me how I am / Making enemies / Black and blue / Last ever lone gunman / If I'd found the right words to say / Batten down the hatch / One night is not enough / Chased by . . . I don't know what / On-off / An olive grove facing the sea / When it's all over we still have to clear up / Make love to me forever / Firelight.		

		Fiction – Polydor	not iss.
Aug 03.	(cd) *(9865408)* **FINAL STRAW** – How to be dead / Wow / Gleaming auction / Whatever's left / Spitting games / Chocolate / Run / Grazed knees / Ways & means / Tiny little fractures / Somewhere a clock is ticking / Same. *(bonus+=)* – We can run away now they're all dead and gone / Half the fun. above album hit UK No.3 in Feb'04		–
Sep 03.	(7") *(980935-1)* **SPITTING GAMES. / STEAL** (cd-s+=) *(980935-0)* – Brave / ('A'-video).	54	–

☐ SOFT BOYS (see under ⇒ HITCHCOCK, Robyn)

☐ SOFT CELL (see under ⇒ ALMOND, Marc)

SOFT MACHINE

Formed: Canterbury, England . . . 1966 by ex-WILDE FLOWERS members ROBERT WYATT and KEVIN AYERS, who met up with Australian beatnik, DAEVID ALLEN and former Oxford University student MIKE RATLEDGE. The others members of The WILDE FLOWERS (PYE HASTINGS & RICHARD COUGHLAN) went on to form CARAVAN. A trip to Majorca in 1966 by ALLEN and AYERS led to a chance meeting with a monied, freak-friendly American by the name of Wes Brunson, who agreed to finance the first incarnation of SOFT MACHINE, the fondly named MR. HEAD. Moving to London, the band regrouped and after phoning WILLIAM BURROUGHS to ask his permission, adopted the SOFT MACHINE moniker. Together with PINK FLOYD, the band formed the vanguard of the psychedelic revolution, playing such legendary London gigs as the International Times launch at the Roundhouse. Early in 1967, they were signed to 'Polydor' by CHAS CHANDLER, who employed the services of SOFTS fan JIMI HENDRIX on the B-side of their debut single, 'LOVE MAKES SWEET MUSIC' (1967). The single was basically a pop song and not entirely representative of the band's live free-form improvisation that took its cue from the avant-jazz of artists like ORNETTE COLEMAN and JOHN COLTRANE. After a gig in St. Tropez (where they played an hour long version of AYERS' 'WE DID IT AGAIN' to the assembled Parisian elite), ALLEN was refused re-entry to the UK due to an expired visa, remaining in France and subsequently forming uber-hippies, GONG. Pared down to a trio, SOFT MACHINE underwent a gruelling tour of America supporting JIMI HENDRIX. During a short break in the middle of the tour, the band recorded their eponymous debut for 'PROBE' records, a US-only affair which incredibly, still hasn't had a full UK release almost 30 years on. A pioneering hybrid of psychedelic jazz improvisation, the album was the first and last to feature KEVIN AYERS, who took off for IBIZA at the end of the US tour. Recruiting HENDRIX roadie HUGH HOPPER, the band recorded another album for 'Probe' to fulfil contractual obligations. 'SOFT MACHINE VOL.2' (1969) was another idiosyncratic classic, containing a backwards rendition of the alphabet and a multitude of highbrow cultural references. Employing such live instrumentation as saxophone, trombone and cornet, the band increasingly moved towards jazz fusion and 'THIRD' (1970) was largely instrumental, save for WYATT's sublime meditation, 'MOON IN JUNE'. The other band members refused to have any serious involvement with the song, a crucial factor in WYATT's eventual split from the group. As SOFT MACHINE moved further into tepid jazz-rock territory, WYATT became increasingly frustrated and was eventually pushed out after 'FOURTH' (1971). While WYATT went on to form MATCHING MOLE before going solo, SOFT MACHINE released a further clutch of noodling albums before splitting in 1981. • **Songwriters:** Either AYERS (on debut lp only), WYATT (on first four albums only), or RATLEDGE and group. • **Trivia:** A John Peel session was recorded on the 21st of June '69 with their seminal 7-piece line-up. They were the first "rock" act to play the normally orchestrated 'Proms' at London's Albert Hall (1970). Non-originals, RATLEDGE and JENKINS became ADIEMUS, who had a UK Top 50 hit with their self-titled single (the theme from the TV ad for Delta Airlines), which featured vocalist MIRIAM STOCKLEY.

Album rating: THE SOFT MACHINE (*6) / SOFT MACHINE VOL.2 (*6) / THIRD (*7) / FOURTH (*6) / SOFT MACHINE FIFTH (*5) / SIX (*5) / SEVEN (*4) / BUNDLES (*4) / SOFTS (*4) / ALIVE AND WELL IN PARIS (*3) / THE LAND OF COCKAYNE (*3) / JET-PROPELLED PHOTOGRAPH early stuff (*6) / THE PEEL SESSIONS (*6) / AS IF . . . (*4) / RUBBER RIFF (*4) / VIRTUALLY (*4)

MIKE RATLEDGE – keyboards / **DAEVID ALLEN** (b. Australia) – guitar / **KEVIN AYERS** (b.16 Aug'45, Herne Bay, England) – bass, vocals (ex-WILDE FLOWERS) / **ROBERT WYATT** (b. ROBERT ELLIDGE, Bristol, England) – drums, vocals (ex-WILDE FLOWERS) / Note:- Other original American-born guitarist LARRY NOLAN left before debut 45.

Polydor not iss.

Feb 67. (7") *(56151)* **LOVE MAKES SWEET MUSIC. / FEELIN' REELIN' SQUEELIN'** [ ] [-]

— trimmed to a trio, when DAEVID ALLEN went to France to form GONG. He was deputised on tour only by ANDY SUMMERS. First 2 albums guest **BRIAN HOPPER** – saxophone (ex-WILDE FLOWERS)

Probe Probe

Nov 68. (7") *<452>* **JOY OF A TOY. / WHY ARE WE SLEEPING** [-] [ ]

Dec 68. (lp) *<PLP 4500>* **THE SOFT MACHINE** [-] [ ]
– Hope for happiness / Joy of a toy / Hope for happiness (reprise) / Why am I so short? / So boot if at all / A certain kind / Save yourself / Priscilla / Lullabye letter / We did it again / Plus belle qu'une poubelle / Why are we sleeping / Box 25-4 LID. *(UK-iss.Mar87 on 'Big Beat' lp/c; WIK A/C 57) (<cd-iss. Oct99 on 'M.C.A.'; MCAD 22064>)*

— **HUGH HOPPER** – bass (ex-WILDE FLOWERS) repl. AYERS who'd went solo

Apr 69. (lp) *(SPB 1002) <PLP 4505>* **SOFT MACHINE VOL.2** [ ] [ ]
– Pataphysical introduction (part I) / A concise British alphabet (part I) / Hibou, Anemone and bear / A concise British alphabet (part II) / Hulloder / Dada was here / Thank you Pierrot Lunaire / Have you ever been green? / Pataphysical introduction (part II) / Out of tunes / As long as he lies perfectly still / Dedicated to you but you weren't listening / Fire engine passing with bells clanging / Pig / Orange skin food / A door opens and closes / 10.30 returns to the bedroom. *(re-iss. 1974 on 'ABC'; ABCL 5004) (re-iss. May87 on 'Big Beat' lp/c; WIK A/C 58) (<cd-iss. Oct99 on 'M.C.A.'; MCAD 22065>)*

— added **ELTON DEAN** – saxophone (ex-BLUESOLOGY) / **LYN DOBSON** – flute, sax / **NICK EVANS** – trombone + **MARK CHARIG** – cornet (ex-BLUESOLOGY) both left before 3rd album. Added guests **JIMMY HASTINGS** – wind / **A.B. SPALL** – violin

C.B.S. Columbia

Jun 70. (d-lp) *(66246) <CGK 30339>* **THIRD** [18] [ ]
– Facelift / Slightly all the time / Moon in June / Out-Bloody-Rageous. *(re-iss. Jun88 on 'Decal' lp/c; LIKD/TCLIKD 35) (cd-iss. Mar93 on 'Beat Goes On'; BGOCD 180) (cd re-iss. Jul96 on 'Columbia'; 471407-2)*

— Now quartet, when LYN departed. Guests **HASTINGS** + **ALAN SKIDMORE** – sax

Feb 71. (lp) *(64280) <30754>* **FOURTH** [32] [ ]
– Teeth / Kings and queens / Fletcher's blemish / Virtually (parts 1-4). *(cd-iss. Apr93 on 'Sony Europe') (re-iss. cd Oct95 on 'One Way')*

— **JOHN MARSHALL** + **PHIL HOWARD** – drums (shared) repl. WYATT who went solo. **ELTON DEAN** added electric piano + **ROY BABBINGTON** – double bass (guested 3)

Jun 72. (lp) *(64806) <31604>* **FIFTH** [ ] [ ]
– All white / Drop / Mc / As if / LBO / Pigling bland / Bone. *(re-iss. 1979 on 'CBS-Embassy'; 31748) (cd-iss. Apr93 on 'Sony Europe') (re-iss. Sep95 on 'One Way')*

— **KARL JENKINS** – piano, saxophone repl. DEAN who stayed with JUST US (above newcomer alongside **RATLEDGE, HOPPER + MARSHALL**)

Feb 73. (d-lp) *(68214) <32260>* **SIX** (half live) [ ] [ ]
– Fanfare / All white / Between / Riff / 37 and a half / Geseolveut / E.P.V. / Lefty / Stumble / 5 from 13 (for Phil Seaman with love and thanks) / Riff II / The soft weed factor / Stanley stamps gibbon album (for B.O.) / Chloe and the pirates / 1983. *(cd-iss. Apr93 on 'Sony Europe')*

— **ROY BABBINGTON** – bass (guest) repl. HUGH HOPPER who went solo

Oct 73. (lp) *(65799) <32716>* **SEVEN** [ ] [ ]
– Nettle bed / Carolyn / Day's eye / Bone fire / Tarabos / D.I.S. / Snodland / Penny hitch / Block / Down the road / The German lesson / The French lesson. *(cd-iss. Apr93 on 'Sony Europe')*

— added **ALAN HOLDSWORTH** – guitar

Harvest not iss.

Apr 75. (lp) *(SHSP 4044)* **BUNDLES** [ ] [-]
– Hazard profile (parts 1-5) / Gone sailing / Bundles / Land of the bag snake / The man who waved at trains / Peff / Four gongs two drums / The floating world. *(re-iss. 1989 on 'See For Miles' lp/cd; SEE/+CD 283)*

— With last original RATLEDGE going solo and HOLDWORTH joining GONG, the remainder (**BABBINGTON, JENKINS + MARSHALL**) were joined by **ALAN WAKEMAN** – saxophone + **JOHN ETHERIDGE** – guitar

Jun 76. (lp) *(SHSP 4056)* **SOFTS** [ ] [-]
– Aubade / The tale of Taliesyn / Bab ban Caliban / Song of Aeolus / Out of season / Second bundle / Kayoo / The Camden tandem / Nexus / One over the eight / Etika. *(reiss.Jan90 on 'See For Miles' lp/cd; SEE/+CD 285)*

— **RIC SAUNDERS** – violin + **STEVE COOKE** – bass repl. WAKEMAN + BABBINGTON

Mar 78. (lp) *(SHSP 4083)* **ALIVE AND WELL – RECORDED IN PARIS** [ ] [-]
– White kite / Eos / Odds, bullets and blades (part 1 & 2) / Song of the sunbird / Puffin, huffin' / Number three / The nodder / Surrounder silence / Soft space. *(cd-iss. Mar90 on 'See For Miles'; SEECD 290) (cd re-iss. Nov95 on 'One Way';)*

Apr 78. (7") *(HAR 5155)* **SOFT SPACE. / (part 2)** [ ] [-]

— Folded 1979, but re-formed for one-off studio outing below. Musicians:- **ETHRIDGE, MARSHALL, HOLDSWORTH** plus sessioners **DICK MORRISSEY** – saxophone / **ALAN PARKER** – guitar / **JOHN TAYLOR** – keyboards / **RAY WARLEIGH** – flute / **JACK BRUCE** – bass

E.M.I. not iss.

Mar 81. (lp) *(EMC 3348)* **THE LAND OF COCKAYNE** [ ] [-]
– Over 'n' above / Lotus groves / Isle of the blessed / Panoramania / Behind the crystal curtain / Palace of glass / Hot biscuit slim / (Black) Velvet mountain / Sly monkey / A lot of what you fancy. *(cd-iss. Nov98 on 'One Way'; OWS 211833-2)*

— finally disbanded after above – until . . .

Elite — not iss.

May 91. (cd/c) *(ELITE 006 CD/MC)* **AS IF . . .** –
– Facelift / Slightly all the time / Kings and queens / Drop / Chloe and the pirates / As if. *(cd-iss. Sep93; same)*

– compilations, others, etc. –

Oct 74. (d-lp) *A.B.C.; (ABC 602)* **THE SOFT MACHINE COLLECTION** –
– (1st 2 albums) *(cd-iss. Sep89 on 'Big Beat'; CDWIKD 920)*

1976. (lp) *De Wolfe; (3331)* **RUBBER RIFF** –
– Crunch / Pavan / Jombles / A little floating music / Hi-power / Little Miss B / Splot / Rubber riff / Sam's short shuffle / Melina / City steps / Gentle turn / Porky / Travelogue. *(cd-iss. Nov94 on 'Voiceprint'; VP 190CD) (cd re-iss. Sep97 on 'Blueprint'; BP 190CD)*

Jan 77. (lp) *Charly; (CR 30014)* **AT THE BEGINNING** –
– That's how much I need you now / Save yourself / I should've / Jet propelled photographs / When I don't want you / Memories / You don't remember / She's gone / I'd rather be with you. *(re-iss. Mar83; CR 30196) (re-iss. Sep87 as 'JET PROPELLED PHOTOGRAPH' on 'Decal'; LIK 35) (cd-iss. Sep89 as 'JET PROPELLED PHOTOGRAPH' on 'Decal'; LIKCD 197) (re-iss. cd Jul97 on 'Charly'; CDGR 188) (cd re-iss. Apr03 on 'Snapper'; SNAP 133CD)*

Mar 77. (t-lp) *Harvest; (SHTW 800)* **TRIPLE ECHO** –

Aug 88. (cd/lp) *Reckless; (CD+/RECK 5)* **LIVE AT THE PROMS (live)** –

Sep 90. (cd/c/d-lp) *Strange Fruit; (SFR CD/MC/LP 201)* **THE COMPLETE PEEL SESSIONS** –

Dec 90. (cd/c/d-lp) *Castle; (CCS CD/MC/LP 281)* **THE UNTOUCHABLE COLLECTION (75-78)** –

Aug 92. (3xcd-box) *Magpie; (MAGPIE 2)* **SOFTS / ALIVE & WELL / BUNDLES** –

Apr 93. (m-cd) *Windsong; (WINCD 031)* **BBC RADIO 1 LIVE IN CONCERT (live)** –

Jun 94. (cd) *Windsong; (WINCD 056)* **BBC RADIO 1 LIVE IN CONCERT (live)** –

Jan 95. (cd) *Movieplay Gold; (MPG 74033)* **LIVE AT THE PARADISO** –
(re-iss. Oct96 on 'Blueprint'; BP 193CD)

Jun 95. (cd) *C5; (C5MCD 623)* **THE BEST OF SOFT MACHINE: THE HARVEST YEARS** –
(re-iss. May97; same)

Nov 96. (cd) *Cuniform; (RUNE 90)* **SPACED** –

Jun 97. (cd; with MARK LEEMAN & DAVEY GRAHAM) *Spalax; (14557)* **LONDON 1967** –

Jun 98. (cd) *Blueprint; (BP 290CD)* **LIVE 1970 (live)** –

Jun 98. (cd) *Cuniform; (RUNE 100)* **VIRTUALLY (live in Bremen)** –

Jan 00. (d-cd) *Cuniform; (<RUNE 130>)* **NOISETTE (live 4th January, 1970)**

Feb 01. (d-cd) *Mooncrest; (CRESTCD 062) / Sanctuary; <80259>* **MAN IN A DEAF CORNER: ANTHOLOGY 1963-1970** Mar01

May 01. (cd) *Neon; (NE 34531)* **THE SOFT MACHINE** –

Jul 01. (cd) *Voiceprint; (<VP 231CD>)* **SOFT MACHINE TURNS ON VOLUME 1**

Jul 01. (cd) *Voiceprint; (<VP 234CD>)* **SOFT MACHINE TURNS ON VOLUME 2**

May 02. (d-cd) *Voiceprint; (<VP 233CD>)* **FACELIFT** (live at Fairfield Hall, Croydon 26/4/1970)

Jun 02. (cd) *Cuniform; (<RUNE 170>)* **BACKWARDS**

Mar 03. (d-cd) *Hux; (<HUX 037>)* **BBC RADIO 1967-1971**

May 03. (d-cd) *Snapper; (<SMDCD 456>)* **KINGS OF CANTERBURY**

Sep 03. (d-cd) *Hux; (<HUX 047>)* **BBC RADIO 1971-1974**

☐ SOMATICS (see under ⇒ ULTRASOUND)

☐ SONIC BOOM (see under ⇒ SPACEMEN 3)

SONIC YOUTH

Formed: New York City, New York, USA ... early 1981 by THURSTON MOORE and KIM GORDON. They replaced an early embryonic rhythm section with LEE RANALDO and RICHARD EDSON. After numerous releases on various US indie labels (notably Glenn Branca's 'Neutral' records), they signed to 'Blast First'in the U.K. First up for the label was 'BAD MOON RISING' in 1985, showing them at their most menacing and disturbing, especially on the glorious 'DEATH VALLEY 69' (a macabre reference to killer Charles Manson) with LYDIA LUNCH providing dual vox. They subsequently secured a US deal with 'S.S.T.', heralding yet another socially passionate thrash effort with 'EVOL'. A sideline project, CICCONE YOUTH, saw KIM and the lads plus MIKE WATT (of fIREHOSE), take off MADONNA's 'INTO THE GROOVE(Y)', which became a surprise dancefloor fave. Two more classic pieces, 'SISTER' (1987) & 'DAYDREAM NATION' (1988), finally secured them a major deal with 'D.G.C.' (David Geffen Company). In the early 90's, they smashed into the UK Top 40 with the album 'GOO', featuring a cameo by CHUCK D (of PUBLIC ENEMY) on the track/single 'KOOL THING'. The album, which sweetened their garage-punk/art-noise collages with melodic hooks, also included their deeply haunting tribute to KAREN CARPENTER, 'TUNIC (SONG FOR KAREN)'. They supported PUBLIC ENEMY that year, also stepping out with NEIL YOUNG on his 'Ragged Glory' tour in '91 (much to the distaste of YOUNG's more conservative fans!). In 1992, many thought 'DIRTY' to be a disappointment, the record being overproduced and overtaken by their new rivals and labelmates NIRVANA. By the mid-late 90's, they had returned to ground roots with acoustic psychedelia and the albums, 'EXPERIMENTAL JET SET' (1994), 'WASHING MACHINE' (1995) and 'A THOUSAND LEAVES' (1998) were again lauded by the alternative music press. All members had also taken on side solo projects, KIM featuring in all-star punk-grunge affair, FREE KITTEN. SONIC YOUTH returned towards the end of the decade with an appropriately-titled set, 'GOODBYE 20th CENTURY' (1999), a record in which they took on the works of avant-garde composers CHRISTIAN WOLFF, JOHN CAGE and CORNELIUS CARDEW. 'NYC GHOSTS & FLOWERS' (2000) was also a tribute of sorts, inspired by the beat poets who once upon a time fed their wayward muse on the Big Apple's mean streets. Featuring an Allen Ginsberg-derived title and William Burroughs cover art, the album was only partly successful in capturing the wild-eyed passion of the era. Their first straight up rock'n'roll album (if SONIC YOUTH could ever be described as dealing in straight up rock'n'roll) in almost five years, 'MURRAY STREET' (2002) found RENALDO and Co (with JIM O'ROURKE now a fully paid up member) reining in much of their tendency to free-form noise experimentation with a refreshingly prudent approach to their too often wearingly familiar craft. • **Songwriters:** MOORE / RANALDO / GORDON compositions, except I WANNA BE YOUR DOG (Stooges) / TICKET TO RIDE + WITHIN YOU WITHOUT YOU (Beatles) / BEAT ON THE BRAT + others (Ramones) / TOUCH ME, I'M SICK (Mudhoney) / ELECTRICITY (Captain Beefheart) / COMPUTER AGE (Neil Young). Their off-shoot CICCONE YOUTH covered INTO THE GROOVE (Madonna) / ADDICTED TO LOVE (Robert Palmer) / IS IT MY BODY (Alice Cooper) / PERSONALITY CRISIS (New York Dolls) / CA PLANE POUR MOI (Plastic Bertrand) / MOIST VAGINA = (MV) (Nirvana). FREE KITTEN covered: OH BONDAGE UP YOURS (X-

Ray Spex). • **Trivia:** Early in 1989, they were featured on hour-long special TV documentary for Melvyn Bragg's 'The South Bank Show'.

Album rating: CONFUSION IS SEX (*6) / KILL YR IDOLS (*4) / BAD MOON RISING (*8) / EVOL (*8) / SISTER (*9) / DAYDREAM NATION (*9) / GOO (*9) / DIRTY (*7) / EXPERIMENTAL JET SET, TRASH AND NO STAR (*6) / WASHING MACHINE (*8) / A THOUSAND LEAVES (*6) / GOODBYE 20th CENTURY (*7) / NYC GHOSTS & FLOWERS (*4) / MURRAY STREET (*6) / Lee Ranaldo: FROM HERE TO INFINITY (*4) / EAST JESUS (*7) / Thurston Moore: PSYCHIC HEARTS (*8) / ROOT (*7)

THURSTON MOORE (b.25 Jul'58, Coral Gables, Florida) – vocals, guitar / **KIM GORDON** (b.28 Apr'53, Rochester, N.Y.) – vocals, bass / **LEE RANALDO** (b. 3 Feb'56, Glen Cove, N.Y.) – vocals, guitar repl. ANN DEMARIS / **RICHARD EDSON** – drums repl. DAVE KEAY

Neutral — not iss.

Feb 84. (m-lp) *(ND 01)* **SONIC YOUTH (live)** [–] German [–]
– The burning spear / I dreamt I dreamed / She's not alone / I don't want to push it / The good and the bad. *(re-iss. cd Oct87 on 'S.S.T.'; SSTCD 097)*

—— **JIM SCLAVUNOS** – drums repl. EDSON

Feb 84. (lp) *(ND 02)* **CONFUSION IS SEX** [–] German [–]
– Inhuman / The world looks red / Confusion is next / Making the nature scene / Lee is free / (She's in a) Bad mood / Protect me you / Freezer burn / I wanna be your dog / Shaking Hell. *(re-iss. cd Oct87 on 'S.S.T.'; SSTCD 096)*

—— **BOB BERT** – drums repl. SCLAVUNOS (still featured on 2 tracks)

Zensor — not iss.

Oct 83. (m-lp) *(ZENSOR 10)* **KILL YR. IDOLS** [–] German [–]
– Protect me you / Shaking Hell / Kill yr. idols / Brother James / Early American.

not iss. — Ecstatic Peace

1984. (c) *<none>* **SONIC DEATH (SONIC YOUTH LIVE)** [–] [ ]
– Sonic Death (side 1) / Sonic Death (side 2). *(UK cd-iss. Jul88 on 'Blast First'; BFFP 32CD>*

not iss. — Iridescence

Dec 84. (12"; by SONIC YOUTH & LYDIA LUNCH) *<1-12>* **DEATH VALLEY '69. / BRAVE MEN (RUN IN MY FAMILY)** [–] [ ]

Blast First — Homestead

Mar 85. (lp) *(BFFP 1) <HMS 016>* **BAD MOON RISING** [ ] [ ]
– Intro / Brave men rule / Society is a hole / I love her all the time / Ghost bitch / I'm insane / Justice is might / Death valley '69. *(cd-iss. Nov86+=; BFFP 1CD)* – Satan is boring / Flower / Halloween. *<US cd re-iss. 1995 on 'Geffen'; 24512>*

Jun 85. (12"ep; by SONIC YOUTH & LYDIA LUNCH) *(BFFP 2) <HMS 012>* **DEATH VALLEY '69. / I DREAMT I DREAMED / INHUMAN / BROTHER JAMES / SATAN IS BORING** [ ] [ ]

Jan 86. (12",12"yellow) *(BFFP 3)* **HALLOWEEN. / FLOWER** [–] [ ]

Jan 86. (7") *(BFFP 3)* **FLOWER. / REWOLF (censored)** [ ] [–]
(12") – ('A'side) / Satan is boring (live).

Mar 86. (etched-12") *(BFFP 3-B)* **HALLOWEEN II** [ ] [–]

—— **STEVE SHELLEY** (b.23 Jun'62, Midland, Michigan) – drums repl. BOB BERT who joined PUSSY GALORE

Blast First — S.S.T.

May 86. (lp/c) *(BFFP 4/+C) <SST/+C/CD 059>* **EVOL** [ ] [ ]
– Green light / Star power / Secret girl / Tom Violence / Death to our friends / Shadow of a doubt / Marilyn Moore / In the kingdom / Madonna, Sean and me. *(cd-iss. Nov86+=; BFFP 4CD)* – Bubblegum. *<US cd re-iss. 1995 on 'Geffen'; 24513>*

Jul 86. (7") *(BFFP 7) <SST 80>* **STAR POWER. / BUBBLEGUM** [ ] [ ]
(12"+=) *(BFFP 7T) <SST 80-12>* – Expressway.

—— added guest **MIKE WATT** – bass (of fIREHOSE)

Nov 86. (12"; as CICCONE YOUTH) *(BFFP 8)* **INTO THE GROOVE(Y). / TUFF TITTY RAP / BURNIN' UP** [ ] [ ]

Jun 87. (lp/c/cd) *(BFFP 20/+C/CD) <SST/+C/CD 134>* **SISTER** [ ] [ ]
– White cross / (I got a) Catholic block / Hot wire my heart / Tuff gnarl / Kotton crown / Schizophrenia / Beauty lies in the eye / Stereo sanctity / Pipeline – killtime / PCH. *(cd+=)* – Master-Dik (original). *<US cd re-iss. 1995 on 'Geffen'; 24514>*

Jan 88. (m-lp) *(BFFP 26T) <SST 155>* **MASTER-DIK** [ ] [ ]
– Master-Dik / Beat on the brat / Under the influence of the Jesus & Mary Chain: Ticket to ride / Ringo – He's on fire – Florida oil / Chines jam / Vibrato – Guitar lick – Funky fresh / Our backyard / Traffik.

Blast First — Capitol

Jan 88. (lp/c/cd; as CICCONE YOUTH) *(BFFP 28/+C/CD) <C1/C4/C2 75402>* **THE WHITEY ALBUM** [63] [ ]
– Needle-gun (silence) / G-force / Platoon II / Macbeth / Me & Jill / Hendrix Cosby / Burnin' up / Hi! everybody / Children of Satan / Third fig / Two cool rock chicks / Listening to Neu! / Addicted to love / Moby-Dik / March of the Ciccone robots / Making the nature scene / Tuff titty rap / Into the groovey. *<US cd re-iss. 1995 on 'Geffen'; 24516>*

Feb 88. (d-one-sided-7"on 'Fierce') *(FRIGHT 015-016)* **STICK ME DONNA MAGICK MOMMA / MAKING THE NATURE SCENE (live)** [ ] [–]
(also soon issued as normal-7")

Blast First — Torso

Oct 88. (d-lp/c/cd) *(BFFP 34/+C/CD) <2602339>* **DAYDREAM NATION** [99] [ ]
– Teenage riot / Silver rocket / The sprawl / 'Cross the breeze / Eric's trip / Total trash / Hey Joni / Providence / Candle? / Rain king / Kissability / Trilogy: The wonder – Hyperstation – Eliminator Jr.

—— Late in '88, KIM teamed up with LYDIA LUNCH and SADIE MAE to form one-off project HARRY CREWS. Their live appearences were issued in Apr 90 as 'NAKED IN GARDEN HILLS' for 'Big Cat' UK + 'Widowspeak' US.

Feb 89. (12") *(BFFP 46)* **TOUCH ME, I'M SICK. / (Halloween; by MUDHONEY)** [ ] [ ]

W.E.A. — D.G.C.

Jun 90. (cd/c/lp) *<(7599 24297-2/-4/-1)>* **GOO** [32] [96]
– Dirty boots / Tunic (song for Karen) / Mary-Christ / Kool thing / Mote / My friend Goo / Disappearer / Mildred Pierce / Cinderella's big score / Scooter + Jinx / Titanium expose. *(re-iss. cd Oct95 on 'Geffen'; GFLD 19297)*

Geffen — Geffen

Sep 90. (7") *(GEF 81)* **KOOL THING. / THAT'S ALL I KNOW (RIGHT NOW)** [ ] [–]
(12"+=) *(GEF 81T)* – ('A'demo version).
(cd-s++=) *(GEF 81CD)* – Dirty boots (rock & roll Heaven version).

—— In Autumn '90, THURSTON was part of 'Rough Trade' supergroup VELVET MONKEYS.

D.G.C. — D.G.C.

Apr 91. (m-lp/m-c/m-cd) *(DGC/+C/D 21634)* **DIRTY BOOTS** (all live, except the title track) [69] [–]
– Dirty boots / The bedroom / Cinderella's big scene / Eric's trip / White kross. *(re-iss. cd Apr92; DGLD 19060)*

—— Early in '92, THURSTON and STEVE also teamed up with RICHARD HELL's off-shoot group The DIM STARS.

Jun 92. (7") *(DGCS 11)* **100%. / CREME BRULEE** [28] [–]
(10"orange+=/12"+=) *(DGC V/T 11)* – Hendrix necro.
(cd-s++=) *(DGCTD 11)* – Genetic.

Jul 92. (d-lp/c/cd) *<(DGC/+C/D 24485)>* **DIRTY** [6] [83]
– 100% / Swimsuit issue / Theresa's sound-world / Drunken butterfly / Shoot / Wish fulfillment / Sugar Kane / Orange rolls, angel's spit / Youth against fascism / Nic fit / On the strip / Chapel Hill / JC / Purr / Creme brulee. *(d-lp+=)* – Stalker. *(re-iss. cd Oct95; GFLD 19296)*

Geffen — D.G.C.

Oct 92. (7") *(GFS 26)* **YOUTH AGAINST FASCISM. / PURR** [52] [–]
(10"colrd+=) *(GFSV 26)* – ('A'version).
(12"++=/cd-s++=) *(GFST/+D 26)* – The destroyed room (radio version)

Apr 93. (7"/c-s) *(GFS/+C 37)* **SUGAR KANE. / THE END OF THE END OF THE UGLY** [26] [–]
(10"blue+=/cd-s+=) *(GFS V/TD 37)* – Is it my body / Personality crisis.

Apr 94. (10"silver/c-s/cd-s) *(GFS V/C/TD 72)* **BULL IN THE HEATHER. / RAZORBLADE** [24] [–]

May 94. (cd/c/blue-lp) *<(GED/GEC/GEF 24632)>* **EXPERIMENTAL JET SET, TRASH AND NO STAR** [10] [34]
– Winner's blues / Bull in the heather / Starfield road / Skink / Self-obsessed and sexxee / Bone / Androgynous mind / Quest for the cup / Waist / Doctor's orders / Tokyo eye / In the mind of the bourgeois reader / Sweet shine.

—— In Sep 94; 'A&M' released CARPENTERS tribute album, which contained their single 'SUPERSTAR'. It was combined with also another cover from REDD KROSS, and reached UK No.45.

Oct 95. (cd/c/d-lp) *<(GED/GEC/GEF 24925)>* **WASHING MACHINE** [39] [58]
– Becuz / Junkie's promise / Saucer-like / Washing machine / Unwind / Little trouble girl / No queen blues / Panty lies / Becuz coda * / Skip tracer / The diamond sea. *(cd+= *)*

Apr 96. (12"/cd-s) *(GRS T/D 22132)* **LITTLE TROUBLE GIRL. / MY ARENA / THE DIAMOND SEA (edit)** [ ] [–]

Feb 98. (12"ep/cd-ep; SONIC YOUTH & JIM O'ROURKE) *<(SYR 003/+CD)>* **INVITO AL CIELO EP**
– Invito al cielo / Hungara vivo / Radio-Amatoroj.
(above issued on own 'Sonic Youth Records')

May 98. (d-cd/d-lp) *<(GED/GEF 25203)>* **A THOUSAND LEAVES** 38 85
– Contre le sexisme / Sunday / Female mechanic now on duty / Wildflower soul / Hoarfrost / French tickler / Hits of sunshine (for Allen Ginsberg) / Karen Koltrane / The ineffable me / Snare / Girl / Heather angel.

Jun 98. (7") *(GFS 22332)* **SUNDAY. / MOIST VAGINA** 72 –
(cd-s+=) *(GFSTD 22332)* – Silver panties / ('A'edit).

— THURSTON collaborated with DON FLEMING and JIM DUNBAR on the freeform/experimental project, FOOT, releasing 'S/T' for 'God Bless'

Smells Like | Smells Like

Nov 99. (d-lp/d-cd) *<(SYR 04/+CD)>* **GOODBYE 20th CENTURY**
– Edges / Six / Six for new time for Sonic Youth / + – / Voice piece for soprano / Pendulum music // Having never written a note for percussion / Six / Burdocks / Four / Piano piece #3 / Enfantine / Treatise.

Geffen | Geffen

May 00. (cd/lp) *<(490665-2/-1)>* **NYC GHOSTS AND FLOWERS**
– Free city rhymes / Renegade princess / Nevermind (what was it anyway) / Small flowers crack concrete / Side 2 side / Streamsonik subway / NYC ghosts and flowers / Lightnin'.

Jun 02. (cd) *<(493319-2)>* **MURRAY STREET**
– The empty page / Disconnection notice / Rain on tin / Karen revisited / Radical adults lick godhead style / Plastic sun / Sympathy for the strawberry.

Narnack | not iss.

Apr 03. (7") *(NACK 002)* **split w/ ERASE ERRATA** –

– compilations, others, etc. –

Feb 92. (cd) *Sonic Death;* <(SD 13001)> **GOO DEMOS LIVE AT THE CONTINENTAL CLUB (live)** Nov89

Mar 95. (cd/c) *Blast First; (BFFP 113 CD/C)* **CONFUSION IS SEX / KILL YR IDOLS** –

Mar 95. (cd) *Warners-Rhino; (8122 71591-2)* **MADE IN THE U.S.A.** (1986 soundtrack)

Apr 95. (cd) *Blast First; (BFFP 119CD)* **SCREAMING FIELDS OF SONIC LOVE**

May 97. (pic-lp) *Sonic Death; (SYLB 1)* **LIVE IN BREMEN (live)** –

Jun 97. (12"ep/cd-ep) *Sonic Youth; (SYR 1/+CD)* **SYR VOL.1** –
– Anagrama / Improvisation ajout'e / Tremens / Mieux: de corrosion.

Jul 98. (cd) *S.Y.R.; (SYR 1)* **SILVER SESSION FOR JASON KNUTH**

Aug 98. (cd) *Goofin' (GOO 2CD)* **HOLD THAT TIGER (live 1987)**

Jul 00. (cd; by SONIC YOUTH & YAMATSUKA EYE) *Ecstatic Peace; <(E 38CD)>* **TV SHIT**

☐ SONNY & CHER (see under ⇒ CHER)

SON VOLT

Formed: Belleville, Illinois, USA ... 1994 by JAY FARRAR and his former UNCLE TUPELO compadre, MIKE HEIDORN; JIM and DAVE BOQUIST joined soon afterwards. Fans yearning for the down-at-heel spirit of UNCLE TUPELO's moodier moments were comforted by the fact that FARRAR himself was still treading the dirt-road backstreets of country's dark underbelly with SON VOLT, releasing 'TRACE' in 1994 and 'STRAIGHTAWAYS' in late '96; 'WIDE SWING TREMELO' (1998) was their most recent set. While some critics railed against what they perceived as the unrelenting miserabilism of FARRAR's approach (especially with regards to the SON VOLT live experience), there was no disputing the quality or honesty of the writing. After 'STRAIGHTAWAYS', FARRAR took time out from SON VOLT (they split 1999) to record 'SEBASTAPOL' (2001) an album of self-conscious beauty, but of beauty all the same. Acoustic numbers such as the whispering 'CLEAR DAY THUNDER' and 'OUTSIDE THE DOOR' evoked that folksy UNCLE TUPELO formula, where as 'BARSTOW' and 'DAMN SHAME' had FARRAR's own personalised stamp. Elsewhere on the set, he had trouble dealing with the process alone (after all he was always best with a collaborator), although the man proved he was still a great contender in the American alt country scene. FARRAR was still meandering down his own ragged path, cutting the austere 'TERROIR BLUES' in 2003. The record found him paring back the arrangements with a ruthlessness unwitnessed since his split from TWEEDY, resulting in one of the most intimate yet exploratory works of his career.

Album rating: TRACE (*7) / STRAIGHTAWAYS (*6) / WIDE SWING TREMELO (*7) / Jay Farrar: SEBASTAPOL (*6) / TERROIR BLUES (*6)

JAY FARRAR – vocals, guitar, organ, harmonica, songwriter / **DAVE BOQUIST** – guitars, fiddle, banjo, lap steel / **JIM BOQUIST** – bass, backing vocals / **MIKE HEIDORN** – drums

Warners | Warners

Oct 95. (cd/c) *<(9362-46010-2/-4)>* **TRACE** Sep95
– Windfall / Live free / Tear stained eye / Route / Ten second news / Drown / Loose string / Out of the picture / Catching on / Too early / Mystifies me.

— with guests **ERIC HEYWOOD** – pedal steel, mandolin / **PAULI RYAN** – tambourine

Aug 97. (cd) *<(9362-46518-2/-4)>* **STRAIGHTAWAYS** May97 44
– Caryatid easy / Back into the world / Picking up the signal / Left a slide / Cresote / Cemetery savior / Last minute shakedown / Been set free / No more parades / Way down Watson.

Oct 98. (cd/c) *<(9362 47059-2/-4)>* **WIDE SWING TREMELO** 93
– Straightface / Driving the view / Jodel / Medicine hat / Strands / Flow / Dead man's clothes / Right on through / Chanty / Carry you down / Question / Streets that time walks / Hanging blue side / Blind hope.

JAY FARRAR

with **DAVID RAWLINGS, TOM RAY, MATT PENCE, JON WURSTER, DADE FARRAR, JOHN AGNELLO, KELLY JOE PHELPS + GILLIAN WELCH**

Epic | Artemis

Oct 01. (cd) *(504570-2) <751093>* **SEBASTAPOL** Sep01
– Feel free / Clear day thunder / Voodoo candle / Barstow / Damn shame / Damaged son / Prelude (make it alright) / Dead promises / Feedkill chain / Make it alright / Fortissimo wah / Drain / Different eyes / Outside the door / Equilibrium / Direction / Vitamins.

Nov 02. (cd-ep) *<751138>* **THIRDSHIFTGROTTOSLACK** –
– Greenwich time / Damn shame / Station to station / Kind of madness / Dues.

Act Resist | Artemis

Jun 03. (cd) *<(ATMCD 51172)>* **TERROIR BLUES**
– No rolling back / Space junk I / Hard is the fall / Fool king's crown / Space junk II / Hanging on to you / Cahokian / Heart on the ground / Out on the road / All of your might / Space junk III / California / Walk you down / Space junk IV / Dent county / Fish fingers Norway / Space junk V / Hanging on to you II / Hard is the fall II / Jam / Heart on the ground II / No rolling back II / Space junk VI.

SOUL ASYLUM

Formed: Minneapolis, Minnesota, USA ... 1981 as LOUD FAST RULES, by ex-AT LAST guitarist DAN MURPHY and ex-SHITS frontman DAVE PIRNER, who were subsequently joined by KARL MUELLER then PAT MORLEY. Very much in the mould of HUSKER DU and The REPLACEMENTS, SOUL ASYLUM joined the latter at 'Twin Tone' records, while the former's BOB MOULD produced their 1984 debut album, 'SAY WHAT YOU WILL'. Later that year, MORLEY departed while the rest of the band took a break, SOUL ASYLUM subsequently returning in 1986 with GRANT YOUNG on their follow-up, 'MADE TO BE BROKEN'. A fusion of 60's pop and 70's punk, the album (also produced by MOULD) showed PIRNER blossoming into a cuttingly perceptive lyricist. Later that year, the band delivered another fine set, 'WHILE YOU WERE OUT', the record attracting major label attention in the form of 'A&M'. Fulfilling their contract with 'Twin Tone', SOUL ASYLUM cut a covers set, 'CLAM DIP AND OTHER DELIGHTS', displaying their wide range of tastes from Barry Manilow's 'MANDY' to Foreigner's 'JUKEBOX HERO'. In 1988, A&M issued the LENNY KAYE and ED STASIUM produced album, 'HANG TIME', an endearing collection of gleaming power-pop nuggets that occasionally veered off the beaten track into country. Their second and final release for A&M, 'SOUL ASYLUM AND THE HORSE THEY RODE IN ON' (1990), saw PIRNER spiral into despair despite the album's critical acclaim. Disillusioned with the major label inertia, the frontman took a break from amplified noise while his colleagues resumed their day jobs. Staking their chances on yet another major label, SOUL ASLYLUM subsequently signed to 'Columbia' and achieved almost instant success with the album 'GRAVE DANCERS UNION' in 1992. This was mainly due to the massive interest in the TOM PETTY-esque 'RUNAWAY TRAIN', a single that hit the American Top 5 in the summer of '93. The track's radio-friendly success paved the way for more typically abrasive numbers such as 'SOMEBODY TO SHOVE' and 'BLACK GOLD', PIRNER landing on his feet as he wooed sultry actress, Winona Ryder (he appeared with her in the film, 'Generation X'). SOUL ASYLUM subsequently became MTV darlings and friends of the stars, such luminaries as BOB DYLAN, PETER BUCK and GUNS N' ROSES professing to fan status. In 1995, they returned with a new drummer, STERLING CAMPBELL, and a new album, 'LET YOUR DIM LIGHT SHINE', another worldwide seller which spawned the melancholy Top 30 gem, 'MISERY'. MURPHY and PIRNER (latter part-time) had also moonlighted in the countrified GOLDEN SMOG with among others the JAYHAWKS' GARY LOURIS and MARC PERLMAN. An EP of covers in '92 was finally followed up by an album in '96, 'DOWN BY THE OLD MAINSTREAM'. A few years later y'all supergroup added BIG STAR's JODY STEPHENS to replace the drumming PIRNER, a second set, 'WEIRD TALES', gaining many plaudits. • **Covers:** MOVE OVER (Janis Joplin) / RHINESTONE COWBOY (Glen Campbell) / BARSTOOL BLUES (Neil Young) / SEXUAL HEALING (Marvin Gaye) / ARE FRIENDS ELECTRIC (Tubeway Army) / SUMMER OF DRUGS (Victoria Williams) / WHEN I RAN OFF AND LEFT HER (Vic Chesnutt).

Album rating: SAY WHAT YOU WILL (*6) / MADE TO BE BROKEN (*6) / WHILE YOU WERE OUT (*6) / HANG TIME (*6) / CLAM DIP AND OTHER DELIGHTS (*5) / SOUL ASYLUM AND THE HORSE THEY RODE IN ON (*8) / GRAVE DANCERS UNION (*7) / LET YOUR DIM LIGHTS SHINE (*6) / CANDY FROM A STRANGER (*5) / BLACK GOLD: THE BEST OF SOUL ASYLUM compilation (*8)

DAVE PIRNER (b.16 Apr'64, Green Bay, Wisconsin) – vocals, guitar / **DAN MURPHY** (b.12 Jul'62, Duluth, Minnesota) – guitar, vocals / **KARL MUELLER** (b.27 Jul'63) – bass / **PAT MORLEY** – drums, percussion

Rough Trade | Twin Tone

Aug 84. (m-lp) *<TT 8439>* **SAY WHAT YOU WILL** [–] [ ]
– Long day / Voodoo doll / Money talks / Stranger / Sick of that song / Walking / Happy / Black and blue / Religiavision. *<US re-iss. May89+=; same>* – Dragging me down / Do you know / Spacehead / Broken glass / Masquerade. *(UK cd-iss. Mar93 as 'SAY WHAT YOU WILL CLARENCE . . . KARL SOLD THE TRUCK' on 'Roadrunner'; RR 9093-2) <(cd re-iss. Mar95 on 'Twin Tone'; TTR 8439-2)> <(cd re-iss. Aug03 on 'Restless'; REST 84039)>*

— **GRANT YOUNG** (b. 5 Jan'64, Iowa City, Iowa) – drums, percussion; repl. MORLEY

Sep 86. (lp) *(ROUGH 102) <TT 8666>* **MADE TO BE BROKEN** [ ] [ ]
– Tied to the tracks / Ship of fools / Can't go back / Another world another day / Made to be broken / Never really been / Whoa! / New feelings / Growing pain / Lone rider / Ain't that tough / Don't it (make your troubles seem small). *(cd-iss. Mar93 on 'Roadrunner'+=; RR 9094-2)* – Long way home. *(cd re-iss. Sep98 on 'R.C.A.'; 74321 60573-20)*

Sep 86. (7") **TIED TO THE TRACKS. /** [–] [ ]

What Goes On | Twin Tone

Mar 88. (lp) *(GOES ON 16) <TT 8691>* **WHILE YOU WERE OUT** [ ] 1987 [ ]
– Freaks / Carry on / No man's land / Crashing down / The judge / Sun don't shine / Closer to the stars / Never too soon / Miracles mile / Lap of luxury / Passing sad daydream. *(cd-iss. Mar93 on 'Roadrunner'; RR 9096-2) <(cd re-iss. Feb95 on 'Twin Tone'; TTR 8691-2)> <(cd re-iss. Aug03 on 'Restless'; REST 86091)>*

May 88. (m-lp) *(GOES ON 22) <TT 8814>* **CLAM DIP AND OTHER DELIGHTS** [ ] 1987 [ ]
– Just plain evil / Chains / Secret no more / Artificial heart / P-9 / Take it to root. *(cd-iss. Mar93 on 'Roadrunner'; RR 9097-2)* – Jukebox hero / Move over / Mandy / Rhinestone cowboy. *<(cd re-iss. Feb95 on 'Twin Tone'; TTR 8814-2)> <(m-cd re-iss. Aug03 on 'Restless'; REST 88144)>*

— split but re-formed adding guest **CADD** – sax, piano

A&M | A&M

Jun 88. (7"/12") *(AM/+Y 447)* **SOMETIME TO RETURN. / PUT THE BOOT IN** [ ] [–]
(12"-iss.Jun91 +=; same) – Marionette.

Jun 88. (lp/c/cd) *(AMA/AMC/CDA 5197) <395197-1/-4/-2>* **HANG TIME** [ ] [ ]
– Down on up to me / Little too clean / Sometime to return / Cartoon / Beggars and choosers / Endless farewell / Standing in the doorway / Marionette / Ode / Jack of all trades / Twiddly dee / Heavy rotation. *(re-iss. Sep93 cd/c; CD/C MID 189)*

Aug 88. (7") *(AM 463)* **CARTOON. / TWIDDLY DEE** [ ] [–]
(12"+=) *(AMY 463)* – Standing in the doorway.

Sep 90. (cd/c/lp) *(5318-2/-4/-1) <75021 5318-2/-4/-1>* **SOUL ASYLUM & THE HORSE THEY RODE IN ON** [ ] [ ]
– Spinnin' / Bitter pill / Veil of tears / Nice guys (don't get paid) / Something out of nothing / Gullible's travels / Brand new shine / Grounded / Don't be on your way / We / All the king's friends. *(re-iss. Sep93 cd/c; CD/C MID 190)*

Jan 91. (7") **EASY STREET. / SPINNING** [ ] [–]
(12"+=) – All the king's friends / Gullible's travels.

Columbia | Columbia

Oct 92. (cd/c/lp) *(472253-2/-4/-1) <48896>* **GRAVE DANCERS UNION** [ ] [11]
– Somebody to shove / Black gold / Runaway train / Keep it up / Homesick / Get on out / New world / April fool / Without a trace / Growing into you / 99% / The Sun maid. *(re-dist.Jul93; hit UK No.52) (UK No.27 early '94)*

Mar 93. (10"ep/cd-ep) *(659 088-0/-2)* **BLACK GOLD. / BLACK GOLD (live) / THE BREAK / 99%** [ ] [ ]

May 93. (c-s,cd-s) *<74966>* **RUNAWAY TRAIN / NEVER REALLY BEEN (live)** [–] [5]

Jun 93. (7"/c-s) *(659 390-7/-4)* **RUNAWAY TRAIN. / BLACK GOLD (live)** [37] [–]
(12"+=) *(659 390-6)* – By the way / Never really been (live).
(cd-s++=) *(659 390-2)* – Everybody loves a winner. (- Black Gold).
(above single returned into UK chart Nov'93 to hit No.7)

Aug 93. (12"ep/cd-ep) *(659 649-6/-2)* **SOMEBODY TO SHOVE / SOMEBODY TO SHOVE (live). / RUNAWAY TRAIN (live) / BY THE WAY (demo)** [34] [–]
(c-ep) *(659 649-4)* – ('A'side) / Black gold (live) / Runaway train (live).

Jan 94. (7"/c-s) *(659 844-7/-4)* **BLACK GOLD. / SOMEBODY TO SHOVE** [26] [–]
(cd-s+=) *(659 844-2)* – Closer to the stairs / Square root.
(cd-s+=) *(659 844-5)* – Runaway train (live).

Mar 94. (7"/c-s) *(660 224-7/-4)* **SOMEBODY TO SHOVE. / BY THE WAY** [32] [–]
(cd-s+=) *(660 224-2)* – Stranger (unplugged) / Without a trace (live).
(cd-s++=) *(660 224-5)* – ('A'mix).

— **STERLING CAMPBELL** – drums; repl. YOUNG

Jun 95. (cd/c) *(480 320-2/-4) <57616>* **LET YOUR DIM LIGHT SHINE** [22] [6]
– Misery / Shut down / To my own devices / Hopes up / Promises broken / Bittersweetheart / String of pearls / Crawl / Caged rat / Eyes of a child / Just like anyone / Tell me when / Nothing to write home about / I did my best.

Jun 95. (c-s,cd-s) *<77959>* **MISERY / HOPE** [-] [20]
Jul 95. (7"white/c-s) *(662 109-7/-4)* **MISERY. / STRING OF PEARLS** [30] [-]
(cd-s+=) *(662 109-2)* – Hope (demo) / I did my best.
Nov 95. (c-s) *(662 478-4)* **JUST LIKE ANYONE / DO ANYTHING YOU WANNA DO (live)** [52] [-]
(cd-s+=) *(662 478-2)* – Get on out (live).
(cd-s) *(662 478-5)* – ('A'side) / You'll live forever (demo) / Fearless leader (demo).
Feb 96. (c-s,cd-s) *<78215>* **PROMISES BROKEN / CAN'T EVEN TELL (live)** [-] [63]

— now a trio of **PIRNER, MURPHY + MUELLER**

May 98. (cd/c) *(487265-2/-4) <67618>* **CANDY FROM A STRANGER** [ ] [ ]
– Creatures of habit / I will still be laughing / Close / See you later / No time for waiting / Blood into wine / Lies of hate / Draggin' out the lake / Blackout / The game / Cradle chain.

– compilations, etc. –

Sep 00. (cd) *Columbia; (499874-2)* **GRAVE DANCERS UNION / LET YOUR DIM LIGHT SHINE** [ ] [ ]
Sep 00. (cd) *Columbia; (498656-2) <63669>* **BLACK GOLD: THE BEST OF SOUL ASYLUM** [ ] [ ]
– Just like anyone / Cartoon / Closer to the stars (live) / Somebody to shove / Close / String of pearls / Tied to the tracks / Runaway train / Sometime to return / Misery / We 3 / Without a trace / I will still be laughing / Black gold / Summer of drugs / Candy from a stranger / Stranger (live) / Can't even tell / Only for you.
Jul 01. (cd) *Sony Special; <52163>* **RUNAWAY TRAIN** [-] [ ]
Dec 02. (d-cd) *Columbia; (499874-2)* **GRAVE DANCERS UNION / LET YOUR DIM LIGHT SHINE** [ ] [-]

SOULFLY

Formed: based – Phoenix, Arizona, USA ... 1997 by ex-SEPULTURA mainman, MAX CAVALERA, the Brazilian enlisting the aid of LUCIO (JACKSON BANDIERA), MARCELO D. RAPP and punk rocker, ROY MAYORGA. MAX had recently found faith in God after his step-son, Dana (also son of wife/manager, Gloria) died; his other sons, Zyon and Igor also had serious illnesses. The man never changed his "ungod"-like vocal chords though, and SOULFLY (under the production of Ross Robinson) unleashed their thrillingly diverse eponymous set in the Spring of '98. The contrast between the tribal 'UMBABARAUMA' and the grinding 'NO' somehow worked, the latter's refreshingly metal assault on the ears and the line, "no motherf***in' HOOTIE & THE BLOWFISH", supplying the definitive "ROCK!!!" highlight of the year! The 'PRIMITIVE' set in 2000 kicked off with the excellent 'BACK TO THE PRIMITIVE', certainly one of the highlights of the year. 'III' (2002) found CAVALERA in as uncompromising form as he's ever been, letting loose a rage which unfortunately dissipated in inarticulacy and blind alleys as often as it seared the senses. With percussion man ROY MAYORGA back in the fold, opener 'BRASIL' resembled a demonic carnaval gone wrong, MAX's spitfire Portuguese raining down like molten hail. While other highlights included the coruscating 'TREE OF PAIN', the gung-ho 'CALL TO ARMS' and a timely cover of Sacred Reich's 'ONE NATION', there was a definite sense that the concept – if not the reality – of SOULFLY needed some fresh creative juice.

Album rating: SOULFLY (*8) / PRIMITIVE (*6) / 3 (*5)

MAX CAVALERA – vocals, 4-string guitar (ex-SEPULTURA) / **JACKSON BANDIERA** (aka LUCIO) – guitars (ex-CHICO SCIENCE) / **MARCELO D. RAPP** – bass (ex-MIST) / **ROY "RATA" MAYORGA** – drums (ex-AGNOSTIC FRONT, ex-SHELTER, ex-NAUSEA, ex-CHAOS USA)

Roadrunner Roadrunner

Mar 98. (ltd;cd-ep) *(RR 2238-3)* **BLEED / NO HOPE = NO FEAR / CANGACEIRO / AIN'T NO FEEBLE BASTARD** [ ] [-]
Apr 98. (cd/c/lp) *(<RR 8748-2/-4/-1>)* **SOULFLY** [16] [79]
– Eye for an eye / No hope = no fear / Bleed / Tribe / Bumba / First commandment / Bumbklaatt / Soulfly / Umbabarauma / Quilombo / Fire / The song remains insane / No / Prejudice / Karmageddon. *(special cd+=; RR 8748-9)* – Cangaceiro / Ain't no feeble bastard / The possibility of life's destruction. *(re-iss. May99 d-cd+=; RR 8748-8)*– Tribe (fuck shit up mix) / Qilombo (extreme ragga dub mix) / Umbabaraumba (World Cup remix) / No hope = no fear (live) / Bleed (live) / Quilombo (live) / The song remains the insane (live) / Eye for an eye (live) / Tribe (tribal terrorism mix) / Umbabaraumba (Brasilia '70 remix) / Quilombo (Zumbi dub remix) / Soulfly (eternal spirit remix).
Jun 98. (ltd;cd-ep) *(RR 2231-3)* **UMBABARAUMA / UMBABARAUMA (World Cup mix) / TRIBE (extended) / UMBABARAUMA (World Cup instrumental)** [ ] [-]
May 99. (cd-s) *(RR 2203-3)* **TRIBE (fuck shit up mix) / QUILOMBO (Zumbi dub mix) / TRIBE (tribal terrorism mix)** [ ] [-]

— **MIKEY DOLING** – guitar; repl. BANDIERA

— **JOE NUNEZ** – drums, percussion; repl. MAYORGA

Sep 00. (cd/pic-lp) *(<RR 8565-2/-1>)* **PRIMITIVE** [45] [32]
– Back to the primitive / Pain / Bring it / Jumpdafuckup / Mulumbo / Son song / Boom / Terrorist / The prophet / Soulfly II / In memory of . . . / Flyhigh. *(special cd+=; RR 8565-5)* – Eye for an eye (live) / Tribe (live) / Soulfire / Soulfly (universal spirit mix).
Dec 00. (cd-s) *(RR 2067-3)* **BACK TO THE PRIMITIVE / TERRORIST (total deconstruction mix) / BACK TO THE PRIMITIVE (dub shit up mix) / BACK TO THE PRIMITIVE (CD-Rom video)** [ ] [-]

— **ROY MAYORGA** – drums; returned to repl. NUNEZ

— added **JACKSON BANDIERA** – guitar

Jun 02. (cd) *<(RR 8455-2)>* **3** [61] [46]
– Downstroy / Seek 'n' strike / Enter faith / One / L.O.T.M. / Brasil / Tree of pain / One nation / 9-11-01 / Call to arms / Four elements / Soulfly III / Sangue de Bairro / Zumbi. *(ltd-cd+=; RR 8455-5)* – I will refuse / Under the sun / Eye for an eye (live at Ozzfest 2000) / Pain (live at Ozzfest 2000).

SOUL II SOUL

Formed: South London, England ... 1982 by BERESFORD ROMEO (aka JAZZIE B) and PHILIP 'DADDAE' HARVEY. Initially operating purely as a sound system, SOUL II SOUL began branching out with the arrival of producer/arranger and erstwhile WILD BUNCH man, NELLEE HOOPER. Having landed a residency at Covent Garden's Africa Centre, the trio began shopping demos around the major labels and were subsequently taken on by 'Virgin' offshoot, 'Ten'. While the outfit's earliest efforts, 'FAIRPLAY' and 'FEEL FREE' only just scraped into the UK Top 75, March 89's sublime 'KEEP ON MOVIN' made the Top 5 and added pop star to a JAZZIE B CV that already included radio presenter (with soon-to-be-commercial pirate station, Kiss FM), record shop proprietor and clothes merchandiser; the collective's famous 'Funky Dred' logo became synonymous with the rise of the club scene in the late 80's. Having whetted peoples' appetites, SOUL II SOUL served up a gourmet platter in the shape of UK No.1 platinum-selling album, 'CLUB CLASSICS VOL.1' (1989); for once the title was no idle boast and an exquisite combination of lavish strings, way heavy dub-style basslines, molten hip hop beats and Afro influences heralded one of the key developments in the British soul/R&B scene. There was also the small matter of CARON WHEELER's steamy diva-esque vocals (alongside other guest singers ROSE WINDROSS and DO'REEN), her tonsils gracing both the aforementioned 'KEEP ON MOVIN' and subsequent No.1 single, 'BACK TO LIFE (HOWEVER DO

YOU WANT ME)'. The track's creamy R&B appeal even translated to the States where the record made the Top 5, a rare feat for an English club-orientated act. While WHEELER went on to a solo career, JAZZIE B and HOOPER used the success as a springboard for high profile production work, their biggest credit coming in early 1990 with SINEAD O'CONNOR's PRINCE-penned No.1, 'Nothing Compares 2 U'. Sophomore album, 'VOL II, A NEW DECADE 1990' arrived the same year, again making No.1 and spawning the singles, 'A DREAM'S A DREAM' and 'MISSING YOU'. With VICTORIA WILSON-JAMES performing on the former and KYM MAZELLE undertaking vocal duties on the latter, SOUL II SOUL had once again perfectly matched up singer and song while the album itself benefitted from the talents of COURTNEY PINE and legendary rapper FAB 5 FREDDIE. 1991 saw HOOPER work with old mates MASSIVE ATTACK on their epochal 'Unfinished Sympathy', arguably the pinnacle of his career (although he went on to work with everyone from BJORK to U2) but also the end of his partnership with JAZZIE B & Co. SOUL II SOUL were back in the Top 5 the following year with 'JOY', their first single to feature a male vocalist (RICHIE STEPHENS). The accompanying album, 'JUST RIGHT VOLUME III' (1992) made the Top 3 but met with a lukewarm critical reception as did 'VOLUME V – BELIEVE' (1995), SOUL II SOUL's parting shot for 'Virgin'. Although the crew moved on to 'Island/4th & Broadway', 'SOUL II SOUL VOL.6 – TIME TO CHANGE' (1997) failed to chart and suggested that the concept had grown just the tiniest bit stale.

Album rating: CLUB CLASSICS – VOLUME ONE (*8) / VOL.II, A NEW DECADE 1990 (*6) / JUST RIGHT VOLUME III (*5) / VOLUME IV – THE CLASSIC SINGLES 88-93 compilation (*7) / VOLUME V – BELIEVE (*5) / SOUL II SOUL VOL.6 – TIME TO CHANGE (*4)

JAZZIE B. (BERESFORD ROMEO) – keyboards, vocals / **NELLEE HOOPER** – keyboards

10-Virgin Virgin

May 88. (7") *(TEN 228)* **FAIRPLAY. / ('A'radio mix)** 63 [ ]
(12"+=) *(TENX 228)* – ('A'bonus beats).
(12") *(TENR 228)* – ('A'side) / Ambition (rap) / ('A'-freestyle horns mix).
above singer & co-composer **ROSE WINDROSS**

Sep 88. (7") *(TEN 239)* **FEEL FREE. / FAIRPLAY** 64 [ ]
(12"+=/cd-s+=) *(TEN X/CD 239)* – ('A'instrumental).
(12"+=) *(TENR 239)* – ('A'-unlimited remix).
above singer **DO'REEN**

Mar 89. (7"/7"w/poster/c-s) *(TEN/+P/C 263)* <99205> **KEEP ON MOVIN'. / ('A'instrumental)** 5 Jun89 11
(12") *(TENX 263)* – ('A'club mix) / ('A'-Big beat acappella) / ('A'-Pianopella) / ('A'instrumental).
(12"/3"cd-s) *(TENR/+D 263)* – ('A'-New York mix) / ('A'-First Movement mix) / ('A'-A dub in the sun mix).
(3"cd-s) *(TENCD 263)* – ('A'side) / ('A'club mix) / Feel free.
above & below singer **CARON WHEELER** (solo artist she co-wrote below 45)

Apr 89. (cd/c/lp) *(DIX/CDIX/DIXCD 82)* <91267> **CLUB CLASSICS – VOLUME ONE** <US-title 'KEEP ON MOVIN'> 1 14
– Keep on movin' (featuring CARON WHEELER) / Fairplay (featuring ROSE WINDROSS) / Holdin' on / Feeling free (live rap) / African dance / Dance / Feel free (featuring DO'REEN) / Happiness (dub) / Back to life (acapella) (featuring CARON WHEELER) / Jazzie's groove. *(cd+=)* – Back to life (however do you want me).

Jun 89. (7"/c-s) *(TEN/+C 265)* <99171> **BACK TO LIFE (HOWEVER DO YOU WANT ME). / BACK TO LIFE (version)** 1 Sep89 4
(12"/c-s) *(TEN X/W 265)* <965370> – ('A'club) / ('A'-Jam on the groove) / ('A'back to the beats).
(3"cd-s) *(TENCD 265)* – ('A'side) / ('A'club) / ('A'-Jam on the groove).

Nov 89. (7"/c-s) *(TEN/+C 284)* <98981> **GET A LIFE. / JAZZIE'S GROOVE (new version)** 3 Apr90 54
('A'club-12"+=) *(TENX 284)* – ('A'bonus beats)/ ('A'piano version).
(ext-12"/12"w/poster) *(TEN R/P 284)* – Back to life (one world mix).
(cd-s+=) *(TENCD 284)* – ('A'club) / Keep on movin' (Teddy Riley remix).
above singer **MARCIE LEWIS** who repl. WHEELER (became solo star)

Apr 90. (7"/c-s/7"box) *(TEN/+C/B 300)* <98955> **A DREAM'S A DREAM. / ('A'instrumental)** 6 Jun90 85
(12"/cd-s) *(TEN X/CD 300)* – ('A'-A night at the opera mix) / ('A'club dub) / Courtney blows (with COURTNEY PINE).
above singer **VICTORIA WILSON-JAMES**

May 90. (cd/c/lp) *(DIXCD/CDIX/DIX 90)* <91367> **VOL II – A NEW DECADE – 1990** 1 21
– Get a life / Love comes through to you / People / Missing you / Courtney blows / 1990 (a new decade) / A dream's a dream / Time / In the heat of the night / Our time has come now.

—— ('PEOPLE' vox – **MARCIE**)

Oct 90. (7"/c-s) *(TEN/+C 345)* **MISSING YOU. / ('A'instrumental)** 22 [ ]
(12"+=) *(TENX 345)* – ('A'-thumpin' bass mix) / ('A'-humanity mix) / People (club).
(12") *(TENR 345)* – ('A'remake) / ('A'-blow Mr. hornsman blow mix) / ('A'-thumpin' bass mix).
(cd-s) *(TENCD 345)* – (the 4 tracks except 7"-b-side).
above singer **KYM MAZELLE**

Apr 92. (7"/c-s) *(TEN/+C 350)* **JOY. / ('A'radio mix)** 4 [ ]
(12"+=) *(TENX 350)* – ('A'instrumental) / ('A'club mix).
(12"++=/cd-s++=) *(TEN R/CD 350)* – ('A'-Brand New Heavies remix).
above singer **RICHIE STEPHENS**

Apr 92. (cd/c/lp) *(BMCDIXD/BMCDIX/10DIX 100)* <91771> **JUST RIGHT – VOLUME III** 3 May92 88
– Joy / Take me higher / Storm / Direction / Just right / Move me no mountain / Intelligence / Future / Mood / Everywhere.
below featured band JELLYFISH

Jun 92. (7"/c-s) *(TEN/+C 400)* **MOVE ME NO MOUNTAIN. / ('A'mix)** 31 [ ]
(12"/cd-s) *(TEN X/CD 400)* – ('A'side) / ('A'club) / ('A'-Hackney E9 mix) / ('A'dub mix) / ('A'removed club mix) / ('A'dum dum dub).
above singer **KOFI**

Sep 92. (7"/c-s) *(TEN/+C 410)* **JUST RIGHT. / ('A'jinx mix)** 38 [ ]
(club;12"+=/cd-s+=) *(TEN X/GD 410)* – ('A'-funky dred mix) / ('A'-Intelligence (9 a.m. mix) / Intelligence (Jazzie II guru mix).
above singer & co-composer **RICK CLARKE**

Virgin Virgin

Oct 93. (7"/c-s) *(VS/+C 1480)* **WISH. / BACK TO LIFE (Masters At Work remix)** 24 [ ]
(10"+=/cd-s+=/cd-s+=) *(VST/VSCDG/VSCDT 1480)* – (2 original mixes).
above singer **MELISSA BELL**

Nov 93. (cd/c)(d-lp) *(CD/TC+/V 2724)* <4036> **VOLUME IV – THE CLASSIC SINGLES 88-93** (compilation) 10 [ ]
– Back to life (however do you want me) / Keep on movin' / Get a life / A dream's a dream / Missing you / Just right / Move me no mountain / People / Fairplay / Jazzie's groove / Wish / Joy / Keep on movin' (Mafia & Fluxy mix) / Fairplay (Ethnic Boys mix) / Back to life (bonus beats). *(cd+=)* – Keep on movin' (Q & Dobie mix)/ Back to life (Masters at work & R&B mixes).

—— now with **PENNY FORD** – vocals (ex-SNAP)

Jul 95. (12"/cd-s) *(VST/VSCDG 1527)* **LOVE ENUFF / ('A'-New York mix) / ('A'-4 wheel drive mix) / ('A'-Todd Terry house mix) / ('A'-Todd Terry horns mix)** 12 –
(cd-s) *(VSCDT 1527)* – ('A'mixes near as above).

Jul 95. (cd/c/lp) *(CD/TC+/V 2739)* <40628> **VOLUME V – BELIEVE** 13 [ ]
– Love enuff / Ride on / How long / Feeling / Universal / Being a man / Zion / Don't you dream / Gane dunn / Sundays / Pride / I care (Soul II Soul) / B groove / Believe. *(d-lp re-iss. Apr01 on 'Simply Vinyl'; SVLP 313)*

Oct 95. (c-s) *(VSC 1560)* **I CARE (SOUL II SOUL) / ('A'-12"master)** 17 –
(12") *(VST 1560)* – ('A'side) / ('A'-Maserati mix) / ('A'-Fred freaky mix) / ('A'-Nu Soul mix) / ('A'-Secret weapon mix).
(cd-s+=) *(VSCDT 1560)* – (includes c-s b-side).

Oct 96. (c-s) *(VSC 1612)* **KEEP ON MOVIN' (remix) / (club mix w/ Caron Wheeler)** 31 –
(cd-s+=) *(VSCDT 1612)* – Feel free (feat. Do'reen).

4th & Broad not iss.

Aug 97. (c-s) *(BRCA 357)* **REPRESENT / (radio)** 39 –
(12"+=/cd-s+=) *(12BRW/BRCD 357)* – (mixes; Katt / soul inside re-worked / full crew).

Island Island

Sep 97. (cd/c/lp) *(CID/ICT/ILPS 8060)* <624> **SOUL II SOUL VOL.6 – TIME TO CHANGE** [ ] [ ]
– Camdino soul / Pleasure dome / Thank you / Dare to differ / Get away /

Love ain't around / Represent / Time for change / I feel love / The limit is the sky.

Oct 97. (c-s) *(CIS 669)* **PLEASURE DOME / ('A'-Booker T mix)** [51] [–]
(12"+=/cd-s+=) *(12IS/CID 669)* – ('A'-Tuff Jam's UVF mix) / ('A'-Dream Team dub).

— SOUL II SOUL had now split for a time

– compilations, etc. –

Sep 98. (cd) *Virgin VIP; (CDVIP 222)* **THE CLUB MIX HITS** [ ] [–]
Mar 99. (cd) *Disky; (VI 85435-2)* **JAZZIE'S GROOVE** [ ] [–]
Sep 99. (cd) *Disky; (VI 24742-2)* **CLUB MIX** [ ] [–]

SOUNDGARDEN

Formed: Seattle, Washington, USA ... 1984 by lead singer CHRIS CORNELL, guitarist KIM THAYIL and bassist HIRO YAMAMOTO. With the addition of drummer MATT CAMERON in '86, the band became one of the first to record for the fledgling 'Sub Pop' label, releasing the 'HUNTED DOWN' single in summer '87. Two EP's, 'SCREAMING LIFE', and 'FOPP' followed, although the group signed to 'S.S.T.' for their debut album, 'ULTRAMEGA OK' (1988). Despite its lack of focus, the record laid the foundations for what was to follow; a swamp-rich miasma of snail-paced, bass-crunch uber-riffing, wailing vocals and punk attitude shot through with bad-trip psychedelia (i.e. not something to listen to last thing at night). And with the Grammy-nominated 'LOUDER THAN LOVE' (1989), the group's major label debut for 'A&M', SOUNDGARDEN harnessed their devilish wares onto infectious melodies and fuck-off choruses; one listen to the likes of 'HANDS ALL OVER', 'LOUD LOVE' and the tongue-in-cheek brilliance of 'BIG DUMB SEX' was enough to convince you that these hairy post-metallers were destined for big, grunge-type things. Success wasn't immediate however, the album failing to make a dent beyond the Sub-Pop in-crowd and a few adventurous metal fans. YAMAMOTO departed soon after the record's release, his replacement being ex-NIRVANA guitarist JASON EVERMAN, who was succeeded in turn by BEN SHEPHERD. CORNELL and CAMERON subsequently got together with future PEARL JAM mambers, EDDIE VEDDER, STONE GOSSARD and JEFF AMENT to form TEMPLE OF THE DOG, releasing an eponymous album in early '91 to critical acclaim. SOUNDGARDEN, meanwhile, finally got their break later that year when 'BADMOTORFINGER' broke the US/UK Top 40. An even more accessible proposition, the record combined a tighter, more driven sound with pop/grunge hooks and their trademark cerebral lyrics to create such MTV favourites as 'JESUS CHRIST POSE' and 'OUTSHINED'. 'RUSTY CAGE' was another juggernaut riffathon, while 'SEARCHING WITH MY GOOD EYE CLOSED' meted out some of the most brutal psychedelia this side of MONSTER MAGNET. A high profile support slot on GUNS N' ROSES' 'Lose Your Illusion' tour afforded the band valuable exposure in the States, their crossover appeal endearing them to the metal hordes on both sides of the Atlantic. Previewed by the Top 20 'SPOONMAN' single, SOUNDGARDEN's masterful fourth set, 'SUPERUNKNOWN' (1994), finally gave the group long overdue success, scaling the US charts and going Top 5 in Britain. Constructed around a head-spinning foundation of acid-drenched retro-rock and JIM MORRISON-esque doom, this epic album spawned the Grammy-winnning 'BLACK HOLE SUN' while 'FELL ON BLACK DAYS' stands as one of their most realised pieces of warped psychedelia to date. Following a world tour with the likes of The SMASHING PUMPKINS, the group began work on 'DOWN ON THE UPSIDE' (1996). Another marathon set boasting sixteen tracks, the record inevitably failed to garner the plaudits of its predecessor; the claustrophobia of old had given way to a marginally more straightforward melodic grunge sound, evidenced to best effect on the likes of 'BURDEN IN MY HAND'. Subversiveness was still the key word; 'TY COBB's mutant country-punk and gonzoid expletive-filled attitude was reminiscent of MINISTRY's seminal 'Jesus Built My Hotrod'. The album ultimately proved to be their swan song, SOUNDGARDEN subsequently pushing up the daisies as of April '97. CORNELL (now in his mid-30's!) returned as a solo artist a few years later, although a largely timid soft-rock debut, 'EUPHORIA MORNING' (1999) – featuring the JEFF BUCKLEY tribute, 'WAVE GOODBYE' – saw the man lose his "metal" credentials. However, the frontman resurfaced – on and off – via post-RAGE AGAINST THE MACHINE project, AUDIOSLAVE; their eponymous debut hitting the Top 20 late 2002. • **Songwriters:** Most by CORNELL and group permutations. Covered SWALLOW MY PRIDE (Ramones) / FOPP (Ohio Players) / INTO THE VOID tune only (Black Sabbath) / BIG BOTTOM (Spinal Tap) / EARACHE MY EYE (Cheech & Chong) / I CAN'T GIVE YOU ANYTHING (Ramones) / HOMOCIDAL SUICIDE (Budgie) / I DON'T CARE ABOUT YOU (Fear) / CAN YOU SEE ME (Jimi Hendrix) / COME TOGETHER (Beatles).

Album rating: ULTRAMEGA OK (*7) / LOUDER THAN LOVE (*8) / BADMOTORFINGER (*9) / SUPERUNKNOWN (*9) / DOWN ON THE UPSIDE (*6) / A-SIDES compilation (*8) / Chris Cornell: EUPHORIA MORNING (*4) / Temple Of The Dog: TEMPLE OF THE DOG (*7)

CHRIS CORNELL (b.20 Jul'64) – vocals, guitar / **KIM THAYIL** (b. 4 Sep'60) – lead guitar / **HIRO YAMAMOTO** (b.13 Apr'61) – bass / **MATT CAMERON** (b.28 Nov'62, San Diego, Calif.) – drums, percussion

not iss. Sub Pop

Jun 87. (7"blue) *<SP 12a>* **NOTHING TO SAY. / HUNTED DOWN** [–] [ ]
Oct 87. (12"ep,orange-12"ep) *<SP 12>* **SCREAMING LIFE** [–] [ ]
– Hunted down / Entering / Tears to forget / Nothing to say / Little Joe / Hand of God.
Aug 88. (12"ep) *<SP 17>* **FOPP** [–] [ ]
– Fopp / Fopp (dub) / Kingdom of come / Swallow my pride.

S.S.T. S.S.T.

Nov 88. (m-lp/c/cd) *<(SST 201/+C/CD)>* **ULTRAMEGA OK** [ ] [ ]
– Flower / All your lies / 665 / Beyond the wheel / 667 / Mood for trouble / Circle of power / He didn't / Smokestack lightning / Nazi driver / Head injury / Incessant mace / One minute of silence. *(re-iss. Oct95;)*
May 89. (12"ep/c-ep/cd-ep) *<(SST 231/+C/CD)>* **FLOWER. / HEAD INJURY / TOY BOX** [ ] [ ]

A&M A&M

Sep 89. (lp/c/cd) *<(AMA/AMC/CDA 5252)>* **LOUDER THAN LOVE** [ ] [ ]
– Ugly truth / Hands all over / Gun / Power trip / Get on the snake / Full on Kevin's mom / Loud love / I awake / No wrong no right / Uncovered / Big dumb sex / Full on (reprise).
Apr 90. (10"ep/cd-ep) *(AM X/CD 560)* **HANDS ALL OVER** [ ] [–]
– Hands all over / Heretic / Come together / Big dumb sex.
Jul 90. (7"ep/12"ep) *(AM/+Y 574)* **THE LOUD LOVE E.P.** [ ] [–]
– Loud love / Fresh deadly roses / Big dumb sex (dub) / Get on the snake.

— **JASON EVERMAN** (b.16 Aug'67) – bass (ex-NIRVANA) repl. HIRO who later formed TRULY after working in a bike shop.

Oct 90. (7",7"purple/green) *<SP 83>* **ROOM A THOUSAND YEARS WIDE. / H.I.V. BABY** [–] [ ]
(above issued on 'Sub Pop')

— **BEN SHEPHERD** (b. HUNTER SHEPHERD, 20 Sep'68, Okinawa, Japan) – bass repl. JASON

Oct 91. (cd/c/lp) *(395374-2/-4/-1) <5374>* **BADMOTORFINGER** [39] [39]
– Rusty cage / Outshined / Slaves & bulldozers / Jesus Christ pose / Face pollution / Somewhere / Searching with my good eye closed / Room a

thousand years wide / Mind riot / Drawing flies / Holy water / New damage.

Mar 92. (7") *(AM 862)* **JESUS CHRIST POSE. / STRAY CAT BLUES** [30] [–]
(cd-s+=) *(AMCD 862)* – Into the void (stealth).

Jun 92. (7"pic-d) *(AM 874)* **RUSTY CAGE. / TOUCH ME** [41] [–]
(12"+=/cd-s+=) *(AM Y/CD 874)* – Show me.
(cd-s+=) *(AMCDX 874)* – Big bottom / Earache my eye.

Nov 92. (7") *(AM 0102)* **OUTSHINED. / I CAN'T GIVE YOU ANYTHING** [50] [–]
(12"+=/cd-s+=) *(AM 0102 T/CD)* – Homocidal suicide.
(cd-s+=) *(AM 0102CDX)* – I don't care about you / Can't you see me.

Feb 94. (7"pic-d/c-s) *(580 538-7/-4)* **SPOONMAN. / FRESH TENDRILS** [20] [–]
(12"clear+=/cd-s+=) *(580 539-1/-2)* – Cold bitch / Exit Stonehenge.

Mar 94. (cd/c/orange-d-lp) *(540215-2/-4/-1) <0198>* **SUPERUNKNOWN** [4] [1]
– Let me drown / My wave / Fell on black days / Mailman / Superunknown / Head down / Black hole Sun / Spoonman / Limo wreck / The day I tried to live / Kickstand / Fresh tendrils / 4th of July / Half / Like suicide / She likes surprises.

Apr 94. (7"pic-d/c-s) *(580594-7/-4)* **THE DAY I TRIED TO LIVE. / LIKE SUICIDE (acoustic)** [42] [–]
(12"etched+=/cd-s+=) *(580595-1/-2)* – Kickstand (live).

Aug 94. (7"pic-d/c-s) *(580736-7/-4)* **BLACK HOLE SUN. / BEYOND THE WHEEL (live) / FELL ON BLACK DAYS (live)** [12] [–]
(pic-cd-s+=) *(580753-2)* – Birth ritual (demo).
(cd-s) *(580737-2)* – ('A'side) / My wave (live) / Jesus Christ pose (live) / Spoonman (remix).

Jan 95. (7"pic-d/c-s) *(580947-7/-4)* **FELL ON BLACK DAYS. / KYLE PETTY, SON OF RICHARD / MOTORCYCLE LOOP** [24] [–]
(cd-s) *(580947-2)* – ('A'side) / Kyle Petty, son of Richard / Fell on black days (video version).
(cd-s) *(580947-5)* – ('A'side) / Girl u want / Fell on black days (early demo).

May 96. (7"red/cd-s) *(581620-7/-4)* **PRETTY NOOSE. / JERRY GARCIA'S FINGER** [14] [–]
(cd-s) *(581620-2)* – ('A'side) / Applebite / An unkind / (interview with Eleven's Alain and Natasha).

May 96. (cd/c/d-lp) *(540526-2/-4/-1) <0526>* **DOWN ON THE UPSIDE** [7] [2]
– Pretty noose / Rhinosaur / Zero chance / Dusty / Ty Cobb / Blow up the outside world / Burden in my hand / Never named / Applebite / Never the machine forever / Tighter & tighter / No attention / Switch opens / Overfloater / An unkind / Boot camp.

Sep 96. (7"/cd-s) *(581854-7/-2)* **BURDEN IN MY HAND. / KARAOKE** [33] [–]
(cd-s) *(581855-2)* – ('A'side) / Bleed together / She's a politician / (Chris Cornell interview).

Dec 96. (7") *(581986-7)* **BLOW UP THE OUTSIDE WORLD. / DUSTY** [38] [–]
(cd-s+=) *(581987-2)* – Gun.
(cd-s) *(581986-2)* – ('A'side) / Get on the snake / Slice of spacejam.

—— split on the 9th of April 1997

– compilations, etc –

Oct 93. (cd) *A&M; (CDA 24118)* **LOUDER THAN LOUD / BADMOTORFINGER** [ ] [ ]

Oct 93. (c/cd) *Sub Pop; (SP/+CD 12)* **SCREAMING LIFE / FOPP** [ ] [ ]

Nov 97. (cd) *A&M; (540833-2) <0833>* **A-SIDES** [ ] [63]
– Nothing to say / Flower / Loud love / Hands all over / Get on the snake / Jesus Christ pose / Outshined / Rusty cage / Spoonman / The day I tried to live / Black hole sun / Fell on black days / Pretty noose / Burden in my hand / Blow up the outside world / Ty Cobb / Bleed together.

CHRIS CORNELL

Sep 99. (cd/c) *<(490412-2/-4)>* **EUPHORIA MORNING** [31] [18]
– Can't change me / Flutter girl / Preaching the end of the world / Follow my way / When I'm down / Mission / Wave goodbye / Moonchild / Sweet euphoria / Disappearing one / Pillow of your bones / Steel rain.

Oct 99. (7") *(497173-7)* **CAN'T CHANGE ME. / FLUTTER GIRL** [62] [–]
(cd-s+=) *(497173-2)* – Nowhere but you.
(cd-s) *(497174-2)* – ('A'side) / When I'm down / ('A'-video).

TEMPLE OF THE DOG

splinter-group feat. **CORNELL + CAMERON** plus **STONE GOSSARD / JEFF AMENT** (both ex-MOTHER LOVE BONE, future PEARL JAM)

A&M A&M

Jun 92. (cd/c/lp) *(395 350-2/-4/-1) <5350>* **TEMPLE OF THE DOG** [ ] [5]
– Say hello to Heaven / Reach down / Hunger strike / Pushing forward back / Call me a dog / Times of trouble / Wooden Jesus / Your saviour / 4-walled world / All night thing.

Oct 92. (7"pic-d/c-s) *(AM 0091/+C)* **HUNGER STRIKE. / ALL NIGHT THING** [51] [ ]
(12"+=/cd-s+=) *(AM 0091 T/CD)* – Your saviour.

□ SOUTHERN DEATH CULT (see under ⇒ CULT)

SPACE

Formed: Liverpool, England . . . 1993 by TOMMY SCOTT, JAMIE MURPHY, FRANNY GRIFFITHS and ANDY PARLE, all seasoned campaigners of the local music scene (TOMMY and FRANNY played in The AUSTRALIANS, whose track, 'THE GIRL WHO LOVED HER MAN ENOUGH TO KILL HIM' appeared on the 'Hit The North' various artists compilation). After a one-off single on the independent 'Home', the band were snapped up by 'Gut', a label which brought us the bare-arsed "pop thrills" of RIGHT SAID FRED. Equally camp in a more masculine kind of Scouse way, SPACE were light years removed from the shower of Brit-pop retro merchants doing the rounds in the mid-90's; the 'NEIGHBOURHOOD' single sounded like ENNIO MORRICONE waltzing round the last chance saloon to an acid-fried Mariachi soundtrack, SCOTT's robotic vocal affectations carrying lyrics cut from the same cloth as PETE SHELLEY's (Buzzcocks) creations. For all his little-boy-lost charm, SCOTT sounded pretty damn scary throughout much of the 'SPIDERS' (1996) album, his tales of losers, freaks and paranoid killers balancing black humour with unhinged Liverpudlian menace. Preceded by the voodoo-xylophone pop genius of 'FEMALE OF THE SPECIES' (a Top 20 hit and arguably one of the singles of the year) and the brassy, bouncy life affirming 'ME & YOU VERSUS THE WORLD' (about as commercial as SPACE get and a nod to native forebears, The Fab Four), the debut was released in late '96 to encouraging reviews and a subsequent Top 5 chart placing. Running the gamut of the band's many influences, from SINATRA and KRAFTWERK to 'South Pacific' and 'Midnight Cowboy', the album even catered for MURPHY's avowed love of techno with an acid freakout, 'GROWLER', bolted on as the closing track. Armed with a further two Top 20 hits in a re-released 'NEIGHBOURHOOD' and 'DARK CLOUDS', SPACE were ready to explore the final frontier where no (sensible) band had gone before i.e. the festival circuit. 1997 proved to be an even more hectic year, one that nearly broke them; JAMIE (at only 21, the stress of it all had played havoc with his peace of mind) pulled out on the eve of an American tour in February, TOMMY mysteriously lost his voice for a couple of months as well as being stalked and the general pressures of slogging round the world turned them into emotional wrecks. No doubt the experiences which formed the basis for follow-up Top 3 album, 'TIN PLANET' (1998), the cadets safely back on earth and ready for a new mission that resulted in two Top 10 hits, 'AVENGING ANGEL' and the tongue-in-cheek duet with CATATONIA's CERYS, 'THE BALLAD OF TOM JONES'. • **Songwriters:** Perm any SCOTT / GRIFFITHS / MURPHY and group except WE GOTTA GET OUT OF THIS PLACE (Animals).

Album rating: SPIDERS (*7) / TIN PLANET (*7) / GREATEST HITS compilation (*7)

TOMMY SCOTT – vocals, guitar / **JAMIE MURPHY** – guitar, vocals / **FRANNY GRIFFITHS** – bass / **ANDY PARLE** – drums

Home | not iss.

Oct 95. (c-s) *(CAHOME 1)* **MONEY / KILL ME** [ ] [–]
(cd-s+=) *(CDHOME 1)* – ('A'club) / ('B'club).
(12") *(12HOME 1)* – ('A'-Lost in space remix) / ('A'-Still lost in space & safe bass mix) / ('A'-Space club mix) / ('A'-instrumental).

Gut | Uptown – Universal

Mar 96. (c-s) *(CAGUT 1)* **NEIGHBOURHOOD / REJECTS** [56] [–]
(cd-s+=) *(CDGUT 1)* – Turn me on to spiders.
(12") *(12GUT 1)* – ('A'-Live it! club) / ('A'-Live it! instrumental club) / ('A'-Pissed up stomp) / ('A'-radio).

Jun 96. (c-s) *(CAGUT 2)* **FEMALE OF THE SPECIES / LOONEY TUNE** [14] [–]
(12"+=/cd-s+=) *(12/CD GUT 2)* – ('A'radio) / Give me something.

Aug 96. (c-s) *(CAGUT 4)* **ME & YOU VERSUS THE WORLD / SPIDERS** [9] [–]
(cd-s+=) *(CDGUT 4)* – Life of a miser / Blow your cover.
(cd-s) *(CXGUT 4)* – ('A'mixes).

Sep 96. (cd/c/lp) *(GUT CD/MC/LP 1)* *<53028>* **SPIDERS** [5] Jan97 [ ]
– Neighbourhood / Mister Psycho / Female of the species / Money / Me & you vs the world / Lovechild of the queen / No-one understands / Voodoo roller / Drop dead / Dark clouds / Major pager / Kill me / Charlie M. / Growler.

— added **DAVE PALMER** – bass

Oct 96. (c-s) *(CAGUT 5)* *<1152>* **NEIGHBOURHOOD / ONLY HALF AN ANGEL** [11] [ ]
(cd-s+=) *(CDGUT 5)* – Crisis / Shut your mouth.
(cd-s) *(CXGUT 5)* – ('A'side) / Welcome to the neighbourhood / Nighthood / Neighbourhood (pissed up stomp mix).

Feb 97. (c-s) *(CAGUT 6)* **DARK CLOUDS / HAD ENOUGH** [14] [–]
(cd-s+=) *(CDGUT 6)* – Children of the night / Influenza.
(cd-s) *(CXGUT 6)* – ('A'side) / Darker clouds / Storm clouds.

Gut | Imprint

Dec 97. (7"blue) *(7GUT 16)* **AVENGING ANGELS. / I AM UNLIKE A LIFEFORM YOU'VE NEVER MET** [6] [–]
(c-s) *(CAGUT 16)* – ('A'side) / Bastard me, bastard you.
(cd-s++=) *(CDGUT 16)* – Theme from "Baretta Vendetta".
(cd-s) *(CXGUT 16)* – ('A'side) / ('A'mixes:- John 'OO' Fleming Theramin mix / Ultra Vegas mix / The Jumping Soundboy mix / Franny's 'Peaceful Devil' mix / Brainbasher's 'Kick Ass Angel' mix / Jonnie Newman's 'Altered State' mix).

— **LEON CAFFREY** – drums (ex-PROPER) repl. PARLE

Feb 98. (7"red; with CERYS of CATATONIA) *(7GUT 18)* **THE BALLAD OF TOM JONES. / NOW SHE'S GONE** [4] [–]
(c-s+=) *(CAGUT 18)* – Happy endings.
(cd-s++=) *(CDGUT 18)* – Stress transmissions.
(cd-s) *(CXGUT 18)* – ('A'mixes:- Cocktail Lounge mix / Dirty Beatniks mix / Sound 5 mix / Sure Is Pure dub mix / SX Dub Scratching Cuckoo mix / Tom Jones Axe To Your Head mix).

Mar 98. (cd/c/lp) *(GUT CD/MC/LP 5)* *<110683>* **TIN PLANET** [3] Jul98 [ ]
– Begin again / Avenging angels / The ballad of Tom Jones / 1 o'clock / Be there / The man / A liddle biddy help from Elvis / The unluckiest man in the world / Piggies / Bad day's / There's no you / Disco dolly / Fran in Japan.

Jun 98. (c-s/cd-s) *(CA/CD GUT 19)* **BEGIN AGAIN / YOU ROMANTIC FOOL / NUMB THE DOUBT / INFLUENZA (flu mix)** [21] [–]
(cd-s) *(CXGUT 19)* – ('A'side) / The ballad of Tom Jones (live) / Female of the species (live) / Avenging angels (live).

Nov 98. (c-s) *(CAGUT 22)* **BAD DAYS EP** [20] [–]
– Bad days / We gotta get out of this place / The unluckiest man in the world.
(cd-s+=) *(CDGUT 22)* – Cold in the city.
(cd-s+=) *(CXGUT 22)* – Yeah right!

— late in 1999, SPACE teamed up with TOM JONES to record 'SUNNY AFTERNOON' on his comeback set, 'Reload'

Jun 00. (c-s/cd-s) *(CA/CD GUT 34)* **DIARY OF A WIMP / IF I EVER / RAYMOND** [49] [–]
(cd-s) *(CXGUT 34)* – ('A'side) / Hell of a girl / Why can't we turn out the lights.

Jul 02. (cd) *(GUTCD 18)* **GREATEST HITS** (compilation) [ ] [–]
– Female of the species / Avenging angels / Neighbourhood / The ballad of Tom Jones (with CERYS MATTHEWS) / Sunny afternoon (with TOM JONES) / Money / Begin again / We gotta get out of this place / Bad days (remix) / Dark clouds / Me & you vs. the world / Diary of a wimp / Gravity / The shit you talk is beautiful / Spiders.

SPACEMEN 3

Formed: Rugby, Warwickshire, England . . . 1983 by SONIC BOOM (PETE KEMBER) and JASON PIERCE. They enlisted PETE BAINES and ROSCO as a rhythm section and through their manager, Gerald Palmer, they signed to indie label, 'Glass'. In 1986, they debuted with 'SOUND OF CONFUSION', a primal embryo for "shoegazers" to come. Their follow-up, 'THE PERFECT PRESCRIPTION', set the world alight (well! the indie world anyway), with some clever pulsating, psychedelic garage-noise intertwined with melancholy bursts of beauty and experimentation, i.e 'WALKIN WITH JESUS' (again!), 'TRANSPARENT RADIATION' and 'TAKE ME TO THE OTHER SIDE'. In 1989, they were back again with a third set, 'PLAYING WITH FIRE', featuring the 10-minute squall of 'SUICIDE', and 'REVOLUTION' (later covered by MUDHONEY). SONIC BOOM's heroin addiction was taking its toll during the early 90's and with JASON having founded SPIRITUALIZED, the group were heading for their own proverbial rocketship to oblivion. Their final outing, 'RECURRING' (1991), recorded amid escalating tension, was a slight disappointment. By this time, SONIC had gone solo, subsequently going under the guise of SPECTRUM. His debut was followed by two albums of patchy, yet somewhat appealing albums, 'SOUL KISS (GLIDE DIVINE)' (1992) and 'HIGH LOWS AND HEAVENLY BLOWS' (1994). The ever prolific KEMBER went on play with mid 90's outfit, JESSAMINE, who to date have released a string of albums including 1997's 'ANOTHER FICTIONALIZED HISTORY'. Around the same time, KEMBER/SONIC simultaneously resurfaced with a SPECTRUM set, 'FOREVER ALIEN', released on the '3rd Stone' imprint. The SPECTRUM posse subsequently indulged their passion for prehistoric analog synth by hooking up with legendary early electronic experimentalists SILVER APPLES. The resulting 'LAKE OF TEARDROPS' (1998) was pretty much what you'd expect from such a collaboration with the respective parties' dedication to retroactivity precluding any startling intergalactic innovation. During the 90's, SONIC BOOM was also part of indie noisesters, EXPERIMENTAL AUDIO RESEARCH alongside (initially) KEVIN SHIELDS (of MY BLOODY VALENTINE) and EDDIE PREVOST (of AMM). EAR – as they were known for short – were primarily concerned with exploring the boundaries where stark ambience meets uncompromising guitar manipulation/noise, making their first lunar mission via a US-only debut CD-album, 'MESMERISED' (1994). Reflecting his love of collectable vinyl, SONIC BOOM decided to release a 5" single, 'POCKET SYMPHONY' a few months later. Subsequently securing a UK deal with 'Big Cat', EAR finally got round to issuing their first studio venture (actually recorded during their formative year), 'BEYOND THE PALE', in 1996. Over the course of the ensuing two years or so, the group were surprisingly prolific, completing a trio of long-players, 'PHENOMENA 256' (1996), 'THE KONER EXPERIMENT' (1997) and 'MILLENNIUM MUSIC' (1998) for three separate labels. Of late, the avant-garde troupe (who had now lost SHIELDS and MARTIN) introduced a revolutionary technique called "circuit bending" on their sixth album, 'DATA RAPE' (1998). 'VIBRATIONS' (2000) continued to tweak the listener into submission, EAR opening their musical account on this occasion with the spaced-out 'KALIMBELL'. • **Songwriters:** KEMBER or PIERCE material until the 90's when KEMBER penned all. Covered; LITTLE DOLL (Stooges) / TRANSPARENT RADIATION (Red Krayola) / IT'S ALRIGHT (Bo Diddley) / CHE + ROCK'N'ROLL IS KILLING MY LIFE (Suicide) / WHEN TOMORROW HITS (Mudhoney) / COME TOGETHER + STARSHIP (MC5) / MARY-ANNE (Juicy Lucy) / ROLLER COASTER (13th Floor Elevators).

Album rating: SOUND OF CONFUSION (*7) / THE PERFECT PRESCRIPTION (*8) / PLAYING WITH FIRE (*8) / RECURRING (*8) / PERFORMANCE posthumous (*7) / DREAM WEAPON – ECSTASY IN SLOW MOTION posthumous: (*7) / TAKING DRUGS TO MAKE MUSIC TO TAKE DRUGS TO posthumous (*5) / SPACEMEN ARE GO! posthumous (*3) / FOR ALL THE FUCKED UP CHILDREN IN THE WORLD posthumous (*4) / TRANSLUCENT FLASHBACKS collection (*6) / Sonic Boom: SPECTRUM (*5) / Spectrum: SOUL KISS (GLIDE DIVINE) (*6) / HIGH LOWS AND HEAVENLY BLOWS (*6) / FOREVER ALIEN (*6) / Experimental Audio Research: MESMERISED (*6) / BEYOND THE PALE (*6) / PHENOMENA 256 (*7) / THE KONER EXPERIMENT (*5) / MILLENNIUM MUSIC (*7) / DATA RAPE (*6) / LIVE AT THE DREAM PALACE (*6) / PESTREPELLER (*5) / VIBRATIONS mini (*5) / CONTINUUM (*6)

SONIC BOOM (b. PETE KEMBER, 19 Nov'65) – vocals / **JASON PIERCE** (b.19 Nov'65) – guitar / **STEWART (ROSCO) ROSSWELL** – keyboards / **PETE (BASSMAN) BAINES** – bass

Glass / not iss.

Jun 86. (lp) *(GLA 018)* **SOUND OF CONFUSION** [ ] [–]
– Losing touch with my mind / Hey man / Roller coaster / Mary Anne / Little doll / 2:35 / O.D. catastrophe. *(re-iss. Sep89 on 'Fire' lp/c/cd; REFIRE CD/MC/LP 5) <US cd-iss. 1994 on 'Taang!'; 93>*

Dec 86. (12"m) *(GLAEP 105)* **WALKIN' WITH JESUS (SOUND OF CONFUSION). / ROLLERCOASTER / FEEL SO GOOD** [ ] [–]

Jul 87. (12"m) *(GLAEP 108)* **TRANSPARENT RADIATION / ECSTASY SYMPHONY / TRANSPARENT RADIATION (FLASHBACK). / THINGS'LL NEVER BE THE SAME / STARSHIP** [ ] [–]

Aug 87. (lp/c) *(GLA LP/MC 026)* **THE PERFECT PRESCRIPTION** [ ] [–]
– Take me to the other side / Walking with Jesus / Ode to street hassle / Ecstasy – Symphony / Feel so good / Things'll never be the same / Come down easy / Call the doctor / Soul 1 / That's just fine. *(re-iss. Dec89 on 'Fire' lp/c/cd; REFIRE LP/MC/CD 6) <US cd-iss. 1994 on 'Taang!'; 94>*

Mar 88. (12") *(GLASS 12-054)* **TAKE ME TO THE OTHER SIDE. / SOUL 1 / THAT'S JUST FINE** [ ] [–]

Jul 88. (lp/cd) *(GLA LP/CD 030)* **PERFORMANCE** (live 1988 Holland) [ ] [–]
– Mary-Anne / Come together / Things'll never be the same / Take me to the other side / Roller coaster / Starship / Walkin' with Jesus. *(re-iss. May91 & Apr02 on 'Fire' cd/c/lp; REFIRE CD/MC/LP 11)*

— **WILLIE B. CARRUTHERS** – bass / **JON MATLOCK** – drums repl. ROSCO + BAINES who formed The DARKSIDE

Fire / not iss.

Nov 88. (7") *(BLAZE 29S)* **REVOLUTION. / CHE** [ ] [–]
(12"+=/cd-s+=) *(BLAZE 29 T/CD)* – May the circle be unbroken.

Feb 89. (lp/c/cd) *(FIRE LP/MC/CD 16)* **PLAYING WITH FIRE** [ ] [–]
– Honey / Come down softly to my soul / How does it feel? / I believe it / Revolution / Let me down gently / So hot (wash away all my tears) / Suicide / Lord can you hear me. *(free-12"ep/cd-ep+=)* – Starship / Revolution / Suicide (live) / Repeater / Live intro theme (xtacy). *<US cd-iss. 1994 on 'Taang'; 97> <d-lp-iss.Sep99 on 'Space Age'; ORBIT 011LP)*

Jul 89. (7") *(BLAZE 36S)* **HYPNOTIZED. / JUST TO SEE YOU SMILE HONEY (part 2)** [ ] [–]
(12"+=/3"cd-s+=) *(BLAZE 36 T/CD)* – The world is dying.
(free 7"flexi w.a) *(CHEREE 5)* – EXTRACTS FROM A CONTEMPORARY SITAR EVENING (with other artists).

Jan 91. (7") *(BLAZE 41)* **BIG CITY. / DRIVE** [ ] [–]
(12"+=/cd-s+=) *(BLAZE 41 T/CD)* – Big City (everybody I know can be found here).
(12"w-drawn) *(BLAZE 41TR)* – ('A'remix) / I love you (remix).

Feb 91. (cd/lp)(s-lp) *(FIRE CD/LP 23)(FIRELP 23S)* **RECURRING** [46] [–]
– Big city (everybody I know can be found here) / Just to see you smile (orchestral) / I love you / Set me free – I've got the key / Set me free (reprise) / Feel so bad (reprise) / Hypnotized / Sometimes / Feelin' just fine (head full of shit) / Billy Whizz – blue 1. *(cd+=)* – When tomorrow hits / Why couldn't I see / Just to see you smile (instrumental) / Feel so sad (demo) / Drive.

— they had already folded June '90.

– compilations, etc. –

Dec 90. (cd/d-lp) *Fierce; (FRIGHT 042/+CD)* **DREAM WEAPON / ECSTASY IN SLOW MOTION** [ ] [–]
(re-iss. Nov95 on 'Space Age' cd/d-lp; ORBIT 001 CD/LP) (cd re-iss. May02 on 'Sympathy For The Record Industry'; SFTRI 211)

Jun 94. (cd/lp) *Taang!; <TAANG 96 CD/LP>* **THE SINGLES** [–] [ ]

Nov 94. (cd) *Bomp; (<BCD 4047>)* **TAKING DRUGS TO MAKE MUSIC TO TAKE DRUGS TO** (demos of 1986) [ ] [ ]
(re-iss. Mar00 on 'Space Age'; ORBIT 023CD)

May 95. (cd/lp) *Sympathy For The Record Industry; (<SFTRI 136 CD/B>)* **FOR ALL FUCKED UP CHILDREN OF THE WORLD WE GIVE YOU . . .** (debut recording session) [ ] [ ]
(cd re-iss. Jun00 & May02; SFTRI 368CD)

May 95. (cd) *Bomp; (<BCD 4044>)* **SPACEMEN ARE GO!** [ ] [ ]
(re-iss. Jun00; same)

Jun 95. (cd/d-lp) *Fire; (FLIP CD/DLP 003)* **TRANSLUCENT FLASHBACKS (THE GLASS SINGLES)** [ ] [–]
(cd re-iss. Aug01; same)

Sep 95. (cd) *Taang; <TAANG 95CD>* **LIVE AT THE MILKWEG 6/2/88 (live)** [–] [ ]
– Mary Ann / Come together / Things'll never be / Take me to the other side / Rollercoaster / Walking with Jesus / Repeater / Starship / Revolution / Suicide.

Oct 95. (cd) *Fierce; (FRIGHT 063)* **THE CHOICE IS REVOLUTIONORHERION** [ ] [–]

Nov 95. (cd/d-lp) *Space Age; (ORBIT 002 CD/LP)* **LIVE IN EUROPE 1989 (live)** [ ] [–]

Mar 97. (d-cd) *Nectar; (NTMCDD 534)* **1 + 1 = 3** [ ] [–]

SONIC BOOM

(**PETE KEMBER** solo with **WILLIE B. CARRUTHERS** and also **PHIL PARFITT + JO WIGGS** of PERFECT DISASTER)

Silvertone / Sympathy

Oct 89. (12"ep/cd-ep) *(ORE T/CD 11)* **ANGEL. / ANGEL (version) / HELP ME PLEASE** [ ] [–]

Feb 90. (cd/c/lp) *(ORE CD/MC/LP 506)* **SPECTRUM** [65] [–]
– Pretty baby / If I should die / Lonely avenue / Help me please / Angel / Rock'n'roll is killing my life / You're the one. *(free 10" w-lp) (SONIC 1)* – DRONE DREAM EP: OCTAVES. / TREMELOS *<US-iss.Oct97 as 'WHEN CAME BEFORE AFTER' on 'Sympathy For The Record Industry'; SFTRI 493>*

Apr 91. (7"colrd) *<SFTRI 75>* **TREMELOS. / ECSTACY (IN SLOW MOTION)** [–] [ ]

Apr 91. (7"; gig freebie) *(SONIC 2)* **(I LOVE YOU) TO THE MOON AND BACK. / CAPO WALTZ (live)** [–] [–]

— SONIC BOOM has now featured in E.A.R. (EXPERIMENTAL AUDIO RESEARCH), who after first low-key album 'MESMERISED' in 1994 on 'Sympathy For The Record Industry), released for 'Big Cat' the 1996 lp/cd 'BEYOND THE PALE' *(ABB 96/+CD)*. It featured KEVIN SHIELDS (of; we still think; MY BLOODY VALENTINE), KEVIN MARTIN (of GOD) and EDDIE PREVOST. SONIC BOOM and E.A.R. released a split 7" in Jul'98 on 'Earworm' (WORM 22)

— In Mar 92, HONEY TONGUE (aka MATTOCK + WIGGS) released lp 'NUDE NUDES' on 'Playtime'; *AMUSE 012CD)*

SPECTRUM

KEMBER, CARRUTHERS, etc

Silvertone / Warners

Jun 92. (7") *(ORE 41)* **HOW YOU SATISFY ME. / DON'T GO (instrumental 2)** [ ] [–]
(12"clear+=/cd-s+=) *(ORE 41 T/CD)* – My life spins around your every smile / Don't go (instrumental 1).

Jun 92. (cd/c/lp) *(ORE CD/C/LP 518)* *<41501>* **SOUL KISS (GLIDE DIVINE)** [ ] [ ]
– How you satisfy me / Lord I don't even know my name / The drunk suite (overture) / Neon sigh / Waves wash over me / (I love you) To the

Moon and back / My love for you never died away but my soul gave out and wit / Sweet running water / Touch the stars / Quicksilver glide divine / The drunk suite / Phase me out (gently). *(re-iss. Apr95; same)*

Sep 92. (7") *(ORE 44)* **TRUE LOVE WILL FIND YOU IN THE END. / MY LIFE SPINS AROUND YOUR EVERY SMILE** [70] [–]
(12"/cd-s) *(ORE T/CD 44)* – ('A'side) / To the moon and back / Waves wash over me.

— now w/ **KEVIN COWAN** – guitar (ex-DARKSIDE) repl. FORMBY

Sep 92. (d7") *<SFTRI 188>* **TRUE LOVE WILL FIND YOU IN THE SUN. / TASTE THE OZONE // DON'T GO (PLEASE STAY). / DRUNK SUITE – QUICKSILVER GLIDE DIVINE** [–] [ ]
Nov 92. (7") *<SFTRI 209>* **SANTA CLAUS (as the Sonics). / CHRISTMAS MESSAGE FROM SONIC BOOM** [–] [ ]
Aug 93. (7") *(ORE 56)* **INDIAN SUMMER. / BABY DON'T YOU WORRY (California lullabye)** [ ] [–]
(12"+=/cd-s+=) *(ORE T/CD 56)* – It's alright / True love will find you in the end.
Oct 94. (12"ep/cd-ep) *(ORE T/CD 65)* **UNDO THE TABOO / IN THE FULLNESS OF TIME. / TURN THE TIDE (SUB AQUA) / GO TO SLEEP** [ ] [–]
Nov 94. (cd/lp) *(ORE CD/LP 532)* **HIGHS, LOWS AND HEAVENLY BLOWS** [ ] [–]
– Undo the taboo / Feedback / Then I just drifted away / Take your time / Soothe me / All night long / Don't pass me by / I know they say / Take me away.

not iss. Sympathy F

Oct 96. (10"ep) *<SFTRI 278>* **SPECTRUM 10** [–] [ ]
– California lullabye / It's alright / Indian summer / True love . . . (alt. version) / Through the rhythm.

— SONIC BOOM also became part of JESSAMINE, an outfit who released a few albums including 'Another Fictionalized History' in '97.

— now with **ALF HARDY** – synthesizers

3rd Stone Reprise

Oct 96. (cd-ep) *<46303>* **SONGS FOR OWSLEY** [–] [ ]
– Owsley / Liquid intentions / Feels like I'm slipping away / Sine study #1 / The new Atlantis.
Aug 97. (d-lp/cd) *(ORBIT 008/+CD)* *<46715>* **FOREVER ALIEN** [ ] [ ]
– Feels like I'm slipping away / The stars are so far (how does it feel?) / Close your eyes and you'll see / Delia Derbyshire / Owsley / Forever alien / Matrix / Like . . . / The new Atlantis / The end. *(UK+=)* – Sounds for a thunderstorm (for Peter Zinovieft) / Liquid intentions / Sine study.
Sep 97. (cd-ep) *(ORBIT 010CD)* **FEELS LIKE I'M SLIPPING AWAY** [ ] [–]
– Feels like I'm slipping away / Forever alien / Dream time / What comes before after? *<US-iss.Jun00; same>*
Oct 98. (cd/lp; as SPECTRUM & SILVER APPLES) *(ORBIT 016 CD/LP)* **A LAKE OF TEARDROPS** [ ] [–]
– Streams of sorrow / Sixth sense / The edge / Second sight / Whirlwind / (I don't care if you) Never come back.
Jun 99. (cd; split w/ IMAJINARY FRIENDS) *(ORBIT 017CD)* **INTERFACE / COME OUT TO PLAY** [ ] [–]
– Against the grain / Taste the night / (5 by other group).

EXPERIMENTAL AUDIO RESEARCH

SONIC BOOM – effects, etc (of SPECTRUM) / **KEVIN SHIELDS** – guitar (of MY BLOODY VALENTINE) / **EDDIE PREVOST** – percussion (of A.M.M.) / **KEVIN MARTIN** – sax, effects (of GOD)

not iss. Sympathy F

Jun 94. (cd) *<SFTRI 279>* **MESMERISED** [–] [ ]
– D.M.T. symphony (overture to an inhabited zone) / Mesmerise 4901 / California nocturne / Guitar feedback manipulation.
Oct 94. (5") **POCKET SYMPHONY** [–] [ ]

Big Cat Big Cat

Jun 96. (lp/cd) *<(ABB 96/+CD)>* **BEYOND THE PALE** (rec.1992) [ ] Feb96 [ ]
– Beyond the pale / The calm before / In the cold light of day / The calm beyond / Dusk / The circle is blue.

not iss. Man's Ruin

Sep 96. (10"; as EAR) *<MR 001>* **DELTA 6 (HYDROPHONIC)** [–] [ ]

— now without SHIELDS; he was repl. by **TOM PRENTICE** – electric viola / **PETE BAIN** – lap steel / **SCOTT RILEY** – hammer guitar

Space Age Sympathy F

Sep 96. (d-lp/cd) *(ORBIT 005/+CD)* *<SFTRI 459>* **PHENOMENA 256** [ ] [ ]
– Delta 6 (hydrophonic) / Space themes part 1 & 2 (tribute to John Cage in C, A, G, E) / Sub aqua (left channel) – Tidal (centre channel) – Lunar (right channel) / Ring modulator / As the night starts closing in / Phenomena 256 (3 piece suite) / Spacestation / Mood for a summer sundown. *(re-iss. Apr98; same)*

— the usual quartet added **THOMAS KONER** + **ANDY MELLWIG** – rhythms

Mille Plateau Mille Plateau

Mar 97. (cd/lp) *(<CDMILLEPLATEAU 36>)* **THE KONER EXPERIMENT** [ ] [ ]
– (track 1-10).

Via Satellite Via Satellite

May 97. (7"split) *(<VSAT 006>)* **SPUTNIK. / Thurston Moore & Don Fleming: TELSTAR** [ ] [ ]

— now **SONIC BOOM, EDDIE PREVOST, PETE BASSMAN (BAIN)** + **TOM PRENTICE**

Atavistic Atavistic

Jan 98. (d-lp; 3-sided/cd) *(<ALP 72/+CD>)* **MILLENIUM MUSIC** [ ] [ ]
– Delysid / Digitana / The enigma coda.

Space Age Space Age

Jul 98. (cd/d-lp) *<(ORBIT 013 CD/LP)>* **DATA RAPE** [ ] [ ]
– Track 1-8.

Earworm not iss.

Aug 98. (7",7"clear) *(WORM 22)* **INTERLUDE. / TRANSISTOR MUSIC** [ ] [–]

Ochre Ochre

Sep 98. (10"ep) *<(OCH 025)>* **DEATH OF A ROBOT** [ ] [ ]
Nov 98. (7"one-sided) *(WORM 35)* **DATA RAPE (part 9)** [ ] [–]
(above iss. on 'Earworm') (below on 'Histrionic')

— now just down to **SONIC BOOM**

Apr 99. (cd; as E.A.R. and JESSAMINE) *<(HIST 02)>* **LIVING SOUND (live)** [ ] [ ]
– Track 1-7.
above with **ANDY BROWN, DAWN SMITHSON, MICHAEL FAETH** + **REX RITTER**
Jul 99. (cd/lp; as E.A.R.) *<(OCH 009 CD/LV)>* **PESTREPELLER** [ ] [ ]
– Beyond the point of no return (part one) / Beyond the point of no return (part two) / Automatic music (for oscillator, ring modulator & filter cluster).
Apr 00. (cd) *<(OCH 015LCD)>* **LIVE AT THE DREAM PALACE, NEW ORLEANS RECORDED 27.11.98 (live)** [ ] [ ]
– Modulo 2 / Song for a seraphim.

Rocket Girl Rocket Girl

Nov 00. (m-lp/m-cd) *(RGIRL 18/+CD)* **VIBRATIONS** [ ] [ ]
– Kalimbell / Ring / Synchrondipity / Wired waves / Tripple.

Space Age Space Age

Oct 01. (cd; as E.A.R.) *<(ORBIT 26CD)>* **CONTINUUM** [ ] [ ]
– Submarine / Buzz / Shimmer / Swing / Ebb / Echo gull / Whisper incantor / See-saw.

SPANDAU BALLET

Formed: Islington, London, England . . . late 1979 by brothers GARY and MARTIN KEMP alongside TONY HADLEY, JOHN KEEBLE and STEVE NORMAN. With their kilts swishing and their fringes flapping, SPANDAU BALLET were initially darlings of the London 'New Romantic' scene, their earliest recordings as haughtily pretentious as their awful moniker. With help from VISAGE man, STEVE STRANGE and RUSTY EGAN (Skids), they found a manager going by the unlikely name of Steve Dagger. The latter famously turned down a deal with 'Island' records, helping the band set up their own label instead, 'Reformation'. A canny move, the group's subsequent output duly being licensed by 'Chrysalis' and a debut single, 'TO CUT A LONG STORY SHORT', making the UK Top 5. This was basically the sole high point of their overwrought debut album, 'JOURNEYS TO GLORY' (1981), one of the first "New Romantic" long players to break the UK Top 5. Their biggest hit to date came later that summer via a collaboration with funksters, BEGGAR & CO., 'CHANT No.1 (I DON'T NEED THIS PRESSURE ON)', a taster for the more commercial leanings of the 'DIAMOND' (1982) opus. The album spawned a further three Top 20 hits, although it was only with the No.1 'TRUE' (1983) album that SPANDAU BALLET really found their calling in musical life; white boy soul/lounge pop with a polished veneer. The new sound was defined with the title track, a massive transatlantic smash upon its release as a single and the SPANDAU's first No.1 hit. 'GOLD' followed suit, a more upbeat effort with HADLEY's coffee table croon no less effective, while 'ONLY WHEN YOU LEAVE' gave the group their third Top 3 hit in succession. 'PARADE' (1984) carried on in much the same vein and was almost as successful, providing a further trio of UK Top 20 hits. Its dismal performance in the States, however, led to the group sueing 'Chrysalis' for lack of promotion, the legal battle keeping SPANDAU BALLET occupied for the whole of 1985. The group eventually re-emerged in late '86 with the embarrassing 'FIGHT FOR OURSELVES', newly signed to 'C.B.S.'. The lighter waving ballad, 'THROUGH THE BARRICADES', gave them their last Top 10 hit, preceding the album of the same name. Though the set also made the Top 10, it was to be the group's final taste of real chart action. Subsequent singles stiffed and 'sunk like a stone' would've been a more accurate title for their 1989 effort, 'HEART LIKE A SKY'. Clearly, SPANDAU BALLET were now a glaring anachronism as the 80's gave way to some decent music in the new decade, wisely splitting in 1990. The KEMP brothers found success in acting, both garnering plaudits for their double lead role in 'The Krays', the 1989 film based on the infamous East End gangsters. GARY subsequently appeared in 'The Bodyguard' alongside Whitney Houston, marrying actress Sadie Frost in real life. He wasn't quite so successful musically, however, a 1995 solo effort predictably stiffing as did HADLEY's early 90's efforts on 'E.M.I.'. The KEMP's were back on show in 1999, while MARTIN (who'd recently suffered a life or death brain operation) starred in Eastenders, GARY was sued by the rest of SPANDAU BALLET for unpaid songwriter royalties; that April, a judge threw out the unwritten agreement in favour of GARY. • **Songwriters:** All written by the KEMP brothers. TONY HADLEY used writers SINFIELD-HILL, CLIMIE-FISHER or DIANE WARREN. HADLEY Covered: ROCK'N'ROLL SUICIDE (David Bowie) / THE BOYS OF SUMMER (Don Henley).

Album rating: JOURNEYS TO GLORY (*5) / DIAMOND (*4) / TRUE (*6) / PARADE (*5) / THE SINGLES COLLLECTION compilation (*7) / THROUGH THE BARRICADES (*6) / HEART LIKE A SKY (*3) / THE BEST OF SPANDAU BALLET compilation (*6)

TONY HADLEY (b. 2 Jun'59) – vocals, synthesizers / **GARY KEMP** (b.16 Oct'60) – keyboards, guitar / **STEVE NORMAN** (b.25 Mar'60) – saxophone, guitar / **MARTIN KEMP** (b.10 Oct'61) – bass / **JOHN KEEBLE** (b. 6 Jul'59) – drums

Chrysalis Chrysalis

Nov 80. (7"/12") *(CHS/+12 2473)* **TO CUT A LONG STORY SHORT. / ('A'instrumental)** 5 □

Jan 81. (7"/ext.12") *(CHS/+12 2486)* **THE FREEZE. / ('A'instrumental)** 17 □

Mar 81. (lp/c) *(<CHR/ZCHR 1331>)* **JOURNEYS TO GLORY** 5 □
– To cut a long story short / Reformation / Mandolin / Musclebound / Age of blows / The freeze / Confused / Toys. *(cd-iss. Dec82; CCD 1331) (cd re-iss. Jul96 on 'EMI Gold'; CDGOLD 1046) (cd re-iss. May97 on 'Disky'; DC 87551-2)*

Mar 81. (7"/12") *(CHS/+12 2509)* **MUSCLEBOUND. / GLOW** 10 □

(c-ep) *(ZCHL 2509)* **ACT 1** – ('A'side) / To cut a long story short / The freeze.

Jul 81. (7"/12") *(CHS/+12 2528)* **CHANT NO.1 (I DON'T NEED THIS PRESSURE ON). / FEEL THE CHANT** 3 □

Nov 81. (7"/12") *(CHS/+12 2560)* **PAINT ME DOWN. / MAN WITH GUITAR (RE-PAINT)** 30 □

Jan 82. (7"/12") *(CHS/+12 2585)* **SHE LOVED LIKE DIAMOND. / ('A'version)** 49 □

Mar 82. (lp/c/4x12"box) *(<CHR/ZCHR/C-BOX 1353>)* **DIAMOND** 15 □
– Chant No.1 (I don't need this pressure on) / Instinction / Paint me down / Coffee club / She loved like diamond / Pharoah / Innocence and science / Missionary. *(cd-iss. Dec82; CDL 1353)*

Apr 82. (7",7"pic-d) *(CHS 2602)* **INSTINCTION. / GENTLY** 10 □
(12"+=) *(CHS/+12 2602)* – Chant No.1 (remix).

Sep 82. (7"/7"pic-d/12") *(CHS/+P/12 2642)* **LIFELINE. / LIVE AND LET LIVE** 7 □

Feb 83. (7"/7"pic-d) *(CHS/+P 2668)* **COMMUNICATION. / COMMUNICATION (part 2)** 12 –
(12"+=) *(CHR12 2668)* – ('A'-edited club mix).

Mar 83. (lp/c) *(<CDL/ZCDL 1403>)* **TRUE** 1 May83 19
– Pleasure / Communication / Code of love / Gold / Lifeline / Heaven is a secret / Foundation / True. *(cd-iss. 1986; CCD 1403) (cd re-iss. Mar94; CD25CR 11)*

Reformation Chrysalis

Apr 83. (7"/7"pic-d) *(SPAN/+P 1)* **TRUE. / LIFELINE** 1 –
(12"+=) *(SPANX 1)* – Lifeline (a capella).

Jul 83. (7") *<42720>* **TRUE. / GENTLY** – 4

Aug 83. (7"/7"pic-d) *(SPAN/+P 2)* **GOLD. / GOLD (part 2)** 2 –
(12"+=) *(SPANX 2)* – Foundation.

Nov 83. (7") *<42743>* **GOLD. / GOLD (live)** – 29

Mar 84. (7") *<42770>* **COMMUNICATION. / ONLY WHEN YOU LEAVE** – 59

May 84. (7"/7"pic-d) *(SPAN/+P 3) <42792>* **ONLY WHEN YOU LEAVE. / PAINT ME DOWN (live)** 3 Jul84 34
(12"+=) *(SPANX 3)* – ('A'live).

Jun 84. (lp/c) *(<CDL/ZCDL 1473>)* **PARADE** 2 Aug84 50
– Only when you leave / Highly strung / I'll fly for you / Nature of the beast / Revenge for love / Always in the back of my mind / With the pride / Round and round. *(cd-iss. Jun87; CCD 1473) (re-iss. Mar96 on 'EMI Gold' cd/c; CD/TC GOLD 1010)*

Aug 84. (7"/7"pic-d; 5-different) *(SPAN/+P 4)* **I'LL FLY FOR YOU. / TO CUT A LONG STORY SHORT (live)** 9 □
(12"+=) *(SPANX 4)* – ('A'live).

Oct 84. (7"silver) *(SPAN 5)* **HIGHLY STRUNG. / (part 2)** 15 □
(12"+=) *(SPANX 5)* – ('A'extended).

Nov 84. (7") *(SPAN 6)* **ROUND AND ROUND. / TRUE (live)** 18 □
(12"+=,12"gold+=) *(SPANX 6)* – Gold (live).

Nov 85. (lp/c) *(SBTV/ZSBTV 1)* **THE SINGLES COLLECTION** (compilation) 3 –
– Gold / Lifeline / Round and round / Only when you leave / Instinction / Highly strung / True / Communication / I'll fly for you / To cut a long story short / Chant No.1 (I don't need this pressure on) / She loved like diamond / Paint me down / The freeze / Musclebound. *(w/free 7") (c+= extra mixes) (cd-iss. Apr86; CCD 1498) (cd re-dist.Apr01)* – hit No.56

C.B.S. Epic

Jun 86. (7") *(QA 7264)* **FIGHT FOR OURSELVES. / FIGHT . . . THE HEARTACHE** 15 –
(12"+=) *(QTA 7264)* – ('A'extended).

Oct 86. (7") *(SPANDS 1)* **THROUGH THE BARRICADES. / WITH THE PRIDE** 6 –
(12"+=) *(SPANDST 1)* – ('A'extended).

Nov 86. (lp/c/cd) *(450259-1/-4/-2)* **THROUGH THE BARRICADES** 7 □
– Barricades – introduction / Cross the line / Man in chains / How many lies / Virgin / Swept / Fight for ourselves / Swept / Snakes and lovers / Through the barricades.

Jan 87. (7") *(SPANDS 2)* **HOW MANY LIES. / COMMUNICATION** 34 –
(12"+=) *(SPANDST 2)* – ('A'extended).

Mar 87. (7") **HOW MANY LIES. / SNAKES AND LOVERS** – □

May 87. (7") **THROUGH THE BARRICADES. / SNAKES AND LOVERS** – □

Aug 87. (7"/7"pic-d) *(SPANS/+P 3)* **RAW. / RAW (flip)** 47 □
(12"+=/cd-s+=) *(SPANS T/C 3)* – Raw (extended).
(pic-cd-s+=) *(SPANSD 3)* – Raw (amnesia mix).

Aug 89. (7") *(SPANS 4)* **BE FREE WITH YOUR LOVE. / ('A'-dance mix edit)** [42] [ ]
(cd-s+=) *(SPANSC 4)* – Through the barricades.
(pic-cd-s+=) *(SPANSD 4)* – Raw (extended).
(12"+=) *(SPANST 4)* – ('A'dub version).

Sep 89. (lp/c/cd) *(463318-1/-4/-2)* **HEART LIKE A SKY** [31] [ ]
– Be free with your love / Crashed into love / Big feeling / A matter of time / Motivator / Raw / Empty spaces / Windy town / A handful of dust.

Nov 89. (7"/c-s) *(SPANS/+M 5)* **EMPTY SPACES. / WITH THE PRIDE – GOLD (live)** [ ] [ ]
(cd-s+=) *(SPANSC 5)* – Chant No.1 (live).
(pic-cd-s+=) *(SPANSD 5)* – True (live).
(12"+=) *(SPANST 5)* – Fight for ourselves (live).

Feb 90. (7"/c-s) *(SPANS/+M 6)* **CRASHED INTO LOVE. / HOW MANY LIES (live)** [ ] [ ]
(12"+=/cd-s+=) *(SPANS T/C 6)* – Through the barricades (live).
(cd-s) *(SPANSD 6)* – ('A'side) / With the pride – Gold (live) / True (live).

— split when the KEMP's became 'The Krays' in the 1990 film. GARY went on to act in 'The Bodyguard' and married actress Sadie Frost before embarking on a solo career in 1995

– compilations, etc. –

(on 'Chrysalis' unless otherwise stated)

Dec 82. (d-c) *(ZCDP 103)* **JOURNEYS TO GLORY / DIAMOND** [ ] [–]

Nov 86. (lp/c) *(SBD/ZSBD 1)* **THE 12" MIXES** [ ] [–]
(cd-iss. Apr87 & Feb94; CCD 1574)

Feb 87. (7") *Old Gold; (OG 9677)* **TO CUT A LONG STORY SHORT. / CHANT NO.1 (I DON'T NEED THIS PRESSURE ON)** [ ] [–]

Feb 87. (7") *Old Gold; (OG 9679)* **TRUE. / GOLD** [ ] [–]
(cd-s iss.Aug95; OG 6319)

Nov 87. (c+book) *(THPA 1232)* **GREATEST HITS** [ ] [–]

Jan 88. (12") *Old Gold; (OG 4037)* **COMMUNICATION. / LIFELINE** [ ] [–]

Aug 91. (7"/c-s) **TRUE. / LIFELINE** [ ] [–]
(12"+=/cd-s+=) – Heaven is a secret / Pleasure.

Sep 91. (cd/c/lp) *(CCD/ZCHR/CHR 1353)* **THE BEST OF SPANDAU BALLET** [44] [–]
– (as THE SINGLES COLLECTION +) Fight for ourselves / Through the barricades / How many lies / Raw / Be free with your love.

Nov 96. (cd) *Disky; (<LAD 87326-2>)* **THE BEST OF SPANDAU BALLET – 18 ORIGINAL HITS** [ ] [ ]

Apr 97. (cd) *EMI Gold; (CDGOLD 1081)* **THE COLLECTION** [ ] [–]

Jul 99. (cd) *Disky; (<HR 85773-2>)* **ORIGINAL GOLD** [ ] [–]

Sep 00. (cd/c) *(526700-2/-4)* **GOLD – THE BEST OF SPANDAU BALLET** [7] [–]

SPARKLEHORSE

Formed: Richmond, Virginia, USA . . . 1995 by former DANCING HOODS member MARK LINKOUS; this New York-based quartet issued two sets, '12 JEALOUS ROSES' (1985) and 'HALLELUJAH ANYWAY' (1988). An alternative to The REPLACEMENTS, the group enjoyed good reviews for their debut, although the long-awaited follow-up – featuring a cover of Leonard Cohen's 'DIAMONDS IN THE MINE' – fell short expectations. LINKOUS would return home to form The JOHNSON FAMILY, which duly evolved into recordless SALT CHUNK MARY. Early SPARKLEHORSE releases on 'Slow River', including 'CHORDS I'VE KNOWN' and 'HAMMERING THE CRAMPS' introduced this drawling southern singer-songwriter. Subsequently securing a deal with 'Capitol', LINKOUS supported labelmates RADIOHEAD in late '95 prior to the release of a debut single, 'SOMEDAY I WILL TREAT YOU GOOD' early the following year. A second single, a re-issue of 'HAMMERING THE CRAMPS', appeared a few months later, both tracks featuring on the tongue twistingly titled debut album, 'VIVADIXIESUBMARINETRANSMISSIONPLOT' (1996). Determinedly lo-fi, melancholic alt-country characterised by LINKOUS' catatonic vocals and influenced by the likes of TOM WAITS, NEIL YOUNG and The AFGHAN WHIGS, the album was an instant hit with the critics and even made a Top 60 showing in the UK charts. A former heroin addict, LINKOUS' health was almost the end of him when he collapsed with a heart attack and badly damaged his legs (he was also confined to a wheelchair for three months) following SPARKLEHORSE's live UK debut. When he eventually resurfaced in 1998 with the acclaimed 'GOOD MORNING SPIDER', several critics suggested that LINKOUS's near-death experience was perhaps a key factor in the vitality of the music. A record of strange beauty, 'GOOD MORNING..' segued from distorted sample-driven noise to passages of forlorn majesty with LINKOUS singing his blues against a lonely acoustic strum. Along with the likes of WILL OLDHAM and SMOG's BILL CALLAHAN, LINKOUS has become an unlikely figurehead for the lo-fi Americana scene with SPARKLEHORSE pushing the genre's boundaries while others are content to recycle. While no relf respecting SPARKLEHORSE afficionado would take the title TOO literally, 'IT'S A WONDERFUL LIFE' (2001) saw at least some sunshine straining at the wonderfully mouldering edges of LINKOUS' stained velvet curtain of sound. Reportedly recorded without the aid of stimulants, the record found a clearer headed LINKOUS getting chummy with the likes of MERCURY REV's DAVID FRIDMANN, PJ HARVEY, The CARDIGANS' NINA PERSSON and even TOM WAITS (the latter on the track 'DOG DOOR'). • **Covered:** WISH YOU WERE HERE (Pink Floyd) / WEST OF ROME (Vic Chesnutt).

Album rating: Dancing Hoods: 12 JEALOUS ROSES (*6) / HALLELUJAH ANYWAY (*4) / Sparklehorse: VIVADIXIESUBMARINETRANSMISSIONPLOT (*9) / GOOD MORNING SPIDER (*8) / IT'S A WONDERFUL LIFE (*8)

DANCING HOODS

MARK LINKOUS – guitar, vocals / **BOB BORTNICK** – vocals, guitar / **ERIC WILLIAMS** – bass / **DON SHORT** – drums

Fun After All / Relativity

Jun 86. (7") *(FAA 104)* **BLUE LETTER. / ANTENNA'S UP** [ ] [–]
(12"+=) *(12FAA 104)* – Pleasure.

Jul 86. (lp) *(AFTER 1) <88561-8055>* **12 JEALOUS ROSES** [ ] Nov85 [ ]
– Pleasure / Impossible years / Build a house / Blue letter / Girl problems / Surfing all over the world / Bye bye Jim / Watching you sleep / (Take my) Chances / She may call you up tonight / Wild and the lonely.

— **MIKE GARACINO** – bass; repl. ERIC

1988. (lp) *<88561-8224>* **HALLELUJAH ANYWAY** [–] [ ]
– Torn away / Baby's got rockets / Better look up / Puppet dancing / Welfare shoes / Border patrol / Diamonds in the mine / Falling down / Tell you something / Crooked angel.

— after the split, LINKOUS formed SALT CHUNK MARY

SPARKLEHORSE

MARK LINKOUS – vocals, guitar / **BOB RUPE** or / **ARMSTEAD WELLEFORD** – bass / **DAVID BUSH** or / **JOHNNY HOTT** – drums / **DAVID CHARLES** – electric guitar, producer

not iss. / Slow River

Apr 95. (7"ep) *<SRR 14>* **CHORDS I'VE KNOWN EP** [–] [ ]
– Heart of darkness / Almost lost my mind / Midget in a junkyard / Dead opera star / Hatchet song.

1995. (7") *<SRR 73>* **SPIRIT DITCH. / WAITING FOR NOTHING** [–] [ ]

1995. (7") *<SRR 74>* **HAMMERING THE CRAMPS. / TOO LATE** [–] [ ]
(UK-iss.Oct96; same)

Capitol / Capitol

Feb 96. (7") *<S7 19167>* **SOMEDAY I WILL TREAT YOU GOOD. / RAINMAKER** [–] [ ]

Feb 96. (7") *(CL 766)* **SOMEDAY I WILL TREAT YOU GOOD. / LONDON** [ ] [–]
(cd-s+=) *(CDCL 766)* – In the dry.

Apr 96. (7") *(CL 770)* **HAMMERING THE CRAMPS. / SPIRIT DITCH** [ ] [ ]
(cd-s+=) *(CDCL 770)* – Dead opera star / Midget in a junkyard.

May 96. (cd/c/d-lp) *(CD/TC+/EST 2280)* *<72438 32816-2/-4>* **VIVADIXIESUBMARINETRANSMISSIONPLOT** [58] Nov95 [ ]
– Homecoming queen / Weird sisters / 850 double pumper Holley / Rainmaker / Spirit ditch / Tears on fresh fruit / Saturday / Cow / Little bastard choo choo / Hammering the cramps / Most beautiful widow in town / Heart of darkness / Ballad of a cold lost marble / Someday I will treat you good / Sad and beautiful world / Gasoline horseys.

— LINKOUS brought in **SCOTT MINOR, PAUL WATSON + SCOTT FITZSIMMONS**

Aug 96. (7") *(CL 777)* **RAINMAKER. / I ALMOST LOST MY MIND** [61] [–]
(cd-s) *(CDCLS 777)* – Intermission.
(cd-s) *(CDCL 777)* – ('A'side) / Homecoming queen (live on KCRW) / Gasoline horseys (live on KCRW).

Feb 98. (7") *<SRR7-32>* **COME ON IN. / BLIND RABBIT CHOIR** [–] [ ]

— <above released on 'Slow River'>

— virtually **LINKOUS** with **MINOR, WATSON + SOFIA MITCHALITSIANOS** – cello / **MELISSA MOORE** – violin / **JOHNNY HOTT** – drums, piano / guests **STEPHEN McCARTHY + DAVID LOWERY + VIC CHESNUTT**

Jul 98. (7") *(CL 806)* **PAINBIRDS. / MARIA'S LITTLE ELBOWS** [ ] [–]
(cd-s+=) *(CDCL 806)* – Wish you were here / Haint / The dirt bike wreck (video).

Jul 98. (cd/lp) *(496014-2/-1)* *<36671>* **GOOD MORNING SPIDER** [30] Feb99 [ ]
– Pig / Painbirds / Saint Mary / Good morning spider / Sick of goodbyes / Box of stars (part one) / Sunshine / Chaos of the galaxy – Happy man / Hey, Joe / Come on in / Maria's little elbows / Cruel sun / All night home / Ghost of his smile / Hundreds of sparrows / Box of stars (part two) / Junebug.

Oct 98. (7"clear) *<(CL 808)>* **SICK OF GOODBYES. / GOOD MORNING SPIDER (session version)** [57] [ ]
(cd-s) *<(CDCL 808)>* – ('A'side) / I shot a dog / Gasoline horseys.
(cd-s) *<(CDCLS 808)>* – ('A'side) / Happy place / Happy pig (session version).

Parlophone Odeon

Jun 00. (cd-ep) *(489505-2)* *<69505>* **DISTORTED GHOST EP** [ ] Feb00 [ ]
– Happy man (Memphis version) / Waiting for nothing / Happy place / My yoke is heavy / Gasoline horsey's (live) / Happy pig (live).

— **LINKOUS** now with **SCOTT MINOR + DAVE FRIDMANN, ADRIAN UTLEY, JOHN PARISH, SOPHIE MICHELITSIANOS, BOB RUPE, JANE SCARPANTONI** etc, + guests **TOM WAITS, PJ HARVEY + NINA PERSSON**

Parlophone Capitol

Jun 01. (cd) *(525616-2)* *<34709>* **IT'S A WONDERFUL LIFE** [49] [ ]
– It's a wonderful life / Gold day / Piano fire / Apple bed / Sea of teeth / King of nails / Eyepennies / Dog door / More yellow birds / Little fat baby / Comfort me / Babies on the sun.

Jul 01. (cd-s) *(CDCL 831)* **GOLD DAY / HELOISE / DEVIL'S NEW / MAXINE** [ ] [–]

– compilations, etc. –

Oct 02. (d-cd) *E.M.I.; (541129-2)* **VIVADIXIESUBMARINE TRANSMISSIONPLOT / GOOD MORNING SPIDER** [ ] [–]

SPARKS

Formed: Los Angeles, California, USA . . . 1968 as HALFNELSON by brothers RON and RUSSELL MAEL. TODD RUNDGREN was sufficiently impressed with a demo tape to get them signed up for Albert Grossman's 'Bearsville' label where he worked as an in-house producer. With EARLE MANKEY, RALPH OSWALD and JOHN HENDERSON completing the line-up, the outfit recorded the eponymous 'HALFNELSON' (1972) under RUNDGREN's guidance. The record sold poorly, however, and the duo changed their name to SPARKS, replacing the rhythm section with JIM MANKEY and HARVEY FEINSTEIN. The resulting 'A WOOFER IN TWEETER'S CLOTHING' (1973) was equally unsuccessful and following an encouraging UK live reception, the brothers relocated to London in 1974, signing to 'Island'. Recruiting a new troupe of backing musicians, RON and RUSSELL were a massive hit (No.2) almost immediately with the pseudo-operatic glam melodrama of 'THIS TOWN AIN'T BIG ENOUGH FOR THE BOTH OF US'. Strikingly eccentric, both visually (RON's unnerving Hitler-esque moodiness and RUSSELL's flouncing, near-falsetto androgyny was quite a match) and musically, it was small wonder the duo were doomed to failure in the States. With Muff Winwood at the controls, the accompanying 'KIMONO MY HOUSE' (1974) developed their arch glam-pop over a whole album and drew inevitable if somewhat inaccurate comparisons with ROXY MUSIC. 'PROPAGANDA' (1974) carried on in the same vein, another Top 10 success which spawned a further two Top 20 hit singles in 'NEVER TURN YOUR BACK ON MOTHER EARTH' and 'SOMETHING FOR THE GIRL WITH EVERYTHING'. By the release of the Tony Visconti-produced 'INDISCREET' (1975), the formula was wearing thin and an expensively disastrous attempt at sub-metal posturing with 'BIG BEAT' (1976) marked the end of the brothers' tenure with 'Island' and a move back to Los Angeles. Meeting electro disco guru, GIORGIO MORODER in Germany the following year, SPARKS collaborated with him on comeback set, 'NUMBER ONE IN HEAVEN' (1979). Released by their new bosses, 'Virgin', the album spawned a couple of major UK hits in 'THE NUMBER ONE SONG IN HEAVEN' and the itchy disco-funk of 'BEAT THE CLOCK', despite barely scraping into the Top 75 itself. Although many 80's outfits owed an obvious debt to SPARKS' innovations, the decade saw them confined to the margins; while they were popular in France, the brothers failed to notch up any hits at all in Britain during this period. Bizarrely enough, SPARKS enjoyed some belated success in the States with the warbling 'ANGST IN MY PANTS' (1982) and 'SPARKS IN OUTER SPACE' (1983) sets. The MAELS' influence on the late 80's/early 90's house scene saw them release a one-off 12" for Scotland's very own 'Finflex' label, 'NATIONAL CRIME AWARENESS WEEK' with dance imprint, 'Logic' subsequently picking them up for the oh-so-cleverly titled 'GRATUITOUS SAX & SENSELESS VIOLINS' (1994). The latter opus actually spawned two minor Top 40 hits, 'WHEN DO I GET TO SING "MY WAY"' and 'WHEN I KISS YOU (I HEAR CHARLIE PARKER PLAYIN')'. With a career incredibly spanning almost thirty years, SPARKS are still showing no signs of pulling the plug, a collaborative revamp (with the late FAITH NO MORE) of the enduring 'THIS TOWN..' making the Top 40 in late '97. The new millennium saw the old SPARKS rekindle once more via a new set, 'BALLS' (2000) – it says it all really. 'LIL' BEETHOVEN' (2002), meanwhile, gathered up various textural strands and ideas from the group's lengthy career, tying them all up with the kind of quasi-classical arrangements suggested by the title. All in, it was their most realised and rewarding release in years, with enough sly humour, wry commentary, chameleon-like energy and musical invention to stake their claim among the cream of contemporary experimentalists. • **Songwriters:** RON MAEL wrote lyrics / music, and they also covered; I WANT TO HOLD YOUR HAND (Beatles) / FINGERTIPS (Stevie Wonder) / etc. • **Trivia:** In 1979, they produced NOEL'S album 'Is There More To Life Than Dancing'. They also worked for ADRIAN MUSSEY, BIJOU + TELEX.

Album rating: HALFNELSON (*4; as Halfnelson) / A WOOFER IN TWEETER'S CLOTHING (*5) / KIMONO MY HOUSE (*7) / PROPAGANDA (*6) / INDISCREET (*5) / BIG BEAT (*4) / THE BEST OF SPARKS compilation (*7) / INTRODUCING SPARKS (*3) / NUMBER ONE IN HEAVEN (*5) / TERMINAL JIVE (*4) / WHOMP THAT SUCKER (*4) / ANGST IN MY PANTS (*5) / SPARKS IN OUTER SPACE (*4) / INTERIOR DESIGN (*3) / MAEL INTUITION: THE BEST OF SPARKS 1974-1976 compilation (*7) / GRATUITOUS SAX AND SENSELESS VIOLINS (*4) / PLAGIARISM (*4) / BALLS (*5) / LIL' BEETHOVEN (*6)

RUSSELL MAEL (b. 5 Oct'55, Santa Monica, Calif.) – vocals, bass / **RON MAEL** (b.12 Aug'50, Culver City, Calif.) – keyboards / **EARLE MANKEY** – guitar / with **RALPH OSWALD** – bass / **JOHN HENDERSON** – drums

Bearsville Bearsville

Feb 72. (lp; as HALFNELSON) *<2048>* **HALFNELSON** –
– Wonder girl / Fa la fa lee / Roger / High C / Fletcher Honorama / Simple ballet / Slowboat / Biology 2 / Saccharin and the war / Big bands / Mr.Nice guys. *(UK-iss.Oct74 as 'SPARKS'; K 45511) (UK cd-iss. Aug93 on 'Rhino'; 8122 71300-2)*

— **JIM MANKEY** – bass + **HARVEY FEINSTEIN** – drums repl. RALPH and JOHN

Nov 72. (7") *(K 15505)* **WONDER GIRL. / (NO MORE) MR.NICE GUYS**

Feb 73. (lp) *(K 45510)* **A WOOFER IN TWEETER'S CLOTHING**
– Girl from Germany / Beaver O'Lindy / Nothing is sacred / Here comes Bob / Moon over Kentucky / Do re mi / Argus desire / Underground / The louvre / Batteries not incuded / Whippings and apologies. *(cd-iss. Aug91 on 'Repertoire'; REP 4051)*

— The **MAELS** moved to London and recruited British musicians **ADRIAN FISHER** – guitar / **MARTIN GORDON** – bass, vocals / **DINKY DIAMOND** – drums / **PETER OXENDALE** – keyboards

Island Island

May 74. (7") *(WIP 6193) <IS 001>* **THIS TOWN AIN'T BIG ENOUGH FOR THE BOTH OF US. / BARBECUTIE** 2 Aug74

May 74. (lp/c) *<(ILPS/ICT 9272)>* **KIMONO MY HOUSE** 4
– This town ain't big enough for the both of us / Amateur hour / Falling in love with myself again / Here in Heaven / Thank God it's not Christmas / Hasta manana Monsieur / Talent is an asset / Complaints / In the family / Equator. *(cd-iss. Aug94; IMCD 198)*

Jul 74. (7") *(WIP 6203)* **AMATEUR HOUR. / LOST AND FOUND** 7 –

Oct 74. (7") *<IS 009>* **TALENT IS AN ASSET. / LOST AND FOUND** –

— **TREVOR WHITE** – guitar repl. PETER / **IAN HAMPTON** – bass (ex-JOOK) repl. MARTIN who joined JET

Oct 74. (7") *(WIP 6211)* **NEVER TURN YOUR BACK ON MOTHER EARTH. / ALABAMY NIGHT** 13 –

Nov 74. (lp/c) *<(ILPS/ICT 9312)>* **PROPAGANDA** 9 Feb75 63
– Propaganda / At home, at work, at play / Reinforcements / B.C. / Thanks but no thanks / Don't leave me alone with her / Never turn your back on Mother Earth / Something for the girl with everything / Achoo / Who don't like kids / Bon voyage. *(cd-iss. Aug94; IMCD 199)*

Jan 75. (7") *(WIP 6221)* **SOMETHING FOR THE GIRL WITH EVERYTHING. / MARRY ME** 17 –

Mar 75. (7") *<IS 023>* **SOMETHING FOR THE GIRL WITH EVERYTHING. / ACHOO** –

Jul 75. (7") *(WIP 6236)* **GET IN THE SWING. / PROFILE** 27 –

Sep 75. (7") *(WIP 6249)* **LOOKS, LOOKS, LOOKS. / PINEAPPLE** 26 –

Oct 75. (lp/c) *<(ILPS/ICT 9345)>* **INDISCREET** 18
– Hospitality on parade / Happy hunting ground / Without using hands / Get in the swing / Under the table with her / How are you getting home / Pineapple / Tits / It ain't 1918 / The lady is lingering / In the future / Looks, looks, looks / Miss the start, miss the end. *(cd-iss. Aug94; IMCD 200)*

Nov 75. (7") *<IS 043>* **LOOKS, LOOKS, LOOKS. / THE WEDDING OF JACQUELINE KENNEDY TO RUSSELL MAEL** –

Mar 76. (7"; w-drawn) *(WIP 6282)* **I WANT TO HOLD YOUR HAND. / ENGLAND** –

— The **MAELS** used session people incl. **SAL MAIDA** – bass (ex-ROXY MUSIC)

Oct 76. (7") *(WIP 6337)* **BIG BOY. / FILL 'ER UP** –

Oct 76. (lp/c) *<(ILPS/ICT 9445)>* **BIG BEAT**
– Big boy / I want to be like everybody else / Nothing to do / I bought the Mississippi River / Fill 'er up / Everybody's stupid / Throw her away / Confusion / Screwed up / White women / I like girls. *(cd-iss. Aug94; IMCD 201)*

Dec 76. (7") *(WIP 6377)* **I LIKE GIRLS. / ENGLAND** –

C.B.S. Columbia

Sep 77. (7") *(CBS 5593)* **A BIG SURPRISE. / FOREVER YOUNG**

Oct 77. (lp/c) *(CBS/40 82284)* **INTRODUCING SPARKS**
– A big surprise / Occupation / Ladies / I'm not / Forever young / Goofing off / Girls on the brain / Over the summer / Those mysteries.

— augmented by **GIORGIO MORODER** – electronics, producer

Virgin Elektra

Mar 79. (7",7"green/12"red,12"blue) *(VS 244/+12)* **THE NUMBER ONE SONG IN HEAVEN. / ('A'-long version)** 14 –

Mar 79. (lp/c) *(V/TCV 2115)* **NO.1 IN HEAVEN** 73
– Tryouts for the human race / Academy award performance / La dolce vita / Beat the clock / My other voice / The number one song in Heaven. *(re-iss. Aug82 on 'Fame' lp/c; FA/TCFA 3035) <(cd-iss. Mar00 on 'Repertoire'; REP 4768)>*

Jul 79. (7"/12",12"various colrd) *(VS 270/+12)* **BEAT THE CLOCK. / ('A'-long version)** 10 –

Oct 79. (7"/12",12"colrd pic-d) *(VS 289/+12)* **TRYOUTS FOR THE HUMAN RACE. / ('A'-long version)** –

Nov 79. (7") **TRYOUTS FOR THE HUMAN RACE. / NO. 1 SONG IN HEAVEN** –

Jan 80. (7") *(VS 319)* **WHEN I'M WITH YOU. / ('A'-long version)** –

Feb 80. (lp/c) *(V/TCV 2137)* **TERMINAL JIVE** –
– When I'm with you / Just because you love me / Rock and roll people in a disco world / When I'm with you (instrumental) / Young girls / Noisy boys / Stereo / The greatest show on Earth.

Apr 80. (7"/ext.12") *(VS 343/+12)* **YOUNG GIRLS. / JUST BECAUSE YOU LOVE ME** –

— added (ex-BATES MOTEL members) **BOB HAAG** – guitar / **LESLIE BOHEM** – bass / **DAVID KENDRICK** – drums

Why-Fi R.C.A.

Apr 81. (7"/12") *(WHY/+T 1)* **TIPS FOR TEENS. / DON'T SHOOT ME** –

May 81. (lp) *(WHO 1) <4091>* **WHOMP THAT SUCKER**
– Tips for teens / Funny face / Where's my girl / Upstairs / I married a Martian / The willys / Don't shoot me / Suzie safety / That's not Nastassia / Wacky women.

Sep 81. (7") *(WHY 4)* **FUNNY FACE. / THE WILLYS** –

— The **MAELS** + **MORODER** added **JAMES GOODWIN** – synths.

Atlantic Atlantic

Jun 82. (7") *(K 11740) <4030>* **I PREDICT. / MOUSTACHE** May82 60

Jun 82. (lp/c) *(K/K4 50888) <19347>* **ANGST IN MY PANTS**
– Angst in my pants / I predict / Sextown U.S.A. / Sherlock Holmes / Nicotina / Mickey mouse / Moustache / Instant weight loss / Tarzan and Jane / The decline and fall of me / Eaten by the monster of love.

1982. (7") **EATEN BY THE MONSTER OF LOVE. / MICKEY MOUSE** –

Jun 83. (7"; SPARKS & JANE WIEDLIN) *() <89866>* **COOL PLACES. / SPORTS** Apr83 49

Jun 83. (lp/c) *(K 780055-1/-4) 80055>* **SPARKS IN OUTER SPACE** 88
– Cool places / Popularity / Prayin' for a party / All you ever think about is sex / Please, baby please / Rockin' girls / I wish I looked a little better / Lucky me, lucky you / A fun bunch of guys from Outer Space / Dance godammit.

Nov 83 (7") *<86990>* **ALL YOU EVER THINK ABOUT IS SEX. / I WISH I LOOKED A LITTLE BETTER** –
(12") *<86990>* – ('A'club) / Dance goddamit (club version) / With all my might (extended club).

Jun 84. (lp/c) *<7-80160-1/-4>* **PULLING RABBITS OUT OF A HAT** –

— MORODER moved on to produce PHIL OAKEY

Jun 84 (7") *<7-89616>* **PRETENDING TO BE DRUNK. / KISS ME QUICK** –

London Curb-MCA

Jun 85. (7"/12") *(LON/+X 69)* **CHANGE. / THIS TOWN AIN'T BIG ENOUGH FOR THE BOTH OF US (acoustic)** [ ] [ ]

— **JOHN THOMAS** – keyboards repl. GOODWIN

Consolidated M.C.A.

Nov 86. (7"/ext.12") *(TOON/+T 2)* **MUSIC THAT YOU CAN DANCE TO. / FINGERTIPS** [ ] [ ]

Nov 86. (lp/c) *(TOONLP 2) <MCA 5780>* **MUSIC THAT YOU CAN DANCE TO** [ ] Aug86 [ ]
– Music that you can to / Rosebud / Fingertips / Armies of the night / The scene / Shopping mall of love / Modesty plays (new version) / Let's get funky. *<US version; 'Armies of the night'; repl. Change>*

Feb 87. (7") *(TOON 4)* **ROSEBUD. / ('A'-Cinematic version)** [ ] [–]
(12") *<TOONT 4>* – ('A'extended) / ('A'-FM mix).

— The MAELS retained **THOMAS + DAVID KENDRICK** introducing **SPENCER SIRCOMBE** – guitar / **HANS CHRISTIAN REUMSCHUSSEL** – bass / **PAMELA STONEBROOK** – vocals

Carrere Fine Art

Jul 88. (7") *(CAR 427)* **SO IMPORTANT. / BIG BRASS RING** [ ] [ ]
(12"+=) *(CART 427)* – ('A'extremely important mix).
(cd-s++=) *CARCD 427)* – Madonna.

— In Aug 88, SPARKS collaborated on 'SINGING IN THE SHOWER'. / 'SMOG' single by French husband and wife duo LES RITA MITSOUKO on 'Virgin' label.

Carrere Rhino

Jul 88. (lp/c/cd) *<R1/R4/R2 70841>* **INTERIOR DESIGN** [ ] Aug88 [ ]
– So important / Just got back from Heaven / Lots of reasons / You got a hold of my heart / Love o rama / The toughest girl in town / Let's make love / Stop me if you've heard this before / A walk down memory lane / Madonna. *(cd+=)* – Madonna (French – German – Spanish; versions) / The big brass ring / So important. *(UK-iss.cd Aug92 on 'Thunderbolt'; CDTB 141)*

Aug 89. (7") *(CAR 431)* **SO IMPORTANT. / JUST GOT BACK FROM HEAVEN** [ ] [–]
(12"+=) *(CART 431)* – ('A'-Extremely Important mix).

— In 1991, the MAELS were working on own feature film 'Mai The Psychic Girl',

Fineflex Fineflex

Nov 93. (12") *(FF 1004)* **NATIONAL CRIME AWARENESS WEEK. / (13 MINUTES OF HEAVEN) / ('A'-Perkins playtime mix)** [ ] [ ]
(cd-s) *(FFCD 1004)* – ('A'side) / (3 other mixes).

Logic-BMG BMG

Oct 94. (12"/c-s/cd-s) *(74321 3446-1/-4/-2)* **WHEN DO I GET TO SING MY WAY. / ('A'-Grid mix) / ('A'-Rapino Brrothers mix)** [38] [ ]
(cd-s) *(74321 3447-2)* – ('A'side) / ('A'-Vince Clarke mixes).

Nov 94. (cd/c) *<(74321 23267-2/-4)>* **GRATUITOUS SAX & SENSELESS VIOLINS** [ ] [ ]
– Gratutous sex / When do I get to sing 'My Way' / (When I kiss you) I hear Charlie Parker playing / Frankly Scarlett I don't give a damn / I thought I told you to wait in the car / Hear no evil, see no evil, speak no evil / Now that I own the BBC / Tsui Hark (featuring TSUI HARK & BILL KONG) / The ghost of Liberace / Let's go surfing / Senseless violins.

Feb 95. (c-s) *(74321 26427-4)* **WHEN I KISS YOU (I HEAR CHARLIE PARKER PLAYIN') / ('A'-Beatmasters mix)** [36] [ ]
(cd-s+=) *(74321 26428-2)* – This town ain't big enough for the both of us.
(12"+=/cd-s+=) *(74321 26427-1/-2)* – ('A'-Bernard Butler mix).

May 95. (c-s) *(74321 27400-4)* **WHEN DO I GET TO SING 'MY WAY' / ('A'-Grid mix)** [32] [ ]
(12"+=) *(74321 27400-1)* – National crime awareness week.
(cd-s++=) *(74321 27400-2)* – (2 extra 'A'mixes).

Feb 96. (c-s) *(74321 34867-4)* **NOW THAT I OWN THE BBC / BEAT THE CLOCK (live)** [60] [ ]
(cd-s) *(74321 34867-2)* – ('A'side) / ('A'mixes) / She's an anchorman.

Roadrunner Roadrunner

Oct 97. (12"/cd-s) *(RR 2262-6/-9)* **THE NUMBER ONE SONG IN HEAVEN. / ('A'mix)** [70] [–]
(cd-s) *(RR 2262-3)* – ('A'remixes with Jimmy Somerville).

Oct 97. (cd) *<(RR 8791-2)>* **PLAGIARISM** (remixes) [ ] [ ]
– Pulling rabbits out of a hat / This town ain't big enough for the both of us / The number one song in Heaven / Funny face / When do I get to sing 'My Way' / Angst in my pants / Change / Popularity / Something for the girl with everything / This town ain't big enough for the both of us / Beat the clock / Big brass ring / Amateur hour / Propaganda / When I'm with you / Something for the girl with everything / Orchestral collage / The number one song in Heaven / Never turn your back on Mother Earth.

Dec 97. (cd-ep; as SPARKS VS FAITH NO MORE) *(RR 2251-3)* **THIS TOWN AIN'T BIG ENOUGH FOR THE BOTH OF US / ('A'version) / SOMETHING FOR THE GIRL WITH EVERYTHING / THE GREAT LEAP FORWARD** [40] [–]

Recognition Oglio

Aug 00. (cd) *(CDREC 5108 B/R/Y/G) <89119>* **BALLS** [ ] [ ]
– Balls / More than a sex machine / Scheherazade / Aeroflot / The calm before the storm / How to get your ass kicked / Bullet train / It's a knockoff / Irreplaceable / It's educational / The angels.

Artful Palm Pics

Nov 02. (cd) *(LILBCD 1) <400009>* **LIL' BEETHOVEN** [ ] [ ]
– The rhythm thief / How do I get to Carnegie Hall? / What are all these bands so angry about? / I married myself / Ride 'em cowboy / My baby's taking me home / Your call's very important to us. Please hold / Ugly guys with beautiful girls / Suburban homeboy.

– compilations, others, etc. –

Jul 74. (7") *Bearsville; (K 15516)* **GIRL FROM GERMANY. / BEAVER O'LINDY** [ ] [–]

Mar 76. (d-lp) *Bearsville; (K 85505)* **TWO ORIGINALS OF SPARKS** [ ] [–]
– (the albums from 1972 + 1973)

Mar 77. (lp/c) *Island; (ILPS/ICT 9493)* **THE BEST OF SPARKS** [ ] [–]
– This town ain't big enough for the both of us / Hasta manana monsieur / Tearing the place apart / At home, at work, at play / Never turn your back on Mother Earth / Get in the swing / Amateur hour / Looks, looks, looks / Thanks but no thanks / Gone with the wind / Something for the girl with everything / Thank God it's not Christmas. *(re-iss. Sep79; same) (cd-iss. Feb90; CID 9493)*

Sep 79. (7") *Island; (WIP 6532)* **THIS TOWN AIN'T BIG ENOUGH FOR THE BOTH OF US. / LOOKS, LOOKS, LOOKS** [ ] [–]

May 83. (12"ep) *Virgin; (VS 590-12)* **THE NUMBER ONE SONG IN HEAVEN / BEAT THE CLOCK. / WHEN I'M WITH YOU / YOUNG GIRLS** [ ] [–]

Nov 81. (lp) *Underdog;* **THE HISTORY OF THE SPARKS** [–] French [–]

May 90. (cd) *Island; (IMCD 88)* **MAEL INTUITION** [ ] [–]

Jun 91. (d-cd) *Rhino; <R2 70731>* **PROFILE: IT'S A MAEL MAEL MAEL MAEL WORLD** [ ] [ ]
(above was re-issue of BEST OF SPARKS)

May 93. (cd/c) *Spectrum; (550065-2/-4)* **IN THE SWING** [ ] [–]

Oct 93. (cd) *Sony;* **THE HEAVEN COLLECTION** [ ] [–]

Oct 93. (cd) *Sony; (473516-2)* **THE HELL COLLECTION** [ ] [–]
(above also issued both as d-cd)

Mar 94. (cd) *Loma; (LOMACD 23)* **SPARKS / A WOOFER IN TWEETER'S CLOTHING** [ ] [–]
(re-iss. Mar99 on 'Essential'; ESMCD 677)

Jul 94. (cd/c) *Success;* **JUST GOT BACK FROM HEAVEN** [ ] [–]

Oct 95. (cd) *Laserlight; (12571)* **SO IMPORTANT** [ ] [–]

Jul 02. (cd) *Repertoire; <(REP 4906)>* **THE BEST OF SPARKS** [ ] [ ]

Sep 02. (cd) *Music Club; (MCCD 503)* **THIS ALBUM'S BIG ENOUGH: THE BEST OF SPARKS** [ ] [–]

☐ SPARROW (see under ⇒ STEPPENWOLF)

☐ SPARTA (see under ⇒ AT THE DRIVE-IN)

Britney SPEARS

Born: 2 Dec'81, Kentwood, Louisiana, USA. Possibly one of the world's most famous teenage divas, the proclaimed "Princess Of Pop" BRITNEY SPEARS was still churning out hit singles come the release of her third album proper 'BRITNEY'. Initiating her paths to superstardom at a very early age, SPEARS was a regular dancer on Disney's 'Mickey Mouse Club', as well as being an avid mumber of her local church choir. The talented youngster attended New York's

Professional Performing Arts school before being a regular presenter on the aforementioned 'Mickey Mouse Club', finally severing her ties with them at age thirteen. SPEARS, with the added persuasion of her determined mother, toured the mid-West shopping mall talent contests before finally signing a deal with 'Jive' records in early 1999. Her debut single, ' . . .BABY ONE MORE TIME' (the infamous video had SPEARS controversially prancing around seductively in a school uniform) was a world-wide smash, hitting the Top of the charts in both the US and the UK and sending the world into BRITNEY hysteria. With its catchy chorus and raunchy lyrics (depending on your poltics), ' . . .BABY . . .' set a new standard for pop songs, with SPEARS herself unleashing two more singles in the same vein, '(YOU DRIVE ME) CRAZY' and 'SOMETIMES'; her debut album ' . . .BABY ONE MORE TIME' (1999) also went platinum. However, she was to mature considerably come her follow-up sophomore set 'OOPS! . . . I DID IT AGAIN' (2000). Gone was the virginal lolita (an image born out of 'Rolling Stone's notorious cover shoot and of SPEARS' "no sex before marriage" clause) and in its place was a fully-matured 18-year-old woman. The album spawned many a hit for the ever-expanding BRITNEY empire, notably the title track 'OOPS! . . .', a bubbling sister track to ' . . .BABY . . .' with SPEARS herself proclaiming "I'm not that innocent", and the fairytale ballad 'LUCKY'. She also appeared in countless television commercials for Pepsi and MTV. BRITNEY also famously covered the Rolling Stones classic '(I CAN'T GET NO) SATISFACTION' – on the aforementioned set – and publicly courted *N SYNC's JUSTIN TIMBERLAKE. Just as she prepared herself for starring in her debut movie 'Crossroads', she also returned to the studio at the end of 2000 to record her most personal album to date, 'BRITNEY' (2001). The long-player, which was backed by the R&B inspired, bump'n'grind single 'I'M A SLAVE 4 U' and a python-clad performance at the MTV awards, had finally demonstrated SPEARS' coming-of-age and fully reinvented the once bubblegum teenybopper's image. The follow-up single, 'I'M NOT A GIRL, NOT YET A WOMAN', spoke for itself, whereas 'OVERPROTECTED' was like a formal message to the press, with SPEARS singing "I can't help the way I feel, 'cause my life has been so overprotected". A global tour followed after she had wrapped up work on the 'Crossroads' movie. SPEARS proved to audiences universally that she was, like MADONNA in her heyday, the new publicly-appointed "Queen Of Pop". After a few missteps including the commercial failure of 2002's 'Crossroads' movie, BRITNEY's ascension to the throne was confirmed with 'IN THE ZONE' (2003), the final stage in her evolution from saccharine teen-popster to fully fledged diva. Unsurprisingly then, the album didn't hold back in attempting to present SPEARS as tough, as independent and as street savvy as a modern day pop- cum-R&B siren should be. With contributions form the likes of MADONNA, MOBY and R. KELLY, the record wasn't quite as cutting edge as she'd perhaps have liked it to have been although the likes of 'TOXIC' (soon to be a chart topper in '04) set her apart from her rival prima donnas.

Album rating: . . .BABY ONE MORE TIME (*6) / OOPS! . . . I DID IT AGAIN (*6) / BRITNEY (*5) / IN THE ZONE (*6)

BRITNEY SPEARS – vocals / with various backers

Jive Jive

Feb 99. (c-s) *(052169-4)* *<42545>* **. . .BABY ONE MORE TIME / AUTUMN GOODBYE** [1] Nov98 [1]
(cd-s+=) *(052275-2)* – ('A'-instrumental).
(cd-s) *(052169-2)* – ('A'side) / ('A'-Sharp platinum vocal remix) / ('A'-Davidson Ospina club mix).

Mar 99. (cd/c) *(052217-2/-4)* *<41651>* **. . .BABY ONE MORE TIME** [2] Jan99 [1]
– . . .Baby one more time / (You drive me) Crazy / Sometimes / Soda pop / Born to make you happy / From the bottom of my broken heart / I will be there / I will still love you / Thinkin' about you / E-mail my heart / The beat goes on.

Jun 99. (c-s) *(052320-4)* *<radio cut>* **SOMETIMES / I'M SO CURIOUS** [3] [21]
(cd-s+=) *(052320-2)* – ('A'-Soul solution mid tempo mix).

Sep 99. (c-s) *(055058-4)* *<42606>* **(YOU DRIVE ME) CRAZY / I'LL NEVER STOP LOVING YOU** [5] [10]
(cd-s) *(055058-2)* – ('A'side) / ('A'-Spacedust dub & club).

Jan 00. (cd-s) *<42653>* **FROM THE BOTTOM OF MY BROKEN HEART / (YOU DRIVE ME) CRAZY** [–] [14]

Jan 00. (7") *(925002-7)* **BORN TO MAKE YOU HAPPY. / (YOU DRIVE ME) CRAZY (Jazzy Jim's hip-hop mix)** [1] [–]
(cd-s+=) *(925002-2)* – ('A'-bonus remix).
(c-s) *(925002-4)* – ('A'side) / ('A'bonus remix) / Baby one more time (answering machine message).

May 00. (c-s) *(925054-4)* *<radio cut>* **OOPS! . . . I DID IT AGAIN / (instrumental) / FROM THE BOTTOM OF MY HEART (Ospina's millennium funk mix)** [1] [9]
(cd-s) *(925054-2)* – (first & third tracks) / Deep in my heart.

May 00. (cd/c) *(922039-2/-4)* *<41704>* **OOPS! . . . I DID IT AGAIN** [2] [1]
– Oops! . . . I did it again / Stronger / Don't go knockin' on my door / (I can't get no) Satisfaction / Don't let me be the last to know / What U see (is what U get) / Lucky / One kiss from you / Where are you now / Can't make you love me / When your eyes say it / Dear diary. *(special cd+=; 922104-2)* – Heart / You got it all / Lucky (video) / Oops! I did it again.

Aug 00. (c-s) *(925102-4)* *<42742>* **LUCKY / OOPS! I DID IT AGAIN (Jack D. Elliot radio mix)** [5] [23]
(cd-s+=) *(925102-2)* – Heart / ('A'-Jack D. Elliot radio mix).

Dec 00. (c-s) *(925150-4)* *<42861>* **STRONGER / WALK ON BY** [7] [14]
(cd-s+=) *(925150-2)* – ('A'-WIP remix).

Mar 01. (c-s/cd-s) *(925198-4/-2)* **DON'T LET ME BE THE LAST TO KNOW / (Hex Hector full & edited mixes)** [12] [–]
(cd-s) *(925203-2)* – ('A'side) / Oops! I did it again (Riprock & Alex G mix) / Stronger (MacQuayle mix show mix).

Oct 01. (c-s) *(925289-4)* *<42967>* **I'M A SLAVE 4 U / (instrumental)** [4] [27]
(cd-s+=) *(925289-2)* – Intimidated.

Nov 01. (cd/c) *(922253-2/-4)* *<41776>* **BRITNEY** [4] [1]
– I'm a slave 4 U / Overprotected / Lonely / I'm not a girl, not yet a woman / Boys / Anticipating / I love rock'n'roll / Cinderella / Let me be / Bombastic love / That's where you take me / When I found you *[bonus track]* / Before the goodbye *[bonus track]* / What it's like to be me. *(cd+=)* – Overprotected (video).

Jan 02. (c-s) *(925307-4)* **OVERPROTECTED / OVERPROTECTED (JS16 remix)** [4] [86]
(cd-s+=) *(925307-2)* *<40027>* – I'm a slave 4 U (Thunderpuss mixshow).

Apr 02. (c-s) *(925347-4)* **I'M NOT A GIRL, NOT YET A WOMAN / I'M NOT A GIRL, NOT YET A WOMAN (Spanish Fly remix)** [2] [–]
(cd-s+=) *(92547-2)* – I run away (version).

Jul 02. (c-s) *(925391-4)* **BOYS / BOYS (album)** [7] [–]
(cd-s+=) *(925391-2)* – Boys (Co Ed instrumental).
(12"+=) *(925391-0)* – I'm a slave 4 U.
(above featured PHARRELL WILLIAMS of N.E.R.D.)

Nov 02. (c-s) *(925420-4)* **I LOVE ROCK'N'ROLL / I LOVE ROCK'N'ROLL (karaoke version)** [13] [–]
(cd-s+=) *(925422-2)* – Overprotected (dark child remix).
(cd-s+=) *(925420-2)* – ('A'video).

Nov 03. (c-s; by BRITNEY SPEARS featuring MADONNA) *(82876 57643-4)* **ME AGAINST THE MUSIC / ME AGAINST THE MUSIC (Rishi Rich's desi kuicha mix)** [2] Oct03 [35]
(12"+=) *(82876 57643-1)* – ('A'-Peter Rauhofer mix) / ('A'-Mad Brit mixshow).
(cd-s+=) *(82876 57643-2)* *<58215>* – ('A'-video).

Nov 03. (cd) *(82876 57644-2)* *<53748>* **IN THE ZONE** [14] [1]
– Me against the music (with MADONNA) / (I got that) Boom boom (with YIN YANG TWINS) / Showdown / Breathe on me / Early mornin' / Toxic / Outrageous / Touch of my hand / The hook up / Shadow / Brave new girl / Everytime. *(UK+=)* – Me against the music (Rishi Rich's desi kuicha remix with MADONNA) / Answer / Don't hang up.

☐ SPECIAL EFFECT (see under ⇒ MINISTRY)

SPECIALS

Formed: Coventry, Midlands, England . . . 1978 by keyboardist JERRY DAMMERS, guitarist LYNVAL GOULDING and bassist HORACE GENTLEMAN. After a brief spell with CLASH manager, Bernie Rhodes, DAMMERS formed the seminal '2-Tone' label in in 1979, releasing a debut single, 'GANGSTERS' (based on the Prince Buster track, 'Al Capone') under The SPECIAL A.K.A. moniker. By this point, the line-up had widened to include frontman TERRY HALL, vocalist/percussionist NEVILLE STAPLES, guitarist RODDY RADIATION and drummer JOHN BRADBURY. Issued as a split single with fellow ska revivalists, The SELECTER, the track almost made the UK Top 5 in the summer of '79, the label – with its unmistakable rude boy logo – quickly becoming the hippest namedrop in Britain as MADNESS debuted with 'The Prince' later that summer. Adding trombonist RICO RODRIGUEZ, the group released a follow-up, 'A MESSAGE TO YOU, RUDY', the mellow warmth of RICO's brass virtually making the track, a socially aware message, as ever, belying the song's easy going feel. An eponymous ELVIS COSTELLO-produced album was released the same month, the record blowing a breath of fresh air through the ashes of the punk scene and heralding one of the most exciting periods in British music since the SEX PISTOLS' heyday. The stand-out track was 'TOO MUCH TOO YOUNG', a frenetic stomp railing against teenage pregnancies and showcasing perfectly the compelling mash-up of reggae, ska, punk and pop which became synonymous with the '2-Tone' label. The song formed part of a live EP released early the following year along with a number of covers including Harry J. All Stars' 'LIQUIDATOR' and Symarip's wonderfully titled 'SKINHEAD MOONSTOMP', the record giving the group their first No.1. Two further Top 10 hits followed in 1980 with 'RAT RACE' and 'STEREOTYPES', along with a second album, 'MORE SPECIALS'. The group's defining moment, however, came during the long hot summer of '81, with the eerily evocative 'GHOST TOWN', the track's plea of "why must the youth fight among themselves?" echoing against a backdrop of inner city rioting in both London and Liverpool. Though the track was easily the best No.1 single released that year, the band splintered soon after, GOULDING, STAPLES and HALL forming The FUN BOY THREE, while RADIATION formed The TEARJERKERS and RICO went solo. DAMMERS and BRADBURY re-adopted the SPECIAL A.K.A. moniker, recruiting RHODA DAKAR, NICKY SUMMERS, JOHN SHIPLEY and DICK CUTHELL. After a couple of minor hits with 'The BOILER' and 'RACIST FRIEND', DAMMERS & Co. were back in the Top 10 with 'FREE NELSON MANDELA' (1984), arguably one of the best pop singles of the 80's, an incredibly inspiring, heartfelt plea for the imprisoned ANC leader, almost gospel-like in its intensity and funky as hell to boot. The accompanying album, 'IN THE STUDIO', wasn't so successful and DAMMERS subsequently split the band, putting his creative talent into political activism. In 1985 he turned up on the 'STARVATION' reggae charity project, formed Artists Against Apartheid in 1986 and played a major role in oraganising the Nelson Mandela 70th Birthday concert at Wembley Stadium in 1988. While a re-formed SPECIALS appeared in 1995, the absence of both DAMMERS (who retired from live work after developing tinnitus) and HALL meant the project lacked credibility. Though they recorded a relatively small body of work, The SPECIALS remain one of the most influential and pivotal bands of the last 20 years. • **Covered:** GUNS OF NAVARONE (Skatelites) / CONCRETE JUNGLE (Bob Marley) / LONG SHOT KICK DE BUCKET (Pioneers) / MONKEY MAN (Maytals) / MAGGIE'S FARM (Bob Dylan).

Album rating: THE SPECIALS (*8) / MORE SPECIALS (*6) / IN THE STUDIO (*6) / THE SPECIALS SINGLES compilation (*9) / TODAY'S SPECIALS (*3)

TERRY HALL (b.19 Mar'59) – vocals / **NEVILLE STAPLES** – vocals, percussion / **LYNVAL GOULDING** (b.24 Jul'51) – guitar, vocals / **JOHN BRADBURY** – drums / **JERRY DAMMERS** (b. GERALD DANKIN, 22 May'54, India) – keyboards / **RODDY RADIATION** (b. RODERICK BYERS) – guitar / **HORACE GENTLEMAN** (b. HORACE PANTER) – bass

2-Tone | not iss.

Jul 79. (7"; SPECIAL A.K.A.) *(TT 1 – TT2)* **GANGSTERS. / The Selecter: THE SELECTER** [6] [–]

— added (on some) guest **RICO RODRIQUEZ** – trombone

Chrysalis – 2-Tone | Chrysalis

Oct 79. (7") *(CHSTT 5)* **A MESSAGE TO YOU RUDY. / NITE CLUB** [10] [ ]

Oct 79. (lp/c) *(CDLTT/ZCDTL 5001)* <1265> **SPECIALS** [4] [84]
– A message to you Rudy / Do the dog / It's up to you / Nite club / Doesn't make it alright / Concrete jungle / Too hot / Monkey man / (Dawning of a) New era / Blank expression / Stupid marriage / Too much too young / Little bitch / You're wondering now. *(US-version with +=)* – Gangsters. *(re-iss. Nov84 on 'Fame' lp/c; FA41 3116-1/-4) (cd-iss. 1991; CCD 5001) (cd re-iss. Mar94; CD25CR 02)*

Jan 80. (7"ep) *(CHSTT 7)* **THE SPECIAL A.K.A. LIVE EP (live)** [1] [ ]
– Too much too young / Guns of Navarone / Long shot kick de bucket / The liquidator / Skinhead moonstomp.

May 80. (7") *(CHSTT 11)* **RAT RACE. / RUDE BOYS OUTA JAIL** [5] [ ]

Sep 80. (7") *(CHSTT 13)* **STEREOTYPES (part 1). / INTERNATIONAL JET SET** [6] [ ]

Sep 80. (lp/c) *(CHRTT/ZCHRT 5003)* <1303> **MORE SPECIALS** [5] [98]
– Enjoy yourself (it's later than you think) / Man at C & A / Hey little rich girl / Do nothing / Pearl's cafe / Sock it to 'em J.B. / Stereotypes / Stereotypes (part 2) / Holiday fortnight / I can't stand it / International jet set / Enjoy yourself (reprise). *(with free 7"; TT 999)* – Roddy Radiation & The Specials: BRAGGIN' AND TRYIN' NOT TO LIE. / Judge Roughneck: RUDE BUOYS OUTA JAIL *(cd-iss. 1991; CCD 5003)*

Jan 81. (7") *(CHSTT 16)* **DO NOTHING. / MAGGIE'S FARM** [4] [ ]

Jun 81. (7"m/12"m) *(CHSTT/+12 17)* **GHOST TOWN. / WHY / FRIDAY NIGHT, SATURDAY MORNING** [1] [ ]

— Only two originals (DAMMERS & BRADBURY) remained, as GOULDING, STAPLES & HALL formed The FUN BOY THREE. RADIATION formed TEARJERKERS. RICO went solo. All repl. by **RHODA DAKAR** – vocals + **NICKY SUMMERS** – bass (ex-BODYSNATCHERS) / **JOHN SHIPLEY** – guitar / **DICK CUTHELL** – saxophone

Jan 82. (7"; RHODA with The SPECIAL A.K.A.) *(CHSTT 18)* **THE BOILER. / THEME FROM THE BOILER** [35] [–]

The SPECIAL A.K.A.

— **HORACE PANTER** – bass returned to repl. SUMMERS who joined The BELLE STARS / **STAN CAMPBELL** (b. 2 Jan'62) – vocals / **NICK PARKER** – violin repl. CUTHELL (same label)

Dec 82. (7"/10") *(CHSTT/+10 23)* **WAR CRIMES (THE CRIME IS STILL THE SAME). / WAR CRIMES** [ ] [ ]

— **RODDY RADIATION** – guitar returned with newcomer **EGIDIO NEWTON** – vox

Aug 83. (7"/7"pic-d) *(CHSTT/CHSTPTT 25)* **RACIST FRIEND. / BRIGHT LIGHTS** [60] [ ]

— **GARY McMANUS** – bass repl. PANTER who joined GENERAL PUBLIC guested on album **DICK CUTHELL** – cornet / **ANDY ADERINTO** – saxophone

Mar 84. (7"/12") *(CHSTT/+12 26)* **NELSON MANDELA. / BREAK DOWN THE DOOR** [9] [ ]

Jun 84. (lp/c) *(<CHRTT/ZCHRT 5008>)* **IN THE STUDIO** [34] [ ]
– Bright lights / Lonely crowd / House bound / War crimes / What I like most about you is your girlfriend / Night on the tiles / Nelson Mandela / War crimes / Rascist friend / Alcohol / Break down the door. *(cd-iss. 1991; CCD 5008)*

Aug 84. (7"/12") *(CHSTT/+12 27)* **WHAT I LIKE MOST ABOUT YOU IS YOUR GIRLFRIEND. / CAN'T GET A BREAK** [51] [ ]

— Folded late '84, STAN CAMPBELL went solo and BRADBURY formed The JB's ALL STARS. DAMMERS turned up on a charity single by STARVATION early 1985.

— In Oct'93, SPECIALS were credited on DESMOND DEKKER single 'Jamaica Sky'.

— re-form with **GOLDING, STAPLES + RADIATION** + featuring **SHEENA STAPLE + KENDELL**

Kuff | not iss.

Jan 96. (c-s/12"/cd-s) *(KUFF C/T/D 3)* **HYPOCRITE / (mixes)** [66] [–]
above a Bob Marley cover and below a Toots & The Maytals number.

Mar 96. (c-s/cd-s) *(KUFF C/D 4)* **PRESSURE DROP / (mixes)** [ ] [–]

Apr 96. (cd/c) *(KUFF CD/MC 2)* **TODAY'S SPECIALS** [ ] [–]
– Take five / Pressure drop / Hypocrite / Goodbye girl / Little bit / The time has come / Somebody got murdered / 007 / Simmer down / Maga dog / Bad boys.

– compilations, etc. –

on 'Chrysalis' unless mentioned otherwise

Dec 82. (d-c) *(ZCDP 104)* **SPECIALS / MORE SPECIALS** [ ] [–]

Feb 87. (12"ep) *Strange Fruit; (SFPS 018)* **THE PEEL SESSIONS** (23.5.79) [ ] [–]
– Gangsters / Too much too young / Concrete jungle / Monkey man.

Feb 87. (7"0 *Old Gold; (OG 9683)* **TOO MUCH TOO YOUNG (live). / RAT RACE** [ ] [–]

Feb 87. (7") *Old Gold; (OG 9686)* **GHOST TOWN. / RAT RACE** [ ] [–]

Jun 88. (7"/12") *(CHS/+12 3276)* **FREE NELSON MANDELA – 70th Birthday re-make). / ('A'original)** [ ] [–]

Aug 91. (cd/c/lp) *(CHRTT/ZCHRT/CCD 5010)* **THE SPECIALS SINGLES** [10] [ ]
– Gangsters / A message to you Rudy / Nite club / Too much too young – Guns of Navarone / Rat race / Rude boys outta jail / Stereotype / International jet set / Do nothing / Ghost town / Why? / Friday night, Saturday morning / Racist friend / Free Nelson Mandela / What I like most about you is your girlfriend.

Oct 91. (7"/cd-s) **GHOST TOWN (REVISITED. / ('A'dub version)** [ ] [–]
(12"+=) – Why / ('A'demo version).

Apr 92. (cd/c/lp) *(CCD/ZCHRITT/CHRITT 5011)* **LIVE AT THE MOONLIGHT CLUB (live)** [ ] [–]

Apr 92. (cd/c/lp) *Receiver;* **TOO MUCH TOO YOUNG** [ ] [–]

— next shared with The SELECTER.

Dec 92. (cd) *Windsong; (WINCD 030)* **BBC RADIO 1 LIVE IN CONCERT (live)** [ ] [–]

Sep 93. (12"ep/c-ep/cd-ep; Various) *(CHS TT/TC/CD)* **THE TWO-TONE EP** [30] [–]
– Gangsters (SPECIAL AKA) / The Prince (MADNESS) / On my radio (SELECTER) / Tears of a clown (BEAT).

Sep 93. (cd) *Receiver; (RR CD/LP 178)* **DAWNING OF A NEW ERA** [ ] [–]

May 96. (cd/c) *EMI Gold; (CD/TC GOLD 1022)* **TOO MUCH TOO YOUNG** [ ] [–]

☐ SPECTRUM (see under ⇒ SPACEMEN 3)

☐ Alexander SPENCE (see under ⇒ MOBY GRAPE)

Jon SPENCER BLUES EXPLOSION

Formed: New York City, New York, USA . . . 1991 by former PUSSY GALORE namesake, JON SPENCER and ex-HONEYMOON KILLERS, JUDAH BAUER and RUSSELL SIMINS. Hardly blues in the conventional sense, SPENCER rather puts the emphasis on EXPLOSION, grinding out a bass-less groove-noise and howling out lip-curled soundbites. It was a formula that had its roots in the primal sludge of PUSSY GALORE and the first instalment in the JSBX saga carried on where that band left off, kind of. Released by 'Caroline' in the States and Virgin subsidiary, 'Hut', in Britain, the eponymous STEVE ALBINI-produced album surfaced in Spring '92, showcasing SPENCER's newly adopted blues drawl and revelling in defiantly dishevelled guitar abuse. Although some critics argued that SPENCER was all mouth and no trousers, so to speak, the man answered in strutting style on the likes of 'BELLBOTTOMS', one of the highlights from 1994's acclaimed 'ORANGE' album; that record, together with its 1993 predecessor, 'EXTRA WIDTH' (both released on 'Matador') really set out the band's manifesto of fractured 70's groove-funk, semi-detached melodies, hand claps, sweat dripping testimonial and sheer distorted noise. Sure, it might've been a style over substance white trash/noise interpretation of delta blues in the loosest sense but SPENCER's tongue was planted firmly in his cheek and following MTV exposure and a tour with The BEASTIE BOYS, JSBX were suddenly big news. A subsequent remix EP roped in such luminaries as BECK and if a move to 'Mute' seemed a little strange, there was no denying the blistering potential of 'NOW I GOT WORRY' (1996). From the delirious swagger of '2KINDSA LOVE' (surely a companion piece, if there ever was one, to MUDHONEY's 'Touch Me I'm Sick') to the disembodied static of Dub Narcotic's 'FUCK SHIT UP', SPENCER sounded as if he'd finally cut that deal down at the crossroads. Still, the man's recorded work only tells half the story; if you really want a baptism by BLUES EXPLOSION fire then you'll have to catch them live. 1998's STEVE ALBINI-produced set, 'ACME', was another adrenalin-fuelled taste of rock'n'roll blues although experimental sidesteps were always on show. Of late, an 'ACME +' remix LP has surfaced while his collaboration with the DUB NARCOTIC SOUND SYSTEM, 'SIDEWAYS SOUL', has also been issued. SPENCER and his crew of blues-blasting hooligans issued the frantic 'PLASTIC FANG' in April of 2002, and, although it covered no new ground whatsoever (and gave guest spots to DR. JOHN and BERNIE WORRELL), it was still a joy to hear SPENCER violently croon away – all in the name of rock'n'roll, baby!
• **Songwriters:** SPENCER/ group except; LOVIN' UP A STORM (Willie Dixon)

Album rating: A REVERSE WILLIE HORTON (aka JON SPENCER BLUES EXPLOSION) (*5) / CRYPT-STYLE collection (*5) / EXTRA WIDTH (*6) / ORANGE (*7) / MO' WIDTH collection (*5) / NOW I GOT WORRY (*7) / ACME (*7) / ACME PLUS out-takes (*5) / PLASTIC FANG (*5)

JON SPENCER – vocals, guitar / **JUDAH BAUER** – guitar / **RUSSELL SIMINS** – drums

not iss. | In The Red

Oct 91. (7") *<ITR 007>* **SHIRT JAC. / LATCH-ON** [–] [ ]

Jan 92. (7") *<ITR 011>* **SON OF SAM. / BENT** [–] [ ]

not iss. | Public Popcam

Feb 92. (lp) *<PORK 1>* **A REVERSE WILLIE HORTON** [–] [ ]
– Write a song / IEV / Exploder / Rachel / Chicken walk / White tail / '78 style / Changed / What to do / Eye to eye / Eliza Jane / History of sex / Come back / Support-a-man / Maynard Ave. / Feeling of love / Vacuum of loneliness / Intro A / Biological / Water man. *<cd-iss. Apr92 as 'BLUES EXPLOSION' on 'Caroline'; CAROLCD 1719> (UK-iss.Dec93 on 'Hut' cd/lp; HUT CD/LP 3) (cd re-iss. Jun97 & Sep98 on 'Caroline'; same as US)*

not iss. | Clawfist

Jun 92. (7"m) *<clawfist 13>* **HISTORY OF SEX. / WRITE A SONG / SMOKE CIGARETTES** [–] mail-o [–]

not iss. | Sub Pop

Nov 92. (7"green) *<SP 180>* **BIG YULE LOG BOOGIE. / MY CHRISTMAS WISH** [–] [ ]

not iss. | In The Red

Mar 93. (7") *<ITR 019>* **TRAIN NO.3. / TRAIN NO.1** [–] [ ]

Matador | Matador

Aug 93. (cd/c/lp; as BLUES EXPLOSION) *<(OLE 052-2/-4/-1)>* **EXTRA WIDTH** [ ] Nov93 [ ]
– Afro / History of lies / Black slider / Soul letter / Soul typecast / Pant leg / Hey mom / Big road / Train No.2 / Inside the world of the blues explosion / The world of sex. *(re-iss. Mar00 on 'Mute' lp/cd; JSBX 1/+CD)*

Feb 94. (7",7"white; as BLUES EXPLOSION) <*(OLE 077-7)*> **AFRO. / RELAX-HER** ☐ Jul93 ☐

Oct 94. (cd/c/lp) <*(OLE 105-2/-4/-1)*> **ORANGE** ☐ ☐
– Bellbottoms / Ditch / Dang / Very rare / Sweat / Cowboy / Orange / Brenda / Dissect / Blues x men / Full grown / Flavor / Greyhound. *(re-iss. Mar00 on 'Mute' lp/cd; JSBX 2/+CD)*

Feb 95. (7"white) *(OLE 111-7)* **BELLBOTTOMS. / MISS ELAINE** ☐ –
(12") *(OLE 111-1)* – ('A'remix) / Flavor 1 / Flavor 2.
(cd-s+=) *(OLE 111-2)* – Soul typecast / Greyhound (part 1 & 2).
(the REMIXES ep of above iss.May95)

Mute / Matador – Capitol

Sep 96. (cd/c/lp) *(cd/c+/stumm 132)* <OLE 193 – 53553> **NOW I GOT WORRY** 50 ☐
– Skunk / Identify / Wail / Fuck shit up / 2Kindsa love / Love all of me / Chicken dog / Rocketship / Dynamite lover / Hot shot / Can't stop / Firefly child / Eyeballin / R.L. got soul / Get over here / Sticky. *(re-iss. May97; same)*

Oct 96. (7") *(MUTE 202)* **2 KINDSA LOVE. / LET'S SMERF** ☐ ☐
(cd-s) *(CDMUTE 202)* – ('A'side) / Fish sauce / Cool Vee.

Nov 96. (7") <*(ITR 42)*> **GET WITH IT. / DOWN LOW** ☐ ☐
(above on 'In The Red')

Apr 97. (7"m) *(MUTE 204)* **WAIL. / JUDAH LOVE THEME / RADIO SPOT** 66 ☐
(7"m) *(LMUTE 204)* – ('A'-Mario C remix) / Afro (live) / Flavor (live).
(cd-s) *(CDMUTE 204)* – ('A'video mix) / Yellow eyes / Buscemi / Turn up Greene.

Oct 98. (cd/lp) *(CD+/STUMM 154)* <OLE 322 – 95566> **ACME** 72 ☐
– Calvin / Magical colours / Do you wanna get heavy? / High gear / Talk about the blues / I wanna make it all right / Lovin' machine / Bernie / Blue green Olga / Give me a chance / Desperate / Torture / Attack. *(cd re-iss. Jul00 on 'Toy's Factory'; TFCK 87163)*

Nov 98. (7"yellow) *(MUTE 222)* **MAGICAL COLOURS. / CONFUSED** ☐ –
(cd-s) *(CDMUTE 222)* – ('A'side) / Bacon / Get down lover.

Mar 99. (7"orange) *(MUTE 226)* **TALK ABOUT THE BLUES. / WAIT A MINUTE (Moby mix)** ☐ –
(12") *(12MUTE 226)* – ('A'side) / Lovin' machine (Automator mix) / Calvin (zebra ranch) / ('A'-Saints and sinners remix).
(cd-s+=) *(CDMUTE 226)* – ('A'-video).

Jun 99. (7") *(SMALL 004)* **NEW YEAR (DESTROYER). / other track by Barry Adamson** ☐ –
(above issued on 'Slut Smalls')

Aug 99. (7") *(MUTE 239)* **HEAVY. / GIVE YA SOME HELL** ☐ ☐
(12") *(12MUTE 239)* – ('A'side) / 2 kindsa love (Duck rock remix) / Attack (Detroit) / Do you wanna get heavy? (Duck rock hip'n'bass remix).
(cd-s) *(CDMUTE 239)* – ('A'side) / 2 kindsa love / Blues power / Attack (Detroit).

Sep 99. (cd/d-lp) *(CD+/STUMM 184)* <OLE 376> **ACME PLUS** (out-takes) ☐ ☐
– Wait a minute / Get down lover / Confused / Magical colors (31 flavors) / Not yet / Get old / Bacon / Blue green / Olga (remix) / Heavy (remix) / Lap dance / Right place, wrong time / Leave me alone so I can rock again / Soul trance / Electricity / New year / Chowder / TATB (for the saints and sinners mix) / Hell / I wanna make it alright (Zebra ranch).

Mar 02. (7") *(MUTE 263)* **SHE SAID. / GHETTO MOM** 58 –
(cd-s) *(CDMUTE 263)* – ('A'side) / Point of view / Do you wanna get it.
(cd-s) *(LCDMUTE 263)* – ('A'side) / Then again I will / Like a bat.

Apr 02. (cd/d-lp) *(CD+/STUMM 199)* <OLE 542> **PLASTIC FANG** ☐ ☐
– Sweet'n'sour / She said / Money rock'n'roll / Killer wolf / The midnight creep / Hold on / Down in the beast / Shakin' rock'n'roll tonight / Over and over / Mother nature / Mean heart / Point of view.

Apr 02. (7") *(ITRJBS 05)* **GHETTO MOM. / DO YOU WANNA GET IT** ☐ ☐
(above issued on 'In The Red')

Jun 02. (7") *(MUTE 271)* **SWEET'N'SOUR. / SHAKIN' ROCK'N'ROLL TONIGHT (live at the VPRO)** 66 –
(cd-s) *(CDMUTE 271)* – ('A'side) / Maureen / Alex.
(cd-s) *(LCDMUTE 271)* – ('A'version) / ('A'-CD-video).

– compilations, others, etc. –

Mar 94. (cd/lp) *Crypt; (EFA 11502-2/-1)* <29> **CRYPT-STYLE** (rec.1991 NYC) ☐ Apr92 ☐
– Lovin' up a storm / Support a man / White tail / Maynard Ave. / '78 style / Chicken walk / Mo' chicken – Let's get funky / Watermain / Like a hawk / Big headed baby / Write a song / Eye to eye / Feeling of love / Kill a man / Rachel / History of sex / Comeback / The vacuum of loneliness.

Feb 97. (lp/cd) *Au Go Go; <(ANDA 166/+CD)>* **MO' WIDTH** ☐ Jan95 ☐
– Afro / Out of luck / Cherry lime / Rob K / Ole man trouble / Wet cat blues / Johnson / There stands the glass / Lion cut / Beat of the traps / Memphis soul typecast.

Oct 97. (7") *Au Go Go; <(ANDA 231)>* **ROCKETSHIP. / CHOCOLATE JOE** – Austra –
(cd-s) <*(ANDA 231CD)*> – ('A'side) / Down low / Dynamite lover / Flavor / Full grown.

1999. (7") *Au Go Go; <ANDA 251>* **CALVIN. / CALVIN (Calvin Hill's T-Ray mix)** – ☐

Mar 00. (lp/cd) *Mute; (JSBX 3/+CD)* **EXPERIMENTAL REMIXES** ☐ –

May 02. (m-cd) *Toys Factory; (TFCK 87285)* **FANG PLASTIQUE** ☐ –
– Maureen / Tore up and broke (with ELLIOTT SMITH) / Mother nature / Do ya wanna get it? (with DR. JOHN) / Point of view (with BERNIE WORRELL) / She said.

☐ SPIDERS (see under ⇒ COOPER, Alice)

SPIRIT

Formed: Los Angeles, California, USA ... 1964 as The RED ROOSTERS, by RANDY CALIFORNIA and his middle-aged, shaven-headed stepfather, ED CASSIDY. The band split in late '65 and later reformed as SPIRITS REBELLIOUS in the Spring of '67, CALIFORNIA returning from New York where he'd traded axe licks with, and been heavily influenced by, a young JIMI HENDRIX. Along with ex-ROOSTERS, MARK ANDES, JOHN LOCKE and JAY FERGUSON, the band became SPIRIT and signed to LOU ADLER's 'Ode' records. Their eponymous debut was released soon after, a mellow melange of jazz and trippy, bluesy rock that marked the band out from the bulk of the folk-rock pack in the L.A. of 1968. SPIRIT also looked different, CASSIDY resembling some ageing hippy Kojak. With the exuberant 'I GOT A LINE ON YOU' single from the follow-up album, 'THE FAMILY THAT PLAYS TOGETHER' (1969), the band scored an unexpected Top 30 hit, although the bulk of the record explored the grey area where jazz, rock and psychedelia met. 'CLEAR SPIRIT' (1969) displayed a harder-edged sound but the band didn't really come into their own until they were paired with NEIL YOUNG producer DAVID BRIGGS and recorded the psychedelic masterwork, 'TWELVE DREAMS OF DR. SARDONICUS' (1971). From the pastoral psychedelia of 'NATURE'S WAY' to the more direct approach of 'MORNING WILL COME' and 'MR. SKIN', this was CALIFORNIA at his most creative in terms of both songwriting and guitar playing. Although it was critically acclaimed upon release, it failed to sell in any great quantity and FERGUSON left shortly after to form JO JO GUNNE. With CALIFORNIA laid up after a road accident and ED CASSIDY the only original remaining member involved in the 'FEEDBACK' (1972) album, it came as no surprise when the record was a resounding failure, creatively, critically and commercially. This was, in effect, the end of the line for the band although a bogus SPIRIT sprang up to haunt them, fronted by the STAEHELY brothers who'd played on 'FEEDBACK'. Meanwhile, CALIFORNIA recorded a minor classic of a solo album, 'KAPT. KOPTER AND THE (FABULOUS) TWIRLYBIRDS'. A rough-hewn set of psychedelic garage-rock, the record featured some inspired covers including The BEATLES' 'RAIN ' and 'DAY TRIPPER'. The original SPIRIT line-up reformed in the mid-70's and recorded a series of albums for 'Mercury', which tried and failed to capture the original vibe. After yet another split and reformation, the band resurrected Kapt. Kopter and recorded a cod-concept album,

'JOURNEY TO POTATOLAND', in 1981 before breaking up again. In the way of these things, the band reformed with differing line-ups throughout the 80's, CALIFORNIA also recording two solo albums. The long 'SPIRIT'-ual journey finally came to an end when CALIFORNIA was tragically drowned off the coast of the Hawaiian island of Molokai, on the 3rd of January, 1997. • **Songwriters:** CALIFORNIA and group, except YESTERDAY (Beatles) / HEY JOE (hit; Jimi Hendrix; c.William Roberts). CALIFORNIA covered solo:- MOTHER AND CHILD REUNION (Paul Simon) / ALL ALONG THE WATCHTOWER (Bob Dylan) / WILD THING (Troggs). • **Trivia:** MARK ANDES played on BORIS PICKETT & THE CRYPT KICKER 5's hit single, 'Monster Mash'. LED ZEPPELIN (Jimmy Page), must have listened to 1968 track, 'TAURUS', before writing 'Stairway To Heaven' (listen?).

Album rating: SPIRIT (*7) / THE FAMILY THAT PLAYS TOGETHER (*7) / CLEAR SPIRIT (*7) / TWELVE DREAMS OF DR SARDONICUS (*8) / FEEDBACK (*4) / THE BEST OF SPIRIT compilation (*8) / SPIRIT OF '76 (*5) / SON OF SPIRIT (*5) / FARTHER ALONG (*5) / FUTURE GAMES (A MAGICAL KAHUANA DREAM) (*4) / SPIRIT LIVE (*3) / JOURNEY TO POTATOLAND (*8) / THE THIRTEENTH DREAM remixes (*4) / Randy California: KAPTAIN KOPTER AND THE (FABULOUS) TWIRLY BIRDS (*5) / EURO AMERICAN (*4) / RESTLESS (*5) / SHATTERED DREAMS (*4) / Randy California's Spirit: RAPTURE IN THE CHAMBERS (*4) / TENT OF MIRACLES (*4) / LIVE AT LA PALOMA (*5) / CALIFORNIA BLUES (*4)

RANDY CALIFORNIA (b. RANDALL CRAIG WOLFE, 20 Feb'51) – guitar, vox / **JAY FERGUSON** (b. JOHN ARDEN FERGUSON, 10 May'47, Burbank, Calif.) – vocals / **MARK ANDES** (b.19 Feb'48, Philadelphia) – bass (ex-YELLOW BALLOON, w /JAY) / **ED CASSIDY** (b. 4 May'22, Chicago, Illinois) – drums (ex-NEW JAZZ TRIO) / **JOHN LOCKE** (b.25 Sep'43) – keyboards (ex-NEW WORLD JAZZ CO.)

C.B.S. Ode

Jun 68. (lp) *(63278)* *<44004>* **SPIRIT** [ ] Jan68 [31]
– Fresh garbage / Uncle Jack / Mechanical world / Taurus / Straight arrow / Topango windows / Gramophone man / Water woman / Great canyon fire in general / Elijah / Girl in your eyes. *(re-iss. Apr79 as 'THE FIRST OF SPIRIT' on 'CBS-Embassy'; 31693) (re-iss. Apr89 on 'Edsel' lp/c/cd; ED/+MC/CD 311) (re-iss. cd Aug95; 480965-2)*

Jun 68. (7") *(3523)* *<257-108>* **UNCLE JACK. / MECHANICAL WORLD** [ ] [ ]

Feb 69. (7") *(3880)* *<257-115>* **I GOT A LINE ON YOU. / SHE SMILED** [ ] Dec68 [25]

Apr 69. (lp) *(63523)* *<44014>* **THE FAMILY THAT PLAYS TOGETHER** [ ] Jan69 [22]
– I got a line on you / Poor Richard / Aren't you glad / It shall be / The drunkard / It's all the same / Dream within a dream / Jewish / So little to say / Silky Sam. *<US re-iss. Jul72; > (re-iss. Mar86 on 'Edsel' lp/c/cd+=; XED/CED/EDCD 162)* – She smiles / Darlin'. *(cd re-iss. Sep94 on 'Rewind';)*

Aug 69. (7") *(4511)* **DARK EYED WOMAN. / ICE** [ ] [–]

Sep 69. (7") *(4565)* *<257-122>* **DARK EYED WOMAN. / NEW DOPE AT TOWN** [ ] [ ]

Oct 69. (lp) *(63729)* *<44016>* **CLEAR SPIRIT** [ ] Jul69 [55]
– Dark eyed woman / Apple orchard / So little time to fly / Groundhog / Cold wind / Policeman's ball / Ice / Give a life, take a life / I'm truckin' / Clear / Caught / New dope in town. *(re-iss. Mar88 on 'Edsel' lp/cd; ED/+CD 268)*

Jan 70. (7") *(4773)* *<257-128>* **1984. / SWEET STELLA BABY** [ ] Dec69 [69]

C.B.S. Epic

Sep 70. (7") *(5149)* *<10648>* **ANIMAL ZOO. / RED LIGHT, ROLL ON** [ ] Aug70 [97]

Oct 70. (7") *<10685>* **MR. SKIN. / SOLDIER** [–] [ ]

Epic Epic

Feb 71. (lp) *(EPC 64191)* *<30267>* **TWELVE DREAMS OF DR. SARDONICUS** [ ] Dec70 [63]
– Nothing to hide / Nature's way / Animal zoo / Love has found a way / Why can't I be free / Mr. Skin / Space child / When I touch you / Sweet worm / Life has just begun / Morning will come / Soldier. *(re-iss. Mar81 lp/c; EPC/40 32006) (re-iss. Apr89 on 'Edsel' lp/c/cd; ED/+MC/CD 313) (re-iss. cd Aug93; 468030-2) (re-iss. cd Apr94; 476603-2)*

—— (Dec70) **JOHN ARLISS** – bass repl. FERGUSON and ANDES who formed JO JO GUNNE (May71) **CASSIDY + LOCKE** recruited new men **AL STAEHELY** – bass (ex-PUMPKIN) / **J.CHRISTIAN** (b.CHRIS STAEHELY) – guitar repl. ARLISS + RANDY who went solo

May 72. (7") *(EPC 8083)* **CADILLAC COWBOYS. / DARKNESS** [ ] [–]

Jun 72. (lp) *(EPC 64507)* *<31175>* **FEEDBACK** [ ] Mar72 [63]
– Chelsea girl / Cadillac / Cowboys / Puesta del scam / Ripe and ready / Darkness / Earth shaker / Mellow morning / Trancas fog-out / The witch.

—— (Aug72) Now a totally 'bogus' SPIRIT, fronted by The STAEHELY brothers. **STU PERRY** – drums repl. CASSIDY (see further below), and LOCKE who went solo. An album 'STA-HAY-LEE', included CASSIDY and LOCKE surfaced in US later? CHRIS was another to join JO JO GUNNE. Regarded as the 'real SPIRIT'

RANDY CALIFORNIA

(solo!) with **TIM McGOVERN** – drums, vocals / **CHARLIE BUNDY** – bass, b.vox / **HENRY MANCHOVITZ** (aka MITCH MITCHELL) – drums / **CLIT McTORIUS** (aka NOEL REDDING) – bass / guests **CASS STRANGE** (aka ED CASSIDY) – bass / **FUZZY KNIGHT** (aka ARRY WEISBER) – keyboards

Sep 72. (7") *<10927>* **WALKIN' THE DOG. / LIVE FOR THE DAY** [–] [ ]

Sep 72. (lp) *(EPC 65381)* *<31755>* **KAPTAIN KOPTER AND THE (FABULOUS) TWIRLY BIRDS** [ ] [ ]
– Downer / Devil / I don't want nobody / Day tripper / Mother and child reunion / Things yet to come / Rain / Rainbow. *(re-iss. Jun80 on 'C.B.S.' lp/c; CBS/40 31829) (re-iss. Nov85 on 'Edsel'+=; ED 164)* – Walkin' the dog / Live for the day. *(cd-iss. Aug93 & May97 on 'Edsel'; EDCD 164)*

—— In 1973, CALIFORNIA attempted suicide by jumping off Chelsea Bridge.

SPIRIT

—— after a few other line-up's in 1974, settled with **CASSIDY, CALIFORNIA + MARK ANDES** who repl. FUZZY KNIGHT. **JOHN LOCKE** re-joined for short spell, until he went into sessions. Also ANDES (who joined FIREFALL) were repl. by **BARRY KEANE** – bass

Mercury Mercury

Jun 75. (d-lp) *(6672 012)* *<804>* **SPIRIT OF '76** [ ] [ ]
– America the beautiful / The times they are a-changin' / Victim of society / Lady of the lakes / Tampa man / Mounalo / What do I have / Sunrise / Walking the dog / Joker on the run / When? / Like a rolling stone / Once again / Feeling in time / Happy / Jack Bond (part 1) / Mr. Road / Thank you Lord / Urantia / Guide me / Veruska / Hey Joe / Jack Bond (part 2) / The star spangled banner. *(re-iss. May88 on 'Edsel'; DED 251) (cd-iss. Mar93; EDCD 251)*

Aug 75. (7") *<73697>* **AMERICA THE BEAUTIFUL. / THE TIMES THEY ARE A-CHANGIN' / LADY OF THE LAKES** [–] [ ]

—— added **MATT ANDES** – guitar (ex-JO JO GUNNE)

Oct 75. (lp) *<SRM1 1053>* **SON OF SPIRIT** [–] [ ]
– Holy man / Looking into darkness / Maybe you'll find / Don't go away / Family / Magic fairy princess / Circle / The other song / Yesterday / It's time now. *(UK-iss.May89 on 'Great Expectations' lp/cd; PIP LP/CD 2)*

Oct 75. (7") *<73722>* **HOLY MAN. / LOOKING INTO DARKNESS** [–] [ ]

Jul 76. (lp) *<(SRM1 1094)>* **FARTHER ALONG** [ ] [ ]
– Farther along / Atomic boogie / World eat world dog / Stoney night / Pineapple / Colossus / Mega star / Phoebe / Don't look up your door / Once with you / Diamond spirit / Nature's way.

Sep 76. (7") *<73837>* **FARTHER ALONG. / ATOMIC BOOGIE** [–] [ ]

—— Now just a trio, when MARK re-joined FIREFALL and MATT & JOHN also left.

Apr 77. (lp) *(9100 036)* *<SRM1 1133>* **FUTURE GAMES (A MAGICAL KAHUANA DREAM)** [ ] [ ]
– CB talk / Stars are love / Kahouna dream / Brued my brain / Bionic unit / So happy now / All along the watchtower / Would you believe / Jack Bond speaks / Star Trek dreaming / Interlude XM / China doll / Hawaiian times / Gorn attack / Interlude 2001 / Detroit City / Freak out frog / The Romulan experiences / Monkey see, monkey do / Mt. Olympus / The journey of Nomad / Ending. *(re-iss. May89 on 'Great Expectations' lp/c/cd; PIP LP/MC/CD 3)*

May 77. (7") *(6167 519)* **ALL ALONG THE WATCHTOWER. / FURTHER ALONG** [ ] [–]

—— **LARRY KNIGHT** – bass returned to repl. KEENE

Illegal / Potato

Dec 78. (7") *(IL 007)* **NATURE'S WAY (live). / STONE FREE (live)** [ ] [–]

Jan 79. (lp) *(ILP 001) <PR 2001>* **SPIRIT LIVE** (live 11th Mar'78, Rainbow, London) [ ] [ ]
– Rock and roll planet / Nature's way / Animal zoo / 1984 / Looking down / It's all the same / I got a line on you / These are words / Hollywood dream.

— disbanded yet again late 1978; RANDY formed own band with **STEVE LAURA** – bass / **JACK WILLOUGHBY** – drums.

— they re-formed to re-record old unissued lost album below. **CALIFORNIA & CASSIDY** (alias KAPTAIN KOPTER & COMMANDER CASSIDY) enlisted **GEORGE VALUCK, JOHN LOCKE, MIKE BUNNELL + KARI NILE** – keys / **JEFF JARVIS, MIKE THORNBURGH + CHUCK SNYDER** – horns / **JOE GREEN** – strings

Beggars Banquet / Rhino

Apr 81. (lp) *(BEGA 23) <RNSP 303>* **JOURNEY TO POTATOLAND** [40] [ ]
– We've got a lot to learn / Potatoland theme / Open up your heart / Morning light / Potatoland prelude / Potatoland intro / Turn to the right / Donut house / Fish fry road / Information / My friend. *(re-iss. 1988 += on 'Chord' lp/c/cd; CHORD/+TC/CD 010) (re-iss. cd Jan91 on 'Line'; LICD 90009-2)*

Apr 81. (7") *(BEGA 45)* **WE'VE GOT A LOT TO LEARN. / FISH FRY ROAD** [ ] [–]

Jun 81. (7") *(BEGA 56)* **TURN TO THE RIGHT. / POTATOLAND THEME** [ ] [–]

— Band toured 1981:- **CALIFORNIA, CASSIDY, VALUCK + STEVE LAURA** (aka LIBERTY)

RANDY CALIFORNIA

— solo including all present SPIRIT members and some past.

Apr 82. (lp) *(BEGA 36)* **EURO-AMERICAN** [ ] [–]
– Easy love / Fearless leader / Five in the morning / Skull and crossbones / Breakout / Hand gun (toy guns) / This is the end / Mon ami / Rude reaction / Calling you / Wild thing. *(free w/7") (RAN 1)* – SHATTERED DREAMS. / MAGIC WAND

Apr 82. (7") *(BEG 76)* **HAND GUNS (TOY GUNS). / THIS IS THE END** [ ] [–]

Aug 82. (7") *(BEG 82)* **ALL ALONG THE WATCHTOWER. / RADIO MAN** [ ] [–]
(12"+=) *(BEG 82T)* – Breakout / Killer weed.

SPIRIT

— originals re-formed re-recording material from that era.

Mercury / not iss.

Jan 84. (7") *(MER 151)* **1984. / ELIJAH** [ ] [–]
(12"+=) *(MERX 151)* – I got a line on you.

Mar 84. (lp) *(MERL 35)* **THE THIRTEENTH DREAM** (remixes) [ ] [–]
– Black satin nights / Mr. Skin / Mechanical world / Pick it up / All over the world / 1984 / Uncle Jack / Natures way / Fresh garbage / I got a line on you. *(c+=)* – Elijah. *(cd-iss. Jul84; 818 514-2)*

Apr 84. (7"/6") *(MER 162/+6)* **FRESH GARBAGE. / MR. SKIN** [ ] [–]

RANDY CALIFORNIA

— solo with live + studio **MIKE SHEPHERD** – bass / **NEIL MURRAY + ADRIAN LEE + NEAL DOUGHTY** – keyboards / **CURLY SMITH** – drums live: **SCOTT MONAHAN** – keys / **LES WARNER** – drums

Vertigo / not iss.

May 85. (7") *(VER 16)* **RUN TO YOUR LOVER. / SECOND CHILD** [ ] [–]
(12"+=) *(VERX 16)* – Shane.

Jun 85. (lp/c) *(VERL 19)* **RESTLESS** [ ] [–]
– Run to your lover / Restless nights / Second child / Jack Rabbit / Shane / One man's Heaven / Murphy's law / Camelot / Battle march of the overlords / Childhood's end.

Jun 85. (7") *(VER 21)* **JACK RABBIT. / SUPER CHILD** [ ] [–]

Line / not iss.

1986. (lp) *(LCD 197)* **SHATTERED DREAMS** [–] German [–]
– Hey Joe (live) / Shattered dreams / All along the watchtower / Don't bother me / Downer / Second child / Man at war / Killer weed / Hand guns (toy guns) / Radio man / Run to your lover.

— In Apr'89, RANDY appeared on Various Artists live d-lp,c,cd,video 'NIGHT OF THE GUITAR', which was on next label.

RANDY CALIFORNIA'S SPIRIT

— gigged with various line-ups, until in 1989 settled with **RANDY, ED + SCOTT** plus **MIKE BUNNELL** – bass

I.R.S. / I.R.S.

Jun 89. (7") *(EIRS 117)* **HARD LOVE. / THE PRISONER** [ ] [–]
(12"+=) *(EIRST 117)* – Hey Joe.

Aug 89. (lp/c/cd) *(EIRS A/C/CD 1014) <13007>* **RAPTURE IN THE CHAMBERS** [ ] [ ]
– Hard love / Love tonight / Thinking of / Rapture in the chambers / Mojo man / Contact / The prisoner / One track mind / Enchanted forest / Human sexuality / Shera, princess of power / End suite.

— now without BUNNELL, repl. by **MIKE NILE**

not iss. / Dolphin

1991. (cd) *<DRG 22001>* **TENT OF MIRACLES** [–] [ ]
– Borderline / Zandu / Love from here / Ship of fools / Burning love / Tent of miracles / Logical answers / Old black magic / Neglected emotion / Imaginary mask / Stuttgart says good-bye / Deep in this land.

not iss. / Phantom

1995. (cd) *<22003>* **LIVE AT LA PALOMA (live)** [–] [ ]
– Life has just begun / Sadana / Mr. Skin / Hey Joe / I got a line on you / Prelude – Nothin' to hide / Like a rolling stone / Going back to Jones / Living in this world / Magic wand / Give a life take a life / La Paloma jam / 1984 / Jamaica jam / Super la Paloma jam / Nature's way.

— SCOTT repl. by **MATT ANDES** – slide guitar / **STEVE LORIA** – bass / **RACHEL ANDES** (daughter of MATT) – vocals

not iss. / C.R.E.W.

Dec 96. (cd) *<2204>* **CALIFORNIA BLUES** [–] [ ]
– California blues / Look over yonder / The river / Call on me / Crossroads / Song for Clyde / Pawn shop blues / Sigar mama / Red house / Gimme some lovin' / We believe / One world / Like a dog / oem for John Lennon / Shoes back on (live '67) / Tell everyone (live '67) / Soundtrack for a moth (live '67).

— On the 3rd of January '97, RANDY was drowned while surfing

– compilations, others, etc. –

— on 'Epic' unless mentioned otherwise

Aug 73. (d-lp) *<31457>* **SPIRIT. / CLEAR SPIRIT** [–] [ ]

Oct 73. (7") *(EPC 7082) <10701>* **MR. SKIN. / NATURE'S WAY** [ ] [92]

Oct 73. (lp) *(EPC 65585) <32271>* **THE BEST OF SPIRIT** [ ] Jul73 [ ]
(re-iss. Sep84; EPC 32516) <US re-iss. May89; >

Dec 91. (d-cd/d-c) *Columbia; (471268-2/-4)* **TIME CIRCLE (1968-72)** [ ] [ ]
– (first 4 albums)

Jan 92. (cd/c) *Castle; (CCS CD/MC 319)* **THE COLLECTION** [ ] [–]

Feb 92. (cd) *Outline; (OLCD 991133)* **CHRONICLES 1967-1982** [ ] [–]

Mar 94. (cd) *Line; (LICD 9000920)* **ADVENTURES OF KAPTAIN KOPTER & COMMANDER CASSIDY IN POTATOLAND** [ ] [–]

Aug 02. (d-cd; by RANDY CALIFORNIA & SPIRIT) *Acadia; <(ACAD 8017)>* **SEA DREAM** [ ] [ ]

SPIRITUALIZED

Formed: Rugby, England, 1990 ... initially as a side project for JASON 'SPACEMAN' PIERCE, who was soon to split from SONIC BOOM and SPACEMEN 3. He retained JON MATTOCK and WILLIE B. CARRUTHERS from the latter outfit and set about getting to grips with a new 90's psychedelia. Their first release was a version of The Troggs' 'ANYWAY THAT YOU WANT ME', which squeezed into the UK Top 75. The debut album, 'LAZER GUIDED MELODIES', was awash with VELVET-tones, recycled, and heavily distorted. A three year hiatus did not deter the British buying public, who also assured the follow-up, 'PURE PHASE', of a Top 30 placing in 1995. It was blessed with a more soulful vibe, while the majestic, lo-fi rhythm lifted it from an ambient crypt. In June '97, they returned to the fold (albeit a month after schedule) with their third album, 'LADIES AND GENTLEMEN WE ARE FLOATING IN SPACE B P'. The delay was due to ELVIS PRESLEY's team of whatnots objecting to the sample of 'Can't Help Falling In Love'. Nevertheless, the album, complete with bizarre prescription pill cd packaging, duly floated into the UK Top 5. Described by one reviewer as 'album of the decade', the record met with almost universal praise while its blissful melange of retro-psych, ambient noise and gospel was a heady tonic for the Dad-rock by numbers peddled by most 'indie' bands. PIERCE and his massive assembly/band gave listeners the chance to hear what it felt like to witness the grandiose SPIRITUALIZED in concert on a double vinyl LP entitled 'ROYAL ALBERT HALL OCTOBER 10 1997' (1998). After firing his band (yes, that's right) and going through a difficult and much publicised drug problem, PIERCE took to writing and recording his next magnum opus; 'LADIES AND GENTLEMEN . . .' part 2, if you will – the brilliant 'LET IT COME DOWN' (2001). Featuring huge gospel choirs and a plethora of musicians, the set boasted fragile songs from the SPIRITUALIZED camp as well as lush orchestrations and sometimes sentimental odes; example the album's finale 'LORD CAN YOU HEAR ME'. Ambitious not just in scope, but also in lyrical content and emotional content, PIERCE would follow this mini-masterpiece in 2003 with a surprisingly stripped-down 'AMAZING GRACE', an album in stark comparison to the lushly orchestrated 'LET IT COME DOWN'. Apparently influenced by the garage rock trashiness of BLACK REBEL MOTORCYCLE CLUB and the bare-bones guitar playing of JACK WHITE, PIERCE ditched the 50-strong choirs and orchestras in favour of aggressive rock, with only the weep-core lament 'THE BALLAD OF RICHIE LEE' and 'LORD LET IT RAIN ON ME' displaying the usual SPIRITUALIZED archetypes. Nevertheless, 'AMAZING GRACE' was undoubtably a JASON PIERCE album and shifted the rock riffage into overdrive on tracks 'CHEAPSTER' and 'SHE KISSED ME (IT FELT LIKE A HIT)'. Superb stuff from a man who never fails to impress. • **Songwriters:** PIERCE, except more covers; BORN NEVER ASKED (Laurie Anderson) / WALKING WITH JESUS (Spacemen 3) / OH HAPPY DAY (Edwin Hawkins Singers). • **Trivia:** In the early 90's, they headlined at the ICA Rock Week sponsored by Irn Bru.

Album rating: LAZER GUIDED MELODIES (*8) / PURE PHASE (*8) / LADIES AND GENTLEMEN WE ARE FLOATING IN SPACE B P (*10) / ROYAL ALBERT HALL OCTOBER 10 1997 (*8) / LET IT COME DOWN (*8) / THE COMPLETE WORKS VOLUME ONE compilation (*7) / AMAZING GRACE (*7)

JASON PIERCE – guitar / **WILLIE B. CARRUTHERS** – bass / **JON MATTOCK** – drums / plus girlfriend **KATE RADLEY** – organ, keyboards, vocals / **MARK REFOY** – guitar, dulcimer

Dedicated R.C.A.

Jun 90. (7") *(ZB 43783)* **ANYWAY THAT YOU WANT ME. / STEP INTO THE BREEZE** [75] [–]
(12"+=/cd-s+=) *(ZT/ZD 43784)* – ('B'-part 2).
(12") *(ZT 43780)* – ('A'remix) / ('B'-parts 2-3) / ('A'demo).

Jun 91. (7") *(FRIGHT 053)* **FEEL SO SAD. / I WANT YOU** [ ] [–]
(above is a gig freebie given away by 'Fierce' re-iss. Apr97)

Aug 91. (7"clear) *(SPIRIT 002)* **RUN. / I WANT YOU** [59] [–]
(12"+=/cd-s+=) *(SPIRIT 002 T/CD)* – Luminescence (stay with me) / Effervescent (chimes).

Nov 91. (7") *(SPIRIT 003)* **WHY DON'T YOU SMILE NOW. / SWAY** [ ] [–]
(12"/cd-s) *(SPIRIT 003 T/CD)* – ('A'extended) / Sway.

Mar 92. (7"ep/cd-ep) *(SPIRIT 004/+CD)* **I WANT YOU. / YOU KNOW IT'S TRUE (instrumental) / 100 BARS (flashback)** [ ] [–]

Apr 92. (cd/c/2x12"lp) *(DED CD/MC/LP 004)* <66035-2/-4> **LAZER GUIDED MELODIES** [27] [ ]
– You know it's true / If I were with her now / I want you / Run / Smiles / Step into the breeze / Symphony space / Take your time / Shine a light / Angel sigh / Sway / 200 bars. *(free-7" at 'Chain With No Name' shops)* – ANY WAY THAT YOU WANT ME / WHY DON'T YOU SMILE NOW *(re-iss. Jul97; same)*

Jul 92. (7"red) *(SPIRIT 005)* **MEDICATION. / SMILES (Peel session)** [55] [–]
(12") *(SPIRIT 005T)* – ('A'side) / Feel so sad (Peel session) / Angel sigh.
(cd-s++=) *(SPIRIT 005CD)* – Space (instrumental).

Jun 93. (7"flexi) *(SPIRIT 006)* **SMILES (live). / 100 BARS (acappella)** [–] [–]

Jun 93. (mail-order cd) *(DEDLP 008)* **F***ED UP INSIDE** [–] [–]

Oct 93. (7"yellow) *(SPIRIT 007)* **GOOD TIMES / LAY BACK IN THE SUN** [49] [–]
(12"ep+=/cd-ep+=) *(SPIRIT 008 T/CD)* – Electric Mainline 1 + 2.

—— now without REFOY, who formed SLIPSTREAM. They issued two albums for 'Che' in 1995; 'SLIPSTREAM' & 'SIDE EFFECTS'.

SPIRITUALIZED ELECTRIC MAINLINE

—— **SPACEMAN (JASON)** + **KATE RADLEY** – keyboards, vox / **SEAN COOK** – bass, harmonica / plus **MARK REFOY** – guitar (guest only) / **JON MATTOCK** – percussion / **LEON HUNT** – banjo / **STEWART GORDON** – violin / **THE BALANESCU QUARTET** – strings / + others on wind instruments

Dedicated Arista

Jan 95. (cd-ep) *(SPIRIT 009CD)* **LET IT FLOW / DON'T GO / STAY WITH ME / DON'T GO / STAY WITH ME (THE INDIVIDUAL)** [30] [–]
(cd-ep) *(SPIRIT 009CD2)* – ('A'side) / Take good care of it / Things will never be the same / Clear rush.
(cd-ep) *(SPIRIT 009CD3)* – ('A'side) / Medication / Take your time / Smile.
(3xbox-cd-ep/10"ep) *(SPIRIT 009BOX/T)* – (all above).

Feb 95. (cd/c/d-lp) *(DED CD/MC/LP 017)* <26035> **PURE PHASE** [20] Mar95 [ ]
– Medication / The slide song / Electric phase / All of my tears / These blues / Let it flow / Take good care of it / Born never asked / Electric mainline / Lay back in the sun / Good times / Pure phase / Spread your wings / Feel like goin' home. *(re-iss. Jul97; same)*

Nov 95. (cd-ep) *(74321 31178-2)* **LAY BACK IN THE SUN / THE SLIDE SONG / SPREAD YOUR WINGS (instrumental) / LAY BACK IN THE SUN (instrumental)** [ ] [–]

Feb 96. (12") *(SPIRT 101T)* **PURE PHASE TONES FOR DJs** [ ] [–]

SPIRITUALIZED

—— **DAMON REECE** – percussion + guests, repl. MATTOCK, HUNT + GORDON

Jun 97. (cd/c/lp) *(DED CD/MC/LP 034)* <18974> **LADIES AND GENTLEMEN WE ARE FLOATING IN SPACE** [4] [ ]
– Ladies and gentlemen we are floating in space / Come together / I think I'm in love / All of my thoughts / Stay with me / Electricity / Home of the brave / The individual / Broken heart / No god only religion / Cool waves / Cop shoot cop . . . *(re-iss. Jan98 as 12xcd-s box; DEDCD 034A)*

Jul 97. (7") *(SPIRIT 012)* **ELECTRICITY. / COOL WAVES (instrumental)** [32] [–]
(cd-s+=) *(SPIRIT 012CD1)* – Take your time (live) / All of my tears (live).
(cd-s) *(SPIRIT 012CD2)* – ('A'album version) / Cop shoot cop (live) / Shine a light (live) / Electric mainline (live).

Feb 98. (7") *(SPIRIT 014)* **I THINK I'M IN LOVE. / ('A'version)** [27] [–]
(12"+=/cd-s+=) *(SPIRIT 014 T/CD)* – ('A'-Chemical Brothers vocal & instrumental mixes).

May 98. (7") *(SPIRIT 015)* <13508> **THE ABBEY ROAD EP** [39] [ ]
– Come together / Broken heart.
(cd-s+=) *(SPIRIT 015CD)* – Broken heart (instrumental).
(12"++=) *(SPIRIT 015T)* – ('A'-Richard Fearless remix) / ('A'-Two Lone Swordsmen remix).

—— **J(ASON) SPACEMAN, DAMON REECE, SEAN COOK, MICHAEL MOONEY, THIGHPAULSANDRA + RAYMOND (MOONSHAKE) DICKATY**

Oct 98. (d-cd/d-lp) *(74321 62285-2/-1)* <19032> **ROYAL ALBERT HALL OCTOBER 10 1997 (live)** [38] Nov98 [ ]
– Intro / Shine a light / Electric mainline / Electricity / Home of the brave / The individual / Medication / Walking with Jesus / Take your time / No

God only religion / Broken heart / Come together / I think I'm in love / Cop shoot cop / Oh happy day.

— COOK, REECE + MOONEY were sacked in June '99 and subsequently formed their own "real" band, LUPINE HOWL, who signed to 'Vinyl Hiss' for releases in early 2000

Spaceman – Arista | Arista

Sep 01. (12") *(OPM 003)* **STOP YOUR CRYING. / ANYTHING MORE (instrumental) / ROCK'N'ROLL** | 18 | –
(cd-s+=) *(OPM 002)* – ('A'-video).

Sep 01. (cd/d-lp) *(OPM 001 CD/LP)* <14722> **LET IT COME DOWN** | 3 |
– On fire / Do it all over again / Don't just do something / Out of sight / The twelve steps / The straight and the narrow / I didn't mean to hurt you / Stop your crying / Anything more / Won't get to Heaven (the state I'm in) / Lord can you hear me.

Nov 01. (12") *(OPM 006)* **OUT OF SIGHT. / DIDN'T MEAN TO HURT YOU (instrumental) / GOING DOWN SLOW** | 65 | –
(cd-s+=) *(OPM 005)* – ('A'-video)>

Feb 02. (7") *(OPM 008)* **DO IT ALL OVER AGAIN. / ROCK AND ROLL (instrumental)** | 31 | –
(cd-s) *(OPM 004)* – ('A'side) / On fire (evening session version) / Amazing grace (peace on earth).
(cd-s) *(OPM 007)* – ('A'side) / Come together (Steve Lamacq session) / Going down slowly / ('A'-video).

Sanctuary | Sanctuary

Aug 03. (12"ep) *(SANEV 220)* **AMAZING GRACE EP 1** | | –
– Cheapster / Hold on / Never goin' back / Power and the glory.

Aug 03. (12"ep) *(SANEV 221)* **AMAZING GRACE EP 2** | | –
– Lord let it rain on me / Oh baby / Rated X / Lay it down slow.

Sep 03. (12"ep) *(SANEV 222)* **AMAZING GRACE EP 2** | | –
– She kissed me (it felt like a hit) / This little life of mine / The ballad of Richie Lee.

Sep 03. (cd-s) *(SANXD 222)* **SHE KISSED ME (IT FELT LIKE A HIT) / (video)** | 38 | –

Sep 03. (cd/lp) *(SAN CD/LP 214)* <84634> **AMAZING GRACE** | 25 |
– This little life of mine / She kissed me (it felt like a hit) / Hold on / Oh baby / Never goin' back / The power and the glory / Lord let it rain on me / The ballad of Richie Lee / Cheapster / Rated X / Lay it down low.

– compilations, others, etc. –

Mar 03. (d-cd) *Spaceman; (OPM 009CD) / Arista;* <50325> **THE COMPLETE WORKS VOLUME ONE** | |
– Anyway that you want me / Step into the breeze (part 1) / Feel so sad (7" single version) / Feel so sad (rhapsodies) / Feel so sad (glides and chimes) / Run (single version) / Luminescence (stay with me) / I want you / Effervescent (chimes) / Why don't you smile now / Sway / 100 bars (acappella) / I want you (instrumental) / Medication / Smiles / Angel sigh / Feel so sad (Medication EP version) / Good dope – Good fun / Lay back in the sun / Good times / Electric mainline (part 1) / Electric mainline (part 2) / 100 bars (flashback).

□ SPLIT ENZ (see under ⇒ CROWDED HOUSE)

Dusty SPRINGFIELD

Born: MARY O'BRIEN, 16 Apr'39, Hampstead, London, England. Taking her early inspiration from the likes of PEGGY LEE, O'BRIEN'S intitial music industry experience came as a member of the LANA SISTERS, an all-female trio who released a handful of singles for 'Fontana'. More successful were The SPRINGFIELDS, a PETER, PAUL & MARY-style folk trio which comprised DUSTY, her brother TOM and friend TIM FIELD. A string of UK hits (inlcuding 'BREAKAWAY', 'BAMBINO', 'ISLAND OF DREAMS' and 'SAY I WON'T BE THERE') established them as one of the most popular British acts of the era and in 1962 the trio even cracked the US Top 20 with 'SILVER THREADS AND GOLDEN NEEDLES'. A subsequent trip to the States introduced DUSTY to the burgeoning girl group craze and, heavily influenced by both Motown and the 'teen symphonies' of PHIL SPECTOR, she embarked on a solo career in 1963. Arranger Ivor Raymonde helped her realise her ambitions and later that year, she hit the UK Top 10 (US Top 20) courtesy of 'I ONLY WANT TO BE WITH YOU', a dizzying pop-soul classic in the trademark SPECTOR mould. A series of transatlantic hits ensued including 'STAY AWHILE', 'I JUST DON'T KNOW WHAT TO DO WITH MYSELF', 'LOSING YOU', 'LITTLE BY LITTLE' and 'WISHIN' AND HOPIN', the latter one of her most successful US singles (Top 10). With an earthier, huskier style than most of the girl groups, SPRINGFIELD was equally adept at carrying off rockier material and the 'British Invasion' led by The BEATLES only served to increase her popularity in the States. While bringing her trademark emotional punch to material by the cream of US writers such as Bacharach & David, Goffin & King, etc., SPRINGFIELD topped the UK chart (US Top5) in 1966 with the epic 'YOU DON'T HAVE TO SAY YOU LOVE ME'. By the late 60's, however, the rise of the "serious" rock artist meant it wasn't enough to simply churn out superior interpretations of other people's songs. Nevertheless, SPRINGFIELD gave it her best – many say greatest – shot with 1969's 'DUSTY IN MEMPHIS' album. Newly signed to 'Atlantic' and ensconced in a Deep South studio with country-soul guru, Jerry Wexler (alongside Tom Dowd and Arif Mardin), the singer reeled off a thrilling set of sultry, smoky soul-pop that invested the work of the aforementioned Bacharach/David, Goffin/King, along with Randy Newman and Mann-Weil (amongst others) with a rare emotional resonance. While supplying SPRINGFIELD with her last major hit (US/UK Top 10) in the classic 'SON OF A PREACHER MAN' (later DUSTY'd down for a new generation courtesy of Quentin Tarantino's 'Pulp Fiction' soundtrack) and the reverance of rock crtics, the album itself was a commercial failure destined for cult acclaim. Subsequently teaming up with the soon-to-be famous Philly writers, Gamble & Huff, she recorded another respectable set of blue-eyed soul in 1970's 'A BRAND NEW ME'. No major hits were forthcoming, however, SPRINGFIELD relocating to L.A. where she recorded one more album, 'CAMEO' (1973) before withdrawing from view as she tackled her spiralling drug dependency. Save for some backing vocals on soulstress ANNE MURRAY's 'Together' album, DUSTY was out of the picture until the late 70's when she made a failed comeback attempt with 'BEGINS AGAIN' (1978) and 'LIVING WITHOUT YOUR LOVE' (1979). Although she did score a minor UK hit with one-off single, 'BABY BLUE', a US-only comeback album, 'WHITE HEAT' (1982), fell flat. It would take the patronage of The PET SHOP BOYS to finally see DUSTY back in the spotlight, the camp synth-pop duo employing her services on their 1987 international smash, 'WHAT HAVE I DONE TO DESERVE THIS'. Early in '89, she had her first Top 20 hit in her own right since the late 60's with 'NOTHING HAS BEEN PROVED', a cut taken from the controversial UK movie, 'Scandal'. The accumulated exposure helped ensure a UK Top 20 placing for her long awaited 'REPUTATION' (1990) album, upon which NEIL TENNANT and CHRIS LOWE returned the favour by producing a couple of tracks. Going way back to her roots, the singer returned to Nashville for 1995's 'A VERY FINE LOVE'. Tragedy struck, however, as she was diagnosed with breast cancer during the album's recording. Sadly, after years of battling, she succumbed to the disease on 2 March, 1999, aged 59. One of the UK's most gifted and charismatic female vocalists, SPRINGFIELD was both loved and respected by fans, musicians and critics across the pop/rock/soul spectrum. It came as little surprise then, when she was inducted into the Rock And Roll Hall Of Fame shortly after her death.

Album rating: A GIRL CALLED DUSTY (*7) / EVERYTHING'S COMING UP DUSTY (*6) / WHERE AM I GOING (*7) / DUSTY DEFINITELY (*6) / DUSTY IN MEMPHIS (*9) / A BRAND NEW ME ((*6) / SEE ALL HER FACES (*5) / CAMEO (*4) / IT BEGINS AGAIN (*5) / LIVING WITHOUT YOUR LOVE (*5) / WHITE HEAT (*4) / REPUTATION (*6) / A VERY FINE LOVE (*4) / GOIN' BACK – THE VERY BEST OF DUSTY SPRINGFIELD compilation (*8)

SPRINGFIELDS

DUSTY SPRINGFIELD – vocals (ex-LANA SISTERS) / **TOM SPRINGFIELD** – vocals / **TIM FIELD** – vocals

Philips Philips

May 61. (7") *(PB 1145)* **DEAR JOHN. / I DONE WHAT THEY TOLD ME TO** [ ] [–]
Aug 61. (7") *(PB 1168)* **BREAKAWAY. / GOOD NEWS** [31] [–]
Nov 61. (7") *(PB 1178)* **BAMBINO. / STAR OF HOPE** [16] [–]
Dec 61. (7"ep) *(SBBE 9068)* **THE SPRINGFIELDS EP** [ ] [–]
– Dear John / I done what they told me to / Breakaway / Good news.
Jan 62. (7") *(PB 1220)* **GOODNIGHT IRENE. / FARAWAY PLACES** [ ] [–]
Apr 62. (7") *(PB 1241) <40038>* **SILVER THREADS AND GOLDEN NEEDLES. / AUNT RHODY** [ ] Jul62 [20]
Apr 62. (lp) *(SBBE 6068) <052>* **KINDA FOLKSY** <US-title 'SILVER THREADS AND GOLDEN NEEDLES'> [ ] Oct62 [91]
– Mambo wimoweh *[not US]* / The black hills of Dakota / Row, row, row *[not US]* / The green leaves of summer / Silver dollar / Allentown jail / Lonesome traveller / Dear hearts and gentle people / They took John away / Eso es al amor *[not US]* / Two brothers / Tzena, tzena, tzena *[not US]*. *<US+=>* – Gotta travel on / Aunt Rhody.
May 62. (7"ep) *(433622 BE)* **KINDA FOLKSY** [ ] [–]
May 62. (7"ep) *(433623 BE)* **KINDA FOLKSY NO.2** [ ] [–]
May 62. (7"ep) *(433624 BE)* **KINDA FOLKSY NO.3** [ ] [–]
Aug 62. (7") *(326536 BF)* **SWAHILI PAPA. / GOTTA TRAVEL ON** [ ] [–]
Oct 62. (7") *<40072>* **DEAR HEARTS AND GENTLE PEOPLE. / GOTTA TRAVEL ON** [–] [95]
Nov 62. (7") *(326557 BF)* **ISLAND OF DREAMS. / THE JOHNSTON BOYS** [5] [–]
Feb 63. (7") *<40092>* **LITTLE BY LITTLE. / WAF-WOOF** [–] [ ]
Mar 63. (7") *(326577 BF)* **SAY I WON'T BE THERE. / LITTLE BOAT** [5] [–]
Apr 63. (7"ep) *(BBE 12538)* **HIT SOUNDS FROM THE SPRINGFIELDS** [ ] [–]
Apr 63. (7") *<40099>* **ISLAND OF DREAMS. / FOGGY MOUNTAIN TOP** [–] [ ]
May 63. (lp) *(632304 BL)* **FOLK SONGS FROM THE HILLS** [ ] [–]
– Settle down / There's a big wheel / Greenback dollar / Midnight special / Wabash cannonball / Alone with you / Cottonfields / Foggy mountain top / Little by little / Maggie / Darling Allalee / Mountain boy.
Jul 63. (7") *(BF 1263)* **COME ON HOME. / PIT-A-PAT** [31] [–]
Nov 63. (7") *<40121>* **LITTLE BOAT. / SAY I WON'T BE THERE** [–] [ ]
Jan 64. (7") *(BF 1306)* **IF I WAS DOWN AND OUT. / MARACAMBA** [ ] [–]
—— The SPRINGFIELDS split when DUSTY went solo (TOM also went solo)
1964. (d-lp) *(BET 606)* **THE SPRINGFIELDS STORY** [ ] [–]

DUSTY SPRINGFIELD

Philips Philips

Nov 63. (7") *(BF 1292) <40162>* **I ONLY WANT TO BE WITH YOU. / ONCE UPON A TIME** [4] Jan64 [12]
Feb 64. (7") *(BF 1313) <40180>* **STAY AWHILE. / SOMETHING SPECIAL** [13] Mar64 [38]
Apr 64. (lp; stereo/mono) *(S+/BL 7594) <PHS600 133>* **A GIRL CALLED DUSTY** <US-title 'STAY WHILE / I ONLY WANT TO BE WITH YOU'> [6] Jun64 [62]
– Mama said / You don't own me / Do re mi / When the lovelight starts shining thru his eyes / My colouring book / Mockingbird / 24 hours from Tulsa / Nothing / Anyone who had a heart / Will you love me tomorrow / Wishin' and hopin' / Don't you know. *(cd re-iss. 1988 on 'Beat Goes On'; BGO 46) (re-iss. May89 cd/c; 842699-2/-4) (cd re-mast.Feb97 on 'Mercury'; 534520-2)*
Jun 64. (7") *<40207>* **WISHIN' AND HOPIN'. / DO RE MI (FORGET ABOUT THE DO AND THINK ABOUT ME)** [–] [6]
Jun 64. (7") *(BF 1348)* **I JUST DON'T KNOW WHAT TO DO WITH MYSELF. / MY COLOURING BOOK** [3] [–]
Sep 64. (7") *<40229>* **ALL CRIED OUT. / I WISH I'D NEVER LOVED YOU** [–] [41]
Oct 64. (7") *(BF 1369)* **LOSING YOU. / SUMMER IS OVER** [5] [–]
Nov 64. (7") *(BF 1382)* **OH HOLY CHILD. / Springfields: JINGLE BELLS** [ ] [–]
Nov 64. (lp) *<PHS600 156>* **DUSTY** [–] [ ]
– All cried out / I wish I'd never loved you / Can I get a witness / Summer is over / Don't say it baby / Guess who? / Live it up / My colouring book / Nothing has been proved / Do re mi (forget about the do and think about me) / Don't you know / I just don't know what to do with myself. *<cd-iss. 1999 on 'Mercury'+=; >* – Every ounce of strength / I'm gonna leave you / Heartbeat.
Jan 65. (7") *<40265>* **GUESS WHO? / LIVE IT UP** [–] [ ]
Feb 65. (7") *(BF 1396)* **YOUR HURTIN' KINDA LOVE. / DON'T SAY IT BABY** [37] [–]
Mar 65. (7") *<40270>* **LOSING YOU. / HERE SHE COMES** [–] [91]
Jun 65. (7") *(BF 1418) <40303>* **IN THE MIDDLE OF NOWHERE. / BABY, DON'T YOU KNOW** [8] Jul65 [ ]
Sep 65. (7") *(BF 1430)* **SOME OF YOUR LOVIN. / I'LL LOVE YOU FOR A WHILE** [8] [–]
Oct 65. (lp; stereo/mono) *(S+/RBL 1002) <PHS600 210>* **EVERYTHING'S COMING UP DUSTY** <US-title 'YOU DON'T HAVE TO SAY YOU LOVE ME'> [ ] Jun66 [77]
– Won't be long / Oh no! not my baby / Long after tonight is all over / La bamba / Who can I turn to? (when nobody needs me) / Doodlin' *[UK only]* / If it don't work out / That's how heartaches are made *[UK only]* / It was easier to hurt him / I've been wrong before / I can't hear you / I had a talk with my man / Packin' up *[UK only]*. *<US+=>* – You don't have to say you love me. *(re-iss. Sep89 on 'Beat Goes On' lp/c/cd; BGO LP/MC/CD 74) (cd re-mast.Mar98 on 'Mercury'; 536852-2)*
Nov 65. (7") *<40319>* **I JUST DON'T KNOW WHAT TO DO WITH MYSELF. / SOME OF YOUR LOVIN'** [–] [ ]
Jan 66. (7") *(BF 1466)* **LITTLE BY LITTLE. / IF IT HADN'T BEEN FOR YOU** [17] [–]
Mar 66. (7") *(BF 1482)* **YOU DON'T HAVE TO SAY YOU LOVE ME. / EVERY OUNCE** [1] [–]
May 66. (7") *<40371>* **YOU DON'T HAVE TO SAY YOU LOVE ME. / LITTLE BY LITTLE** [–] [4]
Jul 66. (7") *(BF 1502)* **GOIN' BACK. / I'M GONNA LEAVE YOU** [10] [–]
Sep 66. (7") *(BF 1510)* **ALL I SEE IS YOU. / GO AHEAD ON** [9] [–]
Sep 66. (7") *<40396>* **ALL I SEE IS YOU. / I'M GONNA LEAVE YOU** [–] [20]
Oct 66. (lp; stereo/mono) *(S+/BL 7737) <PHS600 220>* **GOLDEN HITS** (compilation) [2] Dec66 [ ]
– All I see is you / Wishin' and hopin' / In the middle of nowhere / My colouring book / Goin' back / All cried out / You don't have to say you love me / I only want to be with you / Little by little / Losing you / Stay awhile / I just don't know what to do with myself.
Feb 67. (7") *(BF 1553) <40439>* **I'LL TRY ANYTHING. / THE CORRUPT ONES** [13] Mar67 [40]
May 67. (7") *(BF 1577) <40465>* **GIVE ME TIME. / THE LOOK OF LOVE** [24] [76] [22]
Sep 67. (7") *(BF 1608) <40498>* **WHAT'S IT GONNA BE. / SMALL TOWN GIRL** [ ] Nov67 [49]
Nov 67. (lp; stereo/mono) *(S+/BL 7820)* **WHERE AM I GOING** [40] [–]
– Bring him back / Don't let me lose this dream / I can't wait until I see my baby's face / Take me for a little while / Chained to a memory / Sunny / They long to be close to you / Welcome home / Come back to me / If you go away / Broken blossoms / Where am I going. *(cd/c-iss.May90; 846050-2/-4) (cd re-mast.Mar98; 536962-2)*
Dec 67. (lp) *<PHS600 256>* **THE LOOK OF LOVE** [–] [ ]
– What's it gonna be / The look of love / Give me time / They long to be close to you / If you go away / Sunny / Come back to me / Welcome home / Small town girl / Take me for a little while / Chained to a memory.
Apr 68. (7") *<40547>* **SWEET RIDE. / NO STRANGER AM I** [–] [ ]
Jun 68. (7") *(BF 1682)* **I CLOSE MY EYES AND COUNT TO TEN. / NO STRANGER AM I** [4] [–]
Jul 68. (7") *<40553>* **I CLOSE MY EYES AND COUNT TO TEN. / LA BAMBA** [–] [ ]
Sep 68. (7") *(BF 1706)* **I WILL COME TO YOU. / THE COLOUR OF YOUR EYES** [ ] [–]
Nov 68. (lp; stereo/mono) *(S+/BL 7864)* **DUSTY . . . DEFINITELY** [30] [–]
– Ain't no sun since you've been gone / Take another little piece of

my heart / Another night / Mr. Dream merchant / I can't give back the love I feel for you / Love power / This girl's in love with you / I only wanna laugh / Who (will take my place) / I think it's gonna rain today / Morning / Second time around. *(re-iss. May90 cd/c; 846049-2/-4)*

Philips Atlantic

Nov 68. (7") *(BF 1730) <2580>* **SON OF A PREACHER MAN. / JUST A LITTLE LOVIN' (EARLY IN THE MORNING)** [9] [10]

Feb 69. (7") *<2606>* **DON'T FORGET ABOUT ME. / BREAKFAST IN BED** [–] [64] [91]

Apr 69. (7") *<2623>* **THE WINDMILLS OF YOUR MIND. / I DON'T WANT TO HEAR IT ANYMORE** [–] [31]

Apr 69. (lp) *(SBL 7889) <SD 8214>* **DUSTY IN MEMPHIS** [ ] Mar69 [99]
– Just a little lovin' / So much love / Son of a preacher man / I don't want to hear it anymore / Don't forget about me / Breakfast in bed / Just one smile / The windmills of your mind / In the land of make believe / No easy way down / I can't make it alone. *(re-iss. Sep80 on 'Mercury' lp/c+=; 6381/7215 023)* – I want to be a free girl / I believe in you / What do you do when love dies / Haunted. *(re-iss. Mar85 lp/c; PRICE/PRIMC 83) (cd-iss. Jun89; 836840-2) (cd re-iss. Jul90; 846252-2) (cd re-iss. Sep95 on 'Mercury'+=; 528687-2)*

Jul 69. (7") *<2647>* **WILLIE & LAURA MAE JONES. / THAT OLD SWEET ROLL (HI-DE-HO)** [–] [78]

Sep 69. (7") *<2673>* **IN THE LAND OF MAKE BELIEVE. / SO MUCH LOVE** [–] [ ]

Sep 69. (7") *(BF 1811)* **AM I THE SAME GIRL. / EARTHBOUND GYPSY** [43] [–]

Nov 69. (7") *(BF 1826) <2685>* **A BRAND NEW ME. / BAD CASE OF THE BLUES** [ ] [24]

— In Feb'70, she and brother TOM released 'MORNING PLEASE DON'T COME'

Feb 70. (7") *<2705>* **SILLY, SILLY, FOOL. / JOE** [–] [76]

Apr 70. (lp) *(SBL 7927) <SD 8249>* **FROM DUSTY . . . WITH LOVE** <US-title 'A BRAND NEW ME'> [35] Feb70 [ ]
– Lost / Bad case of the blues / Never love again / Let me in your way / Let's get together soon / A brand new me / Silly, silly, fool / The star of my show / Let's talk it over.

May 70. (7") *<2729>* **LET ME IN YOUR WAY. / I WANNA BE A FREE GIRL** [–] [ ]

Jul 70. (7") *<2739>* **NEVER LOVE AGAIN. / LOST** [–] [ ]

Sep 70. (7") *(6006 045)* **HOW CAN I BE SURE. / SPOOKY** [36] [–]

Nov 70. (7") *<2771>* **WHAT GOOD IS I LOVE YOU. / WHAT DO YOU DO WHEN LOVE DIES** [–] [ ]

Oct 71. (7") *<2825>* **HAUNTED. / NOTHING IS FOREVER** [–] [ ]

Dec 71. (7") *<2841>* **SOMEONE WHO CARED. / I BELIEVE IN YOU** [–] [ ]

Philips Dunhill

May 72. (7") *(6006 214)* **YESTERDAY WHEN I WAS YOUNG. / I START COUNTING** [ ] [–]

Nov 72. (lp) *(6308 117)* **SEE ALL HER FACES** [ ] [–]
– Mixed up girl / Crumbs off the table / Let me down easy / Comfort dream / Girls can't do what the guys do / I start counting / Yesterday when I was young / Girls it ain't easy / What good is I love you / Willie & Laura Mae Jones / Someone who cares / Nothing is forever / See all her faces / That old sweet roll.

Apr 73. (7") *(6006 295) <4341>* **WHO GETS YOUR LOVE. / OF ALL THE THINGS** [ ] Feb73 [ ]

Apr 73. (lp) *(6308 152)* **CAMEO** [ ] [ ]
– Who gets your love / Breakin' up a happy home / Easy evil / Mama's little girl / The other side of life / Coming and going / I just wanna be there / Who could be loving other than me / Tupelo honey / Of all the things / Learn to say goodbye.

Jun 73. (7") *<4357>* **LEARN TO SAY GOODBYE. / MAMA'S LITTLE GIRL** [–] [ ]

Aug 73. (7") *(6006 325)* **LEARN TO SAY GOODBYE. / EASY EVIL** [ ] [–]

Mar 74. (7") *(6006 350)* **WHAT'S IT GONNA BE. / BRING HIM BACK** [ ] [–]

Mercury U.A.

Feb 78. (lp)(c) *(9109 607)(7109 323) <791>* **IT BEGINS AGAIN** [41] [ ]
– Turn me around / Checkmate / I'd rather leave while I'm in love / A love like yours (don't come knocking every day) / Love me by name / Sandra / I found love with you / Hollywood movie girls / That's the kind of love I've got for you.

Mar 78. (7") *(DUSTY 1)* **A LOVE LIKE YOURS (DON'T COME KNOCKING EVERY DAY). / HOLLYWOOD MOVIE GIRLS** [ ] [–]

Mar 78. (7") *<XW 1205>* **SANDRA. / CHECKMATE** [–] [ ]

Jun 78. (7") *(DUSTY 2)* **THAT'S THE KIND OF LOVE I'VE GOT FOR YOU. / SANDRA** [ ] [–]

Jul 78. (7") *<XW 1225>* **GIVE ME THE NIGHT. / CHECKMATE** [–] [ ]

Mar 79. (lp)(c) *(9109 617)(7231 432) <936>* **LIVING WITHOUT YOUR LOVE** [ ] [ ]
– You've really got a hold on me / You can do it / Be somebody / Closet man / Living without your love / Save me, save me / Get yourself to love / I just fall in love again / Dream on / I'm coming home again.

Apr 79. (7") *(DUSTY 3)* **I'M COMING HOME AGAIN. / SAVE ME SAVE ME** [ ] [–]

Jul 79. (7") *<XW 1255>* **LIVING WITHOUT YOUR LOVE. / GET YOURSELF TO LOVE** [–] [ ]

Sep 79. (7"/disc-12") *(DUSTY 4/+12)* **BABY BLUE. / GET YOURSELF TO LOVE** [61] [–]

Jan 80. (7") *(DUSTY 5)* **YOUR LOVE STILL BRINGS ME TO MY KNEES. / I'M YOUR CHILD** [ ] [–]

Jan 80. (7") *<XW 1006>* **LET ME LOVE YOU ONCE BEFORE YOU GO. / I'M YOUR CHILD** [–] [ ]

not iss. 20th Century

1981. (7") *<2457>* **IT GOES LIKE IT GOES. / I WISH THAT LOVE WOULD LAST** [–] [ ]
(above from the movie, 'Norma Rae')

not iss. Casablanca

1982. (7") *<2356>* **DONNEZ MOI (GIVE IT TO ME). / I AM CURIOUS** [–] [ ]

1982. (lp) *<NBLP 7271>* **WHITE HEAT** [–] [ ]
– Donnez moi (give it to me) / I don't think we could ever be friends / Blind sheep / Don't call it love / Time and time again / I am curious / Sooner or later / Losing you / Gotta get used to you / Soft core.

— In Mar'84, she duetted with SPENCER DAVIS on the single 'PRIVATE NUMBER' for 'Allegiance'; (ALES 3)

Hippodrome not iss.

Aug 85. (7") *(HIPPO 103)* **SOMETIMES LIKE BUTTERFLIES. / I WANNA CONTROL YOU** [ ] [–]
(12"+=) *(12HIPPO 103)* – ('A'extended).

— In Aug'87, DUSTY was nearly back at the top when she duetted with The PET SHOP BOYS on their 'WHAT HAVE I DONE TO DESERVE THIS'.

— On a slightly lesser note, she augmented RICHARD CARPENTER on his single, 'SOMETHING IN YOUR EYES'.

Parlophone Enigma

Feb 89. (7"/7"g-f) *(R/RG 6207) <75042>* **NOTHING HAS BEEN PROVED. / (instrumental)** [16] [ ]
(12"+=/cd-s+=) *(12R/CDR 6207)* – ('A'dance mix).

Nov 89. (c-s/7") *(TC+/R 6234)* **IN PRIVATE. / (instrumental)** [14] [–]
(cd-s+=) *(CDR 6234)* – ('A'extended).
(12") *(12R 6234)* – ('A'remix) / ('A'dub) / ('A'bonus beats).

May 90. (7") *(R 6253)* **REPUTATION. / REP U DUB 1** [38] [–]
('A'mix-12"+=) *(12R 6253)* – Rep U dub 2.

Parlophone Alex

Jun 90. (cd/c/lp) *(CD/TC+/PCSD 111) <2013>* **REPUTATION** [18] Jul91 [ ]
– Reputation / Send it to me / Arrested by you / Time waits for no one / I was born this way / In private / Daydreaming / Nothing has been proved / I want to stay here / Occupy your mind. *(cd re-iss. Apr95 on 'Fame'; CDFA 3320)*

Sep 90. (c-s/7") *(TC+/R 6266)* **ARRESTED BY YOU. / (instrumental)** [70] [–]
(ext-12"+=) *(12R 6266)* – Born this way (mix).
(ext-cd-s++=) *(CDR 6266)* – Getting it right.

Columbia Columbia

Oct 93. (7"; by CILLA BLACK & DUSTY SPRINGFIELD) *(659856-7)* **HEART AND SOUL. / (other track by CILLA BLACK)** [75] [–]
(cd-s+=) *(659856-2)* – (a capella mix & instrumental).

Jun 95. (c-s; by DUSTY SPRINGFIELD & DARYL HALL) *(662059-4)* **WHEREVER WOULD I BE / ALL I HAVE TO OFFER YOU IS LOVE** [44] [–]
(cd-s+=) *(662059-2)* – Reputation (alternative mix) / ('A'solo).
(cd-s) *(662059-5)* – ('A'side) / Daydreaming / Arrested by you / ('A'mix).

Jun 95. (cd/c/lp) *(478508-2/-4/-1) <67053>* **A VERY FINE LOVE** [43] [ ]
– Roll away / A very fine love / Wherever would I be / Go easy on me / You are the storm / I can't help the way I don't feel / All I have to offer you is love / Lovin' proof / Old habits die hard / Where is A.

Oct 95. (c-s) *(662368-4)* **ROLL AWAY / OLD HABITS DIE HARD** [68] [–]
(cd-s+=) *(662368-2)* – Your love still brings me to my knees / Born this way.
(cd-s+=) *(662368-5)* – Baby blue / What's it gonna be.

— sadly, on the 2nd March, 1999, DUSTY died of cancer (see above)

– (selective) compilations, etc. –

Oct 81. (lp/c) *K-Tel; (NE1/CE2 139)* **THE VERY BEST OF . . .** [ ] [–]
May 94. (cd/c) *Philips; (848789-2/-4)* **GOIN' BACK – THE VERY BEST OF DUSTY SPRINGFIELD** [5] [ ]
– Wishin' and hopin' / Little by little / All cried out / Losing you / Son of a preacher man / All I see is you / In the middle of nowhere / What have I done to deserve this (with PET SHOP BOYS) / Goin' back / Island of dreams / I'll try anything / Reputation / Stay awhile / In private / Time and time again / I just don't know what to do with myself / I only want to be with you / Windmills of your mind / Silver threads and golden needles (SPRINGFIELDS) / Say I won't be there (SPRINGFIELDS) / Some of your lovin' / The look of love / I close my eyes and count to ten / Nothing has been proved / You don't have to say you love me.
Aug 94. (4xcd-box) *Philips; (522254-2)* **THE LEGEND OF DUSTY SPRINGFIELD** [ ] [–]

Bruce SPRINGSTEEN

Born: 23 Sep'49, Freehold, New Jersey, USA. While still attending college, SPRINGSTEEN formed the short-lived STEEL MILL, three members ('LITTLE STEVEN' VAN ZANDT, DANNY FEDERICI and VINI LOPEZ) subsequently becoming part of his 10-piece back-up group. In May '72, the singer signed to 'Columbia' with the help of legendary A&R man, John Hammond, who had previously signed BOB DYLAN to the same label a decade earlier. The connection didn't stop there, SPRINGSTEEN duly heralded as the latest successor to ZIMMERMAN's singer/songwriter mantle upon the release of his debut album, 'GREETINGS FROM ASBURY PARK, N.J.' Released in early '73, it originally sold poorly, as did the follow-up, 'THE WILD, THE INNOCENT & THE E-STREET SHUFFLE'. Following the latter set's completion, SPRINGSTEEN concentrated on heavy touring with the newly formed E-STREET BAND, the subsequent exposure resurrecting, to some degree, the commercial fortunes of his first two releases, both hitting the US Top 60 in mid-75. It was with much anticipation, then, that a third album, 'BORN TO RUN', eventually hit the shelves later that year. Co-producer and future manager, Jon Landau, had steered the project towards a suitably grandise sound, the starry-eyed romanticism of SPRINGSTEEN's lyrical themes complementing the lavish arrangements. The title track best summed up the mood of the album, teenage rebels following their dreams on the open road; not exactly an original take on rock'n'roll but one which the singer would refine and subvert as his career unfolded. Reaching Top 3 in the USA, the album gave SPRINGSTEEN his first real breakthrough, in the States at least, 'The Boss' (as the Americans soon took to calling him) undertaking a full scale US tour. It would be almost three years before another album as SPRINGSTEEN became embroiled in a legal battle with his former manager, Mike Appel. The latter had attempted to prevent his client working with Landau, an out of court settlement eventually bringing matters to a close and allowing the beleaguered singer to begin recording 'DARKNESS ON THE EDGE OF TOWN' (1978). As the title suggested, the album was an altogether more bleak affair, no doubt inspired by the legal traumas of the preceding few years. Yet it remains one of SPRINGSTEEN's most enduring efforts, establishing him as a sympathetic and cuttingly accurate observer of the gritty realities, hopes and dreams facing ordinary Americans. The spartan echoes of tracks like 'ADAM RAISED A CAIN' would resonate through SPRINGSTEEN's more introspective work throughout his subsequent career. Though the record again made the US Top 5, consolidating SPRINGSTEEN's position as a firm critics' favourite, he only really made a substantial breakthrough with 'THE RIVER' (1980), his first US No.1. A double set, the record could easily have been trimmed down to a single album, brimming as it was with workaday rockers centering on cars, girls, cars and, erm . . . more cars (see 'CADILLAC RANCH', 'RAMROD', 'CRUSH ON YOU', 'DRIVE ALL NIGHT' etc). One of the record's few redeeming factor's was the title track, an aching ode to doomed love which indicated the direction of SPRINGSTEEN's next effort, 'NEBRASKA' (1982). Arguably one of the most darkly powerful modern folk albums of the past twenty years, the record's stark, sublime beauty stood in glaring contrast to the banal excess of its predecessor and could've conceivably been recorded by a different man. Accompanied by a lone acoustic guitar and occasional wailing harmonica, SPRINGSTEEN explored the boundaries between good and evil, right and wrong, through a series of deeply affecting character studies, his whisky throated voice wracked with doubt, frustration and pain. Although the record was a transatlantic Top 3 hit, it somewhat predictably failed to spawn any successful singles. Nevertheless, any readers basing their opinion of 'The Boss' solely on 'BORN IN THE U.S.A.' (1984) and suchlike are urged to give 'NEBRASKA' a spin. 'BORN . . .' saw SPRINGSTEEN's career finally go stratospheric, a record that came to define 80's America as much as it came to define the singer's stadium sound and blue collar image. Though SPRINGSTEEN had simplified his dark musings on the American dream for a wider audience, the message still wasn't clear enough for some people, Ronald Reagan included. Following the latter's attempt to hijack the supposed patriotic sentiments of the record, SPRINGSTEEN made his political allegiances public by supporting environmental and civil right groups. He'd also previously played a number of benefits for Vietnam war veterans, a subject he addressed in the album's raging title track. Elsewhere, songs like 'DOWNBOUND TRAIN' and 'I'M ON FIRE' centred on familiar SPRINGSTEEN themes of human suffering while 'DANCING IN THE DARK' gave him his biggest US hit to date. Despite the lyrical content, however, the bulk of the album was upbeat, infectious and highly commercial, a multi-million seller which precipitated the most extensive touring of SPRINGSTEEN's career. The massive selling live boxed set, 'LIVE 1977-1985' neatly chalked out the end of an era, a markedly different SPRINGSTEEN surfacing in 1987 with 'TUNNEL OF LOVE'. With his marriage under strain, the album was a more personal affair exploring the vagaries of romance. While the likes of 'TOUGHER THAN THE REST' were touchingly direct, overall the album lacked the fire of old. Despite finally parting ways with the E STREET BAND, the concurrently released 'HUMAN TOUCH' and 'LUCKY TOWN' (1992) sets failed to satisfy critics or fans with their formulaic material. More endearing was the poignant 'STREETS OF PHILADELPHIA', which SPRINGSTEEN contributed to the film, 'Philadelphia', a subsequent Grammy Award winner and the singer's biggest hit single for over a decade. The following year saw the low key release of 'THE GHOST OF TOM JOAD' (1995). This was SPRINGSTEEN back doing what he does best, strumming desolate tales of America's lost underclass. With a title taken from Steinbeck's 'Grapes Of Wrath', WOODY GUTHRIE was mentioned in more than one review. It's a comparison not too far off the mark, SPRINGSTEEN never giving up the ghost on documenting the trials of the downtrodden. Many rank the stripped down, one-man shows that accompanied the album's release as among the best of SPRINGSTEEN's career, the singer achieving a newfound authority and maturity. 'LIVE IN NEW YORK CITY' (2001) was a wholly different proposition, a document of SPRINGSTEEN's much lauded millennial reunion with The E STREET BAND. Rather than relying on the big hits, the album featured a clutch of more obscure classics from the late 70's and early 80's such as 'BADLANDS' and 'MANSION ON THE HILL', songs that sound as vital today as they did back then. Of all the American artists who undertook some serious soul-searching after 9/11 – and there were many – it was perhaps SPRINGSTEEN who emerged with the most cohesive, honest and perceptive set of songs. Unlikely as this may have seemed to some, the man's ability to tap into the substrata of American culture and consciousness has been ably demonstrated in the past. Nor did the fact that 'THE RISING' (2002) marked a reunion with The E STREET BAND, detract from the depth and simplicity of the writing. While the band have rarely sounded so powerfully unfettered, it was the hushed grace and spiritual intensity of tracks such as 'MY CITY OF RUINS' which lent the album its root sense of painful catharsis. • **Covered:** JERSEY GIRL (Tom Waits) / WAR (Edwin Starr) / SANTA CLAUS IS COMING TO TOWN (festive trad.) / VIVA LAS VEGAS (Elvis Presley) etc. • **Trivia:** SPRINGSTEEN produced two albums by GARY U.S. BONDS 'Dedication' (1981) and 'On The Line' (1982), records that featured The BOSS's songs. He also provided songs for; SPIRIT IN THE NIGHT + BLINDED BY THE LIGHT for (Manfred Mann's Earth Band) / SANDY (Hollies) / FIRE (Robert Gordon) + (Pointer Sisters) / BECAUSE THE NIGHT (Patti Smith) / FOR YOU (Greg Kihn) / FROM SMALL THINGS (Dave Edmunds) / DANCING IN THE DARK (Big Daddy) / THERE'S A RIOT GOIN' ON (Sly & The Family Stone) / etc. On the 13th of May '85, BRUCE married model/actress, Julianne Phillips, although she filed for divorce in August 1988 after seeing photographic newspaper evidence of a burgeoning relationship between BRUCE and backing singer, PATTI SCIALFA. The latter bore him a child, Evan James, on the 25th of July '90.

Album rating: GREETINGS FROM ASBURY PARK, N.J. (*6) / THE WILD, THE INNOCENT & THE E-STREET SHUFFLE (*6) / BORN TO RUN (*9) / DARKNESS ON THE EDGE OF TOWN (*8) / THE RIVER (*7) / NEBRASKA (*9) / BORN IN THE U.S.A. (*8) / LIVE 1977-1985 (*6) / TUNNEL OF LOVE (*6) / HUMAN TOUCH (*5) / LUCKY TOWN (*5) / IN CONCERT – MTV PLUGGED (*5) / GREATEST HITS compilation (*8) / THE GHOST OF TOM JOAD (*7) / TRACKS early material (*5) / LIVE IN NEW YORK CITY (*5) / THE RISING (*7) / THE ESSENTIAL . . . compilation (*9)

BRUCE SPRINGSTEEN – vocals, guitar / **DAVID SANCIOUS + DANNY FEDERICI** – keyboards / **GARRY TALLENT** – bass / **VINI LOPEZ** – drums / **CLARENCE CLEMENS** – saxophone / **STEVE VAN ZANDT** – lead guitar (left before recording of debut album)

C.B.S. Columbia

Feb 73. (7") *<45805>* **BLINDED BY THE LIGHT. / ANGEL** [–] [ ]

Mar 73. (lp/c) *(CBS/40 65480) <31903>* **GREETINGS FROM ASBURY PARK, N.J.** [ ] Jan73 [ ]
– Blinded by the light / Growin' up / Mary Queen of Arkansas / Does this bus stop at 82nd Street / Lost in the flood / The angel / For you / / Spirit in the night / It's hard to be a saint in the city. *<hit No.60 in the US; Jul75> (re-iss. Nov82 lp/c; CBS/40 32210)* – hit No.41 in Jun85) *(cd-iss. 1986; CD 65480)*

May 73. (7") *<45864>* **SPIRIT IN THE NIGHT. / FOR YOU** [–] [ ]

—— For live appearances The BRUCE SPRINGSTEEN BAND now The E-STREET SHUFFLE. **ERNEST CARTER** – drums repl. LOPEZ

Feb 74. (lp/c) *(CBS/40 65780) <32432>* **THE WILD, THE INNOCENT & THE E-STREET SHUFFLE** [ ] Nov73 [ ]
– The E-Street shuffle / 4th of July, Asbury Park (Sandy) / Kitty's back / Wild Billy's circus story / Incident on 57th Street / Rosalita (come out tonight) / New York City serenade. *<hit No.59 in the US; Jul75> (re-iss. Nov83 lp/c; CBS/40 32363)* – (hit No.33 in Jun85) *(cd-iss. Apr89; CD 32363)*

—— **ROY BITTAN** – piano / **MAX WEINBERG** – drums / and the returning **VAN ZANDT** repl. SANCIOUS and CARTER

Oct 75. (lp/c) *(CBS/40 69170) <33795>* **BORN TO RUN** [17] Sep75 [3]
– Thunder road / Tenth Avenue freeze-out / Night / Backstreets / Born to run / She's the one / Meeting across the river / Jungleland. *(re-iss. Jan87 boxed; BRUCE B2)* (w / free-7") **BECAUSE THE NIGHT. / SPIRIT IN THE NIGHT** *(cd-iss. 1983; CD 69170) (cd re-iss. 1988; CD 80959) (re-iss. cd.Jun93) (lp re-iss. Feb99 on 'Classic'; PC 33795)*

Oct 75. (7") *(A 3661) <10209>* **BORN TO RUN. / MEETING ACROSS THE RIVER** [ ] Sep75 [23]

Feb 76. (7") *(A 3940) <10274>* **TENTH AVENUE FREEZE-OUT. / SHE'S THE ONE** [ ] Jan76 [83]

Jun 78. (7") *(A 6424) <10763>* **PROVE IT ALL NIGHT. / FACTORY** [ ] [33]

Jun 78. (lp/c)<US-pic-d> *(CBS/40 86061) <35318>* **DARKNESS ON THE EDGE OF TOWN** [16] [5]
– Badlands / Adam raised a Cain / Something in the night / Candy's room / Racing in the street / Promised land / Factory / Streets of fire / Prove it all night / Darkness on the edge of town. *(cd-iss. Jul84; CD 66061) (re-iss. Nov84 lp/c; CBS/40 32542)*

Jul 78. (7") *<10801>* **BADLANDS. / STREETS OF FIRE** [–] [42]

Jul 78. (7") *(A 6532)* **BADLANDS. / SOMETHING IN THE NIGHT** [ ] [–]

Oct 78. (7") *(A 6720)* **PROMISED LAND. / STREETS OF FIRE** [ ] [ ]

Oct 80. (d-lp/d-c) *(CBS/40 88510) <36854>* **THE RIVER** [2] [1]
– The ties that bind / Sherry darling / Jackson cage / Two hearts / Independence day / Hungry heart / Out in the street / Crush on you / You can look (but you better not touch) / I wanna marry you / The river / Point blank / Cadillac ranch / I'm a rocker / Fade away / Stolen car / Ramrod / The price you pay / Drive all night / Wreck on the highway. *(d-cd-iss. 1985; CD 88510) (re-iss. d-cd+d-c Oct94 on 'Columbia')*

Nov 80. (7") *(A 9309) <11391>* **HUNGRY HEART. / HELD UP WITHOUT A GUN** [44] [5]

Jan 81. (7") *<11431>* **FADE AWAY. / BE TRUE** [–] [20]

Feb 81. (7") *(A 9568)* **SHERRY DARLING. / BE TRUE** [ ] [–]

May 81. (7") *(A 1179)* **THE RIVER. / INDEPENDENCE DAY** [35] [–]
(12") *(A13 1179)* – ('A'side) / Born to run / Rosalita.

Aug 81. (7") **CADILLAC RANCH. / WRECK ON THE HIGHWAY** [–] [ ]

Sep 82. (lp/c) *(CBS/40 25100) <38358>* **NEBRASKA** [3] [3]
– Nebraska / Atlantic City / Mansion on the hill / Johnny 99 / Highway patrolman / State trooper / Used cars / Open all night / My father's house / Reason to believe. *(cd-iss. 1983; CD 25100) (re-iss. Feb89 lp/c/cd; 463360-1/-4/-2)*

Oct 82. (7") *(A 2794)* **ATLANTIC CITY. / MANSION ON THE HILL** [ ] [ ]

Nov 82. (7") **OPEN ALL NIGHT. / THE BIG PAYBACK** [ ] [ ]

—— **NILS LOFGREN** – lead guitar (Solo artist) repl. VAN ZANDT to solo as LITTLE STEVEN / added **PATTI SCIALFA** – backing vox (ex-SOUTHSIDE JOHNNY)

May 84. (7"/7"sha-pic-d/12") *(A/TA/WA 4436) <04463>* **DANCING IN THE DARK. / PINK CADILLAC** [28] [2]
(re-entered UK charts in Jan85, hit No.4)

Jun 84. (lp/c/cd/pic-lp) *(CBS/40/CD/11 86304) <38653>* **BORN IN THE U.S.A.** [1] [1]
– Born in the U.S.A. / Cover me / Darlington County / Working on the highway / Downbound train / I'm on fire / No surrender / Bobby Jean / I'm goin' down / Glory days / Dancing in the dark / My hometown.

Sep 84. (7") *(A 4662) <04561>* **COVER ME. / JERSEY GIRL (live)** [38] Aug84 [7]
(d7"+=) *(DA 4662)* – Dancing in the dark / Pink Cadillac.
(12"+=) *(TA 4662)* – Dancing in the dark (dub version).

Nov 84. (7") *<04680>* **BORN IN THE U.S.A. / SHUT OUT THE LIGHTS** [–] [9]

Jan 85. (7") *<04772>* **I'M ON FIRE. / JOHNNY BYE BYE** [–] [6]

Mar 85. (7"/7"sha-pic-d) *(A/WA 4662)* **COVER ME. / JERSEY GIRL (live)** [16] [–]
(12"+=) *(QTA 4662)* – Dancing in the dark (dub) / Shut out the light / Cover me (dub).

May 85. (7"/7"sha-pic-d) *(A/WA 6342)* **I'M ON FIRE. / BORN IN THE U.S.A. (Freedom mix)** [5] [–]
(12"+=) *(TA 6342)* – Rosalita / Bye Bye Johnny.

Jul 85. (7") *(A 6375) <04924>* **GLORY DAYS. / STAND ON IT** [17] May85 [5]
(12"+=) *(QTA 6375)* – Sherry darling / Racing in the street.

Aug 85. (7") *<05603>* **I'M GOIN' DOWN. / JANEY, DON'T YOU LOSE HEART** – 9

Dec 85. (7") *(A 6773) <05728>* **MY HOMETOWN. / SANTA CLAUS IS COMIN' TO TOWN** 9 6

Nov 86. (7") *(650 193-7) <06432>* **WAR (live). / MERRY XMAS BABY (live)** 18 8
(12"+=) *(650 193-6)* – Incident on 57th Street (live).
(d7"+=) *(650 193-0)* – My home town (live) / Santa Claus is coming to town (live).

Dec 86. (5xlp-box/3xc-box/3xcd-box) *(450227-1/-4/-2) <40588>* **LIVE 1977-1985 (live)** 4 Nov86 1
– Thunder road / Adam raised a Cain / Fire / Spirit in the night / 4th of July – Asbury Park (Sandy) / Paradise by the 'C' / Growin' up / It's hard to be a saint in the city / Backstreets / Rosalita (come out tonight) / Raise your hand / Hungry heart / Two hearts / Cadillac ranch / You can look (but you better not touch) / War / Candy's room / Badlands / Because the night / Independence day / Johnny 99 / Darkness on the edge of town / Racing in the street / Nebraska / This land is your land / Working on the highway / Reason to believe / Born in the U.S.A. / Seeds / The river / Born to run / Darlington County / Jersey girl / Bobby Jean / Cover me / My hometown / No surrender / I'm on fire / The promised land.

Jan 87. (7") *<06657>* **FIRE (live). / INCIDENT ON 57TH STREET** – 46

Jan 87. (7") *(650 381-7)* **FIRE (live). / FOR YOU (live)** 54 –
(12"+=) *(650 381-6)* – Born to run (live) / No surrender (live) / Tenth avenue freeze-out (live).

May 87. (7"/7"s) *(BRUCE/+BP 2)* **BORN TO RUN (live). / JOHNNY 99 (live)** 16 –
(d7"+=) *(BRUCEB 2)* – Spirit in the night / Because the night (live).
(cd-s+=) *(BRUCEC 2)* – Spirit in the night (live) / Seeds (live).

Sep 87. (7"/7"g-f/12") *(651 141-7/-0/-6) <07595>* **BRILLIANT DISGUISE. / LUCKY MAN** 20 5

Oct 87. (lp/c/cd/pic-lp/pic-cd) *(460 270-1/-4/-2/-0/-9) <40999>* **TUNNEL OF LOVE** 1 1
– Ain't got you / Tougher than the rest / All that Heaven will allow / Spare parts / Cautious man / Walk like a man / Tunnel of love / Two faces / Brilliant disguise / One step up / When you're alone / Valentine's day.

Dec 87. (7"/7"sha-pic-d) *(651 295-7/-0) <07663>* **TUNNEL OF LOVE. / TWO FOR THE ROAD** 45 9
(cd-s+=) *(651 295-6/-2)* – Santa Claus is comin' to town.

Mar 88. (7") *(651 442-7) <07726>* **ONE STEP UP. / ROULETTE** Feb88 13
(12"+=/cd-s+=) *(651 442-6/-2/-0)* – Lucky man.

Jun 88. (7") *(BRUCE 3)* **TOUGHER THAN THE REST. / ROULETTE** 13 –
(12"+=) *(BRUCEQ 3)* – Born to run (live) / Be true (live).
(cd-s+=) *(BRUCEC 3)* – ('A'live) / Born to run (live).

Oct 88. (7") *(BRUCE 4)* **SPARE PARTS. / PINK CADILLAC** 32 –
(cd-s+=/s-cd-s+=) *(BRUCE C/B 4)* – ('A'live version) / Chimes of freedom (live).
(12") *(BRUCEQ 4)* – ('A'side) / Cover me (live) / ('A'live) / I'm on fire (live).

—— new band:- **SHANE FONTAYNE** – guitar / **ZACHERY ALFORD** – drums / **TOMMY SIMMS** – bass / **ROY BITTAN** – keyboards / **CRYSTAL TALIEFERO** – guitar, percussion, vocals / + backing vocalists

Columbia Columbia

Mar 92. (c-s,cd-s) *<74273>* **HUMAN TOUCH / BETTER DAYS** – 16

Mar 92. (7"/c-s) *(657872-7/-4)* **HUMAN TOUCH. / SOULS OF THE DEPARTED** 11 –
(12"+=/cd-s+=/pic-cd-d+=) *(657872-1/-2/-0)* – Long goodbye.

Mar 92. (cd/c/lp) *(471423-2/-4/-1) <53000>* **HUMAN TOUCH** 1 2
– Human touch / Soul driver / 57 channels (and nothin' on) / Cross my heart / Gloria's eyes / With every wish / Roll of the dice / Real world / All or nothin' at al / Man's job / I wish I were blind / Long goodbye / Real man / Pony boy.

Mar 92. (cd/c/lp) *(471424-2/-4/-1) <53001>* **LUCKY TOWN** 2 3
– Better days / Lucky town / Local hero / If I should fall apart / Leap of faith / Big Muddy / Living proof / Book of dreams / Souls of the departed / My beautiful reward.

May 92. (7"/c-s) *(657890-7/-4)* **BETTER DAYS. / TOUGHER THAN THE REST** 34 –
(12"+=/cd-s+=) *(657890-1/-2)* – Part man, part monkey.

Jun 92. (c-s/cd-s) *<74273>* **57 CHANNELS (AND NOTHIN' ON). / PART MAN, PART MONKEY** – 68

Jul 92. (7"/c-s) *(658138-7/-4)* **57 CHANNELS (AND NOTHIN' ON). / STAND ON IT** 32 –
(cd-s+=) *(658138-5)* – Janey don't you lose heart.
(cd-s) *(658138-2)* – ('A'side) / Little Steven mix version 1 / Little Steven mix version 2 / There's a riot goin' on.

Oct 92. (7"/c-s) *(658369-7/-4)* **LEAP OF FAITH. / ('A'version)** 46 –
(cd-s+=) *(658369-2)* – Shut out the light / The big payback.
(cd-s) *(658369-5)* – ('A'side) / 30 days out.

Apr 93. (7"/c-s) *(659228-7/-4)* **LUCKY TOWN (live). / ('A' version)** 48 –
(cd-s+=) *(659228-2)* – Human touch (live).

Apr 93. (cd/c/lp) *(473860-2/-4/-1)* **IN CONCERT – MTV PLUGGED (live)** 4 –
– Red headed woman / Better days / Atlantic city / Darkness on the edge of town / Man's job / Human touch / Lucky town / I wish I were blind / Thunder Road / Light of day / If I should fall behind / Living proof / My beautiful reward.

—— his wife PATTI had their child on the 5th Jan '94.
below from the film 'Philadelphia', which won an Oscar for Tom Hanks.

Mar 94. (7"/c-s/12") *(660065-7/-4/-1) <77354>* **STREETS OF PHILADELPHIA. / IF I SHOULD FALL BEHIND** 2 Feb94 9
(cd-s+=) *(660065-2)* – Growing up (live) / The big Muddy (live).

Feb 95. (cd/c/lp) *(478555-2/-4/-1) <67060>* **GREATEST HITS** (compilation) 1 1
– Born to run / Thunder road / Badlands / The river / Hungry heart / Atlantic city / Dancing in the dark / Born in the U.S.A. / My hometown / Glory days / Brilliant disguise / Human touch / Better days / Streets of Philadelphia / Secret garden / Murder incorporated / Blood brothers / This hard land.

Apr 95. (c-s) *(661295-4) <77847>* **SECRET GARDEN / THUNDER ROAD (plugged live version)** 44 63
(cd-s+=) *(661295-2)* – Murder incorporated.
(cd-s) *(661295-5)* – ('A'side) / Because the night / Pink Cadillac / 4th Of July, Asbury Park (Sandy).

Oct 95. (7"pic-d/c-s) *(662625-7/-4)* **HUNGRY HEART. / STREETS OF PHILADELPHIA** 28
(cd-s+=) *(662 625-2)* – ('A'-Berlin '95 version) / Thunder Road.

Nov 95. (cd/c/lp) *(481650-2/-4/-1) <67484>* **THE GHOST OF TOM JOAD** 16 11
– The ghost of Tom Joad / Straight time / Highway 29 / Youngstown / Sinaola cowboys / The line / Balboa Park / Dry lightning / The new timer / Across the border / Galveston Bay / The best was never good enough.

Apr 96. (7"pic-d) *(663031-7)* **THE GHOST OF TOM JOAD. / STRAIGHT TIME (live)** 26
(cd-s+=) *(663031-2)* – Sinaloa cowboys (live) / Darkness on the edge of town (live).
(cd-s) *(663031-5)* – ('A'side) / Meeting across the river / One step up / Nebraska.

Apr 97. (c-s) *(664324-4)* **SECRET GARDEN / HIGHWAY 29** 17 Jan97 19
(cd-s+=) *(664324-2)* – Missing / High hopes.
(cd-s) *(664324-5)* – ('A'side) / Ghost of Tom Joad / Blood brothers / Streets of Philadelphia.

Apr 00. (cd-s) *<667491>* **SAD EYES / MISSING / MAN AT THE TOP / TAKE 'EM AS THEY COME** –

Apr 01. (d-cd/t-lp) *(500000-2/-1) <85490>* **LIVE IN NEW YORK CITY (live)** 12 5
– My love will not let you down / Prove it all night / Two hearts / Atlantic city / Mansion on the hill / The river / Youngstown / Murder incorporated / Badlands / Out in the street / Tenth Avenue freeze-out / Land of hope and dreams / American skin (41 shots) / Lost in the flood / Born in the U.S.A. / Don't look back / Jungleland / Ramrod / If I should fall behind.

Sep 01. (cd-s) *<67122-2>* **AMERICAN SKIN (live)** –

Jul 02. (cd-s) *<79788>* **THE RISING / LAND OF HOPE AND DREAMS (live at Madison Square Garden)** – 52

Jul 02. (cd/lp) *(508000-2/-1) <86600>* **THE RISING** 1 1
– Lonesome day / Into the fire / Waitin' for a sunny day / Nothing man / Countin' on a miracle / Empty sky / Worlds apart / Let's be friends (skin to skin) / Further on (up the road) / The fuse / Mary's place / You're missing / The rising / Paradise / My city of ruins.

Nov 02. (cd-s) *(673408-2) <67327-2>* **LONESOME DAY / LAND OF HOPE AND DREAMS** 39 Dec02
(cd-s) *(673408-5)* – ('A'side) / Spirit in the night / The rising.

Nov 03. (d-cd) *(513700-2) <90773>* **THE ESSENTIAL BRUCE SPRINGSTEEN** (compilation) 28 14
– Blinded by the light / For you / Spirit in the night / 4th of July, Asbury Park (Sandy) / Rosalita (come out tonight) / Thunder road / Born to run / Jungleland / Badlands / Darkness on the edge of town / The promised land / The river / Hungry heart / Nebraska / Atlantic City / Born in the U.S.A. / Glory days / Dancing in the dark / Tunnel of love /

Brilliant disguise / Human touch / Living proof / Lucky town / Streets of Philadelphia / The ghost of Tom Joad / The rising / Mary's place / Lonesome day / American skin (41 shots) (live) / Land of hope and dreams (live). *(ltd-3xcd+=; 513700-9)* – From small things (big things one day come) / The big paypack / Held up without a gun (live) / Trapped (live) / None but the brave / Missing / Lift me up / Viva Las Vegas / County fair / Code of silence (live) / Dead man walkin' / Countin' on a miracle (acoustic). *(hit UK No.32)*

– compilations, others, etc. –

Date	Release	UK	US
Nov 85.	(4x12"box) *C.B.S.; (BRUCE 1)* **BOXED SET 12" SINGLES**		
Nov 88.	(d-cd) *C.B.S.; (CDBOS 241)* **NEBRASKA / BORN IN THE U.S.A.**		
Mar 93.	(d-cd) *Columbia: (471607-2)* **DARKNESS ON THE EDGE OF TOWN / NEBRASKA** *(re-iss. Feb95; same)*		
Jan 94.	(d-cd/d-c/d-lp) *Dare Int.;* **PRODIGAL SON**		
Oct 96.	(3xcd-box) *Columbia; (485325-2)* DARKNESS ON THE EDGE OF TOWN / GREETINGS FROM ASBURY, N.J. / THE WILD, THE INNOCENT & THE E-STREET SHUFFLE		–
Nov 98.	(4xcd-box) *Columbia; (492605-2) <69475>* **TRACKS** (collection of outtakes, B-sides & rarities)	50	27
Apr 99.	(cd/c) *(494200-2/-4) <69476>* **18 TRACKS**	23	64
May 99.	(c-s) *(667491-4)* **SAD EYES / I WANNA BE WITH YOU**		

TRACKS: – Mary Queen of Arkansas / It's hard to be a saint in the city / Growin' up / Does this bus stop at 52nd Street / Bishop danced / Santa Ana / Seaside bar song / Zero & Blind Terry / Linda let me be the one / Thundercrack / Rendezvous / Give the girl a kiss / Iceman / Bring on the night / So young and in love / Hearts of stone / Don't look back // Restless nights / A good man is hard to find (Pittsburgh) / Roulette / Dollhouse / Where the bands are / Loose ends / Living on the edge of the world / Wages of sin / Take 'em as they come / Be true / Ricky wants a man of her own / I wanna be with you / Mary Lou / Stolen car / Born in the U.S.A. / Johnny bye-bye / Shut out the light // Cynthia / My love will not let you down / This hard land / Frankie / TV movie / Stand on it / Lion's den / Car wash / Rockaway the days / Brothers under the bridges ('83) / Man at the top / Pink Cadillac / Two for the road / Janey don't you lose heart / When you need me / The wish / The honeymooners / Lucky man // Leavin' train / Seven angels / Gave it a name / Sad eyes / My lover man / Over the rise / When the lights go out / Loose change / Trouble in Paradise / Happy / Part man, part monkey / Goin' Cali / Back in your arms / Brothers under the bridge.

SAD EYES: (cd-s+=) *(667491-2)* – Man at the top.
(cd-s) *(667491-5)* – ('A'side) / Born in the USA / Pink Cadillac.

SQUEEZE

Formed: Deptford, South London, England … March '74 by CHRIS DIFFORD and GLENN TILBROOK, the pair initially forming a writing partnership whereby the former penned the lyrics with the latter writing the music. Their genius was subsequently incorporated into a group format as the pair recruited ace pianist, JOOLS HOLLAND, bassist HARRY KAKOULLI and drummer PAUL GUNN, forming SQUEEZE in the process. Early 1977 saw the group's vinyl debut on the independent 'B.T.M.' label with the mock-Egyptian new wave pop/rock of 'TAKE ME I'M YOURS'. Despite the single being subsequently withdrawn, the group replaced GUNN with GILSON LAVIS and proceeded to release the JOHN CALE-produced 'PACKET OF THREE' EP on the 'Deptford Fun City' label. This duly attracted the attentions of 'A&M', keen to get in on the new wave act after their abortive signing of the SEX PISTOLS earlier that year. Immediate Top 20 chart success came with the re-release of 'TAKE ME..', an eponymous debut surfacing soon after. With the addition of JOHN BENTLEY on bass as a replacement for the departing KAKOULLI, the group narrowly missed No.1 in Spring '79 with the cockney wide-boy rap of 'COOL FOR CATS', a similarly titled follow-up album almost breaking the Top 40. The record consolidated the growing reputation of the DIFFORD/TILBROOK songwriting axis; their sagely observed, often darkly amusing social commentary drew inevitable comparisons with prime RAY DAVIES, definitely more accurate than the fanciful LENNON & McCARTNEY references. 'UP THE JUNCTION' was a perfect example, a compelling, hard-bitten tale of love on the breadline leading to broken-hearted disillusionment, a swooning, deceptively melancholy keyboard refrain holding the whole thing together. The song clearly struck a chord in the populace at large, SQUEEZE once again coming within a whisker of No.1. 'ARGYBARGY' (1980) gave the group their first Top 40 album, although the comparatively lowly placings afforded SQUEEZE's long players never really reflected the enduring quality of the songs contained within. Tracks like 'PULLING MUSSELS (FROM THE SHELL)', a brilliant slice of pop genius featuring a rollicking piano break courtesy of the illustrious HOLLAND. The latter left soon after to follow his boogie-woogie muse with JOOLS HOLLAND AND THE MILLIONAIRES and more famously, to present Channel 4's legendary music show, 'The Tube', alongside a young Paula Yates. Finding a replacement in respected vocalist/pianist, PAUL CARRACK (ex-ACE, ex-FRANKIE MILLER etc.), SQUEEZE cut their most successful album to date, 'EAST SIDE STORY' (1981). Co-produced by ELVIS COSTELLO, the album had a rootsier feel, CARRACK's COCKER-esque vocals gracing the grittily soulful 'TEMPTED', while the poignant 'LABELLED WITH LOVE' proved SQUEEZE could 'do' country better than most country artists. The latter song (Top 5) marked the end of their reign as a singles band, however, with the evocative 'BLACK COFFEE IN BED' not even breaching the Top 40. By this point CARRACK had left for a solo career, DON SNOW brought in for a final, patchy album, 'SWEETS FROM A STRANGER' (1982). Though the group were at the height of their popularity, creatively they were beginning to stall and wisely decided to quit while they were still on top. Later that year, the compilation, 'THE SINGLES – 45 AND UNDER', brought the era neatly to a close, a seminal record (no household is complete without a copy!) illustrating why SQUEEZE have aged better than many "new wave" bands of the era. This wasn't the end, though, and after a solo 'DIFFORD & TILBROOK' (1984) album, the pair reunited with HOLLAND, recruiting KEITH WILKINSON on bass. A new album, 'COSI FAN TUTTI FRUTTI' appeared in summer '85, although they didn't really recapture anything resembling the old magic until 'BABYLON AND ON' (1987). That album gave SQUEEZE their first UK Top 20 hit in years with 'HOURGLASS', as well as some belated US chart action, the single reaching No.15 in the States while the album made the Top 40. 'FRANK' (1989) failed to capitalise on the momentum and SQUEEZE were subsequently dealt a double blow when HOLLAND left once again to concentrate on TV work and A&M finally let the band go. The band soldiered on, releasing a sole album, the acclaimed 'PLAY' (1991), for 'Reprise' before eventually regrouping with CARRACK and re-signing with 'A&M' for a further couple of 90's albums, 'SOME FANTASTIC PLACE' (1993) and 'RIDICULOUS' (1995). While the latter set featured at least a handful of bonafide DIFFORD/TILBROOK gems, 'DOMINO' (1998) was something of a career low. If the staleness of the record suggested the writing partnership was past its sell-by date, then 'THE INCOMPLETE GLENN TILBROOK' (2001) offered an opportunity to see what one half of it could achieve on their own. Despite having decided to record alone due to a disagreement over touring rather than writing, TILBROOK grabbed the bull by the proverbial horns nevertheless, turning out a consummately crafted, often charming effort that proved he could go it alone and then some. Although there were contributions from the likes of RON SEXSMITH and AIMEE MANN, the record had TILBROOK's trademarks stamped all over it. Although lyrics were traditionally DIFFORD's bag, TILBROOK proved he was no slouch when it came to wordsmithery. • **Songwriters:** Mostly DIFFORD & TILBROOK compositions, and some by CARRACK who joined late 1980. Covered END OF THE CENTURY (Blur).

Album rating: SQUEEZE (*6) / COOL FOR CATS (*7) / ARGYBARGY (*8) / EAST SIDE STORY (*7) / SWEETS FROM A STRANGER (*4) / THE SINGLES – 45 AND UNDER compilation (*8) / DIFFORD & TILBROOK (*5; as Difford & Tilbrook) / COSI FAN TUTTI FRUTTI (*6) / BABYLON AND ON (*5) / FRANK (*4) / A ROUND AND A BOUT early live (*3) / PLAY (*5) / GREATEST HITS compilation (*8) / SOME FANTASTIC PLACE (*6) / RIDICULOUS (*7) / DOMINO (*5) / THE BIG SQUEEZE – THE VERY BEST OF SQUEEZE compilation (*8)

CHRIS DIFFORD (b. 4 Nov'54) – vocals, guitar / **GLENN TILBROOK** (b.31 Aug'57) – vocals, guitar / **JOOLS HOLLAND** (b.JULIAN, 24 Jan'58) – keyboards / **HARRY KAKOULLI** – bass / **PAUL GUNN** – drums (below 45 withdrawn from release)

B.T.M. | not iss.

Jan 77. (7"; w-drawn) *(SBT 107)* **TAKE ME I'M YOURS. / NO DISCO KID, NO** – | –

— **GILSON LAVIS** (b.27 Jun'51) – drums (ex-MUSTARD) repl. GUNN

Deptford Fun City | not iss.

Aug 77. (7"ep,12"ep) *(DFC 01)* **PACKET OF THREE** | –
– Cat on a wall / Back track / Night ride. *(re-iss. Nov79 12"ep; same)*

A&M | A&M

Feb 78. (7"/12") *(AMS/+P 7335)* **TAKE ME, I'M YOURS. / NIGHT NURSE** 19 |
Mar 78. (lp/c) *(AMLH/CAM 68465)* *<4687>* **SQUEEZE** |
– Sex master / Bang bang / Strong in reason / Wild sewerage tickles Brazil / Out of control / Take me, I'm yours / The call / Model / Remember what / First thing wrong / Hesitation (rool Britania) / Get smart. *(re-iss. Mar82 lp/c; AMID/CMID 122)*
May 78. (7",7"green) *(AMS 7360)* **BANG BANG. / ALL FED UP** 49 | –

— **JOHN BENTLEY** (b.16 Apr'51) – bass; repl. KAKOULLI who went solo (he released an album, 'EVEN WHEN I'M NOT', in 1980 and subsequently released a handful of singles in the first half on the 80's)

Nov 78. (7") *(AMS 7398)* **GOODBYE GIRL. / SAINTS ALIVE** 63 | –
Mar 79. (7",7"pale pink,7"pink,7"red/12"pink) *(AMS/+P 7426)* **COOL FOR CATS. / MODEL** 2 |
Apr 79. (lp/c) *(AMLH/CAM 68503)* *<4759>* **COOL FOR CATS** 45 |
– Slap and tickle / Revue / Touching me, touching you / It's not cricket / It's so dirty / The knack / Hop, skip and jump / Up the junction / Hard to find / Slightly drunk / Goodbye girl / Cool for cats. *(cd-iss. Mar91; CDMID 131)*
May 79. (7",7"lilac) *(AMS 7444)* **UP THE JUNCTION. / IT'S SO DIRTY** 2 | –
Jun 79. (7") *<2168>* **SLIGHTLY DRUNK. / GOODBYE GIRL** – |
Aug 79. (7",7"red) *(AMS 7466)* **SLAP AND TICKLE. / ALL'S WELL** 24 |
Nov 79. (7",7"white) *(AMS 7495)* **CHRISTMAS DAY. / GOING CRAZY** | –
Jan 80. (7",7"clear) *(AMS 7507)* **ANOTHER NAIL IN MY HEART. / PRETTY THING** 17 | –
Feb 80. (7") *<2229>* **IF I DIDN'T LOVE YOU. / PRETTY ONE** – |
Feb 80. (lp/c) *(AMLH/CAM 64802)* *<4802>* **ARGYBARGY** 32 | 71
– Pulling mussels (from the shell) / Another nail in my heart / Separate beds / Misadventure / I think I'm go go / Farfisa beat / Here comes that feeling / Vicky Verky / If I didn't love you / Wrong side of the Moon / There at the top.
Apr 80. (7",7"red) *(AMS 7523)* **PULLING MUSSELS (FROM THE SHELL). / WHAT THE BUTLER SAW** 44 | –
Jun 80. (7") *<2247>* **PULLING MUSSELS (FROM THE SHELL). / PRETTY ONE** – |
Sep 80. (7"m) *<2263>* **ANOTHER NAIL IN MY HEART. / GOING CRAZY / WHAT THE BUTLER SAW** – |
<re-iss. Sep82>

— **PAUL CARRACK** (b. Apr'51, Sheffield, England) – keyboards (ex-ACE, ex-FRANKIE MILLER, ex-ROXY MUSIC) repl. JOOLS who formed his own MILLIONAIRES

Apr 81. (7") *(AMS 8129)* **IS THAT LOVE. / TRUST** 35 | –
May 81. (lp/c) *(AMLH/CAM 64854)* *<4854>* **EAST SIDE STORY** 19 | 44
– In quintessence / Someone else's heart / Tempted / Piccadilly / There's no tomorrow / A woman's world / Is that love / F-hole / Labelled with love / Someone else's bell / Mumbo jumbo / Vanity fair / Messed around. *(cd-iss. Jan87; CDA 3253) (re-iss. cd Mar91; same)*
Jul 81. (7") *(AMS 8147)* **TEMPTED. / YAP YAP YAP** 40 | –
(free 5"w.a.) **ANOTHER NAIL IN MY HEART. / IF I DIDN'T LOVE YOU**
Jul 81. (7") *<2345>* **TEMPTED. / TRUST** – | 49
Sep 81. (7") *(AMS 8166)* **LABELLED WITH LOVE. / SQUABS ON FORTY FAB** 4 |
Oct 81. (7") *<2377>* **MESSED AROUND. / YAP YAP YAP** – |

— **DON SNOW** (b.13 Jan'57, Kenya) – keyboards (ex-VIBRATORS, ex-SINCEROS) repl. CARRACK (now solo)

Apr 82. (7",7"pic-d) *(AMS 8219)* *<2424>* **BLACK COFFEE IN BED. / THE HUNT** 51 Jul82 |
Apr 82. (12") *<2413>* **WHEN THE HANGOVER STRIKES. / I'VE RETURNED** – |
May 82. (lp/c) *(AMLH/CAM 64899)* *<4899>* **SWEETS FROM A STRANGER** 37 | 32
– Out of touch / I can't hold on / Points of view / Stranger than the stranger on the shore / Onto the dance floor / When the hangover strikes / Black coffee in bed / I've returned / Tongue like a knife / His house her home / The very last dance / The elephant ride.
Jul 82. (7",7"pic-d) *(AMS 8237)* **WHEN THE HANGOVER STRIKES. / THE ELEPHANT RIDE** | –
Oct 82. (7") *(AMS 8259)* *<2518>* **ANNIE GET YOUR GUN. / SPANISH GUITAR** 43 Feb83 |
Nov 82. (lp/c) *(AMLH/CAM 68552)* *<4922>* **SINGLES – 45 AND UNDER** (compilation) 3 | 47
– Take me I'm yours / Goodbye girl / Cool for cats / Up the junction / Slap and tickle / Another nail in my heart / Pulling mussels (from the shell) / Tempted / Is that love / Labelled with love / Black coffee in bed / Annie get your gun. *(cd-iss. Dec84; CDA 64922)*
Dec 82. (7") *<2534>* **ANOTHER NAIL IN MY HEART. / GOING CRAZY – WHAT THE BUTLER SAW** – |

— Split at same time of compilation.

DIFFORD & TILBROOK

— carried on as duo, augmented by **KEITH WILKINSON** (b.24 Sep'54, Southfield, England) – bass / + other musicians

Jun 84. (7"/ext.12") *(AM/+X 193)* **LOVE'S CRASHING WAVES. / WITHIN THESE WALLS OF WITHOUT YOU** 57 | –
Jun 84. (lp/c) *(AMLX/CXM 64985)* *<4985>* **DIFFORD & TILBROOK** 47 | 55
– Action speaks faster / Love's crashing waves / Picking up the pieces / On my mind tonight / Man for all seasons / Hope fell down / Wagon train / You can't hurt the girl / Tears for attention / The apple tree.
Jun 84. (7") *<2648>* **PICKING UP THE PIECES. / WITHIN THESE WALLS OF WITHOUT YOU** – |
Oct 84. (7"/12") *(AM/+X 219)* **HOPE FELL DOWN. / ACTION SPEAKS FASTER** | –

SQUEEZE

— re-formed '78 line-up except **KEITH WILKINSON** – bass (- HARRY)

Jun 85. (7"/12") *(AM/+Y 255)* **LAST TIME FOREVER. / SUITE FROM FIVE STRANGERS** 45 |
Aug 85. (lp/c/cd) *(AMLH/AMC/CDA 5085)* *<5085>* **COSI FAN TUTTI FRUTTI** 31 | 57
– Big bang / By your side / King George Street / I learnt how to pray / Last time forever / No place like home / Heartbreakin' world / Hits of the year / Break my heart / I won't ever go drinking again.
Sep 85. (7") *<2776>* **HITS OF THE YEAR. / THE FORTNIGHT SAGA** – |
Sep 85. (7") *(AM 277)* **NO PLACE LIKE HOME. / THE FORTNIGHT SAGA** | –
(12"+=) *(AMY 277)* – Last time forever.
Nov 85. (7") *(AM 291)* **HEARTBREAKING WORLD. / BIG BANG** | –
(10"+=) *(AMY 291)* – Tempted (live) / By your side (live).
Apr 86. (7") *(AM 306)* **KING GEORGE STREET. / LOVE'S CRASHING WAVES (live)** | –
(12"+=) *(AMY 306)* – Up the junction (live).

— added **ANDY METCALFE** – keyboards (ex-SOFT BOYS)

Aug 87. (7") *(AM 400) <2967>* **HOURGLASS. / WEDDING BELLS** [16] [15]
(12"+=) *(AMY 400)* – Splitting into three.

Sep 87. (lp/c/cd) *(<AMA/AMC/CDA 5161>)* **BABYLON AND ON** [14] [36]
– Hourglass / Footprints / Tough love / The prisoner / 853-5937 / In today's room / Trust me to open my mouth / Striking matches / Cigarette of a single man / Who are you? / The waiting game / Some Americans.

Sep 87. (7") *(AM 412)* **TRUST ME TO OPEN MY MOUTH. / TAKE ME, I'M YOURS (live)** [72] [–]
(12"+=) *(AMY 412)* – Black coffee in bed (live).

Nov 87. (7") *(AM 420)* **THE WAITING GAME. / LAST TIME FOREVER** [ ] [ ]
(12"+=) *(AMY 420)* – The prisoner.

Dec 87. (7") *<2994>* **853-5937. / TAKE ME I'M YOURS (live)** [–] [32]

Jan 88. (7"/ext.12") *(AM/+Y 426)* **853-5937. / TOUGH LOVE** [ ] [–]

Apr 88. (7") *<3021>* **FOOTPRINTS. / BLACK COFFEE IN BED (live)** [–] [ ]

Jun 88. (7") *(AM 450)* **FOOTPRINTS. / STRIKING MATCHES (INSTANT BUFF)** [ ] [–]
(ext.12"+=) *(AMY 450)* – In today's room.

— Reverted back to 5-piece when METCALFE departed.

Sep 89. (7") *(AM 350) <1457>* **IF IT'S LOVE. / FRANK'S BAG** [ ] [–]
(12"+=/cd-s+=) *(AMY/CDEE 350)* – Vanity fair (piano version).

Sep 89. (lp/c/cd) *(<AMA/AMC/CDA 5278>)* **FRANK** [58] [ ]
– Frank / If it's love / Peyton Place / Rose I said / Slaughtered, gutted and heartbroken / (This could be) The last time / She doesn't have to shave / Love circles / Melody hotel / Can of worms / Dr. Jazz / Is it too late.

Jan 90. (7") *(AM 535)* **LOVE CIRCLES. / RED LIGHT** [ ] [–]
(12"+=/cd-s+=) *(AMY/CDEE 535)* – Who's that?

Deptford Fun City — I.R.S.

Mar 90. (cd/c/lp) *(DFC CD/MC/LP 1) <82040>* **A ROUND AND A BOUT (live 1974-1989)** [50] [ ]
– Footprints / Pulling mussels (from the shell) / Black coffee in bed / She doesn't have to shave / Is that love / Dr. Jazz / Up the junction / Slaughtered, gutted and heartbroken / Is it too late / Cool for cats / Take me, I'm yours / If it's love / Hourglass / Labelled with love / Annie get your gun / Boogie woogie country girl / Tempted. *(free 7"ep 'PACKET OF THREE')*

— JOOLS left again to go solo and take up more TV work. In 1991 he was repl. by **MATT IRVING + STEVE NIEVE** – keyboards / **TONY BERG** – guitar, keyboards / **BRUCE HORNSBY** – accordion

Reprise — Reprise

Jul 91. (7"/c-s) *(W 0054/+C)* **SUNDAY STREET. / MAIDSTONE** [ ] [–]
(12"+=/cd-s+=) *(W 0054 T/CD)* – Mood swings.

Aug 91. (lp/c)(cd) *(WX 428/+C)(<7599 26644-2>)* **PLAY** [41] [ ]
– Satisfied / Crying in my sleep / Letting go / The day I get home / The truck / House of love / Cupid's toy / Gone to the dogs / Walk a straight line / Sunday street / Wicked and cruel / There is a voice. *(re-iss. cd Feb95; same)*

Nov 91. (7"/c-s) *(W 0071/+C)* **SATISFIED. / HAPPINESS IS KING** [ ] [–]
(12"+=/cd-s+=) *(W 0071 T/CD)* – Laughing in my sleep.

— **DIFFORD + TILBROOK + WILKINSON** plus returning **PAUL CARRACK** – keyboards / **PETE THOMAS** – drums

A&M — A&M

Jul 93. (7"/c-s) *(580334-7/-4)* **THIRD RAIL. / COOL FOR CATS – STRONG IN REASON (live medley)** [39] [–]
(cd-s+=) *(580335-2)* – Take me I'm yours (Paul Dakeyne remix).
(cd-s) *(580337-2)* – ('A'side) / The truth (live) / Melody hotel (live) / Walk a straight line (live).

Aug 93. (7"/c-s) *(580376-7/-4)* **SOME FANTASTIC PLACE. / JUMPING** [73] [–]
(cd-s+=) *(580377-2)* – Dark saloons / Discipline.
(cd-s) *(580379-2)* – ('A'side) / Is that the time? / Don't be a stranger / Stark naked.

Sep 93. (cd/c/lp) *(<540140-2/-4/-1>)* **SOME FANTASTIC PLACE** [26] [ ]
– Everything in the world / Some fantastic place / Third rail / Loving you tonight / It's over / Cold shoulder / Talk to him / Jolly comes home / Images of loving / True colours (the storm) / Pinocchio.

Oct 93. (7"/c-s/12") *(580412-7/-4/-1)* **LOVING YOU TONIGHT. / ('A'edit)** [ ] [–]
(cd-s+=) *(580413-2)* – Tempted (session) / Third rail (session).

Feb 94. (7"/c-s) *(580506-7/-4)* **IT'S OVER. / IS THAT LOVE (live)** [ ] [–]
(cd-s+=) *(580507-2)* – Pulling mussels (from the shell) (live) / Goodbye girl (live).

— they were joined by drummer **KEVIN WILKINSON** (b.1957, Swindon)

A&M — IRS-Capitol

Aug 95. (c-s) *(581189-4)* **THIS SUMMER / GOODBYE GIRL (live)** [47] [–]
(cd-s+=) *(581191-2)* – All the king's horses.
(cd-s) *(581189-2)* – ('A'side) / End of a century (live acoustic) / Periscope.

Nov 95. (c-ep/cd-ep) *(581271-4/-2)* **ELECTRIC TRAINS / CRACKER JACK / FIGHTING FOR PEACE / COLD SHOULDER (live)** [44] [–]
(cd-ep) *(581269-2)* – ('A'side) / Some fantastic place / It's over / Hour glass.

Nov 95. (cd/c) *(540440-2/-4) <38304>* **RIDICULOUS** [50] [ ]
– Electric trains / Heaven knows / Grouch of the day / Walk away / This summer / Got to me / Long face / I want you / Daphne / Lost for words / Great escape / Temptation for love / Sound asleep / Fingertips. *(re-iss. Sep97 cd/c; same)*

Jun 96. (cd-s) *(581605-2)* **HEAVEN KNOWS / GOODBYE GIRL (live) / LABELLED WITH LOVE (live) / IS THAT LOVE? (live)** [27] [–]
(cd-s) *(581607-2)* – ('A'side) / Tempted (live) / Walk away (live) / Some fantastic place (live).
(cd-s) *(581609-2)* – ('A'side) / Take me I'm yours (live) / Annie get your gun (live) / Slap and tickle (live).

Aug 96. (cd-s) *(581837-2)* **THIS SUMMER (remix) / ELECTRIC TRAINS / HEAVEN KNOWS / THIS SUMMER** [32] [–]
(cd-s) *(581839-2)* – ('A'side) / Cool for cats / Up the junction / Black coffee in bed.
(cd-s) *(581841-2)* – ('A'side) / Sweet as a nut / In another lifetime / Never there.

— **DIFFORD, TILBROOK** with **CHRIS HOLLAND** – keyboards, vocals / **HILAIRE PENDA** – bass / **ASHLEY SOAN** – drums, vocals

Quixotic — Valley

May 98. (cd-s) *(QRCSQ 098)* **DOWN IN THE VALLEY / DOWN IN THE VALLEY (mixes; crowd / jug band / instrumental)** [ ] [–]

Nov 98. (cd) *(QRSQD 098) <15046>* **DOMINO** [ ] Sep99 [ ]
– Play on / Bonkers / What's wrong with this picture? / Domino / To be a dad / Donkey talk / Sleeping with a friend / Without you here / In the morning / A moving story / Little king / Short break.

— tragedy struck, when former member KEVIN committed suicide 17 Jul'99

– compilations, etc. –

1981. (10"m-lp) *A&M; <SP 3413>* **SIX SQUEEZE SONGS CRAMMED ONTO ONE TEN INCH RECORD** [–] [ ]

Oct 83. (7") *Old Gold; (OG 9364)* **TAKE ME, I'M YOURS. / UP THE JUNCTION** [ ] [–]

Sep 85. (7") *Old Gold; (OG 9546)* **COOL FOR CATS. / LABELLED WITH LOVE** [ ] [–]

Apr 92. (7"/c-s) *A&M; (AM/+MC 860)* **COOL FOR CATS. / TRUST ME TO OPEN MY MOUTH** [62] [–]
(cd-s+=) *(AMCD 860)* – Squabs on forty fab (medley hits).

May 92. (cd/c/d-lp) *A&M' (397181-2/-4/-1)* **GREATEST HITS** [6] [ ]
– (as THE SINGLES 45 AND UNDER +) Take me, I'm yours / Goodbye girl / Cool for cats / Up the junction / Slap and tickle / Another nail in my heart / Pulling mussels (from the shell) / Tempted / Is that love / Labelled with love / Black coffee in bed / Annie get your gun / King George Street / Last time forever / No place like home / Hourglass / Trust me to open my mouth / Footprints / If it's love / Love circles.

Oct 93. (cd) *A&M; (CDA 24120)* **BABYLON AND ON / EAST SIDE STORY** [ ] [ ]

Aug 96. (cd) *A&M; <540425-2>* **PICCADILLY COLLECTION** [–] [ ]

Nov 96. (d-cd) *A&M; (540651-2)* **EXCESS MODERATION** [ ] [ ]

Oct 97. (6xcd-box) *(540801-2)* **SIX OF ONE** [ ] [ ]

Aug 00. (cd) *Spectrum; (544229-2)* **UP THE JUNCTION** [ ] [–]

Jun 02. (cd) *Universal TV; (493253-2)* **THE BIG SQUEEZE – THE VERY BEST OF SQUEEZE** [8] [–]
– Take me I'm yours / Goodbye girl / Cool for cats / Up the junction / Slap and tickle / Another nail in my heart / Pulling mussels from a shell / Is that love / Tempted / Black coffee in bed / Annie get your gun / Labelled with

love / Last time forever / Hourglass / Some fantastic place / Third rail / This summer / Electric trains / Heaven knows / Domino / Suites from five strangers / Squabs on forty five / Model / Spanish guitar / Elephant girl / Trust / Yap yap yap / Fortnight saga / Wedding bells / What the butler saw / Going crazy / Introvert / Who's that / Vanity fair / Christmas day / Maidstone / Discipline / Periscope / All's well that ends well.

GLENN TILBROOK

with ANDY METCALFE, SIMON HANSON, STEPHEN LARGE, etc

		Quixotic	Valley
Nov 00.	(cd-s) *(QUIXCD 005)* **PARALLEL WORLD / BY THE LIGHT OF THE CASH MACHINE / PARALLEL WORLD**		–
Apr 01.	(cd-s) *(QUIXCD 006)* **THIS IS WHERE YOU AIN'T / THIS IS WHERE YOU AIN'T / SUNDAY BREAKFAST TREAT**		–
May 01.	(cd) *(QUIXCD 007)* *<15144>* **THE INCOMPLETE GLENN TILBROOK**		

– This is where you ain't / Observatory / Parallel world / Morning / One dark moment / G.S.O.H. essential / Up the creek / Other world / Interviewing Randy Newman / You see me / I won't see you / We went thataway.

☐ Chris SQUIRE (see under ⇒ YES)

☐ John SQUIRE (see under ⇒ SEAHORSES)

STAIND

Formed: Springfield, Massachusetts, USA . . . Xmas 1994 by vocalist AARON LEWIS and guitarist MICHAEL MUSHOK, the pair almost immediately hooking up with drummer JON WYSOCKI and an unknown original bassist; JOHNNY APRIL would become their 4-string plucker after their first gig in February '95. In late '96, the quartet self-financed a debut album, 'TORMENTED', its title pretty much giving the game away as to their miserabilist nu-metal approach. Spurred on by healthy sales, the band jumped at the chance to play on the same bill as LIMP BIZKIT in late 1997. While that band's ubiquitous lead singer, FRED DURST, initially took vocal exception to STAIND's quasi-Satanic cover art, an impassioned performance on the night persuaded him they were worthy of his new label. After trying and failing to contact DURST by phone, they travelled to a LIMP BIZKIT gig and left a new demo tape for the man's perusal. He was suitably impressed and soon STAIND were cutting their major label debut for the 'Elektra'-backed 'Flip' imprint with Terry Date (SOUNDGARDEN, DEFTONES, PANTERA etc.) at the production helm. 'DYSFUNCTION' arrived in Spring '99, pulling few punches and even less surprises with a solid if uninspiring set of treacle-thick post-grunge. The record went down a storm nevertheless, spawning three sizeable rock radio hits in 'JUST GO', 'MUDSHOVEL' and 'HOME'. Tours with KID ROCK, KORN and LIMP BIZKIT followed and STAIND were subsequently named as the headline act for MTV's 'Return Of The Rock' jaunt. Amid the media circus and general mayhem, a sophomore album, 'BREAK THE CYCLE', appeared in 2001, the record hitting No.1 in the States (and in Britain) but earning short shrift from the likes of Kerrang! – FRED DURST (of LIMP BIZKIT) featured on the hit track, 'OUTSIDE', while just previously 'IT'S BEEN AWHILE' hit the US Top 10. 2003's '14 SHADES OF GREY' (another US No.1) meditated upon the success of that single, putting the spotlight on LEWIS' angst-ridden navel-gazing rather than the crunching dynamics with which they made their name.

Album rating: TORMENTED (*5) / DYSFUNCTION (*6) / BREAK THE CYCLE (*6) / 14 SHADES OF GREY (*5)

AARON LEWIS – vocals / **MICHAEL MUSHOK** – guitar / **JOHNNY APRIL** – bass / **JON WYSOCKI** – drums

		not iss.	own label
Oct 96.	(cd) **TORMENTED**	–	

– Tolerate / Come again / Break / Painful / Nameless / Mudshuvel / See thru / Question? / No one's kind / Self destruct / Walls.

		Elektra	Elektra
Mar 00.	(cd) *<(7559 62356-2)>* **DYSFUNCTION**		Apr99 74
	– Suffocate / Just go / Me / Raw / Mudshovel / Home / A flat / Crawl / Spleen. *(hidden track+=)* – Excess baggage.		
Feb 01.	(-; as AARON LEWIS of STAIND with FRED DURST) *<radio play>* **OUTSIDE**	–	56
Aug 01.	(cd/c) *<(7559 62626-2/-4)>* **BREAK THE CYCLE**	1	May01 1
	– Open your eyes / Pressure / Fade / It's been awhile / Change / Can't believe / Epiphany / Suffer / Safe place / For you / Take it.		
Sep 01.	(c-s) *(E 7252C)* **IT'S BEEN AWHILE / (acoustic)**	15	Apr01 6
	(cd-s+=) *(E 7252CD1)* *<67228>* – Suffocate (version).		
Oct 01.	(cd-s) *<67259>* **FADE / FADE (album version) / IT'S BEEN AWHILE (live) / SPLEEN (album version)**	–	62
Nov 01.	(c-s) *(E 7277C)* **OUTSIDE / OUTSIDE (live acoustic with FRED DURST) / MUDSHOVEL**	33	–
	(cd-s+=) *(E 7277CD)* – ('A'-CD-Rom).		
Feb 02.	(c-s/cd-s) *(E 7281 C/CD)* *<67281>* **FOR YOU / FOR YOU (lp version) / SUFFER (live)**	55	63
May 03.	(7") *(E 7417)* *<radio>* **PRICE TO PLAY. / CAN'T BELIEVE (live)**	36	66
	(cd-s+=) *(E 7417CD)* – Let it out / ('A'-video).		
May 03.	(cd) *<(7559 62882-2)>* **14 SHADES OF GREY**	16	1
	– Price to play / How about you / So far away / Yesterday / Fray / Zoe Jane / Fill me up / Layne / Falling down / Reality / Tonight / Could it be / Blow away / Intro.		
Sep 03.	(7") *(E 7464)* **SO FAR AWAY. / MUDSHOVEL**		Aug03 24
	(cd-s+=) *(E 7464CD)* *<67450>* – (home grown promo footage).		

☐ Paul STANLEY (see under ⇒ KISS)

Ringo STARR

Born: RICHARD STARKEY, 7 Jul'40, Liverpool, England. Taking up the drums professionally in his late teens, STARKEY played with various skiffle outfits before being invited into The BEATLES fold in August '62. So named due to his predeliction for wearing rings, STARR filled the band's drum stool right through till their messy demise in 1969, occasionally doing a lead vocal and finally penning his own track with the endearing 'DON'T PASS ME BY' (from 1968's classic double set, 'THE BEATLES'). Early in '69, just prior to the band's split, STARR appeared in the movie version of Terry Southern's novel, 'Candy', taking a role alongside Peter Sellers the following year in another Southern adaptation, 'The Magic Christian'. A busy year for the budding actor, STARR also released two post-BEATLES solo albums, 'SENTIMENTAL JOURNEY' and 'BEAUCOUPS OF BLUES'. While the former was a string-laden, George Martin-produced set of Tin Pan Alley standards which made the UK Top 10 (and the US Top 30), the latter was a Nashville-recorded country affair, STARR immersing himself in a genre with which he obviously felt at home (he'd previously sung the few country/rockabilly tunes The BEATLES attempted, while the honky tonk fiddle of the aforementioned 'DON'T PASS..' was an indication of the direction he was headed). Although these sets failed to spawn any hit singles, STARR scored a string of transatlantic Top 10 hits in 1971 with the hard hitting 'IT DON'T COME EASY', 'BACK OFF BOOGALOO' and 'PHOTOGRAPH'. A US chart topper, the latter was featured on the eponymous 'RINGO' (1973), his most successful solo album by a mile. Boasting the musical and songwriting talents of all three former BEATLES, the album was also STARR's most consistent, spawning a further sizeable hit in 'YOU'RE SIXTEEN'. The following year's 'GOODNIGHT VIENNA' included the Top 5 cover of Hoyt Axton's novelty number, 'NO NO SONG', while 'BLAST FROM YOUR PAST' (1975) summed up the first half of STARR's solo career. This half decade was also a purple patch for his acting career, STARR taking a lead role in 'That'll Be The Day' alongside DAVID ESSEX and even making his directing debut with 'Born To Boogie' a rockumentary of MARC BOLAN and T. REX. STARR subsequently signed with 'Atlantic' in 1976, 'RINGO'S ROTOGRAVURE' failing to match the success of his previous efforts, while 'RINGO THE 4TH' (1977) was a commercial failure. An album for 'Portrait', 'BAD BOY' (1978), failed to reverse his ailing fortunes and while he scored a Top 40 hit in 1981 with 'WRACK MY BRAIN', 1983's 'OLD WAVE' was only released in Germany. The 80's proved a difficult time for STARR as he struggled with alcohol and drug abuse, retiring completely from recording and concentrating on TV/film work; he famously narrated celebrated children's TV series, 'Thomas The Tank Engine' in 1984. STARR eventually returned to music full-time at the turn of the decade with 'RINGO STARR & HIS ALL-STARR BAND' (1990), a live set of favourites and cover versions performed with the formidable line-up of DR. JOHN, BILLY PRESTON, NILS LOFGREN, JOE WALSH, RICK DANKO, JIM KELTNER, LEVON HELM and CLARENCE CLEMONS. The collaborative spirit carried over into both 'TIME TAKES TIME' (1992) and 'VERTICAL MAN' (1998), although on the latter he was also joined by contemporary stars like ALANIS MORISSETTE. Not that the album itself was contemporary, merely an update of RINGO's offbeat, unassuming style. 'RINGORAMA' (2003), meanwhile, found the likes of WILLIE NELSON and DAVID GILMOUR pitching in with the amiable studio antics. While STARR's vocal talent may be basic, his patter and wit more often than not makes up for it, and while he displays little of the technical flash of his BEATLES heyday, he remains one of the most solidly reliable drummers in the business. • **Filmography:** BLINDMAN (1971) / 200 MOTELS (1971 with Frank Zappa) / LISZTOMANIA (1975) / SCOUSE THE MOUSE (1977) / PRINCESS DAISY (1983 TV mini-soap with Barbara) / GIVE MY REGARDS TO BROAD STREET (Paul McCartney's film 1984) / WATER (1985) / WILLIE AND THE POOR BOYS (1985 Bill Wyman video) / ALICE IN WONDERLAND (1985 TV). • **Covered:** YOU'RE SIXTEEN (Johnny Burnette) / ONLY YOU (Platters) / SNOOKEROO (Elton John / Bernie Taupin) / IT'S ALL DOWN TO GOODNIGHT VIENNA (John Lennon) / HEY BABY (Bruce Channel). His 1978 album BAD BOY was another covers album. • **Trivia:** In the early 80's, he met actress Barbara Bach, whom he married on 27th of April '81.

Album rating: SENTIMENTAL JOURNEY (*5) / BEAUCOUPS OF BLUES (*5) / RINGO (87) / GOODNIGHT VIENNA (*5) / BLAST FROM YOUR PAST compilation (*6) / RINGO'S ROTOGRAVURE (*5) / RINGO THE 4th (*4) / BAD BOY (*4) / STOP AND SMELL THE ROSES (*5) / OLD WAVE (*3) / STARRSTRUCK: RINGO'S BEST compilation (*6) / RINGO STARR AND HIS ALL-STARR BAND (*6) / TIME TAKES TIME (*6) / RINGO STARR AND HIS ALL-STARR BAND, VOL.2 – LIVE FROM MONTREUX (*5) / VERTICAL MAN (*5)

RINGO STARR – vocals, drums, etc (with session people)

Apple Apple

Mar 70. (lp) *(PCS 7101)* *<3365>* **SENTIMENTAL JOURNEY** [7] [22]
– Sentimental journey / Night and day / Whispering grass / Bye bye blackbird / I'm a fool to care / Stardust / Blue, turning grey over you / Love is a many splendoured thing / Dream / You always hurt the one you love / Have I told you lately that I love you / Let the rest of the world go by. *(cd-iss. May95 on 'E.M.I.';)*

Sep 70. (lp) *(PAS 10002)* *<3368>* **BEAUCOUPS OF BLUES** [ ] [65]
– Beaucoups of blues / Love don't last long / Fastest growing heartache in the west / Without her / Woman of the night / I'd be talking all the time / $15 draw / Wine, women and loud happy songs / I wouldn't have you any other way / Loser's lounge / Waiting / Silent homecoming. *(cd-iss. May95 on 'E.M.I.';)*

Oct 70. (7") *<2969>* **BEAUCOUPS OF BLUES. / COOCHY COOCHY** [–] [87]

Apr 71. (7") *(R 5898)* *<1831>* **IT DON'T COME EASY. / EARLY 1970** [4] [4]

Mar 72. (7") *(R 5944)* *<1849>* **BACK OFF BOOGALOO. / BLINDMAN** [2] [9]

Oct 73. (7") *(R 5992)* *<1865>* **PHOTOGRAPH. / DOWN AND OUT** [8] [1]

Nov 73. (lp/c) *(PCTC 252)* *<3413>* **RINGO** [7] [2]
– You and me (babe) / I'm the greatest / Have you seen my baby / Photograph / Sunshine life for me / You're sixteen / Oh my my / Step lightly / Six o'clock * / Devil woman. *(US track *= extended) (re-iss. Nov80 on 'Music For Pleasure'; MFP 50508) (re-iss. Mar91 on 'E.M.I.' lp/cd;)*

Feb 74. (7") *(R 5995)* *<1870>* **YOU'RE SIXTEEN. / DEVIL WOMAN** [4] Dec73 [8]

Mar 74. (7") *<1872>* **OH MY MY. / STEP LIGHTLY** [–] [5]

Nov 74. (7") *(R 6000)* *<1876>* **ONLY YOU. / CALL ME** [28] [6]

Nov 74. (lp) *(PCS 7168)* *<3417>* **GOODNIGHT VIENNA** [30] [8]
– It's all down to goodnight Vienna / Occapella / Oo-wee / Husbands and wives / Snookeroo / All by myself / Call me / No no song / Only you / Easy for me / Goodnight Vienna (reprise).

Feb 75. (7") *(R 6004)* **SNOOKEROO. / OO-WEE** [ ] [–]

Feb 75. (7") *<1880>* **NO NO SONG. / SNOOKEROO** [–] [3]

Jun 75. (7") *<1882>* **IT'S ALL DOWN TO GOODNIGHT VIENNA. / OO-WEE** [–] [31]

Dec 75. (lp/c) *(PCS 7170)* *<3422>* **BLAST FROM YOUR PAST** (compilation) [ ] [30]
– You're sixteen / No no song / It don't come easy / Photograph / Back off boogaloo / Only you / Beacoups of blues / Oh my my / Early 1970 / I'm the greatest. *(re-iss. Nov81 on 'Music For Pleasure'; MFP 50524) (cd-iss. 1987 on 'E.M.I.'; CDP 746663-2)*

Jan 76. (7") *(R 6011)* **OH MY MY. / NO NO SONG** [ ] [–]

Polydor Atlantic

Sep 76. (7") *(2001 694)* *<3361>* **A DOSE OF ROCK'N'ROLL. / CRYIN'** [ ] [26]

Sep 76. (lp/c) *(2382 040)* *<18193>* **RINGO'S ROTOGRAVURE** [ ] [28]
– A dose of rock'n'roll / Hey baby / Pure gold / Cryin' / You don't know me at all / Cookin' / I'll still love you / This be called a song / La brisas / Lady Gaye. *(re-iss. Jun82 lp/c; 2485 235)(3201 743)*

Nov 76. (7") *(2001 699)* *<3371>* **HEY BABY. / LADY GAYE** [ ] [74]

Sep 77. (7") *<3412>* **DROWNING IN THE SEA OF LOVE. / GROWING** [–] [ ]

Sep 77. (7") *(2001 734)* **DROWNING IN THE SEA OF LOVE. / JUST A DREAM** [ ] [–]

Sep 77. (lp/c) *(2310 556)* *<19108>* **RINGO THE 4th** [ ] [ ]
– Drowning in the sea of love / Tango all night / Wings / Gave it all up / Out on the streets / Can she do it like she dances / Sneaking Sally through the alley / It's no secret / Gypsies in flight / Simple love song.

Oct 77. (lp) *(2480 429)* **SCOUSE THE MOUSE** [ ] [ ]
– (8 children's songs)

Nov 77. (7") *<3429>* **WINGS. / JUST A DREAM** [–] [ ]

Polydor Portrait

Apr 78. (lp/c) *(2310 599)* *<35378>* **BAD BOY** [ ] [ ]
– Who needs a heart / Bad boy / Lipstick traces / Heart on my sleeve / Where did our love go / Hard times / Tonight / Monkey see monkey do / Old time relovin' / A man like me.

May 78. (7"w-drawn) *(2001 782)* *<70015>* **OLD TIME RELOVIN'. / LIPSTICK TRACES (ON A CIGARETTE)** [–] [ ]

Jun 78. (7") *(2001 795)* **TONIGHT. / OLD TIME RELOVIN'** [ ] [–]

Jan 79. (7") *<70018>* **HEART ON MY SLEEVE. / WHO NEEDS A HEART** [–] [ ]

— with NILSSON as COLONEL DOUG BOGIE, he released US single 'OKEY COKEY' / 'AWAY IN A MANGER'; *<ABC Paramount; 12148>*

R.C.A. Boardwalk

Nov 81. (7") *(RCA 166)* *<130>* **WRACK MY BRAIN. / DRUMMING IS MY MADNESS** [ ] [38]

Nov 81. (lp/c) *(LP/K 6022)* *<33246>* **STOP AND SMELL THE ROSES** [ ] [98]
– Private property / Wrack my brain / Drumming is my madness / Attention / Stop and take the time to smell the roses / Dead giveaway / You belong to me / Sure to fall (in love with you) / Nice way / Back off boogaloo.

Feb 82. (7") *<134>* **STOP AND TAKE TIME TO SMELL THE ROSES. / PRIVATE PROPERTY** [–] [ ]

Bellaphon not iss.

Jun 83. (7") *(100.16.012)* **IN MY CAR. / AS FAR AS WE CAN GO** [–] German [–]

Jun 83. (lp) *(260.16.029)* **OLD WAVE** [–] German [–]
– In my car / Hopeless / Alibi / Be my baby / She's about a mover / Keep forgettin' / Picture show life / As far as we can go / Everybody's in a hurry but me / I'm going down.

—— Retired from solo work, guesting on ex-BEATLES' (PAUL McCARTNEY & GEORGE HARRISON solo). In '84, he narrated for children TV series 'Thomas The Tank Engine'. Returned to studio for 1990 album

RINGO STARR & HIS ALL-STARR BAND

DR.JOHN + BILLY PRESTON – keyboards / **NILS LOFGREN + JOE WALSH** – guitar / **RICK DANKO** – bass / **JIM KELTNER** – drums / **LEVON HELM** – percussion / **CLARENCE CLEMONS** – saxophone

E.M.I. Arista

Nov 90. (cd/c/lp) *(CD/TC+/EMC 1375)* **RINGO STARR AND HIS ALL-STARR BAND (live)** [ ] [ ]
– It don't come easy / The no-no song / Iko Iko / The weight / Shine silently / Honey don't / You're sixteen, you're beautiful, and you're mine / Quarter to three / Raining in my heart / Will it go round in circles / Life in the fast lane / Photograph.

Private Private

May 92. (12") *(115392)* **WEIGHT OF THE WORLD. / AFTER ALL THESE YEARS** [74] [ ]

May 92. (cd/c) *<82097-2/-4>* **TIME TAKES TIME** [–] [ ]
– Weight of the world / Don't know a thing about love / Don't go where the road don't go / Golden blunders / All in the name of love / After all these years / I don't believe you / Runaways / In a heartbeat / What goes around.

Rykodisc Rykodisc

Oct 93. (cd/c) *(<RCD2/RAC 0264>)* **RINGO STARR AND HIS ALL-STARR BAND, VOL.2: LIVE FROM MONTREUX (live)** [ ] [ ]
– Really serious introduction (QUINCY JONES & RINGO) / I'm the greatest (RINGO) / Don't go where the rain don't go (RINGO) / Desperado (JOE WALSH) / I can't tell you why (TIMOTHY B.SCHMIT) / Girls talk (DAVE EDMUNDS) / Weight of the world (RINGO) / Bang the drum all day (TODD RUNDGREN) / Walking nerve (NILS LOFGREN) / Black Maria (TODD RUNDGREN) / In the city (JOE WALSH) / American woman (BURTON CUMMINGS) / Boys (RINGO) / With a little help from my friends (RINGO).

—— now with **DUDAS, GRAKAL + HUDSON**

Mercury Mercury

Aug 98. (cd/c) *(558598-2/-4)* *<558400>* **VERTICAL MAN** [ ] Jun98 [61]
– One / What in the . . . world / Mindfield / King of broken hearts / Love me do / Vertical man / Drift away / I was walking / De da / Without understanding / I'll be fine anywhere / Puppet / I'm yours.

Universal Koch

Apr 03. (cd) *(E 238429-2)* *<8429>* **RINGO RAMA** [ ] Mar03 [ ]
– Eye to eye / Missouri loves company / Instant amnesia / Memphis in your mind / Never without you / Imagine me there / I think therefore I rock'n'roll / Trippin' on my own tears / Write one for me / What love wants to be / Love first, ask questions later / Elizabeth reigns / English garden.

– compilations, etc. –

May 84. (7") *EMI Gold; (G45 13)* **IT DON'T COME EASY. / BACK OFF BOOGALOO** [ ] [–]

Feb 89. (lp/c/cd) *Rhino; <R1/R4/R2 70135>* **STARRSTRUCK: RINGO'S BEST** (1976-1983) [–] [ ]
– Wrack my brain / In my car / Cookin' (in the kitchen of love) / I keep forgettin' / Hard times / Hey baby / Attention / A dose of rock'n'roll / Who needs a heart / Private property / Can she do it like she dances / Heart on my sleeve. *(cd+=)* – Sure to fall (in love with you) / Hopeless / You belong to me / She's about a mover.

May 03. (cd) *King Biscuit; (KBCCD 143)* **KING BISCUIT PRESENTS . . .** [ ] [ ]

STARSAILOR

Formed: Wigan, England . . . late 90's by Chorley & Warrington lads JAMES WALSH, JAMES STELFOX and BEN BYRNE with the belated arrival of keyboardist BARRY WESTHEAD. All former music students, the group lifted their name from a TIM BUCKLEY album which obviously proved to be a major influence along with VAN MORRISON and TOM WAITS. The indie quintet debuted at the 'Heavenly Social' in 2000, after having only five songs, three of which were floating around on demo tapes circulating the music industry. Giants 'E.M.I.' eventually won over the band, who were still astonished by the critical response they were receiving, it being so early on in their careers. STARSAILOR were put on tour with fellow indie guitar comrades JJ72 and ALFIE and issued their debut single 'FEVER' which would then spark a sold-out, nationwide headline tour. 'GOOD SOULS', a simple guitar-jangling lullaby followed and word seemed to be spreading as the single was another to crash into the Top 20, earning them an American tour with The DOVES and a spot on nightly comic David Letterman's show. 'LOVE IS HERE' was issued the following year to mixed reviews (one of its harshest critics being MOGWAI's STUART BRAITHWAITE who bravely said: "You can just tell JAMES WALSH would sell his granny for a Brit Award") and boasted the Top 10 single 'ALCOHOLIC', a whinging but endearing lament that would've made even THOM YORKE groan. That said, STARSAILOR obviously had a general appeal and were musically talented enough to climb as high as they did (album hit UK Top 3) in such a short period of time. WALSH displayed his songwriting skills even further on the band's sophomore effort 'SILENCE IS EASY' (2003). With troubled PHIL SPECTOR producing two of the eleven songs on offer, the group weren't moving in any new directions; the soft vocals of WALSH were still present as were the beautiful guitar melodies and poignant lyrics of love and squalor. Although the album wasn't nearly as well received as their debut, perhaps because it sounded a tad over-produced (especialy the SPECTOR tracks), it tended to wear its heart firmly on its sleeve for most of the duration.

Album rating: LOVE IS HERE (*8) / SILENCE IS EASY (*7)

JAMES WALSH (b. 8 Jun'01) – vocals, guitar / **BARRY WESTHEAD** – keyboards / **JAMES STELFOX** – bass / **BEN BYRNE** – drums

Chrysalis Capitol

Feb 01. (cd-s/7"/cd-s) *(CD+/CHS/+S 5123)* **FEVER. / COMING DOWN / LOVE IS HERE** [18] [–]

Apr 01. (c-s/7") *(TC+/CHS 5125)* **GOOD SOULS. / THE WAY YOUNG LOVERS DO** [12] [–]
(c-s+=) *(CDCHS 5125)* – Good souls (Echoboy remix).
(cd-s++=) *(CDCHSS 5125)* – ('A'video).

Sep 01. (7") *(CHS 5130)* **ALCOHOLIC. / LET IT SHINE** [10] [–]
(cd-s+=) *(CDCHS 5130)* – ('A'-original) / ('A'-video).
(c-s+=) *(TCCHS 5130)* – Grandma's hands.
(cd-s) *(CDCHSS 5130)* – ('A'side) / Grandma's hands / Good souls (soulsavers remix).

Oct 01. (cd/c/lp) *(535350-2/-4/-1)* *<7243 5 36448 2 6>* **LOVE IS HERE** [2] Jan02 [ ]
– Tie up my hands / Poor misguided fool / Alcoholic / Lullaby / Way to fall / Fever / She just wept / Talk her down / Love is here / Good souls / Coming down.

Dec 01. (c-s) *(TCCHS 5131)* **LULLABY / FROM A WHISPER TO A SCREAM / TIE UP MY HANDS (live)** [36] [–]
(cd-s+=) *(CDCHS 5131)* – ('A'-video).

Mar 02. (c-s) *(TCCHS 5136)* **POOR MISGUIDED FOOL / BORN AGAIN** [23] [–]
(cd-s+=) *(CDCHS 5136)* – ('A'-soulsavers mix) / ('A'-video).

E.M.I. Capitol

Sep 03. (7") *(EM 625)* **SILENCE IS EASY. / SHE UNDERSTANDS** [9] [–]
(cd-s+=) *(CDEM 625)* – Could you be mine?

Sep 03. (cd/lp) *(590007-2/-1)* <591741> **SILENCE IS EASY** [2] Jan04 [ ]
– Music was saved / Fidelity / Some of us / Silence is easy / Telling them / Shark food / Bring my love / White dove / Four to the floor / Born again / Restless heart. <*US cd+=*> – Could you be mine? / At the end of the show.

Nov 03. (cd-s/7") *(CD+/EM 632)* **BORN AGAIN. / AT THE END OF THE SHOW** [40] [–]
(cd-s) *(CDEMS 632)* – ('A'side) / White dove (original demo) / Silence is easy (live in Cardiff) / ('A'-alt. video).

□ STARSHIP (see under ⇒ JEFFERSON AIRPLANE)

STATIC-X

Formed: based – Los Angeles, California, USA . . . 1996 by WAYNE STATIC and KEN JAY, who'd met while working in a Chicago record store. They soon recruited Japanese-born KOICHI FUKADA and California native TONY CAMPOS, building up a genuine grass roots fanbase in thrall to their guttural, technologically enhanced metal. A subsequent deal with 'Warners' led to the release of a debut album, 'WISCONSIN DEATH TRIP' (1999), earning a fair whack of airtime on US rock radio via the tracks, 'PUSH IT', 'I'M WITH STUPID' and 'BLED FOR DAYS'. By the time the record had gone platinum, FUKADA had been replaced by TRIPP REX EISEN, the erstwhile DOPE guitarist making his debut on sophomore effort, 'MACHINE' (2001). By the release of 2003's hackneyed 'SHADOW ZONE', it was hard to avoid the impression that the alternative rock/metal scene had long left the likes of STATIC-X behind. Displaying a dearth of either lyrical or musical inspiration, the album couldn't hope to compete with the restless innovation of the band's contemporaries.

Album rating: WISCONSIN DEATH TRIP (*5) / MACHINE (*6) / SHADOW ZONE (*4)

WAYNE STATIC (b. WAYNE WELLS, Michigan) – vocals, guitar, programming / **KOICKI FUKADA** – guitar / **TONY CAMPOS** – bass / **KEN JAY** – drums

Warners Warners

Nov 98. (cd-s) **3 SONG EP** [–] [ ]
– Push it / Bled for days / Down.

May 99. (cd/c) <*(9362 47271-2/-4)*> **WISCONSIN DEATH TRIP** [ ] Mar99 [ ]
– Push it / I'm stupid / Bled for days / Love dump / I am / Otsegolation / Stem / Sweat of the bud / Fix / Wisconsin death trip / The trance is the motion / December.

Jan 00. (cd-s) <*44782*> **PUSH IT / BLED FOR DAYS (live) / PUSH IT (JB's death trance mix) / DOWN (demo) / PUSH IT (Mephisto Odyssey crucified dub mix)** [ ] [–]

Sep 00. (12") *(F 1114490-2)* **LOVE DUMP** [ ] [–]
(above issued on Higher Education')

—— **TRIPP REX EISEN** – guitar (ex-DOPE) repl. FUKADA

Jun 01. (cd/c) <*(9362 47948-2/-4)*> **MACHINE** [56] [11]
– Bien venidos / Get to the gone / Permanence / Black and white / This is not / Otsego undead / Cold / Structural defect / . . .In a bag / Burn to burn / Machine / A dios alma perida.

Sep 01. (dvd-s) *(W 560DVD)* **BLACK AND WHITE / ANYTHING BUT THIS / SWEAT OF THE BUD (live)** [65] [–]

Oct 03. (cd) <*(9362 48427-2)*> **SHADOW ZONE** [ ] [20]
– Destroy all / Control it / New pain / Shadow zone / Dead world / Monster / The only / Kill your idols / All in wait / Otsegolectric / So / Transmission / Invincible.

STATUS QUO

Formed: London, England . . . 1962 as The SPECTRES, by schoolboys ALAN LANCASTER, ALAN KEY, MIKE ROSSI (aka FRANCIS) and JESS JAWORSKI. They subsequently added JOHN COGHLAN to replace BARRY SMITH, and, by the mid-60's were playing a residency at Butlin's holiday camp, where ROY LYNES took over from JESS. In July '66, they signed to 'Piccadilly' records but failed with a debut 45, a Leiber & Stoller cover, 'I (WHO HAVE NOTHING)'. They released two more flops, before they changed name in March '67 to The TRAFFIC JAM. After one 45, they chose an alternative moniker, The STATUS QUO, due to the more high profile TRAFFIC making the charts. In October '67, MIKE ROSSI reverted back to his real Christian name, FRANCIS, the band adding a second guitarist, RICK PARFITT. Now re-signed to 'Pye' records, they unleashed their first single, 'PICTURES OF MATCHSTICK MEN', giving them a breakthrough into the UK Top 10 (it also hit No.12 in the States – their only Top 50 hit). This was an attempt to cash-in on the hugely popular psychedelic scene, an enjoyable pastiche nevertheless, which remains one of their most enduring, timeless songs. The following year, they were again in the Top 10 with 'ICE IN THE SUN', another taken from the same blueprint. Soon after, the band shed their psychedelic trappings, opting instead for a blues/boogie hard rock sound a la CANNED HEAT. After two more Top 30 hits in the early 70's, their biggest and best being, 'DOWN THE DUSTPIPE', they jumped ship in 1972, signing to 'Vertigo' records. With their trademark blue jeans and (sometimes) white T-shirts, they became one of the top selling bands of the 70's. Their 3-chord-wonder barrage of rock'n'roll had few variations, a disappointing 1971 set, 'DOG OF TWO HEAD' nevertheless hiding a minor classic in 'MEAN GIRL' (a hit two years later). Flying high once more in early '73, STATUS QUO hit the Top 10 with 'PAPER PLANE', the single lifted from the accompanying album, 'PILEDRIVER' (which featured a cover of The Doors' 'ROADHOUSE BLUES'!). The 'QUO said 'HELLO' in fine fashion nine months later, the chart-topping album widely regarded as ROSSI and Co.'s 12-bar tour de force, the hit single 'CAROLINE' also making the Top 5. The following year, another Top 10'er, 'BREAK THE RULES' (from the 'QUO' album), saw the band rather ironically sticking steadfastly to their tried and tested formula. This same formula served them well throughout the mid 70's, their commercial peak coming with 'DOWN DOWN', a No.1 single from the similarly successful 'ON THE LEVEL' album. They followed this with 'BLUE FOR YOU', a set that was lapped up by the massed ranks of the 'QUO army and featured two classy, almost credible hit singles, 'RAIN' and 'MYSTERY SONG'. A hairy eight-legged hit machine, the band just kept on rockin' oblivious to the punk upstarts; perhaps the song most readily identifiable with STATUS QUO, the cover of John Fogerty's 'ROCKIN' ALL OVER THE WORLD' "rocked" the nation in 1977, everyone from housewives to headbangers getting down with their air-guitar. Although they kept their notoriously die-hard following, the band became something of a reliable joke in the music journals as they veered more and more into R&B-by-numbers pop-rock territory, 1984's cover of Dion's 'THE WANDERER' being a prime example. Two years previous, COGHLAN departed (possibly after hearing the same three chords just once too many), the group bringing in PETE KIRCHNER until 1986 when JEFF RICH replaced him. That same year, yet another founder member, LANCASTER, bailed out, keyboard player, ANDY BOWN (a part-time member since '74) become a full-time fifth member. Hardly recognisable as a 'QUO single, the dreary 'IN THE ARMY NOW' almost took ROSSI, PARFITT and Co. back to the top of the charts in '86 (having earlier wowed the world at LIVE AID). STATUS QUO's past musical misdemeanours paled dramatically against the unforgivable early 90's medley, entitled 'ANNIVERSARY WALTZ' (25th unfortunately). The song found them vying for the knees-up-Mother Brown position previously held by cockney "entertainers", CHAS & DAVE. Enough said. The band redeemed themselves to a certain degree with 'HEAVY TRAFFIC' (2002), claimed by some of their more excitable fans as their best record since the 70's. They had a point, certainly: the record's brutally stripped down, live-in-the-studio, heads down blues-rock suggested that they'd been saving it up for years. The double-disc 'RIFFS' (2003), meanwhile, carried that back-to-basics ethos forward to a lean covers/live set, with spirited interpretations of various good-time rockers. • **Songwriters:** LANCASTER (until his departure) or ROSSI and PARFITT. In the early 70's, ROSSI and tour manager BOB YOUNG took over duties. Covered; SPICKS AND SPECKS (Bee Gees) / GREEN TAMBOURINE (Lemon Pipers) / SHEILA (Tommy Roe) / ICE IN THE SUN + ELIZABETH DREAMS + PARADISE FLAT + others (Marty Wilde – Ronnie Scott) / JUNIOR'S WAILING (Steamhammer) / DOWN THE DUSTPIPE (Carl Grossman) / THE PRICE OF LOVE (Everly Brothers) / WILD SIDE OF LIFE (Tommy Quickly) / IN THE ARMY NOW (Bolland-Bolland) / RESTLESS (Jennifer Warnes) / WHEN YOU WALK IN THE ROOM (Jackie DeShannon) / FUN, FUN, FUN (Beach Boys) / I CAN HEAR THE GRASS GROW (Move) / YOU NEVER CAN TELL (Chuck Berry) / GET BACK (Beatles) / SAFETY DANCE (Men Without Hats) / RAINING IN MY HEART (Buddy Holly) / DON'T STOP (Fleetwood Mac) / PROUD MARY (Creedence Clearwater Revival) / LUCILLE (Little Richard) / JOHNNY AND MARY (Robert Palmer) / GET OUT OF DENVER (Bob Seger) / THE FUTURE'S SO BRIGHT (Timbuk 3) / ALL AROUND MY HAT (Steeleye Span) / etc.

Album rating: PICTURESQUE MATCHSTICKABLE MESSAGES FROM THE STATUS QUO (*5) / SPARE PARTS (*4) / MA KELLY'S GREASY SPOON (*4) / DOG OF TWO HEAD (*6) / PILEDRIVER (*6) / HELLO! (*7) / QUO (*6) / ON THE LEVEL (*6) / BLUE FOR YOU (*5) / STATUS QUO LIVE! (*6) / ROCKIN' ALL OVER THE WORLD (*6) / IF YOU CAN'T STAND THE HEAT (*6) / WHATEVER YOU WANT (*6) / 12 GOLD BARS compilation (*8) / JUST SUPPOSIN' (*6) / NEVER TOO LATE (*5) / 1+9+8+2 (*5) / FROM THE MAKERS OF . . . compilation/live (*6) / BACK TO BACK (*4) / 12 GOLD BARS, VOL.2 compilation (*6) / IN THE ARMY NOW (*6) / AIN'T COMPLAINING (*5) / PERFECT REMEDY (*3) / ROCKIN' ALL OVER THE YEARS compilation (*7) / ROCK 'TIL YOU DROP (*5) / LIVE ALIVE QUO (*4) / THIRSTY WORK (*4) / DON'T STOP (*3) / UNDER THE INFLUENCE (*3) / FAMOUS IN THE LAST CENTURY (*3) / HEAVY TRAFFIC (*5) / RIFFS (*4) / Francis Rossi: KING OF THE DOGHOUSE (*3)

MIKE ROSSI (b. FRANCIS, 29 Apr'49, Forest Hill, London) – vocals, guitar / **ROY LYNES** (b.25 Oct'43, Surrey, Kent) – organ, vocals repl. JESS JAWORSKI / **ALAN LANCASTER** (b. 7 Feb'49, Peckham, London) – bass, vocals / **JOHN COGHLAN** (b.19 Sep'46, Dulwich, London) – drums repl. BARRY SMITH

Piccadilly / not iss.

Sep 66. (7"; as The SPECTRES) *(7N 35339)* **I (WHO HAVE NOTHING). / NEIGHBOUR, NEIGHBOUR** [ ] [–]

Nov 66. (7"; as The SPECTRES) *(7N 35352)* **HURDY GURDY MAN. / LATICA** [ ] [–]

—— (above was not the DONOVAN song)

Feb 67. (7"; as The SPECTRES) *(7N 35368)* **(WE AIN'T GOT) NOTHIN' YET. / I WANT IT** [ ] [–]

Jun 67. (7"; as TRAFFIC JAM) *(7N 35386)* **ALMOST THERE BUT NOT QUITE. / WAIT JUST A MINUTE** [ ] [–]

The STATUS QUO

—— added **RICK PARFITT** (b. RICHARD HARRISON, 12 Oct'48, Woking, Surrey) – guitar, vocals / MIKE now **FRANCIS ROSSI**

Pye / Cadet Concept

Nov 67. (7") *(7N 17449)* *<7001>* **PICTURES OF MATCHSTICK MEN. / GENTLEMAN JOE'S SIDEWALK CAFE** [7] May68 [12]

Apr 68. (7") *(7N 17497)* *<7015>* **BLACK VEILS OF MELONCHOLY. / TO BE FREE** [ ] Jul69 [ ]

Aug 68. (lp) *(NSPL 18220)* *<LSP 315>* **PICTURESQUE MATCHSTICKABLE MESSAGES FROM THE STATUS QUO** (US-title 'MESSAGES FROM THE STATUS QUO') [ ] [ ]
– Black veils of meloncholy / When my mind is not live / Ice in the Sun / Elizabeth dreams / Gentleman Joe's sidewalk cafe / Paradise flat / Technicolour dreams / Spicks and specks / Sheila / Sunny cellophane skies / Green tambourine / Pictures of matchstick men. *(re-iss. Oct87 on 'P.R.T.' lp/c/cd; PYL/PYM/PYC 6020) (cd re-iss. Dec89 on 'Castle'; CLACD 168)*

Aug 68. (7") *(7N 17581)* *<7006>* **ICE IN THE SUN. / WHEN MY MIND IS NOT ALIVE** [8] [70]

Jan 69. (7"w-drawn) *(7N 17650)* **TECHNICOLOR DREAMS. / PARADISE FLAT** [–] [–]

Feb 69. (7") *(7N 17665)* **MAKE ME STAY A BIT LONGER. / AUNTIE NELLIE** [ ] [–]

Mar 69. (7") *<7010>* **TECHNICOLOR DREAMS. / SPICKS AND SPECKS** [–] [ ]

May 69. (7") *(7N 17728)* **ARE YOU GROWING TIRED OF MY LOVE. / SO ENDS ANOTHER LIFE** [46] [–]

Sep 69. (lp) *(NSPL 18301)* **SPARE PARTS** [ ] [–]
– Face without a soul / You're just what I'm looking for / Mr.Mind detector / Antique Angelique / So ends another life / Are you growing tired of my love / Little Miss Nothing / Poor old man / The clown / Velvet curtains / When I awake / Nothing at all. *(re-iss. Oct87 on 'P.R.T.' lp/c/cd; PYL/PYM/PYC 6021) (re-iss. Aug90 on 'Castle' cd/c/lp; CLA CD/MC/LP 205) (re-mast.Aug98 on 'Essential'+=; ESMCD 625)* – (extra tracks).

Oct 69. (7") *(7N 17825)* *<7017>* **THE PRICE OF LOVE. / LITTLE MISS NOTHING** [ ] [ ]

Pye / Janus

Mar 70. (7") *(7N 17907)* *<127>* **DOWN THE DUSTPIPE. / FACE WITHOUT A SOUL** [12] [ ]

Sep 70. (lp) *(NSPL 18344)* *<3018>* **MA KELLY'S GREASY SPOON** [ ] [ ]
– Spinning wheel blues / Daughter / Everything / Shy fly / (April) Spring, Summer and Wednesdays / Junior's wailing / Lakky lady / Need your love / Lazy poker blues / (a) Is it really me – (b) Gotta go home. *(re-iss. Oct87 on 'P.R.T.'; PYL/PYM/PYC 6022) (cd re-iss. Dec89 on 'Castle'; CLACD 169)*

STATUS QUO

—— now a quartet of **ROSSI, PARFITT, LANCASTER + COGHLAN** when LYNES departed

Oct 70. (7") *(7N 17998)* *<141>* **IN MY CHAIR. / GERDUNDULA** [21] [ ]
(re-iss. Jun79)

Pye / Pye

Jun 71. (7") *(7N 45077)* *<65000>* **TUNE TO THE MUSIC. / GOOD THINKING** [ ] [ ]

Dec 71. (lp/c) *(NSPL 18371)* *<3301>* **DOG OF TWO HEAD** [ ] [ ]
– Umleitung / Nanana / Something going on in my head / Mean girl / Nanana / Gerdundula / Railroad / Someone's learning / Nanana. *(cd-iss. 1986 on 'P.R.T.'; CDMP 8837) (re-iss. Oct87 on 'P.R.T.' lp/c/cd; PYL/PYM/PYC 6023) (re-iss. Aug90 on 'Castle' cd/c/lp; CLA CD/MC/LP 206) (re-mast.Aug98 on 'Essential'+=; ESMCD 626)* – (extra tracks).

Vertigo / A&M

Jan 73. (7") *(6059 071)* **PAPER PLANE. / SOFTER RIDE** [8] [–]

Jan 73. (lp) *(6360 082)* *<4381>* **PILEDRIVER** [5] [ ]
– Don't waste my time / O baby / A year / Unspoken words / Big fat mama / Paper plane / All the reasons / Roadhouse blues. *(re-iss. May83 lp/c; PRICE/PRIMC 17) (cd-iss. Feb91; 848 176-2)*

May 73. (7") *<1425>* **DON'T WASTE MY TIME. / ALL THE REASONS** [–] [ ]

Jul 73. (7") *<1443>* **PAPER PLANE. / ALL THE REASONS** [–] [ ]

Sep 73. (7") *(6059 085)* **CAROLINE. / JOANNE** [5] [–]

Sep 73. (lp) *(6360 098)* *<3615>* **HELLO!** [1] [ ]
– Roll over lay down / Claudie / A reason for living / Blue eyed lady / Caroline / Softer ride / And it's better now / Forty-five hundred times. *(re-iss. May83 lp/c; PRICE/PRIMC 16) (cd-iss. Feb91; 848 172-2)*

Feb 74. (7") *<1510>* **CAROLINE. / SOFTER RIDE** [–] [ ]

Apr 74. (7") *(6059 101)* **BREAK THE RULES. / LONELY NIGHT** [8] [–]

May 74. (lp/c) *(9102/7231 001)* *<3649>* **QUO** [2] [ ]
– Backwater / Just take me / Break the rules / Drifting away / Don't think it matters / Fine fine fine / Lonely man / Slow train. *(re-iss. Aug83 lp/c; PRICE/PRIMC 38)*

Vertigo Capitol

Nov 74. (7") *(6059 114)* *<4039>* **DOWN DOWN. / NIGHT RIDE** [1] [ ]

Feb 75. (lp/c) *(9102/7231 002)* *<11381>* **ON THE LEVEL** [1] [ ]
– Little lady / Most of the time / I saw the light / Over and done / Nightride / Down down / Broken man / What to do / Where I am / Bye bye Johnny. *(re-iss. Aug83 lp/c; PRICE/PRIMC 39) (cd-iss. Feb91; 848 175-2)*

Apr 75. (7") *<4125>* **BYE BYE JOHNNY. / DOWN DOWN** [–] [ ]

May 75. (7"ep) *(QUO 13)* **STATUS QUO LIVE! (live)** [9] [–]
– Roll over lay down / Gerdundula / Junior's wailing.

Feb 76. (7") *(6059 133)* **RAIN. / YOU LOST THE LOVE** [7] [ ]

Mar 76. (lp/c) *(9102/7231 006)* *<11509>* **BLUE FOR YOU** <US title 'STATUS QUO'> [1] [ ]
– Is there a better way / Mad about the boy / Ring of a change / Blue for you / Rain / Rolling home / That's a fact / Ease your mind / Mystery song. *(re-iss. Dec83 lp/c; PRICE/PRIMC 55)*

Jul 76. (7") *(6059 146)* **MYSTERY SONG. / DRIFTING AWAY** [11] [ ]

Dec 76. (7") *(6059 153)* **WILD SIDE OF LIFE. / ALL THROUGH THE NIGHT** [9] [ ]

Mar 77. (d-lp)(d-c) *(6641 580)(7599 171)* *<11623>* **LIVE! (live)** [3] [ ]
– Junior's wailing / (a) Backwater, (b) Just take me / Is there a better way / In my chair / Little lady / Most of the time / Forty-five hundred times / Roll over lay down / Big fat mama / Caroline / Bye bye Johnny / Rain / Don't waste my time / Roadhouse blues. *(re-iss. Sep84; d-lp/d-c; PRID/+C 5) (d-cd-iss. Feb92 & Aug98; 510 334-2)*

Oct 77. (7") *(6059 184)* **ROCKIN' ALL OVER THE WORLD. / RING OF A CHANGE** [3] [ ]

Nov 77. (lp)(c) *(9102 014)(7231 012)* *<11749>* **ROCKIN' ALL OVER THE WORLD** [5] [ ]
– Hard time / Can't give you more / Let's ride / Baby boy / You don't own me / Rockers rollin' / Rockin' all over the world / Who am I? / Too far gone / For you / Dirty water / Hold you back. *(re-iss. Aug85 lp/c; PRICE/PRIMC 87) (cd-iss. Feb91; 848 173-2)*

Aug 78. (7") *(QUO 1)* **AGAIN AND AGAIN. / TOO FAR GONE** [13] [–]

Oct 78. (lp)(c) *(9102 027)(7231 017)* **IF YOU CAN'T STAND THE HEAT** [3] [–]
– Again and again / I'm giving up my worryin' / Gonna teach you to love me / Someone show me home / Long legged Linda / Oh! what a night / Accident prone / Stones / Let me fly / Like a good girl. *(cd-iss. see-compilations)*

Nov 78. (7") *(QUO 2)* **ACCIDENT PRONE. / LET ME FLY** [36] [–]

Sep 79. (7") *(6059 242)* **WHATEVER YOU WANT. / HARD RIDE** [4] [–]

Oct 79. (lp)(c) *(9102 037)(7231 025)* **WHATEVER YOU WANT** [3] [–]
– Whatever you want / Shady lady / Who asked you / Your smiling face / Living on an island / Come rock with me / Rockin' on / Runaway / High flyer / Breaking away. *(cd-iss. see-compilations)*

Nov 79. (7") *(6059 248)* **LIVING ON AN ISLAND. / RUNAWAY** [16] [–]

Apr 80. (lp/c) *(QUO TV/MC 1)* **12 GOLD BARS** (compilation) [3] [–]
– Rockin' all over the world / Down down / Caroline / Paper plane / Break the rules / Again and again / Mystery song / Roll over lay down / Rain / The wild side of life / Whatever you want / Living on an island. *(cd-iss. Nov83; 800 062-2)*

Oct 80. (7") *(QUO 3)* **WHAT YOU'RE PROPOSIN'. / AB BLUES** [2] [–]

Oct 80. (lp/c) *(6302/7144 057)* **JUST SUPPOSIN'** [4] [–]
– What you're proposin' / Run to mummy / Don't drive my car / Lies / Over the edge / The wild ones / Name of the game / Coming and going / Rock'n'roll.

Dec 80. (7") *(QUO 4)* **DON'T DRIVE MY CAR. / LIES** [11] [–]

Feb 81. (7") *(QUO 5)* **SOMETHING 'BOUT YOU BABY I LIKE. / ENOUGH IS ENOUGH** [7] [–]

Mar 81. (lp/c) *(6302/7144 104)* **NEVER TOO LATE** [2] [–]
– Never too late / Something 'bout you baby I like / Take me away / Falling in falling out / Carol / Long ago / Mountain lady / Don't stop me now / Enough is enough / Riverside. *(cd-iss. Oct83; 800 053-2)*

Nov 81. (7"m) *(QUO 6)* **ROCK'N'ROLL. / HOLD YOU BACK / BACKWATER** [8] [–]

— **PETE KIRCHNER** – drums (ex-ORIGINAL MIRRORS, ex-HONEYBUS, etc.) repl. COUGHLAN who formed PARTNERS IN CRIME

Mar 82. (7") *(QUO 7)* **DEAR JOHN. / I WANT THE WORLD TO KNOW** [10] [–]

Apr 82. (lp/c) *(6302/7144 189)* **1+9+8+2** [1] [–]
– She don't fool me / Young pretender / Get out and walk / Jealousy / I love rock and roll / Resurrection / Dear John / Doesn't matter / I want the world to know / I should have known / Big man. *(cd-iss. Oct83; 800 035-2)*

Jun 82. (7") *(QUO 8)* **SHE DON'T FOOL ME. / NEVER TOO LATE** [36] [–]

Oct 82. (7"/7"pic-d) *(QUO/+P 10)* **CAROLINE (live). / DIRTY WATER (live)** [13] [–]
(12"+=) *(QUO 10-12)* – Down down (live).

Nov 82. (t-lp/3xlp-box) *(PRO LP/BX 1)* **FROM THE MAKERS OF . . .** (compilation & 2 lp-sides live) [4] [–]
– Pictures of matchstick men / Ice in the Sun / Down the dustpipe / In my chair / Junior's wailing / Mean girl / Gerdundula / Paper plane / Big fat mama / Roadhouse blues / Break the rules / Down down / Bye bye Johnny / Rain / Mystery song / Blue for you / Is there a better way / Again and again / Accident prone / The wild side of life / Living on an island / What you're proposing / Rock and roll / Something 'bout you baby I like / Dear John / Caroline / Roll over lay down / Backwater / Little lady / Don't drive my car / Whatever you want / Hold you back / Rockin' all over the world / Over the edge / Don't waste my time.

Sep 83. (7"/7"blue) *(QUO/+B 11)* **OL' RAG BLUES. / STAY THE NIGHT** [9] [–]
(ext.12"+=) *(QUO 11-12)* – Whatever you want (live).

Oct 83. (lp/c)(cd) *(VERH/+C 10)(814 662-2)* **BACK TO BACK** [9] [–]
– A mess of blues / Ol' rag blues / Can't be done / Too close to the ground / No contrast / Win or lose / Marguerita time / Your kind of love / Stay the night / Going down town tonight. *(cd re-iss. see-compilations)*

Oct 83. (7") *(QUO 12)* **A MESS OF BLUES. / BIG MAN** [15] [–]
(ext.12"+=) *(QUO 12-12)* – Young pretender.

Dec 83. (7"/7"pic-d) *(QUO/+P 14)* **MARGUERITA TIME. / RESURRECTION** [3] [–]
(d7"+=) *(QUO 14-14)* – Caroline / Joanne.

May 84. (7") *(QUO 15)* **GOING DOWN TOWN TONIGHT. / TOO CLOSE TO THE GROUND** [20] [–]

Oct 84. (7"/12"clear) *(QUO/+P 16)* **THE WANDERER. / CAN'T BE DONE** [7] [–]

Nov 84. (d-lp/c)(cd) *(QUO TV/MC 2)(822 985-2)* **12 GOLD BARS VOL.2** (compilation) [12] [–]
– What you're proposing / Lies / Something 'bout you baby I like / Don't drive my car / Dear John / Rock and roll / Ol' rag blues / Mess of the blues / Marguerita time / Going down town tonight / The wanderer. / (includes VOL.1).

— **ROSSI + PARFITT** enlisted **ANDY BOWN** – keyboards (ex-HERD) (He was p/t member since 1974) / **JEFF RICH** – drums (ex-CLIMAX BLUES BAND) repl. KIRCHNER / **RHINO EDWARDS** (r.n.JOHN) – bass (ex-CLIMAX BLUES BAND) repl. LANCASTER

May 86. (7"/7"sha-pic-d) *(QUO/+PD 18)* **ROLLIN' HOME. / LONELY** [9] [–]
(12"+=) *(QUO 18-12)* – Keep me guessing.

Jul 86. (7") *(QUO 19)* **RED SKY. / DON'T GIVE IT UP** [19] [–]
(12"+=)(12"w-poster+=) *(QUO 19-12)(QUOPB 19-1)* – The Milton Keynes medley (live).
(d7"+=) *(QUOPD 19)* – Marguerita time.

Aug 86. (lp/c)(cd) *(VERH/+C 36)(830 049-2)* **IN THE ARMY NOW** [7] [–]
– Rollin' home / Calling / In your eyes / Save me / In the army now / Dreamin' / End of the line / Invitation / Red sky / Speechless / Overdose.

Sep 86. (7"/7"pic-d) *(QUO/PD 20)* **IN THE ARMY NOW. / HEARTBURN** [2] [–]
(d7"+=) *(QUODP 20)* – Marguerita time / What you're proposin'.
('A'-military mix.12"+=) *(QUO 20-12)* – Late last night.

Nov 86. (7") *(QUO 21)* **DREAMIN'. / LONG-LEGGED GIRLS** [15] [–]
('A'-wet mix.12"+=) *(QUO 21-12)* – The Quo Christmas cake mix.

Mar 88. (7"/7"s) *(QUO/+H 22)* **AIN'T COMPLAINING. / THAT'S ALRIGHT** [19] [–]
(ext.12"+=) *(QUO 22-12)* – Lean machine.
(cd-s++=) *(QUOCD 22)* – In the army now (remix).

May 88. (7"/7"s) *(QUO/+H 23)* **WHO GETS THE LOVE?. / HALLOWEEN** [34] [–]
(ext.12"+=) *(QUO 23-12)* – The reason for goodbye.
(cd-s++=) *(QUOCD 23)* – The wanderer (Sharon the nag mix).

Jun 88. (lp/c)(cd) *(VERH/+C 58)(834 604-2)* **AIN'T COMPLAINING** [12] [–]
– Ain't complaining / Everytime I think of you / One for the money /

Another shipwreck / Don't mind if I do / I know you're leaving / Cross that bridge / Cream of the crop / The loving game / Who gets the love? / Burning bridges / Magic.

— (Below single was a re-working of 'ROCKIN' ALL . . . ' for Sport Aid)

Aug 88. (7") *(QUAID 1)* **RUNNING ALL OVER THE WORLD. / MAGIC** 17 –
(12"+=) *(QUAID 1-12)* – ('A'extended).
(cd-s++=) *(QUACD 1)* – Whatever you want.

Nov 88. (7") *(QUO 25)* **BURNING BRIDGES (ON AND OFF AND ON AGAIN). / WHATEVER YOU WANT** 5 –
(ext.12"+=/cd-s+=) *(QUO 25-12/CD25)* – Marguerita time.

Oct 89. (7"/c-s) *(QUO/+MC 26)* **NOT AT ALL. / GONE THRU THE SLIPS** 50 –
(12"+=)(cd-s+=) *(QUO 26-12/CD26)* – Every time I think of you.

Nov 89. (lp/c/cd) *(842 098-1/-4/-2)* **PERFECT REMEDY** 49 –
– Little dreamer / Not at all / Heart on hold / Perfect remedy / Address book / The power of rock / The way I am / Tommy's in love / Man overboard / Going down for the first time / Throw her a line / 1,000 years.

Dec 89. (7"/7"pic-d/c-s) *(QUO/+P/MC 27)* **LITTLE DREAMER. / ROTTEN TO THE BONE** –
(12"+=)(12"g-f+=/cd-s+=) *(QUO 27-12)(QUO X/CD 27)* – Doing it all for you.

Oct 90. (7"/7"silver/c-s) *(QUO/+G/MC 28)* **THE ANNIVERSARY WALTZ – (PART 1). / THE POWER OF ROCK** 2 –
(12"+=/cd-s+=) *(QUO 28-12/CD28)* – Perfect remedy.

Oct 90. (cd/c/d-lp) *(846 797-2/-4/-1)* **ROCKIN' ALL OVER THE YEARS** (compilation) 2 –
– Pictures of matchstick men / Ice in the Sun / Paper plane / Caroline / Break the rules / Down down / Roll over lay down / Rain / Wild side of life / Whatever you want / What you're proposing / Something 'bout you baby I like / Rock'n'roll / Dear John / Ol' rag blues / Marguerita time / The wanderer / Rollin' home / In the army now / Burning bridges / Anniversary waltz (part 1).

Dec 90. (7"/c-s) *(QUO/+MC 29)* **THE ANNIVERSARY WALTZ – (PART 2). / DIRTY WATER (live)** 16 –
(12"+=/cd-s+=) *(QUO 29-12/CD29)* – Pictures of matchstick men – Rock'n'roll music – Lover please – That'll be the day – Singing the blues.

Aug 91. (7"/c-s) *(QUO/+MC 30)* **CAN'T GIVE YOU MORE. / DEAD IN THE WATER** 37 –
(12"+=/cd-s+=) *(QUO 30-12/CD30)* – Mysteries from the ball.

Sep 91. (cd/c/lp) *(510 341-2/-4/-1)* **ROCK 'TIL YOU DROP** 10 –
– Like a zombie / All we really wanna do (Polly) / Fakin' the blues / One man band / Rock 'til you drop / Can't give you more / Warning shot / Let's work together / Bring it on home / No problems. *(cd+=/c+=)* – Good sign / Tommy / Nothing comes easy / Fame or money / Price of love / Forty-five hundred times. *(re-iss. Feb93)*

Jan 92. (7"/c-s) *(QUO/+MC 32)* **ROCK 'TIL YOU DROP. / Awards Medley:- CAROLINE – DOWN DOWN – WHATEVER YOU WANT – ROCKIN' ALL OVER THE WORLD** 38 –
(12"+=/cd-s+=) *(QUO 32-12/CD32)* – Forty-five hundred times.

Polydor / not iss.

Oct 92. (7"/c-s) *(QUO/+MC 33)* **ROADHOUSE MEDLEY (ANNIVERSARY WALTZ 25). / ('A'extended)** 21 –
(cd-s+=) *(QUOCD 33)* – (A'mix).
(cd-s+=) *(QUODD 33)* – Don't drive my car.

Nov 92. (cd/c/lp) *(517 367-2/-4/-1)* **LIVE ALIVE QUO (live)** 37 –
– Roadhouse medley:- Roadhouse blues – The wanderer – Marguerita time – Living on an island – Break the rules – Something 'bout you baby I like – The price of love – Roadhouse blues / Whatever you want / In the army now / Burning bridges / Rockin' all over the world / Caroline / Don't drive my car / Hold you back / Little lady.

— In May 94; their 'BURNING BRIDGES' tune, was used for Manchester United Football Squad's UK No.1 'Come On You Reds'.

Jul 94. (7"colrd/c-s) *(QUO/+MC 34)* **I DIDN'T MEAN IT. / WHATEVER YOU WANT** 21 –
(cd-s+=) *(QUODD 34)* – Down down / Rockin' all over the world.
(cd-s) *(QUOCD 34)* – ('A'side) / ('A'-Hooligan version) / Survival / She knew too much.

Aug 94. (cd/c/lp) *(523607-2/-4/-1)* **THIRSTY WORK** 13 –
– Goin' nowhere / I didn't mean it / Confidence / Point of no return / Sail away / Like it or not / Soft in the head / Queenie / Lover of the human race / Sherri don't fail me now! / Rude awakening time / Back on my feet / Restless / Ciao ciao / Tango / Sorry.

Oct 94. (7"colrd/c-s) *(QUO/+MC 35)* **SHERRI DON'T FAIL ME NOW!. / BEAUTIFUL** 38 –
(cd-s+=) *(QUOCD 34)* – In the army now.
(cd-s) *(QUODD 34)* – ('A'side) / Tossin' and turnin' / Down to you.

Nov 94. (7"/c-s/cd-s) *(QUO/+MC/CD 36)* **RESTLESS (re-orchestrated). / AND I DO** 39 –

PolygramTV / not iss.

Oct 95. (7"/c-s) *(577 512-7/-4)* **WHEN YOU WALK IN THE ROOM. / TILTING AT THE MILL** 34 –
(cd-s+=) *(577 512-2)* – ('A'version).

Feb 96. (7"/c-s; STATUS QUO with The BEACH BOYS) *(576 262-7/-4)* **FUN FUN FUN. / MORTIFIED** 24 –
(cd-s+=) *(576 262-2)* – ('A'mix).

below album features all covers. They sued Radio One for not playing the above hit on their playlist after it charted. The QUO finally lose out in court and faced costs of over £50,000.

Feb 96. (cd/c) *(531 035-2/-4)* **DON'T STOP** 2 –
– Fun, fun, fun (with The BEACH BOYS) / When you walk in the room / I can hear the grass grow / You never can tell (it was a teenage wedding) / Get back / Safety dance / Raining in my heart (with BRIAN MAY) / Don't stop / Sorrow / Proud Mary / Lucille / Johnny and Mary / Get out of enver / The future's so bright (I gotta wear shades) / All around my hat (with MADDY PRIOR).

Apr 96. (7"/c-s) *(576 634-7/-4)* **DON'T STOP. / TEMPORARY FRIEND** 35 –
(cd-s+=) *(576 635-2)* – ('A'extended).

Oct 96. (7"/c-s; STATUS QUO with MADDY PRIOR) *(575 944-7/-4)* **ALL AROUND MY HAT. / I'LL NEVER GET OVER YOU** 47 –
(cd-s+=) *(575 945-2)* – Get out of Denver.

— FRANCIS ROSSI also issued solo releases, the album 'KING OF THE DOGHOUSE' was out in Sept'96

Eagle / Spitfire

Mar 99. (c-s) *(EAGCS 075)* **THE WAY IT GOES / UNDER THE INFLUENCE** 39 –
(cd-s) *(EAGXS 075)* – ('A'side) / Sea cruise.

Mar 99. (cd/c) *(EAG CD/MC 076)* <5035> **UNDER THE INFLUENCE** 26 Jul99
– Twenty wild horses / Under the influence / Round and round / Shine on / Little white lies / Keep 'em coming / Little me and you / Making waves / Blessed are the meek / Roll the dice / Not fade away.

May 99. (c-s) *(EAGCS 101)* **LITTLE WHITE LIES / I KNEW THE BRIDE** 47 –
(cd-s+=) *(EAGXS 101)* – Pictures of matchstick men (1999).

Sep 99. (c-s) *(EAGCS 105)* **TWENTY WILD HORSES / ANALYSE TIME** 53 –
(cd-s+=) *(EAGXS 105)* – Destruction day.

Universal / Universal

Apr 00. (cd/c) *(157814-2/-4)* **FAMOUS IN THE LAST CENTURY** 19 –
– Famous in the last century / Old time rock'n'roll / Way down / Rave on / Roll over Beethoven / When I'm dead and gone / Memphis Tennessee / Sweet home Chicago / Crawling from the wreckage / Good golly Miss Molly / Claudette / Rock'n'me / Hound dog / Runaround Sue / Once bitten twice shy / Mony mony / Famous in the last century (reprise).

May 00. (c-s) *(158013-4)* **MONY MONY / FAMOUS IN THE LAST CENTURY (extended)** 48 –
(cd-s+=) *(158013-2)* – Gerundula (live).

Aug 02. (cd-s) *(019234-2)* **JAM SIDE DOWN / THE MADNESS / JAM SIDE DOWN (video)** 17 –
(cd-s) *(019235-2)* – ('A'side) / Down down (rec. at Top Of The Pops 2) / Rockin' all over the world (rec. at Top Of The Pops 2).

Sep 02. (cd) *(018790-2)* <64435> **HEAVY TRAFFIC** 15
– Blues and rhythm / All stand up (never say never) / The Oriental / Heavy traffic / Solid gold / Green / Jam side down / Diggin' Burt Bacharach / Do it again / Another day / I don't remember anymore / Rhythm of life.

Oct 02. (cd-s) *(019487-2)* **ALL STAND UP (NEVER SAY NEVER) / YOU LET ME DOWN / ALL STAND UP (NEVER SAY NEVER) (video)** 51 –

Nov 03. (cd) *(9813910)* **RIFFS** (covers, etc.) 44 –
– Caroline / I fought the law / Born to be wild / Takin' care of business / Wild one / On the road again / Tobacco road / Centerfold / All day and all of the night / Don't bring me down / Junior's wailing / Pump it up / Down the dustpipe / Whatever you want / Rockin' all over the world. *(ltd cd w/ dvd+=; 9813909)*

– compilations, etc. –

Dec 69. (lp) *Marble Arch; (MALS 1193)* **STATUS QUOTATIONS** –

Mar 73. (7") *Pye; (7N 45229) / <65017>* **MEAN GIRL. / EVERYTHING** 20

May 73. (lp/c) *Pye; (NSPL/ZCP 18402)* **THE BEST OF STATUS QUO** 32 –
– Down the dustpipe / Gerdundula / In my chair / Umleitung / Lakky lady / Daughter / Railroad / Tune to the music / April, Spring, Summer and Wednesdays / Mean girl / Spinning wheel blues. *(cd-iss. 1986 on 'P.R.T.'; CDNSP 7773)*

Jun 73. (lp/c) *Golden Hour; (GH/ZCGH 556)* **A GOLDEN HOUR OF . . .** –
(re-iss. Apr90 on 'Knight' cd/c; KGH CD/MC 110)

Jul 73. (7") *Pye; (7N 45253)* **GERDUNDULA. / LAKKY LADY** –

1975. (lp) *Starline;* **ROCKIN' AROUND WITH** –

Oct 75. (lp/c) *Golden Hour; (GH/ZCGH 604)* **DOWN THE DUSTPIPE: THE GOLDEN HOUR OF . . . VOL.2** 20 –

Sep 76. (lp/c) *Pye; (PKL/ZCPKB 5546)* **THE REST OF STATUS QUO** –

Jan 77. (lp/c) *Pye; (FILD 005)* **THE STATUS QUO FILE SERIES** –
(re-iss. Sep79 on 'P.R.T.';)

Apr 77. (12"ep) *Pye; (BD 103)* **DOWN THE DUSTPIPE / MEAN GIRL. / IN MY CHAIR / GERDUNDULA** –

Apr 78. (lp) *Hallmark; (HMA 257)* **PICTURES OF MATCHSTICK MEN** –

May 78. (lp)(c) *Marble Arch; (HMA 260)(HSC 322)* **STATUS QUO** –

Aug 78. (d-lp/d-c) *Pickwick; (PDA/PDC 046)* **THE STATUS QUO COLLECTION** –

May 79. (7"yellow) *Flashback-Pye; (FBS 2)* **PICTURES OF MATCHSTICK MEN. / DOWN IN THE DUSTPIPE** –
(re-iss. 7"black Apr83 on 'Old Gold'; OG 9298)

Jun 79. (lp,orange-lp/c) *Pye; (NPSL/ZCP 18607)* **JUST FOR THE RECORD** –

Jun 80. (d-lp/d-c) *P.R.T.; (SPOT/ZCSPT 1028)* **SPOTLIGHT ON . . .** –

Sep 80. (d-lp/d-c) *Pickwick; (SSD/+C 8035)* **STATUS QUO** –

Oct 81. (10"lp/c) *P.R.T.; (DOW/ZCDOW 2)* **FRESH QUOTA** (rare) 74 –

Jun 82. (c) *P.R.T.; (ZCTON 101)* **100 MINUTES OF . . .** –

Jul 82. (7") *Old Gold; (OG 9142)* **MEAN GIRL. / IN MY CHAIR** –

Oct 82. (lp/c) *P.R.T.; (SPOT/ZCSPT 1028)* **SPOTLIGHT ON . . . VOL.II** –

Apr 83. (lp/c) *Contour; (CN/+4 2062)* **TO BE OR NOT TO BE** –
(cd-iss. Apr91 on 'Pickwick'; PWKS 4051P)

Jul 83. (10"lp/c) *P.R.T.; (DOW/ZCDOW 10)* **WORKS** –

Jul 84. (lp/c) *Vertigo; (818 947-2/-4)* **LIVE AT THE N.E.C. (live)** 83 Dutch –
(UK cd-iss. Jul91; 818 947-2)

Sep 85. (7") *Old Gold; (OG 9566)* **CAROLINE. / DOWN DOWN** –

Oct 85. (lp/c) *Flashback; (FBLP/ZCFBL 8082)* **NA NA NA** –

Nov 85. (7") *Old Gold; (OG 9567)* **ROCKIN' ALL OVER THE WORLD. / PAPER PLANE** –
(re-iss. Aug89 & Sep90)

Nov 85. (d-lp/c) *Castle; (CCS LP/MC 114)* **THE COLLECTION** –
(cd-iss. 1988; CCSCD 114)

Oct 87. (lp/c/cd) *P.R.T.; (PYL/PYM/PYC 6024)* **QUOTATIONS VOL.1 – (THE EARLY YEARS)** –

Oct 87. (lp/c/cd) *P.R.T.; (PYL/PYM/PYC 6025)* **QUOTATIONS VOL.2 – (ALTERNATIVES)** –

Sep 88. (lp/pic-lp/c/cd) *P.R.T.; (PYZ/PYX/PYM/PYC 4007)* **FROM THE BEGINNING (1966-67)** –

Apr 89. (c)(cd) *Legacy; (C 903)(GHCD 3)* **C90 COLLECTOR** –

Sep 90. (cd/c/d-lp) *Castle; (CCS CD/MC/LP 271)* **B SIDES AND RARITIES** –

Dec 90. (3xcd-box/3xlp-box) *Essential; (ESS CD/LP 136)* **THE EARLY WORKS** –

Feb 91. (cd) *Vertigo; (848 087-2)* **WHATEVER YOU WANT / JUST SUPPOSIN'** –

Feb 91. (cd) *Vertigo; (848 088-2)* **NEVER TOO LATE / BACK TO BACK** –

Feb 91. (cd) *Vertigo; (848 089-2)* **QUO / BLUE FOR YOU** –
(re-iss. Sep97; same)

Feb 91. (cd) *Vertigo; (848 090-2)* **IF YOU CAN'T STAND THE HEAT / 1+9+8+2** –

Sep 91. (d-cd) *Decal; (CDLIK 81)* **BACK TO THE BEGINNING** –

Nov 91. (cd) *Pickwick; (PWKS 4087P)* **THE BEST OF STATUS QUO 1972-1986** –

May 93. (cd/c) *Spectrum; (550002-2/-4)* **A FEW BARS MORE** –

Feb 94. (cd) *Dojo; (EARLD 8)* **THE EARLY YEARS** –

Aug 94. (cd/c) *Matchstick; (MAT CD/MC 291)* **STATUS QUO** –

Sep 94. (cd/c) *Spectrum; (550190-2/-4)* **IT'S ONLY ROCK'N'ROLL** –

Mar 95. (cd) *Connoisseur; (VSOPCD 213)* **THE OTHER SIDE OF STATUS QUO** –

May 95. (cd/c) *Spectrum; (550727-2/-4)* **PICTURES OF MATCHSTICK MEN** –

Jun 95. (cd/c) *Savanna; (SSL CD/MC 204)* **ICE IN THE SUN** –
(re-iss. Apr97 on 'Pulse' cd/c; PLS CD/MC 206)

Jul 96. (cd/c) *Truetrax; (TRT CD/MC 198)* **THE BEST OF STATUS QUO** –

Oct 97. (d-cd/d-c) *Polygram TV; (553507-2/-4)* **WHATEVER YOU WANT – THE VERY BEST OF** 13 –

Mar 99. (cd) *Castle Select; (SELCD 555)* **MATCHSTICK MEN – THE PSYCHEDELIC YEARS** –

Mar 99. (cd) *Spectrum; (554891-2)* **THE ESSENTIAL STATUS QUO VOL.1** –

Aug 99. (cd) *Spectrum; (554896-2)* **THE ESSENTIAL STATUS QUO VOL.2** –

Aug 99. (cd) *Castle Pie; (PIESD 005)* **ICE IN THE SUN** –

Feb 00. (cd) *Spectrum; (554897-2)* **THE ESSENTIAL STATUS QUO VOL.3** –

Jul 00. (cd) *Delta No.10; (CD 23106)* **ROCKIN' ALL OVER THE WORLD** –

Sep 00. (d-cd) *Castle; (CCSCD 821)* **THE SINGLES COLLECTION 1968-1972** –

FRANCIS ROSSI & BERNARD FROST

Vertigo not iss.

Apr 85. (7")(ext-12") *(VER 17)(PROS 1)* **MODERN ROMANCE (I WANT TO FALL IN LOVE AGAIN). / I WONDER WHY** 54 –

Oct 85. (7") **JEALOUSY. / WHERE ARE YOU NOW** –
(ext.12"+=) – That's all right.

FRANCIS ROSSI

Virgin not iss.

Jul 96. (7"pic-d/c-s) *(VSP/VSC 1594)* **GIVE MYSELF TO LOVE / KING OF THE DOGHOUSE** 42 –
(cd-s+=) *(VSCDT 1594)* – Someone show me.

Sep 96. (cd/c) *(CDV/TCV 2809)* **KING OF THE DOGHOUSE** –
– King of the doghouse / I don't know / Darling / Give myself to love / Isaac Ryan / Happy town / Wherever you go / Blue water / The fighter / Someone show me.

□ STEALER'S WHEEL (see under ⇒ RAFFERTY, Gerry)

STEELEYE SPAN

Formed: St. Albans, England . . . 1969 by ex-FAIRPORT CONVENTION bassist, ASHLEY HUTCHINGS, who teamed up with folk duos, MADDY PRIOR / TIM HART and GAY & TERRY WOODS. Under the direction of manager/producer Sandy Robertson, the outfit signed to 'R.C.A.' and recorded a debut album, 'HARK! THE VILLAGE WAIT' (1970). The record comprised largely of traditional reworkings, laying down a blueprint for the distinctive folk-rock hybrid which the group fashioned through the early to mid 70's. By the time sessions had begun on a follow-up, the WOODS had been replaced by PETER KNIGHT and the respected MARTIN CARTHY (the progenitor of the ever impressive

CARTHY folk dynasty), the resulting 'PLEASE TO SEE THE KING' (1971) and 'TEN MAN MOP OR MR. RESERVOIR BUTLER RIDES AGAIN' (1972) seeing the fruition of their experimentation with semi-electrified Olde England folk tunes like 'BLACKSMITH' and 'CAPTAIN COULSTON', the band also overhauling jigs and reels with merry abandon. 1972 saw major changes as CARTHY went solo and founder member, HUTCHINGS, pursued a more traditional folk vocation with The ALBION COUNTRY BAND. Rock scene veterans BOB JOHNSON and RICK KEMP were respectively recruited as replacements and the new-look 'SPAN signed to 'Chrysalis' for the 'BELOW THE SALT' (1972) album. Both this set and 1973's 'PARCEL OF ROGUES' saw the band further stretching the boundaries of the genre, the latter album making the UK Top 30 and even spawning a Top 20 Christmas hit in 'GAUDETTE'. With drummer NIGEL PEGRUM now on board, the band's more rock-centric dynamics were endearing them to a more mainstream audience, 'NOW WE ARE SIX' (1974) making the UK Top 20 and 'COMMONER'S CROWN' (1975) not far behind. It was 1975's Mike Batt-produced 'ALL AROUND MY HAT', however, that became the record most people associate with STEELEYE SPAN, both the album and Top 5 title track cementing the band's name in the public consciousness. Ironically, however, just as the band reached their commercial peak, they began to tread water artistically with the disappointing 'ROCKET COTTAGE' (1976). Even the return of CARTHY for 'STORM FORCE TEN' (1977) couldn't remedy matters and the band officially split in May '78. While the various members went on to further achievements in the folk scene, there were occasional STEELEYE SPAN reformations over the years, most significantly in 1989 with the 'TEMPTED AND TRIED' album. While MADDY PRIOR had more or less maintained a solo career simultaneously with STEELEYE SPAN (both with her TIM HART collaborations and the 1976 'SILLY SISTERS' project with JUNE TABOR), she went on to form the MADDY PRIOR band in the 80's, recording for various labels before going solo once more the following decade. The veteran folk-rockers inaugurated an uncharacteristically prolific spell in the second half of the 90's with 'TIME' (1996), a solid if forgettable album of largely traditional material which seemed to sum up the achievements of the band's latter day incarnations. 'HORKSTOW GRANGE' (1998) carried on where its predecessor left off, again relying on a stoic selection of public domain folk. Boosted by the return of DAVE MATTACKS, 'BEDLAM BORN' (2000) was a considerably stronger and more cohesive collection, its strident rock-centricity conjuring in the spirit of the original British folk-rock explosion without being overtly nostalgic. • **Songwriters:** All members through the years contributed their own songs; i.e. HUTCHINGS, PRIOR & HART, The WOODS, CARTHY, JOHNSON, etc. They also covered traditional Olde England folk tunes, reels and jigs, plus more regular classics RAVE ON (Buddy Holly) / GAUDETE (trad.Latin hymn) / TO KNOW HIM IS TO LOVE HIM (Teddy Bears) / TWINKLE TWINKLE LITTLE STAR (children's song) / etc. MADDY covered RAG DOLL (Four Seasons) / WHO'S SORRY NOW? (Connie Francis) / SWIMMING SONG (Loudon Wainwright III) / BOYS OF BEDLAM (Nick Jones-Dave Morgan) / WINTER WAKENETH (M.Kiszco). • **Trivia:** Their 1974 Top 20 album, 'NOW WE ARE SIX', was produced by IAN ANDERSON (Jethro Tull), and featured DAVID BOWIE playing sax solo on track, 'TO KNOW HIM IS TO LOVE HIM'. Their following album 'COMMONER'S CROWN', saw actor PETER SELLERS play ukelele on 'NEW YORK GIRLS'.

Album rating: HARK! THE VILLAGE WAIT (*7) / PLEASE TO SEE THE KING (*7) / TEN MAN MOP (OR MR. RESERVOIR BUTLER STRIKES AGAIN) (*5) / INDIVIDUALLY AND COLLECTIVELY compilation (*6) / BELOW THE SALT (*8) / PARCEL OF ROGUES (*6) / NOW WE ARE SIX (*8) / COMMONER'S CROWN (*5) / ALL AROUND MY HAT (*6) / ROCKET COTTAGE (*4) / ORIGINAL MASTERS compilation (*7) / STORM FORCE TEN (*5) / LIVE AT LAST (*4) / SAILS OF SILVER (*5) / THE BEST OF STEELEYE SPAN compilation (*7) / BACK IN LINE (*5) / TEMPTED AND TRIED (*5) / TIME (*4) / HORKSTOW GRANGE (*5)

MADDY PRIOR (b.14 Aug'47, Blackpool, England) – vocals / **TIM HART** (b. 9 Jan'48, Lincoln, England) – guitar, vocals / **GAY WOODS** – vocals, concertina / **ASHLEY HUTCHINGS** (b. ? Jan'45, London) – bass (ex-FAIRPORT CONVENTION) / **TERRY WOODS** – guitar, vocals with guest drummers **GERRY CONWAY + DAVE MATTACKS**

R.C.A. Chrysalis

Jun 70. (lp) *(SF 8133)* **HARK! THE VILLAGE WAIT** [ ] 1976 [ ]
– A calling – On song / The blacksmith / Fisherman's wife / Blackleg miner / Dark-eyed sailor / Copshawholme fair / All things are quite silent / The hills of Greenmore / My Johnny was a shoemaker / Lowlands of Holland / Twa corbies / One night as I lay on my bed. *(re-iss. Mar76 on 'Mooncrest'; CREST 22) (re-iss. Jan91 lp/cd; CREST/+CD 003)*

— **MARTIN CARTHY** (b.21 May'41, Hatfield, England) – electric guitar / **PETER KNIGHT** – fiddle repl. TERRY & GAY who formed own self-named duo.

B&C Chrysalis

Mar 71. (lp) *(CAS 1029)* **PLEASE TO SEE THE KING** [45] 1976 [–]
– Blacksmith / Cold, haily, windy night / Bryan O'Lynn (jig) / The hag with the money / Prince Charlie Stuart / Boys of Bedlam / False knight on the road / The lark in the morning / Female drummer / The king / Lonely on the water. *(re-iss. Mar76 on 'Mooncrest'; CREST 8) (re-iss. Mar91 lp/cd; CREST/+CD 003)*

Oct 71. (7") *(CB 164)* **RAVE ON. / REELS / FEMALE DRUMMER** [ ] [–]

Pegasus Chrysalis

Jan 72. (lp) *(PEG 9)* **TEN MAN MOP (OR MR. RESERVOIR STRIKES AGAIN)** [ ] 1976 [–]
– Marrowbones / Captain Coulston / Reels: Dowd's favourite – 10 float – The morning dew / Wee weaver / Skewball / Gower wassail / Jigs: Paddy Clancy's jig – Willie Clancy's fancy / Four nights drunk / When I was on horseback. *(re-iss. Aug91 on 'Mooncrest' lp/cd; CREST/+CD 009)*

— **BOB JOHNSON** – guitar, vocals repl. CARTHY who went solo / **RICK KEMP** (b.15 Nov'41) – bass repl. HUTCHINGS who joined ALBION COUNTRY BAND

Chrysalis Chrysalis

Aug 72. (lp/c) *(<CHR/ZCCHR 1008>)* **BELOW THE SALT** [43] [ ]
– Spotted cow / Rosebuds in June / Jigs / Sheepcrook and black dog / Royal forester / King Henry / John Barleycorn / Saucy sailor. *(cd-iss. Jan97 on 'Beat Goes On'; BGOCD 324)*

Sep 72. (7") *(CHS 2005)* **JOHN BARLEYCORN. / JIGS** [ ] [–]

Nov 73. (7") **GAUDETTE. / ROYAL FORESTER** [–] [ ]

Apr 73. (lp/c) *(<CHR/ZCCHR 1046>)* **PARCEL OF ROGUES** [26] [ ]
– Alison Gross / One misty moisty morning / The bold poacher / The ups and downs / Robbery with violins / The wee wee man / Cam ye o'er fae France / The weaver and the factory maid / Rogues in a nation / Hares on a mountain. *(cd-iss. Dec96 on 'Beat Goes On'; BGOCD 323)*

Nov 73. (7") *(CHS 2026)* **GAUDETE. / THE HOLLY & THE IVY** [14] [ ]

— **PRIOR, HART, KNIGHT, JOHNSON + KEMP** added **NIGEL PEGRUM** – drums, percussion

Feb 74. (lp/c) *(<CHR/ZCCHR 1053>)* **NOW WE ARE SIX** [13] [ ]
– Thomas the rhymer / Two magicians / Edwin / Twinkle twinkle little star / Seven hundred elves / The mooncoin jig / Drink down the Moon / Long a-growing / Now we are six / To know him is to love him. *(cd-iss. Jun91 on 'Beat Goes On'; BGOCD 157)*

Feb 74. (7") *(CHS 2026)* **THOMAS THE RHYMER. / THE MOONCOIN JIG** [ ] [ ]

Jan 75. (lp/c) *(<CHR/ZCCHR 1071>)* **COMMONER'S CROWN** [21] [ ]
– Little Sir Hugh / Bach goes to Limerick / Long Lankin / Dogs and ferrets / Galtee farmer / Demon lover / Elf call / Weary cutters / New York girls. *(cd-iss/Sep96 on 'Beat Goes On'; BGOCD 315)*

Mar 75. (7") *(CHS 2061)* **NEW YORK GIRLS. / TWO MAGICIANS** [ ] [ ]

Oct 75. (7") *(CHS 2078)* **ALL AROUND MY HAT. / BLACK JACK DAVY** [5] [ ]

Oct 75. (lp/c) *(<CHR/ZCCHR 1091>)* **ALL AROUND MY HAT** [7] [ ]
– Black Jack Davy / Hard times of old England / Cadgwith anthem / Sum waves (tunes) / The wife of Usher's Well / Gamble gold (Robin Hood) / All

around my hat / Dance with me / Batchelor's hall. *(re-iss. Jul85 on 'M.F.P.'; 41-57061) (re-iss. Dec92 on 'Beat Goes On'; BGOCD 158) (cd re-iss. Mar94 on 'E.M.I.'; CDP 828785-2) (cd re-iss. Mar96; CDGOLD 1009)*

Jan 76. (7") *(CHS 2085)* **HARD TIMES OF OLD ENGLAND. / CADGWITH ANTHEM**

Sep 76. (7") *(CHS 2107)* **LONDON. / SLIGO MAID**

Oct 76. (lp/c) *(<CHR/ZCCHR 1123>)* **ROCKET COTTAGE** 41
– London / The Bosnian hornpipes / Orfeo / Nathan's reel / The twelve witches / The brown girls / Fighting for strangers / Sligo maid / Sir James the rose / The drunkard. *(cd-iss. Oct96 on 'Beat Goes on'; BGOCD 318)*

Nov 76. (7") *(CHS 2125)* **FIGHTING FOR STRANGERS. / THE BOSNIAN HORNPIPES**

— **MARTIN CARTHY** – guitar, vocals returned to repl. JOHNSON / **JOHN KIRKPATRICK** – accordion repl. KNIGHT who formed duo with JOHNSON. They made one album 'KING OF ELFLAND'S DAUGHTER' in 1978 for 'Chrysalis'.

Nov 77. (7") *(CHS 2192)* **THE BOAR'S HEAD CAROL. / GAUDETE / SOME RIVAL** –

Nov 77. (lp/c) *(<CHR/ZCCHR 1151>)* **STORM FORCE TEN** –
– Awake, awake / Sweep, chimney sweep / The wife of the soldier / The victory / The black freighter / Some rival / Treadmill song / Seventeen come Sunday. *(cd-iss. Apr97 on 'Beat Goes On'; BGOCD 337)*

Nov 78. (lp/c) *(<CHR/ZCCHR 1199>)* **LIVE AT LAST! (live)**
– The Atholl highlanders / Walter Bulwer's polka / Saucy sailor / The black freighter / The maid and the palmer / Hunting the wren / Montrose / Bonnets so blue / The false knight on the road. *(cd-iss. Apr97 on 'Beat Goes On'; BGOCD 342)*

Nov 78. (7") **RAG DOLL. / HUNTING THE WREN** –

— Split May '78 until reformation 1980, **KNIGHT & JOHNSON** returned 1974 line-up

Chrysalis Tacoma

Nov 80. (7") *(CHS 2479)* **SAILS OF SILVER. / SENIOR SERVICE** –

Nov 80. (lp/c) *(<CHR/ZCCHR 1304>)* **SAILS OF SILVER**
– Sails of silver / My love / Barnet fair / Senior service / Gone to America / Where are they now / Let her go now / Longbone / Marigold – Harvest home / Tell me why.

Feb 81. (7") *(CHS 2503)* **GONE TO AMERICA. / LET HER GO DOWN** –

— Disbanded 1981, MADDY PRIOR and TIM HART continued with solo work.

— **STEELEYE SPAN** returned sporadically in the 80's now without HART.

Flutterby Shanachie

Nov 85. (7") *(FLUT 1)* **SOMEWHERE IN LONDON. / LANERCROST** –

May 86. (lp) *(FLUT 2)* *<79063>* **BACK IN LINE**
– Edward / Lanercrost / Lady Diamond / Isabel / A cannon by Telemann / Blackleg miner / Peace on the border / Scarecrow / Take my heart / White man. *(cd re-iss. Aug91 on 'Park'+=; PRKCD 8)* – Spotted cow / One misty moisty morning.

— added **TIM HARRIES** – bass; repl. KEMP

Apr 89. (7") *(FLUT 3)* **PADSTOW. / REDS: THE FIRST HOUSE IN CONNAUGHT – SAILOR'S BONNET** –

Sep 89. (7") *(FLUT 4)* **FOLLOWING ME. / TWO BUTCHERS** –

Dover-Chrysalis Shanachie

Sep 89. (lp/cd) *(ADD/CCD 9)* *<64020>* **TEMPTED AND TRIED**
– Padstow / The fox / Two butchers / Following me / Seagull / The cruel mother / Jack Hall / Searching for lambs / Shaking of the sheets / Reels: The first house in Connaught – Sailor's bonnet – Betsy Bell and Mary Gray.

Park Shanachie

Sep 92. (cd/lp) *(PRK CD/M 010)* *<79080>* **TONIGHT'S THE NIGHT, LIVE (live)**
– Tonight's the night / Ca; the ewes / Gentleman soldier / Tam Lin / Padstow / Fighting for strangers / White man / Weaver / Ten long years / Dawn of the day / Cam ye o'er frae France / All around my hat.

— **GAY WOODS** re-joined

Mar 96. (cd/c) *(PRK CD/MC 34)* *<79099>* **TIME**
– The prickly bush / The old maid in the Garrett (b. Tam Lin (reel)) / Harvest of the moon / Underneath her apron / The Cutty Wren / Go from my window / The elf-knight / The water is wide / You will burn / Corbies / The song will remain.

— In the same year, MADDY augmented STATUS QUO on their version of 'ALL AROUND MY HAT'.

Park Park

Sep 98. (cd/c) *(<PRK CD/MC 44>)* **HORKSTOW GRANGE** May99
– The old turf fire / The tricks of London / Horkstow Grange / Lord Randall / Erin / Queen Mary – Hunsden House / Bonny birdy / Bonny Irish boy / I wish that I never was wed / Austalia / One true love / The parting glass.

Oct 00. (cd) *(<PRKCD 55>)* **BEDLAM BORN**
– Well done liar / Who told the butcher / John of Ditchford / I see his blood upon the rose / Black swan / The beggar / Poor old soldier / Arbour / There was a wealthy merchant / Beyond the dreaming place / We poor labouring men / The Connemara cradle song / Stephen / The white cliffs of Dover.

– compilations, others, etc. –

1972. (lp) *Charisma; (CS 5)* **INDIVIDUALLY AND COLLECTIVELY** –

Sep 76. (7") *Mooncrest; (MOON 50)* **RAVE ON. / FALSE KNIGHT ON THE ROAD** –

1977. (d-lp) *Mooncrest; (CRD 1)* **TIMESPAN** –

May 77. (d-lp) *Chrysalis; (CJT 3)* **ORIGINAL MASTERS** –
(cd-iss. Jan97 on 'Beat Goes On'; BGOCD 322)

Nov 82. (7"ep) *Chrysalis; (CHS 2658)* **ALL AROUND MY HAT / FIGHTING FOR STRANGERS. / GAUDETE / BOAR'S HEAD CAROL** –

Dec 82. (d-c) *Chrysalis;* **ALL AROUND MY HAT / ROCKET COTTAGE** –

Mar 84. (lp/c) *Chrysalis; (CHR/ZCCHR 1467)* **THE BEST OF STEELEYE SPAN** –
(cd-iss. Jul85; CCD 1467)

Oct 88. (d-lp/c/cd) *Chrysalis; (CNW 7)* **PORTFOLIO** –

Nov 79. (c) *Folktracks;* **FOLK ELECTRIC FOLK** –

May 80. (lp) *Hallmark; (SHM 3040)* **STEELEYE SPAN** –

1980. (7") *P.E.L.;* **JIGS AND REELS (REELS MEDLEY). / ('A'version)** –

Sep 84. (d-lp/d-c) *Cambra; (CR 5154)* **STEELEYE SPAN** –

Feb 87. (7") *Old Gold; (OG 9690)* **ALL AROUND MY HAT. / GAUDETE** –

Apr 89. (d-lp/c/cd) *Connoisseur; (VSOP LP/MC/CD 132)* **EARLY YEARS** –

Apr 90. (cd) *Action Replay; (CDAR 1012)* **THE BEST OF AND THE REST OF STEELEYE SPAN** –

Aug 91. (cd/c) *Castle; (CCS CD/MC 292)* **THE COLLECTION** –
– Thomas the rhymer / Alison Gross / John Barleycorn / King Henry / One misty moisty morning / The mooncoin jig / Long Lankin / The fox / Shaking of the sheets / Rougues in a nation / Galtee farmer / All around my hat / Sailor's bonnet / Black Jack Davy / Gaudete / Seven hundred elves / Sligo maid / Following me / Robbery with violins / Seventeen come Sunday.

Nov 94. (cd) *Park; (PRKCD 027)* **THE COLLECTION: STEELEYE SPAN IN CONCERT (live)** –

Mar 95. (d-cd) *Chrysalis; (CDCHR 6093)* **SPANNING THE YEARS** –

Sep 96. (cd) *Mooncrest; (CRESTCD 022)* **THE KING: THE BEST OF STEELEYE SPAN** –

Sep 96. (cd) *Emporio; (EMPRCD 668)* **A STACK OF STEELEYE SPAN** –

Nov 99. (d-cd) *Park; (<PRKCD 52>)* **THE JOURNEY (live)** Sep01

Aug 03. (d-cd) *Castle; (CMDDD 781)* **THE LARK IN THE MORNING: THE EARLY YEARS**

STEELY DAN

Formed: New York, USA . . . by DONALD FAGEN and WALTER BECKER, initially as a writing partnership after leaving Bard's college in 1969. At the turn of the decade the pair toured with JAY & THE AMERICANS as backing musicians as well as recording a soundtrack for the movie, 'YOU GOTTA WALK IT LIKE YOU TALK IT' (starring Richard Pryor). Attempts to hawk their songs to Big Apple publishers proved fruitless however and it was only through meeting independent producer Gary Katz that the duo found their way into a staff job at L.A.'s 'Dunhill-

ABC' label. Katz was also the catalyst for what would become STEELY DAN, a studio outfit comprising FAGEN, BECKER, vocalist DAVID PALMER, DENNY DIAS (a rhythm guitarist with whom they'd previously recorded early demos), ex-HOLY MODAL ROUNDERS guitarist, JEFF 'SKUNK' BAXTER and drummer JIM HODDER, famously naming themselves after a steam-powered(!) dildo in William Burroughs' novel, 'Naked Lunch'. Although a debut single, 'DALLAS', made little impact, the simmering latin-funk rock of 'DO IT AGAIN' made the US Top 10. It also introduced FAGEN's inimitable lyrical wit, a cynical DLYAN-esque worldview which mocked L.A.'s pretensions and would see STEELY DAN hailed as one of the most cuttingly accurate commentators of the 70's. 'CAN'T BUY A THRILL' (1973) nailed the point home with consummate ease, laying down the jazz-rooted, FM-slick blueprint that was endlessly tweaked, polished and perfected with each successive album. The enduring 'REELIN' IN THE YEARS' was lifted as a second single and gave the group another major hit, the track's searing guitar solo, as with 'KINGS', provided by session man, ELLIOTT RANDALL; if there was one critical niggle it was that PALMER couldn't always carry the subtle insinuations of the lyrics. BECKER and FAGEN subsequently took up the task themselves on 'COUNTDOWN TO ECSTACY' (1973), combining even more opaque themes with densely layered, immaculately executed musicianship. Without the help of a hit single, however, the record only just made the Top 40; 'RIKKI DON'T LOSE THAT NUMBER' redressed the balance in fine style, a gorgeously lovelorn Top 5 hit inspired by a HORACE SILVER piano riff and a track which formed the centrepiece of 'PRETZEL LOGIC' (1974). More obviously jazz-influenced (included was a droll cover of Duke Ellington's 'EAST ST. LOUIS TOODLE-OO', while 'PARKER'S BAND' was a tribute to be-bop legend, CHARLIE PARKER) yet more immediately accessible, the album further enhanced their reputation among rock/pop connoiseurs. And it was a reputation that mushroomed without the PR of touring, BECKER and FAGEN refusing to play live after 1974 – although a tour was planned to promote the forthcoming 'KATY LIED' (1975), the idea was abandoned in its early stages. With STEELY DAN now basically a studio entity, both HODDER and BAXTER departed, the latter joining The DOOBIE BROTHERS (ironically enough, an easy rocking, all-American, all-touring hit machine that was essentially the antithesis of the whole SD concept). Coincidentally, BAXTER's replacement was MICHAEL McDONALD, a silky voiced future DOOBIES mentor whose harmony vocals helped sweeten the bite of the aforementioned 'KATY..'. 1976's 'THE ROYAL SCAM' was even more scathing in its lyrical ferocity, taking no prisoners in its portrayal of American society's inherent hypocrisy and monetary greed. But if the sentiments were getting darker, the music was getting slicker; by this point, BECKER and FAGEN were employing the cream of the city's session musicians, recording 'AJA' (1977) in numerous different studios and endlessly remixing it prior to release. Painstakingly crafted but rarely overdone, 'AJA' – for many fans and critics alike – remains the definitive STEELY DAN opus, its dense, lush arrangements rewarding repeated listening. It was also their best seller, a transatlantic Top 5 (at the height of punk in the UK) later plundered by hip hopper's DE LA SOUL ('PEG'), Scotland's very own DEACON BLUE even taking their name from one of its tracks. With 'A.B.C.' coming under the auspices of 'M.C.A.', legal problems led to a three year wait for the final album of STEELY DAN's career, 'GAUCHO' (1980). Criticised for what many detractors saw as cloying slickness, the record was nevertheless another masterstroke of detached observation; the likes of 'BABYLON SISTERS' and 'GLAMOUR PROFESSION' were aimed squarely at the decadence of L.A.'s showbiz elite while 'THIRD WORLD MAN' remains one of the most haunting STEELY DAN compositions. After more than a decade of living in each other's pocket, BECKER and FAGAN parted company; while BECKER went into production, FAGAN penned a solo masterpiece in 'THE NIGHTFLY' (1982), trading in irony for surprisingly upbeat youthful reminiscences. The album's critical and commercial success didn't seem to spur him on to further glories, however, an incredible eleven year gap preceding a belated 90's follow-up, 'KAMAKIRIAD'. FAGAN returned BECKER's production favour on the latter's one and only solo effort, 'ELEVEN TRACKS OF WHACK' (1994), a hard-bitten affair borne of the kind of narcotic strife which would've finished a lesser talent. After appearing live as part of the New York Rock and Soul Revue in the early 90's, BECKER and FAGEN finally reformed STEELY DAN for a series of feverishly anticipated US live dates. Documented on 1995's 'ALIVE IN AMERICA' alive, the tour was an unqualified success despite the duo's misgivings. As the success of the live shows might've predicted, fresh studio set 'TWO AGAINST NATURE' (2000) was a belated comeback well worth waiting for. All the STEELY DAN trademarks – painstakingly crafted arrangements, luxuriant sonic textures, obliquely witty lyrics – were in present and correct, BECKER and FAGEN sounding like their partnership hadn't been interrupted for a single day never mind two decades. Like almost all their works, this was also an album which rewarded the repeated listening necessary to uncover the manifold layers of subtle meaning, shading and tone. Thankfully, fans didn't have to wait another generation for the release of a second latter day studio set. Basically, 'EVERYTHING MUST GO' (2003) continued in a similar vein to its predecessor (it also had nothing whatsoever to do with the MANIC STREET PREACHERS), albeit with a more relaxed vibe and production than any album in their immaculately crafted career. BECKER even made his lead vocal debut, more than thirty years after starting the band, an interesting development even if it was never going to threaten FAGEN's still masterfully insinuating croon.

• **Trivia:** In 1985, BECKER produced CHINA CRISIS' album 'Flaunt The Imperfection'.

Album rating: CAN'T BUY A THRILL (*8) / COUNTDOWN TO ECSTASY (*8) / PRETZEL LOGIC (*9) / KATY LIED (*8) / THE ROYAL SCAM (*6) / AJA (*8) / GREATEST HITS compilation (*9) / GAUCHO (*6) / STEELY DAN GOLD compilation (*8) / REELIN' IN THE YEARS – THE VERY BEST compilation (*9) / ALIVE IN AMERICA (*4) / TWO AGAINST NATURE (*8) / EVERYTHING MUST GO (*6) / Donald Fagen: THE NIGHTFLY (*6) / KAMAKIRIAD (*7) / Walter Becker: ELEVEN TRACKS OF WHACK (*5)

DONALD FAGEN (b.10 Jan'48, Passaic, New Jersey) – keyboards, vocals / **WALTER BECKER** (b.20 Feb'50, New York) – bass, vocals / **DAVID PALMER** – vocals (ex-MIDDLE CLASS) / **DENNY DIAS** – rhythm guitar / **JEFF BAXTER** – guitar (ex-HOLY MODAL ROUNDERS) / **JIM HODDER** – drums (ex-BEAD GAME)

		Probe	A.B.C.
Sep 72.	(7") *(PRO 562)* <11323> **DALLAS. / SAIL THE WATERWAY**	☐	☐
Nov 72.	(7") *(PRO 577)* <11338> **DO IT AGAIN. / FIRE IN THE HOLE**	☐	6
	(re-iss. Sep75 on 'A.B.C.'; 4075); hit UK No.39		
Jan 73.	(lp) *(SPB 1062)* <758> **CAN'T BUY A THRILL**	☐	Nov72 17
	– Do it again / Dirty work / Kings / Midnite cruiser / Only a fool would say that / Reeling in the years / Fire in the hole / Brooklyn (owes the charmer and me) / Change of the guard / Turn that heartbreak over again. *(re-iss. Sep75 on 'A.B.C.' lp/c; ABCL/+C 5034); hit UK No.38) (re-iss. 1983 on 'M.C.A.' lp/c; MCL/+C 1769) (cd-iss. Jul88; DMCL 1769) (cd re-iss. Apr92; MCLD 19017) (cd re-iss. Mar00 on 'M.C.A.'; 111886-2)*		
Mar 73.	(7") *(PRO 587)* <11352> **REELING IN THE YEARS. / ONLY A FOOL WOULD SAY THAT**	☐	11

— **BECKER & FAGEN** now on lead vocals, when PALMER left to BIG WHA-KOO

Jul 73. (7") *(PRO 602)* *<11382>* **SHOWBIZ KIDS. / RAZOR BOY** ☐ 61

Jul 73. (lp) *(SPB 1079)* *<779>* **COUNTDOWN TO ECSTACY** ☐ 35
– Bodhizattva / Razor boy / The Boston rag / Your gold teeth / Showbiz kids / My old school / Pearl of the quarter / King of the world. *(re-iss. Feb82 on 'M.C.A.' lp/c; MCL/+C 1654) (re-iss. Jul83 on 'Fame' lp/c; FA/TC-FA 3069) (cd-iss. Dec88; DMCL 1654) (cd re-iss. Apr92; MCLD 19018) (cd re-iss. Mar00 on 'M.C.A.'; 111887-2)*

Oct 73. (7") *(PRO 606)* *<11396>* **MY OLD SCHOOL. / PEARL OF THE QUARTER** ☐ 63

Mar 74. (lp) *(SPBA 6282)* *<808>* **PRETZEL LOGIC** 37 8
– Rikki don't lose that number / Night by night / Any major dude will tell you / Barrytown / East St.Louis toodle-oo / Parker's bad / Through with buzz / Pretzel logic / With a gun / Charlie Freak / Monkey in your soul. *(re-iss. Oct74 on 'A.B.C.' lp/c; ABCL/+C 5045) (re-iss. Feb84 on 'M.C.A.' lp/c; MCL/+C 1781) (cd-iss. Aug88 on 'M.C.A.; DIDX 371) (cd re-iss. May90; DMCL 1781) (cd re-iss. Jun92; MCLD 19081) (cd re-iss. Mar00 on 'M.C.A.'; 111917-2)*

May 74. (7") *(PRO 622)* *<11439>* **RIKKI DON'T LOSE THAT NUMBER. / ANY MAJOR DUDE WILL TELL YOU** ☐ 4
(re-iss. Oct78 on 'A.B.C.'; ABC 4241); hit UK No.58

A.B.C. A.B.C.

Oct 74. (7") *(ABC 4019)* *<12033>* **PRETZEL LOGIC. / THROUGH WITH BUZZ** ☐ 57

—— **MICHAEL McDONALD** (b.12 Feb'52, St. Louis, Missouri) – keyboards, vocals repl. BAXTER to DOOBIE BROTHERS / **JEFF PORCARO** (b. 1 Apr'54) – drums repl. HODDER

Apr 75. (lp/c) *(ABCL/+C 5094)* *<846>* **KATY LIED** 13 13
– Black Friday / Bad sneakers / Rose darling / Daddy don't live in that New York City no more / Doctor Wu / Everyone's gone to the movies / Your gold teeth II / Chain lightning / Any world (that I'm welcome to) / Throw back the little ones. *(re-iss. Jun84 on 'M.C.A.' lp/c; MCL/+C 1800) (cd-iss. Aug88; DIDX 373) (cd re-iss. Sep90 & Jun92; MCLD 19082) (cd re-iss. Mar00 on 'M.C.A.'; 111916-2)*

May 75. (7") *(ABC 4058)* *<12101>* **BLACK FRIDAY. / THROW BACK THE LITTLE ONES** ☐ 37

Sep 75. (7") *<12128>* **BAD SNEAKERS. / CHAIN LIGHTNING** – ☐

—— When McDONALD joined DOOBIE BROTHERS and PORCARO left later joining TOTO, **BECKER & FAGEN** employed session people incl. **DENNY DIAS** part-time

May 76. (lp/c) *(ABCL/+C 5161>* **THE ROYAL SCAM** 11 15
– Kid Charlemagne / Caves of Altamira / Don't take me alive / Sign in stranger / The fez / Green earrings / Haitian divorce / Everything you did / The royal scam. *(re-iss. Sep82 on 'M.C.A.' lp/c; MCL/+C 1708) (cd-iss. Aug88; DIDX 370) (cd re-iss. Sep91 & Jun92; MCLD 19083) (cd re-iss. Apr00 on 'M.C.A.'; 811708-2)*

May 76. (7") *(ABC 4124)* *<12195>* **KID CHARLEMAGNE. / GREEN EARRINGS** ☐ 82

Sep 76. (7") *<12222>* **THE FEZ. / SIGN IN STRANGER** – 59

Nov 76. (7") *(ABC 4152)* **HAITIAN DIVORCE. / SIGN IN STRANGER** 17 –

Sep 77. (lp/c) *(ABCL/+C 5225)* *<1006>* **AJA** 5 3
– Black cow / Aja / Deacon blues / Peg / Home at last / I got the news / Josie. *(re-iss. 1983 on 'M.C.A.' lp/c; MCL/+C 1745) (cd-iss. 1985; DIDX 55) (cd re-iss. Sep91 & Jul92; MCLD 19145) (cd re-iss. Apr00 on 'M.C.A.'; 811745-2)*

Nov 77. (7") *(ABC 4207)* *<12320>* **PEG. / I GOT THE NEWS** ☐ 11

Apr 78. (7"/12") *(ABC/+12 4217)* *<12355>* **DEACON BLUES. / HOME AT LAST** ☐ Mar78 19

Aug 78. (7") *<12404>* **JOSIE. / BLACK COW** – 26

M.C.A. M.C.A.

Jul 78. (7") *(MCA 374)* *<40894>* **FM (NO STATIC AT ALL). / FM (Reprise)** 49 Jun78 22

Nov 80. (lp/c) *(ABCD/+C 616)* *<6102>* **GAUCHO** 27 9
– Babylon sisters / Hey nineteen / Glamour profession / Gaucho / Time out of mind / My rival / Third world man. *(cd-iss. Jan85; DIDX 56) (re-iss. Sep86 lp/c; MCL/+C 1814) (cd re-iss. Sep91 & Jul92; MCLD 19146)*

Nov 80. (7") *(MCA 659)* *<51036>* **HEY NINETEEN. / BODHISATTVA (live)** ☐ 10

Mar 81. (7") *(MCA 680)* **BABYLON SISTERS. / TIME OUT OF MIND** ☐ –

Mar 81. (7") *<51082>* **TIME OUT OF MIND. / BODHISATTVA** – 22

—— Parted ways after album. FAGEN went solo and BECKER to production.

DONALD FAGEN

Warners Warners

Oct 82. (lp/c) *(923696-1/-4)* *<23696>* **THE NIGHTFLY** 44 11
– New frontier / Walk between the raindrops / Maxine / Green flower street / The goodbye look / The nightfly / I.G.Y. (what a wonderful world). *(cd-iss. Jul88; 923696-2)*

Oct 82. (7") *(W 9900)* *<29900>* **I.G.Y. (WHAT A WONDERFUL WORLD). / WALK BETWEEN THE RAINDROPS** ☐ 26

Jan 83. (7") *(W 9792)* *<29792>* **NEW FRONTIER. / MAXINE** ☐ 70
(12"+=) *(W 9792T)* – The goodbye look.

Apr 83. (7") *(W 9674)* **RUBY BABY. / WALK BETWEEN THE RAINDROPS** ☐ –
(below single from the film 'Bright Lights, Big City')

Apr 88. (7") *(W 7972)* *<27972>* **CENTURY'S END. / SHANGHAI CONFIDENTIAL (instrumental)** ☐ Mar88 83
(3"cd-s+=) *(W 7972CD)* – The nightfly / The goodbye look.

—— with **WALTER BECKER** – bass, solo guitar, co-writer some / **GEORGE WADENIUS** – guitar / **PAUL GRIFFIN** – hamond organ / **LEROY CLOUDEN or CHRISTOPHER PARKER** – drums / **BASHIRI JOHNSON** – percussion / **RANDY BRECKER + others** – horns

Reprise Reprise

May 93. (cd/c/lp) *<(9362 45230-2/-4/-1)>* **KAMAKIRIAD** 3 10
– Trans-island skyway / Countermoon / Springtime / Snowbound / Tomorrow's girls / Florida room / On the dunes / Teahouse on the tracks.

Jun 93. (7"/c-s) *(W 0180/+C)* **TOMORROW'S GIRL. / SHANGHAI CONFIDENTIAL** 46 ☐
(cd-s+=) *(W 0180CDX)* – Confide in me.

Aug 93. (7"/c-s) *(WO 196/+C)* **TRANS-ISLAND SKYWAY. / BIG NOISE, NEW YORK** ☐ ☐
(12"+=/cd-s+=) *(WO 196 T/CD)* – Home at last (live).

Nov 93. (7"/c-s) *(W 0216/+C)* **SNOWBOUND. / TRANS-ISLAND SKYWAY** ☐ ☐
(cd-s+=) *(W 0216CD)* – ('A'mix).

WALTER BECKER

Giant-RCA Giant

Nov 94. (cd/c) *<(74321 22609-2/-4)>* **ELEVEN TRACKS OF WHACK** ☐ ☐
– Down in the bottom / Junkie girl / Surf and or die / Book of liars / Lucky Henry / Hard up case / Cringemaker / Girlfriend / My Waterloo / This moody bastard / Hat too flat.

STEELY DAN

—— duo re-formed for live appearances in the States. They had featured on V/A album 'Live At The Beacon' with The NEW YORK ROCK AND SOUL REVUE

Giant-RCA Giant

Oct 95. (cd/c) *(74321 28691-2/-4)* *<24634>* **ALIVE IN AMERICA (live 1994)** 62 40
– Babylon sister / Green earrings / Bodhisattva / Reelin' in the years / Josie / Book of liars / Peg / Third World man / Kid Charlemagne / Sign in stranger / Aja.

Feb 00. (cd) *(74321 62190-2)* *<24719>* **TWO AGAINST NATURE** 11 6
– Gaslighting Abbie / What a shame about me / Two against nature / Janie runaway / Almost gothic / Jack of speed / Cousin Dupree / Negative girl / West of Hollywood.

Reprise Reprise

Jun 03. (cd/lp) *<(9362 48435-2/-1)>* **EVERYTHING MUST GO** 21 9
– The last mall / Things I miss the most / Blues beach / Godwhacker / Slang of ages / Green book / Pixeleen / Lunch with Gina / Everything must go.

– compilations, others, etc. –

on 'M.C.A.' unless otherwise mentioned

Jan 78. (12"ep) A.B.C.; *(ABE 12-003)* **+ FOUR** ☐ –
– Do it again / Haitian divorce / Dallas / Sail the waterway.

Mar 78. (lp; by BECKER & FAGEN) *Spark; (SRLP 124) <Visa; 7005>* **YOU GOTTA WALK IT (Film Soundtrack)** ☐ 1971 ☐
(cd-iss. Sep92 on 'See For Miles')

Nov 78. (d-lp/c) A.B.C.; *(ABCD/+C 616)* *<1107>* **GREATEST HITS 1972-78** 41 30
(re-iss. Mar82 on 'M.C.A.'; MCLD/+C 608)

Apr 82.	(d-c) *(MCA2 101)* **CAN'T BUY A THRILL / AJA**		–
Jun 82.	(lp/c) *(MCF/+C 3145) <5324>* **GOLD** (w/ free-12") *(re-iss. Aug91 cd/c; MCAD 10387)*	44	
Jul 82.	(7") *(MCA 786)* **FM (NO STATIC AT ALL). / FM (REPRISE)** (12"+=) *(MCAT 786)* – East St. Louis toodle-oo.		–
Apr 83.	(7") *Old Gold; (OG 9321)* **DO IT AGAIN. / RIKKI DON'T LOSE THAT NUMBER**		–
Oct 83.	(d-c) *(MCA2 109)* **KATY LIED / THE ROYAL SCAM**		–
Dec 83.	(12"ep) *(MCAT 852)* **HAITIAN DIVORCE / DO IT AGAIN. / REELING IN THE YEARS / RIKKI DON'T LOSE THAT NUMBER**		–
Mar 84.	(lp) *Aero; <ML 8101>* **THE EARLY YEARS – WALTER BECKER & DONALD FAGEN**	–	
Sep 84.	(d-c) *(MCA2 115)* **COUNTDOWN TO ECSTACY / PRETZEL LOGIC**		–
Aug 85.	(cd) *(DIDX 306)* **DECADE OF STEELY DAN – THE BEST OF STEELY DAN**		
Oct 85.	(lp/c) *(DAN TV/TC 1)* **REELIN' IN THE YEARS – THE VERY BEST OF STEELY DAN** – Do it again / Reelin' in the years / My old school / Bodhisattva / Show biz kids / Rikki don't lose that number / Pretzel logic / Black Friday / Bad sneakers / Doctor Wu / Haitian divorce / Kid Charlemagne / The fez / Peg / Josie / Deacon blues / Hey nineteen / Babylon sisters. *(re-iss. Dec92 d-cd/c; MCLD/MCLC 19147)*	43	–
Nov 85.	(7") *(MSAM 32)* **REELING IN THE YEARS. / RIKKI DON'T LOSE THAT NUMBER**		–
Apr 86.	(c) *Showcase; (SHTC 128)* **SUN MOUNTAIN** (early demos) *(cd-iss. Oct92 on 'Thunderbolt'; CDTB 139)*		–
May 86.	(lp)(cd) *Bellaphon; (230-07-065)(288 07014)* **BERRYTOWN** (demos)	– German	–
May 87.	(lp/c/cd) *Thunderbolt; (THBL/THBL/CDTB 040)* **OLD REGIME** (early material) *(re-iss. Mar94 on 'Prestige' cd/c;)*		–
Oct 87.	(7") *(MCA 1214)* **RIKKI DON'T LOSE THAT NUMBER. / DO IT AGAIN**		–
Oct 87.	(lp/c/cd) *Telstar; (STAR/STAC/TCD 2297)* **DO IT AGAIN – THE VERY BEST OF STEELY DAN**	64	–
Apr 88.	(lp)cd) *Thunderbolt; (THBL 054)(CDTB 056)* **STONE PIANO** (early material)		–
Jun 88.	(d-lp) *Castle; (CCSLP 193)* **BECKER AND FAGEN – THE COLLECTION** *(cd-iss. Nov93; CLACD 365)*		–
Jul 93.	(cd/c) *Charly; (CD CD/MC 116)* **ROARING OF THE LAMB**		–
Sep 93.	(cd/c; as WALTER BECKER & DONALD FAGEN) *Remember; (RMB 7/4 5004)* **FOUNDERS OF STEELY DAN**		–
Nov 93.	(cd/c) *(MCD/MCC 10967)* **REMASTERED – THE BEST OF STEELY DAN**	49	
Dec 93.	(4xcd-box) *(MCAD 410981)* **CITIZEN STEELY DAN (1972-1980)**		
Feb 94.	(cd/c) *Javelin; (HAD CD/MC 103)* **SPOTLIGHT ON STEELY DAN**		–
Jun 94.	(d-cd) *Thunderbolt; (CDTB 503)* **CATALYST (THE ORIGINAL RECORDINGS 1968-71)**		–
Feb 95.	(cd; BECKER & FAGEN) *B.A.M.;* **PEARLS OF THE PAST**		–
1995.	(cd/c) *O.N.N.; (ONN 54 CD/MC)* **STEELY DAN (FEATURING WALTER BECKER & DONALD FAGEN)**		–
Mar 00.	(4xcd-box) *(110981-2)* **CITIZEN 1972-1980 (THE BEST OF STEELY DAN)**		

STEPPENWOLF

Formed: Toronto, Canada ... 1966 as blues band SPARROW, by JOHN KAY, plus MICHAEL MONARCH, GOLDY McJOHN, RUSHTON MOREVE and JERRY EDMONTON. After one-off 45 for 'Columbia', they soon relocated to Los Angeles following a brief stay in New York. There, they met producer Gabriel Mekler, who suggested the STEPPENWOLF name (after a Herman Hesse novel). They quickly signed to 'Dunhill' and recorded their eponymous 1968 debut, which included that summer's No.2 classic biker's anthem, 'BORN TO BE WILD'. This success resurrected the album's appeal, which finally climbed to the higher echelons of the charts. The track was subsequently used on the 1969 film, 'Easy Rider', alongside another from the debut, 'THE PUSHER'. While both songs were enjoyable, hot-wired romps through dusty blues-rock terrain, the pseudo-intellectual musings and less than inspired songwriting of JOHN KAY made the multitude of subsequent STEPPENWOLF releases hard going. Nevertheless, the band hit US Top 3 with the colourful psychedelia of the 'MAGIC CARPET RIDE' (1968) single, its parent album, 'STEPPENWOLF THE SECOND' (1969) notching up a similar placing in the album charts. By the early 70's, the band were experiencing diminishing chart returns and split after the 1972 concept album, 'FOR LADIES ONLY'. KAY recorded a couple of solo albums before reforming STEPPENWOLF in 1974. Signed to 'C.B.S.' then 'Epic', the band failed to resurrect their early momentum, although they continued to inflict their tired biker-rock on an oblivious music world right up until the 90's. • **Songwriters:** KAY written, except; THE PUSHER + SNOW BLIND FRIEND (Hoyt Axton) / SOOKIE SOOKIE (Grant Green) / BORN TO BE WILD (Dennis Edmonton; Jerry's brother) / I'M MOVIN' ON (Hank Snow) / HOOCHIE COOCHIE MAN (Muddy Waters). • **Trivia:** BORN TO BE WILD coined a new rock term in the their lyrics "heavy metal thunder". Early in 1969, they contributed some songs to another cult-ish film, 'Candy'.

Album rating: STEPPENWOLF (*6) / THE SECOND (*6) / AT YOUR BIRTHDAY PARTY (*6) / MONSTER (*7) / STEPPENWOLF 'LIVE' (*5) / STEPPENWOLF 7 (*5) / STEPPENWOLF GOLD – THEIR GREAT HITS compilation (*7) / FOR LADIES ONLY (*5) / FORGOTTEN SONGS AND UNSUNG HEROES (*5; by John Kay) / REST IN PEACE collection (*4) / 16 GREATEST HITS compilation (*7) / MY SPORTIN' LIFE (*4; by John Kay) / SLOW FLUX (*4) / HOUR OF THE WOLF (*3) / SKULLDUGGERY (*3) / REBORN TO BE WILD (*3) / ALL IN GOOD TIME (*3; by John Kay) / John Kay & Steppenwolf: LIVE IN LONDON (*4) / WOLF TRACKS (*3) / ROCK & ROLL REBELS (*4) / RISE & SHINE (*4) / BORN TO BE WILD: A RETROSPECTIVE compilation (*7)

JOHN KAY (b. JOACHIM F. KRAULEDAT, 12 Apr'44, Tilsit, Germany) – vox, guitar / **MICHAEL MONARCH** (b. 5 Jul'50, Los Angeles, California, USA) – guitar / **GOLDY McJOHN** (b. JOHN GOADSBY, 2 May'45) – organ / **RUSHTON MOREVE** (b.1948, Los Angeles) – bass / **JERRY EDMONTON** (b. JERRY McCROHAN, 24 Oct'46, Canada) – drums, vocals

		C.B.S.	Columbia
1966.	(7"; as The SPARROW) *(202342) <43755>* **TOMORROW'S SHIP. / ISN'T IT STRANGE**		
1967.	(7"; as The SPARROW) *<43960>* **GREEN BOTTLE LOVER. / DOWN GOES YOUR LOVE LIFE**	–	
1967.	(7"; as JOHN KAY) *<44769>* **TWISTED. / SQUAREHEAD PEOPLE**	–	

— **JOHN RUSSELL MORGAN** – bass repl. MOREVE. He was killed in car crash on 1st Jul'81.

		R.C.A.	Dunhill
Nov 67.	(7") *<4109>* **A GIRL I KNOW. / THE OSTRICH**	–	
Apr 68.	(7") *(RCA 1679) <4123>* **SOOKIE SOOKIE. / TAKE WHAT YOU NEED**		Jan68
May 68.	(lp; mono/stereo) *(RD/SF 7974) <50029>* **STEPPENWOLF** – Sookie Sookie / Everybody's next one / Berry rides again / Hoochie coochie man / Born to be wild / Your wall's too high / Desperation / The pusher / A girl I knew / Take what you need / The ostrich. *(re-iss. Apr70 on 'Stateside'; SSL 5020); hit No.59 (re-iss. Jun87 on 'M.C.A.' lp/c; MCL/+C 1857) (cd-iss. Jul87; CMCAD 31020) (re-iss. Apr92 cd/c; MCL D/C 19019)*		Jan68 6
Aug 68.	(7") *(RCA 1735) <4138>* **BORN TO BE WILD. / EVERYBODY'S NEXT ONE** *(re-iss. May69 on 'Stateside'; SS 8017); hit No.30*		Jun68 2

Stateside Dunhill

Oct 68. (7") *(SS 8003) <4160>* **MAGIC CARPET RIDE. / SOOKIE SOOKIE** Sep68 3
(re-iss. Sep69; SS 8027)

Jan 69. (lp; stereo/mono) *(S+/SL 5003) <50053>* **STEPPENWOLF THE SECOND** Nov68 3
– Faster than the speed of life / Tighten up your wig / None of your doing / Spiritual fantasy / Don't step on the grass, Sam / 28 / Magic carpet ride / Disappointment number (unknown) / Lost and found by trial and error / Hodge, podge strained through a Leslie / Resurrection / Reflections. *(cd-iss. Jun87 on 'M.C.A.'; CMCAD 31021)*

— **LARRY BYROM** (b.27 Dec'48, USA) – guitar repl. MONARCH / **NICK ST.NICHOLAS** (b. KLAUS KARL KASSBAUM, 28 Sep'43, Pion, Germany) – bass repl. RUSSELL

Mar 69. (7") *(SS 8013) <4182>* **ROCK ME. / JUPITER CHILD** Feb69 10

Jun 69. (lp; stereo/mono) *(S+/SL 5011) <50060>* **AT YOUR BIRTHDAY PARTY** Mar69 7
– Don't cry / Chicken wolf / Lovely meter / Round and down / It's never too late / Sleeping dreaming / Jupiter child / She'll be better / Cat killer / Rock me / God fearing man / Mango juice / Happy birthday.

May 69. (7") *<4192>* **IT'S NEVER TOO LATE. / HAPPY BIRTHDAY** – 51

Aug 69. (7") *<4205>* **MOVE OVER. / POWER PLAY** – 31

Dec 69. (7") *<4221>* **MONSTER. / BERRY RIDES AGAIN** – 39

Jan 70. (7") *(SS 8035)* **MONSTER. / MOVE OVER** –

Jan 70. (lp) *(SSL 5021) <50066>* **MONSTER** 43 Nov69 17
– Monster / Suicide / America / Draft resister / Power play / Move over / Fag / What would you do (if I did that to you) / From here to there eventually. *(cd-iss. Sep91 on 'Beat Goes On'; BGOCD 126)*

Mar 70. (7") *(SS 8038)* **THE PUSHER. / YOUR WALL'S TOO HIGH** –

Jun 70. (7") *(SS 8049) <4234>* **HEY LAWDY MAMA. / TWISTED** Apr70 35

Jun 70. (d-lp) *(SSL 5029) <50075>* **STEPPENWOLF 'LIVE' (live)** 16 Apr70 7
– Sooki, Sooki / Don't step on the grass Sam / Tighten up your wig / Hey lawdy mama / Magic carpet ride / The pusher / Corina, Corina / Twisted / From here to there eventually / Born to be wild. *(re-iss. Oct74 on 'A.B.C.'; ABCL 5007) (cd-iss. Aug98 on 'Beat Goes On'; BGOCD 412)*

Sep 70. (7") *(SS 8056) <4248>* **SCREAMING NIGHT HOG. / SPIRITUAL FANTASY** Aug70 62

Probe Dunhill

Nov 70. (7") *(PRO 510) <4261>* **WHO NEEDS YA. / EARSCHPLITTENLOUDENBOOMER** 54

Nov 70. (lp) *(SPBA 6254) <50090>* **STEPPENWOLF 7** 19
– Ball crusher / Forty days and forty nights / Fat Jack / Renegade / Foggy mental breakdown / Snow blind friend / Who needs ya / Earschplittenloudenboomer / Hippo stomp.

Mar 71. (7") *(PRO 525) <4269>* **SNOW BLIND FRIEND. / HIPPO STOMP** Feb71 60

— **KENT HENRY** – guitar repl. BYROM

— **GEORGE BIONDO** (b. 3 Sep'45, Brooklyn, N.Y.) – bass repl. NICK

Jul 71. (7") *(PRO 534) <4283>* **RIDE WITH ME. / FOR MADMEN ONLY** 52

Oct 71. (7") *(PRO 544) <4292>* **FOR LADIES ONLY. / SPARKLE EYES** 64

Oct 71. (lp) *(SPBA 6260) <50110>* **FOR LADIES ONLY** 54
– For ladies only / I'm asking / Shackles and chains / Tenderness / The night time's for you / Jadet strumpet / Sparkle eyes / Black pit / Ride with me / In hopes of a garden.

— disbanded Feb'72, EDMUNTON and McJOHN formed MANBEAST

JOHN KAY

went solo, augmented by **KENT HENRY + GEORGE BIONDO** plus **HUGH SULLIVAN** – keyboards / **PENTII WHITNEY GLEN** – drums / etc. (same label)

Apr 72. (lp) *(1054) <50120>* **FORGOTTEN SONGS AND UNSUNG HEROES**
– Many a mile / Walk beside me / You win again / To be alive / Bold marauder / Two of a kind / Walking blues / Somebody / I'm moving on.

Apr 72. (7") *<4309>* **I'M MOVIN' ON. / WALK BESIDE ME** – 52

Jul 72. (7") *<4319>* **YOU WIN AGAIN. / SOMEBODY** –

Jul 73. (7") *<4351>* **MOONSHINE. / NOBODY LIVES HERE ANYMORE** –

Jul 73. (lp) *(6274) <50147>* **MY SPORTIN' LIFE**
– Moonshine / Nobody lives here anymore / Drift away / Heroes and devils / My sportin' life / Easy evil / Giles of the river / Dance to my song / Sing with the children.

Sep 73. (7") *(PRO 601) <4360>* **EASY EVIL. / DANCE TO MY SONG**

STEPPENWOLF

re-formed (**KAY, McJOHN, EDMUNTON, BIONDO**) plus **BOBBY COCHRAN** – guitar repl. KENT (first and last with horn section)

C.B.S. Mums

Oct 74. (lp) *(80358) <33093>* **SLOW FLUX** Sep74 47
– Gang war blues / Children of the night / Justice don't be slow / Get into the wind / Jeraboah / Straight shootin' woman / Smokey factory blues / Morning blue / A fool's factory / Fishin' in the dark.

Oct 74. (7") *(MUM 2679) <6031>* **STRAIGHT SHOOTIN' WOMAN. / JUSTICE DON'T BE SLOW** Sep74 29

Jan 75. (7") *<6034>* **GET INTO THE WIND. / MORNING BLUE** –

Apr 75. (7") *(MUM 3147) <6036>* **SMOKEY FACTORY BLUES. / A FOOL'S FANTASY**

— **ANDY CHAPIN** – keyboards repl. McJOHN who went solo

Aug 75. (7") *(MUM 3470) <6040>* **CAROLINE (ARE YOU READY). / ANGEL DRAWERS**

Sep 75. (lp) *(69151) <33583>* **HOUR OF THE WOLF**
– Caroline (are you ready for the outlaw world) / Annie, Annie over / Two for the love of one / Just for tonight / Hard rock road / Someone told a lie / Another's lifetime / Mr. Penny pincher.

— **WAYNE COOK** – keyboards repl. ANDY

Epic Epic

May 77. (lp) *(81328) <34120>* **SKULLDUGGERY**
– Skullduggery / Roadrunner / Rock and roll song / Train of thought / Life is a gamble / Pass it on / Sleep / Lip service.

Dec 77. (lp) *<34382>* **REBORN TO BE WILD** (remixes) –
– Straight shootin' woman / Hard rock road / Another's lifetime / Mr. Penny pincher / Smokey factory blues / Caroline / Get into the wind / Gang war blues / Children of night / Skullduggery.

— Disbanded yet again.

JOHN KAY

with **LARRY BYROM** – slide guitar / **MAC McANALLY** – guitar / **CLAYTON IVEY** – keyboards / **BOB WRAY** – bass / **ROGER CLARK** – drums

Mercury Mercury

Jun 78. (lp) *(9110 054) <1-3715>* **ALL IN GOOD TIME**
– Give me some news I can use / The best is barely good enough / That's when I think of you / Ain't nobody home (in California) / Ain't nothin' like it used to be / Business is business / Show me how you'd like it done / Down in New Orleans / Say you will / Hey, I'm alright.

Jun 78. (7") *<74004>* **GIVE ME SOME NEWS I COULD USE. / SAY YOU WILL** –

Jun 78. (7") *(6167 683)* **GIVE ME SOME NEWS I CAN USE. / BUSINESS IS BUSINESS** –

— In the early 80's, KAY and group toured as

JOHN KAY & STEPPENWOLF

with **MICHAEL PALMER** – guitar / **BRETT TUGGLE** – keyboards / **CHAD PERRY** – bass / **STEVEN PALMER** – drums

not iss. Allegiance

Dec 81. (lp) **LIVE IN LONDON (live)** –
– Sookie Sookie / Give me news I can use / You / Hot night in a cold town / Ain't nothin' like it used to be / Magic carpet ride / Five finger discount / Hey lawdy mama / Business is business / Born to be wild / The pusher.

Dec 81. (7") *<3909>* **HOT TOME IN A COLD TOWN. /** –

— **WELTON GITE** – bass repl. CHAD / added **MICHAEL WILK** – keyboards

not iss. CBS-Sony

1983. (lp) *<DIDZ 10010>* **WOLFTRACKS** –
– All I want is all you got / None of the above / You / Every man for himself / Five finger discount / Hold your head up / Hot night in a cold town / Down to earth / For rock'n'roll / The balance. *(UK-iss.May97 as 'FIVE FINGER DISCOUNT' on 'C.M.C.'; 10045-2)*

— now with **ROCKET RITCHOTTE** – guitar, vocals + **MICHAEL WILK** – keyboards, bass / **RON HURST** – drums, vocals. Finally issued new material 1988.

		Disky		Qwil
May 88.	(lp/c/cd) *(979209-1/-4/-2)* <1560> **ROCK & ROLL REBELS**	☐	Sep87	☐

– Give me life / Rock and roll rebels / Hold on (never give up, never give in) / Man on a mission / Everybody knows you / Rock steady (I'm rough and ready) / Replace the face / Turn out the lights / Give me news I can use / Rage.

		I.R.S.	I.R.S.
Aug 90.	<(cd/c/lp)> *(EIRSA 1037)* <241066-2/-4/-1) **RISE & SHINE**	☐	☐

– Let's do it all / Time out / Do or die / Rise & shine / The wall / The daily blues / Keep rockin' / Rock'n'roll war / Sign on the line / We like it, we love it (we want more of it). *<(cd re-iss. Jul98 on 'C.M.C.'; CMC 823910-2)>*

		not iss.	A-Play
May 97.	(cd) *<CD 10045-2>* **FIVE FINGERS DISCOUNT**	–	☐

– Five fingers discount / You / All I want is what you got / None of the above / Balance / Down to earth / Hot night in a cold town / Hold your head up / For rock'n'roll / Every man for himself.

		C.M.C.		Winter Harvest
Jul 98.	(cd) *(CMC 823908-2)* **PARADOX** (rec.1984)	☐		–

– Watch your innocence / Nothin' is forever / You're the only one / The fixer / Give me news that I can use / Only the strong survive / Ain't nothin' like it used to be / Slender thread of hope / Tell me it's allright / Circles of confusion.

Jul 98.	(cd) *(CMC 823909-2)* <3310> **FEED THE FIRE**	☐	Jul96	☐

– Rock & roll rebels / Rock steady (I'm rough & ready) / Hold on (never give up, never give in) / Everybody knows you / (Give me) News I can use / Replace the face / Bad attitude / Man on a mission / Rage / Feed the fire.

– compilations, others, etc. –

—— on 'Probe' UK / 'Dunhill' US unless mentioned otherwise

Jul 69.	(lp) *Stateside; (5015) / Dunhill; <50060>* **EARLY STEPPENWOLF** (live from 1967 as The SPARROW)	☐		29

– Power play / Howlin' for my baby / Goin' upstairs / Corina Corina / Tighten up your wig / The pusher.

Mar 71.	(lp) *(SPB 1033)* <50099> **STEPPENWOLF GOLD**	☐		24

– Born to be wild / It's never too late / Rock me / Hey lawdy mama / Move over / Who needs ya / Magic carpet ride / The pusher / Sookie Sookie / Jupiter's child / Screaming night hog. *(re-iss. Oct74 on 'A.B.C.'; ABCL 8613) (re-iss. Aug80 on 'M.C.A.'; 1502) (re-iss. Aug81 lp/c; MCM/+C 1619) (re-iss. Jan83 on 'Fame' lp/c; FA/TCFA 3052)*

Jul 72.	(lp) *(SPB 1059)* <50124> **REST IN PEACE**	☐	Jun72	62
Mar 73.	(lp) *(SPB 1071)* <50135> **16 GREATEST HITS**	☐	Feb73	☐

(re-iss. Oct74 on 'A.B.C.'; ABCL 5028) (cd-iss. Feb91 on 'M.C.A.'; MCAD 37049)

Jun 80.	(7") *M.C.A.; (MCA 614)* **BORN TO BE WILD. / THE PUSHER**	☐	☐

(re-iss. Apr83 on 'Old Gold'; OG 9323)

Jul 85.	(lp/c) *M.C.A.; (MCM/+C 5002)* **GOLDEN GREATS**	☐	☐

– Born to be wild / It's never too late / Rock me / Hey lawdy mama / Move over / Who needs ya / Monster / Snow blind friend / Magic carpet ride / The pusher / Sookie sookie / Jupiter's child / Screaming dog night / Ride with me / For ladies only / Tenderness.

1991.	(cd) *M.C.A.; <MCA 10389>* **BORN TO BE WILD: A RETROSPECTIVE**	–	☐
Aug 91.	(cd/c) *Knight; (KN CD/MC 10022)* **NIGHTRIDING**	☐	–
Apr 93.	(cd) *Movieplay Gold; (MPG 74016)* **BORN TO BE WILD**	☐	–
Jan 94.	(cd) *Legacy; <(53044)>* **TIGHTEN UP YOUR WIG – THE BEST OF JOHN KAY & SPARROW**	☐	☐
Dec 96.	(cd) *Beat Goes On; (BGOCD 336)* **AT YOUR BIRTHDAY PARTY / STEPPENWOLF**	☐	–
May 97.	(cd) *Experience; (EXP 029)* **STEPPENWOLF**	☐	–
Feb 99.	(c-s/cd-s) *M.C.A.; (MCS C/TD 48104)* **BORN TO BE WILD / MAGIC CARPET RIDE / ROCK ME**	18	☐
Feb 99.	(cd) *M.C.A.; (MCLD 19386)* **THE BEST OF STEPPENWOLF**	☐	☐
Mar 99.	(cd) *Beat Goes On; (BGOCD 450)* **STEPPENWOLF / STEPPENWOLF II**	☐	–
May 01.	(cd) *Repertoire; (REP 4878)* **COLLECTOR'S ITEM**	☐	–

JOHN KAY

		Crosscut		Cannonball
Jan 02.	(cd) *(CCD 12004)* <29119> **HERETICS & PRIVATEERS**	☐	Mar01	☐

– Heretics and privateers / Don't waste my time / Ain't that a shame / Dodging bullets / She's got the goods / For the women in my life / To be alive / I will not be denied / Endless commercial / The ice age / Sleep with one eye open / The back page.

STEREOLAB

Formed: South London, England . . . late 1990, by ex-indie stalwart/songwriter TIM GANE (mainman for McCARTHY), who invited lyricist girlfriend LAETITIA SADIER to join. They soon completed the initial line-up with MARTIN KEAN and JOE DILWORTH (other past indie veterans), subsequently forming their own label, 'Duophonic Super 45s'. The group released three 45's ('SUPER 45', 'SUPER ELECTRIC' & 'STUNNING DEBUT ALBUM') in 1991, the second of which was for the 'Too Pure' label (these have re-instated vinyl as worthy product, whether for limited edition collectors or just vinyl junkies who hate cd's). The following year, the eclectic ambient-boogie machine that was STEREOLAB topped the indie charts with their actual "stunning debut album", 'PENG!'. The record ran the gamut of the band's minimalist influences including VELVET UNDERGROUND, JOHN CAGE, NEU! and SPACEMEN 3. During this period, the couple introduced four new members; MARY HANSEN, SEAN O'HAGAN, DUNCAN BROWN and ANDY RAMSAY, who helped them with a busy touring schedule. In 1993, they signed to 'Elektra' in the States for a 6 figure-sum, while in the UK, they released several more 45's! and an album, 'TRANSIENT RANDOM-NOISE BURSTS WITH ANNOUNCEMENTS', which, like the classy single, 'JENNY ONDIOLINE', scraped into the UK charts (the track was premiered on Channel 4's "The Word" programme). 1994 saw them unsurprisingly hit the UK Top 20 with another double album, 'MARS AUDIAC QUINTET'. Two years later, with their best offering to date, 'EMPEROR TOMATO KETCHUP', they had established themselves as leaders of the "Metronomic Underground" scene, as the opening track suggested. Over the course of the last three years (including 1997's excellent 'DOTS AND LOOPS'), the band's sound had become increasingly characterised by the dreamy French-style vocals of LAETITIA (pronounced Le-ti-seaya), akin to a spacier SARAH CRACKNELL (of SAINT ETIENNE). Returning to the fold in August '99, STEREOLAB (complete with Gallic songstress, BRIGITTE FONTAINE) issued one of their special limited singles, 'CALIMERO', although it was not a feature on their accompanying album, 'COBRA AND PHASES GROUP PLAY VOLTAGE IN THE MILKY NIGHT'. Officially previewed with yet another single, 'THE FREE DESIGN' (inspired by the obscure outfit of the same name!), the album was a little too twee and lightweight for some, one slightly perturbed (or disturbed?) NME critic in particular panning it enough to give zero out of ten! (a hanging offence in anyone's book). Augmented by main protagonists of the underground post-rock scene, JIM O'ROURKE and TORTOISE leader JOHN McENTIRE, STEREOLAB – after a long gap inbetween "long-playing" records – issued the near fantastic 'SOUND-DUST' (2001), a swirling trip into the uncharted territories for the group. The set matched that of the mini-album, or largely ignored 'THE FIRST OF THE MICROBE HUNTERS' (2000), which separated the band from math-rock wizards to sci-fi pop magicians. On 'SOUND-DUST' SADIER's vocals levitated through soft guitars and echoing bass guitar. Opener 'BLACK ANTS IN SOUND-DUST' was reminiscent of previous 'LAB outings, whereas 'CAPTAIN EASYCHORD' focused on being just a great space lullaby. Tragically, on the 9th of December

2002, at the age of only 36, MARY HANSEN was killed when on a bicycle trip. The band eventually returned to the studio in autumn 2003 to record the 'INSTANT O IN THE UNIVERSE' EP, a much less diffuse affair then their recent albums. While lead track '. . .SUDDEN STARS' harked back to former glories, the record had the feel of a band taking stock rather than retreating.

Album rating: SWITCHED ON collection (*6) / PENG! (*7) / THE GROOP PLAYED "SPACE AGE BATCHELOR PAD MUSIC" (*5) / TRANSIENT RANDOM-NOISE BURSTS WITH ANNOUNCEMENTS (*8) / REFRIED ELECTOPLASM (SWITCHED ON, VOL.2) compilation (*6) / MUSIC FOR THE AMORPHOUS BODY STUDY CENTER (*8) / MARS AUDIO QUINTET (*8) / EMPEROR TOMATO KETCHUP (*9) / DOTS AND LOOPS (*8) / COBRA AND PHASES GROUP PLAY VOLTAGE IN THE MILKY NIGHT (*6) / THE FIRST OF THE MICROBE HUNTERS mini (*6) / SOUND-DUST (*5)

TIM GANE (b.12 Jul'64) – guitar, vox organ, guitar (ex-McCARTHY) / **LAETITIA SADIER** (b. 6 May'68, Paris, France) – vocals, vox organ, guitar, tambourine, moog / **GINA MORRIS** – vocals / **JOE DILWORTH** – drums (of TH' FAITH HEALERS)

Duophonic | not iss.

May 91. (10"ep-mail order) *(DS45-01)* **SUPER 45** [ ] [–]
– The light (that will cease to fail) / Au grand jour / Brittle / Au grand jour!.

— added **MARTIN KEAN** (b.New Zealand) – guitar (ex-CHILLS) / **RUSSELL YATES** – live guitar (of MOOSE). **MICK CONROY** (ex-MOOSE) was also a live member early '92.

Nov 91. (7"clear,7"colrd) *(DS45-02)* **STUNNING DEBUT ALBUM: Doubt / Changer** [ ] [–]

Too Pure | Slumberland

Sep 91. (10"ep) *(PURE 4)* **SUPERELECTRIC / HIGH EXPECTATION. / THE WAY WILL BE OPENING / CONTACT** [ ] [–]

Apr 92. (cd/lp) *(31022)* *<SLR 22>* **SWITCHED ON** (compilation) [ ] Oct92 [ ]
– Super-electric / Doubt / Au grand jour 1 / The way will be opening / Brittle / Contact / Au grand jour / High expectation / The light that will cease to fail / Changer. *(re-iss. Mar97 on 'Duophonic' cd/lp; TBC 25/24) (cd/lp re-iss. Mar99 on 'Too Pure';* PUREL 78 CD/LP)

— GINA departed after above

Too Pure | American

May 92. (cd,c,lp) *(PURE 11)* *<43018>* **PENG!** [ ] [ ]
– Super falling star / Orgiastic / Peng! 33 / K-stars / Perversion / You little shits / The seeming and the meaning / Mellotron / Enivrez-vous / Stomach worm / Surrealchemist.

— added **MARY HANSEN** (b. 11 Jan'66, Brisbane, Australia) – vocals, tambourine, guitar / **ANDY RAMSAY** – percussion, vox organ, bazouki; repl. DILWORTH

Sep 92. (10"ep,10"clear-ep,cd-ep) *(PURE 14)* **LOW FI** [ ] [–]
– Et de votre coeur endormi / (Varoom!) / Laisser-faire / Elektro – He held the world in his iron grip.

— added **SEAN O'HAGAN** – vox organ, guitar (ex-MICRODISNEY, ex-HIGH LLAMAS)

Feb 93. (7",7"pink) *<SLR 24>* **JOHN CAGE BUBBLEGUM. / ELOGE D'EROS** [–] [ ]

— added **DUNCAN BROWN** – bass, guitar, vocals

Mar 93. (cd,c,m-lp) *(PURE 19)* *<43013>* **THE GROOP PLAYED "SPACE AGE BACHELOR PAD MUSIC"** [ ] [ ]
– Avant-garde M.O.R. / Space age bachelor pad music (mellow) / The groop play chord X / Space age bachelor pad music (foamy) / Ronco symphony / We're not adult orientated / UHF-MFP / We're not adult orientated (new wave live).

Duophonic | Elektra

Aug 93. (10"ep/cd-ep) *(DUHF D/CD 01)* *<8815>* **JENNY ONDIOLINE / FRUCTION / GOLDEN BALL / FRENCH DISCO** [75] [ ]

Sep 93. (cd/c/2xlp) *(DUHF CD/DMC/D 02)* *<7559 61536-2>* **TRANSIENT RANDOM-NOISE BURSTS WITH ANNOUNCEMENTS** [62] [ ]
– Tone burst / Our trinitone blast / Pack yr romantic mind / I'm going out of my way / Golden ball / Pause / Jenny Ondioline / Analogue rock / Crest / Lock-groove lullaby.

Nov 93. (7") *(DUHF D01P)* **FRENCH DISKO (new version). / JENNY ONDIOLINE** [ ] [–]

— added **KATHERINE GIFFORD** – synthesizers, keyboards

Jul 94. (7"ltd) *(DUHFD 04S)* **PING PONG. / MOOGIE WONDERLAND** [45] [–]
(10"+=/cd-s+=) *(DUHF D/CD 04)* – Pain et spectacles / Transcoma (live).

Aug 94. (cd/c/d-lp) *(DUHF CD/MC/D 05)* *<61669>* **MARS AUDIAC QUINTET** [16] [ ]
– Three-dee melodie / Wow and flutter / Transona five / Des etoiles electroniques / Ping pong / Anamorphose / Three longers later / Nihilist assault group / International colouring contest / The stars of our destination / Transporte sans bouger / L'enfer des formes / Outer accelerator / New orthophony / Fiery yellow. *(free clear-7" w /d-lp + cd-s on cd) (DUHF D/CD 05X)* – Klang-tang / Ulaan batter.

Oct 94. (7"ltd) *(DUHFD 07S)* **WOW AND FLUTTER. / HEAVY DENIM** [70] [–]
(10"+=/cd-s+=) *(DUHF D/CD 07)* – Nihilist assault group / Narco Martenot.

Apr 95. (10"ep/cd-ep) *(DUHF D/CD 08)* **AMORPHOUS BODY STUDY CENTRE** [59] [–]
– Pop quiz / The extension trip / How to explain your internal organs overnight / The brush descends the length / Melochord seventy five / Space moment.

Sep 95. (cd/c/colrd-d-lp) *(DUHF CD/MC/D 09) / Drag City; <DC 82>* **REFRIED ECTOPLASM (SWITCHED ON – VOLUME II)** (compilation) [30] [ ]
– Harmonium / Lo boob oscillator / Mountain / Revox / French disko / Exploding head movie / Eloge d'eros / Tone burst (country) / Animal or vegetable (a wonderful wooden reason) / John Cage bubblegum / Sadistic / Farfisa / Tempter. *(d-lp re-iss. May98; same as US)*

— **GANE / SADIER / HANSEN / RAMSAY + BROWN** added **MORGANE LHOTE** (guests; SEAN O'HAGAN / JOHN McENTIRE (of TORTOISE) + RAY DICKARTY)

— KATHERINE GIFFORD formed indie supergroup SNOWPONY

Feb 96. (7") *(DUHFD 10S)* **CYBELE'S REVERIE. / BRIGITTE** [62] [–]
(10"+=/cd-s+=) *(DUHF D/CD 10)* – Les yper yper sound / Young lungs.

Mar 96. (d-lp/c/cd) *(DUHF D/MC/CD 11)* *<61640-2>* **EMPEROR TOMATO KETCHUP** [27] Apr96 [ ]
– Metronomic underground / Cybele's reverie / Percolator / Les ypersound / Spark plug / Olv 26 / The noise of carpet / Tomorrow is already here / Emperor tomato ketchup / Monstre sacre / Motoroller scalatron / Slow fast Hazel / Anonymous collective.

Apr 96. (12"ltd.) *(DS 3311)* **SIMPLE HEADPHONE MIND. / (other track by NURSE WITH WOUND)** [ ] [–]
(re-iss. Jun97; same)

— now without BROWN, who was repl. by **RICHARD HARRISON**

Sep 96. (7") *(LISS 15)* **SHE USED TO CALL ME SADNESS. / (other by Fuxa)** [ ] [–]
(above on 'Lissys')

Nov 96. (7"ep)(12"ep/cd-ep) *(DUHFD 14S)(DUHF D/CD 14)* **FLUORESCENCES EP** [ ] [–]
– Fluorescences / Pinball / You used to call me sadness / Soop groove *2.

Dec 96. (12"; STEREOLAB & WAGON CHRIST) *(DUHFD 15)* **METROGNOMIC UNDERGROUND. /** [ ] [–]

Sep 97. (7") *(DUHFD 16S)* **MISS MODULAR. / ALLURES** [60] [–]
(12"+=/cd-s+=) *(DUHF D/CD 16)* – Off-on / Spinal column.

Sep 97. (cd/c/d-lp) *(DUHF CD/C/D 17)* *<62065>* **DOTS AND LOOPS** [19] [ ]
– Brakhage / Miss Modular / The flower called Nowhere / Prisoner of Mars / Rainbo conversation / Refractions in the plastic pulse / Parsec / Ticker-tape of the unconscious / Contronatura.

— **SADIER, GANE, HANSEN, RAMSEY + LHOTE** were joined by **SIMON JOHNS** – bass (ex-CLEARSPOT) / **KEV HOOPER** – musical saw (ex-STUMP) / **ROB MAZUREK** – cornet / **DOMINIC MURCOTT** – marimba / plus guests **JOHN McENTIRE** (of TORTOISE) / **JIM O'ROURKE + SEAN O'HAGAN**

Aug 99. (7"/cd-s; STEREOLAB & BRIGITTE FONTAINE) *(DS45/+CD 25)* **CALIMERO. / (other track 'Cache Cache' by MONADE)** [ ] [–]

Sep 99. (7") *(DUHFD 22S)* **THE FREE DESIGN. / ESCAPE POD (FROM THE WORLD OF MEDICAL OBSERVATIONS)** [ ] [–]
(cd-s+=) *(DUHFCD 22)* – With friends like these / Les aimes des memes.

Sep 99. (cd) *(DUHFCD 23)* **COBRA AND PHASES GROUP PLAY VOLTAGE IN THE MILKY NIGHT** [ ] [–]
– Fuses / People do it all the time / The free design / Blips drips and strips / Italian shoes continuum / Infinity girl / The spiracles / Op hop detonation / Puncture in the radah permutation / Velvet water / Blue

milk / Caleidoscopic gaze / Strobo acceleration / The emergency kisses / Come and play in the milky night.

May 00. (m-lp/m-cd) *(DUHF D/CD 25)* *<62537-2>* **THE FIRST OF THE MICROBE HUNTERS** [ ] [ ]
– Outer Bongolia / Intervals / Barock – plastik / Nomus et phusis / I feel the air (of another planet) / Household names / Retrograde mirror form.

— **O'ROURKE + McENTIRE** were virtually fully-fledged 'LAB techs

Jul 01. (12"/cd-s) *(DUHF D/CD 26)* **CAPTAIN EASYCHORD / LONGLIFE LOVE. / CANNED CANDIES / MOODLES** [ ] [–]

Sep 01. (cd/d-lp) *(DUHF CD/D 27)* *<62676-2>* **SOUND-DUST** [ ] [ ]
– Black ants in sound-dust / Space moth / Captain Easychord / Baby Lulu / The black arts / Hallucinex / Double rocker / Gus the mynah bird / Naught more terrific than man / Nothing to do with me / Suggestion diabolique / Les bons bons des raisons.

— on 9th Dec'02, MARY was killed in a bicycle accident in London

Oct 03. (3x7"ep)(m-cd) *(DUHFD 28S)(DUHFCD 28)* *<62893>* **INSTANT O IN THE UNIVERSE** [ ] [ ]
– . . .Sudden stars / Jaunty Monty and the bubbles of silence / Good is me / Microclimate / Mass riff.

– more very limited singles, etc. –

Jun 92. (7"pink) *B.M.I.; (BMI 025)* **THE LIGHT (THAT WILL CEASE TO FAIL). / AU GRAND JOUR** [ ] [–]

Jul 92. (7"colrd) *Duophonic; (DS45-04)* **HARMONIUM. / FARFISA** [ ] [–]

Oct 93. (10"ep) *Clawfist; (Clawfist 20)* **CRUMB DUCK (with NURSE WITH WOUND)** [ ] [–]
– Animal or vegetable / Exploding head movie.

Oct 93. (7"clear) *Sub Pop; (<SP 107/283>)* **LE BOOB OSCILLATOR. / TEMPTER** [ ] [ ]

Nov 93. (7") *Teenbeat; <Teenbeat 121>* **MOUNTAIN. / ('B'by Unrest)** [–] [ ]

Feb 98. (12"ep/cd-ep; by STEREOLAB & UI) *(DS45/+CD 19)* **FIRES** [ ] [–]
– St. Elmo's fire (mixes) / Less time / Impulse rah. *(re-iss/lp Aug00 on 'Bingo'; BIN 2)*

Oct 98. (d-cd/d-lp) *<DC 159>* **ALUMINIUM TUNES: SWITCHED ON VOL.3** [–] [ ]
– Pop quiz – The extension trip / How to play your internal organs / Brush descends the length / Melochord seventy-five / Space moment / Speedy car / Golden atoms / Olan bator / One small step / Iron man / Long hair of death / You used to call me sadness / New orthophony / One note samba – Surfboard / Cadriopo / Klang tone / Get Carter / 1000 miles an hour / Percolations / Seeperbold / Check and double check / Munich madness / Metronumero underground / Incredible He-woman.

Oct 02. (d-cd) *Strange Fruit; (SFRSCD 111)* **ABC MUSIC: THE RADIO 1 SESSIONS** [ ] [–]

STEREO MC'S

Formed: Clapham, London, England . . . 1985 by DJ/producer NICK HALLAM (aka THE HEAD) and rapper ROB BIRCH. After landing £7,000 from property developers who wanted them to vacate their flat, the enterprising pair used the cash to start up their own label, 'Gee Street'. The operation subsequently gained the backing of New York's '4th & Broadway', as well as a UK deal with 'Island', the duo released their first single, 'MOVE IT', for the label in Spring '88. Although DJ CESARE was initially an integral part of the STEREO MC's set up, he soon departed for a solo career. The debut album, '33-45-78' (1989) introduced the group's distinctive British hip hop sound, earning them a support slot on a HAPPY MONDAYS American tour where they eventually scored their first chart success, 'ELEVATE MY MIND' breaking the US Top 40 singles list in the summer of '91. A follow-up album had appeared the previous year, 'SUPERNATURAL', the record also spawning the classic 'LOST IN MUSIC', still one of the group's best loved tracks. By 1992, the STEREO MC's move towards a completely organic hip hop sound was complete, backing vocalists VERONICA and ANDREA augmenting drummer OWEN IF and vocal stalwart, CATH COFFEY. Previewed by the hypnotic skank of the 'CONNECTED' single, the album of the same name propelled STEREO MC's into the big league. A seamless amalgam of hip hop, soul and funk, the record was a massive crossover hit, pulling in clubbers, rap fiends, indie and pop fans alike, eventually earning the band a Brit Award in 1994 for best group and best album (dance section). One of the few success stories in British rap, the group's universal appeal is obviously grounded in solid songwriting, as well as a fearsome live reputation. The STEREO MC's have also maintained a concurrent career as esteemed remixers, servicing everyone from The JUNGLE BROTHERS to U2, whom they supported for part of their 'Zooropa' tour. With their foot squarely in the MY BLOODY VALENTINE/STONE ROSES studio camp, however, it's was verging on six years since the group's last release, only the occasional remix keeping the STEREO MC's name alive. Nigh on a decade after 'CONNECTED', the group finally got around to releasing a follow-up, 'DEEP, DOWN & DIRTY' (2001). Surely some sort of record(?!) but was the wait worth it? Well, for longtime fans it most certainly was although there were few likely hit singles to mine the charts like the old days. BIRCH sounded as elegantly wasted as ever, the boho bard of latter day souladelica laying off the rapping as he hits middle age. Simultaneously in thrall to black music's golden era while sounding as contemporary as your better than average nu-rap effort, the record once again straddled the fine line between smokers' delight and dancefloor delirium.
• **Songwriters:** BIRCH-HALLAM, except SALSA HOUSE (Richie Rich) / BLACK IS BLACK (Jungle Brothers) / DANCE 4 ME (Queen Lafitah).

Album rating: 33-45-78 (*5) / SUPERNATURAL (*6) / CONNECTED (*8) / DEEP DOWN & DIRTY (*6)

ROB B (b. ROBERT BIRCH, 11 Jun'61, Nottingham, England) – vocals / **THE HEAD** (b. NICK HALLAM, 11 Jun'60, Nottingham) – DJ/producer / **OWEN IF** (b. IAN ROSSITER, 20 Mar'59, Newport, Wales) – drums / **CATH COFFEY** (b. 1965, Kenya) – vocals

4th & Broad 4th & Broad

Mar 88. (7"; STEREO MC'S & CESARE) *(BRW 94)* **MOVE IT. / FEEL SO GOOD** [ ] [–]
(12"+=) *(12BRW 94)* – ('A'mix).
above with CESARE although he left soon after.

Oct 88. (7") *(BRW 119)* **WHAT IS SOUL? / ('A'-Rob B mix)** [ ] [–]
(12"+=) *(12BRW 119)* – ('A'vocal mix) / ('A'instrumental) / ('A'acappella mix).

Jun 89. (7"/c-s) *(BRW/BRCA 134)* **ON 33. / GEE STREET** [ ] [–]
(10"+=) *(10BRW 134)* – Non stop.
(12"+=) *(12BRW 134)* – ('A'-DJ Mark the 45 King mix).

Jul 89. (lp/c/cd) *(BR LP/CA/CD 532)* **33-45-78** [ ] [–]
– On 33 / Use it / Gee Street / Neighbourhood / Toe to toe / What is soul? / Use it (part 2) / Outta touch / Sunday 19th March / This ain't a love song / Ancient concept / On the mike / Back to the future.

Aug 89. (7") *(BRW 148)* **LYRICAL MACHINE. / ON THE MIKE** [ ] [–]
(12"+=) *(12BRW 148)* – Mechanical / Bring it on.

Sep 90. (7") *(BRW 186)* **ELEVATE MY MIND. / SMOKIN' WITH THE MOTHERMAN** [74] [–]
(12"+=/cd-s+=) *(12BRW/BRCD 186)* – ('A'dub).

Sep 90. (cd/c/lp) *(BR CD/CA/LP 556)* *<444032>* **SUPERNATURAL** [ ] [ ]
– I'm a believer / Scene of the crime / Declaration / Elevate my mind / Watcha gonna do / Two horse town / Ain't got nobody / Goin' back to my roots / Lost in music / Life on the line / The other side / Set me loose / What's the word / Early one morning. *(cd+=/c+=)* – Smokin' with the motherman / Relentless. *(cd re-iss. Apr94 on 'Island'; IMCD 185)*

Mar 91. (7"/c-s) *(BRW/BRCA 198)* **LOST IN MUSIC (Ultimatum remix). / EARLY ONE MORNING** [46] [–]
(cd-s+=) *(BRCD 198)* – ('A'instrumental).
(12") *(12BRW 198)* – ('A'side) / ('A'-B.B. mix) / ('A'-B.B. instrumental).

May 91. (c-s,12",cd-s) <447519> **ELEVATE MY MIND. / ('A'-12" version)** - 39

— now a 6-piece, added **VERONICA + ANDREA** – backing vox

4th & Broad Gee Street

Sep 92. (7"/c-s) *(BRW/BRCA 262)* <864744> **CONNECTED. / FEVER** 18 Mar93 20
(cd-s+=) *(BRCD 262)* – ('A'-full version) / Disconnected.

Oct 92. (cd/c/lp) *(BR CD/CA/LP 589)* <514061> **CONNECTED** 2 92
– Connected / Ground level / Everything / Sketch / Fade away / All night long / Step it up / Playing with fire / Pressure / Chicken shake / Creation / The end.

Nov 92. (7"/c-s) *(BRW/BRCA 266)* <862308> **STEP IT UP. / ('A'mix)** 12 Jun93 58
(12"+=/cd-s+=) *(12BRW/BRCD 266)* – Lost in music (US mix).

Feb 93. (7"/c-s) *(BRW/BRCA 268)* **GROUND LEVEL. / EVERYTHING (EVERYTHING GROOVES pt.1)** 19 -
(12"+=/cd-s+=) *(12BRW/BRCD 268)* – ('B'mixes pt.2).

May 93. (7"/c-s) *(BRW/BRCA 276)* **CREATION. / ('A'-Ultimation mix)** 19 -
(12"+=) *(12BRW 276)* – ('A'instrumental).
(cd-s+=) *(BRCD 276)* – All night long.

— the group retired as a unit for several years

Island Island

May 01. (c-s) *(CIS 777)* **DEEP DOWN & DIRTY / (the Jon Carter basement mix)** 17 -
(cd-s+=) *(CID 777)* – Load.
(12") *(12IS 777)* – ('A'side) / ('A'-Two Lone Swordsmen remix).

May 01. (cd/t-lp) *(CID/ILPST 8106)* <586077> **DEEP DOWN & DIRTY** 17
– Deep down & dirty / We belong in this world together / Breeze / Running / Graffiti (part 1) / Graffiti (part 2) / Sofisticated / Traffic / Right effect / Stop at nothing / Unconscious / Shameless / Deliverance. *(t-lp+=)* – (instrumentals).

Aug 01. (12") *(12IS 782)* **WE BELONG IN THIS WORLD TOGETHER. / RHINO / WE BELONG IN THIS WORLD TOGETHER (Chicken lips remix)** 59 -
(cd-s) *(CID 782)* – ('A'side) / ('A'-Chocolate Puma remix) / Deep down & dirty (different gear mix).
(12") *(12ISX 782)* – ('A'mixes).

STEREOPHONICS

Formed: Cwmaman, Mid-Glamorgan, Wales ... late 80's as The TRAGIC LOVE COMPANY by songwriter KELLY JONES, RICHARD JONES and STUART CABLE, initially treading the boards as a teenage covers band. The trio proved they were more than capable of spearheading Richard Branson's new 'V2' label with the release of debut single, 'LOOKS LIKE CHAPLIN', a melodic riffathon that had more in common with trad 70's rock and Seattle grunge than the still dominant Britpop. A Spring '97 follow-up, 'LOCAL BOY IN THE PHOTOGRAPH', came within breathing distance of the Top 50, a dizzying amalgam of the MANICS, RADIOHEAD, OASIS and BUFFALO TOM that managed to sound simultaneously contemporary and classic. JONES confirmed his newfound status as one of Britain's most promising young songwriters as The STEREOPHONICS embarked on an impressive chart run with the Top 40-breaking 'MORE LIFE IN A TRAMP'S VEST'. Late summer saw them nudge closer to the Top 20 with 'A THOUSAND TREES', the opening track on debut album, 'WORD GETS AROUND'. A massive selling UK Top 10 success, the record featured in the upper reaches of many end-of-year polls, helping to net the band a Brit Award (Best New Group) in early '98. Having seen out '97 with the moody magnificence of 'TRAFFIC', JONES and Co began the new year with a Top 20 re-issue of 'LOCAL BOY' prior to a summer of heavy touring. Towards Christmas, The STEREOPHONICS became a household name with Top 3 hit, 'THE BARTENDER & THE THIEF', proving that despite the continued predictions of its imminent demise, good old fashioned guitar-rock and solid songwriting was alive and well in Wales. The following year saw the trio peak both critically and commercially, three massive hits, 'JUST LOOKING', 'PICK A PART THAT'S NEW' and 'I WOULDN'T BELIEVE YOUR RADIO', all squeezed out of an excellent sophomore set, 'PERFORMANCE AND COCKTAILS' (1999). Welsh pop idol, TOM JONES, also called up the services of his fellow countrymen to duet with him on a Top 10 hit of 'Mama Told Me Not To Come'. Everyone's favourite trad-rockers returned in 2001 with 'JUST ENOUGH EDUCATION TO PERFORM', the record's title engendering an unlikely bout of controversy when the band – much to car manufacturer Daimler-Chrysler's disapproval – attempted to abbreviate it to 'J.E.E.P.'. Needless to say, this episode was more unpredictable than any of the meat and potatoes fare on offer within. Which isn't to say The STEREOPHONICS are worthy but dull, just that their acoustic-laced melodic rock lends itself to daytime radio play annoyingly well. Once again, JONES proved himself a master of rock classicism , taking his inspiration from the choicest, most authentic sounding 60's/70's moments and infusing them with the deftest of rootsy flourishes. Thus, try as you might to resist, singles such as 'STEP ON MY OLD SIZE NINES' and the breezy 'HAVE A NICE DAY' slowly but surely shoehorned their way into your consciousness much like that Top Gear compilation your dad used to play. While JONES is a writer who is undoubtedly maturing with age, he still lacks that strain of rugged individuality that marks out a ROD STEWART or a JOHN FOGERTY – 'HANDBAGS & GLADRAGS' indeed. JONES did yet more growing up the hard way with 'YOU GOTTA GO THERE TO COME BACK' (2003), detailing his travails through a series of affecting if often disillusioned vignettes. With the likes of 'NOTHING PRECIOUS AT ALL' and the hit singles 'MADAME HELGA' and 'MAYBE TOMORROW', the band sounded less like they had something to prove and more like they had something to say. In September, STUART CABLE was apparently booted out of the trio. • **Covered:** SUNNY AFTERNOON (Kinks) / POSITIVELY 4th STREET (Bob Dylan) / SOMETHING IN THE WAY (Nirvana) / THE OLD LAUGHING LADY + HEART OF GOLD (Neil Young) / FIRST TIME EVER I SAW YOUR FACE (Ewan MacColl) / I'M ONLY SLEEPING (Beatles) / HANDBAGS & GLADRAGS (Mike D'Abo).

Album rating: WORD GETS AROUND (*7) / PERFORMANCE AND COCKTAILS (*8) / JUST ENOUGH EDUCATION TO PERFORM (*7) / YOU GOTTA GO THERE TO COME BACK (*6)

KELLY JONES (b. 3 Jun'74, Aberdare, Wales) – vocals, guitar / **RICHARD JONES** (b.23 May'74, Aberdare) – bass / **STUART CABLE** (b.19 May'70, Aberdare) – drums

V2 V2

Nov 96. (7") *(SPH 1)* **LOOKS LIKE CHAPLIN. / MORE LIFE IN A TRAMP'S VEST** -
(cd-s+=) *(SPHD 1)* – Raymond's shop.

Mar 97. (7") *(SPH 2)* **LOCAL BOY IN THE PHOTOGRAPH. / TWO MANY SANDWICHES** 51
(cd-s+=) *(SPHD 2)* – Buy myself a small plane.

May 97. (7") *(SPH 4)* **MORE LIFE IN A TRAMP'S VEST. / RAYMOND'S SHOP** 33 -
(cd-s+=) *(SPHD 4)* – Poppy day.
(cd-s) *(SPHDX 4)* – ('A'side) / Looks like Chaplin (live) / Too many sandwiches (live) / Last of the big time drinkers (live).

Aug 97. (7"/c-s) *(VVR 500044-7/-5)* **A THOUSAND TREES. / CARROT CAKE AND WINE** 22 -
(cd-s+=) *(VVR 500044-3)* – ('A'live).
(cd-s) *(VVR 500044-8)* – ('A'acoustic) / Home to me (acoustic) / Looks like Chaplin (acoustic) / Summertime (acoustic).

Aug 97. (cd/c/lp) *(VVR 100043-2/-4/-9)* <27006> **WORD GETS AROUND** 6
– A thousand trees / Looks like Chaplin / More life in a tramps vest / Local

boy in the photograph / Traffic / Not up to you / Check my eyelids for holes / Same size feet / Last of the big time drinkers / Goldfish bowl / Too many sandwiches / Billy Daveys daughter.

Nov 97. (7"/c-s) *(VVR 500094-7/-5)* **TRAFFIC. / TIE ME UP TIE ME DOWN** 20 –
(cd-s+=) *(VVR 500094-3)* – Chris Chambers / ('A'version).
(cd-s) *(VVR 500094-8)* – ('A'live) / More life in a tramp's vest (live) / A thousand trees (live) / Local boy in the photograph (live).

Feb 98. (7"/c-s) *(VVR 500126-7/-5)* **LOCAL BOY IN THE PHOTOGRAPH (remix). / WHO'LL STOP THE RAIN** 14 –
(cd-s+=) *(VVR 500126-3)* – Check my eyelids for holes / ('A'-CD-Rom video).
(cd-s) *(VVR 500126-8)* – ('A'side) / Not up to you (live in session) / The last resort / Traffic (CD-rom video live).

Nov 98. (7"/c-s) *(VVR 500467-7/-5)* **THE BARTENDER AND THE THIEF. / SHE TAKES HER CLOTHES OFF** 3 –
(cd-s+=) *(VVR 500465-3)* – Fiddler's green.
(cd-s) *(VVR 500466-3)* – ('A'live) / Traffic (live) / Raymond's shop (live).

Feb 99. (7"/c-s) *(VVR 500532-7/-5)* **JUST LOOKING. / POSTMEN DO NOT GREAT MOVIE HEROES MAKE (featuring Marco Migliani)** 4 –
(cd-s+=) *(VVR 500530-3)* – Sunny afternoon.
(cd-s) *(VVR 500530-0)* – ('A'side) / Local boy in the photograph (live) / Same size feet (live).

Mar 99. (cd/c/lp) *(VVR 100449-2/-4/-9)* *<27052>* **PERFORMANCE AND COCKTAILS** 1 May99
– Roll up and shine / The bartender and the thief / Hurry up and wait / Pick a part that's new / Just looking / Half the lies you tell ain't true / I wouldn't believe your radio / T-shirt sun tan / Is yesterday, tomorrow, today? / A minute longer / She takes her clothes off / Plastic California / I stopped to fill my car up. *(special cd+=; VVR 100449-8)*

May 99. (7"/c-s) *(VVR 500677-7/-5)* **PICK A PART THAT'S NEW. / NICE TO BE OUT (demo)** 4 –
(cd-s+=) *(VVR 500677-3)* – Positively 4th street / ('A'-CD-Rom video).
(cd-s) *(VVR 500677-8)* – ('A'acoustic) / In my day / Something in the way.

Aug 99. (7"/c-s) *(VVR 500882-7/-5)* **I WOULDN'T BELIEVE YOUR RADIO. / THE BARTENDER AND THE THIEF (bar version)** 11 –
(cd-s+=) *(VVR 500882-3)* – The old laughing lady.
(cd-s) *(VVR 500882-8)* – ('A'live) / Pick a part that's new (live) / T-shirt suntan (live).

Nov 99. (7"/c-s) *(VVR 500932-7/-5)* **HURRY UP AND WAIT. / ANGIE** 11 –
(cd-s+=) *(VVR 500932-3)* – I wouldn't believe your radio.
(cd-s) *(VVR 500932-8)* – ('A'live) / I stopped to fill my car up (live) / Billy Davey's daughter (live) / ('A'-video).

— In Mar'00, the STEREOPHONICS were credited on TOM JONES' UK Top 5 smash, 'Mama Told Me Not To Come'

May 00. (cd-ep) *<70041>* **T-SHIRT SUNTAN EP** –
– I wouldn't believe your radio / The bartender and the thief / Sunny afternoon / Positively 4th Street / Tie me up, tie me down.

— In Sep'00, KELLY JONES collaborated with MANCHILD on their UK Top 60 hit, 'The Cliches Are True'

Mar 01. (7"/c-s) *(VVR 501593-7/-5)* **MR. WRITER. / MARITIM BELLE VUE IN KIEL** 5 –
(cd-s+=) *(VVR 501593-3)* – An audience with Mr. Nice.
(cd-s) *(VVR 501593-8)* – ('A'-live acoustic) / Hurry up and wait (live acoustic) / Don't let me down (live acoustic).

Apr 01. (cd/c/lp) *(VVR 101583-2/-4/-1)* *<27092>* **JUST ENOUGH EDUCATION TO PERFORM** 1
– Vegas two times / Lying in the sun / Mr. Writer / Step on my old size nines / Have a nice day / Nice to be out / Watch them fly Sundays / Everyday I think of money / Maybe / Caravan holiday / Rooftop. *(cd re-iss. Nov01; VVR 101829-2)*

Jun 01. (7"/c-s) *(VVR 501624-7/-4)* **HAVE A NICE DAY. / SURPRISE** 5 –
(cd-s+=) *(VVR 501624-3)* – Piano for a stripper (demo).
(cd-s) *(VVR 501624-8)* – ('A'live acoustic) / Heart of gold (live acoustic) / I stopped to fill my car up (live acoustic).

Sep 01. (c-s) *(VVR 501625-5)* **STEP ON MY OLD SIZE NINES / SHOESHINE BOY** 16 –
(cd-s+=) *(VVR 501625-3)* – I'm only sleeping / ('A'-CD-Rom).
(cd-s) *(VVR 501625-8)* – ('A'side) / Everyday I think of money / Just looking / ('A'live video).

Dec 01. (7"/c-s) *(VVR 501775-7/-5)* **HANDBAGS AND GLADRAGS. / FIRST TIME EVER I SAW YOUR FACE** 4 –
(cd-s+=) *(VVR 501775-3)* – How.
(cd-s) *(VVR 501775-8)* – ('A'live) / Caravan holiday (live) / Nice to be out (live).

Apr 02. (7") *(VVR 501917-7)* **VEGAS TWO TIMES. / VEGAS TWO TIMES (live)** 23 –
(cd-s) *(VVR 501917-3)* – ('A'side) / Mr Writer (live) / Watch them fly Sundays (live).

May 03. (7") *(VVR 502174-7)* **MADAME HELGA. / HIGH AS THE CEILING** 4 –
(cd-s+=) *(VVR 502174-3)* – Royal flush (mono demo).

Jun 03. (cd/c/d-lp) *(VVR 102190-2/-4/-1)* *<80025>* **YOU GOTTA GO THERE TO COME BACK** 1
– Help me (she's out of her mind) / Maybe tomorrow / Madame Helga / You stole my money honey / Getaway / Climbing the wall / Jealousy / I'm alright (you gotta go there to come back) / Nothing precious at all / Rainbows and pots of gold / I miss you now / High as the ceiling / Since I told you it's over. *(ltd-cd+=; VVR 102190-0)* – Lying to myself again.

Jul 03. (7") *(VVR 502189-7)* **MAYBE TOMORROW. / HAVE WHEELS WILL TRAVEL** 3 –
(cd-s+=) *(VVR 502189-3)* – Change changes things.
(cd-s) *(VVR 502189-5)* – ('A'-demo) / Madame Helga (demo) / You stole my money honey (demo).

Nov 03. (7") *(VVR 502262-7)* **SINCE I TOLD YOU IT'S OVER. / MAYBE TOMORROW (live acoustic)** 16 –
(cd-s) *(VVR 502262-3)* – ('A'side) / Nothing precious at all (live acoustic) / Madame Helga (live acoustic).
(cd-s) *(VVR 502262-5)* – ('A'-demo) / Jealousy (demo) / I miss you (demo).

— temp. **STEVE GORMAN** – drums (ex-BLACK CROWES) repl. CABLE

☐ ST. ETIENNE (see under ⇒ SAINT ETIENNE)

Cat STEVENS

Born: STEVEN DEMETRI GEORGIOU, 21 Jul'47, Soho, London, England. Son of Greek restaurant owner and Swedish mother. While studying at Hammersmith college in 1966 he met Mike Hurst (ex-SPRINGFIELDS). He produced first single 'I LOVE MY DOG', after which CAT was signed by Tony Hall to new Decca subsidiary label 'Deram'. It reached the UK Top 30, but was surpassed the next year when follow-up 'MATTHEW AND SON' hit No.2. His songs were soon being covered by many, including P.P.ARNOLD (First Cut Is The Deepest) & TREMELOES (Here Comes My Baby). After a barren chart spell and recuperation from TB two years previous, he signed new deal with 'Island' in 1970 (A&M in America). He scored a comeback Top 10 hit with 'LADY D'ARBANVILLE', which lent on the production skills of ex-YARDBIRD Keith Relf. He stayed for the follow-up to 'MONA BONE JAKON', the 1970 classic album 'TEA FOR THE TILLERMAN'. CAT went on to become one of the biggest stars of the 70's although his output became increasingly stale. 'TEASER AND THE FIRECAT' (1971) was another collection of pleasant but ultimately unsatisfying singer songwriter musings while 'CATCH BULL AT FOUR' (1972) and 'FOREIGNER' (1973) sounded overwrought and cluttered , a failing that marked the remainder of his output for 'Island' until his musical retirement in 1979 when he converted to the muslim faith and changed his name to YUSUF ISLAM. • **Songwriters:** Self-penned except; MORNING HAS BROKEN (Eleanor Farjeon) / ANOTHER SATURDAY NIGHT (Sam Cooke). • **Trivia:** Other STEVENS' songs given new light were; WILD WORLD (Jimmy Cliff – 1970, Maxi Priest – 1988) / FIRST CUT IS THE DEEPEST (Rod Stewart) / PEACE TRAIN (10,000 Maniacs).

Album rating: MATTHEW AND SON (*6) / NEW MASTERS (*5) / MONA BONE JAKON (*6) / TEA FOR THE TILLERMAN (*8) / TEASER AND THE

FIRECAT (*9) / CATCH BULL AT FOUR (*7) / FOREIGNER (*5) / BUDDHA AND THE CHOCOLATE BOX (*6) / GREATEST HITS compilation (*9) / NUMBERS (*3) / IZITSO (*4) / BACK TO EARTH (*3) / FOOTSTEPS IN THE DARK – GREATEST HITS, VOL.2 compilation (*6) / THE VERY BEST OF CAT STEVENS compilation (*9) / REMEMBER CAT STEVENS compilation (*8)

CAT STEVENS – vocals, guitar, keyboards with orchestra

Deram Deram

Sep 66. (7") *(DM 102)* **I LOVE MY DOG. / PORTOBELLO ROAD** [28] [ ]

Dec 66. (7") *(DM 110)* **MATTHEW AND SON. / GRANNY** [2] [ ] *(re-iss. Aug81 on 'Decca')*

Mar 67. (lp; mono/stereo) *(DML/SML 1004)* <18005> **MATTHEW AND SON** [7] [ ]
– Matthew and son / I love my dog / Here comes my baby / Bring another bottle baby / Portobello road / I've found a love / I see a road / Baby get your head screwed on / Granny / When I speak to the flowers / The tramp / Come on and dance / Hummingbird / Lady. *(cd-iss. Jul88 & Nov99 on 'London'; 820 560-2)*

Mar 67. (7") *(DM 118)* **I'M GONNA GET ME A GUN. / SCHOOL IS OUT** [6] [ ]

Jul 67. (7") *(DM 140)* **A BAD NIGHT. / THE LAUGHING APPLE** [20] [ ]

Dec 67. (7") *(DM 156)* **KITTY. / BLACKNESS OF THE NIGHT** [47] [ ]

Dec 67. (lp; mono/stereo) *(DML/SML 1018)* <18010> **NEW MASTERS** [ ] [ ]
– Kitty / I'm so sleepy / Northern wind / The laughing apple / Smash your heart / Moonstone / The first cut is the deepest / I'm gonna be king / Ceylon city / Blackness of the night / Come on baby / I love them all. *(re-iss. Nov84; DOA 5) (cd-iss. Apr89 +=; 820 767-2)* – Image of Hell / Lovely city / Here comes my wife / The view from the top / It's a supa dupa life / Where are you / A bad night.

Feb 68. (7") *(DM 178)* **LOVELY CITY. / IMAGE OF HELL** [ ] [ ]

—— Around early 1968, CAT slowly recovered from tuberculosis.

Oct 68. (7") *(DM 211)* **HERE COMES MY WIFE. / IT'S A SUPA DUPA LIFE** [ ] [–]

Jun 69. (7") *(DM 260)* **WHERE ARE YOU. / THE VIEW FROM THE TOP** [ ] [–]

—— recruited band; **ALUN DAVIES** – guitar / **JOHN RYAN** – bass / **HARVEY BURNS** – drums

Island A&M

Jun 70. (7"m) *(WIP 6086)* **LADY D'ARBANVILLE. / TIME / FILL MY EYES** [8] [–]

Jun 70. (lp) *(ILPS 9118)* <4260> **MONA BONE JAKON** [63] [ ]
– Lady d'Arbanville / Maybe you're right / Pop star / I think I see the light / Trouble / Mona bone Jakon / I wish, I wish / Katmandu / Time – Fill my eyes / Lilywhite. *(re-iss. 1974 & Jan78; same) (cd-iss. Apr87; CID 9118) (cd re-iss. Nov89; IMCD 35) (cd re-mast.May00; IMCD 269)*

Nov 70. (lp) *(ILPS 9135)* <4280> **TEA FOR THE TILLERMAN** [20] Feb71 [8]
– Where do the children play / Hard headed woman / Wild world / Sad Lisa / Miles from nowhere / But I might die tonight / Longer boats / Into white / On the road to find out / Father and son / Tea for the tillerman. *(re-iss. 1974 & Jan78; same) (re-iss. Oct86 lp/c/cd; ILPM/ICM/CID 9135) (cd re-iss. Nov89; IMCD 36) (re-iss. lp Jan94 + May94; same) (cd re-mast.May00; IMCD 268)*

Feb 71. (7") <1231> **WILD WORLD. / MILES FROM NOWHERE** [–] [11]

—— **LARRY STEELE** – bass repl. RYAN

Jun 71. (7") *(WIP 6092)* <1265> **MOON SHADOW. / FATHER AND SON** [22] [30]

Sep 71. (7") *(WIP 6102)* **TUESDAY'S DEAD. / MILES FROM NOWHERE** [ ] [–]

Sep 71. (7") <1291> **PEACE TRAIN. / WHERE DO THE CHILDREN PLAY?** [–] [7]

Sep 71. (lp) *(ILPS 9154)* <4313> **TEASER AND THE FIRECAT** [3] [2]
– The wind / Ruby love / If I laugh / Changes IV / How can I tell you / Tuesday's dead / Morning has broken / Bitterblue / Moon shadow / Peace train. *(re-iss. 1974 & Jan78; same) (re-iss. Oct86 lp/c/cd; ILPM/ICM/CID 9154) (cd re-iss. Mar90; IMCD 104) (cd re-mast.May00; IMCD 267)*

(below 'A'side featured **RICK WAKEMAN** – piano)

Dec 71. (7") *(WIP 6121)* <1335> **MORNING HAS BROKEN. / I WANT TO LIVE IN A WIGWAM** [9] Mar72 [6]

—— In Apr'72, STEVENS contributed tracks to film 'Harold And Maude'.

—— added **JEAN ROUSELL** – piano / **CAT** – some synthesizers repl. WAKEMAN. **ALAN JAMES** – bass repl. LARRY

Sep 72. (lp) *(ILPS 9206)* <4365> **CATCH BULL AT FOUR** [2] [1]
– Sitting / Boy with a moon and star on his head / Angel sea / Silent sunlight / Can't keep it in / 18th Avenue / Freezing steel / O Caritas / Sweet Scarlet / Ruins. *(re-iss. 1974 & Jan78; same) (cd-iss. Oct86; CID 9206) (cd re-iss. Jul89; IMCD 34) (cd re-mast.Aug00; IMCD 271)*

Nov 72. (7") *(WIP 6152)* **CAN'T KEEP IT IN. / CRAB DANCE** [13] [–]

Nov 72. (7") <1396> **SITTING. / CRAB DANCE** [–] [16]

—— CAT now became a tax exile in Brazil and donated money to charity

—— now w / **ROUSSEL, DAVIS, LYNCH + CONWAY** plus loads of sessioners

Jul 73. (7") *(WIP 6163)* <1418> **THE HURT. / SILENT SUNLIGHT** [ ] [31]

Jul 73. (lp) *(ILPS 9240)* <4391> **FOREIGNER** [3] [3]
– Foreigner suite / The hurt / How many times / Later / 100 I dream. *(re-iss. quad.1974) (cd-iss. Nov89; IMCD 72) (cd re-mast.Aug00; IMCE 272)*

—— **BRUCE LYNCH** – bass repl. PAUL

Mar 74. (7") *(WIP 6190)* <1503> **OH VERY YOUNG. / 100 I DREAMS** [ ] [10]

Mar 74. (lp/c) *(ILPS/ICT 9274)* <3623> **BUDDAH AND THE CHOCOLATE BOX** [3] [2]
– Music / Oh very young / Sun – C79 / Ghost town / Jesus / Ready / King of trees / Bad penny / Home in the sky. *(cd-iss. Nov89; IMCD 70) (cd re-mast.Aug00; IMCD 273)*

Jun 74. (lp) <228> **SATURDAY NIGHT (live in Tokyo)** [–] [ ]
– Wild world / Oh very young / Sitting / Where do the children play? / Lady d'Arbanville / Another Saturday night / Hard-headed woman / Peace train / Father & son / King of trees / A bad penny / Bitter blue.

Aug 74. (7") *(WIP 6206)* <1602> **ANOTHER SATURDAY NIGHT. / HOME IN THE SKY** [19] [6]

Dec 74. (7") <1645> **READY. / I THINK I SEE THE LIGHT** [–] [26]

Jul 75. (7") *(WIP 6238)* <1700> **TWO FINE PEOPLE. / BAD PENNY** [ ] [33]

Jul 75. (lp/c) *(ILPS/ICT 9310)* <4519> **GREATEST HITS** (compilation) [2] [6]
– Wild world / Oh very young / Can't keep it in / Hard headed woman / Moonshadow / Two fine people / Peace train / Ready / Father and son / Sitting / Morning has broken / Another Saturday night. *(cd-iss. Apr87; CID 9310) (cd-iss. Mar93; IMCD 168)*

—— now w / **ROUSSEL, DAVIS, LYNCH + CONWAY** plus loads of sessioners

Dec 75. (lp/c) *(ILPS/ICT 9370)* <4555> **NUMBERS** [ ] [13]
– Whistlestar / Novim's nightmare / Majik of majiks / Dry wood / Banapple gas / Land o' free love and goodbye / Jzero / Home / Nomad's anthem. *(cd-iss. Mar01; IMCD 277)*

Mar 76. (7") *(WIP 6276)* <1785> **BANAPPLE GAS. / GHOST TOWN** [ ] Feb76 [41]

Mar 76. (7") <1924> **LAND O' FREE LOVE AND GOODBYE. / (I NEVER WANTED) TO BE A STAR** [–] [ ]

Apr 77. (lp/c) *(ILPS/ICT 9451)* <4702> **IZITSO** [18] [7]
– (Remember the days of the) Old schoolyard / Life / Killin' time / Kypros / Bonfire / To be a star / Crazy / Sweet Jamaica / Was Dog a doughnut / Child for a day. *(cd-iss. Mar01; IMCD 278)*

Jun 77. (7") *(WIP 6387)* **(REMEMBER THE DAYS OF THE) OLD SCHOOLYARD. / DOVES** [44] [–]

Jun 77. (7") <1948> **(REMEMBER THE DAYS OF THE) OLD SCHOOLYARD. / LAND O' FREE LOVE AND GOODBYE** [–] [33]

Nov 77. (7") <1971> **WAS DOG A DOUGHNUT. / SWEET JAMAICA** [–] [70]

Jan 79. (7") <2109> **BAD BRAKES. / NASCIMENTO** [–] [83]

Jan 79. (lp/c) *(ILPS/ICT 9565)* <4735> **BACK TO EARTH** [ ] Dec 78 [33]
– Just another night / Daytime / Bad brakes / Randy / The artist / Last love song / Nascimento / Father / New York times / Never. *(cd-iss. Mar01; IMCD 279)*

Feb 79. (7") *(WIP 6465)* **LAST LOVE SONG. / NASCIMENTO** [ ] [–]

Apr 79. (7") <2126> **RANDY. / NASCIMENTO** [–] [ ]

—— STEVENS retired from the music scene, due to newfound Muslim religion. He changed his name to YUSUF ISLAM and married Fouzia Ali in Sep'79. They lived in London where he taught his faith to local school. In the late 80's, he was back in the limelight, when he condoned the Muslim sanction for the assassination of writer Salman Rushdie.

– compilations, etc. –

Nov 70. (lp) *Decca; (SPA 93)* **THE WORLD OF CAT STEVENS** [ ] [–]

Mar 71. (d-lp) *Deram;* <18005> **MATTHEW AND SON / NEW MASTERS** [–] [ ]
(UK-iss.May75 as 'VIEW FROM THE TOP'; DPA 3019-20)

Jan 72. (lp) *Deram;* <18061> **VERY YOUNG AND EARLY SONGS** [–] [94]

Nov 73. (7") *Deram; (DM 406)* **I LOVE MY DOG. / MATTHEW AND SON** –
(re-iss. Oct83 on 'Old Gold'; OG 9336)

Aug 80. (7"ep) *Deram; (DM 435)* **MATTHEW AND SON / I LOVE MY DOG. / A BAD NIGHT / I'M GONNA GET ME A GUN** –

Aug 81. (lp/c) *Rock Echoes; (TAB/KTAB 25)* **THE FIRST CUT IS THE DEEPEST** –

Nov 83. (7") *Island; (IS 123)* **MORNING HAS BROKEN. / MOON SHADOW** –

Jan 85. (lp/c) *Island; <(ILPS/ICT 3736)>* **FOOTSTEPS IN THE DARK – GREATEST HITS VOL. 2** Dec84
(US version +=) – (3 extra tracks). *(cd-iss. 1988; CD 3736)*

Apr 86. (d-lp/c) *Castle; (CCS LP/MC 127)* **THE COLLECTION** –
(cd-iss. Sep92; CCSCD 127)

Apr 86. (c) *Spot; (SPC 8574)* **CAT STEVENS** –

Jan 88. (cd) *Deram; (820 561-2)* **FIRST CUTS** –

Feb 90. (cd)(lp/c) *Island; (840 148-2)(CATV/+C 1)* **THE VERY BEST OF CAT STEVENS** 4
– Where do the children play / Wild world / Tuesday's dead / Lady D'Arbanville / The first cut is the deepest / Oh very young / Rubylove / Morning has broken / Moonshadow / Matthew and son / Father and son / Can't keep it in / Hard headed woman / (Remember the days of the) Old school yard / I love my dog / Another Saturday night / Sad Lisa / Peace train. *(re-iss. Jul92; same)*

Nov 92. (d-cd) *Island; (ITSCD 12)* **TEA FOR THE TILLERMAN / TEASER & THE FIRECAT** –

Apr 93. (cd) *Pulsar;* **WILD WORLD** –

Sep 93. (cd/c) *Spectrum; (550108-2/-4)* **EARLY TAPES** –

Sep 95. (d-cd/d-c; as YUSUF ISLAM) *Mountain Of Light; (MOL 7001 CD/MC 3)* **THE LIFE OF THE LAST PROPHET** –

Feb 99. (cd; as YUSUF ISLAM) *Mountain Of Light; (MOL 70006CD)* **PRAYERS OF THE LAST PROPHET** –

Nov 99. (cd/c) *Island; (CID/ICT 8079) <524608>* **REMEMBER CAT STEVENS – THE ULTIMATE COLLECTION** 31
– Moon shadow / Father and son / Morning has broken / Wild world / The first cut is the deepest / Lady d'Arbanville / Oh very young / Matthew and son / Sitting / Hard-headed woman / I love my dog / Rubylove / Don't be shy / Can't keep it in / Here comes my baby / Into white / (Remember the days of the) Old schoolyard / Where do the children play / Land o' freelove & goodbye / Another Saturday night / The Foreigner suite (excerpt) / Just another night / Peace train / If you want to sing out, sing out.

Apr 00. (cd) *A&M; <541387>* **THE VERY BEST OF CAT STEVENS** – 58

May 00. (cd/c; as YUSUF ISLAM) *Mountain Of Light; (MOL 70010 CD/MC) / Resurgent; <4707>* **A IS FOR ALLAH** Jul00

Sep 03. (4xcd-box) *(<585285-2>)* **ON THE ROAD TO FIND OUT** Oct03

Oct 03. (cd+dvd) *Universal TV; (9811208)* **THE VERY BEST OF CAT STEVENS** 6 –

Al STEWART

Born: 5 Sep'45, Glasgow, Scotland. Moving to Bournemouth with his widowed mother as a toddler, STEWART later learned guitar alongside ROBERT FRIPP. In the mid-60's, after briefly sharing a flat with fellow (then) budding singer/songwriter folkie, PAUL SIMON, he released a one-off '45, 'THE ELF', for 'Decca', one JIMMY PAGE (then a session musician) playing lead guitar. Signing to 'C.B.S.' in 1967, he debuted with the 'BED-SITTER IMAGES' album the same year, which if nothing else, helped invent the concept of the down-at-heel songwriter poring over angst-ridden ruminations in the safety of his room. STEWART's navel-gazing tales of doomed romance were given free rein on 'ZERO SHE FLIES' (1970) and 'ORANGE' (1972), punctuated by the odd track written from a more historical vein. 1973's quasi-concept affair, 'PAST, PRESENT & FUTURE', took the latter approach to its conclusion and in 'NOSTRADAMUS' featured one of STEWART's most compelling tracks. Subsequently relocating to California, the singer's more Americanised latter 70's output saw him become a fairly major Stateside star. STEWART's first effort for 'R.C.A.', 'YEAR OF THE CAT' (1976) made the US Top 5 (UK Top 40) on the strength of the infectious title track, an American Top 10 hit in its own right. Produced by ALAN PARSONS, the record saw STEWART's fragile, understated style presented in a more accessible pop-folk framework, as did its (almost equally commercially fruitful) successor, 'TIME PASSAGES' (1978). 1980's '24 CARROTS' didn't perform quite so well, STEWART embroiled in business problems for much of the 80's. Comeback set, 'LAST DAYS OF THE CENTURY' (1988), was a synth-enhanced affair embracing STEWART's increasingly fanciful lyrical themes, the singer moving to 'E.M.I.', then 'Permanent' in the 90's for whom he continues to record consistent, if commercially limited material.

Album rating: BED-SITTER IMAGES (*4) / LOVE CHRONICLES (*7) / ZERO SHE FLIES (*6) / ORANGE (*6) / PAST, PRESENT AND FUTURE (*7) / MODERN TIMES (*6) / YEAR OF THE CAT (*8) / TIME PASSAGES (*6) / 24 CARROTS (*5) / LIVE INDIAN SUMMER (*5) / RUSSIANS & AMERICANS (*5) / LAST DAYS OF THE CENTURY (*5) / CHRONICLES: THE BEST OF AL STEWART compilation (*8) / RHYMES IN ROOMS (*5) / FAMOUS LAST WORDS (*5) / BETWEEN THE WARS (*5)

AL STEWART – vocals, guitar with orchestra

Decca / not iss.

Jul 66. (7") *(F 12467)* **THE ELF. / TURN INTO STONE** –

C.B.S. / Columbia

Sep 67. (7") *(CBS 3034)* **BEDSITTER IMAGES. / SWISS COTTAGE MANOEUVRES** –

Oct 67. (lp; stereo/mono) *(S+/BPG 63087)* **BED-SITTER IMAGES** –
– Bedsitter images / Swiss Cottage manoeuvres / Scandinavian girl * / Pretty golden hair * / Denise at 16 / Samuel, oh how you've changed! / Cleave to me * / A long way down from Stephanie / Ivich / Beleeka doodle day. *(re-iss. Jun70 as 'THE FIRST ALBUM (BED-SITTER IMAGES)'; CBS 64023)* – Lover man / Clifton in the rain. *(repl. * tracks)*

Jan 69. (lp; stereo/mono) *(S+/63460)* **LOVE CHRONICLES**
– In Brooklyn / Old Compton Street blues / Ballad of Mary Foster / Life and life only / You should've listened to Al / Love chronicles. *(re-is.May82 on 'RCA International' lp/c; INT S/K 5120)*

Mar 70. (7") *(CBS 4843)* **ELECTRIC LOS ANGELES SUNSET. / MY ENEMIES HAVE SWEET VOICES** –

Mar 70. (lp) *(CBS 64023)* **ZERO SHE FLIES** 40 –
– My enemies have sweet voices / A small fruit song / Gethsemane again / Burbling / Electric Los Angeles sunset / Manuscript / Black hill / Anna / Room of roots / Zero she flies. *(re-iss. Oct85 on 'R.C.A.' lp/c; NL/NK 70874)*

Dec 71. (7") *(CBS 5351)* **THE NEWS FROM SPAIN. / ELVASTON PLACE** –

Feb 72. (7") *(CBS 7763)* **YOU DON'T EVEN KNOW ME. / I'M FALLING** –

Feb 72. (lp) *(CBS 64739)* **ORANGE** –
– You don't even know me / Amsterdam / Songs out of clay / The news from Spain / I don't believe you / Once an orange, always an orange / I'm falling / Night of the 4th of May. *(re-iss. Nov81 lp/c; CBS/40 32061) (cd-iss. Jul96 on 'Columbia'; 484441-2)*

Apr 72. (7") *(CBS 7992)* **AMSTERDAM. / SONGS OUT OF CLAY** –

C.B.S. / Janus

Sep 73. (7") *(CBS 1791)* **TERMINAL EYES. / LAST DAYS OF JUNE 1934** –

Oct 73. (lp) *(CBS 65726) <3063>* **PAST, PRESENT & FUTURE** Jan74
– Old admirals / Warren Harding / Soho (needless to say) / Last days of June 1934 / Post World War Two blues / Roads to Moscow / Terminal eyes / Nostradamus. *(re-iss. Jun81 lp/c; CBS/40 32026) <US cd-iss. 1987 on 'Arista'; ARCD 8359> (cd-iss. Nov92 on 'Beat Goes On'; BGOCD 155)*

Apr 74. (7") *<243>* **NOSTRADAMUS. / TERMINAL EYES** –

— Around Spring'74, toured with backing band HOME

Jun 74. (7") *(CBS 2397)* **NOSTRADAMUS. / SWALLOW WIND** –

— backed w/ **GERRY CONWAY / SIMON NICOL / PAT DONALDSON & SIMON ROUSSEL**

Mar 75. (7") *<250>* **CAROL. / SIRENS OF TITAN** –

Apr 75. (7") *(CBS 3254)* **CAROL. / NEXT TIME** –

Apr 75. (lp/c) *(CBS/40 80477) <7012>* **MODERN TIMES** Feb75 30
– Carol / Sirens of Titan / What's going on / Not the one / Next time /

Apple cider / Re-constitution / The dark and rolling sea / Modern times. *(re-iss. Mar81 lp/c; CBS/40 32019) (cd-iss. Jan93 on 'Beat Goes On'; BGOCD 156)*

R.C.A. Janus

Oct 76. (lp/c) *(RS/ 1082) <7022>* **YEAR OF THE CAT** [38] [5]
– Lord Grenville / On the border / Midas shadow / Sand in your shoes / If it doesn't come naturally, leave it / Flying sorcery / Broadway Hotel / One stage before / Year of the cat. *(re-iss. Sep81 lp/c; RCA LP/K 3015) (cd-iss. Nov84; ND 71493) (re-iss. Dec87 lp/c; NL/NK 71493) (re-iss. Apr91 on 'Fame' cd/c; CD/TC FA 3253) (cd re-mast.Sep01 on 'E.M.I.'; 535456-2)*

Jan 77. (7") *(RCA 2771) <266>* **YEAR OF THE CAT. / BROADWAY HOTEL** [31] Nov76 [8]

Apr 77. (7") *(PB 5019) <267>* **ON THE BORDER. / FLYING SORCERY** [ ] [42]

R.C.A. Arista

Sep 78. (lp/c) *(PL/PK 25173) <4190>* **TIME PASSAGES** [39] [10]
– Time passages / Valentina way / Life in dark water / A man for all seasons / Almost Lucy / Palace of Versailles / Timeless skies / Song on the radio / End of the day. *(re-iss. Sep81 lp/c; RCA LP/K 3026) (re-iss. Aug84 lp/c; PL/PK 70274) (cd-iss. Dec86; PD 70274) (cd re-iss. Oct91 on 'Fame'; CDFA 3312)*

Sep 78. (7") *<0362>* **TIME PASSAGES. / ALMOST LUCY** [–] [7]

Feb 79. (7") *(PB 5139) <0389>* **SONG ON THE RADIO. / A MAN FOR ALL SEASONS** [ ] Jan79 [29]

Aug 80. (7") *(RCA 2)* **MONDO SINISTRO. / MERLIN'S TIME** [ ] [–]

Aug 80. (lp/c) *(PL/PK 25306) <9520>* **24 CARROTS** [55] [37]
– Running man / Midnight rocks / Constantinople / Merlin's time / Mondo sinistro / Murmansk run – Ellis Island / Rocks in the ocean / Paint by numbers / Optical illusion. *(re-iss. Sep81 lp/c; RCA LP/K 3042) (cd-iss. Aug92 on 'E.M.I.'; CZ 512)*

Aug 80. (7") *<0552>* **MIDNIGHT ROCKS. / CONSTANTINOPLE** [–] [24]

Nov 80. (7") *(RCA 17)* **PAINT BY NUMBERS. / OPTICAL ILLUSION** [ ] [ ]

Jan 81. (7") *<0585>* **RUNNING MAN. / MERLIN'S TIME** [–] [ ]

Oct 81. (7") *(RCA 149) <0639>* **INDIAN SUMMER. / PANDORA** [ ] [ ]

Nov 81. (d-lp/d-c) *(RCA LP/K 70257) <8607>* **LIVE – INDIAN SUMMER (live)** [ ] [ ]
– Here in Angola / Pandora / Indian summer / Princess Olivia / Running man / Time passages / Merlin's time / If it doesn't come naturally, leave it / Roads to Moscow / Nostradamus (part 1) – World goes to Riyadah – Nostradamus (part 2) / Soho (needless to say) / On the border / Valentina way / Clarence Frogman Henry / Year of the cat. *(re-iss. 1984 lp/c; PL/PK 70257)*

R.C.A. Passport

May 84. (lp/c) *(PL/PK 70307)* **RUSSIANS AND AMERICANS** [83] [ ]
– Strange girl / Russians and Americans / Cafe society / One, two, three / The candidate / 1-2-3 / Lori, don't go right now * / Rumours of war / The gypsy and the rose * / Accident on 3rd Street. *<US repl. * track>* – The one that got away / Night meeting. *(cd-iss. Jul93 on 'E.M.I.'; CZ 523)*

Jun 84. (7") *(RCA 414)* **LORI, DON'T GO RIGHT NOW. / ACCIDENT ON 3rd STREET** [ ] [–]

May 85. (lp/c) *(PL/PK 70715)* **THE BEST OF AL STEWART** (compilation) [ ] [ ]
– Year of the cat / On the border / If it doesn't come naturally, leave it / Time passages / Almost lucky / Merlin's theme / Valentina way / Running man / Roads to Moscow / Here in Angola / Rumours of war. *<US cd 1988; ARCD 8433> (cd-iss. Feb97 on 'E.M.I.'; CTMCD 310)*

Enigma Enigma

Sep 88. (lp/c/cd) *(ENVLP/TCENV/CDENV 505)* **LAST DAYS OF THE CENTURY** [ ] [ ]
– Last days of the century / Real and unreal / King of Portugal / Red toupee / Where are they now / Bad reputation / Josephine Baker / License to steal / Fields of France / Antartica / Ghostly horses of the plain. *(cd+=)* – Helen and Cassandra. *(re-iss. Jul90 cd/c/lp; 773 316-2/-4/-1)*

Oct 88. (7") *(ENV 4)* **KING OF PORTUGAL. / JOSEPHINE BAKER** [ ] [ ]
(12"+=) *(ENVT 4)* – Bad reputation.
(3"cd-s++=) *(ENVCD 4)* – ('A'-rock mix version).

E.M.I. Mesa

Feb 92. (cd/c/lp) *(CD/TC+/EMC 3613)* **RHYMES IN ROOMS (live)** [ ] [ ]
– Flying sorcery / Soho (needless to say) / Time passages / Josephine Baker / Nostradamus / On the border / Fields of France / Medley:- Clifton in the rain – A small fruit song / Broadway hotel / If it doesn't come naturally, leave it / Year of the cat. *(re-iss. cd Feb95 on 'Fame'; CDFA 3315)*

Mar 92. (7") **RHYMES IN ROOMS (live). / YEAR OF THE CAT (live)** [ ] [ ]
(cd-s+=) – Songs on the radio.

Permanent Mesa

Oct 93. (cd/c) *(PERM CD/MC 15)* **FAMOUS LAST WORDS** [ ] Feb94 [ ]
– Feel like / Angels of mercy / Don't forget me / Peter on the white sea / Genie on a table top / Trespasser / Trains / Necromancer / Charlotte Corday / Hippo song / Night rolls on.

E.M.I. Mesa

Jun 95. (cd/c) *(CD/TC EMC 3710)* **BETWEEN THE WARS** [ ] [ ]
– Night train to Munich / The age of rhythm / Sampan / Lindy comes to town / Three mules / A league of notions / Between the wars / Betty Boop's birthday / Marion the Chatelaine / Joe the Georgian / Always the cause / Laughing into 1939 / The black Danube.

– compilations, etc. –

Apr 78. (lp/c) *R.C.A.; (PL/PK 25131) / Arista; <US-d-lp>* **THE EARLY YEARS** (1967-1970) [ ] [ ]
(re-iss. Oct81 lp/c; INT S/K 5156) (re-iss. Sep86 on 'Fame' lp/c; FA/TC-FA 3165)

1985. (7") *Arista;* **YEAR OF THE CAT / TIME PASSAGES** [–] [ ]

Nov 86. (7") *Old Gold; (OG 9642)* **THE YEAR OF THE CAT. / (other track by Climax Blues Band)** [ ] [–]

Jun 91. (cd/c) *E.M.I.; (CD/TC EMC 3590)* **CHRONICLES: THE BEST OF AL STEWART (1976-81)** [ ] [ ]
– Year of the cat / On the border / If it doesn't come naturally, leave it / Time passages / Almost Lucy / Song on the radio * / Running man * / Merlin's time / In Brooklyn / Soho (needless to say) * / A small fruit song / Manuscript / Roads to Moscow (live) / Nostradamus (part 1) – World goes to Riyadh – Nostradamus (part 2). *(cd+= *)*

Oct 93. (d-cd) *E.M.I.; (CDEM 1511) <27709>* **TO WHOM IT MAY CONCERN (1966-1970)** [ ] [ ]

Apr 97. (3xcd-box) *E.M.I.; (CDOMB 020)* **THE ORIGINALS** [ ] [ ]
– (YEAR OF THE CAT / TIME PASSAGES / RUSSIANS AND AMERICANS)

Sep 97. (cd) *E.M.I.; (CDEMS 1625)* **LIVE AT THE ROXY, LOS ANGELES, 1981** [ ] [–]

Jun 98. (cd) *EMI Gold; (494942-2)* **ON THE BORDER** [ ] [–]

Jun 98. (cd) *E.M.I.; <36973>* **AN ACOUSTIC EVENING WITH . . .** [–] [ ]

Feb 01. (cd) *E.M.I.; (531426-2)* **DOWN IN THE CELLAR** [ ] [–]

Mar 03. (cd) *E.M.I.; (76408-2)* **SINGER / SONGWRITER** [ ] [–]

Mar 03. (cd) *E.M.I.; (581878-2)* **THE ESSENTIAL AL STEWART** [ ] [–]

Jul 03. (cd) *E.M.I.; (INTROCD 7)* **INTRODUCING . . . AL STEWART** [ ] [–]

Rod STEWART

Born: RODERICK DAVID STEWART, 10 Jan'45, Highgate, London, England. Of Scottish parentage, STEWART remains a passionate Scotland supporter and considers himself an adopted Scot. In addition to music, obviously, the singer's other passion is football, the young ROD initially biding his time as an apprentice for Brentford F.C. The lure of the itinerant lifestyle proved irresistible, however, and STEWART subsequently hooked up with folk singer, WIZZ JONES, busking/learning his trade around Europe before eventually being deported for vagrancy in 1963. Upon his return, STEWART threw himself headlong into the burgeoning Brit R&B scene as part of West Midlands group, JIMMY POWELL & The FIVE DIMENSIONS. He then took his feted harmonica blowing skills to London, playing on a live effort by JOHN BALDRY & THE HOOCHIE COOCHIE MEN. This in turn, led to ROD developing his vocal talents and releasing a one-off single for 'Decca' in 1964, 'GOOD MORNING LITTLE

SCHOOLGIRL', before briefly joining BALDRY's new outfit (also featuring BRIAN AUGER, JULIE DRISCOLL and MICK WALLER, the latter a future STEWART collaborator), STEAMPACKET, the following year. After a dispute with BALDRY, STEWART then added a stint with SHOTGUN EXPRESS (alongside a star-studded line-up which boasted a young PETER GREEN and MICK FLEEETWOOD amongst others) to his increasingly impressive CV. The big break finally came in 1967, when JEFF BECK recruited him as a lead singer, ROD's vocals gracing two albums, 'TRUTH' (1968) and 'BECK-OLA' (1969). While still a member of the JEFF BECK GROUP, STEWART signed a solo deal with 'Phonogram', debuting with 'AN OLD RAINCOAT WON'T EVER LET YOU DOWN' in early 1970 (US title, 'THE ROD STEWART ALBUM'). The record was a revelation, the years of practice finally coming together with STEWART rasping his way through a rootsy solo blueprint of folk, country, blues and R&B. Rapidly establishing himself as one of the finest white soul vocalists in the history of rock, STEWART's voice was a unique, compelling combination of bourbon-throated abrasiveness and blue-eyed crooning, equally at home on choice cover material (EWAN MacCOLL's 'Dirty Old Town' and MIKE D'ABO's 'Handbags And Gladrags') as his own brilliant originals, highlights being the gritty 'CINDY'S LAMENT' and the title track. Simultaneously, ROD had joined The FACES (formerly The SMALL FACES) along with RON WOOD, the pair forming the central writing core of the band as they grew from a laddish club act into stadium headliners, WOOD also becoming STEWART's right-hand writing partner through the pioneering early years of the singer's solo career. 'GASOLINE ALLEY' (1970) was a FACES album in all but name, if a bit more downbeat, WOOD, RONNIE LANE and KENNY JONES (IAN McLAGAN absent due to a 'bus strike', apparently!) all playing on a record which launched STEWART in the States (Top 30) and musically, was a companion piece to The FACES' acclaimed 'A Nod Is As Good As A Wink To A Blind Horse' (1971). Kicking in with the plaintive slide guitar moan and emotive reverie of the title track through a cover of ELTON JOHN's 'Country Comfort' and STEWART's own 'LADY DAY', the album also featured the first of his DYLAN cover versions, a sympathetic reading of 'ONLY A HOBO'. With the amplified acoustic double whammy of the 'MAGGIE MAY' / 'REASON TO BELIEVE' single in summer '71, ROD went from critical darling to international superstar overnight, the attendant transatlantic No.1 album, 'EVERY PICTURE TELLS A STORY' (1971) representing the creative pinnacle of his career. Featuring regular contributors such as guitarist, MARTIN QUITTENTON alongside the likes of DANNY THOMPSON and Scot, MAGGIE BELL, the album was a masterclass in roots rock boasting one of his most perfectly conceived originals in the lovely 'MANDOLIN WIND'. The choice of cover material was, as ever, impeccable, STEWART cutting a dash through ARTHUR CRUDUP's 'That's All Right' (a track originally made famous by ELVIS PRESLEY) and wringing a pathos from TIM HARDIN's aforementioned 'Reason To Believe' which even its doomed composer couldn't muster. 'NEVER A DULL MOMENT' (1972) was almost as good, the record taking STEWART's boisterous-lad-with-a-senstitive-side persona to its ultimate conclusion by interspersing a trio of worldly-wise rockers (including the classic 'TRUE BLUE') with a beautiful cover of BOB DYLAN's 'Mama You Been On My Mind', the record also spawning another UK No.1 single with 'YOU WEAR IT WELL'. By 1974, The FACES were buckling under the pressure of STEWART's massive successful solo career although, ironically, this also began to slide inexorably downhill, creatively at least, with the disappointing 'SMILER' set. This was the sound of ROD going through the motions, only 'LOCHINVAR' and 'DIXIE TOOT' approaching previous standards. Worse was to come though, as STEWART jacked in London for America, hooking up with sex bomb actress, Britt Ekland and effecting one of the most extensive and needless musical turnarounds of the 70's. Many rock artists have been accused of 'selling-out' over the years but few managed it with such thoroughness and dearth of integrity. 'ATLANTIC CROSSING' (1975) and 'A NIGHT ON THE TOWN' (1976) had their moments (a cover of DANNY WHITTEN's 'I Don't Want To Talk About It' on the former and a definitive reading of CAT STEVEN's 'The First Cut Is The Deepest' on the latter), although danger signs were on the horizon. While the engaging ballad, 'THE KILLING OF GEORGIE' saw ROD acknowledging his sizeable gay following and the lilting 'TONIGHT'S THE NIGHT' (both major hits from 'A NIGHT . . .') proved ROD could still pen a decent love song, such tasteless nonsense as 'HOT LEGS' and 'D'YA THINK I'M SEXY' saw the singer living his sexist image up to the full as well as indulging his growing passion for pseudo-disco MOR. Predictably, by the release of 'BLONDES HAVE MORE FUN' (1978), STEWART was enjoying more success in America than his home country, the singer trawling a creative trough in the early 80's with the likes of 'FOOLISH BEHAVIOUR' and 'TONIGHT I'M YOURS'. His sales figures remained relatively undiminished however, STEWART enjoying the life of the rock aristocrat, his string of relationships with high profile blondes never far from the gossip columns. Tellingly, the singer's best work of the decade came via a reunion with JEFF BECK, the pair getting together for a brilliant reworking of CURTIS MAYFIELD's 'People Get Ready' (Top 50). The 90's saw STEWART regain at least some critical ground with 'VAGABOND HEART' (1991) while the obligatory 'UNPLUGGED . . . AND SEATED' (1993) saw an entertaining reunion with WOOD. Bizarrely enough, ROD has also exhibited a penchant for covering songs by arch weirdo, TOM WAITS, the latest of which, 'HANG ON ST. CHRISTOPHER', appeared on 'A SPANNER IN THE WORKS' (1995). While this alone signals that STEWART hasn't completely lost the musical plot, the prospect of him ever returning to the downhome brilliance of old looked slimmer with each passing year. However, 1998 saw Rod The Mod turn in a fine batch of covers (bar one of his own) under the title of 'WHEN WE WERE THE NEW BOYS'. At the tender age of 56, ROD crossed over to 'Atlantic' records although things didn't get off to a flyer when the single, 'RUN BACK INTO YOUR ARMS', flopped. However, 'I CAN'T DENY IT' restored the man to the Top 30 and secured a Top 10 spot for his umpteenth set, 'HUMAN' (2001). Moving to an Americanised blend of R&B-pop (BABYFACE and EN VOGUE might've been his template), ROD suffered a backlash of sorts from the critics who thought his previous set was a step forward. Cue the entrance of industry mogul extrordinaire Clive Davis, who came up with the idea of rehabilitating ROD's failing career via an album of standards. Hardly an original concept, granted, but one guaranteed to appeal more to his ageing fanbase than a ridiculous attempt at pseudo-R&B. In the event, 'IT HAD TO BE YOU: THE GREAT AMERICAN SONGBOOK' (2002) sounded pretty much as expected, ROD bringing his battered tonsils to the likes of Gershwin's 'YOU CAN'T TAKE THAT AWAY FROM ME' and Jerome Kern's 'THE WAY YOU LOOK TONIGHT'. Suited up and sounding more at ease than he's done since ' . . . THE NEW BOYS', the singer had seemingly found his latter day vocation. So much so that a second volume was paraded a year later, CHER and QUEEN LATIFAH making unlikely – and somewhat distracting – guest appearances. • **Songwriters:** ROD's cover versions:- STREET

FIGHTING MAN (Rolling Stones) + RUBY TUESDAY / SWEET SOUL MUSIC (Arthur Conley) / I KNOW I'M LOSING YOU (Temptations) / IT'S ALL OVER NOW (Valentinos) / MY WAY OF GIVING (Small Faces) / CUT ACROSS SHORTY (hit; Eddie Cochran) / ANGEL (Jimi Hendrix) / AMAZING GRACE (trad. / hit; Judy Collins) / I'D RATHER GO BLIND (Etta James) / ONLY A HOBO + SWEETHEART LIKE YOU (Bob Dylan) / TWISTIN' THE NIGHT AWAY + BRING IT ON HOME TO ME + YOU SEND ME + HAVING A PARTY + SOOTHE ME (Sam Cooke) / OH NO NOT MY BABY + PRETTY FLAMINGO (Manfred Mann) / COUNTRY COMFORTS + YOUR SONG (Elton John) / WHAT MADE MILWALKEE FAMOUS (hit; Jerry Lee Lewis) / SAILING (Sutherland Brothers) / THIS OLD HEART OF MINE (Isley Brothers) / GET BACK (Beatles) / YOU KEEP ME HANGIN' ON (Supremes) / I DON'T WANT TO TALK ABOUT IT (Crazy Horse member Danny Whitten) / SOME GUYS HAVE ALL THE LUCK (Robert Palmer) / HOW LONG (Ace) / SWEET LITTLE ROCK'N'ROLLER + LITTLE QUEENIE (Chuck Berry) / THE GREAT PRETENDER (Platters) / ALL RIGHT NOW (Free) / TRY A LITTLE TENDERNESS (Otis Redding) / THE MOTOWN SONG (L.J.McNally) / IT TAKES TWO (Marvin Gaye & Tammi Terrell) / DOWNTOWN TRAIN + TOM TRAUBERT'S BLUES (Tom Waits) / BROKEN ARROW (Robbie Robertson) / HAVE I TOLD YOU LATELY THAT I LOVE YOU (Van Morrison) / PEOPLE GET READY (Curtis Mayfield) / SHOTGUN WEDDING (Roy C) / WINDY TOWN (Chris Rea) / DOWNTOWN LIGHTS (Blue Nile) / LEAVE VIRGINIA ALONE (Tom Petty) / OOH LA LA (with The Faces) / CIGARETTES & ALCOHOL (Oasis) / ROCKS (Primal Scream) / SUPERSTAR (Superstar) / SECRET HEART (Ron Sexsmith) / HOTEL CHAMBERMAID (Graham Parker) / SHELLY MY LOVE (Nick Lowe) / WEAK (Skunk Anansie) / WHAT DO YOU WANT ME TO DO (Mike Scott). SIMON CLIMIE began writing for him from 1988. YOU'RE THE STAR single written by Livesey, Lyle & Miller. **Trivia/Blondeography:** BRITT EKLAND (marriage 5 Mar'75-1978) / ALANA HAMILTON (marriage 1979-1984) / KELLY EMBERG (1985-1990) / RACHEL HUNTER (marriage 1990-1999) / PENNY LANCASTER (1999-now).

Album rating: AN OLD RAINCOAT WILL NEVER LET YOU DOWN (*7) / GASOLINE ALLEY (*7) / EVERY PICTURE TELLS A STORY (*9) / NEVER A DULL MOMENT (*8) / SING IT AGAIN ROD (*5) / SMILER (*4) / ATLANTIC CROSSING (*7) / A NIGHT ON THE TOWN (*6) / FOOT LOOSE AND FANCY FREE (*4) / BLONDES HAVE MORE FUN (*5) / GREATEST HITS VOL.1 compilation (*8) / FOOLISH BEHAVIOUR (*3) / TONIGHT I'M YOURS (*6) / ABSOLUTELY LIVE (*3) / BODY WISHES (*3) / CAMOUFLAGE (*3) / EVERY BEAT OF MY HEART (aka ROD STEWART) (*4) / OUT OF ORDER (*5) / STORYTELLER – THE BEST OF ROD STEWART 1964-1990 compilation (*8) / VAGABOND HEART (*6) / UNPLUGGED . . . AND SEATED (*7) / A SPANNER IN THE WORKS (*6) / IF WE FALL IN LOVE TONIGHT (*6) / WHEN WE WERE THE NEW BOYS (*7) / HUMAN (*5) / THE STORY SO FAR compilation (*8) / IT HAD TO BE YOU . . . THE GREAT AMERICAN SONGBOOK (*5) / AS TIME GOES BY . . . THE GREAT AMERICAN SONGBOOK VOLUME II (*4) / CHANGING FACES: THE VERY BEST OF ROD STEWART & THE FACES compilation (*8)

ROD STEWART – vocals with session people

Decca / Press

Oct 64. (7") *(F 11996)* **GOOD MORNING LITTLE SCHOOLGIRL. / I'M GONNA MOVE TO THE OUTSKIRTS OF TOWN**
(re-iss. Mar82)

—— in 1965, ROD joined STEAMPACKET but they issued no 45's; split Mar'66

Columbia / not iss.

Nov 65. (7") *(DB 7766)* **THE DAY WILL COME. / WHY DOES IT GO ON** – –

Apr 66. (7") *(DB 7892)* **SHAKE. / I JUST GOT SOME** – –

—— A month previous, he had joined SHOTGUN EXPRESS who released one 45, 'I COULD FEEL THE WHOLE WORLD TURN AROUND' Oct66 on 'Columbia'.

Immediate / not iss.

Nov 67. (7") *(IM 060)* **LITTLE MISS UNDERSTOOD. / SO MUCH TO SAY** – –
(re-iss. Sep80 on 'Virgin') (re-iss. Feb83)

—— In 1968, he joined JEFF BECK GROUP, appearing on 2 albums; 'TRUTH' & 'BECK-OLA'. Simiultaneously joined The FACES and returned to solo work 1969.

Vertigo / Mercury

Feb 70. (lp) *(VO 4)* *<61237>* **AN OLD RAINCOAT WON'T EVER LET YOU DOWN** <US-title 'THE ROD STEWART ALBUM'>
– Street fighting man / Man of constant sorrow / Blind prayer / Handbags and gladrags / An old raincoat won't ever let you down / I wouldn't ever change a thing / Cindy's lament / Dirty old town. *(re-iss. Aug83 on 'Mercury' lp/c; PRICE/PRIMC 27) (cd-iss. Nov87 & Sep95; 830 572-2) (cd re-iss. Aug98; 558058-2)*

Feb 70. (7") *<73009>* **AN OLD RAINCOAT WON'T LET YOU DOWN. / STREET FIGHTING MAN** –

May 70. (7") *(73031)* **HANDBAGS AND GLADRAGS. / MAN OF CONSTANT SORROW** –
<re-iss. Feb72; *73031*> – hit No.42.

Sep 70. (7") *(6086 002)* *<73095>* **IT'S ALL OVER NOW. / JO'S LAMENT**

Sep 70. (lp) *(6360 500)* *<61264>* **GASOLINE ALLEY** 62 Jun70 27
– Gasoline alley / It's all over now / My way of giving / Country comfort / Cut across Shorty / Lady day / Jo's lament / I don't want to discuss it. *(re-iss. Aug83 on 'Mercury' lp/c; PRICE/PRIMC 28) (cd-iss. Oct84 + Sep95; 824 881-2) (cd re-iss. Aug98; 558059-2)*

Nov 70. (7") *<73115>* **GASOLINE ALLEY. / ONLY A HOBO** –

Jan 71. (7") *<73156>* **CUT ACROSS SHORTY. / GASOLINE ALLEY** –

Mar 71. (7") *<73175>* **MY WAY OF GIVING. /** –

May 71. (7") *<73196>* **COUNTRY COMFORT. / GASOLINE ALLEY** –

Mercury / Mercury

Jul 71. (7") *(6052 097)* *<73224>* **MAGGIE MAY. / REASON TO BELIEVE** 1 1 62
(above was flipped over for BBC Radio One playlist. MAGGIE MAY was now the bigger played hit) *(re-iss. Oct84)*

Jul 71. (lp) *(6338 063)* *<609>* **EVERY PICTURE TELLS A STORY** 1 Jun71 1
– Every picture tells a story / Seems like a long time / That's all right / Tomorrow is such a long time / Amazing Grace / Henry / Maggie May / Mandolin wind / (I know) I'm losing you / Reason to believe. *(re-iss. May83 lp/c; PRICE/PRIMC 15) (cd-iss. Nov87 & Sep95; 822 385-2) (cd re-iss. Aug98; 558060-2)*

Nov 71. (7") *<73244>* **(I KNOW) I'M LOSING YOU. / MANDOLIN WIND** – 24

Jul 72. (lp) *(6499 153)* *<646>* **NEVER A DULL MOMENT** 1 2
– True blue / Lost Paraguayos / Mama you been on my mind / Italian girls / Angel / Interludings / You wear it well / I'd rather go blind / Twisting the night away. *(re-iss. May83 lp/c;) (cd-iss. Nov87 & Sep95; 826 263-2) (cd re-iss. Aug98; 558061-2)*

Aug 72. (7") *(6052 171)* **YOU WEAR IT WELL. / LOST PARAGUAYOS** 1 –

Aug 72. (7") *<73330>***YOU WEAR IT WELL. / TRUE BLUE** – 13

—— Sep72, a ROD STEWART early recording with PYTHON LEE JACKSON; 'In A Broken Dream' hits UK No.3 / US No.56.

Nov 72. (7") *(6052 198)* **ANGEL. / WHAT MADE MILWAUKEE FAMOUS (HAS MADE A LOSER OUT OF ME)** 4 –

Nov 72. (7") *<73344>* **ANGEL. / LOST PARAGUAYOS** – 40

—— May73, older JEFF BECK & ROD STEWART recording 'I'VE BEEN DRINKIN' ' hit 27.

Aug 73. (7") *<73412>* **TWISTING THE NIGHT AWAY. / TRUE BLUE – LADY DAY** – 59

Aug 73. (lp)(c) *(6499 484)(7142 183)* *<680>* **SING IT AGAIN ROD** (compilation of covers) 1 Jul73 31
– Reason to believe / You wear it well / Mandolin wind / Country comforts / Maggie May / Handbags and gladrags / Street fighting man / Twisting the night away / Lost Paraguayos / (I know) I'm losing you / Pinball wizard / Gasoline alley. *(cd-iss. Oct84; 824882-2) (cd re-iss. Aug98; 558062-2)*

Aug 73. (7") *(6052 371)* *<73426>* **OH! NO NOT MY BABY. / JODIE** 6 Oct73 59

Sep 74. (7") *(6167 033)* **FAREWELL. / BRING IT ON HOME TO ME – YOU SEND ME (Medley)** 7 –

Oct 74. (lp)(c) *(9104 001)* *<1017>* **SMILER** 1 13
– Sweet little rock'n'roller / Lochinvar / Farewell / Sailor / Bring it on home to me – You send me (medley) / Let me be your car / A natural man / A natural man / Dixie toot / Hard road / I've grown accustomed to her face / Girl of the North Country / Mine for me. *(cd-iss. Nov87 & Sep95; 832 056-2) (cd re-iss. Aug98; 558063-2)*

Nov 74. (7") *<73636>* **MINE FOR ME. / FAREWELL** – 91

Jan 75. (7") *<73660>* **LET ME BE YOUR CAR. / SAILOR** –

Warners Warners

Aug 75. (7") *(K 16600)* **SAILING. / STONE COLD SOBER** 1 –
(re-activated Sep76, hit UK No.3, re-iss. Jan84) (re-iss. Jun77 on 'Riva') (re-iss. Mar87 for Channel Ferry disaster fund, hit No.41)

Aug 75. (lp/c) *(K/K4 56151)* *<2875>* **ATLANTIC CROSSING** 1 9
– Three time loser / Alright for an hour / All in the name of rock'n'roll / Drift away / Stone cold sober / I don't want to talk about it / It's not the spotlight / This old heart of mine / Still love you / Sailing. *(re-iss. Jan78 on 'Riva' lp/c; RV LP/4 4) (cd-iss. Feb87; K2 56151) (blue-lp Jul77) (cd re-iss. Nov00 on 'WEA'; 9362 47729-2)*

Aug 75. (7") *<8146>* **SAILING. / ALL IN THE NAME OF ROCK'N'ROLL** – 58

Riva Warners

Nov 75. (7") *(1)* **THIS OLD HEART OF MINE. / ALL IN THE NAME OF ROCK'N'ROLL** 4 –

Jan 76. (7") *<8170>* **THIS OLD HEART OF MINE. / STILL LOVE YOU** – 83

May 76. (7") *(RIVA 3)* **TONIGHT'S THE NIGHT. / THE BALLTRAP** 5 –

Jun 76. (lp/c) *(RV LP/4 1)* *<2938>* **A NIGHT ON THE TOWN** 1 2
– Tonight's the night / The first cut is the deepest / Fool for you / The killing of Georgie (part 1 & 2) / The balltrap / Pretty flamingo / Big bayou / The wild side of life / Trade winds. *(re-iss. Jun83 on 'Warner Bros' lp/c; K/K4 56234) (cd-iss. 1989 on 'WEA'; K2 56234) (cd re-iss. Jun93; 7599 27339-2) (cd re-iss. Nov00 on 'WEA'; 9362 47730-2)*

Aug 76. (7") *(RIVA 4)* **THE KILLING OF GEORGIE. / FOOL FOR YOU** 2 –

Sep 76. (7") *<8262>* **TONIGHT'S THE NIGHT. / FOOL FOR YOU** – 1

Nov 76. (7") *(RIVA 6)* **GET BACK. / TRADE WINDS** 11 –

Feb 77. (7") *<8321>* **THE FIRST CUT IS THE DEEPEST. / THE BALLTRAP** – 21

Apr 77. (7") *(RIVA 7)* **THE FIRST CUT IS THE DEEPEST. / I DON'T WANT TO TALK ABOUT IT** 1 –

Apr 77. (7") *<8396>* **THE KILLING OF GEORGIE. / ROSIE** – 30

Oct 77. (7") *(RIVA 11)* *<8476>* **YOU'RE IN MY HEART. / YOU GOT A NERVE** 3 4

Nov 77. (lp/c) *(RV LP/4 5)* *<3092>* **FOOT LOOSE AND FANCY FREE** 3 2
– Hot legs / You're insane / You're in my heart / Born loose / You keep me hangin' on / (If loving you is wrong) I don't want to be right / You got a nerve / I was only joking. *(re-iss. Jun83 on 'Warner Bros.' lp/c; K/K4 56423) (cd-iss. Jun89; K2 56423) (cd re-iss. Nov00 on 'WEA'; 9362 47731-2)*

Jan 78. (7") *(RIVA 10)* **HOT LEGS. / I WAS ONLY JOKING** 5 –

Feb 78. (7") *<8535>* **HOT LEGS. / YOU'RE INSANE** – 28

Apr 78. (7") *<8568>* **I WAS ONLY JOKING. / BORN LOOSE** – 22

May 78. (7"; by ROD STEWART with the SCOTLAND WORLD CUP SQUAD) *(RIVA 15)* **OLE OLA (MUHLER BRASILEIRA). / I'D WALK A MILLION MILES FOR ONE OF YOUR GOALS** 4 –

Nov 78. (7") *(RIVA 17)* **D'YA THINK I'M SEXY?. / DIRTY WEEKEND** 1 –

Dec 78. (7") *<8734>* **D'YA THINK I'M SEXY?. / SCARRED AND SCARED** – 1

Dec 78. (lp/c)<US-pic-lp> *(RV LP/4 8)* *<3261>* **BLONDES HAVE MORE FUN** 3 1
– D'ya think I'm sexy / Dirty weekend / Ain't love a bitch / The best days of my life / Is that the thanks I get / Attractive female wanted / Blondes (have more fun) / Last summer / Standing in the shadows of love / Scarred and scared. *(re-iss. Jun83 on 'Warner Bros.' lp/c; K/K4 56572) (cd-iss. Jan91 on 'Warners'; 7599 27376-2) (cd re-iss. Nov00 on 'WEA'; 9362 47732-2)*

Jan 79. (7") *(RIVA 18)* **AIN'T LOVE A BITCH. / SCARRED AND SCARED** 11 –

Apr 79. (7") *<8810>* **AIN'T LOVE A BITCH. / LAST SUMMER** – 22

Apr 79. (7") *(RIVA 19)* **BLONDES (HAVE MORE FUN). / THE BEST DAYS OF MY LIFE** 63 –

Nov 79. (lp/c) *(RODTV/+4 1)* *<3373>* **GREATEST HITS VOLUME 1** (compilation) 1 22
– Hot legs / Maggie May / a ya think I'm sexy / You're in my heart / Sailing / I don't want to talk about it / Tonight's the night / The killing of Georgie (parts 1 & 2) / Maggie May / The first cut is the deepest / I was only joking. *(re-iss. Jun83 lp/c; K/K4 56744) (cd-iss. Jan84 on 'Warner Bros.'; K2 56744)*

Dec 79. (7") *<49138>* **I DON'T WANT TO TALK ABOUT IT. / THE BEST DAYS OF MY LIFE** – 46

May 80. (7") *(RIVA 23)* **IF LOVING YOU IS WRONG (I DON'T WANT TO BE RIGHT). / LAST SUMMER** 23 –

Nov 80. (7"/ext.12") *(RIVA 26/+T)* *<49617>* **PASSION. / BETTER OFF DEAD** 17 5

Nov 80. (lp/c) *(RV LP/4 11)* *<3485>* **FOOLISH BEHAVIOR** 4 12
– Better off dead / Foolish behaviour / My girl / She won't dance with me / Gi' me wings / So soon we change / Somebody special / Passion / Say it ain't true / Oh God, I wish I was home tonight. *(re-iss. Jun83 on 'Warner Bros.' lp/c; >)*

Dec 80. (7") *(RIVA 28)* **MY GIRL. / SHE WON'T DANCE WITH ME** 32 –

Mar 81. (7"/c-s) *(RIVA 29/+M)* **OH GOD, I WISH I WAS HOME TONIGHT. / SOMEBODY SPECIAL** –

Mar 81. (7") *<49686>* **SOMEBODY SPECIAL. / SHE WON'T DANCE WITH ME** – 71

Oct 81. (7") *<49843>* **YOUNG TURKS. / SONNY** – 5

Oct 81. (7") *(RIVA 33)* **TONIGHT I'M YOURS (DON'T HURT ME). / SONNY** 8 –

Nov 81. (lp/c) *(RV LP/4 14)* *<3602>* **TONIGHT I'M YOURS** 8 11
– Tonight I'm yours (don't hurt me) / Only a boy / Just like a woman / How long / Never give up on a dream / Jealous / Tora, Tora, Tora (out with the boys) / Young Turks / Tear it up / Sonny. *(re-iss. Jun83 lp/c; K/K4 56951) (cd-iss. Jun93 on 'Warners'; 7599 23602-2) (cd re-iss. Nov00 on 'WEA'; 9362 47717-2)*

Dec 81. (7") *(RIVA 34)* **YOUNG TURKS. / TORA, TORA, TORA (OUT WITH THE BOYS)** 11 –

Jan 82. (7") *<49886>* **TONIGHT I'M YOURS (DON'T HURT ME). / TORA, TORA, TORA (OUT WITH THE BOYS)** – 20

Feb 82. (7") *(RIVA 35)* *<50051>* **HOW LONG. / JEALOUS** 41 Apr82 49

Nov 82. (d-lp/d-c) *(RV LP/4 17)* *<23743>* **ABSOLUTELY LIVE (live)** 35 46
– The stripper / Tonight I'm yours / Sweet little rock'n'roller / Hot legs / Tonight's the night / The great pretender / Passion / She won't dance with me / Little Queenie / You're in my heart / Rock my plimsoul / Young Turks / Guess I'll always love you / Gasoline alley / Maggie May / Tear it up / D'ya think I'm sexy / Sailing / I don't want to talk about it / Stay with me. *(re-iss. Mar84 on 'Warner Bros.' d-lp/dc; 923743-1/-4) (cd-iss. Mar87; 923743-2)*

Nov 82. (7") *<29874>* **GUESS I'LL ALWAYS LOVE YOU (live). / ROCK MY PLIMSOUL (live)** –

Warners Warners

May 83. (7") *(W 9608)* *<29608>* **BABY JANE. / READY NOW** 1 14
(12"+=) *(W 9608T)* – If loving you is wrong (live).

Jun 83. (lp/c) *(K 923977-1/-4)* *<23877>* **BODY WISHES** 5 30
– Dancin' alone / Baby Jane / Move me / Body wishes / Sweet surrender / What am I gonna do / Ghetto blaster / Ready now / Strangers again / Satisfied. *(cd-iss. Jul84; K 923977-2)*

Aug 83. (7"/12") *(W 9564/+T)* *<29564>* **WHAT AM I GONNA DO?. / DANCIN' ALONE** 3 35

Dec 83. (7"/67"pic-d) *(W 9440/+P)* **SWEET SURRENDER. / GHETTO BLASTER** 23 –
(12"+=) *(W 9440T)* – Oh God I wish I was home tonight.

May 84. (7") *<29256>* **INFATUATION. / SHE WON'T DANCE WITH ME** – 6

May 84. (7") *(W 9256)* **INFATUATION. / THREE TIME LOSER** 27 –
(12"+=) *(W 9256T)* – Tonight's the night.

Jun 84. (lp/c/cd) *(925095-1/-4/-4)* *<25095>* **CAMOUFLAGE** 8 18
– Infatuation / All right now / Some guys have all the luck / Can we still be friends / Bad for you / Heart is on the line / Camouflage / Trouble. *(free 1-sided 7"pic-d w.a.)* – INFATUATION / (interview).

Jul 84. (7") *(W 9204)* *<29215>* **SOME GUYS HAVE ALL THE LUCK. / I WAS ONLY JOKING** 15 10
(12"+=) *(W 9204T)* – The killing of Georgie.

Nov 84. (7") *(W 9115)* **TROUBLE. / TORA, TORA, TORA (OUT WITH THE BOYS)** [ ] [–]
(12"+=) *(W 9115T)* – This old heart of mine.

Dec 84. (7") *<29112>* **ALL RIGHT NOW. / DANCIN' ALONE** [–] [72]

—— In 1985, he was credited on 45 'PEOPLE GET READY' by JEFF BECK.

Jun 86. (7") *(W 8668) <28668>* **LOVE TOUCH. / HEART IS ON THE LINE** [27] May86 [6]
(12"pic-d+=) *(W 8668TP)* – Hard lesson to learn.

Jun 86. (lp/c)(cd) *(WX 53/+C)(925446-2) <25446>* **EVERY BEAT OF MY HEART** <US-title 'ROD STEWART'> [5] [28]
– Here to eternity / Another heartache / A night like this / Who's gonna take me home / Red hot in black / Love touch / In my own crazy way / Every beat of my heart / Ten days of rain / In my life. *(cd+=)* – Every beat of my heart (remix).

Jul 86. (7") *(W 8625) <28625>* **EVERY BEAT OF MY HEART. / TROUBLE** [2] Nov86 [83]
(12"+=) *(W 8625)* – ('A'mix).
(12"pic-d+=) *(W 8625TE)* – Some guys have all the luck (live)

Sep 86. (7") *(W 8631) <28631>* **ANOTHER HEARTACHE. / YOU'RE IN MY HEART** [54] [52]
(12"+=) *(W 8631T)* – ('A'extended).

Jul 87. (7") *<28303>* **TWISTING THE NIGHT AWAY. / LET'S GET SMALL** [–] [80]
above was issued on 'Geffen' and on film 'Innerspace'.

May 88. (7")<US-c-s> *(W 7927) <27927>* **LOST IN YOU. / ALMOST ILLEGAL** [21] [12]
(12"+=/12"pic-d+=) *(W 7927 T/TP)* – ('A'extended).
(cd-s+=) *(W 7927CD)* – Baby Jane / Every beat of my heart.

May 88. (lp/c)(cd) *(WX 152/+C)(925684-2) <25684>* **OUT OF ORDER** [11] [20]
– Lost in you / The wild horse / Lethal dose of love / Forever young / My heart can't tell you no / Dynamite / Nobody loves you when you're down and out / Crazy about her / Try a little tenderness / When I was your man.

Jul 88. (7") *(W 7796) <27796>* **FOREVER YOUNG. / DAYS OF RAGE** [57] [12]
(12"+=) *(W 7796)* – ('A'extended).
(cd-s+=) *(W 7796CD)* – Every beat of my heart.

Jan 89. (7") **TRY A LITTLE TENDERNESS. / MY HEART CAN'T TELL YOU NO** [–] [ ]

Apr 89. (7") *(W 7729) <27729>* **MY HEART CAN'T TELL YOU NO. / THE WILD HORSE** [49] Nov88 [4]
(12"+=/12"pic-d+=/cd-s+=) *(W 7729 T/TP/CD)* – Passion (live).

May 89. (7"/c-s) *<27657>* **CRAZY ABOUT HER. / DYNAMITE** [–] [11]

Nov 89. (7"/7"pic-d/c-s; with RONALD ISLEY) *(W 2686/+P) <19983>* **THIS OLD HEART OF MINE. / TONIGHT I'M YOURS (DON'T HURT ME)** [51] [–]
(12"+=/cd-s+=/12"pic-d+=) *(W 2686 T/TP/CD)* – Ain't love a bitch.

Nov 89. (d-lp/d-c/d-cd) *(925987-2/-4/-1) <25987>* **STORYTELLER – THE BEST OF ROD STEWART 1964-1990** (compilation) [3] [54]

—— (was also issued UK on (7xlp)(4xc)(4xcd).

Jan 90. (7"/c-s) *(W 2647/+C) <22685>* **DOWNTOWN TRAIN. / THE KILLING OF GEORGIE (pt.1 & 2)** [10] Nov89 [3]
(12"/cd-s) *(W 2647 T/CD)* – ('A'side) / Hot legs.
(12"+=) *(W 2647TE)* – ('A'side) / Cindy incidentally / To love somebody.

Mar 90. (7"; with RONALD ISLEY) *<19983>* **THIS OLD HEART OF MINE. / YOU'RE IN MY HEART** [–] [10]

Mar 90. (cd/c) *<26158>* **DOWNTOWN TRAIN – SELECTIONS FROM STORYTELLER** (compilation) [–] [20]

Nov 90. (7"/c-s; ROD STEWART & TINA TURNER) *(ROD 1/+C)* **IT TAKES TWO. / HOT LEGS (live)** [5] [ ]
(12"+=/cd-s+=) *(ROD 1 T/CD)* – ('A'extended remix).

Mar 91. (7"/c-s) *(W 0017) <19366>* **RHYTHM OF MY HEART. / MOMENT OF GLORY** [3] Feb91 [5]
(12"+=/cd-s+=) *(W 0017 T/CD)* – I don't want to talk about it (re-recording).

Apr 91. (cd)(lp/c) *(<7599 26596-2>)(WX 408/+C)* **VAGABOND HEART** [2] [10]
– Rhythm of my heart / Rebel heart / Broken arrow / It takes two / When a man's in love / You are everything / The Motown song / Go out dancing / No holding back / Have I told you lately that I love you / Moment of glory / Downtown train / If only.

Jun 91. (7"/c-s) *(W 0030/+C) <19322>* **THE MOTOWN SONG. / SWEET SOUL MUSIC (live)** [10] [10]
(12"+=/cd-s+=) *(W 0030 T/CD)* – Try a little tenderness.

Aug 91. (7"/c-s) *(W 0059/+C)* **BROKEN ARROW. / I WAS ONLY JOKING** [54] [–]
(10"+=/cd-s+=) *(W 0059 T/CD)* – The killing of Georgie (parts 1 & 2).

Oct 91. (c-s,cd-s) *<19274>* **BROKEN ARROW / THE WILD HORSE** [–] [20]

Apr 92. (c-s,cd-s) *<865944>* **YOUR SONG / MANDOLIN WIND** [–] [48]

—— <above issued on 'Polydor' US>

Apr 92. (7"/c-s) *(W 0104/+C)* **YOUR SONG. / BROKEN ARROW** [41] [–]
(12"+=/cd-s+=) *(W 0104 T/CD)* – Mandolin wind / The first cut is the deepest.

Nov 92. (7"/c-s) *(W 0104/+C)* **TOM TRAUBERT'S BLUES (WALTZING MATILDA). / NO HOLDING BACK** [6] [–]
(cd-s+=) *(W 0104CD)* – Downtown train.
(cd-s) *(W 0104CDX)* – ('A'side) / Sailing / I don't want to talk about it / Try a little tenderness.

Feb 93. (cd/c/lp) *(<9362 45258-2>)(WX 503/+C)* **ROD STEWART, LEAD VOCALIST** (part compilation) [3] [–]
– I ain't superstitious / Handbags & gladrags / Cindy incidentally / Stay with me / True blue / Sweet Mary lady / Hot legs / Stand back / Ruby Tuesday / Shotgun wedding / First I look at the purse / Tom Traubert's blues.

Feb 93. (7"/c-s) *(W 0158/+C)* **RUBY TUESDAY. / YOU'RE IN MY HEART** [11] [–]
(cd-s+=) *(W 0158CD)* – Out of order / Passion.
(cd-s+=) *(W 0158CDX)* – Crazy about her / Passion.

Apr 93. (7"/c-s) *(W 0171/+C)* **SHOTGUN WEDDING. / EVERY BEAT OF MY HEART** [21] [–]
(cd-s+=) *(W 0171CD)* – Sweet soul music (live).
(cd-s) *(W 0171CDX)* – ('A'side) / Memphis / Maybe I'm amazed / Had me a real goodtime (all 3 by ROD STEWART & THE FACES).
below with special guest **RONNIE WOOD** – guitar plus others **JEFF GOLUB** – guitar / **CARMINE ROJAS** – bass / **CHARLES KENTISS III** – piano, organ / **KEVIN SAVIGAR** – piano, organ & accordion / **JIM CREGAN** – guitar / **DON TESCHNER** – guitar, violin & mandolin / **PHIL PARLAPIANO** – accordion & mandolin / & backing singers

May 93. (cd/c/lp) *(<9362 45289-2/-4/-1>)* **UNPLUGGED . . . AND SEATED (live)** [2] [2]
– Hot legs / Tonight's the night / Handbags and gladrags / Cut across Shorty / Every picture tells a story / Maggie May / Reason to believe / People get ready / Have I told you lately / Tom Traubert's blues (waltzing Matilda) / The first cut is the deepest / Mandolin wind / Highgate shuffle / Stay with me / Having a party.

Jun 93. (7"/c-s) *(W 0185/+C) <18511>* **HAVE I TOLD YOU LATELY THAT I LOVE YOU? / GASOLINE ALLEY** [5] Apr93 [5]
(cd-s+=) *(W 0185CD)* –
(cd-s) *(W 0185CDX)* – ('A'side) / Love wars / One night.

Aug 93. (7"/c-s) *(W 0198/+C) <18427>* **REASON TO BELIEVE (unplugged). / IT'S ALL OVER NOW (unplugged)** [51] [19]
(cd-s+=) *(W 0198CD1)* – Love in the right hands.
(cd-s) *(W 0198CD2)* – ('A'side) / Cindy incidentally / Stay with me (both w / FACES).

—— In Dec '93, ROD & STING, teamed up with BRYAN ADAMS on his US Top 5 hit 'All For Love'.

Dec 93. (7"/c-s) *(W 0226/+C)* **PEOPLE GET READY. / I WAS ONLY JOKING** [45] [–]
(cd-s) *(W 0226CD1)* – ('A'side) / Tonight's the night / If loving you is wrong (I don't want to be right).
(cd-s) *(W 0226CD2)* – ('A'side) / Da ya think I'm sexy / Sweet little rock'n'roller (live) / Baby Jane.

—— Late '93, ROD, BRYAN ADAMS and STING teamed up on a song from 'The Three Musketeers' film; 'ALL FOR LOVE', which hit UK No.2 (early '94) + US No.1.

Dec 93. (c-s,cd-s; ROD STEWART with RONNIE WOOD) *<18427>* **HAVING A PARTY (live unplugged) / SWEET LITTLE ROCK AND ROLLER (live acoustic)** [–] [36]

May 95. (c-s) *(W 0296C)* **YOU'RE THE STAR / SHOCK TO THE SYSTEM** [19] [–]
(cd-s+=) *(W 0296CD)* – Have I told you lately.

May 95. (cd/c/lp) *(<9362 45867-2/-4/-1>)* **A SPANNER IN THE WORKS** [4] [35]
– Windy town / Downtown lights / Leave Virginia alone / Sweetheart like you / This / Lady luck / You're the star / Muddy, Sam and Otis / Hang on St. Christopher / Delicious / Soothe me / Purple heather.

Jun 95. (c-s,cd-s) *<17847>* **LEAVE VIRGINIA ALONE / SHOCK TO THE SYSTEM** [–] [52]

Aug 95. (c-s) *(W 0310C)* **LADY LUCK / HOT LEGS** [56] [–]
(cd-s+=) *(W 0310CD1)* – The groom still waiting at the altar / Young Turks.

(cd-s) *(W 0310CD2)* – ('A'side) / The killing of Georgie / Sailing / The first cut is the deepest.

Jun 96. (c-s/cd-s) *(W 0354 C/CD)* **PURPLE HEATHER / EVERY BEAT OF MY HEART** [16] [ ]

—— The official song for Scotland's Euro '96 football campaign. All proceeds were donated to the families of the Dunblane tragedy.

Nov 96. (cd/c) *(<9362 46467-2/-4>)* **IF WE FALL IN LOVE TONIGHT** [8] [19]
– If we fall in love tonight / Sometimes when we touch / I don't want to talk about it / For the first time / When I need you / Broken arrow / Have I told you lately / Tonight / Forever young / My heart can't tell you no / First cut is the deepest / Tonight's the night / You're in my heart.

Dec 96. (c-s) *(W 0380C) <17459>* **IF WE FALL IN LOVE TONIGHT / TOM TRAUBERT'S BLUES (WALTZING MATILDA)** [58] Nov96 [54]
(cd-s) *(W 0380CD)* – ('A'side) / So far away / I was only joking / Ten days of rain.

—— N-TRANCE featured ROD on their version of 'DA YA THINK I'M SEXY?', which hit UK No.7 in Nov'97.

May 98. (c-s) *(W 0446C) <17195>* **OOH LA LA / A NIGHT LIKE THIS** [16] Jun98 [39]
(cd-s+=) *(W 0446CD)* – Ten days of rain.

Jun 98. (cd/c) *(<9362 46792-2/-4>)* **WHEN WE WERE THE NEW BOYS** [2] [44]
– Cigarettes and alcohol / Ooh la la / Rocks / Superstar / Secret heart / Hotel chambermaid / Shelly my love / When we were the new boys / Weak / What do you want me to do?

Aug 98. (c-s) *(W 0452C)* **ROCKS / STAY WITH ME (live)** [55] [–]
(cd-s+=) *(W 0452CD2)* – Maggie May (live).
(cd-s) *(W 0452CD1)* – ('A'side) / Hot legs (live) / Da ya think I'm sexy? (live).

Dec 98. (c-s/cd-s; w-drawn) *(W 465 C/CD)* **SUPERSTAR** [–] [–]

Universal / not iss.

Apr 99. (c-s) *(UNC 56235)* **FAITH OF THE HEART / Mark Shainman: MAIN TITLE SCORE** [60] [–]
(cd-s+=) *(UND 56235)* – Front porch.

Atlantic / Atlantic

Oct 00. (c-s) *(AT 0088C)* **RUN BACK INTO YOUR ARMS / WHEN WE WERE THE NEW BOYS** [ ] [–]
(cd-s+=) *(AT 0088CD)* – Red hot and black.

Mar 01. (c-s) *(AT 0096C) <85018>* **I CAN'T DENY IT / PEACH** [26] [–]
(cd-s+=) *(AT 0096CD)* – Do wah diddy.

Mar 01. (cd/c) *(<7567 83411-2/-4>)* **HUMAN** [9] Feb01 [50]
– Human / Smitten / Don't come around here / Soul on soul / Loveless / If I had you / Charlie Parker loves me / It was love that we needed / To be with you / Run back into your arms / I can't deny it. *(UK+=)* – Doo wah diddy (if you want me to go) / Peach.

May 01. (c-s; as ROD STEWART & HELICOPTER GIRL) *(AT 0104C)* **DON'T COME AROUND HERE / CUPID** [ ] [–]
(cd-s+=) *(AT 0104CD)* – Charlie Parker loves me.

J – B.M.G. / J – B.M.G.

Oct 02. (cd/c) *(74321 96867-2/-4) <20039>* **IT HAD TO BE YOU . . . THE GREAT AMERICAN SONGBOOK** [8] [4]
– You go to my head / They can't take that away from me / The way you look tonight / It had to be you / That old feeling / These foolish things / The very thought of you / Moonglow / I'll be seeing you / Ev'ry time we say goodbye / The nearness of you / For all we know / We'll be together again / That's all.

Oct 03. (cd) *(82876 57484-2) <55710>* **AS TIME GOES BY . . . THE GREAT AMERICAN SONGBOOK VOLUME II** [4] [2]
– Time after time / I'm in the mood for love / Don't get around much anymore / Bewitched, bothered & bewildered (with CHER) / 'Till there was you / Until the real thing comes along / Where or when / Smile / My heart stood still / Someone to watch over me (with QUEEN LATIFAH) / As time goes by (with QUEEN LATIFAH) / I only have eyes for you / Crazy she calls me / Our love is here to stay.

– compilations, etc. –

Sep 72. (7"; by PYTHON LEE JACKSON) *Youngblood; (YB 1017) / GNP Crescendo; <449>* **IN A BROKEN DREAM. / THE BLUES** [3] [56]
(re-iss. Jul80 /12"+=) – Cloud 9. *(re-iss. Aug87 as "PYTHON LEE JACKSON / ROD STEWART" on 'Bold Reprieve')*

—— PYTHON LEE JACKSON was in fact an Australian 5-piece of the late 60s, headed by keyboard player **DAVID BENTLEY**, who employed ROD to sing on 3 tracks from their lp 'IN A BROKEN DREAM'.

1979. (7") *Lightning;* **IN A BROKEN DREAM. / IF THE WORLD STOPS STILL TONIGHT** [ ] [–]

Below releases on 'Mercury' until otherwise mentioned.

Feb 76. (d-lp/c) *(6672 013)* **THE VINTAGE YEARS 1969-70** [ ] [ ]

Feb 76. (7") *(6086 02)* **IT'S ALL OVER NOW. / HANDBAGS AND GLADRAGS** [ ] [–]

1976. (7") **EVERY PICTURE TELLS A STORY. / WHAT MADE MILWAUKEE FAMOUS (HAS MADE A LOSER OUT OF ME)** [–] [ ]

Jul 76. (lp/c) **RECORDED HIGHLIGHTS AND ACTION REPLAYS** [ ] [ ]

Jun 77. (7"m) *(6160 007)* **MANDOLIN WIND. / GIRL FROM THE NORTH COUNTRY / SWEET LITTLE ROCK'N'ROLLER** [ ] [–]

Jun 77. (d-lp)(d-c) *(6643 030)(7599 141) <7507>* **THE BEST OF ROD STEWART** [18] [90]
(re-iss. Sep85 lp/c; PRID/+C 10)

Jul 77. (c) *(714506-1)* **THE MUSIC OF ROD STEWART (1970-71)** [ ] [–]

Aug 77. (d-lp/d-c) *(661903-1/-4)* **THE BEST OF ROD STEWART VOLUME 2** [ ] [ ]

Dec 78. (lp) *St.Michael;* **REASON TO BELIEVE** [ ] [–]

Nov 79. (7") *(6160 006)* **MAGGIE MAY. / YOU WEAR IT WELL** [ ] [–]
(re-iss. Apr88 on 'Old Gold';)

Sep 80. (lp) *(646306-1)* **HOT RODS** [ ] [–]

May 81. (lp) *(927913-2)* **BEST OF THE BEST** [ ] [–]

Sep 81. (lp/c) *Contour; (CN/+4 2045)* **MAGGIE MAY** [ ] [–]
(cd-iss. Jul90 on 'Pickwick'; PWKS 586)

Oct 82. (lp/c) *Contour; (CN/+4 2059)* **ROD STEWART** [ ] [–]

Jul 83. (d-c) *Cambra;* **ROD STEWART** [ ] [–]

Nov 83. (d-c) *Warners; (923955-2)* **ATLANTIC CROSSING / A NIGHT ON THE TOWN** [ ] [–]

Nov 84. (lp/c) *Astan; (2/4 0119)* **CAN I GET A WITNESS** [ ] [–]

Sep 85. (lp/c) *Contour; (CN/+4 2077)* **THE HITS OF ROD STEWART** [ ] [–]

Jan 87. (lp/c) *Contour; (CN/+4 2082)* **JUKE BOX HEAVEN (14 ROCK'N'ROLL GREATS)** [ ] [–]

Nov 87. (cd) *(925466-2)* **THE ROD STEWART ALBUM** [ ] [–]

Jul 88. (lp/c) *Knight; (KNLP/KNMC 10002)* **NIGHTRIDIN'** [ ] [–]

Feb 89. (c) *Venus; (VENUMC 3)* **THE MAGIC OF ROD STEWART** [ ] [–]

Jun 89. (lp/c/cd) *(830784-1/-4/-2)* **THE ROCK ALBUM** [ ] [–]

Jun 89. (cd) *(830785-2)* **THE BALLAD ALBUM** [ ] [–]

Oct 89. (lp/c/cd) *K-Tel;* **IN A BROKEN DREAM** [ ] 1988 [ ]

Feb 91. (cd/c) *(846 988-2/-4)* **GASOLINE ALLEY / SMILER** [ ] [–]

Oct 92. (7"/c-s) **YOU WEAR IT WELL. / I WOULD RATHER GO BLIND** [ ] [ ]
(cd-s+=) – Angel.

Dec 92. (cd/c) *M Classics; (CJES D/C 2)* **JUST A LITTLE MISUNDERSTOOD** [ ] [–]

Feb 93. (cd; ROD STEWART & STEAMPACKET) *Charly;* **THE FIRST SUPER GROUP** [ ] [–]

Jul 93. (cd/c) *Telstar; (CDSR/TCSR 014)* **THE FACE OF THE SIXTIES** [ ] [–]

Jul 94. (cd/c) *Success;* **COME HOME BABY** [ ] [–]

Jan 95. (cd/c) *K-Tel; (ECD3/EMC2 109)* **THE EARLY YEARS** [ ] [–]

Aug 95. (cd/c) *Spectrum; (551110-2/-4)* **MAGGIE MAY – THE CLASSIC YEARS** [ ] [–]
(re-iss. Sep98; same)

Oct 95. (d-cd) *Mercury; (528 823-2)* **HANDBAGS AND GLADRAGS (The Mercury Recordings 1970-1974)** [ ] [ ]

May 97. (cd) *Experience; (EXP 030)* **ROD STEWART** [ ] [–]

Jul 97. (cd) *Going For A Song; (GFS 061)* **ROD STEWART** [ ] [–]

Aug 98. (cd) *Mercury; (558873-2)* **THE VERY BEST OF ROD STEWART** [ ] [ ]

Oct 99. (cd) *Spectrum; (544165-2)* **REASON TO BELIEVE** [ ] [–]

Jan 00. (cd) *Universal; (E 546836-2)* **UNIVERSAL MASTERS COLLECTION** [ ] [–]

Apr 00. (cd) *A.B.M.; (ABMMCD 1082)* **SHAKE** [ ] [–]

Jul 00. (d-cd+CD-rom) *Burning Airlines; (PILOT 044)* **ROD STEWART 1964-1969** [ ] [–]
(d-lp re-iss. Dec00 on 'Get Back'; GET 578) (re-iss. Nov01; same)

Oct 00. (d-cd) *Universal; (E 536421-2)* **EVERY PICTURE TELLS A STORY / GASOLINE ALLEY** [ ] [–]

Oct 00. (3xcd-box) *Universal; (E 546586-2)* **EVERY PICTURE TELLS A STORY / GASOLINE ALLEY / SMILER** [ ] [–]

Nov 01. (d-cd/d-c) *(8122 73581-2/-4) <78328>* **THE STORY SO FAR – THE VERY BEST OF** [7] [69]

Jun 02. (d-cd; shared w/ ERIC CLAPTON) *Delta Blue; (6305-2)* **WHITE BOY BLUES** [ ] [–]

Oct 03. (d-cd) *Universal; (<9812604>)* **CHANGING FACES: THE VERY BEST OF ROD STEWART & THE FACES** [13] Dec03 [ ]
– Maggie May / Stay with me (FACES) / Reason to believe / You wear it well / In a broken dream (PYTHON LEE JACKSON) / Cut across Shorty / Had a real good time (FACES) / Miss Judy's farm (FACES) / Angel / Oh no not my baby / What made Milwaukee famous (has made a loser out of me) / (I know) I'm losing you / Mandolin wind / Every picture tells a story / I'd rather go blind / Twistin' the night away / Sweet little rock'n'roller / Bring it on home – You send me / Handbags & gladrags / It's all over now / Cindy incidentally (FACES) / Pool hall Richard (FACES) / Street fighting man / Gasoline alley / Let me be your car / That's all right / My way of giving / Italian girls / Lost Paraguayos / True blue / Hard road / (You make me feel like) A natural man / An old raincoat won't ever let you down / Jodie / Man of constant sorrow / You can make me dance, sing or anything (FACES).

STIFF LITTLE FINGERS

Formed: Belfast, N.Ireland . . . 1977 by teenagers JAKE BURNS, HENRY CLUNEY, ALI McMORDIE and GORDON BLAIR, the latter soon being replaced by BRIAN FALOON. Famously taking their name from a line in a VIBRATORS' b-side, the group began life as a CLASH covers band. Taken under the wing of journalist, GORDON OGILVIE (who subsequently became both band manager and BURNS' writing partner), the group began to rely on original material, releasing their incendiary 1978 debut single, 'SUSPECT DEVICE'. / 'WASTED LIFE' on the self-financed 'Rigid Digits' label. Wound tight, both lyrically and musically, with the frustration and anger of living in war-torn Belfast, the record introduced SLF as one of the most visceral and compelling punk bands since The SEX PISTOLS. Championed by the ever vigilant John Peel, the single led to a deal with 'Rough Trade' who jointly released a follow-up single, 'ALTERNATIVE ULSTER', the track rapidly assuming legendary status, although it was originally penned for release as a magazine flexi-disc. A debut album, 'INFLAMMABLE MATERIAL', followed in early '79, a raging, politically barbed howl of punk protest which lined up all the aforementioned tracks alongside such definitive SLF material as 'STATE OF EMERGENCY' and 'JOHNNY WAS'. Storming into the Top 20, the album expanded their already voracious fanbase, the group undertaking their first major headlining tour to promote it. The insistent, bass-heavy pop-punk dynamics of 'GOTTA GETAWAY' marked the debut of JIM REILLY (replacing the departing FALOON on the drum stool) and no doubt fuelled a thousand teenage runaway fantasies while the vicious 'STRAW DOGS' marked the group's major label debut for 'Chrysalis'. Early the following year, SLF scored their sole Top 20 hit with 'AT THE EDGE', another seething account of BURNS' troubled youth in Northern Ireland and arguably one of the group's finest moments. 'NOBODY'S HEROES' (1980) saw a move towards a more varied musical palette and a distinctly melodic feel, notably on the title track although 'TIN SOLDIERS' was as brutal as ever. The seminal live album, 'HANX!' (1980) gave the band their only Top 10 success later that year, surprising given the band's increasingly commercial approach as witnessed on the infectious 'JUST FADE AWAY' (possibly the only song ever written about a woman harassing a man!). A centerpiece of the 'GO FOR IT' (1981) set, the single stood in stark contrast to the insipid cod-reggae that so many punk bands, SLF unfortunately included, were now falling back on. 'NOW THEN' (1982) was an uncomfortable attempt to branch out even further into uncharted pop/rock territory, BURNS leaving soon after to form JAKE BURNS & THE BIG WHEEL. This effectively spelled the end for the band, and after a farewell tour, they called it a day. The live demand for SLF was so strong, however, that they were able to regroup in 1987, new material eventually surfacing in 1991 following the replacement of the disillusioned McMORDIE with ex-JAM bassist BRUCE FOXTON. The album in question, 'FLAGS AND EMBLEMS', hardly set the rock world alight, gigs predictably characterised by diehard fans shouting for old favourites. 'GET A LIFE' (1994) was similarly formulaic and, without being precious, one can't help but wonder how such a vital, influential band are now reduced to basically retreading past glories for a greying audience. That said, 2003's 'GUITAR AND DRUM' (2003), as its title hinted, was a visceral back to basics effort which easily ranked as their hardest hitting and most convincing set of songs since their original early 80's demise. Granted, it wasn't the classic line-up but it came close to sounding like it, with BURNS spitting lyrical venom in fine style (and at the state of the music industry on the title track) but sounding just as passionate when bidding farewell to a legend on 'STRUMMERVILLE'. • **Songwriters:** BURNS penned, some with OGILVIE. They also covered JOHNNY WAS (Bob Marley) / RUNNING BEAR (Johnny Preston) / WHITE CHRISTMAS (Bing Crosby) / LOVE OF THE COMMON PEOPLE (Nicky Thomas) / THE MESSAGE (Grandmaster Flash). • **Trivia:** JAKE once applied for a job as a Radio 1 producer.

Album rating: INFLAMMABLE MATERIAL (*8) / NOBODY'S HEROES (*7) / HANX! (*6) / GO FOR IT (*5) / NOW THEN (*5) / ALL THE BEST compilation (*8) / NO SLEEP TILL BELFAST (*5) / SEE YOU UP THERE! (*5) / FLAGS AND EMBLEMS (*5) / GET A LIFE (*4) / TINDERBOX (*4) / ANTHOLOGY compilation (*8) / GUITAR AND DRUM (*6)

JAKE BURNS – vocals, lead guitar / **HENRY CLUNEY** – guitar / **ALI McMORDIE** – bass / **BRIAN FALOON** – drums; repl. GORDON BLAIR who later joined RUDI

Rigid Digits — not iss.

Mar 78. (7") *(SRD-1)* **SUSPECT DEVICE. / WASTED LIFE** [ ] [–]
(re-iss. Jun78) (re-iss. Mar79 on 'Rough Trade'; RT 006)

Rough Trade — not iss.

Oct 78. (7") *(RT 004)* **ALTERNATIVE ULSTER. / '78 R.P.M.** [ ] [–]

Feb 79. (lp) *(ROUGH 1)* **INFLAMMABLE MATERIAL** [14] [–]
– Suspect device / State of emergency / Here we are nowhere / Wasted life / No more of that / Barbed wire love / White noise / Breakout / Law and order / Rough trade / Johnny was / Alternative Ulster / Closed groove. *(re-iss. Mar89 on 'E.M.I.' lp/c(cd); EMC/TC-EMC 3554)(CDP 792105-2) <US cd-iss. 1992 on 'Restless'; 72363> (cd re-iss. Oct01 on 'E.M.I.'+=; 535886-2)* – Suspect device (single version) / 78 rpm / (Jake Burns interview).

— **JIM REILLY** – drums; repl. FALOON

May 79. (7") *(RT 015)* **GOTTA GETAWAY. / BLOODY SUNDAY** [ ] [–]

Chrysalis — Chrysalis

Sep 79. (7") *(CHS 2368)* **STRAW DOGS. / YOU CAN'T SAY CRAP ON THE RADIO** [44] [–]

Feb 80. (7") *(CHS 2406)* **AT THE EDGE. / SILLY ENCORES: RUNNING BEAR – WHITE CHRISTMAS** [15] [–]

Mar 80. (lp/c) *(CHR/ZCHR 1270)* **NOBODY'S HEROES** [8] [ ]
– Gotta getaway / Wait and see / Fly the flag / At the edge / Nobody's hero / Bloody dub / Doesn't make it alright / I don't like you / No change / Tin soldiers. *(re-iss. Mar89 on 'E.M.I.' lp/c(cd); EMC/TC-EMC 3555)(CDP 792106-2) <US cd-iss. 1992 on 'Restless'; 72364> (cd re-iss. Oct01 on 'E.M.I.'+=; 535887-2)* – Bloody Sunday / Straw dogs / You can't say crap on the radio / (Jake Burns interview).

May 80. (7") *(CHS 2424)* **TIN SOLDIERS. / NOBODY'S HERO** [36] [–]

Jul 80. (7") *(CHS 2447)* **BACK TO FRONT. / MR FIRE COAL-MAN** [49] [–]

Sep 80. (lp/c) *(CHR/ZCHR 1300)* **HANX! (live)** [9] [–]
– Nobody's hero / Gotta getaway / Wait and see / Barbed wire love / Fly the flag / Alternative Ulster / Johnny was / At the edge / Wasted life / Tin soldiers / Suspect device. *(re-iss. Feb89 on 'Fame-EMI' lp/c/cd; FA/TC-FA/CD-FA 3215) <US cd-iss. 1992 on 'Restless'; 72365> (cd re-iss. Oct01 on*

'E.M.I.'+=; 535884-2) – Running bear / White Christmas / (Jake Burns interview).

Mar 81. (7"m) *(CHS 2510)* **JUST FADE AWAY. / GO FOR IT / DOESN'T MAKE IT ALRIGHT (live)** 47 –

Apr 81. (lp/c) *(CHR/ZCHR 1339)* **GO FOR IT** 14 –
– Roots, radicals, rockers and reggae / Just fade away / Go for it / The only one / Hits and misses / Kicking up a racket / Safe as houses / Gate 49 / Silver lining / Piccadilly Circus. *(re-iss. Feb89 on 'Fame-EMI' lp/c/cd+=; FA/TC-FA/CD-FA 3216)* – Back to front. *<US cd-iss. 1992 on 'Restless'; 72366> (cd re-iss. Sep93 on 'Dojo'+=; DOJOCD 148) (<cd re-iss. Oct00 on 'Captain Oi'++=; AHOYCD 151>)* – Mr Fire coal man / Doesn't make it alright (live).

May 81. (7") *(CHS 2517)* **SILVER LINING. / SAFE AS HOUSES** 68 –

— **BRIAN 'DOLPHIN' TAYLOR** – drums (ex-TOM ROBINSON BAND) repl. REILLY

Jan 82. (7"ep) *(CHS 2580)* **R.E.P. PAY 1.10 OR LESS EP** 33 –
– Listen / Sad-eyed people / That's when your blood bumps / Two guitars clash.

Apr 82. (7") *(CHS 2601)* **TALK BACK. / GOOD FOR NOTHING** –

Aug 82. (7"/12") *(CHS/+12 2637)* **BITS OF KIDS. / STANDS TO REASON** 73 –

Sep 82. (lp/c) *(CHR/ZCHR 1400)* **NOW THEN** 24 –
– Falling down / Won't be told / Love of the common people / The price of admission / Touch and go / Stands to reason / Bits of kids / Welcome to the whole week / Big city night / Talkback / Is that what you fought the war for. *(cd-iss. Dec94 on 'Fame'; CDFA 3306) (cd re-iss. Apr97 on 'EMI Gold'; CDGOLD 1090) (<cd re-iss. Oct00 on 'Captain Oi'+=; AHOYCD 152>)* – Listen Sad eyed people / That's when your blood bumps / Two guitars clash / Good for nothing.

Jan 83. (d-lp/d-c) *(CTY/ZCTY 1414)* **ALL THE BEST** (compilation) 19
– Suspect device / Wasted life / Alternative Ulster / '78 R.P.M. / Gotta getaway / Bloody Sunday / Straw dogs / You can't say crap on the radio / At the edge / Running bear / White Christmas / Nobody's hero / Tin soldiers / Back to front / Mr. Fire coal-man / Just fade away / Go for it / Doesn't make it alright / Silver lining / Safe as houses / Sad eyed people / Two guitars clash / Listen / That's when your blood bumps / Good for nothing / Talkback / Stand to reason / Bits of kids / Touch and go / The price of admission / Silly encores *[not on cass]. (d-cd-iss. Jun88; CCD 1414) (re-iss. Sep91 on 'E.M.I.' d-cd/d-c; CD/TC EM 1428) <US d-cd-iss. 1995 on 'One Way'; 18429>*

Feb 83. (7") *(CHS 2671)* **THE PRICE OF ADMISSION. / TOUCH AND GO** –

— Had already disbanded late 1982. McMORDIE joined FICTION GROOVE and DOLPHIN joined SPEAR OF DESTINY after stint with GO WEST.

JAKE BURNS & THE BIG WHEEL

— were formed by **JAKE** plus **NICK MUIR** – keyboards / **SEAN MARTIN** – bass / **STEVE GRANTLEY** – drums

Survival — not iss.

Jul 85. (7"/12") *(SRD/+T 2)* **ON FORTUNE STREET. / HERE COMES THAT SONG AGAIN** –

Mar 86. (7"/12") *(SRD/+T 3)* **SHE GREW UP. / RACE YOU TO THE GRAVE** –

Jive — not iss.

Feb 87. (7"/ext.12") *(JIVE/+T 139)* **BREATHLESS. / VALENTINE'S DAY** –

STIFF LITTLE FINGERS

— re-formed in 1987 by **BURNS, TAYLOR, CLUNEY & McMORDIE**

Link — not iss.

Apr 88. (d-lp,green-d-lp) *(LP 026)* **LIVE AND LOUD (live)** –
– Alternative Ulster / Roots radicals rockers and reggae / Silver lining / Wait and see / Gotta getaway / Just fade away / Wasted life / The only one / Nobody's hero / At the edge / Listen / Barbed wire love / Fly the flag / Tin soldiers / No sleep till Belfast / Suspect device / Johnny was. *(re-iss. May88 as 'NO SLEEP TILL BELFAST' on 'Kaz' c/cd; KAZ MC/CD 6) (cd-iss. Sep89; CD 026) ('NO SLEEP . . .' re-iss. Jun99 on 'Camden'; 74321 67786-2)*

Skunx — not iss.

Jun 88. (12"ep) *(SLFX 1)* **NO SLEEP TILL BELFAST (live)** –
– Suspect device / Alternative Ulster / Nobody's hero.

Virgin — Caroline

Mar 89. (12"ep/cd-ep) *(SLF/+CD 1)* **ST. PATRIX** (the covers live) –
– The wild rover / Love of the common people / Johnny Was.

Apr 89. (d-lp/d-c/d-cd) *(VGD/+C/CD 3515) <CAROL 1377-1/-4/-2>* **SEE YOU UP THERE! (live)**
– (intro: Go for it) / Alternative Ulster / Silver lining / Love of the common people / Gotta getaway / Just fade away / Piccadilly Circus / Gate 49 / Wasted life / At the edge / Listen / Barbed wire love / Fly the flag / Tin soldiers / The wild rover / Suspect device / Johnny was.

— (Mar'91) **BRUCE FOXTON** – bass (ex-JAM, ex-solo) repl. McMORDIE

Essential — Taang!

Oct 91. (cd/c/lp)(pic-lp) *(ESS CD/MC/LP 171)(EPDLP 171)* **FLAGS & EMBLEMS** –
– (It's a) Long way to Paradise (from here) / Stand up and shout / Each dollar a bullet / The cosh / Beirut Moon / The game of life / Human shield / Johnny 7 / Dread burn / No surrender. *(cd re-iss. Jul95 on 'Dojo'; DOJOCD 243)*

Oct 91. (cd-ep) *(ESSX 2007)* **BEIRUT MOON / STAND UP AND SHOUT / (JAKE interview)** –

Jan 94. (12"ep) *(ESS 2035)* **CAN'T BELIEVE IN YOU. / SILVER LINING (unplugged) / LISTEN (unplugged) / WASTED LIFE (unplugged)** –
(cd-ep) *(ESSX 2035)* – ('A'side) / ('A'extended) / Alternative Ulster (featuring RICKY WARWICK of The ALMIGHTY) / Smithers-Jones (live with BRUCE FOXTON vocals).

Feb 94. (cd/c) *(ESS CD/MC 210) <TAANG 100>* **GET A LIFE** Oct94
– Get a life / Can't believe in you / The road to kingdom come / Walk away / No laughing matter / Harp / Forensic evidence / Baby blue ((what have they been telling you?) / I want you / The night that the wall came down / Cold / When the stars fall from the sky / What if I want more? i(re-iss. Apr97; *ESMCD 488)*

Jun 94. (12"/cd-s) *(ESS T/X 2040)* **HARP. / SHAKE IT OFF / NOW WHAT WE WERE (PRO PATRIA MORI)** –

— **STEVE GRANTLEY** – drums (ex-JAKE BURNS . . .) repl. TAYLOR

Spitfire — Taang!

Jun 97. (cd/lp) *(SLF 100 CD/LP) <T 137>* **TINDERBOX** Jul97
– You never hear the one that hits you / (I could) Be happy yesterday / Tinderbox / Dead of night / The message / My ever changing moral stance / Hurricane / You can move mountains / River flowing / You don't believe in me / In your hand / Dust in my eye / Roaring boys (part 1) / Roaring boys (part 2). *(cd re-iss. Mar99; ABT 104CD) (cd re-iss. Oct02 on 'E.M.I.'+=; 543134-2)* – Wasted life / Hope Street / You can get it if you really want it / Fly the flag / Tin soldiers.

E.M.I. — not iss.

Aug 03. (cd) *591480-2)* **GUITAR AND DRUM** –
– Guitar and drum / Strummerville / Can't get away with that / Still burning / Walkin' dynamite / Dead man walking / Empty sky / True to yourself / Best of fools / I waited / Achilles heart / Who died and made you Elvis? / High and low / Protect and serve.

– compilations, etc. –

Sep 86. (12"ep) *Strange Fruit; (SFPS 004)* **THE PEEL SESSIONS** (12.9.78) –
– Johnny was / Law and order / Barbed wire love / Suspect device. *(c-ep-iss.May87; SFPSC 004) (cd-ep-iss.Jul88; SFPCD 004)*

Nov 89. (lp/c/cd) *Strange Fruit; (SFR LP/MC/CD 106) / Dutch East India; <8103>* **THE PEEL SESSIONS**

Oct 89. (12"ep) *Link; (LINK 1203)* **THE LAST TIME. / MR.FIRE-COAL MAN / TWO GUITARS CLASH** –

Apr 91. (cd) *Streetlink; (STRCD 010)* **GREATEST HITS LIVE (live)** –
(re-iss. May93 on 'Dojo'; DOJOCD 110) (re-iss. Feb99 on 'Recall'; SMMCD 538)

Oct 91. (cd) *Link; (AOK 103)* **ALTERNATIVE CHARTBUSTERS** –

Oct 89. (cd/green-lp) *Limited Edition; (LTD EDT 2 CD/LP)* **LIVE IN SWEDEN (live)** –

Dec 92. (cd) *Dojo; (<DOJOCD 75>)* **FLY THE FLAGS – LIVE AT BRIXTON ACADEMY (27/9/91)** Oct94

Aug 93. (cd) *Windsong; (<WINCD 037>)* **BBC RADIO 1 LIVE IN CONCERT (live)**

Mar 95. (cd) *Dojo; (DOJOCD 224)* **PURE FINGERS LIVE – ST.PATRIX 1993** –

Sep 98. (cd) *PinHead; (PINCD 105)* **STAND UP AND SHOUT** –

Feb 99. (d-cd) *E.M.I.; (498816-2)* **AND BEST OF ALL . . . HOPE STREET** [ ] [–]
Mar 99. (cd) *Harry May; (<MAYOCD 105>)* **TIN SOLDIERS (live)** [ ] [ ]
Jun 99. (cd) *Snapper; (SMMCD 516)* **PURE FINGERS LIVE** [ ] [ ]
Mar 00. (d-cd) *Recall; (<SMMCD 276>)* **LIVE INSPIRATION** [ ] [ ]
Apr 01. (cd) *E.M.I.; (532469-2)* **BACK AGAINST THE WALL** [ ] [–]
Mar 02. (3xcd-box) *E.M.I.; (537756-2)* **ANTHOLOGY** [ ] [–]
Apr 02. (cd) *EMI Gold; (538560-2)* **LIVE IN ABERDEEN (live)** [ ] [–]
Aug 02. (cd) *Strange Fruit; (SFRSCD 110)* **THE COMPLETE JOHN PEEL SESSIONS** [ ] [–]
Nov 02. (cd) *Strange Fruit; (SFRSCD 113)* **THE RADIO ONE SESSIONS** [ ] [–]

□ Stephen STILLS / MANASSAS
(see under ⇒ CROSBY, STILLS, NASH & YOUNG)

STING

Born: GORDON MATTHEW SUMNER, 2 Oct'51, Wallsend, nr. Newcastle, England. In the early 70's he gave up his job as a primary school teacher and joined a local group, gaining his nickname in honour of his famous black and yellow hooped T-shirt. STING joined jazz combo, LAST EXIT, in 1974, where he became lead singer on a single, 'WHISPERING VOICES'. Around the same time, the man enrolled with RADA and began occasional TV ad work (he was later to become a successful actor in the 70's). Early in 1977, he formed The POLICE, one of the world's top selling outfits until their demise (and his failed marriage to actress, Frances Tomelty) in 1983. STING had earlier branched out on a solo career, starring in, and scoring the soundtrack for the Dennis Potter film, 'Brimstone & Treacle'. It wasn't until 1985, however, that he released his first solo long player, 'DREAM OF THE BLUE TURTLES'. Employing such noted musicians as BRANFORD MARSALIS and WEATHER REPORT's OMAR HAKIM, STING crafted an endearing set of jazz-influenced, infectiously off-kilter pop songs, highlights being the gaslit noir of 'MOON OVER BOURBON STREET' and the two minor hit singles, 'IF YOU LOVE SOMEBODY SET THEM FREE' and 'SEVENTH WAVE'. The record was a Transatlantic Top 3 hit, STING subsequently touring/promoting with most of the musicians who'd played on the project, 'BRING ON THE NIGHT' (1986) documenting events. Again featuring MARSALIS, in addition to contributions from such luminaries as ERIC CLAPTON, MARK KNOPFLER, GIL EVANS and former colleague, ANDY SUMMERS, 'NOTHING LIKE THE SUN' (1987) was a largely introspective, instrumentally dextrous collection dedicated to STING's recently departed mother. 'AN ENGLISHMAN IN NEW YORK' was quintessential STING, a wry observation on cultural disparity, while the likes of 'FRAGILE' saw STING's work take on a more self-consciously political hue alongside contemporaries like U2 and SIMPLE MINDS. Indeed, most of '89 saw the singer campaigning for Brazilian rainforest projects, STING also championing the efforts of human rights organisation, Amnesty International. Commendable as all this was, many factions of the music press gave the singer a roasting for what they perceived as an often lofty and self-righteous attitude, BONO also coming in for similar flak. Brushing aside such criticism, STING eventually returned to recording with 'THE SOUL CAGES' (1991), a sombre affair informed this time around by the death of his father. Again retaining MARSALIS, STING also employed folk player, KATHRYN TICKELL, her Northumbrian pipes adding to the often bleak atmospherics. Despite its dearth of hit singles, the album gave STING his second UK No.1 in succession, paving the way for the massive selling, and markedly more upbeat 'TEN SUMMONER'S TALES' (1993). As strong a set of songs as STING had yet penned, the record spawned two of his most enduring singles in 'IF I EVER LOSE MY FAITH IN YOU' and the pastoral beauty of 'FIELDS OF GOLD'. Later that year, the singer was back in the upper reaches of the singles chart with the theme tune from the film 'Demolition Man' and a three way collaboration with BRYAN ADAMS and ROD STEWART on the vomit-inducing 'ALL MY LOVE' (the theme from 'The Three Musketeers'. STING even attempted a country/reggae crossover together with PATO BANTON on 'THIS COWBOY SONG', a track culled from 94's greatest hits set, 'FIELDS OF GOLD – THE BEST OF STING 1984-1994'. Not exactly the most prolific of artists, STING's most recent release was the 'MERCURY FALLING' album in 1996. As well as being something of an older guy sex symbol, STING continues to court controversy, his recent comments on the benefits of Ecstasy coming under particular scrutiny. 'BRAND NEW DAY' (1999), was a slight return to his more conventional pop songwriting days, the Top 5 album featuring a title track hit that was certainly his finest number for a long time – it's now used on a TV ad. 'SACRED LOVE' (2003), meanwhile, summarily failed to build on the creative rediscovery of its predecessor despite – or perhaps because of – of the presence of such credible guests as ANOUSHKA SHANKAR and MARY J BLIGE, preening itself on sheen over content. • **Covered:** SPREAD A LITTLE HAPPINESS + SOMEONE TO WATCH OVER ME (George Gershwin) / TUTTI FRUTTI (Little Richard) / NEED YOUR LOVE SO BAD (Little Willie John) / MACK THE KNIFE (Bertold Brecht) / PURPLE HAZE (Jimi Hendrix) / SISTERS OF MERCY (Leonard Cohen) w/ CHIEFTAINS. • **Trivia:** In 1985, he dueted on singles MONEY FOR NOTHING (Dire Straits), which he co-wrote, plus LONG WAY TO GO (Phil Collins). That year, STING also guested on MILES DAVIS' album, 'You're Under Arrest'. He was also another one of the stars on BAND AID and LIVE AID. **Filmography:** QUADROPHENIA (1979) / RADIO ON (1980) / ARTEMIS (1981 TV movie) / BRIMSTONE AND TREACLE (1982) / DUNE (1984) / THE BRIDE (1985) / PLENTY (1985) / STORMY MONDAY (1988) / JULIA JULIA (1987). In 1988, he also narrated Stravinsky's 'Soldier's Tale', which was soon issued on own 'Pangaea' label. He followed this by writing score for the documentary about Quentin Crisp, 'Crisp City'.

Album rating: THE DREAM OF THE BLUE TURTLES (*6) / BRING ON THE NIGHT (*5) / NOTHING LIKE THE SUN (*8) / THE SOUL CAGES (*7) / TEN SUMMONER'S TALES (*8) / FIELDS OF GOLD – THE BEST OF STING 1984-1994 compilation (*8) / MERCURY FALLING (*6) / THE VERY BEST OF STING & THE POLICE compilation (*8) / BRAND NEW DAY (*7) / ALL THIS TIME compilation (*8) / SACRED LOVE (*5)

STING – vocals, bass, etc. (with on set session people)

A&M A&M

Aug 82. (7") *(AMS 8242)* **SPREAD A LITTLE HAPPINESS. / ONLY YOU** [16] [ ]
(above from the film soundtrack 'BRIMSTONE AND TREACLE', released Sep'82 and containing other STING tracks)

—— Enlisted US musicians **KENNY KIRKLAND** – keyboards / **BRANFORD MARSALIS** – sax, percussion / **DARRYL JONES** – bass (ex-MILES DAVIS) / **OMAR HAKIM** – drums (WEATHER REPORT)

May 85. (7") *(AM 258) <2738>* **IF YOU LOVE SOMEBODY SET THEM FREE. / ANOTHER DAY** [26] [3]
(12"+=) *(AMY 258)* – ('A'-Torch song mix) / ('A'-Jellybean dance mix).

Jun 85. (lp)(c/cd) *(DREAM 1)(DRE MC/MD 1) <3750>* **THE DREAM OF THE BLUE TURTLES** [3] [2]
– If you love somebody set them free / Love is the seventh wave / Russians / Children's crusade / Shadows in the rain / We work the black seam /

Consider me gone / The dream of the blue turtles / Moon over Bourbon Street / Fortress around your heart. *(pic-lp Jan86; DREAMP 1) (lp re-iss. Sep99 on 'Simply Vinyl'; SVLP 116)*

Aug 85. (7"/12") *(AM/+Y 272)* **LOVE IS THE SEVENTH WAVE. / CONSIDER ME GONE (live)** 41 –

Aug 85. (7") *<2767>* **FORTRESS AROUND YOUR HEART. / CONSIDER ME GONE (live)** – 8

Oct 85. (7"/12") *(AM/+Y 286)* **FORTRESS AROUND YOUR HEART. / SHADOWS IN THE RAIN** 49 –

Oct 85. (7") *<2787>* **LOVE IS THE SEVENTH WAVE. / DREAM OF THE BLUE TURTLES** – 17

Dec 85. (7") *(AM 292) <2799>* **RUSSIANS. / GABRIEL'S MESSAGE** 12 16
(12"+=) *(AMY 292)* – I burn for you (live).

Feb 86. (7") *(AM 305)* **MOON OVER BOURBON STREET. / MACK THE KNIFE** 44
(12"+=) *(AMY 305)* – Fortress around your heart.

Jul 86. (d-lp/c/cd) *(BRIN G/C/D 1)* **BRING ON THE NIGHT (live)** 16 –
– Bring on the night – When the world is running down you make the best of what's still around / Consider me gone / Low life / We work the black seam / Driven to tears / The dream of the blue turtles – Demolition man / One world (not three) / Love is the seventh wave / Moon over Bourbon street / I burn for you / Another day / Children's crusade / Down so long / Tea in the Sahara.

— he retained **KIRKLAND + MARSALIS,** and recruited **MANU KATCHE** – drums / **MINO CINELU** – percussion, vocoder / **ANDY NEWMARK** – 2nd drummer / plus guests **ERIC CLAPTON, MARK KNOPFLER, ANDY SUMMERS + GIL EVANS**

Oct 87. (7") *(AM 410) <2983>* **WE'LL BE TOGETHER. / CONVERSATION WITH A DOG** 41 7
(12"+=/3"cd-s+=) *(AM Y/CD 410)* – ('A'extended) / ('A'instrumental).

Oct 87. (d-lp/c/cd) *(AMA/AMC/CDA 6402) <6402>* **NOTHING LIKE THE SUN** 1 9
– The Lazarus heart / Be still my beating heart / Englishman in New York / History will teach us nothing / They dance alone (gueca solo) / Fragile / We'll be together / Straight to my heart / Rock steady / Sister Moon / Little wing / The secret marriage.

Jan 88. (7") *<2992>* **BE STILL MY BEATING HEART. / GHOST IN THE STRAND** – 15

Jan 88. (7") *(AM 431)* **ENGLISHMAN IN NEW YORK. / GHOST IN THE STRAND (instrumental)** 51 –
(12"+=/3"cd-s+=) *(AM Y/CD 431)* – Bring on the night – When the world is running down (live).

Mar 88. (7") *<1200>* **ENGLISHMAN IN NEW YORK. / IF YOU'RE THERE** – 84

Mar 88. (7") *(AM 439)* **FRAGILE. / FRAGIL (Portuguese mix)** 70 –
(12"+=/cd-s+=) *(AM Y/CD 439)* – Fragilidad (Spanish mix) / Mariposa libre.

Sep 88. (7") *(AM 458)* **THEY DANCE ALONE. / ELLAS DAMZON SOLAS (GUECA SOLO)**
(12"+=/cd-s+=) *(AM Y/CD 458)* – Si estamos juntos.

Aug 90. (7"/c-s) *(AM/+MC 580)* **ENGLISHMAN IN NEW YORK (Ben Liebrand mix). / IF YOU LOVE SOMEBODY SET THEM FREE** 15 –
(12"+=/cd-s+=/pic-cd-s+=) *(AM Y/CD/CDR 580)* – ('A'original mix) / ('A'-Jellybean dance mix).

— he retained **MARSALIS, KIRKLAND, KATCHE.** New **DOMINIC MILLER** – guitar / **DAVID SANCIOUS** – keyboards / **KATHRYN TICKELL** – pipes / **PAOLA PAPAREUE** – oboe / **RAY COOPER, VINK, BILL SUMMERS, MUNYUNGO JACKSON, SKIP BURNEY, TONY VALCA** – percussion.

Dec 90. (7"/c-s) *(AM/+MC 713)* **ALL THIS TIME. / I MISS YOU, KATE (instrumental)** 22 5
(12"+=/cd-s+=/pic-cd-s+=) *(AM Y/CD/CDR 713) <1541>* – King of pain (live).

Jan 91. (cd/c/lp) *(396 405-2/-4/-1) <6405>* **THE SOUL CAGES** 1 2
– Island of souls / All this time / Mad about you / Jeremiah blues (pt.1) / Why should I cry for you / Saint Agnes and the burning train / The wild wild sea / The soul cages / When the angels fall.

Feb 91. (7"/c-s) *(AM/+MC 721)* **MAD ABOUT YOU (remix). / TEMPTED (live)** 56
(12"+=/cd-s+=) *(AM Y/CDR 721)* – If you love somebody set them free (live).

Apr 91. (7"/c-s) *(AM/+MC 759)* **THE SOUL CAGES. / OH LA LA HUGH** 57 –
(cd-s+=) *(AMCD 759)* – Walking in your footsteps (live).
(12"++=) *(AMY 759)* – Don't stand so close to me (live).
(12") *(AMYR 759)* – ('A'side) / Walking in your footsteps (live) / The Lazarus heart (live) / Too much inforation (live).

Aug 92. (7"/c-s/cd-s; by STING with ERIC CLAPTON) *(AM/+MC/CD 883)* **IT'S PROBABLY ME. / ('A'-long version)** 30

— retained on album **MILLER, SANCIOUS & TICKELL** and brought in **VINNIE COLAIUTA** – drums / **LARRY ADLER + BRENDAN POWER** – chromatic harmonicas / **SIAN BELL** – cello / **DAVE HEATH** – flute / **PAUL FRANKLIN** – pedal steel / **JAMES BOYD** – viola / **KATHRYN GREELEY + SIMON FISCHER** – violins / **GUY BARKER + JOHN BARCLAY** – trumpets / **RICHARD EDWARDS + MARK NIGHTINGALE** – trombone / **DAVID ROXXE** – narration

Feb 93. (7"/c-s) *(AM/+MC 0172) <0111>* **IF I EVER LOSE MY FAITH IN YOU. / ALL THIS TIME (unplugged)** 14 17
(cd-s+=) *(AMCD 0172)* – Mad about you (live) / Every breath you take (live).
(cd-s) *(AMCDR 0172)* – ('A'side) / Message in a bottle (live) / Tea in the Sahara (live) / Walking on the moon (live).

Mar 93. (cd/c/lp) *(540 074-2/-4/-1) <0070>* **TEN SUMMONER'S TALES** 2 2
– Prologue (If I ever lose my faith in you) / Love is stronger than justice (the magnificent seven) / Fields of gold / Heavy cloud no rain / She's too good for me / Seven days / Saint Augustine in Hell / It's probably me / Everybody laughed but you / Shape of my heart / Something the boy said / Epilogue (Nothing 'bout me).

Apr 93. (7"/c-s) *(580 222-7/223-4)* **SEVEN DAYS. / JANUARY STARS** 25 –
(cd-s+=) *(580 223-2)* – Mad about you (live) / Ain't no sunshine (live).
(cd-s) *(580 225-2)* – ('A'side) / Island of souls (live) / The wild wild sea (live) / The soul cages (live).

Jun 93. (7"/c-s) *(580 301-7/302-4) <0258>* **FIELDS OF GOLD. / WE WORK THE BLACK SEAM** 16 23
(cd-s) *(580302-2)* – ('A'side) / King of pain (live) / Fragile (live) / Purple haze (live).
(cd-s) *(580303-2)* – ('A'side) / Message in a bottle (live) / Fortress around your heart (live) / Roxanne (live).

Aug 93. (7"/c-s) *(580353-7-/4)* **SHAPE OF MY HEART. / WALKING ON THE MOON** 57 –
(cd-s) *(580353-2)* – ('A'side) / The soul cages / The wild wild sea / All this time.

Nov 93. (7"/c-s) *(580450-7/-4)* **DEMOLITION MAN. / ('A'mix)** 21 –
(cd-s+=) *(580451-2)* – King of pain (live) / Shape of my heart (live).
(cd-s) *(580453-2)* – ('A'side) / It's probably me (live) / A day in the life of (live).

— Late 1993, he teamed up with BRYAN ADAMS & ROD STEWART to sing theme from 'The Three Musketeers'; ALL FOR LOVE, which hit UK No.2 & US No.1.

Feb 94. (7"/12"/c-s) *(580529-7/-1/-4) <0350>* **NOTHING 'BOUT ME. / IF I EVER LOSE MY FAITH IN YOU** 32 Sep93 57
(cd-s+=) *(580529-2)* – ('B'mixes) / Demolition man (soul power mix).

Oct 94. (c-s) *(580858-4)* **WHEN WE DANCE / FORTRESS AROUND YOUR HEART** 9 –
(cd-s) *(580859-2)* – ('A'side) / If you love somebody set them free (remix) / ('A'remix).
(12"/cd-s) *(580861-1/-2)* – ('A'remixes).

Oct 94. (c-s,cd-s) *<0846>* **WHEN WE DANCE / DEMOLITION MAN** – 38

Nov 94. (cd/c/d-lp) *(540307-2/-4/-1) <0269>* **FIELDS OF GOLD – THE BEST OF STING 1984-1994** (compilation) 2 7
– When we dance / If you love somebody set them free / Fields of gold / All this time / Englishman in New York / Mad about you / It's probably me / They dance alone / If I ever lose my faith in you / Fragile / We'll be together / Nothing 'bout me / Love is the seventh wave / Russians / Seven days / Demolition man / This cowboy song.

— Around same time, Spanish crooner JULIO IGLESIAS covered his 'FRAGILE', which he accompanied with STING.
(below single featured PATO BANTON)

Jan 95. (c-s) *(580957-4)* **THIS COWBOY SONG / IF YOU LOVE SOMEBODY SET THE FREE (Brothers In Rhythm mix)** 15 –
(cd-s+=) *(580957-2)* – Demolition man (Soul Power mix).
(12"++=) *(580965-2)* – If you love somebody set them free (extended).
(cd-s) *(580957-1)* – ('A'side) / ('A'extended) / When we dance (classic) / Take me to the sunshine.

— Jan 96, featured on PATO BANTON's UK Top 40 version of POLICE hit 'SPIRITS IN THE MATERIAL WORLD' from the film 'Ace Ventura II'.

— with band: **MILLER, COLAIUTA / + KENNY KIRKLAND** – keyboards

Feb 96. (c-s) *(581330-4)* *<1456>* **LET YOUR SOUL BE YOUR PILOT / THE BED'S TOO BIG WITHOUT YOU** [15] [86]
(cd-s+=) *(581331-2)* – Englishman in New York.
(12") *(581527-1)* – ('A'mixes).

Mar 96. (cd/c/lp) *(540486-2/-4/-1)* *<0483>* **MERCURY FALLING** [4] [5]
– The hounds of winter / I hung my head / Let your soul be your pilot / I was brought to my senses / You still touch me / I'm so happy I can't stop crying / All four seasons / Twenty five to midnight / La belle dame sans regrets / Valparaiso / Lithium sunset.

Apr 96. (c-s/cd-s) *(581545-4/-2)* *<1582>* **YOU STILL TOUCH ME / TWENTY-FIVE TO MIDNIGHT** [27] [60]
(12"+=/cd-s+=) *(581547-1/-2)* – Lullaby to an anxious child / The pirate's bride.

Jun 96. (c-ep/cd-ep) *(581761-4/-2)* **LIVE AT TFI FRIDAY EP** [53] [–]
– You still touch me / Lithium sunset / Message in a bottle.

Sep 96. (c-s/cd-s) *(581890-4/-2)* **I WAS BROUGHT TO MY SENSES (Steve Lipson remix) / WHEN WE DANCE / IF I EVER LOSE MY FAITH IN YOU / IF YOU LOVE SOMEBODY SET THEM FREE** [31] [–]
(cd-s) *(581889-2)* – ('A'side) / This was never meant to be / The pirate's bride.

Oct 96. (c-s,cd-s) *<1982>* **I'M SO HAPPY I CAN'T STOP CRYING / THIS WAS NEVER MEANT TO BE** [–] [94]

Nov 96. (c-s) *(582029-4)* **I'M SO HAPPY I CAN'T STOP CRYING / FRAGILIDAD** [54] [–]
(cd-s+=) *(582029-2)* – Fields of gold / Englishman in New York.
(cd-s) *(582031-2)* – ('A'side) / Seven days / Moonlight / Giacomo's blues.

— In Dec'97, STING featured on TOBY KEITH's version of 'I'm So Happy I Can't Stop Crying'.

Sep 99. (c-s) *(497153-4)* **BRAND NEW DAY / (lp version)** [13] [ ]
(cd-s) *(497152-2)* – ('A'side) / Windmills of your mind / End of the game (long version).
(cd-s) *(497153-2)* – ('A'side) / Fields of gold / Englishman in New York.

Sep 99. (cd/c) *(490425-2/-5)* *<490443>* **BRAND NEW DAY** [5] [9]
– A thousand years / Desert rose / Big lie small world / After the rain has fallen / Perfect love . . . gone wrong / Tomorrow we'll see / Prelude to the end of the game / Fill her up / Ghost story / Brand new day.

Jan 00. (c-s/12"; as STING featuring CHEB MAMI) *(497240-4/-1)* *<497321>* **DESERT ROSE / (filter dub mix)** [15] May00 [17]
(cd-s) *(497241-2)* – ('A'side + mixes' melodic club x2 / video).
(cd-s) *(497240-2)* – ('A'side) / ('A'CD-Rom) / Fragile (live) / If you love somebody (set them free) (live).

Apr 00. (c-s) *(497325-4)* **AFTER THE RAIN HAS FALLEN / AFTER THE RAIN HAS FALLEN (Tin Tin Out mix)** [31] [ ]
(cd-s+=) *(497325-2)* – Shape of my heart / ('A'-CD-Rom).
(cd-s) *(497326-2)* – ('A'side) / Seven days (live) / Desert rose (version).

Nov 01. (cd) *(493180-2)* *<493169>* **ALL THIS TIME** (compilation) [3] [32]
– Fragile / A thousand years / Perfect love . . . gone wrong / All this time / The hounds of winter / Mad about you *[UK-only]* / Don't stand so close to me / When we dance / Dienda / Roxanne / If you love somebody set them free / Brand new day / Fields of gold / Moon over Bourbon Street / Shape of my heart *[UK-only]* / If I ever lose my faith in you / Every breath you take.

— in May'03, STING featured on CRAIG DAVID's Top 3 hit, 'Rise & Fall'

Sep 03. (cd-s) *(9810103)* **SEND YOUR LOVE / MOON OVER BOURBON STREET (Cornelius mix) / ('A'-Dave Aude remix) / ('A'-video)** [30] [ ]

Sep 03. (cd) *(9860535)* *<87236>* **SACRED LOVE** [3] [3]
– Inside / Send your love / Whenever I say your name (with MARY J. BLIGE) / Dead man's rope / Never coming home / Stolen car (take me dancing) / Forget about the future / This war / The book of my life / Sacred love / Send your love.

Dec 03. (cd-s; by STING & MARY J. BLIGE) *(9815304)* **WHENEVER I SAY YOUR NAME / (Will I am remix) / (Salaam Remi groove mix)** [60] [ ]

– compilations, others, etc. –

on 'A&M' unless mentioned otherwise

Jul 88. (cd-ep) *(AMCD 911)* **COMPACT HITS** [ ] [–]
– Someone to watch over me / Englishman in New York / If you love somebody set them free / Spread a little happiness.

Feb 90. (d-c) *(AMC 24110)* **DREAM OF THE BLUE TURTLES / NOTHING LIKE THE SUN** [ ] [ ]

Nov 91. (cd-box) *(397 171-2)* **ACOUSTIC LIVE IN NEWCASTLE – LIMITED EDITION BOXED SET** [ ] [ ]

Nov 97. (cd/c; STING & THE POLICE) *(540428-2/-4)* **THE VERY BEST OF STING & THE POLICE** [11] [100]
– Message in a bottle / Can't stand losing you / Englishman in New York / Every breath you take / Seven days / Walking on the moon / Fields of gold / Fragile / Every little thing she does is magic / De do do do de da da da / If you love somebody set them free / Let your soul be your pilot / Russians / If I ever lose my faith in you / When we dance / Don't stand so close to me / Roxanne / Roxanne '97 (Puff Daddy remix).

Dec 97. (c-s; STING & The POLICE) *(582455-4)* *<582449>* **ROXANNE '97 (Puff Daddy remix) / ROXANNE (original)** [17] [59]
(12"+=/cd-s+=) *(582455-1/-2)* – Walking on the moon (Roger Sanchez mix).

☐ Sly STONE (see under ⇒ SLY & THE FAMILY STONE)

☐ STONE PONEYS (see under ⇒ RONSTADT, Linda)

STONE ROSES

Formed: Sale & Chorley, Gtr. Manchester, England . . . 1984 by IAN BROWN, JOHN SQUIRE, RENI, ANDY COUZENS and PETER GARNER who took their name from a group called ENGLISH ROSE and The ROLLING STONES. After a MARTIN HANNETT produced 45, they signed a one-off deal with 'Black' records and in 1988, were snapped up by ANDREW LAUDER's 'Jive' subsidiary, 'Silvertone'. They soon became darlings of the music press after the indie success of the single, 'ELEPHANT STONE' (1988), a gloriously uplifting piece of pristine pop. Propelled by RENI's consummate drumming and featuring SQUIRE's dizzy, spiralling guitar, the track was a blueprint for the group's eponymous debut album, released the following year. Surely a contender for album of the decade, the record was flawless, from the ominous opening bass rumble of 'I WANNA BE ADORED' to the orgasmic finale of 'I AM THE RESURRECTION'. This life-affirming hybrid of BYRDS-style psychedelia and shuffling rhythmic flurries remains the definitive indie album, its all-pervading influence more pronounced with each successive crop of guitar bands. Incredibly, the band topped the magic of their debut with the 'FOOL'S GOLD' single, which exploded into the Top 10 later that year. A seminal guitar-funk workout, it was the crowning glory of the 'Baggy' movement with which The STONE ROSES had become so closely affiliated, and marked a creative highpoint in their career. After a few one-off shows (that have since achieved almost mythical status) and a solitary single, 'ONE LOVE', the following year, the band went to ground. In the five years that followed, the band fought a protracted court battle with 'Silvertone', eventually signing with 'Geffen' for a reported record sum of $4,000,000. After much speculation and intrigue into when or if a follow-up would finally appear, the appropriately titled 'SECOND COMING' was eventually released in 1994. A month previously, they had enjoyed a return to the singles chart with the ZEPPELIN-esque 'LOVE SPREADS'. On the album, the effervescent pop of old took second place to riff-heavy guitar workouts, alienating many of their original fans. Nevertheless, the blistering funk-rock of 'BEGGING YOU' partly made up for any excess noodling by SQUIRE. As the STONES ROSES faithful dusted down their flares and beany hats in readiness for the band's headlining spot at the 1995 Glastonbury festival, they were again bitterly disappointed. At the last minute the band pulled out, apparently due to SQUIRE breaking his collarbone, young pretenders OASIS stealing the show in their absence. They had failed to seize the moment and from here on in, it was all downhill.

Despite an ecstatically received Winter tour, SQUIRE shocked the music world by departing the following Spring (RENI had already quit a year earlier). BROWN and MANI bravely soldiered on for a headlining appearance at the 1996 Reading Festival but were given a critical mauling (particularly by the NME), finally splitting later that year. It was a sorry, messy end for a band that had seemed, at one point, to be on the brink of world domination and it remains a bitter irony that their duller Manchester progeny, OASIS, seem to have inherited the success that tragically eluded the 'ROSES. While SQUIRE has gone on to relative success with The SEAHORSES, their sound pales next to the magic of The STONE ROSES, a band that remain as fondly remembered as any in the history of rock. • **Songwriters:** Mainly SQUIRE but with other members also collaborating. The SEAHORSES was mainly SQUIRE, except a few by HELME. one with FLETCHER. NOEL GALLAGHER (Oasis) co-wrote 'LOVE ME AND LEAVE ME'. • **Trivia:** Their debut album artwork was a pastiche of a Jackson Pollock splatter job painted by the multi-talented SQUIRE.

Album rating: THE STONE ROSES (*10) / TURNS INTO STONE collection (*6) / SECOND COMING (*7) / THE COMPLETE STONE ROSES compilation (*8) / GARAGE FLOWER exploitation (*5) / THE VERY BEST OF THE STONE ROSES compilation (*9)

IAN BROWN (b.20 Feb'63, Ancoats, Manchester) – vocals / **JOHN SQUIRE** (b.24 Nov'62, Broadheath, Manchester) – guitar, vocals / **PETER GARNER** – rhythm guitar / **ANDY COUZENS** – bass / **RENI** (b. ALAN WREN, 10 Apr'64) – drums

Thin Line / not iss.

Sep 85. (12") *(THIN 001)* **SO YOUNG. / TELL ME** [ ] [–]

— now a quartet when PETER departed

Revolver / not iss.

May 87. (12"m) *(12REV 36)* **SALLY CINNAMON. / HERE IT COMES / ALL ACROSS THE SANDS** [ ] [–]
(re-iss. Feb89; same) (re-iss. Dec89 cd-ep+=; CDREV 36) – ('A'demo). (hit No.46) *(re-iss. Nov00; REVXD 36)*

— (1987) **GARY 'MANI' MOUNFIELD** (b.16 Nov'62, Crumpsall, Manchester) – bass, vocals repl. COUZENS who later joined The HIGH.

Silvertone / Silvertone

Oct 88. (7") *(ORE 1)* **ELEPHANT STONE. / THE HARDEST THING IN THE WORLD** [ ] [–]
(12"+=) *(ORE 1T)* – Full fathoms five. *(re-iss. Feb90 c-s/cd-s; ORE 1 C/CD);* hit No.8. *(cd-s re-iss. Oct96; same)*

Mar 89. (7") *(ORE 2)* **MADE OF STONE. / GOING DOWN** [ ] [–]
(12"+=) *(ORE 2T)* – Guernica. *(re-iss. Mar90 c-s/cd-s; ORE 2 C/CD);* hit No.20. *(cd-s re-iss. Oct96; same)*

Apr 89. (lp/c/cd) *(ORE LP/MC/CD 502)* <1184-1/-4/-2> **THE STONE ROSES** [19] [86]
– I wanna be adored / She bangs the drum / Waterfall / Don't stop / Bye bye badman / Elizabeth my dear / (Song for my) Sugar spun sister / Made of stone / Shoot you down / This is the one / I am the resurrection. *(re-iss. Aug91 as 2x12"+=; OREZLP 502)* – Elephant stone / Fool's gold. *(cd re-iss. Mar97; same) (d-cd re-iss. as 10th ANNIVERSARY EDITION; 059124-2)* – (w/ extra tracks). – (hit UK No.26)

Jul 89. (7"/7"s) *(ORE/+X 6)* **SHE BANGS THE DRUM. / STANDING HERE** [36] [–]
(12"+=/12"s+=) *(ORE T/Z 6)* – Mersey Paradise.
(c-s++=/cd-s++=) *(ORE C/CD 6)* – Simone. *(re-entered chart Mar90; hit No.34) (cd-s re-iss. Oct96; same)*

Silvertone / Jive

Nov 89. (7"/ext.12") *(ORE/+T 13)* <1315-1> **FOOL'S GOLD. / WHAT THE WORLD IS WAITING FOR** [8] Mar90 [ ]
(c-s+=/cd-s+=) *(ORE C/CD 13)* – ('A'extended). *(flipped over re-entered chart Sep90; hit No.22) (re-iss. remix May92, hit No.73) (cd-s re-iss. Oct96; same)*
(12") *(ORET 13)* – ('A'-The Top Won mix) / ('A'-The Bottom Won mix).

Nov 89. (12"ep) <1301> **I WANNA BE ADORED / (long version) / GOING DOWN / SIMONE** [–] [ ]

Jul 90. (7"/c-s/12"/cd-s) *(ORE/+C/T/CD 17)* <1399-1/-2> **ONE LOVE. / SOMETHING'S BURNING** [4] [ ]
(cd-s re-iss. Oct96; same)

Sep 91. (7"/c-s) *(ORE/+C 31)* **I WANNA BE ADORED. / WHERE ANGELS PLAY** [20] [–]
(12"+=/cd-s+=) *(ORE T/CD 31)* – Sally Cinnamon (live).
(cd-s re-iss. Oct96; same)

Jan 92. (7"/c-s) *(ORE/+C 35)* **WATERFALL (remix). / ONE LOVE (remix)** [27] [ ]
(12"+=/cd-s+=) *(ORE T/CD 35)* – ('A'&'B'extended versions).
(cd-s re-iss. Oct96; same)

Apr 92. (7"/c-s) *(ORE/+C 40)* **I AM THE RESURRECTION. / ('A'-Pan & scan radio version)** [33] [ ]
(12"+=) *(ORET 40)* – Fool's gold (The Bottom Won mix).
(cd-s++=) *(ORECD 40)* – ('A'-5:3 Stoned Out club mix).
(cd-s re-iss. Oct96; same)

Jul 92. (cd/c/lp) *(ORE CD/C/LP 521)* **TURNS INTO STONE** (demos & rare) [32] [–]
– Elephant stone / The hardest thing in the world / Going down / Mersey Paradise / Standing here Where angels play / Simone / Fools gold / What the world is waiting for / One love / Something's burning. *(cd re-iss. Mar97 & Mar99; same)*

Geffen / Geffen

Nov 94. (7"/c-s) *(GFS/+C 84)* **LOVE SPREADS. / YOUR STAR WILL SHINE** [2] [ ]
(cd-s+=) *(GFST 84)* – Breakout.
(12"++=) *(GFSTD 84)* – Groove harder.

Dec 94. (cd/c/lp) <*(GED/GEC/GEF 24503)*> **SECOND COMING** [4] Jan95 [47]
– Breaking into Heaven / Driving south / Ten storey love song / Daybreak / Your star will shine / Straight to the man / Begging you / Tightrope / Good times / Tears / How do you sleep? / Love spreads. *(cd+=)* – (untitled hidden track No.90). *(lp re-iss. Aug99 on 'Simply Vinyl'; SVLP 111)*

Feb 95. (7"/c-s) *(GFS/+C 87)* **TEN STOREY LOVE SONG. / RIDE ON** [11] [ ]
(12"+=/cd-s+=) *(GFST/+D 87)* – Moses.

— In Apr'95, RENI quit and was replaced by **ROBERT MADDIX** (ex-GINA GINA).

Oct 95. (c-s) *(GFSC 22060)* **BEGGING YOU / ('A'-Chic mix)** [15] [ ]
(cd-s+=) *(GFSTD 22060)* – ('A'-Stone Corporation mix) / ('A'-Lakota mix) / ('A'-Young American primitive remix).
(12") *(GFST 22060)* – ('A'-Carl Cox mix) / ('A'-Development Corporation mix).

— Late in March '96, SQUIRE left to pursue new venture, The SEAHORSES. The STONE ROSES continued and in Aug'96, they recruited **AZIZ IBRAHIM** (ex-SIMPLY RED) / **NIGEL IPPINSON** – keyboards

— They officially split in Nov'96, after MANI joined PRIMAL SCREAM. IBRAHIM would join IAN BROWN and eventually issue his solo album in 1999, thoughtfully titled 'AZIZ'.

– compilations, etc. –

on 'Silvertone' unless mentioned; who else?

Jan 92. (8xcd-s-box-set) *(SRBX 1)* **SINGLES BOX** [ ] [–]

Nov 92. (10x12"box-set) *(SRBX 2)* **SINGLES BOX** [ ] [–]

Apr 95. (c-s) *(OREC 71)* **FOOL'S GOLD '95 / ('A'extended mix)** [23] [ ]
(12"+=/cd-s+=) *(ORE T/CD 71)* – ('A'-Tall Paul remix) / ('A'-Cricklewood Ballroom mix).

May 95. (cd/c/lp) *(ORE CD/C/ZLP)* **THE COMPLETE STONE ROSES** [4] [ ]

Nov 96. (cd/c/lp) *(GARAGE CD/C/LP 1)* **GARAGE FLOWER** (early demos) [58] [–]
(cd re-iss. Augg99; same)

Jun 97. (7"ep) *Fierce; (FRIGHT 044)* **SPIKE ISLAND EP** (interviews, etc.) [ ] [–]

Feb 99. (c-s/cd-s) *Jive Electro; (052309-4/-2)* **FOOL'S GOLD / FOOL'S GOLD (Grooverider mix) / RABBIT IN THE MOON** [25] [–]

Oct 00. (cd/d-lp) *(926015-2/-1)* **THE REMIXES** [41] [–]

Nov 02. (cd/d-lp) *(926037-2/-1)* **THE VERY BEST OF THE STONE ROSES** [19] [ ]
– I wanna be adored / She bangs the drums / Ten storey love song / Waterfall / Made of stone / Love spreads / What the world is waiting for / Sally Cinnamon / Fools gold / Begging you / Elephant stone / Breaking into heaven / One love / This is the one / I am the resurrection.

☐ STONE SOUR (see under ⇒ SLIPKNOT)

STONE TEMPLE PILOTS

Formed: Los Angeles, California, USA . . . 1987 as MIGHTY JOE YOUNG by WEILAND and ROBERT DeLEO. Recruiting DeLEO's brother, DEAN and ERIC KRETZ, they opted for the less frenetic San Diego as a musical base, changing their moniker to STONE TEMPLE PILOTS (thankfully changed from the considerably more controversial SHIRLEY TEMPLE'S PUSSY). After a few years on the hard/alternative rock circuit, they finally signed to 'Atlantic', the fruits of their labour, 'CORE' released in '92. Critical raves saw the album climb up the US chart (eventually reaching Top 3), songs like 'SEX TYPE THING' and 'PLUSH' drawing inevitable comparisons with PEARL JAM; WEILAND's vocals especially, were from the EDDIE VEDDER school of gravel-throated cool. After the aforementioned tracks were issued as UK singles, the album surfaced in the British Top 30 a full year on from its original release date, WEILAND's carrot-topped mop marking him out as a distinctive focal point for the band. LED ZEPPELIN and ALICE IN CHAINS were other obvious reference points, a second album, 'PURPLE' (1994), building on these influences to create a more cerebral post-grunge sound. The fact that the album rocketed into the American charts at No.1 was a measure of the group's lofty standing in the echelons of US alt-rock. WEILAND's love of nose candy and associated pleasures was no secret in the music world, the frontman narrowly avoiding a sizeable prison stretch for possession. Early in 1996, STP delivered a third (Top 5) album, 'TINY MUSIC . . . SONGS FROM THE VATICAN GIFT SHOP', accompanying touring commitments were severely disrupted when WEILAND was ordered by the court to attend a rehab centre while awaiting trial (he was later cleared). The following year, WEILAND continued his self-destructive behaviour, STP's future looking bleak as the remaining band members formed TALK SHOW. A WEILAND solo effort, '12 BAR BLUES' (1998), was poorly received by critics and fans alike, while a long 18 months (and after more WEILAND arrests!) saw the group back together on a 'NO.4' set in 1999 – needless to say this type of music had died in Britain ages ago. It was still going strong in the US though, where 'SHANGRI-LA DEE DA' (2001) made the Top 10, a record that faithfully followed the pattern set by its predecessor and further explored their interest in retro-psych. • **Songwriters:** Lyrics: WEILAND + R. DeLEO / KRETZ most of music except covers DANCING DAYS (Led Zeppelin).

Album rating: CORE (*7) / PURPLE (*7) / TINY MUSIC . . . SONGS FROM THE VATICAN GIFT SHOP (*7) / NO.4 (*4) / Talk Show: TALK SHOW (*5) / Scott Weiland: 12 BAR BLUES (*5) / Stone Temple Pilots: SHANGRI-LA DEE DA (*6) / THANK YOU compilation (*8)

(SCOTT) WEILAND (b.27 Oct'67, Santa Cruz, Calif.) – vocals / **DEAN DeLEO** (b.23 Aug'61, New Jersey) – guitar / **ROBERT DeLEO** (b. 2 Feb'66, New Jersey) – bass / **ERIC KRETZ** (b. 7 Jun'66, Santa Cruz) – drums

Atlantic Atlantic

Nov 92. (cd/c/lp) *<(7567 82418-2/-4/-1)>* **CORE** [ ] [3]
– Dead and bloated / Sex type thing / Wicked garden / No memory / Sin / Creep / Piece of pie / Naked Sunday / Plush / Wet my bed / Crackerman / Where the river goes. *(re-dist.Sep93, hit UK No.27) (cd re-iss. Jul00; same)*

Mar 93. (12"/cd-s) *(A 5769 T/CD)* **SEX TYPE THING. / WICKED GARDEN (acoustic) / PLUSH (acoustic)** [60] [–]

Aug 93. (7") *(A 7349)* **PLUSH. / SIN** [23] [–]
(cd-s+=) *(A 7349CD)* – Sex type thing (swing version).
(12"++=) *(A 7349T)* – Plush (acoustic).

Nov 93. (7"/c-s) *(A 7293/+C)* **SEX TYPE THING. / PIECE OF PIE** [55] [–]
(12"+=) *(A 7293TP)* – ('A'-Dead & Bloated mix).
(cd-s++=) *(A 7293CD)* – ('A'live).
(cd-s+=) *(A 7293CDX)* – Wicked garden (live) / Sin (live).

Jun 94. (cd/c/purple-lp) *<(7567 82607-2/-4/-1)>* **PURPLE** [10] [1]
– Meatplow / Vasoline / Lounge fly / Interstate love song / Still remains / Pretty penny / Silvergun Superman / Big empty / Unglued / Army ants / Kitchenware & candybar!. *(cd+=/c+=)* – Gracious melodies.

Aug 94. (12"blue-ep/cd-ep) *(A 5650 T/CD)* **VASOLINE / MEATPLOW. / ANDY WARHOL (MTV unplugged) / CRACKERMAN (unplugged)** [48] [–]

Dec 94. (7"purple/c-s) *(A 7192 K/C)* **INTERSTATE LOVE SONG. / LOUNGE FLY** [53] [–]
(cd-s+=) *(A 7192CD)* – Vasoline (live) / ('A'live).
(cd-s) *(A 7192CDX)* – ('A'side) / Shotgun superman / Army ants.

—— In summer '95, WEILAND was credited on a MAGNIFICENT BASTARDS single, 'Mockingbird Girl'; other tracks by Devo & Stomp.

Mar 96. (cd/c/lp) *<(7567 82871-2/-4/-1)>* **TINY MUSIC . . . SONGS FROM THE VATICAN GIFT SHOP** [31] [4]
– Press play / Pop's love suicide / Tumble in the rough / Big bang baby / Lady picture show / And so I know / Tripping on a hole in a paper heart / Art school girl / Adhesive / Ride the cliche / Daisy / Seven caged tigers. *(cd re-iss. Jul00; same)*

Apr 96. (c-s) *(A 5516C)* **BIG BANG BABY / ADHESIVE** [ ] [–]
(cd-s+=) *(A 5516CD)* – Daisy.

—— the group had to cancel promotion tours due to WEILAND being ordered by a Pasadena court to attend a live-in drug rehabilitation programme. He discharged himself for a few days in July '96 and gave himself up to the LAPD who had issued a warrant for his arrest; WEILAND was subsequently cleared. The other members (ROBERT DeLEO + KRETZ) started working on a side-project VITAMIN, which became TALK SHOW after recruiting frontman DAVID COUTTS

TALK SHOW

—— **ERIC KRETZ + ROBERT DeLEO + DEAN DeLEO / + DAVE COUTTS** – vocals (ex-TEN INCH MEN)

Oct 97. (cd/c) *<(7567 83040-2/-4)>* **TALK SHOW** [ ] [ ]
– Ring twice / Hello hello / Everybody loves my car / Peeling an orange / So long / Wash me down / End of the world / John / Behind / Morning girl / Hide / Fill the fields.

SCOTT WEILAND

plays nearly every instrument, SHERYL CROW guests on accordion!

May 98. (cd/c) *<(7567 83084-2/-4)>* **12 BAR BLUES** [ ] Apr98 [42]
– Desperation #5 / Barbarella / About nothing / Where's the man / Divider / Cool kiss / The date / Son / Jimmy was a stimulator / Lady, your roof brings me down / Mockingbird girl / Opposite octave reaction.

Jun 98. (7"pink/c-s) *(AT 0035/+C)* **BARBARELLA. / MOCKINGBIRD GIRL** [ ] [ ]
(cd-s+=) *(AT 0035CD)* – ('A'-album version).

STONE TEMPLE PILOTS

—— re-formed again

Oct 99. (cd/c) *<(7567 83255-2/-4)>* **NO.4** [ ] [6]
– Down / Heaven and hot rods / Pruno / Church on Tuesday / Sour girl / No way out / Sex and violence / Glide / I got you / MC5 / Atlanta.

Apr 00. (-) *<album cut>* **SOUR GIRL** [–] [78]

Aug 00. (cd/c) *<(7567 83449-2/-4)>* **SHANGRI-LA DEE DA** [ ] Jun00 [9]
– Dumb love / Days of the week / Coma / Hollywood bitch / Wonderful / Black again / Hello it's late / Too cool queenie / Regeneration / Bi-polar bear / Transmissions from a lonely room / A song for sleeping / Long way home.

Sep 01. (c-s) *(AT 0113C)* **DAYS OF THE WEEK / DOWN (live)** [ ] [–]
(cd-s+=) *(AT 0113CD)* – Big empty (live) / ('A'-CD-Rom).

Nov 01. (cd-s) *<7567 85200-2>* **REVOLUTION / (Cd-Rom)** [–] [ ]

– compilations, etc. –

Nov 03. (cd) *<(7567 83586-2)>* **THANK YOU** [ ] [26]
– Vasoline / Down / Wicked garden / Big empty / Plush / Big bang baby / Creep / Lady picture show / Trippin' on a hole in a paper heart / Interstate love song / All in the suit that you wear / Sex type thing / Days of the week / Sour girl / Plush (acoustic).

□ STOOGES (see under ⇒ POP, Iggy)

□ STORM (see under ⇒ JOURNEY)

STRANGLERS

Formed: Chiddington, Surrey, England ... Autumn 1974 as The GUILDFORD STRANGLERS by ex-science teacher, HUGH CORNWELL, history graduate JEAN-JACQUES BURNEL and jazz drummer JET BLACK. Augmented by organist DAVE GREENFIELD in the Spring of '75, they commenced gigging around the pub-rock circuit, developing their boorish, black-clad brand of DOORS/ELECTRIC PRUNES/DR.FEELGOOD retro rock with scant encouragement from the press. Late in '76, after supporting the likes of The FLAMIN' GROOVIES and The RAMONES, The STRANGLERS were signed to 'United Artists' and initially lumped in with the fermenting punk/new wave scene. Released early the following year, '(GET A) GRIP (ON YOURSELF)' found the band at their sneering, leering best, GREENFIELD's churning organ characterising a sound with which they'd stick fairly closely over the early part of their career. The single stalled outside the UK Top 40 – reportedly due to a chart mistake – although its controversial follow-up, 'PEACHES', made the Top 10 and immediately brought the band into conflict with feminists and the more liberal contingent of the music press. It was also banned by the BBC (a slightly modified version was later deemed acceptable), the surrounding controversy the first of many throughout the band's career and one which certainly didn't harm sales of the classic debut album, 'STRANGLERS IV – RATTUS NORVEGICUS' (1977). A Top 5 success comprising both singles and the enduring STRANGLERS favourite, 'HANGING AROUND', the record met with enthusiastic reviews as the group enjoyed the briefest of honeymoon periods with the press. A not entirely convincing attempt at political comment, 'SOMETHING BETTER CHANGE', gave the band a second Top 10 hit later that summer, closely followed by the vicious momentum of 'NO MORE HEROES'. Also released in '77, the album of the same name narrowly missed No.1, another solid set which armed their detractors with more ammunition in the form of 'BRING ON THE NUBILES'; a notorious, stripper-enhanced gig at Battersea Park didn't help matters and The STRANGLERS' were firmly tarred as sexist yobs. Not that their fans cared, helping put a further two singles, 'FIVE MINUTES' and 'NICE 'N' SLEAZY', into the Top 20, both tracks featuring on the album, 'BLACK AND WHITE' (1978). The latter set came free with a limited edition 7" featuring the lads' interesting cover of the BACHARACH/DAVID standard, 'WALK ON BY' tastefully placed side by side with the inimitable 'TITS'. More promising and certainly more memorable was the surprisingly melodic 'DUCHESS', a Top 20 hit lifted from accompanying album, 'THE RAVEN' (1979). That year also saw the release of solo albums from both J.J. BURNEL and HUGH CORNWELL (with ROBERT WILLIAMS), the former's 'EUROMAN COMETH' barely making the Top 40 while the latter's 'NOSFERATU' failed to make any impression on the charts. Worse was to come for CORNWELL when, on the 7th of January 1980, the singer was found guilty of drug possession and sentenced to three months in prison. Later that year, the whole band fell foul of the law, this time in the South of France where they were accused of inciting a riot; although threatened with serious jail terms, they were susbsequently let off with fines, later claiming it was 'NICE IN NICE' on 1986's 'DREAMTIME' album. The STRANGLERS' commercial fortunes didn't fare much better with 'THE MEN IN BLACK' (1981), a tongue-in-cheek (but critically derided nonetheless) pseudo-concept affair about alien undercover agents. Boasting the exquisite harpsichord stylings of 'GOLDEN BROWN', 'LA FOLIE' (1981) was a considerably more successful album, if somewhat pretentious. In line with the prevailing trend, The STRANGLERS' moved perilously closer to synth-pop as the 80's wore on, 'Epic' albums such as 'FELINE' (1983) and 'AURAL SCULPTURE' (1984) seeing the band's hardcore fanbase dwindle. Even a return to their former stamping ground (and the UK Top 10) with a musclebound run-through of The Kinks' 'ALL DAY AND ALL OF THE NIGHT' couldn't rejuvenate them and the subsequent studio album, '10' (1990) was the last to feature CORNWELL. Deciding to carry on with new frontman, JOHN ELLIS, the band recorded for various indie labels in the 90's and although the likes of 'STRANGLERS IN THE NIGHT' (1992) and 'ABOUT TIME' (1995) made the Top 40, most commentators (and many fans) were agreed that the band's glory days were definitely behind them. • **Songwriters:** Mostly CORNWALL-penned except some by BURNEL. They also covered; 96 TEARS (? & The Mysterians).

Album rating: STRANGLERS IV – RATTUS NORVEGICUS (*8) / NO MORE HEROES (*7) / BLACK AND WHITE (*7) / LIVE (X CERT) (*5) / THE RAVEN (*6) THE MEN-IN-BLACK (*5) / LA FOLIE (*7) / THE COLLECTION 1977-1982 compilation (*7) / AURAL SCULPTURE (*6) / DREAMTIME (*6) / ALL LIVE AND ALL OF THE NIGHT (*4) / 10 (*5) / THE STRANGLERS' GREATEST HITS compilation (*9) / STRANGLERS IN THE NIGHT (*4) / SATURDAY NIGHT SUNDAY MORNING (*3) / ABOUT TIME (*4) / WRITTEN IN RED (*4) / THE HIT MEN – THE COMPLETE SINGLES 1977-1990 compilation (*8) / COUP DE GRACE (*4) / PEACHES – THE VERY BEST OF THE STRANGLERS compilation (*8) / JJ Burnel: EUROMAN COMETH (*3) / Dave Greenfield & Jean-Jacques Burnel: FIRE AND WATER (*4) / Hugh Cornwall & Robert Williams: NOSFERATU (*2)

HUGH CORNWALL (b.28 Aug'48, London, England) – vocals, guitar / **JEAN-JAQUES BURNEL** (b.21 Feb'52, London; French parents) – bass, vocals / **DAVE GREENFIELD** (b.29 Mar'49, Brighton, England) – keyboards / **JET BLACK** (b. BRIAN DUFFY, 26 Aug'43, Ilford, England) – drums

U.A. / A&M

Jan 77. (7") *(UP 36211)* **(GET A) GRIP (ON YOURSELF). / LONDON LADY** — 44 / –

Apr 77. (lp/c) *(UAG/UAC 30045) <4648>* **STRANGLERS IV – RATTUS NORVEGICUS** — 4 /
– Sometimes / Goodbye Toulouse / London lady / Princess of the streets / Hanging around / Peaches / (Get a) Grip (on yourself) / Ugly / Down in the sewer: (a) Falling – (b) Down in the sewer – (c) Trying to get out again – (d) Rats rally. *(free ltd.7"w.a.)* **CHOOSEY SUSIE. / IN THE BIG SHITTY (live)** *(re-iss. May82 on 'Fame' lp/c; FA/TC-FA 3001) (cd-iss. Apr88; CDFA 3001) (cd-iss. Feb88 on 'Liberty'; CZ 85) (lp re-iss. Jan01 on 'Simply Vinyl'; SVLP 291) (cd re-iss. Aug01 on 'EMI Gold'+=; 534406-2)* – Choosey Susie / Go buddy go / Peasant in the big shitty (live).

May 77. (7") *(UP 36248)* **PEACHES. / GO BUDDY GO** — 8 / –

—— Jun77; They backed CELIA & THE MUTATIONS on cover single 'MONY MONY'.

Jul 77. (7") *(UP 36277)* **SOMETHING BETTER CHANGE. / STRAIGHTEN OUT** — 9 / –

Sep 77. (7") *(UP 36300)* **NO MORE HEROES. / IN THE SHADOWS** — 8 / –

Oct 77. (lp/c) *(UAG/UAC 30200) <4659>* **NO MORE HEROES** — 2 /
– I feel like a wog / Bitching / Dead ringer / Dagenham Dave / Bring on the nubiles / Something better change / No more heroes / Peasant in the big shitty / Burning up time / English towns / School mam / In the shadows. *(re-iss. 1985 lp/c; ATAK/TC-ATAK 32) (cd-iss. Feb88 on 'E.M.I.'; CDP 746613-2) (re-iss. Sep87 on 'Fame' lp/c; FA/TC-FA 3190) (cd-iss. Aug88; CDFA 3190) (cd re-iss. Aug01 on 'EMI Gold'+=; 534407-2)* – Straighten out / Five minutes / Rok it to the Moon.

Nov 77. (7"pink-ep) **SOMETHING BETTER CHANGE / STRAIGHTEN OUT. / GRIP / HANGIN' AROUND** — – /

Jan 78. (7") *(UP 36350)* **FIVE MINUTES. / ROK IT TO THE MOON** — 11 / –

Apr 78. (7") *(UP 36379)* **NICE 'N' SLEAZY. / SHUT UP** — 18 / Aug78

May 78. (lp/c)<US-grey-lp> *(UAK/TCK 30222) <4706>* **BLACK AND WHITE** — 2 /
– Tank / Nice 'n' sleazy / Outside Tokyo / Mean to me / Hey! (rise of the robots) / Sweden (all quiet on the Eastern Front) / Toiler on the sea / Curfew / Threatened / Do you wanna? / Death and night and blood (Yukio) / Enough time. *(free ltd.7"w.a.) (FREE 9)* **WALK ON BY. / TITS / MEAN TO ME** *(re-iss. Jan86 on 'Epic' lp/c; EPC/40 26439) (cd-iss. Jul88*

on 'E.M.I.'+=; CZ 109) – (free 7" tracks). *(cd re-iss. Aug01 on 'E.M.I.'+=; 534691-2)* – Mean to me / Shut up / Walk on by / Sveridge / Old codger / Tits.

Jul 78. (7"m) *(UP 36429)* **WALK ON BY. / OLD CODGER / TANK** [21] [–]

U.A. I.R.S.

Mar 79. (lp/c) *(UAG/TCK 30224) <70011>* **X-CERT (live)** [7] [ ]
– (Get a) Grip (on yourself) / Dagenham Dave / Burning up time / Dead ringer / Hanging around / I feel like a wog / Straighten out / Do you wanna – Death and night and blood (Yukio) / Five minutes / Go buddy go. *(re-iss. 1985 lp/c; ATAK/TC-ATACK 33) (cd-iss. Jul88 +=; CZ 110)* – In the shadows / Peasant in the big shitty. *(cd re-iss. Aug01 on 'E.M.I.'++=; 534687-2)* – In the shadows / Sometimes / Mean to me / London lady / Goodbye Toulouse / Hangin' around.

Aug 79. (7") *(BP 308)* **DUCHESS. / FOOLS RUSH OUT** [14] [ ]

Sep 79. (lp/c) *(UAG/TCK 30262)* **THE RAVEN** [4] [–]
– Longships / The raven / Dead Loss Angeles / Ice / Baroque bordello / Nuclear device / Shah shah a go go / Don't bring Harry / Duchess / Meninblack / Genetix. *(re-iss. Sep85 on 'Fame' lp/c; FA/TC-FA 3131) (cd-iss. Aug88; CDFA 3131) (cd-iss. Oct87 on 'E.M.I.'+=; CZ 20)* – Bear cage. *(cd re-iss. Aug01 on 'E.M.I.'++=; 534689-2)* – Fools rush out / N'emmenes pas Harry / Yellowcake UFO.

Oct 79. (7") *(BP 318)* **NUCLEAR DEVICE (THE WIZARD OF AUS). / YELLOWCAKE UF6** [36] [–]

Nov 79. (7"ep) *(STR 1)* **DON'T BRING HARRY** [41] [–]
– Don't bring Harry / Wired / Crabs (live) / In the shadows (live).

Liberty I.R.S.

Jan 80. (7") **DUCHESS. / THE RAVEN** [–] [ ]

Jan 80. (lp) *<SP 70011>* **STRANGLERS IV** [–] [ ]
– (5 tracks from 'THE RAVEN', plus recent singles)
(above w/ free 7"ep) – Do The European / Choosie Suzie / Wired / Straighten out.

Mar 80. (7"/12") *(BP/12BP 344)* **BEAR CAGE. / SHAH SHAH A GO GO** [36] [–]

May 80. (7") *(BP 355)* **WHO WANTS THE WORLD. / MENINBLACK** [39] [–]

Jan 81. (7") *(BP 383)* **THROWN AWAY. / TOP SECRET** [42] [–]

Feb 81. (lp/c) *(LBG/TC-LBG 30313)* **THE MEN• IN• BLACK** [8] [–]
– Waltzinblack / Just like nothing on Earth / Second coming / Waiting for the meninblack / Turn the centuries, turn / Two sunspots / Four horsemen / Thrown away / Manna machine / Hallo to our men. *(re-iss. 1985 lp/c; ATAK/TC-ATAK 34) (re-iss. Sep88 on 'Fame' lp/c/cd; FA/TCFA/CDFA 3208)* – Top secret / Maninwhite. *(cd re-iss. Aug01 on 'E.M.I.'++=; 534690-2)* – Tomorrow was hereafter.

Mar 81. (7") *(BP 393)* **JUST LIKE NOTHING ON EARTH. / MANINWHITE** [ ] [–]

Nov 81. (7") *(BP 405)* **LET ME INTRODUCE YOU TO THE FAMILY. / VIETNAMERICA** [42] [–]

Nov 81. (lp/c) *(LBG/TC-LBG 30342)* **LA FOLIE** [11] [–]
– Non stop / Everybody loves you when you're dead / Tramp / Let me introduce you to the family / The man they love to hate / Pin up / It only takes two to tango / Golden brown / How to find true love and happiness in the present day / La folie. *(re-iss. Nov83 on 'Fame' lp/c; FA/TC-FA 3083) (cd-iss. Aug88; CDFA 3083) (cd-iss. Feb88 +=; CZ 86)* – Cruel garden. *(cd re-iss. Aug01 on 'E.M.I.'++=; 534688-2)* – Cocktail nubiles / Vietnamerica / Love 30 / You hold the key to my love in your hands / Strange little girl.

Jan 82. (7") *(BP 407)* **GOLDEN BROWN. / LOVE 30** [2] [–]

Apr 82. (7") *(BP 410)* **LA FOLIE. / WALTZINBLACK** [47] [–]

Jul 82. (7") *(BP 412)* **STRANGE LITTLE GIRL. / CRUEL GARDEN** [7] [–]

Sep 82. (lp/c) *(LBG/TC-LBG 304353)* **THE COLLECTION 1977-1982** (compilation) [12] [–]
– (Get a) Grip (on yourself) / Peaches / Hanging around / No more heroes / Duchess / Walk on by / Waltzinblack / Something better change / Nice'n'sleazy / Bear cage / Who wants the world / Golden brown / Strange little girl / La folie. *(cd-iss. 1985; CDP 746066-2) (re-iss. Aug89 on 'Fame' cd/c/lp; CD/TC+/FA 3230)*

Epic Epic

Nov 82. (7"/7"pic-d) *(EPCA/+11 2893)* **THE EUROPEAN FEMALE. / SAVAGE BEAST** [9] [–]

Jan 83. (lp/c) *(EPC/40 25237) <38542>* **FELINE** [4] [ ]
– Midnight summer dream / It's a small world / Ships that pass in the night / The European female / Let's tango in Paris / Paradise / All roads lead to Rome / Blue sister / Never say goodbye. *(free ltd.one-sided-7"w.a.)* **AURAL SCULPTURE** *(re-iss. Apr86 lp/c; EPC/40 32711) <US lp+=>* – Golden brown. *(cd-iss. Jul97; 484469-2) (cd re-iss. Oct01 +=; 504592-2)* – SAvage breast / Pawsher / Permission / Midnight summer dream / European female (live) / Vladimir and Olga / Aural sculpture manifesto.

Feb 83. (7"/12") *(A/+13 3167)* **MIDNIGHT SUMMER DREAM. / VLADIMIR AND OLGA** [35] [–]

Jul 83. (7") *(A 3387)* **PARADISE. / PAWSHER** [48] [–]
(12"+=) *(A13 3387)* – Permission.

Jul 83. (12") **MIDNIGHT SUMMER DREAM. / PARADISE** [–] [ ]

Sep 84. (7") *(A 4738)* **SKIN DEEP. / HERE AND NOW** [15] [–]
(12"+=) *(TA 4738)* – Vladimir and the beast.

Nov 84. (lp/c) *(EPC/40 26220) <39959>* **AURAL SCULPTURE** [14] [ ]
– Ice queen / Skin deep / Let me down easy / No mercy / North winds / Uptown / Punch & Judy / Spain / Laughing / Souls / Mad Hatter. *(re-iss. May87 lp/c; 450488-1/-4) (cd-iss. 1987; 450488-2) (re-iss. cd Sep93 on 'Sony Collectors'; 983285-2) (cd re-iss. Feb97; 474676-2)*

Nov 84. (7"/7"sha-pic-d) *(A/WA 4921)* **NO MERCY. / IN ONE DOOR** [37] [–]
(12"+=) *(TA 4921)* – Hot club (riot mix).
(d7"++=) *(GA 4921)* – Head on the line.

Feb 85. (7") *(A 6045)* **LET ME DOWN EASY. / ACHILLES HEEL** [48] [–]
(12"+=) *(TA 6045)* – Place des victories.
(12"++=) *(QTA 6045)* – Vladimir goes to Havana / The aural sculpture manifesto.

Aug 86. (7"/12"/7"sha-pic-d) *(650055-7/-6/-0)* **NICE IN NICE. / SINCE YOU WENT AWAY** [30] [–]

Oct 86. (7"/7"sha-pic-d) *(SOLAR/+P 1)* **ALWAYS THE SUN. / NORMAN NORMAL** [30] [–]
(12"+=) *(SOLART 1)* – Soul.
(d7"+=) *(SOLARD 1)* – Nice in Nice / Since you went away.

Oct 86. (lp/c/cd/pic-lp) *(EPC/40/CD/11 26648) <40607>* **DREAMTIME** [16] [ ]
– Always the sun / Dreamtime / Was it you? / You'll always reap what you sow / Ghost train / Nice in Nice / Big in America / Shakin' like a leaf / Mayan skies / Too precious. *(re-iss. Feb89 lp/c/cd; 463366-1/-4/-2) (cd re-iss. Oct01 +=; 504593-2)* – Since you went away / Norman normal / Dry day / Hitman / Was it you / Burnham beaches.

Dec 86. (7"/7"sha-pic-d) *(HUGE/+P 1)* **BIG IN AMERICA. / DRY DAY** [48] [–]
(12"+=) *(HUGET 1)* – Uptown.
(d7"+=) *(HUGED 1)* – Always the sun / Norman normal.

Feb 87. (7"/7"sha-pic-d) *(SHEIK/+P 1)* **SHAKIN' LIKE A LEAF. / HIT MAN** [58] [–]
('A'-Jelly mix-12"+=) *(SHEIKQ 1)* – Was it you?
('A'live-12") *(SHEIKB 1)* – (an evening with Hugh Cornwall).

Dec 87. (7"/7"sha-pic-d) *(VICE/+P 1)* **ALL DAY AND ALL OF THE NIGHT (live). / VIVA VLAD** [7] [ ]
(12"+=) *(VICET 1)* – Who wants the world (live).
(cd-s+=) *(CDVICE 1)* – Strange little girl.

Feb 88. (lp/c/cd) *(460259-1/-4/-2) <44209>* **ALL LIVE AND ALL OF THE NIGHT (live)** [12] [ ]
– No more heroes / Was it you? / Down in the sewer / Always the sun / Golden brown / North winds / The European female / Strange little girl / Nice 'n' sleazy / Toiler on the sea / Spain / London lady / All day and all of the night. *(cd re-iss. Oct01 +=; 504594-2)* – Souls / Uptown / Shakin' like a leaf / Who wants the world / Peaches / Straighten out / Nuclear device / Punch and Judy.

Feb 90. (7"/c-s) *(TEARS/+M 1)* **96 TEARS. / INSTEAD OF THIS** [17] [–]
(12"+=/cd-s+=/pic-cd-s+=) *(TEARS T/C/P 1)* – Poisonality.

Mar 90. (cd/c/lp/pic-lp) *(466483-2/-4/-1/-0)* **10** [15] [–]
– The sweet smell of success / Someone like you / 96 tears / In this place / Let's celebrate / Man of the Earth / Too many teardrops / Where I live / Out of my mind / Never to look back. *(cd re-iss. Oct01 ++; 504595-2)* – Instead of this / Personality / Motorbike / Something / You / Viva Vlad / All day and all of the night (studio) / Always the sun (sunny side up mix).

Apr 90. (7"/c-s/7"pic-d) *(TEARS/+M/P 2)* **THE SWEET SMELL OF SUCCESS. / MOTORBIKE** [65] [–]
(12"+=/cd-s+=) *(TEARS T/C 2)* – Something.

Nov 90. (cd/c/lp/pic-cd) *(467541-2/-4/-1/-9) <47081>* **THE STRANGLERS' GREATEST HITS 1977-1990** (complation) [4] [ ]
– Peaches / Something better change / No more heroes / Walk on by / Duchess / Golden brown / Strange little girl / The European female / Skin deep / Nice in Nice / Always the sun / Big in America / All day and all of the night / 96 tears / No mercy.

Dec 90. (7"/c-s) *(656 430-7/-4)* **ALWAYS THE SUN. / BURNHAM BEECHES** [29] [–]
(12"+=) *(656 430-6)* – Straighten out.
(cd-s) *(656 430-2)* – ('A'side) / Nuclear device (live) / All day and all of the night (live) / Punch and Judy (live).

Mar 91. (7"/c-s) *(656 761-7/-4)* **GOLDEN BROWN (re-mix). / YOU** 68 –
(cd-s+=) *(656 761-2)* – Skin deep (extended) / Peaches.

— (late 1990) **JOHN ELLIS** (b. 1 Jun'52, London) – guitar, vocals (once p/t member) (ex-VIBRATORS, etc.) repl. CORNWALL who has already ventured solo.

— (Jan'91) also added **PAUL ROBERTS** (b.31 Dec'59, London) – vocals (ex-SNIFF 'N' THE TEARS)

China Viceroy

Aug 92. (7") *(WOK 2025)* **HEAVEN OR HELL. / DISAPPEAR** 46 –
(12"+=/c-s+=/cd-s+=) *(WOK T/C/CD 2025)* – Brainbox / Hanging around.

Sep 92. (lp/c/cd) *(WOL/+MC/CD 1030)* *<8007>* **STRANGLERS IN THE NIGHT** 33 Feb93
– Time to die / Sugar bullets / Heaven or Hell / Laughing at the rain / This town / Brainbox / Southern mouintains / Gain entry to your soul / Grand canyon / Wet afternoon / Never see / Leave it to the dogs.

Psycho not iss.

Oct 92. (7"/c-s) *(PSY/+MC 002)* **SUGAR BULLETS. / SO UNCOOL** –
(cd-s+=) *(PSYCD 002)* – ('A'version).

— **TIKAKE TOBE** – drums repl. JET BLACK

Essential Viceroy

Jun 93. (cd/c/lp) *(ESS CD/MC/LP 194)* *<ESM 388>* **SATURDAY NIGHT SUNDAY MORNING (live)** Mar96
– Toiler on the sea / 96 Tears / Always the sun / No more heroes / Golden brown / Tank / Strange little girl / Something better change / Hanging around / All day and all of the night / Duchess / *Medley / Was it you? / Down in the sewer.

— In Jun'93, old Strangler HUGH CORNWALL released album 'WIRED' on 'Transmission' label. Nearly a year earlier as CCW, he, ROGER COOK & AND WEST issued cd 'CCW FEATURING HUGH CORNWALL • ROGER COOK • ANDY WEST' on 'UFO'.

— **JET BLACK** returned

When! Beacon

May 95. (cd/c/lp) *(WEN CD/MC/LP 001)* *<51568>* **ABOUT TIME** 31 Jan96
– Golden boy / Money / Sinister / Little blue lies / Still life / Paradise row / She gave it all / Lies and deception / Lucky finger / And the boat sails by.

Jun 95. (12"/cd-s) *(WEN T/X 1007)* **LIES AND DECEPTION. / SWIM / DANNY COOL** –
(cd-s) *(WENX 1008)* – ('A'side) / Kiss the world goodbye / Bed of nails.

Jan 97. (pic-cd/cd/c) *(WEN PD/CD/MC 009)* **WRITTEN IN RED** 52 –
– Valley of the birds / In Heaven she walks / In a while / Silver into blue / Blue sky / Here / Joy de viva / Miss you / Daddy's riding the range / Summer in the city / Wonderful land. *(cd re-iss. Mar98 on 'Eagle'; EAMCD 001)*

Feb 97. (c-s/cd-s) *(WEN N/X 1018)* **IN HEAVEN SHE WALKS / GOLDEN BROWN (live)** –
(cd-s) *(WENX 1020)* – ('A'side) / Grip (live) / Something better change (live).

Eagle Festival

Oct 98. (cd) *(EAGCD 042)* *<31965>* **COUP DE GRACE** Mar99
– God is good / You don't think that what you've done is wrong / Tonight / Jump over my shadow / Miss you / Coup de grace (S-O-S) / In the end / No reason / Known only unto God / The light.

– compilations, etc. –

Mar 84. (7") *EMI Gold; (G45 6)* **GOLDEN BROWN. / STRANGE LITTLE GIRL** –

Sep 86. (lp/c) *Liberty; (LBG/TCLBG 5001)* **OFF THE BEATEN TRACK** 80 –

Nov 88. (lp/c) *Liberty; (EMS/TCEMS 1306)* **THE RARITIES** –
(cd-iss. Oct02 on 'E.M.I.'; 541079-2)

Jan 89. (7"/7"red) *E.M.I.; (EM/+R 84)* **GRIP '89. / WALTZINBLACK** 33 –
(12"+=) *(12EM 84)* – Tomorrow was thereafter.
(cd-s++=) *(CDEM 84)* – ('A'mix).

Feb 89. (cd/c/lp) *E.M.I.; (CD/TC+/EM 1314)* **THE SINGLES** 57 –

Jun 89. (12"ep) *Nighttracks; (SFNT/+CD 020)* **RADIO 1 SESSION (1982)** –
– The man they love to hate / Nuclear device / Genetix / Down in the sewer.

Dec 90. (3xcd-box) *Epic; (467395-2)* **FELINE / AURAL SCULPTURE / DREAMTIME**
(re-iss. Oct02; 509722-2)

Feb 92. (cd/c/d-lp) *Newspeak; (SPEAK CD/MC/LP 101)* **THE EARLY YEARS 74-75-76, RARE LIVE & UNRELEASED** –

Mar 92. (cd/c) *Epic; (471416-2/-4)* **ALL TWELVE INCHES** –

May 92. (cd/c) *(CDGO/TCGO 2033)* **LIVE AT THE HOPE AND ANCHOR (live)** –
(cd re-iss. Feb95 on 'Fame'; CDFA 3316)

Jul 92. (d-cd) *Epic; (466835-2)* **FELINE / DREAMTIME** –

Dec 92. (4xcd-box) *E.M.I.; CDS 799924-2)* **THE OLD TESTAMENT – THE U.A. STUDIO RECORDINGS (demos)** –

May 94. (cd) *Receiver; (<RRCD 187>)* **DEATH AND NIGHT AND BLOOD**

Jun 94. (cd) *Castle; (CLACD 401)* **THE EARLY YEARS 1974-76** –

Feb 95. (cd) *Receiver; (RRCD 195)* **LIVE IN CONCERT (live w/ FRIENDS)**

Nov 95. (cd) *Essential; <ESM 283>* **RADIO ONE** –

Nov 95. (cd-s) *Old Gold; (12623 6339-2)* **GOLDEN BROWN / NO MORE HEROES** –

Feb 97. (cd/c) *E.M.I.; (CD/TC EMC 3759)* **THE HIT MEN (The Complete Singles 1977-1990)** –

Apr 97. (cd) *EMI Gold; (CDGOLD 171)* **THE COLLECTION** –

Dec 97. (cd) *Rialto; (<RMCD 220>)* **STRANGLERS ARCHIVE LIVE IN LONDON (live)**

Feb 98. (cd) *Disky; (DC 88187-2)* **THE COLLECTION** –

Feb 98. (cd) *Cleopatra; <206>* **FRIDAY THE THIRTEENTH** –

Mar 98. (cd) *Eagle; (EABCD 111)* **THE MASTERS** –

Apr 98. (cd) *Stranglers; (SOF 001CD) / Voiceprint; <1>* **ACCESS ALL AREAS (live)** Jul98

May 98. (cd) *Stranglers; (SOF 002CD)* **FROM BIRTH TO BEYOND** –

Oct 98. (cd) *E.M.I.; (497773-2)* **THE BBC SESSIONS / LIVE AT THE HAMMERSMITH ODEON 1981** –

Jan 00. (cd) *Eagle; (EAGCD 006)* **FRIDAY 13TH (live at the Royal Albert Hall)** –

Feb 01. (cd) *S.P.V.; (SPV 0857105-2)* **5 LIVE VOL.1** –

Jun 01. (10xcd-s; box) *E.M.I.; (889172-2)* **THE U.A. SINGLES 1977-1979** –

Aug 01. (cd) *Armoury; (ARMCD 053)* **THE STRANGLERS** –

Oct 01. (5xcd-box) *Epic; (504596-2)* **THE EPIC YEARS** –

Jan 02. (cd) *Castle; (CMRCD 455)* **DEATH AND NIGHT AND BLOOD – THE STRANGLERS LIVE (live)** –

Jan 02. (cd) *Castle; (CMRCD 459)* **LIVE IN CONCERT (live)** –

Jan 02. (d-cd) *Snapper; (<SMDCD 373>)* **LIES AND DECEPTION (live)**

Mar 02. (cd) *Stable; (STABLE 1)* **CLUBBED TO DEATH – THE GREATEST HITS REMIXED** –

Jun 02. (cd) *Liberty; (540202-2)* **PEACHES – THE VERY BEST OF THE STRANGLERS** 21 –
– Peaches / Golden brown / Walk on by / No more heoes / Skin deep / Hanging around / All day and all of the night / Straighten out / Nice 'n' sleazy / Strange little girl / Who wants the world? / Something better change / Always the sun (sunny side up mix) / European female / Grip (1989 mix) / Five minutes / Don't bring Harry / La folie / 96 tears.

Jul 02. (12") *Tried & Twisted; (TT 2001)* **GOLDEN BROWN (earth loop remix). / GOLDEN BROWN (slipped disco remix)** –

Aug 02. (cd) *Zenith; (ZEN 0031-2)* **LAID BACK** –

Oct 02. (cd) *Epic; (487997-2)* **THE BEST OF THE EPIC YEARS** –

Oct 02. (cd) *Delta; (CD 47103)* **OUT OF THE BLACK** –

Jun o3. (cd) *Nobel Price; (220779)* **MISS YOU**

Aug 03. (cd) *Burning Airlines; (PILOT 177)* **APOLLO REVISITED (Live)**

STRAWBS

Formed: London, England . . . 1967 as The STRAWBERRY HILL BOYS by Leicester University student, DAVE COUSINS and schoolfriend TONY HOOPER, who, along with mandolin player ARTHUR PHILLIPS, initially traded in American-style bluegrass. With the addition of KEN GUDMAND, RON CHESTERMAN and a young SANDY DENNY, they moved towards a British folk revival sound and recorded the 'ALL OUR OWN WORK' album in 1968. This didn't actually see the light of day until 1974 when it was given a full release and credited to SANDY DENNY & THE STRAWBS, by that time of course, DENNY having carved out quite a career for herself. She originally left for FAIRPORT CONVENTION in '69, a core of COUSINS, HOOPER and CHESTERMAN completing 'THE STRAWBS' (1969) with the help of session men. Released on 'A&M', the album was highly regarded among the folk fraternity with its EWAN MacCOLL influenced compositions and exemplary playing. A follow-up, 'DRAGONFLY' (1970) wasn't so well received and the group subsequently pursued a new direction with the addition of ex-VELVET OPERA members, RICHARD HUDSON and JOHN FORD. Another star in the making, RICK WAKEMAN, was also a new addition, the classically trained keyboardist's impetus taking the band closer to electric prog-rock on 1970's 'JUST A COLLECTION OF ANTIQUES AND CURIOS'. Although alienating some of their more traditional fans, the record took The STRAWBS into the UK Top 30 for the first time. 'FROM THE WITCHWOOD' (1971) carried on in much the same vein, although WAKEMAN was feeling increasingly constricted and duly decamped to fledgling prog legends, YES. Ex-AMEN CORNER man, BLUE WEAVER, took his place for the acclaimed 'GRAVE NEW WORLD' (1972), an album which surprisingly failed to spawn a hit single despite its near Top 10 success. Recorded during a temporary split with the band, DAVE COUSINS' solo set, 'TWO WEEKS LAST SUMMER', was released just prior to The STRAWBS' first hit single, 'LAY DOWN'. This was almost immediately followed by the witty 'PART OF THE UNION' early in '73, a track lifted from the band's most creatively and commercially successful (near No.1) album of their career, 'BURSTING AT THE SEAMS'. With HOOPER already out of the picture by this point, internal tensions reached a head during an ill-fated US tour and led to the departure of HUDSON, FORD and WEAVER, a line-up of COUSINS, DAVE LAMBERT (who'd replaced HOOPER prior to 'BURSTING..'), CHAS CRONK, ROD COOMBES and JOHN HAWKEN going on to record a series of increasingly disappointing and poor selling albums right up until 1978. A re-formed STRAWBS, featuring COOPER, HOOPER and HUDSON with a cast of new faces, recorded the lacklustre 'DON'T SAY GOODBYE' in 1987, while varying permutations of the band continued to tour. • **Songwriters:** COUSINS or HUDSON-FORD (the latter pair between 1970 + 1973). • **Trivia:** Off-shoot duo, HUDSON-FORD, had a major Top 10 hit in 1973 with 'PICK UP THE PIECES', followed by a No.15 hit, 'BURN BABY BURN', in '74.

Album rating: THE STRAWBS (*7) / DRAGONFLY (*6) / JUST A COLLECTION OF ANTIQUES AND CURIOS (*6) / FROM THE WITCHWOOD (*6) / GRAVE NEW WORLD (*8) / BURSTING AT THE SEAMS (*7) / HERO AND HEROINE (*6) / STRAWBS BY CHOICE compilation (*6) / GHOSTS (*5) / NOMADNESS (*5) / DEEP CUTS (*5) / BURNING FOR YOU (*5) / DEADLINES (*5) / THE BEST OF THE STRAWBS compilation (*6) / DON'T SAY GOODBYE (*4) / A CHOICE SELECTION OF STRAWBS compilation (*8) / HALCYON DAYS: THE VERY BEST OF . . . compilation (*7) / RINGING DOWN THE YEARS (*4) / GREATEST HITS – LIVE (*5) / HEARTBREAK HILL (*4)

DAVE COUSINS (b. 7 Jan'45, Leicester, England) – vocals, guitar, banjo / **TONY HOOPER** – guitar, vocals / **KEN GUDMAND** – drums / **RON CHESTERMAN** – bass / **ARTHUR PHILLIPS** – mandolin / added **SANDY DENNY** (b. 6 Jan'47, Wimbledon, England) – vocals

— They recorded album 'ALL OUR OWN WORK' as SANDY DENNY & THE STRAWBS which was issued by 'Hallmark' in 1974. DENNY joined FAIRPORT CONVENTION. **DAVE, TONY & RON** employed session men **RONNIE WERRELL** – drums / **ALAN PARKER** – guitar / **ALAN NEIGHBOUR** – bass

A&M A&M

Jun 68. (7") *(AMS 725)* **OH HOW SHE CHANGED. / OR AM I DREAMING** [ ] [–]

Nov 68. (7") *(AMS 738)* **THE MAN WHO CALLED HIMSELF JESUS. / POOR JIMMY WILSON** [ ] [–]

May 69. (lp) *(AMLS 936)* **THE STRAWBS** [ ] [–]
– The man who called himself Jesus / That which was once mine / All the little ladies / Pieces of 79 & 15 / Tell me what you see in me / Oh how she changed / Or am I dreaming / Where is this dream of your youth / Poor Jimmy Wilson / Where am I – I'll show you where to sleep / The battle. *(cd-iss. Apr02 on 'Progressive'; PL 527)*

— basic trio added **CLAIRE DENIZ** – cello

Jul 70. (7") *(AMS 791)* **FOREVER. / ANOTHER DAY** [ ] [–]

Jul 70. (lp) *(AMLS 970)* **DRAGONFLY** [ ] [–]
– The weary song / Dragonfly / I turned my face into the wind / Josephine, for better or for worse / Another day / Till the sun comes shining through / Young again / The vision of the lady of the lake / Close your eyes. *(cd-iss. Nov01 on 'Progressive'; PL 0000503)*

— **RICHARD HUDSON** (b. 9 May'48, London) – drums / **JOHN FORD** (b. 1 Jul'48, London) – bass (both ex-VELVET OPERA) / **RICK WAKEMAN** (b.18 May'48) – keyboards (who guested on last lp) repl. RON + CLAIRE

Nov 70. (lp) *(AMLS 994)* <4288> **JUST A COLLECTION OF ANTIQUES AND CURIOS** [27] [ ]
– Martin Luther King's dream / The antique suite: The reaper – We must cross the river – Antiques and curios – Hey, it's been a long time / Temperament of mind / Fingertips / Song of a sad little girl / Where is this dream of your youth (live). *(cd-iss. Aug98 +=; 540938-2)* – Vision of the lady of the lake / We'll meet again sometime / Forever.

Jan 71. (7") **WHERE IS THE DREAM OF YOUR YOUTH (live). /** [–] [ ]

Jul 71. (lp) *(AMLH 64304)* <4304> **FROM THE WITCHWOOD** [39] [ ]
– A glimpse of Heaven / Witchwood / Thirty days / Flight / The hangman & the papist / Sheep / Canon Dale / The shepherd's song / In amongst the roses / I'll carry on beside you. *(cd-iss. Jul98 +=; 540939-2)* – I'll keep the Devil outside. *(cd re-iss. Nov01 on 'Progressive'; PL 0000516)*

— **BLUE WEAVER** (b.11 Mar'48, Cardiff, Wales) – keyboards (ex-AMEN CORNER) repl. WAKEMAN who joined YES

Feb 72. (lp) *(AMLH 68078)* <4344> **GRAVE NEW WORLD** [11] [ ]
– Benedictus / Hey little man . . .Thursday's child / Queen of dreams / Heavy disguise / New world / Hey little man . . .Wednesday's child / The flower and the young man / Tomorrow / On growing older / Ah me, ah my / Is it today, Lord? / The journey's end. *(cd-iss. Jul98 +=; 540934-2)* – Here it comes / I'm going home.

Feb 72. (7") *(AMS 874)* **BENEDICTUS. / KEEP THE DEVIL OUTSIDE** [ ] [–]

Apr 72. (7") *(AMS 7002)* **HERE IT COMES. / TOMORROW** [ ] [–]

Jun 72. (7") <13645> **BENEDICTUS. / HEAVY DISGUISE** [–] [ ]

— In Sep72, DAVE COUSINS issued a solo single GOING HOME. / WAYS AND MEANS plus an album TWO WEEKS LAST SUMMER for 'A&M'.

— **DAVE LAMBERT** (b. 8 Mar'49, Hounslow, England) – guitar, vocals repl. HOOPER

Oct 72. (7") *(AMS 7035)* **LAY DOWN. / BACKSIDE** [12] [–]

Jan 73. (7") *(AMS 7047)* **PART OF THE UNION. / WILL YOU GO** [2] [–]

Feb 73. (lp/c) *(AMLH/CAM 68144)* <4383> **BURSTING AT THE SEAMS** [2] [ ]
– Flying / Lady Fuchsia / Stormy down / Down by the sea / The river / Part of the union / Tears and Pavan medley / The winter and the summer / Lay down / Thank you. *(cd-iss. Jul98+=; 540936-2)* – Will you go / Back side / Lay down.

Apr 73. (7") <1419> **PART OF THE UNION. / TOMORROW** [–] [ ]

Aug 73. (7") <1451> **LAY DOWN. / THE WINTER AND THE SUMMER** [–] [ ]

— **COUSINS + LAMBERT** recruited new members **CHAS CRONK** – bass / **ROD COOMBES** – drums (ex-STEALER'S WHEEL) repl. HUDSON-FORD who formed own band **JOHN HAWKEN** – keyboards (ex-NASHVILLE TEENS, ex-RENAISSANCE, ex-VINEGAR JOE) repl. BLUE WEAVER

Aug 73. (7") *(AMS 7082)* <1476> **SHINE ON SILVER SUN. / AND WHEREFORE** [34] Nov73 [ ]

Apr 74. (7") *(AMS 7105)* **HERO AND HEROINE. / WHY** [ ] [–]

Apr 74. (7") <1519> **ROUND AND ROUND. / HEROINE'S THEME** [–] [ ]

Apr 74. (lp/c) *(AMLH/CAM 63607)* <3607> **HERO AND HEROINE** [35] Feb74 [94]
– Autumn: (a) Heroine's theme – (b) Deep summer sleep – (c) The winter

long / Sad young man / Just love / Shine on silver sun / Hero and heroine / Midnight sun / Out in the cold / Round and round / Lay a little light on me / Hero's theme. *(cd-iss. Aug98 +=; 540935-2)* – Still small voice / Lay a little light on me (early version).

May 74. (7") *(AMS 7117)* **HOLD ONTO ME (THE WINTER LONG). / WHERE DO YOU GO** [ ] [–]

Aug 74. (lp/c) *(AMLH/CAM 68259)* **BY CHOICE** (compilation) [ ] [ ]
– The man who called himself Jesus / Another day / Forever / Song of a sad little girl / The shepherd's song / Benedictus / Here it comes / The actor / Lay down / Lay a little light on me.

Nov 74. (7") *(AMS 7139)* **GRACE DARLING. / CHANGES ARRANGES** [ ] [–]

Nov 74. (lp/c) *(AMLH/CAM 68277)* <4506> **GHOSTS** [ ] Feb75 [47]
– Ghosts: Sweet dreams – Night light – Guardian angel / Lemon pie / Starshine – Angel wine / Where do you go (when you need a hole to crawl in) / The life auction: Impressions of Southall from the train – The auction / Don't try to change me / Remembering / You and I / Grace darling. *(cd-iss. Aug98 +=; 540937-2)* – Changes arrange us.

Apr 75. (7") *(AMS 7161)* **LEMON PIE. / DON'T TRY TO CHANGE ME** [ ] [–]

Jun 75. (7") *<1687>* **LEMON PIE. / WHERE DO YOU GO (WHEN YOU NEED A HOLE TO CRAWL IN)** [–] [ ]

Nov 75. (7") *<1747>* **LITTLE SLEEPY. / THE GOLDEN SALAMANDER** [–] [ ]

Nov 75. (lp/c) *(AMLH/CAM 68331)* <4544> **NOMADNESS** [ ] Oct75 [ ]
– To be free / Little Sleepy / The golden salamander / Absent friend (how I need you) / Back on the farm / So shall our love die? / Tokyo Rosie / A mind of my own / Hanging in the gallery / The promised land. *(cd-iss. Nov01 on 'Progressive'; PL 0000517)*

Oyster-Polydor — Oyster

Jul 76. (7") *(2066 705)* **I ONLY WANT MY LOVE TO GROW IN YOU. / THINKING OF YOU** [ ] [–]

Sep 76. (lp/c) *(2391-234)* <1603> **DEEP CUTS** [ ] [ ]
– I only want my love to grow in you / Turn me round / Hard, hard winter / My friend Peter / The soldier's tale / Simple visions / Charmer / (Wasting my time) Thinking of you / Beside the Rio Grande / So close and yet so far away.

Oct 76. (7") *(2066 74)* **CHARMER. / BESIDE THE RIO GRANDE** [ ] [–]

Dec 76. (7") *(2066 751)* **SO CLOSE AND YET SO FAR AWAY. / THE SOLDIER'S TALE** [ ] [–]

May 77. (7") *(2066 818)* **BACK IN THE OLD ROUTINE. / BURNING FOR ME** [ ] [–]

Jun 77. (lp/c) *(2391 287)* <1604> **BURNING FOR YOU** [ ] [ ]
– Burning for me / Cut like a diamond / I feel your loving coming on / Barcarole / Alexander The Great / Keep on trying / Back in the old routine / Heartbreaker / Carry me home / Goodbye.

Aug 77. (7") *(2066 846)* **KEEP ON TRYING. / SIMPLE VISIONS** [ ] [–]

Arista — Arista

Jan 78. (7") *(ARIST 159)* **JOEY AND ME. / DEADLY NIGHTSHADE** [ ] [–]

Feb 78. (lp/c) *(SPART/TCARTY 1036)* **DEADLINES** [ ] [ ]
– Deadlines (no return) / Joey and me / Sealed with a traitor's kiss / I don't want to talk about it / The last resort / Time and life / New beginnings / Deadly nightshade / Words of wisdom.

Mar 78. (7") *(ARIST 179)* **NEW BEGINNINGS. / WORDS OF WISDOM** [ ] [–]

Apr 78. (7") **I DON'T WANT TO TALK ABOUT IT. / WORDS OF WISDOM** [–] [ ]

Oct 78. (7") *(ARIST 183)* **I DON'T WANT TO TALK ABOUT IT. / THE LAST RESORT** [ ] [–]

—— Folded in 1978. In Sep79, on 'Slurp' records, COUSINS made another solo album 'OLD SCHOOL SONGS' *(SLURP 1)* augmented by guitarist **BRIAN WILLOUGHBY**. In mid'83, **COUSINS + HOOPER** re-formed **The STRAWBS** with **CHAS CRONK** – bass / **TONY FERNANDEZ** – drums (both of RICK WAKEMAN's band). (below 45 feat. MADDY PRIOR)

L.O. — not iss.

Nov 80. (7") *(LO 1)* **THE KING. / RINGING DOWN THE YEARS** [ ] [–]

—— Early in 1987, **COUSINS, HOOPER, WILLOUGHBY, HUDSON** brought in **CHRIS PARREN** – keyboards (ex-HUDSON-FORD) / **ROD DEMICK** – bass (ex-WHEELS)

not iss. — Virgin

Feb 87. (7") **THAT'S WHEN THE CRYING STARTS. / WE CAN MAKE IT TOGETHER** [–] Canada [–]

Toots — not iss.

May 87. (lp) *(TOOTS 3)* **DON'T SAY GOODBYE** [ ] [–]
– A boy and his dog / Let it rain / We can make it together / Tina dei fada / Big brother / Something for nothing / Evergreen / That's when the crying starts / Beat the retreat. *(re-iss. Oct88 on 'Chord' lp/cd; STRAWBS 001/ CD009)*

Chord — not iss.

Nov 88. (7") *(STRAWBS 101)* **LET IT RAIN. / TINA DEI FADA** [ ] [–]

not iss. — Virgin

1991. (cd) *<CDV 3031>* **RINGING DOWN THE YEARS** [–] Canada [–]
– Might as well be on Mars / The king / Forever ocean blue / Grace darling / Afraid to let you go / Tell me what you see in me / Ringing down the years / Stone cold is the woman's heart / Taking a chance. *(UK-iss.Apr98 d-cd on 'Road Goes On Forever'+=; RGFCD 039)* – DON'T SAY GOODBYE

Road Goes On Forever — not iss.

Oct 93. (cd) *(RGFCD 015)* **GREATEST HITS – LIVE (live 1990)** [ ] [–]
– Cut like a diamond / Something for nothing / The hangman and the papist / Ringing down the years / Stormy down / Afraid to let you go / Grace darling / The river / Down by the sea / Lay down / Part of the union / Hero & heroine. *(re-iss. Jul95; same)*

below featured all The STRAWBS on session plus MARY HOPKIN

Aug 94. (cd; as COUSINS & WILLOUGHBY) *(RGFCD 020)* **THE BRIDGE** [ ] [–]
– You never needed water / Further down the road / Strange day over the hill / Heat of the street / Morning glory / Cry no more / Do you remember / The plain / Oh so sleepy / Song for Alex.

—— line-up:- **COUSINS / CRONK / RICHARDS / FERNANDEZ**

Jul 95. (cd) *(RGFWC 024)* **HEARTBREAK HILL** [ ] [–]
– Something for nothing / Another day without you / We can make it together / Heartbreak Hill / Starting over / Two separate people / Desert song / Let it rain.

– compilations, etc. –

May 73. (lp; SANDY DENNY & THE STRAWBS) *Hallmark; (SHM 813)* **ALL OUR OWN WORK** [ ] [–]
(re-iss. 1991 on 'Hannibal';)

Sep 78. (d-lp) *A&M; (AMLH 66005)* **THE BEST OF THE STRAWBS** [ ] [ ]

Mar 79. (7") *A&M; (AMS 7425)* **PART OF THE UNION. / LAY DOWN** [ ] [–]
(re-iss. Jul82 on 'Old Gold'; OG 9149)

1992. (d-cd) *Road Goes On Forever; (DCD 003)* **PRESERVES UNCANNED** [ ] [–]

Oct 92. (cd) *A&M; (CDMID 173)* **A CHOICE SELECTION OF STRAWBS** [ ] [ ]
– Lay down / Lemon pie / Lady Fuschia / Autumn:- 1- Heroine's theme – 2- Deep summer's sleep – 3- The winter long / A glimpse of Heaven / The hangman and the papist / New world / Round and round / I only want my love to grow in you / Benedictus / Hero and heroine / Song of a sad little girl / Tears and Pavan:- 1- Tears – 2- Pavan / To be free / Part of the union / Down by the sea.

Mar 95. (cd) *Windsong; (WINCD 069)* **STRAWBS IN CONCERT (live)** [ ] [–]

Aug 96. (d-cd) *Road Goes On Forever; (RGFCD 027)* **DEEP CUTS / BURNING FOR YOU** [ ] [–]

Feb 97. (d-cd) *A&M; (540662-2)* **HALYCON DAYS – THE VERY BEST OF THE STRAWBS** [ ] [–]

Jun 99. (cd) *Ranch Life; (RRCC 00706)* **CONCERT CLASSICS** [ ] [–]

Feb 02. (cd) *Witchwood; (WRCD 2004)* **BAROQUE AND ROLL – THE ACOUSTIC STRAWBS** [ ] [ ]

May 02. (cd) *Spectrum; (544706-2)* **THE COLLECTION** [ ] [–]

Sep 02. (cd) *Island; (493369-2)* **TEARS AND PAVAN: AN INTRODUCTION TO THE STRAWBS** [ ] [ ]

Jan 03. (cd) *Progressive; (PL 563)* **PRINCE AND PRINCESS** [ ] [ ]

May 03. (cd) *Witchwood; (WMCD 2008)* **BLUE ANGEL** [ ] [–]

STREETS

Formed: Birmingham, England . . . late 2000 as the brainchild of MIKE SKINNER. All decked out in a hoodie, low-slung cap and white nikes, MIKE took the British Garage scene – not to mention the actual music scene – by storm in 2002 with his debut album 'ORIGINAL PIRATE MATERIAL'. Growing up in a working class household in the suburbs of Birmingham, SKINNER became interested in keyboards at an early age, and, having been raised on a staple diet of hip-hop (apparently his brother was part of the whole VW Beetle medalion-wearing scene in the early '90's) decided to dedicate his life to making music. Setting up a makeshift studio in his bedroom, using a cupboard and a mattress as a vocal booth, the switched-on Brummie invited local MCs around to record and mix tracks. This established The STREETS. Beginning as a collective crew, many soon lost interest, which forced SKINNER to branch out on his own, mixing, recording, mutating styles and sounds, until pirate radio stations and garage DJ's picked up on his immense talent. Hence the album 'ORIGINAL PIRATE MATERIAL', a contender for best album of the year, and one of the most original urban records ever. On the single 'HAS IT COME TO THIS', SKINNER took the speedy garage beat format, mixed it with his own sardonic vocals (a kind of cross between EMINEM and the ARTFUL DODGER) and also added a bit of dancehall ragga to the deck. Standout track 'THE IRONY OF IT ALL' coupled two characters (both played by SKINNER), one being a mouthy lager lout, the other a gentle stoner debating the causes and effects of both drugs with tac-sharp wit and brilliant social observations. At the end of the day, The STREETS were massive amongst kids and students alike; here was an album devoid of the cute, self-indulgent narcissism of mainstream garage and the fake fubbery of the "bling-bling" era – MIKE was taking it back . . . back to the streets.

Album rating: ORIGINAL PIRATE MATERIAL (*9)

MIKE SKINNER (b.27 Nov'78) – vocals, electronics

Locked On | not iss.

May 01. (12") *(LOCKED 035)* **HAS IT COME TO THIS? (mixes)** [ ] [–]

679 | Atlantic

Oct 01. (12"/cd-s) *(679L 001 T/CD1)* **HAS IT COME TO THIS? (mixes; original / Jameson / Zed Bias vocal)** [18] [–]
(cd-s) *(679L 001CD2)* – ('A'side) / Geezers need excitement / Streets score (instrumental).

Mar 02. (cd/c/d-lp) *(0927 43568-2/-4/-1)* <93181> **ORIGINAL PIRATE MATERIAL** [12] Oct02 [ ]
– Turn the page / Has it come to this? / Let's push things forward / Sharp darts / Same old thing / Geezers need excitement / It's too late / Too much brandy / Don't mug yourself / Who got the funk? / The irony of it all / Weak become heroes / Who dares wins / Stay positive.

Apr 02. (12") *(679 005T)* **LET'S PUSH THINGS FORWARD (mixes; Studio Gangsters / Zed Bias vocal / Mystery)** [30] [–]
(cd-s) *(679 005CD1)* – ('A'mixes; original / Studio Gangsters / Zed Bias dub).
(cd-s) *(679 005CD2)* – ('A'-original) / Runnins / Don't mug yourself (instrumental).

Jul 02. (12") *(679L 007TX)* **WEAK BECOME HEROES. / LET'S PUSH THINGS FORWARD (remix featuring ROLL DEEP) / GIVE ME LIGHTER BACK** [27] [–]
(cd-s+=) *(679L 007CD1)* – ('A'-video).
(cd-s) *(679L 007CD2)* – ('A'-Ashley Beadle's love bug vocal) / Same old thing (Outlaw breaks remix) / Same old thing (Morph resurrection remix).

Oct 02. (12") *(679L 008T)* **DON'T MUG YOURSELF. / OUT TAKES / STREETS SCORE** [21] [–]
(cd-s+=) *(679L 008CD1)* – ('A'-video).
(cd-s) *(679L 008CD2)* – ('A'side) / Weak become heroes (Royksopp's memory lane mix) / Has it come to this? (high contrast remix).

Jul 03. (12"/cd-s) <*60393/60543*> **DON'T MUG YOURSELF (Mr. Figit mix). / GIVE ME BACK MY LIGHTER (Jammer mix)** [–] [ ]

☐ STREETWALKERS (see under ⇒ FAMILY)

STROKES

Formed: New York City, New York, USA . . . 1998 by JULIAN CASABLANCAS (son of Elite Model Agency CEO, John Casablancas, and a one-time Miss Denmark), guitarist NICK VALENSI, bass guitarist NIKOLAI FRAITURE and drummer FAB MORETTI; ALBERT HAMMOND JR would be added later. Fed up with the recent import of Nu-metal bands such as LINKIN PARK, LIMP BIZKIT and the soft post-grunge credentials of STAINED, the NME decided to promote a new form of rock music between spring and summer 2001; and The STROKES became virtually overnight the headlining act along with fellow garage rockers WHITE STRIPES. The question begged to be asked, however: if such publicity (and some might've called it hype) wasn't used to promote this youthful garage rock band, would the public and press still deem them to be the saviours of rock? The STROKES began playing – minus HAMMOND – in 1998 where they all attended the upper-class prep school Dwight. It was there that the group discovered their love for garage rock and quickly began pulling ideas together for songs. The sound would be halfway between LOU REED's "ostrich guitar", MC5's thrash meanderings and the tunefulness of TOM PETTY. Surprisingly, the ensemble (now playing in a plush rehearsal room in the lower east side of Manhattan and with the arrival of newcomer HAMMOND) pulled off the technical trickery of the above mentioned, and, through all of the scattered influences, began to develop a sound of their own. They debuted live in spring '99, performing in such venues as NYC's 'Baby Jupiter' and 'LUNA'. Ryan Gentles was finally brought in as manager and helped them require spots at 'Mercury Lounge' and 'Bowery Ballroom'. Things were almost reaching fever pitch for The STROKES, and, alongside THE MOLDY PEACHES and ANDREW W.K., they were becoming the most talked about band in NYC. A tape, including the tracks 'SOMA', 'BARELY LEGAL' and the rip-roaring 'MODERN AGE' was sent to 'Rough Trade' in London. The label (at that time, pulling themselves out of financial difficulty) signed the band, issuing the 'MODERN AGE' EP to critical acclaim. The NME went nuts, urging the record-buying public to go out and listen to this new and exciting group. Bidding wars began in America over The STROKES distribution, with 'R.C.A.' emerging as the champions. The single 'HARD TO EXPLAIN' was issued and reached No.16 in the British charts. Now, it seemed, this group of talented young upstarts were emerging as bonafide rockstars . . . even COURTNEY LOVE wrote a song about CASABLANCAS, entitled 'But Julian, I am much older than you'. With all of the commotion, the humble and ironically titled debut album 'IS THIS IT' was premiered amid much audience anticipation in early September 2001. It reached No.2 in the UK, even with its risqué Helmut Newton-inspired cover (which was refused by Woolworth's and HMV). But as the band watched the Twin Towers collapse from their rehearsal room on September 11, they decided to pull the song 'NYC COPS' from the American release of 'IS THIS IT'. Perhaps not one of their better moves, as the above mentioned song was a blinder; perhaps the best track on the LP, and a genuine audience favourite. 'LAST NITE' appeared on single at the end of 2001, with a video accompanied by Roman Copolla, featuring a live performance from the band. Things were looking bright at the turn of the year, with the addition of a few new tracks, a sold-out tour of Britain and the re-admission of 'NYC COPS' into the live brew. Perhaps The STROKES weren't the saviours of rock, but they were sure pretty damn close. After dabbling with RADIOHEAD producer Nigel Godrich for their sophomore album, the group and Godrich departed citing musical differences, leaving the recording duties up to Gordon Raphael. They worked "soldiers hours" in his basement recording room and churned out their "difficult" sophomore record 'ROOM ON FIRE' in 2003. Going down a storm with the press, The STROKES hadn't suffered from second album syndrome, as tracks such as 'MEET ME IN THE BATHROOM' and hit single 'REPTILIA' beat the living crap out of their critics with their tightly focused arrangements. A sell out tour promptly followed, and many fans and touts (cough-NME-cough!) were sighing a breath of relief that these switched-on fellas weren't just a flash in the pan.

Album rating: IS THIS IT (*9) / ROOM ON FIRE (*7)

JULIAN CASABLANCAS (b.23 Aug'78) – vocals / **NICK VALENSI** (b.16 Jan'81) – guitar / **NIKOLAI FRAITURE** (b.13 Nov'79) – bass / **FAB MORETTI** (b. 2 Jun'80) – drums / added **ALBERT HAMMOND JR** – guitar

		Rough Trade	R.C.A.
Jan 01.	(7"/cd-s) *(RTRADES/+CD 010)* **MODERN AGE. / LAST NIGHT / BARELY LEGAL**		–
	(re-dist.Jun01) – hit UK No.68		
Jun 01.	(7"/cd-s) *(RTRADES/+CD 023)* **HARD TO EXPLAIN. / NEW YORK CITY COPS**	16	–
Aug 01.	(cd/lp) *(RTRADE CD/LP 030)* *<68101>* **IS THIS IT**	2	33
	– Is this it / The modern age / Soma / Barely legal / Someday / Alone, together / Last nite / Hard to explain / New York City cops / Trying your luck / Take it or leave it.		
Nov 01.	(7"/cd-s) *(RTRADES/+CD 041)* **LAST NITE. / WHEN IT STARTED**	14	–
	(cd-s) *(RTRADES 041X)* – ('A'live) / Trying your luck (live) / Take it or leave it (live).		
Apr 02.	(cd-ep) *(RTRADESCD 053)* **HARD TO EXPLAIN / THE MODERN AGE / LAST NITE / WHEN IT STARTED / TAKE IT OR LEAVE IT (live)**	– Irish	–
Jun 02.	(7"clear) *<7863-60554-7>* **HARD TO EXPLAIN. / NEW YORK CITY COPS**	–	
	(cd-s+=) *<60533>* – Take it or leave it / Trying your luck.		
Sep 02.	(7"yellow/cd-s) *(RTRADES/+CD 063)* **SOMEDAY. / ALONE, TOGETHER (home recording) / IS THIS IT (home recording)**	27	–
Apr 03.	(cd-s) *<60611>* **LAST NITE / TRYING YOUR LUCK (live) / LAST NITE (live) / TAKE IT OR LEAVE IT (live)**	–	
Apr 03.	(cd-s) *<60623>* **SOMEDAY / IS THIS IT (version) / ALONE, TOGETHER (version)**	–	
Oct 03.	(7"/cd-s) *(RTRADES/+CD 140)* *<56610>* **12:51. / THE WAY IT IS (home recording)**	7	
Oct 03.	(cd) *(RTRADECD 130)* *<55497>* **ROOM ON FIRE**	2	4
	– What ever happened? / Reptilia / Automatic stop / 12:51 / You talk way too much / Between love & hate / Meet me in the bathroom / Under control / The way it is / The end has no end / I can't win.		

□ Joe STRUMMER (see under ⇒ CLASH)

□ STYLE COUNCIL (see under ⇒ WELLER, Paul)

STYX

Formed: Chicago, Illinois, USA ... 1964 as The TRADEWINDS by DENNIS DE YOUNG and neighbours, the PANOZZO twins (CHUCK and JOHN). After meeting JOHN CURULEWSKI at university and duly recruiting him as guitarist, the group briefly changed their name to TW4 before eventually settling on STYX (after the mythical Greek river). With the line-up augmented by a second guitarist, JAMES YOUNG, the group came to the attention of Bill Traut, who signed them to his 'Wooden Nickel' label. Initially touting a classical/art-rock fusion with overblown vocal arrangements, the group debuted with the eponymous 'STYX' in 1972. Although the album spawned a US Hot 100 single in 'BEST THING', subsequent sets such as 'THE SERPENT IS RISING' (1974) and 'MAN OF MIRACLES' (1974), failed to yield any chart action. Things changed in the mid-70's as CURULEWSKI was replaced with guitarist/vocalist/co-writer, TOMMY SHAW, who, along with DE YOUNG, would help steer the band in a more commercial direction. Widely credited with inventing pomp-rock, STYX only really started to take their falsetto-warbling excess to the masses following a move to 'R.C.A.'. Almost instantaneous success came in late '74/early '75 when the label re-issued 'LADY' (from 1972's 'STYX II'), a strident slice of bombastic pop which marched into the US Top 10. Follow-up sets, 'EQUINOX' (1976) and 'CRYSTAL BALL' (1976) appeared on 'A&M', STYX slowly but surely swelling their fanbase with widescale touring and an increasingly radio-friendly sound. The big break finally came in 1977 with the multi-million selling 'THE GRAND ILLUSION' album and accompanying Top 10 crossover hit, 'COME SAIL AWAY'. The following year's 'PIECES OF EIGHT' (1978) achieved a fine balance between melody, power and stride-splitting vocal histrionics, although it was 'CORNERSTONE' (1980) which furnished the group with their sole No.1 single, the syrupy 'BABE'. A lavishly packaged pomp concept piece, 'PARADISE THEATER' (1980) became the group's first (and only) No.1, even making the Top 10 in Britain(!) Arguably among the group's most affecting work, the record spawned two US Top 10 singles, 'THE BEST OF TIMES' and 'TIME ON MY HANDS'. Yet another concept piece (centering on the increasingly controversial issue of censorship), 'KILROY WAS HERE' (1983), appeared in 1983, the last STYX studio album of the decade. The following year saw both DE YOUNG and SHAW releasing solo debuts, 'DESERT MOON' and 'GIRLS WITH GUNS' respectively. Both sets performed relatively well, although DE YOUNG's poppier affair spawned a Top 10 hit single with the title track. Subsequent mid to late 80's efforts (DE YOUNG's 'BACK TO THE WORLD' and 'BOOMCHILD', SHAW's 'WHAT IF' and 'AMBITION') failed to capture the public's imagination and the inevitable STYX reformation album was released in 1990. Despite the absence of SHAW (his replacement being GLEN BURTNIK), who had joined DAMN YANKEES, 'EDGE OF THE CENTURY' was a relative success, housing a massive US Top 3 hit in 'SHOW ME THE WAY'. Come the late 90's the band were back again with another reformation – this time with SHAW in the ranks – and a live comeback album, 'RETURN TO PARADISE'. While this had consisted largely of old material, 'BRAVE NEW WORLD' (1999) was a set of brand spanking new stuff at least making an attempt to sound contemporary but simultaneously railing against the march of time and the current musical climate. Fans also longing for the old days could torture themselves at will with the self explanatory 'STYX WORLD: LIVE 2001'. With a little help from friends like BRIAN WILSON, BILLY BOB THORNTON and TENACIOUS D, 'CYCLORAMA' (2003) was one of the better reformation-era STYX albums with some of the trademark heavy handedness leavened by the pop smarts of 'KISS YOUR ASS GOODBYE' and the free'n'loose caterwauling of 'BOURGEOIS PIG' (aided and abetted by THORNTON and JACK BLACK respectively).

Album rating: STYX (*4) / STYX II (*6) / THE SERPENT IS RISING (*5) / MAN OF MIRACLES (*6) / EQUINOX (*6) / CRYSTAL BALL (*6) / THE GRAND

ILLUSION (*7) / PIECES OF EIGHT (*7) / THE BEST OF STYX compilation (*6) / CORNERSTONE (*7) / PARADISE THEATER (*8) / KILROY WAS HERE (*6) / CAUGHT IN THE ACT – LIVE (*4) / EDGE OF THE CENTURY (*5) / GREATEST HITS compilation (*8) / RETURN TO PARADISE (*3) / BRAVE NEW WORLD (*3) / STYX WORLD: LIVE 2001 (*3) / CYCLORAMA (*6)

DENNIS DeYOUNG (b.18 Feb'47) – vocals, keyboards / **JOHN CURULEWSKI** – guitar / **JAMES YOUNG** (b.14 Nov'48) – guitar / **CHUCK PANOZZO** (b.20 Sep'47) – bass / **JOHN PANOZZO** – drums

not iss. Wooden Nickel

Sep 72. (lp) *<BXLI 1008>* **STYX** [–] [ ]
– Movement for the common man: Children of the land – Street collage – Fanfare for the common man – Mother Nature's matinee / Right away / What has come between us / Best thing / Quick is the beat of my heart / After you leave me. *(UK-iss.Jul80 as 'STYX 1' on 'R.C.A.'; 3593) (cd re-iss. Jan99 on 'One Way'; OW 35130)*

Sep 72. (7") *<0106>* **BEST THING. / WHAT HAS COME BETWEEN US** [–] [82]

Jul 73. (7") *<0111>* **I'M GONNA MAKE YOU FEEL IT. / QUICK IS THE BEAT OF MY HEART** [–] [ ]

Jul 73. (lp) *<BXLI 1012>* **STYX II** [–] [ ]
– You need love / Lady / A day / You better ask / Little fugue in "G" / Father O.S.A. / Earl of Roseland / I'm gonna make you feel it. *<re-dist.Jan75, hit US No.20> (UK-iss.Jul80 as 'LADY' on 'R.C.A.'; 3594)*

Sep 73. (7") *<0116>* **LADY. / YOU BETTER ASK** [–] [ ]

Feb 74. (lp) *<BXLI 0287>* **THE SERPENT IS RISING** [–] [ ]
– Witch wolf / The grove of Eglantine / Young man / As bad as this / Winner take all / 22 years / Jonas Psalter / The serpent is rising / Krakatoa / Hallelujah chorus. *(UK-iss.Jul80 on 'R.C.A.'; 3595)*

Oct 74. (7") *<10027>* **LIES. / 22 YEARS** [–] [ ]

Nov 74. (lp) *<BWLI 0638>* **MAN OF MIRACLES** [–] [ ]
– Rock & roll feeling / Havin' a ball / Golden lark / A song for Suzanne / A man like me / Best thing / Evil eyes / Southern woman / Christopher Mr. Christopher. *(UK-iss.Jul80 on 'R.C.A.'; 3596)*

R.C.A. R.C.A.

Feb 75. (7") *(RCA 2518) <10102>* **LADY. / CHILDREN OF THE LAND** [ ] Dec74 [6]

Jul 75. (7") *<0252>* **YOUNG MAN. / UNFINISHED SONG** [–] [ ]

May 75. (7") *<10272>* **YOU NEED LOVE. / YOU BETTER ASK** [–] [88]

Nov 75. (7") *<10329>* **BEST THING. / HAVIN' A BALL** [–] [ ]

A&M A&M

Feb 76. (lp) *(AMLH 64559) <4559>* **EQUINOX** [ ] Dec75 [58]
– Light up / Lorelei / Mother dear / Lonely child / Midnight ride / Born for adventure / Prelude 12 / Suite Madame Blue.

Mar 76. (7") *(AMS 7220) <1786>* **LORELEI. / MIDNIGHT RIDE** [ ] Feb76 [27]

Jul 76. (7") *<1818>* **LIGHT UP. / BORN FOR ADVENTURE** [–] [ ]

— **TOMMY SHAW** (b.11 Sep'53, Montgomery, Alabama) – lead guitar repl. CURULEWSKI

Oct 76. (lp) *(AMLH 64604) <4604>* **CRYSTAL BALL** [ ] [66]
– Put me on / Mademoiselle / Jennifer / Crystal ball / Shooz / This old man / Clair de Lune – Ballerina.

Jan 77. (7") *(AMS 7273) <1877>* **MADEMOISELLE. / LIGHT UP** [ ] Nov76 [36]

Feb 77. (7") *<1900>* **JENNIFER. / SHOOZ** [–] [ ]

Jun 77. (7") *(AMS 7299) <1931>* **CRYSTAL BALL. / PUT ME ON** [ ] [ ]

Aug 77. (lp/c) *(AMLH/CAM 64637) <4637>* **THE GRAND ILLUSION** [ ] Jul77 [6]
– The grand illusion / Fooling yourself (the angry young man) / Superstars / Come sail away / Miss America / Man in the wilderness / Castle walls / The grand finale. *(cd-iss. Jul87; CDA 3223)*

Oct 77. (7") *(AMS 7321) <1977>* **COME SAIL AWAY. / PUT ME ON** [ ] Sep77 [8]

Mar 78. (7") *(AMS 7343) <2007>* **FOOLING YOURSELF (THE ANGRY YOUNG MAN). / THE GRAND FINALE** [ ] Feb78 [29]

Sep 78. (lp/c)<US-pic-d> *(AMLH/CAM 64724) <4724>* **PIECES OF EIGHT** [ ] [6]
– Great white hope / I'm O.K. / Sing for the day / The message / Lords of the ring / Blue collar man (long nights) / Queen of spades / Renegade / Pieces of eight / Aku-aku.

Oct 78. (7"/12"colrd) *(AMS/+P 7388) <2087>* **BLUE COLLAR MAN (LONG NIGHTS). / SUPERSTARS** [ ] Sep78 [21]

Mar 79. (7",7"red) *(AMS 7446) <2110>* **RENEGADE. / SING FOR THE DAY** [ ] [16]

[41]

Sep 79. (7") *(AMS 7489) <2188>* **BABE. / I'M OK** [6] Sep79 [1]

Jan 80. (lp/c) *(AMLK/CKM 63711) <3711>* **CORNERSTONE** [36] Oct79 [2]
– Lights / Why me / Babe / Never say never / Boat on the river / Borrowed time / First time / Eddie / Love in the moonlight.

Dec 79. (7") *<2206>* **WHY ME. / LIGHTS** [–] [26]

Mar 80. (7") *<2228>* **BORROWED TIME. / EDDIE** [–] [64]

Mar 80. (7") *(AMS 7512)* **BOAT ON THE RIVER. / COME SAIL AWAY** [ ] [–]

May 80. (7") *(AMS 7528)* **LIGHTS. / RENEGADE** [ ] [–]

Jan 81. (lp/c) *(AML H/K 63719) <3719>* **PARADISE THEATER** [8] [1]
– A.D. 1928 / Rockin' the Paradise / State street Sadie / Too much time on my hands / She cares / Snowblind / Nothing ever goes as planned / The best of times / Half-penny, two-penny / A.D. 1958. *(cd-iss. Jun84; CDA 63719) (re-iss. Oct92 cd/c; CD/C MID 154)*

Jan 81. (7") *(AMS 8102) <2300>* **THE BEST OF TIMES. / LIGHT** [42] [3]
(d-lazer-etched-7") – ('A'side) / PARADISE THEATER

Mar 81. (7",7"colrd) *(AMS 8118) <2323>* **TOO MUCH TIME ON MY HANDS. / QUEEN OF SPADES** [ ] [9]

Jul 81. (7") *<2348>* **NOTHING EVER GOES AS PLANNED. / NEVER SAY NEVER** [–] [54]

Nov 81. (7") *(AMS 8175)* **ROCKIN' THE PARADISE. / SNOWBLIND** [ ] [–]

Feb 83. (lp/c) *(AMLX/CAM 63734) <3734>* **KILROY WAS HERE** [67] [3]
– Mr. Roboto / Cold war / Don't let it end / High time / Heavy metal poisoning / Just get through this night / Double life / Haven't we been here before / Don't let it end (reprise). *(cd-iss. Apr84; CDA 63734)*

Mar 83. (7") *(AMS 8308) <2525>* **MR. ROBOTO. / SNOWBLIND** [ ] Feb83 [3]

May 83. (7"/7"sha-pic-d) *(AM/+P 120) <2543>* **DON'T LET IT END. / ROCKIN' THE PARADISE** [56] Apr83 [6]

Jun 83. (7") *<2560>* **HAVEN'T WE BEEN HERE BEFORE. / DOUBLE LIFE** [–] [ ]

Aug 83. (7") *<2568>* **HIGH TIME. / DOUBLE LIFE** [–] [48]

Apr 84. (d-lp/d-c) *(AMLH/CAM 66704) <6514>* **CAUGHT IN THE ACT – LIVE (live)** [44] [31]
– Music time / Mr. Roboto / Too much time on my hands / Babe / Snowblind / The best of times / Suite Madame Blue / Rockin' the Paradise / Blue collar man (long night) / Miss America / Don't let it end / Fooling yourself (the angry young man) / Crystal ball / Come sail away.

May 84. (7") *(AM 197) <2625>* **MUSIC TIME (live). / HEAVY METAL POISONING (live)** [ ] [40]

— the band rested activities while their main members DeYOUNG and SHAW went solo

— STYX were back, although without SHAW (who joined DAMN YANKEES, and later SHAW BLADES), who was deposed by **GLEN BURTNIK** – lead guitar

Nov 90. (cd/c/lp) *(395327-2/-4/-1) <5327>* **EDGE OF THE CENTURY** [ ] Oct90 [63]
– Love is the ritual / Show me the way / Edge of the century / Love at first sight / All in a day's work / Not dead yet / World tonite / Carrie Ann / Homewrecker / Back to Chicago.

Dec 90. (7"/7"pic-d) *(AM/+X 709) <1525>* **LOVE IS THE RITUAL. / HOMEWRECKER** [ ] Oct90 [80]
(12"+=/cd-s+=) *(AM Y/CD 709)* – Babe.

Feb 91. (7"/c-s) *<1536>* **SHOW ME THE WAY. / BACK TO CHICAGO** [ ] Dec90 [3]
(12"+=/cd-s+=) – Don't let it end.

Mar 91. (c-s,cd-s) *<1548>* **LOVE AT FIRST SIGHT / WORLD TONITE** [–] [25]

— re-formed again with **DeYOUNG, SHAW, YOUNG + PANOZZO**

— **TODD SUCHERMANN** – drums, percussion; repl. PANOZZO who died

S.P.V. C.M.C.

Aug 98. (d-cd) *(SPV 0852918-2) <86212>* **RETURN TO PARADISE (live)** [ ] May97 [ ]
– On my way / Paradise / Rockin' the paradise / Blue collar man / Lady / Too much time on my hands / Snowblind / Suite Madame blue / Crystal ball / The grand illusion / Foolish yourself (the angry young man) / Show me the way / Boat on the river / Lorelei / Babe / Miss America / Come sail away / Renegade / Best of times / Dear John.

C.M.C. C.M.C.

Jun 99. (cd) *<(86275-2)>* **BRAVE NEW WORLD** [ ] [ ]
– I will be your witness / Brave new world / While there's still time /

Number one / Best new face / What have they done to you / Fallen angel / Everything is cool / Great expectations / Heavy water / High crimes and misdemeanors (hip hop-crazy) / Just fell in / Goodbye Roseland / Brave new world (reprise).

—— **LAWRENCE GOWAN** – vocals; repl. DeYOUNG who became ill

Jun 01. (cd) <*(86311-2)*> **STYX WORLD: LIVE 2001 (live)**
– Rockin' the paradise / High enough / Lorelei / A criminal mind / Love is the ritual / Boat on the river / Half-penny, two penny / Sing for the day / Snowblind / Sometimes love just ain't enough / Crystal ball / Miss America / Come sail away.

Sanctuary Sanctuary

Mar 03. (cd) *(SANCD 156)* <*63372*> **CYCLORAMA** Feb03
– Do things my way / Waiting for our time / Fields of the brave / Bourgeois pig / Kiss your ass goodbye / These are the times / Yes I can / More love for the money / Together / Fooling yourself (palm of your hands) / Captain America / Killing the thing that you love / One with everything / Genki desu ka.

– compilations, others, etc. –

Oct 79. (lp/c) *R.C.A.; (PL/PK 13116)* <*3597*> **THE BEST OF STYX**
– You need love / Lady / I'm gonna make you feel it / What has come between us / Southern woman / Rock & roll feeling / Winner take all / Best thing / Witch wolf / The grove of Eglantine / Man of miracles. *(cd-iss. 1992; PD 83597)*

Apr 78. (7"ep) *A&M; (AMS 7355)* **MADEMOISELLE / COME SAIL AWAY. / CRYSTAL BALL / LORELEI** –

1978. (7") *Wooden Nickel-RCA;* <*11205*> **BEST THING. / WINNER TAKE ALL** –

Sep 85. (7") *Old Gold; (OG 9545)* **BABE. / THE BEST OF TIMES** –

Jan 87. (12"ep) *Old Gold; (OG 4013)* **BABE / THE BEST OF TIMES. / (2 by The Tubes)** –

Apr 88. (cd-ep) *A&M; (AMCD 904)* **COMPACT HITS** –
– Babe / Come sail away / Rockin' the Paradise / The best of times.

May 95. (cd) *A&M; (396959-2)* **BOAT ON THE RIVER**

Jul 97. (cd) *A&M; (540465-2)* **THE BEST OF TIMES – THE BEST OF STYX**

Jul 99. (d-cd) *One Way;* <*(OW 35144)*> **THE SERPENT IS RISING / MAN OF MIRACLES**

Oct 00. (cd; shared with REO SPEEDWAGON) *Sanctuary; (SANDD 004)* <*86299*> **ARCH ALLIES: LIVE AT RIVERPORT (live)** Sep00

May 02. (cd) *Universal;* <*(AA69490395-2)*> **THE MILLENNIUM COLLECTION**

Jul 02. (cd) *C.M.C.;* <*86318*> **AT THE RIVER'S EDGE: LIVE IN ST. LOUIS (live)** –

Aug 03. (cd) *Universal;* <*(AAB00007380-2)*> **ROCKERS**

□ SUB SUB (see under ⇒ DOVES)

SUEDE

Formed: London, England . . . 1989 by BRETT ANDERSON, who, by 1992 had put together the final line-up of guitarist BERNARD BUTLER, bassist MATT OSMAN and drummer SIMON GILBERT (ELASTICA prime mover, JUSTINE FRISCHMANN, had also been an early member). After a single, 'BE MY GOD' / 'ART', failed to appear in 1990 on 'RML' (this lost recording was famous for featuring ex-SMITHS drummer, MIKE JOYCE), the band signed to 'Nude', precipitating a storm of media hype and adulation. Featured on the cover of NME before they had even released their debut single, the band became press darlings of a post-grunge/pre-Brit pop music scene desperate for a bit of cheap glamour. Widely touted as spiritual antecedents of The SMITHS, the group were actually closer in style to the camp affectations of mid-period BOWIE, although there was definitely a MORRISSEY-like archness to the lyrics, the glum one actually taking to covering 'MY INSATIABLE ONE' (the B-side of SUEDE's acclaimed debut effort, 'THE DROWNNERS') live. Another couple of singles followed, 'METAL MICKEY' and 'ANIMAL NITRATE', these scoring successively higher chart positions. The media support, together with ANDERSON's sleazy, androgynous posturing, made him, and his band, instant heroes for a new generation of crazy, mixed up kids, the eponymous 1993 debut album quickly reaching No.1. 'Nude's takeover by 'Sony' in early that year gave the act a bit of major label muscle, ironically helping them on their way to becoming one of the biggest "indie" bands in Britain. At the beginning '94, the band scored their biggest hit single to date with the epic 'STAY TOGETHER', the track peaking at No.3. Later that Spring, gay drummer SIMON bravely went to the House Of Commons to air his views on the homosexual laws of consent, which were to be lowered from 21 to either 16 (the heterosexual age) or 18, as it finally turned out. Around the same time, more controversy dogged the group when an American jazz singer called SUEDE won her lawsuit against the band in the US, the upshot of the affair being that from that point on, the band were to be known in America as LONDON SUEDE (lucky for them they didn't come from Leatherhead!). Meantime, the group had won the Mercury Music Prize for their acclaimed debut album and were well on the way to releasing a follow-up, 'DOG MAN STAR' (1994). The last album to feature the departing BUTLER (heralded by some as the UK's most promising guitarist since JOHNNY MARR, BUTLER subsequently went on to a successful, if short lived, collaboration with DAVID McALMONT before signing to 'Creation' and embarking on a solo career), it marked something of a departure in the band's sound, a dense, ambitious set which met with a mixed critical reception. Unbowed, SUEDE swaggered on, recruiting the teenage RICHARD OAKES as BUTLER's replacement and providing a welcome diversion from the laddish excesses of Brit-pop. SUEDE's next effort, 'COMING UP' proved to be their most consistent set to date, spawning the brilliant lowlife anthem, 'TRASH' along with the similarly infectious, organic glam of 'FILMSTAR' and the dislocated melancholy of 'SATURDAY NIGHT'. A stop-gap but worthy collection of rarities and B-sides, 'SCI-FI LULLABIES' (1997) marked time before their return in the Spring of '99. 'ELECTRICITY' sparked off proceedings, the UK Top 5 single also the opening track on their No.1 Steve Osborne-produced 4th album proper, 'HEAD MUSIC' (1999). Three other retro-fied 45's ('SHE'S IN FASHION', 'EVERYTHING WILL FLOW' and 'CAN'T GET ENOUGH') were delivered to an eager kitsch fanbase who were still "into" all things glam:- BOWIE, ROXY, NUMAN, HUMAN . . . A few years in the proverbial wilderness, BRETT and his beloved SUEDE team returned on the scene in summer 2002 (with ex-STRANGELOVE drummer, ALEX LEE, replacing NEIL), releasing 'A NEW MORNING', a set that didn't go straight to No.1; or even make the Top 10, or Top 20! • **Songwriters:** ANDERSON / BUTLER, except; BRASS IN POCKET (Pretenders) / etc.

Album rating: SUEDE (*8) / DOG MAN STAR (*7) / COMING UP (*7) / SCI-FI LULLABIES collection (*6) / HEAD MUSIC (*7) / A NEW MORNING (*6) / SINGLES compilation (*8)

BRETT ANDERSON (b.27 Sep'67, Haywards Heath, Sussex, England) – vocals / **BERNARD BUTLER** (b. 1 May'70) – guitar, piano / **MATT OSMAN** (b. 9 Oct'67) – bass / **SIMON GILBERT** (b.23 May'65) – drums

Nude not iss.

Apr 92. (7") *(nud 1s)* **THE DROWNERS. / TO THE BIRDS** 49 –
(12"+=/cd-s+=) *(nud 1 t/cd)* – My insatiable one.

Sep 92. (7"/c-s) *(nud 3 s/mc)* **METAL MICKEY. / WHERE THE PIGS DON'T FLY** 17 –
(12"+=/cd-s+=) *(nud 3 t/cd)* – He's dead.

Nude-Sony Columbia

Feb 93. (7"/c-s) *(nud 4 s/mc)* **ANIMAL NITRATE. / THE BIG TIME** 7 –
(12"+=/cd-s+=) *(nud 4 t/cd)* – Painted people.

Apr 93. (cd/c/lp) *(nude 1 cd/mc/lp)* <53792> **SUEDE** 1
– So young / Animal nitrate / She's not dead / Moving / Pantomime horse / The drowners / Sleeping pills / Breakdown / Metal Mickey / Animal lover / The next life. *(cd re-iss. Aug02 on 'Epic'; 473735-2)*

May 93. (7"/c-s) *(nud 5 s/mc)* **SO YOUNG. / HIGH RISING** 22 –
(12"+=/cd-s+=) *(nud 5 t/cd)* – Dolly.

Sep 93. (cd-ep) <44K 77172> **THE DROWNERS / MY INSATIABLE ONE / TO THE BIRDS / THE BIG TIME / HE'S DEAD (live)** –

Feb 94. (7"/c-s) *(nud 9 s/mc)* **STAY TOGETHER. / THE LIVING DEAD** 3 –
(ext;12"+=/cd-s+=) *(nud 9 t/cd) – My dark star.*

— An American jazz singer called SUEDE won her lawsuit against the band in the US. They are now to be called LONDON SUEDE, but thankfully only in the States.

Mar 94. (cd-ep) *<CK 64382>* **STAY TOGETHER / THE LIVING DEAD / MY DARK STAR / DOLLY HIGH RISING / STAY TOGETHER (extended)** –

Sep 94. (7"/c-s) *(nud 10 s/mc)* **WE ARE THE PIGS. / KILLING OF A FLASH BOY** 18 –
(12"+=/cd-s+=) *(nud 10 t/cd)* – Whipsnade.

Oct 94. (cd/c/d-lp) *(nude 3 cd/mc/lp)* <66769> **DOG MAN STAR** 3
– Introducing the band / We are the pigs / Heroine / The wild ones / Daddy's speeding / The power / New generation / This Hollywood life / The 2 of us / Black or blue / The asphalt world / Still life. *<US-version +=>* – Modern boys. *(cd re-iss. Aug02 on 'Epic'; 477811-2)*

— (July'94; after rec. album) **RICHARD OAKES** – guitar; repl. BUTLER who went solo

Nov 94. (c-s) *(nud 11mc)* **THE WILD ONES / MODERN BOYS** 18 –
(cd-s+=) *(nud 11cd1)* – This world needs a father.
(12") *(nud 11t)* – ('A'side) / Eno's introducing the band.
(cd-s) *(nud 11cd2)* – (above 2) / Asda town.

Jan 95. (7"/c-s) *(nud 12mc)* **NEW GENERATION. / TOGETHER** 21 –
(12"+=/cd-s+=) *(nud 12 t/cd1)* – Bentswood boys.
(cd-s) *(nud 12cd2)* – ('A'side) / Animal nitrate (live) / The wild ones (live) / Pantomime horse (live).

— added new member **NEIL CODLING** – keyboards, vocals

Jul 96. (c-s) *(nud 2mc)* **TRASH / EUROPE IS OUR PLAYGROUND** 3 –
(cd-s+=) *(nud 21cd1)* – Every Monday morning comes.
(pic-cd-s) *(nud 21cd2)* – ('A'side) / Have you ever been this low? / Another no one.

Sep 96. (cd/c/lp) *(nude 6 cd/mc/lp)* <67911> **COMING UP** 1
– Trash / Filmstar / Lazy / By the sea / She / Beautiful ones / Starcrazy / Picnic by the motorway / The chemistry between us / Saturday night. *(cd re-iss. Aug02 on 'Epic'; 485129-2)*

Oct 96. (c-s) *(nud 23mc)* **BEAUTIFUL ONES / BY THE SEA (demo)** 8 –
(cd-s) *(nud 23 cd1)* – ('A'side) / Young men / The sound of the streets.
(cd-s) *(nud 23 cd2)* – ('A'side) / Money / Sam.

Jan 97. (c-s) *(nud 24mc)* **SATURDAY NIGHT / PICNIC BY THE MOTORWAY (live)** 6 –
(cd-s) *(nud 24cd1)* – ('A'side) / W.S.D. / Jumble sale mums.
(cd-s) *(nud 24cd2)* – ('A'side) / This time / ('A'demo).
(d7") *(nud 24s)* – ('A'side) / This time / Beautiful ones / The sound of the streets.

Apr 97. (c-s) *(nud 27mc)* **LAZY / SHE (live)** 9 –
(cd-s) *(nud 27cd1)* – ('A'side) / These are the sad songs / Feel.
(cd-s) *(nud 27cd2)* – ('A'side) / Sadie / Digging a hole.

Aug 97. (7") *(nud 30s)* **FILMSTAR. / ('A'original demo)** 9 –
(cd-s) *(nud 30cd1)* – ('A'side) / Graffiti women / Duchess. *(w/ free video footage; Beautiful ones / Coming up.*
(cd-s) *(nud 30cd2)* – ('A'side) / Rent / Saturday night / Saturday night (cd-rom).

Oct 97. (d-cd) *(nude 9cd)* <68857> **SCI-FI LULLABIES** (flipsides) 9
– My insatiable one / To the birds / Where the pigs don't fly / He's dead / The big time / High rising / The living dead / My star / Killing of a flash boy / Whipsnade / Modern boys / Together / Bentswood boys / Europe is our playground // Every Monday morning comes / Have you ever been this low? / Another no one / Young men / The sound of the streets / Money / W.S.D. / This time / Jumble sale mums / These are the sad songs / Sadie / Graffiti women / Duchess. *(cd re-iss. Aug02 on 'Epic'; 488851-2)*

Apr 99. (c-s) *(nud 43mc)* **ELECTRICITY / IMPLIMENT, YEAH!** 5 –
(cd-s) *(nud 43cd1)* – ('A'side) / Popstar / Killer.
(cd-s) *(nud 43cd2)* – ('A'side) / See that girl / Waterloo.

May 99. (cd/c/d-lp) *(nude 14 cd/mc/lp)* <69986> **HEAD MUSIC** 1 Jun99
– Electricity / Savoir faire / Can't get enough / Everything will flow / Down / She's in fashion / Asbestos / Head music / Elephant man / Hi-fi / Indian strings / He's gone / Crack in the Union Jack. *(cd re-iss. Aug02 on 'Epic'; 494243-2)*

Jun 99. (c-s) *(nud 44mc)* **SHE'S IN FASHION / DOWN (demo)** 13 –
(cd-s) *(nud 44cd1)* – ('A'side) / Bored / Pieces of my mind.
(cd-s) *(nud 44cd2)* – ('A'side) / Jubilee / God's gift.

Sep 99. (c-s) *(nud 45mc)* **EVERYTHING WILL FLOW / BEAUTIFUL ONES (live)** 24 –
(cd-s) *(nud 45cd1)* – ('A'side) / Weight of the world / Leaving.
(cd-s) *(nud 45cd2)* – ('A'side) / Crackhead / Seascape.

Nov 99. (cd-s) *(nud 47cd1)* **CAN'T GET ENOUGH / LET GO / SINCE YOU WENT AWAY** 23 –
(cd-s) *(nud 47cd2)* – ('A'side) / Situations / Read my mind.
(cd-s) *(nud 47cd3)* – ('A'side) / Everything will flow (Rollo's vocal mix) / She's in fashion (Lironi version) / ('A'-CD video).

— (Mar'01) **ALEX LEE** – drums (ex-BLUE AEROPLANES, ex-STRANGELOVE) repl. NEIL

Epic Sony

Sep 02. (cd-s) *(672949-2)* **POSITIVITY / ONE LOVE / SIMON / POSITIVITY (video)** 16 –
(cd-s) *(672949-5)* – ('A'side) / Superstar / Cheap.

Sep 02. (cd) *(508956-2)* *<649168>* **A NEW MORNING** 24
– Positivity / Obsessions / Lonely girls / Lost in TV / Beautiful loser / Streetlife / Astrogirl / Untitled . . .morning / One hit to the body / When the rain falls. *(special cd+=; 508956-9)* – You belong to me / Oceans.

Nov 02. (cd-s) *(673294-2)* **OBSESSIONS / COOL THING / INSTANT SUNSHINE** 29 –
(cd-s) *(673294-5)* – ('A'side) / UFO / Rainy day girl.

Oct 03. (cd-s) *(674358-2)* **ATTITUDE / GOLDEN GUN / OXYGEN / ATTITUDE (video)** 14 –
(cd-s) *(6743585)* – ('A'-side) / ('A'-demo) / Just a girl / Heroin.

Oct 03. (cd) *(513604-2)* *<70011>* **SINGLES** (compilation) 31
– Beautiful ones / Animal nitrate / Trash / Metal Mickey / So young / The wild ones / Obsessions / Filmstar / Can't get enough / Everything will flow / Stay together / Love the way you love / The drowners / New generation / Lazy / She's in fashion / Attitude / Electricity / We are the pigs / Positivity / Saturday night.

SUGAR

Formed: Minneapolis, USA . . . 1992 by former HUSKER DU frontman/co-writer, BOB MOULD. Upon the demise of the latter act in 1987, MOULD signed to 'Virgin America' and subsequently entered PRINCE's 'Paisley Park' studios to lay down his first solo set, 'WORKBOOK' (1989). Augmented by the former PERE UBU rhythm section of ANTON FIER and TONY MAIMONE and employing cellists JANE SCARPANTONI and STEVE HAIGLER, MOULD confounded expectations with a largely acoustic affair trading in melodic distortion for fragments of contemplative melancholy; only the closing 'WHICHEVER WAY THE WIND BLOWS' acknowledged the sonic assault of prime HUSKER DU. Despite the guaranteed critical plaudits and the more accessible nature of the material, 'WORKBOOK's sales were modest. Perhaps as a reaction, the following year's 'BLACK SHEETS OF RAIN' – again recorded with FIER and MAIMONE – was a searing return to bleaker, noisier pastures; 'HANGING TREE' remains among the most tormented work of MOULD's career, while the likes of 'HEAR ME CALLING' and 'IT'S TOO LATE' combined keening melody with blistering soloing/discordant riffing in patented MOULD fashion. When this album also failed to take off, the singer parted

comapny from 'Virgin' and undertook a low-key acoustic tour. His wilderness period was brief, however, the emerging grunge vanguard citing HUSKER DU as a massive influence and inspiring MOULD to form another melodic power trio. Comprising of fellow songwriter/bassist, DAVE BARBE and drummer MALCOLM TRAVIS, SUGAR signed to 'Creation' and proceeded to cut one of the most feted albums of the era in 'COPPER BLUE' (1992). Leaner, tighter and cleaner, the record's bittersweet pop-hardcore crunch finally provided MOULD with a springboard for commercial success; a UK Top 10 hit, the album even spawned a Top 30 hit single in the sublime 'IF I CAN'T CHANGE YOUR MIND'. 'BEASTER', 1993's mini-album follow-up, took tracks from the 'COPPER BLUE' sessions and buried them in a multi-tiered blanket of howling distortion. Unsurprisingly it failed to spawn a hit, although its Top 3 success was no doubt sweet for the ever contrary MOULD, his follow-up proper, 'FILE UNDER EASY LISTENING (F.U.E.L.)' (1994), suggesting that he'd become bored with the whole concept. MOULD eventually disbanded the project in spring '96, releasing a third solo album the same year, simply titled 'BOB MOULD'. Bowing out of the music industry treadmill with 'THE LAST DOG AND PONY SHOW' (1998), MOULD eventually resurfaced in 2002 with 'MODULATE', an ambitious if ultimately flawed attempt at re-examining his muse through the lens of post-millennial electronica.
• **Songwriters:** MOULD; and now some with others. Covered; SHOOT OUT THE LIGHTS (Richard Thompson).

Album rating: Bob Mould: WORKBOOK (*7) / BLACK SHEETS OF RAIN (*6) / Sugar: COPPER BLUE (*9) / BEASTER mini (*7) / FILE UNDER: EASY LISTENING (*7) / BESIDES collection (*6) / Bob Mould: BOB MOULD (*8) / THE LAST DOG AND PONY SHOW (*7) / MODULATE (*4)

BOB MOULD

BOB MOULD (b.12 Oct'61, Malone, New York) – vocals, guitar, etc (ex-HUSKER DU) / with **ANTON FIER** – drums / **TONY MAIMONE** – bass, (both ex-PERE UBU) / **JANE SCARPANTONI** – cello (of TINY LIGHTS) / **STEVE HAIGLER** – cello

Virgin Virgin

Jun 89. (7") *(VUS 2)* **SEE A LITTLE LIGHT. / ALL THOSE PEOPLE KNOW** [ ] [–]
(12"+=/cd-s+=) *(VUS 2T/CD2)* – Shoot out the lights / Composition for the young and the old (live).

Jul 89. (lp/cd) *(VUS LP/CD 2)* *<91240>* **WORKBOOK** [ ] Apr89 [ ]
– Sunspots / Wishing well / Heartbreak a stranger / See a little light / Poison years / Sinners and their repentances / Lonely afternoon / Brasilia crossed the Tranton / Compositions for the young and old / Dreaming, I amd / Whichever way the wind blows. *(re-iss. Sep90; OVED 340)*

Aug 90. (cd/c/lp) *(VUS CD/MC/LP 21)* *<91395>* **BLACK SHEETS OF RAIN** [ ] May90 [ ]
– Black sheets of rain / Stand guard / It's too late / One good reason / Stop your crying / Hanging tree / The last night / Hear me calling / Out of your life / Disappointed / Sacrifice – let there be peace.

Virgin Virgin

May 94. (cd) *(CDVM 9030)* *<39587>* **THE POISON YEARS** (compilation from first two sets) [ ] Jul94 [ ]

SUGAR

BOB MOULD – vox, guitar, keyboards, percussion / **DAVE BARBE** – bass (ex-MERCYLAND) / **MALCOLM TRAVIS** – drums, percussion (ex-ZULUS)

Creation Rykodisc

Jul 92. (cd-ep) *<1024>* **HELPLESS / NEEDLE HITS E / IF I CAN'T CHANGE YOUR MIND / TRY AGAIN** [–] [ ]

Aug 92. (12"ep)(cd-ep) *(CRE 126T)(CRESCD 126)* **CHANGES / NEEDLE HITS E. / IF I CAN'T CHANGE YOUR MIND / TRY AGAIN** [ ] [–]

Sep 92. (cd/lp)(c) *(CRE CD/LP 129)(C-CRE 129) <RCD/RACS 10239>* **COPPER BLUE** [10] [ ]
– The act we act / A good idea / Changes / Helpless / Hoover dam / The slim / If I can't change your mind / Fortune teller / Slick / Man on the Moon.

Oct 92. (7"ep/c-ep) *(CRE/+CS 143)* *<1030>* **A GOOD IDEA. / WHERE DIAMONDS ARE HALOS / SLICK** [65] [ ]
(12"ep+=)(cd-ep+=) *(CRE 143T)(CRESCD 143)* – Armenia city in the sky.

Jan 93. (7"/c-s) *(CRE/+CS 149)* **IF I CAN'T CHANGE YOUR MIND. / CLOWN MASTER** [30] [ ]
(12"+=) *(CRE 149T) <1031>* – Anyone (live) / Hoover dam (live).
(cd-s) *(CRESCD 149) <1032>* – ('A'side) / The slim / Where diamonds are halos.

Apr 93. (m-cd/m-lp)(m-c) *(CRE CD/LP 153)(C-CRE 153) <50260>* **BEASTER** [3] [ ]
– Come around / Tilted / Judas cradle / JC auto / Feeling better / Walking away.

Aug 93. (7") *(CRE 156)* **TILTED. / JC AUTO (live)** [48] [–]

Aug 94. (7"/c-s) *(CRE/+CS 186)* **YOUR FAVORITE THING. / MIND IS AN ISLAND** [40] [ ]
(12"+=)(cd-s+=) *(CRE 186T)(CRESCD 186) <1038>* – Frustration / And you tell me (T.V. mix).

Sep 94. (cd/lp)(c) *(CRE CD/LP 172)(C-CRE 172) <10300>* **FILE UNDER EASY LISTENING (F.U.E.L.)** [7] [50]
– Gift / Company book / Your favorite thing / What you want it to be / Gee angel / Panama city hotel / Can't help it anymore / Granny cool / Believe what you're saying / Explode and make up.

Oct 94. (7"/c-s) *(CRE/+CS 193)* **BELIEVE WHAT YOU'RE SAYING. / GOING HOME** [73] [ ]
(cd-s+=) *(CRESCD 193) <1039>* – In the eyes of my friends / And you tell me.

Dec 94. (cd-ep) *<RCD5 1040>* **GEE ANGEL / EXPLODE AND MAKE UP / SLIM / AFTER ALL THE ROADS HAVE LED TO . . .** [–] [ ]

Jul 95. (d-cd) *<10321>* **BESIDES** (compilation of b-sides, live, etc) [–] [ ]

— disbanded and BARBE formed BUZZHUNGRY / TRAVIS went to CUSTOMIZED

BOB MOULD

— solo again with various back-up

Creation Rykodisc

Dec 95. (cd-s) *<51050>* **EGOVERRIDE** [–] [ ]

Apr 96. (cd/lp) *(CRE CD/LP 188) <10342>* **BOB MOULD** [52] [ ]
– Anymore time between / I hate alternative rock / Fort Knox, King Solomon / Next time that you leave / Egoverride / Thumbtack / Hair stew / Hair stew / Deep karma canyon / Art crisis / Roll over and die.

— now with **MATT HAMMON** – drums / **ALISON CHESLEY** – cello

Aug 98. (7") *(CRE 206)* **CLASSIFIEDS. / MOVING TRUCKS** [ ] [–]

Aug 98. (cd/lp) *(CRE CD/LP 215) <10443>* **THE LAST DOG AND PONY SHOW** [58] [ ]
– New #1 / Moving trucks / Taking everything / First drag of the day / Classifieds / Who was around? / Skintrade / Vaporub / Sweet serene / Megamaniac / Reflecting pool / Along the way / (interview).

Cooking Vinyl Granary

Apr 02. (cd) *(COOKCD 237) <2021>* **MODULATE** [ ] Mar02 [ ]
– 180 rain / Sunset safety glass / Semper fi / Homecoming parade / Lost zoloft / Without? / Slay – Sway / The receipt / Quasar / Soundonsound / Hornery / Comeonstrong / Trade / Author's lament.

☐ SUGARCUBES (see under ⇒ BJORK)

SUGAR RAY

Formed: Los Angeles, California, USA . . . 1989 out of cover outfit The SHRINKY DINX by MARK McGRATH (of Irish parentage), RODNEY SHEPPARD, MURPHY KARGES, STAN FRAZIER and DJ HOMOCIDE (aka CRAIG BULLOCK). Signed to Atlantic offshoot label 'Lava' in 1994, this dayglo bunch of funky pop-metal funsters debuted the following year with the 'LEMONADE & BROWNIES' set. While that record hinted at an endearing BEASTIES-esque charm, the group only really hit their saucy stride on follow-up set, 'FLOORED' (1997). Trading in hood-down, shout-along metal/rap with a winking undercurrent of dancefloor cheesiness, the record didn't come within a whisker of taking itself seriously (on the majority of tracks anyhow), stretching the limits of good natured fun with a cover of 'STAND AND DELIVER' (Adam & The Ants). While the album received encouraging reviews and the 'FLY' single was an MTV favourite, SUGAR RAY have still to capture the hearts (and groins) of the rock scene at large. Kicking off 1999 with a proverbial bang and now complete with sneakers and loud shirts, SUGAR RAY had a couple of massive American hits beginning with 'EVERY MORNING'. Taken from their sunkissed album, '14:59' (which also contained second Top 10'er, 'SOMEDAY'), the band could do no wrong. The Californians scored their highest charting album (US Top 10) to date in the shape of the eponymous 'SUGAR RAY' (2001), a record even more tinted by that California sunshine than their previous efforts. The beachfront groove of 'WHEN IT'S OVER' was most redolent of their newfound self-possession, a US Top 20 hit that deserved to go higher. 'IN THE PURSUIT OF LEISURE' (2003) played pretty much as its title read, another musical manifesto pledging bushy-tailed alterna-pop fun for anyone not grown up enough to listen. While a modern production sheen made some half hearted attempts at contemporary artifice, the cheeky, slacker-eyed likes of 'CHASIN' YOU AROUND' and 'IN THROUGH THE DOGGIE DOOR' took up where the last album left off. A wildly impressive cover of Joe Jackson's 'IS SHE REALLY GOING OUT WITH HIM' proved their credentials just for the sake of it. • **Covered:** ABRACADABRA (Steve Miller Band).

Album rating: LEMONADE & BROWNIES (*5) / FLOORED (*7) / 14:59 (*6) / SUGAR RAY (*6) / IN THE PURSUIT OF LEISURE (*6)

MARK McGRATH (b.1969) – vocals / **RODNEY SHEPPARD** (b.1966) – guitar / **MURPHY KARGES** (b.1966) – bass (ex-WEIRDOS) / **STAN FRAZIER** (b. CHARLES STANTON FRAZIER, 1968) – drums / **DJ HOMOCIDE** (b. CRAIG BULLOCK, 1971) – turntables (ex-ALCHOLIKS)

		Atlantic	Atlantic
Aug 95.	(7"/c-s) *(A 7143/+C)* **MEAN MACHINE. / WANGO TANGO**		–
	(cd-s+=) *(A 7143CD)* – White minority / Wasted.		
	(re-iss. May96; same)		
Sep 95.	(cd) *<(7567 82743-2)>* **LEMONADE & BROWNIES**		
	– Snug harbor / Iron mic / Rhyme stealer / Hold your eyes / Big black woman / Dance party USA / Danzig needs a hug / 10 seconds down / Streaker / Scuzzboots / Caboose / Drive by / Mean machine / Greatest.		
Feb 96.	(7"/c-s) *(A 7111/+C)* **IRON MIC. / CABOOSE**		–
	(cd-s+=) *(A 7111CD)* – Mean machine (live) / Dr J (live).		
Aug 97.	(cd) *<(7567 83006-2)>* **FLOORED**		Jun97 12
	– R.P.M. / Breathe / Anyone / Fly / Speed home California / High anxiety / Tap, twist, snap / American pig / Stand and deliver / Cash / Invisible / Right direction / Fly (reprise).		
Jan 98.	(7"/c-s) *(AT 0008/+C)* **FLY. / FLY (rock)**	58	–
	(cd-s+=) *(AT 008CD)* – Tap, twist, snap.		
May 99.	(c-s/cd-s) *(AT 0065 C/CD) <84462>* **EVERY MORNING / RIVERS / AIM FOR ME**	10	Jan99 3
Jun 99.	(cd/c) *<(7567 83151-2/-4)>* **14:59**	60	Jan99 17
	– New direction / Every morning / Falls apart / Personal space invader / Live and direct / Someday / Aim for me / Ode to the lonely hearted / Burning dog / Even though / Abracadabra / Glory / New direction.		
Oct 99.	(c-s) *(AT 0071C) <84536>* **SOMEDAY / EVERY MORNING (acoustic)**		Jun99 7
	(cd-s) *(AT 0071CD)* – ('A'acoustic).		
Jan 00.	(-) *<radio>* **FALLS APART**	–	29
Sep 01.	(cd/c) *<(7567 83414-2/-4)>* **SUGAR RAY**		Jun00 6
	– Answer the phone / When it's over / Under the sun / Satellites / Waiting / Ours / Sorry now / Stay on (with NICK HEXUM) / Words to me / Just a little / Disasterpiece.		
Oct 01.	(cd-s) *(AT 0114CD) <radio>* **WHEN IT'S OVER / SOMEDAY (live acoustic) / EVERY MORNING (live acoustic)**	32	May01 13
Jul 03.	(cd) *<(7567 83616-2)>* **IN THE PURSUIT OF LEISURE**		Jun03 29
	– Chasin' you around / Is she really going out with him? / Heaven / Bring me the head of. . . / Mr. Bartender (it's so easy) / Can't start / Photograph of you / 56 Hope Road / Whatever we are / She's different / In through the doggie door / Blues from a gun.		

☐ SUGGS (see under ⇒ MADNESS)

SUICIDE

Formed: New York, USA . . . 1971 by ALAN VEGA and ex-jazz band organist MARTIN REV. After a series of sporadic, performance art-style gigs in the early 70's, the duo laid low until the emergence of the CBGB's punk/new wave scene a few years later. Signed to US independent, 'Red Star' (run by Marty Thau, former manager of The NEW YORK DOLLS), the duo released one of the most influential records of the era in 1977's eponymous 'SUICIDE'. Delivering shock screams and whispered goth-rockabilly vocals over brooding, churning Farfisa organ, the duo laid the foundations for the industrial/electro experimentation of the following decade and in 'ROCKET U.S.A.' and 'FRANKIE TEARDROPS', penned two of the most compelling compositions in the NY avant-garde pantheon. Now almost universally heralded as being ahead of their time, punters of the day weren't always so appreciative; SUICIDE performances were infamous for audience stand-off's, a tour with the CLASH running into trouble while a gig in Belgium ended in a full-on riot (the same gig documented on the 1978 "official bootleg", '24 MINUTES OVER BRUSSELS'). Unperturbed, the pair moved to 'Ze' records ('Island' in the UK) and recorded a follow-up, 'ALAN VEGA / MARTIN REV – SUICIDE' (1980). Produced by CARS mainman, RIC OCASEK, the record presented a slightly more palatable version of SUICIDE's patented synth apocalypse, although sales remained minimal. Subsequently embarking on solo careers, the pair met with little more than cult success, although VEGA's eponymous 1980 solo debut spawned a Top 5 hit in France, 'JUKEBOX BABE'. Following his eponymous 1980 solo debut, REV devoted his time to sculpture with his work exhibited in 1982-83. VEGA continued working with OCASEK, also bringing in a young AL JOURGENSEN (later of MINISTRY fame) for 1983's 'SATURN STRIP' (featuring an unlikely but entertaining cover of Hot Chocolate's 'EVERYONE'S A WINNER') and guesting for SISTERS OF MERCY re-incarnation, The SISTERHOOD in 1986. VEGA and REV eventually reformed SUICIDE in 1988 and recorded 'A WAY OF LIFE' (1989) for 'Wax Trax!' (licensed to 'Chapter 22' in the UK), a label heavily indebted to the duo's pioneering electronics. With the album afforded little interest, VEGA resumed his solo activities on through the 90's, collaborating with STEPHEN LIRONI on his REVOLUTIONARY CORPS OF TEENAGE JESUS project and also ALEX CHILTON on their 1997 set, 'Cubist Blues'. Ironically, there's been something of an upsurge of interest in SUICIDE of late, the duo receiving renewed press attention after their performances with critical darlings SPIRITUALIZED. It was no surprise then, that the inevitable comeback album would appear. The thought-provoking 'AMERICAN SUPREME' (2002), sarcastically waved the stars'n'stripes aloft through the confrontational, snidey words of VEGA and REV. Tracks such as opener 'TELEVISED EXECUTIONS', plus 'SWEARING TO THE FLAG' and 'DACHAU, DISNEY, DISCO', pounded their caustic messages from stark funky beats. Nothing's changed on both fronts then.

Album rating: SUICIDE (*8) / ALAN VEGA – MARTIN REV (*5) / HALF ALIVE exploitation (*6) / GHOST RIDERS exploitation (*5) / A WAY OF LIFE (*7) / Y.B. BLUE (*4) / AMERICAN SUPREME (*4) / Alan Vega: ALAN VEGA (*4) /

COLLISION DRIVE (*5) / SATURN STRIP (*7) / JUST A MILLION DREAMS (*4) / DEUCE AVENUE (*5) / POWER ON TO ZERO HOUR (*4) / NEW RACEION (*4) / DUJANG PRANG (*3) / CUBIST BLUES with Alex Chilton & Ben Vaughn (*5) / Martin Rev: MARTIN REV (*4) / CLOUDS OF GLORY (*6) / CHEYENNE (*5) / SEE ME RIDIN' (*7) / STRANGEWORLD (*4)

ALAN VEGA (b. 1948) – vocals / **MARTIN REV** – keyboards, percussion

Bronze Red Star

Nov 77. (lp) *(BRON 508)* *<RS 1>* **SUICIDE**
– Ghost rider / Rocket U.S.A. / Cheree / Frankie Teardrops / Johnny / Girl / Che. *(re-iss. Sep86 on 'Demon'; FIEND 74) (cd-iss. Jun88; FIENDCD 74)*

Jul 78. (7",12") *(BRO 57)* **CHEREE. / I REMEMBER**
(re-is.Nov86 on 'Demon' 12"; D 1046T)

1978. (lp-ltd; official bootleg) *(FRANKIE 1)* **24 MINUTES OVER BRUSSELS (live)** –

Island Ze

Nov 79. (ext.12"/7") *(12+/WIP 6543)* **DREAM BABY DREAM. / RADIATION** –

May 80. (lp) *(ILPS 7007)* *<7080>* **ALAN VEGA / MARTIN REV – SUICIDE**
– Diamonds, furcoats, champagne / Mr. Ray / Sweetheart / Fast money music / Touch me / Harlem / Be bop kid / Las Vegas man / Shadazz / Dance. *(re-iss. Jun99 on 'Blast First' d-lp/d-cd+=; BFFP 162/+CD)* – Super subway comedian / Dream baby dream / Radiation / Speed queen / Creature feature / Tough guy / Man / Sneakin' around / Too fine for you / See you around / Be my dream / Space blue mambo / Spaceship / Into my eyes / C'mon babe / New city / Do it nice.

—— split partnership in the early 80's and both went solo

ALAN VEGA

with **PHIL HAWK** – guitar

not iss. P.V.C.

1980. (lp) *<PVC 7915>* **ALAN VEGA** –
– Jukebox babe / Fireball / Kung Foo cowboy / Love cry / Speedway / Ice drummer / Bye bye bayou / Lonely.

—— w/band 81-83 **MARK KUGH** – guitar / **LARRY CHAPLAN** – bass / **SESU COLEMAN** – drums

Island Island

Nov 81. (lp) *<(ILPS 9692)>* **COLLISION DRIVE**
– Magdalena 82 / Be bop a lula / Outlaw / Raver / Ghost rider / I believe / Magdalena 83 / Rebel / Viet vet.

Nov 81. (ext.12"/7") *(12+/WIP 6744)* **JUKEBOX BABE. / LONELY** –

—— added **AL JOURGENSEN** – keyboards (of MINISTRY) / **STEPHEN GEORGE** – drums / **GREG HAWKES** – synth, sax (of CARS) / **RIC OCASEK** – guitar, producer (of CARS)

Elektra Elektra

Sep 83. (lp) *(K 960259-1)* *<60259-1>* **SATURN STRIP**
– Saturn drive / Video babe / American dreamer / Wipeout beat / Je t'adore / Angel / Kid Congo / Goodbye darling / Every 1's a winner.

—— retained **OCASEK** + added **KENNAN KEATING** – guitar / **CHRIS LORD** – synth

Oct 85. (7") *(EKR 24)* **ON THE RUN. / CRY FIRE** –
(12"+=) *(EKR 24T)* – Rah rah baby.

Dec 85. (lp/c) *(EKT 15/+C)* *<60434-1/-4>* **JUST A MILLION DREAMS**
– On the run / Shooting for you / Hot fox / Too late / Wild heart / Creation / Cry fire / Ra ra baby.

—— In 1986, VEGA guested for SISTERS OF MERCY re-incarnation, SISTERHOOD

MARTIN REV

not iss. Infidelity

Feb 80. (lp) *<228>* **MARTIN REV** –
– Mari / Baby o baby / Nineteen 86 / Temptation / Jomo / Asia. *<(cd-iss. Nov02 on 'R.O.I.R.'; RUSCD 8279)>* – Coal train / Marvel / 5 to 5 / Wes / Daydreams.

New Rose Red Star

Mar 85. (lp) *(ROSE 52)* *<RS 700>* **CLOUDS OF GLORY**
– Rodeo / Clouds of glory / Metatron / Whisper / Rocking horse / Parade / Island. *(cd-iss. May98 on 'Mau Mau'; MAUCD 648) (cd re-iss. Jun00; RS 700-2>*

SUICIDE

re-formed in 1988

Chapter 22 Wax Trax!

Jan 89. (lp/cd) *(CHAP LP/CD 35)* *<WAX/+CS/CD 7072>* **A WAY OF LIFE**
– Wild in blue / Surrender / Jukebox baby 96 / Rain of ruin / Sufferin' in vain / Dominic Christ / Love so lonely / Devastation.

Feb 89. (12") *(12CHAP 36)* **RAIN OF RUIN. / SURRENDER** –

Brake Out Brake Out

Jun 92. (cd) *<(OUT 108-2)>* **Y B BLUE**
– Why be blue / Cheat-cheat / Hot ticket / Universe / The last time / Play the dream / Pump it / Flashy love / Chewy-chewy / Mujo.

ALAN VEGA

returned to solo work for the 90's. **LIZ LAMERA** – drums

Chapter 22 Infinite Zero

Feb 90. (cd/lp) *(CHAP CD/LP 45)* *<43032>* **DEUCE AVENUE**
– Body bop jive / Sneaker gun fire / Jab Gee / Bad scene / La la bola / Deuce avenue / Faster blaster / Sugee / Sweet sweet money / Love on / No tomorrow / Future sex. *(re-iss. Jun90 on 'Musicdisc' cd/c/lp; 10558-2/-4/-1)*

Musidisc Warners

Jul 91. (cd/c/lp) *(10812-2/-4/-1)* *<43027>* **POWER ON TO ZERO HOUR**
– Bring in the year 2000 / Sucker / Fear / Doomo dance / Automatic terror / Jungle justice / Full force of them nuclear shoes / Believe it / Cry a sea of tears / Quasi.

May 93. (cd/c) *(11012-2/-4)* *<43051>* **NEW RACEION**
– The pleaser / Christ dice / Gamma pop / Viva the legs / Do the job / Junior's little sister's dropped ta cheap / How many lifetimes / Holy skips / Keep it alive / Go Trane go / Just say.

—— next with **LIZ LAMERE** – keyboards, vocals

Thirsty Ear Thirsty Ear

Dec 96. (cd) *<(21308)>* **DUJANG PRANG** Jul96
– Dujang prang / Hammered / Chennaroka / Saturn drive 2 (subtalk) / Jaxson gnome / Life ain't life / Flowers, candles, crucifixes / Big daddy stat's livin' on Tron / Sacrifice / Kiss.

Last Call Thirsty Ear

May 97. (cd; ALAN VEGA, ALEX CHILTON, BEN VAUGHN) *(422466)* *<21314>* **CUBIST BLUES** Oct96
– Fat city / Fly away / Freedom / Candyman / Come on Lord / Promised land / Lover of love / Sister / Too late / Do not do not / Werewolf / Dream baby revisited.

MARTIN REV

Marilyn Alive

Jul 92. (cd) *(FM 1006CD)* *<ALIVE 2>* **CHEYENNE** Jan95
– Wings of the wind / Red Sierra / Dakota / Cheyenne / River of tears / Buckeye / Little Rock / Prairie star / Mustang.

R.O.I.R. R.O.I.R.

Jan 96. (cd) *<(RUSCD 8220)>* **SEE ME RIDIN'**
– See me ridin' / Pillars / I heard your name / No one knows / Be mine / Mari go round / Small talk / Secret teardrops / I made you cry / Here we go / Ten two / Hop and scotch / Told the moon / Yours tonight / Tell me why / Post card.

Sahko Sahko

Mar 00. (cd/lp) *<(efa 50167-2/-1)>* **STRANGEWORLD**
– My strange world / Sparks / Solitude / Funny / Ramplin' / Trouble / Splinters / Cartoons / One track mind / Chalky / Reading my mind / Jacks and aces / Day and night.

SUICIDE

REV + VEGA re-united

Blast First Mute

Oct 02. (lp/cd) *(BFFP 168/+CD)* *<9196>* **AMERICAN SUPREME**
– Televised executions / Misery train / Swearin' to the flag / Beggin' for miracles / American mean / Wrong decisions / Death machine / Power au go-go / Dachau, Disney, disco / Child, it's a new world / I don't know.

– compilations, etc. –

Dec 81. (c) *R.O.I.R.; <(A 103)>* **HALF-ALIVE (half studio)** [ ] [ ]
Oct 86. (c) *R.O.I.R.; <(A 145)>* **GHOST RIDERS (live)** [ ] [ ]
(cd-iss. Apr90 on 'Danceteria'; DANCD 029) (cd-iss. Feb95 on 'ROIR Europe'; RE 145CD)
Mar 96. (cd; by ALAN VEGA) *Infinite Zero; <43069>* **JUKEBOX BABE / COLLISION DRIVE** [–] [ ]
Jan 98. (12"ep) *Blast First; (BFFP 115)* **CHEREE. / HARLEM / I REMEMBER** [ ] [–]

—— Their classic 'FRANKIE TEARDROP' was used by STEPHEN LIRONI (producer and ex- ALTERED IMAGES guy) on project REVOLUTIONARY CORPS, etc

SUM 41

Formed: Ontario, Canada . . .. 41 days into summer '99. DERYCK WHIBLEY, CONE McCASLIN, DAVE BAKSH and STEVE JOCZ all met as members of rival bands and immediately made an impact on the local scene. They were signed to 'Island' that December after releasing their now infamous homemade EPK (Electronic Press Kit). SUM 41 then sharpened their colourful pop-punk aplomb on the road while touring with bands such as OFFSPRING, BLINK 182 and The MIGHTY MIGHTY BOSSTONES. Meanwhile, a debut mini-set, 'HALF HOUR OF POWER' (2000), was unleashed to the North American public, although it made little impact initially. The following May – with producer Jerry Finn in tow – they delivered a second batch of songs, 'ALL KILLER NO FILLER' (2001). A Top 20 entry in both the US and (a little later) the UK charts, the disc featured two major UK hit singles, 'FAT LIP' and 'IN TOO DEEP'. Not content with having one of the most inane names in rock, the Canadian troupe followed on with one of the dullest album titles of the year in 'DOES THIS LOOK INFECTED?' (2002), complete with ridiculous cover art. If you could get past that there was half an hour's worth of witless sub-punk fumbling to torture yourself with.

Album rating: HALF HOUR OF POWER mini (*5) / ALL KILLER NO FILLER (*7) / DOES THIS LOOK INFECTED? (*5)

DERYCK WHIBLEY – vocals, guitar / **DAVE BAKSH** – guitar / **CONE McCASLIN** (b. JAY) – bass / **STEVE JOCZ** – drums

Mercury Island

Jun 00. (m-cd) *<542419-2>* **HALF HOUR OF POWER** [–] [ ]
– Grab the Devil by the horns and fuck him up the ass / Machine gun / What I believe / THT / Makes no difference / Summer / 32 ways to die / Second chance for Max Headroom / Dave's possessed hair / What we're all about / Ride the charlot to the Devil / Another time around. *(UK-iss.Nov01 & May02; same as US)*
Jul 01. (cd) *<(548662-2)>* **ALL KILLER NO FILLER** [7] May01 [13]
– Introduction to destruction / Nothing on my back / Never wake up / Fat lip / Rhythms / Motivation / In too deep / Summer / Handle this / Crazy Amanda Bunkface / All she's got / Heart attack / Pain for pleasure. *(re-iss. Oct01 +=; 548662-9)* – Makes no difference.
Oct 01. (c-s) *(588801-4) <radio cut>* **FAT LIP / CRAZY AMANDA BUNKFACE** [8] Oct01 [66]
(cd-s+=) *(588801-2)* – Machine gun / ('A'-video).
Dec 01. (c-s) *(860982-4)* **IN TOO DEEP / FAT LIP (live)** [13] [–]
(cd-s+=) *(588898-2)* – All she's got (live) / ('A'-video).
Mar 02. (c-s) *(588945-4)* **MOTIVATION / PAIN FOR PLEASURE (live)** [21] [–]
(cd-s+=) *(588945-2)* – What I believe (version) / ('A'-video).
Jun 02. (cd-s) *(672864-2)* **IT'S WHAT WE'RE ALL ABOUT / MOTIVATION / (making of the video – video footage)** [32] [–]
(above issued on 'Columbia')
Nov 02. (c-s) *(63831-4)* **STILL WAITING / IN TOO DEEP (live)** [16] [–]
(cd-s+=) *(63831-2)* – Fat lip (live).
(cd-s) *(63834-2)* – ('A'side) / All messed up (demo) / Motivation (live) / ('A'-video).
Nov 02. (cd) *(63483-2) <06349-2>* **DOES THIS LOOK INFECTED?** [39] [32]
– The Hell song / Over my head (better off dead) / My direction / Still waiting / A.N.I.C. / No brains / All messed up / Mr. Amsterdam / Thanks for nothing / Hyper-insomnia-para-condroid / Billy Spleen / Hooch.
Feb 03. (7") *(063720-7)* **THE HELL SONG. / STILL WAITING (live)** [35] [–]
(cd-s+=) *(063720-2)* – Rhythms (live) / ('A'video).
(cd-s) *(063719-2)* – ('A'side) / Over my head (better off dead) (demo) / My direction (demo) / ('A'-video).

SUNDAYS

Formed: London, England . . . 1988 by HARRIET WHEELER, DAVID GAVURIN and PAUL BRINDLEY, initially playing with a drum machine before recruiting sticksman PATRICK 'Patch' HANNAN. Subsequently signing to 'Rough Trade', the band's fawning music press hype was justified with the release of the semi-classic 'CAN'T BE SURE' single in early '89. A luscious slice of sugary indie, the track's reverberating guitar and fragile, bone-china vocals (courtesy of WHEELER) brought comparisons with "shoegazing" forebears The COCTEAU TWINS, some critics also mentioning THROWING MUSES. Yet The SUNDAYS were in seemingly little hurry to follow-up this indie chart topper (and minor Top 40 hit), almost a full year passing before the release of much anticipated debut album, 'READING, WRITING AND ARITHMETIC' (1990). Its glistening jangle-pop didn't disappoint and The SUNDAYS suddenly found themselves in the UK Top 5, the US Top 40 and the glare of the world's media. An ensuing continent-straddling tour together with the collapse of the band's label conspired to slow down the band's already notoriously relaxed attitude to songwriting and it was late '92 before they re-emerged via a new 'Parlophone' deal. The resulting single, 'GOODBYE', displayed a more world-weary sound (the band even covering The Rolling Stones' mournful classic, 'WILD HORSES' on the B-side) and the accompanying album, 'BLIND', sounded frayed at the edges. While the record's Top 20 placing and the success of the attendant tour suggested that The SUNDAYS' fans hadn't lost interest, their patience would be tested with a subsequent five year gap prior to a third album. When 'STATIC & SILENCE' (1997) finally arrived, critics found fault with what they saw as musical stagnation although loyal fans helped put it into the UK Top 10, proving their enduring appeal. • **Trivia:** An instrumental piece was used on the 1993 series for comedy duo, Newman & Baddiel.

Album rating: READING, WRITING AND ARITHMETIC (*8) / BLIND (*7) / STATIC & SILENCE (*6)

HARRIET WHEELER (b.26 Jun'63, Maidenhead, England) – vocals (ex-JIM JIMINEE) / **DAVID GAVURIN** (b. 4 Apr'63) – guitar / **PAUL BRINDLEY** (b. 6 Nov'63, Loughborough, England) – bass / **PATRICK 'Patch' HANNAN** (b. 4 Mar'66) – drums repl. drum machine

Rough Trade D.G.C.

Feb 89. (7") *(RT 218)* **CAN'T BE SURE. / I KICKED A BOY** [45] [–]
(12"+=/cd-s+=) *(RT 218 T/CD)* – Don't tell your mother.
Jan 90. (lp/c/cd) *(ROUGH/+C/CD 148) <24277>* **READING, WRITING AND ARITHMETIC** [4] [39]
– Skin & bones / Here's where the story ends / Can't be sure / I won / Hideous towns / You're not the only one I know / A certain someone / I kicked a boy / My finest hour / Joy. *(re-iss. May96 cd/c; CD/TC PCS 7378)*
Jan 90. (7") **HERE'S WHERE THE STORY ENDS. / SKIN AND BONES** [–] [ ]

Parlophone D.G.C.

Sep 92. (c-s/7") *(TC+/R 6319)* **GOODBYE. / WILD HORSES** [27] [–]
(cd-s+=) *(CDR 6319)* – Noise.
Oct 92. (cd/c/lp) *(CD/TC+/PCSD 121) <24479>* **BLIND** [15] [ ]
– I feel / Goodbye / Life and soul / Marc / On Earth / God made me / Love /

What do you think? / 24 hours / Blood on my hands / Medieval. *(re-iss. Mar94; same)*

Sep 97. (7") *(R 6475)* **SUMMERTIME. / NOTHING SWEET** [15] [–]
(cd-s+=) *(CDR 6475)* – Gone.
(cd-s) *(CDRS 6475)* – ('A'side) / Skin & bones (live) / Here's where the story ends (live).

Capitol Geffen

Sep 97. (cd/c/lp) *(CD/TC+/EST 2300)* *<25131>* **STATIC & SILENCE** [10] [33]
– Summertime / Homeward / Folk song / She / When I'm thinking about you / I can't wait / Another flavour / Leave this city / Your eyes / Cry / Monochrome.

Nov 97. (c-s) *(TCR 6487)* **CRY / THROUGH THE DARK** [43] [–]
(cd-s+=) *(CDR 6487)* – Life goes on.
(cd-s) *(CDRS 6487)* – ('A'side) / Can't be sure (demo) / You're not the only one I know (demo).

—— the band looked to have disbanded

SUN RA

Born: HERMAN BLOUT, 22 May 1914, Birmingham, Alabama, USA. A child prodigy, he was bought a piano for his 10th birthday by his parents, which he immediately learned to play, while composing some early songs. Majoring at Alabama A&M University, he later went under the name SONNY LEE, playing with a swing band led by FLETCHER HENDERSON. In 1948, he changed his name by deedpoll to LE SONNY'RA, soon shortened to SUN RA. Around this time, he claimed to have been born on Saturn and despatched to Earth as the "creator of the omniverse". By the mid-50's, he had assembled his "ARKESTRA", which included a nucleus of talented musicians; JOHN GILMORE, MARSHALL ALLEN and PAT PATRICK, fusing together be-bop jazz (influenced by THELONIUS MONK or DUKE ELLINGTON), with exotic worldly avant-garde. His/their first recordings were rare, free-form jazz affairs, the band's sound evolving following his move to New York in the early 60's. SUN RA's cult appeal grew, especially after introducing the Moog synthesizer when recording for underground 'E.S.P.' label (home of FUGS). His concerts were of the cosmic funk variety, subsequently developed by the great FUNKADELIC via GEORGE CLINTON. In 1974, the death of his idol DUKE ELLINGTON, seemed to inspire an onslaught of shows, reviving the great man's work (albeit faster and more furiously uptempo). In the late 80's, after releasing many albums over the previous two decades, he signed to UK indie, 'Blast First' (at the time, home to such indie noise merchants as SONIC YOUTH, DINOSAUR JR and The BUTTHOLE SURFERS!), which issued his 1989 and retrospective and a new live album, 'OUT THERE A MINUTE' and 'LIVE IN LONDON 1990' respectively. This led to a contract with his first major, 'A&M', although it was clear his health was fading after suffering a few strokes. On the 4th of July '92, he opened for SONIC YOUTH at New York's Central Park, entering the stage on a wheelchair. He returned to his birthplace late in '92 after he suffered a third stroke, and on the 30th of May 1993, he died. However, his band, under GILMORE's leadership, continued to play SUN RA's music.

Album rating (selective): THE HELIOCENTRIC WORLDS OF SUN RA, I (*9) / THE HELIOCENTRIC WORLDS OF SUN RA II (*8) / SUNRISE IN DIFFERENT DIMENSIONS (*7) / COSMIC TONES FOR MENTAL THERAPY (*7) / BLUE DELIGHT (*8) / THE MAGIC CITY rec.1965 (*8)

SUN RA – piano (with session people)

not iss. Saturn

1955. (7"; by The COSMIC RAYS) *<SR 401/402>* **DREAMING. / DADDY'S GONNA TELL YOU NO LIE** [–] [ ]

1956. (7"; by The COSMIC RAYS with LE SUN RA and his ARKESTRA) *<B 222/223?* **BYE BYE. / SOMEBODY'S IN LOVE** [–] [ ]

1956. (7"; as LE SUN-RA and his ARKISTRA) *<Z 222>* **MEDICINE FOR A NIGHTMARE. / URNACK** [–] [ ]

1956. (7") **A CALL FOR ALL DEMONS. / EMON'S LULLABY** [–] [ ]

1956. (7") **SATURN. / SUPERSONIC JAZZ** [–] [ ]

1956. (7") *<Z 1111>* **SUPER BLONDE. / SOFT TALK** [–] [ ]

1957. (lp) *<H70 P0216>* **SUPER-SONIC JAZZ** [–] [ ]
– India / Sunology / Advice to medics / Sunology part II / Kingdom of Not / Portrait of the living sky / Blues at midnight / El is a sound of joy. *<cd-iss. May92 on 'Evidence'; ECD 22015>*

1959. (7") **SATURN. / VELVET** [–] [ ]

1959. (7") *'ROUND MIDNIGHT. / BACK IN YOUR OWN BACKYARD* [–] [ ]

1959. (lp) *<K 70 P 359 0-1>* **JAZZ IN SILHOUETTE** [–] [ ]
– Hours after / Horoscope / Images / Blues at midnight / Enlightenment / Saturn / Velvet / Ancient Aiethopia.
(cd-iss. May92 on 'Evidence'; 22012-2>

—— note:- SUN RA & HIS ARKESTRA also backed YOCHANAN on a few singles

1960. (7") *<874>* **OCTOBER. / ADVENTUR IN SPACE** [–] [ ]

1960. (7") *<SA-1001>* **THE BLUE SET. / BIG CITY BLUES** [–] [ ]

1961. (7") *<L08W-0114-5>* **SPACE LONELINESS. / STATE STREET** [–] [ ]

1961. (lp) *<HK 5445>* **SUN RA AND HIS SOLAR ARKESTRA VISIT PLANET EARTH; WE TRAVEL THE SPACEWAYS** [–] [ ]
– Eve / Interplanetary music / Tapestry from an asteroid / Velvet / We travel the spaceways / Space loneliness.

1964. (lp) *<408>* **COSMIC TONES FOR MENTAL THERAPY** [–] [ ]
– And otherness / Thither and yon / Adventure – Equation / Moon dance / Voice of space.

1964. (lp) *<KH 9876>* **OTHER PLANES OF THERE** [–] [ ]
– Other planes of there / Sound spectra / Sketch / Pleasure / Spiral galaxy. *<cd-iss. Nov92 on 'Evidence'; ECD 22037-2>*

1960's. (lp) *<9954>* **SECRETS OF THE SUN** [–] [ ]
– Friendly galaxy / Solar differentials / Space aura / Love in outer space / Reflects motion / Solar symbols.

1960's. (lp) *<9956>* **ART FORMS OF DIMENSION TOMORROW** [–] [ ]
– Cluster of galaxies / Ankh / Solar drums / The outer heavens / Infinity of the universe / Lights on a satellite / Kosmos in blue.

not iss. E.S.P.

1965. (lp) *(ESP 1014)* **THE HELIOCENTRIC WORLDS OF SUN RA, VOLUME I** [–] [ ]
– Heliocentric / Outer nothingness / Other worlds / The cosmos / Of heavenly things / Nebulae / Dancing in the sun. *(UK-iss.Apr81; same) (cd-iss. Dec94; ESP 1014-2) (re-iss. Apr97 on 'Get Back'; GET 1004)*

1966. (lp) *(ESP 1017)* **THE HELIOCENTRIC WORLDS OF SUN RA, VOLUME II** [–] [ ]
– The sun myth / A house of beauty / Cosmic chaos. *(UK-iss.Apr81; same) (cd-iss. Dec94; ESP 1017-2) (re-iss. Apr97 on 'Get Back'; GET 1005)*

1968. (lp) *(ESP 1045)* **NOTHING IS** (rec.May '66) [ ] [–]
– Dancing shadows / Imagination / Exotic forest / Sun Ra and his band from outer space / Shadow world / Theme of the stargazers / Outer spaceways incorporated / Next stop Mars. *(UK-iss.Sep84 as 'DANCING SHADOWS' on 'Happy Bird'; B 90130) (cd-iss. Sep92 on 'Giants Of Jazz And Blues'; 30013) (original:- re-iss. Apr97 on 'Get Back'; GET 1007)*

not iss. Saturn

1968. (7") *<3066>* **THE BRIDGE. / ROCKET NUMBER NINE** [–] [ ]

1968. (7") *<911-AR>* **BLUES ON PLANET MARS. / SATURN MOON** [–] [ ]

1969. (lp) *<ESR 507>* **ATLANTIS** (rec.1967) [–] [ ]
– Atlantis / Mu / Lemuria / Yucatan / Bimini. *(UK cd-iss. Nov93 on 'Evidence'+=; ECD 22067-2)* – Yucatan (Impulse version).

1969. (lp) *<ESR 508>* **HOLIDAY FOR SOUL DANCE** [–] [ ]
– Early Autumn / But not for me / Day by day / Holiday for strings / Dorothy's dance / I loves you orgy / Body and soul / Keep your sunny side up. *(UK cd-iss. May92 on 'Evidence'; ECD 22011-2)*

1969. (lp) *<SR 509>* **MONORAILS AND SATELLITES** (rec.1966) [–] [ ]
– Spacetowers / Cognition / Skylight / The alter destiny / Easy street / Blue differentials / Monorails and satellites / The galaxy way. *(UK cd-iss. May92 on 'Evidence'; ECD 22013-2)*

1970's. (lp) <SR 512> **SOUND SUN PLEASURE!!** (rec.1959) [–] [ ]
– 'Round midnight / You never told me that you care / Hour of parting / Back in your own backyard / I could have danced all night. *(UK cd-iss. May92 on 'Evidence'; ECD 22014-2)*

1970's. (lp) <SR 519> **MONORAILS AND SATELLITES VOL.II** (rec.1966) [–] [ ]
– Astro vision / The ninth eye / Solar boats / Perspective prisms of Is / Calundronius.

1970's. (lp) <ESR 520> **CONTINUATION** (rec.1968-69) [–] [ ]
– Continuation to / Jupiter festival / Biosphere blues / Intergalaxtic research / Earth primitive Earth / New planet.

1970's. (lp) <ESR 521> **MY BROTHER THE WIND** [–] [ ]
– My brother the wind / Intergalactic II / To nature's god / The code of independence.

1970's. (lp) <ESR 523> **MY BROTHER THE WIND, VOLUME II** [–] [ ]
– Somewhere else / Contrast / The wind speaks / Sun thoughts / Journey to the stars / World of the myth "I" / The design cosmos II / Otherness blue / Somebody else's world / Pleasant twilight / Walking on the Moon. *(UK cd-iss. Nov92 on 'Evidence'; ECD 22040-2)*

1970's. (lp) <ESR 532> **BAD AND BEAUTIFUL** (rec.late '61) [–] [ ]
– The bad and the beautiful / Ankh / Search light blues / Exotic two / On the blue side / And this is my beloved.

Byg Actuel — not iss.

1972. (lp; as SUN RA & HIS SOLAR-MYTH ARKESTRA) *(529.340)* **THE SOLAR MYTH APPROACH VOL.1** (rec.1968-1970) [–] France [–]
– Spectrum / Realm of lightning / The satellites are spinning / Legend / Seen III, took 4 / They'll come back / The adventures of Bugs Hunter. *(UK-iss.Feb78 on 'Infinity'; AFF 10)*

1971. (lp; as SUN RA & HIS SOLAR-MYTH ARKESTRA) *(529.341)* **THE SOLAR MYTH APPROACH VOL.2** (rec.1968-70) [–] France [–]
– Scene 1, take 1 / Outer spaceways incorporated / The utter nots / Interpretation / Ancient Ethiopia / Strange worlds / Pyramids. *(UK-iss.1983 on 'Affinity'; AFF 76)*

Delmark — Delmark

1974. (lp; as SUN RA ARKESTRA) *(DL 411)* **SUN SONG** [ ] [ ]
– Brainville / Call for all emons / Transition / Possession / Street named Hell / Lullaby for Brainville / Future / Swing a little taste / New horizons / Fall off the log / Sun song. *<US-iss.Dec94; DDCD 411>*

1974. (lp; as SUN RA ARKESTRA) *(DL 414)* **SOUND OF JOY** [ ] [ ]
<US-iss.Dec94; DDCD 414>

Improvising Artists — not iss.

1978. (lp) *(37.38-50)* **SOLO PIANO, VOLUME 1** [ ] [–]
– Sometimes I feel like a motherless child / Cosmo rhythmatic / Yesterdays / Romance of two planets / Irregular galaxy / To a friend. *(cd-iss. Nov92; 123850-2)*

1978. (lp) *(37.38-58)* **ST. LOUIS BLUES: SOLO PIANO (VOLUME 2)** [ ] [–]
– Ohosnisixaeht / St. Louis blues / Three little words / Sky and sun / I am we are I / Thoughts on thoth. *(cd-iss. Nov93; 123858-2)*

Cobra — not iss.

1979. (lp; as SUN RA ARKESTRA) *(COB 37001)* **COSMOS EQUATION** (rec.August '76) [ ] [–]
– The mystery of two / Interstellar low ways / Neo project No.2 / Cosmos / Moonship journey / Journey among the stars / Jazz from an unknown planet. *(cd-iss. Sep92 on 'Giants Of Jazz And Blues'; 30011)*

Inner City — not iss.

Apr 79. (lp) *(IC 1039)* **SUN RA** [ ] [–]
– For the sunrise / Of the other tomorrow / From out where others dwell / On sound infinity spheres / The house of eternal being / Gos of the thunder rain / Lights on a satellite / Take the 'A' train / Prelude / El is the sound of joy / Encore 1 / Encore 2 / We travel the spaceways.

not iss. — Hat Hut

1980. (lp; as SUN RA ARKESTRA) <2R 17> **SUNRISE IN DIFFERENT DIMENSIONS** [–] [ ]
– Lights from a hidden sun / Pin-points of spiral prisms / Silhouettes of the shadow world / Cocktails for two / 'Round midnight / Lady bird – Half Nelson / Big John's special / Yeah man! / Love in outer space * / Provocative celestials / Disguised gods in skullduggery rendezvous / Queer notions / Limehouse blues / King Porter stomp / Take the A train / Lightnin' / On Jupiter * / A helio-hello and goodbye too!. *(cd-iss. Dec91 – =*; ARTCD 6099)*

Y — not iss.

Sep 82. (lp) *(Y 19LP)* **STRANGE CELESTIAL ROAD** (rec.July '79) [ ] [–]
– Celestial road / Say / I'll wait for you. *<US-iss.1988 on 'Rounder' lp/c; ROUNDER 3035/+C> (cd-iss. 1990's cd/c; ROU CD/C 3035)*

Nov 83. (12"; as SUN RA ARKESTRA) *(RA 1)* **NUCLEAR WAR. / SOMETIMES I'M HAPPY** [ ] [–]

Affinity — not iss.

1983. (lp) *(AFF 76)* **SOLAR-MYTH APPROACH VOL.2** [ ] [–]
– The utter nots / Outer spaceways (inc. Scene 1, take 1) / Pyramids / Interpretation / Ancient Ethiopia / Strange worlds. *(cd-iss. both VOLS Jan90; CDAFF 76)*

Praxis — not iss.

May 84. (lp) *(CM 106)* **SUN RA ARKESTRA MEETS SALAM RAGAB IN EGYPT** [–] Greece [–]
– Egypt strut / Dawn / (three others by SALAH RAGAB and The CAIRO JAZZ BAND)

Happy Bird — not iss.

Sep 84. (lp) *(B 90131)* **OTHER WORLDS** [ ] [–]
– Heliocentric / Other nothingness / Other worlds / The cosmos / Of heavenly things / Nebulae dancing in the sun.

Sep 84. (lp) *(B 90132)* **THE SUN MYTH** [ ] [ ]
– The sun myth / House of beauty / Cosmic chaos. *(cd-iss. Sep92 on 'Giants Of Jazz And Blues'; 30012)*

Saturn – Recommended — not iss.

Feb 86. (lp) *(SRRRD 1)* **COSMOS SUN CONNECTION** (live 1984) [ ] [–]
– Fate in a pleasant mood / Cosmo journey blues / Cosmo sun connection / Cosmonaut astronaut rendezvous / As space ships aproach / Pharoah's den.

not iss. — Meltdown

1987. (lp) <MPA-1> **JOHN CAGE MEETS SUN RA** [–] [ ]
– John Cage meets Sun Ra. *<cd-iss. Jan97; MPA-1CD>*

Sep 87. (lp; as SUN RA & HIS COSMO DISCIPLINE ARKESTRA) *Leo; (LR 149)* **NIGHT IN EAST BERLIN (live June '86)** [ ] [–]
– Mystic prophecy / Beyond the wilderness of shadows / Prelude to a kiss / Interstellar low ways / Space is the place – We travel the spaceways / The shadow world / Rocket number nine – Second stop is Jupiter. *(cd-iss. 1987 on 'Leo'; LR 149)*

Black Saint — not iss.

1987. (cd) *(120 101-2)* **REFLECTIONS IN BLUE** [–] Italy [–]
– State street Chicago / Nothin' from nothin' / Yesterdays / Say it isn't so / I dream too much / Reflection in blue.

1987. (cd) *(120 111-2)* **HOURS AFTER** [–] Italy [–]
– But not for me / Hours after / Beautiful love / Dance of the extra terrestrians / Love on a faraway planet.

A&M — A&M

Feb 89. (lp/c/cd) *(AMA/AMC/CDA 5260)* **BLUE DELIGHT** [ ] [ ]
– Blue delight / Out of nowhere / Sunrise / They dwell on other planes / Gone with the wind / Your guest is as good as mine / Nashira / Days of wine and roses.

Jul 90. (cd) *(75021 5324)* **PURPLE NIGHT** [ ] [ ]
– Journey towards stars / Friendly galaxy / Love in outer space / Stars fell on Alabama / Of invisible them / Neverness / Purple night blues.

not iss. — Leo

1991. (cd) <LR 188> **FRIENDLY GALAXY** [–] [ ]
– Intro percussion / Prelude to a kiss / Blue Lou / Lights on a satellite / Alabama / Fate in a pleasant mood / We travel the spaceways / Space is the place / Saturn rings / Friendly galaxy / They'll come back.

1991. (d-cd) <LR 210/211> **PLEIADES** [–] [ ]
– Pleiades / Mythic 1 / Sun procession / Lights on a satellite / Love in outer space / Planet Earth day / Mythic 2 / Blue Lou / Prelude #7 in A major.

1991. (d-cd) <LR 214/215> **LIVE AT THE HACKNEY EMPIRE (live)** [–] [ ]
– Astro black / Other voices / Planet Earth day / Prelude to a kiss / Hocus pocus / Love in outer space / Blue Lou / Face the music / String singhs / Discipline 27-II / I'll wait for you / East of the sun / Somewhere over the rainbow / Frisco fog / Sunset on the Nile / Skimming and loping / Yeah man! / We travel the spaceways / They'll come back.

1992. (cd) <LR 230> **SECOND STAR TO THE RIGHT (SALUTE TO WALT DISNEY)** (rec.April '89) [–] [ ]
– The forest of no return / Someday my prince will come / Frisco fog / Wishing well / Zip-adee-doo-dah / Second star to the right / Heigh ho! heigh ho! / Whistle while you work.

Black Saint / not iss.

Jan 92. (cd) *(12012-2)* **MAYAN TEMPLES** (rec.1990) [–] Italy [–]
– Dance of the language barrier / Bygone / Discipline No.1 / Alone together / Prelude to stargazers / Mayan temples / I'll never be the same / Stardust from tomorrow / El is a sound of joy / Time after time / Opus in springtime / Theme of the stargazers / Sunset on the Nile.

Blast First / not iss.

Jan 92. (cd-s; w/2 videos) *(BFFPCD 101)* **COSMIC VISIONS** [ ] [–]
– I am the instrument.

not iss. / Enja

Jul 92. (cd) *<7071>* **DESTINATION UNKNOWN** (rec. Switzerland) [–] [ ]
– Carefree / Echoes of the future / Prelude to a kiss / Hocus pocus / Theme of the stargazers / Interstellar low ways / Destination unknown / The satellites are spinning / S'wonderful / Space is the place – We travel the spaceways.

— SUN RA died on the 30th of May 1993.

not iss. / Rounder

Jan 94. (cd) *<ROU 3124>* **AT THE VILLAGE VANGUARD (live)** [–] [ ]
– 'Round midnight / Sun Ra blues / Autumn in New York / S'wonderful / Theme of the stargazers.

– (selective) compilations, etc –

Mar 89. (lp/c/cd) *Blast First; (BFFP 42/+C/CD)* **OUT THERE A MINUTE** (rec.in New York 1965-) [ ] [ ]
– Love in Outer Space / Somewhere in Space / Dark clouds with silver linings / Jazz and romantic sounds / When angels speak of love / Cosmo enticement / Song of tree and forest / Other worlds / Journey outward / Lights on a satellite / Starships and solar boats / Out there a minute.

Nov 92. (cd) *Evidence; <ECD 22036-2>* **COSMIC TONES FOR MENTAL THERAPY / ART FORMS OF DIMENSIONS TOMORROW** [–] [ ]

Nov 92. (cd) *Evidence; <ECD 22038-2>* **WE TRAVEL THE SPACEWAYS / BAD AND BEAUTIFUL** [–] [ ]

Nov 92. (cd) *Evidence; <ECD 22039-2>* **SUN RA VISITS PLANET EARTH / INTERSTELLAR LOW WAYS** (rec.1956-58) [–] [ ]
– Two tones / Saturn / Reflections in blue / El Viktor / Planet Earth / Eve / Overtones of China.

May 93. (cd) *Savoy Jazz; (SV 0213)* **THE FUTURISTIC SOUNDS OF SUN RA** (rec.Oct'61) [ ] [–]
– Bassism / Of sounds and something else / What's that? / Where is tomorrow? / The beginning / China gate / New day / Tapestry from an asteroid / Jet flight / Looking outward / Space jazz reverie.

1993. (cd/c) *Rounder; (ROU CD/C 3036)* **SOMEWHERE ELSE** [ ] [ ]
– Priest / Discipline – Tall trees in the sun / S'wonderful / Hole in the sky / Somewhere else (part 1 & 2) / Stardust for tomorrow / Love in outer space / Everything is space / Tristar.

Nov 93. (cd) *Evidence; <ECD 22066-2>* **ANGELS AND DEMONS AT PLAY / THE NUBIANS OF PLUTONIA** (rec.1956-60) [–] [ ]

Nov 93. (cd) *Evidence; <ECD 22068-2>* **FATE IN A PLEASANT MOOD / WHEN SUN COMES OUT** (1960-63) [–] [ ]

Nov 93. (cd) *Evidence; <ECD 22069-2>* **THE MAGIC CITY** (rec.1965) [–] [ ]
– The magic city / The shadow world / Abstract "I" / Abstract eye.

Nov 93. (cd) *Evidence; <ECD 22070-2>* **SPACE IS THE PLACE (original soundtrack)** (rec.1972) [–] [ ]
– It's after the end of the world / Under diferent stars / Discipline 33 / Watusi / Calling planet Earth / I am the alter-destiny / The satellites are spinning (take 1) / Cosmic forces / Outer spaceways incorporated (take 3) / We travel the spaceways / The overseer / Blackman – Love in outer space / Mysterious crystal / I am the brother of the wind / We'll wait for you / Space is the place.

Feb 94. (d-cd; as SUN RA ARKESTRA) *D.I.W.; (DIW 388-2)* **LIVE FROM SOUNDSCAPE (live November 1979)** [–] Japan [–]
– The possibility of altered destiny / Astro black / Pleiades / We're living in the space age / Keep your sunny side up / Discipline #27 / Untitled improvisation / Watusi / Space is the place / We travel the spaceways / Angel race / Destination unknown / On Jupiter.

Mar 94. (cd) *D.I.W.; (DIW 824)* **COSMO OMNIBUS IMAGIABLE ILLUSION: LIVE AT PIT-INN, TOKYO (live 8 August, 1988)** [–] Japan [–]
– Introduction – Cosmo approach prelude / Angel race – I'll wait for you / Can you take it? / If you came from nowhere here / Astro black / Prelude to a kiss / Interstellar low ways.

Jun 96. (cd) *Blast First; (BFFP 60CD)* **LIVE IN LONDON 1990 (live at The Mean Fiddler, 11 June 1990)** [ ] [–]
– Frisco / Shadow world / For the blue people / Prelude to a kiss / Down here on the ground / Blue delight / Cosmo song / Space chants.

May 97. (d-cd; SUN RA & HIS INTERGALAXTIC ARKESTRA) *Leo; (CDLR 235-236)* **STARDUST FROM TOMORROW** [ ] [–]

SUPER FURRY ANIMALS

Formed: Cardiff, Wales ... 1993 by GRUFF RHYS, DAFYDD IEUAN, CIAN CIARAN, GUTO PRYCE and HUW BUNFORD. Emerging from the Welsh underground scene in the mid-90's with a wholly unpronounceable EP on their native 'Ankst' label, the band whipped up a fair bit of interest from the London-based media and industry insiders alike. Alan McGee's 'Creation' subsequently took them on with the proviso that the bulk of their work be in English, the 'FURRY's famously stipulating that they never be made to work on St. David's day. Their first single for the label, 'HOMETOWN UNICORN' appeared in early '96 and dented the Top 50, while the dayglo rampage of 'GOD! SHOW ME MAGIC' made the Top 40 a couple of months later. Hailed by critics as one of the debuts of the year, the accompanying 'FUZZY LOGIC' (1996) album thrilled jaded Brit-pop fans with its dayglo showcase of deranged prog-retro pop/rock; 'MARIO MAN' was their most definitive slice of pseudo psychedelia to date while 'HANGIN' WITH HOWARD MARKS' gave them instant cool – the record's cover art depicted the various guises of "nice guy" one-time drug smuggler, MARKS. A Top 30 hit, the album spawned a further two singles in 'SOMETHING 4 THE WEEKEND' and 'IF YOU DON'T WANT ME TO DESTROY YOU', while the blase brilliance of 'THE MAN DON'T GIVE A FUCK' (repetitive line from the STEELY DAN number, 'Showbiz Kids') drew a swaggering close to a successful but inevitably controversial year, the group having been earlier banned from the Welsh BAFTA awards after a skirmish in the crowd. 1997's follow-up set, 'RADIATOR', made the Top 10, its less intense but equally compelling shenanigans threatening to take the band into the big league (they played the festival circuit that included a return to the rainy 'T In The Park' – Muddy Waters was not even invited). In May '98, after two further Top 30 hits, 'PLAY IT COOL' and 'DEMONS', the band had their biggest hit to date (#12) via non-album cut, 'ICE HOCKEY HAIR'. To end the year, 'OUT-SPACED' (a selection of rare B-sides, etc), marked time as GRUFF RHYS and his crew plotted their return. The 'NORTHERN LITES' single (which reached No.11), previewed unquestionably their finest hour to date, 'GUERILLA' (1999), a Top 10 album that featured xylophones, Caribbean brass, steel guitars, etc over some "way-out" experimental jugband psychedelia. Following the demise of 'Creation', The SUPER FURRIES were free to pursue their own cultural peccadilloes, specifically a Welsh language album on their own 'Placid Casual' imprint. Not just any old Welsh language album though, the first Welsh language record to make the UK Top 20 no less! While the significance of this may be lost on foreign readers, the fact that 'MWNG' (2000) was discussed in the UK parliament demonstrates the precedent it set. More, it was perhaps the band's most readily accessible effort to date, not so ironic when you consider the power of say, Brazilian music; often the melodies are so strong, the lyrics' meaning is besides the point.

They merely function as another instrument. So with The SUPER FURRY ANIMALS and their patented brand of psyched-out leftfield pop exoctica; the melodies soar, the arrangements confound and the hooks reel you in. Although they recorded one of their best efforts on a miniscule budget, a subsequent deal with 'Columbia' presented an opportunity to go for broke on 'RINGS AROUND THE WORLD' (2001). A quasi-concept set based on the earth's ongoing disintegration, the record's technicolour melancholy represented a wild-eyed creative peak for RHYS and Co. Rarely has such digital-era indulgence reaped such endearing rewards. The single 'JUXTAPOSED WITH U' was among the highlights, a deceptive 80's AZTEC CAMERA-style croon which belied a despairing lyric railing against fat cats. From the industrial-strength ELO of the title track to the truly discomforting 'RUN! CHRISTIAN, RUN!', 'RINGS AROUND THE WORLD' truly ran kaleidoscopic rings around its indie competition. Inevitably perhaps, the 'FURRIES reined in the studio excess on their 2003 effort, 'PHANTOM POWER', hooking up with sometime BEASTIE BOYS producer Mario Caldato Jr. The result was a record with a much more easy going, lazy-eyed appeal, insinuating rather than showing off and showcasing a newly Americana-esque twang.

Album rating: FUZZY LOGIC (*8) / RADIATOR (*7) / OUTSPACED collection (*6) / GUERILLA (*9) / MWNG (*7) / RINGS AROUND THE WORLD (*9) / PHANTOM POWER (*7)

GRUFF RHYS (b.18 Jul'70, Bethesda, Gwynedd, Wales) – vocals, guitars (ex-EMILY, ex-FFA COFFI PAWB) / **CIAN CIARAN** (b.16 Jun'76, Isle of Anglesey, Wales) – keyboards / **HUW 'Bumpf' BUNFORD** (b.15 Sep'67, Bath, England) – guitars, vocals / **GUTO PRYCE** (b. 4 Sep'72) – bass / **DAFYDD IEUAN** (b. 1 Mar'69, Isle of Anglesey) – drums, percussion, vocals (ex-ANHREFN, ex-FFA COFFI PAWB)

Ankst — not iss.

Jun 95. (7"ep/cd-ep) *(ANKST 057/+CD)* **LLANFAIRPWLLGWYNGYLLGOGERYCHWYNDROBW-LLANTYSILIOGOGOGOCHOCYNYGOFOD (IN SPACE) EP** [ ] [–]
– Organ yn dy geg / Fix idris / Crys Ti / Blerwytirhwng? *(re-iss. May97; same)*

Oct 95. (7"ep/cd-ep) *(ANKST 062/+CD)* **MOOG DROOG EP** [ ] [–]
– Pam V / God! show me magic / Sali Mali / Focus pocus – Debiel. *(re-iss. May97; same)*

Creation — Sony

Feb 96. (7"/c-s) *(CRE/+CS 222)* **HOMETOWN UNICORN. / DON'T BE A FOOL, BILLY** [47] [–]
(cd-s+=) *(CRESCD 222)* – Lazy life (of no fixed identity).

Apr 96. (7"/c-s) *(CRE/+CS 231)* **GOD! SHOW ME MAGIC. / DIM BENDITH** [33] [–]
(cd-s+=) *(CRESCD 231)* – Death by melody.

May 96. (cd/lp)(c) *(CRE CD/LP 190)(CCRE 190) <67827>* **FUZZY LOGIC** [23] [ ]
– God! show me magic / Fuzzy birds / Something 4 the weekend / Frisbee / Hometown unicorn / Gathering moss / If you don't want me to destroy you / Bad behaviour / Mario man / Hangin' with Howard Marks / Long gone / For now and ever. *(cd re-iss. Feb00; same)*

Jul 96. (7"/c-s) *(CRE/+CS 235)* **SOMETHING 4 THE WEEKEND. / WAITING TO HAPPEN** [18] [–]
(cd-s+=) *(CRESCD 235)* – Arnofio / Glow in the dark.

Sep 96. (7"/c-s/cd-s) *(CRE/+CS/SCD 243)* **IF YOU DON'T WANT ME TO DESTROY YOU. / GUACAMOLE** [18] [–]
(cd-s+=) *(CRESCD 243)* – (Nid) Hon yw'r gan sy'n mynd I achub yr iaith (This song will save the Welsh language (not).

Dec 96. (one-sided-7"blue) *(CRE 247)* **THE MAN DON'T GIVE A FUCK** [22] [–]
(cd-s+=) *(CRESCD 247)* – ('A'-Matthew 'Herbert' Herbert mix) / ('A'-Howard Marks mix).
(12"++=) *(CRE 247T)* – ('A'-Darren Price mix).

—— In Feb'97, HUW BUNFORD was fined £700 on an earlier drug possession charge

Creation — Flydaddy

May 97. (7"/c-s) *(CRE/+CS 252)* **HERMANN LOVES PAULINE. / CALIMERO** [26] [–]
(cd-s+=) *(CRESCD 252)* – Trons Mr. Urdd.

Jul 97. (7"/c-s) *(CRE/+CS 269)* **THE INTERNATIONAL LANGUAGE OF SCREAMING. / WRAP IT UP** [24] [–]
(cd-s+=) *(CRESCD 269)* – Foxy music / O.K.

Aug 97. (cd/c/lp) *(CRECD/CCRE/CRELP 214) <FLY 34CD>* **RADIATOR** [8] [ ]
– Furryvision / The placid casual / The international language of screaming / Demons / Short painkiller / She's got spies / Play it cool / Hermann love's Pauline / Chupacabras / Torra fy ngwallt yn hir / Bass tuned to D.E.A.D. / Down a different river / Download / Mountain people.

Sep 97. (7"/c-s) *(CRE/+CS 275)* **PLAY IT COOL. / PASS THE TIME** [27] [–]
(cd-s+=) *(CRESCD 275)* – Cryndod yn dy lais.

Nov 97. (7"/c-s) *(CRE/+CS 283)* **DEMONS. / HIT AND RUN** [27] [–]
(cd-s+=) *(CRESCD 283)* – Carry the can.

May 98. (7"/c-s) *(CRE/+CS 288)* **ICE HOCKEY HAIR. / SMOKIN'** [12] [–]
(12"+=)(cd-s+=) *(CRE 288T)(CRESCD 288)* – Mu-tron / Let's quit smokin'.

Nov 98. (cd/lp) *(CRE CD/LP 229)* **OUT SPACED** (selected B-sides & rarities 1994-1998) [44] [–]
– The man don't give a fuck / Dim brys dim chwys / Smokin' / Dim bendith / Arnofio – Glo in the dark / Guacamole / Don't be a fool, Billy / Focus pocus – Debiel / Fix Idris / Pam V / Pass the time / Carry the can / Blerwytirhwng? *(ltd-cd; CRECD 229L) (cd re-iss. Sep99 & Feb00; same)*

May 99. (7"/c-s) *(CRE/+CS 314)* **NORTHERN LITES. / RABID DOG** [11] [–]
(cd-s+=) *(CRESCD 314)* – This, that and the other.

Jun 99. (cd/c/lp) *(CRECD/CCRE/CRELP 242) <FLY 36CD>* **GUERILLA** [10] [ ]
– Check it out / Do or die / The turning tide / Northern lites / Night vision / Wherever I lay my phone (that's my home) / A specific ocean / Some things come from nothing / The door to this house remains open / The teacher / Fire in my heart / The sound of life today / Chewing chewing gum / Keep the cosmic trigger happy. *(cd re-iss. Feb00; same)*

Aug 99. (7"/c-s) *(CRE/+CS 323)* **FIRE IN MY HEART. / THE MATTER OF TIME** [25] [–]
(cd-s+=) *(CRESCD 323)* – Mrs Spector.

Jan 00. (7"/c-s) *(CRE/+CS 329)* **DO OR DIE. / MISSUNDERSTANDING (sic)** [20] [–]
(cd-s+=) *(CRESCD 329)* – Colorblind.

Placid Casual — Flydaddy

May 00. (7") *(PC 02)* **YSBEIDIAU HEULOG. / CHARGE** [ ] [–]

May 00. (cd/c/lp)<d-cd> *(PLC 03 CD/MC/LP) <FLY 040>* **MWNG** [11] Jun00 [ ]
– Drygioni / Ymaelodi a'r ymylon / Y gwyneb lau / Dacw hi / Nythod cacwn / Pan ddaw'r wawr / Ysbeidiau heulog / Y teimlad / Sarn Helen / Gwreiddiau dwfn mawrth oer ar y blaned neifion. *<US cd+=>* – Cryndod yn dy lais / Trons mr urdd / Calimero / Sali Mali / (Nid) Hon yw'r gan sy'n mynd I achub yr laith.

Epic — Epic

Jul 01. (12"/c-s) *(671224-6/-4)* **JUXTAPOSED WITH U. / TRADEWINDS / HAPPINESS IS A WORN PUN** [14] [–]
(cd-s+=) *(671224-2)* – ('A'-video).

Jul 01. (cd/c/d-lp) *(<502413-2/-4/-1>)* **RINGS AROUND THE WORLD** [3] [ ]
– Alternate route to Vulcan Street / Sidewalk serfer girl / (Drawing) Rings around the world / It's not the end of the world? / Receptable for the respectable / (A) Touch sensitive / Shoot Doris Day / Miniature / No sympathy / Juxtaposed with U / Presedential suite / Run! Christian, run! / Fragile happiness.

Oct 01. (c-s/12") *(671908-4/-6)* **(DRAWING) RINGS AROUND THE WORLD / EDAM ANCHORMAN / ALL THE SHIT U DO** [28] [–]
(cd-s+=) *(671908-2)* – ('A'video).

Jan 02. (12"/cd-s) *(672175-6/-2)* **IT'S NOT THE END OF THE WORLD? / ROMAN ROAD / GYPSY SPACE MUFFIN** [30] [–]

Epic — X.L.

Jul 03. (7"pic-d/cd-s) *(673906-7/-2)* **GOLDEN RETRIEVER. / SUMMER SNOW / BLUE FRUIT** [13] [–]

Jul 03. (cd/lp) *(512375-2/-1) <85035>* **PHANTOM POWER** [4] [ ]
– Hello sunshine / Liberty belle / Golden retriever / Sex, war & robots / The piccolo snare / Venus & Serena / Father father #1 / Bleed forever / Out of control / Cityscape skybaby / Father father #2 / Valet parking / The undefeated / Slow life.

Oct 03. (7"pic-d) *(674360-7)* **HELLO SUNSHINE. / COWBIRD** [31] [–]
(cd-s+=) *(674360-2)* – Sanitizzzed.

SUPERGRASS

Formed: Oxford, England ... 1991 as The JENNIFERS by schoolboy GAZ COOMBES and DANNY GOFFEY along with brother NICK and ANDY DAVIES. After a sole EP on 'Nude' (home to SUEDE), DAVIES went off to university, COOMBES and DANNY subsequently recruiting MICKEY QUINN and forming SUPERGRASS. Their raucous debut single, 'CAUGHT BY THE FUZZ', complete with a STIFF LITTLE FINGERS-like intro and a snotty, shouty vocal rampage recounting the teenage trauma of being busted for cannabis, could've conceivably come straight out of 1977. Initially released on the small 'Backbeat' label in 1994, the single was eventually re-released by 'Parlophone' after the label promptly snapped the group up in 1994. Although the track narrowly missed the Top 40, a 1995 follow-up, 'MANSIZE ROOSTER', made the Top 20, the MADNESS comparisons inevitable as SUPERGRASS wore their influences proudly on their retro sleeves. Another couple of singles followed in quick succession, 'LOSE IT' as a limited 'Sub Pop' singles club release and 'LENNY' as the group's first Top 10 hit. Few were surprised, then, when the debut album, 'I SHOULD COCO' (1995) made No.1 the following month, a proverbial grab-bag of musical styles from 60's harmony pop to sneering punk. The record's indisputable highlight was 'ALRIGHT', a perfectly formed BEACH BOYS via The YOUNG ONES' pop romp guaranteed to bring a smile to your face and proving that "Brit-pop" didn't necessarily mean second rate STRANGLERS/BLONDIE rip-offs. The song, and especially the Raleigh Chopper-riding exploits of the video, did much to crystallise The SUPERGRASS image, carefree, fun-loving lads with GAZ's wildly impressive sideburns adding to the cartoon appeal. Steven Spielberg was apparently even moved to offer the band the opportunity of starring in a 90's remake of The MONKEES! This was turned down, as was an offer for GAZ to model for Calvin Klein, the group preferring to concentrate solely on the music and downplay the novelty factor. Instead, there were two gems hidden away at the end of 'I SHOULD..' which indicated the direction SUPERGRASS were headed; the intoxicating, slow rolling 70's groove of 'TIME' and the dreamy psychedelia of 'SOFA (OF MY LETHARGY). Save a few live appearances and a solitary single, 'GOING OUT', SUPERGRASS were notably absent in 1996, tucked away once more at Sawmill Studios crafting their acclaimed follow-up, 'IN IT FOR THE MONEY'. Eventually released in Spring '97, the record was something of a departure to say the least. The impetuous buzzsaw punk-pop of old had been replaced by the dark assault of 'RICHARD III' while the bulk of the album fed off warped neo-psychedelia and stark introspection. Horn flourishes were sighted here and there, most satisfyingly on the lazy chug of the aforementioned 'GOING OUT', while parping organs and acoustic strumming were the order of the day. The enigmatic shadow of The BEATLES' 'White Album' loomed large over proceedings, especially on 'YOU CAN SEE ME' and the oom-pa-pa eccentricity of 'SOMETIMES I MAKE YOU SAD'. In fact, the only glimpse of the old SUPERGRASS came with 'SUN HITS THE SKY', a soaring, handclapping, spirit-lifting celebration of good times and faraway places. No matter though, the record's dark charm ensured the band remained a critical favourite, if not quite consolidating the commercial heights of the debut. Clearly, SUPERGRASS were looking at a long term, albums-based career, and on the strength of 'IN IT ...', the future seemed promising. In May '99, the glam BOWIE-esque 'PUMPING ON YOUR STEREO' was the first of three hit singles, the second 'MOVING' ('Dogs' by PINK FLOYD might've been "pumping on their stereo" at the time!?) previewing their self-titled third Top 3 album. However, several critics rated this as a drop in form. ALI G (Boo-y aka SACHA BARON COHEN) subsequently demolished the er, "Super-tramp" GAZ on his cult TV show; the 'SUN HITS THE SKY', indeed. The 'GRASS returned in 2002 with the brilliant 'LIFE ON OTHER PLANETS', a sweeping pop/rock album featuring COMBS' wacky strained vocals and a couple of surefire singles to boot; the infectious 'SAVE YOUR MONEY FOR THE CHILDREN' (which was just 'PUMPING ON YOUR STEREO' reprise) and the power pop punk of 'EVENING OF THE DAY'. In short, it was great to have them back. • **Covered:** STONE FREE (Jimi Hendrix) / ITCHYCOO PARK (Small Faces) / SOME GIRLS ARE BIGGER THAN OTHERS (Smiths).

Album rating: I SHOULD COCO (*9) / IN IT FOR THE MONEY (*8) / SUPERGRASS (*6) / LIFE ON OTHER PLANETS (*7)

JENNIFERS

GAZ COOMBES (b. GARETH, 8 Mar'76, Brighton, England) – vocals, guitar / **NICK GOFFEY** – guitar / **ANDY DAVIES** – bass / **DANNY GOFFEY** (b. DANIEL, 7 Feb'75, London, England) – drums

		Nude-Sony	not iss.
Aug 92.	(12"ep/cd-ep) *(NUD2 T/CD)* **JUST GOT BACK TODAY / ROCKS AND BOULDERS. / DANNY'S SONG / TOMORROW'S RAIN**		–

— **MICK QUINN** (b.17 Dec'69) – guitar; repl. TARA MILTON who had repl. NICK

SUPERGRASS

— now without DAVIES who went to Bristol University

		Parlophone	Capitol
Oct 94.	(7"/c-s) *(R/TCR 6396)* <81769> **CAUGHT BY THE FUZZ. / STRANGE ONES**	43 Feb95	
	(cd-s+=) *(CDR 6396)* – Caught by the fuzz (acoustic).		
Feb 95.	(7"/7"red/c-s) *(R/RS/TCR 6402)* <81964> **MANSIZE ROOSTER. / SITTING UP STRAIGHT**	20 Jun95	
	(cd-s+=) *(CDR 6402)* – Odd.		
Mar 95.	(7"yellow) *(<SP 281>)* **LOSE IT. / CAUGHT BY THE FUZZ (acoustic)**	75	
	(above on 'Sub Pop' also feat. on Jul95 box-set 'HELTER SHELTER') *(re-iss. Sep99; same)*		
Apr 95.	(7"blue/c-s) *(RS/TCR 6401)* **LENNY. / WAIT FOR THE SUN**	9	–
	(cd-s+=) *(CDR 6410)* – Sex!.		
May 95.	(cd/c/lp) *(CD/TC+/PCS 7373)* <33350> **I SHOULD COCO**	1 Jul95	
	– I'd like to know / Caught by the fuzz / Mansize rooster / Alright / Lose it / Lenny / Strange ones / Sitting up straight / She's so loose / We're not supposed to / Time / Sofa (of my lethargy) / Time to go. *(7"free w/ ltd lp)* **STONE FREE. / ODD?**		
Jul 95.	(c-s/7"colrd) *(TC+/R 6413)* <82277> **ALRIGHT. / TIME**	2	
	(cd-s+=) *(CDR 6413)* – Condition / Je suis votre papa sucre.		
	(cd-s+=) *(CDRX 6413)* – Lose it.		
Feb 96.	(c-s/7"burgundy) *(TC+/R 6428)* **GOING OUT. / MELANIE DAVIS**	5	–
	(cd-s+=) *(CDR 6428)* – Strange ones (live).		
Apr 97.	(cd-s/7"yellow) *(CD/+R 6461)* <83820> **RICHARD III. / NOTHING MORE'S GONNA GET IN MY WAY**	2	
	(cd-s+=) *(CDRS 6461)* – 20ft halo.		
	(cd-s) *(CDRS 6461)* – ('A'side) / Sometimes I make you very sad / Sometimes we're very sad.		
Apr 97.	(cd/c/lp) *(CD/TC+/PCS 7388)* <55228> **IN IT FOR THE MONEY**	2 May97	
	– In it for the money / Richard III / Tonight / Late in the day / G-song / Sun hits the sky / Going out / It's not me / Cheapskate / You can see me / Hollow little reign / Sometimes I make you sad.		
Jun 97.	(c-s/7") *(TC+/R 6469)* <84187> **SUN HITS THE SKY. / SOME GIRLS ARE BIGGER THAN OTHERS**	10	
	(cd-s+=) *(CDR 6469)* – ('A'extended).		

Oct 97. (7"gold) *(R 6484) <84758>* **LATE IN THE DAY. / WE STILL NEED MORE (THAN ANYONE CAN GIVE)** [18] [ ]
(cd-s+=) *(CDRS 6484)* – It's not me (demo).
(cd-s) *(CDR 6484)* – ('A'side) / Don't be cruel / The animal.

— while SUPERGRASS took a break from the biz, DANNY moonlighted with the indie superband, LODGER, who issued a few singles in '98

— **GAZ, DANNY + MICK** added **ROBERT COOMBES** – keyboards

May 99. (c-s) *(TCR 6518)* **PUMPING ON YOUR STEREO / YOU'LL NEVER WALK AGAIN** [11] [ ]
(cd-s+=) *(CDRS 6518)* – Sick.
(cd-s) *(CDR 6518)* – ('A'side) / What a shame / Lucky (no fear).

Sep 99. (7") *(R 6524)* **MOVING. / BELIEVER** [9] [ ]
(c-s+=/cd-s+=) *(TCR/CDR 6524)* – Faraway (acoustic).
(cd-s) *(CDRS 6524)* – ('A'side) / You too can play alright / Pumping on your stereo (CD-Rom).

Sep 99. (cd/c) *(5 22056-2/-4) <542388>* **SUPERGRASS** [3] [ ]
– Moving / Your love / What went wrong (in your head) / Beautiful people / Shotover hill / Eon / Mary / Jesus came from outta space / Pumping on your stereo / Born again / Faraway / Mama & papa.

Nov 99. (7"silver) *(R 6531)* **MARY / PUMPING ON YOUR STEREO (live)** [36] [ ]
(c-s+=/cd-s+=) *(TCR/CDR 6531)* – Strange ones (live).
(cd-s+=) *(CDRS 6531)* – Richard III (live) / Sun hits the sky (live).

Parlophone Island

Jul 02. (ltd-7"one-sided) *(R 6583)* **NEVER DONE NOTHING LIKE THAT BEFORE** [75] [–]

Sep 02. (7") *(R 6586)* **GRACE. / VELVETINE** [13] [–]
(cd-s+=) *(CDRS 6586)* – Electric cowboy.
(cd-s) *(CDR 6586)* – ('A'side) / Tishing in windows (kicking down doors) / That old song / ('A'-video).

Sep 02. (cd/lp) *(541800-2/-1) <063685>* **LIFE ON OTHER PLANETS** [9] [ ]
– Za / Rush hour soul / Seen the light / Brecon beacons / Can't get up / Evening of the day / Never done nothing like that before / Funniest thing / Grace / La song / Prophet 15 / Run.

Jan 03. (7"grey) *(R 6592)* **SEEN THE LIGHT. / THE LONER** [22] [–]
(cd-s+=) *(CDR 6592)* – I told the truth.

Aug 03. (7") *(R 6612)* **RUSH HOUR SOUL. / EVERYTIME** [ ] [–]
(cd-s+=) *(CDR 6612)* – ('A'-video).

– compilations, etc. –

Oct 02. (d-cd) *EMI Catalogue; (541103-2)* **SUPERGRASS / I SHOULD COCO** [ ] [–]

SUPERTRAMP

Formed: London, England … 1969 by RICHARD DAVIES. Through the sponsorship of Dutch millionaire, Stanley Miesegaes, he enlisted RICHARD PALMER, BOB MILLER and co-writer, ROBERT HODGSON through a music paper ad. Signing to 'A&M', the band released a largely ignored and directionless eponymous debut in summer 1970, the record's poor critical and commercial reception engendering a personnel reshuffle; HODGSON switched to guitar, recruiting a new rhythm section of FRANK FARRELL and KEVIN CURRIE and adding sax player, DAVE WINTHROP. The resulting album, 'INDELIBLY STAMPED' (1971) was more notable for the tasteless cover shot (a heavily tattooed bust) than any of the music contained within and the group packed it in later that summer. While WINTHROP later joined SECRET AFFAIR, DAVIES and HODGSON resurrected SUPERTRAMP a couple of years later, enlisting the rhythm section of DOUGIE THOMSON and BOB C. BENBERG along with sax/clarinet player JOHN ANTHONY HELLIWELL. The musical chemistry finally clicked and 1974's 'CRIME OF THE CENTURY' album propelled SUPERTRAMP to major league prog-rock/pop status. Complex, insidious and intelligently crafted, the record married conceptually depressing lyrical fare to infectiously melodic hooklines with surprising results. The album itself made the Top 5 while 'DREAMER' was a Top 20 hit single. 'CRISIS? WHAT CRISIS?' (1975) and 'EVEN IN THE QUIETEST MOMENTS' (1977) utilised the same musicians and carried on in much the same vein, solidifying their growing cult fanbase (especially in the US) and even spawning a transatlantic hit single in the acoustic-based 'GIVE A LITTLE BIT'. Increasingly catering to the American AOR market, SUPERTRAMP finally broke through big style with the multi-million selling (US No.1) 'BREAKFAST IN AMERICA' (1979) and its attendant US hits. A living, breathing example of all that punk set out to destroy, this perhaps remains one of the album's charms; while the vocals may have erred towards limp posturing and the lyrics towards irrelevance, there was no denying the record's lasting pop appeal, especially the pompous yet evocative title track. '. . .FAMOUS LAST WORDS' (1982) was the next studio set, carrying on in much the same inoffensive vein without the saving grace of its predecessor's charm. HODGSON left soon after (subsequently recording two mid-80's solo albums, 'IN THE EYE OF THE STORM' and 'HAI HAI'), leaving SUPERTRAMP to complete a further two studio sets, 'BROTHER WHERE YOU BOUND' (1985) and 'FREE AS A BIRD' (1987) amid increasing disinterest. Although they finally folded after a 1988 live effort, they reformed a mere eight years later and recorded an album for 'Chrysalis', 'SOME THINGS NEVER CHANGE' (1997). Unfortunately for SUPERTRAMP, the music scene had changed irrevocably and the record barely scraped a Top 75 placing. To their credit, the HODGSON-less troupe tramped on into the new millennium with 'SLOW MOTION', for the most part failing to capture the exotic, indefinable allure of their best 70's work but nevertheless crafting a passable set of songs destined to placate fans who were still listening. • **Songwriters:** HODGSON and/or DAVIE, except I'M YOUR HOOCHIE COOCHIE MAN (John Lee Hooker).
• **Trivia:** They took their name from a 1910 W.H. Davies book, 'The Autobiography Of A Supertramp'.

Album rating: SUPERTRAMP (*4) / INDELIBLY STAMPED (*4) / CRIME OF THE CENTURY (*8) / CRISIS? WHAT CRISIS? (*6) / EVEN IN THE QUIETEST MOMENTS (*6) / BREAKFAST IN AMERICA (*7) / PARIS (*5) / . . .FAMOUS LAST WORDS (*6) / BROTHER WHERE YOU BOUND (*4) / THE AUTOBIOGRAPHY OF SUPERTRAMP compilation (*8) / FREE AS A BIRD (*4) / LIVE '88 (*4) / SOME THINGS NEVER CHANGE (*5) / SLOW MOTION (*4)

RICHARD DAVIES (b.22 Jul'44) – vocals, keyboards (ex-The JOINT) / **ROGER HODGSON** (b.21 Mar'50) – bass, keyboards, vocals / **RICHARD PALMER** – guitar / **BOB MILLER** – drums

A&M A&M

Aug 70. (lp) *(AMLS 981)* **SUPERTRAMP** [ ] [–]
– Surely / It's a long road / Aubade / And I am not like other birds of prey / Words unspoken / Maybe I'm a beggar / Home again / Nothing to show / Shadow song / Try again / Surely (reprise). *<US-iss.Mar78; 4665> (re-iss. Mar82 lp/c; AMID/CMID 123) (re-iss. May84 on 'Hallmark' lp/c; SHM/HSC 3139) (cd-iss. 1988; CDA 3129) (re-iss. c Jan93)*

— (May'71) **HODGSON** now also lead guitar, vox / **FRANK FARRELL** – bass / **KEVIN CURRIE** – drums repl. PALMER + MILLER / added **DAVE WINTHROP** (b.27 Nov'48, New Jersey) – saxophone

Jun 71. (lp/c) *(AMLS 64306)* **INDELIBLY STAMPED** [ ] [ ]
– Your poppa don't mind / Travelled / Rosie had everything planned / Remember / Forever / Potter / Coming home to see you / Times have changed / Friend in need / Aries. *(cd-iss. 1988; CDA 3149) (re-iss. c Jan93) (cd re-iss. Feb98; 393129-2)*

Oct 71. (7") *<1305>* **FOREVER. / YOUR POPPA DON'T MIND** [–] [ ]

— Disbanded late Summer 1971, WINTHROP later joined SECRET AFFAIR. **DAVIES + HODGSON** re-formed them Aug'73. Recruited **DOUGIE THOMSON** (b.24 Mar'51, Glasgow, Scotland) – bass (ex-ALAN BOWN SET) / **BOB C. BENBERG** (b. SIEBENBERG) – drums (ex-BEES MAKE HONEY) / **JOHN ANTHONY HELLIWELL** (b.15 Feb'45, Todmorden, England) – saxophone, clarinet, vocals (ex-ALAN BOWN SET)

Mar 74. (7") *(AMS 7101)* **LAND HO. / SUMMER ROMANCE** [ ] [–]

Sep 74. (lp/c) *(AMLS/CAM 68258)* *<3647>* **CRIME OF THE CENTURY** [4] [38]
– School / Bloody well right / Hide in your shell / Asylum / Dreamer / Rudy / If everyone was listening / Crime of the century. *(cd-iss. Apr86; CDA 68258) (cd re-iss. May97; 393647-2) (cd re-mast.Sep03; 493346-2)*

Dec 74. (7") *(AMS 7152)* *<1660>* **DREAMER. / BLOODY WELL RIGHT** [13] Mar75 [35]

—— <above B-side was US A-side>

Nov 75. (lp/c) *(AMLH/CAM 68347)* *<4560>* **CRISIS? WHAT CRISIS?** [20] [44]
– Easy does it / Sister Moonshine / Ain't nobody but me / A soapbox opera / Another man's woman / Lady / Poor boy / Just a normal day / The meaning / Two of us. *(cd-iss. Apr86; CDA 4560) (cd re-iss. May97; 394560-2) (cd re-mast.Sep03; 493347-2)*

Nov 75. (7") *(AMS 7201)* *<1793>* **LADY. / YOU STARTED LAUGHING (WHEN I HELD YOU IN MY ARMS)** [ ] [ ]

Jun 76. (7") *<1814>* **SISTER MOONSHINE. / AIN'T NOBODY BUT ME** [–] [ ]

Apr 77. (lp/c) *(AMLK/CAM 64634)* *<4634>* **EVEN IN THE QUIETEST MOMENTS** [12] [16]
– Give a little bit / Lover boy / Even in the quietest moments / Downstream / Babaji / From now on / Fool's overture. *(cd-iss. Apr86; CDA 4634) (cd re-iss. May97; 394634-2) (cd re-mast.Sep03; 493348-2)*

Jun 77. (7") *(AMS 7293)* *<1938>* **GIVE A LITTLE BIT. / DOWNSTREAM** [29] [15]

Nov 77. (7") *<1981>* **FROM NOW ON. / DREAMER** [–] [ ]

Nov 77. (7") *(AMS 7326)* **BABAJI. / FROM NOW ON** [ ] [–]

Mar 79. (lp/c) *(AMLK/CAM 63708)* *<3708>* **BREAKFAST IN AMERICA** [3] [1]
– Gone Hollywood / The logical song / Goodbye stranger / Breakfast in America / Oh darling / Take the long way home / Lord is it mine / Just another nervous wreck / Casual conversations / Child of vision. *(cd-iss. 1983; CDA 63708) (cd re-iss. May97; 393708-2) (lp re-iss. Mar00 on 'Simply Vinyl'; SVLP 184) (cd re-mast.Sep03; 493349-2)*

Mar 79. (7") *(AMS 7427)* *<2128>* **THE LOGICAL SONG. / JUST ANOTHER NERVOUS WRECK** [7] [6]

Jun 79. (7") *(AMS 7451)* **BREAKFAST IN AMERICA. / GONE HOLLYWOOD** [9] [–]

Sep 79. (7") *(AMS 7481)* *<2162>* **GOODBYE STRANGER. / EVEN IN THE QUIETEST MOMENTS** [57] Jul79 [15]

Oct 79. (7") *(AMS 7560)* **TAKE THE LONG WAY HOME. / FROM NOW ON** [ ] [–]

Oct 79. (7") *<2193>* **TAKE THE LONG WAY HOME. / RUBY** [–] [10]

Sep 80. (d-lp/d-c) *(AMLM/CLM 66702)* *<6702>* **PARIS (live 29-11-79)** [7] [8]
– School / Ain't nobody but me / The logical song / Bloody well right / Breakfast in America / You started laughing / Hide in your shell / From now on / Dreamer / Rudy / A soapbox opera / Asylum / Take the long way home / Fool's overture / Two of us / Crime of the century. *(cd-iss. Apr86; CDD 6702) (cd re-iss. May97; 396702-2) (d-cd re-mast.Sep03; 493350-2)*

Sep 80. (7") *<2269>* **DREAMER (live). / FROM NOW ON (live)** [–] [15]

Nov 80. (7") *(AMS 7576)* **DREAMER (live). / YOU STARTED LAUGHING (live)** [ ] [–]

Nov 80. (7") *<2292>* **BREAKFAST IN AMERICA (live). / YOU STARTED LAUGHING (live)** [–] [62]

Oct 82. (7") *(AMS 8255)* *<2502>* **IT'S RAINING AGAIN. / BONNIE** [26] [11]

Oct 82. (lp/c) *(AMLK/CKM 63732)* *<3732>* **. . . FAMOUS LAST WORDS** [6] [5]
– Crazy / Put on your brown school shoes / It's raing again / Bonnie / Know who you are / My kind of lady / C'est la bon / Waiting so long / Don't leave me now. *(cd-iss. 1983; CDA 63732) (cd re-mast.Sep03; 493353-2)*

Jan 83. (7") *(AMS 8301)* *<2517>* **MY KIND OF LADY. / KNOW WHO YOU ARE** [ ] [31]

—— (Nov82) Now a quartet when HODGSON departed to go solo. (Re-joined briefly late'86 tour). HODGSON solo albums: IN THE EYE OF THE STORM ('84) / HAI HAI ('87).

Apr 85. (7") *(AMS 248)* *<2731>* **CANNONBALL. / EVER OPEN DOOR** [ ] [28]

May 85. (lp/c/cd) *(<AMA/AMC/CDA 5014>)* **BROTHER WHERE YOU BOUND** [20] [21]
– Cannonball / Still in love / No inbetween / Better days / Brother where you bound / Ever open door. *(re-iss. Jan93) (cd re-mast.Sep03; 493354-2)*

Jul 85. (7") *(AMS 265)* *<2720>* **STILL IN LOVE. / NO INBETWEEN** [ ] Feb85 [ ]
(12"+=) *(AMY 265)* – Cannonball (dance mix).

Sep 85. (7") *<2760>* **BETTER DAYS. / NO INBETWEEN** [–] [ ]

Nov 86. (lp/c/cd) *(TRAMP/TRAMC/TRACD 1)* **THE AUTOBIOGRAPHY OF SUPERTRAMP** (compilation) [9] [–]
– Goodbye stranger / The logical song / Bloody well right / Breakfast in America / Take the long way home / Crime of the century / Dreamer / From now on / Give a little bit / It's raining again / Cannonball / Ain't nobody but me / Hide in your shell / Rudy. *(cd= 3 extra) (re-iss. cd Jan93 as 'THE VERY BEST OF SUPERTRAMP'+=)*– School.

Oct 87. (7"/12") *(AM/+Y 415)* *<2985>* **I'M BEGGIN' YOU. / NO INBETWEENS** [ ] [ ]

Oct 87. (lp/c/cd) *(<AMA/AMC/CDA 5181>)* **FREE AS A BIRD** [93] [ ]
– It's alright / Not the moment / It doesn't matter / Where I stand / Free as a bird / I'm beggin' you / You never can tell with friends / Thing for you / An awful thing to waste. *(cd re-mast.Sep03; 493355-2)*

Feb 88. (7") *<2996>* **FREE AS A BIRD. / THING FOR YOU** [–] [ ]

Feb 88. (7") *(AM 430)* **FREE AS A BIRD. / I'M BEGGIN' YOU** [ ] [–]

Oct 88. (lp/c/cd) *(<MA/AMC/CDA 3923>)* **LIVE '88 (live)** [ ] [ ]
– You started laughing / It's alright / Not the moment / Oh darling / Breakfast in America / From now on / Just another nervous wreck / The logical song / I'm your hoochie coochie man / Crime of the century / Don't you lie to me. *(re-iss. cd Jan93)*

—— Folded after above, although they reformed 8 years later. Line-up:- **RICK DAVIES** – vocals, keyboards / **MARK HART** – vocals, keyboards, guitars / **JOHN HELLIWELL** – saxophones, woodwind / **CLIFF HUGO** – bass / **BOB SIEBENBERG** – drums / **LEE R. THORNBURG** – trumpet, trombone, vocals / **CARL VERHEYEN** – guitars / **TOM WALSH** – percussion

Chrysalis Oxygen

Apr 97. (cd/c) *(CD/TC CHR 6121)* *<9000-2>* **SOME THINGS NEVER CHANGE** [74] Jun97 [ ]
– It's a hard world / You win, I lose / Get your act together / Live to love you / Some things never change / Listen to me please / Sooner or later / Help me down that road / And the light / Give me a chance / C'est what? / Where there's a will.

—— **JESSE SIEBENBERG** – percussion; repl. WALSH

E.M.I. E.M.I.

Mar 02. (cd) *(<538624-2>)* **SLOW MOTION** [ ] Apr02 [ ]
– Slow motion / Little by little / Broken hearted / Over you / Tenth Avenue breakdown / A sting in the tail / Bee in your bonnet / Goldrush / Dead man's blues.

– compilations, etc. –

on 'A&M' unless mentioned otherwise

May 81. (d-c) *A&M; (CAMCR 7)* **CRISIS? WHAT CRISIS? / EVEN IN THE QUIETEST MOMENTS** [ ] [–]

Sep 85. (7") *Old Gold; (OG 9542)* **DREAMER. / GIVE A LITTLE BIT** [ ] [–]

Sep 86. (7") *(AM 357)* **THE LOGICAL SONG. / GOODBYE STRANGER** [ ] [–]

Aug 88. (cd-ep) *(AMCD 914)* **COMPACT HITS** [ ] [–]
– The logical song / Breakfast in America / Goodbye stranger / Hide in your shell.

Jul 92. (7")(c-s) **GIVE A LITTLE BIT (for Telethon). / ('A' original version)** [ ] [ ]
(cd-s+=) – Breakfast in America.

Aug 92. (cd/c) *(TRA CD/MC 1992)* **THE VERY BEST OF SUPERTRAMP** [24] [ ]
– Schhol / Goodbye stranger / The logical song / Bloody well right / Breakfast in America / Rudy / Take the long way home / Crime of the century / Dreamer / Ain't nobody but me / Hide in your shell / From now on / It's raining again / Give a little bit / Cannonball. *(re-iss. Sep97 hit UK No.8)*

Apr 94. (cd) *Compact Club; (CCV 8919)* **THE SUPERTRAMP SONGBOOK** [ ] [–]

Apr 99. (cd) *E.M.I.; (<499390-2>)* **IT WAS THE BEST OF TIMES** [ ] [ ]

Mar 02. (d-lp) *Fruit Tree; (FT 816)* **IS EVERYBODY LISTENING** (live in Cleveland, Ohio 1976) [ ] [–]

Aug 03. (cd) *King Biscuit; (KBCCD 128)* **IN CONCERT** [ ] [ ]

SUPREMES

Formed: Detroit, Michigan, USA … 1959 as The PRIMETTES by PRIMES (an outfit that included future members of The TEMPTATIONS) manager, Milton Jenkins who originally employed the then quartet of DIANA ROSS, FLORENCE BALLARD, MARY WILSON and BETTY TRAVIS to augment his act on stage. Making a name for themselves around town by guesting on records by established artists, the girls were eventually signed to 'Motown' where label owner, Berry Gordy took them under his wing, renamed them The SUPREMES and singled them out for special treatment. By the release of debut single, 'I WANT A GUY', in late 1960, BETTY had been replaced by BARBARA MARTIN who herself departed the following summer after the release of a second track, 'BUTTERED POPCORN'. Reduced to a trio, the group released a combination of minor hit singles and flops over the ensuing two years including 'LET ME GO THE RIGHT WAY' and 'MY HEART CAN'T TAKE NO MORE'. Many of these tracks had showcased BALLARD's earthy vocal style and the hits only really began piling up when ROSS' cooler, more seductive tones were pushed to the fore. Set to work on material by the crack songwriting team of HOLLAND/DOZIER/HOLLAND, the group scored their first Top 30 hit in late '63 with 'WHEN THE LOVELIGHT STARTS SHINING THROUGH HIS EYES'. The following summer they hit the US top spot (and the UK Top 3) with 'WHERE DID OUR LOVE GO' and over the coming decade racked up an incredible run of classic No.1 singles, becoming in the process the most successful act of the girl group era. Schooled in the legendary Motown way (i.e. choreography, etiquette etc,), The SUPREMES outshone their contemporaries in every department i.e. more glamourous, more professional, more adaptable, more urbane. Above all they had the best tunes and, in DIANA ROSS, a secret weapon of a singer capable of transforming even mediocre material into gold-dust. The run of US No.1's included 'BABY LOVE', 'STOP IN THE NAME OF LOVE', 'BACK IN MY ARMS AGAIN', 'I HEAR A SYMPHONY', 'YOU CAN'T HURRY LOVE' and 'YOU KEEP ME HANGIN' ON', many of these records coming to define the sound of quintessential 60's Motown pop-soul. The classic line-up's final No.1 came with 'THE HAPPENING' in 1967 after which BALLARD departed in messy circumstances (one of Motown's truly tragic characters, she was subsequently cheated out of her severance money and died amid depression, alcoholism and personal problems on the 22nd February '76, aged only 32). Although ex-PATTI LaBELLE & THE BLUE BELLES singer CINDY BIRDSONG was drafted in as a replacement, the next single, 'REFLECTIONS', was released as DIANA ROSS & THE SUPREMES, an indication of ROSS' impending solo career. Having dispensed with the services of HOLLAND/DOZIER/HOLLAND, the hits became thinner on the ground although the social commentary of 'LOVE CHILD' gave them a No.1 in late '68, the group teaming up with old buddies The TEMPTATIONS for a transatlantic Top 3 hit, 'I'M GONNA MAKE YOU LOVE ME' around the same time. Ironically, 'SOMEDAY WE'LL BE TOGETHER' marked their final No.1 in late '69 prior to ROSS' final appearance with the group at a Las Vegas farewell show in early 1970. JEAN TERRELL was the initial replacement, herself succeeded three years later by SCHERRIE PAYNE. In the meantime, the group had only scored one Top 10 hit (discounting the late 1970 collaboration with The FOUR TOPS on a cover of 'RIVER DEEP/MOUNTAIN HIGH') with 'STONED LOVE' in early 1971. LYNDA LAWRENCE had also replaced BIRDSONG and the pattern of personnel upheaval continued amid diminishing chart returns and the indifference of 'Motown' until they finally gave up the ghost in 1977. ROSS, meanwhile, had been paired up with ASHFORD & SIMPSON, who produced her first run of solo hits beginning with 'REACH OUT AND TOUCH (SOMEBODY'S HAND)' in 1970. The eponymous debut album also contained her No.1 cover of 'AIN'T NO MOUNTAIN HIGH ENOUGH' (previously a Top 20 hit in 1967 for MARVIN GAYE & TAMMI TERRELL), setting her up as a polished soul diva in the making. • **Trivia:** Their hits have been covered successfully by many acts. The most popular being YOU CAN'T HURRY LOVE (Phil Collins) / YOU KEEP ME HANGIN' ON (Vanila Fudge) / NATHAN JONES (Bananarama).

Best CD compilation: 40 GOLDEN MOTOWN GREATS (*9)

DIANA ROSS (b.26 Mar'44) – lead vocals / **FLORENCE BALLARD** (b.30 Jun'43) – vocals / **MARY WILSON** (b. 6 Mar44, Greenville, Missouri) – vocals / **BARBARA MARTIN** – vocals; repl. BETTY TRAVIS in 1960

Oriole | Motown

Dec 60. (7") *<54038>* **I WANT A GUY. / NEVER AGAIN** [–] [ ]

Jul 61. (7") *<54045>* **BUTTERED POPCORN. / WHO'S LOVING YOU** [–] [ ]

—— slimmed to a trio when BARBARA left

Jul 62. (7") <1027> **YOUR HEART BELONGS TO ME. / (HE'S) SEVENTEEN** [–] [95]

Nov 62. (7") <1034> **LET ME GO THE RIGHT WAY. / TIME CHANGES THINGS** [–] [90]

Apr 63. (7") <1040> **MY HEART CAN'T TAKE NO MORE. / YOU BRING BACK MEMORIES** [–] [ ]

Jul 63. (7") <1044> **A BREATH TAKING GUY. / (THE MAN WITH THE) ROCK AND ROLL BANJO BAND** [–] [75]

Stateside | Motown

Dec 63. (7") *(SS 257) <1051>* **WHEN THE LOVELIGHT STARTS SHINING THROUGH HIS EYES. / STANDING AT THE CROSSROADS OF LOVE** [ ] Nov63 [23]

Feb 64. (lp) *<606>* **MEET THE SUPREMES** [–] [ ]
– Where did our love go / Your heart belongs to me / Buttered popcorn / Baby, don't go / (The man with the) Rock and roll banjo band / I want a guy / When the lovelight starts shining through his eyes / You bring back memories / Play a sad song / Time changes things / Never again / Standing at the crossroads of love. *(UK-iss.Nov64; SL 10109)* – hit No.8

Mar 64. (7") <1054> **RUN, RUN, RUN. / I'M GIVING YOU YOUR FREEDOM** [–] [93]

Aug 64. (7") *(SS 327) <1060>* **WHERE DID OUR LOVE GO. / HE MEANS THE WORLD TO ME** [3] Jun64 [1]
(re-iss. Aug74) (re-iss. as were most major hit singles; Oct81)

Sep 64. (lp) *<623>* **WHERE DID OUR LOVE GO** [–] [2]
– Where did our love go / Run, run, run / Baby love / When the lovelight starts shining through his eyes / Come see about me / Long gone lover / I'm giving you your freedom / A breath taking guy / He means the world to me / Standing at the crossroads of love / Your kiss of fire / Ask any girl. *(re-iss. Oct81)*

Oct 64. (7") *(SS 350) <1066>* **BABY LOVE. / ASK ANY GIRL** [1] Sep64 [1]

Jan 65. (7") *(SS 376) <1068>* **COME SEE ABOUT ME. / (YOU'RE GONE BUT) ALWAYS IN MY HEART** [27] Nov64 [1]

Tamla Motown | Motown

Jan 65. (lp) *(TML 11002) <623>* **WITH LOVE – FROM US TO YOU** <US-title 'A BIT OF LIVERPOOL'> [ ] Nov64 [21]
– How do you do it / World without love / House of the rising sun / A hard day's night / Because / You've really got a hold on me / You can't do that / Do you love me / Can't buy me love / I want to hold your hand / Bits and pieces.

Mar 65. (7") *(TMG 501) <1074>* **STOP! IN THE NAME OF LOVE. / I'M IN LOVE AGAIN** [7] Feb65 [1]

May 65. (7") *(TMG 516) <1075>* **BACK IN MY ARMS AGAIN. / WHISPER YOU LOVE ME BOY** [40] Apr65 [1]

Jul 65. (lp) *(TML 11012) <629>* **WE REMEMBER SAM COOKE** [ ] Apr65 [75]
– You send me / Nothing can change this love / Cupid / Chain gang / Bring it on home to me / Only sixteen / Havin' a party / Shake / Wonderful world / A change is gonna come / (Ain't that) Good news. *(re-iss. May86 lp/c; WL/WK 72445)*

Jul 65. (7") *(TMG 527) <1080>* **NOTHING BUT HEARTACHES. / HE HOLDS HIS OWN** [ ] [11]

Aug 65. (lp) *(TML 11018) <625>* **THE SUPREMES SING COUNTRY WESTERN AND POP** [ ] Mar65 [79]
– Funny how time slips away / My heart can't take it no more / It makes no difference now / You didn't care / Tears in vain / Tumbling tumbleweeds / Lazy bones / You need me / Baby doll / Sunset / (The man with the) Rock and roll banjo band.

Sep 65. (lp) *(TML 11020) <627>* **MORE HITS BY THE SUPREMES** (compilation) [ ] Aug65 [6]
– Ask any girl / Nothing but heartaches / Mother dear / Honey boy / Back in my arma again / Whisper you love me, boy / The only time I'm happy / He holds his own / Who could ever doubt my love / Heartaches don't last always / I'm in love again.

Nov 65. (7") *(TMG 543) <1083>* **I HEAR A SYMPHONY. / WHO COULD EVER DOUBT MY LOVE** [39] Oct65 [1]

Dec 65. (7") *<1085>* **TWINKLE, TWINKLE LITTLE ME. / CHILDREN'S CHRISTMAS SONG** [–] [ ]

Dec 65. (lp) *<638>* **MERRY CHRISTMAS** (festive songs) [–] [ ]
(UK-iss.Nov82 lp/c; STMS/CSTMS 5084) (re-iss. 1986 lp/c; WL/WK 72117)

Jan 66. (lp; stereo/mono) *(S+/TML 11026) <636>* **THE SUPREMES AT THE COPA (live)** [ ] Nov65 [11]
– Opening introduction: Put on a happy face / I am woman / Baby love / Stop! in the name of love / The boy from Ipanema / Make someone happy / Come see about me / Rock-a-bye your baby with a dixie melody / Queen of the house / Group intro – Somewhere / Back in my arms again / Sam Cooke medley / You're nobody til somebody loves you. *(re-iss. Mar82 lp/c; STMS/CSTMS 5045)*

Feb 66. (7") *(TMG 548) <1089>* **MY WORLD IS EMPTY WITHOUT YOU. / EVERYTHING IS GOOD ABOUT YOU** [ ] Jan66 [5]

May 66. (lp; stereo/mono) *(S+/TML 11028) <643>* **I HEAR A SYMPHONY** [ ] Mar66 [8]
– Stranger in Paradise / Yesterday / I hear a symphony / Unchained melody / With a song in my heart / My world is empty without you / A lover's concerto / Any girl in love (knows what I'm going through) / Wonderful, wonderful / Everything is good about you / He's all I got. *(re-iss. Oct81 lp/c; STMS/CSTMS 5012)*

May 66. (7") *(TMG 560) <1094>* **LOVE IS LIKE AN ITCHING IN MY HEART. / HE'S ALL I GOT** [ ] Apr66 [9]

Aug 66. (7") *(TMG 575) <1097>* **YOU CAN'T HURRY LOVE. / PUT YOURSELF IN MY PLACE** [3] [1]

Oct 66. (7") *<1101>* **YOU KEEP ME HANGIN' ON. / REMOVE THIS DOUBT** [–] [1]

Nov 66. (7") *(TMG 585)* **YOU KEEP ME HANGIN' ON. / COME SEE ABOUT ME** [8] [–]

Dec 66. (lp; stereo/mono) *(S+/TML 11039) <649>* **THE SUPREMES A-GO-GO** [15] Sep66 [1]
– Love is like an itching in my heart / This old heart of mine (is weak for you) / You can't hurry love / Shake me, wake up (when it's over) / Baby I need your loving / These boots are made for walking / I can't help myself / Get ready / Put yourself in my place / Money (that's what I want) / Come and get these memories / Hang on Sloopy. *(re-iss. Oct81 lp/c; STMS/CSTMS 5013) (re-iss. 1986; WL 72072)*

Feb 67. (7") *(TMG 597) <1103>* **LOVE IS HERE AND NOW YOU'RE GONE. / THERE'S NO STOPPING US NOW** [17] Jan67 [1]

Apr 67. (lp; stereo/mono) *(S+/TML 11047) <650>* **THE SUPREMES SING MOTOWN** <US-title 'THE SUPREMES SING HOLLAND-DOZIER-HOLLAND'> [15] Feb67 [6]
– You keep me hangin' on / You're gone, but always in my heart / Love is here and now you're gone / Mother, you smother me / I guess I'll always love you / I'll turn to stone / It's the same old song / Going down for the third time / Love is in our hearts / Remove the doubt / There's no stopping us now / Heatwave. *(re-iss. Oct81 lp/c; STMS/CSTMS 5014) (cd-iss. Sep95)*

May 67. (7") *(TMG 607) <1107>* **THE HAPPENING. / ALL I KNOW ABOUT YOU** [6] Apr67 [1]

Sep 67. (lp; stereo/mono) *(S+/TML 11054) <659>* **THE SUPREMES SING RODGERS AND HART** [25] Jun67 [20]
– The lady is a tramp / Mountain greenery / This can't be love / Where or when / Lover / My funny valentine / My romance / My heart stood still / Falling in love with love / Thou swell / Dancing on the ceiling / Blue moon. *(cd-iss. Nov87; same)* – (extra tracks).

— (May'67) **CINDY BIRDSONG** (b.15 Dec'39, Camden, New Jersey) – vocals (ex-PATTI LaBELLE & THE BLUEBELLES) repl. BALLARD who went solo

DIANA ROSS & THE SUPREMES

Aug 67. (7") *(TMG 616) <1111>* **REFLECTIONS. / GOING DOWN FOR THE THIRD TIME** [5] [2]

Nov 67. (7") *(TMG 632) <1116>* **IN AND OUT OF LOVE. / I GUESS I'LL ALWAYS LOVE YOU** [13] [9]

Jan 68. (lp<d-lp>; stereo/mono) *(S+/TML 11063) <663>* **DIANA ROSS & THE SUPREMES' GREATEST HITS** (compilation) [1] Sep67 [1]
(re-iss. Jan79 & Jun83)

Mar 68. (lp; stereo/mono) *(S+/TML 11070) <676>* **LIVE AT LONDON'S TALK OF THE TOWN (live)** [6] Sep68 [57]
– With a song in my heart / Stranger than Paradise / Wonderful, wonderful / Without a song / Stop! in the name of love / Come and see about me / My world is empty without you / Baby love / Love is here and now you're gone / More / You keep me hangin' on / Michelle / Yesterday / In and out of love / The lady is a tramp / Let's get away from it all / The happening / Thoroughly modern Millie / Second hand Rose / Mame / Reflections / You're nobody till somebody loves you / I hear a symphony. *(re-iss. Jan80 on 'Music For Pleasure'; MFP 50447)*

Mar 68. (7") *(TMG 650) <1122>* **FOREVER CAME TODAY. / TIME CHANGES THINGS** [28] [28]

Jun 68. (7") *(TMG 662) <1126>* **SOME THINGS YOU NEVER GET USED TO. / YOU'VE BEEN SO WONDERFUL TO ME** [34] [30]

Jul 68. (lp; stereo/mono) *(S+/TML 11073) <665>* **REFLECTIONS** [30] Apr68 [18]
– Reflections / I'm gonna make it (I will wait for you) / Forever came today / I can't make it alone / In and out of love / Bah-bah-bah / What the world needs now is love / Up, up and away / Love (makes me do foolish things) / Then / Misery makes its home in my heart / Ode to Billie Joe. *(re-iss. Mar85 lp/c; WL/WK 72368)*

Nov 68. (lp; stereo/mono) *(S+/TML 11088) <672>* **. . .SING AND PERFORM FUNNY GIRL** (from the musical) [–] Sep68 [ ]

Nov 68. (7") *(TMG 677) <1135>* **LOVE CHILD. / THIS WILL BE THE DAY** [15] Oct68 [1]

Jan 69. (lp; stereo/mono) *(S+/TML 11095) <670>* **LOVE CHILD** [8] Dec68 [14]
– Love child / Keep an eye / How long has the evening train been gone / Does your mama know about me / Honey bee (keep on stinging me) / Something you never get used to / He's my sunny boy / You've never been so wonderful to me / (Don't break these) Chains of love / You ain't living til you're lovin' / I'll set you free / Can't shake it loose. *(re-iss. Aug82 lp/c; STMS/CSTMS 5070)*

— Late 1968, The SUPREMES re-united with The TEMPTATIONS on cross-Atlantic Top 3 hit 'I'M GONNA MAKE YOU LOVE ME'. Throughout 1969, they recorded and released a number of other hit 45's and lp's.

Apr 69. (7") *(TMG 695) <1139>* **I'M LIVIN' IN SHAME. / I'M SO GLAD I GOT SOMEBODY (LIKE YOU AROUND)** [14] Jan69 [10]

Apr 69. (7") *<1146>* **THE COMPOSER. / THE BEGINNING OF THE END** [–] [27]

Jun 69. (lp; stereo/mono) *(S+/TML 11114) <689>* **LET THE SUNSHINE IN** [ ] [24]
– The composer / Everyday people / No matter what sign you are / Hey Western Union man / What becomes of the broken hearted? / I'm livin' in shame / Aquarius (medley: Let the sun shine in (in the flesh failures)- Let the music play / With a child's heart / Discover me (and you'll discover love) / Will this be the day / I'm so glad I got somebody (like you around).

Jul 69. (7") *(TMG 704) <1148>* **NO MATTER WHAT SIGN YOU ARE. / THE YOUNG FOLKS** [37] [31] Jun69 [69]

Dec 69. (7") *(TMG 721) <1156>* **SOMEDAY WE'LL BE TOGETHER. / HE'S MY SUNNY BOY** [13] Oct69 [1]

Jan 70. (lp; stereo/mono) *(S+/TML 11137) <694>* **CREAM OF THE CROP** [ ] Nov69 [33]
– Someday we'll be together / Can't you see it's me / You gave me love / Hey Jude / The young folks / Shadows of society / Loving you is better than ever / When it's to the top (still I won't stop giving you love) / Till Johnny comes / Blowin' in the wind / The beginning of the end.

May 70. (lp) *(STML 11146) <702>* **DIANA ROSS & THE SUPREMES' GREATEST HITS VOL.3** (compilation) [ ] Jan70 [31]
– Reflections / Love is here and now you're gone / Someday we'll be together / Love child / Some things you never get used to / Forever came today / In and out of love / The happening / I'm livin' in shame / No matter what sign you are / The composer. *(re-iss. Jul76, Oct81)*

May 70. (d-lp) *(STML 11154)* <708> **FAREWELL** (final concert 14 Jan'70) [ ] [46]
– T.C.B. / Medley: Stop! in the name of love – Come see about me – My world is empty without you – Baby love / Medley: The lady is a tramp – Let's get away from it all / Love is here and now you're gone / I'm gonna make you love me / Can't take my eyes off you / Reflections / My man / Didn't we / It's alright with me / Big spender / Falling in love with love / Love child / Aquarius – Let the sunshine in (the flesh failures) / The impossible dream / Someday we'll be together / (closing dialogue from group).

The SUPREMES

— when DIANA ROSS left to go solo (Jan'70) she was replaced by **JEAN TERRELL** (b.26 Nov'44, Texas) – lead vocals

Apr 70. (7") *(TMG 735)* <1162> **UP THE LADDER TO THE ROOF. / BILL, WHEN ARE YOU COMING BACK** [6] Mar70 [10]

Jun 70. (lp) *(STML 11157)* <705> **RIGHT ON** [ ] May70 [25]
– Up the ladder on the roof / Then we can try again / Everybody's got the right to love / Wait a minute before you leave me / You move me / But I love you more / I got hurt / Baby baby / Take a closer look at me / Then I met you / Bill, when are you coming back / Loving country.

Jul 70. (7") *(TMG 747)* <1167> **EVERYBODY'S GOT THE RIGHT TO LOVE. / BUT I LOVE YOU MORE** [ ] [21]

Nov 70. (lp) *(STML 11175)* <720> **NEW WAYS BUT LOVE STAYS** [ ] Oct70 [68]
– Together we can make such sweet music / Stoned love / It's time to break down / Bridge over troubled water / I wish I were your mirror / Come together / Is there a place (in his heart for me) / Na na hey hey, kiss him goodbye / Shine on me / Thank him for today.

— late 1970, they collaborated with another 'Motown' group The FOUR TOPS. They were to hit US/UK Top 20 with their version of RIVER DEEP – MOUNTAIN HIGH. A few other hits followed in 1971, accompanied by parent albums THE MAGNIFICENT 7 / THE RETURN OF THE MAGNIFICENT 7 / DYNAMITE

Jan 71. (7") *(TMG 760)* <1172> **STONED LOVE. / SHINE ON ME** [3] Nov70 [7]

Aug 71. (7") *(TMG 782)* <1182> **NATHAN JONES. / HAPPY IS A BUMPY ROAD** [5] May71 [16]

Sep 71. (lp) *(STML 11189)* <737> **TOUCH** [40] Jun71 [85]
– This is the story / Nathan Jones / Here comes the sunrise / Love, it came to me first time / Johnny Raven / Have I lost you / Time and love / Touch / Happy (is a bumpy road) / It's so hard for me to say goodbye. *(cd-iss. Nov93; 530211-2)*

Sep 71. (7") <1190> **TOUCH. / IT'S SO HARD FOR ME TO SAY GOODBYE** [–] [71]

Feb 72. (7") *(TMG 804)* <1195> **FLOY JOY. / THIS IS THE STORY** [9] Jan72 [16]

Jun 72. (lp) *(STMLK 11210)* <751> **FLOY JOY** [ ] May72 [54]
– Your wonderful sweet sweet love / Floy joy / A heart like mine / Over and over / Precious little things / Now the bitter, now the sweet / Automatically sunshine / The wisdom of time / Oh be my love.

Jun 72. (7") *(TMG 821)* <1200> **AUTOMATICALLY SUNSHINE. / PRECIOUS LITTLE THINGS** [10] May72 [37]

— **LYNDA LAWRENCE** – vocals; repl. BIRDSONG who was now married

Jul 72. (7") <1206> **YOUR WONDERFUL, SWEET SWEET LOVE. / THE WISDOM OF TIME** [–] [59]

Aug 72. (7") *(TMG 835)* **YOUR WONDERFUL, SWEET SWEET LOVE. / LOVE IT CAME TO ME THIS TIME** [ ] [–]

Nov 72. (lp) *(STML 11222)* <756> **THE SUPREMES (PRODUCED BY JIM WEBB)** [ ] [ ]
– I guess I'll miss the man / 5:30 plane / Tossin' and turnin' / When can Brown begin / Beyond myself / Silent voices / All I want / Once in the morning / I keep it hid / Paradise / Cheap lovin'.

Mar 73. (7") *(TMG 847)* **BAD WEATHER. / IT'S SO HARD FOR ME TO SAY GOODBYE** [37] [–]

May 73. (7") <1225> **BAD WEATHER. / OH BE MY LOVE** [–] [87]

Jun 73. (7") *(TMG 859)* **TOSSIN' AND TURNIN'. / OH BE MY LOVE** [ ] [–]

Jan 74. (7") *(TMG 884)* <1213> **I GUESS I'LL MISS THE MAN. / OVER AND OVER** [ ] Oct72 [85]

— (Jul'73) **MARY + LYNDA** enlisted newcomer **SCHERRIE PAYNE** (b.14 Nov'44) – vocals repl. TERRELL

Jun 75. (lp) *(STML 11293)* <828> **THE SUPREMES** [ ] [ ]
– He's my man / Eary morning love / Where is it I belong / It's been said before / This is why I believe in you / You can't stop a girl in love / Colour my world blue / Give out, but don't give up / Where do I go from here / You turn me around.

Aug 75. (7") *(TMG 950)* <1358> **HE'S MY MAN. / GIVE OUT, BUT DON'T GIVE UP** [ ] [ ]

Nov 75. (7") *(TMG 1012)* **EARLY MORNING LOVE. / WHERE IS IT I BELONG** [ ] [–]

— (1976) **SUSAYNE GREENE** – vocals; repl. CINDY who had repl. LYNDA

— former member FLORENCE BALLARD tragically died on 22nd of Feb'76

May 76. (7") <1391> **I'M GONNA LET MY HEART DO THE WALKING. / EARLY MORNING LOE** [–] [40]

Jun 76. (lp) *(STML 12027)* <863> **HIGH ENERGY** [ ] May76 [42]
– High energy / I'm gonna let my heart do the walking / Only you (can love me like you love me) / You keep me moving on / Don't let my teardrops better you / Till the boat sails away / I don't want to lose you / You're what's missing in my life.

Jul 76. (7") *(TMG 1029)* **I'M GONNA LET MY HEART DO THE WALKING. / COLOUR MY WORLD BLUE** [ ] [–]

Nov 76. (7") <1407> **YOU'RE MY DRIVING WHEEL. / YOU'RE WHAT'S MISSING IN MY LIFE** [–] [85]

Dec 76. (lp) *(STML 12047)* <873> **MARY, SCHERRIE & SUSAYNE** [ ] [ ]
– You're my driving wheel / Sweet dream machine / Let yourself go / Come into my life / We should be closer together / I don't want to be tied down / You are the heart of me / Love I never knew you could feel so good.

Feb 77. (7") <1415> **LET YOURSELF GO. / YOU ARE THE HEART OF ME** [–] [ ]

Mar 77. (7") *(TMG 1064)* **LOVE I NEVER KNEW YOU COULD FEEL SO GOOD. / THIS IS WHY I BELIEVE IN YOU** [ ] [–]

— **KAREN JACKSON** – vocals; repl. MARY WILSON who later toured as MARY WILSON & THE SUPREMES; the real SUPREMES split 1977. On 16th May '83, DIANA, MARY and CINDY re-united for one-off Motown anniversary gig

– (selective) compilations, etc. –

Note; on 'Tamla Motown' unless otherwise mentioned

Jun 74. (t-lp) *(TMSP 6001)* <794> **ANTHOLOGY (1962-1969)** [ ] [66]
(d-cd-iss. Apr93)

Jul 74. (7") *(TMG 915)* **BABY LOVE. / ASK ANY GIRL** [12] [–]

Sep 77. (lp/c) *(EMTV/CEMTV 5)* **DIANA ROSS & THE SUPREMES' 20 GOLDEN GREATS** [1] [–]
(re-iss. Oct81, cd-iss. May86)

Jul 86. (t-lp/d-c/d-cd) <5381> **25th ANNIVERSARY** [–] [ ]

Oct 86. (cd) *(ZD 72423)* **COMPACT COMMAND PERFORMANCES – 20 GREATEST HITS** [ ] [ ]
– When the lovelight starts shining through his eyes / Where did our love go / Baby love / Come see about me / My world is empty without you / Stop in the name of love / Back in my arms again / I hear a symphony / You can't hurry love / Love is like an itching in my heart / You keep me hangin' on / Love is here now you're gone / Reflections / Love child / I'll try something new / I'm gonna make you love me / Someday we'll be together / The ladder to the roof / Stoned love / Nathan Jones.

Nov 86. (cd) *(ZD 72459)* **WHERE DID OUR LOVE GO. / I HEAR A SYMPHONY** [ ] [–]

Nov 86. (cd) *(ZD 73485)* **LOVE CHILD / SUPREMES A GO-GO** [ ] [–]

Dec 86. (cd) *(ZD 72496)* **LET THE SUNSHINE IN / CREAM OF THE CROP** [ ] [–]

Jan 89. (lp/c/cd) *(ZL/ZK/ZD 72701)* **LOVE SUPREME** [10] [ ]
– You can't hurry love / Baby love / The happening / Automatically sunshine / Up the ladder to the roof / Stoned love / Where did our love go? / Love is here and now you're gone / Reflections / In and out of love / Stop! in the name of love / Come see about me / I'm gonna make you love me / Love child / I'm living in shame / Floy joy / You keep me hangin' on / I second that emotion / Nathan Jones / Someday we'll be together.

Feb 89. (7") *(ZB 41963)* **STOP! IN THE NAME OF LOVE. / AUTOMATICALLY SUNSHINE** [62] [–]
(12"+=) *(ZT 41964)* – Automatically sunshine medley.

Oct 98. (d-cd/d-c) *Polygram TV; (530961-2/-4)* **40 GOLDEN MOTOWN GREATS** [35] [–]

DIANA ROSS & THE SUPREMES WITH THE TEMPTATIONS

Jan 69. (7") *(TMG 685)* <1137> **I'M GONNA MAKE YOU LOVE ME. / A PLACE IN THE SUN** [3] Nov68 [2]

Jan 69. (lp; stereo/mono) *(S+/TML 11096)* <679> **DIANA ROSS & THE SUPREMES JOIN THE TEMPTATIONS** 1 Nov68 2
– I'm gonna make you love me / My guy / My girl / Uptight (everything's alright) / Sweet inspiration / I'll try something new / Ain't no mountain high enough / I second that emotion / Why must we fall in love / For better or worse / The weight / I'll be doggone / Stubborn kind of fellow. *(re-iss. Jul81 & Oct82)*

Mar 69. (7",7"red) <1146> **I'LL TRY SOMETHING NEW. / THE WAY YOU DO THE THINGS YOU DO** – 25

Jun 69. (lp; stereo/mono) *(S+/TML 11110)* <682> **TCB** (original soundtrack TV) 11 Dec68 1
– T.C.B. / Stop, in the name of love / You keep me hangin' on / Get ready / The way you do the things you do / A taste of honey / Eleanor Rigby / Do you know the way to San Jose / Mrs.Robinson / Respect / Somewhere / Ain't too proud to beg / Hello young lovers / For once in my life / I know I'm losing you / With a song in my heart / Come see about me / My world is empty without you / Baby love / I hear a symphony / The impossible dream. *(re-iss. Mar82)*

Jul 69. (7";w-drawn) <1150> **STUBBORN KIND OF FELLOW. / TRY IT BABY** – –

Sep 69. (7") *(TMG 709)* **I SECOND THAT EMOTION. / THE WAY YOU DO THE THINGS YOU DO** 18 –

Sep 69. (7") <1153> **THE WEIGHT. / FOR BETTER OR WORSE** – 46

Nov 69. (lp) <699> **ON BROADWAY** (TV Show) – 38

Feb 70. (lp) *(STML 11122)* <692> **TOGETHER** 28 Oct69 28
– Stubborn kind of fellow / I'll be doggone / The weight / Ain't nothing like the real thing / Uptight (everything's alright) / Sing a simple song / My guy, my girl / For better or worse / Can't take my eyes off you / Why (must we fall in love).

Mar 70. (7") *(TMG 730)* **WHY (MUST WE FALL IN LOVE). / UPTIGHT (EVERYTHING'S ALRIGHT)** 31 –

SUPREMES & THE FOUR TOPS

Nov 70. (7") <1173> **RIVER DEEP – MOUNTAIN HIGH. / TOGETHER WE CAN MAKE SUCH SWEET MUSIC** – 14

Jun 71. (7") *(TMG 777)* **RIVER DEEP – MOUNTAIN HIGH. / IT'S GOT TO BE A MIRACLE** 11 –

Jun 71. (lp) *(STML 11179)* <717> **THE MAGNIFICENT 7** 6 Oct70
– River deep – mountain high / Knock on my door / For your love / Without the one you love / Reach out and touch (somebody's hand) / Stoned soul picnic / Baby (you've got what it takes) / Ain't nothing like the real thing / Everyday people / It's got to be a miracle (this thing called love) / A taste of honey / Together we can make such sweet music. *(re-iss. Oct81)*

Nov 71. (7") *(TMG 793)* <1181> **YOU GOTTA HAVE LOVE IN YOUR HEART. / I'M GLAD ABOUT IT** 25 Jul71 55

Nov 71. (lp) *(STML 11192)* <736> **THE RETURN OF THE MAGNIFICENT 7** Jun71

Jan 72. (lp) *(STML 11203)* <745> **DYNAMITE**
– It's impossible / The bigger you love (the harder you fall) / Hello stranger / Love the one you're with / Good lovin' ain't easy to come by / Melodie / If / If I could build my whole world around you / Don't let me lose this dream / Do you love me just a little honey.

SWEET

Formed: London, England ... early 1968 as SWEETSHOP, by BRIAN CONNOLLY and MICK TUCKER (former members of Harrow bubblegum-pop band, WAINWRIGHT'S GENTLEMEN). Completing the line-up with STEVE PRIEST and FRANK TORPY, SWEET released a one-off 45 for 'Fontana', 'SLOW MOTION', before MICK STEWART replaced TORPY. A further three throwaway pop singles (on 'Parlophone') followed with little interest, prior to the band finding a more steady guitarist in ANDY SCOTT and hooking up with the now famous hitmaking/songwriting team of (NICKY) CHINN and (MIKE) CHAPMAN through producer PHIL WAINMAN. Signing to 'R.C.A.', SWEET emerged from their sticky patch with a handful of chartbustin' pure pop nuggets between 1971/72, including 'FUNNY FUNNY', 'CO-CO', 'POPPA JOE', 'LITTLE WILLY' (also a Top 3 Stateside success!) and 'WIG WAM BAM'. One of the pivotal bands of the glam-pop era, SWEET, as with their music, took sugary fashion excess to gender-bending new limits. Early in '73, they followed in the high-heeled footstompin' steps of GARY GLITTER, SLADE, etc, by adopting a slightly harder-edged anthemic approach for the chart-topping 'BLOCKBUSTER'. They repeated this winning formula over the next twelve months, three more singles, 'HELLRAISER', 'BALLROOM BLITZ' and 'TEENAGE RAMPAGE' enjoying a tantalisingly close shave with the No.1 spot. Surprisingly banned from many British ballrooms/concert halls, SWEET subsequently toning down their OTT effeminate image for a more mature "harder" look. The resulting album, 'SWEET FANNY ADAMS' hit the UK Top 30, although no tracks were issued as singles. However, they did score a Top 10 hit later that year with 'THE SIX TEENS' (they also suffered their first flop in some years, 'TURN IT DOWN'), both songs taken from another Top 30 album, 'DESOLATION BOULEVARD'. Early in '75, now without CHINN and CHAPMAN, they particially resurrected their flagging public profile with the self-penned 'FOX ON THE RUN', the single hitting No.2 (and later in the year No.5 in America, 'BALLROOM BLITZ' having achieved a similar feat a few months previous). Alienated from most of their former teenbop fans, SWEET's career began to turn sour, that is, until 'LOVE IS LIKE OXYGEN' breathed some fresh air into their newfound AOR/hard-rock sound, the single a Top 10 transatlantic smash. The internal tensions that had simmered through SWEET's career finally boiled over in 1979, CONNOLLY (younger brother of actor, MARK 'Taggart' McMANUS) striking out on a solo career, while the remaining members recruited GARY MOBERLEY for a handful of forgettable albums, including the aptly-titled 'IDENTITY CRISIS'. The 80's were characterised by countless reformations, tussles over the group name, etc, SWEET effectively finished as a chart commodity and opting instead to trawl the cabaret circuit while SCOTT released a few records under the ANDY SCOTT'S SWEET moniker. Meanwhile, CONNOLLY's health was in terminal decline, any SWEET fans witnessing the TV documentary no doubt shocked by his ravaged appearance. Sadly, CONNOLLY died of heart failure on the 10th of February '97 (he'd previously survived a number of heart attacks) shortly after the programme was made.

Best CD compilation: BALLROOM BLITZ – THE VERY BEST OF SWEET (*8)

BRIAN CONNOLLY (b. BRIAN McMANUS, 5 Oct'45, Hamilton, Scotland) – vocals (ex-WAINWRIGHT'S GENTLEMEN) / **STEVE PRIEST** (b.23 Feb'50, Hayes, Middlesex, England) – bass / **MICK TUCKER** (b.17 Jul'49, Harlesden, London) – drums, vocals (ex-WAINWRIGHT'S GENTLEMEN) / **FRANK TORPY** – guitar

Fontana | not iss.

Jul 68. (7") *(TF 958)* **SLOW MOTION. / IT'S LONELY OUT THERE** –

— **MICK STEWART** – guitar repl. FRANK

Parlophone | not iss.

Sep 69. (7") *(R 5803)* **LOLLIPOP MAN. / TIME** –

Jan 70. (7") *(R 5826)* **ALL YOU'LL EVER GET FROM ME. / THE JUICER** –
(re-iss. May71 flipped over; R 5902)

Jun 70. (7") *(R 5848)* **GET ON THE LINE. / MR. McGALLAGHER** –

— **ANDY SCOTT** (b.30 Jun'51, Wrexham, Wales) – guitar (ex-ELASTIC BAND) repl. STEWART. (employed session people in 71-72)

R.C.A. | Bell

Mar 71. (7") *(RCA 2051)* **FUNNY FUNNY. / YOU'RE NOT WRONG FOR LOVING ME** 13

Jun 71. (7") *(RCA 2087)* **CO-CO. / DONE ME WRONG ALRIGHT** [2] [–]
Jul 71. (7") *<45126>* **CO-CO. / YOU'RE NOT WRONG FOR LOVING ME** [–] [99]
Oct 71. (7") *(RCA 2121)* **ALEXANDER GRAHAM BELL. / SPOTLIGHT** [33] [–]
Nov 71. (lp) *(SF 8288)* **FUNNY HOW SWEET CO-CO CAN BE** [ ] [–]
– Co-Co / Chop chop / Reflections / Honeysuckle love / Santa Monica sunshine / Daydream / Funny funny / Tom Tom turnaround / Jeanie / Sunny sleeps late / Spotlight / Done me wrong all right.
Jan 72. (7") *(RCA 2164)* **POPPA JOE. / JEANIE** [11] [–]
Jun 72. (7") *(RCA 2225) <45251>* **LITTLE WILLY. / MAN FROM MECCA** [4] Jan73 [3]
Sep 72. (7") *(RCA 2260)* **WIG-WAM BAM. / NEW YORK CONNECTION** [4] Dec73 [ ]
Dec 72. (lp) *(SF 8316)* **SWEET'S BIGGEST HITS** (compilation) [ ] [–]
– Wig-wam bam / Little Willy / Done me wrong alright / Poppa Joe / Funny funny / Co-Co / Alexander Graham Bell / Chop chop / You're not wrong for loving me / Jeanie / Spotlight / Tom Tom turnaround.
Jan 73. (7") *(RCA 2305) <45361>* **BLOCKBUSTER. / NEED A LOT OF LOVIN'** [1] Jun73 [73]
Apr 73. (7") *(RCA 2357)* **HELL RAISER. / BURNING** [2] [ ]
Jul 73. (lp) *<1125>* **THE SWEET** [–] [ ]
– Little Willy / New York connection / Wig-wam bam / Done me wrong alright / Hell raiser / Blockbuster / Need a lot of lovin' / Man from Mecca / Spotlight / You're not wrong for loving me. *<re-iss. 1976 on 'Kory'; KK 3009>*

R.C.A. Capitol

Sep 73. (7") *(RCA 2403)* **BALLROOM BLITZ. / ROCK'N'ROLL DISGRACE** [2] [–]
Jan 74. (7") *(LPBO 5004)* **TEENAGE RAMPAGE. / OWN UP, TAKE A LOOK AT YOURSELF** [2] [ ]
Apr 74. (lp) *(LPLI 5039)* **SWEET FANNY ADAMS** [27] [–]
– Set me free / Heartbreak today / No you don't / Rebel rouser / Peppermint twist / Sweet F.A. / Restless / Into the night / AC-DC.
Jul 74. (7") *(LPBO 5037)* **THE SIX TEENS. / BURN ON THE FLAME** [9] [ ]
Nov 74. (7") *(RCA 2480)* **TURN IT DOWN. / SOMEONE ELSE WILL** [41] [ ]
Nov 74. (lp) *(LPLI 5080) <11395>* **DESOLATION BOULEVARD** [ ] Jul75 [25]
– The six teens / Solid gold brass / Turn it down / Medusa / Lady Starlight / Man with the golden arm / Fox on the run / Breakdown / My generation. *<US – version incl. tracks from 'SWEET FANNY ADAMS'> (re-iss. Feb90 on 'Castle' cd/lp; CLA CD/LP 170)*
Mar 75. (7") *(RCA 2524)* **FOX ON THE RUN. / MISS DEMEANOR** [2] [–]
Jun 75. (7") *<4055>* **BALLROOM BLITZ. / RESTLESS** [–] [5]
Jul 75. (7") *(RCA 2578)* **ACTION. / SWEET F.A.** [15] [–]
Nov 75. (d-lp) *(SPC 0001)* **STRUNG UP** (live rec. Dec'73 + hits, etc.) [ ] [–]
– Hell raiser / Burning / Someone else will / Rock'n'roll disgrace / Need a lot of lovin' / Done me wrong alright / You're not wrong for loving me / The man with the golden arm / Action / Fox on the run / Set me free / Miss Deameanour / Ballroom blitz / Burn on the flame / Solid gold brass / The six teens / I wanna be committed / Blockbuster.
Nov 75. (7") *<4157>* **FOX ON THE RUN. / BURN ON THE FLAME** [–] [5]
Jan 76. (7") *(RCA 2641)* **THE LIES IN YOUR EYES. / COCKROACH** [35] [ ]
Feb 76. (7") *<4220>* **ACTION. / MEDUSA** [–] [20]
Mar 76. (lp) *(RS 1036) <11496>* **GIVE US A WINK** [ ] [27]
– The lies in your eyes / Cockroach / Keep it in / 4th of July / Action / Yesterday's rain / White mice / Healer. *(re-iss. Aug91 on 'Repertoire' cd+=)(pic-lp; REP4084WZ)(REP 2084)* – Fox on the run / Lady Starlight / Sweet Fanny Adams / Miss Demeaner.
Oct 76. (7") *(RCA 2748)* **LOST ANGELS. / FUNK IT UP** [ ] [ ]
Feb 77. (7") *(PB 5001)* **FEVER OF LOVE. / DISTINCT LACK OF ANCIENT** [ ] [–]
Mar 77. (lp/c) *(PL/PK 25072) <11636>* **OFF THE RECORD** [ ] [ ]
– Fever of love / Lost angels / Midnight to daylight / Windy city / Live for today / She gimme lovin' / Laura Lee / Hard times / Funk it up (David's song). *(pic-cd.Aug91 on 'Repertoire'+=; REP4085WZ)* – Distinct lack of ancient / Stairway to the stars / Why don't you do it to me.
Mar 77. (7") *<4429>* **FEVER OF LOVE. / HEARTBREAK TODAY** [–] [ ]
Jul 77. (7",12") *<4454>* **FUNK IT UP (DAVID'S SONG). / ('A'disco mix)** [–] [88]
Aug 77. (7") *(PB 5046)* **STAIRWAY TO THE STARS. / WHY DON'T YOU DO IT TO ME** [ ] [–]
Oct 77. (lp/c) *(PL/PK 25111)* **SWEET'S GOLDEN GREATS** (compilation) [ ] [–]
– Blockbuster / Hell raiser / Ballroom blitz / Teenage rampage / The six teens / Turn it down / Fox on the run / Action / Lost angels / The lies in your eyes / Fever of love / Stairway to the stars.

Polydor Capitol

Jan 78. (7") *(POSP 1) <4549>* **LOVE IS LIKE OXYGEN. / COVER GIRL** [9] Feb78 [8]
Jan 78. (lp/c) *(POLD/+C 5001) <11744>* **LEVEL HEADED** [ ] [52]
– Dream on / Love is like oxygen / California nights / Strong love / Fountain / Anthem No.1 / Silverbird / Lettres d'amour / Anthem No.2 / Air on "A" tape loop. *(cd-iss. Aug91 on 'Repertoire'+=; REP 4234WP)* – Love is like oxygen (single) / Cover girl / California nights (single) / Show the way.
Jul 78. (7") *<4610>* **CALIFORNIA NIGHTS. / DREAM ON** [–] [76]

—— **GARY MOBERLEY** – keyboards repl. CONNOLLY who went solo & later formed The NEW SWEET. (ANDY SCOTT was now on lead vocals)

Mar 79. (7") *(POSP 36)* **CALL ME. / WHY DON'T YOU** [ ] [–]
Apr 79. (7") *<4730>* **MOTHER EARTH. / WHY DON'T YOU** [–] [ ]
Aug 79. (7") *(POSP 73)* **BIG APPLE WALTZ. / WHY DON'T YOU** [ ] [–]
Oct 79. (lp/c) *(POLD/+C 5022) <11929>* **CUT ABOVE THE REST** [ ] Apr79 [ ]
– Call me / Play all night / Big Apple waltz / Dorian Gray / Discophony / Eye games / Mother Earth / Hold me / Stay with me.
Apr 80. (7") *(POSP 131)* **GIVE THE LADY SOME RESPECT. / TALL GIRLS** [ ] [–]
Apr 80. (lp/c) *(POLS/+C 1021) <12106>* **WATER'S EDGE** (US-title 'SWEET IV') [ ] [ ]
– Sixties man / Getting in the mood for love / Tell the truth / Own up / Too much talking / Thank you for loving me / At midnight / Water's edge / Hot shot gambler / Give the lady some respect.
Sep 80. (7") *(POSP 160)* **THE SIXTIES MAN. / OH YEAH** [ ] [–]
Sep 80. (7") *<4908>* **THE SIXTIES MAN. / WATER'S EDGE** [–] [ ]

—— **MICK STEWART** – guitar returned to guest on next album.

Nov 82. (lp) *(2311 179)* **IDENTITY CRISIS** [ ] [–]
– Identity crisis / New shoes / Two into one / Love is the cure / It makes me wonder / Hey mama / Falling in love / I wish you would / Strange girl.

—— They had already split Spring 1981, with PRIEST going to the States and SCOTT going into production for heavy metal bands like IRON MAIDEN. He also went solo (see further below). The SWEET re-formed in the mid-80's, with SCOTT, TUCKER plus **PAUL MARIO DAY** – vocals (ex-WILD FIRE) / **PHIL LANZON** – keyboards (ex-GRAND PRIX) / **MAL McNULTY** – bass repl. PRIEST

—— CONNOLLY died of heart failure in the mid 90's

– compilations, etc. –

Dec 70. (lp; one-side by The PIPKINS) *Music For Pleasure; (MFP 5248)* **GIMME DAT THING** [ ] [–]
Jul 78. (lp) *Camden-RCA; (CDS 1168)* **THE SWEET** [ ] [–]
Jun 80. (7"ep) *R.C.A.; (PE 5226)* **FOX ON THE RUN / HELLRAISER. / BLOCKBUSTER / BALLROOM BLITZ** [ ] [–]
Aug 81. (7") *RCA Gold; (524)* **BLOCKBUSTER. / HELLRAISER** [ ] [–]
May 82. (7") *RCA Gold; (551)* **BALLROOM BLITZ. / WIG-WAM BAM** [ ] [–]
Aug 84. (pic-lp/lp) *Anagram; (P+/GRAM 16)* **SWEET 16 – IT'S . . . IT'S . . . SWEET'S HITS** [49] [–]
Sep 84. (7") *Anagram; (ANA 27)* **THE SIX TEENS. / ACTION** [ ] [–]
(12"+=) *(12ANA 27)* – Teenage rampage.
Dec 84. (7"/12") *Anagram; (ANA/12ANA 28)* **IT'S . . . IT'S . . . THE SWEET MIX (Medley; Blockbuster – Fox on the run – Teenage rampage – Hell raiser – Ballroom blitz). / FOX ON THE RUN** [45] [–]
May 85. (7"/12") *Anagram; (ANA/12ANA 29)* **SWEET 2TH – THE WIG-WAM WILLY MIX. / THE TEEN ACTION MIX** [ ] [–]
Apr 87. (7") *Old Gold; (OG 9707)* **BLOCKBUSTER. / LITTLE WILLY** [ ] [–]
Apr 87. (7") *Old Gold; (OG 9709)* **FOX ON THE RUN. / BALLROOM BLITZ** [ ] [–]

Jul 87. (cd/lp) *Zebra; (CDM+/ZEB 11)* **HARD CENTRES – THE ROCK YEARS** –
(re-iss. cd Oct95; CDMZEB 11)
Jan 88. (7") *Old Gold; (OG 9760)* **WIG-WAM BAM. / CO-CO** –
Jan 88. (7") *Old Gold; (OG 9762)* **TEENAGE RAMPAGE. / HELLRAISER** –
Nov 89. (7") *R.C.A.; (PB 43337)* **WIG-WAM BAM. / LITTLE WILLY** –
Dec 89. (lp/c/cd) *R.C.A.; (NL/NK/ND 74313)* **BLOCKBUSTERS** –
– Ballroom blitz / Hell raiser / New York connection / Little Willy / Burning / Need a lot of lovin' / Wig-wam bam / Blockbuster / Rock'n'roll disgrace / Chop chop / Alexander Graham Bell / Poppa Joe / Co-Co / Funny funny.
Dec 89. (d-lp/c/cd) *Castle; (CCS LP/MC/CD 230)* **SWEET COLLECTION** –
Jul 92. (cd-ep) *Old Gold; (OG 6174)* **WIG-WAM BAM / CO-CO / LITTLE WILLY** –
Feb 93. (cd) *Receiver; (RRCD 169)* **ROCKIN' THE RAINBOW** –
Feb 93. Receiver; (cd) *(RRCD 171)* **LAND OF HOPE AND GLORY** –
Jul 93. (cd) *Repertoire; (REP 4140WZ)* **FIRST RECORDINGS 1968-1971** –
Dec 93. (cd) *Receiver; (RRCD 175)* **LIVE FOR TODAY** –
Jul 94. (cd) *Receiver; (RRCD 189)* **BREAKDOWN – THE SWEET LIVE (live)** –
Nov 94. (cd) *Start;* **IN CONCERT** –
Apr 95. (cd) *Receiver; (RRCD 198)* **SET ME FREE** –
Jul 95. (cd) *Aim; (AIM 1041)* **GREATEST HITS LIVE** –
Jan 96. (cd/c) *Polygram; (<535001-2/-4>)* **BALLROOM HITZ – THE VERY BEST OF SWEET** 15
Jan 96. (cd) *Happy Price; (HP 9346-2)* **IN CONCERT** –
Jan 96. (cd) *Music De-Luxe; (MDCD 013)* **BLOCKBUSTER (live on stage)** –
Aug 96. (cd) *KFG; (CDEC 5)* **HITZ, BLITZ, GLITZ** –

□ SWEET 75 (see under ⇒ NIRVANA)

□ David SYLVIAN (see under ⇒ JAPAN)

SYSTEM OF A DOWN

Formed: Los Angeles, California, USA . . . late '94 by expatriot Armenians, SERJ TANKIAN (looks like JELLO BIAFRA with an afro hairdo), DARON MALAKIAN and SHAVO ODADJIAN, the trio almost immediately adding JOHN DOLMAYAN. Produced by RICK RUBIN, their '98 eponymous debut revealed them to be anthemic and politically emotional noise-merchants in the mould of COAL CHAMBER or FAITH NO MORE, stretching punk-metal into jazzy Armenian folk. Largely overlooked until the release of the single 'CHOP SUEY', SYSTEM OF A DOWN's album 'TOXICITY' (2001) smashed the barriers of modern rock, vocalist TANKIAN's scattering lyrics torn between religious connotation and just sheer madness. The group differed from the normal Nu-metal fare; some of the guitar playing was not dissimilar to MOGWAI's more sonic releases, whereas the songs blasted the barriers of popular rock, even interesting the slightly more mellow ARTHUR BAKER into including the group on a recent collection. SYSTEM OF A DOWN proved conclusively they were operating way beyond the confines of anything as restrictive as nu-metal with 'STEAL THIS ALBUM!' (2002), ostensibly an odds'n'sods collection which actually held together better than most of their contemporaries regular albums.

Album rating: SYSTEM OF A DOWN (*8) / TOXICITY (*8) / STEAL THIS ALBUM! collection (*4)

SERJ TANKIAN – vocals / **DARON MALAKIAN** – guitar / **SHAVO ODADJIAN** – bass / **JOHN DOLMAYAN** – drums

American – Columbia / American – Sony

Oct 98. (cd) *(491209-2) <68924>* **SYSTEM OF A DOWN** Sep98
– Suite-pee / Know / Sugar / Suggestions / Spiders / Ddevil / Soil / War? / Mind / Peephole / CUBErt / Darts / P.L.U.C.K. *(re-iss. Aug01; same)*
May 99. (7") *(667478-7)* **SUGAR. / WAR? (live)** –
(cd-s+=) *(667478-2)* – Sugar (live) / Suite-pee (live).
Aug 01. (cd/lp) *(501534-2/-1) <62240>* **TOXICITY** 13 1
– Prison song / Needles / Deer dance / Jet pilot / X / Chop suey / Bounce / Forest / Atwa / Science / Shimmy / Toxicity / Psycho / Aerials. *(bonus track +=)* – Arto. *(d-cd-iss. Jul02 +=; 508383-2)* – Toxicity (video) / Chop suey (live video) / Prison song (live) / Bounce (live).
Oct 01. (7") *(672034-7) <radio>* **CHOP SUEY. / JOHNNY** 17 Dec01 76
(cd-s+=) *(672034-2)* – Know (live).
(cd-s) *(672034-5)* – ('A'side) / Sugar (live) / War (live) / ('A'-video).
Mar 02. (7") *(672502-7) <radio>* **TOXICITY. / STORAGED** 25 70
(cd-s) *(672502-2)* – ('A'side) / X (live) / Suggestions (live) / ('A'-video).
(cd-s) *(672502-5)* – ('A'side) / Marmalade / Metro (explicit).
Jul 02. (7") *(672869-7) <radio>* **AERIALS. / SNOWBLIND** 34 55
(cd-s+=) *(672869-5)* – Streamline / Sugar (live).
(cd-s) *(672869-2)* – ('A'side) / Toxicity (live) / P.L.U.C.K. (live) / ('A'video).
Nov 02. (d-cd) *(510248-2) <87062>* **STEAL THIS ALBUM!** (demos, etc.) 56 15
– Chic 'n' Stu / Innervision / Bubbles / Boom! / Nuguns / A.D.D. / Mr. Jack / I-E-A-I-A-I-O / 36 / Pictures / Highway song / Fuck the system / Ego brain / Thetawaves / Roulette / Streamline.

TINA TURNER

TALKING HEADS

Formed: Manhattan, New York, USA . . . May'75 by former art & design students DAVID BYRNE, TINA WEYMOUTH and CHRIS FRANTZ. Their first gig was supporting The RAMONES at the CBGB's club in New York, circa mid '75. The band were soon spotted by Seymour Stein, who duly signed them to his new US label, 'Sire' and in late 1976 they released their debut 45, 'LOVE GOES TO A BUILDING ON FIRE'. Although this flopped, the following year's '77' album sold well enough to reach the lower regions of the album chart. The record's centerpiece was the spastic, new wave-funk of 'PSYCHO KILLER', BYRNE's compelling eccentricity making the number a live favourite. By this point the band were well established as one of the leading lights in the New York art-punk scene, firing subversively intelligent broadsides at the overblown rock establishment. The follow-up album, 'MORE SONGS ABOUT BUILDINGS AND FOOD' (1978) was produced by BRIAN ENO whom the band had met on a British tour the previous year. Sharing ENO's disregard for the workmanlike, the band were spurred on to new heights, FRANTZ and WEYMOUTH fashioning intricate but gloriously funky rhythms, BYRNE turning around Al Green's 'TAKE ME TO THE RIVER' with his wonderfully idiosyncratic vocal style. ENO stuck around for 'FEAR OF MUSIC' (1979), an album which saw them experimenting with complex ethnic rythms and instrumentation, an area that was further explored on the BYRNE/ENO collaboration, 'MY LIFE IN THE BUSH OF GHOSTS' (1981). Bolstered by a crew of esteemed session musicians, the band cut 'REMAIN IN LIGHT' (1980). Swathed in giddy funk and rooted by African polyrhythms, the album spawned the wondrous 'ONCE IN A LIFETIME' single. The band had now established themselves as a top live draw and were notching up increasing record sales, although it was to be three years before the next TALKING HEADS studio album as the band divided their time between solo projects and live work. Worth the wait, 'SPEAKING IN TONGUES' (1983) was another classy outing, spawning the trance-rock of the 'SLIPPERY PEOPLE' (1984) single and the jittery 'BURNING DOWN THE HOUSE' (1983) which went top 10 in the UK. The Jonathon Demme-directed concert movie 'STOP MAKING SENSE' contained some of the most innovative live footage ever commited to celluloid and further increased The TALKING HEADS' burgeoning reputation. Another groundbreaking piece of film came with the video for 'ROAD TO NOWHERE' (1985), the band's biggest chart hit to date. Its parent album, 'LITTLE CREATURES' (1985), marked a return to a more basic sound. From this point on, the band began to spend an increasing amount of time on solo projects. 'TRUE STORIES' (1986) was a patchy TALKING HEADS version of the soundtrack to the DAVID BYRNE film of the same name while 'NAKED' (1986) came on like an over-produced version of 'REMAIN IN LIGHT'. Following this album, the various 'HEADS went on to do their own thing, BYRNE concentrating on his solo career. The band officially split in 1991, although The HEADS (as WEYMOUTH, FRANTZ and HARRISON were now known) made a comeback album of sorts in '96 entitled 'NO TALKING, JUST HEAD', a record that utilised an array of vocal talent including SHAUN RYDER on the minor hit single, 'DON'T TAKE MY KINDNESS FOR WEAKNESS'. One of the more recent and arguably more compelling BYRNE solo releases was 2003's 'LEAD US NOT INTO TEMPTATION', the soundtrack for the film version of Alex Trocchi's 'Young Adam'. You might say BYRNE went back to his roots in a sense, collaborating with Scottish artists such as MOGWAI and BELLE & SEBASTIAN to create a glowering, autumnal, largely instrumental song cycle perfectly suited to the movie's grainy Caledonian-noir. TOM TOM CLUB also re-emerged in 2002 with 'LIVE @ THE CLUBHOUSE', an animated concert set drawing largely from 2000's 'THE GOOD, THE BAD AND THE FUNKY'. • **Songwriters:** Group compositions except; TAKE ME TO THE RIVER (Al Green) / SLIPPERY PEOPLE (Staple Singers). TOM TOM CLUB:- UNDER THE BOARDWALK (Drifters) / FEMME FATALE (Velvet Underground) / YOU SEXY THING (Hot Chocolate). DAVID BYRNE: – GREENBACK DOLLAR (Hoyt Axton) / GIRLS ON MY MIND (Toquinnho Vinicius) / DON'T FENCE ME IN (Cole Porter). • **Trivia:** FRANTZ and WEYMOUTH (later TOM TOM CLUB) married on the 18th of June '77. BYRNE produced The B-52's on their 1982 album, 'Mesopotamia' and FUN BOY THREE on their 1983, 'Waiting' album. HARRISON produced The VIOLENT FEMMES on 1986 album, 'The Blind Leading The Naked'. TOM TOM CLUB started out producing in 1988 with ZIGGY MARLEY, later working with HAPPY MONDAYS.

Album rating: TALKING HEADS '77 (*9) / MORE SONGS ABOUT BUILDINGS AND FOOD (*8) / FEAR OF MUSIC (*8) / REMAIN IN LIGHT (*8) / THE NAME OF THIS BAND IS TALKING HEADS (*6) / SPEAKING IN TONGUES (*7) / STOP MAKING SENSE (*7) / LITTLE CREATURES (*7) / TRUE STORIES soundtrack (*5) / NAKED (*5) / ONCE IN A LIFETIME – THE BEST OF TALKING HEADS compilation (*9) / Tom Tom Club: TOM TOM CLUB (*5) / CLOSE TO THE BONE (*4) / BOOM BOOM CHI BOOM BOOM (*3) / DARK SNEAK LOVE ACTION (*3) / THE GOOD, THE BAD AND THE FUNKY (*6) / LIVE @ THE CLUBHOUSE (*6) / Jerry Harrison: THE RED AND THE BLACK (*4) / CASUAL GODS (*4) / WALK ON WATER (*4) / Heads: NO TALKING, JUST HEADS (*4) / David Byrne: SONGS FROM 'THE CATHERINE WHEEL' (*6) / MUSIC FOR THE KNEE PLAYS (*6) / REI MOMO (*7) / THE FOREST soundtrack (*4) / UH-OH (*5) / DAVID BYRNE (*4) / FEELINGS (*5) / LOOK INTO THE EYEBALL (*5) / LEAD US NOT INTO TEMPTATION (*7)

DAVID BYRNE (b.14 May'52, Dumbarton, Scotland) – vocals, guitar / **TINA WEYMOUTH** (b.22 Nov'50, Coronado, Calif.) – bass, vocals / **CHRIS FRANTZ** (b. CHARLTON CHRISTOPHER FRANTZ, 8 May'51, Fort Campbell, Kentucky) – drums

		Sire	Sire
Feb 77.	(7") *(6078 604)* *<737>* **LOVE GOES TO A BUILDING ON FIRE. / NEW FEELING**	☐	☐

—— added **JERRY HARRISON** (b.21 Feb'49, Milwaukee, Wisconsin) – guitar, keyboards (ex-JONATHAN RICHMAN & THE MODERN LOVERS)

Sep 77. (lp) *(9103 328)* *<SR 6306>* **TALKING HEADS '77** [60] [97]
– Uh-oh, love comes to town / New feeling / Tentative decisions / Happy day / Who is it? / No compassion / The book I read / Don't worry about the government / First week – last week . . . carefree / Psycho killer / Pulled up. *(re-iss. Sep78; SR 6036) (cd-iss. Feb87; K2 56647)*

Oct 77. (7") *<1002>* **UH-OH, LOVE COMES TO TOWN. / I WISH YOU WOULDN'T SAY THAT** [–] [ ]

Dec 77. (7") *(6078 610)* **PSYCHO KILLER. / I WISH YOU WOULDN'T SAY THAT** [ ] [–]
(12"+=) *(same)* – Psycho killer (acoustic).

Jan 78. (7") *<1013>* **PSYCHO KILLER. / PSYCHO KILLER (acoustic)** [–] [92]

May 78. (7") *(6078 620)* **PULLED UP. / DON'T WORRY ABOUT THE GOVERNMENT** [ ] [–]

Jul 78. (lp/c) *(K/K4 56531)* *<SR 6058>* **MORE SONGS ABOUT BUILDINGS AND FOOD** [21] [29]
– Thank you for sending me an angel / With our love / The good thing / Warning sign / Girls want to be with the girls / Found a job / Artists only / I'm not in love / Stay hungry / Take me to the river / The big country. *(double-play cass. includes debut album) (cd-iss. Jan87; K2 56531)*

Oct 78. (7") *<1032>* **TAKE ME TO THE RIVER. / THANK YOU FOR SENDING ME AN ANGEL** [–] [26]

Jun 79. (7") *(SIR 4004)* **TAKE ME TO THE RIVER. / FOUND A JOB** [ ] [–]
(d7"+=) *(SAM 87)* – Love goes to a building on fire / Psycho killer.

Aug 79. (lp/c) *(K/K4 56707)* *<SRK 6076>* **FEAR OF MUSIC** [33] [21]
– Air / Animals / Cities / Drugs / Electric guitar / Heaven / I Zimbra / Life during wartime / Memories can't wait / Mind / Paper. *(re-iss. Sep79 lp/c; SRK/SRC 6076) (w/ free 7")* – PSYCHO KILLER (live). / NEW FEELING (live) *(cd-iss. Jul84; K2 56707)*

Oct 79. (7") *(SIR 4027)* *<49075>* **LIFE DURING WARTIME. / ELECTRIC GUITAR** [ ] [80]

Feb 80. (7") *(SIR 4033)* **I ZIMBRA. / PAPER** [ ] [–]

Jun 80. (7") *(SIR 4040)* **CITIES. / CITIES (live)** [ ] [–]
(12"+=) *(SIR 4040T)* – Artists only.

—— basic 4 added **BUSTA CHERRY JONES** – bass / **ADRIAN BELEW** – guitar / **BERNIE WORRELL** – keyboards / **STEVEN SCALES** – percussion / **DONETTE McDONALD** – backing vox

Oct 80. (lp/c) *<(SRK/SRC 6095)>* **REMAIN IN LIGHT** [21] [19]
– The great curve / Crosseyed and painless / Born under punches / Houses in motion / Once in a lifetime / Listening wind / Seen and not seen / The overlord. *(cd-iss. Mar84; K2 56867)*

Feb 81. (7"/ext.12") *(SIR 4048/+T)* *<40649>* **ONCE IN A LIFETIME. / SEEN AND NOT SEEN** [14] [ ]

May 81. (7") *<49734>* **HOUSES IN MOTION (remix). / THE OVERLORD** [–] [ ]

May 81. (7") *(SIR 4050)* **HOUSES IN MOTION (remix). / AIR** [50] [–]
(ext.12"+=) *(SIR 4050T)* – ('A'live).

—— In 1981, all 4 diversed into own projects

Mar 82. (7") *(SIR 4055)* **LIFE DURING WARTIME (live). / LIFE DURING WARTIME** [ ] [–]
(12"+=) *(SIR 4055T)* – Don't worry about the government (live).

Apr 82. (d-lp/d-c) *<(SRK/SRC 23590)>* **THE NAME OF THIS BAND IS TALKING HEADS (live)** [22] [31]
– I Zimbra / Drugs / Houses in motion / Life during wartime / Take me to the river / The great curve / Cross-eyed and painless / New feeling / A clean break / Don't worry about the government / Pulled up / Psycho killer / Artists only / Stay hungry / Air / Building on fire / Memories can't wait. *(cd-iss. May87; K2 66112)*

Jun 83. (lp,clear-lp/c/cd) *(923883-1/-4/-2)* *<23883>* **SPEAKING IN TONGUES** [21] [15]
– Burning down the house / Making flippy floppy / Girlfriend is better / Slippery people / I get wild – Wild gravity / Swamp / Moon rocks / Pull up the roots / This must be the place (naive melody). *(c+=/cd+=)* – (6 extra mixes).

Jul 83. (7") *(W 9565)* *<29565>* **BURNING DOWN THE HOUSE. / I GET WILD – WILD GRAVITY** [ ] [9]
(12"+=) *(W 9565T)* – Moon rocks.

Jan 84. (7") *(W 9451)* *<29451>* **THIS MUST BE THE PLACE (NAIVE MELODY). / MOON ROCKS** [51] Oct83 [62]
(ext.d12"+=) *(W 9451T / SAM 176)* – Slippery people (remix) / Making flippy floppy (remix).

Feb 84. (7") *<29163>* **ONCE IN A LIFETIME (live). / THIS MUST BE THE PLACE (live)** [–] [ ]

E.M.I. Sire

Oct 84. (7"/ext.12") *(EMI/12EMI 5504)* **SLIPPERY PEOPLE (live). / THIS MUST BE THE PLACE (NAIVE MELODY) (live)** [68] [–]

Oct 84. (lp/c) *(TAH/+TC 1)* *<25121>* **STOP MAKING SENSE (live)** [37] [41]
– Psycho killer / Swamp / Slippery people / Burning down the house / Girlfriend is better / Once in a lifetime / What a day that was / Life during wartime / Take me to the river. *(cd-iss. Feb85; CDP 746064-2) (c+=/cd+=)* – (extra tracks) *(re-iss. Mar90 cd)(c/lp; CZ 289)(TC+/ATAK 147) (re-iss. Nov93 on 'Fame' cd/c; CD/TC FA 3302) (lp-iss.Apr99 on 'E.M.I.'; 499471-1)*

Nov 84. (7"/ext.12") *(EMI/12EMI 5509)* **GIRLFRIEND IS BETTER (live). / ONCE IN A LIFETIME (live)** [ ] [–]

Dec 84. (7") *<29080>* **STOP MAKING SENSE (GIRLFIRIEND IS BETTER) (live). / HEAVEN** [–] [ ]

May 85. (7"/ext.12") *(EMI/12EMI 5520)* **THE LADY DON'T MIND. / GIVE ME BACK MY NAME** [ ] [–]
(d12"+=) *(12EMID 5520)* – Slippery people (live) / This must be the place (naive melody) (live).

Jun 85. (lp/c)(cd) *(TAH/+TC 2)(CDP 746158-2)* *<25035>* **LITTLE CREATURES** [10] [20]
– And she was / Give me back my name / Creatures of love / The lady don't mind / Perfect world / Stay up late / Walk it down / Television man / Road to nowhere. *(c+=)* – The lady don't mind (extended). *(re-iss. Mar90 cd)(c/lp; CZ 287)(TC+/ATAK 146) (re-iss. Nov93 on 'Fame' cd/c; CD/TC FA 3301) (lp-iss.Dec99 on 'Simply Vinyl'; SVLP 152)*

Jun 85. (7") *<28987>* **ROAD TO NOWHERE. / GIVE ME BACK MY NAME** [–] [ ]

Sep 85. (7") *<28917>* **AND SHE WAS. / ('A'dub)** [–] [54]

Sep 85. (7"/7"pic-d) *(EMI/+P 5530)* **ROAD TO NOWHERE. / TELEVISION MAN** [6] [–]
(d12"+=) *(12EMID 5530)* – Slippery people (extended live) / This must be the place (naive melody) (live).

Feb 86. (7") *(EMI 5543)* **AND SHE WAS. / PERFECT WORLD** [17] [–]
(12"pic-d+=) *(12EMIP 5543)* – ('A'extended).

Apr 86. (7") *<29163>* **ONCE IN A LIFETIME (live). / THIS MUST BE THE PLACE (live)** [–] [91]
(above re-generated from 1984 album & taken from 'Down And Out In Beverly Hills')

Aug 86. (7") *(EMI 5567)* *<28629>* **WILD WILD LIFE. / PEOPLE LIKE US (movie version)** [43] [25]
(12"+=/12"pic-d+=) *(12EMI/+P 5567)* – ('A'extended).

Sep 86. (lp/c)(cd) *(EU/TCEU 3511)(CDP 746345-2)* *<25512>* **TRUE STORIES** [7] [17]
– Love for sale / Puzzlin' evidence / Hey now / Radio head / Papa Legba / Wild wild life / Radio head / Dream operator / People like us / City of dreams. *(cd+=)* – Wild (ET mix). *(re-iss. Sep89 on 'Fame' cd/c/lp; CD/TC+/FA 3231)*

Nov 86. (7") *<28497>* **LOVE FOR SALE. / HEY NOW** [–] [ ]

Nov 86. (lp/c) *(ENC/TCENC 3520)* *<25515>* **SONGS FROM 'TRUE STORIES' (Original DAVID BYRNE Film Soundtrack; w/ other artists)** [ ] [ ]
– Cocktail desperado / Road song / Freeway son / Brownie's theme / Mall muzak: Building a highway – Puppy polka – Party girls / Dinner music / Disco hits / City of steel / Love theme from 'True Stories' / Festa para um Rei Negro / Buster's theme / Soy de Tejas / I love metal buildings / Glass operator.

Apr 87. (7") *(EM 1)* **RADIO HEAD. / HEY NOW (movie version)** [52] [–]
(d7"+=)(12"+=/cd-s+=) *(EMD 1)(12/CD EM 1)* – ('A'remix) / ('B'-Milwaukee remix).

Mar 88. (cd/c/lp) *(CD/TC+/EMD 1005)* *<26654>* **NAKED** [3] [19]
– Blind / Mr. Jones / Totally nude / Ruby dear / (Nothing but) Flowers / The Democratic circus / The facts of life / Mommy daddy you and I / Big daddy / Cool water. *(other cd+=; CDP 790156-2)* – Bill. *(re-iss. Nov93 on 'Fame' cd/c; CD/TC FA 3300)*

Aug 88. (c-s/7") *(TC+/EM 68)* *<27948>* **BLIND. / BILL** [59] [ ]
(ext.12"+=/cd-s+=) *(12/CD EM 68)* – ('A'-Def, dub & blind mix).

Oct 88. (c-s/7") *(TC+/EM 53)* *<27992>* **(NOTHING BUT) FLOWERS. / RUBY DEAR** [ ] Apr88 [ ]
(10"+=) *(10EM 53)* – Facts of life / Mommy, daddy, you and I.
(12") *(12EM 53)* – ('A'extended) / ('B'-Lillywhite mix).
(cd-s) *(CDEM 53)* – ('A'side) / ('B'-bush mix) / Mommy, daddy, you and I / ('A'-Lillywhite mix).

—— cease to function as a group, after last recording. Officially split 1991.

– compilations, others, etc. –

on 'E.M.I.' UK / 'Sire' US unless mentioned otherwise

Apr 81. (c-s) *WEA; (SPC 9)* **TAKE ME TO THE RIVER / PSYCHO KILLER** [ ] [–]

1989. (3"cd-ep) *Sire; (921 135-2)* **LOVE GOES TO A BUILDING ON FIRE / PSYCHO KILLER / ONCE IN A LIFETIME / BURNING DOWN THE HOUSE** [ ] [–]

Oct 92. (c-s/7") *(TC+/EM 250)* **LIFETIME PILING UP. / ROAD TO NOWHERE** [50] [ ]
(cd-s+=) *(CDEM 250)* – Love for sale / The lady don't mind (extended).
(cd-s) *(CDEMS 250)* – ('A'side) / Stay up late / Radio head / Take me to the river.

Oct 92. (d-cd/d-c/d-lp) *(CD/TC+/EQ 5010) <26760>* **POPULAR FAVOURITES 1976-1992** [7] [ ]
– ONCE IN A LIFETIME:- Psycho killer / Take me to the river / Once in a lifetime / Burning down the house / This must be the place (naive melody) / Slippery people (live) / Life during wartime (live) / And she was / Road to nowhere / Wild wild life / Blind / (Nothing but) Flowers / Sax and violins / Lifetime piling up. // SAND IN MY VASELINE:- Sugar on my tongue / I want to live / Love goes to a building on fire / I wish you wouldn't say that / Don't worry about the government / The big country / No compassion / Warning sign / Heaven / Memories can't wait / I Zimbra / Crosseyed and painless / Swamp / Girlfriend is better (live) / Stay up late / Love for sale / City of dreams / Mr. Jones / Gangster of love / Popsicle.

Nov 95. (3xcd-box) *(CDOMB 003)* **THE ORIGINALS** [ ] [–]
– (STOP MAKING SENSE / LITTLE CREATURES / TRUE STORIES). *(re-iss. Mar97; same)*

Sep 99. (cd) *E.M.I.; (522453-2)* **STOP MAKING SENSE: 15th ANNIVERSARY EDITION** [ ] [–]

Sep 00. (3xcd-box) *E.M.I.; (5283722-2)* **LITTLE CREATURES / TRUE STORIES / NAKED** [ ] [–]

Apr 01. (cd) *E.M.I.; (532569-2)* **REMIXED** [ ] [–]

Sep 01. (c-s/12"/cd-s) *(W 571 C/T/CD)* **ONCE IN A LIFETIME** [ ] [–]

DAVID BYRNE

Early in 1981, he had collaborated with BRIAN ENO ⇒ on album 'MY LIFE IN THE BUSH OF GHOSTS'.

Sire Sire

Dec 81. (7") *(SIR 4054)* **BIG BLUE PLYMOUTH (EYES WIDE OPEN). / CLOUD CHAMBER** [ ] [–]
(12") *(SIR 4054T)* – ('A'side) / Leg bells / Light bath.

Jan 82. (lp/c) *(SRK/SRC 3645) <3645>* **SONGS FROM 'THE CATHERINE WHEEL' (Stage score)** [ ] Dec81 [ ]
– His wife refused / Two soldiers / The red house / My big hands (fall through the cracks) / Big business / Eggs in a briar patch / Poison / Cloud chamber / What a day that was / Big blue Plymouth (eyes wide open). *<US d-lp+=)* – Ade / Walking / Under the mountain / Dinosaur / Wheezing / Black flag / Combat / Leg bells / The blue flame / Danse beast / Five golden sections. *(cd-iss. Jan93; 7599 27418-2)*

Feb 82. (12"ep) *<50034>* **THREE BIG SONGS** [–] [ ]
– Big business (remix) / My big hands (fall through the cracks) / Big blue Plymouth (eyes wide open).

E.M.I. ECM

Sep 85. (lp/c) *(EJ 240381-1/-4) <ECM 25022>* **MUSIC FOR THE KNEE PLAYS** [ ] May 85 [ ]
– Tree (today is an important occasion) / In the upper room / The sound of business / Social studies / (The gift of sound) Where the sun never goes down / Theadora is dozing / Admiral Perry / I bid you goodnight / I've tried / Winter / Jungle book / In the future.

— BYRNE recorded a collaboration set with RYUICHI SAKAMOTO on film 'THE LAST EMPEROR'.

— BYRNE (below) now used a plethora of Brazilian musicians, after compiling various artists BELEZA TROPICAL', 'O SAMBA', etc.

Luaka Bop-Sire Luaka Bop

Oct 89. (lp/c)(cd) *(WX 319/+C)(K 925990-2) <25990>* **REI MOMO** [52] [71]
– Independence day / Make believe mambo / The call of the wild / Dirty old town / The rose tattoo / The dream police / Don't want to be part of your world / Marching through the wilderness / Lie to me / Women vs. men / Carnival eyes / I know sometimes a man is wrong.

Dec 89. (7"/ext.12") **MAKE BELIEVE MAMBO. / LIE TO ME** [ ] [ ]

Jun 91. (cd/c) *<(7599 26584-2/-4)>* **THE FOREST (instrumental)** [ ] [ ]
– Ur / Kish / Dura Europus / Nineveh / Ava / Machu picchu / Teotihuaean / Asuka. *(cd+=)* – Samara / Tula. *(re-iss. Jul00; same)*

Aug 91. (m-cd) *<40177>* **FORESTRY** [–] [ ]
– Ava (nu wage remix) / Nineveh (industrial mix) / Ava (less space dance mix edit) / Ava (space dance mix) / Machu picchu (album version).

Mar 92. (cd)(lp/c) *<(7599 26799-2)>(WX 464/+C)* **UH-OH** [26] [ ]
– Now I'm your mom / Girls on my mind / Something ain't right / She's mad / Hanging upside down / Twistin' in the wind / A walk in the dark / The cowboy mambo (hey lookit me now) / Tiny town / Somebody. *(re-iss. Feb95 cd/c; same)*

Apr 92. (7"/c-s) **GIRLS ON MY MIND. / MONKEY MAN** [ ] [ ]
(12"+=/cd-s+=) – Cantode oxum.

May 92. (7"/c-s) *(W 0108/+C)* **HANGING UPSIDE DOWN. / TINY TOWN** [ ] [ ]
(cd-s) *(W 0108CD1)* – ('A'side) / Dirty old town (live) / (Nothing but) Flowers (live) / Girls on my mind (live).
(cd-s) *(W 0108CD2)* – ('A'side) / Something ain't right (live) / Who we're thinking of (live) / Rockin' in the free world (live).

Jul 92. (7"/c-s) *(W 0199/+C)* **SHE'S MAD. / SOMEBODY** [ ] [–]
(12") *(W 0199T)* – ('A'side) / Butt naked (live) / Greenback dollar (live).
(cd-s++=) *(W 0199CD)* – Now I'm your man (live).

— with **PAUL SOCOLOW** – bass, vocals / **TODD TURKISHER** – drum, percussion / **VALERIE NARANJO** – percussion, tambourine (live: MAURO REFOSCO – percussion) / **BILL WARE** – marimba / **ARTO LINDSAY** – guitar / **JOHN MEDESKI** – organ / **BASHIRI JOHNSON** – congas, bongos / **BEBEL GILBERTO** – vocals

May 94. (cd/c) *<(9362 45558-2/-4)>* **DAVID BYRNE** [44] [ ]
– A long time ago / Angels / Crash / A self-made man / Back in the box / Sad song / Nothing at all / My love is you / Lillies of the valley / You & eye / Strange ritual / Buck naked. *(cd re-iss. Jul00; same)*

Jun 94. (7"/c-s) *(W 0253/+C)* **ANGELS. / PRINCESS** [ ] [–]
(12"+=/cd-s+=) *(W 0253 T/CD)* – Ready for this world.

Sep 94. (c-s/cd-s) *(W 0263 C/CD)* **BACK IN THE BOX / GYPSY WOMAN (live) / GIRLS ON MY MIND (live)** [ ] [–]
(US cd-ep) *<41766>* – (first 2 tracks) / Back in the box (mixes) / A woman's secret / Cool water (live).

May 97. (cd/c) *<(9362 46605-2/-4)>* **FEELINGS** [ ] [ ]
– Fuzzy freaky / Miss America / A soft seduction / Dance on vaseline / The gates of Paradise / Amnesia / You don't know me / Daddy go down / Finite = alright / Wicked little doll / Burnt by the sun / The civil wars / They are in love.

Jun 97. (cd-s) *(W 0401CD)* **MISS AMERICA (mixes; clean / album / I love America)** [ ] [–]

Jan 99. (cd) *<2085>* **THE VISIBLE MAN** (remixes) [–] [ ]

Oct 00. (m-cd) **IN SPITE OF WISHING AND WANTING** (soundtrack) [–] [ ]
– Horses / Sleeping up / Speech / Said & the ants / Fear / Danceonvaselinesu – Perextendedremix / Idiot music.

Virgin America Virgin America

May 01. (cd) *(CDVUS 189) <50924>* **LOOK INTO THE THE EYEBALL** [58] [ ]
– UB Jesus / Revolution / Great intoxication / Like humans do / Broken things / Accident / Desconocido soy / Neighbourhood / Smile / Moment of conception / Walk on water / Everyone's in love with you.

Sep 01. (cd-s) *(897529)* **LIKE HUMANS DO / ALL OVER ME / PRINCESS** [ ] [–]

Thrill Jockey Thrill Jockey

Sep 03. (cd/lp) *<(THRILL 133/+LP)>* **LEAD US NOT INTO TEMPTATION: MUSIC FROM THE FILM YOUNG ADAM** [ ] [ ]
– Body in a river / Mnemonic discordance / Seaside smokes / Canal life / Locks & barges / Haitian fight song (by HUNG DRAWN QUARTET) / Sex on the docks / Inexorable / Warm sheets / Dirty hair / Bastard / The lodger / Ineluctable / Speechless / The Great Western Road.

TOM TOM CLUB

CHRIS FRANTZ + TINA WEYMOUTH plus her 2 sisters + **STEVE SCALES** – percussion / **ALEX WEIR** – guitar / **TYRON DOWNIE** – keyboards

Island Sire

Jun 81. (7") *(WIP 6694)* **WORDY RAPPINGHOOD. / YOU DON'T STOP (WORDY RAP)** [7] [ ]
(12"+=) *(12WIP 6694)* – L'elephant.

Sep 81. (7") *(WIP 6735) <49882>* **GENIUS OF LOVE. / LORELEI (instrumental)** [65] Jan82 [31]
(12"+=) *(12WIP 6735)* – Rappa rappa rhythm / Yella.
(re-iss. Oct82; same)

Oct 81. (lp/c) *(ILPS/ICT 9686)* *<SRK 3628>* **TOM TOM CLUB** [78] [23]
– Wordy rappinghood / Genius of love / Tom Tom theme / L'elephant / As above, so below / Lorelei / On, on, on, on . . . / Booming and zooming. *(re-iss. Oct86 lp/c; ILPM/ICM 9686) (cd-iss. May87; CID 9686) (re-iss. cd Apr90; IMCD 103)*

Jul 82. (7") *(WIP 6762)* **UNDER THE BOARDWALK. / ON, ON, ON, ON . . . (remix)** [22] [ ]
(12"+=) *(12WIP 6762)* – Lorelei (remix).

Jul 83. (7"/12") *(IS/12IS 117)* **THE MAN WITH THE 4-WAY HIPS. / ('A'dub version)** [ ] [ ]

Aug 83. (lp/c) *(ILPS/ICT 9738)* *<23916>* **CLOSE TO THE BONE** [ ] [73]
– Pleasure of love / On the line again / This is a foxy world / Bamboo town / The man with the 4-way hips / Measure up / Never took a penny / Atsababy! (life is great).

Dec 83. (7") **NEVER TOOK A PENNY. / PLEASURE OF LOVE** [–] [ ]

— **TINA + CHRIS** added **GARY POZNER** – keyboards / **MARK ROULE** – guitar, percussion

Fontana Sire

Sep 88. (7") *(TCB 1)* **DON'T SAY NO. / DEVIL DOES YOUR DOG BITE?** [ ] [ ]
(12"+=) *(TCBX 1)* – ('A'version) / Beats and pieces.
(cd-s+=) *(TCBCD 1)* – Beats and pieces / Percapella.

Oct 88. (lp/c)(cd) *(SF LP/MC 8)(836 416-2)* *<25888>* **BOOM BOOM CHI BOOM BOOM** [ ] [ ]
– Suboceana / Shock the world / Don't say no / Challenge of the love warriors / Femme fatale / Born for love / Broken promises / She belongs to me / Little Eva / Misty teardrop.

— **KIRSTY MacCOLL** makes a guest vocal appearance on below

Jan 92. (cd/c) *<2-/4-26951>* **DARK SNEAK LOVE ACTION** [–] [ ]
– Love wave / Sunshine and ecstasy / You sexy thing / Who wants an ugly girl? / Say I am / Irrisistable party dip / Dark sneak love action / Innocent sex kiss / Dogs in the trash / My mama told me / As the disco ball turns / Daddy come home.

Rykodisc Rykodisc

Sep 00. (12") *<R 607>* **HAPPINESS CAN'T BUY MONEY** [–] [ ]

Oct 00. (cd) *<(RCD 10603)>* **THE GOOD THE BAD AND THE FUNKY** [ ] Sep00 [ ]
– Time to bounce / Who feelin' it / Happiness can't buy money / Holy water / Soul fire / She's dangerous / She's a freak / (C'mon) Surrender / Love to love you baby / Superdreaming / Lesbians by the lake / Let there be love / Time to bounce / Dangerous dub.

Artist Direct Artist Direct

Apr 03. (cd) *<(IMUCDD 072)>* **LIVE @ THE CLUBHOUSE (live)** [ ] Sep02 [ ]
– Suboceana / Time to bounce / Punk lolita / Soul fire / Who feelin' it / Happiness can't buy money / Sand / She's dangerous / The man with the 4-way hips / Genius of love / Band introduction / You sexy thing / Holy water / Wordy rappinghood / As above so below / 96 tears / Take me to the river.

JERRY HARRISON

Sire Sire

Oct 81. (7") *(SIR 4053)* **THINGS FALL APART. / WORLDS IN COLLISION** [ ] [ ]

Oct 81. (lp/c) *<(SRK/SRC 3631)>* **THE RED AND THE BLACK** [ ] [ ]
– Things fall apart / Slink / The new adventure / Magic hymie / Fast karma / No questions / Worlds in collision / The red nights / No more returns / No warning no alarm. *(cd-iss. Apr96 on 'Warners'; 7599 23631-2)*

Fontana Sire

Feb 88. (7") *(JERRY 1)* **REV IT UP. / BOBBY** [ ] [ ]
(12"+=)(12"pic-d+=)(cd-s+=) *(JERRY 1-12)(JERYP 1-12)(JERCD 1)* – ('A'versions). *(re-iss. Jul88; same)*

Feb 88. (lp/c)(cd) *(SF LP/MC 2)(832992-2)* *<25663>* **JERRY HARRISON: CASUAL GODS** [ ] [78]
– Rev it up / Songs of angels / Man with a gun / Let it come down / Cherokee chief / A perfect lie / Are you running? / Breakdown in the passing lane / A.K.A. love / We're always talkin' / Bobby. *(cd+=)* – Bobby (12"version).

May 88. (7") *(JERRY 2)* **MAN WITH A GUN. / ('A'radio edit)** [ ] [ ]
(12"+=)(cd-s+=) *(JERRY 2-12)(JERCD 2)* – Breakdown on the passing line / Wire always talking.

— backing incl. **BROOKS, WORRELL, BAILEY, SIEGER + WEIR**

Jun 90. (7") *(JERRY 3)* **WALK ON WATER. / MAN WITH A GUN** [ ] [ ]
(12"+=)(cd-s+=) *(JERRY 3-12)(JERCD 3)* – Racing the fire.

Jun 90. (cd/c/lp) *(846321-2/-4/-1)* *<25943>* **WALK ON WATER** [ ] [ ]
– Flying under radar / Cowboy's got to go / Kick start / I don't mind / Sleep angel / Confess / I cry for Iran / Never let it slip / If the rain returns / The doctor's lie.

HEADS

HARRISON, WEYMOUTH, FRANTZ + guest vocalists & lyricists (see below)

Radioactive-MCA M.C.A.

Oct 96. (c-s) *(MCS 48024)* **DON'T TAKE MY KINDNESS FOR WEAKNESS / ('A'mix)** [60] [ ]
(cd-s+=) *(MCSTD 48024)* – ('A'-Lunatic Calm remix).

Nov 96. (cd/c) *<(MCD/MCC 11504)>* **NO TALKING, JUST HEAD** [ ] [ ]
– Damage I've done (w/ JOHNETTE NAPOLITANO) / The king is gone (w/ MICHAEL HUTCHENCE) / No talking just head (w/ DEBBIE HARRY) / Never mind (w/ RICHARD HELL) / No big bang (w/ MARIA McKEE) / Don't take my madness for weakness (w/ SHAUN RYDER) / No more lonely nights (w/ MALIN ANNETEG) / Indie hair (w/ ED KOWALCZYK) / Punk lolita (w/ DEBBIE HARRY, JOHNETTE NAPOLITANO & TINA WEYMOUTH) / Only the lonely (w/ GORDON GANO) / Papersnow (w/ ANDY PARTRIDGE) / Blue blue moon (w/ GAVIN FRIDAY).

□ TALK SHOW (see under ⇒ STONE TEMPLE PILOTS)

TALK TALK

Formed: London, England . . . 1981 by MARK HOLLIS, who, with the help of older brother and session man ED (ex-EDDIE & THE HOT RODS), recruited WEBB, HARRIS and BREMNER. They signed to 'E.M.I.' soon after, manager Keith Aspen hiring producer Colin Thurston to work on the debut album. At the height of New Romantic posturing in the summer of '82, the band broke through with the uptempo keyboard pop of 'TODAY'. Despite reaching No.21 in the charts, the debut album, 'THE PARTY'S OVER' (1982), came across like a more pretentious version of their labelmates DURAN DURAN and unfortunately favoured lip-gloss style over content. It was to be another two years before the next album, 'IT'S MY LIFE' (1984), by which time BREMNER had bowed out and the band had wisely cast off their New Romantic trappings. Spawning three singles which barely breached the charts, the album was nevertheless an improvement on the debut. The band finally broke through with the 1986 single, 'LIFE'S WHAT YOU MAKE IT', a chunky, deliberate piece of moodiness that preceded the classic album, 'THE COLOUR OF SPRING'. Featuring an array of guest musicians that included STEVE WINWOOD and DANNY THOMPSON, the record was a combination of their earlier commercial leanings and a developing talent for abstract rock/pop. Following the album's success, EMI furnished TALK TALK with a larger budget for 1988's 'SPIRIT OF EDEN' and the band embellished their sound with an ensemble of musical exotica that included clarinet, oboe and even The Chelmsford Cathedral Choir (!). This complex sonic tapestry was laced with rich, gliding melodies, a soothing elixir that drew deserved critical praise. EMI didn't quite view things in the same way, however, and the band were dropped in 1989. After being picked up by 'Polydor', the group released 'LAUGHING STOCK' (1991) on the label's jazz imprint, 'Verve'. More heavily orchestrated with cello, viola etc., the album saw TALK TALK move ever further into avant-garde territory. Meanwhile, bassist PAUL WEBB formed 'O' RANG, having left the band in 1990. The debut album, 'HERD OF INSTINCT' (1994) didn't exactly make for easy listening; skeletal percussion, barely audible, vaguely threatening voices, screeching feedback and ethnic chants saw WEBB pushing musical boundaries that his old band hadn't yet encountered. HARRIS and WEBB's sophomore effort, 'FIELD & WAVES' (1996) basically carried on where the debut left off, exploring the grey areas of electronic ambience and the cracks in the pavement of global popular music. A relatively more accessible volume than its predecessor, the magnitude of the experimentalism was often tempered by an oblique sense of melody. In other words, it couldn't be more different than 'MARK HOLLIS' (1998), the long awaited eponymous solo debut from the TALK TALK frontman. Unsurprisingly perhaps, the record dovetailed exquisitely from that band's premature demise, reprising and perfecting the trademark graceful collage of folksy ambience and mystical atmospherics. Of late, PAUL WEBB (aka RUSTIN MAN) – together with other former TALK TALK members – collaborated with PORTISHEAD chanteuse, BETH GIBBONS for the album, 'Out Of Season' (2002). Via a collaboration with dance act, LIQUID PEOPLE, 'IT'S MY LIFE' gave TALK TALK a minor hit in June 2003. • **Songwriters:** Initially group penned, with MARK and brother ED writing most. In 1983, MARK and 4th member TIM FRIESE-GREEN wrote all material. • **Trivia:** The song 'TALK TALK', was first heard in late 1977, when MARK's group, The REACTION, recorded a prototype of the song on the Various Artists album, 'Streets'. A single also surfaced, 'I CAN'T RESIST' / 'I AM A CASE' for 'Island'; (WIP 6437)

Album rating: THE PARTY'S OVER (*5) / IT'S MY LIFE (*6) / THE COLOUR OF SPRING (*8) / SPIRIT OF EDEN (*8) / NATURAL HISTORY – THE VERY BEST OF TALK TALK compilation (*9) / HISTORY REVISITED – THE REMIXES (*5) / LAUGHING STOCK (*8) / THE VERY BEST OF TALK TALK compilation (*8) / LONDON 1986 concert album (*6) / 'O'Rang: HERD OF INSTINCT (*7)

MARK HOLLIS (b.1955) – vocals, piano, guitar (ex-REACTION) / **SIMON BREMNER** – keyboards / **PAUL WEBB** – bass, vocals / **LEE HARRIS** – drums

E.M.I. | EMI America

Feb 82. (7") *(EMI 5265)* **MIRROR MAN. / STRIKE UP THE BAND** [ ] [–]

Apr 82. (7"/ext-12") *(EMI/12EMI 5284)* **TALK TALK. / ('A'version)** [52] [–]

Jun 82. (7"/ext-12") *(EMI/12EMI 5314)* **TODAY. / IT'S SO SERIOUS** [14] [–]

Jul 82. (lp/c) *(EMC/TC-EMC 3413) <17083>* **THE PARTY'S OVER** [21] [ ]
– Talk talk / It's so serious / Today / The party's over / Hate / Have you heard the news? / Mirror man / Another word / Candy. *(re-iss. 1985 lp/c; ATAK/TC-ATAK 65) (cd-iss. Mar87; CDP 746366-2) (re-iss. Sep87 on 'Fame' lp/c; FA/TC-FA 3187) (cd re-iss. Apr88; CDFA 3187) (cd re-mast.Sep97; RETALK 100)*

Oct 82. (7"/7"pic-d) *(EMI/P 5352) <8136>* **TALK TALK (remix). / MIRROR MAN** [23] [75]
(12") *(12EMI 5352)* – ('A'side) / ('A'-BBC version).

Feb 83. (7") *(EMI 5373)* **MY FOOLISH FRIEND. / CALL IN THE NIGHTBOYS** [57] [–]
(12"+=) *(12EMI 5373)* – ('A'extended).

—— Now basic trio when BREMNER departed. His place was taken by 4th member **TIM FRIESE-GREEN** – keyboards, producer, co-composer. Added session people **ROBBIE McINTOSH + HENRY LOWTHER**

Jan 84. (7") *(EMI 5443) <8195>* **IT'S MY LIFE. / DOES CAROLINE KNOW?** [46] [–]
(12"+=) *(12EMI 5443)* – ('A'extended).

Feb 84. (lp/c) *(EMC 240002-1/-4) <17113>* **IT'S MY LIFE** [35] [42]
– Dum dum girl / Such a shame / Renee / It's my life / Tomorrow started / The last time / Call in the night boy / Does Caroline know? / It's you. *(cd-iss. Feb85; CDP 746063-2) (re-iss. 1989 lp/c; ATAK/TC-ATAK 116) (cd re-mast.Sep97; RETALK 101)*

Mar 84. (7") *<8195>* **IT'S MY LIFE. / AGAIN, A GAME AGAIN** [–] [31]

Mar 84. (7") *(EMI 5433) <8215>* **SUCH A SHAME. / AGAIN, A GAME . . . AGAIN** [49] [–]
(12"+=) *(12EMI 5433)* – ('A'extended).
(d7"+=) *(EMID 5433)* – Talk talk (demo) / Mirror man (demo).

Jun 84. (7") *<8215>* **SUCH A SHAME. / CALL IN THE NIGHT BOYS** [–] [89]

Jul 84. (7") *(EMI 5480)* **DUM DUM GIRL. / WITHOUT YOU** [74] [–]
(12"+=) *(12EMI 5480)* – ('A'-US mix) / Such a shame (dub).

Jan 85. (7") *<8244>* **WHY IS IT SO HARD. / IT'S MY LIFE** [–] [ ]

—— guests on next album incl. **DAVID RHODES** – guitar / **DAVID ROACH** – saxophone / **MORRIS PERT** – percussion

Jan 86. (7"/ext.12") *(EMI/12EMI 5540) <8303>* **LIFE'S WHAT YOU MAKE IT. / IT'S GETTING LATE IN THE EVENING** [16] [90]
('A'early mix-12"+=) *(12EMIX 5540)* – ('A'-extended dance mix).
(d12"+=) *(12EMID 5540)* – It's my life / Does Caroline know?.

Feb 86. (lp/c)(cd) *(EMC/TC-EMC 3506)(CDP746228-2) <17179>* **THE COLOUR OF SPRING** [8] [58]
– Happiness is easy / I don't believe in you / Life's what you make it / April 5th / Living in another world / Give it up / Chameleon day / Time it's time. *(re-iss. cd Feb90; CZ 287) (re-iss. Mar90 lp/c; ATAK/TC-ATAK 145) (re-iss. Apr93 on 'Fame' cd/c; CD/TC FA 3291) (re-iss. Feb93; LPCENT 14) (cd re-mast.Sep97; RETALK 102) (lp re-iss. Aug00 on 'Simply Vinyl'; SVLP 232)*

Mar 86. (7"/7"sha-pic-d) *(EMI/+P 5551)* **LIVING IN ANOTHER WORLD. / FOR WHAT IT'S WORTH** [48] [ ]
(12"+=) *(12EMI 5551)* – ('A'extended).
(12"+=) *(12EMIX 5551)* – ('A'-US mix).

Parlophone | EMI America

May 86. (7") *(R 6131)* **GIVE IT UP. / PICTURES OF BERNADETTE** [59] [ ]
(12"+=) *(12R 6131)* – ('A'dance mix).

Nov 86. (7") *(R 6144)* **I DON'T BELIEVE IN YOU. / DOES CAROLINE KNOW? (live)** [ ] [ ]
(12"+=) *(12R 6144)* – Happiness is easy.

—— Basic quartet added ensemble **MARTIN DITCHAM** – percussion (also on last) / **ROBBIE McINTOSH** – dobro, 12-string guitar (also on last lp) / **MARK FELTHAM** – harmonica / **SIMON EDWARDS** – Mexican bass / **HENRY LOWTHER** – trumpet / **NIGEL KENNEDY** – violin / **DANNY THOMPSON** – double bass / **HUGH DAVIS** – shozygs / **MICHAEL JEANS** – oboe / **ANDREW STOWALL** – bassoon / **ANDREW HARRINER** – clarinet / **CHRIS HOOKER** – cor anglais / plus CHOIR OF CHELMSFORD CATHEDRAL

Sep 88. (lp/c)(cd) *(PCSD/TC-PCSD 105)(CDP 746977-2)* **SPIRIT OF EDEN** [19] [ ]
– The rainbow / Eden / Desire / Inheritance / I believe in you / Wealth. *(re-iss. Jun93 on 'Fame' cd/c; CD/TC FA 3293) (cd re-mast.Sep97; RETALK 103) (lp re-iss. Sep00 on 'Simply Vinyl'; SVLP 246)*

Sep 88. (7") *(R 6189)* **I BELIEVE IN YOU. / JOHN COPE** [ ] [ ]
(12"+=/cd-s+=) *(12R/CDR 6189)* – Eden (edit).

Dec 88. (m-lp/c) *<ST/4XT 6542>* **IT'S MY LIFE** (remixes) [–] [ ]

May 90. (7"/c-s) *(R/TCR 6254)* **IT'S MY LIFE (remix). / RENEE (live)** [13] [ ]
(cd-s+=) *(CDR 6254)* – ('A'live).
(12") *(12R 6254)* – ('A'-Tropical Love Forest mix) / ('A'side) / Talk Talk recycled:- Life's what you make it – Living in another world – Such a shame – It's my life.

Jun 90. (cd)(lp/c) *(CDP 793976-2)(PCSD/TC-PCSD 109) <93976>* **NATURAL HISTORY – THE VERY BEST OF TALK TALK** (compilation) [3] Oct90 [ ]
– Today / Talk talk / My foolish friend / Such a shame / Dum dum girl / It's my life / Give it up / Living in another world / Life's what you make it / Happiness is easy / I believe in you / Desire.

Sep 90. (7"/c-s) *(R/TCR 6264)* **LIFE'S WHAT YOU MAKE IT. / ('A'live)** [23] [–]
(cd-s+=) *(CDR 6264)* – Tomorrow started (live).
(12") *(12R 6264)* – ('A'-BBG remix) / ('A'side) / Tomorrow started (live).
(12") *(12RX 6264)* – ('A'-Fluke mix) / ('A'-Dominic Woosey remix).

Nov 90. (7"/c-s) *(R/TCR 6276)* **SUCH A SHAME. / DUM DUM GIRL (live)** [ ] [–]
(12"+=) *(12R 6276)* – ('A'-Gary Miller remix).
(cd-s++=) *(CDR 6276)* – Talk talk (live).

Feb 91. (7"/c-s) *(R/TCR 6282)* **LIVING IN ANOTHER WORLD ('91 remix). / ('A'live remix)** [ ] [–]
(12"+=/cd-s+=) *(12R/CDR 6282)* – ('A'-Mendelsohn mix).

—— Basic quartet only retained **DITCHAM, EDWARDS + LOWTHER** and brought in **LEVINE ANDRADE, STEPHEN TEES, GEORGE ROBERTSON, GAVYN WRIGHT, JACK GLICKMAN, GARFIELD JACKSON + WILF GIBSON** – viola / **ERNEST MOTHLE** – acoustic bass /

ROGER SMITH + PAUL KEGG – cello / **DAVE WHITE** – contra, bass, clarinet

Mar 91. (cd)(lp/c) *(CDP 793976-2)(PCS/TCPCS 7349)* <95965> **HISTORY REVISITED – THE REMIXES** [35] [ ]
– Living in another world '91 / Such a shame / Happiness is easy (dub) / Today / Dum dum girl (spice remix) / Life's what you make it / Talk talk / It's my life (tropical rainforest mix) / Living in another world (curious world dub mix) / Life's what you make it (the Fluke remix).

Verve Verve

Sep 91. (cd/c/lp) *(<847717-2/-4/-1>)* **LAUGHING STOCK** [26] Nov91 [ ]
– Myrrhman / Ascension day / After the flood / Taphead / New grass / Runeii. *(cd re-iss. Mar00 on 'Pond Life'; PLVP 001CD)*

Sep 91. (pic-cd-s) *(TALKD 1)* **AFTER THE FLOOD / MYRRHMAN** [ ] [ ]

Oct 91. (pic-cd-s) *(TALKD 2)* **NEW GRASS. / STUMP** [ ] [ ]

Nov 91. (pic-cd-s) *(TALKD 3)* **ASCENTION DAY. / 5.09** [ ] [ ]

– compilations, etc –

Nov 96. (d-cd) *E.M.I.; (CDEMC 3670)* **ASIDES AND BESIDES** [ ] [ ]

Jan 97. (cd) *E.M.I.; (CDEMC 3763)* **THE VERY BEST OF TALK TALK** [54] [ ]
– It's my life / Talk talk / Dum dum girl / Have you heard the news / Such a shame / For what it's worth / Life's what you make it / Eden / April 5th / Living in another world / I believe in you / Give it up / John Cope / Wealth / Time it's time.

Feb 99. (cd) *Pond Life; (PLVP 001CD)* **LONDON 1986 (live)** [ ] [–]
– Tomorrow started / Life's what you make it / Caroline knows / Living in another world / Give it up / It's my life / Such a shame / Renee.

Jul 00. (cd) *Disky; (<SI 99793-2>)* **THE COLLECTION** [ ] [ ]

Sep 00. (cd) *E.M.I.; (<528559-2>)* **THE COLLECTION** [ ] Jun01 [ ]

Apr 01. (cd) *E.M.I.; (<532570-2>)* **REMIXED** [ ] [ ]

Apr 02. (cd) *Pond Life; (PLVP 004CD)* **MISSING PIECES** [ ] [–]

Jan 03. (12") *Touchy Feely; (TF 02)* **IT'S MY LIFE** [ ] [–]

Mar 03. (cd) *Disky; (<SI 905233>)* **TIME IT'S TIME** [ ] [ ]

Mar 03. (d-cd) *E.M.I.; (582361-2)* **IT'S MY LIFE / SPIRIT OF EDEN** [ ] [–]

Mar 03. (cd) *Essential; (<582164-2>)* **THE ESSENTIAL TALK TALK** [ ] [ ]

Jul 03. (cd) *E.M.I.; (<INTROCD 8>)* **INTRODUCING . . .** [ ] [ ]

'O'RANG

LEE HARRIS + PAUL WEBB

Echo Hit It!

Aug 94. (cd/c/lp) *(ECH CD/MC/LP 002)* <19> **HERD OF INSTINCT** [ ] 1995 [ ]
– Orang / Little brother / Mind on pleasure / All change / Aneon, the oass / Loaded values / Nahoojek – Fogou.

Nov 94. (12"ep/cd-ep) *(7600629)* **SPOOR** [ ] [–]
– Nicolea / Charabanic D.I.P. / An ocean ahead / Core.

Jan 97. (12"ltd) *(ECSYDJ 029)* **P. 53. /** [ ] [–]

Feb 97. (cd/lp) *(ECH CD/LP 010)* <21> **FIELDS AND WAVES** [ ] [ ]
– Barren / Jalap / P.53 / Moider / Seizure / Moratorium / Superculture / Quondam / Forest / Hoo / Boreades / Fields and waves. *(cd re-iss. Feb01; same)*

Feb 98. (12") <23> **REMIXES** [–] [ ]

—— in Oct'02, PAUL WEBB (as RUSTIN MAN) collaborated with PORTISHEAD singer, BETH GIBBONS on the album, 'Out Of Season'

MARK HOLLIS

Polydor Polydor

Feb 98. (cd) *(<537688-2>)* **MARK HOLLIS** [53] [ ]
– The colour of spring / Watershed / Inside looking out / The gift / A life 1895-1915 / Westward bound / The daily planet / A new Jerusalem. *(re-iss. Mar00 on 'Pond Life'; PLVP 003CD)*

TANGERINE DREAM

Formed: Berlin, Germany . . . autumn 1967 by art student EDGAR FROESE, who took the name, TANGERINE DREAM, from lyrics used in The BEATLES' classic, 'Lucy In The Sky With Diamonds'. He was invited to play some classical improvisations by surrealist painter SALVADOR DALI in his Spanish villa, EDGAR subsequently going through many egotistical rock musicians before he finally met KLAUS SCHULZE in '69. Together, they soon found KONRAD SCHNITZLER and JOSEPH BEUYS, who, with other guests, worked on the sessions for the 1970 debut, 'ELECTRONIC MEDITATION'. With others going solo, EDGAR then found CHRIS FRANKE and another album, 'ALPHA CENTAURI' surfaced for UK 'Polydor'. In 1972, PETER BAUMANN joined for their third album, 'ATEM', the record heavily playlisted on John Peel's night-time Radio One show and leading to new entrepeneur, Richard Branson, signing them to his 'Virgin' label. Surprisingly, the following year, 'PHAEDRA' made it into the UK Top 40 lists, much aided by the fact 'Virgin' was now an influential part of the British/continental scene. With this album, TANGERINE DREAM made a departure from their PINK FLOYD-like experimentalism, discovering picturesque, electronic waves of sound, rhythmically haunting and repetitive. 'RUBYCON' (1975) was similarly influential, although from there on in the band started to gravitate towards soundtrack work, their atmospheric mood pieces fitting the genre with ease. Over the course of the following decade, they recorded music for such diverse screen projects as 'SORCERER' (1977), 'THIEF' (1981), 'RISKY BUSINESS' (1983) and 'FIRESTARTER' (1984), although their music increasingly verged upon "New Age" sterility. The group issued their final album for 'Virgin', 'HYPERBOREA' (1983) and, much to fans' delight, the fantastic 'LE PARC' (1985), which many believed was the band's swansong. They continued to experiment with new and exciting ideas (using more samples, loops and electronic wizzardry than before) resulting in the mainly vocal 'TYGER' (1987). SCHMOELLING departed in 1986, his replacement being PAUL HASLINGER first featured on 'UNDERWATER SUNLIGHT' (1986) and more so, 'OPTICAL RACE' (1988). However, it was HASLINGER who subsequently walked out on the group to pursue his career in scoring movies. Replaced by JEROME FROESE, TANGERINE DREAM would encounter their most celebrated album for some time, the seven-times Grammy nominated 'ROCKOON' (1992). Throughout the 90's, they issued a staggering body of work, resulting in perhaps two (new age or soundtrack) albums a year, along with remixes and soundtracks here and there. Among their latter-day work, 'INFERNO' (2002) was one of the most notable recordings, at least in terms of its inspiration and execution. Based on Dante's famous work of the same name, the album was recorded live within the confines of a church, incorporating religious music into their ever expansive electronica agenda.

Album rating: ELECTRONIC MEDITATION (*4) / ALPHA CENTAURI (*4) / ZEIT (*3) / ATEM (*5) / PHAEDRA (*9) / RUBYCON (*9) / RICOCHET (*8) / STRATOSFEAR (*7) / SORCEROR (*7) / ENCORE (*4) / CYCLONE (*5) / FORCE MAJEURE (*6) / TANGRAM (*6) / QUICHOTTE (aka 'PERGAMON – LIVE AT THE PALAST DER REPUBLIK') (*5) / THIEF soundtrack (*4) / EXIT (*6) / WHITE EAGLE (*5) / LOGOS – LIVE (*5) / WAVELENGTH soundtrack (*4) / HYPERBOREA (*4) / RISKY BUSINESS (*4) / FIRESTARTER soundtrack (*4) / POLAND – THE WARSAW CONCERT (*4) / FLASHPOINT soundtrack (*4) / LE PARC (*5) / HEARTBREAKERS soundtrack (*4) / DREAM SEQUENCES compilation (*6) / LEGEND soundtrack with other artists (*3) / UNDERWATER SUNLIGHT (*4) / GREEN DESERT early work (*5) / TYGER (*5) / THREE

O'CLOCK HIGH soundtrack with other artists (*3) / THE TANGERINE DREAM COLLECTION compilation (*7) / NEAR DARK soundtrack (*4) / LIVE MILES (*4) / SHY PEOPLE soundtrack (*4) / OPTICAL RACE (*5) / MIRACLE MILE (*3) / THE BEST OF TANGERINE DREAM compilation (*6) / LILY ON THE BEACH (*4) / MELROSE (*5) / DEAD SOLID PERFECT soundtrack (*3) / THE PARK IS MINE (*3) / ROCKOON (*6) / DEADLY CARE soundtrack (*3) / CANYON DREAMS (*6) / 220 VOLT LIVE (*6) / TURN OF THE TIDES (*6) / TYRANNY OF BEAUTY (*6) / BOOK OF DREAMS collection (*6) / THE DREAM MIXES remixes (*6) / THE DREAM ROOTS COLLECTION compilation (*6) / GOBLIN'S CLUB soundtrack (*6) / OASIS soundtrack (*4) / TOURNADO (*4) / TRANS SIBERIA (*5) / WHAT A BLAST soundtrack (*5) / AMBIENT MONKEYS (*4) / QUINOA (*5) / MARS POLARIS (*7) / GREAT WALL OF CHINA (*5) / THE SEVEN LETTERS FROM TIBET (*4) / INFERNO (*6) / Edgar Froese: AQUA (*6) / EPSILON IN MALAYSIAN PALE (*6) / MACULA TRANSFER (*4) / AGES (*6) / STUNTMAN (*5) / KAMIKAZE 1989 soundtrack (*4) / PINNACLES (*5) / BEYOND THE STORM (*5)

EDGAR FROESE (b. 6 Jun'44, Tilsit, Germany) – guitar, piano, organ (ex-The ONES) / **VOLKER HOMBACH** – flute, violin / **KIRT HERKENBERG** – bass / (Mar69) / **SVEN JOHANNSON** – drums; repl. LANSE HAPRHASH

— In 1970, after HOMBACH became film cameraman for W.R.FASSBINDER, and brief wind instrumentalist STEVE JOLIFFE departed to join STEAMHAMMER. Group reformed **EDGAR FROESE** brought in newcomers **KLAUS SCHULTZE** (b. 4 Aug'47) – drums, percussion / **CONRAD SCHNITZLER** – cello, flute, violin. with guests **JIMMY JACKSON** – organ / **THOMAS VON KEYSERLING** – flute

Ohr — not iss.

Jun 70. (lp) *(OMM 556 004)* **ELECTRONIC MEDITATION** [–] German [–]
– Geburt (Genesis) / Reise durch ein brennendes gehirn (Journey through a burning brain) / Kalter rauch (Cold smoke) / Asche zu asche (Ashes to ashes) / Auferstehung (Resurrection). *(UK cd-iss. Jan87 on 'Jive'; CTANG 4) (cd re-iss. Feb96 on 'Essential'; ESMCD 345)*

— **FROESE** added bass to repertoire, and again supplanted new members **CHRISTOPHER FRANKE** (b. 6 Apr'53) – drums, percussion, synthesizer repl. CONRAD / **STEVE SCHROEDER** – organs repl. KLAUS SCHULTZE who went solo / added new guests **UDO DENNEBORG** – flute, words / **ROLAND PAULICK** – synthesizer

Apr 71. (lp) *(OMM 556 012)* **ALPHA CENTAURI** [–] German [–]
– Sunrise in the third system / Fly and collision of Comas Sola / Alpha Centauri. *(UK-iss.Nov73 on 'Polydor Super'; 2383 314) (cd-iss. Jan87 on 'Jive'; CTANG 5) (re-iss. cd Feb96 on 'Essential'; ESMCD 346)*

— **PETER BAUMANN** – synthesizer, organ repl. SCHROYDER (guested on below)

Feb 72. (7") *(OSS 7006)* **ULTIMA THULE (tell 1). / ULTIMA THULE (tell 2)** [–] German [–]

— More guests were added on next; **FLORIAN FRICKE** – synthesizers / cellists / **CHRISTIAN VALBRACHT / JOCKEN VON GRUMBCOW / HANS JOACHIM BRUNE / JOHANNES LUCKE**

Feb 72. (d-lp) *(OMM 2-556 021)* **ZEIT** [–] German [–]
– 1st movement: Birth of liquid plejades / 2nd movement: Nebulous dawn / 3rd movement: Origins of supernatural probabilities / 4th movement: Zeit. *(UK-iss.Jun76 on 'Virgin'; VD 2503) (cd-iss. Jan87 on 'Jive'; CTANG 3) (cd re-iss. Feb96 on 'Essential'; ESMCD 347)*

Mar 73. (lp) *(OMM 556 031)* **ATEM** [–] German [–]
– Atem / Fauni-Gena / Wahn / Circulation of events. *(UK-iss.Nov73 on 'Polydor Super'; 2383 297) (cd-iss. Jan87 on 'Jive'; CTANG 2) (re-iss. cd Feb96 on 'Essential'; ESMCD 348)*

— In Aug'73, they recorded 'GREEN DESERT' album, unreleased until 1986.

Virgin — Virgin

Mar 74. (lp/c) *(V/TCV 2010) <13108>* **PHAEDRA** [15] [ ]
– Phaedra / Mysterious semblance at the strand of nightmares / Movements of a visionary / Sequent C. *(re-iss. Mar84 lp/c; OVED/+C 25) (cd-iss. Jul87; CDV 2010) (cd re-iss. Feb95; TAND 5)*

— **MICHAEL HOENIG** – synthesizer repl. BAUMANN (on tours only 1974-75)

Mar 75. (lp/c) *(V/TCV 2025) <13166>* **RUBYCON** [12] [ ]
– Rubycon (part 1) / Rubycon (part 2). *(re-iss. Mar84 lp/c; OVED/+C 27) (cd-iss. Jul87; CDV 2025) (cd re-iss. Feb95; TAND 6)*

Dec 75. (lp/c) *(V/TCV 2044)* **RICOCHET (live at Liverpool, Coventry & Yorkminster Cathedrals)** [40] [–]
– Ricochet (part 1) / Ricochet (part 2). *(re-iss. Mar84 lp/c; OVED/+C 26) (cd-iss. Jul87; CDV 204) (cd re-iss. Feb95; TAND 7)*

— **BAUMANN** re-united with outfit, to depose HOENIG

Nov 76. (lp/c) *(V/TCV 2068) <34427>* **STRATOSFEAR** [39] [ ]
– Stratosfear / The big sleep in search of Hades / 3 a.m. at the border of the marsh from Okefnokee / Invisible limits. *(cd-iss. Jul87; CDV 2068) (re-iss. Aug88 lp/c; OVED/+C 70) (cd re-iss. Feb95; TAND 8)*

Jul 77. (lp/c) *(MCF/+C 2806) <2277>* **SORCERER (Soundtrack)** [25] [ ]
– Main title / Search / The call / Creation / Vengeance / The journey / Grind / Rain forest / Abyss / The mountain road / Impressions of Sorcerer / Betrayal (Sorcerer's theme). *(re-iss. Feb82 lp/c; MCL/+C 1646) (cd-iss. Aug92; MCLD 19159)*
(above lp & below 45, were from the MCA film 'Wages Of Fear')

Aug 77. (7") *<40740>* **BETRAYAL. / GRIND** [–] [ ]

Nov 77. (d-lp/d-c) *(VD/TCVD 2506) <35014>* **ENCORE (live)** [55] [ ]
– Cherokee lane / Moonlight / Coldwater canyon / Desert dream. *(cd-iss. Jul87; CDV 2506) (cd re-iss. Apr95; TAND 1)*

Jan 78. (7") *(VS 199)* **ENCORE. / HOBO MARCH** [ ] [–]

Mar 78. (7") *<9516>* **MOONLIGHT. / COLDWATER CANYON** [–] [ ]

— **STEVE JOLIFFE** – vocals, keyboards, wind returned after several years to repl. BAUMANN who went solo. Added **KLAUS KRIEGER** – drums

Mar 78. (lp/c) *(V/TCV 2097)* **CYCLONE** [37] [–]
– Bent cold sidewalk / Rising runner missed by endless sender / Madrigal meridian. *(cd-iss. Jul87; CDV 2097) (re-iss. Aug88 lp/c; OVED/+C 71) (cd re-iss. Apr95)*

Feb 79. (lp,clear-lp/c) *(V/TCV 2111)* **FORCE MAJEURE** [26] [–]
– Force majeure / Cloudburst flight / Thru metamorphic rocks. *(cd-iss. Jul87; CDV 2111) (re-iss. Aug88 lp/c; OVED/+C 111) cd re-iss. Apr95; TAND 10)*

— (now trio) **FROESE + FRANKE** recruited **JOHANNES SCHMOELLING** – keyboards

May 80. (lp/c) *(V/TCV 2147)* **TANGRAM** [36] [–]
– Tangram set 1 / Tangram set 2. *(cd-iss. Oct85; CDV 2147) (re-iss. Aug88 lp/c; OVED/+C 112) (cd-iss. Apr95; TAND 11)*

Virgin — Elektra

Apr 81. (lp/c) *(V/TCV 2198) <521>* **THIEF (Soundtrack)** [43] [ ]
– Beach theme / Dr. Destructo / Diamond diary / Burning bar / Scrap yard / Trap feeling / Igneous / Confrontation. *(re-iss. Aug88 lp/c; OVED/+C 72) (cd-iss. Jun88; CDV 2198) (cd re-iss. Aug95; TAND 12)*

Sep 81. (lp/c) *(V/TCV 2212) <557>* **EXIT** [43] [ ]
– Kiev mission / Pilots of purple twilight / Chronozon / Exit / Network 23 / Remote viewing. *(re-iss. Aug88 lp/c; OVED/+C 166) (cd-iss. Aug88; CDV 2212) (re-iss. cd Aug95; TAND 13)*

Sep 81. (7") *(VS 444)* **CHRONOZON. / NETWORK 23** [ ] [–]

Apr 82. (lp/c) *(V/TCV 2226)* **WHITE EAGLE** [57] [–]
– Midnight in Tulo / Convention of the 24 / White eagle / Mojave plan. *(re-iss. Aug88 lp/c; OVED/+C 150) (cd-iss. Aug88; CDV 2226) (cd re-iss. Aug95; TAND 2)*

Dec 82. (lp/c) *(V/TCV 2257)* **LOGOS – LIVE (At The Dominion)** [ ] [–]
– Logos part 1 / Logos part 2 / Dominion. *(re-iss. Apr86 lp/c; OVED 167) (cd-iss. Jun88; CDV 2257) (re-iss. cd Aug95; TAND 3)*

1983. (lp/c) *<STV/CTV 81207>* **WAVELENGTH (Soundtrack)** [–] [ ]
– Alien voices / Wavelength (main title) / Desert drive / Mojave (end title) / Healing / Breakout / Alien goodbyes / Spaceship / Church theme / Sunset drive / Airshaft / lley walk / Cyro lab / Running through the hills / Campfire theme / Mojave (end title reprise). *(UK cd-iss. Jan89 also on 'Varese Sarabande'; VCD 47223)*

Oct 83. (lp/c/cd) *(V/TCV/CDV 2292)* **HYPERBOREA** [45] [–]
– No man's lannd / Hyperborea / Cinnamon road / Sphinx lightning. *(re-iss. Jun88 lp/c; OVED/+C 175) (re-iss. cd Aug95; TAND 4)*

Dec 83. (lp/c) *(V/TCV 2302) <098620>* **RISKY BUSINESS (Soundtrack)** [ ] [ ]
– The dream is always the same / No future / Love on a real train / Guido the killer pimp / Lana / (tracks by other artists; PHIL COLLINS / JOURNEY / MUDDY WATERS / JEFF BECK / BOB SEGER). *(cd-iss. May87; CDV 2302) (re-iss. Apr90 lp/c; OVED/+C 2302)*

M.C.A. — Varese

Jul 84. (lp/c) *(MCF/+C 3233) <5251>* **FIRESTARTER (Soundtrack)** [ ] [ ]
– Crystal voice / The run / Test lab / Charley the kid / Escaping point / Rainbirds move / Burning force / Between realities / Shop territory / Flash final / Out of the heat. *(re-iss. Jan89; MCA/+C 6163) (cd-iss. Apr90; DMCL 1899)*

Jive Electro — Relativity

Sep 84. (7"/7"sha-pic-d) *(JIVE/+P 74)* **WARSAW IN THE SUN. / POLISH DANCE** [ ] [–]
(12"+=) *(JIVET 74)* – ('A'-part 2) / Rare bird.

Oct 84. (d-lp/d-pic-lp/c) *(HIP/+X/C 22) <826099>* **POLAND – THE WARSAW CONCERT (live)** [90] [ ]
– Poland / Tangent / Barbakane / Horizon. *(cd-iss. 1988; CHIP 22) (re-iss. cd May96 on 'Essential'; ESMCD 365)*
(below album released on 'Heavy Metal' UK / 'EMI America' US)

Feb 85. (lp/pic-lp/c) *(HM1 HP/PD/MC 29) <ST 17141>* **FLASHPOINT (Soundtrack)** [ ] Dec84 [ ]
– Going west / Afternoon in the desert / Plane ride / Mystery tracks / Lost in the dunes / Highway patrol / Love phantasy / Madcap story / Dirty cross-roads / Flashpoint. *(cd-iss. Apr87; HM1 XD 29) (re-iss. cd Sep95 on 'One Way';)*

Aug 85. (lp/c) *(HIP/+C 26) <8043>* **LE PARC** [ ] [ ]
– Bois de Boulogne (Paris) / Central Park (New York) / Gaudi Park (Guell Garden, Barcelona) / Tiergarten (Berlin) / Zen Garden (Myoonj, Temple Kyoto) / Le Parc (L.A. Streethawk) / Hyde Park (London) / The Cliffs of Sydney (Sydney) / Yellowstone Park (Rocky Mountains). *(cd-iss. Mar88; CHIP 26) (re-iss. cd May96 on 'Essential'; ESMCD 364)*

— guest on above album **CLARE TORY** – vocals

Aug 85. (7") *(JIVE 101)* **STREETHAWK. / TIERGARTEN** [ ] [–]
(12"+=) *(JIVET 101)* – Gaudi Park / Warsaw in the sun (part 1 & 2).

1985. (lp) *Virgin; (207 212-620)* **HEARTBREAKERS (soundtrack)** [–] German [–]
– Heartbreakers / Footbridge to Heaven / Twilight painter / Gemeni / Rain in N.Y. city / Pastime / The loser / Breathing the night away / Desire / Thorny affair / Daybreak. *(UK cd-iss. Jun95 on 'Silva Screen'; FILMCD 163)*

— **PAUL HASLINGER** – multi; repl. SCHMOELLING who went solo

Jul 86. (lp/c)(cd) *(HIP/+C 40)(CHIP 40) <8113>* **UNDERWATER SUNLIGHT** [97] [ ]
– Song of the whale / From dawn . . . to dusk / Ride on the ray / Dolphin dance / Underwater sunlight / Scuba scuba. *(cd re-iss. May96 on 'Essential'; ESMCD 366)*

Aug 86. (12"ep) *<88561-8120-1>* **DOLPHIN DANCE. / DOLPHIN SMILE / SONG OF THE WHALE** [–] [ ]

Jive Caroline

Jun 87. (lp/c)(cd) *(HIP/+C 47)(CHIP 47) <CAROL 1341>* **TYGER** [88] [ ]
– Tyger / London / Alchemy of the heart / Smile. *(cd+=)* – 21st century common man I & II. *(cd re-iss. May96 on 'Essential'; ESMCD 367)*

— guest vox – BERNADETTE SMITH

Jun 87. (7") *(JIVE 143)* **TYGER. / 21st CENTURY COMMON MAN II** [ ] [ ]
(12"+=) *(JIVET 143)* – ('A'extended).

1987. (lp) *Atlantic; <47357>* **THREE O'CLOCK HIGH (Soundtrack shared with SYLVESTER LEVAY)** [–] [ ]
– It's Jerry's day today / 46-32-15 / No detention / Any school bully will do / Go to the head of the class / (other artist) / Big bright brass knuckles / Buying paper like it's going out of style / Dangerous trend / Who's chasing who? / Bonding by candlelight / You'll never believe it / Starting the day off right / Weak at the knees / Kill him (the football dummy) / Not so quiet in the library – Get lost in a crowd / (other artists). *(UK cd-iss. Oct90 also on 'Varese Sarabande'; VCD 47307)*

Apr 88. (lp/c)(cd) *(HIP/+C 62)(CHIP 62) <CAROL 1349>* **LIVEMILES (live)** [ ] [ ]
– Live miles: (part 1) – The Albuquerque concert / Live miles: (part 2) – The West Berlin concert. *(re-iss. cd May96 on 'Essential'; ESMCD 368)*

Silva Screen Silva Screen

Feb 88. (lp/c/cd) *(<FILM/+C/CD 026>)* **NEAR DARK (Soundtrack)** [ ] Nov87 [ ]
– Cabeb's blues / Pick up at high noon / Rain in the third house / Bus station / Good times / She's my sister / Father and son / Severin dies / Flight at dawn / Mae's transformation / Mae comes back. *(re-iss. Jun90; same)*

Jul 88. (lp/c/cd) *(<FILM/+C/CD 027>)* **SHY PEOPLE (Soundtrack)** [ ] Nov87 [ ]
– Shy people / Joe's place / The harbor / Nightfal / Dancing on a white moon / Civilized illusion's / Swamp voices / Transparent days / Shy people (reprise).

— now a duo of **FROESE + HASLINGER**

Arista Private Music

Feb 89. (lp/c/cd) *(209/409/259 557) <2042-1/-4/-2 P>* **OPTICAL RACE** [ ] Aug88 [ ]
– Marakesh / Atlas eyes / Mothers of rain / Twin soul tribe / Optical race / Cat scan / Sun gate / Turning of the wheel / The midnight trail / Ghtrezi (long song).

Jul 89. (lp/c/cd) *<209/409/259 887>* **MIRACLE MILE** [–] [ ]
– Teetering scales / One for the book / After the call / On the spur of the moment / All of a dither / Final statement. *(re-iss. cd Feb96; 260.016)*

Dec 89. (lp/c/cd) *<210/410/260 103>* **LILY ON THE BEACH** [–] [ ]
– Too hot for my chinchilla / Lily on the beach / Alaskan summer / Desert drive / Mount Shasta / Crystal curfew / Paradise cove / Twenty nine palms / Valley of the kings / Radio city / Blue mango cafe / Gecko / Long island sunset.

Nov 90. (cd/lp) *(<261/211 105>)* **MELROSE** [ ] Sep90 [ ]
– Melrose / Three bikes in the sky / Dolls in the shadow / Yucatan / Electric lion / Rolling down Cahenga / Art of vision / Desert train / Cool at heart.

Silva Screen Silva Screen

Mar 91. (cd) *(FILMCD 079)* **DEAD SOLID PERFECT (Soundtrack)** [ ] [ ]
– Theme from Dead Solid Perfect / In the pond / Beverly leaves / Of cads and caddies / (Tournament montage) / A whore in one / Sand trap / In the rough / Nine iron / US Open / My name is bad hair / In the hospital room / Welcome to Bushwood / Deja vu / Birdie / Divot / Kenny and Donny montage / Phone to Beverly / Nice shots / Sinking putts / Kenny's winning shot.

Oct 91. (cd) *(FILMCD 080) <1004-2>* **THE PARK IS MINE** [ ] Mar92 [ ]
– The park is mine – main title / Fatal fall – Funeral / The letter (parts 1 & 2) / Taking the park (parts 1 & 2) / Swatting S.W.A.T. / Love theme / Helicopter attack / Morning / We're running out of time / The claymore mine – Stalking / The final confrontation – The park is yours / Finale – End credits.

— Now a duo of **FROESE + JEROME FROESE** his son and **LINDA SPA** – sax / **ZLASLO PERICA** – synth.

Feb 92. Essential; (cd/c/lp) *(ESM CD/MC/LP 403) / Miramar; <2802>* **ROCKOON** [ ] [ ]
– Big city dwarves / Red roadster / Touchwood / Graffiti sreeet / Funky Atlanta / Spanish love / Lifted veil / Penguin reference / Body corporate / Rockoon / Girls on Broadway. *(re-iss. cd Feb96; same) (cd re-iss. Feb00 on 'Tandream'; TDICD 017)*

Dec 92. (cd) *(<FILMCD 121>)* **DEADLY CARE (Soundtrack)** [ ] [ ]
– Main theme / Paddles – Stolen pills / A strong drink – A bad morning / Wasted and sick / Hope for future / The hospital in bed / Annie and father / More pills / In the Head nurse's – At the father's grave / Clean and sober.

Miramar Miramar

Jul 93. (cd) *(<MPCD 2801>)* **CANYON DREAMS** [ ] [ ]
– Shadow flyer / Canyon carver / Water's gift / Canyon voices / Sudden revelation / A matter of time / Purple nightfall / Colorado dawn. *(re-iss. Nov99 on 'Tandream'; TDICD 021)*

Oct 93. (cd/c) *(<MPCD/MPMC 2804>)* **220 VOLT LIVE (live)** [ ] [ ]
– Oriental haze / Two bunch palms / 220 volt / Homeless / Treasure of innocence / Sundance kid / Backstreet hero / The blue bridge / Hamlet / Dreamtime / Purple haze. *(cd re-iss. Nov99 on 'Tandream'; TDICD 018)*

CoastCoast Miramar

Nov 94. (cd) *(CTCZ 108) <2806>* **TURN OF THE TIDES** [ ] [ ]
– Pictures at an exhibition / Firetongues / Galley slave's horizon / Death of a nightingale / Twilight brigade / Jungle journey / Midwinter night / Turn of the tides. *(re-iss. Nov96; same) (cd re-iss. Nov99 on 'Tangerine Dream Int,'; TDICD 019)*

Amp Miramar

Sep 95. (cd) *(23046) <MM 137>* **TYRANNY OF BEAUTY** [ ] [ ]
– Catwalk / Birdwatcher's dream / Little blond in the park of attractions / Living in a fountain pen / Stratosfear 95 / Bride in cold tears / Haze of fame / Tyranny of beauty / Largo / (untitled). *(re-iss. Oct96 on 'Tangerine Dream Int.'; TDI 002CD) (cd re-iss. Nov99; TDICD 020)*

When! Tangerine

Sep 96. (cd) *(<WENCD 011>)* **GOBLIN'S CLUB** [ ] [ ]
– Towards the evening star / At Darwin's motel / On Crane's passage / Rising haul in silence / United goblin's parade / Lamb with radar eyes / Elf June and the midnight patrol / Sad Merlin's Sunday.

Mar 97. (c-s) *(WENM 1022)* **TOWARDS THE EVENING STAR / ('A'mix)** [ ] [–]
(12"+=/cd-s+=) *(WEN T/X 1022)* – ('A'remixes).

Tandream Miramar

Jun 97. (cd) *(TDI 009CD) <63009>* **OASIS** (soundtrack) [ ] Oct97 [ ]
– Flashflood / Zion / Reflections / Cliff dwellers / Waterborne / Cedar breaks / Summer storm / Hopi mesa heart / Chia maroon. *(re-iss. Mar00; same)*

Sep 97. (cd) *(TDI 011CD)* **TOURNADO (live in Europe)** [ ] [–]
– Flashflood / 220 volt / Firetongues / Girls on Broadway / Little blond in the park of attractions / Rising haul in silence / Lamb with radar eyes / Touchwood / Towards the evening star.

Apr 99. (cd) *(TDI 012CD) <63012>* **TRANS SIBERIA** [ ] [ ]
– Yarloslaw station / Smoky Karlow / Siberian lights / Jenissei river / Baikal sunrise / Samowar Juri / Ulan-Ude / Chingan night / Russian soul / The golden horn.

May 99. (cd) *(TDICD 015) <63015>* **WHAT A BLAST** (soundtrack)
– Stoneyard / Silver screen / Beauty of the blast / Dream sculpture / Last trumpet on 23rd Street / Art of destruction / Forced to surrender / TimeSquare (the legendary N.Y. Brix mix) / Jungle journey (the bond of ages mix).

Jul 99. (cd) *(TDI 016CD) <63016>* **MARS POLARIS**
– Comet's figure head / Rim of Schiaparelli / Pilots of the ether belt / Deep space cruiser / Outland (the colony) / Spiral star date / Mars mission encounter / Astrophobia / Tharsis manoeuver / Dies martis (transmercury).

Mar 00. (cd) *(TDI 022CD) <63022>* **GREAT WALL OF CHINA** Jan00
– Meng tian / Summer in Shauxi / The south gate knights / Silence the barking monk / Zhu zhanji / Stranded without shade / No more candles burning / Lights of Beijing / Snow on dragon's peak / Cradle of prodigies / Tiger forest.

Nov 00. (cd) *(TDI 029CD) <63029>* **THE SEVEN LETTERS FROM TIBET** Aug00
– The red blood connection / The orange breath / The golden heart / The green land / The blue pearl / The indigo clouds / The purple of all curtains.

Dec 02. (cd) *(<TDICD 032>)* **INFERNO (live)** Sep02
– Before the closing of the day / The spirit of Virgil / Minotaurae hunt at dawn / Those once broke the first word / Dante in despair / Io non mori / Vidi tre facce / At the deepest point in space / L'omperador del doloroso regno / Voices in a starless night / Fear and longing / Fallen for death / Where all light went silent / Charon, il barchere / La grey de los almas perdidas / Justice of the karma law / As the sun moves towards heaven / Beatrice, l'ame infinie.

– compilations, others, etc. –

—— on 'Virgin' unless mentioned otherwise

Jul 76. (d-lp) *(VD 2504)* **ATEM / ALPHA CENTAURI** –

Dec 80. (4xlp-box) *(VBOX 2)* **TANGERINE DREAM '70-80** –

Nov 85. (t-lp/d-c/d-cd) *(TDLP/TDC/CDTD 1)* **DREAM SEQUENCE** –
(re-iss. d-cd Apr92; same)

Mar 86. (6xlp-box) *Jive Electro; (TANG 1)* **IN THE BEGINNING** –
– (ELECTRONIC MEDITATION / ALPHA CENTAURI / ZEIT (d-lp) / ATEM / GREEN DESERT)

May 86. (lp) *M.C.A.; <6165>* **LEGEND (Soundtrack with other artists)** – 96
– Unicorn theme / Blue room / Darkness / The dance / Goblins / Fairies / The kitchen (medley).

1986. (lp) *(207684620)* **PERGAMON – LIVE AT THE PALAST DER REPUBLIK** *(live & originally issued in East Germany 1980 as 'QUICHOTTE'; Amiga 855891)* – German –
(UK cd-iss. May96 as 'PERGAMON' on 'Essential'; ESMCD 413)

Dec 86. (cd) *Zomba; (CTANG 1)* **GREEN DESERT** (rec.1973) –
(re-iss. May89 on 'Jive' lp/c; HOP/+C 226) (re-iss. Feb96 on 'Essential'; ESMCD 349)

Mar 87. (d-lp/c/cd) *(CCS LP/MC/CD 161)* **THE TANGERINE DREAM COLLECTION** –

Nov 89. (lp/c)(cd) *Jive; (HIP/+C 75)(CHIP 75)* **THE BEST OF TANGERINE DREAM**

Nov 90. (3xcd-box) *(TPAK 11)* **COLLECTORS' EDITION** –
– (CYCLONE / FORCE MAJEURE / ENCORE)

Oct 91. (cd/c) *Music Club; (MC CD/TC 034)* **FROM DAWN . . . TILL DUSK 1973-88** –

Feb 93. (cd) *Private Music; (01005 82105-2)* **THE PRIVATE MUSIC OF TANGERINE DREAM** –

Mar 93. (cd) *Silva Screen; (FILMCD 125)* **DREAM MUSIC**
– from films; THE PARK IS MINE / DEADLY CARE / DEAD SOLID PERFECT.

Oct 94. (5xcd-box) *(CDBOX 4)* **TANGENTS** –

Mar 95. (cd) *Emporio; (EMPRCD 564)* **ATMOSPHERICS** –

Nov 95. (cd) *Silva Screen; (FILMCD 166)* **DREAM MUSIC 2**

Dec 95. (d-cd) *Essential; (EDFCD 353)* **BOOK OF DREAMS** –
– (THE PINK YEARS: 1970-1973) // THE BLUE YEARS: 1983-1987)

Jul 96. (cd) *Tangerine Dream Int.; (TDI 001CD)* **THE DREAM MIXES** –

Nov 96. (5xcd-box) *Essential; (ESFCD 420)* **THE DREAM ROOTS COLLECTION** –

Jan 98. (cd) *Castle; (CCSCD 815)* **THE COLLECTION VOL.1** –

Mar 98. (cd) *Castle; (CCSCD 824)* **THE BEST OF TANGERINE DREAM: THE BLUE YEARS** –

Apr 98. (d-cd) *Cleopatra; (CLP 227)* **THE ANALOGUE SPACE YEARS 1969-1973** –

May 98. (lp; with NEIL NORMAN) *GNP Crescendo; (GNPS 2146)* **MUSIC FROM THE 21st CENTURY** –

Oct 98. (3xcd-box) *Essential; (ESMBX 305)* **ELECTRONIC MEDITATION / ALPHA CENTAURI / ZEIT** –

Mar 99. (cd) *Disky; (VI 87377-2)* **TANGERINE DREAM**

May 99. (cd) *Tandream; (TDICD 014) <63014>* **SOHOMAN (live in Sydney 1982)**

Jun 99. (cd) *Tandream; (TDI 010CD) <63010>* **QUINOA**
– Voxel ux / Quinoa / Lhasa.

Sep 99. (cd) *Castle; (CMP 1005)* **VIDEO DREAM MIXES**

Oct 99. (cd) *Miramar; <23144>* **ARCHITECTURE IN MOTION** –

Mar 00. (cd) *Tandream; (TDICD 001) / Resurgent; <4250>* **AMBIENT MONKEYS (live 1997)** 1998
– Token from Birdland / Symphony in a minor / The seventh propeller of silence / Calyx calamander / Largo / Riddle of the monkey tribe / Moon marble / Concerto in a minor, adagio / Lemon vendor khaly / Campera de mon glyan / Virtue is its own reward / Pantha rhei / Myopia world.

Mar 00. (cd) *Tandream; (TDICD 002) <63002>* **ATLANTIC DREAMS**

Mar 00. (cd) *Tandream; (TDICD 003) <63003>* **ATLANTIC WALLS**

Mar 00. (cd) *Tandream; (TDICD 004) <63004>* **DREAM ENCORES (live)** Jun99
– Order of the ginger guild / Forth Worth runway one / Eleanor Rigby / Oriental haze / Story of the brave / Thief Yang and the tangram seal / Catwalk / Purple haze / The midnight trail / Rolling down Cahuenga / Towards the evening star / Dominion.

Mar 00. (d-cd) *Tandream; (TDICD 005) <63005>* **DREAM MIXES I** –

Mar 00. (cd) *Tandream; (TDICD 006) <63006>* **TIMESQUARE – DREAM MIXES II** (rec. summer 1997)
– Mobocaster / Jungle jacula / Towards the evening star / Digital sister / Pixel pirates / Culpa levis / TimesSquare.

Mar 00. (cd) *Tandream; (TDICD 007) <63007>* **THE HOLLYWOOD YEARS VOL.1**

Mar 00. (cd) *Tandream; (TDICD 008) <63008>* **THE HOLLYWOOD YEARS VOL.2**

Mar 00. (cd) *Tandream; (TDICD 013) <63013>* **VALENTINE WHEELS**

May 00. (d-cd) *Tandream; (TDICD 026) <63026>* **TANG-GO – THE WORLD OF TANGERINE DREAM 1990-2000**

Jun 00. (cd) *(TDI 027CD) <63027>* **SOUNDMILL NAVIGATOR (live at the Philharmonics 1976)** Apr00
– Soundmill navigator.

Aug 00. (cd) *Tandream; (TDICD 028) <63028>* **ANTIQUE DREAMS**

May 01. (cd) *Tandream; (TDICD 031) <63031>* **DM3: DREAM MIXES THREE** Apr01
– Prime time / Astrophobia / Stereolight / Diamonds and dust / Blue spears / Meng tian / Girl on the stairs / The spirit of the czar / The comfort zone.

May 03. (cd) *Tandream; (<TDICD 001>)* **MOTA ATMA**
– The courage to lose / For the summit only / No pleasure no pain / Royal way of privacy / Phoenix burning / Prophet in chains / Snow on angels feather / A fair days wage / Brain offender / A day in Liberty Valley.

EDGAR FROESE

—— solo (all music by himself)

Virgin Virgin

Jun 74. (lp) *(V 2016) <13111>* **AQUA**
– NGC 891 / Upland / Aqua / Panorphelia. *(re-iss. Mar84; OVED 20) (cd-iss. Jun87; CDV 2016)*

Sep 75. (lp) *(V 2040)* **EPSILON IN MALAYSIAN PALE** –
– Epsilon in Malaysian pale / Maroubra Bay. *(re-iss. Mar84; OVED 22) (cd-iss. Jun87; CDV 2040)*

1976. Brain; (lp) *(60.008)* **MACULA TRANSFER** – German –
– Os / Af / Pa / Quantas / If. *(re-iss. Mar82; 0060.008)*

Jan 78. (d-lp) *(VD 2507)* **AGES** –
– Metropolis / Era of the slaves / Tropic of Capricorn / Nights of automatic women / Icarus / Childrens deeper study / Ode to Granny "A" / Pizarro and Atahwallpa / Golgatha and the circle closes. *(cd-iss. Jun97; CDOVD 480)*

Sep 79. (lp) *(V 2139)* **STUNTMAN** ☐ [–]
– Stuntman / It would be like Samoa / Detroit snackbar dreamer / Drunken Mozart in the desert / A Dali-esque sleep fuse / Scarlet score for Mescalero. *(re-iss. Mar84; OVED 21) (cd-iss. Jun87 & Mar94; CDV 2139)*

Oct 82. (lp) *(V 2255)* **KAMIKAZE 1989 (Soundtrack)** ☐ [–]
– Videophonic / Vitamen 'C' / Krismopompas / Polizei disco / Intuition / Polizei therapie center / Blauer panther / Schlangenbad / Underwarter tod / Flying kamikaze / Der konzern / Der 31. stock. *(re-iss. Aug88; OVED 125) (cd-iss. Aug88; CDV 2255)*

Aug 83. (lp) *(V 2277)* **PINNACLES** ☐ [–]
– Specific gravity of smile / The light cone / Walkabout / Pinnacles. *(re-iss. Aug88; OVED 144) (cd-iss. May88; CDV 2277)*

– FROESE compilations, others –

Aug 82. (lp) *Virgin; (V 2197)* **SOLO 1974-1979** ☐ [–]
(re-iss. Mar84; OVED 21) (cd-iss. Aug88; CDV 2197)

Jun 95. (d-cd) *Ambient; (AMBT 5)* **BEYOND THE STORM** ☐ [–]

☐ TAPPI TiKARRASS (see under ⇒ BJORK)

TAPROOT

Formed: Ann Arbor, Michigan, USA . . . 1997 by University of Michigan students STEPHEN RICHARDS, MIKE DeWOLF, PHIL LIPSCOMB and JARROD MONTAGUE. Inspired by the likes of NIRVANA and RAGE AGAINST THE MACHINE, TAPROOT began using the internet for publicity and eventually appropriated a fan's web page as their official site. With a bit of DIY improvement, the site soon generated enough interest for the band to distribute a demo to LIMP BIZKIT mainman FRED DURST. A growing friendship ended in tears after DURST allegedly offered a below par deal and TAPROOT looked elsewhere, resulting in a now infamous answering machine message from the pissed off 'BIZKIT mainman. Undeterred, the group released their self-produced debut album, 'SOMETHING MORE THAN NOTHING' (1998) off their own steam, following it up with the 'MENTOBE' EP. Their internet endeavours together with word of mouth publicity soon attracted major label interest, the band signing with 'Atlantic' for their second album, 'GIFT' (2000). Awarded 5 stars by Kerrang!, the record bore favourable comparison with rap-influenced nu-metal pioneers such as KORN and DEFTONES with a conspicuous lack of any contrived image going in their favour. This very quality perhaps worked against them on 'WELCOME' (2002), another post-grunge by numbers set to add to the avalanche of similar albums clogging up American charts and radio.

Album rating: GIFT (*7) / WELCOME (*5)

STEPHEN RICHARDS – vocals, guitar / **MIKE DeWOLF** – guitar / **PHIL LIPSCOMB** – bass / **JARROD MONTAGUE** – drums

Atlantic Atlantic

Sep 00. (cd) *<(7567 83341-2)>* **GIFT** ☐ Jun00 ☐
– Smile / Again and again / Emotional times / Now / 1 nite stand / Believed / Mentobe / I / Mirror's reflection / Dragged down / Comeback / Impact.

Mar 01. (cd-s) *(AT 0099CD)* **AGAIN AND AGAIN (clean version) / DAY BY DAY / SMILE (clean version)** ☐ [–]

Oct 02. (cd) *<(7567 83561-2)>* **WELCOME** ☐ [17]
– Mine / Poem / Everything / Art / Myself / When / Fault / Sumtimes / Breathe / Like / Dreams / Time.

Oct 02. (cd-s) *(AT 0138CD)* **POEM / TRANSPARENT / FREE** ☐ [–]

☐ TASTE (see under ⇒ GALLAGHER, Rory)

James TAYLOR

Born: 12 Mar'48, Boston, Massachusetts, USA. Despite a privileged upbringing, the troubled TAYLOR admitted himself to a mental institute in 1965, aged only 17. It was during his near-year long stay that the budding singer began writing his own material although it would be early '67 before he'd get the chance to lay some of his ideas down on vinyl. This opportunity presented itself after TAYLOR moved to New York and hooked up with old friend DANNY KORTCHMAR in The FLYING MACHINE, the group subsequently recording two TAYLOR tracks, 'NIGHT OWL' and 'BRIGHTEN YOUR NIGHT WITH MY DAY'. A combination of poor sales and TAYLOR's worsening heroin addiction caused the band to splinter a few months later, the singer subsequently moving to Notting Hill in London the following year. Persuaded to send a demo to Peter Asher, then A&R man at 'Apple' (and future manager of LINDA RONSTADT), TAYLOR soon found himself recording for The BEATLES' fledgling label. His Asher-produced, eponymous debut was released at the tail end of the year, a promising collection of understated strumming and wistful introspection. Almost country-rock but not quite, such memorable originals as 'SOMETHING IN THE WAY SHE MOVES' (NOT the BEATLES song!) and the yearning 'CAROLINA IN MY MIND' marked TAYLOR out as a kind of male JONI MITCHELL, if not quite as adventurous. As it turned out, the pair found they had more in common than just music, TAYLOR and MITCHELL becoming romantically involved in the early 70's. As well as performing together, the couple guested on each other's releases with MITCHELL partly documenting the affair on her landmark 'BLUE' album. Despite its potential, 'JAMES TAYLOR' sank without trace amid the chaotic situation at 'Apple', both TAYLOR and ASHER moving back to the States. After another period in a mental institution, TAYLOR emerged to find himself with a 'Warner Bros' contract, pre-arranged by ASHER (now his manager). Surrounding himself with the likes of RUSS KUNKEL, RANDY MEISNER and CAROLE KING, TAYLOR duly cut a belated follow-up album. Though it took a while to warm up, 'SWEET BABY JAMES' (1970) became one of the best selling US albums of the early 70's as well as a blueprint of sorts for the Laurel Canyon elite (whose tortured musings would come to dominate the American rock scene). Following the Top 3 success of the enduring 'FIRE AND RAIN', the album went on to reside in the upper reaches of the US chart for more than a year, its unassuming confessionals striking at the strife-torn heart of the post-hipppie dream. Not blessed with the most striking of voices, TAYLOR nevertheless relied on it to power his songs, backed by the sparsest of accompaniment, an acoustic strum here, a hint of pedal steel there. What he lacked in impact he made up for in intimacy (although his vocals improved over time), it's just a pity he moved ever further into MOR schmooze-pop. 'MUD SLIDE SLIM AND THE BLUE HORIZON' (1971) consolidated TAYLOR's standing in the L.A. firmament, a transatlantic Top 5 which featured his rather weak reading of CAROLE KING's 'YOU'VE GOT A FRIEND', a US No.1 later that summer. Ironically, many of TAYLOR's subsequent hits would be cover versions although his original material was far more affecting, the lovely 'YOU CAN CLOSE YOUR EYES' for example. This period saw TAYLOR at the height of his fame and apart from the inevitable media attention over his marriage to CARLY SIMON on the 3rd of November '72, he subsequently avoided the spotlight. Both 'ONE MAN DOG' (1972) and 'WALKING MAN' (1974) failed to spawn any major hits, TAYLOR's only Top 5 single during this time a duet with SIMON entitled 'MOCKINGBIRD'. 'GORILLA' (1975) marked a return to form of sorts, the buoyant 'MEXICO' demonstrating what TAYLOR was capable of when he decided to step up a gear. The album's hit was a laboured cover of Marvin Gaye's 'HOW SWEET IT IS TO BE LOVED BY YOU', the song going Top 5 in the summer of '75. Two years on, TAYLOR repeated the success with yet another cover, a strident run-through of the Jimmy Jones & Otis Blackwell's R&B number, 'HANDY MAN'. The album which housed it, 'J.T.' (1977), was TAYLOR's last commercial blockbuster, subsequent releases selling respectably but failing to produce any singles. For the ensuing two years, the singer turned his talents towards collaboration; Autumn '77 saw him produce and play guitar on sister KATE TAYLOR's debut US Top 50 single, 'IT'S IN HIS KISS', while early the folowing year he was credited alongside PAUL SIMON and ART GARFUNKEL on a hit cover of SAM COOKE's 'WONDERFUL WORLD'. 'FLAG' (1979) gave him another Top 10 album although the formula was wearing a mite thin, his marriage with SIMON soon going the same way. In late '78 the couple rode into the Top 40 together with the duet 'DEVOTED TO YOU', but in 1982, CARLY filed for divorce. TAYLOR had hit the US charts the previous year with his last Top 10 album, 'DAD LOVES HIS WORK', the singer spending the first half of the 80's on a massive world tour. Though his albums didn't command the mass audience of yore, TAYLOR retained a loyal following throughout the 80's and beyond. Fans lapped up 'THAT'S WHY I'M HERE' (1986), although he only really hit the mark with 'NEW MOON SHINE' (1991), a strong set which tackled many current issues in impressive fashion and proved that TAYLOR, along with his old mucker, JACKSON BROWNE, could still cut the mustard. A (US) Top 20 live album in 1993 marked his biggest success for years and certainly, it's on a stage in lone acoustic fashion that TAYLOR really comes into his own, the singer playing some rare, warmly received Scottish dates in early '98 at the annual Celtic Connections festival in Glasgow. On the recording front, he finally broke his silence with 'OCTOBER ROAD' (2002), a rich, mellow, intimate album perfectly in tune with his advancing middle age. Unhurried and glowing with contentment without sounding smug, the likes of the title track resurrected well worn themes from his long career, laying his ghosts to rest once and for all. • **Songwriters:** Prolific pensmith, who also covered others; LO AND BEHOLD (Bob Dylan) / MOCKINGBIRD duet (Inez & Charlie Foxx) / DEVOTED TO YOU duet (Everly Brothers) / UP ON THE ROOF (Goffin-King) / DAY TRIPPER (Beatles) / JELLY MAN KELLY (with daughter Sarah) / EVERYDAY (Buddy Holly). • **Trivia:** TAYLOR starred in the 1971 road movie, 'Two Lane Blacktop' and also acted on US TV production, 'Working' (1981).

Album rating: JAMES TAYLOR (*7) / SWEET BABY JAMES (*8) / MUD SLIDE SLIM AND THE BLUE HORIZON (*7) / ONE MAN DOG (*6) / WALKING MAN (*6) / GORILLA (*6) / IN THE POCKET (*5) / GREATEST HITS compilation (*8) / JT (*7) / FLAG (*6) / DAD LOVES HIS WORK (*5) / THAT'S WHY I'M HERE (*6) / BEST OF JAMES TAYLOR – CLASSIC SONGS compilation (*7) / NEVER DIE YOUNG (*5) / NEW MOON SHINE (*6) / (LIVE) (*6) / HOURGLASS (*6) / GREATEST HITS VOLUME 2 compilation (*7) / OCTOBER ROAD (*6) / YOU'VE GOT A FRIEND – THE BEST OF . . . compilation (*8)

JAMES TAYLOR – vocals, acoustic guitar (with session people)

Apple / Apple

Dec 68. (lp) *(SAPCOR 3)* *<3352>* **JAMES TAYLOR** [ ] Sep 70 [62]
– Don't talk now / Something's wrong / Knockin' round the zoo / Sunshine sunshine / Taking it in / Something in the way she moves / Carolina in my mind / Brighten your night with my day / Night owl / Rainy day man / Circle 'round the Sun / The blues is just a bad dream. *(re-iss. Jun71; same) (re-iss. Oct91)*

Apr 69. (7") *<1805>* **CAROLINA ON MY MIND. / SOMETHING'S WRONG** [–] [ ]
<re-iss. Nov70; same> – <hit No.67>

—— now with **DANNY KOOTCH** (b.KORTCHMAR) – guitar / **CAROLE KING** – piano / **RUSS KUNKEL** – drums / **RANDY MEISNER, BOBBY WEST + JOHN LONDON** – bass / **CHRIS DARROW** – fiddle / **RED RHODES** – steel guitar / **JACK BIELAN** – brass arrangement

Warners / Warners

Jul 70. (7") *<7387>* **SWEET BABY JAMES. / SUITE FOR ZOG** [–] [ ]

Sep 70. (7") *<7423>* **FIRE AND RAIN. / ANYWHERE LIKE HEAVEN** [–] [3]

Nov 70. (7") *(WB 6104)* **FIRE AND RAIN. / SUNNY SKIES** [42] [–]

Nov 70. (lp) *(K 46043)* *<1843>* **SWEET BABY JAMES** [7] Mar 70 [3]
– Sweet baby James / Lo and behold / Sunny skies / Steamroller / Country road / Oh, Susannah / Fire and rain / Blossom / Anywhere like Heaven / Oh baby, don't you loose your lip on me / Suite for 20 G. *(re-iss. Dec71, hit UK No.34) (re-iss. Jul88 cd/c; K2/K4 46043)*

Feb 71. (7") *<7460>* **COUNTRY ROAD. / SUNNY SKIES** [–] [37]

—— **LEE SKLAR** – bass repl. 3 bassmen. Guest **JONI MITCHELL** – b.vox (2 – 45's)

May 71. (lp/c) *(K/K4 46085)* *<2561>* **MUD SLIDE SLIM AND THE BLUE HORIZON** [4] [2]
– Love has brought me around / You've got a friend / Places in my past / Riding on a railroad / Soldiers / Mud slide Slim / Hey mister, that's me upon the jukebox / You can close your eyes / Machine gun Kelly / Long ago and far away / Let me ride / Highway song / Isn't it nice to be home again. *(re-iss. Mar72, hit UK No.49) (cd-iss. 1989; K2 56004)*

Aug 71. (7") *(K 16085)* *<7498>* **YOU'VE GOT A FRIEND. / YOU CAN CLOSE YOUR EYES** [4] Jun71 [1]

Sep 71. (7") *<7521>* **LONG AGO AND FAR AWAY. / LET ME RIDE** [–] [31]

Nov 72. (lp/c) *(K/K4 46185)* *<2660>* **ONE MAN DOG** [27] [4]
– One man parade / Nobody but you / Chili dog / Fool for you / Instrumental I / New tune / Back on the street again / Don't let me be lonely tonight / Woh, don't you know / One morning in May / Instrumental II / Someone / Hymn / Fanfare / Little David / Mescalito / Dance / Jig. *(quad-lp US Feb76) (cd-iss. Feb92)*

Nov 72. (7") *(K 16231)* *<7655>* **DON'T LET ME BE LONELY TONIGHT. / WOH, DON'T YOU KNOW** [ ] [14]

Feb 73. (7") *<7682>* **ONE MAN PARADE. / NOBODY BUT YOU** [–] [67]

May 73. (7") *<7695>* **HYMN. / FANFARE** [–] [ ]

—— In Jan'74, did duet with wife CARLY SIMON on UK No.34 / US No.5 hit MOCKINGBIRD.

Jul 74. (lp/c) *(K/K4 56042)* *<2794>* **WALKING MAN** [ ] [13]
– Walking man / Rock'n'roll is music now / Let it fall down / Me and my guitar / Daddy's baby / Ain't no song / Hello old friend / Migration / The promised land / Fading away.

Aug 74. (7") *<8028>* **WALKING MAN. / DADDY'S BABY** [–] [ ]

Aug 74. (7") *(K 16444)* **AIN'T NO SONG. / HELLO OLD FRIEND** [ ] [–]

May 75. (lp/c) *(K/K4 56137)* *<2866>* **GORILLA** [ ] [6]
– Mexico / Music / How sweet it is (to be loved by you) / Wandering / Gorilla / You make it easy / I was a fool to care / Lighthouse / Angry blues / Love song / Sarah Maria. *(cd-iss. Jul88; K 256137) (quad-lp Feb76)*

Jul 75. (7") *(K 16582)* *<8109>* **HOW SWEET IT IS (TO BE LOVED BY YOU). / SARAH MARIA** [ ] Jun75 [5]

Oct 75. (7") *(K 16632)* *<8137>* **MEXICO. / GORILLA** [ ] [49]

Apr 76. (7") *(K 16708)* **WANDERING. / ANGRY BLUES** [ ] [–]

Jun 76. (lp/c) *(K/K4 56197)* *<2912>* **IN THE POCKET** [ ] [16]
– Shower the people / A junkie's lament / Money machine / Slow burning love / Everybody has the blues / Daddy's all gone / Woman's gotta have it / Captain Jim's drunken dream / Don't be sad 'cause your sun is down / Nothing like a hundred miles / Family man / Golden moments.

Jun 76. (7") *(K 16776)* *<8222>* **SHOWER THE PEOPLE. / I CAN DREAM OF YOU** [ ] [22]

Aug 76. (7") *(K 16808)* **EVERYBODY HAS THE BLUES. / I CAN DREAM OF YOU** [ ] [–]

Oct 76. (7") *(K 16819)* **EVERYBODY HAS THE BLUES. / MONEY MACHINE** [ ] [–]

Nov 76. (7") *<8278>* **WOMAN'S GOTTA HAVE IT. / YOU MAKE IT EASY** [–] [ ]

Dec 76. (lp/c) *(K/K4 56309)* *<2979>* **GREATEST HITS** (compilation) [ ] [23]
– Something in the way she moves / Carolina in my mind / Fire and rain / Sweet baby James / Country roads / You've got a friend / Don't let me be lonely tonight / Walking man / How sweet it is (to be loved by you) / Mexico / Shower the people / Steamroller. *(re-iss. Mar82) (re-iss. +cd.Jan87)*

—— Retained **KORTCHMAR, KUNKEL + SKLAR** and recruited **DAVID SANBORN** – sax / **CLARENCE McDONALD** – percussion

C.B.S. Columbia

Jun 77. (7") *(CBS 5363)* *<10557>* **HANDY MAN. / BARTENDER'S BLUES** [ ] [4]

Jul 77. (lp/c) *(CBS/40 86029)* *<34811>* **J.T.** [ ] [4]
– Your smiling face / There we are / Honey don't leave L.A. / Another grey morning / Bartender's blues / Secret of life / Handy man / I was only telling a lie / Looking for love on Broadway / Terra Nova / Traffic jam / If I keep my heart out of sight. *(re-iss. +cd.Feb85) (re-iss. cd+c Oct93 on 'Sony Collectors')*

Oct 77. (7") *(CBS 5737)* *<10602>* **YOUR SMILING FACE. / IF I KEEP MY HEART OUT OF SIGHT** [ ] Sep 77 [20]

—— Autumn'77, saw him produce, play guitar, etc. for sister KATE TAYLOR's debut US Top 50 hit single IT'S IN HIS KISS. Early in 1978, he was credited on another cover hit 45; 'WHAT A WONDERFUL WORLD' with PAUL SIMON & ART GARFUNKEL.

Feb 78. (7") *<10689>* **HONEY DON'T LEAVE L.A. / ANOTHER GREY MORNING** [–] [61]

—— In Sep78, another CARLY SIMON / J.T. duet 'DEVOTED TO YOU' hit US No.36.

Jun 79. (7") *(CBS 7389)* *<11005>* **UP ON THE ROOF. / CHANSON FRANCAISE** [ ] May 79 [28]

Aug 79. (lp/c) *(CBS/40 86091)* *<36058>* **FLAG** [ ] May 79 [10]
– Company man / Johnnie comes back / Day tripper / I will not lie for you / Brother Trucker / Is that the way you look / B.S.U.R. / Rainy day man / Millworker / Up on the roof / Chanson francaise / Slep come free me. *(re-iss. Feb86) (cd-iss. Sep93 on 'Sony Collectors')*

Aug 79. (7") *(CBS 7773)* **B.S.U.R. / SLEEP COME FREE ME** [ ] [ ]

Mar 81. (7"; JAMES TAYLOR & J.D. SOUTHER) *(CBS A1048)* *<60514>* **HER TOWN TOO. / BELIEVE IT OR NOT** [ ] Feb 81 [11]

Apr 81. (lp/c) *(CBS/40 86131)* *<37009>* **DAD LOVES HIS WORK** [ ] Mar 81 [10]
– Hard times / Her town too / Hour that the morning comes / I will follow / Believe it or not / Stand and fight / Only for me / Summer's here / Sugar trade / London town / That lonesome road. *(cd-iss. May87) (cd-iss. Jan94 on 'Sony Europe')*

May 81. (7") *<02093>* **HARD TIMES. / SUMMER'S HERE** [–] [72]

—— Late '85, he duets on RICKY SCAGGS track 'New Star Shining', for current lp

Jan 86. (lp/c/cd) *(CBS/40/CD 25547)* *<40052>* **THAT'S WHY I'M HERE** [ ] Nov 85 [34]
– That's why I'm here / Song for you far away / Only a dream in Rio / Turn away / Going around one more time / Everyday / Limousine driver / Only one / Mona / The man who shot Liberty Valance / That's why I'm here (reprise).

Mar 86. (7") *(CBS A6683)* *<05681>* **EVERYDAY. / LIMOUSINE DRIVER** [ ] Nov85 [61]

Mar 86. (7") *<05785>* **MONA. / ONLY ONE** [–] [ ]

May 86. (7") *<05884>* **THAT'S WHY I'M HERE. / GOING AROUND ONE MORE TIME** [–] [ ]

Sep 86. (7") *<06278>* **ONLY A DREAM IN RIO. / TURN AWAY** [–] [ ]

Feb 88. (lp/c/cd) *(46043-1-4-2)* *<40851>* **NEVER DIE YOUNG** [ ] [25]
– Never die young / T-bone / Baby boom baby / Runaway boy / Valentine's day / Sun on the Moon / Sweet potato pie / Home by another day / Letter in the mail / First of May.

Feb 88. (7") *(651204)* *<07616>* **NEVER DIE YOUNG. / VALENTINE'S DAY** [ ] [80]
(12"+=) *(651 204-1/-2)* – Everyday. *(re-iss. Jun88)*

May 88. (7") *<07948>* **LETTER IN THE MAIL. / BABY BOOM BABY** [–] [ ]

Sep 88. (7") *<08493>* **FIRST OF MAY. / SWEET POTATO PIE** [–] [ ]

Sep 91. (c-s) *<74214>* **(I'VE GOT TO) STOP THINKIN' 'BOUT THAT. / SLAP LEATHER** [–] [ ]

Oct 91. (cd/c/lp) *(468977-2-4-1)* *<46038>* **NEW MOON SHINE** [ ] [37]
– Copperline / Down in the hole / (I've got to) Stop thinkin' 'bout that / Shed a little light / The frozen man / Slap leather / Like every one she knows / One more round to cha cha cha / Native son / Oh brother / The water is wide. *(re-iss. cd Jul94 on 'Sony Europe')*

—— with **CLIFFORD CARTER** – keyboards / **DON GROLNICK** – piano / **JIMMY JOHNSON** – bass / **MICHAEL LANDALL** – guitar / **VALERIE CARTER, DAVID LASLEY, KATE MARKOWITZ & ANDREW McCULLEY** – vocals / **CARLOS VEGA** – drums

Columbia Columbia

Sep 93. (d-cd/d-c) *(474216-2)* *<47056>* **(LIVE)** [ ] Aug93 [20]
– Sweet baby James / Traffic jam / Handy man / Your smiling face / Secret of life / Shed a little light / Everybody has the blues / Steamroller blues / Mexico / Millworker / Country road / Fire and rain / Shower the people / How sweet it is / New hymn / Walking man / Riding on a railroad / Something in the way she moves / Sun on the Moon / Up on the roof / Don't let me be lonely tonight / She thinks I still care / Copperline / Slap leather / Only one / You make it easy / Carolina on my mind / I will follow / That lonesome road / You've got a friend.
('BEST LIVE' of above issued Apr94; *476657-2)*

Jun 97. (cd/c) *(487748-2/-4)* *<67912>* **HOURGLASS** [46] May97 [9]
– Line 'em up / Enough to be your way / Little more time with you / Gaia / Ananas / Jump up behind me / Another day / Up er mei / Up from your life / Yellow and rose / Boatman / Walking my baby back home / Hangnail.

Nov 00. (cd) *<85223>* **GREATEST HITS VOLUME 2** (compilation) [–] [97]
– Secret o' life / Handy man / Your smiling face / Up on the roof / Her town too / That's why I'm here / Only a dream in Rio / Everyday / Song for you far away / Never die young / (I've got to) Stop thinkin' 'bout that / Copperline / Shed a little light / Another day / Little more time with you / Enough to be on your way.

Aug 02. (cd) *(503292-2)* *<63584>* **OCTOBER ROAD** [39] [4]
– September grass / October road / On the 4th of July / Whenever you're ready / Belfast to Bolton / Mean old man / My travelling star / Raised up family / Carry me on my way / Caroline I see you / Baby buffalo / Have yourself a merry little Christmas. *(ltd-cd+=; 503292-9)* – Don't let me be lonely tonight / Sailing to Philadelphia / Benjamin.

– compilations, etc. –

Feb 71. (m-lp) *Euphoria; <2>* **JAMES TAYLOR & THE ORIGINAL FLYING MACHINE** (early material 1967) [–] [ ]
– Night owl / Brighten your night with my day / Kootch's song / Knocking 'round the zoo / Rainy day man / Something's wrong. *(re-iss. Nov76 as 'RAINY DAY MAN' on 'DJM'/'Trip', tracks differed slightly)*

1974. (7"ep) *Warners;* **YOU'VE GOT A FRIEND / SUNNY SKIES. / FIRE AND RAIN / SWEET BABY JAMES** [ ] [–]

Oct 75. (d-lp) *Warners; (K 66029)* **TWO ORIGINALS OF . . .** [ ] [–]
– (contains the 2 albums below)

Oct 82. (d-c) *Warners;* **SWEET BABY JAMES / MUD SLIDE SLIM & THE BLUE HORIZON** [ ] [–]
(d-cd-iss. Apr84)

Mar 86. (7") *Old Gold; (OG 9576)* **YOU'VE GOT A FRIEND. / FIRE AND RAIN** [ ] [–]

Jan 87. (7") *CBS; (YZ 105)* **UP ON THE ROOF. / FIRE AND RAIN** [ ] [–]

Mar 87. (lp/c)(cd) *CBS-WEA TV; (JTV 1/+C)(241 0892)* **THE BEST OF JAMES TAYLOR – CLASSIC SONGS** [53] [–]
– Fire and rain / Mexico / You've got a friend / How sweet it is (to be loved by you) / Carolina on my mind / Something in the way she moves / Shower the people / Sweet baby James / That's why I'm here / Everyday / Up on the roof / Your smiling face / Her town too / Handyman / Don't let me be lonely tonight / Only a dream in Rio.

Sep 03. (cd) *WEA; <(8122 73837-2)>* **YOU'VE GOT A FRIEND – THE BEST OF JAMES TAYLOR** [4] Apr03 [11]
– Something in the way she moves / Sweet baby James / Fire and rain / Country road / You've got a friend / You can close your eyes / Long ago and far away / Don't let me be lonely tonight / Walking man / How sweet it is (to be loved by you) / Mexico / Shower the people / Golden moments / Steamroller blues (live) / Carolina in my mind (1976 version) / Handy man / Your smiling face / Up on the roof / Only a dream in Rio / Bittersweet.

□ John TAYLOR (see under ⇒ DURAN DURAN)

□ Roger TAYLOR (see under ⇒ QUEEN)

□ TEARDROP EXPLODES (see under ⇒ COPE, Julian)

TEARS FOR FEARS

Formed: Bath, Avon, England . . . 1981 by ROLAND ORZABAL and CURT SMITH, childhood friends who had initially played together in ska-pop outfit, GRADUATE. Inspired by psychotherapist Arthur Janov's controversial "primal scream" therapy, ORZABAL and SMITH named the group accordingly, subsequently signing to 'Mercury' on the strength of some demos. After two early singles, 'SUFFER THE CHILDREN' and 'PALE SHELTER (YOU DON'T GIVE ME LOVE), failed to chart, the duo eventually hit the UK Top 3 with the claustrophobic synth-pop of 'MAD WORLD' (produced by CHRIS 'Merrick' HUGHES; ex-ADAM & THE ANTS, as was the debut album). They scored another Top 5 single early the following year with 'CHANGE', the subsequent album, 'THE HURTING' (1983), reaching No.1. Po-faced in true 80's style, with ORZABAL's lyrics centering on mental functioning, therapy, healing etc., the group were often accused of angst-ridden pretension despite their pin-up status. By the release of the million selling 'SONGS FROM THE BIG CHAIR' (1985), however, their focus had widened somewhat, a preceding single, 'SHOUT', surprisingly taking them to the top of the US charts (UK Top 5). The uncharacteristically breezy guitar pop of 'EVERYBODY WANTS TO RULE THE WORLD' was another massive transatlantic hit, further boosting sales of the album. Masterfully crafted, the record displayed a more considered approach to both songwriting and arranging, while ORZABAL and SMITH had more or less ditched the bedsit whine of old. It was to be almost four years before TEARS FOR FEARS released a follow-up, the much anticipated 'THE SEEDS OF LOVE' finally hitting the shelves in the Autumn of '89. A preceding single, 'SOWING THE SEEDS OF LOVE', was a clever take on The BEATLES' 'I AM THE WALRUS', pre-empting OASIS' more cumbersome efforts by a good few years. The whole album, in fact, displayed an even greater level of pop sophistication than its predecessor, boasting contributions from the likes of OLETA ADAMS and JON HASSELL. While the record initially sold well, however, it failed to generate much chart staying power, exacerbating the growing rift between SMITH and ORZABAL. The pair finally split in the early 90's, engendering a covert slanging match similar to the JOHN SQUIRE/IAN BROWN jousting. ORZABAL carried on under the TEARS FOR FEARS moniker, although subsequent releases, 'ELEMENTAL' (1993) and 'RAOUL AND THE KINGS OF SPAIN' (1995) failed to scale the heights of the group's mid-80's heyday, the latter not even breaking the Top 40. • **Songwriters:** All written by ORZABAL, except CREEP (Radiohead) / ASHES TO ASHES (David Bowie).

Album rating: THE HURTING (*7) / SONGS FROM THE BIG CHAIR (*7) / THE SEEDS OF LOVE (*6) / TEARS ROLL DOWN – GREATEST HITS 1982-1992 compilation (*8) / ELEMENTAL (*4) / RAOUL AND THE KINGS OF SPAIN (*4) / SATURNINE, MARSHALL & LUNATIC collection (*4)

GRADUATE

ROLAND ORZABAL (b. ROLAND ORZABAL DE LA QUINTANA, 22 Aug'61, Portsmouth, England) – vocals, guitar / **CURT SMITH** (b.24 Jun'61) – vocals, bass / **JOHN BAKER** – vocals, guitar / **STEVE BUCK** – keyboards, flute / **ANDY MARSDEN** – drums

Precision | not iss.

Mar 80. (7") *(PAR 100)* **ELVIS SHOULD PLAY SKA. / JULIE JULIE** [ ] [–]

May 80. (7") *(PAR 104)* **EVER MET A DAY. / SHUT UP** [ ] [–]

May 80. (10"lp) *(PART 001)* **ACTING MY AGE** [ ] [–]
– Acting my age / Sick and tired / Ever met a day / Dancing nights / Shut up / Elvis should play ska / Watching your world / Love that is bad / Julie Julie / Bad dreams. *(re-iss. Jul86 on 'P.R.T.')*

Oct 80. (7") *(PAR 111)* **AMBITION. / BAD DREAMS** [ ] [–]

Mar 81. (7") *(PAR 117)* **SHUT UP. / EVER MET A DAY** [ ] [–]

TEARS FOR FEARS

ROLAND & CURT with **DAVID LORD** – synthesizers (duo also on synthesizers)

Mercury | Mercury

Nov 81. (7") *(IDEA 1)* **SUFFER THE CHILDREN. / WIND** [ ] [ ]
(remixed-12"+=) *(IDEA 12)* – ('A'instrumental). *(re-iss. Aug85, 7"/12"; same); hit UK No.52)*

—— Trimmed to a basic duo of **ORZABAL & SMITH**

Mar 82. (7") *(IDEA 2)* **PALE SHELTER (YOU DON'T GIVE ME LOVE). / THE PRISONER** [ ] [ ]
(12"+=) *(IDEA 2-12)* – ('A'extended). *(re-iss. Aug85, 7"/12"; same); hit No.73)*

Sep 82. (7") *(IDEA 3)* **MAD WORLD. / IDEAS AS OPIATES** [3] [ ]
(12"+=) *(IDEA 3-12)* – Saxophones as opiates.
(d7"+=) *(IDEA 33)* – ('A'-world remix) / Suffer the children.

Jan 83. (7") *(IDEA 4) <812677>* **CHANGE. / THE CONFLICT** [4] Jun83 [73]
(12"+=) *(IDEA 4-12)* – ('A'extended).

—— augmented by **IAN STANLEY** – keyboards / **MANNY ELIAS** – drums

Mar 83. (lp/c) *(MERS/+C 17) <811039>* **THE HURTING** [1] [73]
– The hurting / Mad world / Pale shelter / Ideas as opiates / Memories fade / Suffer the children / Watch me bleed / Change / The prisoner / Start of the breakdown. *(cd-iss. Sep89; 811039-2) (cd re-mast.Jun99 +=; 558104-2)* – Pale shelter (long version) / The way you are (extended) / Mad world (world remix) / Change (extended).

Apr 83. (7"/7"red/7"green/7"white/7"blue/7"pic-d) *(IDEA 5/+R/G/W/B/P)* **PALE SHELTER. / WE ARE BROKEN** [5] [ ]
(12"+=) *(IDEA 5-12)* – ('A'extended).

Nov 83. (7") *(IDEA 6)* **(THE) WAY YOU ARE. / THE MARAUDERS** [24] [ ]
(ext.12"+=) *(IDEA 6-12)* – Start of the breakdown (live).
(d7"++=) *(IDEAS 6)* – Change (live).

Aug 84. (7",7"green,12"/7"clear-pic-d)(ext.12") *(IDEA/+P 7)(IDEA 7-12) <884638>* **MOTHER'S TALK. / EMPIRE BUILDING** [14] Mar86 [27]

Nov 84. (7"/10") *(IDEA/+C 8) <880294>* **SHOUT. / THE BIG CHAIR** [4] May85 [1]
(12"+=) *(IDEA 8-12)* – ('A'extended).

—— added mainly on tour **WILLIAM GREGORY** – saxophone / **NICKY HOLLAND** – keyboards

Mar 85. (lp/c)(cd) *(MERH/+C 58) <(824300-2)>* **SONGS FROM THE BIG CHAIR** [2] [1]
– Shout / The working hour / Everybody wants to rule the world / Mother's talk / I believe / Broken / Head over heels / Broken (live) / Listen. *(c+=)* – The big chair (mix) / Empire building (mix) / The marauders (mix) / Broken revisited (mix) / The conflict (mix). *(cd re-mast.Jun99 ++=; 558106-2)* – Mothers talk (US remix) / Shout (US remix).

Mar 85. (7"/10") *(IDEA 9/+10) <880659>* **EVERYBODY WANTS TO RULE THE WORLD. / PHAROAHS** [2] [1]
(12"+=) *(IDEA 9-12)* – ('A'extended or urban mix).
(d7"+=) *(IDEA 9-9)* – ('A'-urban mix) / (duo interviewed).

Jun 85. (7"/7"sha-pic-d)(10") *(IDEA/+P 10)(IDEA 10-10) <880899>* **HEAD OVER HEELS (remix). / WHEN IN LOVE WITH A BLIND MAN** [12] Sep85 [3]
(12"+=) *(IDEA 10-12)* – ('A'preacher mix).

Oct 85. (7") *(IDEA 11)* **I BELIEVE (A soulful re-recording). / SEA SONG** [23] [ ]
(10"+=) *(IDEA 11-10)* – I believe (US mix).
(12"++=) *(IDEA 11-12)* – Shout (US mix).
(d7"+=) *(IDEA 11-11)* – Shout (dub) / I believe (original).

May 86. (7"/12") *(RACE 1/+12)* **EVERYBODY WANTS TO RUN THE WORLD. / EVERYBODY . . . (Running version)** [5] [ ]

—— **ORZABAL + SMITH** retained **IAN** and **NICKY** and brought in sessioners **OLETA ADAMS** – some dual vocals, piano / **SIMON CLARK** – organ / **PINO PALLADINO** – bass / **ROBBIE McINTOSH, NEIL TAYLOR + RANDY JACOBS** – guitar / **PHIL COLLINS, CHRIS HUGHES + MANU KATCHE** – drums

Fontana | Fontana

Aug 89. (7"/7"g-f/c-s) *(IDEA/IDEAG/IDMC 12) <874710>* **SOWING THE SEEDS OF LOVE. / TEARS ROLL DOWN** [5] [2]
(ext.12"+=/12"pic-d+=/3"cd-s+=) *(IDEAT/IDPT/IDCD 12)* – Shout (US mix).

Sep 89. (lp/c/cd) *(838730-1/-4/-2) <838730>* **THE SEEDS OF LOVE** [1] [8]
– Woman in chains / Bad man's song / Sowing the seeds of love / Advice for the young at heart / Standing on the corner of the third world / Swords and knives / Year of the knife / Famous last words. *(cd re-mast.Jun99 +=; 558105-2)* – Tears roll down / Always in the past / Music for tables / Johnny Panic and the bible of dreams.

—— (next featured **OLETA ADAMS** – co-vox)

Nov 89. (7"/c-s; as TEARS FOR FEARS featuring OLETA ADAMS) *(IDEA/IDMC 13) <876248>* **WOMAN IN CHAINS. / ALWAYS IN THE PAST** [26] [36]
(12"+=/12"pic-d+=/cd-s+=/3"cd-s+=) *(IDEA/IDPT/IDCD/IDSTN 13)* – ('A'instrumental) / My life in the suicide ranks.

Feb 90. (7"/c-s) *(IDEA/IDMC 14) <876894>* **ADVICE FOR THE YOUNG AT HEART. / JOHNNY PANIC AND THE BIBLE OF DREAMS** [36] [89]
(12"+=/12"pic-d+=/cd-s+=) *(IDPT/IDPIC/IDCD 14)* – Music for tables.
(3"cd-s++=) *(IDCDS 14)* – Johnny Panic (instrumental).

Jul 90. (7") *(IDEA 15)* **FAMOUS LAST WORDS. / MOTHER'S TALK (US remix)**
(c-s+=/12"+=/12"pic-d+=/cd-s+=) *(IDEMC/IDEAT/IDPIC/IDECD 15)* – Listen.

Feb 92. (7"/c-s) *(IDEA/IDMC 17)* **LAID SO LOW. / THE BODY WAH** [17]
(12"pic-d+=/cd-s+=) *(IDEAT/IDCD 17)* – Lord of the Kharma.

Mar 92. (cd/c/lp) *(<510 939-2/-4/-1>)* **TEARS ROLL DOWN – GREATEST HITS 1982-1992** (compilation) [2] [53]
– Sowing the seeds of love / Everybody wants to rule the world / Woman in chains / Shout / Head over heels / Mad world / Pale shelter / I beieve / Laid so low (tears roll down) / Mothers talk / Change / Advice for the young at heart.

Apr 92. (7"/c-s; as TEARS FOR FEARS featuring OLETA ADAMS) *(IDEA/IDMC 16)* **WOMAN IN CHAINS. / BADMAN'S SONG** [57]
(cd-s+=) *(IDCD 16)* – Ghost papa.

—— **ROLAND ORZABAL** now sole survivor, when CURT launched solo career with his album, 'SOUL ON BOARD'.

Mercury Mercury

May 93. (7"/c-s) *(IDEA/IDMC 18) <862330>* **BREAK IT DOWN AGAIN. / BLOODLETTING GO** [20] [25]
(cd-s+=) *(IDECD 18)* – ('A'mix).

Jun 93. (cd/c/lp) *(<514875-2/-4/-1>)* **ELEMENTAL** [5] [45]
– Elemental / Cold / Break it down again / Mr. Pessimist / Dog's a best friend's dog / Fish out of water / Gas giants / Power / Brian Wilson said / Goodnight song.

Jul 93. (7"/c-s) *(IDEA/IDMC 19)* **COLD. / NEW STAR** [72]
(cd-s+=) *(IDECD 19)* – Deja vu / The sins of silence.

Epic Sony

Sep 95. (c-s) *(662 476-4)* **RAOUL AND THE KINGS OF SPAIN / QUEEN OF COMPROMISE** [31]
(cd-s+=) *(662 476-2)* – All of the angels.
(cd-s) *(662 476-5)* – ('A'side) / Creep / The madness of Roland.

Oct 95. (cd/c) *(480 982-2/-4) <67318>* **RAOUL AND THE KINGS OF SPAIN** [41] [79]
– Raoul and the Kings of Spain / Falling down / Secrets / God's mistake / Sketches of pain / Los Reyes Catolicos / Sorry / Humdrum and humble / I choose you / Don't drink the water / Me and my big ideas / Los Reyes Catolicos (reprise).

Jan 96. (c-s/cd-s) *(662 797-4/-2)* **SECRETS / RAOUL AND THE KINGS OF SPAIN (acoustic) / BREAK IT DOWN AGAIN (acoustic)**
(cd-s) *(662 797-5)* – ('A'side) / Until I drown / War of attrition.

Jun 96. (c-s/cd-s) *(663 418-4/-2)* **GOD'S MISTAKE / UNTIL I DROWN** [61] [–]
(cd-s) *(663 418-5)* – ('A'side) / Raoul and the kings of Spain (acoustic) / Break it down again (acoustic).

– compilations, etc. –

Aug 95. (d-cd) *Fontana; (528599-2)* **THE HURTING / SONGS FROM THE BIG CHAIR** [–]

Jun 96. (cd/c) *Fontana; (528114-2/-4)* **SATURNINE, MARSHALL & LUNATIC** (rare material)

Jun 00. (cd) *Universal; <E 542492-2>* **THE BEST OF TEARS FOR FEARS: THE MILLENNIUM COLLECTION** [–]

Oct 00. (d-cd) *Universal; (E 542789-2)* **THE HURTING / THE SEEDS OF LOVE**

Jan 01. (cd) *Universal; (E 548319-2)* **THE UNIVERSAL MASTERS COLLECTION** [–]

May 01. (cd) *Mercury; (548515-2)* **THE WORKING HOUR: AN INTRODUCTION TO TEARS FOR FEARS** [–]

Oct 03. (cd) *Spectrum; (063358-2)* **THE COLLECTION** [–]

TEENAGE FANCLUB

Formed: Glasgow, Scotland . . . 1989 although earlier they had posed as The BOY HAIRDRESSERS. After a one-off single, 'GOLDEN SHOWERS' (1988), bassist GERRY LOVE was recruited and BRENDAN O'HARE replaced FRANCIS MACDONALD (who went off to join that other Glasgow institution, The PASTELS) on the drums. As TEENAGE FANCLUB, they cut the inspired chaos of the 'EVERYTHING FLOWS' (1990) single and followed it up with the debut album, 'A CATHOLIC EDUCATION' later the same year. The term slacker rock was surely coined with this bunch of cheeky Glaswegian wide boys in mind and if it was lazy to compare their honey-in-the-dirt melodic dischord with DINOSAUR JR., that was nothing compared to the laid back, laissez faire philosophy that fuelled (if that's not too strong a word) TEENAGE FANCLUB's ramshackle racket, both on stage and in the studio. By the release of the DON FLEMING-produced 'BANDWAGONESQUE' (1991), ('THE KING' was a sub-standard effort released to fulfil contractual obligations), the band were sounding more professional, crafting an album of langourous harmonies and chiming guitar that was a thinly veiled homage to BIG STAR as well as taking in such obvious reference points as The BYRDS, The BEACH BOYS, BUFFALO SPRINGFIELD etc. Ironically, rather than propelling TEENAGE FANCLUB into the big league, the album seemed instead to merely rekindle interest in BIG STAR's back catalogue and after a honeymoon period of being indie press darlings, the backlash was sharp and swift. The fact that the self-produced 'THIRTEEN' (1993) lacked their trademark inspired sloppiness didn't help matters any. Not that the band were overly concerned, they crafted modern retro more lovingly than most and had a loyal following to lap it up. The FANNIE's – with PAUL QUINN replacing O'HARE – further developed their niche with 'GRAND PRIX' (1995) and if it was that reliably trad, West Coast via Glasgow roots sound you were after then TEENAGE FANCLUB were your band. While they wear their influences more proudly than any other group, (O.K., so I forgot about OASIS . . .) they do it with such verve and style that it'd be churlish to write them off as mere plagiarists and they remain one of Scotland's best loved exports. Their next effort, 'SONGS FROM NORTHERN BRITAIN' (1997) was their most considered release to date, sharpening up their sound and arrangements to an unprecedented degree. But if that's what it takes to come up with something as engagingly swoonsome as 'I DON'T CARE' or 'IS THAT ENOUGH', no one's going to make much of a fuss. Now on the roster of the mighty 'Columbia' records, TEENAGE FANCLUB (complete with former BMX BANDITS man FINLAY McDONALD) returned to the fold via album No.6 proper, 'HOWDY!' (2000). Slightly back to basics and reminiscent of BIG STAR (once again!), the album only just managed to gain a UK Top 40 placing; the appropriately-titled single from it 'I NEED DIRECTION' only just dented the Top 50. Drummer and original member, FRANCIS MACDONALD, subsequently superseded QUINN for a one-off single collaboration 'DUMB DUMB DUMB' with daisy-chain hip hop stars, DE LA SOUL, although this failed miserably with the record buying public.

The group were back to basics again (this time on STEPHEN PASTEL's 'Geographic' imprint) come their short but sweet set, 'WORDS OF WISDOM AND HOPE' (2002), a record that saw them collaborate with US-born songwriter JAD FAIR. Ditching their more commercial rock flair, TFC went for something a bit rougher – all thanks to FAIR – hammering out tracks 'I FEEL FINE', 'VAMPIRE'S CLAW' and 'NEAR TO YOU' (the single) to brilliant effect. • **Songwriters:** BLAKE or BLAKE-McGINLEY or group compositions except; DON'T CRY NO TEARS (Neil Young) / THE BALLAD OF JOHN AND YOKO (Beatles) / LIKE A VIRGIN (Madonna) / LIFE'S A GAS (T.Rex) / FREE AGAIN + JESUS CHRIST (Alex Chilton) / HOW MANY MORE YEARS + NOTHING TO BE DONE (Pastels) / CHORDS OF FAME (Phil Ochs) / PERSONALITY CRISIS (New York Dolls) / HE'D BE A DIAMOND (Bevis Frond) / INTERSTELLAR OVERDRIVE (Pink Floyd) / FALLIN' (Tom Petty) / BAD SEEDS (Beat Happening) / HAVE YOU EVER SEEN THE RAIN? (Creedence Clearwater Revival) / BETWEEN US (Rutles) / I HEARD YOU LOOKING (Yo La Tengo) / OLDER GUYS (Gram Parsons) / FEMME FATALE (Velvet Underground). • **Trivia:** ALEX CHILTON (ex-BOX TOPS) guested on 1992 sessions and contributed some songs.

Album rating: A CATHOLIC EDUCATION (*6) / THE KING instrumental (*5) / BANDWAGONESQUE (*8) / THIRTEEN (*7) / DEEP FRIED FANCLUB collection (*4) / GRAND PRIX (*8) / SONGS FROM NORTHERN BRITAIN (*8) / HOWDY! (*6) / WORDS OF WISDOM AND HOPE with Jad Fair (*6) / FOUR THOUSAND SEVEN HUNDRED AND SIXTY-SIX SECONDS: A SHORT CUT TO TEENAGE FANCLUB compilation (*8)

NORMAN BLAKE (b.20 Oct'65, Bellshill, Scotland) – vocals, guitar (ex-BMX BANDITS) / **RAYMOND McGINLEY** (b. 3 Jan'64, Glasgow) – bass, vocals / **FRANCIS MACDONALD** (b.11 Sep'70, Bellshill, Scotland) – drums / **JOE McALINDEN** – violin / **JIM LAMBIE** – vibraphone

53rd & 3rd not iss.

Jan 88. (12"; as BOY HAIRDRESSERS) *(AGARR 12T)* **GOLDEN SHOWERS. / TIDAL WAVE / THE ASSUMPTION AS AN ELEVATOR** [ ] [–]

— **NORMAN + RAYMOND** – guitars, vocals plus **GERARD LOVE** (b.31 Aug'67, Motherwell, Scotland) – bass, vocals / **BRENDAN O'HARE** (b.16 Jan'70, Bellshill, Scotland) – drums; repl. MACDONALD who joined The PASTELS

Paperhouse Matador

Jun 90. (7"m) *(PAPER 003)* **EVERYTHING FLOWS. / PRIMARY EDUCATION / SPEEEDER** [ ] [–]
(cd-ep+=) *(PAPER 003CD)* – Don't Cry No Tears. *(rel.Feb91)*

Jul 90. (cd/c/lp) *(PAP CD/MC/LP 004)* <OLE 012> **A CATHOLIC EDUCATION** [ ] Aug90 [ ]
– Heavy metal / Everything flows / A catholic education / Too involved / Don't need a drum / Critical mass / Heavy metal II / A catholic education 2 / Eternal light / Every picture I paint / Everybody's fool. *(re-iss. cd Mar95; same) (cd re-iss. Apr02 on 'Fire'; SFIRE 001CD)*

Oct 90. (one-sided-7") *(PAPER 005)* **THE BALLAD OF JOHN AND YOKO** [ ] [–]

Nov 90. (7"m) <OLE 007-7> **EVERYBODY'S FOOL. / PRIMAL EDUCATION / SPEEDER** [–] [ ]

Nov 90. (7") *(PAPER 007)* <OLE 023> **GOD KNOWS IT'S TRUE. / SO FAR GONE** [ ] Jan91 [ ]
(12"+=/cd-s+=) *(PAPER 007 T/CD)* – Weedbreak / Ghetto blaster.

Creation Geffen

Aug 91. (cd/lp) *(CRE CD/LP 096)* **THE KING** (instrumental) [53] [–]
– Heavy metal 6 / Mudhoney / Interstellar overdrive / Robot love / Like a virgin / The king / Opal inquest / The ballad of Bow Evil (slow and fast) / Heavy metal 9.
(above originally only meant for US ears, deleted after 24 hours)

Aug 91. (7") *(CRE 105)* **STAR SIGN. / HEAVY METAL 6** [44] [–]
(12"+=)(cd-s+=) *(CRE 105T)(CRESCD 105)* – Like a virgin / ('A'demo version).
(7"ltd) *(CRE 105L)* – ('A'side) / Like a virgin.

Oct 91. (7"/c-s) *(CRE/+CS 111)* <4370> **THE CONCEPT. / LONG HAIR** [51] Jan92 [ ]
(12"+=)(cd-s+=) *(CRE 111T)(CRESCD 111)* – What you do to me (demo) / Robot love.

Nov 91. (cd)(c/lp) *(CRECD 106)(C+/CRE 106)* <24461> **BANDWAGONESQUE** [22] [ ]
– The concept / Satan / December / What you do to me / I don't know / Star sign / Metal baby / Pet rock / Sidewinder / Alcoholiday / Guiding star / Is this music?. *(cd re-iss. Jan01; same)*

Jan 92. (7"/c-s) *(CRE/+CS 115)* <21708> **WHAT YOU DO TO ME. / B-SIDE** [31] [ ]
(12"+=)(cd-s+=) *(CRE 115T)(CRESCD 115)* – Life's a gas / Filler.

Jun 93. (7"/c-s) *(CRE/+CS 130)* **RADIO. / DON'S GONE COLUMBIA** [31] [ ]
(12"+=)(cd-s+=) *(CRE 130T)(CRESCD 130)* – Weird horses / Chords of fame.

Sep 93. (7"/c-s) *(CRE/+CS 142)* **NORMAN 3. / OLDER GUYS** [50] [–]
(12"+=)(cd-s+=) *(CRE 142T)(CRESCD 142)* – Golden glades / Genius envy.

Oct 93. (cd)(c/lp) *(CRECD 144)(C+/CRE 144)* <24533> **THIRTEEN** [14] Nov93 [ ]
– Hang on / The cabbage / Radio / Norman 3 / Song to the cynic / 120 minutes / Escher / Commercial alternative / Fear of flying / Tears are cool / Ret live dead / Get funky / Gene Clark. *(cd re-iss. Jan01; same)*

— also in 1993, they made a joint single with BIG STAR, 'MINE EXCLUSIVELY' b/w 'PATTI GIRL', proceeds going towards Bosnia, etc

— In Mar'94, they teamed up with DE LA SOUL on single 'FALLIN''. This was from the rock-rap album 'Judgement Day' on 'Epic' records (hit UK 59).

1994. (cd-ep) <21887> **AUSTRALIAN TOUR SAMPLER** [–] [ ]

— **PAUL QUINN** – drums (ex-SOUP DRAGONS) repl. O'HARE who later joined MOGWAI

Mar 95. (7"/c-s) *(CRE/+CS 175)* **MELLOW DOUBT. / SOME PEOPLE TRY TO FUCK WITH YOU** [34] [–]
(cd-s+=) *(CRESCD 175)* – Getting real / About you.
(cd-s) *(CRESCD 175X)* – ('A'side) / Have you ever seen the rain? / Between us / You're my kind.

May 95. (7"/c-s) *(CRE/+CS 201)* **SPARKY'S DREAM. / BURNED** [40] [–]
(cd-s+=) *(CRESCD 201)* – For you / Headstand.
(cd-s) *(CRESCD 201X)* – ('A'-alternative version) / Try and stop me / That's all I need to know / Who loves the sun.

May 95. (cd)(c/lp) *(CRECD 173)(C+/CRE 173)* <24802> **GRAND PRIX** [7] Jul95 [ ]
– About you / Sparky's dream / Mellow doubt / Don't look back / Verisinilitude / Neil Jung / Tears / Discolite / Say no / Going places / I'll make it clear / I gotta know / Hardcore – ballad. *(lp w/ free 7")* – DISCOLITE (demo). / I GOTTA KNOW (demo) *(cd re-iss. Jan01; same)*

Aug 95. (7"/c-s) *(CRE/+CS 210)* **NEIL JUNG. / THE SHADOWS** [62] [–]
(cd-s+=) *(CRESCD 210)* – My life / Every step is a way through love.
(cd-s) *(CRESCD 210X)* – ('A'side) / Traffic jam / Hi-fi / I heard you looking.

Dec 95. (7"ep/c-ep/cd-ep) *(CRE/+CS/SCD 216)* **TEENAGE FANCLUB HAVE LOST IT EP (acoustic)** [53] [–]
– Don't look back / Everything flows / Starsign / 120 mins.

— late in '96, LOVE and McGINLEY joined forces with The VASELINES' EUGENE KELLY to form ASTROCHIMP; one single 'DRAGGIN' for 'Shoeshine'

Creation Sony

Jun 97. (cd-s) *(CRESCD 228)* **AIN'T THAT ENOUGH / KICKABOUT / BROKEN** [17] [–]
(cd-s) *(CRESCD 228X)* – ('A'side) / Femme fatale / Jesus Christ.

Jun 97. (cd/c/lp) *(CRECD/CCRE/CRELP 196)* <68202> **SONGS FROM NORTHERN BRITAIN** [3] [ ]
– Start again / Ain't that enough / Can't feel my soul / I don't want control of you / Planets / It's a bad world / Take the long way round / Winter / I don't care / Mount Everest / Your love is the place where I come from / Speed of light. *(cd re-iss. Jan01; same)*

Aug 97. (7") *(CRE 238)* **I DON'T WANT CONTROL OF YOU. / THE COUNT** [43] [–]
(cd-s+=) *(CRESCD 238)* – Middle of the road.
(cd-s) *(CRESCD 238X)* – ('A'side) / He'd be a diamond / Live my life.

Nov 97. (7") *(CRE 280)* **START AGAIN. / AIN'T THAT ENOUGH (TOTP acoustic)** [54] [–]
(cd-s+=) *(CRESCD 280)* – Take the long way round (radio).
(cd-s) *(CRESCD 280X)* – ('A'side) / How many more years / Nothing to be done.

— added **FINLAY McDONALD** – keyboards (ex-BMX BANDITS, ex-SPEEDBOAT); was p/t on tour

Jun 98. (7") *(CRE 298)* **LONG SHOT. / LOOPS AND STRINGS** [ ] [–]

Columbia Columbia

Oct 00. (7") *(669951-7)* **I NEED DIRECTION. / ON THIS GOOD NIGHT** [48] [–]
(cd-s+=) *(669951-2)* – I lied / Here comes your man.

Oct 00. (cd/lp) *(<500622-2/-1>)* **HOWDY!** [33] Nov00 [ ]
– I need direction / I can't find my way home / Accidental life / Near you / Happiness / Dumb dumb dumb / Town and the city / The sun shines from you / Straight and narrow / Cul de sac / My uptight life / If I never see you again.

—— **FRANCIS MACDONALD** – drums (of Shoeshine records) repl. QUINN who quit during the middle of the last set

Jun 01. (7"; as TEENAGE FANCLUB & DE LA SOUL) *(<671213-7>)* **DUMB DUMB DUMB. / STRAIGHT AND NARROW** [ ] Jan02 [ ]
(cd-s+=) *(671213-2)* – Thaw me / One thousand lights.

TEENAGE FANCLUB & JAD FAIR

Geographic Alternative Tentacles

Feb 02. (7") *(GEOG 013)* **NEAR TO YOU. / ALWAYS IN MY HEART** [68] [–]
(cd-s+=) *(GEOG 013CD)* – Let's celebrate.

Mar 02. (cd/lp) *(GEOG 014 CD/LP) <VIRUS 274>* **WORDS OF WISDOM AND HOPE** [ ] Jan02 [ ]
– Behold the miracle / I feel fine / Near to you / Smile / Crush on you / Cupid / The power of your tenderness / Vampire's claw / Secret heart / You rock / Love's taken over / The good thing.

Nov 02. (7") *(VIRUS 278)* **ALWAYS IN MY HEART. / LET'S CELEBRATE** [ ] [–]

TEENAGE FANCLUB

Poolside JetSet

Jan 03. (cd/lp) *(POOLS 3 CD/LP) <66>* **FOUR THOUSAND SEVEN HUNDRED AND SIXTY-SIX SECONDS** (compilation) [47] [ ]
– The concept / Ain't that enough / The world'll be OK / Everything flows / Star sign / Mellow doubt / I need direction / About you / What you do to me / Empty space / Sparky's dream / I don't want control of you / Hang on / Did I say / Don't look back / Your love is the place where I come from / Neil Jung / Radio / Dumb dumb dumb / Planets / My uptight life.

Aug 03. (7") *(POOLS 5)* **DID I SAY. / THE CABBAGE** [ ] [–]

– compilations, others, etc. –

May 92. (7") *K; <IPU 26>* **FREE AGAIN. / BAD SEEDS** [–] [ ]

Nov 92. (12"ep/cd-ep) *Strange Fruit; (SFPS/+CD 081)* **THE JOHN PEEL SESSION** [ ] [–]
– God knows it's true / Alcoholiday / So far gone / Long hair. *(re-iss. Dec93 & Jul95; same)*

Mar 95. (cd/c) *Snapper; (FLIPCD 002)* **DEEP FRIED FANCLUB** [ ] [–]
– Everything flows / Primary education / Speeder / Critical mass (orig.) / The ballad of John and Yoko / God knows it's true / Weedbreak / So far gone / Ghetto blaster / Don't cry no tears / Free again / Bad seed. *(cd re-iss. Jan03 on 'Fire'; SFIRE 017CD)*

Jul 95. (12"ep/cd-ep; as FRANK BLACK & TEENAGE FANCLUB) *Strange Fruit; (SFPS/+CD 091)* **PEEL SESSION** [ ] [–]
– Handy man / The man who was too loud / The Jacques Tati / Sister Isabel.

Apr 97. (cd) *Nectar; (NTMCD 543)* **FANDEMONIUM** [ ] [–]

Sep 97. (7"ep) *Radiation; (RARE 033)* **TEENAGE FANCLUB EP** [ ] [–]

TELEVISION

Formed: New York City, New York, USA based ... late '73 by TOM VERLAINE, RICHARD HELL and BILLY FICCA who had all been members of The NEON BOYS. In 1975, William Terry Ork gave them a deal on his own self-named indie label, for whom they issued a one-off flop single, 'LITTLE JOHNNY JEWEL'. By this point, HELL (who went on to form the equally seminal RICHARD HELL & THE VOID-OIDS) had been replaced by ex-MC5 man, FRED 'SONIC' SMITH, TELEVISION subsequently signing with 'Elektra' and unleashing their classic debut album, 'MARQUEE MOON'. Although virtually ignored in America (more astute British punk/new wave fans placed it in the UK Top 30) upon its 1977 release, the album has since been acknowledged as a landmark release. The hypnotic near-10 minute title track (also a UK Top 30 hit) breathtakingly showcased the driving/free-form cool guitar interplay between LLOYD and virtuoso VERLAINE (the track first debuted at their early CBGB's shows and perfected/modified over the next couple of years), while the album as a whole testified to VERLAINE's barely disguised passion for The ROLLING STONES, PINK FLOYD and the darker moments of The VELVET UNDERGROUND. While VERLAINE's tortured vocals were reminiscent of LOU REED/PATTI SMITH, his molten-spark histrionics resolutely distinguished the band from the more wilfully amateurish new wave pack and TELEVISION remain the most musically adept band of the era. Unsurprisingly, however, they found it difficult following up such a milestone and although 'ADVENTURE' (1978) contained sporadic moments of genius, TELEVISION were beginning to lose clarity. Ironically, as the New York scene was at its height, LLOYD effectively pulled the plug on the group after walking out mid-tour later that year. VERLAINE tried unsuccessfully to translate his distinctive sound into a more mainstream rock setting with his solo career, retaining his characteristic vocals and of course, his trademark guitar alchemy. TELEVISION eventually re-formed in the 90's with the classic line-up of VERLAINE, LLOYD, SMITH and FICCA, recording the acclaimed 'TELEVISION' (1992) for 'Capitol' and suggesting that what VERLAINE's solo career was lacking was the anchor and foil of LLOYD's rhythm playing. The latter kept himself busy during the 90's with guest spots for the likes of MATTHEW SWEET although parental considerations also took up much of his time. He eventually returned to solo work with 'THE COVER DOESN'T MATTER' (2001), a belated – 15 years (!) – set of pared-back alt-rock recorded with PETER STUART and CHRIS BUTLER. • **Songwriters:** VERLAINE lyrics / group compositions, except early live material; FIRE ENGINE (13th Floor Elevators) / KNOCKIN' ON HEAVEN'S DOOR (Bob Dylan) / SATISFACTION (Rolling Stones). • **Trivia:** VERLAINE played guitar on PATTI SMITH's 1974 single 'Hey Joe'.

Album rating: MARQUEE MOON (*10) / ADVENTURE (*6) / THE BLOW UP exploitation (*4) / TELEVISION (*5) / Tom Verlaine: TOM VERLAINE (*7) / DREAMTIME (*6) / WORDS FROM THE FRONT (*6) / COVER (*7) / FLASH LIGHT (*7) / THE WONDER (*7) / WARM AND COOL (*5) / THE MILLER'S TALE: A TOM VERLAINE ANTHOLOGY compilation (*8)

TOM VERLAINE (b. THOMAS MILLER, 13 Dec'49, Mt.Morris, New Jersey) – vocals, lead guitar / **RICHARD LLOYD** – guitar, vocals / **RICHARD HELL** (b. RICHARD MYERS, 2 Oct'49, Lexington, Kentucky) – bass, vocals / **BILLY FICCA** – drums

not iss. Ork

Oct 75. (7") *<81975>* **LITTLE JOHNNY JEWEL. / (part 2)** [–] [ ]

—— **FRED SMITH** (b.10 Apr'48) – bass, vocals (ex-BLONDIE) repl. RICHARD HELL who went solo

Elektra Elektra

Feb 77. (lp/c) *(K/K4 52046) <7E 1098>* **MARQUEE MOON** [28] [ ]
– See no evil / Venus / Friction / Marquee moon / Elevation / Guiding light / Prove it / Torn curtain. *(cd-iss. Jun89; 960616-2) (lp re-iss. Dec02 on '4 Men With Beards'; 4M 501) <(cd re-mast.Sep03 on 'Rhino'+=; 8122 73920-2)>* – Little Johnny Jewel (pts.1 & 2) / See no evil (alt.) / Friction (alt.) / Marquee moon (alt.) / Untitled instrumental.

Mar 77. (12",2-part-7") *(K 12252)* **MARQUEE MOON (stereo). / MARQUEE MOON (mono)** [30] [–]

Jul 77. (7"/12",12"green) *(K 12262/+T)* **PROVE IT. / VENUS** [25] [–]

Apr 78. (lp,red-lp/c) *(K/K4 52072) <6E 133>* **ADVENTURE** [7] [ ]
– Glory / Days / Foxhole / Careful / Carried away / The fire / Ain't that nothin' / The dream's dream. *(cd-iss. Nov93 on 'WEA'; 7559 60523-2) <(cd re-mast.Sep03 on 'Rhino'+=; 8122 73912-2)>* – Adventure / Ain't that nothin' (single version) / Glory (early version) / Untitled.

Apr 78. (7"/12"red) *(K 12287/+T)* **FOXHOLE. / CAREFUL** [36] [–]
Jul 78. (7") *(K 12306)* **GLORY. / CARRIED AWAY** [ ] [–]
Jul 78. (7") <45516> **GLORY. / AIN'T THAT NOTHIN'** [–] [ ]

—— Broke ranks in Aug'78. FICCA joined The WAITRESSES, FRED joined The PATTI SMITH GROUP and RICHARD LLOYD went solo.

TOM VERLAINE

—— went solo augmented mainly by **FRED SMITH** – bass / **JAY DEE DAUGHERTY** – drums / **BRUCE BRODY** – keyboards / **ALLAN SCHWARTZBERG** – drums, percussion

Elektra Elektra

Sep 79. (lp/c) *(K/K4 52156)* <2156> **TOM VERLAINE** [ ] [ ]
– The grip of love / Souvenir from a dream / Kingdom come / Mr. Bingo / Yonki time / Flash lightning / Red leaves / Last night / Breakin' in my heart.

Warners Warners

Sep 81. (lp/c) *(K/K4 56919)* <BSK 3559> **DREAMTIME** [ ] [ ]
– There's a reason / Penetration / Always / The blue robe / Without a word / Mr. Blur / Fragile / A future in noise / Down on the farm / Mary Marie.
Sep 81. (7"/12") *(K 17855/+T)* **ALWAYS. / THE BLUE ROBE** [ ] [–]

—— **JIMMY RIPP** – guitar; repl. BRODY

Virgin Warners

May 82. (lp/c) *(V/TCV 2227)* <BSK 3685> **WORDS FROM THE FRONT** [ ] [ ]
– Present arrived / Postcard from Waterloo / True story / Clear it away / Words from the front / Coming apart / Days on the mountain. *(cd-iss. Aug88; OVED 87) (re-iss. cd Jun89; CDV 2227)*
May 82. (7"/12") *(VS 501/+12)* **POSTCARD FROM WATERLOO. / DAYS ON THE MOUNTAIN** [ ] [–]
Jun 84. (7") *(VS 696)* **LET'S GO TO THE MANSION. / ('A'version)** [ ] [–]
(12"+=) *(VS 696/+12)* – Lindi Lu.
Aug 84. (7") *(VS 704)* **FIVE MILES OF YOU. / YOUR FINEST HOUR** [ ] [–]
(12"+=) *(VS 704/+12)* – Dissolve reveal.
Sep 84. (lp/c) *(V/TCV 2314)* <25144> **COVER** [ ] [ ]
– Five miles of you / Let's go to the mansion / Travelling / O foolish heart / Dissolve – Reveal / Miss Emily / Rotation / Swim. *(re-iss. Apr86 lp/c; OVED/+C 168) (cd-iss. Jun89; (CDV 2314)*

—— **ANDY NEWMARK** – drums; repl. JAY DEE

Fontana Mercury-IRS

Feb 87. (7") *(FTANA 1)* **A TOWN CALLED WALKER. / SMOOTHER THAN JONES** [ ] [–]
(12"+=) *(FTANA 1-12)* – ('A'version) / Caveman flashlight.
Feb 87. (lp/c)(cd) *(SF LP/MC 1)(830861-2)* <42050> **FLASH LIGHT** [99] [ ]
– Cry mercy, judge / Say a prayer / A town called Walker / Song / The scientist writes a letter / Bomb / 4 a.m. / The funniest thing / Annie's tellin' me / One time at sundown.
Mar 87. (7") *(FTANA 2)* **CRY MERCY JUDGE. / CALL ME THE CIRCLING** [ ] [–]
(12"+=) *(FTANA 2-12)* – At this moment (live) / Lover of the night (live) / Strange things happening.
Jun 87. (7") *(VLANE 3)* **THE FUNNIEST THING. / ONE TIME AT SUNDOWN** [ ] [–]
(12"+=) *(VLANE 3-12)* – Marquee Moon ('87 version).
Aug 87. (7") *(VLANE 4)* **THE SCIENTIST WRITES A LETTER. / ('A'-Paris version)** [ ] [–]
Oct 89. (7") *(VLANE 5)* **SHIMMER. / BOMB** [ ] [–]
(12"+=)(cd-s+=) *(VLANE 5-12)(VLACD 5)* – The scientist writes a letter.
Mar 90. (7") *(VLANE 6)* **KALEIDOSCOPIN'. / SIXTEEN TULIPS** [ ] [–]
(12"+=)(cd-s+=) *(VLANE 6-12)(VLACD 6)* – Vanity fair.
Apr 90. (cd/c/lp) *(842420-2/-4/-1)* **THE WONDER** [ ] [–]
– Kaleidoscopin' / August / Ancient Egypt / Shimmer / Stalingrad / Pillow / Storm / 5 hours from Calais / Cooleridge / Prayer.

Rough Trade Rykodisc

Apr 92. (cd/lp) *(R 288-2/-1)* <10216> **WARM AND COOL** [ ] [ ]
– Those harbour lights / Sleepwalkin' / The deep dark clouds / Saucer crash / Depot (1951) / Boulevard / Harley Quinn / Sor Juanna / Depot (1957) / Spiritual / Little dance / Ore.

– compilation –

Apr 96. (cd) *Virgin; (CDVDM 9034)* **A MILLER'S TALE (The Tom Verlaine Story)** [ ] [–]
– Kingdom come / Souvenir from a dream / Clear it away / Always / Postcard from Waterloo / Penetration / Breakin' in my heart / Marquee moon / Days on the mountain / Prove it / Venus / Glory / The grip of love / Without a word / Words from the front / Let's go to the mansion / Lindi-Lu / O foolish heart / Five miles of you / Your finest hour / Anna / Sixteen tulips / Call me the / At 4 a.m. / Stalingrad / Call Mr. Lee / No glamour for Willi / The revolution.

TELEVISION

—— re-formed for one-off with **VERLAINE, LLOYD, FICCA + SMITH**

Capitol Capitol

Sep 92. (cd/c/lp) <(CD/TC+/EST 2181)> **TELEVISION** [ ] [ ]
– 1880 or so / Shane, she wrote this / In world / Call Mr. Lee / Rhyme / No glamour for Willi / Beauty trip / The rocket / This fire / Mars. *(cd re-iss. Feb99; CDESTV 2181)*

– compilations, others, etc. –

Jan 83. (c) *R.O.I.R.; <A-114>* **THE BLOW UP (live)** [–] [ ]
– The blow up / See no evil / Prove it / Elevation / I don't care / Venus de Milo / Foxhole / Ain't that nothin' / Knockin' on Heaven's door / Little Johnny Jewel / Friction / Marquee moon / Satisfaction. *(UK cd-iss. Feb90 on 'Danceteria'; DANCD 030) (cd re-iss. Nov94 on 'R.O.I.R.'; RE 114CD) <(cd-iss. Apr99; RUSCD 8249)> <(d-lp iss.May01; RUSLP 8249)>*
1979. (12"m) *Ork-WEA; (NYC 1T)* **LITTLE JOHNNY JEWEL (parts 1 & 2). / ('A'live version)** [ ] [–]

☐ TEMPLE OF THE DOG (see under ⇒ SOUNDGARDEN)

TEMPTATIONS

Formed: Birmingham, Alabama, USA ... 1960, initially as The ELGINS, by EDDIE KENDRICKS and PAUL WILLIAMS (from The PRIMES), plus MELVIN FRANKLIN and OTIS WILLIAMS (from The DISTANTS). They moved to Detroit in 1961 after two flop 45's for 'Miracle'. Securing a deal with the Berry 'Gordy' label (aka Tamla Motown), they finally scored their first US hit in 1964 with 'THE WAY YOU DO THE THINGS YOU DO'. By early 1965, 'MY GIRL' had given them their first chart topper. Penned by SMOKEY ROBINSON (who dominated most of the band's songwriting during this period), the song was the first in an incredible run of chart hits that included 'IT'S GROWING', 'SINCE I LOST MY BABY' and 'MY BABY', all released in 1965. Though the act were 'manufactured' to a certain degree by 'Motown', they possessed an impressive three-pronged vocal attack in DAVID RUFFIN's gravel-flecked rasp, EDDIE KENDRICKS' high tenor and PAUL WILLIAMS' heavy baritone. But it was RUFFIN's vocals which were pushed to the fore as producer NORMAN WHITFIELD began to lead the group's sound in a rougher direction, 'AIN'T TOO PROUD TO BEG' (1966), an early example of what was to come. As the band enjoyed a further string of hits including '(I KNOW) I'M LOSING YOU)' (1966), 'YOU'RE MY EVERYTHING' (1967) and 'I WISH IT WOULD RAIN' (1968), RUFFIN became increasingly jealous of the way DIANA ROSS was being nurtured for solo stardom by 'Motown', things coming to a head when RUFFIN failed to show for a gig. The group duly sent him packing, recruiting DENNIS EDWARDS and with the 'CLOUD NINE' (1969) single, hitched a ride on the magic roundabout of "psychedelic soul" pioneered by SLY STONE's thrilling honky hybrids. With WHITFIELD and his partner BARRETT STRONG penning most of the material, the band released a clutch of hard-hitting, socially aware classics like 'PSYCHEDELIC SHACK' (1970), 'BALL OF CONFUSION (THAT'S WHAT THE WORLD IS TODAY)' (1970), the funk getting dirtier and nastier with the hard-bitten tale of a broken home, 'PAPA WAS A ROLLING STONE' (1972). KENDRICKS departed in 1971 after his swansong for the band, 'JUST MY IMAGINATION (RUNNING AWAY WITH ME)' and PAUL WILLIAMS left later the same year, the band drafting in replacements DAMON HARRIS and RICHARD STREET. While the singles dried up, in the pop charts at least, the band still shifted albums up until the late 70's. As their creative muse began to falter, the band extricated itself from 'Motown' and despite a well-received self-produced album, 'THE TEMPTATIONS DO THE TEMPTATIONS' (1976), their two albums for 'Atlantic', 'HEAR TO TEMPT YOU' (1978) and 'BARE BACK' (1978) were marred by insipid disco stylings. EDWARDS had been absent for these albums (replaced by LOUIS PRICE), although he returned towards the end of the decade and the band hooked up with 'Motown' again for a comeback single, 'POWER' (1980) which scraped into the charts. RUFFIN and KENDRICKS returned to the fold for a short-lived reunion in 1982 and following their departure, OTIS WILLIAMS and MELVIN FRANKLIN carried the TEMPTATIONS flame through the 80's and beyond, completing studio and live work with a changing cast of musicians. Although they were inducted into the Rock'n'Roll Hall Of Fame in 1989, the band were merely retreading their 60's heyday, cabaret style. With KENDRICKS dying of cancer in 1992 and MELVIN FRANKLIN dying three years later, WILLIAMS is the sole remaining member from the original group. With a line-up that included OTIS WILLIAMS, ALI WOODSON, RON TYSON and RAY DAVIS, he cut the mid-90's set, 'FOR LOVERS ONLY' and 1998's 'PHOENIX RISING'. Incredibly perhaps, the latter album was the first of their career to hit the platinum sales bracket although it paled next to their classic work. While it's difficult to even contemplate someone coming up with such a cheesy title as 'EAR-RESISTIBLE' (yep, you read that right), this millennial effort featured a clutch of classy ballads that actually did some justice to the group's legacy, earning them a US Top 60 chart placing. 'AWESOME' (c'mon guys, get your titles sorted out!!!) followed in 2001, a pleasant if forgettable addition to their humungous back catalogue. • **Covered:** THE WEIGHT (Band) / I'LL TRY SOMETHING NEW (Miracles) / I'M GONNA MAKE YOU LOVE ME (Madeleine Bell) / etc. • **Trivia:** In 1987, actor and fan, BRUCE WILLIS, invited The TEMPTATIONS to sing back-up on his hit version of The DRIFTERS' 'Under The Boardwalk'.

Album rating: MEET THE TEMPTATIONS (*7) / THE TEMPTATIONS SING SMOKEY (*7) / TEMPTIN' TEMPTATIONS (*7) / GETTIN' READY (*7) / THE TEMPTATIONS GREATEST HITS compilation (*8) / TEMPTATIONS LIVE! (*5) / WITH A LOT OF SOUL (*6) / THE TEMPTATIONS IN A MELLOW MOOD (*6) / WISH IT WOULD RAIN (*7) / DIANA ROSS & THE SUPREMES JOIN THE TEMPTATIONS with Diana Ross & The Supremes (*6) / TCB special with Diana Ross & The Supremes (*6) / LIVE AT THE COPA (*4) / CLOUD NINE (*8) / THE TEMPTATIONS SHOW special (*6) / PUZZLE PEOPLE (*6) / TOGETHER with Diana Ross & The Supremes (*5) / ON BROADWAY special with Diana Ross & The Supremes (*5) / PSYCHEDELIC SHACK (*8) / LIVE AT LONDON'S TALK OF THE TOWN (*5) / TEMPTATIONS GREATEST HITS II compilation (*7) / SKY'S THE LIMIT (*6) / SOLID ROCK (*6) / ALL DIRECTIONS (*6) / MASTERPIECE (*6) / ANTHOLOGY compilation (*8) / 1990 (*6) / A SONG FOR YOU (*5) / HOUSE PARTY (*4) / WINGS OF LOVE (*4) / THE TEMPTATIONS DO THE TEMPTATIONS (*4) / HEAR TO TEMPT YOU (*4) / BARE BACK (*3) / POWER (*5) / ALL THE MILLION SELLERS compilation (*8) / THE TEMPTATIONS (*4) / REUNION (*6) / SURFACE THRILLS (*4) / BACK TO BASICS (*5) / TRULY FOR YOU (*5) / TOUCH ME (*4) / 25th ANNIVERSARY compilation (*7) / TO BE CONTINUED (*5) / TOGETHER AGAIN (*5) / SPECIAL (*4) / MILESTONE (*4) / MOTOWN'S GREATEST HITS compilation (*8) / FOR LOVERS ONLY (*4) / PHOENIX RISING (*5) / GREAT SONGS AND PERFORMANCES ... compilation (*7) / ALL THE MILLION SELLERS compilation (*8) / EAR-RESISTIBLE (*6) / AT THEIR VERY BEST compilation (*8) / AWESOME (*4)

MELVIN FRANKLIN (b. DAVID ENGLISH, 12 Oct'42, Montgomery, Alabama) – vocals / **OTIS WILLIAMS** (b. OTIS MILES, 30 Oct'49, Texarkana, Texas) – vocals / **ELDRIDGE BRYANT** – vocals

not iss. Thelma

1960. (7"; as DISTANTS) <2282> **ANSWER ME. / SAVE ME FROM THIS MISERY** – [ ]

not iss. Northern

1960. (7"; as DISTANTS) <3732> **COME ON. / ALWAYS** – [ ]

not iss. Warwick

1960. (7"; as DISTANTS) <546> **COME ON. / ALWAYS** – [ ]

1960. (7"; as DISTANTS) <577> **ALRIGHT. / OPEN UP YOUR HEART** – [ ]

— added **EDDIE KENDRICKS** (b.17 Dec'39, Union Springs, Alabama) – lead vocals (ex-PRIMES) / **PAUL WILLIAMS** (b. 2 Jul'39) – vocals (ex-PRIMES)

not iss. Miracle

Aug 61. (7") <05> **OH, MOTHER OF MINE. / ROMANCE WITHOUT FINANCE** – [ ]

Nov 61. (7") <12> **CHECK YOURSELF. / YOUR WONDERFUL LIFE** – [ ]

Stateside Gordy

Apr 62. (7") <7001> **DREAM COME TRUE. / ISN'T SHE PRETTY** – [ ]

Sep 62. (7"; as The PIRATES) <*Mel-O-Die; 105*> **MIND OVER MATTER (I'M GONNA MAKE YOY MINE). / I'LL LOVE YOU TILL I DIE** – [ ]

Jan 63. (7") <7010> **PARADISE. / SLOW DOWN HEART** – [ ]

Mar 63. (7") <7015> **I WANT A LOVE I CAN SEE. / THE FURTHER YOU LOOK THE LESS YOU SEE** – [ ]

Jul 63. (7") <7020> **MAY I HAVE THIS DANCE. / FAREWELL MY LOVE** – [ ]

— **DAVID RUFFIN** (b.18 Jan'41, Meridian, Missouri) – vocals (lead in 1965) had already deposed BRYANT

Apr 64. (7") *(SS 278)* <7028> **THE WAY YOU DO THE THINGS YOU DO. / JUST LET ME KNOW** [ ] Jan64 11

— Early 1964, they backed and were credited on LIZ LANDS 'Gordy' single 'MIDNIGHT JOHNNY'. / KEEP ME'. <7030>

Jul 64. (7") *(SS 319)* <7032> **I'LL BE IN TROUBLE. / THE GIRL'S ALRIGHT WITH ME** [ ] May64 33

Oct 64. (7") *(SS 348)* <7035> **GIRL (WHY YOU WANNA MAKE ME BLUE). / BABY BABY I NEED YOU** [ ] Aug64 26

Jan 65. (7") *(SS 378)* <7038> **MY GIRL. / TALKIN' 'BOUT NOBODY BUT MY BABY** 43 Dec64 1

Tamla Motown Gordy

Mar 65. (7") *(TMG 504)* <7040> **IT'S GROWING. / WHAT LOVE HAS JOINED TOGETHER** 45 18

May 65. (lp) **MEET THE TEMPTATIONS** [ ] Apr64 95
– The way you do the things you do / I want a love I can see / Dream come true / Paradise / May I have this dance / Isn't she pretty / Just let me know / Your wonderful love / The further you look the less you see / Check yourself / Slow down heart / Farewell my love. *(cd-iss. Jun99; 549513-2)*

Aug 65. (7") *(TMG 526)* <7043> **SINCE I LOST MY BABY. / YOU'VE GOT TO EARN IT** [ ] Jul65 17

Oct 65. (lp) *(TML 11016)* <912> **TEMPTATIONS SING SMOKEY** [ ] Mar65 35
– The way you do the things you do / Baby baby I need you / You'd lose a precious love / My girl / It's growing / Who's loving you / What love has joined together / What's so good 'bout goodbye. *(re-iss. Feb80 & Oct81 lp/c; STMR/CSTMR 9005) (cd-iss. Mar03; 530930-2)*

Nov 65. (7") *(TMG 541)* <7047> **MY BABY. / DON'T LOOK BABY** [ ] 13 / Oct65 83

Mar 66. (lp; stereo/mono) *(S+/TML 11023)* <914> **TEMPTIN' TEMPTATIONS** [ ] Nov65 11
– Since I lost my babe / Girl's alright with me / Just another lonely night / My baby / You've got to earn it / Everybody needs love / Girl / Don't look back / I gotta know now / Born to love you / I'll be in trouble / You're the one I need. *(cd-iss. Mar03; 530931-2)*

Apr 66. (7") *(TMG 557)* <7049> **GET READY. / FADING AWAY** [ ] Feb66 29

Jun 66. (7") *(TMG 565)* <7054> **AIN'T TOO PROUD TO BEG. / YOU'LL LOSE A PRECIOUS LOVE** 21 May66 13

Sep 66. (lp; stereo/mono) *(S+/TML 11035)* <918> **GETTIN' READY** 40 Jul66 12
– Say you / Little Miss Sweetness / Ain't too proud to beg / Get ready / Lonely, lonely man am I / Too busy thinking about my baby / I've been

good to you / It's a lonely world without your love / Fading away / Who you gonna run to / You're not an ordinary girl / Not now I'll tell you later. *(re-iss. Jul82 on 'Motown') (cd-iss. Jun99; 549514-2)*

Sep 66. (7") *(TMG 578) <7055>* **BEAUTY IS ONLY SKIN DEEP. / YOU'RE NOT AN ORDINARY MAN** 18 Aug66 3

Dec 66. (7") *(TMG 587) <7057>* **(I KNOW) I'M LOSING YOU. / LITTLE MISS SWEETNESS** 19 Nov66 8

May 67. (7") *(TMG 610) <7061>* **ALL I NEED. / SORRY IS A SORRY WORD** [ ] Apr67 8

Jul 67. (lp; stereo/mono) *(S+/TML 11053) <921>* **TEMPTATIONS LIVE! (live)** 20 Mar67 10
– Medley: Girl (why you wanna make me blue) – Girl's alright with me – I'll be in trouble – I want a love I can see / What love has joined together / My girl / Yesterday / What now my love / Beauty is only skin deep / Group introduction / I wish you love / Ain't too proud to beg / Ol' man river / Get ready / Fading away / My baby / Youll lose a precious love / Baby, baby I need you / Don't look back.

Sep 67. (7") *(TMG 620) <7063>* **YOU'RE MY EVERYTHING. / I'VE BEEN GOOD TO YOU** 26 Jul67 6

Oct 67. (lp; stereo/mono) *(S+/TML 11057) <922>* **WITH A LOT O' SOUL** 19 Aug67 7
– You're my everything / All I need / I'm losing you / Ain't no Sun since you've gone / No more water in the well / It's you that I need / Save my love for a rainy day / Just one last look / Sorry is a sorry word / Now that you've won me / Two sides to love / Don't send me away. *(cd-iss. Aug01; 530932-2)*

Dec 67. (7") *(TMG 633) <7065>* **(LONELINESS MADE ME REALISE) IT'S YOU THAT I NEED. / I WANT A LOVE I CAN SEE** [ ] Sep67 14

Feb 68. (7") *(TMG 641) <7068>* **I WISH IT WOULD RAIN. / I TRULY, TRULY BELIEVE** 45 Dec67 4

Mar 68. (lp; stereo/mono) *(S+/TML 11068) <924>* **IN A MELLOW MOOD** [ ] Dec67 13
– Hello young lovers / A taste of honey / For once in my life / Somewhere / Ol' man river / I'm ready for love / Try to remember / Who can I turn to (when nobody needs needs me) / What now my love / That's life / With these hands / The impossible dream. *(cd-iss. Aug01; 530933-2)*

— **DENNIS EDWARDS** (b. 3 Feb'43) – vocals repl. RUFFIN who went solo

May 68. (7") *(TMG 658) <7072>* **I COULD NEVER LOVE ANOTHER (AFTER LOVING YOU). / GONNA GIVE HER ALL THE LOVE I GOT** 47 May68 13

Aug 68. (lp; stereo/mono) *(S+/TML 11079) <927>* **THE TEMPTATIONS WISH IT WOULD RAIN** [ ] Apr68 13
– I could never love another (after loving you) / Cindy / I wish it would rain / Please return your love to me / Fan the flame / He who picks a rose / Why did you leave me darling / I truly, truly believe / This is my beloved / Gonna give her all the love I've got / I've passed this way before / No man can love her like I do.

Jul 68. (7") *<7074>* **PLEASE RETURN YOUR LOVE TO ME. / HOW CAN I FORGET** – 26

Oct 68. (7") *(TMG 671)* **WHY DID YOU LEAVE ME DARLING. / HOW CAN I FORGET** [ ] –

Dec 68. (7") *<7082>* **RUDOLPH, THE RED-NOSED REINDEER. / SILENT NIGHT** – [ ]

— In Jan69 UK / Nov68, they teamed up with DIANA ROSS & THE SUPREMES (see ⇒) on Top 3 single I'M GONNA MAKE YOU LOVE ME. Around the same time the album DIANA ROSS AND THE SUPREMES JOIN THE TEMPTATIONS hit UK No.1 & US No.2. Throughout 1969, this combination also had Top 50 hits with I'LL TRY SOMETHING NEW / I SECOND THAT EMOTION (UK No.18) / THE WEIGHT / WHY (MUST WE FALL IN LOVE) (UK No.31). Their albums TCB (Soundtrack) hit UK No.11 + US No.1 / ON BROADWAY (TV Show) hit US No.38 / TOGETHER hit both UK + US No.38 early 1970.

Feb 69. (7") *(TMG 688)* **GET READY. / MY GIRL** 10 –

May 69. (7") *(TMG 699)* **AIN'T TOO PROUD TO BEG. / FADING AWAY** [ ] –

May 69. (lp; stereo/mono) *(S+/TML 11104) <938>* **LIVE AT THE COPA (live)** [ ] Dec68 15
– (Introduction) / Get ready / You're my everything / I truly, truly believe / I wish it would rain / For once in my life / I could never love another / For once in my life / I could never love another / Hello young lovers / With these hands / Swanee / The impossible dream / Please return your love to me / (I know) I'm losing you.

May 69. (7") *<7086>* **DON'T LET THE JONESES GET YOU DOWN. / SINCE I'VE LOST YOU** – 20

— line-up update:- **MELVIN FRANKLIN, OTIS WILLIAMS, EDDIE KENDRICKS, PAUL WILLIAMS + DENNIS EDWARDS**

Aug 69. (7") *(TMG 707) <7081>* **CLOUD NINE. / WHY DID SHE HAVE TO LEAVE ME (WHY DID SHE HAVE TO GO)** 15 Oct68 6

Sep 69. (lp; stereo/mono) *(S+/TML 11109) <939>* **CLOUD NINE** 32 Mar69 4
– Cloud nine / I heard it through it the grapevine / Why did she have to leave me (why did she have to go) / Runaway child, running wild / Love is a hurtin' thing / Hey girl / I need your lovin' / Don't let him take your love from me / Gonna keep on tryin' till I win your love / I gotta find away (to get you back). *(re-iss. Oct81 lp/c; STML/CSTML 5020) (cd-iss. Aug93; 530153-2)*

Nov 69. (7") *(TMG 716) <7084>* **RUNAWAY CHILD, RUNNING WILD. / I NEED YOUR LOVIN'** [ ] Feb69 6

Jan 70. (7") *(TMG 722) <7093>* **I CAN'T GET NEXT TO YOU. / RUNNING AWAY (AIN'T GONNA HELP ME)** 13 Aug69 1

Feb 70. (lp; stereo/mono) *(S+/TML 11133) <949>* **PUZZLE PEOPLE** 20 Oct69 5
– I can't get next to you / Hey Jude / Don't let the Joneses get you down / Message from a black man / It's your thing / Little green apples / You don't love me no more / Running away (ain't gonna help you) / Since I've lost you / Slave / That's the way love is. *(re-iss. Mar82 lp/c; STML/CSTMS 5050)*

Apr 70. (lp; stereo/mono) *(S+/TML 11141) <953>* **LIVE AT THE (LONDON'S) TALK OF THE TOWN (live)** [ ] Aug70 21
– I'm gonna make you love me / The impossible dream / Run away child running wild / Don't let the Joneses get you down / Love theme from Romeo & Juliet / I can get next to you / This guy's in love with you / I've got to be me / I'm losing you / Cloud nine / Everything is going to be alright. *(re-iss. Jan79 on 'Music For Pleasure' lp/c; MFP/TCMFP 50419)*

Jun 70. (7") *(TMG 741) <7096>* **PSYCHEDELIC SHACK. / THAT'S THE WAY LOVE IS** 33 Jan70 7

Jun 70. (lp) *(STML 11147) <947>* **PSYCHEDELIC SHACK** 56 Mar70 9
– Psychedelic shack / Hum along and dance / War / It's summer / You make your own Heaven and Hell right here on Earth / You need love like I do (don't you) / Take a stroll thru your mind / Friendship train. *(re-iss. Mar82 lp/c; STMS/CSTMS 5051)*

Sep 70. (7") *(TMG 7049) <7099>* **BALL OF CONFUSION (THAT'S WHAT THE WORLD IS TODAY). / IT'S SUMMER** 7 May70 3

Oct 70. (7") *<7102>* **UNGENA ZA ULIMWENGU (UNITE THE WORLD). / HUM ALONG AND DANCE** – 33

Dec 70. (lp) *<951>* **CHRISTMAS CARD** (Festive songs) – [ ]
(UK-iss.1988 on 'Pickwick' lp/c; SHM/HSC 3202)

May 71. (7") *(TMG 773) <7105>* **JUST MY IMAGINATION (RUNNING AWAY WITH ME). / YOU MAKE YOUR OWN HEAVEN AND HELL RIGHT HERE ON EARTH** 8 Jan71 1

— **EDWARDS, FRANKLIN & WILLIAMS** recruited new members **DAMON HARRIS** (b. 3 Jul'50, Baltimore, Maryland) – vocals repl. EDDIE KENDRICKS who went solo.

Jul 71. (7") *<7109>* **IT'S SUMMER. / I'M THE EXCEPTION TO THE RULE** – 51

Aug 71. (lp) *(STML 11184) <957>* **SKY'S THE LIMIT** [ ] Apr71 16
– Gonna keep on tryin' till I win your love / Just my imagination / I'm the exception to the rule / Smiling faces sometimes / Man / Throw a farewell kiss / Ungenza za Ulimwenga / Love can be anything. *(re-iss. May91 cd/c; WD/WK 72743)*

Sep 71. (7") *(TMG 783)* **IT'S SUMMER. / UNGENA ZA ULIMWENGU (UNITE THE WORLD)** [ ] –

— **RICHARD STREET** (b. 5 Oct'42, Detroit) – vocals (ex-DISTANTS) repl. PAUL. He later committed suicide 17 Aug'73.

Jan 72. (7") *(TMG 800) <7111>* **SUPERSTAR (REMEMBER HOW YOU GOT WHERE YOU ARE). / GONNA KEEP ON TRYIN' TILL I WIN YOUR LOVE** 32 Nov71 18

Apr 72. (7") *(TMG 808) <7115>* **TAKE A LOOK AROUND. / SMOOTH SAILING FROM NOW ON** 13 Feb72 30

Apr 72. (lp) *(STML 11202) <961>* **SOLID ROCK** 34 Jan72 30
– Take a look around / Ain't no sunshine / Stop the war now / What it is / Smooth sailing / Superstar (remember how you got where you are) / It's summer / The end of our road.

Jun 72. (7") *<7119>* **MOTHER NATURE. / FUNKY MUSIC SHO NUFF TURNS ME ON** – 92

Oct 72. (7") *(TMG 832)* **MOTHER NATURE. / SMILING FACES SOMETIMES** [ ] –

Jan 73. (7") *(TMG 839) <7121>* **PAPA WAS A ROLLIN' STONE. / ('A'instrumental)** 14 Oct72 1

Dec 72. (lp) *(STML 11218)* <962> **ALL DIRECTIONS** [19] Aug72 [2]
– Funky music sho nuff turns me on / Run Charlie run / I ain't got nothing / Papa was a rollin' stone / Love woke me up this morning / The first time ever I saw your face / Mother nature / It's your thing. *(re-iss. Mar82 lp/c; STMS/CSTMS 5052) (cd-iss. Sep93 & Mar03; 530155-2)*

Apr 73. (7") <TMG 854> <7126> **MASTERPIECE. / ('A'instrumental)** [ ] Feb73 [7]

Jun 73. (lp) *(STML 11229)* <965> **MASTERPIECE** [28] Mar73 [7]
– Masterpiece / Hey girl (I like your style) / Ha / The plastic man / Law of the land / Hurry tomorrow. *(re-iss. Oct81 lp/c; STMS/CSTMS 5021) (cd-iss. Jan93; 530100-2)*

Jun 73. (7") <7129> **THE PLASTIC MAN. / HURRY TOMORROW** [–] [40]

Aug 73. (7") <7131> **HEY GIRL (I LIKE YOUR STYLE). / MA** [–] [35]

Aug 73. (7") *(TMG 866)* **LAW OF THE LAND. / FUNKY MUSIC SHO NUFF TURN ME ON** [41] [–]

Nov 73. (7") <7133> **LET YOUR HAIR DOWN. / AIN'T NO JUSTICE** [–] [27]

Dec 73. (lp) *(STMA 8016)* <966> **1990** [ ] [19]
– Let your hair down / I need you / Heavenly / You've got my soul on fire / Ain't no justice / 1990 / Zoom.

Mar 74. (7") *(TMG 887)* **HEY GIRL (I LIKE YOUR STYLE). / I NEED YOU** [ ] [–]

Apr 74. (7") <7135> **HEAVENLY. / ZOOM** [–] [43]

Jun 74. (7") <7136> **YOU'VE GOT MY SOUL ON FIRE. / I NEED YOU** [–] [74]

— **GLEN LEONARD** – vocals repl. HARRIS

Jan 75. (7") *(TMG 931)* <7138> **HAPPY PEOPLE. / ('A'instrumental)** [ ] [40]

Feb 75. (lp) *(STMA 8021)* <969> **A SONG FOR YOU** [ ] [13]
– Happy people / Glasshouse / Shakey ground / The prophet / Happy people (Instrumental) / A song for you / Memories / I'm a bachelor.

Apr 75. (7") <7142> **SHAKEY GROUND. / I'M A BACHELOR** [–] [26]

May 75. (7") *(TMG 948)* **MEMORIES. / AIN'T NO JUSTICE** [ ] [–]

Aug 75. (7") <7144> **GLASSHOUSE. / THE PROPHET** [–] [37]

— **LOUIS PRICE** – vocals repl. EDWARDS who went solo

Jan 76. (7") <7146> **KEEP HOLDING ON. / WHAT YOU NEED MOST (I DO BEST OF ALL)** [–] [54]

Feb 76. (lp) *(STML 12006)* <973> **HOUSE PARTY** [ ] Nov75 [40]
– Keep holding on / It's just a matter of time / You can't stop a man in love / World of you, love and music / What you need most (I do best of all) / Ways of a grown up man / Johnny Porter / Darling stand by me / If I don't love you this way.

Jun 76. (7") <7150> **UP THE CREEK (WITHOUT A PADDLE). / DARLING STAND BY ME** [–] [94]

Jun 76. (lp) *(STMA 8025)* <971> **WINGS OF LOVE** [ ] Mar76 [29]
– Sweet gypsy Jane / Sweetness in the dark / Up the creek / China doll / Mary Ann / Dream world / Paradise.

Oct 76. (7") *(TMG 1057)* <7152> **WHO ARE YOU. / LET ME COUNT THE WAYS (I LOVE YOU)** [ ] [ ]

Oct 76. (lp) *(STML 12040)* <975> **THE TEMPTATIONS DO THE TEMPTATIONS** [ ] Sep76 [53]
– Why can't you and me get together / Who are you / I'm on fire / Put your trust in me, baby / There's no stopping / Let me count the ways / Is there anybody else / I'll take you in.

Jan 77. (7") *(TMG 1063)* **SHAKEY GROUND. / I'M A BACHELOR** [ ] [–]

Atlantic Atlantic

Nov 77. (7") <3436> **IN A LIFETIME. / I COULD NEVER STOP LOVING YOU** [–] [ ]

Feb 78. (lp) *(K 50413)* <19143> **HEAR TO TEMPT YOU** [ ] Dec77 [ ]
– Think for yourself / In a lifetime / Can we come and share in love / She's all I've got / Snake in the grass / It's time for love / Let's live in peace / Road between the lines / I could never stop loving you.

Feb 78. (7") <3461> **LET'S LIVE IN PEACE. / THINK FOR YOURSELF** [–] [ ]

Aug 78. (7") <3517> **BARE BACK. / I SEE MY CHILD** [–] [ ]

Aug 78. (lp) *(K 50504)* <19188> **BARE BACK** [ ] [ ]
– Bare back / Mystic woman (love me over) / I just don't know how I let you go / That's when you need love / Ever ready love / Wake up to me / You're so easy to love / I see the child / Touch me again.

Sep 78. (7") *(K 11186)* **BARE BACK. / EVER READY LOVE** [ ] [–]

Sep 78. (7") <3538> **EVER READY LOVE. / TOUCH ME AGAIN** [–] [ ]

Jan 79. (7") <3567> **JUST DON'T KNOW HOW TO LET YOU GO. / MYSTIC WOMAN** [–] [ ]

Motown Gordy

May 80. (7"/12") *(TMG/+T 1186)* <7183> **POWER. / ('A'instrumental)** [ ] [43]

Jun 80. (lp/c) *(STML/CSTML 12136)* <994> **POWER** [ ] May80 [45]
– Power / Struck by lightning twice / How can I resist your love / Isn't the night fantastic / Shadow of your love / Go for it / Can't you see sweet thing / I'm coming her.

Aug 80. (7") *(TMG 1197)* <7188> **STRUCK BY LIGHTNING TWICE. / I'M COMING HOME** [ ] [ ]

Jan 81. (7") *(TMG 1216)* **TAKE ME AWAY. / THERE'S MORE WHERE THAT CAME FROM** [ ] [–]

— **DENNIS EDWARDS** returned on lead vocals

Oct 81. (7") *(TMG 1243)* <7208> **AIMING AT YOUR HEART. / LIFE OF A COWBOY** [ ] [67]

Jan 82. (lp/c) *(STML/CSTML 12159)* <1006> **THE TEMPTATIONS** [ ] Aug81 [ ]
– Aiming at your heart / Evil woman (gonna take your love) / The best of both worlds / Ready, willing and able / Oh what a night / Open their eyes / The life of a cowboy / What else / Just ain't havin' fun / Your lovin' is magic.

Feb 82. (7") <7213> **OH, WHAT A NIGHT. / ISN'T THE NIGHT FANTASTIC** [–] [ ]

— **OTIS WILLIAMS, MELVIN FRANKLIN, RICHARD STREET & DENNIS EDWARDS** re-united with **DAVID RUFFIN & EDDIE KENDRICKS** for one-off album

May 82. (lp) <6008> **REUNION** [–] Apr82 [37]
– Standing on the top / You better beware / Lock it in the pocket / I've never been to me / Backstage / More on the inside / Money's hard to get.

May 82. (7"; TEMPTATIONS featuring RICK JAMES) *(TMG 1263)* <1616> **STANDING ON THE TOP. / (part 2)** [53] [66]

Jul 82. (7") <1631> **MORE ON THE INSIDE. / MONEY'S HARD TO GET** [–] [ ]

Nov 82. (7") <1654> **SILENT NIGHT. / EVERYTHING FOR CHRISTMAS** [–] [ ]
<re-iss. Nov83; 1713>

— The quartet added **RON TYSON** (their composer in '78) – vocals

Mar 83. (7"/12") *(TMG/+T 1297)* <1666> **LOVE ON MY MIND TONIGHT. / BRING YOUR BODY HERE** [ ] [88]

Mar 83. (lp/c) *(STML/CSTML 12182)* <6032> **SURFACE THRILLS** [ ] [ ]
– Surface thrills / Love on my mind tonight / One man woman / Show me your love / The seeker / What a way to put it / Made in America / Bring your body here (exercise chant).

May 83. (7") <1683> **SURFACE THRILLS. / MADE IN AMERICA** [–] [ ]

Oct 83. (7") <1707> **MISS BUSY BODY (GET YOUR BODY BUSY). / (part 2)** [–] [ ]

Dec 83. (lp/c) *(STML/CSTML 12196)* <6085> **BACK TO BASICS** [ ] [ ]
– Miss busy body (get your body busy) / Sail away / Outlaw / Stop the world right here (I wanna get off) / The battle song (I'm the one) / Hollywood / Isn't the night fantastic / Make me believe in love again.

Apr 84. (7") <1720> **SAIL AWAY. / ISN'T THE NIGHT FANTASTIC** [–] [54]

— **ALI OLLIE WODSIN** – lead vocals repl. EDWARDS

Nov 84. (7"/12") *(TMG/+T 1365)* <1765> **TREAT HER LIKE A LADY. / ISN'T THE NIGHT FANTASTIC** [12] [48]

Dec 84. (lp/c) *(ZL/ZK 72342)* <6119> **TRULY FOR YOU** [75] Nov84 [55]
– Running / Treat like a lady / How can you say it's over / My life is true (truly for you) / Memories / Just to keep you in my life / Set your love right / I'll keep my light on in my window. *(re-iss. Oct88 lp/c/cd; WL/WK/WD 76244)*

Feb 85. (7") <1781> **MY LOVE IS TRUE (TRULY FOR YOU). / SET YOUR LOVE RIGHT** [–] [ ]

Mar 85. (7") *(TMG 1373)* **MY LOVE IS TRUE (TRULY FOR YOU). / I'LL KEEP A LIGHT ON IN MY WINDOW** [ ] [–]
(12"+=) *(TMGT 1373)* – Treat her like a lady (remix).

Jun 85. (7") <1789> **HOW CAN YOU SAY IT'S OVER. / I'LL KEEP MY LIGHT IN THE WINDOW** [–] [ ]

— In Sep'85, RUFFIN & KENDRICKS were credited on HALL & OATES live album 'LIVE AT THE APOLLO WITH . . . '

Nov 85. (7"/12") *(ZB/ZT 40453)* <1818> **DO YOU REALLY LOVE YOUR BABY. / I'LL KEEP A LIGHT ON IN MY WINDOW** [ ] [ ]

Nov 85. (lp/c) *(ZL/ZK 72413)* <6164> **TOUCH ME** [ ] [ ]
– Magic / Give her some attention / Deeper than love / I'm fascinated /

Touch me / Don't break your promise to me / She got tired of loving me / Do you really love your baby / Oh lover.

Feb 86. (7") *<1834>* **TOUCH ME. / SET YOUR LOVE RIGHT** [–] [ ]

Mar 86. (7"/12") *(ZB/ZT 40622)* **I'M FASCINATED. / HOW CAN YOU SAY IT'S OVER** [ ] [–]

Jun 86. (7") *<1837>* **WISHFUL THINKING. / A FINE MESS** [–] [ ]

Aug 86. (7") *(ZB 40850)* **LADY SOUL. / A FINE MESS** [ ] [–]
(12"+=) *(ZT 40850)* – Papa was a rolling stone.

Sep 86. (lp/c) *(ZL/ZK 72515) <6207>* **TO BE CONTINUED** [ ] Jul86 [74]
– Lady soul / Message to the world / To be continued / Put us together again / Someone / Girls (they like it) / More love, your love / A fine mess / You're the one / Love me right.

Oct 86. (7") *<1856>* **LADY SOUL. / PUT US TOGETHER AGAIN** [–] [47]

Jan 87. (7") *<1871>* **TO BE CONTINUED. / YOU'RE THE ONE** [–] [ ]

Apr 87. (7") *<1881>* **SOMEONE. / LOVE ME RIGHT** [–] [ ]

— **DENNIS EDWARDS** returned again to repl. OTIS

Aug 87. (7") *(ZB 41431)* **PAPA WAS A ROLLIN' STONE (remix). / DON'T SAY NOTHING'S CHANGED** [31] [–]
(12"+=) *(ZT 41431)* – Papa was a rollin' stone (remix 2).

Oct 87. (lp/c/cd) *(ZL/ZK/ZD 72616) <6246>* **TOGETHER AGAIN** [ ] [ ]
– I got your number / Look what you started / I wonder who she's seeing now / 10 x 10 / Do you wanna go with me / Little things / Everytime I close my eyes / Lucky / Put your foot down.

Oct 87. (7"/12") *(ZB/ZT 41547) <1908>* **I WONDER WHO SHE'S SEEING NOW. / GIRLS (THEY LIKE IT)** [ ] [ ]

Jan 88. (7"/c-s) *(ZB/ZV 41734) <1920>* **LOOK WHAT YOU STARTED. / MORE LOVE, YOUR LOVE** [63] [ ]
(12"+=) *(ZT 41734)* – ('A'extended).

Apr 88. (7") *<1933>* **DO YOU WANNA GO WITH ME. / PUT YOUR FOOT DOWN** [–] [ ]

— Late 1987, RUFFIN & KENDRICKS released eponymous duo album on 'RCA'.

— **RON TYSON** – vocals repl. EDWARDS

Oct 89. (7") *(ZB 43233) <1974>* **ALL I WANT FROM YOU. / ('A'instrumental)** [71] [ ]
(12"+=/cd-s+=) *(ZT/ZD 43234)* – Papa was a rollin' stone / Treat her like a lady.

Oct 89. (lp/c/cd) *(ZL/ZK/ZD 72667) <6275>* **SPECIAL** [ ] [ ]
– Friends / Special / All I want from you / She's better than money / One step at a time / Fill me up / Go ahead / Loveline / Soul to soul. *(cd+=)* – O.A.A. lover.

Jan 90. (7") *<2004>* **SPECIAL. / O.A.A. LOVER** [–] [ ]

Mar 90. (7") *<2023>* **SOUL TO SOUL. / ('A'instrumental)** [–] [ ]

Jun 90. (7") *<903>* **ONE STEP AT A TIME. / ('A'instrumental)** [–] [ ]

Jan 92. (cd/c/lp) *(ZD/ZK/ZL 72768) <6331>* **MILESTONE** [ ] [ ]
– Eenie, meenie, minie moe / Any old lovin' (just won't do) / Hoops of fire / We should be makin' love / The Jones' / Get ready / Corner of my heart / Whenever you're ready / Do it easy / Wait a minute. (cd+=) – Celebrate. *(re-iss. cd Apr95; 530005-2)*

Feb 92. (7"/c-s) *(TMG/+C 1403)* **THE JONES'. / ('A'-Surgery mix)** [69] [ ]
(12"+=/cd-s+=) *(TMG T/CD 1403)* – ('A'instrumental).

— sadly, EDDIE KENDRICKS died of cancer in Oct '92

— **THEO PEOPLES** – vocals; repl. STREET

— Later, another original MELVIN FRANKLIN also died on 23rd February 1995.

— **OTIS WILLIAMS, PEOPLES + ALI WOODSON** with **RON TYSON** recruited **RAY DAVIS** (b.29 Mar'40, Sumter, South Carolina, USA)

Sep 95. (cd/c) *<(530568-2/-4)>* **FOR LOVERS ONLY** [ ] [ ]
– Some enchanted evening / I've grown accustomed to her face / At last / Night and day / Time after time / Melvin's interlude / Life is but a dream / What a difference a day makes / I'm glad there is you / South shell interlude / That's why (I love you so) / For your love – You send me.

— **HARRY GILBERRY Jr. + BARRINGTON SCOTT** – vocals; repl. PEOPLES + WOODSON

Oct 98. (cd/c) *<(530937-2/-4)>* **PHOENIX RISING** [ ] Aug98 [44]
– Here after (interlude) / Stay / False faces / How he could hurt you / I'm calling you (interlude) / This is my promise / My love / Tempt me / If I give you my heart / Take me in your arms / That's what friends are for / Just like I told you / Stay.

Sep 00. (cd) *<(157742-2)>* **EAR-RESISTIBLE** [ ] May00 [54]
– I'll just go crazy (intro) / I'm here / Your love / Elevator eyes / Selfish reasons / Kiss me like you miss me / Party / It's alright to be wrong / Proven and true / Got to get on the road / I'll just go crazy / A little bit lonely / One love one world (interlude) / Error of our ways.

Nov 01. (cd) *<(016330-2)>* **AWESOME** [ ] [ ]
– Awesome (intro) / Hurt so bad / 4 days / Lady / Forget about it / Awesome / Race for your heart / Swept away / My baby / Open letter, my one temptation (interlude) / So easy / I want a love I can see / That's how heartaches are made / I feel good.

– (selective) compilations, etc. –

note; on 'Tamla Motown' UK/ 'Gordy' US unless otherwise mentioned

Feb 67. (lp; stereo/mono) *(S+/TML 11042) <919>* **THE TEMPTATIONS' GREATEST HITS** [26] Dec66 [5]
– The way you do the things you do / My girl / Ain't too proud to beg / Don't look back / Get ready / Beauty is only skin deep / Since I lost my baby / The girl's alright with me / My baby / Its growing / I'll be in trouble / Girl (why you wanna make me blue). *(re-iss. Sep88 lp/c/cd; WL/WK/WD 72646)*

Aug 69. (lp) *<933>* **THE TEMPTATIONS SHOW (TV Soundtrack)** [–] [24]

Dec 70. (lp) *(STML 11170) <954>* **THE TEMPTATIONS' GREATEST HITS VOL.2** [35] Sep70 [15]
(re-iss. Sep88 lp/c/cd; WL/WK/WD 72647)

May 74. (d-lp/d-c) *(TMSP/CTMSP 6003) <974>* **ANTHOLOGY 64-73** [ ] Sep73 [65]
(re-iss. Oct82; same)

Oct 80. (d-lp/d-c) *(STML/CSTML 12140)* **20 GOLDEN GREATS** [ ] [–]
(cd-iss. 1986; ZL 72160)

Oct 81. (d-lp/d-c) *(TMSP/CTMSP 6003)* **ALL THE MILLION SELLERS** [ ] [–]
(re-iss. Apr84 lp/c; WL/WK 72096) (cd-iss. Feb86; WD 72096)

Nov 86. (cd) *(ZD 72460)* **CLOUD NINE / PUZZLE PEOPLE** [ ] [–]
(re-iss. Oct00; 159446-2)

Nov 86. (cd) *(ZD 72486)* **PSYCHEDELIC SHACK / ALL DIRECTIONS** [ ] [–]
(re-iss. Oct00; 159445-2)

Dec 86. (cd) *(ZD 72499)* **SONG FOR YOU / MASTERPIECE** [ ] [–]

Jan 87. (cd) *(ZD 72501)* **LIVE AT THE COPA / WITH A LOT O' SOUL** [ ] [–]

Jan 87. (cd) *(ZD 72525)* **ANTHOLOGY 1 & 2** [ ] [–]

Apr 89. (cd) *(WD 72365)* **COMPACT COMMAND PERFORMANCES** [ ] [–]

below from the film 'My Girl' starring McAuley Caulkin.

Feb 92. (7"/c-s/cd-s) *Epic; (657676-7/-4/-2) <74108>* **MY GIRL. / (James Newton Howard theme from 'My Girl')** [2] [ ]

Apr 92. (cd/c) *(530015-2/-4)* **MOTOWN'S GREATEST HITS** [8] [ ]
– My girl / The Jones' / Get ready (new version) / Ain't too proud to beg / Beauty is only skin deep / I wish it would rain / (I know) I'm losing you / Cloud nine / Paa was a rollin' stone / Law of the land / Just my imagination (running away with me) / Take a look around / Ball of confusion (that's what the world is today) / I can't get to you / Psychedelic shack / Treat her like a lady / Get ready / You're my everything / Superstar (remember how you got where you are) / Standing on the top (part 1).

Nov 98. (cd) *<5315>* **GREAT SONGS AND PERFORMANCES THAT INSPIRED THE MOTOWN 25th ANNIVERSARY TELEVISION SPECIAL** [–] [ ]

Feb 00. (cd) *Spectrum; (544255-2)* **PSYCHEDELIC SOUL** [ ] [ ]

Jul 00. (cd) *(153366-2)* **MOTOWN LOST AND FOUND: YOU'VE GOT TO EARN IT – 1962-1968** [ ] [ ]

Oct 00. (cd) *(157519-2)* **LET YOUR HEART BE YOUR GUIDE: AN INTRODUCTION TO THE TEMPTATIONS** [ ] [ ]

Oct 00. (cd) *(159443-2)* **MEET THE TEMPTATIONS / SING SMOKEY** [ ] [ ]

Oct 00. (cd) *(159444-2)* **LIVE AT THE COPA / WITH A LOT O' SOUL** [ ] [ ]

Oct 00. (cd) *(159510-2)* **MASTERPIECE / A SONG FOR YOU** [ ] [ ]

Oct 00. (cd) *(159511-2)* **WISH IT WOULD RAIN / IN A MELLOW MOOD** [ ] [ ]

Jan 01. (d-cd) *Universal TV; (013578-2)* **AT THEIR VERY BEST** [30] [ ]

Oct 01. (cd) *<(AA4400 14594-2)>* **THE BEST OF TEMPTATIONS CHRISTMAS** [ ] [ ]

Apr 02. (d-cd) *<017298>* **MY GIRL: THE VERY BEST OF THE TEMPTATIONS** [–] [ ]
Mar 03. (d-cd) *Universal; (E 530615-2)* **ONE BY ONE: THE BEST OF THE TEMPTATIONS** [ ] [ ]
Jun 03. (d-cd) *Universal; (AAB00005820-2)* **PSYCHEDELIC SOUL** [ ] [ ]

10cc

Formed: Manchester, England . . . early 1970 as HOTLEGS by the experienced ERIC STEWART, LOL CREME and KEVIN GODLEY. STEWART had been a member of WAYNE FONTANA & THE MINDBENDERS between April 1964 and November 1968, (the latter 6 months with pensmith GRAHAM GOULDMAN). GOULDMAN, while a solo artist, had written hits for The YARDBIRDS ('For Your Love', 'Heartful Of Soul' and 'Evil Hearted You'), The HOLLIES ('Bus Stop' and 'Look Through Any Window') and HERMAN'S HERMITS ('No Milk Today'). The aforementioned HOTLEGS scored a 1970 No.2 hit with 'NEANDERTHAL MAN' before folding the following year. In 1972, now trading as 10cc, the trio added GOULDMAN, signing to Jonathan King's newly formed 'UK' imprint. The revamped quartet subsequently became a massive selling outfit, making the Top 3 with the pastiche-like 'DONNA' while the follow-up, 'RUBBER BULLETS', topped the charts. The group amassed an impressive series of hits during the 70's including 'THE DEAN AND I', 'WALL STREET SHUFFLE' and 'LIFE IS A MINESTRONE', although they reached their pinnacle in 1975 (after signing to 'Mercury') with 'I'M NOT IN LOVE', a classy, sophisticated pop ballad lifted from their top selling album, 'THE ORIGINAL SOUNDTRACK'. Further chart success came with 'ART FOR ARTS SAKE' and 'I'M MANDY, FLY ME', although GODLEY & CREME left after the release of the accompanying 'HOW DARE YOU' (1976) set. In typically 70's fashion, the pair then indulged themselves in the luxury of a triple album, 'CONSEQUENCES' (1977), promoting their new "gizmo" guitar device in the process. GODLEY & CREME subsequently went on to become top video directors, producing, amongst others, HERBIE HANCOCK, FRANKIE GOES TO HOLLYWOOD and their own 'CRY' single (a groundbreaking effort featuring a series of human faces morphing into each other). Meanwhile, GOULDMAN and STEWART added TONY O'MALLEY, RICK FENN and STUART TOSH, scoring further hits with 'THE THINGS WE DO FOR LOVE', 'GOOD MORNING JUDGE' and the woeful cod-reggae of 'DREADLOCK HOLIDAY' (their third UK No.1); needless to say, most of the spark had vanished. In the early 80'zzz, GODLEY & CREME notched up further pop hits with 'UNDER YOUR THUMB' and 'WEDDING BELLS', STEWART also producing SAD CAFE while GOULDMAN collaborated with ANDREW GOLD in WAX. The original 10cc line-up re-formed in 1992 for the album, 'MEANWHILE', although all the songs were written by STEWART and GOULDMAN and by the following year's 'MIRROR MIRROR', GODLEY & CREME had left once more.

Album rating: Hotlegs: THINKS: SCHOOL STINKS (*4) / 10cc: 10cc (*6) / SHEET MUSIC (*7) / THE ORIGINAL SOUNDTRACK (*7) / 100cc – THE GREATEST HITS OF 10cc compilation (*6) / HOW DARE YOU! (*5) / DECEPTIVE BENDS (*5) / LIVE AND LET LIVE (*4) / BLOODY TOURISTS (*5) / GREATEST HITS 1972-1978 compilation (*8) / LOOK HEAR! (*4) / TEN OUT OF 10 (*4) / WINDOW IN THE JUNGLE (*3) / MEANWHILE (*3) / MIRROR, MIRROR (*3) / THE VERY BEST OF 10cc compilation (*7) / Eric Stewart: GIRLS (*4) / Graham Gouldman: ANIMALYMPICS (*4) / Godley & Creme: CONSEQUENCES (*4) / L (*4) / FREEZE FRAME (*4) / ISMISM (*5) / BIRDS OF PREY (*4) / THE HISTORY MIX VOLUME 1 (*5) / THE CHANGING FACES OF 10cc AND GODLEY & CREME compilation (*8) / GOODBYE BLUE SKY (*4)

HOTLEGS

ERIC STEWART (b.20 Jan'45) – vocals, guitar, bass (ex-MINDBENDERS) / **LOL CREME** (b. LAWRENCE CREME, 19 Sep'47) – vocals, guitar, keyboards, bass / **KEVIN GODLEY** (b. 7 Oct'45) – drums, vocals (ex-MOCKINGBIRDS, ex-Solo)

Fontana Capitol

Jun 70. (7") *(6007 019) <2886>* **NEANDERTHAL MAN. / YOU DIDN'T LIKE IT** [2] [22]
Mar 71. (7") *<3043>* **HOW MANY TIMES. / RUN BABY RUN** [–] [ ]

Philips Capitol

Mar 71. (lp) *(6308 047) <378>* **THINKS: SCHOOL STINKS** [ ] [ ]
– Neanderthal man / How many times / Desperate Dan / Take me back / Um wah, un woh / Suite F.A. / Fly away / Run baby run / All God's children.
Sep 71. (7") *(6006 140)* **LADY SADIE. / THE LOSER** [ ] [–]

— Split late 1971. A further exploitation lp 'YOU DIDN'T LIKE IT BECAUSE YOU DIDN'T THINK OF IT' was issued 1976 on 'Philips' *(9282 001)*; GOULDMAN guested bass on track 'Today'.

— The trio became . . .

10cc

— adding **GRAHAM GOULDMAN** – bass, vocals (ex-Solo artist, ex-MINDBENDERS)

UK-Decca UK

Sep 72. (7") *(UK 6) <49005>* **DONNA. / HOT SUN ROCK** [2] [ ]
Dec 72. (7") *(UK 22)* **JOHNNY, DON'T DO IT. / 4% OF SOMETHING** [ ] [–]
Apr 73. (7") *(UK 36) <49015>* **RUBBER BULLETS. / WATERFALL** [1] Sep73 [73]
Aug 73. (lp/c) *(UKA L/C 1005) <53105>* **10cc** [36] [ ]
– Rubber bullets / Donna / Johnny, don't do it / Sand in my face / Speed kills / The dean and I / Ships don't disappear in the night (do they?) / The hospital song / Fresh air for my momma / Headline hustler. *(re-iss. Apr82 on 'Philips'; 6359014) (re-iss. Dec83 on 'Mercury' lp/c; PRICE/PRIMC 7)*
Aug 73. (7") *(UK 48)* **THE DEAN AND I. / BEE IN MY BONNET** [10] [–]
Jan 74. (7") *(UK 57)* **THE WORST BAND IN THE WORLD. / 18 CARAT MAN OF MEANS** [ ] [–]
Apr 74. (7") *<49019>* **HEADLINE HUSTLER. / SPEED KILLS** [–] [ ]
Jun 74. (7") *(UK 69) <49023>* **WALL STREET SHUFFLE. / GISMO MY WAY** [10] [ ]
Jun 74. (lp/c) *(UKA L/C 1007) <53107>* **SHEET MUSIC** [9] [81]
– Wall Street shuffle / The worst band in the world / Hotel / Old wild men / Clockwork creep / Silly love / Somewhere in Hollywood / Baron Samedi / The sacro-iliac / Oh! Effendi. *(re-iss. Apr82 on 'Philips'; 6310508) (re-iss. Dec83 on 'Mercury' lp/c; PRICE/PRIMC 8)*
Sep 74. (7") *(UK 77)* **SILLY LOVE. / THE SACRO-ILIAC** [24] [–]

Mercury Mercury

Mar 75. (lp/c) *(9102 500) <SRMI 1029>* **THE ORIGINAL SOUNDTRACK** [4] [15]
– Une nuit a Paris: One night in Paris – The same night in Paris – Later the same night in Paris / I'm not in love / Blackmail / The second sitting for the last supper / Brand new day / Flying junk / Life is a minestrone / The film of my love. *(re-iss. Dec83 lp/c; PRICE/PRIMC 48) (cd-iss. 1988; 830 775-2) (cd re-iss. Aug98 on 'Mobile Fidelity'; USCD 729)*
Mar 75. (7") *(6008 010)* **LIFE IS A MINESTRONE. / CHANNEL SWIMMER** [7] [–]
May 75. (7") *(6008 014)* **I'M NOT IN LOVE. / GOOD NEWS** [1] [–]
May 75. (7") *<73678>* **I'M NOT IN LOVE. / CHANNEL SWIMMER** [–] [2]
(re-iss. Oct84)
Nov 75. (7") *(6080 017) <73725>* **ART FOR ART'S SAKE. / GET IT WHILE YOU CAN** [5] [83]
Jan 76. (lp/c) *(9102 501) <SRMI 1061>* **HOW DARE YOU!** [5] [ ]
– How dare you / Lazy ways / I wanna rule the world / I'm Mandy fly me / Iceberg / Art for art's sake / Rock'n'roll lullaby / Head room / Don't hang up. *(re-iss. Dec83 lp/c; PRICE/PRIMC 60)*
Mar 76. (7") *(6008 019) <73779>* **I'M MANDY FLY ME. / HOW DARE YOU** [6] [60]

— **STEWART + GOULDMAN** carried on with session people including live drummer PAUL BURGESS. They replaced GODLEY & CREME who formed own duo.

Jul 76. (7") *<73805>* **LAZY WAYS. / LIFE IS A MINESTRONE** [–] [ ]
Nov 76. (7") *(6008 022) <73875>* **THE THINGS WE DO FOR LOVE. / HOT TO TROT** [6] [5]

Apr 77. (7") *(6008 025)* **GOOD MORNING JUDGE. / DON'T SQUEEZE ME LIKE TOOTHPASTE** [5] [–]
May 77. (lp/c) *(9102 502)* <SRMI 3702> **DECEPTIVE BENDS** [3] [31]
– Good morning judge / The things we do for love / Marriage bureau rendezvous / People in love / Modern man blues / Honeymoon with B troop / I bought a flat guitar tutor / You've got a cold / Feel the benefit: Reminisce and speculation – A Latin break. *(re-iss. May83; PRICE 5)*
May 77. (7") <73917> **PEOPLE IN LOVE. / DON'T SQUEEZE ME LIKE TOOTHPASTE** [–] [40]
Jun 77. (7") *(6008 028)* **PEOPLE IN LOVE. / I'M SO LAID BACK I'M LAID OUT** [ ] [–]
Jul 77. (7") <73943> **GOOD MORNING JUDGE. / I'M SO LAID BACK I'M LAID OUT** [–] [69]

—— added **RICK FENN** – guitar / **TONY O'MALLEY** – keyboards (ex-ARRIVAL, ex-KOKOMO) / **STUART TOSH** – 2nd drummer (ex-PILOT)

Dec 77. (d-lp/d-c) *(6641698)* <SRM 28600> **LIVE AND LET LIVE (live)** [14] [ ]
– The second sitting for the last supper / You've got a cold / Honeymoon with B troop / Art for art's sake / Wall Street shuffle / Ships don't disappear in the night (do they?) / I'm Mandy fly me / Marriage bureau rendezvous / Good morning judge / Feel the benefit / The things we do for love / Waterfall / I'm not in love / Modern man blues.
Dec 77. (7") <73980> **WALL STREET SHUFFLE (live). / YOU'VE GOT A COLD** [–] [ ]

—— **DUNCAN MACKAY** – keyboards (ex-COCKNEY REBEL) repl. BURGESS

Mercury — Polydor

Jul 78. (7") *(6008 035)* <14511> **DREADLOCK HOLIDAY. / NOTHING CAN MOVE ME** [1] [44]
Sep 78. (lp/c) *(9102 503)* <SRMI 6160> **BLOODY TOURISTS** [3] [69]
– Dreadlock holiday / For you and I / Take these chains / Shock on the tube (don't want love) / Last night / The anonymous alcoholic / Reds in my bed / Life line / Tokyo / Old Mister Time / From Rochdale to Ocho Rios / Everything you've wanted to know about. *(re-iss. May83)*
Oct 78. (7") *(6008 036)* **REDS IN MY BED. / TAKE THESE CHAINS** [ ] [–]
Jan 79. (7") <14528> **FOR YOU AND I. / TAKE THESE CHAINS** [–] [85]
Sep 79. (lp)(c) *(9102 504)(7231 304)* <6244> **GREATEST HITS 1972-1978** (compilation) [5] [ ]
– Rubber bullets / Donna / Silly love / The dean and I / Life is a minestrone / Wall Street shuffle / Art for art's sake / I'm Mandy fly me / Good morning judge / The things we do for love / Dreadlock holiday / I'm not in love.

Mercury — Warners

Feb 80. (7") *(LOOK 1)* **ONE TWO FIVE. / ONLY CHILD** [ ] [ ]
Mar 80. (lp)(c) *(9102 505)(7231 305)* <3442> **LOOK HEAR!** [35] [ ]
– One two five / Welcome to the world / How'm I ever going to say goodbye / Don't send we back / I took you home / It doesn't matter at all / Dressed to kill / Lovers anonymous / I hate to eat alone / Strange lover / L.A. inflatable.

—— At same time ERIC STEWART and GRAHAM GOULDMAN had own solo albums.

May 80. (7") *(LOOK 2)* **IT DOESN'T MATTER AT ALL. / FROM ROCHDALE TO OCHO RIOS** [ ] [–]
May 80. (7") **IT DOESN'T MATTER AT ALL. / STRANGE LOVER** [–] [ ]
May 81. (7") *(TENT 10)* **NOUVEAU RICHE. / I HATE TO EAT ALONE** [ ] [–]
Nov 81. (7") *(MER 86)* **DON'T TURN ME AWAY. / TOMORROW'S WORLD TODAY** [ ] [–]
Nov 81. (lp)(c) *(6350 048)(7150 048)* **TEN OUT OF 10** [ ] [–]
– I don't ask / Overdraft in overdrive / Don't turn me away / Memories / No tell hotel / Les nouveaux riches / Action man in Motown suit / Listen with your eyes / Lying here with you / Survivor. *(cd-iss. 1983)*
Mar 82. (7") *(MER 95)* **THE POWER OF LOVE. / YOU'RE COMING HOME AGAIN** [ ] [–]
Jun 82. (7") **THE POWER OF LOVE. / ACTION MAN IN MOTOWN SUIT** [–] [ ]
Jul 82. (7") *(MER 113)* **RUN AWAY. / ACTION MAN IN MOTOWN SUIT** [50] [–]
Oct 82. (7") *(MER 121)* **WE'VE HEARD IT ALL BEFORE. / OVERNIGHT IN OVERDRIVE** [ ] [–]
Apr 83. (7") *(MER 139)* **24 HOURS. / DREADLOCK HOLIDAY** [ ] [–]
(12"+=) *(MERT 139)* – I'm not in love.
Sep 83. (7") *(MER 143)* **FEEL THE LOVE. / SHE GIVES THE PAIN** [ ] [–]
Oct 83. (lp/c) *(MERL/+C 28)* **WINDOW IN THE JUNGLE** [70] [–]
– 24 hours / Feel the love – Oomachasa ooma / Yes I can / Americana panorama / City lights / Food for thought / Working girls / Taxi! taxi!.

—— split late '83 but reunited 8 years later; originals re-formed in 1991 with STEWART & GOULDMAN

Polydor — not iss.

Apr 92. (7"/c-s/cd-s) **WOMAN IN LOVE. / MAN WITH A MISSION** [ ] [–]
May 92. (cd/c/lp) *(513279-2/-4/-1)* **MEANWHILE** [ ] [–]
– Woman in love / Wonderland / Fill her up / Something special / Welcome to Paradise / The stars didn't show / Green aged monster / Charity begins at home / Shine a light in the dark / Don't break the promises.
Jun 92. (7") **WELCOME TO PARADISE. / DON'T BREAK THE PROMISES** [ ] [–]
(cd-s+=) – Lost in love.

Humbug — not iss.

Feb 94. (cd) *(CMCD 010)* **ALIVE – GREATEST HITS PERFORMED LIVE (live)** [ ] [–]
– The Wall Street shuffle / I'm Mandy fly me / Good morning judge / Welcome to paradise / The things we do for love / Across the universal / The stars didn't show / Art for art's sake / Feel the benefit / Dreadlock holiday / I'm not in love / The bullets medley.

—— GOULDMAN + STEWART acoustic only

Avex — not iss.

Feb 95. (7"/c-s) *(AVEX S/MC 2)* **I'M NOT IN LOVE (acoustic). / BLUEBIRD** [29] [–]
(cd-s+=) *(AVEXCD 2)* – ('A'-the reword of art).
May 95. (c-s/cd-s/12") *(AVEX MC/CD/X 8)* **READY TO GO HOME. / ('A'album mix) / AGE OF CONSENT** [ ] [–]
Sep 95. (cd/c/d-lp) *(AVEX CD/MC/LP 6)* **MIRROR, MIRROR** [ ] [–]
– Yvonne's the one / Code of silence / Blue bird / Age of consent / Take this woman / The monkey and the onion / Everything is not enough / Ready to go home / Grow old with me / Margo wants the mustard / Peace in our time / Why did I break your heart / Now you're gone / I'm not in love (acoustic '95).

– compilations, etc. –

Note; Below 3 on 'UK Decca'.
May 75. (lp/c) *(UKAL/+C 1007)* <53110> **100cc – THE GREATEST HITS OF 10cc** [9] [ ]
May 75. (7") **WATERFALL. / 4% OF NOTHING** [ ] [–]
Jul 87. (7"/12") *(UKP/+T 002)* **THE WORST BAND IN THE WORLD. / HOT SUN ROCK** [ ] [–]
Apr 79. (lp) *Flyover; (RJ 7437)* **THE SONGS WE DO FOR LOVE** [ ] [–]
Sep 79. (7") *Mercury; (6008 043)* **I'M NOT IN LOVE. / FOR YOU AND I** [ ] [–]
1981. (c) *Mercury; (7215 039)* **THE MUSIC OF 10cc (1975-77)** [ ] [–]
Oct 82. (lp) *Contour; (CN 2056)* **10cc IN CONCERT (live)** [ ] [–]
(cd-iss. Apr91 on 'Pickwick'; PWKS 4050P)
Note; below 4 on 'Old Gold'
Jun 88. (7") *(OG 9475)* **I'M NOT IN LOVE. / DREADLOCK HOLIDAY** [ ] [–]
Jun 88. (7") *(OG 9786)* **RUBBER BULLETS. / DONNA** [ ] [–]
Jun 88. (7") *(OG 9788)* **WALL STREET SHUFFLE. / THE DEAN AND I** [ ] [–]
May 92. (cd-s) *(OG 6165)* **I'M NOT IN LOVE / DREADLOCK HOLIDAY / I'M MANDY FLY ME** [ ] [–]
Jul 89. (d-lp/cd) *Castle; (CCS LP/MC 214)* **THE COLLECTION** [ ] [–]
– (albums 10cc + SHEET MUSIC)
Apr 93. (cd/c) *Dojo; (EARLD 12)* **THE EARLY YEARS** [ ] [–]
May 93. (cd/c) *Music Club;* **THE BEST OF THE EARLY YEARS** [ ] [–]
May 93. (cd/c) *Spectrum; (550004-2/-4)* **FOOD FOR THOUGHT** [ ] [–]
Jul 94. (cd/c) *BR Music; (BR CD/MC 126)* **GREATEST HITS** [ ] [–]
Aug 95. (cd-s) *Old Gold; (OG 6307)* **RUBBER BULLETS / THE DEAN AND I** [ ] [–]
Sep 95. (cd-s) *Old Gold; (1262363272)* **DONNA / WALL STREET SHUFFLE** [ ] [–]
Mar 97. (cd/c) *Mercury; (534612-2/-4)* **THE VERY BEST OF 10CC** [37] [–]
Aug 98. (cd) *King Biscuit; (KBFHCD 015)* **KING BISCUIT PRESENTS . . .** [ ] [–]

KEVIN GODLEY & LOL CREME

with guests **PETER COOK + SARAH VAUGHAN** also introduced new Gizmo guitar orchestrator.

Mercury Mercury

Oct 77. (t-lp/d-c) *(CON S/C 017) <1700>* **CONSEQUENCES** [52] [ ]
– Seascape / Wind / Fireworks / Stampede / Burial scene / Sleeping Earth / Honolulu Lulu / The flood / Five o'clock in the morning / When things go wrong / Lost weekend / Rosie / Office chase / Cool, cool, cool / Cool, cool, cool (reprise) / Sailor / Mobilisation / Please, please, please / Blint's tune (movement 1-17). *(re-iss. 1-lp Feb79 as 'MUSIC FROM CONSEQUENCES' tracks *)*

Dec 77. (7") *(SAMP 17)* **FIVE O'CLOCK IN THE MORNING. / THE FLOOD** [ ] [ ]

GODLEY & CREME

—— with guest **ANDY MACKAY** – saxophone

Mercury Polydor

Aug 78. (lp) *(9109611) <6177>* **L** [ ] [ ]
– This sporting life / Sandwiches of you / Art school canteen / Group life / Punchbag / Foreign accents / Hit factory – Business is business.

Jan 79. (7") *(6008104)* **SANDWICHES OF YOU. / FOREIGN ACCENTS** [ ] [ ]

Polydor Mirage

Oct 79. (7") *(POSP 80)* **AN ENGLISHMAN IN NEW YORK. / SILENT RUNNING** [ ] [ ]

Nov 79. (lp/c) *(POLD/+C 5027) <6257>* **FREEZE FRAME** [ ] [ ]
– An Englishman in New York / Random brainwave / I pity inanimate objects / Freeze frame / Clues / Brazilia (wish you were here) / Mugshots / Get well soon. *(re-iss. Aug83 lp/c; SPE LP/C 30) (cd-iss. 1987 & May91; 831 555-2)*

Mar 80. (7") *(POSP 145)* **WIDE BOY. / I PITY INANIMATE OBJECTS** [ ] [-]

Sep 80. (7") *(POSP 171)* **SUBMARINE. / MARCIANO** [ ] [-]

Aug 81. (7") *(POSP 322)* **UNDER YOUR THUMB. / POWER BEHIND THE THRONE** [3] [ ]

Sep 81. (lp/c) *(POLD/+C 5043)* **ISMISM** [29] [-]
– Snack attack / Under your thumb / Joey's camel / The problem / Ready for Ralph / Wedding bells / Lonnie / Sale of the century / The party. *(re-iss. Oct84)*

Nov 81. (7") *(POSP 369)* **WEDDING BELLS. / BABIES** [7] [-]

Feb 82. (7") **WEDDING BELLS. / LONNIE** [-] [ ]
(re-iss. Nov85 on 'Mirage')

Feb 82. (7"/12") *(POSP/+X 412)* **SNACK ATTACK. / STRANGE APPARATUS** [ ] [-]

Sep 82. (7") *(POSP 490)* **SAVE A MOUNTAIN FOR ME. / WELCOME TO BREAKFAST TELEVISION** [ ] [-]

Mar 83. (7") *(POSP 550)* **SAMSON. / SAMSON (dance mix)** [ ] [-]

Apr 83. (lp/c) *(POLD/+C 5070)* **BIRDS OF PREY** [ ] [-]
– My body the car / Worm and the rattlesnake / Cat's eyes / Samson / Save a mountain for me / Madame Guillotine / Woodwork / Twisted nerve / Out in the cold.

May 84. (7"/12") *(POSP/+X 677)* **GOLDEN BOY. / MY BODY THE CAR** [ ] [-]

Mar 85. (7"/12") *(POSP/+X 732) <881786>* **CRY. / LOVE BOMBS** [15] [16]
(re-iss. Aug86, hit UK 66)

Jun 85. (lp/c) *(POLH/+C 22) <825981>* **THE HISTORY MIX VOLUME 1** [ ] [ ]
– Wet rubber soup (recycled from):- Rubber bullets – Minestrone – I'm not in love / Cry: Expanding business – The dare you man – Hum drum boys in Paris – Mountain tension / Light me up / An Englishman in New York / Save a mountain for me / Golden boy. *(cd-iss. May91)*

Sep 85. (7"/12") *(POSP/+X 760)* **GOLDEN BOY (remix). / LIGHT ME UP** [ ] [-]

Dec 87. (7") *(POSP 901)* **A LITTLE BIT OF HEAVEN. / BITS OF BLUE SKY (excerpts)** [ ] [ ]
(12"+=/cd-s+=) *(POSPX/POCD 901)* – ('A'extended).
(c-s++=) *(POSPC 901)* – Rhino rhino. *(re-iss. Jul88)*

Feb 88. (lp/c)(cd) *(POLH/+C 40)(8353482)* **GOODBYE BLUE SKY** [ ] [-]
– H.E.A.V.E.N. / A little piece of Heaven / Don't set fire (to the one I love) / Golden rings / Crime & punishment / The big bang / 10,000 angels / Sweet memory / Airforce one / The last page of history / Desperate times.

Mar 88. (7") *(POSP 913)* **10,000 ANGELS. / HIDDEN HEARTBREAK** [ ] [-]
(12"+=) *(POSPX 913)* – Can't sleep.
(cd-s++=) *(POCD 913)* – Cry.

– compilations, others, etc. –

Aug 82. (d-c) *Polydor;* **FREEZE FRAME / ISMISM** [ ] [-]

Aug 87. (7"/12") *Polydor; (POSP/+X 875)* **SNACK ATTACK. / WET RUBBER SOAP** [ ] [-]

Sep 87. (lp/c)(cd) *Polydor; (TGC LP/MC 1)(8163552)* **CHANGING FACES OF 10 cc & GODLEY AND CREME** [4] [ ]
– Dreadlock holiday / The Wall Street shuffle / Under your thumb (GODLEY & CREME) / Life is a minestrone / An Englishman in New York (GODLEY & CREME) / Art for art's sake / Donna / Snack attack (GODLEY & CREME) / Cry (GODLEY & CREME) / The things we do for love / Wedding bells (GODLEY & CREME) / I'm Mandy, fly me / Good morning judge / Rubber bullets / Save a mountain for me (GODLEY & CREME) / I'm not in love. *(re-iss. Mar94 on 'Polygram TV' cd/c;)*

May 93. (cd/c) *Spectrum; (550007-2/-4)* **IMAGES** [ ] [-]

Apr 95. (cd) *Disky;* **ROCK AND POP LEGENDS** [ ] [-]

10,000 MANIACS

Formed: Jamestown, New York, USA . . . 1981 by NATALIE MERCHANT and J.C. LOMBARDO, who had been part of the band, STILL LIFE. Initially a new wave covers outfit, the group (which was completed by ROBERT BUCK, STEVEN GUSTAFSON, DENNIS DREW and JERRY AUGUSTYNAK) debuted on the obscure 'Christian Burial' label in 1982 with the mini-album, 'HUMAN CONFLICT NUMBER FIVE'. After a further full-length set, 'THE SECRETS OF THE I-CHING' (1984), which scaled the UK indie chart and won praise from Radio 1 guru John Peel, the group secured an international deal with 'Elektra'. Produced by veteran folk man, Joe Boyd, 'THE WISHING CHAIR' (1985) saw the band develop their eclectic, rootsy sound, although it wasn't until the release of 'IN MY TRIBE' (1987) that 10,000 MANIACS began to reap some commercial rewards to match their growing critical acclaim. By this point LOMBARDO had departed after the previous year's heavy touring alongside R.E.M., the group further changing their strategy by enlisting the services of another seasoned producer, Pete Asher. The result was a sparer sound and sharpened songwriting which emphasised MERCHANT's hypnotically plangent vocals, the group scoring minor US hits with 'LIKE THE WEATHER' and 'WHAT'S THE MATTER HERE?'. A cover of Cat Stevens' 'PEACE TRAIN' failed to chart, the band later withdrawing the track from subsequent pressings following hardline Islamic comments made by the former singer/songwriter. Perhaps as a result, the follow-up set, 'BLIND MAN'S ZOO' (1989), took a more political stance, though the enigmatic MERCHANT stopped short of preaching, the album becoming a transatlantic Top 20 hit. Following the accompanying tour, the band took a brief sabbatical, eventually returning in September '92 with another successful set, 'OUR TIME IN EDEN'. The minor hit, 'CANDY EVERYBODY WANTS', was backed with a suitably lugubrious reading of Morrissey's 'EVERYDAY IS LIKE SUNDAY' while CD formats included a MERCHANT/MICHAEL STIPE duet on a version of R.E.M.'s country-tinged classic, 'DON'T GO BACK TO ROCKVILLE'. By the release of the languorous 'UNPLUGGED' (1993) set, however, MERCHANT was disillusioned with the group's attitude and left soon after for a solo career. While 10,000 MANIACS replaced MERCHANT with ex-member, JOHN LOMBARDO and new frontwoman MARY RAMSEY, the group's former focal point almost made the US Top 20 in summer '95 with her debut solo set, 'Tigerlily'. Minus MERCHANT, 10,000 MANIACS carried on regardless, releasing the sorry folk-rock set, 'LOVE AMONG THE RUINS', in 1997. It looked like their next outing, 'EARTH PRESSED FLAT' (1999), would be their last, as ROBERT BUCK sadly died of liver failure in 2000. • **Songwriters:** lyrics – NATALIE / music – JC LOMBARDO until his departure. MERCHANT was then the main writer with DREW or BUCK. Covered: I HOPE THAT I DON'T FALL IN LOVE WITH YOU (Tom Waits) / STARMAN – MOONAGE DAYDREAM (David Bowie) / THESE DAYS (Jackson Browne) / BECAUSE THE NIGHT (Patti Smith Group) / MORE THAN THIS (Bryan Ferry).

Album rating: HUMAN CONFLICT NUMBER FIVE mini (*4) / SECRETS OF THE I-CHING (*5) / THE WISHING CHAIR (*6) / IN MY TRIBE (*8) / BLIND MAN'S ZOO (*7) / HOPE CHEST: THE FREDONIA RECORDINGS 1982-1983 collection (*5) / OUR TIME IN EDEN (*7) / MTV UNPLUGGED (*5) / LOVE AMONG THE RUINS (*5) / THE EARTH PRESSED FLAT (*4) / John And Mary: VICTORY GARDENS (*6) / THE WEEDKILLER'S DAUGHTER (*5)

NATALIE MERCHANT (b.26 Oct'63) – vocals / **ROBERT BUCK** (b. 1 Aug'58) – guitar, synthesizers / **J.C. LOMBARDO** (b. JOHN, 30 Sep'52) – rhythm guitar, bass / **STEVEN GUSTAFSON** (b.10 Apr'57, Madrid, Spain) – bass, guitar / **DENNIS DREW** (b. 8 Aug'57, Buffalo, N.Y.) – organ / **JERRY AUGUSTYNAK** (b. 2 Sep'58, Lackawanna, N.Y.) – drums

not iss. — Christian Burial

1982. (m-lp) **HUMAN CONFLICT NUMBER FIVE** [–] [ ]
– Orange / Planed obsolescence / Anthem for doomed youth / Groove dub / Tension. *(UK-iss.Jun84 on 'Press'; P 2010)*

Jan 84. (lp) **SECRETS OF THE I-CHING** [–] [ ]
– Grey victory / Pour de Chirico / Death of Manolette / Tension / Daktari / Pit viper / Katrina's fair / The Latin one / My mother the war. *(UK-iss.Aug84 on 'Press'; P 3001)*

Reflex — Reflex

Mar 84. (12"m) *(RE 1)* **MY MOTHER THE WAR (remix). / PLANNED OBSOLESCENCE / NATIONAL EDUCATION WEEK** [ ] [ ]

Elektra — Elektra

Jun 85. (7") *(EKR 11)* **CAN'T IGNORE THE TRAIN. / DAKTARI** [ ] [ ]
(12"+=) *(EKR 11T)* – Grey victory / The colonial wing.

Nov 85. (lp/c) *(EKT 14/+C)* **THE WISHING CHAIR** [ ] [ ]
– Can't ignore the train / Just as the tide was a-flowing / Scorpio rising / Lilydale / Maddox table / Everyone a puzzle lover / Arbor day / Back o' the Moon / Tension takes a tangle / Among the Americans / Grey victory / Cotton alley / My mother the war. *(cd-iss. 1989; 960 428-2)*

Nov 85. (7"w/drawn) *(EKR 19)* **JUST AS THE TIDE WAS A-FLOWING. / AMONG THE AMERICANS** [–] [ ]

Jan 86. (7") *(EKR 28)* **SCORPIO RISING. / ARBOR DAY** [ ] [ ]

—— trimmed to a quintet when LOMBARDO departed to form JOHN AND MARY

Aug 87. (7") *(EKR 61)* **PEACE TRAIN. / THE PAINTED DESERT** [ ] [ ]

Aug 87. (lp/c)(cd) *(EKT 41/+C)(960 738-2)* <60738> **IN MY TRIBE** [ ] [37]
– What's the matter here? / Hey Jack Kerouac / Like the weather / Cherry tree / Painted desert / Don't talk / Peace train / Gun shy / Sister Rose / A campfire song / City of angels / Verdi cries. *(initial copies cont. Elektra sampler with X / The CALL; SAM 390)*

Nov 87. (7") *(EKR 64)* **DON'T TALK. / CITY OF ANGELS** [ ] [ ]
(12"+=) *(EKR 64T)* – Goodbye (Tribal outtake).

Mar 88. (7") *(EKR 71)* **WHAT'S THE MATTER HERE?. / VERDI CRIES** [ ] [–]
(12"+=/cd-s+=) *(EKR 71T)* – Like the weather (live) / Gun shy (live).

Jul 88. (7") *(EKR 77)* <69418> **LIKE THE WEATHER. / A CAMPFIRE SONG** [ ] May88 [68]
(12"+=/12"w-poster) *(EKR 77T/+W)* – Poison in the well (live) / Verdi cries (live).

Jul 88. (7") <69388> **WHAT'S THE MATTER HERE? / CHERRY TREE** [–] [80]

May 89. (lp/c)(cd) *(EKT 57/+C)(960 815-2)* <60815> **BLIND MAN'S ZOO** [18] [13]
– Eat for two / Please forgive us / The big parade / Trouble me / You happy puppet / Headstrong / Poison in the well / Dust bowl / The lion's share / Hateful hate / Jubilee.

Jun 89. (7"/c-s) *(EKR 93)* <69298> **TROUBLE ME. / THE LION'S SHARE** [ ] [44]
(12"+=/3"cd-s+=/3"s-cd-s+=) *(EKR 93 T/CD/CDX)* – Party of God.

Sep 89. (7") <69253> **YOU HAPPY PUPPET. / GUNSHY** [–] [ ]

Nov 89. (7"ep) *(EKR 100)* **EAT FOR TWO / WILDWOOD FLOWER. / DON'T CALL US / FROM THE TIME YOU SAY GOODBYE** [ ] [–]
(12"/12"w/poster/3"cd-s) *(EKR 100 T/TW/CD)* – (1st & 2nd track) / Gun shy (acoustic) / Hello in there.
(10") *(EKR 100TE)* – (1st & 4th track) / What's the matter here? (acoustic) / Eat for two (acoustic).

Sep 92. (7"/c-s) *(EKR 156/+C)* *<64700>* **THESE ARE DAYS. / CIRCLE DREAM** [58] [66]
(cd-s+=) *(EKR 156CD)* – I hope that I don't fall in love with you.
(cd-s) *(EKR 156CDX)* – ('A'side) / Medley:- Starman – Moonage daydream / These days.

Sep 92. (cd/c/lp) *<(7559 61385-2/-4/-1)>* **OUR TIME IN EDEN** [33] [28]
– Noah's dove / These are days / Eden / Few and far between / Stockton gala days / Gold rush brides / Jezebel / How you've grown / Candy everybody wants / Circle dream / If you intend / I'm not the man. *(cd+=)* – Tolerance.

Feb 93. (c-s,cd-s) *<64665>* **CANDY EVERYBODY WANTS / I HOPE THAT I DON'T FALL IN LOVE WITH YOU** [–] [67]

Mar 93. (7"/c-s) *(EKR 160/+C)* **CANDY EVERYBODY WANTS. / EVERYDAY IS LIKE SUNDAY** [47] [–]
(cd-s+=) *(EKR 160CD1)* – Don't go back to Rockville (with MICHAEL STIPE co-vocals) / Sally Ann.
(cd-s+=) *(EKR 160CD2)* – Don't go back to Rockville (with MICHAEL STIPE) / ('A' MTV version).
(cd-s) *(EKR 160CD3)* – ('A'side) / Eat for two (live) / My sister Rose (live) / Hey Jack Kerouac (live).

Aug 93. (cd-ep) *<66296>* **FEW AND FAR BETWEEN / CANDY EVERYBODY WANTS / TO SIR WITH LOVE / LET THE MYSTERY BE** [–] [95]

Oct 93. (7"/c-s) *(EKR 175/+C)* **BECAUSE THE NIGHT. / STOCKTON GALA DAYS** [65] [–]
(cd-s+=) *(EKR 175CD)* – Let the mystery be / Sally Ann.

Oct 93. (c-s,cd-s) *<64595>* **BECAUSE THE NIGHT / EAT FOR TWO** [–] [11]

Oct 93. (cd/c) *<(7559 61569-2/-4)>* **MTV UNPLUGGED (live)** [40] [13]
– These are days / Eat for two / Candy everybody wants (MTV version) / I'm not the man / Don't talk / Hey Jack Kerouac / What's the matter here / Gold rush brides / Like the weather / Trouble me / Jezebel / Because the night / Stockton gala days / Noah's dove.

—— 10,000 MANIACS split when NATALIE went solo. The rest re-formed in 1995 and added ex-original JOHN LOMBARDO and his (JOHN AND MARY) partner MARY RAMSEY on vocals and violin.

Geffen — Geffen

Sep 97. (c-s) *(GFSC 22284)* *<19411>* **MORE THAN THIS / BEYOND THE BLUE** [ ] Jul97 [25]
(12"+=/cd-s+=) *(GFST/+D 22284)* – ('A'-Tee's radio mix).

Oct 97. (cd) *<(GED 25009)>* **LOVE AMONG THE RUINS** [ ] Jun97 [ ]
– Rainy day / Love among the ruins / Even with my eyes closed / Girl on a train / Green children / A room for everything / More than this / Big star / You won't find me there / All that never happens / Shining light / Across the fields.

Bar/None — Bar/None

May 99. (cd/c) *<(BARNONE 106)>* **THE EARTH PRESSED FLAT** [ ] Apr99 [ ]
– The Earth pressed flat / Ellen / Once a vity / Glow / On & on (mercy song) / Somebody's Heaven / Cabaret / Beyond the blue / Smallest step / In the quiet morning / Time turns / Hidden in my heart / Who knows where the times goes? *(cd+=)* – Rainbows.

—— ROBERT BUCK died of liver failure in 2000

– compilations, others, etc. –

Oct 90. (lp/c)(cd) *Elektra; (EKT 79/+C)<(7599 60962-2)>* **HOPE CHEST** [ ] [ ]
– (HUMAN CONFLICT NUMBER FIVE / THE SECRETS OF I-CHING)

JOHN AND MARY

JOHN LOMBARDO – vocals, bass, guitars / **MARY RAMSEY** – vocals, keyboards, violin, viola / with **ROBERT BUCK, JEROME AUGUSTYNIAK** – drums / etc.

Rykodisc — Rykodisc

Jul 91. (cd) *<(RCD 10203)>* **VICTORY GARDENS** [ ] [ ]
– Red wooden beads / Azalea festival / Piles of dead leaves / We have nothing / Rags of flowers / I became alone / Open window / July 6th / Pram / Canadien errant.

— guests:- **ALEX CHILTON, MARY MARGARET O'HARA, ANDREW CASE, BOB WISEMAN, SCOTT MILLER, DAVID KANE, JOANNE RAMSEY + BUCK**

Mar 93.	(cd) *<(RCD 10259)>* **THE WEEDKILLER'S DAUGHTER**		

– Two worlds parted / Angels of stone / Your return / Clare's scarf / Cemetery ridge / Nightfall / I wanted you / One step backward / Fly me to the north / Clouds of reason / Maid of mist / Poor murdered woman.

TEN YEARS AFTER

Formed: Nottingham, England . . . summer '65 (originally as covers act The JAYBIRDS in 1961) by ALVIN LEE (vocals and guitar) and LEO LYONS (bass). The following year, they relocated to London, recruiting RIC LEE (drums) and CHICK CHURCHILL (keyboards) and adopting the name, TEN YEARS AFTER. A key forerunner of the forthcoming British blues revival (i.e. FLEETWOOD MAC, CHICKEN, SAVOY BROWN, etc.), LEE, known for his nimble fingered, lightning strike guitar playing, secured a deal (through manager, Chris Wright) with Decca offshoot label, 'Deram'. An eponymous debut set was released in '67, although the prevailing trend for everything flower-power ensured the record met with limited interest. Building up a strong grassroots following through electric stage shows, TEN YEARS AFTER took a calculated risk by releasing a live set recorded at Klook's Kleek, 'UNDEAD' (1968), the album rewarding TYA with a Top 30 breakthrough. Early in '69, they released a third set, 'STONEDHENGE', a surprise Top 10 success (the record also saw them crack the American market) that included their best piece to date, 'HEAR ME CALLING'. To coincide with a forthcoming Woodstock appearance, the band delivered their second set of the year, 'SSSSH', not exactly a hush hush affair but a blistering melange of blues, boogie and country that became the first of three consecutive UK Top 5 albums (US Top 20, well nearly!). LEE's celebrated performance of the epic 11 minute track 'GOIN' HOME' at the aforesaid Woodstock Festival went down in rock history, thrusting the band into the premier league of blues rock acts (the song featured on the subsequent film and soundtrack). The band blazed their way through the early 70's on albums, 'CRICKLEWOOD GREEN' and 'WATT', the former spawning a UK Top 10 hit, 'LOVE LIKE A MAN' in 1970. A subsequent change of both label ('Chrysalis') and music style (following the prevailing trend for electronic progressive rock) for late '71's 'A SPACE IN TIME', saw the band losing substantial ground (critically and commercially). However, due to a Top 40 hit, 'I'D LOVE TO CHANGE THE WORLD', the album still maintained Top 20 status in the US. The ensuing few years saw TEN YEARS AFTER treading water, albums such 'ROCK & ROLL MUSIC TO THE WORLD' (1972), 'TEN YEARS AFTER (RECORDED LIVE)' (1973) and 'POSITIVE VIBRATIONS' (1974) poor reflections of his/their former achievements. It was clear by the last of these that LEE was eager to experiment outside the band framework, a 1973 collaborative project with US gospel singer, MYLON LeFEVRE, resulting in 'ON THE ROAD TO FREEDOM'. The guitarist then formed a new outfit, ALVIN LEE & CO. releasing a handful of unconvincing albums in the mid 70's. From that point on, LEE alternated between various solo incarnations and in 1989 (after a trial at a 4-day German festival the previous year), he re-formed a revamped TEN YEARS AFTER for a one-off album, appropriately titled, 'ABOUT TIME'. LEE continued to spread the blues gospel to an ever faithful band of ageing worldwide disciples. • **Songwriters:** Apart from basic covers act The JAYBIRDS, ALVIN LEE penned and co-wrote with STEVE GOULD in the 80's. Covered; HELP ME (Sonny Boy Williamson) / SPOONFUL (Willie Dixon) / AT THE WOODCHOPPER'S BALL (Woody Herman) / SWEET LITTLE SIXTEEN (Chuck Berry) / GOOD MORNING LITTLE SCHOOLGIRL (Don & Bob) / GOING BACK TO BIRMINGHAM (Little Richard) / etc.

Album rating: TEN YEARS AFTER (*6) / UNDEAD (*7) / STONEDHENGE (*6) / SSSSH (*7) / CRICKLEWOOD GREEN (*7) / WATT (*6) / A SPACE IN TIME (*5) / ALVIN LEE & COMPANY compilation (*6) / ROCK'N'ROLL MUSIC TO THE WORLD (*4) / RECORDED LIVE (*4) / ON THE ROAD TO FREEDOM (*4; by Alvin Lee & Mylon LeFevre) / POSITIVE VIBRATIONS (*4) / IN FLIGHT (*4; by Alvin Lee & Co.) / GOIN' HOME! THEIR GREATEST HITS compilation (*7) / PUMP IRON! (*5; by Alvin Lee & Co.) / LET IT ROCK (*4; by Alvin Lee) / ROCKET FUEL (*4; by Alvin Lee – Ten Years Later) / RIDE ON (*4; Alvin Lee – Ten Years Later) / FREE FALL (*4; by Alvin Lee Band) / RX5 (*3; by Alvin Lee Band) / DETROIT DIESEL (*4; by Alvin Lee) / ABOUT TIME (*5) / ZOOM (*4; by Alvin Lee) / THE ESSENTIAL TEN YEARS AFTER compilation (*7) / NINETEEN NINETY FOUR (*4; by Alvin Lee) / I HEAR YOU ROCKIN' (*3; by Alvin Lee) / LIVE IN VIENNA (*3; by Alvin Lee) / PURE BLUES (*4; by Alvin Lee & Ten Years After)

JAYBIRDS

ALVIN LEE – vocals, guitar / **LEO LYONS** – bass / **DAVE QUICKMIRE** – drums

		Embassy	not iss.
Jan 64.	(7") *(WB 621)* **NOT FADE AWAY. / OVER YOU**		–
Feb 64.	(7") *(WB 624)* **TELL ME WHEN. / YOU CAN'T DO THAT**		–
Mar 64.	(7") *(WB 625)* **CAN'T BUY ME LOVE. / Del Martin: I LOVE YOU BECAUSE**		–
Apr 64.	(7") *(WB 626)* **GOOD GOLLY MISS MOLLY. / WORLD WITHOUT LOVE**		–
May 64.	(7") *(WB 628)* **MOCKIN' BIRD HILL. / HUBBLE BUBBLE (TOIL AND TROUBLE)**		–
May 64.	(7") *(WB 632)* **BABY LET ME TAKE YOU HOME. / Bud Ashton & His Group: RISE AND FALL OF FINGEL BLUNT**		–
Jun 64.	(7") *(WB 635)* **JULIET. / HERE I GO AGAIN**		–
Jul 64.	(7") *(WB 645)* **SOMEDAY WE'RE GONNA LOVE AGAIN. / Ray Pilgrim & The Beatmen: KISSIN' COUSINS**		–
Aug 64.	(7") *(WB 651)* **SHE'S NOT THERE. / Paul Rich: I WOULDN'T TRADE YOU FOR THE WORLD**		–
Oct 64.	(7") *(WB 663)* **ALL DAY & ALL OF THE NIGHT. / GOOGLE EYE**		–
Dec 64.	(7") *(WB 672)* **WHAT HAVE THEY DONE TO THE RAIN. / Bud Ashton & His Group: GENIE WITH THE LIGHT BROWN LAMP**		–
Jan 65.	(7") *(WB 673)* **GO NOW. / Terry Brandon: FERRY 'CROSS THE MERSEY**		–

TEN YEARS AFTER

— (Aug'65) **ALVIN** (b. GRAHAM BARNES, 19 Dec'44) – vocals, guitar + **LEO** (b.30 Nov'43, Bedfordshire) – bass; recruited **RIC LEE** (b.20 Oct'45, Cannock, England) – drums (ex-MANSFIELDS), repl. JAYBIRDS drummer DAVE QUIGMIRE

— added **CHICK CHURCHILL** (b. 2 Jan'49, Mold, Wales) – keyboards

		Deram	Deram
Oct 67.	(lp; mono/stereo) *(DML/SML 1015)* <18009> **TEN YEARS AFTER**		

– I want to know / I can't keep from crying sometimes / Adventures of a young organ / Spoonful / Losing the dogs / Feel it for me / Love until I die / Don't want you woman / Help me. *(cd-iss. May88; 820 532-2)*

Feb 68.	(7") *(DM 176)* <85027> **PORTABLE PEOPLE. / THE SOUNDS**		
Aug 68.	(lp; mono/stereo) *(DML/SML 1023)* <18016> **UNDEAD (live at Klook's Kleek)**	26	

– I may be wrong, but I won't be wrong always / Woodchopper's ball / Spider in my web / Summertime – Shantung cabbage / I'm going home. *(cd-iss. Jun88; 820 533-2)*

Nov 68.	(7") *(DM 221)* <85035> **HEAR ME CALLING. / I'M GOING HOME**		
Feb 69.	(lp; mono/stereo) *(DML/SML 1029)* <18021> **STONEDHENGE**	6	61

– Going to try / I can't live without Lydia / Woman trouble / Skooblyoobly-doobob / Hear me calling / A sad song / Three blind mice / No title / Faro / Speed kills. *(cd-iss. Apr89; 820 534-2) (cd-iss. Jul97 on 'Beat Goes On'; BGOCD 356) (cd re-iss. Jul02; 882898-2)*

Aug 69. (lp) *(SML 1052) <18029>* **SSSSH** [4] [20]
– Bad scene / Two time woman / Stoned woman / Good morning little schoolgirl / If you should love me / I don't know that you don't know my name / The stomp / I woke up this morning. *(re-iss. Jul75 on 'Chrysalis' lp/c; CHR/ZCHR 1083) (cd-iss. Mar94 on 'Chrysalis'; CD25CR 05) (cd re-iss. Feb97 on 'Beat Goes On'; BGOCD 338)*

Apr 70. (lp) *(SML 1065) <18038>* **CRICKLEWOOD GREEN** [4] [14]
– Sugar the road / Working on the road / 50,000 miles beneath my brain / Year 3,000 blues / Me and my baby / Love like a man / Circles / As the sun still burns away. *(re-iss. Jul75 on 'Chrysalis' lp/c; CHR/ZCHR 1084) (re-iss. Dec92 on 'Fame' cd/c; CD/TC FA 3287) (re-iss. Jul94 cd/c; CD/TC CHR 1084) (cd re-iss. Oct96 on 'EMI Gold'; CDGOLD 1052) (lp-iss.Aug00 on 'Simply Vinyl'; SVLP 235) (cd re-mast.Apr02 on 'E.M.I.'+=; 533095-2)* – (bonus tracks).

May 70. (7") *(DM 299) <7529>* **LOVE LIKE A MAN. / LOVE LIKE A MAN (live at 33 rpm)** [10] [98]
(re-iss. while still into UK chart run; DM 310)

Jan 71. (lp) *(SML 1078) <18050>* **WATT** [5] [21]
– I'm coming on / My baby left me / Think about the times / I say yeah / The band with no name / Gonna run / She lies in the morning / Sweet little sixteen. *(re-iss. Jul75 on 'Chrysalis' lp/c; CHR/ZCHR 1085) (cd-iss. Apr97 on 'Beat Goes On'; BGOCD 345)*

Chrysalis Columbia

Nov 71. (lp/c) *(CHR/ZCHR 1001) <30801>* **A SPACE IN TIME** [36] Aug71 [17]
– One of these days / Here they come / I'd love to change the world / Over the hill / Baby won't you let me rock'n'roll you / Once there was a time / Let the sky fall / Hard monkeys / I've been there too / Uncle Jam. *(cd-iss. Jun97 on 'Beat Goes On'; BGOCD 351)*

Sep 71. (7") *<45457>* **I'D LOVE TO CHANGE THE WORLD. / LET THE SKY FALL** [–] [40]

Jan 72. (7") *<45530>* **BABY WON'T YOU LET ME ROCK'N'ROLL YOU. / ONCE THERE WAS A TIME** [–] [61]

Oct 72. (lp/c) *(CHR/ZCHR 1009) <31779>* **ROCK & ROLL MUSIC TO THE WORLD** [27] [43]
– You give me loving / Convention prevention / Turned off T.V. blues / Standing at the station / You can't win them all / Religion / Choo choo mama / Tomorrow I'll be out of town / Rock & roll music to the world. *(cd-iss. May97 on 'Beat Goes On'; BGOCD 348)*

Nov 72. (7") *<45736>* **CHOO CHOO MAMA. / YOU CAN'T WIN THEM ALL** [–] [89]

Feb 73. (7") *<45787>* **TOMORROW, I'LL BE OUT OF TOWN. / CONVENTION PREVENTION** [–] [ ]

Jul 73. (7") *<45915>* **I'M GOING HOME. / YOU GIVE ME LOVING** [–] [ ]

Jul 73. (d-lp/d-c) *(CTY/ZCTY 1049) <32288>* **TEN YEARS AFTER (RECORDED LIVE)** [36] Jun73 [39]
– One of these days / You give me loving / Good morning little schoolgirl / Hobbit / Help me / Classical thing / Scat thing / I can't keep from cryin' sometimes (part 1) / Extension on one chord / I can't keep from cryin' sometimes (part 2) / Silly thing / Slow blues in 'C' / I'm going home / Choo choo mama. *(cd-iss. Apr97 on 'Beat Goes On'; BGOCD 341)*

Apr 74. (lp) *(CHR 1060) <32851>* **POSITIVE VIBRATIONS** [ ] [81]
– Nowhere to run / Positive vibrations / Stone me / Without you / Going back to Birmingham / It's getting harder / You're driving me crazy / Look into my life / Look me straight into the eyes / I wanted to boogie.

Apr 74. (7") *<46061>* **I WANTED TO BOOGIE. / IT'S GETTING HARDER** [–] [ ]

— Disbanded after CHICK CHURCHILL made a solo album 'YOU AND ME' in Feb'74 (CHR 1051).

ALVIN LEE & MYLON LeFEVRE

with the US solo gospel singer plus TRAFFIC members on session plus GEORGE HARRISON and RON WOOD

Nov 73. (7") *<45987>* **SO SAD. / RIFFIN** [–] [ ]

Nov 73. (lp) *(CHR 1054) <32729>* **ON THE ROAD TO FREEDOM** [ ] [ ]
– On the road to freedom / The world is changing / So sad (no love of his own) / Fallen angel / Funny / We will shine / Carry me load / Lay me back / Let 'em say what they will / I can't take it / Riffin / Rockin' til the sun goes down. *(<cd-iss. Mar03 on 'Repertoire'+=; REP 4780>)* – So sad (no love of his own).

Jan 74. (7") *(CHS 2020)* **THE WORLD IS CHANGING. / RIFFIN** [ ] [–]

ALVIN LEE & CO.

with **NEIL HUBBARD** – guitar / **ALAN SPENNER** – bass / **TIM HINKLEY** – keyboards / **IAN WALLACE** – drums / **MEL COLLINS** – saxophone

Nov 74. (d-lp) *(CTY 1069) <33187>* **ALVIN LEE & CO: IN FLIGHT (live gig)** [ ] [65]
– (intro) / Let's get back / Ride my train / There's a feeling / Running around / Mystery train / Slow down / Keep a knocking / How many times / I've got my eyes for you baby / I'm writing you a letter / Got to keep moving / Going through the door / Don't be cruel / Money honey / I'm writing you a letter / You need love love love / Freedom for the stallion / Every blues you've ever heard / All life's trials. *(cd-iss. Jun00 on 'Repertoire'+=; REP 4702)* – Somebody callin' me (live) / Put it in a box.

— touring band **HINKLEY / ANDY PYLE** – bass / **BRYSON GRAHAM** – drums / studio **RONNIE LEAHY** – keyboards / **STEVE THOMPSON** – bass / **IAN WALLACE** – drums

Oct 75. (lp) *(CHR 1094) <33796>* **PUMP IRON!** [ ] Sep75 [ ]
– One more chance / Try to be righteous / You told me / Have mercy / Julian Rice / Time and space / Burnt fungus / The darkest night / It's all right now / Truckin' down the other way / Let the sea burn down. *(cd-iss. Jun00 on 'Repertoire'+=; REP 4703)* – Madness / Midnight special.

— an album 'SAGUITAR' was shelved in 1976

Dec 78. (lp/c; ALVIN LEE) *(CHR/ZCHR 1190)* **LET IT ROCK** [ ] [–]
– Chemicals, chemistry, mystery & more / Love the way you rock me / Ain't nobody / Images shifting / Little boy / Downhill lady racer / World is spinning faster / Through with your lovin' / Time to mediate / Let it rock. *(cd-iss. Jun00 on 'Repertoire'; REP 4704)*

ALVIN LEE – TEN YEARS LATER

with **TOM COMPTON** – drums / **MICK HAWKSWORTH** – bass (ex-ANDROMEDA)

Polydor R.S.O.

Apr 78. (lp) *(2344 103) <3033>* **ROCKET FUEL** [ ] [ ]
– Rocket fuel / Gonna turn you on / Friday the 13th / Somebody's calling me / Ain't nothin' shakin' / Alvin's blue thing / Baby don't you cry / The Devil's screaming. *(cd-iss. Mar00 on 'Repertoire'; REP 4788)*

Sep 79. (lp) *(2310 678) <3049>* **RIDE ON (live studio)** [ ] May79 [ ]
– Ain't nothin' shakin' / Scat encounter / Hey Joe / Going home / Too much / It's a gaz / Ride on cowboy / Sitin' here / Can't sleep at nite. *(cd-iss. Mar00 on 'Repertoire'; REP 4787)*

Sep 79. (7") *(2001 930)* **RIDE ON COWBOY. / SITTIN' HERE** [ ] [–]

Sep 79. (7") *<936>* **RIDE ON COWBOY. / CAN'T SLEEP AT NITE** [–] [ ]

ALVIN LEE BAND

— retained **COMPTON** and added **STEVE GOULD** – guitar (ex-RARE BIRD) / **MICKEY FEAT** – bass (ex-STREETWALKERS)

Avatar Atlantic

Oct 80. (lp) *(AALP 5002)* **FREE FALL** [ ] [ ]
– I don't wanna stop / Take the money / One lonely hour / Heartache / Stealin' / Ridin' truckin' / No more lonely nights / City lights / Sooner or later / Dustbin city. *(cd-iss. Jun00 on 'Repertoire'+=; REP 4705)* – (bonus tracks).

Nov 80. (7") *(AAA 106)* **I DON'T WANNA STOP. / HEARTACHE** [ ] [–]

Mar 81. (7") *<3792>* **RIDIN' TRUCKIN'. / HEARTACHE** [–] [ ]

Jul 81. (7") *(AAA 109)* **TAKE THE MONEY. / NO MORE LONELY NIGHTS** [ ] [–]

Nov 81. (lp) *(AALP 5006) <19306>* **RX5** [ ] [ ]
– Hang on / Lady luck / Can't stop / Wrong side of the law / Nutbush city limits / Rock-n roll guitar picker / Double loser / Fool no more / Dangerous world / High times. *(cd-iss. Jun00 on 'Repertoire'+=; REP 4706)* – Shuffle it.

Dec 81. (7") *(AAA 117)* **ROCK'N'ROLL GUITAR PICKER. / DANGEROUS WORLD** [ ] [–]

Mar 82. (7") *(AAA 122)* **NUTBUSH CITY LIMITS. / HIGH TIMES** [ ] [–]

— **MICK TAYLOR** – guitar (ex-ROLLING STONES) / **FUZZY SAMUELS** – bass (ex-CROSBY, STILLS & NASH) repl. GOULD & FEAT

— split early 1982.

ALVIN LEE

recorded another solo with **LYONS + GEORGE HARRISON**

Viceroy 21 records

Aug 86. (cd) *(VIN 8032-2) <210019>* **DETROIT DIESEL** Feb87
– Detroit diesel / Shot in the dark / Too late to run for cover / Talk don't bother me / Ordinary man / Heart of stone / She's so cute / Back in my arms again / Don't want to fight / Let's go. *(cd-iss. Apr97 on 'Viceroy'; same)*

Sep 86. (7") **DETROIT DIESEL. / LET'S GO** –

Jan 87. (7") **HEART OF STONE. / SHE'S SO CUTE** –

— Signed to 'No Speak' records, but had no releases. In Apr'89, ALVIN guested on Various Artists live cd,c,-d-lp 'NIGHT OF THE GUITAR' for 'I.R.S.' label.

TEN YEARS AFTER

originals re-formed with **ALVIN LEE + STEVE GOULD** plus?

Chrysalis Chrysalis

Nov 89. (lp/c/cd) *(CHR/ZCHR/CCD 1722) <21722>* **ABOUT TIME**
– Highway of love / Let's shake it up / I get all shook up / Victim of circumstance / Going to Chicago / Wild is the river / Saturday night / Bad blood / Working in a parking lot / Outside my window / Waiting for the judgement day.

Nov 89. (7") *(CHS 3447)* **HIGHWAY OF LOVE. / ROCK & ROLL MUSIC TO THE WORLD**

ALVIN LEE

Sequel Domino

Oct 92. (cd/c) *(NED CD/MC 225) <8003>* **ZOOM**
– A little bit of love / Jenny Jenny / Remember me / Anything for you / The price of this love / Real life blues / It don't come easy / Lost in love / Wake up moma / Moving the blues / Use that power. *(re-iss. Oct95 on 'Thunderbolt' cd)(c; CDTB 171)(CTC 0201)*

H.T.D. not iss.

Oct 93. (cd/c) *(HTD CD/MC 14)* **NINETEEN NINETY FOUR** –
– Keep on rockin' / Long legs / I hear you knockin' / I want you (she's so heavy) / I don't give a damn / Give me your love / Play it like it used to be / Take it easy / My baby's come back to me / Boogie all day / Bluest blues / Ain't nobody's business if I do. *(cd re-iss. Mar95 & Sep99 on 'Thunderbolt'; CDTB 150) (cd re-iss. Mar00 on 'Last Call'; 422486)*

Viceroy Viceroy

Mar 94. (cd) *(<VIC 8012-2>)* **I HEAR YOU ROCKIN'**
– Keep on rockin' / Long legs / I hear you knockin' / Ain't nobody's business / Bluest blues / Boogie all day / My baby's come back to me / Take it easy / Play it like it used to play / Give me your love / I don't give a damn / I want you (she's so heavy). *(re-iss. Apr97; same)*

Coast To Coast Viceroy

Mar 95. (cd) *(CTC 0201) <8030>* **LIVE IN VIENNA (live)** Feb96
– Keep on rockin' / Long legs / I hear you knockin' / Hear me calling / Love like a man / Johnny B.Goode / I don't give a damn / Good morning little schoolgirl / Skooboly oobly doobob / Help me baby / Classical thing / Going home / Rip it up. *(re-iss. Apr97 on 'Viceroy'; VIC 80302) (re-iss. Oct98 on 'Thunderbolt'; CDTB 171) (re-iss. Mar00 on 'Last Call'; 422507)*

ALVIN LEE & TEN YEARS AFTER

Chrysalis Capitol

Jul 95. (cd/c) *(CD/TC CHR 6102) <33450>* **PURE BLUES**
– Don't want you woman / Bluest blues / I woke up this morning / Real life blues / Stomp / Slow blues in 'C' / Wake up moma / Talk don't bother me / Every blues you've ever heard / I get all shook up / Lost in love / Help me / Outside my window.

— Aug'95, ALVIN was credited on GUITAR CRUSHER cd 'MESSAGE TO MAN' on 'In-Akustik'; *INAK 9034*

– compilations, others, etc. –

Mar 72. (lp/c; by ALVIN LEE) *Deram; (SML/KSCM 1096)* **ALVIN LEE & COMPANY** 55
– The sounds / Rock your mama / Hold me tight / Standing at the crossroads / Portable people / Boogie on. *(cd-iss. Jan89; 820 566-2)*

Aug 75. (lp/c) *Chrysalis; (CHR/ZCHR 1077) / Deram; <18072>* **GOIN' HOME – THEIR GREATEST HITS** Jul75

Sep 76. (lp/c) *Chrysalis; (CHR/ZCHR 1107)* **ANTHOLOGY**

Feb 77. (lp/c) *Chrysalis; (CHR/ZCHR 1134)* **THE CLASSIC PERFORMANCES OF . . .**
(cd-iss. 1987; CCD 1134)

Feb 79. (c) *Teldec; (CP4 22436)* **GREATEST HITS VOL.1** –

Feb 79. (c) *Teldec; (CP4 23252) GREATEST HITS VOL.2* –

May 80. (lp/c) *Hallmark; (SHM/HSC 3038)* **TEN YEARS AFTER** –

Mar 81. (lp) *Decca; (TAB 12)* **HEAR ME CALLING** –

Oct 83. (7") *Old Gold; (OG 9342)* **LOVE LIKE A MAN. / (B-side by THEM)** –

Nov 85. (d-lp/c) *Castle; (CCS LP/MC 115)* **THE COLLECTION** –
– Hear me calling / No title / Spoonful / I can't keep from crying sometimes / Standing at the crossroads / Portable people / Rock your mama / Love like a man / I want to know / Speed kills / Boogie on / I may be wrong but I won't be wrong always / At the woodchopper's ball / Spider in your web / Summertime / Shantung cabbage / I'm going home. *(re-iss. Jul91 cd/c; CCS CD/MC 293) (cd re-iss. Aug95 on 'Griffin';)*

Feb 87. (lp) *See For Miles; (SEE 80)* **ORIGINAL RECORDINGS: VOL.1** –

Jun 87. (lp) *See For Miles; (SEE 90)* **ORIGINAL RECORDINGS: VOL.2** –
(cd-iss. Nov93; SEECD 387)

May 88. (d-lp/c/cd) *Chrysalis; (CHR/ZCHR/MPCD 1639)* **PORTFOLIO**

Dec 90. (cd/c/lp) *Raw Fruit; (FRS CD/MC/LP 003)* **LIVE AT READING 1983 (live)** –

Oct 92. (cd/c) *Chrysalis; (CD/TC CHR 1857)* **THE ESSENTIAL TEN YEARS AFTER** –

Jul 93. (cd) *Code 90; (NINETY 3)* **LIVE (live)** –

Sep 93. (cd) *Traditional Line; (TL 001327)* **LOVE LIKE A MAN** –

Mar 95. (cd; by ALVIN LEE) *Magnum; (MMGV 064)* **RETROSPECTIVE** –

Nov 95. (3xcd-box) *Chrysalis; (CDOMB 011)* **CRICKLEWOOD GREEN / WATT / A SPACE IN TIME** –

Nov 96. (cd) *Disky; <(DC 86678-2)>* **I'M GOING HOME**

Nov 97. (cd; by ALVIN LEE & TEN YEARS AFTER) *Chrysalis; (CDCHR 6129) / Capitol; <21312>* **SOLID ROCK**

Aug 00. (cd) *Chrysalis; (528499-2)* **THE BEST OF TEN YEARS AFTER**

☐ TERMINATOR X (see under ⇒ PUBLIC ENEMY)

TEXAS

Formed: Glasgow, Scotland . . .1988 by SHARLEEN SPITERI, JOHNNY McELHONE, ALLY McERLAINE and STUART KERR. Initially lumped in with the new wave of young Scottish rock bands tipped for big things (GUN, SLIDE etc.), TEXAS debuted in early '89 with the rootsy pop of 'I DON'T WANT A LOVER', its infectious slide guitar refrain infiltrating the Top 10 but subsequently becoming a millstone round the band's neck as they struggled to shake off the 'one-hit-wonder' tag. The debut album, 'SOUTHSIDE' (1989) was a Top 5 hit nevertheless, a highly listenable set of inoffensive, blues/country-tinged pop/rock which became one of the top selling albums of that year. This was without the help of any further hit singles, both 'THRILL HAS GONE' and 'EVERYDAY NOW' (very reminiscent of BOB DYLAN's 'I Shall Be Released') stalling outside the Top 40. In fact, the group's next major hit single came more than three years later with a cover of Al Green's 'TIRED OF BEING ALONE'. There was certainly no disputing the sensuous beauty and power of SPITERI's voice, or indeed her striking looks and while TEXAS had their critics, they also boasted an extensive grassroots following, especially in their native Scotland where gigs often took on the fervour of religious gatherings. Predictably then, the follow-up set, 'MOTHER'S HEAVEN' (1991), was well received by devotees but failed to convince many waverers. Likewise 'RICK'S ROAD' (1993), an underrated set which leant more on the country-rock side of things. With its BYRDS-esque jangle and gorgeous vocal, 'SO CALLED FRIEND' remains one of TEXAS's most affecting moments, though thousands would no doubt disagree. Many of those thousands, in fact, who probably own a copy of 'WHITE ON BLONDE', TEXAS's million selling 1997 album which must surely rank as one of the most incredible commercial turnarounds in the history of rock. Abandoning the roots trappings for a super slick soul-pop sound, TEXAS transformed themselves from yet another flagging Scottish rock band into an international phenomenon. Buoyed by the success of radio-friendly, highly infectious singles like 'SAY WHAT YOU WANT', 'HALO' and 'BLACK EYED BOY', the album was 1997's ultimate coffee table companion. Not only that, SPITERI was seemingly born again as a style mag sex symbol, her ravishing visage staring out from front cover after front cover. Bizarrely enough, among TEXAS's biggest fans were New York's hardest rap crew, The WU-TANG CLAN, surely resulting in a rather unlikely pairing (of all-time, quite possibly) on a Top 5 version of 'SAY WHAT YOU WANT (ALL DAY AND EVERY DAY)'. Having already topped the charts with their last album, TEXAS repeated the formula with their follow-up, 'THE HUSH' (1999), a deliberately more sensual set of songs that included three massive hits, 'IN OUR LIFETIME, 'SUMMER SON' and 'WHEN WE ARE TOGETHER'. While their commercial stock perhaps wasn't quite what it had been in the preceding half decade or so, SPITERI and Co still breached the UK Top 5 with 'CAREFUL WHAT YOU WISH FOR' (2003), a carefully crafted replica of their previous successes which nevertheless lacked the killer hooks. • **Songwriters:** SPITERI lyrics / McELHONE music; except DIMPLES (John Lee Hooker) / DON'T YOU WANT ME (Human League) / YOU'RE ALL I NEED TO GET BY (Marvin Gaye & Tammi Terrell) / SWEET CHILD O' MINE (Guns N' Roses) / SUSPICIOUS MINDS (Elvis Presley) / ACROSS THE UNIVERSE (Beatles) / WHAT DO I GET (Buzzcocks).

Album rating: SOUTHSIDE (*6) / MOTHER'S HEAVEN (*5) / RICK'S ROAD (*5) / WHITE ON BLONDE (*7) / THE HUSH (*7) / THE GREATEST HITS compilation (*8) / CAREFUL WHAT YOU WISH FOR (*5)

SHARLEEN SPITERI (b. 7 Nov'67) – vocals, guitar / **ALLY McERLAINE** (b. ALISTAIR, 31 Oct'68) – guitar / **JOHNNY McELHONE** (b.21 Apr'63) – bass, vocals (ex-ALTERED IMAGES, ex-HIPSWAY) / **STUART KERR** (b.16 Mar'63) – drums (ex-LOVE AND MONEY)

Mercury Mercury

Jan 89. (7") *(TEX 1) <872350>* **I DON'T WANT A LOVER. / BELIEVE ME** [8] [77]
(ext;12"+=/cd-s+=) *(TEX 1-12/CD1)* – All in vain.

Mar 89. (lp/c/cd) *(<838 171-1/-4/-2>)* **SOUTHSIDE** [3] [88]
– I don't want a lover / Tell me why / Everyday now / Southside / Prayer for you / Faith / The thrill has gone / Fight the feeling / Fool for love / One choice / Future is promises.

Apr 89. (7") *(TEX 2)* **THE THRILL HAS GONE. / NOWHERE LEFT TO HIDE** [60] [–]
(12"+=/12"s+=)(cd-s+=) *(TEX/+P 2-12)(TEXCD 2)* – Dimples.

Jul 89. (7"/c-s) *(TEX/+MC 3)* **EVERYDAY NOW. / WAITING FOR THE FALL** [44] [ ]
(12"+=) *(TEX 3-12)* – Faith.
(cd-s+=) *(TEXCD 3)* – Future is promises (acoustic) / Food for love (live at Radio Clyde).
(12") *(TEXR 3-12)* – ('A'live) / Living for the city (live) / It hurts me too (live).

Nov 89. (7"/c-s) *(TEX/+MC 4)* **PRAYER FOR YOU. / RETURN** [73] [ ]
(12"+=/cd-s+=) *(TEX 4-12/CD4)* – I don't want a lover (live) / ('A'-acoustic).
(12"/cd-s) *(TEX R/CDR 4-12)* – ('A'-Southside & Northside remixes).

Aug 91. (7"/c-s) *(TEX/+MC 5)* **WHY BELIEVE IN YOU. / HOW IT FEELS** [66] [ ]
(12"+=/cd-s+=) *(TEX 5-12/CD5)* – Hold me Lord.
(cd-s) *(TEXCB 5)* – ('A'side) / Is what I do wrong / Hold me LOrd / Living for the city (live).

Sep 91. (cd/c/lp) *(<848 578-2/-4/-1>)* **MOTHER'S HEAVEN** [32] [ ]
– Mother's heaven / Why believe in you / Dream hotel / This will all be mine / Beliefs / Alone with you / In my heart / Waiting / Wrapped in clothes of blue / Return / Walk the dust.

Oct 91. (7"/c-s) *(TEX/+MC 6)* **IN MY HEART. / IS WHAT I DO WRONG** [74] [ ]
(12"+=) *(TEX 6-12)* – Alone with you.
(12"+=/cd-s+=) *(TEX 6-12/CD6)* – You gave me love / ('A'remix).

Feb 92. (7"/c-s) *(TEX/+MC 7)* **ALONE WITH YOU. / DOWN IN THE BATTLEFIELD** [32] [ ]
(cd-s) *(TEXCD 7)* – ('A'side) / Why believe in you / Everyday now / I don't want a lover.
(cd-s) *(TEXCDX 7)* – ('A'live) / Can't get next to you (live) / What goes on (live) / Sweet child o' mine (live).

Apr 92. (7"/c-s) *(TEX/+MC 8)* **TIRED OF BEING ALONE. / WRAPPED IN CLOTHES OF BLUE** [19] [ ]
(cd-s) *(TEXCD 8)* – ('A'side) / Thrill has gone / In my heart (12"mix) / Prayer for you (Northside remix).
(cd-s) *(TEXCB 8)* – ('A'acoustic) / Walk the dust (acoustic) / Why believe in you (acoustic) / Return (acoustic).

— **RICHARD HYND** (b.17 May'68, Aberdeen, Scotland) – drums (ex-SLIDE) repl. KERR

— added **EDDIE CAMPBELL** (b. 6 Jun'65) – keyboards

Vertigo Mercury

Aug 93. (7"/c-s) *(TEX AS/MC 9)* **SO CALLED FRIEND. / YOU'RE THE ONE I WANT IT FOR** [30] [ ]
(cd-s+=) *(TEXCD 9)* – Tonight I stay with you / I've been missing you.
(box;cd-s+=) *(TEXCDP 9)* – Mother's Heaven (French mix) / Tired of being alone.

Oct 93. (7"/c-s) *(TEX AS/MC 10)* **YOU OWE IT ALL TO ME. / DON'T HELP ME THROUGH** [39] [ ]
(cd-s+=) *(TEXCD 10)* – Make me want to scream / Strange that I want you.
(cd-s) *(TEXCL 10)* – ('A'side) / I don't want a lover (acoustic) / So called friend (acoustic) / Revolution (acoustic).

Nov 93. (cd/c/lp) *(<518 252-2/-4/-1>)* **RICK'S ROAD** [18] [ ]
– So called friend / Fade away / Listen to me / You owe it all to me / Beautiful angel / So in love with you / You've got to live a little / I want to go to Heaven / Hear me now / Fearing these days / I've been missing you / Winter's end.

Feb 94. (7"/c-s) *(TEX AS/MC 11)* **SO IN LOVE WITH YOU. / ('A'instrumental)** [28] [ ]
(cd-s) *(TEXCD 11)* – ('A'side) / So called friend / One love / You owe it all to me.
(cd-s) *(TEXCX 11)* – ('A'side) / Why believe in you (live) / Prayer for you (live) / Everyday now (live).

Mercury Mercury

Jan 97. (c-s) *(MERMC 480)* **SAY WHAT YOU WANT / COLD DAY DREAM** [3] [ ]
(cd-s+=) *(MERCD 480)* – Tear it up / ('A'-Boilerhouse remix).
(cd-s) *(MERDD 480)* – ('A'side) / Good advice / ('A'-Rae & Christian mixes).

Feb 97. (cd/c) *(<534 315-2/-4>)* **WHITE ON BLONDE** [1] [ ]
– Halo / Say what you want / Drawing crazy patterns / Put your arms around me / Insane / Black eyed boy / Polo mint city / White on blonde / Postcard / Ticket to lie / Good advice.

Apr 97. (c-s) *(MERMC 482)* **HALO / ASKING FOR FAVOURS** [10] [ ]
(cd-s+=) *(MERCD 482)* – Coming down / ('A'-orchestral version).
(cd-s) *(MERDD 482)* – ('A'side) / ('A'-Rae & Christian mixes) / ('A'-808 mixes).

Aug 97. (c-s) *(MERMC 490)* **BLACK EYED BOY / FAITHLESS** [5] [ ]
(cd-s) *(MERCD 490)* – ('A'side) / Sorry / Black eyed disco (disco boy dub mix) / Say what you want (session).
(cd-s) *(MERDD 490)* – ('A'side) / ('A'-disco/dance mixes).

Nov 97. (c-s) *(MERMC 497)* **PUT YOUR ARMS AROUND ME / NEVER NEVER** [10] [ ]
(cd-s+=) *(MERCD 497)* – You're all I need to get by (session).
(cd-s) *(MERDD 497)* – ('A'mixes; Two Lone Swordsmen & Ballistic Brothers).

Mar 98. (c-s; TEXAS featuring WU-TANG) *(MERMC 499)* **SAY WHAT YOU WANT (ALL DAY EVERY DAY) / INSANE** [4] [ ]
(cd-s+=) *(MERCD 499)* – Polo mint city (extended) / ('A'-Trailermen mix).
(cd-s) *(MERDD 499)* – ('A'extended) / ('B'-The econd scroll) / ('A'&'B'-RZA instrumentals & dub versions).
(12") *(MERX 499)* – ('A'-Trailermen mix) / ('A'-RZA instrumental).

Apr 99. (c-s) *(MERMC 517)* **IN OUR LIFETIME / LOVE DREAM #2** | 4 | – |
(cd-s+=) *(MERDD 517)* – ('A'-enhanced).
(cd-s) *(MERCD 517)* – ('A'side) / ('A'-Jules disco trip mix) ('A'-Return To Tha dub mix).

May 99. (cd/c) *(<538 972-2/-4>)* **THE HUSH** | 1 | |
– In our lifetime / Tell me the answer / Summer son / Sunday afternoon / Move in / When we are together / Day after day / Zero zero / Saint / Girl / The hush / The day before I went away. *(cd hidden+=)* – Let us be thankful.

Aug 99. (c-s) *(MERMC 520)* **SUMMER SON / ('A'-Giorgio Moroder mix)** | 5 | – |
(cd-s+=) *(MERCD 520)* – Don't you want me (live).
(cd-s+=) *(MERDD 520)* – ('A'-Tee's freeze mix).

Nov 99. (c-s) *(MERMC 525)* **WHEN WE ARE TOGETHER / SAY WHAT YOU WANT (ALL DAY AND EVERY DAY) (live)** | 12 | – |
(cd-s+=) *(MERCD 525)* – In our lifetime (live) / ('A'-video).
(cd-s) *(MERDD 525)* – ('A'mixes) / Summer son (Euro bootleg).

Oct 00. (c-s) *(MERMC 528)* **IN DEMAND / EARLY HOURS** | 6 | – |
(cd-s+=) *(MERCD 528)* – Like lovers (holding on) / ('A'-CD-Rom).
(cd-s) *(MERDD 528)* – ('A'-US mix) / ('A'-Sunship mix) / ('A'-Wookie remix) / ('A'-Sunshine dub).
(12") *(MERX 528)* – ('A'-US mix) / ('A'-Wookie remix).

Oct 00. (cd/c) *(548262-2/-4)* **THE GREATEST HITS** (compilation) | 1 | – |
– I don't want a lover / In demand / Say what you want / Summer son / Inner smile / So in love with you / Black eyed boy / So called friend / Everyday now / In our lifetime / Halo / Guitar song / Prayer for you / When we are together / Insane / Tired of being alone / Put your arms around me / Say what you want (all day and every day (with METHOD MAN/RZA). *(d-cd+=; 548227-2)* – (various mixes). *(cd re-iss. Jul01; same)*

Jan 01. (c-s) *(MERMC 531)* **INNER SMILE / ('A'-Moody mix) / ('A'-Stonebridge classic house mix)** | 6 | – |
(cd-s+=) *(MERDD 531)* – ('A'-Jule's club radio mix) / ('A'-Rae & Christian basement mix).
(cd-s) *(MERCD 531)* – ('A'-extended 12" mix) / Across the universe – Inner smile (CD-Rom mix).

Jul 01. (cd-s) *(MERDD 533)* **I DON'T WANT A LOVER (2001 mix) / SUMMER SON (live) / SUSPICIOUS MINDS (live)** | 16 | – |
(c-s+=) *(MERCS 533)* – ('A'-Trailerman mix).
(cd-s) *(MERCD 533)* – ('A'side) / Superwrong / I don't want a lover (Stonebridge bed mix) / ('A'video) / ('A'live).

Oct 03. (cd-s) *(9812253)* **CARNIVAL GIRL / NIGHT FOR DAY / CARNIVAL OF DUB / CARNIVAL GIRL (video)** | 9 | – |
(cd-s) *(9812254)* – ('A'side) / ('A'-feat. Kardinal Offishall).

Oct 03. (cd/c) *(986 5697/5711) <86569>* **CAREFUL WHAT YOU WISH FOR** | 5 | |
– Telephone X / Broken / Carnival girl / I'll see it through / Where did you sleep? / And I dream / Careful what you wish for / Big sleep / Under your skin / Carousel dub / Place in my world / Another day.

Dec 03. (cd-s) *(9815221)* **I'LL SEE IT THROUGH / TIRED OF BEING ALONE** | 40 | – |
(cd-s) *(9815220)* – ('A'side) / What do I get / I'll give it all again / ('A'-Roger Sanchez remix) / ('A'-Guy Chambers mix).

– compilations, etc. –

Sep 95. (d-cd) *Vertigo; (528604-2)* **SOUTHSIDE / RICK'S ROAD** | | – |

THEM

Formed: Belfast, N. Ireland . . . 1963 by VAN MORRISON, BILLY HARRISON, ALAN HENDERSON, ERIC WRIXEN and RONNIE MELLINGS. After their debut single flopped, producers TOMMY SCOTT and BERT BERNS, recruited session men JIMMY PAGE (future LED ZEPPELIN) and PETER BARDENS (future CAMEL) to feature on their hot-wired cover of BIG JOE WILLIAMS' 'BABY PLEASE DON'T GO', the single rocketing into the Top 10 in early '65. The B-side, 'GLORIA' was even more primal, a riotous piece of garage that inspired generations of spotty youths to pick up guitars and has subsequently been covered by everyone from The SHADOWS OF KNIGHT to The DOORS and PATTI SMITH. Although the band found it difficult to equal this incredible double shot, their next single, 'HERE COMES THE NIGHT' climbed to No.2 in the UK charts. The eponymous debut album followed later that summer and although it failed to chart, it was a precocious collection of early VAN-penned originals and incendiary covers. Their fame was short-lived though, as successive singles failed to chart and the second album, 'THEM AGAIN' (1966) lacked the consistency of its predecessor. There were occasional flashes of VAN's maverick genius and it was clear he was the lynchpin holding the thing together. When he left to go solo in 1966, the band inevitably split, only to reform a number of times (minus VAN) around differing line-ups, trading on past glories but predictably producing no new material of any great note. • **Songwriters:** MORRISON penned (until his departure), except HERE COMES THE NIGHT + (IT WON'T HURT) HALF AS MUCH + few early songs (Bert Berns). DON'T START CRYING NOW (Slim Harpo) / BABY PLEASE DON'T GO (Big Joe Williams) / DON'T LOOK BACK (John Lee Hooker) / I PUT A SPELL ON YOU (Screaming Jay Hawkins) / IT'S ALL OVER NOW, BABY BLUE (Bob Dylan), etc.

Album rating: THEM (*7) / THEM AGAIN (*6) / NOW AND THEM (*5) / TIME OUT, TIME IN FOR THEM (*4) / THEM on 'Happy Tiger' (*4) / IN REALITY (*4) / THEM FEATURING VAN MORRISON compilation (*7) / SHUT YOUR MOUTH (*4)

VAN MORRISON (b.GEORGE IVAN, 31 Aug'45) – vocals, harmonica / **BILLY HARRISON** – guitar / **ERIC WRIXEN** – piano, keyboards / **RONNIE MELLINGS** – drums / **ALAN HENDERSON** (b.26 Nov'44) – bass

Decca | Parrot

Aug 64. (7") *(F 11973) <9702>* **DON'T START CRYING NOW. / ONE TWO BROWN EYES** | | |

— **JACKIE McAULEY** – organ + **PATRICK McAULEY** – organ repl. ERIC and RONNIE WRIXEN who joined The WHEELS, while MELLINGS became a milkman.

Dec 64. (7") *(F 12018) <9727>* **BABY PLEASE DON'T GO. / GLORIA** | 10 | Mar65 93 |
<US re-dist.Apr66, flipped over; hit 71> (re-iss. Jul73 on 'Deram'; DM 394) (re-iss. May82; F 13923) (re-iss. Oct83 on 'Old Gold'; OG 9341)

Mar 65. (7") *(F 12094) <9747>* **HERE COMES THE NIGHT. / ALL FOR MYSELF** | 2 | May65 24 |
(re-iss. Sep73 on 'Deram'; DM 400)

Jun 65. (lp; mono/stereo) *(LK 4700) <PS/PAS 6/7 1005>* **THEM** | | Jul65 54 |
– Here comes the night *[US-only]* / Mystic eyes / If you and I could be as two / Little girl / Just a little bit / I gave my love a diamond (UK-only) / Go on home baby / Gloria / You just can't win / Don't look back / I like it like that / Bright lights big city / My little baby *[UK-only]* / Route 66. *(cd-iss. Feb89 on 'London'; 820 563-2) (cd re-mast.Jun98 +=; 844824-2)*
above lp featured sessioners **PETER BARDENS** – keyboards + **JIMMY PAGE** – guitar

— **PETER BARDENS** – keyboards + **JOHN WILSON** (b. 6 Nov'47) – drums now repl. The McAULEY's who formed The BELFAST GYPSIES

Jun 65. (7") *(F 12175)* **ONE MORE TIME. / HOW LONG BABY?** | | – |

Aug 65. (7") *(F 12215) <9784>* **(IT WON'T HURT) HALF AS MUCH. / I'M GONNA DRESS IN BLACK** | | |

Nov 65. (7") *(F 12281) <9796>* **MYSTIC EYES. / IF YOU AND I COULD BE AS TWO** | | Oct65 33 |

— **MORRISON, HENDERSON + WILSON** were joined by **RAY ELLIOTT** (b.13 Sep'43) – piano, sax repl. BARDENS to solo & later CAMEL / **JIM ARMSTRONG** (b.24 Jun'44) – guitar repl. HARRISON

Jan 66. (lp; mono/stereo) *(LK 4751) <PS/PAS 6/7 1008>* **THEM AGAIN** | | |
– Could you would you / Something you got / Call my name / Turn on your love light / I put a spell on you / I can only give you everything / My lonely sad eyes / I got a woman / Out of sight / It's all over now, baby blue / Bad or good / How long baby / Hello Josephine / Don't you

know / Hey girl / Bring 'em on in. *(cd-iss. Feb89 on 'London'; 820 564-2) (cd re-mast.Jun98 +=; 844825-2)*

Mar 66. (7") *(F 12355)* <9819> **CALL MY NAME. / BRING 'EM ON IN** ☐ ☐

— (Jan 66) **TERRY NOONE** – drums repl. WILSON later to TASTE (RORY GALLAGHER) Apr 66, **DAVE HARVEY** – drums repl. NOONE.

May 66. (7") *(F 12403)* <3003> **RICHARD CORY. / DON'T YOU KNOW** ☐ ☐

— Disbanded mid 1966 when VAN MORRISON went solo. In 1967, they re-formed. **KEN McDOWELL** – vocals repl. him

Major Minor not iss.

1967. (7") *(MM 509)* **GLORIA. / FRIDAY'S CHILD** ☐ –

1967. (7") *(MM 513)* **THE STORY OF THEM. / (part 2)** ☐ –

not iss. Tower-Capitol

Jan 68. (lp) <ST 5104> **NOW AND THEM** – ☐

– I'm your witch doctor / What's the matter baby / Truth machine / Square room / You're just what I was looking for today / Dirty old man / At the age of sixteen / Nobody loves you when you're down and out / Walking the Queen's garden / I happen to love you / Come to me. *(UK-iss.Dec88 on 'Zap!'; ZAP 6) (cd-iss. May03 on 'Rev-Ola'+=; CRREV 29)* – Walking in the Queen's garden (mono) / I happen to love you (mono).

Feb 68. (7") <384> **WALKING IN THE QUEEN'S GARDEN. / I HAPPEN TO LOVE YOU** – ☐

Apr 68. (7") <407> **SQUARE ROOM. / BUT IT'S ALRIGHT** – ☐

— trimmed to a quartet when ELLIOTT departed

Nov 68. (lp) <ST 5116> **TIME OUT! TIME IN FOR THEM** – ☐

– Time out for time in / She put a hex on you / Bent over you / Waltz of the flees / Black widow spider / We've all agreed to help / Market place / Just one conception / Young woman / The moth. *(UK-iss.Dec88 on 'Zap!'; ZAP 7)*

Nov 68. (7") <461> **WALTZ OF THE FLIES. / WE ALL AGREED TO HELP** – ☐

Mar 69. (7") <493> **DARK ARE THE SHADOWS. / CORINA** – ☐

— added on session **JERRY COLE** – guitar, vocals / **JOHN STARK** – drums (tour) In 1969, ARMSTRONG, ELLIOT, McDOWELL went off to Chicago to form The TRUTH alongside bassman CURTIS BACHMAN and rummer RENO SMITH. An album 'TRUTH OF TRUTHS' surfaced in 1971 for US 'Oak'. In March '95, an exploitation cd 'OF THEM AND OTHER TALES' was released for 'Epilogue' *(EPI 003)*

not iss. Happy Tiger

1970. (lp) <HT 1004> **THEM** – ☐

– I keep singing / Lonely weekends / Take a little time / You got me good / Jo Ann / Memphis lady / In the midnight hour / Nobody cares / I am waiting / Just a little.

1970. (7") <525> **I AM WAITING. / LONELY WEEKENDS** – ☐

1970. (7") <534> **MEMPHIS LADY. / NOBODY CARES** – ☐

1971. (lp; as THEM featuring ALAN HENDERSON) <HT 1012> **THEM IN REALITY** – ☐

– Gloria / Baby please don't go / Laugh / Let my song through / California man / Lessons of the sea / Rayn / Back to the country / Can you believe.

— **THEM** re-formed originals **HENDERSON, HARRISON & WRIXEN** + **MEL AUSTIN** – vocals / **BILLY BELL** – drums

Decca not iss.

1979. (lp) **SHUT YOUR MOUTH** ☐ –

– Hamburg connection / I'm a lover not a worker / Shut your mouth / Needed on the farm / Streetwalking lady / Firewater / Child of the sixties / Slowdown / Losing you / Weekend entertainer / Holy roller / Cincinnati diceman.

— split 1979 after **JIM ARMSTRONG** – guitar + **BRIAN SCOTT** – keyboards, flute repl. WRIXEN + HARRISON. The latter became BILLY WHO

– (selective) compilations, etc. –

Oct 73. (d-lp; as THEM FEATURING VAN MORRISON) *(DPA 3001-2)* <BP 71053-4> **THEM FEATURING VAN MORRISON** ☐ Jul72 ☐

– Don't start crying now / Baby please don't go / Here comes the night / One more time / It won't hurt half as much / Mystic eyes / Call my name / Richard Cory / One two brown eyes / All for myself / If you and I could be as two / Don't you know / Friday's child / The story of Them (part 1) / Philosophy / How long baby / I'm gonna dress in black / Bring 'em on in / Little girl / I gave my love a diamond / Gloria / You just can't win / Go on home baby / Don't look back / I like it like that / Bright lights big city / My little baby / Route 66.*(re-iss. Jul82; lp/c TAB/KTBC 45) (cd-iss. 1987 on 'London'; 810 165-2)*

Aug 86. (d-lp/d-c; as THEM featuring VAN MORRISON) *Castle; (CCS LP/MC 131)* **THE COLLECTION** ☐ – *(cd-iss. Aug92; CCSCD 131)*

Sep 87. (lp/c) *See For Miles; (SEE/+K 31)* **THE SINGLES** ☐ –

Jan 91. (7"/c-s) *London; (LON/+C 292)* **BABY PLEASE DON'T GO. / GLORIA** 65 ☐

(12"+=/cd-s+=) *(LON X/CD 292)* – Mystic eyes.

Apr 97. (cd) *Spalax; (14967)* **REUNION CONCERT (live)** ☐ –

THERAPY?

Formed: Belfast, N. Ireland . . . summer '89 by ANDY CAIRNS, MICHAEL McKEEGAN and FYFE EWING. After failing to attract major label interest, they took the DIY route and issued a double A-side debut single, 'MEAT ABSTRACT' / 'PUNISHMENT KISS' (1990) on their own bitterly named 'Multifuckingnational' label. With the help of Radio One guru, John Peel and Silverfish's LESLIE RANKINE, the band secured a deal with London indie label, 'Wiiija'. The following year, they released two mini-sets in quick succession, 'BABYTEETH' and 'PLEASURE DEATH', the latter nearly breaking them into the Top 50 (both topping the independent charts). This initial early 90's period was characterised by a vaguely industrial hardcore/proto-grunge sound lying somewhere between American noiseniks, BIG BLACK and HUSKER DU. Their mushrooming street kudos tempted 'A&M' into offering them a deal and in 1992 THERAPY? made their major label debut with the Top 30 single, 'TEETHGRINDER', following it up with their first album proper, 'NURSE'. A Top 40 injection, its blunt combination of metal/punk and ambitious arrangements something of a love-it-or-hate-it affair. The following year, they released a trio of Top 20 singles, starting off with the 'SHORTSHARPSHOCK EP' which opened with the classic 'SCREAMAGER' track. In the first few months of '94, THERAPY? once again crashed into the charts with 'NOWHERE', an adrenaline rush of a single, that preceded their Mercury-nominated Top 5 album, 'TROUBLEGUM'. However, by the release of 1995's 'INFERNAL LOVE', the band affected something of a musical departure from their stock-in-trade indie-metal extremity with aching ballads (including a heart-rending cover of Husker Du's 'DIANE') and string flourishes courtesy of MARTIN McCARRICK. The cellist (who also appeared on their 1994 set) was made full-time member in early 1996, while EWING was replaced by GRAHAM HOPKINS. A long time in the making, the album 'SEMI-DETACHED', was delivered to a muted response from the critics in '98 and was their last for a major label. Although it opened in fine style with Top 30 hit, 'CHURCH OF NOISE', the rest of the tracks were below par. On a new label and – critically at least – on the rack, the Irish rabble rousers came out fighting with the defiantly titled 'SUICIDE PACT: YOU FIRST' (1999). Clearly once again making music for themselves rather than the moguls, the record exhibited an exhilarating disregard for melody, stomping its size 10 jackboot on the juvenile wannabes of the so-called nu-metal scene. For younger fans who missed them first time round, 'SO MUCH FOR THE TEN YEAR PLAN: A RETROSPECTIVE 1990-2000' (2000), collected the choicest, juiciest cuts from THERAPY?'s bloody, bruising back catalogue. As such, it proved an ideal primer for 'SHAMELESS' (2001), another fine testament to the band's creative resurgence and a record that widened and enriched the trademark THERAPY? sonic palette to include post-industrial noise-pop. While THERAPY? had yet another new face behind the drum kit (former BEYOND man, NEIL COOPER) for 2003's 'HIGH ANXIETY', there was nothing SPINAL TAP-like about the Irish veterans' umpteenth instalment of intelligent, incendiary agit-metal. CAIRNS' lyrics were as subversively indelible as ever, while McCARRICK's cello added, quite literally, another string or two to the band's tightly coiled bow. • **Songwriters:** Mostly CAIRNS or group penned, except TEENAGE KICKS (Undertones) / INVISIBLE SUN (Police) / WITH OR WITHOUT YOU (U2) / BREAKING THE LAW (Judas Priest) / C.C. RIDER (hit; Elvis Presley) / ISOLATION (Joy Division) / TATTY SEASIDE TOWN (Membranes) / NICE 'N' SLEAZY (Stranglers) / REUTERS (Wire) / VICAR IN A TUTU (Smiths) / GIMME GIMME GIMME (Abba) / GIMME DANGER (Iggy Pop). • **Trivia:** In 1994, they featured w/ OZZY OSBOURNE on 'IRON MAN' for a BLACK SABBATH tribute album.

Album rating: BABYTEETH mini (*5) / PLEASURE DEATH mini (*6) / NURSE (*7) / TROUBLEGUM (*8) / INFERNAL LOVE (*5) / SEMI-DETACHED (*5) / SUICIDE PACT – YOU FIRST (*5) / SO MUCH FOR THE TEN YEAR PLAN: A RETROSPECTIVE 1990-2000 compilation (*8) / SHAMELESS (*6) / HIGH ANXIETY (*6)

ANDY CAIRNS (b.22 Sep'65, Antrim, N.Ireland) – vocals, guitar / **MICHAEL McKEEGAN** (b.25 Mar'71, Antrim) – bass / **FYFE EWING** – drums

Multifuck-ingnational — not iss.

Aug 90. (7") *(MFN 1)* **MEAT ABSTRACT. / PUNISHMENT KISS** [ ] [–]

Wiiija — not iss.

Jul 91. (m-lp) *(WIJ 9)* **BABYTEETH** [ ] [–]
– Meat abstract / Skyward / Punishment kiss / Animal bones / Loser cop / Innocent X / Dancin' with Manson. *(re-iss. Mar93 + Jun95 on 'Southern' cd/c/red-m-lp; 18507-2/-4/-1)*

Jan 92. (m-lp) *(WIJ 11)* **PLEASURE DEATH** [52] [–]
– Skinning pit / Fantasy bag / Shitkicker / Prison breaker / D.L.C. / Potato junkie. *(re-iss. Sep92 on 'A&M';) (re-iss. Mar93 + Jun95 on 'Southern' cd/c/m-lp; 18508-2/-4/-1)*

A&M — A&M

Oct 92. (7"purple) *(AM 0097)* **TEETHGRINDER. / SUMMER OF HATE** [30] [–]
(12") *(AMY 0097)* – ('A'side) / Human mechanism / Sky high McKay(e).
(cd-s+=) *(AMCD 0097)* – (all four songs above).
(12") – *(AMX 0097)* – ('A'-Tee hee dub mix) / ('A'-Unsane mix).

Nov 92. (cd/c/lp) *(540044-2/-4/-1)* **NURSE** [38] [–]
– Nausea / Teethgrinder / Disgracelands / Accelerator / Neck freak / Perversonality / Gone / Zipless / Deep skin / Hypermania.

Mar 93. (7"pink-ep/c-ep/12"ep/cd-ep) *(AM/+MC/Y/CD 208)* **SHORTSHARPSHOCK EP** [9] [–]
– Screamager / Auto surgery / Totally random man / Accelerator.

—— In May93, they appeared on the B-side of PEACE TOGETHER single 'BE STILL', covered The Police's 'INVISIBLE SUN' on 'Island' records.

Jun 93. (7"grey-ep/c-ep/12"ep/cd-ep) *(580304-7/-4/-1/-2)* **FACE THE STRANGE EP** [18] [–]
– Turn / Speedball / Bloody blue / Neck freak (re-recording).

Aug 93. (7"clearorblue-ep/c-ep/cd-ep) *(580360-7/-4/-2)* **OPAL MANTRA / INNOCENT X (live). / POTATO JUNKIE (live) / NAUSEA (live)** [13] [–]

Sep 93. (cd) *<POCM 1033>* **HATS OFF TO THE INSANE (compilation)** [–] [ ]
– Screamager / Auto surgery / Totally random man / Turn / Speedball / Opal mantra.

Jan 94. (7"ep/c-ep/cd-ep) *(580504-7/-4/-2)* **NOWHERE / PANTOPON ROSE. / BREAKING THE LAW / C.C. RIDER** [18] [–]
(cd-s) *(580 504-2)* – ('A'side) / ('A'-Sabres Of Paradise mix) / ('A'-Therapeutic Distortion mix).

Feb 94. (cd/c/lp,green-lp) *(540196-2/-4/-1)* **TROUBLEGUM** [5] [–]
– Knives / Screamager / Hellbelly / Stop it you're killing me / Nowhere / Die laughing / Unbeliever / Trigger inside / Lunacy booth / Isolation / Turn / Femtex / Unrequited / Brainsaw.
above album guests **PAGE HAMILTON** – lead guitar (of HELMET) / **MARTIN McCARRICK** (b.29 Jul'62, Luton, England) – guitar, cello (of THIS MORTAL COIL) / **LESLEY RANKINE + EILEEN ROSE** – vocals

Feb 94. (7"yellow-ep/c-ep/cd-ep) *(580534-7/-4/-2)* **TRIGGER INSIDE / NICE'N'SLEAZY. / REUTERS / TATTY SEASIDE TOWN** [22] [–]
(12"ep) *(580534-1)* – ('A'side) / ('A'-Terry Bertram mix 1 & 2) / Nowhere (Sabres of Paradise mix 1 & 2).

May 94. (7"red-ep/c-ep/cd-ep) *(580588-7/-4/-2)* **DIE LAUGHING / STOP IT YOU'RE KILLING ME (live). / TRIGGER INSIDE (live) / EVIL ELVIS (the lost demo)** [29] [–]
(12") *(580588-1)* – ('A'-David Holmes mix 1 & 2).

—— In May '95, they hit No.53 UK with remix of 'INNOCENT X', with ORBITAL on the B-side, 'Belfast' / 'Wasted (vocal mix)'.

May 95. (7"orange) *(581504-7)* **STORIES. / STORIES (cello version)** [14] [–]
(c-s+=/cd-s+=) *(581105-4/-2)* – Isolation (Consolidated synth mix).

Jun 95. (cd/c/red-lp) *(540379-2/-4/-1)* **INFERNAL LOVE** [9] [–]
– Epilepsy / Stories / A moment of clarity / Jude the obscene / Bowels of love / Misery / Bad mother / Me vs you / Loose / Diane / 30 seconds.

Jul 95. (c-s/cd-s) *(581163-4/-2)* **LOOSE / OUR LOVE MUST DIE / NICE GUYS / LOOSE (Photek remix)** [25] [–]
(cd-s) *(581165-2)* – ('A'side) / Die laughing (live) / Nowhere (live) / Unbeliever (live).
(7"green/one-sided-12") *(581162-7/-1)* – ('A'side) / ('A'-Photek remix).

Nov 95. (7"red-ep/c-ep/cd-ep) *(581293-7/-4/-2)* **DIANE / JUDE THE OBSCENE (acoustic) / LOOSE (acoustic) / 30 SECONDS (acoustic)** [26] [–]
(cd-ep) *(581291-2)* – ('A'side) / Misery (acoustic) / Die laughing (acoustic) / Screamager (acoustic).

—— Jan 96, **GRAHAM HOPKINS** (b.20 Dec'75, Dublin, Ireland) – drums (ex-MY LITTLE FUNHOUSE) repl. FYFE. Also added full-time **MARTIN McCARRICK**

Mar 98. (7"red) *(582538-7)* **CHURCH OF NOISE. / 60 WATT BULB / ('A'-Messenger mix)** [29] [–]
(cd-s) *(582539-2)* – (first & third tracks) / Suing God / ('A'-CD-Rom video).

Mar 98. (cd/c) *(540891-2/-4)* **SEMI-DETACHED** [21] [–]
– Church of noise / Tightrope walker / Black eye, purple sky / Lonely, cryin', only / Born too soon / Stay happy / Safe / Straight life / Heaven's gate / Don't expect roses / Tramline / The boy's asleep. *(also iss.6x7"box; 582548-7)*

May 98. (7"blue) *(582684-7)* **LONELY, CRYIN', ONLY. / SKYWARD** [32] [–]
(cd-s) *(582685-2)* – ('A'side) / High noon / Diane (new version) / Teethgrinder (new version).
(cd-s) *(044121-2)* – ('A'side) / Kids stuff / Disgracelands / ('A'-CD-Rom video).

Ark 21 — Ark 21

Oct 99. (cd) *(153972-2)* *<810045>* **SUICIDE PACT – YOU FIRST** [61] Feb00 [ ]
– He's not that kind of girl / Wall of mouths / Jam jar jail / Hate kill destroy / Big cave in / Six mile water / Little tongues first / Ten year plan / God kicks / Other people's misery / Sister / While I pursue my way unharmed.

Apr 00. (cd-s) *(156792)* **HATE KILL DESTROY / SIX MILE WATER (live) / SISTER (live)** [–] Europe [–]

Oct 00. (cd) *(ARKCD 1001)* *<810060>* **SO MUCH FOR THE TEN YEAR PLAN: A RETROSPECTIVE 1990-2000** (compilation) [ ] [ ]
– Screamager / Bad karma follows you around / Die laughing / Meat abstract / Straight life / Teethgrinder / Fat camp / Stories / Nausea / Six mile water / Church of noise / He's not that kind of girl / Diane / Nowhere / Potato junkie / Ten year plan. *(d-cd+=; ARKCD 1001X)* – Evil Elvis / Bloody blue (demo) / Summer of hate / Isolation (Consolidated mix) / Where eagles dare / Lunacy booth (string version).

Aug 01. (7"ep) *(ARK7 007)* **GIMME BACK MY BRAIN / GIMME THERAPY. / GIMME SHOCK TREATMENT / GIMME GIMME GIMME** [ ] [–]
(cd-ep) *(ARKCDS 007)* – ('A'side) / Gimme gimme gimme (a man after midnight) / Gimme danger / Gimme nyquill all night.

Sep 01. (cd-s) *(ARKCDS 2A07)* **I AM THE MONEY / TANGO ROMEO (demo) / I AM THE MONEY (full length)** [ ] [–]
(cd-s) *(ARKCD 2B07)* – ('A'side) / Bad karma (live) / Fat camp II.

Oct 01. (cd) *(ARKCD 1007)* *<810073>* **SHAMELESS** [ ] Sep01 [ ]
– Gimme back my brain / Dance / This one's for you / I am the money / Wicked man / Theme from Delorean / Joey / Endless psychology / Alrite / Body bag girl / Tango Romeo / Stalk and stash.

—— **NEIL COOPER** – drums (ex-BEYOND) repl. HOPKINS

Spitfire — Spitfire

Apr 03. (7") *(SPIT7 245)* **IF IT KILLS ME. / RUST** [ ] [–]
(cd-s+=) *(SPITXS 245)* – Mama.

May 03. (cd) *(SPITCD 143) <15143>* **HIGH ANXIETY**
– Hey Satan – you rock / Who knows / Stand in line / Nobody here but us / Watch you go / If it kills me / Not in any name / My voodoo doll / Limbo / Last blast / Rust.

– compilations, etc. –

Mar 92. (cd) *1/4 Stick; <QUARTERSTICK 8>* **CAUCASIAN PSYCHOSIS** [–]
– (BABYTEETH + PLEASURE DEATH)

THE THE

Formed: Swadlincote, Derbyshire, England ... 1979 as a studio project by MATT JOHNSON who was part of post-punk outfit The GADGETS, at the same time. JOHNSON signed to indie label, '4 a.d.' in 1980, unleashing the poignant single, 'CONTROVERSIAL SUBJECT'. JOHNSON released a further debut album for the label in summer '81, 'BURNING BLUE SOUL', although in effect it was a THE THE recording in all but name, JOHNSON being the sole permanent member of the group. Signing briefly to 'Some Bizzare', THE THE released another three singles, 'COLD SPELL AHEAD', 'PERFECT' and the brilliant 'UNCERTAIN SMILE', before securing a deal with 'Epic'. The long awaited and much anticipated 'SOUL MINING' was eventually released in late '83, JOHNSON's critical favour and cult standing seeing the album reach the UK Top 30. An entrancing, ambitious pop record with a brooding undertow, the keening 'THIS IS THE DAY' stands among the best of JOHNSON's work, the album's claustrophobic lyrics marking out JOHNSON as a bedsit commentator par excellence. For live work, JOHNSON recruited the likes of ex-ORANGE JUICE man, ZEKE MANYIKA, JIM THIRLWELL and JOOLS HOLLAND, the latter actually having guested on the album. Three years in the making, 'INFECTED' (1986) was JOHNSON's tour de force, a scathing attack on the industrial, economic and moral wasteland that was Thatcher's Britain. Nowhere was this better articulated than the malignant power of the album's centrepiece, 'HEARTLAND', JOHNSON berating 80's material gain and America's all-pervasive influence through gritted teeth. The pumping electro-soul of the title track, meanwhile, dealt with sexual obsession and the AIDS crisis, the attendant devil-masturbating video causing a storm of controversy. Other highlights included the tortured 'OUT OF THE BLUE (INTO THE FIRE)' and the breathy duet with NENEH CHERRY, 'SLOW TRAIN TO DAWN', JOHNSON's mastery of mood and atmosphere, together with a crack troupe of guest musicians making this one of the most realised albums of the decade. Accompanied by a full-length video/film (which was aired on Channel 4), the record also gave JOHNSON some belated Top 20 success. Spurred on, the restless maverick subsequently recruited a permanent band to turn THE THE into a group proposition, namely DAVID PALMER, JAMES ELLER and ex-SMITHS guitarist JOHNNY MARR. Though the resulting album, 'MIND BOMB' (1989) was THE THE's most successful to date (Top 5), its caustic barrage of political ranting lacked the twisted pop subtlety of its predecessor and left some critics unimpressed (a guest spot from SINEAD O'CONNOR on 'KINGDOM OF RAIN' made up for the pop tones of 'THE BEAT(EN) GENERATION'). Retaining the same core of musicians while adding keyboard player, D.C. COLLARD, THE THE eventually resurfaced with a full length album in the form of 'DUSK' (1993). Previewed by the harmonica howl of 'DOGS OF LUST', the album saw JOHNSON once again wrestling with his inner demons in his disturbingly insinuating way. A mid-life dark-night-of-the-soul, JOHNSON has rarely bared his soul or expressed his despair as affectingly as on the very SMITHS-esque 'SLOW EMOTION REPLAY', MARR literally wringing the pathos from his chiming guitar. This cathartic collection of urban blues nevertheless ended on something of a more hopeful note with 'LONELY PLANET', JOHNSON coming to some kind of peace with himself and the world. The record deservedly reached No.2, becoming the most successful THE THE release to date and making up the critical and commercial ground lost with 'MIND BOMB'. Of course, the ever restless JOHNSON turned his hand to something completely different, so to speak, for his next full-length release; 'HANKY PANKY' (1995) was a tribute album to his hero, country star HANK WILLIAMS, although only the track 'I SAW THE LIGHT' was of much note. Given short shrift by critics (the same ones probably), the record saw JOHNSON going out on a limb, no doubt alienating many of his long-time fans, although he was distant from them after relocating to Sherman Oaks in California. Then again, anyone familiar with the work of this elusive genius knows to expect the unexpected. Not the most prolific of artists these days, JOHNSON emerged blinking into the harsh electronic light of the new millennium with 'NAKEDSELF' (2000). The record (released on Interscope's 'Nothing' records – home to NINE INCH NAILS) only just scraped into the UK Top 50 and featured flop single, 'SHRUNKEN MAN'.

Album rating: Matt Johnson: BURNING BLUE SOUL (*7) / The The: SOUL MINING (*7) / INFECTED (*8) / MIND BOMB (*8) / DUSK (*7) / HANKY PANKY (*4) / NAKEDSELF (*5) / 45 RPM – THE SINGLES OF . . . compilation (*8)

GADGETS

MATT JOHNSON – guitars / **COLIN TUCKER** – synthesizers / **JOHN HYDE** – synthesizers (both ex-PLAIN CHARACTERS)

Final Solution not iss.

Dec 79. (lp) *(FSLP 001)* **GADGETREE** [–]
– Kyleaking / Making cars / Narpath / UFO import No.1 / Slippery / Singing in the rain / Only one me / Shouting 'Nispers' / There over there / Termite mound / Sleep / Devil's dyke / Six mile bottom / UFO import No.2 / Autumn 80 / Duplicate / Bog track / Thin line. *(re-iss. Jun89 on 'Plastic Head' lp/cd; PLAS LP/CD 013)*

— They continued as a studio set-up with MATT's help.

Dec 80. (lp) *(FSLP 002)* **LOVE, CURIOSITY, FRECKLES & DOUBT** [–]
– Bodorgan / Gadget speak / Checking to make sure / Aeron / Leave it to Charlie / Prayers / Happy endido / Quatt / Pictures of you / Aaft / Railway line through blubber houses / She's queen of toyland / Sex / It wasn't that way at all / The death and resurrection of Jennifer Gloom / Bill posters will be prosecuted. *(re-iss. Jun89 on 'Plastic Head' lp/cd; PLAS LP/CD 014)*

— next featured **PETER ASHWORTH** dubbed in instead of MATT

Glass not iss.

Jan 83. (lp/c) *(GLA LP/C 006)* **THE BLUE ALBUM** [–]
– We had no way of knowing / Space in my heart / Bodies without heads / The boyfriend / Uneasy listening / Juice of love / Discuss the sofa / Long empty train / Bite the sawdust / Broken fall. *(re-iss. Jun89 on 'Plastic Head' lp/cd; PLAS LP/CD 016)*

Jun 83. (7"/12"; unissued) *(GLASS/+12 026)* **WE HAD NO WAY OF KNOWING. / ACID BATH** [–] [–]

THE THE

MATT JOHNSON (b.15 Aug'61, Essex, England . . . raised London) – vocals, guitar, etc. (also of The GADGETS) / **KEITH LAWS** – synthesizers, drum machine / **PETER 'Triash' ASHWORTH** – drums / **TOM JOHNSTON** – bass

4 a.d. not iss.

Jul 80. (7") *(AD 10)* **CONTROVERSIAL SUBJECT. / BLACK AND WHITE** [–]

— next with guests **GILBERT & LEWIS** (of WIRE) on 2nd last track

Aug 81. (lp; as MATT JOHNSON) *(CAD 113)* **BURNING BLUE SOUL** [–]
– Red cinders in the sand / Song without an ending / Time again for

the golden sunset / Icing up / Like a Sun risin' thru my garden / Out of control / Bugle boy / Delirious / The river flows east in Spring / Another boy drowning. *(re-iss. Sep83; same) (re-iss. credited to THE THE, Jun93 cd)(c; HAD 113CD)(HADC 113); hit UK No.65 <us cd-iss. 1993 on 'Warners'; 45266>*

Some Bizzare — not iss.

Sep 81. (7") *(BZ 4)* **COLD SPELL AHEAD. / HOT ICE** [ ] [–]
(re-iss. Aug92, 12"pic-d/cd-s;)

— **MATT JOHNSON** was now virtually **THE THE,** although he was augmented by others on tour.

Epic — Epic

Oct 82. (7") *(EPCA 2787)* **UNCERTAIN SMILE. / THREE ORANGE KISSES FROM KAZAN** [68] [–]
(12"+=,12"yellow+=) *(EPC13 2787)* – Waiting for the upturn.

Dec 82. (7") **UNCERTAIN SMILE. / WAITING FOR THE UPTURN** [–] [ ]

Feb 83. (7") *(EPCA 3119)* **PERFECT. / THE NATURE OF VIRTUE** [ ] [–]
(12"+=) *(EPCA13 3119)* – The nature of virtue II.

Sep 83. (7") *(A 3710)* **THIS IS THE DAY. / MENTAL HEALING PROCESS** [71] [ ]
(w/ free-7") *(same)* – Leap into the wind / Absolute liberation.
(12") *(TA 3710)* – ('A'side) / I've been waiting for tomorrow (all of my life).

— added live **ZEKE MANYIKA** – drums (of ORANGE JUICE) / **JIM THIRLWELL / JOOLS HOLLAND** – piano (ex-SQUEEZE) / **THOMAS LEER** – synthesizers, keyboards

Oct 83. (lp/c) *(EPC/40 25525) <EK 39266>* **SOUL MINING** [27] [ ]
– I've been waiting for tomorrow (all of my life) / This is the day / The sinking feeling / Uncertain smile / The twilight hour / Soul mining / Giant. *(free-12"ep.w.a.)* **PERFECT. / SOUP OF MIXED EMOTIONS / FRUIT OF THE HEART** *(c+=)* – Perfect / Three orange kisses from Kazan / Nature of virtue / Fruit of the heart / Soup of mixed emotions / Waiting for the upturn. *(cd-iss. Jun87+=; CD 25525)* – Perfect. *(re-iss. Mar90 cd/c/lp; 466337-2/-4/-1) (cd re-iss. Apr02 +=; 504465-2)*

Nov 83. (7") *(A 3588)* **UNCERTAIN SMILE. / DUMB AS DEATH'S HEAD** [ ] [–]
(12") *(TA 3588)* – ('A'side) / Soul mining.

— guests for next album **ROLI MOSSIMAN / NENEH CHERRY / DAVID PALMER / STEVE HOGARTH / ANNA DOMINO / JAMIE TALBOT / WAYNE LIVESEY / ZEKE MANYIKA** / etc.

May 86. (12"m) *(TRUTH 1)* **SWEET BIRD OF TRUTH. / HARBOUR LIGHTS / SLEEPING JUICE** [ ] [–]

Jul 86. (7") *(TRUTH 2)* **HEARTLAND. / BORN IN THE NEW S.A.** [29] [–]
(12"+=) *(TRUTH T2)* – Flesh and bones.
(d12"++=) *(TRUTH D2)* – Perfect / Fruit of the heart.
(12"+=) *(TRUTH Q2)* – Sweet bird of truth.
(c-s++=) *(TRUTH C2)* – Harbour lights.

Oct 86. (7") *(TRUTH 3)* **INFECTED. / DISTURBED** [48] [ ]
(12"+=/12"uncensored+=) *(TRUTH T/Q 3)* – ('A'-energy mix).
(d12"++=) *(TRUTH D3)* – Soul mining (remix) / Sinking feeling.
(c-s+=) *(TRUTH C3)* – ('A'-Skull crusher mix) / Soul mining / Sinking feeling.

Nov 86. (lp/c/cd) *(EPC/40/CD 26770) <40471>* **INFECTED** [14] [89]
– Infected / Out of the blue (into the fire) / Heartland / Angels of deception / Sweet bird of truth / Slow train to dawn / Twilight of a champion / The mercy beat. *(cd+=)* – ('A'-INFECTED singles remixed) *(TA 3588) (cd re-iss. Apr02; 504466-2)*

Jan 87. (7") *(TENSE 1)* **SLOW TRAIN TO DAWN. / HARBOUR LIGHTS** [64] [ ]
(12"+=/12"w-stencil+=) *(TENSE T/D 3)* – The nature of virtue.

May 87. (7") *(TENSE 2)* **SWEET BIRD OF TRUTH. / SLEEPING JUICE** [55] [ ]
(12"+=) *(TENSE T2)* – Harbour lights.
(c-s++=)(cd-s++=) *(TENSE C2)(CDTHE 2)* – Soul mining (12"mix).

— THE THE were again a group when **MATT** with past session man **DAVID PALMER** – drums (ex-ABC) / recruited **JOHNNY MARR** – guitar (ex-SMITHS) / **JAMES ELLER** – bass (ex-JULIAN COPE)

Feb 89. (7") *(EMU 8)* **THE BEAT(EN) GENERATION. / ANGEL** [18] [ ]
(12"box+=/cd-s+=/3"cd-s+=) *(EMUB/EMUCD/CBEMU 8)* – Soul mining (mix).
(12"+=/pic-cd+=) *(EMUT/CPEMU 8)* – ('A'-Palmer mix) / ('A'-campfire mix).

May 89. (lp/c/cd) *(463319-1/-4/-2) <45241>* **MIND BOMB** [4] [ ]
– Good morning beautiful / Armageddon days are here (again) / The violence of truth / Kingdom of rain / The beat(en) generation / August & September / Gravitate to me / Beyond love. *(cd re-iss. Apr02; 504467-2)*

Jul 89. (7"/c-s) *(EMU/+C 9)* **GRAVITATE TO ME. / THE VIOLENCE OF TRUTH** [63] [ ]
(12"+=/cd-s+=) *(EMUT/CDEMU 9)* – I've been waiting for tomorrow (all of my life).
(etched-12") *(EMUE 9)* – ('A'dub) / I've been waiting for tomorrow.

Sep 89. (7"/c-s) *(EMU/+C 10)* **ARMAGEDDON DAYS ARE HERE (AGAIN). / ('A'orchestral)** [70] [ ]
(12"+=) *(EMUT 10)* – The nature of virtue / Perfect.
(cd-s+=) *(CDEMU 10)* – Perfect / Mental healing process.
(10"ep) *(EMUQT 10)* **THE THE V. THE WORLD EP** – ('A'side) / The nature of virtue / Perfect / Mental healing process.
(etched-12") *(EMUE 10)* – ('A'edit) / Perfect.

Feb 91. (12"/c-s) *(655 798-6/-4)* **JEALOUS OF YOUTH. / ANOTHER BOY DROWNING (live)** [54] [ ]
(cd-s+=) **SHADES OF YOUTH EP** *(655 796-8)* – Solitude / Dolphins.

— added **D.C. COLLARD** – instruments

Jan 93. (7"marble) *(658 457-7)* **DOGS OF LUST. / THE VIOLENCE OF TRUTH** [25] [ ]
(12"pic-d+=/cd-s+=) *(658 457-6/-2)* – Infected (live).
(cd-s) *(658 457-5)* – ('A'side) / Jealous of youth (live) / Beyond love (live) / Armageddon days are here (again) (D.N.A. remix).

Jan 93. (cd/c/lp) *(472468-2/-4/-1) <53164>* **DUSK** [2] [ ]
– True happiness this way lies / Love is stronger than death / Dogs of lust / This is the night / Slow emotion replay / Helpline operator / Sodium light baby / Lung shadows / Bluer than midnight / Lonely planet. *(cd re-iss. Apr02; 504468-2)*

Apr 93. (12"red-ep/cd-ep) *(659 077-6/-9)* **SLOW MOTION REPLAY. / DOGS OF LUST (3 mixes by Jim Thirlwell)** [35] [ ]
(cd-ep) *(659077-0)* – ('A'side) / Scenes from Active Twilight (parts I-V).

Jun 93. (12"ep/cd-ep) *(659 371-6/-2)* **LOVE IS STRONGER THAN DEATH. / THE SINKING FEELING (live) / THE MERCY BEAT (live) / ARMAGEDDON DAYS ARE HERE (AGAIN) (live)** [39] [ ]
(cd-ep) *(659 371-5)* – ('A'side) / Infected / Soul mining / Armageddon days are . . .

Jan 94. (c-ep/12"ep/cd-ep) *(659811-4/-6/-2)* **DIS-INFECTED EP** [17] [ ]
– This was the day / Dis-infected / Helpline operator (sick boy mix) / Dogs of lust (germicide mix).

Jan 95. (c-ep/10"ep/cd-ep) *(661091-0/-6/-9) <61119>* **I SAW THE LIGHT / I'M FREE AT LAST. / SOMEDAY YOU'LL CALL MY NAME / THERE'S NO ROOM IN MY HEART FOR THE BLUES** [31] Aug95 [ ]

Feb 95. (cd/c/10"lp) *(478139-2/-4/-0) <66908>* **HANKY PANKY** [28] [ ]
– Honky tonkin' / Six more miles / My heart would know / If you'll be a baby to me / I'm a long gone daddy / Weary blues from waitin' / I saw the light / Your cheatin' heart / I can't get you off of my mind / There's a tear in my beer / I can't escape from you.

Nothing – Interscope — Nothing – Interscope

Feb 00. (cd) *(<490510-2>)* **NAKEDSELF** [45] [ ]
– Boiling point / Shrunken man / The whisperers / Soul catcher / Global eyes / December sunlight / Swine fever / Diesel breeze / Weather belle / Voidy numbness / Phantom walls / Salt water.

Apr 00. (cd-ep) *(497273-2)* **THE SHRUNKENMAN EP** [ ] [–]
– Shrunken man / (mixes by DAAU / JOHN PARISH / FOETUS).

Jun 02. (cd-s) *(672855-2)* **PILLARBOX RED** [ ] [–]

– compilations, others, etc. –

Dec 88. (d-cd) *Epic; (CDTT 241)* **SOUL MINING / INFECTED** [ ] [–]

May 02. (d-cd) *Epic; (504469-2) / Sony; <86611>* **45 RPM – THE SINGLES OF . . .** [60] [ ]

Jul 02. (4xcd-box) *Epic; (507902-2)* **LONDON TOWN 1983-1993** [ ] [–]

THIN LIZZY

Formed: Dublin, Ireland . . . 1969 by PHIL LYNOTT and BRIAN DOWNEY together with ERIC BELL and ERIC WRIXON (the latter leaving after the first 45). After a debut single for 'Parlophone' Ireland, the group relocated to London in late 1970 at the suggestion of managers, Ted Carroll and Brian Tuite, having already signed to 'Decca'. 'THIN LIZZY' (1971) and 'SHADES OF A BLUE ORPHANAGE' (1972) passed without much notice, although the group scored a surprise one-off UK Top 10 with 'WHISKEY IN THE JAR'. A traditional Irish folk song, THIN LIZZY's highly original adaptation married plangent lead guitar and folk-rock arrangements to memorable effect. The accompanying album, 'VAGABONDS OF THE WESTERN WORLD' (1973), failed to capitalise on the song's success, although it gave an indication of where the band were headed with the hard-edged likes of 'THE ROCKER'. BELL departed later that year, his replacement being ex-SKID ROW axeman GARY MOORE, the first of many sojourns the guitarist would enjoy with 'LIZZY over the course of his turbulent career. He was gone by the Spring tour of the following year (subsequently joining COLOSSEUM II), the trademark twin guitar attack introduced on that tour courtesy of JOHN CANN and ANDY GEE. They were soon replaced more permanently by SCOTT GORHAM and BRIAN ROBERTSON, THIN LIZZY signing a new deal with 'Vertigo' and releasing the 'NIGHTLIFE' set in late '74. Neither that album nor 1975's 'FIGHTING' succeeded in realising the group's potential, although the latter gave them their first Top 60 entry on the album chart. Partly due to the group's blistering live shows and partly down to the massive success of 'THE BOYS ARE BACK IN TOWN', 'JAILBREAK' (1976) was a transatlantic Top 20 smash. One of the band's most consistent sets of their career, it veered from the power chord rumble and triumphant male bonding of 'THE BOYS . . .' to the epic Celtic clarion call of 'EMERALD'. The brooding, thuggish rifferama of the title track was another highlight, LYNOTT's rich, liquor-throated drawl sounding by turns threatening and conspiratorial. 'JOHNNY THE FOX' (1976) followed into the UK Top 20 later that year, a record which lacked the continuity of its predecessor but nevertheless spawned another emotive, visceral hard rock single in 'DON'T BELIEVE A WORD'. This is what marked THIN LIZZY out from the heavy-rock pack; LYNOTT's outlaw-with-a-broken-heart voice and the propulsive economy of the arrangements were light-years away from the warbling and posturing of 70's proto-metal. Accordingly, 'LIZZY were one of the few rock bands who gained any respect from punks and indeed, LYNOTT subsequently formed an extra curricular project with The DAMNED's RAT SCABIES as well as working with ex-SEX PISTOLS, PAUL COOK and STEVE JONES (as The GREEDIES on the Christmas 1980 single, 'A MERRY JINGLE'). A 1977 US tour saw MOORE fill in for ROBERTSON who'd injured his hand in a fight, although the Scots guitarist was back in place for a headlining spot at the 'Reading Festival' later that year. 'BAD REPUTATION' was released the following month, preceded by the R&B-flavoured 'DANCING IN THE MOONLIGHT' single and furnishing the group with their highest chart placing to date (UK Top 5). But it was through blistering live work that THIN LIZZY had made their name and they finally got around to releasing a concert set in 1978. 'LIVE AND DANGEROUS' remains deservedly revered as a career landmark, as vital, razor sharp and unrestrained as any live set in the history of rock. Later that summer, THIN LIZZY again took to the road with MOORE (ROBERTSON departed to form WILD HORSES) undertaking his third stint in the band alongside MARK NAUSEEF who was deputising for an absent DOWNEY. Previewed by the keening exhilaration of 'WAITING FOR AN ALIBI', the 'BLACK ROSE (A ROCK LEGEND)' (1979) set was the last great THIN LIZZY album. Placing all-out rockers alongside more traditionally influenced material, the set produced another two major UK hits in the defiant 'DO ANYTHING YOU WANT TO DO' and the poignant 'SARAH', a beautifully realised tribute to LYNOTT's baby daughter. MOORE, meanwhile, had been enjoying solo chart success with 'PARISIENNE WALKWAYS', the THIN LIZZY frontman guesting on vocals. By late '79, MOORE was out, however, and LYNOTT secured the unlikely services of another Scot, MIDGE URE, to fulfil touring commitments. When the latter subsequently departed to front ULTRAVOX, LYNOTT replaced him with ex-PINK FLOYD man, SNOWY WHITE. 1980 saw LYNOTT marrying Caroline Crowther (daughter of LESLIE) and releasing his first solo set, 'SOLO IN SOHO'. Although it hit the UK Top 30, the record sold poorly, a shame as it contained some of his most endearingly experimental work. The classic 'YELLOW PEARL' (co-written with URE) nevertheless scored a Top 20 placing and was later used as the theme tune for 'Top Of The Pops'. Later that year saw the release of 'CHINATOWN', the title track giving THIN LIZZY yet another hit. A further patchy album, 'RENEGADE' followed in late '81, THIN LIZZY's popularity clearly on the wane as it struggled to break the Top 40. With the addition of ex-TYGERS OF PAN TANG guitarist JOHN SYKES and keyboardist DARREN WHARTON, the group released something of a belated comeback album in 'THUNDER AND LIGHTNING' (1983). It was to be THIN LIZZY's swansong, however; by the release of live set, 'LIFE' (1983), the group had already split, LYNOTT and DOWNEY forming the short-lived GRAND SLAM. LYNOTT eventually carried on with his solo career (he'd previously released a second set, 'THE PHIL LYNOTT ALBUM' in 1982) in 1985, after settling his differences with MOORE. The pair recorded the driving 'OUT IN THE FIELDS', a UK Top 5 hit and a lesson in consummate heavy-rock for the hundreds of dismal 80's bands wielding a guitar and a poodle haircut. A follow-up single, '19', proved to be LYNOTT's parting shot, the Irishman dying from a drugs overdose on the 4th of January '86. As family, rock stars and wellwishers crowded into a small chapel in Southern Ireland for LYNOTT's low-key funeral, the rock world mourned the loss of one of its most talented, charismatic and much-loved figureheads. • **Songwriters:** PHIL LYNOTT and Co. and also covers of ROSALIE (Bob Seger) / I'M STILL IN LOVE WITH YOU (Frankie Miller).

Album rating: THIN LIZZY (*4) / SHADES OF A BLUE ORPHANAGE (*4) / VAGABONDS OF THE WESTERN WORLD (*5) / NIGHTLIFE (*5) / FIGHTING (*6) / JAILBREAK (*8) / JOHNNY THE FOX (*8) / BAD REPUTATION (*6) / LIVE AND DANGEROUS (*9) / BLACK ROSE – A ROCK LEGEND (*6) / CHINATOWN (*5) / ADVENTURES OF THIN LIZZY compilation (*8) / RENEGADE (*5) / THUNDER AND LIGHTNING (*7) / LIFE (*7) / DEDICATION – THE VERY BEST OF THIN LIZZY compilation (*8) / Phil Lynott: SOLO IN SOHO (*4) / THE PHIL LYNOTT ALBUM (*6) / THE BEST OF PHIL LYNOTT & THIN LIZZY – SOLDIER OF FORTUNE compilation (*7)

PHIL LYNOTT (b.20 Aug'51, from Brazillian + Irish parents. Raised from 3 by granny in Crumlin, Dublin) – vocals, bass (ex-ORPHANAGE, ex-SKID ROW brief) / **ERIC BELL** (b. 3 Sep'47, Belfast, N.Ireland) – guitar, vocals (ex-DREAMS) / **BRIAN DOWNEY** (b.27 Jan'51) – drums (ex-ORPHANAGE) / **ERIC WRIXON** – keyboards

		Parlophone	not iss.
1970.	(7"; as THIN LIZZIE) *<DIP 513>* **THE FARMER. / I NEED YOU**	– Ireland	–

—— now a trio (+ without WRIXON)

Decca London

Apr 71. (lp) *(SKL 5082)* *<594>* **THIN LIZZY** [ ] [ ]
– The friendly ranger at Clontarf Castle / Honesty is no excuse / Diddy Levine / Ray-gun / Look what the wind blew in / Eire / Return of the farmer's son / Clifton Grange Hotel / Saga of the ageing orphan / Remembering. *(cd-iss. Jan89 on 'Deram'+=; 820 528-2)* – Dublin / Remembering (part 2) / Old moon madness / Things ain't working out down at the farm.

Aug 71. (7"ep) *(F 13208)* **NEW DAY** [ ] [–]
– Things ain't working out down on the farm / Remembering pt.II / Old moon madness / Dublin.

Mar 72. (lp) *(TXS 108)* **SHADES OF A BLUE ORPHANAGE** [ ] [–]
– The rise and dear demise of the funky nomadic tribes / Buffalo gal / I don't want to forget how to jive / Sarah / Brought down / Baby face / Chatting today / Call the police / Shades of a blue orphanage. *(cd-iss. Nov88 on 'Deram'; 820 527-2)*

Nov 72. (7") *(F 13355)* *<20076>* **WHISKEY IN THE JAR. / BLACK BOYS IN THE CORNER** [6] [ ]

May 73. (7") *(F 13402)* *<20078>* **RANDOLPH'S TANGO. / BROKEN DREAMS** [ ] [ ]

Sep 73. (lp) *(SKL 5170)* *<636>* **VAGABONDS OF THE WESTERN WORLD** [ ] [ ]
– Mama nature said / The hero and the madman / Slow blues / The rocker / Vagabonds (of the western world) / Little girl in bloom / Gonna creep up on you / A song for while I'm away. *(cd-iss. May91 on 'Deram'+=; 820969-2)* – Whiskey in the jar / Black boys on the corner / Randolph's tango / Broken dreams.

Nov 73. (7") *(F 13467)* **THE ROCKER. / HERE I GO AGAIN** [ ] [–]

—— **GARY MOORE** (b. 4 Apr'52, Belfast) – guitar, vocals (ex-SKID ROW) repl. BELL (later MAINSQUEEZE)

Apr 74. (7") *(F 13507)* *<20082>* **LITTLE DARLIN'. / BUFFALO GIRL** [ ] [ ]

—— (on tour May'74) **JOHN CANN** – guitar (ex-ATOMIC ROOSTER, ex-BULLITT) / + **ANDY GEE** – guitar (ex-ELLIS) both repl. GARY MOORE who joined COLOSSEUM II. These temp. guitarists were deposed by **SCOTT GORHAM** (b.17 Mar'51, Santa Monica, Calif.) + **BRIAN ROBERTSON** (b.12 Sep'56, Glasgow, Scotland)

Vertigo Vertigo

Oct 74. (7") *(6059 111)* **PHILOMENA. / SHA LA LA** [ ] [–]

Nov 74. (lp) *(6360 116)* *<SRMI 1107>* **NIGHTLIFE** [ ] [ ]
– She knows / Night life / It's only money / Still in love with you / Frankie Carroll / Showdown / Banshee / Philomena / Sha-la-la / Dear heart. *(re-iss. Aug83 lp/c; PRICE/PRIMC 31) (cd-iss. Jun89; 838029-2)*

Jan 75. (7") *<202>* **SHOWDOWN. / NIGHT LIFE** [–] [ ]

Jun 75. (7") *(6059 124)* **ROSALIE. / HALF CASTE** [ ] [–]

Aug 75. (lp)(c) *(6360 121)(7138 070)* *<SRMI 1108>* **FIGHTING** [60] [ ]
– Rosalie / For those who love to live / Suicide / Wild one / Fighting my way back / King's vengeance / Spirit slips away / Silver dollar / Freedom song / Ballad of a hard man. *(re-iss. Aug83 lp/c; PRICE/PRIMC 32) (cd-iss. Jun89; 842433-2) (cd re-iss. Mar96 on 'Mercury'; 532296-2)*

Oct 75. (7") *(6059 129)* **WILD ONE. / FOR THOSE WHO LOVE TO DIE** [ ] [–]

Nov 75. (7") *<205>* **WILD ONE. / FREEDOM SONG** [–] [ ]

Vertigo Mercury

Mar 76. (lp)(c) *(9102 008)(7138 075)* *<SRMI 1081>* **JAILBREAK** [10] [18]
– Jailbreak / Angel from the coast / Running back / Romeo and the lonely girl / Warriors / The boys are back in town / Fight or fall / Cowboy song / Emerald. *(re-iss. Oct83 lp/c; PRICE/PRIMC 50) (cd-iss. Jun89; 822785-2) (cd re-iss. Mar96 on 'Mercury'; 532294-2)*

Apr 76. (7") *(6059 139)* **THE BOYS ARE BACK IN TOWN. / EMERALD** [8] [–]

Apr 76. (7") *<73786>* **THE BOYS ARE BACK IN TOWN. / JAILBREAK** [–] [12]

Jul 76. (7") *(6059 150)* **JAILBREAK. / RUNNING BACK** [31] [–]

Sep 76. (7") *<73841>* **THE COWBOY SONG. / ANGEL FROM THE COAST** [–] [77]

Oct 76. (lp)(c) *(9102 012)(7138 082)* *<SRMI 1119>* **JOHNNY THE FOX** [11] [52]
– Johnny / Rocky / Borderline / Don't believe a word / Fools gold / Johnny the fox meets Jimmy the weed / Old flame / Massacre / Sweet Marie / Boogie woogie dance. *(re-iss. May83 lp/c; PRICE/PRIMC 11) (cd-iss. May90; 822687-2) (cd re-iss. Mar96 on 'Mercury'; 532295-2)*

Nov 76. (7") *<73867>* **ROCKY. / HALF-CASTE** [–] [ ]

Jan 77. (7") *(LIZZY 1)* **DON'T BELIEVE A WORD. / OLD FLAME** [12] [–]

Jan 77. (7") *<73882>* **JOHNNY THE FOX MEETS JIMMY THE WEED. / OLD FLAME** [–] [ ]

—— BRIAN ROBERTSON became injured, GARY MOORE deputised (on 6 mths. tour only)

Aug 77. (7") *(6059 177)* *<73945>* **DANCING IN THE MOONLIGHT. / BAD REPUTATION** [14] [ ]

Sep 77. (lp)(c) *(9102 016)(7231 011)* *<SRMI 1186>* **BAD REPUTATION** [4] [39]
– Soldier of fortune / Bad reputation / Opium trail / Southbound / Dancing in the moonlight (it's caught me in its spotlight) / Killer without a cause / Downtown sundown / That woman's gonna break your heart / Dear Lord. *(re-iss. May83 lp/c; PRICE/PRIMC 12) (cd-iss. Apr90; 842434-2) (cd re-iss. Mar96 on 'Mercury'; 532298-2)*

Apr 78. (7") *(LIZZY 2)* **ROSALIE; COWBOY'S SONG (live medley). / ME AND THE BOYS** [20] [–]

Vertigo Warners

Jun 78. (d-lp) *(9199 645)* *<3213>* **LIVE AND DANGEROUS (live)** [2] [84]
– Jailbreak / Emerald / South bound / Rosalie – Cowgirls' song / Dancing in the moonlight (it's caught me in its spotlight) / Massacre / Still in love with you / Johnny the fox meets Jimmy the weed / Cowboy song / The boys are back in town / Don't believe a word / Warriors / Are you ready / Suicide / Sha la la / Baby drives me crazy / The rocker. *(re-iss. Nov84; d-lp/d-c; PRID/+C 6) (cd-iss. Jun89; 838030-2) (cd re-iss. Mar96 on 'Mercury'; 532297-2)*

Jul 78. (7") *<8648>* **COWBOY SONG. / JOHNNY THE FOX (MEETS JIMMY THE WEED)** [–] [ ]

—— In Autumn'78 tour, DOWNEY was deputised by MARK NAUSEEF. **GARY MOORE** – guitar, vocals returned to repl. ROBERTSON who formed WILD HORSES

Feb 79. (7") *(LIZZY 3)* **WAITING FOR AN ALIBI. / WITH LOVE** [9] [–]

Apr 79. (lp/c) *(9102/7231 032)* *<3338>* **BLACK ROSE (A ROCK LEGEND)** [2] [81]
– Do anything you want to / Toughest street in town / S & M / Waiting for an alibi / Sarah / Got to give it up / Get out of here / With love / A roisin dubh (Black rose) A rock legend part 1. Shenandoah – part 2. Will you go lassy go – part 3. Danny boy – part 4. The mason's apron. *(re-iss. Sep86 lp/c; PRICE/PRIMC 90) (cd-iss. Jun89; 830392-2) (cd re-iss. Mar96 on 'Mercury'; 532299-2)*

—— Apr'79, LYNOTT's vox feat. on GARY MOORE's Top 10 hit 'Parisienne Walkways'.

Jun 79. (7") *(LIZZY 4)* **DO ANYTHING YOU WANT TO. / JUST THE TWO OF US** [14] [–]

Jun 79. (7") *<49019>* **DO ANYTHING YOU WANT TO. / S & M** [–] [ ]

Sep 79. (7") *(LIZZY 5)* **SARAH. / GOT TO GIVE IT UP** [24] [–]

Sep 79. (7") *<49078>* **WITH LOVE. / GO TO GIVE IT UP** [–] [ ]

—— (for 2 months-late'79) **MIDGE URE** (b. JAMES URE, 10 Oct'53, Glasgow) – guitar (ex-SLIK, ex-RICH KIDS) repl. GARY MOORE who went solo. URE joined ULTRAVOX when repl. by **SNOWY WHITE**

May 80. (7") *(LIZZY 6)* **CHINATOWN. / SUGAR BLUES** [21] [–]

Sep 80. (7") *(LIZZY 7)* **KILLER ON THE LOOSE. / DON'T PLAY AROUND** [10] [–]
(d7"+=) *(LIZZY 7/+701)* – Got to give it up (live) / Chinatown (live).

Oct 80. (lp/c) *(6359/7150 030)* *<3496>* **CHINATOWN** [7] [ ]
– We will be strong / Chinatown / Sweetheart / Sugar blues / Killer on the loose / Having a good time / Genocide (the killing of buffalo) / Didn't I / Hey you. *(re-is.Sep86, cd-iss. Jun89)*

Oct 80. (7") *<49643>* **KILLER ON THE LOOSE. / SUGAR BLUES** [–] [ ]

Nov 80. (7"; as The GREEDIES) *(GREED 1)* **A MERRY JINGLE. / A MERRY JANGLE** [28] [–]
above also featured STEVE JONES + PAUL COOK (ex-SEX PISTOLS)

Feb 81. (7") *<49679>* **WE WILL BE STRONG. / SWEETHEART** [–] [ ]

Apr 81. (7"ep/12"ep) *(LIZZY 8/+12)* **LIVE KILLERS (live)** [19] [–]
– Are you ready / Opium trail / Dear Miss lonely heart / Bad reputation.

Jul 81. (7") *(LIZZY 9)* **TROUBLE BOYS. / MEMORY PAIN** [53] [–]

Nov 81. (lp/c) *(6359/7150 083)* *<3622>* **RENEGADE** [38] [ ]
– Angel of death / Renegade / The pressure will blow / Leave this town / Hollywood (down on your luck) / No one told him / Fats / Mexican blood / It's getting dangerous. *(cd-iss. Jun90; 842435-2)*

Feb 82. (7"/7"pic-d) *(LIZZY/+PD 10)* *<50056>* **HOLLYWOOD (DOWN ON YOUR LUCK). / THE PRESSURE WILL BLOW** [53] [ ]
(10"one-sided) *(LIZZY 10)* – ('A'side only)

— **LYNOTT + DOWNEY** recruited new members **JOHN SYKES** – guitar (ex-TYGERS OF PAN TANG) repl. GORHAM **DARREN WHARTON** – keyboards repl. SNOWY WHITE went solo + re-joined PINK FLOYD

Feb 83. (d7"/12") *(LIZZY 11 11-12/22)* **COLD SWEAT. / BAD HABITS / DON'T BELIEVE A WORD (live). / ANGEL OF DEATH (live)** [27] [–]

Mar 83. (lp/c) *(VERL/+C 3) <23831>* **THUNDER AND LIGHTNING** [4] [ ]
– Thunder and lightning / This is the one / The sun goes down / The holy war / Cold sweat / Someday she is going to hit back / Baby please don't go / Bad habits / Heart attack. *(initial copies with free live 12")* – EMERALD / KILLER ON THE LOOSE. / THE BOYS ARE BACK IN TOWN / HOLLYWOOD *(cd-iss. Jun89; 810490-2)*

Apr 83. (7"/12") *(LIZZY 12/+12)* **THUNDER AND LIGHTNING. / STILL IN LOVE WITH YOU (live)** [39] [–]

Jul 83. (7") *(LIZZY 13)* **THE SUN GOES DOWN (remix). / BABY PLEASE DON'T GO** [52] [–]
(12"+=) *(LIZZY 13/+12)* – ('A'remix).

Nov 83. (d-lp/d-c) *(VERD/+C 6) <23986>* **LIFE (live)** [29] [ ]
– Thunder & lightning / Waiting for an alibi / Jailbreak / Baby please don't go / The holy war / Renegade / Hollywood / Got to give it up / Angel of death / Are you ready / Boys are back in town / Cold sweat / Don't believe a word / Killer on the loose / The sun goes down / Emerald / Roisin dubh (Black rose) A rock legend part 1. Shenandoah – part 2. Will you go lassy go – part 3. Danny boy – part 4. The mason's apron / Still in love with you / The rocker. *(4th side featured past members) (cd-iss. Aug90; 812882-2)*

— Had already concluded proceedings. LYNOTT and DOWNEY formed short-lived GRAND SLAM. Tragically, PHIL LYNOTT died of heart failure due to drugs o.d. on the 4th January '86.

– compilations, others –

Aug 76. (lp/c) *Decca; (SKL/KSKC 5249)* **REMEMBERING – PART ONE** [ ] [–]

Jan 78. (7"m) *Decca; (F 13748)* **WHISKEY IN THE JAR. / SITAMOIA / VAGABOND OF THE WESTERN WORLD** [ ] [–]

Aug 79. (7"m) *Decca; (THIN 1)* **THINGS AIN'T WORKING OUT DOWN ON THE FARM. / THE ROCKER / LITTLE DARLIN'** [ ] [–]

Sep 79. (lp) *Decca; (SKL 5298)* **THE CONTINUING SAGA OF THE AGEING ORPHANS** [ ] [–]

Apr 81. (lp/c) *Vertigo; (LIZ TV/MC 001)* **ADVENTURES OF THIN LIZZY** [6] [–]
– Whiskey in the jar / Wild one / Jailbreak / The boys are back in town / Don't believe a word / Dancing in the moonlight / Waiting for an alibi / Do anything you want to / Sarah / Chinatown / Killer on the loose.

Dec 81. (lp/c) *Decca; (KTBC/TAB 28)* **ROCKERS** [ ] [–]
(re-iss. Oct93 on 'Deram' cd/c; 820 526-2/-4)

Mar 83. (cd) *Vertigo; (800 060-2)* **LIZZY KILLERS** [ ] [–]

Oct 83. (7") *Old Gold; (OG 9330)* **WHISKEY IN THE JAR. / THE ROCKER** [ ] [–]

Nov 83. (lp/c) *Contour; (CN/+4 2066)* **THE BOYS ARE BACK IN TOWN** [ ] [–]

Jan 85. (7") *Old Gold; (OG 9484)* **DANCING IN THE MOONLIGHT. / DON'T BELIEVE A WORD** [ ] [–]

Nov 85. (d-lp/c) *Castle; (CCS LP/MC 117)* **THE COLLECTION** [ ] [–]
(cd-iss. Jul87; CCSCD 117)

Nov 85. (lp/c) *Karussel Gold; (822694-1/-4)* **WHISKEY IN THE JAR** [ ] [–]

Apr 86. (lp/c) *Contour; (CN/+4 2080)* **WHISKEY IN THE JAR** [ ] [–]

Aug 86. (12"ep) *Archive 4;* **WHISKEY IN THE JAR / THE ROCKER. / SARAH / BLACK BOYS ON THE CORNER** [ ] [–]

Nov 87. (lp/c/cd) *Telstar; (STAR/STAC/TCD 2300)* **THE BEST OF PHIL LYNOTT & THIN LIZZY – SOLDIER OF FORTUNE** [55] [–]
– Whiskey in the jar / Waiting for an alibi / Sarah / Parisieene walkways / Do anything you want to / Yellow pearl / Chinatown / King's call / The boys are back in town / Rosalie (cowboy's song) / Dancing in the moonlight / Don't believe a word / Jailbreak. *(cd+=)* – Out in the fields / Killer on the loose / Still in love with you.

Feb 88. (7") *Old Gold; (OG 9764)* **THE BOYS ARE BACK IN TOWN. / ('B'by Bachman-Turner Overdrive)** [ ] [–]

Jun 89. (lp) *Grand Slam; <SLAM 4>* **LIZZY LIVES (1976-84)** [–] [ ]

Jan 91. (7"/c-s) *Vertigo; (LIZZY/LIZMC 14)* **DEDICATION. / COLD SWEAT** [35] [–]
(12"+=/cd-s+=) *(LIZZY1/LIZCD 14)* – Emerald (live) / Still in love with you.
(12"pic-d+=) *(LIZP1 14)* – Bad reputation / China town.

Feb 91. (cd/c/lp) *Vertigo; (848 192-2/-4/-1)* **DEDICATION – THE VERY BEST OF THIN LIZZY** [8] [–]
– Whiskey in the jar / The boys are back in town / Jailbreak / Don't believe a word / Dancing in the moonlight / Rosalie – Cowgirl song (live) / Waiting for an alibi / Do anything you want to / Parisienne walkways (with GARY MOORE) / The rocker / Killer on the loose / Sarah / Out in the fields (with GARY MOORE) / Dedication. *(cd+=/c+=)* – Still in love with you (live) / Bad reputation / Emerald / Chinatown.

Mar 91. (7"/c-s) *Vertigo; (LIZZY/LIZMC 15)* **THE BOYS ARE BACK IN TOWN. / SARAH** [63] [–]
(12"/cd-s) *(LIZZY1/LIZCD 15)* – ('A'side) / Johnny the fox / Black boys on the corner / Me and the boys.

Oct 92. (cd) *Windsong; (WINCD 024)* **BBC RADIO 1 LIVE IN CONCERT** [ ] [–]

Nov 94. (cd/c) *Strange Fruit; (SFR CD/MC 130)* **THE PEEL SESSIONS** [ ] [–]

Jan 96. (cd/c) *Polygram; (528113-2/-4)* **WILD ONE – THE VERY BEST OF THIN LIZZY** [18] [–]

Mar 96. (cd) *Spectrum; (552085-2/-4)* **WHISKEY IN THE JAR** [ ] [–]

Jan 00. (cd) *Universal; (E 844945-2)* **UNIVERSAL MASTERS COLLECTION** [ ] [ ]

Jun 00. (cd) *S.P.V.; (SPV 085-2199-2)* **ONE NIGHT ONLY** [ ] [–]

PHIL LYNOTT

(solo) with THIN LIZZY members

Vertigo Warners

Mar 80. (7"/12") *(SOLO 1/+12)* **DEAR MISS LONELY HEARTS. / SOLO IN SOHO** [32] [–]

Apr 80. (lp)(pic-lp) *(9102 038)(PHIL 1) <3405>* **SOLO IN SOHO** [28] [ ]
– Dear Miss lonely hearts / King's call / A child's lullaby / Tattoo / Solo in Soho / Girls / Yellow pearl / Ode to a black man / Jamaican rum / Talk in '79. *(re-iss. Sep85 lp'c; PRICE/PRIMC 88) (cd-iss. Jul90; 842564-2)*

Jun 80. (7") *(SOLO 2) <49272>* **KING'S CALL. / ODE TO A BLACK MAN** [35] [ ]

Mar 81. (7"yellow) *(SOLO 3)* **YELLOW PEARL. / GIRLS** [56] [–]
(re-iss. Dec81 – 12"; SOLO 3-12)
(above was later the TV theme for 'Top Of The Pops')

Aug 82. (7") *(SOLO 4)* **TOGETHER. / SOMEBODY ELSE'S DREAM** [ ] [–]
(12"+=) *(SOLO 4-12)* – ('A'dance version).

Sep 82. (7") *(SOLO 5)* **OLD TOWN. / BEAT OF THE DRUM** [ ] [–]

Oct 82. (lp/c) *(6359/7150 117)* **THE PHIL LYNOTT ALBUM** [ ] [–]
– Fatalistic attitude / The man's a fool / Old town / Cathleen / Growing up / Together / Little bit of water / Ode to Liberty (the protest song) / Gino / Don't talk about me baby. *(cd-iss. Jul90; 842564-2)*

— May'85, GARY MOORE & PHIL hit UK Top 5 with 'OUT IN THE FIELDS'.

Polydor not iss.

Nov 85. (7") *(POSP 777)* **19. / 19 (dub)** [ ] [–]
(12"+=) *(POSPX 777)* – A day in the life of a blues singer.
(d7"+=; 1 pic-d) *(POSPD 777)* – THIN LIZZY; Whiskey in the jar – The rocker.

– (PHIL LYNOTT) posthumous –

Jan 87. (7") *Vertigo; (LYN 1)* **KING'S CALL. / YELLOW PEARL** [68] [–]
(12"+=) *(LYN 1-12)* – Dear Miss lonely hearts (live).

THIRD EYE BLIND

Formed: San Francisco, California, USA . . . mid-90's by frontman, STEPHAN JENKINS (JASON SLATER, future SNAKE RIVER CONSPIRACY mainman was also a member during TEB's early inception). After supporting OASIS in their home city, TEB signed a lucrative deal with 'Elektra' for whom they delivered their first US Top 5 hit, 'SEMI-CHARMED LIFE'. That Spring of '97 also saw the band gain massive sales for their eponymous debut set which also climbed into the Top 30. Musically, they were nothing startling or adventurous (lying inbetween STEVE MILLER and the SPIN DOCTORS), although classy acoustic alt-rock/pop tunes did help the band achieve some kind of steady fanbase. Sophomore set, 'BLUE' (1999), was another to hit the US Top 40, it sales helped no doubt by the success of single, 'NEVER LET YOU GO', the following year. Their first album since the departure of guitarist/songwriter CADOGAN, 'OUT OF THE VEIN' (2003) showcased a band struggling to replicate the kind of immediacy which had characterised the best of their work thus far. That said, JENKINS sounded as vehement as ever in his pursuit of grandiloquent rock greatness, even if he didn't have the songs to go with the voice.

Album rating: THIRD EYE BLIND (*6) / BLUE (*5) / OUT OF THE VEIN (*5)

STEPHAN JENKINS – vocals, guitar / **KEVIN CADOGAN** – guitar / **REN KLYCE** – keyboards / **ARION SALAZAR** – bass, keyboards

Elektra Elektra

Jun 97. (c-s) *(E 4181C)* *<64137>* **SEMI-CHARMED LIFE. / TATTOO OF THE SUN** [ ] Mar97 [4]
(cd-s+=) *(E 4181CD)* – London.

Jun 97. (cd/c) *<(7559 62012-2/-4)>* **THIRD EYE BLIND** [ ] Apr97 [25]
– Losing a whole year / Narcolepsy / Semi-charmed life / Jumper / Graduate / How's it going to be / Thanks a lot / Burning man / Good for you / London / I want you / Background / Motorcycle drive-by / God of wine.

Sep 97. (7"/c-s) *(E 3907/+C)* **SEMI-CHARMED LIFE. / TATTOO OF THE SUN** [33] [–]
(cd-s+=) *(E 3907CD)* – London.
(re-iss. May98; same)

Nov 97. (7") *(E 3883)* **GRADUATE. / HORROR SHOW** [ ] [ ]
(c-s+=/cd-s+=) *(E 3883 C/CD)* – ('A'remix).

Mar 98. (c-s/cd-s) *(E 3863 C/CD)* *<64130>* **HOW'S IT GOING TO BE / SEMI-CHARMED LIFE / HORROR SHOW** [51] Nov97 [9]

Jul 98. (7") *(E 3832)* **LOSING A WHOLE YEAR. / HORROR SHOW** [ ] [ ]
(cd-s+=) *(E 3832CD)* – Graduate (remix).

Nov 98. (cd-s) *<64058>* **JUMPER / GRADUATE (remix)** [–] [5]

May 00. (cd/c) *<(7559 62415-2/-4)>* **BLUE** [ ] Nov99 [40]
– Anything / Wounded / 10 days late / Never let you go / Deep inside of you / 1000 Julys / Ode to maybe / Red summer sun / Camouflage / Farther / Slow motion / Darkness / Darwin.

Jun 00. (c-s/cd-s) *(E 7050 C/CD)* *<album cut>* **NEVER LET YOU GO / NEVER LET YOU GO (version) / ANYTHING** [ ] Jan00 [14]

Jul 00. (-) *<radio play>* **DEEP INSIDE OF YOU** [–] [69]

— **TONY FREDIANELLI** – guitar; repl. CADOGAN

Jul 03. (cd) *<(7559 62888-2)>* **OUT OF THE VEIN** [ ] May03 [12]
– Faster / Blinded / Forget myself / Danger / Crystal baller / My hit and run / Misfits / Can't get away / Wake for young souls / Palm reader / Self righteous / Company / Good man.

13th FLOOR ELEVATORS

Formed: Austin, Texas, USA . . . 1965 by ROKY ERICKSON and TOMMY HALL, together with STACY SUTHERLAND, BENNY THURMAN and JOHN IKE WALTON. ERICKSON had originally written and recorded 'YOU'RE GONNA MISS ME' with his first band, The SPADES, the single being released on the small 'Zero' label. A local hit, the record gained national notoriety in early '66 after being picked up by the 'International Artists' label. Around this time, self-styled psychedelic explorer, TOMMY HALL, had introduced ERICKSON to the aforementioned musicians (all three were ex-LINGSMEN) and The 13th FLOOR ELEVATORS were launched into orbit. The frenzied garage thrash of 'YOU'RE GONNA MISS ME' stood out from the pack by dint of ERICKSON's apocalyptic vocal threats and HALL's bizarre amplified jug playing. In addition to his idiosyncratic musical accompaniment, HALL penned most of the lyrics, setting out his agenda according to the chemically-enhanced evolution-of-man ethos espoused by the likes of acid guru, TIM LEARY. Debuting with 'THE PSYCHEDELIC SOUNDS OF THE 13TH FLOOR ELEVATORS' in 1966, the band had unleashed nothing less than a musical manifesto for mind expansion. But if the idea was to promote the use of halucinogenics, then the sirens on the DMT-tribute, 'FIRE ENGINE', surely encouraged any sane person never to go near the stuff, sounding more like the tortured wailing of lost, limbo-locked souls. Likewise 'MONKEY ISLAND', with ERICKSON howling like a man possessed. Elsewhere on the album, tracks like 'ROLLERCOASTER' and 'REVERBERATION (DOUBT)' made for thrilling, if uneasy listening, and it was obvious that a trip to the 13th floor with ROCKY and Co. was somewhat different from the rosy hue that the psychedelic experience had taken on in popular mythology. The follow-up, 'EASTER EVERYWHERE' (1967), was a slightly more contemplative affair, opening with the hypnotic brilliance of 'SLIP INSIDE THIS HOUSE' (the subject of an equally essential 90's interpretation by PRIMAL SCREAM) through the trippy 'SHE LIVES (IN A TIME OF HER OWN)' and on to the frantic 'LEVITATION'. Inevitably, the Texan police were none too amused with the band's flagrant advocacy of drugs and after escalating harassment, ERICKSON found himself in court shortly after the album's release. Charged with possession of a small amount of hashish, he was faced with a choice of jail or mental hospital and rather illadvisedly chose the latter. This effectively signalled the end for the band, although a disappointing live album was released the following year and a final studio album appeared in 1969. 'BULL OF THE WOODS' was made up largely of SUTHERLAND-penned tunes although it contained the sublime 'MAY THE CIRCLE REMAIN UNBROKEN', ERICKSON's vocal all the more haunting in light of his tragic incarceration. Subjected to years of mind-numbing drugs and electro shock therapy, ROCKY was finally released in 1972 after a judge declared him sane. Ironically no doubt somewhat less sane after this experience, ERICKSON started making music again, forming a band, BLIWB ALIEN, and immersing himself in B-movie horror nonsense. After a stint in the studio with fellow Texan, DOUG SAHM, of SIR DOUGLAS QUINTET fame, ERICKSON released the inspired psychosis of the 'RED TEMPLE PRAYER (TWO HEADED DOG)' single in 1975. An album, 'ROCKY ERICKSON AND THE ALIENS' surfaced in 1980 and included such wholesome fare as 'DON'T SHAKE ME LUCIFER', 'CREATURE WITH THE ATOM BRAIN' and 'STAND FOR THE FIRE DEMON'. Yet this was no po-faced heavy-metal posturing, ERICKSON actually believed what he was singing about, lending the record a certain level of intensity, despite the cliched hard rock backing. A series of singles and compilations appeared sporadically throughout the 80's, and after ERICKSON was hospitalised again for a short period, 'Warner Bros.' executive and longtime ELEVATORS fan, BILL BENTLEY, masterminded a tribute album, 'Where The Pyramid Meets The Eye', featuring the likes of The JESUS AND MARY CHAIN and JULIAN COPE. Although a collection of early material, 'ALL THAT MAY DO MY RHYME', appeared in 1975 on The BUTTHOLE SURFERS' 'Trance Syndicate' label, ERICKSON appears to have no interest in writing new material. Music biz legend paints the man as an acid casualty, and while he definitely appears to live in a world of his own making, his wayward genius continues to win the respect and admiration of fans the world over.

• **Songwriters:** ERICKSON penned except; I'M GONNA LOVE YOU TOO (Buddy Holly) / HEROIN (Velvet Underground) / BLOWIN' IN THE WIND (Bob Dylan) / etc.

Album rating: THE PSYCHEDELIC SOUNDS OF (*7) / EASTER EVERYWHERE (*6) / LIVE exploitation (*4) / BULL OF THE WOODS exploitation (*5) / THE BEST OF THE 13th FLOOR ELEVATORS compilation (*7) / HIS EYE IS ON THE PYRAMID compilation (*8) / Roky Erickson: ROKY ERICKSON & THE ALIENS (*6) / THE EVIL ONE (*5) / CLEAR NIGHT FOR LOVE mini (*4) / GREMLINS HAVE PICTURES (*4) / DON'T SLANDER ME (*5) / CASTING THE RUNES collection (*4) / THE HOLIDAY INN TAPES fan-club (*4) / OPENERS exploitation (*4) / LIVE AT THE RITZ (*4) / YOU'RE GONNA MISS ME: THE BEST OF ROKY ERICKSON compilation (*7) / MAD DOG compilation (*4) / ALL THAT MAY DO MY RHYME (*6) / NEVER SAY GOODBYE (*7)

The SPADES

— (had already recorded a single 'I NEED A GIRL', before ROKY joined)

— **ROKY ERICKSON** (b. ROGER KYNARD ERICKSON, 15 Jul'47, Dallas, Texas) – vocals, harmonica / **JOHN KERNEY** – guitar, vocals

not iss. Zero

1965. (7") *<10002>* **YOU'RE GONNA MISS ME. / WE SELL SOUL**

13th FLOOR ELEVATORS

— were formed by **ROKY** and **STACEY SUTHERLAND** – lead guitar (ex-LINGSMEN) / **BENNY THURMAN** – bass, electric violin (ex-LINGSMEN) / **JOHN IKE WALTON** – drums (ex-LINGMEN) / **TOMMY HALL** – blow jug, lyrics

not iss. Contact

Jan 66. (7") *<5269>* **YOU'RE GONNA MISS ME. / TRIED TO HIDE**
<re-iss. Apr66 on 'Hanna Barbara'; HBR 492> <re-iss. Jun66 on 'International Artists'; 107>; hit No.55> (UK-iss.Nov78 on 'Radar' 7"green; ADA 13)

— **RONNIE LEATHERMAN** – bass repl. BENNY who formed PLUM NELLY

not iss. Int.Artists

Aug 66. (lp) *<IALP 1>* **THE PSYCHEDELIC SOUNDS OF**
– You're gonna miss me / Roller coaster / Splash 1 / Don't fall down / Reverberation (doubt) / Fire engine / Thru the rhythm / You don't know / Kingdom of Heaven / Monkey island / Tried to hide. *<re-iss. 1977; same> (UK-iss.Nov78 on 'Radar'; RAD 13) (re-iss. Feb88 on 'Decal'; LIK 19) (cd-iss. 1990's on 'Decal-Charly'; CDGR 110) (cd re-iss. Jan99 on 'Spalax'; 14819) (lp re-iss. Nov99; same as US)*

Oct 66. (7") *<111>* **REVERBERATION (DOUBT). / FIRE ENGINE**

— **DAN GALINDO** – bass + **DANNY THOMAS** – drums repl. RONNIE + JOHN IKE

Feb 67. (7") *<113>* **I'VE GOT LEVITATION. / BEFORE YOU ACCUSE ME**

Apr 67. (lp) *<IALP 5>* **EASTER EVERYWHERE**
– Slip inside the house / Slide machine / She lives in a time of her own / Nobody to love / It's all over now, baby blue / Earthquake / Dust / I've got levitation / I had to tell you / Postures (leave your body behind). *<re-iss. 1977; same> (UK-iss.May79 on 'Radar'; RAD 15) (re-iss. Apr88 on 'Decal'; LIK 28) (cd-iss. Jan99 on 'Spalax'; 14888) (lp re-iss. May99; same as US)*

Oct 67. (7") *<121>* **SHE LIVES (IN A TIME OF HER OWN). / BABY BLUE**

Dec 67. (7") *<122>* **SLIP INSIDE THIS HOUSE. / SPLASH 1**

— Disbanded early '68, due to ROKY being imprisoned for possession of a miniscule amount of hash. He once escaped but was then kept there for another 3 years, and suffered thorazine plus electric shock treatment. **DUKE DAVIS** – bass had briefly repl. GALINDO. DANNY THOMAS and DUKE were to become The GOLDEN DAWN. The original 13th FLOOR ELEVATORS reformed in 1972. In 1984, they gigged again with line-up (ERICKSON, WALTON, LEATHERMAN and GREG 'Catfish' FORREST-guitar). In Autumn 1978, STACEY was shot dead by his wife.

– others, compilations, etc. –

on 'International Artists' unless otherwise mentioned

1968. (lp) *<IALP 8>* **LIVE** (studio out-takes, b-sides, demos; with false applause)
– Before you accuse me / She lives in a time of her own / Tried to hide / You gotta take that girl / I'm gonna love you too / Everybody needs somebody to love / I've got levitation / You can't hurt me anymore / Roller coaster / You're gonna miss me. *(UK-iss.May88 on 'Decal'; LIK 30)*

1968. (7") *<126>* **MAY THE CIRCLE BE UNBROKEN. / I'M GONNA LOVE YOU TOO**

1969. (lp) *<IALP 9>* **BULL OF THE WOODS** (rec. early'68)
– Livin' on / Barnyard blues / Till then / Never another / Rose and the thorn / Down by the river / Scarlet and gold / Street song / Doctor Boom / With you / May the circle remain unbroken. *(UK-iss.Jul88 on 'Decal'; LIK 40) (cd-iss. Jan99 on 'Spalax'; 14886) (lp re-iss. Aug99; same as US)*

1969. (7") *<130>* **LIVIN' ON. / SCARLET AND GOLD**

Oct 78. (7"ep) *Austin; <RE 1>* **YOU REALLY GOT ME. / WORD / ROLL OVER BEETHOVEN**

1985. (lp) *Texas Archives; <TAR LP-4>* **FIRE IN MY BONES**

1987. (lp) *Texas Archives; <TAR LP-7>* **ELEVATOR TRACKS (some live 1966)**

1988. (lp) *Big Beat; (WIK 82)* **I'VE SEEN YOUR FACE BEFORE** (live bootleg '66)
(cd-iss. Jun89; CDWIK 82)

1988. (lp) *13th Hour; <(13-LP-1)>* **DEMOS EVERYWHERE**
(US-title 'THE ORIGINAL SOUND OF . . .')

Nov 88. (cd) *Charly; (CDCHARLY 150)* **EASTER EVERYWHERE / BULL OF THE WOODS**

Jun 89. (cd) *Charly; (CDCHARLY 159)* **THE PSYCHEDELIC SOUNDS OF / LIVE**

Aug 91. (4xcd-box) *Decal; (LIKBOX 2)* **THE COLLECTION**
– (all 1960's albums)
<In 1979, these appeared on a 12-lp box of 'International Artists')

Jul 93. (cd) *Thunderbolt; (CDTB 124)* **OUT OF ORDER (LIVE AT THE AVALON BALLROOM)**

Jun 94. (cd) *Thunderbolt; (CDTB 147)* **LEVITATION – IN CONCERT (live)**

Apr 95. (cd) *Thunderbolt; (CDTB 153)* **THE REUNION CONCERT**

Dec 95. (cd) *Nectar; (NTMCD 516)* **THE BEST OF THE 13th FLOOR ELEVATORS**
– You're gonna miss me / Levitation / I had to tell you / She lives (in a time of her own) / Never another / I'm gonna love you too (live) / Thry the rhythm / The kingdom of Heaven / Slip inside this house / Monkey island / Splash 1 / Fire engine / Dr. Doom / Roller coaster / Earthquake / Reverberation (doubt) / May the circle remain unbroken / You're gonna miss me (live). *(re-iss. Jul99 on 'Eva'; 642370)*

Sep 96. (cd) *Thunderbolt; (CDTB 508)* **THE INTERPRETER**
(re-iss. Jun99; CDTB 198)

Nov 97. (cd) *Music Club; (MCCD 324)* **ALL TIME HIGHS**

Nov 97. (cd) *Eagle; (EAGCD 069)* **THE MASTERS**

Oct 99. (cd) *Thunderbolt; (CDTB 199)* **THE INTERPRETER VOL.2**

Nov 99. (d-cd) *Recall; (SMDCD 190)* **HIS EYE IS ON THE PYRAMID**

ROKY ERICKSON

not iss. Mars

1975. (7"; with BLIEB ALIEN) *<1000>* **RED TEMPLE PRAYER (TWO HEADED DOG). / STARRY EYES**

Virgin Rhino

Sep 77. (7") *(VS 180) <003>* **BERMUDA. / INTERPRETER**

Sponge not iss.

Dec 77. (7"ep) *(101)* **TWO HEADED DOG / I HAVE ALWAYS BEEN HERE BEFORE. / MINE, MINE, MIND / CLICK YOUR FINGERS APPLAUDING THE PLAY** France

ROKY ERICKSON AND THE ALIENS

— with **DUANE ASLAKSEN** – guitar / **STEVE BURGESS** – bass / **ANDRE LEWIS** – keyboards / **FUZZY FURIOSO** – drums / **BILL MILLER** – autoharp

C.B.S. not iss.

Aug 80. (7") *(CBS 8888)* **CREATURE WITH THE ATOM BRAIN. / THE WIND AND MORE**

Aug 80. (lp) *(CBS 84463)* **ROKY ERICKSON & THE ALIENS**
– Two headed dog / I think of demons / Don't shake me Lucifer / I walked with a zombie / Night of the vampire / Cold night for alligators / White faces / Creatures with the atom brain / Mine, mine, mind / Stand for the fire demon. *(re-iss. Jan87 as 'I THINK OF DEMONS' on 'Edsel'+=; ED 222)* – (2 tracks). *(cd-iss. Jun97; EDCD 528)*

Oct 80. (7") *(CBS 9055)* **MINE MINE MIND. / BLOODY HAMMER (long version)**

ROKY ERICKSON

not iss. 415 Records

1981. (lp; as ROKY ERICKSON AND THE ALIENS) <0005> **THE EVIL ONE**
– Two-headed dog (red temple prayer) / I think of demons / Creature with the atom brain / Wind and more / Don't shake me Lucifer / Bloody hammer / Stand for the the fire demon / Click your fingers applauding the play / If you have ghosts / I walked with a zombie / Night of the vampire / It's a cold night for alligators / Mine mine mind / Sputnik / White faces. *<cd-iss. 1987 was a compilation on 'Enigma-Pink Dust'; 72212-2>*

not iss. Dynamite

1984. (7") *<DY 002>* **DON'T SLANDER ME. / STARRY EYES**

New Rose not iss.

1985. (m-lp) *(ROSE 69)* **CLEAR NIGHT FOR LOVE** France
– You don't love me yet / Clear night for love / The haunt / Starry eyes / Don't slander me.

One Big Guitar Live Wire

Apr 86. (12") *(OBG 004T)* *<LW 5>* **THE BEAST. / HEROIN (live)** Nov85

Demon Enigma

Jan 87. (lp) *(FIEND 66)* *<72109-1>* **GREMLINS HAVE PICTURES (live 1975-1982 with his bands)** Nov86
– Night of the vampire / Interpreter / Song to Abe Lincoln / John Lawman / Anthem / Warning / Sweet honey pie / Cold night for alligators / I am / Heroin / I have always been there before / Before the beginning / Click your fingers applauding the play / If you have ghosts / Damn thing / Sputnik. *(cd-iss. Oct90 with extra tracks; FIENDCD 66)*

Jun 87. (lp) *(FIEND 86)* **DON'T SLANDER ME**
– (contains some of 'THE EVIL ONE' lp)

Fan Club not iss.

Sep 87. (lp) *(FC 030)* **THE HOLIDAY INN TAPES**

—— next with **WILL SEXTON** + **CHRIS HOLYHAUS** – guitar / **FREDDIE KRC** – drums

1988. (lp) *(FC 046)* **LIVE AT THE RITZ (live Feb'87)**
– You're gonna miss me / Don't slander me / Don't shake me Lucifer / Night of the vampire / Two headed dog / Splash 1 / Take a good look at yourself / Clear night for love / Bloody hammer.

—— next with **ET** (aka EVILHOOK WILDLIFE) **BRIAN S.CURLEY / KERRY GRAFTON / TIM GAGAN + DAVE CAMERON**

Fundam. not iss.

Feb 88. (12") *(PRAY 007)* **CLEAR NIGHT FOR LOVE. / YOU DON'T LOVE ME YET**

Rok not iss.

Dec 88. (7"ep) *(ROK 88)* **ACOUSTIC EP** (field recordings)
– Right track now / Mr. Tambourine man / (interview excerpt 1980) / Creature with the atom brain / For you.

Sympathy.. Sympathy..

1990. (7"colrd) *<SFTRI 152>* **YOU DON'T LOVE ME YET. / I AM HER HERO, SHE IS MY HEROIN**

1992. (7") *<SFTRI 201>* **HASN'T ANYONE TOLD YOU (live). / THE INTERPRETER (live)**

Trance Syndicate Trance Syndicate

Nov 94. (7"ltd.) *(TR 28)* **WE ARE NEVER TALKING. / PLEASE JUDGE (acoustic version)**

Feb 95. (lp/cd) *<(TR 33/+CD)>* **ALL THAT MAY DO MY RHYME**
– I'm gonna free her / Starry eyes / You don't love me yet / Please judge / Don't slander me / We are never talking / For you (I'd do anything) / For you / Clear night for love / Haunt / Starry eyes.

– compilations, others, etc. –

Aug 87. (lp/pic-lp) *5 Hours Back; (TOCK 007/+P)* **CASTING THE RUNES**
(cd-iss. Jan99 on 'R.E.'; RE 1)
(above live Nov79 with The EXPLOSIVES; aka **CAM KING** – lead guitar / **WILLIE COLLIE** – bass / **FREDDIE KRC** – drums)

1987. (7"colrd) *Scatterbrainchild; <SR 07>* **THE HAUNT OF ROKY ERICKSON**
– Cold night for alligators / Can't be brought down.

Mar 88. (lp) *5 Hours Back; (TOCK 010)* **OPENERS**

Jun 88. (red-lp) *5 Hours Back; (TICK 001)* **TWO TWISTED TALES** (interview)

1988. (cd) *Fan Club; (ROKY 1)* **CLICK YOUR FINGERS APPLAUDING THE PLAY**

Sep 91. (cd/c) *Restless; <72532-2/-4>* **YOU'RE GONNA MISS ME: THE BEST OF ROKY ERICKSON**
– Don't shake me Lucifer / Bermuda / Nothing in return / Click your fingers applauding the play / I am / I have always been here before / White faces / Night of the vampire / Don't slander me / Starry eyes / If you have ghosts / Can't be brought down / Creature with the atom brain / I walked with a zombie / Interpreter / Two-headed dog (red temple prayer) / You're gonna miss me / Wake up to rock'n'roll / Gonna die more / I'm a demon / Leave my kitten alone.

May 92. (cd/c) *Swordfish; (SFMD CD/LP 001)* **MAD DOG** (1976-83)

Oct 92. (cd/lp) *New Rose; (422404)* **LIVE DALLAS 1979 (live with The NERVEBREAKERS)**

Feb 93. (cd) *Swordfish; (SFMCD 2)* **LOVE TO SEE YOU BLEED**
– Bloody hammer / Every time I look at you / Miss Elude / Haunt / Laughing things / You don't love me yet / Creature with the atom brain / I think of demons / Two headed dog / Red temple prayer / Bumblebee zombie / Click your fingers applauding / The play / Mine mine mind / Things that go bump in the night / Here today . . . gone tomorrow / Realise your my sweet brown angel eyes / I love to see you bleed / Please don't kill my baby.

Feb 99. (cd) *Emperor Jones; <(EJ 26)>* **NEVER SAY GOODBYE** (rare material)
– Unforced peace / I love the living you / I pledge allegiance / Pushing and pulling / Save me / Think of as one / Birds'd crash / Be and bring me home / I've never known this 'til now / "2 gone and number / I lovbe the blind man / Something extra / You're an unidentified flying object.

Apr 99. (cd) *Triple X; <(TX 70024CD)>* **DEMON ANGEL**

□ 31st FEBRUARY
(see under ⇒ ALLMAN BROTHERS BAND)

□ David THOMAS (see under ⇒ PERE UBU)

Richard THOMPSON

Born: 3 Apr'49, London, England. A founder member of FAIRPORT CONVENTION from 1967 until his departure early in 1971, THOMPSON was an important catalyst in the translation of English folk music into a rock format. He contributed many of FAIRPORT CONVENTION's finest songs including 'MEET ON THE LEDGE' and 'SLOTH'. After session work for ex-FAIRPORT friends, SANDY DENNY and IAIN MATTHEWS, the bearded guitarist finally issued his 1972 debut album, 'HENRY THE HUMAN FLY', for 'Island' records. Just prior to this, he had worked with other recent ex-FAIRPORT members ASHLEY HUTCHINGS and DAVE MATTACKS who, as The BUNCH, released the budget covers lp 'ROCK ON'. The following year, he teamed up both artistically and romantically with Glasgow-born LINDA PETERS, the couple becoming RICHARD & LINDA THOMPSON after their marriage in 1974. Their first of seven albums together, 'I WANT TO SEE THE BRIGHT LIGHTS AGAIN', was acclaimed by many, and by rights, should have provided them with a hit single in the evocative title track. During the recording of their next album, 'HOKEY POKEY' (1975), they converted to Sufism, even initiating their own Sufi community. Over the course of the next seven years, the royal couple of British folk created a string of finely crafted, harmony-laden albums, the pick of which was arguably 1982's 'SHOOT OUT THE LIGHTS'. The album featured the enduring 'WALL OF DEATH', appropriately enough the final track on their final album together, their marriage already having floundered. Picking up the pieces, RICHARD went solo again the following year, recording 'HAND OF KINDNESS' for 'Hannibal'

Records, a set which included the excellent 'TWO LEFT FEET'. After finally achieving a more widespread recognition, he moved to 'Capitol' in the second half of the 80's and made significant inroads with the 1988 set, 'AMNESIA'. THOMPSON gained a belated UK Top 40 solo success with his 1991 album, 'RUMOUR AND SIGH', a wonderfully eclectic set running the gamut of THOMPSON's influences. 1994 saw the release of 'MIRROR BLUE', another critically acclaimed set including highlights such as 'MINGUS EYES' and 'THE WAY THAT IT SHOWS'. His 1996 release, 'YOU? ME? US?', introduced his son, TEDDY, to the proceedings and offered up further classic tracks in the shape of 'COLD KISSES' and 'WOODS OF DARNEY'. His home city of London was the lyrical core of THOMPSON's next work, 'MOCK TUDOR' (1999). His witty tales of the capital's downside, 'WALKING THE LONG MILES HOME' and 'SIGHTS AND SOUNDS OF LONDON TOWN', could have been written years ago (but weren't!) but somehow RICHARD gives them a modern day sheen that his contemporaries can only dream of. After finally being dropped by 'Capitol', THOMPSON took the opportunity of going back to basics on 'THE OLD KIT BAG' (2003), casting an even more economical hand over the writing, recording and production than on its predecessor. With only DANNY THOMPSON, drummer MICHAEL JEROME and singer JUDITH OWEN working alongside him in the studio, the resulting album was simultaneously more intimate and more self-possessed. Lyrically, THOMPSON was also at the top of his game, taking an unflinching look at the more extreme elements of his faith on 'OUTSIDE OF THE INSIDE'. In his time, THOMPSON (now a practising Muslim) has influenced many guitarists including Americans, FRANK BLACK (of The PIXIES) and BOB MOULD (of HUSKER DU) and has come to be regarded as one of England's finest songwriting guitarists. • **Trivia:** A RICHARD THOMPSON tribute album in 1994 featured many top stars, playing their best RT tracks.

Album rating: HENRY THE HUMAN FLY (*7) / Richard & Linda Thompson: I WANT TO SEE THE BRIGHT LIGHTS TONIGHT (*8) / HOKEY POKEY (*7) / POUR DOWN LIKE SILVER (*7) / FIRST LIGHT (*6) / SUNNYVISTA (*5) / SHOOT OUT THE LIGHTS (*9) / Richard Thompson: (guitar, vocal) collection (*4) / STRICT TEMPO! (*4) / HAND OF KINDNESS (*7) / SMALL TOWN ROMANCE (*7) / ACROSS A CROWDED ROOM (*6) / DARING ADVENTURES (*7) / THE MARKSMAN soundtrack for TV with Peter Filleul (*4) / AMNESIA (*6) / RUMOUR AND SIGH (*7) / WATCHING THE DARK (THE HISTORY OF RICHARD THOMPSON 1969-1982) boxed-set (*8) / MIRROR BLUE (*6) / YOU? ME? US? (*6) / INDUSTRY with Danny Thompson (*5) / MOCK TUDOR (*7) / THE BEST OF RICHARD & LINDA THOMPSON compilation (*7) / ACTION PACKED – THE BEST OF THE CAPITOL YEARS compilation (*7) / THE OLD KIT BAG (*7)

RICHARD THOMPSON – vocals, guitar (ex-FAIRPORT CONVENTION) with **LINDA PETERS / PAT DONALDSON** – bass / **TIM DONALD** – drums / plus **SANDY DENNY / ASHLEY HUTCHINGS / JOHN DEFERERI / BARRY DRANSFIELD / DAVID SNELL / CLAY TOYANI / ANDY ROBERTS / SUE DRAHEIM / JEFF COLE**

Island Reprise

Jun 72. (lp/c) *(ILPS/ZCI 9197) <2112>* **HENRY THE HUMAN FLY** ☐ ☐
– Roll over Vaughn Williams / Nobody's wedding / The poor ditching boy / Shaky Nancy / The angels took my racehorse away / Wheely down / The new St. George / Painted ladies / Cold feet / Mary and Joseph / The old changing ways / Twisted. *(re-iss. Jan87 on Hannibal'; HNBL 4405) (re-iss. May87 c/cd; HNBC/HNCD 4405)*

RICHARD & LINDA THOMPSON

husband & wife duo. LINDA (nee. PETERS) (ex-ALBION COUNTRY BAND) with SOUR GRAPES: **SIMON NICOL** – dulcimer / **STEVE BORRELL** – bass / **WILLIAM MURRAY** – drums (ex-KEVIN AYERS)/ plus most of main musicians on above album

Island Island

Jan 74. (7") *(WIP 6186)* **I WANT TO SEE THE BRIGHT LIGHTS TONIGHT. / WHEN I GET TO THE BORDER** ☐ ☐

Apr 74. (lp/c) *(<ILPS/ZCI 9266>)* **I WANT TO SEE THE BRIGHT LIGHTS TONIGHT** ☐ ☐
– When I get to the border / The Calvery Cross / Withered and died / I want to see the bright lights tonight / Down where the drunkards roll / We sing hallelujah / Has he got a friend for me? / The little beggar girl / The end of the rainbow / The Great Valero. *(cd-iss. May88; CID 9266) (re-iss. Oct89 on 'Carthage'; CGLP 4407) (cd re-iss. Mar93 on Island')*

— **IAN WHITEMAN** – keyboards, flute / **ALY BAIN** – fiddle repl. guests

Feb 75. (7") *(WIP 6220)* **HOKEY POKEY. / I'LL REGRET IT ALL IN THE MORNING** ☐ ☐

Mar 75. (lp/c) *(<ILPS/ZCI 9305>)* **HOKEY POKEY** ☐ ☐
– Hokey pokey (the ice-cream song) / I'll regret it all in the morning / Smiffy's glass eye / Egypt room / Never again / Georgie on a spree / Old man inside a young man / The Sun never shines on the poor / A heart needs a home / Mole in a hole. *(re-iss. Jun86 on Hannibal'; HNBL 4408) (re-iss. May89 c/cd; HNBC/HNBD 4408)*

Nov 75. (lp/c) *(<ILPS/ZCI 9348>)* **POUR DOWN LIKE SILVER** ☐ ☐
– Streets of Paradise / For shame of doing wrong / The poor boy is taken away / Night comes in / Jet plane in a rocking chair / Beat the retreat / Hard luck stories / Dimming of the day / Dargai. *(re-iss. Jun86 on Hannibal'; HNBL 4404) (re-iss. May89 c/cd; HNBC/HNBD 4404)*

— Their main band was:- **WILLIE WEEKS** – bass / **ANDY NEWMARK** – drums / **NEIL LARSON** – keyboards / **SIMON NICOL** – guitar, dulcimer / **JOHN KIRKPATRICK** – accordion

Chrysalis Chrysalis

Nov 78. (lp/c) *(<CHR/ZCHS 1177>)* **FIRST LIGHT** ☐ ☐
– Restless highway / Sweet surrender / Don't let a thief steal into your heart / The choice wife / Died for love / Strange affair / Layla / Pavanne / House of cards / First light. *(cd-iss. Jun86; CCD 1177) (re-iss. May89 on 'Carthage' lp/c; CGLP/CGC 4412)*

Jan 79. (7") *(CHS 2278)* **DON'T LET A THIEF STEAL INTO YOUR HEART. / FIRST LIGHT** ☐ ☐

— **TIM DONALD, PAT DONALSON + RABBIT BUNDRICK** repl. NEWMARK, WEEKS + LARSON / guests:- **DAVE MATTACKS** – drums / **DAVE PEGG** – bass

Sep 79. (lp/c) *(<CHR/ZCHS 1247>)* **SUNNYVISTA** ☐ ☐
– Civilization / Borrowed time / Saturday rolling around / You're going to need somebody / Why do you turn your back / Sunnyvista / Lonely hearts / Sisters / Justice in the streets / Traces of my love. *(re-iss. May89 on 'Carthage' lp/c/cd; CGLP/CGC/CGCD 4403)*

Sep 79. (7") *(CHS 2369)* **CIVILIZATION. / GEORGIE ON A SPREE** ☐ [–]

Elixir not iss.

Sep 81. (lp) *(LP 1)* **STRICT TEMPO (RICHARD THOMPSON solo / instrumental)** ☐ [–]
– Scott Skinner medley / Banish misfortune / Dundee hornpipe / Do it for my sake / New fangled flogging reel / Vailance polka militair / Belfast polka / Rockin' in rhythm / The random jig / The grinder / Andalus / Marrakesh / The knife edge. *(re-iss. Jul89 on 'Carthage' lp/c/cd; CGLP/CGC/CGCD 4409)*

— next w / **NICOL / MATTACKS / PEGG / + bassman PETE ZORN**

Hannibal Hannibal

Apr 82. (7") *(HNS 703)* **DON'T RENEGE ON YOUR LOVE. / LIVING IN LUXURY** ☐ [–]

Nov 82. (lp) *(<HNBL 1303>)* **SHOOT OUT THE LIGHTS** ☐ ☐
– Man in need / Walking on a wire / Don't renege on your love / Just the motion / Shoot out the lights / Back street slide / Did she jump or was she pushed / Wall of death. *(re-iss. Jun86 lp/c/cd+=; HNBL/HNBC/HNBD 1303)* – Living in luxury. *(cd-iss. Dec94 on 'Hannibal')*

RICHARD THOMPSON

— returned to solo work after separating with LINDA. He retained last band and label, while LINDA went on in 1985 to release an album ONE CLEAR MOMENT' for Warners'.

Jun 83. (lp) *(<HNBL 1313>)* **HAND OF KINDNESS** ☐ ☐
– A poisoned heart and a twisted memory / Tear stained letter / How I wanted to / Both ends burning / The wrong heartbeat / Hand of kindness / Devonside / Two left feet. *(re-iss. Jun86 lp/c/cd+=; HNBL/HNBC/HNBD 1313)* – Where the wind don't whine.

Jul 83. (7") *(HNS 704)* **THE WRONG HEARTBEAT. / DEVONSIDE** ☐ [–]

Dec 84. (lp) *(<HNBL 1316>)* **SMALL TOWN ROMANCE (live)** –
– Time to ring some changes / Beat the retreat / A heart needs a home / Woman or a man / For shame of doin' wrong / Genesis Hall / Honky tonk blues / Small town romance / I want to see the bright lights tonight / Down where the drunkards roll / Love is bad for business / Never again / The Great Valero / Don't let a thief steal into your heart. i(re-iss. Jun86 lp/c/cd; *HNBL/HNBC/HNBD 1316)*

Polydor Polydor

Mar 85. (lp/c) *(POLD/+C 5175) <825421>* **ACROSS A CROWDED ROOM** 80
– When the spell is broken / You don't say / I ain't going to drag my feet no more / Love in a faithless country / Fire in the engine room / Walking through a wasted land / Little blue number / She twists the knife again / Ghosts in the wind. *(cd-iss. Jun86; 825421-2) (cd re-iss. Jun92 on 'Beat Goes On' cd/c/lp; BGO CD/MC/LP 139)*

Jun 85. (7") *(POSP 750)* **YOU DON'T SAY. / WHEN THE SPELL IS BROKEN**

— now with **MITCHELL FROOM** – organ / **JERRY SCHEFF** – bass / **MICKEY CURRY + JIM KELTNER** – drums / **JOHN KIRKPATRICK** – accordion / **ALEX ACUNA** – percussion

Oct 86. (lp)(cd) *(POLD 5202)(<829728-2>)* **DARING ADVENTURES** 92
– A bone through her nose / Valerie / Missie how you let me down / Dead man's handle / Long dead love / Lover''s lane / Nearly in love / Jennie / Baby talk / Cash down / Never never / How wll I ever be simple again / Al Bowly's in Heaven. *(re-iss. Jun92 on 'Beat Goes On' cd/c/lp; BGO CD/MC/LP 138)*

B.B.C. not iss.

Oct 87. (lp/c; by RICHARD THOMPSON & PETER FILLEUL) *(REB/ZCF 660)* **THE MARKSMAN (TV soundtrack)** –
– My time / Gordon / Rude health / Night school / Cornish pastiche / Crossing the water / The marksman / Kyrie / On yer eyes / Cutters on the run / Don't ever change / Up there.

Capitol Capitol

Oct 88. (cd/c/lp) *(CD/TC/+EST 2075) <48845>* **AMNESIA** 89
– Turning of the tide / Gypsy love songs / Reckless kind / Jerusalem on the jukebox / I still dream / Don't tempt me / Yankee, go home / Can't win / Waiting for dreamers / Pharoah. *(re-iss. Mar91 lp/c; ATAK/TC-ATAK 169) (cd re-iss. Aug91; CZ 399)*

Nov 88. (7") *(CL 516)* **TURNING OF THE TIDE. / PHAROAH**

Sep 89. (7") *(CL 550)* **RECKLESS KIND (live). / TURNING OF THE TIDE (live)**
(12"+=) *(12CL 550)* – Pharoah (live) / Can't win (live).
(cd-s+=) *CDCL 550)* – Jerusalem on the jukebox (live).

May 91. (cd/c/lp) *(CD/TC+/EST 2142)* **RUMOUR AND SIGH** 32
– Read about love / I feel so good / I misunderstood / Behind grey walls / You dream too much / Why must I plead / Vincent / Backlash love affair / Mystery wind / Jimmy Shands / Keep your distance / Mother knows best / God loves a drunk / Psycho Street.

Jun 91. (7") *(CL 617)* **I FEEL SO GOOD. / HARRY'S THEME (from film 'Sweet Talker')** –
(cd-s+=) *(CDCL 617)* – Backlash love affair.

Mar 92. (7") *(CL 638)* **READ ABOUT LOVE. / I MISUNDERSTOOD** –
(cd-s+=) *(CDCL 638)* – I feel so good / The choice wife.

— with **PETE THOMAS** – drums, percussion / **JERRY SCHEFF** – bass, double bass / **MITCHELL FROOM** – keyboards, producer / **ALISTAIR ANDERSON** – concertina, pipes / **TOM McCONVILLE** – fiddle / **MARTIN DUNN** – flute / **PHIL PICKETT** – shawms / **JOHN KIRKPATRICK** – accordion, concertina / **DANNY THOMPSON** – double bass (1) / **CHRISTINE COLLISTER + MICHAEL PARKER** – backing vocals

Jan 94. (cd/c) *(CD/TC EST 2207) <81492>* **MIRROR BLUE** 23
– For the sake of Mary / I can't wake up to save my life / MGB-GT / The way that it shows / Easy there, steady now / King of Bohemia / Shane and Dixie / Mingus eyes / I ride in your slipstream / Beeswing / Fast food / Mascara tears / Taking my business elsewhere.

Apr 96. (d-cd/d-c) *(CD/TC EST 2282) <33704>* **YOU? ME? US?** (part compilation / acoustic) 32 97
– Razor dance / She steers by lightning / Dark hand over my heart / Hide it away / Put it there pal / Business on you / No's not a word / Am I wasting my love on you? / Bank vault in Heaven / The ghost of you walks / Baby don't know what to do with herself / She cut off her long silken hair / Hide it away / Burns supper / Train don't leave / Cold kisses / Sam Jones / Razor dance / Woods of Darney.

Parlophone Hannibal

May 97. (cd; RICHARD & DANNY THOMPSON) *(CDPCS 7383) <1414>* **INDUSTRY** 69
– Chorale / Sweetheart on the barricade / Children of the dark / Big chimney / Kitty "quick get up I can hear clogs going up in the street" / Drifting through the days / Lotteryland / Pitfalls / Saboteur / Mew rhythms / Last shift.

Parlophone Capitol

Aug 99. (cd) *(<4 98860-2>)* **MOCK TUDOR** 28
– METROLAND:- Cooksferry queen / Sibella / Bathsheba smiles / Two-faced love / Hard on me / HEROES IN THE SUBURBS:- Crawl back (under my stone) / Uninhabited man / Dry me tears and move on / Walking the long miles home / STREET CRIES AND STAGE WHISPERS:- Sights and sounds of London town / That's all, amen, close the door / Hope you like the new me. *(d-lp-iss.Nov99 on 'Bongload'; BL 44)*

Cooking Vinyl Cooking Vinyl

Feb 03. (cd) *(COOKCD 251) <74651>* **THE OLD KIT BAG** 52
– THE HAUNTED KEEPSAKE:- Gethsemane / Jealous words / I'll tag along / A love you can't survive / One door opens / First breath / THE PILGRIMS FANCY:- She said it was destiny / Got no right / Pearly Jim / Word unspoken, sight unseen / Outside of the inside / Happy days and Auld Lang Syne.

Jun 03. (cd-s) *(FRYCD 155)* **SHE SAID IT WAS DESTINY / SO BEN MI CA BON TEMPO / HARD ON ME** –

– compilations, etc. –

(below album recorded between 1967-1976)

May 76. (d-lp) *Island; (ICD 8)* **(guitar, vocal)** <US title 'LIVE MORE OR LESS'> –
– A heart needs a home / Flee as a bird / Night comes in / Pitfall / Excursion / Calvery Cross / Time will show the wiser / Throw-away street puzzle / Mr. Lacy / The ballad of Easy Rider / Poor Will and the jolly hangman / Sweet little rock'n'roller / Dark end of the street / I'll be me. *(incl.Live Oxford Street concert & early demos) (re-iss. Jun86 on 'Hannibal'; HNBL 4801) cd-iss. May89; HNBD 4413)*

Apr 93. (3xcd-box) *Hannibal; (HNCD 5303)* **WATCHING THE DARK (THE HISTORY OF RICHARD THOMPSON 1969-1982)** –
– A man in need / Can't win / Waltzing's for dreamers / Crash the party / I still dream / Bird in God's garden / Lost and found / Now be thankful / A sailor's kife / Genesis Hall / The knife-edge / Walking on a wire / Small town romance / Shepherd's march – Maggie Cameron / Wall of death / For shame of doing wrong / Back street slide / Strange affair / The wrong heartbeat / Borrowed time / From Galway to Graceland / Tear-stained letter / Keep your distance / Bogie's bonnie / Poor wee Jockey Clarke / Jet plane in a rocking chair / Dimming of the day / Old man inside a young man / Never again / Hokey pokey (the ice cream song) / A heart needs a home / Beat the retreat / Al Bowlly's in Heaven / Walking through a wasted land / When the spell is broken / Devonside / Little blue number / I ain't going to drag my feet no more / Withered and died / Nobody's wedding / The poor ditching boy / The Great Valerio / The Calvary Cross / Twisted / Jennie / Hand of kindness / Two left feet / Shoot out the lights.

May 93. (cd) *Windsong; (WINCD 034)* **BBC LIVE IN CONCERT** –

Jul 00. (cd) *Capitol; <542456>* **THE BEST OF RICHARD & LINDA THOMPSON: THE ISLAND RECORD YEARS** –
– Roll over Vaughn Williams / The poor ditching boy / When I get to the border / Withered and died / I want to see the bright lights tonight / Down where the drunkards roll / The end of the rainbow / The great Valerio / Hokey pokey / Never again / A heart needs a home / For shame of doing wrong / Night comes in / Beat the retreat / Dimming of the day / Calvary cross (live).

Aug 00. (cd) *Island; (IMCD 271)* **END OF THE RAINBOW: AN INTRODUCTION TO RICHARD & LINDA THOMPSON** –

Apr 01. (cd) *Capitol; (<5 31051-2>)* **ACTION PACKED – THE BEST OF THE CAPITOL YEARS**
– Turning of the tide / Waltzing's for dreamers / 1952 Vincent black lightning / I misunderstood / I feel so good / Keep your distance / Kinf of Bohemia / I can't wake up to save my life / Beeswing / The ghost of you walks / Razor dance / Cool kisses / Bathsheba smiles / Cooksferry queen / Uninhabited man / Walking the long miles home / Persuasion / Mr. Rebound / Fully qualified to be your man. *(<d-lp-iss.Feb01 on 'Bongload'; BL 52>)*

☐ Tracey THORN
(see under ⇒ EVERYTHING BUT THE GIRL)

☐ 3 (see under ⇒ EMERSON, LAKE & PALMER)

3 DOORS DOWN

Formed: Escatawpa, nr. Biloxi, Missouri, USA ... late 90's by vocalist/drummer BRAD ARNOLD, MATT ROBERTS and TODD HARRELL; added CHRIS HENDERSON soon after. Described by some pundits as bland all-American – similar in some respects to drummer/singer PHIL COLLINS – their local radio station WCPR in Biloxi frequently spun their records. Clones to CREED – i.e. big stadium rock and with God on their side; they're all believers – it looked like 3 DOORS DOWN would be another to break in the US but not the UK. After the multi-million selling success of their debut, the tediously named 3 DOORS DOWN once again appealed to the good ol' US of A's hard rocking heartland with 'AWAY FROM THE SUN' (2002), bolstered by the Top 5 success of single, 'WHEN I'M GONE'. Live EP, 'ANOTHER 700 MILES' confirmed their common man credentials and Southern rock references with a cover of Lynyrd Skynyrd's anti-drugs anthem, 'THAT SMELL'.

Album rating: THE BETTER LIFE (*5) / AWAY FROM THE SUN (*5)

BRAD ARNOLD – vocals, drums / **MATT ROBERTS** – guitar / **CHRIS HENDERSON** – guitar / **TODD HARRELL** – bass

		Universal	Universal
Jan 00.	(-) *<radio play>* **KRYPTONITE**	–	3
Sep 00.	(cd) *<(153920-2)>* **THE BETTER LIFE** – Kryptonite / Loser / Duck and run / Not enough / Be like that / Life of my own / The better life / Down poison / By my side / Smack / So I need you.	Feb00	7
Oct 00.	(-) *<radio play>* **LOSER**	–	55

—— added drummer when BRAD took on vocal duties on stage

		M.C.A.	Universal
Apr 01.	(cd-s) *(MCSTD 40251)* **KRYPTONITE / KRYPTONITE (acoustic sic) / KRYPTONITE (video)**		–
Nov 01.	(cd-s) *(MCSTD 40269) <radio cut>* **BE LIKE THAT / BE LIKE THAT (American pie edit) / NOT ENOUGH (live) / BE LIKE THAT (video)**	Jul01	24
Mar 03.	(cd) *(067563-2) <064396>* **AWAY FROM THE SUN** – When I'm gone / Away from the sun / The road I'm on / Ticket to Heaven / Running out of days / Here without you / I feel you / Dangerous game / Changes / Going down in flames / Sarah yellin'.	Nov02	8
Jun 03.	(cd-s) *(MCSTD 40307) <19485>* **WHEN I'M GONE / LIVING A LIE / WASTED ME / WHEN I'M GONE (video)**	Jan03	4
Nov 03.	(m-cd) *<(16030-2)>* **ANOTHER 700 MILES (live)** – Duck and run / When I'm gone (intro) / When I'm gone / Kryptonite / Here without you / It's not me / That smell.		21

311

Formed: Omaha, Nebraska, USA ... 1990 by NICK HEXUM, TIMOTHY J. MAHONEY, P-NUT, CHAD SEXTON and S.A. MARTINEZ. Taking their moniker from the American emergency number, the band signed to the newly resurrected 'Capricorn' label, issuing their debut disc, 'MUSIC' in 1993. Fed mainly on a rap/funk-metal diet of RAGE AGAINST THE MACHINE and RED HOT CHILI PEPPERS, the album, along with their 1994 follow-up, 'GRASSROOTS' built up some local support which translated into a chart call-out two years later with the eponymous US Top 20, '311' set. In 1997, it was all systems go, as 311 were mobilized into the Top 5 with 'TRANSISTOR', although Britain still remained oblivious to their street-chase thrills. Following the 1998 release of disappointing concert set, 'LIVE' , the 311 posse were back on the case with 'SOUNDSYSTEM' (1999), clocking up the decibels with their dizzying meltdown of various attitude-friendly music styles. With erstwhile POLICE producer HUGH PADGHAM lending his expertise, the band reined in most of the excess aural flab which had fleshed out the album's predecessor. With a millennial UK breakthrough seemingly as far off as ever, 311 returned in 2001 with 'FROM CHAOS', their first set for 'Volcano' records. It certainly catapulted the 5-piece back into the US Top 10 where hard-rockin' hip-hop seemed to be more atune to the surroundings. 'EVOLVER' (2003), meanwhile, belied its title with a business as usual set of plucky, swaggering guitar sonics, propped up by limbering rhythms, electronica flourishes and reggae aesthetics. Yet another US Top 10 position merely confirmed 311's position as dependable grandaddys of their own scene.

Album rating: MUSIC (*5) / GRASSROOTS (*5) / 311 (*6) / TRANSISTOR (*6) / LIVE (*4) / SOUNDSYSTEM (*5) / FROM CHAOS (*6) / EVOLVER (*5)

NICK HEXUM – vocals, guitar / **TIMOTHY J. MAHONEY** – guitar / **P-NUT** – bass / **CHAD SEXTON** – drums / **S.A. MARTINEZ** – vocals, turntables

		Capricorn	Capricorn
Nov 93.	(cd/c) *<42008>* **MUSIC** – Welcome / Freak out / Visit / Paradise / Unity / Hydrophonic / My stoney baby / Nix hex / Plain / Feels so good / Do you right / Fat chance.	–	
Jun 95.	(cd/c) *(477894-2/-4) <42026>* **GRASSROOTS** – Lucky / Homebrew / Nutsympton / 8:16 a.m. / Omaha stylee / Apples science / Taiyed / Silver / Grassroots / Salsa / Lose / Six / Offbeat / 1-2-3.	Jul94	
Oct 96.	(cd/c) *(532 530-2/-4) <42041>* **311** – Down / Random / Jack O'Lantern's weather / All mixed up / Hive / Guns / Misdirected hostility / Purpose / Loco / Brodels / Don't stay home / D.L.M.D. / Sweet / T & P combo.	Jul95	12
Nov 96.	(cd-ep) *<10039>* **ENLARGED TO SHOW DETAIL EP** – Tribute / Let the cards fall / Gap / Firewater.	–	95
Aug 97.	(cd) *<(536181-2)>* **TRANSISTOR** – Transistor / Prisoner / Galaxy / Beautiful disaster / Inner light spectrum / Electricity / What was I thinking / Jupiter / Use of time / Continuous life / No control / Running / Color / Light years / Creature feature / Tune in / Rub a dub / Starshines / Strangers / Borders / Stealing happy hour.		4
Nov 98.	(cd) *<(538263-2)>* **LIVE (live)** – Down / Homebrew / Beautiful disaster / Misdirected hostility / Freak out / Nix hex / Applied science / Omaha stylee / Tribute / Galaxy / Light years / Hydrophonic / Who's got the herb? / Feels so good.		77
Oct 99.	(cd) *<(546645-2)>* **SOUNDSYSTEM** – Freeze time / Come original / Large in the margin / Flowing / Can't fade me / Life's not a race / Strong all along / Sever / Eons / Evolution / Leaving Babylon / Mindspin / Livin' and rockin'.		9

		Volcano	Volcano
Aug 01.	(cd) *(921015-2) <32184>* **FROM CHAOS** – You get worked / Sick tight / You wouldn't believe / Full ride / From chaos / I told myself / Champagne / Hostile apostle / Wake your mind up / Amber / Uncalm / I'll be here awhile.	Jun01	10

		Music For Nations	Volcano
Oct 03.	(cd) *(CDMFN 303) <53714>* **EVOLVER** – Creatures (for a while) / Reconsider everything / Crack the code / Same mistake twice / Beyond the gray sky / Seems uncertain / Still dreaming / Give me a call / Don't dwell / Other side of things / Sometimes Jacks rule the realm.	Jul03	7

☐ THREE FISH (see under ⇒ PEARL JAM)

THRILLS

Formed: Dublin, Ireland . . . summer 1999 as The CHEATING HOUSEWIVES by CONOR DEASY and DANIEL RYAN who initially recruited KEVIN HORAN, then BEN CARRIGAN and PADRAIC McMAHON. United in a love of all things musically laid back, soulful and sunkissed, the lads understandably had a bit of a fixation for the classicist sounds of the American West Coast. Though they weren't the first – and no doubt won't be the last – to be influenced by the likes of The BEACH BOYS, The BYRDS, BURT BACHARACH, NEIL YOUNG, PHIL SPECTOR etc, their rock revisionism had less zeal and more heart than the likes of say . . . JET. MORRISSEY of all people – now living in sunny L.A. – took the band under his wing, securing their services for a support slot at the Royal Albert Hall. So far so good, as the band relocated to the USA and began living out the lifestyle they'd only heard about on scratchy old vinyl. A major label deal with 'Virgin' eventually resulted in the acclaimed debut album, 'SO MUCH FOR THE CITY' (2003). From the retro sleeve design to the flawless harmonies and country-tinged, banjo picking roots pop sensibilities, The THRILLS had pulled off one of the last few years' most alluring updates of that elusive 60's/70's vibe. Listening to the likes of hit singles 'BIG SUR', 'SANTA CRUZ (YOU'RE NOT THAT FAR)' and 'ONE HORSE TOWN' floating from the radio, it really was hard to believe The THRILLS weren't California born and bred. • **Covers:** LAST NIGHT I DREAMT THAT SOMEBODY LOVED ME (Smiths).

Album rating: SO MUCH FOR THE CITY (*8)

CONOR DEASY – vocals / **DANIEL RYAN** – guitar, vocals, bass / **KEVIN HORAN** – keyboards / **PADRAIC McMAHON** – bass / **BEN CARRIGAN** – drums

Virgin E.M.I.

Nov 02. (7"white) *(VS 1840) <546885>* **SANTA CRUZ (YOU'RE NOT THAT FAR). / DECKCHAIRS AND CIGARETTES** [ ] Dec02 [ ]
(cd-s+=) *(VSCDT 1840)* – Your love is like Las Vegas / Plans.

Mar 03. (7"yellow) *(VS 1845)* **ONE HORSE TOWN. / DON'T PLAY IT COOL** 18 –
(cd-s+=) *(VSCDT 1845)* – Car crash.

Jun 03. (7"blue) *(VS 1852)* **BIG SUR. / YOUR LOVE IS LIKE LAS VEGAS** 17 –
(cd-s) *(VSCDT 1852)* – ('A'side) / No one likes to be upstaged / One horse town (demo) / ('A'video).

Jun 03. (cd/lp) *(CD+/V 2974) <584968>* **SO MUCH FOR THE CITY** 3 [ ]
– Santa Cruz (you're not that far) / Big Sur / Don't steal our sun / Deckchairs and cigarettes / One horse town / Old friends, new lovers / SAy it ain't so / Hollywood kids / Just travelling through / Your love is like Las Vegas / 'Til the tide creeps in.

Aug 03. (7"plum) *(VS 1862)* **SANTA CRUZ (YOU'RE NOT THAT FAR). / DON'T PLAY IT COOL (orginial version)** 33 –
(cd-s) *(VSCDT 1862)* – ('A'side) / Blue September.

Nov 03. (7") *(VS 1864)* **DON'T STEAL OUR SUN. / THE ONE I LOVE (Radio 1 version)** 45 –
(cd-s) *(VSCDT 1864)* – ('A'side) / One horse town (live).
(cd-s) *(VSCDX 1864)* – ('A'side) / Last night I dreamt that somebody loved me / Santa Cruz (acoustic) / ('A'-video).

THROBBING GRISTLE

Formed: Manchester, England ... Autumn '75 by GENESIS P-ORRIDGE and girlfriend COSEY FANNI TUTTI, a nude model, the couple having previously met at an art exhibition in Hull. Defiantly unconventional from day one, their early live shows boasted some dubious attractions such as COSEY going topless, P-ORRIDGE and other member CHRIS CARTER slashing themselves and a backdrop of stomach-churning slides. In 1977, along with PETER CHRISTOPHERSON, the act set up their own independent label, 'Industrial', as a means of issuing limited edition material. A debut album, '2ND ANNUAL REPORT', was given a low-key release at the height of punk in '77. Although revelling in the genre's subversiveness, P-ORRIDGE & Co. were more interested in monotonic electronic textures than three-chord rock. Beloved of the more arty avant-garde post-punk set, THROBBING GRISTLE were largely a vehicle for the bizarre P-ORRIDGE's psycho-sexual narratives, usually set to pioneering synth-musak (CABARET VOLTAIRE and SUICIDE were mining a similar seam). A doubled-header single, 'UNITED' / 'ZYKLON B ZOMBIE' emerged the following summer, pursued by a second set, 'D.O.A.', at the end of '78. The following year, THROBBING GRISTLE made a vague stab at commerciality with the cynically titled '20 JAZZ FUNK GREATS', unearthing the wild 'PERSUASION' and the tortuously ponderous 'CONVINCING PEOPLE'. The record unsurprisingly failed to win the band any new admirers, especially in the music press, a swansong album, 'HEATHEN EARTH' (1980), paving the way for new ground; the group split two ways, P-ORRIDGE forming PSYCHIC TV, while CHRIS AND COSEY formed their own duo. • **Songwriters:** GENESIS P-ORRIDGE or mainly group compositions. • **Trivia:** Many or all performance / art gigs were recorded on tape and video.

Album rating: GREATEST HITS: ENTERTAINMENT THROUGH PAIN compilation (*7) / 20 JAZZ FUNK GREATS (*7) / D.O.A. (*8)

GENESIS P-ORRIDGE (b. NEIL ANDREW MEGSON, 22 Feb'50) – vox, electric violin, bass (ex-PORK DUKES) / **COSEY FANNI TUTTI** – guitar, cornet, effects / **CHRIS CARTER** – synthesizers, keyboards / **PETER 'Sleazy' CHRISTOPHERSON** – tapes, synthesizers, trumpet

Industrial not iss.

Dec 76. (ltd-c) *(IR 0001)* **BEST OF VOLUME II** [ ] –
– Slug bait / Very friendly / We hate you / Seers of E / etc. *(cd-iss. Jun91 on 'Grey Area-Mute'; TGCD 1)*

Nov 77. (ltd-lp) *(IR 0002)* **SECOND ANNUAL REPORT** (some live) [ ] –
– Industrial introduction / Slug bait (ICA) / Slug bait (live at Southampton) / Slug bait (live at Brighton) / Maggot death (live at the Rat Club) / Maggot death (live at Southampton) / Maggot death (live at Brighton) / After cease to exist – The original soundtrack of the Coum transmission film. *(re-iss. Nov78 + Apr79; same) (re-iss. Jun81 on 'Fetish'; FET 2001) (re-iss. Apr83 + Nov83 on 'Mute'; MIR 1) (cd-iss. Jul91 on 'Grey Area-Mute'+=; TGCD2)* – Zyklon B Zombie / United. *<US cd-iss. 1993 on 'Mute-Warners'; 61093>*

Jun 78. (7"/7"white) *(IR 0003/+U)* **UNITED. / ZYKLON B ZOMBIE** [ ] –
(re-iss. Jan80; same) – B-side longer.

Dec 78. (lp) *(IR 0004)* **D.O.A. – THE THIRD AND FINAL REPORT** [ ] –
– I.B.M. / Hit by a rock / United / The valley of the shadow of death / Dead on arrival / Weeping / Hamburger lady / Hometime / Ab-7a / E-Coli / Death threats / Walls of sound / Blood on the floor. *(re-iss. Nov83 on 'Mute'; MIR 002) (cd-iss. Jul91 on 'Grey Area-Mute'; TGCD 3) <US cd-iss. 1993 on 'Mute-Warners'+=; 61094>* – Five knuckle shuffle / We hate you (little girls).

Jul 79. (7") *<SS45 001>* **WE HATE YOU (LITTLE GIRLS). / FIVE KNUCKLE SHUFFLE** – French –
(above on 'Sordid Sentimentale') *<US-iss.Sep81 on 'Adolescent'; ARTI 010>*

Oct 79. (lp) *(IR 0008)* **20 JAZZ FUNK GREATS** [ ] –
– 20 jazz funk greats / Beach Head / Still walking / Tanith / Convincing people / Exotica / Hot on the heels of love / Persuasion / Walkabout / What a day / Six six sixties. *(re-iss. Nov83 on 'Mute'; MIR 3) (cd-iss. Jul91 on 'Grey Area-Mute'+=; TGCD 4)* – Discipline (Berlin) / Discipline (Manchester). *<US cd-iss. 1993 on 'Mute-Warners'; 61095>*

Jun 80. (lp,blue-lp) *(IR 0009)* **HEATHEN EARTH** [ ] –
– Heathen Earth (pts 1-8) / Adrenalin / Subhuman *(re-iss. Nov83 on 'Mute'; MIR 004) (cd-iss. Jul91 on 'Grey Area-Mute'; TGCD 5)* – (also on video). *<US cd-iss. 1993 on 'Mute-Warners'; 61696>*

Sep 80. (7") *(IR 0013)* **SUBHUMAN. / SOMETHING CAME OVER ME**

Sep 80. (7") *(IR 0015)* **ADRENALIN. / DISTANT DREAMS (Part Two)** Fetish Fetish

May 81. (12") *(FET 006)* **DISCIPLINE (live in Manchester). / DISCIPLINE (live in Berlin)**

—— dissolved in 1981 when P-ORRIDGE and CHRISTOPHERSON formed PSYCHIC TV; the other two formed duo CHRIS & COSEY

– compilations, others, etc. –

Oct 81. (lp) *Mute; <61001-2>* **GREATEST HITS: ENTERTAINMENT THROUGH PAIN**
– Hamburger lady / Hot on the heels of love / Subhuman / Ab 7a / Six six sixties / Blood on the floor / 20 jazz funk greats / Tiab guls / United / What a day / Adrenalin. *(UK-iss.Dec84 on 'Rough Trade'; ROUGHUS 23) (cd-iss. Oct90 & Jul91 on 'Grey Area-Mute'; TGCD 7) (<re-iss. Feb93 on 'Grey Area-Mute' c; 961001-4>)*

Nov 81. (lp) *Zensor; (ZENSOR 1D)* **FUNERAL IN BERLIN** Germ'y
– Stained by dead horses / Trained condition of obedience zero's death / Nomon / Raudive bunker experiment / Denial of death / Funeral in Berlin / Trade deficit.

Feb 82. (5xlp-box) *Fetish; (FX 1)* **A BOXED SET**
– (5 original albums) *(cd's 1988 on 'Mute')*

1982. (ltd-lp) *Death; (01)* **MUSIC FROM THE DEATH FACTORY, MAY '79 (live)**

1982. (ltd-lp) *Walter Ulbricht; (001)* **JOURNEY THROUGH THE BODY**
(cd-iss. Oct93 on 'Grey Area-Mute'; TGCD 8)

1982. (ltd-lp) *Power Focus; (001)* **ASSUMING POWER FOCUS** (most rec.1975) fanclub
– Debris of murder / Freedom is a sickness / His arm was her leg / What a day! / Dead'd / Last exit / Propaganda yogananga / Sunstroke militia / Heathen earth / Urge to kill / Epping forest / Persuasion / Leeds ripper. *(<cd-iss. Oct95 on 'Paragoric'; PA 016CD>) (<cd re-iss. Apr98 on 'Triple X'; TX 6001CD>)*

Nov 82. (d-lp) *Karnage; (KILL 1)* **THEE PSYKICK SACRIFICE**
(re-iss. Aug86 as 'SACRIFICE' on 'Dojo'; DOJOLP 29)

1983. (lp) *Expanded;* **MISSION IS TERMINATED: NICE TRACKS**
(free-12"w.a.) **DAMURA SUNRISE. / YOU DON'T KNOW**

1983. (10"lp) *Phonograph;* **FUHRER DER MEIN SHEAT**

1983. (lp) *Illuminated; (SJAMS 31S)* **EDITIONS FRANKFURT – BERLIN**

Nov 83. (lp) *Mute; (MIR 5)* **MISSION OF DEAD SOULS (THE LAST LIVE PERFORMANCE OF THROBBING GRISTLE) (live San Francisco)**
– Dead souls / Guts on the floor / Circle of animals / Looking for the Oto / Vision and voice / Funeral rites / Spirits flying / Persuasion U.S.A. / Process / Discipline / Distant dreams / Something came over me. *(cd-iss. Jul91 on 'Grey Area-Mute'; TGCD 6) <US cd-iss. Feb93 on 'Mute-Warners'; 61097>*

Feb 84. (lp) *Illuminated; (JAMS 35)* **IN THE SHADOW OF THE SUN (Soundtrack)**
(cd-iss. Oct93 on 'Grey Area-Mute'; TGCD 9)

Apr 84. (lp) *Casual Abandon; (CAS 1J)* **ONCE UPON A TIME**

May 84. (c) *Cause For Concern; (CFC 001)* **NOTHING SHORT OF TOTAL WAR**
(lp-iss.Oct87; CFC 016)

1984. (lp) *Mental Decay; (MD 01-1)* **SPECIAL TREATMENT**
(re-iss. May88; same)

1980's. (lp) *Sprut; (001)* **VERY FRIENDLY – THE FIRST ANNUAL REPORT OF T.G.**
(cd-iss. Oct96 on 'New Millennium'; CDTG 23) (cd re-iss. Apr01 on 'Yeaah'; YEAAH 50) (lp re-iss. Dec01 on 'Get Back'; GET 83)

1980's. (4xc-box) *Industrial; (IRC 1-IRC 24)* **24 HOURS**

Apr 93. (cd) *Grey Area-Mute; (TGCD 10)* **LIVE – VOLUME 1 (live 1976-1978)**

Apr 93. (cd) *Grey Area-Mute; (TGCD 11)* **LIVE – VOLUME 2 (live 1977-1978)**

Apr 93. (cd) *Grey Area-Mute; (TGCD 12)* **LIVE – VOLUME 3 (live 1978-1979)**

Apr 93. (cd) *Grey Area-Mute; (TGCD 13)* **LIVE – VOLUME 4 (live 1979-1980)**

Dec 93. (cd) *Dossier; (EFA 08450CD)* **FUNK BEYOND JAZZ**

Oct 94. (cd) *Dossier; (EFA 08458-2)* **GIFTGAS**

Dec 95. (cd) *Dossier; (EFA 08448-2)* **BLOOD PRESSURE**

Oct 96. (cd) *New Millennium; (CDTG 24)* **GRIEF**
(re-iss. Jul01 on 'Yeaah'; YEAAH 51)

Oct 97. (cd) *Dossier; (<EFA 08490-2>)* **KREEME HORN**
– Careless idle chatter / Merely nodding / Raw mode of life / Rumour and dishonour / Ugliness is a form of genius.

Dec 98. (cd) *Dossier; (<EFA 08493-2>)* **DIMENTIA IN EXCELSIS (live first US gig)** Sep98

Nov 99. (cd) *Tin Toy; (TTCD 010)* **RAFTERS**

Jan 02. (cd) *Dressed To Kill; (MIDRO 849)* **FINAL MUSAK**

THROWING MUSES

Formed: Boston, Massachusetts, USA . . . 1983 by KRISTIN HERSH and her half-sister, TANYA DONELLY, who duly recruited a rhythm section of ELAINE ADAMEDES and BECCA BLUMEN; DAVID NARCIZO replaced the latter in '84. After an independently released US-only EP, the group were signed up (alongside fellow Bostonians, The PIXIES) to British indie label, '4 a.d.', the first American band to be bestowed such an honour. Produced by Gil Norton, the band's eponymous debut album (featuring new bassist LESLIE LANGSTON) centred around the emotional anguish of chief writer HERSH; her tortured, BUFFY SAINTE-MARIE-like wailing and oblique lyrics conjured up an air of ill-defined unease on the likes of 'RABBIT'S DYING' and 'SOUL SOLDIER' while the twisting, folk-noir minimalism of the music lent proceedings an uncomfortable unpredictability. Raved over in Britain (John Peel was a particularly vocal fan) but largely ignored at home, the 'MUSES consolidated their cult appeal with a further couple of EP's the following year before 1988's slightly disappointing follow-up proper, 'HOUSE TORNADO'. The record signalled a move towards the more accessible territory staked out in 'HUNKPAPA' (1989), US college radio's increasing influence seeing their native fanbase mushrooming. Feeling creatively stifled by HERSH's lion's share of the songwriting, DONELLY subsequently formed her own outfit, The BREEDERS while simultaneously working on her final 'MUSES album, 'THE REAL RAMONA' (1991). A breakthrough set which contained some of the group's most immediate compositions ('COUNTING BACKWARDS' was perhaps the nearest HERSH has come to writing a pop song), DONELLY's contributions a blueprint for the more straightforward alternative pop she would perfect in BELLY. Taking then 'MUSES bassist, ABONG with her, DONELLY finally left the band in 1992, leaving a core of HERSH and NARCIZO. Welcoming LANGSTON back into the fold, HERSH proved THROWING MUSES was still a going concern with the soft grunge-friendly distortion of 'RED HEAVEN' (1992), the band's highest (UK) charting album to date. Nevertheless, the 'MUSES' muse took time out in 1994 to complete a solo debut, 'HIPS AND MAKERS'. Produced by LENNY KAYE and featuring a guest appearance from MICHAEL STIPE, the album found HERSH probing her troubled psyche through a skewed, childlike lens, distorting the sparse acoustic backing and making for compelling listening. Hailed by critics, the record made the UK Top 10 and saw the singer gaining belated recognition from an often reluctant music press. 1995 saw the release of the sixth THROWING MUSES album, 'UNIVERSITY', another fine set which maintained the hi-octane approach of its predecessor. The following years' 'LIMBO' was exactly that, the group becoming a little directionless and stale, although its highlights were the minor hit, 'SHARK'. During the last two years of the decade, KRISTIN delivered a couple of fine long-players, 'STRANGE ANGELS' (1998) and 'SKY MOTEL' (1999), the latter her best work to date; it also was a truly "solo" affair. HERSH's fourth solo set was concentrated on the folky side of her muse, the veteran singer/songwriter once again handling all the instrumental and arranging duties. While this lent the album a singular grace and a feeling of continuity, there was little of the sonic juxtaposition so effectively employed by the 'MUSES. Highlights included a cover of Cat Stevens' 'TROUBLE' and the tense '37 HOURS'. 2003's 'THE GROTTO' found HERSH as abstrusely compelling as ever, certainly lyrically and partly musically as well, her luminous, literate vignettes only fully revealing their secrets with repeated listening. The singer/songwriter's oblique charms were amplified this time around by the presence of semi-legendary desert-rock guru HOWE GELB. • **Songwriters:** KRISTIN lyrics / group compositions except; AMAZING GRACE (trad. hit Judy Collins) / CRY BABY CRY (Beatles) / RIDE INTO THE SUN (Velvet Underground) / MANIC DEPRESSION (Jimi Hendrix) / WHEN THE LEVEE BREAKS (Led Zeppelin) / CRAYON SUN + IF (Latin Playboys) / JAK (Mission Of Burma). HERSH solo:- PANIC PURE (Vic Chesnutt) / JESUS CHRIST (Alex Chilton) / CAN THE CIRCLE BE UNBROKEN (. . . Carter) / PENNYROYAL TEA (Nirvana) / EVERYBODY'S GOT SOMETHING TO HIDE EXCEPT ME AND MY MONKEY (Beatles).

Album rating: THROWING MUSES (*8) / THE FAT SKIER mini (*6) / HOUSE TORNADO (*6) / HUNKPAPA (*5) / THE REAL RAMONA (*8) / RED HEAVEN (*7) / THE CURSE (*5) / UNIVERSITY (*7) / LIMBO (*6) / Kristin Hersh: HIPS AND MAKERS (*6) / STRANGE ANGELS (*6) / SKY MOTEL (*8) / SUNNY BORDER BLUE (*6) / THE GROTTO (*5)

KRISTIN HERSH (b. 7 Aug'66, Atlanta, Georgia) – vocals, lead guitar, piano / **ELAINE ADAMEDES** – bass / **TANYA DONELLY** (b.14 Jul'66) – rhythm guitar, vocals / **DAVID NARCIZO** (b. 6 May'66) – drums, percussion, vocals; repl. BECCA BLUMEN

not iss. Throwing Muses

Nov 85. (7"ep) *<NONTM 1>* **STAND UP / DIRT IS ON THE FLOOR. / THE PARTY / SANTA CLAUS** [–]

—— **LESLIE LANGSTON** (b. 1 Apr'64) – bass, vocals; repl. ELAINE

4 a.d. 4ad-Sire

Sep 86. (lp/c)(cd) *(CAD/+C 607)(CAD 607CD)* **THROWING MUSES** [–]
– Call me / Green / Hate my way / Vicky's box / Rabbit's dying / America (she can't say no) / Fear / Stand up / Soul soldier / Delicious cutters.

Mar 87. (12"ep/c-ep) *(BAD 701/+C)* **CHAINS CHANGED**
– Cry baby cry / Finished / Reel / Snail head.

Aug 87. (m-lp/c) *(CAD/+C 706) <25640>* **THE FAT SKIER**
– Soul soldier / Garoux des larmes / Pool in eyes / A feeling / You cage / Soap and water / And a she-wolf after the war.

Mar 88. (lp/c)(cd) *(CAD/+C 802)(CAD 802CD) <25710>* **HOUSE TORNADO**
– Colder / Mexican woman / The river / Juno / Marriage tree / Run letter / Saving grace / Drive / Downtown / Giant / Walking in the dark. *(cd+=)* – THE FAT SKIER

Jan 89. (lp/c)(cd) *(CAD/+C 901)(CAD 901CD) <25855>* **HUNKPAPA** [59]
– Devil's roof / Bea / Dizzy / No parachutes (say goodbye) / Dragonhead / Fall down / I'm alive / Angel / Mania / The burrow. *(c+=)* – Take. *(cd++=)* – Santa Claus.

Feb 89. (7") *(AD 903)* **DIZZY. / SANTA CLAUS** [–]
(12"+=/10"+=)(cd-s+=) *(BAD/+D 903)(BAD 903CD)* – Mania (live) / Downtown (live).

—— TANYA with DAVID (only in '89) formed off-shoot The BREEDERS. She stayed with the MUSES until next album's completion. **FRED ABONG** – bass repl. her

Jan 91. (7") *(AD 7001) <21833>* **COUNTING BACKWARDS. / AMAZING GRACE** [70]
(12"+=/cd-s+=) *(BAD/+CD 1001)* – Some sun / Cotton mouth.

Feb 91. (cd)(lp/c) *(CAD 1002CD)(CAD/+C 1002) <26489>* **THE REAL RAMONA** [26]
– Counting backwards / Him dancing / Red shoes / Graffiti / Golden thing / Ellen West / Dylan / Hook in her head / Not too soon / Honey chain / Say goodbye / Two step.

Nov 91. (7") *(AD 1015) <40135>* **NOT TOO SOON. / CRY BABY CRY**
(12"+=/cd-s+=) *(BAD 1015/+CD)* – Dizzy (remix) / Him dancing (remix).

—— (Sep'91) DONELLY and ABONG had now quit to form BELLY in 1992

—— **KRISTIN + NARCIZO** recruited newcomer **BERNARD GEORGES** (b.29 Mar'65, Gonaive, Haiti) – bass

Jul 92. (12"ep/cd-ep) *(BAD 2012/+CD)* **FIREPILE / MANIC DEPRESSION. / SNAILHEAD / CITY OF THE DEAD** [46] [–]
(12"ep)(cd-ep) *(BADR 2012)(BAD 2012CDR)* – ('A'remix) / Jack / Ride into the Sun / Handsome woman.

Aug 92. (cd)(lp/c) *(CAD 2013CD)(CAD/+C 2013) <26897>* **RED HEAVEN** [13]
– Furious / Firepile / Die / Dirty water / Stroll / Pearl / Summer Street / Vic / Backroad / The visit / Dovey / Rosetta stone / Carnival wig. *(free-lp w.a.)* **LIVE (live)** – Juno / Marriage tree / Pearl / Stand up – Dovey – Mexican woman / Run letter / Soap and water / Rabbit dying / Cry baby cry / Counting backwards – Handsome woman / Take / Soul soldier / Bea / Delicate cutters.

Nov 92. (cd) *(TAD 2019CD)* **THE CURSE (live)** [74] [–]
– Manic depression / Counting backwards / Fish / Hate my way / Furious / Devil's roof / Snailhead / Firepile / Finished / Take / Say goodbye / Mania / Two step / Delicate cutters / Cottonmouth / Pearl / Vic / Bea.

Dec 94. (7") *(AD 4018)* **BRIGHT YELLOW GUN. / LIKE A DOG** [51] [–]
(12"+=/cd-s+=) *(BAD 4018/+CD)* – Red eyes / Crayon sun.

Jan 95. (cd)(lp/c) *(CAD 5002CD)(CAD/+C 5002) <45796>* **UNIVERSITY** [10]
– Bright yellow gun / Start / Hazing / Shimmer / Calm down, come down / Crabtown / No way in Hell / Surf cowboy / That's all you wanted / Teller / University / Snake face / Fever few.

Jul 96. (7") *(AD 6016)* **SHARK. / TAR MOOCHERS** [53] [–]
(7") *(ADD 6016)* – ('A'side) / Limbobo.
(cd-s++=) *(BAD 6016CD)* – Serene swing.

4 a.d. Rykodisc

Aug 96. (cd)(lp/c) *(CAD 6014CD)(CAD/+C 6014) <10354>* **LIMBO** [36]
– Buzz / Ruthie's knocking / Freefloader / The field / Limbo / Tar kisser / Tango / Serene / Mr. Bones / Night driving / Cowbirds / Shark.

Sep 96. (7"etched) *(TAD 6017) <51052>* **RUTHIE'S KNOCKING**

Jan 97. (cd-s) *(NONTM 12) <51055>* **FREELOADER / IF / TAKE / HEEL TOE** [–]

—— disbanded later in '97

– compilations, etc. –

Jul 98. (d-cd) *4 a.d.; (DAD 8014CD) / Rykodisc; <8017>* **IN A DOGHOUSE** [–]
– (THROWING MUSES album tracks) / (CHAINS CHAINED ep tracks) / Call me / Sinkhole / Green / Hate my way / Vicky's box / America (she can't say no) / Fear / Raise the roses / And a she wolf after the war / Fish / Catch / Lizzie Sage / Clear and great / Doghouse / People.

KRISTIN HERSH

first below featured **MICHAEL STIPE** (R.E.M.) / **JANE SCARPANTONI** – cello

4 a.d. Sire

Jan 94. (12"ep/cd-ep) *(BAD 4001/+CD)* **YOUR GHOST / THE KEY. / UNCLE JUNE AND AUNT KIYOTI / WHEN THE LEVEE BREAKS** [45] [–]

Feb 94. (cd)(lp/c) *(CAD 4002CD)(CAD/+C 4002) <45413>* **HIPS AND MAKERS** [7]
– Your ghost / Beestung / Teeth / Sundrops / sparky / Houdini blues / A loon / Velvet days / Close your eyes / Me and my charms / Tuesday night / The letter / Lurch / The cuckoo / Hips and makers. *(cd re-iss. Jul98; same)*

Apr 94. (7"/c-s) *(AD 4006) <45667>* **A LOON. / VELVET DAYS** [60] Jun94
(12"ep+=/cd-ep+=) *(BAD 4006/+CD)* **STRINGS EP** – Sundrops / Me and my charms.

4 a.d. Rykodisc

Dec 95. (cd-ep) *(TAD 5017CD) <1049>* **THE HOLY SINGLE** [–]
– Jesus Christ / Amazing grace / Sinkhole / Can the circle be unbroken.

Feb 98. (cd) *(CAD 8003CD) <10429>* **STRANGE ANGELS** [64]
– Home / Like you / Aching for you / Cold water coming / Some catch flies / Stained / Shake / Hope / Pale / Baseball field / Heaven / Gazebo tree / Gut pageant / Rock candy brains / Cartoons.

Mar 98. (cd-ep) *(TAD 8005CD)* **LIKE YOU / SHAKE (live to tape) / YOUR GHOST (live to tape)** [–]

Jun 99. (7") *(AD 9007)* **ECHO. / PENNYROYAL TEA** [–]
(cd-s+=) *(BAD 9007CD)* – Everybody's got something to hide except for me and my monkey.

Jun 99. (cd) *(CAD 9008CD)* <79010> **SKY MOTEL** [ ] [ ]
– Echo / White trash moon / Fog / Costa Rica / A cleaner light / San Francisco / Cathedral heat / Husk / Caffeine / Spring / Clay feet / Faith.

Nov 99. (cd-s; promo) *<01>* **A CLEANER LIGHT / HATE MY WAY (acoustic) / GAROUX DES LARMES (acoustic) / A CRY BABY CRY (acoustic)** [–] [–]
4 a.d. 4 a.d.

Mar 01. (cd) *<(CAD 2102CD)>* **SUNNY BORDER BLUE** [ ] [ ]
– Your dirty answer / Spain / 37 hours / Silica / William's cut / Summer salt / Trouble / Candyland / Measure / White suckers / Ruby / Flipside / Listerine.

Mar 03. (cd) *<(CAD 2302CD)>* **THE GROTTO** [ ] [ ]
– Sno cat / Deep Wilson / Snake oil / Vanishing twin / SRB / Silver sun / Vitamins V / Arnica Montana / Milk street / Ether.

Johnny THUNDERS

Born: JOHN ANTHONY GENZALE, 15 Jul'52, Leesburg, Florida, USA. Having been an integral part of The NEW YORK DOLLS in the first half of the 70's, vocalist/guitarist THUNDERS formed new wave/punk act, The HEARTBREAKERS alongside ex-'DOLLS drummer, JERRY NOLAN and ex-TELEVISION bassist, RICHARD HELL. After an initial gig as a trio, they picked up extra guitarist, WALTER LURE, although this incarnation was short-lived as RICHARD promptly departed to form his own RICHARD HELL & THE VOID-OIDS. Filling the void with BILLY RATH, they were invited to London by ex-'DOLLS manager, MALCOLM McLAREN, who offered them a support slot with his punk proteges, The SEX PISTOLS (on their 'Anarchy' tour of late '76). The HEARTBREAKERS subsequently signed to UK label, 'Track', issuing their debut 45, 'CHINESE ROCKS' (a tribute to oriental narcotics co-written with DEE DEE RAMONE), in early '77; both the lead track and the B-side, 'BORN TO LOSE', drawled out with inimitably wasted NY cool. In September of that "Jubilee" year, the group released their much-anticipated debut album, 'L.A.M.F.' (New York street slang for 'Like A Mother F***** '), and although it suffered from terrible production provided by SPEEDY KEEN (ex-THUNDERCLAP NEWMAN), the set still managed a Top 60 placing in Britain. So bad was the record's sound that NOLAN left in protest, further calamity befalling the band as they found themselves on the wrong side of the immigration authorities having abandoned their label. Deported back to NY, the band inevitably splintered despite having recruited a replacement drummer, TY STYX. THUNDERS subsequently returned to London where he recorded a solo album, 'SO ALONE' (1978) aided and abetted by the cream of the UK new wave scene including PETER PERRETT (The Only Ones), CHRISSIE HYNDE (Pretenders), PAUL COOK and STEVE JONES (Sex Pistols) and even PHIL LYNOTT (Thin Lizzy)! In the interim, THUNDERS teamed up with SID VICIOUS in the ill-fated, unfortunately named, The LIVING DEAD (SID was to die shortly afterwards). Just prior to the turn of the decade, The HEARTBREAKERS regrouped in New York with THUNDERS masterminding the affair and prefixing the band name with his own; the resulting stage set, 'LIVE AT MAX'S KANSAS CITY' stands as testament to what might have been. In the 80's, THUNDERS released a series of sporadic albums/singles mostly for UK indie label, 'Jungle', although he never managed to shake off the cult legend tag. Sadly, THUNDERS died in New Orleans on the 23rd of April 1991, the circumstances remaining shrouded in mystery until a subsequent autopsy revealed what most people suspected, that he'd overdosed on heroin. • **Covered:** CAN'T KEEP MY EYES OFF YOU (Andy Williams) / DO YOU LOVE ME (Brian Poole & The Tremeloes) / DOWNTOWN (Petula Clark) / LIKE A ROLLING STONE (Bob Dylan) / CRAWFISH (Elvis Presley) / QUE SERA, SERA (hit; Doris Day). 'COPY CATS' was a complete covers album.

Album rating: Heartbreakers: L.A.M.F. (*7) / Johnny Thunders: SO ALONE (*7) / Johnny Thunders & The Heartbreakers: LIVE AT MAX'S KANSAS CITY (*7) / D.T.K. (*6) / Johnny Thunders: IN COLD BLOOD (*5) / TOO MUCH JUNKIE BUSINESS collection (85) / HURT ME (*6) / QUE SERA, SERA (*5) / STATIONS OF THE CROSS collection (*4) / COPY CATS with Patti Palladin (*5) / GANG WAR (*4) / BOOTLEGGING THE BOOTLEGGERS (*4)

HEARTBREAKERS

JOHNNY THUNDERS – vocals, guitar / **JERRY NOLAN** (b. 7 May'46) – drums / **WALTER LURE** (b.22 Apr'49) – guitar, vocals / **BILLY RATH** – bass, vocals repl. RICHARD HELL who formed his own group

Track not iss.

May 77. (7"/12") *(2094 135/+T)* **CHINESE ROCKS. / BORN TO LOSE** [ ] [–]

Sep 77. (lp) *(2409 218)* **L.A.M.F.** [55] [–]
– Born to lose / Baby talk / All by myself / I wanna be loved / It's not enough / Get off the phone / Chinese rocks / Pirate love / One track mind / I love you / Goin' steady / Let go. *(re-iss. May85 as 'L.A.M.F. – REVISITED' on 'Jungle' lp,pink-lp/pic-lp; FREUD 4/+P) <(re-iss. Sep96 as 'THE LOST '77 MIXES' cd/c/lp; FREUD CD/C/LP 044)> (cd re-iss. Oct00; FREUDCD 044E)*

Nov 77. (7") *(2094 137)* **ONE TRACK MIND. / CAN'T KEEP MY EYES OFF YOU (live) / DO YOU LOVE ME (live)** [ ] [–]

Mar 78. (7"w-drawn) *(2094 142)* **IT'S NOT ENOUGH. / LET GO** [ ] [–]

— split early '78 after being deported back to New York, NOLAN joined SNATCH, while RATH and LURE disappeared

JOHNNY THUNDERS

— returned to London and went solo using session people

Real-W.E.A. not iss.

May 78. (7") *(ARE 1)* **DEAD OR ALIVE. / DOWNTOWN** [ ] [–]

Sep 78. (7"/12"pink,12"blue) *(ARE 3/+T)* **YOU CAN'T PUT YOUR ARMS AROUND A MEMORY. / HURTIN'** [ ] [–]

Oct 78. (lp) *(RAL 1)* **SO ALONE** [ ] [–]
– Pipeline / You can't put your arms around a memory / Great big kiss / Ask me no questions / Leave me alone / Daddy rolling stone / London boys / Untouchable / Subway train / Downtown. *<(re-iss. Jul92 & Feb95 on 'Warners' lp/cd; 7599 26982-2)>*

JOHNNY THUNDERS & THE HEARTBREAKERS

— re-formed '79, with **WALTER, BILLY / + STYX** – drums

Beggars Banquet Max's Kansas

Jul 79. (7") *(BEG 21)* **GET OFF THE PHONE (live). / I WANNA BE LOVED (live)** [ ] [–]

Sep 79. (lp) *(BEGA 9) <DTK 213>* **LIVE AT MAX'S KANSAS CITY (live)** [ ] [ ]
– (intro) / Milk me / Chinese rocks / Get off the phone / London / Take a chance / One track mind / All by myself / Let go / I love you / Can't keep my eyes on you / I wanna be loved / Do you love me?. *(cd-iss. Jul91; BBL 9CD) <(cd-iss. Dec95 on 'ROIR USA'; RUSCD 8219)>*

— Split again '79. In 1980, THUNDERS joined WAYNE KRAMER'S GANG WAR.

JOHNNY THUNDERS

solo again with **WALTER LURE** – guitar / **BILLY ROGERS** – drums

New Rose not iss.

Dec 82. (7") *(NEW 14)* **IN COLD BLOOD / ('A'live)** [–] France [–]

Jan 83. (d-lp) *(NR 18)* **IN COLD BLOOD** (some live) [–] France [–]
– In cold blood / Just another girl / Green onions / Diary of a lover / Look at my eyes / Live: (intro) / Just another girl / Too much junkie business / Sad vacation / Louie Louie / Gloria / Treat me like a nigger / Do you love me / Green onions / 10 commandments. *(re-iss. Apr94 lp/cd; 422367) (re-iss. cd Jun95 on 'Dojo'; DOJOCD 221) <(cd re-iss. Aug97 on 'Essential'; ESMCD 589)> (lp re-iss. Mar98 on 'Munster'; MR 142)*

Jan 84. (7"m) *(NEW 27)* **HURT ME. / IT'S NOT ENOUGH / LIKE A ROLLING STONE** [ ] [-]

Jan 84. (lp) *(ROSE 26)* **HURT ME** [ ] [-]
– So alone / It ain't me babe / Eve of destruction / You can't put your arms round a memory / You're so strange / I'm a boy in a girl / Lonely planet boy / Sad vacation / Hurt me / Diary of a lover / Ask me no questions. *(cd-iss. May94; 422366) (re-iss. cd Jul95 on 'Dojo'; DOJOCD 217) <cd re-iss. Aug97 on 'Essential'; ESMCD 588> (lp re-iss. Mar98 on 'Munster'; MR 142)*

Jungle not iss.

Oct 85. (7"/7"pic-d; by JOHNNY THUNDERS with PATTI PALLADIN) *(JUNG 23/+P)* **CRAWFISH. / TIE ME UP (LOVE KNOT)** [ ] [-]
(ext.12"+=) *(JUNG 23T)* – ('A'-Bayou mix).

— with **PATTI PALLADIN** – vocals (ex-SNATCH, FLYING LIZARDS)

Dec 85. (lp) *(FREUD 9)* **QUE SERA, SERA** [ ] [-]
– Que sera, sera / Short lives / M.I.A. / I only wrote this song for you / Little bit of whore / Cool operator / Blame it on mom / Tie me up / Alone in a crowd / Billy boy / Endless party. *(pic-lp iss.Jun87; FREUDP 09) <(cd-iss. Dec94; FREUDCD 49)> (cd re-iss. Apr01; FREUDCD 49E)*

Jun 87. (7") *(JUNG 33)* **QUE SERA SERA. / SHORT LIVES** [ ] [-]
(12"+=) *(JUNG 33T)* – I only wrote this song.

JOHNNY THUNDERS & PATTI PALLADIN

May 88. (7") *(JUNG 38)* **SHE WANTS TO MAMBO. / UPTOWN** [ ] [ ]
(12"+=) *(JUNG 38T)* – Love is strange.

Jun 88. (lp/c/cd) *(FREUD/+C/CD 20)* **YEAH, YEAH, I'M A COPY CAT** [ ] [-]
– Can't seem to make you mine / Baby it's you / She wants to mambo / Treat her right / Uptown to Harlem / Crawfish / Alligator wine / Two time loser / Love is strange / (I was) Born to cry / He cried (she cried) / Let me entertain you (part 1 & 2). *(re-iss. cd Nov96; same)*

Jan 89. (7") *(JUNG 43)* **(I WAS) BORN TO CRY. / TREAT HER RIGHT** [ ] [-]
(12"+=) *(JUNG 43T)* – Can't seem to make her mine.

— THUNDERS died on the 23rd April '91, aged 38. He left three children from his first marriage plus another 3 year-old daughter, Jamie, conceived while he'd lived in Sweden with his girlfriend, Suzanne. JERRY NOLAN died on the 14th January '92 of a stroke (aged 45) after a bout of pneumonia and meningitis. Original drummer, BILLY MURCIA, also died in the 90's.

– compilations, etc. –

on 'Jungle' unless otherwise mentioned

Nov 82. (lp,pink-lp,white-lp/pic-lp) *(FREUD/+P 1)* **D.T.K. – LIVE AT THE SPEAKEASY (live)** [ ] [-]
<(cd-iss. Aug94 on 'Receiver'; R 191)>

May 83. (7"ep) *(JUNG 1)* **VINTAGE '77** [ ] [-]
– Let go / Chinese rocks / Born to lose.

1983. (c) *R.O.I.R.; <A 118>* **TOO MUCH JUNKIE BUSINESS** [-] [ ]
(cd-iss. Feb95 on 'ROIR Europe'; same) <US 'Combat'; 5029>

Mar 84. (7"/7"pic-d) *(JUNG 14/+P)* **GET OFF THE PHONE. / ALL BY MYSELF** [ ] [-]
(12"+=) *(JUNG 14X)* – Pirate love.

Jun 84. (lp) *A.B.C.; (ABCLP 2)* **LIVE AT THE LYCEUM BALLROOM 1984 (live)** [ ] [-]
<(re-iss. Jun91 on 'Receiver' lp/c/cd; RR LP/LC/CD 134)>

Feb 85. (7") *Twins; (T 1702)* **BORN TO LOSE. / IT'S NOT ENOUGH** [ ] [-]

May 85. (7"ep/12"ep) *(JUNG 18/+X)* **CHINESE ROCKS / BORN TO LOSE / ONE TRACK MIND / I WANNA BE LOVED** [ ] [-]

Feb 87. (c) *R.O.I.R.; (A 146) / Combat; <5028>* **STATIONS OF THE CROSS** [-] [ ]
(re-iss. cd Jul94 on 'Receiver'; RRCD 188) (re-iss. cd Feb95 on 'ROIR Europe'; same)

May 88. (box-lp) *(JTBOX 1)* **THE JOHNNY THUNDERS ALBUM COLLECTION** [ ] [-]

Feb 90. (lp/cd) *(FREUD/+CD 30)* **BOOTLEGGIN' THE BOOTLEGGERS** [ ] [-]

Jan 92. (cd) *Fan Club;* **LIVE AT MOTHERS (live)** [ ] [-]
(re-iss. Mar98 on 'Munster'; MR 140)

Feb 92. (cd) *Bomp; <(BCD 4039)>* **WHAT GOES AROUND (live)** [ ] [ ]

Oct 92. (cd) *Fan Club; (422365)* **HAVE FAITH (live solo)** [ ] [-]
<(re-iss. Aug96 on 'Mutiny'; MUT 8005CD)>

Dec 93. (cd) *Anagram; (CDGRAM 70)* **CHINESE ROCKS – THE ULTIMATE LIVE COLLECTION (live)** [ ] [-]
(lp-iss.Sep99 on 'Get Back'; GET 49) (re-iss. Nov02; same)

Sep 94. (cd) *Skydog; (62251)* **VIVE LE REVOLUTION – LIVE PARIS, 1977 (live JOHNNY THUNDERS & THE HEARTBREAKERS)** [ ] [-]

Nov 94. (cd) *Essential; (ESDCD 226)* **ADD WATER AND STIR – LIVE IN JAPAN 1991 (live)** [ ] [ ]

Apr 96. (cd) *Dojo; (DOJOCD 231)* **THE STUDIO BOOTLEGS** [ ] [ ]

Oct 97. (cd) *Anagram; (CDMGRAM 117)* **BELFAST ROCKS** [ ] [ ]
(re-iss. Jul00 on 'Triple X'; TX 0031CD)

Feb 99. (cd) *Mogul; (MNR 003)* **LIVE CRISIS** [ ] [ ]

Apr 99. (d-cd) *Receiver; <(RRDCD 009)>* **SAD VACATION** [ ] [ ]

May 99. (cd) *Sonic; (SRCD 0020)* **INTERNAL POSSESSION** [ ] [ ]

Sep 99. (7"pink) *(JUNG 62)* **CHINESE ROCKS. /** [ ] [-]

Sep 99. (7") *(JUNG 63)* **ONE TRACK MIND. /** [ ] [-]

Oct 99. (d-cd) *Jungle; (FREUDCD 60)* **BORN TO LOSE** [ ] [ ]

May 00. (cd) *Amsterdamned; (TX 70030CD)* **IN THE FLESH** [ ] [ ]

May 00. (cd) *Receiver; <(RRCD 288)>* **PLAY WITH FIRE – JOHNNY THUNDERS LIVE** [ ] [ ]

Nov 00. (cd) *Receiver; <(RRCD 297)>* **LIVE AND WASTED – UNPLUGGED 1990 (live)** [ ] [ ]

Apr 01. (cd) *Triple X; <(TX 70032CD)>* **ENDLESS PARTY** [ ] [ ]

Apr 02. (cd) *Captain Trip; (CTCD 359)>* **THUNDERSTORM IN DETROIT – LIVE AT THE SILVERBIRD 21/12/80 (live)** [ ] [ ]

Jun 02. (3xcd-box) *Castle; <(CMETD 468)>* **YOU CAN'T PUT YOUR ARMS AROUND A MEMORY** [ ] [ ]
– (L.A.M.F. REVISITED / LIVE AT THE LYCEUM / LIVE & WASTED).

THURSDAY

Formed: New Brunswick, New Jersey, USA . . . 1997 by frontman GEOFF RICKLY, along with guitarists STEVE PEDULLA, TOM KEELEY and rhythm men TIM PAYNE and TUCKER RULE. Forging their melodious emo-core rock into the American mainstream through two CURE-esque sets, 'WAITING' (2000) and 'FULL COLLAPSE' (2001), THURSDAY delivered the 5-song EP, 'FIVE STORIES FALLING', a year later. This epitomised their uniformed, hard-edged sound via four live faves, 'AUTOBIOGRAPHY OF A NATION', 'UNDERSTANDING OF A CAR CRASH', 'STANDING ON THE EDGE OF SUMMER' and 'PARIS IN FLAMES'. It was no surprise when 'Island' records took up the reins and set the ball rolling again with their third full-set, 'WAR ALL THE TIME' (2003). With shades of U2 at their anthemic and grandiose (example 'THIS SONG BROUGHT TO YOU BY A FALLING BOMB' and 'SIGNALS OVER THE AIR'), the critically acclaimed album raced into the US Top 10 and into the minds and souls of a new breed of American youth.

Album rating: WAITING (*5) / FULL COLLAPSE (*5) / WAR ALL THE TIME (*7)

GEOFF RICKLY – vocals / **STEVE PEDULLA** – guitar, vocals / **TOM KEELEY** – guitar, vocals / **TIM PAYNE** – bass, vocals / **TUCKER RULE** – drums, vocals

not iss. Eyeball

Jan 00. (cd) *<EB 015CD>* **WAITING** [-] [ ]
– Porcelain / This side of brightness / Ian Curtis / Introduction / Streaks in the sky / In transmission / Dying in New Brunswick / The dotted line / Where the circle ends. *(UK-iss.Sep02; same as US)*

Victory Victory

Apr 01. (lp/cd) *<VR 145/+CD>* **FULL COLLAPSE** [ ] [ ]
– A0001 / Understanding in a car / Concealer / Autobiography of a nation / A hole in the world / Cross out the eyes / Paris in flames / I am the killer / Standing on the edge of summer / Wind-up / How long is the night? / I1100.

Oct 02. (cd-ep) *<VR 189CD>* **FIVE STORIES FALLING (live)** [ ] [ ]
– Autobiography of a nation / Understanding in a car crash / Standing on the edge of summer / Paris in flames / Jet black New Year (studio).

		Universal	Island
Sep 03.	(cd)(lp) *(9860874)(0772931)* <2930-2/-1> **WAR ALL THE TIME**	62	7

– For the workforce, drowning / Between rupture and rapture / Division St. / Signals over the air / Marches and manoeuvres / Asleep in the chapel / This song brought to you by a falling bomb / Steps ascending / War all the time / M. Shepard / Tomorrow I'll be you.

Oct 03.	(7") *(9812291)* **SIGNALS OVER THE AIR. / NY BATTERI**	62	

(cd-s) <(9 812292)> – ('A'side) / Division St. (acoustic) / Hole in the world (acoustic) / ('A'-video).

☐ TIGER LILY (see under ⇒ ULTRAVOX)

☐ Glenn TILBROOK (see under ⇒ SQUEEZE)

☐ 'TIL TUESDAY (see under ⇒ MANN, Aimee)

Justin TIMBERLAKE

Born: 31 Jan'81, Memphis, Tennessee, USA. *NSYNC member, former BRITNEY SPEARS beau and all around suave smoothie, JUSTIN TIMBERLAKE's curly afro could be seen as far back as the late 80's, when – alongside SPEARS and AGUILERA – he featured heavily on the bubble-gum pop of Disney's Mickey Mouse Club. After forming the immensely successful boyband *NSYNC (with CHRIS KIRKPATRICK, JOEY FATONE, JOSH CHASEZ and LANCE BASS) in Florida in 1996, the group went on to sell millions of units, the most notable being candy-pop hits 'Tearing Up My Heart' and 'I Want You Back' and the multi-platinum selling sophomore set 'No Strings Attached' (2000). After the group's third release, 2001's 'Celebrity', JUSTIN underwent an image makeover, and changed his musical direction for the release of his solo debut 'JUSTIFIED' in 2002. Gone was the Art Garfunkel-esque hairdo (shaved, with a stripe was more the thing) and in was super producers The NEPTUNES (N.E.R.D.) and TIMBALAND for what was to become one of the biggest selling albums in recent years. Lead single, 'LIKE I LOVE YOU' confirmed this almost straight away, with JT dancing in MICHAEL JACKSON, 'Off The Wall' period stylee, breakbeats, acoustic guitars and weird keyboard hooks – the man was a star. The emotion-fuelled second single, 'CRY ME A RIVER', shone light on JT's much publicised split with BRITNEY. Thank goodness for 'ROCK YOUR BODY' and 'SENORITA', following in quick succession. Two uptempo tracks, the former featured cut'n'paste beatboxing, the latter with a coda which included a concert inspired crowd separation technique ("They don't do this anymore", says JT) where JUSTIN encourages the ladies to sing one vocal harmony and the men the other. All singles were inevitably big hits, the real star here was TIMBERLAKE, with many people wondering, after his massive success and new-found bachelor sex-appeal, how could he go back to the uncool and uninspiring manufactured boyband *NSYNC?

Album rating: JUSTIFIED (*7)

JUSTIN TIMBERLAKE – vocals / with session people

		Jive	Jive
Oct 02.	(c-s) *(925434-4)* **LIKE I LOVE YOU / (instrumental)**	2 Sep02	11

(12"+=/cd-s+=) <25434> *(925434-0/-2)* – ('A'extended club mix).

Nov 02.	(cd/d-lp) *(922463-2/-1)* <41823> **JUSTIFIED**	1	2

– Senorita / Like I love you / (Oh no) What you got / Take it from here / Cry me a river / Rock your body / Nothin' else / Last night / Still on my brain / (And she said) Take me now / Right for me / Let's take a ride / Never again.

Feb 03.	(c-s) *(925461-4)* **CRY ME A RIVER / (Dirty Vegas vocal mix) / LIKE I LOVE YOU (Basement Jaxx vocal mix)**	2 Dec02	3

(cd-s) *(925461-2)* – (first 2 tracks) / (Bill Hamel vocal mix).

(12") *(925461-0)* <40073> – ('A'-Dirty Vegas vocal mix) / Like I love you (Basement Jaxx vocal) / Like I love you (Deep Dish zigzag mix).

(cd-s) *(925463-2)* – ('A'-Johnny Fiasco mix) / Like I love you (Basement Jaxx vocal mix) / Like I love you (Deep Dish mix).

—— in Mar'03, JUSTIN featured on NELLY's Top 10 hit, 'Work It'

May 03.	(c-s) *(925495-4)* **ROCK YOUR BODY / WORTHY OF**	2	5

(12"+=) *(925495-0)* <25496> – ('A'-Sander Kleinberg radio mix) / ('A'-Paul Oakenfold mix).

(cd-s++=) *(925495-0)* – ('A'-instrumental).

Sep 03.	(cd-s) *(82876 56344-2)* <52255> **SENORITA / I'M LOVIN' IT / SENORITA (Eddie's crossover mix)**	13	27

(12") *(82876 56344-0)* – (first 2 tracks) / ('A'-Dr Octavo 2 step mixes).

(cd-s) *(82876 56395-2)* – ('A'-NUM edit) / ('A'-thick vocal mix) / ('A'-E smoove house mix).

TINDERSTICKS

Formed: Nottingham, England . . . 1988 as ASPHALT RIBBONS, by STUART STAPLES, DAVE BOULTER and DICKON HINCHCLIFFE, the line-up completed by NEIL FRASER, MARK COLWILL and AL McCAULEY. Abandoning their previous TRIFFIDS/GO-BETWEENS-esque indie attempts, the group adopted a darkly brooding hybrid of faded-glamour easy listening and semi-acoustic strumming, incorporating swooning strings, mournful violin, frantic flamenco and hints of country. Surely the heartbroken, doomed romantic to top all doomed romantics, STAPLES' low-key mumblings were somehow utterly compelling, his often barely audible melange of NICK CAVE, LEE HAZLEWOOD and TOM WAITS capable of expressing every nuance in the music regardless of what he was actually saying. The TINDERSTICKS came to critical notice with only their second single, 'MARBLES', a lo-fi STAPLES monologue cosetted by an aching melody. Released on their own 'Tippy Toe' label, the track was unanimously awarded Single Of The Week by both NME and Melody Maker, creating a buzz which would eventually see the group sign to the newly formed 'This Way Up' label. Previewed by the string-drenched melancholy of the 'CITY SICKNESS' single, the eponymous 'TINDERSTICKS' was released in late '93. A dense, bleakly beautiful, seedily glamorous near 80-minute epic, the record was so strikingly different from anything else around (save for maybe GALLON DRUNK or NICK CAVE) it sounded timeless. From the edgy resignation of 'WHISKEY & WATER' to the lovelorn lament of 'RAINDROPS', this was one of the most luxuriantly dark albums of the 90's, reeking of failed relationships and nicotine-stained despair. With gushing praise from the music press, both for the album and their hypnotic live shows, The TINDERSTICKS even managed to scrape a Top 60 chart placing. Released simultaneously with the album was a cover of John Barry's 'WE HAVE ALL THE TIME IN THE WORLD' alongside GALLON DRUNK on a 'Clawfist' 7", the latter group's TERRY EDWARDS having guested on the album and subsequently adding string arrangements on their next long player. Preceded by a cover of the late Townes Van Zandt's 'KATHLEEN', 'TINDERSTICKS' (same title, different album) was finally released in Spring '95, its grainy noir narratives and downtrodden country enhanced with exquisite orchestration. There were no great stylistic leaps, just a further exploration and refinement of the blurred shadows and twilit corners that graced the debut. An undisputed highlight was the goose-bump country duet with The WALKABOUTS' CARLA TORGERSON, 'TRAVELLING LIGHT', released as a single that summer. The TINDERSTICKS were also in the process of refining their live sound, or rather expanding it, with the help of a full orchestra; the gorgeous results can be heard on concert set, 'THE BLOOMSBURY THEATRE 12.3.95'. Unable to sustain such a money draining enterprise for too long, The TINDERSTICKS-plus-orchestra phase reached its zenith during a hugely successful week long residency at London's ICA theatre in late '96. The same year also saw the group's first foray into soundtrack work, scoring the music for French art film, 'Nenette et Boni'. Largely instrumental, the piano and bass-led main theme was fleshed out with the moving 'TINY TEARS' (or 'PETITES GOUTTES D'EAU' in French) from the second album; hardly essential but a pleasant listen all the same. Following the group's own fears that the fragile balance of The TINDERSTICKS' muse was becoming unworkable, the difficult third album, 'CURTAINS' was finally completed in a fevered rush of creativity and released in Summer '97. Less sprawling and more cohesive than previous efforts, it was also bolder and more accessible, STAPLES actually singing comprehensibly on the bulk of the tracks. Predictably, there were also more strings than ever, HINCHCLIFFE's orchestral flourishes crescendoing majestically on 'DON'T LOOK DOWN' and achieving a pathos only previously glimpsed before on 'LET'S PRETEND', JESUS ALEMANY's mariachi-style trumpet a bittersweet counterpart. There was even another country duet, 'BURIED BONES', a brilliantly executed NANCY/LEE-style sparring match featuring the velvet tones of BONGWATER's ANNE MAGNUSON. Lyrically, the themes remained reliably unchanged, tales of everyday lust and disillusionment dripping from STAPLES' lips like the honey from his claws as described in the gripping, unsettling 'BEARSUIT'. And, with 'BALLAD OF TINDERSTICKS', STAPLES indicated that they don't take this music business lark TOO seriously. After a stop-gap 'best of' album, 'DONKEYS' was released in '98, TINDERSTICKS were back to their mournful best courtesy of 1999's 'SIMPLE PLEASURE'. Opening with the minor hit, 'CAN WE START AGAIN?' and then a cover of Odyssey's dancefloor hit(!), 'IF YOU'RE LOOKING FOR A WAY OUT', it was clear to see the familiar 'STICKS territory had been given a modern day injection. Switching to another label was perhaps the best possible thing to happen to TINDERSTICKS who issued their dark melancholic set 'CAN OUR LOVE . . .' in 2001. A jazzy, but yet still tortoise speed release, STAPLES' crooning, brooding, COHEN-esque vocals reached new heights of intimacy on songs such as 'DYING SLOWLY' and 'SWEET RELEASE'. The group returned one year later to issue the soundtrack to Claire Denis' post-feminist, cannibal movie 'TROUBLE EVERY DAY', which marked the group's second collaboration with the director after her debut film 'Nenette et Boni'. As usual, the tone set was a dark one, STAPLES providing only one vocal track, to much eerie and frightening effect. If there was any justice, TINDERSTICKS would be bigger than OASIS; as it is they remain a treasured secret for anyone who's ever glimpsed the universe through the bottom of a wine glass. With 'WAITING FOR THE MOON' (2003), the band signalled both their ability and willingness to follow their dark musical whims seemingly indefinitely, with only occasional fine tuning. And if they can still create sound-lyric atmospherics as menacingly vivid as opener 'UNTIL THE MORNING COMES', that can only be a good thing.

• **Other covers:** KOOKS (David Bowie) / I'VE BEEN LOVING YOU TOO LONG (Otis Redding & Jerry Butler) / HERE (Pavement).

• **Trivia:** JON LANGFORD of The THREE JOHNS, produced early ASPHALT RIBBONS material.

Album rating: Asphalt Ribbons: OLD HORSE & OTHER SONGS (*4) / Tindersticks: TINDERSTICKS (*8) / THE SECOND TINDERSTICKS ALBUM (*7) / THE BLOOMSBURY THEATRE 12.3.95 (*6) / NANETTE ET BONI soundtrack (*6) / CURTAINS (*8) / DONKEYS 92-97 compilation (*7) / SIMPLE PLEASURE (*8) / CAN OUR LOVE (*7) / TROUBLE EVERY DAY (*6) / WAITING FOR THE MOON (*6)

ASPHALT RIBBONS

STUART STAPLES – vocals / **DICKON HINCHCLIFFE** – violin / **DAVE BOULTER** – keyboards / **BLACKHOUSE** – guitar / **FRASER** – bass / **WATT** – drums

In-Tape | not iss.

Oct 89. (7"ep) *(IT 063)* **THE ORCHARD** | | –
– Over again / Red sauce / Greyhound / I used to live T.

May 90. (7"m) *(IT 068)* **GOOD LOVE. / LONG LOST UNCLE / THE DAY I TURNED BAD** | | –

— (Alongside new stablemates MY LIFE WITH PATRICK, their new label below issued a free flexi sampler with 'Zip Code' fanzine; cat no. LILY 001)

Tiger Lily | not iss.

Apr 91. (12"ep) *(LILY 002)* **PASSION, COOLNESS, INDIFFERENCE, BOREDOM, MOCKERY, CONTEMPT, DISGUST** | | –

E.T.T. | not iss.

Aug 91. (m-lp) *(E 101)* **OLD HORSE & OTHER SONGS** | | –
– Rosemarie / Old horse / State inside / The distance between us / Strong hands / Downside. *(cd-iss. Apr92; E 101-2)*

TINDERSTICKS

— were formed by **STUART, DICKON and DAVE**, plus Londoners **NEIL FRASER** – guitar / **MARK COLWILL** – bass / **AL McCAULEY** – drums

Tippy Toe | No.6

Nov 92. (7") *(TIPPY TOE 1)* **PATCHWORK. / MILKY TEETH** | | –

Mar 93. (10"ep) *(TIPPY TOE – che 2)* **MARBLES / JOE STUMBLE. / FOR THOSE . . . / BENN** | | –

— Below featured dual vox of **NIKI SIN** of HUGGY BEAR.

Rough Trade Sing. Club | not iss.

Mar 93. (7") *(45REV 16)* **A MARRIAGE MADE IN HEAVEN. / (instrumental)** | | –

Domino | No.6

Jul 93. (7"ep) *(RUG 6)* **UNWIRED E.P.** | | –
– Feeling relatively good / Rottweilers and mace / She / Kooks.

Sep 93. (7") <*KAR 028*> **MARBLES. / FOR THOSE NOT BEAUTIFUL** | – |

This Way Up | Bar None

Sep 93. (7"/cd-s) *(WAY 1811/1833)* **CITY SICKNESS. / UNTITLED / THE BULLRING** | | –

Oct 93. (cd/c/lp) *(518306-2/-4/-1)* <*46*> **TINDERSTICKS** | 56 |
– Nectar tyed / Sweet, sweet man (pt.1) / Whiskey & water / Blood / City sickness / Patchwork / Marbles / The Walt blues / Milky teeth (pt.2) / Sweet, sweet man (pt.2) / Jism / Piano song / Tie dye / Raindrops / Sweet, sweet man (pt.3) / Her / Tea stain / Drunk tank / Paco de Renaldo's dream / The not knowing. *(lp+=)* – Fruitless. *(re-iss. Jun97; same)*

Oct 93. (7") *(XPIG 21)* **WE HAVE ALL THE TIME IN THE WORLD – JAMES BOND THEME. / (other by Gallon DRunk)** | | –
(above issued on 'Clawfist')

— 'Tippy Toe' also gave away 7" 'LIVE IN BERLIN' at gigs.

Jan 94. (7"ep/10"ep/cd-ep) *(WAY 2811/2888/2833)* **KATHLEEN EP** | 61 | –
– Kathleen / Summat Moon / A sweet sweet man / E-type Joe.

— In Aug'94, they appeared on Various Artists EP on 'Blue Eyed Dog'; track 'LOVE BITES', and others by STRANGELOVE / GOD MACHINE + BREED.

This Way Up | London

Mar 95. (7") *(WAY 38-11)* **NO MORE AFFAIRS. / (instrumental)** | 58 | –
(cd-s+=) *(WAY 38-33)* – Fruitless.

Apr 95. (cd/c/d-lp) *(526303-2/-4/-1)* <*6303*> **THE SECOND TINDERSTICKS ALBUM** | 13 | Oct95
– El diablo en el ojo / My sister / Tiny tears / Snowy in F minor / Seaweed / Vertrauen 2 / Talk to me / No more affairs / Singing / Travelling light / Cherry blossoms / She's gone / Mistakes / Vertraven 3 / Sleepy song. *(ltd.lp w/ free one-sided-7")* – PLUS DE LIAISONS

Jun 95. (7") <*SP 297*> **THE SMOOTH SOUNDS OF TINDERSTICKS** | – |
– Here / Harry's dilemma.

— <above issued for 'Sub Pop'>

Jul 95. (7"/cd-s) *(WAY 45-11)* **TRAVELLING LIGHT. / WAITING 'ROUND YOU / I'VE BEEN LOVING YOU TOO LONG** [51] [–]

Oct 95. (cd/d-10"lp) *(528597-2/-1)* **THE BLOOMSBURY THEATRE 12.3.95 (live)** [32] [–]
– El diablo en el ojo / A night in / Talk to me / She's gone / My sister * / No more affairs / City sickness / Vertrauen II / Sleepy song / Jism / Drunk tank / Mistakes / Tiny tears / Raindrops / For those . . . *(d-lp+= *)*

This Way Up · Bar None

Oct 96. (cd/lp) *(524300-2/-1)* <99> **NENETTE ET BONI (Original Soundtrack)** [ ] [ ]
– Ma souer / La passerelle / Les gateaux / Camions / Nenette est la / Petites chiennes / Nosterfrau / Petites gouttes d'eau / Les Cannes a peche / La mort de Felix / Nenette s'en va / Les bebes / Les fleurs / Rumba.

This Way Up · Polygram

May 97. (12"ep/cd-ep) *(WAY 61-22/-33)* **BATHTIME. / MANALOW / SHADOWS / PACO'S THEME** [38] [–]
(cd-ep) *(WAY 61-66)* – ('A'side) / Kathleen / Here / Tyed.

Jun 97. (cd/c/lp) *(<524344-2/-4/-1>)* **CURTAINS** [37] [ ]
– Another night in / Rented rooms / Don't look down / Dick's slow song / Fast one / Ballad of Tindersticks / Dancing / Let's pretend / Desperate man / Buried bones / Bearsuit / (Tonight) Are you trying to fall in love again / I was your man / Bathtime / Walking.

Oct 97. (7") *(WAY 65-22)* **RENTED ROOMS. / ('A'-Swing version)** [56] [ ]
(cd-s+=) *(WAY 65-33)* – Make believe.
(cd-s) *(WAY 65-66)* – ('A'side) / Cherry blossoms (live) / She's gone (live) / Rhumba (live).

Island · Island

Sep 98. (cd/lp) *(CID/ILPS 8074)* *<524588>* **DONKEYS 92-97 (A COLLECTION OF SINGLES ° RARITIES ° UNRELEASED RECORDINGS)** (compilation) [ ] [ ]
– Patchwork / Marbles / Her / City sickness / Travelling light / I've been loving you too long / Plus de liaisons / Here / Tiny tears / Bathtime / A marriage made in Heaven / For those . . .

Aug 99. (7") *(IS 756)* **CAN WE START AGAIN? / ONE WAY STREET** [54] [–]
(cd-s+=) *(CID 756)* – A little time.
(cd-s) *(CIDX 756)* – ('A'demo) / Puppy fat / Desperate man (alternate version).

Aug 99. (cd) *(CID 8085)* *<546372>* **SIMPLE PLEASURE** [36] [ ]
– Can we start again? / If you're looking for a way out / Pretty words / From the inside / If she's torn / Before you close your eyes / (You take) This heart of mine / I know that loving / CF GF. *(lp-iss.Sep99 on 'Simply Vinyl'; SVLP 112)*

Beggars Banquet · Beggars Banquet

Dec 00. (7"/cd-s) *(SINS 001/1CD)* **WHAT IS A MAN. / (instrumental)** [ ] [–]

May 01. (cd/lp) *(BBQ CD/LP 222)* <80222> **CAN OUR LOVE . . .** [47] [ ]
– Dying slowly / People keep comin' around / Tricklin' / Can our love . . . / Sweet release / Don't ever get tired / No man in the world / Chilitetime.

Oct 01. (cd/lp) *(BBQ CD/LP 225)* *<80225>* **TROUBLE EVERY DAY** (original soundtrack) [ ] [ ]
– Opening titles / Dream / Houses / Maid theme 1 / Room 321 / Computer / Notre Dame / Killing theme / Taxi to Core / Core on stairs – Love theme (Shane and June) / Maid theme (end) / Closing titles / Killing theme (alternate version) / Trouble every day.

May 03. (12"ep/cd-ep) *(BBQ 367 T/CD)* **DON'T EVEN GO THERE EP** [ ] [–]
– Trying to find a home / Sexual funk / Everything changes / I want you.

Jun 03. (cd/lp) *(BBQ CD/LP 232)* *<80232>* **WAITING FOR THE MOON** [ ] [ ]
– Until the morning comes / Say goodbye to the city / Sweet memory / 4.48 psychosis / Waiting for the moon / Trying to find a home / Sometimes it hurts / My oblivion / Just a dog / Running wild.

below featured **LHASA DE SELA**

Jul 03. (7"/cd-s) *(BBQ 369/+CD)* **SOMETIMES IT HURTS. / MY AUTUMN'S DONE COME** [60] [–]

Oct 03. (12"/cd-s) *(BBQ 372 T/CD)* **MY OBLIVION. / NOW IT'S OVER / RUNNING WILD (instrumental)** [ ] [–]

☐ TIN MACHINE (see under ⇒ BOWIE, David)

☐ TOM TOM CLUB (see under ⇒ TALKING HEADS)

☐ TONES ON TAIL (see under ⇒ BAUHAUS)

TOOL

Formed: Hollywood, California, USA . . . 1990 by ADAM JONES, MAYNARD JAMES KEENAN, PAUL D'AMOUR and DANNY CAREY. Signing to 'Zoo' records, TOOL showcased their claustrophobic, nihilistic nu-metal on the 1992 mini-set, 'OPIATE'. Creating a buzz with high-profile supports to the likes of HENRY ROLLINS, TOOL subsequently hammered out a full album's worth of HELMET-like savage intensity with 'UNDERTOW' (1993), a record with such bluntly titled tracks as 'PRISON SEX' (also a single), 'INTOLERANCE' and 'BOTTOM' (the latter featuring the aforementioned ROLLINS). The album went on to sell over a million copies in the States, having only reached the Top 50. Three years later, after extensive touring, they resurfaced in dramatic fashion with 'AENIMA', the record bolting straight to No.2, surprising many who had yet to acquire a taste for TOOL. An ensuing legal battle with 'Freeworld Entertainment' lasted two years before the band agreed a joint deal for subsequent recordings. While TOOL then underwent a hard earned sabbatical, KEENAN hooked up with BILLY HOWERDEL (TOOL guitar tech), PAZ LENCHANTIN, TOY VAN LEEUWEN and JOSH FREESE to form A PERFECT CIRCLE. After making their debut at L.A.'s Viper Room in summer '99, the group released the 'MER DE NOMS' album in 2000. With songwriting duties shared by KEENAN and HOWERDEL, the record carried on in the dark spirit of TOOL while drawing a string-enhanced gothic cloak (or cape, even) around KEENAN's emotionally ravaged vocals. Following the release of the millennial 'SALIVAL' box set, TOOL themselves re-entered the fray in 2001 with the widely acclaimed 'LATERALUS', an ineffably complex work of shifting textures, oblique mood and inscrutable lyrics carrying the mystical torch of its predecessor into a parallel sonic universe. Kerrang! hailed it as one of the greatest albums ever recorded, grand claims which will no doubt leave those humble TOOL lads unfazed. A PERFECT CIRCLE returned in 2003 with the ominously titled 'THIRTEENTH STEP' album, featuring former MARILYN MANSON bassist JEORDIE OSBORNE WHITE (who stepped into the breach after the departure of LENCHANTIN) and guitarist DANNY LOHNER, who was the immediate stand-in for VAN LEEUWEN and was himself later replaced by ex-SMASHING PUMPKINS man JAMES IHA. Produced by HOWERDEL, the record sought to deepen and enhance the sinister atmospherics of the debut, relying on skilfully wrought, sonic light and shade rather than dynamic bludgeon.

Album rating: OPIATE mini (*5) / UNDERTOW (*6) / AENIMA (*7) / SALIVAL live (*6) / LATERALUS (*8) / A Perfect Circle: MER DE NOMS (*6) / THIRTEENTH STEP (*6)

MAYNARD JAMES KEENAN – vocals / **ADAM JONES** – guitar / **PAUL D'AMOUR** – bass / **DANNY CAREY** – drums

Zoo-RCA · Zoo

Jul 92. (m-cd/m-c/m-lp) <*(72445 11027-2/-4/-1)*> **OPIATE** [ ] [ ]
– Sweat / Hush / Part of me / Cold and ugly (live) / Jerk-off (live) / Opiate.

Apr 93. (cd/c) <*(72445 11052-2/-4)*> **UNDERTOW** [ ] [50]
– Intolerance / Prison sex / Sober / Bottom / Crawl away / Swamp song / Undertow / 4 degrees / Flood / Disgustipated.

Mar 94. (12"grey/cd-s) *(74321 19432-1/-2)* **PRISON SEX. / UNDERTOW (live) / OPIATE (live)** [ ] [ ]

Jul 94. (12"/cd-s) *(74321 22043-1/21849-2)* **SOBER. / INTOLERANCE** [ ] [ ]

—— **JUSTIN CHANCELLOR** – bass; repl. D'AMOUR

Oct 96. (cd/c/lp) *(61422 31144-2/-4/-1)* *<72445 11087-2/-4/-1>* **AENIMA** [ ] [2]
– Stinkfist / Eulogy / H. / Useful idiot / Forty six & 2 / Message to Harry

Manback / Hooker with a penis / Intermission / Jimmy / Die eier von Satan / Pushit / Cesaro summability / Aenima / (-)Ions / Third eye.

A PERFECT CIRCLE

MAYNARD JAMES KEENAN – vocals / **BILLY HOWERDEL** – guitar, keyboards, programming, vocals / **PAZ LENCHANTIN** – bass / **TROY VAN LEEUWEN** – guitar (ex-FAILURE, ex-ENEMY) / **JOSH FREESE** – drums (ex-GUNS N' ROSES, ex-VANDALS)

Virgin Virgin

May 00. (cd/lp) *(CDVUS/VUSLP 173)* *<49253>* **MER DE NOMS** [55] [4]
– The hollow / Magdalena / Rose / Judith / Orestes / 3 Libras / Sleeping beauty / Thomas / Renholder / Thinking of you / Brena / Over.

Jul 00. (cd-s) *(VUSCD 168)* **JUDITH / MAGDALENA (live) / BRENA (live) / ORESTES (demo)** [ ] [–]
(7"/7") *(VUS/+X 168)* – (same tracks).

Nov 00. (7"/cd-s) *(VUS/+DX 181)* **THE HOLLOW. / THE HOLLOW (Bunk mix)** [72] [–]
(cd-s) *(VUSCD 181)* – ('A'side) / ('A'-Constantly consuming mix) / Judith (Danny Lohner mix).

Jan 01. (7") *(VUS 184)* **3 LIBRAS. / MAGDALENA (live)** [49] [ ]
(cd-s) *(VUSCD 184)* – ('A'side) / ('A'-All main courses remix) / Judith (live) / ('A'-CD ROM).
(cd-s) *(VUSDX 184)* – ('A'live) / ('A'-Feel my ice dub) / Sleeping beauty (live).

TOOL

—— were back (see last line-up)

Music For Nations Volcano

Feb 01. (cd-set; w/dvd/vhs) *(DVDMFN/VFN 18)* *<31159>* **SALIVAL** [ ] [38]
– Third eye (live) / Part of me (live) / Pushit (live) / Message to Harry Manback II / Merkarba (live) / You lied (live) / No quarter / L.A.M.C. / Sober (video) / Prison sex (video) / Aenima (video) / Stinkfist (video).

Volcano Volcano

May 01. (cd/c) *(921013-2)* *<31160>* **LATERALUS** [16] [1]
– The grudge / Eon blue apocalypse / The patient / Mantra / Schism / Parabol / Parabola / Tricks and leeches / Lateralus / Disposition / Reflection / Triad / Faaip de Oiad.

May 01. (-) *<radio>* **SCHISM** [–] [67]

A PERFECT CIRCLE

HOWERDEL + KEENAN + FREESE recruited **DANNY LOHNER** – guitar; repl. TROY (on most) / **JEORDIE OSBORNE WHITE** – bass (ex-MARILYN MANSON) repl. PAZ / added **JAMES IHA** – guitar (ex-SMASHING PUMPKINS)

Virgin Virgin

Sep 03. (cd) *(CDVUS 247)* *<80918>* **THIRTEENTH STEP** [27] [2]
– The package / Weak and powerless / The noose / Blue / Vanishing / A stranger / The outsider / Crimes / The nurse who loved me / Pet / Lullaby / Gravity.

Dec 03. (cd-s) *<38888>* **WEAK AND POWERLESS / BLUE** [–] [ ]

TOPLOADER

Formed: Eastbourne, England ... mid-90's by JOSEPH WASHBOURN, JULIAN DEANE, DAN HIPGRAVE, MATT KNIGHT and ROB GREEN. An inspiring group of cannabis smokers, it's no surprise that the name TOPLOADER originates from a term meaning: a spliff-greedy scoundrel who laces (for himself) one end of the ciggy with drugs passing it nonchalantly to his "too-stoned-to-notice" smoking buddies. After years of chilling and jamming, the five unsung heroes found themselves stranded with the likes of NOEL GALLAGHER and PAUL WELLER on the latter's previous tour in 1999. TOPLOADER signed to 'Sony Soho 2' and unleashed their debut single, 'ACHILLES HEEL', in May of the same year. Much like OASIS, OCEAN COLOUR SCENE, The JAM and a string of other indie bands, the textures never differed from soaring guitars, uplifting melodies and general feelgood pub-rock. In short, the band sounded like EMBRACE on a good summer's morning. Like ARAB STRAP, the ensemble ridiculed their native town, only this time launching an attack on Eastbourne's elderly (tisk, tisk, the young don't have any respect these days!), forcing the rascals to flit to London, where they doubled as session musicians for acts such as JAMIROQUAI and STEVIE WONDER! 'LET THE PEOPLE KNOW' was delivered in July of 1999 and celebrated within the anthemic, happy-go-lucky, rock song trait. After hitting the UK Top 20 with remixes of both 'DANCING IN THE MOONLIGHT' and 'ACHILLES HEEL', the quintet finally delivered their debut album, the ridiculously titled 'ONKA'S BIG MONKA' in 2000. The former track even managed to peak higher in the charts (Top 10) when re-issued later in the year via a TV commercial. Elsewhere, the album was patchy although it displayed a fantastic berth of electric keyboards, STEVIE WONDER-esque vocal turns and DAN's booming bass guitar. Speaking of which, DAN the man hit the headlines around the same time by marrying gorgeous Scots lass/TV presenter, Gail Porter. Everybody's favourite dad-rockers were back in 2002 with that difficult second album, 'MAGIC HOTEL'. While the feelgood factor wasn't quite primed for another 'DANCING IN THE MOONLIGHT', it wasn't exactly flagging either. Top 20 single, 'TIME OF MY LIFE', came closest in the anthem stakes, while 'LADY LET ME SHINE' hinted at the sensitive songwriter cowering beneath WASHBOURN's regulation cheerfulness.

Album rating: ONKA'S BIG MONKA (*6) / MAGIC HOTEL (*5)

JOSEPH WASHBOURN – vocals / **JULIAN DEANE** – guitar / **DAN HIPGRAVE** – guitar / **MATT KNIGHT** – bass / **ROB GREEN** – drums

Sony Soho 2 Sony

May 99. (cd-s) *(667161-2)* **ACHILLES HEEL / COMING HOME / YOU IN STONE** [64] [–]
(cd-s) *(667161-5)* – ('A'side) / As big as a house (live) / Lucy (live).

Jul 99. (cd-s) *(667713-2)* **LET THE PEOPLE KNOW / AS BIG AS A HOUSE / IF SIX WAS EIGHT** [52] [–]
(cd-s) *(667713-5)* – ('A'side) / ('A'-acoustic) / Do you know what the future will be (xmf acoustic session).

Feb 00. (c-s) *(668941-4)* **DANCING IN THE MOONLIGHT / LUCY** [19] [–]
(cd-s+=) *(668941-2)* – Jack.
(7") *(668941-7)* – ('A'side) / Man with a plan / Times like these.

May 00. (c-s) *(669187-4)* **ACHILLES HEEL / ALIEN** [8] [–]
(cd-s+=) *(669187-2)* – Colour me / ('A'-Cd-Rom).
(cd-s) *(669187-5)* – ('A'side) / You in stone / Dancing in the moonlight (radio edit) / ('A'-CD-Rom).

May 00. (cd/c/lp) *(494780-2/-4/-1)* *<85792>* **ONKA'S BIG MONKA** [4] Jul00 [ ]
– Let the people know / Dancing in the moonlight / Achilles heel / Breathe / Do you know what your future will be? / Only for a while / Higher state / High flying bird / Summer cycle / Just about living / Floating away (in a bath tub). *(re-iss. Sep00; same)* – Just hold on.

Aug 00. (c-s) *(669624-4)* **JUST HOLD ON / ACHILLES HEEL (live)** [20] [–]
(cd-s+=) *(669624-5)* – Do you know what the future will be? (live) / Achilles heel (live CD-Rom).
(cd-s) *(669624-2)* – ('A'side) / This is our home / The heat within / ('A'-CD-Rom).

Nov 00. (c-s) *(669985-4)* **DANCING IN THE MOONLIGHT / DANCING IN THE MOONLIGHT (Stargate radio mix)** [7] [–]
(cd-s+=) *(669985-2)* – ('A'-Alliance DC vocal) / ('A'-live).

Apr 01. (c-s) *(670861-4)* **ONLY FOR A WHILE / CLOUD 9** [19] [–]
(cd-s+=) *(670861-2)* – You keep me hanging on (video).

Jul 02. (cd-s) *(672886-2)* **TIME OF MY LIFE / HAVE AND TO HOLD / HERO UNDERGROUND / TIME OF MY LIFE (video)** [18] [–]
(cd-s) *(672886-5)* – ('A'side) / Man I know I am / Stepping stone.

Aug 02. (cd/lp) *(508471-2/-1)* **MAGIC HOTEL** [3] [–]
– Time of my life / Cloud 8 / Never forgotten / Leave me be / Lady let me shine / Stupid games / Following the sun / Only desire / Promised tide / The Midas touch / Some kind of wonderful.

Oct 02. (cd-s) *(673162-2)* **SOME KIND OF WONDERFUL / SOMETHING / ONLY DESIRE (acoustic version) / ('A'video)** [ ] [-]
(cd-s) *(673162-5)* – ('A'side) / Time of my life (acoustic) / Promised tide (acoustic).

—— split a little time after above

□ TORCH SONG (see under ⇒ ORBIT, William)

TORTOISE

Formed: Chicago, Illinois, USA . . . 1990 by DOUG McCOMBS and JOHN HERNDON, who started jamming together with JOHN McENTIRE, BUNDY K BROWN and DAN BITNEY. This cult outfit initially crawled out of their collective shell with a series of early 90's EP's before finally unleashing their eponymous debut in '94. Remixed by STEVE ALBINI on the following year's blistering EP, 'RHYTHMS, RESOLUTIONS & CLUSTERS', the record proved TORTOISE to be the foremost purveyors of cut'n'mix avant-jazz. In 1996, their second album, 'MILLIONS NOW LIVING WILL NEVER DIE' (featuring the STEREOLAB trio of TIM, LAETITIA and MARY) was even better, opening with the psychedelic/Krautrock marathon of 'DJED'. This 20-minute track was subsequently given the 'Mo Wax' treatment, the extent of the band's appeal illustrated by their impressive run of collaborations over the course of the next year. The hard-working McENTIRE, who was also a part-time member of RED CRAYOLA and The SEA AND CAKE, returned to the studio at the end of the year, beavering away on what was yet another classic TORTOISE set, 'TNT' (1998). A segued journey from cool avant-jazz rock that unsuspectingly flowed into complex rhythmical landscapes, the record proved a hard listen for alt-rock buffs. JOHN McENTIRE (who also sidelined with the SEA AND CAKE), subsequently found his niche in soundtrack work, although 'REACH THE ROCK' (1999) was too pretentious and complex for some. After a one-off collaboration ('IN THE FISHTANK') with Dutch indie-meisters, The EX, TORTOISE resumed their position as electronica's top groovesters via their fourth album proper, 'STANDARDS' (2001) – their first for the seminal UK imprint, 'Warp'. McENTIRE and the group "prog"-ressed with every mixed-up, well-rehearsed bass and vibraphone beat, although it didn't quite match the experimentation of their previous work. The trio of PARKER, HERNDON and BITNEY were also behind ISOTOPE 217, an inevitable TORTOISE offshoot which catered to the guys' jazzier urges. Also featuring MATT LUX, ROB MAZUREK and SARA P. SMITH, the ensemble debuted in 1997 with 'THE UNSTABLE MOLECULE', a supple, low-key excursion into the kind of fusion territory which even most Chicago outfits, never mind conventional lo-fi experimentalists, wouldn't dare to venture. 'UTONIAN AUTOMATIC' (1999) extended their intrepid musical brief while the 'COMMANDER MINDFUCK/DESIGNER' remix EP, released the same year, offered up dynamic reworkings of selected live performances. 'WHO STOLE THE I WALKMAN?' followed in 2000.

Album rating: TORTOISE (*8) / RHYTHMS, RESOLUTIONS & CLUSTERS remixes (*6) / MILLIONS NOW LIVING WILL NEVER DIE (*9) / DIGEST COMPENDIUM OF . . . compilation (*7) / TNT (*8) / IN THE FISHTANK mini; with The Ex (*5) / STANDARDS (*7) / Isotope 217: THE UNSTABLE MOLECULE mini (*7) / COMMANDER MINDFUCK mini (*6) / UTONIAN AUTOMATIC (*6) / WHO STOLE THE I WALKMAN? (*4) / John McEntire: REACH THE ROCK soundtrack (*5)

JOHN McENTIRE – synthesizers, drums, vibraphone (ex-BASTRO, ex-SHRIMP BOAT) / **BUNDY K BROWN** – guitar, bass (ex-GASTR DE SOL) / **DOUG McCOMBS** – bass (ex-ELEVENTH DREAM DAY) / **JOHNNY HERNDON** – drums, synthesizers, vibraphone (ex-POSTER CHILDREN) / **DAN BITNEY** – synthesizers, percussion, multi (ex-TAR BABIES) / 6th member **CASEY RICE** – soundman

not iss. | Torsion

1993. (7") <003> **MOSQUITO. / ONIONS WRAPPED IN RUBBER / GOOSENECK** [-] [ ]

not iss. | Soul Static

1994. (7") <SOUL 7> **WHY WE FIGHT. / WHITEWATER** [-] [ ]
(UK-iss.Jan95; same)

City Slang | Thrill Jockey

1994. (12") *<THRILL 006>* **LONESOME SOUND. / RESERVOIR / SHEETS** [-] [ ]

Jan 95. (cd/lp) *(EFA 04950-2/-1) <THRILL 013>* **TORTOISE** [ ] [ ]
– Magnet pulls through / Night air / Ry Cooder / Onions wrapped in rubber / Tin cans and twine / Spiderwebbed / His second story island / On noble / Flyrod / Cornpole brunch. *(cd-iss. remixed May97; TKCB 71016) (lp re-iss. Jun97 on 'Thrill Jockey'; THRILL 013)*

Apr 95. (12") *(Dodgey Beast; DS 3309)* **GAMERA. / CLIFF DWELLER SOCIETY** [ ] [ ]
(12") *(DS 3309S)* – ('A'mixes).

Jun 95. (m-cd/m-lp) *(EFA 04957-2/-1) <THRILL 019>* **RHYTHMS, RESOLUTIONS & CLUSTERS: REMIXED AND RARE** [ ] [ ]
– Alcohall / Your new rod / Cobwebbed / Match incident / Not quite east of the Ryan / Initial gesture protraction.

—— **DAVE PAJO** – guitar (ex-SLINT) repl. BUNDY who formed DIRECTIONS IN MUSIC for one eponymous set; he and McCOMBS were also part of alt-supergroup, PULLMAN.

Jan 96. (cd/lp) *(EFA 04972-2/-1) <THRILL 025>* **MILLIONS NOW LIVING WILL NEVER DIE** [ ] [ ]
– Djed / Glass museum / A survey / The taut and the tame / Dear grandma and grandpa / Along the banks of rivers. *(cd-iss. Japanese version May97; TKCB 70931)*

Apr 96. (12"; by TORTOISE Vs U.N.K.L.E./JOHN McENTIRE) *(SHELL 001) <TJ 12.1>* **DJED (bruise blood mix). / TJED** [ ] [ ]

Jul 96. (12"; by TORTOISE Vs BUNDY BROWN) *<TJ 12.2>* **ROME** [-] [ ]

Jul 96. (12"; by TORTOISE Vs OVAL) *(SHELL 002) <TJ 12.3>* **MUSIC FOR WORK GROUPS EP** [ ] [ ]
– The bubble economy (mix by Marcus Popp) / Learning curve (mix by Marcus Popp).

Sep 96. (12"; by TORTOISE VS SPRING HEEL JACK) *(SHELL 003) <TJ 12.4>* **GALAPAGOS 1 (Spring Heel Jack remix). / REFERENCE RESISTANCE GATE (Jim O'Rourke remix)** [ ] [ ]
(re-iss. Jun97 on 'Thrill Jockey'; TJ 124)

Oct 96. (12"; by TORTOISE Vs LUKE VIBERT/BUNDY K BROWN) *(SHELL 004) <TJ 12.5>* **THE TAUT AND THE TAME. / FIND THE ONE (WAIT, ABSTRACTION NO . . .)** [ ] [ ]

—— In 1996, they also shared a single with STEREOLAB, 'VAUS' / 'SPEEDY CAR', released on 'Duophonic'; *D-UHF-D12)*

—— **JEFF PARKER** – guitar; repl. PAJO who formed AERIAL M

Mar 98. (cd/d-lp) *(EFA 08705-2/-1) <THRILL 050>* **TNT** [ ] [ ]
– Swung from the gutters / Ten-day interval / I set my face to the hillside / The equator / A simple way to go faster than light that does not work / The suspension bridge at Iguazu Falls / Four-day interval / In Sarah, Mencken, Christ, and Beethoven there were women and men / Almost always is nearly enough / Jetty / Everglade.

Jul 98. (ltd-12"; TORTOISE VS. DERRICK CARTER) *(087096)* **IN SARAH, MENCKEN, CHRIST, AND BEETHOVEN THERE WERE WOMEN AND MEN** [ ] [-]
– (D's winter crazy mix) / (D's winter outtake).
(above issued on 'Rephlex') (below on 'Fishtank/Konkurrent')

May 99. (m-cd/m-lp; by TORTOISE & THE EX) *(FISH 5 CD/LP)* **IN THE FISHTANK** [ ] [ ]
– Lawn of the limb / Pooh song / Central heating / Pleasure as usual / Did you comb / Huge hidden spaces.

Warp | Thrill Jockey

Feb 01. (cd/lp) *(WARP CD/LP 081) <THRILL 089>* **STANDARDS** [ ] [ ]
– Seneca / Eros / Benway / Firefly / Six pack / Eden 2 / Monica / Blackjack / Eden 1 / Speakeasy.

– compilations, others, etc. –

May 97. (cd) *Thrill Jockey;* *<(TKCB 70932)>* **A DIGEST COMPENDIUM OF TORTOISE'S WORLD** ☐ 1996 ☐
– Tin cans & twine / Alcohall / Night air / Gooseneck / Onions wrapped in rubber / Spiderwebbed / Cobnebbed / Your new rod / Ry Cooder (the beer incident) / Not quite east of the Ryan / Reservoir / Cornpone brunch / Whitewater / Initial gesture protraction.

Apr 98. (cd) *Thrill Jockey;* *<(TKCB 71016)>* **TORTOISE REMIXED** (all the 4 collaboration/Vs singles) ☐ 1996 ☐

Oct 01. (m-cd) *Thrill Jockey;* *<(THRILL 122-2)>* **GENTLY CUPPING THE CHIN OF THE APE** ☐ ☐
– Waihopai / Peering / Seneca (video) / Tortoise 98 (video) / Rehearsal 2001 (video).

ISOTOPE 217

JEFF PARKER – guitar / **JOHN HERNDON** – percussion / **DAN BITNEY** – percussion / **MATT LUX** – bass (of HEROIC DOSES) / **ROB MAZUREK** – trumpet (of CHICAGO UNDERGROUND DUO) / **SARA P. SMITH** – trombone

Thrill Jockey | Thrill Jockey

Jan 98. (lp/cd) *<(THRILL 049/+CD)>* **THE UNSTABLE MOLECULE** ☐ Nov97 ☐
– Kryptonite smokes the red line / Beneath the undertow / La jetee / Phonometrics / Prince Namor / Audio boxing.

Mar 99. (m-cd) *<(ASTO 6 CD/LP)>* **COMMANDER MINDFUCK** ☐ ☐
– Hodah / User password: Lebar.
(above credited DESIGNER – CASEY RICE – and issued on 'Aesthetics')

Aug 99. (lp/cd) *<(THRILL 063/+2)>* **UTONIAN AUTOMATIC** ☐ ☐
– Luh / Audio champion / New beyond / Rest for the wicked / Looking after life on Mars / Solaris / Real MC's.

Aug 00. (lp/cd) *<(THRILL 080/+CD)>* **WHO STOLE THE I WALKMAN?** ☐ ☐
– Ham-o-lodge / Space krikts / Meta bass / Moonlex / Kidtronix / (untitled) / Moot ang / Sint_D / Input / (untitled) / (untitled).

JOHN McENTIRE

—— his debut solo album (although shared with others)

Hefty | Hefty

Feb 99. (7"pic-d) *<(HEF 13)>* **split w/ SEA AND CAKE** ☐ ☐

Mar 99. (cd) *<(HEFT 14CD)>* **REACH THE ROCK** (Original Soundtrack) ☐ ☐
– In a thimble (TORTOISE) / Criminal record / Overview / Stolen car / Drift (BUNDY K. BROWN) / Quinn goes to town / Window lights (SEA AND CAKE) / Reverse migraine (POLVO) / Lise arrives / The kiss / Main title / Dreams of being king (DIANOGAH). *(lp-iss.Nov99; HEFT 014LP)*

Peter TOSH

Born: WINSTON HUBERT MacINTOSH, 9 Oct'44, Westmoreland, Jamaica. A founding member of The WAILERS alongside BOB MARLEY in 1962, TOSH was as equally pivotal as his more famous peer in spreading the reggae gospel if not more so. During his time with The WAILERS, he maintained a prolific recording schedule for the famous 'Studio One' label, eventually founding his own imprint, 'Intel-Diplo H.I.M.' in 1971. This became the main outlet for TOSH's music following his break with MARLEY & Co; throughout his lengthy spell with the band, TOSH had provided them with consistently quality material, his last contribution being 'GET UP STAND UP' on the 'Burnin' (1973) album. His career only really got off the ground again, however, when 'Virgin' signed him in 1976, his debut album proper, 'LEGALIZE IT' (1976) nearly hitting the UK Top 50. TOSH made no bones about what exactly he proposed to legalize, his hardline Rasta stance, booming baritone voice and bass-quaking reggae/dub sound winning die hard fans across the whole musical spectrum. Recorded with backing band, WORD, SOUND & POWER, 'EQUAL RIGHTS' (1977) was an even more fiercely political set featuring such scathing missives as 'DOWNPRESSOR MAN', 'STEPPING RAZOR' and a tuffed-up revamp of 'GET UP STAND UP'. One of the man's more famous admirers was MICK JAGGER of The ROLLING STONES, who signed TOSH to his own label and even provided (clearly audible) backing vocals on his first Top 50 hit single, 'DON'T LOOK BACK'. The track was featured on the 'BUSH DOCTOR' (1978) set, one of a trio of albums for The 'STONES label alongside 'MYSTIC MAN' (1979) and 'WANTED DREAD & ALIVE' (1981). After signing to 'E.M.I.' in the early 80's, he scored a further minor hit single with a cover of Chuck Berry's 'JOHNNY B. GOODE' and although his mainstream successes were few and far between, the man remained one of the scene's most visible figures. Tragically, 1987 protest set, 'NO NUCLEAR WAR', was to become the man's swansong; TOSH was shot dead on 11th September the same year during a robbery at his Kingston home. Speculation that the killing was politically motivated has continued to flourish, however, TOSH having clashed with both the Government and police in the past. He was only 42, his death coming as a sore loss to a movement that had lost figurehead, BOB MARLEY only six years earlier. • **Songwriters:** Writes himself, except several including; DON'T LOOK BACK (Temptations).

Album rating: LEGALIZE IT (*7) / EQUAL RIGHTS (*7) / BUSH DOCTOR (*7) / MYSTIC MAN (*6) / WANTED, DREAD & ALIVE (*6) / MAMA AFRICA (*5) / CAPTURED LIVE (*5) / NO NUCLEAR WAR (*6) / THE TOUGHEST compilation (*7) / THE GOLD COLLECTION compilation (*7)

PETER TOSH – vocals, keyboards, guitar (ex-WAILERS) / with some ex-WAILERS, SLY & ROBBIE, etc.

Virgin | Virgin

Mar 76. (7") *(VS 140)* **LEGALIZE IT. / BRAND NEW SECOND HAND** ☐ –

Aug 76. (lp/c) *(V/TCV 2061)* *<34253>* **LEGALIZE IT** 54 ☐
– Legalize it / Burial / Watcha gonna do / No sympathy / Why must I care / Igziabeher (let jah be praised) / Ketchy shuby / Till your well runs dry / Brand new second hand. *(re-iss. Aug88; OVED 108) (cd-iss. Oct88; CDV 2061) (lp re-iss. Apr01 on 'Simply Vinyl'; SVLP 316)*

Apr 77. (7") *(VS 179)* **AFRICAN. / STEPPING RAZOR** ☐ –

Apr 77. (lp/c) *(V/TCV 2081)* *<34670>* **EQUAL RIGHTS** (with WORDS, SOUND & POWER) ☐ ☐
– Get up, stand up / Downpressor man / I am that I am / Stepping razor / Equal rights / African / Jah guide / Apartheid. *(re-iss. Aug88; OVED 109) (cd-iss. Oct88; CDV 2081) (lp re-iss. Apr01 on 'Simply Vinyl'; SVLP 308)*

E.M.I. | Columbia

Sep 78. (7") *(EMI 2859)* *<19308>* **(YOU GOTTA WALK) DON'T LOOK BACK. / SOON COME** 43 81
above featured duet with MICK JAGGER

Rolling Stones | Rolling Stones

Nov 78. (lp/c) *(CUN 39109)* *<39109>* **BUSH DOCTOR** ☐ ☐
– (You gotta walk) Don't look back / Pick myself up / I'm the toughest / Soon come / Moses the prophet / Bush doctor / Stand firm / Dem ha fe get a beatin' / Creation. *(re-iss. Nov85 on 'Fame' lp/c; FA 41 3139-1/-4) (cd-iss. Oct88 on 'E.M.I.'; CDP 791085-2) (cd re-iss. Nov90 on 'Trojan'; CDTRP 100)*

Mar 79. (7") *(RSR 103)* **I'M THE TOUGHEST. / TOUGHEST (version)** ☐ ☐
(12"+=) *(12RSR 103)* – Word, sound and power.

Aug 79. (7") *(RSR 104)* **BUK-IN-HAMM PALACE. / THE DAY THE DOLLAR DIE** ☐ ☐

Aug 79. (lp/c) *(CUN 39111)* *<39111>* **MYSTIC MAN** ☐ ☐
– Mystic man / Recruiting soldiers / Can't you see / Fight on / Jah say no / Buk-in-hamm Palace / The day the dollar die / Crystal ball / Rumours of war.

Sep 80. (7") (RSR 107) **NOTHING BUT LOVE. (w/ GWEN GUTHRIE) / COLD BLOOD** ☐ ☐

Rolling Stones | EMI America

Jun 81. (7"/12") *(RSR/12RSR 107)* **NOTHING BUT LOVE. / COLD BLOOD** ☐ ☐

Jun 81. (lp/c) *(CUN/TC-CUN 39113)* *<17055>* **WANTED DREAD & ALIVE** ☐ 91

– Coming in hot / Nothing but love / Reggaemylitis / Rock with me / Oh bumbo klaat / Wanted dread and alive / Rastafari is / Guide me from my friends / Fools die. *(cd-iss. Jun98 on 'E.M.I.'; 791670-2)*

Radic-EMI | EMI America

Mar 83. (7") *(RIC 115) <8159>* **JOHNNY B. GOODE. / PEACE TREATY** [48] [84]
Apr 83. (lp/c) *(RDC/TCRDC 2005) <17095>* **MAMA AFRICA** [ ] [59]
– Mama Africa / Glasshouse / Not gonna give it up / Stop that train / Johnny B. Goode / Where you gonna run / Peace treaty / Feel no way / Maga dog.
May 83. (7") *(RIC 116)* **WHERE YOU GONNA RUN. / STOP THAT TRAIN** [ ] [–]
Sep 83. (7"/10") *(RIC/10RIC 117)* **MAMA AFRICA. / NOT GONNA GIVE IT UP** [ ] [–]

E.M.I. | EMIAmerica

Jul 84. (lp) *(PTOSH 1) <17126>* **CAPTURED LIVE (live)** [ ] [ ]
– Coming in hot / Bush doctor / African / Get up, stand up / Johnny B. Goode / Equal rights – Downpresser man / Rastafari is.

Parlophone | EMI America

Jul 87. (7") *(R 6156)* **IN MY SONG. / COME TOGETHER** [ ] [–]
(12"+=) *(12R 6156)* – Nah goa jail.
Sep 87. (cd/c/lp) *(CD/C+/PCS 7309) <46700>* **NO NUCLEAR WAR** [ ] [ ]
– No nuclear war / Nah goa jail / Fight apartheid / Vampire / In my song / Lesson in my life / Testify / Come together.

—— TOSH was shot dead on the 11th September, 1987

– compilations, others, etc. –

Oct 79. (7") *Virgin; (VS 304)* **STEPPING RAZOR. / LEGALIZE IT** [ ] [–]
Mar 88. (cd/c/lp) *Parlophone; (CD/MC+/PCS 7318)* **THE TOUGHEST** [ ] [ ]
– Coming in hot / (You gotta walk) Don't look back / Pick myself up / Crystal ball / Mystic man / Reggaemythilis / Bush doctor / Mega dog / Johnny B. Goode / Equal rights / Downpressed man / In my song. *(cd re-iss. Mar96 on 'Heartbeat'; CDHB 150)*
Mar 96. (cd/c) *EMI Gold; (CD/TC GOLD 1007)* **THE GOLD COLLECTION** [ ] [–]
– Johnny B. Goode / Bush doctor / (You gotta walk) Don't look back / No nuclear war / Come together / Na Goa jail / Coming in hot / Pick myself up / In my song / Reggaemylitis / Equal rights / Crystal ball / Vampire / Lesson in my life / Testify / Maga dog.
Sep 97. (cd) *E.M.I.; (CTMCD 334)* **THE CENTENARY COLLECTION: THE BEST OF PETER TOSH** [ ] [–]
Sep 97. (3xcd-box) *Columbia; (C3K 65064)* **HONORARY CITIZEN** [ ] [ ]
May 00. (cd) *Trojan; (CDTRL 436)* **ARISE BLACK MAN** [ ] [–]
Mar 01. (cd) *Music Club; (MCCD 448)* **ARISE: THE BEST OF PETER TOSH** [ ] [–]

TOTO

Formed: Los Angeles, California, USA . . . 1977 by noted ex-session men, brothers JEFF and STEVE PORCARO, BOBBY KIMBALL, STEVE LUKATHER, DAVID PAICH and DAVID HUNGATE, taking their name partly from the dog in the 'Wizard Of Oz' and partly from KIMBALL's real name (TOTEAUX). The band signed a worldwide deal on 'CBS-Epic' in 1978, their debut single, 'HOLD THE LINE', breaking through into the US and UK Top 20 in early 1979 and selling over a million copies in the process. Their eponymous debut album also became a massive seller, their blend/bland of airbrushed melody and supersession soft-rock going down a storm in America's heartlands. Enjoyed further moderate success until 1982, when they released the monster selling, 'TOTO IV', a record which became their most successful album to date and turned over three million copies in America alone. Highlights included 'ROSANNA' (a song written about actress, Rosanna Arquette) which lodged at the US No.2 spot for 5 weeks, and AOR classic, 'AFRICA', which became another million seller and furnished them with their first US No.1 the following year. TOTO's fortunes declined as the decade wore on, key group members bailing out along the way. Undoubtedly the biggest blow came with the mysterious (heart-attack) death of JEFF PORCARO in 1992, the band nevertheless opting to carry on in various incarnations. Their first post-JEFF PORCARO release, 'TAMBU' (1995), fell foul of the kind of directionless and unremarkable if well executed soft-rock and convoluted lyrical chin-scratching beloved of many ageing AOR acts. Matters hardly improved with 'MINDFIELDS' (1999), proffering even more artless lyrics and competently vacuous studio rock, while 2002's 'THROUGH THE LOOKING GLASS' was an enjoyable enough if ultimately pointless set of tastefully selected covers including Steely Dan's 'BODHISATTVA', Bob Dylan's 'IT TAKES A LOT TO LAUGH, IT TAKES A TRAIN TO CRY', Elton John's 'BURN DOWN THE MISSION' and even Elvis Costello's 'WATCHING THE DETECTIVES'. • **Songwriters:** PAICH was main songwriter, with others contributing, with group taking more of a hand in the 90's. Covered; WITH A LITTLE HELP FROM MY FRIENDS + WHILE MY GUITAR GENTLY WEEPS (Beatles) / COULD YOU BE LOVED (Bob Marley) / SUNSHINE OF YOUR LOVE (Cream) / HOUSE OF THE RISING SUN (trad.) / LIVING FOR THE CITY (Stevie Wonder) / MAIDEN VOYAGE – BUTTERFLY (Herbie Hancock) / I CAN'T GET NEXT TO YOU (Temptations).

Album rating: TOTO (*6) / HYDRA (*5) / TURN BACK (*4) / TOTO IV (*7) / ISOLATION (*5) / DUNE soundtrack (*2) / FAHRENHEIT (*4) / THE SEVENTH ONE (*5) / PAST TO PRESENT: 1977 TO 1990 compilation (*7) / KINGDOM OF DESIRE (*3) / ABSOLUTELY LIVE (*2) / TAMBU (*4) / MINDFIELDS (*3) / THROUGH THE LOOKING GLASS (*4)

BOBBY KIMBALL (b. ROBERT TOTEAUX, 29 Mar'47, Vinton, Louisiana) – vocals / **STEVE LUKATHER** (b.21 Oct'57) – lead guitar, vocals / **STEVE PORCARO** (b. 2 Sep'57) – keyboards, vocals / **JEFF PORCARO** (b. 1 Apr'54) – drums, percussion (ex-RURAL LIFE) / **DAVID PAICH** (b.25 Jun'54) – keyboards, vocals (ex-RURAL LIFE) / **DAVID HUNGATE** – bass

C.B.S. | Columbia

Jan 79. (7") *(CBS 6784) <10830>* **HOLD THE LINE. / TAKIN' IT BACK** [14] Sep78 [5]
Mar 79. (lp/c) *(CBS/40 83148) <35317>* **TOTO** [37] Oct78 [9]
– Child's anthem / I'll supply the love / Georgy porgy / Manuela run / You are the flower / Girl goodbye / Takin' it back / Rockmaker / Hold the line / Angela. *(re-iss. Jun84 lp/c; CBS/40 32165) (cd-iss. Oct86; CD83148) (cd re-iss. May94 on 'Sony'; 982730-2)*
Mar 79. (7") *(CBS 7157) <10898>* **I'LL SUPPLY THE LOVE. / YOU ARE THE FLOWER** [ ] Feb79 [45]
Apr 79. (7",7"pic-d) *<10944>* **GEORGY PORGY. / CHILD'S ANTHEM** [–] [48]
Jun 79. (7") *(CBS 7378)* **GEORGY PORGY. / (part 2)** [ ] [–]
Dec 79. (7",7"pic-d) *<11040>* **ST. GEORGE AND THE DRAGON. / WHITE SISTER** [–] [ ]
Jan 80. (7") *(CBS 8085)* **ST. GEORGE AND THE DRAGON. / A SECRET LOVE** [ ] [–]
Feb 80. (7") *(CBS 8132) <11173>* **99. / HYDRA** [ ] Dec79 [26]
Feb 80. (lp/c) *(CBS/40 83900) <36229>* **HYDRA** [ ] Nov79 [37]
– Hydra / St. George and the dragon / 99 / Lorraine / All us boys / Mama / White sister / A secret love. *(re-iss. Feb85 lp/c; CBS/40 32222)*
Mar 80. (7") *<11238>* **ALL US BOYS. / HYDRA** [–] [ ]
Feb 81. (7") *(CBS 9492) <11437>* **GOODBYE ELENORE. / TURN BACK** [ ] [ ]
Apr 81. (7") *<01056>* **TURN BACK. / IT'S THE LAST NIGHT** [–] [ ]
Apr 81. (lp/c) *(CBS/40 84609) <36813>* **TURN BACK** [ ] Jan81 [41]
– Gift with a golden gun / English eyes / Live for today / A million miles away / Goodbye Elenore / I think I could stand you forever / Turn back / If it's the last night. *(cd-iss. May87; CD 84609)*
Apr 82. (lp/c) *(CBS/40 85529) <37728>* **TOTO IV** (peaked UK Feb'83) [4] [4]
– Rosanna / Make believe / I won't hold you back / Good for you / It's a feeling / Afraid of love / Lovers in the night / We made it / Waiting for your love / Africa. *(cd-iss. Mar83; CD 85529) (re-iss. Nov86 lp/c; 450088-1/-4) (cd re-iss. Mar91; 450088-2) (cd re-iss. Dec95 on 'Columbia'; CK 64423)*

Apr 82. (7"/7"pic-d) *(A/WA 2079) <02811>* **ROSANNA. / IT'S A FEELING** [ ] [2]
(re-iss. Mar83; same) – hit UK No.12

Oct 82. (7") *(A 2868) <03143>* **MAKE BELIEVE. / WE MADE IT** [ ] Aug82 [30]

Oct 82. (7") *<03335>* **AFRICA. / GOOD FOR YOU** [–] [1]

Jan 83. (7"/7"sha-pic-d) *(A/WA 2510)* **AFRICA. / WE MADE IT** [3] [–]

Jun 83. (7"/7"pic-d) *(A/WA 3392) <03597>* **I WON'T HOLD YOU BACK. / AFRAID OF LOVE** [37] Mar83 [10]
(12"+=) *(TA 3392)* – 99 / Hold the line / Goodbye Elenore.

Jul 83. (7") *(A 3627) <03981>* **WAITING FOR YOUR LOVE. / LOVERS IN THE NIGHT** [ ] [73]

— (late'82) **MIKE PORCARO** (b.29 May'55) – bass had already repl. HUNGATE

— (In '84) **DENNIS 'Fergie' FREDRICKSON** (b.15 May'51) – vocals repl. KIMBALL who later became part of the awful FAR CORPORATION

Nov 84. (7"/12") *(A/TX 4461) <04672>* **STRANGER IN TOWN. / CHANGE OF HEART** [ ] [30]

Nov 84. (lp/c) *(CBS/40 86305) <38962>* **ISOLATION** [67] [42]
– Carmen / Lion / Stranger in town / Angel don't cry / How does it feel / Endless / Isolation / Mr. Friendly / Change of heart / Holyanna. *(cd-iss. 1988; CD 86305)*

— Dec '84, saw their instrumental 'DUNE' (Film Soundtrack) released on 'Polydor' <823770>. It was accompanied by The VIENNA SYMPHONY ORCHESTRA and it flopped. Around this time they laid down backing instruments for USA IN AFRICA single.

Jan 85. (7") *<04752>* **HOLYANNA. / MR. FRIENDLY** [–] [71]

Feb 85. (7") *(A 6043)* **HOW DOES IT FEEL. / MR. FRIENDLY** [ ] [–]

Apr 85. (7") *(A 6174)* **ENDLESS. / ISOLATION** [ ] [–]

— **JOSEPH WILLIAMS** – vocals (ex-Solo artist) repl. FREDRICKSON

Oct 86. (7") *(650043-7) <06280>* **I'LL BE OVER YOU. / IN A WORD** [ ] Aug86 [11]
(12"+=) *(650043-6)* – Africa / 99.

Oct 86. (lp/c/cd) *(CBS/40/CD 57091) <40273>* **FAHRENHEIT** [99] Sep86 [40]
– Till the end / We can make it tonight / Without your love / Can't stand it any longer / I'll be over you / Fahrenheit / Somewhere tonight / Could this be love / Lea / Don't stop me now.

Dec 86. (7") *<06570>* **WITHOUT YOUR LOVE. / CAN'T STAND IT ANY LONGER** [–] [38]

— trimmed to quintet, when STEVE PORCARO went solo

Mar 87. (7") *<07030>* **TILL THE END. / DON'T STOP ME NOW** [–] [ ]

Feb 88. (7") *<07715>* **PAMELA. / THE SEVENTH ONE** [–] [ ]

Feb 88. (7"/7"pic-d) *(651411-7/-0)* **STOP LOVING YOU. / THE SEVENTH ONE** [ ] [–]
(12"+=) *(651411-6)* – ('A'version).
(cd-s+=) *(651411-2)* – I'll be over you.

Mar 88. (lp/c/cd) *(460645-1/-4/-2) <40873>* **THE SEVENTH ONE** [73] [64]
– Pamela / You got me / Anna / Stop loving you / Mushanga / Stay away / Straight for the heart / Only the children / A thousand years / These chains / Home of the brave.

Apr 88. (7") *<07945>* **STRAIGHT FROM THE HEART. / THE SEVENTH ONE** [–] [ ]

May 88. (7") *(651607-7)* **PAMELA. / STAY AWAKE** [ ] [–]
(12"+=) *(651607-6)* – America.
(cd-s+=) *(651607-2)* – Africa / Rosanna.

— **KIMBALL** returned Sep'88 but was repl. by temp. **TOMMY NELSON** ; he in turn was deposed by **JEAN-MICHEL BYRON** (b.South Africa) – vocals

Sep 90. (7"/c-s/12") **CAN YOU HEAR WHAT I'M SAYING. / AFRICA** [ ] [ ]
(cd-s+=) – Georgy porgy / Waiting for your love.

Oct 90. (cd/c/lp) *(465988-2/-4/-1) <45368>* **PAST TO PRESENT: 1977 TO 1990** (compilation) [ ] Sep90 [ ]
– Love has the power / Africa / Hold the line / Out of love / Georgy Porgy / I'll be over you / Can you hear what I'm saying / Rosanna / I won't hold you back / Stop loving you / 99 / Pamela / Animal.

— **KIMBALL** returned to repl. BYRON who formed self-named group. In Aug'92, JEFF died mysteriously of either poisoning or a heart attack.

Columbia Columbia

Sep 92. (cd/c/lp) *(471633-2/-4/-1)* **KINGDOM OF DESIRE** [ ] [ ]
– Gypsy train / Don't chain my heart / Never enough / How many times / 2 hearts / Wings of time / She knows the Devil / The other side / Only you / Jake to the bone.

Nov 93. (d-cd/d-c) *(474514-2/-4)* **ABSOLUTELY LIVE (live)** [ ] [ ]
– Hydra / Rosanna / Kingdom of desire / Georgy Porgy / 99 / I won't hold you back / Don't stop me now / Africa / Don't chain my heart / I'll be over you / Home of the brave / Hold the line / With a little help from my friends.

— **SIMON PHILLIPS** – drums; repl. PORCARO

Oct 95. (cd/c) *(481202-2/-4) <64957>* **TAMBU** [ ] May95 [ ]
– Gift of faith / I will remember / Slipped away / If you belong to me / Baby, he's your man / The other end of time / The turning point / Time is the enemy / Drag him to the roof / Just can't get to you / Dave's gone skiing / The road goes on. *(cd+=)* – Hold the line / Africa / Rosanna / I won't hold you back / I'll be over you.

Nov 95. (c-s) *(662655-4)* **I WILL REMEMBER / DAVE'S GONE SKIING** [64] [ ]
(cd-s) *(662655-2)* – ('A'side) / Rosanna / Africa / Georgy porgy.

Apr 99. (cd/c) *(493245-2/-4) <69607>* **MINDFIELDS** [ ] [ ]
– Cruel / Caught in the balance / After you've gone / Mysterious ways / Last love / Mindfields / Selfish / No love / High price of hate / Mad about you / Melanie / One road / Better world (pts. 1, 2 & 3) / Spanish steps.

Oct 99. (d-cd) *(4962049)* **LIVEFIELDS (1999 live)** [ ] [–]
– (intro) / Caught in the balance / Tale of a man / Rosanna / (Steve Lukather solo) / A million miles away / Jake to the bone / (Simon Phillips solo) / Dave's gone skiing / Acoustic set: Out of love – Mama – You are the flower – The road goes on / Better world / (David Paich solo) / Girl goodbye / White sister / I will remember / Hold the line / I won't hold you back / Cruel / Melanie (video) / Tale of a man.

E.M.I. Capitol

Feb 03. (cd) *<(5 41457-2)>* **THROUGH THE LOOKING GLASS** [ ] Nov02 [ ]
– Could you be loved / Bodhisattva / While my guitar gently weeps / I can't get next to you / Living for the city / Maiden voyage – Butterfly / Burn down the mission / Sunshine of your love / House of the rising sun / Watching the detectives / It takes a lot to laugh, it takes a train to cry.

– compilations, etc. –

Sep 84. (lp/c) *Hallmark; (SHM/HSC 3152))* **HOLD THE LINE** [ ] [–]

Sep 85. (7") *Old Gold; (OG 9555)* **HOLD THE LINE. / ROSANNA** [ ] [–]

Mar 90. (7") *Old Gold; (OG 9867)* **AFRICA. / I WON'T HOLD YOU BACK** [ ] [–]

Dec 90. (3xcd-box) *C.B.S.; (467386-2)* **TOTO / TURN BACK / HYDRA** [ ] [ ]

Nov 91. (3xcd-box) *C.B.S.; (468331-2)* **FAHRENHEIT / TOTO IV / SEVENTH ONE** [ ] [ ]

Sep 01. (3xcd-box) *Columbia; (485326-2)* **IV / THE SEVENTH ONE / KINGDOM OF DESIRE** [ ] [–]

Sep 03. (3xcd-box) *Epic; (496015-2)* **TOTO / TURN BACK / HYDRA** [ ] [–]

Sep 03. (cd) *Eagle; (EAGCD 266)* **25th ANNIVERSARY: LIVE IN AMSTERDAM (live)** [ ] [–]

□ TOURISTS (see under ⇒ EURYTHMICS)

□ Pete TOWNSHEND (see under ⇒ WHO)

TRAFFIC

Formed: based Midlands, England … April '67, by STEVE WINWOOD, DAVE MASON, JIM CAPALDI and CHRIS WOOD. Initially, TRAFFIC purveyed musically accomplished, thinking man's psychedelia, debuting with the yearning 'PAPER SUN' (1967) single after signing to 'Island'. Utilising MASON's lilting, sitar-like guitar playing, the record perfectly anticipated the mood of the times and duly hit the Top 5. Dippy but delightful, the follow-up, 'HOLE IN MY SHOE' (1967) (later covered with great affection by NIGEL PLANER aka 'NEIL' of 'Young Ones' comedy fame) hit No.2 and after their third Top 10 hit in a row, 'HERE WE GO ROUND THE MULBERRY BUSH' (from the film of the same name), the band released their debut album, 'MR

FANTASY' (1967). The record was a well crafted melting pot of ideas and genres put through the psychedelic blender and given a soulful reading by WINWOOD's wholesome vocal chords. The conspicuous absence of any of the previous hit singles, however, signalled that, as was the wont of group in those serious muso days, TRAFFIC wished to be considered an 'Albums' band. Around this time, MASON split, only to return another six months later whence the band fashioned their second album, 'TRAFFIC' (1968), a marked progression that highlighted the band's instrumental dexterity and flowering songwriting talent. Once again, MASON came up with one of the record's most memorable tunes, 'FEELIN' ALRIGHT', later covered by JOE COCKER amongst others. The ever dependable MASON upped sticks and left once more during the recording of TRAFFIC's third album, 'LAST EXIT' (1969). Aptly titled, this careless rag-bag of below par live and studio tracks did indeed mark the end of MASON's time with the band (save for a brief spell of live work in the early 70's), in fact the end of the band itself, for the time being at least. After a spell in short-lived 'supergroup', BLIND FAITH, WINWOOD went in to the studio to commence the recording of a mooted solo album with a working title of 'MAD SHADOWS'. When WOOD and CAPALDI were drafted in for work on the sessions, the project became a fully fledged TRAFFIC concern. The resulting album, re-titled 'JOHN BARLEYCORN MUST DIE' (1970) was a triumphant return to form, mixing up folk, R&B and jazz into a prog-rock classic. In the year or so before their next album, the band recruited bassist RICK GRECH (ex-FAMILY/BLIND FAITH), African percussionist REEBOP KWAKU-BAAH, drummer JIM GORDON (ex-DEREK AND THE DOMINOES) and their old mucker DAVE MASON. 'WELCOME TO THE CANTEEN' (1971) was fairly heavy going but no less self-indulgent than your average early 70's live effort, while the next studio outing, 'THE LOW SPARK OF HIGH HEELED BOYS' (1971) saw the band add to their not inconsiderable studio accomplishments despite the cringe-inducing title. DAVID HOOD and ROGER HAWKINS (both of whom had played on CAPALDI's solo project, 'OH HOW WE DANCED') replaced GRECH and GORDON for 1973's 'SHOOT OUT AT THE FANTASY FACTORY'. The 'Muscle Shoals' veterans had tightened up the rhythm section considerably, cutting it on stage and in the studio, as evidenced by the best live album of TRAFFIC's career, 'ON THE ROAD' (1973). By 1974's 'WHEN THE EAGLE FLIES', TRAFFIC were beginning to sound congested, finally stalling the following year. CAPALDI and WINWOOD both went on to successful solo careers, resurrecting TRAFFIC briefly in 1994. WINWOOD's output, in particular was undeniable coffee table rock at its shiniest, though surprisingly, he was given top billing at the 1997 Glastonbury festival. In the event he didn't show, apparently due to illness, his place taken by KULA SHAKER. • **Songwriters:** Individually or group compositions, except GIMME SOME LOVIN' (Spencer Davis Group). CAPALDI covered LOVE HURTS (Everly Brothers).

Album rating: MR. FANTASY (*8) / TRAFFIC (*9) / LAST EXIT (*5) / THE BEST OF TRAFFIC compilation (*8) / JOHN BARLEYCORN MUST DIE (*7) / WELCOME TO THE CANTEEN (*5) / THE LOW SPARK OF THE HIGH HELED BOYS (*7) / SHOOT OUT AT THE FANTASY FACTORY (*6) / ON THE ROAD (*5) / WHEN THE EAGLE FLIES (*5) / HEAVY TRAFFIC compilation (*7) / MORE HEAVY TRAFFIC compilation (*5) / SMILING PHASES compilation (*9) / FAR FROM HOME (*5)

STEVE WINWOOD (b.12 May'48, Birmingham, England) – vocals, keyboards (ex-SPENCER DAVIS GROUP) / **DAVE MASON** (b.10 May'47, Worcester, England) – guitar, vocals (ex-HELLIONS) / **JIM CAPALDI** (b.24 Aug'44, Evesham, England) – drums, vocals (ex-HELLIONS) / **CHRIS WOOD** (b.24 Jun'44, Birmingham) – flute, sax (ex-SOUNDS OF BLUE)

Island U.A.

May 67. (7") *(WIP 6002) <50195>* **PAPER SUN. / GIVING TO YOU** [5] Aug67 [94]

Aug 67. (7") *(WIP 6017) <50218>* **HOLE IN MY SHOE. / SMILING PHASES** [2] [ ]

Nov 67. (7") *(WIP 6025) <50232>* **HERE WE GO ROUND THE MULBERRY BUSH. / COLOURED RAIN** [8] [ ]

Dec 67. (lp; mono/stereo) *(ILP/+S 9061) <6651>* **MR. FANTASY** [8] Apr68 [88]
– Heaven is in your mind / Berkshire poppies / House for everyone / No name, no face, no number / Dear Mr. Fantasy / Dealer / Utterly simple / Coloured rain / Hope I never find me there / Giving to you. *<US version +=)* – Paper sun / Hole in my shoe. *(re-iss. 1970; same) (re-iss. Feb87 lp/c; ILPM/ICM 9061) (cd-iss. Nov87; CID 9061) (cd re-iss. Sep89; IMCD 43) <US version-iss.Aug92; 3DCID 1003> (cd re-mast.Oct99 +=; IMCD 264)<546496>* – Paper sun / Dealer / Coloured rain / Hole in my shoe / No face, no name, no number / Heaven is in your mind / House for everyone / Berkshire poppies / Giving to you / Smiling phases / Dear Mr. Fantasy / We're a fade, you missed this.

Feb 68. (7") *(WIP 6030)* **NO NAME, NO FACE, NO NUMBER. / ROAMIN' IN THE GLOAMIN' WITH 40,000 HEADMEN** [40] [–]

Feb 68. (7") *<50261>* **NO NAME, NO FACE, NO NUMBER. / HEAVEN IS IN YOUR MIND** [–] [ ]

Sep 68. (7") *(WIP 6041) <50460>* **FEELIN' ALRIGHT. / WITHERING TREE** [ ] [ ]

Oct 68. (lp; mono/stereo) *(ILPS 9081/+T) <6676>* **TRAFFIC** [9] [17]
– You can all join in / Pearly queen / Don't be sad / Who knows what tomorrow may bring / Feelin' alright / Vagabond virgin / Forty thousand headmen / Cryin' to be heard / No time to live / Means to an end. *(re-iss. Feb87 lp/c; ILPM/ICM 9081) (cd-iss. Nov87; CID 9081) (cd re-iss. Sep89; IMCD 45) (<cd re-mast.Oct99 +=; IMCD 265>)* – Here we go 'round the mulburry bush / Am I what I was or am I what I am / Withering tree / Medicated goo / Shanghai noodle factory.

Dec 68. (7") *(WIP 6050)* **MEDICATED GOO. / SHANGHAI NOODLE FACTORY** [ ] [–]

Jan 69. (7") *<50500>* **MEDICATED GOO. / PEARLY QUEEN** [–] [ ]

—— Below album was recorded before their split late 1968.

May 69. (lp; mono/stereo) *(ILP/+S 9097) <6702>* **LAST EXIT (some live)** [ ] [19]
– Just for you / Shanghai noodle factory / Something's got a hold of my toe / Withering tree / Medicated goo / Feelin' good / Blind man. *(cd-iss. May88; CID 9097) (cd re-iss. Sep89; IMCD 41)*

Oct 69. (lp; mono/stereo) *(ILP/+S 9112) <5500>* **THE BEST OF TRAFFIC** (compilation) [ ] [48]
– Paper Sun / Heaven is in your mind / No face, no name, no number / Coloured rain / Smiling phases / Hole in my shoe / Medicated goo / Forty thousand headmen / Feelin' alright / Shanghai noodle factory / Dear Mr. Fantasy. *(cd-iss. Mar93; IMCD 169)*

—— In 1969, WINWOOD formed BLIND FAITH with ERIC CLAPTON and GINGER BAKER. WOOD also joined the latter's group AIRFORCE. WOOD, MASON and CAPALDI then formed WOODEN FROG. DAVE MASON went solo as TRAFFIC re-formed as a trio.

Jul 70. (lp) *(ILPS 9116) <5504>* **JOHN BARLEYCORN MUST DIE** [5] [11]
– Glad / Freedom rider / Empty pages / Stranger to himself / John Barleycorn / Every mother's son. *(re-iss. Sep86 lp/c/cd; ILPM/ICM/CID 9116) (cd-iss. Sep89; IMCD 40) (cd re-mast.Oct99 +=; IMCD 266)<548541>* – I just want you to know / Sittin' here thinkin' of my love / Backstage and introduction / Who knows what tomorrow may bring (live) / Glad (live).

Aug 70. (7") *<50692>* **EMPTY PAGES. / STRANGER TO HIMSELF** [–] [74]

—— added **RIC GRECH** (b. 1 Nov'46) – bass (ex-FAMILY, ex-BLIND FAITH, ex-GINGER BAKER'S AIRFORCE) / **REEBOP KWAKU-BAAH** (b. Konongo, Ghana) – percussion (ex-GINGER BAKER'S AIRFORCE) / **JIM GORDON** – drums (ex-DEREK & THE DOMINOES) / **DAVE MASON** guested on some live.

Sep 71. (lp) *(ILPS 9166) <5550>* **WELCOME TO THE CANTEEN (live)** [ ] [26]
– Medicated goo / Sad and deep as you / 40,000 headmen / Shouldn't have took more than you gave / Dear Mr. Fantasy / Gimme some lovin'. *(cd-iss. May88; CID 9166) (cd re-iss. Sep89; IMCD 39) (<cd re-mast.Apr02 +=; 586847-2>)* – (extended tracks).

Oct 71. (7") *<50841>* **GIMME SOME LOVIN'. / (part 2)** [–] [68]

Island Island

Dec 71. (lp/c) *(ILPS/ZCI 9180) <9306>* **THE LOW SPARK OF THE HIGH HEELED BOYS** [ ] [7]
– Hidden treasure / The low spark of the high heeled boys / Light up or leave me alone / Rock & roll stew / Many a mile to freedom / Rainmaker. *(re-iss. Sep86 lp/c; ILPM/ICM 9180) (cd-iss. Nov87; CID 9180) (cd re-iss. Sep89; IMCD 42) (<cd re-mast.Apr02 +=; 548827-2>)* – Rock & roll stew (parts 1 & 2).

Jan 72. (7") *<1201>* **ROCK & ROLL STEW. / (part 2)** [–] [93]

— **DAVID HOOD** – bass + ROGER HAWKINS – drums (both of JIM CAPALDI band) repl. JIM GORDON and GRECH. (The latter formed KGB)

Feb 73. (lp/c) *(ILPS/ZCI 9224) <9323>* **SHOOT OUT AT THE FANTASY FACTORY** [ ] [6]
– Shoot out at the fantasy factory / Roll right stone / Evening blue / Tragic magic / (Sometimes I feel so) Uninspired. *(cd-iss. May88; CID 9224) (cd re-iss. Sep89; IMCD 44) (<cd re-mast.Jun03; ISL 842781>)*

— added **BARRY BECKETT** – keyboards

Oct 73. (d-lp)(d-c) *(ILSD 2)(ZCID 102) <9336>* **ON THE ROAD (live)** [40] [29]
– Glad – Freedom rider / Tragic magic / (Sometimes I feel so) Uninspired / Shoot out at the fantasy factory / Light up or leave me alone / The low spark of the high heeled boys. *(cd-iss. Jun88; CIDD 2) (cd re-iss. Aug91 & Apr94; IMCD 183) (<cd re-mast.Jun03; ISL 63434>)*

Dec 73. (7") *<50883>* **GLAD. / (part 2)** [–] [ ]

— **WINWOOD, CAPALDI & WOOD** enlisted **ROSKO GEE** – bass (ex-GONZALES)

Island Asylum

Sep 74. (lp/c) *(ILPS/ZCI 9273) <7E 1020>* **WHEN THE EAGLE FLIES** [31] [9]
– Something new / Dream Gerrard / Graveyard people / Walking in the wind / Memories of a rock and rolla / Love / When the eagle flies. *(cd-iss. Jun88; CID 9273) (re-iss. Aug91 cd)(c; IMCD 142)(ICM 9273) (<cd re-mast.Jun03; ISL 548826>)*

Oct 74. (7") *(WIP 6207)* **WALKING IN THE WIND. / WALKING IN THE WIND (instrumental)** [ ] [ ]

— Disbanded early 1975. STEVE WINWOOD went solo, also collaborating with STOMU YAMASHTA. WOOD and GEE took up session work. On 12 Jul'83, CHRIS WOOD died of liver failure. JIM CAPALDI continued his solo career

TRAFFIC

— **WINWOOD + CAPALDI** re-formed for the studio

Virgin Virgin

May 94. (cd/c) *(CD/TC V 2727) <39490>* **FAR FROM HOME** [29] [ ]
– Riding high / Here comes a man / Far from home / Nowhere is their freedom / Holy ground / Some kinda woman / Every night, every day / This train won't stop / State of grace / Mosambique. *(cd re-iss. Nov02 on 'Disky'; VI 905179)*

May 94. (7"/c-s) *(VS/+C 1494)* **HERE COMES A MAN. / GLAD (live)** [ ] [–]
(cd-s+=) *(VSCDG 1494)* – ('A'mix).

Sep 94. (c-s) *(VSC 1506)* **SOME KINDA WOMAN. / FORTY THOUSAND HEADMEN (live)** [ ] [–]
(cd-s+=) *(VSCDX 1506)* – Low spark of high heeled boys (live)/ ('A'mix).

– compilations, etc. –

— on 'Island' unless stated otherwise

May 74. (7") **HOLE IN MY SHOE. / HERE WE GO ROUND THE MULBERRY BUSH** [–] [ ]

May 75. (lp) *United Artists; <4211>* **HEAVY TRAFFIC** [–] [ ]

Sep 75. (lp) *United Artists; <LA 526>* **MORE HEAVY TRAFFIC** [–] [ ]

Mar 78. (7"ep,7"pic-d-ep) *(IEP 7)* **EXTENDED PLAY** [ ] [–]
– I'm a man / Hole in my shoe / Gimme some lovin' / No name, no face, no number.

Jun 92. (d-cd) *(IMCCD 158)* **SMILING PHASES** [ ] [–]
– Paper sun / Hole in my shoe / Smiling phases / Heaven is in your mind / Coloured rain / No face, no name, no number / Here we go round the mulbury bush / Dear Mr. Fantasy / You can all join in / Feelin' alright / Pearly queen / Forty thousand headmen / Vagabond virgin / Shanghai noodle factory / Withering tree / Medicated goo / Glad / Freedom rider / Empty pages / John Barleycorn / The low spark of the high heeled boys / Light up or leave me alone / Rock & roll stew / Shoot out at the fantasy factory / Walking in the wind / When the eagle flies.

Nov 98. (cd) *(IMCD 257)* **HEAVEN IS IN YOUR MIND: AN INTRODUCTION TO TRAFFIC** [ ] [ ]

Feb 00. (cd) *What's Up; (PLG 54227-2)* **FEELIN' ALRIGHT: THE VERY BEST OF TRAFFIC** [ ] [–]

Jun 01. (cd) *Spectrum; (544558-2)* **THE BEST OF TRAFFIC** [ ] [–]

TRAIN

Formed: San Francisco, California, USA ... 1993 by PATRICK MONAHAN and ex-APOSTLES frontman ROB HOTCHKISS. The two became friends after a chance meeting and the soon began playing acoustic-driven pop in the local coffee houses of the city's Bay Area. The pair decided to invite other APOSTLE casualties, JIMMY STAFFORD, CHARLIE COLIN and percussionist SCOTT UNDERWOOD to form what would ultimately become TRAIN. After self-financing their debut recording, the eponymous 'TRAIN' in 1996, 'Columbia' records (through offshoot imprint 'Aware') took them on board, giving the record a whole new lease of life when (re-)issuing it early '98. Guitar driven ballads such as 'FREE' and 'I AM' began to receive heavy rotation on college radio, while 'MEET VIRGINIA' finally dented the US Top 20 a year later. Like the COUNTING CROWS before them, TRAIN dealt in soft, tingling American sentimentality that became overtly hyberbolated come the release of their sophomore set 'DROPS OF JUPITER' (2001). Paul Buckmaster, who was the main driving force on ELTON JOHN's recent classical/string arrangements, finely-tuned the more heart-felt tracks, whereas pop guitar songs such as 'GET AWAY' and 'HOPELESS' became a tad mundane after two or three listenings. The aforementioned album slowly climbed into the US and British Top 10, while its classy radio-friendly title track did the same. The new kings of MOR roots rock were back in 2003 with the Brendan O'Brien-produced 'MY PRIVATE NATION', another solid US Top 10 album which rarely veered from their tried and tested sound and earnest lyrical themes. The record's more interesting moments came courtesy of O'Brien, who co-wrote a handful of tracks.

Album rating: TRAIN (*6) / DROPS OF JUPITER (*7) / MY PRIVATE NATION (*4)

PATRICK MONAHAN – vocals / **ROB HOTCHKISS** – guitar / **JIMMY STAFFORD** – guitar / **CHARLIE COLIN** – bass / **SCOTT UNDERWOOD** – drums

Columbia Columbia

Feb 98. (cd) *<38052>* **TRAIN** [–] [ ]
– Meet Virginia / I am / If you leave / Homesick / Free / Blind / Eggplant / Idaho / Days / Rat / Swaying / Train / Heavy. *<re-dist.Jun99; same>* – hit No.76 *(UK-iss.Feb02; 496289-2)*

1999. (cd-ep) **LIVE FROM FANTASY STUDIOS (live)** [–] [ ]
– Eggplant / I am / Train / If you leave.

1999. (cd-ep) **ONE AND A HALF ep** [–] [ ]
– Counting on you / Hopeless / Ramble on (acoustic) / Sweet rain / The highway / Meet Virginia (acoustic).

Sep 99. (cd-s; promo) *<41775>* **MEET VIRGINIA / (+ 4 mixes)** [–] [20]

Dec 99. (cd-s; promo) *<42830>* **I AM / (+ 2 mixes)** [–] [ ]

Jul 01. (c-s) *(671447-4) <radio>* **DROPS OF JUPITER (TELL ME) / THIS IS NOT YOUR LIFE** [10] Mar01 [5]
(cd-s) *(671447-2)* – ('A'side) / It's love / ('A'-CD-Rom).

Aug 01. (cd) *(5023069) <69888>* **DROPS OF JUPITER** [8] Apr01 [6]
– She's on fire / I wish you would / Drops of Jupiter (tell me) / It's about you / Hopeless / Respect / Let it roll / Something more / Whipping boy / Getaway / Mississippi.

Nov 01. (c-s) *(672041-4)* **SOMETHING MORE / I WISH YOU WOULD (live)** [ ] [–]
(cd-s+=) *(672041-2)* – Eggplant (live) / Free (live).

Feb 02. (c-s) *(672281-4)* **SHE'S ON FIRE / DROPS OF JUPITER (TELL ME) (live)** [49] [ ]
(cd-s+=) *(672281-2)* – Meet Virginia (live) / ('A'-video).

Jun 03. (cd) *(511222-9) <86593>* **MY PRIVATE NATION** [ ] [6]
– Calling all angels / All American girl / When I look to the sky / Save the day / My private nation / Get to me / Counting airplanes / Following Rita / Your every colour / Lincoln Avenue / I'm about to come alive.

Jul 02. (cd-s) *(674028-2)* <*radio*> **CALLING ALL ANGELS / DROPS OF JUPITER (live) / CALLING ALL ANGELS (vide)** [ ] [19]

TRAVELING WILBURYS

Formed: Los Angeles, California, USA . . . 1988 by ageing superstars BOB DYLAN, TOM PETTY, GEORGE HARRISON, JEFF LYNNE and ROY ORBISON. The various members originally came together to record a B-side for HARRISON's 'WHEN WE WAS FAB' single, the session going sufficiently well that they subsequently decided to take things further. The resulting debut album, ' . . . VOLUME 1' (1988) unsurprisingly became a huge seller, the hit single, 'HANDLE WITH CARE', one of the easy rocking highlights alongside 'TWEETER AND THE MONKEY MAN'. Each member of the band took on a pseudonym, mainly to get round contract difficulties; DYLAN was LUCKY WILBURY, PETTY became CHARLIE T. WILBURY JR, HARRISON changed to NELSON WILBURY, LYNNE took the moniker OTIS WILBURY and ORBISON was LEFTY WILBURY. ROGER McGUINN subsequently declined the offer to take over from the deceased ROY ORBISON before the release of their second (yes, second!) album, 'TRAVELING WILBURYS VOLUME 3' (1990). Their blend of good-time adult-rock took up where the previous set left off and although no hit singles were forthcoming, fans could content themselves with such enjoyable fare as 'COOL DRY PLACE' and 'NEW BLUE MOON'. This time around the names had changed to BOO (DYLAN), SPIKE (HARRISON), CLAYTON (LYNNE) and MUDDY WILBURY (PETTY), although by now the concept was wearing as thin as their crowns.

Album rating: TRAVELING WILBURYS VOLUME I (*6) / VOLUME 3 (*5)

BOB DYLAN (b.ROBERT ALLAN ZIMMERMAN, 24 May'41, Duluth, Minnesota, USA) – vocals, guitar (also solo artist) / **GEORGE HARRISON** (b.25 Feb'43, Liverpool, England) – vocals, guitar (ex-BEATLES, also solo artist) / **ROY ORBISON** (b.23 Apr'36, Vernon, Texas, USA) – vocals, guitar (solo artist) / **TOM PETTY** (b.20 Oct'53, Gainsville, Florida, USA) – vocals, guitar (solo . . .) / **JEFF LYNNE** (b.30 Dec'47, Birmingham, England) – vocals, guitar (solo artist, ex-ELECTRIC LIGHT ORCHESTRA)

Warners Warners

Oct 88. (7") *(W 7637)* <*27732*> **HANDLE WITH CARE. / MARGARITA** [21] [45]
(12"+=/cd-s+=) *(W 7732 T/CD)* – ('A'extended).

Oct 88. (lp/c)(cd) *(WX 224/+C)(925769-2)* <*25796*> **TRAVELING WILBURYS VOLUME 1** [16] [3]
– Handle with care / Dirty world / Rattled / Last night / Not alone anymore / Conratulations / Heading for the light / Margarita / Tweeter and the monkey man / End of the line.

Feb 89. (7"/12"/cd-s) *(W 7637/+T/CD)* <*27637*> **END OF THE LINE. / CONGRATULATIONS** [52] [63]

—— now augmented by **JIM KELTNER** – drums, percussion / **JIM HORN** – saxophone / **RAY COOPER** – percussion (and a quartet, after the death of ROY O)

Jun 90. (7") *(W 9773)* **NOBODY'S CHILD. / ('B'by 'Dave Stewart & The Spiritual Cowboy')** [44] [ ]
(12"+=/cd-s+=) *(W 9773 T/CD)* – (track by 'Ringo Starr').
Above single was from The ARMENIAN DISASTER album by Various Artists.

Nov 90. (7"/c-s) **SHE'S MY BABY. / NEW BLUE MOON** [ ] [ ]
(12"+=/cd-s+=) – Runaway.

Nov 90. (lp/c)(cd) *(WX 384/+C)*<*(7599 26324-2)*> **TRAVELING WILBURYS VOLUME 3** [14] [11]
– She's my baby / Inside out / If you belonged to me / The Devil's been busy / 7 deadly sins / Poor house / Where were you last night? / Cool dry place / New blue moon / You took my breath away / Wilbury twist.

Mar 91. (7"/c-s) **WILBURY TWIST. / NEW BLUE MOON (instrumental)** [ ] [ ]
(12"+=/cd-s+=) – Cool dry place.

—— all members subsequently returned to their normal solo work

TRAVIS

Formed: Glasgow, Scotland . . . 1991 as GLASS ONION by ANDY DUNLOP and NEIL PRIMROSE, who'd both been members of RUNNING RED. Songwriting singer FRAN HEALY was invited to join the fresh-faced guitar-pop quintet (with the MARTYN brothers), replacing the original female vocalist soon after. In 1993, FRAN's mother advanced the lads some cash to cut a demo and this led to a publishing contract with 'Sony'. Winning a trip to the New Music Seminar in New York via first place in a talent contest might've given them an early break had they attended, although they did manage to squeeze out an eponymous EP the same year. With the band going nowhere fast, changes had to be made and by March '96, the MARTYN brothers had made way for FRAN's Glasgow School Of Art chum, DOUGIE PAYNE (ANDY had also been a student); TRAVIS were now in circulation. Following a self-financed debut single, 'ALL I WANT TO DO IS ROCK', the quartet were taken under the wing of (ex-Go! Discs man) Andy McDonald's 'Independiente' (still through 'Sony') early in '97. Subsequently relocating to London, TRAVIS released their controversial follow-up single, 'U16 GIRLS', apparently a paeon to the charms of underage females. A re-vamp of their hard-to-find debut single followed it into the Top 40 and suddenly TRAVIS were one of the hippest new names on the block. Though HEALY was a charismatic frontman, the Top 10 debut album, 'GOOD FEELING', illustrated at the time the one-dimensional nature of much of their material. Nevertheless, the record did spawn two further Top 40 hits, 'TIED TO THE 90's' and 'HAPPY', indicating that there was at least some potential for the future. After a relatively quiet '98 – although 'MORE THAN US' became their biggest hit to date at No.16 – TRAVIS were back the following March. Taking a softer, laid back approach (70's BREAD come to mind!), the quartet achieved a deserved second Top 20 spot with the beautiful ballad 'WRITING TO REACH YOU'. Further successes came in the shape of 'DRIFTWOOD', 'WHY DOES IT ALWAYS RAIN ON ME?' and 'TURN', all songwriting masterpieces from the critically acclaimed No.1 follow-up set, 'THE MAN WHO' (1999). TRAVIS were fast becoming the United Kingdom's No.1 band and by the start of the year 2000 they were given that accolade by winning the now prestigious Brit award. OASIS (who had been tops until recently!) invited nice guy HEALY and Co to support them on a US tour, the American audiences eventually being won over by their sheer honest enthusiasm and talent. While many critics predictably put the boot in, you could bet your bottom dollar they had a secret copy of UK chart-topper 'THE INVISIBLE BAND' (2001) hidden away for furtive listening pleasure. TRAVIS simply write great songs, occasionally something more but rarely anything less. On first listen, the deceptively simple single, 'SING' may sound trite, but its subtle, banjo inflected power deepens with every spin, enveloping you in a dizzying aura of elemental truth. Similarly the lyrics of 'SIDE' were the butt of cheap jibes yet their sentiment leaks into the consciousness like a zen koan. The band's lack of image and endearing avoidance of any flirtations with the vagaries of musical fashion merely accentuates the strength of the material.

While there was nothing on the album that matched the searing melancholy of say, 'WRITING TO REACH YOU', chances are you'll still be playing this album next year, and the next, and the next . . . However, disaster struck the band on the 9th of July 2002, when drummer PRIMROSE accidently hit his upper torso on the bottom of a swimming pool in France. He underwent extensive surgery to his neck, accumulating in the cancellation of the group's entire European tour (as well as V2002). All was said to be well, though, with PRIMROSE making a slow but steady recovery, the group being set to enter the studio. All was said to be well, though, as the band entered the studio to record their fourth album, the darker and more agitated '12 MEMORIES' in 2003. Probably hoping to match COLDPLAY's emotional, piano-driven songwriting, TRAVIS seemed to be slowly running out of steam, with HEALY's ballady content becoming more and more moot. However, for fans of TRAVIS their was much to admire here: the attack on American ignorance entitled 'THE BEAUTIFUL OCCUPATION' and the spunky UK hit 'RE-OFFENDER' were two that stood out. • **Covered:** BE MY BABY (Ronettes) / BABY ONE MORE TIME (Britney Spears) / ALL THE YOUNG DUDES (Mott The Hoople) / HERE COMES THE SUN (Beatles).

Album rating: GOOD FEELING (*7) / THE MAN WHO (*8) / THE INVISIBLE BAND (*7) / 12 MEMORIES (*6)

GLASS ONION

FRAN HEALY (b. Stafford, England) – vocals, guitar; repl. female / **ANDY DUNLOP** – guitar / **NEIL PRIMROSE** – drums / **. . . MARTYN** – bass / **. . . MARTYN** – keyboards

own label not iss.

Nov 93. (cd-ep) *(GLASSCD 001)* **GLASS ONION** [ ] [ ]
– Dream on / The day before / Free soul / Whenever she comes around.

TRAVIS

—— **DOUGIE PAYNE** – bass; repl. the MARTYN brothers

Red Telephone not iss.

Oct 96. (10"ep) *(PHONE 001)* **ALL I WANT TO DO IS ROCK. / THE LINE IS FINE / FUNNY THING** [ ] [–]

Independiente-Independiente

Mar 97. (7"pic-d/c-s) *(ISOM 1 S/CS)* **U16 GIRLS. / HAZY SHADES OF GOLD / GOOD TIME GIRLS** [40] [–]
(c-s+=/cd-s+=) *(ISOM 1MS)* – Good feeling.

Jun 97. (7") *(SOM 3S) <6080>* **ALL I WANT TO DO IS ROCK. / BLUE ON A BLACK WEEKEND** [39] Apr98 [ ]
(cd-s+=) *(ISOM 3MS)* – Combing my hair.
(cd-s) *(ISOM 3SMS)* – ('A'side) / "20" / 1922.

Aug 97. (7"/cd-s) *(ISOM 5S/+MS) <6084>* **TIED TO THE 90's. / ME BESIDE YOU** [30] Apr98 [ ]
(cd-s) *(ISOM 5MS)* – ('A'side) / City in the rain / Whenever she comes around / Standing on my own.

Sep 97. (cd/c/lp) *(ISOM 1 CD/MC/LP) <68239>* **GOOD FEELING** [9] Oct97 [ ]
– All I want to do is rock / U16 girls / Line is fine / Good day to die / Good feeling / Midsummer nights dreamin' / Tied to the 90's / I love you anyways / Happy / More than us / Falling down / Funny thing. *(re-iss. Nov99; same) (re-dist.Jun01)* – hit No.19

Oct 97. (c-s) *(ISOM 6CS) <6081>* **HAPPY / UNBELIEVERS** [38] Apr98 [ ]
(cd-s+=) *(ISOM 6MS)* – Everyday faces.
(cd-s) *(ISOM 6SMS)* – ('A'side) / When I'm feeling blue (days of the week) / Mother.

Mar 98. (7"ep/c-ep/cd-ep) *(ISOM 11 S/CS/MS)* **MORE THAN US E.P.** [16] [–]
– More than us (with Anne Dudley) / Give me some truth / All I want to do is rock (with Noel Gallagher) / Funny thing (mixed by Tim Simenon).
(cd-s) *(ISOM 11SMS)* – (lead track) / Beautiful bird (demo version) / Reason (with Susie Hug) / More than us (acoustic version).

Mar 99. (7"/c-s) *(ISOM 22 S/CS)* **WRITING TO REACH YOU. / ONLY MOLLY KNOWS** [14] [–]
(cd-s+=) *(ISOM 22MS)* – Green behind the ears.
(cd-s) *(ISOM 22SM)* – ('A'side) / Yeah yeah yeah yeah / High as a kite.

May 99. (c-s) *(ISOM 27CS)* **DRIFTWOOD / WRITING TO REACH YOU (Deadly Avenger remix)** [13] [–]
(cd-s+=) *(ISOM 27SMS)* – Wtiting to reach you (Deadly Avenger instrumental remix).
(cd-s) *(ISOM 27MS)* – ('A'side) / Be my baby / Where is the love.

May 99. (cd/c/lp) *(ISOM 9 CD/MC/LP) <62151>* **THE MAN WHO** [1] Apr00 [ ]
– Writing to reach you / The fear / As you are / Driftwood / The last laugh of the laughter / Turn / Why does it always rain on me? / Luv / She's so strange / Slide show. *(lp w/free 12"; ISOM 27T)* – WRITING TO REACH YOU (Deadly Avenger mixes). *(special ltd-cd+=; ISOM 9CDX)* – Blue flashing light / Writing to reach you / Driftwood. *(cd re-iss. Aug02; same)*

Aug 99. (c-s) *(ISOM 33CS)* **WHY DOES IT ALWAYS RAIN ON ME? / VILLAGE MAN** [10] [–]
(cd-s+=) *(ISOM 33MS)* – Driftwood (live).
(cd-s) *(ISOM 33SMS)* – ('A'side) / The urge for going / Slide show (live).

Nov 99. (c-s) *(ISOM 39CS)* **TURN / DAYS OF OUR LIVES** [8] [–]
(cd-s+=) *(ISOM 39MS)* – River.
(cd-s) *(ISOM 39SMS)* – ('A'side) / We are monkeys / Baby one more time.

Jun 00. (7"/c-s) *(ISOM 45 S/CS)* **COMING AROUND. / CONNECTION** [5] [ ]
(cd-s+=) *(ISOM 45MC)* – Just the faces change.
(cd-s) *(ISOM 45SMS)* – ('A'side) / Rock'n'(salad) roll / The weight.

May 01. (7"/c-s) *(ISOM 49 S/CS)* **SING. / KILLER QUEEN** [3] [ ]
(cd-s+=) *(ISOM 49MS)* – Ring out the bell.
(cd-s) *(ISOM 49SMAS)* – ('A'side) / You don't know what I'm like / Beautiful.

Jun 01. (cd/c/lp) *(ISOM 25 CD/MC/LP) <85788>* **THE INVISIBLE BAND** [1] [39]
– Sing / Dear diary / Side / Pipe dreams / Flowers in the window / The cage / Safe / Follow the light / Last train / Afterglow / Indefinitely / The Humpty Dumpty love song.

Sep 01. (7"/c-s) *(ISOM 54 S/CS)* **SIDE. / ALL THE YOUNG DUDES (live)** [14] [–]
(cd-s) *(ISOM 54MS)* – ('A'side) / Driftwood (live).
(cd-s) *(ISOM 54SMS)* – ('A'side) / You're a big girl now / Ancient train.

Mar 02. (c-s) *(ISOM 56CS)* **FLOWERS IN THE WINDOW / A LITTLE BIT OF SOUL** [18] [–]
(cd-s+=) *(ISOM 56MS)* – Here comes the sun.
(cd-s) *(ISOM 56SMS)* – ('A'side) / Central station / No cigar.
(7") *(ISOM 56S)* – ('A'side) / Here comes the sun.

Sep 03. (7") *(ISOM 78S)* **RE-OFFENDER. / DEFINITION OF WRONG** [7] [–]
(cd-s+=) *(ISOM 78SMS)* – Enemy.
(cd-s) *(ISOM 78MS)* – ('A'side) / The sea / Don't be shy.

Oct 03. (cd/c/lp) *(ISOM 40 CD/MC/LP) <90672>* **12 MEMORIES** [3] [41]
– Quicksand / The beautiful occupation / Re-offender / Peace the fuck out / How many hearts / Paperclips / Somewhere else / Love will come through / Mid-life Krysis / Happy to hang around / Walking down the hill. *(clean cd; ISOM 40CDX)*

Dec 03. (7") *(ISOM 81S)* **THE BEAUTIFUL OCCUPATION. / I DIDN'T MEAN TO GET HIGH** [48] [–]
(cd-s+=) *(ISOM 81MS)* – Score.
(cd-s) *(ISOM 81SMS)* – ('A'side) / Distraction / Back in the day.

☐ T. REX (see under ⇒ BOLAN, Marc)

a TRIBE CALLED QUEST

Formed: Queens, New York, USA . . . 1988 by ALI, PHIFE, JAROBI and Q-TIP. They had met at high school, while Q-TIP had already sung alongside DE LA SOUL and The JUNGLE BROTHERS. Two 1989/90 singles floated by, before debut album 'PEOPLE'S INSTINCTIVE TRAVELS' cracked the US charts. It gained further success in Britain, due to hit singles 'BONITA APPLEBUM' and 'CAN I KICK IT?', which sampled LOU REED's 'Walk On The Wild Side'. Afro-centric hip-hop pioneers of acid-jazz (R&B psychedelia) influenced by JUNGLE BROTHERS, their next album 'LOW END THEORY', was their breakthrough into the US Top 50 and featured jazz veteran, RON CARTER, on upright bass. Q-TIP and others were requested by many (DEEE-LITE – 'Groove Is In The Heart', JUNGLE BROTHERS and DE LA SOUL) as guest artists, while they surfaced once again in 1993 with 'MIDNIGHT MARAUDERS'. This went to the top of the R&B charts, while gaining a US Top 10 spot, a feat easily surpassed when 1996's 'BEATS, RHYMES AND LIFE' topped the chart. After another Top 3 set, 'THE MOVEMENT' (1998), the 'QUEST was over. • **Songwriters:** Group penned (DAVIS / TAYLOR / JONES / MUHAMMAD). Samples; SIR DUKE (Stevie Wonder) / INNER CITY BLUES (Marvin Gaye) / Others:- Grace Jones + Carly Simon on 'BONITA APPLEBUM'.

Album rating: PEOPLE'S INSTINCTIVE TRAVELS AND THE PATHS OF RHYTHM (*6) / LOW END THEORY (*7) / REVISED QUEST FOR THE SEASONED TRAVELLER remixes (*4) / MIDNIGHT MARAUDERS (*7) / BEATS, RHYMES AND LIFE (*8) / THE LOVE MOVEMENT (*6) / THE ANTHOLOGY compilation (*7)

Q-TIP (b. JONATHAN DAVIS, 20 Nov'70) – vocals / **ALI** (b. ALI SHAHEED MUHAMMAD, 11 Aug'70) – DJ / **PHIFE** (b. MALIK TAYLOR, 10 Apr'70) – vocals / **JAROBI** – vocals

Jive Jive

Aug 89. (7") *(JIVE 215)* *<1241>* **DESCRIPTION OF A FOOL (talkie). / ('A'instrumental)** [ ] [ ]
(12"+=) *(JIVET 215)* – ('A'-silent version).

Mar 90. (12") *(JIVET 242)* **PUBIC ENEMY. / (mix)** [ ] [-]

May 90. (cd)(lp/c) *(CHIP 96)(HIP/+C 96)* *<1331>* **PEOPLE'S INSTINCTIVE TRAVELS AND THE PATHS OF RHYTHM** [54] Apr90 [91]
– Push it along / Luck of Lucien / After hours / Footprints / I left my wallet in El Segundo / Bonita Applebum / Can I kick it? / Youthful expression / Rhythm (devoted to the art of moving butts) / Mr. Muhammad / Ham 'n' eggs / Go ahead in the rain / Description of a fool. *(cd re-iss. Mar97 & Aug99; same)*

Aug 90. (7")<c-s> *(JIVE 256)* *<1368>* **BONITA APPLEBUM. / ('A'mix)** [47] [ ]
(12"+=/cd-s+=) *(JIVE T/CD 256)* *<1384>* – Between the sheets.

Jan 91. (7"/c-s) *(JIVE/+C 265)* *<1430>* **CAN I KICK IT?. / ('A'-Boilerhouse mix)** [15] [ ]
(12"+=/cd-s+=) *(JIVE T/CD 265)* *<1400>* – ('A'-Phase 5 mix) / ('A'-If the tapes come remix).

Mar 91. (7"/c-s)<c-s> *(JIVE/+C 270)* *<1300>* **I LEFT MY WALLET IN EL SEGUNDO. / ('A'-talkie)** [ ] [ ]
(12"+=/cd-s+=) *(JIVE T/CD 270)* – ('A'-Vampire mix) / ('A'-Silent mix).

—— now without JAROBI

Sep 91. (7") *(JIVE 284)* *<42011>* **CHECK THE RHIME. / ('A'instrumental)** [ ] [ ]
(12"+=/cd-s+=) *(JIVE T/CD 284)* – ('A'mixes).

Sep 91. (lp/c/cd) *(HIP/+C/CD 117)* *<1418>* **LOW END THEORY** [58] [45]
– Excursions / Buggin' out / Rap promoter / Butter / Verses from the abstract / Show business / Vibes and stuff / The infamous date rape / Check the rhime / Everything is fair / Jazz (we've got) / Skypager / Scenario. *(cd re-iss. Mar97; same)*

Dec 91. (12"ep/cd-ep) *(JIVE T/CD)* **JAZZ (WE'VE GOT) (4 versions) / BUGGIN' OUT** [ ] [ ]

May 92. (12"ep/cd-ep) *(JIVE T/CD 302)* *<42065>* **SCENARIO (MC mix). / (8 mixes)** [ ] [57]

Sep 92. (7") *(JIVE 317)* **LUCK OF LUCIEN. / BUTTER** [ ] [ ]
(12"+=/cd-s+=) *(JIVE T/CD 317)* – ('A'mixes).

Oct 92. (cd)(lp/c) *(CHIP 130)(HIP/+C 130)* **REVISED QUEST FOR THE SEASONED TRAVELLER** (remixes) [ ] [-]
– Bonita Applebum / I left my wallet in El Segundo / Description of a fool / Pubic enemy / Check the rhyme / Luck of Lucien / Can I kick it / Scenario / If the papers came/ Jazz (we've got) / Butter. *(cd re-iss. Mar97; same)*

Nov 92. (7") *(JIVE 324)* **CAN I KICK IT?. / HOT SEX** [ ] [ ]
(12"+=/cd-s+=) *(JIVE T/CD 324)* – ('A'-Boilerhouse extended) / ('A'side again).

Oct 93. (cd)(d-lp/c) *(CHIP 143)(HIP/+C 143)* *<42197>* **MIDNIGHT MARAUDERS** [70] [8]
– Midnight marauders tour guide / Steve Biko (stir it up) / Award tour / 8 million stories / Sueka nigga / Midnight / We can get down / Electric relaxation (relax yourself girl) / (interlude) / Clap your hands / Oh my God / (interlude) / Keep it rollin' / The chase pt.II / Lyrics to go / God lives through / Hot sex. *(cd re-iss. Mar97; same)*

Nov 93. (c-s) *(JIVEC 344)* *<42187>* **AWARD TOUR. / THE CHASE (pt.II)** [ ] [47]
(cd-s+=) *(JIVECD 344)* – ('A'instrumental).
(12"++=) *(JIVET 344)* – ('A'radio mix).

Feb 94. (12"ep/cd-ep) *(JIVE T/CD 351)* *<42179>* **ELECTRIC RELAXATION (RELAX YOURSELF GIRL) / ('A'version) / MIDNIGHT / ('B'version)** [ ] [65]

May 94. (12"/c-s) *(JIVE T/C 355)* **OH MY GOD. / ('A'-UK flavour radio mix)** [68] [ ]
(cd-s) *(JIVECD 355)* – ('A'side) / Bonita Applebum / Can I kick it? / Left my wallet in El Segundo.

Nov 94. (7"ep/12"ep/cd-ep) *(JIVE/+T/CD 374)* **A TRIBE CALLED QUEST EP** [ ] [-]
– We can get down / Clap your hands / Verses from the abstract / Footprints.

Jul 96. (12"/cd-s) *(JIVE T/CD 399)* **1NCE AGAIN. / ('A'radio) / ('A'instrumental) / I left my wallet in El Segundo** [34] [ ]
(cd-s) *(JIVERCD 399)* – ('A'side) / Bonita applebum / Can I kick it? / Scenario (remix).

Aug 96. (cd)(lp/c) *(CHIP 170)(HIP/+C 170)* *<41587>* **BEATS, RHYMES AND LIFE** [28] [1]
– Phony rappers / Get a hold / Motivators / Jam / Crew / The pressure / 1nce again (featuring TAMMY LUCAS) / Mind power / The hop / Keeping it moving / Baby Phife's return / Separate – together / What really goes on / Word play / Stressed out (featuring FAITH EVANS).

Nov 96. (c-s; by A TRIBE CALLED QUEST featuring FAITH EVANS & RAPHAEL SAADIQ) *(JIVEC 404)* **STRESSED OUT / ('A'mix)** [33] [ ]
(12"/cd-s) *(JIVE T/CD 404)* – ('A'mixes).

—— Mar'97, credited on FUGESS Top 3 hit 'Rumble In The Jungle'.

Aug 97. (12"ep/cd-ep) *(JIVE TCD 427)* **THE JAM EP** [61] [ ]
– Jam / Get a hold / Mardi gras at midnight / Same ol' thing.

Aug 98. (c-s) *(051898-4)* *42534>* **FIND A WAY / STEPPIN' IT UP (with BUSTA RHYMES & REDMAN)** [41] [71]
(12"+=/cd-s+=) *(051898-0/-2)* – ('A'instrumental).

Sep 98. (cd/c/lp) *(052103-2/-4/-1)* *<41638>* **THE LOVE MOVEMENT** [38] [3]
– Start it up / Find a way / Da booty / Steppin' it up / Like it like that / Common ground (get it goin' on) / Moms / His name is Mutty Ranks / Give me / Pad & pen / Busta's lament / Hot 4 U / Against the world / Love / Rock rock y'all / Scenario / Money maker / Hot sex / Oh my God / Jazz (we've got) / One two s**t.

—— split later in 1998

– compilations, etc. –

Oct 99. (d-cd/t-lp) *Jive; (052384-2/-1)* *<41679>* **THE ANTHOLOGY** [ ] [81]
– Check the rhime / Bonita applebum / Award tour / Can I kick it? / Scenario / Buggin' out / If the papes come / Electric relaxation / Jazz (we've got) / I left my wallet in El Segundo / Hot sex / Oh my God / Stressed out / Luck of Lucien / Description of a fool / Keep it moving / Find a way / Sucka nigga / Vibrant thing / Bonita applebum / I left my wallet in El Segundo / Public enemy / Can I kick it? / Scenario / Bonita applebum / Oh my God.

Jul 03. (cd+dvd) *Jive; (8287 654348-2)* *<41839>* **HITS, RARITIES & REMIXES** [ ] Jun03 [ ]

TRICKY

Born: ADRIAN THAWES, 27 Jan'68, Knowle West, Bristol, England. After a troubled youth growing up on one of Bristol's poorer housing estates, THAWES began spending less time lawbreaking and more time busying himself with the city's club culture, helping run sound systems and hanging out with The WILD BUNCH, a loose collective of musicians and DJ's that icluded MASSIVE ATTACK and famed producer NELLEE HOOPER. In between trips to court in OXFORD, where he was defending an assault charge, TRICKY KID (as he was nicknamed by his Bristolian cohorts) occasionally collaborated with MASSIVE ATTACK on their seminal 'BLUE LINES' album, contributing stoned raps on several tracks. He also contributed to MASSIVE's follow-up,

'PROTECTION', although his first solo effort was a 'Betty Blue'-sampling track entitled 'LOYALTY IS VALUABLE', engineered by future PORTISHEAD mainman GEOFF BARROWS and featured on the 1991 Sickle Cell charity album, 'HARD SELL', alongside the likes of MASSIVE ATTACK, SMITH & MIGHTY etc. Yet the track that brought him to the attention of a discerning public was the sublime claustrophobia of 'AFTERMATH'. Eventually released in early '94, the track had previously been recorded a couple of years earlier with TRICKY's musical partner, MARTINA, predating the trip-hop scene that TRICKY would later be lumped in with. Next came the jarring loops and nervous paranoia of 'PONDEROSA', another taster for the pioneering debut album, 'MAXINQUAYE' (1994), released later that summmer. A dense, brooding collection of slow motion beat-poetry from the darkside, the record was immediately hailed as a classic. Taking bastardised hip-hop beats as his raw material then suffocating them with layers of samples, disjointed rhythms, freak instrumental lines and obscure noises, TRICKY created music that was wired yet lethargic, with lyrics equally contradictory and ambiguous to match. Collaborating with TERRY HALL, NENEH CHERRY and ALISON MOYET amongst others, TRICKY released his 'NEARLY GOD' project in 1996. The album revisited the dark intensity of 'MAXINQUAYE' without quite the same effect, possibly a case of too many cooks (or too many spliffs) spoiling the broth. 'PRE-MILLENNIUM TENSION', released later the same year, was on a par with 'MAXINQUAYE' and if it didn't exactly break new ground, the album illustrated that TRICKY's wellspring of paranoid psychosis was far from running dry. Tracks like 'BAD THINGS', 'MAKES ME WANNA DIE' and 'MY EVIL IS STRONG' speak for themselves, and though it's a well worn cliche, it would appear that this man really does suffer for his art. Then again, maybe he shouldn't smoke so much. 1999 was a busy year for TRICKY, everything from making "real" gangster LP, 'PRODUCT OF THE ENVIRONMENT' (with Mad Frankie Fraser for one!) to delivering his final album for 'Island', 'JUXTAPOSE'. The latter – which was recorded with DJ MUGGS (of CYPRESS HILL) and GREASE – achieved the usual plaudits, its return to his experimental trip-hop roots gaining him a near UK Top 30 place. TRICKY was to fall out with his label 'Island' one year later. Comeback set, 'BLOWBACK', was finally unleashed by 'Epitaph' (once home to BAD RELIGION and their ilk) wasn't thought ready until summer 2001. A slightly disappointing set, the album displayed TRICKY's usual mix of hip-hop beats and chilled-out smoking rhymes. From the Red Hot Chili Peppers' 'GIRLS' to collaboration dabblings with HAWKMAN (a toaster from Jamaica), ED KOWALCZYK (of LIVE) and AMBERSUNSHOWER (an obscure new age diva), the album certainly had its moments.
• **Songwriters:** Self-penned & samples except; BLACK STEEL + THE MOMENT I FEARED (Public Enemy) / PONDEROSA (co-with HOWIE B) / HELL IS ROUND THE CORNER (same source that PORTISHEAD found 'Glory Box'?) / SINGING THE BLUES (Mary McReary) / POP MUZIK (M) / he also sampled a song by Billie Holiday on 'Carriage For Two'.

Album rating: MAXINQUAYE (*9) / NEARLY GOD (*7; as Nearly God) / PRE-MILLENNIUM TENSION (*7) / ANGELS WITH DIRTY FACES (*7) / JUXTAPOSE (*7) / BLOWBACK (*6) / A RUFF GUIDE compilation (*8) / VULNERABLE (*7)

TRICKY – vocals (ex-MASSIVE ATTACK) / with **MARTINE TOPLEY-BIRD** – vocals / and others

4th & Broad 4th & Broad

Jan 94. (7") *(BRW 288)* *<590>* **AFTERMATH. / ('A'-I could be looking for people mix)** [69] [ ]
(12"+=) *(12BRW 288)* – ('A'mix).
(cd-s++=) *(BRCD 288)* – ('A'mix).

Apr 94. (7") *(BRW 299)* *<595>* **PONDEROSA. / ('A'-Dobie's roll pt.1 mix)** [ ] Jul94 [ ]
(12"+=/cd-s+=) *(12BRW/BRCD 299)* – (3 'A'mixes; Ultragelic / Original / Dobie's roll pt.2).

Jan 95. (7"/c-s) *(BR W/CA 304)* **OVERCOME. / ABBA ON FAT TRACKS** [34] [–]
(12"+=/cd-s+=) *(12BRW/BRCD 304)* – ('A'-Zippy & Bungle mix).

—— guests on below ALISON GOLDFRAPP + RAGGA – vocals / PETE BRIQUETTE – bass / MARK SAUNDERS – keyboards / FTV – guitar, drums / TONY WRAFTER – flute / JAMES STEVENSON – guitar

Feb 95. (cd/c/lp) *(BR CD/CA/LP 610)* *<524089>* **MAXINQUAYE** [3] Apr95 [ ]
– Overcome / Ponderosa / Black steel / Hell is round the corner / Pumpkin / Aftermath / Abbaon fat tracks / Brand new you're retro / Suffocated love / You don't / Strugglin' / Feed me.

Mar 95. (c-s) *(BRCA 320)* **BLACK STEEL. / ('A'-Been caught stealing mix)** [28] [–]
(12"+=/cd-s+=) *(12BRW/BRCD 320)* – ('A'live) / ('A'-In the draw mix).
(cd-s++=) *(BRCDX 320)* – ('A'edit).

Jul 95. (7"pic-d-ep/12"red-ep/cd-ep; as TRICKY VS. THE GRAVEDIGGAZ) *(BRW/12BRW/BRCD 326)* *<383>* **THE HELL E.P.** [12] [ ]
– Hell is round the corner (original) / ('A'-Hell and water mix) / Psychosis / Tonite is a special nite (chaos mass confusion mix).

Nov 95. (c-s) *(BRCA 330)* **PUMPKIN / MOODY BROODY BUDHIST CAMP / NEW KINGDOM** [26] [ ]
(cd-s+=) *(BRCD 330)* – Brand new you're retro (Alex Reece mix).
(12"colrd) *(12BRW 330)* – ('A'side) / (above track) / Slick 66.

NEARLY GOD

TRICKY with **TERRY HALL / MARTINE / BJORK / NENEH CHERRY / ALISON MOYET + CATH COFFEY**

Durban Poison Island

Apr 96. (7") *(DP 003)* **POEMS / CHILDREN'S STORY** [28] [ ]
(12"+=/cd-s+=) *(DP X/CD 003)* – ('A'extended).

Apr 96. (cd/c/lp) *(DP CD/MC/LP 1001)* *<531064>* **NEARLY GOD** [11] [ ]
– Tattoo / Poems / Together now / Keep your mouth shut / I be the prophet / Make a chane / Black cofee / Bubbles / I sing for you / Yoga.
above was to have been under his DURBAN POISON project.

—— Aug 96, TRICKY PRESENTS GRASS ROOTS 12"ep for 'Ultra'.

TRICKY

—— with a plethora of musicians incl. **PATRICE CHEVALIER** – guitar / **JOHN TONKS** – drums / **PAT McMANUS** – piano, violin

4th & Broad Island

Oct 96. (7"pic-d) *(BRW 340)* **CHRISTIANSANDS. / FLYNN** [36] [ ]
(12"+=/cd-s+=) *(12BRW/BRCD 340)* – Ghetto youth.

Nov 96. (cd/c/lp) *(BR CD/CA/LP 623)* *<524302>* **PRE-MILLENNIUM TENSION** [30] [ ]
– Vent / Christiansands / Tricky kid / Bad dreams / Makes me wanna die / Ghetto youth / Sex drive / Bad things / Lyrics of fury / My evil is strong / Piano. *(d-cd-iss. ; BRCDX 623)*

—— late '96, featured on the hit single by GARBAGE; 'Milk'.

Dec 96. (cd-ep) *(BRCDX 341)* **TRICKY KID. / MAKES ME WANNA DIE (Tricky's extremix) / GRASS ROOTS** [28] [ ]
(12"ep+=) *(12BRW 341)* – Smoking Beagles (Sub Sub vs Tricky).
(cd-ep) *(BRCD 341)* – ('A'side) / Devils helper / Smoking Beagles (Sub Sub vs Tricky) / Suffocated love (live on 'Later with Jools').

Apr 97. (cd-s) *(BRCDX 348)* **MAKES ME WANNA DIE / MAKES ME WANNA DIE (The Weekend mix – remixed by The Stereo MC's) / PIANO (the Green sticky mix remixed by A Guy Called Gerald)** [29] [ ]
(12"clear+=) *(BRX 348)* – Here comes the aliens (AFRIKA IZLAM & TRICKY).
(cd-s) *(BRCD 348)* – ('A'side) / ('A'acoustic) / Here come the aliens (AFRIKA IZLAM & TRICKY).

Island Island

May 98. (7"; TRICKY featuring POLLY JEAN HARVEY) *(IS 701)* **BROKEN HOMES. / MONEY GREEDY** [25] [–]
(cd-s+=) *(CID 701)* – Anti histamine / Taxi.
(cd-s+=) *(CIDX 701)* – 360 degrees.

May 98. (cd/c/d-lp) *(CID/ICT/ILPS 8071)* *<524520>* **ANGELS WITH DIRTY FACES** [23] Jun98 [84]
– Money greedy / Mellow / Singing the blues / Broken homes / 6 minutes /

Analyze me / The moment I feared / Talk to me (angels with dirty faces) / Carriage for two / Demise / Tear out my eyes / Record companies / Peyote sings / Taxi.

Dec 98. (cd-s) *<572515>* **6 MINUTES (mixes)** [–] [ ]

Aug 99. (12"/cd-s) *(12IS/CID 753)* **FOR REAL (mixes; Hip Hop / Genaside II / Rollo)** [45] [–]
(cd-s) *(CIDX 753)* – ('A'side) / Bombing bastards / Pop muzik.

Aug 99. (cd/lp; by TRICKY with DJ MUGGS & GREASE) *(CID/ILPS 8087) <546432>* **JUXTAPOSE** [22] [ ]
– For real / Bom bom diggy / Contradictive / She said / I like the girls / Hot like a sauna / Call me / Wash my soul / Hot like a sauna (metal mix) / Scrappy love.

Anti Hollywood

Nov 00. (12"ep/cd-ep) *(6595-1/-2)* **MISSION ACCOMPLISHED EP** [ ] [–]
– Mission accomplished / Crazy claws / Tricky versus Lynx (live) / Divine comedy.

—— next with guests ED KOWALCZYK, HAWKMAN, ANTHONY KEIDIS, JOHN FRUSCIANTE, FLEA, AMBERSUNSHOWER, CYNDI LAUPER

Anti Hollywood

Jul 01. (cd/d-lp) *(6596-2/-1) <162285>* **BLOWBACK** [34] [ ]
– Excess / Evolution revolution love / Over me / Girls / You don't wanna / 1da woman / Your name / Diss never (dig up we history) / Bury the evidence / Something in the way / Five days / Give it to 'em / Song for Yukiko. *(ltd d-cd-iss. Jul02 +=; 6645-2)* – Excess / My head / Costanza / Five days (instrumental) / Suffocating / Divine comedy / I da woman / Unofficial.

Anti Sanctuary

May 03. (cd) *(6686-2) <84618>* **VULNERABLE** [ ] Jun03 [ ]
– Stay / Antimatter / Ice pick / Car crash / Dear God / How high / What is wrong / Hollow / Moody / Wait for God / Where I'm from / The love cats / Search, search, survive. *(cd w/ dvd+=)* – Antimatter (Jimmy & T remix) / Receive us / You don't wanna (with RADAGON).

Jul 03. (12") *(1101-1)* **ANTIMATTER / (mixes; ragga / Jimmy & T / Ollie)** [ ] [–]
(cd-s+=) *(1101-2)* – ('A'-video).

– compilations, etc. –

May 02. (cd) *Island; (CID 8114) <586872>* **A RUFF GUIDE** [ ] [ ]
– Aftermath / Poems (NEARLY GOD) / For real / Black steel / Pumpkin / Broken homes / Wash my soul / I be the prophet / Makes me wanna die / Tricky kid / Scrappy love / Ponderosa / Christiansands / Hell is around the corner / Singing the blues / Bubbles (NEARLY GOD) / Overcome / Aftermath (I could be looking for people remix) / Black steel (in the draw mix).

□ TRIPPING DAISY (see under ⇒ POLYPHONIC SPREE)

TROGGS

Formed: Andover, Hampshire, England … 1964 briefly as The TROGLODYTES, by REG BALL (PRESLEY), CHRIS BRITTON, PETE STAPLES and RONNIE BOND. In 1965, they were signed by KINKS manager, Larry Page, who leased them to 'C.B.S.' in early '66 for the debut single, 'LOST GIRL'. Their second 45, 'WILD THING', with TV exposure on 'Thank Your Lucky Stars', gave them a No.2 hit, which also went on to become a US No.1. This primal three-chord assault carried on where 'LOUIE LOUIE' left off, the band taking on American garage-rock in a bizarre inversion of the British invasion. It has since become one of the most covered songs ever, a blueprint for almost any band with a guitar and an amp that went up to 11. They then went No.1 with the harmony-laden, 'WITH A GIRL LIKE YOU', which again featured PRESLEY's grizzled drawl of a vocal. Their next single, 'I CAN'T CONTROL MYSELF', gave them their third consecutive Top 3 hit, closely followed by another CHIP TAYLOR-penned song (like 'WILD THING'), 'ANY WAY THAT YOU WANT ME'. They continued in their bid for chart domination with a further string of Top 50 hits, the band's sound rapidly evolving with the onset of psychedelia. One of the aforementioned 45's, 'LOVE IS ALL AROUND', became an even bigger smash in 1994, when Scots popsters WET WET WET took it to the top for several weeks. This subsequently furnished PRESLEY with enough money to indulge his crop circle obsession. Previously in 1990, The TROGGS' profile was raised somewhat, through a collaboration with R.E.M. on an album, 'AU' (this also featured 'LOVE IS ALL AROUND'). • **Songwriters:** PRESLEY was the main writer, except HI HI HAZEL (Geno Washington) / GOOD VIBRATIONS (Beach Boys) / I CAN'T GET NO SATISFACTION (Rolling Stones) / THE KITTY CAT SONG (Hal Roach-Allen Toussaint) / RIDE YOUR PONY (Aaron Neville) / EVIL (… Singleton) / LOUIE LOUIE (Richard Berry) / JAGUAR AND THUNDERBIRD + MEMPHIS + NO PARTICULAR PLACE TO GO (Chuck Berry) / GOT LOVE IF YOU WANT IT (Slim Harpo) / WALKING THE DOG (Rufus Thomas) / etc. • **Trivia:** Their 1990's reformation included collaborations with R.E.M. on single 'Nowhere Road'.

Album rating: FROM NOWHERE … THE TROGGS (*7) / TROGGLODYNAMITE (*7) / BEST OF THE TROGGS compilation (*7) / CELLOPHANE (*7) / LOVE IS ALL AROUND (*6) / MIXED BAG (*5) / BEST OF THE TROGGS, VOL.II compilation (*6) / TROGGLOMANIA (*5) / CONTRASTS (*4) / TROGGS (*3) / THE TROGGS TAPES (*2) / LIVE AT MAX'S KANSAS CITY (*2) / BLACK BOTTOM (*3) / AU (*4) / ATHENS ANDOVER (*5) / ARCHEOLOGY (1967-1977) boxed-set compilation (*8)

REG BALL (b.12 Jun'43; became REG PRESLEY after hit) – vocals, ocamna / **CHRIS BRITTON** (b.21 Jun'45, Watford, England) – guitar repl. TONY MANSFIELD / **PETE STAPLES** (b. 3 May'44) – bass (ex-TEN FOOT FIVE) repl. DAVID WRIGHT / **RONNIE BOND** (b. 4 May'43) – drums

C.B.S. not iss.

Feb 66. (7") *(202038)* **LOST GIRL. / THE YELLA IN ME** [ ] [–]

Fontana Fontana

Apr 66. (7") *(TF 689) <1548>* **WILD THING. / FROM HOME** [2] Jun66 [1]
<above & below 'A' was also double 'A'side on 'Atco'; 6415>

Jul 66. (7") *(TF 717) <1552>* **WITH A GIRL LIKE YOU. / I WANT YOU** [1] [29]

Jul 66. (lp; stereo/mono) *(S+/TL 5355)* **FROM NOWHERE… THE TROGGS** [6] [–]
– Wild thing / The kitty cat song / Ride your pony / Hi hi Hazel / I just sing / Evil / The yella in me / With a girl like you / Our love will still be there / Louie Louie / Jingle jangle / When I'm with you / From home / Jaguar and Thunderbird / I can't control myself / Night of the long grass. *(cd-iss. 1989; 832957-2)*

Aug 66. (lp) *<67556><Atco; SD 33193>* **WILD THING** [–] [52]
– Wild thing / From home / Just sing / Hi hi Hazel / Lost girl / Evil / With a girl like you / I want you / Your love / Our love will be there.

Page One Atco

Sep 66. (7") *(POF 001) <6444>* **I CAN'T CONTROL MYSELF. / GONNA MAKE YOU MINE** [2] [43]
<also on US 'Fontana'; 1557>

Page One Fontana

Dec 66. (7") *(POF 010) <1585>* **ANY WAY THAT YOU WANT ME. / 6-5-4-3-2-1** [8] Apr67 [ ]

Feb 67. (7") *(POF 015) <1576>* **GIVE IT TO ME. / YOU'RE LYIN'** [12] [ ]

Feb 67. (lp) *(POL 001)* **TROGGLODYNAMITE** [10] [–]
– I can only give you everything / Last summer / Meet Jacqueline / Oh no / It's too late / No.10 Downing Street / Mona / I want you to come into my life / Let me tell you babe / Little Queenie / Cousin Jane / You can't beat it / Baby come closer / It's over.

May 67. (7") *(POF 022) <1593>* **NIGHT OF THE LONG GRASS. / GIRL IN BLACK** [17] Jun67 [ ]

Jul 67. (lp) *(FOR 001)* **BEST OF THE TROGGS** (compilation) [24] [–]
– Night of the long grass / Gonna make you / Anyway that you want me / 6-5-4-3-2-1 / I want you / With a girl like you / I can't control myself / Girl in black / Give it to me / You're lying / From home / Wild thing. *(re-iss. Feb85 on 'Rhino'+ 1988 on 'Bigtime')*

Jul 67. (7") *(POF 030)* **HI HI HAZEL. / AS I RIDE BY** [42] [–]

Oct 67. (7") *(POF 040) <1607>* **LOVE IS ALL AROUND. / WHEN WILL THE RAIN COME** [5] Feb68 [7]

Dec 67. (lp; mono/stereo) *(POL/S 003)* **CELLOPHANE** [ ] [–]
– Little red donkey / Too much of a good thing / Butterflies and bees / All

of my time / Seventeen / Somewhere my girl is waiting / It's showing / Her emotion / When will the rain come / My lady / Come the day / Love is all around.

Feb 68. (7") *(POF 056)* **LITTLE GIRL. / MAYBE THE MADMEN** 37 –

May 68. (7") *(POF 064)* **SURPRISE SURPRISE. / MARBLES AND SOME GUM?** –

May 68. (lp) <67576> **LOVE IS ALL AROUND** –
– Love is all around / Night of the long grass / Gonna make you / Anyway that you want me / 6-5-4-3-2-1 / When will the rain come / Little girl / I can't control myself / Girl in black / Give it to me / Cousin Jane.

Aug 68. (7") *(POF 082)* *<1622>* **YOU CAN CRY IF YOU WANT TO. / THERE'S SOMETHING ABOUT YOU**

Sep 68. (7") *<1630>* **SURPRISE SURPRISE. / COUSIN JANE** –

Oct 68. (7") *(POF 092)* *<1634>* **HIP HIP HOORAY. / SAY DARLIN'!**

Dec 68. (lp) *(POLS 012)* **MIXED BAG** –

Page One — Page One

Jan 69. (7") *(POF 114)* **EVIL WOMAN. / SWEET MADELAINE** –

Jan 69. (lp) *(FOR 007)* **BEST OF THE TROGGS VOL.II** (compilation)
– I can only give you everything / Meet Jacqueline / Jingle jangle / I want you to come into my life / Cousin Jane / Louie Louie / Love is all around / From home / Jaguar and the thunderbird / Hi hi Hazel / Mona.

Feb 69. (7") *<21026>* **EVIL WOMAN. / HEADS OR TAILS** –

— Split Mar'69.

Mar 69. (7"; by RONNIE BOND) *(POF 123)* **ANYTHING FOR YOU. / CAROLYN** –

Apr 69. (7"; by REG PRESLEY) *(POF 131)* **LUCINDA LEE. / WICHITA LINEMAN** –

— CHRIS BRITTON also issued solo album 'AS I AM' in 1969.

— The TROGGS re-formed. **TONY MURRAY** – bass (ex-PLASTIC PENNY) repl. PETE

Feb 70. (7") *(POF 164)* *<21030>* **EASY LOVIN'. / GIVE ME SOMETHING**

1970. (lp) *(POS 602)* **TROGGLOMANIA (live)**
– Give it to me / Jingle jangle / No.10 Downing Street / Wild thing / Oh no / Last Summer / Anyway that you want me / Hi hi Hazel / With a girl like you / Mona / Baby come closer / Cousin Jane / I can't control myself / I want you to come into my life / I just sing.

May 70. (7") *(POF 171)* *<21032>* **LOVER. / COME NOW**

Jul 70. (7") *(POF 182)* *<21035>* **THE RAVER. / YOU**

— **RICHARD MOORE** – guitar repl. BRITTON

D.J.M. — Silverline

1970. (lp) *(DJML 009)* **CONTRASTS** (1966-70)
– I can't control myself / The raver / Surprise, surprise (I need you) / Evil woman / Lover / Wild thing / Love is all around / Little girl / You can cry if you want to / I've waited for someone / Easy loving / Any way that you want me *(re-iss. Nov76; same)*

Jun 71. (7") *(DJS 248)* **LAZY WEEKEND. / LET'S PULL TOGETHER**

Jam — not iss.

Nov 72. (7"m) *(JAM 25)* **WILD THING (new version). / WITH A GIRL LIKE YOU / LOVE IS ALL AROUND** –

Pye — Pye

1972. (7") *(7N 45147)* **EVERYTHING'S FUNNY. / FEELS LIKE A WOMAN** –

Pye — Bell

1973. (7") *(7N 45244)* *<45405>* **LISTEN TO THE MAN. / QUEEN OF SORROW**

Oct 73. (7") *(7N 45295)* *<45426>* **STRANGE MOVIES. / I'M ON FIRE**

Penny Farthing — Pye

Dec 74. (7") *(PEN 861)* **GOOD VIBRATIONS. / PUSH IT UP TO ME**

May 75. (7") *(PEN 884)* **WILD THING (reggae version). / JENNY COME DOWN** –

Jul 75. (7") *(PEN 889)* **SUMMERTIME. / JENNY COME DOWN**

1975. (lp) *(PEN 543)* **TROGGS**
– I got lovin' if you want it / Good vibrations / No particular place to go / Summertime / Satisfaction / Full blooded band / Memphis Tennessee / Peggy Sue / Jenny come down / Wild thing.

Nov 75. (7") *(PEN 901)* **(I CAN'T GET NO) SATISFACTION. / MEMPHIS, TENNESSEE**

Jun 76. (lp) *(PELS 551)* **THE TROGGS TAPES** –
– Get you tonight / We rode through the night / A different me / Downsouth to Georgia / Gonna make you / Supergirl / I'll buy you an island / Rolling stone / After the rain / Rock and roll lady / Walkin' the dog.

Jun 76. (7") *(PEN 919)* **I'LL BUY YOU AN ISLAND. / SUPERGIRL** –

1977. (7") *(PEN 929)* **FEELING FOR LOVE. / SUMMERTIME** –

Raw — not iss.

1978. (7") *(RAW 25)* **JUST A LITTLE TOO MUCH. / THE TRUE TROGG TAPES** –

— added **COLIN 'Dill' FLETCHER** – rhythm guitar

Max's Kansas City — Basement

Mar 81. (lp) *(MKC 100)* **LIVE AT MAX'S KANSAS CITY (live)** — 1980
– Got love if you want it / Satisfaction / Love is all around / Feels like a woman / Strange movies / Summertime / Walking the dog / Memphis / No particular place to go / Wild thing / Gonna make you. *(cd-iss. Oct94 on 'President'+=; MKCD 1001)* – I do I do / Call me.

New Rose — not iss.

Mar 82. (lp) *(ROSE 4)* **BLACK BOTTOM** –
(cd-iss. Mar85; ROSE 4CD)

Mar 82. (7") *(NEW 6)* **I LOVE YOU BABY. /** –

Stage Coach — not iss.

May 82. (7") *(MAIL 38)* **BLACK BOTTOM. / WITH YOU** –

10-Virgin — not iss.

1984. (7") *(TEN 21)* **EVERY LITTLE THING. / BLACKJACK AND POKER** –
(7"pic-d+=/12"+=) *(TEN T/Y 21)* – With a girl like you.

— In 1986, REG featured on SUZI QUATRO's version of 'WILD THING'.

— **PRESLEY + BOND** recruited **PETER LUCAS** – bass / **DAVE MAGGS** – drums

Big Wave — not iss.

Nov 89. (7"/12") *(BWR/+T 27)* **WILD THING '89. / FROM HOME** –

New Rose — not iss.

May 90. (lp/cd) *(ROSE/+CD 186)* **AU** –
– Always something there to remind me / Walking the dog / Wild thing / Love is all around / With a girl like you / I can't control myself / Strange movies / Maximum overdrive / The Disco Kid versus Sid Chicane / What you doing here. *(re-iss. cd Dec95 on 'Javelin'; HADCD 195)*

— now without BOND

Essential — Rhino

Feb 92. (7"/c-s/12"/cd-s) **DON'T YOU KNOW. / NOWHERE ROAD**

Mar 92. (cd/c/lp) *(ESS CD/MC/LP 180)* **ANTHENS ANDOVER**
– Crazy Annie / Together / Tuned into love / Deja vu / Nowhere road / Dust bowl / I'm in control / Don't you know / What's your game / Suspicious / Hot stuff. *(cd re-iss. Aug96; same)*

Lifetime — not iss.

Nov 92. (7"/c-s; by TROGS featuring OLIVER REED & HURRICANE HIGGINS) *(LIF/+C 37)* **WILD THING. / ('A'mix)** –
(12"+=/cd-s+=) *(LIF T/CD 37)* – ('A'original). *(re-is.Oct94; same)*

Weekend — not iss.

Oct 93. (cd-s; TROGGS featuring WOLF) *(CDWEEK 103)* **WILD THING. / (other by EDWIN STARR & SHADOW)** 69 –

– (selective) compilations, etc. –

1976. (d-lp) *Sire; <SASH 3714-2>* **VINTAGE YEARS** –

Jul 76. (lp) *D.J.M.; (44314)* **THE (ORIGINAL) TROGGS TAPES** –

Feb 93. (3xcd-box) *Fontana; (514 423-2)* **ARCHEOLOGY (1967-1977)**

Mar 94. (cd) *Charly; (CDCD 1147)* **WILD THING** –

Jul 94. (cd/c) *Polygram TV; (522 739-2/-4)* **GREATEST HITS** 27 –

Jun 96. (cd/c) *Music Club; (MC CD/TC 242)* **ATHENS GEORGIA AND BEYOND** –

Nov 96. (cd) *See For Miles; (SEECD 453)* **THE E.P. COLLECTION** –

Feb 97. (cd) *Beat Goes On; (BGOCD 340)* **FROM NOWHERE / TROGGLODYNAMITE** [ ] [-]
Apr 97. (cd/c) *Prism; (PLA TCD/C 203)* **WILD THING** [ ] [-]
Apr 97. (cd) *Beat Goes On; (BGOCD 343)* **CELLOPHANE / MIXED BAG** [ ] [-]
Apr 97. (cd) *Prestige; (CDSGP 0337)* **ALL THE HITS PLUS MORE** [ ] [-]

Robin TROWER

Born: 9 Mar'45, London, England. TROWER had an initial period with 60's outfit The PARAMOUNTS, who subsequently metamorphosed into PROCOL HARUM. He had been an integral part of this rock act since the 'HOMBURG' hit single, staying for five albums, 'PROCOL HARUM' (1967), 'SHINE ON BRIGHTLY' (1968), 'A SALTY DOG' (1969), 'HOME' (1970) and 'BROKEN BARRICADES' (1971), before the now HENDRIX-inspired TROWER set up his own band, JUDE. This deeply blues-rooted short-lived supergroup featured FRANKIE MILLER on husky vox, CLIVE BUNKER (ex-JETHRO TULL) on drums and JAMES DEWAR (ex-STONE THE CROWS) on bass. The latter was re-united with TROWER when the guitarist launched his solo career after re-signing to 'Chrysalis' (incidentally, also the home of PROCOL HARUM) in 1972. A debut album, 'TWICE REMOVED FROM YESTERDAY', appeared the following year featuring REG ISADORE on drums plus DEWAR on bass and soulful vocals!, TROWER (face-contortionist extroadinaire) nearly having his first solo breakthrough into the US Top 100. 1974's 'BRIDGE OF SIGHS' made up for it tenfold, this and his 1975 set, 'FOR EARTH BELOW' (1975) both cracking the US Top 10. ISADORE had been replaced on the latter by former SLY & THE FAMILY STONE man, BILL LORDAN and a live set in 1976 repeated the same feat. TROWER and his band continued to gain further album chart experience, sets such as 'LONG MISTY DAYS' (1976), 'IN CITY DREAMS' (1977), 'CARAVAN TO MIDNIGHT' (1978) and 'VICTIMS OF THE FURY' (1980), all making the US Top 40 (also selling moderately well in Britain). In 1981, TROWER and LORDAN teamed up with JACK BRUCE (ex-CREAM), delivering yet another success story, 'B.L.T.', while the following year's 'TRUCE' was strictly a BRUCE / TROWER effort. The rest of the 80's plodded on a bit for the man with the souped-up Fender Stratocaster, a change of labels to 'GNP Crescendo' in '86 giving him his last US Top 100 appearance with his umpteenth set, 'PASSION'. Another shift two years later, this time to 'Atlantic' was not so fruitful, albums 'TAKE WHAT YOU NEED' and 'IN THE LINE OF FIRE' (1990) for the TROWER or blues connoisseur only. More recently, TROWER, who had rejoined PROCOL HARUM for a reunion set, 'THE PRODIGAL STRANGER' in 1991/92, made two albums for UK 'Demon' records, '20th CENTURY BLUES' (1994) and 'SOMEDAY BLUES' (1997). The millennium began in fine style courtesy of return to form set, 'GO MY WAY', a record that opened with a classy 9 minute title track. He continued to produce and work with BRYAN FERRY on his solo releases, (i.e. 'Frantic'), having previously featured on his 'Taxi' and 'Mamouna' sets in the mid 90's. • **Songwriters:** Mostly TROWER-DEWAR compositions, except; MAN OF THE WORLD (Fleetwood Mac) / ROCK ME BABY (B.B. King) / I CAN'T WAIT MUCH LONGER (Frankie Miller) / FURTHER ON UP THE ROAD (BB King) / SAILING (Sutherland Brothers) / RECONSIDER BABY (Lowell Folsom) / etc.

Album rating: TWICE REMOVED FROM YESTERDAY (*6) / BRIDGE OF SIGHS (*7) / FOR EARTH BELOW (*6) / ROBIN TROWER LIVE! (*7) / LONG MISTY DAYS (*5) / IN CITY DREAMS (*4) / CARAVAN TO MIDNIGHT (*4) / VICTIMS OF THE FURY (*5) / B.L.T. (*5; as B.L.T.) / TRUCE with Jack Bruce (*4) / BACK IT UP (*5) / BEYOND THE MIST (*5) / PASSION (*5) / PORTFOLIO compilation (*7) / TAKE WHAT YOU NEED (*5) / IN THE LINE OF FIRE (*4) / 20th CENTURY BLUES (*5) / SOMEDAY BLUES (*4) / GO MY WAY (*6)

ROBIN TROWER – guitar (ex-JUDE, ex-PROCOL HARUM) / **JAMES DEWAR** (b.12 Oct'46, Glasgow, Scotland) – vocals, bass (ex-JUDE, ex-STONE THE CROWS) / **REG ISADORE** (b. West Indies) – drums (ex-QUIVER)

Chrysalis Chrysalis

Mar 73. (lp/c) *(<CHR/ZCHR 1039>)* **TWICE REMOVED FROM YESTERDAY** [ ] [ ]
– I can't wait much longer / Daydream / Hannah / Man of the world / I can't stand it / Rock me baby / Twice removed from yesterday / Sinner's song / Ballerina.

Mar 73. (7") *(CHS 2009)* **MAN OF THE WORLD. / TAKE A FAST TRAIN** [ ] [ ]

Mar 74. (7") **TOO ROLLING STONED. / MAN OF THE WORLD** [-] [ ]

Apr 74. (lp/c) *(<CHR/ZCHR 1057>)* **BRIDGE OF SIGHS** [ ] [7]
– Day of the eagle / Bridge of sighs / In this place / The fool and me / Too rolling stoned / About to begin / Lady love / Little bit of sympathy. *(re-iss. Jan82; same) (cd-iss. Mar94; CD25CR 15)*

May 74. (7") *(CHS 2046)* **TOO ROLLING STONED. / LADY LOVE** [ ] [-]

—— **BILL LORDAN** – drums (ex-SLY & THE FAMILY STONE) repl. REG to HUMMINGBIRD

Feb 75. (lp/c) *(<CHR/ZCHR 1073>)* **FOR EARTH BELOW** [26] [5]
– Shame the devil / It's only money / Confessin' midnight / Fine day / Alethea / A tale untold / Gonna be more suspicious / For Earth below.

Mar 76. (lp/c) *(<CHR/ZCHR 1089>)* **ROBIN TROWER LIVE! (live)** [15] [10]
– Too rolling stoned / Daydream / Rock me baby / Lady love / I can't wait much longer / Alethea / Little bit of sympathy.

Oct 76. (lp/c) *(<CHR/ZCHR 1107>)* **LONG MISTY DAYS** [31] [24]
– Some rain falls / Long misty days / Hold me / Caledonia / Pride / Sailing / S.M.O. / I can't live without you / Messin' the blues.

Nov 76. (7") *(CHS 2124)* **CALEDONIA. / MESSIN' THE BLUES** [ ] [82]

—— added **RUSTEE ALLEN** – bass (ex-SLY & THE FAMILY STONE)

Sep 77. (lp/c) *(<CHR/ZCHR 1148>)* **IN CITY DREAMS** [58] [25]
– Somebody calling / Sweet wine of love / Bluebird / Falling star / Further up the road / Smile / Little girl / Love's gonna bring you round / In city dreams.

—— added **PAULHINO DACOSTA** – percussion

Aug 78. (lp/c) *(<CHR/ZCHR 1189>)* **CARAVAN TO MIDNIGHT** [ ] [37]
– My love (burning love) / Caravan to midnight / I'm out to get you / Lost in love / Fool / It's for you / Birthday boy / King of the dance / Sail on.

Sep 78. (7",7"red) *(CHS 2247)* **IT'S FOR YOU. / MY LOVE (BURNING LOVE) / IN CITY DREAMS** [ ] [ ]

Jan 79. (7") *(CHS 2256)* **IT'S FOR YOU. / MY LOVE (BURNING LOVE)** [ ] [ ]

—— reverted to the trio of the mid-70's; (**TROWER, DEWAR + LORDAN**)

Jan 80. (7") *(CHS 2402)* **VICTIMS OF THE FURY. / ONE IN A MILLION** [ ] [ ]

Jan 80. (lp/c) *(<CHR/ZCHR 1215>)* **VICTIMS OF THE FURY** [61] [34]
– Jack and Jill / Roads to freedom / Victims of the fury / The ring / Only time / Into the flame / The shout / Madhouse / Ready for the taking / Fly low.

Apr 80. (7") *(CHS 2423)* **JACK AND JILL. / THE SHOUT** [ ] [ ]

—— **JACK BRUCE** (b.14 May'43, Glasgow, Scotland) – vocals, bass (ex-CREAM, ex-JOHN MAYALL'S BLUESBREAKERS, ex-Solo artist) repl. DEWAR

Feb 81. (lp/c; as B.L.T.) *(<CHR 1324>)* **B.L.T.** [ ] [37]
– Into money / What it is / Won't let you down / No island lost / It's too late / Life on earth / Once the bird has flown / Carmen / Feel the heat / End game.

Feb 81. (7"; as B.L.T.) *(CHS 2497)* **WHAT IT IS. / INTO MONEY** [ ] [ ]

—— trimmed to a duo plus with drummer **REG ISADORE**

Jan 82. (lp/c; by JACK BRUCE & ROBIN TROWER) *(<CHR/ZCHR 1352>)* **TRUCE** [ ] [ ]
– Gonna shut you down / Gone too far / Thin ice / The last train to the stars / Take good care of yourself / Fall in love / Fat gut / Shadows touching / Little boy lost.

ROBIN TROWER

— went solo again, augmented by **DEWAR / DAVE BRONZE** – bass / **BOBBY CLOUTER + ALAN CLARKE** – drums

Sep 83. (lp/c) *(<CHR/ZCHR 1420>)* **BACK IT UP**
– Back it up / River / Black to red / Benny dancer / Time is short / Islands / None but the brave / Captain midnight / Settling the score. *(cd-iss. Jul99 on 'Beat Goes On'; BGOCD 426)*

Music For Nations — Passport

Jun 85. (lp/c) *(MFN/TMFN 51)* *<PB/+C/CD 6049>* **BEYOND THE MIST**
– The last time / Keeping a secret / The voice (live) / Beyond the mist (live) / Time is short (live) / Back it up (live) / Bridge of sighs (live).

— still retained **BRONZE,** and also with **DAVEY PATTISON** – vox (ex-GAMMA) / **PETE THOMPSON** – drums

P.R.T. — GNP Cres..

Feb 87. (lp/c/cd) *(PRTN/ZCN/PRTCD 6563)* *<GNPD 2187>* **PASSION** — Dec86 **100**
– Caroline / Secret doors / If forever / Won't even think about you / Passion / No time / Night / Bad time / One more world. *(cd-iss. GNPD 2187)*

— retained **PATTISON**

Atlantic — Atlantic

Jun 88. (lp/c/cd) *(781 838-1/-4/-2)* *<81838>* **TAKE WHAT YOU NEED** — May88
– Tear it up / Take what you need (from me) / Love attack / I want you home / Shattered / Over you / Careless / Second time / Love won't wait forever.

— now with **PATTISON** – vox / **JOHN REGAN** – bass / **AL FRITSCH + PEPPY CASTRO** – backing vocals / **BOBBY MAYO + MATT NOBLE** – keyboards / **TONY BEARD** – drums

Mar 90. (cd/c/lp) *<782 080-2/-4/-1>* **IN THE LINE OF FIRE** — -
– Sea of love / Under the gun / Turn the volume up / Natural fact / If you really want to find love / Every body's watching you now / Isn't it time / (I would) Still be here for you / All that I want / (Let's) Turn this fight into a brawl / Climb above the rooftops.

— ROBIN then re-joined the reformed PROCOL HARUM in 1991

— now w/ **LIVINGSTONE BROWNE** – bass / **CLIVE MAYUYU** – drums

Demon — V-12

Nov 94. (cd/c) *(FIEND CD/C 753)* *<50001>* **20th CENTURY BLUES**
– 20th century blues / Prisoner of love / Precious gift / Whisper up a storm / Extermination blues / Step into the dark / Rise up like the Sun / Secret place / Chase the bone / Promise you the stars / Don't lose faith in tomorrow / Reconsider baby.

Jun 97. (cd) *(FIENDCD 931)* *<50020>* **SOMEDAY BLUES**
– Next in line / Feel so bad / Someday blues / Crossroads / I want you to love me / Inside out / Shining through / Looking for a true love / Extermination blues / Sweet little angel.

Orpheus — V2

Jul 00. (cd) *(7576 670600-2)* *<50040>* **GO MY WAY** — Jun00
– Go my way / Breathless / Into dust / Run with the wolves / Too much joy / Blue soul / This old world / On your own / Take this river / Long hard game / In my dream.

– compilations, etc. –

Jul 87. (d-lp/c)(cd) *Chrysalis; (CNW/ZCNW 3)(MPCD 1600)* **PORTFOLIO**
– Bridge of sighs / Too rolling stoned / For Earth below / Caravan to midnight / Day of the eagle / Shame the Devil / Fine day / Daydream (live) / Lady Love (live) / Alethea (live) / Caledonia (live) / Messin' the blues / Blue bird / Victims of fury / Madhouse / Into money / Gonna shut you down / Thin ice / Benny dancer. *(re-iss. cd Mar93; same)*

Aug 91. (cd/c/d-lp) *Castle; (CCS CD/MC/LP 291)* **THE ROBIN TROWER COLLECTION** — -

Apr 92. (cd) *Windsong; (WINCD 013)* **BBC RADIO 1 LIVE IN CONCERT (live)** — -

May 94. (cd) *Connoisseur; (VSOPCD 197)* **ANTHOLOGY** — -

Feb 97. (cd) *Beat Goes On; (BGOCD 339)* **TWICE REMOVED FROM YESTERDAY / BRIDGE OF SIGHS** — -

Mar 97. (cd) *Beat Goes On; (BGOCD 347)* **FOR EARTH BELOW / ROBIN TROWER LIVE!** — -

Apr 97. (cd) *Beat Goes On; (BGOCD 349)* **LONG MISTY DAYS / IN CITY DREAMS** — -

May 97. (cd) *Beat Goes On; (BGOCD 352)* **CARAVAN TO MIDNIGHT / VICTIMS OF THE FURY** — -

Aug 98. (cd) *Beat Goes On; (BGOCD 411)* **BLT / TRUCE** — -

Oct 98. (cd) *King Biscuit; (<KBFHCD 020>)* **KING BISCUIT PRESENTS . . .**

Feb 01. (cd) *E.M.I.; (576227-2)* **GUITAR LEGENDS**

May 02. (cd) *Disky; (SI 79416-2)* **TOO ROLLING STONE** — -

Apr 03. (cd) *King Biscuit; (KBCCD 123)* **IN CONCERT**

TUBES

Formed: Phoenix, Arizona, USA . . . 1972 by BILL SPOONER, VINCE WELNICK and ex-drama student FEE WAYBILL, who moved the outfit to the Bay Area, San Francisco, the line-up completed by RICK ANDERSON, MICHAEL COTTEN, ROGER STEEN, PRAIRIE PRINCE and REG STYLES. Coming on like a perverted, pseudo-punk precursor to MEAT LOAF's theatrical overload, the group became infamous for their garish shows which placed scantily clad ladies against such unsavoury stage characters as Dr. Strangekiss and Quay Lude. Signed to 'A&M', their debut single was the legendary 'WHITE PUNKS ON DOPE', a UK Top 30 hit some three years later when Britain was in the grip of three-chord fever. The accompanying AL KOOPER-produced, eponymous debut album narrowly missed the US Top 100, while follow-up, 'YOUNG AND RICH' (produced by KEN SCOTT), broke them into the US Top 50 in 1976. But the music often took second place to the theatrics and in 1979, obviously bored with the limitations of the genre, swapped anthemic punk/new wave for easier going pop/rock on that year's TODD RUNDGREN-produced 'REMOTE CONTROL' album. A proposed 1980 set, 'SUFFER FOR SOUND', was shelved by 'A&M' prior to the band being dropped. Inking a new deal with 'Capitol', the group moved even further towards the mainstream with 'THE COMPLETION BACKWARD PRINCIPLE' (1981), an album which spawed a one-off Top 10 hit in 'SHE'S A BEAUTY'. After a final couple of albums, 'OUTSIDE INSIDE' (1983) and 'LOVE BOMB' (1986), The TUBES realised the joke had run its course and packed it in. Having already released a solo set, 'READ MY LIPS' (1984), WAYBILL went on to write material for RICHARD MARX (!), while SPOONER and WELNICK subsequently went on to work with Bay Area veterans, The GRATEFUL DEAD. Just when you thought WAYBILL and Co had fully retired from their musical extravaganzas, The TUBES were back on tour for a series of American and European dates c.1993. An album, 'GENIUS OF AMERICA' (1996), found little friends among the critics and their die-hard, loyal fanbase; 2000's 'TUBES WORLD TOUR 2001' album (yes, 2001) was worth the price of a ticket at least. • **Songwriters:** WAYBILL penned except I SAW HER STANDING THERE (Beatles) / etc. • **Trivia:** In 1980, they undertook a cameo performance in the film, 'Xanadu', soundtrack courtesy of ELECTRIC LIGHT ORCHESTRA and OLIVIA NEWTON-JOHN.

Album rating: THE TUBES (*5) / YOUNG AND RICH (*6) / NOW (5) / WHAT DO YOU WANT FROM LIVE (*5) / REMOTE CONTROL (*4) / THE COMPLETION BACKWARD PRINCIPLE (*6) / T.R.A.S.H. (TUBES RARITIES AND SMASH HITS) compilation (*7) / OUTSIDE INSIDE (*5) / LOVE BOMB (*4) / THE BEST OF THE TUBES compilation (*7) / GENIUS OF AMERICA (*3) / THE TUBES WORLD TOUR 2001 (*5) / Fee Waybill: READ MY LIPS (*3)

FEE WAYBILL (b. JOHN WALDO, 17 Sep'50, Omaha, Nebraska) – vocals / **BILL 'Sputnik' SPOONER** (b.16 Apr'49) – guitar / **VINCE WELNICK** (b.21 Feb'51) – keyboards / **RICK ANDERSON** (b. 1 Aug'47, St. Paul, Minnesota) – bass / **MICHAEL COTTEN** (b.25 Jan'50, Kansas City, Missouri) – synthesizer / **ROGER STEEN** (b.13 Nov'49, Pipestone, Minnesota) – guitar / **PRAIRIE PRINCE** (b. 7

May'50, Charlotte, New Connecticut) – drums / **REG STYLES** (b. 3 Mar'50) – vocals, guitar

A&M A&M

Jul 75. (7") *<1733>* **WHITE PUNKS ON DOPE. / (part 2)** [–] [ ]

Jul 75. (lp/c) *(AMLH/CAM 64534) <4534>* **THE TUBES** [ ] [ ]
– Up from the deep / Haloes / Space baby / Malaguena Salerosa / Mondo bondage / What do you want from life / Boy crazy / White punks on dope. *(re-iss. May83 on 'Fame') (d-cd-iss. Dec85 on 'Mobile Fidelity', incl.next album)*

Nov 75. (7") **WHAT DO YOU WANT FROM LIFE. / SPACE BABY** [–] [ ]

Jan 76. (7") *(AMS 7209)* **WHAT DO YOU WANT FROM LIFE. / WHITE PUNKS ON DOPE** [ ] [–]

May 76. (lp/c) *(AMLH/CAM 64580) <4580>* **YOUNG AND RICH** [ ] [46]
– Tubes world tour / Brighter day / Pimp / Stand up and shout / Don't touch me there / Slipped my disco / Proud to be an American / Poland whole / Madam I'm Adam / Young and rich.

Jun 76. (7") *(AMS 7239) <1826>* **DON'T TOUCH ME THERE. / PROUD TO BE AMERICAN** [ ] [61]

Jan 77. (7") **YOUNG AND RICH. / LOVE WILL KEEP US TOGETHER** [–] [ ]

—— added **MINGO LEWIS** – percussion

May 77. (lp/c) *(AMLH/CAM 64632) <4632>* **THE TUBES NOW** [ ] [ ]
– Smoke (la vie en fumer) / Hit parade / Strung out on strings / Golden boy / My head is my house (unless it rains) / God-bird-change / I'm just a mess / Cathy's clone / This town / Pound of flesh / You're no fun.

Aug 77. (7") *<1956>* **I'M JUST A MESS. / THIS TOWN** [–] [ ]

Nov 77. (7"m/12"m) *(AMS 7323)* **WHITE PUNKS ON DOPE. / DON'T TOUCH ME THERE / WHAT DO YOU WANT FROM LIFE** [28] [–]

Feb 78. (d-lp/d-c) *(AMLM/CLM 68460) <6003>* **WHAT DO YOU WANT FROM LIVE (live)** [38] [82]
– (overture) / Got yourself a deal / Show me a reason / What do you want from life / God-bird-change / Special ballet / Don't touch me there / Mondo bondage / Smoke (la vie en fumer) / Crime medley: (themes from 'Dragnet' – 'Peter Gunn' – 'Perry Mason' – 'The Untouchables') / I was a punk before you were a punk / I saw her standing there / (drum solo) / Boy crazy / You're no fun / Stand up and shout / White punks on dope. *(cd-iss. Apr97; 396003-2)*

Apr 78. (7") *(AMS 7349)* **SHOW ME A REASON (live). / MONDO BONDAGE (live)** [ ] [–]

Jul 78. (7") *<2037>* **SHOW ME A REASON (live). / I SAW HER STANDING THERE (live)** [–] [ ]

Feb 79. (7")(7"colrd-7 diff.) *(AMS 7423,) <2120>* **PRIME TIME. / NO WAY OUT** [ ] [34]

May 79. (lp/c) *(AMLH/CAM 64751) <4751>* **REMOTE CONTROL** [40] Mar 79 [46]
– Turn me on / TV is king / Prime time / I want it all / No way out / Getoverture / No mercy / Only the strong survive / Be mine tonight / Love's a mystery (I don't understand) / Telecide.

May 79. (7") *<2149>* **LOVE'S A MYSTERY (I DON'T UNDERSTAND). / TELECIDE** [–] [ ]

Jul 79. (7")(7"yellow) *(AMS 7462,)* **TV IS KING. / TELECIDE** [ ] [ ]

—— trimmed slightly when LEWIS + STYLES left.

Capitol Capitol

May 81. (7") *<5016>* **TALK TO YA LATER. / POWER TOOLS** [–] [ ]

May 81. (7") *(CL 201)* **TALK TO YA LATER. / WHAT'S WRONG WITH ME** [ ] [–]

May 81. (lp/c) *(EST/TCEST 26285) <12151>* **THE COMPLETION BACKWARD PRINCIPLE** [ ] [36]
– Talk to ya later / Let's make some noise / Matter of pride / Mr. Hate / Attack of the fifty foot woman / Think about me / Sushi girl / Don't want to wait anymore / Power tools / Amnesia. *(re-iss. Mar91 on 'Beat Goes On' cd/lp; BGO CD/LP 100)*

Jul 81. (7") *(CL 208) <5007>* **DON'T WANT TO WAIT ANYMORE. / THINK ABOUT ME** [60] Jun81 [35]

Oct 81. (7") *(CL 219)* **SUSHI GIRL. / MR. HATE** [ ] [ ]

Apr 83. (7") *(CL 288) <5217>* **SHE'S A BEAUTY. / WHEN YOU'RE READY TO COME** [ ] [10]
(12"+=) *(12CL 288)* – Fantastic delusion.

May 83. (lp/c) *<(EST/TCEST 12260)>* **OUTSIDE INSIDE** [77] Apr83 [18]
– She's a beauty / No not again / Out of the business / The monkey time / Glass house / Wild women of Wongo / Tip of my tongue / Fantastic delusion / Drums / Theme park / Outside lookin' inside. *(cd-iss. Jul92 on 'Beat Goes On'; BGOCD 133)*

above feat. guests **MAURICE WHITE** (of EARTH, WIND & FIRE) + **MARTHA DAVIS** – vocals (of MOTELS)

Jul 83. (7") *<5258>* **TIP OF MY TONGUE. / KEYBOARD KIDS** [–] [52]

Sep 83. (7") *<5254>* **THE MONKEY TIME. / SPORTS FAN** [–] [68]

—— In 1984, WAYBILL released a solo album, 'READ MY LIPS'

Mar 85. (7") *<5443>* **PIECE BY PIECE. / NIGHT PEOPLE** [–] [87]

May 85. (lp) *<12381>* **LOVE BOMB** [–] [87]
– Piece by piece / Stella / Come as you are / One good reason / Bora Bora 2000 – Love bomb / Night people / Say hey / Eyes / Muscle girls / Theme from a wooly place – Wooly bully – Theme from a summer place / For a song / Say hey (part 2) / Feel it / Night people (reprise). *(cd-iss. Aug93 on 'Beat Goes On'; BGOCD 188)*

—— group disbanded after above album. WAYBILL continued to write and guest on albums by RICHARD MARX (1988). WELNICK joined GRATEFUL DEAD. The TUBES re-formed in 1993; **WAYBILL, STEEN, PRINCE, ANDERSON / + GARY CAMBRA** – vocals, keyboards / **JENNIFER McFEE + AMY FRENCH** – vocals

Brilliant Popular Critique

Oct 96. (cd) *<12007>* **GENIUS OF AMERICA** [–] [ ]
– Genius of America / Arms of the enemy / Say what you want / How can you live with yourself / Big brothers still watching you / After all you said / Fishhouse / The fastest gun alive / I never saw it comin' / Who names the hurricanes / It's too late / Around the world.

Nov 99. (cd) *(BT 33028)* **HOODS FROM OUTER SPACE** [ ] [–]
– Hoods from Outer Space / I know you / Say what you want / Around the world / Genius of America / Who names the hurricanes / It's too late / How can you live with yourself / I never saw it comin' / Arms of the enemy / Fishhouse / Big Brother's still watching you / The fastest gun alive / After all you said. *(re-iss. Mar02; same)*

Sanctuary C.M.C.

Oct 00. (cd) *(SANCD 007) <86300>* **THE TUBES WORLD TOUR 2001 (live)** [ ] [ ]
– Introduction / The Tubes World Tour / She's a beauty / Digi-doll / T.V. king / Don't touch me there / Tip of my tongue / Loveline / Wild women of Wongo / Mondo bondage / White punks on dope / Talk to ya later.

– compilations, etc. –

Nov 81. (lp/c) *A&M; (AMLH/CAM 64870) <4870>* **T.R.A.S.H. (TUBES RARITIES AND SMASH HITS)** [ ] [ ]
– Drivin' all night / What do you want from life / Turn me on / Slipped my disco / Mondo bondage / Love will keep us together / I'm just a mess / Only the strong survive / Don't touch me there / White punks on dope / Prime time.

Sep 85. (7") *Old Gold; (OG 9545)* **PRIME TIME. / (B-side by STYX)** [ ] [–]

Jan 87. (7") *Old Gold; (OG 9545)* **(above tracks)** [ ] [–]
(12"+=) *(OG 4013)* – White punks on dope / (other by 'Styx').

Nov 86. (lp) *Plastic Head; (PLASLP 006)* **PRIME TIME** [ ] [–]

Apr 93. (cd) *Capitol; (C 298359)* **THE BEST OF THE TUBES** [ ] [ ]

Oct 96. (d-cd) *A&M; (540564-2)* **GOING DOWN . . . THE TUBES** [ ] [–]

Feb 98. (cd) *Disky; <(DC 88611-2)>* **DON'T WANT TO WAIT ANYMORE** [ ] [ ]

Feb 00. (cd) *Hux; (HUX 017) <91263>* **INFOMERCIAL: HOW TO BECOME TUBULAR (live)** [ ] [ ]

Aug 00. (cd) *Spectrum; (544352-2)* **WHITE PUNKS ON DOPE** [ ] [–]

Oct 00. (cd) *Universal; (AA69 490766-2)* **THE MILLENNIUM COLLECTION: THE BEST OF THE TUBES** [ ] [–]

☐ TUBEWAY ARMY (see under ⇒ NUMAN, Gary)

TURIN BRAKES

Formed: Balham, London, England . . . 1998 by OLLIE KNIGHTS and GALE PARADJANIAN (a guy). Acting as Britain's own KINGS OF CONVENIENCE, TURIN BRAKES have been fighting the NAM (New Acoustic Movement) war since the release of their 1999 EP 'THE DOOR'. Comprising of hushed acoustic tracks with multi-talented OLLIE KNIGHTS on vocals and PARADJANIAN playing whatever took his fancy, the set helped them grab the attention of independent label 'Source', who issued two EP's 'FIGHT OR FLIGHT' and 'THE STATE OF THINGS' in 2000, whilst re-issuing 'THE DOOR'. After much attention from the music press and MTV's own 'alternative' music channel MTV2, the duo had a Top 40 chart position with their debut album 'THE OPTIMIST LP' (2001). The set, with added percussion, piano and emotive strings, spawned three further Top 40 singles, the best being the sublime 'MIND OVER MONEY', with KNIGHTS' vocal gymnastics being a particular highlight. The quietly confident duo would return in 2003 to issue possibly their best work to date, the delicate 'ETHER SONG', another to add to the post-millennium canon of soft melodic rock. Producer, Tony Hoffer, brought out the best in KNIGHTS earnest songwriting, with tracks 'PAINKILLER' and the gorgeous 'AVERAGE MAN' setting the tone quiet nicely. Elsewhere on the album 'CLEAN BLUE SKY' was TURIN BRAKES at their lo-fi indie best, while the title track soared with majestic grace, proving that the group had not lost the verve and reverence displayed on their earlier material.

Album rating: THE OPTIMIST LP (*8) / ETHER SONG (*8)

OLLIE KNIGHTS – vocals, guitar / **GALE PARADJANIAN** – multi

Anvil — not iss.

Jun 99. (ltd;7"ep/cd-ep) *(ANV 027/+CDS)* **'THE DOOR' EP** [ ] [–]
– The door / By TV light / Nowhere / The road.

Source — Astralwerks

Aug 00. (d7"ep/cd-ep) *(SOUR V/CDS 008)* **THE STATE OF THINGS EP** [ ] [–]
– The boss / Balham to Brooklyn / All away / The state of things.

Oct 00. (7"ep/cd-ep) *(SOUR V/CDS 012)* **FIGHT OR FLIGHT EP** [ ] [–]
– Mind over money / Nine to five / Emergency 72 / Christine.

Feb 01. (7"ep/cd-ep) *(SOUR V/CDS 024)* **THE DOOR EP** [67] [–]
– The door / Reach out / Boss.

Mar 01. (cd/lp) *(SOUR CD/LP 023)* <30696> **THE OPTIMIST LP** [27] May01 [ ]
– Feeling oblivion / Underdog (save me) / Emergency 72 / Future boy / The door / The state of things / By TV light / Slack / Starship / The road / Mind over money / The optimist.

Apr 01. (7") *(SOURV 015)* **UNDERDOG (SAVE ME). / BALHAM TO BROOKLYN** [39] [–]
(cd-s+=) *(SOURCDS1 015)* – The door (live).
(cd-s) *(SOURCDS2 015)* – ('A'side) / Nowhere / Feeling oblivion (live) / ('A'-video).

Jul 01. (7") *(SOUR 038)* **MIND OVER MONEY. / STONE** [31] [–]
(cd-s+=) *(SOURCDX 038)* – Tunnel.
(cd-s) *(SOURCD 038)* – ('A'extended) / Road (session) / Sunjets – Heavy 2 (instrumental) / ('A'-video).

Oct 01. (7") *(SOUR 041)* **EMERGENCY 72. / EVERYBODY KNOWS** [41] [–]
(cd-s+=) *(SOURCDX 041)* – The first time / ('A'video).
(cd-s) *(SOURCD 041)* – ('A'extended) / The last time / Lasso.

Oct 02. (7") *(SOUR 064)* **LONG DISTANCE. / LOST AND FOUND** [22] [–]
(cd-s+=) *(SOURCD 064)* – ('A'-The Bees remix).
(cd-s) *(SOURCDX 064)* – ('A'side) / ('A'-Max Tundra remix) / Soul less (home recording).

Feb 03. (7") *(SOUR 068)* **PAIN KILLER. / LITTLE BROTHER (demo)** [5] [–]
(cd-s) *(SOURCD 068)* – ('A'side) / Where's my army (home recording) / ('A'-video).

Feb 03. (cd/d-lp) *(CDSOUR/SOURLP 054)* <82407> **ETHER SONG** [4] Mar03 [ ]
– Blue hour / Average man / Long distance / Self help / Falling down / Stone thrown / Clean blue air / Pain killer (summer rain) / Full of stars / Panic attack / Little brother / Rain city. *(hidden +=)* – Ether song. *(ltd d-cd+=; CDSOURX 054)* – Blue hour (home recording) / Self help (SBN session) / Long distance (SBN session) / Bright golden lights (home recording) / Ether song (EPK video). *(ltd d-cd-iss. Oct03 +=; CDSOURXX 054)* – 5 mile (these are the days) / The boss / Piano instrumental / Long distance (VARA Radio 3FM) / Falling down (SBN session) / Pain killer (RTL2 acoustic). *(re-iss. Nov03 +=; CDSOURY 054)* – Ether song / 5 mile (these are the days).

May 03. (7") *(SOUR 085)* **AVERAGE MAN. / WHERE I'VE BEEN (XFM acoustic session)** [35] [–]
(cd-s+=) *(SOURCD 085)* – Pain killer (Today FM acoustic).

Sep 03. (7") *(SOUR 089)* **5 MILE (THESE ARE THE DAYS). / SELF HELP (WFUV acoustic version)** [31] [–]
(cd-s) *(SOURCD 089)* – ('A'side) / Pain killer (RTL2 acoustic). (cd-s) *(SOURCDX 089)* – ('A'side) / The door (KEXP acoustic) / Stone thrown (acoustic) / ('A'-video).

(Ike &) Tina TURNER

Initiated: 1956-58, when billed as "IKE TURNER, CARLSON OLIVER & LITTLE ANN" they recorded a 1958 single, 'BOXTOP' for 'Tune Town' records. LITTLE ANN was renamed TINA TURNER the following year, although the couple weren't married until 1962(!), having conceived a child in '59. TINA was born ANNIE MAE BULLOCK, 26th November '38, Brownsville, Tennessee, USA, although she was raised in Nutbush and became a local choir singer. IKE TURNER was born on 5th November '31, Clarksville, Mississippi, USA where he became a regular DJ aged ony sixteen. In 1950, with solid session work behind him, the crack blues guitarist formed his own 5-piece outfit, IKE & THE KINGS OF RHYTHM (WILLIE WIZARD, EUGENE FOX, JACKIE BENSTON and one other). They made a couple of singles for 'Chess'; 'HEARTBROKEN AND WORRIED' / 'I'M LONESOME BABY' plus 'ROCKET 88' / 'COME BACK WHERE YOU BELONG' before signing to Sam Phillips management, the 'Sun' head honcho taking on the role of both producer and A&R man. Five years later, IKE flitted from Memphis to St. Louis where he was to strike up a working and loving partnership with TINA (after she persuaded him to let her have a go at fronting his band) and in 1960, now billed as IKE & TINA TURNER, they hit the US Top 30 with 'A FOOL IN LOVE'. As well as presenting a much feted stage show (which served to highlight both IKE's musical and choreographic skills alongside TINA's raunchy vocals and stunning appearance), the duo proceeded to notch up a string of R&B hits, even hitting the pop charts the following year with their Top 20 smash hit, 'IT'S GONNA WORK OUT FINE'. After one further major hit, things dried up until the mid-60's, when they were introduced to the legendary PHIL SPECTOR. He produced their magnus-opus, 'RIVER DEEP MOUNTAIN HIGH', a "wall of sound" soul classic which, although a relative flop in the States, peaked at No.3 in the UK. With varying degrees of fortune, they moved from one label to another, finally scoring a massive Top 5 US hit on 'Liberty' in early '71 with an earthy cover of JOHN FOGERTY's classic 'PROUD MARY'. The enthusiastic patronage of The ROLLING STONES did much to raise their profile (the pair performed at the ill-fated Altamont gig in 1969) and they finally broke out again in 1973 when TINA's autobiographical composition, 'NUTBUSH CITY LIMITS', was a massive seller on both sides of the Atlantic. In 1974, she landed the part of 'The Acid Queen' in The WHO's rock opera, 'TOMMY', her new-found independence giving her time to reflect on her well-documented ill-treatment by IKE. In 1976, after converting to Buddhism, she finally divorced him, in effect ending not only their marriage but their lucrative musical partnership. After a time on welfare (US equivalent of the dole), she began to make tentative moves to carving out a solo career, already having released an impressive album of covers, 'ACID QUEEN', the previous year. Yet although she remained a star attraction on the live club circuit scene, she still found it hard to sell records. Until that is, 'Capitol' contracted her late in '82 following some show-stopping support slots for The 'STONES. Following the surprise international success of her Al Green cover, 'LET'S STAY TOGETHER' in late '83, the multi-million 'PRIVATE DANCER' album was rush-recorded and released in summer '84. The record included her recent Grammy winner and US No.1, 'WHAT'S LOVE GOT TO WITH IT' alongside the Top 10 title track and the Top 5 'BETTER BE GOOD TO ME, going platinum in both America and Britain. It also showcased a more sophisticated, smoother approach although TURNER's range was as impressive as ever and incredibly, she was looking better than many female stars half her age. In '85, she starred in the film 'Mad Max: Beyond The Thunderdome', receiving an award by NAACP for best actress; TURNER was also reputed to have turned down the offer of a major part in the film, 'The Color Purple'. She was now arguably the most famous female Rock & Pop singer on Earth, a claim to which the 180,000 audience attending the Rio De Janeiro January '86 concert would testify. In contrast with her continuing triumphs – TURNER went on to release further million selling 80's albums, 'BREAK EVERY RULE' (1986) and 'FOREIGN AFFAIR' (1989) – IKE was unceremoniously sentenced to a year in prison in 1988 after admitting his dealings with cocaine. The troubled history of IKE and TINA's former partnership was documented in the 1993 biopic, 'WHAT'S LOVE GOT TO DO WITH IT' (based on TINA's book), the accompanying soundtrack topping the UK charts. • **Songwriters:** IKE wrote most of the early material, but with (selective) covers interspersed I'VE BEEN LOVING YOU TOO LONG (Otis Redding) / PLEASE PLEASE PLEASE (James Brown) / COME TOGETHER (Beatles) / I WANT TO TAKE YOU HIGHER (Sly & The Family Stone) / HONKY TONK WOMAN + LET'S SPEND THE NIGHT TOGETHER + UNDER MY THUMB (Rolling Stones) / OOH POO PAH DOO (Jesse Hill) / SAVE THE LAST DANCE FOR ME (Drifters) / etc. TINA's solo covers; ACID QUEEN + I CAN SEE FOR MILES (Who) / SOMETIME WHEN WE TOUCH (Dan Hill) / THE BITCH IS BACK (Elton John) / VIVA LA MONEY (Allen Toussaint) / EARTHQUAKE AND HURRICANE (Willie Dixon) / FIRE DOWN BELOW (Bob Seger) / WHOLE LOTTA LOVE (Led Zeppelin) / FUNNY HOW TIME SLIPS AWAY (. . . Nelson) / BACKSTABBERS (O'Jays) / HELP! + COME TOGETHER (Beatles) / TAKE ME TO THE RIVER (Al Green) / I CAN'T STAND THE RAIN (Ann Peebles) / TONIGHT I'LL BE STAYING HERE WITH YOU (Bob Dylan) / PRIVATE DANCER (Mark Knopfler) / WHAT'S LOVE GOT TO DO WITH IT? (Terry Britten, her co-producer & Graham Lyle; ex-Gallagher & Lyle) / ADDICTED TO LOVE (Robert Palmer) / IN THE MIDNIGHT HOUR (Wilson Pickett) / STEAMY WINDOWS (Tony Joe White) / IT TAKE TWO (Marvin Gaye & Tammi Terrell) / WHY MUST WE WAIT UNTIL TONIGHT (Bryan Adams – Mutt Lange) / GOLDEN EYE (U2) / etc. • **Trivia:** In the 60's, The IKETTES also had US hits with I'M BLUE (THE GONG-GONG SONG) (No.19, Feb62) / PEACHES'N'CREAM (No.36, Apr65). In 1981, TINA appeared on BEF's (HEAVEN 17) various vocalists album 'MUSIC OF QUALITY . . . ' re-actifying The Temptations number BALL OF CONFUSION.

Album rating: PROUD MARY: BEST OF IKE & TINA TURNER (best CD compilation; *7) / Tina Turner: TINA TURNS THE COUNTRY ON (*4) / ACID QUEEN (*5) / ROUGH (*4) / LOVE EXPLOSION (*4) / PRIVATE DANCER (*7) / BREAK EVERY RULE (*6) / TINA LIVE IN EUROPE (*4) / FOREIGN AFFAIR (*6) / SIMPLY THE BEST compilation (*8) / WHAT'S LOVE GOT TO DO WITH IT soundtrack (*6) / WILDEST DREAMS (*6) / TWENTY FOUR SEVEN (*5)

IKE & TINA TURNER

IKE TURNER – guitar, vocals / **TINA TURNER** – vocals plus sessioners & singing group The IKETTES (aka **P.P.ARNOLD, MERRY CLAYTON & BONNIE BRAMLETT** and loads more at various times).

		London	Sue
Nov 60.	(7") *(HLU 9226)* <730> **A FOOL IN LOVE. / THE WAY YOU LOVE ME**		Aug 60 27
Dec 60.	(7") *<735>* **I IDOLISE YOU. / LETTER FROM TINA**	–	82
1961.	(7") **I'M JEALOUS. / YOU'RE MY BABY**	–	
1961.	(lp) *<2001>* **THE SOUL OF IKE & TINA TURNER**	–	

– I'm jealous / I idolize you / If / Letter from Tina / You can't love two / I had a motion / A fool in love / Sleepless / Chances are / You're my baby / The way you love me. *(UK-iss.Apr84 on 'Kent')*

Oct 61.	(7") *(HL 94510) <749>* **IT'S GONNA WORK OUT FINE. / WON'T YOU FORGIVE ME**		Jul 61 14
Nov 61.	(7") *<753>* **POOR FOOL. / YOU CAN'T BLAME ME**	–	38
1962.	(lp) *<2005>* **DON'T PLAY ME CHEAP**	–	

– Wake up / I made a promise up above / Desire / Those ways / Mamma tell him / Pretend / Don't play me cheap / The real me / Forever mine / No amending / Love letters / My everything to me.

Mar 62.	(7") *<757>* **TRA LA LA LA LA. / PUPPY LOVE**	–	
Jun 62.	(7") *<765>* **YOU SHOULD'VE TREATED ME RIGHT. / SLEEPLESS**	–	89
1962.	(lp) *<2007>* **IT'S GONNA WORK OUT FINE**	–	

– Gonna find me a substitute / Mojo queen / Kinda strange / Why should I / Tinarro / I'm gonna cut you loose / Foolish / It's gonna work out fine / I'm fallin' in love / This man's crazy / Good good lovin' / The rooster / Steel guitar rag / Trackdown twist / Going home.

		Sue	Kent
Nov 62.	(7") **I IDOLIZE YOU. / TINA'S DILEMMA**	–	
1963.	(7") **MIND IN A WHIRL. / THE ARGUMENT**	–	
1963.	(7") **PLEASE DON'T HURT ME. / WORRIED AND HURTIN' INSIDE**	–	
1963.	(7") **DON'T PLAY ME CHEAP. / WAKE UP**	–	
Feb 64.	(7"ep) *(IEP 706)* **THE SOUL OF IKE & TINA TURNER**		–
Aug 64.	(7") *(SR 322)* **THE ARGUMENT. / POOR FOOL**		–
Nov 64.	(7") *(SR 350) <402>* **I CAN'T BE BELIEVE WHAT YOU SAY (FOR SEEING WHAT YOU DO). / MY BABY NOW**		Sep 64 95
Nov 64.	(lp) <> **IKE & TINA TURNER REVUE!!! (live)**	–	

– Please, please, please / Feel so good / The love of my man / Think / Drown in my own tears / I love the way you love / Your precious love / All in my mind / I can't believe what you say. *(UK-iss.Jul66 on 'Ember') (re-iss. Dec72 on 'New World') (cd-iss. Jul93 on 'Kent')*

May 65.	(7") *(SR 376)* **PLEASE PLEASE PLEASE. / AM I A FOOL IN LOVE**		–

—— They had already signed to . . .

		Warners	Warners
Jan 65.	(7") *(WB 153)* **FINGER POPPIN'. / OOH POO PAH DOO**		
Jan 65.	(7"ep) *(WEP 619)* **THE IKE & TINA TURNER SHOW (live)**		
Apr 65.	(lp) *(W 1579) <1579>* **LIVE! THE IKE & TINA TURNER SHOW (live)**		Feb 65

– Finger poppin' / Down in the valley / Good times / You are my sunshine / Good time tonight / Twist and shout / Something's got a hold on me / I know (you don't want me no more) / (Tight pants) High heel sneakers / My man he's a loving man / I can't stop loving you / Tell the truth. *(re-iss. Jul66) (re-iss. May70 on 'Valient') (cd-iss. Apr85 on 'Edsel')*

Jan 66.	(7"ep) *(WEP 620)* **SOMEBODY NEEDS YOU**		

—— Warners continued to issue material after 1966 success and new dealings . . .

Jul 66.	(7") *(WB 5753)* **TELL HER I'M NOT HOME. / FINGER POPPIN'**	48	
Nov 66.	(7") *(WB 5766)* **SOMEBODY (SOMEWHERE) NEEDS YOU. / JUST TO BE WITH YOU**		
Feb 67.	(lp) *(WB 5904) <1568>* **THE IKE & TINA TURNER SHOW VOL.II (live)**		

– Shake a tail feather / You must believe in me / Ooh poo pah doo / Early in the morning / All I can do is cry / Somebody somewhere needs you / Keep on pushing / It's all over / You're no good / Fool for you.

—— Signed to different labels at same time . . .

		H.M.V.	Tangerine
Aug 66.	(7") *(POP 1544)* **ANYTHING THAT YOU WASN'T BORN WITH. / BEAUTY IS JUST SKIN DEEP**		

Mar 67. (7") *(POP 1583)* **I'M HOOKED. / DUST MY BROOM**

Stateside Modern

Oct 66. (7") *(SS 551)* **GOODBYE, SO LONG. / HURT IS ALL YOU GAVE ME**

London Philles

May 66. (7") *(HLU 10046)* *<131>* **RIVER DEEP, MOUNTAIN HIGH. / I'LL KEEP YOU HAPPY** [3] [88]
(re-iss. Dec 69 on 'A & M' US)

Sep 66. (lp) *(HAU 8396)* **RIVER DEEP MOUNTAIN HIGH** [27] [–]
– River deep, mountain high / I idolize you / A love like yours (don't come knockin' every day) / A fool in love / Make 'em wait / Hold on baby / I'll never need more than this / Save the last dance for me / Oh! baby (things ain't what they used to be) / Every day I have to cry / Such a fool for you / It's gonna work out fine. *(US-iss.Sep 69 on 'A&M', UK-re-iss. Mar70 +cd.1988) (UK re-iss. 1974 on 'Mayfair-A&M', Jan 75 on 'Hamlet-A&M', Dec79 on 'M.F.P.', re-iss. +c.May 84 on 'Spot', cd-iss. 1988 on 'Mobile Fidelity') (re-iss. cd+c Sep 93 on 'Yesterday's Gold')*

Oct 66. (7") *(HLU 10083)* **A LOVE LIKE YOURS (DON'T COME KNOCKIN' EVERY DAY). / HOLD ON BABY** [16]

Sep 67. (7") *(HLU 10155)* **I'LL NEVER NEED MORE THAN THIS. / SAVE THE LAST DANCE FOR ME**

Apr 68. (7") *(HLU 10189)* **SO FINE. / SO BLUE OVER YOU**

Aug 68. (7") *(HLU 10217)* **WE NEED AN UNDERSTANDING. / IT SHO' AIN'T ME**

Jan 69. (lp) *(SHU 8370)* *<6000>* **SO FINE**
– Bet'cha can't kiss me (just one time) / T'ain't nobody's business / It sho' ain't me / Too hot to hold / A fool in love / Poor little fool / I better get ta steppin' / Shake a tail feather / So fine / We need an understanding / You're so fine / Poor Sam. *(cd-iss. Sep87 on 'Entertainer')*

— Were again on the books of 2 labels.

Minit Minit

Apr 69. (7") *(MLF 11016)* *<32060>* **I'M GONNA DO ALL I CAN (TO DO RIGHT BY MY MAN). / YOU'VE GOT TOO MANY TIES THAT BIND** [98]

Jun 69. (7") **I WISH IT WOULD RAIN. / WITH A LITTLE HELP FROM MY FRIENDS** [–]

Sep 69. (7") **I WANNA JUMP. / TREATING US FUNKY** [–]

Oct 69. (lp) *(40014)* *<24018>* **IN PERSON (live)** Jul 69
– Everyday people / Gimme some lovin' / Sweet soul music / Son of a preacher man / I heard it through the grapevine / Respect / Medley: There was a time – African boo's / Funky street / A fool in love / Medley: The summit – All I could do was cry – Please, please, please – Baby I love you / Goodbye, so long.

Feb 70. (7") *(LBF 15303)* **COME TOGETHER. / HONKY TONK WOMAN** [–] [57]

Harvest Blue Thumb

May 69. (7") *<101>* **I'VE BEEN LOVING YOU TOO LONG. / GRUMBLING** [–] [68]

Jul 69. (7") *<102>* **THE HUNTER. / CRAZY 'BOUT YOU BABY** [–] [93]

Nov 69. (7") *<104>* **BOLD SOUL SISTER. / I KNOW** [–] [59]

May 70. (7") *(HAR 5018)* **THE HUNTER. / BOLD SOUL SISTER** [–]

Sep 70. (lp) *(LBS 83350)* *<7637>* **COME TOGETHER** May 70
– It ain't right / Too much woman (for a henpecked man) / Unlucky creature / Young and dumb / Honky tonk woman / Come together / Why can't we be happy / Contact high / Keep on walkin' / I want to take you higher / Evil man / Doin' it.

Sep 70. (lp) *(SHSP 4001)* *<11>* **THE HUNTER** Nov 69
– The hunter / You don't love me (yes I know) / You got me running / Bold soul sister / I smell trouble / Things I used to do / Early in the morning / You're still my baby / I know.

Liberty Blue Thumb

Jun 69. (lp) *(LBS 83241)* *<5>* **OUTTA SEASON** Apr 69
– I've been loving you too long / Mean old world / 3 o'clock im the morning blues / Five long years / Dust my broom / Grumbling / I am a motherless child / Crazy 'bout your baby / Reconsider baby / Honest I do / Please love me / My babe / Rock me baby. *(re-iss. Sep73 on 'Sunset')*

Jul 69. (7") *(LBF 15223)* **CRAZY ABOUT YOU BABY. / I'VE BEEN LOVIN' YOU TOO LONG** Apr 69

Liberty Liberty

Jun 70. (7") *(LBF 15367)* *<56177>* **I WANT TO TAKE YOU HIGHER. / CONTACT HIGH** May 70 [34]

Sep 70. (7") **WORKIN' TOGETHER. / THE WAY YOU LOVE ME** [–]

Jan 71. (7") *(LBF 15432)* *<56216>* **PROUD MARY. / FUNKIER THAN MOSQUITA'S TWEETER** [4]

Feb 71. (lp) *(LBS 83455)* *<7650>* **WORKIN' TOGETHER** Dec 70 [25]
– Workin' together / Get you when I want you / Get back / The way you love me / You can have it / Game of love / Funkier than a mosquito's tweeter / Ooh poo pah doo / Proud Mary / Goodbye so long / Let it be. *(cd-iss. Dec95 on 'EMI Europe')*

U.A. U.A.

Jun 71. (7") *(UP 35245)* *<50782>* **OOH POO PAH DOO. / I WANNA JUMP** [60]

Sep 71. (d-lp) *(UAD 600056)* *<9953>* **LIVE AT THE CARNEGIE – WHAT YOU HEAR IS WHAT YOU GET (live)** Jul 71 [25]
– Piece of my heart / Everyday people / Doin' The Tina Turner / Sweet soul music / Ooh poo pah doo / Honky tonk women / A love like yours (don't come knockin' every day) / Proud Mary / I smell trouble / Ike's tune / I want to take you higher / I've been loving you too long / Respect / What you see is what you get.

Nov 71. (7") *(UP 35310)* **I'M YOURS. / DOIN' IT**

Jan 72. (7") *(UP 35219)* **CRAZY ABOUT YOU BABY. / I'VE BEEN LOVIN' YOU TOO LONG**

Mar 72. (lp/c) *(UAG 29256)* *<5530>* **'NUFF SAID** Dec 71
– I love what you do to me / Baby (what you want me to do) / Sweet flustrations / What you don't see (is better yet) / Nuff said (part 1) / Tell the truth / Pick me up (take me where your home is) / Moving into hip style – A trip child / I love baby / Can't you hear me callin' / Nuff said (part 2).

Feb 72. (7") *<50881>* **UP IN HEAH. / DOO WAH DIDDY** [–] [83]

Jun 72. (7") *(UP 35373)* **FEEL GOOD. / OUTRAGEOUS**

Oct 72. (lp) *(UAS 29377)* *<5598>* **FEEL GOOD** Jul 72
– Chopper / Kay got laid, Joe got paid / Feel good / I like it / If you can hully gully (I can hully gully too) / Black coffee / She came in through the bathroom window / If I knew then (what I know now) / You better think of something.

Oct 72. (7") *(UP 9)* **LET ME TOUCH YOUR MIND. / CHOPPER**

Feb 73. (lp) *(UAS 29423)* *<5660>* **LET ME TOUCH YOUR MIND**
– Let me touch your mind / Annie had a baby / Don't believe her / I had a notion / Popcorn / Early one morning / Help him / Up on the roof / Born free / Heaven help us all

Jul 73. (7") *(UP 35550)* **WORK ON ME. / BORN FREE**

Oct 73. (7") *(UP 35582)* *<298>* **NUTBUSH CITY LIMITS. / HELP HIM** [4] Sep 73 [22]

Nov 73. (lp/c) *(UA S/C 29557)* *<180>* **NUTBUSH CITY LIMITS**
– Nutbush city limits / Make me over / Drift away / That's my purpose / Fancy Annie / River deep mountain high / Get it out of your mind / Daily bread / You are my sunshine / Club Manhattan.

Dec 73. (7") *(UP 35632)* **FANCY ANNIE. / RIVER DEEP MOUNTAIN HIGH**

Apr 74. (7") *(UP 35650)* **SWEET RHODE ISLAND RED. / GET IT OUT OF YOUR MIND**

Sep 74. (7") *(UP 35726)* *<528>* **SEXY IDA. / (part 2)** [65]

Oct 74. (lp/c) **SWEET RHODE ISLAND RED**
– Let me be there / Living for the city / I know / Mississippi rolling stone / Sugar hill / Sweet Rhode Island red / Ready for you baby / Smooth out the wrinkles / Doozie / Higher ground.

Jul 75. (7") *(UP 35766)* *<598.* **BABY-GET IT ON. / ('A'disco version)** Jun 75 [88]

Oct 75. (7") *(UP 36028)* **DELILAH'S POWER. / THAT'S MY PURPOSE**

Mar 77. (lp/c) *(UA S/C 30040)* *<707>* **DELILAH'S POWER**
– Delilah's power / Never been to Spain / Unhappy birthday / (You've got to) Put something into it / Nothing comes to you when you're asleep but a dream / Stormy weather (keeps rainin' all the time) / Sugar sugar / Too much for one woman / Trying to find my mind / Pick me up (take me where your home is) / Too many women / I want to take you higher. *(cd-iss. Feb01 on 'EMI Plus'; 576099-2)*

— Above album was already recorded mid 70's, before their divorce/split.

TINA TURNER

— went solo in 1974 with session people

U.A. U.A.

Aug 74. (lp/c) *<200>* **TINA TURNS THE COUNTRY ON**
– Bayou song / Help me make it through the night / Tonight I'll be staying here with you / If you love me (let me know) / He belongs to me / Don't talk now / Long long time / I'm moving on / There'll always be music / The love that lights our way.

Oct 75. (lp/c) *(UN S/C 29875) <495>* **ACID QUEEN** [ ] Sep75 [ ]
– Under my thumb / Let's spend the night together / Acid queen / I can see for miles / Whole lotta love / Baby git it on / Bootsey Whitelaw / Pick me tonight / Rockin' and rollin'. *(cd-iss. May96 on 'EMI Gold'; CDGOLD 1026)*

Jan 76. (7") *(UP 36043)* **ACID QUEEN. / ROCKIN' AND ROLLIN'** [ ] [ ]

Sep 78. (lp/c) *(UAG/UAC 30211)* **ROUGH** [ ] [ ]
– Fruits of the night / The bitch is back / The woman I'm supposed to be / Viva la money / Funny how time slips away / Earthquake & hurricane / Root toot undisputable rock'n'roller / Fire down below / Sometimes when we touch / A woman in a man's world / Night time is the right time. *(cd-iss. Aug95; CDP 795213-2)*

Feb 79. (7") *(UP 36485)* **ROOT TOOT UNDISPUTABLE ROCK'N'ROLLER. / FIRE DOWN BELOW** [ ] [ ]

Mar 79. (lp/c) *(UA G/C 30267)* **LOVE EXPLOSION** [ ] [ ]
– Love explosion / Fool for your love / Sunset on sunset / Music keeps me dancin' / I see home / Backstabbers / Just a little lovin' (early in the morning) / You get what I'm gonna get / On the radio.

Apr 79. (7") *(UP 36513)* **SOMETIMES WHEN WE TOUCH. / EARTHQUAKE AND HURRICANE** [ ] [ ]

Nov 79. (7") *(BP 322)* **BACKSTABBERS. / SUNSET ON SUNSET** [ ] [ ]

— In May'82, she sang on BALL OF CONFUSION single by 'BEF' (aka HEAVEN 17).

Capitol Capitol

Nov 83. (7")(12")(12"pic-d) *(CL/12CL/12CLP 316) <5322>* **LET'S STAY TOGETHER. / I WROTE A LETTER** [6] Jan 84 [26]

Feb 84. (7"/12"/7"pic-d) *(CL/12CL/CLP 325)* **HELP!. / ROCK'N'ROLL WIDOW** [40] [ ]

May 84. (7") *<5354>* **WHAT'S LOVE GOT TO DO WITH IT. / ROCK'N'ROLL WIDOW** [–] [1]

Jun 84. (7"/'A'ext-12"/12"pic-d) *(CL/12CL/12CLP 334)* **WHAT'S LOVE GOT TO DO WITH IT. / DON'T RUSH THE GOOD THINGS** [3] [–]

Jun 84. (lp/c)(cd) *(TINA/TCTINA 1)(CDP 7460412) <12330>* **PRIVATE DANCER** [2] [3]
– I might have been queen / What's love got to do with it / Show some respect / Private dancer / I can't stand the rain / Let's stay together / Better be good to me / Steel claw / Help! / 1984. *(pic-lp Apr85) (special cd-iss. Aug00 +=; CDCNTAV 1)* – (extra tracks).

Sep 84. (7")(12")(7"sha-pic-d) *(CL/12CL/CLP 338) <5387>* **BETTER BE GOOD TO ME. / WHEN I WAS YOUNG** [45] [5]

Nov 84. (7"/12") *(CL/12CL 343) <5433>* **PRIVATE DANCER. / NUTBUSH CITY LIMITS** [26] [7]

Feb 85. (7"/12") *(CL/12CL 352)* **I CAN'T STAND THE RAIN. / LET'S PRETEND WE'RE MARRIED** [57] [ ]

Apr 85. (7") *<5461>* **SHOW SOME RESPECT. / LET'S PRETEND WE'RE MARRIED** [–] [37]

Jun 85. (7"/12"/7"pic-d/7"sha-pic-d) (CL/12CL/CLP 364) <5491> *(CL 364)* **WE DON'T NEED ANOTHER HERO (THUNDERDOME). / ('A'instrumental)** [3] [2]

— Above + below 45s, from her film 'Mad Max: Beyond The Thunderdome'.

Sep 85. (7"/12") *(CL/12CL 376) <5518>* **ONE OF THE LIVING. / (part 2)** [55] [15]

— In Oct85, teamed up with BRYAN ADAMS on UK No.29 + US 19 hit IT'S ONLY LOVE

Aug 86. (7") *(CL 419) <5615>* **TYPICAL MALE. / DON'T TURN AROUND** [33] [2]
('A'extended-12"+=) *(12CL 419)* – ('A'dub version).
(12"++=)(12"pic-d++=) *(12CLP 419,)* – ('A'dance mix).

Sep 86. (lp/c)(cd) *(EST/TCEST 2018)(CDP 7463232) <12530>* **BREAK EVERY RULE** [2] [4]
– Typical male / What you get is what you see / Two people / Till the right man comes along / Afterglow / Girls / Back where you started / Break every rule / Overnight sensation / Paradise is here / I'll be thunder.

Oct 86. (7"/12") *(CL/12CL 430) <5644>* **TWO PEOPLE. / HAVIN' A PARTY** [43] [30]
(d12"+=) *(12CLD 430)* – Let's stay together (live) / Private dancer (live).

Feb 87. (7"/12") *(CL/12CL 439) <5668>* **WHAT YOU GET IS WHAT YOU SEE. / TINA TURNER MONTAGE MIX – I Can't Stand The Rain – Two People – We Don't Need Another Hero – What's Love Got To Do With It – Typical Male – Let's Stay Together** [30] [13]
(d7"+=) *(7CLD 439)* – ('A'live) / Take me to the river.

Apr 87. (7") *<44003>* **BREAK EVERY RULE. / TAKE ME TO THE RIVER** [–] [74]

May 87. (7"/7"sha-pic-d) *(CL/+P 452)* **BREAK EVERY RULE. / GIRLS** [43] [–]

Sep 87. (7"/12"/7"pic-d) *(CL/12CL/CLP 459)* **PARADISE IS HERE. / IN THE MIDNIGHT HOUR** [ ] [ ]

Mar 88. (7") *(CL 484)* **ADDICTED TO LOVE (live). / OVERNIGHT SENSATION (live)** [71] [ ]
(12"+=/cd-s+=) *(12CL/CDCL 484)* – Legs (live).

Mar 88. (d-c/d-cd/d-lp) *(TC/CD+/ESTD 1) <90126>* **TINA LIVE IN EUROPE (live)** [8] [86]
– What you get is what you see / Break every rule / I can't stand the rain / Two people / Girls * / Typical male / Back where you started * / Better be good to me / Addicted to love / Private dancer / We don't need another hero (Thunderdome) / What's love got to do with it / Let's stay together / Show some respect / Land of 1,000 dances / In the midnight hour / 634-5789 (with ROBERT CRAY) / A change is gonna come / River deep, mountain high * / Tearing us apart (with ERIC CLAPTON) / Proud Mary / Help! / Tonight + Let's dance (with DAVID BOWIE) / Overnight sensation * / It's only love (with BRYAN ADAMS) / Nutbush city limits / Paradise is here. *(c+cd+= *)*

Jun 88. (7"/12") *(CL/12CL 495)* **A CHANGE IS GONNA COME (live). / NUTBUSH CITY LIMITS (live)** [ ] [ ]

Aug 89. (7"/c-s) *(CL/TCCL 543) <44442>* **THE BEST. / UNDERCOVER AGENT FOR THE BLUES** [5] [15]
(12"+=)(cd-s+=) *(12CL/CDCL 543)* – Bold and reckless.

Sep 89. (c/cd/lp) *(TC/CD+/ESTU 2103) <91873>* **FOREIGN AFFAIR** [1] [31]
– Steamy windows / The best / You know who (is doing you know what) / Undercover agent for the blues / Look me in the heart / Be tender with me baby / You can't stop me loving you / Ask me how I feel / Falling like rain / I don't wanna lose you / Not enough romance / Foreign affair. *(re-iss. Sep94)*

Oct 89. (7"/c-s) *(CL/TCCL 553)* **I DON'T WANNA LOSE YOU. / NOT ENOUGH ROMANCE** [8] [ ]
(12"+=/12"pic-d+=) *(12CL/+P 553)* – Stronger than the wind.
(cd-s+=) *(CDCL 553)* – We don't need another hero.

Jan 90. (7") *(CL 560) <44473>* **STEAMY WINDOWS. / THE BEST (muscle mix)** [13] Nov89 [39]
('B'extended-cd-s+=) *(CDCL 560)* – ('A'house mix).
(12")(c-s) *(12CL/TCCL 560)* – ('A'side) / ('A'vocal mix) / ('A'house mix).

Jul 90. (c-s,cd-s) <>>**LOOKMEINTHEHEART/STRONGER THAN THE WIND** [–] [ ]

Aug 90. (7"/c-s) *(CL/TCCL 584)* **LOOK ME IN THE HEART. / STEEL CLAW (live)** [31] [–]
(12"+=)(cd-s+=) *(12CL/CDCL 584)* – ('A'instrumental).
('A'remixed-cd-s) *(CDCLX 584)* – ('A'instrumental) / Tina Turner montage mix.

Oct 90. (7"/c-s/7"pic-d) *(CL/TCCL/CLP 593)* **BE TENDER WITH MY HEART. / ('A'live)** [28] [ ]
(12"+=/cd-s+=) *(12CL/CDCL 593)* – You know who is doing you know what.

— In Nov90, she teamed up with ROD STEWART on hit single IT TAKES TWO.

Sep 91. (7"/c-s) *(CL/TCCL 630)* **NUTBUSH CITY LIMITS (THE 90's VERSION). / THE BEST** [23] [ ]
(12"+=/cd-s+=) *(12/CD CL 630)* – Addicted to love (live) / Nutbush city limits ('91).

Oct 91. (cd/c/d-lp) *(CD/TC+/ESTV 1) <97152>* **SIMPLY THE BEST** – (compilation) [1] [ ]

Nov 91. (7"/c-s) *(CL/TCCL 637)* **WAY OF THE WORLD. / I DON'T WANNA LOSE YOU** [13] [ ]
(12"+=)(cd-s+=) *(12CL/CDCL 637)* – Foreign affair.

Feb 92. (7") *(CL 644)* **LOVE THING. / I'M A LADY** [29] [ ]
(c-s+=/cd-s+=) *(TC/CD CL 644)* – It's only love / Private dancer (live).

May 92. (7"/c-s) *(CL/TCCL 659)* **I WANT YOU NEAR ME. / LET'S STAY TOGETHER** [22] [ ]
(cd-s+=) *(CDCL 659)* – Tonight + Let's dance (live with DAVID BOWIE).
(cd-s) *(CDCLX 659)* – ('A'side) / Land of a 1,000 dances / In the midnight hour / 634-5789 (live with ROBERT CRAY).

Parlophone Virgin

May 93. (7"/c-s) *(R/TCR 6346)* **I DON'T WANNA FIGHT. / THE BEST** [7] [–]
(cd-s+=) *(CDR 6346)* – I don't wanna lose you / What's love got to do with it.
(cd-s) *(CDRS 6346)* – ('A'side) / Tina's wish / ('A'urban mix).

May 93. (c-s,cd-s) *<12652>* **I DON'T WANNA FIGHT / TINA'S WISH** [–] [9]

Jun 93. (cd/c/lp) *(CD/TC+/PCSD 128)* <88189> **WHAT'S LOVE GOT TO DO WITH IT (soundtrack)** [1] [17]
– I don't wanna fight / Rock me baby / Disco inferno / Why must we wait until tonight / Stay awhile / Nutbush city limits / You know I love you / Proud Mary / A fool in love / It's gonna work out fine / Shake a tail feather / I might have been Queen / What's love got to do with it (live) / Tina's wish.
– (a selection of new recordings of old & new songs from her biopic film)

Aug 93. (7"/c-s) *(R/TCR 6357)* **DISCO INFERNO. / I DON'T WANNA FIGHT** [12] [ ]
(12"+=/cd-s+=) *(12R/CDR 6357)* – ('A'mixes).

Oct 93. (7"/c-s) *(R/TCR 6366)* <12683> **WHY MUST WE WAIT UNTIL TONIGHT? / SHAKE A TAIL FEATHER** [16] [97]
(cd-s+=) *(CDR 6366)* – The best.
(cd-s++=) *(CDRS 6366)* – ('A'remix).

Nov 95. (7"/c-s) *(R/TCR 0071001)* **GOLDENEYE. / ('A'-Morales club mix)** [10] [ ]
(cd-s+=) *(CDR 0071001)* – ('A'-urban mix) / ('A'-A/C mix) / ('A'-urban A/C mix).

Mar 96. (c-s) *(TCR 6429)* **WHATEVER YOU WANT / GOLDENEYE** [23] [ ]
(cd-s+=) *(CDR 6429)* – ('A'-extended Olympic mix).
(cd-s+=) *(CDRS 6429)* – Unfinished sympathy.

Apr 96. (cd/c) *(CD/TC+/EST 2279)* <41920> **WILDEST DREAMS** [4] Sep96 [61]
– Missing you / In your wildest dreams / Whatever you want / Do what you do / Thief of hearts / On silent wings / Something beautiful remains / Confidential / The difference between us / All kinds of people / Unfinished symphony / Goldeneye / Dancing in my dreams.

May 96. (c-s/cd-s) *(TCR/CDR 6434)* **ON SILENT WINGS / PRIVATE DANCER / THE BEST / I DON'T WANNA LOSE YOU** [13] [ ]
(cd-s) *(CDRS 6434)* – ('A'side) / Whatever you want / Do something.

Jul 96. (c-s) *(TCR 6441)* **MISSING YOU / WHATEVER YOU WANT** [12] [–]
(cd-s+=) *(CDR 6441)* – The difference between us.
(cd-s) *(CDRS 6441)* – ('A'side) / We don't need another hero (live) / What's love got to do with it (live).

Sep 96. (c-s,cd-s) <38553> **MISSING YOU / DO SOMETHING** [–] [84]

Oct 96. (c-s) *(TCR 6448)* **SOMETHING BEAUTIFUL REMAINS / ADDICTED TO LOVE (live)** [27] [ ]
(cd-s) *(CDR 6448)* – ('A'side) / Steamy windows / Better be good to me.
(cd-s) *(CDRS 6448)* – ('A'mixes).

Dec 96. (c-s; by TINA TURNER featuring BARRY WHITE) *(TCR 6451)* **IN YOUR WILDEST DREAMS / WHAT'S LOVE GOT TO DO WITH IT?** [32] [ ]
(cd-s+=) *(CDR 6451)* – Goldeneye (live) / Missing you (live).
(cd-s) *(CDRS 6451)* – ('A'side) / ('A'mixes).

Oct 99. (c-s; as TINA) *(TCR 6529)* **WHEN THE HEARTACHE IS OVER / ('A'-Metro mix)** [10] [ ]
(cd-s+=) *(CDR 6529)* – ('A'-7th district club mix).
(cd-s) *(CDRS 6529)* – ('A'mix) / I can't stand the rain (live) / On silent wings (live).

Nov 99. (cd/c) *(523180-2/-4)* <23180> **TWENTY FOUR SEVEN** [9] Feb00 [21]
– Whatever you need / All the woman / When the heartache is over / Absolutely nothing's changed / Talk to my heart / Don't leave me this way / Go ahead / Without you / Falling / Will be there / Twenty four seven. *(d-cd-iss. Jul00; 527213-0)*

Jan 00. (c-s) *(TCR 6532)* **WHATEVER YOU NEED / (mix)** [27] [ ]
(cd-s) *(CDRS 6532)* – ('A'side) / The best (live) / River deep mountain high (live).
(cd-s) *(CDR 6532)* – ('A'live) / What's love got to do with it (live) / Steamy windows (live).

– (IKE & TINA) compilations, etc. –

Jan 69. (7") *London; (HLU 10242)* **RIVER DEEP MOUNTAIN HIGH. / SAVE THE LAST DANCE FOR ME** [33] [–]

May 76. (lp/c) *United Artists; (UA S/C 29948)* **THE VERY BEST OF IKE & TINA TURNER** [ ] [ ]

Feb 88. (cd) *Edsel; (ED 243)* **FINGER POPPIN' – THE WARNER BROS YEARS** [ ] [–]

Dec 88. (c) *Capitol; (4XLL 9191)* **PROUD MARY AND OTHER HITS** [ ] [–]
– A fool in love / I idolize you / I'm jealous / It's gonna work out fine / Poor fool / Tra la la la la / You shoulda treated me right / Come together / Honky tonk woman / I want to take you higher / Workin' together / Proud Mary / Funkier than a mosquito's tweeter / Ooh poo pah doo / I'm yours (use me any way you wanna) / Up in heah / River deep, mountain high / Nutbush city limits / Sweet Rhode Island red / Sexy Ida (parts 1 & 2) / Baby – Get it on / Acid queen. *(re-iss. Oct91 as 'PROUD MARY – THE BEST OF IKE & TINA TURNER' on 'EMI')*

Nov 94. (3xcd-box) *Capitol; (CDEST 2240)* **THE COLLECTED RECORDINGS** [ ] [–]

Jul 96. (cd) *EMI Gold; (CDGOLD 1049)* **18 CLASSIC TRACKS** [ ] [ ]

Sep 96. (3xcd-box) *Disky; (SA 87270-2)* **WORKIN' TOGETHER** [ ] [ ]

Nov 96. (3xcd-box) *Disky; (LAD 87330-2)* **THE BEST OF IKE & TINA TURNER: 18 ORIGINIAL HITS** [ ] [–]

Feb 97. (cd/c) *Platinum; (PLA TCD/C 211)* **BOLD SOUL SISTER** [ ] [ ]

May 97. (cd/c) *A-Play; (10176-2/-4)* **LIVING FOR THE CITY** [ ] [ ]

Oct 97. (cd/c) *Castle Pulse; (PLS CD/MC 253)* **LET THE GOOD TIMES ROLL** [ ] [ ]

Nov 97. (d-cd) *Eagle; (EDMCD 016)* **THE MASTERS** [ ] [ ]

Nov 98. (d-cd) *Disky; (HR 85303-2)* **ORIGINAL GOLD** [ ] [ ]

Dec 98. (d-cd) *Double Classics; (DC 31017)* **THE STORY OF . . .** [ ] [ ]

May 99. (cd) *Platinum; (PLATCD 507)* **THE VERY BEST OF IKE & TINA TURNER** [ ] [ ]

Aug 99. (d-cd) *K-Box; (KBOX 244)* **IKE & TINA TURNER** [ ] [ ]

Nov 99. (cd) *Laserlight; (21330)* **ROCKIN' AND ROLLIN'** [ ] [ ]

Jan 00. (cd) *Universal; (E 112167-2)* **UNIVERSAL MASTERS COLLECTION** [ ] [ ]

Apr 00. (cd) *Disky; (SI 99035-2)* **THE BEST OF THE 70'S** [ ] [ ]

May 00. (cd) *Kent; (CDKEND 182)* **THE KENT YEARS** [ ] [ ]

Jun 00. (d-cd) *Snapper; (SMDCD 290)* **TWO TOUGH** [ ] [ ]

Jun 00. (cd) *Starburst; (CDSB 017)* **LET THE GOOD TIMES ROLL** [ ] [ ]

Sep 00. (cd) *Members Edition; (UAE 31252)* **IKE & TINA TURNER** [ ] [ ]

Nov 00. (3xcd-box) *Goldies; (GLD 25407)* **RIVER DEEP MOUNTAIN HIGH** [ ] [ ]

Jan 01. (cd) *Bianco; (BIA 4043)* **LIVING FOR THE CITY** [ ] [ ]

Feb 01. (cd) *EMI Plus; (576074-2)* **WORKIN' TOGETHER** [ ] [ ]

Jul 01. (d-cd) *Laserlight; (24697)* **BABY GET IT ON** [ ] [ ]

Oct 01. (cd) *Platinum; (PLATCD 696)* **ROCKIN' AND ROLLIN': 20 HIP SHAKING FAVOURITES** [ ] [ ]

Dec 01. (cd) *Prestige; (CDSGP 058)* **IT'S ALL OVER** [ ] [ ]

Feb 02. (d-cd) *Universe; (UV 035)* **PORTRAIT IN BLUES** [ ] [ ]

Apr 02. (d-cd) *Platinum; (PLATBX 2217)* **ROCKIN' AND ROLLIN' / THE VERY BEST OF IKE & TINA TURNER** [ ] [ ]

Jun 02. (cd) *Stateside; (537960-2)* **FUNKIER THAN A MOSQUITO'S TWEETER** [ ] [ ]

Feb 03. (cd) *Mystic; (MYSCD 143)* **ULTIMATE MAXIMUM** [ ] [ ]

Mar 03. (3xcd-box) *Trilogie; (20595-2)* **I WANNA TAKE YOU HIGHER** [ ] [–]

Jun 03. (d-cd) *Gemini; (220444)* **I WANNA TAKE YOU HIGHER** [ ] [ ]

Jul 03. (d-cd) *Blacl Box; (BB 208)* **NUTBUSH CITY LIMITS** [ ] [ ]

☐ Jeff TWEEDY (see under ⇒ WILCO)

2PAC

Born: LESANE PARISH CROOKS, 16 Jun'71, Brooklyn, New York, USA. The son of a Black Panther member, after a successful start to his career as a member of West Coast rap act, DIGITAL UNDERGROUND, the "re-christened" TUPAC AMARU SHAKUR signed to 'Interscope' in 1991, making his solo debut with '2PACALYPSE NOW' (1992). A veritable journey into the heart of black inner city darkness, the record combined the bleak violence of gangsta with strong pro-Afro-American sentiments, as did the follow-up, 'STRICTLY 4 MY N.I.G.G.A.Z.' (1993), 2PAC almost breaking the US Top 10 with the 'I GET AROUND' single. He also had a penchant for getting on the wrong side of the law, running up an incredible string of charges including shooting two off-duty police officers, forceful sodomy (not with the police officers!) and attacking the co-director of the film, 'Menace II Society', Allen Hughes (2PAC had already made appearances in 'Juice', 'Under The Rim' and an acclaimed role in 'Poetic Justice'). While the shooting charge was dropped, 2PAC was subsequently sentenced to spend some time in prison for the sexual assault, ironically beginning his sentence while his third album, the aptly titled 'ME AGAINST THE WORLD' (1995) went to the top of the Billboard charts. The following year, the rapper was back at No.1 in defiant form with the landmark double set, 'ALL EYEZ ON ME', answering his many critics with 'ONLY GOD CAN JUDGE ME'. The album also spawned a No.1 single in the epochal 'CALIFORNIA LOVE', an utterly compelling 70's style pimp-rolling groove singing the praises of 2PAC's beloved home state, cut in collaboration with ex-ZAPP frontman, ROGER TROUTMAN. But if 2PAC was pro-Cali, he was viciously anti-New York, or at least its rap contingency, as witnessed on the track 'HIT 'EM UP' (included on the CD single of 'HOW DO YOU WANT IT'), a ferocious litany of hate primarily directed against his one-time friend, BIGGIE SMALLS (tried to shoot him?) but also stretching to MOBB DEEP and 'Bad Boy' records, the label at the centre of the East v West feud along with DR DRE's 'Death Row'. It had to end in tears of course, and it came as little surprise when 2PAC was shot and killed in a drive-by incident (13 September, 1996). Although no-one was subsequently charged with the murder, the rapper's list of enemies was almost as big as his police charge sheet and it was probably inevitable that a man who lived so closely by the gun wouldn't live to see 30. Violence and politics aside, there's no getting around the fact that 2PAC was an immensely talented artist, having scored his third US No.1 album in a row with 'THE DON KILLUMANATI: THE 7 DAY THEORY' (1996) under the alias MAKAVELI. His status as an American cultural icon was underlined recently when a US college introduced a 2PAC course, exploring the man's life and work. Crazy? Well, certainly no crazier than the esteem afforded the Kray Twins in Britain, and besides, did they pen anything as groovy as 'CALIFORNIA LOVE' (?!). In common with JEFF BUCKLEY, TUPAC's profile has remained high after his death through the regular release of half-finished, work in progress, the most recent being 'UNTIL THE END OF TIME' (2001). Also in common with BUCKLEY, the bulk of this material is of prime interest largely to hardcore fans who've got the time and inclination to muse over what the finished article would've sounded like. 2002's 'BETTER DAYZ' ranked as one of the more enduring posthumous releases, a sprawling double set of largely unreleased material which attempted some kind of focus by splitting the music up into one disc of hardcore and one of more accessible tracks. Of the two, the harder material perhaps left the deepest impression, the likes of 'F*** 'EM ALL' – a collaboration with OUTLAWZ – generating the kind of brooding portent that sounded all the more menacing in the light of subsequent events. One year on and fans were still being supplied with songs from beyond the grave, this time in the shape of the 'TUPAC: RESURRECTION' (2003) soundtrack. Another essential purchase for diehards, the record gathered together more obscure tracks from TUPAC's bulging back catalogue, a brace of which benefitted from EMINEM's production genius. The most poignant moment had to be the long lost collaboration with NOTORIOUS B.I.G., 'RUNNIN' (DYING TO LIVE)', an echo of happier days.

Album rating: 2PACALYPSE NOW (*6) / STRICTLY 4 MY N.I.G.G.A.Z. (*7) / VOLUME 1 by Thug Life (*6) / ME AGAINST THE WORLD (*7) / ALL EYEZ ON ME (*7) / DON KILLUMMINATI: THE 7 DAY THEORY (*4; as Makeveli) / R U STILL DOWN (REMEMBER ME) (*5) / IN HIS OWN WORDS (*5) / GREATEST HITS compilation (*8) / UNTIL THE END OF TIME (*6) / BETTER DAYZ (*7) / NU-MIXX KLAZZICS remixes (*3) / RESURRECTION soundtrack (*6)

TUPAC SHAKUR – vocals (with various guests, etc)

Interscope Interscope

Feb 92. (cd/c) *<(IND/INC 91767)>* **2PACALYPSE NOW** 64
– Young black male / Trapped / Soulja's story / I don't give a fuck / Violent / Words of wisdom / Something wicked / Crooked ass nigga / If my home calls / Brenda's got a baby / Lunatic / Rebel of the underground / Part time mutha. *(cd re-iss. Feb97; same) (cd re-iss. Mar98 on 'Jive'; CHIP 199)*

Feb 93. (cd/c) *<(IND/INC 92209)>* **STRICTLY 4 MY N.I.G.G.A.Z.** 24
– Holler if ya hear me / 2Pac's theme / Point the finga / Something 2 die 4 / Last wordz / Souljah's revenge / Peep game / Strugglin' / Guess who's back / Representin' / Keep ya head up / Strictly 4 my N.I.G.G.A.Z. / Streetz R deathrow / I get around / Papa'z song / Five deadly venomz. *(cd re-iss. Feb97; same) (cd re-iss. Mar98 on 'Jive'; CHIP 197)*

Jun 93. (c-s,cd-s) *<98372>* **I GET AROUND / NOTHING BUT LOVE** – 11
<with free c-s+=; 96036> – KEEP YA HEAD UP *<hit No.12>*

Apr 94. (c-s,cd-s) *<98303>* **PAPA'Z SONG / ('A'instrumental)** – 87

—— **2PAC** briefly set up THUG LIFE with **SKYE, MOPREME, MACADOSHIS + THE RATED R**

Nov 94. (cd/c; as THUG LIFE) *<(6544 92360-2/-4)>* **THUG LIFE VOLUME 1** 42
– Bury me a G / Don't get it twisted / Shit don't stop (THUG LIFE & YNV) / Pour out a little liquor / Stay true / How long will they mourn me? (THUG LIFE & NATE DOGG) / Under pressure / Street fame / Cradle to the grave / Str8 ballin'. *(cd re-iss. Feb97; IND 92360) (cd re-iss. Mar98 on 'Jive'; CHIP 198)*

Mar 95. (cd/c/lp) *<(6544 92399-2/-4/-1)>* **ME AGAINST THE WORLD** 1
– Intro / If I die 2nite / Me against the world / So many tears / Temptations / Young niggaz / Heavy in the game / Lord knows / Dear mama / It ain't easy / Can U get away / Old school / Fuck the world / Death around the corner / Outlaw. *(cd re-iss. Feb97; IND 92399) (cd re-iss. Mar98 on 'Jive'; CHIP 200)*

Jun 95. (c-s,cd-s) *<95748>* **SO MANY TEARS / (track by Dramacydal)** – 44

Aug 95. (c-s) *(A 8156C)* **DEAR MAMA / OLD SCHOOL** Mar95 9
(12"+=/cd-s+=) *(A 8156 T/CD)* – ('A'mixes).
(above on 'Atlantic' UK)

Sep 95. (12",cd-s) *<98120>* **TEMPTATIONS (mixes) / ME AGAINST THE WORLD (mixes)** – 68

Death Row Death Row

Mar 96. (d-cd/d-c) *(524249-2/-4)* *<524204>* **ALL EYEZ ON ME** 33 Feb96 1
– Book 1:- Ambitionz az a ridah / All bout u / Skandalouz / Got my mind made up / How do u want it / 2 of Amerikaz most wanted / No more pain / Heartz of men / Life goes on / Only God can judge me / Tradin war stories / California love / I ain't mad at cha / What'z ya phone # // Book 2:- Can't c me / Shorty wanna be a thug / Holla at me / Wonda why they call U bitch / When we ride / Thug passion / Picture me rollin' / Check out time / Ratha be ya nigga / All eyez on me / Run tha streetz / Ain't hard 2 find / Heaven ain't hard 2 find. *(d-cd-iss. Sep02)* – hit UK No.65

Apr 96. (c-s; 2PAC featuring DR.DRE) *(DRWMC 3)*
CALIFORNIA LOVE / (instrumental) 6 –
(12"+=/cd-s+=) *(12DRW/DRWCD 3)* – ('A'mixes)

Jul 96. (c-s; 2PAC featuring KC and JOJO / 2PAC featuring DR.DRE and ROGER TRAUTMAN) *(DRWMC 4)*
<854652> **HOW DO U WANT IT / CALIFORNIA LOVE** 17 1
6
(12"+=/cd-s+=) *(12DRW/DRWCD 4)* – 2 of Amerikaz most wanted / Hit 'em up.

—— 2PAC was shot dead on the 13th September, 1996 (below were posthumous releases)

Nov 96. (c-s) *(DRWMC 5)* **I AIN'T MAD AT CHA / SKANDALOUZ** 13 –
(12"+=) *(12DRW 5)* – Got my mind made up.
(cd-s++=) *(DRWCD 5)* – Heartz of men.

Jive Amaru – Death Row – Interscope

Nov 97. (d-cd/d-c) *(CHIP/HIPC 195)* *<41630>* **R U STILL DOWN? (REMEMBER ME)** 44 2
– Redemption / Open fire / R U still down? (remember me) / Hellrazor / Thug style / I wonder if Heaven got a ghetto / Nothing to lose / I'm gettin' money / Lie to kick it / Fuck all y'all / Let them thangs go / Definition of a thug nigga // Ready 4 whatever / When I get free / Hold on be strong / I'm losin' it / Fake ass bitches / Do for love / Enemies with me / Nothin'

but love / 16 on death row / I wonder if Heaven got a ghetto (hip hop version) / When I get free II / Black starry night / Only fear of death.

Dec 97. (c-s) *(JIVEC 446)* *<42500>* **I WONDER IF HEAVEN GOT A GHETTO / WHEN I GET FREE** [21] [67]
(12"+=/cd-s+=) *(JIVE T/CD 446)* – ('A'mixes).

Jun 98. (c-s) *(051851-4)* *<42516>* **DO FOR LOVE / BRENDA'S GOT A BABY** [12] Mar98 [21]
(12"+=/cd-s+=) *(051851-6/-2)* – ('A'mixes; soul society / Pic-a-dil-yo!).
(above credited in the States to 2PAC featuring ERIC WILLIAMS)

Nov 98. (d-cd/d-c/q-lp) *Jive; (052266-2/-4/-1) / Amaru – Death Row – Interscope; <490307>* **GREATEST HITS** (compilation) [17] [3]
– Keep ya head up / 2 of Americaz most wanted / Temptations / God bless the dead / Hail Mary / Me against the world / How do you want it? / So many tears / Unconditional love / Trapped / Life goes on / Hit 'em up // Troublesome '96 / Brenda's got a baby / I ain't mad at cha / I get around / Changes / California love / Picture me rollin' / How long will they mourn me / Toss it up (remix) / Dear mama / All bout U (w/ TOPP DOGG) / To live & die in L.A. / Heartz of men. *(d-cd re-iss. Jul01; same)* – hit UK No.25

Feb 99. (c-s) *(052283-4)* *<radio cut>* **CHANGES / ('A'mix)** [3] Nov98 [32]
(12"+=/cd-s+=) *(052283-0/-2)* – ('A'mixes).

Jun 99. (c-s) *(052334-4/-2)* **DEAR MAMA / (instrumental)** [27] [–]
(cd-s) *(052370-2)* – (2-'A'mixes by Moe Z).

Dec 99. (cd/c; by 2PAC + OUTLAWZ) *<(490413-2/-4)>* **STILL I RISE** [75] [6]
– Letter to the president / Still I rise / Secretz of war / Baby don't cry (keep ya head up II) / As the world turns / Black Jesuz / Homeboyz / Hell 4 a hustler / High speed / The good die young / Killuminati / Teardrops and closed caskets / Tattoo tears / U can be touched / Y'all don't know us. *<(clean version; 490417-2)>*

Feb 00. (-; by 2PAC + OUTLAWZ) *<radio cut>* **BABY DON'T CRY (KEEP YOUR HEAD UP II)** [–] [72]

Apr 01. (d-cd) *<(490840-2)>* **UNTIL THE END OF TIME** [33] [1]
– Ballad of a dead soulja / Fuck friendz / Lil' homies / Let 'em have it / Good life / Letter 2 my unborn / Breathin' / Happy home / All out / Fuckin' wit the wrong nigga / Thug n U thug n me (remix) / Everything they owe / Until the end of time / M.O.B. / World wide mob figgaz / Big skye (intelude) / My closest roaddogz / Niggaz nature (remix) / When thugz cry / U don't have to worry / This ain't livin' / Why U turn me on / Lastonesleft / Thug n U thug me (Hutch mix) / Words 2 my first born / Let 'em have it (committee mix) / Runnin' on E / When I get free / Until the end of time (RP remix).

Jun 01. (c-s/12") *(497581-1/-4)* *<radio cut>* **UNTIL THE END OF TIME. / THUG N THUG N ME / BABY DON'T CRY (KEEP YA HEAD UP)** [4] Apr01 [52]
(cd-s+=) *(497581-2)* – ('A'-video).

Oct 01. (c-s) *(497614-4)* **LETTER 2 MY UNBORN / UNTIL THE END OF TIME** [21] [–]
(12") *(497614-1)* – ('A'side) / Hell 4 a hustler / ('A'0instrumental).
(cd-s+=) *(497614-2)* – ('A'-video).

Nov 02. (d-cd) *<(497070-2)>* **BETTER DAYZ** [68] [5]
– Intro / Still ballin (with TRICK DADDY) / When we ride on our enemies / Changed man (with JAZZE PHA, T.I. & JOHNTA' AUSTIN) / Fuck em all (with OUTLAWZ) / Never B peace (with E.D.I. & KASTRO) / Mama's just a little girl (with KIMMY HILL) / Street fame / Whatcha gonna do (with KASTRO & YOUNG NOBLE) / Fair xchange (with JAZZE PHA) / Late night (with DJ QUIK & OUTLAWZ) / Ghetto star (with NUTSO) / Thugz mansion (with NAS & J. PHOENIX) / My block (remix) / Thugz mansion (with ANTHONY HAMILTON) / Never call U bitch again (with TYRESE) / Better dayz (with MR. BIGGS) / U can call (with JAZZE PHA) / Military minds (with CO CO BROTHERS & BUCKSHOT) / Fame (with KADAFI, KASTRO, NAPOLEON & YOUNG NOBLE) / Fair xchange (remix with MYA) / Catching feelins (with MUSSAMILL, E.D.I., NAPOLEON & YOUNG NOBLE) / There U go (with KADAFI, E.D.I., KASTRO & NAPOLEON) / This life I lead (with OUTLAWZ) / Who do U believe in (with KADAFI) / They don't give a fuck about us (with OUTLAWZ).

Feb 03. (c-s) *(497854-4)* **THUGZ MANSION / THUGZ MANSION (explicit with NAS)** [24] [19]
(12"+=) *(497854-1)* – Fuck em all (explicit).
(cd-s+=) *(497854-2)* – ('A'-video).

Universal Amaru

Oct 03. (cd-s; with NOTORIOUS B.I.G.) *<11042>* **RUNNIN' (DYING TO LIVE) / (version)** [–] [47]

Nov 03. (cd; as TUPAC) *(9861159)* *<154302>* **RESURRECTION** [62] [2]
– Intro / Ghost / One day at a time (with EMINEM & OUTLAWZ) / Death around the corner / Secretz of war / Runnin' (dying to live) (with NOTORIOUS B.I.G.) / Holler if ya' hear me / Starin' through my rear view / Bury me a G / Same song (with DIGITAL UNDERGROUND) / Panther power / Str8 ballin / Rebel of the underground / The realist killaz (with 50 CENT).

– compilations, etc. –

Sep 97. (cd) *Aim; (AIM 4001CD)* **1 IN 2 1 (2PAC – A TUPAC SHAKUR STORY)** [ ] [ ]

Jun 98. (cd; as 2PAC & NOTORIOUS B.I.G.) *Cashmoneybruthas; (CMBCD 1)* **WHO SHOT YA** [ ] [ ]

Jul 98. (c-s; 2PAC & NOTORIOUS B.I.G.) *Black Jam; (BJAM 9005)* **RUNNIN'** (rec.1995) / ('A'mixes) [15] [ ]
(12"+=/cd-s+=) *(BJAM 1205/6605)* – ('A'mixes).

Jul 98. (cd/c) *Eagle; (EAG CD/MC 050)* **IN HIS OWN WORDS** [65] [ ]

Nov 98. (12"/c-s/cd-s) *Eagle; (EAG CS/12/XS 058)* **HAPPY HOME (mixes)** [17] [ ]

Sep 99. (cd; as 2PAC & The NOTORIOUS B.I.G.) *ZYX; (20531-2)* **THE HERE AFTER** [ ] [ ]

Nov 00. (cd; by TUPAC SHAKUR & Various Artists) *Polydor; <(490813-2)>* **THE ROSE THAT GREW FROM CONCRETE VOL.1** [ ] [89]

Oct 03. (cd) *Koch; <(23 9530-2)>* **NU MIXX KLAZZICS** [ ] [15]

MAKAVELI

Interscope Interscope

Nov 96. (cd/c) *<(IND/INC 90039)>* **THE DON KILLUMINATI: THE 7 DAY THEORY** [53] [1]
– (intro) – Bomb first (my second reply) / Hail Mary / Toss it up / To live & die in L.A. / Blasphemy / Life of an outlaw / Just like daddy / Krazy / White man'z world / Me and my girlfriend / Hold ya head / Against all odds. *(re-iss. Feb97 on 'Interscope' cd/c; same)*

— In Jan'97, 2PAC plus NOTORIOUS B.I.G., RADIO, DRAMACYDAL & STRETCH, released collaboration single, 'RUNNIN', which hit US No.84

Apr 97. (c-s) *(INC 95529)* **TO LIVE & DIE IN L.A. / (album mix)** [10] [ ]
(12"+=/cd-s+=) *(INT/IND 95529)* – Just like daddy.

— In Apr'97, 2PAC & SNOOP DOGGY DOGG had a combined UK No.16 hit 'WANTED DEAD OR ALIVE'. 2PAC then guested on the SCARFACE single 'Smile' which hit No.12 US.

Aug 97. (c-s) *(INC 95521)* **TOSS IT UP / (album mix)** [15] [ ]
(12"+=) *(INT 95521)* – ('A'-instrumental).
(cd-s++=) *(IND 95521)* – ('A'-video).

Feb 98. (c-s) *(INC 95575)* **HAIL MARY / (album mix)** [43] [ ]
(12"+=) *(INT 95575)* – ('A'-instrumental).
(cd-s++=) *(IND 95575)* – Life of an outlaw.

TYPE O NEGATIVE

Formed: Brooklyn, New York, USA ...1988 by PETER STEELE (ex-CARNIVORE). One of the more compelling original bands skulking around the fringes of the metal scene, TYPE O NEGATIVE caused controversy from the off with the shocking artwork for the unambiguously titled debut album, 'SLOW, DEEP, HARD' (1991). Issued by 'Roadracer', the record's sleeve resembled a phallic symbol (talking of symbols, sex ones that is, the musclebound STEELE appeared naked in the August '95 edition of Playgirl!). A follow-up, meanwhile, 'THE ORIGIN OF THE FECES' (1992), featured a cover which left even less to the imagination, while music contained within its grooves lent the band's goth/industrial NIN-esque metal hybrid a demonic ambience. With something of a cult building around the band, 'BLOODY KISSES' (1993), became their most successful to date, while 1996's 'OCTOBER RUST' made it into the UK Top 30. In the more experimental climate of the mid 90's metal scene, TYPE O NEGATIVE emerged from the margins to become a significant player. Autumn '97 saw the release of an EP devoted to different mixes of TYPE O's Neil Young cover, 'CINNAMON GIRL'. Select the wittily titled 'Depressed Mode' mix for maximum black humour value. Their fifth set, 'WORLD COMING DOWN' (1999), was another to reach both the US and UK Top 50. • **Covered:** BLACK SABBATH (Black Sabbath) / SUMMER BREEZE (Seals & Croft).

Album rating: SLOW, DEEP AND HARD (*6) / THE ORIGIN OF THE FECES (*5) / BLOODY KISSES (*7) / OCTOBER RUST (*6) / WORLD COMING DOWN (*5) / THE LEAST WORST OF TYPE O NEGATIVE compilation (*7)

PETE STEELE – vocals, bass / **JOSH SILVER** – keyboards / **KENNY HICKEY** – guitar

Roadracer Roadracer

May 91. (cd/lp) *<(RO 9313-2/-1)>* **SLOW, DEEP AND HARD** ☐ ☐
– Unsuccessfully coping with the natural beauty of infidelity / Der untermensch / Xero tolerance / Prelude to agony / Glass walls of limbo (dance mix) / The misinterpretation of silence and its disastrous consequences / Gravitational constant: G = 6.67 x 10-8 cm 3 gm-1 sec-2.

Roadrunner Roadrunner

Feb 92. (cd/lp) *<(RR 9006-2/-4)>* **THE ORIGIN OF THE FECES (live)** ☐ ☐
– I know you're fucking someone someone else / Are you afraid / Gravity / Pain / Kill you tonight / Hey Pete / Kill you tonight (reprise) / Paranoid. *(re-iss. Nov94 cd/c; same) (cd re-iss. Nov97; RR 8762-2)*

—— added **JOHNNY KELLY** – drums

Aug 93. (cd/c/lp) *<(RR 9100-2/-4/-1)>* **BLOODY KISSES** ☐ ☐
– Machine screw * / Christian woman / Black No.1 (Little Miss Scare-all) / Fay Wray come out to play * / Kill all the white people * / Summer breeze / Set me on fire / Dark side of the womb * / We hate everything * / Bloody kisses (a death in the family) / 3.0.1.F. * / Too late: Frozen / Blood & fire / Can't lose you. *(cd+=/c+= *) (lp+=)* – Suspended in dusk.

Feb 94. (cd-s) *(RR 2378-3)* **CHRISTIAN WOMAN / ('A'mixes) / SUSPENDED IN DUSK** ☐ -

Aug 96. (cd-ep) *(promo)* **MY GIRLRIEND'S GIRLFRIEND / BLACK SABBATH (from 'The Satanic Perspective') / BLOOD & FIRE (remix)** ☐ ☐

Sep 96. (cd/c/d-lp) *<(RR 8874-2/-4/-1)>* **OCTOBER RUST** 26 42
– Bad ground / Love you to death / Be my druidess / Green man / Red water (Christmas mourning) / My girlfriend's girlfriend / Die with me / Burnt flowers fallen / In praise of Bacchus / Cinnamon girl / The glorious liberation of the people's technocratic republic of Vinnland by the combined forces of the United Territories of Europe / Wolf moon (including zoanthrobe paranoia) / Haunted / Outro.

Nov 96. (cd-ep) *(promo)* **LOVE YOU TO DEATH (radio) / SUMMER BREEZE (rejected radio) / LOVE YOU TO DEATH (album)** - mail-o -

Sep 97. (cd-ep) *(RR 2270-3)* **CINNAMON GIRL (Depressed Mode mix) / CINNAMON GIRL (US radio mix) / CINNAMON GIRL (extended mix)** ☐ -

Sep 99. (cd) *<(RR 8660-2)>* **WORLD COMING DOWN** 49 39
– Skip it / White slavery / Sinus / Everyone I love is dead / Who will save the sane? / Liver / World coming down / Creepy green light / Everything dies / Lung / Pyretta blaze / All hallows eve / Day tripper (medley).

Nov 99. (cd-s) *<(RR 2130-3)>* **EVERYTHING DIES / 12 BLACK RAINBOWS / EVERYTHING DIES (album version)** ☐ Jan00 ☐

Oct 00. (cd) *<(RR 85105-5)>* **THE LEAST WORST OF TYPE O NEGATIVE** (compilation) ☐ 99
– The misinterpretation of silence and its disastrous consequences (wombs & tombs mix) / Everyone I love is dead / Black No.1 (little miss-scare all mix) / It's never enough / Love you to death / Black sabbath (from the satanic perspective) / Christian woman / 12 black rainbows / My girlfriend's girlfriend / Hey Pete / Everything dies / Cinnamon girl (depressed mode mix) / Unsuccessfully coping with the natural beauty of infidelity / Stay out of my dreams.

☐ TYRANNOSAURUS REX

(see under ⇒ BOLAN, Marc)

U2

UB40

Formed: Mosley, Birmingham, England . . . early 1979 by ALI and ROBIN, sons of Scots folk singer, IAN CAMPBELL. The self-taught brothers built around them a multi-racial ensemble, who, due to their own jobless status and the country's unemployment figures, decided to name themselves after the dole card form, UB40. BRIAN TRAVERS, EARL FALCONER and JIM BROWN had been in their band while at Art College in 1977 and around two years later (including a lengthy stint playing in local pubs and clubs), they signed to David and Susan Virr's new label, 'Graduate'. Their protest reggae style was introduced to a wider audience as the group embarked on a prestigious tour with The PRETENDERS and 1980 saw UB40 hitting the UK Top 5 with the classic double A-side, 'FOOD FOR THOUGHT' / 'KING'. A Top 10 follow-up, 'THE EARTH DIES SCREAMING', was preceded by a Bob Lamb-produced debut album, appropriately enough titled 'SIGNING OFF' (as one does after procuring employment). In 1981, they formed their own label, 'DEP International' and recording studio, 'The Abbatoir', where they laid down the material for a second album, 'PRESENT ARMS'. The cosmopolitan reggae conglomerate continued to have massive hits throughout the 80's, including two chart topping covers, 'RED RED WINE' (from the pen of NEIL DIAMOND) and the CHRISSIE HYNDE collaboration, 'I GOT YOU BABE' (previously a 60's No.1 for SONNY & CHER). The former was taken from their album of cover versions, 'LABOUR OF LOVE' (1983) and marked their first real inroads into the lucrative US market. UB40 consolidated their position as Britain's foremost mainstream reggae act with an impressive run of hit singles and albums, continuing to translate traditional Jamaican stylings into more chart friendly pop. A temporary change in personnel was required in July 1988 when bassist FALCONER was jailed for six months on a drink driving charge. Upon his return UB40 went on to achieve further success in the 90's, their version of the ELVIS PRESLEY hit 'CAN'T HELP FALLING IN LOVE' topping the charts and a definite highlight of their equally successful long player, 'PROMISES AND LIES' (1993). ALI went solo in 1995, releasing the 'BIG LOVE' album before returning to the band for UB40's umpteenth outing, 'GUNS IN THE GHETTO' (1997). While 'LABOUR OF LOVE III' (1998) featured the usual set of covers, although a third instalment was perhaps milking the cash cow just a bit too hard and there were precious few moments of inspiration to refute that conclusion. After an extended break punctuated by a millennial 'BEST OF . . .' detailing their 20-year career, Birmingham's veteran reggae revivalists returned with 'COVER UP' (2001), the title track a reference to AIDS prevention rather than an indication of a covers set. 'HOMEGROWN' (2003) was notable mainly for the inclusion of UB40's highly unlikely contribution to England's Rugby World Cup hopes, 'SWING LOW SWEET CHARIOT', although there were hints at the brooding brilliance of old on the likes of 'YOUNG GUNS', a swipe at hip-hop's culture of violence. • **Songwriters:** ALI penned most material except singles I THINK IT'S GOING TO RAIN TODAY (Randy Newman) / MANY RIVERS TO CROSS (Jimmy Cliff) / CHERRY OH BABY (Eric Donaldson) / PLEASE DON'T MAKE ME CRY (Junior Tucker) / SMALL AXE + SOUL REBEL (Bob Marley) / KEEP ON MOVING (Mayfield-Marley) / JOHNNY TOO BAD (Wilson, Bedford, Bailey & Crooks) / VERSION GIRL (R.Thompson aka-Dandy Livingstone) / BREAKFAST IN BED (Dusty Springfield) / HOMELY GIRL (Chi-Lites) / KINGSTON TOWN (Andy Patrick) / HERE I AM (Al Green) / THE WAY YOU DO THE THINGS YOU DO (Smokey Robinson) / HOLLY HOLY (Neil Diamond). LABOUR OF LOVE and LABOUR OF LOVE II & III were cover albums featuring some already mentioned. ALI CAMPBELL covered HAPPINESS (Stevie Wonder-Syreeta) / SOMETHIN' STUPID (hit; Frank & Nancy Sinatra) / THAT LOOK IN YOUR EYE (Starks-Grey) / YOU CAN CRY ON MY SHOULDER (Berry Gordy) / LET YOUR YEAH BE YEAH (Jimmy Cliff) / DRIVE IT HOME (Ernest Ranglin).

Album rating: SIGNING OFF (*8) / PRESENT ARMS (*7) / PRESENT ARMS IN DUB (*5) / THE SINGLES ALBUM compilation (*7) / UB44 (*6) / LABOUR OF LOVE (*8) / GEFFREY MORGAN (*7) / BAGGARIDDIM (*6) / RAT IN THE KITCHEN (*7) / CCCP: LIVE IN MOSCOW (*4) / THE BEST OF UB40 VOLUME 1 compilation (*7) / UB40 (*7) / LABOUR OF LOVE II (*6) / PROMISES AND LIES (*6) / THE BEST OF UB40 VOL.2 compilation (*7) / GUNS IN THE GHETTO (*6) / LABOUR OF LOVE III (*5) / THE VERY BEST OF UB40 1980-2000 compilation (*8) / COVER UP (*5) / . . .PRESENT THE FATHERS OF REGGAE (*5) / HOMEGROWN (*4) / Ali Campbell: BIG LOVE (*5)

ALI CAMPBELL (b.ALISTAIR, 15 Feb'59) – vocals, guitar / **ROBIN CAMPBELL** (b.25 Dec'54) – guitar, vocals / **ASTRO** (b. TERENCE WILSON, 24 Jun'57) – toaster/**vocals** repl. YOMI BABAYEMI / **MICHAEL VIRTUE** (b.19 Jan'57) – keyboards repl. JIMMY LYNN / **EARL FALCONER** (b.23 Jan'59) – bass / **BRIAN TRAVERS** (b. 7 Feb'59) – saxophone / **JIM BROWN** (b.20 Nov'57) – drums / **NORMAN HASSAN** (b.26 Jan'58) – percussion

		Graduate	Sound
Jan 80.	(7") *(GRAD 6)* **FOOD FOR THOUGHT. / KING**	4	
Jun 80.	(7"/12") *(GRAD/12GRAD 8)* **MY WAY OF THINKING. / I THINK IT'S GOING TO RAIN TODAY**	6	
Aug 80.	(lp/c) *(GRAD LP/C 2)* **SIGNING OFF**	2	
	– Tyler / King / 12 bar / Burden of shame / Adella / I think it's going to rain today / 25% / Food for thought / Little by little / Signing off. *(free-12"ep w.a.)* **MADAM MEDUSA. / STRANGE FRUIT / REEFER MADNESS** *(cd-iss. 1986 on 'Target')*		
Oct 80.	(7"/12") *(GRAD/12GRAD 10)* **THE EARTH DIES SCREAMING. / DREAM A LIE**	10	
	(all above 45's re-iss. 1984)		
		DEP Inter.	A & M
May 81.	(7"/12") *(DEP 1/112)* **DON'T LET IT PASS YOU BY. / DON'T SLOW DOWN**	16	–
May 81.	(lp/c) *(LP/CA DEP 1)* **PRESENT ARMS**	2	–
	– Present arms / Sardonicus / Don't let it pass you by / Wild cat / One in ten / Don't slow down / Silent witness / Lambs bread. *(free 12" w.a.)*		

DON'T WALK ON THE GRASS. / DOCTOR X *(lp re-iss. Jan83) (cd-iss. Apr88 on 'Virgin')*

Jul 81. (7") *(DEP 2)* **ONE IN TEN. / PRESENT ARMS IN DUB** [7] [–]

Oct 81. (lp/c) *(LP/CA DEP 2)* **PRESENT ARMS IN DUB** [38] [–]
– Present arms / Smoke it / B-line / Kings Row / Return of Doctor X / Walk out / One in ten / Neon haze. *(re-iss. Jan83)*

Feb 82. (7"/12") *(DEP 3/+12)* **I WON'T CLOSE MY EYES. / FOLITICIAN** [32] [–]

May 82. (7") *(DEP 4)* **LOVE IS ALL IS ALRIGHT. / HOT-CROSS DUB** [29] [–]
(12"+=) *(DEP 412)* – ('A'live version).

Aug 82. (7") *(DEP 5)* **SO HERE I AM. / SILENT WITNESS** [25] [–]
(12"+=) *(DEP 512)* – Doctor X (live).

Sep 82. (lp/c) *(LP/CA DEP 3)* **UB44** [4] [–]
– So here I am / I won't close my eyes / Forget the cost / Love is all is alright / The piper calls the tune / The key / Don't do the crime / Folitician / The prisoner. *(re-iss. Jan83) (re-iss. +cd.remixed Apr86)*

—— DEP International were now distributed by 'Virgin'.

Jan 83. (7") *(DEP 6)* **I'VE GOT MINE. / DUBMOBILE** [45] [–]
(12"+=) *(DEP 612)* – Forget the cost.

Feb 83. (lp/c) *(LPCA DEP 4)* **UB40 LIVE (live in Ireland)** [44] [–]
– Food for thought / Sardonicus / Don't slow down / Folitician / Tyler / Present arms / The piper calls the tune / Love is all is alright / Burden of shame / One in ten. *(re-iss. Aug84) (cd-iss. 1988)*

Aug 83. (7"/12") *(DEP 7/+12)* *<2600>* **RED RED WINE. / SUFFERING** [1] Nov 83 [34]
(US re-iss. Aug88, hit No.1) (at same time, below album hits US No.14)

Sep 83. (lp/c) *(LP/CA DEP 5)* *<4980>* **LABOUR OF LOVE** [1] Nov 83 [39]
– Cherry oh baby / Keep on moving / Please don't make me cry / Sweet sensation / Johnny too bad / Red red wine / Guilty / She caught the train / Version girl / Many rivers to cross. *(cd-iss. Jul86)*

Oct 83. (7"/12") *(DEP 8/+12)* **PLEASE DON'T MAKE ME CRY. / SUFFERING (featuring NYA & NATTY)** [10] [–]

Dec 83. (7") *(DEP 9)* **MANY RIVERS TO CROSS. / FOOD FOR THOUGHT (live)** [16] [ ]
(12"+=) *(DEP 9-12)* – Johnny Too Bad (version).

Feb 84. (7") **CHERRY OH BABY. / FOOD FOR THOUGHT** [–] [ ]

Mar 84. (7"/12")(10"pic-d) *(DEP 10/+12)(DEPY 10)* **CHERRY OH BABY. / FRILLA** [12] [ ]

Apr 84. (7") **PLEASE DON'T MAKE ME CRY. / FOOD FOR THOUGHT** [–] [ ]

Sep 84. (7"/12") *(DEP 11/+12)* **IF IT HAPPENS AGAIN. / NKOMO A GO-GO** [9] [ ]

Oct 84. (lp/c)(cd) *(LP/CA DEP 6)(DEPCD 6)* *<5033>* **GEFFERY MORGAN** [3] [60]
– Riddle me / As always you were wrong again / If it happens again / D.U.B. / The pillow / Nkomo a go-go / Seasons / You're not an army / I'm not fooled so easily / Your eyes were open.

Nov 84. (7"/12") *(DEP 15/+12)* **RIDDLE ME. / D.U.B. (dub)** [59] [ ]

—— In Feb85, they appeared on charity single STARVATION with various BEAT members, etc. Released on 'Zarjazz' label, it hit UK No.33.

Mar 85. (7"/12") *(DEP 16/+12)* **I'M NOT FOOLED. / THE PILLOW** [ ] [ ]

Jul 85. (7"; UB40 & CHRISSIE HYNDE) *(DEP 20)* **I GOT YOU BABE. / THEME FROM LABOUR OF LOVE** [1] [–]
(12"+=) *(DEP 2012)* – Up and coming MC.

Jul 85. (7"; UB40 & CHRISSIE HYNDE) *<2758>* **I GOT YOU BABE. / NKOMO A GO-GO** [–] [28]

Aug 85. (m-lp/c)(cd) *<5090>* **LITTLE BAGGARIDM** [–] [40]
– Don't break my heart / I got you babe / Hip hop lyrical robot / One in ten.

Sep 85. (lp/c)(cd) *(LP/CA DEP 10)(DEPCD 10)* **BAGGARIDDIM** [14] [–]
– The king step mk.1 / The buzz feeling / Lyric officer mk.2 / Demonstrate / Two in a one mk.1 / Hold your position mk.3 / Hip hop lyrical robot / Style mk.4 / Fight fe come in mk.2 / V's version. (12"w.a.) **DON'T BREAK MY HEART. / I GOT YOU BABE / MI SPLIFF** *(re-iss. Apr90)*

Oct 85. (7"/12") *(DEP 22/+12)* **DON'T BREAK MY HEART. / MEK YA ROK** [3] [ ]

Jun 86. (7"/12") *(DEP 23/+12)* **SING OUR OWN SONG. / ('A' instrumental)** [5] [ ]

Jul 86. (lp/c)(cd) *(LP/CA DEP 11)(DEPCD 11)* *<5137>* **RAT IN THE KITCHEN** [8] [53]
– All I want to do / You could meet somebody / Tell it like this / The elevator / Watchdogs / Rat in me kitchen / Looking down at my reflection / Don't blame me / Sing our own song.

Sep 86. (7"/12") *(DEP 24/+12)* **ALL I WANT TO DO. / ('A'version)** [41] [ ]

Jan 87. (7"/12") *(DEP 25/+12)* **RAT IN MI KITCHEN. / ('A' long version)** [12] [ ]

Apr 87. (7") *(DEP 26)* **WATCHDOGS. / DON'T BLAME ME** [39] [ ]
(12"+=) *(DEP 26-12)* – ('A'live version).

Aug 87. (lp/c/cd) *<5168>* **CCCP: LIVE IN MOSCOW (live)** [–] [ ]
– All I want to do / Cherry oh baby / Keep on moving / Watchdogs / Don't blame me / Tell it like it is / Please don't make me cry / Johnny too bad / I got you babe / Don't break my heart / If it happens again / Rat in me kitchen / Sing our own song.

Sep 87. (7") *(DEP 27)* **MAYBE TOMORROW. / DREAD DREAD TIME** [14] [ ]
(12"+=)(c-s+=) *(DEP 27-12)(DEPC 27)* – Anything mi chat.

May 88. (7"; UB40 & CHRISSIE HYNDE) *(DEP 29)* **BREAKFAST IN BED. / ('A'instrumental)** [6] [ ]
(12"+=)(cd-s+=) *(DEP 29-12)(DEPX 29)* – ('A'other versions).

May 88. (lp/c)(cd) *(LP/CA DEP 13)(DEPCD 13)* *<5213>* **UB40** [12] [44]
– Dance with the Devil / Come out to play / Breakfast in bed / You're always pulling me down / I would do for you / 'Cause it isn't true / Where did I go wrong / Contaminated minds / Matter of time / Music so nice / Dance with the Devil (reprise). *(pic-cd.Dec88)*

Aug 88. (7") *(DEP 30)* **WHERE DID I GO WRONG. / ('A'instrumental)** [26] [–]
(12"+=) *(DEP 3012)* – Contaminated dub.
(cd-s++=) *(DEPX 30)* – Hit it (instrumental).

Nov 88. (7") <> **WHERE DID I GO WRONG. / DANCE WITH THE DEVIL** [–] [ ]

—— **LARRY BUSHELL** – bass temp.repl. EARL for 4 mths. Jul88.

Nov 88. (7"/c-s) *(DEP/+C 31)* **COME OUT TO PLAY. / CONTAMINATED MINDS** [ ] [ ]
(12"+=) *(DEP 31-12)* – Sing our own song (live).
(10"++=) *(DEP 31-10)* – ('A'instrumental).
(cd-s+=) *(DEPX 31)* – Dance with the Devil / Rat in mi kitchen.

Jun 89. (7"/c-s) *(DEP/+C 32)* **I WOULD DO FOR YOU. / HIT IT** [45] [ ]
(12"+=)(3"cd-s+=) *(DEP 32-12)(DEPX 32)* – ('B'version).

DEP Int. Virgin

Nov 89. (7"/c-s) *(DEP/+C 33)* **HOMELY GIRL. / GATOR** [6] [ ]
(12"+=)(3"cd-s+=) *(DEP 33-12)(DEPX 33)* – ('A'extended).

Dec 89. (lp/c)(cd) *(LP/CA DEP 14)(DEPCD 14)* *<91324>* **LABOUR OF LOVE II** [4] [30]
– Here I am (come and take me) / Tears from my eyes / Groovin' / The way you do the things you do / Wear you to the ball / Singer man / Kingston Town / Baby / Wedding day / Sweet Cherrie / Stick by me / Just another girl / Homely girl / Impossible love.

Jan 90. (7"/c-s) *(DEP/+C 34)* **HERE I AM (COME AND TAKE ME). / CRISIS** [46] [–]
(12"+=)(cd-s+=) *(DEP 34-12)(DEPX 34)* – ('B'dub version).

Mar 90. (7"/c-s) *(DEP/+C 35)* **KINGSTON TOWN. / LICKWOOD** [4] [ ]
(12"+=)(cd-s+=) *(DEP 35-12)(DEPXT 35)* – ('A'extended mix).

Jul 90. (7"/c-s) *(DEP/+C 36)* **WEAR YOU TO THE BALL. / SPLUGIN** [35] [ ]
(12"+=)(cd-s++=) *(DEP 36-12)(DEPXT 36)* – ('A'extended)./ / ('A'dub version).

Sep 90. (c-s,cd-s) *<98978>* **THE WAY YOU DO THE THINGS YOU DO** [–] [6]

—— (Oct90, teamed up with ROBERT PALMER on UK No.6 I'LL BE YOUR BABY TONIGHT)

Nov 90. (7"/c-s) *(DEP/+C 37)* **IMPOSSIBLE LOVE. / FIRST SHOT** [47] [ ]
(12"+=)(cd-s+=) *(DEP 37-12)(DEPXT 37)* – Council house.

Jan 91. (7"/c-s) *(DEP/+C 38)* **THE WAY YOU DO THE THINGS YOU DO. / MISSPENT YOUTH** [49] [–]
(cd-s+=) *(DEPXT 38)* – ('A'remix).

Mar 91. (c-s,cd-s) *<99141>* **HERE I AM (COME AND TAKE ME) / GATOR** [–] [7]

Nov 91. (7"/c-s) *(DEP/+C 39)* **BABY. / SHE CAUGHT THE TRAIN** [ ] [ ]
(12"+=)(cd-s+=) *(DEP 39-12)(DEPXT 39)* – Here I am (come and take me) (mix) / Dubmobile (live).

Nov 91. (c-s,cd-s) *<98654>* **GROOVIN' / COUNCIL HOUSE** [–] [90]

—— In Nov'92, teamed up with 808 STATE on a UK Top 20 version of 'ONE IN TEN'.

May 93. (7"/c-s) *(DEP/+C 40) <12653>* **(I CAN'T HELP) FALLING IN LOVE WITH YOU. / JUNGLE LOVE** [1] [1]
(12"+=)/ /(cd-s++=) *(DEP 40-12)/ /(DEPDG 40)* – ('A'extended)./ / Red red wine.

Jul 93. (cd/c)(lp) *(LP/CA DEP 15)(DEPCD 15) <88229>* **PROMISES AND LIES** [1] [6]
– C'est la vie / Desert sand / Promises and lies / Bring me your cup / Higher ground / Reggae music / Can't help falling in love / Now and then / Things ain't what they used to be / It's a long long way / Sorry.

Aug 93. (7"/c-s) *(DEP/+C 41) <12681>* **HIGHER GROUND. / CHRONIC** [8] Oct93 [45]
(12"+=)(cd-s+=) *(DEP 4112)(DEPD 41)* – Punjab dub (mix).

Nov 93. (7"/c-s) *(DEP/+C 42)* **BRING ME YOUR CUP. / BAD EKKO** [24] [ ]
(cd-s+=) *(DEPD 42)* – ('A'mixes).

Mar 94. (7"/c-s) *(DEP/+C 43)* **C'EST LA VIE. / PROMISES AND LIES (live)** [37] [ ]
(12"+=)(cd-s+=) *(DEP 43-12)(DEPD 43)* – Tyler.

Aug 94. (7"/c-s) *(DEP/+C 44)* **REGGAE MUSIC. / MATTER OF TIME** [28] [ ]
(cd-s+=) *(DEPDG 44)* – Things ain't like they used to be.

—— In Oct94, they featured on UK No.1 'Baby Come Back' by PATO BANTON.

Oct 95. (c-s) *(DEPC 45)* **UNTIL MY DYING DAY / ('A'instrumental)** [15] [ ]
(cd-s+=) *(DEPD 45)* – Sorry (live) / Bring me your cup (live).
(cd-s+=) *(DEPDX 45)* – ('A'-C.J.'s closet mix).

Oct 95. (cd/c) *(DUBTV/UBTVC 2)* **THE BEST OF UB 40 VOL.2** (compilation) [12] [-]
– Breakfast in bed / Where did I go wrong / I would do for you / Homely girl / Here I am (come and take me) / Kingston Town / Wear you to the ball / Can't help falling in love / Higher ground / Bring me your cup / C'est la vie / Reggae music / Superstition / Until my dying day.

Jul 97. (cd/c) *(DEPCD/CADEP/LPDEP 16) <44402>* **GUNS IN THE GHETTO** [7] [ ]
– Always there / Hurry come on up / I love it when you smile / I've been missing you / Guns in the ghetto / Tell me is it true / Oracabessa moonshine / Friendly fire / I really can't say / Lisa.

Aug 97. (c-s/cd-s) *(DEP C/DE 48)* **TELL ME IS IT TRUE / IT'S TRUE** [14] [ ]
(12"+=/cd-s+=) *(DEP X/D 48)* – ('A'mixes; Fugees / Sly & Robbie).

Nov 97. (cd-s) *(DEPDE 49)* **ALWAYS THERE / MAGIC CARPET (pincers)** [53] [-]
(c-s+=) *(DEPC 49)* – ('A'-remixed by Gogglehead).
(cd-s===) *(DEPDC 49)* – Hills and valley (Ninjaman).

May 98. (cd/c) *(DEP CD/C 17)* **UB40 present THE DANCEHALL ALBUM** [ ] [-]
– Magic carpet (with PINCHERS) / Force ripe (with MERCILESS) / Smile for me (with GENERAL DEGREE) / Waw waw waw (with Lt. STITCHIE) / More opportunity (with ANTHONY B) / Oh no baby don't go (with PETER METRO) / Love that I need (with BEENIE MAN) / Ladda bay (with MAD COBRA) / More love (with RED DRAGON) / Nuff love (with LADY SAW) / Who (SPRAGGA BENZ) / Hills and valley (with NINJA MAN) / No stray (with ROUNDHEAD).

Sep 98. (c-s) *(DEPC 50)* **COME BACK DARLING / IN THE PARK** [10] [-]
(cd-s+=) *(DEPD 50)* – ('A'instrumental).

Oct 98. (cd/c) *(DEPCD/CADEP 18) <48469>* **LABOUR OF LOVE III** [8] [ ]
– Holly holy / It's my delight / Come back darling / Never let you go / Soul rebel / My best girl / Good ambition / The train is coming / Blood and fire / Mr. Fix it / Stay a little bit longer / Someone like you / The time has come / Crying over you / Legalise it.

Dec 98. (c-s) *(DEPC 51)* **HOLLY HOLY / KING OF THE HILL** [31] [-]
(cd-s+=) *(DEPD 51)* – Legalise it (mixes) / Now you see it.
(cd-s+=) *(DEPX 51)* – Legalise it (high grade mix).

Apr 99. (c-s/cd-s) *(DEP C/D 52)* **THE TRAIN IS COMING / MISPENT YOUTH / THE WAY YOU DO THE THINGS YOU DO (remix)** [30] [-]
(cd-s) *(DEPDX 52)* – ('A'side) / Tyler / King.

Oct 00. (cd/c) *(DUBTVX/UBTVCX 3) <50525>* **THE VERY BEST OF UB40 – 1980-2000** (compilation) [7] Nov00 [ ]
– One in ten / Red red wine / Kingston town / Higher ground / King / Cherry oh baby / I got you babe / Come back darling / The Earth dies screaming / If it happens again / Don't break my heart / Can't help falling in love / Watchdogs / Tell me it is true / Rat in mi kitchen / Homely girl / Light my fire / Bring me your cup / Food for thought / Sing our own song. *(d-lp iss.Nov00 on 'Simply Vinyl'; SVLP 274)*

Nov 00. (cd-s) *(DEPD 53)* **LIGHT MY FIRE / KING (snipers remix) / HIGH ON A BREEZE** [63] [-]
(12") *(DEP 53-12)* – ('A'side) / King (instrumental).

DEP Int. E.M.I.

Oct 01. (cd-s; by UB40 featuring LADY SAW) *(DEPD 55)* **SINCE I MET YOU LADY / SPARKLE OF MY EYES / SINCE I MET YOU LADY (Oracabessa original)** [38] [-]

Oct 01. (cd) *(DEPCD 19) <811298>* **COVER UP** [29] [ ]
– Rudie / Sparkle of my eyes / Really / The day I broke the law / Let me know / Cover up / Walk on me land / Something more than this / Everytime / I'm on the up / Look at me / Since I met you lady / Walked in the rain / Write off the debt.

Feb 02. (cd-s) *(DEPD 56)* **COVER UP / COUVRE LA / DON'T FORGET TO SMELL THE ROSES** [54] [-]

Aug 02. (cd) *(DEPCD 20) <812675>* **UB40 PRESENT THE FATHERS OF REGGAE** [ ] Sep02 [ ]
– You could meet somebody (with MIGHTY DIAMONDS) / You're always pulling me down (with FREDDIE McGREGOR) / Bring me your cup (with GREGORY ISAACS) / Silent witness (with BRENT DOWE) / Always there (with HONEY BOY) / I love it when you smile (with ANTON ELLIS) / Don't do the crime (with JACKIE ROBINSON) / Watchdogs (with MAX ROMEO) / Love is all is alright (with BOB ANDY) / The earth dies screaming (with KEN BOOTHE) / Don't slow down (with WINSTON GROOVY) / Higher ground (with LEROY SIBBLES) / Pillow (with JOHN HOLT) / C'est la vie (with TOOTS HIBBERT).

Oct 03. (cd-s; by UB40 & UNITED COLOURS OF SOUND) *(DEPD 54)* **SWING LOW SWEET CHARIOT / SO DESTRUCTIVE (dub)** [17] [-]
(cd-s) *(DEPX 54)* – ('A'-stadium mix) / ('A'-acappella mix) / ('A'-video).

Nov 03. (cd) *(DEPCD 22) <593124>* **HOMEGROWN** [49] [ ]
– So destructive / I knew you / Drop on by / Someone like me / Freestyler / Everything is better now / Just be good / Young guns / Hand that rocks the cradle / Nothing without you / Nothing without you (dub). *(UK+=)* – Swing low sweet chariot.

– compilations, others, etc. –

Aug 82. (lp/c) *Graduate; (GRAD LP/C 3)* **THE SINGLES ALBUM** [17] [-]
– Food for thought / King / My way of thinking / I think it's going to rain today / Dream a lie / Tyler / Adella / Little by little / The earth dies screaming.

Feb 83. (12"m) *Graduate; (12GRAD 15)* **TYLER. / ADELLA / LITTLE BY LITTLE** [ ] [-]
(re-iss. 1984)

Mar 85. (d-lp/c) *Graduate; (VGD/+C 3511)* **THE UB40 FILE** [ ] [-]
(cd-iss. Jul86; VGDCD 3511)

Oct 87. (lp/c/cd) *Virgin TV; (UBTV/UBTVC/DUBTV 1)* **THE BEST OF UB40 VOLUME 1** [3] [-]
– Red red wine / I got you babe / One in ten / food for thought / Rat in mi kitchen / Don't break my heart / Cherry oh baby / Many rivers to cross / Please don't make me cry / If it hapens again / Sing our own song / Maybe tomorrow / My way of thinking / King. (cd+=extra tracks) *(re-iss. +cd.Jan89) (re-iss. cd+c Aug93, hit UK No.51)*

Nov 91. (d-cd) *Virgin; (DEPDDX 1)* **LABOUR OF LOVE I & II** [ ] [ ]
(re-iss. Nov94, hit UK No.6)

Oct 94. (3xcd-box) *Virgin;* **THE COMPACT COLLECTION** [ ] [-]

Jun 03. (3xcd-box) *DEP Int.; (DEPCDX 21)* **LABOUR OF LOVE VOL.1-3** [7] [-]

ALI CAMPBELL

Virgin Virgin

May 95. (7"/c-s) *(KUFF/+C 1)* **THAT LOOK IN YOUR EYE. / DRIVE IT HOME** [5] [-]
(cd-s+=) *(KUFFDG 1)* – ('A'mix).

Jun 95. (cd/c/d-lp) *(CD/TC/+V 2783) <40458>* **BIG LOVE** [6] [ ]
– Big love (intro) / Happiness / That look in your eye / Let your yeah be yeah / You can cry on my shoulder / Somethin' stupid / Big love / You could meet somebody / Talking blackbird / Pay the rent / Drive it home / Stop the guns.

Aug 95. (7"/c-s) *(KUFF/+C 2)* **LET YOUR YEAH BE YEAH. / YOU COULD MEET SOMEBODY** [25] [-]
(10"+=/cd-s+=) *(KUFF A/D 2)* – ('A'version).

Nov 95. (c-s; as ALI & KIBIBI CAMPBELL) *(KUFFC 5)* **SOMETHIN' STUPID / PAY THE RENT** [30] [-]
(cd-s+=) *(KUFFD 5)* – ('A'version).

U.F.O.

Formed: North London, England . . . 1969 initially as HOCUS POCUS, by PHIL MOGG, PETE WAY, MICK BOLTON and ANDY PARKER. Gaining a deal with 'Beacon' records in the early 70's, UFO had a surprising degree of success in Japan and Germany, where their blend of boogified space-rock (embellished with extended jams) sold like hotcakes. Their version of Eddie Cochran's 'C'MON EVERYBODY' (1972) was a massive hit in the far east, although Britain had previously shunned their pretentiously unremarkable first two albums, the thoughtfully titled 'UFO 1' and 'UFO 2 – FLYING' (both 1971). When BOLTON departed in 1972, his place was filled by a succession of guitarists, MICHAEL SCHENKER (ex-SCORPIONS) finally getting the permanent job the following year when BERNIE MARSDEN (who had replaced LARRY WALLIS; ex-PINK FAIRIES) departed for a bit of WILD TURKEY. Signing to 'Chrysalis' in 1974, UFO changed their style dramatically, hard-rock becoming their paymaster with classic songs such as 'DOCTOR, DOCTOR' and 'ROCK BOTTOM' featuring "heavily" on their label debut that year, 'PHENOMENON'. Between mid '74 and early '75, they added a fifth member, PAUL CHAPMAN (ex-SKID ROW), although the group soon reverted to a quartet when the guitarist joined LONE STAR. 'FORCE IT' was pushed out in the same year, the album immediately securing a Top 75 placing in the States where SCHENKER's fingering on his "Flying V" style guitar was as much talked about as the record. For their follow-up set, the mildly disappointing 'NO HEAVY PETTIN'' (1976), they added keyboard player, DANNY PEYRONEL, although he was subsequently replaced by PAUL RAYMOND on the 1977 disc, 'LIGHTS OUT'. A definite improvement, UFO landed in America properly this time, hitting their Top 30 with a blistering attack on tracks such as 'TOO HOT TO HANDLE' and a cover of Love's 'ALONE AGAIN OR'. 1978's 'OBSESSION' (featuring the classic hard-rock anthem, 'ONLY YOU CAN ROCK ME'), was again plucked from the stars, although after a live set, 'STRANGERS IN THE NIGHT' (1979), SCHENKER decided to return to The SCORPIONS. PAUL CHAPMAN returned for one GEORGE MARTIN-produced album, 'NO PLACE TO RUN' (1980), although it was clear the only thing taking off in UFO was the group members. PAUL RAYMOND joined SCHENKER in his new group and was replaced by NEIL CARTER prior to the recording of their 1981 set, 'THE WILD, THE WILLING AND THE INNOCENT', an aggressive piece of class that made its mark in Britain. All seemed well after 'MECHANIX' peaked at No.8 in the British charts in '82, however, PETE WAY was another to jump ship, the bassist eventually reappearing in his WAYSTED outfit. Former punk PAUL GRAY (from The DAMNED and EDDIE & THE HOT RODS), filled in on the 1983 set, 'MAKING CONTACT', although this was hardly the standard their fans had come to expect. They split soon after, MOGG and cohorts reforming many times over the next decade but never quite getting off the ground. • **Songwriters:** Mostly WAY / MOGG or CHAPMAN / MOGG, with both variations sometimes adding SCHENKER or CARTER. • **Trivia:** PHIL MOGG's nephew, NIGEL MOGG, became relatively famous in the band, The QUIREBOYS.

Album rating: U.F.O. 1 (*2) / U.F.O. 2 – FLYING (*3) / LIVE IN JAPAN (*5) / PHENOMENON (*6) / FORCE IT (*6) / NO HEAVY PETTIN' (*5) / LIGHTS OUT (*7) / OBSESSION (*8) / STRANGERS IN THE NIGHT (*8) / NO PLACE TO RUN (*6) / THE WILD, THE WILLING + THE INNOCENT (*8) / MECHANIX (*6) / MAKING CONTACT (*5) / HEADSTONE – THE BEST OF U.F.O. compilation (*7) / MISDEMEANOUR (*4) / AIN'T MISBEHAVIN' (*4) / HIGH STAKES AND DANGEROUS MEN (*5) / LIGHTS OUT IN TOKYO (*5) / WALK ON WATER (*3) / COVENANT (*4) / Mogg/Way: EDGE OF THE WORLD (*5) / CHOCOLATE BOX (*4)

PHIL MOGG (b.1951) – vocals / **PETE WAY** – bass / **MICK BOLTON** – guitar / **ANDY PARKER** – drums

Beacon | Rare Earth

1970. (7") *(BEA 161)* **SHAKE IT ABOUT. / EVIL** [ ] [–]

Jan 71. (lp) *(BES 12)* <524> **UFO** [ ] [ ]
– Unidentified flying object / Boogie / C'mon everybody / Shake it about / Melinda / Timothy / Follow you home / Treacle people / Who do you love / Evito. *(cd-iss. Apr91 on 'Line'; GACD 900691) (cd re-iss. Feb99 on 'Repertoire'; RR 4742)*

Jan 71. (7") *(BEA 165)* **COME AWAY MELINDA. / UNIDENTIFIED FLYING OBJECT** [ ] [–]

Jun 71. (7") *(BEA 172)* **BOOGIE FOR GEORGE. / TREACLE PEOPLE** [ ] [–]

Oct 71. (7") *(BEA 181)* **PRINCE KAJUKU. / THE COMING OF PRINCE KAJUKU** [ ] [–]

Oct 71. (lp) *(BEAS 19)* **UFO 2 – FLYING** [ ] [–]
– Silver bird / Star storm / Prince Kajuku / Coming of Prince Kajuku / Flying. *(re-iss. Feb72; same) (cd-iss. Apr91 on 'Line'; GACD 900694) (cd re-iss. Feb99 on 'Repertoire'; RR 4743)*

Nova | not iss.

1972. (lp) *(621454>* **UFO: LIVE (live in Japan)** [–] German [–]
– C'mon everybody / Who do you love / Loving cup / Prince Kajaku – The coming of Prince Kajuku / Boogie for George / Follow you home. *(UK-iss.1982 on 'AKA'; AKP 2) (cd-iss. Oct98 on 'Repertoire'; RR 4698)*

— In 1972, they issued a few 45's in Japan, incl. 'C'MON EVERYBODY'.

— (Jun'73) **MICHAEL SCHENKER** (b.10 Jan'55, Savstedt, Germany) – guitar repl. BERNIE MARSDEN to WILD TURKEY. BERNIE had repl. LARRY WALLIS (Nov'72) who had repl. BOLTON (Feb'72). WALLIS went on to PINK FAIRIES

Chrysalis | Chrysalis

Mar 74. (7") *(CHS 2040)* **DOCTOR DOCTOR. / LIPSTICK TRACES** [ ] [ ]

May 74. (lp/c) *(<CHR/ZCHR 1059>)* **PHENOMENON** [ ] [ ]
– Too young to know / Crystal light / Doctor doctor / Space child / Rock bottom / Oh my / Time on my hands / Built for comfort / Lipstick traces / Queen of the deep. *(cd-iss. Oct91 on 'Episode'; LUSCD 10) (cd re-iss. Feb00 on 'Liberty'; 524628-2)*

Jul 75. (lp/c) *(<CHR/ZCHR 1074>)* **FORCE IT** [ ] [71]
– Let it roll / Shoot shoot / High flyer / Love lost love / Out in the street / Mother Mary / Too much of nothing / Dance your life away / This kid's – Between the walls. *(cd-iss. Feb00 on 'Liberty'; 524599-2)*

— (Sep'75) added **DANNY PEYRONEL** – keyboards (ex-HEAVY METAL KIDS)

May 76. (lp/c) *(<CHR/ZCHR 1103>)* **NO HEAVY PETTING** [ ] [ ]
– Natural thing / I'm a loser / Can you roll her / Belladonna / Reasons love / Highway lady / On with the action / A fool in love / Martian landscape.

— (Jul'76) **PAUL RAYMOND** – keyboards, guitar (ex-SAVOY BROWN) repl. DANNY

Apr 77. (7") *(CHS 2146)* **ALONE AGAIN OR. / ELECTRIC PHASE** [ ] [ ]

May 77. (lp/c) *(<CHR/ZCHR 1127>)* **LIGHTS OUT** [54] [23]
– Too hot to handle / Just another suicide / Try me / Lights out / Gettin' ready / Alone again or / Electric phase / Love to love. *(cd-iss. 1987; ACCD 1127) (cd-re-iss. Jul91 on 'Episode'; LUSCD 9) (cd re-iss. Aug99 on 'EMI'; 521309-2)*

Jun 77. (7") **TOO HOT TO HANDLE. / ELECTRIC PHASE** [–] [ ]

Jun 78. (lp/c) *(<CDL/ZCDL 1182>)* **OBSESSION** [26] [41]
– Only you can rock me / Pack it up (and go) / Arbory Hill / Ain't no baby / Lookin' out for No.1 / Hot 'n' ready / Cherry / You don't fool me / Lookin' out for No.1 (reprise) / One more for the rodeo / Born to lose. *(cd-iss. Sep91 on 'Episode'; LUSCD 11) (cd re-iss. Aug99 on 'EMI'; 521310-2)*

Jul 78. (7"red) *(CHS 2241)* **ONLY YOU CAN ROCK ME. / CHERRY / ROCK BOTTOM** [50] [ ]

Dec 78. (d-lp/d-c) *(CJT/ZCJT 1)* <1209> **STRANGERS IN THE NIGHT (live)** [8] [42]
– Natural thing / Out in the street / Only you can rock me / Doctor doctor / Mother Mary / This kid's / Love to love / Lights out / Rock bottom / Too hot to handle / I'm a loser / Let it roll / Shoot shoot. *(cd-iss. Sep91; CCD 1209) (cd re-iss. Mar94; CD25CR 22)*

Jan 79. (7"clear) *(CHS 2287)* **DOCTOR DOCTOR (live). / ON WITH THE ACTION (live) / TRY ME** [35] [ ]

Mar 79. (7"clear) *(CHS 2318)* **SHOOT SHOOT (live). / ONLY YOU CAN ROCK ME (live) / I'M A LOSER (live)** 48

— (Nov'78) **PAUL CHAPMAN** – guitar returned to repl. SCHENKER who joined The SCORPIONS and later formed his own self-named group.

Jan 80. (7"red) *(CHS 2399)* **YOUNG BLOOD. / LIGHTS OUT** 36

Jan 80. (lp/c) *(<CDL/ZCDL 1239>)* **NO PLACE TO RUN** 11 51
– Alpha Centauri / Lettin' go / Mystery train / This fire burns tonight / Gone in the night / Young blood / No place to run / Take it or leave it / Money money / Anyday.

— (Aug'80) **WAY, MOGG, CHAPMAN + PARKER** recruited **NEIL CARTER** – keyboards, guitar (ex-WILD HORSES) repl. PAUL RAYMOND who joined MICHAEL SCHENKER GROUP

Oct 80. (7"clear) *(CHS 2454)* **COULDN'T GET IT RIGHT. / HOT 'N' READY (live)**

Jan 81. (lp/c) *(<CHR/ZCHR 1307>)* **THE WILD, THE WILLING AND THE INNOCENT** 19 77
– Chains chains / Long gone / The wild, the willing and the innocent / It's killing me / Makin' moves / Lonely heart / Couldn't get it right / Profession of violence.

Jan 81. (7"clear) *(CHS 2454)* **LONELY HEART. / LONG GONE** 41

Jan 82. (7"clear) *(CHS 2576)* **LET IT RAIN. / HEEL OF A STRANGER / YOU'LL GET LOVE** 62

Feb 82. (lp/c) *(<CHR/ZCHR 1360>)* **MECHANIX** 8 82
– The writer / Something else / Back into my life / You'll get love / Doing it all for you / We belong to the night / Let it rain / Terri / Feel it / Dreaming.

Apr 82. (7"/7"pic-d) *(CHS/+P 2607)* **BACK INTO MY LIFE. / THE WRITER**

— (Jun'82) on tour **BILLY SHEEHAN** – bass (ex-TALAS) repl. PETE WAY who formed FASTWAY and briefly joined OZZY OSBOURNE (later WAYSTED)

Jan 83. (lp/c) *(<CHR/ZCHR 1402>)* **MAKING CONTACT** 32
– Blinded by a lie / Diesel in the dust / A fool for love / You and me / When it's time to rock / The way the wild wind blows / Call my name / All over you / No getaway / Push, it's love.

Mar 83. (7"/7"pic-d) *(CHS/+P 2672)* **WHEN IT'S TIME TO ROCK. / EVERYBODY KNOWS** 70
(12"+=) *(CHS12 2672)* – Push it's love.

— Disbanded when MOGG suffered a nervous breakdown on stage. He resurrected the band in 1984 with **PAUL RAYMOND / PAUL GRAY** – bass (ex-DAMNED) / **JIM SIMPSON** – drums (ex-MAGNUM) / **ATOMIK TOMMY M.** – guitar (b. Japan)

Oct 85. (7"/7"sha-pic-d) *(UFO/+P 1)* **THIS TIME. / THE CHASE** –
(12"+=) *(UFOX 1)* – ('A'extended).

Nov 85. (lp/c) *(<CHR/ZCHR 1518>)* **MISDEMEANOR** 74
– This time / One heart / Night run / The only ones / Meanstreets / Name of love / Blue / Dream the dream / Heaven's gate / Wreckless.

Feb 86. (7"red) *(UFO 2)* **NIGHT RUN. / HEAVEN'S GATE**
(12"+=) *(UFOX 2)* – ('A'extended).

— (late '86) **DAVID 'Jake' JACOBSON** – guitar (ex-ERIC MARTIN) repl. RAYMOND

FM Revolver / not iss.

Mar 88. (lp/c/cd) *(WKFM LP/MC/XD 107)* **AIN'T MISBEHAVIN'** –
– Between a rock and a hard place / Another Saturday night / At war with the world / Hunger in the night / Easy money / Rock boyz, rock. *(cd+=)* – Lonely cities (of the heart). *(pic-lp Jan89; WKFMHP 107)*

— Disbanded Spring 1988. PHIL went into production mainly for his nephew NIGEL MOGG's new band QUIREBOYS

— **MOGG + WAY** re-united **UFO** adding **LAURENCE ARCHER** – guitar (ex-GRAND SLAM) / **CLIVE EDWARDS** – drums (ex-WILD HORSES) / **JEM DAVIS** – keyboards

Essential / Victory

Nov 91. (12"ep/cd-ep) **ONE OF THOSE NIGHTS. / AIN'T LIFE SWEET / LONG GONE** –

Feb 92. (cd/c/lp) *(ESM CD/MC 178)* **HIGH STAKES AND DANGEROUS MEN** –
– Borderline / Primed for time / She's the one / Ain't life sweet / Don't want to lose you / Burnin' fire / Running up the highway / Back door man / One of those nights / Revolution / Love deadly love / Let the good times roll. *(cd re-iss. Mar00; ESMCD 864)*

Feb 93. (cd/c) *(ESS CD/MC 191)* *<VICP 5204>* **LIGHTS OUT IN TOKYO LIVE (live)** Nov92
– Running up the highway / Borderline / Too hot to handle / She's the one / Cherry / Back door man / One of those nights / Love to love / Only you can rock me / Lights out / Doctor, doctor / Rock bottom / Shoot, shoot / C'mon everybody. *(cd re-iss. Apr95; ESSCD 386) (cd re-iss. Mar00; ESMCD 863)*

— The UFO who released '3RD PERSPECTIVE' in 1997 was not the same group

Eagle / C.M.C.

Nov 95. (cd/c) *(EAG CD/MC 009)* *<86239>* **WALK ON WATER**
– A self made man / Venus / Pushed to the limit / Stopped by a bullet (of love) / Darker days / Running on empty / Knock, knock / Dreaming of summer / Doctor, doctor / Lights out / Fortune town / I will be there / Public enemy #1. *(re-iss. Jan00; same)*

MOGG/WAY

Roadrunner / Roadrunner

Nov 97. (cd) *(<RR 8804-2>)* **EDGE OF THE WORLD**
– Change brings a change / All out of luck / Gravy train / Fortune town / Highwire / Saving me from myself / Mother Mary / House of pain / It's a game / History of flames / Spell on you / Totaled. *(re-iss. May99; same)*

S.P.V. / S.P.V.

Oct 99. (cd) *(<085-2155-2>)* **CHOCOLATE BOX**
– Muddy's gold / Jerusalem / Too close to the sun / This is a life / Lying and dying / King of the city / Death in the family / Whip that groove / Last man in space / Sparkling wine.

UFO

— re-formed yet again

S.P.V. / Shrapnel

Jul 00. (d-cd) *(087-2189-2)* *<SH 1142-2>* **COVENANT**
– Love is forever / Unreveled / Miss the lights / Midnight train / Fool's gold / In the middle of madness / The smell of money / Rise again / Serenade / Cowboy joe / The world and his dog / Mother Mary / Let it roll / This kids / Love to love / Out in the street / Pushed to the limit / Venus.

– compilations, others, etc. –

1973. (d-lp) *Decca; (SD 30311/2)* **U.F.O. 1 / FLYING** –

Dec 82. (d-c) *Chrysalis; (ZCDP 107)* **MECHANIX / LIGHTS OUT** –

Aug 83. (d-lp/d-c) *Chrysalis; (CTY/ZCTY 1437)* **HEADSTONE – THE BEST OF U.F.O.** 39 –
– Doctor doctor / Rock bottom / Fool for your loving / Shoot shoot / Too hot to handle / Only you can rock me / Love drive (SCORPIONS) / She said she said (LONE STAR) / Lights out / Armed and ready (MICHAEL SCHENKER GROUP) / Young blood / Criminal tendencies / Lonely heart / We belong to the night / Let it rain / Couldn't get it right / Electric phase / Doing it all for you.

Nov 85. (d-lp/d-c) *Castle; (CCS LP/MC 101)* **THE COLLECTION** –

Apr 87. (d-lp/c/cd) *Raw Power; (RAW LP/TC/CD 029)* **ANTHOLOGY** –
– Rock bottom / Built for comfort / Highway lady / Can you roll her / Fool for love / Shoot shoot / Too hot to handle / Gettin' ready / Only you can rock me / Looking for number one / Hot 'n' ready / Mystery train / No place to run / Profession and violence / Chains chains / Something else / Doing it for all of you / When it's time to rock / Diesel in the dust. *(cd re-iss. Jan94; CCSCD 316)*

Sep 89. (cd) *Line; (GACD 900704)* **SPACE METAL** –

Apr 92. (cd) *Windsong; (WINCD 016)* **BBC LIVE IN CONCERT (live)** –

Oct 92. (cd/c) *Chrysalis; (CD/TC CHR 1888)* **ESSENTIAL U.F.O.** –

Nov 92. (cd) *Dojo; (EARLD 9)* **EARLY YEARS** –

Mar 94. (cd/c) *Music Club; (MC CD/TC 153)* **TOO HOT TO HANDLE: THE BEST OF U.F.O.** –

May 94. (cd) *Beat Goes On; (BGOCD 229)* **OBSESSION / NO PLACE TO RUN** –

Jun 94. (cd) *Essential; (ESDCD 218)* **TNT (live in Texas)** –
(re-iss. Mar00; ESMCD 862)

Aug 94. (cd) *Beat Goes On; (BGOCD 228)* **NO HEAVY PETTING / LIGHTS OUT** –

Sep 94. (cd) *Beat Goes On; (BGOCD 230)* **THE WILD, THE WILLING AND THE INNOCENT / MECHANIX** –

Oct 94. (cd) *Beat Goes On; (BGOCD 227)* **PHENOMENOM / FORCE IT** –

May 95. (cd) *Spectrum; (550743-2)* **DOCTOR, DOCTOR** –

Nov 95. (cd) *M&M; (M&MCD 1)* **HEAVEN'S GATE LIVE (live)** [ ] [-]
(re-iss. May98 on 'Indelible'; INDELCD 18)
Jul 96. (cd) *EMI Gold; (CDGOLD 1050)* **THE BEST OF U.F.O.** [ ] [-]
Jul 96. (cd) *Beat Goes On; (BGOCD 319)* **MAKING CONTACT / MISDEMEANOUR** [ ] [-]
May 97. (d-cd) *Snapper; (SMDCD 122)* **THE X-FACTOR – OUT THERE . . . AND BACK** [ ] [-]
Feb 98. (cd) *Disky; <(WB 88595-2)>* **UNIDENTIFIED FLYING OBJECT** [ ] [ ]
Oct 98. (d-cd) *Repertoire; (RR 4720)* **TIME TO ROCK** [ ] [ ]
Apr 99. (cd) *EMI; (499403-2)* **BBC SESSIONS / IN CONCERT** [ ] [ ]
Jun 99. (cd) *Zoom Club; (ZCRCD 1)* **ON WITH THE ACTION (live at the Roundhouse 1976)** [ ] [ ]
Sep 99. (d-cd) *Zoom Club; (ZCRCD 20)* **WEREWOLVES OF LONDON (live 1988)** [ ] [ ]
May 00. (cd) *Brilliant; (BT 33037)* **UFO LIVE IN LONDON (live)** [ ] [-]
Aug 00. (cd) *EMI; (528502-2)* **THE BEST OF U.F.O.** [ ] [ ]
Jan 02. (cd) *Zoom Club; (ZDRCD 75)* **REGENERATOR – LIVE 1972 (live)** [ ] [ ]
Sep 02. (cd) *S.P.V.; (085-7431-2) / Shrapnel; <SH 1156>* **SHARKS** [ ] [ ]

ULTRASOUND

Formed: Newcastle, England . . . early 90's by the bulky (ex-POSSESSION) singer, TINY and guitarist RICHARD GREEN, whom he had met at a music course at Wakefield College. The pair decided to form wacky CARDIACS-induced outfit, SLEEPY PEOPLE, adding drummer ANDY PEACE in the process. Relocating to London (Acton, actually), they added VANESSA BEST on bass and MATT JONES on keyboards, although times were tough playing gigs for next to nothing and trying to explain that to the dole office the next day. TINY, with a look between EDDIE IZZARD on a very bad night and a chubby MORRISSEY, began to attract the right people to ULTRASOUND gigs. Among the A&R pack was 'Virgin' supremo himself, Richard Branson, who was enticed to go and see them perform by staff at his offshoot imprint, 'V2'. Fortunately, they played at NME's Unsigned Bands Gig early the following year, releasing a debut 45, 'SAME BAND', for 'Fierce Panda' soon after. This in turn, led to 'Nude' records subsequently giving them a deal, their second single, 'BEST WISHES', breaking the hard working quintet into the UK Top 75. In the summer of '98, they cracked the Top 30 with the excellent 'STAY YOUNG', although 'I'LL SHOW YOU MINE IF YOU SHOW ME YOURS', failed to register. Released the following March, 'FLOOTLIT WORLD' (a non-album cut) continued ULTRASOUND's chart campaign and previewed the double-CD debut album, 'EVERYTHING PICTURE'. A tad ambitious, overblown and retro 70's (especially in format!), the 100-minute plus set was just too much for the average punter although it did break into the Top 30. ULTRASOUND split soon after in October 1999. GREEN had already instigated The SOMATICS, a psychedelic guitar outfit with STEPHANIE GREEN and BRUCE RENSHAW. They issued the single 'LAST DAYS OF AN OLD TOWN' on Oxford's 'Shifty Disco' label in 2000, subsequently followed by the Chris Blair-produced, debut self-titled album in 2001. • **Covered:** Neil Young's 'HEY, HEY, MY, MY (INTO THE BLACK)', Pere Ubu's 'FINAL SOLUTION' and the Beatles' 'GETTING BETTER'.

Album rating: EVERYTHING PICTURE (*6) / Somatics: THE SOMATICS (*6)

TINY (b. ANDREW VICTOR WOOD, 1962, Birkenhead, Liverpool) – vocals / **RICHARD GREEN** – guitar / **MATT JONES** – keyboards / **VANESSA BEST** – bass / **ANDY PEACE** – drums

Fierce Panda / not iss.

Jul 97. (ltd-7"/cd-s) *(NING 35/+CD)* **SAME BAND. / OVER THERE / FLOODLIT WORLD** [ ] [-]

Nude / not iss.

Feb 98. (ltd;10"/cd-s) *(NUD 33 T/CD)* **BEST WISHES / KURT RUSSELL / BLACK HOLE** [68] [-]
Jun 98. (7") *(NUD 35S)* **STAY YOUNG. / UNDERWATER LOVE STORY** [30] [-]
(cd-s+=) *(NUD 35CD1)* – Can't say no.
(cd-s) *(NUD 35CD2)* – ('A'side) / Football meat / Hey, hey, my, my (into the black).
Oct 98. (12"/cd-s) *(NUD 39 T/CD)* **I'LL SHOW YOU MINE IF YOU SHOW ME YOURS. / LOVESICK / ONE PLUS ONE / FINAL SOLUTION** [ ] [-]
Mar 99. (7") *(NUD 41S)* **FLOODLIT WORLD. / DEATH OF A DRAG RACER** [39] [-]
(cd-s+=) *(NUD 41CD1)* – We will find love / Getting better.
(cd-s+=) *(NUD 41CD2)* – I'll show you mine (CD-Rom).
Apr 99. (d-cd/c/d-lp) *(NUDE 12 CDX/MC/LP)* **EVERYTHING PICTURE** [23] [-]
– Cross my heart / Same band / Stay young / Suckle / Fame thing / Happy times (are coming) // Aire & Calder / Sentimental song / Floodlit world / My impossible dream / Everything picture.

— ULTRASOUND disbanded in October 1999; MATT JONES would subsequently become MINUTEMAN who released an technoid album, 'RESIGNED TO LIFE' (2002). VANESSA BEST tried to embark on a solo career, while WOOD and PEACE reunited for a few ULTRASOUND outings; most got back together as SLEEPY PEOPLE to make one set, 'BURST NAILS IN A SHARP WALL' (1999).

SOMATICS

RICHARD GREEN – vocals, guitar / **STEPHANIE GREEN** – vocals, bass / **BRUCE RENSHAW** – drums, percussion

Shifty Disco / not iss.

Jun 01. (cd-s) *(DISCO 0106)* **LAST DAYS IN AN OLD TOWN / ASHES TO COAL** [ ] [-]

Beggars Banquet / not iss.

Apr 02. (7") *(BBQ 359)* **LEMONADE. / KILL TIME (OR IT KILLS YOU)** [ ] [-]
(cd-s+=) *(BBQ 359CD)* – Almost an introduction.
May 02. (cd/lp) *(BBQ CD/LP 227)* **THE SOMATICS** [ ] [-]
– For Claudette / Lemonade / Last days in an old town / LS2 9LZ / There is a happy land / Quietly / Come on heal me / Urban 45 / Guilt trip / Goodbye 25.

ULTRAVOX

Formed: London, England . . . mid '76 out of TIGER LILY (whose one and only single was a bizarre cover of Fats Waller's 'AIN'T MISBEHAVIN', subsequently withdrawn from release) comprising frontman JOHN FOXX, CHRIS CROSS, STEVE SHEARS, BILLY CURRIE and WARREN CANN. With the addition of violin (courtesy of CURRIE) and added synth power, the group became ULTRAVOX, initially with a ! at the end!. The fact that the band were picked up by 'Island' records and their eponymous 1977 debut album produced by BRIAN ENO says a lot about where ULTRAVOX! were coming from; artsy avant-pop combining elements of a punked-up ROXY MUSIC, the group were something of a cult live act. This didn't translate into sales, however, and despite an improved second effort, 'HA! HA! HA!' (1977), the group languished in relative obscurity. With ROBIN SIMON replacing SHEARS, they decamped to Germany to begin work on a third set under the auspices of electronic maestro, CONNY PLANK. The underwhelming result, 'SYSTEMS OF ROMANCE' (1978), failed to change the group's fortunes and by the Spring of '79, FOXX had abandoned ship for a solo career while SIMON went on to join MAGAZINE. The ubiquitous MIDGE URE was brought in as lead man, the singer having already cut his music business teeth in such diverse outfits as SLIK, The RICH KIDS and THIN LIZZY. He was also an integral part of moody synth-poppers, VISAGE, co-writing some of their material alongside mainman, STEVE STRANGE. Ironically, all this upheaval seemed to work wonders for all concerned, FOXX going his experimental electronic way and scoring a Top 40 hit almost immediately with the brilliant 'UNDERPASS' (early '80), while the newly revamped ULTRAVOX (now without a ! and signed to 'Chrysalis') broke the Top 30 that summer with 'SLEEPWALK'. 'VIENNA' (1980; again produced by CONNY PLANK) was released later that year, its Top 5 placing indicating that the new-look outfit had effectively cornered the burgeoning new romantic/electropop market. This was confirmed early in '81 when the album's title track narrowly missed the UK No.1 spot, its chilly, grandiose Euro feel and indelible melody managing to combine pretentiousness with mass public appeal. This was a talent which was to serve the group well over the ensuing five years, ULTRAVOX scoring an impressive run of seven Top 10 albums and a string of Top 30 hits. 'RAGE IN EDEN' (1981) was another Top 5 success, spawning three Top 20 singles including the po-faced 'ALL STOOD STILL'. The album also marked the end of the group's tenure with PLANK, GEORGE MARTIN overseeing production duties on 'QUARTET' (1982). The result was a markedly warmer sound and more commercial appeal, evident on the preceding single, 'REAP THE WILD WIND'. By the release of 'LAMENT' (1984), ULTRAVOX were a fully fledged pop band, the evocative heartbreak of 'DANCING WITH TEARS IN MY EYES' giving the group their biggest hit since 'VIENNA'. A bonus new track on the best selling compilation, 'THE COLLECTION' (1984), 'LOVE'S GREAT ADVENTURE', was another pop odyssey, its rolling synth crescendos a taster for the latest chapter in URE's solo career. Strangely enough, ULTRAVOX's last hit single was the sombre 'ALL FALL DOWN', its subject matter the war-torn Northern Ireland, an almost militaristic rhythm and uillean pipes utilised for greater effect. The track was lifted from the 'U-VOX' (1986) set, an album featuring the drumming talents of BIG COUNTRY's MARK BRZEZICKI. Realising they'd reached a creative impasse, ULTRAVOX disbanded the following year, URE taking up the solo career that had begun so successfully in 1982 with a Top 10 cover of Tom Rush's 'NO REGRETS' (made famous by the WALKER BROTHERS) and continued with the soaring pop of 'IF I WAS', a No.1 single in summer '85 (URE had also helped to mastermind the Band Aid single, 'Do They Know It's Christmas). He struggled, however, to resurrect his flagging solo career, the 1988 set, 'ANSWERS TO NOTHING' barely scraping into the Top 40 while a Spring '89 single, 'SISTERS AND BROTHERS' was withdrawn by 'Chrysalis'. Subsequently securing a new contract with 'Arista', URE returned in 1991 with the Top 20 hit, 'COLD COLD HEART' and a Top 40 album, 'PURE'. While ULTRAVOX made a low-key comeback in 1993 with a new singer, TONY FENELLE, and a new album, 'REVELATION', URE was conspicuous by his absence from the charts for most of the 90's. • **Songwriters:** FOXX and group until URE replaced FOXX. Covered only KING'S LEAD HAT (Brian Eno). MIDGE URE's solo career included THE MAN WHO SOLD THE WORLD (David Bowie) / STRANGE BREW (Cream).

Album rating: ULTRAVOX! (*5) / HA! HA! HA! (*5) / SYSTEMS OF ROMANCE (*5) / THREE INTO ONE compilation (*7) / VIENNA (*7) / RAGE IN EDEN (*6) / QUARTET (*5) / MONUMENT – THE SOUNDTRACK (*4) / LAMENT (*5) / THE COLLECTION compilation (*7) / U-VOX (*4) / REVELATION (*3) / INGENUITY (*2) / Midge Ure: THE GIFT (*6) / ANSWERS TO NOTHING (*5) / PURE (*4) / IF I WAS: THE VERY BEST OF MIDGE URE & ULTRAVOX compilation (*7) / BREATHE (*5)

TIGER LILY

DENNIS LEIGH (JOHN FOXX) – vocals / **STEVE SHEARS** – guitar / **BILLY CURRIE** (b. 1 Apr'52, Huddersfield, Yorkshire, England) – keyboards / **WARREN CANN** (b.20 May'52, Victoria, Canada) – drums / **CHRIS ST. JOHN** (b. CHRISTOPHER ALLEN, 14 Jul'52) – bass

Gull — not iss.

Mar 75. (7") *(GULS 12)* **AIN'T MISBEHAVIN'. / MONKEY JIVE** [–] w-drawn [–]
(re-iss. Oct77; GULS 54) (re-iss. Oct80 on 'Dead Good'; DEAD 11)

ULTRAVOX!

LEIGH became **JOHN FOXX** and ST.JOHN now **CHRIS CROSS.** (CURRIE now added violin, synthesizers.)

Island — Antilles

Feb 77. (7") *(WIP 6375)* **DANGEROUS RHYTHM. / MY SEX** [ ] [–]
Mar 77. (lp/c) *(ILPS/ICT 9449)* **ULTRAVOX!** [ ] [–]
– Saturday night in the city of the dead / Life at Rainbow End (for all the tax exiles on Main Street) / Slip away / I want to be a machine / Wide boys / Dangerous rhythm / The lonely hunter / The wild the beautiful and the damned / My sex. *(cd-iss. Jul92; IMCD 146)*
May 77. (7") *(WIP 6392)* **YOUNG SAVAGE. / SLIPAWAY** [ ] [–]
Oct 77. (7") *(WIP 6404)* **ROCKWROK. / HIROSHIMA MON AMOUR** [ ] [–]
(all 3 ULTRAVOX! singles were re-iss. Jul81)
Oct 77. (lp/c) *(ILPS/ICT 9505)* **HA! HA! HA!** [ ] [–]
– Rockwrok / The frozen ones / Fear in the western world / Distant smile / The man who dies every day / Artificial life / While I'm still alive / Hiroshima mon amour. *(free-7"w.a.)–* **QUIRKS. / MODERN LOVE (live).** *(cd-iss. Jul92; IMCD 147)*
Feb 78. (7"ep) *(IEP 8)* **RETRO E.P. (live)** [ ] [–]
– The wild the beautiful and the damned / Young savage / My sex / The man who dies every day.

— **ROBIN SIMON** – guitar (ex-NEO) repl. SHEARS to COWBOYS INTERNATIONAL

Aug 78. (7"/12"violet) *(WIP/12WIP 6454)* **SLOW MOTION. / DISLOCATION** [ ] [ ]
Sep 78. (lp/c) *(ILPS/ICT 9555) <7069>* **SYSTEMS OF ROMANCE** [ ] [ ]
– Slow motion / I can't stay long / Someone else's clothes / Blue light / Some of them / Quiet men / Dislocation / Maximum acceleration / When you walk through me / Just for a moment. *(cd-iss. Aug92; IMCD 148)*
Oct 78. (7"/12"white) *(WIP/12WIP 6459)* **QUIET MEN. / CROSS FADE** [ ] [ ]

— (Apr79) **MIDGE URE** (b.JAMES, 10 Oct'53, Cambuslang, Scotland) – vocals, guitar (ex-SLIK, ex-RICH KIDS, ex-THIN LIZZY, ex-VISAGE) repl. JOHN FOXX who went solo. ROBIN also departed to MAGAZINE. Now as ULTRAVOX, after dropping the exclamation mark!

Chrysalis — Chrysalis

Jun 80. (7",7"clear) *(CHS 2441)* **SLEEPWALK. / WAITING** [29] [ ]
Sep 80. (7",7"clear/12") *(CHS 2457/122457)* **PASSING STRANGERS. / SOUND ON SOUND** [57] [ ]
Oct 80. (lp/c) *(CHR/ZCHR 1296) <1296>* **VIENNA** [3] [ ]
– Astradyne / New Europeans / Private lives / Passing strangers / Sleepwalk / Mr. X / Western promise / Vienna / All stood still. *(cd-iss. 1985; CCD 1296) (re-iss. Dec92 on 'Fame' cd/c; CDFA/TCFA 3283) (re-iss. cd Mar94 + Jul94; same) (cd re-iss. Apr00 on 'EMI Gold'; 5255230)*
Jan 81. (7",7"clear) *(CHS 2481)* **VIENNA. / PASSIONATE REPLY** [2] [ ]
(12"+=) *(CHS 122481) - Herr X.*
Apr 81. (7",7"clear) *(CHS 2457)* **PASSING STRANGERS. / FACE TO FACE** [ ] [–]
(12"+=) *(CHA 122457)* – King's lead hat.
May 81. (7",7"clear) *(CHS 2522)* **ALL STOOD STILL. / ALLES KLAR** [8] [ ]
(12"+=) *(CHS 122522)* – Keep talking.
Aug 81. (7",7"clear/ext-12") *(CHS 2549/122549)* **THE THIN WALL. / I NEVER WANTED TO BEGIN** [14] [ ]
Sep 81. (lp/c) *(CHR/ZCHR 1338) <1338>* **RAGE IN EDEN** [4] [ ]
– The voice / We stand alone / Rage in Eden / I remember (death in the afternoon) / The thin wall / Stranger within / Accent on youth / The ascent / Your name has slipped my mind again. *(cd-iss. Jun87; CPCD 1338) (cd re-iss. Sep97 on 'EMI Gold'; CDGOLD 1097)*
Nov 81. (7",7"clear) *(CHS 2559)* **THE VOICE. / PATHS AND ANGELS** [16] [ ]

(12"+=,12"clear+=) *(CHS 122559)* – All stood still (live) / Private lives (live).

Sep 82. (7",7"clear/c-s/12") *(CHS 2639/122639)* *<42682>* **REAP THE WILD WIND. / HOSANNA (IN EXCELIS DEO)** [12] Mar 83 [71]

Oct 82. (lp/c/pic-lp) *(CDL/ZCDL/PCDL 1394)* *<1394>* **QUARTET** [6] Mar83 [61]
– Reap the wild wind / Serenade / Mine for life / Hymn / Visions of blue / When the scream subsides / We came to dance / Cut and run / The song (we go). *(cd-iss. 1988; CCD 1394) (cd re-iss. Sep98 on 'EMI Gold'; 496823-2)*

Nov 82. (7",7"clear) *(CHS 2557)* **HYMN. / MONUMENT** [11] [ ]
(12"+=,12"clear+=) *(CHS 122557)* – The thin wall.

Mar 83. (7",7"clear,7"pic-d) *(CHS 2676)* **VISIONS IN BLUE. / BREAK YOUR BACK** [15] [ ]
(12"+=,12"clear+=) *(CHS 122676)* – Reap the wild wind.

May 83. (7",7"pic-d,7"clear/12",12"clear) *(VOX/+X 1)* **WE CAME TO DANCE. / OVERLOOK** [18] [ ]

Oct 83. (lp/c) *(CUX/ZCUX 1452)* **MONUMENT – THE SOUNDTRACK (live)** [9] [ ]
– Monument / Reap the wild wind / The voice / Vienna / Mine for life / Hymn. *(cd-iss. 1986 +=; CCD 1452)* – Passing strangers / Visions in blue. *(cd re-iss. Jul96 on 'EMI Gold'; CDGOLD 1025)*

Feb 84. (7",7"clear/12") *(VOX/+X 2)* **ONE SMALL DAY. / EASTERLY** [27] [ ]

Apr 84. (lp/c/pic-lp/cd) *(CDL/ZCDL/PCDL/CCD 1459)* *<41459>* **LAMENT** [8] [ ]
– White China / One small day * / Dancing with tears in my eyes / Lament * / Man of two worlds / Heart of the country / When the time comes / A friend I called Desire. *(c+=/cd+=)* – (tracks * remixed). *(cd re-iss. Sep99 on 'EMI Gold'; 521834-2)*

May 84. (7",7"clear/12") *(UV/+X 1)* **DANCING WITH TEARS IN MY EYES. / BUILDING** [3] [ ]

Jul 84. (7",7"clear) *(UV 2)* **LAMENT. / HEART OF THE COUNTRY** [22] [ ]
(12"+=) *(UVX 2)* – ('A'instrumental).

Oct 84. (7",7"clear,7"pic-d/12") *(UV/+X 3)* **LOVE'S GREAT ADVENTURE. / WHITE CHINA** [12] [ ]

Nov 84. (lp/c/cd) *(UTV/ZUTV 1)(CCD 1490)* **THE COLLECTION** (compilation) [2] [ ]
– Dancing with tears in my eyes / Hymn / The thin wall / The voice / Vienna / Passing strangers / Sleepwalk / Reap the wild wind / All stood still / Visions in blue / We came to dance / One small day / Love's great adventure / Lament. *(w/ free 12")*

— guest **MARK BRZEZICKI** (b.21 Jun'57) – drums (of BIG COUNTRY) repl. CANN to HELDEN

Sep 86. (7",7"clear,7"pic-d) *(UV 4)* **SAME OLD STORY. / 3** [31] [ ]
(12",12"clear) *(UVX 4)* – ('A'side) / All in one day.

Oct 86. (lp/c/cd) *(CDL/ZCDL/CCD 1545)* *<207934>* **U-VOX** [9] [ ]
– Same old story / Sweet surrender / Dream on / The prize / All fall down / Time to kill / Moon madness / Follow your heart / All in one day. *(cd re-iss. Oct00 on 'EMI Gold'; 525611-2)*

Nov 86. (7",7"clear) *(UV 5)* **ALL FALL DOWN. / DREAM ON** [30] [ ]
(12"+=) *(UVX 5)* – ('A'version).

May 87. (7",7"clear) *(UV 6)* **ALL IN ONE DAY. / THE PRIZE (live)** [ ] [–]
(12"+=) *(UVX 6)* – Stateless.

— disbanded 1987, although U-VOX was formed by BILLY CURRIE, ROBIN SIMON and MARCUS O'HIGGINS – vocals; they toured 1989 playing ULTRAVOX songs

— **TONY FENELLE** – vocals; repl. MIDGE URE who was by now continuing solo

D.S.B. — not iss.

May 93. (cd/c/lp) *(DSB 3098-2/-4/-1)* **REVELATION** [ ] [–]
– I am alive / Revelation / Systems of love / Perfecting the art of common ground / The great outdoors / The closer I get to you / No turning back / True believer / Unified / The new frontier. *(cd re-iss. Sep02 on 'Puzzle'; PZLCD 106)*

Jun 93. (7"/c-s/7"clear) *(DSB 3097-7/-3/-1)* **I AM ALIVE. / SYSTEMS OF LOVE** [ ] [ ]
(cd-s+=) *(DSB 30975)* – ('A'extended).

— line-up: **CURRIE / BLUE / BURNS**

Resurgence — not iss.

Nov 95. (cd) *(RES 109CD)* **INGENUITY** [ ] [–]
– Ingenuity / There goes a beautiful world / Give it all back / Future picture forever / The silent cries / Distance / Ideals / Who'll save you / A way out, a way through / Majestic. *(re-iss. Mar02 on 'Puzzle'; PZLCD 105)*

– compilations, others, etc. –

Jun 80. (lp/c) *Island/ US= Antilles; (ILPS/ICM 9614) <7079>* **THREE INTO ONE** [ ] [ ]
– Young savage / Rockwrok / Dangerous rhythm / The man who dies every day / The wild the beautiful and the damned / Slow motion / Just for a moment / My sex / Quiet men / Hiroshima mon amour. *(re-iss. Nov86, cd-iss. 1989; IMCD 30)*

Mar 81. (12"ep,12"clear-ep) *Island; (DWIP 6691)* **SLOW MOTION / DISLOCATION. / QUIET MEN / HIROSHIMA MON AMOUR** [33] [–]

Dec 82. (d-c) *Chrysalis; (ZCDP 109)* **VIENNA / RAGE IN EDEN** [ ] [–]

Feb 87. (7") *Old Gold; (OG 9675)* **VIENNA. / THE VOICE** [ ] [–]

Apr 87. (7") *Old Gold; (OG 9698)* **DANCING WITH TEARS IN MY EYES. / REAP THE WILD WIND** *(12"-iss.Jan88)* [ ] [–]

Apr 88. (12"ep) *Strange Fruit; (SFPS 047)* **THE PEEL SESSIONS** (21.7.77) [ ] [–]
– My sex / Artificial life / Young savage.

Sep 93. (cd/c) *Spectrum; (550112-2/-4)* **SLOW MOTION** [ ] [–]

Aug 94. (cd) *Chrysalis; (CDCHR 6053)* **RARE VOLUME 2** [ ] [ ]

Jun 95. (cd) *Receiver; (RRCD 199)* **FUTURE PICTURE** [ ] [–]

Aug 95. (cd-s) *Old Gold;* **VIENNA / REAP THE WILD WIND** [ ] [–]

Oct 95. (cd) *MFP; (CDMFP 6175)* **DANCING WITH TEARS IN MY EYES** [ ] [–]

Nov 95. (3xcd-box) *Island; (5241522)* **ULTRAVOX! / HA! HA! HA! / SYSTEMS OF ROMANCE** [ ] [–]

Feb 98. (cd) *EMI Gold; (493465-2)* **EXTENDED – A COLLECTION OF 12" REMIXES** [ ] [–]

Nov 98. (d-cd) *Disky; (HR 85380-2)* **ORIGINAL GOLD** [ ] [–]

Mar 99. (cd) *Spectrum; (554898-2)* **THE ISLAND YEARS** [ ] [–]

Jul 00. (cd) *Disky; (SI 25080-2)* **THE BEST OF THE 80'S** [ ] [–]

Aug 01. (cd) *Armoury; (ARMCD 043)* **GREATEST HITS LIVE (live)** [ ] [–]

MIDGE URE

— had already started own solo career. Debut w / ex-COCKNEY REBEL **STEVE HARLEY** – dual vocals

Chrysalis — Chrysalis

Mar 82. (7") **I CAN'T EVEN TOUCH YOU. / I CAN'T BE ANYONE** [ ] [–]

Jun 82. (7"/12") *(CHS 2618/122618)* **NO REGRETS. / MOOD MUSIC** [9] [ ]

Jul 83. (7"/12") *(FEST/+X 1)* **AFTER A FASHION ("MIDGE URE & MICK KARN"). / TEXTURES** [39] [–]
Above 45 on 'Musicfest' w / ex-JAPAN bassist

— Dec'84 saw MIDGE co-write and create BAND AID with BOB GELDOF (BOOMTOWN RATS). They hit UK No.1 with famine relief single DO THEY KNOW IT'S CHRISTMAS.

Aug 85. (7",7"clear) *(URE 1)* **IF I WAS. / PIANO** [1] [ ]
(12"+=,12"clear+=) *(UREX 1)* – The man who sold the world.

Oct 85. (lp/c/cd) *(CHR/ZCHR/CCD 1508)* **THE GIFT** [2] [ ]
– If I was / When the winds blow / Living in the past / That certain smile / The gift / Antilles / Wastelands / Edo / The chieftain / The gift (reprise). *(re-iss. cd+c Apr93)*

Nov 85. (7",7"clear/7"pic-d) *(URE/+P 2)* **THAT CERTAIN SMILE. / THE GIFT** [28] [ ]
(12"+=,d12"+=,12"clear+=) *(UREX 2)* – ('A'instrumental) / Fade to grey.

Jan 86. (7",7"clear) *(URE 3)* **WASTELANDS. / THE CHIEFTAIN** [46] [ ]
(12"+=,12"clear+=) *(UREX 3)* – Dancer.

May 86. (7",7"clear) *(URE 4)* **CALL OF THE WILD. / WHEN THE WIND BLOWS** [27] [ ]
(12"+=,12"clear+=) *(UREX 4)* – After a fashion (w/ MICK KARN).

Aug 88. (7",7"clear) *(URE 5)* **ANSWERS TO NOTHING. / HONORARE** [49] [ ]
(12"+=,12"clear+=) *(UREX 5)* – Oboe.
(cd-s++=) *(URECD 5)* – (excerpts from lp below).

Sep 88. (lp/c/cd) *(CDL/ZCHR/CCD 1649)* *<41649>* **ANSWERS TO NOTHING** [30] [88]
– Answers to nothing / Take me home / Sister and brother / Dear God / The leaving (so long) / Just for you / Hell to Heaven / Lied / Homeland / Remembrance day. *<US cd re-iss. Aug98 on 'EMI'; 96824>*

Nov 88. (7",7"clear) *(URE 6)* *<43319>* **DEAR GOD. / MUSIC 1** [55] [95]
(12"+=) *(UREX 6)* – All fall down (live) / Strange brew (live).
(cd-s+=) *(URECD 6)* – Remembrance day.

— In Apr'89, SISTERS AND BROTHERS single was withdrawn.

— URE now with **MARK BRZEZICKI** – drums / **STEVE BRZEZICKI + JEREMY MEEHAN** – bass / **ROBBIE KILGORE** – keys / **SIMON PHILLIPS** – drums / **STEVE WILLIAMS** – perc./ etc

Arista | R.C.A.

Aug 91. (7") *(114 555)* **COLD COLD HEART. / FLOWERS** 17 | –
(12"+=/cd-s+=) – Supernatural *(written by GREEN; SCRITTI POLITTI)*

Sep 91. (cd/lp) *(261/211 922)* *<61010>* **PURE** 36 | –
– I see hope in the morning light / Cold, cold heart / Pure love / Sweet 'n' sensitive thing / Let it go? / Rising / Light in your eyes / Little one / Hands around my heart / Waiting days / Tumbling down.

Oct 91. (7"/c-s) **I SEE HOPE IN THE MORNING LIGHT. / THE MAN I USED TO BE** – | –
(12"+=/cd-s+=) – Madame de Sade.

May 96. (c-s) *(74321 37117-4)* **BREATHE / COLD COLD HEART (live)** 70 | –
(cd-s+=) *(74321 37117-2)* – No regrets / Trail of tears (live).

Jun 96. (cd/c) *(74321 34629-2/-4)* **BREATHE** – | –
– Breathe / Fields of fire / Fallen angel / Free / Guns and arrows / Lay my body down / Sinner man / Live forever / Trail of tears / May your good Lord / Maker.

Oct 96. (c-s) *(74321 42316-4)* **GUNS & ARROWS / TRAIL OF TEARS (demo)** – | –
(cd-s+=) *(74321 42316-2)* – Trail of tears (demo) / Man of the world (live).

not iss. | Orchard

Oct 00. (cd) *<7226>* **WENT TO CONEY ISLAND** (instrumental soundtrack) – | –
– The Gabby variations / High noon on 103rd Street / Surgery / Stan's disco / Stealing candy / Arriving at Coney / Midday suite / Bumper cars – Locket stealing / Pawnshop – Jerry Mahoney / Finding Richie again / Allegra / Richie calls his mom / Wedding / Lost point / Return to Skeeball.

Curb | Arista-MI5

May 01. (cd) *(CURCD 100)* *<03484>* **MOVE ME** – | –
– You move me / Beneath a Spielberg sky / Words / Strong / Let me go / Alone / Monster / Absolution sometime! / The refugee song / Four / Somebody. *(ltd-bonus disc)*

Jul 01. (cd-s) *(CUBC 070)* **BENEATH A SPIELBERG SKY** – | –

– (MIDGE URE & ULTRAVOX) compilations, etc. –

on 'Chrysalis' unless mentioned otherwise

Jan 93. (7"/c-s) *(TCCHS 3936)* **VIENNA. / WASTELANDS** 13 | –
(cd-s+=) *(CDCHS 3936)* – Answers to nothing / The voice.
(cd-s) *(CDCHSS 3936)* – ('A'side) / Call of the wild / One small day / Hymn.

Feb 93. (cd/c/lp) *(CD/TC/+CHR 1987)* **IF I WAS: THE VERY BEST OF MIDGE URE & ULTRAVOX** 10 | –
– If I was / No regrets / Love's great adventure / Dear God / Cold cold heart / Vienna / Call of the wild / Dancing with tears in my eyes / All fall down / Yellow pearl / Fade to grey / Reap the wild wind / Answers to nothing / Do they know it's Christmas? (BAND AID). *(cd+=)* – After a fashion (with MICK KARN) / That certain smile.

Oct 01. (cd) *(535811-2)* **THE VERY BEST OF MIDGE URE & ULTRAVOX** 45 | –

UNCLE KRACKER

Born: MATTHEW SHAFER, 6 Jun'74, Mount Clemens, Michigan, USA. Having met and bonded with KID ROCK back in 1987, SHAFER soon became the Rap-Rock superbrat's right hand man and made his vinyl debut via a contribution to ROCK's 1991 album, 'Grits Sandwiches For Breakfast'. He also had a hand in the writing of his sidekick's massive 'DEVIL WITHOUT A CAUSE' opus and generally paved the way for his own solo career. Signed to KID ROCK's 'Atlantic' subsidiary, 'Top Dog', SHAFER – in the guise of UNCLE KRACKER – finally unleashed his own album in the shape of 'DOUBLE WIDE' (2001). A finger lickin' deep fry-up of twangin hang-dog country, shit-kicking hard rock and hick hip-hop with a dollop of Detroit humour, the album was a mite more accessible than his compadres' recent outings although that didn't stop KID ROCK and his TWISTED BROWN TUCKER crew making their mark.

Album rating: DOUBLE WIDE (*6) / NO STRANGER TO SHAME (*6)

UNCLE KRACKER – rapping, DJ / with **JIMMIE BONES** – keyboards, vocals / **JASON KRAUSE + KENNY OLSON** – guitar / **MICHAEL BRADFORD** – bass / **STEFANIE EULINBERG** – drums

Atlantic | Atlantic

Jul 01. (cd/c) *<(7567 83279-2/-4)>* **DOUBLE WIDE** 40 Apr01 | 7
– Intro / Better days / What 'chu lookin' at? / Follow me / Heaven / Steaks 'n shrimp / Who's your uncle? / Whiskey & Walter / I can, I can, I can / Aces & 8's / You can't take me.

Aug 01. (c-s) *(AT 0108C)* *<radio play>* **FOLLOW ME / (album version)** 3 Feb01 | 5
(cd-s+=) *(AT 0108CD)* – ('A'-DJ Homicide remix).

Oct 01. (cd-s) *<85158>* **YEAH, YEAH, YEAH / (radio) / (album) / FOLLOW ME (ultimix)** – | –

Sep 02. (cd) *<(7567 83542-2)>* **NO STRANGER TO SHAME** – | 43
– Keep it comin' / Thunderhead Hawkins / In a little while / I wish I had a dollar / Drift away / Baby don't cry / I do / Memphis soul song / I don't know / To think I used to love you / Letter to my daughters / No stranger to shame. *(hidden+=)* – After school special.

Oct 02. (cd-s) *(AT 140CD)* *<85357>* **IN A LITTLE WHILE / (version) / I DON'T KNOW** – Sep02 | 59

2003. (-) *<radio>* **DRIFT AWAY** – | 9

UNCLE TUPELO

Formed: Belleville, Illinois, USA ... 1987 by schoolmates JEFF TWEEDY and JAY FARRAR (who had played in punk outfit, The PRIMITIVES – US), MIKE HEIDORN completing the line-up. A band that have achieved almost legendary status among alternative country afficionados, UNCLE TUPELO christened a whole movement with the release of their seminal debut album, 'NO DEPRESSION' (1990). Issued on the small 'Rockville' label, the record translated the raw expression and sonic assault of punk into a contemporary country context; the spirit of what TWEEDY and FARRAR were trying to do was best illustrated on the title track, an impressive excavation of an ancient CARTER FAMILY song yearning for the sanctuary of Heaven, performed with as much conviction as any bonafide gospel act. Follow-up set, 'STILL FEEL GONE' (1991) continued in the same vein, developing and updating country in a fashion a damn sight closer to GRAM PARSONS' cosmic vision than the polished dross coming out of Nashville. Yet it was the stark testimony of the PETER BUCK-produced 'MARCH 16-20' (1992) that really cut to the heart of American roots tradition, a breathtaking album of grainy originals and hard-bitten folk covers. While the quality of the songwriting arguably outstripped almost anything released under the banner of country/alt-country in the past twenty years, it was the bruised beauty of the vocals (especially FARRAR) that really brought on the goose-bumps and belied UNCLE TUPELO's relative youthfulness. The likes of 'GRINDSTONE', 'BLACK EYE' and the traditional 'MOONSHINER' resonated with what sounded like the careworn resignation of a lifetime's toil and trouble, the whole album religious in its rawness. Released to rave reviews, it didn't take long for word to spread and with major labels eager for a piece of the action, FARRAR and TWEEDY opted to sign for 'Reprise' (home to spiritual forefathers PARSONS and NEIL YOUNG amongst others). With FARRAR and TWEEDY maintaining a hard-drinking, volatile relationship at the best of times, 'ANODYNE' (1993) proved to be the final product of their mercurial partnership. A return to more upbeat material, the album featured a rousing cover of Doug Sahm's 'GIVE BACK THE KEY TO MY HEART' (featuring the cult Texan roots man on guitar) alongside more reflective fare like the gorgeously plaintive 'SLATE', one of the most perfectly formed compositions in the FARRAR/TWEEDY canon with fiddle arrangements to break the hardest heart. While many mourned the band's passing, fans could look forward to the prospect of two solo projects, FARRAR's SON VOLT and TWEEDY's WILCO. • **Songwriters:** All compositions FARRAR – TWEEDY except arrangements of traditional tunes, plus covers: I WANNA DESTROY YOU (Soft Boys) / NO DEPRESSION (Carter Family) / JOHN HARDY (Leadbelly) / ATOMIC POWER (Louvin Brothers) / BLUE EYES (Gram Parsons) / SIN CITY (Flying Burrito Brothers) / I WANNA BE YOUR DOG (Stooges) / EFFIGY (Creedence Clearwater Revival).

Album rating: NO DEPRESSION (*8) / STILL FEEL GONE (*9) / MARCH 16-20 (*7) / ANODYNE (*8) / 1989-1993: AN ANTHOLOGY (*8)

JEFF TWEEDY (b.25 Aug'67) – vocals, guitar, bass / **JAY FARRAR** (b.26 Dec'66) – vocals, guitar / **MICHAEL HEIDORN** – drums

Rockville Rockville

Aug 90. (lp) *<ROCK 6050-1>* **NO DEPRESSION** [-] [ ]
– Graveyard shift / That year / Before I break / No depression / Factory belt / Whiskey bottle / Outdone / Train / Life worth livin' / Flatness / So called friend / Screen door / John Hardy. *(UK cd-iss. Sep97; ROCK 6050-2)*

Sep 90. (7") *<ROCK 6055-7>* **I GOT DRUNK. / SIN CITY** [-] [ ]

Sep 91. (7") *<ROCK 6069-7>* **GUN. / I WANNA DESTROY YOU** [-] [ ]

Sep 91. (lp) *<ROCK 6070-1>* **STILL FEEL GONE** [-] [ ]
– Gun / Looking for a way out / Fall down easy / Nothing / Still be around / Watch me fall / Punch drunk / Postcard / D. Boon / True to life / Cold shoulder / Discarded / If that's alright. *(UK-iss.cd Nov92 on 'Yellow Moon'; BUFF 001CD)*

Nov 92. (7") *<(ROCK 6089-7)>* **SAUGET WIND. / LOOKING FOR A WAY OUT (acoustic) / TAKE MY WORD** [ ] [ ]

Mar 93. (cd/c/lp) *<(ROCK 6110-2/-4/-1)>* **MARCH 16-20, 1992** [ ] Aug92 [ ]
– Grindstone / Coalminers / Wait up / Criminals / Shaky ground / Satan, your kingdom must come down / Black eye / Moonshiner / I wish my baby was born / Atomic power / Lilli Schull / Warfare / Fatal wound / Sandusky / Wipe the clock.

—— **KEN COOMER** – drums + **JOHN STIRRATT** – bass; repl. HEIDORN

Warners Sire

Oct 93. (cd/c) *(9362 45330-2/-4) <45424>* **ANODYNE** [ ] [ ]
– Slate / Acuff-Rose / The long cut / Give back the key to my heart / Chickamauga / New Madrid / Anodyne / We've been had / Fifteen keys / High water / No sense in lovin' / Steal the crumbs.

—— arguments arose, FARRAR subsequently forming SON VOLT with MICHAEL HEIDORN, TWEEDY took STIRRATT + COOMER and formed WILCO

– compilations, etc. –

May 95. (c) *Dutch East; <6110>* **STILL FEEL GONE / MARCH 16-20, 1992** [-] [ ]

May 02. (cd) *Sony; (507612-2) <62223>* **1989-1993: AN ANTHOLOGY** [ ] Mar02 [ ]
– No depression / Screen door / Graveyard shift / Whiskey bottle / Outdone / I got drunk / I wanna be your dog / Gun / Still be around / Looking for a way out (acoustic) / Watch me fall / Sauget wind / Black eye / Moonshiner / Fatal wound / Grindstone / Effigy / The long cut / Chickamuuga / New Madrid / We've been had (live). *<(d-lp-iss.Jun02 on 'Sundazed'; SCLP 5153)>*

UNDERTONES

Formed: Londonderry, N. Ireland . . . late '75 by the O'NEILL brothers, DAMIAN and JOHN, alongside FEARGAL SHARKEY, MIKE BRADLEY and BILLY DOHERTY. Taking up the offer of a one-off singles deal with Belfast label, 'Good Vibrations', they released a debut EP in September '78 with the seminal 'TEENAGE KICKS' as the lead track. Immediately championed by DJ John Peel, this compelling slice of adolescent angst reached the collective ear of 'Sire' records leading to a prestigious deal. Their major label debut, 'GET OVER YOU', scraped into the Top 60 although they eventually cracked the chart later that Spring with 'JIMMY JIMMY', a boisterous post-punk stomper reminiscent of a wittier, more laid-back SHAM 69. This was closely followed by an eponymous debut album, establishing The UNDERTONES as one of the most promising and intelligent new-wave punk/pop bands in the UK. Like a more hyperactive KINKS, the band chronicled the nitty gritty, highs and lows of everyday life in such unforgettable pop nuggets as 'HERE COMES THE SUMMER', 'TRUE CONFESSIONS' and 'FAMILY ENTERTAINMENT'. Arguably, 'YOU'VE GOT MY NUMBER (WHY DON'T YOU USE IT), remains The UNDERTONES' finest moment, a jarring, insistent riff marking it out from the group's standard pop rush. While the song barely made the UK Top 40, The UNDERTONES were back in the Top 10 the following year with the sneering 'MY PERFECT COUSIN', a humorous tale of a goody-two-shoes relative which obviously struck a chord with more than a few disaffected youngsters. The accompanying album, 'HYPNOTISED' (1980), consolidated the group's standing, critically and commercially, a more assured set which also spawned another classic single in 'WEDNESDAY WEEK'. Inevitably, however, along with many of their contemporaries, The UNDERTONES increasingly moved away from the roughshod charm of old to a more refined sound. This was evident in the group's third album, 'THE POSITIVE TOUCH' (1981), only one track making the Top 20 ('IT'S GOING TO HAPPEN') despite such enduring material as the lovely 'JULIE OCEAN'. By 1983's 'THE SIN OF PRIDE', FEARGAL's quavering vocals and the group's boy-next-door image had been shelved for a blend of "alternative soul". Predictably, this didn't sit well with the group's more traditional fans who were unsurprisingly becoming increasingly critical of The UNDERTONES newfound sophistication. The imminent split eventually came in mid '83 with SHARKEY initially hooking up with VINCE CLARKE in The ASSEMBLY before launching a solo career. The O'NEILL brothers, meanwhile, formed the critically acclaimed THAT PETROL EMOTION, alongside with CIARAN McLAUGHLIN, REAMANN O'GORMAN and US-born frontman, STEVE MACK. Basing themselves in London from the mid-80's onwards, the TPE made their vinyl debut in summer '85 with the independently released 'KEEN'. A further indie single, 'V2' followed a few months later before 'Demon' took them on for a critically acclaimed ROLI MOSSIMAN-produced debut album, 'MANIC POP THRILL' (1986). Strikingly different from The UNDERTONES' three-chord rush, THAT PETROL EMOTION dealt in a more caustic, politicised brand of alternative pop/rock which embraced elements of 60's garage and psychedelia, their potential subsequently recognised by 'Polydor'. The major label backing paid almost immediate dividends as the band narrowly missed the UK Top 40 with their next single, 'BIG DECISION'. A follow-up album, 'BABBLE' (1987) appeared a couple of months later and landed the band their first and only Top 30 success; despite vocal support from the likes of John Peel and the NME, THAT PETROL EMOTION seemed unable to convert their potential into sales. Moving on to 'Virgin', they came up with the more experimental 'END OF THE MILLENNIUM PSYCHOSIS BLUES' (1988), featuring O'NEILL's political coup de grace, 'CELLOPHANE'. Yet he was unhappy with the life of a professional musician and subsequently moved back to Derry. A potentially fatal blow was overcome with the recruitment of JOHN MARCHINI and the songwriting development of McLAUGHLIN, the group attempting a final shot at pop glory with the 'SENSITIZE' and 'HEY VENUS' singles. Both were culled from 1990's 'CHEMICRAZY' album and both fell cruelly short of the Top 40 to the exasperation of the band, their label and their many advocates in the media. Dropped by 'Virgin', the band stuck it out for one final set, 'FIREPROOF' (1993) on their own 'Koogat' label before finally throwing in the towel. The O'NEILL's continued with the short-lived project, RARE. Following that band's demise, the pair, together with DOHERTY, BRADLEY and newly installed frontman, PAUL McLOONE, re-formed The UNDERTONES and released 'GET WHAT YOU NEED' (2003), the Derry outfit's first album of new material in two decades. Despite the absence of SHARKEY's petulant yelp, the new look band proved they could still bang out two-minute blasts of hormonal, adrenalised pop despite nudging their mid-forties. • **Songwriters:** O'NEILL brothers except UNDER THE BOARDWALK (Drifters) / ME AND BABY BROTHER (War) / FOR WHAT IT'S WORTH (Buffalo Springfield) / NON-ALIGNMENT PACT (Pere Ubu) / ZIGZAG WANDERER (Captain Beefheart) / HEY BULLDOG (Beatles) / CINNAMON GIRL (Neil Young) / FUNTIME (Iggy Pop).

Album rating: THE UNDERTONES (*9) / HYPNOTISED (*7) / POSITIVE TOUCH (*6) / THE SIN OF PRIDE (*5) / ALL WRAPPED UP compilation (*7) / CHER O'BOWLES – THE PICK OF THE UNDERTONES compilation (*8) / That Petrol Emotion: MANIC POP THRILL (*7) / BABBLE (*8) / END OF THE MILLENNIUM PSYCHOSIS BLUES (*6) / CHEMICRAZY (*5) / FIREPROOF (*6) / Undertones: TEENAGE KICKS – THE BEST OF . . . compilation (*9) / GET WHAT YOU NEED (*7)

FEARGAL SHARKEY (b.13 Aug'58) – vocals / **DAMIAN O'NEILL** (b.15 Jan'61, Belfast, N.Ireland) – guitar, bass / **JOHN O'NEILL** (b.26 Aug'57) – guitar / **MIKE BRADLEY** (b.13 Aug'59) – bass / **BILLY DOHERTY** (b.10 Jul'58, Larne, N.Ireland) – drums

Good Vibrations — not iss.

Sep 78. (7"ep) *(GOT 4)* **TEENAGE KICKS / TRUE CONFESSIONS. / SMARTER THAN U / EMMERGENCY CASES** [ ] [–]
(re-iss. Oct78 on 'Sire'; SIR 4007) – hit No.31 *(re-iss. Jul83 on 'Ardeck';* ARDS 1) – hit 60 *(re-iss. on 7"ep/cd-ep Apr94 on 'Dojo'; TONES/+CD 1)*

Sire — Sire

Jan 79. (7"m) *(SIR 4010)* **GET OVER YOU. / REALLY REALLY / SHE CAN ONLY SAY NO** [57] [ ]
Apr 79. (7",7"lime green) *(SIR 4015)* **JIMMY JIMMY. / MARS BARS** [16] [ ]
May 79. (lp/c) *(SRK/+C 6071) <6081>* **THE UNDERTONES** [13] Jan 80 [ ]
– Family entertainment / Girls don't like it / Male model / I gotta getta / Teenage kicks / Wrong way / Jump boys / Here comes the summer / Get over you / Billy's third / Jimmy Jimmy / True confessions / She's a runaround / I know a girl / Listening in. *(re-iss. Jul83 on 'Ardeck'; ARDM 164739-1) (re-iss. Oct87 on 'Fame' lp/c/cd; FA/TCFA/CDFA 3188) (re-iss. May94 on 'Dojo' cd/c/lp; DOJO CD/MC/LP 191)* – Smarter than u / Emergency cases / Top twenty / Really really / Mars Bars / She can only say no / One way love. *(cd re-iss. Mar97 on 'Essential'; ESMCD 484) (re-iss. Feb00; ESMCD 831)*
Jul 79. (7"m) *(SIR 4022)* **HERE COMES THE SUMMER. / ONE WAY LOVE / TOP TWENTY** [34] [ ]
Sep 79. (7") *(SIR 4024)* **YOU'VE GOT MY NUMBER (WHY DON'T YOU USE IT). / LET'S TALK ABOUT GIRLS** [32] [ ]
Mar 80. (7"m) *(SIR 4038)* **MY PERFECT COUSIN. / HARD LUCK / I DON'T WANNA SEE YOU AGAIN** [9] [ ]
(d7"+=) *(SIR 4038)* – Here comes the summer.
Apr 80. (lp/c) *(SRK/+C 6088) <6088>* **HYPNOTISED** [6] [ ]
– More songs about chocolate and girls / There goes Norman / Hypnotised / See that girl / Whizz kids / Under the boardwalk / The way girls talk / Hard luck / My perfect cousin / Boys will be boys / Tearproof / Wednesday week / Nine times out of ten / Girls that don't talk / What's with Terry?. *(re-iss. Jul83 on 'Ardeck'; ARDM 164742-1) (re-iss. Mar86 on 'Fame' lp/c; FA/TCFA 3145) (re-iss. May94 on 'Dojo' cd+=/c/lp; DOJO CD/MC/LP 192)* – You've got my number (why don't you use it?) / Hard luck (again) / Let's talk about girls / I told you so / I don't want to see you again. *(cd re-iss. Mar97 on 'Essential'; ESMCD 486) (cd re-iss. Feb00; ESMCD 832)*
Jun80. (7") *(SIR 4042)* **WEDNESDAY WEEK. / I TOLD YOU SO** [11] [ ]

Ardeck-EMI — Rykodisc

Apr 81. (7") *(ARDS 8)* **IT'S GOING TO HAPPEN. / FAIRLY IN THE MONEY NOW** [18] [–]
May 81. (lp/c) *(ARD/TCARD 103) <12159>* **THE POSITIVE TOUCH** [17] [ ]
– Fascination / Life's too easy / You're welcome / The positive touch / Julie Ocean / Crisis of mine / His good looking friend / When Saturday comes / It's going to happen / Sigh and explode / I don't know / Hannah Doot / Boy wonder / Forever Paradise. *(re-iss. Apr84 on 'E.M.I.' lp/c; ATAK/TCATAK 46) (re-iss. May94 on 'Dojo' cd+=/c/lp; DOJO CD/MC/LP 193)* – Kiss in the dark / Beautiful friend / Life's too easy / Fairly in the money now. *(cd re-iss. Mar97 on 'Essential'; ESMCD 485) (cd re-mast.Apr00; ESMCD 853)*
Jul 81. (7") *(ARDS 9)* **JULIE OCEAN. / KISS IN THE DARK** [41] [ ]
Feb 82. (7") *(ARDS 10)* **BEAUTIFUL FRIEND. / LIFE'S TOO EASY** [ ] [–]
Jan 83. (7") *(ARDS 11)* **THE LOVE PARADE. / LIKE THAT** [ ] [–]
(12"+=) *(12ARDS 11)* – You're welcome / Family entertainment / Crises of mine.
Mar 83. (7") *(ARDS 12)* **GOT TO HAVE YOU BACK. / TURNING BLUE** [ ] [–]
(12"+=) *(12ARDS 12)* – Bye bye baby blue.
Mar 83. (lp/c) *(ARD/TCARD 104)* **THE SIN OF PRIDE** [43] [–]
– Got to have you back / Valentine's treatment / Luxury / Love before romance / Untouchable / Bye bye baby blue / Conscious / Chain of love / Soul seven / The love parade / Save me / The sin of pride. *(re-iss. Aug85 on 'E.M.I.' lp/c; ATAK/TCATAK 47) (re-iss. May94 on 'Dojo' cd+=/c/lp; DOJO CD/MC/LP 194)* – Turning blue / Like that / Window shopping for new clothes / Bitter sweet / You stand so close (but you're never there) / I can only dream. *(cd re-iss. Mar97 on 'Essential'; ESMCD 487) (cd re-mast.Apr00; ESMCD 854)*
Apr 83. (7") *(ARDS 13)* **CHAIN OF LOVE. / WINDOW SHOPPING FOR NEW CLOTHES** [ ] [–]

—— split mid '83 with FEARGAL SHARKEY joining The ASSEMBLY; (see YAZOO) before going solo. The O'NEILL brothers formed THAT PETROL EMOTION

THAT PETROL EMOTION

STEVE MACK (b.19 May'63, New York City, USA) – vocals / (ex-EAGER SIN BABIES) / **SEAN O'NEILL** – guitar / **DAMIAN O'NEILL** – bass, keyboards / **REAMANN O'GORMAIN** (b. 7 Jun'61) – guitar / **CIARAN McLAUGHLIN** (b.18 Nov'62) – drums

Pink — not iss.

Jun 85. (7") *(PINKY 004)* **KEEN. / A GREAT DEPRESSION ON SLUM NIGHT** [ ] [–]
(re-iss. Oct86; PINKY 13T)

Noise A Noise — not iss.

Oct 85. (7") *(NAN 1)* **V2. / THE GONEST THING** [ ] [–]
(12"+=) *(NAN 1T)* – Happiness drives me round the bend.

Demon — Demon

Apr 86. (7") *(D 1042)* **IT'S A GOOD THING. / THE DEADBEAT** [ ] [–]
(12"+=) *(D 1042T)* – Mine.
May 86. (lp/c/cd)<US-orange-lp> *(<FIEND/+CASS/+CD 70>)* **MANIC POP THRILL** [84] [ ]
– Fleshprint / Can't stop / Lifeblood / Natural kind of joy / It's a good thing / Circusville / Mouth crazy / Tight lipped / A million miles away / Lettuce / Cheepskate / Blind spot. *(cd+=)* – V2 / Jesus said / The deadbeat. *(cd re-iss. Mar97 on Diabolo'; DIAB 823)*
Jul 86. (7") *(D 1043)* **NATURAL KIND OF JOY. / CAN'T STOP** [ ] [–]
(12"+=) *(D 1043T)* – Non-alignment pact / Jesus said.

Polydor — Polydor

Mar 87. (7"/12") *(TPE/+X 1)* **BIG DECISION. / SOUL DEEP** [43] [–]
(ext.10"+=) *(TPE/+T 1)* – Split!
May 87. (lp/c/cd) *(TPELP/+MC/+CD 1) <833132-1/-4/-2>* **BABBLE** [30] [ ]
– Swamp / Spin cycle / For what it's worth / Big decision / Static / Split! / Belly bugs / In the playpen / Inside / Chester Burnette / Creeping to the cross. *(cd re-mast.Feb01 +=; 549565-2)* – Big decision (12" mix) / Swamp (12" mix) / Creeping to the cross (7" mix) / Soul deep / Dance your ass off.
Jun 87. (7") *(TPE 2)* **SWAMP. / DANCE YOUR ASS OFF** [64] [–]
(12"+=) *(TPEX 2)* – Creeping to the cross (live).
(7"ep++=) *(TPEE 2)* – Me and baby brother (live).

Virgin Virgin

Oct 87. (7") *(VS 1022)* **GENIUS MOVE. / PARTY GAMES** [65] [–]
(12"+=) *(VST 1022)* – Mouthcrazy.

Sep 88. (lp/c/cd) *(V/TCV/CDV 2550) <91019-1/-4/-2>* **END OF THE MILLENNIUM PSYCHOSIS BLUES** [53] [ ]
– Sooner or later / Every little bit / Cellophane / Candy love satellite / Here it is . . . take it! / The price of my soul / Groove check / The bottom line / Tension / Tired shattered man / Goggle box / Under the sky.

Oct 88. (7") *(VS 1116)* **CELLOPHANE. / THINK OF A WOMAN** [ ] [–]
(12"+=/cd-s+=) *(VST/VSCD 1116)* – Hot head / Fast 'n' bullbous.

— **JOHN MARCHINI** – bass; repl. SEAN O'NEILL (only temporary until 1989 then full-time)

Feb 89. (10"ep/3"cd-ep) *(VSA/VSCD 1159)* **GROOVE CHECK / CHEMICRAZY. / TENSION (live) / UNDER THE SKY (live)** [ ] [ ]

Mar 90. (7") *(VS 1242)* **ABANDON. / FAT MOUTH CREED** [73] [–]
(12"+=) *(VST 1242)* – Jewel.
(cd-s+=) *(VSCD 1242)* – ('A'-Boys own mix) / Headstaggered.

Apr 90. (cd/c/lp) *(CD/TC+/V 2618) <91354-2/-4/-1>* **CHEMICRAZY** [62] [ ]
– Hey Venus / Blue to black / Mess of words / Sensitize / Another day / Gnaw mark / Scum surfin' / Compulsion / Tingle / Head staggered / Abandon / Sweet shiver burn.

May 90. (7") *(VS 1261)* **SENSITIZE. / CHEMICRAZY (revitalized)** [ ] [–]
(10"+=/12"+=/cd-s+=) *(VSAX/VST/VSCDT 1261)* – Abandon (Boys Own mix) / Groove check this groove.

Aug 90. (7") *(VS 1290)* **HEY VENUS. / ('A'-Mad Thatcher mix)** [49] [–]
(12"+=/cd-s+=) *(VST/VSCD 1290)* – (2-'A'mixes).

— **FRANK TREISCHLER** – bass (ex-YOUNG GODS) repl. MARCHINI

Jan 91. (7") *(VS 1312)* **TINGLE. / ('A'-Hard bop edit)** [49] [–]
(12"+=) *(VST 1312)* – ('A'mix).
(cd-s+=) *(VSCD 1312)* – Light and shade / Hey Bulldog.
(12") *(VSTX 1312)* – ('A'-Christmas mix) / 'A'-Jazz tup mix).

Apr 91. (7"ep/12"ep) *(VS/+T 1261)* **SENSITIZE. / ABANDON (mix) / GROOVE CHECK** [55] [–]
(10"ep+=/c-ep+=/cd-ep+=) *(VS X/C/CD 1261)* – Cinnamon girl.

— **MARCHINI** now returned to substitute TREICHE who went back to the YOUNG GODS

Koogat Rykodisc

Mar 93. (12"ep/cd-ep) *(GAT 1 T/CDS)* **DETONATE MY DREAMS. / BLUE TO BLACK (extended) / BIG HUMAN THING** [ ] [–]

Apr 93. (cd/c/lp) *(GAT 1 CD/MC/LP) <RCD/RAC+/10289>* **FIREPROOF** [ ] Feb94 [ ]
– Detonate my dreams / Catch a fire / Last of the true believers / Too late blues / 7th wave / Infinite thrill / Speed of light / Shangri-la / Heartbeat mosaic / Metal mystery. *(cd re-mast.Aug00 on 'Essential'; ESMCD 903)*

Jul 93. (12"ep/cd-ep) *(GAT 2 T/CDS)* **CATCH A FIRE (re-mix). / FUN TIME / LITTLE BIKINI / CHROME** [ ] [–]

— disbanded at the end of April 1994; the O'NEILL brothers formed RARE

– compilations, others, etc. –

Oct 87. (12"ep) *Strange Fruit; (SFPS 038)* **THE PEEL SESSIONS** [ ] [–]
– Blind spot / Lettuce / V2 / Can't stop.

Dec 89. (m-lp/m-cd) *Strange Fruit; (SFPMA/+CD 205) / Dutch East India; <DEI 8401>* **DOUBLE PEEL SESSIONS II** [ ] [ ]

Aug 00. (cd) *Essential; (ESMCD 902)* **LIVE (live)** [ ] [–]

UNDERTONES

re-formed **PAUL McLOONE** – vocals (not FEARGAL!)

Sanctuary Sanctuary

Oct 03. (cd) *(SANCD 210) <84646>* **GET WHAT YOU NEED** [ ] [ ]
– Thrill me / I need your love the way it used to be / Everything but you / Ride the rough escalator / You can't say that / Enough / Touch / Girl like you / The cruellest thing / Oh please / Winter sun / Joyland / Shut down.

– compilations, others, etc. –

Nov 83. (d-lp)(c) *Ardeck-EMI; (ARD 1654283)(1654289)* **ALL WRAPPED UP** [67] [–]
– Teenage kicks / Get over you / Jimmy Jimmy / Here comes the summer / You've got my number (why don't you use it) / My perfect cousin / Wednesday week / It's going to happen / Julie Ocean / Beautiful friend / The love parade / Got to have you back / Chain of love.

— (note: all singles were re-iss. on 'Ardeck-EMI')

May 86. (lp/c) *Ardeck-EMI; (EMS/TCEMS 1172)* **CHER O'BOWLIES – THE PICK OF THE UNDERTONES** [96] [–]
– Teenage kicks / True confessions / Get over you / Family entertainment / Jimmy Jimmy / Here comes the Summer / You got my number (why don't you use it) / My perfect cousin / See that girl / Tearproof / Wednesday week / It's going to happen / Julie Ocean / You're welcome / Forever Paradise / Beautiful friend / Save me / The love parade / Valentine's treatment / Love before romance. *(re-iss. Oct89 on 'Fame' cd/c/lp; CD/TC+/FA 3226)*

Jun 86. (7") *Ardeck-EMI; (ARDS 14)* **SAVE ME. / TEARPROOF** [ ] [–]
(12"+=) *(12ARDS 14)* – I know a girl.

Dec 86. (12"ep) *Strange Fruit; (SFPS 016)* **THE PEEL SESSIONS (21.1.79)** [ ] [–]
– Listening in / Family entertainment / Here comes the summer / Billy's third. *(cd-ep iss.Mar88)*

Dec 89. (lp/c/cd) *Strange Fruit; (SFR LP/MC/CD 103)* **DOUBLE PEEL SESSIONS** [ ] [–]
(re-iss. cd Mar94 as 'THE PEEL SESSIONS ALBUM'; same)

Sep 93. (cd/c) *Castle; (CTV CD/MC 121) / Rykodisc; <RCD 20297>* **THE BEST OF THE UNDERTONES – TEENAGE KICKS** [45] [ ]
(cd re-iss. Jan97 on 'Renaissance'; CCSCD 808)

Jul 95. (cd-ep) *Dojo; (TONESCD 1)* **HERE COMES THE SUMMER / GET OVER YOU / JIMMY JIMMY / YOU'VE GOT MY NUMBER (WHY DON'T YOU USE IT)** [ ] [–]

Sep 99. (d-cd) *Essential; (ESDCD 788)* **TRUE CONFESSIONS: SINGLES A's & B's** [ ] [–]

Jun 00. (12xcd-s) *Essential; (ESFCD 893)* **THE SINGLES BOX SET** [ ] [–]

Sep 03. (cd) *Sanctuary; (TVSAN 005)* **TEENAGE KICKS – THE BEST OF THE UNDERTONES** [35] [–]

UNDERWORLD

Formed: Romford, London, England . . . 1987 by RICK SMITH, KARL HYDE, ALFIE THOMAS and BRYN BURROWS, who had all been in Cardiff outfit FREUR (which was actually a symbol translated into a word!; no, PRINCE wasn't the first!). Even before this, RICK and KARL had played in synth-pop band, The SCREEN GEMS. In 1987, they took on the more conventional moniker, UNDERWORLD and hit America in the late 80's after signing for Seymour Stein's 'Sire' records. After a No.1 smash, 'RADAR', in Australia, they toured the States supporting EURYTHMICS, but it was clear this was not the direction for them. After recruiting DJ DARREN EMERSON, the band signed with the 'Boys Own' label, releasing the seminal techno crescendo of 'REZ' in February '93. They followed this up with the critically acclaimed, early '94 album, 'DUBNOBASSWITHMYHEADMAN', a nouveau-psychedelic classic climaxing with the delirious trance-athon of 'COWGIRL'. However, their big break came with the track 'BORN SLIPPY', a song featured on the 'Trainspotting' soundtrack. When re-released as a single in 1996, the track stormed to No.2, boosting sales of their recently released follow-up album, 'SECOND TOUGHEST IN THE INFANTS'. The band remain one of Britain's best loved techno acts, and with the Stateside success of The PRODIGY, there was still a chance that the band might break in America. Indeed, 1999's long-awaited 'BEAUCOUP FISH' took them into the US Top 100 having already made Top 3 in Britain. Highlights from the set were undoubtably hit singles, 'PUSH UPSTAIRS', 'JUMBO' and 'SHUDDER – KING OF SNAKE', while 'MOANER' (theme from 1997's 'Batman & Robin' movie) was its 10-star pièce de resistance. The first live album of their

decade+ career, 'EVERYTHING, EVERYTHING' (2000) was as thrilling a recreation of UNDERWORLD's unique techno meets rock'n'roll concert experience as you could hope for, featuring a fair clutch (with some notable omissions nevertheless) of their best loved dancefloor marathons including 'REZ' and 'BORN SLIPPY'. EMERSON officially departed in spring 2000. The first post-EMERSON album, 'A HUNDRED DAYS OFF', followed in 2002, a strangely muted affair undoubtedly affected by the alteration in group chemistry. There were still touches of the sly genius of old, notably on the marathon, near 10-minute 'TWO MONTHS OFF'.
• **Songwriters:** SMITH / HYDE / THOMAS then SMITH / HYDE / EMERSON. • **Trivia:** Produced by RUPERT HINES in 1988. HYDE worked on a 1991 'Paisley P.' album with TERRI NUNN (ex-Berlin). GEOFF DUGMORE (ex-ART OF NOISE) was a guest on 1989 album. Also appeared on WILLIAM ORBIT's 'Watch From A Vine Leaf' & ORBITAL's 'Lush 3' and remixed BJORK's 'Human Behaviour'.

Album rating: Freur: DOOT DOOT (*4) / GET US OUT OF HERE (*4) / Underworld: UNDERNEATH THE RADAR (*5) / CHANGE THE WEATHER (*4) / DUBNOBASSWITHMYHEADMAN (*8) / SECOND TOUGHEST IN THE INFANTS (*8) / BEAUCOUP FISH (*8) / A HUNDRED DAYS OFF (*4) / 1992-2002 compilation (*8)

FREUR

RICK SMITH (b.25 May'59, Ammanford, Wales) – keyboards, vocals / **KARL HYDE** (b.10 May'57, Worcester, England) – vocals, guitar / **ALFIE THOMAS** – guitar, vocals / **JOHN WARWICKER LE BRETON** – synthesizers / **BRYN B. BURROWS** – drums

C.B.S. | Epic

Mar 83. (7"pic-d/ext.12") *(WA/A13 3141)* **DOOT DOOT. / HOLD ME MOTHER** [59] [ ]
Jun 83. (7"/7"pic-d) *(A/WA 3456)* **MATTERS OF THE HEART. / YOU'RE A HOOVER** [ ] [ ]
(12"+=) *(TA 3456)* – ('A'extended).
Sep 83. (7"/12") **RUNAWAY. / YOU'RE A HOOVER** [–] [ ]
Nov 83. (lp/c) *(CBS/40 25522)* *<81566>* **DOOT DOOT** [ ] [ ]
– Doot doot / Runaway / Riders in the night / Theme from the film of the same name / Tender surrender / Matters of the heart / My room / Steam machine / Whispering / All too much.
Jan 84. (7"/ext.12") *(A/TA 4073)* **DOOT DOOT. / HOLD ME MOTHER** [ ] [ ]
Apr 84. (7") *(A 4333)* **RIDERS IN THE NIGHT. / INNOCENCE** [ ] [ ]
(12"+=) *(TA 4333)* – This is the way I like to live my life.

— added **JAKE BOWIE** – bass

Oct 84. (7") *(A 4726)* **DEVIL AND DARKNESS. / JAZZ 'N' KING** [ ] [ ]
(12"+=) *(TX 4726)* – ('A'extended).
Feb 85. (7") *(A 4983)* **LOOK IN THE BACK FOR ANSWERS. / HEY HO AWAY WE GO** [ ] [ ]
(12"+=) *(TX 4983)* – Uncle Jeff.
Feb 85. (lp/c/cd) **GET US OUT OF HERE** [ ] [ ]
– Look in the back for answers / Emeralds and pearls / Kiss me / A.O.K.O. / The Devil and darkness / The piano song / Happiness / Endless groove / This is the way I'd like to live my life / Bella Donna.

UNDERWORLD

— **BAZ ALLEN** – bass; repl. JOHN

Sire | Sire

Mar 88. (lp/c/cd) *(<925627-1/-4/-2>)* **UNDERNEATH THE RADAR** [ ] [ ]
– Glory! glory! / Call me No.1 / Rubber ball (space kitchen) / Show some emotion / Underneath the radar / Miracle party / I need a doctor / Bright white flame / Pray / The God song.
Jul 88. (7") *(W 7968)* *<27968>* **UNDERNEATH THE RADAR. / BIG RED X** [ ] Apr88 [74]
(12"+=) *(W 7968T)* – ('A'dub version).
Aug 88. (7") **SHOW SOME EMOTION. / SHOCK THE DOCTOR** [–] [ ]

— **PASCAL CONSOLI** – percussion, drums repl. BURROWS who joined WORLDWIDE ELECTRIC

Aug 89. (7"/c-s) *(W 2854/+C)* *<22852>* **STAND UP. / OUTSKIRTS** [ ] [67]
(12") *(W 2854T)* – Stand up (and dance) / Stand up (ya house) / Outskirts.
(cd-s) *(W 2854CD)* – (all mixes & B-side)
Sep 89. (lp/c)(cd) *(WX 289/+C)(K 925945-2)* *<25945>* **CHANGE THE WEATHER** [ ] [ ]
– Change the weather / Stand up / Fever / Original song / Mercy / Mr. Universe / Texas / Thrash / Sole survivor / Beach.
Nov 89. (7") **CHANGE THE WEATHER. / TEXAS** [–] [ ]

— ALLEN + CONSOLI became D-INFLUENCE

— **SMITH** + **HYDE** brought in **DARREN EMERSON** (b.30 Apr'71, Hornchurch, Essex, England) – keyboards

Tomato | not iss.

1992. (12") *(PLUM 2001)* **MOTHER EARTH / MOTHER EARTH (FM mix). / THE HUMP / THE HUMP (groove without a doubt mix)** [ ] [–]

Boys Own | not iss.

Jan 93. (12"ep/cd-ep) *(BOI X/CD 13)* **MMM . . . SKYSCRAPER I LOVE YOU. / ('A'-Telegraph mix 6.11.92) / ('A'-Jamscraper mix)** [ ] [–]
1993. (12"/12"pink) *(Collect 002/+P)* **REZ. / WHY WHY WHY** [ ] [–]

Junior Boys Own | Wax Trax!

1993. (12"; as LEMON INTERRUPT) *(JBO 12-002)* **ECLIPSE. / BIGMOUTH** [ ] [–]
1993. (12"; as LEMON INTERRUPT) *(JBO 7-12)* **DIRTY / MINNEAPOLIS. / MINNEAPOLIS (AIRWAVES)** [ ] [–]
Sep 93. (12"/cd-s) *(JBO 13/+CD)* **COWGIRL. / REZ** [ ] [–]
(re-iss. Aug95 on 'Junior Boys Own'; JBO 1001)
Dec 93. (12"/cd-s) *(JBO 17/+CD)* **SPIKEE. / DOGMAN GO WOOF** [60] [ ]
Feb 94. (cd/c/d-lp) *(JBO CD/CS/LP 1)* *<7217>* **DUBNOBASSWITHMYHEADMAN** [12] [ ]
– Dark and long / Mmm . . . skyscraper I love you / Surf boy / Spoon man / Tongue / Dirty epic / Cowgirl / River of bass / M.E. *(cd re-iss. May97; same)*
Jun 94. (cd-ep) *(JBO 19CDS)* **DARK & LONG (mixes)** [57] [–]
– Hall's mix / Dark train / Most 'ospitable / 215 miles.
(12") *(JB 019)* – ('A'-spoon deep mix) / ('A'-thing in a back mix).
(12") *(JB 019X)* – ('A'-dark train mix) / ('A'-Burt's mix).
(re-iss. Sep99 12"/cd-s; JBO 501027-3/-6)
Dec 94. (cd-ep) *<8722>* **DIRTY EPIC (mixes; dirty guitar / dirty mix / album) / COWGIRL (mixes; Irish pub in Kyoto / winjer / album) / REZ / RIVER OF BASS** [–] [ ]
Jan 95. (12") *<8724-0>* **COWGIRL (mixes; album / Winjer / Irish pub in Kyoto)** [–] [ ]
May 95. (12") *(JBO 29)* **BORN SLIPPY (telenatic). / COWGIRL (Vinjer mix)** [52] [ ]
(12") *(JBO 29R)* – ('A'side) / ('A'-Nuxx mix).
(cd-s) *(JBO 29CDS)* – (above 2) / ('A'side again).
Mar 96. (cd/c/d-lp) *(JBO CD/MC/LP 4)* *<7240>* **SECOND TOUGHEST IN THE INFANTS** [9] [ ]
– Juanita – Kiteless – To dream of love / Banstyle – Sappys curry / Confusion the waitress / Rowla / Pearls girl / Air towel / Blueski / Stagger. *(cd re-iss. May97; same)*
May 96. (12"ep) *(JBO 38)* **PEARLS GIRL. / MOSAIC / DEEP ARCH** [24] [–]
(cd-ep) *(JBO 38CDS1)* – ('A'-Carp Dreams . . . Koi) / Oich oich / Cherry pie.
(cd-ep) *(JBO 38CDS2)* – ('A'mixes).

Junior Boys Own | TVT

Jun 96. (12") *<8737>* **ROWLA. / JUANITA** [–] [ ]
Jul 96. (12"/cd-s) *(JBO 44/+CDS1)* *<8731>* **BORN SLIPPY. / ('A'mixes)** [2] [ ]
(cd-s) *(JBO 38CDS2)* – ('A'side) / ('A'-Deep pan mix) / ('A'-Darren Price mix) / ('A'-Darren Price remix).
(re-iss. Apr99 on 'Junior Boys Own-V2' 12"/cd-s/cd-s; JBO 50056 2-6/0-3/1-3)
Oct 96. (12"/cd-s) *(JBO 45/+CDS1)* *<8748>* **PEARLS GIRL. / ('A'mixes; Puppies / Oich oich / Cherry Pie)** [22] Feb97 [ ]
(cd-s) *(JBO 45CDS2)* – ('A'mixes; Mosaic / Deep arch).
1997. (cd-ep) *(9362 43905-2)* **MOANER (short) / (album) / (relentless legs) / (long)** [ ] [ ]
(above from the Warners movie, 'Batman & Robin')

Junior Boys Own – V2 | V2

Mar 99. (cd/c/d-lp) *(JBO 100543-2/-4/-1)* <27042> **BEAUCOUP FISH** [3] [93]
– Cups / Push upstairs / Jumbo / Shudder – King of snake / Winjer / Skym / Bruce Lee / Kittens / Push downstairs / Something like a mama / Moaner.

Mar 99. (12"/cd-s) *(JBO 500544-6/-3)* **PUSH UPSTAIRS (mixes; The Large Unit / Darren Price) / PLEASE HELP ME** [12] [ ]
(cd-s) *(JBO 500617-3)* – ('A'mixes).

May 99. (12"/cd-s) *(JBO 500719-6/-3)* **JUMBO (mixes; edit / Rob Rives & Francois K Main Dish / Jedis Electro dub)** [21] [ ]
(cd-s) *(JBO 500720-3)* – ('A'mixes).

Aug 99. (cd-s) *(JBO 500879-3)* **KING OF SNAKE (mixes; Straight (Mate) / Fatboy Slim / Slam)** [17] [ ]
(12"/cd-s) *(JBO 500879-6/-8)* – ('A'mixes) / Shudder – King of snake.

Nov 99. (12"/cd-s) *(JBO 501003-6/-3)* **BRUCE LEE (Micronauts remixes) / CUPS (Salt City Orchestra mix)** [ ] [–]

Aug 00. (12"/cd-s) *(JBO 501251-6/-3)* **COWGIRL (mixes; radio / Bedrock / Futureshock) / REZ – COWGIRL (live)** [24] [–]
(cd-s) *(JBO 501251-8)* – (mixes).

Sep 00. (cd/c) *(JBO 101254-2/-4)* <27078> **EVERYTHING, EVERYTHING (live)** [22] [ ]
– Juanita – Kiteless / Cups / Push upstairs / Pearls girl / Jumbo / Shudder – King of snake / Born slippy nuxx / Rez – Cowgirl.

—— EMERSON left in April 2000

Sep 02. (cd-s) *(JBO 502009-3)* **TWO MONTHS OFF / TWO MONTHS OFF (KIng Unique sunspots – vocal) / HEADSET** [12] [ ]
(cd-s) *(JBO 502009-8)* – ('A'side) / ('A'-John Ciafone vocal) / Tiny clicks.
(12") *(JBO 502009-6)* <27764-1> – (2 'A'-mixes).

Sep 02. (cd/d-lp) *(JBO 102010-2/-1)* <27137> **A HUNDRED DAYS OFF** [16] [ ]
– Mo move / Two months off / Twist / Sola sistim / Little speaker / Trim / Ess Gee / Dinosaur adventure 3D / Ballet lane / Luetin.

Jan 03. (cd-s) *(JBO 502052-3)* **DINOSAUR ADVENTURE 3D / ANSUM** [34] [–]
(12"/cd-s) *(JBO 502052-6/-8)* – ('A'mixes).

Oct 03. (cd-s) *(JBO 502470-3)* **BORN SLIPPY NUXX (mixes; Rick Smith / Atomic Hooligan / Paul Oakenfold)** [27] [–]
(12") *(JBO 502470-0)* – ('A'-mixes; Atomic Hooligan / London Elektricity).

Nov 03. (d-cd/q-lp) *(JBO 102469-2/-1)* <27175> **1992-2002** (compilation) [43] Dec03 [ ]
– Big mouth / Dirty / Mmm skyscraper I love you / Rez / Spikee / Dirty epic / Dark and long (dark train) // Cowgirl / Born slippy NUXX / Pearls girl / Jumbo / Push upstairs / Moaner / Shudder – King of snake / 8 ball / Two months off.

– compilations, etc. –

Oct 97. (cd) *April; <002>* **DARK & LONG** [–] [ ]

Mar 99. (cd-s) *TVT; (8722-2)* **DIRTY EPIC / COWGIRL / REZ** [ ] [–]

Sep 02. (12") *T.V.T.; (TVT 87180)* **COWBOY. / REX** [ ] [–]
(12") *(TVT 87420)* – ('A'-mixes; album / Winjer / Irish pub in Kyoto).

□ UNIFIED THEORY (see under ⇒ BLIND MELON)

U.N.K.L.E.

Formed: London, England ... 1994 by JAMES LAVELLE (head honcho of 'Mo Wax'), along with TIM GOLDSWORTHY (from New York) and Japanese label boss KUDO (of 'Major Force' and psychedelic electronic outfit SKYLAB). The collective – not so much of a band – gathered acclaim due to their classy remixes, which included the likes of TORTOISE and The JON SPENCER BLUES EXPLOSION. LAVELLE, already a renowned producer and label boss, was planning a special "all-star" concept album to go under the UNKLE banner. He enlisted the help of DJ SHADOW, moved out to a studio in Los Angeles and effectively began work on his epic 'PSYENCE FICTION' set. KUDO, due to work commitments had left the project, leaving SHADOW to do most of the work on the sampling and the music side of things. They enlisted some of the in-demand musicians of the moment – noteably THOM YORKE who had just delivered RADIOHEAD's groundbreaking album 'OK Computer', RICHARD ASHCOFT (ex-of THE VERVE) and MIKE D (of the BEASTIE BOYS). The resulting aforementioned set was a cross-breed of jazz, electronica, hip-hop and trip-hop with the standout track being YORKE's contribution 'RABBIT IN YOUR HEADLIGHTS', a strange off-kilter, free-jazz time signature, with a mellow piano and memorable voice sample from the movie 'Jacob's Ladder'. LAVELLE toured the album, not with SHADOW, but with the not-so-well-known SCRATCH PERVERTS and set to work on its follow-up. Fans had a long time to wait as it eventually arrived in 2003 under the title 'NEVER, NEVER, LAND'. It featured guests IAN BROWN, 3D (from MASSIVE ATTACK) and JOSH HOMME (of The QUEENS OF THE STONE AGE). However, unlike its Top 5 predecessor, the set went practicaly unnoticed, although it did hit the UK Top 30.

Album rating: PSYENCE FICTION (*8) / NEVER, NEVER, LAND (*6)

JAMES LAVELLE plus **DJ SHADOW** + **TIM GOLDSWORTHY** + **MASAYUKI KUDO** (Major Force West)

Mo' Wax | Universal

Jan 95. (12"/12"pic-d) <*(MW 028/+P)*> **THE TIME HAS COME (mixes)** [ ] [–]
(re-iss. May96 w/cd-ep; MW 028CD)

Feb 97. (12"/cd-s) <*(MW 069/+CD)*> **BERRY MEDITATION (mixes; original / last ever / the darker the berry . . .)** [ ] [–]
(12"clear) *(MW 069L)* – ('A'remixes).

Mar 97. (12"/cd-s) <*(MW 070/+CD)*> **ROCK ON (mixes)** [ ] [–]

—— **LAVELLE** + **DJ SHADOW** with guests vocalists **THOM YORKE** (Radiohead) / **RICHARD ASHCROFT** (Verve) / **MIKE D** (Beastie Boys) / **MARK HOLLIS** (ex-Talk Talk) / **ALICE TEMPLE** (Eg And Alice) / **BADLY DRAWN BOY** + **KOOL G RAP**

Aug 98. (lp/c/cd) *(MW 085/+MC/CD)* <540970> **PSYENCE FICTION** [4] [ ]
– Intro – Guns blazing (drums of death, pt.1) / UNKLE main title theme / Blood stain / Unreal / Lonely soul / Getting ahead in the field of artistic management / Nursery rhyme – Breather / Celestial annihilation / The knock (drums of death, pt.2) / Chaos / Rabbit in your headlights / Outro. *(also ltd;d-cd/d-lp; MW 085 CDS/S)*

Oct 98. (12"ep/cd-ep) *(MW 103/+CD)* **RABBIT IN YOUR HEADLIGHTS / (instrumental) / (Underdog mix) / (Underdog instrumental) / (30 mix 'reverse light') / (30 mix 'reverse light' instrumental) / (Suburban hell remix)** [–] nochart [–]

Feb 99. (12"/cd-s; UNKLE featuring IAN BROWN) *(MW 108/+CD1)* **BE THERE (mixes; original / Underdog / Underdog instrumental)** [8] [–]
(cd-s) *(MW 108CD2)* – ('A'side) / The knock (drums of Zep) (Noel Gallagher mix) / Rabbit in your headlights (video).

—— DJ SHADOW was now not part of the UNKLE set-up

—— **LAVELLE** + **RICHARD FILE** + **ANTHONY GLENN** recruited numerous guests (see biog)

Aug 03. (cd-s) *(CID 826)* **AN EYE FOR AN EYE (mixes)** [31] [–]
(12"/cd-s) *(12IS/CIDX 826)* – ('A'mixes).
(12"/12"/12"/12") *(12IS W/X/Y/Z 826)* – (various mixes).
(above on 'Island' records)

Sep 03. (cd) *(MWU 001CD)* <986554> **NEVER, NEVER, LAND** [24] [ ]
– Back and forth / Eye for an eye / In a state / Safe in mind (UNKLE & JOSH HOMME) / I need something stronger / What are you to me? / Panic attack / Invasion (UNKLE & 3D) / Reign (UNKLE & IAN BROWN) / Glow (UNKLE & JOE CADBURY) / Inside. *(d-lp-iss.Nov03 +=; MWU 001LP)* – Awake the unkind.

Nov 03. (12") *(MWU 002TX)* **IN A STATE. / (Sasha remix)** [44] [–]
(12") *(MWU 002TY)* – ('A'-DFA remix) / ('A'-Meat Katie & Elite Force remix).
(cd-s) *(CID 839)* – (all above +).

□ Midge URE (see under ⇒ ULTRAVOX)

URIAH HEEP

Formed: London, England . . . early 1970 by guitarist MICK BOX and vocalist DAVID BYRON, who had both cut their proverbial teeth in mid 60's outfit, The STALKERS (BYRON had also featured in a cover version hits compilation singing alongside REG DWIGHT, er . . . ELTON JOHN!). In 1968, the pair became SPICE, having found musicians PAUL NEWTON (ex-GODS), ROY SHARLAND and ALEX NAPIER. A solitary 45 was issued on 'United Artists', 'WHAT ABOUT THE MUSIC' failing to sell in any substantial quantities, although it has since become very rare. Taking their new moniker, URIAH HEEP, from a character in Dickens' 'David Copperfield' novel, the band enlisted some seasoned musicians, KEN HENSLEY (ex-GODS, ex-TOE FAT) and NIGEL OLLSON (ex-SPENCER DAVIS GROUP, ex-PLASTIC PENNY) to replace ROY SHARLAND and ALEX NAPIER. Now signed to 'Vertigo' and on a hefty diet of hard rock that critics lambasted for allegedly plagiarising LED ZEPPELIN, URIAH HEEP delivered their debut album, 'VERY 'EAVY, VERY 'UMBLE', in 1970. Although this did little to change music press opinions, the record contained at least two gems, 'GYPSY' and a cover of Tim Rose's 'COME AWAY MELINDA'. Drummer KEITH BAKER filled in for the ELTON JOHN bound OLLSON, prior to their follow-up set, 'SALISBURY' (1971), which, like its predecessor sold better in Germany and other parts of Europe. People were beginning to take BYRON's at times, high-pitched warblings seriously, the classic track 'BIRD OF PREY' (which was criminally left off the US version), being a perfect example. Later that year, 'LOOK AT YOURSELF' (on the new 'Bronze' imprint and featuring new drummer, IAIN CLARK) was released to some decent reviews, the celebrated 10 minute plus epic, 'JULY MORNING' (with an outstanding guest synth/keys spot from MANFRED MANN), helping it to touch the UK Top 40, while breaking the US Top 100. A steadier formation was found while recording their fourth album, 'DEMONS AND WIZARDS' (1972), GARY THAIN (ex-KEEF HARTLEY) took over from short-stop, MARK CLARKE (who had replaced NEWTON in November '71), while HENSLEY's old mate, LEE KERSLAKE superseded CLARKE. The results were outstanding, the disc going Top 30 and gold on both sides of the Atlantic, with tracks such as 'THE WIZARD' and 'EASY LIVIN' (also a US Top 40 hit), URIAH HEEP standards. 'THE MAGICIAN'S BIRTHDAY' (1972) did much of the same, lifted from the record, 'SWEET LORRAINE' and 'BLIND EYE' both became minor US favourites. 1973 saw another two gold albums being released, a live one and their first for 'Warner Bros' in the States, 'SWEET FREEDOM', while HENSLEY even found time to release a solo set, 'PROUD WORDS ON A DUSTY SHELF'. Their live disc contained a live rock'n'roll medley, featuring their interpretations of ROLL OVER BEETHOVEN, BLUE SUEDE SHOES, MEAN WOMAN BLUES, HOUND DOG, AT THE HOP and WHOLE LOTTA SHAKIN' GOIN' ON, some of their more discerning fans awaiting 1974's more sombre studio set, 'WONDERWORLD'. A bad period indeed for URIAH HEEP, THAIN was near-fatally electrocuted on stage in Dallas, Texas, subsequently resulting in major conflicts with the manager, Gerry Bron. His personal problems and drug-taking (while recovering from his injuries) led to URIAH HEEP being kept in a state of limbo for some months and after lengthy group discussions, THAIN was finally asked to leave in February '75 (tragically, on the 19th of March, 1976, he died of a drug overdose). Another bloke with considerable talents, JOHN WETTON (ex-KING CRIMSON, ex-FAMILY, ex-ROXY MUSIC etc.), was quickly drafted in to record 'RETURN TO FANTASY' (1975) and although the record hit the UK Top 10, it barely scratched out a Top 100 US placing. HENSLEY delivered a second solo set that year, 'EAGER TO PLEASE'. Appropriately titled, it failed to get off the starting blocks, a thing that could be said of 'HEEP's next album, 'HIGH AND MIGHTY' (1976), which only checked in at No.55 in the British charts. Disillusioned by their lack of success and the sacking of BYRON (he had formed ROUGH DIAMOND), WETTON too decided to jump ship. Their places were filled by vocalist, JOHN LAWTON and bassist more famous to BOWIE fans, TREVOR BOLDER; the 'HEEP that the band had become soldiered on while punk rock in '77 became yet another stumbling block. Subsequent albums (with various comings and goings) 'FIREFLY' (1977), 'INNOCENT VICTIM' (1977), 'FALLEN ANGEL' (1978) and 'CONQUEST' (1980) all failed both commercially and critically. After a break from music in the early 80's, URIAH HEEP returned with a new line-up, BOX enlisting the services of LEE KERSLAKE, PETE GOALBY (vocals), JOHN SINCLAIR (keyboards) and BOB DAISLEY (bass) to complete a comeback album of sorts, 'ABOMINOG', a record that returned them to the charts on both sides of the Atlantic in 1982. Another, 'HEAD FIRST' (1983), showed the rock world they had not given up just yet, in fact, URIAH HEEP were still going strong a decade and a half later, although their output has led to derision from all circles except that of a loyal fanbase in Kerrang!. They even became the first ever heavy-rock act to play in the U.S.S.R. A few years later, the band plucked up some degree of courage in covering a heavy rock version of Argent's 'HOLD YOUR HEAD UP', which became a track on the 1989 set, 'RAGING SILENCE'. URIAH HEEP will be best remembered for their "very 'eavy, very 'ard" 70's sound and style, much mimicked by a plethora of 80's rock acts too numerous and risky to mention (apart from SPINAL TAP, maybe). • **Songwriters:** Majority by HENSLEY or BOX/THAIN. In 1976 all members took share of work.

Album rating: VERY 'EAVY . . . VERY 'UMBLE (*5) / SALISBURY (*5) / LOOK AT YOURSELF (*6) / DEMONS AND WIZARDS (*7) / MAGICIAN'S BIRTHDAY (*6) / URIAH HEEP LIVE! (*5) / SWEET FREEDOM (*5) / WONDERWORLD (*5) / RETURN TO FANTASY (*5) / THE BEST OF URIAH HEEP compilation (*7) / HIGH AND MIGHTY (*5) / FIREFLY (*4) / INNOCENT VICTIM (*3) / FALLEN ANGEL (*3) / CONQUEST (*3) / ABOMINOG (*4) / HEAD FIRST (*4) / EQUATOR (*4) / LIVE IN MOSCOW (*3) / RAGING SILENCE (*4) / STILL HEAVY, STILL PROUD (*4) / DIFFERENT WORLD (*4) / SEA OF LIGHT (*4) / SPELLBINDER (*4) / SONIC ORIGAMI (*5) / THE BEST OF URIAH HEEP, VOL.1 compilation (*6) / Ken Hensley: PROUD WORDS ON A DUSTY SHELF (*5) / EAGER TO PLEASE (*4) / FREE SPIRIT (*4) / ANTHOLOGY compilation (*5) / David Byron: TAKE NO PRISONERS (*4)

DAVID BYRON (b.29 Jan'47, Epping, Essex, England) – vocals / **MICK BOX** (b. 8 Jun'47, London, England) – guitar, vocals / **ROY SHARLAND** – organ / **PAUL NEWTON** – bass, vocals / **ALEX NAPIER** – drums

U.A. | not iss.

Dec 68. (7"; as SPICE) *(UP 2246)* **WHAT ABOUT THE MUSIC. / IN LOVE** [ ] [–]

—— now without SHARLAND who joined ARTHUR BROWN, etc. / added **KEN HENSLEY** (b.24 Aug'45) – keyboards, guitar, vox (ex-GODS, ex-TOE FAT) / **NIGEL OLSSON** – drums (ex-SPENCER DAVIS GROUP, ex-PLASTIC PENNY) repl. NAPIER (on all lp except 2 tracks)

Vertigo | Mercury

Jun 70. (lp) *(6360 006)* *<61294>* **VERY 'EAVY . . . VERY 'UMBLE** <US-title 'URIAH HEEP'>
– Gypsy / Walking in your shadow / Come away Melinda / Lucy blues / Dreammare / Real turned on / I'll keep on trying / Wake up (set your sights). *(re-iss. 1971 on 'Bronze'; ILPS 9142) (re-iss. Apr77 on 'Bronze'; BRNA 142) (re-iss. Apr86 on 'Castle' lp/c; CLA LP/MC 105) (cd-iss. Dec90;) (re-iss. cd Jan96 on 'Essential'+=; ESMCD 316)* – Gypsy / Come away Melinda / Born in a trunk. *(cd re-mast.Jan03 on 'Castle'+=; CMRCD 642)* – Born in a trunk (vocal) / Dreammare (BBC session) / Gypsy (BBC session) / Come

away Melinda (BBC session) / Born in a trunk (instrumental) / Lucy blues (alt.) / Gypsy (alt.).

Jul 70. (7") *<73103>* **GYPSY. / REAL TURNED ON** [–] [ ]

Nov 70. (7") *<73145>* **COME AWAY MELINDA. / WAKE UP (SET YOUR SIGHTS)** [–] [ ]

— **KEITH BAKER** – drums (ex-BAKERLOO) repl. OLSSON who joined ELTON JOHN

Jan 71. (7") *<73174>* **HIGH PRIESTESS. /** [–] [ ]

Jan 71. (lp) *(6360 028) <61319>* **SALISBURY** [ ] [ ]
– Bird of prey * / The park / Time to live / Lady in black / High Priestess / Salisbury. *<US copies repl. *, with =)* – Simon the bullet freak. *(re-iss. 1971 on 'Bronze'; ILPS 9152) (re-iss. Jul77 on 'Bronze'; BRNA 152) (re-iss. Apr86 on 'Castle' lp/c; CLA LP/MC 106) (cd-iss. Apr89; CLACD 106) (re-iss. cd Jan96 on 'Essential'+=; ESMCD 317)* – Simon the bullet freak / High priestess. *(cd re-mast.Jan03 on 'Castle'+=; CMRCD 643)* – Simon the bullet freak / Here am I / Bird of prey (BBC session) / Salisbury (BBC session) / High priestess (single version).

Mar 71. (7") *(6059 037)* **LADY IN BLACK. / SIMON THE BULLET FREAK** [ ] [–]

— **IAIN CLARK** – drums (ex-CRESSIDA) repl. BAKER

— guest was **MANFRED MANN** – moog synthesizer / keyboards

Bronze Mercury

Nov 71. (lp) *(ILPS 9169) <614>* **LOOK AT YOURSELF** [39] Sep71 [93]
– Look at yourself / I wanna be free / July morning / Tears in my eyes / Shadows of grief / What should be done / Love machine. *(re-iss. Apr77; BRNA 169) (re-iss. Apr86 on 'Castle' lp/c; CLA LP/MC 107) (cd-iss. Apr89; CLACD 107) (re-iss. cd Jan96 on 'Essential'+=; ESMCD 318)* – Look at yourself (single version) / What's within my heart. *(cd re-mast.Mar03 on 'Castle'+=; CMRCD 671)* – What's within my heart / Why (extended) / Look at yourself (alt.) / Tears in my eyes (extended) / What should be done (alt.) / Look at yourself (BBC session) / What should be done (BBC session).

Dec 71. (7") *(WIP 6111)* **LOOK AT YOURSELF. / SIMON THE BULLET FREAK** [ ] [–]

Dec 71. (7") *<73243>* **LOVE MACHINE. / LOOK AT YOURSELF** [–] [ ]

Feb 72. (7") *<73254>* **I WANNA BE FREE. / WHAT SHOULD BE DONE** [–] [ ]

— (Nov71) **LEE KERSLAKE** – drums, vocals (ex-GODS, ex-TOE FAT) repl. IAN (Feb'72) / **GARY THAIN** (b. New Zealand) – bass, vocals (ex-KEEF HARTLEY) repl. MARK CLARKE (ex-COLOSSEUM to TEMPEST) who had repl. NEWTON (Nov'71)

May 72. (lp) *(ILPS 9193) <630>* **DEMONS AND WIZARDS** [20] [23]
– The wizard / Traveller in time / Easy livin' / Poet's justice / Circle of hands / Rainbow demon / All my life / (a) Paradise – (b) The spell. *(re-iss. Apr77; BRNA 193) (re-iss. Apr86 on 'Castle' lp/c; CLA LP/MC 108) (cd-iss. Apr89; CLACD 108) (re-iss. cd Jan96 on 'Essential'+=; ESMCD 319)* – Why (single version) / Home again to you. *(lp re-iss. Jan97 on 'Original'; ORRLP 003) (cd re-mast.Mar03 +=; CMRCD 672)* – Why (extended) / Home again to you / Green eye / Rainbow demon / Untitled (demo).

May 72. (7") *<73271>* **THE WIZARD. / WHY** [–] [ ]

Jun 72. (7") *(WIP 6126)* **THE WIZARD. / GYPSY** [ ] [–]

Jul 72. (7") *<73307>* **EASY LIVIN' / ALL MY LIFE** [–] [39]

Aug 72. (7") *(WIP 6140)* **EASY LIVIN'. / WHY** [ ] [–]

Nov 72. (lp) *(ILPS 9213) <652>* **THE MAGICIAN'S BIRTHDAY** [28] [31]
– Sunrise / Spider woman / Blind eye / Echoes in the dark / Rain / Sweet Lorraine / Tales / The magician's birthday. *(re-iss. Jul77; BRNA 213) (re-iss. Apr86 on 'Castle' lp/c; CLA LP/MC 109) (cd-iss. Apr89; CLACD 109) (re-iss. cd Jan96 on 'Essential'+=; ESMCD 339)* – Silver white man / Crystal ball. *(cd re-mast.Aug03 on 'Castle'++=; CMRCD 771)* – Gary's song / Silver white man (demo) / Echoes in the dark (part 1 & 2) / Proud words / Rain / Happy birthday / Sunrise.

Jan 73. (7") *<73349>* **BLIND EYE. / SWEET LORRAINE** [–] [97] [91]

May 73. (d-lp) *(ISLD 1) <7503>* **URIAH HEEP LIVE (live)** [23] [37]
– Sunrise / Sweet Lorraine / Traveller in time / Easy livin' / July morning / Tears in my eyes / Gypsy / Circle of hands / Look at yourself / The magician's birthday / Love machine / Rock'n'roll medley:- Roll over Beethoven – Blue suede shoes – Mean woman blues – Hound dog – At the hop – Whole lotta shakin' goin' on. *(re-iss. Apr77; BRSP 1) (cd-iss. Jun96 on 'Essential'; ESMCD 320) (cd re-mast.Aug03 on 'Castle'; CMDDD 772)*

May 73. (7") *<73406>* **JULY MORNING (live). / TEARS IN MY EYES (live)** [–] [ ]

Bronze Warners

Sep 73. (lp) *(ILPS 9245) <2724>* **SWEET FREEDOM** [18] [33]
– Dreamer / Stealin' / One day / Sweet freedom / If I had the time / Seven stars / Circus / Pilgrim. *(re-iss. Apr77; BRNA 245) (cd-iss. Jan96 on 'Essential'+=; ESMCD 338)* – Sunshine / Stealin' / Seven stars.

May 74. (7") *(BRO 7) <7738>* **STEALIN'. / SUNSHINE** [ ] Oct73 [91]

Jun 74. (lp) *(ILPS 9280) <2800>* **WONDERWORLD** [23] [38]
– Wonderworld / Suicidal man / The shadows and the winds / So tired / The easy road / Something or nothing / I won't mind / We got we / Dreams. *(re-iss. Apr77; BRNA 280) (cd-iss. May96 on 'Essential'; ESMCD 380)*

Aug 74. (7") *(BRO 10) <8013>* **SOMETHING OR NOTHING. / WHAT CAN I DO** [ ] [ ]

— **JOHN WETTON** (b.12 Jul'49, Derby, England) – bass, vocals (ex-KING CRIMSON, ex-ROXY MUSIC, ex-FAMILY) repl. THAIN (He died of a drug overdose 19 May'76) Line-up now **BYRON, BOX, HENSLEY, KERSLAKE & WETTON**

Jun 75. (lp) *(ILPS 9335) <2869>* **RETURN TO FANTASY** [7] [85]
– Return to fantasy / Shady lady / Devil's daughter / Beautiful dream / Prima Donna / Your turn to remember / Showdown / Why did you go / A year or a day. *(re-iss. Jul77; BRNA 385) (cd-iss. May96 on 'Essential'; ESMCD 381)*

Jun 75. (7") *<8132>* **PRIMA DONNA. / STEALIN'** [–] [ ]

Jun 75. (7") *(BRO 17)* **PRIMA DONNA. / SHOUT IT OUT** [ ] [–]

May 76. (lp) *(ILPS 9384) <2949>* **HIGH AND MIGHTY** [55] [ ]
– One way or another / Weep in silence / Misty eyes / Midnight / Can't keep a good band down / Woman of the world / Footprints in the snow / Can't stop singing / Make a little love / Confession. *(re-iss. Apr77; BRNA 384) (re-iss. Mar91 on 'Castle' cd/lp; CLA CD/LP 191) (re-mast.Jul97 on 'Essential'; ESMCD 468)*

Jun 76. (7") *(BRO 27)* **ONE WAY OR ANOTHER. / MISTY EYES** [ ] [ ]

— **JOHN LAWTON** – vocals (ex-LUCIFER'S FRIEND) repl. BYRON to ROUGH DIAMOND / **TREVOR BOLDER** – bass (ex-David Bowie's SPIDERS FROM MARS, ex-WISHBONE ASH) repl. WETTON who joined BRYAN FERRY BAND, and later UK and ASIA

Feb 77. (lp) *(ILPS 9483) <3013>* **FIREFLY** [ ] [ ]
– Been away too long / Sympathy / Who needs me / Wise man / The hanging tree / Rollin' on / Do you know / Firefly. *(re-iss. Apr77; BRNA 483) (re-iss. Mar91 on 'Castle' cd/lp; CLA CD/LP 190) (re-mast.Jul97 on 'Essential'; ESMCD 559)*

Apr 77. (7") *(BRO 37)* **WISE MAN. / CRIME OF PASSION** [ ] [–]

Oct 77. (7") *(BRO 47) <8581>* **FREE ME. / MASQUERADE** [ ] [ ]

Nov 77. (lp) *(BRON 504) <3145>* **INNOCENT VICTIM** [ ] [ ]
– Keep on ridin' / Flyin' high / Roller / Free 'n' easy / Illusion / Free me / Cheat 'n' lie / The dance / Choices. *(re-iss. Dec90 on 'Castle' cd/lp; CLA CD/LP 210)*

Bronze Chrysalis

Sep 78. (lp) *(BRNA 512) <1204>* **FALLEN ANGEL** [ ] [ ]
– Woman of the night / Falling in love / One more night (last farewell) / Put your lovin' on me / Come back to me / Whad'ya say / Save it / Love or nothing / I'm alive / Fallen angel. *(re-iss. Feb90 on 'Castle' cd/c/lp; CLA CD/MC/LP 176) (re-mast.Jul97 on 'Essential'; ESMCD 561)*

Oct 78. (7") *(BRO 62)* **COME BACK TO ME. / CHEATER** [ ] [ ]

— **JOHN SLOMAN** – vocals (ex-LONE STAR) repl. LAWTON / **CHRIS SLADE** (b.30 Oct'46) – drums (ex-MANFRED MANN'S EARTH BAND) repl. LEE to OZZY OSBOURNE

Jan 80. (7") *(BRO 88)* **CARRY ON. / BEING HURT** [ ] [–]

Feb 80. (lp/c) *(BRON/+C 524)* **CONQUEST** [ ] [–]
– No return / Imagination / Feelings / Fools / Carry on / Won't have to wait too long / Out on the street / It ain't easy. *(re-iss. Dec90 on 'Castle' cd/lp; CLA CD/LP 208) (re-mast.Aug97 on 'Essential'; ESMCD 570)*

Jun 80. (7") *(BRO 96)* **LOVE STEALER. / NO RETURN** [ ] [ ]

— **GREGG DETCHETT** – keyboards (ex-PULSAR) repl. HENSLEY to solo & BLACKFOOT

Jan 81. (7") *(BRO 112)* **THINK IT OVER. / MY JOANNA NEEDS TUNING** [ ] [–]

— split 1981 when SLOMAN developed a throat infection (he later formed BADLANDS). CHRIS SLADE joined GARY NUMAN then DAVID GILMOUR and later joined The FIRM. DETCHETT later joined MIKE + THE MECHANICS. BOLDER re-joined WISHBONE ASH. Early 1982, URIAH HEEP re-formed with **BOX** bringing back **LEE KERSLAKE** plus new **PETE GOALBY** – vocals (ex-TRAPEZE) / **JOHN SINCLAIR** – keyboards (ex-HEAVY METAL KIDS) / **BOB DAISLEY** – bass (ex-OZZY OSBOURNE, ex-RAINBOW, ex-WIDOWMAKER, etc)

Bronze Mercury

Feb 82. (7"ep) *(BRO 143)* **THE ABOMINATOR JUNIOR EP** [ ] [–]
– On the rebound / Tin soldier / Song of a bitch.

Mar 82. (lp/c) *(BRON/+C 538)* <4057> **ABOMINOG** [34] [56]
– Too scared to run / Chasing shadows / On the rebound / Hot night in a cold town / Running all night (with the lion) / That's the way that it is / Prisoner / Hot persuasion / Sell your soul / Think it over. *(re-iss. Apr86 on 'Castle' lp/c; CLA LP/MC 110) (cd-iss. Apr89; CLACD 110) (re-mast.Aug97 on 'Essential'; ESMCD 571)*

May 82. (7") *(BRO 148)* **THAT'S THE WAY THAT IT IS. / HOT PERSUASION** [ ] [-]

May 82. (7") *<76177>* **THAT'S THE WAY THAT IT IS. / SON OF A BITCH** [-] [ ]

May 83. (lp/c) *(BRON/+C 545)* <812313> **HEAD FIRST** [46] [ ]
– The other side of midnight / Stay on top / Lonely nights / Sweet talk / Love is blind / Roll-overture / Red lights / Rollin' the rock / Straight through the heart / Weekend warriors. *(re-iss. Dec90 on 'Castle' cd/lp; CLA CD/LP 209) (re-mast.Jul97 on 'Essential'; ESMCD 572)*

Jun 83. (7"/7"pic-d) *(BRO/+P 166)* **LONELY NIGHTS. / WEEKEND WARRIORS** [ ] [-]

Aug 83. (7") *(BRO 168)* **STAY ON TOP. / PLAYING FOR TIME** [ ] [-]
(d7"+=) *(BROG 168)* – Gypsy / Easy livin' / Sweet Lorraine / Stealin'.

— **TREVOR BOLDER** – bass returned to repl. DAISLEY

Portrait CBS Assoc.

Mar 85. (7"/7"sha-pic-d) *(TA/WA 6103)* **ROCKERAMA. / BACK STAGE GIRL** [ ] [ ]

Mar 85. (lp) *(PRT 26414)* **EQUATOR** [79] [ ]
– Rockarama / Bad blood / Lost one love / Angel / Holding on / Party time / Poor little rich girl / Skools burnin' / Heartache city / Night of the wolf. *(cd-iss. Feb99 on 'Columbia'; 493339-2)*

May 85. (7"/7"pic-d) *(A/WA 6309)* **POOR LITTLE RICH GIRL. / BAD BLOOD** [ ] [-]

— **BERNIE SHAW** – vocals (ex-GRAND PRIX, ex-PRAYING MANTIS) repl. GOALBY / **PHIL LANZON** – keyboards (ex-GRAND PRIX, etc) repl. SINCLAIR (above 2 now alongside **BOX, BOLDER, KERSLAKE**)

Legacy Legacy-Sony

Jul 88. (lp/c/cd) *(LLP/LLK/LLCD 118)* <848811> **LIVE IN MOSCOW (live)** [ ] [ ]
– Bird of prey / Stealin' / Too scared to run / Corrina / Mister Majestic / The wizard / July morning / Easy livin' / That's the way that it is / Pacific highway. *(cd+=)* – Gypsy. *(cd re-iss. 1992 on 'Castle'; CLACD 276) (cd re-iss. Mar98 on 'Essential'; ESMCD 611)*

Sep 88. (7") *(LGY 65)* **EASY LIVIN' (live). / CORRINA (live)** [ ] [-]
(12"red+=) *(LGYT 65)* – Gypsy (live).

Apr 89. (7") *(LGY 67)* **HOLD YOUR HEAD UP. / MIRACLE CHILD** [ ] [-]
(12"+=) *(LGYT 67)* – ('A'extended).

Apr 89. (lp/pic-lp/c/cd) *(LLP/LLPPD/LLK/LLCD 120)* <848812> **RAGING SILENCE** [ ] [ ]
– Hold your head up / Blood red roses / Voice on my TV / Rich kid / Cry freedom / Bad bad man / More fool you / When the war is over / Lifeline / Rough justice. *(cd re-iss. Feb93 on 'Castle'; CLACD 277) (cd re-iss. Mar98 on 'Essential'; ESMCD 612)*

Jul 89. (7") *(LGY 101)* **BLOOD RED ROSES. / ROUGH JUSTICE** [ ] [-]
(12"+=) *(LGYT 101)* – Look at yourself.

1990. (cd) *(LLCD 133)* **STILL 'EAVY, STILL PROUD (live)** [-] Swedish [-]
– Gypsy / Lady in black / July morning / Easy livin' / The easy road / Free me / The other side of midnight / Mr Majestic / Rich kid / Blood red roses.

Feb 91. (cd) *(LLCD 137)* **DIFFERENT WORLD** [ ] [-]
– Blood on stone / Which way will the wind blow / All God's children / All for one / Different world / Step by step / Seven days / First touch / One on one / Cross that line / Stand back. *(UK re-iss. 1990's on 'Castle'; CLACD 279) <US-iss.Nov94 on 'Griifin'; 239> (cd re-iss. Mar98 on 'Essential'; ESMCD 614)*

H.T.D. H.T.D.

Apr 95. (cd/c/lp) *(<HTD CD/MC/LP 33>)* **SEA OF LIGHT** [ ] [ ]
– Against the odds / Sweet sugar / Time of revelation / Mistress of all time / Universal wheels / Fear of falling / Spirit of freedom / Logical progression / Love in silence / Words in the distance / Fires of hell / Dream on. *(cd re-iss. Dec96 on 'S.P.V.'; 085-7695-2)*

Oct 95. (cd-s) *(CDHTD 102)* **DREAM ON /** [ ] [-]

S.P.V. Spitfire

Jul 96. (cd) *(0857699-2)* <5034> **SPELLBINDER (live)** [ ] Jun99 [ ]
– Devil's daughter / Stealin' / Bad bad man / Rainbow demon / Words in a distance / The wizard / Circle of hands / Gypsy / Look at yourself / Lady in love / Easy livin'.

Eagle Spitfire

Sep 98. (cd) *(EAGCD 043)* **SONIC ORIGAMI** [ ] [ ]
– Between two worlds / I hear voices / Protect little heart / Heartless land / Only the young / In the moment / Question / Change / Shelter from the rain / Everything in life / Across the miles / Feels like / The golden palace / Sweet pretender.

– compilations, etc. –

Nov 75. (lp) *Bronze; (ILPS 9375) / Mercury; <1070>* **THE BEST OF URIAH HEEP** [ ] [ ]
– Gypsy / Bird of prey / July morning / Look at yourself / Easy livin' / The wizard / Sweet Lorraine / Stealin' / Lady in black / Return to fantasy. *(re-iss. Apr77; BRNA 375) (cd-iss. Apr90 on 'Sequel';)*

1983. (12"ep) *Bronze; (HEEP 1)* **EASY LIVIN' / SWEET LORRAINE. / GYPSY / STEALIN'** [ ] [-]

Apr 86. (d-lp/c/cd) *Raw Power; (RAW LP/TC/CD 012)* **ANTHOLOGY** [ ] [-]

1986. (cd) *Legacy; (LLHCD 3003)* **ANTHOLOGY** [ ] [-]

Mar 87. (lp/c/cd) *Raw Power; (RAW LP/MC/CD 030)* **LIVE IN EUROPE 1979 (live)** [ ] [-]

May 88. (d-lp/c/cd) *That's Original; (TFO LP/MC/CD 7)* **LOOK AT YOURSELF / VERY 'EAVY, VERY 'UMBLE** [ ] [-]

1988. (d-lp/c) *Castle; (CCS LP/MC 177)* **THE URIAH HEEP COLLECTION** [ ] [-]

Dec 88. (cd-ep) *Special Edition; (CD 3-16)* **LADY IN BLACK / JULY MORNING / EASY LIVIN'** [ ] [-]

Dec 88. (lp/c/cd) *Castle; (HEEP LP/TC/CD 1)* **LIVE AT SHEPPERTON '74 (live)** [ ] [-]
(re-iss. Dec90 cd/lp; CLA CD/LP 192) (re-mast.Jul97 on 'Essential'; ESMCD 590)

Aug 89. (d-lp/c/cd) *Castle; (CCS LP/MC/CD 226)* **THE COLLECTION** [ ] [-]

Jun 90. (3xcd/5xlp) *Essential; (ESB CD/LP 022)* **TWO DECADES IN ROCK** [ ] [-]

Jul 90. (cd/c) *Raw Power; (RAW CD/MC 041)* **URIAH HEEP LIVE (live)** [ ] [-]

Oct 91. (cd/c) *Elite; (ELITE 020 CD/MC)* **ECHOES IN THE DARK** [ ] [-]
– Echoes in the dark / The wizard / Come away Melinda / Devil's daughter / Hot persuasion / Showdown / I'm alive / Look at yourself / Spider woman / Woman of the night / I want to be free / Gypsy / Sunrise / Bird of prey / Love machine / Lady in black *(re-iss. Sep93; same)*

Nov 91. (cd) *Sequel; (NEXCD 184)* **EXCAVATIONS FROM THE BRONZE AGE** [ ] [-]

Feb 92. (3xcd-box) *Castle; (CLABX 903)* **3 ORIGINALS** [ ] [-]
– (FIREFLY / HEAD FIRST / DEMONS AND WIZARDS)

Jan 95. (cd) *Spectrum; (550 730-2)* **LADY IN BLACK** [ ] [-]

May 95. (cd) *Spectrum; (550 731-2)* **FREE ME** [ ] [-]

Oct 95. (d-cd) *H.T.D.; (CDHTD 561)*

Mar 96. (4xcd-box) *Essential; (ESFCD 298)* **A TIME OF REVELATION – 25 YEARS ON** [ ] [-]

May 96. (cd) *Red Steel; (RMCCD 0193)* **THE LANSDOWNE TAPES** [ ] [-]

Oct 96. (cd) *Essential; (<ESMCD 418>)* **THE BEST OF URIAH HEEP, VOL.1** [ ] [ ]

Oct 97. (cd) *Essential; (<ESMCD 594>)* **THE BEST OF URIAH HEEP, VOL.2** [ ] [ ]

May 98. (cd) *King Biscuit; (KBFHCD 008)* <88027-2> **URIAH HEEP IN CONCERT (live)** [ ] Jun97 [ ]

Oct 98. (3xcd-box) *Essential; (ESMBX 306)* **VERY 'EAVY, VERY 'UMBLE / SALISBURY / LOOK AT YOURSELF** [ ] [-]

Oct 98. (3xcd-box) *Essential; (ESMBX 307)* **FIREFLY / INNOCENT VICTIM / FALLEN ANGEL** [ ] [-]

Jan 00. (d-cd) *Essential; (<ESDCD 818>)* **ANTHOLOGY** [ ] [ ]

Jan 00. (d-cd) *Essential; (<ESDCD 819>)* **LIVE IN EUROPE 1979** [ ] [ ]

Jan 00. (cd) *Members Edition; (UAE 3089-2)* **URIAH HEEP** [ ] [-]

Jul 00. (cd) *S.P.V.; (31021920)* **SEA OF LIGHT / SPELLBINDER** [ ] [ ]

Sep 01. (d-cd) *Classic Rock; (CRL 0731)* **2 SIDES OF . . .** [ ] [-]

☐ UTOPIA (see under ⇒ AMON DUUL II)

☐ UTOPIA (see under ⇒ RUNDGREN, Todd)

U2

Formed: Dublin, Ireland . . . 1977 by BONO (b. PAUL HEWSON), THE EDGE (b. DAVID EVANS), ADAM CLAYTON and LARRY MULLEN. Indisputably one of the biggest and the most talked about 'musical phenomenon's of the last two decades, U2 nevertheless graduated from humble beginnings as a covers band. Finally adopting the U2 moniker in 1978, they subsequently attracted the attention of Paul McGuinness, one of the most respected managers in the business. It wasn't long before they found themselves signed to 'C.B.S.' Ireland via A&R man, Jackie Hayden, releasing a debut single, 'U2-3' in late '79. The track scaled the Irish charts, as did a follow-up, 'ANOTHER DAY', the group subsequently snapped up by 'Island' records for a worldwide deal. Initially, U2 made little impact, singles '11 O'CLOCK TICK TOCK' and 'A DAY WITHOUT ME' failing to chart. By the release of the Steve Lillywhite-produced debut album, 'BOY' (1980), however, U2 were already assuming the mantle of cult status. Strikingly original, the group carved out their own plot of fertile territory within the suffocatingly oversubscribed rock format, cultivating a watertight, propulsive minimalism to partner their politically direct lyrics. Carried equally by BONO's crusading vocal theatrics, THE EDGE's serrated guitar cascades and the ryhthmic drive of CLAYTON and MULLEN, the likes of 'I WILL FOLLOW' was a blueprint for the U2 formula. And it was a formula which seemed to command devotion; those who followed the band did so with the same zeal as U2 set out their humanitarian agenda, the group eschewing party politics for a more expansive but no less focused commentary on the world's ills with an overriding religious/spiritual bent. Live, the group were also being hailed as one of the most innovative and exciting acts to emerge from the post-punk morass. Though 'OCTOBER' (1981) almost broke into the Top 10, the album failed to spawn any major hits, the clarion call of 'GLORIA' surprisingly stiffing outside the Top 50. So it was then, that U2 seemed to come out of nowhere in early '83 with a Top 10 single, the highly emotive 'NEW YEAR'S DAY' (inspired by the Lech Walenska's Polish Solidarity Union) and a No.1 album, 'WAR'. U2's first masterstroke, the album was consistently compelling, through the rousing rhythmic militarism of 'SUNDAY BLOODY SUNDAY' (interpreted by many as a republican rebel song, BONO famously declared otherwise when introducing the track live) and the celebratory 'TWO HEARTS BEAT AS ONE' to the more meditative acoustics of 'DROWNING MAN'. The record's anthemic Irish qualities also appealed to the Americans, 'WAR' almost making the US Top 10; from the electric atmosphere of the live 'UNDER A BLOOD RED SKY' (1983), it certainly seemed U2's sound could galvanise a transatlantic audience, probably (and eventually) a world audience. Previewed by perhaps U2's most anthemic, politically pointed song, 'PRIDE (IN THE NAME OF LOVE)' (a tribute to assassinated black civil rights hero, Martin Luther King), 'THE UNFORGETTABLE FIRE' (1984) consolidated the band's commerical and creative maturity. For the most part, however, the record took a completely different approach, BRIAN ENO presiding over a collection of more exploratory, occasionally near-ambient excursions, the highlight arguably being the epic atmospherics of the stunning title track. Equally evocative was 'BAD', an almost hymn-like incantation with which U2 entranced the world at Live Aid in summer '85. One of the key events in the band's career, their celebrated performance undoubtedly won them a massive new audience almost overnight, much in the same way as QUEEN rejuvenated their career through the concert. Understandably, then, the anticipation for U2's next album, 'THE JOSHUA TREE' (1987), was fevered. Fortunately it was also justified, U2 delivering what was undeniably the most accomplished set of their career and probably one of the greatest rock albums ever released. Like many such masterworks, U2 scaled this pinnacle of creativity by means of a subtle balance, between panoramic euphoria and hushed reflection, between the personal and the political and between insinuation and crystal clarity. The record's undertow of spiritual soul searching evident on the likes of 'I STILL HAVEN'T FOUND WHAT I'M LOOKING FOR' (a US No.1) obviously struck a chord in a decade more concerned with ruthless material gain, while the air of soft-focus melancholy permeating 'WITH OR WITHOUT YOU' and 'RUNNING TO STAND STILL' further enhanced the album's almost tangible warmth. Even the more full-on tracks such as 'WHERE THE STREETS HAVE NO NAME' and 'IN GOD'S COUNTRY' seemed to emanate from a deep-seated yearning through the shards of THE EDGE's guitar scree. 'THE JOSHUA TREE' was a transatlantic No.1 (a worldwide No.1), facilitating U2's move to the top of the world premier league. As well as being a formidable commercial proposition, U2 were hailed by some commentators as the most 'important' rock group on the planet, both lyrically and musically. Of course, such inflated claims were matched by equally vociferous critics of the group's perceived pomposity and preaching self-importance. Such criticism was nothing new, although it reached its height in the aftermath of 'THE JOSHUA TREE' and its attendant tour, when BONO was being hailed as some kind of messiah. The sight of the singer charging around the stage with a floodlight and a white flag, together with his increasingly politicised between song (or even half-way through) speeches became too much for some, although in a music scene bereft of direction or purpose, BONO probably made up for the prevailing insipidness. Attempting to follow up this musical landmark, U2 released a kind of stop-gap half-live/half-studio affair, 'RATTLE AND HUM' (1988). A soundtrack to the rockumentary of the same name which marked the culmination of the group's obsession with America, the album was accused of being half-baked in parts. Possibly, but the gut-level punch of 'GOD PART II' and the bleakly beautiful 'VAN DIEMEN'S LAND' were unquestionably full-baked, if oddities nonetheless. Following the poignant love song, 'ALL I WANT IS YOU' (a UK Top 5) in summer '89, U2 went to ground, hard at work on a new strategy. Sporting wraparound shades and skin-tight black leather, BONO finally emerged in late '91 with 'THE FLY', a grinding guitar groove with urgent, hoarsely whispered lyrics. The track entered the UK chart at No.1, paving the way for the massively successful 'ACHTUNG BABY' (1991). Stylistically diverse, the album marked the beginnings of U2's flirtation with dance culture, a sign that the band were wary of falling into the rock dinosaur mould. BONO had also obviously been listening to his critics, changing his persona from earnest poet to lounge lizard sophisticate. Though the likes of 'WHO'S GONNA RIDE YOUR WILD HORSES' and the deeply affecting 'ONE' (probably the most intimate song the group have ever penned) signalled a move into more personal lyrical territory, the album's attendant 'Zoo TV' tour was themed around political events in Europe, albeit with a more post-modern, multi-media stoked irony. Inspired by the tour, 'ZOOROPA' (1993) was U2's most contemporary release to date, a fractured, dance-orientated affair which rather unfairly received a bit of a pasting from more short-sighted critics. Following on from the celebrated dance mixes of 'EVEN BETTER THAN THE REAL THING' (from 'ACHTUNG BABY'), the 12' remix of 'LEMON' was hot property when originally released in limited lemon coloured vinyl. As well as catering for dance trainspotters, U2 even recorded a duet with JOHNNY CASH, the darkly brilliant 'THE WANDERER', in effect kickstarting the aging country star's career. In the ensuing two years, BONO popped up with GAVIN FRIDAY on the theme to the acclaimed 'IN THE NAME OF THE FATHER', while U2 scored a UK No.2 hit with 'HOLD ME, THRILL ME, KISS ME, KILL ME' from the huge box office smash, 'Batman Forever'. This fascination with soundtrack music continued via the PASSENGERS project, a collaboration between U2, BRIAN ENO, italian opera singer PAVAROTTI and Glaswegian beatz guru HOWIE B. Entitled 'ORIGINAL SOUNDTRACKS VOL.1' (1995), a few of the album's tracks (highlight being the hit single, 'MISS SARAJEVO') were actually written as themes to avant-garde films while the remainder were written for imaginary celluloid pieces. As low-key as U2 have ever dared go, the album passed by without much fuss, its ambient noodlings not really indicating a new direction as such but proving that the group were firmly committed to constant experimentation. For their next album proper, U2 retained HOWIE B as co-producer, crafting an album that once again used dance music as a touchstone. Preview single, 'DISCOTHEQUE', sounded like a watered-down 'FLY' although the accompanying VILLAGE PEOPLE-pastiche video showed, shock horror!, U2 having a right old laugh! Despite this newfound sense of humour, the 'POP' (1996) album met with mixed reviews, some hailing it as a bold new dawn, others accusing the band of treading water. The record certainly had its moments, the searing desolation of 'STARING AT THE SUN' and the apocalyptic 'LAST NIGHT ON EARTH' (the video featuring an appearance from counter-culture guru, William Burroughs, just weeks before his death, U2 having previously persuaded the voraciously anti-rock Charles Bukowski to attend a gig, no mean feat!) for example, but there was a feeling of incompleteness to the whole affair. Likewise, the accompanying 'Pop Mart' tour which got off to a shaky start in Las Vegas, its consumerist theme carried by another media extravaganza, albeit downscaled from the Zoo TV era. While U2 undoubtedly lead the way in terms of stadium rock, constantly innovative in new ways to keep the medium fresh, they arguably need to rediscover themselves musically and give up recycling second hand ideas. Whether they have either the willingness or ability to do this is another matter, although being past masters of coming out fighting in the face of adversity, it's highly likely. With a new decade, a new millennium and a new album, 'ALL THAT YOU CAN'T LEAVE BEHIND' (2000), U2 arguably did rediscover themselves although only in terms of the strident, open sound which defined their approach during the 80's. This revisionism works (often spectacularly) well within a modern – or even post-modern – context, most obviously on the massive singles, 'BEAUTIFUL DAY' and 'ELEVATION'. BONO's recently stated intention to reclaim U2's position as the world's top dogs matched the overarching reach of the album, resuming normal service for the Irish veterans. The inevitable best-of surfaced in 2002 although it could've been much more thoughtfully put together. While classics like 'THE FLY' and 'LEMON' were missing altogether, the tendency to replace original songs with inferior – and usually pointless – remixes only underlined a missed opportunity. • **Songwriters:** All written by BONO / THE EDGE, except HELTER SKELTER (Beatles) / ALL ALONG THE WATCHTOWER (Bob Dylan) (hit; Jimi Hendrix) / STAR SPANGLED BANNER (US National anthem) / DANCING BAREFOOT (Patti Smith) / NIGHT AND DAY (Cole Porter) / PAINT IT BLACK (Rolling Stones) / FORTUNATE SON (Creedence Clearwater Revival) / HALLELUJAH (Leonard Cohen) by BONO. • **Trivia:** BONO contributed vox to BAND AID single late '84. That year, the band also started own record label, mainly for other Irish groups and was a starter for HOTHOUSE FLOWERS, CACTUS WORLD NEWS etc. In 1988, BONO and THE EDGE co-wrote for ROY ORBISON on his last living studio album, 'Mystery Girl'. They wrote the theme for the James Bond film 'GoldenEye', which became a hit for TINA TURNER in 1995.

Album rating: BOY (*8) / OCTOBER (*6) / WAR (*9) / UNDER A BLOOD RED SKY (*6) / THE UNFORGETTABLE FIRE (*9) / WIDE AWAKE IN AMERICA (*6) / THE JOSHUA TREE (*10) / RATTLE & HUM (*8) / ACHTUNG BABY (*8) / ZOOROPA (*9) / ORIGINAL SOUNDTRACKS 1 (*7; as the Passengers) / POP (*6) / THE BEST OF 1980-1990 compilation (*9) / ALL THAT YOU CAN'T LEAVE BEHIND (*7) / THE BEST OF 1990-2000 + THE B-SIDES compilation (*7)

BONO VOX (b. PAUL HEWSON, 10 May'60) – vocals / **THE EDGE** (b. DAVID EVANS, 8 Aug'61, Barking, Essex) – guitar, keyboards / **ADAM CLAYTON** (b.13 Mar'60, Chinnor, Oxfordshire, England) – bass / **LARRY MULLEN** (b. LAURENCE MULLEN, 31 Oct'61) – drums

C.B.S. — not iss.

Oct 79. (7"ep/12"ep) *(CBS/+12 7951)* **U2: THREE** [–] Irish [–]
– Out of control / Stories for boys / Boy-girl. *(re-iss. 1980 7"orange,yellow,white; same) (re-iss. c-ep 1985; CBS 40-7951)*

Feb 80. (7",7"yellow,7"orange,7"white) *(CBS 8306)* **ANOTHER DAY. / TWILIGHT (demo)** [–] Irish [–]

Island — Island

May 80. (7") *(WIP 6601)* **11 O'CLOCK TICK TOCK. / TOUCH** [ ] [–]

Aug 80. (7") *(WIP 6630)* **A DAY WITHOUT ME. / THINGS TO MAKE AND DO** [ ] [–]

Oct 80. (7") *(WIP 6656)* **I WILL FOLLOW. / BOY-GIRL (live)** [ ] [–]

Nov 80. (lp/c) *(ILPS/ICT <9646>)* **BOY** [52] Feb81 [63]
– I will follow / Twilight / An cat dubh / Into the heart / Out of control / Stories for boys / The ocean / A day without me / Another time, another place / The Electric Co. / Shadows and tall trees. *(cd-iss. May86; CID 110) (re-iss. May95 cd)(c)(lp; IMCD 211)(ILPM 9646)*

Apr 81. (7") **I WILL FOLLOW. / OUT OF CONTROL** [–] [ ]

Jul 81. (7") *(WIP 6679)* **FIRE. / J. SWALLO** [35] [ ]
(d7"+=) *(U-WIP 6679)* – 11 o'clock tick tock (live) / The ocean (live) / Cry (live) / The Electric Co. (live).

Sep 81. (7") *(WIP 6733)* **GLORIA. / I WILL FOLLOW (live)** [55] [ ]

Oct 81. (lp/c) *(ILPS/ICT <9680>)* **OCTOBER** [11] [ ]
– Gloria / I fall down / I threw a brick through a window / Rejoice / Fire / Tomorrow / October / With a shout / Stranger in a strange land / Scarlet / Is that all?. *(cd-iss. May86; CID 111) (re-dist.Jun92; same) (cd re-iss. Mar96; IMCD 223)*

Mar 82. (7") *(WIP 6770)* **A CELEBRATION. / TRASH, TRAMPOLENE AND THE PARTY GIRL** [47] [ ]

Jan 83. (7") *(WIP 6848)* *<99915>* **NEW YEAR'S DAY. / TREASURE (WHATEVER HAPPENED TO PETE THE CHOP)** [10] [53]
(d7"+=/12"+=) *(U-WIP/12WIP 6848)* – Fire (live) / I threw a brick through the window (live) / A day without me (live).

Feb 83. (lp/c) *(ILPS/ICT 9733)* *<90067>* **WAR** [1] [12]
– Sunday bloody Sunday / Seconds / Like a song / New Year's day / Two hearts beat as one / The refugee / Drowning man / Red light / '40' / Surrender. *(cd-iss. Dec85; CID 112) (re-iss. Aug91 cd/c; IMCD/ICT 141; hit No.51 Jun92, hit UK No.38 Aug93)*

Mar 83. (7") *(IS 109)* *<99861>* **TWO HEARTS BEAT AS ONE. / ENDLESS DEEP** [18] [ ]
(d7"+=) *(ISD 109)* – Two hearts beat as one (U.S. remix) / New Year's day (U.S. remix).
(12") *(12IS 109)* – ('A'-club mix) / New Year's day (U.S. remix) / ('A'-U.S. remix).

Nov 83. (lp/c) *(IMA/IMC 3)* *<90127>* **UNDER A BLOOD RED SKY (live)** [2] [28]
– Gloria / 11 o'clock tick tock / I will follow / Party girl / Sunday bloody Sunday / The Electric Co. / New Year's day / '40'. *(cd-iss. May86; CID 113) (re-dist.Jun92; same)*

Dec 83. (7") *<99789>* **I WILL FOLLOW (live). / TWO HEARTS BEAT AS ONE (live)** [–] [81]

Sep 84. (7"/7"pic-d) *(IS/+P 202)* *<99704>* **PRIDE (IN THE NAME OF LOVE). / BOOMERANG 2** [3] [33]
(d7"+=/c-s+=/12"white+=) *(ISD/CIS/12IS 202)* – 4th of July / Boomerang 1.

(12"blue+=) *(12ISX 202)* – Boomerang 1 / 11 o'clock tick tock (extended) / Touch.

Oct 84. (lp/c)(cd) *(U2/+C 5)(CID 102)* <90231> **THE UNFORGETTABLE FIRE** [1] [12]
– A sort of homecoming / Pride (in the name of love) / Wire / The unforgettable fire / Promenade / 4th of July / Bad / Indian summer sky / Elvis Presley and America / MLK. *(re-dist.Jun92 hit No.38 UK; same)*

May 85. (7"/7"sha-pic-d) *(IS/+P 220)* **THE UNFORGETTABLE FIRE. / A SORT OF HOMECOMING (live)** [6] [ ]
(12"+=) *(12IS 220)* – The three sunrises / Bass trap / Love comes tumbling.
(d7"+=) *(ISD 220)* – The three sunrises / Love comes tumbling / 60 seconds in kingdom come.

May 85. (m-lp/c) *(ISSP/+C 22)* <90279> **WIDE AWAKE IN AMERICA** [11] [37]
– Bad (live) / A sort of homecoming (live) / The three sunrises / Love comes tumbling. *(cd-iss. Oct87; CIDU 22) (cd re-iss. Nov89; IMCD 75)*

— Later in the year, BONO guested for CLANNAD on hit 'IN A LIFETIME'. In Sep'86, THE EDGE issued soundtrack album CAPTIVE (see further below).

Mar 87. (7"/c-s/12"/cd-s) *(IS/CIS/12IS/CID 319)* <99469> **WITH OR WITHOUT YOU. / LUMINOUS TIMES (HOLD ON TO LOVE) / WALK TO THE WATER** [4] [1]

Mar 87. (lp/c)(cd) *(U2/+C 6)(CIDU 26)* <90581> **THE JOSHUA TREE** [1] [1]
– Where the streets have no name / I still haven't found what I'm looking for / With or without you / Bullet the blue sky / Running to stand still / Red Hill mining town / In God's country / Trip through your wires / One tree hill / Exit / Mothers of the disappeared. *(also on 4x7"box) (re-charted UK Jan92, peaked Jun92 at No.19) (re-iss. Aug93 cd/c/lp, hit UK No.27; same)*

May 87. (7"/c-s/12") *(IS/CIS/12IS 328)* <99430> **I STILL HAVEN'T FOUND WHAT I'M LOOKING FOR. / SPANISH EYES / DEEP IN THE HEART** [6] [1]

Sep 87. (7") *(IS 340)* <99408> **WHERE THE STREETS HAVE NO NAME. / SILVER AND GOLD / SWEETEST THING** [4] [13]
(c-s+=/12"+=/cd-s+=) *(CIS/12IS/CID 340)* – Race against time.

Jan 88. (7"-US-imp) <7-99385> **IN GOD'S COUNTRY. / BULLET THE BLUE SKY / RUNNING TO STAND STILL** [48] Nov87 [44]

Sep 88. (7") *(IS 400)* <99250> **DESIRE. / HALLELUJAH (HERE SHE COMES)** [1] [3]
(12"+=/12"g-f+=/pic-cd-s+=) *(12IS/12ISG/CIDP 400)* – ('A'-Hollywood remix).

Oct 88. (d-lp/c)(cd) *(U2/+C 7)(CIDU 27)* <91003> **RATTLE AND HUM** (some live) [1] [1]
– Helter skelter / Hawkmoon 269 / Van Diemen's land / Desire / Angel of Harlem / I still haven't found what I'm looking for / When love comes to town / God part II / Bullet the blue sky / Silver and gold / Love rescue me / Heartland / Star spangled banner / All I want is you / Freedom for my people / All along the watchtower / Pride (in the name of love). *(re-charted UK No.37 on Jun92) (re-iss. Aug93, hit UK No.34)*

Oct 88. (7") *(IS 402)* <99254> **ANGEL OF HARLEM. / A ROOM AT THE HEARTBREAK HOTEL** [9] [14]
(12"+=/pic-cd-s+=/US-3"cd-s+=) *(12IS/CIDP/CIDX 402)* – Love rescue me (live with KEITH RICHARDS & ZIGGY MARLEY).

Apr 89. (7"/c-s; U2 & B.B. KING) *(IS 411)* <99225> **WHEN LOVE COMES TO TOWN. / DANCING BAREFOOT** [6] [68]
(12"+=/pic-cd-s+=/US-3"cd-s+=) *(12IS/CIDP/CIDX 411)* – ('A'-live from the kingdom mix) / God part II (the hard metal dance mix).

Jun 89. (7"/7"box/c-s) *(IS/ISB/CIS 422)* <99199> **ALL I WANT IS YOU. / UNCHAINED MELODY** [4] [83]
(ext;12"+=/12"box+=) *(12IS/+B 422)* – Everlasting love.
(pic-cd-s++=) *(CIDP 422)* – ('A'extended).

Oct 91. (c-s/7") *(C+/IS 500)* <868885> **THE FLY. / ALEX DESCENDS INTO HELL FOR A BOTTLE OF MILK / KOROVA 1** [1] [61]
(12"+=/cd-s+=) *(12IS/CID 500)* – The Lounge Fly mix.

Nov 91. (cd)(lp/c) *(CIDU 28)(U2/+C 8)* <10347> **ACHTUNG BABY** [2] [1]
– Zoo station / Even better than the real thing / One / Until the end of the world / Who's gonna ride your wild horses / So cruel / The fly / Mysterious ways / Tryin' to throw your arms around the world / Ultra violet (light my way) / Acrobat / Love is blindness. *(re-iss. Aug93, hit UK No.17; same)*

Dec 91. (c-s/7") *(C+/IS 509)* <866188> **MYSTERIOUS WAYS. / ('A'-solar plexus magic hour remix)** [13] Nov91 [9]
(12"+=) *(12IS 509)* – ('A'-Apollo 440 remix) / ('A'-Tabla Motown remix).
(pic-cd-s++=) *(CID 509)* – ('A'-Solar Plexus extended club mix).
(12") *(12ISX 509)* – ('A'-Perfecto mix) / ('A'-Ultimatum mix) / ('A'-Apollo 400 Magic Hour remix) / ('A'-Solar Plexus extended club mix).

Feb 92. (c-s/7") *(C+/IS 515)* <866533> **ONE. / LADY WITH THE SPINNING HEAD (UVI)** [7] [10]
(12"+=) *(12IS 515)* – Satellite of love.
(cd-s++=) *(CID 515)* – Night and day (steel string remix).

Jun 92. (c-s/7") *(C+/IS 525)* <866977> **EVEN BETTER THAN THE REAL THING. / SALOME** [12] [32]
(12"+=/cd-s+=) *(12IS/CID 525)* – Where did it all go wrong (demo) / Lady with the spinning head (UVI) (extended dance mix).

Jul 92. (12") *(REAL U2)* **EVEN BETTER THAN THE REAL THING (the perfecto mix) / ('A'-trance mix) / ('A'-sexy dub mix)** [8] [–]
(cd-s) *(CREAL 2)* – (first 2) / ('A'-Apollo 440 Stealth Sonic remix) / ('A'-V16 Exit Wound remix) / ('A'-Apollo 440 vs. U2 instrumental remix).

Nov 92. (c-s/7") *(C+/IS 550)* <864521> **WHO'S GONNA RIDE YOUR WILD HORSES. / PAINT IT BLACK** [14] [35]
(cd-s+=) *(CID 550)* – Fortunate son / ('A'version).
(pic-cd-s+=) *(CIDX 550)* – Salome (Zooromancer remix) / Can't help falling in love (Triple Peaks remix).

Jun 93. (12"ltd-promo) *(12LEMDJ 1)* **LEMON. / SALOME (Boys Own Mix)** [–] [–]

Jul 93. (cd)(lp/c) *(CIDU 29)(U2/+C 9)* <518047> **ZOOROPA** [1] [1]
– Zooropa / Babyface / Numb / Lemon / Stay (faraway, so close!) / Daddy's gonna pay for your crashed car / Some days are better than others / The first time / Dirty day / The wanderer.

Aug 93. (video-ep) *(088 162-3)* **NUMB / NUMB (video remix) / LOVE IS BLINDNESS** [–] [–]

Nov 93. (c-s/7") *(C+/IS 578)* <858076> **STAY (FARAWAY, SO CLOSE!). / FRANK SINATRA WITH BONO: I'VE GOT YOU UNDER MY SKIN** [4] [61]
(cd-s+=) *(CID 578)* – Lemon (Bad Yard club) / Lemon (Perfecto mix).
(pic-cd-s) *(CIDX 578)* – ('A'side) / Slow dancing / Bullet the blue sky (live) / Love is blindness (live).

— In Mar 94, BONO teamed up with GAVIN FRIDAY (Virgin Prunes) on single 'IN THE NAME OF THE FATHER' from the film of the same name. It made No.46 in UK and was taken from soundtrack album. (below from the 'Batman Forever' movie released on 'Atlantic' UK)

Jun 95. (7"red/c-s) *(A 7131/+C)* <87131> **HOLD ME, THRILL ME, KISS ME, KILL ME / (other artist)** [2] [16]
(cd-s+=) *(A 7131CD)* – (other artist).

PASSENGERS

— aka U2, ENO + guests incl. vocalists PAVAROTTI + HOLI

Island Island

Nov 95. (cd/c/lp) *(CID/ICT/ILPS 8043)* <524166> **ORIGINAL SOUNDTRACKS 1** [12] [76]
– United colours / Slug / Your blue room / Always forever now / A different kind of blue / Beach sequence / Miss Sarajevo / Ito Okashi / One minute warning / Corpse (these chains are way too long) / Elvis ate America / Plot 180 / Theme from the swan / Theme from let's go native.

Nov 95. (c-s/7") *(C+/IS 625)* **MISS SARAJEVO. / ONE (live)** [6] [ ]
(cd-s+=) *(CID 625)* – Bottoms (Watashitachi No Ookina Yume) (Zoo Station remix) / Viva Davidoff.

U2

Feb 97. (c-s) *(CIS 649)* <7316> **DISCOTHEQUE / HOLY JOE (Garage mix)** [1] [10]
(cd-s+=) *(CID 649)* – Holy Joe (Guilty mix).
(cd-s) *(CIDX 649)* – ('A'-DM Deep Club mix) / ('A'-Howie B, hairy mix) / ('A'-Hexidecimal mix) / ('A'-DM Tec radio mix).
(3x12"box) *(12IST 649)* – 1:- (David Morales mixes; 4) // 2:- (12"version & David Holmes mix) // 3:- (Howie B & Steve Osborne's Hexidecimal mix).

Mar 97. (cd/c/d-lp) *(CIDU/UC/U 210)* <524334> **POP** [1] [1]
– Discotheque / Do you feel loved / Mofo / If God will send his angels / Staring at the sun / Last night on Earth / Gone / Miami / The Playboy mansion / If you wear that velvet dress / Please / Wake up dead man.

Apr 97. (c-s) *(CIS 658)* <854972> **STARING AT THE SUN / NORTH AND SOUTH (OF THE RIVER)** [3] [26]
(cd-s+=) *(CID 658)* – Your blue room.
('A'-Monster Truck mix; cd-s+=) *(CIDX 658)* – ('A'-Sad bastards mix) / ('A'-Lab rat mix).

Jul 97. (c-s) *(CIS 664)* <572053> **LAST NIGHT ON EARTH / POP MUZIK (Pop Mart mix)** [10] [57]
(cd-s+=) *(CID 664)* – Happiness is a warm gun (the gun mix).

('First Night In Hell mix; cd-s+=) *(CIDX 664)* – Numb (the Soul Assassins mix) / Happiness is a warm gun (the Danny Saber mix).
(12") *(12IS 664)* – ('A'mixes).

Sep 97. (c-s) *(CIS 673)* *<572195>* **PLEASE / DIRTY DAY (JUNK DAY)** [7] Nov97 [ ]
(cd-s+=) *(CID 673)* – Dirty day (bitter kiss) / I'm not your baby (Sky splintered mix).
(cd-ep) **POPHEART EP** *(CIDX 673)* – ('A'live) / Where the streets have no name (live) / With or without you (live) / Staring at the sun (live).

Dec 97. (c-s) *(CIS 684)* *<572189>* **IF GOD WILL SEND HIS ANGELS / MOFO (Romin remix)** [12] Mar98 [ ]
(cd-s) *(CID 684)* – ('A'side) / Slow dancing (with WILLIE NELSON) / Two shots of happy, one shot of sad / Sunday bloody Sunday (live with THE EDGE on vox).
(cd-s) *(CIDX 684)* – ('A'-The Grand Jury mix) / Mofo (Phunk Phorce mix) / Mofo (Mother's mix).
(12") *(12IS 684)* – Mofo (Funk Force mix) / (Black hole dub) / (Mothers mix) / (House flava mix) / (Roamin' mix).

Oct 98. (c-s) *(CIS 727)* *<radio cut>* **SWEETEST THING / STORIES FOR BOYS (live 1981)** [3] [63]
(cd-s+=) *(CIDX 727)* – Out of control (live 1981).
(cd-s) *(CID 727)* – ('A'side) / Twilight (live 1983) / An cat dubh (live 1983).

Nov 98. (cd/c/d-lp) *(CIDU/UC/U 211)* *<524612>* **THE BEST OF 1980-1990** (compilation) [1] [2]
– Pride (in the name of love) / New years day / With or without you / I still haven't found what I'm looking for / Sunday bloody Sunday / Bad / Where the streets have no name / I will follow / The unforgettable fire / Sweetest thing (new recording) / Desire / When love comes to town / Angel of Harlem / All I want is you. *(also on d-cd; CIDDU 211)<524613>* – (hit UK No.8 & US No.45).

Oct 00. (c-s) *(CIS 766)* *<562972>* **BEAUTIFUL DAY / SUMMER RAIN** [1] Sep00 [21]
(cd-s+=) *(CID 766)* – Always.
(cd-s) *(CIDX 766)* – ('A'side) / Discotheque (live) / If you wear that velvet dress (live).

Oct 00. (cd/c/lp) *(CIDU/UC/U 212)* *<524653>* **ALL THAT YOU CAN'T LEAVE BEHIND** [1] Nov00 [3]
– Beautiful day / Stuck in a moment you can't get out of / Elevation / Walk on / Kite / In a little while / Wild honey / Peace on Earth / When I look at the world / New York / Grace / Ground beneath her feet.

Jan 01. (c-s) *(CIS 770)* *<radio cut>* **STUCK IN A MOMENT YOU CAN'T GET OUT OF / BIG GIRLS ARE BEST** [2] Sep01 [52]
(cd-s+=) *(CID 770)* – Beautiful day (Quincey & Sonance remix).
(cd-s) *(CIDX 770)* – ('A'side) / Beautiful day (live) / New York (live).

Jul 01. (cd-s) *(CID 780)* **ELEVATION (Tomb Raider mix) / ELEVATION (escalation mix) / ELEVATION (Vandit club mix)** [3] [–]
(cd-s) *(CIDX 780)* – ('A'side) / Last night on Earth (live) / Don't take your guns to town.
(d12"+=) *(12ISD 780)* – Beautiful day (remixes).

Nov 01. (cd-s) *(CID 788)* **WALK ON / WHERE THE STREETS HAVE NO NAME (live) / STAY (FARAWAY SO CLOSE) (live)** [5] [–]
(cd-s) *(CIDX 788)* – ('A'side) / Stuck in a moment you can't get out of (acoustic) / Stuck in a moment you can't get out of (CD-Rom).

Oct 02. (cd-s) *(CID 808)* *<radio>* **ELECTRICAL STORM (William Orbit mix) / NEW YORK NEW YORK (nice mix) / NEW YORK NEW YORK (nasty mix)** [5] [77]
(cd-s) *(CIDX 808)* – ('A'side) / Bad – 40 – Where the streets have no name (medley live).

Nov 02. (cd/c/d-lp) *(CIDU/UC/U 213)* *<063438>* **THE BEST OF 1990-2000 / THE B-SIDES** (compilation) [2] [3]
– Even better than the real thing / Mysterious ways / Beautiful day / Electrical storm (William Orbit mix) / One / Miss Sarajevo (PASSENGERS) / Stay (faraway, so close!) / Stuck in a moment you can't get out of / Gone (Mike Hedges mix) / Until the end of the world / The hands that built America (theme from Gangs Of New York) / Discotheque (Mike Hedges mix) / Hold me, thrill me, kiss me, kill me / Staring at the sun (Mike Hedges mix) / Numb (Mike Hedges mix) / The first time / Fly *[UK cd+=]. (THE B-SIDES d-cd+=; CIDTU 213)* – Lady with the spinning head (extended dance mix) / Dirty day / Summer rain / Electrical storm / North and south of the river / Your blue room / Happiness is a warm gun / Salome (Zooromancer remix) / Even better than the real thing / Numb (gimme some more dignity mix) / Mysterious ways (solar plexus club mix) / If God will send his angels / Lemon (jeep mix) / Discotheque (hexidecimal mix). *(dvd++=)* – (videos, etc.)
– (hit UK No.37 + US 34)

The EDGE

with guest **SINEAD O'CONNOR** – vocals

Virgin Atlantic

Sep 86. (cd/c/lp) *(CD/TC+/V 2401)* *<90609>* **CAPTIVE (Soundtrack)** [ ] 1987 [ ]
– Rowena's theme / Heroine (theme from 'Captive') / One foot in Heaven / The strange party / Hiro's theme 1 & 2 / Drift / The dream theme / Djinn / Island.

Sep 86. (7"/12") *(VS/+T 897)* **HEROINE. / HEROINE (mix II)** [ ] [–]

— In 1983, The EDGE had collaborated with JAH WOBBLE & HOLGER CZUKAY on m-lp 'SNAKE CHARMER'.

ADAM CLAYTON & LARRY MULLEN

Mother Mother

May 96. (c-s) *(MUMSC 75)* *<576670>* **THEME FROM "MISSION: IMPOSSIBLE" / "MISSION: IMPOSSIBLE" THEME (MISSION ACCOMPLISHED)** [7] [7]
(12"+=/cd-s+=) *('A'-Junior's hard mix) / ('A'-cut the red not the blue mix) / ('A'-Dave Clarke remix).*

VELVET UNDERGROUND

V

Steve VAI

Born: STEVEN CIRO VAI, 6 Jun'60, Carve Place, Long Island, New Jersey, USA. Taught as a young teenager by the great JOE SATRIANI (his neighbour), he went on to join FRANK ZAPPA's ever-changing band of musicians, playing on albums from 'Tinseltown Rebellion' (1981) to 'Frank Zappa Meets The Mothers Of Prevention' (1986). During a ZAPPA interim (and there's not many of these!), VAI found time to issue a solo album, 'FLEX-ABLE', which, after its initial copies were sold out on the small 'Akashic', went like hotcakes on the larger stable, 'Relativity'. Now much in demand, the superb axeman became part of ALCATRAZZ, briefly replacing YNGWIE MALMSTEEN for one album in '85. During a spell of activity that would even put ZAPPA to shame, the young man played the guitar-grinding Devil in Walter Hill's movie 'Crossroads', while also finding time to lay down all the six-string work for PUBLIC IMAGE LTD.'s 'Album' set. The egocentric DAVID LEE ROTH was the next person to seek out his services, VAI staying and co-writing on two albums, 'Eat 'Em And Smile' (1986) and 'Skyscraper' (1987) before moving on to WHITESNAKE and playing on their 'Slip Of The Tongue' (1989) set. The following year, while still a member of the aforementioned outfit, VAI released his long-awaited follow-up, 'PASSION AND WARFARE', a remarkable and innovative disc which brought delightfully fresh experimentation to the world of guitarslinging hard-rock. Its reviews and his consummate CV ensured it a Top 20 placing on both sides of the Atlantic, marking out VAI, alongside his teacher, SATRIANI as one of the greatest young guitarists in the world. In 1993, he turned his head to more commercially viable roots, his band VAI taking on an old ZAPPA vocalist, TERRY BOZZIO for the album, 'SEX & RELIGION'. Over the course of the next few years, VAI released a few more sets, 'ALIEN LOVE SECRETS' (1995) and 'FIRE GARDEN' (1996), both moderate sellers in Britain. More recently, VAI has turned up on a collaboration live set, '3G' alongside ERIC JOHNSON and who else but JOE SATRIANI. After disappointing efforts like the 'THE ULTRA ZONE' (1999) and 'THE 7th SONG' (2000), VAI came up with the most ambitious project of his career, to write a series of songs about different countries and record them in the countries concerned. 'ALIVE IN AN ULTRA WORLD' (2001) was the result, both a global grand tour and a journey through VAI's feverishly inventive mind.

Album rating: FLEX-ABLE mini (*6) / PASSION AND WARFARE (*7) / SEX & RELIGION (*5) / ALIEN LOVE SECRETS (*5) / FIRE GARDEN (*6) / G3: LIVE IN CONCERT with Joe Satriani & Eric Johnson (*7) / THE ULTRA ZONE (*5) / THE 7th SONG (*5) / ALIVE IN AN ULTRA WORLD (*5)

STEVE VAI – guitar, keyboards, bass, etc.

Music For Nations | Akashic

1984. (lp) *(MFN 31)* **FLEX-ABLE** [ ] [ ]
– Little green men / Viva women / Lovers are crazy / The boy / Salamanders in the sun / Girl song / Attitude song / Call it sleep / Junkie / Bill is private parts / Next stop Earth / There's something dead in here. *(re-iss. Sep86 on 'Food For Thought' lp/c; GRUB/TGRUB 3) (cd-iss. 1989; CDGRUB 3) (cd re-iss. Jun97 on 'Relativity-Epic'; 487871-2) (cd re-iss. Mar01 on 'Favored Nations'; FN 2777-2>*

—— now with **DAVE ROSENTHAL** – keyboards / **STU HAMM** – bass / **CHRIS FRAZIER** – drums

Food For Thought | Relativity

May 90. (cd/c/lp) *(CD/C+/GRUB 17) <1037>* **PASSION AND WARFARE** [8] [18]
– Liberty / Erotic nightmares / The animal / Answers / The riddle / Ballerina 12-24 / For the love of God / The audience is listening / I would love to / Blue powder / Greasy kid's stuff / Alien water kiss / Sisters / Love secrets. *(pic-lp Nov90; GRUB 17P) (re-iss. Oct93 on 'Epic' cd/c; 467109-2/-4)*

—— His new band were **TIM STEVENS** – bass / **TERRY BOZZIO** – drums / with **DEVIN TOWNSEND** – vocals / **WILL RILEY** – keyboards / **SCOTT THUNES** – bass / **ABE LABORIEL JR.** – drums

Relativity-Epic | Relativity-Epic

Jul 93. (cd/c/lp; as VAI) *(473947-2/-4/-1) <1132>* **SEX & RELIGION** [17] [48]
– An earth dweller's return / Here & now / In my dreams with you / Still my bleeding heart / Sex and religion / Dirty black hole / Touching tongues / State of grace / Survive / Pig / The road to Mt.Calvary / Deep down into the pain / Rescue me or bury me.

Aug 93. (12"pic-ep/cd-ep) *(659491-6/-2)* **DEEP DOWN INTO THE PAIN. / JUST CARTILAGE / DEEP DOWN IN THE PAIN (edit)** [ ] [ ]

Nov 93. (12"pic-ep/cd-ep) *(659614-6/-2)* **IN MY DREAMS WITH YOU. / EROTIC NIGHTMARES / I WOULD LOVE TO** [ ] [ ]

Apr 95. (cd/c) *(478586-2/-4) <1245>* **ALIEN LOVE SECRETS** [39] [ ]
– Mad horsie / Juice / Die to live / The boy from Seattle / Ya yo gakk / Kill the guy with the ball – The God eaters / Tender surrender.

Sep 96. (cd/c) *(485062-2/-4) <67776>* **FIRE GARDEN** [41] [ ]
– There's a fire in my house / Crying machine / Dyin' day / Whookam / Blowfish / Mysterious murder of Christian Tierra's lover / Hand on heart / Bangkok / Fire garden suite / Deepness / Little alligator / All about Eve / Aching burger / Brother / Damn you / When I was a little boy / Genocide / Warm regards.

Jun 97. (cd/c; shared with JOE SATRIANI & ERIC JOHNSON) *(487539-2/-4) <67920>* **G3 LIVE IN CONCERT** (live 2nd November, 1996 at the Northrop Auditorium, Minneapolis) [ ] [ ]
– (tracks by JOE SATRIANI) / (tracks by ERIC JOHNSON) / Answers / For the love of God / The attitude song / The jam songs (featuring all 3 G's):- Going down. *(video+=)* – My guitar wants to kill your mama / Red house.

Sep 99. (cd/c) *<69817>* **THE ULTRA ZONE** [–] [ ]
– Blood & tears / The ultra zone / Oooo / Frank / Jiboom / Voodoo acid / Windows to the soul / Silent within / I'll be around / Lucky charms / Fever dream / Here I am / Asian sky.

Jul 01. (d-cd) *(501539-2) <85183>* **ALIVE IN AN ULTRA WORLD** [ ] [ ]
– Giants balls of gold / Burning rain / The black forest / Alive in an ultra world / Devil's food / Blood and glory / Whispering a prayer / Iberian jewel / The power of bombos / Incantation / Light of the Moon /

Babushka / Being with you (in Paris) / Principessa / Brandos costumes (gentle ways).

– compilations, etc. –

Dec 98. (cd) *Relativity; (492858-2)* **FLEX-ABLE LEFTOVERS**

Nov 00. (3xcd-box) *Epic; (496016-2)* **ALIEN LOVE SECRETS / SEX AND RELIGION / PASSION AND WARFARE**

Dec 00. (cd) *Epic; (501093-2) <85182>* **THE 7th SONG – ENCHANTING GUITAR MELODIES: ARCHIVE VOL.1**
– For the love of God / Touching tongues / Windows to the soul / Burnin' down the mountain / Tender surrender / Hand on heart / Melissa's garden / Call it sleep / Christmas time is here / The wall of light / Boston rain melody.

Dec 02. (d-cd) *Relativity; (509427-2)* **PASSION AND WARFARE / SEX AND RELIGION**

Sep 03. (cd) *Favored Nations; <(FN 2350-2)>* **MYSTERY TRACKS ARCHIVES VOL.3**

Oct 03. (cd) *Favored Nations; <(FN 2360-2)>* **MYSTERY TRACKS ARCHIVES VOL.4**

□ VALENTINOS (see under ⇒ WOMACK, Bobby)

VAN DER GRAAF GENERATOR

Formed: Manchester, England ... 1967 by PETER HAMMILL, CHRIS 'JUDGE' SMITH and NICK PEAME, who met at Manchester University. A one-off 45, 'THE PEOPLE YOU WERE GOING TO', surfaced in 1968, before they disbanded. Re-grouping soon after with a slightly modified line-up, HAMMILL and SMITH enlisted the more experienced KEITH ELLIS, GUY EVANS and NICK BANTON. However, it wasn't long before SMITH left HAMMILL as the focal point and sole remaining founder member. This line-up recorded what was initially intended to be a HAMMILL solo album, 'AEROSOL GREY MACHINE', which surprisingly only saw a full release in the States. It was a remarkable debut, showcasing cuts such as 'NECROMANCER', 'RUNNING BACK' and 'AFTERWARDS', in which HAMMILL exercised his wide-ranging vocal talent to startling effect. A change of line-up ensued, with NIC POTTER (like EVANS, he had played in The MISUNDERSTOOD) replacing the JUICY LUCY bound ELLIS. Signing to 'Charisma', they released their conceptual follow-up, 'THE LEAST WE CAN DO IS WAVE TO EACH OTHER', which dented the UK Top 50 in early 1970. The album saw the band developing a hybrid of pseudo-gothic lyrics and progressive rock styles, the stand-out tracks being 'REFUGEEES' and 'AFTER THE FLOOD'. POTTER departed during their next project, 'H TO HE', a record which featured the services of the (then) in-demand guitarist ROBERT FRIPP (KING CRIMSON). He also contributed session work to their subsequent effort, 'PAWN HEARTS' (1971), which included the 20-minute piece, 'A PLAGUE OF LIGHTHOUSE KEEPERS'. The composition traversed a varying degree of moods and tempos, hitting a breathtaking finale. After a GEORGE MARTIN (yes, that one!) penned 45, 'THEME ONE', failed to sell, they disbanded for the second time in the summer of '72. With the help of some VAN DER GRAAF members, HAMMILL had previously recorded a solo album, 'FOOL'S MATE', returning to the studio once again for a follow-up, 'CHAMELEON IN THE SHADOW OF THE NIGHT', released in 1972. For a few years, HAMMILL continued in an increasingly experimental and inventive vein, much in evidence on his 1975 album, 'NADIR'S BIG CHANCE'. VAN DER GRAAF reformed around this time, releasing three albums during the next two years, one of which was the highly regarded 'WORLD RECORD' (1976). After the plug was finally pulled on the 'GENERATOR, HAMMILL went to work on a series of solo albums, bringing in his group K. His work was quite prolific in the 80's and was virtually VAN DER GRAAF in all but name. He has been an inspiration to many alternative acts, JOHN LYDON citing HAMMILL's vocal technique as a guiding influence. Still going strong with a string of albums behind him (including 1988's 'SITTING TARGETS'), PETER moved into the millennium with two further sets, 'NONE OF THE ABOVE' (2000) and 'WHAT, NOW?' (2001). • **Trivia:** Named after a generator built by Dr. Robert Jemison Van Der Graaf.

Album rating: AEROSOL GREY MACHINE (*8) / THE LEAST WE CAN DO IS WAVE TO EACH OTHER (*7) / H TO HE, WHO AM THE ONLY ONE (*6) / PAWN HEARTS (*6) / Peter Hammill: FOOL'S MATE (*6) / CHAMELEON IN THE SHADOW OF THE NIGHT (*6) / THE SILENT CORNER AND THE EMPTY STAGE (*6) / IN CAMERA (*5) / NADIR'S BIG CHANCE (*7) / Van Der Graaf Generator: GODBLUFF (*6) / STILL LIFE (*6) / WORLD RECORD (*7) / Van Der Graaf: THE QUIET ZONE – THE PLEASURE DOME (*6) / VITAL (*5) / REPEAT PERFORMANCE posthumous collection (*7) / Peter Hammill: OVER (*6) / THE FUTURE NOW (*6) / pH7 (*6) / A BLACK BOX (*6) / SITTING TARGETS (*7) / ENTER K (*6) / LOOPS AND REELS (*5) / PATIENCE (*6) / THE LOVE SONGS collection (*6) / THE MARGIN – LIVE (*6) / SKIN (*6) / AND CLOSE AS THIS (*6) / SPUR OF THE MOMENT with Guy Evans (*5) / IN A FOREIGN TOWN (*6) / OUT OF WATER (*6) / THE FALL OF THE HOUSE OF USHER (*3) / FIRESHIPS (*4) / THE NOISE (*4) / THE CALM (AFTER THE STORM) compilation (*6) / THE STORM (BEFORE THE CALM) compilation (*6) / THERE GOES THE DAYLIGHT (*6) / ROARING FORTIES (*6) / ROOM TEMPERATURE LIVE (*6) / X MY HEART (*6) / SONIX (*5) / EVERYONE YOU HOLD (*5) / THIS (*5) / TYPICAL (*6) / NONE OF THE ABOVE (*5) / WHAT, NOW? (*5)

PETER HAMMILL (b. 5 Nov'48, London, England) – vocals, guitar, piano /**NICK PEAME** – organ / **CHRIS JUDGE SMITH** – drums, vocals, oricanos

Polydor / Mercury

Jan 69. (7") *(56758)* **PEOPLE YOU WERE GOING TO. / FIREBRAND** [ ] [–]

—— **HUGH BANTON** – keyboards, repl. PEAME

—— added **KEITH ELLIS** – bass (ex-KOOBAS) / **GUY EVANS** – drums (ex-MISUNDERSTOOD)

—— Now a quartet when CHRIS formed HEEBALOB. He later wrote for HAMMILL

not iss. / Mercury

Jan 69. (lp) *<SR 61238>* **AEROSOL GREY MACHINE** [–] [ ]
– Afterwards / Orthenthian St. (part 1 & 2) / Running back / Into a game / Aerosol grey machine / Black smoke yen / Aguarian / Necromancer / Octopus. *(UK-iss.Feb75 on 'Fontana'; 6430 083) (cd-iss. Mar97 on 'Repertoire'+=; RR 4647)* – People you were going to / Firebrand. *(cd re-iss. May97 on 'Fie!'+=; FIE 9116)* – Ferret / Featherbird / Giant squid.

Apr 69. (7") *<72979>* **AFTERWARDS. / NECROMANCER** [–] [ ]

—— **NIC POTTER** – bass (ex-MISUNDERSTOOD) repl. ELLIS who joined JUICY LUCY / added **DAVE JACKSON** – saxophone (ex-HEEBALOB)

Charisma / Dunhill

Feb 70. (lp) *(CAS 1007)* **THE LEAST WE CAN DO IS WAVE TO EACH OTHER** [47] [ ]
– Darkness / Refugees / White hammer / Whatever would Robert have said / Out of my book / After the flood. *(re-iss. Aug82 lp/c; CHC/+MC 5) (cd-iss. Apr87; CASCD 1007)*

Apr 70. (7") *(CB 122)* **REFUGEES. / THE BOAT OF MILLIONS OF YEARS** [ ] [ ]

—— A quartet again, when POTTER left only completing half of next album. Guest on next 2 albums **ROBERT FRIPP** – guitar (of KING CRIMSON)

Dec 70. (lp) *(CAS 1027) <50097>* **H TO HE, WHO AM THE ONLY ONE** [ ] [ ]
– Killer / House with no door / The emperor in his war-room: The emperor – The room / Lost: Dance in sand and sea – Dance in frost / The pioneers over C. *(re-iss. Jun81 & Sep83 on 'Polydor'; 6321 126) (cd-iss. Nov88; CASCD 1027)*

Charisma / Mercury

Oct 71. (lp) *(CAS 1051)* **PAWN HEARTS** [ ] [–]
– Lemmings / Man-erg / A plague of lighthouse keepers: 1) Eyewitness – 2) Pictures – Lighthouse – 3) Eyewitness – 4) S.H.M. – 5) Presence of the

night – 6) Kosmos tours – 7) (Custards) Last stand – 8) The clot chickens – 9) Lands End – 10) We go now. *(re-iss. Oct86; CHC 54) (cd-iss. Apr88; CASCD 1051)*

Feb 72. (7") *(CB 175)* **THEME ONE. / W**

PETER HAMMILL

had by this time gone solo when VAN DER GRAAF split. He continued to use VDGG members.

Charisma Charisma

Jul 71. (lp) *(<CAS 1037>)* **FOOL'S MATE**
– Imperial zeppelin / Candle / Happy / Solitude / Vision / Re-awakening / Sunshine / Child / Summer song (in the autumn) / Viking / The birds / I once wrote some poems. *(re-iss. Sep83 lp/c; CHC/+MC 2) (cd-iss. Oct88; CASCD 1037)*

May 73. (lp) *(<CAS 1067>)* **CHAMELEON IN THE SHADOW OF THE NIGHT**
– German overalls / Slender threads / Rock and role / In the end / What's it worth / Easy to slip away / Dropping the torch / In the black room / The tower. *(cd-iss. Apr89; CASCD 1067)*

Feb 74. (lp) *(<CAS 1083>)* **THE SILENT CORNER AND THE EMPTY STAGE**
– Modern / Wilhemina / The lie (Bernini's Saint Teresa) / Forsaken gardens / Red shift / Rubicon / A louse is not a home. *(re-iss. Oct86; CHC 61) (cd-iss. Nov88; CASCD 1083)*

Sep 74. (lp) *(<CAS 1089>)* **IN CAMERA**
– Ferret and featherbed / (No more) The sub-mariner / Tapeworm / Again / Faintheart and the sermon / The comet, the course. the tail / Gog Magog (in bromine chambers). *(re-iss. Nov80 on 'Polydor'; 9198 770) (re-iss. Aug88 lp/c; CHC/+MC 33) (cd-iss. Nov88; CASCD 1089)*

Feb 75. (lp) *(<CAS 1099>)* **NADIR'S BIG CHANCE**
– Nadir's big chance / The institute of mental health's burning / Open your eyes / Nobody's business / Been alone so long / Pompeii / Shingle song / Airport / People you were going to / Birthday special / Two or three spectres. *(re-iss. Mar83 lp/c; CHC/+MC 19) (cd-iss. Nov88; CASCD 1099)*

Apr 75. (7") *(CB 245)* **BIRTHDAY SPECIAL. / SHINGLE SONG**

— **HAMMILL, BANTON, JACKSON + EVANS** reformed

VAN DER GRAAF GENERATOR

Charisma Mercury

Oct 75. (lp) *(CAS 1109) <1069>* **GODBLUFF**
– The undercover man / Scorched Earth / Arrow / The sleepwalkers. *(re-iss. Mar83 lp/c; CHC/+MC 13) (cd-iss. Apr88; CASCD 1109)*

Apr 76. (lp)(c) *(CAS 1116)(7208 605) <1096>* **STILL LIFE**
– Pilgrims / Still life / La rossa / My room (waiting for Wonderland) / Childlike faith in childhood's end. *(re-iss. Oct86; CHC 55) (cd-iss. Apr87; CASCD 1116)*

Oct 76. (lp)(c) *(CAS 1120)(7208 610) <1116>* **WORLD RECORD**
– When she comes / A place to survive / Masks / Meurglys III (the songwriters guild) / Wondering. *(re-iss. Aug88; CHC 62) (cd-iss. 1988; CASCD 1120)*

Oct 76. (7") *(CB 297)* **WONDERING. / MEURGLYS III**

VAN DER GRAAF

GRAHAM SMITH – violin (ex-STRING DRIVEN THING) repl. JACKSON / **NIC POTTER** – bass returned after US session work to repl. BANTON

Sep 77. (lp) *(CAS 1131)* **THE QUIET ZONE – THE PLEASURE DOME**
– Lizard play / The habit of the broken heart / The siren song / Last frame / The wave / Yellow fever (running) / The sphinx in the face / Chemical world / The sphinx returns. *(re-iss. 1987 lp/c; CHC/+MC 32) (cd-iss. 1987; CASCD 1131)*

— added **DAVE JACKSON** who returned w / **CHARLES DICKIE** – cello, piano

Charisma P.V.C.

Jul 78. (d-lp) *(CVLD 101)* **VITAL (live)**
– Ship of fools / Still life / Mirror images / Medley: Parts of A plague of lighthouse keepers and Sleepwalkers / Pioneers over C / Door / Urban / Nadir's big chance. *(cd-iss. Apr89; CVCLD 101) (re-iss. cd Mar94 on 'Virgin';)*

– compilations, etc. –

Aug 72. (lp) *Charisma; (CS 2)* **68-71** –

Aug 80. (lp/c) *Charisma; (BG/+C 3)* **REPEAT PERFORMANCE** –
– Afterwards / Refugees / The boat of millions of years / W / White hammer / Necromancer / The Emperor in his war room / The empereor / The room / Manerg. *(c+=)* – The clot thickens (extended).

Mar 83. (d-c) *Charisma; (CASMC 106)* **PAWN HEARTS / STILL LIFE** –

May 85. (lp) *Demi-Monde; (DM 003)* **TIME VAULTS** (rare) –
(cd-iss. Apr97 on 'Spalax'; 14847)

Feb 87. (cd) *Virgin; (COMCD 2)* **FIRST GENERATION** –

Feb 87. (cd) *Virgin; (COMCD 3)* **SECOND GENERATION** –

May 88. (lp/cd) *Thunderbolt; (THBL/CDTB 042)* **NOW AND THEN** –

Sep 93. (cd) *Virgin; (CDVM 9026)* **I PROPHESY DISASTER** –

Jun 94. (cd) *Band Of Joy; (BOJCD 008)* **MAIDA VALE** –

PETER HAMMILL

went solo after the VDGG split

Charisma Charisma

Sep 76. (lp) *(<CAS 1125>)* **OVER**
– Crying wolf / Autumn / Time heals / Alice (letting go) / This side of the looking-glass / Betrayed (on Tuesdays she used to) / Yoga / Lost and found. *(cd-iss. Feb91; CASCD 1125)*

Charisma P.V.C.

Sep 78. (lp) *(CAS 1137) <2202>* **THE FUTURE NOW**
– The future now / Still in the dark / Mediaevil / A motor-bike in Africa / The cut / Palinurus / Pushing thirty / The second hand / Trappings / The mousetrap (caught in) / Energy vampires / If I could. *(re-iss. Oct86; CHC 59) (cd-iss. Nov88; CASCD 1137)*

Nov 79. (lp) *(CAS 1146) <2205>* **pH7**
– My favourite / Careering / Porton Down / Mirror images / Handicap and equality / Not for Keith / The old school tie / Time for a change / Imperial walls / Mr. X gets tense / Faculty X. *(cd-iss. Apr89; CASCD 1146)*

Nov 79. (7"; as RICKY NADIR) *(CB 339)* **THE POLAROID. / THE OLD SCHOOL TIE** –

Mercury not iss.

1980. (lp) *(6302 067)* **A BLACK BOX** – Europe –
– Golden promise / Losing faith in words / The Jargon king / Fog walking / The spirit / In slow time / The wipe / Flight: Flying blind – White cave fandango – Control – Cockpit – Silk worm wings / Nothing is nothing – A black box. *(UK-iss.Jun83; same) (re-iss. Aug88 on 'Virgin' lp/cd; OVED/CDOVD 140)*

Virgin not iss.

May 81. (7") *(VS 424)* **MY EXPERIENCE. / GLUE** –

Jun 81. (lp) *(V 2205)* **SITTING TARGETS** –
– Breakthrough / My experience / Ophelia / Empress's clothes / Glue / Hesitation / Sitting targets / Stranger still / Sign / What I did for love / Central hotel. *(re-iss. Aug88; OVED 139) (cd-iss. Oct88; CDV 2205)*

— **HAMMILL** with **GUY EVANS / NIC POTTER** plus **JOHN ELLIS** – guitar (ex-VIBRATORS), formed **K**

Naive not iss.

Sep 82. (7") *(NAV 3)* **PARADOX DRIVE. / NOW MORE THAN EVER** –

Oct 82. (lp/c) *(NAV L/C 1)* **ENTER K** –
– Paradox Drive / The unconscious life / Accidents / The great experiments / Don't tell me / She wraps it up / Happy hour / Seven wonders. *(cd-iss. May92 on 'Fie!'; FIE 9101)*

Sep 83. (lp) *(NAVL 3)* **PATIENCE** –
– Labour of love / Film noir / Just good friends / Jeunesse D'Oree / Traintime / Now more than ever / Comfortable / Patient. *(cd-iss. May92 on 'Fie!'; FIE 9102) (above 2 re-iss. Jan86 on 'Spartan' d-lp/d-c; SPD P/C 1)*

Sep 83. (7") *(NAV 8)* **FILM NOIR. / SEVEN WONDERS** –

Foundry not iss.

Feb 85. (d-lp) *(FONDL 1)* **THE MARGIN (live)** –
– Future now / Porton Down / Stranger still / Sign / The Jargon king / The second hand / Empress's clothes / The sphinx in the face / Labour of love / Sitting targets / Patience / Flight. *(cd-iss. Feb91 on 'Virgin'; CDOVD 345)*

Mar 86. (lp/c) *(FOND L/C 3)* **SKIN** –
– Skin / After the show / Painting by numbers / Shell / All said and done / A perfect date / Four pails / New lover. *(cd-iss. Nov87 on 'Line'; DACD 900145) (cd re-iss. Feb91 on 'Virgin'; CDOVD 344)*

Mar 86. (7") *(FOUND 3)* **PAINTING BY NUMBERS. / YOU HIT ME WHERE I LIVE** –
(ext.12"+=) *(FOUND 3-12)* – Shell.

Virgin not iss.

Nov 86. (lp/c) *(V/TCV 2409)* **AND CLOSE AS THIS** ☐ ⊟
– Too many of my yesterdays / Faith / Empire of delight / Silver / Beside the one you love / Other old cliches / Confident / Sleep now. *(cd-iss. Nov88; CDV 2409) (cd re-iss. 1989 on 'Line'; DACD 900254)*

Red Hot not iss.

Jun 88. (c/cd; PETER HAMMILL & GUY EVANS) *(ZCRH/CDR 102)* **SPUR OF THE MOMENT** ☐ ⊟
– Sweating it out / Little did he know / Without a glitch / Anatol's proposal / You think not? / Multiman / Deprogramming Archie / Always so polite / An imagined brother / Bounced / Roger and out. *(re-iss. May93; same)*

Enigma Restless

Nov 88. (lp/c/cd) *(ENVLP/TCENV/CDENV 512) <72337>* **IN A FOREIGN TOWN** ☐ ☐
– Hemlock / Invisible ink / Sci-finance (re-visited) / This book / Time to burn / Auto / Vote brand X / Sun City night life / The play's the thing / Under cover names. *(c+=/cd+=)* – Smile / Time to burn (instrumental). *(cd re-iss. Jun95 on 'Fie!'; FIE 9108)*

Feb 90. (cd/c/lp) *(CDENV/TVENVENVLP 1003) <73540>* **OUT OF WATER** ☐ ☐
– Evidently goldfish / Not the man / No Moon in the water / Our oyster / Something about Ysabel's dance / Green fingers / On the surface / A way out. *(cd re-iss. Jun95 on 'Fie!'; FIE 9109)*

Some Bizzare not iss.

Nov 91. (cd/c/lp) *(SBZ CD/MC/LP 007)* **THE FALL OF THE HOUSE OF USHER** ☐ ⊟
– An unenviable role / That must be the house / Architecture / The sleeper / One thing at a time / I shun the light / Leave this house / Dreaming / A chronic catalepsy / The herbalist / The evil that is done / Five years ago / It's over now / An influence / No rot / She is dead / Beating of the heart / The haunted palace / I dared not speak / She comes towards the door / The fall. *(cd re-iss. Nov99 on 'Fie!'; FIE 9121)*

Fie! Fie!

Mar 92. (cd/c) *(FIE/+C 9103)* **FIRESHIPS** ☐ ⊟
– I will find you / Curtains / His best girl / Oasis / Incomplete surrender / Fireship / Given time / Reprise / Gaia.

Mar 93. (cd/c) *(FIE/+C 9104)* **THE NOISE** ☐ ⊟
– A kick to kill the kiss / Like a shot / The entertainer / Noise / Celebrity kissing / Where the mouth is / Great European department store / Planet Coventry / Primo on the carpet.

Nov 93. (cd; as PETER HAMMILL & THE NOISE) *(FIE 9106)* **THERE GOES THE DAYLIGHT (live)** ☐ ⊟
– Sci-finance (revisited) / The habit of a broken heart / Sign / I will find you / Lost and found / Planet Coventry / Empress's clothes / Cat's eye – Yellow fever / Primo on the parapet / Central hotel.

Sep 94. (cd) *FIE 9107)* **ROARING FORTIES** ☐ ⊟
– Sharply unclear / The gift of fire / You can't want what you always get / A headlong stretch / Your tall ship.

Jun 95. (d-cd) *(FIE 9110)* **ROOM TEMPERATURE (live)** ☐ ⊟
– Wave / Just good friends / Vision / Time to burn / Four pails / The comet, the course, the tail / Ophelia / Happy hour / If I could / Something about Ysabel's dance / Patient / Cat's eye, yellow fever (running) / Running / Skin / Hemlock / Our oyster / Unconscious life / After the snow / Way out / Future now / Traintime / Modern.

Mar 96. (cd) *(FIE 9111)* **X MY HEART** ☐ ⊟
– Better time / Amnesiac / Ram origami / Forest of pronouns / Earthbound / Narcissus (bar & grill) / Material possession / Come clean.

Nov 96. (cd) *(FIE 9114)* **SONIX** ☐ ⊟
– Emmene moi bare theme / Walk in the dark / In the Polish house / Dark matter / Hospital silence / Four to the floor / Exercise for Louise / Labyrinthe dreams / Emmene moi full theme.

Oct 97. (cd) *(<FIE 9117>)* **EVERYONE YOU HOLD** ☐ ☐
– Everyone you hold / Personality / Nothing comes / From the safe house / Phosphorescence / Falling open / Bubble / Can do / Tenderness.

Oct 98. (cd) *(FIE 9118)* **THIS** ☐ ⊟
– Frozen in place (fragment) / Unrehearsed / Stupid / Since the kids / Nightman / Fallen (the city of night) / Unready (fragment) / Always is next / Unsteady (fragment) / The light continent.

Apr 99. (d-cd) *(FIE 9119)* **TYPICAL (live 1992)** ☐ ⊟
– My room / Curtains / Just good friends / Too many of my yesterdays / Vision / Time to burn / The comet, the course, the tail / I will find you / Ophelia / Given time / Modern / Time for a change / Patient / Stranger still / Our oyster / Shell / A way out / Traintime / The future now.

May 00. (cd) *(FIE 9122)* **NONE OF THE ABOVE** ☐ ⊟
– Touch and go / Naming the rose / Hoe far I fell / Somebody bad enough / Tango for one / Like Veronica / In a bottle / Astart.

Jun 01. (cd) *(FIE 9123)* **WHAT, NOW?** ☐ ⊟
– Here come the talkies / Far-flung (across the sky) / The American girl / Wendy and the lost boy / Lunatic in knots / Edge of the road / Fed to the wolves / Enough.

– compilations, etc. –

1978. (lp) *G.I.R.; <9211 1016>* **VISION** ⊟ ☐
1983. (c) *Sofa;* **LOOPS AND REELS** ☐ ⊟
(cd-iss. Nov93 on 'Fie!'; FIE 9105)

Aug 84. (lp) *Charisma; (CAS 1166)* **THE LOVE SONGS** (remixes) ☐ ⊟
– Just good friends / My favourite / Been alone so long / Ophelia / Again / If I could / Vision / Don't tell me / The birds / (THis side of) The looking glass. *(re-iss. Jun88 lp/c; CHC/+MC 69) (cd-iss. Nov88; CASCD 1166)*

May 85. (7") *Charisma; (CB 414)* **JUST GOOD FRIENDS. / ('A'instrumental)** ☐ ⊟

Jul 93. (cd) *Virgin; (CDVM 9017)* **THE CALM (AFTER THE STORM)** ☐ ⊟

Jul 93. (cd) *Virgin; (CDVM 9018)* **THE STORM (BEFORE THE CALM)** ☐ ⊟

Jan 95. (cd) *Golden Hind; (GH 70112)* **OFFENSICHTLLICH GOLDFISCH** ☐ ⊟
– Offensichtilich goldfisch / Dich zu finden / Die kalte killt den kub / Favorit / Kaufhaus Europa / Der larm / Oase / Die prominenz kubt sich / Die tunte verlischt / Auto (wieder im wagen) / Gaia / Schlaft nun.

Nov 95. (cd) *Strange Fruit; (SFRCD 136)* **THE PEEL SESSIONS** ☐ ⊟
Jan 96. (cd) *Virgin; (CDOVD 460)* **AFTER THE SHOW** ☐ ⊟
Sep 96. (cd) *Fie!; (FIE 9112)* **PAST GO: COLLECTED** ☐ ⊟
– A kick to kill the kiss / I will find you / Accidents / His best girl / Sharply unclear / Patient / Planet Coventry / A ritual mask / The noise / The gift of fire / Traintime / Gaia / Your tall ship.

Sep 96. (cd) *Sine; (SINE 006)* **TIDES** ☐ ⊟
– My room / Too many yesterdays / Just good friends / Mirror images / Time to burn / Untitled / Stranger / Where the actors go.

Feb 02. (cd) *Fie!; (FIE 9103)* **FIRESHIPS** ☐ ⊟

VANGELIS

Born: EVANGELOS PAPATHANASSIOU, 29 Mar'43, Volos, Greece. A child prodigy, the young VANGELIS was performing his own compositions in front of a large audience from the age of six. Groomed by his artistic parents, he subsequently studied classical music alongside other areas of the Arts at The Academy Of Fine Arts in Athens. Having already cultivated a love of jazz, like many other budding musicians of the day, he was inspired by the revoltionary pop takeover of The BEATLES. In 1963, he duly instigated a 6-piece beat combo, The FORMINX, who scored a major hit in Greece with the single, 'YENKA BEAT'. They continued for four years, becoming one of their country's leading popular music acts and initiated a dance craze with their biggest hit, 'JERONIMO YANKA' in 1965. Following the band's demise, VANGELIS PAPATHANASSIOU took on board a more keyboard-orientated style, the result being a solo single, 'THE CLOCK', in 1968. Working with him at this time were drummer LUCAS SIDERAS and vocalist/bassist DEMIS ROUSSOS, this trio soon evolving into APHRODITE'S CHILD. A classical adaptation of PACHELBEL's 'Canon' (similar in style to PROCOL HARUM's 'A Whiter Shade Of Pale'), 'RAIN AND TEARS' was released by 'Mercury' in 1968, the single denting the UK Top 30 after being a Europe-wide hit. An album soon followed, 'END OF THE WORLD', being an unlikely hybrid of progressive rock and Latin-styled folk. Further singles appeared, although VANGELIS was eager to branch into more complex solo work. He scored the soundtrack for a soft-porn movie, 'Sex Power', released under the name, 'L'APOCALYPSE DES ANIMAUX' (1971). The following year, APHRODITE'S CHILD surfaced from their Paris studio, delivering the double set, '666', which explored the Bible's Book Of Revelations against a prog-rock backdrop. It was a critical success, although DEMIS ROUSSOS took off for a fruitful solo career (e.g. the chart-topper, 'Forever And Ever'). VANGELIS signed to 'R.C.A.' in 1974, enjoying a revived chart success with his UK debut for the label, 'HEAVEN AND HELL' (1975), which featured vocals by JON ANDERSON (of YES fame) on the track 'SO LONG AGO, SO CLEAR'. 'ALBEDO 0.39' (1976) was an overly ambitious, jazzy concept album while 'BEAUBOURG' (1978) saw VANGELIS in similarly abstruse territory, the album featuring only one track, divided into two parts. In 1979, he again hooked up with JON ANDERSON to form the duo JON AND VANGELIS, recording three successful albums, 'SHORT STORIES' (1980), 'SEE YOU LATER' (1980) and 'THE FRIENDS OF MR. CAIRO' (1981), before splitting in 1983. Meanwhile, VANGELIS recorded his masterstroke with the 1981 soundtrack, 'CHARIOTS OF FIRE'. The regal, whooshing electronica of the title track was an international smash, leading to more soundtrack work for a host of movies throughout the 80's and 90's, including 'MASK' (1985), 'ANTARTICA' (1988) and '1492: THE CONQUEST OF PARADISE' (1992). He also recorded a further one-off album with JON ANDERSON in 1991, 'PAGE OF LIFE'. • **Trivia:** In 1975, he was asked but refused to take the place of RICK WAKEMAN in YES, instead of PATRICK MORAZ. In 1985, he also wrote the ballet score for new version of 'Frankenstein'.

Album rating: Aphrodite's Child: END OF THE WORLD – RAIN AND TEARS (*4) / IT'S FIVE O'CLOCK (*4) / 666 (**8**) / Vangelis: SEX POWER (*4) / FAIS QUE TON REVE SOIT PLUS LONG QUE LA NUIT (*4) / THE DRAGON bootleg (*4) / L'APOCALYPSE DES ANIMAUX (*4) / EARTH (*5) / HEAVEN & HELL (**8**) / ALBEDO 0.39 (*6) / SPIRAL (*5) / HYPOTHESIS early work (*4) / BEAUBOURG (*4) / CHINA (*5) / SHORT STORIES by Jon & Vangelis (*6) / SEE YOU LATER (*4) / CHARIOTS OF FIRE soundtrack (*7) / THE FRIENDS OF MR. CAIRO by Jon & Vangelis (*5) / OPERA SAUVAGE – COSMOS (*4) / TO THE UNKNOWN MAN collection (*6) / PRIVATE COLLECTION by Jon & Vangelis (*5) / THE BEST OF JON & VANGELIS compilation (*6) / SOIL FESTIVITIES (*4) / MASK soundtrack (*3) / INVISIBLE CONNECTIONS (*4) / RHAPSODIES (*4) / DIRECT (*4) / THEMES compilation (*5) / THE CITY (*4) / PAGE OF LIFE by Jon & Vangelis (*4) / 1492: THE CONQUEST OF PARADISE soundtrack (*6) / BLADE RUNNER soundtrack (*6) / PORTRAIT (SO LONG AGO, SO CLEAR) compilation (*6) / VOICES (*4) / OCEANIC (*4) / EL GRECO (*4) / ODYSSEY: THE DEFINITIVE COLLECTION compilation (*7)

FORMINX

VANGELIS – keyboards / **TASSOS PAPASTHAMATIS** – vocals / **VASILLIS BAKOPOULOS** – rhythm guitar / **SOTORIS ARNIS** – bass / **KOSTAS SKODOS** – drums / **NIKOS MASTORASKIS** – co-songs

Vocalion | not iss.

Apr 65. (7") *(V 9235)* **JENKA BEAT. / GERONIMO JENKA** [ ] [–]

— also issued a number of Greek 45's; an LP finally surfacing in 1975

APHRODITE'S CHILD

VANGELIS PAPATHANASSIOU (b. EVANGELOS, 15 Jun'47, Velos) – keyboards, wind, percussion / **DEMIS ROUSSOS** (b.15 Jun'47, Alexandria, Egypt) – vocals, bass / **LUCAS SIDERAS** (b. 5 Dec'44, Athens) – drums, vocals

Mercury | Mercury

Oct 68. (7") *(MF 1039)* **RAIN AND TEARS. / DON'T TRY TO CATCH A RIVER** [30] [ ]

Feb 69. (7") *(MF 1075)* **END OF THE WORLD. / YOU ALWAYS STAND IN THE WAY** [ ] [ ]

Feb 69. (lp) *(SMCL 20140)* **END OF THE WORLD / RAIN AND TEARS** [ ] [ ]
– End of the world / Don't try to catch a river / Mister Thomas / Rain and tears / The grass is not green / Valley of sadness / You always stand in my way / The shepherd and the Moon / Day of the fool.

Polydor | Polydor

Jun 69. (7") *(BM 56769)* <15005> **I WANT TO LIVE. / MAGIC MIRROR** [ ] [ ]

Nov 69. (7") *(BM 56785)* **LET ME LOVE, LET ME LIVE. / MARIE JOLIE** [ ] [–]

Mar 70. (7") *(BM 56791)* **IT'S FIVE O'CLOCK. / FUNKY MARY** [ ] [–]

Jan 70. (lp) *(238 4005)* **IT'S FIVE O'CLOCK** [ ] [–]
– It's five o'clock / Wake up / Take your time / Annabella / Let me love, let me live / Funky Mary / Good time so fine / Marie Jolie / Such a funny night. *(re-iss. Jul78 on 'Impact'; 6886 650)*

1970. (7") *(6033 003)* **SPRING, SUMMER, WINTER AND FALL. / AIR** [–] France [–]

— Disbanded for a time, until reappeared adding **SILVER KOULOURIS** – guitar, percussion. Guests **HARRIS HALKITIS** – bass, saxophone, percussion, vocals / **MICHEL RIPOCHE** – trombone, saxophone/ **JOHN FORST** – narration / **YANNIS TSAROUCHIS** – Greek text / **IRENE PAPAS** – vox on (1).

Vertigo | Vertigo

Jun 72. (d-lp) *(6673 001)* <500> **666** [ ] [ ]
– The system / Babylon / Loud, loud, loud / The four horsemen / The lamb / The seventh seal / Aegian Sea / Seven bowls / The wakening beast / Lament / The marching beast / The battle of the locusts / Do it / Tribulation / The beasts / Ofis / / Seven trumpets / Altamont / The wedding of the lamb / The capture of the beast / oo / Hic and nunc / All the seats were occupied / Break. *(re-iss. Feb77; 6641 581)* (re-iss. May83 on 'Impact' d-lp/c; *6673/7528 001) (cd-iss. Aug98 on 'Mercury'; 838430-2)*

Aug 72. (7") <107> **BREAK. / BABYLON** [–] [ ]
(UK-iss.Jun75; 6032 900)

— Disbanded again in 72/73. VANGELIS went solo, as did DEMIS ROUSSOS.

– compilations, etc. –

Jun 75. (lp) *Vertigo; (6333 002)* **THE BEST OF APHRODITE'S CHILD – FEATURING DEMIS ROUSSOS** [ ] [–]
– End of the world / Valley of sadness / Marie Jolie / Rain and tears / Good time so fine / It's five o'clock / I want to live / Such a funny night / Annabella / Break.

Jun 75. (lp) *Philips; (6483 025)* **RAIN AND TEARS** [ ] [–]
(re-iss. Aug81 as 'GREATEST HITS 1968-1970' on 'Fontana' lp/c; 6420 006)(7240 955)

VANGELIS

VANGELIS – keyboards, synthesizers, etc.

Philips | not iss.

1968. (7") **THE CLOCK. / OUR LOVE SLEEPS ON THE WATERS** [–] Greece [–]

1969. (7") **DJEMILLA. / THIRD LOVE** [–] Greece [–]

1970. (lp; as VANGELIS PAPATHANASSIOU) *(6397 013)* **SEX POWER** (soundtrack) [–] French [–]
– (part 1) / (part 2).

WEA | not iss.

1971. (lp; as VANGELIS PAPATHANASSIOU) *(54009)* **FAIS QUE TON REVE SOIT PLUS LONG QUE LA NUIT** [–] French [–]
– C'est une nuit verte / Celle des barricades / Nuit verte ou rouge ou bleue ou noire / Qu'importe mon ami / Cela importe mon ami / L'espoir de la victoire / Le reve est realite / Jouissez sans entraves / Vivez sans temps morts / Baisez sans carottes.

Charly | not iss.

1971. (lp; bootleg) *(CRL 5013)* **THE DRAGON** [ ] [–]
– The dragon / Stuffed aubergine / Stuffed tomato. *(re-iss. 1980)*

Polydor | not iss.

1973. (lp) *(2393 058)* **L'APOCALYPSE DES ANIMAUX (Soundtrack)** [–] French [–]
– Apocalypse des animaux – Generique / La petite fille de la mer / Le singe bleu / La mort du loup / L'ours musicien / Creation du monde / La mer recommencee. *(re-iss. Oct76; 2489 113) (re-iss. Apr84 lp/c; SPE LP/MC 72) (cd-iss. 1988; 831 503-2)*

1973. (7") **COME ON. / HE-O** [–] French [–]

— he now moved to London and signed to . . .

Vertigo | Vertigo

1974. (lp) *(6499 693)* <1019> **EARTH** [ ] [ ]
– Come on / We were all uprooted / Sunny Earth / He-o / Ritual / Let it happen / The city / My face in the rain / Watch out / A song.

R.C.A. R.C.A.

Nov 75. (lp/c) *(RS 1025) <5110>* **HEAVEN & HELL** [31] [ ]
– Heaven and Hell pt.1 – Bacchanale symphony to the powers of B – 2nd movement – 3rd movement – So long ago so clear * / Heaven and Hell pt.2 – Intestinal heart – Needles and bones – 12 o'clock – Aries – Away. *(re-iss. Sep81; 3012) (re-iss. 1984 lp/c; PL/PK 70009) (re-iss. Oct86 lp/c; NL/NK 71148) (cd-iss. Sep89; ND 71148)*
above featured The ENGLISH CHAMBER CHOIR and VANA VEROUTIS – lead vocals (track* was first to use vocals of **JON ANDERSON** (of YES)

Aug 76. (7") *<10733>* **SO LONG AGO, SO CLEAR. / HEAVEN AND HELL THEME** [–] [ ]

Sep 76. (lp/c) *(RS/RC 1080) <5136>* **ALBEDO 0.39** [18] [ ]
– Pulstar / Freefall / More tranquilillitatis / Main sequence / Sword of Orion / Alpha / Nucleogenesis (pt.1 & 2) / Albedo 0• 39. *(re-iss. Sep81 lp/c; RCA LP/K 3017) (re-iss. Sep89 lp/c/cd; NL/NK/ND 74208)*

Oct 76. (7") *(RCA 2762) <10882>* **PULSTAR. / ALPHA** [ ] [ ]

Dec 77. (lp/c) *(PL2 5116) <2627>* **SPIRAL** [ ] [ ]
– Spiral / Ballad / Dervish D / To the unknown man / 3 plus 3. *(re-iss. Sep81 + Nov84 lp/c; NL/NK 70568) (cd-iss. Oct89; ND 70568)*

Jan 78. (7") *(PB 5064)* **TO THE UNKNOWN MAN. / (part 2)** [ ] [–]

Jul 78. (lp/c) *(PL2/PK2 5155) <3020>* **BEAUBOURG** [ ] [ ]
– Beaubourg (part 1) / Beaubourg (part 2). *(re-iss. Sep86 on 'Fame' lp/c; FA/TC-FA 3168) (re-iss. Feb90 cd/c; ND/NK 74516)*

Polydor Polydor

Apr 79. (lp/c) *(POLD/+C 5018) <6199>* **CHINA** [ ] [ ]
– Chung Kuo / The long march / The dragon / The plum blossom / The Tao of love / The little fete / Yin and Yang / Himalaya / Summit. *(re-iss. Aug83 lp/c)(cd; SPE LP/MC 19)(813653-2)*

May 79. (7") *(POSP 57)* **THE LONG MARCH. / (part 2)** [ ] [–]

JON & VANGELIS

JON = **JON ANDERSON** – vocals (also of YES)

Polydor Polydor

Dec 79. (7") *(POSP 96) <2098>* **I HEAR YOU NOW. / THUNDER** [8] Aug80 [58]

Jan 80. (lp/c) *(POLD/+C 5030) <PD1 6272>* **SHORT STORIES** [4] [ ]
– Curious electic / Each and everyday / Bird song / I hear you now / The road / Far away in Bagdhad / Love is / One more time / Thunder / A play within a play. *(cd-iss. 1983; 800027-2) (re-iss. Jun87 lp/c; SPE LP/MC 105)*

Feb 80. (7") *<2130>* **ONE MORE TIME. / THE ROAD** [–] [ ]

VANGELIS

solo (same label until stated)

Jun 80. (7") *(2001 973)* **MY LOVE. / DOMESTIC LOGIC 1** [ ] [–]

Nov 80. (lp)(c) *(2302 101)(3100 567)* **SEE YOU LATER** [ ] [ ]
– I can't take it anymore / Multitrack suggestion / Memories of green / Not a bit – all of it / Suffocation / See you later.

Mar 81. (lp/c) *(POLS/+C 1026) <PD1 6335>* **CHARIOTS OF FIRE (Original Motion Picture Soundtrack)** [5] Oct81 [1]
– Titles / Five circles / Abraham's theme / Eric's theme / 100 metres / Jerusalem / Chariots of fire. *(re-iss. Apr84; POLD 5160); hit UK No.39) (cd-iss. 1983; 8000202-2)*

Apr 81. (7") *(POSP 246) <2189>* **CHARIOTS OF FIRE – TITLES. / ERIC'S THEME** [12] Dec81 [1]
(re-prom.UK Feb82 hit UK No.41 & re-iss. Aug84; same)

JON & VANGELIS

May 81. (7") *(POSP 258) <2181>* **THE FRIENDS OF MR. CAIRO. / BESIDE** [ ] [ ]

Jul 81. (lp/c) *(POLD/+C 5039) <PD1 6326>* **THE FRIENDS OF MR. CAIRO** [6] [64]
– The friends of Mr. Cairo / Back to school boogie / Outside of this (inside of that) / State of independence / Beside / The Mayflower. *(cd-iss. May83; 800021-2) (re-iss. Oct89 lp/c; POLD/+C 5053)*

Jul 81. (7") *(POSP 323)* **STATE OF INDEPENDENCE. / BESIDE** [ ] [ ]

Nov 81. (7") *(JV 1)* **I'LL FIND MY WAY HOME. / BACK TO SCHOOL BOOGIE** [6] [–]

Apr 82. (7") *<2205>* **I'LL FIND MY WAY HOME. / I HEAR YOU NOW** [–] [51]

—— In 1982, he wrote unissued vinyl score for film 'Blade Runner'.

May 83. (7") *(JV 3)* **AND WHEN THE NIGHT COMES. / SONG IS** [ ] [–]

May 83. (lp/c)(cd) *(POLH/+C 4)(813174-2) <813174>* **PRIVATE COLLECTION** [22] [ ]
– He is sailing / And when the night comes / Deborah / The king is coming / Horizon.

Jul 83. (7") *(JV 4)* **HE IS SAILING. / POLANAISE** [61] [ ]
(12"+=) *(JVX 4)* – Song is.

—— Above was last collaboration between the duo, until 1991.

Aug 84. (7"/12") *(JV/+X 5)* **STATE OF INDEPENDENCE. / THE FRIENDS OF MR. CAIRO** [67] [ ]

Aug 84. (lp/c/cd) *(POLH/+C 6)(821929-2)* **THE BEST OF JON & VANGELIS** (compilation) [42] [ ]
– Italian song / I'll find my way home / State of independence / One more time / Play within a play / The friends of Mr. Cairo / Outside of this (inside of that) / He is sailing / I hear you now.

VANGELIS

continued solo. BOUNTY Soundtrack was also unissued. He continued to write unissued soundtracks throughout the 80's as well as below.

Oct 84. (lp/c)(cd) *(POLH/+C 11)(823396-2)* **SOIL FESTIVITIES** [55] [ ]
– Movements 1-5. *(re-iss. Jun87 lp/c; SPE LP/MC 106)*

Mar 85. (lp/c)(cd) *(POLH/+C 19)(825245-2)* **MASK (Soundtrack)** [69] [ ]
– Movements 1-6.

Deutsche not iss.

Mar 85. (lp/c/cd) *(415196-1/-4/-2)* **INVISIBLE CONNECTIONS** [–] [–]
– Invisible connections / Atom blaster / Thermo vision.

1986. (lp/c/cd) **RHAPSODIES** [ ] [ ]
– Ti ipermacho stratigo / O! gliki mou ear / Ton nimfona sou vlepo / Rapsodia / Tin oreotita tis partenias sou / Christos anesti / Asma asmaton.

Arista not iss.

Sep 88. (lp/c/cd) *(209/409/259 149)* **DIRECT** [ ] [–]
– The motion of stars / The will of the wind / Metallic rain / Elsewhere / Glorianna (hymn a la femme) / Rotations logic / The oracle of Apollo / Ave / First approach / Dial out / Intergallactic radio station / Message.

Sep 88. (c-s) *(111 767)* **WILL OF THE WIND / INTERGALACTIC RADIO STATION** [ ] [–]
(12"+=/cd-s+=) *(611/661 767)* – Metallic rain.

JON & VANGELIS

Aug 91. (7") **WISDOM CHAIN. / PAGE OF LIFE** [ ] [ ]
(cd-s+=) – ('A'full version) / Sing with your eyes.

Sep 91. (cd/c/lp) *(261/411/211 373)* **PAGE OF LIFE** [ ] [ ]
– Wisdom chain / Page of life / Money / Garden of senses / Is it love / Anyone can light a candle / Journey to Ixtlan / Shine for me / Genevieve.

VANGELIS

East West Atlantic

Nov 90. (cd)(lp/c) *(903173026-2)(WX 398/+C) <82248>* **THE CITY** [ ] [ ]
– Dawn / Morning papers / Nerve centre / Side streets / Good to see you / Twilight / Red lights / Procession. *(re-iss. cd Nov93 & Feb95; same)*

Oct 92. (cd)(c) *(4509 91014-2)(WX 497C) <82432>* **1492: THE CONQUEST OF PARADISE (Soundtrack)** [33] [ ]
– Opening theme / 1492: The conquest of Paradise / Monastery of la Rabida / City of Isabel / Light and shadow / Deliverance / West across the ocean sea / Eternity / Hispanola / Moxica and the horse / 28th parallel / Pinta, Nina, Santa Maria (into eternity) *(re-iss. cd Jun94).*

Oct 92. (7"/c-s) *(YZ 704C)* **CONQUEST OF PARADISE. / MOXICA AND THE HORSE** [60] [–]
(cd-s+=) *(YZ 704CD)* – Line open / Landscape. *(re-iss. May95; same)*

Mar 93. (c-s/cd-s) *(YZ 736 C/CD)* **28th PARALLEL / WEST ACROSS THE OCEAN SEA** [ ] [–]

Oct 95. (c-s) *(EW 007C)* **VOICES / VOICES II (ECHOES)** [ ] [–]
(cd-s+=) *(EW 007CD)* – Voices III.

Feb 96. (cd/c) *(0630 12786-2/-4) <82853>* **VOICES** [58] [ ]
– Voices / Echoes / Come to me / P.S. / Ask the mountains / Prelude / Losing sleep (still, my heart) / Messages / Dream in an open place.
above featured PAUL YOUNG on vocals

Mar 96. (c-s; as VANGELIS & STINA NORDENSTAM) *(EW 031C)* **ASK THE MOUNTAINS / SLOW PIECE** [ ] [–]
(cd-s+=) *(EW 031CD)* – ('A'-Album version).

Oct 96. (cd/c) *(0630 16761-2/-4) <82953>* **OCEANIC** [ ] [ ]
– Bon voyage / Sirens' whispering / Dreams of surf / Spanish harbour /

Islands of the Orient / Fields of coral / Aquatic dance / Memories of blue / Song of the seas.

below featured MONSERRAT CABELLE (soprano); – about 16th century master painter

Nov 98. (cd) *(3984 25107-2) <83161>* **EL GRECO**
– Movements:- I / II / III / IV / V / VI / VII / VIII / IX / X (epilogue). Sony Sony

Oct 01. (cd) *(<SK 89191>)* **MYTHODEA: MUSIC FOR THE NASA MISSION: 2001 MARS ODYSSEY**
– Movements:- I / II / III / IV / V / VI / VII / VIII / IX / X / XI / special edit).

– compilations, others, etc. –

—— on 'R.C.A.' unless mentioned otherwise

1978. (lp/c) *(PL2 5174)* **THE BEST OF VANGELIS**
(re-iss. Sep81 lp/c; RCA LP/K 3028) (cd-iss. May93; 74321 13885-2)

May 78. (cd) *Affinity; (AFF 11)* **HYPOTHESIS** (rec.1971) –

Jul 81. (7") *B.B.C.; (BBC 1)* **HEAVEN AND HELL, THIRD MOVEMENT (THEME FROM THE BBC-TV SERIES – THE COSMOS). / ALPHA** 48 –

Aug 81. (lp) *Polydor; (AFL1 4003)* **OPERA SAUVAGE – COSMOS** –
(re-iss. Nov84 lp/c; SPE LP/MC 81) (cd-iss. 1987; 829663-2) <US-iss.Dec86; 829663> hit No.42>

Aug 82. (d-c; JON & VANGELIS) *Polydor; (3574 139)* **SHORT STORIES / THE FRIENDS OF MR. CAIRO** –

Nov 82. (d-lp/d-c) *(RCA LP/K 1002-3) <4397>* **TO THE UNKNOWN MAN VOLS.1 & 2** –

1982. (7") *<13402>* **TO THE UNKNOWN MAN. / (part 2)** –

Nov 82. (t-lp) *Polydor; (BOX 1)* **CHARIOTS OF FIRE / CHINA / OPERA SAUVAGE** –

1983. (lp) *(PL 30036)* **THE SAVAGE BEAST** –

Jun 84. (c) *(NK 70345)* **MAGIC MOMENTS** –

Jul 84. (lp) *(NL 70078)* **GREATEST HITS** –

1984. (7") *B.B.C.; (RESL 144)* **FRAME OF THE DAY: BBC SNOOKER THEMES (TO THE UNKNOWN MAN) (part 1). / (part 2)** –

Jun 88. (7"; JON & VANGELIS) *Old Gold; (OG 9785)* **I HEAR YOU NOW. / I'LL FIND MY WAY HOME** –

Nov 88. (lp/c/cd) *Polydor; (815 732-1/-4/-2)* **ANTARCTICA (Original Soundtrack)** –

Jul 89. (lp/c)(cd) *Polydor; (LP/MC VGTV 1)(839518-2)* **THEMES**
– (excerpts from films, including some from previously unissued)

Oct 89. (cd-box/c-box) *(VGPK 1)* **SPIRAL / ALBEDO 0• 39 / HEAVEN AND HELL** –

Apr 93. (cd) *C.A.M.;* **ENTENDS-TU LES CHEINS** –

Jun 94. (cd/c) *East West; (4509 96574-2/-4)* **BLADE RUNNER (Soundtrack)** 20

Aug 94. (cd/c) *(74321 22415-2/-4)* **THE COLLECTION** –

Sep 94. (cd/c; JON & VANGELIS) *Spectrum; (550196-2/-4)* **CHRONICLES** –

Apr 95. (cd) *(74321 25954-2)* **ALBEDO 0.39 / HEAVEN AND HELL** –

Apr 96. (cd/c) *Polydor; (531154-2/-4)* **PORTRAIT (SO LONG AGO, SO CLEAR)** 14
– To the unknown man / Italian song / Pulsar / La petite fille de la mer / Alpha / I hear you now / I'll find my way home / State of indepenence / Himalaya / Conquest of Paradise / Hymn / Antartica / Sauvage et beau / Chariots of fire / So long ago, so clear.

Jun 96. (cd) *Camden; (74321 39337-2)* **GIFT . . . THE BEST OF VANGELIS** –

Aug 96. (cd/c) *Autograph; (MAC CD/MC 246)* **CHARIOTS OF FIRE (THE MUSIC OF VANGELIS)** –

Oct 99. (cd/c) *Reprise; <(3984 98288-2/-4)>* **REPRISE 1990-1999**

Oct 00. (d-cd) *Universal; (E 539269-2)* **CHINA / ANTARTICA** –

Oct 03. (cd) *Universal TV; (9813149) / Hip-O; <1427>* **ODYSSEY: THE DEFINITIVE COLLECTION** 20 Nov03
– Pulstar / Hymn / Chariots of fire (main theme) / Missing (main theme) / Blade runner (love theme) / Blade runner (end titles) / The Tao of love / Antartica (main theme) / Cafavy (main theme) / Mutiny on the bounty (opening titles) / Conquest of Paradise / La petite fille de la mer / L'enfant / Alpha / Celtic dawn / Mythodea (movement 1). *(bonus tracks+=)* – I'll find my way home (JON & VANGELIS) / State of independence (JON & VANGELIS).

VAN HALEN

Formed: Pasadena, California, USA . . . 1975 by brothers ALEX and EDDIE VAN HALEN. Recruiting blonde-maned high priest of metal cool, DAVE LEE ROTH, and bass player MICHAEL ANTHONY, the quartet initially traded under the MAMMOTH moniker. As VAN HALEN, the group built up a solid reputation as a covers outfit on L.A.'s Sunset Strip, gradually introducing original material into their set. Eventually signed to 'Warners' after being spotted by in-house producer, Ted Templeman, the group released their eponymous debut album in 1977. Coming at a time when hard rock was in seemingly terminal stagnation with punk snapping at its heels, 'VAN HALEN' redefined the boundaries of the genre; from the back cover shot of a shirtless ROTH (chest-wig de rigueur!) sporting leather flares to the opening three chord mash-up of The KINKS' 'YOU REALLY GOT ME', VAN HALEN dripped effortless cool, the golden elixir of sun-bleached California coursing through their collective veins. Then there was 'AIN'T TALKIN' 'BOUT LOVE', EDDIE casually reeling off the razor-edged, caterwauling riff (recently resurrected by dance bods, APOLLO FOUR FORTY) while ROTH drawled his most lascivious, sneering drawl. And basically, this was what set VAN HALEN apart from the spandex pack; ROTH actually sang rather than screeching like an asphyxiated budgie, while in EDDIE VAN HALEN, the group boasted one of the most inventive and single-mindedly talented guitarists in the history of metal. O.K., 'ERUPTION' may be responsible for countless fret-wank crimes but it's still impossible not to be impressed by the man's vision, his innovations (flying-fingered hammer-ons, leaving a still smoking cigarette nudged in at the top of the fretboard etc.) becoming base material for any aspiring 80's guitar hero. Essentially, VAN HALEN were glamourous as opposed to glam, and for a few heady years they made heavy metal desirable. Though the debut album barely nudged into the US Top 20, it would go on to sell in excess of five million copies and remains one of THE classic hard-rock releases. A follow-up, 'VAN HALEN II' (1979) didn't pack quite the same punch, although it made the US Top 10 and spawned the group's first hit single, the dreamy 'DANCE THE NIGHT AWAY'. 'WOMEN AND CHILDREN FIRST' (1980) and 'FAIR WARNING' (1981) consolidated the band's standing, both commercially and critically although it wasn't until 'DIVER DOWN' (1982) that VAN HALEN began to cast their net wider. A cover of Roy Orbison's 'PRETTY WOMAN' gave them another US Top 20 hit, the album going Top 5 as a result. The following year, EDDIE famously flashed his fretboard skills on MICHAEL JACKSON's 'Beat It', gaining valuable crossover exposure although by this point, VAN HALEN were already one of the biggest hard rock acts in the world. This was proved with the massive success of the '1984' (released in 1984, funnily enough!) opus and attendant synth-heavy No.1 single, 'JUMP'. For many people, especially in Britain, this was the first time they'd witnessed "Diamond" DAVE in action, the loose-limbed singer, as ever, performing death-defying feats of stage acrobatics in the accompanying video. While the album saw VAN HALEN successfully tackling obligatory 80's experimentation (which did for many of their peers), the likes of 'HOT FOR TEACHER' carried on the grand tradition of tongue-in-cheek lewdness and six-string trickery. Incredibly, at the peak of their success, ROTH buggered off for a solo career, taking his not inconsiderable wit, charisma and sly humour with him. Though VAN HALEN chose to rumble on, it was a rather different beast which reared its head in early '86 with the single, 'WHY CAN'T

THIS BE LOVE'. With ex-MONTROSE man, SAMMY HAGAR on vocals, VAN HALEN had created their most consistently accessible and musically ambitious set to date in '5150' (1986), although the absence of ROTH's cheeky innuendo was glaringly obvious. If not gone completely, the group chemistry had been irrevocably altered, in effect, making VAN HALEN just another hard rock band, albeit highly professional and massively successful. '5150' gave the revamped group their first US No.1 album, the record not doing too badly in the UK either. 'OU812' (1988) was another multi-million selling No.1, VAN HALEN now virtually a US institution guaranteed multi-platinum sales with every successive release. 'FOR UNLAWFUL CARNAL KNOWLEDGE' (1991), or 'F.U.C.K.' in its abbreviated form (very clever, lads) saw the group adopt a heavier approach although this didn't prevent it from selling in bucketloads, VAN HALEN holding their own in the age of grunge when many of their contemporaries suddenly seemed embarrassingly outdated. A long overdue live album, 'RIGHT HERE, RIGHT NOW', finally appeared in 1993, while a rare European tour no doubt helped boost UK sales of 'BALANCE' (1995), yet another US No.1 album and their first Top 10 placing in Britain. DAVE LEE ROTH returned during the same year; however after a compilation set in which he appeared on a few new songs, the man departed once more, this time to be replaced by ex-EXTREME frontman, GARY CHERRONE. • **Covered:** FAIR WARNING (Aerosmith) / A POLITICAL BLUES (Little Feat) / WON'T GET FOOLED AGAIN (Who). • **Trivia:** In April '81, EDDIE married actress Valerie Bertinelli.

Album rating: VAN HALEN (*8) / VAN HALEN II (*7) / WOMEN AND CHILDREN FIRST (*7) / FAIR WARNING (*6) / DIVER DOWN (*6) / 1984 (*7) / 5150 (*5) / OU812 (*6) / FOR UNLAWFUL CARNAL KNOWLEDGE (*6) / LIVE: RIGHT HERE, RIGHT NOW (*6) / BALANCE (*5) / THE BEST OF: VOLUME ONE compilation (*8) / VAN HALEN III (*5)

EDDIE VAN HALEN (b.26 Jan'57, Nijmegen, Netherlands) – guitar / **DAVID LEE ROTH** (b.10 Oct'55, Bloomington, Indiana) – vocals / **MICHAEL ANTHONY** (b.20 Jun'55, Chicago, Illinois) – bass / **ALEX VAN HALEN** (b. 8 May'55, Nijmegen) – drums

Warners Warners

Feb 78. (7") *(K 17107) <8515>* **YOU REALLY GOT ME. / ATOMIC ROCK PUNK** [ ] Jan78 [36]

Apr 78. (lp/c) *(K/K4 56470) <3075>* **VAN HALEN** [34] Feb78 [19]
– Runnin' with the Devil / Eruption / You really got me / Ain't talkin' 'bout love / I'm the one / Jamie's cryin' / Atomic punk / Feel your love tonight / Little dreamer / Ice cream man / On fire. *(cd-iss. Jul86; K2 56470) (cd re-iss. Feb95; K2 56470) (cd re-iss. Jan01; 9362 47737-2)*

Apr 78. (7") *(K 17162) <8556>* **RUNNIN' WITH THE DEVIL. / ERUPTION** [ ] [84]

Jul 78. (7") *<8631>* **JAMIE'S CRYIN'. / I'M THE SAME** [–] [ ]

Sep 78. (7") *<8707>* **AIN'T TALKIN' BOUT LOVE. / FEEL YOUR LOVE TONIGHT** [–] [ ]

Apr 79. (lp/c) *(K/K4 56616) <3312>* **VAN HALEN II** [23] [6]
– You're no good / Dance the night away / Somebody get me a doctor / Bottoms up! / Outta love again / Light up the sky / Spanish fly / D.O.A. / Women in love / Beautiful girls. *(cd-iss. Mar87; K2 56616) (cd re-iss. Jan01; 9362 47738-2)*

May 79. (7"/7"pic-d) *(K 17371/+P) <8823>* **DANCE THE NIGHT AWAY. / OUTTA LOVE AGAIN** [ ] Apr79 [15]

Sep 79. (7") *<49035>* **BEAUTIFUL GIRLS. / D. O. A.** [–] [84]

Apr 80. (lp/c) *(K/K4 56793) <3415>* **WOMEN AND CHILDREN FIRST** [15] [6]
– And the cradle will rock . . . / Everybody wants some / Fools / Romeo delight / Tora! Tora! / Loss of control / Take your whiskey home / Could this be magic? / In a simple rhyme. *(cd-iss. Jun89; K 923415-2) (cd re-iss. Jan01; 9362 47739-2)*

Apr 80. (7") *<49501>* **AND THE CRADLE WILL ROCK. / COULD THIS BE MAGIC** [–] [55]

Aug 80. (7") *(K 17645)* **AND THE CRADLE WILL ROCK. / EVERYBODY WANTS SOME!!** [ ] [–]

May 81. (7") *<49751>* **SO THIS IS LOVE. / HEAR ABOUT IT LATER** [–] [ ]

May 81. (lp/c) *(K/K4 56899) <3540>* **FAIR WARNING** [49] [6]
– Mean street / Dirty movies / Sinner's swing / Hear about it later / Unchained / Push comes to shove / So this is love? / Sunday afternoon in the dark / One foot out of the door. *(cd-iss. Jun89; K 923540-2) (cd re-iss. Jan01; 9362 47740-2)*

Feb 82. (7") *(K 17909) <50003>* **(OH) PRETTY WOMAN. / HAPPY TRAILS** [ ] Jan82 [12]

May 82. (7") *<29986>* **DANCING IN THE STREET. / THE BULL BUG** [–] [38]

May 82. (lp/c) *(K/K4 57003) <3677>* **DIVER DOWN** [36] [3]
– Where have all the good times gone / Hang 'em high / Cathedral / Secrets / Intruder / (Oh) Pretty woman / Dancing in the street / Little guitars (intro) / Little guitars / Big bad Bill (is sweet William now) / The bull bug / Happy trails. *(cd-iss. Jan84; K2 57003) (cd re-iss. Jan01; 9362 47718-2)*

May 82. (7") *(K 17957)* **DANCING IN THE STREET. / BIG BAD BILL (IS SWEET WILLIAM NOW)** [ ] [–]

Aug 82. (7") *<29929>* **BIG BAD BILL (IS SWEET WILLIAM NOW). / SECRETS** [–] [ ]

Jan 84. (lp/c/cd) *(923985-1/-4/-2) <23985>* **1984 (MCMLXXXIV)** [15] [2]
– 1984 / Jump / Panama / Top Jimmy / Drop dead legs / Hot for teacher / I'll wait / Girl gone bad / House of pain. *(re-iss. cd/c Feb95; same) (cd re-iss. Jan01; 9362 47741-2)*

Jan 84. (7") *<29384>* **JUMP. / HOUSE OF PAIN** [–] [1]

Jan 84. (7") *(W 9384)* **JUMP. / RUNNIN' WITH THE DEVIL** [7] [–]
(12"+=) *(W 9384T)* – House of pain.

Apr 84. (7") *<29307>* **I'LL WAIT. / GIRL GONE BAD** [–] [13]

Apr 84. (7") *(W 9273) <29250>* **PANAMA. / GIRL GONE BAD** [61] Jun84 [13]
(12"+=) *(W 9273T)* – Dance the night away.

Jun 84. (7") *(W 9213)* **I'LL WAIT. / DROP DEAD LEGS** [ ] [–]
(12"+=) *(W 9213T)* – And the cradle will rock / (Oh) Pretty woman.

Jun 85. (7") *(W 9199) <29199>* **HOT FOR TEACHER. / LITTLE PREACHER** [ ] Oct84 [56]
(12"+=) *(W 9199T)* – Hear about it later.

—— (Jun'85) Trimmed to a trio, when DAVID LEE ROTH went solo full-time. Early '86 added **SAMMY HAGAR** (b.13 Oct'47, Monterey, Calif.) – vocals (ex-MONTROSE, ex-Solo Artist)

Mar 86. (7"/7"sha-pic-d/12") *(W 8740/+P/T) <28740>* **WHY CAN'T THIS BE LOVE. / GET UP** [8] [3]

Apr 86. (lp/c)(cd) *(W 5150/+C)(925394-2) <25394>* **5150** [16] [1]
– Good enough / Why can't this be love / Get up / Dreams / Summer nights / Best of both worlds / Love walks in / "5150" / Inside. *(re-iss. cd/c Feb95; same)*

Jun 86. (7"/7"sha-pic-d/12") *(W 8642/+P/T) <28702>* **DREAMS. / INSIDE** [62] May86 [22]

Aug 86. (7") *<28626>* **LOVE WALKS IN. / SUMMER NIGHTS** [–] [22]

Oct 86. (7") *<28505>* **BEST OF BOTH WORLDS. / ('A'live)** [–] [ ]

May 88. (7"/12") *(W 7891/+T) <27891>* **BLACK AND BLUE. / APOLITICAL BLUES** [ ] [34]

Jun 88. (lp/c)(cd) *(WX 177/+C)(K 925732-2) <25732>* **OU812** [16] [1]
– Mine all mine / When it's love / A.F.U. (naturally wired) / Cabo wabo / Source of infection / Feels so good / Finish what ya started / Black and blue / Sucker in a 3-piece. *(cd+=)* – Apolitical blues.

Jul 88. (7") *<27827>* **WHEN IT'S LOVE. / CABO WABO** [–] [5]

Jul 88. (7") *(W 7816)* **WHEN IT'S LOVE. / APOLITICAL BLUES** [28] [–]
(12"+=/12"pic-d+=/cd-s+=) *(W 7816 T/TP/CD)* – Why can't this be love.

Sep 88. (7") *<27746>* **FINISH WHAT YA STARTED. / SUCKER IN A 3-PIECE** [–] [13]

Feb 89. (7") *(W 7565) <27565>* **FEELS SO GOOD. / SUCKER IN A 3 PIECE** [63] Jan89 [35]
(12"+=/cd-s+=) *(W 7565 T/CD)* – Best of both worlds (live).

Jun 91. (7"/c-s) *(W 0045/+C)* **POUNDCAKE. / PLEASURE DOME** [74] [–]
(12"+=/cd-s+=) *(W 0045 T/CD)* – (interview).

Jul 91. (cd)(lp/c) *(7599 26594-2)(WX 420/+C) <26594>* **FOR UNLAWFUL CARNAL KNOWLEDGE** [12] [1]
– Poundcake / Judgement day / Spanked / Runaround / Pleasure dome / In 'n' out / Man on a mission / The dream is over / Right now / 316 / Top of the world.

Sep 91. (7") *<19151>* **TOP OF THE WORLD. / POUNDCAKE** [–] [27]

Oct 91. (7"/c-s) *(W 0066/+C)* **TOP OF THE WORLD. / IN 'N' OUT** [63] [–]
(cd-s+=) *(W 0066CD)* – Why can't this be love (extended) / When it's love / Dreams.

Feb 92. (c-s,cd-s) *<19059>* **RIGHT NOW / MAN ON A MISSION** [–] [55]

Feb 93. (d-cd/d-c) *<(9362 45198-2/-4)>* **LIVE: RIGHT HERE, RIGHT NOW (live)** [24] [5]
– Poundcake / Judgement day / When it's love / Spanked / Ain't talkin' 'bout love / In'n'out / Dreams / Man on a mission / Ultra bass / Pressure dome – Drum solo / Panama / Love walks in / Runaround/ / Right now / One way to rock / Why can't this be love / Give to love / Finished what ya started / Best of both worlds / 316 / You really got me – Cabo wabo / Won't get fooled again / Jump / Top of the world.

Mar 93. (7"/c-s/cd-s) *(W 0155/+C/CD)* **JUMP (live). / LOVE WALKS IN (live)** [26] [–]
(cd-s+=) *(W 0155CDX)* – Eagles fly (live) / Mine, all mine (live).

Jan 95. (7"purple/c-s) *(W 0280 X/C)* **DON'T TELL ME (WHAT LOVE CAN DO). / BALUCHITHERIUM** [27] [–]
(cd-s+=) *(W 0280CD)* – Why can't this be love (live)/ Poundcake (live)/ Panama (live).
(cd-s) *(W 0280CDX)* – ('A'side)/ Judgement day (live)/ Dreams (live)/ Top of the world (live).

Jan 95. (cd/c/lp) *<(9362 45760-2/-4/-1)>* **BALANCE** [8] [1]
– The seventh seal / Can't stop lovin' you / Don't tell me (what love can do) / Amsterdam / Big fat money / Strung out / Not enough / Aftershock / Doin' time / Baluchitherium / Take me back (deja vu) / Feelin'.

Mar 95. (7"/c-s) *(W 0288/+C) <17909>* **CAN'T STOP LOVIN' YOU. / CROSSING OVER** [33] [30]
(cd-s+=) *(W 0288CD)* – Man on a mission / Right now.
(cd-s) *(W 0288CDX)* – ('A'side) / Best of both worlds (live) / One way to rock (live) / When it's love (live).

Jun 95. (c-s) *(W 0302C)* **AMSTERDAM / RUNAROUND (live)** [ ] [–]
(cd-s) *(W 0302CDX)* – ('A'side) / Finish what ya started (live).

Aug 95. (c-s,cd-s) *<17810>* **NOT ENOUGH / AMSTERDAM** [–] [97]

— **DAVID LEE ROTH** returned on 2 tracks below ('Me Wise Magic' & 'Can't Get This Stuff No More') to repl. HAGAR

Oct 96. (cd/c) *<(9362 46474-2/-4)>* **THE BEST OF: VOLUME ONE** (compilation) [45] [1]

— ROTH's ego led to the old reunion failing. **GARY CHERONE** (ex-EXTREME) became frontman and co-writer.

Mar 98. (cd/c) *<(9362 46662-2/-4)>* **VAN HALEN III** [43] [4]
– Neworld / Without you / One I want / From afar / Dirty water dog / Once / Fire in the hole / Josephina / Year to the day / Primary / Ballot or the bullet / How many say I.

– others, etc. –

Jun 80. (7") *Atlantic; (HM 10)* **RUNNIN' WITH THE DEVIL. / D.O.A.** [52] [–]

VANILLA FUDGE

Formed: New York City, New York, USA ... 1965 as The PIGEONS. They became VANILLA FUDGE in late '66, and after their debut at The Village Theater (Fillmore East), they were signed up by 'Atlantic'. Their po-faced, psychedelic-symphonic rock often degenerated into dirty, leaden dirges and VANILLA SLUDGE would've been a more accurate name for this proto-metallic band. Nevertheless, in 1967 they were unique, if nothing else than for their unqualified heaviness and they enjoyed chart success with their first release, a characteristically over the top and drawn out rendition of The SUPREMES' 'YOU KEEP ME HANGIN' ON'. The self-titled debut album followed later that summer and contained similarly overblown and amusing covers, The BEATLES' 'ELEANOR RIGBY' and 'TICKET TO RIDE' among them. Follow-up albums were inconsistent, the band's original material falling woefully short of matching the strength of the covers they'd made their name with and, after the band split in mid '69, TIM BOGERT and CARMINE APPICE formed the short lived CACTUS with RUSTY DAY and JIM McCARTY. Purveying straight-down-the-line hard rock, the band cut three albums, 'CACTUS' (1970), 'ONE WAY ...OR ANOTHER' (1971) and 'RESTRICTIONS' (1972) before BOGERT and APPICE joined JEFF BECK in the supergroup BECK, BOGERT & APPICE. • **Songwriters:** STEIN or group compositions, with mainly other covers :- BANG BANG (Cher) / SEASON OF THE WITCH (Donovan) / I CAN'T MAKE IT ALONE (Goffin-King) / THE WINDMILLS OF YOUR MIND (Legrand-Bergyan). CACTUS also covered several standards. • **Trivia:** In the summer of '69, they played the Seattle Pop Festival at Woodenville, Washington.

Album rating: VANILLA FUDGE (*7) / THE BEAT GOES ON (*5) / RENAISSANCE (*5) / NEAR THE BEGINNING (*5) / ROCK & ROLL (*4) / Cactus: CACTUS (*5) / ONE WAY ... OR ANOTHER (*4) / RESTRICTIONS (*3) / 'OT 'N' SWEATY (*3) / Vanilla Fudge: MYSTERY (*3) / THE BEST OF (PSYCHEDELIC SUNDAE) compilation (*7)

MARK STEIN (b.11 Mar'47, Bayonne, New Jersey) – vocals, organ / **VINCE MARTELL** (b.11 Nov'45, Bronx, NY) – guitar, vocals / **TIM BOGERT** (b.27 Aug'44) – bass, vocals / **CARMINE APPICE** (b.15 Dec'46, Staten Island, NY) – drums, vocals

Atlantic Atco

Jun 67. (7") *<6590>* **YOU KEEP ME HANGIN' ON. / COME BY DAY, COME BY NIGHT** [–] [67]
<US re-prom.Jul68, hit No.6>

Jul 67. (7") *(584 123) <6590>* **YOU KEEP ME HANGIN' ON. / TAKE ME FOR A LITTLE WHILE** [18] [–]

Sep 67. (lp; mono/stereo) *(587/588 086) <33224>* **VANILLA FUDGE** [31] [6]
– Ticket to ride / People get ready / She's not there / Bang bang / Illusions of my childhood – part one / You keep me hanging on / Illusions of my childhood – part two / Take me for a little while / Illusions of my childhood – part three / Eleanor Rigby. *(cd-iss. May93; 7567 90390-2)*

Oct 67. (7") *(584 139)* **ILLUSIONS OF MY CHILDHOOD. / ELEANOR RIGBY** [ ] [–]

Feb 68. (lp; mono/stereo) *(587/588 100) <33237>* **THE BEAT GOES ON** [ ] [17]
– Sketch / Variation on a theme from Mozart's Divertimento No.13 in F / Old black Joe / Don't fence me in / 12th Street rag / In the mood / Hound dog / I want to hold your hand – I feel fine – Day tripper – She loves you / The beat goes on / Beethoven's fur Elise and theme from Moonlight Sonata / The beat goes on / Voices in time: – Neville Chamberlain – Winston Churchill – F.D. Roosevelt – Harry S. Truman – John F.Kennedy / Merchant / The game is over / The beat goes on. *(cd-iss. Jun92 & Jul93 on 'Repertoire'+=; RR 4261) <(cd re-iss. Nov98 on 'Sundazed'; SC 6142)>*

Apr 68. (7") *(584 179) <6554>* **WHERE IS MY MIND?. / THE LOOK OF LOVE** [ ] Jan68 [73]

Jun 68. (lp; mono/stereo) *(587/588 110) <33244>* **RENAISSANCE** [ ] [20]
– The sky cried – When I was a boy / Thoughts / Paradise / That's what makes a man / The spell that comes after / Faceless people / Season of the witch. *(cd-iss. Jul93 on 'Repertoire'+=; REP 4126)* – You keep me hangin' on (7" version) / Come by day, come by night / People. *<(cd re-iss. Nov98 on 'Sundazed'; SC 6143)>*

Sep 68. (7") *<6616>* **TAKE ME FOR A LITTLE WHILE. / THOUGHTS** [–] [38]

Nov 68. (7") *<6632>* **SEASON OF THE WITCH. / (part 2)** [–] [65]

Atco Atco

Feb 69. (lp) *(228 020) <33278>* **NEAR THE BEGINNING** (half studio / half live) [ ] [16]
– Shotgun / Some velvet morning / Where is happiness / Break song. *(cd-iss. Jul93 on 'Repertoire'+=; REP 4127)* – Good good lovin' (unedited) / Shotgun (single version) / People (single version). *<(cd re-iss. Nov98 on 'Sundazed'; SC 6144)>*

Mar 69. (7") *(584 257) <6655>* **SHOTGUN. / GOOD GOOD LOVIN'** [ ] [68]

Jun 69. (7") *<6679>* **SOME VELVET MORNING. / PEOPLE** [–] [ ]

Jul 69. (7") *(584 276)* **SOME VELVET MORNING. / THOUGHTS** [ ] [–]

Oct 69. (lp) *(228 029) <33303>* **ROCK & ROLL** [ ] [34]
– Need love / Lord in the country / I can't make it alone / Street walking woman / Church bells of St. Martin's / The windmills of your mind / If you gotta make a fool of somebody. *(cd-iss. Jul93 on 'Repertoire'+=; REP 4168)* – Good good lovin' / Shotgun / Where is my mind / Need love (7" version). *<(cd re-iss. Nov98 on 'Sundazed'; SC 6145)>*

Nov 69. (7") *<6703>* **I CAN'T MAKE IT ALONE. / NEED LOVE** [–] [ ]

Jan 70. (7") *<6728>* **LORD IN THE COUNTRY. / THE WINDMILLS OF YOUR MIND** –

—— Had already folded mid '69. STEIN formed BOOMERANG and MARTELL retired.

CACTUS

were formed Feb'70 by **BOGERT & APPICE** with **RUSTY DAY** – vocals, mouth harp (ex-AMBOY DUKES / TED NUGENT) / **JIM McCARTY** – guitar (not of YARDBIRDS)

Atlantic Atco

Jul 70. (lp) *(2400 020) <SD 33340>* **CACTUS** 54
– Parchman farm / My lady from south of Detroit / Bro. Bill / You can't judge a book by the cover / Let me swim / No need to worry / Oleo / Feel so good. *(cd-iss. Jan96; 7567 80290-2)*

Oct 70. (7") *<6792>* **YOU CAN'T JUDGE A BOOK BY THE COVER. / BRO BILL** –

Mar 71. (7") *<6811>* **LONG TALL SALLY. / ROCK'N'ROLL CHILDREN** –

Jul 71. (lp) *(2400 114) <SD 33356>* **ONE WAY . . . OR ANOTHER** Mar71 88
– Long tall Sally / Rock out whatever you feel like / Rock'n'roll children / Big mam boogie / Feel so bad / Hometown bust / One way . . .or another.

Sep 71. (7") *<6842>* **TOKEN CHOKIN'. / ALASKA** –

—— (May71) added **DUANE HITCHINGS** – piano

Jan 72. (7") *<6872>* **EVIL. / SWEET SIXTEEN** –

Apr 72. (lp) *(K 40307) <SD 33377>* **RESTRICTIONS** Nov71
– Restrictions / Token chokin' / Guiltness glider / Evil / Alaska / Sweet sixteen / Bag drag / Mean night in Cleveland. *(cd-iss. Jul93 on 'Repertoire')*

—— **PETE FRENCH** – vocals (ex-ATOMIC ROOSTER) McCARTY and DAY

Oct 72. (lp) *(K 50013) <SD 7011>* **'OT & SWEATY** (live/studio)
– Swim / Bad mother boogie / Our lil' rock and roll thing / Bad stuff / Bring me down / Bedroom Mazurka / Telling you / Underneath / The arches.

Oct 72. (7") *<6901>* **BAD MOTHER BOOGIE. / BRINGING ME DOWN** –

—— Disbanded and DUANE retained some of name NEW CACTUS BAND issuing an album, 'SON OF CACTUS' and single 'BILLIE GYPSY WOMAN' in 1973. TIM and CARMINE teamed up with JEFF BECK ⇒ in supergroup BECK, BOGERT & APPICE. CARMINE joined MIKE BLOOMFIELD's band KGB in the mid-70's. He later joined ROD STEWART and in the 80's with RICK DERRINGER formed DNA.

VANILLA FUDGE

re-formed originals 1982 and again in 1984.

Atco Atco

Jul 84. (lp/c) *<(90149-1/-4)>* **MYSTERY**
– Golden age dreams / Jealousy / Mystery / Under suspicion / It gets stronger / Walk on by / My world is empty / Don't stop now / Hot blood / The stranger.

Jul 84. (7") *<99729>* **MYSTERY. / THE STRANGER** –

—— Folded again, although they briefly got together for Atlantic 40 year bash mid-'88.

– compilations, others, etc. –

1970. (lp; as PIGEONS) *Wand; <687>* **WHILE THE WORLD WAS EATING** –

1974. (lp) *Midi; (MID 0033)* **STAR COLLECTION** –

1982. (lp/c) *Atco; <90006-2>* **GREATEST HITS** –

1991. (cd) *Rhino; <R2 70798>* **VANILLA FUDGE LIVE (live)** –

Mar 93. (cd) *Atlantic; (8122 71154-2)* **THE BEST OF VANILLA FUDGE (PSYCHEDELIC SUNDAE)**
– You keep me hangin' on / Where is my mind? / The look of love / Ticket to ride / Come by day, come by night / Take me for a little while / That's what makes a man / Season of the witch / Shotgun / Thoughts / Faceless people / Good good lovin' / Some velvet morning / I can't make it alone / Lord in the country / Need love / Street walking woman / All in your mind.

Aug 95. (cd) *Atlantic; (7567 90006-2)* **THE BEST OF VANILLA FUDGE** –

Jul 94. (cd/c) *Success;* **YOU KEEP ME HANGIN' ON** –

Jul 96. (cd; CACTUS) *Atlantic; (8122 72411-2)* **CACTOLOGY**

Townes VAN ZANDT

Born: JOHN TOWNES VAN ZANDT, 7 Mar'44, Fort Worth, Texas, USA. Born into a Texas oil dynasty, VAN ZANDT's upbringing was characterised by constant relocation as his family moved around from state to state. As a teenager he also spent an unhappy couple of years in military school where he was allegedly diagnosed as a manic depressive, later dropping out of college courses in both Colorado and Houston in order to devote himself to writing and performing. Inspired initially by HANK WILLIAMS and later ELVIS PRESLEY, VAN ZANDT had begun learning the guitar before he'd even reached his teens. By the time he'd started making a name for himself on the mid 60's Houston folk circuit, BOB DYLAN was a glaring influence as – judging by the wry 'TALKIN' KARATE BLUES' – was DYLAN's own mentor, WOODY GUTHRIE. The latter track appeared on TOWNES' debut album, 'FOR THE SAKE OF THE SONG' (1968), a promising set produced by semi-legendary Nashville veteran, Jack Clement. Set up with the help of songwriter, MICKIE NEWBURY (whom VAN ZANDT had befriended on the Houston scene along with up and coming singer/songwriters GUY CLARK and JERRY JEFF WALKER), the sessions resulted in such enduring classics as 'TECUMSEH VALLEY' and the Spanish-tinged title track. While not blessed with the strongest of voices, VAN ZANDT's vocals resonated with the painful honesty of the archetypal tortured artist. The chilling 'WAITIN' AROUND TO DIE' could possibly be construed as morbidly prophetic with regards to VAN ZANDT's premature demise and yet while his lyrics told of a constant struggle with depression, the songs were rarely depressing in themselves. Equally, the enigmatic Texan was no archetype, rather a lone-wolf troubadour who set striking lyrical images to subtle, introspective country-folk melodies, gaining a substantial cult following over the course of his all too short life. The small 'Poppy' label was once again home for VAN ZANDT's sophomore effort, 'OUR MOTHER THE MOUNTAIN' (1969), generally considered by critics and fans alike to be his finest hour and featuring the dark, orchestrated beauty of 'KATHLEEN' (recently covered by the mighty TINDERSTICKS) as well as 'ST. JOHN THE GAMBLER'. An incredibly prolific period for the singer, he released his eponymous third album later that year, a record that revisited the finest tracks of the debut alongside a clutch of new material including the heart-rending 'NONE BUT THE RAIN'. Another of TOWNES' early mentor's was LIGHTNIN' HOPKINS, whose influence hovers over 1971's 'DELTA MOMMA BLUES' while 'HIGH LOW AND IN BETWEEN' (1972) found the surprisingly versatile Texan getting a gospel groove going on 'TWO HANDS'. His final early period album, 'THE LATE, GREAT TOWNES VAN ZANDT' (1973) featured the first incarnation of his classic outlaw ballad, 'PANCHO AND LEFTY', subsequently the subject of a sublime cover by EMMYLOU HARRIS (on her 1977 album, 'Luxury Liner') while WILLIE NELSON and MERLE HAGGARD also got to grips with it atop the country chart. By this point, the 'outlaw' movement had permanently altered the course of country music (well, at least for a while) and VAN ZANDT had definitely played his part. Yet in reality he was more hermit than outlaw, holeing up in the hills for weeks at a time as his albums lingered in obscurity amid label distribution problems and bankruptcy. He continued to perform though and in 1977 released a typically low-key concert set, 'LIVE AT THE OLD QUARTER, HOUSTON, TEXAS'. His next set of bonafide new material came with the following year's 'FLYIN' SHOES', its haunting title track (with rare piano accompaniment) arguably the man's finest composition. After another period in the wilderness, TOWNES was back with an album on 'Sugar Hill', 'AT MY WINDOW' (1987), followed by an all too rare UK tour. 1989 saw the release of 'LIVE AND OBSCURE', its title a typical example of VAN ZANDT's self-deprecating sense of humour and ambivalent attitude to the machinations of the music industry. Tragically, although he continued to occasionally perform and record into the 90's, VAN ZANDT died suddenly on New Year's day, 1997; he was only 52. Following his death, there've been a slew of posthumous releases including 'Arista's 'FAR CRY FROM DEAD' (1999) featuring previously unreleased material.

Album rating: FOR THE SAKE OF THE SONG (*6) / OUR MOTHER THE MOUNTAIN (*8) / TOWNES VAN ZANDT (*7) / DELTA MOMMA BLUES (*6) / HIGH, LOW AND INBETWEEN (*8) / THE LATE, GREAT TOWNES VAN ZANDT (*8) / LIVE AT THE OLD QUARTER, HOUSTON, TEXAS (*9) / FLYING SHOES (*6) / AT MY WINDOW (*8) / LIVE AND OBSCURE (*6) / RAIN ON A CONGA DRUM (*7) / THE NASHVILLE SESSIONS (*6) / REAR VIEW MIRROR (*6) / ROADSONGS (*6) / NO DEEPER BLUE (*6) / THE BEST OF . . . compilation (*7) / THE HIGHWAY KIND (*6) / LAST RIGHTS: THE LIFE & TIMES OF . . . compilation (*7) / A FAR CRY FROM DEAD compilation (*7) / TEXAS TROUBADOUR boxed set (*8)

TOWNES VAN ZANDT – vocals, acoustic guitar

R.C.A. Poppy

1968. (7") *<506>* **WAITIN' AROUND TO DIE. / TALKING KARATE BLUES** – –

1968. (lp) *<PYS 40.001>* **FOR THE SAKE OF THE SONG** –
– For the sake of the song / Tecumseh valley / Many a fine lady / Quick silver daydreams of Maria / Waitin' around to die / I'll be there in the morning / Sad Cinderella / The velvet voices / Talkin' karate blues / All your young servants / Sixteen summers, fifteen falls. *(UK cd-iss. Aug93 on Tomato'; 598 109129) <cd-iss. 1994 on 'Rhino'; R2 71541> (cd-iss. Jun98 on 'Charly'; CDGR 241)*

1969. (7") *<510>* **SECOND LOVERS SONG. / TECUMSEH VALLEY** –

1969. (lp) *(SF 8040) <PYS 40.004>* **OUR MOTHER THE MOUNTAIN**
– Be here to love me / Kathleen / She came and she touched me / Like a summer Thursday / Our mother the mountain / Second lovers song / St. John the gambler / Tecumseh valley / Snake mountain blues / My proud mountains / Why she's acting this way. *<re-iss. Mar79 on 'Tomato'; TOM 7015> (UK-iss.Jan88 on 'Decal' lp/c; LIK/TCLIK 17) (cd-iss. Jan88 on 'Charly'; CDCHARLY 104) <cd-iss. 1994 on 'Rhino'; R2 71241> (cd re-iss. Mar98 on 'Charly'; CDGR 211)*

1970. (lp) *<PYS 40.007>* **TOWNES VAN ZANDT** –
– For the sake of the song / Columbine / Waiting around to die / Don't take it too bad / Colorado girl / Lungs / I'll be here in the morning / Fare thee well, Miss Carousel / (Quick silver daydreams of) Maria / None but the rain. *<re-iss. Mar79 on 'Tomato'; TOM 7014> (UK-iss.Jun88 on 'Decal' lp/c; LIK/TCLIK 32) (cd-iss. Jun88 on 'Charly'; CDCHARLY 119) <cd-iss. 1994 on 'Rhino'; R2 71240> (cd re-iss. Mar98 on 'Charly'; CDGR 212)*

1971. (7") *<90104>* **COME TOMORROW. / DELTA MAMA BLUES** –

1971. (lp) *<PYS 40.012>* **DELTA MOMMA BLUES** –
– FFV / Delta momma blues / Only him or me / Turnstyled, junkpiled / Tower song / Come tomorrow / Brand new companion / Where I lead me / Rake / Nothin'. *<(UK + re-iss. Mar79 on 'Tomato'; TOM 7013)> (re-iss. Apr88 on 'Decal'; LIK/TCLIK 25) (cd-iss. Apr88 on 'Charly'; CDCHARLY 110) <cd-iss. 1994 on 'Rhino'; R2 71244> (cd re-iss. Nov97 on 'Musidisc'; 17404-2) (cd re-iss. Jun98 on 'Charly'; CDGR 213)*

1971. (lp) *<PYS 5700>* **HIGH, LOW AND INBETWEEN** –
– Two hands / You are not needed now / Greensboro woman / Highway kind / Standin' / No deal / To live is to fly / When he offers his hand / Mr. Gold and Mr. Mudd / Blue ridge mountains / High, low and inbetween. *<(UK + re-iss. Mar79 on 'Tomato'; TOM 7012)> (UK re-iss. Nov88 on 'Decal' lp/c; LIK/TCLIK 50) (cd-iss. Nov88 on 'Charly'; CDCHARLY 151) <cd-iss. 1994 on 'Rhino'; R2 71243> (cd re-iss. Aug98 on 'Charly'; CDGR 214)*

1972. (7") *<90108>* **GREENSBORO WOMAN. / STAND IN** –

U.A. Poppy

1972. (7") *<90113>* **IF I NEEDED YOU. / SUNSHINE BOY** –

1972. (7") *<90116>* **HONKY TONKIN'. / SNOW DON'T FALL** –

1973. (lp) *(UAS 29442) <LA 004>* **THE LATE, GREAT TOWNES VAN ZANDT** 1972
– No lonesome tune / Sad Cinderella / German mustard / Don't let the sunshine fool you / Honky tonkin' / Snow don't fall / Fraulein / Poncho and Lefty / If I needed you / Silver ships of Andilar / Heavenly houseboat blues. *<(UK + re-iss. Mar79 on 'Tomato'; TOM 7011)> (UK-iss.Aug88 on 'Edsel'; ED 293) (re-iss. Oct88 on 'Decal' lp/c; LIK/TCLIK 49) (cd-iss. Oct88 on 'Charly'; CDCHARLY 145) <cd-iss. 1994 on 'Rhino'; R2 71242> (cd re-iss. Nov97 on 'Charly'; CDGR 215)*

1973. (7") *<90124>* **PONCHO AND LEFTY. / IF I NEEDED YOU** –

not iss. Tomato

1977. (d-lp) *<TOM 7001>* **LIVE AT THE OLD QUARTER, HOUSTON, TEXAS (live)** –
– Announcement / Pancho and Lefty / Mr. Mudd and Mr. Gold / Don't you take it too bad / Two girls / Fraternity blue / If I needed you / Brand new companion / White freightliner blues / To live is to fly / She came and touched me / Talking thunderbird blues / Rex's blues / Nine pound hammer / For the sake of the song / No place to fall / Loretta / Kathleen / Tower song / Waiting 'round to die / Tecumseh valley / Lungs / Only him or me. *(UK-iss.Oct89 on 'Decal' d-lp/d-c; LIKD/TCLIKD 57) (d-cd-iss. Oct89 on 'Charly'; CDCHARLY 183) <cd-iss. 1994 on 'Rhino'; R2 71245> (d-cd-iss. Aug98 on 'Charly'; CDGR 216)*

1978. (7") *<10003>* **WHO DO YOU LOVE. / DOLLAR BILL BLUES** –

1978. (lp) *<TOM 7017>* **FLYING SHOES** –
– Loretta / No place to fall / Flyin' shoes / Who do you love / When she don't need me / Dollar bill blues / Rex's blues / Pueblo waltz / Brother flower / Snake song. *(UK-iss.Jul89 on 'Decal' lp/c; LIK/TCLIK 59) (cd-iss. Jul89 on 'Charly'; CDCHARLY 193) <cd-iss. 1994 on 'Rhino'; R2 71291> (cd re-iss. Nov98 on 'Charly'; CDGR 217)*

1978. (7") *<10005>* **WHEN SHE DON'T NEED ME. / NO PLACE TO FALL** –

Heartland Sugar Hill

Nov 87. (lp/cd) *(HLD/+CD 003) <SH 1020/+CD>* **AT MY WINDOW**
– Snowin' on Baton / Blue wind blew / At my window / For the sake of the song / Ain't leavin' your love / Buckskin stallion blues / Little sundance / Still lookin' for you / Gone gone blues / The catfish song. *(cd re-iss. May92 on 'Edsel'; EDCD 351)*

Nov 89. (lp/cd) *(HLD/+CD 004) <SH 1026/+CD>* **LIVE AND OBSCURE (live in Nashville 1985)**
– Dollar bill blues / Many a fine lady / Nothin' / Pueblo waltz / Talking Thunderbird blues / Rex's blues / White freight liner blues / Loretta / Snake mountain blues / Waitin' round to die / Tecumseh valley / Panch and Lefty / You are not needed now. *(cd re-iss. Mar92 as 'PANCHO AND LEFTY (LIVE AND OBSCURE)' on 'Edsel'; EDCD 244)*

Exile – Silenz not iss.

Oct 91. (lp – c/cd) *(EXLP 02 – 269575-4/-2)* **RAIN ON A CONGA DRUM (live in Berlin)** –
– Mr. Mudd and Mr. Gold / If I needed you / Buckskin stallion blues / Short haired woman blues / Ain't leavin' your love / Pancho and Lefty / Dollar bill blues / Fraulein / Shrimp song / Blaze's blues / No place to fall / To live is to fly / Lungs / Tecumseh valley / Dead flowers / White freightliner blues / Catfish blues.

Sugar Hill Sugar Hill

Apr 94. (cd/c) *<(SH 1042 CD/C)>* **ROADSONGS** (live covers rec.1976) 1993
– Ira Hayes / Dead flowers / Automobile blues / Coo coo / Fraulein hello / Central Indian cowboy / Racing in the streets / My starter won't start this morning / Texas river song / Wabash cannonball / Short haired woman blues / Man gave names to all the animals / Little Willie the gambler / Cocaine / You win again / High, low and inbetween / When he offers his hand. *(cd re-iss. Feb97 on 'Normal'; NORMAL 195)*

Aug 95. (cd) *<(SHCD 1046)>* **NO DEEPER BLUE** 1994
– Song for / Blaze's blues / Hole / Marie / Goin' down to Memphis / Hey Willy boy / Niles river blues / Nilly, Boney and ma / Katie Belle Vue / If I was Washington / Lover's lullaby / Cowboy Junkies lament / BW railroad blues / Gone too long. *(re-iss. Jun96 on 'Intercord'; IRS 993151)*

—— TOWNES died on the 1st of January, 1997 leaving behind posthumous . . .

Apr 97. (cd) *<(SHCD 1056)>* **THE HIGHWAY KIND**
– Lost highway / My proud mountains / The highway kind / Dublin blues / Blaze's blues / Wreck on the highway / Hole / (I heard that) Lonesome whistle / Rake / Banks of the Ohio / Ira Hayes / Darcey Farrow / Song for / Still lookin' for you / Joke / No deal / At my window.

– compilations, etc. –

Dec 90.	(c) *Charly; (TCAD 21)* **TOWNES / LIVE IN THE LATIN QUARTER**		
Aug 93.	(cd) *Tomato; <(598 107929)>* **THE NASHVILLE SESSIONS** – At my window / Rex's blues / No place to fall / Buckskin stallion / White freight liner / The snake song / Loretta / Two girls / The spider song / When she don't need me / Pueblo waltz / Upon my soul.		
1993.	(cd/c) *Sundown; <SD 2100-2/-4>* **REAR VIEW MIRROR (live renditions)** *(UK-iss.Jun96 on 'Intercord'; IRS 993150) (re-iss. Feb97 on 'Sugar Hill'; SHCD 1054) (re-iss. Nov97 on 'Normal'; NORMAL 203)*	–	
Jun 96.	(cd) *Charly; <(CPCD 8176)>* **THE BEST OF TOWNES VAN ZANDT** – Kathleen / St. John the gambler / Waiting 'round to die / Don't take it too bad / Colorado girl / I'll be here in the morning / Delta momma blues / Tower song / Brand new companion / Two hands / Standin' / No deal / To live is to fly / No lonesome tune / Honky tonkin' / Pancho and Lefty / If I needed you / Heavenly houseboat blues / Loretta / No place to fall / Flying shoes.		1999
Oct 96.	(cd) *Return To Sender; <(RTS 24)>* **ABNORMAL** *(re-iss. Aug98 on 'Normal'; NORMAL 216CD)*		
Oct 96.	(cd) *Capitol; <53930>* **HIGH, LOW AND INBETWEEN / THE LATE, GREAT TOWNES VAN ZANDT**	–	
Jul 97.	(cd) *Normal; (NORMAL 211CD)* **DOCUMENTARY**		–
Nov 97.	(cd) *Eagle; (EABCD 043)* **THE MASTERS**		–
Feb 98.	(d-cd) *Charly; (CDGR 207-2)* **ANTHOLOGY 1968-1979**		–
Mar 98.	(cd) *Gregor; (GREGORCD 41290)* **LAST RIGHTS: THE LIFE & TIMES OF TOWNES VAN ZANDT**		–
May 99.	(7") *Exile; (EX7 013)* **RIDING THE RANGE. / DIRTY OLD TOWN**		–
Jul 99.	(cd) *Arista; <(07822 18888-20)>* **A FAR CRY FROM DEAD** – Dollar bill blues / To live is to fly / Rex's blues / Sanitarium blues / Ain't leavin' your love / Greensboro woman / Snake mountain blues / Pancho and Lefty / For the sake of the song / Waitin' round to die / Many a fine lady / Tower song / Squash.		Jun99
Oct 99.	(cd/lp) *Normal; <(NORMAL 225 CD/LP)>* **IN PAIN (live)**		
Jun 00.	(d-cd) *Snapper; (SMDCD 288)* **DRAMA FALLS LIKE TEARDROPS**		–
Aug 01.	(cd) *Return To Sender; <(RTS 32)>* **LIVE AT McCABE'S (live)**		
Sep 01.	(4xcd-box) *Snapper; (SNAB 903CD)* **TEXAS TROUBADOUR**		–
Jul 02.	(cd) *Dualtone; <(01119)>* **A GENTLE EVENING WITH TOWNES VAN ZANDT (live at Carnegie Hall 26/11/1969)**		
Mar 03.	(cd) *Normal; <(N 211CD)>* **DOCUMENTARY**		

—— TOWNES also featured alongside STEVE EARLE and GUY CLARK on the shared set, 'TOGETHER AT THE BLUEBIRD'

Stevie Ray VAUGHAN

Born: 3 Oct'54, Dallas, Texas, USA. No white bluesman, not even ERIC CLAPTON, enjoyed the amount of peer adulation afforded STEVIE RAY, the closest probably being ALAN 'BLIND OWL' WILSON of CANNED HEAT. He idolised ALBERT KING, HOWLIN' WOLF and MUDDY WATERS and his early career mirrored that of JOHNNY WINTER in that he arrived with a sensational impact, consumed an equally sensational amount of alcohol followed by collapse and eventual rehabilitation. VAUGHAN moved to Austin in 1972, playing in local bands including the NIGHTCRAWLERS and PAUL RAY & THE COBRAS (with whom he recorded 'TEXAS CLOVER' in 1974). BUDDY GUY, JOHN LEE HOOKER, MUDDY WATERS and ALBERT KING were among VAUGHAN's admirers after seeing him play at Antone's in Austin where his blend of HENDRIX, ALBERT KING, HUBERT SUMLIN and LONNIE MACK was the best show in town. His band, DOUBLE TROUBLE, (which, after many personnel changes numbered JOHNNY RENO on sax, JACKIE NEWHOUSE on bass, FREDDIE PHAROAH on drums and LOU ANN BARTON on vocals) started out, in 1976, as the TRIPLE THREAT REVUE, co-starring BARTON and local bluesman W.C. CLARK. However, the band wasn't big enough for both VAUGHAN and BARTON, the latter leaving for a solo deal with 'Elektra'/'Asylum' records and taking RENO with her (PHARAOH also left, his replacement being CHRIS 'WHIPPER' SMITH). DOUBLE TROUBLE's final line-up was finally completed with the addition of TOMMY SHANNON in place of NEWHOUSE. STEVIE RAY was then introduced to JERRY WEXLER and secured a spot at the 1982 Montreux Jazz Festival through his contacts (a feat unheard of for an unsigned band although VAUGHAN certainly didn't disgrace himself), while JACKSON BROWNE offered them some free time in his L.A. studio after hearing that they were still without a deal. JOHN HAMMOND, hearing tapes of the Montreux show and the rough mixes from BROWNE's studio, signed him for 'Epic' and BOWIE procured his services for the 'LET'S DANCE' sessions. VAUGHAN left BOWIE before the Serious Moonlight tour, either through loyalty to his own band or through BOWIE's insistance on an exclusive contract, going on to tour in his own right and promote his first album, 1983's 'TEXAS FLOOD'. An earthy, no-nonsense blues album containing the classic 'PRIDE AND JOY', the record sold half a million copies, reaching Top 40 in the States and winning a Grammy for Best Traditional Blues recording. After DOUBLE TROUBLE played at the Reading Festival in 1983, they went into the studio to record the follow-up, 'COULDN'T STAND THE WEATHER', another US Top 40 money spinner. VAUGHAN became a sought after guest and played on albums by JAMES BROWN, JOHNNY COPELAND and LONNIE MACK, while the awards continued to pile up. Although the band became a tighter unit on 'COULDN'T STAND..' and its 1985 follow-up, 'SOUL TO SOUL' and VAUGHAN was stretching his talent further, the pressures of the music biz, together with his father's death, pushed him into a spiral of cocaine and booze intake that ended in him collapsing during a European tour. STEVIE subsequently retreated into a rehabilitation clinic to re-assess his life; the 1986 album 'LIVE ALIVE', which included a 9-minute version of Jimi Hendrix's 'VOODOO CHILE', was later considered by the band to be their worst, mainly because they were out of their heads on cocaine and alcohol when it was recorded and mixed, although many fans thought that it was better than the studio albums which preceded it. His marriage and management relationship suffered but after a slow recovery he reappeared in 1989 with his life and talent still intact and his first studio album in four years, 'IN STEP' (his finest work yet and a US Top 40 success with tracks such as 'THE HOUSE IS ROCKIN'', 'CROSSFIRE', 'TIGHTROPE' and 'WALL OF DENIAL' forming the record's backbone). The following year, he recorded the NILE RODGERS-produced 'FAMILY STYLE' with brother JIMMIE, (ex-FABULOUS THUNDERBIRDS), under the banner of The VAUGHAN BROTHERS. His recording career was to last little more than seven years, for only minutes after blowing ERIC CLAPTON, BUDDY GUY, ROBERT CRAY and JIMMIE off the stage at a show in Alpine Valley, Wisconsin on the 27th of August 1990, his helicopter crashed into a man-made hill on leaving the gig, killing all on board. His death instigated an outpouring of grief and the great artists who inspired him, from JOHN LEE HOOKER and BUDDY GUY (who dedicated their next albums to him), to JEFF BECK and ERIC CLAPTON, queued up to pay tribute to the guy who played the beat-up Stratocaster and who inspired a new generation of blues fans and artists. JACKSON BROWNE, STEVIE

WONDER and BONNIE RAITT sang 'AMAZING GRACE' during the memorial service at Oak Cliff, Dallas four days after his death and his hometown of Austin erected a nine foot bronze statue of him in 1992. 'COULDN'T STAND THE WEATHER' became his first million seller and 'THE SKY IS CRYING', an album of out-takes from his first four studio albums (including everything from Lonnie Mack's 'WHAM' – the first record that VAUGHAN ever bought – to Jimi Hendrix's 'LITTLE WING') reached US No.10. Other albums also did well after his death, notably 'FAMILY STYLE' which made the US Top 10. In 1997, the Fender guitar company paid VAUGHAN the ultimate honour by issuing a signature Stratocaster.

• **Songwriters:** Wrote half the material except TEXAS FLOOD (Davis-Scott) / CHANGE IT + LOOKING OUT THE WINDOW (D.Bramhall) / LOOK AT LITTLE SISTER (Hank Ballard) / YOU'LL BE MINE (Willie Dixon) / COME ON (E.King) / TAXMAN (George Harrison) / etc.

Album rating: TEXAS FLOOD (*6) / COULDN'T STAND THE WEATHER (*6) / SOUL TO SOUL (*7) / LIVE ALIVE (*5) / IN STEP (*6) / FAMILY STYLE (*6; as the Vaughan Brothers) / posthumous:- THE SKY IS CRYING (*7) / IN THE BEGINNING (*5) / GREATEST HITS compilation (*8) / LIVE AT CARNEGIE HALL (*5) / THE REAL DEAL: GREATEST HITS VOLUME 2 compilation (*6) / BLUES AT SUNRISE compilation (*6) / SRV boxed compilation (*6)

STEVIE RAY VAUGHAN & DOUBLE TROUBLE

STEVIE RAY VAUGHAN – vocals, guitar / **TOMMY SHANNON** – bass (ex-JOHNNY WINTER) / **CHRIS 'Whipper' LAYTON** – drums (ex-GREAZY BROTHERS)

Epic Epic

Jul 83. (7") *<04031>* **PRIDE AND JOY. / RUDE MOOD** [–] [ ]

Aug 83. (lp/c) *(EPC/40 25534) <38734>* **TEXAS FLOOD** [ ] Jul83 [38]
– Love struck baby / Pride and joy / Texas flood / Tell me / Testify / Rude mood / Mary had a little lamb / Dirty pool / I'm cryin' / Lenny. *(cd-iss. Jul89; CD 25534) (re-iss. Apr91 cd/c; 460951-2/-4) (cd re-iss. Mar99 on 'Legacy'; 494129-2)*

Aug 83. (7") *(EPC 3689)* **LOVE STRUCK BABY. / RUDE MOOD** [ ] [–]

— added brother **JIMMIE VAUGHAN** – guitar, bass

Jun 84. (lp/c) *(EPC/40 25940) <39304>* **COULDN'T STAND THE WEATHER** [ ] [31]
– Scuttle buttin' / Couldn't stand the weather / The things (that) I used to do / Voodoo chile (slight return) / Cold shot / Tin Pan alley / Honey bee / Stang's swang. *(cd-iss. Jul89; CD 25940) (re-iss. Apr91 cd/c; 465571-2/-4) (cd-iss. Feb95; EK 64425) (cd re-iss. Mar99 on 'Legacy'; 494130-2)*

— **JOE SUBLETT** – saxophone; repl. JIMMIE

— added **REESE WYNANS** – keyboards

Sep 85. (lp/c) *(EPC/40 26441) <40036>* **SOUL TO SOUL** [ ] [34]
– Say what! / Lookin' out the window / Look at little sister / Ain't gone 'n' give up on love / Gone home / Change it / You'll be mine / Empty arms / Come on (part III) / Life without you. *(cd-iss. Apr86; CD 26441) (re-iss. Apr91 cd/c; 466330-2/-4) (cd re-iss. Mar99 on 'Legacy'; 494131-2)*

Sep 85. (7") *<05731>* **CHANGE IT. / LOOK AT LITTLE SISTER** [–] [ ]

Mar 86. (7") *<06601>* **SUPERSTITION (live). / PRIDE AND JOY (live)** [–] [ ]

Jan 87. (7") *<06696>* **WILLIE THE WIMP. / SUPERSTITION** [–] [ ]

Jan 87. (d-lp/d-c/cd) *(450238-1/-4/-2) <40511>* **LIVE ALIVE (live)** [ ] Dec86 [52]
– Say what! / Ain't gone 'n' give up on love / Pride and joy / Mary had a little lamb / Superstition / I'm leaving you (commit a crime) / Cold shot / Willie the wimp / Look at little sister / Texas flood / Voodoo chile (slight return) / Love struck baby / Change it / Life without you. *(re-iss. Apr93 cd/c; 466839-2/-4)*

Jun 87. (7") *<07340>* **LOVE STRUCK BABY. / PIPELINE (W/ DICK DALE)** [–] [ ]

Jun 89. (7") *<69025>* **TRAVIS WALK. / CROSSFIRE** [–] [ ]

Jul 89. (lp/c/cd) *(463395-1/-4/-2) <45024>* **IN STEP** [63] Jun89 [33]
– The house is rockin' / Crossfire / Tightrope / Let me love you baby / Leave my girl alone / Travis walk / Wall of denial / Scratch-n-sniff / Love me darlin' / Riviera paradise. *(cd re-iss. Mar99 on 'Legacy'; 494132-2)*

Aug 89. (7") *<73212>* **THIS HOUSE IS ROCKIN'. / TIGHTROPE** [–] [ ]

— Late in the 80's, STEVIE jammed with The ERIC CLAPTON Band. On 27 Aug'90, after a concert in Alpine Valley, Wisconsin, STEVIE and other travellers were killed in a helicopter crash. He and brother JIMMIE had just cut album below.

VAUGHAN BROTHERS

Epic Epic

Oct 90. (cd/c/lp) *(467014-2/-4/-1) <46225>* **FAMILY STYLE** [63] [7]
– Hard to be / White boots / D-FW / Good Texan / Hillbillies from Outer Space / Long way from home / Tick tock / Telephone song / Baboom / Mama said / Brothers.

Oct 90. (c-s) *<73576>* **TICK TOCK. / BROTHERS** [–] [65]

Jan 91. (c-s) *<73673>* **GOOD TEXAN. / MAMA SAID / BABOOM** [–] [ ]

– (STEVIE RAY VAUGHAN) compilations, etc. –

on 'Legacy-Epic' unless mentioned otherwise

Nov 91. (cd/c/lp) *(468649-2/-4/-1) <47390>* **THE SKY IS CRYING** [ ] [10]
– Boot hill / The sky is crying / Empty arms / Little wing / Wham / May I have a talk with you / Chitlins con carne / So excited / Life by the drop. *(cd re-iss. Apr00; same)*

Nov 92. (7") *<74142>* **THE SKY IS CRYING. / CHITLINS CON CARNE** [–] [ ]

Oct 92. (cd/c/lp) *(472624-2/-4/-1) <53168>* **IN THE BEGINNING (live 1st April, 1980)** [ ] [58]
– In the open / Slide thing / They call me guitar Hurricane / All your love (I miss loving) / Tin pan alley / Love struck baby / Tell me / Shake for me / Live another day.

Jan 93. (7") **EMPTY ARMS. / WHAM** [–] [ ]

Nov 95. (cd/c) *(481023-2/-4) <66217>* **GREATEST HITS** [ ] [39]
– Taxman / Texas flood / The house is rockin' / Pride and joy / Tightrope / Little wing / Crossfire / Change it / Cold shot / Couldn't stand the weather / Life without you. *(cd re-iss. Feb01; same)*

Aug 97. (cd/c) *(488206-2/-4) <68163>* **LIVE AT CARNEGIE HALL (live)** [ ] [40]
– (intro) / Scuttle buttin' / Testifyin' / Love struck baby / Honey bee / Cold shot / Letter to my girl / Dirty pool / Pride and joy / Things that I used to do / C.O.D. / Iced over / Lenny / Rude mood.

Mar 99. (cd/c) *(494133-2/-4) <65873>* **THE REAL DEAL: GREATEST HITS VOLUME 2** [ ] [53]
– Lovestruck baby / Ain't gonna give up on love / Scuttle buttin' / Wall of denial / Lenny / Superstition / Empty arms / Riviera paradise / Look at little sister / Willie the wimp / Pipeline / Shake for me / Leave my girl alone / Telephone song / Voodoo chile (slight return) / Life by the drop.

Apr 00. (cd) *(497858-2) <63842>* **BLUES AT SUNRISE** [ ] [80]

Nov 00. (3xcd-box) *(495368-2)* **SOUL TO SOUL / TEXAS FLOOD / COULDN'T STAND THE WEATHER** [ ] [–]

Dec 00. (3xcd-box w/dvd) *(5009302-4) <65714>* **SRV** [ ] [ ]

☐ Alan VEGA (see under ⇒ SUICIDE)

Suzanne VEGA

Born: 12 Aug'59, Upper West Side, New York, USA. Studying dance at the High School of Performing Arts, VEGA spent her spare time gaining valuable musical experience in the folk clubs of New York's Greenwich Village. Hooking up with managers Ron Fierstein and Steve Addabbo, VEGA eventually secured a contract with 'A&M', Addabbo and LENNY KAYE (ex-PATTI SMITH GROUP and 'Nuggets' curator) overseeing production duties on her eponymous 1985 debut album. Critically acclaimed, this starkly compelling folk set saw VEGA hailed as the new JONI MITCHELL with some observers drawing comparisons with LAURA NYRO and even DORY PREVIN. Highly intelligent and acutely observed, VEGA's musings were reminiscent of LEONARD COHEN although she possessed a distinctive lyrical voice with a delicately understated vocal to match. Buoyed by the UK success (on its second release) of 'MARLENE ON THE WALL', the album almost made the British Top 10 although it struggled to penetrate the US Top 100. A couple of months later, she scored another UK Top 40 with the moodily intense 'LEFT OF CENTER', written for the soundtrack of 80's movie, 'Pretty In Pink' and featuring JOE JACKSON on piano. VEGA finally broke through in her home country with 'LUKA', a poignant character portrayal of an abused child which made No.3 in the American charts. The accompanying album, 'SOLITUDE STANDING' (1987) consolidated VEGA's standing as one of the most promising young talents in the new singer/songwriter movement alongside the likes of TRACY CHAPMAN etc. One track, the acappella 'TOM'S DINER', only a minor UK hit upon its original release in 1987, was later reworked by dance act, D.N.A., its success prompting a remixed version credited to SUZANNE VEGA & D.N.A. This in turn was even more successful, going Top 5 in Britain and America and leading to an album of the same name featuring interpretations of various VEGA tracks by such esteemed artists as R.E.M. A third album proper, 'DAYS OF OPEN HAND' (1990), met with mixed reactions however, its more ambitious jazz arrangements and enigmatic lyrics standing in contrast to the economical simplicity of her earlier work. No hit singles were forthcoming although the success of the aforementioned 'TOM'S DINER' track made sure VEGA's career stayed on the commercial straight and narrrow. No doubt indspired by the rhythmic innovation applied to the track, her fourth set, '99.9F' (1992) saw VEGA experimenting with all manner sound effects. The result was arguably her most consistent set since the debut, the likes of 'BLOOD MAKES NOISE' and 'FAT MAN & DANCING GIRL' fastening spiky rhythmic structures to VEGA's trademark sound, while the more traditional 'WHEN HEROES GO DOWN' showed VEGA could still pen affecting folk-pop. In 1997, SUZANNE was back with her most accessible work to date, 'NINE OBJECTS OF DESIRE', one of tracks featured on the record, NO CHEAP THRILL' even appearing on Britain's lottery show! While the 90's were characterised by an experimentalism in large part due to the influence of husband/producer Mitchell Froom, her subsequent divorce made for both rich songwriting material and a back to basics approach on the Rupert Hine-produced 'SONGS IN RED AND GRAY' (2001). Very much a return to the sparse, confessional style which made her name back in the 80's, the record analysed the breakdown of her marriage in oblique yet emotionally loaded style. • **Covered:** CHINA DOLL (Grateful Dead) / STORY OF ISAAC (Leonard Cohen). • **Trivia:** In 1987, she contributed two song lyrics for a PHILIP GLASS album, 'Songs From Liquid Days'.

Album rating: SUZANNE VEGA (*8) / SOLITUDE STANDING (*7) / DAYS OF OPEN HAND (*5) / 99.9 F (*6) / NINE OBJECTS OF DESIRE (*6) / THE BEST OF SUZANNE VEGA – TRIED AND TRUE compilation (*8) / SONGS IN RED AND GRAY (*6) / RETROSPECTIVE: THE BEST OF . . . double compilation (*8)

SUZANNE VEGA – vocals, guitar with **JIM GORDON** – guitar / **FRANK CHRISTIAN** – guitar / **PAUL DUGAN + FRANK GRAVIS** – bass / **SUE EVANS** – drums / **C.P. ROTH** – synth She replaced above with touring + studio band from mid'85-late 80's. **MARC SHULMAN** – guitar / **MIKE VISCEGLIA** – bass / **ANTON SANKO** – keyboards / **STEPHEN FERRARA** – percussion / **SUE EVANS** – drums

A&M A&M

Jul 85. (lp/c) *<(AMA/AMC 5072)>* **SUZANNE VEGA** [11] Jun85 [91]
– Cracking / Freeze tag / Marlene on the wall / Small blue thing / Straight lines / Undertow / Some journey / The queen and the soldier / Knight moves / Neighborhood girls. *(cd-iss. Feb86 & Mar93; CDA 5072) (lp re-iss. Apr00 on 'Vivante'; VPLP 006)*

Aug 85. (7") *(AM 275) <2759>* **MARLENE ON THE WALL. / NEIGHBORHOOD GIRLS** [ ] [ ]

Jan 86. (7") *(AM 294)* **SMALL BLUE THING. / THE QUEEN AND THE SOLDIER** [65] [–]
(d7"+=) *(DAM 294)* – Some journey / Black widow station.

Feb 86. (7") *<2834>* **SMALL BLUE THING. / LEFT OF CENTER** [–] [ ]

Mar 86. (7") *(AM 309)* **MARLENE ON THE WALL. / SMALL BLUE THING** [21] [–]
(10"+=) *(AMY 309)* – Neighborhood girls / Straight lines (live).

May 86. (7") *(AM 320)* **LEFT OF CENTER. / UNDERTOW** [32] [–]
(10"+=) *(AMX 320)* – ('A'live) / Freeze tag (live).
(cd-s+=) *(CDQ 320)* – Cracking.
(above 'A'side featured JOE JACKSON – piano). SUE EVANS had now left.

Oct 86. (7") *(AM 349)* **GYPSY. / CRACKING (live)** [ ] [–]
(12"+=) *(AMY 349)* – Knight movies (live).

May 87. (lp/c/cd) *(SUZ LP/MC/CD 2) <5136>* **SOLITUDE STANDING** [2] [11]
– Tom's diner / Luka / Ironbound / Fancy poultry / In the eye / Night vision / Solitude standing / Calypso / Language / Gypsy / Wooden horse.

May 87. (7") *<2937>* **LUKA. / NIGHT VISION** [–] [3]

May 87. (7") *(VEGA 1)* **LUKA. / STRAIGHT LINES (live)** [23] [–]
(12"+=) *(VEGA 12)* – Neighbourhood girls.
(10"+=/c-s+=) *(VEGA 10/C10)* – Cracking (alternative mix).

Jul 87. (7") *(VEGA 2)* **TOM'S DINER. / LEFT OF CENTER** [58] [–]
(10"+=/12"+=) *(VEGA 210/212)* – Luka (live).
(cd-s+=) *(VEGCD 2)* ('A'live).

Sep 87. (7") *<2960>* **SOLITUDE STANDING. / TOM'S DINER** [–] [94]

Nov 87. (7") *<2888>* **GYPSY. / LEFT OF CENTER** [–] [ ]

Nov 87. (7"/c-s) *(VEGA/+C 3)* **SOLITUDE STANDING. / LUKA** [ ] [–]
(12"+=) *(VEGA 3-12)* – Ironbound – Fancy poultry.
(10"/cd-s) *(VEG A3-10/CD 3)* – ('A'side) / Marlene on the wall (live) / Some journey (live).

—— **FRANK VILARDI** – drums repl. FERRARA

—— added **MICHAEL BLAIR** – percussion

Apr 90. (cd/c/lp) *(CDA/AMC/AMA 5293) <15293>* **DAYS OF OPEN HAND** [7] [50]
– Tired of sleeping / Men in a war / Rusted pipe / Institution green / Book of dreams / Those whole girls (run in grace) / Room off the street / Big space / Predictions / Fifty-fifty chance / Pilgrimage. *(re-iss. cd May95; 395293-2)*

Apr 90. (7"/c-s) *(AM/+MC 559)* **BOOK OF DREAMS. / BIG SPACE** [66] [ ]
(cd-s+=) *(AMCD 559)* – Marlene on the wall (live) / Ironbound (live).
(10"++=) *(AMX 559)* – Fancy poultry.

Jun 90. (7") *(AM 565)* **TIRED OF SLEEPING. / THOSE WHOLE GIRLS (RUN IN GRACE)** [ ] [ ]
(10"+=/cd-s+=) *(AM X/CD 565)* – Left of center / Room off the street.

Jul 90. (7"/c-s; D.N.A. featuring SUZANNE VEGA) *(AM/+MC 592) <1592>* **TOM'S DINER. / ('A'version)** [2] Sep90 [5]
(12"+=/cd-s+=) *(AM X/CD 592)* – (2 other mixes by the Bristol duo).

Sep 90. (7"/c-s) *(AM/+MC 584)* **MEN IN A WAR. / UNDERTOW (live)** [ ] [ ]
(12"+=/cd-s+=) *(AM X/CD 584)* – ('A'live).

Aug 92. (7"/c-s) *(AM/+C 0029)* **IN LIVERPOOL. / SOME JOURNEY** [52] [ ]
(cd-s+=) *(AMCD 0029)* – The Queen and the soldier / Luka.

Sep 92. (cd/c/lp) *(540012-2/-4/-1) <0005>* **99.9 F** [20] [86]
– Rock in this pocket (song of David) / Blood makes noise / In Liverpool / 99.9 F / Blood sings / Fat man & dancing girl / (If you were) In my movie / As a child / Bad wisdom / When heroes go down / As girls go / Songs of sand / Private goes public.

Oct 92. (7"/c-s) *(AM/+C 0085)* **99.9 F. / MEN WILL BE MEN** [46] [–]
(cd-s+=) *(AMCD 0085)* – Rock in this pocket (acoustic) / In Liverpool (acoustic).
(cd-s) *(AMCDX 0085)* – ('A'side) / Tired of sleeping / Straight lines / Tom's diner (all live).

Dec 92. (7"/c-s) *(AM/+C 0112)* **BLOOD MAKES NOISE. / TOM'S DINER** [60] [–]
(cd-s) *(AMCD 0112)* – ('A'side) / Neighbourhood girls / Predictions / China doll.
(12") *(AMY 0112)* – ('A'side) / ('A'-Mitchell Froom remix) / ('A'house mix) / ('A'master mix).

Feb 93. (7"/c-s) *(AM/+C 0158)* **WHEN HEROES GO DOWN. / KNIGHT MOVES (live)** [58] [–]
(cd-s+=) *(AMCD 0158)* – Men in a war (live) / Gypsy (live).

(cd-s) *(AMCDX 0158)* – ('A'side) / Marlene on the wall / Luka / Left of center.

Feb 97. (c-ep/cd-ep) *(581869-4/-2)* **NO CHEAP THRILL / LUKA / MARLENE ON THE WALL / TOM'S DINER** 40 –

Feb 97. (cd/c) *(540583-2/-4)* **NINE OBJECTS OF DESIRE** 43 Sep96 92
– Birth-day (love made real) / Headshots / Caramel / Stockings / Casual match / Thin man / No cheap thrill / World before Columbus / Lolita / Honeymoon suite / Tombstone / My favorite plum.

Jun 97. (c-s) *(582269-4)* **BIRTH-DAY (LOVE MADE REAL) / WOMEN ON A TIER** –
(cd-s) *(582267-2)* – ('A'side) / Caramel / Small blue thing / Blood makes noise.
(cd-s) *(582269-2)* – ('A'side) / Casual match / World before Columbus.

Oct 98. (cd/c) *<(540945-2/-4)>* **THE BEST OF SUZANNE VEGA – TRIED AND TRUE** (compilation) 46
– Luka / Tom's diner (DNA featuring SUZANNE VEGA) / Marlene on the wall / Caramel / 99.9f / Small blue thing / Blood makes noise / Left of the center / In Liverpool / Gypsy / Book of dreams / No cheap thrill / World before Columbus / When heroes go down / The queen and the soldier / Book & a cover / Rosemary.

Sep 01. (cd) *<(493111-2)>* **SONGS IN RED AND GRAY**
– Penitent / Widow's walk / (I'll never be) Your Maggie May / It makes me wonder / Soap and water / Songs in red and gray / Last year's troubles / Priscilla / If I were a weapon / Harbor song / Machine ballerina / Solitaire / St. Clare.

Universal Universal

Jul 03. (cd) *(9808884) <493670>* **RETROSPECTIVE: THE BEST OF . . .** 27 Apr03
– Luka / Tom's diner (DNA featuring SUZANNE VEGA) / Marlene on the wall / Caramel / 99.9F / Tired of sleeping / Small blue thing / Blood makes noise / Left of center / (I'll never be) Your Maggie May / In Liverpool / Gypsy / Book of dreams / No cheap thrill / Calypso / World before Columbus / Solitude standing / Penitent / Rosemary / The queen and the soldier (live) / Woman on the tier (I'll see you through). *(UK cd w/bonus cd+=)* – Caramel (live) / Widow's talk (live) / Solitude standing (live) / Blood makes noise (live) / In Liverpool (a short reading from The Passionate Eye) / In Liverpool (live) / Anniversary (demo) / Tom's diner (original).

– more compilations, others, etc. –

Oct 88. (cd-ep) *A&M; (AMCD 912)* **COMPACT HITS** –
– Luka / Left of center / Neighbourhood girls / The queen and the soldier.

Sep 91. (cd/c/lp; Various Artists) *A&M; (395363-2/-4/-1)* **TOM'S ALBUM**
– (contained re-workings by other artists of the track TOM'S DINER)

VELVET UNDERGROUND

Formed: New York City, New York, USA . . . early 1965, by LOU REED and JOHN CALE, who nearly hit as The PRIMITIVES with the single, 'The Ostrich'. They met modern pop artist, ANDY WARHOL, who invited German chanteuse NICO to join the set-up alongside STERLING MORRISON and MO TUCKER. Early in 1966, they signed to 'MGM-Verve', and soon began work on what was to be their debut album, 'THE VELVET UNDERGROUND AND NICO'. The album was a revelation, strikingly different from the love and peace psychedelia of the day, The VELVETS vision was decidedly darker and more disturbing. Combining sublime melodies and nihilistic noise, it featured eleven superb ahead-of-their-time classics, notably the brutally frank and frenetic 'HEROIN', the S&M 'VENUS IN FURS' and the garage raunch of 'WAITING FOR THE MAN'. It also contained three NICO sung beauties, 'FEMME FATALE', 'ALL TOMORROW'S PARTIES' and 'I'LL BE YOUR MIRROR'. The record only managed a brief stay in the US Top 200, as did the 1967 follow-up, 'WHITE LIGHT, WHITE HEAT', which included the 17-minute white noise freak-out of 'SISTER RAY'. With CALE now out of the picture, the focus fell on REED's songwriting for the self-titled third album. An altogether mellower set of more traditionally structured songs, the highlight was undoubtedly REED's beautiful lullaby, 'PALE BLUE EYES'. The band's last studio album, 'LOADED', was the closest The VELVET UNDERGROUND ever came to mainstream rock and an indicator of the direction REED would take in his solo career. 'SWEET JANE' and 'ROCK 'N' ROLL' marked his creative peak, a final glorious burst of guitar noise before the group disbanded and the myth started to crystallise. And that was that. Except it wasn't, not come 1992 anyway, when many a precious, pasty faced obsessive went even whiter with horror as The VELVET UNDERGROUND reformed. Many more fans, however, eagerly shelled out their hard earned cash for a reunion tour and album as CALE and REED became buddies once more. The live shows were apparently rather joyous and the accompanying vinyl document, 'LIVE MCMXCIII' (1993), was an enjoyable romp through all the favourites. After the death of STERLING MORRISON in 1995, however, the prospect of further VELVETS activity looked doubtful. Yet despite the reunion, despite LOU REED's dodgy hairdo, despite everything, The VELVET UNDERGROUND of the 60's remain perennially cool and insidiously influential. Basically, alternative music begins and ends with VU and they have been cited as the inspiration for punk rock. A decade after that, a generation of indie groups (i.e. JESUS & MARY CHAIN, early PRIMAL SCREAM, MY BLOODY VALENTINE, etc.) paid barely disguised homage to their heroes. • **Songwriters:** REED compositions, except some by group. Many rock acts have covered their material, but so far not surprisingly, none have managed to score a major chart hit yet. • **Miscellaneous:** In 1990, REED and CALE re-united on a tribute album to the deceased ANDY WARHOL. NICO had earlier died on the 18th of July '88 after suffering a brain haemorrhage due to a fall from her bike while on holiday in Ibiza. • **Trivia:** Their debut LP sleeve featured a gimmick peeling-banana-skin sticker. They reformed for a gig in Paris, 15 June 1990. UK's Channel 4 featured a night-long session of all their previous work.

Album rating: THE VELVET UNDERGROUND AND NICO (*10) / WHITE LIGHT – WHITE HEAT (*9) / THE VELVET UNDERGROUND (*8) / LOADED (*8) / ANDY WARHOL'S VELVET UNDERGROUND FEATURING NICO compilation (*7) / LIVE AT MAX'S KANSAS CITY exploitation (*2) / SQUEEZE (*3) / THE VELVET UNDERGROUND AND LOU REED compilation (*6) / 1969 – THE VELVET UNDERGROUND LIVE exploitation (*7) / GREATEST HITS compilation (*6) / V.U. unreleased set (*7) / ANOTHER VIEW exploitation (*4) / THE BEST OF THE VELVET UNDERGROUND (THE WORDS AND MUSIC OF LOU REED) compilation (*7) / LIVE MCMXCIII reunion (*5)

LOU REED (b. LOUIS FIRBANK, 2 Mar'44, Long Island, N.Y.) – vocals, guitar (ex-JADES, ex-PRIMITIVES) / **JOHN CALE** (b. 9 Dec'42, Garnant, Wales) – bass, viola, vocals, etc. / **STERLING MORRISON** – guitar / **MAUREEN TUCKER** – drums / plus **NICO** (b. CHRISTA PAFFGEN, 16 Oct'38, Cologne, Germany) – vocals (also – Solo artist)

Verve Verve

Oct 66. (7") *<10427>* **ALL TOMORROW'S PARTIES. / I'LL BE YOUR MIRROR** –

Dec 66. (7") *<10466>* **SUNDAY MORNING / FEMME FATALE** –

Oct 67. (lp; stereo/mono) *(S+/VLP 9184) <5008>* **THE VELVET UNDERGROUND AND NICO** Dec66
– Sunday morning / I'm waiting for the man / Femme fatale / Venus in furs / Run run run / All tomorrow's parties / Heroin / There she goes again / I'll be your mirror / Black angel's death song / European son to Delmore Schwartz. *(re-iss. Oct71 on 'M.G.M.; 2315 056) (re-iss. Aug83 on 'Polydor' lp/c; SPE LP/MC 20) (cd-iss. 1986 on 'Polydor'; 823 290-2) (cd re-iss. May96 on 'Polydor'; 531 250-2) (lp re-iss. Jun99 on 'Simply Vinyl'; SVLP 90) <(d-cd-iss. Apr02 on 'Polydor'+=; MLST 756)>* – (NICO tracks) / (mono versions) / (various versions). *(hit UK No.59)*

—— trimmed to a quartet when NICO preferred the solo life

Jan 68. (7") *<10543>* **WHITE LIGHT – WHITE HEAT. / HERE SHE COMES NOW** –

Mar 68. (7") *<10560>* **I HEARD HER CALL MY NAME. / HERE SHE COMES NOW** –

Jun 68. (lp; stereo/mono) *(S+/VLP 9201)* *<5046>* **WHITE LIGHT / WHITE HEAT** □ Dec67 □
– White light – white heat / The gift / Lady Godiva's operation / Here she comes now / I heard her call my name / Sister Ray. *(re-iss. Oct71 on 'MGM Select'; 2353 024) (re-iss. Apr84 on 'Polydor' lp/c; SPE LP/MC 73) (cd-iss. 1986 on 'Polydor'; 825 119-2) (cd re-iss. May96 on 'Polydor'; 531 251-2) (lp re-iss. Apr00 on 'Simply Vinyl'; SVLP 200)*

—— **DOUG YULE** – bass, vocals, keyboards, guitar; repl. CALE who went solo

M.G.M. M.G.M.

Apr 69. (lp) *(CS 8108)* *<4617>* **THE VELVET UNDERGROUND** □ Mar 69 □
– Candy says . . . / What goes on / Some kinda love / Pale blue eyes / Jesus / Beginning to see the light / I'm set free / That's the story of my life / The murder mystery / Afterhours. *(re-iss. Nov71 on 'MGM Select'; 2353 022) (re-iss. Mar76;) (re-iss. Sep83 on 'Polydor'; SPE LP/MC 39) <US re-iss. Apr85; 815454> (cd-iss. May96 on 'Polydor'; 531 252-2)*

May 69. (7") *<14057>* **JESUS. / WHAT GOES ON** – □

—— **BILLY YULE** – drums repl. TUCKER who had a baby. **MO TUCKER** returned in 1970 and BILLY only appeared on MAX's live album (see compilations)

Atlantic Cotillion

Jan 71. (7") *<44107>* **WHO LOVES THE SUN? / OH! SWEET NUTHIN'** – □

Apr 71. (lp) *(2400 111)* *<9034>* **LOADED** □ Aug70 □
– Who loves the sun? / Sweet Jane / Rock and roll / Cool it down / New age / Head held high / Lonesone cowboy Bill / I found a reason / Train around the bend / Oh! sweet nuthin'. *(re-iss. 1972 lp/c; K/K4 40113) (cd-iss. Jun88 & Feb93 on 'Warners'; 7567 90367-2) (d-cd-iss. May97 as 'LOADED (THE FULLY LOADED EDITION)' on 'Rhino'+=; 8122 72563-2)* – (diff.mixes & demos, etc.) *(lp re-iss. Oct97 on 'Simply Vinyl'; SVLP 22)*

Apr 71. (7") *(2091 008)* **WHO LOVES THE SUN. / SWEET JANE** □ –

—— (Aug70) now with no originals The **YULE's** brought in newcomers **WALTER POWERS** – bass repl. LOU REED who went solo in 1971. (1971) **WILLIE ALEXANDER** – guitar repl. MORRISON who took a doctorate in English. MO TUCKER finally departed to raise her new family and eventually had five children in total, before going solo in 1980.

Polydor not iss.

Feb 73. (lp) *(2383 180)* **SQUEEZE** □ –
– Little Jack / Mean old man / She'll make you cry / Wordless / Dopey Joe / Crash / Friends / Jack and Jane / Send no letter / Louise.

—— Folded soon after above, DOUG sessioned for ELLIOTT MURPHY and later joined AMERICAN FLYER.

—— they re-formed early in 1993; **REED, CALE, MORRISON + TUCKER**

Sire Sire

Oct 93. (d-cd/d-c) *<(9362 45464-2/-4)>* **LIVE MCMXCIII (live 1993)** 70 □
– We're gonna have a good time together / Venus in furs / Guess I'm falling in love / After hours / All tomorrow's parties / Some kinda love / I'll be your mirror / Beginning to see the light / The gift / I heard her call my name / Femme fatale / Hey Mr. Rain / Sweet Jane / Velvet nursery rhyme / White light – white heat / I'm sticking with you / Black angel's death song / Rock'n'roll / I can't stand it / I'm waiting for the man / Heroin / Pale blue eyes / Coyote.

Feb 94. (7"/c-s) *(W 0224/+C)* **VENUS IN FURS (live). / I'M WAITING FOR THE MAN (live)** 71 □
(cd-s+=) *(W 0224CD)* – Heroin (live) / Sweet Jane (live).

—— On the 30th August 1995, STERLING MORRISON died of lymphoma.

—— Group inducted into the Rock'n'roll Hall Of Fame, and performed 'LAST NIGHT I SAID GOODBYE TO A FRIEND', REED's tribute to recently deceased STERLING.

– compilations, others, etc. –

Dec 71. (d-lp) *M.G.M.; (2683 006)* **ANDY WARHOL'S VELVET UNDERGROUND FEATURING NICO** □ –
– I'm waiting for the man / Candy says / Run, run, run / White light – white heat / All tomorrow's parties / Sunday morning / I heard her call my name / Femme fatale / Heroin / Here she comes now / There she goes again / Sister Ray / Venus in furs / European son / Pale blue eyes / Black angel's death song / Beginning to see the light.

Aug 72. (lp) *Atlantic; (K 30022) / Cotillion; <9500>* **LIVE AT MAX'S KANSAS CITY (live 22 Aug'70)** □ May72 □
– I'm waiting for the man / Sweet Jane / Lonesome Cowboy Bill / Beginning to see the light / I'll be your mirror / Pale blue eyes / Sunday morning / New age / Femme fatale / After hours. *(cd-iss. Jun93 on 'Warners'; 7567 90370-2)*

Jun 73. (7"m; as LOU REED & VELVET UNDERGROUND) *M.G.M.; (2006 283)* **CANDY SAYS. / I'M WAITING FOR THE MAN / RUN RUN RUN** □ –

Aug 73. (7") *Atlantic; (K 10339)* **SWEET JANE (live). / ROCK AND ROLL** (live) □ –

Oct 73. (lp) *Verve; (2315 258) / Pride; <0022>* **THE VELVET UNDERGROUND AND LOU REED** □ □

1974. (lp) *M.G.M.; <4950>* **ARCHETYPES** – □

1976. (ltd-7"m) *A.E.B.;* **FOGGY NOTION – INSIDE YOUR HEART. / I'M STICKING WITH YOU / FERRYBOAT BILL** □ –

Feb 79. (d-lp) *Mercury; (6643 900) <SRM2 7504>* **1969 – THE VELVET UNDERGROUND LIVE (live)** □ Apr74 □
– I'm waiting for the man / Lisa says / What goes on / Sweet Jane / We're gonna have a real good time together / Femme fatale / New age / Rock and roll / Beginning to see the light / Ocean / Pale blue eyes / Heroin / Some kinda love / Over you / Sweet Bonnie Brown – It's just too much / I'll be your mirror / White light – white heat. *(re-iss. Nov84; PRID 7) (re-iss. 1987; 834 823-1) (re-iss. 1988 as 'VOL.1' & 'VOL.2' cd/c; 834823-2/-4 & 834824-2/-4)*

Nov 80. (d-lp)(d-c) *Polydor; (2664 438)(3578 485)* **GREATEST HITS** □ –

Oct 82. (12"ep) *Polydor; (POSPX 603)* **HEROIN / VENUS IN FURS. / I'M WAITING FOR THE MAN / RUN RUN RUN** □ –

Feb 85. (lp/c) *Polydor; (POLD/+C 5167) <823721>* **V.U.** (rare rec.68-69) 47 85
– I can't stand it / Stephanie says / She's my best friend / Lisa says / Ocean / Foggy notion / Temptation inside your heart / One of these days / Andy's chest / I'm sticking with you. *(cd-iss. Jun87; 825 092-2)*

May 86. (5xlp-box)(5xcd-box) *Polydor; (VUBOX 1)(815 454-2)* **BOXED SET** □ □
– (first 3 albums, plus V.U. & ANOTHER VIEW)

Aug 86. (lp/c/cd) *Polydor; (829 405-1/-4/-2)* **ANOTHER VIEW** □ □
– We're gonna have a good time together / I'm gonna move right in / Hey Mr. Rain (version 1) / Ride into the Sun / Coney Island steeplechase / Guess I'm falling in love / Hey Mr. Rain (version 2) / Ferryboat Bill / Rock and roll (original).

Feb 88. (12") *Old Gold; (OG 4049)* **I'M WAITING FOR THE MAN. / HEROIN** □ –

Mar 88. (12") *Old Gold; (OG 4051)* **VENUS IN FURS. / ALL TOMORROW'S PARTIES** □ –

Sep 88. (lp) *Plastic Inevitable; <FIRST 1>* **THE VELVET UNDERGROUND ETC.** – □
– The ostrich / Cycle Annie / Sneaky Pete / Noise.

Sep 88. (lp) *Plastic Inevitable; <SECOND 1>* **THE VELVET UNDERGROUND AND SO ON** – □
– It's alright (the way you live) / I'm not too sorry / Stephanie says.

Oct 89. (lp/c/cd) *Verve; <(841 164-1/-4/-2)>* **THE BEST OF THE VELVET UNDERGROUND (THE WORDS AND MUSIC OF LOU REED)** □ □
– I'm waiting for the man / Femme fatale / Run run run / Heroin / All tomorrow's parties / I'll be your mirror / White light – white heat / Stephanie says / What goes on / Beginning to see the light / Pale blue eyes / I can't stand it / Lisa says / Sweet Jane / Rock and roll.

Oct 95. (cd/c) *Global; (RAD CD/MC 21)* **THE BEST OF LOU REED & VELVET UNDERGROUND** 56 □

Oct 95. (4xcd-box) *Polydor; <(527887-2)>* **PEEL SLOWLY AND SEE** □ Sep95 □

Oct 00. (cd) *Universal; <(AA314 549133-2)>* **THE MILLENNIUM COLLECTION: THE BEST OF . . .** □ □

Jul 01. (cd) *Polydor; (549690-2)* **ROCK AND ROLL: AN INTRODUCTION TO THE VELVET UNDERGROUND** □ –

Aug 01. (4xcd-box) *Captain Trip; (CTCD 35053)* **FINAL VU 1971-1973 (live)** □ –
– (LIVE IN LONDON 1971 / LIVE IN THE NETHERLANDS 1971 / LIVE IN WALES 1972 / MASSACHUSETTS 1973).

Oct 01. (3xcd-box) *Polydor; <(557665-2)>* **BOOTLEG SERIES VOL.1: THE QUINE TAPES** □ □

—— (see also LOU REED discography for other tracks on comps & B's)

—— Also tribute albums 'HEAVEN AND HELL' 1, 2 & 3 were issued Oct'90-Feb'92, all on 'Imaginary' records, as was another '15 MINUTES'.

☐ VENT 414 (see under ⇒ WONDER STUFF)

☐ Tom VERLAINE (see under ⇒ TELEVISION)

VERTICAL HORIZON

Formed: Boston, Massachusetts, USA ... 1991 by Georgetown University graduates MATTHEW SCANNELL and KEITH KANE. Sleek and radio-friendly, VERTICAL HORIZON broke through with their fourth, rock orientated album, but this was not always the group's signature sound. They independently issued the album 'THERE AND BACK AGAIN', a collection of wispy folk songs before releasing their sophomore set, 'RUNNING ON ICE' to critical, but not commercial acclaim. The album featured CARTER BEAUFORD of the DAVE MATTHEWS BAND as well as some very stern nods towards a sound that JAMES TAYLOR would have been proud of. A live album entitled 'LIVE STAGES' followed in 1997 and this included songs from the band's first two albums. The decibel level had been somewhat turned up, SCANNELL and KANE rocking their way through songs such as 'ON THE SEA' and 'FALLING DOWN'. This paved the way to the group's fourth and most commercially viable album to date, 'EVERYTHING YOU WANT' (1999), which as said previously saw the band head in a rock-orientated direction not unlike that of peers the DAVE MATTHEWS BAND. The songs were all neatly produced with catchy choruses and repetitive guitar hooks, in other words, very staid and uninspiring.

Album rating: THERE AND BACK AGAIN (*5) / RUNNING ON ICE (*6) / LIVE STAGES (*5) / EVERYTHING YOU WANT (*5)

MATTHEW SCANNELL – vocals, guitars, keyboards, bass, drum programming / **KEITH KANE** – acoustic guitar, vocals

not iss. Rhythmic

Feb 93. (cd) *<7771>* **THERE AND BACK AGAIN** [–] [ ]
– Trying to find a purpose / Children's lullaby / Footprints in the snow / Love's light / Mountain song / Prayer for an innocent man / Lines upon your face (for the Aylesbury Road gang) / Willingly / On the sea / Liberty. *(UK-iss.Nov00 on 'R.C.A.'; 07863 67779-2)*

— added guests **CARTER BEAUFORD** – drums (of DAVE MATTHEWS BAND) / bass:- **RYAN FISHER + STEVE SIDLEY**

Apr 95. (cd) *<7772>* **RUNNING ON ICE** [–] [ ]
– Heart in hand / Wash away / Fragments / Famous / The man who would be Santa / Angel without wings / Answer me / Life in the city / Japan / Call it even / Sunrays and Saturdays / Candyman / Falling down / Goodnight my friends. *(UK-iss.Nov00 on 'R.C.A.'; 07863 67780-2)*

— added **SEAN HURLEY** – bass + **ED TOTH** – drums

Jan 97. (cd) *<7773>* **LIVE STAGES (live)** [–] [ ]
– The man who would be Santa / The ride / Falling down / On the sea / Japan / It's only me / Candyman / Fragments / The unchosen one / Heart in hand / Wash away / Great divide. *(UK-iss.Nov00 on 'R.C.A.'; 07863 67781-2)*

R.C.A. R.C.A.

Aug 00. (c-s) *(74321 74869-4) <65981>* **EVERYTHING YOU WANT (modern rock mix) / THE MAN WHO WOULD BE SANTA (live)** [42] Oct99 [1]
(cd-s+=) *(74321 74869-2)* – Heart in hand (live).

Aug 00. (cd/c) *(74321 78005-2/-4) <67818>* **EVERYTHING YOU WANT** [ ] Jan00 [40]
– We are / You're a god / Everything you want / Best I ever had (grey sky morning) / You say / Finding me / Miracle / Send it up / Give you back / All of you / Shackled.

Nov 00. (c-s) *(74321 79243-4) <radio cut>* **YOU'RE A GOD / WASH AWAY** [ ] Aug00 [23]
(cd-s+=) *(74321 79966-2)* – ('A'-album version).

Feb 01. (-) *<radio cut>* **BEST I EVER HAD (GREY SKY MORNING)** [–] [58]

VERVE

Formed: Wigan, England . . . 1990 by local college lads RICHARD ASHCROFT (the main writer), NICK McCABE, SIMON JONES and PETER SALISBURY. They were soon supporting the likes of RIDE and SPIRITUALIZED, signing to 'Hut' in 1991. The following year, they released three singles, the spiralling psychedelia of 'ALL IN THE MIND', 'SHE'S A SUPERSTAR' & 'GRAVITY GRAVE'. In early summer of '93, they had a minor hit with 'BLUE', a taster for the debut album, 'A STORM IN HEAVEN', which made the UK Top 30. The album delivered on the promise of the early singles; an amorphous melange of trippy rock and liquid space-jazz ambience. Ambitious and cocksure, they toured the States, subsequently coming unstuck with US label VERVE, who forced them to slightly change their name to THE VERVE. In 1995, they unleashed a second album, 'A NORTHERN SOUL', a much darker, more intense affair featuring more conventional song structures. Although the album went Top 20, they announced they were splitting several months later, the 'HISTORY' single apparently their swan song. Just when the band were poised to enter the big league, it looked as if they'd missed the boat, McCABE and ASHCROFT's quarreling, together with well documented drug problems, seemingly to blame for the band's demise. By February '97, however, they got it together sufficiently to reform and their first single of the year was to many, their best song yet, the grandiose, string-laden 'BITTER SWEET SYMPHONY' (written by MICK JAGGER and KEITH RICHARDS for The ANDREW LOOG OLDHAM ORCHESTRA). The song crashed into the UK chart at No.2 thanks to a glorious video featuring a tense, jaywalking ASHCROFT barging into everyone in sight! A follow-up, 'THE DRUGS DON'T WORK', went straight in at No.1, as did parent album, 'URBAN HYMNS' (1997). It seemed THE VERVE could do no wrong, although tensions between ASHCROFT and the others were coming to a head; McCABE would subsequently announce his retirement from stage work in July '98 (veteran pedal steel man BJ COLE was enlisted). The Americans had already taken the band into their hearts by this time, the aforementioned third set hitting the Top 30 and going platinum in the process. However by May 1999, THE VERVE were history, "astral man" ASHCROFT opting for a solo career with his SPIRITUALIZED wife KATE RADLEY in tow. And what a picture of domestic bliss he painted on 'ALONE WITH EVERYBODY' (2000), his first solo set and a marked transition from the anguished soul-searching of his best work with THE VERVE. Eloquent string arrangements, folky strumming and contented musings on life's basic essentials made for one of the best solo debuts in years. A lucky man? It certainly seemed so. ASHCROFT returned in 2002 to deliver 'HUMAN CONDITIONS', a slighty bitter sophomore record, that seemed to isolate VERVE fans even more. Reverting into a world of deliberate melancholy, ASHCROFT even dabbled with the world's smallest violin. Themes of God, lost love and difficult relationships have all been explored before by ASHCROFT et al, nevertheless it reached UK No.3. Yet its only saving grace remained in the brilliant closing track 'NATURE IS THE LAW' (excuse the cheesy title), which featured BRIAN WILSON on backing harmonies.

Album rating: A STORM IN HEAVEN (*7) / NO COME DOWN collection (*6) / A NORTHERN SOUL (*8) / URBAN HYMNS (*9) / Richard Ashcroft: ALONE WITH EVERYBODY (*7) / HUMAN CONDITIONS (*6)

RICHARD ASHCROFT (b.11 Sep'71) – vocals, guitar / **NICK McCABE** (b.14 Jul'71) – lead guitar / **SIMON JONES** (b.29 Jul'72) – bass / **PETER SALISBURY** (b.24 Sep'71) – drums

Hut / Vernon Yard

Mar 92. (7") *(HUT 12)* **ALL IN THE MIND. / ONE WAY TO GO** [ ] [–]
(12"+=/cd-s+=) *(HUT T/CD 12)* – A man called Sun.

Jun 92. (7"/ext-12"/ext-cd-s) *(HUT/+H/CD 16)* **SHE'S A SUPERSTAR. / FEEL** [66] [–]

Oct 92. (10"ep) *(HUTEN 21)* **GRAVITY GRAVE EP** [ ] [–]
– Gravity grave / Endless life / She's a superstar (live).
(12"+=/cd-s++) *(HUT T/CD 21)* – ('A'extended) / Endless life / A man called Sun (live).

Jan 93. (m-cd) *(<HUTUS 1>)* **THE VERVE E.P.** (compilation) [–] [ ]
– Gravity grave / A man called Sun / She's a superstar / Endless life / Feel. *(UK-iss.Sep97 on 'Vernon Yard'; YARDCD 001)*

May 93. (12"ep) *(HUTT 29)* **BLUE. / TWILIGHT / WHERE THE GEESE GO** [69] [–]
(10"ep+=/cd-ep+=) *(HUT EN/CD 29)* – No come down.

Jun 93. (cd/c/lp) *(CDHUT/HUTMC/HUTLP 10) <87950>* **A STORM IN HEAVEN** [27] [ ]
– Star sail / Slide away / Already there / Beautiful mind / The sun, the sea / Virtual world / Make it 'til Monday / Blue / Butterfly / See you in the next one (have a good time).

Sep 93. (7"pink) *(HUT 35)* **SLIDE AWAY. / 6 O'CLOCK** [ ] [–]
(12"/cd-s) *(HUT T/CD 35)* – ('A'side) / Make it 'til Monday (acoustic) / Virtual world (acoustic).

May 94. (cd) *(CDHUT 18)* **NO COMEDOWN** (rare / b-sides) [ ] [–]
– No come down / Blue (USA mix) / Make it 'til Monday (acoustic) / Butterfly (acoustic) / Where the grease go / 6 o'clock / One way to go / Gravity grave (live) / Twilight. *(re-iss. Sep97 on 'Vernon Yard'; YARDCD 007)*

THE VERVE

Apr 95. (7"burgundy) *(HUT 54)* **THIS IS MUSIC. / LET THE DAMAGE BEGIN** [35] [–]
(12"+=/cd-s+=) *(HUT T/CD 54)* – You and me.

Jun 95. (7"green/c-s) *(HUT/+C 55)* **ON YOUR OWN. / I SEE THE DOOR** [28] [–]
(cd-s+=) *(HUTCD 55)* – Little gem / Dance on your bones.

Jul 95. (cd/c/d-lp) *(CDHUT/HUTMC/HUTLP 27) <40437>* **A NORTHERN SOUL** [13] [ ]
– A new decade / This is music / On your own / So it goes / A northern soul / Brainstorm interlude / Drive you home / History / No knock on my door / Life's an ocean / Stormy clouds / Stormy clouds (reprise).

Sep 95. (c-s) *(HUTC 59)* **HISTORY / BACK ON MY FEET AGAIN** [24] [–]
(cd-s+=) *(HUTCD 59)* – On your own (acoustic) / Monkey magic (Brainstorm mix).
(cd-s) *(HUTDX 59)* – ('A'extended) / Grey skies / Life's not a rehearsal.

— originals re-formed adding **SIMON TONG** – guitar, keyboards

Hut / Virgin

Jun 97. (7") *(HUTLH 82) <38634>* **BITTER SWEET SYMPHONY. / SO SISTER** [2] Mar98 [12]
('A'extended; cd-s+=) *(HUTDX 82)* – Echo bass.
(c-s/cd-s) *(HUT C/DG 82)* – ('A'side) / Lord I guess I'll never know / Country song / ('A'radio version).

Sep 97. (c-s/cd-s) *(HUT C/DG 88)* **THE DRUGS DON'T WORK / THREE STEPS / THE DRUGS DON'T WORK (original demo)** [1] [ ]
(cd-s) *(HUTDX 88)* – ('A'extended) / Bitter sweet symphony (James Lavelle remix) / The crab / Stamped.

Sep 97. (cd/c/lp) *(<44913-2/-4/-1>)* **URBAN HYMNS** [1] [23]
– Bitter sweet symphony / Sonnet / The rolling people / The drugs don't work / Catching the butterfly / Neon wilderness / Space and time / Weeping willow / Lucky man / One day / This time / Velvet morning / Come on.

Nov 97. (c-s/cd-s) *(HUT C/DG 92)* **LUCKY MAN / NEVER WANNA SEE YOU CRY / HISTORY** [7] [ ]
(cd-s) *(HUT DX 92)* – ('A'side) / MSG / The longest day / Lucky man (happiness more or less).

Feb 98. (cd-ep) *<13112-2>* **FIVE BY FIVE** [–] [ ]
– Come on / The rolling people / Lucky man (radio edit) / Catching the butterfly / Space and time.

— THE VERVE announced their demise in '99; JONES (and later TONG) formed The SHINING

– compilations, etc. –

Mar 98. (ltd-12"ep) **BITTER SWEET SYMPHONY (original) / LORD I GUESS I'LL NEVER KNOW. / BITTER SWEET SYMPHONY (James Lavelle mix) / COUNTRY SONG** [ ] [–]

Mar 98. (ltd-12"ep) **THE DRUGS DON'T WORK / THREE STEPS. / THE DRUGS DON'T WORK (demo) / THE CRAB** [ ] [–]

Mar 98. (ltd-12"ep) **LUCKY MAN / NEVER WANNA SEE YOU CRY. / MSG / THE LONGEST DAY** [ ] [–]

Mar 98. (ltd-12"ep) **SONNET / STAMPED. / SO SISTER / ECHO BASS** [ ] [–]
(the import cd-single version of the above single <895075-2> actually hit UK No.74 in May'98)

RICHARD ASHCROFT

— with various session people incl. **PETER SALISBURY**

Hut / Virgin

Apr 00. (c-s) *(HUTC 128)* **A SONG FOR THE LOVERS / PRECIOUS STONE** [3] [–]
(12"+=/cd-s+=) *(HUT T/CD 128)* – Could be a country thing city thing blues thing.

Jun 00. (c-s) *(HUTC 136)* **MONEY TO BURN / XXYY** [17] [–]
(12"+=/cd-s+=) *(HUT T/CD 136)* – Leave me high.

Jun 00. (cd/c/lp) *(CDHUTX/HUTMCX/HUTDLP 63) <49494>* **ALONE WITH EVERYBODY** [1] Jul00 [ ]
– A song for the lovers / I get my beat / Brave new world / New York / You on my mind in my sleep / Crazy world / On a beach / Money to burn / Slow was my heart / C'mon people (we're making it now) / Everybody.

Sep 00. (c-s) *(HUTC 138)* **C'MON PEOPLE (WE'RE MAKING IT NOW) / A SONG FOR THE LOVERS (remix)** [21] [–]
(12"+=/cd-s+=) *(HUT T/CD 138)* – Make a wish.

Oct 02. (7") *(HUT 161)* **CHECK THE MEANING. / MIRACLE** [11] [–]
(cd-s+=) *(HUTCD 161)* – ('A'-Chris Potter remix) / ('A'-video).

Oct 02. (cd/d-lp) *(CDHUT/HUTDLP 77) <13383>* **HUMAN CONDITIONS** [3] [ ]
– Check the meaning / Buy it in bottles / Bright lights / Paradise / God in the numbers / Science of silence / Man on a mission / Running away / Lord I've been trying / Nature is the law.

Jan 03. (7") *(HUT 163)* **SCIENCE OF SILENCE. / GET UP NOW** [14] [–]
(cd-s+=) *(HUTCD 163)* – Check the meaning (freelance hellraiser remix) / ('A'-video).

Apr 03. (7") *(HUT 167)* **BUY IT IN BOTTLES. / DON'T TAKE ME IN** [26] [–]
(cd-s+=) *(HUTCD 167)* – The journey's just begun / ('A'-video).

□ VICTOR (see under ⇒ RUSH)

Gene VINCENT

Born: EUGENE VINCENT CRADDOCK, 11 Feb'35, Norfolk, Virginia, USA. In 1955, he left the US Navy after suffering leg injuries in a serious motor-cycle crash. Incidentally, this never fully healed, and after a year in plaster, he had a leg-brace fitted and took up singing during his recuperation, often sitting in with WCMS Radio house band, The VIRGINIANS. Early in 1956, he briefly married 15 year-old Ruth Ann Hand, also gaining a contract for 'Capitol' in April. He formed The BLUE CAPS (name taken from President Eisenhower's favourite blue golf cap) for tour work, his live commitments becoming more extensive after the US Top 10 success of his debut single (B-side), 'BE-BOP-A-LULA' (which ELVIS PRESLEY's mother reportedly thought was her own son singing). VINCENT subsequently became a cult star in the 50's, his black leather-clad image and sporadic chart appearances (his last US chart single was 'DANCE TO THE BOP' in January 1958) fueling the myth. Later that year, the media attention focused on his recent drinking bouts which made him irritable to everyone bar his great friend, EDDIE COCHRAN; late in 1959, he toured the UK with EDDIE, resurrecting his chart status in the process with 'PISTOL PACKIN MAMA' (with GEORGIE FAME on piano) and 'SHE SHE LITTLE SHEILA'. Tragedy struck however, on the 17th of April 1960, when EDDIE was killed in a London cab, with GENE and EDDIE's fiancee sustaining injuries. Shaken but vowing to continue, he had a short series of UK hits that year although success soon eluded him and his last UK chart single was 1961's 'I'M GOING HOME'. The following year, he appeared on a bill at The Cavern Club with an up and coming beat combo, The BEATLES, although his 'Capitol' contract expired in '63 and was not renewed. He married for a fourth time in 1965, signing to US label 'Challenge', although his move into country rock'n'roll in 1966 was treated with apathy. In the early 70's, his career took off again when UK BBC Radio DJ John Peel contracted him to his newly formed 'Dandelion' imprint, releasing 'I'M BACK AND I'M PROUD' in the same year. VINCENT then signed to 'Kama Sutra' in the US and released his final albums, 'GENE VINCENT' and 'THE DAY THE WORLD TURNED BLUE', and although critically well received, the records failed to sell. After more hard-living and domestic problems, GENE VINCENT died on the 12th of October 1971 (of a burst stomach ulcer) in Newall hospital California. Many had copied his image including The BEATLES and ALVIN STARDUST and there were many tributes, none more poignant than IAN DURY's 'SWEET GENE VINCENT'. • **Songwriters:** His first hit, was written by fellow hospital patient in the same ward. He then wrote own material, except covers OVER THE RAINBOW (Judy Garland) / SUMMERTIME (Gershwin) / FRANKIE & JOHNNY (?) / ANOTHER SATURDAY NIGHT (Sam Cooke) / SLIPPIN' AND SLIDIN' + LONG TALL SALLY + GOOD GOLLY MISS MOLLY (Little Richard) / SUSIE Q (Dale Hawkins) / YOU ARE MY SUNSHINE (hit; Ray Charles) / WHITE LIGHTNING (Big Bopper) / etc. • **Trivia:** He and his BLUE CAPS made appearances in the film 'The Girl Can't Help It' & 'Hot Rod Gang'.

Best CD compilation: THE SCREAMING END: THE BEST OF . . . (*8)

GENE VINCENT & HIS BLUE CAPS

GENE VINCENT – vocals, guitar / **CLIFF GALLUP** – lead guitar / **WILLIE WILLIAMS** – acoustic rhythm guitar / **JACK NEAL** – upright bass / **DICKIE HARRELL** – drums

Capitol Capitol

Jun 56. (7",78) *(CL 14599)* <3450> **BE BOP A LULA. / WOMAN LOVE** 16 May 56 7

(above B-side, was originally the A, until BE BOP . . . was radio playlisted)

Aug 56. (7",78) *(CL 14628)* <3530> **RACE WITH THE DEVIL. / GONNA BACK UP MY BABY** 28 Jul 56 96

Oct 56. (7",78) *(CL 14637)* <3558> **BLUE JEAN BOP. / WHO SLAPPED JOHN?** 16 Sep 56 49

Nov 56. (lp) *<(T 764)>* **BLUE JEAN BOP** Sep 56 16

– Blue jean bop / Jezebel / Who slapped John / Ain't she sweet / I flipped / Waltz of the wind / Jump back, honey, jump back / That old gang of mine / Jumps, giggles and shouts / Up a lazy river / Bop street / Peg o' my heart. *(re-iss. 1983 on 'E.M.I.') (cd-iss. Jan03 on 'E.M.I.'+=; 540685-2)* – Woman love / Be-bop-a-lula / Race with the Devil / Gonna back up my baby / Well I knocked him bam bam / Crazy legs.

— **PAUL PEAK** – rhythm guitar, vocals repl. WILLIAMS. (NEAL now on bass)

Mar 57. (7",78) *(CL 14693)* <3617> **CRAZY LEGS. / IMPORTANT WORDS** Nov 56

Jan 57. (7",78) *(CL 14681)* **JUMPS, GIGGLES AND SHOUTS. / WEDDING BELLS** –

Apr 57. (lp) *<(T 811)>* **GENE VINCENT AND HIS BLUE CAPS**

– Red blue jeans and a pony tail / Hold me, hug me, rock me / Unchained melody / You told a fib / Cat man / You better believe / Cruisin' / Double talkin' baby / Blues stay away from me / Pink Thunderbird / I sure miss you / Pretty, pretty baby. *(re-iss. 1983 on 'E.M.I.') (cd-iss. Jan03 on 'E.M.I.'+=; 540684-2)* – Important words (version 1) / Bi-bickey-bi-bo-bo-go / Five days, five days / Teenage partner (version 1) / Five feet of lovin' (version 1).

— On tour **RUSSELL WILAFORD** then **TEDDY CRUTCHFIELD** had repl. GALLUP

May 57. (7",78) *(CL 14722)* <3678> **BI-BICKEY-BI-BO-BO-GO. / FIVE DAYS, FIVE DAYS**

— **JOHNNY MEEKS** – lead guitar repl. GALLUP **BOBBY LEE JONES** – bass repl. BILLY MACK who had repl. NEAL (PEEK was now relegated to clapper boy alongside TOMMY FACIENDA)

Sep 57. (7",78) *(CL 14763)* <3763> **LOTTA LOVIN'. / WEAR MY RING** Jul 57 13

Nov 57. (7",78) *(CL 14808)* <3839> **DANCE TO THE BOP. / I GOT IT** 23

Dec 57. (lp) *<(T 970)>* **GENE VINCENT ROCKS AND THE BLUE CAPS ROLL**

– Brand new beat / By the light of the silvery Moon / You'll never walk alone / Frankie and Johnny / In my dreams / Flea brain / Rollin' Dany / You belong to me / Your cheatin' heart / Time will bring you everything / Should I ever love again / It's no lie. *(cd-iss. Oct00 on 'Magic'; 499271-2)*

— briefly on tour **DUDE KAHN** – drums had repl. HARRELL until quick return. / added **MAX LIPSCOMB** – rhythm guitar, piano

Feb 58. (7",78) *(CL 14830)* <3874> **I GOT A BABY. / WALKING HOME FROM SCHOOL WITH YOU**

— **CLIFF SIMMONS** – piano + GRADY OWEN – drums repl. MAX, PAUL & TOMMY

Apr 58. (7") *(CL 14868)* <3959> **BABY BLUE. / TRUE TO YOU**

1958. (lp) *<(T 1059)>* **A GENE VINCENT RECORD DATE**

– Five feet of lovin' / The wayward mind / Somebody help me / Keep it a secret / Hey good lookin' / Git it / Teenage partner / Peace of mind / Look what you gone and done to me / Summertime / I can't help it / I love you. *(cd-iss. Nov99 on 'Magic'; 520757-2)*

— on tour **JUVEZ GOMEZ** – drums repl. HARRELL

— **BLUE CAPS:- HOWARD REED** – lead guitar / **BILL MACK** – bass / **MAX LIPSCOMB** – rhythm guitar / **CLIFF SIMMONS** – piano / **GRADY OWEN** – bass / **DUDE KAHN** – drums

Aug 58. (7") *(CL 14908)* <4010> **ROCKY ROAD BLUES. / YES I LOVE YOU BABY**

— (Sep58) **JOHNNY MEEKS** – lead guitar returned to repl. REED / **CLYDE PENNINGTON** – drums repl. KAHN and D.J.FONTANA. (sax – **JACKIE KELSO**)

Oct 58. (7") *(CL 14935)* <4051> **GIT IT. / LITTLE LOVER**

Oct 58. (lp)*<(T 1207)>* **SOUNDS LIKE GENE VINCENT**

–] My baby don't 'low / I can't believe you wanna leave / I might have known / In love again / You are the one for me / Ready Teddy / I got to you yet / Vincent's blues / Now is the hour / My heart / Maybelline.

Jan 59. (7") *(CL 14974)* <4105> **SAY MAMA. / BE BOP BOOGIE BOY**

Mar 59. (7") *(CL 15000)* <4153> **WHO'S PUSHIN' YOUR SWING. / OVER THE RAINBOW**

Jun 59. (7") *(CL 15035)* **SUMMERTIME. / FRANKIE AND JOHNNY** –

— The BLUE CAPS had already disbanded late 1958,

GENE VINCENT

now solo augmented by **JACKIE MERRITT** – guitar / **SANDY NELSON** – drums / **JACKIE KELSO** – sax

Aug 59. (7") *(CL 15053)* <4237> **RIGHT NOW. / THE NIGHT IS LONELY**

Dec 59. (7") *(CL 15099)* <4313> **WILD CAT. / RIGHT HERE ON EARTH** 21

Feb 60. (7") *(CL 15115)* <7P 159> **MY HEART. / I'VE GOT TO GET TO YOU YET** 16

May 60. (7") *(CL 15136)* **PISTOL PACKIN' MAMA. / WEEPING WILLOW** 15 –

May 60. (lp) *<(T 1342)>* **CRAZY TIMES** 12 Sep 59

– Crazy times / She she little Sheila / Darlene / Everybody's got a date but me / Why don't you people learn how to drive / Green back dollar / Big fat Saturday night / Mitchiko from Tokyo / Hot dollar / Accentuate the postive / Blue eyes crying in the rain / Pretty Pearly. *(re-iss. +c.1970's on 'M.F.P.', re-iss. Oct87 on 'Tower')*

Oct 60. (7") <4442> **ANNA ANNABELLE. / PISTOL PACKIN' MAMA** –

Nov 60. (7") *(CL 15169)* **ANNA ANNABELLE. / ACCENT-TCHUATE THE POSITIVE** –

Jan 61. (7") *(CL 15179)* **JEZEBEL. / MAYBE**
Feb 61. (7") *(CL 15185)* <4525> **IF YOU WANT LOVIN'. / MISTER LONELINESS**
May 61. (7") *(CL 15202)* **SHE SHE LITTLE SHEILA. / HOT DOLLAR** 22 Jul 60
Aug 61. (7") *(CL 15215)* **I'M GOING HOME. / LOVE OF A MAN** 36
Nov 61. (7") *(CL 15231)* **BRAND NEW BEAT. / UNCHAINED MELODY**
Mar 62. (7") *(CL 15243)* **LUCKY STAR. / BABY DON'T BELIEVE HIM**
Aug 62. (7") *(CL 15264)* **KING OF FOOLS. / BE BOP A LULA 2 (with The CHARLES BLACKWELL ORCHESTRA)**
Feb 63. (7") *(CL 15290)* **HELD FOR QUESTIONING. / YOU'RE STILL IN MY HEART**
Jul 63. (7") *(CL 15307)* **CRAZY BEAT. / HIGH BLOOD PRESSURE**
Aug 63. (lp) <*(T 20453)*> **THE CRAZY BEAT OF GENE VINCENT**
– Crazy beat / Important words / It's been nice / Lonesome boy / Good lovin' / I'm gonna catch me a rat / Rip it up / High blood pressure / That's the trouble with love / Weeping willow / Tear drops / Gone, gone, gone. *(re-iss. 1983 as 'CRAZY BEAT' on 'E.M.I.') (cd-iss. Nov99 on 'Magic'; 523015-2)*

—— now w / **TIM BATES** – guitar, vocals / **JOHN REECE** – bass, vocals / **JEM FIELD** – tenor sax, vocals / **ERIC BAKER** – keyboards / **VICTOR CLARK** – drums, percussion

Columbia Columbia

Nov 63. (7") *(DB 7174)* **WHERE HAVE YOU BEEN ALL MY LIFE. / TEMPTATION BABY**
Apr 64. (7") *(DB 7218)* **HUMPITY DUMPITY. / LOVE 'EM LEAVE 'EM KINDA GUY**
Jul 64. (7") *(DB 7293)* **LA DEN LA DEN DA DA. / BEGINNING OF THE END**
Sep 64. (7") *(DB 7343)* **PRIVATE DETECTIVE. / YOU ARE MY SUNSHINE**
Oct 64. (lp) *(33SX 1646)* **SHAKIN' UP A STORM**
– Hey-hey-hey-hey / Lavender blue / Private detective / Shimmy shammy shingle / Someday (you'll want me to want you) / Another Saturday night / Slippin' and slidin' / Long tall Sally / Send me some lovin' / Love love love / Good golly, miss Molly / Baby blue / Susie Q / You are my sunshine. *(re-iss. +c.Jun83 as 'PLAYIN' UP A STORM' on 'E.M.I.') (cd-iss. Aug97 on 'E.M.I.'; DORIG 124) (cd re-iss. Feb02 on 'Magic'; 3930159)*

London Challenge

Sep 66. (7") *(HLH 10079)* **BIRD DOGGIN'. / AIN'T THAT MUCH TO DO**
Dec 66. (7") *(HLH 10099* **LONELY STREET. / I'VE GOT MY EYES ON YOU**
Sep 67. (lp) *(HAH 8333)* **GENE VINCENT**
– I've got my eyes on you / Ain't that too much / Bird doggin' / Love is a bird / Lonely street / Hurtin' for you baby / Poor man's prison / Born to be a rolling stone / Hi lili hi lo / I'm a lonesome fugitive. *(re-iss. +c.Aug82 as 'BIRD-DOGGIN'' on 'Bulldog')*
1967. (7") **BORN TO BE A ROLLING STONE. / HURTIN' FOR YOU BABY** –
(re-iss. later on 'Playground')

not iss. Forever

1968. (7") **STORY TO THE ROCKERS. / PICKIN' POPPIES** –

—— w / **MARS BONFIRE** – guitar / **GRANT JOHNSON** – keyboards / **RED RHODES** – steel guitar / **SKIP BATTIN** – bass / **JIM GORDON** – drums

Dandelion Elektra

1969. (7") *(S 4596)* **BE BOP A LULA '69. / RUBY BABY** –
Jan 70. (7") *(S 4974)* **WHITE LIGHTNING. / SCARLET RIBBONS** –
Jan 70. (lp) *(63754)* <102> **I'M BACK AND I'M PROUD** –
– Rockin' Robin / In the pines / Be bop a lula / Rainbow at midnight / Black letter / White lightning / Sexy ways / Ruby baby / Lotta lovin' / Circle never broken / I heard that lonesome whistle / Scarlet ribbons. *(cd-iss. 1987 on 'Nightlife Communications') (cd-iss. Dec94 on 'See For Miles')*

—— now w/several musicians incl. **CHRIS DARROW**

Kama Sutra Kama Sutra

1970. (lp) *(2361009)* <2019> **IF ONLY YOU COULD SEE ME TODAY**
– Sunshine / I need woman's love / Slow times comin' / Danse Colinda / Geese / 500 miles / Listen to the music / If only you could see me today / A million shades of blue.
Jan 70. (7") **SUNSHINE. / GEESE** –
above was recorded with UK band KANSAS HOOK early in Oct'71.
Nov 70. (7") *(2013 018)* **THE DAY THE WORLD TURNED BLUE. / HIGH OF LIFE** –
Jan 71. (lp) <*(KSBS2027)*> **THE DAY THE WORLD TURNED BLUE**
– How I love them old songs / High on life / North Carloina line / You can make it if you try / Our souls / Looking back / The day the world turned blue / Boppin' the blues / There is something on your mind / Oh lonesome me / The woman in black.
Jan 71. (7") **THE DAY THE WORLD TURNED BLUE. / HOW I LOVE THEM OLD SONGS** –

—— Sadly on the 12th Oct'71, GENE VINCENT died of a bleeding ulcer. He was just 36.

– (selective) compilations, etc. –

all below on 'Capitol' unless otherwise stated

Oct 85. (lp/c) *(EG 260760-/-4)* **THE BEST OF GENE VINCENT AND HIS BLUE CAPS**
– Race with the Devil / Be-bop-a-lula / Woman love / I sure miss you / Crazy legs / Gonna back up baby / Who slapped John / Important words / Rollin' Dany / In my dreams / Baby blues '57 / Git it / Somebody help me / Summertime / Beautiful brown eyes / Say mama. *(cd-iss. Jul88)*
Jul 88. (lp/c/cd) *See For Miles; (SEE/+K/+CD 233)* **INTO THE SEVENTIES** –
(cd re-iss. Sep00; same) (below cd re-iss. May02; same)
May 89. (lp/c/cd) *See For Miles; (SEE/+K/+CD 253)* **THE EP COLLECTION** –
Aug 90. (6xcd-box) *(CDS 7945932)* **THE GENE VINCENT CD BOXED SET: THE COMPLETE CAPITOL & COLUMBIA RECORDINGS 1956-64**
– (BE BOP A LULA / DANCE TO THE BOP / GIT IT / SAY MAMA / WILD CAT / KING OF . . .)
Nov 92. (cd) *Magnum Force; (CDMF 087)* **REBEL HEART VOL.1**
Apr 95. (cd) *Magnum Force; (CDMF 093)* **REBEL HEART VOL.2**
Apr 96. (cd) *Magnum Force; (CDMF 096)* **REBEL HEART VOL.3**
Feb 97. (cd) *Razor & Tie;* <*(RE 2123)*> **THE SCREAMING END: THE BEST OF GENE VINCENT** Jan97
Mar 97. (cd) *Magnum Force; (CDMF 097)* **REBEL HEART VOL.4**
Jan 98. (cd) *Camden; (74321 55844-2)* **500 MILES**
Feb 98. (cd) *Disky; (TO 86094-2)* **THE ORIGINAL**
Mar 98. (cd) *Eagle; (EDMCD 028)* **THE MASTERS** –
Apr 98. (cd) *Rollercoaster; (RCCD 3031)* **THE LOST DALLAS SESSIONS 1957-1958**
Apr 98. (cd) *Magnum Force; (CDMF 099)* **REBEL HEART VOL.5**
Jun 98. (cd) *See For Miles; (SEECD 492)* **THE EP COLLECTION**
Apr 99. (cd) *Magnum Force; (CDMF 101)* **REBEL HEART VOL.6**
Jan 00. (cd) *Magnum Force; (CDMF 020)* **ON THE ROAD AGAIN**
Mar 00. (cd) *Magnum Force; (CDMF 089)* **THE LEGENDARY BLUE CAPS**
Apr 00. (cd) *Magnum Force; (CDMF 102)* **REBEL HEART VOL.7**
Oct 00. (cd) *Members Edition; (UAE 31292)* **GENE VINCENT**
Feb 01. (cd) *EMI Plus; (5761420)* **THE STORY**
Mar 01. (cd/c) *Castle Pulse; (PLS CD/MC 383)* **BE-BOP-A-LULA**
Jul 01. (cd) *E.M.I.; (533632-2)* **BLUE JEAN BOP / GENE VINCENT ROCKS**
Oct 01. (10"lp) *Stomper Time; (STEN 7)* **THE BE BOP BOOGIE BOY** –
May 02. (cd) *Magnum Force; (CDMF 109)* **BIRD DOGGIN': THE COMPLETE CHALLENGE SESSIONS**
Jul 03. (cd) *Magnum Force; (CDMF 108)* **REBEL HEART VOL.8**

VINES

Formed: Sydney, Australia . . . late 1999 by frontman CRAIG NICHOLLS, a NIRVANA-obsessed McDonalds worker who pulled together PATRICK MATTHEWS, RYAN GRIFFITHS and DAVID OLLIFFE. Named after NICHOLLS' dad's band from the 60's (although they were called The VYNES), the group began performing at house parties where they would amuse the guests with

NIRVANA and MUDHONEY covers. It wasn't until 2001 that they issued their debut single, a roaring number entitled 'FACTORY', which sounded like a lost song from COBAIN and crew, with screeching vocals aplenty and a chorus to die for. This led to their signing with 'Heavenly' in the UK, and The VINES were shipped off to L.A. to record their debut album, all the while being compared to Jesus by the ever reliable NME. It wasn't until summer 2002 that the ensemble would return, clutching a handful of admittedly great rock songs with the unfettering of the album 'HIGHLY EVOLVED'. 'GET FREE', the debut single was grunge from the very first note, with NICHOLLS even singing in unison with his guitar – just like COBAIN. The hollowed out sound of 'OUTTATHAWAY' was much more intense, and the 90-minute pop/punk blast of 'HIGHLY EVOLVED' was just a smack in the face. However it was not all grind-core grunge; the group also showed their 'sensitive' side (with NICHOLLS basically saying "look how tortured I am") with such trite stuff as 'AUTUMN SHADE' and the cringeworthy 'HOMESICK', all pianos and welling tears. During interviews with the group NICHOLLS also admitted that his two favourite things were "a McDonalds meal and a SUEDE album". McDonalds was bad enough, but SUEDE!

Album rating: HIGHLY EVOLVED (*7)

CRAIG NICHOLLS – vocals, guitar / **PATRICK MATTHEWS** – bass, vocals / **DAVID OLLIFFE** – drums

		Rex	not iss.
Oct 01.	(ltd-7") *(REKD 195)* **FACTORY. / AIN'T NO ROOM / DROWN THE BAPTISTS**	☐	–
		Heavenly	Capitol
Apr 02.	(7"/cd-s) *(HVN 112/+CD)* **HIGHLY EVOLVED. / SUN CHILD**	32	–

—— **HAMISH ROSSER** – drums; repl. OLLIFFE

—— added **RYAN GRIFFITHS** – guitar

Jun 02.	(7") *(HVN 113)* **GET FREE. / BLUES RIFF** (cd-s) *(HVN 113CD) <550942>* – ('A'side) / Down at the club / Hot leather.	24	Jul02 ☐
Jul 02.	(lp/cd) *(HVNLP 36/+CD) <537527>* **HIGHLY EVOLVED** – Highly evolved / Autumn shade / Outtathaway / Sunshinin' / Homesick / Get free / Country yard / Factory / In the jungle / Mary Jane / Ain't no room / 1969.	3	☐
Oct 02.	(7") *(HVN 120)* **OUTTATHAWAY. / MS. JACKSON** (cd-s+=) *(HVN 120CDS) <551223>* – Country yard (live) / ('A'-David LaChapelle video). (cd-s) *(HVN 120CD) <551215>* – ('A'side) / Don't go (demo) / Get free (live) / ('A'-Alastair McKevitt US film video).	20	☐

☐ VIOLET INDIANA (see under ⇒ COCTEAU TWINS)

☐ VIVA SATURN (see under ⇒ RAIN PARADE)

VON BONDIES

Formed: Detroit, Michigan, USA ... 2000 out of The BABY KILLERS by JASON STOLLSTEIMER (ex-COBRA YOUTH), MARCIE BOLEN, CARRIE SMITH and DON BLUM. Garage rock didn't come any dirtier and rawer than The VON BONDIES style of thrash'n'tickle. Influenced by peers The DIRTBOMBS, SOLEDAD BROTHERS and, of course, JACK WHITE of The WHITE STRIPES, the ensemble recorded cuts 'IT CAME FROM JAPAN' (a deafening experience) and 'NITE TRAIN', before being snapped up by 'Sympathy For The Record Industry' in 2001 and sent on a whirlwind tour across the US. Word had already hit the streets in Britain, and along with The WHITE STRIPES came promise of The VON BONDIES and their sonic attack. JACK WHITE produced the album 'LACK OF COMMUNICATION' (2001), a messy, fractured, skeletal record that possessed infinite passion and harked back to the good ol' days of MC5. Lying somewhere between GUITAR WOLF's searing, screeching guitars and BLONDIE's proto-punk New Wave days, the set switched from one style to the next; EDDIE COCHRAN's in there somewhere, and so was the grinding rhythm'n'blues of JIMMY REED. Yet, it was a very Detroit kind of record – dirty, polluted and very impassioned. Things just came together for a lot of bands from the State of Detroit at the turn of the new millennium, proving that their New Yorker cousins weren't getting away with having all the fun. • **Covered:** BRING IT ON HOME TO ME (Sam Cooke).

Album rating: LACK OF COMMUNICATION (*7)

JASON STOLLSTEIMER – vocals, guitar / **MARCIE BOLEN** – guitar, vocals (ex-SLUMBER PARTY) / **LAUREN WILCOX** – bass / **DON BLUM** – drums

		not iss.	D-wreckEd-hiT
2000.	(7") *<DET 001>* **NITE TRAIN. / GOIN' DOWN**	–	☐

—— **CARRIE SMITH** – bass; repl. WILCOX

		Sympathy F	Sympathy F
2001.	(7") *<SFTRI 667>* **IT CAME FROM JAPAN. / RED HEAD DEVIL** *(UK-iss.Sep02 on 'Sweet Nothing' c-s; CSSN 012)*	–	☐
Jul 01.	(lp/cd) *<(SFTRI 658/+CD)>* **LACK OF COMMUNICATION** – Lack of communication / It came from Japan / Shallow grave / Going down / Cass and Henry / Nite train / No sugar mama / Cryin' / In the act / Please please man / Sound of terror. *(hidden cd track+=)* – Bring it on home to me. *(re-iss. Apr02 on 'Sweet Nothing'; SNCD/SNLP 015)*	☐	☐
Dec 01.	(7"clear-ep) *(FLB 118)* **X-MAS SURPRISE PACKAGE VOLUME 4** – Ain't no chimney in the big house / SOLEDAD BROTHERS: Hang my star / MISTREATERS: Santa stole my baby. (above on 'Flying Bomb', below on 'Must Destroy')	☐	☐
Nov 02.	(ltd-7"one-sided) *(DESTROYER 2)* **TELL ME WHAT YOU SEE**	☐	–

– compilations, etc. –

Jul 03.	(cd) *Dim Mak; <(DMK 210053)>* **RAW AND RARE (live)**	☐	Jun03 ☐

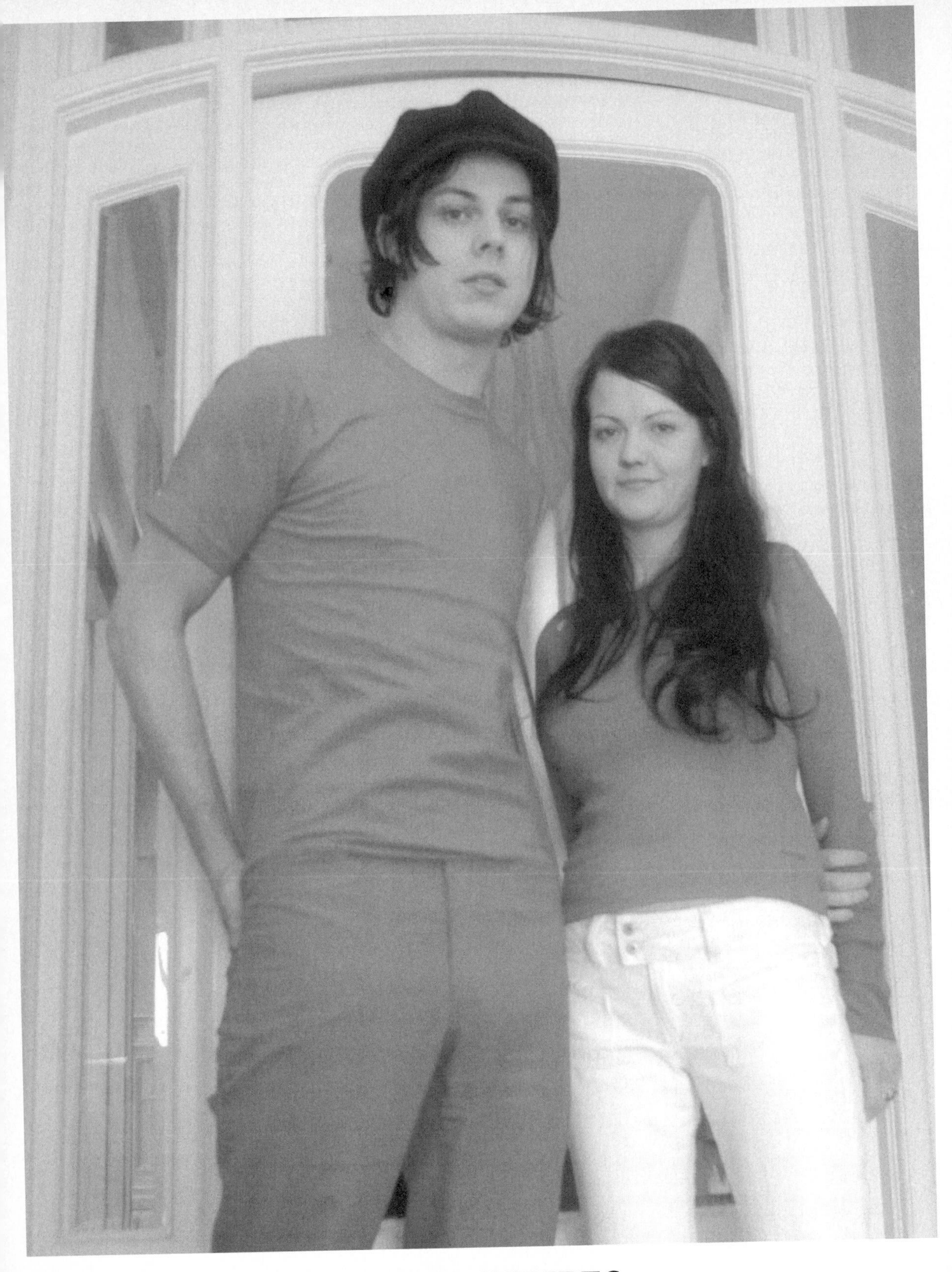

WHITE STRIPES

☐ WAILERS (see under ⇒ MARLEY, Bob)

Loudon WAINWRIGHT III

Born: 5 Sep '46, Chapel Hill, North Carolina, USA. The son of a journalist, WAINWRIGHT served his musical apprenticeship on the US college and folk-club circuit following in the footsteps of BOB DYLAN and JOAN BAEZ. The budding singer/songwriter (hailed as the new DYLAN and later as the Woody Allen of folk, the Charlie Chaplin of rock and the male MELANIE!) hitched to San Francisco in 1967 and signed to 'Atlantic' two years later, soon becoming publicly recognised. After moving to 'Columbia' in 1973, he scored a US Top 20 hit with the novelty song, 'DEAD SKUNK' (which allegedly took 15 minutes to write), lifted from the helpfully titled 'ALBUM III'. His subsequent efforts, 'ATTEMPTED MOUSTACHE' and 'UNREQUITED', failed to consolidate his position, although the former contained some excellent material including 'SWIMMING SONG'. After an unsuccessful move to 'Arista', WAINWRIGHT relocated to London and spent five years on 'Demon/Rounder', sometimes augmented by RICHARD THOMPSON on albums such as 'FAME AND WEALTH', 'I'M ALRIGHT' and 'MORE LOVE SONGS'. Although still critically lauded, these albums were met with diminishing commercial returns; while WAINWRIGHT was admittedly not the greatest of singers, his inimitable comic satire usually compensated. Continuing to release fine material into the 90's, WAINWRIGHT's last effort to date was the 1995 set, 'GROWN MAN', featuring the hilarious 'IWIWAL (I WISH I WAS A LESBIAN)' which almost equalled his hit 'DEAD SKUNK' (this one took him eight! minutes to write) for deadpan humour. 1999's 'SOCIAL STUDIES' was pretty much what the title suggested although the tone was inimitably sardonic rather than academic, many of these topical sketches written especially for America's National Public Radio. A different beast altogether, 'LAST MAN ON EARTH' (2001) was an intensely personal and emotionally fraught affair written after the death of his mother. 'SO DAMN HAPPY' (2003) was back to irreverent business for LOUDON, with his first live set in a decade. Featuring material culled largely from the 80's and 90's, and recorded at separate venues in California, the album was a highly enjoyable jaunt through the man's back pages with help from the likes of RICHARD THOMPSON and VAN DYKE PARKS. • **Trivia:** In the mid-70's, he appeared on a couple of TV episodes of comedy Korean War series, 'M.A.S.H.'. WAINWRIGHT resurrected an intended acting career in the 80's by appearing in stage productions, 'Pump Boys & Dinettes' and 'Owners'. In '88, he featured in the film, 'Jacknife'.

Album rating: LOUDON WAINWRIGHT III (*6) / ALBUM II (*6) / ALBUM III (*6) / ATTEMPTED MOUSTACHE (*5) / UNREQUITED (*5) / T-SHIRT (*4) / FINAL EXAM (*4) / A LIVE ONE (*7) / FAME AND WEALTH (*6) / I'M ALRIGHT (*6) / MORE LOVE SONGS (*6) / THERAPY (*6) / HISTORY (*8) / CAREER MOVES (*6) / GROWN MAN (*6) / LITTLE SHIP (*5) / SOCIAL STUDIES (*7) / LAST MAN ON EARTH (*6) / SO DAMN HAPPY (*6)

LOUDON WAINWRIGHT III – vocals, acoustic guitar

Atlantic Atlantic

May 71. (lp) *(2400 103)* <8260> **LOUDON WAINWRIGHT III** ☐ Nov70 ☐
– School days / Hospital lady / Ode to a Pittsburgh / Glad to see you've got religion / Uptown / Black Uncle Remus / Four is a magic number / I don't care / Central Square song / Movies are a mother to me / Bruno's place. *(re-iss. 1972; K 40107)*

Sep 71. (lp) *(2400 142)* <8291> **ALBUM II** ☐ ☐
– Me and my friend the cat / Motel blues / Nice Jewish girls / Be careful / Plane too / Cook that diner, Dora / There's a baby in the house / I know I'm unhappy / Suicide song / Glenville reel / Saw your name in the paper / Samson and the warden / Plane, too / Cook that dinner, Dora / Old friend / Old paint / Winter song. *(re-iss. 1974; K 40272) (re-iss. May89 on 'Edsel'; ED 310)*

— added **RICHARD CROOKS** – drums / to session people from last album.

C.B.S. Columbia

Jan 73. (lp) *(CBS 65238)* <31462> **ALBUM III** ☐ ☐
– Dead skunk / Red guitar / East Indian princess / Muse blues / Hometeam crowd / B side / Needless to say / Smokey Joe's cafe / New paint / Trilogy (circa 1967) / Drinking song / Say that you love me. *(re-iss. Dec85 on 'Edsel' lp/c; ED/CED 168) (cd-iss. Feb91; EDCD 168)*

Jun 73. (7") *(CBS 1120)* <45726> **DEAD SKUNK. / NEEDLESS TO SAY** ☐ Jan73 16

Aug 73. (7") <45849> **SAY THAT YOU LOVE ME. / NEW PAINT** – ☐

Feb 74. (lp) *(CBS 65837)* <32710> **ATTEMPTED MOUSTACHE** ☐ ☐
– The swimming song / A.M. world / Bell bottom pants / Liza / I am the way / Clockwork chartreuse / Down drinking at the bar / The man who couldn't cry / Come a long way / Nocturnal stumblebutt / Dialated to meet you / Lullaby. *(re-iss. May88 on 'Edsel'; ED 269)*

May 74. (7") *(CBS 2172)* <45949> **DOWN DRINKING AT THE BAR. / I AM THE WAY** ☐ ☐

Jul 74. (7") <46064> **THE SWIMMING SONG. / BELL BOTTOM PANTS** – ☐

Mar 75. (lp) *(CBS 80696)* <33369> **UNREQUITED** ☐ ☐
– Sweet nothings / The lowly tourist / Kings and queens / Kick in the head / Whatever happened to us / Crime of passion / Absence makes the heart grow fonder / On the rocks / Guru / Mr. Guilty / Untitled (aka The Hardy boys at the Y) / Unrequited to the Nth degree / Old friends / Rufus is a tit man. *(re-iss. May88 on 'Edsel'; ED 273) (cd-iss. Mar91; EDCD 273)*

— Now with band: **ELLIOTT RANDALL** – guitar / **RICHARD DAVIS** – bass / **R.CROOKS** / **ERIC WEISSBERG** – banjo / **STEPHEN TUBIN + GLEN MITCHELL** – keyboards / etc.

Arista Arista

Apr 76. (7") *(ARIST 53)* <0174> **BICENTENNIAL (SUMMER'S ALMOST OVER). / TALKING THE BIG APPLE '75** ☐ ☐

Jun 76. (lp) *(ARTY 127)* <4063> **T-SHIRT** ☐ ☐
– Bicentennial / Summer's almost over / Hollywood hopeful / Reciprocity / At both ends / Wine with dinner / Hey Packy / California prison blues / Talking big apple / Prince Hal's dirge / Just like President Thieu.

Apr 78. (lp) *(SPART 1042)* <4173> **FINAL EXAM** ☐ ☐
– Final exam / Mr.Guilty / Pen pal blues / Golfin' blues / The heckler / Natural disaster / Fear with flying / Heaven and mud / Two-song set / Pretty little Martha / Watch me rock I'm over thirty.

May 78. (7") <0340> **FINAL EXAM. /** – ☐

— Next featured singing trio The ROCHES.

Radar Rounder

Sep 79. (lp) *(RAD 24) <ROUNDER 3050>* **A LIVE ONE (live)**
– Motel blues / Hollywood hopeful / Whatever happened to us? / Natural disaster / Suicide song / School days / Kings and queens / Down drinking at the bar / B-side / Nocturnal stumblebutt / Red guitar / Clockwork chartreuse / Lullaby. *(re-iss. Jun87 on 'Edsel' lp/c; ED/CED 223) <US re-iss. Aug88; same> <US cd-iss. Aug88; CD 3050> (cd-iss. Jul92 on 'Demon';)*

Demon Rounder

Apr 83. (lp) *(FIEND 5) <ROUNDER 3076>* **FAME AND WEALTH**
– Reader and advisor / The Grammy song / Dump the dog / Thick and thin / Revenge / Five years old / Ingenue / Idttywim / Westchester County / Saturday morning fever / April Fools Day morn / Fame and wealth. *<US re-iss. Aug88; same> <cd-iss. Aug88; CD 3076>*

Apr 83. (7") *(D 1016)* **FIVE YEARS OLD. / RAMBUNCTIOUS**

—— Now collborated with **RICHARD THOMPSON** – producer, guitar

Jul 85. (7") *(D 1039)* **CARDBOARD BOXES. / COLOURS**

Sep 85. (lp) *(FIEND 54) <ROUNDER 3096>* **I'M ALRIGHT**
– One man guy / Lost love / I'm alright / Not John / Cardboard boxes / Screaming issue / How old are you? / Animal song / Out of this world / Daddy take a nap / Ready or not (so ripe) / Career moves. *<US re-iss. Aug88; same> <cd-iss. Aug88; CD 3096>*

Aug 86. (7") *(D 1044)* **UNHAPPY ANNIVERSARY. / THE ACID SONG**

Sep 86. (lp/c/cd) *(FIEND/+CASS/CD 79) <ROUNDER 3106/+C/CD>* **MORE LOVE SONGS**
– Hard day on the Planet / Synchronicity / Your mother and I / I eat out / No / The home stretch / Unhappy anniversary / Man's world / Vampire blues / Overseas calls / Expatriot / The back nine. *(cd+=)* – The acid song. *<(cd re-iss. Mar03 on 'Diablo'; DIAB 8046)>*

Sep 87. (7") *(D 1051)* **YOUR MOTHER AND I. / AT THE END OF A LONG LONELY DAY** –

Silvertone Silvertone

May 89. (lp/c/cd) *(ORE LP/C/CD 500) <1203>* **THERAPY**
– Therapy / Bill of goods / T.S.D.H.A.V. (This Song Don't Have A Video) / Harry's wall / Aphrodisiac / Fly paper / Nice guys / Thanksgiving / Your father's car / Me and all the other mothers / You don't want to know / Mind read (it belonged to you) / This year.

Sep 89. (7") *(ORE 15)* **T.S.D.H.A.V. (THIS SONG DON'T HAVE A VIDEO). / NICE GUYS**

—— with **CHAIM TANNENBAUM** – banjo, harmonica / **DAVID MANSFIELD** – fiddle, mandolin

Virgin Virgin

Sep 92. (cd/c/lp) *(CD/TC+/V 2703) <86416>* **HISTORY**
– People in love / Men / The picture / When I'm at your house / The doctor / Hitting you / I'd rather be lonely / Between / Talking new Bob Dylan / So many songs / 4 x 10 / A father and a son / Sometimes I forget / Handful of dust.

Jul 93. (cd/c) *(CD/TC 2718) <87273>* **CAREER MOVES (live)**
– Road ode / I'm alright / Five years old / Your mother and I / Westchester County / He said, she said / Christmas rap / Suddenly it's Christmas / Thanksgiving / A fine Celtic name / T.S.M.N.W.A. / some balding guys / The swimming song / Absence makes the heart grow fonder / Happy birthday Elvis / Unhappy anniversary / I'd rather be lonely / Just say no / April fool's Day morn / The man who couldn't cry / The acid song / Tip that waitress / Career moves.

Oct 95. (cd/c) *(CD/TC 2789) <40625>* **GROWN MAN**
– The birthday present / Grown man / That hospital / Housework / Cobwebs / A year / Father / Father – daughter dialogue / 1994 / Iwiwal / Just a John / I suppose / Dreaming / The end has begun / Human cannonball / Treasure untold.

Oct 97. (cd) *(CDV 2844) <44879>* **LITTLE SHIP** Feb98
– Breakfast in bed / Four mirrors / Mr. Ambivalent / O.G.M. / Our own war / So damn happy / Primrose hill / Underwear / World /What are families for / Bein' a dad / Birthday present / I can't stand myself / Little ship / Song.

Hannibal Hannibal

Jul 99. (cd) *<(HNCD 1442)>* **SOCIAL STUDIES**
– What gives / Tonya's twirls / New street people / Carmine street / O.J. / Leap of faith / Conspiracies / Christmas morning / Y2k / Number one / Bad man / Inaugural blues / Our boy Bill / Jesse don't like it / Pretty good day.

Evangeline Red House

Sep 01. (cd) *(GEL 4025) <158>* **LAST MAN ON EARTH**
– Missing you / Livin' alone / White winos / Fresh fossils / I'm not gonna cry / Out of reach / Bridge / Surviving twin / Donations / Graveyard / Bed / Last man on earth / Homeless.

Sanctuary Sanctuary

Aug 03. (cd) *(SANCD 197) <84627>* **SO DAMN HAPPY (live)**
– Much better bets / So damn happy / Between / The picture / Cobwebs / Heaven / Something for nothing / Dreaming / Westchester County / Tonya's twirls / A year / You never phone / 4x10 / The shit song / Primrose Hill / The home stretch / Men.

– compilations, etc. –

Jan 92. (cd) *Demon; (FIENDCD 711)* **FAME & WEALTH / I'M ALRIGHT** –

Jul 94. (cd/c) *Music Club; (MC CD/TC 166)* **ONE MAN GUY (THE BEST OF LOUDON WAINWRIGHT III (1983-1986)** –

Nov 98. (cd) *Strange Fruit; (SFRSCD 073)* **THE BBC SESSIONS** –

Rufus WAINWRIGHT

Born: 22 Jul'73, Rhinebeck, New York, USA. The son of LOUDON WAINWRIGHT III and KATE McGARRIGLE, RUFUS was raised in Canada following his parents' divorce. Steeped in music from an early age, by the time he reached his teens RUFUS was touring with his folk singing family. It'd be the lure of classic torch singing, cabaret and opera, however, which was to really fire the piano player through his formative years. These were influences which he carried over to his pop career, which received an early boost after his father passed (via the legendary VAN DYKE PARKS) a demo to an impressed 'DreamWorks' head Larry Waronker. The label subsequently issued WAINWRIGHT's eponymous 1998 debut album to almost unanimous critical acclaim, RUFUS' incredible voice investing the record's intimate, baroque chamber pop (arrangements by that man PARKS) with a profound emotional charge. Sophomore set, 'POSES' (2001) featured contributions from his sister MARTHA and another second generation musician TEDDY THOMPSON (son of RICHARD and LINDA) as well as the likes of PROPELLERHEADS' ALEX GIFFORD. Less personal then, than his debut but cut from the same singular cloth and basking in that same neo-operatic glow which surrounds RUFUS' songs. 'WANT ONE' followed in 2003, confirming his unique position in contemporary pop. • **Covered:** ACROSS THE UNIVERSE (Beatles).

Album rating: RUFUS WAINWRIGHT (*8) / POSES (*7) / WANT ONE (*5)

RUFUS WAINWRIGHT – vocals, acoustic guitar / w/ session people

Dreamworks Dreamworks

Aug 98. (cd) *<(DRD 50039)>* **RUFUS WAINWRIGHT** May98
– Foolish love / Danny boy / April fools / In my arms / Millbrook / Baby / Beauty mark / Barcelona / Matinee idol / Damned ladies / Sally Ann / Imaginary love.

Jun 01. (cd) *<(450237-2)>* **POSES**
– Cigarettes and chocolate milk / Greek song / Poses / Shadows / California / The tower of learning / Grey gardens / Rebel prince / The consort / One man guy / Evil angel / In a graveyard / Cigarettes and chocolate milk (reprise). *<re-iss. Feb02 +=; 450369-2>* – Across the universe (remix).

Sep 03. (cd) *(4505041) <89612>* **WANT ONE** 60
– Oh what a world / I don't know what it is / Vicious world / Movies of myself / Pretty things / Go or go ahead / Vibrate / 14th street / Natasha / Harvester of hearts / Beautiful child / Want / 11:11 / Dinner at eight. *(UK+=)* – Es mus sein / Velvet curtain rag.

Tom WAITS

Born: 7 Dec'49, Pomona, California, USA. Signed to 'Asylum' in 1973, after being spotted at the Troubadour club. His debut album 'CLOSING TIME' produced by Jerry Yester (ex-LOVIN' SPOONFUL), didn't sell greatly, but it did contain 'OL '55' which was soon covered by The EAGLES on their album 'On The Border'. 'THE HEART OF SATURDAY NIGHT' (1974) was more proficient, his downtrodden JACK KEROUAC meets CHARLES BUKOWSKI persona beginning to develop. With his distinctive Billy Goat Gruff vocals he sounded frighteningly like he'd been drinking industrial strength paint stripper since childhood. A born raconteur, his sharply observed tales of American lowlife were set against a musical backdrop of smokey blues and jazz stylings. The live album 'NIGHTHAWKS AT THE DINER' (1975) was WAITS in his element, reeling off wry vignettes with casual ease. 'SMALL CHANGE' (1976) was a confident step forward, his booze-sodden recollections more focused and his songwriting more complex on tracks like 'TOM TRAUBERT'S BLUES'. He even attempted to cultivate his parched vocals on 'FOREIGN AFFAIR' (1977), duetting with BETTE MIDLER for 'I NEVER TALK TO STRANGERS'. With 'BLUE VALENTINE' (1978) and 'HEARTATTACK AND VINE' (1980), WAITS opted for a combination of supple R&B tracks and heartbroken love ballads, the latter set spawning the haunting 'JERSEY GIRL' which was later covered by BRUCE SPRINGSTEEN. This was the end of an era for the maverick singer/songwriter as he signed to 'Island' and employed a more experimental strategy. The gloriously titled 'SWORDFISHTROMBONES' (1983) introduced the new WAITS sound, a surrealistic cut up of mutant jazz, skewed rhythms, jarring guitar and wildly inspired lyrics. 'RAIN DOGS' (1985) advanced this formula, again employing an array of session musicians to realise his eccentric musical vision. Adapted from a song on 'SWORDFISHTROMBONES', 'FRANK'S WILD YEARS' (1987) was the soundtrack to a musical stage show that included the brilliant horn-driven weirdness of 'HANG ON ST. CHRISTOPHER'. 'BIG TIME' (1988) was similar in tone, taking material from all his 'Island' recordings to date. With a string of acting credits already behind him as well as 1983's 'ONE FROM THE HEART' soundtrack, he scored JIM JARMUSCH'S 'NIGHT ON EARTH' in 1992. His next album proper was 'BONE MACHINE', released later the same year. The title was apt, a stark collection of minimalistic clankings and dark, muted musings. 'BLACK RIDER' (1993) held the musical fruits of a collaboration between director ROBERT WILSON and uber-Beat poet WILLIAM BURROUGHS. It was six long years before WAITS returned to the fold, the 'Epitaph' label (more identified with today's hardcore/punk scene) astonishingly taking up the reins for his marvellous comeback set, 'MULE VARIATIONS' (1999); if his gruff vox could be singled out as one type of music, it would indeed be "hard core". Now nearly fifty years of age (and looking every part of it!), WAITS had his first UK Top 10 success with 'MULE . . .', and even more importantly, his debut into the American Top 30. WAITS is an artist with defiantly singular vision and is a rare commodity in a marketplace where so often the blind lead the blind in a musical wild goose chase for the next trend. Why bother with a double set when two simultaneously-released single albums will do, May 2002's 'BLOOD MONEY' and 'ALICE', gave WAITS another cross-Atlantic success. • **Songwriters:** Pens own songs except; WHAT KEEPS MAN ALIVE (Kurt Weill) / HEIGH-HO (from 'Snow White') / IT'S ALL RIGHT WITH ME (Cole Porter). From 1987, his material was co-written with wife and Irish playwright Kathleen Brennan, whom he married on the 31st December '81. • **Filmography:** PARADISE ALLEY (bit-part 1978) / WOLFEN (cameo 1979) / STONE BOY (cameo 1980) / ONE FROM THE HEART (1981 cameo + soundtrack) / THE OUTSIDERS (1983) / RUMBLEFISH (1983) / THE COTTON CLUB (1984 cameo) / DOWN BY LAW (1986) / IRONWEED (1988) / COLD FEET (1989) / SHORT CUTS (1993) / THE FISHER KING (1990). • **Trivia:** In the late 70's, he parted company with girlfriend/singer RICKIE LEE JONES. In 1991, he sued a radio ad company for using a soundalike in a chips commercial and won nearly $2.5 million.

Album rating: CLOSING TIME (*7) / THE HEART OF SATURDAY NIGHT (*6) / NIGHTHAWKS AT THE DINER (*6) / SMALL CHANGE (*8) / FOREIGN AFFAIRS (*6) / BLUE VALENTINE (*6) / HEARTATTACK AND VINE (*7) / BOUNCED CHECKS compilation (*6) / ONE FROM THE HEART soundtrack with Crystal Gayle (*6) / SWORDFISHTROMBONES (*9) / THE ASYLUM YEARS compilation (*8) / RAIN DOGS (*9) / FRANKS WILD YEARS soundtrack (*7) / BIG TIME (*7) / NIGHT ON EARTH soundtrack (*5) / BONE MACHINE (*8) / THE BLACK RIDER (*5) / BEAUTIFUL MALADIES – THE ISLAND YEARS compilation (*8) / MULE VARIATIONS (*7) / BLOOD MONEY (*7) / ALICE (*7)

TOM WAITS – vocals, piano, accordion

Asylum | Elektra

May 73. (lp) *(SYL 9007)* *<SD 5061>* **CLOSING TIME**
– Ol' 55 / I hope that I don't fall in love with you / Virginia Ave/ Old shoes (and picture postcards) / Midnight lullaby / Martha / Rosie / Lonely / Ice cream man / Little trip to Heaven (on the wings of your love) / Grapefruit moon / Closing time. *(re-iss. Jun76; K 53030) (cd-iss. Feb93 on 'WEA'; 960836-2)*

May 73. (7") **OL '55. / MIDNIGHT LULLABY** –

Jan 74. (lp) *(K 53035)* *<7E 1015>* **THE HEART OF SATURDAY NIGHT**
– New coat of paint / San Diego serenade / Semi suite / Shiver me timbers / Diamonds on my windshield / (Looking for) The heart of Saturday night / Fumblin' with the blues / Please call me baby / Depot, depot / Drunk on the Moon / The ghosts of Saturday night (after hours at Napoleon's pizza house). *(re-iss. Jun76; same) (cd-iss. 1989 on 'WEA'; 960 597-2)*

Mar 74. (7") *<45213>* **DIAMONDS ON MY WINDSHIELD. / SAN DIEGO SERENADE** –

Jun 75. (7") *<45233>* **NEW COAT OF PAINT. / BLUE SKIES** –

Oct 75. (7") *<45262>* **(LOOKING FOR) THE HEART OF SATURDAY NIGHT. / DIAMONDS ON MY WINDSHIELD** –

—— with **MIKE MELVOIN** – piano / **JIM HUGHART** – bass / **BILL GOODWIN** – drums

Dec 75. (d-lp) *(SYSP 903)* *<7E 2008>* **NIGHTHAWKS AT THE DINER (live)** Oct75
– (opening intro) / Emotional weather report / (intro) / On a foggy night / (intro) / Eggs and sausage / (intro) / Better off without a wife / Nighthawk postcards (from Easy street) / (intro) / Warm beer and cold women / (intro) / Puttnam County / Spare parts 1 (a nocturnal emission) / Nobody / (intro) / Big Joe and Phantom 309 / Spare parts 2 and closing. *(re-iss. Jun76; K 63002) (cd-iss. 1989 on 'WEA'; 960 620-2)*

—— retained **HUGHART** + new **SHELLY MANNE** – drums / **LEW TABACKIN** – tenor sax

Nov 76. (7") *<45371>* **STEP RIGHT UP. / THE PIANO HAS BEEN DRINKING (NOT ME)** –

May 77. (lp) *(K 52050)* *<7E 1078>* **SMALL CHANGE** Nov 76 89
– Tom Traubert's blues / Step right up / Jitterbug boy / I wish I was in New Orleans / The piano has been drinking (not me) / Invitation to the blues / Pasties and a g-string / Bad liver and a broken heart / The one that got away / Small change / I can't wait to get off work. *(cd-iss. 1989 on 'WEA'; 960 612-2)*

—— **FRANK VICARI** – tenor sax / **JACK SHELDON** – trumpet repl. TABACKIN

Oct 77. (lp) *(K 53068)* *<7E 1117>* **FOREIGN AFFAIRS**
– Cinny's waltz / Muriel / I never talk to strangers / Jack and Neal – California here I come / A sight for sore eyes / Potter's field / Burma shave / Barber shop / Foreign affair. *(cd-iss. Mar95 on 'WEA'; 7559 60618-2)*

—— **RICK LAWSON** – drums repl. MANNE / added **ROLAND BAUTISTA** + **RAY CRAWFORD** – guitar / **BYRON MILLER** – bass / **DA WILLIE CONGA** – piano / **HAROLD BATTISTE** – piano

Apr 79. (7") *<45539>* **SOMEWHERE. / RED SHOES BY THE DRUGSTORE** –

Aug 79. (lp) *(K 53088)* *<6E 162>* **BLUE VALENTINE**
– Somewhere / Red shoes by the drugstore / Christmas card from a hooker

in Minneapolis / Romeo is bleeding / Wrong side of the road / Whistlin' past the graveyard / Kentucky Avenue / A sweet little bullet from a pretty blue gun / Blue valentines. *(cd-iss. Feb93; 7559 60533-2)*

— retained **HUGHART + BAUTISTA** + new **LARRY TAYLOR** – upright bass / **RONNIE BARRON** – organ / **GREG COHEN** – bass / **PLAS JOHNSON** – sax / **BIG JOHN THOMASSIE** – drums

Oct 80. (lp/c) *(K/K4 52252) <6E 295>* **HEARTATTACK AND VINE** [ ] [96]
– Saving all my love for you / On the nickel / In shades / Downtown / Jersey girl / Til the money runs out / Mr. Segal / Ruby's arms. *(cd-iss. 1989 on 'WEA') (re-iss. cd May93; 7559 60547-2)*

Dec 80. (7") *<47077>* **JERSEY GIRL. / HEARTATTACK AND VINE** [–] [ ]

Nov 81. (lp/c) *(K/K4 52316)* **BOUNCED CHECKS** (compilation, some live) [ ] [–]
– Heartattack and vine / Jersey girl / Eggs and sausage / I never talk to strangers / The piano has been drinking (not me) / Whistlin' past the graveyard / Mr. Henry / Diamonds on my windshield / Burma shave / Tom Traubert's blues.

— now with many session people from above incl.**VICTOR FELDMAN** – percussion

C.B.S. Columbia

Feb 83. (lp; TOM WAITS & CTYSTAL GAYLE) *(70215) <37703>* **ONE FROM THE HEART (Film Soundtrack)** [ ] [ ]
– (opening montage): Tom's piano intro – Once upon a town – The wages of love / Is there any way out of this dream / Picking up after you / Old boyfriends / Broken bicycles / I beg your pardon / Little boy blue / (instrumental montage): The tango – Circus girl / You can't unring a bell / This one's from the heart / Take me home / Presents / *(others by CRYSTAL GAYLE only). (cd-iss. Jan91)*

— **FRED TACKETT** – guitar + **STEPHEN TAYLOR HODGES** – drums repl. BAUTISTA + LAWSON / added **FRANCIS THUMM** – pump organ / **RANDY ALDCROFT** – horns

Island Island

Sep 83. (lp/c) *(ILPS/ICM 9762) <90095>* **SWORDFISHTROMBONES** [62] [ ]
– Underground / Shore leave / Dave the butcher / Johnsburg, Illinois / 16 shells from a thirty-ought-six / Town with no cheer / In the neighbourhood / Just another sucker on the vine / Frank's wild years / Swordfishtrombones / Down, down, down / Soldier's things / Gin soaked boy / Trouble's braids / Rainbirds. *(re-iss. Sep86 lp/c; same) (cd-iss. Nov87; CID 9762) (re-iss. cd Jun89; IMCD 48) (re-iss. lp Jan94 + May94; ILPM 9762)*

Oct 83. (7") *(IS 141)* **IN THE NEIGHBOURHOOD. / FRANK'S WILD YEARS** [ ] [ ]

— **MARC RIBOT** – guitar + **MICHAEL BLAIR** – drums, percussion repl. TACKETT, THUMM + HODGES / **WILLIAM SCHIMMEL** – piano / **RAPLH CARNEY** – sax, clarinet + **BOB FUNK** – trombone repl. FELDMAN + ALDCROFT

Oct 85. (lp/c)(cd) *(ILPS/ICT 9803)(CID 131) <90299>* **RAIN DOGS** [29] [ ]
– Singapore / Clap hands / Cemetery polka / Jockey full of bourbon / Tango till they're sore / Big black Mariah / Diamonds and gold / Hang down your head / Time / Rain dogs / Midtown / Ninth and headpin / Gun Street girl / Union square / Blind love / Walking Spanish / Downtown train / Bride of Rain dog / Anywhere I lay my head. *(re-iss. cd.Aug89 & Apr91; IMCD 49)*

Nov 85. (7"/12") *(IS/12IS 253)* **DOWNTOWN TRAIN. / TANGO 'TILL THEY'RE SORE** [ ] [ ]

Feb 86. (7") *(IS 260)* **IN THE NEIGHBOURHOOD. / SINGAPORE** [ ] [ ]
(d7"+=) *(ISD 260)* – Tango till they're sore (live) / Rain dogs (live).
(12") *(12IS 260)* – ('A'side) / Jockey full of bourbon / Tango till they're sore (live) / 16 shells from a thirty-ought-six (live).

— Past live group **FRED TACKETT** – guitar / **RICHIE HAYWARD** – drums / **LARRY TAYLOR** – upright bass. Retained only **TAYLOR, CARNEY, SCHIMMEL** / new: **MORRIS TEPPER** – guitar / **FRANCIS THUMM** – pump organ (on some) / guest **DAVID HIDALGO** – accordion

Aug 87. (lp/c/cd) *(ITW/+C/CD 3) <90572>* **FRANKS WILD YEARS (soundtrack)** [20] [ ]
– Hang on St. Christopher / Straight to the top (rhumba) / Blow wind blow / Temptation / Innocent when you dream (barroom) / I'll be gone / I'll take New York / Telephone call from Istanbul / Cold cold ground / Train song / Yesterday is here / Please wake me up / Frank's theme / More than rain / Way down in the hole / Straight to the top (Vegas). *(re-iss. cd.Jun89 & Apr91; IMCD 50)*

— 1988 live band **WILLIE SCHWARZ** – keyboards, accordion repl. SCHIMMEL + TEPPER

Sep 88. (lp/c/cd) *(ITW/+C/CD 4) <90987>* **BIG TIME (live)** [84] [ ]
– 16 shells from a thirty-ought-six / Red shoes / Cold cold ground / Way down in the hole / Falling down / Strange weather / Big black Mariah / Rain dogs / Train song / Telephone call from Istanbul / Gun street girl / Time. *(cd+=)* – Underground / Straight to the top / Yesterday is here / Johnsburg, Illinois / Ruby's arms / Clap hands. *(cd-iss. Mar97; IMCD 249)*

Sep 88. (7") *(IS 370)* **16 SHELLS FROM A THIRTY-OUGHT-SIX (live). / BIG BLACK MARIAH (live)** [ ] [ ]
(12"+=) *(12IS 370)* – Ruby's arms (live).

May 92. (cd/c) *<(510929-2/-4)>* **NIGHT ON EARTH (soundtrack)** [ ] [ ]
– Back in the good old world / Los Angeles mood (chromium descentions) / Los Angeles theme (another private dick) / New York theme (hey, you can have that heart attack outside, buddy) / New York mood (a new haircut and a busted lip) / Baby, I'm not a baby anymore (Beatrice theme) / Good old world (waltz) / Carnival (Brunello del Montalcino) / On the old side of the world (vocal) / Good old world (gypsy instrumental) / Paris mood (un de fromage) / Dragging a dead priest / Helsinki mood / Carnival Bob's confession / Good old world (waltz vocal) / On the other side of the world (instrumental).

Aug 92. (7") *(IS 537)* **GOIN' OUT WEST. / A LITTLE RAIN** [ ] [–]
(10"+=/cd-s+=) *(10IS/CID 537)* – The ocean doesn't want me / Back in the good old world (gypsy).

Sep 92. (cd/c/lp) *(CID/ICT/ILPS 9993) <512580>* **BONE MACHINE** [26] [ ]
– Earth died screaming / Dirt in the ground / Such a scream / All stripped down / Who are you / The ocean doesn't want me / Jesus gonna behave / A little rain / In the Colosseum / Goin' out west / Murder in the red barn / Black wings / Whistle down the wind / I don't wanna grow up / Let me get up on it / That feel.

Nov 93. (cd/c/lp) *(CID/ICT/ILPS 8021) <518559>* **THE BLACK RIDER** [47] [ ]
– Lucky day overture / The black rider / November / Just the right bullets / Black box theme / 'T ain't no sin / Flash pan hunter intro / That's the way / The briar and the rose / Russian dance / Gospel train-orchestra / I'll shoot the Moon / Flash pan hunter / Crossroads / Gospel train / Interlude / Oily night / Lucky day / The last rose of summer / Carnival.

— 3 of above tracks were co-written with author WILLIAM S. BURROUGHS

Epitaph Epitaph

Apr 99. (cd/c/lp) *<(8 6547-2/-4/-1)>* **MULE VARIATIONS** [9] [30]
– Big in Japan / Lowside of the road / Hold on / Get behind the mule / House where nobody lives / Cold water / Pony / What's he building? / Black market baby / Eyeball kid / Picture in a frame / Chocolate Jesus / Georgia Lee / Filipino box spring hog / Take it with me / Come on up to the house.

Jun 99. (cd-s) *(1020-2)* **HOLD ON / BIG IN JAPAN / FLEDDERJON** [ ] [ ]

Anti- Anti-

May 02. (cd/lp) *<(8 6629-2/-1)>* **BLOOD MONEY** [21] [32]
– Misery is the river of the world / Everything goes to hell / Coney Island baby / All the world is green / God's away on business / Another man's vine / Knife chase / Lullaby / Starving in the belly of a whale / The part you throw away / Woe / Calliope / A good man is hard to find.

May 02. (cd/lp) *<(8 6632-2/-1)>* **ALICE** [20] [33]
– Alice / Everything you can think / Flower's grave / No one knows I'm gone / Kommienezuspadt / Poor Edward / Table top Joe / Lost in the harbour / We're all mad here / Watch her disappear / Reeperbahn / I'm still here / Fish & bird / Barcarolle / Fawn.

– compilations, etc. –

Apr 84. (d-lp/c) *Asylum; (960 321-1/-4)* **THE ASYLUM YEARS** [ ] [ ]
– Diamonds on my windshield / (Looking for) The heart of Saturday night / Martha / The ghosts of Saturday night / Grapefruit Moon / Small change / Burma slave / I never talk to strangers / Tom Traubert's blues / Blue valentine / Potter's field / Kentucky avenue / Somewhere / Ruby's arms. *(cd-iss. Oct86; 960 494-2)* – (omitted 9 tracks but added 3 others).

Jul 91. (cd/c/lp) *Edsel; (ED/C+/ED 332)* **THE EARLY YEARS** (rare & demos) [ ] [–]
– Goin' down slow / Poncho's lament / I'm your late night evening prostitute / Had me a girl / Ice cream man / Rockin' chair / Virginia Ave. / Midnight lullabye / When you ain't got nobody / Little trip to Heaven / Frank's song / Looks like I'm up shit creek again / So long I'll see you. *(re-iss. Feb97 & Mar98 on 'Manifesto'; PT 340601)*

Nov 92. (d-cd) *Island; (ITSCD 5)* **SWORDFISHTROMBONES / RAIN DOGS** ☐ ☐
Feb 93. (cd/c) *Edsel; (ED CD/MC 371)* **THE EARLY YEARS VOL.2** ☐ -
– Hope I don't fall in love with you / Ol' 55 / Mockin bird / In between love / Blue skies / Nobody / I want you / Shiver me timbers / Grapefruit moon / Diamonds on my windshield / Please call me, baby / So it goes / Old shoes. *(re-iss. Feb97 & Mar98 on 'Manifesto'; PT 340602)*
Mar 93. (7"/c-s) *Elektra; (EKR 162/+C)* **HEARTATTACK AND VINE. / BLUE VALENTINES** ☐ ☐
(cd-s+=) *(EKR 162CD)* – On a foggy night (live) / Intro to a foggy night (live).
Jun 98. (d-cd) *Island; (524 519-2)* **BEAUTIFUL MALADIES – THE ISLAND YEARS** 63 ☐
– Hang on St. Christopher / Temptation / Clap hands / The back rider / Underground / Jockey full of bourbon / Earth died screaming / Innocent when you dream (78) / Straight to the top / Frank's wild years / Singapore / Shore leave / Johnsburg, Illinois / Way down in the hole / Strange weather (live) / Cold, cold ground (live) / November / Downtrain train / 16 shells from a thirty-ought six / Jesus gonna be here / Good old world (waltz) / I don't wanna grow up / Time.
Nov 01. (cd) *Burning Airlines; (PILOT 082)* **DIME STORE NOVELS VOL.1** ☐ -
Mar 02. (cd) *Rhino; <(8122 78351-2)>* **USED SONGS 1973-1980** ☐ ☐

Rick WAKEMAN

Born: 18 May'49, Perivale, Middlesex, England. Aged 16, he attended The Royal College of Music, although interest in playing live and doing sessions led to him dropping out. His in-demand pop session work (i.e. WHITE PLAINS, EDISON LIGHTHOUSE, etc.), saw him working on albums by CAT STEVENS, DAVID BOWIE, T.REX, etc. In 1970, he joined The STRAWBS, but the following year he couldn't turn down YES, as they matched his classical ambitions. He was an on-off YES member during the 70's, subsequently starting his own solo career on 'A&M' records. Prior to this, he had augmented The JOHN SCHROEDER ORCHESTRA on the 1971 'Polydor lp, 'PIANO VIBRATIONS'; (2460 135). Taking themes of history, fiction and legend, he released three well-received (at the time) Top 10 albums between 1973-1975. His second album, 'JOURNEY TO THE CENTRE OF THE EARTH' (an adaptation of the Jules Verne classic), was premiered live at The Royal Festival Hall in January '74, topping the UK charts upon its release that year. With orchestra and choir in tow, he performed it at an open-air Crystal Palace Garden Party, subsequently touring the show around major US venues. His virtuoso, exhibitionist keyboard-playing and flash-rock image (long blonde hair and ankle-length silver capes) was perfectly suited to the live arena, a comparison that could be made with the other famous keys-basher of the era, KEITH EMERSON. Nevertheless, this gruelling tour took its toll, when RICK suffered a minor heart attack nearing the end of the pocket-draining extravaganza. On his recovery, he released the third of these epics, 'KING ARTHUR' in 1975, regarded by many as overblown pomp-rock, although it did have its redeeming moments (i.e. 'MERLIN THE MAGICIAN' and 'SIR LANCELOT & THE BLACK KNIGHT'). Following a move into soundtrack work, notably on Ken Russell's 'LISZTOMANIA' (starring ROGER DALTREY) and 'WHITE ROCK' (a docu-film focussing on the 1976 Winter Olympics), he found time to squeeze in his fourth studio set, 'NO EARTHLY CONNECTION', a record that still managed a Top 10 placing. WAKEMAN returned in 1977 with his '. . . CRIMINAL RECORD', which was a failure both critically and commercially, leading to public attention drifting somewhat, thus his steady decline. He continued to release a plethora of albums, most taking a neo-classical rock/pop or new-age stance. He will probably be remembered in the next century, not for his theatrical rock indulgence, but for the romantic classical style he helped revive. • **Songwriters:** All his own work, interspersed with little snatches of past classical works. • **Trivia:** Most distinguished session work included; LIFE ON MARS (David Bowie) / CHANGES (Black Sabbath) / MORNING HAS BROKEN (Cat Stevens) / LOU REED's debut album. WAKEMAN was married in the 70's to Ros and settled down in a Buckingham mansion alongside his collection of Rolls Royce's. The couple had three children before their divorce. In the 80's, RICK married ex-model, NINA CARTER, (also of twin-sister outfit, BLONDE ON BLONDE). He fathered another two kids (so far), later finding Christianity. BILL ODDIE (of the GOODIES TV programme) contributed vocals on WAKEMAN's 'JOURNEY' and 'CRIMINAL RECORD'.

Album rating: THE SIX WIVES OF HENRY VIII (*8) / JOURNEY TO THE CENTRE OF THE EARTH (*7) / THE MYTHS & LEGENDS OF KING ARTHUR . . . (*6) / LISZTOMANIA soundtrack (*4) / NO EARTHLY CONNECTION (*5) / WHITE ROCK soundtrack (*5) / RICK WAKEMAN'S CRIMINAL RECORD (*4) / RHAPSODIES (*4) / 1984 (*4) / THE BURNING soundtrack (*3) / ROCK'N'ROLL PROPHET (*3) / G'OLE soundtrack (*3) / THE COST OF LIVING (*4) / SILENT NIGHTS (*3) / LIVE AT HAMMERSMITH (*4) / COUNTRY AIRS (*5) / THE GOSPELS (*3) / CRIMES OF PASSION soundtrack (*4) / THE FAMILY ALBUM (*4) / A SUITE OF GODS with Ramon Remedios (*4) / ZODIAQUE with Tony Fernandez (*4) / TIME MACHINE (*4) / SEA AIRS (*4) / NIGHT AIRS (*4) / ASPIRANT SUNSET (*4) / ASPIRANT SUNRISE (*4) / BLACK KNIGHTS IN THE COURT OF FERNINAND IV with Mario Fasciano (*4) / PHANTOM POWER soundtrack (*4) / SOFTSWORD: KING JOHN AND THE MAGNA CHARTER (*4) / A WORLD OF WISDOM with Norman Wisdom (*3) / 2000 A.D. INTO THE FUTURE (*4) / AMBIENT SUNSHADOWS (*4) / WAKEMAN WITH WAKEMAN with Adam Wakeman (*4) / HERITAGE SUITE (*4) / AFRICAN BACH (*4) / NO EXPENSE SPARED with Adam (*4) / ROMANCE OF THE VICTORIAN AGE with Adam (*4) / THE SEVEN WONDERS OF THE WORLD (*3) / CIRQUE SURREAL – STATE CIRCUS OF IMAGINATION (*6) / VISIONS (*4) / VOYAGE: THE VERY BEST RICK WAKEMAN compilation (*7)

RICK WAKEMAN – keyboards (a member of YES; Aug71-Jun74, Nov76-Mar80, 1990+)

— now used various YES people on sessions plus numerous choirs & ensembles.

A&M A&M

Feb 73. (lp/c) *(AMLH/CAM 64361)* **THE SIX WIVES OF HENRY VIII** 7 30
– Catherine of Aragon / Anne of Cleves / Catherine Howard / Jane Seymour / Anne Boleyn / Catherine Parr. *(quad-lp; QU-84361) (cd-iss. 1988; CDA 3229) (re-iss. cd Aug89; 393 229-2) (re-iss. cd Jan92; CDMID 136)*
Mar 73. (7") *(AMS 7061)* **CATHERINE. / ANNE** ☐ -
(below A-side was an excerpt of 'CATHERINE PARR')

— Introduced **ASHLEY HOLT** – vocals / **ROGER NEWELL** – bass / **BARNEY JAMES** – drums / plus The ENGLISH ROCK ENSEMBLE with The LONDON SYMPHONY ORCHESTRA. Narration by actor DAVID HEMMINGS.

May 74. (lp/c) *(AMLH/CAM 63621)* **JOURNEY TO THE CENTRE OF THE EARTH** 1 3
– The journey / Recollections / The battle / The forest. *<US quad-lp 1974; SPQU 3621> (re-iss. Feb85 on 'Hallmark' lp/c; SHM/HSC 3164) (cd-iss. Jan88; CDA 3156) <US cd-iss. 1988 on 'Mobile Fidelity'; MFCD 848> (re-iss. cd Jan92; CDMID 161) (re-iss. May93 on 'Spectrum' cd/c; 550 061-2/-4)*
Oct 74. (7") **THE JOURNEY. / THE RETURN** - ☐
Dec 74. (7") **THE BATTLE. / AND NOW A WORD FROM OUR SPONSOR** - ☐
Apr 75. (lp/c) *(AMLH/CAM 64515)* **THE MYTHS AND LEGENDS OF KING ARTHUR AND THE KNIGHTS OF THE ROUND TABLE** 2 21
– Arthur / Lady of the lake / Guinevere / Sir Lancelot & the Black Knight / Merlin the magician / Sir Galahad / The last battle. *<US quad-lp 1975; SPQU 54515> (cd-iss. 1988; CDA 3230) (re-iss. cd; CDMID 135)*
Jun 75. (7") **MERLIN THE MAGICIAN. / SIR GALAHAD** - ☐
(below 1975 releases with ROGER DALTREY on vocals)
Nov 75. (lp) *(AMLH 64546)* **LISZTOMANIA (Soundtrack)** ☐ ☐
– Rienzi / Chopsticks fantasia / Love's dream / Dante period / Orpheus song / Hell / Hibernation / Excelsior song / Master race / Rape, pillage and clap funerailles / Free song / Peace at last.
Nov 75. (7") *(AMS 7206)* **ORPHEUS SONG. / LOVE'S DREAM** ☐ ☐

— For North & South American tour he trimmed his ENGLISH ROCK ENSEMBLE down to **ASHLEY HOLT** – vocals / **JOHN DUNSTERVILE** – guitar / **ROGER NEWELL** – bass / **TONY FERNANDEZ** – drums / **REG BROOKS + MARTYN SHIELDS** – brass section

Apr 76. (lp/c) *(AMLK/CLK 64583)* **NO EARTHLY CONNECTION** [9] [67]
– Music reincarnate: (part 1) The warning – (part 2) The maker – (part 3) The spaceman – (part 4) The realization – (part 5) The reaper / The prisoner / The lost cycle.

Jan 77. (lp/c) *(AMLH/CAM 64614)* **WHITE ROCK (Film Soundtrack)** [14] [ ]
– White rock / Searching for gold / The loser / The shoot / Lax'x / After the ball / Montezuma's revenge / Ice run. *(cd-iss. 1988; CDA 4614)*
(above from 1976 Winter Olympics docu-film, narrated by James Coburn)

Jun 77. (7") *<1937>* **AFTER THE BALL. / WHITE ROCK** [-] [ ]

Nov 77. (lp/c) *(AMLH/CAM 64660)* **RICK WAKEMAN'S CRIMINAL RECORD** [25] [ ]
– Statute of justice / Crime of passion / Chamber of horrors / Birdman of Alcatraz / The breathalizer / Judas Iscariot. *(re-iss. Mar82 lp/c; AMID/CMID 125)*

Apr 79. (7") *(AMS 7435)* **BIRDMAN OF ALCATRAZ (theme from My Son My Son). / FALCONS DE NEIGE** [ ] [-]

Apr 79. (7") *<2010>* **BIRDMAN OF ALCATRAZ. / AND NOW A WORD FROM OUR SPONSOR** [-] [ ]

May 79. (d-lp/c) *(AMLX/CXM 68508)* **RHAPSODIES** [25] [ ]
– Pedra da Gavea / Front line / Bombay duck / Animal showdown / Big Ben / Rhapsody in blue / Wooly Willy tango / The pulse / Swan lager / March of the gladiators / Flacons de Neige / The flasher / The palais / Stand by / Sea horses / Half holiday / Summertime.

May 79. (7"/7"pic-d) *(AMS/+P 7436)* **ANIMAL SHOWDOWN. / SEA HORSES** [ ] [-]

Nov 79. (7") *(AMS 7497)* **SWAN LAGER. / WOOLLY WILLY TANGO** [ ] [-]

Feb 80. (7") *(AMS 7510)* **I'M SO STRAIGHT I'M A WEIRDO. / DO YOU BELIEVE IN FAIRIES?** [ ] [-]

WEA not iss.

Oct 80. (7") *(K 18354)* **THE SPIDER. / DANIELLE** [ ] [-]
featured **FERNANDEZ / STEVE BARNACLE** – bass / **GARY BARNACLE** – sax / **TIM STONE** – guitar / etc.

Charisma Charisma?

Jun 81. (lp)(c) *(CDS 4022)(7144 136)* **1984** [24] [ ]
– 1984 overture – part 1 & 2 / War games / Julia / The hymn / The room – part 1 & 2 / Robot man / Sorry / No name / 1984 / Forgotten memories / The proles / 1984. *(re-iss. Jun88; CHC 41)*
(below vocals by; CORI JOSIAS)

Jul 81. (7"; by The RICK WAKEMAN BAND) *(CB 384)* **JULIA. / SORRY** [ ] [-]

Nov 81. (7"; by The RICK WAKEMAN BAND) *(CB 392)* **ROBOT MAN. / 1984 OVERTURE (part 1)** [ ] [-]

Jan 82. (lp) *(CLASS 12)* **THE BURNING (soundtrack)** [ ] [ ]
– Themes from 'The Burning' / The chase continues / Variations on the fire / Sheer terror and more / The burning (end title theme) / Campfire story / The fire / Doin' it / Devil's creek breakdown / The chase / Sheer terror.

Moon not iss.

Nov 82. (7") *(LUNA 6)* **I'M SO STRAIGHT I'M A WEIRDO. / MAYBE '80 (edit)** [ ] [-]

Dec 82. (lp/c) *(LUNLP/ZCLUN 1)* **ROCK'N'ROLL PROPHET** (rec.1979) [ ] [-]
– I'm so straight I'm a weirdo / The dragon / Dark / Maybe '80 / Early warning / Spy of '55 / Do you believe in fairies? / Rock'n'roll prophet. *(cd-iss. Apr93 on 'President'; RWCD 12)(+=)* – Return of the prophet / Alpha sleep / March of the child soldiers / Stalemate.

— solo with music from 1982 football World Cup in Spain

Charisma not iss.

Apr 83. (7") *(CB 411)* **LATIN REEL (theme from G'OLE). / NO POSSIBLA** [ ] [-]

Apr 83. (lp/c) *(CAS/+MC 1162)* **G'OLE (film soundtrack)** [ ] [-]
– International flag / The dove / Wayward spirit / Red island / Latin reel (theme from G'ole) / Spanish holiday / No possibla / Shadows / Black pearls / Frustration / Spanish montage / G'ole.

Jun 83. (lp) *(CAS 1163)* **THE COST OF LIVING** [ ] [ ]
– Twij / Pandomonia / Gone but not forgotten / One for the road / Bedtime stories / Happening man / Shakespeare's run / Monkey nuts / Elegy (written in a country church yard). *(re-iss. Aug88; CHC 63) (cd-iss. Jun97 on 'Griffin'; GCDWR 1892)*

— Oct '84, WAKEMAN collaborated on album BEYOND THE PLANETS by KEVIN PEEK (Sky); hit UK No.64

— His Spring 1985 tour band: **TONY FERNANDEZ** – drums / **CHAS CRONK** – bass / **RICK FENN** – lead guitar / **GORDON NEVILLE** – vocals / **LYNN SHEPHERD** – b.vocals

President not iss.

Dec 84. (7") *(WAKE 1)* **GLORY BOYS. / GHOST OF A ROCK AND ROLL STAR** [ ] [-]
(12"+=) *(12WAKE 1)* – Elgin mansions.

Mar 85. (lp/c) *(RW/+K 1)* **SILENT NIGHTS** [ ] [-]
– Tell 'em all you know / The opening line / The opera / Man's best friend / Glory boys / Silent nights / Ghost of a rock and roll star / The dancer / That's who I am. *(cd-iss. Jan87; RWCD 1)* – Elgin mansions.

Jun 85. (7"/12") *(WAKE/12WAKE 2)* **THE THEME FROM 'LYTTON'S DIARY'. / DATABASE** [ ] [-]

Dec 85. (lp) *(RW 2)* **LIVE AT HAMMERSMITH (live)** [ ] [-]
– Arthur / Three wives of Henry VIII / The journey / Merlin the magician. *(cd-iss. Jan87; RWCD 2) (re-iss. Nov93)*

Coda not iss.

Apr 86. (lp/c)(cd) *(NAGE/+C 10)(NAGE 10CD)* **COUNTRY AIRS** [ ] [-]
– Dandelion dreams / Stepping stones / Ducks and drakes / Morning haze / Waterfalls / Quite valleys / Nature trail / Heather carpets / Wild moors / Lakeland walks. *(re-iss. Oct92 on 'Art Of Language' cd/c; NAGE 102CD) (re-iss. re-recorded cd Dec92 on 'President'; RWCD 10)* – The spring / Green to gold / Harvest festival / The glade.

Apr 86. (7") *(CODS 19)* **WATERFALLS. / HEATHER CARPETS** [ ] [-]

Stylus not iss.

Nov 86. (d-lp/d-c/d-cd) *(SMR/SMC/SMD 729)* **THE GOSPELS** [94] [-]
– The baptism / The welcoming / The sermon on the mount / The Lord's Prayer / The way / The road to Jerusalem / Trial and error / Galilee / The gift / The magnificat / Welcome a star / Power (the acts of the apostles) / The word / The hour / The children of mine / The last verse. *(re-iss. d-cd Mar94 on 'Fragile'; BM 2-3)*

President not iss.

Mar 87. (lp/c/cd) *(RW/+K/CD 3)* **CRIMES OF PASSION (Soundtrack)** [ ] [-]
– It's a lovely life (featuring MAGGIE BELL) / Eastern shadows / Joanna / The stretch / Policeman's ball / Stax / Taken in hand / Paradise lost / The box / Web of love. *(cd+=)* – Dangerous woman (featuring MAGGIE BELL). *(re-iss. cd Feb93)*

Aug 87. (lp/c/cd) *(RW/+K/CD 4)* **THE FAMILY ALBUM** [ ] [-]
– Adam (Rick's second son) / Black Beauty (black rabbit) / Jemma (Rick and Nina's daughter) / Benjamin (Rick's third son) / Oscar (Rick & Nina's son) / Oliver (Rick's eldest son) / Nina (Rick's wife) / Chloe (German shepherd) / Rookie (cat) / Tilly (Golden Retriever) / Mum / Dad. *(c+=)* – Wiggles (black & white rabbit). *(cd++=)* – The day after the fair / Mackintosh.

Feb 88. (lp/c/cd; RICK WAKEMAN & RAMON REMEDIOS) *(RW/+K/CD 5)* **A SUITE OF GODS** [ ] [-]
– Dawn of time / The oracle / Pandora's box / Chariot of the sun / The flood / The voyage of Ulysses / Hercules.

Apr 88. (lp/c/cd; RICK WAKEMAN & TONY FERNANDEZ) *(RW/+K/CD 6)* **ZODIAQUE** [ ] [-]
– Sagittarius / Capricorn / Gemini / Cancer / Pisces / Aquarius / Aries / Libra / Leo / Virgo / Taurus / Scorpio.

— retained **FERNANDEZ** + recruited **DAVEY PATON** – bass / **JOHN KNIGHTSBRIDGE** – guitar (2) / guest vocals **TRACEY ACKERMAN** + **ASHLEY HOLT**
below vocals by ROY WOOD (A-side) / JOHN PARR (B-side)

Jul 88. (7") *(WAKE 3)* **CUSTER'S LAST STAND. / OCEAN CITY** [ ] [-]

Jul 88. (lp/c/cd) *(RW/+K/CD 7)* **TIME MACHINE** [ ] [-]
– Custer's last stand / Ocean city / Angel of time * / Slaveman * / Ice / Open up your eyes * / Elizabethan rock / Make me a woman * / Rock age *. *(cd has extended versions of *)*

Nov 89. (lp/c/cd) *(RW/+K/CD 8)* **SEA AIRS** [ ] [-]
– Harbour lights / The pirate / Storm clouds / Last at sea / The mermaid / Waves / The fisherman / Flying fish / The Marie Celeste / Time and tide / The lone sailor / The sailor's lament.

Nov 90. (lp/c/cd) *(RW/+K/CD 9)* **NIGHT AIRS** [ ] [-]
– The sad dream / Twilight / The sleeping child / Mr. Badger / Jack Frost / The lone star / Rain shadows / Fox by night / Night owls / An evening romance.

— (in the US; he released cd 'IN THE BEGINNING' for 'Asaph'; *<AR-1049>*, which received a UK date Dec91). In 1991, the 'Badger' label issued cassette 'THE SUN TRILOGY'; *AMB 4MC)*

Ambient / not iss.

Nov 90. (cd) *(AMB1-MCD)* **ASPIRANT SUNSET** [ ] [-]
– Floating clouds / Still waters / The dream / The sleeping village / Sea of tranquility / Peace / Sunset / Dying embers / Dusk / Evening moods. *(re-iss. 1992 on 'Rio Digital'; RIOCD 1008) (re-iss. Jun93 on 'President'; RWCD 18)*

Nov 90. (cd) *(AMB2-MCD)* **ASPIRANT SUNRISE** [ ] [-]
– Thoughts of love / Gentle breezes / Whispering cornfields / Peaceful beginnings / Dewy morn / Musical dreams / Distant thoughts / The dove / When time stood still / Secret moments / Peaceful. *(re-iss. 1992 on 'Rio Digital'; RIOCD 1009) (re-iss. Jun93 on 'President'; RWCD 17)*

Jan 91. (lp/cd; by RICK WAKEMAN & MARIO FASCIANO) *(A-IOM-2/+CD)* **BLACK KNIGHTS IN THE COURT OF FERNINAND IV** [ ] [-]
(re-iss. cd Nov92 on 'Rio Digital'; RIOCD 1002) (re-iss. cd Jun94 on 'West Coast'; WCPCD 1009)

Feb 91. (lp/cd) *(A-IOM-2/+CD)* **PHANTOM POWER** [ ] [-]
– The visit / Heaven / The rat / The stiff / Evil love / The voice of love / Heat of the moment / Fear of love / The love trilogy:- One night – The dream sequence – One night of love / The hangman / The sand-dance / You can't buy my love / Phantom power / The chase. *(re-iss. cd Nov92 on 'Rio Digital'; RIOCD 1003)*

May 91. (lp/cd) *(A-IOM-3/+CD)* **SOFTSWORD: KING JOHN AND THE MAGNA CHARTER** [ ] [-]
– Magna charter / After prayers / Battle sonata / The siege / Rochester college / The story of love (King John) / March of time / Don't fly away / Isabella / Softsword / Hymn of hope. *(re-iss. cd Nov92 on 'Rio Digital'; RIOCD 1001) (re-iss. cd Feb94 on 'President'; RWCD 24)*

Sep 91. (lp/cd) *(A-IOM-5/+CD)* **A WORLD OF WISDOM** [ ] [-]
(re-iss. cd Feb94 on 'D-Sharp'; DSHCD 7013)
(above credited to veteran English comedian/singer NORMAN WISDOM)

Oct 91. (7"; by RICK WAKEMAN featuring CHRISSIE HAMMOND) *(A-IOMS 1)* **DON'T FLY AWAY. / AFTER PRAYERS** [ ] [-]

Nov 91. (cd) **2000 A.D. INTO THE FUTURE** [ ] [-]
– Into the future / Toward peace / 2000 A.D. / A.D rock / The time tunnel / Robot dance / A new beginning / Forward past / The seventh dimension. *(re-iss. Dec92 on 'Rio Digital'; RIOCD 1007) (re-iss. Sep93 on 'President'; RWCD 21)*

Rio Digital / not iss.

1992. (cd) *(RIOCD 1010)* **AMBIENT SUNSHADOWS** [ ] [-]
– The nightwind / Churchyard / Tall shadows / Shadowlove / Melancholy mood / Mount Fuji by night / Hidden reflections / The evening harp / The moonraker pond / The last lamplight / Japanese sunshadows. *(re-iss. Jul93 as 'ASPIRANT SUNSHADOWS' on 'President'; RWCD 19)*

Nov 92. (cd; RICK WAKEMAN & ADAM WAKEMAN) *(RIOCD 1011)* **WAKEMAN WITH WAKEMAN** [ ] [-]
– Lure of the wild / The beach comber / Meglomania / Raga and rhyme / Sync or swim / Jigajig / Caesarea / After the atom / The suicide shuiffle / Past and present / Paint it black. *(re-iss. Feb93 on 'President'; RWCD 11)*
(above was with son ADAM)

Myrrh / not iss.

May 93. (cd) *(MYRCD 1296)* **PRAYERS** [ ] [-]

President / not iss.

May 93. (cd) *(RWCD 16)* **HERITAGE SUITE** [ ] [-]
– The chasms / Thorwald's cross / St.Michael's isle / Spanish head / The Ayres / Mona's isle / The Dhoon / The bee orchid / Chapel Hill / The Curraghs / The painted lady / The Peregrine falcon.

Aug 93. (cd) *(RWCD 17)* **AFRICAN BACH** (rec.& rel.South Africa 1991) [ ] [-]
– African Bach / Message of mine / My homeland / Liberty / Anthem / Brainstorm / Face in the crowd / Just a game / Africa east / Don't touch the merchandise.

Nov 93. (cd; by WAKEMAN WITH WAKEMAN) *(RWCD 22)* **NO EXPENSE SPARED** [ ] [-]

May 94. (cd-ep; by RICK WAKEMAN & HIS BAND) *(WAKEY 4)* **LIGHT UP THE SKY / SIMPLY FREE / STARFLIGHT / THE BEAR** [ ] [ ]

Nov 94. (cd; by WAKEMAN WITH WAKEMAN) *(RWCD 25)* **ROMANCE OF THE VICTORIAN AGE** [ ] [-]
– Burlington arcade / If only / The last teardrop / Still dreaming / Memories of the Victorian age / Lost in words / A tale of love / Mysteries unfold / Forever in my heart / Days of wonder / The swans / Another mellow day / Dance of the elves.

Jun 95. (cd) *(RWCD 27)* **THE SEVEN WONDERS OF THE WORLD** (with narration) [ ] [-]
– The Pharoahs Of Alexandria / The Colossus Of Rhodes / The Pyramids Of Egypt / The Gardens Of Babylon / The Temples Of Artemis / The Statue Of Zeus / The Mausoleum At Halicarnassus.

Jul 95. (cd) *(DSHLCD 7018)* **CIRQUE SURREAL – STATE CIRCUS OF IMAGINATION** [ ] [-]
– Gnash / Balance of power / Wings of fortune / Static / Party / Wired for sound / Juliet / Tubular balls / Carlos / Love that I know / The jig.
(above released on 'D-Sharp' label)

Oct 95. (cd) *(RWCD 28)* **VISIONS** [ ] [-]
– Fantasy / Peace of mind / Innermost thoughts / Vision of light / Higher planes / Astral traveller / Dream on / Thought waves / Drifting patterns / Future patterns / Levitation / Moondreams.

Nov 96. (cd; by RICK & ADAM WAKEMAN) *(RWCD 30)* **VIGNETTES** [ ] [-]
– Waiting alone / Wish I was you / Sun comes crying / A breath of Heaven / Moment in time / Artist's dream / Change of face / Madman blues / A painting of our love / Riverside / Need you / Simply acoustic / Just another tear.

Hope / not iss.

Mar 97. (cd) *(HRHCD 004)* **LIGHT AT THE END OF THE TUNNEL** [ ] [-]

Mar 97. (cd) *(HRHCD 005)* **CAN YOU HEAR ME?** [ ] [-]

EMI Classics / EMI Classics

Mar 99. (cd/lp) *(<CDC/EX 556763-2/-1>)* **RETURN TO THE CENTRE OF THE EARTH** [34] [ ]
– A vision / The return overture / Mother Earth: Shadow of June – Gallery – Avenue of prismed light – Earthquake / Buried alive (with OZZY OSBOURNE) / The enigma / Is anybody there? (with BONNIE TYLER) / The ravine / Dance of a thousand lights / The shephard / Mr Slow / Bridge of time / Never is a long time (with TREVOR RABIN) / Tales of the Lidenbrook sea – River of hope – Hunter and hunted – Fight for life / The kill / Timeless history / Still waters run deep (with JUSTIN HAYWARD) / Time within time / The ebbing tide – Electric storm / Ride of your life (with KATRINA LESKANICH) / Globes of fire – Cascades of fear / Floodflames / The volcano: Tongues of fire – Blue mountains / The end of the return.

– compilations, others, etc. –

1978. (lp) *A&M; (AMLX 68447)* **THE ROYAL PHILHARMONIC ORCHESTRA PERFORMING BEST KNOWN WORKS OF RICK WAKEMAN** [ ] [-]

May 81. (d-c) *A&M; (CAMCR 8)* **THE SIX WIVES OF HENRY VIII / THE MYTHS AND LEGENDS OF KING ARTHUR . . .** [ ] [-]

Feb 89. (4xcd-box) *A&M; (RWCD 20)* **20th ANNIVERSARY** [ ] [-]
– (THE SIX WIVES OF HENRY VIII / JOURNEY TO THE CENTRE OF THE EARTH / THE MYTHS AND LEGENDS OF KING ARTHUR AND THE KNIGHTS OF THE ROUND TABLE / WHITE ROCK)

Mar 83. (d-c) *Charisma; (CASMC 111)* **1984 / THE BURNING** [ ] [-]

May 91. (cd) *Ambient; (A-IOM-4CD)* **THE PRIVATE COLLECTION** [ ] [-]
(re-iss. Nov92 on 'Rio Digital'; RIOCD 1004) (re-iss. Feb94 on 'President'; RWCD 23)

Oct 91. (d-cd) *Ambient; (AMB5-MCD)* **THE CLASSICAL CONNECTION** [ ] [-]
(re-iss. Dec92 on 'Rio Digital'; RIOCD 1005) (re-iss. 1-cd May93 on 'President'; RWCD 13)

Oct 91. (cd) *Ambient; (A-IOM-6MCD)* **THE CLASSICAL CONNECTION II** [ ] [-]
(re-iss. Dec92 on 'Rio Digital'; RIOCD 1006) (re-iss. May93 on 'President'; RWCD 14)

Sep 93. (cd) *Icon; (ICONCD 005)* **THE VERY BEST OF RICK WAKEMAN – CHRONICLES** [ ] [-]
– (see below cd for tracks, although not YES songs)

Dec 93. (d-cd) *Fragile; (CDFRL 001)* **RICK WAKEMAN'S GREATEST HITS** (some with YES) [ ] [-]
– Roundabout / Wondrous stories / Don't kill the whale / Going for the one / Siberian khatru / Madrigal / Starship trooper/ / Overture / The journey / The Hansbach / Lost in time / The recollection / Stream of voices / The battle / Liddenbrook / The forest / Mount Etna / Journey's end / Sea horses / Catherine of Aragon / Gone but not forgotten / Merlin the magician.

Apr 94. (cd/c) *Prestige; (CDSGP 115)* **THE CLASSIC TRACKS** [ ] [-]

Jun 94. (d-cd; WAKEMAN WITH WAKEMAN) *Cyclops; (CYCLD 006)* **THE OFFICIAL LIVE BOOTLEG** [ ] [–]
(re-iss. Mar95 on 'Griffin'; GCDRW 156)
Dec 94. (cd; as RICK WAKEMAN & THE ENGLISH ROCK ENSEMBLE) *Windsong; (WHISCD 007)* **LIVE ON THE TEST (live)** [ ] [–]
Jun 95. (cd) *Disky; (RPCD 13)* **ROCK AND POP LEGENDS** [ ] [–]
Sep 95. (d-cd) *Hope; (HR 001)* **THE NEW GOSPELS** [ ] [–]
Oct 95. (cd) *Essential; (ESSCD 322)* **THE PIANO ALBUM – LIVE (live)** [ ] [–]
Nov 96. (cd) *A&M; <5852>* **VOYAGE: THE VERY BEST OF RICK WAKEMAN** [–] [ ]
– Catherine of Aragon / Catherine Howard / Jane Seymour / Anne Boleyn / Arthur / Merlin the magician / The last battle / White rock / Searching for gold / After the ball / Ice run / March of the gladiators / Summertime / Temperament of mind / Journey – Recollection / The battle – The forest / Crime of passion / Judas Iscariot / Hibernation / Free song / Maker.
May 97. (cd) *RP Media; (CDRPM 0018)* **TRIBUTE** [ ] [–]
May 99. (3xcd-box) *Music Fusion: (MFCD 001)* **NATURAL WORLD TRILOGY** [ ] [–]
May 99. (3xcd-box) *Music Fusion; (MFCD 002)* **ART IN MUSIC TRILOGY** [ ] [–]
– (THE SCULPTOR / THE WRITER / SKETCHES)
May 99. (2xcd-box) *Music Fusion; (MFCD 003)* **OFFICIAL LIVE BOOTLEG (live)** [ ] [–]
Jun 99. (cd) *Music Fusion; (MFCD 004)* **WHITE ROCK VOL.2** [ ] [–]
Jun 99. (d-cd) *Eagle; (EDMCD 086)* **THE MASTERS** [ ] [–]

Scott WALKER / The WALKER BROTHERS

Formed: Los Angeles, California, USA . . ..1964 as The WALKER BROTHERS by GARY LEEDS, SCOTT ENGEL and JOHN MAUS. LEEDS was a drummer for P.J. PROBY (previously a co-founder of The STANDELLS) and ENGEL and MAUS were playing bass and lead guitar respectively for The DALTON BROTHERS. After signing to 'Smash' Records, they were advised to try their luck in Britain and they subsequently relocated to London. Their debut single, 'PRETTY GIRLS EVERYWHERE' (with MAUS on lead vocal) flopped although their second, 'LOVE HER'(1965), scraped into the UK Top 20. After SCOTT took over on vocals they soon made No.1 twice in the UK with the 1965-66 cult easy-listening classics, 'MAKE IT EASY ON YOURSELF' (US Top 20) and 'THE SUN AIN'T GONNA SHINE ANYMORE' (also US Top 20 and written by FRANKIE VALLI). Their debut album, 'TAKE IT EASY WITH THE WALKER BROTHERS' (1966) hit the UK Top 5, followed by further smashes, 'PORTRAIT' (1966) and 'IMAGES' (1967). Later in '67, SCOTT WALKER left JOHN MAUS and GARY LEEDS (after some arguments with JOHN) and went solo, hitting the heights until the 70's (his melancholy ballads later influencing the likes of JULIAN COPE). SCOTT scored late 60's solo hits with the controversial 'JACKIE', 'JOANNA' and 'LIGHTS OF CINCINATTI' as well as the albums, 'SCOTT' (1967), 'SCOTT 2' (1968; a UK No.1) and 'SCOTT 3' (1969). He also contributed backing vocals to The BEATLES' 'All You Need Is Love' world broadcast in 1967, by this point even hosting his own TV show on BBC1. With the release of cult classic, 'SCOTT 4' (1969), however, he faded from popular stardom and languished in MOR hell for much of the early 70's. The man briefly re-emerged mid-decade as part of a reformed WALKER BROTHERS, enjoying a UK Top 10 with a cover of Tom Rush's 'NO REGRETS'. SCOTT eschewed the lure of the beckoning nostalgia circuit, however, leading the band in a radically different direction for 1978's 'NITE FLIGHTS' (the brothers' final album together). WALKER eventually resurfaced in solo mode with the tortured 'CLIMATE OF HUNTER' in 1984, hardly a record to kickstart his career. 'Virgin' were suitably unimpressed with the commercial returns and he subsequently signed to 'Fontana' in 1985. Although he recorded with BRIAN ENO, the project was never completed; similarly, SCOTT's collaborative work with former JAPAN warbler, DAVID SYLVIAN produced no concrete results. It would be a further eleven years before he came out with new work in the form of 95's 'TILT'. As out-there as WALKER has yet ventured, fans and critics alike agreed that while he mightn't be the most prolific artist, his darkly compelling experiments are worth waiting for. • **Songwriters:** WALKER BROTHERS covered (45's only); LOVE HER (Mann-Weill) / MAKE IT EASY ON YOURSELF (Jerry Butler) / MY SHIP IS COMING IN (Jimmy Radcliffe) / THE SUN AIN'T GONNA SHINE ANYMORE (Frankie Valli) / LOVE MINUS ZERO (Bob Dylan) / ANOTHER TEAR FALLS (Gene McDaniels) / STAY WITH ME BABY (Lorraine Ellison) / WALKING IN THE RAIN (Ronettes) / NO REGRETS (Tom Rush) / etc. SCOTT WALKER covers; JACKIE and others from 'SCOTT 2' lp (Jacques Brel). JOANNA (Tony Hatch & Jackie Trent). On his 'STRETCH' country roots album, several songs were written by BILLY JOE SHAVER. • **Trivia:** In 1987, SCOTT appeared in TV ads for Britvic juice.

Best CD compilation(s): Walker Brothers: AFTER THE LIGHTS GO OUT: THE BEST OF 1965-1967 (*7) / NO REGRETS: THE BEST OF . . . (*6; shared with Scott Walker)

Album rating: SCOTT (*7) / SCOTT 2 (*8) / SCOTT (*7) / . . .SINGS SONGS FROM HIS TV SERIES special (*4) / SCOTT 4 (*8) / 'TIL THE BAND COMES IN (*6) / THE MOVIEGOER (*4) / ANY DAY NOW (*4) / STRETCH (*4) / WE HAD IT ALL (*4) / FIRE ESCAPE IN THE SKY: THE GODLIKE GENIUS OF SCOTT WALKER compilation (*7) / SCOTT WALKER SINGS JACQUES BREL collection (*6) / CLIMATE OF HUNTER (*7) / BOY CHILD; THE BEST OF SCOTT WALKER 1967-1970 compilation (*8) / TILT (*5) / POLA X soundtrack (*6)

SCOTT ENGEL

(aka SCOTT WALKER) – vocals

		Vogue	Orbit
Aug 58.	(7") *<511>* **CHARLIE BOP. / ALL I DO IS DREAM OF YOU**	–	
Oct 58.	(7") *(V 9125)* **BLUEBELL. / PAPER DOLL**		
Jun 59.	(7") *(V 9145) <506>* **THE LIVIN' END. / GOOD FOR NOTHIN'**	Jun58	
Sep 59.	(7") *<537>* **SUNDAY. / GOLDEN RULE OF LOVE**	–	
Nov 59.	(7") **I DON'T WANNA KNOW. / COMIN' HOME**	–	

—— Continued to do session work until 1962 when he joined The ROUTERS alongside JOHN STEWART. They released 2 singles late 62-early 63, 'LET'S GO WITH THE ROUTERS' & 'MAKE IT SNAPPY'. After a spell with the SANDY NELSON band, he and JOHN joined The MOONGOONERS. They issued singles MOONGOON STOMP and MOONGOON TWIST in 1963. The following year, they became The DALTONS duo releasing one 45, 'I ONLY CAME TO DANCE WITH YOU'. SCOTT was now part of the famous trio.

WALKER BROTHERS

SCOTT ENGEL (WALKER)(b. 9 Jan'44, Hamilton, Ohio) – vocals, bass, keyboards / **JOHN MAUS** (WALKER)(b.12 Nov'43, New York City, N.Y.) – vocals, guitar / **GARY LEEDS** (WALKER) (b. 3 Sep'44, Glendale, Calif.) – drums, vocals

		Philips	Smash
Feb 65.	(7") *<1952>* **PRETTY GIRLS EVERYWHERE. / DOIN' THE JERK**	–	
Apr 65.	(7") *(BF 1409) <1976>* **LOVE HER. / THE SEVENTH DAWN**	20	
Aug 65.	(7") *(BF 1428) <2000>* **MAKE IT EASY ON YOURSELF. / BUT I DO**	1 Jul65	
Sep 65.	(7") *<2009>* **MAKE IT EASY ON YOURSELF. / DOIN' THE JERK**	–	16
Nov 65.	(7") *(BF 1454) <2016>* **MY SHIP IS COMING IN. / YOU'RE ALL AROUND ME**	3	63

Dec 65. (lp) *(SBL 7691)* **TAKE IT EASY WITH THE WALKER BROTHERS** [4] [–]
– Make it easy for yourself / There goes my baby / First love never dies / Dancing in the street / Lonely winds / The girl I lost in the rain / Land of 1000 dances / You're all around me / Love minus zero / I don't want to hear it anymore / Here comes the night / Tell the truth.

Feb 66. (7") *(BF 1473) <2032>* **THE SUN AIN'T GONNA SHINE ANYMORE. / AFTER THE LIGHTS GO OUT** [1] [13]

Jul 66. (7") *(BF 1497) <2048>* **(BABY) YOU DON'T HAVE TO TELL ME. / MY LOVE IS GROWING** [13] [ ]

Aug 66. (lp) *(SBL 7732)* **PORTRAIT** [3] [ ]
– In my room / Saturday's child / Just for a thrill / Hurting each other / Old folks / Summertime / People get ready / I can see it now / Where's the girl / Living above your head / Take it like a man / No sad songs for me.

Sep 66. (7") *(BF 1514) <2063>* **ANOTHER TEAR FALLS. / SADDEST NIGHT IN THE WORLD** [12] [ ]

Nov 66. (7") *(BF 1537)* **DEADLIER THAN THE MALE (theme from the film). / ARC ANGEL** [34] [–]

Jan 67. (7") *(BF 1548)* **STAY WITH ME BABY. / TURN OUT THE MOON** [26] [–]

Mar 67. (lp) *(SBL 7770)* **IMAGES** [6] [ ]
– Everything under the sun / Once upon a summertime / Experience / Blueberry Hill / Orpheus / Stand by me / I wanna know / I willwait for you / It makes no difference now / I can't let it happen to you / Genevieve / Just say goodbye.

May 67. (7") *(BF 1576)* **WALKING IN THE RAIN. / BABY MAKE IT THE LAST TIME** [26] [–]

— Disbanded May '67

SCOTT WALKER

re-issued old recordings

Liberty | Liberty

1966. (7"ep; as SCOTT ENGEL) *(LEP 2261)* **SCOTT ENGEL** [ ] [–]
– I broke my own heart / What do you say / Are these really mine / Crazy in love with you.

Capitol | Capitol

May 66. (7"; with JOHN STEWART) *(CL 15440)* **I ONLY CAME TO DANCE WITH YOU. / GREENS** [ ] [ ]

Philips | not iss.

Dec 66. (7"ep; 1-side by JOHN MAUS) *(BE 12597)* **SOLO SCOTT – SOLO JOHN** [ ] [–]
– (SCOTT WALKER:- The gentle rain / Mrs. Murphy.

— solo after the WALKER BROTHERS split

Philips | Smash

Aug 67. (lp; stereo/mono) *(S+/BL 7816)* **SCOTT** [3] [ ]
– Mathilde / Montague Terrace (in blue) / Angelica / Lady came from Baltimore / When Joanna loved me / My death / Through a long and sleepless night / The big hurt / Such a small love / You're gonna hear from me / Always coming back to me / Amsterdam. *(re-iss. Mar92 & Jun00 on 'Fontana' cd/c; 510 879-2/-4)*

Nov 67. (7") *(BF 1628) <2156>* **JACKIE. / THE PLAGUE** [22] [ ]

Mar 68. (lp; stereo/mono) *(S+/BL 7840)* **SCOTT 2** [1] [ ]
– Jackie / Best of both worlds / The amorous Humphrey Plugg / Black sheep boy / Next / The girls from the street / Plastic palace people / Wait until dark / The girls and the dogs / Windows of the world / The bridge / Come next Spring. *(re-iss. Aug92 & Jun00 on 'Fontana' cd/c; 510 880-2/-4)*

Apr 68. (7") *(BF 1662) <2168>* **JOANNA. / ALWAYS COMING BACK TO YOU** [7] [ ]

Mar 69. (lp) *(SBL 7882)* **SCOTT 3** [3] [ ]
– It's raining today / Copenhagen / Rosemary / Big Louise / We came through / Butterfly / Two ragged soldiers / 30th century man / Winter night / Two weeks since you've gone / Sons of / Funeral tango / If you go away. *(re-iss. Aug92 & Jun00 on 'Fontana' cd/c; 510 881-2/-4)*

Jun 69. (7") *(BF 1793) <2228>* **LIGHTS OF CINCINNATI. / TWO WEEKS SINCE YOU'VE GONE** [13] [ ]

Jun 69. (lp) *(SBL 7900)* **. . . SINGS SONGS FROM HIS TV SERIES** [7] [ ]
– I have dreamed / The impossible dream / Will you still be mine / When the world was young / Who (will take my place) / If she walked into my life / The song is you / The look of love / Country girl / Someone to light up my life / Only the young / Lost in the stars.

Nov 69. (lp; as NOEL SCOTT ENGEL) *(SBL 7913)* **SCOTT 4** [ ] [ ]
– The seventh seal / On your own again / World's strongest man / Angels of ashes / Boy child / The old man's back again / Hero of the war / Duchess / Get behind me / Rhymes of goodbye. *(re-iss. Aug92 & Jun00 on 'Fontana' cd/c; 510 882-2/-4)*

Dec 70. (lp) *(6308 035)* **'TIL THE BAND COMES IN** [ ] [ ]
– Prologue / Little things (that keep us together) / Jean the machine / Joe / Thanks for Chicago, Mr. James / Long about now / Time operator / Cowbells shakin' / 'Til the band comes in / The war is over / Stormy / The hills of yesterday / What are you doing the rest of your life / Rueben James / It's over. *(cd-iss. Aug96 on 'Beat Goes On'; BGOCD 320)*

Oct 71. (7") *(6006 168)* **I STILL SEE YOU. / MY WAY HOME** [ ] [–]

Oct 72. (lp) *(6308 127)* **THE MOVIEGOER** [ ] [–]
– This way Mary / Speak softly love / Glory road / That night / The summer of '42 / Easy come easy go / The ballad of Sacco and Vanzetti (here's to you) / Face in the crowd / Joe Hill / All his children / Come Saturday morning / The look of love. *(re-iss. on 'Contour'; 6870 633)*

May 73. (7") *(6006 311)* **THE ME I NEVER KNEW. / THIS WAY MARY** [ ] [ ]

May 73. (lp) *(6308 148)* **ANY DAY NOW** [ ] [ ]
– Any day now / All my love's laughter / Do I love you / Ain't no sunshine / Maria Bethania / Cowboy / When you get right down to it / The me I never knew / If ships were made to sail / We could be flying.

C.B.S. | Columbia

Oct 73. (7") *(1795)* **A WOMAN LEFT LONELY. / WHERE LOVE HAS DIED** [ ] [ ]

Nov 73. (lp) *(65725)* **STRETCH** [ ] [ ]
– Sunshine / Just one smile / A woman left lonely / No easy way down / That's how I got to Memphis / Use me / Frisco depot / Someone who cared / Where does brown begin / Where love has died / I'll be home.

Jul 74. (7") *(2521)* **DELTA DAWN. / WE HAD IT ALL** [ ] [–]

Aug 74. (lp) *(80254)* **WE HAD IT ALL** [ ] [ ]
– Low down freedom / We had it all / Black rose / Ride me down easy / You're young and you'll forget / The house song / Old five and dimers like me / Whatever happened to Saturday night / Sundown / Delta dawn.

— SCOTT shelved solo career when the WALKERS re-formed in 1975

WALKER BROTHERS

— (SCOTT, JOHN & GARY) / on session were **BIG JIM SULLIVAN** – guitar / **ALAN SKIDMORE / BRIAN BENNETT + CHRIS MERCER**

G.T.O. | G.T.O.

Oct 75. (lp) *(GTLP 007)* **NO REGRETS** [49] [ ]
– No regrets / Hold an old friend's hand / I've got to have you / Boulder to Birmingham / Lover's lullaby / Walkers' in the Sun / Half break your heart / Everything that touches you / Lovers / Burn our bridges. *(re-iss. Jul77; same) (re-iss. May94 on 'Sony' cd/c; 983276-2/-4) (cd re-iss. Sep94 on 'Rewind'; 477354-2)*

Nov 75. (7") *(GT 42)* **NO REGRETS. / REMEMBER ME** [7] [ ]

Jul 76. (lp) *(GTLP 014)* **LINES** [ ] [ ]
– Lines / Taking it all in stride / Inside of you / Have you seen my baby / We're all alone / Many rivers to cross / Hard to be friends / First day / Brand new Tennessee waltz / Dreaming as one. *(cd-iss. Mar96 on 'Columbia'; 483674-2)*

Sep 76. (7") *(GT 67)* **LINES. / FIRST DAY** [ ] [–]

Jun 77. (7") *(GT 78)* **WE'RE ALL ALONE. / HAVE YOU SEEN MY BABY** [ ] Nov76 [ ]

Jul 78. (7") *(GT 230)* **THE ELECTRICIAN. / DEN HAAGUE** [ ] [–]

Jul 78. (lp) *(GTLP 033)* **NITE FLIGHTS** [ ] [–]
– Shutout / Fat mama kick / Nite flights / The electrician / Death of romance / Den Haague / Rhythms of vision / Child of flames / Disciples of death / Fury and the fire. *(cd-iss. Jul96 on 'Epic'; 484438-2)*

— Split again in 1978 for the last time.

– (selected WALKERs) compilations, etc. –

Sep 67. (d-lp) *Philips; (DBL 002)* **THE WALKER BROTHERS STORY** [9] [ ]

Dec 91. (cd/c/lp) *Fontana; (510831-2/-4/-1)* **NO REGRETS – THE BEST OF SCOTT WALKER AND THE WALKER BROTHERS 1965-1976** [4] [ ]
– (* denotes SCOTT WALKER track) – No regrets / Make it easy on yourself / The Sun ain't gonna shine anymore / My ship is comin' in / * Joanna / * Lights of Cincinatti / Another tear falls / * Boy child / * Montague Terrace in blue / * Jackie / Stay with me baby / * If you go away / First love never dies / Love her / Walking in the rain / (Baby) You don't have to tell me / Deadlier than the male / We're all alone. *(re-dist.Jul00)* – hit UK No.55

SCOTT WALKER

— went solo again in '84

Virgin Virgin

Mar 84. (7") *(VS 666)* **TRACK 3. / BLANKET ROLL BLUES**

Mar 84. (lp/c) *(T/TCV 2303)* **CLIMATE OF HUNTER** [60]
– Rawhide / Dealer / Track 3 / Sleepwalker's woman / Track 5 / Track 6 / Track 7 / Blanket roll blues. *(re-iss. Aug88 lp/c; OVED/+C 149) (cd-iss. Nov89; CDV 2303)*

— retired from music until . . .

Fontana Drag City

May 95. (cd/lp) *(526 859-2/-1)* <DC 134CD> **TILT** [27] Nov97
– Farmer in the city / The cockfighter / Bouncer see bouncer . . . / Manhattan / Face on breast / Bolivia '95 / Patriot (a single) / Tilt / Rosary.

Barclay not iss.

Jun 00. (cd) *(547608-2)* **POLA X** (soundtrack) [–] French [–]
– The time is out of joint / Light / Meadow / The darkest forest / Extra blues (by SMOG) / Never again / Iza kana zanbi (by FAIRUZ) / Trang mo ben suo / Zai na yao yuan de di fang / The church of the apostles / Bombupper / River of blood / Blink (by SONIC YOUTH) / Running / Closing / Isabel.

– (selective SCOTT) compilations, etc. –

on 'Philips' unless otherwise stated

Dec 67. (lp) *Ember; (EMB 3393)* **LOOKING BACK WITH SCOTT WALKER** [–]
(cd-iss. Nov00 & Jul02 on 'Repertoire'; REP 4604)

Jan 70. (lp) *(SBL 7910)* **THE BEST OF SCOTT WALKER** [–]
(re-iss. Nov71 as 'THIS IS SCOTT WALKER'; 6382 007) (re-iss. Jun82; 6381 073) (re-iss. Oct83; PRICE 43)

Oct 72. (lp) *(6382 052)* **THIS IS SCOTT WALKER – VOL.2** [–]

Nov 81. (lp) *(6359 090)* **SINGS JAQUES BREL** [–]
(cd-iss. Sep92 on 'Fontana' cd/c; 838212-2/-4)

Sep 81. (lp) *Zoo; (ZOO 2)* **FIRE ESCAPE IN THE SKY – THE GODLIKE GENIUS OF SCOTT WALKER** [–]

Jun 90. (cd/c/lp) *Fontana; <(842832-2/-4/-1)>* **BOY CHILD: 67-70** 1992
– Montague Terrace (in blue) / Such a small love / The amorous Humphrey Plugg / The girl from the streets / Plastic palace people / The bridge / It's raining today / Copenhagen / Big Louise / We came through / The seventh seal / On your own again / Boy child / The old man's back again (dedicated to the neo-Stalinist regime) / Angels of ashes / Prologue / Little things (that keep us together) / Time operator / Epilogue, the war is over (sleepers). *(re-iss. Jun00; 542705-2)*

Dec 96. (cd) *Razor & Tie; (RE 2120-2)* **IT'S RAINING TODAY: THE SCOTT WALKER STORY 1967-1970** [–]

May 97. (cd) *Beat Goes On; <(BGOCD 358)>* **STRETCH / WE HAD IT ALL**

Dec 97. (cd) *Spalax; (14566)* **EARLY TEN YEARS** [–]

Mar 99. (cd) *Fontana; (538609-2)* **SCOTT ON SCREEN** [–]

Mar 01. (cd/c) *Castle Pulse; (PLS CD/MC 367)* **IN THE BEGINNING** [–]

Jul 01. (cd) *Platinum; (PLATCD 672)* **14 ORIGINAL RECORDINGS** [–]

WALLFLOWERS

Formed: New York, USA ... 1990 by frontman and more significantly, the son of BOB DYLAN, JAKOB DYLAN. With the line-up completed by RAMI JAFFE, TOBY MILLER, BARRY MAGUIRE and PETER YANOWITZ, The WALLFLOWERS had no problem securing a major label contract ('Virgin') with which to release their eponymous 1992 debut. Sounding pretty much like you'd expect for the son of rock's great roots man, the album met with a fair amount of critical praise in their native America although the lack of a bonafide hit single led to marginal sales. Following major internal changes at Virgin, the band were conspicuous by their absence from the music scene over the course of the next few years as they set up a new contract with 'Interscope' and recruited newcomers MICHAEL WARD and MARIO CALIRE. DYLAN Jnr & Co. eventually resurfaced in '96 with a T-BONE BURNETT-produced follow-up, 'BRINGING DOWN THE HORSE', a slow burning gem which featured contributions from such alt-country figureheads as GARY LOURIS (of The JAYHAWKS) and COUNTING CROWS. Residing in the US charts for over a year, the album finally peaked at No.4 as word spread among roots-rock afficionados. After an extended lay-off, the WALLFLOWERS returned with '(BREACH)' (2000), further evidence, if any was needed, that JAKOB has not only emerged completely from the towering shadow of his father but has inherited that seemingly indestructable songwriting gene that will see him stay the course. Given the ultimately disappointing reception afforded '(BREACH)', the band strove to smooth out the rough edges and sharpen the hooks on 'RED LETTER DAYS' (2002), presumably in an attempt to woo back the fans who'd strayed since the mid-90's. DYLAN's songwriting still stood head and shoulders above his contemporaries, it's just a pity it wasn't more appreciated.

Album rating: THE WALLFLOWERS (*5) / BRINGING DOWN THE HORSE (*7) / (BREACH) (*7) / RED LETTER DAYS (*6)

JAKOB DYLAN (b. 1970) – vocals, guitar / **RAMI JAFFE** – keyboards / **TOBI MILLER** – guitar / **BARRIE MAGUIRE** – bass / **PETER YANOWITZ** – drums

Virgin America Virgin

Sep 92. (cd/c) *(CDVUS/VUSMC 54)* <86293> **THE WALLFLOWERS** Aug92
– Shy of the moon / Sugarfoot / Sidewalk Annie / Hollywood / Be your own girl / Another one in the dark / Ashes to ashes / After the blackbird sings / Somebody else's money / Asleep at the wheel / Honeybee / For the love of me.

— **GREG RICHLING** – bass; repl. MAGUIRE

— **MICHAEL WARD** – guitar; repl. MILLER

— **MARIO CALIRE** – drums; repl. YANOWITZ

Interscope Interscope

Aug 96. (cd/c) *<(IND/INC 90055)>* **BRINGING DOWN THE HORSE** May96 [4]
– One headlight / 6th Avenue heartache / Bleeders / Three Marlenas / Difference / Invisible city / Laughing out loud / Josephine / God don't make lonely girls / Angel on my bike / I wish I felt nothing. *(re-iss. Jun97 hit UK No.58; same)*

Jun 97. (7") *(INS 95532)* **ONE HEADLIGHT. / 6th AVENUE HEARTACHE** [54] Mar97
(cd-s+=) *(IND 95532)* – Angel on my bike (live).

Mar 98. (c-s) *(INC 95574)* **THREE MARLENAS / ONE HEADLIGHT**
(cd-s+=) *(IND 95574)* – ('A'live).

Dec 98. (cd-s) <66416> **HEROES / INVISIBLE CITY** [–]
(above issued on 'Sony')

Oct 00. (-) <radio cut> **SLEEPWALKER** [–] [73]

Oct 00. (cd) *(490817-2)* <490745> **(BREACH)** Sep00 [13]
– Letters from the wasteland / Hand me down / Sleepwalker / I've been delivered / Witness / Some flowers bloom dead / Mourning train / Up from under / Murder 101 / Birdcage. *(UK+=)* – Sleepwalker (demo) / Sleepwalker (video).

— now without WARD; repl. by session guitarists

Nov 02. (cd) *<(493491-2)>* **RED LETTER DAYS** [32]
– When you're on top / How good it can get / Closer to you / Everybody out of the water / Three ways / Too late to quit / If you never got sick / Health and happiness / See you when I get there / Feels like summer again / Everything I need / Here in Pleasantville. *(hidden track+=)* – Empire of my mind.

Joe WALSH

Born: 20th Nov'47, Wichita, Kansas, USA, the classically-trained son of a piano playing mother. In 1969, having spent the previous four years imitating the fret work of guitar idols, JEFF BECK and JIMMY PAGE, while studying at Kent State University (in Cleveland, Ohio), WALSH joined The JAMES GANG. He quit the 'GANG for a solo career late in '71, after contributing his much lauded star quality to three studio albums, 'YER ALBUM', 'RIDES AGAIN' and 'THIRDS'. Keeping his hard-rock roots firmly intact and adding harmonies, WALSH named his new backing band, BARNSTORM (KENNY PASSARELLI on bass and JOE VITALE on drums), also the title of his debut US Top 100 album released in '72. A follow-up, the strangely-titled 'THE SMOKER YOU DRINK, THE PLAYER YOU GET' (with the addition of ROCKE GRACE on keyboards and JOE LALA on percussion), thundered up the American charts into the Top 10. The single from it, 'ROCKY MOUNTAIN WAY' (Top 30), complete with his new 'talkbox', became a classic in its own right, the guitar work and countrified wail of WALSH making him a focal point par excellence. His third set, 'SO WHAT' (1974), featured guest spots from The EAGLES, J.D. SOUTHER and DAN FOGELBERG (JW produced and performed on his 'Souvenirs'), while BARNSTORM took a back seat on around half the tracks. The record just failed to match its predecessor, WALSH subsequently forming a new stage band comprising of drummer RICKY FATAAR (ex-BEACH BOYS), bassist BRYAN GAROFALO and keyboard players DAVID MASON and PAUL HARRIS, a concert set, 'YOU CAN'T ARGUE WITH A SICK MIND', belatedly reaching the Top 20 in the Spring of '76. By this time, WALSH had shocked the rock world, taking the place of BERNIE LEADON in The EAGLES, his contributions to their classic 'Hotel California' (1976), certainly giving the once proud kings of country-rock a harder edge. He remained with the group for the rest of the 70's, reactivating his solo career in 1978 with the celebrated hit single 'LIFE'S BEEN GOOD' taken from another platinum album, 'BUT SERIOUSLY FOLKS . . .'. From 1980 to 1988, he became a semi-serious candidate at the US presidential elections, his recording work understandably a little sporadic and unremarkable during this time (although he did find time to perform a cameo appearance in the 'Blues Brothers' film). Mellowed-down soft-rock albums such as 'THERE GOES THE NEIGHBORHOOD' (1981), 'YOU BOUGHT IT – YOU NAME IT' (1983), 'THE CONFESSOR' (1985) and 'GOT ANY GUM' (1987). all sold moderately well in the States, the former more successful due to the appearance of another major hit, 'LIFE OF ILLUSION'. In 1991, WALSH released his umpteenth set, 'ORDINARY AVERAGE GUY', probably never a truer self-analysis of one of the great guitarists of the 70's. A few years later, the man was back on the "Vote For Me" campaign trail, subsequently rejoining The EAGLES on a reunion set; the album did little to win back the critics, although their concerts sold out everywhere. • **Covered:** WILL YOU STILL LOVE ME TOMORROW? (Goffin-King) / WE GOTTA GET YOU A WOMAN (Todd Rundgren) / IN-A-GADDA-DA-VIDA (Iron Butterfly) / SHAKE YOUR BOOTY (KC & The Sunshine Band) / etc.

Album rating: BARNSTORM (*6) / THE SMOKER YOU DRINK, THE PLAYER YOU GET (*7) / SO WHAT (*5) / YOU CAN'T ARGUE WITH A SICK MIND (*6) / BUT SERIOUSLY FOLKS . . . (*5) / SO FAR SO GOOD – THE BEST OF JOE WALSH compilation (*8) / THERE GOES THE NEIGHBOURHOOD (*5) / YOU BOUGHT IT – YOU NAME IT (*4) / THE CONFESSOR (*4) / GOT ANY GUM? (*4) / ORDINARY AVERAGE GUY (*5) / SONGS FOR A DYING PLANET (*3) / A FUTURE TO THIS LIFE (*3) / LOOK WHAT I DID: THE JOE WALSH ANTHOLOGY compilation (*8)

JOE WALSH – vocals, guitar (ex-JAMES GANG) with his band BARNSTORM: **KENNY PASSARELLI** – bass / **JOE VITALE** – drums

Probe — Dunhill

Oct 72. (7") *<4327>* **MOTHER SAYS. / I'LL TELL THE WORLD ABOUT YOU** [–] [ ]

Jan 73. (lp) *(6268) <50130>* **BARNSTORM** [ ] Oct72 [79]
– Here we go / Midnight visitor / One and one / Giant bohemoth / Mother says / Birdcall morning / Home / I'll tell the world about you / Turn to stone / Comin' down. *(re-iss. Oct74 on 'A.B.C.'; ABCL 5022)*

—— added **ROCKE GRACE** – keyboards / **JOE LALA** – percussion

Aug 73. (7") *(PRO 600) <4361>* **ROCKY MOUNTAIN WAY. / (DAYDREAM) PRAYER** [ ] [23]
(UK-iss.Jul75 on 'A.B.C.'; 4061)

Sep 73. (lp) *<50140>* **THE SMOKER YOU DRINK, THE PLAYER YOU GET** [ ] Jun73 [6]
– Rocky mountain way / Bookends / Wolf / Midnight moodies / Happy ways / Meadows / Dreams / Days gone by / (Daydream) Prayer. *(re-iss. quad.Oct74 on 'A.B.C.'; ABCL 5033) (cd-iss. Apr92 on 'M.C.A.'; MCLD 19020)*

Jan 74. (7") *(PRO 611) <4373>* **MEADOWS. / BOOKENDS** [ ] Dec73 [89]
(re-iss. Mar76 on 'A.B.C.'; 4105)

—— In 1974, he sessioned for EAGLES, B.B. KING, etc., and produced DAN FOGELBERG

—— Solo; used past BARNSTORM members on a couple of tracks, plus new studio & live line-up **DAVID MASON** + **PAUL HARRIS** – keyboards / **BRYAN GAROFOLO** – bass / **RICKY FATAAR** – drums (ex-BEACH BOYS) / **TOM STEPHENSON** – keyboards

Anchor — Dunhill

Dec 74. (lp) *(ABCL 5055) <50171>* **SO WHAT** [ ] [11]
– Welcome to the club / Falling down / Pavane / Time out / All night laundromat blues / Turn to stone / Help me thru the night / County fair / Song for Emma.

Feb 75. (7") *(ABC 4035) <15026>* **TURN TO STONE. / ALL NIGHT LAUNDROMAT BLUES** [ ] [93]

—— although he was still a solo artist, WALSH joined EAGLES late '75.

A.B.C. — A.B.C.

Apr 76. (lp) *(ABLC 5156) <932>* **YOU CAN'T ARGUE WITH A SICK MIND (live)** [28] [20]
– Walk away / Meadows / Rocky mountain way / Tell me / Help me through the night / Turn to stone. *(re-iss. Jan83 on 'Fame' lp/c; FA/TCFA 3051) <US cd-iss. Jun88; 31120>*

Apr 76. (7") *<12115>* **TIME OUT (live). / HELP ME THRU THE NIGHT (live)** [–] [ ]

Jun 76. (7") *(ABC 4121)* **WALK AWAY (live). / HELP ME THRU THE NIGHT (live)** [ ] [–]

—— WALSH used mainly session people + VITALE

Asylum — Asylum

Jun 78. (7") *(K 13129) <45493>* **LIFE'S BEEN GOOD. / THEME FROM BOAT WEIRDOS** [14] [12]

Jun 78. (lp/c) *(K/K4 53081) <141>* **BUT SERIOUSLY, FOLKS . . .** [16] [8]
– Over and over / Second hand store / Indian summer / At the station / Tomorrow / Inner tube / Theme from Boat Weirdos / Life's been good. *(cd-iss. Feb93 on 'WEA'; 7559 60527-2)*

Nov 78. (7") *(K 13141) <45536>* **OVER AND OVER. / AT THE STATION** [ ] [ ]
below from the film 'Urban Cowboy'. B-side by GILLEY'S URBAN COWBOY BAND. On 'Full Moon' in America.

Jun 80. (7") *(K 79146) <46639>* **ALL NIGHT LONG. / ORANGE BLOSSOM SPECIAL / HOEDOWN** [ ] May80 [19]

—— now an ex-EAGLES man after that group's split

May 81. (7") *<47144>* **A LIFE OF ILLUSION. / ROCKETS** [–] [34]

May 81. (7") *(K 12533)* **A LIFE OF ILLUSION. / DOWN ON THE FARM** [ ] [–]

May 81. (lp/c) *(K/K4 52285) <523>* **THERE GOES THE NEIGHBORHOOD** [ ] [20]
– Things / Made your mind up / Down on the farm / Rivers (of the hidden funk) / A life of illusion / Bones / Rockets / You never know.

Jul 81. (7") *<47197>* **MADE YOUR MIND UP. / THINGS** [–] [ ]

Jan 82. (7") *<69951>* **WAFFLE STOMP. / THINGS** [–] [ ]

Full Moon — Warners

Jun 83. (7") *<29611>* **SPACE AGE WHIZ KIDS. / THEME FROM ISLAND WEIRDOS** [–] [52]

Jul 83. (lp/c) *(923884-1/-4) <23884>* **YOU BOUGHT IT – YOU NAME IT** [ ] [48]
– I can play that rock & roll / Told you so / Here we are now / The worry song / I.L.B.T.'s / Space age whiz kids / Love letters / Class of '65 / Shadows / Theme from Island weirdos. *(cd-iss. Jul84; 923884-2) (cd re-iss. Jul96 on 'WEA'; 7559 23884-2)*

Aug 83. (7") *<29519>* **I CAN PLAY THAT ROCK & ROLL. / HERE WE ARE NOW** [–] [ ]

Sep 83. (7") *(W 9841)* **LOVE LETTERS. / TOLD YOU SO** [ ] [–]

Nov 83. (7") *<29454>* **LOVE LETTERS. / I.L.B.T.'s** [–] [ ]

Jun 85. (7") *<28910>* **I BROKE MY LEG. / GOOD MAN DOWN** [–] [ ]

Jun 85. (lp/c) *(925281-1/-4) <25281>* **THE CONFESSOR** [ ] May85 [65]
– Problems / I broke my leg / Bubbles / Slow dancing / 15 years / Confessor / Rosewood bitters / Good man down / Dear John. *(cd-iss. Jul88; 925606-2)*

— now with **CHAD CROMWELL** – drums / **DAVID COCHRAN + RICK THE . . . PLAYER** – bass / **MARK RIVERA** – saxophone / **JOHN DAVID SOUTHER + JIMI JAMISON** – backing vocals

Aug 87. (lp/c/cd) *(925606-1/-4/-2) <25606>* **GOT ANY GUM?** [ ] Jul87 [ ]
– The radio song / Fun / In my car / Malibu / Half of the time / Got any gum? / Up to me / No peace in the jungle / Memory lane / Time. *(cd re-iss. Jan96 on 'WEA'; 7599 25606-2)*

Aug 87. (7") *<28304>* **THE RADIO SONG. / HOW YA DOIN'** [–] [ ]

Nov 87. (7") *<28225>* **IN MY CAR. / HOW YA DOIN'** [–] [ ]

Epic Pyramid-Epic

Jul 91. (cd/c/lp) *(468128-2/-4/-1) <47384>* **ORDINARY AVERAGE GUY** [ ] May91 [ ]
– Two sides to every story / Ordinary average guy / The gamma goochee / All of a sudden / Alphabetical order / Look at us now / I'm actin' different / Up all night / You might need somebody / Where I grew up (prelude to schooldays).

Jul 91. (7") *<73843>* **ORDINARY AVERAGE GUY. / ALPHABETICAL ORDER** [–] [ ]

May 92. (cd/c) *<ZK 78916>* **SONGS FOR A DYING PLANET** [–] [ ]
– Shut up / Fairbanks, Alaska / Coyote love / I know / Certain situations / Vote for me / Theme from baroque weirdos / Friend song / It's all right / Will you still you love me tomorrow? / Decades / Song for a dying planet.

Apr 95. (cd-ep; JOE WALSH & LITA FORD) **A FUTURE TO HIS LIFE /** [–] [ ]

Apr 95. (cd) *<71888>* **A FUTURE TO THIS LIFE** (ROBOCOP: THE SERIES SOUNDTRACK) [–] [ ]
– A future to this life / Guilty of the crime / Fire and brimstone / Chutes and ladders / Flannel / Jacket / We gotta get you a woman / I only have eyes for you / Stuff ya gotta watch / In-a-gadda-da-vida / Shake your booty / Robocop adventure.

– compilations, others, etc. –

Jun 77. (7") *A.B.C.; (12426>* **ROCKY MOUNTAIN WAY. / TURN TO STONE** [–] [ ]

Jun 77. (12"ep) *A.B.C.; (ABE 12-002)* **PLUS FOUR EP** [39] [–]
– Rocky mountain way / Turn to stone / Meadows / Walk away.

Oct 78. (lp/c) *A.B.C.; (ABCL/+C 5240) <1083>* **SO FAR SO GOOD – THE BEST OF JOE WALSH** [ ] [71]
– Rocky mountain way / Welcome to the club / Bookends / Walk away / Mother says / Turn to stone / Here we go / Pavane / Time out / Meadows. *(re-iss. 1983 on 'M.C.A.' lp/c; MCL/+C 1751) (cd-iss. 1987; MCAD 1601) (cd re-iss. Jun97 on 'Half Moon'; HMNCD 007)*

Aug 82. (7") *M.C.A.; (MCA 787)* **ROCKY MOUNTAIN WAY. / TURN TO STONE** [ ] [–]
(12"pic-d+=) *(MCATP 787)* – Funk 49.

Apr 86. (7") *Old Gold; (OG 9599)* **ROCKY MOUNTAIN WAY. / (b-side by Poco)** [ ] [–]

Oct 87. (d-cd) *M.C.A.; (DMCL 1874)* **THE SMOKER YOU DRINK . . . / YOU CAN'T ARGUE WITH A SICK MIND** [ ] [–]
(re-iss. Apr92; MCLD 19020) (re-iss. Jul96; MCD 33728)

Sep 89. (lp/c) *Raw Power; (RAW LP/TC 036)* **WELCOME TO THE CLUB** [ ] [–]

May 94. (cd/c; JOE WALSH & THE JAMES GANG) *Pickwick; (PWK S/MC 4207)* **ALL THE BEST** [ ] [–]

Jul 95. (d-cd) *M.C.A.; (MCD 11233)* **LOOK WHAT I DID: THE JOE WALSH ANTHOLOGY** [ ] [–]
– Tuning, part 1 / Take a look around / Funk #48 / Bomber / Tend my garden / Funk #49 / Ashes, the rain and I / Walk away / It's all the same / Midnight man / Here we go / Midnight visitor / Mother says / Turn to stone / Comin' down / Meadows / Rocky mountain way / Welcome to the club / All night laundry mat blues / Country fair / Help me thru the night / Life's been good / Over and over / A life of illusion / Theme from the Island Weirdos / I can play that rock and roll / I.L.B.T.'s / Space age whiz kids / Rosewood bitters / Shut up / Decades / Song for a dying planet / Ordinary average guy (live with GLENN FREY).

Jun 97. (cd) *Half Moon; (HMNCD 007)* **THE BEST OF JOE WALSH** [ ] [ ]

WAR

Formed: 1969 . . . out of Compton/South Bay, L.A. outfit The CREATORS. An eclectic R&B combo with a strong Latino influence, The CREATORS released a few singles in the mid-60's but failed to make much of an impact outside of their native California. They did, however, pre-figure their soul/blues/rock partnership with white R&B merchant ERIC BURDON by hooking up with LOVE sax player TJAY CONTRELLI for a series of L.A. club dates (actual recordings of this bizarre partnership are rumoured to exist although they've never been commercially released). In 1968, The CREATORS metamorphasised into The NIGHTSHIFT, the group subsequently backing up American football figurehead, Deacon Jones, who was attempting to re-invent himself as a club crooner. WAR were saved from such a fate by producer/songwriter Jerry Goldstein, who introduced the band to ex-ANIMALS singer ERIC BURDON, fresh from England and looking to get hip to the West Coast scene. Renaming themselves WAR, the group (who at this stage comprised LONNIE JORDAN, HOWARD SCOTT, CHARLES MILLER, HAROLD BROWN, LEE OSKAR, B.B. DICKERSON and PAPA DEE ALLEN) recorded two albums with BURDON, 'ERIC BURDON DECLARES WAR' (1970) and 'BLACK MAN'S BURDON' (1971; 1970 US). Though the strangely infectious rhythms of Top 3 hit, 'SPILL THE WINE', boded well, the debut sounded stodgy and directionless despite its US Top 20 success. The group nevertheless toured America and Europe to critical acclaim and mass adulation, while the follow-up album showed more promise. The union was to be short-lived however, and following the death of close friend JIMI HENDRIX in September 1970, BURDON bailed out of the tour. WAR battled on alone, fulfilling their live commitments and beginning work on their own album. Although the group were still officially working as BURDON's backing band, Goldstein (now their manager) secured them a separate deal with 'United Artists'. 'WAR' was released in Spring '71, a promising collection of soul, funk, gospel and jazz, underpinned with the group's trademark latino rhythms. The album opened with 'SUN OH SON', mellow flute, harmonica and close harmonies kicking into a stone-heavy bass/organ groove; dynamic tactics which would see WAR develop into one of the fiercest progressive soul combos of the 70's. One of WAR's secret weapons was the Danish-born OSKAR, his harmonica playing at its bittersweet best on the beautiful 'BACK HOME', a sun-kissed, hymn-like ballad which stands among the cream of WAR's mellower work. Their more experimental tendencies emerged on 'WAR DRUMS' and 'FIDEL'S FANTASY', the latter a bizarre spoken monologue berating Cuban leader Fidel Castro, its mocking message driven on a hypnotic groundswell of insistent piano and latin percussion. There were apparently fears for ALLEN's (writer and narrator) safety after the record's release; WAR were certainly big enough to attract unwanted attention, especially after the considerable success of 'ALL DAY MUSIC' (1971). For many fans the consummate WAR set, it was certainly their most consistent, boasting the seminal spookiness of 'SLIPPIN' INTO DARKNESS', a shadowy blues/funk epic which had the atmosphere of an old-time confessional, alongside the defiant funk clarion call of 'GET DOWN' and the groovy 'NAPPY HEAD'. 'THAT'S WHAT LOVE WILL DO', meanwhile, was an old CREATORS tune, updated in moody, melancholy style. Again produced by Goldstein, some of the flab had been trimmed off since the debut, resulting in a leaner more radio-friendly sound. Upon its release as a single, 'SLIPPIN' . . .' eventually hit the Top 20, becoming WAR's first gold release as well as boosting sales of the album and cementing the group's position as one of the foremost funk/soul attractions in America. It came as little surprise then, when WAR scaled the US charts with their third set, 'THE WORLD IS A GHETTO' (1973), the record spawning two Top 10 singles in the compelling mock-Western fantasy of 'CISCO KID' and the title track. 'DELIVER THE WORD' (1973) and 'WHY CAN'T WE BE FRIENDS' (1975) both went Top 10, continuing WAR's singles chart success with a gold disc for the latter's title track (a heartfelt plea for an end to racial segregation which was even beamed into space for US and Russian astronauts' listening pleasure!). The brilliant 'LOW RIDER' meanwhile, became one of only two WAR singles to break the UK Top 20. Things started to go awry in the latter half of the decade, beginning with a move to 'Blue Note'. Though 'PLATINUM JAZZ' (1977) was the label's only platinum release, musically it fell way short of expectations with its noodling, instrumental hotch-potch of old and previously unreleased tracks. 'GALAXY' (1978) wasn't much of an improvement, the group found all at sea attempting to come to grips with the all-pervasive disco revolution. The 80's were a barren time for WAR as sax maestro MILLER was murdered during a robbery and the group tried in vain for a successful comeback on 'R.C.A.' with 'OUTLAW' (1982). Further strife came as ALLEN died from a brain aneurysm on stage, the group having split from Goldstein and given up recording. WAR were eventually coaxed back into the studio in 1995 for 'PEACE SIGN', their profile having been revived via an extensive re-issue programme for 'ARG' records (through BMG in the UK) and the continuing patronage of various hip hop artists. At their leanest, WAR were among the most adventurous, exciting black musicians of their day, it's just a pity their passion for social justice and racial integration is so often substituted for "bitches" and "uzis" among their musical descendants.

Album rating: Eric Burdon & War: ERIC BURDON DECLARES WAR (*6) / THE BLACK MAN'S BURDON (*5) / War: WAR (*6) / ALL DAY MUSIC (*7) / THE WORLD IS A GHETTO (*8) / DELIVER THE WORD (*6) / WAR LIVE! (*4) / WHY CAN'T WE BE FRIENDS? (*8) / GREATEST HITS compilation (*7) / PLATINUM JAZZ collection (*5) / GALAXY (*6) / YOUNGBLOOD soundtrack (*4) / THE MUSIC BAND (*4) / THE MUSIC BAND 2 (*4) / OUTLAW (*5) / LIFE (IS SO STRANGE) (*4) / THE BEST OF WAR . . . AND MORE remixes (*5) / WAR ANTHOLOGY 1970-1994 compilation (*8) / PEACE SIGN (*4)

LONNIE JORDAN (b.LEROY JORDAN, 21 Nov'48, San Diego, Calif.) – keyboards / **HOWARD SCOTT** (b.15 Mar'46, San Pedro, Calif.) – guitar, vocals / **CHARLES MILLER** (b. 2 Jun'39, Olathe, Kansas) – saxophone, clarinet / **HAROLD BROWN** (b.17 Mar'46) – drums, percussion / **LEE OSKAR** (b.24 Mar'46, Copenhagen, Denmark) – harmonica / **B.B.DICKERSON** (b. MORRIS, 3 Aug'49, Torrance, Calif.) – bass, vocals repl. PETER ROSEN who died drug overdose mid '69. / **PAPA DEE ALLEN** (b. THOMAS SYLVESTER ALLEN, 18 Jul'31, Wilmington, Delaware) – keyboards

Recorded 2 albums in 1970 + 71 with (ex-ANIMALS ⇒) vocalist ERIC BURDON. 'ERIC BURDON DECLARES WAR' & 'THE BLACK MAN'S BURDON' both hit UK/US charts.

U.A. U.A.

Apr 71. (7") *(LBF 15443)* <50746> **SUN OH SON. / LONELY FEELIN'** [ ] [ ]

May 71. (lp) *(LBG 83478)* <5508> **WAR** [ ] Apr71 [ ]
– Sun oh son / Lonely feelin' / Back home / War drums / Vibeka / Fidel's fantasy. *(re-iss. Jun76 on 'Island'; ILPS 9164) (re-iss. Oct79 on 'M.C.A.'; MCG 4003)*

Aug 71. (7") *(UP 35281)* <50815> **ALL DAY MUSIC. / GET DOWN** [ ] [35]

Oct 71. (lp) *(UAS 29269)* <5546> **ALL DAY MUSIC** [ ] [16]
– All day music / Get down / That's what love will do / There must be a reason / Nappy need / Slipping into darkness / Baby brother. *(re-iss. Jun76 on 'Island'; ILPS 9177) (re-iss. Oct79 on 'MCA'; MCF 3020) (cd-iss. Oct95 on 'Avenue'; 74321 30520-2)*

Apr 72. (7") *(UP 35327)* <50867> **SLIPPIN' INTO DARKNESS. / NAPPY HEAD** [ ] Jan72 [16]
(re-iss. Nov76;)

Dec 72. (7") *(UP 35469)* <50975> **THE WORLD IS A GHETTO. / FOUR CORNERED ROOM** [ ] Nov72 [7]

Jan 73. (lp/c) *(UAS/+C 29400)* <5652> **THE WORLD IS A GHETTO** [ ] Nov72 [1]
– The Cisco kid / Where was you at / City, country city / Four cornered room / The world is a ghetto / Beetles in a bog. *(re-iss. Oct79 on 'MCA'; MCF 3021) (cd-iss. Oct95 on 'Avenue'; 74321 130521-2)*

Mar 73. (7") *(UP 35521)* <163> **THE CISCO KID. / BEETLES IN THE BOG** [ ] [2]

Aug 73. (7") *(UP 35576)* <281> **GYPSY MAN. / DELIVER THE WORD** [ ] Jul73 [8]

Aug 73. (lp/c) *(UAS/+C 29521)* <128> **DELIVER THE WORD** [ ] [6]
– Three dog night eyes / Gypsy man / Me and baby brother / Deliver the word / Southern part of Texas / Blisters. *(re-iss. Oct79 on 'MCA'; MCF 3022) (cd-iss. Oct95 on 'Avenue'; 74321 30522-2)*

Dec 73. (7") *(UP 35623)* <350> **ME AND BABY BROTHER. / IN YOUR EYES** [ ] Nov73 [15]
(UK re-iss. Jun76; WIP 6303) – hit No.21

Apr 74. (d-lp/c) *(UAD/+C 60067/8)* <193> **WAR LIVE! (live)** [ ] Mar74 [13]
– (introductions by E.Rodney Jones) / Sun oh son / The Cisco kid / Slippin' into darkness / All day music / Ballero / Lonely feelin' / Intro – Get down / Get down. *(re-iss. Jun76 on 'Island'; ILSD 8) (re-iss. Oct79 on 'MCA'; MCF 3040)*

Apr 74. (7") <432> **BALLERO (live). / SLIPPIN' INTO DARKNESS (live)** [–] [33]

Jul 75. (7") *(UP 35836)* <629> **WHY CAN'T WE BE FRIENDS?. / IN MAZATLAN** [ ] May75 [6]
(re-iss. Mar76 on 'Island'; WIP 6289)

Jul 75. (lp/c) *(UAG/+C 29843)* <441> **WHY CAN'T WE BE FRIENDS?** [ ] Jun76 [8]
– Don't let no one get you down / Lotus blossom / Heartbeat / Leroy's Latin lament: Lonies dream – The dream – The way we feel – La fiesta – Lament / Smile happy / So / Low rider / In Mazatlan / Why can't we be friends. *(re-iss. Jun76 on 'Island'; ILPS 9378) (re-iss. Oct79 on 'MCA'; MCF 3023) (cd-iss. Oct95 on 'Avenue'; 74321 30523-2)*

Island U.A.

Jan 76. (7") *(WIP 6267)* <706> **LOW RIDER. / SO** [12] Sep75 [7]

Aug 76. (7") *(WIP 6315)* <834> **SUMMER. / ALL DAY MUSIC** [ ] Jul76 [7]

Sep 76. (lp/c) *(ILPS/ICT 9413)* <648> **GREATEST HITS** (compilation) [ ] [6]
– All day music / Slippin' into darkness / The world is a ghetto / The Cisco kid / Gypsy man / Me and baby brother / Southern part of Texas / Why can't we be friends? / Low rider / Summer. *(re-iss. Jul76 on 'Island'; ILPS 9413) (re-iss. Oct79 on 'MCA'; MCF 3030)*

Island Blue Note

Jul 77. (d-lp) <690> **PLATINUM JAZZ** [–] [23]
– (compilation) War is coming / Slowly we walk together / Platinum jazz / I got you / L.A. sunshine / River Niger / H2 overture / City, country, city / Smile happy / Deliver the word / Nappy head / Four cornered room. *(re-iss. Sep77 as 'PLATINUM FUNK' on 'Island'; ILPS 9507) (re-iss. Oct79 on 'MCA'; MCSP 305) (cd-iss. Oct95 on 'Avenue'; 74321 30524-2)*

Jul 77. (7") <1009> **L.A.SUNSHINE. / SLOWLY WE WALK TOGETHER** [–] [45]

M.C.A. M.C.A.

Dec 77. (7") *(MCA 339)* <40820> **GALAXY. / ('A'instrumental)** [14] [39]

Jan 78. (lp/c) *(MCF/+C 2822)* <3030> **GALAXY** [ ] Nov77 [15]
– Galaxy / Baby Face (she said do do do do) / Sweet fighting lady / Hey senorita / The seven tin soldiers.

Mar 78. (7"/12") *(MCA/+T 359)* <40883> **HEY SENORITA. / SWEET FIGHTING LADY** [40] [ ]

Jul 78. (lp/c) *(MCF/+C 2804)* <904> **YOUNGBLOOD (Soundtrack)** [ ] [69]
– Youngblood / Sing a happy song / Keep on movin' / The Kingsmen sign / Walking to war / This funky music makes you feel good / Junk yard / Superdude / Youngblood & Sybil / Flying machine / Searching for Youngblood & Rommel / Youngblood (rerise). *(re-iss. Dec79 on 'MCA'; MCF 2804)*

Aug 78. (7") *(MCA 383)* **BABY FACE (SHE SAID DO DO DO DO). / ('A'version)** [ ] [–]

Oct 78. (7"/12") *(MCA/+T 399)* <1213> **YOUNGBLOOD. / ('A'version)** [ ] [ ]

—— added **ALICE TWEED SMYTH** – vocals + **LUTHER RABB** – bass

Apr 79. (7"/12") *(MCA/+T 418)* **GOOD GOOD FEELIN'. / SWEET FIGHTIN' LADY** [ ] [–]

Apr 79. (lp/c) *(MCG/+C 4001)* <3085> **THE MUSIC BAND** [ ] [41]
– The music band / Corns & callouses / I'm the one who understands /

Good good feelin' / Millionaire / All around the world. *(re-iss. Oct79 on 'MCA'; MCF 3050)*

Aug 79. (7"/12") *(MCA/+T 514)* <41061> **I'M THE ONE WHO UNDERSTANDS. / CORNS & CALLOUSES**

— added **PAT RIZZO** – horns / **RON HAMMOND** – percussion to repl. DICKERSON.

Jan 80. (7"/12") *(MCA/+T 557)* **THE WORLD IS A GHETTO. / I'LL TAKE CARE OF YOU** – –

Jan 80. (lp/c) *(MCF/+C 3050)* <3193> **THE MUSIC BAND 2** Dec 79
– Don't take it away / I'll take care of you / The world is a ghetto / I'll be around / Night people / The music band 2. Don't take it away / I'll take care of you / The world is a ghetto / I'll be around / Night people / The music band 2.

May 80. (7") *(MCA 593)* <41209> **I'LL BE AROUND. / THE MUSIC BAND 2**

Nov 80. (lp) <5156> **THE MUSIC BAND – LIVE (live)** –
– Spill the wine / All day music / Slippin' into darkness / Low rider / Cisco kid / All night long / Gypsy man / Why can't we be friends.

R.C.A. Lax

Mar 82. (7"/12") *(RCA/+T 201)* <13061> **YOU GOT THE POWER. / CINCO DE MAYO** 58 66

Mar 82. (lp/c) *(RCA LP/K 3050)* <4208> **OUTLAW** 48
– You got the power / Outlaw / The jungle (medley):- Beware it's a jungle out there – The street of walls – The street of lights – The street of now / Just because / Baby it's cold outside / I'm about somebody / Cinco de Mayo.

May 82. (7") <13238> **OUTLAW. / I'M ABOUT SOMEBODY** – 94

Jul 82. (7") *(RCA 240)* **JUST BECAUSE. / I'M ABOUT SOMEBODY** –

— SMYTH + MILLER now departed

Jun 83. (lp/c) *(RCA LP/K 3113)* <4598> **LIFE (IS SO STRANGE)**
– Life (is so strange) / Happiness / W.W.III (medley) / The dawning of night / Waiting at the church / When the nightmare comes / Shaking it down / Summer dreams / U-2 (medley):- U-2 (part 1) – Automatic eyes – U-2 (part 2) – U-2 (part 3)

— **RICKY GREEN** – bass repl. RABB

Bluebird not iss.

Mar 85. (7"/12") *(BR/T 16)* **GROOVIN'. / ('A'instrumental)** 43 –
(re-iss. Aug86)

Lax Lax

May 87. (7") *(XLAX 1)* **LOW RIDER (remix). / SLIPPIN' INTO DARKNESS** –
(12"+=) *(XLAX 100)* – ('A'original mix).
(cd-s+=) *(CDLAX 100)* – Galaxy / Me and baby brother.

— **JORDAN** moved to bass when GREEN departed

— In Aug'91, LATIN ALLIANCE featuring WAR hit the US Top 60 with 'LOWRIDER (ON THE BOULEVARD)'

— now without OSKAR

Avenue Avenue

1992. (cd) <R2 71040> **RAP DECLARES WAR** –

— added **BROWN / TETSUYA NAKAMURA / RAE VALENTINE / KERRY CAMPBELL / SAL RODRIGUEZ + CHARLES GREEN**

Jun 95. (cd) <76024> **PEACE SIGN** 1994
– Peace sign / East L.A. / Wild Rodriguez / I'm the one (who understands) / Da roof / The smuggler (the light in the window) / U B O K / Let me tell you / Smile for me / What if / Angel / Homeless hero.

– compilations, etc. –

1983. (lp) *MCA;* **THE MUSE BAND – JAZZ** –

Jun 87. (lp) *Thunderbolt; (THBL 1041)* **ON FIRE** –

May 87. (cd) *Chord; (CDLAX 100) / Priority; <9467>* **THE BEST OF WAR & MORE – THE REMIXES**
(re-iss. Apr92 on 'Avenue-Rhino'; 70072>

Oct 94. (d-cd) *Rhino; <71774>* **WAR ANTHOLOGY: 1970-1994** –
– Tobacco road / Spill the wine / They can't take away our music / Sun oh son / Lonely feelin' / All day music / Get down / Slippin' into darkness / Cisco kid / The world is a ghetto / City, country, city / Where was you at / Gypsy man / Me and my baby brother / Deliver the word / Ballero / Why can't we be friends? / Low rider / Don't let no one get you down / Summer / L.A. sunshine / River Niger / Galaxy / Youngblood (livin' in the streets) / This funky music makes you feel good / Music band / Outlaw / You got the power / Cinco de Mayo / Life (is so strange) / Don't let no one get you down / Peace sign.

WATERBOYS

Formed: London, England . . . 1982 by Scots-born MIKE SCOTT, Englishman ANTHONY THISTLETHWAITE and Welshman KARL WALLINGER. SCOTT had previously fronted Edinburgh new wave outfit, ANOTHER PRETTY FACE, along with old Ayr school pals, JOHN CALDWELL and JIM GEDDES. Taking their name from a track on LOU REED's sleaze-noir masterpiece, 'Berlin', The WATERBOYS soon secured a deal with the Irish-run label, 'Ensign', following the release of a self-financed debut single in Spring '83, 'A GIRL CALLED JOHNNY'. A tribute to punk priestess, PATTI SMITH (an obvious early influence), the track received a fair amount of airplay and almost broke into the lower regions of the charts. An eponymous debut album followed later that summer, an esoteric set of avant folk/rock which drew comparisons with TIM BUCKLEY's more ambitious meanderings and introduced SCOTT as a promising singing/songwriting seer. Embellished by additional instrumentation such as horns and violin, 'A PAGAN PLACE' (1984) was a confident follow-up, SCOTT venturing ever further out on his spiritual journey with the likes of 'THE BIG MUSIC' and 'CHURCH NOT MADE WITH HANDS'. A burgeoning live reputation and gushing critical praise saw The WATERBOYS' third set, 'THIS IS THE SEA' (1985) break into the UK Top 40, its centerpiece epic, 'THE WHOLE OF THE MOON', becoming the group's first Top 30 single. Despite this overdue success, WALLINGER subsequently departed to form his own outfit, WORLD PARTY. Relocating to Galway, Ireland for an extended sabbatical at the behest of fiddler, STEVE WICKHAM (who'd played on 'THIS..'), SCOTT and THISTLETHWAITE increasingly infused their music with traditional Irish folk influences. It was an earthier WATERBOYS, then, who eventually emerged in late '88 with the acclaimed 'FISHERMAN'S BLUES', SCOTT seemingly having at last found his true musical calling. From the strident Celtic clarion call of the title track to the soulful cover of Van Morrison's 'SWEET THING', it sounded as if The WATERBOYS had been playing this music for centuries. The record almost made the UK Top 10, an album which established The WATERBOYS as a major league act and which remains their biggest seller. 'ROOM TO ROAM' (1990) continued in the same vein, making the UK Top 5 although it lacked the depth of its predecessor. Bang on cue, 'Ensign' re-released 'THE WHOLE OF THE MOON' to massive success (Top 3), the track being played to death by radio all over again. By this point, however, the original WATERBOYS line-up had splintered following a final UK tour (wherein the group drew criticism for their return to an all-out rock sound), THISTLETHWAITE forming The BLUE STARS while SCOTT eventually moved to New York and gathered together a new group of musicians. Now signed to 'Geffen', he recorded 'DREAM HARDER' (1993), the sixth WATERBOYS album but a SCOTT solo set in all but name. Exploring many familiar themes, the album spawned two Top 30 singles in 'THE RETURN OF PAN' and 'GLASTONBURY SONG', even boasting a brief contribution from Scots comedy legend, BILLY CONNOLLY. Although SCOTT released two solo albums, 'BRING 'EM ALL IN' (1995) and 'STILL BURNING' (1997), the WATERBOYS had been out of action nigh on seven years. 'A ROCK IN THE WEARY LAND', put this to rights. Fusing psychedelia, folk-rock and pop, the album was a lacklustre attempt to break back into the mainstream, although it did have its moments. SCOTT harboured the current trend of rock'n'roll nihilism on opening track 'LET IT HAPPEN', while 'CROWN' remained quietly poignant. It's easy to see why

SCOTT still carries on despite critical disapproval from some of the press. He at least enjoys what he does as do his dedicated fanbase who'll never forget what the man and his group have achieved. An odds'n'sods collection of outtakes and unreleased material from the band's early days, 'TOO CLOSE TO HEAVEN' (2001) was a fascinating document of MIKE SCOTT's genesis from punk beat poet to fledgling folk mystic. Named after a theatre run by Scotland's very own Findhorn Foundation (which remains very much a place of inspiration for SCOTT), 'UNVERSAL HALL' (2003) was markedly different from its predecessor. Heavily accented with spiritual and religious concerns, albeit not in the dogmatic fashion that such themes can be in lesser hands, the record was closest in spirit – if not exactly in feel – to VAN MORRISON's (an obvious comparison but one which continues to be relevant) latter day quasi-religious searching. • **Covered:** LOST HIGHWAY (Hank Williams) / DEATH IS NOT THE END (Bob Dylan) / WAYWARD WIND (Lebawsky-Newman) / BECAUSE THE NIGHT (Patti Smith – Bruce Springsteen) / PURPLE RAIN (Prince) / and a several traditional renditions.

Album rating: THE WATERBOYS (*6) / A PAGAN PLACE (*6) / THIS IS THE SEA (*7) / FISHERMAN'S BLUES (*6) / ROOM TO ROAM (*6) / THE BEST OF THE WATERBOYS compilation (*9) / DREAM HARDER (*5) / THE SECRET LIFE OF THE WATERBOYS early stuff (*4) / A ROCK IN THE WEARY LAND (*7) / TOO CLOSE TO HEAVEN collection (*5) / UNIVERSAL HALL (*6) / Mike Scott: BRING 'EM ALL IN (*6) / STILL BURNING (*5)

ANOTHER PRETTY FACE

MIKE SCOTT (b.14 Dec'58, Edinburgh, Scotland) – vocals, guitar, piano / **JOHN CALDWELL** – guitar / **JIM GEDDES** – bass / **CRIGG** (b.IAN WALTER GREIG) – drums

New Pleasures — not iss.

May 79. (7") *(Z1)* **ALL THE BOYS LOVE CARRIE. / THAT'S NOT ENOUGH** [ ] [–]

Virgin — not iss.

Feb 80. (7") *(VS 320)* **WHATEVER HAPPENED TO THE WEST?. / GODDBYE 1970's** [ ] [–]

—— trimmed to basic duo of **SCOTT** + **CALDWELL** plus **MAIRI ROSS** – bass / added **ADRIAN JOHNSON** – drums

Chicken Jazz — not iss.

Dec 80. (7") *(JAZZ 1)* **ONLY HEROES LIVE FOREVER. / HEAVEN GETS CLOSER EVERY DAY** [ ] [–]

Mar 81. (c-ep) *(JAZZ 2)* **I'M SORRY THAT I BEAT YOU, I'M SORRY THAT I SCREAMED, FOR A MOMENT THERE I REALLY LOST CONTROL(live)** [ ] [–]
– This could be Hell / My darkest hour / Lightning that strikes twice / Graduation day / Carrie. *(on most copies, studio tracks +=)* – Another kind of circus / Only heroes live forever / Out of control.

Apr 81. (7") *(JAZZ 3)* **SOUL TO SOUL. / A WOMAN'S PLACE / GOD ON THE SCREEN** [ ] [–]

FUNHOUSE

—— were formed by **SCOTT** + **CALDWELL**

Ensign — not iss.

Feb 82. (7"/ext.12") *(ENY/+T 222)* **OUT OF CONTROL. / THIS COULD BE HELL** [ ] [–]

The WATERBOYS

MIKE SCOTT plus **ANTHONY THISTLETHWAITE** (b. 8 Aug'55, Leicester, England) – saxophone (ex-ROBYN HITCHCOCK / of SOFT BOYS) / **KARL WALLINGER** (b.19 Oct'57, Prestatyn, Wales) – keyboards, bass

Chicken Jazz — not iss.

May 83. (7") *(CJ 1)* **A GIRL CALLED JOHNNY. / THE LATE TRAIN TO HEAVEN** [ ] [–]
(12") *(CJT 1)* – ('A'side) / Ready for the monkey house / Somebody might wave back / Out of control (APF; John Peel session).

Ensign — Chrysalis

Jul 83. (lp/c) *(ENC L/C 1)* **THE WATERBOYS** [ ] [–]
– December / A girl called Johnny / The three day man / Gala / I will not follow / It should have been you / The girl in the swing / Savage Earth heart. *(re-iss. Aug86 on 'Chrysalis-Ensign' lp/c; CHEN/ZCHEN 1) (cd-iss. Feb87; CCD 1541) <US cd-iss. 1987; 21541> (cd re-mast.Mar02 on 'Chrysalis'+=; 537703-2)* – (extra tracks).

Sep 83. (7") *(ENY 506)* **DECEMBER. / WHERE ARE YOU NOW WHEN I NEED YOU** [ ] [–]
(12") *(12ENY 506)* – ('A'side) / Red army blues / The three day man (Peter Powell session).

—— added **KEVIN WILKINSON** – drums / **RODDY LORIMER** (b. Glasgow, Scotland) – trumpet / **TIM BLANTHORN** – violin

Apr 84. (7") *(ENY 508)* **THE BIG MUSIC. / THE EARTH ONLY ENDURES** [ ] [–]
(12"+=) *(12ENY 508)* – Bury my heart.

May 84. (lp/c) *(ENC L/C 3)* **A PAGAN PLACE** [100] [–]
– Church not made with hands / All the things she gave me / The thrill is gone / Rags / Somebody might wave back / The big music / Red army blues / A pagan place. *(re-iss. Aug86 on 'Chrysalis-Ensign' lp/c; CHEN/ZCHEN 2) (cd-iss. Feb87 & Jul94; CCD 1542) <US cd-iss. 1987; 21542> (cd re-mast.Mar02 on 'Chrysalis'+=; 537704-2)* – (extra tracks).

—— (Oct84) **MIKE** + **KARL** recruited new people for tour/lp **TERRY MANN** – bass / **CHARLIE WHITTEN** – drums / **STEVE WICKHAM** (b. Dublin, Ireland) – violin / **LORIMER** / **DELAHAYE** – organ

Sep 85. (lp/c) *(ENC L/C 5)* **THIS IS THE SEA** [37] [–]
– Don't bang the drum / The whole of the Moon / Spirit / The pan within / Medicine bow / Old England / Be my enemy / Trumpets / This is the sea. *(re-iss. Aug86 on 'Chrysalis-Ensign' lp/c; CHEN/ZCHEN 3) (cd-iss. Feb87; CCD CCD 1543) (re-iss. cd Mar94;) <US cd-iss. 1987; 21543> (lp re-iss. Aug00 on 'Simply Vinyl'; SVLP 234)*

Oct 85. (7") *(ENY 502)* **THE WHOLE OF THE MOON. / MEDICINE BOW** [26] [ ]
(ext.12"+=) *(12ENY 520)* – Spirit (extended) / The girl in the swing (live).

—— **MIKE SCOTT** now only original survivor (retained THISTLETHWAITE + HUTCHISON), when KARL formed WORLD PARTY.

—— additional band **STEVE WICKHAM** – violin (ex-IN TUA NUA) / **J.D. DOHERTY** – drums / **COLIN BLAKEY** (b. Falkirk, Scotland) – flute (ex-WE FREE KINGS) /('88) added **SHARON SHANNON** (b. Ireland) – accordion / **NOEL BRIDGEMAN** (b. Dublin, Ireland) – drums repl. DOHERTY

Nov 88. (lp/c)(cd) *(CHEN/ZCHEN 5)(CCD 1589) <41589>* **FISHERMAN'S BLUES** [13] [76]
– Fisherman's blues / We will not be lovers / Strange boat / World party / Sweet thing / And a bang on the ear / Has anybody here seen Hank? / When we will be married? / When ye go away / The stolen child. *(cd+=)* – The lost highway. *(lp re-iss. Sep00 on 'Simply Vinyl'; SVLP 245)*

Dec 88. (7"/12"/cd-s) *(ENY/+X/CD 621)* **FISHERMAN'S BLUES. / THE LOST HIGHWAY** [32] [–]

Jun 89. (7"/c-s/12"/cd-s) *(ENY/+MC/X/CD 624)* **AND A BANG ON THE EAR. / THE RAGGLE TAGGLE GYPSY** [51] [–]

—— **MIKE SCOTT** / **THISTLETHWAITE** / **HUTCHISON** / + **KEV BLEVINS** – drums repl. last additional band members

Sep 90. (cd)(c/lp) *(CCD 1768)(Z+/CHEN 16) <21768>* **ROOM TO ROAM** [5] [ ]
– In search of a rose / Songs from the edge of the world / A man is in love / Bigger picture / Natural bridge blues / Something that is gone / The star and the sea / Life on Sundays / Island man / The raggle taggle gypsy / How long will I love you? / Upon the wind and waves / Spring rooms to Spiddal / Further up, further in / Trip to Broadford / Room to roam. *(cd+=)* – The kings of Kerry. *(re-iss. Sep94 cd/c;)*

Mar 91. (7"/c-s) *(ENY/+MC 642) <Alex; 1516>* **THE WHOLE OF THE MOON. / A GOLDEN AGE** [3] Jul91 [ ]
(12"+=/cd-s+=) *(ENY X/CD 642)* – Higher in time / High far soon / Soon as I get home.

Apr 91. (cd)(c/lp) *(CCD 1845)(Z+/CHEN 19) <21845>* **THE BEST OF THE WATERBOYS ('81-'90)** (compilation) [2] [ ]
– A girl called Johnny / The big music / All the things she gave me / The whole of the Moon / Spirit / Don't bang the drum / Fisherman's blues / Killing my heart / Strange boat / And a bang on the ear / Old England / A man is in love. *(cd re-iss. Aug00; same)*

May 91. (7"/c-s) *(ENY/+MC 645) <Alex; 1581>* **FISHERMAN'S BLUES. / LOST HIGHWAY** [75] Jun91 [ ]
(12"+=/cd-s+=) *(ENY X/CD 645)* – Medicine bow (live).

—— disbanded soon after last studio album above. In mid'91, MIKE SCOTT re-formed group and signed for US-based label 'Geffen'. THISTLETHWAITE formed The BLUE STARS.

— **MIKE SCOTT** with **CHRIS BRUCE** – guitars / **SCOTT THUNES** – bass / **CARLA AZAR** – drums / **BASHIRI JOHNSON** – percussion / **LJUBISA 'Lubi' RISTIC** – sitar / **GEORGE STATHOS** – Greek clarinet / **JAMES CAMPAGNOLA** – saxophone / **JERE PETERS** – rattles / **PAL SHAZAR** + **JULES SHEAR** – backing vox / **BILLY CONNOLLY**– guest 10 second voiceover

Geffen Geffen

May 93. (7"/c-s) *(GFS/+C 42)* **THE RETURN OF PAN. / KARMA** [24] [ ]
(12"+=/cd-s+=) *(GFS T/CD 42)* – Mister Powers / ('A'demo).

May 93. (cd/c/lp) *(<GED/GEC/GEF 24476>)* **DREAM HARDER** [5] [ ]
– The new life / Glastonbury song / Preparing to fly / The return of Pan / Corn circles / Suffer / Winter winter / Love and death / Spiritual city / Wonders of Lewis / The return of Jimi Hendrix / Good news. *(cd re-iss. Jul96; GFLD 19318)*

Jul 93. (7"/c-s) *(GFS/+C 49)* **GLASTONBURY SONG. / CHALICE HILL** [29] [–]
(12"+=/cd-s+=) *(GFS T/CD 49)* – Burlington Bertie – Accrington Stanley / Corn circle symphony (extended).

— MIKE SCOTT split the band after above

MIKE SCOTT

— mostly all solo with some guests

Chrysalis Chrysalis

Sep 95. (c-s/7") *(TC+/CHS 5025)* <58503> **BRING 'EM ALL IN. / CITY FULL OF GHOSTS (DUBLIN)** [56] Nov95 [ ]
(cd-s+=) *(CDCHS 5025)* – Mother Cluny / Beatles reunion blues.

Sep 95. (cd/c/lp) *(<CD/TC+/CHR 6108>)* **BRING 'EM ALL IN** [23] [ ]
– Bring 'em all in / Iona song / Edinburgh Castle / What do you want me to do? / I know she's in the building / City full of ghosts (Dublin) / Wonderful disguise / Sensitive children / Learning to love him / She is so beautiful / Wonderful disguise (reprise) / Long way to the light / Building the city of light.

Nov 95. (7") *(CHS 5026)* **BUILDING THE CITY OF LIGHT. / WHERE DO YOU WANT THE BOOMBOX, BUDDY** [60] [–]
(cd-s+=) *(CDCHSS 5026)* – Goin' back to Glasters (live) / The whole of the Moon (live).
(cd-s) *(CDCHS 5026)* – ('A'side) / Two great waves / My beautiful guide / Building the city of light (Universal Hall demo).

— now with **CHRIS BRUCE** – lead guitar / **PINO PALLADINO** – bass / **JIM KELTNER** – drums / **JAMES HALLAWELL** – organ / etc

Sep 97. (c-s) *(TCCHS 5064)* **LOVE ANYWAY / KING OF STARS** [50] [–]
(cd-s) *(CDCHS 5064)* – ('A'side) / King electric (including Moonage Daydream) / Blues is my business.
(cd-s) *(CDCHSS 5064)* – ('A'side) / Big lover / Careful with the mellotron, Eugene / Since I found my school.

Oct 97. (cd/c) *(<CD/TC CHR 6122>)* **STILL BURNING** [34] [ ]
– Questions / My dark side / Open / Love anyway / Rare, precious and gone / Dark man of my dreams / Personal / Strawberry man / Sunrising / Everlasting arms.

Feb 98. (cd-ep) *(CDCHSS 5073)* **RARE, PRECIOUS AND GONE / KISS THE WIND / WHEN WILL WE BE MARRIED (live) / LOVE ANYWAY (demo)** [74] [–]
(cd-ep) *(CDCHS 5073)* – ('A'side) / All things she gave me (live) / She is so beautiful (live) / Nectar (7 days).

WATERBOYS

MIKE SCOTT re-formed the band with **LIVINGSTON BROWN** + **MARK SMITH** – bass / **JEREMY STACEY** – drums / **ANTHONY THISTLETHWAITE** – electric slide mandolin / + others on session

R.C.A. R.C.A.

Sep 00. (cd/c) *(<74321 78305-2/-4>)* **A ROCK IN THE WEARY LAND** [47] Nov00 [ ]
– Let it happen / My love is my rock in the weary land / It's all gone / Is she conscious? / We are Jonah / Malediction / Dumbing down the world / His word is not his bond / Night falls on London / The charlatan's lament / The wind in the wires / Crown.

Oct 00. (7") *(74321 79417-7)* **MY LOVE IS MY ROCK IN THE WEARY LAND. / YOUR BABY AIN'T YOUR BABY ANYMORE (with the Half Mast Flag Country & Western Band)** [ ] [–]
(cd-s) *(74321 79417-2)* – ('A'side) / Lucky day – Bad advice / Time space and the bride's bed.
(cd-s) *(74321 79418-2)* – ('A'side) / Trouble down yonder / Send him down to Waco.

Feb 01. (m-cd) *(74321 83649-2)* **IS SHE CONSCIOUS?** [ ] [–]
– Is she conscious? (album version) / Sad procession / Faeries prisoner / Is she conscious? / Savage earth heart / My Lord what a morning / Is she conscious (video).

Apr 01. (7") *(74321 84870-7)* **WE ARE JONAH. / TIME, SPACE AND THE BRIDE'S BED** [ ] [–]
(cd-s) *(74321 84870-2)* – ('A'side) / Lucky day – Bad advice / Dumbing down the world (live at Glastonbury 2000).
(cd-s) *(74321 84871-2)* – ('A'side) / Martin descent / Send him down to Waco.

Sep 01. (cd) *(<74321 88152-2>)* **TOO CLOSE TO HEAVEN** (rarities) [ ] Jan02 [ ]
– On my way to heaven / Higher in time / The ladder / Too close to Heaven / Good man gone / Blues for your baby / Custer's blues / A home in the meadow / Tenderfootin' / Lonesome old wind.

— **SCOTT** brought back **STEVE WICKHAM** – fiddle / + new **RICHARD NAIFF** – flute, piano

Puck Minty Fresh

Jun 03. (cd) *(PUCK 1)* <70053> **UNIVERSAL HALL** [74] May03 [ ]
– This light is for the world / The Christ in you / Silent fellowship / Every breath is yours / Peace of Iona / Ain't no words for the things I'm feeling / Seek the light / I've lived here before / Always dancing, never getting tired / The dance at the crossroads / E.B.O.L. / Universal hall.

– compilations, etc. –

Oct 94. (cd/c) *Ensign; (CD/TC CHEN 35)* **THE SECRET LIFE OF THE WATERBOYS** (81-85 material) [ ] [ ]
(cd re-iss. Sep97; same)

Aug 98. (d-cd) *Griffin; <40>* **LIVE ADVENTURES OF THE WATERBOYS (live)** [–] [ ]
– Death is not the end / Earth only endures / Medicine bow / Fisherman's blues / This is the sea / Meet me at the station / We will not be lovers / Wayward wind / A girl called Johnny / Purple rain / Be my enemy / Old England / The thrill is gone – And the healing has begun / Pain within (including Because the night) / Whole of the moon / Spirit / Savage earth heart / Saints and angels. *(UK-iss.Jul00 on 'Burning Airlines' d-cd/t-lp; PILOT 040/+LP)*

Sep 98. (cd) *Chrysalis; (496505-2)* **THE WHOLE OF THE MOON – THE BEST OF MIKE SCOTT & THE WATERBOYS** [ ] [–]

Sep 00. (3xcd-box) *EMI; (528661-2)* **A PAGAN PLACE / THIS IS THE SEA / FISHERMAN'S BLUES** [ ] [–]

Mar 03. (cd) *E.M.I.; (582226-2)* **THE ESSENTIAL WATERBOYS** [ ] [–]

Muddy WATERS

Born: McKINLEY MORGANFIELD, 4th April 1915, Rolling Fork, Mississippi, USA. While perhaps not as widely celebrated as his peers, JOHN LEE HOOKER and BB KING, it was WATERS who was the main catalyst in converting blues to urban electric and then to rock'n'roll. Brought up by his mother in Clarksdale (birthplace of HOOKER), he began singing and playing harmonica at the age of 7, acquired his nickname due to his fondness for playing in a nearby muddy creek. By his late teens, WATERS had switched to guitar and was supplementing his wages as a cotton picker (although he had ambitions beyond that – in his late teens he was running his own whisky still!) by playing at local juke joints and parties. Initially, his style was a combination of CHARLEY PATTON, SON HOUSE (his mentor and tutor) and his hero, ROBERT JOHNSON (although he never met him, he once saw him play, the experience apparently changing his life) although he had evolved his own approach to the blues by the time he'd moved to Chicago in 1943. Another turning point came in 1941 when ALAN LOMAX visited the plantation where MUDDY worked; LOMAX had already recorded SON HOUSE and wanted to record ROBERT JOHNSON for the Library Of Congress, unaware that JOHNSON was already dead. When he found out, he asked about ELMORE JAMES and finally ended up recording the young MUDDY WATERS, both solo and in a band with the SON SIMS FOUR (the recorded songs were 'I BE'S TROUBLED' and 'COUNTRY BLUES'). WATERS was suitably impressed with the sound of the recordings to decide on a career as a professional musician. In Chicago he worked in a paper mill by day and played in clubs at night (encouraged by BIG BILL BROONZY and SUNNYLAND SLIM), quickly discovering that his acoustic guitar wasn't loud enough for these venues and subsequently going electric. WATERS gradually assembled the finest blues band of the era, featuring, at various times, MARVIN 'LITTLE WALTER' JACOBS (harmonica/vocals), OTIS SPANN (piano) and WILLIE DIXON (bass), among others; his bands attracted the greatest talents, WATERS giving them a platform to develop their reputations (even allowing them to record their own music during his studio time) and training them to be leaders in their own right. When LITTLE WALTER, JIMMY ROGERS, OTIS SPANN and JAMES COTTON set off on their own he wished them the best and simply replaced them. He recorded briefly for 'Columbia' in 1946 ('HARD DAY BLUES' displayed signs of what was to come) before signing to 'Aristocrat' (later 'Chess' in 1950) although he didn't start recording under his own name until 1948. Such was the strength of WATERS' reputation that his first single, 'I CAN'T BE SATISFIED' sold out its first pressing within 24 hours while the follow up, 'I FEEL LIKE GOING HOME' saw him making his R&B chart debut. WATERS' first 'Chess' single was 'ROLLIN STONE' in 1950, the bluesman achieving his second major R&B success with 'LOUISIANA BLUES' (WATERS had a further thirteen R&B hits up to 1956) the following year. His band toured the UK in 1958 and although critics weren't so supportive, viewers of the shows were taken aback by the power of the performances which effected an incalculable impact upon a future generation of British performers including ALEXIS KORNER and CYRIL DAVIES, who were inspired to form BLUES INCORPORATED. Songs like 'HOOCHIE COOCHIE MAN', 'ROLLIN' AND TUMBLIN', 'BABY PLEASE DON'T GO', 'I GOT MY MOJO WORKING', 'I JUST WANT TO MAKE LOVE TO YOU' and 'MANNISH BOY', many written by WILLIE DIXON, became standards among early UK R&B bands while The ROLLING STONES, The MOJOS, The HOOCHIE COOCHIE MEN and The MANNISH BOYS even took their name from WATERS songs. He also had a direct influence on JUNIOR WELLS, BUDDY GUY, JIMI HENDRIX and ERIC CLAPTON. Yet it took a long time for him to reap the financial benefits (he was often out-sold by JIMMY REED, JIMMY ROGERS and LITTLE WALTER) and at the end of the 50's Chess decided to market WATERS as an album based performer, released two albums in 1960 including 'MUDDY WATERS AT NEWPORT' (arguably his finest live album). When the 'STONES arrived to record at the Chess studios in 1964 (the year that saw the release of the all-acoustic 'MUDDY WATERS, FOLK SINGER') they famously found WATERS up a ladder, painting the studio(!); some of the musicians he had inspired subsequently recorded collaborative albums with him. They were of inconsistent quality, but they did, at least, get WATERS noticed outwith blues circles. 'FATHERS & SONS' was a joint effort with MIKE BLOOMFIELD, PAUL BUTTERFIELD, DONALD 'DUCK' DUNN, BUDDY MILES and OTIS SPANN, marking his only entry to the US Top 100. 'THE LONDON MUDDY WATERS SESSIONS' featuring RORY GALLAGHER, GEORGIE FAME, MITCH MITCHELL, RICK GRECH and STEVE WINWOOD also helped him break out of the blues ghetto. In an attempt to keep WATERS in the public eye, 'Chess' rather ill-advisedly persuaded him to record such projects as the psychedelic 'ELECTRIC MUD' (which included a version of The STONES' 'LET'S SPEND THE NIGHT TOGETHER') album in the late 60's. Nevertheless, he won Grammy's in 1972 for 'THEY CALL ME MUDDY WATERS' and 'LONDON SESSIONS' although tragedy struck the following year when he was seriously injured in a car crash; the accident left three people dead and put him into semi-retirement for two years. The guitarist returned with the Grammy Award winning 'MUDDY WATERS WOODSTOCK ALBUM' and performed 'MANNISH BOY' at The BAND's farewell concert. WATERS left 'Chess' (after the CHESS brothers sold out to a New York corporation) in 1977 and signed to STEVE PAUL's 'Blue Sky' (PAUL was the manager of JOHNNY WINTER) imprint. WINTER, who had long idolised WATERS, jumped at the chance to work with his hero and set about recreating the veteran bluesman's 50's recording sound aided by the likes of JAMES COTTON, WALTER HORTON, LUTHER JOHNSON, JIMMY ROGERS, PINETOP PERKINS and WILLIE 'BIG EYES' SMITH. Four albums, 'HARD AGAIN', 'I'M READY', 'MUDDY MISSISSIPPI WATERS' (all Grammy winners) and 'I'M A KING BEE' were released between 1977 and 1980. 'HARD AGAIN' was recorded amid a great atmosphere, lots of excitement at the end of each track as the band went through classics like 'I WANT TO BE LOVED', 'I CAN'T BE SATISFIED' (with WINTER on slide guitar), 'DEEP DOWN IN FLORIDA' and 'MANNISH BOY'. Incidentally, it was this recording of 'MANNISH BOY' that was used for a Levi jeans TV advert in 1988 and was subsequently released as a single, becoming WATERS' only UK chart entry at number 51. By 1980, he had moved from the south side to a comfortable home in the suburbs with his 25 year old wife and numerous grandchildren. WATERS died peacefully in his sleep on the 30th of April 1983 (only after his death it was discovered that he had contracted cancer), receiving a posthumous induction to the Rock And Roll Hall Of Fame in 1987 and a Lifetime Achievement Award at the Grammy's in 1992.

Best CD compilation: MUDDY WATERS – THE CHESS BOX box-set (*9)

MUDDY WATERS – vocals, guitar; with **SUNNYLAND SLIM** – piano

		not iss.	Aristocrat
1948.	(78) *<1302>* **GYPSY WOMAN. / LITTLE ANNA MAE**	–	
1948.	(78) *<1305>* **I CAN'T BE SATISFIED. / FEEL LIKE GOIN' HOME**		
1948.	(78) *<1306>* **TRAIN FARE HOME. / SITTIN' HERE AND DRINKIN'**	–	
1949.	(78) *<1307>* **YOU'RE GONNA MISS ME. / MEAN RED SPIDER**	–	
1949.	(78) *<1310>* **STREAMLINE WOMAN. / MUDDY JUMPS ONE**	–	
1949.	(78) *<1311>* **LITTLE GENEVA. / CANARY BIRD**	–	
1949.	(78) *<406>* **SCREAMIN' AND CRYIN'. / WHERE'S MY WOMAN BEEN**	–	
1951.	(78) *<412>* **ROLLIN' AND TUMBLIN'. / (pt. 2)**	–	

—— with band **JIMMY RODGERS** – guitar / **WILLIE DIXON** – bass / **LITTLE WALTER** – harmonica / **LEONARD CHESS** – drums / **ERNEST CRAWFORD** – bass

		not iss.	Chess
1950.	(78) *<1434>* **YOU'RE GONNA NEED MY HELP I SAID. / SAD LETTER BLUES** *(UK-iss.May52 on 'Vogue Coral'; V 2101)*	–	
1951.	(78) *<1441>* **LOUISIANA BLUES. / EVAN'S SHUFFLE**	–	
1951.	(78) *<1452>* **LONG DISTANCE CALL. / TOO YOUNG TO KNOW** *(UK-iss.Nov54 on 'Vogue Coral'; V 2273)*	–	
1951.	(7") *<1468>* **HONEY BEE. / APPEALING BLUES** *(UK-iss.May56 on 'Vogue Coral'; V 2372)*	–	

1951. (78) <1480> **MY FAULT. / STILL A FOOL**

—— ELGIN EVANS – drums repl. CHESS

1952. (78) <1490> **SHE MOVES ME. / EARLY MORNING BLUES**

1952. (78) <1509> **ALL NIGHT LONG. / COUNTRY BOY**

1952. (78) <1514> **PLEASE HAVE MERCY. / I CAN'T BE SATISFIED (LOOKING FOR MY BABY)**

1952. (78) <1526> **STANDING AROUND CRYING. / GONE TO MAIN STREET**

1953. (78) <1537> **SHE'S ALL RIGHT. / SAD, SAD DAY**

1953. (78) <1542> **TURN THE LAMP DOWN LOW. / WHO'S GONNA BE YOUR SWEET MAN**

1953. (78) <1550> **BLOW WIND BLOW. / MAD LOVE (I JUST WANT YOU TO LOVE ME)**

—— **OTIS SPANN** – piano (to mid-60's) repl. SLIM

1954. (78) <1560> **HOOCHIE COOCHIE MAN. / SHE'S SO PRETTY**

1954. (78) <1571> **I JUST WANT TO MAKE LOVE TO YOU. / OH YEAH**

1954. (78) <1579> **I'M READY. / I DON'T KNOW WHY**

1954. (78) <1585> **I'M A NATURAL BORN LOVER. / LOVING MAN**

Mar 55. (7"ep) *Vogue; (EPV 1046)* **MUDDY WATERS WITH LITTLE WALTER**
– I can't be satisfied / Louisiana blues / Evans shuffle / I feel like going home.

1955. (78) <1596> **I WANT TO BE LOVED. / MY EYES (KEEP ME IN TROUBLE)**

1955. (78) <1602> **MANNISH BOY. / YOUNG FASHIONED WAYS**

1955. (78) <1612> **SUGAR SWEET. / TROUBLE NO MORE**

1956. (78) <1620> **40 DAYS AND 40 NIGHTS. / ALL ABOARD**

1956. (78) <1630> **DON'T GO NO FURTHER. / DIAMONDS AT YOUR FEET**

1956. (78) <1644> **JUST TO BE WITH YOU. / I GOT TO FIND MY BABY**

London — Chess

Oct 56. (7"ep) *(RU-E 1060)* **MISSISSIPPI BLUES**
– All aboard / 40 days and 40 nights / Mannish boy / Young fashioned ways.

1957. (7") <1652> **GOT MY MOJO WORKING. / ROCK ME**

1957. (7") <1667> **GOOD NEWS. / COME HOME BABY**

1957. (7") <1680> **EVIL. / I LIVE THE LIFE I LOVE**

1958. (7") <1692> **I WON'T GO. / SHE'S GOT IT**

1958. (7") <1704> **SHE'S 19 YEARS OLD. / CLOSE TO YOU**

1958. (7") <1718> **WALKING THRU THE PARK. / MEAN MISTREATER**

1958. (7") <1724> **CLOUDS IN MY HEART. / OOH WEE**

1959. (7") <1733> **TAKE THE BITTER WITH THE SWEET. / SHE'S INTO SOMETHING**

1959. (7") <1739> **TELL ME BABY. / LOOK WHAT YOU'VE DONE**

1959. (7") <1748> **WHEN I GET TO THINKING. / I FEEL SO GOOD**

1960. (7") <1752> **I'M YOUR DOCTOR. / READ WAY BACK**

1960. (7") <1758> **LOVE AFFAIR. / RECIPE FOR LOVE**

—— **WALTER HORTON** – repl. LITTLE WALTER until **JAMES COTTON** repl. HORTON / **PAT HARE** came in on drums and ROGERS departed. He toured in the UK.

Mar 59. (lp) *(LJZ-M 15152)* **THE BEST OF MUDDY WATERS** (compilation)
– I just want to make love to you / Long distance call / Louisiana blues / Honey bee / Rollin' stone / I'm ready / Hoochie coochie / She moves me / I want you to love me / Standing around crying / Still a fool / I can't be satisfied. *(re-iss. Oct87 lp/c; GCH/+K7 8044) (cd-iss. Jun88; CDCHESS 1012)*

—— toured now with **FRANCIS CLAY** – drums / **ANDREW STEPHENSON** – bass / **PAT HARE** – guitar / **SPANN** + **COTTON**

Jun 60. (7") <1765> **TIGER IN YOUR TANK. / MEANEST WOMAN**

Aug 60. (7") <1774> **GOT MY MOJO WORKING (pt.1). / WOMAN WANTED**

1961. (7") <1796> **LONESOME ROOM BLUES. / MESSIN' WITH THE MAN**

Pye Jazz — Chess

Sep 61. (lp) *(NJL 34)* <1449> **MUDDY WATERS AT NEWPORT (live 1960)** — 1960
– Tiger in your tank / I've got my mojo working / I got my brand on you / Baby, please don't go / Soon forgotten / I feel so glad / Goodbye Newport blues. *(re-iss. Nov65 on 'Chess'; CRL 4513) (re-iss. Jan67 on 'Marble Arch'; MAL 661) (re-iss. 1973 on 'Checker') (cd-iss. Jun96 on 'Beat Goes On'; BGOCD 314)*

1962. (7") <1819> **TOUGH TIMES. / GOING HOME**

1962. (7") <1827> **YOU SHOOK ME. / MUDDY WATERS TWIST**

1962. (7") <1839> **YOU NEED LOVE. / LITTLE BROWN BIRD**

1963. (7") <1862> **FIVE LONG YEARS. / TWENTY FOUR HOURS**

1964. (7") <1895> **THE SAME THING. / YOU CAN'T LOSE WHAT YOU NEVER HAD**

Pye Inter. — Chess

May 64. (lp) *(NPL 28038)* <1483> **MUDDY WATERS – FOLK SINGER**
– My home is my delta / Long distance / My captain / Good morning little schoolgirl / You're gonna need my help / Cold weather blues / Peg leg woman / Country boy / Feel like going home. *(re-iss. Aug87 on 'Chess'; GCH/+K7 8040)*

Sep 64. (lp) *(NPL 28040)* **MUDDY WATERS**
– I got my brand on you / Baby, please don't go / Tiger in your tank / I've got my mojo working (part 1) / Goodbye Newport blues / The same thing / Sittin' and thinkin' / 19 years old / I'm your hoochie coochie man / Soon forgotten / I feel so good / I've got my mojo working (part 2) / Long distance call / Wee wee baby / Clouds in my heart. *(cd-iss. Mar90 on 'Roots'; RTS 33018)*

Chess — Chess

Feb 65. (7") *(CRS 8001)* <1914> **MY JOHN THE CONQUER ROOT. / SHORT DRESS WOMAN**

1965. (7") <1921> **PUT ME IN YOUR LAY-A-WAY. / STILL A FOOL**

Aug 65. (7"ep) *(CRE 6006)* **I'M READY**
– She moves me / I can't be satisfied / I want you to love me.

Aug 65. (7") *(CRS 8019)* <1937> **I GOT A RICH MAN'S WOMAN. / MY DOG CAN'T BARK**

Jan 66. (lp) *(CRL 4515)* <1501> **THE REAL FOLK BLUES**
– Mannish boy / Screamin' and cryin' / Just to be with you / Walking in the park / Same thing / Walking blues / Canary bird / Gypsy women / Rollin' and tumblin' / Forty days and forty nights / You can't lose what you never had / Little Geneva.

May 66. (7"ep) *(CRE 6022)* **THE REAL FOLK BLUES VOL.4**
– I just want to make love to you / Louisiana blues / Still a fool / Standing around crying.

1966. (7") <1973> **CORINA, CORINA. / HOOTCHI KOOTCHIE MAN**

Jan 67. (lp) *(CRL 4525)* <1507> **MUDDY, BRASS AND THE BLUES**
– Corrine, Corrina / Piney brown blues / Black night / Trouble in mind / Goin' back to Memphis / Betty and Dupree / Sweet little angel / Take me advice / Trouble / Hard loser.

Aug 67. (lp; MUDDY WATERS, BO DIDDLEY & LITTLE WALTER) *(CRL 4529)* **SUPERBLUES**

1967. (7") <2018> **BIRDNEST ON THE GROUND. / WHEN THE EAGLE FLIES**

May 68. (lp; MUDDY WATERS, BO DIDDLEY & HOWLIN' WOLF) *(CRL 4537)* <LPS 3010> **THE SUPER BLUES BAND**

Chess — Cadet

Jan 69. (lp) *(CRL 4542)* <314> **ELECTRIC MUD** — Nov68
– I just want to make love to you / Hoochie coochie man / Let's spend the night together / She's all right / I'm a man / Herbert Harper's free press / Tom cat / Same thing. *(cd-iss. Apr97 on 'Chess-MCA'; MCD 09364)*

Jan 69. (7") *(CRS 8083)* **LET'S SPEND THE NIGHT TOGETHER. / I'M A MAN**

Aug 69. (lp) *(CRL 4553)* <320> **AFTER THE RAIN**
– I a the blues / Ramblin' mind / Rollin and tumblin' / Bottom of the sea / Honey bee / Blues and trouble / Hurtin' soul / Screamin' and cryin'

Oct 69. (d-lp) *(CRL 4556)* <127> **FATHERS AND SONS (live with PAUL BUTTERFIELD & MIKE BLOOMFIELD)** — Sep69 — 70
– All aboard / Mean disposition / Blow wind blow / Can't lose what you ain't never had / Walking through the park / 40 days and 40 nights /

Standin' round crying / I'm ready / Twenty four hours / Sugar sweet / Long distance call / Baby, please don't go / Honey bee / The same thing / Got my mojo working (pt.1 & 2). *(cd-iss. Oct01 on 'Universal'+=; AA8811 2648-2)* – (extra tracks).

(above also featured **BUDDY MILES + PHIL UPCHURCH**)

1970. (7") *<2085>* **GOING HOME. / I FEEL SO GOOD** –

Chess Chess

1972. (7") *<2107>* **MAKING FRIENDS. / TWO STEPS FORWARD** –

Jul 72. (lp) *(6310 121) <60013>* **THE LONDON MUDDY WATERS SESSIONS**

– Blind man blues / Key to the highway / Walkin' blues / I'm gonna move to the outskirts of town / Who's gonna be your sweet man when I'm gone / Young fashioned ways / Sad sad day / I don't know why. *(re-iss. Apr82 on 'Charly'; CXMP 2005) (re-iss. May92 on 'Chess-MCA'; CHLD/CHLC 19105)*

—— On 11 Oct'73, he was involved in a car accident which 3 people were killed. After releasing one more album, he went into semi-retirement for 2 years. Released 'LONDON REVISITED' Jan74 with HOWLIN' WOLF.

Nov 73. (7") *<2143>* **CAN'T GET NO GRINDIN'. / GARBAGE MAN** –

Jan 74. (lp) *(6310 129) <50023>* **CAN'T GET NO GRINDIN'**

– Can't get no grindin' / Mothers bad luck / Funky butt / Sad letter / Someday I'm gonna kitch you / Love weapon / Garbage man / After hours / Whiskey ain't no good / Muddy Waters' shuffle. *(re-iss. Sep90 lp/cd; CH/+D 9319)*

Mar 74. (lp) *<60031>* **"UNK" IN FUNK** –

Blue Sky Blue Sky

Apr 77. (lp) *(SKY 81853) <34449>* **HARD AGAIN** Feb77

– Mannish boy / Bus driver / I want to be loved / Jealous-hearted man / I can't be satisfied / The blues had a baby, and they named it rock'n'roll / Deep down in Florida / Crosseyed cat / Little girl. *(re-iss. Sep83; 32357) (cd-iss. Mar91) (re-iss. Feb94 on 'Columbia' cd/c; CD/40 32357)*

Feb 78. (lp) *(SKY 82235) <34928>* **I'M READY**

– I'm ready / 33 years / Who do you trust / Cooper Brown / I'm your hoochie coochie man / Mame / Rock me / Screamin' and cryin' / Good morning little schoolgirl. *(cd-iss. Nov91 on 'Beat Goes On';)*

Jan 79. (lp) *(SKY 83422) <35712>* **MUDDY MISSISSIPPI WATERS LIVE (live)**

– Mannish boy / She's 19 years old / Nine below zero / Streamline woman / Howling wolf / Baby please don't go / Deep down in Florida. *(cd-iss. Mar91 on 'Beat Goes On';)*

May 81. (lp) *(SKY 84918) <37064>* **KING BEE**

– I'm a king bee / Too young to know / Mean old Frisco blues / Forever lonely / I feel like goin' home / Champagne and reefer / Sad sad day / My eyes keep me in trouble / Deep down in Florida / No escape from the blues.

—— On the 30th Apr'83, MUDDY died of a heart attack in his Chicago home.

– (selective) compilations, etc. –

Nov 64. (lp) *Pye; (NPL 28048)* **MUDDY SINGS BIG BILL (BROONZY)**
(re-iss. Nov67 on 'Marble Arch'; MAL 723)

Jan 67. (lp) *Chess; <1511>* **MORE REAL FOLK BLUES** –

May 70. (lp) *Syndicate/ US= Chess; (SC 002) <002>* **GOOD NEWS**

– Trouble no more / Don't go no further / Diamonds at your feet / Evil / All aboard / I love the life I live / Mean mistreater / Recipe for love / Good news / Come home baby / I won't go / She's got it / Close to you. *(re-iss. 1979)*

Jun 70. (lp) *Syndicate; (SC 005) / Chess; <005>* **WE THREE KINGS ("with HOWLIN' WOLF & LITTLE WALTER")**
(re-iss. Sep82)

Feb 71. (lp) *Chess; <1553>* **THEY CALL ME MUDDY WATERS** –
(cd-iss. Jan98 on 'Summit'; SUMCD 4173)

Aug 92. (9xcd-box) *Chess; (CDREDBOX 3)* **THE COMPLETE MUDDY WATERS: 1947-1967**

Jan 92. (cd) *Quality; (QSCD 6004)* **THE ESSENTIAL RECORDINGS** –

Aug 92. (cd) *Columbia; (4768922)* **BLUE SKIES**
(re-iss. Nov02; 509315-2)

Nov 92. (cd/c) *Charly; (CD/TC BM 10)* **ROCK ME** –

Feb 93. (cd/c) *Charly; (CD/TC BM 39)* **FUNKY BUTT** –

Feb 93. (cd) *Charly; (CDCD 1039)* **GOT MY MOJO WORKING** –

Jul 93. (cd) *Charly; (CDCD 1100)* **HOOCHIE COOCHIE MAN** –

Sep 93. (cd) *See For Miles; (SEECD 379)* **THE EP COLLECTION (1-side by HOWLIN' WOLF)** –

May 94. (cd) *Charly; (CDTT 3)* **TWO ON ONE (w/JOHN LEE HOOKER)** –

Aug 94. (cd) *Charly;* **LIVE AT NEWPORT (live w/OTIS SPANN)** –

Nov 94. (cd) *Charly;* **CHICAGO 1979 (live)** –

Apr 95. (cd) *Charly; (CDRB 15)* **ELECTRIC MUD & MORE** –

Apr 95. (4xcd-box+book) *Charly; (CDDIG 9)* **THE KING OF CHICAGO BLUES** –

Apr 96. (cd) *Imp; (IMP 305)* **BABY PLEASE DON'T GO (live)**
(re-iss. May01 on 'I.T.M.'; ITM 960006)

Apr 97. (cd) *Chess-MCA; (MCD 09344)* **THE COMPLETE PLANTATION RECORDINGS**

Apr 97. (cd) *Chess-MCA; (MCD 09348)* **ONE MORE MILE**

Jul 97. (cd) *Chess-MCA; (MCD 09370)* **THE BEST OF MUDDY WATERS 1947-1955**

Feb 98. (cd) *Just A Memory; (JAM 9130-2)* **GOIN' WAY BACK**

Aug 98. (cd) *Beat Goes On; (BGOCD 397)* **MUDDY WATERS SINGS BILL BROONZY / FOLK SINGER**

Jan 99. (cd) *Beat Goes On; (BGOCD 436)* **REAL FOLK BLUES / MORE REAL FOLK BLUES**

Sep 99. (cd) *Just A Memory; (JAM 9142-2)* **HOOCHIE COOCHIE MAN: LIVE AT THE RISING CLUB 1977**

Jan 00. (cd) *I.T.M.; (ITM 960014)* **AFTER HOURS**

Mar 00. (d-cd) *Snapper; (SMDCD 249)* **TAKE A WALK WITH ME**

May 00. (cd) *Music Club; (MCCD 425)* **MOJO**

Jul 00. (cd) *Zircon Bleu; (BLEU 506)* **ARISTOCRAT OF THE BLUES 1946-1948**

Oct 00. (cd) *Play Me..; (PBCD 20510)* **PLAY ME THE BLUES VOL.10: THE LEGENDARY BLUES SINGERS**

Nov 00. (3xcd-box) *Golden Stars; (GSS 5293)* **BLUES LEGEND**

Jan 01. (cd) *Catfish; (KATCD 117)* **STREAMLINED WOMAN**

Feb 01. (cd) *Pablo; (PACD 5302-2)* **PARIS 1972**

Sep 01. (d-cd) *M.C.A.; (112649-2)* **THE ANTHOLOGY: 1947-1972**

Jul 02. (cd/c) *Castle Pulse; (PLS CD/MC 594)* **KINGS OF THE BLUES**

Jul 03. (cd) *Apreggio Blues; (ARB 001)* **OL' MAN MUD**

Roger WATERS

Born: 6 Sep'44, Great Bookham, Cambridge, England. A founding member of PINK FLOYD in 1965, WATERS became the outfit's mainman in 1968 following SYD BARRETT's break with reality. PINK FLOYD's frontman and main contributor until his departure in 1983, he put together the soundtrack to the film 'THE BODY' in 1970 together with synth/keys man, RON GEESIN. With PINK FLOYD absent from the recording front in the mid-80's, fans locked onto WATERS for worthwhile material. His debut album, 'PROS & CONS OF HITCH HIKING' (1984) didn't exactly set the world alight but managed a UK Top 20 placing. Not straying too far from latter day PF territory, WATERS carried on in even more lugubrious fashion with 1987's 'RADIO KAOS' set. Come the turn of the decade, with The BERLIN WALL being dismantled, ROGER thought it necessary to revive the 1979 PINK FLOYD album, 'THE WALL'. With an array of famous guests, he played there to a live audience of 200,000, plus TV millions all contributing to The Disaster Relief Fund. Almost ten years on from the release of studio set, 'AMUSED TO DEATH', WATERS released concert set, 'IN THE FLESH LIVE' (2000), a document of his turn of the decade American tour. For the first time since his break with PINK FLOYD – save his Berlin effort – WATERS revisited his favourite tracks from the band's glory heyday. • **Songwriters:** WATERS wrote all material. • **Trivia:** In 1987, WATERS took the existing members of PINK FLOYD to court, for their use of group name.

Album rating: THE BODY soundtrack with Ron Geesin (*4) / THE PROS AND CONS OF HITCH HIKING (*7) / RADIO K.A.O.S. (*5) / THE WALL: LIVE IN BERLIN (*4) / AMUSED TO DEATH (*5) / IN THE FLESH – LIVE (*5) / FLICKERING FLAME compilation (*7)

ROGER WATERS – vocals, bass, etc. (ex-PINK FLOYD) with **ERIC CLAPTON** – guitar / **ANDY NEWMARK** – drums / **RAY COOPER** – percussion / **MADELINE BELL** – vocals

Harvest Columbia

Apr 84. (7") *(HAR 5228)* **5:01 a.m. (THE PROS AND CONS OF HITCH HIKING). / 4:30 a.m. (APPARENTLY THEY WERE TRAVELLING ABROAD)** [ ] [ ]
(12"+=) *(12HAR 5228)* – 4:33 a.m. (Running shoes).

May 84. (lp/c/cd) *(SHVL 240105-1/-4/-2) <39290>* **THE PROS AND CONS OF HITCH HIKING** [13] [31]
– 4:30 a.m. (Apparently they were travelling abroad) / 4:33 a.m. (Running shoes) / 4:37 a.m. (Arabs with knives and West German skies) / 4:39 a.m. (For the first time today) / 4:41 a.m. (Sexual revolution) / 4:47 a.m. (The remains of our love) / 4:50 a.m. (Go fishing) / 4:56 a.m. (For the first time today pt.2) / 4:58 a.m. (Dunroamin' duncarin' dunlivin') / 5:06 a.m. (Every strangers eyes) / 5:11 a.m. (The moment of clarity).

Jun 84. (7") *(HAR 5230)* **5:06 a.m. (EVERY STRANGERS EYES). / 4:39 a.m. (FOR THE FIRST TIME TODAY)** [ ] [ ]

—— In Oct'86, WATERS and his BLEEDING HEART BAND featured on 1 side of 'WHEN THE WIND BLOWS' album / animated cartoon film on 'Virgin'.

—— His new band: **ANDY FAIRWEATHER-LOW** – guitar / **JAY STAPLEY** – electric guitar / **MEL COLLINS** – sax / **IAN RITCHIE** – keyboards, drum prog. / **GRAHAM BROAD** – drums

E.M.I. Columbia

May 87. (7") *(EM 6)* **RADIO WAVES (edit). / GOING TO LIVE IN L.A.** [74] [ ]
(12"+=/cd-s+=) *(12/CD EM 6)* – ('A'demo version).

Jun 87. (cd/c/lp) *(CD/TC+/KAOS 1) <40795>* **RADIO KAOS** [25] [50]
– Radio waves / Who needs information / Me or him / The powers that be / Sunset Strip / Home / Four minutes / The tide is turning.

Nov 87. (7") *(EM 37)* **THE TIDE IS TURNING (After Live Aid). / GET BACK ON THE RADIO (demo)** [54] [ ]
(12"+=/cd-s+=) *(12/CD EM 37)* – Money (live).

Mercury Mercury

Sep 90. (d-cd/d-c/d-lp; ROGER WATERS AND THE BLEEDING HEART BAND) *(<846611-2/-4/-1>)* **THE WALL: LIVE IN BERLIN (live)** [27] [56]
– In the flesh? (SCORPIONS) / The thin ice (UTE LEMPER) / Another brick in the wall – part 1 / The happiest days of our lives (JOE CHEMAY) / Another brick in the wall – part 2 (CYNDI LAUPER) / Mother (SINEAD O'CONNOR) / Goodbye blue sky (JONI MITCHELL) / Empty spaces + Young lust (BRYAN ADAMS) / One of my turns / Don't leave me now / Another brick in the wall – part 3 / Goodbye cruel world / Hey you (PAUL CARRACK) / Is there anybody out there? (MICHAEL KAMEN /The RUNDFUNK ORCHESTRA +*) / Nobody home / Vera (*) / Bring the boys back home / Comfortably numb (VAN MORRISON) / In the flesh? (*) / Run like Hell / Waiting for the worms (*) / Stop to / The trial (TIM CURRY & THOMAS DOLBY) / The tide is turning (The COMPANY). *(re-iss. d-cd Sep95)*

Sep 90. (7"/12") **ANOTHER BRICK IN THE WALL (part 2). / RUN LIKE HELL (live)** [ ] [ ]
(cd-s+=) – ('A'extended).

Columbia Columbia

Aug 92. (7"/c-s) *(658 139-7/-4)* **WHAT GOD WANTS, PART 1. / ('A'video edit)** [35] [ ]
(cd-s+=) *(658 139-2)* – What God wants, part III.

Sep 92. (cd/c/lp) *(468761-2/-4/-1) <47127>* **AMUSED TO DEATH** [8] [21]
– The ballad of Bill Hubbard / What God wants, part 1 / Perfect sense, part I & II / The bravery of being out of range / Late home tonight, part I & II / Too much rope / What God wants, part II & III / Watching TV / Three wishes / It's a miracle / Amused to death. *(cd re-iss. Jan99; same)*

Dec 92. (7"/c-s) *(658 819-7/-4)* **THE BRAVERY OF BEING OUT OF RANGE. / WHAT GOD WANTS (part 1)** [ ] [ ]
(cd-s+=) *(658 819-2)* – Perfect sense (part 1).

—— ROGER semi-retired for several years

Dec 00. (d-cd) *(501137-2) <85235>* **IN THE FLESH – LIVE (live)** [ ] [ ]
– In the flesh / The happiest days of our lives / Another brick in the wall (part 2) / Mother / Get your filthy hands off my desert / Southampton dock / Pigs on the wing (part 1) / Dogs / Welcome to the machine / Wish you were here / Shine on you crazy diamond (parts 1-8) / Set the controls for the heart of the sun / Breathe (in the air) / Time / Money / The pros and cons of hitch hiking (part 2) / Perfect sense (parts 1 & 2) / The bravery of being out of range / It's a miracle / Amused to death / Brain damage / Eclipse / Comfortably numb / Each small candle.

– compilations, etc. –

May 02. (cd) *Columbia; (<5 07906-2>)* **FLICKERING FLAME: THE SOLO YEARS VOLUME 1** [ ] [ ]
– Knockin' on Heaven's door / Too much rope / The tide is turning / Perfect sense (pts.1 & 2) / Three wishes / 5.06 a.m. (every stranger's eyes) / Who needs information / Each small candle / Flickering flame / Towers of faith / Radio waves / Lost boys calling (original demo).

Johnny "Guitar" WATSON

Born: 3 Feb'35, Houston, Texas, USA. Taught piano by his father, the teenage WATSON soon became more concerned with playing electric guitar. Inspired by such local heroes as CLARENCE 'GATEMOUTH' BROWN, WATSON subsequently relocated to L.A. and became involved with the thriving blues/R&B scene. Although his first vinyl appearance was with CHUCK HIGGINS' MELLOTONES, he made his solo debut for 'Federal' in 1953 as YOUNG JOHN WATSON. All the while developing his axe skills, he was dubbed JOHNNY "GUITAR" WATSON by 'Modern' records, for whom he recorded during the mid 50's. During his tenure with the label, he scored a one-off R&B hit with a version of Earl King's 'THOSE LONELY LONELY NIGHTS', moving on to cut sides for a variety of imprints and recording the original version of 'GANGSTER OF LOVE' (later famously covered by STEVE MILLER) in 1968. More hits followed in the early 60's with 'King', WATSON hooking up with LARRY WILLIAMS (who had briefly challenged LITTLE RICHARD's rock'n'roll crown in the late 50's) throughout the 60's and scoring a few collaborative hits for 'Okeh'. The early 70's proved a pivotal time for WATSON as he headed out on his own, re-evaluated his direction and began incorporating elements of a more experimental sonic palate, initially with 'Fantasy' and then with UK label, 'DJM', previously home to ELTON JOHN. He scored almost immediately with the brassy, breezy pop-funk of 'I NEED IT', tipping a hat to the likes of the AVERAGE WHITE BAND. The accompanying album, 'AIN'T THAT A BITCH' (1976), confirmed the veteran guitarist's move towards a more contemporary sound, a ploy that duly earned him his first gold record. A man not scared to admit he was a 'SUPERMAN LOVER', WATSON's run of success continued with the albums 'A REAL MOTHER' (1977), 'FUNK BEYOND THE CALL OF DUTY' (1977) and 'LOVE JONES' (1980) amongst others, moogs, fender rhodes piano and vocoders the order of the day alongside the patented fret work. One listen to the revamped 'GANGSTER OF LOVE' from 1978's 'GIANT' was enough to dispel any blues purists' fears of WATSON forgetting his roots. With the death of his longtime friend WILLIAMS in 1980, however, along with the changing musical climate, WATSON made a retreat from the music biz frontline after a one-off album for 'A&M', 'THAT'S WHAT TIME IT IS' (1981). Save a few low profile live appearances, the man remained absent from the scene until 1994, when he made something of a comeback with the 'BOW WOW' album. Tragically, however, on the 17th of May 1996, the Guitar man suffered a fatal heart attack onstage at the Yokohama Blues Cafe in Japan.

Album rating: JOHNNY GUITAR WATSON (*5) / BLUES SOUL (*4) / BAD (*4) / TWO FOR THE PRICE OF ONE (*4) / IN THE FATS BAG (*4) / LISTEN (*5) / I DON'T WANT TO A LONE RANGER (*5) / AIN'T THAT A BITCH

(*8) / A REAL MOTHER FOR YA (*7) / FUNK BEYOND THE CALL OF DUTY (*6) / MASTER FUNK by Watsonian Institute (*4) / GIANT (*4) / WHAT THE HELL IS THIS (*5) / LOVE JONES (*4) / . . . AND THE FAMILY CLONE (*4) / THAT'S WHAT TIME IT IS (*4) / STRIKE ON COMPUTERS (*3) / BOW WOW (*6) / GANGSTER OF LOVE – THE BEST OF JOHNNY "GUITAR" WATSON compilation (*7)

JOHNNY "GUITAR" WATSON – vocals, guitar / with various

not iss. — Federal

1953. (78; as YOUNG JOHN WATSON) *<12175>* **SPACE GUITAR. / HALF PINT A WHISKEY** –
1954. (78; as YOUNG JOHN WATSON) *<12183>* **YOU CAN'T TAKE IT WITH YOU. / GETTIN' DRUNK** –

—— unsure of his recordings for 'Modern' in the mid-late 50's

not iss. — King

1958. (lp) **GANGSTER OF LOVE** –
Oct 61. (7") *<5536>* **EMBRACEABLE YOU. / POSIN'** –
Jan 62. (7") *<5579>* **CUTTIN' IN. / BROKE AND LONELY** –
Mar 62. (7") *<5607>* **I JUST WANT ME SOME LOVE. / THE NEARNESS OF YOU** –
Aug 62. (7") *<5666>* **WHAT YOU DO TO ME. / SWEET LOVIN' MAMA** –
Mar 63. (7") *(5716>* **COLD, COLD HEART. / THAT'S THE CHANCE YOU'VE GOT TO TAKE** –
Aug 63. (7") *<5774>* **GANGSTER OF LOVE. / IN THE EVENING** –
Dec 63. (7") *<5833>* **YOU BETTER LOVE ME. / I SAY, I LOVE YOU** –
1960's. (lp) *<857>* **JOHNNY "GUITAR" WATSON** –
(cd-iss. May97 on 'Experience'; EXP 045)

not iss. — Chess

1960's. (lp) *<1490>* **BLUES SOUL** –

Decca — not iss.

May 65. (7"; by LARRY WILLIAMS & JOHNNY "GUITAR" WATSON) *(F 12151)* **SWEET LITTLE BABY. / SLOW DOWN** –
1965. (lp; by LARRY WILLIAMS & JOHNNY "GUITAR" WATSON) *(LK 4691)* **THE LARRY WILLIAMS SHOW** –

Columbia — Okeh

1966. (lp) *<OKS 14118>* **BAD** –
Feb 67. (7"; by LARRY WILLIAMS & JOHNNY "GUITAR" WATSON) *(DB 8140) <7274>* **MERCY, MERCY, MERCY. / A QUITTER NEVER QUITS** 96
1967. (lp) *<OKS 14122>* **TWO FOR THE PRICE OF ONE** –
1968. (lp) *<OKS 14124>* **IN THE FATS BAG** –

—— now included band incl. **EMERY THOMAS** – drums

Fantasy — Fantasy

1973. (lp) *(038-61279) <9437>* **LISTEN**
– If I had the power / You've got a hard head / Lovin' you / It's all about you / You're the sweetest thing I've ever had / I get a feeling / Why don't you treat me like I'm your man / You bring love / You stole my heart. *(cd-iss. Sep92 on 'Ace-Charly'; CDCHD 408)*
Feb 76. (7") *(FTC 124) <FTC 739>* **I DON'T WANT TO BE A LONE RANGER. / YOU CAN STAY BUT THE NOISE MUST GO** Sep75 99
Mar 76. (lp) *<9484>* **I DON'T WANT TO BE A LONE RANGER** –
– I don't want to be a lone ranger / Your new love is a player / Tripping / Lonely man's prayer / You make my heart want to sing / It's way too late / Love is sweet misery / You can stay but the noise must go / Strong vibrations.

D.J.M. — D.J.M.

Jul 76. (7") *(DJS 10694) <1013>* **I NEED IT. / SINCE I MET YOU BABY** 35 Jun76
Sep 76. (lp/c) *(DJF2/DJH4 0485) <3>* **AIN'T THAT A BITCH** Jul76 52
– I need it / I want to ta-ta you baby / Superman lover / Ain't that a bitch / Since I met you baby / We're no exception / Won't you forgive me baby. *(re-iss. Nov81 lp/c; 2/4 2100) (cd-iss. Jan96 on 'Sequel'; NEMCD 774)*
Oct 76. (7") *(DJS 10722) <1019>* **SUPERMAN LOVER. / WE'RE NO EXCEPTION**
Dec 76. (7") *<1020>* **AIN'T THAT A BITCH. / WON'T YOU FORGIVE ME BABY** –
Apr 77. (7") *(DJS 10762) <1024>* **A REAL MOTHER FOR YA. / NOTHING LEFT TO BE DESIRED** 44 41
May 77. (lp/c) *(DJF2/DJH4 0505) <7>* **A REAL MOTHER FOR YA** Apr77 20
– A real mother for ya / Nothing left to be desired / Your love is my love / The real deal / Tarzan / I wanna thank you / Lover Jones. *(re-iss. Nov81 lp/c; 2/4 2105) (cd-iss. 1988; 825363-2) (cd re-iss. Jan96 on 'Sequel'; NEMCD 775)*
Jun 77. (7") *<1029>* **LOVER JONES. / TARZAN** –
Jul 77. (7") *(DJS 10790)* **THE REAL DEAL. / TARZAN** –
Jan 78. (7") *(DJS 10838) <1034>* **IT'S A DAMN SHAME. / LOVE THAT WILL NOT DIE**
Jan 78. (lp/c) *(DJF2/DJH4 0525) <714>* **FUNK BEYOND THE CALL OF DUTY** Dec77 84
– Funk beyond the call of duty / It's about the dollar bill / Give me my love / It's a damn shame / I'm gonna get you / Barn door / Love that will not die. *(re-iss. Nov81 lp/c; 2/4 2101) (cd-iss. Jan96 on 'Sequel'; NEMCD 776)*
Apr 78. (7"; as WATSONIAN INSTITUTE) *<1100>* **THE INSTITUTE. / VIRGINIA'S PRETTY FUNKY** –
Apr 78. (lp/c; as WATSONIAN INSTITUTE) *(DJF2/DJH4 0529) <13>* **MASTER FUNK**
– The institute / Master funk / The funk if I know / Lady voodoo / De John's delight / Coming round / Virginia's pretty funky.
Oct 78. (7") *(DJS 10881)* **MISS FRISCO (QUEEN OF THE DISCO). / TU JOURS AMOUR** –
Nov 78. (lp/c) *(DJS2/DJH4 0551) <19>* **GIANT** Oct78
– Miss Frisco (queen of the disco) / Tu jours amour / Gangster of love / Guitar disco / Wrapped in black mink / You can stay but the noise can go / Baby face. *(re-iss. Nov81 lp/c; 2/4 2102)*
Dec 78. (7") *<1101>* **GUITAR DISCO. / GANGSTER OF LOVE** –
Jan 79. (7")(12") *(DJS 10890)(DJR 18004)* **YOU CAN STAY BUT THE NOISE MUST GO. / GANGSTER OF LOVE** –
Jul 79. (7") *<1106>* **WHAT THE HELL IS THIS. / CAN YOU HANDLE IT** –
Aug 79. (lp/c) *(DJS2/DJH4 0557) <24>* **WHAT THE HELL IS THIS**
– What the hell is this / In the world / Proud of you / Cop and blow / I don't want to be president / Mother in law / Strung out. *(re-iss. Nov81 lp/c; 2/4 2103) (cd-iss. Nov87 on 'Mercury'; 832839-2)*
Jun 80. (7") *<1304>* **LOVE JONES. /** –
Jun 80. (7") *(DJS 10943)* **BOOTY OOTY. / JET PLANE** –
(12") *(DJR 18011)* – ('A'side) / Love Jones.
Jul 80. (lp/c) *(DJS2/DJH4 0568) <31>* **LOVE JONES** Jun80
– Booty ooty / Love Jones / Going up in smoke / Close encounters / Asante sana / Telephone bill / Lone ranger / Jet plane / Children of the universe. *(re-iss. Nov81 lp/c; 2/4 2104)*
Nov 80. (7") *<1305>* **TELEPHONE BILL. /** –
Jun 81. (lp/c) *(DJS2/DJH4 0574) <501>* **JOHNNY "GUITAR" WATSON AND THE FAMILY CLONE**
– Clone information / Family clone / Forget the Joneses / Ain't movin' / Come and dance with me / Rio dreamin' / What is love? / Voodoo what you do.
Oct 81. (lp/c) *(DJS2/DJH4 0576)* **THE VERY BEST OF JOHNNY "GUITAR" WATSON** (compilation) –
– Gangster of love / Booty ooty / Ain't that a bitch / Love Jones / What the hell is this / It's about the dollar bill / Ain't movin' / I need it / A mother for ya / Strung out. *(cd-iss. 1988; 825364-2)*

A&M — not iss.

Dec 81. (lp) *(AMLH 64880)* **THAT'S WHAT TIME IT IS** –
– Do the guitar / The planet funk / You sexy thing / That's what time it is / Flip it / Go for it / At the wishing well / First Timothy six / I miss your kiss.

Stomp Off — not iss.

Jul 87. (lp/c/cd) *(SOS/+MC/CD 2001)* **STRIKE ON COMPUTERS** –
– You do me bad so good / Boogie down party down / Scratching "85" / Let's get together / Strike on computers / Byrd ball train / Statue of liberty / Please send me someone to love.

S.P.V. — Bellmark

Oct 96. (cd) *(SPV 084-4207-2) <6863951007-2>* **BOW WOW** 1994
– Johnny G. is back / Bow wow / Never too late / My funk / It takes 2 / Time change / Doing wrong woman / What's up with you / Hook me up / I don't think so. *(re-iss. Jun00 on 'Bellmark'; same as US)*

– compilations, others, etc. –

Jul 76. (7"; by LARRY WILLIAMS & JOHNNY "GUITAR" WATSON) *Epic; (EPC 4421)* **TOO LATE. / TWO FOR THE PRICE OF ONE**

Nov 81. (d-c) *D.J.M.; (TWO 417)* **THE VERY BEST OF . . . / MR. GUITAR**

Sep 82. (lp) *Red Lightnin'; (RL 0013)* **THE GANGSTER IS BACK** (1955-61)
– Too tired / Don't touch me / Hot little mama / Blues side / I love to love you / Oh baby / Someone cares of me / She moves me / Love me baby / Gangster of love / One room country shack / Acoustic instrumental / One more kiss / Johnny Guitar / Looking back / The eagle is back.

Jul 83. (lp) *Ace-Charly; (CH 70)* **HIT THE HIGHWAY**

Oct 83. (7") *D.J.M.; (DJS 4)* **GANGSTER OF LOVE. / I NEED IT**
(12") *(DJR 4)* – ('A'side) / Ain't that a bitch / A real mother for ya.

Jul 85. (lp/c) *Charly; (CRB/TC-CRB 1101)* **I HEARD THAT**
(cd-iss. Jan87; CDCHARLY 48)

Jan 87. (lp/c) *Chess; (GCH/+K7 8017)* **GETTIN' DOWN WITH . . .**

Mar 87. (cd) *Ace; (CDCH 909)* **THREE HOURS PAST MIDNIGHT**

Jul 88. (lp) *Bellaphon; (BID 8013)* **GANGSTER OF LOVE**
(cd-iss. Feb91 on 'Charly'; CDCHARLY 267) (cd re-iss. Aug95 on 'Castle'; CCSCD 802) (cd re-iss. Oct99 on 'King'; KCD 6004)

Sep 96. (cd) *Ace-Charly; (CDCHD 621)* **HOT JUST LIKE T.N.T.**

Feb 00. (cd) *Sequel; (NEMCD 467)* **GANGSTER OF LOVE – THE BEST OF JOHNNY "GUITAR" WATSON**

□ Ben WATT (see under ⇒ EVERYTHING BUT THE GIRL)

Jimmy WEBB

Born: 15 Aug'46, Elk City, Oklahoma. Son of a baptist preacher/minister, WEBB had learned piano as a kid and, inspired by the California surf boom, had already begun writing songs by the time he signed up for a course at San Bernardino college in 1963. Jacking it in shortly after to ply his trade as a songwriter, he soon found himself working for 'Jobete' music, the publishing wing of 'Tamla Motown'. A subsequent move to L.A. eventually led to a job with a similar company set up by JOHNNY RIVERS, the singer unsuccessfully covering WEBB's haunting 'BY THE TIME I GET TO PHOENIX'. A classic example of this farmer turned songwriter's orchestral L.A. sound, the track was later given a definitive reading by easy rocking country celeb GLEN CAMPBELL. WEBB's first real success had actually come around the same time when black soul-pop outfit, FIFTH DIMENSION took 'UP, UP AND AWAY' into the US Top 10. TWA subsequently used the track on a commercial and WEBB's career went stratospheric almost overnight. A keen student of the PHIL SPECTOR/BRIAN WILSON school of production technique, WEBB's highly distinctive, expansive arrangements were indelibly marked with the desolation and panoramic melancholy of his native Oklahoma. You could hear it in 'WITCHITA LINEMAN', another WEBB weepie transformed by the golden tonsils of GLEN CAMPBELL, the singer completing his hat trick in 1969 when he carried 'GALVESTON' into the Top 5. The previous year RICHARD HARRIS had narrowly missed the top of the US charts with WEBB's 'MACARTHUR PARK', the most deliciously overwrought composition of his songwriting career and a song subsequently covered by artists as diverse as DIANA ROSS and WAYLON JENNINGS. As for WEBB's own recording career (not including a one-one 45 with bubblegum trio, The STRAWBERRY CHILDREN), 'Epic' kickstarted it without telling him in 1968 with 'JIM WEBB SINGS JIM WEBB', a collection of early demos. With the rise of the singer songwriter brigade in the early 70's, WEBB quite understandably attempted to cut himself a piece of the action as the role of the traditional songwriter diminished. Signed to L.A. powerhouse, 'Reprise', he finally released a debut album proper, 'WORDS AND MUSIC', in 1970. Markedly more lo-fi than the grandiose pieces that had made him famous, the album made little impact. A further two albums of excellent singer songwriter fare, 'AND SO ON' (1971) and 'LETTERS' (1972), were similarly overlooked and ultimately WEBB failed to make the transition from backroom to centre stage undertaken so successfully by his former East coast contemporary, CAROLE KING. He nevertheless enjoyed at least some sporadic chart grace as ART GARFUNKEL hit in 1973 with 'ALL I KNOW', no doubt helping to ease the pressure of being dropped by 'Reprise'. Briefly taken under the wing of 'Asylum' for 'LAND'S END' (1974), WEBB's recording fortunes failed to improve and even his production forays fell by the wayside as an attempted FIFTH DIMENSION reunion project stiffed in the mid-70's. Although he continued to write for film and television, WEBB's profile was almost non existent for the bulk of the 80's following 1982's 'ANGEL HEART' album. It was more than a decade before he released another album of songs, 1993's well received 'SUSPENDING DISBELIEF'. The man behind some of America's most evocative and enduring songs, WEBB's place in music biz history is assured even if he's never actually been a household name. He still tours occasionally and even played some rare UK dates in 1998, performing timeless songs to an ageing audience.

Album rating: JIM WEBB SINGS JIM WEBB (*3) / WORDS AND MUSIC (*5) / AND SO ON (*5) / LETTERS (*4) / LAND'S END (*4) / EL MIRAGE (*7) / ANGEL HEART (*4) / ARCHIVE compilation (*8) / SUSPENDED DISBELIEF (*5) / TEN EASY PIECES (*7)

JIMMY WEBB – vocals, acoustic guitar / (with various others)

Liberty — Soul City

1967. (7"; by The STRAWBERRY CHILDREN) *(LBF 15012)* *<758>* **LOVE YEARS COMING. / ONE STANDS HERE**

C.B.S. — Epic

Jul 68. (lp; as JIM WEBB) *(63335)* *<26401>* **JIM WEBB SINGS JIM WEBB** (unauthorised demos)
– I keep it hid / You're so young / I'll be back / Life is hard / I need you / Our time is running out / I can do it on my own / Then / I'm in need / Run, run, run.

Aug 68. (7"; as JIM WEBB) *(3672)* *<10329>* **I KEEP IT HID. / I NEED YOU**

Reprise — Reprise

Jan 71. (7"; as JIMMY L. WEBB) *<(RS 20-978)>* **P.F. SLOAN. / PSALM ONE-FIVE-O**

Jan 71. (lp; as JIMMY L. WEBB) *<(RSLP 6421)>* **WORDS AND MUSIC** — Feb70
– Words and music / Sleepin' in the daytime / P.F. Sloan / Love song / Careless weed / Psalm one-five-o / Music for an unmade movie part 1:- Songseller – part 2:- Dorothy Chandler blues – part 3:- Jerusalem / Three songs:- Let it be me – Never my love – I wanna be free / Once before I die. *(re-iss. 1971; K 44101)*

Aug 71. (lp) *(K 44134)* *<RSLP 6448>* **AND SO ON**
– Met her on a plane / All night show / All my love's laughter / Highpockets / Marionette / Laspitch / One lady / If ships were made to sail / Pocketful of keys / See you then.

Sep 72. (lp) *(K 44173)* *<RSLP 2055>* **LETTERS**
– Galveston / Campo de Encino / Love hurts / Hurt me well / Once in the morning / Catharsis / Song seller / When can brown begin / Piano. *<US cd-iss. 1999 on 'WEA Int.'; 10305>*

Sep 72. (7") *<1116>* **CAMPO DE ENCINO. / LOVE HURTS**

Jul 73. (7") *(K 14279)* **CAMPO DE ENCINO. / ONCE IN THE MORNING**

Asylum — Asylum

Nov 73. (7") *<11027>* **CRYING IN MY SLEEP. / OCEAN IN HIS EYES**

May 74. (7") *<11042>* **FEET IN THE SUNSHINE. / LADY FITS HER BLUE JEANS**

May 74. (7") *(AYM 529)* **FEET IN THE SUNSHINE. / OCEAN IN HIS EYES** –

Jul 74. (lp) *(SYL 9014)* <5070> **LAND'S END** Apr74
– Ocean in his eyes / Feet in the sunshine / Cloudman / Lady fits her blue jeans / Just this one time / Crying in my sleep / It's a sin / Alyce blue gown / Land's end – Asleep on the wind.

Atlantic Atlantic

Apr 77. (7") *(K 10931)* **THE HIGHWAYMAN. / CHRISTIAN NO** –

May 77. (lp) *(K 50370)* <18218> **EL MIRAGE**
– The highwayman / If you see me getting smaller I'm leaving / Mixed-up guy / Christian no / Moment in a shadow / Sugarbird / Where the universes are / P.F. Sloan / Dance to the radio. *<US cd-iss. 1999 on 'WEA Int.'; 2768>*

Jun 77. (7") <3407> **IF YOU SEE ME GETTING SMALLER I'M LEAVING. / CHRISTIAN NUMBER** –

Jul 77. (7") *(K 10978)* **WHERE THE UNIVERSES ARE. / THE MOON IS A HARSH MISTRESS** –

Aug 77. (7") <3426> **THE HIGHWAYMAN. / THE MOON IS A HARSH MISTRESS** –

— in 1979, JIMMY featured on the 1979 film, 'Voices'.

not iss. Columbia

Aug 82. (lp) <FC 37695> **ANGEL HEART** –
– Angel heart / God's gift / One of the few / Scissors cut / Work for a dollar / His world / Our movie / Nasty love / In cars / Old wing mouth. *<cd-iss. 1992 on 'Sony'; 66654>*

WEA WEA

Oct 93. (cd/c) <(7559 61506-2/-4)> **SUSPENDED DISBELIEF** Sep93
– Too young to die / I don't know how to love you anymore / Elvis and me / It won't bring her back / Sandy cove / Friends to burn / What does a woman see in a man / Postcards from Paris / Just like always / Adios / I will arise.

Guardian-EMI Guardian-EMI

Oct 97. (cd) <(8 52826-2)> **TEN EASY PIECES** (re-takes) Oct96
– Galveston / The highwayman / Wichita lineman / The moon is a harsh mistress / By the time I get to Phoenix / If these walls could speak / Didn't we? / The worst thing that could happen / All I know / MacArthur Park.

— A Various Artists tribute, 'AND SOMEONE LEFT THE CAKE OUT IN THE RAIN', was issued by 'Debutante' early '98

– compilations, etc. –

Jul 93. (cd) *WEA; (9548 32063-2)* **ARCHIVE** (1970-1977) –
– P.F. Sloan / Love song / Three songs / Met her on a plane / All my love's laughter / One lady / If ships were made to sail / Galveston / Once in the morning / When brown can begin / Piano / The highwayman / Christian no / Where the universes are / The moon is a harsh mistress / Feet in the sunshine / Lady fits her blue jeans / Just this one time / Crying in my sleep / Land's end – Asleep on the wind.

WEDDING PRESENT

Formed: Leeds, England . . . 1984 by ex-teachers DAVID GEDGE and PETE SOLOWKA (father Ukrainian) along with KEITH GREGORY and SHAUN CHARMAN. They gained a deal with local indie label, 'Reception', in 1985 and, with appearances on John Peel's radio 1 show, quickly grew into a cult act. Debut album, 'GEORGE BEST' (1987) was one of the key 80's indie releases, GEDGE's tunefully challenged monotone combining with the fast and furious punk-jangle racket to somehow create something more than the sum of its parts. Towards the end of the decade, they were finally signed to a major record company, 'R.C.A.', their first release on the label, 'UKRAINSKI . . .', surprising many with its marriage of Ukranian folk styles and indie-rock. GEDGE reverted to his trademark lovelorn lyrical fashion for follow-up proper, 'BIZARRO', a record that disappointed many longtime fans. Nevertheless, The WEDDING PRESENT were nothing if not prolific, even achieving the accolade of a Guinness Book Of Records entry in 1992 when every one of their monthly single (7"only) releases hit the UK Top 30 (The 12 hits also contained an unusual cover version on the B-side, see below). Despite the departure of all founding members save GEDGE (SALOWKA left in the early 90's to form The UKRAINIANS), 1994's 'WATUSI' again found the band in favour with the critics if not commanding the fanbase they once had. In 1998, GEDGE re-invented himself as a SERGE GAINSBOURG or BURT BACHARACH-type crooner in the project/duo, CINERAMA, alongside SALLY MURRELL, his sort of JANE BIRKIN, you could say. An album, 'VA VA VOOM', was a marked change of direction from the WEDDOES bust-a-gut blasts, into EDWYN COLLINS glutty vocals. CINERAMA completed their second batch, 'DISCO VOLANTE' (2000), while the romantic GEDGE and MURRELL returned all 'STARRY EYED' (one of the tracks incidentally) on 2002's 'TORINO'. • **Songwriters:** GEDGE compositions, except GETTING NOWHERE FAST (Girls At Our Best) / WHAT BECOME OF THE BROKEN HEARTED (Jimmy Ruffin) / I FOUND THAT ESSENCE RARE (Gang Of Four) / IT'S NOT UNUSUAL (Tom Jones) / FELICITY (Orange Juice) / MAKE ME SMILE (COME UP AND SEE ME) (Steve Harley & Cockney Rebel) / BOX ELDER (Pavement) / SHE'S MY BEST FRIEND (Velvet Underground) / MOTHERS (Jean Michel Satre) / CUMBERLAND GAP (Leadbelly) / CATTLE AND CANE (Go-Betweens) / DON'T CRY NO TEARS (Neil Young) / THINK THAT IT MIGHT (Altered Images) / FALLING (Julee Cruise) / PLEASANT VALLEY SUNDAY (Monkees) / LET'S MAKE SOME PLANS (Close Lobsters) / ROCKET (Mud) / THEME FROM SHAFT (Isaac Hayes) / CHANT OF THE EVER CIRCLING SKELETAL FAMILY (Bowie) / GO WILD IN THE COUNTRY (Bow Wow Wow) / U.F.O. (Barry Gray) / STEP INTO CHRISTMAS (Elton John) / JUMPER CLOWN (Marc Riley). CINERAMA covered: LONDON (Smiths) / ELENORE (Turtles) / YESTERDAY ONCE MORE (Carpenters) / DIAMONDS ARE FOREVER (John Barry). • **Trivia:** STEVE ALBINI (ex-BIG BLACK) produced their early 90s material.

Album rating: GEORGE BEST (*9) / TOMMY collection (*8) / UKRAINSKI VISTUPU V JOHNA PEELA (*5) / BIZARRO (*7) / SEAMONSTERS (*7) / THE HIT PARADE 1 compilation (*7) / THE HIT PARADE 2 compilation (*6) / WATUSI (*5) / MINI (*4) / SATURNALIA (*5) / Cinerama: VA VA VOOM (*6) / DISCO VOLANTE (*5) / THIS IS CINERAMA collection (*6) / JOHN PEEL SESSIONS collection (*5) / TORINO (*5) / CINERAMA HOLIDAY collection (*5)

DAVID GEDGE (b.23 Apr'60) – vocals, guitar / **PETE SOLOWKA** (b. Manchester) – guitar / **KEITH GREGORY** (b. 2 Jan'63, County Durham) – bass / **SHAUN CHARMAN** (b.Brighton) – drums

Reception not iss.

May 85. (7") *(REC 001)* **GO OUT AND GET 'EM BOY. / (THE MOMENT BEFORE) EVERYTHING'S SPOILED AGAIN** –
(re-iss. Sep85 on 'City Slang'; CSL 001)

Feb 86. (7") *(REC 002)* **ONCE MORE. / AT THE EDGE OF THE SEA** –

Apr 86. (12"ep) *(REC 002-12)* **DON'T TRY AND STOP ME MOTHER** –
– Go out and get 'em boy / (The moment before) Everything's spoiled again / Once more / At the edge of the sea.

Jul 86. (7") *(REC 003)* **THIS BOY CAN'T WAIT. / YOU SHOULD ALWAYS KEEP IN TOUCH WITH YOUR FRIENDS** –
(ext.12"+=) *(REC 003-12)* – Living and learning.

Feb 87. (7",7"white/12") *REC 005/+12)* **MY FAVOURITE DRESS. / EVERY MOTHER'S SON / NEVER SAID** –
(2,000 copies of above single were also given free with debut lp)

Sep 87. (7") *(REC 006)* **ANYONE CAN MAKE A MISTAKE. / ALL ABOUT EVE** –
(c-s+=/12"+=) *(REC 006 C/12)* – Getting nowhere fast.

Oct 87. (lp/c/cd) *(LEEDS 001/+C/CD)* **GEORGE BEST** 47 –
– Everyone thinks he looks daft / What did your last servant die of? / Don't be so hard / A million miles / All this and more / Getting nowhere fast * / My favourite dress / Shatner / Something and nothing / It's what you

want that matters / Give my love to Kevin / Anyone can make a mistake / You can't moan can you / All about Eve *. *(c+=/cd+= * tracks) (<cd re-iss. Oct97 on 'Cooking Vinyl' 4x10"lp-box++/cd+=; COOK/+CD 134>)* – Nobody's twisting your arm / Nothing comes easy / Don't laugh / I'm not always so stupid / Why are you being so reasonable now? / Not from where I'm standing / Give my love to Kevin / Getting better / Pourquoi es tu devenue si raisonnable?

—— **SIMON SMITH** (b. 3 May'65, Lincolnshire) – drums repl. SHAUN to POPGUNS

Feb 88. (7") *(REC 009)* **NOBODY'S TWISTING YOUR ARM. / I'M NOT ALWAYS SO STUPID** [46] [–]
(12"+=/cd-s+=) *(REC 009 12/CD)* – Nothing comes easy / Don't laugh.

Jul 88. (lp/c/cd) *(LEEDS 002/+C/CD)* **TOMMY** (compilation 4 singles + Peel sessions) [42] [–]
– Go out and get 'em boy / (The moment before) Everything's spoiled again / Once more / At the edge of the sea / Living and learning / This boy can't wait / You should always keep in touch with your friends / Felicity / What becomes of the broken hearted? / Never said / Every mother's son / My favourite dress. *(<cd-iss. Oct97 on 'Cooking Vinyl'; COOKCD 135>)*

Sep 88. (7") *(REC 011)* **WHY ARE YOU BEING SO REASONABLE NOW?. / NOT FROM WHERE I'M STANDING** [42] [–]
(12"+=) *(REC 011-12)* – Give my love to Kevin (acoustic) / Getting better.
(c-s++=/cd-s++=) *(REC 011 C/CD)* – Pourquoi es tu devenue si raisonable?.
(s7") *(REC 011F)* – Pourquoi es tu devenue si raisonable?. / Give my love to Kevin (acoustic).

—— added guest **LEN LIGGINS** – vocals, violin (ex-SINISTER CLEANERS, Solo artist) others played assortment of instruments in Ukrainian style.

R.C.A. R.C.A.

Apr 89. (lp/c/cd) *(PL/PK/PD 74104)* **UKRAINSKI VISTUPI V JOHNA PEELA** (Ukrainian style John Peel sessions) [22] [–]
– Davny chasy / Yikhav kozak za dunai / Tiutiunyk / Zadmav didochok svitit misyats / Katrusyai Vasya vasyl'ok / Hude dn ipro hude Verkhovyno. *(was to have been issued as 10"m-lp, Nov88 on 'Reception'; REC 010) (cd re-iss. Sep00 as 'UKRAINIAN JOHN PEEL SESSIONS' on 'Fresh Air'; FRESHCD 100)*

—— reverted to usual 4-piece & style

Sep 89. (7"/c-s) *(PB/PK 43117)* **KENNEDY. / UNFAITHFUL** [33] [–]
(c-s+=/12"+=/cd-s+=) *(PT/PK/PD 43118)* – One day all this will all be yours / It's not unusual.

Oct 89. (lp/c/cd) *(PL/PK/PD 74302)* *<2173>* **BIZARRO** [22] [ ]
– Brassneck / Crushed / No / Thanks / Kennedy / What have I said now / Granadaland / Bewitched / Take me / Be honest. *(cd+=)* – Brassneck (extended) / Box elder / Don't talk, just kiss / Gone. *(cd re-mast.Aug01 on 'Camden'++=; 74321 86965-2)* – One day this will all be yours / Unfaithful / It's not unusual.

Feb 90. (7"/c-s) *(PB/PK 43403)* **BRASSNECK. / DON'T TALK, JUST KISS** [24] [–]
(c-s+=/12"+=/cd-s+=) *(PK/PT/PD 43404)* – Gone / Box elder.

Sep 90. (7"ep/c-ep)(12"ep/cd-ep) *(PB/PK 44021)(PT/PD 44022)* **THE 3 SONGS EP** [25] [–]
– Corduroy / Make me smile (come up and see me) / Crawl.
(10"+=) *(PJ 44022)* – Take me (live).

R.C.A. First Warning

Apr 91. (7") *(PB 44495)* **DALLIANCE. / NIAGARA** [29] [–]
(c-s+=)(12"+=/cd-s+=) *(PK 44495)(PT/PD 44496)* – She's my best friend.
(10"++=) *(PJ 44495)* – What have I said now? (live).

May 91. (cd/c/lp) *(PD/PK/PL 75012)* *<75708>* **SEAMONSTERS** [13] [ ]
– Dalliance / Dare / Suck / Blonde / Rotterdam / Lovenest / Corduroy / Carolyn / Heather / Octopussy. *(cd+=)* – Niagara / Dan Dare / Fleshworld. *(cd re-mast.Aug01 on 'Camden'++=; 74321 86966-2)* – Make me smile (come up and see me) / She's my best friend.

Jul 91. (12"ep/cd-ep) *(PT/PD 44750)* **LOVENEST (edit) / MOTHERS. / DAN DARE / FLESHWORLD** [58] [–]

—— **PAUL DORRINGTON** – guitar (ex-TSE TSE FLY, ex-AC TEMPLE) repl. SOLOWKA to UKRAINIANS

Jan 92. (7") *(PB 45185)* **BLUE EYES. / CATTLE AND CANE** [26] [–]
Feb 92. (7") *(PB 45183)* **GO-GO DANCER. / DON'T CRY NO TEARS** [20] [–]
Mar 92. (7") *(PB 45181)* **THREE. / THINK THAT IT MIGHT** [14] [–]
Apr 92. (7") *(PB 45311)* **SILVER SHORTS. / FALLING** [14] [–]
May 92. (7") *(PB 45313)* **COME PLAY WITH ME. / PLEASANT VALLEY SUNDAY** [10] [–]
Jun 92. (7") *(PB 45313)* **CALIFORNIA. / LET'S MAKE SOME PLANS** [16] [–]
Jun 92. (cd/c/lp) *(PD/PK/PL 75343)* *<75711>* **THE HIT PARADE 1** (compilation of last 6 singles) [22] [ ]
(cd re-iss. Sep96 on 'Camden'; 74321 40073-2)
Jul 92. (7") *(PB 10115)* **FLYING SAUCER. / ROCKET** [22] [–]
Aug 92. (7") *(PB 10117)* **BOING!. / THEME FROM SHAFT** [19] [–]
Sep 92. (7") *(PB 10116)* **LOVESLAVE. / CHANT OF THE EVER CIRCLING SKELETAL FAMILY** [17] [–]
Oct 92. (7") *(PB 11691)* **STICKY. / GO WILD IN THE COUNTRY** [17] [–]
Nov 92. (7") *(PB 11692)* **THE QUEEN OF OUTER SPACE. / U.F.O.** [23] [–]
Dec 92. (7"red) *(PB 11693)* **NO CHRISTMAS. / STEP INTO CHRISTMAS** [25] [–]

—— The above 12 singles, were limited to 15,000 copies, and hit peak chart position on its first week of issue.

Jan 93. (cd/c/lp) *(PD/PK/PL 74321)* *<75711>* **THE HIT PARADE 2** [19] [ ]
– (all last 6 'A'&'B' singles above) (free lp w/lp+=) **BBC SESSIONS** – (all 12 of the years' A-sides).

—— **DARREN BELK** – guitar, bass; repl. GREGORY who later formed CHA CHA COHEN

Island Polygram

Sep 94. (c-ep/12"ep/cd-ep) *(CIS/12IS/CID 585)* **YEAH YEAH YEAH YEAH YEAH / THE BIKINI / FLAME ON / HIM OR ME (WHAT'S IT GONNA BE)** [51] [–]
(cd-ep) *(CIDX 585)* – ('A'side) / Gazebo / So long baby / Spangle.

Sep 94. (cd/c/lp) *(CID/ICT/ILPS 8014)* *<524044>* **WATUSI** [47] [ ]
– So long, baby / Click click / Yeah yeah yeah yeah yeah / Let him have it / Gazebo / Shake it / Spangle / It's a gas / Swimming pools, movie stars / Big rat / Catwoman / Hot pants.

Nov 94. (c-s/7") *(C+/IS 591)* **IT'S A GAS. / BUBBLES** [ ] [–]
(12"purple+=/cd-s+=) *(12IS/CID 591)* – ('A'acoustic) / Jumper clown.

—— SMITH was another turn up in CHA CHA COHEN

Cooking Vinyl Cooking Vinyl

Jan 96. (10"m-lp/m-cd) *(<COOK/+CD 094>)* **MINI** [ ] [ ]
– Drive / Love machine / Go, man, go / Mercury / Convertible / Sports car. *(cd+=)* – Sucker / Waiting on the guns / Jet girl.

—— line-up now **DAVID GEDGE + SIMON SMITH** plus newcomers **SIMON CLEAVE** – guitar (ex-TSE TSE FLY) / + guest on last mini-cd **JAYNE LOCKEY** – bass, vocals (ex-TSE TSE FLY)

Aug 96. (7") *(FRY 048)* **2, 3, GO. / UP** [67] [–]
(cd-s+=) *(FRYCD 048)* – Jet girl / Real thing.

Sep 96. (2x10"lp/c/cd) *(<COOK/+C/CD 099>)* **SATURNALIA** [36] [ ]
– Venus / Real thing / Dreamworld / 2, 3, go / Snake eyes / Hula doll / Big boots / Montreal / Skin diving / Jet girl / Kansas / 50s.

Jan 97. (7") *(FRY 063)* *<5053>* **MONTREAL. / PROJECT CENZO** [40] [ ]
(7") *(FRY 053X)* – ('A'side) / Where everybody knows your name.
(cd-s) *(FRYCD 053)* – ('A'side) / Sports car / My favourite dress (live) / Brassneck (live).

—— they officially split after above

– compilations, etc. –

Oct 86. (12"ep) *Strange Fruit; (SFPS 009)* **THE PEEL SESSIONS** (26.2.86) [ ] [–]
– What becomes of the broken hearted / This boy can't wait / Felicity / You should always keep in touch with your friends. *(c-ep iss.Jun87; SFPSC 009) (cd-ep iss.Aug88; SFPSC 009)*

Nov 88. (12"ep/cd-ep) *Nighttracks; (SFNT/+CD 016)* **THE EVENING SHOW SESSIONS** (20.4.86) [ ] [–]
– Everyone thinks he looks daft / I found that essence rare / Shatner / My favourite dress.

Oct 93. (lp/cd) *Strange Fruit; (SFR LP/CD 122)* **JOHN PEEL SESSIONS 1987-1990** [ ] [–]
– Give my regards to Kevin / Getting nowhere fast / A million miles / Something and nothing / Take me I'm yours / Unfaithful / Why are you being so reasonable now? / Happy birthday / Dalliance / Heather Blonde / Niagara.

Jun 97. (cd) *Strange Fruit; (<SFRSCD 029>)* **THE EVENING SESSIONS 1986-1994** [ ] [ ]

Apr 98. (cd) *Cooking Vinyl; (<COOKCD 146>)* **JOHN PEEL SESSIONS 1992-1995** [ ] [ ]

Sep 99. (cd) *Cooking Vinyl; (COOKCD 184) / SpinArt; <SPIN 78>* **SINGLES 1995-1997** [ ] Oct99 [ ]
Nov 99. (4xcd-box) *Cooking Vinyl; (COOKCD 117) / SpinArt; <SPIN 75>* **REGISTRY** [ ] [ ]
– (GEORGE BEST / TOMMY / MINI / SATURNALIA)

CINERAMA

DAVID LEWIS GEDGE – vocals, guitar / **SALLY MURRELL** – vocals, programming / with **DARE MASON** – guitar, theremin / **MARTY WILLSON-PIPER** – guitar (of The CHURCH) / **ANTHONY COOTE** – bass (of ANIMALS CAN SWIM) / **DAVEY RAY MOORE** – keyboards (of PUSHA) / **RICHARD MARKANGELO + CHE ALBRIGHTON** – drums, percussion / **JULIA PALMER + ABIGAIL TRUNDLE** – cello / **RACHEL DAVIES** – violin / **DUNCAN BRIDGEMAN** – flute / **THIBAULT DE MONTFORT** – oboe / **DEREK CRABTREE** – trumpet / **EMMA POLLOCK** – vocals (of DELGADOS)

Cooking Vinyl SpinArt

Jul 98. (7") *(FRY 072)* **KERRY KERRY. / 7X** [71] [–]
(7") *(FRY 072X)* – ('A'side) / Mr Kiss Kiss Bang Bang.
(cd-s) *(FRYCD 072)* – ('A'side) / Love / Au pair.
Aug 98. (lp/cd) *(COOK/+CD 150) <68>* **VA VA VOOM** [ ] Oct98 [ ]
– Maniac / Comedienne / Hate / Kerry Kerry / Barefoot in the park / You turn me on / Ears / Me next / Hard, fast and beautiful / Dance, girl, dance / Honey rider.
Oct 98. (7") *(FRY 077)* **DANCE, GIRL, DANCE. / EARS (acoustic version)** [ ] [–]
(cd-s) *(FRYCD 077)* – ('A'side) / Crusoe / Model spy.
(cd-s) *(FRYCD 077X)* – Pacific / King's Cross.

Elefant not iss.

Aug 99. (ltd-7") *(ER 210)* **PACIFIC. / KING'S CROSS** [ ] [–]

— **SIMON CLEAVE** – guitar (ex-TSE TSE FLY) was added to duo

— + added **TERRY DE CASTRO** – bass (ex-GOYA DRESS) / **SIMON PEARSON** – drums (ex-GOYA DRESS)

Scorpitones Manifesto

Feb 00. (cd-s) *(TONECD 001)* **MANHATTAN / LONDON / FILM** [ ] [–]
Jun 00. (cd-s) *(TONECD 002)* **WOW / 10 DENIER / GIGOLO** [ ] [–]
Aug 00. (cd-s) *(TONECD 003)* **LOLLOBRIGIDA / SEE THRU / SLY CURL** [ ] [–]
Sep 00. (cd/lp) *(TONE CD/LP 004) <42401>* **DISCO VOLANTE** [ ] Oct00 [ ]
– 146 degrees / Lollobrigida / Your charms / Heels / Unzip / Apres ski / Superman / Because I'm beautiful / Let's pretend / Wow (extended) / Your time startys here.
Nov 00. (cd-s) *(TONECD 005)* **YOUR CHARMS / REEL 2 DIALOGUE / GIRL ON A MOTORCYCLE** [ ] [–]
Apr 01. (cd) *(TONECD 006) <42402>* **JOHN PEEL SESSIONS** (1998-2000) [ ] [ ]
– Comedienne / Maniac / You turn me on / Honey rider / Pacific / Dance, girl, dance (acoustic) / 146 degrees / Reel 2 dialogue 2 / Film / Elenore / Kerry Kerry (live) / Hard fast and beautiful (live).
Apr 01. (7"m) *(TONE 007)* **SUPERMAN. / SUPERMAN (Spanish version) / HARD FAST AND BEAUTIFUL (Spanish version)** [ ] [–]
(cd-s) *(TONECD 007)* – ('A'side) / Starry eyed / Yesterday once more.

— session strings repl. PEARSON

Oct 01. (7"m) *(TONE 008)* **HEALTH AND EFFICIENCY. / HEALTH AND EFFICIENCY (French version) / LOLLOBRIGIDA (French version)** [ ] [–]
(cd-s) *(TONECD 008)* – ('A'side) / Swim / Diamonds are forever.
Jun 02. (cd-s) *(TONECD 010)* **QUICK BEFORE IT MELTS / EARS (acoustic) / AS IF** [ ] [–]
Jul 02. (cd) *(TONECD 011) <42404>* **TORINO** [ ] [ ]
– And when was she bad / Two girls / Estrella / Cat girl tights / Airborne / Quick, before it melts (extended) / Tie me up / Careless / Close up / Starry eyed / Get up and go / Get smart / Health and efficiency.
Aug 02. (cd-s) *(TONECD 012)* **CARELESS / THIS ISN'T WHAT IT LOOKS LIKE / SPARKLE LIPSTICK** [ ] [–]
Sep 02. (cd) *(TONECD 013)* **CINERAMA HOLIDAY** (compilation) [ ] [–]
– Wow / 10 denier / Gigolo / Lollobrigida / See thru / Sly curls / Your charms / Reel 2 dialogue 2 / Girl on a motorcycle / Superman / Starry eyed / Yesterday one more / Superman (Spanish version) / Dura rapida y hermosa.

– compilations, etc. –

Oct 00. (cd) *Cooking Vinyl; (COOKCD 180) / SpinArt; <SPIN 82>* **THIS IS CINERAMA** [ ] [ ]
– Kerry Kerry / Love / Au pair / 7x / Mr. kiss kiss bang bang / Dance, girl, dance / Model spy / Crusoe / Pacific / King's Cross / Manhattan / Film / London / Ears.

WEEZER

Formed: Los Angeles, California, USA ... 1993 by RIVERS CUOMO, MATT SHARP and PATRICK WILSON. Signing to 'Geffen' and recruiting final member, BRIAN BELL, the group released their eponymous RIC OCASEK-produced debut album in September '94. Helped by the transatlantic success of singles such as 'UNDONE – THE SWEATER SONG' and the pogo-pop of 'BUDDY HOLLY', the album became one of the year's biggest sellers. Often described as The PIXIES meeting The BEACH BOYS, their blaring college 'nerd'-rock saw WEEZER riding the crest of an American 'new wave' triggered by the likes of GREEN DAY and OFFSPRING. Meanwhile, MATT SHARP was also busy with a side project, The RENTALS (comprising CHERIELYNN WESTRICH, ROD CERVERA, PETRA HADEN, PAT WILSON and JIM RICHARDS), releasing an album of New Wave-esque songs in 'RETURN OF THE RENTALS' (1995/96). A second WEEZER album, 'PINKERTON' (1996), was much of the same, although it brought the band a bit of grief when the American security firm of the same name brought legal action. WEEZER released their third long-awaited set, 'THE GREEN ALBUM', in May 2001, bringing back geek-rock to the masses. After a year of touring, self-produced 'MALADROIT' (2002), a sort of companion piece to 'THE GREEN ALBUM' was released into the US Top 5. Short, sweet and very melodic (as always), CUOMO and crew had created another half-an-hour blast of guitar pop that was impossible not to like. Reasons why? Well, the faux-thrash metal piss-take 'DEATH AND DESTRUCTION', or jangling opener 'AMERICAN GIGOLO' or the catchy head-bopping single 'KEEP FISHING', which featured the entire cast of The Muppets in its video. Reasons to be cheerful, 1, 2, 3! • **Songwriters:** CUOMO, a few w/ WILSON.

Album rating: WEEZER (*7) / PINKERTON (*7) / THE GREEN ALBUM (*8) / MALADROIT (*6) / Rentals: RETURN OF THE RENTALS (*5) / SEVEN MORE MINUTES (*6)

RIVERS CUOMO – vocals / **BRIAN BELL** – guitar, vocals / **MATT SHARP** – bass, vocals / **PATRICK WILSON** – drums

Geffen D.G.C.

Jan 95. (7"blue) *(GFS 85) <19378>* **UNDONE – THE SWEATER SONG. / HOLIDAY** [35] Sep94 [57]
(c-s+=/cd-s+=) *(GFS C/TD 85)* – Mykel & Carli / Susanne.
Feb 95. (cd/c/lp) *<(GED/GEC/GEF 24629)>* **WEEZER** [23] Aug94 [16]
– My name is Jonas / No one else / The world has turned and left me here / Buddy Holly / Undone – the sweater song / In the garage / Holiday / Only in dreams. *(lp re-iss. Mar02 on 'Universal'; AA694 93045-1)*
Apr 95. (7"/c-s) *(GFS/+C 88)* **BUDDY HOLLY. / JAMIE** [12] [–]
(cd-s+=) *(GFSTD 88)* – My name is Jonas / Surf wax America.
Jul 95. (10"ep/c-ep/cd-ep) *(GFS V/C/TD 95)* **SAY IT AIN'T SO (remix). / NO ONE ELSE (live acoustic) / JAMIE (live acoustic)** [37] [ ]
Sep 96. (7"/c-s) *(GFS/+C 22167)* **EL SCORCHO. / YOU GAVE YOUR LOVE TO ME SOFTLY** [50] [–]
(cd-s+=) *(GFSTD 22167)* – Devotion.
Oct 96. (cd/c) *<(GED/GEC 25007)>* **PINKERTON** [43] [19]
– Tired of sex / Getchoo / No other one / Why bother / Across the sea / Good life / El Scorcho / Pink triangle / Falling for you / Butterfly.

RENTALS

MATT SHARP – vocals, bass, Moog synthesizer / plus **CHERIELYNN WESTRICH** – vocals / **ROD CERVERA** – guitar / **PETRA HADEN** – violin, vocals / **JIM RICHARDS** – keyboards / **PAT WILSON** – drums

Warners Maverick

Jan 96. (cd/c) *<9362 46093-2/-4>* **RETURN OF THE RENTALS** [ ] Nov95 [ ]
– Love I'm searching for / Waiting / Friends of P. / Move on / Please let that be you / My summer girl / Brilliant boy / Naive / These days / Sweetness and tenderness.

Mar 96. (c-s) *(W 0340C)* **FRIENDS OF P. / SO SOON** [ ] [ ]
(cd-s+=) *(W 0340CD)* – Love I'm searching for.

Sire Sire

Apr 99. (cd/c) *<9362 46680-2/-4>* **SEVEN MORE MINUTES** [ ] [ ]
– Getting by / Hello hello / She says it's alright / Cruise / Barcelona / Say goodbye forever / Overlee / Big daddy C / Keep sleeping / The man with two brains / Must be wrong / Insomnia / She says it's alright (reprise) / My head is in the sun / Jumping around.

WEEZER

—— re-formed for 2001

Geggen Interscope

May 01. (cd) *(493061-2)* *<493045>* **THE GREEN ALBUM** [31] [4]
– Don't let go / Photograph / Hash pipe / Island in the sun / Crab / Knock-down drag-out / Smile / Simple pages / Glorious days / O girlfriend / I do *[UK-only]*.

Jul 01. (7") *(497567-7)* **HASH PIPE. / TEENAGE VICTORY SONG** [21] [–]
(c-s) *(497567-4)* – ('A'side) / Starlight.
(cd-s+=) *(497564-2)* – ('A'-Jimmy Pop remix) / ('A'-video).

Oct 01. (7") *(497616-7)* **ISLAND IN THE SUN. / ALWAYS** [31] [–]
(cd-s+=) *(497610-2)* – Oh Lisa / ('A'-video).
(cd-s) *(297616-2)* – ('A'side) / Sugar booger / My best friends are gone.

May 02. (cd) *(493325-2)* *<493241>* **MALADROIT** [16] [3]
– American gigolo / Dope noise / Keep fishin' / Take control / Death and destruction / Slob / Burndt jamb / Space rock / Slave / Fall together / Possibilities / Love explosion / December *(UK+=)* – Living without you (version) / Island in the sun (version). *(lp-iss.May02; same as US)*

Sep 02. (7") *(497771-7)* **KEEP FISHIN'. / PHOTOGRAPH (live)** [29] [–]
(cd-s+=) *(497771-2)* – Death and destruction (live) / ('A'-video).
(cd-s) *(497792-2)* – ('A'side) / Slob (live) / Knockdown drag out (live).

☐ Scott WEILAND
(see under ⇒ STONE TEMPLE PILOTS)

☐ WE KNOW WHERE YOU LIVE
(see under ⇒ WONDER STUFF)

Paul WELLER

Born: 25 May'58, Woking, Surrey, England. (see The JAM for further details). Formed STYLE COUNCIL in early '83 with former MERTON PARKAS keys player, MICK TALBOT, and talented young sticksman, STEVE WHITE. Though it was merely a matter of months since WELLER had folded The JAM, The STYLE COUNCIL followed a radical new direction, taking the agit-soul of CURTIS MAYFIELD as their inspiration and fashioning a very 80's hybrid of cocktail jazz, breezy pop and white funk. Scoring immediately with the Top 5 'SPEAK LIKE A CHILD', the group went Top 3 later that year with the 'LONG HOT SUMMER' EP, its sultry lead track arguably the best the group ever penned and the creative pinnacle of what they were trying to achieve. Previewing The STYLE COUNCIL's debut album, 'CAFE BLEU' (1984), the mellow atmospherics of 'MY EVER CHANGING MOODS' gave the group another huge hit in early '84. The album itself was a lush fusion of summery jazz and easy soul, the keening strum of 'YOU'RE THE BEST THING' making the Top 5. WELLER became increasingly political as the decade wore on, the rousing soul/funk of 'SHOUT TO THE TOP' and 'WALLS COME TUMBLING DOWN' an indication of the direction The JAM may have taken had they still been in existence. With the miners strike in full effect, politics were very much still an issue in rock/pop and WELLER and Co. released a benefit single, 'SOUL DEEP', at Christmas '84 under the COUNCIL COLLECTIVE banner. With production handled by HEAVEN 17's MARTYN WARE, the project included the likes of JIMMY RUFFIN, JUNIOR (GISCOMBE), VAUGHN TOULOUSE, DIZZY HEIGHTS and DEE C. LEE. The latter became not only WELLER's other half but a full-time backing singer for The STYLE COUNCIL, her sweet soul tones helping make 'OUR FAVOURITE SHOP' (1985) a mid-80's classic. The overall sound was more satisfying and the writing was sharper; 'COME TO MILTON KEYNES' was WELLER's most cutting slice of social commentary since The JAM heyday. Come 1986, The STYLE COUNCIL became heavily involved in the 'Red Wedge' movement alongside the likes of The COMMUNARDS and BILLY BRAGG, attempting to educate music fans into voting for the right party in the upcoming elections i.e. Labour. Such an openly party political stance was probably doomed to failure from the start, the attendant tour floundering and the Tories of course, predictably romping home. It was the last time WELLER would lay his beliefs on the line and the failure of the project seemed to lie at the heart of the lugubrious meanderings of the double set, 'THE COST OF LOVING' (1987). The following year's 'CONFESSIONS OF A POP GROUP' (1988) was similarly lacking in focus, its string arrangements and classical pretensions seeing The STYLE COUNCIL sinking in a mire of self-indulgence. The record failed to spawn any major hits and didn't even make the Top 10; when 'Polydor' refused to release a proposed fifth set, WELLER finally adjourned the 'COUNCIL and retired to re-evaluate his career. Now without a band or a recording deal, WELLER eventually regained his thirst for music via the low-key PAUL WELLER MOVEMENT, a band comprising STEVE WHITE, JACKO PEAKE, PAUL FRANCIS, MAX BEESLEY, DAMON BROWN, CHRIS LAWRENCE and DJ PAULO HEWITT along with backing singers DEE C.LEE, DR. ROBERT and CAMELLE HINDS. The subsequent early late 1990/early 1991 shows saw the singer once again armed with a guitar and suggested that he'd been reacquainting himself with his record collection, more specifically late 60's R&B and psychedelia. The 'MOVEMENT released a sole single, 'INTO TOMORROW' on the DIY 'Freedom High' label. It squeezed into the Top 40 nonetheless and WELLER eventually whittled down the bulk of the group for a more basic sound, signing with 'Go! Discs' and debuting with 'UH HUH OH YEH' in late summer '92. Hailed as the best thing he'd done in years, the single went into the Top 20 and the PAUL WELLER revival was up and running. The music press had given the singer a wide berth since the heyday of The STYLE COUNCIL and as the plaudits began to roll in for his eponymous debut album, were eventually forced to admit that, yes, WELLER was undergoing something of a creative rebirth. Matching the visceral, emotional punch of the music, the lyrics were of a decidedly more personal nature, eschewing politics for matters of the soul and the heart. With the ebullient 'SUNFLOWER' single and the attendant 'WILD WOOD' (1993) album, WELLER's star was most definately in the ascendant. Characterised by a crisp, uncluttered Brendan Lynch production, the record saw WELLER distill his influences into vintage singer/songwriter maturity. With his voice now sufficiently rough around the edges to complement such material, the likes of the resonating, meditative folkiness of the title track assumed a greater depth. The album reached No.2, featuring in many end of year polls (Mercury Prize), the chino wearing ghost of The STYLE COUNCIL now finally laid to rest. While the UK music press were still largely fixated on US grunge, WELLER was nothing if not instrumental in the upcoming Brit-pop debacle. Cited by the likes of OASIS as a guiding influence, the Modfather, as WELLER came to be known, was everything that the hordes of mop-topped chancers aspired to. It was a role that WELLER fitted into naturally, OCEAN COLOUR SCENE's STEVE CRADDOCK was already a regular musical collaborator, while NOEL GALLAGHER would guest on WELLER's forthcoming No.1 album, 'STANLEY ROAD'. Released in Spring '95 as Brit-pop was reaching its zenith, the album was earthier than anything WELLER had recorded in his career to date. Again produced by LYNCH, the record was previewed by the blistering single, 'THE CHANGINGMAN', its lyrics signalling an even more personal bent to WELLER's writing as the looking-good-for-30-something star even began appearing in the British style press. Elsewhere on the album, WELLER covered Dr. John's 'I WALK ON GILDED SPLINTERS' although it was the spirit of ERIC CLAPTON or NEIL YOUNG that most often came to mind. WELLER was at his most affecting on the ballads, the deeply felt 'YOU DO SOMETHING TO ME', the beautiful gospel-soul of album closer 'WINGS OF SPEED' and the brilliantly evocative hammond/wurlitzer musings of 'BROKEN STONES'. Of course, a backlash was inevitable, and certain sections of the music press derided WELLER's new material as tired 'Dad-rock', an incestuous Brit-pop conspiracy which continually looked to the past instead of breaking new ground. While this may have been true to a certain degree, and WELLER was partly responsible for the vexing success of the terminally workmanlike OCEAN COLOUR SCENE, the man was simply integrating retro influences into his muse as he'd done all the way through his career; it's the fact that these influences changed which seems to annoy some writers. Keeping his profile high with various festival appearances (as well as a predictable guest spot at OASIS' Knebworth show), WELLER (now signed to 'Island' following the demise of 'Go! Discs' eventually returned to the fray in summer '97 with the storming 'BRUSHED' single. Arguably standing among the best of WELLER's work to date, the track was propelled by a stone solid/funky as hell rhythmic thrust (courtesy of WHITE), combining mod, psychedelia and rock in a fashion that he's only previously hinted at. 'Raw' is probably the best word to describe it and the best word to describe the accompanying album, 'HEAVY SOUL' (1997), WELLER's voice as impressive as ever on a set which nevertheless too often relies on 'authentic' sound over songwriting. 1998, saw the release of two Top 30 singles, 'BRAND NEW DAY' and the 'WILD WOOD' remixes EP, mainly to complement the delivery of his best of package, 'MODERN CLASSICS – THE GREATEST HITS'. Come the new millennium the doggedly determined WELLER underwent yet another creative renaissance with the acclaimed 'HELIOCENTRIC' (2000). The record mightn't have struck a zeitgeist-style chord like 'STANLEY ROAD' but it confirmed his ever changing muse was still as fertile as ever. It was also one of the most PAUL WELLER-sounding albums he'd ever done, a rich, life affirming blend of soulful, occasionally psychedelic retro influences. That very richness was the key ingredient of 'DAYS OF SPEED' (2001), a document of WELLER's recent solo tour which – in its pared down acoustica (and included old JAM numbers!) – served to underline the sheer breadth and consistency of the man's songwriting. Just to note, PAUL was cleared of all rape charges in October 2000 (from four years previous) and stated at the time the unfairness of the anonymity law not protecting the innocently accused. On the music front once again, WELLER released his umpteenth solo set, 'ILLUMINATION' (No.1 in September 2002), a soulful and back to basics album that featured the Top 10 single, 'IT'S WRITTEN IN THE STARS'. • **Songwriters:** WELLER penned except for TALBOT's STYLE COUNCIL instrumentals. They also covered MOVE ON UP (Curtis Mayfield) / PROMISED LAND (Joe Smooth) / OHIO (Neil Young). WELLER solo:- FEELIN' ALRIGHT (Traffic) / SEXY SADIE (Beatles) / I'M ONLY DREAMING (Small Faces) / I SHALL BE RELEASED (Bob Dylan).

Album rating: Style Council: CAFE BLEU (*5) / OUR FAVOURITE SHOP (*6) / HOME AND ABROAD – LIVE (*4) / THE COST OF LOVING (*5) / CONFESSIONS OF A POP GROUP (*3) / THE SINGULAR ADVENTURES OF THE STYLE COUNCIL compilation (*7) / HERE'S SOME THAT GOT AWAY collection (*4) / Paul Weller: PAUL WELLER (*6) / WILD WOOD (*9) / LIVE WOOD (*6) / STANLEY ROAD (*8) / HEAVY SOUL (*7) / MODERN CLASSICS – THE GREATEST HITS compilation (*8) / HELIOCENTRIC (*7) / DAYS OF SPEED (*6) / ILLUMINATION (*6) / FLY ON THE WALL – B-SIDES & RARITIES compilation (*5)

STYLE COUNCIL

PAUL WELLER (b.25 May'58, Woking, Surrey, England) – vocals, guitar (ex-JAM) / **MICK TALBOT** (b.11 Sep'58) – keyboards (ex-MERTON PARKAS) / **STEVE WHITE** – drums / plus various guests.

Polydor Polydor

Mar 83. (7") *(TSC 1)* **SPEAK LIKE A CHILD. / PARTY CHAMBERS** 4 [ ]

May 83. (7") *(TSC 2)* **MONEY GO ROUND. / (part 2)** 11 [ ]
(12") *(TSCX 2)* – ('A'side) / Headstart for happiness / Mick's up.

Aug 83. (7"ep/12"ep) *(TSC/+X 3)* **LONG HOT SUMMER / PARTY CHAMBERS. / PARIS MATCH / LE DEPART** 3 [ ]

Nov 83. (7") *(TSC 4)* **SOLID BOND IN YOUR HEART. / IT JUST CAME TO PIECES IN MY HAND / ('A'instrumental)** 11 [ ]

Oct 83. (m-lp) *<815277>* **INTRODUCING THE STYLE COUNCIL** – [ ]
– (above songs)

Polydor Geffen

Feb 84. (7") *(TSC 5)* *<29359>* **MY EVER CHANGING MOODS. / MICK'S COMPANY** 5 29
(12"+=) *(TSCX 5)* – Spring, Summer, Autumn.

Mar 84. (lp/c)(cd) *(TSC LP/MC 1)(817535-2)* *<4029>* **CAFE BLEU** <US-title 'MY EVER CHANGING MOODS'> 2 56
– Mick's blessings / My ship came in / Blue cafe / The Paris match / My ever changing moods / Dropping bombs on the Whitehouse / A gospel / Strength of your nature / You're the best thing / Here's the one that got away / Headstart for happiness / Council meetin'. *(cd+=)* – The whole point of no return. *(re-iss. cd Sep95; same)*

May 84. (7") *(TSC 6)* *<29248>* **YOU'RE THE BEST THING. / BIG BOSS GROOVE** 5 76
(12") *(TSCX 6)* – ('A'dub version).

Oct 84. (7") *(TSC 7)* **SHOUT TO THE TOP. / GHOSTS OF DACHAU** 7 [ ]
(12"+=) *(TSCX 7)* – Piccadilly trail / ('A'instrumental).

Dec 84. (7"; as COUNCIL COLLECTIVE) *(MINE 1)* **SOUL DEEP. / (part 2)** 24 –
(12"+=) *(MINEX 1)* – ('A'version) / (striking miner's interview).
(above single gave proceeds to miner's strike & the deceased miner David Wilkie's widow) The COLLECTIVE featured guests JIMMY RUFFIN, JUNIOR GISCOMBE, VAUGHN TOULOUSE, DEE C.LEE and DIZZY HEIGHTS. Production handled by MARTYN WARE (Heaven 17).

May 85. (7"ep/12"ep) *(TSC/+X 8)* **WALLS COME TUMBLING DOWN. / THE WHOLE POINT II / BLOODSPORTS** 6 –

Jun 85. (lp/c)(cd) *(TSC LP/MC 2)(825700-2)* *<24061>* **OUR FAVOURITE SHOP** <US title 'INTERNATIONALISTS'> 1 [ ]
– Homebreakers / All gone away / Come to Milton Keynes / Internationalists / A stone's throw away / The stand up comic's instructions / Boy who cried wolf / A man of great promise / Down in

the Seine / The lodgers / Luck / With everything to lose / Our favourite shop / Walls come tumbling down. *(cd+=)* – Shout to the top. *(c+=)* – (interview). *(cd re-iss. Aug90; same)*

Jun 85. (7") *(TSC 9)* **COME TO MILTON KEYNES. / WHEN YOU CALL ME** [23] [–]
(12"+=) *(TSCG 9)* – Our favourite shop / ('A'club) / The lodgers (club mix).

Aug 85. (7") *<28941>* **OUR FAVOURITE SHOP. / BOY WHO CRIED WOLF** [–] [ ]

Sep 85. (7") *(TSC 10)* **THE LODGERS (remix). / YOU'RE THE BEST THING (live)** [13] [ ]
(d7"+=) *(TSCDP 10)* – Big boss groove (live) / Long hot summer (live).
(12"+=) *(TSC?? 10)* – Big boss groove (live) / Move on up (live).
(12"+=) *(TSCX 10)* – Medley: Money go round – Soul deep – Strength of your nature.

Mar 86. (7"ep/12"ep) *(CINEX 1/+12)* **HAVE YOU EVER HAD IT BLUE. / MR. COOL'S DREAM** [14] [ ]

May 86. (lp/c)(cd) *(TCS LP/MC 3)(829143-2)* **HOME AND ABROAD – LIVE (live)** [8] [–]
– The big boss groove * / My ever changing moods / The lodgers / Headstart for happiness / (When you) Call me / The whole point of no return / Our favourite shop * / With everything to lose / Homebreakers / Shout to the top / Walls come tumbling down / Internationalists. *(cd+= *) (cd re-iss. Aug90; same)*

Jun 86. (7") *<28674>* **INTERNATIONALISTS. / (WHEN YOU) CALL ME** [–] [ ]

Polydor Polydor

Jan 87. (7"/12") *(TSC/+X 12)* **IT DIDN'T MATTER. / ALL YEAR ROUND** [9] [ ]

Feb 87. (2x12"lp/c)(cd) *(TSC LP/MC 4)(<831433-2>)* **THE COST OF LOVING** [2] [ ]
– It didn't matter / Right to go / Waiting / Walking the night / The cost of loving / Heaven's above / Fairy tales / Angel / A woman's song. *(re-iss. Oct90)*

Mar 87. (7") *(TSC 13)* **WAITING. / FRANCOISE** [52] [ ]
(12"+=) *(TCSX 13)* – Theme from 'Jerusalem'.

Oct 87. (7") *(TSC 14)* **WANTED (FOR WAITER). / THE COST OF LOVING** [20] [ ]
(12"+=/c-s+=) (TSC X/CS 14) – There's soup in my flies.
(cd-s++=) – The cost.

May 88. (7") *(TSC 15)* **LIFE AT A TOP PEOPLE'S HEALTH FARM. / SWEET LOVING WAYS** [28] [ ]
(12"+=/cd-s+=) *(TSC X/CD 15)* – Spark (live) / ('A'version).

Jun 88. (lp/c)(cd) *(TSC LP/MC 5)(<835785-2>)* **CONFESSIONS OF A POP GROUP** [15] [ ]
– It's a very deep sea / The story of someone's shoe / Changing of the guard / The little boy in a castle – A dove flew down from the elephant / The gardener of Eden (a three piece suite):- In the beginning – The gardener of Eden – Mourning the passing of time / Life at a top people's health farm / Why I went missing / How she threw it all away / I was a doledads toyboy / Confessions of a pop group (parts 1, 2 & 3) / Confessions of a pop group. *(cd re-iss. Oct90; same)*

Jul 88. (7"ep/12"ep) *(TSC 16)* **HOW SHE THREW IT ALL AWAY / IN LOVE FOR THE FIRST TIME. / LONG HOT SUMER / I DO LIKE TO BE B-SIDE THE A-SIDE** [41] [ ]

Feb 89. (7") *(TSC 17)* **PROMISED LAND. / CAN YOU STILL LOVE ME** [27] [ ]
(12") *(TSCXS 17)* – ('A'-Joe Smooth's alternate club) / ('B'club) / ('B'dub).
(cd-s) *(TSCCD 17)* – ('A'-Juan Atkins mix) / ('A'-Pianopella mix) / ('B'-dub).
(cd-s) *(TSCD 17)* – ('A'side) / ('A'extended) / ('B'vocal) / ('B'dub).
(7"box) *(TSCB 17)* – ('A'-Juan Atkins mix) / ('B'side).

Mar 89. (lp/c)(cd) *(TSC TV/TC 1)(837896-2)* **THE SINGULAR ADVENTURES OF THE STYLE COUNCIL** (compilation) [3] [–]
– You're the best thing / Have you ever had it blue (extended) / Money go round (parts 1 & 2) / My ever changing moods (extended) / Long hot summer (extended) / The lodgers / Walls come tumbling down / Shout to the top / Wanted / It didn't matter / Speak like a child / A solid bond in your heart / Life at a top people's health farm / Promised land. *(c+=/cd+=)* – How she threw it all away / Waiting.

May 89. (7") *(LHS 1)* **LONG HOT SUMMER ('89 mix). / EVERYBODY'S ON THE RUN** [48] [–]
(12"+=/cd-s+=) *(LHS X/CD 1)* – ('A'&'B' different mixes).

—— Disbanded Mar'90. WELLER went solo, see below.

– compilations, etc. –

on 'Polydor' unless mentioned otherwise

Nov 87. (cd-ep) *(TSCCD 101)* **CAFE BLEU** [ ] [–]
– Headstart for happiness / Here's one that got away / Blue cafe / Strength of your nature.

Nov 87. (cd-ep) *(TSCCD 102)* **BIRDS AND BEES** [ ] [–]
– Piccadilly trail / It just came to pieces in my hands / Spin drifting / Spring, Summer, Autumn.

Nov 87. (cd-ep) *(TSCCD 103)* **MICK TALBOT IS AGENT '88** [ ] [–]
– Mick's up / Party chambers / Mick's blessing / Mick's company.

Jan 90. (7") *Old Gold; (OG 9924)* **LONG HOT SUMMER. / SPEAK LIKE A CHILD** [ ] [–]

Jan 90. (7") *Old Gold; (OG 9929)* **YOU'RE THE BEST THING. / MY EVER CHANGING MOODS** [ ] [–]

Jul 93. (cd/c) *(519 372-2/-4)* **HERE'S SOME THAT GOT AWAY** [39] [–]

Feb 96. (cd/c) *(529 483-2/-4)* **THE STYLE COUNCIL COLLECTION** [60] [–]

Aug 00. (cd)(d-lp) *(557900-2)(549134-1)* **GREATEST HITS** [28] [–]

PAUL WELLER

with **STEVE WHITE** – drums, percussion / **JACKO PEAKE** – sax, flute, b.vox / **DEE C.LEE, DR.ROBERT + CAMELLE HINDS** – b.vox

Freedom High London

May 91. (7"/c-s; as PAUL WELLER MOVEMENT) *(FHP/+C 1)* **INTO TOMORROW. / HERE'S A NEW THING** [36] 1992 [ ]
(12"+=/cd-s+=) *(FHP T/CD 1)* – That spiritual feeling / ('A'demo).

Go! Discs London

Aug 92. (7"/c-s) *(GOD/+MC 86)* **UH HUH OH YEH. / FLY ON THE WALL** [18] [–]
(12"+=/cd-s+=) *(GOD X/CD 86)* – Arrival time / Always there to fool you.

Sep 92. (cd/c/lp) *(<828 343-2/-4/-1>)* **PAUL WELLER** [8] Oct92 [ ]
– Uh huh oh yeh / I didn't mean to hurt you / Bull-rush / Round and round / Remember how we started / Above the clouds / Clues / Into tomorrow / Amongst butterflies / The strange museum / Bitterness rising / Kosmos. *(re-iss. Apr94; same)*

Oct 92. (7"/c-s) *(GOD/+MC 91)* **ABOVE THE CLOUDS. / EVERYTHING HAS A PRICE TO PAY** [47] [–]
(12"+=/cd-s+=) *(GOD X/CD 91)* – All year round (live) / Feelin' alright.

—— now with **STEVE WHITE** – drums, percussion / **MARCO NELSON** – bass

Go! Discs Go! Discs

Jul 93. (7"/c-s) *(GOD/+MC 102)* **SUNFLOWER. / BULL-RUSH – MAGIC BUS (live)** [16] [–]
(12"+=/cd-s+=) *(GOD X/CD 102)* – Kosmo's sxdub 2000 / That spiritual feeling (new mix).

Aug 93. (7"/c-s/10"/cd-s) *(<GOD/+MC/T/CD 104>)* **WILD WOOD. / ENDS OF THE EARTH** [14] [ ]

Sep 93. (cd/c/lp) *(<828 435-2/-4/-1>)* **WILD WOOD** [2] Oct93 [ ]
– Sunflower / Can you heal us (holy man) / Wild wood – instrumental (pt.1) / All the pictures on the wall / Has my fire really gone out? / Country / 5th season / The weaver – instrumental (pt.2) / Foot of the mountain / Shadow of the Sun – Holy man (reprise) / Moon on your pyjamas. *(re-iss. Apr94 +=; same)* – Hung up.

Nov 93. (7"ep/c-ep/10"ep/cd-ep) *(GOD/+MC/T/CD 107)* **THE WEAVER EP** [18] [–]
– The weaver / This is no time / Another new day / Ohio (live).

Mar 94. (7"ep/c-ep/12"ep/cd-ep) *(GOD/+MC/X/CD 111)* **HOME OF THE CLASSIC EP** [11] [–]
– Hung up / Foot of the mountain (live from Albert Hall) / The loved / Kosmos (Lynch Mob bonus beats).

Sep 94. (cd/c/lp) *(828 561-2/-4/-1) <00601>* **LIVE WOOD (live)** [13] [ ]
– Bull rush – Magic bus / This is no time / All the pictures on the wall / Remember how we started? / Dominoes / Above the clouds / Wild wood / Shadow of the Sun / (Can you hear us) Holy man – War / 5th season / Into tomorrow / Fool of the mountains / Sunflower / Has the fire really gone out?.

Oct 94. (7"ep/c-ep/12"ep/cd-ep) *(GOD/+MC/X/CD 121)* **OUT OF THE SINKING. / SUNFLOWER (Lynch Mob dub) / SEXY SADIE** [20] [–]

—— with **STEVE WHITE** – drums / **DR.ROBERT** – bass, vocals (ex-BLOW MONKEYS) / **STEVE CRADDOCK** – guitar / **MARK NELSON** – bass / **HELEN TURNER** – strings, organ / **BRENDAN LYNCH** – organ, co-producer / + guests **MICK TALBOT / CARLEEN ANDERSON /**

STEVE WINWOOD / NOEL GALLAGHER / YOLANDA CHARLES / CONSTANTINE WEIR

Apr 95. (12"ep/c-ep/cd-ep) *(GOD X/MC/CD 127)* **THE CHANGINGMAN / I'D RATHER GO BLIND / IT'S A NEW DAY, BABY / I DIDNT MEAN TO HURT YOU (live)** 7 [ ]

May 95. (cd/c/lp)(6x7"pack) *(<828 619-2/-4/-1>)(850070-7)* **STANLEY ROAD** 1 [ ]
– The changingman / Porcelain gods / I walk on gilded splinters / You do something to me / Woodcutter's son / Time passes / Stanley Road / Broken stones / Out of the sinking / Pink on white walls / Whirlpool's end / Wings of speed.

Jul 95. (7"ep/c-ep/cd-ep) *(GOD/+MC/CD 130)* **YOU DO SOMETHING TO ME / A YEAR LATE. / MY WHOLE WORLD IS FALLING DOWN / WOODCUTTER'S SON** 9 –

Sep 95. (7"/c-s) *(GOD/+MC 132)* **BROKEN STONES. / STEAM** 20 [ ]
(cd-s+=) *(GODCD 132)* – Whirlpool's end / Porcelain gods.

— WELLER was also part of one-off supergroup The SMOKIN' MOJO FILTERS alongside PAUL McCARTNEY and NOEL GALLAGHER. They had a Top 20 hit late '95 with 'COME TOGETHER'.

Feb 96. (7"ep/cd-ep) *(GOD/+CD 143)* **OUT OF THE SINKING EP** 16 –
– Out of the sinking / I shall be released / Porcelain gods / Broken stones.

Aug 96. (7"/c-s/cd-s) *(GOD/+MC/CD 149)* **PEACOCK SUIT. / EYE OF THE STORM** 5 –

Island Polygram

Jun 97. (cd/c/lp) *(CID/ICT/ILPS 8058)* *<524277>* **HEAVY SOUL** 2 Aug97 [ ]
– Heavy soul / Peacock suit / Up in Suzie's room / Brushed / Driving nowhere / I should have been there to inspire you / Heavy soul (part 2) / Friday Street / Science / Golden sands / As you lean into the light / Mermaids.

Aug 97. (7"ep/c-ep/cd-ep) *(IS/CIS/CID 666)* **BRUSHED EP** 14 –
– Brushed / Ain't no love in the heart of the city / Shoot the dove / As you lean into the light.

Oct 97. (7"ep/c-ep/cd-ep) *(CIS/IS/CID 676)* **FRIDAY STREET EP** 21 –
– Friday street / Sunflower (live) / Brushed (live) / Mermaids (live).

Nov 97. (c-s/cd-s/7") *(CIS/CID/IS 683)* **MERMAIDS. / EVERYTHING HAS A PRICE TO PAY ('97 version) / SO YOU WANT TO BE A DANCER** 30 –

Nov 98. (c-s/7") *(C+/IS 711)* **BRAND NEW START. / RIGHT UNDERNEATH IT** 16 [ ]
(cd-s+=) *(CID 711)* – The riverbank (new version).

Nov 98. (cd/c/d-lp) *(CID/ICT/ILPSD 8080)* *<524558>* **MODERN CLASSICS – THE GREATEST HITS** (compilation) 7 [ ]
– Out of the sinking / Peacock suit / Sunflower / The weaver / Wild wood / Above the clouds / Uh huh oh yeh / Brushed / The changingman / Friday Street / You do something to me / Brand new start / Hung up / Mermaids / Broken stones / Into tomorrow. *(lp-box; IBX 8080) (d-cd; CIDD 8080)*

Dec 98. (7"ep/12"ep/cd-ep) *(IS/12IS/CID 734)* **WILD WOOD EP** 22 –
– Wild wood (mixes; original / Portishead / Science (Psychonauts).

Apr 00. (cd/c/lp) *(CID/ICT/ILPS 8093)* *<542394>* **HELIOCENTRIC** 2 May00 [ ]
– He's the keeper / Frightened / Sweet pea, my sweet pea / A whale's tale / Back in the fire / Dust and rocks / There is no drinking after you're dead / With time and temperance / Picking up sticks / Love-less.

May 00. (12"/cd-s) *(12IS/CID 760)* **HE'S THE KEEPER. / HELIOCENTRIC / BANG-BANG** [ ] –

Aug 00. (12"/cd-s) *(12IS/CID 764)* **SWEET PEA, MY SWEET PEA. / BACK IN THE FIRE (BBC session) / THERE IS NO DRINKING AFTER YOU'RE DEAD (noonday underground mix)** 44 –

Independiente Epic

Oct 01. (cd/d-lp) *(ISOM 26 CD/LP)* *<80703>* **DAYS OF SPEED (live)** 3 [ ]
– Brand new start / Loved / Out of the sinking / Clues / English rose / Above the clouds / You do something to me / Amongst butterflies / Science / Back in the fire / Down in the Seine / That's entertainment / Love-less / There's no drinking after you're dead / Everything has a price to pay / Wild wood / Headstart for happiness / A town called Malice. *(cd re-iss. Aug02; same)*

— in summer 2002, WELLER featured on NOONDAY UNDERGROUND's single, 'I'll Walk Right In'.

Sep 02. (10"m/cd-s) *(ISOM 63 TE/MS)* **IT'S WRITTEN IN THE STARS. / HORSESHOE DRAMA / PUSH BUTTON AUTOMATIC** 7 –
(cd-s) *(ISOM 63SMS)* – ('A'side) / The butterfly collector / Carnation.

Sep 02. (cd/lp) *(ISOM 33 CD/LP)* *<892000>* **ILLUMINATION** 1 [ ]
– Going places / A bullet for everyone / Leafy mysteries / It's written in the stars / Who brings joy / Now the night is here / Spring (at last) / One x one / Bag man / All good books / Call me No.5 / Standing out in the universe / Illumination.

Nov 02. (cd-s) *(ISOM 65S)* **LEAFY MYSTERIES / TALISMAN / WILD WOOD (live)** 23 –
(cd-s) *(ISOM SMS)* – ('A'side) / Broken stones (live) / Peacock suit (live).

– compilations, etc. –

Aug 03. (t-cd) *Polydor-Universal; (<063527-2>)* **FLY ON THE WALL – B-SIDES & RARITIES** (1991-2000) 22 [ ]

☐ Leslie WEST (see under ⇒ MOUNTAIN)

☐ Paul WESTERBERG (see under ⇒ REPLACEMENTS)

☐ WESTERN ELECTRIC (see under ⇒ LONG RYDERS)

☐ WHAM! (see under ⇒ MICHAEL, George)

WHEATUS

Formed: Long Island, New York, USA . . . late 90's by frontman/songwriter BRENDAN BROWN together with his brother PETER, PHIL JIMENEZ and RICH LEIGEY (subsequently replaced by MIKE McCABE). Trailed by the massive US hit single, 'TEENAGE DIRTBAG' (with a video featuring 'American Pie' stars Jason Biggs and Mena Suvari), the band's eponymous major label debut album hit the shops in summer 2000. Bursting with spunky 3 minute volleys of clever teenage commentary, the record covered familiar power-pop/punk territory with the requisite big choruses and geeky attitude although a surprise inclusion was an apparently sincere cover of Erasure's 80's hit, 'A LITTLE RESPECT'. The aforementioned 'TEENAGE . . .' was subsequently featured in the film 'Loser' and went on to hit the UK Top 10 in early 2001; probably youth's anthem of the millennium so far – annoyingly catchy to the max and a namecheck for IRON MAIDEN to boot. Follow-up set, 'HAND OVER YOUR LOVED ONES' (2003), was a threat no one. Enough said.

Album rating: WHEATUS (*6) / HAND OVER YOUR LOVED ONES (*3)

BRENDAN BROWN – vocals, guitar / **PHIL JIMENEZ** – keyboards, percussion / **RICH LEIGEY** – bass / **PETER BROWN** – drums

Columbia Sony

Jul 00. (12") *<79468>* **TEENAGE DIRTBAG. / (other track by Prozzak)** – [ ]

Jan 01. (cd/c) *(499605-2/-4)* *<62146>* **WHEATUS** 7 Aug00 76
– Truffles / Sunshine / Teenage dirtbag / A little respect / Hump 'em n' dump 'em / Leroy / Hey, Mr. Brown / Love is a mutt from Hell / Punk ass bitch / Wannabe gangster. *(cd+=)* – Teenage dirtbag (video).

— (Jul'00) **MIKE McCABE** – bass; repl. LEIGEY

Feb 01. (c-s) *(670796-4)* **TEENAGE DIRTBAG / NEVER WRITE A SONG / MR. BROWN (with club audience)** 2 –
(cd-s+=) *(670796-2)* – ('A'-CD-Rom).

Jul 01. (c-s) *(671428-4)* **A LITTLE RESPECT / SUNSHINE (X-ecutioners mix)** 3 [ ]
(cd-s+=) *(671428-2)* – Teenage dirtbag (live).

Jan 02. (c-s; as WHEATUS featuring BRUCE DICKINSON) *(672127-4)* **WANNABE GANGSTER / LEROY (Brendan's remix) / WANNABE GANGSTER (Soulchild remix)** 22 [ ]

(cd-s+=) *(672127-5)* – ('A'-video).
(cd-s) *(672127-2)* – ('A'side) / Leroy (live from V2001) / Hey Mr. Brown / ('A'-video).

Aug 03. (cd-s) *(674107-2)* **AMERICAN IN AMSTERDAM / I'D NEVER WRITE A SONG ABOUT YOU (live) / A LITTLE RESPECT (live) / ('A'-video)** 59 –
(cd-s) *(674107-5)* – Fair weather friend (live) / Teenage dirtbag (live).

Sep 03. (cd) *(509846-2)* **HAND OVER YOUR LOVED ONES** – – American in Amsterdam / The song that I wrote when you dissed me / Anyway / Freak on / Lemonade / Dick / Fair weather friend / Randall / Whole amoeba / Dynamite satchel of pain / Song that I wrote when you dissed me (demo part 1) / Song that I wrote when you dissed me (demo part 2).

WHISKEYTOWN

Formed: Raleigh, North Carolina, USA ... 1994 by singer/songwriter, DAVID RYAN ADAMS (not the "Reckless" lad from Canada!), straight out of Jacksonville punk outfit, PATTY DUKE SYNDROME – one split single/EP alongside GLAMOUR PUSS exists while the lad (at 15 year-old) played drums for BLANK LABEL in the early 90's. Recruiting guitarist, PHIL WANDSCHER, violin-player CAITLIN CARY and a rhythm section, this much feted alt-country rock outfit delivered their debut set, 'FAITHLESS STREET' (1996), a deep intoxicating journey into the badlands where the ROLLING STONES or the REPLACEMENTS might have veered off track had it not been for the love of raw blues. A plethora of major record labels came a-knockin', Geffen's newish imprint, 'Outpost', winning their signatures in '96. A year later, WHISKEYTOWN were dragged from the proverbial boozer to record their long-awaited follow-up, 'STRANGERS ALMANAC', a much-lauded dozen songs of a country-grunge-esque nature (it also featured singing by ALEJANDRO ESCOVEDO – ex-DILS, ex-NUNS). After their third album was shelved for almost two years, WHISKEYTOWN, once champions of the alt country scene were fast fading into obscurity when 'Universal' refused to issue the excellent and tender 'PNEUMONIA'. It finally saw the light of day in 2001. The set was a big treat for WHISKEYTOWN fans, and was highly regarded as their lost classic. Gone was the angst rock'n'roll country of GRAM PARSONS and in its place was the mellow and bittersweet folk of ADAMS, who was splitting with his girlfriend and trying desperately to stay away from booze and drugs. This can be heard on ballads such as 'PAPER MOON' and the strange wurlitzer loop of 'WHAT THE DEVIL WANTED'. Of course, ADAMS went on to do great things on his own (see the ADAMS discography), and although CARY and ETHAN helped produce his debut solo album 'Heartbreaker' in 2000, the rest of the band disappeared from the scene altogether. • **Covered:** WITHERED & DIED (Richard Thompson) / NERVOUS BREAKDOWN (Greg Ginn) / BLANK GENERATION (Richard Hell).

Album rating: FAITHLESS STREET (*6) / STRANGERS ALMANAC (*8) / PNEUMONIA (*7)

DAVID RYAN ADAMS – vocals, guitars, banjo, piano, percussion / **PHIL WANDSCHER** – guitar, vocals, organ, percussion / **CAITLIN CARY** – violin, vocals / **STEVE GROTHMAN** – bass / **ERIC 'SKILLET' GILMORE** – drums

Mood Food Mood Food

May 95. (7"ep) <*MFR 001-7*> **ANGELS EP** –
– Angels are messengers from God / Captain Smith / Tennessee square / Take your guns to town.

Jan 96. (cd) **FAITHLESS STREET** –
– Midway park / Drank like a river / Too drunk to dream / What may seem like love / Faithless street / Mining town / If he can't have you / Black arrow, bleeding heart / Matrimony / Hard luck story / Top dollar / Oklahoma. <*re-iss. 1996 on 'Outpost-Geffen'+=; OPD 30002*> – (baseball park sessions):- Empty baseball park / Here's to the rest of the world / 16 days / Yesterday's news / Factory girl. *(UK-iss.Oct98 ++=; same)* – Tennessee Square / Excuse me while I break my own heart tonight / Desperate ain't lonely / Lo-fi Tennessee mountain angel (for Kathy Poindexter).

— **JEFF RICE** – bass; repl. STEVE

Apr 97. (7"ep) <*BS 021*> **WHISKEYTOWN EP** –
– Theme for a trucker / My heart is broken / The strip / Houses on the hill. *(UK-iss.Jun97 + on US label, 'Bloodshot')*

Jun 97. (m-cd) <*(MFR 008-2)*> **RURAL FREE DELIVERY**
– Take your guns to town / Nervous breakdown / Tennessee square / Captain Smith / Macon, Georgia county line / Pawn shop ain't no place for a wedding ring / Oklahoma / Angels are messengers from God.

— **STEVE TERRY** – drums; repl. ERIC

Outpost – Geffen Outpost – Geffen

Jan 98. (cd) <*(OPD 30005)*> **STRANGERS ALMANAC** Nov97
– Inn town / Excuse me while I break my own heart tonight / Yesterday's news / 16 days / Everything I do / Houses on the hill / Turn around / Dancing with the women at the bar / Waiting to derail / Avenues / Losering / Somebody remembers the rose / Not home anymore.

— **CHRIS LANEY** – bass; repl. RICE

1998. (7"ep) <*BS 037*> **HIGHWAY 145. / Neko Case & The Sadies: MY '63** –
(above also issued on 'Bloodshot')

— now down to a trio of **ADAMS, CARY + MIKE DALY** – multi

— split in 1999; CARY went solo (one set, 'WALTZIE' in 2000), while RYAN ADAMS became a star in his own right

Lost Highway Lost Highway

May 01. (cd) <*(170199-2)*> **PNEUMONIA**
– Ballad of Carol Lynn / Don't wanna know why / Jacksonville skyline / Reason to lie / Don't be sad / Sit & listen to the rain / Under your breath / Mirror, mirror / Paper moon / What the Devil wanted / Crazy about you / My hometown / Easy hearts / Bar lights.

CAITLIN CARY

Yep Roc Yep Roc

Aug 00. (cd) <*(YEP 2018)*> **WALTZIE**
– Sorry / Rosemary Moore / Nursery lie / Big town / Withered & died (live).

☐ Alan WHITE (see under ⇒ YES)

WHITESNAKE

Formed: London, England ... late 70's by ex-DEEP PURPLE vocalist, DAVID COVERDALE (b.22 Sep'49, Saltburn-On-Sea, Yorkshire, England). After leaving 'PURPLE, COVERDALE recorded two fine sets of bluesy hard-rock, 'DAVID COVERDALE'S WHITESNAKE' (1977) and 'NORTHWINDS' (1978), taking the name for his new outfit from the former and retaining a core of musicians which included such seasoned veterans as MICKY MOODY, BERNIE MARSDEN and NEIL MURRAY. Signing to 'EMI International', he/they debuted with the 'SNAKEBITE' EP in summer '78, the record's highlight being a smoky cover of Bobby Bland's 'AIN'T NO LOVE IN THE HEART OF THE CITY'. The group subsequently hit the UK Top 50 with their debut album, 'TROUBLE' (1978), the record adding the keyboard skills of ex-DP man, JON LORD. While they followed it up with the overlooked 'LOVE HUNTER' in 1979, they only really broke through with the 'READY AN' WILLING' (1980) set, the success of its attendant single pushing the album into the UK Top 10. The band were certainly ready, willing and able to fill the gap in the market left by the now defunct DEEP PURPLE, their musical prowess securing them an enviable live reputation if not quite measuring up in the songwriting department. Consequently then, the band's only official concert set, 'LIVE . . . IN THE HEART OF THE CITY' (1980), ranks as one of the most consistent recordings of their career. However their most successful album to date (narrowly missing No.1), 'COME AN' GET IT' (1981) was something of a disappointment, the group moving away from their bluesy roots towards a neutered hard-rock sound. Critics also rounded on COVERDALE's notoriously sexist, cliche-ridden lyrics, complaints which were water off a duck's back to the blonde-maned, mouth-full-of-plums cock-rocker. Despite personnel shuffles which saw new faces such as MEL GALLEY, COLIN 'Bomber' HODGKINSON and COZY POWELL, 'SAINTS AN' SINNERS' (1982) failed to remedy matters although it went Top 10 nevertheless. With the addition of ex-TYGERS OF PAN TANG guitarist, JOHN SYKES, COVERDALE had finally found a sympathetic writing partner as evidenced on the much improved 'SLIDE IT IN' (1984). Blatant innuendo was still high on the agenda, but then again, that's what COVERDALE excelled at, his panting and moaning all over the shop on the epic climax-blues stomp, 'SLOW AN' EASY', actually as effective as it was hilarious. Never the most stable of bands, the tour that followed saw WHITESNAKE eventually reduced to SYKES and COVERDALE, even LORD bogging off to join the reformed DEEP PURPLE. Recruiting TONY FRANKLIN and CARMINE APPICE, the group eventually returned with the eponymous 'WHITESNAKE 1987' (1987, funnily enough), sleeker, (some might say) sexier, and considerably more commercial than ever before. Previewed by the Top 10 LED ZEPELLIN-esque, 'STILL OF THE NIGHT', the album stormed both the British and US charts. The latter track was the hardest fare on offer, however, the bulk of the album made up of limp MTV ballads like 'IS THIS LOVE' and ravamps of old songs, the infectious reworking of 'HERE I GO AGAIN' (the original can be found on 'SAINTS AN' SINNERS') giving the group their first and only No.1. While the album no doubt alienated many of their previously loyal older fans, it sold millions, finally giving COVERDALE the success he'd long been after. It didn't do much for the group's stability, however, as SYKES split for BLUE MURDER and COVERDALE once again recruited a whole new line-up numbering ADRIAN VANDENBURG, RUDY SARZO, TOMMY ALDRIDGE and VIVIAN CAMPBELL. Guitar wizard STEVE VAI subsequently replaced CAMPBELL and this line-up gave a rather lacklustre headlining performance at the 1989 Monsters Of Rock Festival, the highly anticipated 'SLIP OF THE TONGUE' (1989) equally uninspiring. Unsurprisingly, the record failed to match the giddy commercial heights of its predecessor and COVERDALE put the band on ice while he subsequently hooked up with JIMMY PAGE for the successful 'COVERDALE ° PAGE' album in 1993. Last sighted on a tour of Europe in support of a 1994 greatest hits collection, DAVID COVERDALE & WHITESNAKE delivered a UK Top 40 comeback album, 'RESTLESS HEART' in 1997. With the metal/hard-rock scene changing almost beyond recognition, it looks unlikely that WHITESNAKE can repeat the glory days of the late 80's . . . the nostalgia circuit beckons. Well, maybe not quite yet, it seems there's life in the old dog yet. While his new image may shock a few of his older fans, not to mention a few small children, the song, basically remains the same on COVERDALE's 2000 solo set, 'INTO THE LIGHT'. His first since 'NORTHWINDS' back in '78, the record featured a solid if unadventurous selection of the man's trademark bluesy hard rock and histrionic balladry, co-written largely with veteran guitarist EARL SLICK. • **Trivia:** On the 17th of February '89, COVERDALE married actress Tawny Kittaen, who had previously featured on their video of 'IS THIS LOVE'.

Album rating: NORTHWINDS (*7; by David Coverdale) / TROUBLE (*5) / LOVEHUNTER (*6) / READY AN' WILLING (*6) / LIVE . . . IN THE HEART OF THE CITY (*6) / COME AND GET IT (*6) / SAINTS 'N' SINNERS (*4) / SLIDE IN IT (*5) / 1987 (*5) / SLIP OF THE TONGUE (*5) / WHITESNAKE'S GREATEST HITS compilation (*8) / BEST OF compilation (*7) / COVERDALE – PAGE (*5) / RESTLESS HEART (*5) / David Coverdale: INTO THE LIGHT (*5)

DAVID COVERDALE

(solo) – vocals (ex-DEEP PURPLE) with **MICK MOODY** – guitar (ex-JUICY LUCY, ex-SNAFU) / **TIM HINKLEY** – keyboards / **SIMON PHILLIPS** – drums / **DELISLE HARPER** – bass / plus **RON ASPERY** – sax / **ROGER GLOVER** – producer, bass, keyboards

Purple — not iss.

May 77. (lp) *(TPS 3509)* **DAVID COVERDALE'S WHITESNAKE** [ ] [–]
– Lady / Blindman / Goldie's place / Whitesnake / Time on my side / Peace lovin' man / Sunny days / Hole in the sky / Celebration. *(cd-iss. Aug00 on 'Connoisseur'+=; VSOPCD 313)* – Peace lovin' man (version) / Sunny days (version).

May 77. (7") *(PUR 133)* **HOLE IN THE SKY. / BLINDMAN** [ ] [–]

— **COVERDALE** retained only **MOODY** and recruited **BERNIE MARSDEN** – guitar (ex-PAICE, ASHTON & LORD, ex-UFO, ex-WILD TURKEY) / **NEIL MURRAY** – bass (ex-COLOSSEUM, ex-NATIONAL HEALTH) / **BRIAN JOHNSON** – keyboards + **DAVID DOWELL** – drums (both ex-STREETWALKERS)

Feb 78. (7") *(PUR 136)* **BREAKDOWN. / ONLY MY SOUL** [ ] [–]

Mar 78. (lp) *(TPS 3513)* **NORTHWINDS** [ ] [–]
– Keep on giving me love / Northwinds / Give me kindness / Time & again / Queen of hearts / Only my soul / Say you love me / Breakdown. *(re-iss. Apr84 on 'Fame' lp/c; FA41 3097-1/-4) (cd-iss. Aug00 on 'Connoisseur'+=; VSOPCD 314)* – Shame the Devil / Sweet mistreater.

Jun 78. (7") **BREAKDOWN. / BLOODY MARY** [–] [ ]

DAVID COVERDALE'S WHITESNAKE

PETE SOLLEY – keyboards repl. JOHNSTON

EMI Int. — Sunburst

Jun 78. (lp) *<5C 062-61290>* **SNAKEBITE** [ ] [–]
– Come on / Bloody Mary / Ain't no love in the heart of the city / Steal away / Keep on giving me love / Queen of hearts / Only my soul / Breakdown.

Jun 78. (7"ep,7"white-ep) *(INEP 751) <915>* **SNAKEBITE EP** [61] [ ]
– Bloody Mary / Steal away / Come on / Ain't no love in the heart of the city.

— **JON LORD** (b. 9 Jun'41, Leicester, England) – keyboards (ex-PAICE, ASHTON & LORD, ex-DEEP PURPLE) repl. SOLLEY

Oct 78. (7") *(INT 568)* **LIE DOWN. / DON'T MESS WITH ME** [ ] [–]

Oct 78. (lp) *(INS 3022) <937>* **TROUBLE** [50] [ ]
– Take me with you / Love to keep you warm / Lie down (a modern love song) / Day tripper / Night hawl (vampire blues) / The time is right for love / Trouble / Belgian Tom's hat trick / Free flight / Don't mess with me. *(re-iss. Sep80 on 'United Artists'; UAG 30305) (re-iss. May82 on 'Fame' lp/c; FA/TCFA 3002) (re-iss. May90 cd/c/lp; CD/TC+/FA 3234) (re-iss. Jun87 on 'E.M.I.' lp/c; EMS/TCEMS 1257) (cd-iss. Apr88 on 'E.M.I.'; CZ 9)*

Mar 79. (7") *(INT 578)* **THE TIME IS RIGHT FOR LOVE. / COME ON (live)** [ ] [–]

Apr 79. (7") **THE TIME IS RIGHT FOR LOVE. / BELGUIN TOM'S HAT TRICK** [–] [ ]

U.A. — U.A.

Oct 79. (lp/c) *(UAG 30264) <981>* **LOVE HUNTER** [29] [ ]
– Long way from home / Walking in the shadow of the blues / Help me thro' the day / Medicine man / You 'n' me / Mean business / Love hunter / Outlaw / Rock'n'roll women / We wish you well. *(re-iss. Apr84 on 'Fame' lp/c; FA/TCFA 3095) (cd-iss. Apr88; CDFA 3095) (cd re-iss. Jul94 on 'E.M.I.'; CDEMS 1529)*

Oct 79. (7"m) *(BP 324)* **LONG WAY FROM HOME. / TROUBLE (live) / AIN'T NO LOVE IN THE HEART OF THE CITY (live)** [55] [–]

Nov 79. (7") **LONG WAY FROM HOME. / WE WISH YOU WELL** [–] [ ]

WHITESNAKE

— with **IAN PAICE** (b.29 Jun'48, Nottingham, England) – drums (ex-PAICE, ASHTON & LORD, ex-DEEP PURPLE) repl. DOWELL

U.A. Mirage-Atlantic

Apr 80. (7"m) *(BP 352)* **FOOL FOR YOUR LOVING. / MEAN BUSINESS / DON'T MESS WITH ME** 13 –

Jun 80. (lp/c) *(UAG 30302)* <19276> **READY AN' WILLING** 6 90
– Fool for your loving / Sweet talker / Ready an' willing / Carry your load / Blindman / Ain't gonna cry no more / Love man / Black and blue / She's a woman. *(re-iss. Sep85 on 'Fame' lp/c; FA/TCFA 3134) (cd-iss. Apr88; CDFA 3134) (cd re-iss. Jul94 on 'E.M.I.'; CDEMS 1526) (cd re-iss. Feb00 on 'Axe Killer';* **AXE 305526CD)**

Jul 80. (7"m) *(BP 363)* **READY AN' WILLING. / NIGHT HAWK (VAMPIRE BLUES) / WE WISH YOU WELL** 43 –

Jul 80. (7") *<3672>* **FOOL FOR YOUR LOVING. / BLACK AND BLUE** – 53

Oct 80. (7") *<3766>* **SWEET TALKER. / AIN'T GONNA CRY NO MORE** –

Nov 80. (d-lp/d-c) *(SNAKE/TC2SNAKE 1) <19292>* **LIVE . . . IN THE HEART OF THE CITY (live)** 5
– Come on * / Sweet talker / Walking in the shadow of the blues / Love hunter / Fool for your loving / Ain't gonna cry no more / Ready an' willing / Take me with you * / Might just take your life / Lie down * / Ain't no love in the heart of the city / Trouble * / Mistreated. *<cd-iss. Jul88 on 'Underdog'; CDS 790860-2>* – <omits *> *(re-iss. Nov91 on 'Fame' cd/c; CD/TC FA 3265) (re-iss. Jul94 on 'E.M.I.' cd/c; CD/TC EMS 1525)*

Nov 80. (7"/12") *(BP/12BP 381) <3794>* **AIN'T NO LOVE IN THE HEART OF THE CITY (live). / TAKE ME WITH YOU (live)** 51

Liberty Atlantic

Apr 81. (7") *(BP 395)* **DON'T BREAK MY HEART AGAIN. / CHILD OF BABYLON** 17 –

Apr 81. (lp/c) *(LBG/TCLBG 30327) <16043>* **COME AN' GET IT** 2
– Come an' get it / Hot stuff / Don't break my heart again / Lonely days, lonely nights / Wine, women an' song / Child of Babylon / Would I lie to you / Girl / Hit an' run / Till the day I die. *(re-iss. May89 on 'Fame' cd/c/lp; CD/TC+/FA 3219) (re-iss. Jul94 on 'E.M.I.' cd/c; CD/TC EMS 1528)*

May 81. (7") *(BP 399)* **WOULD I LIE TO YOU. / GIRL** 37 –

Jun 81. (7") *<3844>* **DON'T BREAK MY HEART AGAIN. / LONELY DAYS, LONELY NIGHTS** –

— **COVERDALE** retained **MOODY + LORD** and brought in **MEL GALLEY** – guitar (ex-TRAPEZE) repl. MARSDEN who formed ALASKA / **COLIN 'Bomber' HODGKINSON** (b.14 Oct'45) – bass (ex-BACK DOOR) repl. MURRAY to GARY MOORE / **COZY POWELL** (b.29 Dec'47, Cirencester, England) – drums (ex-JEFF BECK, ex-RAINBOW, Solo Artist, ex-BEDLAM) repl. PAICE who joined GARY MOORE

Liberty Geffen

Oct 82. (7"pic-d) *(BP 416)* **HERE I GO AGAIN. / BLOODY LUXURY** 34 –

Nov 82. (lp/c/pic-lp) *(LBG/TCLBG/LBGP 30354) <2-24173>* **SAINTS AN' SINNERS** 9
– Young blood / Rough an' ready / Blood luxury / Victim of love / Crying in the rain / Here I go again / Love an' afection / Rock'n'roll angels / Dancing girls / Saints an' sinners. *(re-iss. 1985 lp/c; ATAK/TCATAK 10) (re-iss. May87 on 'Fame' lp/c; FA/TCFA 3177) (cd-iss. Apr88; CDFA 3177) (cd re-iss. Jul94 & Jul98 on 'E.M.I.'; CDEMS 1521)*

Aug 83. (7"/7"sha-pic-d) *(BP/+P 420)* **GUILTY OF LOVE. / GAMBLER** 31 –

— now a quintet, when MICK MOODY departed

Jan 84. (7"/12") *(BP/12BP 422)* **GIVE ME MORE TIME. / NEED YOUR LOVE SO BAD** 29 –

— **NEIL MURRAY** – bass returned to repl. HODGKINSON / added **JOHN SYKES** (b.29 Jul'59) – guitar (ex-TYGERS OF PAN TANG)

Feb 84. (lp/c) *(WHITE/TCWHITE 1) <4018>* **SLIDE IT IN** 9 Aug84 40
– Gambler / Slide it in / Standing in the shadow / Give me more time / Love ain't no stranger / Slow an' easy / Spit it out / All or nothing / Hungry for love / Guilty of love. *(cd-iss. Apr88 on 'E.M.I.'; CZ 88) (pic-lp 1984 w/extra US mixes; LBGP 240-000-0)*

Apr 84. (7"/7"pic-d) *(BP/+P 423)* **STANDING IN THE SHADOWS. / ALL OR NOTHING (US mix)** 62 –
(12"+=) – ('A'-US remix).

Aug 84. (7") *<29171>* **LOVE AIN'T NO STRANGER. / GUILTY OF LOVE** –

Feb 85. (7"/12") *(BP/12BP 424)* **LOVE AIN'T NO STRANGER. / SLOW AN' EASY** 44 –
(12"white+=) *(BP12 424)* – Slide it in.

— split for a while in 1984 when JON LORD re-joined DEEP PURPLE. **WHITESNAKE** were re-formed by **COVERDALE + SYKES** and new musicians **TONY FRANKLIN** – bass (ex-The FIRM) repl. MURRAY and GALLEY / **CARMINE APPICE** – drums (ex-BECK, BOGERT & APPICE) repl. POWELL to E.L.P.

EMI Int. Geffen

Mar 87. (7"/7"white) *(EMI/+W 5606)* **STILL OF THE NIGHT. / HERE I GO AGAIN (1987)** 16 –
(12"+=/12"pic-d+=) *(12EMI/+P 5606)* – You're gonna break my heart again.

Apr 87. (cd/c/lp) *(CD/TC+/EMC 3528) <24099>* **WHITESNAKE 1987** 8 2
– Still of the night / Bad boys / Give me all your love / Looking for love / Crying in the rain / Is this love / Straight for the heart / Don't turn away / Children of the night. *(also on pic-lp; EMCP 3528) (cd+=)* – Here I go again '87 / You're gonna break my heart again. *(re-iss. Jul94 cd/c; CD/TC EMS 1531)*

May 87. (7"/7"sha-pic-d) *(EM/+P 3)* **IS THIS LOVE. / STANDING IN THE SHADOWS** 9 –
(12"+=/12"white+=) *(12EM/+P 3)* – Need your love so bad.
(cd-ep++=/7"ep++=) *(EMX/CDEM 3)* – Still of the night.

Jun 87. (7") *<28331>* **STILL OF THE NIGHT. / DON'T TURN AWAY** – 79

Jul 87. (7") *<28339>* **HERE I GO AGAIN. / CHILDREN OF THE NIGHT** – 1

Oct 87. (7") *<28233>* **IS THIS LOVE. / BAD BOYS** – 2

Oct 87. (c-s/12"/7") *(TC/12+/EM 35)* **HERE I GO AGAIN '87 (US mix). / GUILTY OF LOVE** 9 –
(7"etched/10"white/cd-s) *(EMP/10EM/CDEM 35)* – ('A'side) / ('A'-US remix).

Jan 88. (7"/7"white) *(EM/+W 23)* **GIVE ME ALL YOUR LOVE. / FOOL FOR YOUR LOVING** 18 –
(12"+=/12"white) *(12EMP/+W 23)* – Don't break my heart again.
(3"cd-s+=) *(CDEM 23)* – Here I go again (USA remix).

Jan 88. (7") *<28103>* **GIVE ME ALL YOUR LOVE. / STRAIGHT FROM THE HEART** – 48

— **COVERDALE** completely re-modelled line-up when SYKES formed BLUE MURDER. He was replaced by **ADRIAN VANDENBURG** (b. Netherlands) – guitar (ex-VANDENBERG) / **RUDY SARZO** (b. 9 Nov'52, Havana, Cuba) – bass (ex-OZZY OSBOURNE, ex-QUIET RIOT) repl. FRANKLIN / **TOMMY ALDRIDGE** – drums (ex-OZZY OSBOURNE, ex-BLACK OAK ARKANSAS) repl. APPICE (Dec88) / **STEVE VAI** (b. 6 Jun'60, Carle Place, N.Y.) – guitar (solo Artist, ex-FRANK ZAPPA, DAVID LEE ROTH) repl. VIVIAN CAMPBELL

Nov 89. (cd/c/lp) *(CD/TC+/EMD 1013) <24249>* **SLIP OF THE TONGUE** 10 10
– Slip of the tongue / Cheap an' nasty / Fool for your loving / Now you're gone / Kitten's got claws / Wings of the storm / The deeper the love / Judgement day / Slow poke music / Sailing ships. *(re-iss. Jul94 cd/c; CD/TC EMS 1527)*

Nov 89. (7"/7"s)<US-c-s> *(EM/+P 123) <22715>* **FOOL FOR YOUR LOVING ('89). / SLOW POKE MUSIC** 43 37
(c-s+=) *(TCEM 123)* – ('A'version).
(12"+=/12"white+=) *(12EM+/P 1243)* – Walking in the shadow of the blues.

Jan 90. (7") *<19951>* **THE DEEPER THE LOVE. / SLIP OF THE TONGUE** – 28

Feb 90. (c-s/7"/7"pic-d) *(TC+/EM/+PD 128)* **THE DEEPER THE LOVE. / JUDGEMENT DAY** 35 –
(12"white+=) *(12EMS 128)* – Sweet lady luck.
(12"++=/cd-s++=) *(12/CD EM 128)* – Fool for your lovin' (Vai voltage mix).

Aug 90. (c-s/7"/7"sha-pic-d) *(TC+/EM+/PD 150) <19976>* **NOW YOU'RE GONE (remix). / WINGS OF THE STORM** 31 May90 96
(12"+=/12"pic-d+=/cd-s+=) *(12EM/12EMPS/CDEM 150)* – Kittens got claws / Cheap an' nasty.

DAVID COVERDALE

Epic Epic

Sep 90. (7"/c-s) *(656 292-7/-4)* **THE LAST NOTE OF FREEDOM. / (track by HANS ZIMMER)**
(12"+=) *(656 292-6)* – (track by other artist).
(cd-s++=) *(656 292-2)* – ('A'version).

COVERDALE• PAGE

DAVID COVERDALE – vocals / **JIMMY PAGE** – guitar (ex-LED ZEPPELIN, ex-solo artist) / **JORGE CASAS** – bass / **DENNY CARMASSI** – drums (ex-

MONTROSE) / **RICKY PHILIPS** – bass / **LESTER MENDEL** – keyboards / **JOHN HARRIS** – acoustic harmonica / **TOMMY FUNDERBUCK** – backing vocals

E.M.I. Geffen

Mar 93. (cd/c/lp) *(CD/TC+/EMD 1041) <24487>* **COVERDALE• PAGE** [4] [5]
– Shake my tree / Waiting on you / Take me for a little while / Pride and joy / Over now / Feeling hot / Easy does it / Take a look at yourself / Don't leave me this way / Absolution blues / Whisper a prayer for the dying *(re-iss. Jul94 cd/c; same)*

Jun 93. (c-s/12"pic-d) *(12EMPD/TCEM 270)* **TAKE ME FOR A LITTLE WHILE. / EASY DOES IT** [29] [ ]
(cd-s) *(CDEM 270)* – ('A'side) / ('A'acoustic) / Shake my tree (the crunch mix) / ('A'edit).

Sep 93. (7"pic-d/c-s) *(EMPD/TCEM 279)* **TAKE A LOOK AT YOURSELF. / WAITING ON YOU** [ ] [ ]
(cd-s+=) *(CDEM 279)* – ('A'acoustic) / ('A'girls version).

DAVID COVERDALE & WHITESNAKE

E.M.I. E.M.I.

May 97. (c-s/cd-s) *(TC/CD EM 471)* **TOO MANY TEARS / THE DEEPER THE LOVE / IS THIS LOVE** [46] [–]
(cd-s) *(CDEMS 471)* – ('A'part 1) / Can't stop now / ('A'part 2).

Jun 97. (cd/c) *(CD/TCEMD 1104) <56806>* **RESTLESS HEART** [34] Jun98 [ ]
– Don't fade away / All in the name of love / Restless heart / Too many tears / Crying / Stay with me / Can't go on / You're so fine / Your precious love / Take me back again / Woman trouble blues.

Oct 97. (c-s) *(TCEM 495)* **DON'T FADE AWAY / OI** [ ] [–]
(cd-s+=) *(CDEM 495)* – Anything you want / Don't fade away.

DAVID COVERDALE

—— with various session people

E.M.I. Dragonfly

Sep 00. (cd-s) *(CDEM 574)* **LOVE IS BLIND / LOVE IS BLIND (radio) / SHE GIVE ME** [ ] [–]

Sep 00. (cd) *(528124-2) <12251>* **INTO THE LIGHT** [75] Oct00 [ ]
– Into the light / River song / She give me / Don't you cry / Love is blind / Slave / Cry for love / Living on love / Midnight blue / Too many tears / Don't lie to me / Where you may go.

– compilations, etc. –

Apr 88. (d-lp/c/cd) *Connoisseur; (VSOP LP/MC/CD 118)* **THE CONNOISSEUR COLLECTION** [ ] [–]
– (DAVID COVERDALE's first 2 solo albums)

Jun 88. (d-lp) *Polydor; <9244/5>* **GREATEST HITS** [–] [ ]

Jul 94. (cd/c/lp) *E.M.I.; (CD/TC+/EMD 1065) / Geffen; <24620>* **WHITESNAKE'S GREATEST HITS** [4] [ ]
– Still of the night / Here I go again / Is this love / Love ain't no stranger / Looking for love / Now you're gone / Slide it in / Slow an' easy / Judgement day / You're gonna break my heart again / The deeper the love / Crying in the rain / Fool for your loving / Sweet lady luck.

Jul 94. (7"/7"white/c-s) *E.M.I.; (EM/EMS/TCEM 329)* **IS THIS LOVE. / SWEET LADY LUCK** [25] [ ]
(cd-s+=) *(CDEM 329)* – Now you're gone.

Nov 95. (3xcd-box) *E.M.I.; (CDOMB 016)* **SLIDE IT IN / 1987 / SLIP OF THE TONGUE** [ ] [ ]

Mar 99. (cd) *E.M.I.; (499508-2)* **STARKERS IN TOKYO** [ ] [ ]

Jun 00. (d-cd) *Axe Killer; (AXE 3055482CD)* **1987 / SLIP OF THE TONGUE** [ ] [ ]

Mar 03. (cd) *E.M.I.; (581245-2)* **BEST OF** [44] [–]
– Fool for your loving / Don't break my heart again / Love ain't no stranger / Is this love / Now you're gone / Give me all your love / Ready and willing / Guilty of love / Would I lie to you / Long way from home / The deeper the love / Ain't no love in the heart of the city / Too many tears / Give me more time / Standing in the shadow / Here I go again / Still of the night.

Apr 03. (cd) *Polydor; <2580>* **BEST!** [–] [ ]

May 03. (d-cd) *E.M.I.; (<581694-2>)* **THE SILVER ANNIVERSARY COLLECTION** [ ] [ ]

WHITE STRIPES

Formed: Detroit, Michigan, USA . . . 1997 by husband and wife duo JACK and MEG WHITE; JACK (aka JOHN GILLIS) took his wife's surname when they married in October 1996. Mystery surrounding their relationship (many including myself and other biographers were fooled) thought that they were brother and sister! JACK began his musical career in Michigan's local outfit GO, before recruiting his partner MEG to play percussion in what would ultimately become The WHITE STRIPES. Clad in matching red and white clothes (apparently they even smoke Embassy Royals because of their clever color scheme), the duo debuted with the single 'LET'S SHAKE HANDS' (1997), issued on the 'Italy' imprint, after whipping up a storm on the local garage/underground rock circut. Two more singles followed and the group flitted to champions of the independent scene 'Sympathy For The Record Industry', where their self-titled album was released in 1999. It was good enough to generate column inches and critics seemed most impressed with covers of blues classics 'STOP BREAKING DOWN BLUES' and 'ST. JAMES INFIRMARY BLUES'. Whilst still borrowing a variation of sounds from the likes of The WHO and MC5, JACK's love for the blues was apparent: he continuously cited giant of the genre CHARLEY PATTON as his immediate influence, and frequently covered some of his songs in The STRIPES' live sets. This love of country blues was even more obvious come the sophomore LP 'DE STIJL' (2000), named after the abstract art movement led by Dutch artist Gerrit Rietveld. Stand-out tracks included the rock-steady 'LITTLE BIRD', 'TRUTH DON'T MAKE A NOISE' and a worthy Son House cover 'DEATH LETTER'. A break was imminent and JACK took to producing some of the scene's most promising acts during the period between 1999-2000. Shortly before the release of 'DE STIJL' – March 2000, to be precise – the couple officially divorced having lived separately for just over a year. The VON BONDIES and The SOLEDAD BROTHERS were just two of the groups that had impressed him, and judging by the cover of the latter's debut album, he was happy to dress up as Uncle Sam, get propped up against a wall and shot by a firing squad (but don't worry, ladies and gents, he didn't really suffer for his art). That aside, it was time for him and MEG to venture back into the studio to record what was to become their breakthrough album, 'WHITE BLOOD CELLS' (2001). On the eve of its premiere, the NME claimed that the WHITE STRIPES, along with fellow garage rockers The STROKES, were destined to become the future of rock music. Even the tabloids caught on, with the Sun hailing them as "Stripe-tastic". Meanwhile, normally MOR radio station Radio 4 caught the STRIPE's buzz, as did John Peel, who casually compared them to The SEX PISTOLS. Rolling Stone magazine reckoned that Detroit was the new Seattle, but JACK STRIPE was unfazed, claiming he'd rather hang-out with fellow musicians The VON BONDIES than pay attention to the hype. A sold-out tour followed, plus a reputed $1m move to 'X.L.' records, once home to The PRODIGY. Singles 'HOTEL YOBA'- named after a "doss-house" – and 'FELL IN LOVE WITH A GIRL' followed, both charting in the Top 20. Going from strength to strength, The WHITE STRIPES' trail-blazing success saw them entering the US Top 10 and the UK No.1 spot with their indispensable set 'ELEPHANT' (2003). A stonking mix of blues, acoustic folk and downright dirty riffage, it saw the duo initiate a worldwide anthem with the single 'SEVEN NATION ARMY'. Hinged solely on one guitar hook and MEG WHITE's booming drum kit, it was the envy of all guitarists and probably the song which will replace 'Smells Like Teen Spirt' when kids tested out new guitars in music shops (much to the annoyance of the employees). That aside, the album had much more on offer; the BACHARACH cover of 'I JUST DON'T KNOW WHAT TO DO WITH MYSELF' (coupled with a Kate Moss pole-dancing video), the start/stop ferocity of 'HARDEST BUTTON TO BUTTON' and the complex blues jam 'BALL AND BISCUIT'. Dark, moody and slightly harsh on the ears, 'ELEPHANT' also had its fun moments, most notably the warm three-way acoustic stop of 'IT'S TRUE THAT WE LOVE ONE ANOTHER', with MEG and first lady of Garage rock HOLLY GOLIGHTLY sharing vocal duties with JACK. Mostly recorded live by Liam Watson on reel-to-reel tape at his studio in London's Abbey Road, 'ELEPHANT' is as punk as is comes with a band who are were literally in the throes of international and critical acclaim. Darlings they ain't! • **Covers:** LOOK ME OVER CLOSELY (Marlene Dietrich) / JOLENE (Dolly Parton) / ONE MORE CUP OF COFFEE (Bob Dylan) / STOP BREAKING DOWN (Robert Johnson) / ST. JAMES INFIRMARY BLUES (Cab Calloway) / LORD, SEND ME AN ANGEL + YOUR SOUTHERN CAN IS MINE (Blind Willie McTell) / DEATH LETTER (Son House) / PARTY OF SPECIAL THINGS TO DO + CHINA PIG + ASHTRAY HEART (Captain Beefheart) / RATED X (Loretta Lynn) / BLACK JACK DAVEY (trad.) / GOOD TO ME (Brendan Benson) / WHO'S TO SAY? (Blanche) / ST. IDES OF MARCH (Soledad Brothers).

Album ratings: THE WHITE STRIPES (*7) / DE STIJL (*7) / WHITE BLOOD CELLS (*8) / ELEPHANT (*9)

JACK WHITE (b. JOHN ANTHONY GILLIS, 9 Jul'75) – vocals, guitar, piano, etc / **MEG WHITE** (b. MEGAN MARTHA WHITE, 10 Dec'74) – drums, tambourine

not iss. | Italy

1997. (7"red,7") *<IR 003>* **LET'S SHAKE HANDS. / LOOK ME OVER CLOSELY** [–] [ ]

1998. (7"white,7") *<IR 006>* **LAFAYETTE BLUES. / SUGAR NEVER TASTED SO GOOD** [–] [ ]

Sympathy F | Sympathy F

Jun 99. (lp/cd) *<(SFTRI 577/+CD)>* **THE WHITE STRIPES** [ ] [ ]
– Jimmy the exploder / Stop breaking down / The big three killed my baby *[cd-only]* / Suzy Lee / Sugar never tasted so good *[cd-only]* / Wasting my time / Cannon / Astro / Broken bricks / When I hear my name / Do / Screwdriver / One more cup of coffee *[cd-only]* / Little people / Slicker drips / St. James infirmary blues / I fought piranhas. *(UK re-iss. Apr01; same) <(re-iss. Sep01 on 'X.L.' lp/cd; XLLP/XLCD 149)>*

Jun 99. (7"red) *<SFTRI 578>* **THE BIG THREE KILLED MY BABY. / RED BOWLING BALL RUTH** [–] [ ]
(UK-iss.Jan02; same as US)

Jun 00. (lp/cd) *<(SFTRI 609/+CD)>* **DE STIJL** [ ] [ ]
– You're pretty good looking / Hello operator / Little bird / Apple blossom / I'm bound to pack it up / Death letter / Sister, do you know my name? / Truth doesn't make a noise / A boy's best friend / Let's build a home / Jumble, jumble / Why can't you be nicer to me? / Your southern can is mine. *(UK re-iss. Apr01; same) <(re-iss. Sep01 on 'X.L.' lp/cd; XLLP/XLCD 150)>*

Aug 00. (7"pic-d,7") *<SFTRI 619>* **HELLO OPERATOR. / JOLENE** [–] [ ]
(UK-iss.Jan02; same as US)

Nov 00. (7"red,7"; tour) *<SFTRI 645>* **LORD, SEND ME AN ANGEL. / YOU'RE PRETTY GOOD LOOKING (trendy American remix)** [–] Austra [–]
(UK-iss.Jan02; same)

Jan 01. (7") *<SP 527>* **PARTY OF SPECIAL THINGS TO DO. / CHINA PIG / ASHTRAY HEART** [–] [ ]

—— <above issued for 'Sub Pop' singles club>

Jul 01. (lp/cd) *<(SFTRI 660/+CD)>* **WHITE BLOOD CELLS** [55] [ ]
– Dead leaves and the dirty ground / Hotel Yorba / I'm finding it harder to be a gentleman / Fell in love with a girl / Expecting / Little room / The union forever / The same boy you've always known / We're going to be friends / Offend in every way / I think I smell a rat / Aluminium / I can't wait / Now Mary / I can learn / This protector. *<(re-iss. Sep01 on 'X.L.' lp/cd; XLLP/XLCD 151)> <US cd re-iss. 2002 on 'V2'; 27124>* – hit No.61

X.L. | X.L.

Nov 01. (7") *<(XLS 139)>* **HOTEL YORBA (live at the Hotel Yorba). / RATED X (live at the Hotel Yorba)** [26] [ ]
(cd-s+=) *<(XLS 139CD)>* – ('A'-video).

Feb 02. (7") *(XLS 142)* **FELL IN LOVE WITH A GIRL. / I JUST DON'T KNOW WHAT TO DO WITH MYSELF** [21] [–]
(cd-s+=) *(XLS 142CD2)* – Lovesick (live) / ('A'-video).
(cd-s) *(XLS 142CD)* – ('A'side) / Let's shake hands / Lafayette blues.

Sep 02. (7") *(XLS 148)* **DEAD LEAVES AND THE DIRTY GROUND. / STOP BREAKING DOWN** [25] [–]
(cd-s+=) *(XLS 148CD)* – Suzy Lee.

X.L. | V2

Mar 03. (cd/d-lp) *(XLCD/XLLP 162) <27148>* **ELEPHANT** [1] Apr03 [6]
– Seven nation army / Black math / There's no home for you here / I just don't know what to do with myself / In the cold, cold night / I want to the boy to warm your mother's heart / You've got her in your pocket / Ball and biscuit / The hardest button to button / Little acorns / Hypnotize / The air near my fingers / Girl, you have no faith in medicine / Well it's true that we love each other.

Apr 03. (7") *(XLS 162) <radio>* **SEVEN NATION ARMY. / GOOD TO ME** [7] [76]
(cd-s+=) *(XLS 162CD)* – Black Jack Davey.

Sep 03. (7") *(XLS 166)* **I JUST DON'T KNOW WHAT TO DO WITH MYSELF. / WHO'S TO SAY** [13] [–]
(cd-s+=) *(XLS 166CD)* – I'm finding it harder to be a gentlemen.

Nov 03. (7") *(XLS 173)* **THE HARDEST BUTTON TO BUTTON. / ST IDES OF MARCH** [23] [–]
(cd-s+=) *(XLS 173CD)* – ('A'-video).

WHITE ZOMBIE

Formed: New York City, New York, USA . . . early 1985 by frontman ROB ZOMBIE and female bassist SEAN YSEULT. Guitarist TOM GUAY and drummer IVAN DePRUME were drafted in a few years later after early members (ENA KOSTABI, PETER LANDAU and TIM JEFFS) had departed. Fresh from an unhealthy diet of BLACK SABBATH and horror B-movies, this cartoon-esque bunch of schlock-rockers set out on their demonic trail in 1987 with a debut mini-set, 'PSYCHO-HEAD BLOWOUT', for the US indie 'Silent Explosion'. A year later, their first full-length album, 'SOUL CRUSHER', was unleashed to an unsuspecting public, although the British still awaited their landing party by early '89. A third set, 'MAKE THEM DIE SLOWLY' came out around this time, produced by the seasoned BILL LASWELL and released on 'Caroline' records, its funky death-metal slowly unearthing itself and finding underground success from both metal and alternative rock audiences. J (JOHN RICCI) had replaced GUAY at this point, although his stay was short-lived when he was in turn superseded by JAY YUENGER. In the early 90's and now on the bulging, money-spinning roster of 'Geffen', WHITE ZOMBIE went to work on a new album with producer, ANDY WALLACE. The results were mindblowing in every conceivable sense, 'LA SEXORCISTO: DEVIL MUSIC VOLUME 1' (1992), being the musical carcass that The STOOGES and KISS once spewed out. Inevitably, twisted tracks such as 'WELCOME TO PLANET MOTHERFUCKER (PSYCHOHOLIC SLAG)', 'THUNDERKISS '65', etc. (lyrics, care of the warped brain of ROB), saw the band reach the American Top 30, cracking open the skull of any youth into terror-metal (even "real" cartoon pair, Beavis & Butt-head loved them, 'ZOMBIE being a highlight on the duo's various artists album). The band were rewarded with a heavy metal Grammy the following year as the band went on a mighty touring schedule across the globe, only halting to find a replacement for the departing DePLUME. In 1995, having substituted temp PHILO with (ex-TESTAMENT) drummer JOEY TEMPESTA, they rooted out a second long-player for the label,

'ASTROCREEP 2000: SONGS OF LOVE, DESTRUCTION, AND OTHER SYNTHETIC DELUSIONS OF THE ELECTRIC HEAD' (whew!). Conceptual and groundbreaking yet again, it duly scurried up the charts and into the Top 10 (also cracked the UK Top 30), demented titles such as 'EL PHANTASMO AND THE CHICKEN-RUN BLAST-O-RAMA' carrying off where the predecessor left off. During the summer of '96, they surprised many by issuing some danceable remixes of earlier tracks going under the title of 'SUPER SEXY SWINGIN' SOUNDS', a Top 20 hit in their own country. WHITE ZOMBIE split in 1997, although the solo ROB ZOMBIE (retaining TEMPESTA) released an album, 'HELLBILLY DELUXE' (1998) and after failing to come up with the score for 'The Crow 3' movie, launched his own label, 'Zombie A Go-Go'. Meanwhile, YSEULT resurrected her moonlighting project, FAMOUS MONSTERS, releasing a second CRAMPS/B-52's style 45, 'KNOCK KNOCK HALLOWEEN' (the first, 'MONSTER GIRLS – ARE GO!', was issued a few years previously) and a debut album, 'IN THE NIGHT' (1998). Following on from 1999's 'HELLBILLY DELUXE' remix set, 'AMERICAN MADE MUSIC TO STRIP BY', the undead one was back with 'THE SINISTER URGE' (2001). If that urge is to keep on making music as menacingly camp, humourously twisted and downright swinging as he managed here then we can only hope it's never satisfied. The likes of OZZY OSBOURNE and SLAYER's KERRY KING put in their tuppence worth although as ever, ROB ZOMBIE was the undisputed star of his own freakshow. • **Covers:** STRAKER/ZOMBIE except CHILDREN OF THE GRAVE (Black Sabbath) / GOD OF THUNDER (Kiss). FM covered CLOCK STRIKES TEN (Cheap Trick).

Album rating: PSYCHO-HEAD BLOWOUT mini (*4) / SOUL CRUSHER (*4) / LA SEXORCISTO: DEVIL MUSIC VOLUME 1 (*7) / ASTROCREEP 2000: SONGS OF LOVE AND DESTRUCTION . . . (*6) / SUPER SEXY SWINGIN' SOUNDS dance remixes (*7) / Rob Zombie: HELLBILLY DELUXE (*6) / SINISTER URGE (*7) / PAST, PRESENT & FUTURE compilation (*7)

ROB ZOMBIE (b. ROBERT CUMMINGS, 12 Jan'66, Haverhill, Mass.) – vocals, guitar / **ENA KOSTABI** – guitar / **SEAN YSEULT** – bass / **PETER LANDAU** – drums

not iss. — Silent Explosion

Feb 86. (7"ep) *<none>* **GODS ON VOODOO MOON** [–]
– Gentlemen junkie / King of souls / Tales from the scarecrow man / Cat's eye resurrection / Black Friday / Dead or alive.

— **IVAN DePRUME** – drums; repl. PETER

— **TIM JEFFS** – guitar; repl. ENA

Dec 86. (7") *<none>* **SLAUGHTER THE GREY. / PIG HEAVEN** [–]

Feb 87. (m-lp) *<SILENT 001>* **PSYCHO-HEAD BLOWOUT** [–]
– Eighty eight / Fast jungle / Gun crazy / Kick / Memphis / Magdalen / True crime / God of thunder.

— **TOM GUAY** – guitar; repl. TIM

Jan 88. (lp) *<(SILENT 002)>* **SOUL CRUSHER**
– Ratmouth / Shack of hate / Drowning the collosus / Crow III / Die, zombie, die / Skin / Truck on fire / Future shock / Scum-kill / Diamond ass.

— **J** (b. JOHN RICCI) – guitar; repl. TOM

Caroline — Caroline

Feb 89. (lp/c/cd) *<CAR LP/C/CD 3)>* **MAKE THEM DIE SLOWLY**
– Demonspeed / Disaster blaster / Murderworld / Revenge / Acid flesh / Power hungry / Godslayer.

Mar 89. (7") **GOD OF THUNDER. / LOVE RAZOR / DISASTER BLASTER** [–]

— **JAY YUENGER** (b.1967, Chicago, Illinois) – guitar; repl. RICCI

Jul 89. (12"ep) *(CLNT 1)* **GOD OF THUNDER. / LOVE RAZOR / DISASTER BLASTER 2**

Geffen — Geffen

Mar 92. (lp/c/cd) *<(GEF/+C/D 24460)>* **LA SEXORCISTO: DEVIL MUSIC VOL.1** [26]
– Welcome to Planet Motherfucker (psychoholic slag) / Knuckle duster (Radio 1-A) / Thunderkiss '65 / Black sunshine / Soul-crusher / Cosmic monsters inc. / Spiderbaby (yeah-yeah-yeah) / I am legend / Knuckle duster (Radio 2-B) / Thrust! / One big crunch / Grindhouse (a go-go) / Starface / Warp asylum.

— **JOHN TEMPESTA** – drums (ex-TESTAMENT, ex-EXODUS) repl. PHILO (PHIL BUERSTATTE), who had briefly repl. DePRUME

May 95. (c-s) *(GFSC 92)* **MORE HUMAN THAN HUMAN / BLOOD, MILK AND SKY (KERO KERO KEROPFI AND THE SMOOTH OPERATOR)** [51] [–]
(10"+=/cd-s+=) *(GFST/+D 92)* – ('A'-Jeddak of the Tharks super mix).

May 95. (cd/c/lp) *(GED/GEC/GEF 24806)>* **ASTROCREEP 2000: SONGS OF LOVE AND DESTRUCTION AND OTHER SYNTHETIC DELUSIONS OF THE ELECTRIC HEAD** [25] [6]
– Electric head part I (the agony) / Super charger Heaven / Real solution No.9 / Creature of the wheel / Electric head part II (the ecstasy) / Grease paint and monkey brains / I, zombie / More human than human / El Phantasmo and the chicken-run blast-o-rama / Blur the technicolor / Blood, milk and sky. *(c+=/cd+=)* – The sidewalk ends where the bug parade begins.

May 96. (12"ep) *(GFST 22140)* **ELECTRIC HEAD PART II (THE ECSTASY) / EL PHANTASMO AND THE CHICKEN-RUN BLAST-O-RAMA. / SUPER CHARGER HEAVEN / MORE HUMAN THAN HUMAN (The Warlord Of Mars mega mix)** [31] [–]
(cd-ep) *(GFSTD 22140)* – (first 2 tracks) / More human than human (Princess of Helium ultra) / Blood, milk & sky (Im-Ho-Tep 3,700 year old boogie mix).
(cd-ep) *(GFSXD 22140)* – (tracks except second) / Thunder kiss '65 (Swinging Lovers extended mix).

Oct 96. (cd/c) *<(GED/GEC 24976)>* **SUPERSEXY SWINGIN' SOUNDS** (dance remixes!) Aug96 [17]
– Phantasmo / Blood, milk & sky / Real solution / Electronic head pt.1 / I'm your boogie man / Electronic head pt.2 / More human than human / I, zombie / Grease paint & monkey brains / Blur the technicolour / Super charger Heaven.

— WHITE ZOMBIE looked to have split, J YUENGER went on to produce FU MANCHU while YSEULT moonlighted in the all-girl surf-rock act, FAMOUS MONSTERS

ROB ZOMBIE

— with **TEMPESTA** + **DANNY LOHNER** – guitar (ex-NINE INCH NAILS, ex-SKREW) / **BLASKO** – bass

Aug 98. (cd/c) *<(GED/GEC 25212)>* **HELLBILLY DELUXE** [37] [5]
– Call of the zombie / Superbeast / Dragula / Living dead girl / Perversion / Demonoid phenomenon / Spookshow baby / How to make a monster / Meet the creeper / The ballad of resurrection Joe and Rosa Whore / What lurks on Channel X? / Return of the phantom stranger / Beginning of the end.

Dec 98. (7"pic-d) *(GFS 22367) <1213>* **DRAGULA. / DRAGULA (Hot Rod Herman mix)** [44]
(cd-s+=) *(GFSTD 22367)* – ('A'-video).
(7"pic-d) *(GFX 22367)* – ('A'side) / Halloween (she's so mean).

Interscope — Interscope

Oct 99. (cd) *<(490349-2)>* **AMERICAN MADE MUSIC TO STRIP BY** (HELLBILLY DELUXE remixed) [38]

Nov 01. (cd) *<(493147-2)>* **SINISTER URGE** [8]
– Sinners Inc. / Demon speeding / Dead girl superstar / Never gonna stop / Iron head / (Go to) California / Feel so numb / Transylvania transmissions (pt.1) / Bring her down (to Crippletown) / Scum of the earth / House of 1000 corpses.

Sep 03. (cd) *<(104100)>* **PAST, PRESENT & FUTURE** (compilation) [11]
– Thunder kiss '65 (WHITE ZOMBIE) / Black sunshine (WHITE ZOMBIE & IGGY POP) / Feed the gods (WHITE ZOMBIE) / More human than human (WHITE ZOMBIE) / Super charger heaven (WHITE ZOMBIE) / I'm your boogieman (WHITE ZOMBIE) / Hands of death (burn baby burn) (with ALICE COOPER) / The great American nightmare (with HOWARD STERN) / Dragula / Living dead girl / Superbeast / Feel so numb / Never gonna stop (the red red kroovy) / Demon speeding / Brick house 2003 (with LIONEL RICHIE & TRINA) / Pussy liquor / Blitzkrieg bop. *(+dvd+=; 98612090)* – (bonus tracks).

WHO

Formed: Chiswick & Hammersmith, London, England ... 1964 as The HIGH NUMBERS, by ROGER DALTREY, PETE TOWNSHEND, JOHN ENTWISTLE and DOUG SANDOM. After making his impromptu mid-set debut at an early gig, manic sticksman, KEITH MOON, was immediately recruited in favour of the struggling SANDERS. At his first show proper, MOON reportedly mystified colleagues by roping his drums to some pillars before the show. All became clear when the drummer proceeded to knock seven shades of proverbial shit out of them during a solo, the kit actually bouncing off the floor! And thus was completed the line-up that would make their mark as one of the most pivotal, not to mention aggressive bands in rock history. Manager PETE MEADON introduced the band to the burgeoning "Mod" scene and shaped their image accordingly as a musical voice for the sharply dressed, scooter-riding young rebels, a movement that TOWNSHEND in particular felt a strong affinity with, and whose frustrations he'd document in his early, indignant blasts of raw rock'n'roll. A strutting, gloriously arrogant piece of R&B, the band's debut one-off 45 for 'Fontana', 'I'M THE FACE', was released the same month as the experienced managerial team of KIT LAMBERT and CHRIS STAMP took the reins from MEADON and began a concerted campaign for chart domination. Later that year, the band were re-christened The WHO and by this time had begun to perfect their powerful stageshow, TOWNSHEND developing his ferocious "windmilling" power-chord guitar style while the band courted controversy and delighted crowds by smashing their instruments in a cathartic rage. Rejected by major labels, they eventually secured a deal with 'Decca' US, through producer SHEL TALMY. Released in Britain via 'Decca's' UK subsidiary, 'Brunswick', 'I CAN'T EXPLAIN' (1965) introduced a more melodic sound and gave the band their first chart hit. The single climbed into the top 10 after TV appearances on 'Ready Steady Go' (which later adopted the track as its theme tune) and Top Of The Pops, 'ANYWAY, ANYHOW, ANYWHERE' following it later that summer. For most people however, The WHO really arrived with the seminal rebel anthem, 'MY GENERATION'. A stuttering, incredibly focused piece of amphetamine aggression, it galvanised legions of disaffected youths and only The SEX PISTOLS ever equalled it for sheer snide factor. It reached No.2 and was closely followed by the similarly titled debut album which included 'THE KIDS ARE ALRIGHT', probably TOWNSHEND's most explicit alignment with his "Mod" following. But if the kids were alright, The WHO's deal with SHEL TALMY certainly wasn't, or at least that's what the band thought, and after releasing their next single, 'SUBSTITUTE' (1966), on a new label, they became embroiled in a court battle over TALMY's right to produce the group. Despite TALMY winning a royalty on all the band's recordings for another five years, The WHO came out fighting, releasing a string of hits including 'I'M A BOY' (1966), 'HAPPY JACK' (1966) and the wistful ode to masturbation, 'PICTURES OF LILY' (1967). The title track from 'A QUICK ONE' (1966) was a patchy, prototype of the rock opera concept TOWNSHEND would later refine towards the end of the decade. Elsewhere on the album, tracks like ENTWISTLE's 'BORIS THE SPIDER' and TOWNSHEND's 'HAPPY JACK' possessed the same quirky Englishness that was the essence of The KINKS, and The WHO only really began to make some headway in America after their incendiary performance at The Monterey Pop Festival in the summer of '67. 'THE WHO SELL OUT' (1967), a mock concept album, contained the sublime 'I CAN SEE FOR MILES', a spiralling piece of neo-psychedelia that had a spiritual partner in the equally trippy 'ARMENIA CITY IN THE SKY'. With 'TOMMY' (1969), TOWNSHEND ushered in the dreaded concept of the 'Rock Opera'. Yet with his compelling story of a "deaf, dumb and blind kid" who finds release through pinball, he managed to carry the whole thing off. 'PINBALL WIZARD' and 'SEE ME, FEEL ME' were classic TOWNSHEND. The album was even made into a film by maverick director Ken Russell and later into a successful West End show. After this artful tour de force, the band released the legendary 'LIVE AT LEEDS' (1970) album while they worked on TOWNSHEND's latest idea, the 'LIFEHOUSE' project. An ambitious attempt at following up 'TOMMY', the venture was later aborted, although some of the material was used as the basis for the landmark 'WHO'S NEXT' album. Released in 1971, the record heralded a harder rocking sound with the anthemic 'WON'T GET FOOLED AGAIN' and 'BABA O'REILLY'. Immaculately produced, it still stands as The WHO's most confident and cohesive work and only No.1 album. TOWNSHEND finally created a follow-up to TOMMY with 'QUADROPHENIA' in 1973. A complex, lavishly embellished piece that saw him retrospectively examining the Mod sub-culture he'd so closely identified with. The project was later made into a film, inspiring a whole new wave of neo-Mod bands at the turn of the decade. 'THE WHO BY NUMBERS' (1975) was exactly that, a confused set that found the band treading water while trying to find direction in a music scene that was to become increasingly dominated by punk rock. While 'WHO ARE YOU' (1978) sounded more assured, the album's release was marred by the death of KEITH MOON, whose hard drinking and drugging ways finally proved his undoing. Speculation of a split was rife but ex-FACE, KENNY JONES, was drafted in and the band eventually came up with 'FACE DANCES' in 1981. Neither this album, nor 1982's 'IT'S HARD' were successful in rekindling The WHO spark of old and, already demoralised after a number of fans were crushed at a gig in Cincinatti, the band finally called it a day in 1983. The WHO have since occasionally reformed for one-off live appearances including 'Live Aid' and as DALTREY has mainly concentrated on his acting career, TOWNSHEND is the only ex-WHO member who's maintained a serious solo career. His most recent release was the critically acclaimed 'PSYCHODERELICT' (1993) album which was a rock opera of sorts updated for the 90's and included material from the shelved 'LIFEHOUSE' project. 1999's 'PETE TOWNSHEND LIVE: A BENEFIT FOR MARYVILLE ACADEMY' documented a 1998 charity concert at Chicago's House Of Blues with the WHO veteran giving it large on a selection of golden oldies and a few oddities including a cover of Canned Heat's 'ON THE ROAD AGAIN'. More interesting, at least for diehard WHO fans was 'THE OCEANIC CONCERTS' (2001), a document of obscure late 70's live material performed for TOWNSHEND's spiritual guru, Meher Baba. The album was co-credited to RAPHAEL RUDD (of RENAISSANCE fame) who accompanied PETE on meditative, stripped down covers of WHO classics performed for a select audience of Baba devotees. Meanwhile, The WHO (featuring ZAK STARKEY on drums) were still filling stadiums all around the world. 'LIVE AT THE ROYAL ALBERT HALL' (2003), a one-off charity concert renunion, featured a line-up of DALTREY, TOWNSHEND, ENTWISTLE amd JOHN 'RABBIT' BUNDRICK , belting out the cream of the band's back catalogue with surprising verve and vitality, and featuring guest spots from the likes of PAUL WELLER and EDDIE VEDDER. It was to be the last time ENTWISTLE would appear on record with the band, the bassist dying in a hotel room in Las Vegas on the 22nd of July 2002. On another rather sour note, TOWNSHEND was arrested in January 2003 on child pornography charges, his website computers confiscated while police looked at his claims – although he did use his credit card – that he was only looking at indecent images for novel research purposes. We await the outcome. • **DALTREY's filmography:** LISZTOMANIA (1975) / THE LEGACY (1979) / McVICAR (1980) / BUDDY (1991 TV serial + 1992 film). • **Songwriters:** TOWNSHEND wrote most of material except, I'M THE FACE (Slim Harpo's 'Got Live If You Want It') / I'M A MAN (Bo Diddley) / IN THE CITY (Speedy Keen; aka of Thunderclap Newman) / BARBARA ANN (Beach Boys) / BABY DON'T YOU DO IT (Marvin Gaye) / THE LAST TIME + UNDER MY THUMB (Rolling Stones) / SUMMERTIME BLUES (Eddie Cochran). KEITH MOON's only album was comprised wholly of cover versions. DALTREY's solo career started with songs written for him by LEO SAYER and DAVE COURTNEY. • **Trivia:** DALTREY continues to run a trout farm in Dorset. The WHO were inducted into the Guinness Book Of Records after performing the loudest concert (120 decibels) at Charlton Athletic's Football Club.

Album rating: MY GENERATION (*7) / A QUICK ONE (*6) / THE WHO SELL OUT (*7) / MAGIC BUS – THE WHO ON TOUR (*5) / TOMMY (*8) / THE WHO LIVE AT LEEDS (*8) / WHO'S NEXT (*10) / MEATY, BEATY, BIG AND BOUNCY compilation (*9) / QUADROPHENIA (*9) / ODDS AND SODS collection (*5) / THE WHO BY NUMBERS (*5) / THE STORY OF THE WHO compilation (*7) / WHO ARE YOU (*6) / THE KIDS ARE ALRIGHT docu-soundtrack (*6) / FACE DANCES (*5) / IT'S HARD (*4) / WHO'S BETTER WHO'S BEST compilation (*8) / MY GENERATION – THE VERY BEST OF THE WHO compilation (*9) / THE ULTIMATE COLLECTION compilation (*9) / LIVE AT THE ROYAL ALBERT HALL (*5) / Pete Townshend: WHO CAME FIRST (*6) / ROUGH MIX with Ronnie Lane (*6) / EMPTY GLASS (*7) / ALL THE BEST COWBOYS HAVE CHINESE EYES (*4) / SCOOP rarities (*4) / WHITE CITY – A NOVEL (*4) / PETE TOWNSHEND'S DEEP END LIVE! (*3) / THE IRON MAN a musical (*4) / ANOTHER SCOOP rarities (*3) / PSYCHODERELICT (*5) / THE BEST OF PETE TOWNSHEND – COOLWALKINGSMOOTH . . . compilation (*7) / Roger Daltrey: DALTREY (*5) / RIDE A ROCK HORSE (*6) / ONE OF THE BOYS (*5) / McVICAR soundtrack (*4) / THE BEST OF . . . compilation (*6) / PARTING SHOULD BE PAINLESS (*4) / UNDER A RAGING MOON (*5) / CAN'T WAIT TO SEE THE MOVIE (*3) / John Entwistle: THE OX (*4) / WHISTLE RHYMES (*4) / RIGOR MORTIS SETS IN (*5) / MAD DOG (*4) / TOO LATE THE HERO (*3) / Keith Moon: TWO SIDES OF THE MOON (*2)

ROGER DALTREY (b. 1 Mar'45) – vocals / **PETE TOWNSHEND** (b.19 May'45) – guitar, vocals / **JOHN ENTWISTLE** (b. 9 Oct'44) – bass, vocals / **KEITH MOON** (b.23 Aug'47) – drums, vocals repl. DOUG SANDOM

Fontana — not iss.

Jul 64. (7"; as The HIGH NUMBERS) *(TF 480)* **I'M THE FACE. / ZOOT SUIT** [ ] [–]
(re-iss. Feb65) (re-iss. Mar80 on 'Back Door', hit UK No.49) (US re-iss. Mar80 as The WHO on 'Mercury')

Brunswick — Decca

Jan 65. (7") *(05926)* *<31725>* **I CAN'T EXPLAIN. / BALD HEADED WOMAN** [8] Feb65 [93]
(US re-iss. 1973 on 'MCA')

May 65. (7") *(05935)* **ANYWAY ANYHOW ANYWHERE. / DADDY ROLLING STONE** [10] [–]

Jun 65. (7") *<31801>* **ANYWAY ANYHOW ANYWHERE. / ANYTIME YOU WANT ME** [–] [ ]

Oct 65. (7") *(05944)* **MY GENERATION. / SHOUT & SHIMMY** [2] [–]

Nov 65. (7") *<31877>* **MY GENERATION. / OUT IN THE STREET** [–] [74]

Dec 65. (lp) *(LAT 8616)* *<74664>* **MY GENERATION** [5] [ ]
– Out in the street / I don't mind / The good's gone / La-la-la-lies / Much too much / My generation / The kid's are alright / Please please please / It's not true / I'm a man / A legal matter / The ox. *(US title 'THE WHO SING MY GENERATION') (UK re-iss. Oct80 on 'Virgin' lp/c; V/TCV 2179)* – (hit UK No.20) *(cd-iss. 1990;) (deluxe d-lp edition iss.Sep02 +=; 133981-1)* – Circles / I can't explain / Bald headed woman / Daddy rolling stone / Leaving here / Lubie (come back home) / Shout and shimmy / Love is like a heat wave / Motoring / Anytime you want it / Anyhow anywhere anyway / Instant party mixture / I don't mind / Good's gone / My generation (instrumental) / Anytime you want me. *(deluxe d-cd edition ++=; 112926-2)* – A legal matter / My generation (mono). *(hit UK No.47)*

Reaction — Decca

Mar 66. (7") *(591 001)* *<6409>* **SUBSTITUTE. / WALTZ FOR A PIG ("The WHO ORCHESTRA")** [5] [ ]
—— (some copies 'INSTANT PARTY' or 'CIRCLES' on b-side)
<above on US 'Atco'; re-iss. Aug67; 6509>

Aug 66. (7") *(591 004)* *<32058>* **I'M A BOY. / IN THE CITY** [2] Dec66 [ ]

Dec 66. (7") *(591 010)* **HAPPY JACK. / I'VE BEEN AWAY** [3] [–]

Dec 66. (lp) *(593 002)* *<74892>* **A QUICK ONE** <US-title 'HAPPY JACK'> [4] May67 [67]
– Run run run / Boris the spider / Whiskey man / I need you / Heatwave / Cobwebs and strange / Don't look away / See my way / So sad about us / A quick one, while he's away. *(re-iss. Aug88 on 'Polydor' lp/c)(cd); (SPE LP/MC 114)(835 782-2) (cd re-iss. Jun95 & Apr97; 527758-2)*

Mar 67. (7") *<32114>* **HAPPY JACK. / WHISKEY MAN** [–] [24]

Track — Decca

Apr 67. (7") *(604 002)* *<32156>* **PICTURES OF LILY. / DOCTOR DOCTOR** [4] Jun67 [51]

Jul 67. (7") *(604 006)* **THE LAST TIME. / UNDER MY THUMB** [44] [–]

Oct 67. (7") *(604 011)* **I CAN SEE FOR MILES. / SOMEONE'S COMING** [10] [–]

Oct 67. (7") *<32206>* **I CAN SEE FOR MILES. / MARY ANN WITH THE SHAKY HANDS** [–] [9]

Jan 68. (lp; mono/stereo) *(612/613 002)* *<74950>* **THE WHO SELL OUT** [13] [48]
– Armenia, city in the sky / Heinz baked beans / Mary Anne with the shaky hands / Odorono / Tattoo / Our love was, is / I can see for miles / I can't reach you / Medac / Silas Stingy / Sunrise / Tattoo / Rael (1 and 2). *(re-iss. Aug88 on 'Polydor' lp/c)(cd; (SPE LP/MC 115) (cd re-iss. Jun95 & Apr97 on 'Polydor'; 527 759-2)*

Mar 68. (7") *<32288>* **CALL ME LIGHTNING. / DR. JEKYLL & MR. HIDE** [–] [40]

Jun 68. (7") *(604 023)* **DOGS. / CALL ME LIGHTNING** [25] [–]

Jul 68. (7") *<32362>* **MAGIC BUS. / SOMEONE'S COMING** [–] [25]

Oct 68. (7") *(604 024)* **MAGIC BUS. / DR. JEKYLL & MR. HIDE** [26] [–]

Oct 68. (lp) *<75064>* **MAGIC BUS – (THE WHO ON TOUR) (live)** [–] [39]
– Disguises / Run run run / Dr. Jekyll & Mr. Hyde / I can't reach you / Our love was, is / Call me Lightning / Magic bus / Someone's coming / Doctor doctor / Bucket T. / Pictures of ily.

Nov 68. (lp; mono/stereo) *(612/613 006)* **DIRECT HITS** (compilation) [ ] [–]
– Bucket T. / I'm a boy / Pictures of Lily / Doctor doctor / I can see for miles / Substitute / Happy Jack / The last time / In the city / Call me Lightning / Mary-Anne with the shaky hand / Dogs.

Mar 69. (7") *(604 027)* *<32465>* **PINBALL WIZARD. / DOGS (part 2)** [4] [19]
<US re-iss. 1973 on 'MCA'>

May 69. (d-lp) *(613 013-014)* *<7205>* **TOMMY** [2] [4]
– Overture / It's a boy / 1921 / Amazing journey / Sparks / Eyesight for the blind / Miracle cure / Sally Simpson / I'm free / Welcome / Tommy's holiday camp / We're not gonna take it / Christmas / Cousin Kevin / The acid queen / Underture / Do you think it's alright / Fiddle about / Pinball wizard / There's a doctor / Go to the mirror / Tommy can you hear me / Smash the mirror / Sensation. *(re-iss. Jul84 on 'Polydor'; 2486 161/2) (d-cd-iss. Apr89; 800 077-2)*

Jul 69. (7") *<32519>* **I'M FREE. / WE'RE NOT GONNA TAKE IT** [–] [37]

Mar 70. (7") *(604 036)* *<32670>* **THE SEEKER. / HERE FOR MORE** [19] [44]

May 70. (lp) *(2406 001)* *<79175>* **LIVE AT LEEDS (live)** [3] [4]
– Young man / Substitute / Summertime blues / Shakin' all over / My generation / Magic bus. *(re-iss. Nov83 on 'Polydor' lp/c; SPE LP/MC 50) (cd-iss. May88 on 'Polydor'; 825 339-2) (cd re-iss. Feb95 on 'Polydor', hit No.59 & Apr97; 527 169-2)*

Jul 70. (7") *(2094 002)* **SUMMERTIME BLUES (live). / HEAVEN AND HELL** [38] [–]

Jul 70. (7") *<32708>* **SUMMERTIME BLUES (live). / HERE FOR MORE** [–] [27]

Sep 70. (7") *<32729>* **SEE ME, FEEL ME. / WE'RE NOT GONNA TAKE IT / OVERTURE FROM TOMMY** [–] [12]
<US re-iss. 1973 on 'MCA'>

Sep 70. (7"w-drawn) *(2094 004)* **SEE ME, FEEL ME. / OVERTURE FROM TOMMY** [–] [–]

Jul 71. (7") *(2094 009)* *<32846>* **WON'T GET FOOLED AGAIN. / I DON'T EVEN KNOW MYSELF** 9 15

Sep 71. (lp) *(2408 102)* *<79182>* **WHO'S NEXT** 1 Aug71 4
– Baba O'Riley / Bargain / Love ain't for keeping / My wife / Song is over / Getting in tune / Going mobile / Behind blue eyes / Won't get fooled again. *(re-iss. Nov83 on 'Polydor' lp/c)(cd; SPE LP/MC 49)(813 651-2) (cd re-iss. Aug96; 527760-2)*

Oct 71. (7") *(2094 012)* **LET'S SEE ACTION. / WHEN I WAS A BOY** 16 –

Nov 71. (7") *<32888>* **BEHIND BLUE EYES. / MY WIFE** – 34

Dec 71. (lp/c) *(2406/3191 006)* *<79184>* **MEATY, BEATY, BIG AND BOUNCY** (compilation) 9 Nov71 11
– I can't explain / The kids are alright / Happy Jack / I can see for miles / Pictures of Lily / My generation / The seeker / Anyway, anyhow, anywhere / Pinball wizard / A legal matter / Boris the spider / Magic bus / Substitute / I'm a boy. *(re-iss. 1974)*

Jun 72. (7") *(2094 102)* *<32983>* **JOIN TOGETHER. / BABY DON'T YOU DO IT** 9 17

— In Oct72, PETE TOWNSHEND was another like ENTWISTLE to issue debut solo album 'WHO CAME FIRST'. It scraped into UK Top30. He issued more throughout 70's-80's (see . . .) In Apr'73, ROGER DALTREY hit the singles chart with GIVING IT ALL AWAY. It was a cut from debut album DALTREY.

Jan 73. (7") *(2094 106)* *<33041>* **RELAY. / WASPMAN** 21 Dec72 39

Track M.C.A.

Oct 73. (7") *(2094 115)* **5:15. / WATER** 20 –

Oct 73. (7") *<40152>* **5:15. / LOVE REIGN O'ER ME** –

Nov 73. (d-lp) *(2657 002)* *<10004>* **QUADROPHENIA** 2 2
– I am the sea / The real me / Quadrophenia / Cut my hair / The punk and the godfather / I'm one / Dirty jobs / Helpless dancer / Is it in my head? / I've had enough / 5:15 / Sea and sand / Drowned / Bell boy / Doctor Jimmy / The rock / Love, reign o'er me. *(re-iss. Sep79 on 'Polydor' d-lp)(d-c; 2657013)(3526001) (d-cd-iss. Jan87 on 'Polydor'; 831074-2)*

Nov 73. (7") *<40152>* **LOVE, REIGN O'ER ME. / WATER** – 76

Jan 74. (7") *<40182>* **THE REAL ME. / I'M ONE** – 92

— In Apr75, KEITH MOON was the last WHO member to release solo vinyl. The dismal 'TWO SIDES OF THE MOON' sold poorly.

Polydor M.C.A.

Oct 75. (lp/c) *(2490/3194 129)* *<2161>* **THE WHO BY NUMBERS** 7 8
– Slip kid / However much I booze / Squeeze box / Dreaming from the waist / Imagine a man / Success story / They are all in love / Blue, red and grey / How many friends / In a hand or a face. *(re-iss. Mar84 lp/c; SPE LP/MC 68) (cd-iss. Jul89; 831552-2)*

Jan 76. (7") *(2121 275)* *<40475>* **SQUEEZE BOX. / SUCCESS STORY** 10 Nov75 16

Aug 76. (7") *<40603>* **SLIP KID. / DREAMING FROM THE WAIST** –

Sep 76. (d-lp)(d-c) *(2683 069)(3519 020)* **THE STORY OF THE WHO** (compilation) 2 –
– Magic bus / Substitute / Boris the spider / Run run run / I'm a boy / Heatwave / My generation / Pictures of Lily / Happy Jack / The seeker / I can see for miles / Bargain / Squeeze box / Amazing journey / The acid queen / Do you think it's alright / Fiddle about / Pinball wizard / I'm free / Tommy's holiday camp / We're not gonna take it / See me, feel me / Summertime blues / Baba O'Riley / Behind blue eyes / Slip kid / Won't get fooled again.

Jul 78. (7") *(WHO 1)* *<40948>* **WHO ARE YOU?. / HAD ENOUGH** 18 14

— On 5th Aug'78, manager PETE MEADON committed suicide.

Sep 78. (lp/c)<US-red/pic-lp> *(WHOD/+C 5004)* *<3050>* **WHO ARE YOU** 6 2
– New song / Had enough / 905 / Sister disco / Music must change / Trick of the light / Guitar and pen / Love is coming down / Who are you. *(re-iss. Aug84 lp/c; SPE LP/MC 77) (cd-iss. Jul89; 831557-2)*

— After a party on 7th Sep'78, KEITH MOON died on an overdose of heminevrin.

Dec 78. (7") *<40978>* **TRICK OF THE LIGHT. / 905** –

— Early'79, **KENNY JONES** (b.16 Sep'48) – drums (ex-SMALL FACES, ex-FACES) took place of KEITH. Added 5th tour member **JOHN 'Rabbit' BUNDRICK** – keyboards

Polydor Warners

Feb 81. (7") *(WHO 4)* *<49698>* **YOU BETTER YOU BET. / THE QUIET ONE** 9 18

Mar 81. (lp/c) *(WHOD/+C 5037)* *<3516>* **FACE DANCES** 2 4
– You better you bet / Don't let go the coat / Cache cache / The quiet one / Did you steal my money / How can you do it alone / Daily records / You / Another tricky day. *(re-iss. May88 lp/c; SPE LP/MC 112) (re-iss. cd Jun93;) (cd re-iss. May97; 537695-2)*

May 81. (7") *(WHO 5)* *<49743>* **DON'T LET GO THE COAT. / YOU** 47 84

Sep 82. (lp/c) *(WHOD/+C 5066)* *<23731>* **IT'S HARD** 11 8
– Athena / It's your turn / Cooks county / It's hard / Dangerous / Eminence front / I've known no war / One life's enough / One at a time / Why did I fall for that / A man is a man / Cry if you want. *(cd-iss. 1983 & Jun93; 800 106-2) (cd re-iss. May97; 537696-2)*

Sep 82. (7"/7"pic-d) *(WHO/+P 6)* **ATHENA. / A MAN IS A MAN** 40 –
(12"+=/12"pic-d+=) *(WHO X/PX 6)* – Won't get fooled again.

Sep 82. (7") *<29905>* **ATHENA. / IT'S YOUR TURN** – 28

Dec 82. (7") *<29814>* **EMINENCE FRONT. / ONE AT A TIME** – 68

Feb 83. (7") *<29731>* **IT'S HARD. / DANGEROUS** –

— They officially split late 1983 from studio work. They occasionally returned for one-off live work.

– (selective) compilations, etc. –

below 4 on 'Brunswick' label.

Mar 66. (7") *(05956)* **A LEGAL MATTER. / INSTANT PARTY** 32 –

Aug 66. (7") *(05965)* **THE KIDS ARE ALRIGHT. / THE OX** 41 –

Aug 66. (7") *<31988>* **THE KIDS ARE ALRIGHT. / A LEGAL MATTER** –

Nov 66. (7") *(05968)* **LA LA LA LIES. / THE GOOD'S GONE** –

Nov 66. (7"ep) *Reaction; (592 001)* **READY STEADY WHO** –
– Circles / Disguises / Batman / Bucket 'T' / Barbara Ann. *(re-iss. Nov83 on 'Reaction-Polydor'; WHO 7); hit 58*

Oct 74. (lp/c) *Track; (2406/3191 116)* *<2126>* **ODDS AND SODS** (rarities) 10 15
– Postcard / Now I'm a farmer / Put the money down / Little Billy / Too much of anything / Glow girl / Pure and easy / Faith in something bigger / I'm the face / Naked eye / Long live rock. *(cd-iss. Jun93; 517946-2)*
below with guest singers ELTON JOHN, TINA TURNER, OLIVER REED, ANN-MARGRET, etc

Aug 75. (d-lp/d-c) *Polydor; (2657/5326 007)* *<9502>* **TOMMY (Film Soundtrack)** 30 Mar75 2
– Prologue / Captain Walker – It's a boy / Bernie's holiday camp / 1951 – What about the boy? / Amazing journey / Christmas / Eyesight to the blind / Acid queen / Do you think it's alright / Cousin Kevin / Do you think it's alright / Fiddle about / Do you think it's alright / Sparks / Extra, extra, extra / Pinball wizard / Champagne / There's a doctor / Go to the mirror / Tommy can you hear me / Smash the mirror / I'm free / Mother and son / Sensation / Miracle cure / Sally Simpson / Welcome / T.V. studio / Tommy's holiday camp / We're not gonna take it / Listening to you – See me, feel me.

— Note; below on 'Polydor' UK/ 'MCA' US, unless mentioned otherwise

Oct 76. (7"m) *(2058 803)* **SUBSTITUTE. / I'M A BOY / PICTURES OF LILY** 7 –

Apr 79. (7"m) *(WHO 2)* *<41053>* **LONG LIVE ROCK. / I'M THE FACE / MY WIFE** 48 54

Jun 79. (d-lp)(d-c)<US-pic-d-lp> *(2675 179)(3577 343)* *<11005>* **THE KIDS ARE ALRIGHT** 26 8
– (some live tracks with interviews) *(re-iss. cd Jun93)*

Sep 79. (7") *<2022>* **I'M ONE. / 5:15** b-side 45

Sep 79. (d-lp)(d-c) *(2625 037)(3577 352)* *<6235>* **QUADROPHENIA (Film Soundtrack)** 23 46
– (includes tracks by other artists)

Feb 81. (lp)(c) *(2486 140)(3195 235)* **MY GENERATION (compilation)** –

Oct 81. (lp/c) *<MCA/+C 212001>* **HOOLIGANS** – 52
(UK-iss.Dec88; same)

May 83. (lp) *<5408>* **WHO'S GREATEST HITS** – 94

Nov 84. (d-lp/d-c) *(WHO/+C 1)* *<8018>* **WHO'S LAST** 48 81
(cd-iss. Dec88; DWHO 1)

Oct 85. (d-lp/d-c) *Impression; (IMDP/IMDK 1)* **THE WHO COLLECTION** 44 –
(d-cd-iss. Oct88; IMCD 41)

Feb 88. (7") *(POSP 907)* **MY GENERATION. / SUBSTITUTE** 68
(12"+=/c-s+=/cd-s+=) *(POSPX/POSPC/POCD 907)* – Baba O'Riley / Behind blue eyes.

Mar 88. (lp/c)(cd) *(WTV/+C 1)(835 389-2)* *<MCAD 8031>* **WHO'S BETTER WHO'S BEST** 10 Nov88
– My generation / Anyway, anyhow, anywhere / The kids are alright /

Substitute / I'm a boy / Happy Jack / Pictures of Lily / I can see for miles / Who are you / Won't get fooled again / Magic bus / Pinball wizard / I'm free / I can't explain / See me feel me / Squeeze box / Join together / You better you bet. *(cd+=)* – Baba O'Riley.

Mar 90. (cd/d-c/d-lp) *Virgin; (CD/TC+/VDT 102) / M.C.A.; <19501>* **JOIN TOGETHER** [59] [ ]
– (contains some solo material)

Jul 94. (4xcd-box) *(521751-2) <11020>* **THIRTY YEARS OF MAXIMUM R&B** [48] [ ]

Jul 96. (7"/c-s) *(863918-7/-4)* **MY GENERATION. / PINBALL WIZARD (live)** [31] [–]
(cd-s+=) *(854637-2)* – Boris the spider.

Aug 96. (cd/c) *(533150-2/-4) <11462>* **MY GENERATION – THE VERY BEST OF** [11] [ ]
– I can't explain / Anyway, anyhow, anywhere / My generation / Substitute / I'm a boy / Boris the spider / Hapy Jack / Pictures of Lily / I can see for miles / Magic bus / Pinball wizard / The seeker / Baba O'Riley / Won't get fooled again / Let's see action / 5.15 / Join together / Squeeze box / Who are you / You better you bet.

Feb 00. (cd/c/d-lp) *(547727-2/-4/-1) <111960>* **BBC SESSIONS** (1965-73) [24] [ ]
– My generation / Anyway, anyhow, anywhere / Good lovin' / Just you and me, darling / Leaving here / My generation / The good's gone / La-la lies / Substitute / Dancing in the street / Disguises / I'm a boy / Run run run / Boris the spider / Happy Jack / See my way / Pictures of Lily / A quick one, while he's away / Substitute / The seeker / I'm free / Shakin' all over / The relay / Long live rock / Boris the spider (Radio 1 jingle).

Oct 02. (d-cd) *Universal TV; (065234-2) <112877>* **THE ULTIMATE COLLECTION** [17] Jun02 [31]
– I can't explain / Anyway, anyhow, anywhere / My generation / The kids are alright / A legal matter / Substitute / I'm a boy / Boris the spider / Happy Jack / Pictures of Lily / I can see for miles / Call me lightning / Magic bus / Pinball wizard / I'm free / See me feel me / The seeker / Summertime blues (live) / My wife / Baba O'Riley / Bargain / Behind blue eyes / Won't get fooled again / Let's see action / Pure and easy / Join together / Long live rock / The real me / 5.15 / Love reign o'er me / Squeeze box / Who are you / Had enough / Sister disco / You better you bet / Don't let go the coat / The quiet one / Another tricky day / Athena / Eminence front. *(t-cd+=; 0655300-2)* – Substitute (rare US single version) / I'm a boy (early version) / Happy Jack (acoustic) / Magic bus (UK single) / Baba O'Riley (CD-Rom) / Substitute (CD-Rom).

Jun 03. (3xcd-box) *S.P.V.; (<093 7488-2>)* **LIVE AT THE ROYAL ALBERT HALL (live in November 2000)** [72] Jul03 [ ]
– I can't explain / Anyway anyhow anywhere / Pinball wizard / Relay / My wife / The kids are alright / Mary Anne with the shaky hand / Bargain / Magic bus / Who are you / Baba O'Riley / Drowned / A heart to hang onto / So sad about us / I'm one / Getting in tune / Behind blue eyes / You better you bet / The real me / 5.15 / Won't get fooled again / Substitute / Let's see action / My generation / See me feel me / Listening to you / I'm free / I don't even know myself / Summertime blues / Young man blues.

PETE TOWNSHEND

(solo). Before his 1972 official debut, TOWNSHEND issued 2 lp's on 'Universal'; HAPPY BIRTHDAY (1970) & I AM (1972).

Track / Track

Oct 72. (lp) *(2408 201) <79189>* **WHO CAME FIRST** [30] [69]
– Pure and easy / Evolution / Forever's no time at all / Let's see action / Time is passing / There's a heartache followin' me / Sheraton Gibson / Content / Parvardigar. *(cd-iss. Oct92 & Mar97 on 'Rykodisc'; RCD 20246)*

— next collaboration with Solo artist and ex-SMALL FACES bassman and singer.

PETE TOWNSHEND & RONNIE LANE

Polydor / M.C.A.

Sep 77. (7") *<40818>* **MY BABY GIVES IT AWAY. / APRIL FOOL** [–] [ ]

Sep 77. (lp) *(2442 147) <2295>* **ROUGH MIX** [44] [45]
– My baby gives it away / Nowhere to run / Rough mix / Annie / Keep me turning / Catmelody / Misunderstood / April fool / Street in the city / Heart to hang on to / Till the rivers all run dry. *(re-iss. Nov80 & Nov83)*

Nov 77. (7") *(2058 944)* **STREET IN THE CITY. / Ronnie Lane: ANNIE** [ ] [–]

Nov 77. (7") *<40878>* **NOWHERE TO RUN . / KEEP ME TURNING** [–] [ ]

PETE TOWNSHEND

Island / not iss.

Dec 79. (12"ep) *(12WIP 6598)* **THE SECRET POLICEMAN'S BALL** (the songs) [ ] [–]
– Drowned / Pinbal wizard / Won't get fooled again.

Atco / Atco

Mar 80. (7") *(K 11460) <7318>* **ROUGH BOYS. / AND I MOVED** [39] Nov80 [89]

Apr 80. (lp/c) *(K/K4 50699) <32100>* **EMPTY GLASS** [11] [5]
– Rough boys / I am an animal / And I moved / Let my love open your door / Jools and Jim / Keep on working / Cat's in the cupboard / A little is enough / Empty glass / Gonna get ya. *(cd-iss. 1984; K 250 699) (cd re-iss. Nov93 & Oct95; 7567 9038-2-2)*

Jun 80. (7") *<7217>* **LET MY LOVE OPEN THE DOOR. / AND I LOVED** [–] [9]

Jun 80. (7"m) *(K 11486)* **LET MY LOVE OPEN THE DOOR. / CLASSIFIED / GREYHOUND GIRL** [46] [–]

Sep 80. (7") *<7312>* **A LITTLE IS ENOUGH. / CAT'S IN THE CUPBOARD** [–] [72]

Oct 80. (7") *(K 11609)* **KEEP ON WORKING. / JOOLS AND JIM** [ ] [–]

May 82. (7") *(K 11734) <99989>* **FACE DANCES (pt.2). / MAN WATCHING** [ ] [ ]

Jun 82. (lp/c) *(K/K4 50889) <38149>* **ALL THE BEST COWBOYS HAVE CHINESE EYES** [32] [26]
– The sea refuses no river / Communication / Exquisitely bored / North country girl / Slit skirts / Uniforms / Prelude / Somebody saved me / Face dances 2 / Stardom in action / Stop hurting people. *(cd-iss. 1984; K 250 699) (cd re-iss. Nov93 & Oct95 & Jul00; 7567 82812-2)*

Aug 82. (7",7"pic-d) *(K 11751)* **UNIFORMS (CORPS D'ESPRIT). / DANCE IT ALL AWAY** [48] [–]
(12",12"pic-d) *(K 11751T)* – ('A'side) / Stop hurting people.

Aug 82. (7") *<99973>* **UNIFORMS (CORPS D'ESPRIT). / SLIT SKIRTS** [–] [ ]

Apr 83. (7") *<99884>* **BARGAIN. / DIRTY WATER** [–] [ ]

Oct 85. (7"/12") *(U/UT 8859)* **FACE THE FACE. / HIDING OUT** [ ] [26]

Nov 85. (lp/c/cd) *(252392-1/-4/-2) <90473>* **WHITE CITY – A NOVEL** [70] [26]
– Give blood / Brilliant blues / Face the face / Hiding out / Secondhand love / Crashing by design / I am secure / White City fighting Come to mama. *(re-iss. cd Nov93; same)*

Jan 86. (7") *<99553>* **SECOND HAND LOVE. / WHITE CITY FIGHTING** [–] [ ]

Apr 86. (7") *(U 8744)* **GIVE BLOOD. / MAGIC BUS (live)** [ ] [–]
(12"+=) *(UT 8744)* – Won't get fooled again.

May 86. (7") *<99499>* **BEHIND BLUE EYES. / BAREFOOTIN'** [–] [ ]

Oct 86. (lp,c,cd) *<90553>* **PETE TOWNSEND'S DEEP END LIVE! (live)** [–] [98]
– Barefootin' / After the fire / Behind blue eyes / Stop hurtin' people / I'm one / I put a spell on you / Save it for later / Pinball wizard / Little is enough / Eyesight to the blind.

— Next featured singers JOHN LEE HOOKER (Iron Man) / NINA SIMONE (The Dragon) / DALTREY + JOHN ENTWISTLE who play on 2 new WHO tracks.

Virgin / Atlantic

Jun 89. (lp/c/cd) *(CD/TC+/V 2592) <81996>* **THE IRON MAN (The Musical)** [ ] [58]
– I won't run anymore / Over the top / Man machines / Dig / A friend is a friend / I eat heavy metal / All shall be well / Was there life / Fast food / A fool says . . . / Fire / New life (reprise). *(re-iss. Mar91 lp/c; OVED/+C 355)*

Jul 89. (7"/c-s) *(VS/+C 1198)* **A FRIEND IS A FRIEND. / MAN MACHINES** [ ] [ ]
(12"+=/12"g-f+=/3"cd-s+=) *(VS T/TG/CD 1198)* – Real world.

Nov 89. (7"/12"/12"g-f) *(VS/+T/TG 1209)* **I WON'T RUN ANYMORE. / A FOOL SAYS . . .** [ ] [ ]

Atlantic / Atlantic

Jul 93. (cd/c) *<(7567 82494-2/-4)>* **PSYCHODERELICT** [ ] [ ]
– English boy / Meher Baba M3 / Let's get pretentious / Meher Baba M4 (signal box) / Early morning dreams / I want that thing / Introduction to outlive the dinosaur / Outlive the dinosaur / Flame (demo) / Now and then / I am afraid / Don't try to make me real / Introduction to predictable / Predictable / Flame / Meher Baba M5 (Vivaldi) / Fake it / Introduction to now and then (reprise) / Now and then (reprise) / Baba O'Riley (demo) / English boy (reprise). *(cd re-iss. Jan97; same)*

Jul 93. (7"/c-s) *(A 7370/+C)* **ENGLISH BOY. / ('A'-dialogue mix)** [ ] [–]
(cd-s+=) *(A 7370CD1)* – Fake it / Psycho montage.
(cd-s+=) *(A 7370CD2)* – ('A'dialogue version) / Fake it / Flame / Early morning dreams.

May 96. (cd/c) *(<7567-82712-2/-4>)* **THE BEST OF PETE TOWNSHEND – COOLWALKINGSMOOTHSTRAIGHTSMOKINGFIRESTOKING** (compilation) [ ] [ ]
– Rough boys / Let my love open the door / Mis understood / Give blood / A friend is a friend / Sheraton Gibson / English boy / Street in the city / Pure and easy / Slit skirts / The sea refuses no river / A little is enough / Face the face / Uneasy street / Let my love open the door (E. Cola mix).

Jun 96. (c-s) *(A 5511C)* **LET MY LOVE OPEN THE DOOR / ROUGH BOYS** [ ] [–]
(cd-s+=) *(A 5511CD)* – ('A'-E. Cola mix; long version).

Platinum Platinum

Jun 00. (cd) *(<15095 9555-2>)* **LIVE: A BENEFIT FOR MARYVILLE ACADEMY – HOUSE OF THE BLUES CHICAGO** [ ] Sep99 [ ]
– On the road again / Anyway, anyhow, anywhere / A little is enough / Drowned / Now and then / North country girl / Let my love open the door / Won't get foled again / Magic bus / I'm one / Magic bus / Heart to hang onto.

Rhino Rhino

Oct 01. (cd; by PETE TOWNSHEND & RAPHAEL RUDD) *(<8122 74289-2>)* **OCEANIC CONCERTS (live)** [ ] [ ]
– Raga / Drowned / The seeker / Magic grace / Who is Meher Baba? / The ferryman / Kitty's theme / A little is enough / Contact in solitude / Sleeping dog / Sound barrier / Bargain / Longing for the beloved / Tattoo / Let my love open the door / Awakening / Western (American) Arti / O'Parvardigar.

– (other PETE TOWNSHEND compilations, etc.) –

Apr 83. (d-lp) *Atco; (B 0063) <90063>* **SCOOP** [ ] [35]
– (unfinished WHO demos and solo rarities)
Jul 89. (d-lp/d-c) *Polydor; (839350-1/-4)* **ANOTHER SCOOP** [ ] [ ]
Jun 00. (cd) *Redline; (70001)* **LIFEHOUSE ELEMENTS (SAMPLER)** [ ] [ ]
Dec 01. (cd) *Compact; <13>* **SCOOP3** [–] [ ]

ROGER DALTREY

Track Track

Apr 73. (7") *(2094 110) <40053>* **GIVING IT ALL AWAY. / THE WAY OF THE WORLD** [5] [83]
Apr 73. (lp) *(2406 207) <328>* **DALTREY** [ ] [45]
– One man band / The way of the world / You are yourself / Thinking / You and me / It's a hard life / Giving it all away / The story so far / When the music stops / Reasons. *(re-iss. Aug82 lp/c; 2485/3201 219) (cd-iss. Apr95 on 'Polydor') (cd re-iss. Mar00 on 'Repertoire'; REP 4636)*
Jun 73. (7") *(ODS 66302) <Ode; 66040>* **I'M FREE. / (OVERTURE)** [13] [ ]
Sep 73. (7") *(2094 014) <40084>* **THINKING. / THERE IS LOVE** [ ] [ ]
Nov 73. (7") *(2094 016)* **IT'S A HARD LIFE. / ONE MAN BAND** [ ] [ ]

Polydor M.C.A.

Mar 75. (7") *(2001 561)* **LISTENING TO YOU. / (OVERTURE)** [ ] [–]
May 75. (7") **COME AND GET YOUR LOVE. / THE WORLD OVER** [ ] [–]
Jul 75. (lp)(c) *(2442 135)(2660 111) <2147>* **RIDE A ROCK HORSE** [14] [28]
– Come and get your love / Hearts right / Oceans away / Proud / The world over / Near to surrender / Feeling / Walking the dog / Milk train / I was to sing your song. *(cd-iss. Mar00 on 'Repertoire'; REP 4642)*
Jul 75. (7") *(2058 628)* **WALKING THE DOG. / PROUD** [ ] [–]
Sep 75. (7") *<40453>* **COME AND GET YOUR LOVE. / FEELING** [–] [68]
Nov 75. (7") *<40512>* **OCEANS AWAY. / FEELING** [–] [ ]
Oct 75. (7") *<1779>* **ORPHEUS SONG. / LOVE'S DREAM** [ ] [ ]
—— (above from the Ken Russell film LISTZOMANIA. Released at the same time, it was scored by RICK WAKEMAN for 'A&M' *(AMLH 64546)* and featured some with DALTREY vocals).
Apr 77. (7") *(2121 319)* **WRITTEN ON THE WIND. / DEAR JOHN** [46] [–]
May 77. (7") *<40761>* **ONE OF THE BOYS. / DOING IT ALL AGAIN** [–] [ ]
May 77. (lp) *(2441 146) <2271>* **ONE OF THE BOYS** [45] [46]
– Parade / Single man's dilemma / Avenging Annie / The prisoner / Leon / One of the boys / Giddy / Written on the wind / Satin and lace / Doing it all again. *(cd-iss. Mar00 on 'Repertoire'; REP 4643)*
Jun 77. (7") *(2058 896)* **ONE OF THE BOYS. / TO PUT SOMETHING BETTER INSIDE ME** [ ] [–]
Jul 77. (7") *<40765>* **SAY IT ISN'T SO, JOE. / SATIN AND LACE** [–] [ ]
Sep 77. (7") *<40800>* **AVENGING ANNIE. / THE PRISONER** [–] [88]
Jan 78. (7") *<40862>* **THE PRISONER. / LEON** [–] [ ]
Feb 78. (7") *(2058 986)* **SAY IT AIN'T SO, JOE. / THE PRISONER** [ ] [–]

Polydor Polydor

Jul 80. (7") *(2001 980) <2105>* **FREE ME. / McVICAR** [39] Jun80 [53]
Jul 80. (lp/c) *(POLD/+C 5034) <6284>* **McVICAR (Soundtrack)** [39] [22]
– Bitter and twisted / Just a dream away / Escape (part 1) / White City lights / Free me / My time is gonna come / Waiting for a friend / Escape (part 2) / Without your love / McVicar. *(cd-iss. Apr95; 527341-2)*
Sep 80. (7") *<2121>* **WITHOUT YOUR LOVE. / ESCAPE (part 2)** [–] [20]
Oct 80. (7") *(POSP 181)* **WITHOUT YOUR LOVE. / SAY IT AIN'T SO, JOE. / FREE ME** [55] [–]
Jan 81. (7") *<2153>* **WAITING FOR A FRIEND. / BITTER AND TWISTED** [–] [ ]

Polydor M.C.A.

Mar 82. (lp/c) *(2490/3194 162) <5301>* **THE BEST OF ROGER DALTREY** <US-title 'BEST BITS'>(compilation) [ ] [ ]
– Martyrs and madmen / Say it isn't so, Joe / Oceans away / Treasury / Free me / Without your love / It's a hard life / Giving it all away / Avenging Annie / Proud / You put something better inside me. *(UK cd-iss. May91)*
Apr 82. (7") *<52051>* **MARTYRS AND MADMEN. / AVENGING ANNIE** [–] [ ]

WEA Atlantic

Feb 84. (7") *(U 9686) <89704>* **WALKING IN MY SLEEP. / SOMEBODY TOLD ME** [56] [62]
(12"+=) *(U 9686T)* – Gimme some lovin'.
Feb 84. (lp) *(2502 981) <80128>* **PARTING SHOULD BE PAINLESS** [ ] [ ]
– Walking in my sleep / Parting would be painless / Is there anybody out there / Would a stranger do / Going strong / Looking for you / Somebody told me / How does the cold wind cry / Don't wait on the stairs.
Jun 84. (7") *(U 9541) <89667>* **PARTING SHOULD BE SO PAINLESS. / IS THERE ANYBODY OUT THERE** [ ] [ ]
(12"+=) *(U 9541T)* – I won't be the one to say goodbye.

Ten-Virgin Atlantic

Sep 85. (7") *(TEN 69) <89491>* **AFTER THE FIRE. / IT DON'T SATISFY ME** [50] [48]
(12"+=) *(TEN 69-12)* – Love me like you do.
Oct 85. (lp/c/cd) *(DIX/CDIX/DIXCD 17) <81269>* **UNDER A RAGING MOON** [52] [42]
– After the fire / Don't talk to strangers / Breaking down Paradise / The pride you hide / Move better in the night / Let me down easy / Fallen angel / It don't satisfy me / Rebel / Under a raging moon. *(cd+=)* – Behind blue eyes / 5:15 / Won't get fooled again. *(re-iss. 1989 lp/c; XID/CXID 22)*
Dec 85. (7") *<89471>* **LET ME DOWN EASY. / FALLEN ANGEL** [–] [86]
Feb 86. (7"/12") *(TEN 81/+12)* **UNDER A RAGING MOON. / MOVE BETTER IN THE NIGHT** [43] [–]
(d7"+=) *(TEND 81)* – Behind blue eyes / 5:15 / Won't get fooled again.
Apr 86. (7") *<89457>* **QUICKSILVER LIGHTNING. / LOVE ME LIKE YOU DO** [–] [ ]
May 86. (7") *(TEN 103)* **THE PRIDE YOU HIDE. / BREAK OUT** [ ] [–]
(d7"+=/12"+=) *(TEN D/T 103)* – Don't talk to strangers (live) / Pictures of Lily (live).
Jun 86. (7") *<89419>* **UNDER A RAGING MOON. / THE PRIDE YOU HIDE** [–] [ ]
Jun 87. (7") *(TEN 147)* **HEARTS OF FIRE. / LOVERS STORM** [ ] [ ]
(12"+=) *(TENT 147)* – Quick silver lightning.
Jul 87. (lp/c/cd) *(DIX/CDIX/DIXCD 54) <81759>* **CAN'T WAIT TO SEE THE MOVIE** [ ] [ ]
– Hearts of fire / When the thunder comes / Ready for love / Balance on wires / Miracle of love / The price of love / The heart has its reasons / Alone in the night / Lover's storm / Take me home.

Jul 87. (7") *(TEN 202)* **DON'T LET THE SUN GO DOWN ON ME. / THE HEART HAS ITS REASONS**
(12"+=) *(TENT 202)* – ('A'extended).

— next featured **GERARD McMAHON**

not iss. Rhino

Jul 92. (cd) *<72846>* **ROCKS IN THE HEAD** –
– Who's gonna walk on water / Before my time is up / Times changed / You can't call it love / Mirror mirror / Perfe t world / Love is / Blues man's road / Everything a heart could ever want / Days of light / Unforgettable opera.

not iss. Continuum

1994. (cd) *<19402>* **A CELEBRATION: THE MUSIC OF PETE TOWNSHED & THE WHO** –

– compilations, etc. –

Jul 97. (cd) *Rhino;* **MARTYRS & MADMEN: THE BEST OF ROGER DALTREY** –
Mar 00. (cd) *Repertoire; (REP 4670)* **ANTHOLOGY**

JOHN ENTWISTLE

Track Decca

Nov 70. (lp; The WHO) *(2407 014)* **THE OX: BACKTRACK 14** (ENTWISTLE songs by The WHO) –
– Heinz baked beans / Heaven & Hell / Dr. Jekyll & Mr. Hyde / Fiddle about / Cousin Kevin / Doctor, doctor / Medac / Boris the spider / I've been away / Whiskey man / In the city / Someone's coming / Silas Stingy.
May 71. (lp) *(2406 005) <2024>* **SMASH YOUR HEAD AGAINST THE WALL**
– My size / Pick me up (big chicken) / What kind of people are they? / Heaven and Hell / Ted end / You're mine / No.29 (external youth) / I believe in everything. *(cd-iss. Sep97 on 'Sundazed'; SC 6116) (cd re-iss. Mar97 & May00 on 'Repertoire'; REP 4613)*
May 71. (7") *(2094 008)* **I BELIEVE IN EVERYTHING. / MY SIZE**

— ENTWHISTLE with RIGOR MORTIS:- **BRYAN WILLIAMS** – keyboards / **ALAN ROSS** – guitar / **HOWIE CASEY** – sax / **GRAHAM DEACON** – drums / **TONY ASHTON** – percussion

Track Track

Nov 72. (lp) *(2406 104) <79190>* **WHISTLE RHYMES**
– Ten little friends / Mr. Bones & Mrs. Apron strings / And I feel better / Thinking it over / Who cares / I wonder now / I was just being friendly / The window shopper / I found out / Nightmare. *(cd-iss. Sep97 on 'Sundazed'; SC 6117) (cd re-iss. May00 on 'Repertoire'; REP 4618)*
Nov 72. (7") *<33052>* **WHO CARES. / I WONDER NOW** –

Track M.C.A.

Jun 73. (lp) *(2406 106) <321>* **RIGOR MORTIS SETS IN**
– Give me that rock and roll / Mr. Bass man / Do the dangle / Hound dog / Made in Japan / My wife / Roller skate Kate / Peg leg Peggy / Lucille / Big black Cadillac. *(cd-iss. May97 & Mar00 on 'Repertoire'; REP 4621)*
Jun 73. (7") *(2094 107)* **MADE IN JAPAN. / HOUND DOG** –
Jun 73. (7") *<40066>* **MADE IN JAPAN. / ROLLER SKATE KATE** –

— with **DEACON, ASHTON & CASEY** plus **JIM RYAN** – guitar / **MIKE WEDGWOD** – guitar / **EDDIE JOBSON** – keyboards (guest)
Feb 75. (7"; as JOHN ENTWISTLE'S OX) *(FR 13567)* **MAD DOG. / CELL NO.7**
Mar 75. (lp; as JOHN ENTWISTLE'S OX) *(2129)* **MAD DOG**
– I fall to pieces / Cell number seven / You can be so mean / Lady killer / Who in the hell? / Mad dog / Jungle bunny / I'm so scared / Drowning. *(cd-iss. Mar97 & May00 on 'Repertoire'; REP 4629)*

— (solo, with session stars incl. **JOE WALSH** – guitar

WEA Atco

Sep 81. (7",7"pic-d) *(K 79249)* **TOO LATE THE HERO. / COMIN' BACK**
Nov 81. (lp/c) *(K/K4 99179) <38142>* **TOO LATE THE HERO** 71
– Try me / Talk dirty / Lovebird / Sleepin man / I'm coming back / Dancing master / Fallen angel / Love is a heart attack / Too late the hero. *(cd-iss. Mar97 & Apr00 on 'Repertoire'; RR 4634)*
Dec 81. (7") **TALK DIRTY. /** –

— next with HENRY SMALL, ZAK STARKEY, TIM GORMAN, DEVIN POWERS, etc

not iss. Griffin

Aug 96. (cd) *<615>* **THE ROCK** –
– Stranger in a strange land / Love doesn't last / Suzie / Bridges under the water / Heartache / Billy / Life after love / Hurricane / Too much too soon / Last song / Country hurricane. *(UK-iss.Jul98 on 'Repertoire'; REP 4696)*

J-Bird J-Bird

Jul 99. (cd; as The JOHN ENTWISTLE BAND) *(<JBD 80286>)* **LEFT FOR LIVE (live)**
– Horror rock / The real me / Darker side of night / Success story / 5.905 / I'll try again today / Under a raging moon / Endless vacation / Too late the hero / Had enough / Shakin' all over / Young man blues. *(re-iss. Jan01 on 'Bianca'; BIA 300-2)*

not iss. Pulsar

2000. (cd) *<30012>* **MUSIC FROM VAN-PIRES** (soundtrack) –
– Horror rock / Darker side of night / Sometimes / Bogeyman / Good and evil / When you see the light / Back on the road / Left for dead / When the sun comes up / Rebel without a car / Don't be a sucker / Endless vacation / I'll try again today / Face the fear.

– compilations, etc. –

Oct 96. (cd) *Rhino; <72570>* **THUNDERFINGERS: THE BEST OF JOHN ENTWISTLE** –
May 98. (cd) *King Biscuit; (<KBFHCD 006>)* **KING BISCUIT PRESENTS . . .** Jun97
Apr 00. (cd) *Repertoire; (REP 4600) / Alex; <5737>* **ANTHOLOGY** Aug96

KEITH MOON

Polydor M.C.A.

Apr 75. (lp) *(2442 134) <2136>* **TWO SIDES OF THE MOON**
– Crazy like a fox / Solid gold / Don't worry baby / One night stand / The kid's are alright / Move over Ms. L / Teenage idol / Back door Sally / In my life / Together. *(cd-iss. Apr00 on 'Repertoire'+=; REP 4635)* – US radio spot / I don't suppose / Naked man / Do me good / Real emotion / Teenage idol / Together rap.
May 75. (7") *(2058 584)* **DON'T WORRY BABY. / TOGETHER** –
May 75. (7") *<40316>* **DON'T WORRY BABY. / TEENAGE IDOL** –
Jul 75. (7") *<40387>* **MOVE OVER MS. L. / SOLID GOLD** –
Sep 75. (7") *<40433>* **CRAZY LIKE A FOX. / IN MY LIFE** –

WILCO

Formed: Belleville, Illinois, USA . . . 1994 out of UNCLE TUPELO members JEFF TWEEDY, JAY BENNETT, JOHN STIRRATT and veterans MAX JOHNSTON and KEN COOMER. WILCO were off the starting block with 1994's 'A.M.', an enjoyable enough set of uptempo country-rock. It was nevertheless eclipsed by the 1996 follow-up, 'BEING THERE', a sprawling double set drawing comparisons with The 'STONES 'Exile On Main Street' and hailed as one of the albums of the year. Reaching far beyond TWEEDY's patented musical boundaries to encompass everything from bar-room belters to Spector-esque rock/pop, the record proved conclusively that FARRAR's other half was blessed with his own distinct musical vision. While former writing partner JAY FARRAR continued to come up with the goods, the prospect of an UNCLE TUPELO reunion was (at the time) still tantalisingly within reach. However, WILCO returned in the summer of '98, an unlikely collaboration with English bard BILLY BRAGG on a memorable WOODY GUTHRIE tribute album, 'MERMAID AVENUE', kept the duo ticking over fine style. The following March, the leaders of the alt-country/folk scene released their long-awaited third set, 'SUMMERTEETH' (1999), a UK Top 40 record (Top 100 in the US) that boasted some breezy old tales opening with minor

UK hit, 'CAN'T STAND IT'. A second volume of GUTHRIE re-writes, 'MERMAID AVENUE VOL.2' (2000) couldn't come up with anything quite as affecting as say, 'CALIFORNIA STARS' but it had its moments. WILCO's penchant for uptempo roots-rock wasn't always the best vehicle for presenting the legendary socialist's humourous protest-folk, BRAGG often stealing the limelight. TWEEDY moved even further from both his old sparring partner and his musical roots with 'YANKEE HOTEL FOXTROT' (2002), a record the band believed in so much they spent a hefty sum buying it back from 'Reprise'. While JIM O'ROURKE's off-kilter production opened up angles seemingly irreconcilable with their limited roots-rock sound of yore, the results were never less than intriguing and often brilliantly conceived. Released around the same time was the soundtrack to Ethan Hawke's 'CHELSEA WALLS' (2002), composed in large part by TWEEDY and new WILCO drummer GLENN KOTSCHE. While the bulk of the music consisted of pared-down, instrumental mood pieces well out of WILCO's normal orbit, there were a couple of previously unreleased offcuts: one from 'MERMAID AVENUE' ('WHEN THE ROSES BLOOM AGAIN') and one from the WILCO vaults ('PROMISING'). Add those to a cover of John Lennon's 'Jealous Guy' by Jimmy Scott, and you had a mixed bag to say the least. Seemingly in thrall to his newly expanded musical horizons, TWEEDY went on to cut an album's worth of off-kilter experiments with O'ROURKE and KOTSCHE. An eponymous set released under the LOOSE FUR banner in early 2003, the record spliced the various musical personalities in intriguing and often frustrating fashion. • **Other info:** TWEEDY was also an integral part of y'allternative supergroup, GOLDEN SMOG, alongside members of the JAYHAWKS, SOUL ASYLUM, RUN WESTY RUN and BIG STAR.

Album rating: A.M. (*8) / BEING THERE (*8) / SUMMERTEETH (*8) / YANKEE HOTEL FOXTROT (*6) / Jeff Tweedy: CHELSEA WALLS soundtrack (*4) / Loose Fur: LOOSE FUR (*6)

JEFF TWEEDY – vocals, guitar (ex-UNCLE TUPELO) / **JOHN STIRRATT** – ORGAN, guitars, bass, vocals (ex-UNCLE TUPELO) / **KEN COOMER** – drums (ex-UNCLE TUPELO) / with others

Warners Reprise

Apr 95. (cd) *<(9362 45857-2)>* **A.M.**
– I must be high / Casino queen / Box full of letters / Shouldn't be ashamed / Pick up the change / I thought IU held you / That's not the issue / It's just that simple / Should've been in love / Passenger side / Dash 7 / Blue eyed soul / Too far apart.

Jul 95. (c-s) *(W 0306MC)* **BOX FULL OF LETTERS / I AM NOT WILLING** [–]
(cd-s+=) *(W 0306)* – Who were you thinking of (live).

—— added **JAY BENNETT** – guitar

Feb 97. (d-cd) *<(9362 46236-2)>* **BEING THERE** Nov96 [73]
– Misunderstood / Forget the flowers / I got you (at the end of the century) / Red eyed and blue / (Was I) In your dreams / Dreamer in my dreams / Lonely one / Why would you wanna live / Kingpin / Someone else's song / Outta mind (outta sight) / Someday soon / Sunken treasure / Say you miss me / Hotel Arizona / What's the world got in store / Far far away / Monday.

Apr 97. (cd-ep) *(W 0397CD)* **OUTTA SIGHT (OUTTA MIND) / OUTTA MIND (OUTTA SIGHT) / THIRTEEN / A LASTING FONDER** [–]

—— In the middle of '98, WILCO collaborated with BILLY BRAGG on a tribute album ('MERMAID AVENUE') to WOODY GUTHRIE

Mar 99. (cd/c/lp) *<(9362 47282-2/-4/-1)>* **SUMMERTEETH** [38] [78]
– Can't stand it / She's a jar / A shot in the arm / We're just friends / I'm always in love / Nothing'severgonnastandinmyway (again) / Pieholden suite / How to fight loneliness / Via Chicago / ELT / My darling / When you wake up feeling old / Summer teeth / In a future age.

Apr 99. (cd-s) *(W 475CD1)* **CAN'T STAND IT / STUDENT LOAN ZERO / TRIED AND TRUE** [67]
(cd-s) *(W 475CD2)* – ('A'side) / Sunken treasure (solo acoustic) / I'm always in love (solo acoustic).

Jun 99. (c-s/cd-s) *(W 496 C/CD2)* **A SHOT IN THE ARM / VIA CHICAGO (demo) / SHE'S A JAR**
(cd-s) *(W 496CD1)* – ('A'side) / ELT (demo) / True love will find you in the end.

—— a 2nd 'MERMAID AVENUE' (VOL.2) was issued with BILLY BRAGG in mid'00

—— **GLENN KOTCHE** – drums; repl. COOMER

—— **LEROY BACH** – guitar; repl. BENNETT

Nonesuch Nonesuch

Apr 02. (cd) *<(7559 79669-2)>* **YANKEE HOTEL FOXTROT** [40] [13]
– I am trying to break your heart / Kamera / Radio cure / War on war / Jesus, etc. / Ashes of American flags / Heavy metal drummer / I'm the man who loves you / Pot kettle black / Poor places / Reservations. *(d-lp-iss.Nov02 on 'Sundazed'; SCLP 5161)>*

May 02. (cd-s) *(NONE 001CD)* **WAR ON WAR / THE GOOD PART / I'M THE MAN WHO LOVES YOU (live)** [–]

JEFF TWEEDY

with **GLENN KOTCHE** – drums, percussion

Rykodisc Rykodisc

Apr 02. (cd) *<(RCD 10624)>* **CHELSEA WALLS** (soundtrack)
– Opening titles / Red elevator / Promising / Frank's dream / When the roses bloom again / Jealous guy / The wallman / The lonely 1 / Hello, are you there? / Softly and tenderly Jesus is calling / Finale / End credits.

LOOSE FUR

JEFF TWEEDY + GLENN KOTCHE + JIM O'ROURKE

Domino Drag City

Jan 03. (cd/lp) *(WIG CD/LP 119) <DC 203>* **LOOSE FUR**
– Laminated cat / Elegant transaction / So long / You were wrong / Liquidation totale / Chinese apple.

☐ WILDBUNCH (see under ⇒ ELECTRIC SIX)

WILDHEARTS

Formed: London, England . . . 1989 by Northern-born guitarist GINGER, guitarist CJ (CHRIS JADGHAR), vocalist SNAKE, bassist JULIAN and drummer STIDI (ANDREW STIDOLPH): all veterans of the late 80's hard-rock/glam-metal scene. STIDI and SNAKE subsequently dropped out the following year, GINGER taking over lead vocal duties, while a guy called PAT filled in on drums prior to BAM (of DOGS D'AMOUR fame) grabbing the sticks. By the summer of '91, a new line-up introduced 19 year-old DANNY McCORMICK to the proceedings and after difficulties with their initial record label, 'Atco', they signed to 'East West' (GINGER would later slate them at most opportunities!). The following year, The WILDHEARTS were finally on their hard-rockin' way with the much-touted, 'MONDO-AKIMBO-A-GO-GO', an EP that was premiered while supporting their mates, The MANIC STREET PREACHERS. Like a punk/metal fusion of The RUTS, The CULT or The MANICS, GINGER and Co. delivered a mini-set, 'DON'T BE HAPPY . . . JUST WORRY' (a play on words from a Bobby McFerrin hit!), featuring the gorefest, 'SPLATTERMANIA'. Slagging everyone from IZZY STRADLIN of GUNS N' ROSES (he chucked them off his tour after only one gig!) to their producer, Simon Efeny, the wild ones toasted the release of their first full-length effort, 'EARTH VS THE WILDHEARTS' (1993), a set that saw the return of STIDI. The record managed to scrape into the UK Top 50, aided by some loveable tracks such as 'GREETINGS FROM SHITSVILLE', 'TV TAN' and a near Top 30 hit, 'CAFFEINE BOMB'. Much of 1994 was spent in personnel turmoil; STIDI was substituted by RITCH BATTERSBY, while CJ was in and out of the band more times than even he could recall. McCORMACK too had his moments, the hardy bassman dislocating his knee during their first number at the Reading Festival, while six months later, he smashed the computer of a Kerrang! journalist, who had said he was about to leave the band. Meanwhile, at the start of '95, a couple of singles had torn into the UK charts, 'IF LIFE IS LIKE A LOVE BANK I WANT AN OVERDRAFT' and 'I WANNA GO WHERE THE PEOPLE GO', the latter one of the many highlights on their glorious Top 10 "comeback" album, 'P.H.U.Q.'. CJ's departure had caused a few problems, none more so when interim (ex-SENSELESS THINGS) guitarist MARK KEDS was posted missing in Japan causing the band to cancel a Phoenix Festival spot; they subsequently found JEFF STREATFIELD. Growing hostility between them and their record company (who issued the 'FISHING FOR LUCKIES' set just one too many times), led to The WILDHEARTS branching out on their own label, 'Round', issuing two hit singles, 'SICK OF DRUGS' and 'RED LIGHT – GREEN LIGHT' in '96. Late the following year, and now on 'Mushroom' records, the group released a couple of Top 30 singles, 'ANTHEM' and 'URGE', which surprisingly didn't push up the sales of third album proper, 'ENDLESS, NAMELESS'. With The WILDHEARTS out of the way by the end of the year, GINGER looked to other pursuits. However, a five week stint in a Bangkok prison put paid to any musical activity; he was arrested for being drunk after missing his flight home. Licking his wounds, he was back early in '99 with a new project, CLAM ABUSE, a duo that featured American ALEX KANE (or CLINT ABUSE, as he was better known at the time). Six years on from their last album, the WILDHEARTS returned with most of the original line-up for 'THE WILDHEARTS MUST BE DESTROYED' (2003), a less immediate, less frenetic and more mature collection which balanced the recklessness of old with something approaching wisdom and shock, horror, even a ballad! ('ONE LIFE, ONE LOVE, ONE GIRL'). • **Songwriters:** GINGER, except some by others. • **Trivia:** In 1993, the group featured in a Channel 4 play, 'Comics'.

Album rating: DON'T BE HAPPY . . . JUST WORRY (*6) / EARTH VERSUS THE WILDHEARTS (*6) / P.H.U.Q. (*8) / THE BEST OF THE WILDHEARTS compilation (*8) / ENDLESS, NAMELESS (*5) / Clam Abuse: STOP THINKING (*4) / Wildhearts: THE WILDHEARTS MUST BE DESTROYED (*7)

GINGER (b. DAVID WALLS, 17 Dec'64, South Shields, England) – vocals, guitar (ex-QUIREBOYS) / **BAM** – drums (ex-DOGS D'AMOUR) / **CJ** (CHRIS JAGDHAR) – guitar, vocals (ex-TATTOOED LOVE BOYS) / **DANNY McCORMACK** (b.28 Feb'72, South Shields) – bass, vocals (ex-ENERGETIC KRUSHER)

East West East West

Mar 92. (12"ep/12"white-ep/cd-ep) *(YZ 669 T/TX/CD)* **MONDO- AKIMBO-A-GO-GO** [ ] [–]
– (Nothing ever changes but the) Shoes / Turning American / Crying over nothing / Liberty cap.

Nov 92. (2xm-cd/c/2x12"m-lp) *(4509 91202-2/-4/-1)* **DON'T BE HAPPY . . . JUST WORRY** [ ] [–]
– (above 4 tracks; with 4 new ones:-) Splattermania / Weekend (5 days long) / etc. *(cd w/ anti-dance mixes of 'MONDO . . .') (re-iss. Apr 94 cd/c; 4509 96067-2/-4)*

—— **ANDREW 'STIDI' STIDOLPH** – drums; returned to repl. BAM who returned to DOGS D'AMOUR

Sep 93. (cd/c/lp) *(4509 93201-2/-4/-1) <92315>* **EARTH VERSUS THE WILDHEARTS** [46] [ ]
– Greetings from Shitsville / TV tan / Everlone / Shame on me / Loveshit / The miles away girl / My baby is a headf*** / Suckerpunch / News of the world / Love u til I don't. *(cd+=/c+=)* – Drinking about life. *(re-iss. Feb94 cd/c; 4509 94859-2/-4)*

Oct 93. (7"brown) *(YZ 773)* **GREETINGS FROM SHITSVILLE. / THE BULLSHIT GOES ON** [ ] [–]

Nov 93. (7"pic-d/c-s) *(YZ 784 P/C)* **TV TAN. / SHOW A LITTLE EMOTION** [53] [ ]
(12"+=/cd-s+=) *(YZ 784 T/CD)* – Dangerlust / Down on London.

—— **RITCH BATTERSBY** (b.RICHARD, 29 Jun'68, Birmingham, England) – drums (ex-RADIO MOSCOW) repl. STIDI

Feb 94. (7"green/c-s) *(YZ 794/+C)* **CAFFEINE BOMB / GIRLFRIENDS CLOTHES** [31] [–]
(12"+=/cd-s+=) *(YZ 794 T/CD)* – Shut your fuckin' mouth and use your fuckin' brain / And the bullshit goes on.

—— added on tour **WILL DOWNING** – keyboards (ex-GRIP) on tour

Jun 94. (etched10"ep/c-ep/cd-ep) *(YZ 828 TE/C/CD)* **SUCKERPUNCH / BEAUTIFUL THING YOU. / TWO-WAY IDIOT MIRROR / 29 x THE PAIN** [38] [–]

—— (Jul'94) temp **DEVON TOWNSEND** – guitar (ex-STEVE VAI) repl. CJ who formed, although only briefly, HONEYCRACK. He returned for the Reading Festival August 1994 before taking WILL to the aforementioned outfit

Dec 94. (mail order m-cd) *(4509 99039-2)* **FISHING FOR LUCKIES** [–] [–]
– Sky babies / Inglorious / Do the channel bop / Shizophronic / Geordie in wonderland / If life is like a love bank I want an overdraft.

Jan 95. (10"ep/c-ep/cd-ep/s-cd-ep) *(YZ 874 TEX/C/CD/CDX)* **IF LIFE IS LIKE A LOVE BANK I WANT AN OVERDRAFT / GEORDIE IN WONDERLAND. / HATE THE WORLD DAY / FIRE UP** [31] [–]

Apr 95. (10"ep/c-ep/cd-ep/s-cd-ep) *(YZ 923 TEX/C/CD/CDX)* **I WANNA GO WHERE THE PEOPLE GO / SHANDY BANG. / CAN'T DO RIGHT FOR DOING WRONG / GIVE THE GIRL A GUN** [16] [–]

May 95. (cd/c/lp)(s-cd) *(0630 10404-2/10653-4/10654-1)(0630 10437-2)* **P.H.U.Q.** [6] [–]
– I wanna go where the people go / V-day / Rust in lust / Baby strange / Nita nitro / Jonesing for Jones / Woah shit, you got through / Cold patootie tango / Caprice / Be my drug / Naivety play / In Lilly's garden / Getting it.

—— **MARK KEDS** – guitar (ex-SENSELESS THINGS) finally repl. C.J.

Jul 95. (10"ep/c-ep/cd-ep/cd-ep) *(YZ 967 TEX/C/CD/CDX)* **JUST IN LUST / MINDSLIDE. / FRIEND FOR FIVE MINUTES / S.I.N. (IN SIN)** [28] [–]

—— **JEF STREATFIELD** (b. 8 Jun'71, Southampton, England) – guitar repl. KEDS who went AWOL in July

Nov 95. (cd/c)(lp) *(0630 14855-2/-4)(0630 14888-1)* **FISHING FOR MORE LUCKIES** [ ] [–]

—— disbanded at the end of '95 although they quickly reformed

Round – East West not iss.

Apr 96. (c-ep/cd-ep) *(WILD 1 C/CD)* **SICK OF DRUGS / UNDERKILL / BAD TIME TO BE HAVING A BAD TIME / SKY CHASER HIGH** [14] [ ]
(cd-ep) *(WILD 1CDX)* –

May 96. (3D-cd/c/d-lp) *(0630 14855-2/-4/-1)* **FISHING FOR LUCKIES** (re-issue from late '94) [16] [–]
– Inglorious / Sick of drugs / Red light – green light / Schitzophonic / Soul searching on Planet Earth / Do the channel bop / Mood swings & roundabouts / In like Flynn / Sky babies / Nite songs.

Jun 96. (7"ep/c-ep/cd-ep) *(WILD 2/+C/CD)* **RED LIGHT – GREEN LIGHT EP** [30] [–]
– Red light – green light / Got it on Tuesday / Do anything / The British all-American homeboy crowd.

Nov 96. (cd/c) *(0630 17212-2/-4)* **THE BEST OF THE WILDHEARTS** (compilation) [ ] [–]
– I wanna go where the people go / T.V. tan / Sick of drugs / 29 x the pain / Caffeine bomb / Geordie in wonderland / Suckerpunch / Just in lust / Greetings from Shitsville / In Lilly's garden / My baby is a headfuck / If life is like a love bank I want an overdraft / Nothing ever changes but the shoes / Red light – green light / Beautiful me, beautiful you / Splattermania.

Mushroom not iss.

Aug 97. (7") *(MUSH 6S)* **ANTHEM. / HE'S A WHORE** [21] [–]
(cd-s) *(MUSH 6CD)* – ('A'side) / So good to be back home / Time to let you go.
(cd-s) *(MUSH 6CDX)* – ('A'side) / The song formerly known as / White lies.

Oct 97. (7") *(MUSH 14S)* **URGE. / FUGAZI (DO THE FAKE)** [26] [–]
(cd-s+=) *(MUSH 14CDS)* – Kill me to death.

Oct 97. (cd/c) *(MUSH 13 CD/MC/LP)* **ENDLESS, NAMELESS** [41] [–]
– Junkenstein / Nurse maximum / Anthem / Urge / Pissjoy / Soundog Babylon / Now is the colour / Heroin / Why you lie / Thunderfuck.

—— split after above, DANNY formed The YO-YO'S (with TOM, NEIL and BLADS) in '98, releasing their debut single, 'OUT OF MY MIND', in December; he is currently in a band called The CHASERS. GINGER subsequently joined the band, SUPERSHIT 666, alongside DREGEN (Backyard Babies) and NICKE ANDERSON (Hellacopters). Meanwhile, BATTERSBY helped form GRAND THEFT AUDIO.

– compilations, etc. –

Mar 98. (cd/d-lp) *Kuro Neko; (NKEK/+LP 3)* **ANARCHIC AIRWAVES – THE WILDHEARTS AT THE BBC** [ ] [–]

Sep 98. (cd) *Kuro Neko; (KNEK 4)* **LANDMINES & PANTOMIMES – THE LAST OF THE WILDHEARTS . . .?** [ ] [–]

CLAM ABUSE

GINGER (aka CLAM SAVAGE) + **CLINT ABUSE** (b. ALEX KANE)

Infernal Global Warning — not iss.

Jul 99. (cd) *(INFERNAL 001CD)* **STOP THINKING** [ ] [–]
– Sing like a girl / I think I love you / Message to Geri / Unlucky in love / .com together / Falling in bed with you / Sunday driving on a Thursday afternoon / For that girl, everything is groovy / Barney sings the blues / She's so taboo / There's always someone more fucked up than you.

WILDHEARTS

re-formed with **GINGER** + **CJ** + **STIDI** etc

Snapper — not iss.

Sep 02. (7") *(SMASLP 048)* **VANILLA RADIO. / BETTER THAN CABLE** [26] [–]
(cd-s) *(SMASCD 048)* – ('A'side) / Putting it on / Looking for the one.
(cd-s) *(SMASCD 048X)* – ('A'side) / O.C.D/ / Let's go.

Jan 03. (cd-s) *(SMASCD 049)* **STORMY IN THE NORTH KARMA IN THE SOUTH / BANG / IF I DECIDE** [17] [–]
(cd-s) *(SMASCD 049X)* – ('A'side) / You've got to get through what you've got to get through ((to get what you want but you've got to know what you want to get through what you want to get through) / Move on.

Gut — not iss.

May 03. (7"red) *(7GUT 49)* **SO INTO YOU. / DANCIN' (instrumental) / RETURN TO ZERO** [22] [–]
(cd-s) *(CDGUT 49)* – (first 2 tracks) / Lake of piss.
(cd-s) *(CXGUT 49)* – ('A'-Gordon Raphael mix) / Action panzer / The people that life forgot.

Aug 03. (cd/lp) *(GUT CD/LP 25)* **THE WILDHEARTS MUST BE DESTROYED** [54] [–]
– Nexus icon / Only love / Someone that won't le me go / Vanilla radio / One love, one life, one girl / Get your groove on / So into you / There's only one hell / It's all up to me / Out from the inside / Top of the world.

Nov 03. (cd-s) *(CDGUT 54)* **TOP OF THE WORLD / 6:30 ONWARDS / EAGER TO LEAVE 'ER** [26] [–]
(cd-s) *(CXGUT 54)* – ('A'side) / Hit it on the world / ('A'-video).
(cd-s) *(CYGUT 54)* – ('A'side) / Cheers / L.T.D.

☐ WILD TCHOUPITOULAS
(see under ⇒ NEVILLE BROTHERS)

WILLARD GRANT CONSPIRACY

Formed: Boston, Massachusetts, USA . . . 1996 out of The FLOWER TAMERS and The LAUGHING ACADEMY, initially as an informal weekly get together for various local musicians/songwriters. The group (California-rasised ROBERT FISHER, PAUL AUSTIN and Co.) eventually took on a more permanent nature for the recording of a self-financed debut album, '3 A.M. SUNDAY @ FORTUNE OTTO'S'. Following in the brooding shadow of such mood masters as NICK CAVE, TINDERSTICKS and The WALKABOUTS, WILLARD GRANT CONSPIRACY revel in detailing life's seedier side to a rootsy, downbeat musical backdrop incorporating such traditional instrumentation as mandolin, bouzouki, etc. Their self-styled "swamp noir" sound was finally brought to a UK audience via 1998's 'FLYING LOW' on the influential 'Slow River' label. One of last year's finest alt-country releases, highlights included loser's anthem, 'EVENING MASS', a grim meditation on life's hardships also featured on the brilliant 'Uncut' magazine compilation, 'Sounds Of The New West'. The desert doomsters were back with more neo-Gothic roots manoeuvres on 1999's 'MOJAVE', alternating their bleak alt-country with a snatch of heart of darkness punk and – on, marathon coda, 'THE VISITOR' – striking out into more exploratory, quasi-psychedelic territory. WGC love their dark irony and 'EVERYTHING'S FINE' (2001) proffered more monochrome snapshots of lives in desperate need of salvation, the revelatory, sonorous timbre of FISHER's vocal reverberating through the dense instrumentation like a distant thunderclap. On paper a seemingly irreconcilable partnership, the pairing of WGC and Dutch electronicists TELE:FUNK was fascinating in practice. Released as part of Amsterdam label 'Konkurrent's series of intriguing collaborations, the 'IN THE FISHTANK' (2001) EP proved that the grainy stamp of tradition resonated perhaps even more deeply when availed of technology's organic pulse. ROBERT FISHER and his band of merry men (er, joke!) returned in 2003 with the sombre 'REGARD THE END', perhaps the group's best work since 'MOJAVE'. Recorded in London, but very much an Americana record, this was the territory of LAMBCHOP's KURT WAGNER, the doomy wit of the HANDSOME FAMILY, or the twisted backwoods stories of murder and revenge from the likes of the RICHMOND FONTAINE. Yet, from the opener, 'PINES IN THE RIVER', the listener could see that the album belonged very much to WILLARD GRANT CONSPIRACY and to its sole author FISHER. However, lending a delicate hand (or two) was the ever reliable HILLMAN, CURRY and KRISTEN HERSH. Another great big black ball in WGC's beautiful canon.

Album rating: 3 A.M. SUNDAY @ FORTUNE OTTO'S (*6) / FLYING LOW (*6) / MOJAVE (*5) / EVERYTHING'S FINE (*6) / IN THE FISHTANK with Telefunk (*6) / REGARD THE END (*7)

ROBERT FISHER – vocals, guitar / **PAUL AUSTIN** – guitars / **SEAN O'BRIEN** – guitar

not iss. — Dahlia

1996. (cd) **3 A.M. SUNDAY @ FORTUNE OTTO'S** [–] [ ]
– (opening remarks) / Morning is the end of the day / Clockwork timing device / The ostrich song / Siren on the rocks / The only story I tell / Child's prayer / Unrequited / If Bojangles couldn't dance / Oh Mary / Bring it down. <*(re+UK-iss.Jun99 on 'Slow River'+=; SRRCD 40)*> – Chines New Year (New York).

1997. (7") <*DHL 0020*> **WAKE ME WHEN I'M UNDER** [–] [ ]
– (track by CHRIS & CARLA) / Arch's lullabye.

—— added for next **JAMES APT** – guitars / **DAVID MICHAEL CURRY** – viola / **ERICH GROAT** – mandolin / **MATT GRIFFIN** – bass

Slow River — Slow River

Mar 98. (cd) <*(SRRCD 35)*> **FLYING LOW** [ ] Aug98 [ ]
– The smile at the bottom of the ladder / Evening mass / August list / St. John Street / House is not a home (Palmdale, CA) / Bring the monster inside / No such thing as clean / It doesn't matter / Eephus pitch / Water / Split tender.

—— added guests **CHRIS BROKAW** (of COME), **MALCOLM TRAVIS** (ex-SUGAR) + **EDITH FROST** (solo artist)

May 99. (cd) <*(SRRCD 46)*> **MOJAVE** [ ] [ ]
– Another lonely night / Color of the sun / The work song / How to get to Heaven / Archy's lullaby / Go, Jimmy, go / I miss you best / Cat nap in the boom boom room / Front porch / Love has no meaning / Sticky / Right on time / The visitor.

1999. (cd-ep) **COLOR OF THE SUN** [–] [ ]
– Color of the sun / The work song / Love doesn't / Sticky (alt. version) / Massachusetts.

Oct 00. (cd) <*(SRRCD 58)*> **EVERYTHING'S FINE** [ ] Feb01 [ ]
– Notes from the waiting room / Christmas in Nevada / Kite flying / Wicked / Hesitation / Ballad of John Parker / Southend of a northbound

train / The beautiful song / Drunkard's prayer / Closing time / Massachusetts.

Fishtank Fishtank

Jan 02. (m-cd; by WILLARD GRANT CONSPIRACY & TELEFUNK) *<(FISH 8CD)>* **IN THE FISHTANK** ☐ ☐
– Twistification / Cuckoo / Grun grun / Near the cross / Just a little rain / Dig a hole in the meadow.

— AUSTIN would subsequently team up with TERRI MOELLER (of WALKABOUTS) to form TRANSMISSIONARY 6; they released an eponymous set in 2002

Vinyl Junkie Kimchee

Jun 03. (cd) *(VJCD 142) <30>* **REGARD THE END** ☐ May03 ☐
– River in the pines / The trials of Harrison Hayes / Beyond the shore / Ghost of the girl in the well / Twistification / Another man is gone / Soft hand / Rosalee / Fare thee well / Day is past and gone / The suffering song.

☐ WILLIAM (see under ⇒ JESUS & MARY CHAIN)

Hank WILLIAMS

Born: HIRAM WILLIAMS, 17 Sep'23, Garland, Alabama, USA. From the age of seven, WILLIAMS was raised by his domineering mother, Lillybelle after his father had finally left the recession-hit household having suffered one too many beatings at the hands of his wife (what about zero tolerance, eh?!). HANK, together with his mother and older sister, Irene, subsequently moved to Georgiana, where he bunked school to do odd jobs and learn guitar from an older negro friend, Tee Tot. In 1937, the family moved again, this time to Montgomery, where Lily opened a boarding house. There, she took in many male guests, too many for HANK's liking and he soon took off for a singing career on local radio. Even in his teens, WILLIAMS was drinking heavily, mainly to alleviate the pain of a chronic back ailment. He subsequently formed a band, The DRIFTING COWBOYS, who toured the Honky Tonk saloon bars as the 30's turned into the 40's. When the US of A decided to join the Second World War, HANK was fortunate enough not to be called up due to his bad back and he soon met soon-to-be divorced Audrey, whom he married in 1944. It was she who pestered publisher FRED ROSE to listen to him singing in a hotel lobby. The famous partner of ROY ACUFF was duly impressed and in 1946, after the war had ended, he was asked to scout out a new country star by 'Sterling' records. ROSE, of course, sent them HANK, who shortly after cut his first discs (see below). Three singles later, he was taken by Frank Walker to the new 'M.G.M.' stable in 1947, where they released 'MOVE IT ON OVER'. Walker then had him booked into the Louisiana Hayride, a weekly country radio show that was second only to The Grand Ole Opry. Troubles at home took precedence, however, as his wife and mother argued about his late night drinking binges. It wasn't only booze that was taking him over but a cocktail of uppers and downers. Early in 1949, he entered the country charts with standard, 'LOVESICK BLUES', propelling him overnight to Opry status. Following the birth of his son, HANK Jnr., he brought the house down at the Opry and made history with six encores, the country charts littered with HANK's songs over the period 1949-1950. Around this time, he had reluctantly agreed to kickstart his wife's singing career by convincing 'Decca' (who had earlier turned him down!) to record and release two of her songs in addition to two from his own pen; at the time HANK was writing with friend Vic McAlpin although he subsequently bought out the latter's half credit for 500 dollars. The following year, the rising country star co-authored a book, 'HOW TO WRITE COUNTRY AND FOLK MUSIC TO SELL' while Tony Bennett topped the pop charts with HANK's 'COLD COLD HEART'. In 1952 his relationship with Audrey had deteriorated to such an extent that he was drinking himself into oblivion and turning up on stage completely out of it. When Audrey and Hank Jnr. moved out of the family home, his drinking took over completely. By the time he returned to the studio in June of that year, however, the songs were coming thick and fast; classics 'JAMBALAYA', 'YOUR CHEATIN' HEART' and 'YOU WIN AGAIN' were all recorded during these sessions, demonstrating the troubled WILLIAMS at his heartbreaking best. Although he was fired from The Grand Ole Opry shows in August he returned to the Hayride to promote his new C&W No.1, 'JAMBALAYA'. He also met a young divorcee, Billie Jean, whom he married in October. He tried desperately to beat his alcoholism by spending time at a detox sanitarium, all to no avail. Tragically, in the early hours of the 1st January 1953, his 17 year-old chauffeur Charles Carr found him dead in the back seat. Two days previously, while his plane was being delayed due to bad weather, he had downed a bottle of spirits while taking morphine in his Knoxville hotel room. Desperate to make an Ohio gig, he had phoned Carr to pick his Cadillac up and drive him there. Mystery then, shrouded his death, when a rushed coroner gave a verdict as heart failure, although many still think it was an attempted suicide slow to hit fatal impact. Several others had also suspected murder, although this seems unlikely. Meanwhile, his record company 'M.G.M.' announced he was killed in a car crash! It wasn't laid to rest there, as even at his well attended funeral (estimated 20,000+), he wasn't even buried in his plot as it was too small!. Instead they dug up two nearby graves and put him in there!. A few days later, legal battles ensued between the unusual alliance of his ex-wife Audrey and his mother Lily, who fought out court battles with his recent wife Billie Jean. After around 20 pain-staking years (although not for their lawyers), Billie Jean won his estate. To make matters even crazier, a biopic film 'YOUR CHEATIN' HEART' was released early in 1965, starring GEORGE HAMILTON as HANK; his son HANK WILLIAMS Jnr. sang the soundtrack of his fathers' material. Billie Jean duly sued 'M.G.M.', claiming it portrayed her as a slut, although this was hardly surprising as ex-wife Audrey was employed as the film's technical advisor! HANK Jnr. carried on with his own solo career over the next 30 years, recording many of his fathers' classics (grandson HANK WILLIAMS III has also emerged in the late 90's!). Leaving this sometimes troubled 29-year legacy aside, the late great HANK has been a towering inspiration for many, including JERRY LEE LEWIS, BOB DYLAN, JOHN FOGERTY, BRUCE SPRINGSTEEN and even THE THE (aka MATT JOHNSON) who released a whole album attributed to the great man. Countless other artists have also made vast sums of money after hitting the pop charts with his songs. Here are a list:- JAMBALAYA (ON THE BAYOU) for (Fats Domino) (Carpenters) (John Fogerty) / YOU WIN AGAIN for (Fats Domino) / YOUR CHEATING HEART + TAKE THESE CHAINS FROM MY HEART for (Ray Charles) / HEY GOOD LOOKIN' for (Bo Diddley) / etc, etc. Many rock historians and commentators hold that HANK's premature demise represented the first bonafide rock'n'roll death, a grisly portent to the countless drug/alcohol deaths during rock's 60's/70's heyday.

Best CD compilation: THE ORIGINAL SINGLES COLLECTION box-set (*9)

HANK WILLIAMS – vocals, acoustic guitar with session people
— (all records before his death were 78 r.p.m.)

not iss. Sterling

Dec 46. (78) *<201>* **CALLING YOU. / NEVER AGAIN WILL I KNOCK ON YOUR DOOR** ☐ – ☐

Dec 46. (78) *<204>* **WEALTH WON'T SAVE YOUR SOUL. / WHEN GOD COMES AND (F)GATHERS HIS JEWELS**

Mar 47. (78) *<208>* **I DON'T CARE (IF TOMORROW NEVER COMES). / MY LOVE FOR YOU (HAS TURNED TO HATE)**

May 47. (78) *<210>* **HONKY TONKIN'. / PAN AMERICAN**

M.G.M. M.G.M.

Jul 47. (78) *<10033>* **MOVE IT ON OVER. / LAST NIGHT I HEARD YOU CRYING IN YOUR SLEEP**

Sep 47. (78) *<10073>* **FLY TROUBLE. / ON THE BANKS OF THE OLD PONTCHARTRAIN**

Feb 48. (78) *<10124>* **ROOTIE TOOTIE. / MY SWEET LOVE AIN'T AROUND**

Apr 48. (78) *<10171>* **HONKY TONKIN'. / I'LL BE A BACHELOR TILL I DIE**

Jun 48. (78) *<10212>* **I'M A LONG GONE DADDY. / BLUES COME AROUND**

Jul 48. (78) *<10226>* **PAN AMERICAN. / I DON'T CARE IF TOMORROW NEVER COMES**

Sep 48. (78) *<10271>* **I SAW THE LIGHT. / SIX MORE MILES (TO THE GRAVEYARD)**

Dec 48. (78) *<10328>* **MANSION ON THE HILL. / I CAN'T GET YOU OFF MY MIND**

Feb 49. (78) *<10352>* **LOVESICK BLUES. / NEVER AGAIN WILL I KNOCK ON YOUR DOOR**

Apr 49. (78) *<10401>* **WEDDING BLUES. / I'VE JUST TOLD MAMA GOODBYE**

May 49. (78; by "HANK AND AUDREY") *<10434>* **DEAR BROTHER. / LOST ON THE RIVER**

Jul 49. (78) **MIND YOUR OWN BUSINESS. / THERE'LL BE NO TEARDROPS TONIGHT**

Sep 49. (78) *<10506>* **YOU'RE GONNA CHANGE (OR I'M GONNA LEAVE). / LOST HIGHWAY**

Nov 49. (78) *<10560>* **MY BUCKET'S GOT A HOLE IN IT. / I'M SO LONESOME I COULD CRY**

Jan 50. (78) *<10609>* **I JUST DON'T LIKE THIS KIND OF LIVING. / MAY YOU NEVER BE ALONE**

Feb 50. (78; as LUKE THE DRIFTER) *<10630>* **THE FUNERAL. / BEYOND THE SUNSET**

Late in 1949, his wife AUDREY WILLIAMS signed to 'Decca' and released 2 singles with the aid of HANK. These were 'I LIKE THAT KIND'. / 'MY TIGHT WAD DADDY', and his songs 'HOW CAN YOU REFUSE HIM NOW'. / HELP ME UNDERSTAND'.

Mar 50. (78) *(MGM 269)* **LOVESICK BLUES. / WEDDING BELLS**

Mar 50. (78) *<10645>* **LONG GONE LONESOME BLUES. / MY SON CALLS ANOTHER MAN DADDY**

May 50. (78) *<10696>* **WHY DON'T YOU LOVE ME. / A HOUSE WITHOUT LOVE**

Jun 50. (78; as LUKE THE DRIFTER) *10718>* **EVERYTHING'S OKAY. / TOO MANY PARTIES**

Aug 50. (78) *<10760>* **THEY'L NEVER TAKE HER LOVE AWAY FROM ME. / WHY SHOULD WE TRY ANYMORE**

Oct 50. (78; as "LUKE THE DRIFTER") *<10806>* **NO NO JOE. / HELP ME UNDERSTAND**

Oct 50. (78; as "HANK AND AUDREY") *<10813>* **I HEARD MY MOTHER PRAYING FOR ME. / JESUS REMEMBERED ME**

Oct 50. (78) *<10832>* **MOANIN' THE BLUES. / NOBODY'S LONESOME FOR ME**

Dec 50. (78) *<10904>* **DEAR JOHN. / COLD, COLD HEART**

Mar 51. (78; as LUKE THE DRIFTER) **JUST WAITIN'. / MEN WITH BROKEN HEARTS**

Mar 51. (78) *(MGM 381)* **MOANIN' THE BLUES. / BLUES COME AROUND**

Apr 51. (78) *<10961>* **HOWLIN' AT THE MOON. / I CAN'T HELP IT (IF I'M STILL IN LOVE WITH YOU)**

Jun 51. (78) *<11000>* **HEY GOOD LOOKIN'. / MY HEART WOULD KNOW**

Jun 51. (78) *(MGM 405)* **DEAR JOHN. / FLY TROUBLE**

Jul 51. (78; as LUKE THE DRIFTER) *<11017>* **I'VE BEEN DOWN THAT ROAD BEFORE. / I DREAMED ABOUT MAMA LAST NIGHT**

Sep 51. (78) *<11054>* **LONESOME WHISTLER. / CRAZY HEART**

Nov 51. (78) *<11100>* **BABY WE'RE REALLY IN LOVE. / I'D STILL WANT YOU**

Dec 51. (78; as LUKE THE DRIFTER) *<11120>* **RAMBLIN' MAN. / PICTURE FROM LIFE'S OTHER SIDE**

Nov 51. (78) *(MGM 454)* **HEY, GOOD LOOKIN'. / HOWLING AT THE MOON**

Dec 51. (78) *(MGM 459)* **COLD, COLD HEART. / I'M A LONG GONE DADDY**

Feb 52. (78) *(MGM 471)* **I CAN'T HELP IT (IF I'M STILL IN LOVE WITH YOU). / BABY, WE'RE REALLY IN LOVE**

Mar 52. (78) *<11202>* **HALF AS MUCH. / LET'S TURN BACK THE YEARS**

Mar 52. (78) *(MGM 483)* **WHY DON'T YOU LOVE ME. / I'D STILL WANT YOU**

May 52. (78) *(MGM 505) <11160>* **HONKY-TONK BLUES. / I'M SORRY FOR YOU, MY FRIEND** Feb 52

Jul 52. (78) *(MGM 527)* **HALF AS MUCH. / LONG GONE LONESOME BLUES**

Jul 52. (78) *<11283>* **JAMBALAYA (ON THE BAYOU). / WINDOW SHOPPING**

Aug 52. (78; as LUKE THE DRIFTER) *<11309>* **WHY DON'T YOU MAKE UP YOUR MIND. / BE CAREFUL OF STONES THAT YOU THROW**

Sep 52. (78) *<11318>* **SETTIN' THE WOODS ON FIRE. / YOU WIN AGAIN**

Sep 52. (78) *(MGM 553)* **NOBODY'S LONESOME FOR ME. / MIND YOUR OWN BUSINESS**

Oct 52. (10"lp) *(D 105)* **HANK WILLIAMS SINGS**
– A house without love / Wedding bells / The mansion on the hill / Wealth won't save your soul / I saw the light / Six more miles (to the graveyard) / Lost highway / I've just told mama goodbye.

Oct 52. (78) *(MGM 566)* **JAMBALAYA (ON THE BAYOU). / SETTIN' THE WODS ON FIRE**

Dec 52. (78) *(SP 1016) <11366>* **I'LL NEVER GET OUT OF THIS WORLD ALIVE. / I COULD NEVER BE ASHAMED OF YOU** Oct 52

— tragically the above 'A'side was poignantly true, when, in the early hours of New Year's Day 1953, he was found dead

– (selective) compilations, etc. –

Apr 57. (10"lp) *(D 144)* **MOANIN' THE BLUES**
– Someday you'll call my name / Weary blues / Alone and forsaken / Moanin' the blues / I'm so lonely I could cry / Honky tonk blues / Lovesick blues / The blues come around / I'm a lone gone daddy / Long gone lonesome blues.

Jan 78. (d-lp/d-c) *(2683 071)(3271 302)* **40 GREATEST HITS**
– Baby, we're really in love / Cold, cold heart / Crazy heart / Dear John / Half as much / Hey, good lookin' / Honky tonk blues / Howlin' at the Moon / I can't help it / I just don't like this kind of living / I saw the light / I won't be home no more / I'll never get out of this world alive / I'm so lonesome I could cry / I'm sorry for you my friend / Jambalaya (on the bayou) / Kaw-liga / Lonesome whistle / Long gone lonesome blues / Lost highway / Lovesick blues / A mansion on the hill / Mind your own business / Moanin' the blues / Move it on over / My bucket's got a hole in it / My son calls another man daddy / Nobody's lonesome for me / Ramblin' man / Settin' the woods on fire / Take these chains from my heart / They'll never take her love from me / Weary blues / Wedding bells / Why don't you love me / Why should we try anymore / Window shopping / You win again / Your cheatin' heart / You're gonna change. *(d-cd iss.Mar89 on 'Polydor'; 821 233-2)*

Mar 91. (d-cd/d-c) *Polydor; (847194-2/-4)* **THE ORIGINAL SINGLES COLLECTION . . . PLUS**

Jan 96. (cd) *Polydor; (528037-2)* **ALONE AND FORSAKEN**

Apr 98. (cd) *Spectrum; (554381-2)* **THE BEST OF HANK WILLIAMS**

Sep 98. (10xcd-box) *Mercury; (536077-2)* **THE COMPLETE HANK WILLIAMS**

Mar 99. (cd) *Charly; (CPCD 8356)* **HONKY TONKIN'**

May 99. (cd/c) *Castle Pulse; (PLS CD/MC 328)* **FAMOUS COUNTRY MUSIC MAKERS**

Sep 99. (3xcd-box) *Goldies; (GLD 25351)* **LOVESICK BLUES**

Oct 99. (d-cd) *Mercury; (546466-2)* **LIVE AT THE GRAND OLE OPRY (live)**

Nov 99. (4xcd-box) *Chrome Dreams; (ABCD 021)* **THE HANK WILLIAMS STORY**

Mar 00. (cd) *Country Stars; (CTS 55456)* **LOVESICK BLUES**

Jul 00. (cd) *Music; (CD 6222)* **LOST HIGHWAY**
Sep 00. (cd) *Flapper; (PASTCD 7848)* **HONKY TONKIN'**
Nov 00. (3xcd-box) *Golden Stars; (GSS 5279)* **MOVE IT ON OVER**
Jan 01. (cd) *Living Era; (CDAJA 5461)* **JAMBALAYA: 28 ORIGINAL MONO RECORDINGS 1946-1952**
Jan 01. (cd) *Living Era; (CDAJA 5371)* **LOVESICK BLUES: 25 ORIGINAL MONO RECORDINGS 1947-1950**
Mar 01. (cd) *K-Tel; (ECD 3635)* **THE GREATEST COUNTRY SINGER OF ALL TIME**
May 01. (cd) *Catfish; (KATCD 194)* **BLUES COME AROUND**
Jul 01. (cd) *Country Stars; (CTS 5543-2)* **MOVE IT ON OVER**
Jul 01. (cd) *Arpeggio; (ARC 001)* **PRODIGAL SON**
Feb 02. (d-cd) *Snapper; (SMDCD 381)* **LONG GONE DADDY**
Mar 02. (4xcd-box) *Proper; (PROPERBOX 39)* **HILLBILLY HERO**
Jun 02. (cd) *Spectrum; (544650-2)* **THE COLLECTION**
Feb 03. (cd) *Mercury; (170315-2)* **AN INTRODUCTION TO HANK WILLIAMS: COME SEPTEMBER**
Mar 03. (cd) *Platinum; (PLATCD 926)* **YOU WIN AGAIN: THE LEGENDARY HANK WILLIAMS – 26 ORIGINAL RECORDINGS**
Mar 03. (4xcd-box) *Universal; (AA 847194-2)* **THE ORIGINAL SINGLES COLLECTION . . . PLUS**
Jun 03. (d-cd) *Metro; (METRDCD 519)* **THE ESSENTIAL HANK WILLIAMS**
Jun 03. (3xcd-box) *Disky; (MP 905617)* **GOLDEN GREATS**
Jul 03. (cd) *Country Stars; (CTS 55480)* **COLD COLD HEART**
Aug 03. (cd) *Castle Pulse; (PLS CD/MC 649)* **COUNTRY AND FOLK ROOTS**

Lucinda WILLIAMS

Born: 26 Jan'53, Lake Charles, Louisiana, USA. The daughter of an English lit prof/poet, WILLIAMS' childhood was spent in such diverse locations as Texas, Mexico City and the Chilean capital, Santiago. Influenced primarily by both the literature and music of the deep South, WILLIAMS began playing in her teens around the clubs of Houston (where the likes of TOWNE VAN ZANDT and GUY CLARK had founded a burgeoning folk-country scene) and Austin. By the release of her debut album, 'RAMBLIN' ON MY MIND' (1979), she was already on the way to becoming a seasoned performer and the record's trad country/blues standards – mainly borrowed from ROBERT JOHNSON, HANK WILLIAMS and MEMPHIS MINNIE – reflected her apprenticeship. In contrast, the following year's 'HAPPY WOMAN BLUES' comprised entirely of original material backed up by a full acoustic band. After a brief flirtation with the Greenwich Village folk scene and a further period down South, she eventually settled in L.A. where she concentrated on writing, performing and building up a permanent band. Deflecting regular major label offers, WILLIAMS' insistence on full creative control finally led her to a deal with UK indie, 'Rough Trade', who issued the long awaited 'LUCINDA WILLIAMS' early in 1989. While the music married the unmistakable influence of L.A.'s rock'n'roll heart with her trademark take on rootsy Americana, many of the lyrics centered on her recent divorce (from the Long Ryders' GREG SOWDERS) and the likes of 'PASSIONATE KISSES' and 'THE NIGHT'S TOO LONG' made for compelling listening. The former track was later covered by MARY-CHAPIN CARPENTER while PATTI LOVELESS took the latter into the country charts. WILLIAMS herself sold her work by the sheer hard graft of touring rather than any singles success although her stock with critics and roots fans had never been higher. The collapse of 'Rough Trade' certainly didn't help raise her profile, however, and after a doomed dalliance with 'R.C.A.', she again signed to an indie label, 'Chameleon'. The result was 1992's 'SWEET OLD WORLD', a roots-rock masterclass which managed to be both accomplished and inventively diverse, even pulling off a NICK DRAKE cover ('WHICH WILL'). Incredibly, her label went bust yet again and WILLIAMS moved on to Rick Rubin's 'American' before settling at 'Mercury'. She'd also based herself in Nashville and 1998's acclaimed 'CAR WHEELS ON A GRAVEL ROAD' was arguably the best thing to come out of music city in a good few years. Grittier than the likes of SHERYL CROW and certainly a lot more credible than SHANIA TWAIN, the record was roundly praised by both the rock and country camps, cropping up in many end of year polls and enjoying a prolonged stay in Mojo magazine's playlist. While her profile remains lower than it really should be, WILLIAMS' unquestionable musical integrity continues to endear her to critics and roots afficionados alike. That integrity was perhaps even more evident on 'ESSENCE' (2001), a much more personal, delicate record that explored human frailty and possibility with a keeness and sympathy rarely witnessed on record. A brave step after the forthright country-rock of 'CAR WHEELS . . .' but one which longtime fans will relish. 'WORLD WITHOUT TEARS' (2003), meanwhile, was probably an even braver step, as raw and visceral a statement as she's yet put together. Sonically stark and roughly split between brooding balladry and driving, cathartic country/blues-rock, the record made no concessions whatsoever to either commercial considerations or the expectations of her fans (or at least a proportion of them) given her career path thus far. Lyrically unflinching in the dissection of love's destructive power and obsessional dark side, the likes of 'THOSE THREE DAYS' laid bare her soul like never before.

Album rating: RAMBLIN' (*4) / HAPPY WOMAN BLUES (*6) / LUCINDA WILLIAMS (*7) / SWEET OLD WORLD (*8) / CAR WHEELS ON A GRAVEL ROAD (*7) / ESSENCE (*6) / WORLD WITHOUT TEARS (*7)

LUCINDA WILLIAMS – vocals, acoustic guitar / with **JOHN GRIMAUDO** – guitar

not iss. Heartbeat

1979. (lp) <*3507*> **RAMBLIN' ON MY MIND** – –
– Ramblin' on my mind / Me and my chauffeur / Motherless children / Malted milk blues / Disgusted / Jug band music / Stop breaking down / Drop down daddy / Little darlin' pal of mine / Make me a pallet on the floor / Jambalaya (on the bayou) / Great speckled bird / You're gonna need that pure religion / Satisfied mind. *<(cd/c-iss.1991 & UK Dec94/Dec98 as 'RAMBLIN' on 'Smithsonian-Folkways'; SFW CD/MC 40042)>*

— she was now backed by session people

not iss. Folkways

1980. (lp) <*FTS 31067*> **HAPPY WOMAN BLUES** –
– Lafayette / I lost it / Maria / Happy woman blues / King of hearts / Rolling along / One night stand / Howlin' at midnight / Hard road / Louisiana man / Sharp cutting wings (song to a poet). *(UK cd-iss. 1990 on 'Network'; NETCD 12) <(cd/c-iss.1990 & UK Dec94/Dec98 on 'Simthsonian-Folkways'; SFW CD/MC 40003)>*

— although she continued to work, she awaited a decent recording deal

— next with **GURF MORLIX** – guitar / **JOHN CIAMBOTTI** – bass / **DONALD LINDLEY** – drums / + session people

Rough Trade Rough Trade

Jan 89. (lp/c/cd) *(ROUGH/+C/CD 130) <ROUGHUS 47/+C/CD>* **LUCINDA WILLIAMS**
– I just wanted to see you so bad / The night's too long / Abandoned / Big red sun blues / Like a rose / Changed the locks / Passionate kisses / Am I too blue / Crescent city / Side of the road / Price to pay / I asked for water (he gave me gasoline). *(cd re-iss. Jul94 +=; R 316-2)* – Nothing in rambling / Disgusted / Goin' back home / Something what happens when we talk / Sundays / Side of the road. *(cd re-iss. Jun98 on 'Kock Int.'; 38005-2)*
Apr 89. (7"/12") *(RT/+T 224)* **I JUST WANTED TO SEE YOU SO BAD. /** –
Aug 89. (7"/12") *(RT/+T 232)* **PASSIONATE KISSES. / SIDE OF THE ROAD** –
(cd-ep+=) *(RT 232CD) <ROUGHUS 66CD>* – Nothing in rambling (live) / Goin' back home (live) / Disgusted (live). *<re-iss. 1992 on 'Chameleon'; 61387-2>*

Chameleon-WEA Chemeleon-WEA

Jan 93. (cd/c) *<(3705 61351-2/-4)>* **SWEET OLD WORLD** Aug92
– Six blocks away / Something about what happens when we talk / He never got enough love / Sweet old world / Little angel, little brother / Pineola / Lines around your eyes / Prove my love / Sidewalks of the city / Memphis pearl / Hot blood / Which will.

Mercury Mercury

Jul 98. (cd) *<(558338-2)>* **CAR WHEELS ON A GRAVEL ROAD** 65
– Right in time / Car wheels on a gravel road / 2 kool 2 be 4-gotten / Drunken angel / Concrete and barbed wire / Lake Charles / Can't let go / I lost it / Metal firecracker / Greenville / Still I long for your kiss / Joy / Jackson.

Lost Highway Lost Highway

Jun 01. (cd) *<(170197)>* **ESSENCE** 63 28
– Lonely girls / Steal your love / I envy the wind / Blue / Out of touch / Are you down / Essence / Reason to cry / Get right with God / Bus to Baton Rouge / Broken butterflies.

Apr 03. (cd/d-lp) *<(170355-2/-1)>* **WORLD WITHOUT TEARS** 48 18
– Fruits of my labor / Righteously / Ventura / Real live bleeding fingers and broken guitar strings / Over time / Those three days / Atonement / Sweet side / Minneapolis / People talkin' / American dream / World without tears / Words fell.

☐ Michelle WILLIAMS (see under ⇒ DESTINY'S CHILD)

☐ Pharrell WILLIAMS (see under ⇒ N*E*R*D)

Robbie WILLIAMS

Born: 13 Feb'74, Stoke-On-Trent, England. As the cheeky chappy of legendary Manchester boy band TAKE THAT, WILLIAMS enjoyed massive chart success from the early innocence of the 'Take That And Party' era through to the more risqué bare-arsed antics of the band's latter days. Yet even the adoration of schoolgirl legions wasn't enough to tether the boy wonder to the restrictions of the manufactured pop industry; as WILLIAMS embarked on an extended booze-athon with rock'n'roll bad boys OASIS etc., his position as a boy band popster was deemed untenable and he soon found himself looking at solo prospects. After eventually recovering from his much publicised indulgences, the singer launched his revamped career with a hugely successful cover of George Michael's 'FREEDOM', subsequently hooking up with songwriter GUY CHAMBERS to pen the likes of 'OLD BEFORE I DIE' and 'LAZY DAYS'. While the former was a sunny, vaguely humorous stab at deflating the rock'n'roll myth, the latter showed our ROBBIE could be mean'n'moody when he wanted to be. Along with fourth single, 'SOUTH OF THE BORDER', all the tracks (save 'FREEDOM') were included on his 1997 debut album, 'LIFE THRU A LENS', the general critical concensus being that WILLIAMS was having the last laugh, beating his former TAKE THAT cronies hands down (both GARY BARLOW and MARK OWEN were taking the solo road with middling success) and winning over a cross section of musical palates with his irrepressible style. He sealed his success that Christmas with the tearjerking ballad, 'ANGELS', a massive Top 5 hit which proved conclusively, if any further proof was needed, that the lad was most definitely back for good. 'LET ME ENTERTAIN YOU' (complete with QUEEN/KISS-style video) was ROBBIE's next single to reach the Top 3 (America still took a backseat for a while). In September '98, the classy JOHN BARRY ('You Only Live Twice')-styled 'MILLENNIUM', deservedly topped the UK chart for a week – ROBBIE now kitted out in James Bond tin flute. The track was also one of the highlights on his sophomore set, 'I'VE BEEN EXPECTING YOU' (1998), a record that boasted three further Top 5 hits, 'NO REGRETS', 'STRONG' and 'SHE'S THE ONE'. The latter was a recent WORLD PARTY track, having failed to be issued as a single by KARL WALLINGER and Co it was now a No.1 smash all around Europe. 1999 was not all party-time for the reformed Mr. WILLIAMS, celebrations were probably subdued a little when he lost a court battle with former TAKE THAT manager, Nigel Martin-Smith; the £90,000 claim would turn into £1 million adding of course legal fees, commission, interest and probably a counter damage claim. Still, there was no holding down the roguish heart-throb for long, 'SING WHEN YOU'RE WINNING' (2000) sticking to the well established blueprint. Thus we were treated to the infectious but ultimately turgid 'ROCK DJ', the even more turgid 'SUPREME' and a string of "heartfelt" album tracks baring the star's manly but oh-so sensitive side. Anyone suffering from ROBBIE overkill no doubt blanched when they heard of his next conceit, an easy listening tribute to Rat Pack stars like FRANK SINATRA and DEAN MARTIN. 'SWING WHEN YOU'RE WINNING' (2001) was tailor-made to please his simpering fans, ROBBIE's swell guy persona gorging itself on chestnuts like 'WELL, DID YOU EVAH' and 'SOMETHIN' STUPID' (the latter a Xmas No.1 duet with actress NICOLE KIDMAN). We await the American-networked ROBBIE soap with glazed eyes. If his work had been tiresome if admittedly professional up to this point, 2002's 'ESCAPOLOGY' signalled that even the sheen of songwriting polish which had kept him in the charts thus far was beginning to dull. Save for the trite 'SOMETHING BEAUTIFUL' hit single, there were no stadium singalongs to speak of. Even his formidable force of personality couldn't mask the tiredness in these songs. Despite the album's lack of lighter waving anthems, ROBBIE persisted in trundling out a selection on 'LIVE AT KNEBWORTH' (2003), a document of those mammoth summer gigs which even eclipsed his old pals' OASIS' former record at the English country estate. • **Songwriters:** Self-penned except collaborations and covers; MAKING PLANS FOR NIGEL (Xtc) / KOOKS (David Bowie) / I WOULDN'T NORMALLY DO THIS KIND OF THING (Pet Shop Boys) / EV'RY TIME WE SAY GOODBYE (Cole Porter) / ANT MUSIC (Adam & The Ants) / etc.

Album rating: LIFE THRU A LENS (*7) / I'VE BEEN EXPECTING YOU (*7) / SING WHEN YOU'RE WINNING (*7) / SWING WHEN YOU'RE WINNING (*5) / ESCAPOLOGY (*6) / LIVE AT KNEBWORTH (*5)

Chrysalis Capitol

Aug 96. (c-s) *(TCFREE 1)* **FREEDOM '96 / ('A'-The Next Big Gen mix) / ('A'-Arthur Baker's Shake and Bake mix)** 2 –
(cd-s+=) *(CDSFREE 1)* – (interview part 2).
(cd-s) *(CDFREE 1)* – ('A'side) / ('A'-Arthur Baker mix) / ('A'instrumental) / (interview part 1).

Apr 97. (c-s/cd-s) *(TCCHS/CDCHSS 5055)* **OLD BEFORE I DIE / KOOKS / MAKING PLANS FOR NIGEL** 2 –
(cd-s) *(CDCHS 5055)* – ('A'side) / Better days / Average B side.

Jun 97. (c-s/cd-s) *(TC/CD CHS 5063)* **LAZY DAYS / TEENAGE MILLIONAIRE / FALLING IN BED (AGAIN)** 8 –
(cd-s) *(CDCHSS 5063)* – ('A'side) / She makes me high / Everytime we say goodbye..

Sep 97. (c-s/cd-s) *(TC/CD CHS 5068)* **SOUTH OF THE BORDER / ('A'-Mother's milkin' it mix) / CHEAP LOVE SONG** 14 –
(cd-s) *(CDCHSS 5068)* – ('A'side) / Cheap love song / ('A'-187 Lockdown mix) / ('A'-Phil "The Kick Drum" Dane & Mart Smith's nosebag dub).

Oct 97. (cd/c) *(CD/TC CHR 6127)* **LIFE THRU A LENS** 1 –
– Lazy days / Life thru a lens / Ego a go go / Angels / South of the border / Old before I die / One of God's better people / Let me entertain you / Killing me / Clean / Baby girl window. *(lp-iss.Jun01 on 'Simply Vinyl'; SVLP 329)*

Dec 97. (7") *(CHSLH 5072)* **ANGELS. / SOUTH OF THE BORDER** 4 –

(c-s/cd-s) *(TC/CD CHS 5072)* – ('A'side) / Back for good (live) / Walk this sleigh.
(cd-s) *(CDCHSS 5072)* – ('A'side) / Karaoke overkill / ('A'acoustic) / Get the joke.

Mar 98. (7") *(CHSLH 5080)* **LET ME ENTERTAIN YOU. / LAZY DAYS** 3 –
(c-s/cd-s) *(TCCHS/CDCHSS 5080)* – The Full Monty medley: Make me smile (come up and see me) – You can leave your hat on – Land of a 1000 dances) / I wouldn't normally do this kind of thing / I am the (res)erection.
(cd-s) *(CDCHS 5080)* – ('A'extended) / ('A'-Stretch'n'Vern's rock'n'roll mix) / ('A'-Amethyst's dub) / ('A'-Robbie loves his mother mix) / ('A'-The Bizarro mix).

Sep 98. (c-s/cd-s) *(TC/CD CHS 5099)* *<radio cut>* **MILLENNIUM / LAZY DAYS (original) / ANGELS (live)** 1 May99 72
(cd-s) *(CDCHSS 5099)* – ('A'side) / Love cheat (demo) / Rome Munich Rome (demo).

Oct 98. (cd/c) *(497837-2/-4)* **I'VE BEEN EXPECTING YOU** 1 –
– Strong / No regrets / Millennium / Phoenix from the flames / Win some lose some / Grace / Jesus in a camper van / Heaven from here / Karma killer / She's the one / Man machine / These dreams. *(cd+=)* – Stand your ground / Stalker's day.

Nov 98. (7") *(CHS 5100)* **NO REGRETS. / ANTMUSIC** 4 –
(c-s+=/cd-s+=) *(TCCHS/CDCHSS 5100)* – Deceiving is believing.
(cd-s) *(CDCHS 5100)* – ('A'side) / There she goes / Sexed up.

Mar 99. (c-s/cd-s) *(TC/CD CHS 5107)* **STRONG / LET ME ENTERTAIN YOU (live at The Brit Awards) / HAPPY SONG** 5 –

Jul 99. (cd) *<97726-2>* **THE EGO HAS LANDED** (compilation) – 63

Nov 99. (-) *<album cut>* **ANGELS** – 53

Nov 99. (c-s) *(TCCHS 5112)* **SHE'S THE ONE / IT'S ONLY US / MILLENNIUM (live)** 1 –
(cd-s+=) *(CDCHS 5112)* – ('A'video).
(cd-s) *(CDCHSS 5112)* – ('A'side) / Coke and tears / It's only us / It's only us (video).

Jul 00. (c-s) *(TCCHS 5112)* **ROCK DJ / TALK TO ME** 2 –
(cd-s+=) *(CDCHS 5112)* – ('A'-Player One remix).

Aug 00. (cd/c/d-lp) *(528125-2/-4/-1)* *<29024>* **SING WHEN YOU'RE WINNING** 1 Oct00
– Let love be your energy / Better man / Rock DJ / Supreme / Kids / If it's hurting you / Singing for the lonely / Love calling Earth / Knutsford city limits / Forever Texas / By all means necessary / The road to Mandalay. *(cd re-iss. Dec00 +=; 528125-0)* – live:- Often / Sing when you're winning / Phoenix from the flames.

Oct 00. (c-s; by ROBBIE WILLIAMS & KYLIE MINOGUE) *(TCCHS 5119)* **KIDS / JOHN'S GAY / OFTEN** 2 –
(cd-s+=) *(CDCHS 5119)* – ('A'-video).
(cd-s) *(CDCHSS 5119)* – ('A'side) / Karaoke star / Kill me or cure me.

Dec 00. (c-s/cd-s) *(TC/CD CHS 5120)* **SUPREME / DON'T DO LOVE / COME TAKE ME OVER** 4 –
(cd-s) *(CDCHSS 5120)* – ('A'side) / United / ('A'live).

Apr 01. (c-s) *(TCCHS 5124)* **LET LOVE BE YOUR ENERGY / MY WAY** 10 –
(cd-s+=) *(CDCHS 5124)* – Rollin' stone / My way (video).

Jul 01. (c-s) *(TCCHS 5126)* **ETERNITY / THE ROAD TO MANDALAY** 1 –
(cd-s+=) *(CDCHS 5126)* – Toxic.

Nov 01. (cd/c/lp) *(<536826-2/-4/-1>)* **SWING WHEN YOU'RE WINNING** 1
– I will talk and Hollywood will listen / Mack the knife / Somethin' stupid / Do nothin' 'til you hear from me / It was a very good year / Straighten up and fly right / Well, did you evah / Mr. Bojangles / One for my baby / Things / Ain't that a kick in the head / They can't take that away from me / Have you met Miss Jones? / Me and my shadow / Beyond the sea.

Dec 01. (c-s; by ROBBIE WILLIAMS & NICOLE KIDMAN) *(TCCHS 5132)* **SOMETHIN' STUPID / ETERNITY (orchestral version) / MY WAY (live)** 1 –
(cd-s+=) *(CDCHS 5132)* – ('A'video).

Chrysalis Virgin

Nov 02. (cd/c/lp) *(543994-2/-4/-1)* *<81777>* **ESCAPOLOGY** 1 Apr03 43
– How peculiar / Feel / Something beautiful / Monsoon / Sexed up / Get a little high *[US-only]* / Love somebody / Revolution / Handsome man / Come undone / One fine day *[US-only]* / Me and my monkey / World's most handsome man *[US-only]* / Song 3 *[UK-only]* / Hot fudge *[UK-only]* / Cursed *[UK-only]* / Nan's song / How peculiar (reprise) / I tried love *[UK-only]*.

Dec 02. (c-s) *(TCCHS 5150)* **FEEL / NOBODY SOMEDAY / YOU'RE HISTORY** 4 –
(cd-s+=) *(CDCHS 5150)* – ('A'-video).

Apr 03. (c-s) *(TCCHS 5151)* **COME UNDONE / ONE FINE DAY / HAPPY EASTER (WAR IS COMING)** 4 –
(cd-s+=) *(CDCHS 5151)* – (the making of . . .).

Jul 03. (c-s) *(TCCHS 5152)* **SOMETHING BEAUTIFUL / BERLINER STAR / COFFEE TEA AND SYMPATHY** 3 –
(cd-s+=) *(CDCHS 5152)* – ('A'-video).

Sep 03. (cd) *(594637-2)* **LIVE AT KNEBWORTH (live)** 2 –
– Let me entertain you / Let love be your energy / We will rock you / Monsoon / Come undone / Me and my monkey / Hot fudge / Mr. Bojangles / She's the one / Kids / Better man / Nan's song / Feel / Angels.

Nov 03. (cd-s) *(CDCHS 5153)* **SEXED UP / GET A LITTLE HIGH / APPLIANCE OF SCIENCE** 10 –

Sonny Boy WILLIAMSON

Born: WILLIE 'RICE' MILLER on the 5th of December 1901, Glendora, Mississippi, USA. He mastered harmonica early in life and could also play guitar and drums, and if he had had more belief in himself then he would have gone on to be one of the most respected post-war bluesmen. During the 30's he used many names such as LITTLE BOY BLUE, WILLIE WILLIAMSON, WILLIE WILLIAMS and WILLIE MILLER (after his brother) but he decided in 1941, who knows why, to borrow the name of an established fellow harpist, JOHN LEE 'SONNY BOY' WILLIAMSON (who could do nothing about the interloper) and after the latter's death in 1948, MILLER actually claimed to be the original SONNY BOY WILLIAMSON. WILLIAMSON started to host the 'King Biscuit Time' radio show (sponsored by the King Biscuit flour company) on KFFA Radio, West Helena, Arkansas in 1941. He was a unique stylist with a resonating baritone and piercing harp; what's more, he was a better performer than the man whose name he had taken. WILLIAMSON made his first records (of which 'MIGHTY LONG TIME' was one of his finest) in 1951, for Lillian McMurray's 'Trumpet' label in Jackson, Mississippi along with WILLIE LOVE and ELMORE JAMES. He was already a seasoned performer by then, having played with ROBERT JOHNSON as well as teaching harmonica to his brother-in-law, HOWLIN' WOLF in exchange for guitar lessons. WILLIAMSON had also frequently crossed the paths of ELMORE JAMES, JOHNNY SHINES, SUNNYLAND SLIM and ROBERT 'JR.' LOCKWOOD, with whom he worked frequently during the 30's and who played lead guitar on many of his late 50's 'Chess' recordings. Although he had the reputation as a mean, bitter man, he was, in actual fact, generous to up and coming musicians; B.B. KING owed his start to a spot on WILLIAMSON's radio show while he virtually adopted JAMES COTTON as a son. SONNY subsequently moved to Chicago where he started to record for 'Chess' (who bought his contract from a third party after 'Trumpet' had sold it on). By 1955, he was in the studio with MUDDY WATERS, OTIS SPANN, JIMMY ROGERS and WILLIE DIXON backing him on his first 'Chess' single, 'DON'T START ME TALKIN'. This was a minor hit and he became a cult figure in Europe during the 60's, choosing to relocate to London in 1963 and recruiting The ANIMALS and The YARDBIRDS as backing bands. He returned to the Delta in 1964 and was found dead in his bed in Helena, Arkansas by drummer PECK CURTIS on the 25th of May 1965. His album 'DOWN AND OUT BLUES' went into the UK Top 20 one month after his death. • **Please note:** Not to be confused with another bluesman of the same name. The other was born JOHN LEE WILLIAMSON, 30 Mar'14, Jackson, Tennessee, USA, who as a teenager augmented other musicians HOMESICK JAMES WILLIAMSON and SLEEPY JOHN ESTES. He moved to Chicago in the late 30's, releasing classic songs 'GOOD MORNING LITTLE SCHOOLGIRL' and 'SUGAR MAMA' for the 'RCA-Bluebird' label. This SONNY BOY was to die on the 1st of June '48 after being attacked and robbed.

Best CD compilation: VERY BEST OF SONNY BOY WIILIAMSON box (*7)

SONNY BOY WILLIAMSON (RICE MILLER) – vocals, guitar, harmonica with **CLIFF BIVENS** – bass / **FROCK** – drums

not iss. Trumpet

Feb 51. (78) *<129>* **EYESIGHT TO THE BLIND. / CRAZY ABOUT YOU BABY** [–] [ ]

— added **DAVE CAMPBELL** – piano / **JOE WILLIE WILKINS** – guitar

Jun 51. (78) *<139>* **COOL, COOL BLUES. / DO IT IF YOU WANNA** [–] [ ]

Jul 51. (78) *<140>* **STOP CRYING. / COME ON BACK HOME** [–] [ ]

Nov 51. (78) *<144>* **WEST MEMPHIS BLUES. / I CROSS MY HEART** [–] [ ]

— **CLARENCE LONNIE** – piano; repl. CAMPBELL (after next w/out BIVENS)

Dec 51. (78) *<145>* **PONTIAC BLUES. / SONNY BOY'S CHRISTMAS BLUES** [–] [ ]

Apr 52. (78) *<166>* **NINE BELOW ZERO. / MIGHT LONG TIME** [–] [ ]

Jun 52. (78) *<168>* **STOP NOW BABY. / MR. DOWNCHILD** [–] [ ]

— **DUKE HUDDLESTON** – tenor sax / **OLIVER HARRIS** – bass / **S.P.** – drums; repl. LONNIE + FROCK

Dec 53. (78) *<212>* **CAT HOP. / TOO CLOSE TOGETHER** [–] [ ]

Mar 54. (78) *<215>* **GETTIN' OUT OF TOWN. / SHE BROUGHT LIFE BACK TO THE DEAD** [–] [ ]

May 54. (78) *<216>* **GOING IN YOUR DIRECTION. / RED HOT KISSES** [–] [ ]

— now w/ **CLARENCE LONNIE** – piano / **B.B. KING** – guitar / **GLEN RICKETTS** – drums

Oct 54. (78) *<228>* **EMPTY BEDROOM. / FROM THE BOTTOM** [–] [ ]

— now w/ **DAVE CAMPBELL + WILKINS**

not iss. Ace

Dec 54. (78) *<511>* **NO NIGHTS BY MYSELF. / BOPPIN' WITH SONNY** [–] [ ]

— now w/ **OTIS SPANN** – piano / **JIMMY ROGERS + MUDDY WATERS** – guitar / **FRED BELOW** – drums

not iss. Checker

Mar 55. (7") *<824>* **DON'T START ME TO TALKIN'. / ALL MY LOVE IN VAIN** [–] [ ]

— **ROBERT LOCKWOOD + Jr. LUTHER TUCKER** – guitar / **WILLIE DIXON** – bass repl. WATERS + ROGERS + SPANN

Jul 55. (7") *<834>* **LET ME EXPLAIN. / YOUR IMAGINATION** [–] [ ]

1956. (7") *<847>* **KEEP IT TO YOURSELF. / THE KEY TO YOUR DOOR** [–] [ ]

1957. (7") *<864>* **FATTENING FROGS FOR SNAKES. / I DON'T KNOW** [–] [ ]

— added **OTIS SPANN** – piano

1957. (7") *<883>* **BORN BLIND. / NINETY NINE** [–] [ ]

1958. (7") *<894>* **YOUR FUNERAL AND MY TRIAL. / WAKE UP BABY** [–] [ ]

1958. (7") *<910>* **CROSS MY HEART. / DISSATISFIED** [–] [ ]

1959. (7") *<927>* **LET YOUR CONSCIENCE BE YOUR GUIDE. / UNSEEING EYE** [–] [ ]

1959. (7") *<943>* **THE GOAT. / IT'S SAD TO BE ALONE** [–] [ ]

1960. (7") *<956>* **TEMPERATURE 110. / LONESOME CABIN** [–] [ ]

1960. (7") *<963>* **TRUST ME BABY. / TOO CLOSE TOGETHER** [–] [ ]

1961. (7") *<975>* **STOP RIGHT NOW. / THE HUNT** [–] [ ]

1961. (7") *<1003>* **ONE WAY OUT. / NINE BELOW ZERO** [–] [ ]

— now w/ **LAFAYETTE LEAKE** – organ / **MATT MURPHY** – guitar / **MILTON RECTOR** – bass / **AL DUNCAN** – drums

Pye Int. Checker

Apr 63. (7") *(7N 25191) <1036>* **HELP ME. / BYE BYE BIRD** [ ] [ ]

Oct 63. (7") *<1065>* **TRYING TO GET BACK ON MY FEET. / DECORATION DAY** [–] [ ]

1963. (lp) *<1417>* **ONE WAY OUT** [–] [ ]
– Born blind / Work with me / Your killing me / Keep it to yourself / Don't lose your eye / Good evening everybody / Too close together / Let your conscience be your guide / I wonder why / This is my apartment / One way out / Like Wolf / Have you ever been in love / Cool disposition / I know what love is all about. *(re-iss. Aug86 lp/c; GCH/+K7 8006) (re-iss. Sep90 c/cd; CH/+D 9116) (cd re-iss. Sep92; CHLD 19174) (cd-iss. Feb93 on 'Charly'; CDCD 1070)*

— **BUDDY GUY** – guitar / **JACK MEYERS** – bass / **CLIFTON JAMES; repl. all except LEAKE**

Dec 63. (7") *<1080>* **I WANT YOU CLOSE TO ME. / MY YOUNGER DAYS** [–] [ ]

Feb 64. (7") *<1134>* **DOWN CHILD. / BRING IT ON HOME** [–] [ ]

May 64. (lp) *(NPL 28036) <1437>* **DOWN AND OUT BLUES** [20] [ ]
– Don't start me talkin' / I don't know / All my love in vain / The key / Keep it to yourself / Dissatisfied / Fattening frogs for snakes / Wake up baby / Your funeral and my trial / 99 / Cross my heart / Let me explain. *(re-iss. Jan67 on 'Marble Arch'; MAL 662) (cd-iss. Jun88 on 'Chess'; CHD 31272) (cd re-iss. Jul90 on 'Chess'; CH 9257) (cd re-iss. Oct92; CHLD 19106)*

Oct 64. (7") *(7N 25268)* **LONESOME CABIN. / THE GOAT** [ ] [–]

Nov 64. (7"ep) *(NEP 44037)* **SONNY BOY WILLIAMSON** [ ] [–]

— SONNY died on 25 May'65

– (selective) compilations, etc. –

Dec 86. (cd) *Greenline-Chess; (CDCHESS 35)* **THE BEST OF SONNY BOY WILLIAMSON** [ ] [–]
– Don't start me to talkin' / All my love in vain / Let me explain / Keep it to yourself / The key (to your door) / Fattening frogs for snakes / Cross my heart / Born blind / Ninety nine / Your funeral and my trial / Let your conscience be your guide / The goat / It's sad to be alone / Checkin' up on my baby / Lonesome cabin / Trust my baby / Too close together / Nine below zero / Help me / Bring it on home / Decoration day / One way out.

1987. (4xlp-box) *Chess; (BOX 1)* **THE CHESS YEARS** [ ] [ ]
(4xcd-box iss.Feb91; CDREDBOX 1)

Oct 89. (6xlp-box) *Chess; (CXHT 109)* **SONNY BOY WILLIAMSON** [ ] [ ]

Aug 92. (lp/c/cd) *Alligator; (AL/+CS/CD 4787)* **KEEPIN' IT TO OURSELVES** [ ] [ ]
(re-iss. Aug99 on 'Analogue'; APB 036/+CD)

Mar 94. (cd) *See For Miles; (SEECD 395)* **THE EP COLLECTION VOL.2** [ ] [–]

Jul 94. (cd) *Alligator; (AL 2803)* **GOIN' IN YOUR DIRECTION** [ ] [ ]

Feb 95. (cd) *The Collection; (COL 044)* **THE COLLECTION** [ ] [–]

Jul 95. (3xcd-box; with other artists) *Charly; (VBCD 304)* **THE VERY BEST OF SONNY BOY WILLIAMSON** [ ] [–]

Jul 95. (cd) *Charly; (CDRB 21)* **LIVE IN ENGLAND** [ ] [–]

Sep 96. (cd) *Charly; (CHLDD 19330)* **THE ESSENTIAL SONNY BOY WILLIAMSON** [ ] [–]

Jul 97. (cd) *M.C.A.; (MCD 09377)* **HIS BEST** [ ] [ ]

May 98. (cd; with GRAHAM BOND) *Spalax; (14552)* **ROCK GENERATION** [ ] [–]

Jul 00. (cd) *Spectrum; (544277-2)* **THE BEST OF SONNY BOY WILLIAMSON** [ ] [ ]

Oct 01. (cd) *Catfish; (KATCD 212)* **EYESIGHT TO THE BLIND** [ ] [ ]

☐ Brian WILSON (see under ⇒ BEACH BOYS)

Jackie WILSON

Born: JACK LEROY WILSON, 9 Jun'34, Detroit, Michigan, USA. His first taste of fame (albeit minor) came in 1950 when he won an American amateur 'Golden Gloves' boxing title; due to his young age he was registered under a false name, Sonny Wilson. His mother, however, was more interested in directing him towards the musical arena and the teenage WILSON joined The EVER READY GOSPEL SINGERS the same year. He subsequently went on to sing alongside The THRILLERS and HANK BALLARD before being spotted by L.A. R&B mainstay, JOHNNY OTIS; he was introduced to BILLY WARD, who in turn recruited WILSON for his band, The DOMINOES. He nevertheless cut a one-off solo single – as

JACKIE WILSON – in 1951 on DIZZY GILLESPIE's 'Dee Gee' label, a straining pop cover of Irish traditional standard, 'DANNY BOY'. In April '53 he took over as The DOMINOES lead singer following the departure of CLYDE McPHATTER (to form The DRIFTERS). Although WILSON was a more than adequate replacement, the group managed only one Top 20 hit ('ST. THERESE OF THE ROSES') during his tenure. In late '56 JACKIE departed for a solo career, scoring a sizeable UK Top 10 late the following year with 'REET PETITE (THE FINEST GIRL YOU EVER WANT TO KNOW)'. Co-penned by Berry Gordy Jr. (future 'Motown' guru), this strutting slice of pop/R&B was to make the record books in 1986 when it became a re-issued UK chart topper 29 years after its original release. In the meantime, a follow-up, 'TO BE LOVED', made both the US and UK Top 30 although it'd be America where WILSON would make a lasting impression on the charts. One of his biggest and most enduring hits came in late '58 with the classic 'LONELY TEARDROPS' while the near-operatic dimension to his vocal style (many of his 60's songs were adapted from operas or classical works) was showcased on 1960's Top 5 'NIGHT'. Although he continued to score minor hits throughout the early 60's, his only entry into the Top 10 was 1963's 'BABY WORKOUT', a proto-soul belter that went a long way to capturing the excitement of the JACKIE WILSON live experience. A ball of sexually kinetic energy as potent as JAMES BROWN, WILSON's loose-footed athleticism and sweat-stained, gospel-rooted fervor made him a magnetic performer who attracted legions of female fans. The man almost came a cropper in 1961 when one of those fans, Juanita Jones, attempted to shoot herself in JACKIE's New York apartment; when WILSON intervened he was shot in the stomach and spent a long period in hospital. If his studio output didn't always live up to expectations, WILSON was guaranteed to pull off at least the occasional powerful performance; a link-up with veteran Windy City producer, Carl Davis, resulted in the near Top 10 'WHISPERS' (1966) and the joyous near Top 5 '(YOUR LOVE KEEPS LIFTING ME) HIGHER AND HIGHER' (1967). In 1969, JACKIE was back in the British charts (with the latter track) for the first time in almost a decade while summer 72's 'I GET THE SWEETEST FEELING' made the UK Top 10. Ironically, longtime fan VAN MORRISON scored a minor US chart hit at almost exactly the same time with his sublime WILSON tribute, 'JACKIE WLISON SAID (I'M IN HEAVEN WHEN YOU SMILE)'. Tragically, on September 29th 1975 (by which time WILSON was touring the oldies circuit), the singer suffered a heart attack onstage; he'd been midway through 'LONELY TEARDROPS', performing as part of a Dick Clark Revue at the Latin Casino in Cherry Hill, New Jersey. He never fully regained his faculties due to brain damage and spent over eight years in hospital before his death on 21st January 1984. BARRY WHITE and The SPINNERS were among the stars who performed benefit concerts to pay for his hospital bills although the $60,000 that was raised actually went towards a $300,000 unpaid tax demand. • **Songwriters:** JACKIE wrote most of material himself and collaborating with others, notably ALONZO TUCKER in 1962-65. BERRY GORDY JR. & TYRAN CARLO (alias cousin BILLY DAVIS), penned his late 1950's 'Brunswick' songs. Many of his 1960's songs were adapted from operas or classical works. Covered:- DANNY BOY (Irish trad.) / SHAKE A HAND (Faye Adams) / THINK TWICE (Brook Benton) / FOR YOUR PRECIOUS LOVE (Impressions) / CHAIN GANG (Sam Cooke) / I GET THE SWEETEST FEELING (co-with; Van McCoy) / FOR ONCE IN MY LIFE (Stevie Wonder) / YOU GOT ME WALKING (Eugene Record; Chi-Lites) / etc. • **Trivia:** In 1959, he appeared in the Alan Freed film 'Go Johnny Go'.

Best CD compilation: THE VERY BEST OF JACKIE WILSON (*8)

JACKIE WILSON – vocals (with various personnel)

		not iss.	Dee Gee
1952.	(78) **RAINY DAY BLUES. / ROCKAWAY ROCK**	–	
1952.	(78) **DANNY BOY. / BULLDOZER BLUES**	–	

—— In Apr'53, he replaced CLYDE McPHATTER in The DOMINOES.

		not iss.	Federal
1953.	(78) **WHERE NOW, LITTLE HEART. / YOU CAN'T KEEP A GOOD MAN DOWN**	–	
1953.	(78) **RAGS TO RICHES. / DON'T THANK ME**	–	
1953.	(78) **CHRISTMAS IN HEAVEN. / RING IN A BRAND NEW YEAR**	–	
1954.	(78) **UNTIL THE REAL THING COMES ALONG. / MY BABY'S 3-D**	–	
1954.	(78) **TOOTSIE ROLL. / I'M GONNA MOVE TO THE OUTSKIRT OF TOWN**	–	
1954.	(78) **TENDERLY. / A LITTLE LIE**	–	
1954.	(78) **THREE COINS IN A FOUNTAIN. / I REALLY DON'T WANNA KNOW**	–	
1954.	(78) **ABOVE JACOB'S LADDER. / LITTLE BLACK RAIN**	–	
1955.	(78) **IF I NEVER GET TO HEAVEN. / CAN'T DO SIXTY NO MORE**	–	
1955.	(78) **LOVE ME NOW OR LET ME GO. / CAVEMAN**	–	
1955.	(78) **MAY I NEVER LOVE AGAIn. / LEARNIN' THE BLUES**	–	
1956.	(78) **GIVE ME YOU. / OVER THE RAINBOW**	–	
1956.	(78) **BOBBY SOX BABY. / HOW LONG, HOW LONG BLUES**	–	

—— The DOMINOES to 'Jubilee' in '54 – released a handful of singles

		not iss.	Decca
1956.	(78) **ST. THERESE OF THE ROSES. / HOME IS WHERE YOU HANG YOUR HEART**	–	
1956.	(78) **WILL YOU REMEMBER. / COME ON SNAKE LET'S CRAWL**	–	
1956.	(78) **HALF A LOVE. / EVERMORE**	–	
1957.	(78) **ROCK, PLYMOUTH ROCK. / 'TIL KINGDOM COME**	–	
1957.	(78) **TO EACH HIS OWN. / I DON'T STAND A GHOST OF A CHANCE**	–	
1957.	(78) **SEPTEMBER SONG. / WHEN THE SAINTS GO MARCHING IN**	–	

—— **JACKIE WILSON** reverted to solo career

		Coral		Brunswick
Nov 57.	(7",78) *(Q 72290) <55024>* **REET PETITE (THE FINEST GIRL YOU EVER WANT TO KNOW). / BY THE LIGHT OF THE SILVERY MOON**	6	Oct57	62
Mar 58.	(7",78) *(Q 72306) <55052>* **TO BE LOVED. / COME BACK TO ME**	23		22
Sep 58.	(7",78) *(Q 72332) <55070>* **I'M WANDERIN'. / AS LONG AS I LIVE**			
Oct 58.	(lp) *(LVA 9087) <54042>* **HE'S SO FINE** – Etc., etc. / To be loved / Come back to me / If I can't have you / As long as I live / Reet petite / It's too bad we had to say goodbye / Why can't you be mine / I'm wanderin' / Right now / Danny boy / He's so fine.			
Oct 58.	(7",78) *(Q 72338) <55086>* **WE HAVE LOVE. / SINGING A SONG**		Sep58	93
Dec 58.	(7",78) *(Q 72347) <55105>* **LONELY TEARDROPS. / IN THE BLUE OF EVENING**		Nov58	7
May 59.	(7",78) *(Q 72366) <55121>* **THAT'S WHY (I LOVE YOU SO). / LOVE IS ALL**		Mar59	13
Jul 59.	(7",78) *(Q 72372) <55136>* **I'LL BE SATISFIED. / ASK**		Jun59	20
Sep 59.	(lp) *(LVA 9108) <54045>* **LONELY TEARDROPS** – Lonely teardrops / Each time (I love you more) / (That's why) I love you so / In the blue of the evening / The joke (is not on me) / Someone to need me / You better know it / By the light of the silvery moon / Singing a song / Love is all We have love / Hush-a-bye.			
Oct 59.	(7",78) *(Q 72380) <55149>* **YOU BETTER KNOW IT. / NEVER GO AWAY**		Sep59	37
Dec 59.	(7",78) *(Q 72384) <55165>* **TALK THAT TALK. / ONLY YOU, ONLY ME**		Nov59	34
Mar 60.	(7") *<55166>* **NIGHT. / DOGGIN' AROUND**	–		4 15
Apr 60.	(7") *(Q 72393)* **DOGGIN' AROUND. / THE MAGIC OF LOVE**			–

May 60. (lp) *(LVA 9121) <754050>* **SO MUCH** [ ] [ ]
– I know I'll always be in love with you / Happiness / Only you, only me / The magic of love / Wishing well / Talk that talk / Ask / I'll be satisfied / It's all a part of love / Never go away / Thrill of love.

Sep 60. (7") *(Q 72407) <55167>* **(YOU WERE MADE FOR) ALL MY LOVE. / A WOMAN, A LOVER, A FRIEND** [ ] [12] Jul60 [15]

Sep 60. (lp) *(LVA 9130) <754055>* **JACKIE SINGS THE BLUES** [ ] Jul60 [ ]
– Please tell me why / Doggin' around / New girl in town / Nothin' but the blues / Passin' through / Excuse me for lovin' / She done me wrong / Sazzle dazzle / Please stick around / Come on and love me baby / Comin' to your house / It's been a long time.

Nov 60. (7") *(Q 72412) <55170>* **ALONE AT LAST. / AM I THE MAN** [50] [8] Oct60 [32]

Dec 60. (lp) *(LVA 9135) <754058>* **MY GOLDEN FAVOURITES** (compilation) [ ] [ ]
– Reet petite / To be loved / I'll be satisfied / Only you, only you / Talk that talk / Ask / (That's why) I love you so much / It's all a part of love / Lonely teardrops / I'm wanderin' / You better know it / We have love.

Jan 61. (7") *(Q 72421) <55201>* **MY EMPTY ARMS. / THE TEAR OF THE YEAR** [ ] [9] [44]

Feb 61. (7") *(Q 72424)* **THE TEAR OF THE YEAR. / YOUR ONE AND ONLY LOVE** [ ] [–]

Mar 61. (7") *<55208>* **PLEASE TELL ME WHY. / YOUR ONE AND ONLY LOVE** [–] [20] [40]

May 61. (lp) *(LVA 9144) <754059>* **A WOMAN, A LOVER, A FRIEND** [ ] [ ]
– A woman, a lover, a friend / Your one and only love / You cried / The river / When you add religion to love / One kiss / Night / (You were made for) All my love / Am I the man / Behind a smile is a tear / We kissed / (So many) Cute little girls.

May 61. (7") *(Q 72430)* **CUTE LITTLE GIRLS. / PLEASE TELL ME WHY** [ ] [ ]

Jul 61. (7") *(Q 72434) <55216>* **I'M COMING ON BACK TO YOU. / LONELY LIFE** [ ] [19] Jun61 [80]

Sep 61. (lp) *(LVA 9148) <754100>* **YOU AIN'T HEARD NOTHIN' YET** [ ] [ ]
– Toot, toot, tootsie goodbye / Sonny boy / California, here I come / Keep smiling at trouble (trouble's a bubble) / You made me love you (I didn't want to do it) / My Yiddishe momme / Swane / April showers / Anniversary song / Rock-a-bye with a Dixie melody / For me and my gal / In our house.

Sep 61. (7") *(Q 72439) <55219>* **YEARS FROM NOW. / YOU DON'T KNOW WHAT IT MEANS** [ ] [37] Aug61 [79]

Nov 61. (7") *(Q 72444) <55220>* **THE WAY I AM. / MY HEART BELONGS TO ONLY YOU** [ ] [58] Oct61 [65]

Feb 62. (7") *(Q 72450) <55221>* **THE GREATEST HURT. / THERE'LL BE NO NEXT TIME** [ ] [34] Jan62 [75]

Apr 62. (lp) *(LVA 9151) <754101>* **BY SPECIAL REQUEST** [ ] [ ]
– Cry / My heart belongs to only you / Stormy weather / Tenderly / Lonely life / The way I am / Try a little tenderness / Mood indigo / You belong to my heart / Indian love call / One more time / I'm comin' on back to you

May 62. (7"; by JACKIE WILSON & LINDA HOPKINS) *<55224>* **I FOUND LOVE. / THERE'S NOTHING LIKE LOVE** [ ] Apr62 [93]

May 62. (7") *<55225>* **HEARTS. / SING** [–] [58]

Aug 62. (7") *(Q 72454) <55229>* **I JUST CAN'T HELP IT. / THE TALE OF WOE** [ ] Jun62 [70]

Sep 62. (lp) *(LVA 9202) <754105>* **BODY AND SOUL** [ ] [ ]
– Body and soul / I don't know you anymore / I apologize / I got it bad (and that ain't good) / The greatest hurt / I'll always be in love with you / Crazy she calls me / The tear of the year / Blue Moon / I'll be around / There'll be no next time / We'll be together.

Sep 62. (7") *<55233>* **FOREVER AND A DAY. / BABY, THAT'S ALL** [–] [82]

Jan 63. (7") *<55236>* **WHAT GOOD AM I WITHOUT YOU?. / A GIRL NAMED TAMIKO** [–] [ ]

Feb 63. (lp) *(LVA 9209) <754108>* **AT THE COPA (live)** [ ] Nov62 [ ]
– Tonight / Medley: Body and soul – I apologize / Love for sale / And this is my beloved / The way I am / I love them all (part 1): What'd I say – Night – That's why (I love you so) / I love them all (part 2): Danny boy – Doggin' around – To be loved – Lonely teardrops / St. James infirmary / A perfect day.

Mar 63. (7") *<55239>* **BABY WORKOUT. / I'M GOING CRAZY (GOTTA GET YOU OFF MY MIND)** [–] [5]

Mar 63. (7") *(Q 72460)* **BABY WORKOUT. / WHAT GOOD AM I WITHOUT YOU** [ ] [–]

Apr 63. (lp) *<754110>* **BABY WORKOUT** [–] [36]
– Shake! shake! shake! / The kictapoo / Yeah! yeah! yeah! / You only live once / Say you will / Baby workout / It's not my fault / Love train / Now that I want her / (I feel like I'm in) Paradise / (So many) Cute little girls / What good am I without you.

Jun 63. (7") *(Q 72464) <55243>* **SHAKE A HAND. ("JACKIE WILSON & LINDA HOPKINS") / SAY I DO** [ ] May63 [42]

Aug 63. (7") *(Q 72465) <55246>* **SHAKE! SHAKE! SHAKE!. / HE'S A FOOL** [ ] Jul63 [33]

Sep 63. (lp; mono/stereo) *(LVA/SVL 9214) <754106>* **SINGS THE WORLD'S GREATEST MELODY** [ ] [ ]
– Forever and a day / Take my heart / Pianissmo / My eager heart / I dream of you / My tale of woe / A girl named Tamiko / All my love / A heart of love / Alone at last / A thing of beauty.

Nov 63. (7") *(Q 72467) 55250> BABY GET IT (AND DON'T QUIT IT). / THE NEW BREED* [ ] Sep63 [61]

Dec 63. (7") *<55254>* **SILENT NIGHT. / O HOLY NIGHT** [–] [ ]

Jan 64. (7") *<55260>* **I'M TRAVELIN' ON. / HAUNTED HOUSE** [–] [ ]

Mar 64. (7") *<55263>* **CALL HER UP. / THE KICKAPOO** [–] [ ]

Jun 64. (7") *(Q 72474) <55266>* **BIG BOSS LINE. / BE MY GIRL** [ ] May64 [94]

Jun 64. (lp; by JACKIE WILSON & LINDA HOPKINS) *<754113>* **SHAKE A HAND** [–] [ ]
– Swing low sweet cariot / Nobody knows the trouble I've seen / Yes indeed / Joshua fit the battle of Jericho / Old time religion / Shake a hand / He's got the whole world in his hands / When the saints go marching in / Do Lord / Everytime I feel the spirit / Dry bones / Down by the riverside.

Sep 64. (7") *(Q 72476) <55269>* **SQUEEZE HER, TEASE HER (BUT LOVE HER). / GIVE ME BACK MY HEART** [ ] Aug64 [89]

Nov 64. (7") *<55273>* **SHE'S ALRIGHT. / WATCH OUT** [–] [ ]

Feb 65. (7") *<55277>* **DANNY BOY. / SOUL TIME** [–] [94]

Mar 65. (lp) *<754117>* **SOMETHIN' ELSE** [–] [ ]
– Big boss line / Groovin' / Deep down love / Take one step / Love (is where you find it) / Give me back my heart / Squeeze her – tease her (but love her) / Be my girl / Baby (I just can't help it) / Rebecca / My best friend's girl / Twistin' and shoutin' (doing the monkey).

May 65. (7"; by JACKIE WILSON & LINDA HOPKINS) *(Q 72480) <55278>* **YES INDEED. / WHEN THE SAINTS GO MARCHING IN** [ ] [ ]

Aug 65. (7") *(Q 72481) <55280>* **NO PITY (IN THE NAKED CITY). / I'M SO LONELY** [ ] Jun65 [59]

Sep 65. (lp) *<754118>* **SOUL TIME** [–] [ ]
– No pity / Danny boy / An ocean I'll cry / Teardrop avenue / She'll be there / Star dust / A kiss, a thrill and goodbye / Mama of my song / She's all right / Better play it safe / No time out.

Nov 65. (7") *(Q 72482) <55283>* **I BELIEVE I'LL LOVE ON. / LONELY TEARDROPS** [ ] Oct65 [96]

Jan 66. (lp) *(LVA 9231) <754119>* **SPOTLIGHT ON JACKIE WILSON** [ ] [ ]
– Over the rainbow / Pledging my love / Georgia on my mind / Georgia on my mind / You'll never walk alone / Rags to riches / You don't know me / What kind of fool am I / I wanna be around / Until the real thing comes along / I apologize / Lonely teardrops / We have love.

Jan 66. (7"; by JACKIE WILSON & LAVERN BAKER) *<55287>* **THINK TWICE. / PLEASE DON'T HURT ME** [–] [93]

May 66. (7") *(Q 72484)* **TO MAKE A BIG MAN CRY. / BE MY LOVE** [ ] [–]

Jul 66. (lp; mono/stereo) *(LVA/SVL 9232) <754120>* **SOUL GALORE** [ ] [ ]
– Brand new thing / 3 days 1 hour 30 minutes / I've got to get back (country boy) / So you say you wanna dance (workout #2) / Stop lying / Let me build / Brand new thing (2) / Soul galore / What's done in the dark / I got my mind made up / Everything's gonna be fine / Your loss, my gain.

Jul 66. (7") *<55289>* **I'VE GOT TO GET BACK (COUNTRY BOY). / 3 DAYS, 1 HOUR, 30 MINUTES** [–] [ ]

Aug 66. (7") *<55290>* **BRAND NEW THING. / SOUL GALORE** [–] [ ]

Sep 66. (7") *<55294>* **I BELIEVE. / BE MY LOVE** [–] [ ]

Nov 66. (7") *(Q 72487) <55300>* **WHISPERS (GETTIN' LOUDER). / THE FAIREST OF THEM ALL** [ ] Oct66 [11]

Feb 67. (7") *<55309>* **JUST BE SINCERE. / I DON'T WANT TO LOSE YOU** [–] [91]

[84]

Apr 67. (7") *<55321>* **I'VE LOST YOU. / THOSE HEARTACHES** [–] [82]

Jul 67. (lp) *(LVA 9235) <754122>* **WHISPERS** [ ] Jan67 [ ]
– I don't want to lose you / My heart is calling / Who am I / Whispers (gettin' louder) / The fairest of them all / (Too much) Sweet loving / I can do better / Just be sincere / Only your love can save me / To make a man cry / I've gotta talk to you / Tears will tell it all.

Sep 67. (7") *(Q 72493) <55336>* **(YOUR LOVE KEEPS LIFTING ME) HIGHER AND HIGHER. / I'M THE ONE TO DO IT** [ ] Aug67 [6]

Dec 67. (7") *(Q 72496) <55354>* **SINCE YOU SHOWED ME HOW TO BE HAPPY. / THE WHO WHO SONG** [ ] Nov67 [32]

M.C.A. Brunswick

Mar 68. (7"; by JACKIE WILSON & COUNT BASIE) *(MU 10140) <55365>* **FOR YOUR PRECIOUS LOVE. / UPTIGHT** [ ] Feb68 [49]

Apr 68. (lp; mono/stereo) *(MUP/+S 304) <754130>* **HIGHER AND HIGHER** [ ] Dec67 [ ]
– (Your love keeps lifting me) Higher and higher / I don't need you around / I've lost you / Those heartaches / Soulville / Open the door to your heart / I'm the one to do it / You can count on me / I need your loving / Somebody up there likes you / When will our day come.

Apr 68. (7"; by JACKIE WILSON & COUNT BASIE) *<55373>* **CHAIN GANG. / FUNKY BROADWAY** [–] [84]

Jul 68. (7") *<55381>* **I GET THE SWEETEST FEELING. / NOTHING BUT HEARTACHES** [–] [34]

Sep 68. (lp; mono/stereo; as JACKIE WILSON & COUNT BASIE) *(MUP/MUPS 333) <754134>* **TOO MUCH** <US-title 'MANUFACTURERS OF SOUL'> [ ] Jun68 [ ]
– Funky Broadway / For your precious love / In the midnight hour / Ode to Bilie Joe / Chain gang / I was made to love her / Uptight (everything's alright) / I never loved a woman (the way I love you) / Respect / Even when you cry / My girl. *(UK re-iss. Feb74)*

Oct 68. (7") *<55393>* **FOR ONCE IN MY LIFE. / YOU BROUGHT ABOUT A CHANGE IN ME** [–] [70]

Apr 69. (lp) *(MUPS 361) <754138>* **I GET THE SWEETEST FEELING** [ ] [ ]
– You keep me hangin' on / Once in a lifetime / Who can I turn to (when nobody needs me) / People / Don't go to strangers / I get the sweetest feeling / You brought about the change in me / Nothing but blue skies / A woman needs to be loved / Growin' tall / Since you showed me how to be happy.

Apr 69. (7") *(MU 1131)* **(YOUR LOVE KEEPS LIFTING ME) HIGHER AND HIGHER. / WHISPERS (GETTIN' LOUDER)** [11] [–]

Dec 69. (7") *(MU 1105) <55418>* **HELPLESS. / DO IT THE RIGHT WAY** [ ] [ ]

Feb 70. (7") *<55423>* **WITH THESE HANDS. / (WHY DON'T YOU) DO YOUR THING** [–] [ ]

Apr 70. (7") *<55435>* **LET THIS BE A LETTER (TO MY BABY). / DIDN'T I** [–] [91]

Jun 70. (lp) *(MUPS 405) <754154>* **DO YOUR THING** [ ] [ ]
– To change my love / This guy's in love with you / Why don't you do your thing / This better Earth / Helpless / Light my fire / That lucky old Sun (just rolls around Heaven all day) / With these hands / Hold on, I'm coming / Eleanor Rigby.

Dec 70. (7") *<55443>* **(I CAN FEEL THOSE VIBRATIONS) THIS LOVE IS REAL. / LOVE UPRISING** [–] [56]

Apr 71. (7") *<55449>* **SAY YOU WILL. / THIS GUY'S IN LOVE WITH YOU** [–] [ ]

Nov 71. (7") *<55461>* **LOVE IS FUNNY THAT WAY. / TRY IT AGAIN** [–] [95]

Feb 72. (7") *<55467>* **YOU GOT ME WALKING. / THE FOUNTAIN** [–] [93]

Jul 72. (7"m) *(MU 1160)* **I GET THE SWEETEST FEELING. / GALORE / SOUL GALORE** [9] [–]

Brunswick Brunswick

May 73. (7") *<55467>* **YOU GOT ME WALKING. / THE FOUNTAIN** [–] [ ]

Jul 73. (7") *<55475>* **FOREVER AND A DAY. / THE GIRL TURNED ME ON** [–] [ ]

Aug 73. (lp) *(BRLS 3001) <754172>* **YOU GOT ME WALKING** [ ] [ ]
– You got me walking / What a lovely day / You left the fire burning / My way / Try it again / Forever and a day / The girl turned me on Hard to get a thing called love / Love is funny that way / The fountain.

Oct 73. (7") *<55480>* **WHAT A LOVELY DAY. / YOU LEFT THE FIRE BURNING** [–] [ ]

Mar 74. (7") *(BR 3) <55490>* **BEAUTIFUL DAY. / WHAT'CHA GONNA DO ABOUT LOVE** [ ] [ ]

Apr 74. (lp) *<754189>* **BEAUTIFUL DAY** [–] [ ]
– Beautiful day / Because of you / Go away / Pretty little angel eyes / Let's love again / It's all over / I get lonely sometimes / This love is mine / Don't you know I love you / What'cha gonna do about me.

1974. (7") *<55495>* **BECAUSE OF YOU. / GO AWAY** [–] [ ]

1974. (7") *<55499>* **NO MORE GOODBYES. / SING A LITTLE SONG** [–] [ ]

Apr 75. (7") *(BR 18)* **I GET THE SWEETEST FEELING. / (YOUR LOVE KEEPS LIFTING ME) HIGHER AND HIGHER** [25] [–]

Jul 75. (7") *<55504>* **IT'S ALL OVER. / SHAKE A LEG** [–] [ ]

Nov 75. (7"; by JACKIE WILSON & The CHI-LITES) *(BR 28) <55522>* **DON'T BURN NO BRIDGES / ('A'instrumental)** [ ] [ ]

Jan 76. (7") *<55536>* **NOBODY BUT YOU. / I'VE LEARNED ABOUT LOVE** [–] [ ]

—— On the 29th September '75, JACKIE had a heart attack. He lapsed into a coma and due to brain damage stayed in the same state until his death on 21st of January '84.

– (selective) compilations, etc. –

Aug 75. (lp) *Brunswick; (BRLS 3016)* **THE VERY BEST OF JACKIE WILSON** [ ] [–]
– Reet petite / Lonely teardrops / That's why I love you so / Night / You better know it / Talk that talk / To be loved / I'l be satisfied / Whispers (gettin' louder) / Your love keeps lifting me higher and higher / I get the sweetest feeling / Doggin' around / Am I the man / I'm comin' on back to you / A woman a lover a friend / No pity (in the naked city).

Mar 85. (7"m) *Skratch; (SKM 1)* **I GET THE SWEETEST FEELING. / WHISPERS (GETTIN' LOUDER) / (YOUR LOVE KEEPS LIFTING ME) HIGHER AND HIGHER** [ ] [–]
(12"+=) *(SKM12 1)* – The who who song / Nothin' but blue skies. *(UK re-iss. Feb87; same)* – hit No.3

Mar 85. (7"m/12"m) *Skratch; (SKM/+12 3)* **REET PETITE. / YOU BROUGHT ABOUT A CHANGE IN ME / I'M THE ONE TO DO IT** [ ] [–]
(UK re-iss. Nov86; same) – hit No.1

Mar 85. (lp/c) *Ace; (CH/+C 125)* **REET PETITE** [ ] [–]
(cd-iss. May86; CDCH 902)

Jun 87. (7"/12") *Skratch; (SKM 10/+12)* **(YOUR LOVE KEEPS LIFTING ME) HIGHER AND HIGHER. / THE WHO WHO SONG** [15] [–]

Oct 95. (cd) *Charly; (JWCD 1)* **THE JACKIE WILSON STORY – THE NEW YORK YEARS, VOLUME 1** [ ] [–]

Oct 95. (cd) *Charly; (JWCD 2)* **THE JACKIE WILSON STORY – THE NEW YORK YEARS, VOLUME 2** [ ] [–]

Oct 95. (cd) *Charly; (JWCD 5)* **THE JACKIE WILSON STORY – THE CHICAGO YEARS, VOLUME 1** [ ] [–]

Oct 95. (cd) *Charly; (JWCD 6)* **THE JACKIE WILSON STORY – THE CHICAGO YEARS, VOLUME 2** [ ] [–]

Jun 96. (cd) *Charly; (JWCD 3)* **THE JACKIE WILSON STORY – THE NEW YORK YEARS, VOLUME 3** [ ] [–]

Jul 96. (d-cd) *Double Gold; (DBG 53035)* **THE JACKIE WILSON STORY** [ ] [–]

Sep 96. (cd) *Charly; (JWCD 4)* **THE JACKIE WILSON STORY – THE NEW YORK YEARS, VOLUME 4** [ ] [–]

Nov 96. (cd) *More Music; (MOCD 3018)* **THE VERY BEST OF JACKIE WILSON** [ ] [–]

Jul 99. (cd) *Music Club; (MCCD 395)* **SWEETEST FEELIN': THE VERY BEST OF . . .** [ ] [ ]

Nov 01. (d-cd) *Brunswick; (BICD 1001)* **THE BRUNSWICK ANTHOLOGY** [ ] [ ]

Oct 02. (cd) *Metro; (METRCD 083)* **BEST OF JACKIE WILSON** [ ] [ ]

Feb 03. (cd) *Westside; (WESM 596)* **UPTOWN AND UPNORTH: FINGERSNAPPERS FLOATERS & FLOORSHAKERS – THE ORIGINAL BRUNSWICK RECORDINGS** [ ] [ ]

Aug 03. (cd) *Disky; (SI 901046)* **JACKIE'S GREATEST** [ ] [ ]

☐ WINGS (see under ⇒ McCARTNEY, Paul)

Edgar WINTER

Born: 28 Dec'46, Beaumont, Texas, USA. Having spent the latter half of the 60's playing in his older brother JOHNNY's bands including BLACK PLAGUE, the albino keyboard wizard (strapped to his shoulder on stage!) went solo in 1969. His debut album, 'ENTRANCE' (1970) scraped into the US Top 200 and in 1972, after forming WHITE TRASH, he made the Top 30 with double live set, 'ROADWORK' (a record oft cited as one of the seminal progressive rock releases). The following year, he surpassed brother JOHNNY's triumphs when the EDGAR WINTER GROUP topped the US charts with the classic instrumental 45, 'FRANKENSTEIN', a track lifted from his finest album, 'THEY ONLY COME OUT AT NIGHT'. Mainstream success was to be relatively short-lived, however and WINTER parted company with 'Epic' following the release of 'SHOCK TREATMENT' in 1974, signalling the end of the high profile period of his career. He subsequently re-joined JOHNNY, recording 'TOGETHER' (1976) and signing to 'Blue Sky' Records, releasing albums that showed a return to his blues and jazz roots. Arguably ahead of his time, WINTER's maverick streak effectively prevented him from becoming the star that his talent merited. Nevertheless, his band has provided a launching pad for many a future star including BOZ SCAGGS, DAN HARTMAN, RICK DERRINGER and RONNIE MONTROSE. WINTER belatedly came in from the commercial wilderness in the late 90's, appearing in a series of US TV ads that led to a new recording contract (with the 'Pyramid' label) and a comeback album. 'WINTER BLUES' (1999) featured guest spots from his brother JOHNNY, LEON RUSSELL, EDDIE MONEY, RICK DERRINGER and DR. JOHN, its workmanlike blues-rock catering to the tastes of longtime fans rather than trying to win over any new ones. • **Covered:** I CAN'T TURN YOU LOOSE (Otis Redding) / TOGETHER album with JOHNNY featured loads of covers.

Album rating: ENTRANCE (*6) / EDGAR WINTER'S WHITE TRASH (*6) / ROADWORKS (*7) / THEY ONLY COME OUT AT NIGHT (*7) / SHOCK TREATMENT (*6) / JASMINE NIGHTDREAMS (*4) / THE EDGAR WINTER GROUP WITH RICK DERRINGER (*5) / RECYCLED (*4) / THE EDGAR WINTER ALBUM (*3) / STANDING ON ROCK (*4) / HARLEM NOCTURNE (*4) / THE BEST OF EDGAR WINTER compilation (*6) / LIVE IN JAPAN (*4) / NOT A KID ANYMORE (*3) / THE REAL DEAL (*4)

EDGAR WINTER – (solo) – keyboards, saxophone, all (ex-JOHNNY WINTER) except guests **JOHNNY WINTER + RANDAL DOLANON** – guitar / **JIMMY GILLEN** – drums / **RAY AVONGE, EARL CHAPIN + BROOKS TILLOTSON** – horns

Epic | Epic

Jun 70. (lp) *(EPC 64083)* *<26503>* **ENTRANCE**
– Entrance / Where have you gone / Rise to fall / Fire and ice / Hung and up / Back in the blues / Re-entrance / Tobacco Road / Jump right out / Peace pipe / A different game / Jimmy's gospel.

Jun 70. (7") *<10618>* **TOBACCO ROAD. / NOW IS THE TIME** –

EDGAR WINTER'S WHITE TRASH

EDGAR with **JERRY LaCROIX** – vox, sax / **JON ROBERT SMITH** – sax, vox / **MIKE McLELLAN** – trumpet, vox / **GEORGE SHECK** – bass / **FLOYD RADFORD** – guitar / **BOBBY RAMIREZ** – drums also **RICK DERRINGER** – guitar

May 71. (7") *(EPC 7269)* *<10740>* **WHERE WOULD I BE. / GOOD MORNING MUSIC**

Jun 71. (lp) *(EPC 81191)* *<30512>* **EDGAR WINTER'S WHITE TRASH** Apr 71
– Give it everything you got / Fly away / Where would I be / Let's get it on / I've got news for you / Save the planet / Dying to live / Keep playin' that rock'n'roll / You were my light / Good morning music. *(cd-iss. Oct93 on 'Sony Europe')*

Nov 71. (7") *(EPC 7550)* *<10788>* **KEEP PLAYIN' THAT ROCK'N'ROLL. / DYING TO LIVE** 70

May 72. (d-lp) *(EPC 67244)* *<31249>* **ROADWORK (live)** Mar72 23
– Save the planet / Jive jive jive / I can't turn you loose / Still alive & well / Back in the U.S.A. / Rock and roll hoochie koo / Tobacco Road / Cool fool / Do yourself a favour / Turn on your lovelight.

Jun 72. (7") *(EPC 8136)* *<10855>* **I CAN'T TURN YOU LOOSE. / COOL FOOL** May72 81

— WHITE TRASH folded when on 24th Jul'72, RAMIREZ was killed in pub brawl.

EDGAR WINTER GROUP

added synthesizer to his new line-up **DAN HARTMAN** – vocals, bass / **RONNIE MONTROSE** – guitar / **CHUCK RUFF** – drums / + **RICK**

Aug 72. (7") *(EPC 8315)* **FREE RIDE. / CATCHIN' UP**

Jan 73. (lp) *(EPC 65074)* *<31584>* **THEY ONLY COME OUT AT NIGHT** Nov72 3
– Hangin' around / When it comes / Alta Mira / Free ride / Frankenstein / Autumn / Round and round / Rock'n'roll boogie woogie blues / We all had a really good time. *(re-iss. quad.Sep84; EPC 32518)*

Jan 73. (7") *(EPC 1064)* *<10922>* **ROUND AND ROUND. / CATCHIN' UP** Nov72

Jan 73. (7") *<10945>* **FRANKENSTEIN. / HANGIN' AROUND** –

May 73. (7") *(EPC 1440)* *<10967>* **FRANKENSTEIN. / UNDERCOVER MAN** 18 Mar73 1

Aug 73. (7") *(EPC 1712)* *<11024>* **FREE RIDE. / WHEN IT COMES** 14

Feb 74. (7") *(EPC 2031)* *<1069>* **HANGIN' AROUND. / WE ALL HAD A REAL GOOD TIME** Dec73 65

— Billed on tour as EDGAR WINTER GROUP Featuring RICK DERRINGER

RICK – guitars, vocals, etc. (ex-JOHNNY WINTER, ex-McCOYS) repl. JERRY WEEMS. In Oct'74, WEEMS had repl. RONNIE who formed own band MONTROSE

Jul 74. (lp/c) *(EPC/40 65640)* *<32461>* **SHOCK TREATMENT** May74 13
– Some kinda animal / Easy street / Sundown / Miracle of love / Do like me / Rock & roll woman / Someone take my heart away / Queen of my dreams / Maybe someday you'll call my name / River's risin' / Animal.

Jul 74. (7") *(EPC 2537)* *<11143>* **RIVER'S RISIN'. / ANIMAL** 33

Nov 74. (7") *(EPC 2802)* *<50034>* **EASY STREET. / DO LIKE ME** Oct74 83

Feb 75. (7") *(EPC 3146)* *<50060>* **SOMEONE TAKE MY HEART AWAY. / MIRACLE OF LOVE**

EDGAR WINTER

(solo) with **HARTMAN, RUFF, DERRINGER + J.WINTER**

Blue Sky | Blue Sky

Jun 75. (7") *<2758>* **JASMINE NIGHTDREAMS. / ONE DAY TOMORROW** –

Jun 75. (lp/c) *(SKY/40 80772)* *<33483>* **JASMINE NIGHTDREAMS** 69
– One day tomorrow / Little brother / Hello mellow feelin' / Tell me in a whisper / Shuffle-low / Keep on burnin' / How do you like your love / I always wanted you / Outa control / All out / Sky train / Solar strut.

Sep 75. (7") *<2761>* **I ALWAYS WANTED YOU. / OUTA CONTROL** –

The EDGAR WINTER GROUP WITH RICK DERRINGER

Nov 75. (7") *<2762>* **COOL DANCE. / PEOPLE MUSIC** –

Nov 75. (lp/c) *(SKY/40 69181)* *<33798>* **THE EDGAR WINTER GROUP WITH RICK DERRINGER**
– Cool dance / People music / Good shot / Nothin' good comes easy / Infinite peace in rhythm / Paradise skies / Diamond eyes / Modern love / Let's do it together again / Can't tell one from the other / J.A.P. (Just another punk) / Chainsaw.

May 76. (7") *(SKY 4217)* *<2763>* **DIAMOND EYES. / INFINITE PEACE IN RHYTHM**

— Next set was a collaboration, 'TOGETHER' with his brother, JOHNNY

EDGAR WINTER'S WHITE TRASH

1977. (7") <2769> **PUTTIN' IT BACK. / STICKIN' IT OUT** -
1977. (lp/c) *(SKY/40 82228)* <34858> **RECYCLED**
– Puttin' it back / Leftover love / Shake it off / Stickin' it out / New wave / Open up / Parallel love / The in and out of love blue / Competition.

EDGAR WINTER GROUP

in 1979 with different line-up **CRAIG SNYDER** – guitar / **JAMES WILLIAMS** – bass / **KEITH BENSON** – drums / **LARRY WASHINGTON** – percussion (same label)

Aug 79. (7") *(SKY 7803)* <2780> **IT'S YOUR LIFE TO LIVE. / FOREVER IN LOVE**
Sep 79. (lp/c) *(SKY/40 83648)* <35989> **THE EDGAR WINTER ALBUM**
– It's your life to live / Above and beyond / Take it the way it is / Dying to live / Please don't stop / Make it last / Do what / It took your love to bring me out / Forever in blue.
Mar 80. (7"/12") *(SKY/+12 8246)* <2786> **ABOVE AND BEYOND. / ('A'instrumental)**

— now with **AL FERRANTE** – guitar / **GREG CARTER** – drums / **SCOTT SPRAY** – bass / **RONNIE LAWSON** – keyboards, vocals / **MONIQUE WINTER** – backing vocals

1981. (lp) *(SKY 84503)* <36494> **STANDING ON ROCK**
– Step garbage / Standing on rock / Love is everywhere / Martians / Rock'n'roll revival / In love / Everyday man / Tomorrowland.

— EDGAR retired from solo work for the rest of the 80's

Thunderbolt Goldcastle

Nov 90. (cd) *(CDTB 089)* **HARLEM NOCTURNE** -
– Searching / Tingo tango / Cry me a river / Save your love for me / Quiet gas / Satin doll / Jordu / Girl from Ipanema / Harlem nocturne / Come back baby / Before the sunset / Who dunnit / Please come home for Christmas. *(re-iss. Aug99 on 'MagMid'; MM 034)*
Nov 91. (cd; EDGAR WINTER & RICK DERRINGER) *(CDTB 134)* <71352> **LIVE IN JAPAN (live)**
– Keep playing that rock and roll / Teenage love affair / Free ride / Fly away / Blood from a stone / Undercover man / Jump jump jump / Hang on Sloopy / Against the law / Play guitar / Rock and roll hoochie koo / Frankenstein. *(re-iss. Jul01 on 'Cleopatra'; CLP 1116CD)*

Thunderbolt Intersound

Jan 94. (cd) *(CDTB 152)* <9125> **NOT A KID ANYMORE**
– Way down south / I'm not a kid anymore / Against the law / Brother's keeper / I wanta rock / Crazy / Just like you / Big city woman / Innocent lust / Wild man / Frankenstein. *(re-iss. Aug97 on 'S.P.V.'; SPV 0844664-2)*

— In Apr 94; his former keyboard wizard, DAN HARTMAN, died of a brain tumour.

May 97. (cd) *(CDTB 182)* <9222> **THE REAL DEAL**
– Hoochie coo / The real deal / We can't win / Good ol' rock'n'roll / Nitty gritty / Eye of the storm / Sanctuary / Hot passionate love / Music is you / What do I tell my heart.

Eagle Rhino

Jun 99. (cd) *(EAGCD 041)* <75808> **WINTER BLUES**
– Good ol' shoe / Nu-orlins / Texas / New millennium / On the tip of my tongue / White man's blues / They only come out at night / It's only money / Show your love / You are my song.

– compilations, etc. –

1975. (7") *Epic; (152337)* **FRANKENSTEIN. / FREE RIDE** -
Jul 91. (cd/c; with JOHNNY) *Elite;* **BROTHERS IN ROCK'N'ROLL**
(re-iss. Sep93)
Apr 91. (cd/c/lp) *Columbia; (467507-2/-4/-1)* **THE BEST OF EDGAR WINTER** -
Aug 93. (cd) *Rhino; (8122 70709-2)* **MISSION EARTH**
May 95. (cd) *Rhino; (8122 70895-2)* **THE COLLECTION** -
Mar 98. (cd; with RICK DERRINGER) *Eagle; (EABCD 078)* **THE MASTERS** -

Johnny WINTER

Born: JOHN DAWSON WINTER III, 23 Feb'44, Leland, Mississippi, USA. Something of a musical child prodigy, WINTER grew up in Beaumont, Texas on a diet of blues and hard rock, gigging anywhere (often backed by bands including younger brother, EDGAR on piano and sax) and churning out singles for small local labels, sounding like anyone from BOB DYLAN to BOBBY 'BLUE' BLAND (an early band, JOHNNY AND THE JAMMERS, released the single 'SCHOOLDAY BLUES' on 'Dart' in 1959). WINTER hammered out power blues at amazing velocity and played some of the most ferocious slide guitar ever laid down on vinyl, a compression of MUDDY WATERS, ROBERT JOHNSON and ELMORE JAMES sped up to breakneck speed. By the late 60's he was totally into the blues, fronting a power trio including TOMMY SHANNON (bass – later to back STEVIE RAY VAUGHAN) and drummer JOHN 'RED' TURNER. This was the combination with which he made his major label breakthrough, signing to 'Columbia' on a five year, $300,000 contract in 1969 (a bargain as WINTER became the top live act of the early 70's). 'Imperial' Records stole 'Columbia's' thunder by releasing 'THE PROGRESSIVE BLUES EXPERIMENT' (a US Top 50 hit) as a one-off album prior to WINTERS' new company getting a record out. After two albums, the eponymous debut and 'SECOND WINTER', his manager steered him towards hard rock and, dumping SHANNON and TURNER, teamed him up with the 60's teen band, The McCOYS, to form, JOHNNY WINTER AND .... Two albums later (including the eponymous set which was to become his biggest seller outwith the US and included such choice fare as 'ROCK N ROLL HOOCHIE KOO', 'STORMY MONDAY' and Eddie Floyd's 'FIVE LONG YEARS), WINTER was in rehab with a severe heroin habit. His creative capacity was obviously suffering judging by the patchy-at-best quality of 'STILL ALIVE AND WELL' (1973) and 'JOHN DAWSON WINTER III' (1974), his first couple of releases for new label, 'Blue Sky'. He was subsequently reunited with brother, EDGAR for 'TOGETHER' in 1976 (a rag-bag of soul and old time rock'n'roll favourites). WINTER duly re-emerged with a renewed commitment to the blues and his biggest 70's achievements were the production of MUDDY WATERS' post 'Chess' albums beginning with 1977's 'HARD AGAIN' and his own 'NOTHIN BUT THE BLUES', recorded with the same band during the same sessions. 1978's 'WHITE HOT AND BLUE' marked the guitarist's final US chart entry (Top 200) for six years; a new band comprising WINTER, JON PARIS on bass and BOBBY TORDELLO on drums was formed for 'RAISIN CAIN' in 1980, subsequently signing to 'Alligator' Records prior to 1984's 'WHOOPIN'. 'GUITAR SLINGER', 'SERIOUS BUSINESS' and 'THIRD DEGREE' (a Grammy winner) followed over the next two years and although they were his best blues albums in years, they all failed to chart. WINTER subsequently attempted to re-enter the rock market with 'MCA's 'WINTER OF 88'; the results were poor and the man now records blues for 'Point Blank', his first release for the label being 1991's Grammy-nominated 'LET ME IN'. The Dick Shurman-produced album was a blistering return to form for the veteran bluesman. The same year he featured on JOHN LEE HOOKER's 'Mr. Lucky' and in 1992, sang 'HIGHWAY 61 REVISITED' at the BOB DYLAN Anniversary Tribute in Madison Square Garden. The 1992 follow-up, 'HEY WHERE'S YOUR BROTHER' (it's title a reference to brother EDGAR) was almost as good, following a similar formula and using the same production team. A gap of five years ensued before the release of 'LIVE IN NYC '97' (1998), a concert set documenting a performance at the Big Apple's 'Bottom Line' put together with the help of WINTERS' fan club. No surprise then, that the setlist was designed with longtime fans in mind, featuring a mix of classics and covers. Although WINTERS has been concentrating on touring for the past few years, a new studio album is planned for 2002. WINTER may not be the greatest white blues guitarist although he probably should have been and can still take the breath away on a good night. • **Songwriters:** J.WINTER or DERRINGER, with mostly covers; JUMPIN' JACK FLASH + SILVER TRAIN + LET IT BLEED + STRAY CAT BLUES + SILVER TRAIN (Rolling Stones) / HIGHWAY 101 (Van Morrison) / IT'S ALL OVER NOW (Bobby & Shirley Womack) / GREAT BALLS OF FIRE + WHOLE LOTTA SHAKIN' GOIN' ON (Jerry Lee Lewis) / LONG TALL SALLY + SLIPPIN' & SLIDIN' (Little Richard) / BONY MORONIE (Larry Williams) / JOHNNY B. GOODE + THIRTY DAYS (Chuck Berry) / ROCK & ROLL PEOPLE (John Lennon) / IT'S MY OWN FAULT (B.B. King) / HIGHWAY 61 REVISITED (Bob Dylan) / SHAME SHAME SHAME (Shirley Ellis) / RAISED ON ROCK (Elmore James) / ROCK ME BABY (Big Bill Broozy-Arthur Crudup) / GOOD MORNING LITTLE SCHOOLGIRL (Don & Bob) / BAREFOOTIN' (Robert Parker) / PLEASE COME HOME FOR CHRISTMAS (Charles Brown) / GOT MY BRAND ON YOU (Muddy Waters) / etc.

Album rating: WINTER, THE PROGRESSIVE BLUES EXPERIMENT (*4) / JOHNNY WINTER (*7) / SECOND WINTER (*8) / JOHNNY WINTER AND . . . (*7) / JOHNNY WINTER AND . . . LIVE (*6) / STILL ALIVE AND WELL (*6) / SAINTS AND SINNERS (*6) / JOHN DAWSON WINTER III (*5) / CAPTURED LIVE! (*5) / TOGETHER with Edgar Winter (*5) / NOTHIN' BUT THE BLUES (*6) / WHITE, HOT & BLUE (*4) / RAISIN' CAIN (*4) / WHOOPIN' (*4) / GUITAR SLINGER (*6) / SERIOUS BUSINESS (*5) / 3RD DEGREE (*4) / WINTER OF '88 (*5) / LET ME IN (*4) / HEY, WHERE'S YOUR BROTHER? (*5) / A ROCK'N'ROLL COLLECTION compilation (*7) / LIVE IN NYC '97 (*6)

JOHNNY WINTER – vocals, guitar, mandolin / with **EDGAR WINTER** – keyboards, alto saxophone / **TOMMY SHANNON** – bass, ukelele / **JOHN 'Red' TURNER** – percussion

Liberty Imperial

May 69. (lp) *(LBS 83240)* <12431> **WINTER, THE PROGRESSIVE BLUES EXPERIMENT** [ ] Apr69 [49]
– Rollin' and tumblin' / Tribute to Muddy / I got love if you want it / Bad luck and trouble / Help me / Mean town blues / Broke down engine / Black cat bones / It's my own fault / Forty-four. *(re-iss. 1973 on 'Sunset'; 50264) (re-iss. Oct79 on 'Liberty'; LBR 1001) (re-iss. Nov86 on 'Razor'; MACH 7) (cd-iss. Sep93 on 'I.T.M.')*

C.B.S. Columbia

Jun 69. (lp) *(CBS 63619)* <9826> **JOHNNY WINTER** [ ] May69 [24]
– I'm yours and I'm hers / Be careful with a fool / Dallas / Mean mistreater / Leland Mississippi blues / Good morning little schoolgirl / When you got a good friend / I'll drown in my tears / Back door friend. *(re-iss. Jan76; same) (re-iss. Nov85 on 'Edsel' lp/c; ED/CED 163) (cd-iss. Jan97 on 'Columbia'; 471218-2)*

Jul 69. (7") *(CBS 4386)* <44900> **I'M YOURS AND I'M HERS. / I'LL DROWN IN MY TEARS** [ ] [ ]

Jan 70. (d-lp;3-playing sides) *(CBS 66231)* <9947> **SECOND WINTER** [59] Nov69 [55]
– Memory pain / I'm not sure / The good love / Slippin' and slidin' / Miss Ann / Johnny B. Goode / Highway 61 revisited / I love everybody / Hustled down in Texas / I hate everybody / Fast life rider. *(re-iss. 1974; same) (re-iss. Apr89 on 'Edsel' lp/cd; ED/CD 312)*

Jan 70. (7") *(CBS 4794)* <45058> **JOHNNY B.GOODE. / I'M NOT SURE** [ ] Dec69 [92]

— band now **RICK DERRINGER** – guitar, producer repl. EDGAR who went solo / **RANDY JO HOBBS** – bass / **RANDY ZEHRINGER** (RICK's bro) – drums (all ex-McCOYS)

Oct 70. (lp) *(CBS 64117)* <30221> **JOHNNY WINTER AND** [29] Sep70 [ ]
– Guess I'll go away / Ain't that a kindness / No time to live / Rock and roll hoochie koo / Am I here? / Look up / Prodigal son / On the limb / Let the music play / Nothing left / Funky music. *(re-iss. Sep91 on 'Beat Goes On' lp/cd; BGO LP/CD 105)*

Nov 70. (7") <45260> **ROCK AND ROLL HOOCHIE KOO. / 21st CENTURY MAN** [–] [ ]

— **BOBBY CALDWELL** – drums repl. RANDY

May 71. (lp) *(CBS 64289)* <64289> **JOHNNY WINTER AND LIVE (live)** [20] Mar71 [40]
– Good morning little schoolgirl / It's my own fault / Jumpin' Jack Flash / Rock'n'roll medley: Great balls of fire – Long tall Sally – Whole lotta shakin' goin' on – Mean town blues – Johnny B.Goode. *(re-iss. 1974; same) (re-iss. Jan89 on 'Beat Goes On'; BGOLP 29) (cd-iss. Jun92; BGOCD 29)*

May 71. (7") *(CBS 7227)* <45368> **JUMPIN' JACK FLASH (live). / GOOD MORNING LITTLE SCHOOLGIRL (live)** [ ] Apr71 [89]

— Due to drugs problems, JOHNNY semi-retired. DERRINGER joined EDGAR WINTER Re-united w/DERRINGER in 1973, **RICHARD HUGHES** – drums repl. CALDWELL

Apr 73. (lp) *(CBS 65484)* <32188> **STILL ALIVE AND WELL** [ ] [22]
– Rock me baby / Can't you feel it / Cheap tequila / All tore down / Rock and roll / Silver train / Ain't nothing to me / Still alive and well / Too much seconal / Let it bleed. *(also on quad.Sep74; CQ 32188) (cd-iss. Apr93 on 'Sony Europe')*

Jun 73. (7") *(CBS 1620)* <45860> **SILVER TRAIN. / ROCK AND ROLL** [ ] [ ]

Sep 73. (7") <45899> **CAN YOU FEEL IT. / ROCK AND ROLL** [–] [ ]

Mar 74. (7") <46036> **BONY MORONIE. / HURTIN' SO BAD** [–] [ ]

Mar 74. (lp/c) *(CBS/40 65842)* <32715> **SAINTS AND SINNERS** [ ] Feb74 [42]
– Stone County / Blinded by love / Thirty days / Stray cat blues / Bad luck situation / Rollin' cross the country / Riot in cell block #9 / Hurtin' so bad / Bony Moronie / Feedback on Highway 101. *(cd-iss. Apr93 on 'Sony Europe') (cd-iss. Jul94; CK 66420)*

Apr 74. (7") *(CBS 2162)* <46006> **STONE COUNTY. / BAD LUCK SITUATION** [ ] Jan74 [ ]

Blue Sky Blue Sky

Nov 74. (7") *(CBS 2800)* **MIND OVER MATTER. / PICK UP ON MY MOJO** [ ] [–]

Dec 74. (lp/c) *(SKY/40 80586)* <33292> **JOHN DAWSON WINTER III** [ ] [78]
– Rock & roll people / Golden days of rock & roll / Self-destructable blues / Raised on rock / Stranger / Mind over matter / Roll with me / Love song to me / Pick up on my mojo / Lay down your sorrows / Sweet Papa John. *(cd-iss. Apr93 on 'Sony Europe')*

Dec 74. (7") <2754> **RAISED ON ROCK. / PICK UP ON MY MOJO** [–] [ ]

Feb 75. (7") <2756> **GOLDEN DAYS OF ROCK & ROLL. / STRANGER** [–] [ ]

— **FLOYD RADFORD** – guitar repl. DERRINGER.

Mar 76. (lp/c) *(SKY/40 69230)* <33944> **CAPTURED LIVE! (live)** [ ] [93]
– Bony Moronie / Roll with me / Rock & roll people / It's all over now / Highway 61 revisited / Sweet Papa John.

— Mid'76, teamed up with brother EDGAR on below set

— + **RICK DERRINGER** + **FLOYD RADFORD** – guitar / **CHUCK RUFF** + **RICHARD HUGHES** – drums / **RANDY JO HOBBS** – bass (DAN HARTMAN was now solo disco artist)

Jul 76. (lp/c; JOHNNY & EDGAR WINTER) *(SKY/40 81338)* <34033> **TOGETHER (live)** [ ] [89]
– Harlem shuffle / Soul man / You've lost that lovin' feeling / Rock'n'roll medley:- Slippin' & slidin' – Jailhouse rock – Tutti frutti – Sick & tired – I'm ready – Reelin' and rockin' – Blue sude shoes – Jenny take a ride – Good golly Miss Molly / Let the good times roll / Mercy, mercy / Baby whatcha want me to do. *(cd-iss. Jun93 on 'Sony Europe')*

Aug 76. (7") <2764> **SOUL MAN. / LET THE GOOD TIMES ROLL** [–] [ ]

— Early 1977, JOHNNY also produced and joined MUDDY WATERS band.

— with **CHARLES CALMESE** – bass / **WILLIE SMITH** – drums / **MUDDY WATERS** – guitar

Aug 77. (lp/c) *(SKY/40 82141)* <34813> **NOTHIN' BUT THE BLUES** [ ] Jul77 [ ]
– Tired of tryin' / TV mama / Everybody's blues / Sweet love and evil woman / Drinkin' blues / Mad blues / It was rainin' / Blondie Mae / Walking thru the park. *(re-iss. Aug91 on 'Beat Goes On' lp/cd; BGO LP/CD 104)*

— with **BOBBY TORELLO** – drums / **I.P.SWEAT** – bass / **PAT RUSH** – guitar / + **EDGAR**

Aug 78. (lp/c) *(SKY/40 82963) <35475>* **WHITE, HOT AND BLUE**
– Walkin' by myself / Slidin' in / Divin' duck blues / One stop at a time / Nickel blues / E-Z rider / Last night / Messin' with the kid / Honest I do. *(cd-iss. Jun93 on 'Sony Europe')*

— now with **BOBBY TORTELLO** – drums / **JON PARIS** – bass, etc.

May 80. (lp/c) *(SKY/40 84103) <36343>* **RAISIN' CAIN**
– The crawl / Sitting in this jail house / Like a rolling stone / New York, New York / Talk is cheap / Rollin' and tumblin' / Don't hide your love. *(cd-iss. Apr93 on 'Sony Europe')*

Sonet Alligator

Mar 84. (lp) **WHOOPIN'**
– I got my eyes on you / Sonny's whoopin' the doop / Burnt child / Whoee whoee / Crow Jane / So tough with me / Whoo wee baby / I think I got the blues / Ya ya / Roll me baby.

Aug 84. (lp) *(SNTF 914) <4735>* **GUITAR SLINGER**
– It's my life baby / Don't like advantage / Iodine in my coffee / Trick bag / Mad dog / Boothill / I smell trouble / Lights out / My soul / Kiss tomorrow goodbye. *(cd-iss. Oct86; SNTCD 914) <US cd-iss. 1990's; ALCD 4735>*

Sep 85. (lp) *(SNTF 948) <4742>* **SERIOUS BUSINESS**
– Master mechanic / Sound the bell / Murdering the blues / It ain't your business / Good time woman / Unseen eye / My time after a while / Serious as a heart attack / Give it back / Route 90. *(re-iss. Jun88 cd/c; SNTCD/ZCSN 948) <US cd-iss. 1988; ALCD 4742>*

Oct 86. (lp/cd) *(SNT F/CD 965) <4748>* **3RD DEGREE**
– Mojo boogie / Love, life and money / Evil on my mind / See see baby / Tin pan alley / I'm good / Third degree / Shake your moneymaker / Bad girl blues / Broke and lonely.

— now with **JON PARIS** – bass / **TOM COMPTON** – drums

M.C.A. Voyager-MCA

Nov 88. (lp/c/cd) *(MCF/MCFC/DMCF 3436) <42241>* **WINTER OF '88**
– Close to me / Stranger blues / Lightning / Anything for your love / Rain / Ain't that just like a woman / Looking for trouble / Look away.

Point Blank Virgin

Aug 91. (cd/lp) *(VPB CD/LP 5) <91744>* **LET ME IN**
– Illustrated man / Barefootin' / Life is hard / Hey you / Blue mood / Sugarlee / Medicine man / You're humbuggin' me / If you got a good woman / Got to find my baby / Shame shame shame / Let me in. *(cd+=)* – You lie too much.

— with **JEFF GANZ** – bass / **TOM COMPTON** – drums, percussion / guests **EDGAR** – sax / **BILLY BRANCH** – harmonica

Sep 92. (cd/c/lp) *(VPB CD/TC/LP 11) <86512>* **HEY, WHERE'S YOUR BROTHER?**
– Johnny Guitar / She likes to boogie real low / White line blues / Please come home for Christmas / You must have a twin / You keep sayin' that you're leavin' / Hard way / Sick and tired / Blues this bad / no more dogin' / Check out her mama / Got my brand on you. *(cd+=)* – One step forward (two steps back).

Mar 98. (cd) *(VPBCD 43) <45527>* **LIVE IN NYC '97 (live)**
– Hideaway / Sen-sa-shun – Got my mojo working / She likes to boogie real low / Blackjack / Just a little bit / The sun is shining / The sky is crying / Johnny Guitar / Drop the bomb.

– compilations, etc. –

1969. (7") *GRT;* **ROADRUNNER. / GANGSTER OF LOVE** –
1971. (lp) *Marble Arch; / GRT; <10010>* **THE JOHNNY WINTER STORY** Sep69
1970. (lp) *Buddah; (2359 011)* **FIRST WINTER** –
1971. (lp) *Janus; <3008>* **ABOUT BLUES** –
1971. (lp) *Janus; <3023>* **EARLY TIMES** –
Feb 81. (d-lp) *Blue Sky; (SKY 88457)* **THE JOHNNY WINTER STORY – RAISED ON ROCK**
Jul 84. (lp) *President; (PRCV 116)* **EARLY WINTER** –
(cd-iss. Jan87; PRCD 116)
Apr 86. (lp) *Showcase; (SHLP/SHTC 132)* **LIVIN' IN THE BLUES** –
(cd-iss. Oct90 on 'Thuderbolt'; CDTB 083)
Mar 87. (lp/c)(cd) *Topline; (TOP/KTOP 168)(TOPCD 515)* **OUT OF SIGHT** –
1988. (d-lp/c/cd) *Castle; (CCS LP/MC/CD 167)* **THE JOHNNY WINTER COLLECTION** –
– Rock and roll hoochie koo / Cheap tequila / On the lamb / Slippin' and slidin' / Johnny B.Goode / Rock me baby / Let it bleed / Stray cat blues / Riot in cell block 9 / Bony Moronie / Highway 61 revisited / Raised on rock / Pick up on my mojo / Thirty days / Good morning little school girl / Jumpin' Jack Flash / It's my own fault / Medley:- Great balls of fire – Long tall Sally – Whole lotta shakin' goin' on.

Jan 89. (lp) *Relix;* **BIRDS CAN'T ROW BOATS** –
Nov 89. (lp/cd) *Thunderbolt; (THBL/CDTB 073)* **FIVE AFTER 4 A.M.** –
Apr 90. (cd/lp; JOHNNY WINTER & UNCLE JOHN TURNER) *(THBL/CDTB 077)* **BACK IN BEAUMONT** –
Jul 91. (cd) *Thunderbolt; (CDTB 100)* **LIVE IN HOUSTON, BUSTED IN AUSTIN (live)** –
Feb 92. (cd; JOHNNY WINTER & CALVIN JOHNSON) *Thunderbolt; (CDTB 126)* **RAW TO THE BONE**
Aug 92. (cd/c) *Sony; (471661-2/-4)* **SCORCHIN' BLUES**
Nov 92. (cd) *Fan Club;* **LIVE AT LIBERTY HALL, HOUSTON, TX. 1972 (live with JIMMY REED)**
Feb 93. (cd) *Charly; (CDCD 1033)* **THE TEXAS TORNADO** –
Apr 93. (cd) *Pulsar;* **THE GOLDEN DAYS OF ROCK'N'ROLL** –
Nov 93. (cd) *Thunderbolt; (CDTB 149)* **WHITE LIGHTNING** –
Jul 94. (cd/c) *Success;* **LIVIN' THE BLUES** –
Jun 96. (cd) *Sony; (483897-2)* **A ROCK AND ROLL COLLECTION** –
Jan 97. (cd) *Thunderbolt; (CDTB 509)* **ELECTRIC BLUES MAN** –
Mar 96. (cd) *Thunderbolt; (CDTB 165) / Magnum; <41>* **BROKE AND LONELY**
Jan 97. (cd) *Sundazed; (SC 6070)* **LIVIN' IN THE BLUES** –
Jan 97. (cd) *Sundazed; (SC 6071)* **EASE MY PAIN** –
Feb 97. (cd) *Castle; (CCSCD 445)* **WINTER BLUES** –
Apr 97. (cd) *Carlton; (303600085-2)* **JOHNNY B. GOODE** –
Feb 98. (d-cd) *Snapper; (SMDCD 185)* **TEXAS BLUES**

Steve WINWOOD

Born: 12 May'48, Birmingham, Warwickshire, England. The young WINWOOD had his first encounter with rock'n'roll via his music loving uncle before beginning his illustrious career with his father's band. At the age of 15 (already an accomplished vocalist, guitarist and keyboard player), he joined The SPENCER DAVIS GROUP with brother MUFF, where he had three massive hits on the fledgling 'Island' records between 1963 and April 1967; the brilliant 'KEEP ON RUNNING', 'SOMEBODY HELP ME' and 'GIMME SOME LOVING'. Around this time he formed TRAFFIC and scored three more, newly psychedelicised UK Top 10 smashes, 'PAPER SUN', 'HOLE IN MY SHOE' and 'HERE WE GO ROUND THE MULBERRY BUSH'. In 1969, (still only 21) WINWOOD joined ERIC CLAPTON, GINGER BAKER and RIC GRECH in the short-lived supergroup, BLIND FAITH. Early the following year, he joined GINGER BAKER's AIRFORCE, subsequently returning to TRAFFIC in 1971. WINWOOD's first solo album was to have been 'MUD SHADOWS' in 1970 although it eventually surfaced as TRAFFIC album, 'JOHN BARLEYCORN MUST DIE', following the input of JIM CAPALDI and CHRIS WOOD. After leaving TRAFFIC, he made session appearances for TOOTS & THE MAYTALS, The SUTHERLAND BROTHERS and SANDY DENNY plus a guest spot on 'GO' by STOMU YAMASHTA. Having re-signed to 'Island' in 1976, his first solo venture (released at the onset of punk) was an undistinguished eponymous effort in 1977. His second release (taking two years to complete) 'ARC OF A DIVER' (1981) was produced, engineered and performed by WINWOOD himself with excellent results (the album and the extracted single 'WHILE YOU SEE A CHANCE' both reached US Top 10 while the album hit the UK Top 20). 'TALKING BACK TO THE NIGHT' (1982) was similar to the preceding album and had, in 'VALERIE', an outstanding highlight. 1986 saw WINWOOD joining the 80's tasteful coffee table elite with 'BACK IN THE HIGH LIFE', a record which sold three million copies in the US alone. One of the set's standouts, 'HIGHER LOVE' (with guest vocals by CHAKA KHAN), topped the US singles chart and earned him a Grammy. His contract with 'Island' expired shortly after and the label were outbid by 'Virgin', who reportedly secured WINWOOD's artistic services with an offer worth 13 million. His first release for the label, 'ROLL WITH IT', saw him teaming up with The MEMPHIS HORNS, such enduring songs as 'DANCING SHOES' and the fantastic title track ensured that WINWOOD would enjoy the fruits of his first No.1 album. The 1990 follow-up, 'REFUGEES OF THE HEART' was extremely disappointing, however, and together with CAPALDI, WINWOOD re-formed TRAFFIC for one set in 1994. It seemed that the short-lived TRAFFIC reformation hadn't exactly rejuvenated WINWOOD's muse judging by the insipid blandness of 'JUNCTION SEVEN' (1997). Co-produced by veteran knob-twiddler Narada Michael Walden, the album was coffee table soul-pop without the soul. It was a much more natural sounding WINWOOD who emerged in 2003 with 'ABOUT TIME', the first album for his own 'Wincraft' label. The downscaling seemed to have done him good, presumably inspiring him to also pare things back both in terms of arrangements and production. In place of the airbrushed fodder of his last effort was an easy going selection of jazzy, small-band R&B influenced by the chops of his latin sidemen: if it wasn't quite a VAN MORRISON, it does seem as if WINWOOD is headed back to his roots as he gets older. • **Songwriters:** For his debut in 1977, he co-wrote with JIM CAPALDI (an ex-member of TRAFFIC). He collaborated on some further releases with lyricist VIV STANSHALL, WILL JENNINGS and JOE WALSH. • **Trivia:** He was also a renowned session man, having played on albums by JIMI HENDRIX (1968 + 1970) / JOE COCKER (1969) / McDONALD & GILES (1970) / LEON RUSSELL (1970) / HOWLIN' WOLF (1971) / ALVIN LEE (1973) / JOHN MARTYN (1973) / AMAZING BLONDEL (1973) / JADE WARRIOR (1975) / TOOTS & THE MAYTALS (1976) / SANDY DENNY (1977) / VIVIAN STANSHALL (1978) / GEORGE HARRISON (1979) / MARIANNE FAITHFULL (1979) / PIERRE MOERLEN'S GONG (1979) / etc. (see other 'Island' label artists).

Album rating: STEVE WINWOOD (*7) / ARC OF A DIVER (*8) / TALKING BACK TO THE NIGHT (*6) / BACK IN THE HIGH LIFE (*8) / CHRONICLES compilation (*7) / ROLL WITH IT (*6) / REFUGEES OF THE HEART (*6) / THE FINER THINGS boxed-set compilation/history (*8) / JUNCTION SEVEN (*4) / ABOUT TIME (*5)

STEVE WINWOOD (debut solo recording was actually compiled from his past bands' work)

Island U.A.

May 71. (d-lp) *(ILPS 9964) <9950>* **WINWOOD** [ ] [93]
– (tracks by SPENCER DAVIS GROUP / TRAFFIC / BLIND FAITH / AIRFORCE)

— Later that year, WINWOOD reformed TRAFFIC and went into numerous session work mainly for 'Island' artists. In 1976, he and ex-SANTANA drummer MIKE SHRIEVE collaborated with solo classical percussionist STOMU YAMASH'TA. As **"GO"**, they issued eponymous live album in Jun76. When WINWOOD was releasing solo albums, GO also issued live 12" CROSSING THE LINE. Another album GO LIVE IN PARIS (live), was given light in Spring'78. (see STOMU YAMASH'TA discography)

STEVE WINWOOD

STEVE WINWOOD – vocals, keyboards solo with **WILLIE WEEKS** – bass / **ANDY NEWMARK** – drums / **REEBOP KWAKU BANU** – congas

Island Island

Jun 77. (7")*(WIP 6394)* **TIME IS RUNNING OUT. / PENULTIMATE ZONE** [ ] [–]
Jul 77. (7") **TIME IS RUNNING OUT. / HOLD ON** [–] [ ]
Jul 77. (lp/c) *(ILPS/ZCI <9494>)* **STEVE WINWOOD** [12] [22]
– Hold on / Time is running out / Midland maniac / Vacant chair / Luck's in / Let me make something in your life. *(cd-iss. May87; CID 9494) (re-iss. cd Mar93; IMCD 161)*

— His next projects/albums featured WINWOOD on all instruments, vocals

Dec 80. (lp/c) *(ILPS/ICT <9576>)* **ARC OF A DIVER** [13] [3]
– While you see a chance / Arc of a diver / Second-hand woman / Slowdown sundown / Spanish dancer / Night train / Dust. *(cd-iss. May87; CID 9576)*
Dec 80. (7"/c-s) *(WIP/CWIP 6655) <49656>* **WHILE YOU SEE A CHANCE. / VACANT CHAIR** [45] [7]
Mar 81. (7"/12") *(WIP/12WIP 6680)* **SPANISH DANCER (remix). / HOLD ON** [ ] [ ]
May 81. (7") *<49726>* **ARC OF A DIVER. / DUST** [–] [48]
Sep 81. (7"/12") *(WIP/12WIP 6710)* **NIGHT TRAIN. / ('A'instrumental)** [ ] [ ]
Nov 81. (7") *(WIP 6747)* **THERE'S A RIVER. / TWO WAY STRETCH** [ ] [ ]
Jul 82. (7") *(WIP 6786) <29940>* **STILL IN THE GAME. / DUST** [ ] [47]
Aug 82. (lp/c) *(ILPS/ICT <9777>)* **TALKING BACK TO THE NIGHT** [6] Jul82 [28]
– Valerie / Big girls walk away / And I go / While there's a candle burning / Still in the game / It was happiness / Help me angel / Talking back to the night / There's a river. *(cd-iss. May87; CID 9777)*
Sep 82. (7"/12") *(WIP/12WIP 6818) <29879>* **VALERIE. / SLOWDOWN SUNDOWN** [51] [70]
Jun 83. (7") *(WIP 6849)* **YOUR SILENCE IS YOUR SONG. / ('A'instrumental)** [ ] [ ]

— Around the mid-80's, his work took a back seat as his marriage broke down. In 1986, he brought in session musicians to augment.

Jun 86. (7") *(IS 288) <28710>* **HIGHER LOVE. / AND I GO** [13] [1]
(ext.12"+=) *(12IS 288)* – ('A'instrumental).
(c-s+=) *(CIS 288)* – Valerie / While you see a chance / Talking back to the night.
Jul 86. (lp/c/cd) *(ILPS/ICT/CID 9844) <25448>* **BACK IN THE HIGH LIFE** [8] [3]
– Higher love / Take it as it comes / Freedom overspill / Back in the high life again / The finer things / Wake me up on judgement day / Split decision / My love's leavin'.
Aug 86. (7") *<28595>* **FREEDOM OVERSPILL. / HELP ME ANGEL** [–] [20]
Aug 86. (7") *(IS 294)* **FREEDOM OVERSPILL. / SPANISH DANCER** [69] [–]
(some w/ c-s+=) *(IS 294)* – (last lp excerpts & interview).
(12"+=) *(12IS 294)* – ('A'-Liberty mix).
(12"w/ free 7") *(ISG 294)* – Low spark of high heeled boys / Gimme some lovin'.
(d7"+=) *(ISD 294)* – Higher love / And I go.
Jan 87. (7") *(IS 303)* **BACK IN THE HIGH LIFE AGAIN. / HELP ME ANGEL** [53] [–]
(12"+=) *(12IS 303)* – Night train (instrumental).
Feb 87. (7") *<28498>* **THE FINER THINGS. / NIGHT TRAIN** [–] [8]
May 87. (7") *<28472>* **BACK IN THE HIGH LIFE AGAIN. / NIGHT TRAIN (instrumental)** [–] [13]
Sep 87. (7") *(IS 336) <28231>* **VALERIE (remix). / TALKING BACK TO THE NIGHT (instrumental)** [19] [9]
(c-s+=/12"+=/cd-s+=) *(CIS/12IS/CID 336)* – The finer things.
Oct 87. (lp)(c)(cd) *(SSW/+MC/CD 1) <25660>* **CHRONICLES** (compilation) [12] [26]
– Wake me up on judgement day / While you see a chance / Vacant chair / Help me angel / My love's leavin' / Valerie / Arc of a diver / Higher love / Spanish dancer / Talking back to the night.
Feb 88. (7") *<28122>* **TALKING BACK TO THE NIGHT. / THERE'S A RIVER** [–] [57]

Virgin Virgin

May 88. (7"/ext.12") *(VS/+T 1085) <99326>* **ROLL WITH IT. / THE MORNING SIDE** [53] [1]
(cd-s+=) *(VSCD 1085)* – ('A'extended).
(c-s+=) *(VSTC 1085)* – ('A'dub version).
Jun 88. (cd/c/lp) *(CD/TC+/V 2532) <90946>* **ROLL WITH IT** [4] [1]
– Roll with it / Holding on / The morning side / Put on your dancing shoes / Don't you know what the night can do? / Hearts on fire / One more morning / Shining song.
Aug 88. (7") *(VS 1107) <99290>* **DON'T YOU KNOW WHAT THE NIGHT CAN DO? (remix). / ('A'instrumental)** [ ] [6]
(12"+=) *(VST 1107)* – ('A'extended).
(cd-s+=) *(VSCD 1107)* – Roll with it.
Oct 88. (7") *(VS 1135) <99261>* **HOLDING ON. / ('A'instrumental)** [ ] [11]
(3"cd-s+=/12"+=) *(VS T/CD 1135)* – ('A'dance version) / Go Juan.

Mar 89. (7") *<99234>* **HEARTS ON FIRE. / (instrumental)** [–] [53]

Oct 90. (7") *(VS 1299) <98892>* **ONE AND ONLY MAN. / ALWAYS** [ ] [18]
(12"+=/cd-s+=) *(VST/+CD 1299)* – ('A'extended).

Nov 90. (cd/c/lp) *(CD/TC+/V 2650) <91405>* **REFUGEES OF THE HEART** [26] [27]
– You'll keep on searching / Every day (oh Lord) / One and only man / I will be here / Another deal goes down / Running on / Come out and dance / In the light of day.

Apr 91. (7"/12") *(VS/+T 1317)* **I WILL BE HERE. / IN THE LIGHT OF DAY (Instrumental)** [ ] [–]

Mar 97. (c-s/cd-s) *(VSC/+DT 1642)* **SPY IN THE HOUSE OF LOVE / COME OUT AND DANCE** [ ] [–]

Jun 97. (cd/c) *(CDV/TCV 2832) <44059>* **JUNCTION SEVEN** [32] [ ]
– Spy in the house of love / Angel of mercy / Just wanna have some fun / Let your love come down / Real love / Fill me up / Gotta get back to my baby / Someone like you / Family affair / Plenty lovin' / Lord of the street.

Sanctuary Wincraft

Jun 03. (cd) *(SANCD 130) <1>* **ABOUT TIME** [ ] [ ]
– Different light / Cigano (for the gypsies) / Take it to the final hour / Why can't we live together / Domingo morning / Now that you're alive / Bully / Phoenix rising / Horizon / Walking on / Silvia (who is she?).

– compilations, others –

May 65. (7"; by ANGLOS) *Fontana; (TF 589)* **INCENSE. / YOU'RE FOOLING ME** [ ] [–]
(re-iss. May69 on 'Island'; WIP 6061)

Aug 91. (cd/c/lp) *Island; (CID/ICT/ILPS 9975)* **KEEP ON RUNNING** [ ] [ ]
– (tracks by SPENCER DAVIS GROUP / TRAFFIC / BLIND FAITH / + 2 solo) *(re-iss. cd Mar96; IMCD 224)*

Mar 95. (4xcd-box) *Island; (IBXCD 2)* **THE FINER THINGS** [ ] [ ]
– (tracks by SPENCER DAVIS GROUP / ERIC CLAPTON & POWERHOUSE / BLIND FAITH / TRAFFIC / STOMU YAMASH'TA's GO / solo)

WIRE

Formed: London, England . . . October '76, by GRAHAM LEWIS, COLIN NEWMAN, BRUCE GILBERT and ROBERT GOTOBED. WIRE made their vinyl debut in April '77 when safety pin-pierced ears were subjected to their punk anthems, '12XU' and 'LOWDOWN' on the seminal Various Artists lp, 'Live At The Roxy'. The EMI backed label 'Harvest', desperate for some hip punk credibility, decided to give WIRE a contract and although unsuccessful with their first single attempt ('MANNEQUIN'), unleashed the Mike Thorne-produced 'PINK FLAG' at the end of '77. The record contained 21 short, sharp shocks of minimalist punk rock/new wave, possessed of a musical intelligence that dwarfed their more retro-fixated contemporaries. Early in 1978, they followed this with the classic 'I AM THE FLY', lyrically a simple piece of what can only be described as progressive punk. After another fruitless stab at the charts with 'DOT DASH', they returned with an even more engaging second set, the oblique, atmospheric 'CHAIRS MISSING'. This record surely deserved better than its Top 50 placing, featuring as it did the classy avant-punk tunes, 'PRACTICE MAKES PERFECT', 'I FEEL MYSTERIOUS TODAY' and the "minor" hit 45, 'OUTDOOR MINER'. In the Autumn of '79, WIRE's third set, '154' hit the Top 40, effectively displaying an even more experimental side to the one-time three-chord wonders. Sadly, however, it was their final outing for 'Harvest', the group moving on to the more appropriate indie label, 'Rough Trade', who released the 1981 single, 'OUR SWIMMER'. An anti-commercial, unproduced live set appeared around the same time, the band members having already taken off for solo projects. One of these, DOME (aka GILBERT & LEWIS), had been in the pipeline for some time, while NEWMAN went on to indie success with several albums. In 1986, the much-in-demand WIRE returned, completing a few EP's for top indie, 'Mute' before the following year's 'THE IDEAL COPY' album. They continued to enjoy cult success, which even spread across the Atlantic, the band signing to US label, 'Enigma'. In 1991, GOTOBED retired (to Bedfordshire, no doubt?!) and the band became WIR, releasing the disappointing 'THE FIRST LETTER' that year. For the remainder of the 90's, each took on individual projects, all fairly obscure of course. With the nasty 90's out of the way, WIRE were back with the internet-friendly series releases, 'READ & BURN 01' (2002), a record that opened with the basic and incise 'IN THE ART OF STOPPING'. This track was the opener on their long-awaited full-set, 'SEND' (2003), a transitional, energetic return to form which also included new greats such as 'SPENT' and 'MR. MARX'S TABLE'. • **Songwriters:** Group compositions. • **Trivia:** COLIN NEWMAN produced The VIRGIN PRUNES in 1982 and FAD GADGET in 1984. He moved to India at this time, returning after a few years to live in Belgium where he founded 'Crammed Discs' records.

Album rating: PINK FLAG (*8) / CHAIRS MISSING (*9) / 154 (*7) / DOCUMENT AND EYEWITNESS: ELECTRIC BALLROOM (*3) / THE IDEAL COPY (*7) / A BELL IS A CUP . . . UNTIL IT IS STRUCK (*5) / ON RETURNING (1977-1979) compilation (*8) / IT'S BEGINNING TO & BACK AGAIN (*6) / MANSCAPE (*5) / THE FIRST LETTER (*4; as Wir) / SEND (*7)

COLIN NEWMAN (b.16 Sep'54, Salisbury, England) – vox, guitar, keyboards / **BRUCE GILBERT** (b.18 May'46, Watford, England) – guitar, vocals, synths. / **GRAHAM LEWIS** (b.22 Feb'53, Grantham, England) – bass, vocals, synthesizers / **ROBERT GOTOBED** (b. MARK FIELD, 1951, Leicester, England) – drums, percussion (ex-SNAKES, ex-ART ATTACKS) / **GEORGE GILL** – guitar (left before debut)

Harvest Harvest

Nov 77. (7"m) *(HAR 5144)* **MANNEQUIN. / 12XU / FEELING CALLED LOVE** [ ] [–]

Nov 77. (lp/c) *(SHSP/TC-SHSP 4076) <11757>* **PINK FLAG** [ ] [ ]
– Reuters / Field day for the Sundays / Three girl rhumba / Ex-lion tamer / Lowdown / Start to move / Brazil / It's so obvious / Surgeon's girl / Pink flag / The commercial / Straight line / 106 beats that / Mr. Suit / Strange / Fragile / Mannequin / Different to me / Champs / Feeling called love / 12XU. *(cd-iss. 1990 on 'Restless'+=; 72360)* – Options R. *(re-iss. cd Aug94 on 'E.M.I.'; CDGO 2063) <cd-iss. 1995 on 'Capitol'; 29857-2>*

Feb 78. (7") *(HAR 5151)* **I AM THE FLY. / EX-LION TAMER** [ ] [–]

Jun 78. (7") *(HAR 5161)* **DOT DASH. / OPTIONS R** [ ] [–]

Sep 78. (lp/c) *(<SHSP/TC-SHSP 4093>)* **CHAIRS MISSING** [48] [ ]
– Practice makes perfect / French film blurred / Another the letter / Men 2nd / Marooned / Sand in my joints / Being sucked in again / Heartbeat / Mercy / Outdoor miner / I am the fly / I feel mysterious today / From the nursery / Used to / Too late. *(cd-iss. 1990 on 'Restless'+=; 72361)* – Go ahead / A question of degree / Former airline. *(re-iss. cd Aug94 on 'E.M.I.'; CDGO 2065) <cd-iss. 1995 on 'Capitol'; 29858-2>*

Jan 79. (7",7"white) *(HAR 5172)* **OUTDOOR MINER. / PRACTICE MAKES PERFECT** [51] [–]

Harvest Warners

Jun 79. (7") *(HAR 5187)* **A QUESTION OF DEGREE. / FORMER AIRLINE** [ ] [–]

Sep 79. (lp/c) *(SHSP/TC-SHSP 4105) <3398>* **154** [39] [ ]
– I should have known better / Two people in a room / The 15th / The other window / Single k.o. / A touching display / On returning / A mutual friend / Blessed state / Once is enough / Map reference 41°N, 93°W / Indirect enquiries / 40 versions. *(free-7"ep w.a) (Dome; PSR 444)* – Song 2 / Get down (parts 1 & 2) / Let's panic / Later / Small electric piece. *(cd-iss. 1990 on 'Restless'+= 72362)* – (7"ep above). *(re-iss. cd Aug94 on 'E.M.I.'; CDGO 2064) <cd-iss. 1995 on 'Capitol'; 39859> (cd re-iss. Jul99; CDGO 2064)*

Oct 79. (7") *(HAR 5192)* **MAP REFERENCE 41°N 93°W. / GO AHEAD** [ ] [–]

— In 1980, WIRE also diverged into own activities; GILBERT & LEWIS became CUPOL and DOME, etc. The pair also joined THE THE. COLIN NEWMAN went solo taking ROBERT GOTOBED with him. The latter also became member of FAD GADGET. (see further on for these activities)

Rough Trade — not iss.

May 81. (7") *(RT 079)* **OUR SWIMMER. / MIDNIGHT BAHNHOF CAFE** – –

Jul 81. (lp) *(ROUGH 29)* **DOCUMENT AND EYEWITNESS: ELECTRIC BALLROOM (live)** – –
– 5 10 / 12XU (fragment) / Underwater experiences / Zegk hoqp / Everything's going to be nice / Instrumental (thrown bottle) / Piano tuner (keep strumming those guitars) / And then . . . / We meet under tables / Revealing trade secrets / Eels sang lino / Eastern standard / Coda. *(free 12"m-lp)* **DOCUMENT AND EYEWITNESS: NOTRE DAME HALL (live)** – Underwater experiences / Go ahead / Ally in exile / Relationship / Our swimmer / Witness to the fact / 2 people in a room / Heartbeat. *(re-iss. 1984 lp/c; same/ COPY 004) (cd-iss. Apr91 on 'Grey Area-Mute'; WIRE 80CD)*

Mar 83. (12"m) *(RTT 123)* **CRAZY ABOUT LOVE. / SECOND LENGTH (OUR SWIMMER) / CATAPULT 30** – –

—— WIRE were now back to full-time membership.

Mute — Enigma

Nov 86. (12"ep) *(12MUTE 53)* <72245> **SNAKEDRILL**
– A serious of snakes / Advantage in height / Up to the sun / Drill.

Mar 87. (7") *(MUTE 57)* **AHEAD. / FEED ME (live)** – –
(12"+=) *(12MUTE 57)* – Ambulance chasers (live) / Vivid riot of red (live).

Apr 87. (cd/c/lp) *(CD/C+/STUMM 42)* <273270> **THE IDEAL COPY** 87
– Points of collapse / Ahead / Madman's honey / Feed me / Ambitious / Cheeking tongues / Still shows / Over theirs. *(cd+=)* – Ahead II / SNAKEDRILL EP tracks.

Mar 88. (7") *(MUTE 67)* **KIDNEY BONGOS. / PIETA**
(3"cd-s+=) *(CDMUTE 67)* – Drill (live).
(12"++=) *(12MUTE 67)* – Over theirs (live).

May 88. (cd/c/lp) *(CD/C+/STUMM 54)* <73314-1> **A BELL IS A CUP . . . UNTIL IT IS STRUCK**
– Silk skin paws / The finest drops / The queen of Ur and the king of Um / Free falling divisions / It's a boy / Boiling boy / Kidney bongos / Come back in two halves / Follow the locust / A public place. *(cd+=)* – The queen of Ur and the king of Um (alternate take) / Pieta / Over theirs (live) / Drill (live).

Jun 88. (7") *(MUTE 84)* **SILK SKIN PAWS. / GERMAN SHEPHERDS**
(12"+=) *(12MUTE 84)* – Ambitious (remix).
(3"cd-s+=) *(CDMUTE 84)* – Come back in two halves.

Apr 89. (7"clear; withdrawn) *(MUTE 87)* **EARDRUM BUZZ. / THE OFFER** 68
(12"+=) *(12MUTE 87)* – It's a boy (instrumental).
(cd-s) *(CDMUTE 87)* – ('A'side) / Silk skin paws / A serious of snakes / Ahead (extended).
(live-12") *(LMUTE 87)* – BUZZ BUZZ BUZZ – Eardrum buzz / Ahead / Kidney bongos.

Mute — Mute

May 89. (cd/c/lp) *(CD/C+/STUMM 66)* <73516-2> **IT'S BEGINNING TO AND BACK AGAIN (live)**
– Finest drops / Eardrum buzz / German shepherds / Public place / It's a boy / Illuminated / Boiling boy / Over theirs / Eardrum buzz (12"version) / The offer / In vivo.

Jul 89. (7") *(MUTE 98)* **IN VIVO. / ILLUMINATED**
(12"+=/cd-s+=) *(12/CD MUTE 98)* – Finest drops (live).

May 90. (7"; w-drawn) *(MUTE 107)* **LIFE IN THE MANSCAPE. / GRAVITY WORSHIP** –
(12"+=/cd-s+=) *(12/CD MUTE 107)* – Who has wine.

May 90. (cd/c/lp) *(CD/C+/STUMM 80)* <73559-2> **MANSCAPE**
– Patterns of behaviour / Goodbye ploy / Morning bell / Small black reptile / Torch it / Other moments / Sixth sense / What do you see? / Where's the deputation? / You hung your lights in the trees – A craftman's touch. <US cd+=> – Life in the manscape / Stampede / Children of groceries.

Apr 91. (cd/c/lp) *(CD/C+/STUMM 74)* **DRILL**
– (7 versions of out-takes from last album)

WIR

—— slightly different name when GOTOBED left

Sep 91. (7") *(MUTE 107)* **SO AND SLOW IT GOES. / NICE FROM HERE** –
(12") *(12MUTE 107)* – ('A'side) / ('A'-Orb mix) / Take it (LFO mix)
(cd-s+=) *(CDMUTE 107)* – (all 4 tracks).

Oct 91. (cd/c/lp) *(CD/C+/STUMM 87)* <61238> **THE FIRST LETTER**
– Take it (for greedy) / So and slow it goes (extended) / A bargain at 3 and 20 yeah! / Rootsi-rootsy / Ticking mouth / It continues / Looking at me (stop!) / Naked, whooping and such-like / Tailor made / No cows on the ice / A big glue canal.

—— allo 4 members were back again

pinkflag.www — pinkflag.www

Nov 00. (7") *(VPF 3)* **TWELVE TIMES YOU. / X U (version)** –

May 02. (m-cd) *(<PF 4>)* **READ & BURN 01**
– In the art of stopping / I don't understand / Comet / Germ ship / 1st fast / The Agfers of Kodack.

Apr 03. (cd) *(<PF 6CD>)* **SEND** May03
– In the art of stopping / Mr Marx's table / Being watched / Comet / The Agfers of Kodack / Nice streets above / Spent / Read and burn / You can't leave now / Half eaten / 99.9.

– compilations, others, etc. –

Mar 86. (m-lp) *Pink; (PINKY 7)* **PLAY POP** –

Aug 86. (lp) *Dojo; (DOJOLP 36)* **IN THE PINK (live)** –

Nov 87. (12"ep) *Strange Fruit; (SFPS 041)* **THE PEEL SESSIONS** (18.1.78) –
– I am the fly / Culture vultures / Practice makes perfect / 106 beats that.

Jul 89. (cd)(c/lp) *Harvest; (CDP 792 535-2)(TC+/SHSP 4127) / Restless; <72358-1>* **ON RETURNING (1977-1979)**
– 12XU / It's so obvious / Mr. Suit / Three girl rhumba / Ex lion tamer / Lowdown / Strange / Reuters / Feeling called love / I am the fly / Practise makes perfect / French film blurred / I feel mysterious today / Marooned / Sand in my joints / Outdoor miner / A question of degree / I should have known better / The other window / 40 versions / A touching display / On returning. *(cd+=)* – Straight line / 106 beats that / Field day for the Sundays / Champs / Dot dash / Another the letter / Men 2nd / Two people in a room / Blessed state. *(cd re-iss. Feb00; same)*

Feb 90. (cd/c/lp) *Strange Fruit; (SFR CD/MC/LP 108)* **DOUBLE PEEL SESSIONS** –
(cd re-iss. May96; same)

May 93. (cd/c/d-lp) *Mute; (CD/C+/STUMM 116)* **1985-1990 THE A LIST** –

Sep 94. (cd; w/book) *Audioglobe; (SCONC 25)* **EXPLODING VIEWS** –

May 95. (cd) *E.M.I.; (CDGO 2066)* **BEHIND THE CURTAIN** –

Dec 95. (12"; WIRE with HAFLER TRIO) *Touch; (TONE 5)* **THE FIRST LETTER / THE LAST LAST NUMBER** –

May 96. (cd) *W.M.O.; (WMO 004CD)* **TURNS AND STROKES** –
– Safe / Lorries / Panamanian craze / Remove for improvement / Spare one / Over my head / 12XU / Inventory / Ritual view / Part of our history / Second length (our swimmer) / Catapult 30.
(d-lp-iss.Apr97; same)

Oct 97. (cd) *W.M.O.; (WMO 014CD) / World Domination; <67>* **COATINGS**
– Ambulance chasers / Series of snakes / Ambitious / Madman's honey / Kidney bongos / It's a boy / German shepherds / Boling boy / Drill / In vivo / Who has nine? / It can't be true can it? / Gravity worship. *(w/ free cd-s)* – AMBITIOUS

Sep 00. (3xcd-box) *E.M.I.; (528357-2)* **PINL FLAG / CHAIRS MISSING / 154** –

WISHBONE ASH

Formed: Torquay, Devon, England . . . summer 1969 out of the EMPTY VESSELS, by MARTIN TURNER and STEVE UPTON. They quickly moved to London with two new members; ANDY POWELL and TED TURNER (no relation). In 1970, they signed to 'M.C.A.' and delivered their eponymous debut into the UK Top 40. They were described at the time as Britain's answer to The ALLMAN BROTHERS, albeit with a mystical lyrical element. Fusing heavy-rock with fine harmonies and self-indulgent solos, the second album, the Top 20 'PILGRIMAGE' was more of the same. Their third album, 'ARGUS' (1972) broke them through big time, a compelling hybrid of arcane medieval themes and water-tight prog-rock. This classic Top 3 album featured, 'WARRIOR', 'THE KING WILL COME' and 'THROW DOWN THE SWORD' alongside the more freely flowing, 'BLOWIN' FREE' (a record that should have given them a hit). 'WISHBONE FOUR' was completed the following year, a mellower set with a rootsier country-rock feel, especially on the track, 'BALLAD OF THE BEACON'. After a double live set in '73, they took an even more down-home approach on 'THERE'S THE RUB', although it did contain one highlight, 'F*U*B*B*' (Fucked Up Beyond Belief). Although they managed to retain some (very!) loyal fans, by the end of the decade they had lost all their credibility when most of the original members left. In 1981, they even drafted in folky/new-age vocalist, CLAIRE HAMILL, in an attempt to develop other areas of their sound. They are still treading the boards, churning out new versions of their once classic songs, two live albums of recent material being recorded in Chicago and Geneva respectively. • **Songwriters:** Group compositions / TURNER's.

Album rating: WISHBONE ASH (*5) / PILGRIMAGE (*6) / ARGUS (*8) / WISHBONE FOUR (*6) / LIVE DATES (*8) / THERE'S THE RUB (*5) / LOCKED IN (*4) / NEW ENGLAND (*4) / CLASSIC ASH compilation (*8) / FRONT PAGE NEWS (*5) / NO SMOKE WITHOUT FIRE (*5) / JUST TESTING (*4) / LIVE DATES II (*5) / NUMBER THE BRAVE (*4) / TWIN BARRELS BURNING (*4) / RAW TO THE BONE (*4) / NOUVEAU CALLS (*4) / HERE TO HEAR (*4) / STRANGE AFFAIR (*4) / THE ASH LIVE IN CHICAGO (*4) / BLOWIN' FREE – THE VERY BEST OF . . . compilation (*7) / LIVE IN GENEVA (*4) / ILLUMINATIONS (*3) / TRANCE VISIONARY (*4) / PSYCHIC TERRORISM (*4) / BONAFIDE (*5)

MARTIN TURNER (b. 1 Oct'47) – vocals, bass / **ANDY POWELL** (b. 8 Feb'50) – guitar, vocals repl. GLEN TURNER (no relation) / **TED TURNER** (b.DAVID, 2 Aug'50) – guitar, vocals (ex-KING BISCUIT) / **STEVE UPTON** (b.24 May'46, Wrexham, Wales) – drums

M.C.A. Decca

Dec 70. (lp) *(MKPS 2014)* *<75249>* **WISHBONE ASH** 34
– Blind eye / Lady Whiskey / Error of my ways / Queen of torture / Handy / Phoenix. *(re-iss. Feb74 lp/c; MCG/TCMCG 3507) (re-iss. 1980; MCA 2343) (cd-iss. Jul91) (cd-iss. Dec94 on 'Beat Goes On'; BGOCD 234)*

Jan 71. (7") *(MK 5061)* *<32826>* **BLIND EYE. / QUEEN OF TORTURE**

Sep 71. (lp) *(MDKS 8004)* *<75295>* **PILGRIMAGE** 14
– Vas dis / The pilgrim / Jail bait / Alone / Lullaby / Valediction / Where were you tomorrow. *(re-iss. Feb74 lp/c; MCG/TCMCG 3504) (re-iss. Dec83 lp/c; MCL/+C 1762) (cd-iss. Jul91; DMCL 1762) (cd re-iss. 1990's; MCLD 19084) (+=)* – Baby what you want me to do / Jail bait (live).

Oct 71. (7") *<32902>* **JAIL BAIT. / VAS DIS** –

May 72. (lp) *(MDKS 8006)* *<75437>* **ARGUS** 3
– Time was / Sometime world / Blowin' free / The king will come / Leaf and stream / Warrior / Throw down the sword. *(re-iss. Feb74 lp/c; MCG/TCMCG 3510) (re-iss. Feb84 lp/c; MCL/+C 1787) (re-iss. 1987 on 'Castle' lp/c; CLA LP/MC 140) (cd-iss. 1991; DMCL 1787) (cd re-iss. 1990's; MCLD 19085) (cd re-mast.Mar02; 112816-2)*

Jun 72. (7") *(MKS 5097)* *<33004>* **BLOWIN' FREE. / NO EASY ROAD**

M.C.A. M.C.A.

May 73. (lp) *(MDKS 8011)* *<327>* **WISHBONE FOUR** 12 44
– So many things to say / Ballad of the beacon / No easy road / Everybody needs a friend / Doctor / Sorrel / Sing out the song / Rock and roll widow. *(re-iss. Feb74 lp/c; MCG/TCMCG 3505)*

Jul 73. (7") *<40041>* **ROCK AND ROLL WIDOW. / NO EASY ROAD** –

Jul 73. (7") *(MUS 1210)* **SO MANY THINGS TO SAY. / ROCK'N'ROLL WIDOW** –

Dec 73. (d-lp) *(ULD 1-2)* *<2-8006>* **LIVE DATES (live)** Nov73 82
– The king will come / Warrior / Throw down the sword / Rock'n'roll widow / Ballad of the beacon / Baby what you want me to do / The pilgrim / Blowin' free / Jail bait / Lady Whiskey / Phoenix. *(re-iss. Jun74 d-lp/c; MCSP/+C 254) (cd-iss. Sep95 on 'Beat Goes On'; BGOCD 293)*

— (Jun'74) **LAURIE WISEFIELD** – guitar (ex-HOME) repl. TED who found religion

Nov 74. (7") *(MCA 165)* **HOMETOWN. / PERSEPHONE** –

Nov 74. (lp/c) *(MCF/TCMCF 2585)* *<464>* **THERE'S THE RUB** 16 88
– Silver shoes / Don't come back / Persephone / Hometown / Lady Jay / F*U*B*B.

Feb 75. (7") *(MCA 176)* *<40362>* **SILVER SHOES. / PERSEPHONE**

— added on session **PETER WOODS** – keyboards

M.C.A. Atlantic

Mar 76. (lp/c) *(MCF/TCMCF 2750)* *<18164>* **LOCKED IN** 36
– Rest in peace / No water in the well / Moonshine / She was my best friend / It started in Heaven / Half past lovin' / Trust in you / Say goodbye. *(cd-iss. Nov02 on 'Repertoire'; REP 4557)*

Nov 76. (lp/c) *(MCG/TCMCG 3523)* *<18200>* **NEW ENGLAND** 22
– Mother of pearl / (In all of my dreams) You rescue me / Runaway / Lorelei / Outward bound / Prelude / When you know love / Lonely island / Candle-light. *(re-iss. Jul82 lp/c; MCL/+C 1699)*

Nov 76. (7") *(MCA 261)* *<3381>* **OUTWARD BOUND. / LORELEI**

M.C.A. M.C.A.

Sep 77. (7") *(MCA 326)* **FRONT PAGE NEWS. / DIAMOND JACK** –

Oct 77. (lp/c) *(MCG/+C 3524)* *<2311>* **FRONT PAGE NEWS** 31
– Front page news / Midnight dancer / Goodbye baby hello friend / Surface to air / 714 / Come in from the rain / Right or wrong / Heart beat / The day I found your love / Diamond Jack. *(re-iss. Feb82 lp/c; MCL/+C 1655)*

Oct 77. (7") *<40829>* **FRONT PAGE NEWS. / GOODBYE BABY, HELLO FRIEND** –

Nov 77. (7") *(MCA 327)* **GOODBYE BABY, HELLO FRIEND. / COME IN FROM THE RAIN** –

Sep 78. (7"/12") *(MCA/12MCA 392)* **YOU SEE RED. / BAD WEATHER BLUES (live)** –

Oct 78. (lp/c) *(MCG/+C 3528)* *<3060>* **NO SMOKE WITHOUT FIRE** 43
– You see red / Baby the angels are here / Ships in the sky / Stand and deliver / Anger in harmony / Like a child / The way of the world (part 1 & 2) / A stormy weather. *(w/ free live 7")* – COME IN FROM THE RAIN. / LORELEI *(cd-iss. May98; MCLD 19374)*

Aug 79. (7") *(MCA 518)* **COME ON. / FAST JOHNNY**

Jan 80. (7") *<41214>* **HELPLESS. / INSOMNIA** –

Jan 80. (7") *(MCA 549)* **LIVING PROOF. / JAIL BAIT (live)** –

Jan 80. (lp/c) *(MCF/TCMCF 3052)* **JUST TESTING** 41
– Living proof / Haunting me / Insomnia / Helpless / Pay the price / New rising star / Master of disguise / Lifeline. *(cd-iss. May98; MCLD 19375)*

Apr 80. (7"/12") *(MCA/+T 577)* **HELPLESS (live). / BLOWIN' FREE (live)** –

Oct 80. (d-lp/c) *(MCG/+C 4012)* **LIVE DATES II (live)** 40
– Doctor / Living proof / Runaway / Helpless / F*U*B*B / The way of the world / Lorelei / Persephone / You rescue me / Time was / Goddbye baby hello friend / No easy road. *(ltd. w/ free live lp) (re-iss. Jun84; MCL 1799)*

— **JOHN WETTON** – bass, vocals (ex-URIAH HEEP, ex-FAMILY, ex-KING CRIMSON) repl. MARTIN TURNER to production. / added **CLAIRE HAMILL** – vocals (solo artist)

Mar 81. (7") *(MCA 695)* **UNDERGROUND. / MY MIND IS MADE UP** –

Apr 81. (lp/c) *(MCF/+C 3103)* **NUMBER THE BRAVE** 61
– Loaded / Where is the love / Underground / Kicks on the street / Open road / Get ready / Rainstorm / That's that / Rollercoaster / Number the brave.

May 81. (7") *(MCA 726/+/MCL 14)* **GET READY. / KICKS ON THE STREET** –

May 81. (7") *<51149>* **GET READY. / LOADED** –

— **UPTON, POWELL + WISEFIELD** recruited new member **TREVOR BOLDER** – bass (ex-SPIDERS FROM MARS / Bowie, ex-URIAH HEEP, etc. repl. WETTON to ASIA, etc.

A.V.M. Fantasy

Oct 82. (7") *(WISH 1)* **ENGINE OVERHEAT. / GENEVIEVE** –

Nov 82. (lp/c) *(ASH/+C 1)* *<F 9629>* **TWIN BARRELS BURNING** 22 1983
– Engine overheat / Can't fight love / Genevieve / Me and my guitar / Hold on / Streets of shame / No more lonely nights / Angels have mercy / Wind up. *(cd-iss. Aug93 on 'Castle'; CLACD 389)*

Dec 82. (7") *(1002)* **NO MORE LONELY NIGHTS. / STREETS OF SHAME** –

— **MERVYN 'Spam' SPENCER** – bass (ex-TRAPEZE) repl. BOLDER to URIAH HEEP

Neat not iss.

Jan 85. (lp/pic-lp/c) *(NEAT/+P/C 1027)* **RAW TO THE BONE** –
– Cell of fame / People in motion / Don't cry / Love is blue / Long live the night / Rocket in my pocket / It's only love / Don't you mess / Dreams (searching for an answer) / Perfect timing. *(re-iss. Aug93 on 'Castle'; CLACD 390)*

— **ANDY PYLE** – bass (ex-SAVOY BROWN, ex-BLODWYN PIG) repl. SPENCE

— Originals (**ANDREW, STEVE, MARTIN & TED**) reformed WISHBONE ASH.

I.R.S.-MCA I.R.S.-MCA

Feb 88. (lp/c/cd) *(MIRF/CMIRF/DMIRF 1028) <42101>* **NOUVEAU CALLS** (instrumental)
– Tangible evidence / Closseau / Flags of convenience / From Soho to Sunset / Arabesque / In the skin / Something's happening in Room 602 / Johnny left home without it / The spirit flies free / A rose is a rose / Real guitars have wings. *(re-iss. 1990 lp/c/cd; ILP/+MC/CD 39) (cd re-iss. Aug99 on 'Power Bright'; PBVP 005CD) (cd re-iss. Mar03 on 'Talking Elephant'; TECD 050)*

May 88. (7") *(IRM 164)* **IN THE SKIN. / TANGIBLE EVIDENCE** –

— In Apr89, TED & ANDY guested on their labels' Various Artists live cd,c,d-lp, video 'NIGHT OF THE GUITAR'.

I.R.S. I.R.S.

Jun 89. (7") *(EIRS 104)* **COSMIC JAZZ. / T-BONE SHUFFLE** –
(12"+=) *(EIRST 104)* – Bolan's monument.

Aug 89. (lp/c/cd) *(EIRSA/+C/CD 1006) <82006>* **HERE TO HEAR**
– Cosmic jazz / Keeper of the light / Mental radio / Walk on water / Witness on wonder / Lost cause in Paradise / Why don't we / In the case / Hole in my heart (part 1 & 2). *(cd re-iss. Feb03 on 'Talking Elephant'; TECD 049)*

— **RAY WESTON** – drums; repl. MARTIN

May 91. (lp/c/cd) *(EIRSA/+C/CD 1045)* **STRANGE AFFAIR** –
– Strange affair / Wings of desire / Dream train / You / Hard times / Standing in the rain / Renegade / Say you will / Rollin' / Some conversion. *(cd re-iss. Feb03 on 'Talking Elephant'; TECD 048)*

— **POWELL + TED TURNER + RAY** bring in **ANDY PYLE** – bass / **DAN C. GILLOGLY** – keyboards

Permanent Griffin

Mar 92. (cd/c/lp) *(PERM CD/MC/LP 6) <476>* **THE ASH LIVE IN CHICAGO (live)** Dec95
– The king will come / Strange affair / Standing in the rain / Lost cause in Paradise / Keeper of the light / Throw down the sword / In the skin / Why don't we? / Hard times / Blowing free / Living proof. *(cd re-iss. Jun99 as 'LIVING PROOF . . .' on 'Right'; RIGHT 005) (cd re-iss. Sep02 on 'Platinum'; PLATCD 909)*

— **POWELL** recruited an entire new line-up:- **ROGER FILGATE** – guitar / **TONY KISHMAN** – bass / **MIKE STRURGIS** – drums

Hengest Pavement

Mar 96. (cd) *(HNRCD 03) <32255>* **LIVE IN GENEVA (live)** Mar97
– The king will come / Strange affair / Thrown down the sword / In the skin / Hard times / Blowin' free / Keeper of the light / Medley: Blind eye – Lady Whiskey – Jail bait – Phoenix – The pilgrim / Runaway / Sometime world / Vas dis. *(re-iss. Jul99 on 'S.P.V.'; 076-1846-2)*

— **MARK TEMPLETON + MIKE MINDEL** – keyboards (FILGATE now bass); repl. KISHMAN

H.T.D. Renaissance

Oct 96. (cd) *(HTDCD 67) <181>* **ILLUMINATIONS** Nov96
– Mountainside / On your own / Top of the world / No joke / Tales of the wise / Another time / A thousand years / The ring / Comfort zone / Mystery man / Wait out the storm / The crack of dawn. *(re-iss. Jul01 on 'Talking Elephant'; TECD 012)*

Invisible Hands Resurgent

Apr 98. (cd) *(IHCD 12) <140>* **TRANCE VISIONARY** Jun99
– Numerology / Wonderful stash / Heritage / Interfaze / Powerbright (black and white screen) / Remnants of a paranormal managerie / Narcissus nervosa / Trance visionary / Flutterby / Banner headlines / The loner / Powerbright volition / Gutterfly / Wronged by righteousness.

Ration-L Resurgent

Oct 00. (d-cd) *(RALVP 004CD) <4580>* **PSYCHIC TERRORISM** Apr00
– Translitetion / Narcissus stash / Sleeps eternal slave / Monochrome / Breaking out / The son of righteousness / Psychic terrorism / How many times / Bloodline / Back page muse / Powerbright conclusion // Powerbright industrial / Dub visionary / X-ert heritage / Original powerbright / Wonderful nervosa / Powerthrack / Wrong or write / Wonderful stash.

— **POWELL** now with **BEN GRANFELT** – guitar, vocals / **BOB SKEAT** – bass, keyboards, vocals / **RAY WESTON** – drums

Talking Elephant not iss.

May 02. (cd) *(TECD 040)* **BONAFIDE** –
– Almighty blues / Enigma / Faith, hope and love / Ancient remedy / Changing tracks / Shoulda, woulda, coulda / Bonafide / Difference in time / Come rain, come shine / Peace.

– compilations, others, etc. –

— on 'M.C.A.' unless stated otherwise

Apr 77. (7"ep) *(MCA 291)* **PHOENIX. / BLOWIN' FREE / JAIL BAIT** –

May 77. (lp/c) *(MCF/TCMCF 2795)* **CLASSIC ASH**
– Blind eye / Phoenix / The pilgrim / Blowin' free / The king will come / Rock'n'roll widow / Persephone / Outward bound / Throw down the sword (live). *(re-iss. Aug81 lp/c; MCL/+C 1621) (re-iss. Jan83 on 'Fame' lp/c; FA/TCFA 3053)*

Jan 82. (lp) *(5283-27126)* **HOT ASH** –

Apr 82. (d-c) *(MCA 2103)* **PILGRIMAGE / ARGUS** –

May 82. (lp) *(MCF 3134)* **THE BEST OF WISHBONE ASH**

Oct 91. (cd) *Windsong; (WINCD 004)* **LIVE IN CONCERT (live)** –

1993. (d-cd) *<MCAD2 10765>* **TIME WAS** (w/ remixed 'ARGUS') –

Mar 94. (cd/c) *Nectar; (NTR CD/MC 014)* **BLOWIN' FREE – THE VERY BEST OF WISHBONE ASH** –

Sep 94. (cd/c) *(MCLD/MCLC 19249)* **THERE'S THE RUB / LOCKED IN** –

Nov 94. (cd) *Start; (HP 93452)* **IN CONCERT** –

Jan 97. (cd) *Receiver; (RRCD 216)* **LIVE – TIMELINE (live)** –

Nov 97. (cd) *Rialto; (RMCD 224)* **ARCHIVE** –

Feb 98. (cd) *(<MCAD 11620>)* **THE BEST OF WISHBONE ASH** Jul97
– Blind eye / Phoenix / The pilgrim / Lorelei (live) / Sometime world / Warrior / Throw down the sword / Persephone / F.U.B.B. / Blowin' free / Living proof.

Apr 98. (cd) *Culture Press; (CP 1002)* **MOTHER OF PEARL (live)** –

Jun 98. (4xcd-box) *Repertoire; (REP 4649WX)* **DISTILLATION**

Nov 98. (cd) *Power Bright; (PBVP 001CD)* **FROM THE ARCHIVES VOL.1** –

Nov 98. (cd) *Power Bright; (PBVP 002CD)* **FROM THE ARCHIVES VOL.2** –

Jan 99. (cd) *Power Bright; (PBVP 003CD)* **FROM THE ARCHIVES VOL.3** –

Mar 99. (cd) *Beat Goes On; (BGOCD 405)* **NEW ENGLAND / FRONT PAGE NEWS** –

Mar 99. (cd) *Strange Fruit; (SFRSCD 021)* **ON AIR: THE BBC SESSIONS** –

Oct 99. (cd) *Receiver; (<RRCD 276>)* **THE KING WILL COME – LIVE**

Nov 99. (cd) *H.T.D.; (HTDCD 104) / Silverline; <288088>* **BARE BONES** Feb00
– Wings of desire / Errors of my way / Master of disguise / You won't take me down / Love abuse / (Won't you give him) One more chance / Baby don't mind / Living proof / Hard times / Strange affair / Everybody needs a friend. *(re-iss. Aug01 on 'Talking Elephant'; TECD 022) (cd re-iss. Apr02 on 'Castle'; TRACD 332)*

Feb 01. (cd) *Eagle; (EAGCD 172)* **LIVE DATES 3 (live)** –

Oct 01. (cd) *(MCLD 19401)* **BLOWIN' FREE: AN INTRODUCTION TO . . .** –

Mar 02. (cd) *Angel Air; (SJPCD 112)* **LIVE IN WINDY CITY (live)** –

Oct 02. (d-cd) *Talking Elephant; (TECD 045)* **RAW TRACKS** –

Mar 03. (cd) *Spectrum; (113066-2)* **THE COLLECTION** –

Sep 03. (cd) *Classic Rock Legends; (CRP 1139)* **ALMIGHTY BLUES – LONDON & BEYOND (live)** –

Oct 03. (d-cd) *Snapper; (<SMDCD 483>)* **WARRIORS** Jan04

Nov 03. (d-cd) *Talking Elephant; (TECD 056)* **TRACKS VOL.2** –

Nov 03. (cd) *Classic Rock Legends; (CRP 1045)* **LIVE IN BRISTOL** –

Bill WITHERS

Born: 4 Jul'38, Slab Fork, West Virginia, USA. The youngest child in a family whose offspring ran into double figures, WITHERS came to the music industry relatively late in life. He joined the navy in his teens and began singing and writing songs during his nine year tenure, settling in Los Angeles upon his discharge in the mid-60's. While working full-time in an aerospace factory, BILL did the rounds of the major West Coast record companies and publishers with his own demo tape although his efforts proved fruitless. His talent was finally recognised by Sussex Records who financed the recording of a debut album with BOOKER T JONES at the helm. The result was 'JUST AS I AM' (1971), its title indicative of the thirty-something singer/songwriter's lack of gimmick or pretence. WITHERS' acoustic, Sunday morning folk-soul possessed a gnarly, lived-in authenticity that saw the likes of 'AIN'T NO SUNSHINE' make the US Top 3. A million seller, this classic track featured backing from the MG's DONALD "DUCK" DUNN and AL JACKSON as well as STEPHEN STILLS, symptomatic of WITHERS' closer proximity – at least musically – to L.A.'s white troubadours than its handful of genuine soul acts. The album itself nudged into the Top 40 although follow-up 'GRANDMA'S HANDS' stalled just outside. 1972's sophomore long player, 'STILL BILL' was just as strong, spawning the timeless, universally themed 'LEAN ON ME'. This gospel flavoured favourite topped both the pop and R&B charts in the summer of '72 and has since been covered by everyone from TERRY CALLIER and BETH ORTON to CLUB NOUVEAU. The latter's 1987 remake resulted in WITHERS' receiving a belated Grammy award (his third) in recognition of his songwriting skills. Second single 'USE ME' was almost as big (narrowly missing No.1) if not quite so enduring. At the height of his fame the singer brought the house down at at Carnegie Hall, an event documented in 1973's 'LIVE AT CARNEGIE HALL'. 1974 saw the release of his final Sussex effort, '+JUSTMENTS' as well as a performance alongside the likes of JAMES BROWN and B.B. KING at Muhammad Ali's legendary 'Rumble In The Jungle' in Zaire. Although WITHERS subsequently signed to 'Columbia', albums such as 'MAKING MUSIC' (1975), 'NAKED AND WARM' (1976) and 'MENAGERIE' (1977) veered increasingly towards MOR/adult contemporary territory. The latter set spawned another of WITHERS' languid calling cards, 'LOVELY DAY', a US Top 30 hit first time round and a belated UK hit just over a decade later (after it was used in a TV commercial). 1979's 'BOUT LOVE', meanwhile, was a collection of romantic musings co-penned by gospel pianist PAUL SMITH. Although he wasn't to release another solo set until 1985's 'WATCHING YOU WATCHING ME', in the meantime the man shared his vocal talents with jazz-funk artists such as The CRUSADERS and GROVER WASHINGTON Jr, earning a Grammy for his 1981, near chart-topping duet ('JUST THE TWO OF US') with WASHINGTON. Save the aforementioned mid-80's album, WITHERS has been notable by his absence from the music scene although he continues to tour and his classic early 70's work is still treasured by many.

Album rating: JUST AS I AM (*8) / STILL BILL (*7) / LIVE AT CARNEGIE HALL (*5) / +'JUSTMENTS (*5) / MAKING MUSIC: THE BEST OF BILL WITHERS compilation (*7) / NAKED & WARM (*5) / MENAGERIE (*5) / 'BOUT LOVE (*5) / BILL WITHERS' GREATEST HITS compilation (*6) / WATCHING YOU WATCHING ME (*4) / LEAN ON ME: THE BEST OF . . . (*8)

BILL WITHERS – vocals, guitar / with session people/band

A&M | Sussex

May 71. (7") *(AMS 845)* **EVERYBODY'S TALKIN'. / HARLEM** — [ ] [ ]

Aug 71. (lp) *(AMLS 65002)* <7006> **JUST AS I AM** — [ ] Jun71 [39]

– Harlem / Ain't no sunshine / Grandma's hands / Sweet Wanomi / Everybody's talkin' / Do it good / Hope she'll be happier / Let it be / I'm her daddy / In my heart / Moanin and groanin / Better off dead.

Sep 71. (7") *(AMS 858)* <219> **AIN'T NO SUNSHINE. / HARLEM** — [ ] Jul71 [3]

Oct 71. (7") <227> **GRANDMA'S HANDS. / SWEET WANOMI** — [–] [42]

Jul 72. (7") *(AMS 7004)* <235> **LEAN ON ME. / BETTER OFF DEAD** — [18] Apr72 [1]

Aug 72. (lp) *(AMLH 68107)* <7014> **STILL BILL** — [ ] May72 [4]

– Lonely town, lonely street / Let me in your life / Who is he / Use me / Lean on me / Kissing my love / I don't know / Another day to run / I don't want you on my mind / Take it all in and check it all out.

Oct 72. (7") *(AMS 7038)* <241> **USE ME. / LET ME IN YOUR LIFE** — [ ] Aug72 [2]

Nov 72. (7") <247> **LET US LOVE. / THE GIFT OF GIVING** — [–] [47]

Mar 73. (7") *(AMS 7055)* <250> **KISSING MY LOVE. / I DON'T KNOW** — [ ] Jan73 [31]

May 73. (7") *(AMS 7068)* **LOOK WHAT I FOUND. / THE LADY IS WAITING** — [ ] [–]

Jul 73. (d-lp) *(AMLD 3001)* <7025> **LIVE AT CARNEGIE HALL (live)** — [ ] Apr73 [63]

– Use me / Friend of mine / Ain't no sunshine / Grandma's hands / The world keeps going around / Let me in your life / Better off dead / For my friend / I can't write left handed / Lean on me / Lonely town, lonely street / Hope she'll be happier / Let us love / Harlem – Cold baloney. *(cd-iss. Nov97 on 'Columbia'; 488987-2)*

Jun 73. (7") <257> **FRIEND OF MINE. / LONELY TOWN, LONELY STREET** — [–] [80]

Sep 73. (7"m) *(AMS 7080)* **AIN'T NO SUNSHINE. / HARLEM / GRANDMA'S HANDS** — [ ] [–]

Apr 74. (7") *(AMS 7108)* <513> **THE SAME LOVE THAT MADE ME LAUGH. / MAKE A SMILE FOR ME** — [ ] [50]

Jun 74. (lp) *(AMLH 68230)* <8032> **+'JUSTMENTS** — [ ] Mar74 [67]

– You / The same love that made me laugh / Stories / Green grass / Ruby Lee / Heartbreak road / Can we pretend / Liza / Make a smile for me / Railroad man.

Sussex | Sussex

Feb 75. (7") *(SXX 7)* <629> **HEARTBREAK ROAD. / RUBY LEE** — [ ] Dec74 [89]

Apr 75. (7") *(SXX 9)* **LEAN ON ME. / USE ME** — [ ] [–]

Jul 75. (lp) *(LPSX 10)* <8037> **BEST OF BILL WITHERS** (compilation) — [ ] May75 [ ]

C.B.S. | Columbia

Dec 75. (7") <10255> **MAKE LOVE TO YOUR MIND. / I LOVE YOU DAWN** — [–] [76]

Dec 75. (lp) *(CBS 69183)* <33704> **MAKING MUSIC** — [ ] Oct75 [81]

– I wish you well / The best you can / Make love to your mind / I love you Dawn / She's lonely / Sometimes a song / Paint your pretty picture / Family table / Don't you want to stay / Hello like before.

Dec 76. (lp/c) *(CBS/40 81580)* <34327> **NAKED & WARM** — [ ] Oct76 [ ]

– Close to me / Naked & warm / Oh heaven / Where are you? / Dreams / If I didn't mean you well / I'll be with you / City of the angels / My imagination.

Nov 77. (7") *(CBS 5773)* <10627> **LOVELY DAY. / IT AIN'T BECAUSE OF ME BABY** — [7] [30]

Jan 78. (lp/c) *(CBS/40 82265)* <34903> **MENAGERIE** — [27] Oct77 [39]

– Lovely day / I want to spend the night / Lovely night for dancing / Then you smile at me / She wants to (get on down) / It ain't because of me baby / Tender things / Wintertime / Let me be the one you need. *(re-iss. Nov85 lp/c; CBS/40 32694)*

Mar 78. (7") *(CBS 6193)* **LOVELY NIGHT FOR DANCING. / LET ME BE THE ONE YOU NEED** — [ ] [ ]

Mar 79. (7") *(CBS 7052)* **DON'T MAKE IT BETTER. / LOVE IS** — [ ] [ ]

Apr 79. (lp/c) *(CBS/40 83176)* <35596> **'BOUT LOVE** — [ ] [ ]

– All because of you / Dedicated to you my love / Don't it make it better / You got the stuff / Look to each other for love / Love love is / Memories are that way.

—— in Feb'81, BILL featured on GROVER WASHINGTON's hit single, 'Just The Two Of Us'

Jun 81. (7") *(A 1403)* **I WANT TO SPEND THE NIGHT. / MEMORIES ARE THAT WAY** — [ ] [ ]

Jun 81. (lp/c) *(CBS/40 84710)* <37199> **BILL WITHERS' GREATEST HITS** (compilation) — [ ] May81 [ ]

– Who is he what is he to you / Use me / Ain't no sunshine / Harlem / I want to spend the night / Grandma's hands / City of the angels / Tender things / Lovely day / Lean on me. *(re-iss. 1987; CBS/40 32343) (cd re-iss. Oct94 on 'Columbia'; 477503-2)*

Feb 82. (7") *(A 2000)* **U.S.A. / PAINT YOUR PRETTY PICTURE** [ ] [ ]

— in Aug'84, he featured on RALPH McDONALD's hit, 'In The Name Of Love'

May 85. (7") *(A 6154)* **OH YEAH! / JUST THE FIRST TIME** [60] [ ]
(12"+=) *(TA 6154)* – Ain't no sunshine.

Jun 85. (lp/c) *(CBS/40 26200)* <39887> **WATCHING YOU WATCHING ME** [60] May85 [ ]
– Oh yeah! / Something that turns you on / Don't make me wait / Heart in your life / Watching you watching me / We could be sweet lovers / You just can't smile it away / Steppin' right along / Whatever happens / You try to find a love.

— BILL retired from the biz except for the odd tour

– compilations, etc. –

released on 'Columbia' ('CBS' before 1989) unless mentioned otherwise

Aug 80. (7") *(CBS 8865)* **LOVELY DAY. / LOVELY NIGHT FOR DANCING** [ ] [–]

Jul 82. (7") *Old Gold; (OG 9186)* **LEAN ON ME. / AIN'T NO SUNSHINE** [ ] [–]

1987. (7") *Old Gold; (OG 9729)* **LOVELY DAY. / OH YEAH!** [ ] [–]

Jul 87. (7") *(650992-7)* **LOVELY DAY. / LOVELY NIGHT FOR DANCING** [ ] [–]
(12"+=) *(650992-6)* – Lean on me.

Aug 88. (7") *(653001-7)* **LOVELY DAY (sunshine remix). / (original version)** [4] [–]
(12"+=/cd-s+=) *(653001-6/-2)* – Lean on me / Ain't no sunshine.

Sep 88. (lp/c/cd) *(CBS/40/CD 32343)* **GREATEST HITS** [90] [ ]
(cd/c re-iss. Jun99; same)

Apr 89. (lp/c/cd) *Blatant; (BLAT LP/MC/CD 13)* **THE SOUND OF SOUL** [ ] [–]

Apr 90. (cd/c/lp) *(466824-2/-4/-1)* **LOVELY DAYS** [ ] [ ]
– Lovely day (sunshine mix) / Use me / Ain't no sunshine (eclipse mix) / Harlem / Kissing my love / Lean on me / Steppin' right along / Grandma's hands / Lonely town, lonely street / Who is he and what is he to you?

May 95. (cd) *(480506-2)* **LEAN ON ME – THE BEST OF BILL WITHERS** [ ] [ ]
– Ain't no sunshine / Grandma's hands / Lean on me / Use me / Kissing my love / Who is he and what is he to you? / I don't want you on my mind / Same love that made me laugh / Hello like before / Lovely day / Let me be the one you need / I want to spend the night / Stepping right along / Whatever happens / Watching you watching me / Heart is your life / Try to find a love / Just the two of us.

Oct 98. (cd) *(491961-2)* **LOVELY DAY: THE BEST OF BILL WITHERS** [ ] [ ]

Jan 01. (3xcd-box) *(500604-2)* **THE ULTIMATE BILL WITHERS COLLECTION** [ ] [ ]

☐ WIZZARD (see under ⇒ MOVE)

Andrew W.K.

Born: ANDREW WILKES-KRIER, 9 May'79, Los Angeles, California, USA. Like all very eccentric or barmy musicians who unwittingly debut on to any scene, ANDREW W.K. was deemed as an industry joke, either set up by DAVE GROHL (one rumour suggested that GROHL wrote all of W.K.'s tracks) or orchestrated by a very intelligent comedian who wanted to prove to the world that people would lap up anything that was hyped up enough – even if it was thrash stadium rock. But looking closer at W.K. the press and public realised enough that, like Forrest Gump running across America for no apparent reason, the long-haired rocker had no intention of hoaxing anyone, he was just a rocking, partying, hard-working madman. Raised in Michigan, ANDREW finally moved to New York where he became synonymous with the trendy underground scene. Although he didn't fit in with the poetic, garage angst of The STROKES or the anti-folk meanderings of The MOLDY PEACHES, W.K. created such a buzz with his debut single, the brilliantly titled 'GIRLS OWN JUICE' (from the 'AWKGOJ' EP) in May 2000. 'PARTY TILL YOU PUKE' was issued at the end of the year and W.K. performed live for the first time in a Starbucks cafe with electro-clash wizards FISHERSPOONER. Mixing 80's spandex rock with the outright disgrace of The BEASTIE BOYS' '(You Gotta) Fight For Your Right (To Party)', and if one person deserved to have a custom-made, notch 11 amp, then it was W.K., as he thrashed his way through the dumb-as-shit rock tracks that nobody would have paid attention to five years ago. On this alone, he secured a deal with 'Mercury' records and issued the 'PARTY HARD' single in 2001, a smash-it-up, thrash-glam record with classical piano amid the IRON MAIDEN/VAN HALEN riffs. Its catchy chorus ("We do what we like and we like what we do!" and stonking guitars and drums no doubt helped it enter the UK Top 20 while a sold-out tour of the country warmed his audiences up for the release of his absolutely insane debut album 'I GET WET' (2001) – sleeve complete with a bloody-lipped W.K. By the time he came to release sophomore set, 'WOLF' (2003), everybody and their dog were doing unembarrassingly unreconstructed cock-rock. Which only made Mr W.K. sound even more innovative than he (n)ever really was, easing into his role as an aberrant, latter-day AXL ROSE with a dash of BON JOVI-style stadium savvy, lyrical platitudes and all.

Album rating: I GET WET (*8) / THE WOLF (*7)

ANDREW W.K. – vocals, arranger / **JEFF HOLMES** – keyboards, etc / **TONY ALLEN** – drums

not iss. / Bulb

May 00. (cd-ep) <BLB 068> **AWKGOJ EP** [–] [ ]
– Girls own juice / Don't ever stop the noise / We want fun / Music or die / Make sex.

Dec 00. (12"ep) <BLB 073> **PARTY TIL YOU PUKE** [–] [ ]
– Party til you puke (3 version) / Old man / Dance party / I want to kill.

— now with **F.T. THOMAS** – guitar / **CHRIS CHANEY** – bass / **GARY NOVAK** – drums

Mercury / Mercury

Oct 01. (7") *(588813-7)* **PARTY HARD. / VIOLENT LIFE** [19] [–]
(cd-s+=) *(588813-2)* – Make sex / ('A'-video).

Nov 01. (cd) <(586588-2)> **I GET WET** [71] [84]
– It's time to party / Party hard / Girl's own love / Ready to die / Take it off / I love NYC / She is beautiful / Party 'til you puke / Fun night / Got to do it / I get wet / Don't stop living in the red. *(lp-iss.Mar03; AA314 586588-1)*

Feb 02. (7") *(588973-7)* **SHE IS BEAUTIFUL. / WE WANT FUN** [55] [–]
(cd-s+=) *(588952-2)* – AWK / ('A'-video).

Mercury / Island

Sep 03. (cd) *(9860814)* <105102> **THE WOLF** [ ] [61]
– Victory strikes again / Long live the party / Tear it up / Free jumps / Never let down / Your rules / The song / Make sex / Totally stupid / Really in love / The end of our lives / I love music.

Bobby WOMACK

Born: 4 Mar'44, Cleveland, Ohio, USA. Along with his four siblings, CECIL, CURTIS, HARRIS, FRIENDLY Jnr and BOBBY formed The WOMACK BROTHERS as a gospel quintet in 1959. It wasn't long before he met SAM COOKE who subsequently snapped him up to play guitar in his own gospel outfit, The SOUL STIRRERS. In early 1960, COOKE formed the L.A.-based 'SAR' label with manager J.W. Alexander and promptly added the brothers to his roster, renaming them The VALENTINOS after the following year's debut single, 'SOMEBODY'S WRONG'. A handful of classy R&B singles followed while two of them, 'IT'S ALL OVER NOW' and 'LOOKIN' FOR A LOVE' became major hits for The ROLLING

STONES and The J.GEILS BAND respectively. After SAM COOKE's controversial death in 1964, Alexander had a dispute with COOKE's widow, Barbara (whom BOBBY married three months later) and subsequently shut down 'SAR'. Although The VALENTINOS soon followed suit, BOBBY's songwriting and performing credentials were already well established and although he began recording for new label, 'Him', most of his time was taken up by session work for the likes of ARETHA FRANKLIN, RAY CHARLES and WILSON PICKETT. As well as playing on the latter's 'Funky Broadway' single, WOMACK penned a series of tracks for PICKETT including 'I'M IN LOVE' and 'I'M A MIDNIGHT MOVER'. The two also became great buddies and it isn't difficult to hear similarities in their gritty soul-shout vocal style; WOMACK himself was nicknamed 'The PREACHER'. After a brief spell at 'Chess', he signed to Liberty's R&B subsidiary, 'Minit', where he cut a series of fair to middling solo singles, none of which were big hits. His final effort for the label was 'THE WOMACK LIVE (LIVE '68)', a Hollywood-recorded concert set that pitted masterful interpretations of soul classics like Sam Cooke's 'LAUGHING AND CLOWNING' and Percy Mayfield's 'TO LIVE THE PAST' against his characteristic penchant for seemingly incongruous cover material i.e. The Mamas And The Papas' 'CALIFORNIA DREAMIN' and Fred Neil's 'Everybody's Talkin'. The square-spectacled soul man had more success with his 'United Artists' (who took over over 'Liberty') recordings which he kicked off in late 1971 with his first (US) Top 30 hit, 'THAT'S THE WAY I FEEL ABOUT 'CHA'. WOMACK's impressive development as both a singer and songwriter was illustrated the following year with the release of two great albums, 'COMMUNICATION' and 'UNDERSTANDING', the latter featuring BOBBY's fond ode to his brother HARRY (who was subsequently stabbed to death by his own wife in 1978), 'HARRY HIPPIE'. 1972 was also the year of SLY & THE FAMILY STONE's seminal 'There's A Riot Goin' On', to which WOMACK added his famous wah-wah guitar; his well documented friendship with the wayward SLY STONE led them both off the rails in the early 70's as they became increasingly dependent on drugs and the high-rolling L.A. lifestyle. Following the lead of contemporaries MARVIN GAYE and CURTIS MAYFIELD, WOMACK cut a blaxploitation soundtrack in 1973 for the movie, 'ACROSS 110th STREET' and although the classic title track remains arguably one of the finest marriages of soul and pop ever committed to vinyl, the project failed to bring BOBBY the same fame as ISAAC HAYES' 'Shaft' which was screened around the same time. A series of back to basics Muscle Shoals-recorded efforts followed in the form of 'FACTS OF LIFE' (1973), 'LOOKIN' FOR A LOVE AGAIN' (1974), 'I DON'T KNOW WHAT THE WORLD IS COMING TO' (1975) and 'SAFETY ZONE' (1976) although only the old VALENTINOS song, 'LOOKIN' FOR A LOVE' was a major hit (US Top 10) in 1974. 1976, meanwhile saw the release of his brave country-soul set, 'B.W. GOES C & W', one of the poorest selling albums of his career. Things didn't get much better as he recorded another couple of flop albums for 'Columbia', 'HOME IS WHERE THE HEART IS' (1977) and 'PIECES' (1978), closing the decade with a patchy one-off set for 'Arista', 'ROADS OF LIFE' (1979) as he tried to come to terms with the cot death of his baby son. Salvation came in the form of CRUSADERS man, WILTON FELDER who asked WOMACK to sing on his solo album, 'Inherit The Wind'; the title track was a UK hit and its success provided the impetus for BOBBY's creative and critical rebirth with 'THE POET' (1982). One of that sterile decade's few soul records of any lasting worth, WOMACK had succeeded in updating his classic soulman stance without being swamped by new technology, singing his pain on the massive R&B hit, 'IF YOU THINK YOU'RE LONELY NOW'. Yet more strife followed however as he fought a protracted court battle with his new label, 'Beverly Glen' over non-payment of royalties. Nevertheless, a second instalment, 'THE POET II' (1984), finally emerged on 'Motown', hitting the UK Top 40 and enjoying further critical acclaim due in part to some stunning duets with PATTI LaBELLE. Following another collaboration with FELDER, WOMACK returned to his Memphis roots for 'WOMAGIC' (1986), hooking up with veteran country-soul man, Chips Moman. For the remainder of the decade, WOMACK kept a low profile, occasionally popping up on other artist's albums (notably the ROLLING STONES' 'Dirty Work'). The 90's brought another period of personal upheaval before the true soul survivor finally re-emerged with 'RESURRECTION' (1994). • **Songwriters:** All his own work, except covers:- CALIFORNIA DREAMIN' (Mamas & The Papas) / SWEET CAROLINE (Neil Diamond) / I WISH IT WOULD RASIN (Temptations) / LIVING IN A BOX (Living In A Box) / etc. • **Trivia:** His brother CECIL became part of WOMACK & WOMACK team with wife LINDA.

Album rating: FLY ME TO THE MOON (*6) / MY PRESCRIPTION (*6) / THE WOMACK "LIVE" (*5) / COMMUNICATION (*6) / UNDERSTANDING (*6) / ACROSS 110th STREET soundtrack (*6) / FACTS OF LIFE (*6) / LOOKIN' FOR A LOVE AGAIN (*5) / BOBBY WOMACK'S GREATEST HITS compilation (*6) / I DON'T KNOW WHAT THE WORLD IS COMING TO (*5) / SAFETY ZONE (*5) / BW GOES C&W (*4) / HOME IS WHERE THE HEART IS (*4) / PIECES (*4) / ROADS OF LIFE (*4) / THE POET (*7) / THE POET II (*8) / SOMEDAY WE'LL ALL BE FREE (*4) / SO MANY RIVERS (*5) / WOMAGIC (*4) / THE SOUL MAN (*4) / MIDNIGHT MOVER: THE BOBBY WOMACK COLLECTION compilation (*8)

VALENTINOS

BOBBY, CECIL, CURTIS, HARRY + FRIENDLY Jnr

		not iss.	S.A.R.
Nov 61.	(7"; as WOMACK BROTHERS) *<118>* **SOMEBODY'S WRONG. / YIELD NOT TO TEMPTATION**	–	
Jul 62.	(7") *<132>* **LOOKIN' FOR A LOVE. / SOMEWHERE THERE'S A GIRL**	–	72
Sep 62.	(7") *<137>* **I'LL MAKE IT ALRIGHT. / DARLING COME BACK HOME**	–	97
Feb 63.	(7") *<144>* **SHE'S SO GOOD TO ME. / BABY, LOT'S OF LUCK**	–	
Jun 64.	(7") *<152>* **IT'S ALL OVER NOW. / TIRED OF LIVING IN THE COUNTRY** *(UK-iss.1968 on 'Soul City'; SC 106)*	–	94
Sep 64.	(7") *<155>* **EVERYBODY WANTS TO FALL IN LOVE. / BITTER DREAMS**	–	

—— they split later in the year. On February '65, BOBBY married SAM COOKE's widow, BARBARA. That year, he recorded for new label 'Him', but time was mostly taken up by session work for RAY CHARLES, WILSON PICKETT and other 'Atlantic' artists. In 1966, he signed for the label, but he mainly wrote for PICKETT before briefly moving to 'Chess'.

BOBBY WOMACK

		Minit	Minit
Sep 67.	(7") *<32024>* **TRUST ME. / BABY, I CAN'T STAND IT**	–	
Feb 68.	(7") *(MLF 11001) <32030>* **BROADWAY WALK. / SOMEBODY SPECIAL**		
Apr 68.	(7") *(MLF 11005) <32037>* **WHAT IS THIS. / WHAT YOU GONNA DO (WHEN YOUR LOVE HAS GONE)**		
Sep 68.	(7") *(MLF 11010) <32048>* **FLY ME TO THE MOON. / TAKE ME**		Aug68 52
Dec 68.	(lp) *<24014>* **FLY ME TO THE MOON** – Fly me to the Moon / Baby, you oughta think it over / I'm a midnight mover / What is this / Somebody special / Take me / Moonlight in Vermont / Love, the time is now / I'm in love / California dreamin' / No money in my pocket / Lillie-Mae.	–	
Jan 69.	(7") *(MLF 11012) <32055>* **CALIFORNIA DREAMIN'. / BABY! YOU OUGHTA THINK IT OVER**		Nov68 43

Apr 69. (7") *<32059>* **I LEFT MY HEART IN SAN FRANCISCO. / LOVE, THE TIME IS NOW** –

Jul 69. (7") *<32071>* **IT'S GONNA RAIN. / THANK YOU** –

Nov 69. (7") *<32081>* **HOW I MISS YOU BABY. / TRIED AND CONVICTED** – 93

Feb 70. (lp) *<24027>* **MY PRESCRIPTION** –
– How I miss you baby / More than I can stand / It's gonna rain / Everyone's gone to the Moon / I can't take it like a man / I left my heart in San Francisco / Arkansas state prison / I'm gonna forget about you / Don't look back / Tired and convicted / Fly me to the Moon / Thank you.

Apr 70. (7") *<32093>* **MORE THAN I CAN STAND. / ARKANSAS STATE PRISON** – 90

not iss. Liberty

Jun 70. (7") *<56186>* **I'M GONNA FORGET ABOUT YOU. / DON'T LOOK BACK** –

Dec 70. (7") *<56206>* **SOMETHING (live). / EVERYBODY'S TALKIN' (live)** –

Apr 71. (lp) *<7645>* **THE WOMACK "LIVE" (live '68)** –
– Intro – Let it out / Oh how I miss you baby / California dreamin' / Something / Everybody's talking / Laughin' and clownin' / To live the past / I'm a midnight mover / More than I can stand. *(UK-iss.Feb89 on 'Charly' lp/c; CRB/TCCRB 1201) (cd; CDCHARLY 155)*

— with a number of exceptions, his band over the 70's included **ROGER HAWKINS** – drums / **CLAYTON IVEY** – keyboards / **JIMMY JOHNSON** – guitar / **BARRY BECKETT** – keyboards / **TRUMAN THOMAS** – bass

U.A. U.A.

Feb 72. (7") *(UP 35339) <50847>* **THAT'S THE WAY I FEEL ABOUT CHA. / COME L'AMORE** Nov71 27

Jun 72. (lp) *(UAS 29306) <5539>* **COMMUNICATION** Nov71 83
– Communication / Come l'amore / Fire and rain / (If you don't want my love) Give it back / (They long to be) Close to you / Everything is beautiful / That's the way I feel about cha / Held not to temptation.

Jul 72. (7") *(UP 35375) <50902>* **WOMAN'S GOT TO HAVE IT. / (IF YOU DON'T WANT MY LOVE) GIVE IT BACK** Apr72 60

Sep 72. (lp) *(UAG 29365) <5577>* **UNDERSTANDING** Jun72 43
– I can understand it / Woman's gotta have it / And I love her / Got to get you back / Simple man / Ruby Dean / A thing called love / Sweet Caroline (good times never seemed so good) / Harry hippie. *(re-iss. Jan75 as 'I CAN UNDERSTAND IT'; UAG 29715)*

Aug 72. (7") *<50946>* **SWEET CAROLINE (GOOD TIMES NEVER SEEMED SO GOOD). / HARRY HIPPIE** – 51 31

Dec 72. (7") *(UP 35456)* **HARRY HIPPIE. / I CAN UNDERSTAND IT** –
(re-iss. Jan75 but flipped over; UP 36462)

Apr 73. (7") *(UP 35512) <196>* **ACROSS 110th STREET. / HANG ON IN THERE** Mar73 56

May 73. (lp) *(UAS 29451) <5225>* **ACROSS 110th STREET (Soundtrack)** Jan73 50
– Across 110th Street / If you don't want my love give it back / Quicksand / Do it right / Hang on in there / Across 110th Street / Harlem clavinet (J.J. JOHNSON ORCHESTRA) / Harlem love theme (J.J. JOHNSON ORCHESTRA). *(cd-iss. May98 on 'Charly'; CPCD 8340)*

Jul 73. (7") *(UP 35565) <255>* **NOBODY WANTS YOU WHEN YOU'RE DOWN AND OUT. / I'M THROUGH TRYING TO PROVE MY LOVE TO YOU** Jun73 29

Sep 73. (lp) *(UAS 29456) <LA 043>* **FACTS OF LIFE** Jun73 37
– Nobody wants you when you're down and out / I'm through trying to prove my love to you / If you can't give her love give her up / That's Heaven to me / Holdin' on to my baby's love / Nobody (reprise) / Facts of life / He'll be there when the sun goes down / Can't stop a man in love / The look of love / Natural man / All along the watchtower / Interlude No.1.

Mar 74. (7") *(35644) <375>* **LOOKIN' FOR A LOVE. / LET IT ALL HANG OUT** Jan74 10

Apr 74. (lp) *(UAS 29574) <LA 199>* **LOOKIN' FOR A LOVE AGAIN** Jan74 85
– Lookin' for a love / I don't wanna be hurt by your love again / Doing it my way / Let it all hang out / Point of no return / You're welcome, stop on by / You're messing up a good thing / Don't let me down / Copper kettle / There's one thing that beats falling. *(re-iss. Aug88 on 'Edsel'; ED 291) (re-iss. Jan89 on 'Charly' lp/c; CRB/TCRB 1193) (cd; CDCHARLY 153)*

Jun 74. (7") *<439>* **YOU'RE WELCOME, STOP ON BY. / I DON'T WANNA BE HURT BY YA LOVE AGAIN** – 59

Nov 74. (lp) *<LA 346>* **BOBBY WOMACK'S GREATEST HITS** (compilation) –

May 75. (lp) *(UAG 29762) <LA 353>* **I DON'T KNOW WHAT THE WORLD IS COMING TO**
– I don't know – (interlude 1 & 2) / Superstar / I want my love, put something down on it / Git it / What's your world / Check it out / Interlude No.2 / Jealous love / It's all over now / Yes Jesus loves me.

Jun 75. (7") *(UP 35859) <621>* **CHECK IT OUT. / INTERLUDE No.2** Apr75 91

Jul 75. (7") *<674>* **GIT IT. / IT'S ALL OVER NOW** –

Jan 76. (7") *(UP 36042) <735>* **WHERE THERE'S A WILL THERE'S A WAY. / EVERYTHING'S GONNA BE ALRIGHT** Nov75

Feb 76. (lp) *(UAG 29907) <LA 544>* **SAFETY ZONE** Jan76
– Everything's gonna be alright / I wish it would rain / Trust me / Where there's a will there's a way / Love ain't something you can get for free / Something you got / Daylight / I feel a groove comin' on / Don't make this the last date for you and me.

Mar 76. (7") *(UP 36098) <763>* **DAYLIGHT. / TRUST ME**

Aug 76. (lp) *(UAS 29979) <LA 638>* **B.W. GOES C & W** Apr76
– Behind closed doors / Bouquet of roses / Tired of living in the country / Tarnished rings / Big bayou / Song of the mockingbird / I'd be ahead if I could quit while I'm behind / You / I take it on home.

Sep 76. (7") *<804>* **TRUST ME. / I FEEL A GROOVE COMIN' ON** –

C.B.S. Columbia

Jan 77. (7"; as BOBBY WOMACK & BROTHERHOOD) *(CBS 4827) <10437>* **HOME IS WHERE THE HEART IS. / WE'VE ONLY JUST BEGUN** Oct76

Feb 77. (lp/c) *(CBS/40 81693) <34384>* **HOME IS WHERE THE HEART IS** Sep76
– Home is where the heart is / A little bit salty / Standing in the safety zone / One more chance on love / How long (has this been goin' on) / I could never be satisfied / Something for my head / A change is gonna come / We've only just begun. *(re-iss. Feb86 on 'Edsel' lp/c; ED/CED 172) (cd-iss. Feb91; EDCD 172)*

Mar 77. (7"; as BOBBY WOMACK & BROTHERHOOD) *<10493>* **STANDING IN THE SAFETY ZONE. / A CHANGE IS GONNA COME** –

Apr 78. (7") *<10672>* **TRUST YOUR HEART. / WHEN LOVE BEGINS, FRIENDSHIP ENDS** –

Jun 78. (7") *<10732>* **WIND IT UP. / STOP BEFORE WE START** –

Jul 78. (lp) *<39083>* **PIECES** –
– It's party time / Trust your heart / Stop before we start / When love begins, friendship ends / Wind it up / Is this the thanks I get / Caught up in the middle / Never let nothing get the best of you.

Arista Arista

Jun 79. (7") *<0421>* **I HONESTLY LOVE YOU. / HOW COULD YOU BREAK MY HEART** –

Jul 79. (lp) *(ARTY 165) <4222>* **ROADS OF LIFE**
– Roads of life / How could you break my heart / Honey dripper boogie / Roots in me / What are you doin' / Give it up / Mr. D.J. don't stop the music / I honestly love you. *(cd-iss. Aug97 on 'Razor & Tie'; RE 2140)*

Aug 79. (7") *<0446>* **ROADS OF LIFE. / GIVE IT UP** –

— took time out to stifle increasing drug intake, re-actifying again after his brother Harris was murdered. Oct'80, he provided the vocals for WILTON FELDER's (of The CRUSADERS) hit single 'INHERIT THE WIND'.

Motown Beverly Glen

Jun 82. (lp) *(STML 12168) <BG 10000>* **THE POET** Dec81 29
– So many sides of you / Lay your lovin' on me / Secrets / Just my imagination / Stand up / Games / If you think you're lonely now / Where do we go from here. *(cd-iss. Jul87 on 'Pacific'; BGD 10000) (re-iss. Sep94 on 'M.C.I.' cd/c; MUS CD/MC 505) (cd re-iss. Jun96 on 'Razor & Tie'; RE 2029) (cd-iss. May99 on 'Charly'; CPCD 8054) (cd re-iss. Jul99 on 'Sequel'; NEMCD 437)*

Jul 82. (7"/12") *(TMG/+T 1267)* **SO MANY SIDES OF YOU. / JUST MY IMAGINATION** –

Sep 82. (7") *(TMG 1278) <2000>* **SECRETS. / STAND UP** Feb82

Sep 82. (7") *<2001>* **WHERE DO WE GO FROM HERE. / JUST MY IMAGINATION** –

— In 1982, BOBBY took 'Beverly Glen' label owner Otis Smith to court, fighting literally over non-payment of royalties.

Mar 84. (7"; by BOBBY WOMACK and PATTI LaBELLE) *<2012>* **LOVE HAS FINALLY COME AT LAST. / AMERICAN DREAM** – 88

Apr 84. (lp/c) *(ZL/ZK 72205) <BG 10003>* **THE POET II** 31 Mar84 60
– Love has finally come at last / It takes a lot of strength to say goodbye /

Through the eyes of a child / Surprise surprise / Tryin' to get over you / Tell me why / Who's foolin' who / I wish I had someone to go home to / American dream. *(cd-iss. Jul87 on 'Pacific'; BGD 10003) (re-iss. Sep94 on 'M.C.I.' cd/c; MUS CD/TC 506) (cd re-iss. Jun96 on 'Razor & Tie'; RE 2030) (cd re-iss. Jul99 on 'Sequel'; NEMCD 438)*

Jun 84. (7"/12") *(TMG/+T 1339)* <2014/2015> **TELL ME WHY. / THROUGH THE EYES OF A CHILD** [60] [ ]

Sep 84. (7") *(TMG 1353)* **SURPRISE SURPRISE. / AMERICAN DREAM** [ ] [–]
(12"+=) *(TMGT 1353)* – If you think you're lonely now.

Sep 84. (7"; by BOBBY WOMACK and PATTI LaBELLE) *<2018>* **IT TAKES A LOT OF STRENGTH TO SAY GOODBYE / WHO'S FOOLIN' WHO** [–] [ ]

Jan 85. (7") *<2021>* **I WISH I HAD SOMEONE TO GO HOME TO. / SOMEDAY WE'LL ALL BE FREE** [–] [ ]

Feb 85. (lp) *<BG 10006>* **SOMEDAY WE'LL ALL BE FREE** [–] [ ]
– I'm so proud / Someday we'll all be free / Gifted one / Falling in love again / Searching for my love / In over my heart / I wish I had someone to go home to / Someday we'll all be free (acoustic) / Gifted one (acoustic). *(cd-iss. Jul99 as 'THE POET VOL.3' on 'Sequel; NEMCD 439)*

Mar 85. (7") *<2023>* **SEARCHING FOR MY LOVE. / I'M SO PROUD** [–] [ ]

— early in 1985, he re-united with WILTON FELDER on 7+12" '(NO MATTER HOW HIGH I GET) I WILL STILL BE LOOKING UP TO YOU'.

M.C.A. M.C.A.

Sep 85. (lp/c) *(MCF/+C 3282)* *<5617>* **SO MANY RIVERS** [ ] [66]
– I wish he didn't trust me so much / So baby don't leave home without it / So many rivers / Got to be with you tonight / Whatever happened to the times / Let me kiss it where it hurts / The only survivor / That's where it's at / Check it out / Gypsy woman. *(cd-iss. 1986; DMCF 3282) (cd re-iss. Aug89; DMCL 1894) (cd-iss. Mar93; MCLD 19136)*

Sep 85. (7"/12") *(MCA/+T 944)* **I WISH HE DIDN'T TRUST ME SO MUCH. / GOT TO BE WITH YOU TONIGHT** [64] [ ]

May 86. (7"/12") *(MCA/+T 1050)* **GYPSY WOMAN. / WHATEVER HAPPENED TO THE TIMES** [ ] [ ]

Nov 86. (lp/c) *(MCG/+C 6020)* *<5899>* **WOMAGIC** [ ] Jul86 [ ]
– I wanna make love to you / When the weekend comes / All the things you do / I can't stay mad too long / Hear the music / Outside myself / I ain't got to live nobody else / More than love / It ain't me. *(cd-iss. Nov87; DMCG 6020)*

Jan 87. (7"/12") *(MCA/+T 1108)* **I WANNA MAKE LOVE TO YOU. / WHATEVER HAPPENED TO THE TIMES** [ ] [ ]

Oct 87. (7") *(MCA 1210)* **LIVING IN A BOX. / ('A'instrumental)** [70] [ ]
(12"+=) *(MCAT 1210)* – ('A'-Another box) / ('A'-Hacienda mix).

Nov 87. (lp/c/cd) *(MCF/MCFC/DMCF 3408)* *<42097>* **THE LAST SOUL MAN** [ ] [ ]
– Living in a box / When the weekend comes / I still love you / Gina / A world where no one cries / A woman likes to hear that / Real love please stand up / The things we do (when we're lonely) / Falling in love again / Outside myself.

— In Nov'89, WOMACK teamed up with SHIRLEY BROWN on the single, 'AIN'T NOTHIN' LIKE THE LOVIN' WE GOT' on 'Chrysalis' ('Cooltempo' US)

— In Mar'93, he was credited on the LULU single, 'I'm Back For More', which hit the UK Top 30

Continuum Continuum

Aug 94. (c-s/12"/cd-s) *(T/12/CD CTUM 105)* **FOREVER LOVE / COLOUR HIM FATHER / (other mixes)** [ ] [–]

Sep 94. (cd/c) *(CD/T CTUM 8)* *<19401>* **RESURRECTION** [ ] [ ]
– Good ole days / You made me love again / So high on your love / Don't break your promise (too soon) / Forever love / Please change your mind / Trying not to break down / Cousin Henry / Centerfield / Goin' home / Walking on the wildside / Cry myself to sleep / Wish / Color him father.

— In May'95, he collaborated with JEANIE TRACY on the single, 'IT'S A MAN'S MAN'S WORLD' on 'Pulse'.

not iss. Capitol

Jul 99. (cd) *<98584>* **BACK TO MY ROOTS** (gospel) [–] [ ]

– (selective) compilations, etc. –

Nov 89. (d-lp/c)(cd) *Charly; (CDX/TCCDX 47)(CDCHARLY 199)* **SAFETY ZONE / B.W. GOES C&W** [ ] [–]

May 91. (cd/c/lp) *Essential; (ESD CD/MC/LP 141)* **SUPER SOUL SEDUCTION** [ ] [–]

Jun 91. (cd/c) *Music Club; (MC CD/TC 018)* **THE VERY BEST OF BOBBY WOMACK** [ ] [–]
– I can understand it / Harry hippie / I'm a midnight mover / What is this / Somebody special / That's the way I feel about cha / Communication / California dreaming / If you don't want my love give it back / I wish it would rain / Nobody wants you when you're down and out / Across 110th Street / If you want my love, put something down on it / Lookin' for a love / I don't wanna be hurt by ya love again / Got to get you back / Woman's gotta have it / There's one thing that beats failing / You're messing up a good thing / Love ain't something you can get for free.

Mar 94. (d-cd) *E.M.I.; (CDEM 1514)* **MIDNIGHT MOVER – THE BOBBY WOMACK STORY** [ ] [ ]

Apr 94. (cd/c) *Castle; (CCS CD/MC 404)* **THE COLLECTION** [ ] [–]
(re-iss. May03 on 'Spectrum'; 113125-2)

Jul 94. (3xcd-box) *Charly; (CPCD 80803)* **THE POET TRILOGY** [ ] [–]

Jun 96. (cd) *Razor & Tie; (RE 2009)* **LOOKIN' FOR A LOVE (THE BEST OF BOBBY WOMACK 1968-1975)** [ ] [–]

Nov 96. (d-cd) *Charly; (CPCD 8255-2)* **THE VERY BEST OF BOBBY WOMACK** [ ] [–]

Apr 97. (cd) *M.C.A.; (MCLD 19355)* **THE ONLY SURVIVOR (THE M.C.A. YEARS)** [ ] [–]

Sep 97. (cd) *Charly; (CDGR 165)* **FLY ME TO THE MOON / MY PRESCRIPTION** [ ] [–]

Nov 97. (d-cd) *Eagle; (EDMCD 020)* **THE MASTERS** [ ] [–]

Nov 97. (cd) *Charly; (CDGR 179)* **LOOKIN' FOR A LOVE / B.W. GOES C.W.** [ ] [–]

Jan 98. (cd) *Sequel; (NEMCD 996)* **SOUL SENSATION** [ ] [–]

Feb 98. (cd) *Charly; (CDGR 183)* **UNDERSTANDING / COMMUNICATION** [ ] [ ]

Mar 98. (cd) *Charly; (CDGR 208)* **FACTS OF LIFE / I DON'T KNOW WHAT THE WORLD IS COMING TO** [ ] [ ]

Jun 98. (cd) *Charly; (CDGR 237)* **SAFETY ZONE / THE WOMACK "LIVE"** [ ] [ ]

Jun 98. (cd) *Charly; (CDGR 255)* **GREATEST HITS** [ ] [–]

Aug 98. (cd) *Columbia; (487394-2)* **AT HOME IN MUSCLE SHOALS** [ ] [ ]

Jul 99. (d-cd) *Sequel; (NXTCD 319)* **THE BEST OF THE POETS** [ ] [ ]

Oct 99. (cd) *Sequel; (NEMCD 453)* **SAVE THE CHILDREN** [ ] [ ]

Nov 99. (d-cd) *Charly; (CDVAL 1092)* **THE ULTIMATE COLLECTION** [ ] [ ]

Feb 00. (cd) *Castle Pie; (PIESD 189)* **SOUL BROTHER** [ ] [ ]

Mar 00. (cd) *Neon; (NE 3452-2)* **THE VERY BEST OF BOBBY WOMACK** [ ] [ ]

Sep 00. (cd) *Music Club; (MCCD 432)* **THE BEST OF THE POET TRILOGY** [ ] [ ]

Nov 00. (cd) *Indigo; (IGOXCD 525)* **THE CHRISTMAS ALBUM** [ ] [ ]

Nov 02. (cd) *Disky; (SI 905178)* **LOOKIN' FOR A LOVE** [ ] [ ]

Feb 03. (d-cd) *Black Box; (BB 256)* **HOW I MISS YOU BABY** [ ] [ ]

Jun 03. (d-cd) *Excellence; (EXCEL 2114)* **TWENTY LEGENDARY R&B MASTERPIECES** [ ] [–]

Jun 03. (cd) *Castle; (CMRCD 652)* **THE BEST OF BOBBY WOMACK** [ ] [ ]

Jul 03. (cd) *E.M.I.; (584936-2)* **LOOKIN' FOR A LOVE: THE BEST OF BOBBY WOMACK 1068-1976** [ ] [ ]

Stevie WONDER

Born: STEVELAND JUDKINS MORRIS, 13 May'50, Saginaw, Michigan, USA. Blind since birth, he became a member of his local Baptist choir, and in 1960 he also formed a duo with JOHN GLOVER, who recommended him to his cousin; MIRACLES singer RONNIE WHITE. He in turn contacted, BERRY GORDY, who immediately signed STEVIE for a long-term contract to 'Tamla Motown' and gave him the famous title of (LITTLE) STEVIE WONDER. After two albums and a few flop 45's, STEVIE broke through in 1963 with US chart-topper, 'FINGERTIPS – Pt.2', an updated version of a track from his debut album that featured STEVIE's dazzling harmonica playing. This preceded the No.1 album, 'RECORDED LIVE – THE 12 YEAR OLD GENIUS' (1963), a record which featured the child prodigy in concert playing an array of instruments with breathtaking ease. After a few years of mediocre fortunes, and now somewhat older, he emerged as simply STEVIE WONDER, notching up a top 3 hit with the high-octane soul of 'UPTIGHT' (1966). The album of the same name was released later the same year and included an early indication of WONDER's developing social awareness and eclectic diversity with a cover of Bob Dylan's 'BLOWIN' IN THE WIND'. 'I WAS MADE TO LOVE HER' (1968) contained some passionately executed covers, while the goose-bump gem of a title track was a Top 10 hit in its own right. The celebratory title track from 'FOR ONCE IN MY LIFE' (1969) was similarly successful while the sun-ripened loveliness of 'MY CHERIE AMOUR' went Top 5 on both sides of the Atlantic. 'SIGNED, SEALED, DELIVERED (I'M YOURS)' (1970) saw WONDER begin taking more control of his affairs in the studio, handling the whole operation almost single-handedly. This self-determination was consolidated in 1971 when he turned 21 and renegotiated his contract with 'Motown'. Setting up his own publishing operation, WONDER made sure that he'd never be on the wrong end of a bum deal again, especially one where he received only one million dollars out of the thirty million he'd earned at 'Motown' in his youth. 'MUSIC OF MY MIND' (1972) was the first album to fully realise WONDER's kaleidoscopic vision, fusing jazz, rock and soul with pioneering synthesizer sounds and ethnic rhythms while still maintaining an overt pop sensibility. That summer he toured with The ROLLING STONES, bringing his music to a predominantly white rock audience who subsequently lapped up WONDER's heaviest offering to date, the taut funk of 'SUPERSTITION' (1973). The album 'TALKING BOOK' was released the same month and was the first of STEVIE's mercurial 70's masterpieces. From the heart-melting opening chords of 'YOU ARE THE SUNSHINE OF MY LIFE' to the gospel-like closer, 'I BELIEVE (WHEN I FALL IN LOVE IT WILL BE FOREVER)', WONDER had created one of the most accomplished, searching albums in the soul pantheon. It was a hard act to follow but follow it he did, in fine style with 'INNERVISIONS' (1973), a similarly spiritual journey of epic proportions. 'HIGHER GROUND' kept the funk intact while 'VISIONS' and 'JESUS CHILDREN OF AMERICA' were meditative quests for truth. 'LIVING FOR THE CITY' was a hard-bitten knot of genius while the closing 'HE'S MISSTRA KNOW-IT-ALL' featured some beautifully careworn piano playing. These themes were developed on 'FULFILLINGNESS' FIRST FINALE' (1974), an album that repeated 'INNERVISIONS' Grammy Award winning success and included the defiantly anti-Nixon 'YOU HAVEN'T DONE NOTHIN' as well as a rare nod to sexuality on 'BOOGIE ON REGGAE WOMAN'. WONDER completed this quadruple whammy with his groundbreaking double album, 'SONGS IN THE KEY OF LIFE' (1976). A breathtaking summation of all that WONDER had been working towards up to that point, it embraced everything from jazz and funk ('SIR DUKE' and 'I WISH' repectively, both American No.1's) to charming MOR with 'ISN'T SHE LOVELY'. The ominously chiding 'PASTIME PARADISE' was later reinterpreted by rapper COOLIO to massive success. In many ways, releasing another double album, especially one as esoteric and lacking in focus as 'THE SECRET LIFE OF PLANTS' (1979) was commercial suicide. The album was a moderate success however, and stil outshone WONDER's contemporaries. Returning to more commercial fare with a vengeance on 'HOTTER THAN JULY' (1980), WONDER offered up the reggae-flavoured 'MASTERBLASTER (JAMMIN')' (1980) and the anthemic Martin Luther King tribute, 'HAPPY BIRTHDAY' (1980). A string of singles followed, among them the duet with PAUL McCARTNEY, 'EBONY AND IVORY' (1982) and the similarly radio-friendly 'I JUST CALLED TO SAY I LOVE YOU' (1984), which won an oscar the following year. While 1985's 'IN SQUARE CIRCLE' produced the No.1 hit 'PART-TIME LOVER', it was generally inconsistent and along with 'CHARACTERS' (1987) and his soundtrack to Spike Lee's 'JUNGLE FEVER' (1991) failed to capture the pioneering spirit of his 70's work. WONDER's most recent album, 1995's 'CONVERSATION PEACE' contained flashes of brilliance but fans are still waiting (probably in vain) for another 'TALKING BOOK' or 'INNERVISIONS'. Live, WONDER is still worth selling your granny for the ticket price, his charismatic energy rarely failing to deliver the goods. As well as being a tireless promoter of worthy causes he remains one of the most respected figures in the music industry, and his influence on the course of popular music is incalculable. • **Songwriters:** STEVIE wrote all his own work except, when in the 60's he collaborated with producer HENRY COSBY. His cover versions were; MR. TAMBOURINE MAN (Bob Dylan) / WE CAN WORK IT OUT (Beatles) / SIXTEEN TONS (Ernie Ford) / CAN I GET A WITNESS (Marvin Gaye) / PLEASE, PLEASE, PLEASE (James Brown) / RESPECT (Otis Redding) / MY GIRL (Temptations) / LIGHT MY FIRE (Doors) / GOD BLESS THE CHILD (Billie Holiday) / BRIDGE OVER TROUBLED WATER (Simon & Garfunkel). The album 'TRIBUTE TO UNCLE RAY', had many covers of RAY CHARLES' songs. • **Miscellaneous:** On the 14th September '70, STEVIE married singer, SYREETA WRIGHT, who became his co-writer in the early 70's. They split-up 4 years later and STEVIE found new girlfriend, YOLANDA SIMMONS, who moved with him and their new daughter, to Manhattan. On the 6th August '73, STEVIE was nearly killed in a serious road accident. He recovered from head injuries, after spending a few days in a coma. STEVIE also wrote million sellers for Minnie Riperton (LOVIN' YOU) & Rufus (TELL ME SOMETHING GOOD).

Album rating: TRIBUTE TO UNCLE RAY (*5) / THE JAZZ SOUL OF LITTLE STEVIE (*5) / THE 12 YEAR OLD GENIUS (RECORDED LIVE) (*6) / WITH A SONG IN MY HEART (*4) / AT THE BEACH (HEY HARMONICA MAN) (*4) / UP-TIGHT EVERYTHING'S ALRIGHT (*6) / DOWN TO EARTH (*5) / I WAS MADE TO LOVE HER (*7) / GREATEST HITS compilation (*8) / FOR ONCE IN MY LIFE (*7) / MY CHERIE AMOUR (*7) / STEVIE WONDER LIVE (AT THE TALK OF THE TOWN) (*6) / SIGNED SEALED & DELIVERED (*7) / WHERE I'M COMING FROM (*7) / STEVIE WONDER'S GREATEST HITS, VOL.2 compilation (*8) / MUSIC OF MY MIND (*7) / TALKING BOOK (*9) / INNERVISIONS (*10) / FULFILLINGNESS' FIRST FINALE (*7) / SONGS IN THE KEY OF LIFE (*8) / LOOKING BACK (aka ANTHOLOGY) compilation (*8) / JOURNEY THROUGH THE SECRET LIFE OF PLANTS (*6) / HOTTER THAN JULY (*7) / ORIGINAL MUSIQUARIUM 1 compilation (*9) / WOMAN IN RED soundtrack with others (*4) / IN SQUARE CIRCLE (*5) / CHARACTERS (*4) / JUNGLE FEVER soundtrack (*5) / CONVERSATION PEACE (*4) / NATURAL WONDER – LIVE IN CONCERT (*4) / THE DEFINITIVE COLLECTION double compilation (*8)

LITTLE STEVIE WONDER

– vocals, piano, harmonica

		Oriole	Tamla
Aug 62.	(7") *<54061>* **I CALL IT PRETTY MUSIC (BUT OLD PEOPLE CALL IT THE BLUES). / (part 2)**	–	
1962.	(lp) *<232>* **TRIBUTE TO UNCLE RAY**	–	

– Hallelujah I love her so / Ain't that love / Don't you know / Sunset / Frankie and Johnny / Drown in my own tears / Come back baby / Mary Ann / My baby's gone / (I'm afraid) The masquerade is over. *(UK-iss.Aug63 on 'Oriole'; PS 40049) (re-iss. May82 on 'Motown') (cd-iss. Sep95)*

		Oriole	Tamla
Oct 62.	(7") *<54070>* **LITTLE WATER BOY (w/ CLARENCE PAUL). / LA LA LA LA LA**	–	
1963.	(lp) *<233>* **THE JAZZ SOUL OF LITTLE STEVIE**	–	

– Fingertips / Square / Soul bongo / Manhattan at six / Some other time / Wandering / Session number 112 / Bam. *(UK-iss.May64 on 'Stateside'; SL 10078) (re-iss. Mar82 on 'Motown')*

Dec 62. (7") *<54074>* **CONTRACT ON LOVE. / SUNSET** –

Aug 63. (7") *(CBA 1853) <54080>* **FINGERTIPS (part 2). / FINGERTIPS (part 1)** Jun63 1

Aug 63. (lp) *(PS 40050) <240>* **THE 12 YEAR OLD GENIUS (RECORDED LIVE) (live)** Jul63 1
– Fingertips / Soul bongo / Drown in my own tears / La la la la / (I'm afraid) The masquerade is over / Hallelujah I love her so / Don't you know. *(re-iss. Oct81 on 'Motown')*

Stateside Tamla

Nov 63. (7") *(SS 238) <54086>* **WORKOUT STEVIE, WORKOUT. / MONKEY TALK** Oct63 33

Jan 64. (lp) *<250>* **WITH A SONG IN MY HEART** –
– Dream / With a song in my heart / Get happy / Put on a happy face / When you wish upon a star / Smile / Make someone happy / Without a song / On the sunny side of the street / Give your heart a chance. *(UK-iss.Oct81 on 'Motown')*

Apr 64. (7") *(SS 285) <54090>* **CASTLES IN THE SAND. / THANK YOU (FOR LOVING ME ALL THE WAY)** Feb64 52

STEVIE WONDER

Aug 64. (7") *(SS 323) <54096>* **HEY HARMONICA MAN. / THIS LITTLE GIRL** Jun64 29

Sep 64. (7") *<54103>* **SAD BOY. / HAPPY STREET** –

Jan 65. (lp) *(SL 10108)* **AT THE BEACH (HEY HARMONICA MAN)**
– Red sails in the sunset / Party at the beach house / Happy Street / Beachcomber / Castles in the sand / Beyond the sea / Sad boy / Beach stomp / Hey, harmonica man.

Tamla Motown Tamla

Jan 65. (7") *<54108>* **PRETTY LITTLE ANGEL. / TEARS IN VAIN** –

Mar 65. (7") *(TMG 505)* **KISS ME BABY. / TEARS IN VAIN**

Sep 65. (7") *(TMG 532) <54119>* **HIGH HEEL SNEAKERS. / MUSIC TALK** Aug65 59

Jan 66. (7") *(TMG 545) <54124>* **UPTIGHT (EVERYTHING'S ALRIGHT). / PURPLE RAINDROPS** 14 Dec65 3

Apr 66. (7") *(TMG 558) <54130>* **NOTHING'S TOO GOOD FOR MY BABY. / WITH A CHILD'S HEART** Mar66 20

Aug 66. (7") *(TMG 570) <54136>* **BLOWIN' IN THE WIND. / AIN'T THAT ASKING FOR TROUBLE** 36 Jun66 9

Nov 66. (lp) *(TML 11036)* **UP-TIGHT EVERYTHING'S ALRIGHT** Jun 66 33
– Love a go-go / Hold me / Blowin' in the wind / Nothing's too good for my baby / Teach me tonight / Uptight (everything's alright) / Ain't that asking for trouble / I want my baby back / Pretty little angel / Music talk / Contract on love / With a child's heart. *(re-iss. Oct81) (re-iss. 1973 on 'M.F.P.')*

Dec 66. (7") *(TMG 588) <54139>* **A PLACE IN THE SUN. / SYLVIA** 20 Oct66 9

Dec 66. (7") *<54142>* **SOME DAY AT CHRISTMAS. / THE MIRACLE OF CHRISTMAS** –

Apr 67. (lp) *(TML 11045) <272>* **DOWN TO EARTH** Jan67 92
– A place in the Sun / Bang bang / Thank you love / Mr. Tambourine man / Hey love / Sixteen tons / Down to Earth / Sylvia / Lonesome road / The world is empty without you / Angel baby (don't you ever leave me) / Be cool, be calm (and keep yourself together). *(re-iss. Oct81)*

Apr 67. (7") *(TMG 602) <54147>* **TRAVELLIN' MAN. / HEY LOVE** 32
Mar67 90

Jul 67. (7") *(TMG 613) <54151>* **I WAS MADE TO LOVE HER. / HOLD ME** 5 Jun 67 2

Oct 67. (7") *(626) <54157>* **I'M WONDERING. / EVERY TIME I SEE YOU I GO WILD** 22 12

Apr 68. (lp) *(TML 11059) <279>* **I WAS MADE TO LOVE HER** Sep67 45
– I was made to love her / Send me some lovin' / I'd cry / Everybody needs somebody (I need you) / Respect / My girl / Baby don't you do it / A fool for you / Can I get a witness / I pity the fool / Please, please, please / Every time I see you I go wild. *(re-iss. Oct81)*

Apr 68. (7") *(TMG 653) <54165>* **SHOO-BE-DOO-BE-DOO-DA-DAY. / WHY DON'T YOU LEAD ME TO LOVE** 46 9

Aug 68. (lp) *(TML 11075) <282>* **STEVIE WONDER'S GREATEST HITS** (compilation) 25 Apr68 37
– Shoo-be-doo-be-doo-da-day / A place in the Sun / Uptight (everything's alright) / Travellin' man / High heel sneakers / Sad boy / Kiss me, baby / Workout Stevie, workout / Fingertips (part 2) / Hey, harmonica man / Contract on love / Castles in the sand / Nothing's too good for my baby / I was made to love her / Blowin' in the wind / I'm wonderin'. *(re-iss. Oct81 & 1986) (cd-iss. 'VOL.1' Sep89) (cd-iss. Nov93 & Oct98; 530941-2)*

Aug 68. (7") *(TMG 666) <54168>* **YOU MET YOUR MATCH. / MY GIRL** Jul68 35

Dec 68. (7") *(TMG 679) <54174>* **FOR ONCE IN MY LIFE. / ANGIE GIRL** 3 Oct68 2
(re-iss. Oct81)

Feb 69. (lp) *(TML 11098) <291>* **FOR ONCE IN MY LIFE** Oct68 50
– For once in my life / Shoo-be-ddo-be-doo-da-day / You met your match / I wanna make her love me / I'm more than happy (I'm satisfied) / I don't know why (I love you) / Sunny / I'd be a fool right now / Ain't no lovin' / God bless the child / Do I love her / The house on the hill. *(re-iss. Oct81) (cd-iss. Aug88) (cd re-iss. Mar03; AA374635234-2)*

Mar 69. (7") *(TMG 690) <54180>* **I DON'T KNOW WHY (I LOVE YOU). / MY CHERIE AMOUR** 14 Feb69 39
(above flipped over Jun69 hit both UK + US No.4) (re-iss. Oct81)

Nov 69. (7") *(TMG 717) <54188>* **YESTER-ME, YESTER-YOU, YESTERDAY. / I'D BE A FOOL RIGHT NOW** 2 Oct69 7

Nov 69. (lp) *(TML 11128) <296>* **MY CHERIE AMOUR** 17 Oct69 34
– My Cherie amour / Hello young lovers / At last / Light my fire / The shadow of your smile / You and me / Pearl / Somebody knows, somebody cares / Yester-me, yester-you, yesterday / Angie girl / Give your love / I've got you. *(re-iss. Oct81 & Apr84, cd-iss. Aug88)*

Mar 70. (7") *(TMG 731) <54191>* **NEVER HAD A DREAM COME TRUE. / SOMEBODY KNOWS, SOMEBODY CARES** 6 Feb70 26

Mar 70. (lp) *(TML 11164) <298>* **LIVE (AT THE TALK OF THE TOWN)** Apr70 81
– Pretty world / Never had a dream come true / Shoo-be-doo-be-doo-da-day / My Cherie amour / Alfie / (drum solo) / Bridge over troubled water / I was made to love her / Yester-me, yester-you, yesterday / For once in my life / Signed, sealed, delivered (I'm yours). *(re-iss. Oct81)*

Jun 70. (7") *(TMG 744) <54196>* **SIGNED, SEALED, DELIVERED (I'M YOURS). / I'M MORE THAN HAPPY (I'M SATISFIED)** 15 3

Nov 70. (lp) *(TML 11169) <304>* **SIGNED, SEALED, DELIVERED (I'M YOURS)** Aug70 25
– Never had a dream come true / We can work it out / Signed, sealed, delivered (I'm yours) / Heaven help us all / You can't judge a book by it's cover / Sugar / Don't wonder why / Anything you want me to do / I can't let my Heaven walk away / Joy (takes over me) / I gotta have a song / Something to say. *(re-iss. Oct81, re-iss. +cd.Aug88)*

Nov 70. (7") *(TMG 757) <54200>* **HEAVEN HELP US ALL. / I GOTTA HAVE A SONG** 29 Oct70 9

Mar 71. (7") *<54202>* **WE CAN WORK IT OUT. / NEVER DREAMED YOU'D LEAVE ME IN SUMMER** – 13
78

May 71. (7") *(TMG 772)* **WE CAN WORK IT OUT. / DON'T WONDER WHY** 27 –

Jul 71. (7") *(TMG 779)* **NEVER DREAMED YOU'D LEAVE ME IN SUMMER. / IF YOU REALLY LOVE ME** –

Jul 71. (lp) *(TML 11183) <308>* **WHERE I'M COMING FROM** May71 62
– Look around / Do yourself a favour / Think of me as your soldier / Something out of the blue / If you really love me / I wanna talk to you / Take up a course in happiness / Never dreamed you'd leave me in Summer / Sunshine in their eyes. *(re-iss. Jul81) (re-iss. +cd.Apr91) (cd-iss. Sep93)*

Nov 71. (7") *<54214>* **WHAT CHRISTMAS MEANS TO ME. / BEDTIME FOR TOYS** –

Jan 72. (7") *(TMG 798) <54208>* **IF YOU REALLY LOVE ME. / THINK OF ME AS YOUR SOLDIER** 20 Aug71 8

Jan 72. (lp) *(STML 11196) <313>* **GREATEST HITS VOL.2** (compilation) 30 Nov71 69
– Signed, sealed, delivered (I'm yours) / We can work it out / For once in my life / If you really love me / You met your match / My Cherie amour / Yester-me, yester-you, yesterday / Never had a dream come true / Heaven help us all / Don't know why I love you / Never dreamed you'd leave in Summer. *(re-iss. Oct81 & 1986) (cd-iss. Sep89 as 'VOL.2') (cd-iss. Nov93 & Oct98; 530942-2)*

May 72. (7") *<54216>* **SUPERWOMAN (WHERE WERE YOU WHEN I NEEDED YOU). / I LOVE EVERY LITTLE THING ABOUT YOU** –

May 72. (lp/c) *(STMA/TC-STMA 8002) <314>* **MUSIC OF MY MIND** Mar72 21
– Love having you around / Superwoman (where were you when I needed you) / I love every thing about you / Sweet little girl / Happier than the

morning sun / Girl blue / Seems so long / Keep on running / Evil. *(re-iss. Oct81) (cd-iss. Nov87 & Jul92 & May00; 157353-2) (lp re-iss. Apr01 on 'Simply Vinyl'; SVLP 228)*

Sep 72. (7") *(TMG 827)* **SUPERWOMAN (WHERE WERE YOU WHEN I NEEDED YOU). / SEEMS SO LONG** [ ] [–]

Sep 72. (7") *<54223>* **KEEP ON RUNNING. / EVIL** [–] [90]

Jan 73. (7") *(TMG 841) <54226>* **SUPERSTITION. / YOU'VE GOT IT BAD GIRL** [11] Nov72 [1]

Jan 73. (lp/c) *(STMA/TC-STMA 8007) <319>* **TALKING BOOK** [16] Nov72 [3]
– You are the sunshine of my life / Maybe your baby / You and I / Tuesday heartbreak / You've got it bad girl / Superstition / Big brother / Blame it on the sun / Lookin' for another pure love / I believe (when I fall in love it will be forever). *(re-iss. Oct81) (cd-iss. May86 & Jul92 & May00; 157354-2) (lp re-iss. Apr01 on 'Simply Vinyl'; SVLP 229)*

Mar 73. (7") *<54232>* **YOU ARE THE SUNSHINE OF MY LIFE. / TUESDAY HEARTBREAK** [–] [1]

May 73. (7") *(TMG 852)* **YOU ARE THE SUNSHINE OF MY LIFE. / LOOK AROUND** [7] [–]
(re-iss. Oct81)

Aug 73. (lp/c) *(STMA/TC-STMA 8011) <326>* **INNERVISIONS** [8] [4]
– Too high / Visions / Living for the city / Golden lady / Higher ground / Jesus children of America / All in love is fair / Don't you worry 'bout a thing / He's a misstra know-it-all. *(re-iss. Ocr81) (cd-iss. Oct87 & Jul92 & May00; 157355-2) (lp re-iss. Apr01 on 'Simply Vinyl'; SVLP 230)*

Sep 73. (7") *(TMG 869) <54235>* **HIGHER GROUND. / TOO HIGH** [29] Aug73 [4]

Dec 73. (7") *(TMG 881) <54242>* **LIVING FOR THE CITY (edit). / VISIONS** [15] Nov73 [8]

Apr 74. (7") *(TMG 892)* **HE'S MISSTRA KNOW IT ALL. / YOU CAN'T JUDGE A BOOK BY IT'S COVER** [10] [–]
(re-iss. Oct81)

Apr 74. (7") *<54245>* **DON'T YOU WORRY 'BOUT A THING. / BLAME IT ON THE SUN** [–] [16]

Jul 74. (7") *(TMG 908)* **DON'T YOU WORRY 'BOUT A THING. / DO YOURSELF A FAVOUR** [ ] [–]

Aug 74. (lp/c) *(STMA/TCSTMA 8019)* **FULFILLINGNESS' FIRST FINALE** [5] [1]
– Smile please / Heaven is 10 zillion light years away / Too shy to say / Boogie on reggae woman / Creepin' / You haven't done nothin' / It ain't no use / They won't go when I go / Bird of beauty / Please don't go. *(re-iss. Oct81) (cd-iss. Oct87 & Nov93 & May00; 157356-2)*

Aug 74. (7") *<54252>* **YOU HAVEN'T DONE NOTHIN? / BIG BROTHER** [–] [1]

Oct 74. (7") *(TMG 921)* **YOU HAVEN'T DONE NOTHIN'. / HAPPIER THAN THE MORNING SUN** [30] [–]

Nov 74. (7") *<54254>* **BOOGIE ON REGGAE WOMAN. / SEEMS SO LONG** [–] [3]

Dec 74. (7") *(TMG 928)* **BOOGIE ON REGGAE WOMAN. / EVIL** [12] [–]

Oct 76. (d-lp/d-c) *(TMPS/TC-TMSP 6002) <340>* **SONGS IN THE KEY OF LIFE** [2] [1]
– Love's in need of love today / Have a talk with God / Village ghetto land / Confusion / Sir Duke / Isn't she lovely / Joy inside my tears / Black man / I wish / Knocks me off my feet / Pastime Paradise / Summer soft / Ordinary pain / Ngiculela es una historia – I am singing / If it's magic / As / Another star. *(7"ep w.a.) (re-iss. Oct81, d-cd-iss. 1988 & Jul92 & May00; 157357-2)*

Dec 76. (7") *(TMG 1054) <54274>* **I WISH. / YOU AND I** [5] Nov76 [1]

Mar 77. (7") *<54281>* **SIR DUKE. / HE'S MISSTRA KNOW-IT-ALL** [–] [1]

Mar 77. (7") *(TMG 1068)* **SIR DUKE. / TUESDAY HEARTBREAK** [2] [–]

Aug 77. (7") *(TMG 1083) <54286>* **ANOTHER STAR. / CREEPIN'** [29] [32]

Nov 77. (7") *(TMG 1091) <54291>* **AS. / CONFUSION** [ ] [36]
(last 5 singles, except Aug77 re-iss. Oct81)

Jan 79. (t-lp) *<M-804 LP3>* **LOOKING BACK** (compilation) [–] [34]

—— In Feb79, STEVIE WONDER teamed up with DIANA ROSS, MARVIN GAYE & SMOKEY ROBINSON on minor hit single POPS WE LOVE YOU.

Nov 79. (d-lp/d-c) *(TMSP/+TC-TMSP 6009) <371>* **STEVIE WONDER'S JOURNEY THROUGH THE SECRET LIFE OF PLANTS** [8] [4]
– Earth's creation / The first garden / Voyage to India / Same old story / Venus' flytrap and the bug / Ai no sono / Seasons / Power flower / Send one your love / Race babbling / Outside my window / Black orchid / Ecclesiates / Kesse ye lolo de ye / Come back as a flower / A seed's a star – Tree (medley) / The secret life of plants / Tree / Seasons. *(d-cd-iss. 1986 & Sep95; 530106-2)*

Nov 79. (7") *(TMG 1146) <54303>* **SEND ONE YOUR LOVE. / ('A'instrumental)** [52] [4]

Jan 80. (7") *(TMG 1173* **BLACK ORCHID. / BLAME IT ON THE SUN** [63] [–]

Mar 80. (7") *(TMG 1179) <54308>* **OUTSIDE MY WINDOW. / SAME OLD STORY** [52] Feb80 [52]

Sep 80. (7")(12") *(TMG 1204) <54317>* **MASTERBLASTER (JAMMIN'). / MASTERBLASTER (dub)** [2] [5]
(last 3 singles re-iss. Oct81)

Oct 80. (lp/c) *(STMA/TC-STMA 8035) <373>* **HOTTER THAN JULY** [2] [3]
– Did I hear you say you love me / All I do / Rocket love / I ain't gonna stand for it / As if you read my mind / Masterblaster (jammin') / Do like you / Cash in your face / Lately / Happy birthday. *(re-iss. Oct81) (cd-iss. Oct87 & Apr00; E 157363-2)*

Dec 80. (7") *(TMG 1215) <54320>* **I AIN'T GONNA STAND FOR IT. / KNOCKS ME OFF MY FEET** [10] [11]

Feb 81. (7") *(TMG 1226) <54323>* **LATELY. / IF IT'S MAGIC** [3] [64]
(re-iss. Oct81)

May 81. (7") *<54328>* **DID I HEAR YOU SAY YOU LOVE ME. / AS IF YOU READ MY MIND** [–] [ ]

Jul 81. (7"/12") *(TMG/+T 1235)* **HAPPY BIRTHDAY. / HAPPY BIRTHDAY (SINGALONG)** [2] [–]

Jan 82. (7") *(TMG 1254) <1602>* **THAT GIRL. / ALL I DO** [39] [4]

—— In Mar82, hit UK/US No.1 with PAUL McCARTNEY on single EBONY AND IVORY.

May 82. (7"/12") *(TMG/+T 1269/) <1612>* **DO I DO. / ROCKET LOVE** [10] [13]

May 82. (d-lp/d-c) *(TMSP/TC-TMSP 6012) <6002>* **ORIGINAL MUSIQUARIUM 1** (compilation) [8] [ ]
– Superstition / You haven't done nothin' / Living for the city / Front line / Superwoman (where were you when I needed you) / Send one your love / You are the sunshine of my life / Ribbon in the sky / Higher ground / Sir Duke / Master blaster / Boogie on reggae woman / That girl / I wish / isn't she lovely / Do I do. *(re-iss. +d-cd-'2 VOLUMES' Nov84 & Jul92)*

Sep 82. (7"/12") *(TMG/+T 1280)* **RIBBON IN THE SKY. / THE SECRET LIFE OF PLANTS** [45] [–]

Sep 82. (7") *<1639>* **RIBBON IN THE SKY. / BLACK ORCHID** [–] [54]
Dec 82, he & other Motown artist CHARLENE had US Top50 hit with USED TO BE.

Jan 83. (7"/12") *(TMG/+T 1289)* **FRONT LINE. / ('A'instrumental)** [ ] [–]

—— In Aug83, STEVIE co-wrote and sang on GARY BYRD's UK Top 10 hit 12" 'The CROWN'. Early next year, he guested on ELTON JOHN's 'I GUESS THAT'S WHY THEY..'.

Aug 84. (7"/12") *(TMG/+T 1349) <1745>* **I JUST CALLED TO SAY I LOVE YOU. / ('A'instrumental)** [1] [1]

—— Shared half of next lp with DIONNE WARWICK (also duet on *)

Sep 84. (lp/c) *(ZL/ZK 72285) <6108>* **WOMAN IN RED – SELECTIONS FROM ORIGINAL MOTION PICTURE SOUNDTRACK** [2] [4]
– The woman in red / It's you (with DIONNE WARWICK) / It's more than you / I just called to say I love you / Love light in flight / Weakness (with DIONNE WARWICK) / Don't drive drunk / Moments aren't moments (DIONNE WARWICK solo). *(cd-iss. Oct87)*

Nov 84. (7"/12") *(TMG/+T 1364) <1769>* **LOVE LIGHT IN FLIGHT. / IT'S MORE THAN YOU** [44] [17]

Dec 84. (7"/12") *(TMG/+T 1372)* **DON'T DRIVE DRUNK. / ('A'instrumental)** [62] [–]

—— In Mar85, STEVIE featured on USA FOR AFRICA charity single WE ARE THE WORLD

Aug 85. (7"/12") *(ZB/ZT 40351) <1808>* **PART-TIME LOVER. / ('A'instrumental)** [3] [1]

Sep 85. (lp/c/cd) *(ZL/ZK/ZD 72005) <6134>* **IN SQUARE CIRCLE** [5] [5]
– Part-time lover / I love you too much / Whereabouts / Stranger on the shore of love / Never in the sun / Spiritual walkers / Land of la la / Go home / Overjoyed / It's wrong (apartheid). *(re-iss. cd.Nov92 & Mar96; 530046-2)*

Nov 85. (7"/12") *(ZB/ZT 40501) <1817>* **GO HOME. / ('A'instrumental)** [67] [10]

Feb 86. (7"/12") *(ZB/ZT 40567) <1832>* **OVERJOYED. / ('A'instrumental)** [17] [24]

Jun 86. (7"/12") *(WOND/+T 1) <1846>* **LAND OF LA LA. / (‘A’instrumental)** [ ] [86]

Jan 87. (7"/12") *(WOND/+T 2)* **STRANGER ON THE SHORE OF LOVE. / DID I HEAR YOU SAY YOU LOVE ME** [55] [–]

Oct 87. (7"/12"/c-s) *(ZB/ZT/ZC 41439) <1907>* **SKELETONS. / (‘A’instrumental)** [59] [19]

Nov 87. (lp/c/cd) *(ZL/ZK/ZD 72001) <6248>* **CHARACTERS** [33] [17]
– You will know / Dark ‘n’ lovely / In your corner / With each part of my heart / One of a kind / Skeletons / Get it / Galaxy Paradise / Cryin’ through the night. *(c+=/cd+=)* – Come let me make your love come down / My eyes don’t cry.

Jan 88. (7"/12") *(ZB/ZT 41723) <1919>* **YOU WILL KNOW. / (‘A’instrumental)** [ ] [77]
(cd-s+=) *(ZD 41723)* – (interview).

— In Feb88, collaborated with JULIO IGLESIAS on single MY LOVE.

May 88. (7"/12"; STEVIE WONDER & MICHAEL JACKSON) *(ZB/ZT 41883) <1930>* **GET IT. / GET IT (instrumental)** [37] [80]

Oct 88. (7") *(ZB 42259)* **MY EYES DON’T CRY. / (‘A’instrumental)** [ ] [ ]
(12"/cd-s) *(ZT/ZD 42260)* – (‘A’side) / (‘A’dub) / (‘A’radio edit).

May 89. (7"/c-s) *(ZB/ZK 42855)* **FREE. / HAPPY BIRTHDAY** [49] [ ]
(12"+=/cd-s+=) *(ZT/ZD 42856)* – It’s wrong (aparteid).

Oct 90 (7"/c-s) **KEEP YOUR LOVE ALIVE. / (‘A’instrumental)** [ ] [ ]
(12"+=)(cd-s+=) – (‘A’version).

May 91. (cd/c/lp) *(ZD/ZK/ZL 71750) <6291>* **JUNGLE FEVER (Soundtrack)** [56] [24]
– Fun day / Queen in the black / These three words / Each other’s throats / If she breaks your hearts / Gotta have you / Make sure you’re sure / Jungle fever / I go sailing / Chemical love / Lighting up the candles.

Jun 91. (7"/c-s) *<2081>* **GOTTA HAVE YOU. / FEEDING OFF THE LOVE OF THE LAND** [ ] [92]
(12"+=/cd-s+=) – (‘A’extended mix).

Sep 91. (7"/c-s) *(ZB/ZK 44957)* **FUN DAY. / (‘A’instrumental)** [63] [ ]
(12"+=/cd-s+=) *(ZT/ZD 44958)* – (‘A’remix) / (‘A’club mix).

Feb 95. (7"/c-s) *(TMG/+CS 1437) <0290>* **FOR YOUR LOVE. / (‘A’mix)** [23] [53]
(cd-s+=) – My Cherie amour/ Uptight (everything’s alright).

Mar 95. (cd/c) *(530238-2/-4) <0238>* **CONVERSATION PEACE** [8] [16]
– Rain your love down / Edge of eternity / Taboo to love / Take the time out / I’m new / My love is with you / Treat myself / Tomorrow Robins will sing / Sensuous whisper / For your love / Cold chill / Sorry / Conversation peace.

Jul 95. (c-s) *(860 356-4)* **TOMORROW ROBINS WILL SING / (‘A’-Wonder West side version)** [71] [ ]
(12") *(860 373-1)* – (‘A’-Ronin smooth) / (‘A’-Dance Hall) / (‘A’-Slo jungle).
(cd-s) *(860 373-2)* – (‘A’side) / (above 3 tracks).

Oct 95. (c-s) *(860 464-4)* **COLD CHILL / (‘A’mix)** [ ] [ ]
(12"+=/cd-s+=) *(860 465-1/-2)* – (‘A’mixes).

Oct 95. (d-cd/d-c) *(530546-2/-4) <0546>* **NATURAL WONDER – LIVE IN CONCERT (live)** [ ] [ ]
– Love’s in need of love today / Master blaster (jammin’) / Higher ground / Rocket love / Ribbon in the sky / Pastime paradise / If it’s magic / Village ghetto land / Tomorrow robins will sing / Overjoyed / My Cherie amour / Signed, sealed, delivered (I’m yours) / Living for the city / Sir Duke / I wish / You are the sunshine of my life / Superstition / I just called to say I love you / For your love / Another star / Stevie Ray blues / Ms. and Mr. little ones / Stay gold.

— in Dec’03, STEVIE (& ANGIE STONE) featured on BLUE’s cover of ‘Signed, Sealed, Delivered (I’m Yours)’

– (selective) compilations, etc. –

note; on ‘Tamla Motown’ until otherwise stated

Dec 77. (d-lp/d-c) *(M9 804) <804>* **ANTHOLOGY** [ ] [ ]
(both above re-iss. Oct81)

Oct 86. (cd) *(ZD 72489)* **FOR ONCE IN MY LIFE / UPTIGHT** [ ] [ ]

Oct 86. (cd) *(ZD 72453)* **MY CHERIE AMOUR / SIGNED, SEALED, DELIVERED, I’M YOURS** [ ] [ ]

Jun 87. (d-lp/d-c/d-cd) *(WL/WK/ZD 72585)* **THE ESSENTIAL** [ ] [ ]
(d-cd re-iss. Jan93; 530047-2)

Jul 87. (cd) *(ZD 72558)* **DOWN TO EARTH / I WAS MADE TO LOVE YOU** [ ] [ ]

Nov 84. (lp/c) *Telstar; (STA R/C 2251)* **LOVE SONGS – 16 CLASSIC HITS** [20] [–]
(re-iss. +cd.Jul86 & Jan 93 as ‘20 CLASSIC HITS’ on ‘Motown’; 530037-2) – (4 extra tracks).

Nov 96. (cd/c) *(530757-2/-4)* **SONG REVIEW – A GREATEST HITS COLLECTION** [19] [ ]

Jan 00. (cd) *(153928-2)* **THE BALLAD COLLECTION** [ ] [ ]

Jan 00. (cd) *Universal; (E 157261-2)* **UNIVERSAL MASTERS COLLECTION** [ ] [ ]

Feb 00. (cd) *Spectrum; (544211-2)* **MOTOWN EARLY CLASSICS** [ ] [ ]

Mar 00. (4xcd-box) *(153992-2)* **AT THE CLOSE OF THE CENTURY** [ ] [ ]

Oct 00. (d-cd) *Universal; (E 159048-2)* **INNERVISIONS / FULFILLINGNESS FIRST FINALE** [ ] [ ]

Oct 00. (d-cd) *Universal; (E 159049-2)* **TALKING BOOK / MUSIC OF MY MIND** [ ] [ ]

Oct 02. (d-cd) *Universal TV; <(066502-2)>* **THE DEFINITIVE COLLECTION** [16] [ ]
– Superstition / Sir Duke / I wish / Masterblaster (jammin’) / Isn’t she lovely / I just called to say I love you / Ebony and ivory (with PAUL McCARTNEY) / As / Never had a dream come true / I was made to love her / Heaven help us all / Overjoyed / Lately / For your love / If you really love me / Higher ground / Do I do / Living for the city / Part-time lover / For once in my life / Uptight (everything’s alright) / We can work it out / Signed, sealed, delivered (I’m yours) / Yester-me, yester-you, yesterday / I’m wondering / My cherie amour / You are the sunshine of my life / I don’t know why (I love you) / A place in the sun / Blowin’ in the wind / Send one your love / Pastime paradise / I ain’t gonna stand for it / Fingertips (parts 1-2) / Boogie on reggae woman / You haven’t done nothin’ / He’s misstra know it all / Happy birthday.

Oct 02. (cd) *<AA440 066164-2>* **THE DEFINITIVE COLLECTION** [–] [35]
– Fingertips part 2 (live) / Uptight (everything’s alright) / Hey love / I was made to love her / For once in my life / My cherie amour / Signed, sealed, delivered (I’m yours) / You are the sunshine of my life / Superstition / Higher ground / Living for the city / You haven’t done nothin’ / Boogie on reggae woman / I wish / Sir Duke / Masterblaster (jammin’) / That girl / Do I do / I just called to say I love you / Overjoyed / Part-time lover.

WONDER STUFF

Formed: Stourbridge, Midlands, England . . .early 1986 by ex-EDEN drummer turned frontman, MILES HUNT, together with MALCOLM TREECE, THE BASS THING and MARTIN GILKS. After a couple of EP’s on their own ‘Farout’ label, the group signed to ‘Polydor’ in late ’87, initially lumped in with contemporaries like POP WILL EAT ITSELF and CRAZYHEAD under the music press-created ‘grebo’ banner. It soon became clear, however, that The WONDER STUFF were a unique proposition in their own right, as evidenced on the debut album, ‘THE EIGHT LEGGED GROOVE MACHINE’ (1988), a diverse collection of sparkling, hard-edged indie pop. HUNT was as bitingly uncompromising in his lyrics as he was in his relations with the media, the sardonic singer ever reliable for a controversial comment. While ‘A WISH AWAY’ narrowly missed the Top 40, another single, the wry ‘IT’S YER MONEY I’M AFTER BABY’, just nosed its way into the chart, the track backed by the self-explanatory ‘ASTLEY IN THE NOOSE’. ‘WHO WANTS TO BE THE DISCO KING?’ asked HUNT in his inimitable bad attitude style, taking the WONDER STUFF into the Top 30 for the first time in early ’89. A comparatively sensitive side was glimpsed on the jaunty ‘DON’T LET ME DOWN’ later that year, a Top 20 hit and a taster for the follow-up album, ‘HUP’ (1989). With the addition of JAMES TAYLOR on organ and MARTIN BELL on banjo/mandolin (no, not THAT JAMES TAYLOR and not THAT MARTIN BELL!), the record combined their high-octane pop/rock with a loose folky feel. It also marked their first major success, reaching the Top 5 and establishing the group as a headlining act. The success brought internal tensions to a head, however, with THE BASS THING (aka ROB JONES) departing for New York where he later formed 8-piece outfit The BRIDGE AND THE TUNNEL CREW (JONES subsequently died from heart problems in 1993). With PAUL CLIFFORD coming in as a replacement, the group entered the most high profile period of their career. Following on from the Top 20 success of the groovy 'CIRCLESQUARE' single, The WONDER STUFF scored a massive hit with the insanely catchy and ultimately annoying 'SIZE OF A COW'. A third set, 'NEVER LOVED ELVIS' (1991), made the Top 3 later that summer, a more mature set which neverthless lacked the raw charm of old. A marriage made in heaven/hell (delete according to taste), The WONDER STUFF teamed up with comedic loonies VIC REEVES & BOB MORTIMER for a cover of TOMMY ROE's 'DIZZY', giving the group their one and only No.1 single later that year. With the help of rootsy chanteuse KIRSTY MacCOLL, the 'WELCOME TO THE CHEAP SEATS' EP (1992) contined the band's folk/indie hybrid, as did the group's final album, 'CONSTRUCTION FOR THE MODERN IDIOT' (1993). Increasingly disillusioned by their failure to break the American market and the direction of the British music scene, The WONDER STUFF finally signed off with the surprisingly ebullient 'HOT LOVE NOW! EP' (1994) and a farewell performance at the 1994 Phoenix festival. While HUNT went on to work as a presenter for MTV before forming VENT 414, the other members subsequently founded the group WEKNOWWHEREYOULIVE. Towards the end of the millennium, MILES HUNT was back in solo form, releasing 'COMMON THREADS' and 'HAIRY ON THE INSIDE' during this spell. • **Songwriters:** Group music / HUNT lyrics except; GIMME SOME TRUTH (John Lennon) / THAT'S ENTERTAINMENT (Jam) / INSIDE YOU (Pop Will Eat Itself) / COZ I LUV YOU (Slade).

Album rating: THE EIGHT LEGGED GROOVE MACHINE (*6) / HUP (*6) / NEVER LOVED ELVIS (*7) / CONSTRUCTION FOR THE MODERN IDIOT (*5) / IF THE BEATLES HAD READ HUNTER . . . THE SINGLES compilation (*8) / CURSED WITH INSINCERITY (*6)

MILES HUNT – vocals, guitar / **MALCOLM TREECE** – guitar, vocals / **THE BASS THING** (b.ROB JONES) – bass / **MARTIN GILKS** – drums, percussion (ex-MIGHTY LEMON DROPS)

Farout · not iss.

Feb 87. (7"ep) *(GONE ONE)* **IT'S NOT TRUE . . . / A WONDERFUL DAY. / LIKE A MERRY GO ROUND / DOWN HERE** [ ] [–]

Sep 87. (7") *(GONE 002)* **UNBEARABLE. / TEN TRENCHES DEEP** [ ] [–]
(12"+=) *(GOBIG 002)* – I am a monster / Frank.

Polydor · Polygram

Apr 88. (7") *(GONE 3)* **GIVE GIVE GIVE ME MORE MORE MORE. / A SONG WITHOUT AN END** [72] [–]
(12"+=/cd-s+=) *(GONE X/CD 3)* – Meaner than mean / See the free world.

Jul 88. (7") *(GONE 4)* **A WISH AWAY. / JEALOUSY** [43] [–]
(12"+=/cd-s+=) *(GONE X/CD 4)* – Happy-sad / Goodbye fatman.

Aug 88. (lp/c)(cd) *(GON LP/MC 1)(837135-2) <837802>* **THE EIGHT LEGGED GROOVE MACHINE** [18] [ ]
– Redbury joy town / No for the 13th time / It's yer money I'm after baby / Rue the day / Give give give me more more more / Like a merry go round / The animals and me / A wish away / Grin / Mother and I / Some sad someone / Ruby horse / Unbearable / Poison. *(cd-iss. Apr95; same) (cd re-mast.Oct00; 549263-2)*

Sep 88. (7"ep/12"ep/cd-ep) *(GONE/+X/CD 5)* **IT'S YER MONEY I'M AFTER BABY / ASTLEY IN THE NOOSE. / OOH, SHE SAID / RAVE FROM THE GRAVE** [40] [–]

Feb 89. (7") *(GONE 6)* **WHO WANTS TO BE THE DISCO KING?. / UNBEARABLE (live)** [28] [–]
(12"+=/cd-s+=) *(GONEX/GONCD 6)* – Ten trenches deep (live) / No for the 13th time (live).

— added guests **JAMES TAYLOR** – organ (ex-PRISONERS) / **MARTIN BELL** – banjo

Sep 89. (7"/c-s) *(GONE/GONCS 7)* **DON'T LET ME DOWN, GENTLY. / IT WAS ME** [19] [–]
(12"+=/cd-s+=) *(GONEX/GONCD 7)* – ('A'extended).

Oct 89. (lp/c/cd) *(841 187-1/-4/-2)* **HUP** [5] [–]
– 30 years in the bathroom / Radio ass kiss / Golden green / Let's be other people / Piece of sky / Can't shape up / Good night though / Don't let me down, gently / Cartoon boyfriend / Unfaithful / Them, big oak trees / Room 410. *(re-iss. cd Apr95; same) (cd re-mast.Oct00; 549264-2)*

Nov 89. (7"/c-s) *(GONE/GONCS 8)* **GOLDEN GREEN. / GET TOGETHER** [33] [–]
(12"+=/cd-s+=) *(GONEX/GONCD 8)* – Gimme some truth.

— (Mar'90) **PAUL CLIFFORD** – bass; finally repl. The BASS THING (left '89); he later formed 8-piece The BRIDGE AND THE TUNNEL CREW.

May 90. (7"/c-s) *(GONE/GONCS 10)* **CIRCLESQUARE. / OUR NEW SONG** [20] [–]
(12"+=/cd-s+=) *(GONEX/GONCD 10)* – ('A'-Paranoia mix).

Mar 91. (7"/c-s) *(GONE/GONCD 11)* **THE SIZE OF A COW. / RADIO ASS KISS (live)** [5] [–]
(12"+=/cd-s+=) *(GONEX/GONCD 11)* – Give give give me more more more (live).

May 91. (7"/c-s) *(GONE/GONCS 12)* **CAUGHT IN MY SHADOW. / GIMME SOME TRUTH (live)** [18] [–]
(12"+=/cd-s+=) *(GONEX/GONCD 12)* – ('A'extended).

Jun 91. (cd/c/lp) *(847 252-2/-4/-1)* **NEVER LOVED ELVIS** [3] [–]
– Mission drive / Play / False start / Welcome to the cheap seats / The size of a cow / Sleep alone / Reaction / Inertia / Maybe / Grotesque / Here come everyone / Caught in my shadow / Line poem. *(re-iss. cd Apr95; same) (cd re-iss. Oct00; 549265-2)*

Aug 91. (7"/c-s) *(GONE/GONCS 13)* **SLEEP ALONE. / EL HERMANO DE FRANK** [43] [–]
(12"+=/cd-s+=) *(GONEX/GONCD 13)* – The takin' is easy.

— In Oct'91, they teamed up with comedian VIC REEVES (& BOB MORTIMER) on No.1 hit cover of Tommy Roe's 'DIZZY'. Next single with guest, KIRSTY MacCOLL

Jan 92. (7"ep/c-ep) *(GONE/GONCS 14)* **WELCOME TO THE CHEAP SEATS** [8] [–]
– Welcome to the cheap seats / Me, my mum, my dad and my brother / Will the circle be unbroken / That's entertainment.
(cd-ep+=) *(GONECD 14)* – ('A'naked mix) / Caught in my shadw (bare mix) / Circlesque (butt naked mix) / Can't shape up again.

— added **MARTIN BELL** – fiddle, accordion, mandolin, guitar, sitar, keyboards and 6th member **PETE WHITTAKER** – keyboards

Sep 93. (7"ep/c-ep/12"ep/cd-ep) *(GONE/GONCS/GONEX/GONCD 15)* **ON THE ROPES EP** [10] [–]
– On the ropes / Professional disturber of the peace / Hank and John / Whites.

Oct 93. (cd/c/lp) *(519 894-2/-4/-1)* **CONSTRUCTION FOR THE MODERN IDIOT** [4] [–]
– Change every light bulb / I wish them all dead / Cabin fever / Hot love now / Full of life (happy now) / Storm drain / On the ropes / Your big assed mother / Swell / A great drinker / Hush / Sing the absurd. *(cd re-mast.Oct00; 549266-2)*

Nov 93. (7") *(GONE 16)* **FULL OF LIFE (HAPPY NOW). / CLOSER TO FINE** [28] [–]
(cd-s+=) *(GONCD 16)* – Burger standing / A curious weird and ugly scene.
(cd-s) *(GONCDX 16)* – ('A'-Dignity mix) / Change every light bulb (dub mix) / I wish them all dead (dub mix).

— Note: Ex-member ROB JONES (THE BASS THING) died mysteriously on 30 Jul'93 in his New York apartment.

Mar 94. (7"ep/c-ep/cd-ep) *(GONE/GONEX/GONCD 17)* **HOT LOVE NOW! EP** [19] [–]
– Hot love now! / Just helicopters / I must've had something really useful to say / Room 512, all the news that's fit to print.
(cd-ep) *(GONCDX 17)* – ('A'cardinal error mix) / Unrest song / Flour babies / The Tipperary triangle.

— disbanded after July Phoenix Festival; MILES went on to work for MTV and form VENT 414 and go solo

WE KNOW WHERE YOU LIVE

— **TREECE / CLIFFORD / GILKS / + ANGE** – vocals (ex-EAT)

H.M.D. · not iss.

Nov 95. (7"ep/cd-ep) *(HMD 0016/0012)* **DON'T BE TOO HONEST. / CONFESSIONS OF A THUG / EXCUSE ME?** [ ] [–]

Noise Factory not iss.

Jun 96. (7") *(NFRS 002)* **DRAPED. / MENTAL HYGIENE (demo version)** –
(cd-s+=) *(NFRCD 002)* – Crude manipulator (crude version).

VENT 414

— **MILES HUNT** – vocals, guitar / **MORGAN NICHOLLS** – bass (ex-SENSELESS THINGS) / **PETE HOWARD** – drums (ex-EAT)

Polydor not iss.

Sep 96. (7"/c-s) *(575328-7/-4)* **FIXER. / KISSING THE MIRROR** 71 –
(cd-s+=) *(575328-2)* – Give it whole / Dimki pense.
(12"+=) *(575326-6)* – Shimmy.

Oct 96. (cd/c/lp) *(533048-2/-4/-1)* **VENT 414** –
– Fixer / Fits and starts / At the base of the fire / The last episode / Laying down with / life before you / Correctional / Easy to talk / Night out with a foreign fella / Kissing the mirror / At one / 2113 / Guess my god.

Nov 96. (7"/c-s) *(575534-7/-4)* **LIFE BEFORE YOU. / THE LAST EPISODE** –
(cd-s+=) *(575535-2)* – Your latest innuendo / Manifold 36 boro.

MILES HUNT

— w/ **MALCOLM TREECE** – guitar, vocals + **MARTIN BELL** – violin

Gig Orchard

Mar 99. (cd) *(GIG 1002-2)* **COMMON THREADS (live)** –
– Don't let me down gently / Give, give, give, me more, more, more / It's your money I'm after, baby / (blah, blah one) / Manna from Heaven / (blah, blah two) / Your latest innuendo / Fixer / Circle square / Caught in my shadow / Mission drive / (blah, blah three) / A wish away. *(re-iss. Dec00 as 'BY THE TIME I GOT TO JERSEY'; GIG 1007-2) <US-iss.Mar00 on 'Orchard' with new title; 689>*

May 99. (cd) *(GIG 1012-2)* <868> **HAIRY ON THE INSIDE** Mar00
– Manna from Heaven / Everything is not okay / Immortalising chase / Getting over you / Let's hope I get it right this time / The slow drowning / Four to the floor / Someone like the kingbird / Amongst the old reliables / Not in my plans. *(hidden track)*

Mar 00. (cd-ep) <5008> **LIFE'S GREAT!** –
– The truth at last / A quick fix / The feeling I've been waiting for / Smoked / Yes and a no.

Gig Gig

Dec 00. (cd-ep) <7707> **5 SONGS** –
– How many saints / The terrible / Straight lines / Line 'em up / Muzzle.

WONDER STUFF

HUNT, GILKS, JONES + TREECE re-formed for a reunion gig

Eagle not iss.

Jun 01. (d-cd) *(EDGCD 179)* **CURSED WITH INSINCERITY (live 2000)** –
– Can't shape up / A wish away / Unbearable / Full of life (happy now) / Caught in my shadow / Cartoon boyfriend / Here comes everyone / Circle Square / Golden green / Welcome to the cheap seats / The size of a cow / Red berry joy town / Ruby horse / Sleep alone / Donation / Room 512, all the news that's fit to print / On the ropes / Who wants to be the disco king? / Ten trenches deep / Mission drive / Give, give, give, me more, more, more / It's your money I'm after, baby / No, not for the 13th time / Don't let me down gently / A song without an end / Good night though.

– compilations, etc. –

Sep 94. (7"/c-s/cd-s) *Polydor; (GONE/GONCS/GONCD 18)* **UNBEARABLE. / INSIDE YOU / HIT BY A CAR** 16 –
(cd-s) *(GONCDX 18)* – ('A'original) / Ten trenches deep / I am a monster / Frank.

Sep 94. (cd/c) *Polydor; (521 397-2/-4/-1)* **IF THE BEATLES HAD READ HUNTER . . . THE SINGLES** 8 –
– Welcome to the cheap seats / A wish away / Caught in my shadow / Don't let me gently / Size of a cow / Hot love now! / Dizzy / Unbearable / Circlesquare / Who wants to be the disco king? / Golden green / Give give give me more more more / Sleep alone / Coz I luv you / Full of life / On the ropes / It's yer money I'm after baby / It's not true.

Jul 95. (cd) *Windsong; (WINCD 074)* **LIVE IN MANCHESTER (live)** 74 –

Nov 00. (d-cd) *Polydor; (549454-2)* **LOVE BITES AND BRUISES: THE WONDER STUFF ANTHOLOGY** –

MILES HUNT CLUB

HUNT with **MICHAEL FERENTINO** – bass, guitars, keyboards, vocals + **ANDRES KARU** – drums, percussion, keyboards

Eagle Red Ink

Mar 02. (cd-s) *(EAGXS 217)* **EVERYTHING IS NOT OKAY / THE TERRIBLE SELVES / MUZZLE** –

Apr 02. (cd) *(EAGCD 197)* <19351> **THE MILES HUNT CLUB** Aug02
– Everything is not okay / Traces / Not in my plans / Diluted / Straight lines / Amongst the old reliables / Smoked / The truth at last / The feeling I've been waiting for / Line 'em up / Love can make you sorry / Flapping on the pier (pt.2).

□ Roy WOOD (see under ⇒ MOVE)

Link WRAY

Born: LINCOLN WRAY, 2 May'30, Dunn, North Carolina, USA. The (part Shawnee Indian) guitarist's first music venture was a country band (LUCKY WRAY & THE LAZY PINE WRANGLERS) consisting of his brothers DOUG and VERNON; the trio – who subsequently renamed themselves LUCKY WRAY & THE PALOMINO RANCH HANDS – recruited SHORTY HORTON and cut a debut EP for the local 'Kay' label. After losing a lung from TB in the Korean War, WRAY increasingly concentrated on his guitar technique; by the release of 1958's 'RUMBLE' (a one-off debut for 'Cadence'), he'd developed a primitive yet pioneering style of 6-string distortion which would see the aforementioned track have a seismic influence on the development of white guitar-rock and in turn, Heavy Metal. A Top 20 US hit, LINK WRAY & HIS WRAYMEN moved on to 'Epic' for their follow-up, 'RAW-HIDE', another classic Top 30 instrumental that was again slated for apparently appealing to juvenile delinquents. After the major label failed to tone the man down for popular consumption, WRAY set up his own 'Rumble' records and released the original version of 'JACK THE RIPPER'. The Philadelphia-based 'Swan' imprint turned this platter into a minor hit in 1963, although subsequent 45's would fail to impress the majority of the American record buying public. He made several attempts to revive his flagging career, although all were in vain (probably too busy looking after his nine children from three marriages). 1971's eponymous comeback set (which included a version of Willie Dixon's 'TRAIL DRAGGER') was recorded in his home studio (a converted chicken coop), a more mellow effort that attempted to resurrect the various American Roots traditions. Having spent a short spell on Richard Branson's 'Virgin' label in the mid-70's, WRAY was back in the spotlight in '77 after scoring a minor hit ('RED HOT') with rockabilly punk man ROBERT GORDON (ex-TUFF DARTS). With groups like The CRAMPS, The GUN CLUB, etc, citing him as a major influence, WRAY was never short of a recording contract (or three . . .), 1993's 'INDIAN CHILD' recorded in Denmark where he now resides.

Album rating: LINK WRAY & THE WRAY MEN (*5) / JACK THE RIPPER (*5) / LINK WRAY (*8) / BE WHAT YOU WANT TO (*5) / BEANS AND FATBACK (*4) / RUMBLE! – THE BEST OF LINK WRAY compilation (*8) / INTERSTATE 10 (*4) / STUCK IN GEAR (*5) / BULLSHOT (*4) / LIVE AT THE PARADISO (*4) / LIVE IN '85 (*4) / GROWLING GUITAR (*4) / INDIAN CHILD (*6)

LINK WRAY & HIS RAY MEN

between 1957-1964, his WRAYMEN were; **DOUG WRAY** – drums, sax, flute / **SHORTY HORTON** – bass (added in 1963; **VERNON WRAY** – keyboards)

London Cadence

May 58. (7") *(HLA 8623)* <1347> **RUMBLE. / THE SWAG** Apr58 16

not iss. — Epic

Jan 59. (7") *<9300>* **RAW-HIDE. / THE DIXIE-DOODLE** – 23
(UK-iss.1975; 15-2210)

1959. (7") *<9321>* **COMMANCHE. / LILLIAN** –

1959. (7") *<9343>* **SLINKY. / RENDEZVOUS** –

1960. (7") *<9361>* **GOLDEN STRINGS. / TRAIL OF THE LONESOME PINE** –

1960. (7") *<9419>* **MARY ANN. / AIN'T THAT LOVIN' YOU BABY** –

1960. (lp) *<LN 3661>* **LINK WRAY & THE WRAY MEN** –
– The Dixie-doodle / Ramble / Caroline / Raw-hide / Right turn / Golden strings / Comanche / Hambone / Mary Ann / Rumble mambo / Ain't that lovin' you baby / Slinky / Hand clapper / Lillian / Radar / Studio blues. *(UK version iss.1973 + Apr76 as 'ROCKIN' AND HANDCLAPPIN' on 'Epic'; EPC 63627) (UK-iss.Jun85 on 'Edsel'; ED 149) (cd-iss. Jan88; EDCD 149)*

1961. (7") *<9454>* **EL TORO. / TIAJUANA** –

not iss. — Rumble

1962. (7") *<1000>* **JACK THE RIPPER. / THE STRANGER** –

Stateside — Swan

Aug 63. (7") *(SS 217) <4137>* **JACK THE RIPPER. / THE BLACK WIDOW** Jun63 64

1963. (lp) *<SLP 510>* **JACK THE RIPPER** –
– Mr guitar / My Beth / Deacon Jones / Steel trap / Cross ties / Jack the Ripper / Ace of spades / Hidden charms / Fat back / Run chicken run / Dinosaur / Big Ben / Mash potato party / I'll do anything for you / Rendez-vous / Slinky *(UK-iss.Jun90 on 'Hangman'; HANG 033UP)*

Sep 63. (7") *<4154>* **TURNPIKE U.S.A. / WEEKEND** –

Nov 63. (7") *<4163>* **THE SWEEPER. / RUN CHICKEN RUN** –

Jan 64. (7") *(SS 256)* **THE SWEEPER. / WEEKEND** –

Feb 64. (7"ep) *(SE 1015)* **MR. GUITAR** –
– Mr. Guitar / Dinosaur / Run chicken run / Rumble.

1964. (7") *<4171>* **THE SHADOW KNOWS. / MY ALBERTA** –

1964. (7") *<4187>* **DEUCES WILD. / SUMMER DREAM** –

—— **BOBBY HOWARD** – vocals; repl. VERNON

Mar 65. (7") *(SS 397) <4201>* **GOOD ROCKIN' TONIGHT. / I'LL DO ANYTHING FOR YOU**

LINK WRAY

1965. (7") *<4211>* **BRANDED. / HANG ON** –

1965. (7") *<4232>* **GIRL FROM NORTH COUNTRY. / YOU HURT ME SO** –

1966. (7") *<4239>* **ACE OF SPADES. / THE FUZZ** –

1966. (7") *<4244>* **BATMAN THEME. / ALONE** –

1966. (7") *<4261>* **HIDDEN CHARMS. / ACE OF SPADES** –

1967. (7") *<4273>* **LET THE GOOD TIMES ROLL. / SOUL TRAIN** –

1967. (7") *<4284>* **JACK THE RIPPER. / I'D DO ANYTHING FOR YOU** –

not iss. — Heavy

1968. (7") *<101>* **RUMBLE '68. / BLOW YOUR MIND** –

not iss. — Mr.G

1969. (7") *<101>* **RUMBLE '69. / BLOW YOUR MIND** –

—— returned for the 70's, w/**DOUG + BOBBY + BILLY HODGES** – keyboards / **STEVE VERROCA** – drums

Polydor — Polydor

Sep 71. (lp) *(2489 029) <244064>* **LINK WRAY** Jul71
– La de da / Take me home Jesus / Jukebox mama / Rise and fall of Jimmy Stokes / Fallin' rain / Fire and brimstone / Ice people / God out west / Crowbar / Black river swamp / Tail dragger.

Sep 71. (7") *(2066 120) <14084>* **FIRE AND BRIMSTONE. / JUKEBOX MAMA**

Nov 71. (7") *<14096>* **FALLIN' RAIN. / JUKE BOX MAMA** –

—— w/loads on session incl. guests **PETER KAUKONEN + COMMANDER CODY**

Jul 73. (lp) *(2391 063) <5047>* **BE WHAT YOU WANT TO**
– Be what you want to / All cried out / Lawdy Miss Clawdy / Tucson, Arizona / Riverbed / You walked by / Walk easy, walk slow / All the love in my life / You realy got a hold on me / Shine the light / Morning.

Aug 73. (7") *<14188>* **LAWDY MISS CLAWDY. / SHINE THE LIGHT**

Nov 73. (7") *<14256>* **SHE'S THAT KIND OF WOMAN. / I GOT TO RUMBLE** –

—— w/1971 line-up, except **MORDICAI JONES** – piano, mandolin repl. BOBBY

Virgin — not iss.

Sep 73. (lp) *(V 2006)* **BEANS & FATBACK** –
– Beans and fatback / I'm so glad / Shaw Nee tribe / Hobo man / Georgia pines / Alabama circus / Water boy / From Tulsa to North Carolina / Right or wrong / In the pines / Take my hand.

Nov 73. (7") *(VS 103)* **I'M SO GLAD I'M SO PROUD. / SHAWNEE TRIBE** –

Apr 75. (lp) *(C 1511)* **INTERSTATE 10** – French –
(above issued on 'Caroline')

—— LINK now w/**ARCHIE LEGGAT** – bass / **FREDDIE SMITH** – drums, percussion / **GORDON SMITH** – steel guitar / **RUAN O'LOCHLAINN** – keyboards, alto sax

Mar 76. (lp) *(V 2050)* **STUCK IN GEAR** –
– Southern lady / Tecolote / Quicksand / I know you're leaving me now / Did you see the man / Midnight lover / Cottoncandy apples / Bo Jack / Jack the ripper.

Apr 76. (7") *(VS 142)* **I KNOW YOU'RE LEAVING ME NOW. / QUICKSAND** –

—— between 1977 & 1978, LINK WRAY teamed up with ex-TUFF DARTS singer ROBERT GORDON on two albums, 'ROBERT GORDON WITH LINK WRAY' and 'FRESH FISH SPECIAL'; the single 'THE WAY I WALK' was also a dual effort.

—— now with **ANTON FIG** – drums / **CHRIS ROBINSON** – keyboards, synthesizers / + producer **RICHARD GOTTEHEIR** – piano, etc.

Chiswick — not iss.

Mar 78. (7"; w-drawn) *(NS 32)* **BATMAN THEME. / HIDDEN CHARMS** – –

Charisma — Visa

May 79. (7"blue) *(CB 333)* **IT'S ALL OVER NOW, BABY BLUE. / JUST THAT KIND OF SWITCHBLADE** –

May 79. (lp) *(CAS 1143) <7009>* **BULLSHOT**
– Good good lovin' / Fever / Snag / Just that kind of switchblade / It's all over now, baby blue / Rawhide / Wild party / The sky is falling / Don't. *(cd-iss. Nov89 on 'Line'; LICD 9.00142)*

—— w/**ANTON FIG** / + **JIMMY LOWELL** – bass

Magnum Force — Visa

Oct 80. (lp) *(MFLP 008) <7010>* **LIVE AT THE PARADISO (live)**
– Blue suede shoes / Ace of spades / Walk away from love / I saw her standing there / Run chicken run / She's no good / Rumble / Rawhide / Subway blues / Money / Shake, rattle and roll / Be bop a lula. *(re-iss. Jul82; MFM 012) (cd-iss. Apr91; CDMF 008)*

—— w/ **KEITH LENTIN** – bass, vocals / **MARTY FEIER** – drums

Big Beat — not iss.

Jan 86. (lp) *(WIKM 42)* **LIVE IN '85 (live)** –
– Rumble / It's only words / Fire / Mystery train / I gotta woman / Baby let's play house / Jack the ripper / Love me / King Creole / I'm counting on you / Rawhide / Born to be wild.

Sep 87. (lp) *(WIK 65)* **GROWLING GUITAR** (60's tracks) –
– Climbing a high wall / Genocide / The Earth is crying / Growlin' guts / Hungry / Ace of spades / Ruby baby / Hang on / Summer dreams / Sorrento / Peggy Sue / Alone / Girl from North Country / You hurt me so / The fuzz. *(cd-iss. May91+=; CDWIK 972)* – LIVE IN '85

—— with **KIM HYTTEL** – keyboards / **FLEMMING NILSSON** – percussion / **SHAKY GROUND band: JAN MOLS** – rhythm guitar, vocals / **CARSTEN EGHOLM** – bass / **ERIK LODBERG** – drums (he now writes music & lyrics with wife OLIVE

Ball Product — Sony Denmark

Jun 93. (cd) *(SHED 001CD)* **INDIAN CHILD**
– Torture / Trying to find your love / Indian child / God's litle baby / I apologize / Saving all my love / Diamonds and pearls / It was Elvis / Guitar man from New Orleans / Bring on the night.

– (selective) compilations, etc. –

Mar 79. (lp) *Ace-Chiswick; (CH 6)* **THE EARLY RECORDINGS** –

Apr 79. (lp) *Charly; (CR 30171)* **ROCK'N'ROLL RUMBLE** –
(re-iss. May83 as 'GOOD ROCKIN' TONITE' on 'Ace'; CH 69)

Nov 89. (cd) *Ace; (CDCH 924)* **THE ORIGINAL RUMBLE** –

Jun 90. (cd) *Ace; (CDCHD 931)* **APACHE / WILD SIDE OF THE CITY LIGHTS** –

Apr 91. (cd) *Big Beat; (CDWIK 972)* **LIVE IN 85 / GROWLING GUITAR** –

May 93. (cd) *Columbia; (472866-2)* **WALKING WITH LINK**

Apr 96. (cd) *Polydor; (527717-2)* **GUITAR PREACHER: THE POLYGRAM YEARS**
Jan 97. (cd) *Ace-Charly; (CDCHD 638)* **SHADOWMAN**
Feb 97. (cd) *Visionary; (VICD 010)* **WALKING DOWN A STREET CALLED LOVE: THE RUMBLE MAN LIVE IN LONDON AND MANCHESTER (live)**
(re-iss. Mar03 on 'Cherry Red'; CDMRED 227)
Sep 97. (d-cd) *Norton; (CED 242)* **MR. GUITAR**
Oct 97. (cd) *Rollercoaster; (CDROLL 3011)* **THE SWAN SINGLES COLLECTION**
May 98. (cd) *Rollercoaster; (RCCD 3032)* **THEY'RE OFF AND RUMBLIN'**
Sep 00. (cd) *Ace; (CDCHD 770)* **BARBED WIRE**
Feb 02. (d-cd) *Sundazed; <(SC 11098)>* **SLINKY: THE EPIC SESSIONS 1958-1961**
Mar 02. (cd) *Ace; (CDCHD 837)* **LAW OF THE JUNGLE**
Mar 03. (cd) *Disky; (EMI 76404-2)* **GUITAR LEGENDS**

☐ Richard WRIGHT (see under ⇒ PINK FLOYD)

WU-TANG CLAN

Formed: Staten Island, New York, USA . . . 1992 by the RZA (aka THE ABBOT) and a posse of several young rappers under the pseudonyms; METHOD MAN, GENIUS/GZA, CHEF RAEKWON, OL' DIRTY BASTARD, GHOSTFACE KILLAH and U-GOD. The RZA was originally a solo artist (who at one point stood trial for murder) and the man responsible for forming GRAVEDIGGAZ, a gothic hip hop outfit who later worked with TRICKY. All chess-loving, blunt-smoking wordsmiths, the 'CLAN were highly influenced by martial art movies and took their name from the WU-TANG or SHAOLIN sword. In 1991, GENIUS released a debut album for 'Cold Chillin', 'WORDS FROM THE GENIUS', followed a year later by the 'CLAN's first single, the self-financed, 'PROTECT YA NECK'. The following year, the conglomerate signed for 'R.C.A.', although each member was allowed to retain his separate contract, if he had one. In 1993, complete with Kung-Fu style movie samples, WU-TANG CLAN's acclaimed debut 'ENTER THE WU-TANG (36 CHAMBERS)', scaled the US charts and showed the socially aware, wise-cracking gang in full flow. With their lavish use of sampled jazz/soul, loping beats and breathtaking, expletive-filled spitfire rapping, the crew opened up a whole new chapter of the ever unfolding hip hop saga and, for a while at least, breathed some spliff-heavy air into a stagnant scene. However, in March the following year, tragedy struck when U-GOD's toddler son, Dante, was seriously injured by a bullet in a crossfire battle. 1995 proved to be a busy and commercially fruitful year for most of the gang, especially OL' DIRTY BASTARD, METHOD MAN, CHEF RAEKWON and GENIUS/GZA, the latter unleashing the highly praised 'LIQUID SWORDS' set later that year. WU-TANG themselves made a belated return in 1997 with the feverishly anticipated 'WU-TANG FOREVER', an album which broke records by gatecrashing/topping both the US and UK charts simultaneously, an incredible feat for a hip hop act. Even more surprisingly, the set was a double; on reflection, the material could have been pared down to a blistering single disc although the schizophrenic combination of melodic but hard-bitten soul and frenetic rapping was rarely less engaging. Early in '98, GHOSTFACE KILLAH was jailed for three months on a 1995! attempted robbery charge, while on June 30th, OL' DIRTY BASTARD was wounded in the back and arm after being shot by an intruder (in his cousin's New York apartment); he er, discharged himself a day later! ODB was up on a number of separate charges the following year in which he was alleged to have threatened security guards then (a few months later) his girlfriend before topping it all off with a shoot-out with the police; the latter would see him charged with attempted murder, although after a short-stay in jail (a six-figure bail was paid) this case – and later the others – was thrown out due to lack of evidence. Were they out to get 'im, who knows? The rapper (who was admitted to a drug rehabilitation center in August '99) was back on the record front soon after, 'N***A PLEASE' (1999) the RICK JAMES-meets-IGGY POP-stylings making it the best WU-TANG platter for some time. In fact, mostly all the 'CLAN were at the solo game in the last few years, INSPECTAH DECK philosophising with his 'UNCONTROLLED SUBSTANCE' (in September also), the GENIUS/GZA swordsman with 'BENEATH THE SURFACE' (in July '99) and master CLANsman RZA with their 'HITS' package (also in July) – RZA, wrote, produced, directed and starred in his own movie, 'BOBBY DIGITAL', which also featured WU-TANG members and was released late in '98. Around the same time, METHOD MAN made a re-appearance with 'TICAL 2000: JUDGEMENT DAY', while KILLAH PRIEST (via 'HEAVY MENTAL') and CAPPADONNA (via 'THE PILLAGE') were both out and about in March of 1998 – note also that GHOSTFACE KILLAH issued his solo 'IRONMAN' in October '96. Phew! and is if that wasn't enough, towards the end of the decade, CHEF RAEKWON added 'IMMOBILARITY' to WU-TANG's stock-pile release schedule, while METHOD MAN (and "outsider" REDMAN) had their 'BLACKOUT!' collaboration – all albums, monster sellers in the big U.S. of A. Come the new millennium, it was only fitting that the apocalyptically inclined CLAN get back together for another dose of street-poet doom-mongering. 'THE W' (2000) pared both the running time and sound back to a digestible level, resulting in a tighter, tougher and ultimately more menacing rhythmic and lyrical flow. It also focused and concentrated their brooding essence, which had arguably been dispersed in the avalanche of solo projects. The surfeit of guest collaborators (everyone from SNOOP DOGG to JUNIOR REID) may have detracted from RZA's sonic originality but when it resulted in such gutter-scarred ferocity as 'LET MY NIGGAS LIVE', this seemed a minor quibble. GHOSTFACE KILLAH released his feisty sophomore effort, 'SUPREME CLIENTELE' (2000), the same year, utilising a raft of producers to create a comfortingly belligerent sound absent on the tarted-up 'BULLETPROOF WALLETS' (2001). The WU-TANG CLAN no doubt surprised even themselves by getting their shit together two years in a row. Even more surprising, perhaps, 'IRON FLAG' (2001) – with ODB – was another focused effort, RZA keeping the production frills to a minimum on a set that was closer in spirit to their East Coast roots. Solo outings in 2001 came courtesy of RZA's BOBBY DIGITAL ('DIGITAL BULLET'), while the same man brought out two sets, the Various Artists 'THE WORLD ACCORDING TO RZA' and the "real" solo 'BIRTH OF A PRINCE'; he also contributed to Quentin Tarantino's 'Kill Bill Vol.1' martial arts movie. A year previous to this saw ODB branch out on his own label 'D-3' (having been dissed by 'Elektra' after his drug busts) for the extremely disappointing 'THE TRIALS AND TRIBULATIONS OF RUSSELL JONES' (2002).

Album rating: ENTER THE WU-TANG (36 CHAMBERS) (*8) / WU-TANG FOREVER (*7) / WU-TANG RECORDS PRESENTS: WU-CHRONICLES various artists compilation (*5) / Genius/GZA: WORDS FROM THE GENIUS (*6) / LIQUID SWORDS (*8) / BENEATH THE SURFACE (*7) / Ol' Dirty Bastard: RETURN TO THE 36 CHAMBERS (*7) / N***A PLEASE (*8) / THE DIRTY STORY compilation (*6) / THE TRIALS AND TRIBULATIONS OF RUSSELL JONES (*4) / Method Man: TICAL (*7) / TICAL 2000: JUDGEMENT DAY (*7) / BLACKOUT! with Redman (*6) / Chef Raekwon: ONLY BUILT 4 CUBAN LINX (*7) / IMMOBILARITY (*5) / Ghostface Killah: IRONMAN (*7) / SUPREME CLIENTELE (*6) / BULLETPROOF WALLETS (*4) / Killah Priest: HEAVY

MENTAL (*6) / RZA: RZA AS BOBBY DIGITAL IN STEREO (*6) / THE RZA HITS various artists compilation (*7) / DIGITAL BULLET (*6) / THE WORLD ACCORDING TO RZA Various Artists (*4) / BIRTH OF A PRINCE (*5) / Inspectah Deck: UNCONTROLLED SUBSTANCE (*7) / Wu-Tang Clan: THE W (*7) / IRON FLAG (*6)

RZA (b. ROBERT DIGGS, 22 Aug'66) – producer, mixer / rappers **GENIUS** (aka GZA and MAXIMILLIAN) (b. GARY PRICE, 22 Aug'66) **METHOD MAN** (aka JOHNNY BLAZE and SHAQUAN) (b. CLIFFORD SMITH, 1 Apr'71) / **OL' DIRTY BASTARD** (aka DIRT McDIRT and OSIRIS) (b. RUSSELL JONES, 15 Nov'68) / **RAEKWON** (aka CHEF and LEX DIAMONDS) (b. COREY WOODS) / **GHOSTFACE KILLAH** (aka TONY STARKS) (b. DENNIS COLES, 9 May'70) / **U-GOD** (aka GOLDEN ARMS) (b. LAMONT HAWKINS) / **INSPECTAH DECK** (aka REBEL INS) (b. JASON HUNTER) / **CAPPADONNA** (aka CAPPUCCINO and TRACK SLASHER) (b. DARRYL HILL) / with other early members **MASTA KILLAH** (aka NOODLES and JAMAL) (b. ELGIN TURNER) / **SHYLEIM THE RUGGED PRINCE (PAUL) / DOLLY FINGERS / DREDDY KRUGER / KILLAH PRIEST** (b. WILLIAM REED) (of SUNZ OF MAN) / **4th DISCIPLE**

Loud-RCA Loud-RCA

May 93. (c-s)(12",cd-s) *<62544>* *<62530>* **PROTECT YA NECK. / (mixes)** [–] [ ]

Sep 93. (c-s,cd-s) *<62544>* **METHOD MAN / PROTECT YA NECK** [–] [69]

Feb 94. (c-s,12",cd-s) *<62829>* **C.R.E.A.M. (CASH RULES EVERYTHING AROUND ME). / DA MYSTERY OF CHESSBOXIN'** [–] [60]

May 94. (cd/c) *(74321 20367-2/-4)* *<66336>* **ENTER THE WU-TANG (36 CHAMBERS)** [ ] Nov93 [41]
– Bring da ruckus / Shame on a nigga / Clan in da front / Wu-Tang: 7th chamber / Can it all be so simple / (intermission) / Da mystery of chessboxin' / Wu-Tang Clan ain't nuthing ta f'wit / C.R.E.A.M. / Method Man / Protect ya neck / Tearz / Wu-Tang: 7th chamber – part II. *(cd+=)* – Method Man (skunk mix) / (conclusion).

—— were back (**RZA The Abbott / GZA The Genius / DIRTY Osirus / U-GOD Golden Arms / METHOD MAN Hott Nikkels / RAEKWON Lex Diamonds / GHOSTFACE KILLAH Ironman / INSPECTAH DECK Fifth Brother / MASTA KILLAH High Chief / CAPPADONNA Jaybird,** plus STREET LIFE, TEKITHA or POPPA WU and UNCLE PETE / **TRUEMASTER** (b. DAVID HARRIS) a new member now on tour

Jun 97. (d-cd/d-c) *(74321 45769-2/-4)* *<66905>* **WU-TANG FOREVER** [1] [1]
– Wu-revolution / Reunited / For Heaven's sake / Cash still rules – Scary hours (still don't nothing move but the money) / Visionz / As high as Wu-Tang get / Severe punishment / Older gods / Maria / A better tomorrow / It's yourz / / Intro / Triumph / Impossible / Little ghetto boys / Deadly melody / The city / The projects / Bells of war / The M.G.M. / Dog sh*t / Duck seazon / Hellz wind staff / Heaterz / Black shampoo / Second coming / The closing / Sunshower / Projects international remix.

Aug 97. (12"/cd-s) *(74321 49678-1/-2)* **TRIUMPH. / PROJECTS INTERNATIONAL** [ ] [ ]
(cd-s+=) *(74321 51021-2)* – Diesel.
(above featured CAPPADONNA)

—— In Mar'98, the WU-TANG CLAN featured on TEXAS's new UK Top 5 version of 'SAY WHAT YOU WANT'

Aug 98. (cd/c/d-lp; as RZA presents WU-TANG KILLA BEES) *<(50013)>* **THE SWARM VOLUME 1** [ ] Jul98 [4]
– (Various cuts from some of the WU-TANG CLAN and new talents including SUNZ OF MAN and BLACK KNIGHTS OF THE NORTH STAR)

Mar 99. (cd/d-lp) *(WT 004 CD/LP)* *<51143>* **WU-TANG RECORDS PRESENTS: WU-CHRONICLES** (V/A compilation) [ ] [25]
(above 2 issued on 'Wu-Tang Records')

Nov 00. (c-s) *(670518-4)* **GRAVEL PIT / PROTECT YA NECK (THE JUMP OFF) (dirty)** [6] [ ]
(12"+=) *(670518-6)* – Protect ya neck (the jump off) (Dirty DJ mix).
(cd-s++=) *(670518-2)* – ('A'-video).

Nov 00. (cd/c/d-lp) *(499576-2/-4/-1)* *<62193>* **THE W** [19] [5]
– Intro (Shaolin finger jab) – Chamber music / Careful (click, click) / Hollow bones / Redbull (with REDMAN) / One blood under W (with JUNIOR READ) / Conditioner (with SNOOP DOGG) / Protect ya neck (the jump off) / Let my niggas live (with NAS) / I can't go to sleep (with ISAAC HAYES) / Do you really (thang, thang) (with ISAAC HAYES) / Monument (with BUSTA RHYMES) / Gravel pit / Jah world (with JUNIOR READ).

Dec 01. (cd) *(504752-2)* *<86236>* **IRON FLAG** [ ] [32]
– In the hood / Rules / Chrome wheels / Soul power (black jungle) / Uzi (pinky ring) / One of these days / Ya'll been warned / Babies / Radioactive (four assassins) / Back in the game (with RON ISLEY) / Iron flag / Dashing (reasons).

– other associated releases, etc. –

OL' DIRTY BASTARD

Elektra Elektra

Feb 95. (c-s,cd-s) *<64477>* **BROOKLYN ZOO / ('A'remix)** [–] [54]

Mar 95. (cd/c) *<(7559 61659-2/-4)>* **RETURN TO THE 36 CHAMBERS** (dirty version) [ ] [7]
– Intro / Shimmy shimmy ya / Baby c'mon / Brooklyn zoo / Hippa to da hoppa / Raw hide / Damage / Don't u know / The stomp / Goin' down / Drunk game (sweet sugar pie) / Snakes / Brooklyn zoo II (tiger crane) / Proteck ya neck II the zoo / Cuttin' headz / Dirty dancin' / Harlem world. *(cd+=)* – (2 extra).

May 95. (c-s,12"/cd-s) *<66419>* **SHIMMY SHIMMY YA. / ('A'version)** [–] [62]

—— In Jun'97, ODB featured on The ALKOHOLIKS minor US hit, 'Hip Hop Drunkies'. A month later, he was also on the BLACKstreet hit single, 'Fix'.

Sep 99. (cd/c) *<(7559 62414-2/-4)>* **N***A PLEASE** [ ] [10]
– Recognize / I can't wait / Cold blooded / Got your money / Rollin' wit' you / Getting high / You don't want to fuck with me / Nigga please / Dirt dog / I want pussy / Good morning heartache / All in together now.

Nov 99. (c-s/12"/cd-s; as OL' DIRTY BASTARD featuring KELIS) *(E 3719 C/T/CD)* *<radio cut>* **GOT YOUR MONEY / ROLLIN' WITH YOU** [ ] Oct99 [33]

Jun 00. (c-s/12"/cd-s; by OL' DIRTY BASTARD featuring KELIS) *(E 7077 C/T/CD)* **GOT YOUR MONEY (mixes)** [11] [ ]

Oct 01. (cd/lp) *<(7559 62683-2/-1)>* **THE DIRTY STORY: THE BEST OF OL' DIRTY BASTARD** (compilation) [ ] [ ]

—— he left the CLAN before 'IRON FLAG'; ODB hit US No.33 with his next set, 'THE TRIALS AND TRIBULATIONS OF RUSSELL JONES' (2002)

METHOD MAN

—— with RZA on co-writing credits

Def Jam Def Jam

Nov 94. (c-s,cd-s) *<85-3964>* **BRING THE PAIN / ('A'radio version)** [–] [45]

Apr 95. (12") *(12DEF 6)* *<85-4184>* **RELEASE YO' DELF / (3 'A'mixes)** [46] Feb95 [98]
(cd-s+=) *(DEFCD 6)* – (2 'A'mixes) / Bring the pain (remix).

Jul 95. (cd-s; METHOD MAN featuring MARY J. BLIGE) *(DEFDX 11)* *<85-1878>* **I'LL BE THERE FOR YOU / YOU'RE ALL I NEED TO GET BY** [10] Apr95 [3]
(12"+=) *(12DEF 11)* – Bring the pain (remix).
(cd-s++=) *(DEFCD 11)* – Release yo' delf.

Aug 95. (cd/c) *(529 174-2/-4)* *<523839>* **TICAL** [ ] [4]
– Tical / Biscuits / Bring the pain / All I need / What the blood clot / Meth Vs. Chef / Sub crazy / Release yo' delf / P.L.O. style / I get my thang in action / Mr. Sandman / Stimulation / Method Man (remix) / I'll be there for you – You're all I need to get by (featuring MARY J. BLIGE).

—— In Aug'95, METHOD MAN was credited with REDMAN on the single, 'HOW HIGH', which hit US No.13. In Oct'95, MM featured on CAPLETON's minor hit 'Wings Of The Morning'. Below from the movie, 'Batman Forever' on 'Atlantic' records.

Oct 95. (c-s,cd-s) *<87100>* **THE RIDDLER / ('A'-Riddler Hide-Out mix)** [–] [56]

Nov 98. (cd/d-lp) *<(558 920-2/-1)>* **TICAL 2000: JUDGEMENT DAY** [49] [2]
– 1999: Judgement day (intro) / Perfect world / Cradle rock (featuring LEFT EYE) / Dangerous grounds (featuring STREETLIFE) / Sweet love (skit) / Sweet love (featuring CAPPADONNA & STREETLIFE) / Shaolin what (skit) / Torture / Where's Method Man? (skit featuring ED LOVER) / Suspect chin music (featuring STREETLIFE) / Retro godfather / Dooney boy / Spazzola (featuring STREETLIFE, RAEKWON, MASTA KILLA, KILLER SIN & INSPECTAH DECK) / Check writer (skit) / 2000: You play too much (CHRIS ROCK & METHOD MAN) / Party crasher / Grid iron rap (featuring STREETLIFE) / Step by step / Play IV keeps (featuring INSPECTAH DECK, STREETLIFE & MOBB DEPP) / Donald Trump / Snuffed out (skit featuring STREETLIFE) / Elements (featuring STAR & POLITE) / Killin' fields / Big dogs (featuring REDMAN) / Break ups 2

make ups (featuring D'ANGELO) / Message from Penny / Judgement day / C.E.O.utro.

Feb 99. (c-s/cd-s; as METHOD MAN featuring D'ANGELO) *<563405>* **BREAK UPS 2 MAKE UPS / DANGEROUS GROUNDS (featuring Streetlife) / I'LL BE THERE FOR YOU – YOU'RE ALL I NEED TO GET BY** [–] [98]

Mar 99. (12"/cd-s) *(566 851-1/845-2)* **JUDGEMENT DAY / (mixes)** [ ] [ ]

May 99. (12"/cd-s; by METHOD MAN featuring D'ANGELO) *(870927-1/-2)* **BREAK UPS 2 MAKE UPS (mixes).** [33] [–]
(cd-s) *(870929-2)* – (mixes).

Sep 99. (cd/lp; by METHOD MAN & REDMAN) *<(546609-2/-1)>* **BLACKOUT!** [45] [3]
– A special joint (intro) / Tear it off / Mi casa / Maaad crew / The? / Cheka / 1, 2, 1, 2 / Da rockwilder / Run 4 cover / 4 seasons / Dat's dat shit / Blackout / Y.O.U. / Cereal killer / Fire ina hole / Where we at (skit) / Well all rite cha / Big dogs / How high.

—— in Nov'99, METHOD MAN featured on US singles by D'ANGELO ('Left & Right') and LIMP BIZKIT ('N 2 Gether Now')

Dec 01. (cd-s; by METHOD MAN & REDMAN) *<588891>* **PART II** [–] [72]

—— also in May'01, METHOD MAN featured on JONELL's hit, 'Round & Round'

CHEF RAEKWON

Loud-RCA Loud-RCA

Jul 95. (c-s,cd-s) *<64375>* **GLACIERS OF ICE / CRIMINOLOGY** [–] [43]

Aug 95. (cd/c) *<(07863 66663-2/-4)>* **ONLY BUILT 4 CUBAN LINX . . .** [ ] [4]
– Striving for perfection / Knuckleheadz / Knowledge god / Criminology / Incarcerated scarfaces / Rainy dayz / Guillotine (swordz) / Can it all be so simple (remix) / Shark niggas (biters) / Ice water / Glaciers of ice / Verbal intercourse / Wisdom body / Spot rusherz / Ice cream / Wu-Gambinos / Heaven G Hell. *(cd+=)* – North Star (jewels).

Oct 95. (c-s,cd-s) *<64426>* **INCARCERATED SCARFACES / ICE CREAM** [–] [37] [71]

—— RAEKWON featured on FAT JOE's minor US hit 'FIREWATER' / 'ENVY'

Loud-Epic Loud-Columbia

Nov 99. (cd/c/lp) *(496361/-2/-4/-1) <63844>* **IMMOBILARITY** [ ] [9]
– Intro / Yae yo / Casablanca / 100 rounds / Real life / Power / Skit No.1 / All I got is you pt.II / Jury / Fuck them / Skit No.2 / Live from New York / My favourite dred / Friday / The table / Sneakers / Raw / Pop shit / Heart to heart / Forecast / Outro.

GENIUS/GZA

with some of the posse

Geffen Geffen

Oct 95. (c-s)(cd-s) *<19390>* **LIQUID SWORDS / LABELS** [–] [48]

Nov 95. (cd/c/lp) *<(GED/GEC/GEF 24813)>* **LIQUID SWORDS** [73] [9]
– Killah Hills 10304 / Liquid swords / Living in the world today / Investigative reports / Duel of the Iron Mic / Labels / Cold world / Gold / I gotcha back / Swordsman / 4th chamber / Shadowboxin' / B.I.B.L.E. (Basic Instructions Before Leaving Earth) / Hell's wind staff / Unexplained.

Feb 96. (c-s; GENIUS/GZA featuring Inspektah Deck a.k.a. Rollie Fingers) *(GFSC 2214) <19391>* **COLD WORLD (RZA mix) / COLD WORLD (power mix)** [40] Dec95 [97]
(12"+=/cd-s+=) *(GFST/+D 2214)* – B.I.B.L.E.
above featuring D'ANGELO

Mar 96. (c-s,cd-s; GENIUS/GZA featuring METHOD MAN) *<19396>* **SHADOWBOXIN' / (instrumental) / SHADOWBOXIN' (2 versions)** [–] [67]

M.C.A. M.C.A.

Jul 99. (cd/d-lp as GZA) *<(MCD/MCA 11969)>* **BENEATH THE SURFACE** [56] [9]
– Intro / Amplified sample / Beneath the surface / Skit 1 / Skit 2 / Crash your crew / Breaker breaker / High price small reward / Hip hop fury / Skit 3 / 1112 / Skit 4 / Victim / Publicity / Feel like an enemy / Stingplay (like dis – like dat) / Mic trippin' / Outro.

RZA

not iss. Big Beat

Aug 96. (c-s,cd-s; RZA featuring METHOD MAN & CAPPADONNA) *<98045>* **WU-WEAR: THE GARMENT RENAISSANCE / GET DOWN FOR MINE (REAL LIVE)** [–] [60]
(above from the film, 'High School High')

Gee Street V2

Nov 98. (cd/d-lp) *(GEE 100380-2/-1) <32521>* **RZA AS BOBBY DIGITAL IN STEREO** [70] [16]
– Intro / B.O.B.B.Y. / Unspoken word / Slow grind African / Airwaves / Love Jones / N.Y.C. everything / Mantis / Slow grind French / Holocaust (silkworm) / Terrorist / Bobby did it (Spanish fly) / Handwriting on the wall / Kiss of a black widow / Slow grindi Italian / My lovin' is digi / Domestic violence / Project talk / Lab drunk / Fuck what you think / Daily routine.

Epic Epic

Jun 99. (cd/c) *(492542-2/-4) <69610>* **THE RZA HITS** (V/A compilation) [ ] [61]
– RZA: (narration) / WU-TANG CLAN: Wu-Tang Clan ain't nothin' to fuck with / Protect ya neck / OL' DIRTY BASTARD: Shimmy / GENIUS/GZA: Liquid swords / METHOD MAN: Method man / RAEKWON THE CHEF: Incarcerated surfaces / Ice cream / RZA: (narration) / METHOD MAN: Bring the pain / GHOSTFACE KILLAH; Winter warz / OL' DIRTY BASTARD: Brooklyn zoo / METHOD MAN: All I need / WU-TANG CLAN: Cream / GHOSTFACE KILLAH: All that I got is you / RZA: (narration) / WU-TANG CLAN: Wu wear the garment renaissance.

Koch Int. Koch Int.

Sep 01. (cd-s; as BOBBY DIGITAL) *(KOCDS 8335)* **LA RHUMBA / LA RHUMBA (dirty) / LA RHUMBA (instrumental) / LA RHUMBA (acappella) / SHOW U LOVE (dirty)** [ ] [ ]

Sep 01. (cd/lp; RZA as BOBBY DIGITAL) *<(KOC CD/LP 8182)>* **DIGITAL BULLET** [ ] [24]
– Show U love / Can't loose / Glocko pop / Must be Bobby / Brooklyn babies / Domestic violence (part 2) / Do U / Fools / La rhumba / Black widow (part 2) / Shady / Break bread / Bong bong / Throw your flag up / Be a man / Righteous way / Build strong / Sickness.

Virgin E.M.I.

Apr 03. (cd/d-lp; Various Artists) *(CD/LP VIR 207) <584255>* **THE WORLD ACCORDING TO RZA** [ ] [ ]

Sanctuary Sanctuary

Oct 03. (cd) *(SANCD 231) <84652>* **THE BIRTH OF A PRINCE** [ ] [49]
– Bob n' L / The grunge / We pop / Grits / Fast cars / Chi kung / You'll never know / Drink, smoke + fcuk / The whistle / The drop off / Wherever I go / Koto chotan / A day to God is 1,000 years / Cherry range / The birth / See the joy.

Nov 03. (cd-s; by RZA & OL' DIRTY BASTARD) *(SANXD 241) <9934>* **WE POP (mixes)** [ ] [ ]

GHOSTFACE KILLAH

Razor Sharp – Epic Razor Sharp – Epic

Oct 96. (cd/c) *(485389-2/-4) <67729>* **IRONMAN** [38] [2]
– Iron maiden / Wildflower / Faster blade / 260 / Assassination day / Poisonous darts / Winter warz / Box in hand / Fish / Camay / Daytona 500 / Motherless child / Black Jesus / After the smoke is clear / All that I got is you / Soul controller / Marvel. *(cd re-iss. Apr00; same)*

Jun 97. (c-s) *(664684-4)* **ALL THAT I GOT IS YOU / DAYTONA 500** [11] [ ]
(12"+=/cd-s+=) *(664684-6/-2)* – Camay.

Feb 00. (cd/lp) *(491955-2/-1) <69325>* **SUPREME CLIENTELE** [ ] [7]
– Intro / Nutmeg (with RZA) / One / Saturday nite / Ghost Deini (with SUPERB) / Apollo kids (with RAEKWON) / The grain (with RZA) / Buck 50 / Mighty healthy / Woodrow the base head / Stay true (with 60 SECOND ASSASSIN) / We made it (with SUPERB) / Stroke of death / Iron's theme / Malcolm / Who would you fuck / Child's play / Cherchez LaGhost / Wu banga / Clyde Smith (skit) / Iron's theme (conclusion).

Jul 00. (cd-s) *<79464>* **CHERCHEZ LaGHOST (mixes; clean / instrumental / album)** [–] [98]

—— in 2000, KILLAH featured on the MOS DEF hit single, 'Miss Fat Booty – part II'

Nov 01. (cd) *(501941-2)* **BULLETPROOF WALLETS** [ ] [ ]
– (intro) / Maxine / Flowers (with RAEKWON, METHOD MAN & SUPERB) / Never be the same again (with CARL THOMAS &

RAEKWON) / (Teddy skit) / Theodore (with TRIFE & TWITZ) / Ghostshowers / Strawberry (with KILLAH SIN) / The forest / The juks (pop your collar) (with TRIFE & SUPERB) / Walking thru darkness (with TAKITHA) / Jealousy / The Hilton (with RAEKWON) / (interlude) / Love session (with RUFF ENDZ) / Street chemistry.

INSPECTAH DECK

Loud-Epic Loud-Columbia

Oct 99. (cd/c) *(496180-2/-4) <1865>* **UNCONTROLLED SUBSTANCES** [ ] [19]
– Intro / Movas & shakers / 9th chamber / Uncontrolled substance / Femme fatale / Grand prix / Forget me not / Longevity / Word on the street / Elevation / Lovin you / Trouble man / R.E.C. room / Friction / Hyperdermix / Show n prove / Cause.

Robert WYATT

Born: ROBERT ELLIDGE, 28 Jan'45, Bristol, England. While at school he formed The WILDE FLOWERS with the HOPPER brothers, which soon spliced into two groups, CARAVAN and SOFT MACHINE. The latter was the band WYATT joined in 1966, but after four albums ('THE SOFT MACHINE', 'VOLUME 2', 'THIRD' & 'FOURTH'), he estranged himself from the group in '71, forming his own MATCHING MOLE. The previous year, his record label 'C.B.S.', had issued his first solo album, 'THE END OF THE EAR', which was assisted by fellow SOFT MACHINE members supplying the jazz-rock feel. In the summer of '73, WYATT was paralysed from the waist down after falling from a window, convalescing for several months at Stoke Mandeville hospital. He returned the following year (now confined to a wheel-chair), his single, a version of The MONKEES' 'I'M A BELIEVER' hitting the Top 30. Richard Branson had given him a break on 'Virgin' records earlier in the year, WYATT subsequently critically heralded for his NICK MASON-produced album, 'ROCK BOTTOM' (1974). The set featured such gems as 'SEA SONG' and 'LITTLE RED RIDING HOOD HITS THE ROAD' (in two parts). His second for the label, 'RUTH IS STRANGER THAN RICHARD' (1975), showed an even deeper side, WYATT covering CHARLIE HAYDEN's jazz track, 'SONG FOR CHE'. In 1977, he had another stab at the pop charts, a dire cover version of CHRIS ANDREWS' 'YESTERDAY MAN' being his final recording for some time. He signed to indie, 'Rough Trade' in 1980, releasing a number of singles prior to his comeback album, 'NOTHING CAN STOP US NOW' (1982). This featured his classy re-working of ELVIS COSTELLO and CLIVE LANGER's 'SHIPBUILDING'. In 1983, through constant airplay by Radio 1 DJ John Peel, the anti-Falklands war song gained a Top 40 placing. He continued to spread his political messages through his music, although he has never been one to preach, his songs retaining an intensely personal quality. He returned to penning his own material with a vengeance on 1985's 'OLD ROTTENHAT', titles such as 'THE UNITED STATES OF AMNESIA', 'VANDALUSIA' and 'EAST TIMOR' pretty much indicative of the record's brooding political atmospherics. While 'DONDESTAN' (1991) also had its quota of skeletal, subtly barbed commentaries, there were a clutch of co-writing credits for his wife Alfreda Benge, whose more abstruse poetic sensibilities lent the album's somber keyboard-led minimalism some balance. 'DONDESTAN (REVISITED)' (1998), meanwhile, was a remixed version of the record which attempted to flesh out the sparest songs and, in slightly rearranging the running order, sandwich the collaborations with his wife between the political commentary. The result was a less oppressive listen, one which drew out more of the record's quiet humour. 1997's 'SHLEEP' continued the songwriting collaboration with Benge, lending the record even more of a phantasmagorical sheen than usual. PAUL WELLER was also among the songwriting credits, penning the brief but memorable coda 'WHOLE POINT OF NO RETURN'. The WELLER association carried over into the brilliant 'CUCKOOLAND' (2003), where WYATT was also joined by the likes of BRIAN ENO, DAVID GILMOUR, PHIL MANAZANERA and ANNIE WHITEHEAD. If the compelling avant-jazz wiles of 'TRICKLE DOWN' and 'OLD EUROPEAN' were anything to go by, fans should probably be grateful that WYATT's record collection apparently doesn't stretch much beyond the post-bop era. Ditto the searching cover of the Tom Jobim/Víncius de Moraes bossa classic, 'INSENSATEZ', as graceful in its own way as his reading of the Boudleaux Bryant's tearjerker 'RAINING IN MY HEART'. • **Songwriters:** WYATT penned except: GRASS (Ivor Cutler) / STRANGE FRUIT (Billie Holiday) / AT LAST I AM FREE (Chic) / STALIN WASN'T STALLIN' (Golden Gate Quartet) / BIKO (Peter Gabriel). • **Trivia:** WYATT also provided session drums for SYD BARRETT (1969) / KEVIN AYERS (early 70's) / HENRY COW (1975) / NICK MASON (1981) / RAINCOATS (1981 and '83).

Album rating: THE END OF AN EAR (*6) / Matching Mole: MATCHING MOLE (*6) / MATCHING MOLE'S LITTLE RED RECORD (*6) / Robert Wyatt: ROCK BOTTOM (*7) / RUTH IS STRANGER THAN RICHARD (*7) / NOTHING CAN STOP US (*8) / ANIMALS mini (*4) / OLD ROTTENHAT (*6) / DONDESTAN (*6) / A SHORT BREAK mini (*5) / FLOTSAM JETSAM collection (*5) / GOING BACK A BIT: A LITTLE HISTORY OF ROBERT WYATT compilation (*8) / SHLEEP (*7) / DONDESTAN (REVISTED) (*6) / EPS BY ROBERT WYATT compilation (*6) / CUCKOOLAND (*8) / SOLAR FLARES BURN FOR YOU collection (*7)

ROBERT WYATT (solo) – vocals, drums (ex-SOFT MACHINE) w / **DAVID SINCLAIR** – oboe (of CARAVAN) / **MARK CHARIG** – cornet (of SOFT MACHINE) / **ELTON DEAN** – sax / plus **NEVILLE WHITEHEAD** – bass / **CYRIL AYERS** – percussion

C.B.S. Columbia

Oct 70. (lp) *(64189) <31846>* **THE END OF AN EAR** [ ] [ ]
– Las Vegas tango (part 1) / To Mark everywhere / To saintly Bridget / To Oz alien Daevyd and Gilly / To Nick everyone / To caravan and Brother Jim / To the old world (thank you for the use of your body) / To Carla, Marsha and Caroline (for making everything beautifuller) / Las Vegas tango (part 2). *(re-iss. Aug80 on 'Embassy' lp/c; CBS/40 31846) (cd-iss. Apr93 on 'Sony Europe') (cd re-iss. Nov02 on 'Columbia'; 493342-2)*

MATCHING MOLE

WYATT with retained guest **D.SINCLAIR** and band **DAVE McRAE** – keyboards / **BILL McCORMICK** – bass (ex-QUIET SUN) / **PHIL MILLER** – guitar (ex-DYBLE, COXHILL & THE MB's) (same label)

Apr 72. (lp) *(64850) <32148>* **MATCHING MOLE** [ ] [ ]
– O Caroline / Instant pussy / Signed curtain / Part of the dance / Instant kitten / Dedicated to Hugh, but you weren't listening / Beer as in braindeer / Immediate curtain. *(re-iss. Mar82; CBS 32105) (cd-iss. Mar93 on 'Beat Goes On'; BGOCD 175)*

Apr 72. (7") *(8101)* **O CAROLINE. / SIGNED CURTAIN** [ ] [–]

Oct 72. (lp) *(65260)* **MATCHING MOLE'S LITTLE RED RECORD** [ ] [ ]
– Gloria gloom / God song / Flora fidgit / Smoke signal / Starting in the middle of the day we can drink all our politics away / Marchides / Nan's true hole / Righteous rumba / Brandy as in Benji. *(cd-iss. Jul93 on 'Beat Goes On'; BGOCD 174) (cd re-iss. Mar97 on 'Columbia Rewind'; 471488-2)*

— In the summer of '73, WYATT was paralysed from the waist down after falling from a window. After a year convalescing, but still in a wheelchair;

ROBERT WYATT

returned as solo vocalist. He was augmented by guests/friends **FRED FRITH** – percussion / **HUGH HOPPER** – bass / **GARY WINDO** – wind / **LAURIE ALLEN** – drums / **MIKE OLDFIELD** – guitar / **RICHARD SINCLAIR** – bass / **IVOR CUTLER** – vox, keyboards / **ALFREDA BENGE** – vocals

		Virgin	Virgin
Jul 74.	(lp/c) *(V/TCV 2017) <13112>* **ROCK BOTTOM** – Sea song / A last straw / Little Red Riding Hood hits the road (part 1) / Alifib / Alife / Little Red Riding Hood hit the road (part 2). *(cd-iss. Feb89; CDV 2017)*	☐	☐
Sep 74.	(7") *(VS 114)* **I'M A BELIEVER. / MEMORIES**	29	☐

—— **WYATT** retained **FRITH, ALLEN & WINDO** and contributions from **PHIL MANZANERA** – guitar / **BILL McCORMICK** – bass / **BRIAN ENO** – synthesizers / **JOHN GREAVES** – bass / **MONEZI FEZI** – trumpet / **GEORGE KHAN** – saxophone

May 75.	(lp/c) *(V/TCV 2034)* **RUTH IS STRANGER THAN RICHARD** – Muddy house: (a) Solar flames – (b) Five black notes and one white tone – (c) Muddy mouth / Soup song / Sonia / Team spirit 1 & 2 / Soup for Che. *(cd-iss. Feb89; CDV 2034)*	☐	☐
Apr 77.	(7") *(VS 115)* **YESTERDAY MAN. / SONJA**	☐	–

—— accompanied only by **McCORMICK** – bass / **HARRY BECKETT** – flugelhorn (B-side)

		Rough Trade	not iss.
Mar 80.	(7") *(RT 037)* **ARAUCO. / CAIMENERA**	☐	–

—— now used only **MOGOTSI MOTHLE** – double bass / **FRANK ROBERTS** – keyboards

Nov 80.	(7") *(RT 052)* **AT LAST I AM FREE. / STRANGE FRUIT**	☐	–
Feb 81.	(7") *(RT 046)* **STALIN WASN'T STALLIN'. / STALINGRAD (P. Blackman)**	☐	–

—— now with **ESMAIL SHEK** – tabla / **KADIR DURUESH** – shenzi

Aug 81.	(7") *(RT 81)* **GRASS. / TRADE UNION (Dishari featuring Abdus Salique)**	☐	–
Apr 82.	(lp) *(ROUGH 35)* **NOTHING CAN STOP US** – Born again cretin / At last I am free / Quantanera / Grass / Stalin wasn't stalling / The red flag / Strange fruit / Arauco / Strange fruit / Trade union / Stalingrad. *(re-iss. Apr83 lp+=/c+=; ROUGH/+C 35)* – Shipbuilding. *(cd-iss. May87; ROUGHCD 35)*	☐	–

—— Above album featured musicians as 1980-82.

—— In Apr'82, WYATT was credited on BEN WATT ep 'SUMMER INTO WINTER'.

—— guests **STEVE NIEVE** – piano / **MARK BEDDERS** – double bass / **MARTIN HUGHES** – drums / **CLIVE LANGER** – organ / **ELVIS COSTELLO** – b.vox

Aug 82.	(7") *(RT 115)* **SHIPBUILDING. / MEMORIES OF YOU** *(12"-iss.Nov82+=; RTT 115)* – Round midnight. *(re-iss. Apr83; same); hit No.35)*	☐	–

—— now with ? plus **HUGH HOPPER**, etc.

May 84.	(m-lp) *(ROUGH 40)* **THE ANIMAL FILM (Soundtrack)** – (no tracks listed) *(cd-iss. Jul94)*	☐	–
Aug 84.	(12"ep) *(RTT 149)* **WORK IN PROGRESS** – Biko / Amber and the amberines / Yolanda / Te rescuerdo Amanda.	☐	–
Oct 85.	(7"/12"; ROBERT WYATT with The SWAPO SINGERS) *(RT/+T 168)* **THE WIND OF CHANGE. / NAMIBIA**	☐	–

		Rough Trade	Gramavision
Dec 85.	(lp/c) *(ROUGH/+C 69) <18 8604-1/-4>* **OLD ROTTENHAT** – Alliance / The United States of amnesia / East Timor / Speechless / The age of self / Vandalusia / The British road / Mass medium / Gharbzadegi / P.L.A. *(cd-iss. Nov86; ROUGHCD 69) (cd re-iss. Jun98 on 'Hannibal'; HNCD 1434)*	☐	☐

below with one side by/with BENGE

Sep 91.	(cd/c/lp) *(R 274-2/-4/-1)* **DONDESTAN** – Costa / The sight of the wind / Worship / Catholic architecture / Shrink rap / Left on man / Lisp service / CP jeebies / Dondestan.	☐	☐

		Blueprint	not iss.
Nov 92.	(cd+book) *(BP 108CD)* **A SHORT BREAK** – A short break / Tubab / Kutcha / Ventilatir / Unmasked. *(re-iss. Apr96; same)*	☐	–

		Trade 2	not iss.

—— the next A-side featured **PAUL WELLER** – guitars, vocals

Sep 97.	(7") *(TRDSC 010)* **FREE WILL AND TESTAMENT. / THE SIGHT OF THE WIND**	☐	–

		Hannibal	Thirsty Ear
Sep 97.	(cd) *(HNCD 1418) <57040>* **SHLEEP** – Heaps of sheeps / The duchess / Maryan / Was a friend / Free will and testament / September the ninth / Alien / Out of season / A Sunday in Madrid / Blues in Bob minor / The whole point of no return.	☐	Nov97 ☐
Oct 98.	(cd) *(HNCD 1436) <57057>* **DONDESTAN (REVISITED)** – CP jeebies / N.I.O. (New Information Order) / Donestan / Sight of the wind / Shrinkwrap / Catholic architecture / Worship / Costa (memories of under-development) / Left on man / Lisp service.	☐	Nov98 ☐

		Hannibal	Hannibal
Sep 03.	(cd) *(<HNCD 1468>)* **CUCKOOLAND** – Just a bit / Old Europe / Tom Hay's fox / Forest / Beware / Cuckoo madame / Raining in my heart / Lullaby for Hamza – Silence / Trickle down / Insensatez / Mister E / Lullaloop / Life is sheep / Foreign accents / Brian the fox / La ahada yalam (No-one knows).	☐	Oct03 ☐

– compilations, others, etc. –

Mar 81.	(d-lp) *Virgin; (VGD 3505)* **ROCK BOTTOM / RUTH IS STRANGER THAN RICHARD**	☐	–
Apr 82.	(7"ep; ROBERT WYATT & MEMBERS OF CAST) *Virgin; (VS 499)* **FROM MAN TO WOMAN**	☐	–
Dec 84.	(lp) *Rough Trade; (RTSP 25)* **1982-1984**	–	☐
Feb 85.	(12") *Recommended; (RE 1984)* **THE LAST NIGHTINGALE. / ON THE BEACH AT CAMBRIDGE**	☐	–

—— next 'B'side by "The GRIMETHORPE COLLIERY BAND".

Sep 85.	(7") *T.U.C.;* **THE AGE OF SELF. / RAISE YOUR BANNERS HIGH**	☐	–
Sep 87.	(12"ep) *Strange Fruit; (SFPS 037)* **THE PEEL SESSIONS** (10.9.74) – Soup song / Sea song / Alife / I'm a believer.	☐	–
Jan 93.	(cd) *Rough Trade; (R 2952)* **MID EIGHTIES**	☐	☐
Jul 94.	(cd; by MATCHING MOLE) *Windsong; (WINCD 063)* **BBC RADIO 1 LIVE IN CONCERT (live)**	☐	–
Jul 94.	(d-cd) *Virgin; (CDVM 9031)* **GOING BACK A BIT: A LITTLE HISTORY OF . . .**	☐	–
Aug 94.	(cd) *Rough Trade; (R 3112)* **FLOTSAM AND JETSAM** (rare 1968-1990)	☐	–
Feb 99.	(5xcd-ep;box) *Hannibal; (HNCD 1440) / Thirsty Ear; <57062> EPS BY ROBERT WYATT*	☐	☐
Sep 03.	(cd) *Cuniform; (RUNE 175)* **SOLAR FLARES BURN FOR YOU** (sessions)	☐	☐

☐ Steve WYNN (see under ⇒ DREAM SYNDICATE)

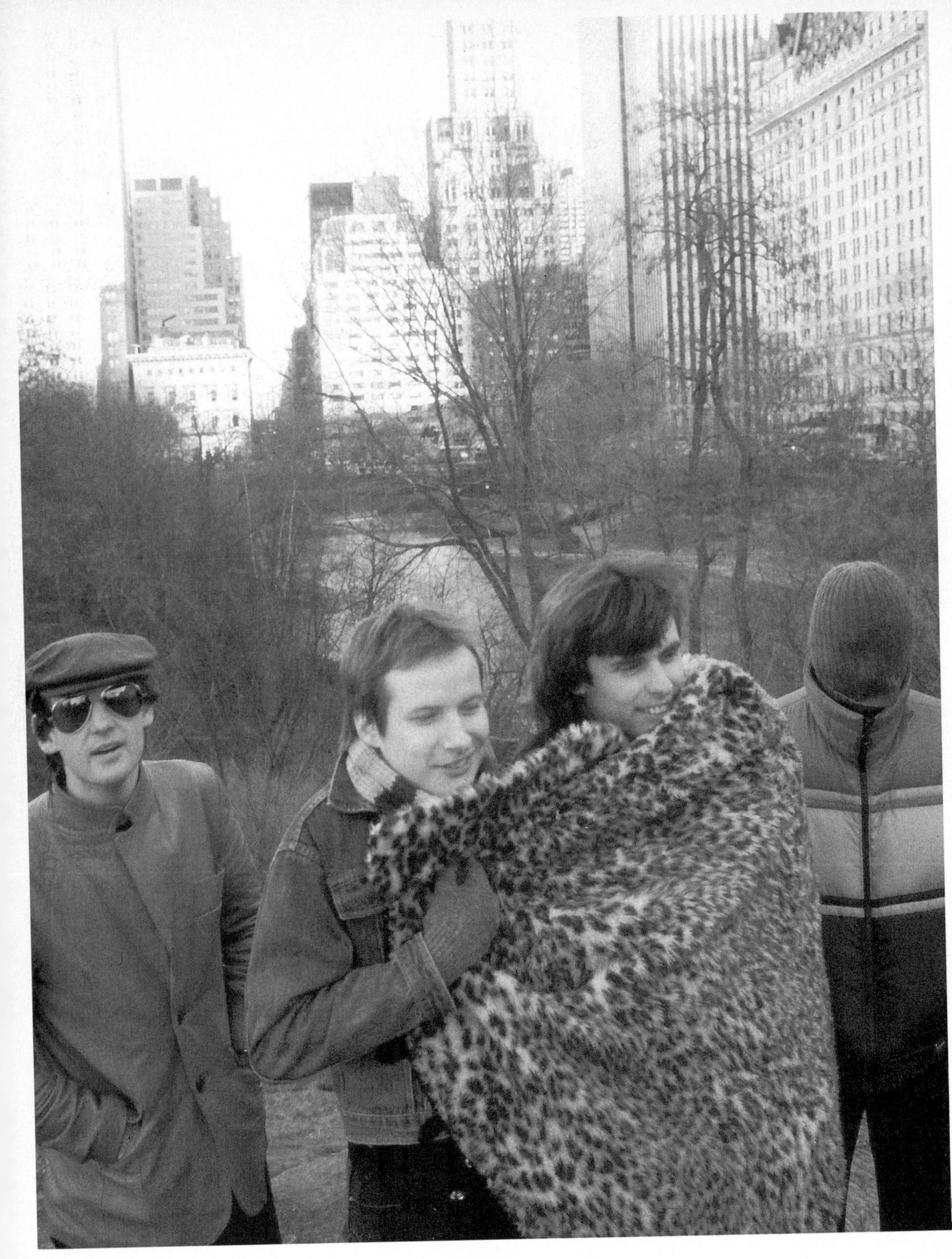

XTC

X

Formed: Los Angeles, California, USA ... 1977 by EXENE CERVENKA, BILLY ZOOM, JOHN DOE and original drummer MICK BASHER (the latter subsequently replaced by DJ BONEBRAKE). After a one-off debut in 1978, 'ADULT BOOKS' (for the US 'Dangerhouse' imprint), X marked their spot with the then newly formed indie label, 'Slash'. Pioneers of the cowpunk scene alongside WALL OF VOODOO, The GUN CLUB, etc, the quartet enlisted the help of RAY MANZAREK, the former DOORS organist producing their debut set, 'LOS ANGELES' (1980). A rock hybrid of country and raw punk, X were obviously influenced by 60's garage punks the FUGS and MC5 with a tone of 50's rockabilly, this combination of musical styles used most effectively on follow-up set, 'WILD GIFT' (also recorded with MANZAREK at the helm). The MANZAREK connection continued when X moved to 'Elektra', their third album, 'UNDER THE BIG BLACK SUN' (1982) breaking them into the US Top 100. A fourth set, 'MORE FUN IN THE NEW WORLD' (1983), fared just as well commercially, although the band were in turn accused of selling out. The previous year, EXENE and LYDIA LUNCH had a book of poetry, 'Adulterers Anonymous' (with that title, it's not surprising that EXENE and JOHN were divorced in '84) published in the States, the X frontwoman subsequently teaming up with DOE, DAVE ALVIN (Blasters), HENRY ROLLINS (Black Flag) and JONNY RAY BARTEL to form country-rock outfit, The KNITTERS. The latter project obviously had an effect on X themselves (ALVIN had now replaced ZOOM), who emerged with a more countrified sound on 1985's 'AIN'T LOVE GRAND'. The following year ALVIN was deposed by ex-LONE JUSTICE guitarist, TONY GILKYSON, a fuller heavy sound beginning to manifest itself on 1987's 'SEE HOW WE ARE'. A commercially disastrous double-live set was their last for some time, although the band returned after other solo projects with a disappointing comeback set, 'HEY ZEUS!' (1993). • **Covered:** WILD THING (Troggs) / ALL OR NOTHING (Small Faces) / IT'S IN HIS KISS (Betty Everett) / SOUL KITCHEN (Doors) / POSITIVELY 4th STREET (Bob Dylan) / U.S. MALE (hit; Elvis Presley) / HOME MOTEL (Willie Nelson).

Album rating: LOS ANGELES (*8) / WILD GIFT (*8) / UNDER THE BIG BLACK SUN (*6) / MORE FUN IN THE NEW WORLD (*5) / AIN'T LOVE GRAND (*6) / SEE HOW WE ARE (*5) / LIVE AT THE WHISKEY A GO-GO (*5) / HEY ZEUS! (*4) / UNCLOGGED (*4)

EXENE CERVENKA (b. CHRISTINE CERVENKA, 1 Feb'56, Chicago, Illinois) – vocals / **BILLY ZOOM** – guitar / **JOHN DOE** (b. JOHN NOMMENSEN, 25 Feb'53, Decatur, Illinois) – bass, vocals / **D.J. BONEBRAKE** (b. DON, 8 Dec'55, Hollywood, Calif.) – drums repl. MICK BASHER

not iss. / Dangerhouse

Jun 78. (7") *<D 88>* **ADULT BOOKS. / WE'RE DESPERATE** [–] [ ]

not iss. / Slash

Jun 80. (lp) *<SR 104>* **LOS ANGELES** [–] [ ]
– Your phone's off the hook, but you're not / Johnny hit and run Pauline / Soul kitchen / Nausea / Sugarlight / Los Angeles / Sex and dying in high society / The unheard music / The world's a mess / It's in my kiss. *<(cd-iss. Sep01 on 'Rhino'+=; 8122 74370-2)>* – I'm coming over / Adult books (demo) / Delta 88 (demo) / Cyrano De Berger's back (rehearsal) / Los Angeles (dangerhouse version).

May 81. (lp) *<SR 107>* **WILD GIFT** [–] [ ]
– The once over twice / We're desperate / Adult books / Universal corner / I'm coming over / It's who you know / In this house that I call home / Some other time / White girl / Beyond and back / Back 2 the base / When our love passed out on the coach / Year 1. *<(cd-iss. Sep01 on 'Rhino'+=; 8122 74371-2)>* – Beyond and back (live) / Blue spark (demo) / We're desperate (single) / Back 2 the base (live) / Heater (rehearsal) / White girl (single) / The once over twice (single).

Aug 81. (7") *<SRS 106>* **WHITE GIRL. / YOUR PHONE'S OFF THE HOOK** [–] [ ]

Elektra / Elektra

Jul 82. (7") *<69885>* **BLUE SPARK. / DANCING WITH TEARS IN MY EYES** [ ] [ ]

Jul 82. (lp) *(K 52401) <60150>* **UNDER THE BIG BLACK SUN** [ ] [76]
– The hungry wolf / Motel room in my bed / Riding with Mary / Come back to me / Under the big black sun / Because I do / Blue spark / Dancing with tears in my eyes / Real child of Hell / How I (learned my lesson) / The have nots. *<(cd-iss. Sep01 on 'Rhino'; 8122 74372-2)>* – Riding with Mary (single) / X rewrites "El Paso" (rehearsal) / Because I do (instrumental) / Universal corner (live) / Breathless (single) / How I (learned my lesson) (live).

Jun 83. (7") *<69825>* **BREATHLESS. / RIDING WITH MARY** [–] [ ]

Sep 83. (lp/c) *(K 960283-1/-4) <60283>* **MORE FUN IN THE NEW WORLD** [ ] [86]
– The new world / We're having much more fun / True love / Poor girl / Make the music go bang / Breathless / I must not think bad thoughts / Devil doll / Painting the town blue / Hot house / Drunk in my past / I see red / True love #2. *<(cd-iss. May02 on 'Rhino'+=; 8122 78257-2)>* – Poor girl (demo) / True love #2 (demo) / Devil doll (demo) / I must not think bad thoughts (demo).

Jan 84. (7") *(E 9779)* **THE NEW WORLD. / I MUST NOT THINK BAD THOUGHTS** [ ] [ ]

Jun 84. (12") *<66966>* **WILD THING. / TRUE LOVE (part 2)** [ ] [–]

Jun 84. (7") *<69709>* **WILD THING. / DEVIL DOLL** [–] [ ]

— In 1985, JOHN DOE splintered with country-western project The KNITTERS. They included HENRY ROLLINS (of BLACK FLAG), DAVE ALVIN (of BLASTERS) + JOHNNY RAY BARTEL and made one album POOR LITTLE CRITTER ON THE ROAD. In fact, X brought in **DAVE ALVIN** – guitar to repl. BILLY

Aug 85. (7") *(EKR 18)* **BURNING HOUSE OF LOVE. / LOVE SHACK** [ ] [ ]
(12"+=) *(EKRT 18)* – Wild thing.

Sep 85. (lp) *(EKT 12) <60430>* **AIN'T LOVE GRAND** [ ] Aug85 [89]
– Burning house of love / Love shack / My soul cries your name / My goodness / Around my heart / What's wrong with me . . . / All or nothing / Watch the sun go down / I'll stand up for you / Little honey / Supercharged. *<(cd-iss. May02 on 'Rhino'+=; 8122 78258-2)>* – Wild thing (extended) / I will dare (demo) / My goodness (demo) / All or nothing.

— **TONY GILKYSON** (b. 6 Aug'52) – guitar (ex-LONE JUSTICE) repl. ALVIN who went solo

Jul 87. (lp/c) *(K 960492-1/-4) <60492>* **SEE HOW WE ARE** [ ] [ ]
– I'm lost / You / 4th of July / In the time it takes / Anyone can fill your shoes / See how we are / Left & right / When it rains . . . / Holiday

story / Surprise surprise / Cyrano de Bergerac's back. <*(cd-iss. May02 on 'Rhino'+=; 8122 78259-2)*> – Holiday story (demo) / I'm lost (demo remix) / Highway 61 revisited (rough take) / In the time it takes (demo) / See how we are (alt. take).

Jul 87. (7") *<69462>* **4th OF JULY. / POSITIVELY 4th STREET** –

May 88. (d-lp/c/cd) *(K 960788-1/-4/-2) <60788>* **LIVE AT THE WHISKEY A GO-GO ON THE FABULOUS SUNSET STRIP (live)**
– Los Angeles / House I call home / The new world / Around my heart / Surprise surprise / Because I do / Burning house of love / My goodness / Blue spark / The once over twice / In the time it takes / Devil doll / Hungry wolf / Just another perfect day / Unheard music / Riding with Mary / The world's a mess / True love / White girl / Skin deep town / So long / Call of the wreckin' ball / Year 1 / Johnny hit a run / Pauline.

R.C.A. D.G.C.

Oct 89. (7") **WILD THING. / (part 2)**
(ext;12"+=/cd-s+=) – Oh you angel / U.S. male.

— split after this final flop, although they re-formed in 1993

Big Life Mercury

Jun 93. (cd/c) *<519261-2/-4>* **HEY ZEUS!** –
– Someone's watching / Big blue house / Clean like tomorrow / New life / Country at war / Arms for hostages / Into the light / Lettuce and vodka / Everybody / Baby you lied / Drawn in the dark.

Jul 93. (c-s) *(BLRC 94)* **COUNTRY AT WAR / YOU WOULDN'T TELL ME** –
(12"+=/cd-s+=) *(BLR T/D 94)* – Drawn in the dark (acoustic).

not iss. Infidelity

Jun 95. (cd) *<10812>* **UNCLOGGLED** (acoustic live) –
– White girl / Because I do / Lying in the road / Unheard music / I must not think bad thoughts / Burning house of love / Stage / See how we are / True love / Have nots / The world's a mess, it's in my kiss / I see red / What's wrong with me.

— when they finally split, EXENE fronted the band AUNTIE CHRIST who had signed to 'Lookout!'; included in their ranks, MATT FREEMAN (of RANCID).

– compilations, etc. –

Oct 97. (d-cd) *Elektra; <62103>* **BEYOND & BACK: THE X ANTHOLOGY** –
– Los Angeles / The world's a mess, it's in his kiss / Yr ignition / Year one / Hungry wolf / We're desperate / Beyond and back / Back 2 the base / Blue spark / Some other time / Sex and dying in high society / Motel room in my bed / Heater / Once over twice / Because I do / In this house I call home / Soul kitchen / Universal corner / Delta 88 / Real child of hell / I'm coming over / White girl / Nausea / Johnny hit and run Paulene / You phone's off the hook but you're / Riding with Mary / New world / Breathless / Poor girl / What's wrong with me / How I (learned my lesson) / Have nots / Someone like you / Stage / See how we are / Surprise, surprise / 4th of July / Arms for hostages – Country at war / Wild thing / Burning house of love / Devil doll / True love / Call of the wreckin' ball / In the time it takes / I must not think bad thoughts.

Feb 00. (cd) *Ascension; (XCD 1)* **LIVE AT THE STAGEDOOR TAVERN (live)**

Jul 01. (lp/cd) *Drop Kick; <(BEHIND 016/+CD)>* **LIVE AT THE CIVIC 1979 (live)**

XTC

Formed: Swindon, Wiltshire, England . . . 1976 after 3 years of calling themselves The HELIUM KIDZ. Not an early version of acid house as the name might suggest, XTC traded in a quirky blend of pop that owed more to quintessential English psychedelia than the nihilistic three chord assault of their punk peers. Nevertheless, they were picked up by 'Virgin' in the signing scramble that followed The SEX PISTOLS early success in 1977. The debut album, 'WHITE MUSIC' (1978), introduced their tentative art-pop sound, PARTRIDGE's songwriting talent much in evidence even at this early stage. The JOHN LECKIE produced 'GO 2' (1978) was a more sonically adventurous follow-up, heavily influenced by BRIAN ENO and moulding their pop with quirky electronica. Soon after the record's release, ANDREWS left to join ROBERT FRIPP's 'LEAGUE OF GENTLEMEN' and was replaced by DAVE GREGORY. The new improved unit cut the successful 'DRUMS AND WIRES' (1979) album which spawned a top 20 hit single, the hypnotic, MOULDING-penned 'MAKING PLANS FOR NIGEL'. The rest of the tracks were just as catchy in their distinctive, left-of-centre way. This signalled the onset of a punishing touring/recording schedule during which time the band released a succession of impressive singles, some of which went top 20 and an album, 'BLACK SEA' (1980), that hinted at the psychedelic nostalgia which would characterise their later output. 'ENGLISH SETTLEMENT' (1982) is generally held to be band's finest hour. A double set, the record artfully blended rustic folk, ethnic rhythms and synthesizer pop, all shot through with the spectral hue of psychedelia. Although the stellar single, 'SENSES WORKING OVERTIME' was one of the band's biggest hits and XTC looked to be headed for the big time, PARTRIDGE, never comfortable with live performance, was dreading the inevitable round of touring. In the event, after a few disastrous shows he decided he could suffer it no longer and shortly after, announced that the band would never tour again. CHAMBERS promptly left, unhappy with such a prospect and although PARTRIDGE was now suffering from Agoraphobia, the band struggled on. With no full-time drummer and a string of producers, 'MUMMER' (1983) and 'THE BIG EXPRESS' (1983) were inconsistent and lacking in direction although 'EVERYDAY STORY OF SMALLTOWN' from the latter set was a charming piece of nostalgia-pop. It was clear the band needed some fresh inspiration and with the help of JOHN LECKIE they cut the '25 O'CLOCK' mini-album in 1985 under the pseudonym DUKES OF STRATOSPHERE. More overtly psychedelic than any previous XTC material, PARTRIDGE was given free range to indulge his obvious passions. Re-energised, the band were paired with TODD RUNDGREN for 'SKYLARKING' (1986) and although there were some well documented clashes between PARTRIDGE and the maverick American, the resultant album was a triumphant return to form. Embellishing the gentle hybrid of 'ENGLISH SETTLEMENT' with a 'PET SOUNDS'-like sonic richness, the album spawned the sultry single 'GRASS'. Its B-side, the semi-acoustic sweep of 'DEAR GOD' was picked up by American radio, with the end result that 'SKYLARKING' was a considerable stateside success. After a final DUKES OF STRATOSPHERE album, 'PSONIC PSUNSPOT', XTC began work on the 'ORANGES AND LEMONS' set. Released in 1989, the album was another resounding success, creatively at least, and spawned the charming 'MAYOR OF SIMPLETON' single. While the album was a relative success in America, it failed to make any lasting impact in the UK and after 'NONESUCH' (1992) stiffed completely, XTC faded into obscurity. Although sightings are rare, PARTRIDGE has surfaced occasionally, notably on the HAROLD BUDD collaboration, 'THROUGH THE HILL', in 1994. Without even an inkling that songwriters PARTRIDGE and MOULDING were about to unleash a new episode of quirky pop tunes, the public were happy to find out XTC were once again planning their comeback. Delivered early '99 for 'Cooking Vinyl', 'APPLE VENUS VOLUME 1' saw Swindon's finest regain the ground they had lost while securing a Top 30 entry in the process. The record's swelling, organic orchestrations delighted many longtime fans and whetted appetites for a follow-up. In the event, 'WASP STAR (APPLE VENUS, PT.2)' (2000) was a more straightforward XTC album rather than a continuation of its predecessor's grandiose pop, concentrating on the kind of nuts and bolts material that the band have long made their own. • **Covered:** ALL ALONG THE WATCHTOWER (Bob Dylan) / ELLA GURU (Captain Beefheart).

Album rating: WHITE MUSIC (*8) / GO 2 (*4) / DRUMS AND WIRES (*8) / BLACK SEA (*7) / ENGLISH SETTLEMENT (*8) / WAXWORKS (SOME SINGLES 1977-82) compilation (*8) / BEESWAX (SOME B-SIDES 1977-82) compilation (*5) / MUMMER (*7) / THE BIG EXPRESS (*7) / SLYLARKING (*8) / THE COMPACT XTC – THE SINGLES 1978-1985 (*8) / ORANGES AND LEMONS (*7) / EXPLODE TOGETHER (THE DUB EXPERIMENTS '78-'80) exploitation (*4) / RAG 'N' BONE BUFFET collection (*5) / NONESUCH (*8) / FOSSIL FUEL: THE XTC SINGLES 1977-1992 compilation (*8) / APPLE VENUS VOLUME 1 (*7) / WASP STAR – APPLE VENUS VOLUME 2 (*6) / Andy Partridge: TAKE AWAY (THE LURE OF SALVAGE) (*5) / Dukes Of Stratosfear: 25 O'CLOCK mini (*4) / PSONIC PSUNSPOT (*5)

ANDY PARTRIDGE (b.11 Dec'53) – vocals, guitar / **COLIN MOULDING** (b.17 Aug'55) – bass, vocals / **BARRY ANDREWS** (b.12 Sep'56, London) – keyboards repl. JONATHAN PERKINS / **TERRY CHAMBERS** (b.18 Jul'55) – drums

Virgin Virgin-Epic

Oct 77. (7") *(VS 188)* **SCIENCE FRICTION. / SHE'S SO SQUARE** –
(12"ep+=) *(VS 188-12)* **3-D** – Dance band.

Jan 78. (7") *(VS 201)* **STATUE OF LIBERTY. / HANG ON TO THE NIGHT** –

Feb 78. (lp/c) *(<V/TCV 2095>)* **WHITE MUSIC** 38
– Radios in motion / Cross wires / This is pop? / Do what you do / Statue of liberty / All along the watchtower / Into the atom age / I'll set myself on fire / I'm bugged / New town animal in a furnished cage / Neon shuffle. *(re-iss. Mar84 lp/c; OVED/+C 60) (cd-iss. Mar87 +=; CDV 2095)* – Science friction / She's so square / Dance band / Hang on to the night / Heatwave / Traffic light rock / Instant tunes. *(cd re-iss. Jun01 +=; CDVX 2095) <US cd-iss. May02 on 'Caroline'+=; 50691>*

Apr 78. (7") *(VS 209)* **THIS IS POP?. / HEATWAVE** –

Oct 78. (7") *(VS 231)* **ARE YOU RECEIVING ME. / INSTANT TUNES** –

Oct 78. (lp/c) *(<V/TCV 2108>)* **GO 2** 21
– Mekanic dancing (oh we go!) / Battery brides / Buzzcity talking / Crowded room / The rhythm / Beatown / My weapon / Life is good in the greenhouse / Jumping in Gomorrah / My weapon / Super-tuff. *(free-12"ep w/ lp)* **GO +** – Dance with me Germany / Beat the bible / A dictionary of modern marriage / Clap, clap, clap / We kill the beast. *(re-iss. Mar84 lp/c; OVED/+C 61) (cd-iss. Jul87 +=; CDV 2108)* – Are you receiving me. *(cd re-iss. Jun01 +=; CDVX 2108) <US cd-iss. Jun02 on 'Caroline'+=; 50666>*

— **DAVE GREGORY** – synthesizers, guitar repl. ANDREWS who joined LEAGUE OF GENTLEMEN (w/ ROBERT FRIPP). He later went solo and formed SHRIEKBACK

May 79. (7",7"clear) *(VS 259)* **LIFE BEGINS AT THE HOP. / HOMO SAFARI** 54 –

Virgin Virgin Atlantic

Aug 79. (lp/c) *(V/TCV 2129) <VA 13134>* **DRUMS AND WIRES** 34
– Making plans for Nigel / Helicopter / Life begins at the hop / When you're near me I have difficulty / Ten feet tall / Roads girdle the globe / Reel by reel / Millions / That is the way / Outside world / Scissor man / Complicated game. *(free-7"w/ lp)* – LIMELIGHT. / CHAIN OF COMMAND *(re-iss. 1986 lp/c; OVED/+C 113) (cd-iss. Jun88 +=; CDV 2129)* – Limelight / Chain of command. *(cd re-mast.Jun01 +=; CDVX 2129) <US cd-iss. Aug02 on 'Caroline'; 50653>*

Sep 79. (7"m) *(VS 282)* **MAKING PLANS FOR NIGEL. / BUSHMAN PRESIDENT (HSS 2) / PULSING, PULSING** 17 –

Nov 79. (7") **TEN FEET TALL. / HELICOPTER / THE SOMNAMBULIST** –

Feb 80. (7"m) *<VA 67009>* **MAKING PLANS FOR NIGEL. / THIS IS POP? / MEKANIC DANCING (OH WE GO!)** –

Mar 80. (7") *(VS 322)* **WAIT TILL YOUR BOAT GOES DOWN. / TEN FEET TALL (U.S. version)**

Aug 80. (7") *(VS 365)* **GENERALS AND MAJORS. / DON'T LOSE YOUR TEMPER** 32
(d7"+=) *(VS 365)* – Smokeless zone. / The somnambulist.

Sep 80. (lp/c) *(V/TCV 2173) <VA 13147>* **BLACK SEA** 16 41
– Respectable Street / General and majors / Living through another Cuba / Love at first sight / Rocket from a bottle / No language in our lungs / Towers of London / Paper and iron (notes and coins) / Burning with optimism's flames / Sgt. Rock (is going to help me) / Travels in Nihilon. *(re-iss. 1986 lp/c; OVED/+C 83) (cd-iss. Mar87 +=; CDV 2172)* – Smokeless zone / Don't lose your temper / The somnambulist. *(cd re-mast.Jun01 +=; CDVX 2173) <US cd-iss. Jun02 on 'Caroline'+=; 50636>*

Oct 80. (7") *(VS 372)* **TOWERS OF LONDON. / SET MYSELF ON FIRE (live)** 31
(d7"+=) *(VS 372)* – Battery brides (live) / Scissor man.

Oct 80. (7"; as The COLONEL) *(VS 380)* **TOO MANY COOKS IN THE KITCHEN. / I NEED PROTECTION** –
(above by The COLONEL; aka MOULDING + CHAMBERS)

Nov 80. (7") *(RSO 71)* **TAKE THIS TOWN. / (b-side by The Ruts)**
(above single was from 'Times Square' film soundtrack on 'R.S.O.')

Dec 80. (7") **LOVE AT FIRST SIGHT. / ROCKET FROM A BOTTLE** –

Jan 81. (7"m) *(VS 384)* **SGT. ROCK (IS GOING TO HELP ME). / LIVING THROUGH ANOTHER CUBA (live) / GENERALS AND MAJORS (live)** 16

Mar 81. (7"m) *(VS 407)* **RESPECTABLE STREET. / STRANGE TALES, STRANGE TAILS / OFFICER BLUE**

Virgin Epic

Jan 82. (7"m) *(VS 462)* **SENSES WORKING OVERTIME. / BLAME THE WEATHER / TISSUE TIGERS** 10 –
(12"+=) *(VS 462-12)* – Egyptian solution (HSS 3).

Feb 82. (d-lp/c)<US-lp> *(V/TCV 2223) <37943>* **ENGLISH SETTLEMENT** 5 Mar82 48
– Runaways / Ball and chain / Senses working overtime / Jason and the Argonauts / No thugs in our house / Yacht dance / All of a sudden (it's too late) / Melt the guns / ** Leisure * / It's nearly Africa * / Knuckle down * / Fly on the wall * / ** Down in the cockpit * / English roundabout / Snowman. *<US single-lp version omits *> (cd-iss. Jun88; CDV 2223)*; omits tracks **) *(cd re-iss. Jun01 +=; CDVX 2223)*

Mar 82. (7"m) *(VS 482)* **BALL AND CHAIN. / PUNCH AND JUDY / HEAVEN IS PAVED WITH BROKEN GLASS** 58
(12"+=) *(VS 482-12)* – Cockpit dance mixture.

May 82. (7"ep,9"ep) *(VS 490)* **NO THUGS IN OUR HOUSE / CHAIN OF COMMAND. / LIMELIGHT / OVER RUSTY WALLS** –

May 82. (7") **SENSES WORKING OVERTIME. / ENGLISH ROUNDABOUT** –

Nov 82. (lp/c) *(V/TCV 2251)* **WAXWORKS (SOME SINGLES 1977-82)** (compilation) 54 –
(free lp w/ above) **BEESWAX (SOME B-SIDES 1977-82)** (re-iss. Dec82 lp/c; *OVED/+C 9)*

— trimmed to basic trio of **PARTRIDGE, MOULDING + GREGORY** plus on session **PETER PHIPPES** – drums (ex-GLITTER BAND) (CHAMBERS emigrated to Australia)

Virgin Geffen

Apr 83. (7") *(VS 553)* **GREAT FIRE. / GOLD** –
(12"+=) *(VS 553-12)* – Frost circus (HSS 5) / Procession towards learning land (HSS 6).

Jul 83. (7"/7"pic-d) *(VS/+Y 606)* **WONDERLAND. / JUMP**

Aug 83. (lp/c) *(V/TCV 2264) <4027>* **MUMMER** 51
– Beating of hearts / Wonderland / Love on a farmboy's wages / Great fire / Deliver us from the elements / Human alchemy / Ladybird / In loving memory of a name / Me and the wind / Funk pop a roll. *(re-iss. 1986 lp/c; OVED/+C 142) (cd-iss. Mar87 +=; CDV 2264)* – Frost circus (HSS 5) / Jump / Toys / Gold / Procession towards learning land (HSS 6) / Desert island. *(cd re-iss. Jun01 +=; CDVX 2264) <US cd-iss. Aug02 on 'Caroline'+=; 50672>*

Sep 83. (7") *(VS 613)* **LOVE ON A FARMBOY'S WAGES. / IN LOVING MEMORY OF A NAME** 50
(d7"+=) *(VS 613)* – Desert island / Toys.
(12") *(VS 613-12)* – ('A'side) / Burning with optimism's flames (live / English roundabout (live) / Cut it out (live).

Nov 83. (7"; as THREE WISE MEN) *(VS 642)* **THANKS FOR CHRISTMAS. / COUNTDOWN TO CHRISTMAS PARTYTIME** –

Sep 84. (7") *(VS 709)* **ALL YOU PRETTY GIRLS. / WASHAWAY** 55 –
(12"+=) *(VS 709-12)* – Red brick dream.

Oct 84. (lp/c) *(V/TCV 2325) <24054>* **THE BIG EXPRESS** 38
– Wake up / All you pretty girls / Shake you donkey up / Seagulls screaming kiss her, kiss her / This world over / The everyday story of Smalltown / I bought myself a liarbird / Reign of blows / You're the wish you are I had / I remember the sun / Train running low on soul coal. *(cd-iss. 1987 +=; CDV 2325)* – Red brick dreams / Washaway / Blue overall. *(re-iss. 1988 lp/c; OVED/+C 182) (cd re-iss. Jun01 +=; CDVX 2325)*

Oct 84. (7"/12") *(VS 721/+12)* **THIS WORLD OVER. / BLUE OVERALL**

Jan 85. (7"m) *(VS 746)* **WAKE UP. / TAKE THIS TOWN / MANTIS ON PAROLE (HSS 4)**
(12"+=) *(VS 746-12)* – Making plans for Nigel / Sgt. Rock (is going to help me) / Senses working overtime.

— **IAN GREGORY** (DAVE's brother) – drums repl. PHIPPES

DUKES OF STRATOSPHEAR

Apr 85. (7") *(VS 763)* **THE MOLE FROM THE MINISTRY. / MY LOVE EXPLODES** [-]
Apr 85. (m-lp/c) *(WOW/+C 1)* **25 O'CLOCK**
– 25 o'clock / Bike ride to the Moon / My love explodes / What in the world . . . / Your gold dress / The mole from the ministry.

XTC

Aug 86. (7") *(VS 882)* **GRASS. / DEAR GOD**
(12"+=) *(VS 882-12)* – Extrovert.
Oct 86. (lp/c/cd) *(V/TCV/CDV 2399)* *<24117>* **SKYLARKING** [90] [70]
– Summer's cauldron / Grass / The meeting place / That's really super, Supergirl / Ballet for a rainy day / 1000 umbrellas / Season cycle / Earn enough for us / Big day / Another satellite / Mermaid smiled * / The man who sailed around his soul / Dying / Sacrificial bonfire. *<re-iss. 1987; 'Dear God' repl. *> (cd re-iss. Jun01 +=; CDVX 2399)*
Jan 87. (7"/7"clear) *(VS/+Y 912)* **THE MEETING PLACE. / THE MAN WHO SAILED AROUND HIS SOUL**
(12"+=) *(VS 912-12)* – Terrorism.
Jun 87. (7") *(VS 960)* **DEAR GOD. / BIG DAY** [-]
(12"+=) *(VS 960-12)* – Another satellite (live).
(cd-s) *(CDEP 3)* – ('A'side) / Homo safari series (HSS 1-6):- Homo safari / Bushman president / Egyptian solution / Mantis on parole / Frost circus / Procession towards learning land.
Jul 87. (7") **DEAR GOD. / MERMAID SMILED** [-]

DUKES OF STRATOSPHEAR

Jul 87. (7"/7"colrd) *(VS/+Y 982)* **YOU'RE A GOOD MAN ALBERT BROWN (CURSE YOU RED BARREL). / VANISHING GIRL** [-]
(12"+=) *(VS 982-12)* – The mole from the ministry / My love explodes.
Aug 87. (lp/colrd-lp/c) *(V/VP/TCV 2440)* **PSONIC PSUNSPOT**
– Vanishing girl / Have you seen Jackie? / Little lighthouse / You're a good man Albert Brown (curse you red barrel) / Collideascope / You're my drug / Shiny cage / Brainiac's daughter / The affiliated / Pale and precious.
1989. (cd) *(COMCD 11)* **CHIPS FROM THE CHOCOLATE FIREBALL**
– (25 O'CLOCK / PSONIC PSUNSPOT)

XTC

— **PAT MASTELOTTO** – drums (of MR. MISTER) repl. IAN
Jan 89. (7") *(VS 1158)* **THE MAYOR OF SIMPLETON. / ONE OF THE MILLIONS** [46] [72]
(12"+=) *(VST 1158)* – Ella guru.
(3"cd-s) *(VSCD 1158)* – ('A'side) / Ella guru / Living in a haunted heart / The good thing.
(12") *(VSR 1158)* – ('A'side) / Dear God / Senses working overtime / Making plans for Nigel.
Feb 89. (d-lp/c/cd) *(V/TCV/CDV 2581)* *<24218>* **ORANGES AND LEMONS** [28] [44]
– Garden of earthly delights / The Mayor of Simpleton / King for a day / Here comes President Kill again / The loving / Poor skeleton steps out / One of the millions / Scarecrow people / Merely a man / Cynical days / Across this antheap / Hold me my daddy / Pink thing / Miniature sun / Chalkhills and children. *(re-iss. Oct89, 3xcd-ep-box; CDVT 2581) (cd re-iss. Jun01; CDVX 2581)*
Apr 89. (7") *(VS 1177)* **KING FOR A DAY. / HAPPY FAMILIES** [-]
(12"+=) *(VST 1177)* – ('A'extended).
(c-s+=) *(VSC 1177)* – Generals and majors / Towers of London.
(3"cd-s) *(VSCD 1177)* – ('A'extended) / ('A'side) / My paint heroes (home demo) / Skeletons (home demo).
Aug 89. (7") *(VS 1201)* **THE LOVING. / CYNICAL DAYS** [-]
(c-s) *(VSC 1201)* – ('A'side) / The world is full of angry young men.
(12"/cd-s) *(VS T/CD 1201)* – (all 3 tracks).
Sep 89. (cd-ep) *<9-21236-2>* **KING FOR A DAY (Czar mix) / ('A' Versailles mix) / TOYS / DESERT ISLAND** [-]

Mar 92. (7"/c-s) *(VS/+C 1404)* **THE DISAPPOINTED. / THE SMARTEST MONKEYS** [33] [-]
(10"+=) *(VST 1404)* – Humble Daisy.
(cd-s++=) *(VSCD 1404)* ('B'demo).
May 92 (cd/c/d-lp) *(CD/TC+/V 2699)* *<24474>* **NONESUCH** [28] [97]
– The ballad of Peter Pumpkinhead / My bird performs / Dear Madam Barnum / Humble Daisy / The smartest monkeys / The dismal / Holly up on poppy / Crocodile / Rook / Omnibus / That wave / Then she appeared / War dance / Wrapped in grey / The ugly underneath / Bungalow / Books are burning. *(cd re-iss. Jun01; CDVX 2699)*
Jun 92. (7"/c-s) *(VS/+C 1415)* **THE BALLAD OF PETER PUMPKINHEAD. / WAR DANCE** [71] [-]
(cd-s+=) *(VSCD1 1415)* – Down a peg (demo) / ('A'demo).
(cd-s+=) *(VSCD2 1415)* – My bird performs (demo) / Always winter never Christmas (demo).

— **PARTRIDGE + MOULDING** re-formed six years later

— additional musicians **DAVE GREGORY, PRAIRIE PRINCE**, etc

Cooking Vinyl T.V.T.

Feb 99. (lp/c/cd) *(COOK/+C/CD 172)* *<3250>* **APPLE VENUS VOLUME 1** [42]
– River of orchids / I'd like that / Easter theatre / Knights in shining karma / Frivolous tonight / Greenman / Your dictionary / Fruit nut / I can't own her / Harvest festival / Last balloon.
Apr 99. (cd-s) *(FRYCD 080)* **EASTER THEATRE / EASTER THEATRE (home demo) / HOW EASTER THEATRE CAME TO BE** [-]
Jun 99. (cd-s) *(FRYCD 083)* **I'D LIKE THAT / I'D LIKE THAT (home demo) / HOW I'D LIKE THAT CAME TO B** [-]
Sep 99. (lp/cd) *(COOK/+CD 188)* **HOMESPUN (APPLE VENUS VOLUME 1 HOME DEMOS)** [-]
May 00. (lp/c/cd) *(COOK/+C/CD 194)* *<3260>* **WASP STAR – APPLE VENUS VOLUME 2** [40]
– Playground / Stupidly happy / In another life / My brown guitar / Boarded up / I'm the man who murdered love / We're all light / Standing in for Joe / Wounded horse / You and the clouds will still be beautiful / Church of women / The wheel and the maypole.
Jul 00. (cd-s) *(FRYCD 095)* **I'M THE MAN WHO MURDERED LOVE (mixes) / DIDN'T HURT A BIT** [-]

– compilations, others, etc. –

on 'Virgin' unless otherwise mentioned
Jan 87. (cd) *(CDV 2251)* **THE COMPACT XTC – THE SINGLES 1978-1985** [-]
– Science friction / Statue of liberty / This is pop? / Are you receiving me / Life begins at the hop / Making plans for Nigel / Wait till your boat goes down / Generals and majors / Towers of London / Sgt. Rock (is going to help me) / Senses working overtime / Ball and chain / Great fire / Wonderland / Love on a farmboy's wages / All you pretty girls / This world over / Wake up.
Jul 88. (3"cd-ep) *(VSCDT 9)* **SENSES WORKING OVERTIME / BLAME THE WEATHER / TISSUE TIGERS** [-]
Nov 88. (7") *Old Gold; (OG 9819)* **MAKING PLANS FOR NIGEL. / SENSES WORKING OVERTIME** [-]
Aug 90. (cd) *(CDOVD 308)* **EXPLODE TOGETHER (THE DUB EXPERIMENTS 78-80)** [-]
– (included the ANDY PARTRIDGE album below)
Aug 90. (cd) *(CDOVD 311) / Geffen; <24417>* **RAG & BONE BUFFET** (rare)
Nov 94. (cd) *Night Tracks; (CDNT 008)* **DRUMS AND WIRELESS: BBC RADIO SESSIONS 77-89** [-]
Jun 96. (d-cd) *Geffen; <25137>* **UPSY DAISY ASSORTMENT (A SELECTION OF SWEETEST HITS)** [-]
Sep 96. (cd/c) *(CD/TC VD 2811)* **FOSSIL FUEL: THE XTC SINGLES 1977-92** [33]
– (nearly same tracks as 1987 collection + add more recent) *(d-cd; CDVDX 2811)*
Nov 98. (4xcd-box) *Cooking Vinyl; (COOKCD 152) / TVT; <3240>* **TRANSISTOR BLAST: BEST OF THE BBC SESSIONS**
Mar 02. (4xcd-box) *Virgin; (XTCBOX 1) / Caroline; <CAROL 11900>* **A COAT OF MANY CUPBOARDS**

MR. PARTRIDGE

Feb 80. (lp/c) *(V/TCV 2145)* **TAKE AWAY (THE LURE OF SALVAGE)** [ ] [–]
– Commerciality / The day the pulled the North Pole down / Cairo / Madhattan / The forgotten language of light / Steam fist futurist / The rotary / Shore leave ornithology (another 1950) / I sit in the snow / Work away Tokyo day / New broom. *(re-iss. Aug88; OVED 130)*

— In Jun'94, ANDY PARTRIDGE co-released with HAROLD BUDD the cd 'THROUGH THE HILL' for 'All Saints' label.

— Also in '94, PARTRIDGE with MARTIN NEWELL, issued album 'THE GREATEST LIVING ENGLISHMAN' for 'Pipeline'.

XZIBIT

Born: ALVIN NATHANIEL JOINER, Detroit, Michigan, USA; but raised in New Mexico. A member of notorious rap posse THA ALKAHOLICS, underground rapper XZIBIT blasted onto the mainstream after word-of-mouth hype followed his two, largely unnoticed solo albums. After departing from the group in 1995, XZIBIT issued 'AT THE SPEED OF LIFE' on the independent hip-hop label 'Loud' records in 1996. He soon became a rising talent on the West Coast scene. '40 DAYZ & 40 NIGHTZ' was issued two years later to critical acclaim, with fan SNOOP DOGGY DOGG inviting the promising rapper to appear on the DRE produced 'Top Dog'. The song became a massive hit all over the world, thus propelling XZIBIT into near megastardom. After featuring on DRE's own '2001' LP and EMINEM's sophomore set, the rapper – who had BUSTA RHYMES' gravel-tinged vocals but with the flair of KOOL KEITH and the aggression of 2PAC – issued his debut album 'RESTLESS' (2000). The set featured the fantasic car-bouncing single 'X', also aided by SNOOP DOGG's free-flow rhyming skills, which went on to become a Top 20 hit. The third album didn't disappoint fans, old and new, as it contained the same strength and passion seen on the first two, but with a tighter production and a whole host of guests. XZIBIT also accompanied DRE, ICE CUBE, EMINEM, D-12 and SNOOP DOGG on the nationwide 'Up In Smoke' tour, where his womanising antics could be seen in the tour's 'home video'. 2002 saw the man bounce back with a plethora of superstar helpers, SNOOP DOGG, EMINEM, DRE and ERICK SERMON, alongside usual suspects, THA LIKS, SAAFIR and RAS KASS for his follow-up set, 'MAN VS. MACHINE'. This guaranteed his first US Top 3 placing although critics were less than enthusiastic about raunchy titles such as 'CHOKE ME, SPANK ME (PULL MY HAIR)' and the minor hit 'MULTIPLY', the latter with NATE DOGG.

Album rating: AT THE SPEED OF LIFE (*6) / 40 DAYZ & 40 NIGHTZ (*6) / RESTLESS (*7) / MAN VS. MACHINE (*5)

XZIBIT – vocals / with various backing

Loud – RCA | Loud – RCA

May 96. (12"/cd-s) *<64535/65>* **PAPARAZZI (mixes; radio / club / instrumental / acapella)** [–] [83]

Sep 96. (12") *<64631-1>* **EYES MAY SHINE** [–] [ ]

Oct 96. (cd) *<(07863 66816-2)>* **AT THE SPEED OF LIFE** [ ] [74]
– Grand opening (interlude) / At the speed of life / Just maintain (with HURRICANE GEE) / Eyes may shine / Positively negative (with KING TEE) / Don't hate me (interlude) / Paparazzi / The foundation / Mrs. Crabtree (interlude) / Bird's eye view (with CATASHTRAPHE & J-RO) / Hit and run (part 2) / Carry the weight / Plastic surgery (with RAS KASS & SAAFIR) / Enemies and friends / Last words (interlude). *(re-iss. Feb00 on 'Loud-Epic; 497672-2) (d-lp-iss.Mar01 on 'Loud-Epic'; 497672-1)*

Nov 96. (12"/cd-s) *<64707/8>* **THE FOUNDATION (mixes; radio / album / instrumental)** [–] [ ]

Jul 98. (12"/cd-s) *<65506/7>* **WHAT U SEE IS WHAT U GET / 3 CARD MOLLY** [–] [50]

Aug 98. (cd/d-lp) *<(07863 67578-2/-1)>* **40 DAYZ & 40 NIGHTZ** [ ] [58]
– The last night intro / Chamber music / 3 card Molly (with RAS KASS & SAAFIR) / What U see is what U get / Handle your business (with DEFARI HERUT) / Nobody soundz like me (with MONTAGEONE) / Pussy pop (with JAYO FELONY & METHOD MAN) / Chronic keeping 101 / Shroomz / Focus / Jason (48 months interlude) (with E SWIFT) / Deeper / Los Angeles times / Inside job / Let it rain (with THA ALKAHOLIKS & KING TEE) / Recycled assassins (with MONTAGEONE) / Outro. <US+=> – Don't let the money make you. *(cd re-iss. Jan01 on 'Loud-Epic'; 498839-2) (d-lp re-iss. Mar01; 498839-1)*

Sep 98. (12") *<65466-1>* **3 CARD MOLLY (mixes)** [–] [ ]

Nov 98. (12"/cd-s) *<63615-1/-2>* **PUSSY POP (mixes; clean / LP / instrumental) / HANDLE YOUR BUSINESS** [–] [ ]

Loud – Epic | Loud – Sony

Mar 00. (12"; by XZIBIT & JONATHAN DAVIS) *<79368>* **YEAR 2000 (mixes)** [–] [ ]
(above featured on the 'Black And White' soundtrack)

Dec 00. (cd/lp) *(498913-2/-1)* *<1885>* **RESTLESS** [27] [12]
– Restless intro / Front 2 back / Been a long time (with NATE DOGG) / U know (with DR. DRE) / X / Alkaholik (with ERICK SERMON, J-RO & TASH) / Kenny Parker show 2001 (with KRS-ONE) / D.N.A. (Drugs-N-Alkahol) (with SNOOP DOGG) / Double time / Don't approach me / Rimz & tirez (with DEFARI, GOLDIE LOC & KOKANE) / Fuckin' you right / Best of things / Get your walk on / Sorry I'm away so much (with DJ QUIK & SUGAFREE) / Loud & clear (with BUTCH CASSIDY & DEFARI).

Mar 01. (c-s) *(670907-4)* *<1968>* **X / X (explicit)** [14] [76]
(12"+=) *(670907-6)* – Year 2000 (remix).
(cd-s++=) *(670907-2)* – ('A'-video).

May 01. (12"/cd-s) *<1997>* **FRONT 2 BACK (explicit) / ALKOHOLIK (explicit feat. Erick Sermon, J-Ro & Tash of Tha Liks) / XZIBIT "X" (Howie Beno mix) / FRONT 2 BACK (instrumental)** [–] [ ]

Jan 02. (cd-s) *<672065>* **GET YOUR WALK ON (mixes; explicit / remix / instrumental)** [–] [ ]

Loud – Epic | Columbia

Oct 02. (cd/d-lp) *(504753-2/-1)* *<85925>* **MAN VS. MACHINE** [43] [3]
– Release date / Symphony in X major (with DR. DRE) / Multiply (with NATE DOGG) / Break yourself / Heart of man / Harder (with GOLDEN STATE PROJECT) / Paul / Choke me, spank me (pull my hair) / Losin' your mind (with SNOOP DOGG) / BK to LA (with M.O.P.) / My name is (with EMINEM & NATE DOGG) / The gambler (with ANTHONY HAMILTON) / Missin' U / Right on / Bitch and nigga (with EDDIE GRIFFIN) / Enemies / My life, my world / What a mess / (Hit U) Where it hurts.

Nov 02. (12"; by XZIBIT & NATE DOGG) *(673155-6)* **MULTIPLY (explicit) / MULTIPLY (clean) / GET YOUR WALK ON (remix) / MULTIPLY (instrumental)** [39] [ ]
(cd-s) *(673155-2)* – ('A'-video).

Dec 02. (cd-s) **SYMPHONY IN X MAJOR (mixes) / GET YOUR WALK ON (explicit)** [–] [ ]

NEIL YOUNG

YARDBIRDS

Formed: Richmond, Surrey, England ... 1963, by KEITH RELF and PAUL SAMWELL-SMITH (both ex-METROPOLITAN BLUES QUARTET) together with JIM McCARTY, CHRIS DREJA and ANTHONY TOPHAM. The latter was soon replaced by ERIC CLAPTON and after a residency at Richmond's 'Crawdaddy' club backing bluesman, SONNY BOY WILLIAMSON, the YARDBIRDS were signed up by EMI's 'COLUMBIA' label in early '64. After two well received singles that year, 'I WISH YOU WOULD' and 'GOOD MORNING LITTLE SCHOOLGIRL', the band released the acclaimed 'FIVE LIVE YARDBIRDS' the following year. Recorded at London's Marquee club, the album was a thrilling snapshot of the group's pioneering, souped-up blues and R&B sound. Although it contained no original material, the band marked interpretations of standards like 'SMOKESTACK LIGHTNING' and 'RESPECTABLE' with an indelible stamp. But this line-up promptly came to an end upon the release of the classic 'FOR YOUR LOVE' (1965) single. Considering the record a betrayal of the band's blues roots, CLAPTON upped sticks and left for JOHN MAYALL'S BLUESBREAKERS. Enter JEFF BECK, another supremely gifted guitarist, and the band embarked upon the most successful period of their career, notching up hits with the likes of 'HEART FULL OF SOUL', 'EVIL HEARTED YOU', 'STILL I'M SAD' and 'SHAPES OF THINGS'. BECK had brought a new spirit of experimentation to the band and employed such psychedelic tactics as Eastern-style guitar mantras, distortion and Gregorian Chant. With 'THE YARDBIRDS' (1966), the band further embraced psychedelia and the album stands as a career pinnacle, innovative while maintaining the essence of their R&B heritage. This was especially evident on the single, 'OVER UNDER SIDEWAYS DOWN' (1966), which was backed by another of the album's best tracks, the self explanatory 'JEFF'S BOOGIE'. SAMWELL-SMITH, who'd produced the album, departed soon after and was replaced by yet another future guitar God, JIMMY PAGE. Soon shifting from bass to co-lead alongside BECK, the new line-up cut the electrifying psychedelia of 'HAPPENINGS TEN YEARS AGO' (1966). This honeymoon period was short-lived however, as BECK parted ways with the band during a particularly laborious US tour. 'LITTLE GAMES' (1967) was an ill-advised attempt at commerciality while covers of MANFRED MANN's 'HA! HA! SAID THE CLOWN' and NILSSON's 'TEN LITTLE INDIANS' were equally puzzling. Though these releases achieved a modicum of success in America, the band split in mid '68, PAGE and DREJA going on to form The NEW YARDBIRDS which in turn evolved into LED ZEPPELIN. The inevitable reunion took place in the mid-80's and under the BOX OF FROGS moniker, a line-up of BECK, McCARTY, DREJA, SAMWELL-SMITH, RORY GALLAGHER and MAX MIDDLETON cut a self-titled album in 1984 and the 'STRANGE LAND' lp in 1986. • **Songwriters:** RELF wrote some, except covers, I WISH YOU WOULD (Billy Boy Arnold) / SMOKESTACK LIGHTNING (Howlin' Wolf) / A CERTAIN GIRL (Ernie K-Doe) / GOOD MORNING LITTLE SCHOOLGIRL (Don & Bob) / TRAIN (Johnny Burnette) / FOR YOUR LOVE + HEART FULL OF SOUL (c. Graham Gouldman, ⇒ 10cc) / I'M A MAN (Bo Diddley) / THE SUN IS SHINING (Elmore James) / plus loads of other blues greats. • **Trivia:** Made two group appearances in the 66/67 films 'SWINGING LONDON' & 'BLOW-UP'. Early in 1966, manager GIORGIO GOMELSKY was replaced by SIMON NAPIER-BELL.

Album rating: FIVE LIVE YARDBIRDS (*8) / FOR YOUR LOVE (*6) / HAVING A RAVE UP WITH THE YARDBIRDS (*5) / SONNY BOY WILLIAMSON & THE YARDBIRDS exploitation (*5) / THE YARDBIRDS (aka OVER UNDER SIDEWAYS DOWN) (*5) / GREATEST HITS compilation (*7) / LITTLE GAMES (*(*5) / THE VERY BEST OF THE YARDBIRDS (*9)

KEITH RELF (b.22 Mar'43, Richmond) – vocals, harmonica / **ERIC CLAPTON** (b.30 Mar'45, Ripley, England) – lead guitar, vocals repl. ANTHONY TOPHAM / **CHRIS DREJA** (b.11 Nov'45, Surbiton, Surrey) – rhythm guitar / **PAUL SAMWELL-SMITH** (b. 8 May'43, Richmond) – bass / **JIM McCARTY** (b.25 Jul'43, Liverpool) – drums

Columbia | Epic

Jun 64. (7") *(DB 7283)* <9709> **I WISH YOU WOULD. / A CERTAIN GIRL** — [ ] | Oct64 [ ]

Oct 64. (7") *(DB 7391)* **GOOD MORNING LITTLE SCHOOLGIRL. / I AIN'T GOT YOU** — [44] | [–]

Feb 65. (lp) *(33SX 1677)* **FIVE LIVE YARDBIRDS (live)** — [ ] | [–]
– Too much monkey business / I got love if you want it / Smokestack lightning / Good morning little schoolgirl / Respectable / Five long years / Pretty girl / Louise / I'm a man / Here 'tis. *(re-iss. Aug79 on 'Charly' lp)(c; CR 30173)(CFK 1017) (re-iss. Aug89; LIK 55) (cd-iss. on 'Charly'; CDCHARLY 182)*

Mar 65. (7") *(DB 7499)* <9790> **FOR YOUR LOVE. / GOT TO HURRY** — [3] | May65 [6]
(re-iss. Aug76 on 'Charly'; CYS 1012)

Jul 65. (lp; mono/stereo) <LN24/BN26 167> **FOR YOUR LOVE** — [–] | [96]
– For your love / I'm not talking / Putty (in your hands) / I ain't got you / Got to hurry / I ain't done wrong / I wish you would / A certain girl / Sweet music / Good morning little schoolgirl / My girl Sloopy.

—— (Mar65) **JEFF BECK** (b.24 Jun'44, Surrey) – lead guitar repl. CLAPTON who joined JOHN MAYALL's BLUESBREAKERS. He later formed CREAM and went solo

Jul 65. (7") *(DB 7594)* <9823> **HEART FULL OF SOUL. / STEELED BLUES** — [2] | [9]

Oct 65. (7") *(DB 7706)* **EVIL HEARTED YOU. / STILL I'M SAD** — [3] | [–]
(re-iss. Jul82 on 'Old Gold'; OG 9111)

Nov 65. (7") <9857> **I'M A MAN. / STILL I'M SAD** — [–] | [17]

Jan 66. (lp; mono/stereo) *(export; SCXC 28)* <LN24/BN26 177> **HAVING A RAVE UP WITH THE YARDBIRDS (live)** — [–] | Dec65 [53]
– You're a better man than I / Evil hearted you / I'm a man / Still I'm sad / Heart full of soul / The train kept a-rollin' / Smokestack lightning / Respectable / I'm a man / Here 'tis. *(last 4 tracks from 'FIVE LIVE YARDBIRDS')*

Feb 66. (7") *(DB 7848)* **SHAPES OF THINGS. / YOU'RE A BETTER MAN THAN I** [3] [–]

Mar 66. (7") *<10006>* **SHAPES OF THINGS. / NEW YORK CITY BLUES** [–] [11]

—— (Feb66) **JIMMY PAGE** (b. 9 Jan'44, Middlesex, England) – guitar (ex-session man, solo artist) repl. SAMWELL-SMITH who became producer. (DREJA moved to bass) KEITH issued solo 45 in May.

May 66. (7") *(DB 7928) <10035>* **OVER, UNDER, SIDEWAYS, DOWN. / JEFF'S BOOGIE** [10] Jun66 [13]

Jul 66. (lp; mono/stereo) *(SX/SCX 6063) <LN24/BN26 210>* **THE YARDBIRDS** (US title 'OVER UNDER SIDEWAYS DOWN') [20] [52]
– Lost women / Over, under, sideways, down / The Nazz are blue / I can't make your way / Rack my mind / Farewell / Hot house of Omagarashid / Jeff's boogie / He's always there / Turn into earth / What do you want / Ever since the world began. *(re-iss. Feb83 as 'ROGER THE ENGINEER' on 'Edsel' lp; mono/stereo)(c; ED 116 M/S)(CED 116) (cd-iss. 1986+=; EDCD 116)* – Happenings ten years time ago / Psycho daisies. *(cd-iss. Feb92 on 'Raven-Topic' US version;)*

Oct 66. (7") *(DB 8024)* **HAPPENINGS TEN YEARS TIME AGO. / PSYCHO DAISIES** [43] [–]

Nov 66. (7") *<10094>* **HAPPENINGS TEN YEARS TIME AGO. / THE NAZZ ARE BLUE** [–] [30]

—— (Oct66) Trimmed to a quartet when JEFF BECK left to go solo.

Apr 67. (7") *(DB 8165) <10156>* **LITTLE GAMES. / PUZZLES** [ ] [51]

Apr 67. (lp; mono/stereo) *<LN24/BN26 246>* **GREATEST HITS** (compilation) [–] [28]
– Shapes of things / Still I'm sad / New York City blues / For your love / Over, under, sideways, down / I'm a man / Happenings ten years time ago / Heart full of soul / Smokestack lightning / I'm not talking.

Jun 67. (7") *<10204>* **HA HA SAID THE CLOWN. / TINKER, TAILOR, SOLDIER, SAILOR** [–] [45]

Aug 67. (lp; mono/stereo) *<LN24/BN26 313>* **LITTLE GAMES** [–] [80]
– Little games / Smile on me / White summer / Tinker, tailor, soldier, sailor / Glimpses / Drinking muddy water / No excess baggage / Stealing, stealing / Only the black rose / Little soldier boy. *(UK-iss.May85 on 'Fame' lp/c; FA 41 3124-1/-4) (re-iss. Apr91 on 'E.M.I.'; CDEMS 1389) (cd re-iss. Oct96 on 'Gold'; CDGOLD 1068)*

Oct 67. (7") *<10248>* **TEN LITTLE INDIANS. / DRINKIN' MUDDY WATER** [–] [96]

Mar 68. (7"w-drawn) *(DB 8368) <10303>* **GOODNIGHT SWEET JOSEPHINE. / THINK ABOUT IT** [–] [ ]

—— Disbanded mid'68. PAGE and DREJA formed NEW YARDBIRDS, but when DREJA departed, PAGE formed LED ZEPPELIN. RELF and McCARTY formed the original RENAISSANCE. On 14 May'76, RELF was electrocuted when touching a faulty amp. In the early 90s, McCARTY was also part of PRETTY THINGS / YARDBIRD BLUES BAND collaboration.

– (selective) compilations, etc. –

Jan 66. (lp; mono/stereo) *Fontana; (TL 5277) / Mercury; <MG2/SR6 1071>* **SONNY BOY WILLIAMSON AND THE YARDBIRDS (live)** [ ] Feb66 [ ]
– Bye bye bird / Mr. Downchild / The river Rhine / 23 hours too long / Out on the water coast / Baby don't worry / Pontiac blues / Take it easy baby / I don't care no more / Do the Weston. *(re-iss. 1968; SFJL 960) (re-iss. Jun75 on 'Philips'; 6435 011)*

Aug 77. (lp) *Charly; (CR 30013)* **THE YARDBIRDS FEATURING JEFF BECK** [ ] [–]
(re-iss. Mar83; CR 30195) (re-iss. Feb85 on 'Cambra'; CR 107)

Nov 84. (lp-box) *Charly; (BOX 104)* **SHAPES OF THINGS – COLLECTION OF CLASSIC RECORDINGS 1964-66** [ ] [–]
– (lp's) THE FIRST RECORDINGS / SONNY BOY WILLIAMSON & . . . / FIVE LIVE YARDBIRDS / FOR YOUR LOVE / HAVING A RAVE . . . / SHAPES OF THINGS / ODDS AND SODS *(4xcd-box Jun91 on 'Decal'; CDLIKBOX 1)*

Jun 91. (cd) *Music Club; (MCCD 023)* **THE VERY BEST OF THE YARDBIRDS** [ ] [–]
– For your love / Heart full of soul / Good morning little schoolgirl / Still I'm sad / Evil hearted you / A certain girl / Jeff's blues / I wish you would / New York City / I'm not talking / You're a better man than I / Shapes of things / I'm a man / Boom boom / Smokestack lightning (live) / Let it rock (live) / You can't judge a book by it's cover (live) / Who do you love (live) / Too much monkey business (live) / Respectable (live) / Pretty girl (live) / Stroll on.

Apr 91. (cd/c/lp) *Band Of Joy; (BOJ CD/MC/LP 20)* **ON AIR** (65-67) [ ] [–]

Apr 93. (4xcd-box) *Decal; (CDLIKBOX 3)* **THE BLUES WAILING YARDBIRDS – THE COMPLETE GIORGIO GOMELSKY SESSIONS** [ ] [–]

Mar 97. (cd) *Nectar; (NTMCD 527)* **THE BEST OF THE LEGENDARY YARDBIRDS** [ ] [–]

YAZOO

Formed: Basildon, Essex, England . . . late 1981 by VINCE CLARKE and ALISON MOYET. Electro maestro CLARKE was retained by 'Mute' after leaving DEPECHE MODE and, hooking up with MOYET, the pair crashed into the UK charts in Spring '82 with the bittersweet 'ONLY YOU'. YAZOO again made the Top 3 later that summer with the hypnotic synthesised power-blues of 'DON'T GO'. The album 'UPSTAIRS AT ERIC'S' (1982) ranked as one of the best albums of the year, YAZOO rising above the synth-pop pack by dint of CLARKE's robotic yet seductively melodic keyboard lines and MOYET's gritty, diva-like vocal impact and stunning range. The following year the duo repeated the success with No.1 album, 'YOU AND ME BOTH', a more ambitious and consistent set which spawned the classic 'NOBODY'S DIARY', another UK Top 3 hit. MOYET was again the focal point of the record, her not inconsiderable charisma and womanly presence asserting itself with a force that was rarely visible on her later, more ponderous mainstream material. Despite their enormous success and a growing groundswell of interest in America, the duo decided to split while the going was good, MOYET going on to a highly successful solo career, while CLARKE eventually hooked up with ANDY BELL to form the equally successful ERASURE. • **Trivia:** Due to a record company of the same name in the States, they had to be called YAZ. Acappella group, The FLYING PICKETS, had a UK Christmas 1983 No.1 with their version of 'ONLY YOU'.

Album rating: UPSTAIRS AT ERIC'S (*8) / YOU AND ME BOTH (*7) / ONLY YAZOO – THE BEST OF YAZOO compilation (*8)

ALISON MOYET (b. GENEVIEVE ALISON-JANE MOYET, 18 Jun'61, Billericay, Essex, England) – vocals (ex-VICARS, ex-SCREAMING ABDABS) / **VINCE CLARKE** (b. 3 Jul'61, South Woodford, England) – keyboards, synthesizers (ex-DEPECHE MODE)

Mute Sire

May 82. (7"/ext.12") *(7/12 MUTE 020)* **ONLY YOU. / SITUATION** [2] [–]

Jul 82. (7") *(7 YAZ 001)* **DON'T GO. / WINTER KILLS** [3] [ ]
(remix-12"+=) *(12 YAZ 001)* – ('A'remix).

Aug 82. (lp/c) *(STUMM/CSTUMM 7) <23737>* **UPSTAIRS AT ERIC'S** [2] [92]
– Don't go / Too pieces / Bad connection / I before E except after C / Midnight / In my room / Only you / Goodbye 70's / Tuesday / Winter kills / Bring your love down (didn't I). *(cd-iss. Jan87 & Jun95+=) (CDSTUMM 7)* – The other side of love / Situation (12"mixes).

Sep 82. (7") *<29953>* **SITUATION. / WINTER KILLS** [–] [73]

Nov 82. (7"/remix-12") *(7/12 YAZ 002)* **THE OTHER SIDE OF LOVE. / ODE TO BOY** [13] [ ]

Apr 83. (7"/ext.12") *(7/12 YAZ 003)* **NOBODY'S DIARY. / STATE FARM** [3] [ ]
(12") *(L12 YAZ 003)* – ('A'side) / Situation (re-recorded).

Jul 83. (lp/c) *(STUMM/CSTUMM 12) <23930>* **YOU AND ME BOTH** [1] [69]
– Nobody's diary / Softly over / Sweet thing / Mr. Blue / Good times / Walk away from love / Ode to boy / Unmarked / Anyone / Happy people / And on. *(cd-iss. Jan87 & Jun95; CDSTUMM 12)*

—— split summer 1983, MOYET went solo and VINCE formed ASSEMBLY (see)

– compilations, others, etc. –

on 'Mute' unless mentioned otherwise

Nov 90. (7") *(7 YAZ 4)* **SITUATION (deadline remix). / STATE FARM (madhouse mix)** [14] [–]

(12"+=/cd-s+=) *(12/CD YAZ 4)* – ('A'-aggressive mix) / ('A'-space mix).
(cd-s+=) *(LCD YAZ 4)* – ('A'&'B'-original & US remixes).

Aug 99. (c-s/cd-s) *(C/LCD YAZ 5)* **ONLY YOU (1999 remix) / DON'T GO (Tee's radio mix)** 38 –
(cd-s+=) *(CDYAZ 5)* – Winter kills.
(cd-s+=) *(LCDYAZ 5)* – Don't go (Digital Blonde instrumental).
(12"+=) *(12YAZ 5)* – ('A'mixes; Todd's freeze / Tee's dub).

Sep 99. (cd/c) *(CD/C MUTEL 6)* **ONLY YAZOO – THE BEST OF YAZOO** 22
– Only you / Ode to a boy / Nobody's diary / Midnight / Goodbye 70's / Anyone / Don't go / Mr. Blue / Tuesday / Winter kills / State farm / Situation / Don't go (Todd Terry mix) / Situation / Only you (1999 mix).

Nov 99. (12"/cd-s) *(12/CD YAZ 6)* **SITUATION (mixes; Club 69 speed / Richard 'Humpty' Vission instrumental)** –
(12") *(L12YAZ 6)* – ('A'-Dave Ralph's tea freaks english breakfast mix) / ('A'-Club 69 speed mix).

The ASSEMBLY

VINCE CLARKE plus **FEARGAL SHARKEY** – vocals (ex-UNDERTONES) / **E.C. RADCLIFFE** – drums (ex-FAD GADGET)

Mute / Intercord

Nov 83. (7") *(TINY 1)* **NEVER NEVER. / STOP START** 4

VINCE CLARKE & PAUL QUINN

QUINN (b. Scotland) – vox (ex-BOURGIE BOURGIE)

Mute / not iss.

Jun 85. (7"/12") *(TAG/12TAG 1)* **ONE DAY. / SONG FOR** –

— In 1985, VINCE formed ERASURE with ANDY BELL

YEAH YEAH YEAHS

Formed: New York City, New York, USA ... 2000 by KAREN O, a student from Ohio who flitted to NY and subsequently met guitarist NICK ZINNER and drummer BRAIN CHASE. Dubbed the "Strokes' favourite new band" (Christ, isn't everyone!), because one of them wore a YEAH YEAH YEAHS' badge while playing on an American chatshow, this 3-piece outfit didn't deserve being introduced like that in the wake of NYC's other trendy garage rockers. However, if one could describe the sound of O and her cohorts, it would most likely include a ROYAL TRUX's rock-out sludginess and POLLY JEAN HARVEY's precise eroticism mixed with garage guts and slut-chic. After a handful of support gigs with the likes of The WHITE STRIPES and BOSS HOG, they recorded and issued their self-titled EP in 2001, which was produced by JERRY TEEL, himself a member of BOSS HOG. After touring even more, another EP arrived on 'Touch and Go' records, entitled 'MACHINE' (in 2002), and displayed KAREN O's raw, sexually driven grind-house stompers (barely backed by only guitar and drums), which were harshly reminiscent of early BIKINI KILL, especially on screamers such as 'ART STAR' and 'BANG'. It was all worth the hype when the band issued their debut album 'FEVER TO TELL' in 2003. Backed by the hit single 'PIN', the no-wave funky garage of the YEAH YEAH YEAHS was a million miles away from the LOU REED-esque narcissism of The STROKES. Hit single 'DATE WITH THE NIGHT's abruptness was startling, while elsewhere, 'COLD LIGHT's heavy drone was very much reminiscent of fellow rockers The KILLS.

Album rating: FEVER TO TELL (*8)

KAREN O – vocals / **NICK ZINNER** – guitar / **BRIAN CHASE** – drums

Wichita / Shifty

Apr 02. (12"ep/cd-ep) *(WEBB 029 T/CD)* <05> **YEAH YEAH YEAHS EP** Nov01
– Bang / Mystery girl / Art star / Miles away / Our time. *<(US re-iss. Mar02 + UK-iss.Jan03 on 'Touch & Go'; T&G 238)>*

Wichita / Touch & Go

Nov 02. (7"ep/cd-ep) *(WEBB 036 S/CD)* *<T&G 244/+CD>* **MACHINE EP** 37
– Machine / Graveyard / Pin (remix). *(UK-iss.May03; same)*

Polydor / Interscope

Apr 03. (7") *(65744-7)* **DATE WITH THE NIGHT. / YEAH! NEW YORK** 16 –
(cd-s+=) *(65744-2)* – Bang (remix) / ('A'-video).

Apr 03. (cd/lp) *(76061-2/-1)* *<03490-2/-1>* **FEVER TO TELL** 13 May03 67
– Rich / Date with the night / Man / Tick / Black tongue / Pin / Cold light / No no no / Maps / Y control / Modern romance. *(hidden tracks+=)* – Yeah! New York / Date with the night (video).

Jun 03. (12") *(980808-6)* **PIN. / RICH (Pandaworksforthecops remix) / MR. YOU'RE ON FIRE MR.** 29 –
(cd-s+=) *(980808-5)* – ('A'-video).

Sep 03. (cd-s) *(981141-3)* **MAPS / COUNTDOWN / MILES AWAY (Radio 1 John Peel session) / ('A'-video)** 26 –

YES

Formed: London, England ... mid '68 by veterans of the 60's beat era; JON ANDERSON and CHRIS SQUIRE. They added BILL BRUFORD, PETE BANKS and TONY KAYE, soon signing to 'Atlantic' after opening for CREAM at their farewell concert at London's Royal Albert Hall. In the summer of 1969, their self-titled debut album was released, a set of original material such as 'SURVIVAL', interspersed with two covers ('I SEE YOU' – Byrds & 'EVERY LITTLE THING' – Beatles). In 1970, the follow-up, 'TIME AND A WORD', also included a version of Stephen Stills' 'NO OPPORTUNITY NECESSARY', alongside the more accomplished title track and the single, 'SWEET DREAMS'. A UK Top 50 hit, it was surpassed early the next year by 'THE YES ALBUM', their first release to feature the innovative guitar-work of STEVE HOWE; BANKS having moved on to the group FLASH. The record featured four meticulously-crafted tracks, 'YOURS IS NO DISGRACE', 'STARSHIP TROOPER', 'PERPETUAL CHANGE' and 'I'VE SEEN ALL GOOD PEOPLE', which went some way to crystallising the typical YES sound, ANDERSON's high-pitched choirboy vocals providing the focal point. The more stylish and flamboyant keyboard-wizard, RICK WAKEMAN was then drafted in to replace KAYE on their 4th album, 'FRAGILE'. A little self-indulgent, it nonetheless garnered widespread critic acclaim and was the first to feature ROGER DEAN's fantasy sleeve artwork. The record's sales were boosted by the Top 20 smash, 'ROUNDABOUT', a US-only single in 1972. Later in the year, they unleashed their progressive tour de force, 'CLOSE TO THE EDGE', an exuberant, atmospheric set which utilised a high-tech multi-layered sound. A triple live set, 'YESSONGS', peaked at No.1 in the UK, also hitting Top 20 in America. During this period, they returned with a double studio concept piece, 'TALES FROM TOPOGRAPHIC OCEANS' which was subsequently lambasted by certain sections of the music press for its overly long tracks. This, and other minor details (such as WAKEMAN not toeing the vegetarian line and being partial to a few beers), led to his departure (he had already released a solo album 'THE SIX WIVES OF HENRY VIII'). His replacement was PATRICK MORAZ (ex-REFUGEE) who took over in time for the 1974 album, 'RELAYER'. Each of the individual group members then took the opportunity to have their own solo outing (see below for details). In 1977, when punk rock was king, YES re-grouped once more with RICK WAKEMAN back in the fold for comeback album, 'GOING FOR THE ONE'. By this stage, the pomp-rock excesses had been slimmed down somewhat to accommodate a more commercial sound, much in evidence on the hit single (first in the UK), 'WONDROUS STORIES'. They failed to emulate this success, critically at least, on their follow-up, 'TORMATO', although it did provide a minor hit, 'SAVE THE WHALE'. In the early 80's, two of their most fundamental creative forces, WAKEMAN and ANDERSON, split ranks, leaving YES to pick up the pieces. However, fans were aghast at the pieces they picked up, i.e. The BUGGLES (TREVOR HORN and GEOFFREY DOWNES), who had previously topped the pop charts with the novelty hit, 'Video Killed The Radio Star'. Despite the initial shock, fans still parted with their hard-earned cash for the resultant 'DRAMA' album. YES split again in 1982, when HOWE and DOWNES joined the soon-to-be successful British supergroup ASIA. ANDERSON returned from a solo career (including a lucrative collaboration with VANGELIS on the hit 45 'I Hear You Now') to a newly reformed YES the following year. The new line-up also included old hands TONY KAYE, CHRIS SQUIRE, ALAN WHITE and a new guitarist, the South African born TREVOR RABIN. Retaining TREVOR HORN on production duties only, they recorded the '90125' album, which spawned the US No.1, 'OWNER OF A LONELY HEART. After RABIN dominated the songwriting on their 1987 set, 'THE BIG GENERATOR', ANDERSON departed yet again. Over the next two years, a bitter dispute was fought over the rights to the YES name. SQUIRE and the last remaining members in 1987 won, while ANDERSON, BRUFORD, WAKEMAN & HOWE were forced to record a surprisingly successful album under their own surnames. Come 1991, the two opposing camps had reconciled their differences, recording the appropriately-titled 'UNION' together. The '90125' line-up was then resurrected for the 1994 'TALK' album, a more lightweight affair which was yet another pointless exercise in dinosaur rock. The second half of the 90's have seen YES deliver some well below par recordings, the concert pair 'KEYS TO ASCENSION' 1 & 2 (1996/97), 'OPEN YOUR EYES' (1997) and Top 40 entry! 'THE LADDER' (1999). With the millennial 'MAGNIFICATION' (2001), YES went for broke and did what they've always probably secretly wanted to do, record a whole album in conjunction with a full blown symphony orchestra. A lowly chart placing of UK Top75 suggested that fans weren't exactly thrilled with the results. • **Other covers:** I'M DOWN (Beatles) / SOMETHING'S COMING (Sondheim-Bernstein) / AMERICA (Simon & Garfunkel) / AMAZING GRACE (trad).

Album rating: YES (*6) / TIME AND A WORD (*6) / THE YES ALBUM (*9) / FRAGILE (*8) / CLOSE TO THE EDGE (*10) / YESSONGS (*7) / TALES FROM TOPOGRAPHIC OCEANS (*7) / RELAYER (*6) / YESTERDAYS collection (*5) / GOING FOR THE ONE (*7) / TORMATO (*3) / DRAMA (*4) / YESSHOWS (*4) / CLASSIC YES compilation (*8) / 90125 (*6) / 90125 – THE SOLOS (*3) / BIG GENERATOR (*5) / ANDERSON BRUFORD WAKEMAN HOWE (*5) / UNION (*4) / TALK (*5) / KEYS TO ASCENSION (*5) / KEYS TO ASCENSION, VOL.2 (*3) / OPEN YOUR EYES (*4) / THE LADDER (*4) / MAGNIFICATION (*4) / THE ULTIMATE YES double compilation (*5) / Steve Howe: BEGINNINGS (*5) / THE STEVE HOWE ALBUM (*3) / TURBULENCE (*4) / THE GRAND SCHEME OF THINGS (*4) / VOYAGERS (*4) / Chris Squire: FISH OUT OF WATER (*4) / Alan White: RAMSHACKLED (*2) / Jon Anderson: OLIAS OF SUNHILLOW (*6) / SONG OF SEVEN (*7) / ANIMATION (*6) / 3 SHIPS (*3) / IN THE CITY OF ANGELS (*4) / CHANGE WE MUST (*4)

JON ANDERSON (b.25 Oct'44, Accrington, England) – vocals (ex-WARRIORS, ex-MABEL GREER'S TOY SHOP) / **TONY KAYE** (b.11 Jan'46, Leicester, England) – keyboards (ex-FEDERALS, ex-BITTER SWEET) / **PETER BANKS** (b. 7 Jul'47, Barnet, England) – guitar (ex-SYN, ex-MABEL GREER'S TOYSHOP) / **CHRIS SQUIRE** (b. 4 Mar'48, Nth. London) – bass, vocals (ex-SYN, ex-MABEL GREER'S TOYSHOP) / **BILL BRUFORD** (b.17 May'48, Seven Oaks, London, England) – drums, percussion (ex-SAVOY BROWN BLUES BAND)

Atlantic Atlantic

Jun 69. (7") *(584 280)* **SWEETNESS. / SOMETHING'S COMING** –

Jul 69. (lp) *(588 190) <8243>* **YES** Oct69
– Beyond and before / I see you / Yesterday and today / Looking around / Harold land / Every little thing / Sweetness / Survival. *(re-iss. Dec71 lp/c; K/K4 40034) (cd-iss. Oct94 on 'East West'; 7567 82680-2)*

Oct 69. (7"w-drawn) *(584 298)* **LOOKING AROUND. / EVERYDAYS** – –

Jan 70. (7") *<2709>* **SWEETNESS / EVERY LITTLE THING** –

Mar 70. (7") *(584 323)* **TIME AND A WORD. / THE PROPHET** –

Jun 70. (lp) *(2400 006) <8273>* **TIME AND A WORD** 45 Nov70
– No opportunity neccessary, no experience needed / Then / Everydays / Sweet dreams / The prophet / Clear days / Astral traveller / Time and a word. *(re-iss. Dec71 lp/c; K/K4 40085) (cd-iss. Oct94 on 'East West'; 7567 82681-2)*

Jun 70. (7") *(2091 004)* **SWEET DREAMS. / DEAR FATHER** –

— **STEVE HOWE** (b. 8 Apr'47) – guitar (ex-TOMORROW, ex-IN CROWD, ex-SYNDICATS, ex-BODAST) repl. BANKS who joined BLODWYN PIG and later FLASH

Mar 71. (lp) *(2400 101) <8283>* **THE YES ALBUM** 7 May71 40
– Yours is no disgrace / The clap / Starship trooper; (a) Life seeker – (b) Disiilusion – (c) Wurm / I've seen good people (a) Your move – (b) All good people / A venture / Perpetual change. *(re-iss. Dec71 lp/c; K/K4 40106) (cd-iss. Jul87; SD 19131-2) (cd re-iss. Aug94 on 'East West'; 7567 82665-2)*

Aug 71. (7") *<2819>* **YOUR MOVE. / THE CLAP** – 40
<re-iss. 1974; 3141>

— **RICK WAKEMAN** (b.18 May'49) – keyboards (ex-STRAWBS) repl. KAYE who formed BADGER

Nov 71. (lp) *(2401 019) <7211>* **FRAGILE** 7 Jan72 4
– Roundabout / Cans and Brahms / We have Heaven / South side of the sky / Five per cent of nothing / Long distance runaround / The fish (Shindleria Praematurus) / Mood for a day / Heart of the sunrise. *(re-iss. Dec71 lp/c; K/K4 50009) (cd-iss. Dec86; K2 50009) (cd re-iss. Aug94 on 'East West'; 7567 82667-2)*

Jan 72. (7") *<2854>* **ROUNDABOUT. / LONG DISTANCE RUNAROUND** – 13

Jul 72. (7") *<2899>* **AMERICA. / TOTAL MASS RETAIN** – 46

Sep 72. (lp/c) *(K/K4 50012) <7244>* **CLOSE TO THE EDGE** 4 3
– Close to the edge; (a) The solid time of change – (b) Total mass retain – (c) I get up I get down – (d) Seasons of man / And you and I; (a) Cord of life – (b) Eclipse – (c) The preacher the teacher – (d) The apocalypse / Siberian Khatru. *(cd-iss. Dec86; K2 50012) (cd re-iss. Aug94 on 'East West'; 7567 82666-2)*

Oct 72. (7") *<2920>* **AND YOU AND I (part II). / (part I)** – 42

— (Aug72) **ANDERSON, HOWE, WAKEMAN + SQUIRE** brought in **ALAN WHITE** (b.14 Jun'44, Pelton, Durham, England) – drums (ex-John Lennon's PLASTIC ONO BAND, ex-HAPPY MAGAZINE) repl. BRUFORD who joined KING CRIMSON, etc. (both appeared on live album below)

May 73. (t-lp/d-c) *(K/K4 60045) <100>* **YESSONGS (live)** 1 12
– (opening excerpt from 'Firebird Suite') / Siberian Khatru / Heart of the sunrise / Perpetual change / And you and I; (a) Cord of life – (b) Eclipse – (c) The preacher the teacher – (d) The apocalypse / Mood for a day / (excerpts from 'The Six Wives Of Henry VIII') / Roundabout / I've seen all good people; Your move – All good people / Long distance runaround / The fish (Shindleria Praematurus) / Close to the edge (a) The solid time of change – (b) Total mass retain – (c) I get up I get down – (d) Seasons of man / Yours is no disgrace / Starship trooper (a) Life seeker – (b) Disillusion – (c) Wurm. *(d-cd-iss. Feb87; K2 60045) (re-iss. d-cd Oct94 on 'East West'; 7567 82682-2)*

Dec 73. (d-lp/c) *(K/K4 80001) <2908>* **TALES FROM TOPOGRAPHIC OCEANS** 1 6
– The revealing science of God / The remembering / The ancient / Ritual. *(cd-iss. Sep89; K 781325) (re-iss. d-cd Oct94 on 'East West'; 7567 82683-2)*

Jan 74. (7") *(K 10407)* **ROUNDABOUT (live). / AND YOU AND I (live)** –

— **PATRICK MORAZ** (b.24 Jun'48, Morges, Switzerland) – keyboards (ex-REFUGEE) repl. WAKEMAN who continued solo

Nov 74. (lp/c) *(K/K4 50096) <18122>* **RELAYER** 4 Dec74 5
– The gates of delirium / Sound chaser / To be over. *(cd-iss. Jul88; K2 50096) (re-iss. cd Oct94 on 'East West'; 7567 82664-2)*

Dec 74. (7") *<3222>* **SOON (from 'Gates of Delirium'). / SOUND CHASER** –

— Temporarily disbanded to release solo albums.

STEVE HOWE

augmented by **WHITE, BRUFORD, MORAZ** + many including **GRAEME TAYLOR** – guitar / **MALCOLM BENNETT + COLIN GIBSON** – bass / **DAVID OBERLE** – drums

		Atlantic	Atlantic
Nov 75.	(lp/c) *(K/K4 50151) <SD 18154>* **BEGINNINGS** – Doors of sleep / Australia / The nature of the sea / The lost symphony / Beginnings / Will o' the wisp / Ram / Pleasure stole the night / Break away from it all. *(cd-iss. Oct94 on 'East West'; 7567 80319-2)*	22	63

CHRIS SQUIRE

augmented by **BILL BRUFORD** – drums / **ANDREW BRYCE JACKMAN + BARRY ROSE** – keyboards / **MEL COLLINS** – sax / **PATRICK MORAZ** – keyboards, synthesizers / **JIMMY HASTINGS** – flute

		Atlantic	Atlantic
Nov 75.	(lp/c) *(K/K4 50203) <SD 18159>* **FISH OUT OF WATER** – Hold out your hand / You by my side / Silently falling / Lucky seven / Safe (canon song). *(cd-iss. Feb96 on 'WEA'; 7567 81500-2)*	25	69

ALAN WHITE

augmented by **PETER KIRTLEY** – guitar, vocals / **COLIN GIBSON** – bass / **KENNY CRADDOCK** – keyboards, vocals / **ANDY PHILIPS** – steel drums / **ALAN MARSHALL** vocals / **HENRY LOWTHER** – trumpet / **STEVE GREGORY + BUD BEADLE** – wind

		Atlantic	Atlantic
Mar 76.	(lp/c) *(K/K4 50217) <SD 18167>* **RAMSHACKLED** – Oooh! baby (going to pieces) / One way rag / Avakak / Spring – Song of innocence / Giddy / Silly woman / Marching into a bottle / Everybody / Darkness (parts 1, 2 & 3). *(cd-iss. Jan96 on 'WEA'; 7567 80396-2)*	41	
Apr 76.	(7") *(K 10747)* **OOOH! BABY (GOING TO PIECES). / ONE WAY RAG**		–

JON ANDERSON

augmented **BRIAN GAYLOR** – synths / **KEN FREEMAN** – strings

		Atlantic	Atlantic
Jun 76.	(lp/c) *(K/K4 50261) SD 18180>* **OLIAS OF SUNHILLOW** – Ocean song / Meeting (Garden of Geda) – Sound of the galleon / Dance of Ranyart – Olias (to build the Moorglade) / Qoquag en transic – Naon – Transic to / Flight of the Moorglade / Solid space / Moon Ra – Chords – Song of search / To the runner. *(cd-iss. Feb96 on 'WEA'; 7567 80273-2)*	8	47
Oct 76.	(7") *(K 10840)* **FLIGHT OF THE MOORGLADE. / TO THE RUNNER**		–

— PATRICK MORAZ also hit UK Top 30 with his 'I, PATRICK MORAZ' album for 'Charisma'. He had now departed YES to continue solo work & join MOODY BLUES.

YES

re-formed the 1973 line-up w / **RICK WAKEMAN** returning, to repl. MORAZ

Jul 77.	(lp/c/3x12") *(K/K4/DSK 50379) <19106>* **GOING FOR THE ONE** – Going for the one / Turn of the century / Parallels / Wondrous stories / Awaken. *(cd-iss. Jul88; K2 50379) (cd re-iss. Aug94 on 'East West'; 7567 82670-2)*	1	8
Sep 77.	(12"blue) *(K 10999)* **WONDROUS STORIES. / PARALLELS**	7	–
Sep 77.	(7") *<3416>* **WONDEROUS STORIES. / AWAKEN**	–	
Nov 77.	(12") *(K 11047)* **GOING FOR THE ONE. / AWAKEN (part 1)**	24	–
Sep 78.	(7") *(K 11184)* **DON'T KILL THE WHALE. / ABILENE**	36	–
Sep 78.	(lp/c) *(K/K4 50518) <19202>* **TORMATO** – Future times / Rejoice / Don't kill the whale / Madrigal / Release, release / Arriving UFO / Circus of Heaven / Onward / On the silent wings of freedom. *(cd-iss. Aug94 on 'East West'; 7567 82671-2)*	8	10
Nov 78.	(7") *<3534>* **RELEASE, RELEASE. / DON'T KILL THE WHALE**	–	

— They shocked their fans, when they replaced (solo seeking once more) WAKEMAN and ANDERSON with (ex-BUGGLES duo) :-**TREVOR HORN** (b.15 Jul'49, Hertfordshire, England) – vocals, bass / + **GEOFF DOWNES** – keyboards

Aug 80.	(lp/c) *(K/K4 50736) <16019>* **DRAMA** – Machine messiah / White car / Does it really happen? / Into the lens / Run through the light / Tempus fugit. *(cd-iss. Oct94 on 'East West'; 7567 82685-2)*	2	18
Oct 80.	(7") *(K 11622) <3767>* **INTO THE LENS. / DOES IT REALLY HAPPEN?**		
Jan 81.	(7") *<3801>* **RUN THROUGH THE LIGHT. / WHITE CAR**	–	

— YES split again.

Nov 81.	(7"; CHRIS SQUIRE & ALAN WHITE / or / CAMERA) *(K 11695)* **RUN WITH THE FOX. / RETURN OF THE FOX**		–

above partnership brought back **ANDERSON + KAYE,** plus newcomer **TREVOR RABIN** (b.13 Jan'54, Johannesburg, South Africa) – guitar, vocals. They repl. DOWNES + HOWE (to ASIA) / and HORN who was retained as producer.

		Atco	Atco
Nov 83.	(7"/7"colrd-sha-pic-d/c-s) *(B9817/+P/C) <99817>* **OWNER OF A LONELY HEART. / OUR SONG**	28	1
Nov 83.	(lp/c/cd) *(790 125-1/-4/-2) <90125>* **90125** – Owner of a lonely heart / Hold on / It can happen / Changes / Cinema / Leave it / Our song / City of love / Hearts.	16	5
Mar 84.	(7") *(B 9787) <99787>* **LEAVE IT. / LEAVE IT (acappella)** (12"+=) *(B 9787T)* – ('A'version). (c-s+=)<US cd-s+=> *<B 9789C>* – ('A'-hello goodbye mix) / Owner of a lonely heart.	56	24
Jun 84.	(7") *(B 9745) <99745>* **IT CAN HAPPEN. / IT CAN HAPPEN (live)**		51
Mar 86.	(m-lp/c) *(790 474-1/-4) <90474>* **9012LIVE – THE SOLOS (live)** – Hold on / Si / Solly's beard / Soon / Changes / Amazing Grace / Whitefish.	44	Dec85 81
Sep 87.	(7") *(A 9449) <99449>* **LOVE WILL FIND A WAY. / HOLY LAMB** (ext.12"+=) *(A 9449T)* – ('A'-Rise & fall mix).	73	30
Sep 87.	(lp/c)(cd) *(WX 70/+C)(790 522-2) <90522>* **BIG GENERATOR** – Rhythm of love / Big generator / Shoot high aim low / Almost like love / Love will find a way / Final eyes / I'm running / Holy love.	17	15
Dec 87.	(12"ep) *<99419>* **RHYTHM OF LOVE (dance mix) – ('A'move mix) / ('A'dub) / CITY OF LOVE** (live)	–	40

— In-house squabbles led to splinter of YES . . .

ANDERSON BRUFORD WAKEMAN HOWE

		Arista	Arista
Jun 89.	(lp/c/cd) *(209/409/259 970) <90126>* **ANDERSON BRUFORD WAKEMAN HOWE** – Themes: Sound – Second attention – Soul warrior / Fist of fire / Brother of mine: The big dream – Nothing can come between us – Long lost brother of mine / Quartet: I wanna learn – She gives me love – Who was the first – I'm alive / Birthright / The meeting / Teakbois / Order of the universe: Order theme – Rock gives courage – It's so hard to grow – The universe / Let's pretend. *(lp tracks edited) (re-iss. Dec91 cd/c; 262/412 155)*	14	30
Jun 89.	(7") *(112444)* **BROTHER OF MINE. / THEMES: SOUND** (12"+=) *(612379)* – Themes: Second attention – Soul warrior. (3"cd-s+=/5"cd-s+=)(10"+=)(c-s+=) *(1/6 62379)(260018)(410017)* – Vultures (in the city).	63	–
Jun 89.	(cd-s) *<9852>* **BROTHER OF MINE: THE BIG DREAM – NOTHING CAN COME BETWEEN US – LONG LOST BROTHER OF MINE / VULTURES**	–	
Aug 89.	(7") *<9898>* **LET'S PRETEND. / QUARTET: I'M ALIVE**	–	
Nov 89.	(7"/c-s) *(112618)* **ORDER OF THE UNIVERSE. / FIST OF FIRE** (12"+=)(cd-s+=) *(612618)(662693)* – ('A'extended).		–

YES

now settled dispute by combining last line-up of **ANDERSON, BRUFORD, HOWE, WAKEMAN** with present YES men **SQUIRE, WHITE, RABIN + KAYE**

		Arista	Arista
May 91.	(cd/c/lp) *(261/411/211 558) <8643>* **UNION** – I would have waited forever / Shock to the system / Masquerade / Lift me up / Without hope you cannot start the day / Saving my heart / Miracle of life / Silent talking / The more we live-let go / Dangerous / Holding on / Evensong. *(c+=/cd+=)* – Angkor wat / Take the water to the mountain / Give and take.	7	15
Jun 91.	(7") *(114 553)* **SAVING MY HEART. / LIFT ME UP (edit)** (cd-s+=) *(664 553)* – America.		–

Aug 91. (c-s) <2218> **LIFT ME UP / AMERICA** [–] [86]
(cd-s+=) <2218> – Give and take.

Nov 91. (c-s) **SAVING MY HEART. / THE MORE WE LIVE – LET GO** [–] [ ]

Victory London

Mar 94. (cd/c) *(828 489-2/-4)* <480033> **TALK** [20] [33]
– Calling / I am waiting / Real love / State of play / Walls / Where will you be / Endless dream (Silent spring – Talk – Endless dream).

Essential CMC Int.

Oct 96. (cd/c) *(EDF CD/MC 417)* <86204> **KEYS TO ASCENSION (live)** [48] [99]
– Siberia / Revealing science / America / Onward / Awaken / Roundabout / Starship trooper / Be the one / That, that is.

Essential Cleopatra

Nov 97. (d-cd/d-c) *(EDF CD/MC 457)* <159> **KEYS TO ASCENSION (2) (live)** [62] [ ]
– All good people / Going for the one / Time and a word / Close to the edge / Turn of the century / And you and I / Mind drive / Foot prints / Bring to the power / Lightning / Children of the light / Lifeline / Sign language.

Eagle Beyond

Nov 97. (cd/c) *(EAG CD/MC 013)* <3074> **OPEN YOUR EYES** [ ] [ ]
– New state of mind / Open your eyes / Universal garden / No way we can lose / Fortune seller / Man in the moon / Wonderlove / From the balcony / Love shine / Somehow . . . someday / The solution.

—— **ANDERSON, HOWE, SQUIRE, WHITE / + BILLY SHERWOOD** – guitar, vocals + **IGOR KHOROSHEV** – keyboards, vocals

Eagle Damian

Sep 99. (cd/d-lp) *(EAG CD/12 088)* <78046> **THE LADDER** [36] [ ]
– Homeworld (the ladder) / It will be a good day (the river) / Lightning strikes / Can I? / Face to face / If only you knew / To be alive (hep yadda) / Finally / The messenger / New language / Nine voices (longwalker).

—— **ANDERSON, HOWE, SQUIRE + WHITE**

Eagle Beyond

Sep 01. (cd) *(EAGCD 189)* <578205> **MAGNIFICATION** [71] [ ]
– Magnification / Spirit of survival / Don't go / Give love each day / Can you imagine / We agree / Soft as a dove / Dreamtime / In the presence of: 1. Deeper – 2. Death of . . . / Time is time.

– compilations, others, etc. –

Note; on 'Atlantic' unless otherwise stated.

Feb 75. (lp/c) *(K/K4 50048)* <18103> **YESTERDAYS** (early rare) [27] [17]
– America / Looking around / Time and a word / Sweet dreams / Then / Survival / Astral traveller / Dear father. *(re-iss. cd Oct94)*

Dec 81. (lp/c) *(K/K4 50842)* <19320> **CLASSIC YES** [ ] [ ]
– Heart of the sunrise / Wondrous stories / Yours is no disgrace / Roundabout / Starship trooper (a) Life seeker (b) Disillusion (c) Wurm / Long distance runaround / The fish (schindleria praematurus) / And you and I; (a) Cord of life (b) Eclipse (c) The preacher the teacher (d) The apocalypse / I've seen all good people; (a) Your move (b) All good people. *(w/ free 7")* ROUNDABOUT (live). / I'VE SEEN ALL GOOD PEOPLE (live) *(cd-iss. Dec86; 250842-2) (re-iss. cd Oct94 on 'East West'; 7567 82687-2)*

Dec 80. (d-lp/c) *Atco; (K 60142)* <510> **YESSHOWS (live 1976-1978)** [22] [43]
(cd-iss. Oct94; 7567 91747-2)

Oct 82. (d-c) *(K4 60166)* **FRAGILE / CLOSE TO THE EDGE** [ ] [–]

Aug 91. (4xcd-box) *Atco; (<7567 91644-2>)* **YESYEARS** [ ] [ ]

Oct 91. (d-cd/d-c/t-lp) *East West; (<7567 91747-2/-4/-1>)* **THE YES STORY** [ ] [ ]

Nov 91. (7"/c-s) *East West; (B 8713/+C)* **OWNER OF A LONELY HEART. / ('A'-wonderous mix)** [ ] [ ]
(12"/cd-s) *(B 8713 T/CD)* – ('A'side) / ('A'-Not Fragile mix) / ('A'-Move Yourself mix) / ('A'-Close To The Edge mix).

Sep 93. (cd) *Connoisseur; (VSOPCD 190)* **FAMILY ALBUM AFFIRMATIVE** (YES family tree) [ ] [–]
– Small beginnings (FLASH) / Feels good to me (BRUFORD) / Catherine Howard / Merlin the magician (RICK WAKEMAN) / Ocean song / All in a matter of time (JON ANDERSON) / I HEAR YOU NOW (JON & VANGELIS) / SPRING SONG OF INNOCENCE (ALAN WHITE) / Nature of the sea / Ram (STEVE HOWE) / Cahcaca (PATRICK MORAZ) / Hold out your hand (CHRIS SQUIRE) / Wind of change (BADGER) / Etoile noir (TREVOR RABIN).

Sep 93. (cd/c) *(7567 82517-2/-4)* **HIGHLIGHTS – THE VERY BEST OF YES** [ ] [ ]

Dec 93. (d-cd/video) *Fragile;* **AN EVENING OF YES MUSIC . . . PLUS** [ ] [ ]

Jul 03. (d-cd) *WEA; (8122 73702-2)* **THE ULTIMATE YES – 35th ANNIVERSARY COLLECTION** [10] Jan04 [ ]

JON ANDERSON

with more solo releases. Earlier in the year 1980, he (JON) and VANGELIS ⇒ had hit UK No.8 with single 'I HEAR YOU NOW', and 'SHORT STORIES' lp hit No.4.

—— with a plethera of session people.

Atlantic Atlantic

Sep 80. (7") *(K 11619)* **SOME ARE BORN. / DAYS** [ ] [ ]

Nov 80. (lp/c) *(K/K4 50756)* <16021> **SONG OF SEVEN** [38] [ ]
– For you for me / Some are born / Don't forget (nostalgia) / Heart of the matter / Hear it / Everybody loves you / Take your time / Days / Song of seven. *(cd-iss. May96 on 'WEA'; 7567 81475-2)*

Nov 80. (7") *(K 11641)* **TAKE YOUR TIME. / HEART OF THE MATTER** [ ] [ ]

—— Around mid'81, JON & VANGELIS released album 'THE FRIENDS OF MR. CAIRO' which hit UK No.6. Lifted from it 'I'LL FIND MY WAY HOME' also managed to hit UK No.6 / US No.51 in Nov '81. These and his next solo releases were issued on

Polydor Mercury

Apr 82. (7") *(POSP 393)* **SURRENDER. / SPIDER** [ ] [ ]

May 82. (lp/c) *(POLD/+C 5044)* <19355> **ANIMATION** [43] [ ]
– Olympia / Animation / All in a matter of time / Unlearning / Boundaries / Pressure point / Much better reason / All Gods children.

Nov 82. (7") *(POSP 465)* **ALL IN A MATTER OF TIME. / SPIDER** [ ] [ ]

—— May83, sees another JON & VANGELIS album 'PRIVATE COLLECTION' hit UK No.22. Their compilation album 'THE BEST OF . . . ' hit UK No.42 in Aug84.

Elektra Elektra

Nov 85. (7"/12") *(EKR 31/+T* **EASIER SAID THAN DONE. / DAY OF DAYS** [ ] [ ]

Dec 85. (lp/c) *(EKT/+C 22)* **3 SHIPS** [ ] [–]
– Save all your love / Easier said than done / 3 ships / Forest of fire / Ding dong merrily on high / Save all your love (reprise) / The holly and the ivy / Day of days / 2,000 years / Where were you / Oh holy night / How it hits you / Jingle bells.

—— In 1986, he guested on MIKE OLDFIELD'S album 'SHINE'.

Epic Atlantic

Jun 88. (7"/12") *(651514-7/-1)* **HOLD ON TO LOVE. / SUN DANCING (FOR THE HOPI-NAVAJO ENERGY)** [ ] [ ]
(cd-s+=) *(651514-2)* – In a lifetime.

Jun 88. (lp/c/cd) *(460693-1/-4/-2)* <40910> **IN THE CITY OF ANGELS** [ ] [ ]
– Hold on to love / If it wasn't for love (oneness family) / Sun dancing (for the Hopi-Navajo energy) / Is it me / In a lifetime / For you / New civilization / It's on fire / Betcha / Top of the world (the glass bead game) / Hurry home (soon from the Pleiades).

Aug 88. (7") *(652947-7)* **IS IT ME. / TOP OF THE WORLD (GLASS BEAD GAME)** [ ] [ ]
(12"+=/cd-s+=) *(652947-6/-2)* – For you.

—— Later that year he provided vocals for charity 45 'WHATEVER YOU BELIEVE' accompanying STEVE HARLEY & MIKE BATT.

E.M.I. not iss.

Oct 94. (c-s/7") *(TC+/JON 1)* **CHANGE WE MUST. / STATE OF INDEPENDENCE** [ ] [ ]
(cd-s+=) *(CDJON 1)* – ('A'mixes) / (interview).

Oct 94. (cd/c) *(CDL/EL 555088-2/-4)* **CHANGE WE MUST** [ ] [ ]
– State of independence / Shaker loops / Hearts / Alive and wel / Kiss / Chagall duet / Run on, Jon / Candle song / View from the coppice / Hurry home / Under the sun / Change we must.

STEVE HOWE

with in 1979; **PATRICK MORAZ** – keyboards / **ALAN WHITE + BILL BRUFORD + CLIVE BUNKER** – drums / **RONNIE LEAHY** – keyboards / **GRAHAM PRESKETT** – violin / **CLAIRE HAMILL** – vocals

Atlantic Atlantic

Oct 79. (lp/c) *(K/K4 50621)* <19243> **THE STEVE HOWE ALBUM** [68] [ ]
– Pennants / Cactus boogie / All's a chord / Look over your shoulder /

Diary of a man who disappeared / Meadow rag / The continental / Surface tension / Double rondo / Concerto in D (second movement). *(cd-iss. Oct94 on 'East West'; 7567 81559-2)*

Roadrunner Roadrunner

Jan 92. (cd/c/lp) *(RR 9233-2/-4/-1)* **TURBULENCE** ☐ ☐
– Turbulence / Hint hint / Running the human race / The inner battle / Novalis / Fine line / Sensitive chaos / Corkscrew / While Rome's burning / From a place where time runs slow.

Sep 93. (cd/c) *(RR 9086-2/-4)* **THE GRAND SCHEME OF THINGS** ☐ ☐
– The grand scheme of things / Desire comes first / Blinded by science / Beautiful ideas / The valley of rocks / At the gates of the new world / Wayward course / Reaching the point / Common ground / Luck of the draw / The fall of civilization / Passing phase / Georgia's theme / Too much is taken and not enough is given / Maiden voyage / Road to one's self.

– others, etc –

Apr 90. (cd; with BODAST) *C5; (C5 528)* **THE EARLY YEARS** ☐ –

Jun 95. (cd) *Thunderbird-R.P.M.; (CSA 104)* **NOT NECESSARILY ACOUSTIC** ☐ –

Mar 96. (cd; STEVE HOWE & PAUL SUTIN) *S.P.V.; (SPV 0768956-2)* **SEREAPHIM** ☐ –

Mar 96. (cd) *S.P.V.; (SPV 0768957-2)* **VOYAGERS** ☐ –

Jun 96. (cd) *R.P.M.; (RPM 164)* **HOMEBREW** ☐ –

—— For RICK WAKEMAN releases, see under own solo entry.

☐ Y KANT TORI READ (see under ⇒ AMOS, Tori)

Neil YOUNG

Born: 12 Nov'45, Toronto, Canada. He was raised in Winnipeg until 1966, when he drove to America in his Pontiac hearse. NEIL had cut his teeth in local instrumental outfit, The SQUIRES, who released one '45 'THE SULTAN'. / 'AURORA' for 'V' records in September '63. The following year, NEIL formed The MYNHA BIRDS and joined forces with RICKY JAMES MATTHEWS (later to become RICK JAMES). Although many songs were recorded, only one saw the light of day; 'MYNHA BIRD HOP' for 'Columbia' Canada. They signed to 'Motown' (first white people to do so) but were soon dropped when they found out that RICKY had dodged the draft. He subsequently met up with past acquaintance, STEPHEN STILLS, and formed BUFFALO SPRINGFIELD. Constant rivalry led to YOUNG departing for a solo venture after signing for new label, 'Reprise', in Spring '68. His eponymous debut with arranger/producer JACK NITZSCHE, then DAVID BRIGGS, was finally issued in early 1969. A fragile, acoustic affair, the album was a tentative start to YOUNG's mercurial solo career, songs like 'THE OLD LAUGHING LADY' and 'THE LONER' hinting at the genius to come. The album was also a guinea pig for 'Warners' (then) new 'CSG' recording process, YOUNG later complaining bitterly about the resulting sound quality. 'EVERYBODY KNOWS THIS IS NOWHERE' (1969), however, was the sound of YOUNG in full control. Hooking up with a bunch of hard-bitten rockers going by the name of CRAZY HORSE, the record marked the beginning of a long and fruitful partnership that's still going strong almost thirty years on. With 'CINNAMON GIRL', DOWN BY THE RIVER' and 'COWGIRL IN THE SAND', this bruising musical synergy saw YOUNG scaling cathartic new heights and the guitar interplay would become a template for the primal improvisation of YOUNG's live work. Although 'AFTER THE GOLDRUSH' (1970) was partly recorded with CRAZY HORSE and featured the blistering 'SOUTHERN MAN', most of the album was by turns melancholy, bittersweet and charming in the style of the gorgeous ballad, 'HELPLESS', he'd contributed some months earlier to the CSN&Y album, 'DEJA VU'. 'BIRDS' and 'I BELIEVE IN YOU' stand as two of the most poignant love songs of YOUNG's career while the title track was a compelling lament of surreal poetry, based on a script written by actor DEAN STOCKWELL. The album gave YOUNG his breakthrough, going Top 10 in Britain and America but it was the 1972 single, 'HEART OF GOLD' and subsequent album, 'HARVEST', which made YOUNG a household name. Most of the tracks were recorded in Nashville with a band called The STRAY GATORS, piano and production duties falling to JACK NITZSCHE. His biggest selling album to date, the finely crafted country crooning of 'OUT ON THE WEEKEND' and 'HEART OF GOLD' was the closest YOUNG ever came to MOR and true to his contrary style, the next few years saw him trawling the depths of his psyche for some of the most uncompromising and uncommercial material of his career. After the fierce sonic assault of the live 'TIME FADES AWAY' (1973) album, YOUNG went back into the studio with CRAZY HORSE to record a tribute to DANNY WHITTEN, their sad-voiced singer who'd overdosed on heroin the previous year. Just as YOUNG was due to begin recording, another of his friends, BRUCE BERRY (STEPHEN STILLS' guitar roadie), succumbed to smack the morose, drunken confessionals that resulted from those sessions eventually appeared a couple of years later as the 'TONIGHT'S THE NIGHT' (1975) album. Arguably YOUNG's most essential release, this darkly personal chronicle of drug oblivion veered from the resigned melancholy of 'ALBUQUERQUE' to the detached, twisted country of 'TIRED EYES', while the visceral catharsis of 'COME ON, BABY, LET'S GO DOWNTOWN' (an earlier live recording with a WHITTEN vocal) cranked up the guitars to match the unrelenting intensity level. Following 'Warners' reluctance to release the album, YOUNG set about writing yet another batch of hazy confessionals upon his return from touring the 'TONIGHT'S THE NIGHT' material. Deeply troubled by his increasing estrangement from actress CARRIE SNODGRASS (with whom he'd had a son, ZEKE), he shacked himself up in his new Malibu pad and penned 'ON THE BEACH' (1974). When every other rock star in L.A. was desperately trying to forget they'd ever hung out with CHARLES MANSON, YOUNG wrote 'REVOLUTION BLUES' in response to the Manson Family killings. 'AMBULANCE BLUES' was just as darkly compelling and the album remains an obscure classic. After a brief, ill-starred reunion with CROSBY, STILLS & NASH, YOUNG came up with a set entitled 'HOMEGROWN', which 'Warners' deemed too downbeat to release. Instead, they relented to the belated issue of 'TONIGHT'S THE NIGHT'. Come 1975, YOUNG was back in the studio with CRAZY HORSE, who'd recently recruited FRANK 'PANCHO' SAMPEDRO on guitar as a permanent replacement for WHITTEN. The resulting album, 'ZUMA' (1975), bore the first raw fruits of this new guitar partnership, the lucid imagery and meditative ruminations of 'CORTEZ THE KILLER' bringing the album to a darkly resonant climax while 'DON'T CRY NO TEARS' and 'BARSTOOL BLUES' found YOUNG more animated then he'd sounded for years. Following a disappointing album, 'LONG MAY YOU RUN' (1976), and aborted tour with STEPHEN STILLS, YOUNG cut the 'AMERICAN STARS 'N' BARS' (1977) album. A competent set of country rock, the record featured one of his best loved songs, an aching, soaring testament to the power of romantic obsession entitled 'LIKE A HURRICANE'. With 'COMES A TIME' (1978), he reverted to 'HARVEST'-style mellow country, duetting with then girlfriend, NICOLETTE LARSON. But YOUNG's more abrasive side couldn't be suppressed for long and, rejuvenated by the energy of the punk explosion, YOUNG reunited with CRAZY HORSE once more for the 'RUST NEVER SLEEPS' (1979) album. An electrifying set of passionate rockers and lean acoustic songs, it included such enduring live favourites as 'MY MY, HEY HEY (OUT OF THE BLUE)/(INTO THE BLACK)' (written about SEX PISTOL, JOHNNY ROTTEN) and the wounded 'POWDERFINGER'. The former was YOUNG's own comment on the "live fast, die young" rock'n'roll school of thought (it came back to haunt him when KURT COBAIN quoted the song in his suicide note). 'LIVE RUST' (1979) was the corrosive companion album capturing NEIL YOUNG & CRAZY HORSE live in all their frayed magnificence. Towards the end of 1978, YOUNG's new love, PEGI MORTON, had borne him a second child, BEN. While YOUNG's first son, ZEKE, had been born with cerebral palsy, BEN was a spastic. A stunned YOUNG began to clam up emotionally, with the result that much of his 80's work sounded confused and directionless. After 'REACTOR' (1981) stiffed, YOUNG moved to 'Geffen' where he recorded 'TRANS' (1983), an album that attempted to reflect his son's communication problems. Using a vocoder, YOUNG succeeded in rendering the lyrics almost unintelligible and while the album was almost universally panned, tracks like 'TRANSFORMER MAN' remain oddly affecting. The remainder of his time at 'Geffen' marked an all-time low in his career, both commercially and creatively, during which time he made ill-advised forays into rockabilly and stagnant, MOR country as well as making embarrassing pro-Reagan statments in interviews. Testing his fans to the limit, he was eventually sued by 'Geffen' for making records that didn't sound like NEIL YOUNG! He didn't really get back on track until 1989's 'FREEDOM' album, 'ROCKIN' IN THE FREE WORLD' (on 'Reprise') and 'CRIME IN THE CITY' marking YOUNG's return to searing rock'n'roll. With CRAZY HORSE, he cut 'RAGGED GLORY' (1990) the following year, a frenetic guitar mash-up that was staggering in its intensity for such an elder statesman of rock. 'WELD' (1991), a live document of the subsequent tour, saw YOUNG championed by the new "grunge" vanguard and revered once more by the indie/rock press as the epitome of guitar cool. Influenced by SONIC YOUTH (who supported him for part of the tour), he even recorded a CD collage of feedback, 'ARC', available in a limited quantity as a bonus disc with the 'WELD' double set. His critical rebirth now complete, 'HARVEST MOON' (1992) gave him his biggest commercial success since the 70's. A lilting, careworn set of country-folk, it was billed as a belated follow-up to 1972's 'HARVEST'. Of course, the MTV 'UNPLUGGED' (1993) set was now obligatory, but rather than give the audience a predictable run through of acoustic numbers, he presented radically altered versions of old numbers like 'TRANSFORMER MAN' and 'LIKE A HURRICANE'. 'SLEEPS WITH ANGELS' (1994) was a downbeat elegy for KURT COBAIN while 'MIRRORBALL' (1995) was a misguided collaboration with grunge band, PEARL JAM. The 'DEAD MAN' soundtrack was interesting although 'BROKEN ARROW' (1996) and the live 'YEAR OF THE HORSE' (1997) were given short shrift by the press. In truth, the records were far too inconsistent to warrant parting with hard earned cash. The man's long awaited 'SILVER & GOLD' (2000) went some way towards redressing the balance although it wasn't quite the dazzling return to form many had hoped for. Much of the album meandered along in a similar fashion to the trio of acoustic songs YOUNG had contributed to the previous year's CSN&Y reunion set, 'Looking Forward'. Bearing in mind that these tracks were by far the most memorable, it follows that 'SILVER & GOLD' is an enjoyable enough listen without ever hitting those plateaus of inspiration integral to YOUNG's best work. A less obvious comparison than 'HARVEST MOON' might be his transitional 1978 effort, 'COMES A TIME'. New fans could do worse than starting with the 'DECADE' (1977) compilation, a stunning triple set (double CD) gathering the best of YOUNG's earlier work and including such obscure gems as the beautiful 'WINTERLONG'. With 2002's 'ARE YOU PASSIONATE', YOUNG extended his relationship with BOOKER T & THE MG's to the studio, cutting a straight-up Southern soul set. While this might've confounded his more rock-centric converts, it came as little surprise to long time fans who've learned to take YOUNG's stylistic whims in their stride. Like VAN MORRISON, the ageing troubadour seems more and more content to indulge lifelong passions than keep on top of his muse. The result was pleasant if unstartling; it all seemed a long way away from his feedback experimentation of the early 90's. More than a decade after 'WELD', YOUNG finally tried his hand at something more ambitious with 'GREENDALE' (2003), a bizarre quasi-concept set which, if not exactly holding together as a narrative (the convoluted plot centres on a fictional American town of the title, and more specifically on the troubles of one of the community's familys) at least found the singer flexing his creative muscle for a change. • **Songwriters:** As said, 99% of material is his own with contributions from CRAZY HORSE members, except; FARMER JOHN (Harris-Terry). The album 'EVERYBODY'S ROCKIN'' was full of covers.

Album rating: NEIL YOUNG (*7) / EVERYBODY KNOWS THIS IS NOWHERE (*8; with Crazy Horse) / AFTER THE GOLD RUSH (*10) / HARVEST (*9) / JOURNEY THROUGH THE PAST soundtrack (*3) / TIME FADES AWAY (*6) / ON THE BEACH (*9) / TONIGHT'S THE NIGHT (*8) / ZUMA (*8; with Crazy Horse) / AMERICAN STARS 'N BARS (*5) / DECADE compilation (*8) / COMES A TIME (*6) / RUST NEVER SLEEPS (*9; with Crazy Horse) / LIVE RUST (*7; with Crazy Horse) / HAWKS & DOVES (*6) / RE-AC-TOR (*5; with Crazy Horse) / TRANS (*5) / EVERYBODY'S ROCKIN' (*4; as Neil & The Shocking Pinks) / OLD WAYS (*5) / LANDING ON WATER (*3) / LIFE (*4; with Crazy Horse) / THIS NOTE'S FOR YOU (*6; as Neil Young & The Bluenotes) / FREEDOM (*7) / RAGGED GLORY (*8; with Crazy Horse) / WELD (*8; with Crazy Horse) / HARVEST MOON (*8) / LUCKY THIRTEEN compilation (*6) / UNPLUGGED (*6) / SLEEPS WITH ANGELS (*8; with Crazy Horse) / MIRRORBALL (*6) / DEAD MAN soundtrack (*4) / BROKEN ARROW (*5; with Crazy Horse) / THE YEAR OF THE HORSE (*5; with Crazy Horse) / SILVER & GOLD (*6) / ARE YOU PASSIONATE? (*5) / GREENDALE (*7; with Crazy Horse)

NEIL YOUNG – vocals, guitar (ex-BUFFALO SPRINGFIELD) with **JIM MESSINA** – bass / session men, etc.

Reprise Reprise

Jan 69. (lp) *<(RSLP 6317)>* **NEIL YOUNG** [ ] [ ]
– The Emperor of Wyoming / The loner / If I could have her tonight / I've been waiting for you / The old laughing lady / String quartet from Whiskey Boot Hill / Here we are in the years / What did I do to my life / I've loved her so long / The last trip to Tulsa. *(re-iss. 1971 lp/c; K/K4 44059) (cd-iss. 1987; K2 44059)*

Mar 69. (7") *<0785>* **THE LONER. / SUGAR MOUNTAIN** [–] [ ]

Sep 69. (7") *(RS 23405)* **THE LONER. / EVERYBODY KNOWS THIS IS NOWHERE** [ ] [–]

NEIL YOUNG with CRAZY HORSE

— with **DANNY WHITTEN** – guitar / **BILLY TALBOT** – bass / **RALPH MOLINA** – drums / **BOBBY NOTKOFF** – violin

Jul 69. (lp) *<(RSLP 6349)>* **EVERYBODY KNOWS THIS IS NOWHERE** [ ] May69 [24]
– Cinnamon girl / Everybody knows this is nowhere / Round and round (it won't be long) / Down by the river / The losing end (when you're on) / Running dry (requiem for the rockets) / Cowgirl in the sand. *(re-iss. 1971 lp/c; K/K4 44073) (cd-iss. 1988; K2 44059)*

Jul 69. (7") *<0836>* **DOWN BY THE RIVER (edit). / THE LOSING END (WHEN YOU'RE ON)** [–] [ ]

— Late 1969, NEIL YOUNG was also added to CROSBY, STILLS, NASH (& YOUNG).

Aug 70. (7") *(RS 23462)* **DOWN BY THE RIVER (edit). / CINNAMON GIRL (alt.take)** [ ] [–]

NEIL YOUNG

— with **NILS LOFGREN** – guitar (of GRIN) repl. NOTKOFF

Aug 70. (7") *<0898>* **OH LONESOME ME (extended). / I'VE BEEN WAITING FOR YOU (alt.mix)** [–] [ ]

Sep 70. (lp) *<(RSLP 6383)>* **AFTER THE GOLD RUSH** [7] [8]
– Tell me why / After the gold rush / Only love can break your heart / Southern man / Till the morning comes / Oh lonesome me / Don't let it bring you down / Birds / When you dance I can really love / I believe in you / After the goldrush / Cripple Creek ferry. *(re-iss. 1971 lp/c; K/K4 44088) (cd-iss. Jul87; K2 44088)*

Sep 70. (7") *(RS 20861)* **OH LONESOME ME (extended). / SUGAR MOUNTAIN** [ ] [–]

Jun 70. (7") *<0911>* **CINNAMON GIRL (alt.mix). / SUGAR MOUNTAIN** [–] [55]

Oct 70. (7") *(RS 20958) <0958>* **ONLY LOVE CAN BREAK YOUR HEART. / BIRDS** [ ] [33]

Jan 71. (7") *<0992>* **WHEN YOU DANCE I CAN REALLY LOVE. / SUGAR MOUNTAIN** [–] [93]

Feb 71. (7") *(RS 23488)* **WHEN YOU DANCE I CAN REALLY LOVE. / AFTER THE GOLDRUSH** [ ] [–]

— solo with The STRAY GATORS. (CRAZY HORSE now recorded on their own). NEIL's musicians: **JACK NITZSCHE** – piano / **BEN KEITH** – steel guitar / **TIM DRUMMOND** – bass / **KENNY BUTTREY** – drums. guests included **CROSBY, STILLS & NASH, LINDA RONSTADT, JAMES TAYLOR** plus The LONDON SYMPHONY ORCHESTRA

Feb 72. (7") *(K 14140) <1065>* **HEART OF GOLD. / SUGAR MOUNTAIN** [10] [1]

Mar 72. (lp/c) *(K/K4 54005) <MS 2032>* **HARVEST** [1] [1]
– Out on the weekend / Harvest / A man needs a maid / Heart of gold / Are you ready for the country? / Old man / There's a world / Alabama / The needle and the damage done / Words (between the lines of age). *(cd-iss. May83; K 244131)*

Apr 72. (7") *(K 14167) <1084>* **OLD MAN. / THE NEEDLE AND THE DAMAGE DONE** [ ] [31]

Jun 72. (7"; by NEIL YOUNG & GRAHAM NASH) *<1099>* **WAR SONG. / THE NEEDLE AND THE DAMAGE DONE** [–] [61]

— **JOHNNY BARBATA** – drums (ex-CROSBY, STILLS & NASH) repl. BUTTREY

Sep 73. (lp/c) *(K/K4 54010) <MS 2151>* **TIME FADES AWAY (live)** [20] [22]
– Time fades away / Journey through the past / Yonder stands the sinner / L.A. / Love in mind / Don't be denied / The bridge / Last dance.

Oct 73. (7") *<1184>* **TIME FADES AWAY (live). / LAST TRIP TO TULSA (live)** [–] [ ]

— now used session people including **CRAZY HORSE** members **BEN KEITH** – steel guitar; had now repl. WHITTEN who o.d.'d August 1972

Jul 74. (7") *(K/K4 54014) <R 2180>* **ON THE BEACH** [42] [16]
– Walk on / See the sky about to rain / Revolution blues / For the turnstiles / Vampire blues / On the beach / Motion pictures (for Carrie) / Ambulance blues. *<(cd-iss. Jul03; 9362 48497-2)>* – hit UK No.42

Jul 74. (7") *(K 14360) <1209>* **WALK ON. / FOR THE TURNSTILES** [ ] [69]

— Had just earlier in 1974, re-united with CROSBY, STILLS & NASH

— recorded solo lp in '73. Musicians: **NILS LOFGREN / BEN KEITH / BILLY TALBOT / RALPH MOLINA**

Jun 75. (lp/c) *(K/K4 54040) <MS 2221>* **TONIGHT'S THE NIGHT** [48] [25]
– Tonight's the night (part I) / Speakin' out / World on a string / Borrowed tune / Come on baby let's go downtown / Mellow my mind / Roll another number (for the road) / Albuquerque / New mama / Lookout Joe / Tired eyes / Tonight's the night (part II). *(cd-iss. Jul93; 7599 27221-2)*

NEIL YOUNG with CRAZY HORSE

— (Mar'75) **FRANK 'Poncho' SAMPEDRO** – guitar, vocals repl. KEITH + LOFGREN The latter earlier went solo, and later joined BRUCE SPRINGSTEEN band.

Nov 75. (lp/c) *(K/K4 54057) <MS 2242>* **ZUMA** [44] [25]
– Don't cry no tears / Danger bird / Pardon my heart / Lookin' for a love / Barstool blues / Stupid girl / Drive back / Cortez the killer / Through my sails. *(cd-iss. Jul93; 7599 27222-2)*

Mar 76. (7") *<K 14416) <1344>* **LOOKIN' FOR A LOVE. / SUGAR MOUNTAIN** [ ] Dec75 [ ]

Mar 76. (7") *<1350>* **DRIVE BACK. / STUPID GIRL** [–] [ ]

May 76. (7") *(K 14431)* **DON'T CRY NO TEARS. / STUPID GIRL** [ ] [–]

— Mid 1976, he teamed up as STILLS-YOUNG BAND with STEPHEN STILLS on album 'LONG MAY YOU RUN'; *K/K4 54081 <MS 2253>*. (see under ⇒ CROSBY, STILLS, NASH & YOUNG).

Jun 77. (lp/c) *(K/K4 54088) <MSK 2261>* **AMERICAN STARS 'N BARS** [17] [21]
– The old country waltz / Saddle up the Palomino / Hey babe / Hold back the tears / Bite the bullet / Star of Bethlehem / Will to love / Like a hurricane / Homegrown. *(cd-iss. Dec96; 7599 27234-2)*

Jul 77. (7") *<1390>* **HEY BABE. / HOMEGROWN** [–] [ ]

Sep 77. (7") *(K 14482) <1391>* **LIKE A HURRICANE (edit). / HOLD BACK THE TEARS** [ ] [ ]

NEIL YOUNG

— solo with loads on session incl.**NICOLETTE LARSON** – vox

Oct 78. (7") *<1395>* **COMES A TIME. / MOTORCYCLE MAMA** [–] [ ]

Oct 78. (lp/c) *(K/K4 54099) <2266>* **COMES A TIME** [42] [7]
– Goin' back / Comes a time / Look out for my love / Lotta love / Peace of mind / Human highway / Already one / Field of opportunity / Motorcycle mama / Four strong winds. *(cd-iss. Jul93; 7599 27235-2)*

Nov 78. (7") *(K 14493)* **FOUR STRONG WINDS. / MOTORCYCLE MAMA** [57] [–]

Dec 78. (7") *<1396>* **FOUR STRONG WINDS. / HUMAN HIGHWAY** [–] [61]

NEIL YOUNG with CRAZY HORSE

— (YOUNG w / **SAMPEDRO, TALBOT & MOLINA**)

Jun 79. (lp/c) *(K/K4 54105) <2295>* **RUST NEVER SLEEPS** [13] [8]
– My my, hey hey (out of the blue) / Thrasher / Ride my llama / Pocahontas / Sail away / Powderfinger / Welfare mothers / Sedan delivery / Hey hey, my my (into the black). *(cd-iss. Jul93; 7599 27249-2)*

Aug 79. (7") *(K 14498) <49031>* **HEY HEY, MY MY (INTO THE BLACK). / MY MY, HEY HEY (OUT OF THE BLUE)** [ ] [79]

Nov 79. (d-lp/d-c) *(K/K4 64041) <2296>* **LIVE RUST (live)** [55] [15]
– Sugar mountain / I am a child / Comes a time / After the gold rush / My my, hey hey (out of the blue) / When you dance I can really love / The loner / The needle and the damage done / Lotta love / Sedan delivery / Powderfinger / Cortez the killer / Cinnamon girl / Like a hurricane / Hey hey, my my (into the black) / Tonight's the night. *(re-iss. cd Jul93; 7599 27250-2)*

Dec 79. (7") *<49189>* **CINNAMON GIRL (live). / THE LONER (live)** [–] [ ]

NEIL YOUNG

— solo with **TIM DRUMMOND + DENNIS BELFIELD** – bass / **LEVON HELM + GREG THOMAS** – drums / **BEN KEITH** – steel, dobro / **RUFUS THIBODEAUX** – fiddle

Oct 80. (lp/c) *(K/K4 54109) <2297>* **HAWKS & DOVES** [34] [30]
– Little wing / The old homestead / Lost in space / Captain Kennedy / Stayin' power / Coastline / Union power / Comin' apart at every nail / Hawks & doves.

Nov 80. (7") *(K 14508) <49555>* **HAWKS & DOVES. / UNION MAN** [ ] [ ]

Feb 81. (7") *<49641>* **STAYIN' POWER. / CAPTAIN KENNEDY** [–] [ ]

NEIL YOUNG with CRAZY HORSE

— (see last CRAZY HORSE line-up)

Oct 81. (lp/c) *(K/K4 54116) <2304>* **RE• AC• TOR** [69] [27]
– Opera star / Surfer Joe and Moe the sleaze / T-bone / Get back on it / Southern Pacific / Motor city / Rapid transit / Shots.

Nov 81. (7"/10"shaped-red) *<498 70/95>* **SOUTHERN PACIFIC. / MOTOR CITY** [–] [70]

Jan 82. (7") *<50014>* **OPERA STAR. / SURFER JOE AND MOE THE SLEAZE** [–] [ ]

NEIL YOUNG

— solo adding synthesizers, drum machine (sessioners) **BRUCE PALMER** – bass (ex-BUFFALO SPRINGFIELD)

Geffen Geffen

Jan 83. (7") *(GEF 2781)* <29887> **LITTLE THING CALLED LOVE. / WE R IN CONTROL** — Dec82 71

Jan 83. (lp/c) *(GEF/+C 25019)* <2018> **TRANS** 29 19
– Little thing called love / Computer age / We r in control / Transformer man / Computer cowboy (aka Syscrusher) / Hold on to your love / Sample and hold / Mr. Soul / Like an Inca. *(re-iss. Sep86 lp/c; 902018-1/-4) (cd-iss. Apr97; GFLD 19357)*

Jan 83. (12") <20105> **SAMPLE AND HOLD (extended). / MR SOUL (extended) / SAMPLE AND HOLD** – –

Feb 83. (7") <29707> **MR. SOUL. / MR. SOUL (part 2)** – –

—— w / **BEN KEITH** – guitar / **TIM DRUMMOND** – bass / **KARL HIMMEL** – drums / **LARRY BYROM** – piano, vocals / **RICK PALOMBI + ANTHONY CRAWFORD** – b.vocals

Sep 83. (lp/c; as NEIL & THE SHOCKING PINKS) *(GEF/+C 25590)* <4013> **EVERYBODY'S ROCKIN'** 50 Aug83 46
– Betty Lou's got a new pair of shoes / Rainin' in my heart / Payola blues / Wonderin' / Kinda fonda Wanda / Jellyroll man / Bright lights, big city / Cry, cry, cry / Mystery train / Everybody's rockin'. *(re-iss. Sep86 lp/c/cd; 904013-1/-4/-2)*

Sep 83. (7") *(GEF 3581)* <29574> **WONDERIN'. / PAYOLA BLUES**

Oct 83. (7") <29433> **CRY, CRY, CRY. / PAYOLA BLUES** –

—— Jul85, with country singer WILLIE NELSON he duets on his ARE THERE ANY MORE REAL COWBOYS single issued on 'Columbia'.

—— solo again with loads of session people.

Aug 85. (lp/c) *(GEF/40 26377)* <24068> **OLD WAYS** 39 75
– The wayward wind / Get back to the country / Are there any more real cowboys? / Once an angel / Misfits / California sunset / Old ways / My boy / Bound for glory / Where is the highway tonight? *(cd-iss. Apr97; GFLD 19356)*

Sep 85. (7") <28883> **BACK TO THE COUNTRY. / MISFITS** –

Nov 85. (7") <28753> **OLD WAYS. / ONCE AN ANGEL** –

—— w / **STEVE JORDAN** – drums, synths, vox / **DANNY KORTCHMAR** – guitar, synth

Aug 86. (lp/c/cd) *(924109-1/-4/-2)* <24109> **LANDING ON WATER** 52 46
– Weight of the world / Violent side / Hippie dream / Bad news beat / Touch the night / People on the street / Hard luck stories / I got a problem / Pressure / Drifter. *(re-iss. Apr91;) (cd-iss. Nov96; GED 24109)*

Sep 86. (7"/12") *(GEF/+T 7)* <28623> **WEIGHT OF THE WORLD. / PRESSURE** — Jul86

NEIL YOUNG & CRAZY HORSE

—— (see last **CRAZY HORSE, + BRYAN BELL** – synth)

May 87. (lp/c)(cd) *(WX 108/+C)(924154-2)* <24154> **LIFE** 71 75
– Mideast vacation / Long walk home / Around the world / Inca queen / Too lonely / Prisoners of rock'n'roll / Cryin' eyes / When your lonely heart breaks / We never danced.

Jun 87. (7") <28196> **MIDEAST VACATION. / LONG WALK HOME** –

Jun 87. (7") *(GEF 25)* **LONG WALK HOME. / CRYIN' EYES** –

NEIL YOUNG & THE BLUENOTES

—— with **SAMPEDRO** – keyboards plus others **CHAD CROMWELL** – drums / **RICK ROSAS** – bass / **STEVE LAWRENCE** – tenor sax / **BEN KEITH** – alto sax / **LARRY CRAIG** – baritone sax / **CLAUDE CAILLIET** – trombone / **JOHN FUMO** – trumpet / **TOM BRAY** – trumpet

Reprise Reprise

Apr 88. (7") <27908> **TEN MEN WORKIN'. / I'M GOIN'** –

May 88. (lp/c/cd) *(WX 168/+C)(925719-2)* <25719> **THIS NOTE'S FOR YOU** 56 61
– Ten men workin' / This note's for you / Coupe de ville / Life in the city / Twilight / Married man / Sunny inside / Can't believe you're lyin' / Hey hey / One thing. *(re-iss. cd Feb95)*

May 88. (7") <27848> **THIS NOTE'S FOR YOU (live). / THIS NOTE'S FOR YOU** –

—— Nov88, NEIL re-joined CROSBY, STILLS, NASH & YOUNG for 'AMERICAN DREAM' lp.

NEIL YOUNG

—— solo again with **SAMPEDRO, ROSAS, CROMWELL,** etc.

Oct 89. (lp/c/cd) *(WX 257/+C)(K 925899-2)* <25899> **FREEDOM** 17 35
– Rockin' in the free world / Crime in the city (sixty to zero part 1) / Don't cry / Hangin' on a limb / Eldorado / The ways of love / Someday / On Broadway / Wreckin' ball / No more / Too far gone / Rockin' in the free world (live). *(re-iss. cd/c Feb95)*

Apr 90. (7") *(W 2776)* <22776> **ROCKIN' IN THE FREE WORLD. / ('A'live)** — Aug89
(12"+=/cd-s+=) *(W 2776 T/CD)* – Cocaine eyes.

NEIL YOUNG & CRAZY HORSE

—— with **SAMPEDRO, TALBOT + MOLINA**

Sep 90. (cd)(lp/c) <(7599-26315-2)>*(WX 374/+C)* **RAGGED GLORY** 15 31
– Country home / White line / Fuckin' up / Over and over / Love to burn / Farmer John / Mansion on the hill / Days that used to be / Love and only love / Mother Earth (natural anthem). *(re-iss. cd/c Feb95)*

Sep 90. (cd-s) <7599-21759-2> **MANSION ON THE HILL (edit) / MANSION ON THE HILL / DON'T SPOOK THE HORSE** –

Oct 91. (d-cd/d-c/d-lp) <(7599 26671-2/-4/-1)> **WELD (live)** 20
– Hey hey, my my (into the black) / Crime in the city / Blowin' in the wind / Live to burn / Welfare mothers / Cinnamon girl / Mansion on the hill / F+!#in' up / Farmer John / Cortez the killer / Powderfinger / Love and only love / Roll another number / Rockin' in the free world / Like a hurricane / Tonight's the night. *(free-cd-ep w.a.+=)* – ARC EP – (feedback).

NEIL YOUNG

solo, with The STRAY GATORS (**KENNY BUTTREY, TIM DRUMMOND, BEN KEITH & SPOONER OLDHAM**) plus **JAMES TAYLOR, LINDA RONSTADT, NICOLETTE LARSON, ASTRID YOUNG & LARRY CRAGG** – backing vocals

Oct 92. (cd/c/lp) <(9362 45057-2/-4/-1)> **HARVEST MOON** 9 16
– Unknown legend / From Hank to Hendrix / You and me / Harvest moon / War of man / One of these days / Such a woman / Old king / Dreamin' man / Natural beauty.

Feb 93. (7"/c-s) *(W 0139/+C)* **HARVEST MOON. / WINTERLONG** 36
(cd-s+=) *(W 0139CD)* – Deep forbidden lake / Campaigner.
(cd-s) *(W 0139CDX)* – ('A'side) / Old king / The needle and the damage done / Goin' back.

Jun 93. (cd/c/lp) <(9362 45310-2/-4/-1)> **UNPLUGGED** 4 23
– The old laughing lady / Mr. Soul / World on a string / Pocahontas / Strongman / Like a hurricane / The needle and the damage done / Helpless / Harvest Moon / Transformer man / Unknown legend / Look out for my love / Long may you run / From Hank to Hendrix.

Jul 93. (7"/c-s) *(W 0191/+C)* **THE NEEDLE AND THE DAMAGE DONE (live). / YOU AND ME** 75
(cd-s+=) *(W 0191CD)* – From Hank to Hendrix.

Oct 93. (7"/c-s) *(W 207/+C)* **LONG MAY YOU RUN (live). / SUGAR MOUNTAIN (live)** 71
(cd-s+=) *(W 0207CD)* – Cortez the killer (live) / Cinnamon girl (live).

Feb 94. (7"/c-s) *(W 0231/+C)* **ROCKIN' IN THE FREE WORLD. / ('A'mixes)**
(cd-s+=) *(W 0231CD)* – Weld.

Apr 94. (7"/c-s) *(W 0242/+C)* **PHILADELPHIA. / SUCH A WOMAN** 62
(12"+=/cd-s+=) *(W 0242 T/CD)* – Stringman (unplugged).

—— Above 'A'side was another to be taken from the film 'Philadelphia'.

NEIL YOUNG & CRAZY HORSE

Aug 94. (cd/c/d-lp) <(9362 45749-2/-4/-1)> **SLEEPS WITH ANGELS** 2 9
– My heart / Prime of life / Drive by / Sleeps with angels / Western hero / Change your mind / Blue Eden / Safeway cart / Train of love / Trans Am / Piece of crap / A dream that can last. *(re-iss. Jan97; same)*

Aug 94. (c-s/cd-s) *(W 0261 C/CD)* **PIECE OF CRAP / TONIGHT'S THE NIGHT** –

Oct 94. (c-s) *(W 0266C)* **MY HEART / ROLL ANOTHER NUMBER (FOR THE ROAD)**
(cd-s+=) *(W 0266CD)* – Tired eyes.

Nov 94. (c-s) *(W 0276C)* **CHANGE YOUR MIND / SPEAKIN' OUT** [ ] [–]
(cd-s+=) *(W 0276CD)* – ('A'-full 14 minute version).

NEIL YOUNG

— with backing from all of PEARL JAM; 8th track written w/ EDDIE VEDDER

Jun 95. (cd/c/lp) *<(9362 45934-2/-4/-1)>* **MIRRORBALL** [4] [5]
– Song X / Act of love / I'm the ocean / Big green country / Truth be known / Downtown / What happened yesterday / Peace and love / Throw your hatred down / Scenery / Fallen angel.

Sep 95. (c-s) *(W 0314C)* **DOWNTOWN / BIG GREEN COUNTRY** [ ] [ ]
(cd-s+=) *(W 0314CD)* – ('A'-lp version).

Feb 96. (cd) *<(9362 46171-2)>* **DEAD MAN** [ ] [ ]
– Guitar solo, No.1 / The round stones beneath the earth / Guitar solo, No.2 / Why does thou hide thyself, clouds / Organ solo / Do you know how to use this weapon? / Guitar solo, No.3 / Nobody's story / Guitar solo, No.4 / Stupid white men / Guitar solo, No.5 / Time for you to leave, William Blake / Guitar solo, No.6.
above was instrumental YOUNG, and based on Jim Jarmusch's film starring Johnny Depp.

NEIL YOUNG WITH CRAZY HORSE

Jun 96. (cd/c) *<(9362 46291-2/-4)>* **BROKEN ARROW** [17] [31]
– Big time / Loose change / Slip away / Changing highways / Scattered (let's think about livin') / This town / Music arcade / Baby what you want me to do.

Jun 97. (cd/c) *<(9362 46652-2/-4)>* **THE YEAR OF THE HORSE (live)** [36] [57]
– When you dance / Barstool blues / When your lonely heart breaks / Mr. Soul / Big time / Pocahontas / Human highway / Slip away / Scattered / Danger bird / Prisoners / Sedan delivery.

NEIL YOUNG

— with **BEN KEITH, JIM KELTNER, DONALD "DUCK" DUNN, SPOONER OLDHAM**

Apr 00. (cd/c) *<(9362 47305-2/-4)>* **SILVER & GOLD** [10] [22]
– Good to see you / Silver and gold / Daddy went walkin' / Buffalo Springfield again / The great divide / Horseshoe man / Red sun / Distant camera / Razor love / Without rings.

— next with backing from **BOOKER T & THE MG'S** (house band), etc.

Apr 02. (cd) *<(9362 48111-2)>* **ARE YOU PASSIONATE?** [24] [10]
– You're my girl / Mr. Disappointment / Differently / (Quit) Don't say you love me / Let's roll / Are you passionate? / Goin' home / When I hold you in my arms / Be with you / Two old friends / She's a healer. *(d-lp-iss.May02; 9362 48111-1)*

NEIL YOUNG & CRAZY HORSE

Aug 03. (cd) *<(9362 48543-2)>* **GREENDALE** [24] [22]
– Falling from above / Double E / Devil's sidewalk / Leave the driving / Carmichael / Bandit / Grandpa's interview / Bringin' down dinner / Sun green / Be the rain. *<(ltd-cd w/dvd+=; 9362 48543-2)>*

– compilations, others, etc. –

Note; on 'Reprise' until otherwise stated.

1971. (7") *<0746>* **CINNAMON GIRL (alt.mix). / ONLY LOVE CAN BREAK YOUR HEART** [–] [ ]

Nov 72. (d-lp) *(K 64015)* *<2XS 6480>* **JOURNEY THROUGH THE PAST (Soundtrack featuring live & rare material with past bands)** [ ] [45]
– For what it's worth – Mr. Soul / Rock & roll woman / Find the cost of freedom / Ohio / Southern man / Are you ready for the country / Let me call you sweetheart / Alabama / Words / Relativity invitation / Handel's Messiah / King of kings / Soldier / Let's go away for a while.

Jan 73. (7") *<1152>* **HEART OF GOLD. / OLD MAN** [–] [ ]

Mar 74. (7") *(K 14319)* **ONLY LOVE CAN BREAK YOUR HEART. / AFTER THE GOLDRUSH** [ ] [–]

May 74. (7"ep) *(K 14350)* **SOUTHERN MAN / TILL MORNING COMES. / AFTER THE GOLDRUSH / HEART OF GOLD** [ ] [–]

Nov 77. (t-lp) *(K 54088)* *<3RS 2257>* **DECADE** [46] [43]
– Down to the wire + Burned + Mr.Soul + Broken arrow + Expecting to fly (BUFFALO SPRINGFIELD) / Sugar mountain / I am a child / The loner / The old laughing lady / Cinnamon girl / Down by the river / Cowgirl in the sand / I believe in you / After the goldrush / Southern man / Helpless + Ohio (CROSBY, STILLS, NASH & YOUNG) / A man needs a maid / Harvest / Heart of gold / Star of Bethlehem / The needle and the damage done / Tonight's the night (part 1) / Turnstiles / Winterlong / Deep forbidden lake / Like a hurricane / Love is a rose / Cortez the killer / Campaigner / Long may you run (with STEPHEN STILLS). *(re-iss. d-cd Jul93; 7559 27233-2) (d-cd-iss. Jul02 as 'DECADE – THE VERY BEST OF 1968-1976'; same)* – hit UK No.15

Jan 78. (7") *<1393>* **SUGAR MOUNTAIN. / THE NEEDLE AND THE DAMAGE DONE** [–] [ ]

Oct 82. (d-c) *(K4 64043)* **NEIL YOUNG / EVERYBODY KNOWS THIS IS NOWHERE** [ ] [–]

Oct 82. (d-c) *(K4 64044)* **AFTER THE GOLDRUSH / HARVEST** [ ] [–]

Feb 87. (cd) *(925271-2)* **THE BEST OF NEIL YOUNG** [ ] [ ]

Jan 93. (cd) *Movieplay Gold; (MPG 74011)* **THE LOST TAPES** [ ] [–]

Jan 93. (cd/c) *Geffen; (GED/GEC 24452)* **LUCKY THIRTEEN** (80's material) [69] [ ]
– Sample and hold / Transformer man / Depression blues / Get gone / Don't take your love away from me / Once an angel / Where is the highway tonight / Hippie dream / Pressure / Around the world / East vacation / Ain't it the truth / This note's for you. *(cd re-iss. Sep96; GFLD 19328)*

Dec 00. (cd) *Reprise; <48036>* **ROAD ROCK V1 (live)** [–] [ ]

— Note that 1980's 'Where The Buffalo Roam' film contained several YOUNG songs

FRANK ZAPPA

Frank ZAPPA

Born: FRANK VINCENT ZAPPA, 21 Dec'40, Baltimore, Maryland, USA, from Sicilian and Greek parents, who moved to California in 1950. In 1956, he formed The BLACKOUTS with school chum DON VAN VLIET (aka CAPTAIN BEEFHEART). After marrying in the late 50's, he wrote a soundtrack for B-movie, 'The World's Greatest Sinner'. In 1963, after writing another B-movie soundtrack, 'Run Home Slow', he set up his own Studio Z. He also initiated local groups, The MASTERS and The SOUL GIANTS, who recorded some extremely rare 45's. In 1964, he was arrested and sentenced to 10 days in prison and put on probation for 3 years, having made a pornographic tape. He moved to Los Angeles and reformed The SOUL GIANTS, who soon evolved into The MOTHERS OF INVENTION. Early in 1966, after a residency at The Whiskey A-Go-Go, they were signed to 'M.G.M.' by producer Tom Wilson. Their debut album (a double!), 'FREAK OUT!', peaked at No.130 in the States, an avant-garde, satirical piece, that combined psych-pop/rock of songs such as, 'WHO ARE THE BRAIN POLICE' and 'HELP, I'M A ROCK'. The following year (1967), FRANK and his MOTHERS, unleashed another set of weird but wonderful songs on the 'ABSOLUTELY FREE' album. This contained seminal work with equally bizarre titles, 'CALL ANY VEGETABLE', 'SON OF SUZY CREAMCHEESE' and 'BROWN SHOES DON'T MAKE IT', the album nearly scratching the surface of the Top 40. On the 23rd of September '67, The MOTHERS played London's Albert Hall with a 15-piece orchestra, an arrangement he would take further on future albums. His third album, 'WE'RE ONLY IN IT FOR THE MONEY' was an obvious swipe at The BEATLES and their sleeve design for 'Sgt. Pepper's'. This was certainly FRANK and the band's most inventive work to date, the album taking a uniquely anti-drug/hippie stance. The tracks 'LET'S MAKE THE WATER TURN BLACK', 'MOM AND DAD' and 'FLOWER PUNK' being his swipe at America and the 60's counter-cultural establishment. His work continued apace, 'LUMPY GRAVY', 'CRUISING WITH RUBEN AND THE JETS' and 'UNCLE MEAT' all hitting the shelves in the space of a year. Late in 1969, FRANK released his first solo album, 'HOT RATS', which gave him deserved widespread critical acclaim, hitting Top 10 in Britain! The album forsook doo-wop and sardonic pastiche, for a more rock-based guitar extravaganza, the tracks 'PEACHES EN REGALIA' and the BEEFHEART-led 'WILLIE THE WIMP', becoming future ZAPPA jewels. For a few years to come, he combined MOTHERS albums with solo releases (normally with his entourage anyway), the best of these came in the form of live sets, including the double, 'FILLMORE EAST – JUNE 1971'. His commercial fortunes declined however, until The MOTHERS (who had just re-united) came back with the almost pornographic, 'OVERNITE SENSATION', which included the squealing, 'DINAH MOE HUMM'. A year later in 1974, he attacked the US charts once more with the Top 10 return to form, 'APOSTROPHE (')', which featured the cautionary, 'DON'T EAT THE YELLOW SNOW'. His work was now gaining more attention and a live album with his old buddy CAPTAIN BEEFHEART, reconciled their egotistical differences. In 1976, after securing a new deal with 'Warners', he unleashed another fine effort, 'ZOOT ALLURES', which contained some more risqué ditties in the shape of the rocking, 'DISCO BOY' and 'FRIENDLY LITTLE FINGER'. After releasing a few instrumental albums, he was back again in 1979 with the 'SHEIK YERBOUTI' set, which included another dig at dance music, 'DANCIN' FOOL' and the cheeky 'BOBBY BROWN GOES DOWN'. The album 'JOE GARAGE' (ACTS 1, II & III) was split over two albums and a lot more was to come in the 80's. Although his work was still quite excellent during this period (i.e. 'SHIP ARRIVING TOO LATE TO SAVE A DROWNING WITCH' and 'THE MAN FROM UTOPIA' being his best), he returned to his favourite pastime of jazz and classical. In the early 90's, he was diagnosed with prostate cancer, and sadly he was to die on the 4th of December '93. • **Songwriters:** ZAPPA compositions, augmented by MOTHERS. Covered WHIPPING POST (Allman Brothers Band) / STAIRWAY TO HEAVEN (Led Zeppelin) / etc. • **Trivia:** In 1969, he married for a second time and was soon the father of sons, DWEEZIL (who became a guitarist in the 80's), AHMET RODAN, and daughters MOON UNIT and DIVA. In 1976, ZAPPA produced GRAND FUNK on their lp, 'Good Singin', Good Playin''.

Album rating: FREAK OUT (*8) / ABSOLUTELY FREE (*8) / WE'RE ONLY IN IT FOR THE MONEY (*8) / LUMPY GRAVY (*6) / CRUISING WITH RUBEN AND THE JETS (*6) / MOTHERMANIA – THE BEST OF THE MOTHERS compilation (*8) / UNCLE MEAT (*7) / HOT RATS (*8) / BURNT WEENY SANDWICH (*6) / WEASELS RIPPED MY FLESH (*7) / CHUNGA'S REVENGE (*7) / FILLMORE EAST: JUNE 1971 (*6) / 200 MOTELS (*3) / JUST ANOTHER BAND FROM L.A. (*5) / WAKA – JAWAKA (*6) / THE GRAND WAZOO (*6) / OVER-NITE SENSATION (*8) / APOSTROPHE (') (*8) / ROXY & ELSEWHERE (*6; by Frank Zappa – Mothers) / ONE SIZE FITS ALL (*8; as Frank Zappa & The Mothers Of Invention) / BONGO FURY (*6; as Frank Zappa, Captain Beefheart & The Mothers) / ZOOT ALLURES (*7) / ZAPPA IN NEW YORK (*6) / STUDIO TAN (*5) / SLEEP DIRT (*4) / SHEIK YERBOUTI (*6) / ORCHESTRAL FAVORITES (*4) / JOE'S GARAGE, ACT I (*7) / JOE'S GARAGE, ACTS II & III (*6) / TINSEL TOWN REBELLION (*7) / YOU ARE WHAT YOU IS (*7) / SHIP ARRIVING TO LATE TO SAVE A DROWNING WITCH (*6) / SHUT UP 'N PLAY YER GUITAR (*6) / THE MAN FROM UTOPIA (*5) / THEM OR US (*8) / THING FISH (*6) / DOES HUMOR BELONG IN MUSIC (*6) / FRANK ZAPPA MEETS THE MOTHERS OF PREVENTION (*5) / JAZZ FROM HELL (*4) / THE LONDON SYMPHONY ORCHESTRA VOL.II out-takes (*3) / GUITAR exploitation (*4) / YOU CAN'T DO THAT ON STAGE ANYMORE, VOL.1 collection (*6) / YOU CAN'T DO THAT ON STAGE ANYMORE, VOL.2 collection (*6) / BROADWAY THE HARD WAY (*5) / BABY SNAKES soundtrack (*3) / YOU CAN'T DO THAT ON STAGE ANYMORE, VOL.3 collection (*6) / THE BEST BAND YOU NEVER HEARD IN YOUR LIFE collection (*6) / MAKE A JAZZ NOISE HERE collection (*4) / YOU CAN'T DO THAT ON STAGE ANYMORE, VOL.4 collection (*6) / BEAT THE BOOTS boxed bootlegs (*5) / BEAT THE BOOTS #2 boxed bootlegs (*5) / YOU CAN'T DO THAT ON STAGE ANYMORE, VOL.5 collection (*6) / YOU CAN'T DO THAT ON STAGE ANYMORE, VOL.6 collection (*6) / AHEAD OF THEIR TIME early stuff (*5) / THE YELLOW SHARK

(*7) / STRICTLY COMMERCIAL – THE BEST OF FRANK ZAPPA (*9) / LOST EPISODES (*7) / LATHER (*5) / HAVE I OFFENDED SOMEONE collection (*7) / STRICTLY GENTEEL: A CLASSICAL INTRODUCTION collection (*7)

The MOTHERS OF INVENTION

FRANK ZAPPA – guitar, vocals / with **RAY COLLINS** – vocals (had been temp.repl. by JIM GUERCIO; later a producer) / **ELLIOTT INGBER** – guitar repl. JIM FIELDER + STEVE MANN who had repl. HENRY VESTINE. Before he moved onto CANNED HEAT he had repl. MOTHERS original ALICE STUART. / **ROY ESTRADA** – bass / **JIM BLACK** – drums

Verve — Verve-MGM

1966. (7") *<10418>* **HELP, I'M A ROCK. / HOW COULD I BE SUCH A FOOL?** [–] [ ]

Nov 66. (7") *(VS 545)* **IT CAN'T HAPPEN HERE. / HOW COULD I BE SUCH A FOOL?** [ ] [–]

1966. (7") *<10458>* **TROUBLE EVERY DAY. / WHO ARE THE BRAIN POLICE?** [–] [ ]

Mar 67. (lp; stereo/mono) <US; d-lp+=*> *(S+/VLP 9154)* *<5005>* **FREAK OUT!** [ ] Aug66 [ ]
– Hungry freaks, daddy / I ain't got no heart / Who are the brain police? / Go cry on somebody else's shoulder * / Motherly love / How could I be such a fool * / Wowie Zowie / You didn't try to call me / Any way the wind blows * / I'm not satisfied / You're probably wondering why I'm here / Trouble comin' every day / Help, I'm a rock / The return of the son of monster magnet. *(UK re-iss. Dec71 on 'Verve-Polydor' d-lp; 2683 004) (cd-iss. Oct87 on 'Zappa'; CDZAP 1) <Rykodisc'US> (cd re-iss. May95 on 'Rykodisc'; RCD 10501)*

— **JIM 'MOTORHEAD' SHERWOOD** – sax repl. INGBER who joined FRATERNITY OF MAN. He later changed his name and joined CAPTAIN BEEFHEART / added **BILLY MUNDI** – drums / **DON PRESTON** – keyboards / **BUNK GARDNER** – horns

Apr 67. (7") *(VS 557)* **BIG LEG EMMA. / WHY DON'T YOU DO ME RIGHT?** [ ] [–]

Oct 67. (lp; stereo/mono) *(S+/VLP 9174) <5013>* **ABSOLUTELY FREE** [ ] May67 [41]
– Plastic people / The duke of prunes / Amnesia vivace / The Duke regains his chops / Call any vegetable / Invocation and ritual dance of the young pumpkin / Soft-cell conclusion and ending of side 1 / America drinks / Status back baby / Uncle Bernie's farm / Son of Suzy Creamcheese / Brown shoes don't make it / America drinks and goes home. *(re-iss. Jun72 on 'Verve-Polydor'; 2317 035) (cd-iss. Jan89 on 'Zappa'; CDZAP 12) ('Rykodisc' US version +=) (cd re-iss. May95 on 'Rykodisc'+=; RCD 10502)* – Big leg Emma / Why don'tcha do me right?.

— **ZAPPA, ESTRADA, MUNDI, PRESTON, GARDNER & JIMMY CARL BLACK** plus **IAN UNDERWOOD** – piano, wind repl. COLLINS

Dec 67. (7") *<10570>* **MOTHER PEOPLE. / LONELY LITTLE GIRL (version)** [–] [ ]

Jun 68. (lp; stereo/mono) *(S+/VLP 9199) <5045>* **WE'RE ONLY IN IT FOR THE MONEY** [32] Jan68 [30]
– Are you hung up? / Who needs the peace corps? / Concentration Moon / Mom and dad / Telephone conversation / Bow tie daddy / Harry, you're a beast / What's the ugliest part of your body? / Absolutely free / Flower punk / Hot poop / Nasal retentive calliope music / Let's make the water turn black / The idiot bastard son / Lonely little girl / Take your clothes off when you dance / What's the ugliest part of your body (reprise) / Mother people / The chrome plated megaphone of destiny. *(re-iss. Jun72 on 'Verve-Polydor'; 2317 034) (re-iss. cd/c/lp Apr95 on 'Rykodisc'; RCD/RAC/RALP 10503)*

— (now with The ABNUCEALS EMUUKHA ELECTRIC SYMPHONY ORCHESTRA & CHORUS; a 50+ piece orchestra incl. GARDNER + GUERIN + some other MOTHERS in choir)

Oct 68. (lp; stereo/mono; by FRANK ZAPPA) *(S+/VLP 9223)* *<8741>* **LUMPY GRAVY** [ ] May68 [ ]
– Lumpy gravy (part one): The way I see it, Barry – Duodenum – Oh no – Bit of nostalgia – It's from Kansas – Bored out 90 over – Almost Chinese – Switching girls – Oh no again – At the gas station – Another pickup – I don't know if I can go through this again / Lumpy gravy (part two): Very distrautening – White ugliness – Amen – Just one more time – A vicious circle – King Kong – Drums are too noisy – Kangaroos – Envelopes the bath tub – Take your clothes off. *(re-iss. Jun72 on 'Verve-Polydor'; 2317 046) (cd-iss. Apr95 on 'Rykodisc'; RCD 10504)*

— **ARTHUR TRIPP III** – drums repl. MUNDI who formed RHINOCEROS / added again **RAY COLLINS** – vocals

Dec 68. (7") **DESERI. / JELLY ROLL GUM DROP** [–] [ ]

Feb 69. (lp; stereo/mono) *(S+/VLP 9237) <5055>* **CRUISING WITH RUBEN & THE JETS** [ ] Nov68 [ ]
– Cheap thrills / Love of my life / How could I be such a fool / Deseri / I'm not satisfied / Jelly roll gum drop / Anything / Later that night / You didn't try to call me / Fountain of love / No no no / Anyway the wind blows * / Stuff up the cracks. *(re-iss. Jun73 on 'Verve-Polydor'; 2317 069) (cd-iss. Oct87 on 'Zappa'; CDZAP 4) ('Rykodisc'US) (re-iss. cd May95 on 'Rykodisc'; RCD 10505)*

Apr 69. (lp; stereo/mono) *(S+/VLP 9239) <5068>* **MOTHERMANIA: THE BEST OF THE MOTHERS** (compilation) [ ] Mar68 [ ]
– Brown shoes don't make it / Mother people / Duke of prunes / Call any vegetable / The idiot bastard son / It can't happen here / You're probably wondering why I'm here / Who are the brain police? / Plastic people / Hungry freaks, daddy / America drinks and goes home. *(re-iss. Feb72 on 'Verve-Polydor'; 2317 047) (re-iss. Jul73 on 'Verve-Polydor'; 2352 017)*

— added **RUTH KOMANOFF** (UNDERWOOD) – marimba, vibes / **NELCY WALKER** – soprano vocals (on 2)

Transatla. — Bizarre

Sep 69. (d-lp) *(TRA 197) <2024>* **UNCLE MEAT** [ ] Apr69 [43]
– Uncle Meat (main title theme) / The voice of cheese / Nine types of industrial pollution / Zolar Czakl / Dog breath in the year of the plague / The legend of the golden arches / Louie Louie (at the Royal Albert Hall in London) / The dog breath variations / Sleeping in a jar / Our bizarre relationship / The Uncle Meat variations / Electric Aunt Jemima // Prelude to King Kong / God bless America (live at the Whisky A Go Go) / A pound for a brown on the bus / Ian Underwood whips it out (live on stage in Copenhagen) / Mr. Green genes / We can shoot you / If we'd all been living in California / The air / Project X / Cruising for burgers / Uncle Meat film excerpt part 1 * / Tengo na minchia tanta * / Uncle Meat film excerpt part II * / King Kong itself (as played by The Mothers in a studio) / King Kong II (it's magnificence as interpreted by Dom Dewild) / King Kong III (as Motorhead explains it) / King Kong IV (the Gardner varieties) / King Kong V (as played by 3 deranged good humor trucks) / King Kong VI (live on a flat bed diesel in the middle of a race track at a Miami pop festival . . . the Underwood ramifications). *(d-cd-iss. Oct87 on 'Zappa' +=; CDZAP 3) (cd-iss. May95 on 'Rykodisc'; RCD 10506-7)*

Sep 69. (7") *<0840>* **MY GUITAR. / DOG BREATH** [–] [ ]

FRANK ZAPPA

— solo guitar w/ **UNDERWOOD** plus **CAPTAIN BEEFHEART** – vocals / **JEAN-LUC PONTY + SUGAR-CANE HARRIS** – violin / **MAX BENNETT + SHUGGY OTIS** – bass / **PAUL HUMPHREY + RON SELICO + JOHN GUERIN** – drums

Reprise — Reprise

Jan 70. (7") *<0889>* **PEACHES EN REGALIA. / LITTLE UMBRELLAS** [–] [ ]

Feb 70. (lp) *(RSLP <6356>)* **HOT RATS** [9] Oct69 [ ]
– Peaches en regalia / Willie the pimp / Son of Mr. Green genes / Little umbrellas / The Gumbo variations / It must be a camel. *(re-iss. Jul71; K 44078) (remixed cd-iss. Oct87 on 'Zappa'; CDZAP 2) (cd-iss. May95 on 'Rykodisc'; RCD 10508)*

The MOTHERS OF INVENTION

— (see last MOTHERS line-up) + add **BUZZ GARDNER** – horns / **SUGAR-CANE HARRIS** – violin (now without KOMANOFF)

Mar 70. (lp) *(RSLP <6370>)* **BURNT WEENY SANDWICH** [17] Feb70 [94]
– WPLJ / Igor's boogie – phase 1 / Overture to a holiday in Berlin / Theme from Burnt Weenie Sandwich / Igor's boogie – phase 2 / Holiday in Berlin, full blown / Aybe sea / The little house I used to live in / Valarie. *(re-iss. Jul71; K 44083) (cd-iss. Nov91 on 'Zappa'; CDZAP 35) (re-iss. cd May95 on 'Rykodisc'; RCD 10509)*

Mar 70. (7") *<0892>* **WPLJ. / MY GUITAR** [–] [ ]
(below album used rare material from 1967-69, as The MOTHERS OF INVENTION officially disbanded Oct69) guest LOWELL GEORGE – guitar

Sep 70. (lp) *(RSLP <2028>)* **WEASELS RIPPED MY FLESH** [28] [ ]
– Didja get any onya? / Directly from my heart to you / Prelude to the afternoon of a sexually aroused gas mask / Toads of the short forest / Get a little / Eric Dolphy memorial barbecue / Dwarf Nebula processional march and dwarf Nebula / My guitar wants to kill your mama / oh no / The Orange County lumber truck / Weasels ripped my flesh. *(re-iss. Jul71; K 44019) (cd-iss. May95 on 'Rykodisc'; RCD 10510)*

— LOWELL and ROY formed LITTLE FEAT. ART TRIPP became ED MARIMBA and joined CAPTAIN BEEFHEART & HIS MAGIC BAND.

BUNK GARDNER and JIMMY CARL BLACK formed GERONIMO BLACK.

FRANK ZAPPA

— formed solo band with **IAN UNDERWOOD, SUGAR-CANE HARRIS & MAX BENNETT**. He introduced **JEFF SIMMONS** – bass / **JOHN GUERIN** – drums / **AYNSLEY DUNBAR** – drums / **GEORGE DUKE** – keyboards, trombone / **MARK VOLMAN + HOWARD KAYLAN** (aka The PHLORESCENT LEECH AND EDDIE) – vocals (ex-TURTLES)

Nov 70. (lp) *(RSLP <2030>)* **CHUNGA'S REVENGE** [43] [ ]
– Transylvania boogie / Road ladies / Twenty small cigars / The Nancy and Mary music (part 1, 2 & 3) / Tell me you love me / Would you go all the way? / Chunga's revenge / The clap / Rudy wants to buy yez a drink / Sharleena. *(re-iss. Jul71; K 44020) (cd-iss. Jun90 on 'Zappa'; CDZAP 23) (cd-iss. May95 on 'Rykodisc'; RCD 10511)*

Nov 70. (7") *<0967>* **TELL ME YOU LOVE ME. / WOULD YOU GO ALL THE WAY?** [–] [ ]

The MOTHERS

— re-formed early 1971 and retained **DON PRESTON** – mini moog / **DUNBAR / VOLMAN & KAYLAN and recruited JIM PONS** – bass (ex-TURTLES) / **BOB HARRIS** – keyboards

Aug 71. (lp) *(K 44150) <2042>* **FILLMORE EAST – JUNE 1971 (live)** [ ] [38]
– Little house I used to live in / The mud shark / What kind of girl do you think we are? / Bwana Dik / Latex solar beef / Willie the pimp (part 1) / Do you like my new car? / Happy together / Lonesome electric turkey / Peaches en regalia / Tears began to fall. *(cd-iss. Jun90 on 'Zappa'; CDZAP 29) (cd re-iss. May95 on 'Rykodisc'; RCD 10512)*

Aug 71. (7") *(K 14100) <1052>* **TEARS BEGAN TO FALL. / JUNIER MINTZ BOOGIE** [ ] [ ]

FRANK ZAPPA

— solo, with MOTHERS:- **IAN + RUTH UNDERWOOD / GEORGE DUKE / AYNSLEY DUNBAR / VOLMAN + KAYLAN / MARTIN LICKERT** – bass / guests were **JIM PONS + JIMMY CARL BLACK / THEODORE BIKEL** – narrator + ROYAL PHILHARMONIC ORCHESTRA

U.A. U.A.

Oct 71. (d-lp) *(UDF 50003) <9956>* **200 MOTELS (live studio soundtrack)** [ ] [59]
– Semi-fraudulent – Direct-from-Hollywood overture / Mystery roach / Dance of the rock & roll interviewers / This town is a sealed tuna sandwich (prologue) / Tuna fish promenade / Dance of the just plain folks / This town is a sealed tuna fish sandwich (reprise) / The sealed tuna bolero / Lonesome cowboy Burt / Touring can make you crazy / Would you like a snack? / Redneck eats / Centerville / She painted up her face / Janet's big dance number / Half a dozen provocative squats / Mysterioso / Shove it right in / Lucy's seduction of a bored violinist & postlude / I'm stealing the towels / Dental hygeine dilemma / Does this kind of life look interesting to you? / Daddy, daddy, daddy / Penis dimension / What will this evening bring me this morning / A nun suit painted on some old boxes / Magic fingers / Motorhead's midnight ranch / Dew on the newts we got / The lad searches the night for his newts / The girl wants to fix him some broth / The girl's dream / Little green scratchy sweaters & corduroy ponce / Strictly genteel (the finale). *(re-iss. Jan89 on 'M.C.A.' d-lp/c; MCA/+C 24183)*

Oct 71. (7") *<50857>* **MAGIC FINGERS. / DADDY, DADDY, DADDY** [–] [ ]

Nov 71. (7") *(UP 35319)* **WHAT WILL THIS EVENING BRING ME THIS MORNING?. / DADDY, DADDY, DADDY** [ ] [–]

— now with a plethera of musicians (see next solo also), including some MOTHERS

Reprise Reprise

Aug 72. (lp) *(K 44203) <2094>* **WAKA/JAWAKA: HOT RATS** [ ] [ ]
– Big Swifty / Your mouth / It just might be a one-shot deal / Waka-Jawaka. *(cd-iss. Jan89 on 'Zappa'; CDZAP 10) (re-iss. cd May95 on 'Rykodisc'; RCD 10516)*
(above featured **PRESTON, DUNBAR, DUKE, SIMMONS** & others also on next).

The MOTHERS

— recorded live 7th August'71. (see last ZAPPA line-up) Re-formed earlier that year minus BOB HARRIS

Reprise Bizarre

Jun 72. (lp) *(K 44179) <2075>* **JUST ANOTHER BAND FROM L.A.** [ ] [85]
– Billy the mountain / Call any vegetable / Eddie, are you kidding? / Magdalena / Dog breath. *(cd-iss. Jun90 on 'Zappa'; CDZAP 10515) (cd re-iss. May95 on 'Rykodisc'; RCD 10515)*

— The MOTHERS added **TONY DURAN** – slide guitar / **ERRONEOUS** – bass repl. SIMMONS / **KEN SHROYER** – trombone / **JOEL PESKIN** – tenor saxophone / **SAL MARQUEZ** – timpani / **BILL BYERS** – trombone / **MIKE ALTSCHUL** – wind / **JANET NEVILLE-FERGUSON** – vocals / **CHUNKY** – vocals / **EARL DUMLER, FRED JACKSON + TONY ORTEGA** – wind / **ERNIE WATTS** – sax / **ERNIE TACK + MALCOLM McNABB** – horns / **JOHNNY ROTELLA, BOB ZIMMITTI + LEE CLEMENT** – percussion / **JOANNE CALDWELL McNABB** – violin

Dec 72. (lp) *(K 44209)* **THE GRAND WAZOO** [ ] [–]
– The grand Wazoo / For Calvin (and his next two hitch-hikers) / Cletus-awreetus-awrightus / Eat that question / Blessed relief. *(cd-iss. Sep90 on 'Zappa'; CDZAP 31) (cd re-iss. May95 on 'Rykodisc'; RCD 10517)*

Dec 72. (7") *<1127>* **CLETUS-AWREETUS-AWRIGHTUS. / EAT THAT QUESTION** [–] [ ]

— **ZAPPA** brought back **IAN + RUTH UNDERWOOD** (They were on '72 tour) / **GEORGE DUKE / JEAN-LUC PONTY / SAL MARQUEZ.** He introduced **TOM FOWLER** – bass / **BRUCE FOWLER** – trombone / **RALPH HUMPHREY** – drums

DiscReet DiscReet

Jan 73. (lp) *(K 41000) <2149>* **OVERNITE SENSATION** [ ] [32]
– Camarillo brillo / I'm the slime / Dirty love / Fifty-fifty / Zomby woof / Dinah-Moe humm / Montana. *<cd-iss. Oct87 w / 'APOSTROPHE' tracks on 'Rykodisc'> (cd-iss. Jul90 on 'Zappa'; CDZAP 36) (re-iss. cd/c Apr95 on 'Rykodisc'; RCD/RAC 10518)*

Feb 73. (7") *<1180>* **I'M THE SLIME. / MONTANA** [–] [ ]

FRANK ZAPPA

— solo retaining current MOTHERS. He also brought back past MOTHERS: **AYNSLEY DUNBAR / RAY COLLINS / ERRONEOUS / JOHN GUERIN / SUGAR CANE HARRIS / RUBEN GUEVARA + ROBERT CAMARENA** – b.vocals (of RUBEN &..JETS) **NAPOLEON BROCK** – saxophone / guest **JACK BRUCE** – bass (ex-CREAM)

May 74. (lp/c) *(K/K4 59201) <2175>* **APOSTROPHE (')** [ ] Apr74 [10]
– Don't eat the yellow snow / Nanook rubs it / St. Alfonzo's pancake breakfast / Father O'Blivion / Cosmik debris / Excentrifugal forz / Apostrophe' / Uncle Remus / Stink-foot. *(re-iss. cd/c Apr95 on 'Rykodisc'; RCD/RAC 10519) (cd-version-iss.Jun96; RCD 80519)*

Aug 74. (7") *<1312>* **DON'T EAT THE YELLOW SNOW. / COSMIK DEBRIS** [–] [86]

Aug 74. (7") *(K 19201)* **COSMIK DEBRIS. / UNCLE REMUS** [ ] [–]

Sep 74. (7") *(K 19202)* **DON'T EAT THE YELLOW SNOW. / CAMARILLO BRILLO** [ ] [–]

— were now basically **GEORGE DUKE / TOM FOWLER / NAPOLEON / RUTH UNDERWOOD** and new drummer **CHESTER THOMPSON.** Temp. old members were also used **DON PRESTON / BRUCE + WALT FOWLER / JEFF SIMMONS + RALPH HUMPHREY**

Oct 74. (d-lp/c; ZAPPA / MOTHERS) *(K/K4 69201) <2202>* **ROXY & ELSEWHERE (live + unreleased)** [ ] Sep74 [27]
– Preamble / Penguin in bondage / Pygmy twylyte / Dummy up / Preamble / Village of the sun / Echidna's arf (of you) / Don't you ever wash that thing? / Preamble / Cheepnis / Son of Orange County / More trouble every day / Be-bop tango (of old Jazzmen's church). *(cd-iss. Feb92 on 'Zappa'; CDZAP 39) (re-iss. cd/c May95 on 'Rykodisc'; RCD/RAC 10520)*

— temp.members above repl. by **JOHNNY GUITAR WATSON** – vocals / **JAMES YOUMAN** – bass / **BLOODSHOT ROLLIN RED** (DON WATSON) – harmonica

Aug 75. (lp; by FRANK ZAPPA & THE MOTHERS OF INVENTION) *(K 59207) <2216>* **ONE SIZE FITS ALL** [ ] [26]
– Inca roads / Can't afford no shoes / Sofa No.1 / Po-jama people / Florentine pogen / Evelyn, a modified dog / San Ber'dino / Andy / Sofa No.2. *<(cd-iss. Jan89 on 'Zappa'; RCD 10095 / CDZAP 11)> (re-iss. cd May95 on 'Rykodisc'; RCD 10521)*

Sep 75. (7"; by FRANK ZAPPA & THE MOTHERS OF INVENTION) *(K 19205)* **STINK-FOOT. / DU BIST MEIN SOFA** [ ] [–]

— next a collaboration with **CAPTAIN BEEFHEART** with also **DUKE / FOWLER's / BROCK / THOMPSON** plus **TERRY BOZZIO** – drums / **DENNY WALLEY**– slide guitar

Nov 75. (lp; by FRANK ZAPPA, CAPTAIN BEEFHEART & THE MOTHERS) *(K 59209; w-drawn) <2234>* **BONGO FURY (live + 2 studio)** [–] [66]
– Debra Kadabra / Caroline hard-core ecstasy / Sam with the showing scalp flat top / Poofter's froth Wyoming plans ahead / 200 years old / Cucamonga / Advance romance / Man with the woman head / Muffin man. *(cd-iss. Jan89 on 'Zappa'; CDZAP 15) <US 'Rykodisc'; RY 10097> (re-iss. cd May95 on 'Rykodisc'; RCD 10522)*

FRANK ZAPPA

— finally disbanded The MOTHERS and went solo. Augmented by **TERRY BOZZIO** – drums / **ROY ESTRADA, DAVE PARLATO + RUTH UNDERWOOD** – marimba, synth / **DAVEY MOIRE** – b.vocals / **LU ANN NEIL** – harp / **ANDRE LEWIS** – backing vocals

Warners Warners

Oct 76. (7") *<8296>* **FIND HER FINER. / ZOOT ALLURES** [–] [ ]
Nov 76. (lp/c) *(K/K4 56298) <2970>* **ZOOT ALLURES** [ ] [61]
– Wind up workin' in a gas station / Black napkins / The torture never stops / Ms. Pinky / Find her finer / Friendly little finger / Wonderful wino / Zoot allures / Disco boy. *(cd-iss. Jun90 on 'Zappa'; CDZAP 22) (re-iss. cd May95 on 'Rykodisc'; RCD 10523)*
Dec 76. (7") *<8342>* **DISCO BOY. / MS. PINKY** [–] [ ]

— His basic band were **EDDIE JOBSON** – keyboards, violin (ex-ROXY MUSIC) / **RAY WHITE** – guitar, vocals / **PAT O'HEARN** – bass / **RUTH UNDERWOOD** – / **TERRY BOZZIO** – drums. Plus brass section – **RANDY + MICHAEL BRECKER / LOU MARINI / RONNIE CUBER / TOM MALONE / DAVID SAMUELS** – percussion

DiscReet DiscReet

Jun 78. (d-lp) *(K 69204) <2290>* **ZAPPA IN NEW YORK (live 1976)** [55] [57]
– Titties & beer / Cruisin' for burgers * / I promise not to come in your mouth / Punky's whips *[not on some]* / Honey, don't you want a man like me? / The Illinois enema bandit // I'm the slime * / Pound for a brown * / Manx needs women / The black page drum solo – Black page #1 / Big leg Emma / Sofa / Black page #2 / The torture never stops * / The purple lagoon – approximate. *(d-cd-iss. Sep91 on 'Zappa'; CDDZAP 37) (cd re-iss. May95 on 'Rykodisc'+= *; RCD 10524-5)*
Nov 78. (lp/c) *(K/K4 59210) <2291>* **STUDIO TAN** (2 instrumental 74-76) [ ] [ ]
– The adventures of Greggery Peccary / Revised music for guitar and low budget orchestra / Lemme take you to the beach / RDNZL. *(cd-iss. May95 on 'Rykodisc'; RCD 10526)*
Feb 79. (lp/c) *(K/K4 59211) <2292>* **SLEEP DIRT** (mostly instrumental 74-76) [ ] [ ]
– Filthy habits / Flambay / Spider of destiny / Regyptian strut / Time is money / Sleep dirt / The ocean is the ultimate solution. *(cd-iss. Oct91 on 'Zappa'; CDZAP 43) (cd re-iss. May95 on 'Rykodisc'; RCD 10527)*

— He retained only **BOZZIO + O'HEARN,** bringing back **NAPOLEON, ANDRE LEWIS + MOIRE.** New musicians:- **ADRIAN BELEW** – rhythm guitar, some lead vox / **TOMMY MARS** – keyboards, vocals / **PETER WOLF** – keyboards / **ED MANN** – percussion, vocals / **RANDY THORNTON** – b.vocals / **DAVID OCKER** – clarinet (1)

Zappa-CBS Zappa

Mar 79. (d-lp/d-c) *(CBS/40 88339) <1501>* **SHEIK YERBOUTI** [32] [21]
– I have been in you / Flakes / Broken hearts are for assholes / I'm so cute / Jones crusher / What ever happened to all the fun in the world / Rat tomago / Wait a ninute / Bobby Brown goes down / Rubber shirt / The Sheik Yerbouti tango / Baby snakes / Tryin' to grow a chin / City of tiny lites / Dancin' fool / Jewish princess / Wild love / Yo' mama. *(re-iss. Feb86 on 'E.M.I.' d-lp/d-c; EN/TCEN 5001) (cd-iss. Apr88; CDEN 5001) (cd re-iss. Jun91 on 'Zappa'; CDZAP 28) (re-iss. cd/c May95 on 'Rykodisc'; RCD/RAC 10528)*
Apr 79. (7") *(SCBS 7261) <10>* **DANCIN' FOOL. / BABY SNAKES** [ ] [45]

— **WARREN CUCURULLO** – rhythm guitar repl. BELEW (later to BOWIE + TALKING HEADS) /**IKE WILLIS** – lead vocals / **ARTHUR BARROW** – bass repl. O'HEARN / **VINNIE COLAIUTA** – drums repl. TERRY BOZZIO. Others in line-up **DALE BOZZIO** – vocals / **DENNIS WALLEY** – slide guitar / **MARGINAL CHAGRIN** – sax / **WOLF + MANN.**
Sep 79. (lp/c) *(CBS/40 86101) <1603>* **JOE'S GARAGE ACT I** [62] [27]
– Central scrutinizer / Joe's garage / Catholic girls / Crew slut / Fembot in a wet T-shirt / On the bus / Why does it hurt when I pee? / Lucille has messed my mind up / Scrutinizer postlude. *<d-cd-iss. Oct87 on 'Rykodisc'; RCD 10060> (UK d-cd-iss. Sep90 on 'Zappa'; CDZAP 20) (d-cd re-iss. May95; RCD 10530-31)*

Jan 80. (7") **JOE'S GARAGE. / CENTRAL SCRUTINIZER** [–] [ ]
Jan 80. (7") *(SCBS 7950)* **JOE'S GARAGE. / CATHOLIC GIRLS** [ ] [–]

— now without DALE, MARS + CHAGRIN
Jan 80. (d-lp/d-c) *(CBS/40 88475) <1502>* **JOE'S GARAGE ACT II & III** [75] [53]
– ACT II:- A token of my extreme / Stick it out / Sy Borg / Dong work for Yuda / Keep it greasey / Outside now / ACT III:- He used to cut the grass / Packard goose / Watermelon in Easter hay / A little green Rosetta. *<US d-cd-iss. Oct87 on 'Rykodisc'; RCD 10061>*
Jun 80. (7") *(SCBS 8652) <ZR 1001>* **I DON'T WANT TO GET DRAFTED. / ANCIENT ARMAMENTS** [ ] [ ]

— now with **STEVE VAI + RAY WHITE + IKE WILLIS** – rhythm guitar, vocals / **TOMMY MARS** – keyboards / **BOB HARRIS** – keyboards, trumpet, high vox / **ED MANN / BARROW** – bass / **COLAIUTA / WOLF**

CBS CBS

May 81. (d-lp/d-c) *(CBS/40 88516) <37336>* **TINSELTOWN REBELLION (live)** [55] [66]
– Fine girl / Easy meat / For the young sophisticate / Love of my life / I ain't got no heart / Panty rap / Tell me you love me / Now you see it – now you don't / Dance contest / The blue light / Tinseltown rebellion / Pick me, I'm clean / Bamboozled by love / Brown shoes don't make it / Peaches III. *(re-iss. Feb86 on 'E.M.I.' d-lp/d-c; EN/TCEN 5002) (d-cd-iss. Apr88; CDEN 5002) (cd-iss. Jun90 on 'Zappa'; CDZAP 26) (re-iss. cd May95 on 'Rykodisc'; RCD 10532)*

— **JIMMY CARL BLACK** – guest vocals returned (+ daughter MOON, son AHMET) to repl. CUCURULLO / WOLF / COLAIUTA and O'HEARN. new members:- **DAVID OCKER** – – clarinet / **PAT O'HEARN** – bass / **SHERWOOD** – sax (returned) / **DAVID LOGEMAN** – drums
Oct 81. (d-lp/d-c) *(CBS/40 88560) <37537>* **YOU ARE WHAT YOU IS** [51] [93]
– Teenage wind / Harder than your husband / Doreen / Goblin girl / Theme from the 3rd movement of sinister footwear / Society pages / I'm a beautiful guy / Beauty knows no pain / Charlie's enormous mouth / Any downers? / Conehead / You are what you is / Mudd club / The meek shall inherit nothing / Dumb all over / Heavenly bank account / Suicide chump / Jumbo go away / If only she woulda / Drafted again. *(re-iss. Feb86 on 'E.M.I.' d-lp/d-c; EN/TCEN 5000) (d-cd-iss. Apr88; CDEN 5000) (cd-iss. Jun90 on 'Zappa'; CDZAP 27) (re-iss. cd May95 on 'Rykodisc'; RCD 10536)*
Nov 81. (12"pic-d) *<BPRP 114>* **GOBLIN GIRL. / PINK NAPKINS** [–] [ ]
Feb 82. (7") *(A 1622)* **YOU ARE WHAT YOU IS. / HARDER THAN YOUR HUSBAND** [ ] [ ]
(12"pic-d+=) *(A12 1622)* – Pink napkins / Soup'n'old clothes.

— added **SCOTT THUNES** – bass / **CHAD WACKERMAN** – drums / **BOBBY MARTIN** – keyboards, sax / vocalists ROY ESTRADA, LISA POPIEL / MOON, who replaced WALLEY, LOGEMAN, SHERWOOD, OCKER, STEWART, BLACK + AHMET
Jun 82. (lp/c) *(CBS/40 85804) <38066>* **SHIP ARRIVING TOO LATE TO SAVE A DROWNING WITCH** [61] [23]
– No not now / Valley girl / I come from nowhere / Drowning witch / Envelopes / Teen-age prostitute. *(free 7"w.a.) (XPS 147)* – SHUT UP 'N' PLAY YER GUITAR. / VARIATION ON THE C. SANTANA SECRET *(re-iss. Feb86 on 'E.M.I.' lp/c; EMC/TCEMC 3501) (re-iss. Jun87 on 'Fame' lp/c; FA/TCFA 3180) (cd-iss. Aug91 on 'Zappa'; CDZAP 42) (re-iss. cd May95 on 'Rykodisc'; RCD 10537)*
Jul 82. (7")(12") *<02972><03069>* **VALLEY GIRL. / YOU ARE WHAT YOU IS** [–] [32]
Aug 82. (7"; by FRANK & MOON ZAPPA) *(A 2412) <02972>* **VALLEY GIRL. / TEENAGE PROSTITUTE** [ ] [–]

— **MYRTY KRYSTALL** – sax repl.MOON + POPIEL / **DICK FEGY** – mandolin / also added **CRAIG STEWARD** – harmonica
Jun 83. (lp/c) *(CBS/40 25251) <38403>* **THE MAN FROM UTOPIA** [87] [ ]
– Cocaine decisions / Sex / Tink walks amok / The radio is broken / We are not alone / The dangerous kitchen / The man from Utopia meets Mary Lou / Stick together / The jazz discharge party hats / Luigi & the wise guys * / Moggio. *(re-iss. Feb86 on 'E.M.I.' lp/c; EMC/TCEMC 3500) (re-iss. Apr88 on 'Fame' lp/c)(cd; FA/TCFA 3203)(CDP 790074-2) (cd-iss. Feb93 on 'Zappa'+= *; CDZAP 53) (re-iss. cd May95 on 'Rykodisc'; RCD 10538)*

— **JOHNNY GUITAR WATSON + NAPOLEON MURPHY BROCK** – vocals repl. STEWARD, FEGY, KRISTALL (+ COLAIUTA) other guest his son DWEEZIL ZAPPA – guitar solos (2)

E.M.I. Rykodisc

Sep 84. (7") *(EMI 5499)* **BABY TAKE YOUR TEETH OUT. / STEVIE'S SPANKING**

Oct 84. (d-lp/d-c) *(FZD/+TC 1)* *<R 40027>* **THEM OR US** 53
– The closer you are / In France / Ya hozna / Sharleena / Sinister footwear II / Truck driver divorce / Stevie's spanking / Baby take your teeth out / Marqueson's chicken / Planet of my dreams / Be in my video / Them or us / Frogs with dirty, little lips / Whippin' post. *(cd-iss. Apr88; CDEN 24) (cd re-iss. Apr91 on 'Zappa'; CDZAP 30) (re-iss. cd May95 on 'Rykodisc'; RCD 10543)*

1984. (lp) **FRANCESCO ZAPPA** (classical) –
(UK cd-iss. May92 on 'Zappa'; CDZAP 48) (cd re-iss. May95 on 'Rykodisc'; RCD 10546)
(above was conducted by FRANK, and taken from pieces of music from an Italian musician circa 1973-1988)

— **ZAPPA** with band: **VAI, MARS, WHITE, MANN, WACKERMAN, BARROW, THUNES** plus **STEVE DE FURIA & DAVID OCKER** – synclavier programmer. Characters: **IKE WILLIS** (Thing Fish) / **TERRY BOZZIO** (Harry) / His wife **DALE BOZZIO** (Rhonda) / **NAPOLEON MURPHY BROCK** (Evil Prince) / **BOB HARRIS** (Harry as a boy) / **JOHNNY GUITAR WATSON** (Brown Moses) / **RAY WHITE** (Owl Gonkwin Jane Cowhoon)

E.M.I. Capitol

Mar 85. (t-lp/d-c) *(EX240294-1/-4)* *<R 10020>* **THING FISH**
– Prologue / The mammy nuns / Harry & Rhonda / Galoot up-date / The 'torchum' never stops / That evil prince / You are what you is / Mudd club / The meek shall inherit nothing / Clowns on velvet / Harry-as-a-boy / He's so gay / The massive improve'lence / Artificial Rhonda / The crab-grass baby / The white boy troubles / No not now / Briefcase boogie / Brown Moses / Wistful wit a fist-full / Drop dead / Won ton on. *(d-cd-iss. Apr88; CDFZ 3) (d-cd-iss. Feb90 on 'Zappa'; CDDZAP 21) (re-iss. d-cd May95 on 'Rykodisc'; RCD 10544-45)*

— In Jun'85, PIERRE BOULEZ released his versions of ZAPPA, under the title 'THE PERFECT STRANGER – BOULEZ CONDUCTS ZAPPA'. Later issued in the UK on cd on 'Rykodisc'; *RCD 10542)*

— musicians; as last but without BOZZIO's, BARROW, BROCK, HARRIS

— **BOBBY MARTIN** – vocals, keyboards repl. DE FURIA + OCKER

Mar 86. (lp/c) *(EMC/TCEMC 3507)* *<ST 74203>* **FRANK ZAPPA MEETS THE MOTHERS OF PREVENTION**
– Porn wars / We're turning again / Alien orifice / Aerobics in bondage / I don't even care * / Little beige sambo / What's new in Baltimore / One man, one vote * / H.R. 2911 *. *(cd-iss. Sep90 on 'Zappa'; CDZAP 33)* – repl. Porn wars; w/ *) *(cd-iss. May95 on 'Rykodisc' all tracks; RCD 10547)*

— now ZAPPA on synclavier only + one live from '82. others:- **VAI, WHITE, MARS, MARTIN, MANN, THUNES, WACKERMAN**

E.M.I. Barking P.

Dec 86. (lp/c) *(EMC/TCEMC 3521)* *<74205>* **JAZZ FROM HELL**
– Night school / The Beltway bandits / While you were art II / Jazz from Hell / G-spot tornado / Damp ankles / St.Etienne / Massaggio galore. *(cd-iss. Sep90 on 'Zappa'; CDZAP 32) (cd-iss. May95 on 'Rykodisc'; RCD 10549)*

— **FRANK** still with **WILLIS, WACKERMAN, THUNES, MANN, MARTIN,** plus new **MIKE KENEALLY** – guitar, synth., vocals repl. VAI who went solo, etc. / **WALT FOWLER** – trumpet / **BRUCE FOWLER** – trombone / **PAUL CARMAN** – alto sax / **ALBERT WING** – tenor sax / **KURT McGETTRICK** – baritone sax / guest vox – **ERIC BUXTON**

Zappa Zappa

Dec 88. (lp/c/cd) *<(ZAPPA/TZAPPA/CDZAP 14)>* **BROADWAY THE HARD WAY (live)**
– Elvis has just left the building / Planet of the baritone women / Any kind of pain / Dickie's such an asshole / When the lie's so big / Rhymin' man / Promiscuous / The untouchables / Why don't you like me? * / Bacon fat * / Stolen moments * / Murder by numbers * / Jezebel boy * / Outside now * / Hot plate heaven at the green hotel * / What kind of a girl? * / Jesus thinks you're a jerk. *(cd+= *) (re-iss. cd May95 on 'Rykodisc'; RCD 10552)*

— Late '91, it was announced FRANK had been diagnosed with prostrate cancer. He was to die of this on 4th Dec'93.

Feb 93. (12"/cd-s) *(12/CD FRANK 101)* **STAIRWAY TO HEAVEN. / BOLERO** –

— next with the ENSEMBLE MODERN, conducted by himself & PETER RUNDEL

Oct 93. (cd/c) *<(CDZAP/TZAPPA 57)>* **YELLOW SHARK (live)**
– Intro / Dog breath variations / Uncle Meat / Outrage at Valdez / Times beach II / III revised / The girl in the magnesium dress / Be bop tango / Ruth is sleeping / None of the above / Pentagon afternoon / Questi cazzi di piccione / Times beach III / Food gathering in post industrial America 1992 / Welcome to the united States / Pound for a brown / Exercise 4 / Get Whitey / G-spot tornado. *(re-iss. cd/c May95 on 'Rykodisc'; RCD/RAC 40560)*

— an opera-pantomime with pre-recorded voices and music supplied by THE PIANO PEOPLE: **F.Z. / SPIDER / JOHN / MOTORHEAD / LARRY / ROY / LOUIS / MONICA / GILLY / GIRL 1 / GIRL 2 / MOON / MIKE / ALI / TODD / DARYL / JESUS**

Feb 95. (d-cd/d-c) *<(CDDZAP/TZAPPA 56)>* **CIVILIZATION PHAZE III**
– ACT ONE; This is phaze III / Put a motor in yourself / Oh-umm / They made me eat it / Reagan at Bitburg / A very nice body / Navanax / How the pigs' music works / Xmas values / Dark water / Amnerika / Have you ever heard their band / Religious superstition / Saliva can only take so much / Buffalo voice / Someplace else right now / Get a life / A kayak (on snow) / N-lite (I) Negative light (II) Venice submerged (III) The new world order (IV) The lifestyle you deserve (V) Creationism (VI) He is risen / / ACT TWO; I wish Motorhead would come back / Secular humanism / Attack! attack! attack! / I was in a drum / A different octave / This ain't CNN / The pigs' music / A pig with wings / This is all wrong / Hot & putrid / Flowing inside-out / I had a dream about that / Gross man / A tunnel into muck / Why not? / Put a little motor in 'em / You're just insultin' me, aren't you! / Cold light generation / Dio fa / That would be the end of that / Beat the reaper / Waffenspiel.

– compilations, others, etc. –

1975. (lp; by ZAPPA & THE MOTHERS) *Verve-Polydor; (2352 057)* **ROCK FLASHBACKS** –

Jun 79. (lp/c) *DiscReet; (K/K4 59212)* *<2294>* **ORCHESTRAL FAVORITES (live 1975)**
– Strictly genteel / Pedro's dowry / Naval aviation in art? / Duke of prunes / Bogus pomp. *(cd-iss. May95 on 'Rykodisc')*

— Next vocal-less **ZAPPA** – lead guitar plus usual ensemble.

Aug 82. (t-lp) *Barking Pumpkin-CBS; (66368)* **SHUT UP 'N PLAY YER GUITAR** (rec.1977-80 live)
– Five, five, five / Hog heaven / Pink napkins / Stucco homes / Variations on the C. Santana secret chord progression / Gee I like your pants / Soup 'n old clothes / The deathless horsie / Shut up 'n play yer guitar (x2) / Heavy duty Judy / The return of shut up 'n play yer guitar / Canard du joir / While you were out / Pinocchio's furniture / Beat it with your fist / Why Johnny can't read / Canarsie / Treacherous cretins. *(re-iss. Apr88 on 'E.M.I.' t-lp/d-cd; FZAP/CDFZ 2) (d-cd-re-iss. Jan90 on 'Zappa'; CDDZAP 19) (re-iss. t-cd May95 on 'Rykodisc'; RCD 10533-34-35)*

Feb 86. (cd) *E.M.I.; (CDP 746188-2)* **DOES HUMOR BELONG IN MUSIC**
(re-iss. Apr95 on 'Rykodisc' cd/c; RCD/RAC 10548)

Jul 87. (lp-box) *Barking Pumpkin; (BPR 7777)* **OLD MASTERS – BOX ONE**
– FREAK OUT / ABSOLUTELY FREE / WE'RE ONLY IN IT FOR THE MONEY / LUMPY GRAVY / CRUISIN' WITH RUBEN & THE JETS / (Mystery Disc – rare).

Jul 87. (lp-box) *Barking Pumpkin; (BPR 8888)* **OLD MASTERS – BOX TWO**
– UNCLE MEAT / HOT RATS / BURNT WEENIE SANDWICH / WEASELS RIPPED MY FLESH / CHUNGA'S REVENGE / LIVE AT THE FILLMORE EAST / JUST ANOTHER BAND FROM L.A. / (Mystery Disc – live in London 1968).

Oct 87. (cd) *Rykodisc; <RCD 40025>* **APOSTROPHE / OVERNIGHT SENSATION** –

Oct 87. (3"cd-ep) *Rykodisc;* **PEACHES EN REGALIA / I'M NOT SATISFIED / LUCILLE HAS MESSED UP MY MIND** –

Nov 87. (lp-box) *Barking Pumpkin; (BPR 9999)* **OLD MASTERS – BOX THREE**
– OVERNITE SENSATION / ONE SIZE FITS ALL / WAKA JAWAKA / THE GRAND WAZOO / APOSTROPHE / BONGO FURY / ZOOT ALLURES / ROXY AND ELSEWHERE.

Jan 88. (lp/c/cd) *Zappa; (ZAPPA/TZAPPA/CDDZAP 5)* **THE LONDON SYMPHONY ORCHESTRA VOL.II**
(out-takes from '200 MOTELS')
– Bob in Dacron / Strictly genteel / Bogus bomp. *(cd+=)* – (2 extra tracks).

Apr 88. (d-lp/c/cd) *Zappa/ US= Barking Pumpkin; (ZAPPA/TZAPPA/CDDZAP 6)* **GUITAR** (rec.live 1979-84) 82
– Sexual harassment in the workplace / Which one is it? * / Republicans /

Do not pass go / Chalk pie * / In-a-gadda-Stravinsky * / That's not really reggae / When no one was no one / Once again, without the net / Outside now (original solo) / Jim and Tammy's upper room / Were we ever really safe in San Antonio? / That ol' G minor thing again / Hotel Atlanta incidentals * / That's not really a shuffle * / Move it or park it / Sunrise redeemer // Variations on sinister #3 * / Orrin Hatch on skis * / But who was Fulcanelli? / For Duane / Goa / Winos do not march / Swans? what swans? * / Too ugly for show business * / Systems of edges / Do not try this at home * / Things that look like meat / Watermelon in Easter hay / Canadian customs * / Is that all there is? * / It ain't necessarily the St. James Infirmary *. *(cd+= *) (re-iss. cd May95 on 'Rykodisc'; RCD 10550-51)*

Apr 88. (cd) *EMI/ US= Capitol;* **THE MAN FROM UTOPIA / SHIP ARRIVING TOO LATE TO SAVE THE DROWNING WITCH** ☐ [–]

Apr 88. (2xt-lp-box) *E.M.I.; (FZAP 1)* **JOE'S GARAGE ACTS I / II / III / SHUT UP AND PLAY YER GUITAR** ☐ ☐

Apr 88. (d-lp) *Zappa; (ZAPPA 7)* **YOU CAN'T DO THAT ON STAGE ANYMORE SAMPLER** ☐ ☐
(d-cd-iss. Jan90; CDZAP 7)

Apr 88. (3"cd-s) *Rykodisc;* **SEXUAL HARASSMENT IN THE WORKPLACE / WATERMELON IN EASTER HAY** [–] ☐

May 88. (3"cd-s) *Rykodisc;* **ZOMBY WOOF / YOU DIDN'T TRY TO CALL ME** [–] ☐

May 88. (3"cd-s) *Rykodisc;* **MONTANA (WHIPPING FLOSS) / CHEEPNIS** [–] ☐

May 88. (d-cd) *Zappa; (CDZAP 8)* **YOU CAN'T DO THAT ON STAGE ANYMORE VOL.2** ☐ ☐
(re-iss. Jul95 on 'Rykodisc'; RCD 10561-62)

May 88. (cd) *E.M.I.; (CDP 790078-2)* **ZAPPA MEETS THE MOTHERS OF PREVENTION / JAZZ FROM HELL** ☐ [–]

Oct 88. (d-cd) *Zappa; (CDDZAP 9)* **YOU CAN'T DO THAT ON STAGE ANYMORE VOL.2** ☐ ☐
(re-iss. May95 on 'Rykodisc'; RCD 10563-64)

Dec 88. (d-cd) *Zappa; (CDZAP 13) / Rykodisc; <RCD 40024>* **WE'RE ONLY IN IT FOR THE MONEY / LUMPY GRAVY** ☐ ☐

Jan 89. (cd) *Zappa; (CDZAP 16)* **BABY SNAKES** (live 1977) ☐ ☐
(re-iss. May95 on 'Rykodisc'; RCD 10539)

Jan 90. (t-cd) *Zappa; (CDDZAP 20)* **JOE'S GARAGE ACT I / II / III** ☐ [–]

— FRANK decided to bootleg the bootleggers by releasing 10 best sellers that had fleeced him in the past. They were limited on 'Rhino'.

Apr 91. (d-cd/d-c) *Zappa; (CDDZAP/TZAPPA 38)* **THE BEST BAND YOU NEVER HEARD IN YOUR LIFE** (live 1988) ☐ ☐
(re-iss. May95 on 'Rykodisc'; RCD 10653-54)

Jun 91. (d-cd/d-c) *Zappa; (CDDZAP/TZAPA 41)* **MAKE A JAZZ NOISE HERE** (live 1988) ☐ ☐
(re-iss. d-cd May95 on 'Rykodisc'; RCD 10555-56)

Jun 91. (d-cd) *Zappa; (CDDZAP 17)* **YOU CAN'T DO THAT ON STAGE ANYMORE VOL.3** ☐ ☐
(re-iss. d-cd May95 on 'Rykodisc'; RCD 10565-66)

Jun 91. (d-cd/d-c) *Zappa; (CDDZAP/TZAPPA 40)* **YOU CAN'T DO THAT ON STAGE ANYMORE VOL.4** ☐ ☐
(re-iss. May95 on 'Rykodisc'; RCD 10567-68)
Note; below former bootleg releases on 'Essential-Zappa' UK/ 'Rykodisc' US. Released Aug91 as 'BEAT THE BOOTS' 10-lp box; *70907*

Sep 91. (cd) *(ESMCD 956) <70537>* **AS AN AM (live 1981)** ☐ ☐

Sep 91. (cd) *(ESMCD 957) <70538>* **THE ARK (live Boston 1968)** ☐ ☐

Sep 91. (cd) *(ESMCD 958) <70539>* **FREAKS & MOTHERFU*£'%!** ☐ ☐

Sep 91. (cd) *(ESMCD 959) <70540>* **UNMITAGATED AUDACITY** ☐ ☐

Sep 91. (d-cd) *(ESMCD 960) <70541>* **ANYWAY THE WIND BLOWS** ☐ ☐

Sep 91. (cd) *(ESMCD 961) <70542>* **'TIS THE SEASON TO BE JELLY** ☐ ☐

Sep 91. (cd) *(ESMCD 962) <70543>* **SAARBRUCKEN 1978** ☐ ☐

Sep 91. (cd) *(ESMCD 963) <70544>* **PIQUANTIQUE** ☐ ☐
(above 'Essential' releases of 1991 were re-iss. May97; same)

May 92. (cd) *Zappa; (CDZAP 49)* **BOULEZ CONDUCTS ZAPPA: THE PERFECT STRANGER** (Various Artists) ☐ ☐
(re-iss. May95 on 'Rykodisc'; RCD 10542)

Jul 92. (8xcd-box/7xc-box/11xlp-box) *Rykodisc; <R2/R4/R1 70372>* **BEAT THE BOOTS II** [–] ☐
– (DISCONNECTED SYNAPSES / TENGO NA MINCHIA TANTA / ELECTRIC AUNT JEMIMA / AT THE CIRCUS / SWISS CHEESE (double) / FIRE (double) / OUR MAN IN NIRVANA / CONCEPTUAL CONTINUITY)

Nov 92. (d-cd) *Zappa; (CDDZAP 55)* **PLAYGROUND PSYCHOTICS** (live 1971) ☐ ☐
(re-iss. May95 on 'Rykodisc'; RCD 10557-58)

Nov 92. (d-cd) *Zappa; (CDDZAP 46)* **YOU CAN'T DO THAT ON STAGE ANYMORE VOL.5** ☐ ☐
(re-iss. May95 on 'Rykodisc'; RCD 10569-70)

Nov 92. (d-cd) *Zappa; (CDDZAP* **YOU CAN'T DO THAT ON STAGE ANYMORE VOL.6** ☐ ☐
(re-iss. May95 on 'Rykodisc'; RCD 10571-72)

Mar 93. (cd) *Zappa; (CDZAP 51)* **AHEAD OF THEIR TIME** (live 1968) ☐ ☐
(re-iss. May95 on 'Rykodisc'; RCD 10559)

Jul 93. (12"/cd-s) *Zappa; (12/CD FRANK 102)* **VALLEY GIRLS. / YOU ARE WHAT YOU IS** ☐ ☐

Apr 95. (d-cd) *Rykodisc; (RCD 10540-41)* **LONDON SYMPHONY ORCHESTRA VOLUMES 1 & 2** ☐ ☐

May 95. (cd; w/mag) *Sonora;* **MAGAZINE & CD** ☐ ☐

Aug 95. (cd/c/d-lp) *Rykodisc; (RCD/RAC/RALP 40600)* **STRICTLY COMMERCIAL (THE BEST OF FRANK ZAPPA)** [45] ☐
– Peaches en regalia / Don't eat the yellow snow / Dancin' fool / San Ber'dino / Dirty love / My guitar wants to kill your mama / Cosmik debris / Trouble every day / Disco boy / Fine girl / Sexual harassment in the workplace / Let's make the water turn black / I'm the slime / Joe's garage / Bobby Brown goes down / Montana / Valley girl / Be in my video / Muffin man.

Feb 96. (cd/c) *Rykodisc; (RCD/RAC 40573)* **THE LOST EPISODES** ☐ ☐

Sep 96. (t-cd) *Rykodisc; (RCD 10574-75)* **LATHER** ☐ ☐

Apr 97. (cd) *Rykodisc; (RCD 10577)* **HAVE I OFFENDED SOMEONE?** ☐ [–]

Nov 99. (7"; as FRANK ZAPPA & JOHN TRUBEE) *Musical Tragedies; (efa 126047)* **LETTER FROM JEEPERS** ☐ [–]

☐ ZEE (see under ⇒ PINK FLOYD)

ZERO 7

Formed: North London, England . . . 1997 by HENRY BINNS and SAM HARDAKER. Both began working in a London studio making tea for producers and visiting artists. They watched engineers work the desks and soon picked up the procedures for recording, testing their trade with a few low-key remixes; RADIOHEAD's 'Climbing Up The Walls' and TERRY CALLIER's ' . . .Spartacus'. The duo assembled a collection of songs, issued in early 2000 as 'EP1'. The record sold its limited pressing of 1000 in days. With support from Radio One DJ GILLES PETERSON, the band issued the highly anticipated second EP, the aptly titled 'EP2'. This preceded their debut set, 'SIMPLE THINGS', in May 2001. The album boasted a light and breezy psychedelic take-on of jazz, funk and lounge, with inevitable comparisons to AIR, although the album came across more like a hybrid mix of GROOVE ARMADA, BOARDS OF CANADA and the loungey musings of JIM O'ROURKE's recent material, all backed by chilled-out beats and the occasional soaring female vocal. The record featured the Top 30 hit 'DESTINY' plus sophomore single 'IN THE WAITING LINE' and, as well as winning the Mercury Music Award, went gold in September 2001. The pair also remixed LAMBCHOP's immortal 'UP WITH PEOPLE', turning it from a choir-driven country/soul classic, to a sparkling laid-back summer anthem with looped guitars, horns and climbing cresendos over thick drawn-out beats. ZERO

7 weren't in any way "Britain's answer to AIR", nor were they the next generation's MASSIVE ATTACK, they simply were two very talented, like-minded producers whose futures were the next beat.

Album rating: SIMPLE THINGS (*8)

HENRY BINNS – electronics / **SAM HARDAKER** – electronics

		Zero 7	not iss.
Jan 00.	(12"ltd) **ZERO 7 EP** – Out of town / This world / Likufanele (Zero 7 remix) / Low / One arm break.	☐	–
		Ultimate Dilemma	Palm Pictures
Nov 00.	(12"ep/cd-ep) *(UDR/+CDS 040)* **ZERO 7 EP 2** – Give it away / Polaris / Distractions / Monday night.	☐	–

—— with also vocals from:- SIA FURLER, SOPHIE BARKER + MOZEZ

May 01.	(cd/lp) *(UDR CD/LP 016)* *<5007>* **SIMPLE THINGS** – I have seen / Polaris / Destiny / Give it away / Simple things / Red dust / Distractions / In the waiting line / Out of town / This world / Likufanele / End theme / Salt water sound / Spining.	28	Jun01 ☐
Jun 01.	(12"/cd-s) *(UDR/+CDS 041)* **I HAVE SEEN. / SALT WATER SOUND / SPINNING**	☐	–
Aug 01.	(12"/cd-s; by ZERO 7 featuring SIA & SOPHIE) *(UDR/+CDS 043)* **DESTINY. / DESTINY (Photek mix) / END THEME (Roni Size remix)** (cd-s) *(UDRCDSX 043)* – ('A'extended) / ('A'-Hefner's destiny chill mix) / ('A'-Simian remix).	30	–
Oct 01.	(ltd-12") *(UDR 042)* **END THEME (Roni Size tear it up remix). / END THEME (Roni Size tear it down remix)**	☐	–
Nov 01.	(12"/cd-s) *(UDR/+CDS 045)* **IN THE WAITING LINE. / IN THE WAITING LINE (Dorfmeister con Madrid de los Austrias dub) / SIMPLE THINGS (live)** (cd-s) *(UDRCDSX 045)* – ('A'-original) / This world / Likufanele.	47	–
Mar 02.	(12"/cd-s) *(UDR/+CDR 046)* **DISTRACTIONS (mixes; radio / Bugz in the attic / DJ Spinna)** (12"?cd-s) *(UDRX/+CDS 046)* – ('A'-mixes; radio / idjut / Madlib / Block 16).	45	–

Warren ZEVON

Born: 24 Jan'47, Chicago, Illinois, USA. The son of immigrant Russian parents, ZEVON was a classical music child prodigy. In time honoured fashion, however, he succumbed to the lure of rock after catching an earful of BOB DYLAN, his first break coming in 1969 when his song, 'HE QUIT ME MAN', was used on the classic 'Midnight Cowboy' soundtrack. A debut album, 'WANTED DEAD OR ALIVE' (1969) didn't perform quite so well and he returned to writing songs for other artists, TV jingles and some session piano work for The EVERLY BROTHERS. In 1976, ZEVON released a comeback album on 'Asylum', featuring such enduringly dark material as 'POOR POOR PITIFUL ME' (subsequently recorded by LINDA RONSTADT) and the heart-rending 'CARMELITA'. Produced by JACKSON BROWNE and featuring contributions from such West Coast luminaries as The EAGLES and the BUCKINGHAM/NICKS FLEETWOOD MAC axis, the record established ZEVON's L.A.-noir writing style and immediately marked him out from the navel-gazing songwriting pack. In 1978, he deservedly broke through when 'WEREWOLVES OF LONDON' hit the US Top 30 and the accompanying album, 'EXCITABLE BOY' reached the Top 10, another unsavoury trip through the back alleys of ZEVON's fevered muse which brought further comparisons with the twisted narratives of RANDY NEWMAN. A subsequent descent into alcohol abuse indicated that ZEVON's battle with his demons was intensifying and first album of the new decade, 'BAD LUCK STREAK IN DANCING SCHOOL' (1980) was heavy going to say the least. 'STAND IN THE FIRE' (1981) channelled all this frustrated energy into a blistering live set while 'THE ENVOY' (1982) found ZEVON in more reflective, world-weary wise mode. Still battling with the drink and stranded in the commercial wilderness, ZEVON's profile was given a bit of a boost via the HINDU LOVE GODS single, a project which saw the man hooking up with R.E.M.'s PETER BUCK, BILL BERRY and MIKE MILLS. Cleaned up and armed with a new contract ('Virgin America'), he released the rocking 'SENTIMENTAL HYGIENE' (1987). With the R.E.M trio again lending a hand alongside stalwarts like NEIL YOUNG and BOB DYLAN, ZEVON turned in a hard-bitten set born of hard-won conviction ('DETOX MANSION' said it all). Yet ZEVON seemed doomed to commercial oblivion, his cause not helped any by the dense, pseudo concept effort, 'TRANSVERSE CITY' (1990). Entering the 90's with an expired 'Virgin' contract, ZEVON reunited with The HINDU LOVE GODS, signed to 'Giant' records and released an eponymously titled, sporadically enjoyable album of covers including a fine version of Prince's 'RASPBERRY BERET'. The following year's solo set, 'MR. BAD EXAMPLE', found ZEVON in comfortingly indignant mood and as far from mainstream acknowledgement as ever. He nevertheless commands a diehard band of admirers, the kind of rock solid fanbase which allowed the man to sign yet another major label deal in the mid-90's, this time for 'R.C.A.' The resulting 'MUTINEER' was relatively laid-back, suggesting that the L.A. firebrand (now in his 50's) is approaching old age with at least some kind of contentment. The millennial release from the master of sharp-eyed sardonica, 'LIFE'LL KILL YA' (2000) found ZEVON's worldview as reassuringly ironic as ever, a cover of Steve Winwood's 'BACK IN THE HIGH LIFE AGAIN' summing up the L.A. minstrel's ability to reflect life through his own curiously refracted lens. 2002's 'MY RIDE'S HERE' wasn't quite so incisive, with its cast of literary collaborators – including the novelist Carl Hiaasen, legendary journo Hunter S. Thompson and even David Letterman – often serving to detract from the strength of the writing rather than adding to it. Shortly after the record's release, ZEVON was diagnosed with a severe form of lung cancer and told he he had only months to live. As single-minded as ever, the singer set about filling his remaining time with a last album. Boasting a credits list that reads like a roll-call of classic American rock – with the likes of RY COODER, DON HENLEY, JACKSON BROWNE, BRUCE SPRINGSTEEN, TOM PETTY, EMMYLOU HARRIS and T-BONE BURNETT guesting amongst others – 'THE WIND' (2003) was an epitaph every bit as cynical, emotionally raw and unrepentant as he would presumably have wanted it. Even the poignant cover of Bob Dylan's 'KNOCKIN' ON HEAVEN'S DOOR' bore no trace of regret or self-pity. Sadly, WARREN ZEVON died on 7th September 2003, a matter of weeks after the album's release. • **Covered:** JESUS WAS A CROSS MAKER (Judy Sill).

Album rating: WANTED – DEAD OR ALIVE (*4) / WARREN ZEVON (*7) / EXCITABLE BOY (*6) / BAD LUCK STREAK IN DANCING SCHOOL (*5) / STAND IN THE FIRE (*5) / THE ENVOY (*6) / A QUIET NORMAL LIFE – THE BEST OF WARREN ZEVON compilation (*8) / SENTIMENTAL HYGIENE (*7) / TRANSVERSE CITY (*6) / MR. BAD EXAMPLE (*5) / LEARNING TO FLINCH (*6) / MUTINEER (*5) / LIFE'LL KILL YA (*4) / MY RIDE'S HERE (*4) / THE WIND (*8)

WARREN ZEVON – vocals, piano + sessioners

		Liberty	Imperial
1969.	(lp) *(LBS 83357)* **WANTED – DEAD OR ALIVE** – Wanted dead or alive / Hitchhikin' woman / She quit me / Calcutta / Iko-Iko / Traveling in the lightning / Tule's blues / A bullet for Ramona / Gorilla / Fiery emblems.	☐	☐

—— semi-retired into jingle-land and sessions.

Asylum Asylum

Jun 76. (lp/c) *(K/K4 52039)* *<1060>* **WARREN ZEVON** [ ] [ ]
– Frank and Jesse James / Mama couldn't be persuaded / Backs turned looking down the path / Hasten down the wind / Poor poor pitiful me / The French inhaler / Mohammed's radio / I'll sleep when I'm dead / Carmelita / Join me in L.A. / Desperados under the eaves.

Aug 76. (7") *<45356>* **HASTEN DOWN THE WIND. / MOHAMMED'S RADIO** [–] [ ]

Oct 76. (7") *(K 13060)* **I'LL SLEEP WHEN I'M DEAD. / MOHAMMED'S RADIO** [ ] [–]

Oct 77. (7") *(K 13111)* **WEREWOLVES OF LONDON. / TENDERNESS ON THE BLOCK** [ ] [–]

Feb 78. (lp/c) *(K/K4 53073)* *<118>* **EXCITABLE BOY** [ ] [8]
– Johnny strikes up the band / Roland the headless Thompson gunner / Excitable boy / Werewolves of London / Accidently like a martyr / Nighttime in the switching yard / Veracruz / Tenderness on the block / Lawyers, guns and money. *(re-iss. cd/c Sep95 on 'Warners'; 7559 60521-2/-4)*

Mar 78. (7"/12"pic-d) *<45472>* **WEREWOLVES OF LONDON. / ROLAND THE HEADLESS THOMPSON GUNNER** [–] [21]

May 78. (7") *(K 13124)* **NIGHTTIME IN THE SWITCHING YARD. / ROLAND THE HEADLESS THOMPSON GUNNER** [ ] [–]

May 78. (7") *<45498>* **LAWYERS, GUNS AND MONEY. / VERACRUZ** [–] [ ]

Aug 78. (7") *<45526>* **NIGHTTIME IN THE SWITCHING BOARD. / JOHNNY STRIKES UP THE BAND** [–] [ ]

Oct 78. (7") *(K 13140)* **EXCITABLE BOY. / VERACRUZ** [ ] [–]

Feb 80. (7") *(K 12431)* **GORILLA, YOU'RE A DESPERADO. / EMPTY-HANDED HEART** [ ] [–]

Feb 80. (lp/c) *(K/K4 52191)* *<509>* **BAD LUCK STREAK IN DANCING SCHOOL** [ ] [20]
– Bad luck streak in dancing school / A certain girl / Jungle work / Empty-handed heart / Interlude No.1 / Play it all night long / Jeannie needs a shooter / Interlude No.2 / Bill Lee / Gorilla, you're a desperado / Bed of coals / Wild age. *(cd-iss. Sep95; 7559 60561-2)*

Mar 80. (7") *<46610>* **A CERTAIN GIRL. / EMPTY-HANDED HEART** [–] [57]

May 80. (7") *(K 12437)* **A CERTAIN GIRL. / JUNGLE WORK** [ ] [–]

Jul 80. (7") *(K 12464)* **JEANNIE NEEDS A SHOOTER. / INTERLUDE No.2** [ ] [–]

Jan 81. (lp/c) *(K/K4 52265)* *<519>* **STAND IN THE FIRE (live)** [ ] [80]
– Stand in the fire / Jeannie needs a shooter / Excitable boy / Mohammed's radio / Werewolves of London / Lawyers, guns and money / The sin / Poor poor pitiful me / I'll sleep when I'm dead / Bo Diddley's a gunslinger – Bo Diddley.

Jan 81. (7") *<47118>* **LAWYERS, GUNS AND MONEY (live). / DOWN ON MY LUCK** [–] [ ]

Aug 82. (7") *(K 13193)* *<69946>* **LET NOTHING COME BETWEEN US. / THE HULA HULA BOYS** [ ] [ ]

Aug 82. (lp/c) *(K/K4 53073)* *<60159>* **THE ENVOY** [ ] [93]
– The envoy / The overdraft / The hula hula boys / Jesus mentioned / Let nothing come between you / Ain't that pretty at all / Charlie's medicine / Looking for the next best thing / Never too late for love.

Nov 86. (lp/c)(cd) *(WX 81/+C)(960503-2)* **A QUIET NORMAL LIFE – THE BEST OF WARREN ZEVON** (compilation) [ ] [–]
– Werewolves of London / Play it all night long / Roland the headless Thompson gunner / The envoy / Mohammed's radio (live) / Desperados under the eaves / I'll sleep when I'm dead / Lawyers, guns and money / Ain't that pretty at all / Poor poor pitiful me / Accidentally like a martyr / Looking for the next big thing.

Elektra Elektra

Mar 87. (7") *(EKR 52)* **WEREWOLVES OF LONDON. / JESUS MENTIONED** [ ] [ ]
(12"+=) *(EKRT 52)* – Poor, poor pitiful me.

—— next album feat R.E.M. minus STIPE

Virgin America Virgin

Jun 87. (7") *(VS 976)* **LEAVE MY MONKEY ALONE. / NOCTURNE** [ ] [ ]
(12"+=/cd-s+=) *(VS T/CD 976)* – ('A'Latin version). *<US; b-side>*

Jun 87. (cd/c/lp) *(CD/TC+/V 2433)* *<90603>* **SENTIMENTAL HYGIENE** [ ] [63]
– Sentimental hygiene / Boom boom Mancini / The factory / Trouble waiting to happen / Reconsider me / Detox mansion / Bad karma / Even a dog can shake hands / The heartache / Leave my monkey alone. *(cd re-iss. Mar91; same)*

Jul 87. (7") *(VS 995)* **SENTIMENTAL HYGIENE. / THE FACTORY** [ ] [–]
(12"+=) *(VST 995)* – Leave my monkey alone.

Oct 87. (7") *(VS 1021)* **BAD KARMA. / BOOM BOOM MANCINI** [ ] [–]
(12"+=) *(VST 1021)* – Leave my monkey alone.

Feb 88. (7") *(VS 1055)* **RECONSIDER ME. / THE FACTORY** [ ] [ ]
(12"+=) *(VST 1055)* – Bad karma.

—— next featured **NEIL YOUNG, RITCHIE HAYWARD, JERRY GARCIA, BOBBY TENCH, DAVID GILMOUR,** etc.

Jan 90. (cd/c/lp) *(CDVUS/VUSMC/VUSLP 9)* *<91068>* **TRANSVERSE CITY** [ ] Oct89 [ ]
– Transverse city / Run straight down / The long arm of the law / Turbulence / They moved the Moon / Splendid isolation / Networking / Gridlock / Down in the mall / Nobody's in love this year.

Jan 90. (7") **SPLENDID ISOLATION. / EVEN A DOG CAN SHAKE HANDS** [ ] [ ]
(12"+=/cd-s+=) – Bad karma / Gridlock.

—— Later 1990, he provided vox for HINDU LOVE GODS splinter band of R.E.M. ⇒

Giant Giant

Nov 91. (cd/c) *<(7599 24431-2/-4)>* **MR. BAD EXAMPLE** [ ] [ ]
– Finishing touches / Susie Lightning / Model citizen / Angel dressed in black / Mr. Bad example / Renegade / Heartache spoken here / Quite ugly one morning / Things to do in Denver / Searching for a heart.

Oct 93. (cd/c) *<(7599 24493-2/-4)>* **LEARNING TO FLINCH** [ ] [ ]
– Splendid isolation / Lawyer's, guns & money / Mr.Bad example / Excitable boy / Hasten down the wind / The French inhaler / Warrior king / Roland chorale / Roland the headless Thompson gunner / Searching for a heart / Boom boom Mancini / Jungle work / Piano fighter / Werewolves of London / The indifference of Heaven / Poor poor pitiful me / Play it all night long.

R.C.A. R.C.A.

Jul 95. (cd) *<(74321 27685-2)>* **MUTINEER** [ ] [ ]
– Seminole bingo / Something bad hapened to a clown / Similar to rain / The indifference of Heaven / Jesus was a cross maker / Poisonous lookalike / Piano fighter / Rottweiler blues / Monkey wash donkey rinse / Mutineer.

Artemis Artemis

Jan 00. (cd) *<(497629-2)>* **LIFE'LL KILL YA** [ ] [ ]
– I was in the house when the house burned down / Life'll kill ya / Porcelain monkey / For my next trick I'll need a volunteer / I'll slow you down / Hostage-o / Dirty little religion / Back in the high life again / My shit's fucked up / Fistful of rain / Ourselves to know / Don't let us get sick. *<(re-iss. Nov03 on 'Rykodisc'; RCD 17007)>*

Mar 01. (cd-s) *<751069>* **HIT SOMEBODY (THE HOCKEY SONG) / FOR MY NEXT TRICK I'LL NEED A VOLUNTEER** [–] [ ]

Epic Artemis

May 02. (cd) *(507838-2)* *<751124>* **MY RIDE'S HERE** [ ] [ ]
– Sacrificial lambs / Basket case / Lord Byron's luggage / Macgillycuddy's reeks / You're a whole different person when . . .. / Hit somebody! (the hockey song) / Genius / Laissez-moi tranquille / I have to leave / My ride's here. *<(re-iss. Nov03 on 'Rykodisc'; RCD 17008)>*

Rykodisc Artemis

Sep 03. (cd) *(RCD 17001)* *<51156>* **THE WIND** [57] Aug03 [12]
– Dirty life and times / Disorder in the house / Knockin' on Heaven's door / Numb as a statue / She's too good for me / Prison grove / El amor de mi vida / The rest of the night / Please stay / Rub me raw / Keep me in your heart.

—— tragically, ZEVON died on the 7th September, 2003

– compilations, etc. –

Sep 96. (d-cd) *Rhino;* *<73510>* **I'LL SLEEP WHEN I'M DEAD: AN ANTHOLOGY** [–] [ ]

☐ Rob ZOMBIE (see under ⇒ WHITE ZOMBIE)

ZOMBIES

Formed: St. Albans, England . . . 1963 by ROD ARGENT, COLIN BLUNSTONE, HUGH GRUNDY and PAUL ATKINSON. In early 1964, after winning a local band competition, they signed to 'Decca' and soon had a massive worldwide hit with the classic 'SHE'S NOT THERE'. With its distinctive churning organ and portentous overtones, the single instantly marked the band out from the rest of the Brit-Beat pack, especially in America where the song climbed to No.2. The equally classy 'TELL HER NO', again reaped success across the Atlantic but strangely stiffed in the UK. Despite a fine debut album, 'BEGIN HERE' (1965) and a string of well-crafted singles, the band met with zero success in the UK and even their early success in America wasn't repeated. 'Decca' duly declined to renew their contract and they signed to 'C.B.S.' in 1967. Although The ZOMBIES split in frustration before its release, 'ODESSEY AND ORACLE' (deliberate spelling mistake!) was their masterstroke. A concept album of sorts, the record boasted an exquisitely arranged combination of sublime harmonies and jazz-inflected instrumentation, BLUNSTONE's unmistakable high vocals floating overhead. Though the album barely scraped into the top 100, it was an ironic twist of fate when the compelling 'TIME OF THE SEASON' single became an American million seller. The band reformed briefly (minus BLUNSTONE and WHITE) and released a couple of singles without success, ARGENT going on to form, funnily enough, ARGENT, while BLUNSTONE carved out a fairly successful solo career. • **Songwriters:** ARGENT-WHITE penned, except for the ubiquitous covers; GOT MY MOJO WORKING (Muddy Waters) / YOU'VE REALLY GOT A HOLD ON ME (Smokey Robinson) / ROADRUNNER (Bo Diddley) / SUMMERTIME (Gershwin) / GOIN' OUT OF MY HEAD (Little Anthony & The Imperials) / etc. • **Trivia:** Early in 1966, they made a cameo appearance in the film, 'Bunny Lake Is Missing'. They were known as the most intelligent pop group of the mid-60's, after leaving school with over fifty 'O' and 'A' levels between them.

Album rating: BEGIN HERE (*6) / ODESSEY & ORACLE (*8) / NEW WORLD (*3) / THE BEST OF THE ZOMBIES compilation (*8)

COLIN BLUNSTONE (b.24 Jun'45, Hatfield, England) – vocals / **ROD ARGENT** (b.14 Jun'45, St.Albans) – piano, keyboards, vocals / **PAUL ATKINSON** (b.19 Mar'46, Cuffley, England) – guitar / **CHRIS WHITE** (b. 7 Mar'43, Barnet, England) – bass repl. PAUL ARNOLD / **HUGH GRUNDY** (b. 6 Mar'45, Winchester, England) – drums

Decca — Parrot

Jul 64. (7") *(F 11940)* <9695> **SHE'S NOT THERE. / YOU MAKE ME FEEL GOOD** — 12 — Oct64 2

Oct 64. (7") *(F 12004)* **LEAVE ME BE. / WOMAN** — — –

Jan 65. (7") *(F 12072)* <9723> **TELL HER NO. / WHAT MORE CAN I DO** — 42 — 6

Mar 65. (7") *(F 12125)* <9747> **SHE'S COMING HOME. / I MUST MOVE** — — 58

Apr 65. (lp) *(LK 4679)* <7001> **BEGIN HERE** <US-title 'THE ZOMBIES'> — — Feb65 39
– Roadrunner / Summertime / I can't make up my mind / The way I feel inside / Work 'n' play / You've really got a hold on me / She's not there / Sticks and stones / Can't nobody love you / Woman / I don't want to know / I remember when I loved her / What more can I do / I got my mojo working. *(re-iss. Nov84; DOA 4) (re-iss. Jul86 on 'See For Miles' US version) (cd-iss. Aug92 & May01 on 'Repertoire'+=; REP 4939)* – You make me feel good / Leave me be / Tell her no / She's coming home / I must move / Kind of girl / It's alright with me / Sometimes / Whenever you're ready / I love you / Is this the dream / Don't go away / Remember you / Just out of reach / Indication / How we were before / I'm going home. *(cd re-iss. Apr99 on 'Big Beat'; CDWIKD 191)*

Jun 65. (7") <9769> **I WANT YOU BACK AGAIN. / ONCE UPON A TIME** — – — 95

Sep 65. (7") *(F 12225)* <9786> **WHENEVER YOU'RE READY. / I LOVE HER** — —

Nov 65. (7") *(F 12296)* <9821> **IS THIS A DREAM. / DON'T GO AWAY** — — Apr66

Jan 66. (7") *(F 12322)* <9797> **REMEMBER YOU. / JUST OUT OF REACH** — —

Jun 66. (7") *(F 12426)* <3004> **INDICATION. / HOW WE WERE BEFORE** — —

Nov 66. (7") *(F 12495)* **GOTTA GET A HOLD ON MYSELF. / THE WAY I FEEL INSIDE** — — –

Mar 67. (7") *(F 12584)* **GOIN' OUT OF MY HEAD. / SHE DOES EVERYTHING FOR ME** — — –

May 67. (7") *(F 12798)* **I LOVE YOU. / THE WAY I FEEL INSIDE** — — –

C.B.S. — Columbia

Sep 67. (7") *(2960)* **FRIENDS OF MINE. / BEECHWOOD PARK** — — –

Nov 67. (7") *(3087)* <44363> **CARE OF CELL 44. / MAYBE AFTER HE'S GONE** — —
(re-iss. Mar74 on 'Epic';)

—— disbanded late '67; posthumous release below resurrected group in '69

C.B.S. — Date

Apr 68. (lp; stereo/mono) *(S+/BPG 63280)* <4013> **ODYSSEY AND ORACLE** — — Mar69 95
– Care of Cell 44 / A rose for Emily / Maybe after he's gone / Beechwood park / Brief candles / Hung up on a dream / Changes / I want her she wants me / This will be our year / Butcher's tale (Western Front 1914) / Friends of mine / Time of the season. *(re-iss. Dec86 on 'Razor';) (cd-iss. Aug92 & Sep02 on 'Repertoire'+=; REP 4940)* – I call you mine / She loves the way they love her / Imagine the swan / Smokey day / If it don't work out / I know she will / Don't cry for me / Walking in the sun / Conversation off Floral Street / I want you back again / Gotta get hold of myself / Goin' out of my head / She does everything for me / Nothing's changed / I could spend the day / Girl help me. *(re-iss. Apr98 on 'Big Beat' cd/lp; CD+/WIKD 181)*

Apr 68. (7") *(3380)* <1604> **TIME OF THE SEASON. / I'LL CALL YOU MINE** — —

Jul 68. (7") <1612> **THIS WILL BE OUR YEAR. / BUTCHERS TALE (WESTERN FRONT 1914)** — – —

Feb 69. (7") <1628> **TIME OF THE SEASON. / FRIENDS OF MINE** — – — 3

—— (Mar'69) With them riding high in US Top 3, they decided to re-form but without BLUNSTONE (who went solo) / WHITE (who went into producing) + ATKINSON. ARGENT + GRUNDY recruited **RICK BIRKETT** – guitar / **JIM RODFORD** – bass

May 69. (7") <1644> **IMAGINE THE SWAN. / CONVERSATIONS OF FLORAL STREET** — – —

Jul 69. (7") <1648> **IF IT DON'T WORK OUT. / DON'T CRY FOR ME** — – —

—— Didn't last long, when ROD and JIM decided to form ARGENT. The ZOMBIES reformed for one-off in the early 90's

Essential — not iss.

Apr 91. (cd/c/lp) *(ESS CD/MC/LP 131)* **NEW WORLD** — — –
– New world (my America) / Love breaks down / I can't be wrong / Lula Lula / Heaven's gate / Time of the season / Moonday morning dance / Blue / Losing you / Alone in Paradise / Knowing you / Love conquers all / Nights on fire. *(cd re-iss. Jun94 on 'Castle'; CLACD 348) (cd re-iss. Aug03 on 'Ace'; CDWIKM 234)*

– (selective) compilations, etc. –

Feb 86. (lp) *Rhino; (RNLP 120)* **LIVE ON THE BBC 1965-67 (live)** — — –

Sep 87. (lp/c) *See For Miles; (SEE/K 30)* **THE SINGLES A's & B's** — — –
(cd-iss. Sep88 & May97; SEECD 30)

Aug 88. (d-lp/c/cd) *Castle; (CCS LP/MC/CD 196)* **THE COLLECTION** — — –
– Goin' out of my head / Leave me be / Gotta get a hold on myself / I can't make up my mind / Kind of girl / Sticks and stones / Summertime / Woman / I got my mojo working / Roadrunner / You really got a hold on me / Nothing's changed / You make me feel good / She's not there / Don't go away / How we were before / Tell her no / Whenever you're ready / Just out of reach / Remember you / Indication / She does everything for me / Time of the season / I love you.

Feb 91. (cd/c) *Music Club; (MC CD/TC 002)* **BEST OF THE ZOMBIES** — — –

Jul 91. (3xcd-box) *Razor; (RAZCDBOX 1)* **THE ZOMBIES** ☐ -
Nov 92. (cd) *See For Miles; (SEECD 358)* **THE EP COLLECTION** ☐ -
Feb 95. (cd/c) *More Music; (MO CD/MC 3009)* **THE ZOMBIES 1964-67** ☐ -
Apr 96. (cd) *Disky; (DC 86272-2)* **THE ZOMBIES** ☐ ☐
Nov 97. (4xcd-box) *Big Beat; (ZOMBOX 7)* **ZOMBIE HEAVEN** ☐ ☐
Jul 99. (cd) *Varese Sarabande; (VSD 1039)* **ABSOLUTELY THE BEST** ☐ ☐
Jan 00. (cd) *Chiswick; (CDWIKD 200)* **THE SINGLES** ☐ ☐
Apr 00. (cd) *Disky; (SI 99076-2)* **THE BEST OF THE SIXTIES** ☐ ☐
Sep 02. (d-cd) *Repertoire; (REP 4985)* **SINGLES A'S AND B'S** ☐ ☐
Nov 02. (d-cd) *Big Beat; (CDWIK2 225)* **THE DECCA STEREO ANTHOLOGY** ☐ ☐
Mar 03. (cd) *Disky; (EMI 760160)* **THE STORY OF THE ZOMBIES** ☐ ☐
Apr 03. (cd) *Repertoire; (REP 4790)* **LIVE AT THE BBC** ☐ ☐

☐ ZWAN (see under ⇒ SMASHING PUMPKINS)

ZZ TOP

Formed: Houston, Texas, USA . . . as garage band, THE MOVING SIDEWALKS by BILLY GIBBONS, the now infamous trio/line-up finally emerging in 1970 with the addition of DUSTY HILL and FRANK BEARD. Having initially released a debut single on manager Billy Ham's new 'Scat' label (prior to the arrival of messrs. BEARD and HILL), ZZ TOP subsequently secured a deal with 'London' records. 'FIRST ALBUM' appeared in 1971, its stark title matching the raw simplicity of the southern blues/boogie contained within the grooves. This straightforward approach also extended to the group's music biz masterplan; ZZ TOP were first and foremost a live band, their punishing touring schedule, largely in the American South initially, would eventually turn grassroots support into record sales as well as honing their musical skills for future glories. A follow-up set, 'RIO GRANDE MUD' (1972) spawned the group's first (US) hit single in 'FRANCENE' although ZZ TOP only really began to make an impact with 1973's 'TRES HOMBRES'. Occasionally reminiscent of 'EXILE . . .'-era 'STONES (see the the smokin' 'LA GRANGE' single), the group had begun to perfect their combination of boot-leather riffing and Texas blues drawl, GIBBONS' nifty axe-work oiling the beast nicely (he'd previously drawn public praise from none other than JIMI HENDRIX). By 1976, the group were popular enough to take their 'Wordwide Texas Tour' on the road, a mammoth operation which certainly equalled The ROLLING STONES in terms of stage set and ticket sales, ZZ TOP now one of America's biggest grossing homegrown acts. The classic 70's grind of 'TUSH' was the group's highest charting single of the decade (Top 20 in '75), although ZZ TOP didn't really garner widespread critical acclaim until the release of 'DEGUELLO' in 1979, their first album for 'Warners'. The record's gristly blues licks and knowing, often surreal sense of humour demonstrating that ZZ TOP were considerably more sussed than the backwoods caricatures which they were often portrayed as (a perception which they often perpetuated), the deadpan 'CHEAP SUNGLASSES' a blistering cover of ELMORE JAMES' 'DUST MY BROOM' and a version of Isaac Hayes' 'I THANK YOU' proving highlights. 'EL LOCO' (1981) was almost as good, the boys insisting that what a woman really wanted was, ahem . . . a 'PEARL NECKLACE'. The tongue-in-cheek smut only really got underway with 'ELIMINATOR' (1983), however, the gleaming videos for the likes of the pounding 'GIMME ALL YOUR LOVIN'', 'SHARP DRESSED MAN' and of course, 'LEGS', featuring more leggy lovelies than a ROBERT PALMER video. These MTV staples also introduced ZZ TOP's famous red Ford coupe, the fearsome motor becoming as much of an 80's icon as FRANKIE GOES TO HOLLYWOOD t-shirts. Musically, the album was almost a complete departure, turbo-charging the guitars way up in the mix and boosting the overall sound with a synthesized throb. This trademark electro-boogie would see ZZ TOP through the best part of a decade. Deservedly, the record was a massive worldwide success, a multi-million seller which marked the first instalment in a three-album semi-concept affair, built around the 'Eliminator' car. For 'AFTERBURNER' (1985), the car, don't laugh!, had turned into a space rocket flying high above the earth although it seemed as if they'd also jettisoned the cocksure stomp of old. 'SLEEPING BAG' and 'VELCRO FLY' were competent enough, the videos ensuring another MTV bonanza and healthy sales. 'RECYCLER' (1990) continued in much the same vein, although relatively poor sales subsequently saw the group parting with 'Warners' and starting afresh with 'R.C.A.'. Never the most prolific band, ZZ TOP only released a further four albums in the 90's, the compilation 'ZZ TOP GREATEST HITS' (1992; and including 'VIVA LAS VEGAS' made famous by Elvis), 'ANTENNA' (1994), 'RHYTHMEEN' (1996) and 'XXX' (1999), at last abandoning their outdated 80's sound in favour of a leaner, meaner return to their roots. The 'TOP strode boldly into the new millennium with 'MESCALERO' (2003), not quite the ever anticipated return to tequila-swilling cross-border boogie which its title suggested but at least another tentative step in the right direction. They mightn't sell as many records these days but they've still got beards (save FRANK BEARD, that is!) as long and grizzly as a DEEP PURPLE guitar solo, and that's what counts! • **Songwriters:** Group penned (plus some early with manager BILL HAM) except; FRANCINE (trad.) / JAILHOUSE ROCK (hit; Elvis Presley)

Album rating: FIRST ALBUM (*6) / RIO GRANDE MUD (*6) / TRES HOMBRES (*8) / FANDANGO (*7) / TEJAS (*6) / THE BEST OF ZZ TOP compilation (*8) / DEGUELLO (*8) / EL LOCO (*6) / ELIMINATOR (*8) / AFTERBURNER (*6) / RECYCLER (*5) / ZZ TOP'S GREATEST HITS compilation (*9) / ANTENNA (*5) / ONE FOOT IN THE BLUES collection (*4) / RHYTHMEEN (*4) / XXX (*3) / MESCALERO (*4)

MOVING SIDEWALKS

BILLY GIBBONS (b.12 Dec'49) – vocals, guitar / **TOM MOORE** – keyboards / **DON SUMMERS** – bass / **DAN MITCHELL** – drums

not iss. Tantara

1967. (7") <3101> **99th FLOOR. / WHAT ARE YOU GOING TO DO?** - ☐
<re-iss. 1967 on 'Wand'; 1156>

not iss. Wand

1967. (7") <1167> **NEED ME. / EVERY NIGHT A NEW SURPRISE** - ☐
<above tracks were re-iss. 1980 as EP on 'Moxie'; 1030>

— **LANIER GREIG** – keyboards repl. MOORE

not iss. Tantara

1968. (7") <3108> **I WANT TO HOLD YOUR HAND. / JOE BLUES** - ☐
1968. (lp) <6919> **FLASH** - ☐
– Flashback / Crimson witch / Pluto – Sept.31 / Eclipse / Scoun da be / No good to cry / You don't know the life / You make me shake / Reclipse.
1969. (7") <3113> **FLASHBACK. / NO GOOD TO CRY** - ☐

ZZ TOP

(GIBBONS, MITCHELL & GREIG)

not iss. Scat

1970. (7") <45-500> **SALT LICK. / MILLER'S FARM** - ☐
<re-iss. later 1970 on 'London'; 45-131>

— **GIBBONS** now sole survivor when LANIER and DAN departed. Newcomers were **DUSTY HILL** (b.JOE, 1949) – bass, vocals (ex-WARLOCKS, ex-AMERICAN BLUES) / **FRANK BEARD** (b.10 Dec'49) – drums (ex-CELLAR DWELLARS)

London London

Jan 71. (lp) *<PS 584>* **FIRST ALBUM** [–] [ ]
– (Somebody else been) Shaking your tree / Brown sugar / Squank / Goin' down to Mexico / Old man / Neighbor, neighbor / Certified blues / Bedroom thang / Just got back from baby's / Backdoor love affair. *<re-iss. 1980 on 'Warners'; WB 3268> (UK-iss.Sep84 on 'Warners' lp/c; K/K4 56601) (cd-iss. Jan87; K2 56601)*

Feb 71. (7") *<45-138>* **(SOMEBODY ELSE BEEN) SHAKING YOUR TREE. / NEIGHBOR, NEIGHBOR** [–] [ ]

May 72. (7") *<45-179>* **FRANCENE. / FRANCENE (Spanish)** [–] [69]

Jul 72. (lp) *(SHU 8433) <PS 612>* **RIO GRANDE MUD** [ ] Apr72 [ ]
– Francene / Just got paid / Mushmouth shoutin' / Ko ko blue / Chevrolet / Apologies to Pearly / Bar-b-q / Sure got cold after the rain fell / Whiskey'n mama / Down Brownie. *<US re-iss. 1980 on 'Warners'; BSK 3269> (re-iss. Sep84 on 'Warners' lp/c; K/K4 56602) (cd-iss. Jan87; K2 56602) (cd re-iss. Mar94 on 'Warners'; 7599 27380-2)*

Jul 72. (7") *(HLU 10376)* **FRANCENE. / DOWN BROWNIE** [ ] [–]

Nov 73. (lp) *(SHU 8459) <PS 631>* **TRES HOMBRES** [ ] Aug73 [8]
– Waitin' for the bus / Jesus just left Chicago / Beer drinkers & Hell raisers / Master of sparks / Hot, blue and righteous / Move me on down the line / Precious and Grace / La Grange / Sheik / Have you heard?. *<US re-iss. 1980 on 'Warners'; BSK 3270> (re-iss. Nov83 on 'Warners' lp/c; K/K4 56603)*

Jun 74. (7") *(HLU 10458)* **BEER DRINKERS & HELL RAISERS. / LA GRANGE** [ ] [–]

Jan 75. (7") *(HLU 10475) <45-179>* **LA GRANGE. / JUST GOT PAID** [ ] Mar74 [41]

Jun 75. (lp) *(SH 8482) <PS 656>* **FANDANGO! (live Warehouse, New Orleans + studio)** [60] May75 [10]
– Thunderbird / Jailhouse rock / Back door medley: Backdoor love affair – Mellow down easy – Backdoor love affair No.2 – Long distance boogie / Nasty dogs and funky kings / Blue jean blues / Balinese / Mexican blackbird / Heard it on the X / Tush. *<US re-iss. 1980 on 'Warners'; BSK 3271> (re-iss. Nov83 on 'Warners' lp/c; K/K4 56604) (cd-iss. Jan87; K2 56604)*

Jul 75. (7") *(HLU 10495) <5N-220>* **TUSH. / BLUE JEAN BLUES** [ ] [20]

Aug 76. (7") *(HLU 10538) <5N-241>* **IT'S ONLY LOVE. / ASLEEP IN THE DESERT** [ ] [44]

Feb 77. (lp) *(LDU 1) <PS 680>* **TEJAS** [ ] Jan77 [17]
– It's only love / Arrested for driving while blind / El Diablo / Snappy kakkie / Enjoy and get it on / Ten dollar man / Pan Am highway blues / Avalon hideaway / She's a heartbreaker / Asleep in the desert. *<US re-iss. 1980 on 'Warners'; BSK 3272> (re-iss. Sep84 on 'Warners' lp/c; K/K4 56605) (cd-iss. Mar87; K2 56605) (cd re-iss. Mar94 on 'Warners'; 7599 27383-2)*

Mar 77. (7") *<5N-251>* **ARRESTED FOR DRIVING WHILE BLIND. / IT'S ONLY LOVE** [–] [91]

Apr 77. (7") *(HLU 10547)* **ARRESTED FOR DRIVING WHILE BLIND. / NEIGHBOUR, NEIGHBOUR** [ ] [–]

May 77. (7") *<5N-252>* **EL DIABLO. / ENJOY AND GET IT ON** [–] [ ]

Dec 77. (lp) *<PS 706>* **THE BEST OF ZZ TOP** (compilation) [–] [94]
– Tush / Waitin' for the bus / Jesus just left Chicago / Francene / Just got paid / La grange / Blue jean blues / Backdoor love affair / Beer drinkers and Hell raisers / Heard it on the X. *<re-iss. 1980 on 'Warners'; BSK 3273> (UK-iss.Dec83 on 'Warners' lp/c; K/K4 56598) cd-iss. Jan86; K2 56598)*

Warners Warners

Dec 79. (lp/c) *(K/K4 56701) <HS 3361>* **DEGUELLO** [ ] Nov79 [24]
– I thank you / She loves my automobile / I'm bad, I'm nationwide / A fool for your stockings / Manic mechanic / Dust my broom / Lowdown in the street / Hi fi mama / Cheap sunglasses / Esther be the one. *(re-iss. Jan85 lp/cd; same/K2 56701) (re-iss. Mar94 on 'Warners' cd/c; K2/K4 56701)*

Mar 80. (7") *(K 17516) <WB 49163>* **I THANK YOU. / A FOOL FOR YOUR STOCKINGS** [ ] Jan80 [34]

Jun 80. (7") *<WB 49220>* **CHEAP SUNGLASSES. / ('A'live)** [–] [89]

Jun 80. (7") *(K 17647)* **CHEAP SUNGLASSES. / ESTHER BE THE ONE** [ ] [–]

Jul 81. (7") *<WB 49782>* **LEILA. / DON'T TEASE ME** [–] [77]

Jul 81. (lp/c) *(K/K4 56929) <BSK 3593>* **EL LOCO** [88] [17]
– Tube snake boogie / I wanna drive you home / Ten foot pole / Leila / Don't tease me / It's so hard / Pearl necklace / Groovy little hippy pad / Heaven, Hell or Houston / Party on the patio. *(cd-iss. Mar87; K2 56929) (cd re-iss. Mar94 on 'Warners'; 7599 23593-2)*

Jan 82. (7") *<WB 49865>* **TUBE SNAKE BOOGIE. / HEAVEN, HELL OR HOUSTON** [–] [ ]

Jun 83. (7"/7"sha-pic-d) *(W 9693/+P) <WB 29693>* **GIMME ALL YOUR LOVIN'. / IF I COULD ONLY FLAG HER DOWN** [61] Mar83 [37]
(12") *(W 9693T)* – ('A'side) / Jesus just left Chicago / Heard it on the x / Arrested for driving while blind.

Jun 83. (lp/c) *(W 3774/+4) <23774-1/-4>* **ELIMINATOR** [3] Apr83 [9]
– Gimme all your lovin' / Got me under pressure / Sharp dressed man / I need you tonight / I got the six / Legs / Thug / TV dinners / Dirty dog / If I could only flag her down / Bad girl. *(cd-iss. 1984; 9-3774-2) (pic-lp Aug85; W 3774P)*

Nov 83. (7") *(WB 9576) <WB 29576>* **SHARP DRESSED MAN. / I GOT THE SIX** [53] Jul83 [56]
(12"+=) *(WB 9576T)* – La Grange.

Mar 84. (7") *(WB 9334)* **TV DINNERS. / CHEAP SUNGLASSES** [67] [–]
(c-s+=/d12"+=) *(W 9334 C/T)* – A fool for your stockings.

Sep 84. (single re-issue) *(same)* **GIMME ALL YOUR LOVIN'** [10] [–]

Dec 84. (single re-issue) *(same)* **SHARP DRESSED MAN** [22] [–]

Feb 85. (7") *(W 9272) <WB 29272>* **LEGS (remix). / BAD GIRL** [16] May84 [8]
('A'-Metal mix-12") *(W 9272T)* – A fool for your stockings.

Jul 85. (7"ep/c-ep/12"ep) *(W 8946/+C/T)* **THE ZZ TOP SUMMER HOLIDAY EP** [51] [–]
– Tush / Got me under pressure / Beer drinkers and hell raisers / I'm bad, I'm nationwide.

Oct 85. (7"/7"sha-pic-d/7"interlocking jigsaw pic-d pt.1) *(W 2001/+P/DP) <WB 28884>* **SLEEPING BAG. / PARTY ON THE PATIO** [27] [8]
(12"+=) *(W 2001T)* – Blue jean blues.
(d7+=) *(W 2001D)* – Sharp dressed man / I got the six.

Nov 85. (lp/c)(cd) *(WX 27/+C)(925342-2) <25342>* **AFTERBURNER** [2] [4]
– Sleeping bag / Stages / Woke up with wood / Rough boy / Can't stop rockin' / Planet of women / I got the message / Velcro fly / Dipping low (in the lap of luxury) / Delirious.

Feb 86. (7"/7"jigsaw pic-d pt.2) <US-12"> *(W 2002/+BP) <WB 28810T>* **STAGES. / HI-FI MAMA** [43] Jan86 [21]
(12"+=) *(W 2002T)* – ('A'extended).

Apr 86. (7"/7"pic-d,7"jigsaw pic-d pt.3) *(W 2003/+FP) <WB 28733>* **ROUGH BOY. / DELIRIOUS** [23] Mar86 [22]
(12"shrinkwrapped w/ free jigsaw 'SLEEPING BAG' pic-d+=) – Legs (mix).

Jul 86. (7") *<WB 28650>* **VELCRO FLY. / CAN'T STOP ROCKIN'** [–] [35]

Sep 86. (7") *(W 8515)* **VELCRO FLY. / WOKE UP IN WOOD** [54] [–]
(12"+=) *(W 8515T)* – Can't stop rockin' ('86 remix).

Jul 90. (7"/c-s/12") *(W 9812/+C/T) <19812>* **DOUBLEBACK. / PLANET OF WOMEN** [29] May90 [50]
(cd-s+=) *(W 9812CD)* – ('A'-AOR mix).

Oct 90. (cd)(lp/c) *(7599 26265-2)(WX 390/+C) <26265>* **RECYCLER** [8] [6]
– Concrete and steel / Lovething / Penthouse eyes / Tell it / My head's in Mississippi / Decision or collision / Give it up / 2000 blues / Burger man / Doubleback. *(re-iss. Mar94 cd/c)*

Nov 90. (7"/c-s) *(W 9509/+C)* **GIVE IT UP. / SHARP DRESSED MAN** [ ] [–]
(12"+=/cd-s+=) *(W 9509 T/CD)* – Cheap sunglasses (live).

Jan 91. (c-s,cd-s) *<19470>* **GIVE IT UP / CONCRETE AND STEEL** [–] [79]

Apr 91. (7"/7"sha-pic-d/c-s) *(W 0009/+P/C)* **MY HEAD'S IN MISSISSIPPI. / A FOOL FOR YOUR STOCKINGS** [37] [–]
(12"+=/cd-s+=) *(W 0009 T/CD)* – Blue Jean blues.

Mar 92. (7"/c-s) *(W 0098/+C) <18979>* **VIVA LAS VEGAS. / 2000 BLUES** [10] [ ]
(cd-s+=) *(W 0098CD)* – Velcro fly / Stages / Legs.

May 92. (cd/c/lp) *<(7599 26846-2/-4/-1)>* **GREATEST HITS** (compilation) [5] [9]
– Gimme all your lovin' / Sharp dressed man / Rough boy / Tush / My head's in Mississippi / Pearl necklace / I'm bad, I'm nationwide / Viva Las Vegas / Doubleback / Gun love / Got me under pressure / Give it up / Cheap sunglasses / Sleeping bag / Planet of women / La Grange / Tube snake boogie / Legs.

Jun 92. (7"/c-s) *(W 0111/+C)* **ROUGH BOY. / VIVA LAS VEGAS (remix)** [49] [–]
(cd-s+=) *(W 0111CD)* – Velcro fly (extended) / Doubleback (AOR mix).
(cd-s) *(W 0111CDX)* – ('A'side) / TV dinners / Jesus has just left Chicago / Beer drinkers and Hell raisers.

R.C.A. R.C.A.

Jan 94. (7"/c-s/cd-s) *(74321 18473-7/-4/-2)* **PINCUSHION. / CHERRY RED** [15] [ ]
(cd-s+=) *(74321 18261-2)* – ('A'mix).

Jan 94. (cd/c/lp) *(74321 18260-2/-4/-1) <66317>* **ANTENNA** [3] [14]
– Pincushion / Breakaway / World of swirl / Fuzzbox voodoo / Girl in a T-shirt / Antenna head / PCH / Cherry red / Cover your rig / Lizard life /

Deal goin' down / Everything.

Apr 94. (c-s/12"/cd-s) *(74321 19228-4/-1/-2)* **BREAKAWAY. / MARY'S / BREAKAWAY (version)** 60

Jun 96. (7"m) *(74321 39482-7)* **WHAT'S UP WITH THAT. / STOP BREAKIN' DOWN BLUES (live) / NASTY DOGS AND FUNKY KINGS (live)** 58

(cd-s+=) *(74321 39482-2)* – ('A'version).

Sep 96. (cd/c) *(74321 39466-2/-4)* <66958> **RHYTHMEEN** 32 29

– Rhythmeen / Bang bang / Black fly / What's up with that / Vincent Price blues / Zipper job / Hairdresser / She's just killing me / My mind is gone / Loaded / Prettyhead / Hummbucking, part 2.

—— ZZ were back in the UK Top 30 in Oct'99, albeit credited on MARTAY's version of their 'GIMME ALL YOUR LOVIN' 2000'

May 00. (cd/c) *(74321 69377-2)* <67850-2> **XXX** Sep99 100

– Poke chop sandwich / Crucifixx-a-flatt / Fearless boogie / 36-22-36 / Made into a movie / Beatbox / Trippin' / Dreadmonboogaloo / Introduction by Ross Mitchell / Sinpusher / (Let me be your) Teddy bear / Hey Mr. Millionaire / Belt buckle.

Apr 03. (cd) *(82876 51654-2)* <51168> **MESCALERO** 57

– Mescalero / Two ways to play / Alley-gator / Buck nekkid / Goin' so good / Me so stupid / Piece / Punk ass boyfriend / Stackin' paper / What would you do / What it is kid / Que lastima / Tramp / Crunchy / Dusted / Liquor.

– compilations, others, etc. –

on 'Warners' unless mentioned otherwise

Nov 83. (d-c) *(K4 66121)* **TRES HOMBRES / FANDANGO** –

1987. (3xcd-box) *(K 925661-2)* **FIRST ALBUM / RIO GRANDE MUD / / TRES HOMBRES / FANDANGO! / / TEJAS / EL LOCO**

Nov 94. (cd/c) <*(9362 45815-2/-4)*> **ONE FOOT IN THE BLUES**

Dec 02. (3xcd-box) *R.C.A.; (74321 95370-2)* **ANTENNA / RHYTHMEEN / XXX**